D1428896

OFFICIAL SCRABBLE® DICTIONARY

William Collins' dream of knowledge for all began with the publication of his first book in 1819. A self-educated mill worker, he not only enriched millions of lives, but also founded a flourishing publishing house. Today, staying true to this spirit, Collins books are packed with inspiration, innovation, and practical expertise. They place you at the centre of a world of possibility and give you exactly what you need to explore it.

Language is the key to this exploration, and at the heart of Collins Dictionaries is language as it is really used. New words, phrases, and meanings spring up every day, and all of them are captured and analysed by the Collins Word Web. Constantly updated, and with over 2.5 billion entries, this living language resource is unique to our dictionaries.

Words are tools for life. And a Collins Dictionary makes them work for you.

Collins. Do more.

OFFICIAL SCRABBLE® DICTIONARY

Collins

HarperCollins Publishers
Westerhill Road
Bishopbriggs
Glasgow
G64 2QT

First Edition 2005

ISBN-13 978-0-00-721310-8
ISBN-10 0-00-721310-7

www.collins.co.uk

A catalogue record for this book is available from the British Library.

Typeset by Wordcraft

Printed and bound in Germany by Bercker

Acknowledgements
We would like to thank those authors and publishers who kindly gave permission for copyright material to be used in the Collins Word Web. We would also like to thank Times Newspapers Ltd for providing valuable data.

Collins

Contents

EDITORIAL STAFF

SCRABBLE® CONSULTANTS
Allan Simmons
Darryl Francis

EDITORS
Katharine Coates
Kay Cullen
Justin Crozier
Susan Gillespie
Lorna Gilmour
Alice Grandison
Penny Hands
Andrew Holmes
Cordelia Lilly
Cormac McKeown
Mike Munro
Elspeth Summers

COMPUTING SUPPORT
Thomas Callan

CORPUS RESEARCH
Nigel Rochford

FOR THE PUBLISHERS
Morven Dooner
Elaine Higgleton
Lorna Knight

roduction

ins **Official SCRABBLE® Dictionary** is the most complete **SCRABBLE®** rence in existence, comprising the game's complete wordlist together with nitions for words of up to nine letters. As such, the Dictionary is an invaluable for any competitive or club player, as well as the ultimate authority for ling disputes between those who play with their friends and family.

aggering 267,977 words are listed in this Dictionary – representing an austive list of every valid play in **SCRABBLE®**. The book is divided into two ions: Section One contains every word of between two and nine letters, with er a definition or a cross-reference to a defined root word, while Section Two tains words of ten to fifteen letters, without definitions. In any **SCRABBLE®** ne, most words will be between two and nine letters, with longer words being ned only very rarely. Therefore, while this book lists every word that could ceivably be played on the **SCRABBLE®** board, the main focus is on words that ers are likely to have the opportunity to form from the seven letters on their and the words that are placed on the board during the game.

tion One thus allows every **SCRABBLE®** player, whether a beginner or veteran, ess to the definitions of all the most useful words in **SCRABBLE®**, enabling m to learn words by meaning rather than simply as combinations of letters. many players definitions are the key to remembering words, and to using m in **SCRABBLE®**, and the ability to check meanings, inflections, and variant llings will add interest to most social games.

initions in Section One are succinct and practical. In many cases, only a single nition is given, and in general only those parts of speech necessary for ting inflections are included. Cross-referred words include noun plurals, verb ections, the comparative and superlative forms of adjectives, and variant llings. Adjectives formed with obvious suffixes, such as *-like* and *-less*, are also ss-referred to the root word when the meaning is easily deduced.

Section Two contains all of the longer words permissible in **SCRABBLE®**, from ten to fifteen letters in length. Most of these words will only rarely appear on the board, due to their length, which is why definitions are not provided. The main function of this section of the book is to act as an indisputable authority when such longer words are played. Players may also wish to explore ways in which they can 'build' on words on the board by consulting Section Two. By exploring the way in which shorter words can be combined with common suffixes such as *-man*, *-woman*, *-like*, *-less*, *-ness*, and *-lessness*, and prefixes such as *non-*, *un-*, *over-*, and *under-*, the keen **SCRABBLE®** player can add an extra dimension to his or her game.

Unlike a conventional dictionary, every word in each section is listed in strict alphabetical order, regardless of the relationship between words. Thus there may be several, or many, words between the singular form of a noun and its plural. This strict alphabetization allows rapid checking of words – which is particularly important during **SCRABBLE®** tournaments.

Collins would like to give warm thanks to Darryl Francis and Allan Simmons for their enormous contribution to the wordlist in this dictionary. They worked tirelessly with the editorial team to get this right. Any errors – and all the definitions in this book – are the responsibility of the publisher.

ıg the Official SCRABBLE® Dictionary

ːy word eligible for SCRABBLE® is listed in this book. The first section includes ·layable words of two to nine letters in length, in one straight alphabetical These words are either defined or cross-referred. Cross-referred words include noun als, verb inflections, the comparative and superlative forms of adjectives, and variant lings. Adjectives formed with obvious suffixes, such as *-like* and *-less* are also s-referred to the root word.

ollins SCRABBLE® Dictionary, only a single definition is given for each part of speech, in general only those parts of speech necessary for existing inflections are included. ıe definitions have been sourced from **Collins English Dictionary, Complete and bridged**, and other definitions have been written specially for this dictionary. While ıave shortened many of the **Collins English Dictionary** definitions for the purpose of this book, / are fuller than the others.

:d order — **Collins SCRABBLE® Dictionary** is in strict alphabetical order.

ɜnsive terms — there may be words in **Collins SCRABBLE® Dictionary** that most or some players might consider derogatory, offensive, or even taboo.

ents — as English language SCRABBLE® tiles are not accented, no accents are shown in **Collins SCRABBLE® Dictionary.**

n entry words — printed in bold capitals, eg

AA

All entry words,
in one alphabetical
sequence, eg

AA
AAH
AAHED
AAL
AALI

ts of Speech — shown in italics as an abbreviation, eg

AA *n*

When more than one part
of speech is given, the
change of part of speech is
shown after an arrow, eg

ABANDON *vb* desert or leave
▷ *n* lack of inhibition

Cross-references

noun plurals, verb inflections, comparatives and superlatives, and derivatives are all cross-referred to their root form

ABASH *vb* cause or feel ill at ease, embarrassed, or confused

...

ABASHES > ABASH
ABASHING > ABASH
ABASHLESS > ABASH
ABASHMENT > ABASH

Variant forms

variant forms and synonyms are cross-referred to the most commonly-used form of a word, eg

CAFTAN *same as* > KAFTAN

noun plurals, verb inflections, comparitives, superlatives, and derivatives of the variant form are all cross-referred to the root form of that particular variant, eg

CAFTAN *same as* > KAFTAN
...

CAFTANS > CAFTAN

Phrases

when a word is most comonly used in a phrase, the phrase is given in italics and defined, eg

BANGALORE as in *bangalore torpedo* explosive device in a long metal tube, used to blow gaps in barbed-wire barriers

Aa

AA *n* volcanic rock consisting of angular blocks of lava with a very rough surface
AAH *vb* exclaim in pleasure or surprise
AAHED > AAH
AAHING > AAH
AAHS > AAH
AAL *n* Asian shrub or tree
AALII *n* bushy sapindaceous shrub, *Dodonaea viscosa*, of Australia, Hawaii, Africa, and tropical America, having small greenish flowers and sticky foliage
AALIIS > AALII
AALS > AAL
AARDVARK *n* S African anteater with long ears and snout
AARDVARKS > AARDVARK
AARDWOLF *n* nocturnal mammal, *Proteles cristatus*, that inhabits the plains of southern Africa and feeds on termites and insect larvae: family *Hyaenidae* (hyenas), order *Carnivora* (carnivores)
AARGH *interj* cry of pain
AARRGH *interj* cry of pain
AARRGHH *interj* cry of pain
AARTI *n* Hindu ceremony in which lights with wicks soaked in ghee are lit and offered up to one or more deities
AARTIS > AARTI
AAS > AA
AASVOGEL *n* South African bird of prey
AASVOGELS > AASVOGEL
AB *n* abdominal muscle
ABA *n* type of cloth from Syria, made of goat hair or camel hair
ABAC *n* mathematical diagram
ABACA *n* Philippine plant, *Musa textilis*, related to the banana: family *Musaceae*. Its leafstalks are the source of Manila hemp
ABACAS > ABACA
ABACI > ABACUS
ABACK *adv* towards the back; backwards
ABACS > ABAC
ABACTINAL *adj* (of organisms showing radial symmetry) situated away from or opposite to the mouth
ABACTOR *n* cattle thief
ABACTORS > ABACTOR
ABACUS *n* beads on a wire frame, used for doing calculations
ABACUSES > ABACUS
ABAFT *adv* closer to the rear of (a ship) ▷ *adj* closer to the stern of a ship
ABAKA *n* abaca
ABAKAS > ABAKA
ABALONE *n* edible sea creature with a shell lined with mother of pearl
ABALONES > ABALONE
ABAMP *same as* > ABAMPERE
ABAMPERE *n* cgs unit of current in the electromagnetic system
ABAMPERES > ABAMPERE
ABAMPS > ABAMP
ABAND *vb* abandon
ABANDED > ABAND
ABANDING > ABAND
ABANDON *vb* desert or leave (one's wife, children, etc) ▷ *n* lack of inhibition
ABANDONED *adj* deserted
ABANDONEE *n* person to whom something is formally relinquished, esp an insurer having the right to salvage a wreck
ABANDONER > ABANDON
ABANDONS > ABANDON
ABANDS > ABAND
ABAPICAL *adj* away from or opposite the apex
ABAS > ABA
ABASE *vb* humiliate or degrade (oneself)
ABASED > ABASE
ABASEDLY > ABASE
ABASEMENT > ABASE
ABASER > ABASE
ABASERS > ABASE
ABASES > ABASE
ABASH *vb* cause to feel ill at ease, embarrassed, or confused
ABASHED *adj* embarrassed and ashamed
ABASHEDLY > ABASHED
ABASHES > ABASH
ABASHING > ABASH
ABASHLESS > ABASH
ABASHMENT > ABASH
ABASIA *n* disorder affecting ability to walk
ABASIAS > ABASIA
ABASING > ABASE
ABASK *adv* in pleasant warmth
ABATABLE > ABATE
ABATE *vb* make or become less strong
ABATED > ABATE
ABATEMENT *n* diminution or alleviation
ABATER > ABATE
ABATERS > ABATE
ABATES > ABATE
ABATING > ABATE
ABATIS *n* rampart of felled trees bound together, placed with their branches outwards
ABATISES > ABATIS
ABATOR *n* person who effects an abatement
ABATORS > ABATOR
ABATTIS *same as* > ABATIS
ABATTISES > ABATTIS
ABATTOIR *n* place where animals are killed for food
ABATTOIRS > ABATTOIR
ABATTU *adj* dejected
ABATURE *n* trail left by hunted stag
ABATURES > ABATURE
ABAXIAL *adj* facing away from the axis, as the surface of a leaf
ABAXILE *adj* away from the axis
ABAYA *n* Arab outer garment
ABAYAS > ABAYA
ABB *n* yarn used in weaving
ABBA *n* title for a bishop in the Coptic Church
ABBACIES > ABBACY
ABBACY *n* office or jurisdiction of an abbot or abbess
ABBAS > ABBA
ABBATIAL *adj* of or relating

to an abbot, abbess, or abbey
ABBE *n* French abbot
ABBED *adj* displaying well-developed abdominal muscles
ABBES > ABBE
ABBESS *n* nun in charge of a convent
ABBESSES > ABBESS
ABBEY *n* dwelling place of, or a church belonging to, a community of monks or nuns
ABBEYS > ABBEY
ABBOT *n* head of an abbey of monks
ABBOTCIES > ABBOT
ABBOTCY > ABBOT
ABBOTS > ABBOT
ABBOTSHIP > ABBOT
ABBS > ABB
ABCEE *n* alphabet
ABCEES > ABCEE
ABCOULOMB *n* cgs unit of electric charge in the electromagnetic system
ABDABS *n* highly nervous state
ABDICABLE > ABDICATE
ABDICANT > ABDICATE
ABDICATE *vb* give up (the throne or a responsibility)
ABDICATED > ABDICATE
ABDICATES > ABDICATE
ABDICATOR > ABDICATE
ABDOMEN *n* part of the body containing the stomach and intestines
ABDOMENS > ABDOMEN
ABDOMINA > ABDOMEN
ABDOMINAL > ABDOMEN
ABDUCE *vb* abduct
ABDUCED > ABDUCE
ABDUCENS as in *abducens nerve* either of the sixth pair of cranial nerves, which supply the lateral rectus muscle of the eye
ABDUCENT *adj* (of a muscle) abducting
ABDUCES > ABDUCE
ABDUCING > ABDUCE
ABDUCT *vb* carry off, kidnap
ABDUCTED > ABDUCT
ABDUCTEE > ABDUCT
ABDUCTEES > ABDUCT
ABDUCTING > ABDUCT
ABDUCTION *n* act of taking someone away by force or cunning
ABDUCTOR > ABDUCT
ABDUCTORS > ABDUCT
ABDUCTS > ABDUCT
ABEAM *adj* at right angles to the length of a ship or aircraft
ABEAR *vb* bear or behave
ABEARING > ABEAR
ABEARS > ABEAR
ABED *adv* in bed
ABEGGING *adj* in the act of begging for money etc
ABEIGH *adv* aloof
ABELE *n* white poplar tree
ABELES > ABELE
ABELIA *n* garden plant with pink or white flowers
ABELIAN > ABELIA
ABELIAS > ABELIA
ABELMOSK *n* tropical bushy malvaceous plant, *Hibiscus abelmoschus*, cultivated for its yellow-and-crimson flowers and for its musk-scented seeds, which yield an oil used in perfumery
ABELMOSKS > ABELMOSK
ABERNETHY *n* crisp unleavened biscuit
ABERRANCE > ABERRANT
ABERRANCY > ABERRANT
ABERRANT *adj* showing aberration ▷ *n* person whose behaviour is considered to be aberrant
ABERRANTS > ABERRANT
ABERRATE *vb* deviate from what is normal or correct
ABERRATED > ABERRATE
ABERRATES > ABERRATE
ABESSIVE *n* grammatical case indicating absence
ABESSIVES > ABESSIVE
ABET *vb* help or encourage in wrongdoing
ABETMENT > ABET
ABETMENTS > ABET
ABETS > ABET
ABETTAL > ABET
ABETTALS > ABET
ABETTED > ABET
ABETTER > ABET
ABETTERS > ABET
ABETTING > ABET
ABETTOR > ABET
ABETTORS > ABET
ABEYANCE *n* state of being suspended or put aside temporarily
ABEYANCES > ABEYANCE
ABEYANCY *n* abeyance
ABEYANT > ABEYANCE
ABFARAD *n* cgs unit of capacitance in the electromagnetic system
ABFARADS > ABFARAD
ABHENRIES > ABHENRY
ABHENRY *n* cgs unit of inductance in the electromagnetic system
ABHENRYS > ABHENRY
ABHOR *vb* detest utterly
ABHORRED > ABHOR
ABHORRENT *adj* hateful, loathsome
ABHORRER > ABHOR
ABHORRERS > ABHOR
ABHORRING > ABHOR
ABHORS > ABHOR
ABID > ABIDE
ABIDANCE > ABIDE
ABIDANCES > ABIDE
ABIDDEN > ABIDE
ABIDE *vb* endure, put up with
ABIDED > ABIDE
ABIDER > ABIDE
ABIDERS > ABIDE
ABIDES > ABIDE
ABIDING *adj* lasting ▷ *n* action of one who abides
ABIDINGLY > ABIDING
ABIDINGS > ABIDING
ABIES *n* fir tree
ABIETIC *adj* pertaining to fir trees
ABIGAIL *n* maid for a lady
ABIGAILS > ABIGAIL
ABILITIES > ABILITY
ABILITY *n* competence, power
ABIOGENIC *adj* abiogenetic
ABIOSES > ABIOSIS
ABIOSIS *n* absence of life
ABIOTIC > ABIOSIS
ABJECT *adj* utterly miserable ▷ *vb* throw down
ABJECTED > ABJECT
ABJECTING > ABJECT
ABJECTION > ABJECT
ABJECTLY > ABJECT
ABJECTS > ABJECT
ABJOINT *vb* cut off
ABJOINTED > ABJOINT
ABJOINTS > ABJOINT
ABJURE *vb* deny or renounce on oath
ABJURED > ABJURE
ABJURER > ABJURE
ABJURERS > ABJURE
ABJURES > ABJURE
ABJURING > ABJURE
ABLATE *vb* remove by ablation
ABLATED > ABLATE
ABLATES > ABLATE
ABLATING > ABLATE
ABLATION *n* surgical removal of an organ or part
ABLATIONS > ABLATION
ABLATIVAL > ABLATIVE
ABLATIVE *n* case of nouns in Latin and other languages, indicating source, agent, or instrument of action ▷ *adj* (in certain inflected languages such as Latin) denoting a case of nouns, pronouns, and adjectives indicating the agent in passive sentences or the instrument, manner, or place of the action described by the verb
ABLATIVES > ABLATIVE
ABLATOR *n* heat shield of a space vehicle, which melts or wears away during re-entry into the earth's atmosphere
ABLATORS > ABLATOR
ABLAUT *n* vowel gradation, esp in Indo-European languages
ABLAUTS > ABLAUT
ABLAZE *adj* burning fiercely ▷ *adv* on fire
ABLE *adj* capable, competent ▷ *vb* enable
ABLED *adj* having a range of physical powers as specified
ABLEGATE *n* papal envoy
ABLEGATES > ABLEGATE
ABLEISM *n* discrimination against disabled or handicapped people
ABLEISMS > ABLEISM
ABLEIST > ABLEISM
ABLEISTS > ABLEISM
ABLER > ABLE
ABLES > ABLE
ABLEST > ABLE
ABLET *n* freshwater fish
ABLETS > ABLET
ABLING > ABLE
ABLINGS *adv* possibly
ABLINS *adv* Scots word meaning perhaps
ABLOOM *adj* in flower
ABLOW *adj* blooming
ABLUENT *n* substance used for cleansing
ABLUENTS > ABLUENT
ABLUSH *adj* blushing
ABLUTED *adj* washed thoroughly
ABLUTION *n* ritual washing of a priest's hands or of sacred vessels
ABLUTIONS > ABLUTION
ABLY *adv* competently or skilfully
ABMHO *n* unit of electrical conductance
ABMHOS > ABMHO
ABNEGATE *vb* deny to oneself
ABNEGATED > ABNEGATE
ABNEGATES > ABNEGATE
ABNEGATOR > ABNEGATE
ABNORMAL *adj* not normal or usual ▷ *n* abnormal person or thing
ABNORMALS > ABNORMAL
ABNORMITY > ABNORMAL
ABNORMOUS > ABNORMAL
ABO *offensive name for* > ABORIGINE
ABOARD *adv* on, in, onto, or into (a ship, train, or plane) ▷ *adj* on, in, onto, or into (a ship, plane, or train)
ABODE *n* home, dwelling ▷ *vb* forebode
ABODED > ABODE
ABODEMENT > ABODE
ABODES > ABODE
ABODING > ABODE
ABOHM *n* cgs unit of resistance in the electromagnetic system: equivalent to 10^{-9} ohm
ABOHMS > ABOHM
ABOIDEAU *n* dyke with a sluicegate that allows flood water to drain but keeps the sea water out
ABOIDEAUS > ABOIDEAU
ABOIDEAUX > ABOIDEAU
ABOIL *adj* boiling
ABOITEAU *same as* > ABOIDEAU

ABOITEAUS > ABOITEAU
ABOITEAUX > ABOITEAU
ABOLISH *vb* do away with
ABOLISHED > ABOLISH
ABOLISHER > ABOLISH
ABOLISHES > ABOLISH
ABOLITION *n* act of abolishing or the state of being abolished
ABOLLA *n* Roman cloak
ABOLLAE > ABOLLA
ABOLLAS > ABOLLA
ABOMA *n* South American snake
ABOMAS > ABOMA
ABOMASA > ABOMASUM
ABOMASAL > ABOMASUM
ABOMASI > ABOMASUS
ABOMASUM *n* fourth and last compartment of the stomach of ruminants, which receives and digests food from the psalterium and passes it on to the small intestine
ABOMASUS *n* abomasum
ABOMINATE *vb* dislike intensely
ABONDANCE *same as* > ABUNDANCE
ABOON *Scots word for* > ABOVE
ABORAL *adj* away from or opposite the mouth
ABORALLY > ABORAL
ABORD *vb* accost
ABORDED > ABORD
ABORDING > ABORD
ABORDS > ABORD
ABORE > ABEAR
ABORIGEN *n* aborigine
ABORIGENS > ABORIGEN
ABORIGIN *n* aborigine
ABORIGINE *n* original inhabitant of a country or region, esp Australia
ABORIGINS > ABORIGIN
ABORNE *adj* Shakespearean form of auburn
ABORNING > ABEAR
ABORT *vb* have an abortion or perform an abortion on ▷ *n* premature termination or failure of (a space flight, military operation, etc)
ABORTED > ABORT
ABORTEE *n* woman having an abortion
ABORTEES > ABORTEE
ABORTER > ABORT
ABORTERS > ABORT
ABORTING > ABORT
ABORTION *n* operation to end a pregnancy
ABORTIONS > ABORTION
ABORTIVE *adj* unsuccessful
ABORTS > ABORT
ABORTUARY *n* place where abortions are carried out
ABORTUS *n* aborted fetus
ABORTUSES > ABORTUS
ABOS > ABO
ABOUGHT > ABY
ABOULIA *same as* > ABULIA
ABOULIAS > ABOULIA
ABOULIC > ABOULIA
ABOUND *vb* be plentiful
ABOUNDED > ABOUND
ABOUNDING > ABOUND
ABOUNDS > ABOUND
ABOUT *adv* nearly, approximately
ABOUTS *prep* about
ABOVE *adv* over or higher (than) ▷ *n* something that is or appears above
ABOVES > ABOVE
ABRACHIA *n* condition of having no arms
ABRACHIAS > ABRACHIA
ABRADABLE > ABRADE
ABRADANT > ABRADE
ABRADANTS > ABRADE
ABRADE *vb* scrape away or wear down by friction
ABRADED > ABRADE
ABRADER > ABRADE
ABRADERS > ABRADE
ABRADES > ABRADE
ABRADING > ABRADE
ABRAID *vb* awake
ABRAIDED > ABRAID
ABRAIDING > ABRAID
ABRAIDS > ABRAID
ABRAM *adj* auburn
ABRASAX *same as* > ABRAXAS
ABRASAXES > ABRASAX
ABRASION *n* scraped area on the skin
ABRASIONS > ABRASION
ABRASIVE *adj* harsh and unpleasant in manner ▷ *n* substance for cleaning or polishing by rubbing
ABRASIVES > ABRASIVE
ABRAXAS *n* ancient charm composed of Greek letters: originally believed to have magical powers and inscribed on amulets, etc, but from the second century AD personified by Gnostics as a deity, the source of divine emanations
ABRAXASES > ABRAXAS
ABRAY *vb* awake
ABRAYED > ABRAY
ABRAYING > ABRAY
ABRAYS > ABRAY
ABRAZO *n* embrace
ABRAZOS > ABRAZO
ABREACT *vb* alleviate (emotional tension) through abreaction
ABREACTED > ABREACT
ABREACTS > ABREACT
ABREAST *adj* side by side
ABREGE *n* abridgment
ABREGES > ABREGE
ABRI *n* shelter or place of refuge, esp in wartime
ABRICOCK *n* apricot
ABRICOCKS > ABRICOCK
ABRIDGE *vb* shorten by using fewer words
ABRIDGED > ABRIDGE
ABRIDGER > ABRIDGE
ABRIDGERS > ABRIDGE
ABRIDGES > ABRIDGE
ABRIDGING > ABRIDGE
ABRIM *adj* full to the brim
ABRIN *n* poisonous compound
ABRINS > ABRIN
ABRIS > ABRI
ABROACH *adj* (of a cask, barrel, etc) tapped
ABROAD *adv* in a foreign country ▷ *adj* (of news, rumours, etc) in general circulation ▷ *n* foreign place
ABROADS > ABROAD
ABROGABLE *adj* able to be abrogated
ABROGATE *vb* cancel (a law or agreement) formally
ABROGATED > ABROGATE
ABROGATES > ABROGATE
ABROGATOR > ABROGATE
ABROOKE *vb* bear or tolerate
ABROOKED > ABROOKE
ABROOKES > ABROOKE
ABROOKING > ABROOKE
ABROSIA *n* condition involving refusal to eat
ABROSIAS > ABROSIA
ABRUPT *adj* sudden, unexpected ▷ *n* abyss
ABRUPTER > ABRUPT
ABRUPTEST > ABRUPT
ABRUPTION *n* breaking off of a part or parts from a mass
ABRUPTLY > ABRUPT
ABRUPTS > ABRUPT
ABS > AB
ABSCESS *n* inflamed swelling containing pus ▷ *vb* form a swelling containing pus
ABSCESSED > ABSCESS
ABSCESSES > ABSCESS
ABSCIND *vb* cut off
ABSCINDED > ABSCIND
ABSCINDS > ABSCIND
ABSCISE *vb* separate or be separated by abscission
ABSCISED > ABSCISE
ABSCISES > ABSCISE
ABSCISIN *n* plant hormone
ABSCISING > ABSCISE
ABSCISINS > ABSCISIN
ABSCISS *n* cutting off
ABSCISSA *n* cutting off
ABSCISSAE > ABSCISSA
ABSCISSAS > ABSCISSA
ABSCISSE *n* cutting off
ABSCISSES > ABSCISSE
ABSCISSIN *n* plant hormone
ABSCOND *vb* leave secretly
ABSCONDED > ABSCOND
ABSCONDER > ABSCOND
ABSCONDS > ABSCOND
ABSEIL *vb* go down a steep drop by a rope fastened at the top and tied around one's body ▷ *n* instance of abseiling
ABSEILED > ABSEIL
ABSEILING > ABSEIL
ABSEILS > ABSEIL
ABSENCE *n* being away
ABSENCES > ABSENCE
ABSENT *adj* not present ▷ *vb* stay away
ABSENTED > ABSENT
ABSENTEE *n* person who should be present but is not
ABSENTEES > ABSENTEE
ABSENTER > ABSENT
ABSENTERS > ABSENT
ABSENTING > ABSENT
ABSENTLY *adv* in an absent-minded or preoccupied manner
ABSENTS > ABSENT
ABSEY *n* alphabet
ABSEYS > ABSEY
ABSINTH *same as* > ABSINTHE
ABSINTHE *n* strong green aniseed-flavoured liqueur
ABSINTHES > ABSINTHE
ABSINTHS > ABSINTH
ABSIT *n* overnight leave from college
ABSITS > ABSIT
ABSOLUTE *adj* complete, perfect ▷ *n* something that is absolute
ABSOLUTER > ABSOLUTE
ABSOLUTES > ABSOLUTE
ABSOLVE *vb* declare to be free from blame or sin
ABSOLVED > ABSOLVE
ABSOLVENT *n* something that absolves
ABSOLVER > ABSOLVE
ABSOLVERS > ABSOLVE
ABSOLVES > ABSOLVE
ABSOLVING > ABSOLVE
ABSONANT *adj* unnatural and unreasonable
ABSORB *vb* soak up (a liquid)
ABSORBANT *n* absorbent substance
ABSORBATE *n* absorbed substance
ABSORBED *adj* engrossed
ABSORBENT *adj* able to absorb liquid ▷ *n* substance that absorbs
ABSORBER *n* person or thing that absorbs
ABSORBERS > ABSORBER
ABSORBING *adj* occupying one's interest or attention
ABSORBS > ABSORB
ABSTAIN *vb* choose not to do something
ABSTAINED > ABSTAIN
ABSTAINER > ABSTAIN
ABSTAINS > ABSTAIN
ABSTERGE *vb* cleanse
ABSTERGED > ABSTERGE
ABSTERGES > ABSTERGE
ABSTINENT *adj* refraining from a certain activity
ABSTRACT *adj* existing as a quality or idea rather

than a material object ▷ *n* summary ▷ *vb* summarize
ABSTRACTS > ABSTRACT
ABSTRICT *vb* release
ABSTRICTS > ABSTRICT
ABSTRUSE *adj* not easy to understand
ABSTRUSER > ABSTRUSE
ABSURD *adj* incongruous or ridiculous ▷ *n* conception of the world, esp in Existentialist thought, as neither designed nor predictable but irrational and meaningless
ABSURDER > ABSURD
ABSURDEST > ABSURD
ABSURDISM *n* belief that life is meaningless
ABSURDIST > ABSURDISM
ABSURDITY > ABSURD
ABSURDLY > ABSURD
ABSURDS > ABSURD
ABTHANE *n* ancient Scottish church territory
ABTHANES > ABTHANE
ABUBBLE *adj* bubbling
ABUILDING *adj* being built
ABULIA *n* pathological inability to take decisions
ABULIAS > ABULIA
ABULIC > ABULIA
ABUNA *n* male head of Ethiopian family
ABUNAS > ABUNA
ABUNDANCE *n* copious supply
ABUNDANCY *n* abundance
ABUNDANT *adj* plentiful
ABUNE *Scots word for* > ABOVE
ABURST *adj* bursting
ABUSABLE > ABUSE
ABUSAGE *n* wrong use
ABUSAGES > ABUSAGE
ABUSE *vb* use wrongly ▷ *n* prolonged ill-treatment
ABUSED > ABUSE
ABUSER > ABUSE
ABUSERS > ABUSE
ABUSES > ABUSE
ABUSING > ABUSE
ABUSION *n* wrong use or deception
ABUSIONS > ABUSION
ABUSIVE *adj* rude or insulting
ABUSIVELY > ABUSIVE
ABUT *vb* be next to or touching
ABUTILON *n* any shrub or herbaceous plant of the malvaceous genus *Abutilon*, such as the flowering maple, that have showy white, yellow, or red flowers
ABUTILONS > ABUTILON
ABUTMENT *n* construction that supports the end of a bridge
ABUTMENTS > ABUTMENT
ABUTS > ABUT
ABUTTAL *same as* > ABUTMENT
ABUTTALS > ABUTTAL
ABUTTED > ABUT
ABUTTER *n* owner of adjoining property
ABUTTERS > ABUTTER
ABUTTING > ABUT
ABUZZ *adj* noisy, busy with activity etc
ABVOLT *n* cgs unit of potential difference in the electromagnetic system
ABVOLTS > ABVOLT
ABWATT *n* cgs unit of power in the electromagnetic system, equal to the power dissipated when a current of 1 abampere flows across a potential difference of 1 abvolt: equivalent to 10^{-7} watt
ABWATTS > ABWATT
ABY *vb* pay the penalty for
ABYE *same as* > ABY
ABYEING > ABYE
ABYES > ABYE
ABYING > ABY
ABYS > ABY
ABYSM *archaic word for* > ABYSS
ABYSMAL *adj* extremely bad, awful
ABYSMALLY > ABYSMAL
ABYSMS > ABYSM
ABYSS *n* very deep hole or chasm
ABYSSAL *adj* of or belonging to the ocean depths, esp below 2000 metres (6500 feet)
ABYSSES > ABYSS
ACACIA *n* tree or shrub with yellow or white flowers
ACACIAS > ACACIA
ACADEME *n* place of learning
ACADEMES > ACADEME
ACADEMIA *n* academic world
ACADEMIAS > ACADEMIA
ACADEMIC *adj* of an academy or university ▷ *n* lecturer or researcher at a university
ACADEMICS > ACADEMIC
ACADEMIES > ACADEMY
ACADEMISM *n* adherence to rules and traditions in art, literature, etc
ACADEMIST > ACADEMY
ACADEMY *n* society to advance arts or sciences
ACAI *n* berry found in Brazilian rainforest
ACAIS > ACAI
ACAJOU *n* type of mahogany used by cabinet-makers in France
ACAJOUS > ACAJOU
ACALCULIA *n* inability to make simple mathematical calculations
ACALEPH *n* any of the coelenterates of the former taxonomic group *Acalephae*, which included the jellyfishes
ACALEPHAE > ACALEPH
ACALEPHAN > ACALEPH
ACALEPHE *n* acaleph
ACALEPHES > ACALEPHE
ACALEPHS > ACALEPH
ACANTH *n* acanthus
ACANTHA *n* thorn or prickle
ACANTHAE > ACANTHA
ACANTHAS > ACANTHA
ACANTHI > ACANTHUS
ACANTHIN *n* organic chemical used in medicine
ACANTHINE *adj* of or resembling an acanthus
ACANTHINS > ACANTHIN
ACANTHOID *adj* resembling a spine
ACANTHOUS *adj* of an acanthus
ACANTHS > ACANTH
ACANTHUS *n* prickly plant
ACAPNIA *n* lack of carbon dioxide
ACAPNIAS > ACAPNIA
ACARBOSE *n* diabetes medicine
ACARBOSES > ACARBOSE
ACARI > ACARUS
ACARIAN > ACARUS
ACARIASES > ACARIASIS
ACARIASIS *n* infestation of the hair follicles and skin with acarids, esp mites
ACARICIDE *n* any drug or formulation for killing acarids
ACARID *n* any of the small arachnids of the order *Acarina* (or *Acari*), which includes the ticks and mites ▷ *adj* of or relating to the order *Acarina*
ACARIDAN *same as* > ACARID
ACARIDANS > ACARIDAN
ACARIDEAN > ACARID
ACARIDIAN > ACARID
ACARIDS > ACARID
ACARINE *n* acarid
ACARINES > ACARINE
ACAROID *adj* resembling a mite or tick
ACAROLOGY *n* study of mites and ticks
ACARPOUS *adj* (of plants) producing no fruit
ACARUS *n* any of the free-living mites of the widely distributed genus *Acarus*, several of which, esp *A. siro*, are serious pests of stored flour, grain, etc
ACATER *n* buyer of provisions
ACATERS > ACATER
ACATES *n* provisions
ACATOUR *n* buyer of provisions
ACATOURS > ACATOUR
ACAUDAL *adj* having no tail
ACAUDATE *same as* > ACAUDAL
ACAULINE *adj* having no stem
ACAULOSE *same as* > ACAULINE
ACAULOUS *adj* having a short stem or no stem
ACCA *n* academic
ACCABLE *adj* dejected or beaten
ACCAS > ACCA
ACCEDE *vb* consent or agree (to)
ACCEDED > ACCEDE
ACCEDENCE > ACCEDE
ACCEDER > ACCEDE
ACCEDERS > ACCEDE
ACCEDES > ACCEDE
ACCEDING > ACCEDE
ACCEND *vb* set alight
ACCENDED > ACCEND
ACCENDING > ACCEND
ACCENDS > ACCEND
ACCENSION > ACCEND
ACCENT *n* distinctive style of pronunciation of a local, national, or social group ▷ *vb* place emphasis on
ACCENTED > ACCENT
ACCENTING > ACCENT
ACCENTOR *n* any small sparrow-like songbird of the genus *Prunella*, family *Prunellidae*, which inhabit mainly mountainous regions of Europe and Asia
ACCENTORS > ACCENTOR
ACCENTS > ACCENT
ACCENTUAL *adj* of, relating to, or having accents
ACCEPT *vb* receive willingly
ACCEPTANT *adj* receiving willingly
ACCEPTED *adj* generally approved
ACCEPTEE *n* person who has been accepted
ACCEPTEES > ACCEPTEE
ACCEPTER > ACCEPT
ACCEPTERS > ACCEPT
ACCEPTING > ACCEPT
ACCEPTIVE *adj* ready to accept
ACCEPTOR *n* person or organization on which a draft or bill of exchange is drawn after liability has been accepted, usually by signature
ACCEPTORS > ACCEPTOR
ACCEPTS > ACCEPT
ACCESS *n* means of or right to approach or enter ▷ *vb* obtain (data) from a computer
ACCESSARY *same as* > ACCESSORY
ACCESSED > ACCESS
ACCESSES > ACCESS
ACCESSING > ACCESS
ACCESSION *n* taking up of an office or position ▷ *vb* make a record of

(additions to a collection)
ACCESSORY *n* supplementary part or object ▷ *adj* supplementary
ACCIDENCE *n* inflectional morphology
ACCIDENT *n* mishap, often causing injury
ACCIDENTS > ACCIDENT
ACCIDIA *same as* > ACCIDIE
ACCIDIAS > ACCIDIA
ACCIDIE *n* spiritual sloth
ACCIDIES > ACCIDIE
ACCINGE *vb* put a belt around
ACCINGED > ACCINGE
ACCINGES > ACCINGE
ACCINGING > ACCINGE
ACCIPITER *n* any hawk of the genus *Accipiter*, typically having short rounded wings and a long tail
ACCITE *vb* summon
ACCITED > ACCITE
ACCITES > ACCITE
ACCITING > ACCITE
ACCLAIM *vb* applaud, praise ▷ *n* enthusiastic approval
ACCLAIMED > ACCLAIM
ACCLAIMER > ACCLAIM
ACCLAIMS > ACCLAIM
ACCLIMATE *vb* adapt or become accustomed to a new climate or environment
ACCLIVITY *n* upward slope, esp of the ground
ACCLIVOUS > ACCLIVITY
ACCLOY *vb* choke or clog
ACCLOYED > ACCLOY
ACCLOYING > ACCLOY
ACCLOYS > ACCLOY
ACCOAST *vb* accost
ACCOASTED > ACCOAST
ACCOASTS > ACCOAST
ACCOIED > ACCOY
ACCOIL *n* welcome ▷ *vb* gather together
ACCOILS > ACCOIL
ACCOLADE *n* award or praise ▷ *vb* give an award or praise
ACCOLADED > ACCOLADE
ACCOLADES > ACCOLADE
ACCOMPANY *vb* go along with
ACCOMPT *vb* account
ACCOMPTED > ACCOMPT
ACCOMPTS > ACCOMPT
ACCORAGE *vb* encourage
ACCORAGED > ACCORAGE
ACCORAGES > ACCORAGE
ACCORD *n* agreement, harmony ▷ *vb* fit in with
ACCORDANT *adj* in conformity or harmony
ACCORDED > ACCORD
ACCORDER > ACCORD
ACCORDERS > ACCORD
ACCORDING *adj* in proportion
ACCORDION *n* portable musical instrument played by moving the two sides apart and together, and pressing a keyboard or buttons to produce the notes
ACCORDS > ACCORD
ACCOST *vb* approach and speak to, often aggressively ▷ *n* greeting
ACCOSTED > ACCOST
ACCOSTING > ACCOST
ACCOSTS > ACCOST
ACCOUNT *n* report, description ▷ *vb* judge to be
ACCOUNTED > ACCOUNT
ACCOUNTS > ACCOUNT
ACCOURAGE *vb* encourage
ACCOURT *vb* entertain
ACCOURTED > ACCOURT
ACCOURTS > ACCOURT
ACCOUTER *same as* > ACCOUTRE
ACCOUTERS > ACCOUTER
ACCOUTRE *vb* provide with equipment or dress, esp military
ACCOUTRED > ACCOUTRE
ACCOUTRES > ACCOUTRE
ACCOY *vb* soothe
ACCOYED > ACCOY
ACCOYING > ACCOY
ACCOYLD > ACCOIL
ACCOYS > ACCOY
ACCREDIT *vb* give official recognition to
ACCREDITS > ACCREDIT
ACCRETE *vb* grow or cause to grow together
ACCRETED > ACCRETE
ACCRETES > ACCRETE
ACCRETING > ACCRETE
ACCRETION *n* gradual growth
ACCRETIVE > ACCRETION
ACCREW *vb* accrue
ACCREWED > ACCREW
ACCREWING > ACCREW
ACCREWS > ACCREW
ACCROIDES *n* red alcohol-soluble resin
ACCRUABLE > ACCRUE
ACCRUAL *n* act of accruing
ACCRUALS > ACCRUAL
ACCRUE *vb* increase gradually
ACCRUED > ACCRUE
ACCRUES > ACCRUE
ACCRUING > ACCRUE
ACCUMBENT *adj* (of plant parts and plants) lying against some other part or thing
ACCURACY *n* faithful representation of the truth
ACCURATE *adj* exact, correct
ACCURSE *vb* curse
ACCURSED *adj* under a curse
ACCURSES > ACCURSE
ACCURSING > ACCURSE
ACCURST *same as* > ACCURSED
ACCUSABLE > ACCUSE
ACCUSABLY > ACCUSE
ACCUSAL *n* accusation
ACCUSALS > ACCUSAL
ACCUSANT *n* person who accuses
ACCUSANTS > ACCUSANT
ACCUSE *vb* charge with wrongdoing
ACCUSED *n* person or people accused of a crime in a court
ACCUSER > ACCUSE
ACCUSERS > ACCUSE
ACCUSES > ACCUSE
ACCUSING > ACCUSE
ACCUSTOM *vb* make used to
ACCUSTOMS > ACCUSTOM
ACE *n* playing card with one symbol on it ▷ *adj* excellent ▷ *vb* serve an ace in racquet sports
ACED > ACE
ACEDIA *same as* > ACCIDIE
ACEDIAS > ACEDIA
ACELDAMA *n* place with ill feeling
ACELDAMAS > ACELDAMA
ACELLULAR *adj* not made up of or containing cells
ACENTRIC *adj* without a centre ▷ *n* acentric chromosome or fragment
ACEPHALIC *n* having no head or one that is reduced and indistinct, as certain insect larvae
ACEQUIA *n* irrigation ditch
ACEQUIAS > ACEQUIA
ACER *n* any tree or shrub of the genus *Acer*, often cultivated for their brightly coloured foliage
ACERATE *same as* > ACERATED
ACERATED *adj* having sharp points
ACERB *adj* bitter
ACERBATE *vb* embitter or exasperate
ACERBATED > ACERBATE
ACERBATES > ACERBATE
ACERBER > ACERB
ACERBEST > ACERB
ACERBIC *adj* harsh or bitter
ACERBITY *n* bitter speech or temper
ACEROLA *n* cherry-like fruit
ACEROLAS > ACEROLA
ACEROSE *adj* shaped like a needle, as pine leaves
ACEROUS *same as* > ACEROSE
ACERS > ACER
ACERVATE *adj* growing in heaps or clusters
ACERVULI > ACERVULUS
ACERVULUS *n* spore-producing part of plant
ACES > ACE
ACESCENCE > ACESCENT
ACESCENCY > ACESCENT
ACESCENT *adj* slightly sour or turning sour ▷ *n* something that is turning sour
ACESCENTS > ACESCENT
ACETA > ACETUM
ACETABULA *n* deep cuplike cavities on the side of the hipbones that receive the head of the thighbone
ACETAL *n* 1,1-diethoxyethane
ACETALS > ACETAL
ACETAMID *same as* > ACETAMIDE
ACETAMIDE *n* white or colourless soluble deliquescent crystalline compound
ACETAMIDS > ACETAMID
ACETATE *n* salt or ester of acetic acid
ACETATED *adj* combined with acetic acid
ACETATES > ACETATE
ACETIC *adj* of or involving vinegar
ACETIFIED > ACETIFY
ACETIFIER > ACETIFY
ACETIFIES > ACETIFY
ACETIFY *vb* become or cause to become acetic acid or vinegar
ACETIN *n* type of acetate
ACETINS > ACETIN
ACETONE *n* colourless liquid used as a solvent
ACETONES > ACETONE
ACETONIC > ACETONE
ACETOSE *same as* > ACETOUS
ACETOUS *adj* containing, producing, or resembling acetic acid or vinegar
ACETOXYL *n* medicine used to treat acne
ACETOXYLS > ACETOXYL
ACETUM *n* solution that has dilute acetic acid as solvent
ACETYL *n* of, consisting of, or containing the monovalent group CH_3CO-
ACETYLATE *vb* introduce an acetyl group into (a chemical compound)
ACETYLENE *n* colourless flammable gas used in welding metals
ACETYLIC > ACETYL
ACETYLIDE *n* any of a class of carbides in which the carbon is present as a diatomic divalent ion (C_2^{2-}). They are formally derivatives of acetylene
ACETYLS > ACETYL
ACH *interj* Scots expression of surprise
ACHAENIA > ACHAENIUM
ACHAENIUM *n* achene
ACHAGE *n* pain
ACHAGES > ACHAGE
ACHALASIA *n* failure of the cardiac sphincter of the oesophagus to relax, resulting in difficulty in

swallowing
ACHARNE *adj* furiously violent
ACHARYA *n* prominent religious teacher and spiritual guide
ACHARYAS > ACHARYA
ACHATES *same as* > ACATES
ACHE *n* dull continuous pain ▷ *vb* be in or cause continuous dull pain
ACHED > ACHE
ACHENE *n* dry one-seeded indehiscent fruit with the seed distinct from the fruit wall. It may be smooth, as in the buttercup, or feathery, as in clematis
ACHENES > ACHENE
ACHENIA > ACHENIUM
ACHENIAL > ACHENE
ACHENIUM *n* achene
ACHENIUMS > ACHENIUM
ACHES > ACHE
ACHIER > ACHY
ACHIEST > ACHY
ACHIEVE *vb* gain by hard work or ability
ACHIEVED > ACHIEVE
ACHIEVER > ACHIEVE
ACHIEVERS > ACHIEVE
ACHIEVES > ACHIEVE
ACHIEVING > ACHIEVE
ACHILLEA *n* any plant of the N temperate genus *Achillea*, with white, yellow, or purple flowers, some species of which are widely grown as garden plants: family *Asteraceae* (composites)
ACHILLEAS > ACHILLEA
ACHIMENES *n* any plant of the tropical S American tuberous-rooted perennial genus *Achimenes*, with showy red, blue, or white tubular flowers, some of which are grown as greenhouse plants: family *Gesneriaceae*
ACHINESS > ACHY
ACHING > ACHE
ACHINGLY > ACHE
ACHINGS > ACHE
ACHIOTE *n* annatto
ACHIOTES > ACHIOTE
ACHIRAL *adj* of a tuber producing arrowroot
ACHKAN *n* man's coat in India
ACHKANS > ACHKAN
ACHOLIA *n* condition involving lack of bile secretion
ACHOLIAS > ACHOLIA
ACHOO *interj* sound of a sneeze
ACHROMAT *n* lens designed to bring light of two chosen wavelengths to the same focal point, thus reducing chromatic aberration
ACHROMATS > ACHROMAT
ACHROMIC *adj* colourless
ACHROMOUS *same as* > ACHROMIC
ACHY *adj* affected by a continuous dull pain
ACICULA *n* needle-shaped part, such as a spine, prickle, or crystal
ACICULAE > ACICULA
ACICULAR > ACICULA
ACICULAS > ACICULA
ACICULATE *adj* having aciculae
ACICULUM *n* needle-like bristle that provides internal support for the appendages (chaetae) of some polychaete worms
ACICULUMS > ACICULUM
ACID *n* one of a class of compounds, corrosive and sour when dissolved in water, that combine with a base to form a salt ▷ *adj* containing acid
ACIDEMIA *n* abnormally high level of acid in blood
ACIDEMIAS > ACIDEMIA
ACIDER > ACID
ACIDEST > ACID
ACIDFREAK *n* person taking LSD regularly
ACIDHEAD *n* person who uses LSD
ACIDHEADS > ACIDHEAD
ACIDIC *adj* containing acid
ACIDIER > ACID
ACIDIEST > ACID
ACIDIFIED > ACIDIFY
ACIDIFIER > ACIDIFY
ACIDIFIES > ACIDIFY
ACIDIFY *vb* convert into acid
ACIDITIES > ACIDITY
ACIDITY *n* quality of being acid
ACIDLY > ACID
ACIDNESS > ACID
ACIDOPHIL *adj* (of cells or cell contents) easily stained by acid dyes ▷ *n* acidophil organism
ACIDOSES > ACIDOSIS
ACIDOSIS *n* condition characterized by an abnormal increase in the acidity of the blood and extracellular fluids
ACIDOTIC > ACIDOSIS
ACIDS > ACID
ACIDULATE *vb* make slightly acid or sour
ACIDULENT *same as* > ACIDULOUS
ACIDULOUS *adj* rather sour
ACIDURIA *n* abnormally high level of acid in urine
ACIDURIAS > ACIDURIA
ACIDY > ACID
ACIERAGE *n* iron-plating of metal
ACIERAGES > ACIERAGE
ACIERATE *vb* change (iron) into steel
ACIERATED > ACIERATE
ACIERATES > ACIERATE
ACIFORM *adj* shaped like a needle
ACINAR *adj* of small sacs
ACING > ACE
ACINI > ACINUS
ACINIC > ACINUS
ACINIFORM *adj* shaped like a bunch of grapes
ACINOSE > ACINUS
ACINOUS > ACINUS
ACINUS *n* any of the terminal saclike portions of a compound gland
ACKEE *n* sapindaceous tree, *Blighia sapida*, native to tropical Africa and cultivated in the Caribbean for its fruit, edible when cooked
ACKEES > ACKEE
ACKER *same as* > ACCA
ACKERS > ACKER
ACKNEW > ACKNOW
ACKNOW *vb* recognize
ACKNOWING > ACKNOW
ACKNOWN > ACKNOW
ACKNOWNE *adj* aware
ACKNOWS > ACKNOW
ACLINIC *adj* unbending
ACMATIC *adj* highest or ultimate
ACME *n* highest point of achievement or excellence
ACMES > ACME
ACMIC *same as* > ACMATIC
ACMITE *n* chemical with pyramid-shaped crystals
ACMITES > ACMITE
ACNE *n* pimply skin disease
ACNED *adj* marked by acne
ACNES > ACNE
ACNODAL > ACNODE
ACNODE *n* point whose coordinates satisfy the equation of a curve although it does not lie on the curve
ACNODES > ACNODE
ACOCK *adv* cocked
ACOELOUS *adj* not having a stomach
ACOEMETI *n* order of monks
ACOLD *adj* feeling cold
ACOLUTHIC *adj* of an afterimage
ACOLYTE *n* follower or attendant
ACOLYTES > ACOLYTE
ACOLYTH *n* acolyte
ACOLYTHS > ACOLYTH
ACONITE *n* poisonous plant with hoodlike flowers
ACONITES > ACONITE
ACONITIC > ACONITE
ACONITINE *n* poison made from aconite
ACONITUM *same as* > ACONITE
ACONITUMS > ACONITUM
ACORN *n* nut of the oak tree
ACORNED *adj* covered with acorns
ACORNS > ACORN
ACOSMISM *n* belief that no world exists outside the mind
ACOSMISMS > ACOSMISM
ACOSMIST > ACOSMISM
ACOSMISTS > ACOSMISM
ACOUCHI *n* any of several South American rodents of the genus *Myoprocta*, closely related to the agoutis but much smaller, with a white-tipped tail: family *Dasyproctidae*
ACOUCHIES > ACOUCHY
ACOUCHIS > ACOUCHI
ACOUCHY *same as* > ACOUCHI
ACOUSTIC *adj* of sound and hearing
ACOUSTICS *n* science of sounds
ACQUAINT *vb* make familiar, inform
ACQUAINTS > ACQUAINT
ACQUEST *n* something acquired
ACQUESTS > ACQUEST
ACQUIESCE *vb* agree to what someone wants
ACQUIGHT *vb* acquit
ACQUIGHTS > ACQUIGHT
ACQUIRAL > ACQUIRE
ACQUIRALS > ACQUIRE
ACQUIRE *vb* gain, get
ACQUIRED > ACQUIRE
ACQUIREE *n* one who acquires
ACQUIREES > ACQUIREE
ACQUIRER > ACQUIRE
ACQUIRERS > ACQUIRE
ACQUIRES > ACQUIRE
ACQUIRING > ACQUIRE
ACQUIST *n* acquisition
ACQUISTS > ACQUIST
ACQUIT *vb* pronounce (someone) innocent
ACQUITE *vb* acquit
ACQUITES > ACQUITE
ACQUITING > ACQUITE
ACQUITS > ACQUIT
ACQUITTAL *n* deliverance and release of a person appearing before a court on a charge of crime, as by a finding of not guilty
ACQUITTED > ACQUIT
ACQUITTER > ACQUIT
ACRASIA *n* lack of willpower
ACRASIAS > ACRASIA
ACRASIN *n* chemical produced by slime moulds
ACRASINS > ACRASIN
ACRATIC > ACRASIA
ACRAWL *adv* crawling
ACRE *n* measure of land, 4840 square yards (4046.86 square metres)
ACREAGE *n* land area in acres ▷ *adj* of or relating to a large allotment of land, esp in a rural area
ACREAGES > ACREAGE

ACRED *adj* having acres of land
ACRES > ACRE
ACRID *adj* pungent, bitter
ACRIDER > ACRID
ACRIDEST > ACRID
ACRIDIN *n* acridine
ACRIDINE *n* colourless crystalline solid
ACRIDINES > ACRIDINE
ACRIDINS > ACRIDIN
ACRIDITY > ACRID
ACRIDLY > ACRID
ACRIDNESS > ACRID
ACRIMONY *n* bitterness and resentment felt about something
ACRITARCH *n* type of fossil
ACRITICAL *adj* not critical
ACROBAT *n* person skilled in gymnastic feats requiring agility and balance
ACROBATIC > ACROBAT
ACROBATS > ACROBAT
ACRODONT *adj* (of the teeth of some reptiles) having no roots and being fused at the base to the margin of the jawbones ▷ *n* acrodont reptile
ACRODONTS > ACRODONT
ACRODROME *adj* (of the veins of a leaf) running parallel to the edges of the leaf and fusing at the tip
ACROGEN *n* any flowerless plant, such as a fern or moss, in which growth occurs from the tip of the main stem
ACROGENIC > ACROGEN
ACROGENS > ACROGEN
ACROLECT *n* most correct form of language
ACROLECTS > ACROLECT
ACROLEIN *n* colourless or yellowish flammable poisonous pungent liquid
ACROLEINS > ACROLEIN
ACROLITH *n* (esp in ancient Greek sculpture) a wooden, often draped figure with only the head, hands, and feet in stone
ACROLITHS > ACROLITH
ACROMIA > ACROMION
ACROMIAL > ACROMION
ACROMION *n* outermost edge of the spine of the shoulder blade
ACRONIC *adj* acronical
ACRONICAL *adj* occurring at sunset
ACRONYCAL *same as* > ACRONICAL
ACRONYM *n* word formed from the initial letters of other words, such as NASA
ACRONYMIC > ACRONYM
ACRONYMS > ACRONYM
ACROPETAL *adj* (of leaves and flowers) produced in order from the base upwards so that the youngest are at the apex
ACROPHOBE *n* person afraid of heights
ACROPHONY *n* use of symbols to represent sounds
ACROPOLIS *n* citadel of an ancient Greek city
ACROSOMAL > ACROSOME
ACROSOME *n* structure at the tip of a sperm cell
ACROSOMES > ACROSOME
ACROSPIRE *n* first shoot developing from the plumule of a germinating grain seed
ACROSS *adv* from side to side (of)
ACROSTIC *n* lines of writing in which the first or last letters of each line spell a word or saying
ACROSTICS > ACROSTIC
ACROTER *n* plinth bearing a statue, etc, at either end or at the apex of a pediment
ACROTERIA *n* acroters
ACROTERS > ACROTER
ACROTIC *adj* of a surface
ACROTISM *n* absence of pulse
ACROTISMS > ACROTISM
ACRYLATE *n* chemical compound in plastics and resins
ACRYLATES > ACRYLATE
ACRYLIC *adj* (synthetic fibre, paint, etc) made from acrylic acid ▷ *n* man-made fibre used for clothes and blankets
ACRYLICS > ACRYLIC
ACRYLYL *n* type of monovalent group
ACRYLYLS > ACRYLYL
ACT *n* thing done ▷ *vb* do something
ACTA *n* minutes of meeting
ACTABLE > ACT
ACTANT *n* (in valency grammar) a noun phrase functioning as the agent of the main verb of a sentence
ACTANTS > ACTANT
ACTED > ACT
ACTIN *n* protein that participates in many kinds of cell movement, including muscle contraction, during which it interacts with filaments of a second protein, myosin
ACTINAL *adj* of or denoting the oral part of a radiate animal, such as a jellyfish, sea anemone, or sponge, from which the rays, tentacles, or arms grow
ACTINALLY > ACTINAL
ACTING *n* art of an actor ▷ *adj* temporarily performing the duties of
ACTINGS > ACTING
ACTINIA *n* any sea anemone of the genus *Actinia*, which are common in rock pools
ACTINIAE > ACTINIA
ACTINIAN *n* sea-anemone
ACTINIANS > ACTINIAN
ACTINIAS > ACTINIA
ACTINIC *adj* (of radiation) producing a photochemical effect
ACTINIDE *n* member of the actinide series
ACTINIDES > ACTINIDE
ACTINISM > ACTINIC
ACTINISMS > ACTINIC
ACTINIUM *n* radioactive chemical element
ACTINIUMS > ACTINIUM
ACTINOID *adj* having a radiate form, as a sea anemone or starfish ▷ *n* member of the actinide series
ACTINOIDS > ACTINOID
ACTINON *same as* > ACTINIDE
ACTINONS > ACTINON
ACTINOPOD *n* any protozoan of the phylum *Actinopoda*, such as a radiolarian or a heliozoan, having stiff radiating cytoplasmic projections
ACTINS > ACTIN
ACTION *n* process of doing something ▷ *vb* put into effect
ACTIONED > ACTION
ACTIONER *n* film with a fast-moving plot, usually containing scenes of violence
ACTIONERS > ACTIONER
ACTIONING > ACTION
ACTIONIST *n* activist
ACTIONS > ACTION
ACTIVATE *vb* make active
ACTIVATED > ACTIVATE
ACTIVATES > ACTIVATE
ACTIVATOR > ACTIVATE
ACTIVE *adj* moving, working ▷ *n* active form of a verb
ACTIVELY > ACTIVE
ACTIVES > ACTIVE
ACTIVISE *same as* > ACTIVIZE
ACTIVISED > ACTIVISE
ACTIVISES > ACTIVISE
ACTIVISM *n* policy of taking direct and often militant action to achieve an end, esp a political or social one
ACTIVISMS > ACTIVISM
ACTIVIST > ACTIVISM
ACTIVISTS > ACTIVISM
ACTIVITY *n* state of being active
ACTIVIZE *vb* make active
ACTIVIZED > ACTIVIZE
ACTIVIZES > ACTIVIZE
ACTON *n* jacket or jerkin, originally of quilted cotton, worn under a coat of mail
ACTONS > ACTON
ACTOR *n* person who acts in a play, film, etc
ACTORISH > ACTOR
ACTORLY *adj* of or relating to an actor
ACTORS > ACTOR
ACTRESS *n* woman who acts in a play, film, broadcast, etc
ACTRESSES > ACTRESS
ACTRESSY *adj* exaggerated and affected in manner
ACTS > ACT
ACTUAL *adj* existing in reality
ACTUALISE *same as* > ACTUALIZE
ACTUALIST *n* person dealing in hard fact
ACTUALITE *n* humorous word for truth
ACTUALITY *n* reality
ACTUALIZE *vb* make actual or real
ACTUALLY *adv* really, indeed
ACTUALS *pl n* commercial commodities that can be bought and used
ACTUARIAL > ACTUARY
ACTUARIES > ACTUARY
ACTUARY *n* statistician who calculates insurance risks
ACTUATE *vb* start up (a device)
ACTUATED > ACTUATE
ACTUATES > ACTUATE
ACTUATING > ACTUATE
ACTUATION > ACTUATE
ACTUATOR > ACTUATE
ACTUATORS > ACTUATE
ACTURE *n* action
ACTURES > ACTURE
ACUATE *adj* sharply pointed
ACUITIES > ACUITY
ACUITY *n* keenness of vision or thought
ACULEATE *adj* cutting
ACULEATED *same as* > ACULEATE
ACULEI > ACULEUS
ACULEUS *n* prickle or spine, such as the thorn of a rose
ACUMEN *n* ability to make good judgments
ACUMENS > ACUMEN
ACUMINATE *adj* narrowing to a sharp point, as some types of leaf ▷ *vb* make pointed or sharp
ACUMINOUS > ACUMEN
ACUPOINT *n* any of the specific points on the body where a needle is inserted in acupuncture or pressure is applied in acupressure
ACUPOINTS > ACUPOINT
ACUSHLA *n* Irish endearment

ACUSHLAS > ACUSHLA
ACUTANCE *n* physical rather than subjective measure of the sharpness of a photographic image
ACUTANCES > ACUTANCE
ACUTE *adj* severe ▷ *n* accent (´) over a letter to indicate the quality or length of its sound, as in café
ACUTELY > ACUTE
ACUTENESS > ACUTE
ACUTER > ACUTE
ACUTES > ACUTE
ACUTEST > ACUTE
ACYCLIC *adj* not cyclic
ACYCLOVIR *n* drug used against herpes
ACYL *n* member of the monovalent group of atoms RCO-
ACYLATE *vb* introduce an acyl group into a compound
ACYLATED > ACYLATE
ACYLATES > ACYLATE
ACYLATING > ACYLATE
ACYLATION *n* introduction into a chemical compound of an acyl group
ACYLOIN *n* organic chemical compound
ACYLOINS > ACYLOIN
ACYLS > ACYL
AD *n* advertisement
ADAGE *n* wise saying, proverb
ADAGES > ADAGE
ADAGIAL > ADAGE
ADAGIO *adv* (piece to be played) slowly and gracefully ▷ *n* movement or piece to be performed slowly
ADAGIOS > ADAGIO
ADAMANCE *n* being adamant
ADAMANCES > ADAMANCE
ADAMANCY *n* being adamant
ADAMANT *adj* unshakable in determination or purpose ▷ *n* any extremely hard or apparently unbreakable substance
ADAMANTLY > ADAMANT
ADAMANTS > ADAMANT
ADAMSITE *n* yellow poisonous crystalline solid that readily sublimes
ADAMSITES > ADAMSITE
ADAPT *vb* alter for new use or new conditions
ADAPTABLE > ADAPT
ADAPTED > ADAPT
ADAPTER *same as* > ADAPTOR
ADAPTERS > ADAPTER
ADAPTING > ADAPT
ADAPTION *n* adaptation
ADAPTIONS > ADAPTION
ADAPTIVE > ADAPT
ADAPTOGEN *n* any of various natural substances used in herbal medicine to normalize and regulate the systems of the body
ADAPTOR *n* device for connecting several electrical appliances to a single socket
ADAPTORS > ADAPTOR
ADAPTS > ADAPT
ADAW *vb* subdue
ADAWED > ADAW
ADAWING > ADAW
ADAWS > ADAW
ADAXIAL *adj* facing towards the axis, as the surface of a leaf that faces the stem
ADAYS *adv* daily
ADD *vb* combine (numbers or quantities)
ADDABLE > ADD
ADDAX *n* large light-coloured antelope, *Addax nasomaculatus*, having ribbed loosely spiralled horns and inhabiting desert regions in N Africa: family *Bovidae*, order *Artiodactyla*
ADDAXES > ADDAX
ADDEBTED *adj* indebted
ADDED > ADD
ADDEDLY > ADD
ADDEEM *vb* adjudge
ADDEEMED > ADDEEM
ADDEEMING > ADDEEM
ADDEEMS > ADDEEM
ADDEND *n* any of a set of numbers that is to be added
ADDENDA > ADDENDUM
ADDENDS > ADDEND
ADDENDUM *n* addition
ADDENDUMS > ADDENDUM
ADDER *n* small poisonous snake
ADDERS > ADDER
ADDERWORT *n* plant of the dock family
ADDIBLE *adj* addable
ADDICT *n* person who is unable to stop taking drugs ▷ *vb* cause (someone or oneself) to become dependent (on something, esp a narcotic drug)
ADDICTED > ADDICT
ADDICTING > ADDICT
ADDICTION *n* condition of being abnormally dependent on some habit, esp compulsive dependency on narcotic drugs
ADDICTIVE *adj* causing addiction
ADDICTS > ADDICT
ADDIES > ADDY
ADDING *n* act or instance of addition ▷ *adj* of, for, or relating to addition
ADDIO *interj* farewell ▷ *n* cry of addio
ADDIOS > ADDIO
ADDITION *n* adding
ADDITIONS > ADDITION
ADDITIVE *n* something added, esp to a foodstuff, to improve it or prevent deterioration ▷ *adj* characterized or produced by addition
ADDITIVES > ADDITIVE
ADDITORY *adj* adding to something
ADDLE *vb* make or become confused or muddled ▷ *adj* indicating a confused or muddled state
ADDLED > ADDLE
ADDLEMENT > ADDLE
ADDLES > ADDLE
ADDLING > ADDLE
ADDOOM *vb* adjudge
ADDOOMED > ADDOOM
ADDOOMING > ADDOOM
ADDOOMS > ADDOOM
ADDORSED *adj* back to back
ADDRESS *n* place where a person lives ▷ *vb* mark the destination, as on an envelope
ADDRESSED > ADDRESS
ADDRESSEE *n* person addressed
ADDRESSER > ADDRESS
ADDRESSES > ADDRESS
ADDRESSOR > ADDRESS
ADDREST > ADDRESS
ADDS > ADD
ADDUCE *vb* mention something as evidence or proof
ADDUCED > ADDUCE
ADDUCENT > ADDUCE
ADDUCER > ADDUCE
ADDUCERS > ADDUCE
ADDUCES > ADDUCE
ADDUCIBLE > ADDUCE
ADDUCING > ADDUCE
ADDUCT *vb* (of a muscle) to draw or pull (a leg, arm, etc) towards the median axis of the body ▷ *n* compound formed by direct combination of two or more different compounds or elements
ADDUCTED > ADDUCT
ADDUCTING > ADDUCT
ADDUCTION > ADDUCT
ADDUCTIVE > ADDUCE
ADDUCTOR *n* muscle that adducts
ADDUCTORS > ADDUCTOR
ADDUCTS > ADDUCT
ADDY *n* e-mail address
ADEEM *vb* cancel
ADEEMED > ADEEM
ADEEMING > ADEEM
ADEEMS > ADEEM
ADEMPTION *n* failure of a specific legacy, as by a testator disposing of the subject matter in his lifetime
ADENINE *n* purine base present in tissues of all living organisms as a constituent of the nucleic acids DNA and RNA and of certain coenzymes
ADENINES > ADENINE
ADENITIS *n* inflammation of a gland or lymph node
ADENOID *adj* of or resembling a gland
ADENOIDAL *adj* having a nasal voice caused by swollen adenoids
ADENOIDS *pl n* tissue at the back of the throat
ADENOMA *n* tumour, usually benign, occurring in glandular tissue
ADENOMAS > ADENOMA
ADENOMATA > ADENOMA
ADENOSES > ADENOSIS
ADENOSINE *n* nucleoside formed by the condensation of adenine and ribose
ADENOSIS *n* disease of glands
ADENYL *n* enzyme
ADENYLIC as in *adenylic acid* nucleotide consisting of adenine, ribose or deoxyribose, and a phosphate group
ADENYLS > ADENYL
ADEPT *n* very skilful (person) ▷ *adj* proficient in something requiring skill
ADEPTER > ADEPT
ADEPTEST > ADEPT
ADEPTLY > ADEPT
ADEPTNESS > ADEPT
ADEPTS > ADEPT
ADEQUACY > ADEQUATE
ADEQUATE *adj* sufficient, enough
ADERMIN *n* vitamin
ADERMINS > ADERMIN
ADESPOTA *n* anonymous writings
ADESSIVE *n* grammatical case denoting place
ADESSIVES > ADESSIVE
ADHAN *n* call to prayer
ADHANS > ADHAN
ADHARMA *n* wickedness
ADHARMAS > ADHARMA
ADHERABLE > ADHERE
ADHERE *vb* stick (to)
ADHERED > ADHERE
ADHERENCE > ADHERE
ADHEREND *n* something attached by adhesive
ADHERENDS > ADHEREND
ADHERENT *n* devotee, follower ▷ *adj* sticking or attached
ADHERENTS > ADHERENT
ADHERER > ADHERE
ADHERERS > ADHERE
ADHERES > ADHERE
ADHERING > ADHERE
ADHESION *n* sticking (to)
ADHESIONS > ADHESION

ADHESIVE *n* substance used to stick things together ▷ *adj* able to stick to things
ADHESIVES > ADHESIVE
ADHIBIT *vb* administer or apply
ADHIBITED > ADHIBIT
ADHIBITS > ADHIBIT
ADHOCRACY *n* management that responds to urgent problems rather than planning to avoid them
ADIABATIC *adj* (of a thermodynamic process) taking place without loss or gain of heat ▷ *n* curve or surface on a graph representing the changes in two or more characteristics (such as pressure and volume) of a system undergoing an adiabatic process
ADIAPHORA *n* matters of indifference
ADIEU *n* goodbye
ADIEUS > ADIEU
ADIEUX > ADIEU
ADIOS *sentence substitute* Spanish for goodbye
ADIPIC as in *adipic acid* colourless crystalline solid used in the preparation of nylon
ADIPOCERE *n* waxlike fatty substance formed during the decomposition of corpses
ADIPOCYTE *n* fat cell that accumulates and stores fats
ADIPOSE *adj* of or containing fat ▷ *n* animal fat
ADIPOSES > ADIPOSIS
ADIPOSIS *n* obesity
ADIPOSITY > ADIPOSE
ADIPOUS *adj* made of fat
ADIPSIA *n* complete lack of thirst
ADIPSIAS > ADIPSIA
ADIT *n* almost horizontal shaft into a mine, for access or drainage
ADITS > ADIT
ADJACENCE > ADJACENT
ADJACENCY > ADJACENT
ADJACENT *adj* near or next (to) ▷ *n* side lying between a specified angle and a right angle in a right-angled triangle
ADJACENTS > ADJACENT
ADJECTIVE *n* word that adds information about a noun or pronoun ▷ *adj* additional or dependent
ADJIGO *n* yam plant, *Dioscorea hastifolia*, native to SW Australia that has edible tubers
ADJIGOS > ADJIGO
ADJOIN *vb* be next to
ADJOINED > ADJOIN
ADJOINING *adj* being in contact
ADJOINS > ADJOIN
ADJOINT *n* type of mathematical matrix
ADJOINTS > ADJOINT
ADJOURN *vb* close (a court) at the end of a session
ADJOURNED > ADJOURN
ADJOURNS > ADJOURN
ADJUDGE *vb* declare (to be)
ADJUDGED > ADJUDGE
ADJUDGES > ADJUDGE
ADJUDGING > ADJUDGE
ADJUNCT *n* something incidental added to something else
ADJUNCTLY > ADJUNCT
ADJUNCTS > ADJUNCT
ADJURE *vb* command (to do)
ADJURED > ADJURE
ADJURER > ADJURE
ADJURERS > ADJURE
ADJURES > ADJURE
ADJURING > ADJURE
ADJUROR > ADJURE
ADJURORS > ADJURE
ADJUST *vb* adapt to new conditions
ADJUSTED > ADJUST
ADJUSTER > ADJUST
ADJUSTERS > ADJUST
ADJUSTING > ADJUST
ADJUSTIVE > ADJUST
ADJUSTOR > ADJUST
ADJUSTORS > ADJUST
ADJUSTS > ADJUST
ADJUTAGE *n* nozzle
ADJUTAGES > ADJUTAGE
ADJUTANCY > ADJUTANT
ADJUTANT *n* army officer in charge of routine administration
ADJUTANTS > ADJUTANT
ADJUVANCY > ADJUVANT
ADJUVANT *adj* aiding or assisting ▷ *n* something that aids or assists
ADJUVANTS > ADJUVANT
ADLAND *n* advertising industry and the people who work in it
ADLANDS > ADLAND
ADMAN *n* man who works in advertising
ADMASS *n* mass advertising
ADMASSES > ADMASS
ADMEASURE *vb* measure out (land, etc) as a share
ADMEN > ADMAN
ADMIN *n* administration
ADMINICLE *n* something contributing to prove a point without itself being complete proof
ADMINS > ADMIN
ADMIRABLE *adj* deserving or inspiring admiration
ADMIRABLY > ADMIRABLE
ADMIRAL *n* highest naval rank
ADMIRALS > ADMIRAL
ADMIRALTY *n* office or jurisdiction of an admiral
ADMIRANCE *n* admiration
ADMIRE *vb* regard with esteem and approval
ADMIRED > ADMIRE
ADMIRER > ADMIRE
ADMIRERS > ADMIRE
ADMIRES > ADMIRE
ADMIRING > ADMIRE
ADMISSION *n* permission to enter
ADMISSIVE > ADMISSION
ADMIT *vb* confess, acknowledge
ADMITS > ADMIT
ADMITTED > ADMIT
ADMITTEE *n* one who admits
ADMITTEES > ADMITTEE
ADMITTER > ADMIT
ADMITTERS > ADMIT
ADMITTING > ADMIT
ADMIX *vb* mix or blend
ADMIXED > ADMIX
ADMIXES > ADMIX
ADMIXING > ADMIX
ADMIXT > ADMIX
ADMIXTURE *n* mixture
ADMONISH *vb* reprove sternly
ADMONITOR > ADMONISH
ADNASCENT *adj* growing with something else
ADNATE *adj* growing closely attached to an adjacent part or organ
ADNATION > ADNATE
ADNATIONS > ADNATE
ADNEXA *pl n* organs adjoining the uterus
ADNEXAL > ADNEXA
ADNOMINAL *n* word modifying a noun ▷ *adj* of or relating to an adnoun
ADNOUN *n* adjective used as a noun
ADNOUNS > ADNOUN
ADO *n* fuss, trouble
ADOBE *n* sun-dried brick
ADOBELIKE > ADOBE
ADOBES > ADOBE
ADOBO *n* Philippine dish
ADOBOS > ADOBO
ADONIS *n* beautiful young man
ADONISE *vb* adorn
ADONISED > ADONISE
ADONISES > ADONISE
ADONISING > ADONISE
ADONIZE *vb* adorn
ADONIZED > ADONIZE
ADONIZES > ADONIZE
ADONIZING > ADONIZE
ADOORS *adv* at the door
ADOPT *vb* take (someone else's child) as one's own
ADOPTABLE > ADOPT
ADOPTED *adj* having been adopted
ADOPTEE *n* one who has been adopted
ADOPTEES > ADOPTEE
ADOPTER *n* person who adopts
ADOPTERS > ADOPTER
ADOPTING > ADOPT
ADOPTION > ADOPT
ADOPTIONS > ADOPT
ADOPTIOUS *adj* adopted
ADOPTIVE *adj* related by adoption
ADOPTS > ADOPT
ADORABLE *adj* very attractive
ADORABLY > ADORABLE
ADORATION *n* deep love or esteem
ADORE *vb* love intensely
ADORED > ADORE
ADORER > ADORE
ADORERS > ADORE
ADORES > ADORE
ADORING > ADORE
ADORINGLY > ADORE
ADORN *vb* decorate, embellish
ADORNED > ADORN
ADORNER > ADORN
ADORNERS > ADORN
ADORNING > ADORN
ADORNMENT > ADORN
ADORNS > ADORN
ADOS > ADO
ADOWN *adv* down
ADOZE *adv* asleep
ADPRESS *vb* press together
ADPRESSED > ADPRESS
ADPRESSES > ADPRESS
ADRAD *adj* afraid
ADREAD *vb* dread
ADREADED > ADREAD
ADREADING > ADREAD
ADREADS > ADREAD
ADRED *adj* filled with dread
ADRENAL *adj* near the kidneys ▷ *n* adrenal gland
ADRENALIN *n* hormone secreted by the adrenal glands in response to stress
ADRENALLY > ADRENAL
ADRENALS > ADRENAL
ADRIFT *adv* drifting
ADROIT *adj* quick and skilful
ADROITER > ADROIT
ADROITEST > ADROIT
ADROITLY > ADROIT
ADRY *adj* dry
ADS > AD
ADSCRIPT *n* serf
ADSCRIPTS > ADSCRIPT
ADSORB *vb* (of a gas or vapour) condense and form a thin film on a surface
ADSORBATE *n* substance that has been or is to be adsorbed on a surface
ADSORBED > ADSORB
ADSORBENT *adj* capable of adsorption ▷ *n* material, such as activated charcoal, on which adsorption can occur
ADSORBER > ADSORB
ADSORBERS > ADSORB

ADSORBING > ADSORB
ADSORBS > ADSORB
ADSUKI *same as* > ADZUKI
ADSUKIS > ADSUKI
ADSUM *sentence substitute* I am present
ADUKI *same as* > ADZUKI
ADUKIS > ADUKI
ADULARIA *n* white or colourless glassy variety of orthoclase
ADULARIAS > ADULARIA
ADULATE *vb* flatter or praise obsequiously
ADULATED > ADULATE
ADULATES > ADULATE
ADULATING > ADULATE
ADULATION *n* uncritical admiration
ADULATOR > ADULATE
ADULATORS > ADULATE
ADULATORY *adj* expressing praise, esp obsequiously
ADULT *adj* fully grown, mature ▷ *n* adult person or animal
ADULTERER *n* person who has committed adultery
ADULTERESS *n* female adulterer
ADULTERY *n* sexual unfaithfulness of a husband or wife
ADULTESE *n* language spoken by adults
ADULTESES > ADULTESE
ADULTHOOD > ADULT
ADULTLIKE > ADULT
ADULTLY > ADULT
ADULTNESS > ADULT
ADULTS > ADULT
ADUMBRAL *adj* shadowy
ADUMBRATE *vb* outline
ADUNC *adj* hooked
ADUNCATE *adj* hooked
ADUNCATED *adj* hooked
ADUNCITY *n* quality of being hooked
ADUNCOUS *adj* hooked
ADUST *vb* dry up or darken by heat
ADUSTED > ADUST
ADUSTING > ADUST
ADUSTS > ADUST
ADVANCE *vb* go or bring forward ▷ *n* forward movement ▷ *adj* done or happening before an event
ADVANCED *adj* at a late stage in development
ADVANCER > ADVANCE
ADVANCERS > ADVANCE
ADVANCES > ADVANCE
ADVANCING > ADVANCE
ADVANTAGE *n* more favourable position or state
ADVECT *vb* move horizontally in air
ADVECTED > ADVECT
ADVECTING > ADVECT
ADVECTION *n* transferring of heat in a horizontal stream of gas
ADVECTIVE > ADVECTION
ADVECTS > ADVECT
ADVENE *vb* add as extra
ADVENED > ADVENE
ADVENES > ADVENE
ADVENING > ADVENE
ADVENT *n* arrival
ADVENTIVE *adj* (of a species) introduced to a new area and not yet established there ▷ *n* such a plant or animal
ADVENTS > ADVENT
ADVENTURE *n* exciting and risky undertaking or exploit ▷ *vb* take a risk or put at risk
ADVERB *n* word that adds information about a verb, adjective, or other adverb
ADVERBIAL *n* word or group of words playing the grammatical role of an adverb, such as *in the rain* in the sentence *I'm singing in the rain* ▷ *adj* of or relating to an adverb or adverbial
ADVERBS > ADVERB
ADVERSARY *n* opponent or enemy
ADVERSE *adj* unfavourable
ADVERSELY > ADVERSE
ADVERSER > ADVERSE
ADVERSEST > ADVERSE
ADVERSITY *n* very difficult or hard circumstances
ADVERT *n* advertisement ▷ *vb* draw attention (to)
ADVERTED > ADVERT
ADVERTENT *adj* heedful
ADVERTING > ADVERT
ADVERTISE *vb* present or praise (goods or services) to the public in order to encourage sales
ADVERTIZE *same as* > ADVERTISE
ADVERTS > ADVERT
ADVEW *vb* look at
ADVEWED > ADVEW
ADVEWING > ADVEW
ADVEWS > ADVEW
ADVICE *n* recommendation as to what to do
ADVICEFUL > ADVICE
ADVICES > ADVICE
ADVISABLE *adj* prudent, sensible
ADVISABLY > ADVISABLE
ADVISE *vb* offer advice to
ADVISED *adj* considered, thought-out
ADVISEDLY > ADVISED
ADVISEE *n* person receiving advice
ADVISEES > ADVISEE
ADVISER *n* person who offers advice, e.g. on careers to students or school pupils
ADVISERS > ADVISER
ADVISES > ADVISE
ADVISING > ADVISE
ADVISINGS > ADVISE
ADVISOR *same as* > ADVISER
ADVISORS > ADVISOR
ADVISORY *adj* giving advice ▷ *n* statement giving advice or a warning
ADVOCAAT *n* liqueur with a raw egg base
ADVOCAATS > ADVOCAAT
ADVOCACY *n* active support of a cause or course of action
ADVOCATE *vb* propose or recommend ▷ *n* person who publicly supports a cause
ADVOCATED > ADVOCATE
ADVOCATES > ADVOCATE
ADVOCATOR *n* person who advocates
ADVOUTRER *n* adulterer
ADVOUTRY *n* adultery
ADVOWSON *n* right of presentation to a vacant benefice
ADVOWSONS > ADVOWSON
ADWARD *vb* award
ADWARDED > ADWARD
ADWARDING > ADWARD
ADWARDS > ADWARD
ADWARE *n* type of computer software that collects information about a user's browsing patterns in order to display relevant advertisements in his or her Web browser
ADWARES > ADWARE
ADWOMAN *n* woman working in advertising
ADWOMEN > ADWOMAN
ADYNAMIA *n* loss of vital power or strength, esp as the result of illness
ADYNAMIAS > ADYNAMIA
ADYNAMIC > ADYNAMIA
ADYTA > ADYTUM
ADYTUM *n* most sacred place of worship in an ancient temple from which the laity was prohibited
ADZ *same as* > ADZE
ADZE *n* tool with an arched blade at right angles to the handle ▷ *vb* use an adze
ADZED > ADZE
ADZES > ADZE
ADZING > ADZE
ADZUKI *n* leguminous plant, *Phaseolus angularis*, that has yellow flowers and pods containing edible brown seeds and is widely cultivated as a food crop in China and Japan
ADZUKIS > ADZUKI
AE *determiner* one
AECIA > AECIUM
AECIAL > AECIUM
AECIDIA > AECIDIUM
AECIDIAL > AECIDIUM
AECIDIUM *same as* > AECIUM
AECIUM *n* globular or cup-shaped structure in some rust fungi in which aeciospores are produced
AEDES *n* any mosquito of the genus *Aedes* (formerly *Stegomyia*) of tropical and subtropical regions, esp *A. aegypti*, which transmits yellow fever and dengue
AEDICULE *n* opening such as a door or a window, framed by columns on either side, and a pediment above
AEDICULES > AEDICULE
AEDILE *n* magistrate of ancient Rome in charge of public works, games, buildings, and roads
AEDILES > AEDILE
AEDINE *adj* of a species of mosquito
AEFALD *adj* single
AEFAULD *adj* single
AEGIRINE *n* green mineral
AEGIRINES > AEGIRINE
AEGIRITE *n* green mineral
AEGIRITES > AEGIRITE
AEGIS *n* sponsorship, protection
AEGISES > AEGIS
AEGLOGUE *n* eclogue
AEGLOGUES > AEGLOGUE
AEGROTAT *n* (in British and certain other universities, and, sometimes, schools) a certificate allowing a candidate to pass an examination although he has missed all or part of it through illness
AEGROTATS > AEGROTAT
AEMULE *vb* emulate
AEMULED > AEMULE
AEMULES > AEMULE
AEMULING > AEMULE
AENEOUS *adj* brass-coloured or greenish-gold
AENEUS *n* aquarium fish
AEOLIAN *adj* of or relating to the wind
AEOLIPILE *n* device illustrating the reactive forces of a gas jet: usually a spherical vessel mounted so as to rotate and equipped with angled exit pipes from which steam within it escapes
AEOLIPYLE > AEOLIPILE
AEON *n* immeasurably long period of time
AEONIAN *adj* everlasting
AEONIC > AEON
AEONS > AEON
AEPYORNIS *n* any of the large extinct flightless birds of the genus *Aepyornis*, remains of which have been found in Madagascar
AEQUORIN *n* type of protein
AEQUORINS > AEQUORIN
AERATE *vb* put gas into (a

liquid), as when making a fizzy drink
AERATED > AERATE
AERATES > AERATE
AERATING > AERATE
AERATION > AERATE
AERATIONS > AERATE
AERATOR > AERATE
AERATORS > AERATE
AERIAL *adj* in, from, or operating in the air ▷ *n* metal pole, wire, etc, for receiving or transmitting radio or TV signals
AERIALIST *n* trapeze artist or tightrope walker
AERIALITY > AERIAL
AERIALLY > AERIAL
AERIALS > AERIAL
AERIE *a variant spelling (esp US) of* > EYRIE
AERIED *adj* in a very high place
AERIER > AERY
AERIES > AERIE
AERIEST > AERY
AERIFIED > AERIFY
AERIFIES > AERIFY
AERIFORM *adj* having the form of air
AERIFY *vb* change or cause to change into a gas
AERIFYING > AERIFY
AERILY > AERY
AERO *n* of or relating to aircraft or aeronautics
AEROBAT *n* person who does stunt flying
AEROBATIC *adj* pertaining to stunt flying
AEROBATS > AEROBAT
AEROBE *n* organism that requires oxygen to survive
AEROBES > AEROBE
AEROBIA > AEROBIUM
AEROBIC *adj* designed for or relating to aerobics
AEROBICS *n* exercises designed to increase the amount of oxygen in the blood
AEROBIONT *n* organism needing oxygen to live
AEROBIUM *same as* > AEROBE
AEROBOMB *n* bomb dropped from aircraft
AEROBOMBS > AEROBOMB
AEROBRAKE *vb* use airbrakes to slow aircraft
AEROBUS *n* type of monorail
AEROBUSES > AEROBUS
AERODART *n* metal arrow dropped from an aircraft as a weapon
AERODARTS > AERODART
AERODROME *n* small airport
AERODUCT *n* air duct
AERODUCTS > AERODUCT
AERODYNE *n* any heavier-than-air machine, such as an aircraft, that derives the greater part of its lift from aerodynamic forces
AERODYNES > AERODYNE
AEROFOIL *n* part of an aircraft, such as the wing, designed to give lift
AEROFOILS > AEROFOIL
AEROGEL *n* colloid that has a continuous solid phase containing dispersed gas
AEROGELS > AEROGEL
AEROGRAM *n* airmail letter on a single sheet of paper that seals to form an envelope
AEROGRAMS > AEROGRAM
AEROGRAPH *n* airborne instrument recording meteorological conditions
AEROLITE *n* stony meteorite consisting of silicate minerals
AEROLITES > AEROLITE
AEROLITH *n* meteorite
AEROLITHS > AEROLITH
AEROLITIC > AEROLITE
AEROLOGIC > AEROLOGY
AEROLOGY *n* study of the atmosphere, particularly its upper layers
AEROMANCY *n* using weather observation to foretell the future
AEROMETER *n* instrument for determining the mass or density of a gas, esp air
AEROMETRY *n* branch of physics concerned with the mechanical properties of gases, esp air
AEROMOTOR *n* aircraft engine
AERONAUT *n* person who flies in a lighter-than-air craft, esp the pilot or navigator
AERONAUTS > AERONAUT
AERONOMER *n* scientist studying atmosphere
AERONOMIC > AERONOMY
AERONOMY *n* science of the earth's upper atmosphere
AEROPAUSE *n* region of the upper atmosphere above which aircraft cannot fly
AEROPHAGY *n* spasmodic swallowing of air
AEROPHOBE *n* person suffering from aerophobia
AEROPHONE *n* wind instrument
AEROPHORE *n* device for playing a wind instrument
AEROPHYTE *another name for* > EPIPHYTE
AEROPLANE *n* powered flying vehicle with fixed wings
AEROPULSE *n* type of jet engine
AEROS > AERO
AEROSAT *n* communications satellite
AEROSATS > AEROSAT
AEROSCOPE *n* device for observing the atmosphere
AEROSHELL *n* parachute used to slow spacecraft
AEROSOL *n* pressurized can from which a substance can be dispensed as a fine spray
AEROSOLS > AEROSOL
AEROSPACE *n* earth's atmosphere and space beyond ▷ *adj* of rockets or space vehicles
AEROSTAT *n* lighter-than-air craft, such as a balloon
AEROSTATS > AEROSTAT
AEROTAXES > AEROTAXIS
AEROTAXIS *n* movement away from or towards oxygen
AEROTONE *n* bath incorporating air jets for massage
AEROTONES > AEROTONE
AEROTRAIN *n* train driven by a jet engine
AERUGO *(esp of old bronze) another name for* > VERDIGRIS
AERUGOS > AERUGO
AERY *adj* lofty, insubstantial, or visionary
AESC *n* rune
AESCES > AESC
AESCULIN *n* chemical in horse-chestnut bark
AESCULINS > AESCULIN
AESIR *n* chief of the Norse gods
AESTHESES > AESTHESIS
AESTHESIA *n* normal ability to experience sensation, perception, or sensitivity
AESTHESIS *variant of* > ESTHESIS
AESTHETE *n* person who has or affects an extravagant love of art
AESTHETES > AESTHETE
AESTHETIC *adj* relating to the appreciation of art and beauty ▷ *n* principle or set of principles relating to the appreciation of art and beauty
AESTIVAL *adj* of or occurring in summer
AESTIVATE *vb* pass the summer
AETHER *same as* > ETHER
AETHEREAL *a variant spelling of* > ETHEREAL
AETHERIC > AETHER
AETHERS > AETHER
AETIOLOGY *n* philosophy or study of causation
AFALD *adj* single
AFAR *adv* at, from, or to a great distance ▷ *n* great distance
AFARA *n* African tree
AFARAS > AFARA
AFARS > AFAR
AFAWLD *adj* single
AFEAR *vb* frighten
AFEARD *an archaic or dialect word for* > AFRAID
AFEARED *same as* > AFEARD
AFEARING > AFEAR
AFEARS > AFEAR
AFEBRILE *adj* without fever
AFF *adv* off
AFFABLE *adj* friendly and easy to talk to
AFFABLY > AFFABLE
AFFAIR *n* event or happening
AFFAIRE *n* love affair
AFFAIRES > AFFAIRE
AFFAIRS *pl n* personal or business interests
AFFEAR *vb* frighten
AFFEARD > AFFEAR
AFFEARE *vb* frighten
AFFEARED > AFFEAR
AFFEARES > AFFEARE
AFFEARING > AFFEAR
AFFEARS > AFFEAR
AFFECT *vb* act on, influence ▷ *n* emotion associated with an idea or set of ideas
AFFECTED *adj* displaying affectation
AFFECTER > AFFECT
AFFECTERS > AFFECT
AFFECTING *adj* arousing feelings of pity
AFFECTION *n* fondness or love
AFFECTIVE *adj* relating to affects
AFFECTS > AFFECT
AFFEER *vb* assess
AFFEERED > AFFEER
AFFEERING > AFFEER
AFFEERS > AFFEER
AFFERENT *adj* bringing or directing inwards to a part or an organ of the body, esp towards the brain or spinal cord ▷ *n* nerve that conveys impulses towards an organ of the body
AFFERENTS > AFFERENT
AFFIANCE *vb* bind (a person or oneself) in a promise of marriage ▷ *n* solemn pledge, esp a marriage contract
AFFIANCED > AFFIANCE
AFFIANCES > AFFIANCE
AFFIANT *n* person who makes an affidavit
AFFIANTS > AFFIANT
AFFICHE *n* poster or advertisement, esp one drawn by an artist, as for the opening of an exhibition
AFFICHES > AFFICHE
AFFIDAVIT *n* written statement made on oath
AFFIED > AFFY
AFFIES > AFFY
AFFILIATE *vb* (of a group) link up with a larger group ▷ *n* person or organization that is affiliated with

another
AFFINAL > AFFINE
AFFINE *adj* of, characterizing, or involving transformations which preserve collinearity, esp in classical geometry, those of translation, rotation and reflection in an axis ▷ *n* relation by marriage
AFFINED *adj* closely related
AFFINELY > AFFINE
AFFINES > AFFINE
AFFINITY *n* close connection or liking
AFFIRM *vb* declare to be true
AFFIRMANT > AFFIRM
AFFIRMED > AFFIRM
AFFIRMER > AFFIRM
AFFIRMERS > AFFIRM
AFFIRMING > AFFIRM
AFFIRMS > AFFIRM
AFFIX *vb* attach or fasten ▷ *n* word or syllable added to a word to change its meaning
AFFIXABLE > AFFIRM
AFFIXAL > AFFIX
AFFIXED > AFFIX
AFFIXER > AFFIX
AFFIXERS > AFFIX
AFFIXES > AFFIX
AFFIXIAL > AFFIX
AFFIXING > AFFIX
AFFIXMENT > AFFIX
AFFIXTURE > AFFIX
AFFLATED *adj* inspired
AFFLATION *n* inspiration
AFFLATUS *n* impulse of creative power or inspiration, esp in poetry, considered to be of divine origin
AFFLICT *vb* give pain or grief to
AFFLICTED > AFFLICT
AFFLICTER *n* one who afflicts
AFFLICTS > AFFLICT
AFFLUENCE *n* wealth
AFFLUENCY *n* affluence
AFFLUENT *adj* having plenty of money ▷ *n* tributary stream
AFFLUENTS > AFFLUENT
AFFLUENZA *n* guilt or lack of motivation experienced by people who have made or inherited large amounts of money
AFFLUX *n* flowing towards a point
AFFLUXES > AFFLUX
AFFLUXION *n* flow towards something
AFFOORD *vb* consent
AFFOORDED > AFFOORD
AFFOORDS > AFFOORD
AFFORCE *vb* strengthen
AFFORCED > AFFORCE
AFFORCES > AFFORCE
AFFORCING > AFFORCE
AFFORD *vb* have enough money to buy
AFFORDED > AFFORD
AFFORDING > AFFORD
AFFORDS > AFFORD
AFFOREST *vb* plant trees on
AFFORESTS > AFFOREST
AFFRAP *vb* strike
AFFRAPPED > AFFRAP
AFFRAPS > AFFRAP
AFFRAY *n* noisy fight, brawl ▷ *vb* frighten
AFFRAYED > AFFRAY
AFFRAYER > AFFRAY
AFFRAYERS > AFFRAY
AFFRAYING > AFFRAY
AFFRAYS > AFFRAY
AFFRENDED *adj* brought back into friendship
AFFRET *n* furious attack
AFFRETS > AFFRET
AFFRICATE *n* composite speech sound consisting of a stop and a fricative articulated at the same point, such as the sound written *ch*, as in *chair*.
AFFRIGHT *vb* frighten ▷ *n* sudden terror
AFFRIGHTS > AFFRIGHT
AFFRONT *n* insult ▷ *vb* hurt someone's pride or dignity
AFFRONTE *adj* facing
AFFRONTED > AFFRONT
AFFRONTEE *adj* facing
AFFRONTS > AFFRONT
AFFUSION *n* baptizing of a person by pouring water onto his head
AFFUSIONS > AFFUSION
AFFY *vb* trust
AFFYDE > AFFY
AFFYING > AFFY
AFGHAN *n* type of biscuit
AFGHANI *n* standard monetary unit of Afghanistan, divided into 100 puli
AFGHANIS > AFGHANI
AFGHANS > AFGHAN
AFIELD *adj* away from one's usual surroundings or home
AFIRE *adj* on fire
AFLAJ *n* Arabian irrigation channel
AFLAME *adj* burning
AFLATOXIN *n* toxin produced by the fungus *Aspergillus flavus* growing on peanuts, maize, etc, causing liver disease (esp cancer) in man
AFLOAT *adj* floating ▷ *adv* floating
AFLUTTER *adv* in or into a nervous or excited state
AFOOT *adj* happening, in operation ▷ *adv* happening
AFORE *adv* before
AFOREHAND *adv* beforehand
AFORESAID *adj* referred to previously
AFORETIME *adv* formerly
AFOUL *adj* in or into a state of difficulty, confusion, or conflict (with)
AFRAID *adj* frightened
AFREET *n* powerful evil demon or giant monster
AFREETS > AFREET
AFRESH *adv* again, anew
AFRIT *same as* > AFREET
AFRITS > AFRIT
AFRO *n* bush-like frizzy hairstyle
AFRONT *adv* in front
AFROS > AFRO
AFT *adv* at or towards the rear of a ship or aircraft ▷ *adj* at or towards the rear of a ship or aircraft
AFTER *adv* at a later time
AFTERBODY *n* any discarded part that continues to trail a satellite, rocket, etc, in orbit
AFTERCARE *n* support given to a person discharged from a hospital or prison
AFTERCLAP *n* unexpected consequence
AFTERDAMP *n* poisonous gas formed after the explosion of firedamp in a coal mine
AFTERDECK *n* unprotected deck behind the bridge of a ship
AFTEREYE *vb* gaze at someone or something that has passed
AFTEREYED > AFTEREYE
AFTEREYES > AFTEREYE
AFTERGAME *n* second game that follows another
AFTERGLOW *n* glow left after a source of light has gone
AFTERHEAT *n* heat generated in a nuclear reactor after it has been shut down, produced by residual radioactivity in the fuel elements
AFTERINGS *n* last of the milk drawn in milking
AFTERLIFE *n* life after death
AFTERMATH *n* results of an event considered together
AFTERMOST *adj* closer or closest to the rear or (in a vessel) the stern
AFTERNOON *n* time between noon and evening
AFTERPAIN *n* pain that comes after a while
AFTERPEAK *n* space behind the aftermost bulkhead, often used for storage
AFTERS *n* sweet course of a meal
AFTERSHOW *n* party held after a public performance of a play or film
AFTERSUN *n* moisturizing lotion applied to the skin to soothe sunburn and avoid peeling
AFTERSUNS > AFTERSUN
AFTERTAX *adj* after tax has been paid
AFTERTIME *n* later period
AFTERWARD *adv* after an earlier event or time
AFTERWORD *n* epilogue or postscript in a book, etc
AFTMOST *adj* furthest towards rear
AFTOSA *n* foot-and-mouth disease
AFTOSAS > AFTOSA
AG *n* agriculture
AGA *n* title of respect, often used with the title of a senior position
AGACANT *adj* irritating
AGACANTE *adj* irritating
AGACERIE *n* coquetry
AGACERIES > AGACERIE
AGAIN *adv* once more
AGAINST *prep* in opposition or contrast to
AGALACTIA *n* absence or failure of secretion of milk
AGALLOCH *another name for* > EAGLEWOOD
AGALLOCHS > AGALLOCH
AGALWOOD *n* eaglewood
AGALWOODS > AGALWOOD
AGAMA *n* any small terrestrial lizard of the genus *Agama*, which inhabit warm regions of the Old World: family *Agamidae*
AGAMAS > AGAMA
AGAMETE *n* reproductive cell, such as the merozoite of some protozoans, that develops into a new form without fertilization
AGAMETES > AGAMETE
AGAMI *n* South American bird
AGAMIC *adj* asexual
AGAMID *same as* > AGAMA
AGAMIDS > AGAMID
AGAMIS > AGAMI
AGAMOGONY *n* asexual reproduction in protozoans that is characterized by multiple fission
AGAMOID *n* lizard of the agamid type
AGAMOIDS > AGAMOID
AGAMONT *another name for* > SCHIZONT
AGAMONTS > AGAMONT
AGAMOUS *adj* without sex
AGAPAE > AGAPE
AGAPAI > AGAPE
AGAPE *adj* (of the mouth) wide open ▷ *n* love feast among the early Christians
AGAPEIC > AGAPE
AGAPES > AGAPE

AGAR *n* jelly-like substance obtained from seaweed and used as a thickener in food
AGARIC *n* fungus with gills on the underside of the cap, such as a mushroom
AGARICS > AGARIC
AGAROSE *n* gel used in chemistry
AGAROSES > AGAROSE
AGARS > AGAR
AGAS > AGA
AGAST *adj* aghast
AGATE *n* semiprecious form of quartz with striped colouring ▷ *adv* on the way
AGATES > AGATE
AGATEWARE *n* ceramic ware made to resemble agate or marble
AGATISE *same as* > AGATIZE
AGATISED > AGATISE
AGATISES > AGATISE
AGATISING > AGATISE
AGATIZE *vb* turn into agate
AGATIZED > AGATIZE
AGATIZES > AGATIZE
AGATIZING > AGATIZE
AGATOID *adj* like agate
AGAVE *n* tropical American plant with tall flower stalks and thick leaves
AGAVES > AGAVE
AGAZE *adj* gazing at something
AGAZED *adj* amazed
AGE *n* length of time a person or thing has existed ▷ *vb* make or grow old
AGED *adj* old
AGEDLY > AGED
AGEDNESS > AGED
AGEE *adj* awry, crooked, or ajar ▷ *adv* awry
AGEING *n* fact or process of growing old ▷ *adj* becoming or appearing older
AGEINGS > AGEING
AGEISM *n* discrimination against people on the grounds of age
AGEISMS > AGEISM
AGEIST > AGEISM
AGEISTS > AGEISM
AGELAST *n* someone who never laughs
AGELASTIC > AGELAST
AGELASTS > AGELAST
AGELESS *adj* apparently never growing old
AGELESSLY > AGELESS
AGELONG *adj* lasting for a very long time
AGEMATE *n* person the same age as another person
AGEMATES > AGEMATE
AGEN *archaic form of* > AGAIN
AGENCIES > AGENCY
AGENCY *n* organization providing a service
AGENDA *n* list of things to be dealt with, esp at a meeting
AGENDAS > AGENDA
AGENDUM > AGENDA
AGENDUMS *same as* > AGENDA
AGENE *n* chemical used to whiten flour
AGENES > AGENE
AGENESES > AGENESIS
AGENESIA *n* imperfect development
AGENESIAS > AGENESIA
AGENESIS *n* (of an animal or plant) imperfect development
AGENETIC > AGENESIS
AGENISE *same as* > AGENIZE
AGENISED > AGENISE
AGENISES > AGENISE
AGENISING > AGENISE
AGENIZE *vb* whiten using agene
AGENIZED > AGENIZE
AGENIZES > AGENIZE
AGENIZING > AGENIZE
AGENT *n* person acting on behalf of another ▷ *vb* act as an agent
AGENTED > AGENT
AGENTIAL > AGENT
AGENTING > AGENT
AGENTINGS > AGENT
AGENTIVAL *adj* of the performer of an action
AGENTIVE *adj* (in some inflected languages) denoting a case of nouns, etc, indicating the agent described by the verb ▷ *n* agentive case
AGENTIVES > AGENTIVE
AGENTRIES > AGENTRY
AGENTRY *n* acting as agent
AGENTS > AGENT
AGER *n* something that ages
AGERATUM *n* any tropical American plant of the genus *Ageratum*, such as *A. houstonianum* and *A. conyzoides*, which have thick clusters of purplish-blue flowers
AGERATUMS > AGERATUM
AGERS > AGER
AGES > AGE
AGEUSIA *n* lack of the sense of taste
AGEUSIAS > AGEUSIA
AGGADA *n* explanation in Jewish literature
AGGADAH *same as* > AGGADA
AGGADAHS > AGGADAH
AGGADAS > AGGADA
AGGADIC *adj* of aggada
AGGADOT > AGGADA
AGGADOTH > AGGADA
AGGER *n* earthwork or mound forming a rampart, esp in a Roman military camp
AGGERS *adj* aggressive
AGGIE *n* American agricultural student
AGGIES > AGGIE
AGGRACE *vb* add grace to
AGGRACED > AGGRACE
AGGRACES > AGGRACE
AGGRACING > AGGRACE
AGGRADE *vb* build up the level of (any land surface) by the deposition of sediment
AGGRADED > AGGRADE
AGGRADES > AGGRADE
AGGRADING > AGGRADE
AGGRATE *vb* gratify
AGGRATED > AGGRATE
AGGRATES > AGGRATE
AGGRATING > AGGRATE
AGGRAVATE *vb* make worse
AGGREGATE *n* total ▷ *adj* gathered into a mass ▷ *vb* combine into a whole
AGGRESS *vb* attack first or begin a quarrel
AGGRESSED > AGGRESS
AGGRESSES > AGGRESS
AGGRESSOR *n* person or body that engages in aggressive behaviour
AGGRI *adj* of African beads
AGGRIEVE *vb* grieve
AGGRIEVED *adj* upset and angry
AGGRIEVES > AGGRIEVE
AGGRO *n* aggressive behaviour
AGGROS > AGGRO
AGGRY *adj* of African beads
AGHA *same as* > AGA
AGHAS > AGHA
AGHAST *adj* overcome with amazement or horror
AGILA *n* eaglewood
AGILAS > AGILA
AGILE *adj* nimble, quick-moving
AGILELY > AGILE
AGILENESS > AGILE
AGILER > AGILE
AGILEST > AGILE
AGILITIES > AGILE
AGILITY > AGILE
AGIN *prep* against, opposed to
AGING *same as* > AGEING
AGINGS > AGING
AGINNER *n* someone who is against something
AGINNERS > AGINNER
AGIO *n* difference between the nominal and actual values of a currency
AGIOS > AGIO
AGIOTAGE *n* business of exchanging currencies
AGIOTAGES > AGIOTAGE
AGISM *same as* > AGEISM
AGISMS > AGISM
AGIST *vb* care for and feed (cattle or horses) for payment
AGISTED > AGIST
AGISTER *n* person who grazes cattle for money
AGISTERS > AGISTER
AGISTING > AGIST
AGISTMENT > AGEISM
AGISTOR *n* person who grazes cattle for money
AGISTORS > AGISTOR
AGISTS > AGIST
AGITA *n* acid indigestion
AGITABLE > AGITATE
AGITANS as in *paralysis agitans* Parkinson's disease
AGITAS > AGITA
AGITATE *vb* disturb or excite
AGITATED *adj* anxious or worried > AGITATE
AGITATES > AGITATE
AGITATING > AGITATE
AGITATION *n* state of excitement, disturbance, or worry
AGITATIVE > AGITATE
AGITATO *adv* (to be performed) in an agitated manner
AGITATOR *n* person who agitates for or against a cause, etc
AGITATORS > AGITATOR
AGITPOP *n* use of pop music to promote political propaganda
AGITPOPS > AGITPOP
AGITPROP *n* political agitation and propaganda
AGITPROPS > AGITPROP
AGLARE *adj* glaring
AGLEAM *adj* glowing
AGLEE *same as* > AGLEY
AGLET *n* metal sheath or tag at the end of a shoelace, ribbon, etc
AGLETS > AGLET
AGLEY *adj* awry
AGLIMMER *adj* glimmering
AGLITTER *adj* sparkling, glittering
AGLOO *same as* > AGLU
AGLOOS > AGLOO
AGLOSSAL > AGLOSSIA
AGLOSSATE > AGLOSSIA
AGLOSSIA *n* congenital absence of the tongue
AGLOSSIAS > AGLOSSIA
AGLOW *adj* glowing
AGLU *n* breathing hole made in ice by a seal
AGLUS > AGLU
AGLY *Scots word for* > WRONG
AGLYCON *n* chemical compound
AGLYCONE *n* chemical compound
AGLYCONES > AGLYCONE
AGLYCONS > AGLYCON
AGMA *n* symbol used to represent a velar nasal consonant
AGMAS > AGMA
AGMINATE *adj* gathered or clustered together
AGNAIL *another name for* > HANGNAIL
AGNAILS > AGNAIL

AGNAME *n* name additional to first name and surname
AGNAMED *adj* having an agname
AGNAMES > AGNAME
AGNATE *adj* related by descent from a common male ancestor ▷ *n* male or female descendant by male links from a common male ancestor
AGNATES > AGNATE
AGNATHAN *n* any jawless eel-like aquatic vertebrate of the superclass *Agnatha*, which includes the lampreys and hagfishes ▷ *adj* of, relating to, or belonging to the superclass *Agnatha*
AGNATHANS > AGNATHAN
AGNATHOUS *adj* (esp of lampreys and hagfishes) lacking jaws
AGNATIC > AGNATE
AGNATICAL > AGNATE
AGNATION > AGNATE
AGNATIONS > AGNATE
AGNISE *vb* acknowledge
AGNISED > AGNISE
AGNISES > AGNISE
AGNISING > AGNISE
AGNIZE *vb* acknowledge
AGNIZED > AGNIZE
AGNIZES > AGNIZE
AGNIZING > AGNIZE
AGNOMEN *n* fourth name or second cognomen occasionally acquired by an ancient Roman
AGNOMENS > AGNOMEN
AGNOMINA > AGNOMEN
AGNOMINAL > AGNOMEN
AGNOSIA *n* loss or diminution of the power to recognize familiar objects or people, usually as a result of brain damage
AGNOSIAS > AGNOSIA
AGNOSIC > AGNOSIA
AGNOSTIC *n* person who believes that it is impossible to know whether God exists ▷ *adj* of agnostics
AGNOSTICS > AGNOSTIC
AGO *adv* in the past
AGOG *adj* eager or curious
AGOGE *n* ancient Greek tempo
AGOGES > AGOGE
AGOGIC *n* musical accent
AGOGICS > AGOGIC
AGOING *adj* moving
AGON *n* (in ancient Greece) a festival at which competitors contended for prizes. Among the best known were the Olympic, Pythian, Nemean, and Isthmian Games
AGONAL *adj* of agony
AGONE *an archaic word for* > AGO
AGONES > AGON
AGONIC *adj* forming no angle
AGONIES > AGONY
AGONISE *same as* > AGONIZE
AGONISED > AGONISE
AGONISES > AGONISE
AGONISING > AGONISE
AGONIST *n* any muscle that is opposed in action by another muscle
AGONISTES *n* person suffering inner struggle
AGONISTIC *adj* striving for effect
AGONISTS > AGONIST
AGONIZE *vb* worry greatly
AGONIZED > AGONIZE
AGONIZES > AGONIZE
AGONIZING > AGONIZE
AGONS > AGON
AGONY *n* extreme physical or mental pain
AGOOD *adv* seriously or earnestly
AGORA *n* marketplace in Athens, used for popular meetings, or any similar place of assembly in ancient Greece
AGORAE > AGORA
AGORAS > AGORA
AGOROT > AGORA
AGOROTH *n* agorot
AGOUTA *n* Haitian rodent
AGOUTAS > AGOUTA
AGOUTI *n* any hystricomorph rodent of the genus *Dasyprocta*, of Central and South America and the Caribbean: family *Dasyproctidae*. Agoutis are agile and long-legged, with hooflike claws, and are valued for their meat
AGOUTIES > AGOUTI
AGOUTIS > AGOUTI
AGOUTY *n* agouti
AGRAFE *same as* > AGRAFFE
AGRAFES > AGRAFE
AGRAFFE *n* fastening consisting of a loop and hook, formerly used in armour and clothing
AGRAFFES > AGRAFFE
AGRAPHA > AGRAPHON
AGRAPHIA *n* loss of the ability to write, resulting from a brain lesion
AGRAPHIAS > AGRAPHIA
AGRAPHIC > AGRAPHIA
AGRAPHON *n* saying of Jesus not in Gospels
AGRARIAN *adj* of land or agriculture ▷ *n* person who favours the redistribution of landed property
AGRARIANS > AGRARIAN
AGRASTE > AGGRACE
AGRAVIC *adj* of zero gravity
AGREE *vb* be of the same opinion
AGREEABLE *adj* pleasant and enjoyable
AGREEABLY > AGREEABLE
AGREED *adj* determined by common consent
AGREEING > AGREE
AGREEMENT *n* agreeing
AGREES > AGREE
AGREGE *n* winner in examination for university teaching post
AGREGES > AGREGE
AGREMENS *n* amenities
AGREMENT *n* diplomatic approval of a country
AGREMENTS *n* amenities
AGRESTAL *adj* (of uncultivated plants such as weeds) growing on cultivated land
AGRESTIAL *adj* agrestal
AGRESTIC *adj* rural
AGRIA *n* appearance of pustules
AGRIAS > AGRIA
AGRIMONY *n* yellow-flowered plant with bitter-tasting fruits
AGRIN *adv* grinning
AGRIOLOGY *n* study of primitive peoples
AGRISE *vb* fill with fear
AGRISED > AGRISE
AGRISES > AGRISE
AGRISING > AGRISE
AGRIZE *vb* fill with fear
AGRIZED > AGRIZE
AGRIZES > AGRIZE
AGRIZING > AGRIZE
AGRODOLCE *n* Italian sweet-and-sour sauce
AGROLOGIC > AGROLOGY
AGROLOGY *n* scientific study of soils and their potential productivity
AGRONOMIC > AGRONOMY
AGRONOMY *n* science of soil management and crop production
AGROUND *adv* onto the bottom of shallow water ▷ *adj* on or onto the ground or bottom, as in shallow water
AGRYPNIA *n* inability to sleep
AGRYPNIAS > AGRYPNIA
AGRYZE *vb* fill with fear
AGRYZED > AGRYZE
AGRYZES > AGRYZE
AGRYZING > AGRYZE
AGS > AG
AGTERSKOT *n* final payment to a farmer for crops
AGUACATE *n* avocado
AGUACATES > AGUACATE
AGUE *n* periodic fever with shivering
AGUED *adj* suffering from fever
AGUELIKE > AGUE
AGUES > AGUE
AGUEWEED *n* North American gentianaceous plant, *Gentiana quinquefolia*, that has clusters of pale blue-violet or white flowers
AGUEWEEDS > AGUEWEED
AGUISE *vb* dress
AGUISED > AGUISE
AGUISES > AGUISE
AGUISH > AGUE
AGUISHLY > AGUE
AGUISING > AGUISE
AGUIZE *vb* dress
AGUIZED > AGUIZE
AGUIZES > AGUIZE
AGUIZING > AGUIZE
AGUTI *n* agouti
AGUTIS > AGUTI
AH *vb* say ah
AHA *interj* exclamation expressing triumph, surprise, etc, according to the intonation of the speaker
AHCHOO *interj* sound made by someone sneezing
AHEAD *adv* in front
AHEAP *adv* in a heap
AHED > AH
AHEIGHT *adv* at height
AHEM *interj* clearing of the throat in order to attract attention
AHEMERAL *adj* not constituting a full 24-hour day
AHENT *adv* behind
AHI *n* yellowfin tuna
AHIGH *adv* at height
AHIMSA *n* (in Hindu, Buddhist, and Jainist philosophy) the law of reverence for, and nonviolence to, every form of life
AHIMSAS > AHIMSA
AHIND *adv* behind
AHING > AH
AHINT *adv* behind
AHIS > AHI
AHISTORIC *adj* not related to history; not historical
AHOLD *n* holding
AHOLDS > AHOLD
AHORSE *adv* on horseback
AHOY *interj* hail used to call a ship
AHS > AH
AHULL *adv* with sails furled
AHUNGERED *adj* very hungry
AHUNGRY *adj* very hungry
AHURU *n* small pink cod, *Auchenoceros punctatus*, of SW Pacific waters
AHURUHURU *same as* > AHURU
AI *n* shaggy-coated slow-moving animal of South America
AIA *n* female servant in East
AIAS > AIA
AIBLINS *Scots word for* > PERHAPS
AID *n* (give) assistance

or support ▷ *vb* help financially or in other ways
AIDANCE *n* help
AIDANCES > AIDANCE
AIDANT *adj* helping
AIDE *n* assistant
AIDED > AID
AIDER > AID
AIDERS > AID
AIDES > AIDE
AIDFUL *adj* helpful
AIDING > AID
AIDLESS *adj* without help
AIDMAN *n* military medical assistant
AIDMEN > AIDMAN
AIDOI *adj* of the genitals
AIDOS *Greek word for* > SHAME
AIDS > AID
AIERIES > AIERY
AIERY *n* eyrie
AIGA *n* Māori word for family
AIGAS > AIGA
AIGLET *same as* > AGLET
AIGLETS > AIGLET
AIGRET *same as* > AIGRETTE
AIGRETS > AIGRET
AIGRETTE *n* long plume worn on hats or as a headdress, esp one of long egret feathers
AIGRETTES > AIGRETTE
AIGUILLE *n* rock mass or mountain peak shaped like a needle
AIGUILLES > AIGUILLE
AIKIDO *n* Japanese system of self-defence employing similar principles to judo, but including blows from the hands and feet
AIKIDOS > AIKIDO
AIKONA *interj* South African expression meaning no
AIL *vb* trouble, afflict
AILANTHIC > AILANTHUS
AILANTHUS *n* E Asian simaroubaceous deciduous tree, *Ailanthus altissima*, planted in Europe and North America, having pinnate leaves, small greenish flowers, and winged fruits
AILANTO *n* Asian tree
AILANTOS > AILANTO
AILED > AIL
AILERON *n* movable flap on an aircraft wing which controls rolling
AILERONS > AILERON
AILETTE *n* shoulder armour
AILETTES > AILETTE
AILING *adj* sickly
AILMENT *n* illness
AILMENTS > AILMENT
AILS > AIL
AIM *vb* point (a weapon or missile) or direct (a blow or remark) at a target ▷ *n* aiming
AIMED > AIM
AIMER > AIM
AIMERS > AIM
AIMFUL *adj* with purpose or intention
AIMFULLY > AIMFUL
AIMING > AIM
AIMLESS *adj* having no purpose
AIMLESSLY > AIMLESS
AIMS > AIM
AIN *variant of* > AYIN
AINE *adj* French word for elder (male)
AINEE *adj* French word for elder (female)
AINGA *n* Māori word for village
AINGAS > AINGA
AINS > AIN
AINSELL *n* Scots word meaning own self
AINSELLS > AINSELL
AIOLI *n* garlic mayonnaise
AIOLIS > AIOLI
AIR *n* mixture of gases forming the earth's atmosphere ▷ *vb* make known publicly
AIRBAG *n* safety device in a car, consisting of a bag that inflates automatically in an accident to protect the driver or passenger
AIRBAGS > AIRBAG
AIRBASE *n* centre from which military aircraft operate
AIRBASES > AIRBASE
AIRBOAT *n* shallow-draught boat powered by an aeroplane engine on a raised structure for use in swamps
AIRBOATS > AIRBOAT
AIRBORNE *adj* carried by air
AIRBOUND *adj* heading into the air
AIRBRICK *n* brick with holes in it, put into the wall of a building for ventilation
AIRBRICKS > AIRBRICK
AIRBRUSH *n* atomizer that sprays paint by compressed air ▷ *vb* paint using an airbrush
AIRBURST *n* explosion of a bomb, shell, etc, in the air
AIRBURSTS > AIRBURST
AIRBUS *n* commercial passenger aircraft
AIRBUSES > AIRBUS
AIRBUSSES > AIRBUS
AIRCHECK *n* recording of a radio broadcast
AIRCHECKS > AIRCHECK
AIRCOACH *n* bus travelling to and from an airport
AIRCRAFT *n* any machine that flies, such as an aeroplane
AIRCREW *n* crew of an aircraft
AIRCREWS > AIRCREW
AIRDATE *n* date of a programme broadcast
AIRDATES > AIRDATE
AIRDRAWN *adj* imaginary
AIRDROME *same as* > AERODROME
AIRDROMES > AIRDROME
AIRDROP *n* delivery of supplies, troops, etc, from an aircraft by parachute ▷ *vb* deliver (supplies, etc) by an airdrop
AIRDROPS > AIRDROP
AIRED > AIR
AIRER *n* device on which clothes are hung to dry
AIRERS > AIRER
AIREST > AIR
AIRFARE *n* money for an aircraft ticket
AIRFARES > AIRFARE
AIRFIELD *n* place where aircraft can land and take off
AIRFIELDS > AIRFIELD
AIRFLOW *n* flow of air in a wind tunnel or past a moving aircraft, car, train, etc
AIRFLOWS > AIRFLOW
AIRFOIL *same as* > AEROFOIL
AIRFOILS > AIRFOIL
AIRFRAME *n* body of an aircraft, excluding its engines
AIRFRAMES > AIRFRAME
AIRGAP *n* gap between parts in an electrical machine
AIRGAPS > AIRGAP
AIRGLOW *n* faint light from the upper atmosphere in the night sky, esp in low latitudes
AIRGLOWS > AIRGLOW
AIRGRAPH *n* photographic reduction of a letter for sending airmail
AIRGRAPHS > AIRGRAPH
AIRHEAD *n* person who is stupid or incapable of serious thought
AIRHEADED > AIRHEAD
AIRHEADS > AIRHEAD
AIRHOLE *n* hole that allows the passage of air
AIRHOLES > AIRHOLE
AIRIER > AIRY
AIRIEST > AIRY
AIRILY *adv* in a light-hearted and casual manner
AIRINESS *n* quality or condition of being fresh, light, or breezy
AIRING *n* exposure to air for drying or ventilation
AIRINGS > AIRING
AIRLESS *adj* stuffy
AIRLIFT *n* transport of troops or cargo by aircraft when other routes are blocked ▷ *vb* transport by airlift
AIRLIFTED > AIRLIFT
AIRLIFTS > AIRLIFT
AIRLIKE > AIR
AIRLINE *n* company providing scheduled flights for passengers and cargo
AIRLINER *n* large passenger aircraft
AIRLINERS > AIRLINER
AIRLINES > AIRLINE
AIRLOCK *n* air bubble blocking the flow of liquid in a pipe
AIRLOCKS > AIRLOCK
AIRMAIL *n* system of sending mail by aircraft ▷ *adj* of, used for, or concerned with airmail ▷ *vb* send by airmail
AIRMAILED > AIRMAIL
AIRMAILS > AIRMAIL
AIRMAN *n* member of the air force
AIRMEN > AIRMAN
AIRMOBILE *adj* using aircraft as transport
AIRN *Scots word for* > IRON
AIRNED > AIRN
AIRNING > AIRN
AIRNS > AIRN
AIRPARK *n* car park at airport
AIRPARKS > AIRPARK
AIRPLANE *same as* > AEROPLANE
AIRPLANES > AIRPLANE
AIRPLAY *n* broadcast performances of a record on radio
AIRPLAYS > AIRPLAY
AIRPORT *n* airfield for civilian aircraft, with facilities for aircraft maintenance and passengers
AIRPORTS > AIRPORT
AIRPOST *n* system of delivering mail by air
AIRPOSTS > AIRPOST
AIRPOWER *n* strength of a nation's air force
AIRPOWERS > AIRPOWER
AIRPROOF *vb* make something airtight
AIRPROOFS > AIRPROOF
AIRS *pl n* manners put on to impress people
AIRSCAPE *n* picture or view of sky
AIRSCAPES > AIRSCAPE
AIRSCREW *n* aircraft propeller
AIRSCREWS > AIRSCREW
AIRSHAFT *n* shaft for ventilation
AIRSHAFTS > AIRSHAFT
AIRSHED *n* air over a particular geographical area
AIRSHEDS > AIRSHED
AIRSHIP *n* lighter-than-air

self-propelled aircraft
AIRSHIPS > AIRSHIP
AIRSHOT *n* (in golf) shot that misses the ball completely, but counts as a stroke
AIRSHOTS > AIRSHOT
AIRSHOW *n* occasion when an air base is open to the public and a flying display and, usually, static exhibitions are held
AIRSHOWS > AIRSHOW
AIRSICK *adj* nauseated from travelling in an aircraft
AIRSIDE *n* part of an airport nearest the aircraft
AIRSIDES > AIRSIDE
AIRSPACE *n* atmosphere above a country, regarded as its territory
AIRSPACES > AIRSPACE
AIRSPEED *n* speed of an aircraft relative to the air in which it moves
AIRSPEEDS > AIRSPEED
AIRSTOP *n* helicopter landing-place
AIRSTOPS > AIRSTOP
AIRSTREAM *n* wind, esp at a high altitude
AIRSTRIKE *n* attack by military aircraft
AIRSTRIP *n* cleared area where aircraft can take off and land
AIRSTRIPS > AIRSTRIP
AIRT *n* direction or point of the compass, esp the direction of the wind ▷ *vb* direct
AIRTED > AIRT
AIRTH *same as* > AIRT
AIRTHED > AIRTH
AIRTHING > AIRTH
AIRTHS > AIRTH
AIRTIGHT *adj* sealed so that air cannot enter
AIRTIME *n* time allocated to a particular programme, topic, or type of material on radio or television
AIRTIMES > AIRTIME
AIRTING > AIRT
AIRTS > AIRT
AIRWARD *adj* into air
AIRWARDS *adv* into air
AIRWAVE *n* radio wave used in radio and television broadcasting
AIRWAVES > AIRWAVE
AIRWAY *n* air route used regularly by aircraft
AIRWAYS > AIRWAY
AIRWISE *adv* towards the air
AIRWOMAN > AIRMAN
AIRWOMEN > AIRMAN
AIRWORTHY *adj* (of aircraft) fit to fly
AIRY *adj* well-ventilated
AIS > AI
AISLE *n* passageway separating seating areas in a church, theatre, etc, or row of shelves in a supermarket
AISLED > AISLE
AISLELESS > AISLE
AISLES > AISLE
AISLEWAY *n* aisle
AISLEWAYS > AISLEWAY
AISLING *Irish word for* > DREAM
AISLINGS > AISLING
AIT *n* islet, esp in a river
AITCH *n* letter *h* or the sound represented by it
AITCHBONE *n* cut of beef from the rump bone
AITCHES > AITCH
AITS > AIT
AITU *n* half-human half-divine being
AITUS > AITU
AIVER *n* a working horse
AIVERS > AIVER
AIZLE *n* Scots word for hot ashes
AIZLES > AIZLE
AJAR *adv* (of a door) partly open ▷ *adj* not in harmony
AJEE *same as* > AGEE
AJIVA *n* Jainist term for non-living thing
AJIVAS > AJIVA
AJOWAN *n* plant related to caraway
AJOWANS > AJOWAN
AJUGA *n* garden plant
AJUGAS > AJUGA
AJUTAGE *n* nozzle
AJUTAGES > AJUTAGE
AJWAN *n* plant related to caraway
AJWANS > AJWAN
AKA *n* vine, *Metrosideros scandens*, found in New Zealand
AKARYOTE *n* cell without a nucleus
AKARYOTES > AKARYOTE
AKARYOTIC > AKARYOTE
AKATEA *n* vine with white flowers, *Metrosideros diffusa*, found in New Zealand
AKATHISIA *n* inability to sit still because of uncontrollable movement caused by reaction to drugs
AKE *vb* old spelling of ache
AKEAKE *n* New Zealand tree
AKEAKES > AKEAKE
AKED > AKE
AKEDAH *n* binding of Isaac in Bible
AKEDAHS > AKEDAH
AKEE *same as* > ACKEE
AKEES > AKEE
AKELA *n* adult leader of a pack of Cub Scouts
AKELAS > AKELA
AKENE *same as* > ACHENE
AKENES > AKENE
AKENIAL > ACHENE
AKES > AKE
AKHARA *n* (in India) gymnasium
AKHARAS > AKHARA
AKIMBO *adj* *with arms akimbo* with hands on hips and elbows projecting outwards
AKIN *adj* related by blood
AKINESES > AKINESIS
AKINESIA *n* loss of power to move
AKINESIAS > AKINESIA
AKINESIS *n* loss of power to move
AKINETIC > AKINESIA
AKING > AKE
AKIRAHO *n* small New Zealand shrub, *Olearia paniculata*, with white flowers
AKITA *n* large powerfully-built dog of a Japanese breed with erect ears, a typically white coat, and a large full tail carried curled over its back
AKITAS > AKITA
AKKAS *slang word for* > MONEY
AKOLUTHOS *n* leader of Byzantine Varangian Guard
AKRASIA *n* weakness of will
AKRASIAS > AKRASIA
AKRATIC > AKRASIA
AKVAVIT *same as* > AQUAVIT
AKVAVITS > AKVAVIT
AL *same as* > AAL
ALA *n* wing or flat winglike process or structure, such as a part of some bones and cartilages
ALAAP *n* part of raga in Indian music
ALAAPS > ALAAP
ALABAMINE *old name for* > ASTATINE
ALABASTER *n* soft white translucent stone ▷ *adj* of or resembling alabaster
ALACHLOR *n* type of herbicide
ALACHLORS > ALACHLOR
ALACK *archaic or poetic word for* > ALAS
ALACKADAY *same as* > ALACK
ALACRITY *n* speed, eagerness
ALAE > ALA
ALAIMENT *old spelling of* > ALLAYMENT
ALAIMENTS > ALAIMENT
ALALAGMOI > ALALAGMOS
ALALAGMOS *n* ancient Greek war cry
ALALIA *n* complete inability to speak
ALALIAS > ALALIA
ALAMEDA *n* public walk or promenade lined with trees, often poplars
ALAMEDAS > ALAMEDA
ALAMO *n* poplar tree
ALAMODE *n* soft light silk used for shawls and dresses, esp in the 19th century
ALAMODES > ALAMODE
ALAMORT *adj* exhausted and downcast
ALAMOS > ALAMO
ALAN *n* member of ancient European nomadic people
ALAND *vb* come onto land
ALANDS > ALAND
ALANE *Scots word for* > ALONE
ALANG *n* type of grass in Malaysia
ALANGS > ALANG
ALANIN *n* alanine
ALANINE *n* nonessential aliphatic amino acid that occurs in many proteins
ALANINES > ALANINE
ALANINS > ALANIN
ALANNAH *interj* my child: used as a term of address or endearment ▷ *n* cry of alannah
ALANNAHS > ALANNAH
ALANS > ALAN
ALANT *n* flowering plant used in herbal medicine
ALANTS > ALANT
ALANYL *n* chemical found in proteins
ALANYLS > ALANYL
ALAP *n* Indian vocal music without words
ALAPA *n* part of raga in Indian music
ALAPAS > ALAPA
ALAPS > ALAP
ALAR *adj* relating to, resembling, or having wings or alae
ALARM *n* sudden fear caused by awareness of danger ▷ *vb* fill with fear
ALARMABLE > ALARMABLE
ALARMED > ALARM
ALARMEDLY > ALARM
ALARMING > ALARM
ALARMISM > ALARMIST
ALARMISMS > ALARMIST
ALARMIST *n* person who alarms others needlessly ▷ *adj* causing needless alarm
ALARMISTS > ALARMIST
ALARMS > ALARM
ALARUM *n* alarm, esp a call to arms ▷ *vb* raise the alarm
ALARUMED > ALARUM
ALARUMING > ALARUM
ALARUMS > ALARUM
ALARY *adj* of, relating to, or shaped like wings
ALAS *adv* unfortunately, regrettably
ALASKA *n* dessert made of cake and ice cream

ALASKAS >ALASKA
ALASTOR *n* avenging demon
ALASTORS >ALASTOR
ALASTRIM *n* form of smallpox
ALASTRIMS >ALASTRIM
ALATE *adj* having wings or winglike extensions ▷ *n* winged insect
ALATED *adj* having wings
ALATES >ALATE
ALATION *n* state of having wings
ALATIONS >ALATION
ALAY *vb* allay
ALAYED >ALAY
ALAYING >ALAY
ALAYS >ALAY
ALB *n* long white robe worn by a Christian priest
ALBA *n* song of lament
ALBACORE *n* tuna found in warm seas, eaten for food
ALBACORES >ALBACORE
ALBARELLI >ALBARELLO
ALBARELLO *n* jar for drugs
ALBAS >ALBA
ALBATA *n* variety of German silver consisting of nickel, copper, and zinc
ALBATAS >ALBATA
ALBATROSS *n* large sea bird with very long wings
ALBE *old word for* >ALBEIT
ALBEDO *n* ratio of the intensity of light reflected from an object, such as a planet, to that of the light it receives from the sun
ALBEDOES >ALBEDO
ALBEDOS >ALBEDO
ALBEE *archaic form of* >ALBEIT
ALBEIT *conj* even though
ALBERGHI >ALBERGO
ALBERGO *n* Italian word for inn
ALBERT *n* kind of watch chain usually attached to a waistcoat
ALBERTITE *n* black solid variety of bitumen that has a conchoidal fracture and occurs in veins in oil-bearing strata
ALBERTS >ALBERT
ALBESCENT *adj* shading into, growing, or becoming white
ALBESPINE *old name for* >HAWTHORN
ALBESPYNE *old name for* >HAWTHORN
ALBICORE *n* species of tunny
ALBICORES >ALBICORE
ALBINAL >ALBINO
ALBINESS *n* female albino
ALBINIC >ALBINO
ALBINISM >ALBINO
ALBINISMS >ALBINO
ALBINO *n* person or animal with white skin and hair and pink eyes
ALBINOISM >ALBINO
ALBINOS >ALBINO
ALBINOTIC >ALBINO
ALBITE *n* colourless, milky-white, yellow, pink, green, or black mineral
ALBITES >ALBITE
ALBITIC >ALBITE
ALBITICAL >ALBITE
ALBITISE *vb* turn into albite
ALBITISED >ALBITISE
ALBITISES >ALBITISE
ALBITIZE *vb* turn into albite
ALBITIZED >ALBITIZE
ALBITIZES >ALBITIZE
ALBIZIA *n* mimosa
ALBIZIAS >ALBIZIA
ALBIZZIA *n* mimosa
ALBIZZIAS >ALBIZZIA
ALBRICIAS *interj* Spanish expression of welcome
ALBS >ALB
ALBUGO *n* opacity of the cornea
ALBUGOS >ALBUGO
ALBUM *n* book with blank pages for keeping photographs or stamps in
ALBUMEN *same as* >ALBUMIN *n* egg white
ALBUMENS >ALBUMEN
ALBUMIN *n* protein found in blood plasma, egg white, milk, and muscle
ALBUMINS >ALBUMIN
ALBUMOSE *the US name for* >PROTEOSE
ALBUMOSES >ALBUMOSE
ALBUMS >ALBUM
ALBURNOUS >ALBURNUM
ALBURNUM *former name for* >SAPWOOD
ALBURNUMS >ALBURNUM
ALBUTEROL *n* drug used to treat lung diseases
ALCADE *same as* >ALCALDE
ALCADES >ALCADE
ALCAHEST *same as* >ALKAHEST
ALCAHESTS >ALCAHEST
ALCAIC *n* verse consisting of strophes with four tetrametric lines
ALCAICS >ALCAIC
ALCAIDE *n* commander of a fortress or castle
ALCAIDES >ALCAIDE
ALCALDE *n* (in Spain and Spanish America) the mayor or chief magistrate in a town
ALCALDES >ALCALDE
ALCARRAZA *n* Spanish water container
ALCATRAS *n* pelican
ALCAYDE *n* alcaide
ALCAYDES >ALCAYDE
ALCAZAR *n* any of various palaces or fortresses built in Spain by the Moors
ALCAZARS >ALCAZAR
ALCHEMIC >ALCHEMY
ALCHEMIES >ALCHEMY
ALCHEMISE *same as* >ALCHEMIZE
ALCHEMIST *n* person who practises alchemy
ALCHEMIZE *vb* alter (an element, metal, etc) by alchemy
ALCHEMY *n* medieval form of chemistry concerned with trying to turn base metals into gold and to find the elixir of life
ALCHERA *n* (in the mythology of Australian Aboriginal peoples) mythical Golden Age of the past
ALCHERAS >ALCHERA
ALCHYMIES >ALCHYMY
ALCHYMY *old spelling of* >ALCHEMY
ALCID *n* bird of the auk family
ALCIDINE *adj* of, relating to, or belonging to the *Alcidae*, a family of sea birds including the auks, guillemots, puffins, and related forms
ALCIDS >ALCID
ALCO *same as* >ALKO
ALCOHOL *n* colourless flammable liquid present in intoxicating drinks
ALCOHOLIC *adj* of alcohol ▷ *n* person addicted to alcohol
ALCOHOLS >ALCOHOL
ALCOLOCK *n* breath-alcohol ignition-interlock device, which is fitted to the ignition in certain motor vehicles. The driver must blow into a tube and, if his or her breath contains too much alcohol, a lock is activated to prevent the vehicle starting
ALCOLOCKS >ALCOLOCK
ALCOOL *n* form of pure grain spirit distilled in Quebec
ALCOOLS >ALCOOL
ALCOPOP *n* alcoholic drink that tastes like a soft drink
ALCOPOPS >ALCOPOP
ALCORZA *n* Spanish sweet
ALCORZAS >ALCORZA
ALCOS >ALCO
ALCOVE *n* recess in the wall of a room
ALCOVED *adj* with or in an alcove
ALCOVES >ALCOVE
ALDEA *n* Spanish village
ALDEAS >ALDEA
ALDEHYDE *n* one of a group of chemical compounds derived from alcohol by oxidation
ALDEHYDES >ALDEHYDE
ALDEHYDIC >ALDEHYDE
ALDER *n* tree related to the birch
ALDERFLY *n* insect with large broad-based hind wings, which produces aquatic larvae
ALDERMAN *n* formerly, senior member of a local council
ALDERMEN >ALDERMAN
ALDERN *adj* made of alder wood
ALDERS >ALDER
ALDICARB *n* crystalline compound used as a pesticide
ALDICARBS >ALDICARB
ALDOL *n* colourless or yellowish oily liquid
ALDOLASE *n* enzyme present in the body
ALDOLASES >ALDOLASE
ALDOLS >ALDOL
ALDOSE *n* sugar that contains the aldehyde group or is a hemiacetal
ALDOSES >ALDOSE
ALDOXIME *n* oxime formed by reaction between hydroxylamine and an aldehyde
ALDOXIMES >ALDOXIME
ALDRIN *n* brown to white poisonous crystalline solid
ALDRINS >ALDRIN
ALE *n* kind of beer
ALEATORIC *same as* >ALEATORY
ALEATORY *adj* dependent on chance
ALEBENCH *n* bench at alehouse
ALEC *same as* >ALECK
ALECITHAL *adj* (of an ovum) having little or no yolk
ALECK *n* irritatingly oversmart person
ALECKS >ALECK
ALECOST *another name for* >COSTMARY
ALECOSTS >ALECOST
ALECS >ALEC
ALECTRYON *n* New Zealand tree
ALEE *adj* on or towards the lee
ALEF *n* first letter of Hebrew alphabet
ALEFS >ALEF
ALEFT *adv* at or to left
ALEGAR *n* malt vinegar
ALEGARS >ALEGAR
ALEGGE *vb* alleviate
ALEGGED >ALEGGE
ALEGGES >ALEGGE
ALEGGING >ALEGGE
ALEHOUSE *n* public house
ALEHOUSES >ALEHOUSE
ALEMBIC *n* anything that distils or purifies, esp an obsolete vessel used for distillation
ALEMBICS >ALEMBIC

ALEMBROTH *n* mercury compound in alchemy
ALENCON *n* elaborate lace worked on a hexagonal mesh
ALENCONS >ALENCON
ALENGTH *adv* at length
ALEPH *n* first letter in the Hebrew alphabet
ALEPHS >ALEPH
ALEPINE *n* type of cloth
ALEPINES >ALEPINE
ALERCE *n* wood of the sandarac tree
ALERCES >ALERCE
ALERION *n* eagle in heraldry
ALERIONS >ALERION
ALERT *adj* watchful, attentive ▷ *n* warning of danger ▷ *vb* warn of danger
ALERTED >ALERT
ALERTER >ALERT
ALERTEST >ALERT
ALERTING >ALERT
ALERTLY >ALERT
ALERTNESS >ALERT
ALERTS >ALERT
ALES >ALE
ALETHIC *adj* of or relating to such philosophical concepts as truth, necessity, possibility, contingency, etc
ALEURON *n* outer protein-rich layer of certain seeds, esp of cereal grains
ALEURONE *same as* >ALEURON
ALEURONES >ALEURONE
ALEURONIC >ALEURON
ALEURONS >ALEURON
ALEVIN *n* young fish, esp a young salmon or trout
ALEVINS >ALEVIN
ALEW *n* cry to call hunting hounds
ALEWASHED *adj* showing effects of beer drinking
ALEWIFE *n* North American fish
ALEWIVES >ALEWIFE
ALEWS >ALEW
ALEXANDER *n* cocktail made with creme de cacao
ALEXIA *n* disorder of the central nervous system characterized by impaired ability to read
ALEXIAS >ALEXIA
ALEXIC >ALEXIA
ALEXIN *n* complement
ALEXINE *same as* >ALEXIN
ALEXINES >ALEXINE
ALEXINIC >ALEXIN
ALEXINS >ALEXIN
ALEYE *vb* allay
ALEYED >ALEYE
ALEYES >ALEYE
ALEYING >ALEYE
ALF *n* uncultivated Australian
ALFA *n* type of grass
ALFAKI *n* expert in Muslim law
ALFAKIS >ALFAKI
ALFALFA *n* kind of plant used to feed livestock
ALFALFAS >ALFALFA
ALFAQUI *n* expert in Muslim law
ALFAQUIN *n* expert in Muslim law
ALFAQUINS >ALFAQUIN
ALFAQUIS >ALFAQUI
ALFAS >ALFA
ALFERECES >ALFEREZ
ALFEREZ *n* Spanish standard-bearer
ALFILARIA *n* plant with finely divided leaves and small pink or purplish flowers
ALFILERIA *same as* >ALFILARIA
ALFORJA *n* saddlebag made of leather or canvas
ALFORJAS >ALFORJA
ALFREDO *adj* cooked with a cheese and egg sauce
ALFRESCO *adj* in the open air ▷ *adv* in the open air
ALFS >ALF
ALGA *n* unicellular or multicellular organism formerly classified as a plant
ALGAE >ALGA
ALGAECIDE *n* substance for killing algae
ALGAL >ALGA
ALGAROBA *same as* >ALGARROBA
ALGAROBAS >ALGAROBA
ALGARROBA *n* edible pod of these trees
ALGARROBO *n* carob
ALGAS >ALGA
ALGATE *adv* anyway
ALGATES *adv* anyway
ALGEBRA *n* branch of mathematics using symbols to represent numbers
ALGEBRAIC *adj* of or relating to algebra
ALGEBRAS >ALGEBRA
ALGERINE *n* soft striped woollen cloth
ALGERINES >ALGERINE
ALGESES >ALGESIS
ALGESIA *n* capacity to feel pain
ALGESIAS >ALGESIA
ALGESIC >ALGESIA
ALGESIS *n* feeling of pain
ALGETIC >ALGESIA
ALGICIDAL >ALGICIDE
ALGICIDE *n* any substance that kills algae
ALGICIDES >ALGICIDE
ALGID *adj* chilly or cold
ALGIDITY >ALGID
ALGIDNESS >ALGID
ALGIN *n* gelatinous solution obtained as a by-product in the extraction of iodine from seaweed
ALGINATE *n* salt or ester of alginic acid
ALGINATES >ALGINATE
ALGINIC as in *alginic acid* powdery substance extracted from kelp
ALGINS >ALGIN
ALGOID *adj* resembling or relating to algae
ALGOLOGY *n* branch of biology concerned with the study of algae
ALGOMETER *n* instrument for measuring sensitivity to pressure or to pain
ALGOMETRY >ALGOMETER
ALGOR *n* chill
ALGORISM *n* Arabic or decimal system of counting
ALGORISMS >ALGORISM
ALGORITHM *n* logical arithmetical or computational procedure for solving a problem
ALGORS >ALGOR
ALGUACIL *n* Spanish law officer
ALGUACILS >ALGUACIL
ALGUAZIL *n* Spanish law officer
ALGUAZILS >ALGUAZIL
ALGUM *n* type of wood mentioned in Bible
ALGUMS >ALGUM
ALIAS *adv* also known as ▷ *n* false name
ALIASES >ALIAS
ALIASING *n* error in a vision or sound signal arising from limitations in the system that generates or processes the signal
ALIASINGS >ALIASING
ALIBI *n* plea of being somewhere else when a crime was committed ▷ *vb* provide someone with an alibi
ALIBIED >ALIBI
ALIBIES >ALIBI
ALIBIING >ALIBI
ALIBIS >ALIBI
ALIBLE *adj* nourishing
ALICANT *n* wine from Alicante in Spain
ALICANTS >ALICANT
ALICYCLIC *adj* (of an organic compound) having aliphatic properties, in spite of the presence of a ring of carbon atoms
ALIDAD *same as* >ALIDADE
ALIDADE *n* surveying instrument used in plane-tabling for drawing lines of sight on a distant object and taking angular measurements
ALIDADES >ALIDADE
ALIDADS >ALIDAD
ALIEN *adj* foreign ▷ *n* foreigner ▷ *vb* transfer (property, etc) to another
ALIENABLE *adj* able to be transferred to another owner
ALIENAGE >ALIEN
ALIENAGES >ALIEN
ALIENATE *vb* cause to become hostile
ALIENATED >ALIENATE
ALIENATES >ALIENATE
ALIENATOR >ALIENATE
ALIENED >ALIEN
ALIENEE *n* person to whom a transfer of property is made
ALIENEES >ALIENEE
ALIENER >ALIEN
ALIENERS >ALIEN
ALIENING >ALIEN
ALIENISM *n* study and treatment of mental illness
ALIENISMS >ALIENISM
ALIENIST *n* psychiatrist who specializes in the legal aspects of mental illness
ALIENISTS >ALIENIST
ALIENLY >ALIEN
ALIENNESS >ALIEN
ALIENOR *n* person who transfers property to another
ALIENORS >ALIENOR
ALIENS >ALIEN
ALIF *n* first letter of Arabic alphabet
ALIFORM *adj* wing-shaped
ALIFS >ALIF
ALIGARTA *n* alligator
ALIGARTAS >ALIGARTA
ALIGHT *vb* step out of (a vehicle) ▷ *adj* on fire ▷ *adv* on fire
ALIGHTED >ALIGHT
ALIGHTING >ALIGHT
ALIGHTS >ALIGHT
ALIGN *vb* bring (a person or group) into agreement with the policy of another
ALIGNED >ALIGN
ALIGNER >ALIGN
ALIGNERS >ALIGN
ALIGNING >ALIGN
ALIGNMENT *n* arrangement in a straight line
ALIGNS >ALIGN
ALIKE *adj* like, similar ▷ *adv* in the same way
ALIKENESS >ALIKE
ALIMENT *n* something that nourishes or sustains the body or mind ▷ *vb* support or sustain
ALIMENTAL >ALIMENT
ALIMENTED >ALIMENT
ALIMENTS >ALIMENT
ALIMONIED *adj* provided with alimony
ALIMONIES >ALIMONY
ALIMONY *n* allowance paid under a court order to a separated or divorced

spouse
ALINE *a rare spelling of* >ALIGN
ALINED >ALINE
ALINEMENT >ALINE
ALINER >ALINE
ALINERS >ALINE
ALINES >ALINE
ALINING >ALINE
ALIPED *n* animal, like the bat, whose toes are joined by a membrane that serves as a wing ▷ *adj* (of bats and similar animals) having the digits connected by a winglike membrane
ALIPEDS >ALIPED
ALIPHATIC *adj* (of an organic compound) having an open chain structure
ALIQUANT *adj* denoting or belonging to a number that is not an exact divisor of a given number
ALIQUOT *adj* of or denoting an exact divisor of a number ▷ *n* exact divisor
ALIQUOTS >ALIQUOT
ALISMA *n* marsh plant
ALISMAS >ALISMA
ALISON *same as* >ALYSSUM
ALISONS >ALISON
ALIST *adj* leaning over
ALIT *rare past tense and past participle of* >ALIGHT
ALITERACY >ALITERATE
ALITERATE *n* person who is able to read but disinclined to do so ▷ *adj* of or relating to aliterates
ALIUNDE *adj* from a source extrinsic to the matter, document, or instrument under consideration
ALIVE *adj* living, in existence
ALIVENESS >ALIVE
ALIYA *n* immigration to Holy Land
ALIYAH *n* immigration to the Holy Land
ALIYAHS >ALIYAH
ALIYAS >ALIYA
ALIYOS *n* remission of sin in Jewish faith
ALIYOT >ALIYAH
ALIYOTH >ALIYAH
ALIZARI *n* madder from Middle East
ALIZARIN *n* brownish-yellow powder or orange-red crystalline solid
ALIZARINE *n* alizarin
ALIZARINS >ALIZARIN
ALIZARIS >ALIZARI
ALKAHEST *n* hypothetical universal solvent sought by alchemists
ALKAHESTS >ALKAHEST
ALKALI *n* substance which combines with acid and neutralizes it to form a salt
ALKALIC *adj* (of igneous rocks) containing large amounts of alkalis, esp sodium and potassium
ALKALIES >ALKALI
ALKALIFY *vb* make or become alkaline
ALKALIN *adj* leaning over
ALKALINE *adj* having the properties of or containing an alkali
ALKALIS >ALKALI
ALKALISE *same as* >ALKALIZE
ALKALISED >ALKALISE
ALKALISER >ALKALISE
ALKALISES >ALKALISE
ALKALIZE *vb* make alkaline
ALKALIZED >ALKALIZE
ALKALIZER >ALKALIZE
ALKALIZES >ALKALIZE
ALKALOID *n* any of a group of organic compounds containing nitrogen
ALKALOIDS >ALKALOID
ALKALOSES >ALKALOSIS
ALKALOSIS *n* abnormal increase in the alkalinity of the blood and extracellular fluids
ALKALOTIC >ALKALOSIS
ALKANE *n* any saturated hydrocarbon with the general formula $C\mathit{n}H_{2}\mathit{n}+2$
ALKANES >ALKANE
ALKANET *n* European boraginaceous plant, *Alkanna tinctoria*, the roots of which yield a red dye
ALKANETS >ALKANET
ALKANNIN *same as* >ALKANET
ALKANNINS >ALKANNIN
ALKENE *n* type of unsaturated hydrocarbon
ALKENES >ALKENE
ALKIE *same as* >ALKY
ALKIES >ALKY
ALKINE *n* alkyne
ALKINES >ALKINE
ALKO *n* heavy drinker or alcoholic
ALKOS >ALKO
ALKOXIDE *n* chemical compound containing oxygen
ALKOXIDES >ALKOXIDE
ALKOXY *adj* of type of chemical compound containing oxygen
ALKY *n* heavy drinker or alcoholic
ALKYD *n* synthetic resin
ALKYDS >ALKYD
ALKYL *n* of, consisting of, or containing the monovalent group $C\mathit{n}H_{2}\mathit{n}+1$
ALKYLATE *vb* add alkyl group to a compound
ALKYLATED >ALKYLATE
ALKYLATES >ALKYLATE
ALKYLIC >ALKYL
ALKYLS >ALKYL
ALKYNE *n* any unsaturated aliphatic hydrocarbon
ALKYNES >ALKYNE
ALL *adj* whole quantity or number (of) ▷ *adv* wholly, entirely ▷ *n* entire being, effort, or property
ALLANITE *n* rare black or brown mineral
ALLANITES >ALLANITE
ALLANTOIC >ALLANTOIS
ALLANTOID *adj* relating to or resembling the allantois
ALLANTOIN *n* chemical used in cosmetics
ALLANTOIS *n* membranous sac growing out of the ventral surface of the hind gut of embryonic reptiles, birds, and mammals. It combines with the chorion to form the mammalian placenta
ALLATIVE *n* word in grammatical case denoting movement towards
ALLATIVES >ALLATIVE
ALLAY *vb* reduce (fear or anger)
ALLAYED >ALLAY
ALLAYER >ALLAY
ALLAYERS >ALLAY
ALLAYING >ALLAY
ALLAYINGS >ALLAY
ALLAYMENT *n* mitigation
ALLAYS >ALLAY
ALLCOMERS *n* everyone who comes
ALLEDGE *vb* allege
ALLEDGED >ALLEDGE
ALLEDGES >ALLEDGE
ALLEDGING >ALLEDGE
ALLEE *n* avenue
ALLEES >ALLEE
ALLEGE *vb* state without proof
ALLEGED *adj* stated but not proved
ALLEGEDLY *adv* reportedly
ALLEGER >ALLEGE
ALLEGERS >ALLEGE
ALLEGES >ALLEGE
ALLEGGE *vb* alleviate
ALLEGGED >ALLEGGE
ALLEGGES >ALLEGGE
ALLEGGING >ALLEGGE
ALLEGIANT *n* loyalty
ALLEGING >ALLEGE
ALLEGORIC *adj* used in, containing, or characteristic of allegory
ALLEGORY *n* story with an underlying meaning as well as the literal one
ALLEGRO *adv* (piece to be played) in a brisk lively manner ▷ *n* piece or passage to be performed in a brisk lively manner
ALLEGROS >ALLEGRO
ALLEL *n* form of gene
ALLELE *n* any of two or more genes that are responsible for alternative characteristics, such as smooth or wrinkled seeds in peas
ALLELES >ALLELE
ALLELIC >ALLELE
ALLELISM >ALLELE
ALLELISMS >ALLELE
ALLELS >ALLEL
ALLELUIA *n* song of praise to God
ALLELUIAH *interj* alleluia
ALLELUIAS >ALLELUIA
ALLEMANDE *n* first movement of the classical suite, composed in a moderate tempo in a time signature of four-four
ALLENARLY *adv* solely
ALLERGEN *n* substance capable of causing an allergic reaction
ALLERGENS >ALLERGEN
ALLERGIC *adj* having or caused by an allergy ▷ *n* person suffering from an allergy
ALLERGICS >ALLERGIC
ALLERGIES >ALLERGY
ALLERGIN *n* allergen
ALLERGINS >ALLERGIN
ALLERGIST *n* physician skilled in the diagnosis and treatment of diseases or conditions caused by allergy
ALLERGY *n* extreme sensitivity to a substance, which causes the body to react to it
ALLERION *n* eagle in heraldry
ALLERIONS >ALLERION
ALLETHRIN *n* clear viscous amber-coloured liquid
ALLEVIANT *n* medical treatment that reduces pain but does not cure the underlying problem
ALLEVIATE *vb* lessen (pain or suffering)
ALLEY *n* narrow street or path
ALLEYCAT *n* homeless cat that roams in back streets
ALLEYCATS >ALLEYCAT
ALLEYED *adj* having alleys
ALLEYS >ALLEY
ALLEYWAY *n* narrow passage with buildings or walls on both sides
ALLEYWAYS >ALLEYWAY
ALLHEAL *n* any of several plants reputed to have healing powers, such as selfheal and valerian
ALLHEALS >ALLHEAL
ALLIABLE *adj* able to form an alliance
ALLIANCE *n* state of being allied
ALLIANCES >ALLIANCE
ALLICE *n* species of fish
ALLICES >ALLICE
ALLICHOLY *n* melancholy

ALLICIN *n* chemical found in garlic
ALLICINS > ALLICIN
ALLIED *adj* joined, as by treaty, agreement, or marriage
ALLIES > ALLY
ALLIGARTA *n* alligator
ALLIGATE *vb* join together
ALLIGATED > ALLIGATE
ALLIGATES > ALLIGATE
ALLIGATOR *n* reptile of the crocodile family, found in the southern US and China
ALLIS *n* species of fish
ALLISES > ALLIS
ALLIUM *n* any plant of the genus *Allium*, such as the onion, garlic, shallot, leek, or chive: family *Alliaceae*
ALLIUMS > ALLIUM
ALLNESS *n* being all
ALLNESSES > ALLNESS
ALLNIGHT *adj* lasting all night
ALLOBAR *n* form of element
ALLOBARS > ALLOBAR
ALLOCABLE > ALLOCATE
ALLOCARPY *n* production of fruit through cross-fertilization
ALLOCATE *vb* assign to someone or for a particular purpose
ALLOCATED > ALLOCATE
ALLOCATES > ALLOCATE
ALLOCATOR > ALLOCATE
ALLOD *same as* > ALLODIUM
ALLODIA > ALLODIUM
ALLODIAL *adj* (of land) held as an allodium
ALLODIUM *n* lands held in absolute ownership, free from such obligations as rent or services due to an overlord
ALLODIUMS > ALLODIUM
ALLODS > ALLOD
ALLOGAMY *n* cross-fertilization in flowering plants
ALLOGENIC *adj* having different genes
ALLOGRAFT *n* tissue graft from a donor genetically unrelated to the recipient
ALLOGRAPH *n* document written by a person who is not a party to it
ALLOMERIC *adj* of similar crystalline structure
ALLOMETRY *n* study of the growth of part of an organism in relation to the growth of the entire organism
ALLOMONE *n* chemical substance secreted externally by certain animals, such as insects, affecting the behaviour or physiology of another species detrimentally
ALLOMONES > ALLOMONE
ALLOMORPH *n* any of the phonological representations of a single morpheme
ALLONGE *n* paper extension to bill of exchange
ALLONGES > ALLONGE
ALLONS *interj* French word meaning let's go
ALLONYM *n* name, often one of historical significance or that of another person, assumed by a person, esp an author
ALLONYMS > ALLONYM
ALLOPATH *n* person who practises or is skilled in allopathy
ALLOPATHS > ALLOPATH
ALLOPATHY *n* orthodox method of treating disease, by using drugs that produce an effect opposite to the effect of the disease being treated, as contrasted with homeopathy
ALLOPATRY *n* condition of taking place or existing in areas that are geographically separated from one another
ALLOPHANE *n* variously coloured amorphous mineral consisting of hydrated aluminium silicate and occurring in cracks in some sedimentary rocks
ALLOPHONE *n* any of several speech sounds that are regarded as contextual or environmental variants of the same phoneme
ALLOPLASM *n* part of the cytoplasm that is specialized to form cilia, flagella, and similar structures
ALLOSAUR *n* any large carnivorous bipedal dinosaur common in North America in late Jurassic times
ALLOSAURS > ALLOSAUR
ALLOSTERY *n* condition of an enzyme in which the structure and activity of the enzyme are modified by the binding of a metabolic molecule
ALLOT *vb* assign as a share or for a particular purpose
ALLOTMENT *n* distribution
ALLOTROPE *n* any of two or more physical forms in which an element can exist
ALLOTROPY *n* existence of an element in two or more physical forms
ALLOTS > ALLOT
ALLOTTED > ALLOT
ALLOTTEE *n* person to whom something is allotted
ALLOTTEES > ALLOTTEE
ALLOTTER *n* person who allots
ALLOTTERS > ALLOTTER
ALLOTTERY *n* something allotted
ALLOTTING > ALLOT
ALLOTYPE *n* additional type specimen selected because of differences from the original type specimen, such as opposite sex or morphological details
ALLOTYPES > ALLOTYPE
ALLOTYPIC > ALLOTYPE
ALLOTYPY *n* existence of allotypes
ALLOVER *n* fabric completely covered with a pattern
ALLOVERS > ALLOVER
ALLOW *vb* permit
ALLOWABLE *adj* permissible
ALLOWABLY > ALLOWABLE
ALLOWANCE *n* amount of money given at regular intervals
ALLOWED > ALLOW
ALLOWEDLY *adv* by general admission or agreement
ALLOWING > ALLOW
ALLOWS > ALLOW
ALLOXAN *n* chemical found in uric acid
ALLOXANS > ALLOXAN
ALLOY *n* mixture of two or more metals ▷ *vb* mix (metals)
ALLOYED > ALLOY
ALLOYING > ALLOY
ALLOYS > ALLOY
ALLOZYME *n* any one of a number of different structural forms of the same enzyme encoded by a different allele
ALLOZYMES > ALLOZYME
ALLS > ALL
ALLSEED *n* any of several plants that produce many seeds, such as knotgrass
ALLSEEDS > ALLSEED
ALLSORTS *n* assorted sweets
ALLSPICE *n* spice made from the berries of a tropical American tree
ALLSPICES > ALLSPICE
ALLUDE *vb* refer indirectly to
ALLUDED > ALLUDE
ALLUDES > ALLUDE
ALLUDING > ALLUDE
ALLURE *n* attractiveness ▷ *vb* entice or attract
ALLURED > ALLURE
ALLURER > ALLURE
ALLURERS > ALLURE
ALLURES > ALLURE
ALLURING *adj* extremely attractive
ALLUSION *n* indirect reference
ALLUSIONS > ALLUSION
ALLUSIVE *adj* containing or full of allusions
ALLUVIA > ALLUVIUM
ALLUVIAL *adj* of or relating to alluvium ▷ *n* soil consisting of alluvium
ALLUVIALS > ALLUVIAL
ALLUVION *n* wash of the sea or of a river
ALLUVIONS > ALLUVION
ALLUVIUM *n* fertile soil deposited by flowing water
ALLUVIUMS > ALLUVIUM
ALLY *vb* unite or be united, esp formally, as by treaty, confederation, or marriage ▷ *n* country, person, or group allied with another
ALLYING > ALLY
ALLYL *n* of, consisting of, or containing the monovalent group CH_2: $CHCH_2$
ALLYLIC > ALLYL
ALLYLS > ALLYL
ALLYOU *pron* all of you
ALMA *n* Egyptian dancing girl
ALMAGEST *n* medieval treatise concerning alchemy or astrology
ALMAGESTS > ALMAGEST
ALMAH *n* Egyptian dancing girl
ALMAHS > ALMAH
ALMAIN *n* German dance
ALMAINS > ALMAIN
ALMANAC *n* yearly calendar with detailed information on anniversaries, phases of the moon, etc
ALMANACK *same as* > ALMANAC
ALMANACKS > ALMANACK
ALMANACS > ALMANAC
ALMANDINE *n* deep violet-red garnet
ALMANDITE *n* form of garnet
ALMAS > ALMA
ALME *n* Egyptian dancing girl
ALMEH *n* Egyptian dancing girl
ALMEHS > ALMEH
ALMEMAR *n* (in Ashkenazic usage) the raised platform in a synagogue on which the reading desk stands
ALMEMARS > ALMEMAR
ALMERIES > ALMERY
ALMERY *n* cupboard for church vessels
ALMES > ALME
ALMIGHTY *adj* all-powerful ▷ *adv* extremely
ALMIRAH *n* cupboard
ALMIRAHS > ALMIRAH
ALMNER *n* almoner

ALMNERS > ALMONER
ALMOND *n* edible oval-shaped nut which grows on a small tree
ALMONDS > ALMOND
ALMONDY > ALMOND
ALMONER *n* formerly, a hospital social worker
ALMONERS > ALMONER
ALMONRIES > ALMONRY
ALMONRY *n* house of an almoner, usually the place where alms were given
ALMOST *adv* very nearly
ALMOUS *Scots word for* > ALMS
ALMS *pl n* gifts to the poor
ALMSGIVER *n* one who gives alms
ALMSHOUSE *n* (formerly) a house, financed by charity, which offered accommodation to the poor
ALMSMAN *n* person who gives or receives alms
ALMSMEN > ALMSMAN
ALMSWOMAN *n* woman who gives or receives alms
ALMSWOMEN > ALMSWOMAN
ALMUCE *n* fur-lined hood or cape formerly worn by members of certain religious orders, more recently by canons of France
ALMUCES > ALMUCE
ALMUD *n* Spanish unit of measure
ALMUDE *n* Spanish unit of measure
ALMUDES > ALMUDE
ALMUDS > ALMUD
ALMUG *n* type of wood mentioned in Bible
ALMUGS > ALMUG
ALNAGE *n* measurement in ells
ALNAGER *n* inspector of cloth
ALNAGERS > ALNAGER
ALNAGES > ALNAGE
ALNICO *n* alloy of various metals including iron, nickel, and cobalt
ALNICOS > ALNICO
ALOCASIA *n* any of various tropical plants of the genus *Alocasia*
ALOCASIAS > ALOCASIA
ALOD *n* feudal estate with no superior
ALODIA > ALODIUM
ALODIAL > ALODIUM
ALODIUM *same as* > ALLODIUM
ALODIUMS > ALODIUM
ALODS > ALOD
ALOE *n* plant with fleshy spiny leaves
ALOED *adj* containing aloes
ALOES *another name for* > EAGLEWOOD
ALOETIC > ALOE
ALOETICS > ALOE
ALOFT *adv* in the air ▷ *adj* in or into a high or higher place
ALOGIA *n* inability to speak
ALOGIAS > ALOGIA
ALOGICAL *adj* without logic
ALOHA *a Hawaiian word for* > HELLO
ALOHAS > ALOHA
ALOIN *n* bitter crystalline compound derived from various species of aloe: used as a laxative and flavouring agent
ALOINS > ALOIN
ALONE *adv* without anyone or anything else
ALONELY > ALONE
ALONENESS > ALONE
ALONG *adv* forward
ALONGSIDE *adv* beside (something)
ALONGST *adv* along
ALOOF *adj* distant or haughty in manner
ALOOFLY > ALOOF
ALOOFNESS > ALOOF
ALOPECIA *n* loss of hair
ALOPECIAS > ALOPECIA
ALOPECIC > ALOPECIA
ALOPECOID > ALOPECIA
ALOUD *adv* in an audible voice ▷ *adj* in a normal voice
ALOW *adj* in or into the lower rigging of a vessel, near the deck
ALOWE *Scots word for* > ABLAZE
ALP *n* high mountain
ALPACA *n* Peruvian llama
ALPACAS > ALPACA
ALPACCA *same as* > ALPACA
ALPACCAS > ALPACCA
ALPARGATA *n* Spanish sandal
ALPEEN *n* Irish cudgel
ALPEENS > ALPEEN
ALPENGLOW *n* reddish light on the summits of snow-covered mountain peaks at sunset or sunrise
ALPENHORN *same as* > ALPHORN
ALPHA *n* first letter in the Greek alphabet
ALPHABET *n* set of letters used in writing a language
ALPHABETS > ALPHABET
ALPHAS > ALPHA
ALPHASORT *vb* arrange in alphabetical order
ALPHORN *n* wind instrument used in the Swiss Alps, consisting of a very long tube of wood or bark with a cornet-like mouthpiece
ALPHORNS > ALPHORN
ALPHOSIS *n* absence of skin pigmentation, as in albinism
ALPHYL *n* univalent radical
ALPHYLS > ALPHYL
ALPINE *adj* of high mountains ▷ *n* mountain plant
ALPINELY > ALPINE
ALPINES > ALPINE
ALPINISM > ALPINIST
ALPINISMS > ALPINIST
ALPINIST *n* mountain climber
ALPINISTS > ALPINIST
ALPS > ALP
ALREADY *adv* before the present time
ALRIGHT *adj* all right
ALS > AL
ALSIKE *n* clover native to Europe and Asia
ALSIKES > ALSIKE
ALSO *adv* in addition, too
ALSOON *same as* > ALSOONE
ALSOONE *adv* as soon
ALT *n* octave directly above the treble staff
ALTAR *n* table used for Communion in Christian churches
ALTARAGE *n* donations placed on altar for priest
ALTARAGES > ALTARAGE
ALTARS > ALTAR
ALTARWISE *adv* in the position of an altar
ALTER *vb* make or become different
ALTERABLE > ALTER
ALTERABLY > ALTER
ALTERANT *n* alternative
ALTERANTS > ALTERANT
ALTERCATE *vb* argue, esp heatedly
ALTERED > ALTER
ALTERER > ALTER
ALTERERS > ALTER
ALTERING > ALTER
ALTERITY *n* quality of being different
ALTERN *adj* alternate
ALTERNANT *adj* alternating
ALTERNAT *n* practice of deciding precedence by lot
ALTERNATE *vb* (cause to) occur by turns ▷ *adj* occurring by turns ▷ *n* person who substitutes for another in his absence
ALTERNATS > ALTERNAT
ALTERNE *n* neighbouring but different plant group
ALTERNES > ALTERNE
ALTERS > ALTER
ALTESSE *n* French word for highness
ALTESSES > ALTESSE
ALTEZA *n* Spanish word for highness
ALTEZAS > ALTEZA
ALTEZZA *n* Italian word for highness
ALTEZZAS > ALTEZZA
ALTHAEA *n* plant such as the hollyhock, having tall spikes of showy white, yellow, or red flowers
ALTHAEAS > ALTHAEA
ALTHEA *same as* > ALTHAEA
ALTHEAS > ALTHEA
ALTHO *conj* short form of although
ALTHORN *n* valved brass musical instrument belonging to the saxhorn or flügelhorn families
ALTHORNS > ALTHORN
ALTHOUGH *conj* despite the fact that; even though
ALTIGRAPH *n* instrument that measures altitude
ALTIMETER *n* instrument that measures altitude
ALTIMETRY *n* science of measuring altitudes, as with an altimeter
ALTIPLANO *n* high plateau
ALTISSIMO *adj* (of music) very high in pitch
ALTITUDE *n* height above sea level
ALTITUDES > ALTITUDE
ALTO *n* (singer with) the highest adult male voice ▷ *adj* denoting such an instrument, singer, or voice
ALTOIST *n* person who plays the alto saxophone
ALTOISTS > ALTOIST
ALTOS > ALTO
ALTRICES *pl n* altricial birds
ALTRICIAL *adj* (of the young of some species of birds after hatching) naked, blind, and dependent on the parents for food ▷ *n* altricial bird, such as a pigeon
ALTRUISM *n* unselfish concern for the welfare of others
ALTRUISMS > ALTRUISM
ALTRUIST > ALTRUISM
ALTRUISTS > ALTRUISM
ALTS > ALT
ALUDEL *n* pear-shaped vessel, open at both ends, formerly used with similar vessels for collecting condensates, esp of subliming mercury
ALUDELS > ALUDEL
ALULA *n* tuft of feathers attached to the first digit of a bird
ALULAE > ALULA
ALULAR > ALULA
ALUM *n* double sulphate of aluminium and potassium
ALUMIN *n* aluminium oxide
ALUMINA *n* aluminium oxide
ALUMINAS > ALUMINA
ALUMINATE *n* salt of the ortho or meta acid forms of aluminium hydroxide
ALUMINE *n* French word for alumina

ALUMINES > ALUMINE
ALUMINIC *adj* of aluminium
ALUMINISE *same as* > ALUMINIZE
ALUMINIUM *n* light silvery-white metal that does not rust
ALUMINIZE *vb* cover with aluminium
ALUMINOUS *adj* resembling aluminium
ALUMINS > ALUMIN
ALUMINUM *same as* > ALUMINIUM
ALUMINUMS > ALUMINUM
ALUMISH *adj* like alum
ALUMIUM *old name for* > ALUMINIUM
ALUMIUMS > ALUMIUM
ALUMNA *n* female graduate of a school, college, etc
ALUMNAE > ALUMNA
ALUMNI > ALUMNUS
ALUMNUS *n* graduate of a college
ALUMROOT *n* North American plants having small white, reddish, or green bell-shaped flowers and astringent roots
ALUMROOTS > ALUMROOT
ALUMS > ALUM
ALUMSTONE *same as* > ALUNITE
ALUNITE *n* white, grey, or reddish mineral
ALUNITES > ALUNITE
ALURE *n* area behind battlements
ALURES > ALURE
ALVEARIES > ALVEARY
ALVEARY *n* beehive
ALVEATED *adj* with vaults like beehive
ALVEOLAR *adj* of, relating to, or resembling an alveolus ▷ *n* alveolar consonant, such as the speech sounds written *t*, *d*, and *s* in English
ALVEOLARS > ALVEOLAR
ALVEOLATE *adj* having many alveoli
ALVEOLE *n* alveolus
ALVEOLES > ALVEOLE
ALVEOLI > ALVEOLUS
ALVEOLUS *n* any small pit, cavity, or saclike dilation, such as a honeycomb cell, a tooth socket, or the tiny air sacs in the lungs
ALVINE *adj* of or relating to the intestines or belly
ALWAY *same as* > ALWAYS
ALWAYS *adv* at all times
ALYSSUM *n* garden plant with small yellow or white flowers
ALYSSUMS > ALYSSUM
AM *see* > BE
AMA *n* vessel for water
AMABILE *adj* sweet
AMADAVAT *same as* > AVADAVAT
AMADAVATS > AMADAVAT
AMADODA *pl n* grown men
AMADOU *n* spongy substance made from certain fungi, such as *Polyporus* (or *Fomes*) *fomentarius* and related species, used as tinder to light fires, in medicine to stop bleeding, and, esp formerly, by anglers to dry off dry flies between casts
AMADOUS > AMADOU
AMAH *n* (in the East, formerly) a nurse or maidservant
AMAHS > AMAH
AMAIN *adv* with great strength, speed, or haste
AMALGAM *n* blend or combination
AMALGAMS > AMALGAM
AMANDINE *n* protein found in almonds
AMANDINES > AMANDINE
AMANDLA *n* political slogan calling for power to the Black population
AMANDLAS > AMANDLA
AMANITA *n* type of fungus
AMANITAS > AMANITA
AMANITIN *n* poison from amanita
AMANITINS > AMANITIN
AMARACUS *n* marjoram
AMARANT *n* amaranth
AMARANTH *n* imaginary flower that never fades
AMARANTHS > AMARANTH
AMARANTIN *n* protein
AMARANTS > AMARANT
AMARELLE *n* variety of sour cherry that has pale red fruit and colourless juice
AMARELLES > AMARELLE
AMARETTI > AMARETTO
AMARETTO *n* Italian liqueur with a flavour of almonds
AMARETTOS > AMARETTO
AMARNA *adj* pertaining to the reign of the Pharaoh Akhenaton
AMARONE *n* strong dry red Italian wine
AMARONES > AMARONE
AMARYLLID *n* plant of the amaryllis family
AMARYLLIS *n* lily-like plant with large red, pink, or white flowers
AMAS > AMA
AMASS *vb* collect or accumulate
AMASSABLE > AMASS
AMASSED > AMASS
AMASSER > AMASS
AMASSERS > AMASS
AMASSES > AMASS
AMASSING > AMASS
AMASSMENT > AMASS
AMATE *vb* match
AMATED > AMATE
AMATES > AMATE
AMATEUR *n* person who engages in a sport or activity as a pastime rather than as a profession ▷ *adj* not professional
AMATEURS > AMATEUR
AMATING > AMATE
AMATION *n* lovemaking
AMATIONS > AMATION
AMATIVE *a rare word for* > AMOROUS
AMATIVELY > AMATIVE
AMATOL *n* explosive mixture of ammonium nitrate and TNT, used in shells and bombs
AMATOLS > AMATOL
AMATORIAL *same as* > AMATORY
AMATORIAN > AMATORY
AMATORY *adj* relating to romantic or sexual love
AMAUROSES > AMAUROSIS
AMAUROSIS *n* blindness, esp when occurring without observable damage to the eye
AMAUROTIC > AMAUROSIS
AMAUT *n* hood on an Inuit woman's parka for carrying a child
AMAUTS > AMAUT
AMAZE *vb* surprise greatly, astound
AMAZED > AMAZE
AMAZEDLY > AMAZE
AMAZEMENT *n* incredulity or great astonishment
AMAZES > AMAZE
AMAZING *adj* causing wonder or astonishment
AMAZINGLY > AMAZING
AMAZON *n* any tall, strong, or aggressive woman
AMAZONIAN > AMAZON
AMAZONITE *n* green variety of microcline used as a gemstone
AMAZONS > AMAZON
AMBACH *same as* > AMBATCH
AMBACHES > AMBACH
AMBAGE *n* ambiguity
AMBAGES > AMBAGE
AMBAGIOUS > AMBAGE
AMBAN *n* Chinese official
AMBANS > AMBAN
AMBARI *same as* > AMBARY
AMBARIES > AMBARY
AMBARIS > AMBARI
AMBARY *n* tropical Asian malvaceous plant, *Hibiscus cannabinus*, that yields a fibre similar to jute
AMBASSAGE *n* embassy
AMBASSIES > AMBASSY
AMBASSY *n* embassy
AMBATCH *n* tree or shrub of the Nile Valley, *Aeschynomene elaphroxylon*, valued for its light-coloured pithlike wood
AMBATCHES > AMBATCH
AMBEER *n* saliva coloured by tobacco juice
AMBEERS > AMBEER
AMBER *n* clear yellowish fossil resin ▷ *adj* brownish-yellow
AMBERED *adj* fixed in amber
AMBERGRIS *n* waxy substance secreted by the sperm whale, used in making perfumes
AMBERIES > AMBERY
AMBERINA *n* type of glassware
AMBERINAS > AMBERINA
AMBERITE *n* powder like amber
AMBERITES > AMBERITE
AMBERJACK *n* any of several large carangid fishes of the genus *Seriola*, esp *S. dumerili*, with golden markings when young, occurring in tropical and subtropical Atlantic waters
AMBEROID *n* synthetic amber made by compressing pieces of amber and other resins together at a high temperature
AMBEROIDS > AMBEROID
AMBEROUS *adj* like amber
AMBERS > AMBER
AMBERY *adj* like amber
AMBIANCE *same as* > AMBIENCE
AMBIANCES > AMBIANCE
AMBIENCE *n* atmosphere of a place
AMBIENCES > AMBIENCE
AMBIENT *adj* surrounding ▷ *n* ambient music
AMBIENTS > AMBIENT
AMBIGUITY *n* possibility of interpreting an expression in more than one way
AMBIGUOUS *adj* having more than one possible meaning
AMBIPOLAR *adj* (of plasmas and semiconductors) involving both positive and negative charge carriers
AMBIT *n* limits or boundary
AMBITION *n* desire for success
AMBITIONS > AMBITION
AMBITIOUS *adj* having a strong desire for success
AMBITS > AMBIT
AMBITTY *adj* crystalline and brittle
AMBIVERT *n* person who is intermediate between an extrovert and an introvert
AMBIVERTS > AMBIVERT
AMBLE *vb* walk at a leisurely pace ▷ *n* leisurely walk or pace
AMBLED > AMBLE
AMBLER > AMBLE
AMBLERS > AMBLE
AMBLES > AMBLE

AMBLING *n* walking at a leisurely pace

AMBLINGS > AMBLING

AMBLYOPIA *n* impaired vision with no discernible damage to the eye or optic nerve

AMBLYOPIC > AMBLYOPIA

AMBO *n* either of two raised pulpits from which the gospels and epistles were read in early Christian churches

AMBOINA *same as* > AMBOYNA

AMBOINAS > AMBOINA

AMBONES > AMBO

AMBOS > AMBO

AMBOYNA *n* mottled curly-grained wood of an Indonesian leguminous tree, *Pterocarpus indicus*, used in making furniture

AMBOYNAS > AMBOYNA

AMBRIES > AMBRY

AMBROID *same as* > AMBEROID

AMBROIDS > AMBROID

AMBROSIA *n* anything delightful to taste or smell

AMBROSIAL > AMBROSIA

AMBROSIAN > AMBROSIA

AMBROSIAS > AMBROSIA

AMBROTYPE *n* early type of glass negative that could be made to appear as a positive by backing it with black varnish or paper

AMBRY *n* recessed cupboard in the wall of a church near the altar, used to store sacred vessels, etc

AMBSACE *n* double ace, the lowest throw at dice

AMBSACES > AMBSACE

AMBULACRA *n* radial bands on the ventral surface of echinoderms, such as the starfish and sea urchin, on which the tube feet are situated

AMBULANCE *n* motor vehicle designed to carry sick or injured people

AMBULANT *adj* moving about from place to place

AMBULANTS > AMBULANT

AMBULATE *vb* wander about or move from one place to another

AMBULATED > AMBULATE

AMBULATES > AMBULATE

AMBULATOR *n* person who walks

AMBULETTE *n* motor vehicle designed for transporting ill or handicapped people

AMBUSCADE *n* ambush ▷ *vb* ambush or lie in ambush

AMBUSCADO *n* ambuscade

AMBUSH *n* act of waiting in a concealed position to make a surprise attack ▷ *vb* attack from a concealed position

AMBUSHED > AMBUSH

AMBUSHER > AMBUSH

AMBUSHERS > AMBUSH

AMBUSHES > AMBUSH

AMBUSHING > AMBUSH

AMEARST *old form of* > AMERCE

AMEBA *same as* > AMOEBA

AMEBAE > AMEBA

AMEBAN > AMEBA

AMEBAS > AMEBA

AMEBEAN *same as* > AMOEBEAN

AMEBIASES > AMEBIASIS

AMEBIASIS *n* disease caused by amoeba

AMEBIC > AMEBA

AMEBOCYTE *n* any cell having properties similar to an amoeba, such as shape, mobility, and ability to engulf particles

AMEBOID *same as* > AMOEBOID

AMEER *n* (formerly) the ruler of Afghanistan

AMEERATE *n* country ruled by an ameer

AMEERATES > AMEERATE

AMEERS > AMEER

AMEIOSES > AMEIOSIS

AMEIOSIS *n* absence of pairing of chromosomes during meiosis

AMELCORN *n* variety of wheat

AMELCORNS > AMELCORN

AMELIA *n* congenital absence of arms or legs

AMELIAS > AMELIA

AMEN *n* term used at the end of a prayer or religious statement ▷ *vb* say amen

AMENABLE *adj* likely or willing to cooperate

AMENABLY > AMENABLE

AMENAGE *vb* tame

AMENAGED > AMENAGE

AMENAGES > AMENAGE

AMENAGING > AMENAGE

AMENAUNCE *n* person's bearing

AMEND *vb* make small changes to correct or improve (something)

AMENDABLE > AMEND

AMENDE *n* public apology and reparation made to satisfy the honour of the person wronged

AMENDED > AMEND

AMENDER > AMEND

AMENDERS > AMEND

AMENDES > AMENDE

AMENDING > AMEND

AMENDMENT *n* improvement or correction

AMENDS *n* recompense or compensation given or gained for some injury, insult, etc

AMENE *adj* pleasant

AMENED > AMEN

AMENING > AMEN

AMENITIES > AMENITY

AMENITY *n* useful or enjoyable feature

AMENS > AMEN

AMENT *n* mentally deficient person

AMENTA > AMENTUM

AMENTAL > AMENTUM

AMENTIA *n* severe mental deficiency, usually congenital

AMENTIAS > AMENTIA

AMENTS > AMENT

AMENTUM *same as* > AMENT

AMERCE *vb* punish by a fine

AMERCED > AMERCE

AMERCER > AMERCE

AMERCERS > AMERCE

AMERCES > AMERCE

AMERCING > AMERCE

AMERICIUM *n* white metallic element artificially produced from plutonium

AMESACE *same as* > AMBSACE

AMESACES > AMESACE

AMETHYST *n* bluish-violet variety of quartz used as a gemstone ▷ *adj* purple or violet

AMETHYSTS > AMETHYST

AMETROPIA *n* loss of ability to focus images on the retina, caused by an imperfection in the refractive function of the eye

AMETROPIC > AMETROPIA

AMI *n* male friend

AMIA *n* species of fish

AMIABLE *adj* friendly, pleasant-natured

AMIABLY > AMIABLE

AMIANTHUS *n* any of the fine silky varieties of asbestos

AMIANTUS *n* amianthus

AMIAS > AMIA

AMICABLE *adj* friendly

AMICABLY > AMICABLE

AMICE *n* rectangular piece of white linen worn by priests around the neck and shoulders under the alb or, formerly, on the head

AMICES > AMICE

AMICI > AMICUS

AMICUS *n* Latin for friend

AMID *prep* in the middle of, among ▷ *n* same as > AMIDE

AMIDASE *n* enzyme

AMIDASES > AMIDASE

AMIDE *n* any organic compound containing the group $-CONH_2$

AMIDES > AMIDE

AMIDIC > AMIDE

AMIDIN *n* form of starch

AMIDINE *n* crystalline compound

AMIDINES > AMIDINE

AMIDINS > AMIDIN

AMIDMOST *adv* in the middle

AMIDO *adj* containing amide

AMIDOGEN *n* chemical compound derived from ammonia

AMIDOGENS > AMIDOGEN

AMIDOL *n* chemical used in developing photographs

AMIDOLS > AMIDOL

AMIDONE *n* pain-killing drug

AMIDONES > AMIDONE

AMIDS *same as* > AMID

AMIDSHIP *adj* in the middle of a ship

AMIDSHIPS *adv* at or towards the middle of a ship ▷ *adj* at, near, or towards the centre of a vessel

AMIDST *same as* > AMID

AMIE *n* female friend

AMIES > AMIE

AMIGA *n* Spanish female friend

AMIGAS > AMIGA

AMIGO *n* friend

AMIGOS > AMIGO

AMILDAR *n* manager in India

AMILDARS > AMILDAR

AMIN *same as* > AMINE

AMINE *n* organic base formed by replacing one or more of the hydrogen atoms of ammonia by organic groups

AMINES > AMINE

AMINIC > AMINE

AMINITIES > AMINITY

AMINITY *n* amenity

AMINO *n* of, consisting of, or containing the group of atoms $-NH_2$

AMINS > AMIN

AMIR *n* (formerly) the ruler of Afghanistan

AMIRATE > AMIR

AMIRATES > AMIR

AMIRS > AMIR

AMIS > AMI

AMISES > AMI

AMISS *adv* wrongly, badly ▷ *adj* wrong, faulty ▷ *n* evil deed

AMISSES > AMISS

AMISSIBLE *adj* likely to be lost

AMISSING *adj* missing

AMITIES > AMITY

AMITOSES > AMITOSIS

AMITOSIS *n* unusual form of cell division in which the nucleus and cytoplasm divide by constriction without the formation of chromosomes

AMITOTIC > AMITOSIS

AMITROLE *n* pesticide

AMITROLES > AMITROLE
AMITY *n* friendship
AMLA *n* species of Indian tree
AMLAS > AMLA
AMMAN *same as* > AMTMAN
AMMANS > AMMAN
AMMETER *n* instrument for measuring electric current
AMMETERS > AMMETER
AMMINE *n* compound that has molecules containing one or more ammonia molecules bound to another molecule, group, or atom by coordinate bonds
AMMINES > AMMINE
AMMINO *adj* containing ammonia molecules
AMMIRAL *old word for* > ADMIRAL
AMMIRALS > AMMIRAL
AMMO *n* ammunition
AMMOCETE *n* ammocoete
AMMOCETES > AMMOCETE
AMMOCOETE *n* larva of primitive jawless vertebrates, such as the lamprey, that lives buried in mud and feeds on microorganisms
AMMON *n* Asian wild sheep
AMMONAL *n* explosive made by mixing TNT, ammonium nitrate, and aluminium powder
AMMONALS > AMMONAL
AMMONATE *same as* > AMMINE
AMMONATES > AMMONATE
AMMONIA *n* strong-smelling alkaline gas containing hydrogen and nitrogen
AMMONIAC *n* strong-smelling gum resin obtained from the stems of the N Asian umbelliferous plant *Dorema ammoniacum* and formerly used as an expectorant, stimulant, perfume, and in porcelain cement
AMMONIACS > AMMONIAC
AMMONIAS > AMMONIA
AMMONIATE *vb* unite or treat with ammonia
AMMONIC *adj* of or concerned with ammonia or ammonium compounds
AMMONICAL > AMMONIC
AMMONIFY *vb* treat or impregnate with ammonia or a compound of ammonia
AMMONITE *n* fossilized spiral shell of an extinct sea creature
AMMONITES > AMMONITE
AMMONITIC > AMMONITE
AMMONIUM *n* type of monovalent chemical group
AMMONIUMS > AMMONIUM
AMMONO *adj* using ammonia
AMMONOID *n* type of fossil
AMMONOIDS > AMMONOID
AMMONS > AMMON
AMMOS > AMMO
AMNESIA *n* loss of memory
AMNESIAC > AMNESIA
AMNESIACS > AMNESIA
AMNESIAS > AMNESIA
AMNESIC > AMNESIA
AMNESICS > AMNESIA
AMNESTIC *adj* relating to amnesia
AMNESTIED > AMNESTY
AMNESTIES > AMNESTY
AMNESTY *n* general pardon for offences against a government ▷ *vb* overlook or forget (an offence)
AMNIA > AMNION
AMNIC *adj* relating to amnion
AMNIO *n* amniocentesis
AMNION *n* innermost of two membranes enclosing an embryo
AMNIONIC > AMNION
AMNIONS > AMNION
AMNIOS > AMNIO
AMNIOTE *n* any vertebrate animal, such as a reptile, bird, or mammal, that possesses an amnion, chorion, and allantois during embryonic development
AMNIOTES > AMNIOTE
AMNIOTIC *adj* of or relating to the amnion
AMNIOTOMY *n* breaking of the membrane surrounding a fetus to induce labour
AMOEBA *n* microscopic single-celled animal able to change its shape
AMOEBAE > AMOEBA
AMOEBAEAN *adj* of or relating to lines of verse dialogue that answer each other alternately
AMOEBAN > AMOEBA
AMOEBAS > AMOEBA
AMOEBEAN *same as* > AMOEBAEAN
AMOEBIC > AMOEBA
AMOEBOID *adj* of, related to, or resembling amoebae
AMOK *n* state of murderous frenzy, originally observed among Malays
AMOKS > AMOK
AMOKURA *n* white pelagian bird, *Paethon rubricauda*, of tropical latitudes in the Indian and Pacific oceans, with a red beak and long red tail feathers
AMOLE *n* American plant
AMOLES > AMOLE
AMOMUM *n* plant of ginger family
AMOMUMS > AMOMUM
AMONG *prep* in the midst of
AMONGST *same as* > AMONG
AMOOVE *vb* stir someone's emotions
AMOOVED > AMOOVE
AMOOVES > AMOOVE
AMOOVING > AMOOVE
AMORAL *adj* without moral standards
AMORALISM > AMORAL
AMORALIST > AMORAL
AMORALITY > AMORAL
AMORALLY > AMORAL
AMORANCE *n* condition of being in love
AMORANCES > AMORANCE
AMORANT > AMORANCE
AMORCE *n* small percussion cap
AMORCES > AMORCE
AMORET *n* sweetheart
AMORETS > AMORET
AMORETTI > AMORETTO
AMORETTO *n* (esp in painting) a small chubby naked boy representing a cupid
AMORETTOS > AMORETTO
AMORINI > AMORINO
AMORINO *same as* > AMORETTO
AMORISM > AMORIST
AMORISMS > AMORIST
AMORIST *n* lover or a writer about love
AMORISTIC > AMORIST
AMORISTS > AMORIST
AMORNINGS *adv* each morning
AMOROSA *n* lover
AMOROSAS > AMOROSA
AMOROSITY *n* quality of being amorous
AMOROSO *adv* (to be played) lovingly ▷ *n* rich sweetened sherry of a dark colour
AMOROSOS > AMOROSO
AMOROUS *adj* feeling, showing, or relating to sexual love
AMOROUSLY > AMOROUS
AMORPHISM > AMORPHOUS
AMORPHOUS *adj* without distinct shape
AMORT *adj* in low spirits
AMORTISE *same as* > AMORTIZE
AMORTISED > AMORTISE
AMORTISES > AMORTISE
AMORTIZE *vb* pay off (a debt) gradually by periodic transfers to a sinking fund
AMORTIZED > AMORTIZE
AMORTIZES > AMORTIZE
AMOSITE *n* form of asbestos
AMOSITES > AMOSITE
AMOTION *n* act of removing
AMOTIONS > AMOTION
AMOUNT *n* extent or quantity ▷ *vb* be equal or add up to
AMOUNTED > AMOUNT
AMOUNTING > AMOUNT
AMOUNTS > AMOUNT
AMOUR *n* (secret) love affair
AMOURETTE *n* minor love affair
AMOURS > AMOUR
AMOVE *vb* stir someone's emotions
AMOVED > AMOVE
AMOVES > AMOVE
AMOVING > AMOVE
AMOWT *same as* > AMAUT
AMOWTS > AMOWT
AMP *n* ampere ▷ *vb* excite or become excited
AMPASSIES > AMPASSY
AMPASSY *n* ampersand
AMPED > AMP
AMPERAGE *n* strength of an electric current measured in amperes
AMPERAGES > AMPERAGE
AMPERE *n* basic unit of electric current
AMPERES > AMPERE
AMPERSAND *n* character (&), meaning and
AMPERZAND *n* ampersand
AMPHIBIA *n* class of amphibians
AMPHIBIAN *n* animal that lives on land but breeds in water ▷ *adj* of, relating to, or belonging to the class *Amphibia*
AMPHIBOLE *n* any of a large group of minerals consisting of the silicates of calcium, iron, magnesium, sodium, and aluminium
AMPHIBOLY *n* ambiguity of expression, esp where due to a grammatical construction
AMPHIGORY *n* piece of nonsensical writing in verse or, less commonly, prose
AMPHIOXI > AMPHIOXUS
AMPHIOXUS *another name for the* > LANCELET
AMPHIPATH *adj* of or relating to a molecule that possesses both hydrophobic and hydrophilic elements
AMPHIPOD *n* any marine or freshwater crustacean of the order *Amphipoda*, such as the sand hoppers, in which the body is laterally compressed: subclass *Malacostraca* ▷ *adj* of, relating to, or belonging to the *Amphipoda*
AMPHIPODS > AMPHIPOD
AMPHOLYTE *n* electrolyte that can be acid or base
AMPHORA *n* two-handled ancient Greek or Roman jar
AMPHORAE > AMPHORA
AMPHORAL > AMPHORA

AMPHORAS > AMPHORA
AMPHORIC *adj* resembling the sound produced by blowing into a bottle. Amphoric breath sounds are heard through a stethoscope placed over a cavity in the lung
AMPING > AMP
AMPLE *adj* more than sufficient
AMPLENESS > AMPLE
AMPLER > AMPLE
AMPLEST > AMPLE
AMPLEXUS *n* mating in amphibians
AMPLIDYNE *n* magnetic amplifier
AMPLIFIED > AMPLIFY
AMPLIFIER *n* device used to amplify a current or sound signal
AMPLIFIES > AMPLIFY
AMPLIFY *vb* increase the strength of (a current or sound signal)
AMPLITUDE *n* greatness of extent
AMPLOSOME *n* stocky body type
AMPLY *adv* fully or generously
AMPOULE *n* small sealed glass vessel containing liquid for injection
AMPOULES > AMPOULE
AMPS > AMP
AMPUL *n* ampoule
AMPULE *same as* > AMPOULE
AMPULES > AMPULE
AMPULLA *n* dilated end part of certain tubes in the body
AMPULLAE > AMPULLA
AMPULLAR > AMPULLA
AMPULLARY > AMPULLA
AMPULS > AMPUL
AMPUTATE *vb* cut off (a limb or part of a limb) for medical reasons
AMPUTATED > AMPUTATE
AMPUTATES > AMPUTATE
AMPUTATOR > AMPUTATE
AMPUTEE *n* person who has had a limb amputated
AMPUTEES > AMPUTEE
AMREETA *same as* > AMRITA
AMREETAS > AMREETA
AMRIT *n* sanctified solution of sugar and water used in the Amrit Ceremony
AMRITA *n* ambrosia of the gods that bestows immortality
AMRITAS > AMRITA
AMRITS > AMRIT
AMSINCKIA *n* Californian herb
AMTMAN *n* magistrate in parts of Europe
AMTMANS > AMTMAN
AMTRAC *n* amphibious tracked vehicle
AMTRACK *n* amphibious tracked vehicle
AMTRACKS > AMTRACK
AMTRACS > AMTRAC
AMU *n* unit of mass
AMUCK *same as* > AMOK
AMUCKS > AMUCK
AMULET *n* something carried or worn as a protection against evil
AMULETIC > AMULET
AMULETS > AMULET
AMUS > AMU
AMUSABLE *adj* capable of being amused
AMUSE *vb* cause to laugh or smile
AMUSEABLE *same as* > AMUSABLE
AMUSED > AMUSE
AMUSEDLY > AMUSE
AMUSEMENT *n* state of being amused
AMUSER > AMUSE
AMUSERS > AMUSE
AMUSES > AMUSE
AMUSETTE *n* type of light cannon
AMUSETTES > AMUSETTE
AMUSIA *n* inability to recognize musical tones
AMUSIAS > AMUSIA
AMUSING *adj* mildly entertaining
AMUSINGLY > AMUSING
AMUSIVE *adj* deceptive
AMYGDAL *n* almond
AMYGDALA *n* almond-shaped part, such as a tonsil or a lobe of the cerebellum
AMYGDALAE > AMYGDALA
AMYGDALAS > AMYGDALA
AMYGDALE *n* vesicle in a volcanic rock, formed from a bubble of escaping gas, that has become filled with light-coloured minerals, such as quartz and calcite
AMYGDALES > AMYGDALE
AMYGDALIN *n* white soluble bitter-tasting crystalline glycoside extracted from bitter almonds
AMYGDALS > AMYGDAL
AMYGDULE *same as* > AMYGDALE
AMYGDULES > AMYGDULE
AMYL *n* of, consisting of, or containing any of eight isomeric forms of the monovalent group C_5H_{11}-
AMYLASE *n* enzyme, present in saliva, that helps to change starch into sugar
AMYLASES > AMYLASE
AMYLENE *another name (no longer in technical usage) for* > PENTENE
AMYLENES > AMYLENE
AMYLIC *adj* of or derived from amyl
AMYLOGEN *n* soluble part of starch
AMYLOGENS > AMYLOGEN
AMYLOID *n* complex protein resembling starch, deposited in tissues in some degenerative diseases ▷ *adj* starchlike
AMYLOIDAL > AMYLOID
AMYLOIDS > AMYLOID
AMYLOPSIN *n* enzyme of the pancreatic juice that converts starch into sugar
AMYLOSE *n* minor component (about 20 per cent) of starch, consisting of long unbranched chains of glucose units. It is soluble in water and gives an intense blue colour with iodine
AMYLOSES > AMYLOSE
AMYLS > AMYL
AMYLUM *another name for* > STARCH
AMYLUMS > AMYLUM
AMYOTONIA *another name for* > MYOTONIA
AMYTAL *n* barbiturate
AMYTALS > AMYTAL
AN *adj* form of **a** used before vowels, and sometimes before 'h'
ANA *adv* (of ingredients in a prescription) in equal quantities ▷ *n* collection of reminiscences, sketches, etc, of or about a person or place
ANABAENA *n* any freshwater alga of the genus *Anabaena*, sometimes occurring in drinking water, giving it a fishy taste and smell
ANABAENAS > ANABAENA
ANABANTID *n* any of various spiny-finned fishes constituting the family *Anabantidae* and including the fighting fish, climbing perch, and gourami ▷ *adj* of, relating to, or belonging to the family *Anabantidae*
ANABAS *n* type of fish
ANABASES > ANABASIS
ANABASIS *n* march of Cyrus the Younger and his Greek mercenaries from Sardis to Cunaxa in Babylonia in 401 BC
ANABATIC *adj* (of air currents) rising upwards, esp up slopes
ANABIOSES > ANABIOSIS
ANABIOSIS *n* ability to return to life after apparent death
ANABIOTIC > ANABIOSIS
ANABLEPS *n* any of various cyprinodont fishes constituting the genus *Anableps*, which includes the four-eyed fishes
ANABOLIC *adj* of or relating to anabolism
ANABOLISM *n* metabolic process in which body tissues are synthesized from food
ANABOLITE *n* product of anabolism
ANABRANCH *n* stream that leaves a river and enters it again further downstream
ANACHARIS *n* water plant
ANACLINAL *adj* (of valleys and similar formations) progressing in a direction opposite to the dip of the surrounding rock strata
ANACLISES > ANACLITIC
ANACLISIS > ANACLITIC
ANACLITIC *adj* of or relating to relationships that are characterized by the strong dependence of one person on others or another
ANACONDA *n* large S American snake which kills by constriction
ANACONDAS > ANACONDA
ANACRUSES > ANACRUSIS
ANACRUSIS *n* one or more unstressed syllables at the beginning of a line of verse
ANADEM *n* garland for the head
ANADEMS > ANADEM
ANAEMIA *n* deficiency in the number of red blood cells
ANAEMIAS > ANAEMIA
ANAEMIC *adj* having anaemia
ANAEROBE *n* organism that does not require oxygen
ANAEROBES > ANAEROBE
ANAEROBIA *same as* > ANAEROBES
ANAEROBIC *adj* not requiring oxygen
ANAGLYPH *n* stereoscopic picture consisting of two images of the same object, taken from slightly different angles
ANAGLYPHS > ANAGLYPH
ANAGLYPHY > ANAGLYPH
ANAGOGE *n* allegorical or spiritual interpretation, esp of sacred works such as the Bible
ANAGOGES > ANAGOGE
ANAGOGIC > ANAGOGE
ANAGOGIES > ANAGOGY
ANAGOGY *same as* > ANAGOGE
ANAGRAM *n* word or phrase made by rearranging the letters of another word or phrase
ANAGRAMS > ANAGRAM
ANAL *adj* of the anus
ANALCIME *same as* > ANALCITE
ANALCIMES > ANALCIME
ANALCIMIC > ANALCIME
ANALCITE *n* white, grey, or

colourless zeolite mineral
ANALCITES >ANALCITE
ANALECTA *same as* >ANALECTS
ANALECTIC >ANALECTS
ANALECTS *pl n* selected literary passages from one or more works
ANALEMMA *n* graduated scale shaped like a figure of eight that indicates the daily declination of the sun
ANALEMMAS >ANALEMMA
ANALEPTIC *adj* (of a drug, etc) stimulating the central nervous system ▷ *n* any drug, such as doxapram, that stimulates the central nervous system
ANALGESIA *n* absence of pain
ANALGESIC *adj* (drug) relieving pain ▷ *n* drug that relieves pain
ANALGETIC *n* painkilling drug
ANALGIA *same as* >ANALGESIA
ANALGIAS >ANALGIA
ANALITIES >ANALITY
ANALITY *n* quality of being psychologically anal
ANALLY >ANAL
ANALOG *same as* >ANALOGUE
ANALOGA >ANALOGON
ANALOGIC >ANALOGY
ANALOGIES >ANALOGY
ANALOGISE *same as* >ANALOGIZE
ANALOGISM >ANALOGIZE
ANALOGIST >ANALOGY
ANALOGIZE *vb* use analogy
ANALOGON *n* analogue
ANALOGONS >ANALOGON
ANALOGOUS *adj* similar in some respects
ANALOGS >ANALOG
ANALOGUE *n* something that is similar in some respects to something else ▷ *adj* displaying information by means of a dial
ANALOGUES >ANALOGUE
ANALOGY *n* similarity in some respects
ANALYSAND *n* any person who is undergoing psychoanalysis
ANALYSE *vb* make an analysis of (something)
ANALYSED >ANALYSE
ANALYSER >ANALYSE
ANALYSERS >ANALYSE
ANALYSES >ANALYSIS
ANALYSING >ANALYSE
ANALYSIS *n* separation of a whole into its parts for study and interpretation
ANALYST *n* person skilled in analysis
ANALYSTS >ANALYST
ANALYTE *n* substance that is being analyzed
ANALYTES >ANALYTE
ANALYTIC *adj* relating to analysis ▷ *n* analytical logic
ANALYTICS >ANALYTIC
ANALYZE *same as* >ANALYSE
ANALYZED >ANALYZE
ANALYZER >ANALYZE
ANALYZERS >ANALYZE
ANALYZES >ANALYZE
ANALYZING >ANALYZE
ANAMNESES >ANAMNESIS
ANAMNESIS *n* ability to recall past events
ANAMNIOTE *n* any vertebrate animal, such as a fish or amphibian, that lacks an amnion, chorion, and allantois during embryonic development
ANAN *interj* expression of failure to understand
ANANA *n* pineapple
ANANAS *n* plant related to the pineapple
ANANASES >ANANAS
ANANDROUS *adj* (of flowers) having no stamens
ANANKE *n* unalterable necessity
ANANKES >ANANKE
ANANTHOUS *adj* (of higher plants) having no flowers
ANAPAEST *n* metrical foot of three syllables, the first two short, the last long
ANAPAESTS >ANAPAEST
ANAPEST *same as* >ANAPAEST
ANAPESTIC >ANAPEST
ANAPESTS >ANAPEST
ANAPHASE *n* third stage of mitosis, during which the chromatids separate and migrate towards opposite ends of the spindle
ANAPHASES >ANAPHASE
ANAPHASIC >ANAPHASE
ANAPHOR *n* word referring back to a previous word
ANAPHORA *n* use of a word such as a pronoun that has the same reference as a word previously used in the same discourse
ANAPHORAL >ANAPHORA
ANAPHORAS >ANAPHORA
ANAPHORIC *adj* of or relating to anaphorism
ANAPHORS >ANAPHOR
ANAPLASIA *n* reversion of plant or animal cells to a simpler less differentiated form
ANAPLASTY *n* plastic surgery
ANAPTYXES >ANAPTYXIS
ANAPTYXIS *n* insertion of a short vowel between consonants in order to make a word more easily pronounceable
ANARCH *n* instigator or personification of anarchy
ANARCHAL >ANARCHY
ANARCHIAL >ANARCHY
ANARCHIC >ANARCHY
ANARCHIES >ANARCHY
ANARCHISE *vb* make anarchic
ANARCHISM *n* doctrine advocating the abolition of government
ANARCHIST *n* person who advocates the abolition of government
ANARCHIZE *vb* make anarchic
ANARCHS >ANARCH
ANARCHY *n* lawlessness and disorder
ANARTHRIA *n* loss of the ability to speak coherently
ANARTHRIC >ANARTHRIA
ANAS >ANA
ANASARCA *n* generalized accumulation of serous fluid within the subcutaneous connective tissue, resulting in oedema
ANASARCAS >ANASARCA
ANASTASES >ANASTASIS
ANASTASIS *n* Christ's harrowing of hell
ANASTATIC >ANASTASIS
ANATA *n* (in Theravada Buddhism) the belief that since all things are constantly changing, there can be no such thing as a permanent, unchanging self
ANATAS >ANATA
ANATASE *n* rare blue or black mineral
ANATASES >ANATASE
ANATHEMA *n* detested person or thing
ANATHEMAS >ANATHEMA
ANATMAN *same as* >ANATA
ANATMANS >ANATMAN
ANATOMIC >ANATOMY
ANATOMIES >ANATOMY
ANATOMISE *same as* >ANATOMIZE
ANATOMIST *n* expert in anatomy
ANATOMIZE *vb* dissect (an animal or plant)
ANATOMY *n* science of the structure of the body
ANATOXIN *n* bacterial toxin used in inoculation
ANATOXINS >ANATOXIN
ANATROPY *n* (of a plant ovule) condition of being inverted during development by a bending of the stalk (funicule) attaching it to the carpule
ANATTA *n* annatto
ANATTAS >ANATTA
ANATTO *same as* >ANNATTO
ANATTOS >ANATTO
ANAXIAL *adj* asymmetrical
ANBURIES >ANBURY
ANBURY *n* soft spongy tumour occurring in horses and oxen
ANCE *dialect form of* >ONCE
ANCESTOR *n* person from whom one is descended
ANCESTORS >ANCESTOR
ANCESTRAL *adj* of or inherited from ancestors ▷ *n* relation that holds between *x* and *y* if there is a chain of instances of a given relation leading from *x* to *y*
ANCESTRY *n* lineage or descent
ANCHO *n* chili pepper
ANCHOR *n* heavy hooked device attached to a boat by a cable and dropped overboard to fasten the ship to the sea bottom ▷ *vb* fasten with or as if with an anchor
ANCHORAGE *n* place where boats can be anchored
ANCHORED >ANCHOR
ANCHORESS >ANCHORITE
ANCHORET *n* achorite
ANCHORETS >ANCHORET
ANCHORING >ANCHOR
ANCHORITE *n* religious recluse
ANCHORMAN *n* broadcaster in a central studio who links up and presents items from outside camera units and other studios
ANCHORMEN >ANCHORMAN
ANCHORS *pl n* brakes of a motor vehicle
ANCHOS >ANCHOS
ANCHOVETA *n* small anchovy, *Cetengraulis mysticetus*, of the American Pacific, used as bait by tuna fishermen
ANCHOVIES >ANCHOVY
ANCHOVY *n* small strong-tasting fish
ANCHUSA *n* any Eurasian plant of the boraginaceous genus *Anchusa*, having rough hairy stems and leaves and blue flowers
ANCHUSAS >ANCHUSA
ANCHUSIN *same as* >ALKANET
ANCHUSINS >ANCHUSIN
ANCHYLOSE *same as* >ANKYLOSE
ANCIENT *adj* dating from very long ago ▷ *n* member of a civilized nation in the ancient world, esp a Greek, Roman, or Hebrew
ANCIENTER >ANCIENT
ANCIENTLY *adv* in ancient times
ANCIENTRY *n* quality of being ancient
ANCIENTS >ANCIENT
ANCILE *n* mythical Roman shield

ANCILIA > ANCILE
ANCILLA *n* Latin word for servant
ANCILLAE > ANCILLA
ANCILLARY *adj* supporting the main work of an organization ▷ *n* subsidiary or auxiliary thing or person
ANCILLAS > ANCILLA
ANCIPITAL *adj* flattened and having two edges
ANCLE *old spelling of* > ANKLE
ANCLES > ANCLE
ANCOME *n* inflammation
ANCOMES > ANCOME
ANCON *n* projecting bracket or console supporting a cornice
ANCONAL > ANCON
ANCONE *same as* > ANCON
ANCONEAL > ANCON
ANCONES > ANCONE
ANCONOID > ANCON
ANCORA *adv* Italian for encore
ANCRESS *n* female anchorite
ANCRESSES > ANCRESS
AND *n* additional matter or problem
ANDANTE *adv* (piece to be played) moderately slowly ▷ *n* passage or piece to be performed moderately slowly
ANDANTES > ANDANTE
ANDANTINI > ANDANTINO
ANDANTINO *adv* slightly faster or slower than andante ▷ *n* passage or piece to be performed in this way
ANDESINE *n* feldspar mineral of the plagioclase series
ANDESINES > ANDESINE
ANDESITE *n* fine-grained tan or grey volcanic rock
ANDESITES > ANDESITE
ANDESITIC > ANDESITE
ANDESYTE *n* andesite
ANDESYTES > ANDESYTE
ANDIRON *n* iron stand for supporting logs in a fireplace
ANDIRONS > ANDIRON
ANDOUILLE *n* spicy smoked pork sausage with a blackish skin
ANDRADITE *n* yellow, green, or brownish-black garnet
ANDRO *n* type of sex hormone
ANDROECIA *n* stamens of flowering plants collectively
ANDROGEN *n* any of several steroids, produced as hormones by the testes or made synthetically, that promote development of male sexual organs and male secondary sexual characteristics
ANDROGENS > ANDROGEN
ANDROGYNE *n* person having both male and female sexual characteristics and genital tissues
ANDROGYNY *n* condition of having male and female characteristics
ANDROID *n* robot resembling a human ▷ *adj* resembling a human being
ANDROIDS > ANDROID
ANDROLOGY *n* branch of medicine concerned with diseases and conditions specific to men
ANDROMEDA *n* type of shrub
ANDROS > ANDRO
ANDS > AND
ANDVILE *old form of* > ANVIL
ANDVILES > ANDVILE
ANE *Scots word for* > ONE
ANEAR *adv* nearly ▷ *vb* approach
ANEARED > ANEAR
ANEARING > ANEAR
ANEARS > ANEAR
ANEATH *Scots word for* > BENEATH
ANECDOTA *n* unpublished writings
ANECDOTAL *adj* containing or consisting exclusively of anecdotes rather than connected discourse or research conducted under controlled conditions
ANECDOTE *n* short amusing account of an incident
ANECDOTES > ANECDOTE
ANECDOTIC > ANECDOTE
ANECDYSES > ANECDYSIS
ANECDYSIS *n* period between moults in arthropods
ANECHOIC *adj* having a low degree of reverberation of sound
ANELACE *same as* > ANLACE
ANELACES > ANELACE
ANELASTIC *adj* not elastic
ANELE *vb* anoint, esp to give extreme unction to
ANELED > ANELE
ANELES > ANELE
ANELING > ANELE
ANEMIA *n* anaemia
ANEMIAS > ANEMIA
ANEMIC *same as* > ANAEMIC
ANEMOGRAM *n* record produced by anemograph
ANEMOLOGY *n* study of winds
ANEMONE *n* plant with white, purple, or red flowers
ANEMONES > ANEMONE
ANEMOSES > ANEMOSIS
ANEMOSIS *n* cracking in timber caused by wind affecting growing tree
ANENST *dialect word for* > AGAINST
ANENT *prep* lying against
ANERGIA *n* anergy
ANERGIAS > ANERGIA
ANERGIC > ANERGY
ANERGIES > ANERGY
ANERGY *n* lack of energy
ANERLY *Scots word for* > ONLY
ANEROID *adj* not containing a liquid ▷ *n* barometer that does not contain liquid
ANEROIDS > ANEROID
ANES > ANE
ANESTRA > ANESTRUS
ANESTRI > ANESTRUS
ANESTROUS > ANESTRUS
ANESTRUM *n* anestrus
ANESTRUS *same as* > ANOESTRUS
ANETHOL *n* substance derived from oil of anise
ANETHOLE *n* white water-soluble crystalline substance with a liquorice-like odour
ANETHOLES > ANETHOLE
ANETHOLS > ANETHOL
ANETIC *adj* medically soothing
ANEUPLOID *adj* (of polyploid cells or organisms) having a chromosome number that is not an exact multiple of the haploid number ▷ *n* cell or individual of this type
ANEURIN *a less common name for* > THIAMINE
ANEURINS > ANEURIN
ANEURISM *same as* > ANEURYSM
ANEURISMS > ANEURISM
ANEURYSM *n* permanent swelling of a blood vessel
ANEURYSMS > ANEURYSM
ANEW *adv* once more
ANGA *n* a part in Indian music
ANGAKOK *n* Inuit shaman
ANGAKOKS > ANGAKOK
ANGARIA *n* species of shellfish
ANGARIAS > ANGARIA
ANGARIES > ANGARY
ANGARY *n* right of a belligerent state to use the property of a neutral state or to destroy it if necessary, subject to payment of full compensation to the owners
ANGAS > ANGA
ANGASHORE *n* miserable person given to complaining
ANGEKKOK *n* Inuit shaman
ANGEKKOKS > ANGEKKOK
ANGEKOK *n* Inuit shaman
ANGEKOKS > ANGEKOK
ANGEL *n* spiritual being believed to be an attendant or messenger of God ▷ *vb* provide financial support for
ANGELED > ANGEL
ANGELFISH *n* South American aquarium fish with large fins
ANGELHOOD *n* state of being an angel
ANGELIC *adj* very kind, pure, or beautiful
ANGELICA *n* aromatic plant
ANGELICAL *same as* > ANGELIC
ANGELICAS > ANGELICA
ANGELING > ANGEL
ANGELS > ANGEL
ANGELUS *n* series of prayers recited in the morning, at midday, and in the evening, commemorating the Annunciation and Incarnation
ANGELUSES > ANGELUS
ANGER *n* fierce displeasure or extreme annoyance ▷ *vb* make (someone) angry
ANGERED > ANGER
ANGERING > ANGER
ANGERLESS > ANGER
ANGERLY *adv* old form of angrily
ANGERS > ANGER
ANGICO *n* South American tree
ANGICOS > ANGICO
ANGINA *n* heart disorder causing sudden severe chest pains
ANGINAL > ANGINA
ANGINAS > ANGINA
ANGINOSE > ANGINA
ANGINOUS > ANGINA
ANGIOGRAM *n* X-ray picture obtained by angiography
ANGIOLOGY *n* branch of medical science concerned with the blood vessels and the lymphatic system
ANGIOMA *n* tumour consisting of a mass of blood vessels or lymphatic vessels
ANGIOMAS > ANGIOMA
ANGIOMATA > ANGIOMA
ANGKLUNG *n* Asian musical instrument
ANGKLUNGS > ANGKLUNG
ANGLE *n* space between or shape formed by two lines or surfaces that meet ▷ *vb* bend or place (something) at an angle
ANGLED > ANGLE
ANGLEDUG *n* earthworm
ANGLEDUGS > ANGLEDUG
ANGLEPOD *n* American wild flower
ANGLEPODS > ANGLEPOD
ANGLER *n* person who fishes with a hook and line
ANGLERS > ANGLER

ANGLES > ANGLE
ANGLESITE *n* white or grey secondary mineral
ANGLEWISE > ANGLE
ANGLEWORM *n* earthworm used as bait by anglers
ANGLICE *adv* in English
ANGLICISE *same as* > ANGLICIZE
ANGLICISM *n* word, phrase, or idiom peculiar to the English language, esp as spoken in England
ANGLICIST *n* expert in or student of English literature or language
ANGLICIZE *vb* make or become English in outlook, form, etc
ANGLIFIED > ANGLIFY
ANGLIFIES > ANGLIFY
ANGLIFY *same as* > ANGLICIZE
ANGLING *n* art or sport of fishing with a hook and line
ANGLINGS > ANGLING
ANGLIST *same as* > ANGLICIST
ANGLISTS > ANGLIST
ANGLO *n* White inhabitant of the US not of Latin extraction
ANGLOPHIL *n* person having admiration for England or the English
ANGLOS > ANGLO
ANGOLA *same as* > ANGORA
ANGOPHORA *n* Australian tree related to the eucalyptus
ANGORA *n* variety of goat, cat, or rabbit with long silky hair
ANGORAS > ANGORA
ANGOSTURA *n* bitter aromatic bark
ANGRIER > ANGRY
ANGRIES > ANGRY
ANGRIEST > ANGRY
ANGRILY > ANGRY
ANGRINESS > ANGRY
ANGRY *adj* full of anger ▷ *n* angry person
ANGST *n* feeling of anxiety
ANGSTIER > ANGSTY
ANGSTIEST > ANGSTY
ANGSTROM *n* unit of length used to measure wavelengths
ANGSTROMS > ANGSTROM
ANGSTS > ANGST
ANGSTY *adj* displaying or feeling angst, esp in a self-conscious manner
ANGUIFORM *adj* shaped like a snake
ANGUINE *adj* of, relating to, or similar to a snake
ANGUIPED *adj* having snakes for legs
ANGUIPEDE *adj* having snakes for legs
ANGUISH *n* great mental pain ▷ *vb* afflict or be afflicted with anguish
ANGUISHED *adj* feeling or showing great mental pain
ANGUISHES > ANGUISH
ANGULAR *adj* (of a person) lean and bony
ANGULARLY > ANGULAR
ANGULATE *adj* having angles or an angular shape ▷ *vb* make or become angular
ANGULATED > ANGULATE
ANGULATES > ANGULATE
ANGULOSE *adj* having angles
ANGULOUS *adj* having angles
ANHEDONIA *n* inability to feel pleasure
ANHEDONIC > ANHEDONIA
ANHEDRAL *n* downward inclination of an aircraft wing in relation to the lateral axis
ANHINGA *n* type of bird
ANHINGAS > ANHINGA
ANHUNGRED *adj* very hungry
ANHYDRASE *n* enzyme that catalyzes the removal of water
ANHYDRIDE *n* substance that combines with water to form an acid
ANHYDRITE *n* colourless or greyish-white mineral found in sedimentary rocks
ANHYDROUS *adj* containing no water
ANI *n* any of several gregarious tropical American birds of the genus *Crotophaga:* family *Cuculidae* (cuckoos). They have a black plumage, long square-tipped tail, and heavily hooked bill
ANICCA *n* (in Theravada Buddhism) the belief that all things, including the self, are impermanent and constantly changing: the first of the three basic characteristics of existence
ANICCAS > ANICCA
ANICONIC *adj* (of images of deities, symbols, etc) not portrayed in a human or animal form
ANICONISM > ANICONIC
ANICONIST > ANICONIC
ANICUT *n* dam in India
ANICUTS > ANICUT
ANIDROSES > ANIDROSIS
ANIDROSIS *n* absence of sweating
ANIGH *adv* near
ANIGHT *adv* at night
ANIL *n* West Indian shrub, from which indigo is obtained
ANILE *adj* of or like a feeble old woman
ANILIN *n* aniline
ANILINE *n* colourless oily liquid obtained from coal tar and used for making dyes, plastics, and explosives
ANILINES > ANILINE
ANILINGUS *n* sexual stimulation involving oral contact with the anus
ANILINS > ANILIN
ANILITIES > ANILE
ANILITY > ANILE
ANILS > ANIL
ANIMA *n* feminine principle as present in the male unconscious
ANIMACIES > ANIMACY
ANIMACY *n* state of being animate
ANIMAL *n* living creature with specialized sense organs and capable of voluntary motion, esp one other than a human being ▷ *adj* of animals
ANIMALIAN > ANIMAL
ANIMALIC > ANIMAL
ANIMALIER *n* painter or sculptor of animal subjects, esp a member of a group of early 19th-century French sculptors who specialized in realistic figures of animals, usually in bronze
ANIMALISE *same as* > ANIMALIZE
ANIMALISM *n* preoccupation with physical matters
ANIMALIST > ANIMALISM
ANIMALITY *n* animal instincts of human beings
ANIMALIZE *vb* make (a person) brutal or sensual
ANIMALLY *adv* physically
ANIMALS > ANIMAL
ANIMAS > ANIMA
ANIMATE *vb* give life to ▷ *adj* having life
ANIMATED *adj* interesting and lively
ANIMATELY > ANIMATE
ANIMATER *same as* > ANIMATOR
ANIMATERS > ANIMATER
ANIMATES > ANIMATE
ANIMATIC *n* animated film sequence
ANIMATICS > ANIMATIC
ANIMATING > ANIMATE
ANIMATION *n* technique of making cartoon films
ANIMATISM *n* belief that inanimate objects have consciousness
ANIMATIST > ANIMATISM
ANIMATO *adv* (to be performed) in a lively manner
ANIMATOR *n* person who makes animated cartoons
ANIMATORS > ANIMATOR
ANIME *n* type of Japanese animated film with themes and styles similar to manga comics
ANIMES > ANIME
ANIMI > ANIMUS
ANIMIS > ANIMI
ANIMISM *n* belief that natural objects possess souls
ANIMISMS > ANIMISM
ANIMIST > ANIMISM
ANIMISTIC > ANIMISM
ANIMISTS > ANIMISM
ANIMOSITY *n* hostility, hatred
ANIMUS *n* hatred, animosity
ANIMUSES > ANIMUS
ANION *n* ion with negative charge
ANIONIC > ANION
ANIONS > ANION
ANIS > ANI
ANISE *n* plant with liquorice-flavoured seeds
ANISEED *n* liquorice-flavoured seeds of the anise plant
ANISEEDS > ANISEED
ANISES > ANISE
ANISETTE *n* liquorice-flavoured liqueur made from aniseed
ANISETTES > ANISETTE
ANISIC > ANISE
ANISOGAMY *n* type of sexual reproduction in which the gametes are dissimilar, either in size alone or in size and form
ANISOLE *n* colourless pleasant-smelling liquid used as a solvent
ANISOLES > ANISOLE
ANKER *n* old liquid measure for wine
ANKERITE *n* greyish to brown mineral that resembles dolomite
ANKERITES > ANKERITE
ANKERS > ANKER
ANKH *n* T-shaped cross with a loop on the top, which symbolized eternal life in ancient Egypt
ANKHS > ANKH
ANKLE *n* joint between the foot and leg ▷ *vb* move
ANKLEBONE *the nontechnical name for* > TALUS
ANKLED > ANKLE
ANKLES > ANKLE
ANKLET *n* ornamental chain worn round the ankle
ANKLETS > ANKLET
ANKLING > ANKLE
ANKLONG *n* Asian musical instrument
ANKLONGS > ANKLONG
ANKLUNG *n* Asian musical instrument

ANKLUNGS > ANKLUNG
ANKUS *n* stick used, esp in India, for goading elephants
ANKUSES > ANKUS
ANKUSH *n* Indian weapon
ANKUSHES > ANKUSH
ANKYLOSE *vb* (of bones in a joint, etc) to fuse or stiffen by ankylosis
ANKYLOSED > ANKYLOSE
ANKYLOSES > ANKYLOSE
ANKYLOSIS *n* abnormal immobility of a joint, caused by a fibrous growth
ANKYLOTIC > ANKYLOSIS
ANLACE *n* medieval short dagger with a broad tapering blade
ANLACES > ANLACE
ANLAGE *n* organ or part in the earliest stage of development
ANLAGEN > ANLAGE
ANLAGES > ANLAGE
ANLAS *same as* > ANLACE
ANLASES > ANLAS
ANN *n* old Scots word for a widow's pension
ANNA *n* former Indian coin worth one sixteenth of a rupee
ANNAL *n* recorded events of one year
ANNALISE *vb* record in annals
ANNALISED > ANNALISE
ANNALISES > ANNALISE
ANNALIST > ANNAL
ANNALISTS > ANNAL
ANNALIZE *vb* record in annals
ANNALIZED > ANNALIZE
ANNALIZES > ANNALIZE
ANNALS > ANNAL
ANNAS > ANNA
ANNAT *n* singular of annates
ANNATES *pl n* first year's revenue of a see, an abbacy, or a minor benefice, paid to the pope
ANNATS > ANNAT
ANNATTA *n* annatto
ANNATTAS > ANNATTA
ANNATTO *n* small tropical American tree, *Bixa orellana*, having red or pinkish flowers and pulpy seeds that yield a dye
ANNATTOS > ANNATTO
ANNEAL *vb* toughen (metal or glass) by heating and slow cooling ▷ *n* act of annealing
ANNEALED > ANNEAL
ANNEALER > ANNEAL
ANNEALERS > ANNEAL
ANNEALING > ANNEAL
ANNEALS > ANNEAL
ANNECTENT *adj* connecting
ANNELID *n* worm with a segmented body, such as an earthworm ▷ *adj* of, relating to, or belonging to the *Annelida*
ANNELIDAN > ANNELID
ANNELIDS > ANNELID
ANNEX *vb* seize (territory)
ANNEXABLE > ANNEX
ANNEXE *n* extension to a building
ANNEXED > ANNEX
ANNEXES > ANNEXE
ANNEXING > ANNEX
ANNEXION *n* old form of annexation
ANNEXIONS > ANNEXION
ANNEXMENT > ANNEX
ANNEXURE *n* something that is added
ANNEXURES > ANNEXURE
ANNICUT *n* dam in India
ANNICUTS > ANNICUT
ANNO *adv* Latin for in the year
ANNONA *n* American tree or shrub
ANNONAS > ANNONA
ANNOTATE *vb* add notes to (a written work)
ANNOTATED > ANNOTATE
ANNOTATES > ANNOTATE
ANNOTATOR > ANNOTATE
ANNOUNCE *vb* make known publicly
ANNOUNCED > ANNOUNCE
ANNOUNCER *n* person who introduces radio or television programmes
ANNOUNCES > ANNOUNCE
ANNOY *vb* irritate or displease
ANNOYANCE *n* feeling of being annoyed
ANNOYED > ANNOY
ANNOYER > ANNOY
ANNOYERS > ANNOY
ANNOYING *adj* causing irritation or displeasure
ANNOYS > ANNOY
ANNS > ANN
ANNUAL *adj* happening once a year ▷ *n* plant that completes its life cycle in a year
ANNUALISE *same as* > ANNUALIZE
ANNUALIZE *vb* calculate (a rate) for or as if for a year
ANNUALLY > ANNUAL
ANNUALS > ANNUAL
ANNUITANT *n* person in receipt of or entitled to an annuity
ANNUITIES > ANNUITY
ANNUITY *n* fixed sum paid every year
ANNUL *vb* declare (something, esp a marriage) invalid
ANNULAR *adj* ring-shaped ▷ *n* ring finger
ANNULARLY > ANNULAR
ANNULARS > ANNULAR
ANNULATE *adj* having, composed of, or marked with rings ▷ *n* annelid
ANNULATED > ANNULATE
ANNULATES > ANNULATE
ANNULET *n* moulding in the form of a ring, as at the top of a column adjoining the capital
ANNULETS > ANNULET
ANNULI > ANNULUS
ANNULLED > ANNUL
ANNULLING > ANNUL
ANNULMENT *n* formal declaration that a contract or marriage is invalid
ANNULOSE *adj* (of earthworms, crustaceans, and similar animals) having a body formed of a series of rings
ANNULS > ANNUL
ANNULUS *n* area between two concentric circles
ANNULUSES > ANNULUS
ANOA *n* type of small cattle
ANOAS > ANOA
ANOBIID *n* any type of beetle
ANOBIIDS > ANOBIID
ANODAL > ANODE
ANODALLY > ANODE
ANODE *n* positive electrode in a battery, valve, etc
ANODES > ANODE
ANODIC > ANODE
ANODISE *same as* > ANODIZE
ANODISED > ANODISE
ANODISES > ANODISE
ANODISING > ANODISE
ANODIZE *vb* coat (metal) with a protective oxide film by electrolysis
ANODIZED > ANODIZE
ANODIZES > ANODIZE
ANODIZING > ANODIZE
ANODONTIA *n* congenital absence of teeth
ANODYNE *n* something that relieves pain or distress ▷ *adj* relieving pain or distress
ANODYNES > ANODYNE
ANODYNIC > ANODYNE
ANOESES > ANOESIS
ANOESIS *n* feeling without understanding
ANOESTRA > ANOESTRUS
ANOESTRI > ANOESTRUS
ANOESTRUM > ANOESTRUS
ANOESTRUS *n* period of sexual inactivity between two periods of oestrus in many mammals
ANOETIC > ANOESIS
ANOINT *vb* smear with oil as a sign of consecration
ANOINTED > ANOINT
ANOINTER > ANOINT
ANOINTERS > ANOINT
ANOINTING > ANOINT
ANOINTS > ANOINT
ANOLE *n* type of lizard
ANOLES > ANOLE
ANOLYTE *n* part of electrolyte around anode
ANOLYTES > ANOLYTE
ANOMALIES > ANOMALY
ANOMALOUS *adj* different from the normal or usual order or type
ANOMALY *n* something that deviates from the normal, irregularity
ANOMIC > ANOMIE
ANOMIE *n* lack of social or moral standards
ANOMIES > ANOMIE
ANOMY *same as* > ANOMIE
ANON *adv* in a short time, soon
ANONYM *n* anonymous person or publication
ANONYMA *n* promiscuous woman
ANONYMAS > ANONYMA
ANONYMISE *same as* > ANONYMIZE
ANONYMITY > ANONYMOUS
ANONYMIZE *vb* organize in a way that preserves anonymity
ANONYMOUS *adj* by someone whose name is unknown or withheld
ANONYMS > ANONYM
ANOOPSIA *n* squint in which the eye turns upwards
ANOOPSIAS > ANOOPSIA
ANOPHELES *n* any of various mosquitoes constituting the genus *Anopheles*, some species of which transmit the malaria parasite to man
ANOPIA *n* inability to see
ANOPIAS > ANOPIA
ANOPSIA *n* squint in which the eye turns upwards
ANOPSIAS > ANOPSIA
ANORAK *n* light waterproof hooded jacket
ANORAKS > ANORAK
ANORECTAL *adj* of the anus and rectum
ANORECTIC > ANOREXIA
ANORETIC *n* anorectic
ANORETICS > ANORETIC
ANOREXIA *n* psychological disorder characterized by fear of becoming fat and refusal to eat
ANOREXIAS > ANOREXIA
ANOREXIC > ANOREXIA
ANOREXICS > ANOREXIA
ANOREXIES > ANOREXY
ANOREXY *old name for* > ANOREXIA
ANORTHIC *another word for* > TRICLINIC
ANORTHITE *n* white to greyish-white or reddish-white mineral
ANOSMATIC > ANOSMIA
ANOSMIA *n* loss of the sense of smell, usually as the result of a lesion of the olfactory nerve, disease in another organ or part, or obstruction of the nasal

passages
ANOSMIAS > ANOSMIA
ANOSMIC > ANOSMIA
ANOTHER *adj* one more
ANOUGH *adj* enough
ANOUROUS *adj* having no tail
ANOVULANT *n* drug preventing ovulation
ANOVULAR *adj* without ovulation
ANOW *adj* old form of enough
ANOXAEMIA *n* deficiency in the amount of oxygen in the arterial blood
ANOXAEMIC > ANOXAEMIA
ANOXEMIA *same as* > ANOXAEMIA
ANOXEMIAS > ANOXEMIA
ANOXEMIC > ANOXEMIA
ANOXIA *n* lack or absence of oxygen
ANOXIAS > ANOXIA
ANOXIC > ANOXIA
ANSA *n* either end of Saturn's rings
ANSAE > ANSA
ANSATE *adj* having a handle or handle-like part
ANSATED *adj* ansate
ANSERINE *adj* of or resembling a goose ▷ *n* chemical compound
ANSERINES > ANSERINE
ANSEROUS *same as* > ANSERINE
ANSWER *n* reply to a question, request, letter, etc ▷ *vb* give an answer (to)
ANSWERED > ANSWER
ANSWERER > ANSWER
ANSWERERS > ANSWER
ANSWERING > ANSWER
ANSWERS > ANSWER
ANT *n* small insect living in highly-organized colonies
ANTA *n* pilaster attached to the end of a side wall or sometimes to the side of a doorway
ANTACID *n* substance that counteracts acidity, esp in the stomach ▷ *adj* having the properties of this substance
ANTACIDS > ANTACID
ANTAE > ANTA
ANTALGIC *n* pain-relieving drug
ANTALGICS > ANTALGIC
ANTALKALI *n* substance that neutralizes alkalis
ANTAR *old word for* > CAVE
ANTARA *n* South American panpipes
ANTARAS > ANTARA
ANTARCTIC *adj* relating to Antarctica
ANTARS > ANTAR
ANTAS > ANTA
ANTBEAR *n* aardvark
ANTBEARS > ANTBEAR
ANTBIRD *n* any of various dull-coloured South American passerine birds that typically feed on ants
ANTBIRDS > ANTBIRD
ANTE *n* player's stake in poker ▷ *vb* place (one's stake) in poker
ANTEATER *n* mammal which feeds on ants by means of a long snout
ANTEATERS > ANTEATER
ANTECEDE *vb* go before, as in time, order, etc
ANTECEDED > ANTECEDE
ANTECEDES > ANTECEDE
ANTECHOIR *n* part of a church in front of the choir, usually enclosed by screens, tombs, etc
ANTED > ANTE
ANTEDATE *vb* precede in time ▷ *n* earlier date
ANTEDATED > ANTEDATE
ANTEDATES > ANTEDATE
ANTEED > ANTE
ANTEFIX *n* carved ornament at the eaves of a roof to hide the joint between the tiles
ANTEFIXA > ANTEFIX
ANTEFIXAE > ANTEFIX
ANTEFIXAL > ANTEFIX
ANTEFIXES > ANTEFIX
ANTEING > ANTE
ANTELOPE *n* deerlike mammal with long legs and horns
ANTELOPES > ANTELOPE
ANTELUCAN *adj* before daylight
ANTENATAL *adj* during pregnancy, before birth ▷ *n* examination during pregnancy
ANTENATI *n* people born before certain date
ANTENNA *n* insect's feeler
ANTENNAE > ANTENNA
ANTENNAL > ANTENNA
ANTENNARY > ANTENNA
ANTENNAS > ANTENNA
ANTENNULE *n* one of a pair of small mobile appendages on the heads of crustaceans in front of the antennae, usually having a sensory function
ANTEPAST *n* appetizer
ANTEPASTS > ANTEPAST
ANTERIOR *adj* the front
ANTEROOM *n* small room leading into a larger one, often used as a waiting room
ANTEROOMS > ANTEROOM
ANTES > ANTE
ANTETYPE *n* earlier form
ANTETYPES > ANTETYPE
ANTEVERT *vb* displace (an organ or part) by tilting it forward
ANTEVERTS > ANTEVERT
ANTHELIA > ANTHELION
ANTHELION *n* faint halo sometimes seen in polar or high altitude regions around the shadow of an object cast onto a thick cloud bank or fog
ANTHELIX *n* prominent curved fold of cartilage just inside the outer rim of the external ear
ANTHEM *n* song of loyalty, esp to a country ▷ *vb* provide with an anthem
ANTHEMED > ANTHEM
ANTHEMIA > ANTHEMION
ANTHEMIC > ANTHEM
ANTHEMING > ANTHEM
ANTHEMION *n* floral design, used esp in ancient Greek and Roman architecture and decoration, usually consisting of honeysuckle, lotus, or palmette leaf motifs
ANTHEMS > ANTHEM
ANTHER *n* part of a flower's stamen containing pollen
ANTHERAL > ANTHER
ANTHERID *n* antheridium
ANTHERIDS > ANTHERID
ANTHERS > ANTHER
ANTHESES > ANTHESIS
ANTHESIS *n* time when a flower becomes sexually functional
ANTHILL *n* mound of soil, leaves, etc, near the entrance of an ants' nest, carried and deposited there by the ants while constructing the nest
ANTHILLS > ANTHILL
ANTHOCARP *n* fruit developing from many flowers
ANTHOCYAN *n* any of a class of water-soluble glycosidic pigments
ANTHODIA > ANTHODIUM
ANTHODIUM *another name for* > CAPITULUM
ANTHOID *adj* resembling a flower
ANTHOLOGY *n* collection of poems or other literary pieces by various authors
ANTHOTAXY *n* arrangement of flowers on a stem or parts on a flower
ANTHOZOAN *n* any of the solitary or colonial sessile marine coelenterates of the class *Anthozoa*, including the corals, sea anemones, and sea pens, in which the body is in the form of a polyp ▷ *adj* of or relating to the class *Anthozoa*
ANTHOZOIC > ANTHOZOAN
ANTHRACES > ANTHRAX
ANTHRACIC *adj* of anthrax
ANTHRAX *n* dangerous disease of cattle and sheep, communicable to humans
ANTHRAXES > ANTHRAX
ANTHROPIC *adj* of or relating to human beings
ANTHURIUM *n* any of various tropical American aroid plants constituting the genus *Anthurium*, many of which are cultivated as house plants for their showy foliage and their flowers, which are borne in a long-stalked spike surrounded by a flaring heart-shaped white or red bract
ANTI *adj* opposed (to) ▷ *n* opponent of a party, policy, or attitude
ANTIABUSE *adj* designed to prevent abuse
ANTIACNE *adj* inhibiting the development of acne
ANTIAGING *adj* resisting the effects of ageing
ANTIAIR *adj* countering attack by aircraft or missile
ANTIALIEN *adj* designed to prevent foreign animal or plant species from becoming established
ANTIAR *another name for* > UPAS
ANTIARIN *n* poison derived from antiar
ANTIARINS > ANTIARIN
ANTIARMOR *adj* designed or equipped to combat armoured vehicles
ANTIARS > ANTIAR
ANTIATOM *n* atom composed of antiparticles, in which the nucleus contains antiprotons with orbiting positrons
ANTIATOMS > ANTIATOM
ANTIAUXIN *n* substance acting against auxin
ANTIBIAS *adj* countering bias
ANTIBLACK *adj* hostile to black people
ANTIBODY *n* protein produced in the blood, which destroys bacteria
ANTIBOSS *adj* acting against bosses
ANTIBUG *adj* acting against computer bugs
ANTIBUSER *n* person who opposes the policy of transporting students to faraway schools to achieve racial balance
ANTIC *n* actor in a ludicrous or grotesque part ▷ *adj* fantastic
ANTICAL *adj* (of the position of plant parts) in front of or above another part
ANTICALLY > ANTICAL

ANTICAR *n* opposed to cars
ANTICHLOR *n* substance used to remove chlorine from a material after bleaching or to neutralize the chlorine present
ANTICISE *same as* > ANTICIZE
ANTICISED > ANTICISE
ANTICISES > ANTICISE
ANTICITY *adj* opposed to cities
ANTICIVIC *adj* opposed to citizenship
ANTICIZE *vb* play absurdly
ANTICIZED > ANTICIZE
ANTICIZES > ANTICIZE
ANTICK *vb* perform antics
ANTICKE *adj* old form of antique
ANTICKED > ANTICK
ANTICKING > ANTICK
ANTICKS > ANTICK
ANTICLINE *n* fold of rock raised up into a broad arch so that the strata slope down on both sides
ANTICLING *adj* acting against clinging
ANTICLY *adv* grotesquely
ANTICODON *n* element of RNA
ANTICOLD *adj* preventing or fighting the common cold
ANTICOUS *adj* on the part of a flower furthest from the stem
ANTICRACK *adj* protecting a computer against unauthorized access
ANTICRIME *adj* preventing or fighting crime
ANTICS *pl n* absurd acts or postures
ANTICULT *n* organisation that is opposed to religious cults
ANTICULTS > ANTICULT
ANTIDORA *n* bread used in Russian Orthodox Communion
ANTIDOTAL > ANTIDOTE
ANTIDOTE *n* substance that counteracts a poison ▷ *vb* counteract with an antidote
ANTIDOTED > ANTIDOTE
ANTIDOTES > ANTIDOTE
ANTIDRAFT *adj* opposed to conscription
ANTIDRUG *adj* intended to discourage illegal drug use
ANTIDUNE *n* sand hill or inclined bedding plane that forms a steep slope against the direction of a fast-flowing current
ANTIDUNES > ANTIDUNE
ANTIELITE *adj* opposed to elitism
ANTIENT *old spelling of* > ANCIENT
ANTIENTS > ANTIENT
ANTIFAT *adj* acting to remove or prevent fat
ANTIFLU *adj* acting against influenza
ANTIFOAM *adj* allowing gas to escape rather than form foam
ANTIFOG *adj* preventing the buildup of moisture on a surface
ANTIFRAUD *adj* acting against fraud
ANTIFUR *adj* opposed to the wearing of fur garments
ANTIGANG *adj* designed to restrict the activities of criminal gangs
ANTIGAY *adj* hostile to homosexuals
ANTIGEN *n* substance causing the blood to produce antibodies
ANTIGENE *n* antigen
ANTIGENES > ANTIGENE
ANTIGENIC > ANTIGEN
ANTIGENS > ANTIGEN
ANTIGLARE *adj* cutting down glare
ANTIGRAFT *adj* designed to reduce corruption
ANTIGUN *adj* opposed to the possession of guns
ANTIHELIX *same as* > ANTHELIX
ANTIHERO *n* central character in a book, film, etc, who lacks the traditional heroic virtues
ANTIHUMAN *adj* inhuman
ANTIJAM *adj* preventing jamming
ANTIKING *n* rival to an established king
ANTIKINGS > ANTIKING
ANTIKNOCK *n* substance added to motor fuel to reduce knocking in the engine caused by too rapid combustion
ANTILABOR *adj* opposed to labor interests
ANTILEAK *adj* preventing leaks
ANTILEFT *adj* opposed to the left wing in politics
ANTILIFE *adj* in favour of abortion
ANTILIFER *n* person in favour of abortion
ANTILOCK *adj* designed to prevent overbraking
ANTILOG *n* number whose logarithm to a given base is a given number
ANTILOGS > ANTILOG
ANTILOGY *n* contradiction in terms
ANTIMACHO *adj* opposed to macho attitudes
ANTIMALE *adj* opposed to men
ANTIMAN *adj* opposed to men
ANTIMASK *n* interlude in a masque
ANTIMASKS > ANTIMASK
ANTIMERE *n* part or organ of a bilaterally or radially symmetrical organism that corresponds to a similar structure on the other side of the axis, such as the right or left limb of a four-legged animal
ANTIMERES > ANTIMERE
ANTIMERIC > ANTIMERE
ANTIMINE *adj* designed to counteract landmines
ANTIMONIC *adj* of or containing antimony in the pentavalent state
ANTIMONY *n* brittle silvery-white metallic element
ANTIMONYL *n* of, consisting of, or containing the monovalent group SbO-
ANTIMUON *n* antiparticle of a muon
ANTIMUONS > ANTIMUON
ANTIMUSIC *n* music intended to overthrow traditional conventions and expectations
ANTIMYCIN *n* antibiotic drug
ANTING *n* placing or rubbing of ants by birds on their feathers. The body fluids of the ants are thought to repel parasites
ANTINGS > ANTING
ANTINODAL > ANTINODE
ANTINODE *n* point at which the amplitude of one of the two kinds of displacement in a standing wave has maximum value. Generally the other kind of displacement has its minimum value at this point
ANTINODES > ANTINODE
ANTINOISE *n* sound generated so that it is out of phase with a noise, such as that made by an engine, in order to reduce the noise level by interference
ANTINOME *n* opposite
ANTINOMES > ANTINOME
ANTINOMIC > ANTINOMY
ANTINOMY *n* contradiction between two laws or principles that are reasonable in themselves
ANTINOVEL *n* type of prose fiction in which conventional elements of the novel are rejected
ANTINUKE *same as* > ANTINUKER
ANTINUKER *n* person who is opposed to nuclear weapons or energy
ANTINUKES > ANTINUKE
ANTIPAPAL *adj* opposed to the pope
ANTIPARTY *adj* opposed to a political party
ANTIPASTI > ANTIPASTO
ANTIPASTO *n* appetizer in an Italian meal
ANTIPATHY *n* dislike, hostility
ANTIPHON *n* hymn sung in alternate parts by two groups of singers
ANTIPHONS > ANTIPHON
ANTIPHONY *n* antiphonal singing of a musical composition by two choirs
ANTIPILL *adj* opposed to the use of the contraceptive pill
ANTIPODAL *adj* of or relating to diametrically opposite points on the earth's surface
ANTIPODE *n* exact or direct opposite
ANTIPODES *pl n* any two places diametrically opposite one another on the earth's surface
ANTIPOLAR > ANTIPOLE
ANTIPOLE *n* opposite pole
ANTIPOLES > ANTIPOLE
ANTIPOPE *n* pope set up in opposition to the one chosen by church laws
ANTIPOPES > ANTIPOPE
ANTIPORN *adj* opposed to pornography
ANTIPOT *adj* opposed to illegal use of marijuana
ANTIPRESS *adj* hostile to the news media
ANTIPYIC *n* drug acting against suppuration
ANTIPYICS > ANTIPYIC
ANTIQUARK *n* antiparticle of a quark
ANTIQUARY *n* student or collector of antiques or ancient works of art
ANTIQUATE *vb* make obsolete or old-fashioned
ANTIQUE *n* object of an earlier period, valued for its beauty, workmanship, or age ▷ *adj* made in an earlier period ▷ *vb* give an antique appearance to
ANTIQUED > ANTIQUE
ANTIQUELY > ANTIQUE
ANTIQUER *n* collector of antiques
ANTIQUERS > ANTIQUE
ANTIQUES > ANTIQUE
ANTIQUEY *adj* having the appearance of an antique
ANTIQUING > ANTIQUE
ANTIQUITY *n* great age
ANTIRADAR *adj* preventing detection by radar
ANTIRAPE *adj* protecting against rape
ANTIRED *adj* of a particular colour of antiquark
ANTIRIOT *adj* (of police officers, equipment,

measures, etc) designed for or engaged in the control of crowds
ANTIROCK *adj* designed to prevent a vehicle from rocking
ANTIROLL *adj* designed to prevent a vehicle from tilting
ANTIROYAL *adj* opposed to the monarchy
ANTIRUST *adj* (of a product or procedure) effective against rust ▷ *n* substance or device that prevents rust
ANTIRUSTS > ANTIRUST
ANTIS > ANTI
ANTISAG *adj* preventing sagging
ANTISCIAN *n* person living on other side of equator
ANTISENSE *adj* acting in opposite way to RNA
ANTISERA > ANTISERUM
ANTISERUM *n* blood serum containing antibodies used to treat or provide immunity to a disease
ANTISEX *adj* opposed to sexual activity
ANTISHARK *adj* protecting against sharks
ANTISHIP *adj* designed for attacking ships
ANTISHOCK *n* one of a pair of walking poles designed to reduce stress on the knees
ANTISKID *adj* intended to prevent skidding
ANTISLEEP *adj* acting to prevent sleep
ANTISLIP *adj* acting to prevent slipping
ANTISMOG *adj* reducing smog
ANTISMOKE *adj* preventing smoke
ANTISMUT *adj* opposed to obscene material
ANTISNOB *n* person opposed to snobbery
ANTISNOBS > ANTISNOB
ANTISOLAR *adj* opposite to the sun
ANTISPAM *adj* intended to prevent spam
ANTISPAST *n* group of four syllables in poetic metre
ANTISTAT *n* substance preventing static electricity
ANTISTATE *adj* opposed to state authority
ANTISTATS > ANTISTAT
ANTISTICK *adj* preventing things from sticking to a surface
ANTISTORY *n* story without a plot
ANTISTYLE *n* style that rejects traditional aesthetics
ANTITANK *adj* (of weapons) designed to destroy military tanks
ANTITAX *adj* opposed to taxation
ANTITHEFT *adj* (of a device, campaign, system, etc) designed to prevent theft
ANTITHET *n* example of antithesis
ANTITHETS > ANTITHET
ANTITOXIC > ANTITOXIN
ANTITOXIN *n* (serum containing) an antibody that acts against a toxin
ANTITRADE *n* wind blowing in the opposite direction to a trade wind
ANTITRAGI *n* cartilaginous projections of the external ear opposite the tragus
ANTITRUST *adj* (of laws) opposing business monopolies ▷ *n* regulating or opposing trusts, monopolies, cartels, or similar organizations, esp in order to prevent unfair competition
ANTITUMOR *adj* acting against tumours
ANTITYPAL > ANTITYPE
ANTITYPE *n* person or thing that is foreshadowed or represented by a type or symbol, esp a character or event in the New Testament prefigured in the Old Testament
ANTITYPES > ANTITYPE
ANTITYPIC > ANTITYPE
ANTIULCER *adj* used to treat ulcers
ANTIUNION *adj* opposed to union
ANTIURBAN *adj* opposed to city life
ANTIVENIN *n* antitoxin that counteracts a specific venom, esp snake venom
ANTIVENOM *n* venom antidote
ANTIVIRAL *adj* inhibiting the growth of viruses ▷ *n* any antiviral drug: used to treat diseases caused by viruses, such as herpes infections and AIDS
ANTIVIRUS *adj* relating to software designed to protect computer files from viruses ▷ *n* such a piece of software
ANTIWAR *adj* opposed to war
ANTIWEAR *adj* preventing wear
ANTIWEED *adj* killing or preventing weeds
ANTIWHITE *adj* hostile to white people
ANTIWOMAN *adj* hostile to women
ANTIWORLD *n* hypothetical or supposed world or universe composed of antimatter
ANTLER *n* branched horn of a male deer
ANTLERED *adj* having antlers
ANTLERS > ANTLER
ANTLIA *n* butterfly proboscis
ANTLIAE > ANTLIA
ANTLIATE *adj* relating to antlia
ANTLIKE *adj* of or like an ant or ants
ANTLION *n* any of various neuropterous insects of the family *Myrmeleontidae*, which typically resemble dragonflies and are most common in tropical regions
ANTLIONS > ANTLION
ANTONYM *n* word that means the opposite of another
ANTONYMIC > ANTONYM
ANTONYMS > ANTONYM
ANTONYMY *n* use of antonyms
ANTRA > ANTRUM
ANTRAL > ANTRUM
ANTRE *n* cavern or cave
ANTRES > ANTRE
ANTRORSE *adj* directed or pointing upwards or forwards
ANTRUM *n* natural cavity, esp in a bone
ANTRUMS > ANTRUM
ANTS > ANT
ANTSIER > ANTSY
ANTSIEST > ANTSY
ANTSINESS > ANTSY
ANTSY *adj* restless, nervous, and impatient
ANTWACKIE *adj* old-fashioned
ANUCLEATE *adj* without a nucleus
ANURAL *adj* without a tail
ANURAN *n* any of the vertebrates of the order *Anura* (or *Salientia*), characterized by absence of a tail and very long hind legs specialized for hopping: class *Amphibia* (amphibians). The group includes the frogs and toads ▷ *adj* of, relating to, or belonging to the order *Anura*
ANURANS > ANURAN
ANURESES > ANURESIS
ANURESIS *n* inability to urinate even though urine is formed by the kidneys and retained in the urinary bladder
ANURETIC > ANURESIS
ANURIA *n* complete suppression of urine formation, often as the result of a kidney disorder
ANURIAS > ANURIA
ANURIC > ANURIA
ANUROUS *adj* lacking a tail
ANUS *n* opening at the end of the alimentary canal, through which faeces are discharged
ANUSES > ANUS
ANVIL *n* heavy iron block on which metals are hammered into particular shapes ▷ *vb* forge on an anvil
ANVILED > ANVIL
ANVILING > ANVIL
ANVILLED > ANVIL
ANVILLING > ANVIL
ANVILS > ANVIL
ANVILTOP *n* type of stormcloud formation
ANVILTOPS > ANVILTOP
ANXIETIES > ANXIETY
ANXIETY *n* state of being anxious
ANXIOUS *adj* worried and tense
ANXIOUSLY > ANXIOUS
ANY *adj* one or some, no matter which ▷ *adv* at all
ANYBODIES > ANYBODY
ANYBODY *n* any person at random
ANYHOW *adv* anyway
ANYMORE *adv* at present
ANYON *n* (in mathematics) projective representation of a Lie group
ANYONE *pron* any person ▷ *n* any person at random
ANYONES > ANYONE
ANYONS > ANYON
ANYPLACE *adv* in, at, or to any unspecified place
ANYROAD *a northern English dialect word for* > ANYWAY
ANYTHING *pron* any object, event, or action whatever ▷ *n* any thing at random
ANYTHINGS > ANYTHING
ANYTIME *adv* at any time
ANYWAY *adv* at any rate, nevertheless
ANYWAYS *nonstandard word for* > ANYWAY
ANYWHEN *adv* at any time
ANYWHERE *adv* in, at, or to any place
ANYWHERES *nonstandard word for* > ANYWHERE
ANYWISE *adv* in any way or manner
ANZIANI *n* Italian word for councillors
AORIST *n* tense of the verb in classical Greek and in certain other inflected languages, indicating past action without reference to whether the action involved was momentary or continuous

AORISTIC > AORIST
AORISTS > AORIST
AORTA *n* main artery of the body, carrying oxygen-rich blood from the heart
AORTAE > AORTA
AORTAL > AORTA
AORTAS > AORTA
AORTIC > AORTA
AORTITIS *n* inflammation of the aorta
AOUDAD *n* wild mountain sheep, *Ammotragus lervia*, of N Africa, having horns curved in a semicircle and long hair covering the neck and forelegs
AOUDADS > AOUDAD
APACE *adv* swiftly
APACHE *n* Parisian gangster or ruffian
APACHES > APACHE
APADANA *n* ancient Persian palace hall
APADANAS > APADANA
APAGE *interj* Greek word meaning go away
APAGOGE *n* reduction to absurdity
APAGOGES > APAGOGE
APAGOGIC > APAGOGE
APAID > APAY
APANAGE *same as* > APPANAGE
APANAGED *adj* having apanage
APANAGES > APANAGE
APAREJO *n* kind of packsaddle made of stuffed leather cushions
APAREJOS > APAREJO
APART *adv* to pieces or in pieces
APARTHEID *n* former official government policy of racial segregation in S Africa
APARTMENT *n* room in a building
APARTNESS > APART
APATETIC *adj* of or relating to coloration that disguises and protects an animal
APATHATON *old word for* > EPITHET
APATHETIC *adj* having or showing little or no emotion
APATHIES > APATHY
APATHY *n* lack of interest or enthusiasm
APATITE *n* pale green to purple mineral, found in igneous rocks
APATITES > APATITE
APATOSAUR *n* long-necked dinosaur
APAY *vb* old word meaning satisfy
APAYD > APAY
APAYING > APAY
APAYS > APAY
APE *n* tailless monkey such as the chimpanzee or gorilla ▷ *vb* imitate
APEAK *adj* in a vertical or almost vertical position
APED > APE
APEDOM *n* state of being an ape
APEDOMS > APEDOM
APEEK *adv* nautical word meaning vertically
APEHOOD *n* state of being ape
APEHOODS > APEHOOD
APELIKE > APE
APEMAN *n* extinct primate thought to have been the forerunner of true humans
APEMEN > APEMAN
APEPSIA *n* digestive disorder
APEPSIAS > APEPSIA
APEPSIES > APEPSY
APEPSY *n* apepsia
APER *n* person who apes
APERCU *n* outline
APERCUS > APERCU
APERIENT *adj* having a mild laxative effect ▷ *n* mild laxative
APERIENTS > APERIENT
APERIES > APERY
APERIODIC *adj* not periodic
APERITIF *n* alcoholic drink taken before a meal
APERITIFS > APERITIF
APERITIVE *n* laxative
APERS > APER
APERT *adj* open
APERTNESS > APERT
APERTURAL > APERTURE
APERTURE *n* opening or hole
APERTURED *adj* having an aperture
APERTURES > APERTURE
APERY *n* imitative behaviour
APES > APE
APETALIES > APETALOUS
APETALOUS *adj* (of flowering plants) having no petals
APETALY > APETALOUS
APEX *n* highest point
APEXES > APEX
APGAR as in *apgar score* system for determining the condition of an infant at birth
APHAGIA *n* refusal or inability to swallow
APHAGIAS > APHAGIA
APHAKIA *n* absence of the lens of an eye, congenital or otherwise
APHAKIAS > APHAKIA
APHANITE *n* any fine-grained rock, such as a basalt, containing minerals that cannot be distinguished with the naked eye
APHANITES > APHANITE
APHANITIC > APHANITE
APHASIA *n* disorder of the central nervous system that affects the ability to speak and understand words
APHASIAC > APHASIA
APHASIACS > APHASIA
APHASIAS > APHASIA
APHASIC > APHASIA
APHASICS > APHASIA
APHELIA > APHELION
APHELIAN > APHELION
APHELION *n* point of a planet's orbit that is farthest from the sun
APHELIONS > APHELION
APHERESES > APHERESIS
APHERESIS *n* omission of a letter or syllable at the beginning of a word
APHERETIC > APHERESIS
APHESES > APHESIS
APHESIS *n* gradual disappearance of an unstressed vowel at the beginning of a word, as in *squire* from *esquire*
APHETIC > APHESIS
APHETISE *vb* lose a vowel at the beginning of a word
APHETISED > APHETISE
APHETISES > APHETISE
APHETIZE *vb* lose a vowel at the beginning of a word
APHETIZED > APHETIZE
APHETIZES > APHETIZE
APHICIDE *n* substance for killing aphids
APHICIDES > APHICIDE
APHID *n* small insect which sucks the sap from plants
APHIDES > APHIS
APHIDIAN > APHID
APHIDIANS > APHID
APHIDIOUS > APHID
APHIDS > APHID
APHIS *n* any of various aphids constituting the genus *Aphis*, such as the blackfly
APHOLATE *n* type of pesticide
APHOLATES > APHOLATE
APHONIA *n* loss of the voice caused by damage to the vocal tract
APHONIAS > APHONIA
APHONIC *adj* affected with aphonia ▷ *n* person affected with aphonia
APHONICS > APHONIC
APHONIES > APHONY
APHONOUS > APHONIA
APHONY *same as* > APHONIA
APHORISE *same as* > APHORIZE
APHORISED > APHORISE
APHORISER > APHORISE
APHORISES > APHORISE
APHORISM *n* short clever saying expressing a general truth
APHORISMS > APHORISM
APHORIST > APHORISM
APHORISTS > APHORISM
APHORIZE *vb* write or speak in aphorisms
APHORIZED > APHORIZE
APHORIZER > APHORIZE
APHORIZES > APHORIZE
APHOTIC *adj* characterized by or growing in the absence of light
APHRODITE *n* North American butterfly
APHTHA *n* small ulceration on a mucous membrane, as in thrush, caused by a fungal infection
APHTHAE > APHTHA
APHTHOUS > APHTHA
APHYLLIES > APHYLLOUS
APHYLLOUS *adj* (of plants) having no leaves
APHYLLY > APHYLLOUS
APIACEOUS *adj* parsley-like
APIAN *adj* of, relating to, or resembling bees
APIARIAN *adj* of or relating to the breeding and care of bees ▷ *n* apiarist
APIARIANS > APIARIAN
APIARIES > APIARY
APIARIST *n* beekeeper
APIARISTS > APIARIST
APIARY *n* place where bees are kept
APICAL *adj* of, at, or being an apex ▷ *n* sound made with the tip of the tongue
APICALLY > APICAL
APICALS > APICAL
APICES *plural of* > APEX
APICIAN *adj* of fine or dainty food
APICULATE *adj* (of leaves) ending in a short sharp point
APICULI > APICULUS
APICULUS *n* short sharp point
APIECE *adv* each
APIMANIA *n* extreme enthusiasm for bees
APIMANIAS > APIMANIA
APING > APE
APIOL *n* substance formerly used to assist menstruation
APIOLOGY *n* study of bees
APIOLS > APIOL
APISH *adj* stupid or foolish
APISHLY > APISH
APISHNESS > APISH
APISM *n* behaviour like an ape
APISMS > APISM
APIVOROUS *adj* eating bees
APLANAT *n* aplanatic lens
APLANATIC *adj* (of a lens or mirror) free from spherical aberration
APLANATS > APLANAT
APLANETIC *adj* (esp of some algal and fungal spores) nonmotile or lacking a motile stage

APLASIA *n* congenital absence or abnormal development of an organ or part
APLASIAS > APLASIA
APLASTIC *adj* relating to or characterized by aplasia
APLENTY *adv* in plenty
APLITE *n* light-coloured fine-grained acid igneous rock with a sugary texture, consisting of quartz and feldspars
APLITES > APLITE
APLITIC > APLITE
APLOMB *n* calm self-possession
APLOMBS > APLOMB
APLUSTRE *n* stern ornament on an ancient Greek ship
APLUSTRES > APLUSTRE
APNEA *same as* > APNOEA
APNEAL > APNEA
APNEAS > APNEA
APNEIC > APNEA
APNEUSES > APNEUSIS
APNEUSIS *n* protracted gasping inhalation followed by short inefficient exhalation, which can cause asphyxia
APNEUSTIC *adj* of or relating to apneusis
APNOEA *n* temporary inability to breathe
APNOEAL > APNOEA
APNOEAS > APNOEA
APNOEIC > APNOEA
APO *n* type of protein
APOAPSES > APOAPSIS
APOAPSIS *n* point in an orbit furthest from the object orbited
APOCARP *n* apocarpous gynoecium or fruit
APOCARPS > APOCARP
APOCARPY *n* presence of many carpels
APOCOPATE *vb* omit the final sound or sounds of (a word)
APOCOPE *n* omission of the final sound or sounds of a word
APOCOPES > APOCOPE
APOCOPIC > APOCOPE
APOCRINE *adj* denoting a type of glandular secretion in which part of the secreting cell is lost with the secretion, as in mammary glands
APOCRYPHA *n* writings or statements of uncertain authority
APOD *n* animal without feet
APODAL *adj* (of snakes, eels, etc) without feet
APODE *n* animal without feet
APODES > APODE
APODICTIC *adj* unquestionably true by virtue of demonstration
APODOSES > APODOSIS
APODOSIS *n* consequent of a conditional statement, as *the game will be cancelled* in *if it rains the game will be cancelled*
APODOUS *same as* > APODAL
APODS > APOD
APOENZYME *n* protein component that together with a coenzyme forms an enzyme
APOGAEIC > APOGEE
APOGAMIC > APOGAMY
APOGAMIES > APOGAMY
APOGAMOUS > APOGAMY
APOGAMY *n* type of reproduction, occurring in some ferns, in which the sporophyte develops from the gametophyte without fusion of gametes
APOGEAL > APOGEE
APOGEAN > APOGEE
APOGEE *n* point of the moon's or a satellite's orbit that is farthest from the earth
APOGEES > APOGEE
APOGEIC > APOGEE
APOGRAPH *n* exact copy
APOGRAPHS > APOGRAPH
APOLLO *n* strikingly handsome youth
APOLLOS > APOLLO
APOLOG *same as* > APOLOGUE
APOLOGAL > APOLOGUE
APOLOGIA *n* formal written defence of a cause
APOLOGIAE > APOLOGIA
APOLOGIAS > APOLOGIA
APOLOGIES > APOLOGY
APOLOGISE *same as* > APOLOGIZE
APOLOGIST *n* person who formally defends a cause
APOLOGIZE *vb* make an apology
APOLOGS > APOLOG
APOLOGUE *n* allegory or moral fable
APOLOGUES > APOLOGUE
APOLOGY *n* expression of regret for wrongdoing
APOLUNE *n* point in a lunar orbit when a spacecraft is at its greatest distance from the moon
APOLUNES > APOLUNE
APOMICT *n* organism, esp a plant, produced by apomixis
APOMICTIC > APOMIXIS
APOMICTS > APOMICT
APOMIXES > APOMIXIS
APOMIXIS *n* (esp in plants) any of several types of asexual reproduction, such as parthenogenesis and apogamy, in which fertilization does not take place
APOOP *adv* on the poop deck
APOPHASES > APOPHASIS
APOPHASIS *n* device of mentioning a subject by stating that it will not be mentioned
APOPHATIC *adj* of theology that says God is indescribable
APOPHONY *n* change in the quality of vowels
APOPHYGE *n* outward curve at each end of the shaft of a column, adjoining the base or capital
APOPHYGES > APOPHYGE
APOPHYSES > APOPHYSIS
APOPHYSIS *n* process, outgrowth, or swelling from part of an animal or plant
APOPLAST *n* nonprotoplasmic component of a plant, including the cell walls and intercellular material
APOPLASTS > APOPLAST
APOPLEX *vb* afflict with apoplexy
APOPLEXED > APOPLEX
APOPLEXES > APOPLEX
APOPLEXY *n* stroke
APOPTOSES > APOPTOSIS
APOPTOSIS *n* programmed death of some of an organism's cells as part of its natural growth and development
APOPTOTIC > APOPTOSIS
APORETIC > APORIA
APORIA *n* doubt, real or professed, about what to do or say
APORIAS > APORIA
APORT *adj* on or towards the port side
APOS > APO
APOSITIA *n* unwillingness to eat
APOSITIAS > APOSITIA
APOSITIC > APOSITIA
APOSPORIC > APOSPORY
APOSPORY *n* development of the gametophyte from the sporophyte without the formation of spores
APOSTACY *same as* > APOSTASY
APOSTASY *n* abandonment of one's religious faith or other belief
APOSTATE *n* person who has abandoned his or her religion, political party, or cause ▷ *adj* guilty of apostasy
APOSTATES > APOSTATE
APOSTATIC > APOSTATE
APOSTIL *n* marginal note
APOSTILLE *n* apostil
APOSTILS > APOSTIL
APOSTLE *n* one of the twelve disciples chosen by Christ to preach his gospel
APOSTLES > APOSTLE
APOSTOLIC *adj* of or relating to the Apostles or their teachings
APOTHECE *n* obsolete word for shop
APOTHECES > APOTHECE
APOTHECIA *n* cup-shaped structures that contain the asci, esp in lichens
APOTHEGM *n* short cryptic remark containing some general or generally accepted truth; maxim
APOTHEGMS > APOTHEGM
APOTHEM *n* perpendicular line or distance from the centre of a regular polygon to any of its sides
APOTHEMS > APOTHEM
APOZEM *n* medicine dissolved in water
APOZEMS > APOZEM
APP *n* application program
APPAID > APPAY
APPAIR *vb* old form of impair
APPAIRED > APPAIR
APPAIRING > APPAIR
APPAIRS > APPAIR
APPAL *vb* dismay, terrify
APPALL *same as* > APPAL
APPALLED > APPALL
APPALLING *adj* dreadful, terrible
APPALLS > APPALL
APPALOOSA *n* North American horse breed
APPALS > APPAL
APPALTI > APPALTO
APPALTO *n* Italian word for contact
APPANAGE *n* land or other provision granted by a king for the support of a member of the royal family, esp a younger son
APPANAGED *adj* having appanage
APPANAGES > APPANAGE
APPARAT *n* Communist Party organization in the former Soviet Union and other states
APPARATS > APPARAT
APPARATUS *n* equipment for a particular purpose
APPAREL *n* clothing ▷ *vb* clothe, adorn, etc
APPARELED > APPAREL
APPARELS > APPAREL
APPARENCY *old word for* > APPARENT
APPARENT *adj* readily seen, obvious ▷ *n* heir apparent
APPARENTS > APPARENT
APPARITOR *n* officer who summons witnesses and executes the orders of an ecclesiastical and (formerly) a civil court
APPAY *old word for* > SATISFY
APPAYD > APPAY
APPAYING > APPAY

APPAYS > APPAY
APPEACH *old word for* > ACCUSE
APPEACHED > APPEACH
APPEACHES > APPEACH
APPEAL *vb* make an earnest request ▷ *n* earnest request
APPEALED > APPEAL
APPEALER > APPEAL
APPEALERS > APPEAL
APPEALING *adj* attractive or pleasing
APPEALS > APPEAL
APPEAR *vb* become visible or present
APPEARED > APPEAR
APPEARER > APPEAR
APPEARERS > APPEAR
APPEARING > APPEAR
APPEARS > APPEAR
APPEASE *vb* pacify (a person) by yielding to his or her demands
APPEASED > APPEASE
APPEASER > APPEASE
APPEASERS > APPEASE
APPEASES > APPEASE
APPEASING > APPEASE
APPEL *n* stamp of the foot, used to warn of one's intent to attack
APPELLANT *n* person who makes an appeal to a higher court
APPELLATE *adj* of appeals
APPELLEE *n* person who is accused or appealed against
APPELLEES > APPELLEE
APPELLOR *n* person initiating a law case
APPELLORS > APPELLOR
APPELS > APPEL
APPEND *vb* join on, add
APPENDAGE *n* thing joined on or added
APPENDANT *adj* attached, affixed, or added ▷ *n* person or thing attached or added
APPENDED > APPEND
APPENDENT *same as* > APPENDANT
APPENDING > APPEND
APPENDIX *n* separate additional material at the end of a book
APPENDS > APPEND
APPERIL *old word for* > PERIL
APPERILL *old word for* > PERIL
APPERILLS > APPERILL
APPERILS > APPERIL
APPERTAIN *vb* belong to
APPESTAT *n* neural control centre within the hypothalamus of the brain that regulates the sense of hunger and satiety
APPESTATS > APPESTAT
APPETENCE *n* craving or desire
APPETENCY *same as* > APPETENCE
APPETENT *adj* eager
APPETIBLE *adj* old word meaning desirable
APPETISE *vb* stimulate the appetite
APPETISED > APPETISE
APPETISER *same as* > APPETIZER
APPETISES > APPETISE
APPETITE *n* desire for food or drink
APPETITES > APPETITE
APPETIZE *vb* stimulate the appetite
APPETIZED > APPETIZE
APPETIZER *n* thing eaten or drunk to stimulate the appetite
APPETIZES > APPETIZE
APPLAUD *vb* show approval of by clapping one's hands
APPLAUDED > APPLAUD
APPLAUDER > APPLAUD
APPLAUDS > APPLAUD
APPLAUSE *n* approval shown by clapping one's hands
APPLAUSES > APPLAUSE
APPLE *n* round firm fleshy fruit that grows on trees
APPLECART *n* cart used to carry apples
APPLEJACK *n* brandy made from apples
APPLES > APPLE
APPLET *n* computing program that runs within a page on the World Wide Web
APPLETS > APPLET
APPLEY *adj* resembling or tasting like an apple
APPLIABLE *adj* applicable
APPLIANCE *n* device with a specific function
APPLICANT *n* person who applies for something
APPLICATE *adj* applied practicably
APPLIED *adj* (of a skill, science, etc) put to practical use
APPLIER > APPLY
APPLIERS > APPLY
APPLIES > APPLY
APPLIQUE *n* decoration or trimming of one material sewn or otherwise fixed onto another ▷ *vb* sew or fix (a decoration) on as an appliqué
APPLIQUED > APPLIQUE
APPLIQUES > APPLIQUE
APPLY *vb* make a formal request
APPLYING > APPLY
APPOINT *vb* assign to a job or position
APPOINTED > APPOINT
APPOINTEE *n* person who is appointed
APPOINTER > APPOINT
APPOINTOR *n* person to whom a power to nominate persons to take property is given by deed or will
APPOINTS > APPOINT
APPORT *n* production of objects by apparently supernatural means at a spiritualists' seance
APPORTION *vb* divide out in shares
APPORTS > APPORT
APPOSABLE *adj* capable of being apposed or brought into apposition
APPOSE *vb* place side by side or near to each other
APPOSED > APPOSE
APPOSER > APPOSE
APPOSERS > APPOSE
APPOSES > APPOSE
APPOSING > APPOSE
APPOSITE *adj* suitable, apt
APPRAISAL *n* assessment of the worth or quality of a person or thing
APPRAISE *vb* estimate the value or quality of
APPRAISED > APPRAISE
APPRAISEE *n* person being appraised
APPRAISER > APPRAISE
APPRAISES > APPRAISE
APPREHEND *vb* arrest and take into custody
APPRESS *vb* press together
APPRESSED > APPRESS
APPRESSES > APPRESS
APPRISE *vb* make aware (of)
APPRISED > APPRISE
APPRISER > APPRISE
APPRISERS > APPRISE
APPRISES > APPRISE
APPRISING > APPRISE
APPRIZE *same as* > APPRISE
APPRIZED > APPRIZE
APPRIZER > APPRIZE
APPRIZERS > APPRIZE
APPRIZES > APPRIZE
APPRIZING > APPRIZE
APPRO *n* approval
APPROACH *vb* come near or nearer (to) ▷ *n* approaching or means of approaching
APPROBATE *vb* accept as valid
APPROOF *old word for* > TRIAL
APPROOFS > APPROOF
APPROS > APPRO
APPROVAL *n* consent
APPROVALS > APPROVAL
APPROVE *vb* consider good or right
APPROVED > APPROVE
APPROVER > APPROVE
APPROVERS > APPROVE
APPROVES > APPROVE
APPROVING > APPROVE
APPS > APP
APPUI *n* support
APPUIED > APPUY
APPUIS > APPUI
APPULSE *n* very close approach of two celestial bodies so that they are in conjunction but no eclipse or occultation occurs
APPULSES > APPULSE
APPULSIVE > APPULSE
APPUY *vb* support
APPUYED > APPUY
APPUYING > APPUY
APPUYS > APPUY
APRACTIC > APRAXIA
APRAXIA *n* disorder of the central nervous system caused by brain damage and characterized by impaired ability to carry out purposeful muscular movements
APRAXIAS > APRAXIA
APRAXIC > APRAXIA
APRES *prep* French word for after
APRICATE *vb* bask in sun
APRICATED > APRICATE
APRICATES > APRICATE
APRICOCK *old word for* > APRICOT
APRICOCKS > APRICOT
APRICOT *n* yellowish-orange juicy fruit like a small peach ▷ *adj* yellowish-orange
APRICOTS > APRICOT
APRIORISM *n* philosophical doctrine that there may be genuine knowledge independent of experience
APRIORIST > APRIORISM
APRIORITY *n* condition of being innate in the mind
APRON *n* garment worn over the front of the body to protect the clothes ▷ *vb* equip with an apron
APRONED > APRON
APRONFUL *n* amount held in an apron
APRONFULS > APRONFUL
APRONING > APRON
APRONLIKE > APRON
APRONS > APRON
APROPOS *adv* appropriate(ly)
APROTIC *adj* (of solvents) neither accepting nor donating hydrogen ions
APSARAS *n* Hindu water sprite
APSARASES > APSARAS
APSE *n* arched or domed recess, esp in a church
APSES > APSE
APSIDAL > APSIS
APSIDES > APSIS
APSIDIOLE *n* small arch
APSIS *n* either of two points lying at the extremities of the elliptical orbit of a planet or satellite
APSO *n* Tibetan terrier
APSOS > APSO
APT *adj* having a specified tendency ▷ *vb* be fitting

APTED > APT
APTER > APT
APTERAL *adj* (esp of a classical temple) not having columns at the sides
APTERIA > APTERIUM
APTERISM > APTEROUS
APTERISMS > APTEROUS
APTERIUM *n* bare patch on the skin of a bird
APTEROUS *adj* (of insects) without wings, as silverfish and springtails
APTERYX *n* kiwi (the bird)
APTERYXES > APTERYX
APTEST > APT
APTING > APT
APTITUDE *n* natural ability
APTITUDES > APTITUDE
APTLY > APT
APTNESS > APT
APTNESSES > APT
APTOTE *n* noun without inflections
APTOTES > APTOTE
APTOTIC > APTOTE
APTS > APT
APYRASE *n* enzyme
APYRASES > APYRASE
APYRETIC > APYREXIA
APYREXIA *n* absence of fever
APYREXIAS > APYREXIA
AQUA *n* water
AQUABATIC *adj* of gymnastic feats in water
AQUABOARD *n* board used to ride on water
AQUACADE *same as* > AQUASHOW
AQUACADES > AQUACADE
AQUADROME *n* venue for water sports
AQUAE > AQUA
AQUAFARM *vb* cultivate fish or shellfish
AQUAFARMS > AQUAFARM
AQUAFER *n* aquifer
AQUAFERS > AQUAFER
AQUALUNG *n* mouthpiece attached to air cylinders, worn for underwater swimming
AQUALUNGS > AQUALUNG
AQUANAUT *n* person who lives and works underwater
AQUANAUTS > AQUANAUT
AQUAPHOBE *n* person afraid of water
AQUAPLANE *n* board on which a person stands to be towed by a motorboat ▷ *vb* ride on an aquaplane
AQUAPORIN *n* any one of a group of proteins in cell membranes that allow the passage of water across the membrane
AQUARELLE *n* method of watercolour painting in transparent washes
AQUARIA > AQUARIUM
AQUARIAL *adj* > AQUARIUM
AQUARIAN *n* person who keeps an aquarium
AQUARIANS > AQUARIAN
AQUARIIST *n old form of* AQUARIST
AQUARIST *n* curator of an aquarium
AQUARISTS > AQUARIST
AQUARIUM *n* tank in which fish and other underwater creatures are kept
AQUARIUMS > AQUARIUM
AQUAROBIC *adj* pertaining to exercises performed standing up in a swimming pool
AQUAS > AQUA
AQUASHOW *n* exhibition of swimming and diving, often accompanied by music
AQUASHOWS > AQUASHOW
AQUATIC *adj* living in or near water ▷ *n* marine or freshwater animal or plant
AQUATICS *pl n* water sports
AQUATINT *n* print like a watercolour, produced by etching copper ▷ *vb* etch (a block, etc) in aquatint
AQUATINTA *n* aquatint
AQUATINTS > AQUATINT
AQUATONE *n* fitness exercise in water
AQUATONES > AQUATONE
AQUAVIT *n* grain- or potato-based spirit from the Scandinavian countries, flavoured with aromatic seeds and spices, esp caraway
AQUAVITS > AQUAVIT
AQUEDUCT *n* structure carrying water across a valley or river
AQUEDUCTS > AQUEDUCT
AQUEOUS *adj* of, like, or containing water
AQUEOUSLY > AQUEOUS
AQUIFER *n* deposit of rock, such as sandstone, containing water that can be used to supply wells
AQUIFERS > AQUIFER
AQUILEGIA *another name for* > COLUMBINE
AQUILINE *adj* (of a nose) curved like an eagle's beak
AQUILON *n* name for the north wind
AQUILONS > AQUILON
AQUIVER *adv* quivering
AR *n* letter R
ARAARA *another name for* > TREVALLY
ARAARAS > ARAARA
ARABA *n* Asian carriage
ARABAS > ARABA
ARABESK *same as* > ARABESQUE
ARABESKS > ARABESK
ARABESQUE *n* ballet position in which one leg is raised behind and the arms are extended ▷ *adj* designating, of, or decorated in this style
ARABIC as in *gum arabic* gum exuded by certain acacia trees
ARABICA *n* high-quality coffee bean
ARABICAS > ARABICA
ARABICISE *same as* > ARABICIZE
ARABICIZE *vb* make or become Arabic
ARABILITY *n* suitability of land for growing crops
ARABIN *n* essence of gum arabic
ARABINOSE *n* pentose sugar in plant gums
ARABINS > ARABIN
ARABIS *n* any plant of the annual or perennial genus *Arabis*, some of which form low-growing mats with downy grey foliage and white flowers: family *Brassicaceae* (crucifers)
ARABISE *vb* make or become Arab
ARABISED > ARABISE
ARABISES > ARABISE
ARABISING > ARABISE
ARABIZE *vb* make or become Arab
ARABIZED > ARABIZE
ARABIZES > ARABIZE
ARABIZING > ARABIZE
ARABLE *adj* suitable for growing crops on ▷ *n* arable land or farming
ARABLES > ARABLE
ARACEOUS *same as* > AROID
ARACHIS *n* Brazilian plant
ARACHISES > ARACHIS
ARACHNID *n* eight-legged invertebrate, such as a spider, scorpion, tick, or mite
ARACHNIDS > ARACHNID
ARACHNOID *n* middle of the three membranes that cover the brain and spinal cord ▷ *adj* of or relating to the middle of the three meninges
ARAGONITE *n* generally white or grey mineral, found in sedimentary rocks
ARAISE *vb* old form of raise
ARAISED > ARAISE
ARAISES > ARAISE
ARAISING > ARAISE
ARAK *same as* > ARRACK
ARAKS > ARAK
ARALIA *n* any plant of the genus *Aralia* of trees, shrubs, and herbaceous plants. The greenhouse and house plant generally known as aralia is *Schefflera elegantissima* of a related genus, grown for its decorative evergreen foliage: family *Araliaceae*
ARALIAS > ARALIA
ARAME *n* Japanese edible seaweed
ARAMES > ARAME
ARAMID *n* synthetic fibre
ARAMIDS > ARAMID
ARANEID *n* any of numerous arachnids constituting the order *Araneae* (or *Araneida*), which comprises the spiders
ARANEIDAN > ARANEID
ARANEIDS > ARANEID
ARANEOUS *adj* like a spider's web
ARAPAIMA *n* very large primitive freshwater teleost fish that occurs in tropical S America
ARAPAIMAS > ARAPAIMA
ARAPONGA *n* South American bird with a bell-like call
ARAPONGAS > ARAPONGA
ARAPUNGA *n* South American bird with a bell-like call
ARAPUNGAS > ARAPUNGA
ARAR *n* African tree
ARAROBA *n* Brazilian leguminous tree, *Andira araroba*
ARAROBAS > ARAROBA
ARARS > ARAR
ARAUCARIA *n* any tree of the coniferous genus *Araucaria* of South America, Australia, and Polynesia, such as the monkey puzzle and bunya-bunya
ARAYSE *vb* old form of raise
ARAYSED > ARAYSE
ARAYSES > ARAYSE
ARAYSING > ARAYSE
ARB *short for* > ARBITRAGE
ARBA *n* Asian carriage
ARBALEST *n* large medieval crossbow, usually cocked by mechanical means
ARBALESTS > ARBALEST
ARBALIST *same as* > ARBALEST
ARBALISTS > ARBALIST
ARBAS > ARBA
ARBELEST *n* arbalest
ARBELESTS > ARBELEST
ARBITER *n* person empowered to judge in a dispute
ARBITERS > ARBITER
ARBITRAGE *n* purchase of currencies, securities, or commodities in one market for immediate resale in others in order to profit from unequal prices
ARBITRAL *adj* of or relating to arbitration
ARBITRARY *adj* based on personal choice or chance rather than reason

ARBITRATE *vb* settle (a dispute) by arbitration
ARBITRESS *n* female arbitrator
ARBITRIUM *n* power to decide
ARBLAST *n* arbalest
ARBLASTER > ARBLAST
ARBLASTS > ARBLAST
ARBOR *n* revolving shaft or axle in a machine
ARBOREAL *adj* of or living in trees
ARBORED *n* having arbors
ARBOREOUS *adj* thickly wooded
ARBORES > ARBOR
ARBORET *n* old name for an area planted with shrubs
ARBORETA > ARBORETUM
ARBORETS > ARBORET
ARBORETUM *n* place where rare trees or shrubs are cultivated
ARBORIO as in *arborio rice* variety of round-grain rice used for making risotto
ARBORISE *same as* > ARBORIZE
ARBORISED > ARBORISE
ARBORISES > ARBORISE
ARBORIST *n* specialist in the cultivation of trees
ARBORISTS > ARBORIST
ARBORIZE *vb* give or take on a treelike branched appearance
ARBORIZED > ARBORIZE
ARBORIZES > ARBORIZE
ARBOROUS *adj* of trees
ARBORS > ARBOR
ARBOUR *n* glade sheltered by trees
ARBOURED *adj* having arbours
ARBOURS > ARBOUR
ARBOVIRAL > ARBOVIRUS
ARBOVIRUS *n* any one of a group of viruses that cause such diseases as encephalitis and dengue and are transmitted to humans by arthropods, esp insects and ticks
ARBS > ARB
ARBUSCLE *n* small tree
ARBUSCLES > ARBUSCLE
ARBUTE *old name for* > ARBUTUS
ARBUTEAN > ARBUTUS
ARBUTES > ARBUTE
ARBUTUS *n* evergreen shrub with strawberry-like berries
ARBUTUSES > ARBUTUS
ARC *n* part of a circle or other curve ▷ *vb* form an arc
ARCADE *n* covered passageway lined with shops ▷ *vb* provide with an arcade
ARCADED > ARCADE
ARCADES > ARCADE
ARCADIA *n* traditional idealized rural setting
ARCADIAN *n* person who leads a rural life
ARCADIANS > ARCADIAN
ARCADIAS > ARCADIA
ARCADING > ARCADE
ARCADINGS > ARCADE
ARCANA *n* either of the two divisions of a pack of tarot cards
ARCANAS > ARCANA
ARCANE *adj* mysterious and secret
ARCANELY > ARCANE
ARCANIST *n* person with secret knowledge
ARCANISTS > ARCANIST
ARCANUM *n* profound secret or mystery known only to initiates
ARCANUMS > ARCANUM
ARCATURE *n* small-scale arcade
ARCATURES > ARCATURE
ARCCOS *same as* > ARCCOSINE
ARCCOSES > ARCCOS
ARCCOSINE *n* trigonometric function
ARCED > ARC
ARCH *n* curved structure supporting a bridge or roof ▷ *vb* (cause to) form an arch ▷ *adj* superior, knowing
ARCHAEA *n* order of prokaryotic microorganisms
ARCHAEAL > ARCHAEAN
ARCHAEAN *n* type of microorganism
ARCHAEANS > ARCHAEAN
ARCHAEI > ARCHAEUS
ARCHAEON *variant of* > ARCHAEAN
ARCHAEUS *n* spirit believed to inhabit a living thing
ARCHAIC *adj* ancient
ARCHAICAL *same as* > ARCHAIC
ARCHAISE *same as* > ARCHAIZE
ARCHAISED > ARCHAISE
ARCHAISER > ARCHAISE
ARCHAISES > ARCHAISE
ARCHAISM *n* archaic word or phrase
ARCHAISMS > ARCHAISM
ARCHAIST > ARCHAISM
ARCHAISTS > ARCHAISM
ARCHAIZE *vb* give an archaic appearance or character to, as by the use of archaisms
ARCHAIZED > ARCHAIZE
ARCHAIZER > ARCHAIZE
ARCHAIZES > ARCHAIZE
ARCHANGEL *n* chief angel
ARCHDUCAL *adj* of or relating to an archduke, archduchess, or archduchy
ARCHDUCHY *n* territory of an archduke or archduchess
ARCHDUKE *n* duke of specially high rank
ARCHDUKES > ARCHDUKE
ARCHED *adj* provided with or spanned by an arch or arches
ARCHEI > ARCHEUS
ARCHENEMY *n* chief enemy
ARCHER *n* person who shoots with a bow and arrow
ARCHERESS *n* female archer
ARCHERIES > ARCHERY
ARCHERS > ARCHER
ARCHERY *n* art or sport of shooting with a bow and arrow
ARCHES > ARCH
ARCHEST > ARCH
ARCHETYPE *n* perfect specimen
ARCHEUS *n* spirit believed to inhabit a living thing
ARCHFIEND *n the.* the chief of fiends or devils
ARCHFOE *n* chief enemy
ARCHFOES > ARCHFOE
ARCHICARP *n* female reproductive structure in ascomycetous fungi that consists of a cell or hypha and develops into the ascogonium
ARCHIL *a variant spelling of* > ORCHIL
ARCHILOWE *n* treat given in return
ARCHILS > ARCHIL
ARCHIMAGE *n* great magician or wizard
ARCHINE *n* Russian unit of length equal to about 71 cm
ARCHINES > ARCHINE
ARCHING > ARCH
ARCHINGS > ARCH
ARCHITECT *n* person qualified to design and supervise the construction of buildings
ARCHITYPE *n* primitive original from which others derive
ARCHIVAL > ARCHIVE
ARCHIVE *n* collection of records or documents ▷ *vb* store (documents, data, etc) in an archive or other repository
ARCHIVED > ARCHIVE
ARCHIVES > ARCHIVE
ARCHIVING > ARCHIVE
ARCHIVIST *n* person in charge of archives
ARCHIVOLT *n* moulding around an arch, sometimes decorated
ARCHLET *n* small arch
ARCHLETS > ARCHLET
ARCHLUTE *n* old bass lute
ARCHLUTES > ARCHLUTE
ARCHLY > ARCH
ARCHNESS > ARCH
ARCHOLOGY *n* study of the origins of things
ARCHON *n* (in ancient Athens) one of the nine chief magistrates
ARCHONS > ARCHON
ARCHONTIC > ARCHON
ARCHOSAUR *n* early type of dinosaur
ARCHRIVAL *n* chief rival
ARCHWAY *n* passageway under an arch
ARCHWAYS > ARCHWAY
ARCHWISE *adv* like an arch
ARCIFORM *adj* shaped like an arch
ARCING > ARC
ARCINGS > ARC
ARCKED > ARC
ARCKING > ARC
ARCKINGS > ARC
ARCMIN *n* 1/60 of a degree of an angle
ARCMINS > ARCMIN
ARCO *adv* musical direction meaning with bow
ARCOGRAPH *n* instrument used for drawing arcs without using a central point
ARCOLOGY *n* architecture blending buildings with the natural environment
ARCS > ARC
ARCSEC *n* 1/3600 of a degree of an angle
ARCSECOND *n* unit used in astronomy
ARCSECS > ARCSEC
ARCSIN *same as* > ARCSINE
ARCSINE *n* trigonometrical function
ARCSINES > ARCSINE
ARCSINS > ARCSIN
ARCTAN *n* trignometrical function
ARCTANS > ARCTAN
ARCTIC *adj* very cold ▷ *n* high waterproof overshoe with buckles
ARCTICS > ARCTIC
ARCTIID *n* any moth of the family *Arctiidae*, which includes the footman, ermine, and tiger moths
ARCTIIDS > ARCTIID
ARCTOID *adj* like a bear
ARCTOPHIL *n* arctophile
ARCUATE *adj* shaped or bent like an arc or bow
ARCUATED *same as* > ARCUATE
ARCUATELY > ARCUATE
ARCUATION *n* use of arches or vaults in buildings
ARCUS *n* circle around the cornea of the eye
ARCUSES > ARCUS
ARD *n* primitive plough
ARDEB *n* unit of dry measure used in Egypt and other Middle Eastern countries. In Egypt it is approximately equal to 0.195 cubic metres

ARDEBS > ARDEB
ARDENCIES > ARDENT
ARDENCY > ARDENT
ARDENT *adj* passionate
ARDENTLY > ARDENT
ARDOR *same as* > ARDOUR
ARDORS > ARDOR
ARDOUR *n* passion
ARDOURS > ARDOUR
ARDRI *n* Irish high king
ARDRIGH *n* Irish high king
ARDRIGHS > ARDRIGH
ARDRIS > ARDRI
ARDS > ARD
ARDUOUS *adj* hard to accomplish, strenuous
ARDUOUSLY > ARDUOUS
ARE *n* unit of measure, 100 square metres ▷ *vb* used as the singular form with *you*
AREA *n* part or region
AREACH *vb* old form of reach
AREACHED > AREACH
AREACHES > AREACH
AREACHING > AREACH
AREAD *vb* old word meaning declare
AREADING > AREAD
AREADS > AREAD
AREAE > AREA
AREAL > AREA
AREALLY > AREA
AREAR *n* old form of arrear
AREAS > AREA
AREAWAY *n* passageway between parts of a building or between different buildings
AREAWAYS > AREAWAY
ARECA *n* any of various tall palms of the genus *Areca*, which are native to SE Asia and have white flowers and orange or red egg-shaped nuts
ARECAS > ARECA
ARECOLINE *n* drug derived from betel nut
ARED > AREAD
AREDD > AREAD
AREDE *vb* old word meaning declare
AREDES > AREDE
AREDING > AREDE
AREFIED > AREFY
AREFIES > AREFY
AREFY *vb* dry up
AREFYING > AREFY
AREG *a plural of* > ERG
AREIC *adj* relating to area
ARENA *n* seated enclosure for sports events
ARENAS > ARENA
ARENATION *n* use of hot sand as a medical poultice
ARENE *n* aromatic hydrocarbon
ARENES > ARENE
ARENITE *n* any arenaceous rock
ARENITES > ARENITE
ARENITIC > ARENITE
ARENOSE *adj* sandy
ARENOUS *adj* sandy
AREOLA *n* small circular area, such as the coloured ring around the human nipple
AREOLAE > AREOLA
AREOLAR > AREOLA
AREOLAS > AREOLA
AREOLATE > AREOLA
AREOLATED *adj* areolate
AREOLE *n* space outlined on a surface, such as an area between veins on a leaf or on an insect's wing
AREOLES > AREOLE
AREOLOGY *n* study of the planet Mars
AREOMETER *n* instrument for measuring the density of liquids
AREOSTYLE *n* building with widely-spaced columns
AREPA *n* Colombian cornmeal cake
AREPAS > AREPA
ARERE *adv* old word meaning backwards
ARES > ARE
ARET *vb* old word meaning entrust
ARETE *n* sharp ridge separating two cirques or glacial valleys in mountainous regions
ARETES > ARETE
ARETHUSA *n* North American orchid, *Arethusa bulbosa*, having one long narrow leaf and one rose-purple flower fringed with yellow
ARETHUSAS > ARETHUSA
ARETS > ARET
ARETT *vb* old word meaning entrust
ARETTED > ARETT
ARETTING > ARETT
ARETTS > ARETT
AREW *adv* old word meaning in a row
ARF *n* barking sound
ARFS > ARF
ARGAL *same as* > ARGALI
ARGALA *n* Indian stork
ARGALAS > ARGALA
ARGALI *n* wild sheep, *Ovis ammon*, inhabiting semidesert regions in central Asia: family *Bovidae*, order *Artiodactyla*. It is the largest of the sheep, having massive horns in the male, which may almost form a circle
ARGALIS > ARGALI
ARGALS > ARGAL
ARGAN *n* Moroccan tree
ARGAND *n* lamp with a hollow circular wick
ARGANDS > ARGAND
ARGANS > ARGAN
ARGEMONE *n* prickly poppy
ARGEMONES > ARGEMONE
ARGENT *n* silver
ARGENTAL *adj* of or containing silver
ARGENTIC *adj* of or containing silver in the divalent or trivalent state
ARGENTINE *adj* of, relating to, or resembling silver ▷ *n* type of small silver fish
ARGENTITE *n* dark grey mineral that consists of silver sulphide, usually in cubic crystalline forms, and occurs in veins, often with native silver. It is found esp in Mexico, Nevada, and Saxony and is an important source of silver. Formula: Ag_2S
ARGENTOUS *adj* of or containing silver in the monovalent state
ARGENTS > ARGENT
ARGENTUM *an obsolete name for* > SILVER
ARGENTUMS > ARGENTUM
ARGHAN *n* agave plant
ARGHANS > ARGHAN
ARGIL *n* clay, esp potters' clay
ARGILLITE *n* any argillaceous rock, esp a hardened mudstone
ARGILS > ARGIL
ARGINASE *n* type of enzyme
ARGINASES > ARGINASE
ARGININE *n* essential amino acid of plant and animal proteins, necessary for nutrition and for the production of excretory urea
ARGININES > ARGININE
ARGLE *vb* quarrel
ARGLED > ARGLE
ARGLES > ARGLE
ARGLING > ARGLE
ARGOL *n* crude potassium hydrogentartrate, deposited as a crust on the sides of wine vats
ARGOLS > ARGOL
ARGON *n* inert gas found in the air
ARGONAUT *n* paper nautilus
ARGONAUTS > ARGONAUT
ARGONON *n* inert gas
ARGONONS > ARGONON
ARGONS > ARGON
ARGOSIES > ARGOSY
ARGOSY *n* large merchant ship
ARGOT *n* slang or jargon
ARGOTIC > ARGOT
ARGOTS > ARGOT
ARGUABLE *adj* capable of being disputed
ARGUABLY *adv* it can be argued that
ARGUE *vb* try to prove by giving reasons
ARGUED > ARGUE
ARGUER > ARGUE
ARGUERS > ARGUE
ARGUES > ARGUE
ARGUFIED > ARGUFY
ARGUFIER > ARGUFY
ARGUFIERS > ARGUFY
ARGUFIES > ARGUFY
ARGUFY *vb* argue or quarrel, esp over something trivial
ARGUFYING > ARGUFY
ARGUING > ARGUE
ARGULI > ARGULUS
ARGULUS *n* parasite on fish
ARGUMENT *n* quarrel
ARGUMENTA *n* appeals to reason
ARGUMENTS > ARGUMENT
ARGUS *n* any of various brown butterflies
ARGUSES > ARGUS
ARGUTE *adj* shrill or keen
ARGUTELY > ARGUTE
ARGYLE *adj* made of knitted or woven material with a diamond-shaped pattern of two or more colours ▷ *n* sock made of this
ARGYLES > ARGYLE
ARGYLL *n* sock with diamond pattern
ARGYLLS > ARGYLL
ARGYRIA *n* staining of skin by exposure to silver
ARGYRIAS > ARGYRIA
ARGYRITE *n* mineral containing silver sulphide
ARGYRITES > ARGYRITE
ARHAT *n* Buddhist, esp a monk who has achieved enlightenment and at death passes to nirvana
ARHATS > ARHAT
ARHATSHIP > ARHAT
ARHYTHMIA *n* irregular heartbeat
ARHYTHMIC > ARHYTHMIA
ARIA *n* elaborate song for solo voice, esp one from an opera
ARIARY *n* currency of Madagascar
ARIAS > ARIA
ARID *adj* parched, dry
ARIDER > ARID
ARIDEST > ARID
ARIDITIES > ARID
ARIDITY > ARID
ARIDLY > ARID
ARIDNESS > ARID
ARIEL *n* Arabian gazelle, *Gazella arabica* (or *dama*)
ARIELS > ARIEL
ARIETTA *n* short relatively uncomplicated aria
ARIETTAS > ARIETTA
ARIETTE *same as* > ARIETTA
ARIETTES > ARIETTE
ARIGHT *adv* rightly
ARIKI *n* first-born male or female in a notable family
ARIL *n* appendage on certain seeds, such as those of the yew and nutmeg, developed from or near the funicle of the ovule and often brightly coloured and fleshy

ARILED *adj* having an aril
ARILLARY *adj* having an aril
ARILLATE > ARILLATED
ARILLATED *adj* having an aril
ARILLI > ARILLUS
ARILLODE *n* structure in certain seeds that resembles an aril but is developed from the micropyle of the ovule
ARILLODES > ARILLODE
ARILLOID *adj* of or like an aril
ARILLUS *n* aril
ARILS > ARIL
ARIOSE *adj* songlike
ARIOSI > ARIOSO
ARIOSO *n* recitative with the lyrical quality of an aria
ARIOSOS > ARIOSO
ARIOT *adv* riotously
ARIPPLE *adv* in ripples
ARIS *n* Cockney slang for buttocks
ARISE *vb* come about
ARISEN > ARISE
ARISES > ARISE
ARISH *n* field that has been mown
ARISHES > ARISH
ARISING > ARISE
ARISTA *n* stiff bristle such as the awn of some grasses and cereals
ARISTAE > ARISTA
ARISTAS > ARISTA
ARISTATE > ARISTA
ARISTO *n* aristocrat
ARISTOS > ARISTO
ARISTOTLE *n* bottle
ARK *n* boat built by Noah, which survived the Flood ▷ *vb* place in an ark
ARKED > ARK
ARKING > ARK
ARKITE *n* passenger in ark
ARKITES > ARKITE
ARKOSE *n* sandstone consisting of grains of feldspar and quartz cemented by a mixture of quartz and clay minerals
ARKOSES > ARKOSE
ARKOSIC > ARKOSE
ARKS > ARK
ARLE *vb* make downpayment
ARLED > ARLE
ARLES > ARLE
ARLING > ARLE
ARM *n* either of the upper limbs from the shoulder to the wrist ▷ *vb* supply with weapons
ARMADA *n* large number of warships
ARMADAS > ARMADA
ARMADILLO *n* small S American mammal covered in strong bony plates
ARMAGNAC *n* dry brown brandy
ARMAGNACS > ARMAGNAC
ARMAMENT *n* military weapons
ARMAMENTS > ARMAMENT
ARMATURE *n* revolving structure in an electric motor or generator, wound with coils carrying the current
ARMATURED > ARMATURE
ARMATURES > ARMATURE
ARMBAND *n* band of material worn round the arm, such as one bearing an identifying mark, etc, or a black one indicating mourning
ARMBANDS > ARMBAND
ARMCHAIR *n* upholstered chair with side supports for the arms ▷ *adj* taking no active part
ARMCHAIRS > ARMCHAIR
ARMED *adj* equipped with or supported by arms, armour, etc
ARMER > ARM
ARMERS > ARM
ARMET *n* close-fitting medieval visored helmet with a neck guard
ARMETS > ARMET
ARMFUL *n* as much as can be held in the arms
ARMFULS > ARMFUL
ARMGAUNT *adj* word in Shakespeare of uncertain meaning
ARMHOLE *n* opening in a garment through which the arm passes
ARMHOLES > ARMHOLE
ARMIES > ARMY
ARMIGER *n* person entitled to bear heraldic arms, such as a sovereign or nobleman
ARMIGERAL > ARMIGER
ARMIGERO *n* armiger
ARMIGEROS > ARMIGERO
ARMIGERS > ARMIGER
ARMIL *n* bracelet
ARMILLA *n* bracelet
ARMILLAE > ARMILLA
ARMILLARY *adj* of or relating to bracelets
ARMILLAS > ARMILLA
ARMILS > ARMIL
ARMING *n* act of taking arms or providing with arms
ARMINGS > ARMING
ARMISTICE *n* agreed suspension of fighting
ARMLESS > ARM
ARMLET *n* band worn round the arm
ARMLETS > ARMLET
ARMLIKE > ARM
ARMLOAD *n* amount carried in the arms
ARMLOADS > ARMLOAD
ARMLOCK *vb* grip someone's arms
ARMLOCKED > ARMLOCK
ARMLOCKS > ARMLOCK
ARMOIRE *n* large cabinet, originally used for storing weapons
ARMOIRES > ARMOIRE
ARMONICA *n* glass harmonica
ARMONICAS > ARMONICA
ARMOR *same as* > ARMOUR
ARMORED *same as* > ARMOURED
ARMORER *same as* > ARMOURER
ARMORERS > ARMORER
ARMORIAL *adj* of or relating to heraldry or heraldic arms ▷ *n* book of coats of arms
ARMORIALS > ARMORIAL
ARMORIES > ARMORY
ARMORING > ARMOR
ARMORIST *n* heraldry expert
ARMORISTS > ARMORIST
ARMORLESS > ARMOR
ARMORS > ARMOR
ARMORY *same as* > ARMOURY
ARMOUR *n* metal clothing formerly worn to protect the body in battle ▷ *vb* equip or cover with armour
ARMOURED *adj* having a protective covering
ARMOURER *n* maker, repairer, or keeper of arms or armour
ARMOURERS > ARMOURER
ARMOURIES > ARMOURY
ARMOURING > ARMOUR
ARMOURS > ARMOUR
ARMOURY *n* place where weapons are stored
ARMOZEEN *n* material used for clerical gowns
ARMOZEENS > ARMOZEEN
ARMOZINE *n* material used for clerical gowns
ARMOZINES > ARMOZINE
ARMPIT *n* hollow under the arm at the shoulder
ARMPITS > ARMPIT
ARMREST *n* part of a chair or sofa that supports the arm
ARMRESTS > ARMREST
ARMS > ARM
ARMSFUL > ARMFUL
ARMURE *n* silk or wool fabric with a small cobbled pattern
ARMURES > ARMURE
ARMY *n* military land forces of a nation
ARMYWORM *n* caterpillar of a widely distributed noctuid moth
ARMYWORMS > ARMYWORM
ARNA *n* Indian water buffalo
ARNAS > ARNA
ARNATTO *n* annatto
ARNATTOS > ARNATTO
ARNICA *n* any N temperate or arctic plant of the genus *Arnica*, typically having yellow flowers: family *Asteraceae* (composites)
ARNICAS > ARNICA
ARNOTTO *n* annatto
ARNOTTOS > ARNOTTO
ARNUT *n* plant with edible tubers
ARNUTS > ARNUT
AROBA *n* Asian carriage
AROBAS > AROBA
AROHA *n* love, compassion, or affection
AROHAS > AROHA
AROID *adj* of, relating to, or belonging to the *Araceae*, a family of plants having small flowers massed on a spadix surrounded by a large petaloid spathe. The family includes arum, calla, and anthurium ▷ *n* any plant of the *Araceae*
AROIDS > AROID
AROINT *vb* drive away
AROINTED > AROINT
AROINTING > AROINT
AROINTS > AROINT
AROLLA *n* European pine tree
AROLLAS > AROLLA
AROMA *n* pleasant smell
AROMAS > AROMA
AROMATASE *n* enzyme involved in the production of oestrogen
AROMATIC *adj* having a distinctive pleasant smell ▷ *n* something, such as a plant or drug, that gives off a fragrant smell
AROMATICS > AROMATIC
AROMATISE *same as* > AROMATIZE
AROMATIZE *vb* make aromatic
AROSE *past tense of* > ARISE
AROUND *adv* on all sides (of)
AROUSABLE > AROUSE
AROUSAL > AROUSE
AROUSALS > AROUSE
AROUSE *vb* stimulate, make active
AROUSED > AROUSE
AROUSER > AROUSE
AROUSERS > AROUSE
AROUSES > AROUSE
AROUSING > AROUSE
AROW *adv* in a row
AROYNT *vb* old word meaning to drive away
AROYNTED > AROYNT
AROYNTING > AROYNT
AROYNTS > AROYNT
ARPEGGIO *n* notes of a chord played or sung in quick succession
ARPEGGIOS > ARPEGGIO
ARPEN *n* old French measure of land
ARPENS > ARPEN
ARPENT *n* former French

unit of length equal to 190 feet (approximately 58 metres)
ARPENTS > ARPENT
ARPILLERA *n* Peruvian wall-hanging
ARQUEBUS *n* portable long-barrelled gun dating from the 15th century
ARRACACHA *n* S American plant
ARRACK *n* alcoholic drink distilled from grain or rice
ARRACKS > ARRACK
ARRAH *interj* Irish exclamation
ARRAIGN *vb* bring (a prisoner) before a court to answer a charge
ARRAIGNED > ARRAIGN
ARRAIGNER > ARRAIGN
ARRAIGNS > ARRAIGN
ARRANGE *vb* plan
ARRANGED > ARRANGE
ARRANGER > ARRANGE
ARRANGERS > ARRANGE
ARRANGES > ARRANGE
ARRANGING > ARRANGE
ARRANT *adj* utter, downright
ARRANTLY > ARRANT
ARRAS *n* tapestry wall-hanging
ARRASED *adj* having an arras
ARRASENE *n* material used in embroidery
ARRASENES > ARRASENE
ARRASES > ARRAS
ARRAUGHT > AREACH
ARRAY *n* impressive display or collection ▷ *vb* arrange in order
ARRAYAL > ARRAY
ARRAYALS > ARRAY
ARRAYED > ARRAY
ARRAYER > ARRAY
ARRAYERS > ARRAY
ARRAYING > ARRAY
ARRAYMENT *n* act of arraying
ARRAYS > ARRAY
ARREAR *n* singular of arrears
ARREARAGE *same as* > ARREARS
ARREARS *pl n* money owed
ARRECT *adj* pricked up
ARREEDE *vb* old word meaning declare
ARREEDES > ARREEDE
ARREEDING > ARREEDE
ARREST *vb* take (a person) into custody ▷ *n* act of taking a person into custody
ARRESTANT *n* substance that stops a chemical reaction
ARRESTED > ARREST
ARRESTEE *n* arrested person
ARRESTEES > ARRESTEE
ARRESTER *n* person who arrests
ARRESTERS > ARRESTER
ARRESTING *adj* attracting attention, striking
ARRESTIVE *adj* making something stop
ARRESTOR *n* person or thing that arrests
ARRESTORS > ARRESTOR
ARRESTS > ARREST
ARRET *n* judicial decision
ARRETS > ARRET
ARRHIZAL *adj* without roots
ARRIAGE *n* Scottish feudal service
ARRIAGES > ARRIAGE
ARRIBA *interj* exclamation of pleasure or approval
ARRIDE *vb* old word meaning gratify
ARRIDED > ARRIDE
ARRIDES > ARRIDE
ARRIDING > ARRIDE
ARRIERE *adj* French word meaning old-fashioned
ARRIERO *n* Spanish word for mule driver
ARRIEROS > ARRIERO
ARRIS *n* sharp edge at the meeting of two surfaces at an angle with one another, as at two adjacent sides of a stone block
ARRISES > ARRIS
ARRISH *n* corn stubble
ARRISHES > ARRISH
ARRIVAL *n* arriving
ARRIVALS > ARRIVAL
ARRIVANCE *n* old word meaning people who have arrived
ARRIVANCY *n* arrivance
ARRIVE *vb* reach a place or destination
ARRIVED > ARRIVE
ARRIVER > ARRIVE
ARRIVERS > ARRIVE
ARRIVES > ARRIVE
ARRIVING > ARRIVE
ARRIVISME *n* unscrupulous ambition
ARRIVISTE *n* person who is unscrupulously ambitious
ARROBA *n* unit of weight used in some Spanish-speaking countries
ARROBAS > ARROBA
ARROGANCE > ARROGANT
ARROGANCY > ARROGANT
ARROGANT *adj* proud and overbearing
ARROGATE *vb* claim or seize without justification
ARROGATED > ARROGATE
ARROGATES > ARROGATE
ARROGATOR > ARROGATE
ARROW *n* pointed shaft shot from a bow
ARROWED *adj* having an arrow pattern
ARROWHEAD *n* pointed tip of an arrow
ARROWING > ARROW
ARROWLESS > ARROW
ARROWLIKE > ARROW
ARROWROOT *n* nutritious starch obtained from the root of a W Indian plant
ARROWS > ARROW
ARROWWOOD *n* any of various trees or shrubs, esp certain viburnums, having long straight tough stems formerly used by N American Indians to make arrows
ARROWWORM *n* any small marine invertebrate of the genus *Sagitta*, having an elongated transparent body with fins and prehensile oral bristles
ARROWY *adj* like an arrow
ARROYO *n* steep-sided stream bed that is usually dry except after heavy rain
ARROYOS > ARROYO
ARS > AR
ARSE *n* buttocks or anus ▷ *vb* play the fool
ARSED > ARSE
ARSEHOLE *n* anus
ARSEHOLES > ARSEHOLE
ARSENAL *n* place where arms and ammunition are made or stored
ARSENALS > ARSENAL
ARSENATE *n* salt or ester of arsenic acid
ARSENATES > ARSENATE
ARSENIATE *n* arsenate
ARSENIC *n* toxic grey element ▷ *adj* of or containing arsenic
ARSENICAL *adj* of or containing arsenic ▷ *n* drug or insecticide containing arsenic
ARSENICS > ARSENIC
ARSENIDE *n* compound in which arsenic is the most electronegative element
ARSENIDES > ARSENIDE
ARSENIOUS *adj* of or containing arsenic in the trivalent state
ARSENITE *n* salt or ester of arsenous acid, esp a salt containing the ion $A_5O_3^{3-}$
ARSENITES > ARSENITE
ARSENO *adj* containing arsenic
ARSENOUS *same as* > ARSENIOUS
ARSES > ARSIS
ARSEY *adj* aggressive, irritable, or argumentative
ARSHEEN *n* old measure of length in Russia
ARSHEENS > ARSHEEN
ARSHIN *n* old measure of length in Russia
ARSHINE *n* old measure of length in Russia
ARSHINES > ARSHINE
ARSHINS > ARSHIN
ARSIER > ARSY
ARSIEST > ARSY
ARSINE *n* colourless poisonous gas used in the manufacture of organic compounds, to dope transistors, and as a military poisonous gas
ARSINES > ARSINE
ARSING > ARSE
ARSINO *adj* containing arsine
ARSIS *n* (in classical prosody) the long syllable or part on which the ictus falls in a metrical foot
ARSON *n* crime of intentionally setting property on fire
ARSONIST > ARSON
ARSONISTS > ARSON
ARSONITE *n* person committing arson
ARSONITES > ARSONITE
ARSONOUS *adj* of arson
ARSONS > ARSON
ARSY *same as* > ARSEY
ART *n* creation of works of beauty, esp paintings or sculpture
ARTAL *a plural of* > ROTL
ARTEFACT *n* something made by human beings
ARTEFACTS > ARTEFACT
ARTEL *n* (in the former Soviet Union) a cooperative union or organization, esp of producers, such as peasants
ARTELS > ARTEL
ARTEMISIA *n* any herbaceous perennial plant of the genus *Artemisia*, of the N hemisphere, such as mugwort, sagebrush, and wormwood: family *Asteraceae* (composites)
ARTERIAL *adj* of an artery ▷ *n* major road
ARTERIALS > ARTERIAL
ARTERIES > ARTERY
ARTERIOLE *n* any of the small subdivisions of an artery that form thin-walled vessels ending in capillaries
ARTERITIS *n* inflammation of an artery
ARTERY *n* one of the tubes carrying blood from the heart
ARTESIAN as in *artesian well* well sunk through impermeable strata receiving water from an area at a higher altitude than that of the well
ARTFUL *adj* cunning, wily
ARTFULLY > ARTFUL
ARTHRITIC > ARTHRITIS
ARTHRITIS *n* painful inflammation of a joint or

joints
ARTHRODIA *n* joint
ARTHROPOD *n* animal, such as a spider or insect, with jointed limbs and a segmented body
ARTHROSES > ARTHROSIS
ARTHROSIS *n* disease of joint
ARTI *n* ritual performed in homes and temples in which incense and light is offered to a deity
ARTIC *n* articulated vehicle
ARTICHOKE *n* flower head of a thistle-like plant, cooked as a vegetable
ARTICLE *n* written piece in a magazine or newspaper ▷ *vb* bind by a written contract
ARTICLED > ARTICLE
ARTICLES > ARTICLE
ARTICLING > ARTICLE
ARTICS > ARTIC
ARTICULAR *adj* of or relating to joints
ARTIER > ARTY
ARTIES > ARTY
ARTIEST > ARTY
ARTIFACT *same as* > ARTEFACT
ARTIFACTS > ARTIFACT
ARTIFICE *n* clever trick
ARTIFICER *n* craftsman
ARTIFICES > ARTIFICE
ARTILLERY *n* large-calibre guns
ARTILY > ARTY
ARTINESS > ARTY
ARTIS > ARTI
ARTISAN *n* skilled worker, craftsman
ARTISANAL > ARTISAN
ARTISANS > ARTISAN
ARTIST *n* person who produces works of art, esp paintings or sculpture
ARTISTE *n* professional entertainer such as a singer or dancer
ARTISTES > ARTISTE
ARTISTIC *adj* of or characteristic of art or artists
ARTISTRY *n* artistic skill
ARTISTS > ARTIST
ARTLESS *adj* free from deceit or cunning
ARTLESSLY > ARTLESS
ARTS > ART
ARTSIER > ARTSY
ARTSIES > ARTSY
ARTSIEST > ARTSY
ARTSINESS > ARTSY
ARTSMAN *old word for* > CRAFTSMAN
ARTSMEN > ARTSMAN
ARTSY *adj* interested in the arts ▷ *n* person interested in the arts
ARTWORK *n* all the photographs and illustrations in a publication
ARTWORKS > ARTWORK
ARTY *adj* having an affected interest in art ▷ *n* person interested in art
ARUGOLA *n* salad plant
ARUGOLAS > ARUGOLA
ARUGULA *another name for* > ROCKET
ARUGULAS > ARUGULA
ARUHE *n* edible root of a fern
ARUM *n* any plant of the ariod genus *Arum*
ARUMS > ARUM
ARUSPEX *variant spelling of* > HARUSPEX
ARUSPICES > ARUSPEX
ARVAL *adj* of ploughed land
ARVICOLE *n* water rat
ARVICOLES > ARVICOLE
ARVO *n* afternoon
ARVOS > ARVO
ARY *dialect form of* > ANY
ARYBALLOS *n* ancient Greek flask
ARYL *n* of, consisting of, or containing an aromatic group
ARYLS > ARYL
ARYTENOID *adj* denoting either of two small cartilages of the larynx that are attached to the vocal cords ▷ *n* arytenoid cartilage or muscle
ARYTHMIA *n* any variation
ARYTHMIAS > ARYTHMIA
ARYTHMIC > ARYTHMIA
AS *adv* used to indicate amount or extent in comparisons ▷ *n* ancient Roman unit of weight
ASAFETIDA *n* bitter resin with an unpleasant onion-like smell
ASANA *n* any of various postures in yoga
ASANAS > ASANA
ASAR > AS
ASARUM *n* dried strong-scented root of the wild ginger plant: a flavouring agent and source of an aromatic oil used in perfumery, formerly used in medicine
ASARUMS > ASARUM
ASBESTIC > ASBESTOS
ASBESTINE > ASBESTOS
ASBESTOS *n* fibrous mineral which does not burn
ASBESTOUS > ASBESTOS
ASBESTUS *n* asbestos
ASCARED *adj* afraid
ASCARID *n* any parasitic nematode worm of the family *Ascaridae*, such as the common roundworm of man and pigs
ASCARIDES > ASCARID
ASCARIDS > ASCARID
ASCARIS *n* ascarid
ASCAUNT *adv* old word meaning slantwise
ASCEND *vb* go or move up
ASCENDANT *adj* dominant or influential
ASCENDED > ASCEND
ASCENDENT *same as* > ASCENDANT
ASCENDER *n* part of certain lower-case letters, such as *b* or *h*, that extends above the body of the letter
ASCENDERS > ASCENDER
ASCENDEUR *n* metal grip that is threaded on a rope and can be alternately tightened and slackened as an aid to climbing the rope: used attached to slings for the feet and waist
ASCENDING *adj* moving upwards
ASCENDS > ASCEND
ASCENSION *n* act of ascending
ASCENSIVE *adj* moving upwards
ASCENT *n* ascending
ASCENTS > ASCENT
ASCERTAIN *vb* find out definitely
ASCESES > ASCESIS
ASCESIS *n* exercise of self-discipline
ASCETIC *adj* (person) abstaining from worldly pleasures and comforts ▷ *n* person who abstains from worldly comforts and pleasures
ASCETICAL ascetic
ASCETICS > ASCETIC
ASCI > ASCUS
ASCIAN *n* person living in the tropics
ASCIANS > ASCIAN
ASCIDIA > ASCIDIUM
ASCIDIAN *n* any minute marine invertebrate animal of the class *Ascidiacea*, such as the sea squirt, the adults of which are degenerate and sedentary
ASCIDIANS > ASCIDIAN
ASCIDIATE > ASCIDIUM
ASCIDIUM *n* part of a plant that is shaped like a pitcher, such as the modified leaf of the pitcher plant
ASCITES *n* accumulation of serous fluid in the peritoneal cavity
ASCITIC > ASCITES
ASCITICAL > ASCITES
ASCLEPIAD *n* Greek verse form
ASCLEPIAS *n* any plant of the perennial mostly tuberous genus *Asclepias*; some are grown as garden or greenhouse plants for their showy orange-scarlet or purple flowers: family *Asclepiadaceae*
ASCOCARP *n* (in some ascomycetous fungi) a globular structure containing the asci
ASCOCARPS > ASCOCARP
ASCOGONIA *n* female reproductive bodies in some fungi
ASCONCE *adv* old form of askance
ASCORBATE *n* salt of ascorbic acid
ASCORBIC as in *ascorbic acid* white crystalline vitamin present in plants, esp citrus fruits, tomatoes, and green vegetables
ASCOSPORE *n* one of the spores (usually eight in number) that are produced in an ascus
ASCOT *n* cravat with wide square ends, usually secured with an ornamental stud
ASCOTS > ASCOT
ASCRIBE *vb* attribute, as to a particular origin
ASCRIBED > ASCRIBE
ASCRIBES > ASCRIBE
ASCRIBING > ASCRIBE
ASCUS *n* saclike structure that produces (usually) eight ascospores during sexual reproduction in ascomycetous fungi such as yeasts and mildews
ASDIC *an early form of* > SONAR
ASDICS > ASDIC
ASEA *adv* towards the sea
ASEISMIC *adj* denoting a region free of earthquakes
ASEITIES > ASEITY
ASEITY *n* existence derived from itself, having no other source
ASEPALOUS *adj* (of a plant or flower) having no sepals
ASEPSES > ASEPSIS
ASEPSIS *n* aseptic condition
ASEPTATE *adj* not divided into cells or sections by septa
ASEPTIC *adj* free from harmful bacteria ▷ *n* aseptic substance
ASEPTICS > ASEPTIC
ASEXUAL *adj* without sex
ASEXUALLY > ASEXUAL
ASH *n* powdery substance left when something is burnt ▷ *vb* reduce to ashes
ASHAKE *adv* shaking
ASHAME *vb* make ashamed
ASHAMED *adj* feeling shame
ASHAMEDLY > ASHAMED
ASHAMES > ASHAME
ASHAMING > ASHAME

ASHCAKE *n* cornmeal bread
ASHCAKES > ASHCAKE
ASHCAN *n* large metal dustbin
ASHCANS > ASHCAN
ASHED > ASH
ASHEN *adj* pale with shock
ASHERIES > ASHERY
ASHERY *n* place where ashes are made
ASHES > ASH
ASHET *n* shallow oval dish or large plate
ASHETS > ASHET
ASHFALL *n* dropping of ash from a volcano
ASHFALLS > ASHFALL
ASHIER > ASHY
ASHIEST > ASHY
ASHINE *adv* old word meaning shining
ASHINESS > ASHY
ASHING > ASH
ASHIVER *adv* shivering
ASHKEY *n* winged fruit of the ash
ASHKEYS > ASHKEY
ASHLAR *n* square block of hewn stone used in building ▷ *vb* build with ashlars
ASHLARED > ASHLAR
ASHLARING > ASHLAR
ASHLARS > ASHLAR
ASHLER *same as* > ASHLAR
ASHLERED > ASHLER
ASHLERING > ASHLER
ASHLERS > ASHLER
ASHLESS > ASH
ASHMAN *n* man who shovels ashes
ASHMEN > ASHMAN
ASHORE *adv* towards or on land ▷ *adj* on land, having come from the water
ASHPLANT *n* walking stick made from an ash sapling
ASHPLANTS > ASHPLANT
ASHRAM *n* religious retreat where a Hindu holy man lives
ASHRAMA *n* stage in Hindu spiritual life
ASHRAMAS > ASHRAMA
ASHRAMITE *n* person living in an ashram
ASHRAMS > ASHRAM
ASHTRAY *n* receptacle for tobacco ash and cigarette butts
ASHTRAYS > ASHTRAY
ASHY *adj* pale greyish
ASIAGO *n* either of two varieties (ripened or fresh) of a cow's-milk cheese produced in NE Italy
ASIAGOS > ASIAGO
ASIDE *adv* one side ▷ *n* remark not meant to be heard by everyone present
ASIDES > ASIDE
ASINICO *n* old Spanish word for fool
ASINICOS > ASINICO
ASININE *adj* stupid, idiotic
ASININELY > ASININE
ASININITY > ASININE
ASK *vb* say or write (something) in a form that requires an answer
ASKANCE *adv* with an oblique glance ▷ *vb* turn aside
ASKANCED > ASKANCE
ASKANCES > ASKANCE
ASKANCING > ASKANCE
ASKANT *same as* > ASKANCE
ASKANTED > ASKANT
ASKANTING > ASKANT
ASKANTS > ASKANT
ASKARI *n* (in East Africa) a soldier or policeman
ASKARIS > ASKARI
ASKED > ASK
ASKER > ASK
ASKERS > ASK
ASKESES > ASKESIS
ASKESIS *n* practice of self-discipline
ASKEW *adj* one side, crooked
ASKEWNESS > ASKEW
ASKING > ASK
ASKINGS > ASK
ASKLENT *Scots word for* > ASLANT
ASKOI > ASKOS
ASKOS *n* ancient Greek vase
ASKS > ASK
ASLAKE *vb* slake
ASLAKED > ASLAKE
ASLAKES > ASLAKE
ASLAKING > ASLAKE
ASLANT *adv* at a slant (to), slanting (across)
ASLEEP *adj* sleeping
ASLOPE *adj* sloping
ASLOSH *adj* awash
ASMEAR *adj* smeared
ASMOULDER *adv* old word meaning smouldering
ASOCIAL *n* person who avoids social contact
ASOCIALS > ASOCIAL
ASP *n* small poisonous snake
ASPARAGUS *n* plant whose shoots are cooked as a vegetable
ASPARKLE *adv* sparkling
ASPARTAME *n* artificial sweetener
ASPARTATE *n* enzyme found in blood
ASPARTIC as in *aspartic acid* nonessential amino acid that is a component of proteins and acts as a neurotransmitter
ASPECT *n* feature or element ▷ *vb* look at
ASPECTED > ASPECT
ASPECTING > ASPECT
ASPECTS > ASPECT
ASPECTUAL *adj* of or relating to grammatical aspect
ASPEN *n* kind of poplar tree ▷ *adj* trembling
ASPENS > ASPEN
ASPER *n* former Turkish monetary unit, a silver coin, worth 1/120 of a piastre
ASPERATE *adj* (of plant parts) having a rough surface due to a covering of short stiff hairs ▷ *vb* make rough
ASPERATED > ASPERATE
ASPERATES > ASPERATE
ASPERGE *vb* sprinkle
ASPERGED > ASPERGE
ASPERGER > ASPERGE
ASPERGERS > ASPERGE
ASPERGES > ASPERGE
ASPERGILL *n* perforated instrument used to sprinkle holy water
ASPERGING > ASPERGE
ASPERITY *n* roughness of temper
ASPERMIA *n* failure to form or emit semen
ASPERMIAS > ASPERMIA
ASPEROUS *same as* > ASPERATE
ASPERS > ASPER
ASPERSE *vb* spread false rumours about
ASPERSED > ASPERSE
ASPERSER > ASPERSE
ASPERSERS > ASPERSE
ASPERSES > ASPERSE
ASPERSING > ASPERSE
ASPERSION *n* disparaging or malicious remark
ASPERSIVE > ASPERSE
ASPERSOIR *n* sprinkler for holy water
ASPERSOR > ASPERSE
ASPERSORS > ASPERSE
ASPERSORY *n* sprinkler for holy water
ASPHALT *n* black hard tarlike substance used for road surfaces etc ▷ *vb* cover with asphalt
ASPHALTED > ASPHALT
ASPHALTER *n* person who lays asphalt
ASPHALTIC > ASPHALT
ASPHALTS > ASPHALT
ASPHALTUM *n* asphalt
ASPHERIC *adj* not spherical
ASPHODEL *n* plant with clusters of yellow or white flowers
ASPHODELS > ASPHODEL
ASPHYXIA *n* suffocation
ASPHYXIAL > ASPHYXIA
ASPHYXIAS > ASPHYXIA
ASPHYXIES > ASPHYXY
ASPHYXY *n old form of* > ASPHYXIA
ASPIC *n* savoury jelly used to coat meat, eggs, fish, etc
ASPICK *old word for* > ASP
ASPICKS > ASPICK
ASPICS > ASPIC
ASPIDIA > ASPIDIUM
ASPIDIOID > ASPIDIUM
ASPIDIUM *n* variety of fern
ASPINE *old word for* > ASPEN
ASPINES > ASPINE
ASPIRANT *n* person who aspires ▷ *adj* aspiring or striving
ASPIRANTS > ASPIRANT
ASPIRATA *n* rough stop
ASPIRATAE > ASPIRATA
ASPIRATE *vb* pronounce with an *h* sound ▷ *n* *h* sound ▷ *adj* (of a stop) pronounced with a forceful and audible expulsion of breath
ASPIRATED > ASPIRATE
ASPIRATES > ASPIRATE
ASPIRATOR *n* device for removing fluids from a body cavity by suction
ASPIRE *vb* yearn (for), hope (to do or be)
ASPIRED > ASPIRE
ASPIRER > ASPIRE
ASPIRERS > ASPIRE
ASPIRES > ASPIRE
ASPIRIN *n* drug used to relieve pain and fever
ASPIRING > ASPIRE
ASPIRINS > ASPIRIN
ASPIS *n* horned viper
ASPISES > ASPIS
ASPISH *adj* like an asp
ASPLENIUM *n* type of fern
ASPORT *vb* old word meaning take away
ASPORTED > ASPORT
ASPORTING > ASPORT
ASPORTS > ASPORT
ASPOUT *adv* spouting
ASPRAWL *adv* sprawling
ASPREAD *adv* spreading
ASPRO *n* associate professor at an academic institution
ASPROS > ASPRO
ASPROUT *adv* sprouting
ASPS > ASP
ASQUAT *adv* squatting
ASQUINT *adj* with a glance from the corner of the eye, esp a furtive one
ASRAMA *n* stage in Hindu spiritual life
ASRAMAS > ASRAMA
ASS *n* donkey
ASSAGAI *same as* > ASSEGAI
ASSAGAIED > ASSAGAI
ASSAGAIS > ASSAGAI
ASSAI *adv* (usually preceded by a musical direction) very ▷ *n* any of several Brazilian palm trees of the genus *Euterpe*, esp *E. edulis*, that have small dark purple fleshy edible fruit
ASSAIL *vb* attack violently
ASSAILANT *n* person who attacks another, either physically or verbally
ASSAILED > ASSAIL
ASSAILER > ASSAIL
ASSAILERS > ASSAIL

ASSAILING > ASSAIL
ASSAILS > ASSAIL
ASSAIS > ASSAI
ASSAM *n* (in Malaysia) tamarind as used in cooking
ASSAMS > ASSAM
ASSART *vb* clear ground for cultivation
ASSARTED > ASSART
ASSARTING > ASSART
ASSARTS > ASSART
ASSASSIN *n* person who murders a prominent person
ASSASSINS > ASSASSIN
ASSAULT *n* violent attack ▷ *vb* attack violently
ASSAULTED > ASSAULT
ASSAULTER > ASSAULT
ASSAULTS > ASSAULT
ASSAY *n* analysis of a substance, esp a metal, to ascertain its purity ▷ *vb* make such an analysis
ASSAYABLE > ASSAY
ASSAYED > ASSAY
ASSAYER > ASSAY
ASSAYERS > ASSAY
ASSAYING > ASSAY
ASSAYINGS > ASSAY
ASSAYS > ASSAY
ASSED *adj* motivated
ASSEGAAI *same as* > ASSEGAI
ASSEGAAIS > ASSEGAI
ASSEGAI *n* slender spear used in S Africa ▷ *vb* spear with an assegai
ASSEGAIED > ASSEGAI
ASSEGAIS > ASSEGAI
ASSEMBLE *vb* collect or congregate
ASSEMBLED > ASSEMBLE
ASSEMBLER *n* person or thing that assembles
ASSEMBLES > ASSEMBLE
ASSEMBLY *n* assembled group
ASSENT *n* agreement or consent ▷ *vb* agree or consent
ASSENTED > ASSENT
ASSENTER *n* person supporting another's nomination
ASSENTERS > ASSENTER
ASSENTING > ASSENT
ASSENTIVE > ASSENT
ASSENTOR *n* any of the eight voters legally required to endorse the nomination of a candidate in a parliamentary or local election in addition to the nominator and seconder
ASSENTORS > ASSENTOR
ASSENTS > ASSENT
ASSERT *vb* declare forcefully
ASSERTED > ASSERT
ASSERTER > ASSERT
ASSERTERS > ASSERT
ASSERTING > ASSERT
ASSERTION *n* positive statement, usu. made without evidence
ASSERTIVE *adj* confident and direct in dealing with others
ASSERTOR > ASSERT
ASSERTORS > ASSERT
ASSERTORY *adj* making affirmation
ASSERTS > ASSERT
ASSES > ASS
ASSESS *vb* judge the worth or importance of
ASSESSED > ASSESS
ASSESSES > ASSESS
ASSESSING > ASSESS
ASSESSOR *n* person who values property for taxation or insurance purposes
ASSESSORS > ASSESSOR
ASSET *n* valuable or useful person or thing
ASSETLESS > ASSET
ASSETS > ASSET
ASSEVER *vb* old form of asseverate
ASSEVERED > ASSEVER
ASSEVERS > ASSEVER
ASSEZ *adv* (as part of a musical direction) fairly
ASSHOLE *same as* > ARSEHOLE
ASSHOLES > ASSHOLE
ASSIDUITY *n* constant and close application
ASSIDUOUS *adj* hard-working
ASSIEGE *vb* old form of besiege
ASSIEGED > ASSIEGE
ASSIEGES > ASSIEGE
ASSIEGING > ASSIEGE
ASSIENTO *n* slave trade treaty between Britain and Spain
ASSIENTOS > ASSIENTO
ASSIGN *vb* appoint (someone) to a job or task ▷ *n* person to whom property is assigned
ASSIGNAT *n* paper money issued by the Constituent Assembly in 1789, backed by the confiscated land of the Church and the émigrés
ASSIGNATS > ASSIGNAT
ASSIGNED > ASSIGN
ASSIGNEE *n* person to whom some right, interest, or property is transferred
ASSIGNEES > ASSIGNEE
ASSIGNER > ASSIGN
ASSIGNERS > ASSIGN
ASSIGNING > ASSIGN
ASSIGNOR *n* person who transfers or assigns property
ASSIGNORS > ASSIGNOR
ASSIGNS > ASSIGN
ASSIST *vb* give help or support ▷ *n* pass by a player which enables another player to score a goal
ASSISTANT *n* helper ▷ *adj* junior or deputy
ASSISTED > ASSIST
ASSISTER > ASSIST
ASSISTERS > ASSIST
ASSISTING > ASSIST
ASSISTIVE *adj* providing a means of reducing a physical impairment
ASSISTOR > ASSIST
ASSISTORS > ASSIST
ASSISTS > ASSIST
ASSIZE *n* sitting of a legislative assembly or administrative body
ASSIZED > ASSIZE
ASSIZER *n* weights and measures official
ASSIZERS > ASSIZER
ASSIZES > ASSIZE
ASSIZING > ASSIZE
ASSLIKE > ASS
ASSOCIATE *vb* connect in the mind ▷ *n* partner in business ▷ *adj* having partial rights or subordinate status
ASSOIL *vb* absolve
ASSOILED > ASSOIL
ASSOILING > ASSOIL
ASSOILS > ASSOIL
ASSOILZIE *vb* old Scots word meaning absolve
ASSONANCE *n* rhyming of vowel sounds but not consonants
ASSONANT > ASSONANCE
ASSONANTS > ASSONANCE
ASSONATE *vb* show assonance
ASSONATED > ASSONATE
ASSONATES > ASSONATE
ASSORT *vb* arrange or distribute into groups of the same type
ASSORTED *adj* consisting of various types mixed together
ASSORTER > ASSORT
ASSORTERS > ASSORT
ASSORTING > ASSORT
ASSORTIVE > ASSORT
ASSORTS > ASSORT
ASSOT *vb* old word meaning make infatuated
ASSOTS > ASSOT
ASSOTT *vb* besot
ASSOTTED > ASSOT
ASSOTTING > ASSOT
ASSUAGE *vb* relieve (pain, grief, thirst, etc)
ASSUAGED > ASSUAGE
ASSUAGER > ASSUAGE
ASSUAGERS > ASSUAGE
ASSUAGES > ASSUAGE
ASSUAGING > ASSUAGE
ASSUASIVE > ASSUAGE
ASSUETUDE *n* state of being accustomed
ASSUMABLE > ASSUME
ASSUMABLY > ASSUME
ASSUME *vb* take to be true without proof
ASSUMED *adj* false
ASSUMEDLY > ASSUME
ASSUMER > ASSUME
ASSUMERS > ASSUME
ASSUMES > ASSUME
ASSUMING *adj* expecting too much ▷ *n* action of one who assumes
ASSUMINGS > ASSUMING
ASSUMPSIT *n* (before 1875) an action to recover damages for breach of an express or implied contract or agreement that was not under seal
ASSURABLE > ASSURE
ASSURANCE *n* assuring or being assured
ASSURE *vb* promise or guarantee
ASSURED *adj* confident ▷ *n* beneficiary under a life assurance policy
ASSUREDLY > ASSURED
ASSUREDS > ASSURED
ASSURER > ASSURE
ASSURERS > ASSURE
ASSURES > ASSURE
ASSURGENT *adj* (of leaves, stems, etc) curving or growing upwards
ASSURING > ASSURE
ASSUROR > ASSURE
ASSURORS > ASSURE
ASSWAGE *old spelling of* > ASSUAGE
ASSWAGED > ASSWAGE
ASSWAGES > ASSWAGE
ASSWAGING > ASSWAGE
ASTABLE *adj* not stable
ASTARE *adv* staring
ASTART *old word for* > START
ASTARTED > ASTART
ASTARTING > ASTART
ASTARTS > ASTART
ASTASIA *n* inability to stand
ASTASIAS > ASTASIA
ASTATIC *adj* not static
ASTATIDE *n* binary compound of astatine with a more electropositive element
ASTATIDES > ASTATIDE
ASTATINE *n* radioactive nonmetallic element
ASTATINES > ASTATINE
ASTATKI *n* fuel derived from petroleum
ASTATKIS > ASTATKI
ASTEISM *n* use of irony
ASTEISMS > ASTEISM
ASTELIC > ASTELY
ASTELIES > ASTELY
ASTELY *n* lack of central cylinder in plants
ASTER *n* plant with daisy-like flowers
ASTERIA *n* gemstone with starlike light effect
ASTERIAS > ASTERIA

ASTERID *n* variety of flowering plant
ASTERIDS > ASTERID
ASTERISK *n* star-shaped symbol (*) used in printing or writing to indicate a footnote, etc ▷ *vb* mark with an asterisk
ASTERISKS > ASTERISK
ASTERISM *n* three asterisks arranged in a triangle to draw attention to the text that follows
ASTERISMS > ASTERISM
ASTERN *adv* at or towards the stern of a ship ▷ *adj* at or towards the stern of a ship
ASTERNAL *adj* not connected or joined to the sternum
ASTEROID *n* any of the small planets that orbit the sun between Mars and Jupiter ▷ *adj* of, relating to, or belonging to the class *Asteroidea*
ASTEROIDS > ASTEROID
ASTERS > ASTER
ASTERT *vb* start
ASTERTED > ASTERT
ASTERTING > ASTERT
ASTERTS > ASTERT
ASTHENIA *n* abnormal loss of strength
ASTHENIAS > ASTHENIA
ASTHENIC *adj* of, relating to, or having asthenia ▷ *n* person having long limbs and a small trunk
ASTHENICS > ASTHENIC
ASTHENIES > ASTHENY
ASTHENY *same as* > ASTHENIA
ASTHMA *n* illness causing difficulty in breathing
ASTHMAS > ASTHMA
ASTHMATIC *adj* of, relating to, or having asthma ▷ *n* person who has asthma
ASTHORE *n* Irish endearment
ASTHORES > ASTHORE
ASTICHOUS *adj* not arranged in rows
ASTIGMIA *n* defect of a lens resulting in the formation of distorted images
ASTIGMIAS > ASTIGMIA
ASTILBE *n* any perennial saxifragaceous plant of the genus *Astilbe* of E Asia and N America: cultivated for their ornamental spikes or panicles of pink or white flowers
ASTILBES > ASTILBE
ASTIR *adj* out of bed
ASTOMATAL *adj* having no stomata
ASTOMOUS *adj* having no mouth
ASTONE *vb old form of* > ASTONISH
ASTONED > ASTONE
ASTONES > ASTONE
ASTONIED *adj* stunned
ASTONIES > ASTONY
ASTONING > ASTONE
ASTONISH *vb* surprise greatly
ASTONY *vb old form of* > ASTONISH
ASTONYING > ASTONY
ASTOOP *adv* stooping
ASTOUND *vb* overwhelm with amazement
ASTOUNDED > ASTOUND
ASTOUNDS > ASTOUND
ASTRACHAN *same as* > ASTRAKHAN
ASTRADDLE *adj* with a leg on either side of something
ASTRAGAL *n* small convex moulding, usually with a semicircular cross section
ASTRAGALI *n* bones of the ankles that articulate with the leg bones to form ankle joints
ASTRAGALS > ASTRAGAL
ASTRAKHAN *n* dark curly fleece of lambs from Astrakhan in Russia
ASTRAL *adj* of stars ▷ *n* oil lamp
ASTRALLY > ASTRAL
ASTRALS > ASTRAL
ASTRAND *adv* on shore
ASTRANTIA *n* flowering plant
ASTRAY *adv* off the right path
ASTRICT *vb* bind, confine, or constrict
ASTRICTED > ASTRICT
ASTRICTS > ASTRICT
ASTRIDE *adv* with a leg on either side (of) ▷ *adj* with a leg on either side
ASTRINGE *vb* cause contraction
ASTRINGED > ASTRINGE
ASTRINGER *n* person who keeps goshawks
ASTRINGES > ASTRINGE
ASTROCYTE *n* any of the star-shaped cells in the tissue supporting the brain and spinal cord (neuroglia)
ASTRODOME *n* transparent dome on the top of an aircraft, through which observations can be made, esp of the stars
ASTROFELL *n* plant in Spenser's poetry
ASTROID *n* hypocycloid having four cusps
ASTROIDS > ASTROID
ASTROLABE *n* instrument formerly used to measure the altitude of stars and planets
ASTROLOGY *n* study of the alleged influence of the stars, planets, and moon on human affairs
ASTRONAUT *n* person trained for travelling in space
ASTRONOMY *n* scientific study of heavenly bodies
ASTROPHEL *n* plant in Spenser's poetry
ASTRUT *adv* old word meaning in a protruding way
ASTUCIOUS *adj* old form of astute
ASTUCITY *n* quality of being astute
ASTUN *vb* old form of astonish
ASTUNNED > ASTUN
ASTUNNING > ASTUN
ASTUNS > ASTUN
ASTUTE *adj* perceptive or shrewd
ASTUTELY > ASTUTE
ASTUTER > ASTUTE
ASTUTEST > ASTUTE
ASTYLAR *adj* without columns or pilasters
ASUDDEN *adv* old form of suddenly
ASUNDER *adv* into parts or pieces ▷ *adj* into parts or pieces
ASWARM *adj* filled, esp with moving things
ASWAY *adv* swaying
ASWIM *adv* floating
ASWING *adv* swinging
ASWIRL *adv* swirling
ASWOON *adv* swooning
ASYLA > ASYLUM
ASYLLABIC *adj* not functioning in the manner of a syllable
ASYLUM *n* refuge or sanctuary
ASYLUMS > ASYLUM
ASYMMETRY *n* lack of symmetry
ASYMPTOTE *n* straight line closely approached but never met by a curve
ASYNAPSES > ASYNAPSIS
ASYNAPSIS *n* failure of pairing of chromosomes at meiosis
ASYNDETA > ASYNDETON
ASYNDETIC *adj* (of a catalogue or index) without cross references
ASYNDETON *n* omission of a conjunction between the parts of a sentence
ASYNERGIA *n* lack of coordination between muscles or parts, as occurs in cerebellar disease
ASYNERGY *same as* > ASYNERGIA
ASYSTOLE *n* absence of heartbeat
ASYSTOLES > ASYSTOLE
ASYSTOLIC > ASYSTOLE
AT *n* Laotian monetary unit worth one hundredth of a kip
ATAATA *n* grazing marine gastropod
ATAATAS > ATAATA
ATABAL *n* N African drum
ATABALS > ATABAL
ATABEG *n* Turkish ruler
ATABEGS > ATABEG
ATABEK *n* Turkish ruler
ATABEKS > ATABEK
ATABRIN *n* drug formerly used for treating malaria
ATABRINE *same as* > ATABRIN
ATABRINES > ATABRINE
ATABRINS > ATABRIN
ATACAMITE *n* mineral containing copper
ATACTIC *adj* (of a polymer) having a random sequence of the stereochemical arrangement of groups on carbon atoms in the chain
ATAGHAN *a variant of* > YATAGHAN
ATAGHANS > ATAGHAN
ATALAYA *n* watchtower in Spain
ATALAYAS > ATALAYA
ATAMAN *n* elected leader of the Cossacks
ATAMANS > ATAMAN
ATAMASCO *n* N American lily
ATAMASCOS > ATAMASCO
ATAP *n* palm tree of S Asia
ATAPS > ATAP
ATARACTIC *adj* able to calm or tranquillize ▷ *n* ataractic drug
ATARAXIA *n* calmness or peace of mind
ATARAXIAS > ATARAXIA
ATARAXIC *same as* > ATARACTIC
ATARAXICS > ATARAXIC
ATARAXIES > ATARAXY
ATARAXY *same as* > ATARAXIA
ATAVIC > ATAVISM
ATAVISM *n* recurrence of a trait present in distant ancestors
ATAVISMS > ATAVISM
ATAVIST > ATAVISM
ATAVISTIC *adj* of or relating to reversion to a former or more primitive type
ATAVISTS > ATAVISM
ATAXIA *n* lack of muscular coordination
ATAXIAS > ATAXIA
ATAXIC > ATAXIA
ATAXICS > ATAXIA
ATAXIES > ATAXY
ATAXY *same as* > ATAXIA
ATCHIEVE *vb old form of* > ACHIEVE
ATCHIEVED > ATCHIEVE
ATCHIEVES > ATCHIEVE
ATE *past tense of* > EAT
ATEBRIN *n* drug formerly used to treat malaria

ATEBRINS > ATEBRIN
ATECHNIC *adj* without technical ability
ATELIC *adj* of action without end
ATELIER *n* workshop, artist's studio
ATELIERS > ATELIER
ATEMOYA *n* tropical fruit tree
ATEMOYAS > ATEMOYA
ATEMPORAL *adj* not governed by time
ATENOLOL *n* type of beta-blocker
ATENOLOLS > ATENOLOL
ATES *n* shop selling confectionery
ATHAME *n* (in Wicca) witch's ceremonial knife, usually with a black handle, used in rituals rather than for cutting or carving
ATHAMES > ATHAME
ATHANASY *n* absence of death
ATHANOR *n* alchemist's furnace
ATHANORS > ATHANOR
ATHEISE *vb* speak atheistically
ATHEISED > ATHEISE
ATHEISES > ATHEISE
ATHEISING > ATHEISE
ATHEISM *n* belief that there is no God
ATHEISMS > ATHEISM
ATHEIST > ATHEISM
ATHEISTIC > ATHEISM
ATHEISTS > ATHEISM
ATHEIZE *vb* speak atheistically
ATHEIZED > ATHEIZE
ATHEIZES > ATHEIZE
ATHEIZING > ATHEIZE
ATHELING *n* (in Anglo-Saxon England) a prince of any of the royal dynasties
ATHELINGS > ATHELING
ATHEMATIC *adj* not based on themes
ATHENAEUM *n* institution for the promotion of learning
ATHENEUM *same as* > ATHENAEUM
ATHENEUMS > ATHENEUM
ATHEOLOGY *n* opposition to theology
ATHEOUS *adj* without a belief in god
ATHERINE *n* small fish
ATHERINES > ATHERINE
ATHEROMA *n* fatty deposit on or within the inner lining of an artery, often causing an obstruction to the blood flow
ATHEROMAS > ATHEROMA
ATHETESES > ATHETESIS
ATHETESIS *n* dismissal of a text as not genuine
ATHETISE *vb* reject as not genuine
ATHETISED > ATHETISE
ATHETISES > ATHETISE
ATHETIZE *vb* reject as not genuine
ATHETIZED > ATHETIZE
ATHETIZES > ATHETIZE
ATHETOID > ATHETOSIS
ATHETOSES > ATHETOSIS
ATHETOSIC > ATHETOSIS
ATHETOSIS *n* condition characterized by uncontrolled rhythmic writhing movement, esp of fingers, hands, head, and tongue, caused by cerebral lesion
ATHETOTIC > ATHETOSIS
ATHIRST *adj* having an eager desire
ATHLETA *n old form of* > ATHLETE
ATHLETAS > ATHLETA
ATHLETE *n* person trained in or good at athletics
ATHLETES > ATHLETE
ATHLETIC *adj* physically fit or strong
ATHLETICS *n* track and field events
ATHODYD *another name for* > RAMJET
ATHODYDS > ATHODYD
ATHRILL *adv* feeling thrills
ATHROB *adv* throbbing
ATHROCYTE *n* cell able to store matter
ATHWART *adv* transversely
ATIGI *n* type of parka worn by the Inuit in Canada
ATIGIS > ATIGI
ATILT *adj* in a tilted or inclined position
ATIMIES > ATIMY
ATIMY *n* loss of honour
ATINGLE *adv* tingling
ATISHOO *n* sound of a sneeze
ATISHOOS > ATISHOO
ATLANTES > ATLAS
ATLAS *n* book of maps
ATLASES > ATLAS
ATLATL *n* Native American throwing stick
ATLATLS > ATLATL
ATMA *same as* > ATMAN
ATMAN *n* personal soul or self
ATMANS > ATMAN
ATMAS > ATMA
ATMOLOGY *n* study of aqueous vapour
ATMOLYSE *vb* separate gases by filtering
ATMOLYSED > ATMOLYSE
ATMOLYSES > ATMOLYSIS
ATMOLYSIS *n* method of separating gases that depends on their differential rates of diffusion through a porous substance
ATMOLYZE *vb* separate gases by filtering
ATMOLYZED > ATMOLYZE
ATMOLYZES > ATMOLYZE
ATMOMETER *n* instrument for measuring the rate of evaporation of water into the atmosphere
ATMOMETRY > ATMOMETER
ATOC *n* skunk
ATOCIA *n* inability to have children
ATOCIAS > ATOCIA
ATOCS > ATOC
ATOK *n* skunk
ATOKAL *adj* having no children
ATOKE *n* part of a worm
ATOKES > ATOKE
ATOKOUS *adj* having no children
ATOKS > ATOK
ATOLL *n* ring-shaped coral reef enclosing a lagoon
ATOLLS > ATOLL
ATOM *n* smallest unit of matter which can take part in a chemical reaction
ATOMIC *adj* of or using atomic bombs or atomic energy
ATOMICAL > ATOMIC
ATOMICITY *n* state of being made up of atoms
ATOMICS *n* science of atoms
ATOMIES > ATOMY
ATOMISE *same as* > ATOMIZE
ATOMISED > ATOMISE
ATOMISER *same as* > ATOMIZER
ATOMISERS > ATOMISER
ATOMISES > ATOMISE
ATOMISING > ATOMISE
ATOMISM *n* ancient philosophical theory that the ultimate constituents of the universe are atoms
ATOMISMS > ATOMISM
ATOMIST > ATOMISM
ATOMISTIC > ATOMISM
ATOMISTS > ATOMISM
ATOMIZE *vb* reduce to atoms or small particles
ATOMIZED > ATOMIZE
ATOMIZER *n* device for discharging a liquid in a fine spray
ATOMIZERS > ATOMIZER
ATOMIZES > ATOMIZE
ATOMIZING > ATOMIZE
ATOMS > ATOM
ATOMY *n* atom or minute particle
ATONABLE > ATONE
ATONAL *adj* (of music) not written in an established key
ATONALISM > ATONAL
ATONALIST > ATONAL
ATONALITY *n* absence of or disregard for an established musical key in a composition
ATONALLY > ATONAL
ATONE *vb* make amends (for sin or wrongdoing)
ATONEABLE > ATONE
ATONED > ATONE
ATONEMENT *n* something done to make amends for wrongdoing
ATONER > ATONE
ATONERS > ATONE
ATONES > ATONE
ATONIA *n* lack of normal muscle tone
ATONIAS > ATONIA
ATONIC *adj* (of a syllable, word, etc) carrying no stress ▷ *n* unaccented or unstressed syllable, word, etc, such as *for* in *food for thought*
ATONICITY > ATONIC
ATONICS > ATONIC
ATONIES > ATONY
ATONING > ATONE
ATONINGLY > ATONE
ATONY *n* lack of normal tone or tension, as in muscles
ATOP *adv* on top
ATOPIC *adj* of or relating to hereditary hypersensitivity to certain allergens
ATOPIES > ATOPY
ATOPY *n* hereditary tendency to be hypersensitive to certain allergens
ATRAMENT *n* old word meaning black liquid
ATRAMENTS > ATRAMENT
ATRAZINE *n* white crystalline compound
ATRAZINES > ATRAZINE
ATREMBLE *adv* trembling
ATRESIA *n* absence of or unnatural narrowing of a body channel
ATRESIAS > ATRESIA
ATRESIC > ATRESIA
ATRETIC > ATRESIA
ATRIA > ATRIUM
ATRIAL > ATRIUM
ATRIP *adj* (of an anchor) no longer caught on the bottom
ATRIUM *n* upper chamber of either half of the heart
ATRIUMS > ATRIUM
ATROCIOUS *adj* extremely cruel or wicked
ATROCITY *n* wickedness
ATROPHIA *n* wasting disease
ATROPHIAS > ATROPHIA
ATROPHIC > ATROPHY
ATROPHIED > ATROPHY
ATROPHIES > ATROPHY
ATROPHY *n* wasting away of an organ or part ▷ *vb* (cause to) waste away
ATROPIA *n* atropine
ATROPIAS > ATROPIA
ATROPIN *same as* > ATROPINE
ATROPINE *n* poisonous alkaloid obtained from

deadly nightshade
ATROPINES > ATROPINE
ATROPINS > ATROPIN
ATROPISM *n* condition caused by using belladonna
ATROPISMS > ATROPISM
ATROPOUS *adj* growing straight
ATT *n* old Siamese coin
ATTABOY *sentence substitute* expression of approval or exhortation
ATTACH *vb* join, fasten, or connect
ATTACHE *n* a specialist attached to a diplomatic mission
ATTACHED *adj* fond of
ATTACHER > ATTACH
ATTACHERS > ATTACH
ATTACHES > ATTACH
ATTACHING > ATTACH
ATTACK *vb* launch a physical assault (against) ▷ *n* act of attacking
ATTACKED > ATTACK
ATTACKER > ATTACK
ATTACKERS > ATTACK
ATTACKING > ATTACK
ATTACKMAN *n* attacking player in sport
ATTACKMEN > ATTACKMAN
ATTACKS > ATTACK
ATTAGIRL *humorous feminine version of* > ATTABOY
ATTAIN *vb* achieve or accomplish (a task or aim)
ATTAINDER *n* (formerly) the extinction of a person's civil rights resulting from a sentence of death or outlawry on conviction for treason or felony
ATTAINED > ATTAIN
ATTAINER > ATTAIN
ATTAINERS > ATTAIN
ATTAINING > ATTAIN
ATTAINS > ATTAIN
ATTAINT *vb* pass judgment of death or outlawry upon (a person) ▷ *n* dishonour
ATTAINTED > ATTAINT
ATTAINTS > ATTAINT
ATTAP *n* palm tree of South Asia
ATTAPS > ATTAP
ATTAR *n* fragrant oil made from roses
ATTARS > ATTAR
ATTASK *old word for* > CRITICIZE
ATTASKED > ATTASK
ATTASKING > ATTASK
ATTASKS > ATTASK
ATTASKT > ATTASK
ATTEMPER *vb* modify by blending
ATTEMPERS > ATTEMPER
ATTEMPT *vb* try, make an effort ▷ *n* effort or endeavour
ATTEMPTED > ATTEMPT
ATTEMPTER > ATTEMPT
ATTEMPTS > ATTEMPT
ATTEND *vb* be present at
ATTENDANT *n* person who assists, guides, or provides a service ▷ *adj* accompanying
ATTENDED > ATTEND
ATTENDEE *n* person who is present at a specified event
ATTENDEES > ATTENDEE
ATTENDER > ATTEND
ATTENDERS > ATTEND
ATTENDING > ATTEND
ATTENDS > ATTEND
ATTENT *old word for* > ATTENTION
ATTENTAT *n* attempt
ATTENTATS > ATTENTAT
ATTENTION *n* concentrated direction of the mind
ATTENTIVE *adj* giving attention
ATTENTS > ATTENT
ATTENUANT *adj* causing dilution or thinness, esp of the blood ▷ *n* attenuant drug or agent
ATTENUATE *vb* weaken or become weak ▷ *adj* diluted, weakened, slender, or reduced
ATTERCOP *n* spider
ATTERCOPS > ATTERCOP
ATTEST *vb* affirm the truth of, be proof of
ATTESTANT > ATTEST
ATTESTED *adj* (of cattle) certified to be free from a disease, such as tuberculosis
ATTESTER > ATTEST
ATTESTERS > ATTEST
ATTESTING > ATTEST
ATTESTOR > ATTEST
ATTESTORS > ATTEST
ATTESTS > ATTEST
ATTIC *n* space or room within the roof of a house
ATTICISE *same as* > ATTICIZE
ATTICISED > ATTICISE
ATTICISES > ATTICISE
ATTICISM *n* elegant, simple, and clear expression
ATTICISMS > ATTICISM
ATTICIST > ATTICISM
ATTICISTS > ATTICISM
ATTICIZE *vb* conform or adapt to the norms of Attica
ATTICIZED > ATTICIZE
ATTICIZES > ATTICIZE
ATTICS > ATTIC
ATTIRE *n* fine or formal clothes ▷ *vb* dress, esp in fine elegant clothes
ATTIRED > ATTIRE
ATTIRES > ATTIRE
ATTIRING > ATTIRE
ATTIRINGS > ATTIRE
ATTITUDE *n* way of thinking and behaving
ATTITUDES > ATTITUDE
ATTOLASER *n* high-power laser capable of producing pulses with a duration measured in attoseconds
ATTOLLENS *adj* (of muscle) used to lift
ATTOLLENT *adj* muscle used in lifting
ATTONCE *adv* old word for at once
ATTONE *vb* old word meaning appease
ATTONES > ATTONE
ATTORN *vb* acknowledge a new owner of land as one's landlord
ATTORNED > ATTORN
ATTORNEY *n* person legally appointed to act for another
ATTORNEYS > ATTORNEY
ATTORNING > ATTORN
ATTORNS > ATTORN
ATTRACT *vb* arouse the interest or admiration of
ATTRACTED > ATTRACT
ATTRACTER > ATTRACT
ATTRACTOR > ATTRACT
ATTRACTS > ATTRACT
ATTRAHENS *adj* (of muscle) drawing towards
ATTRAHENT *adj* something that attracts
ATTRAP *vb* adorn
ATTRAPPED > ATTRAP
ATTRAPS > ATTRAP
ATTRIBUTE *vb* regard as belonging to or produced by ▷ *n* quality or feature representative of a person or thing
ATTRIST *vb* old word meaning to sadden
ATTRISTED > ATTRIST
ATTRISTS > ATTRIST
ATTRIT *vb* wear down or dispose of gradually
ATTRITE *vb* wear down
ATTRITED > ATTRITE
ATTRITES > ATTRITE
ATTRITING > ATTRITE
ATTRITION *n* constant wearing down to weaken or destroy
ATTRITIVE > ATTRITION
ATTRITS > ATTRIT
ATTRITTED > ATTRIT
ATTUENT *adj* carrying out attuition
ATTUITE *vb* perceive by attuition
ATTUITED > ATTUITE
ATTUITES > ATTUITE
ATTUITING > ATTUITE
ATTUITION *n* way of mentally perceiving something
ATTUITIVE > ATTUITION
ATTUNE *vb* adjust or accustom (a person or thing)
ATTUNED > ATTUNE
ATTUNES > ATTUNE
ATTUNING > ATTUNE
ATUA *n* spirit or demon
ATUAS > ATUA
ATWAIN *adv* old word meaning into two parts
ATWEEL *Scots word for* > WELL
ATWEEN *an archaic or Scots word for* > BETWEEN
ATWITTER *adv* twittering
ATWIXT *old word for* > BETWEEN
ATYPIC *adj* not typical
ATYPICAL *adj* not typical
AUA *n* yellow-eye mullet
AUBADE *n* song or poem appropriate to or greeting the dawn
AUBADES > AUBADE
AUBERGE *n* inn or tavern
AUBERGES > AUBERGE
AUBERGINE *n* dark purple tropical fruit, cooked and eaten as a vegetable
AUBRETIA *same as* > AUBRIETIA
AUBRETIAS > AUBRETIA
AUBRIETA *same as* > AUBRIETIA
AUBRIETAS > AUBRIETA
AUBRIETIA *n* trailing plant with purple flowers
AUBURN *adj* (of hair) reddish-brown ▷ *n* moderate reddish-brown colour
AUBURNS > AUBURN
AUCEPS *n* old word meaning person who catches hawks
AUCEPSES > AUCEPS
AUCTION *n* public sale in which articles are sold to the highest bidder ▷ *vb* sell by auction
AUCTIONED > AUCTION
AUCTIONS > AUCTION
AUCTORIAL *adj* of or relating to an author
AUCUBA *n* Japanese laurel
AUCUBAS > AUCUBA
AUDACIOUS *adj* recklessly bold or daring
AUDACITY > AUDACIOUS
AUDAD *n* wild African sheep
AUDADS > AUDAD
AUDIAL *adj* of sound
AUDIBLE *adj* loud enough to be heard ▷ *n* change of playing tactics called by the quarterback when the offence is lined up at the line of scrimmage ▷ *vb* call an audible
AUDIBLED > AUDIBLE
AUDIBLES > AUDIBLE
AUDIBLING > AUDIBLE
AUDIBLY > AUDIBLE
AUDIENCE *n* group of spectators or listeners
AUDIENCES > AUDIENCE
AUDIENCIA *n* court in S America

AUDIENT *n* person who hears
AUDIENTS > AUDIENT
AUDILE *n* person who possesses a faculty for auditory imagery that is more distinct than his visual or other imagery ▷ *adj* of or relating to such a person
AUDILES > AUDILE
AUDING *n* practice of listening to try to understand
AUDINGS > AUDING
AUDIO *adj* of sound or hearing ▷ *n* of or relating to sound or hearing
AUDIOBOOK *n* recorded reading of a book
AUDIOGRAM *n* graphic record of the acuity of hearing of a person obtained by means of an audiometer
AUDIOLOGY *n* scientific study of hearing, often including the treatment of persons with hearing defects
AUDIOPHIL *n* audiophile
AUDIOS > AUDIO
AUDIOTAPE *n* tape for recording sound
AUDIPHONE *n* type of hearing aid consisting of a diaphragm that, when placed against the upper teeth, conveys sound vibrations to the inner ear
AUDIT *n* official examination of business accounts ▷ *vb* examine (business accounts) officially
AUDITABLE > AUDIT
AUDITED > AUDIT
AUDITEE *n* one who is audited
AUDITEES > AUDITEE
AUDITING > AUDIT
AUDITION *n* test of a performer's ability for a particular role or job ▷ *vb* test or be tested in an audition
AUDITIONS > AUDITION
AUDITIVE *n* person who learns primarily by listening
AUDITIVES > AUDITIVE
AUDITOR *n* person qualified to audit accounts
AUDITORIA *n* areas of concert halls, theatres, schools, etc, in which audiences sit
AUDITORS > AUDITOR
AUDITORY *adj* of or relating to hearing
AUDITRESS *n* female auditor
AUDITS > AUDIT
AUE *interj* Māori exclamation
AUF *old word for* > OAF
AUFGABE *n* word used in psychology to mean task
AUFGABES > AUFGABE
AUFS > AUF
AUGEND *n* number to which another number, the addend, is added
AUGENDS > AUGEND
AUGER *n* tool for boring holes
AUGERS > AUGER
AUGHT *adv* in any least part ▷ *n* less common word for NOUGHT (zero)
AUGHTS > AUGHT
AUGITE *n* black or greenish-black mineral
AUGITES > AUGITE
AUGITIC > AUGITE
AUGMENT *vb* increase or enlarge ▷ *n* (in Greek and Sanskrit grammar) a vowel or diphthong prefixed to a verb to form a past tense
AUGMENTED > AUGMENT
AUGMENTER > AUGMENT
AUGMENTOR > AUGMENT
AUGMENTS > AUGMENT
AUGUR *vb* be a sign of (future events) ▷ *n* (in ancient Rome) a religious official who observed and interpreted omens and signs to help guide the making of public decisions
AUGURAL > AUGUR
AUGURED > AUGUR
AUGURER *old word for* > AUGUR
AUGURERS > AUGURER
AUGURIES > AUGURY
AUGURING > AUGUR
AUGURS > AUGUR
AUGURSHIP > AUGUR
AUGURY *n* foretelling of the future
AUGUST *same as* > AUGUSTE *adj* dignified and imposing
AUGUSTE *n* type of circus clown who usually wears battered ordinary clothes and is habitually maladroit or unlucky
AUGUSTER > AUGUST
AUGUSTES > AUGUSTE
AUGUSTEST > AUGUST
AUGUSTLY > AUGUST
AUGUSTS > AUGUST
AUK *n* northern sea bird with short wings and black-and-white plumage
AUKLET *n* any of various small auks of the genera *Aethia* and *Ptychoramphus*
AUKLETS > AUKLET
AUKS > AUK
AULA *n* hall
AULARIAN *n* Oxford University student belonging to hall
AULARIANS > AULARIAN
AULAS > AULA
AULD *a Scots word for* > OLD
AULDER > AULD
AULDEST > AULD
AULIC *adj* relating to a royal court
AULNAGE *n* measurement in ells
AULNAGER *n* inspector of cloth
AULNAGERS > AULNAGER
AULNAGES > AULNAGE
AULOI > AULOS
AULOS *n* ancient Greek pipes
AUMAIL *old word for* > ENAMEL
AUMAILED > AUMAIL
AUMAILING > AUMAIL
AUMAILS > AUMAIL
AUMBRIES > AUMBRY
AUMBRY *same as* > AMBRY
AUMIL *n* manager in India
AUMILS > AUMIL
AUNE *n* old French measure of length
AUNES > AUNE
AUNT *n* father's or mother's sister
AUNTER *old word for* > ADVENTURE
AUNTERS > AUNTER
AUNTHOOD > AUNT
AUNTHOODS > AUNT
AUNTIE *n* aunt
AUNTIES > AUNTY
AUNTLIER > AUNTLY
AUNTLIEST > AUNTLY
AUNTLIKE > AUNT
AUNTLY *adj* of or like an aunt
AUNTS > AUNT
AUNTY *same as* > AUNTIE
AURA *n* distinctive air or quality of a person or thing
AURAE > AURA
AURAL *adj* of or using the ears or hearing
AURALITY > AURAL
AURALLY > AURAL
AURAR *plural of* > EYRIR
AURAS > AURA
AURATE *n* salt of auric acid
AURATED *adj* combined with auric acid
AURATES > AURATE
AUREATE *adj* covered with gold, gilded
AUREATELY > AUREATE
AUREI > AUREUS
AUREITIES > AUREITY
AUREITY *n* attributes of gold
AURELIA *n* large jellyfish
AURELIAN *n* person who studies butterflies and moths
AURELIANS > AURELIAN
AURELIAS > AURELIA
AUREOLA *same as* > AUREOLE
AUREOLAE > AUREOLA
AUREOLAS > AUREOLA
AUREOLE *n* halo
AUREOLED > AUREOLE
AUREOLES > AUREOLE
AUREOLING > AUREOLE
AURES > AURIS
AUREUS *n* gold coin of the Roman Empire
AURIC *adj* of or containing gold in the trivalent state
AURICLE *n* upper chamber of the heart
AURICLED > AURICLE
AURICLES > AURICLE
AURICULA *n* alpine primrose with leaves shaped like a bear's ear
AURICULAE > AURICULA
AURICULAR *adj* of, relating to, or received by the sense or organs of hearing ▷ *n* auricular feather
AURICULAS > AURICULA
AURIFIED > AURIFY
AURIFIES > AURIFY
AURIFORM *adj* shaped like an ear
AURIFY *vb* turn into gold
AURIFYING > AURIFY
AURIS *n* medical word for ear
AURISCOPE *n* medical instrument for examinig the external ear
AURIST *a former name for* > AUDIOLOGY
AURISTS > AURIST
AUROCHS *n* recently extinct European wild ox
AUROCHSES > AUROCHS
AURORA *n* bands of light sometimes seen in the sky in polar regions
AURORAE > AURORA
AURORAL > AURORA
AURORALLY > AURORA
AURORAS > AURORA
AUROREAN *adj* of dawn
AUROUS *adj* of or containing gold, esp in the monovalent state
AURUM *n* gold
AURUMS > AURUM
AUSFORM *vb* temper steel
AUSFORMED > AUSFORM
AUSFORMS > AUSFORM
AUSLANDER *n* German word meaning foreigner
AUSPEX *same as* > AUGUR
AUSPICATE *vb* inaugurate with a ceremony intended to bring good fortune
AUSPICE *n* patronage or guidance
AUSPICES > AUSPICE
AUSTENITE *n* solid solution of carbon in face-centred-cubic gamma iron, usually existing above 723°C
AUSTERE *adj* stern or severe
AUSTERELY > AUSTERE
AUSTERER > AUSTERE
AUSTEREST > AUSTERE
AUSTERITY *n* state of being austere
AUSTRAL *adj* southern ▷ *n* former monetary unit of

Argentina equal to 100 centavos, replaced by the peso
AUSTRALES > AUSTRAL
AUSTRALIS *adj* Australian
AUSTRALS > AUSTRAL
AUSUBO *n* tropical tree
AUSUBOS > AUSUBO
AUTACOID *n* any natural internal secretion, esp one that exerts an effect similar to a drug
AUTACOIDS > AUTACOID
AUTARCH *n* absolute ruler
AUTARCHIC > AUTARCHY
AUTARCHS > AUTARCH
AUTARCHY *n* absolute power or autocracy
AUTARKIC > AUTARKY
AUTARKIES > AUTARKY
AUTARKIST > AUTARKY
AUTARKY *n* policy of economic self-sufficiency
AUTECIOUS *adj* (of parasites, esp the rust fungi) completing the entire life cycle on a single species of host
AUTECISM > AUTECIOUS
AUTECISMS > AUTECIOUS
AUTEUR *n* director whose creative influence on a film is so great as to be considered its author
AUTEURISM > AUTEUR
AUTEURIST > AUTEUR
AUTEURS > AUTEUR
AUTHENTIC *adj* known to be real, genuine
AUTHOR *n* writer of a book etc ▷ *vb* write or originate
AUTHORED > AUTHOR
AUTHORESS *n* female author
AUTHORIAL > AUTHOR
AUTHORING *n* creation of documents, esp multimedia documents
AUTHORISE *same as* > AUTHORIZE
AUTHORISH > AUTHOR
AUTHORISM *n* condition of being author
AUTHORITY *n* power to command or control others
AUTHORIZE *vb* give authority to
AUTHORS > AUTHOR
AUTISM *n* disorder characterized by lack of response to people and limited ability to communicate
AUTISMS > AUTISM
AUTIST *n* autistic person
AUTISTIC > AUTISM
AUTISTICS > AUTISM
AUTISTS > AUTIST
AUTO *n* automobile ▷ *vb* travel in an automobile
AUTOBAHN *n* German motorway
AUTOBAHNS > AUTOBAHN
AUTOBUS *n* motor bus
AUTOBUSES > AUTOBUS
AUTOCADE *another name for* > MOTORCADE
AUTOCADES > AUTOCADE
AUTOCAR *n* motor car
AUTOCARP *n* fruit produced through self-fertilization
AUTOCARPS > AUTOCARP
AUTOCARS > AUTOCAR
AUTOCIDAL *adj* (of insect pest control) effected by the introduction of sterile or genetically altered individuals into the wild population
AUTOCLAVE *n* apparatus for sterilizing objects by steam under pressure ▷ *vb* put in or subject to the action of an autoclave
AUTOCOID *n* hormone
AUTOCOIDS > AUTOCOID
AUTOCRACY *n* government by an autocrat
AUTOCRAT *n* ruler with absolute authority
AUTOCRATS > AUTOCRAT
AUTOCRIME *n* crime of stealing a car
AUTOCRINE *adj* relating to self-stimulation through production of a factor and its receptor
AUTOCROSS *n* motor-racing over a rough course
AUTOCUE *n* electronic television prompting device
AUTOCUES > AUTOCUE
AUTOCUTIE *n* young and attractive but inexperienced female television presenter
AUTOCYCLE *n* bicycle powered or assisted by a small engine
AUTODYNE *adj* denoting or relating to an electrical circuit in which the same elements and valves are used as oscillator and detector ▷ *n* autodyne circuit
AUTODYNES > AUTODYNE
AUTOECISM *n* (of a parasite) completion of an entire lifecycle on a single species of host
AUTOED > AUTO
AUTOFLARE *n* automatic landing systen in aircraft
AUTOFOCUS *n* camera system in which the lens is focused automatically
AUTOGAMIC > AUTOGAMY
AUTOGAMY *n* self-fertilization in flowering plants
AUTOGENIC *adj* produced from within
AUTOGENY *n* hypothetical process by which living organisms first arose on earth from nonliving matter
AUTOGIRO *n* self-propelled aircraft resembling a helicopter but with an unpowered rotor
AUTOGIROS > AUTOGIRO
AUTOGRAFT *n* tissue graft obtained from one part of a patient's body for use on another part
AUTOGRAPH *n* handwritten signature of a (famous) person ▷ *vb* write one's signature on or in
AUTOGUIDE *n* traffic information transmission system
AUTOGYRO *same as* > AUTOGIRO
AUTOGYROS > AUTOGYRO
AUTOHARP *n* zither-like musical instrument
AUTOHARPS > AUTOHARP
AUTOICOUS *adj* (of plants, esp mosses) having male and female reproductive organs on the same plant
AUTOING > AUTO
AUTOLATRY *n* self-worship
AUTOLOGY *n* study of oneself
AUTOLYSE *vb* undergo or cause to undergo autolysis
AUTOLYSED > AUTOLYSE
AUTOLYSES > AUTOLYSE
AUTOLYSIN *n* any agent that produces autolysis
AUTOLYSIS *n* destruction of cells and tissues of an organism by enzymes produced by the cells themselves
AUTOLYTIC > AUTOLYSIS
AUTOLYZE *same as* > AUTOLYSE
AUTOLYZED > AUTOLYZE
AUTOLYZES > AUTOLYZE
AUTOMAKER *n* car manufacturer
AUTOMAN *n* car manufacturer
AUTOMAT *n* vending machine
AUTOMATA > AUTOMATON
AUTOMATE *vb* make (a manufacturing process) automatic
AUTOMATED > AUTOMATE
AUTOMATES > AUTOMATE
AUTOMATIC *adj* (of a device) operating mechanically by itself ▷ *n* self-loading firearm
AUTOMATON *n* robot
AUTOMATS > AUTOMAT
AUTOMEN > AUTOMAN
AUTOMETER *n* small device inserted in a photocopier to enable the process of copying to begin and to record the number of copies made
AUTONOMIC *adj* occurring involuntarily or spontaneously
AUTONOMY *n* self-government
AUTONYM *n* writing published under the real name of an author
AUTONYMS > AUTONYM
AUTOPEN *n* mechanical device used to produce imitation signatures
AUTOPENS > AUTOPEN
AUTOPHAGY *n* consumption of one's own tissue
AUTOPHOBY *n* reluctance to refer to oneself
AUTOPHONY *n* medical diagnosis by listening to vibration of one's own voice in patient
AUTOPHYTE *n* autotrophic plant, such as any green plant
AUTOPILOT *n* automatic pilot
AUTOPISTA *n* Spanish motorway
AUTOPOINT *n* point-to-point race in cars
AUTOPSIA *n* autopsy
AUTOPSIAS > AUTOPSIA
AUTOPSIC > AUTOPSY
AUTOPSIED > AUTOPSY
AUTOPSIES > AUTOPSY
AUTOPSIST > AUTOPSY
AUTOPSY *n* examination of a corpse to determine the cause of death
AUTOPTIC > AUTOPSY
AUTOPUT *n* motorway in the former Yugoslavia
AUTOPUTS > AUTOPUT
AUTOROUTE *n* French motorway
AUTOS > AUTO
AUTOSCOPY *n* hallucination in which one sees oneself
AUTOSOMAL > AUTOSOME
AUTOSOME *n* any chromosome that is not a sex chromosome
AUTOSOMES > AUTOSOME
AUTOSPORE *n* nonmotile algal spore that develops adult characteristics before being released
AUTOTELIC *adj* justifying itself
AUTOTIMER *n* device for turning a system on and off automatically at times predetermined by advance setting
AUTOTOMIC > AUTOTOMY
AUTOTOMY *n* casting off by an animal of a part of its body, to facilitate escape when attacked
AUTOTOXIC > AUTOTOXIN
AUTOTOXIN *n* any poison or toxin formed in the organism upon which it acts
AUTOTROPH *n* organism

capable of manufacturing complex organic nutritive compounds from simple inorganic sources
AUTOTUNE *n* software package that automatically manipulates a recording of a vocal track until it is in tune regardless of whether or not the original performance was in tune
AUTOTUNES > AUTOTUNE
AUTOTYPE *n* photographic process for producing prints in black and white, using a carbon pigment ▷ *vb* process using autotype
AUTOTYPED > AUTOTYPE
AUTOTYPES > AUTOTYPE
AUTOTYPIC > AUTOTYPE
AUTOTYPY > AUTOTYPE
AUTOVAC *n* vacuum pump in a car petrol tank
AUTOV > AUTOVAC
AUTUMN *n* season between summer and winter
AUTUMNAL *adj* of, occurring in, or characteristic of autumn
AUTUMNS > AUTUMN
AUTUMNY *adj* like autumn
AUTUNITE *n* yellowish fluorescent radioactive mineral
AUTUNITES > AUTUNITE
AUXESES > AUXESIS
AUXESIS *n* growth in animal or plant tissues resulting from an increase in cell size without cell division
AUXETIC *n* something that promotes growth
AUXETICS > AUXETIC
AUXILIAR *old word for* > AUXILIARY
AUXILIARS > AUXILIAR
AUXILIARY *adj* secondary or supplementary ▷ *n* person or thing that supplements or supports
AUXIN *n* any of various plant hormones, such as indoleacetic acid, that promote growth and control fruit and flower development. Synthetic auxins are widely used in agriculture and horticulture
AUXINIC > AUXIN
AUXINS > AUXIN
AUXOCYTE *n* any cell undergoing meiosis, esp an oocyte or spermatocyte
AUXOCYTES > AUXOCYTE
AUXOMETER *n* instrument for measuring magnification
AUXOSPORE *n* diatom cell before its silicaceous cell wall is formed
AUXOTONIC *adj* (of muscle contraction) occurring against increasing force
AUXOTROPH *n* mutant strain of microorganism having nutritional requirements additional to those of the normal organism
AVA *adv* at all ▷ *n* Polynesian shrub
AVADAVAT *n* either of two Asian weaverbirds of the genus *Estrilda*, esp *E. amandava*, having a red plumage: often kept as cagebirds
AVADAVATS > AVADAVAT
AVAIL *vb* be of use or advantage (to) ▷ *n* use or advantage
AVAILABLE *adj* obtainable or accessible
AVAILABLY > AVAILABLE
AVAILE *old word for* > LOWER
AVAILED > AVAIL
AVAILES > AVAILE
AVAILFUL *old word for* > USEFUL
AVAILING > AVAIL
AVAILS > AVAIL
AVAL *adj* of a grandparent
AVALANCHE *n* mass of snow or ice falling down a mountain ▷ *vb* come down overwhelmingly (upon)
AVALE *old word for* > LOWER
AVALED > AVALE
AVALES > AVALE
AVALING > AVALE
AVANT *prep* before
AVANTI *interj* forward!
AVANTIST *n* proponent of the avant-garde
AVANTISTS > AVANTIST
AVARICE *n* greed for wealth
AVARICES > AVARICE
AVAS > AVA
AVASCULAR *adj* (of certain tissues, such as cartilage) lacking blood vessels
AVAST *sentence substitute* stop! cease!
AVATAR *n* appearance of a god in animal or human form
AVATARS > AVATAR
AVAUNT *sentence substitute* go away! depart! ▷ *vb* go away; depart
AVAUNTED > AVAUNT
AVAUNTING > AVAUNT
AVAUNTS > AVAUNT
AVE *n* expression of welcome or farewell
AVEL *a variant of* > OVEL
AVELLAN *adj* of hazelnuts
AVELLANE *adj* of hazelnuts
AVELS > AVEL
AVENGE *vb* take revenge in retaliation for (harm done) or on behalf of (a person harmed)
AVENGED > AVENGE
AVENGEFUL > AVENGE
AVENGER > AVENGE
AVENGERS > AVENGE
AVENGES > AVENGE
AVENGING > AVENGE
AVENIR *n* future
AVENIRS > AVENIR
AVENS *n* any of several temperate or arctic rosaceous plants
AVENSES > AVENS
AVENTAIL *n* front flap of a helmet
AVENTAILE *n* avantail
AVENTAILS > AVENTAIL
AVENTRE *old word for* > THRUST
AVENTRED > AVENTRE
AVENTRES > AVENTRE
AVENTRING > AVENTRE
AVENTURE *old form of* > ADVENTURE
AVENTURES > AVENTURE
AVENTURIN *n* dark-coloured glass, usually green or brown, spangled with fine particles of gold, copper, or some other metal
AVENUE *n* wide street
AVENUES > AVENUE
AVER *vb* state to be true
AVERAGE *n* typical or normal amount or quality ▷ *adj* usual or typical ▷ *vb* calculate the average of
AVERAGED > AVERAGE
AVERAGELY > AVERAGE
AVERAGES > AVERAGE
AVERAGING > AVERAGE
AVERMENT > AVER
AVERMENTS > AVER
AVERRABLE > AVER
AVERRED > AVER
AVERRING > AVER
AVERS > AVER
AVERSE *adj* disinclined or unwilling
AVERSELY > AVERSE
AVERSION *n* strong dislike
AVERSIONS > AVERSION
AVERSIVE *n* tool or technique intended to repel animals etc
AVERSIVES > AVERSIVE
AVERT *vb* turn away
AVERTABLE > AVERT
AVERTED > AVERT
AVERTEDLY > AVERT
AVERTER > AVERT
AVERTERS > AVERT
AVERTIBLE > AVERT
AVERTING > AVERT
AVERTS > AVERT
AVES > AVE
AVGAS *n* aviation fuel
AVGASES > AVGAS
AVGASSES > AVGAS
AVIAN *adj* of or like a bird ▷ *n* bird
AVIANISE *same as* > AVIANIZE
AVIANISED > AVIANISE
AVIANISES > AVIANISE
AVIANIZE *vb* modify microorganisms in a chicken embryo
AVIANIZED > AVIANIZE
AVIANIZES > AVIANIZE
AVIANS > AVIAN
AVIARIES > AVIARY
AVIARIST *n* person who keeps an aviary
AVIARISTS > AVIARIST
AVIARY *n* large cage or enclosure for birds
AVIATE *vb* pilot or fly in an aircraft
AVIATED > AVIATE
AVIATES > AVIATE
AVIATIC *adj* pertaining to aviation
AVIATING > AVIATE
AVIATION *n* art of flying aircraft
AVIATIONS > AVIATION
AVIATOR *n* pilot of an aircraft
AVIATORS > AVIATOR
AVIATRESS > AVIATOR
AVIATRICE > AVIATOR
AVIATRIX > AVIATOR
AVICULAR *adj* of small birds
AVID *adj* keen or enthusiastic
AVIDER > AVID
AVIDEST > AVID
AVIDIN *n* protein, found in egg-white, that combines with biotin to form a stable compound that cannot be absorbed, leading to a biotin deficiency in the consumer
AVIDINS > AVIDIN
AVIDITIES > AVIDITY
AVIDITY *n* quality or state of being avid
AVIDLY > AVID
AVIDNESS > AVID
AVIETTE *n* aeroplane driven by human strength
AVIETTES > AVIETTE
AVIFAUNA *n* all the birds in a particular region
AVIFAUNAE > AVIFAUNA
AVIFAUNAL > AVIFAUNA
AVIFAUNAS > AVIFAUNA
AVIFORM *adj* like a bird
AVIGATOR *another word for* > AVIATOR
AVIGATORS > AVIGATOR
AVINE *adj* of birds
AVION *n* aeroplane
AVIONIC > AVIONICS
AVIONICS *n* science and technology of electronics applied to aeronautics and astronautics
AVIONS > AVION
AVIRULENT *adj* (esp of bacteria) not virulent
AVISANDUM *n* consideration of a law case by a judge
AVISE *old word for* > ADVISE
AVISED > AVISE

AVISEMENT > AVISE
AVISES > AVISE
AVISING > AVISE
AVISO *n* boat carrying messages
AVISOS > AVISO
AVITAL *adj* of a grandfather
AVIZANDUM *n* judge's or court's decision to consider a case privately before giving judgment
AVIZE *old word for* > ADVISE
AVIZED > AVIZE
AVIZEFULL > AVIZE
AVIZES > AVIZE
AVIZING > AVIZE
AVO *n* Macao currency unit
AVOCADO *n* pear-shaped tropical fruit with a leathery green skin and yellowish-green flesh
AVOCADOES > AVOCADO
AVOCADOS > AVOCADO
AVOCATION *n* occupation
AVOCET *n* long-legged wading bird with a long slender upward-curving bill
AVOCETS > AVOCET
AVODIRE *n* African tree
AVODIRES > AVODIRE
AVOID *vb* prevent from happening
AVOIDABLE > AVOID
AVOIDABLY > AVOID
AVOIDANCE *n* act of keeping away from or preventing from happening
AVOIDANT *adj* (of behaviour) demonstrating a tendency to avoid intimacy or interaction with others
AVOIDED > AVOID
AVOIDER > AVOID
AVOIDERS > AVOID
AVOIDING > AVOID
AVOIDS > AVOID
AVOISION *n* nonpayment of tax
AVOISIONS > AVOISION
AVOS > AVO
AVOSET *n* avocet
AVOSETS > AVOSET
AVOUCH *vb* vouch for
AVOUCHED > AVOUCH
AVOUCHER > AVOUCH
AVOUCHERS > AVOUCH
AVOUCHES > AVOUCH
AVOUCHING > AVOUCH
AVOURE *old word for* > AVOWAL
AVOURES > AVOURE
AVOUTERER *old word for* > ADULTERER
AVOUTRER *old word for* > ADULTERER
AVOUTRERS > AVOUTRER
AVOUTRIES > AVOUTRY
AVOUTRY *old word for* > ADULTERY
AVOW *vb* state or affirm
AVOWABLE > AVOW
AVOWABLY > AVOW
AVOWAL > AVOW
AVOWALS > AVOW
AVOWED > AVOW
AVOWEDLY > AVOW
AVOWER > AVOW
AVOWERS > AVOW
AVOWING > AVOW
AVOWRIES > AVOWRY
AVOWRY *old word for* > AVOWAL
AVOWS > AVOW
AVOYER *n* former Swiss magistrate
AVOYERS > AVOYER
AVRUGA *n* herring roe with a smoky flavour, sometimes used as a less expensive alternative to caviar
AVRUGAS > AVRUGA
AVULSE *vb* take away by force
AVULSED > AVULSE
AVULSES > AVULSE
AVULSING > AVULSE
AVULSION *n* forcible tearing away or separation of a bodily structure or part, either as the result of injury or as an intentional surgical procedure
AVULSIONS > AVULSION
AVUNCULAR *adj* (of a man) friendly, helpful, and caring towards someone younger
AVYZE *old word for* > ADVISE
AVYZED > AVYZE
AVYZES > AVYZE
AVYZING > AVYZE
AW variant of > ALL
AWA *adv* away
AWAIT *vb* wait for
AWAITED > AWAIT
AWAITER > AWAIT
AWAITERS > AWAIT
AWAITING > AWAIT
AWAITS > AWAIT
AWAKE *vb* emerge or rouse from sleep ▷ *adj* not sleeping
AWAKED > AWAKE
AWAKEN *vb* awake
AWAKENED > AWAKEN
AWAKENER > AWAKEN
AWAKENERS > AWAKEN
AWAKENING *n* start of a feeling or awareness in someone
AWAKENS > AWAKEN
AWAKES > AWAKE
AWAKING > AWAKE
AWAKINGS > AWAKE
AWANTING *adj* missing
AWARD *vb* give (something, such as a prize) formally ▷ *n* something awarded, such as a prize
AWARDABLE > AWARD
AWARDED > AWARD
AWARDEE > AWARD
AWARDEES > AWARD
AWARDER > AWARD
AWARDERS > AWARD
AWARDING > AWARD
AWARDS > AWARD
AWARE *adj* having knowledge, informed
AWARENESS > AWARE
AWARER > AWARE
AWAREST > AWARE
AWARN *vb* old form of warn
AWARNED > AWARN
AWARNING > AWARN
AWARNS > AWARN
AWASH *adv* washed over by water ▷ *adj* washed over by water
AWATCH *adv* watching
AWATO *n* New Zealand caterpillar
AWAVE *adv* in waves
AWAY *adv* from a place ▷ *adj* not present ▷ *n* game played or won at an opponent's ground
AWAYDAY *n* day trip taken for pleasure
AWAYDAYS > AWAYDAY
AWAYES *old word for* > AWAY
AWAYNESS > AWAY
AWAYS > AWAY
AWDL *n* traditional Welsh poem
AWDLS > AWDL
AWE *n* wonder and respect mixed with dread ▷ *vb* fill with awe
AWEARIED *old word for* > WEARY
AWEARY *old form of* > WEARY
AWEATHER *adj* towards the weather
AWED > AWE
AWEE *adv* for a short time
AWEEL *interj* Scots word meaning well
AWEIGH *adj* (of an anchor) no longer hooked onto the bottom
AWEING > AWE
AWELESS > AWE
AWES > AWE
AWESOME *adj* inspiring awe
AWESOMELY > AWESOME
AWESTRIKE *vb* inspire awe in
AWESTRUCK *adj* filled with awe
AWETO *n* New Zealand caterpillar
AWETOS > AWETO
AWFUL *adj* very bad or unpleasant ▷ *adv* very
AWFULLER > AWFUL
AWFULLEST > AWFUL
AWFULLY *adv* in an unpleasant way
AWFULNESS > AWFUL
AWHAPE *old word for* > AMAZE
AWHAPED > AWHAPE
AWHAPES > AWHAPE
AWHAPING > AWHAPE
AWHATO *n* New Zealand caterpillar
AWHEEL *adv* on wheels
AWHEELS *same as* > AWHEEL
AWHETO *n* New Zealand caterpillar
AWHILE *adv* for a brief time
AWHIRL *adv* whirling
AWING > AWE
AWKWARD *adj* clumsy or ungainly
AWKWARDER > AWKWARD
AWKWARDLY > AWKWARD
AWL *n* pointed tool for piercing wood, leather, etc
AWLBIRD *n* woodpecker
AWLBIRDS > AWLBIRD
AWLESS > AWE
AWLS > AWL
AWLWORT *n* small stemless aquatic plant, *Subularia aquatica*, of the N hemisphere, having slender sharp-pointed leaves and minute, often submerged, white flowers: family *Brassicaceae* (crucifers)
AWLWORTS > AWLWORT
AWMOUS *Scots word for* > ALMS
AWMRIE *n* cupboard for church vessels
AWMRIES > AWMRIE
AWMRY *n* cupboard for church vessels
AWN *n* any of the bristles growing from the flowering parts of certain grasses and cereals
AWNED > AWN
AWNER *n* machine for removing awns
AWNERS > AWNER
AWNIER > AWNY
AWNIEST > AWNY
AWNING *n* canvas roof supported by a frame to give protection against the weather
AWNINGED *adj* sheltered with awning
AWNINGS > AWNING
AWNLESS > AWN
AWNS > AWN
AWNY *adj* having awns
AWOKE *past tense of* > AWAKE
AWOKEN > AWAKE
AWOL *n* person who is absent without leave
AWOLS > AWOL
AWORK *adv* old word meaning at work
AWRACK *adv* in wrecked condition
AWRONG *adv* old word meaning wrongly
AWRY *adj* with a twist to one side, askew
AWSOME *adj* old form of awesome
AX *same as* > AXE
AXAL *adj* of an axis
AXE *n* tool with a sharp blade for felling trees or chopping wood ▷ *vb* dismiss (employees), restrict (expenditure), or

terminate (a project)
AXEBIRD *n* nightjar of northern Queensland and New Guinea with a cry that sounds like a chopping axe
AXEBIRDS > AXEBIRD
AXED > AXE
AXEL *n* jump in which the skater takes off from the forward outside edge of one skate, makes one and a half, two and a half, or three and a half turns in the air, and lands on the backward outside edge of the other skate
AXELS > AXEL
AXEMAN *n* man who wields an axe, esp to cut down trees
AXEMEN > AXEMAN
AXENIC *adj* (of a biological culture or culture medium) free from other microorganisms
AXES > AXIS
AXIAL *adj* forming or of an axis
AXIALITY > AXIAL
AXIALLY > AXIAL
AXIL *n* angle where the stalk of a leaf joins a stem
AXILE *adj* of, relating to, or attached to the axis
AXILEMMA *same as* > AXOLEMMA
AXILEMMAS > AXILEMMA
AXILLA *n* area on the undersurface of a bird's wing corresponding to the armpit
AXILLAE > AXILLA
AXILLAR *same as* > AXILLARY
AXILLARS > AXILLAR
AXILLARY *adj* of, relating to, or near the armpit ▷ *n* one of the feathers growing from the axilla of a bird's wing
AXILLAS > AXILLA
AXILS > AXIL
AXING > AXE
AXINITE *n* crystalline substance
AXINITES > AXINITE
AXIOLOGY *n* theory of values, moral or aesthetic
AXIOM *n* generally accepted principle
AXIOMATIC *adj* containing axioms
AXIOMS > AXIOM
AXION *n* type of hypothetical elementary particle
AXIONS > AXION
AXIS *n* (imaginary) line round which a body can rotate or about which an object or geometrical figure is symmetrical
AXISED *adj* having an axis
AXISES > AXIS
AXITE *n* type of gunpowder
AXITES > AXITE
AXLE *n* shaft on which a wheel or pair of wheels turns
AXLED *adj* having axle
AXLES > AXLE
AXLETREE *n* bar fixed across the underpart of a wagon or carriage that has rounded ends on which the wheels revolve
AXLETREES > AXLETREE
AXLIKE > AX
AXMAN *same as* > AXEMAN
AXMEN > AXMAN
AXOID *n* type of curve
AXOIDS > AXOID
AXOLEMMA *n* membrane that encloses the axon of a nerve cell
AXOLEMMAS > AXOLEMMA
AXOLOTL *n* aquatic salamander of central America
AXOLOTLS > AXOLOTL
AXON *n* long threadlike extension of a nerve cell that conducts nerve impulses from the cell body
AXONAL > AXON
AXONE *same as* > AXON
AXONEMAL > AXONEME
AXONEME *n* part of cell consisting of proteins
AXONEMES > AXONEME
AXONES > AXONE
AXONIC > AXON
AXONS > AXON
AXOPLASM *n* part of cell
AXOPLASMS > AXOPLASM
AXSEED *n* crown vetch
AXSEEDS > AXSEED
AY *adv* ever ▷ *n* expression of agreement
AYAH *n* (in parts of the former British Empire) a native maidservant or nursemaid
AYAHS > AYAH
AYAHUASCA *n* type of Brazilian plant
AYAHUASCO *n* South American vine
AYATOLLAH *n* Islamic religious leader in Iran
AYE *n* affirmative vote or voter ▷ *adv* always
AYELP *adv* yelping
AYENBITE *old word for* > REMORSE
AYENBITES > AYENBITE
AYES > AYE
AYGRE *old word for* > EAGER
AYIN *n* 16th letter in the Hebrew alphabet
AYINS > AYIN
AYONT *adv* beyond
AYRE *old word for* > AIR
AYRES > AYRE
AYRIE *old word for* > EYRIE
AYRIES > AYRIE
AYS > AY
AYU *n* small Japanese fish
AYURVEDA *n* ancient medical treatise on the art of healing and prolonging life
AYURVEDAS > AYURVEDA
AYURVEDIC > AYURVEDA
AYUS > AYU
AYWORD *n* old word meaning byword
AYWORDS > AYWORD
AZALEA *n* garden shrub grown for its showy flowers
AZALEAS > AZALEA
AZAN *n* call to prayer five times a day, usually by a muezzin from a minaret
AZANS > AZAN
AZEDARACH *n* astringent bark of the chinaberry tree, formerly used as an emetic and cathartic
AZEOTROPE *n* mixture of liquids that boils at a constant temperature, at a given pressure, without a change in composition
AZEOTROPY > AZEOTROPE
AZERTY *n* common European version of typewriter keyboard layout with the characters a, z, e, r, t, and y positioned on the top row of alphabetic characters at the left side of the keyboard
AZIDE *n* type of chemical compound
AZIDES > AZIDE
AZIDO *adj* containing an azide
AZIMUTH *n* arc of the sky between the zenith and the horizon
AZIMUTHAL > AZIMUTH
AZIMUTHS > AZIMUTH
AZINE *n* any organic compound having a six-membered ring containing at least one nitrogen atom
AZINES > AZINE
AZIONE *n* musical drama
AZIONES > AZIONE
AZLON *n* fibre made from protein
AZLONS > AZLON
AZO *adj* of, consisting of, or containing the divalent group -N:N-
AZOIC *adj* without life
AZOLE *n* organic five-membered ring compound containing one or more atoms in the ring, the number usually being specified by a prefix
AZOLES > AZOLE
AZOLLA *n* tropical water fern
AZOLLAS > AZOLLA
AZON *n* type of drawing paper
AZONAL *adj* not divided into zones
AZONIC *adj* not confined to a zone
AZONS > AZON
AZOTAEMIA *a less common name for* > URAEMIA
AZOTAEMIC > AZOTAEMIA
AZOTE *an obsolete name for* > NITROGEN
AZOTED > AZOTE
AZOTEMIA *same as* > AZOTAEMIA
AZOTEMIAS > AZOTEMIA
AZOTEMIC > AZOTAEMIA
AZOTES > AZOTE
AZOTH *n* panacea postulated by Paracelsus
AZOTHS > AZOTH
AZOTIC *adj* of, containing, or concerned with nitrogen
AZOTISE *same as* > AZOTIZE
AZOTISED > AZOTISE
AZOTISES > AZOTISE
AZOTISING > AZOTISE
AZOTIZE *vb* combine or treat with nitrogen or a nitrogen compound
AZOTIZED > AZOTIZE
AZOTIZES > AZOTIZE
AZOTIZING > AZOTIZE
AZOTOUS *adj* containing nitrogen
AZOTURIA *n* presence of excess nitrogen in urine
AZOTURIAS > AZOTURIA
AZUKI *same as* > ADZUKI
AZUKIS > AZUKI
AZULEJO *n* Spanish porcelain tile
AZULEJOS > AZULEJO
AZURE *n* (of) the colour of a clear blue sky ▷ *adj* deep blue
AZUREAN *adj* azure
AZURES > AZURE
AZURINE *n* blue dye
AZURINES > AZURINE
AZURITE *n* azure-blue mineral associated with copper deposits
AZURITES > AZURITE
AZURN *old word for* > AZURE
AZURY *adj* bluish
AZYGIES > AZYGY
AZYGOS *n* biological structure not in a pair
AZYGOSES > AZYGOS
AZYGOUS *adj* developing or occurring singly
AZYGY *n* state of not being joined in pair
AZYM *n* unleavened bread
AZYME *n* unleavened bread
AZYMES > AZYME
AZYMITE *n* member of a church using unleavened bread in the Eucharist
AZYMITES > AZYMITE
AZYMOUS *adj* unleavened
AZYMS > AZYM

Bb

BA *n* symbol for the soul in Ancient Egyptian religion
BAA *vb* make the characteristic bleating sound of a sheep ▷ *n* cry made by a sheep
BAAED > BAA
BAAING > BAA
BAAINGS > BAA
BAAL *n* any false god or idol
BAALEBOS *n* master of the house
BAALIM > BAAL
BAALISM > BAAL
BAALISMS > BAAL
BAALS > BAAL
BAAS *South African word for* > BOSS
BAASES > BAAS
BAASKAAP *same as* > BAASKAP
BAASKAAPS > BAASKAAP
BAASKAP *n* (in South Africa) control by Whites of non-Whites
BAASKAPS > BAASKAP
BAASSKAP *same as* > BAASKAP
BAASSKAPS > BAASSKAP
BABA *n* small cake of leavened dough, sometimes mixed with currants and usually soaked in rum
BABACO *n* greenish-yellow egg-shaped fruit
BABACOOTE *n* large lemur
BABACOS > BABACO
BABALAS *adj* drunk
BABAS > BABA
BABASSU *n* Brazilian palm tree, *Orbignya martiana* (or *O. speciosa*), having hard edible nuts that yield an oil used in making soap, margarine, etc
BABASSUS > BABASSU
BABBELAS *same as* > BABALAS
BABBITRY > BABBITT
BABBITT *vb* line (a bearing) or face (a surface) with Babbitt metal or a similar soft alloy
BABBITTED > BABBITT
BABBITTRY > BABBITT
BABBITTS > BABBITT
BABBLE *vb* talk excitedly or foolishly ▷ *n* muddled or foolish speech
BABBLED > BABBLE
BABBLER *n* person who babbles
BABBLERS > BABBLER
BABBLES > BABBLE
BABBLIER > BABBLE
BABBLIEST > BABBLE
BABBLING > BABBLE
BABBLINGS > BABBLE
BABBLY > BABBLE
BABE *n* baby
BABEL *n* confused mixture of noises or voices
BABELDOM > BABEL
BABELDOMS > BABEL
BABELISH > BABEL
BABELISM > BABEL
BABELISMS > BABEL
BABELS > BABEL
BABES > BABE
BABESIA *n* parasite causing infection in cattle
BABESIAS > BABESIA
BABICHE *n* thongs or lacings of rawhide
BABICHES > BABICHE
BABIED > BABY
BABIER > BABY
BABIES > BABY
BABIEST > BABY
BABIRUSA *n* wild pig, *Babyrousa babyrussa*, inhabiting marshy forests in Indonesia. It has an almost hairless wrinkled skin and enormous curved canine teeth
BABIRUSAS > BABIRUSA
BABIRUSSA *same as* > BABIRUSA
BABKA *n* cake
BABKAS > BABKA
BABLAH *n* type of acacia
BABLAHS > BABLAH
BABOO *same as* > BABU
BABOOL *n* type of acacia
BABOOLS > BABOOL
BABOON *n* large monkey with a pointed face and a long tail
BABOONERY *n* uncouth behaviour
BABOONISH *adj* uncouth
BABOONS > BABOON
BABOOS > BABOO
BABOOSH *same as* > BABOUCHE
BABOOSHES > BABOOSH
BABOUCHE *n* Middle-Eastern slipper
BABOUCHES > BABOUCHE
BABU *n* (in India) a title or form of address more or less equivalent to *Mr*, placed before a person's full name or after his first name
BABUCHE *same as* > BABOUCHE
BABUCHES > BABUCHE
BABUDOM > BABU
BABUDOMS > BABU
BABUISM > BABU
BABUISMS > BABU
BABUL *n* any of several leguminous trees of the genus *Acacia*, esp *A. arabica* of N Africa and India, which bear small yellow flowers and are a source of gum arabic, tannin, and hardwood
BABULS > BABUL
BABUS > BABU
BABUSHKA *n* headscarf tied under the chin, worn by Russian peasant women
BABUSHKAS > BABUSHKA
BABY *n* very young child or animal ▷ *adj* comparatively small of its type ▷ *vb* treat as a baby
BABYDOLL *n* woman's short nightdress
BABYDOLLS > BABYDOLL
BABYFOOD *n* puréed food for babies
BABYFOODS > BABYFOOD
BABYHOOD > BABY
BABYHOODS > BABY
BABYING > BABY
BABYISH > BABY
BABYISHLY > BABY
BABYPROOF *adj* safe for babies to handle ▷ *vb* make babyproof
BABYSAT > BABYSIT
BABYSIT *vb* look after a child in its parents' absence
BABYSITS > BABYSIT
BAC *n* baccalaureate

BACALAO *n* dried salt cod
BACALAOS > BACALAO
BACCA *n* berry
BACCAE > BACCA
BACCARA *same as* > BACCARAT
BACCARAS > BACCARA
BACCARAT *n* card game involving gambling
BACCARATS > BACCARAT
BACCARE *same as* > BACKARE
BACCAS > BACCA
BACCATE *adj* like a berry in form, texture, etc
BACCATED > BACCATE
BACCHANAL *n* follower of Bacchus ▷ *adj* of or relating to Bacchus
BACCHANT *n* priest or votary of Bacchus
BACCHANTE *n* priestess or female votary of Bacchus
BACCHANTS > BACCHANT
BACCHIAC > BACCHIUS
BACCHIAN *same as* > BACCHIC
BACCHIC *adj* riotously drunk
BACCHII > BACCHIUS
BACCHIUS *n* metrical foot of one short syllable followed by two long ones
BACCIES > BACCY
BACCIFORM *adj* shaped like a berry
BACCO *n* tobacco
BACCOES > BACCO
BACCOS > BACCO
BACCY *n* tobacco
BACH *same as* > BATCH
BACHA *n* Indian English word for young child
BACHARACH *n* German wine
BACHAS > BACHA
BACHCHA *n* Indian English word for young child
BACHCHAS > BACHCHA
BACHED > BACH
BACHELOR *n* unmarried man
BACHELORS > BACHELOR
BACHES > BACH
BACHING > BACH
BACHS > BACH
BACILLAR *same as* > BACILLARY
BACILLARY *adj* of or caused by bacilli
BACILLI > BACILLUS
BACILLUS *n* rod-shaped bacterium
BACK *n* rear part of the human body, from the neck to the pelvis ▷ *vb* (cause to) move backwards ▷ *adj* situated behind ▷ *adv* at, to, or towards the rear
BACKACHE *n* ache or pain in one's back
BACKACHES > BACKACHE
BACKARE *interj* instruction to keep one's distance; back off
BACKBAND *n* back support
BACKBANDS > BACKBAND
BACKBEAT *n* second and fourth beats in music written in even time or, in more complex time signatures, the last beat of the bar
BACKBEATS > BACKBEAT
BACKBENCH *n* lower-ranking seats in Parliament
BACKBEND *n* gymnastic exercise in which the trunk is bent backwards until the hands touch the floor
BACKBENDS > BACKBEND
BACKBIT > BACKBITE
BACKBITE *vb* talk spitefully about an absent person
BACKBITER > BACKBITE
BACKBITES > BACKBITE
BACKBLOCK *n* singular of backblock: bush or remote farming area
BACKBOARD *n* board that is placed behind something to form or support its back
BACKBOND *n* legal document
BACKBONDS > BACKBOND
BACKBONE *n* spinal column
BACKBONED > BACKBONE
BACKBONES > BACKBONE
BACKBURN *vb* clear (an area of bush) by creating a fire that burns in the opposite direction from the wind ▷ *n* act or result of backburning
BACKBURNS > BACKBURN
BACKCAST *n* backward casting of fishing rod
BACKCASTS > BACKCAST
BACKCHAT *n* impudent replies
BACKCHATS > BACKCHAT
BACKCHECK *vb* (in ice hockey) return from attack to defence
BACKCLOTH *n* painted curtain at the back of a stage set
BACKCOMB *vb* comb (the hair) towards the roots to give more bulk to a hairstyle
BACKCOMBS > BACKCOMB
BACKCOURT *n* part of the court between the service line and the baseline
BACKCROSS *vb* mate (a hybrid of the first generation) with one of its parents ▷ *n* offspring so produced
BACKDATE *vb* make (a document) effective from a date earlier than its completion
BACKDATED > BACKDATE
BACKDATES > BACKDATE
BACKDOOR *adj* secret, underhand, or obtained through influence
BACKDOWN *n* abandonment of an earlier claim
BACKDOWNS > BACKDOWN
BACKDRAFT *n* reverse movement of air
BACKDROP *vb* provide a backdrop to (something)
BACKDROPS > BACKDROP
BACKDROPT > BACKDROP
BACKED *adj* having a back or backing
BACKER *n* person who gives financial support
BACKERS > BACKER
BACKET *n* shallow box
BACKETS > BACKET
BACKFALL *n* fall onto the back
BACKFALLS > BACKFALL
BACKFIELD *n* quarterback and running backs in a team
BACKFILE *n* archives of a newspaper or magazine
BACKFILES > BACKFILE
BACKFILL *vb* refill an excavated trench, esp (in archaeology) at the end of an investigation ▷ *n* soil used to do this
BACKFILLS > BACKFILL
BACKFIRE *vb* (of a plan) fail to have the desired effect ▷ *n* (in an engine) explosion of unburnt gases in the exhaust system
BACKFIRED > BACKFIRE
BACKFIRES > BACKFIRE
BACKFISCH *n* young girl
BACKFIT *vb* overhaul nuclear power plant
BACKFITS > BACKFIT
BACKFLIP *n* backwards somersault
BACKFLIPS > BACKFLIP
BACKFLOW *n* reverse flow
BACKFLOWS > BACKFLOW
BACKHAND *n* stroke played with the back of the hand facing the direction of the stroke ▷ *adv* with a backhand stroke ▷ *vb* play (a shot) backhand
BACKHANDS > BACKHAND
BACKHAUL *vb* transmit data
BACKHAULS > BACKHAUL
BACKHOE *n* digger ▷ *vb* dig with a backhoe
BACKHOED > BACKHOE
BACKHOES > BACKHOE
BACKHOUSE *n* toilet
BACKIE *n* ride on the back of someone's bicycle
BACKIES > BACKIE
BACKING *n* support
BACKINGS > BACKING
BACKLAND *n* undeveloped land behind a property
BACKLANDS > BACKLAND
BACKLASH *n* sudden and adverse reaction ▷ *vb* create a sudden and adverse reaction
BACKLESS *adj* (of a dress) low-cut at the back
BACKLIFT *n* backward movement of bat
BACKLIFTS > BACKLIFT
BACKLIGHT *vb* illuminate (something) from behind
BACKLIST *n* publisher's previously published books that are still available ▷ *vb* put on a backlist
BACKLISTS > BACKLIST
BACKLIT *adj* illuminated from behind
BACKLOAD *n* load for lorry on return journey ▷ *vb* load a lorry for a return journey
BACKLOADS > BACKLOAD
BACKLOG *n* accumulation of things to be dealt with
BACKLOGS > BACKLOG
BACKLOT *n* area outside a film or television studio used for outdoor filming
BACKLOTS > BACKLOT
BACKMOST *adj* furthest back
BACKOUT *n* instance of withdrawing (from an agreement, etc)
BACKOUTS > BACKOUT
BACKPACK *n* large pack carried on the back ▷ *vb* go hiking with a backpack
BACKPACKS > BACKPACK
BACKPAY *n* pay received by an employee from an increase awarded retrospectively
BACKPAYS > BACKPAY
BACKPEDAL *vb* retract or modify a previous opinion, principle, etc
BACKPIECE *n* tattoo on the back
BACKRA *n* white person
BACKRAS > BACKRA
BACKREST *n* support for the back of something
BACKRESTS > BACKREST
BACKROOM *n* place where research or planning is done, esp secret research in wartime
BACKROOMS > BACKROOM
BACKRUSH *n* seaward return of wave
BACKS > BACK
BACKSAW *n* small handsaw stiffened along its upper edge by a metal section
BACKSAWS > BACKSAW
BACKSEAT *n* seat at the back, esp of a vehicle
BACKSEATS > BACKSEAT
BACKSET *n* reversal
BACKSETS > BACKSET
BACKSEY *n* sirloin
BACKSEYS > BACKSEY
BACKSHISH *same as* > BAKSHEESH
BACKSHORE *n* area of beach

above high tide mark
BACKSIDE *n* buttocks
BACKSIDES > BACKSIDE
BACKSIGHT *n* sight of a rifle nearer the stock
BACKSLAP *vb* demonstrate effusive joviality
BACKSLAPS > BACKSLAP
BACKSLASH *n* slash which slopes to the left
BACKSLID > BACKSLIDE
BACKSLIDE *vb* relapse into former bad habits
BACKSPACE *vb* move a typewriter carriage or computer cursor backwards ▷ *n* typewriter key that effects such a movements
BACKSPEER *same as* > BACKSPEIR
BACKSPEIR *vb* interrogate
BACKSPIN *n* backward spin given to a ball to reduce its speed at impact
BACKSPINS > BACKSPIN
BACKSTAB *vb* attack deceitfully
BACKSTABS > BACKSTAB
BACKSTAGE *adj* behind the stage in a theatre ▷ *adv* behind the stage in a theatre ▷ *n* area behind the stage in a theatre
BACKSTAIR *adj* underhand
BACKSTALL *n* backward flight of a kite
BACKSTAMP *n* mark stamped on the back of an envelope ▷ *vb* mark with a backstamp
BACKSTAY *n* stay leading aft from the upper part of a mast to the deck or stern
BACKSTAYS > BACKSTAY
BACKSTOP *n* screen or fence to prevent balls leaving the playing area ▷ *vb* provide with backing or support
BACKSTOPS > BACKSTOP
BACKSTORY *n* events assumed before a story begins
BACKSWEPT *adj* slanting backwards
BACKSWING *n* backward movement of a bat, etc
BACKSWORD *same as* a broad-bladed sword
BACKTRACK *vb* return by the same route by which one has come
BACKUP *n* support or reinforcement
BACKUPS > BACKUP
BACKVELD *n* (in South Africa) remote sparsely populated area
BACKVELDS > BACKVELD
BACKWARD *same as* > BACKWARDS
BACKWARDS *adv* towards the rear
BACKWASH *n* water washed backwards by the motion of a boat ▷ *vb* remove oil from (combed wool)
BACKWATER *n* isolated or backward place or condition ▷ *vb* reverse the direction of a boat, esp to push the oars of a rowing boat
BACKWOOD > BACKWOODS
BACKWOODS *pl n* remote sparsely populated area
BACKWORD *n* act or an instance of failing to keep a promise or commitment
BACKWORDS > BACKWORD
BACKWORK *n* work carried out under the ground
BACKWORKS > BACKWORK
BACKWRAP *n* back support
BACKWRAPS > BACKWRAP
BACKYARD *n* yard at the back of a house, etc
BACKYARDS > BACKYARD
BACLAVA *same as* > BAKLAVA
BACLAVAS > BACLAVA
BACLOFEN *n* drug used to treat stroke victims
BACLOFENS > BACLOFEN
BACON *n* salted or smoked pig meat
BACONER *n* pig that weighs between 83 and 101 kg, from which bacon is cut
BACONERS > BACONER
BACONS > BACON
BACS > BAC
BACTERIA *pl n* large group of microorganisms
BACTERIAL > BACTERIA
BACTERIAN > BACTERIA
BACTERIAS > BACTERIA
BACTERIC > BACTERIA
BACTERIN *n* vaccine prepared from bacteria
BACTERINS > BACTERIN
BACTERISE *same as* > BACTERIZE
BACTERIUM singular form of > BACTERIA
BACTERIZE *vb* subject to bacterial action
BACTEROID *adj* resembling a bacterium ▷ *n* any rodlike bacterium of the genus *Bacteroides*, occurring in the gut of man and animals
BACULA > BACULUM
BACULINE *adj* relating to flogging
BACULITE *n* fossil
BACULITES > BACULITE
BACULUM *n* bony support in the penis of certain mammals, esp the carnivores
BACULUMS > BACULUM
BAD *adj* not good ▷ *n* unfortunate or unpleasant events collectively ▷ *adv* badly
BADASS *n* tough or aggressive person ▷ *adj* tough or aggressive
BADASSED > BADASS
BADASSES > BADASS
BADDER > BAD
BADDEST > BAD
BADDIE *n* bad character in a story, film, etc, esp an opponent of the hero
BADDIES > BADDY
BADDISH > BAD
BADDY *same as* > BADDIE
BADE > BID
BADGE *n* emblem worn to show membership, rank, etc ▷ *vb* put a badge on
BADGED > BADGE
BADGELESS > BADGE
BADGER *n* nocturnal burrowing mammal of Europe, Asia, and N America with a black and white head ▷ *vb* pester or harass
BADGERED > BADGER
BADGERING > BADGER
BADGERLY > BADGER
BADGERS > BADGER
BADGES > BADGE
BADGING > BADGE
BADINAGE *n* playful and witty conversation ▷ *vb* engage in badinage
BADINAGED > BADINAGE
BADINAGES > BADINAGE
BADINERIE *n* name given in the 18th century to a type of quick, light movement in a suite
BADIOUS *adj* chestnut; brownish-red
BADLAND > BADLANDS
BADLANDS *pl n* any deeply eroded barren area
BADLY *adv* poorly
BADMAN *n* hired gunman, outlaw, or criminal
BADMASH *n* evil-doer ▷ *adj* naughty or bad ▷ *n* hooligan
BADMASHES > BADMASH
BADMEN > BADMAN
BADMINTON *n* game played with rackets and a shuttlecock, which is hit back and forth over a high net
BADMOUTH *vb* speak unfavourably about (someone or something)
BADMOUTHS > BADMOUTH
BADNESS > BAD
BADNESSES > BAD
BADS > BAD
BAEL *n* spiny Indian rutaceous tree, *Aegle marmelos*
BAELS > BAEL
BAETYL *n* magical meteoric stone
BAETYLS > BAETYL
BAFF *vb* strike ground with golf club
BAFFED > BAFF
BAFFIES *pl n* slippers
BAFFING > BAFF
BAFFLE *vb* perplex or puzzle ▷ *n* device to limit or regulate the flow of fluid, light, or sound
BAFFLED > BAFFLE
BAFFLEGAB *n* insincere speech
BAFFLER > BAFFLE
BAFFLERS > BAFFLE
BAFFLES > BAFFLE
BAFFLING *adj* impossible to understand
BAFFS > BAFF
BAFFY *n* golf club
BAFT *n* coarse fabric
BAFTS > BAFT
BAG *n* flexible container with an opening at one end ▷ *vb* put into a bag
BAGARRE *n* brawl
BAGARRES > BAGARRE
BAGASS *same as* > BAGASSE
BAGASSE *n* pulp remaining after the extraction of juice from sugar cane or similar plants: used as fuel and for making paper, etc
BAGASSES > BAGASSE
BAGATELLE *n* something of little value
BAGEL *n* hard ring-shaped bread roll
BAGELS > BAGEL
BAGFUL *n* amount (of something) that can be held in a bag
BAGFULS > BAGFUL
BAGGAGE *n* suitcases packed for a journey
BAGGAGES > BAGGAGE
BAGGED > BAG
BAGGER *n* person who packs groceries
BAGGERS > BAGGER
BAGGIE *n* plastic bag
BAGGIER > BAGGY
BAGGIES > BAGGY
BAGGIEST > BAGGY
BAGGILY > BAGGY
BAGGINESS > BAGGY
BAGGING > BAG
BAGGINGS > BAG
BAGGIT *n* unspawned salmon
BAGGITS > BAGGIT
BAGGY *same as* > BAGIE
BAGH *n* (in India and Pakistan) a garden
BAGHOUSE *n* dust-filtering chamber
BAGHOUSES > BAGHOUSE
BAGHS > BAGH
BAGIE *n* turnip
BAGIES > BAGIE
BAGLESS *adj* (esp of a vacuum cleaner) not containing a bag
BAGLIKE > BAG
BAGMAN *n* travelling salesman
BAGMEN > BAGMAN
BAGNETTE *variant of* > BAGUETTE

BAGNETTES > BAGNETTE
BAGNIO *n* brothel
BAGNIOS > BAGNIO
BAGPIPE *vb* play the bagpipes
BAGPIPED > BAGPIPE
BAGPIPER > BAGPIPES
BAGPIPERS > BAGPIPES
BAGPIPES *pl n* musical wind instrument with reed pipes and an inflatable bag
BAGPIPING > BAGPIPE
BAGS > BAG
BAGSFUL > BAGFUL
BAGUET *same as* > BAGUETTE
BAGUETS > BAGUET
BAGUETTE *n* narrow French stick loaf
BAGUETTES > BAGUETTE
BAGUIO *n* hurricane
BAGUIOS > BAGUIO
BAGWASH *n* laundry that washes clothes without drying or pressing them
BAGWASHES > BAGWASH
BAGWIG *n* 18th-century wig with hair pushed back into a bag
BAGWIGS > BAGWIG
BAGWORM *n* type of moth
BAGWORMS > BAGWORM
BAH *interj* expression of contempt or disgust
BAHADA *same as* > BAJADA
BAHADAS > BAHADA
BAHADUR *n* title formerly conferred by the British on distinguished Indians
BAHADURS > BAHADUR
BAHT *n* standard monetary unit of Thailand, divided into 100 satang
BAHTS > BAHT
BAHUT *n* decorative cabinet
BAHUTS > BAHUT
BAHUVRIHI *n* class of compound words consisting of two elements the first of which is a specific feature of the second
BAIDARKA *n* narrow hunting boat
BAIDARKAS > BAIDARKA
BAIGNOIRE *n* low-level theatre box
BAIL *n* money deposited with a court as security for a person's reappearance in court ▷ *vb* pay bail for (a person)
BAILABLE *adj* eligible for release on bail
BAILBOND *n* document in which a prisoner and one or more sureties guarantee that the prisoner will attend the court hearing of the charges against him if he is released on bail
BAILBONDS > BAILBOND
BAILED > BAIL
BAILEE *n* person to whom the possession of goods is transferred under a bailment
BAILEES > BAILEE
BAILER > BAIL
BAILERS > BAIL
BAILEY *n* outermost wall or court of a castle
BAILEYS > BAILEY
BAILIE *n* (in Scotland) a municipal magistrate
BAILIES > BAILIE
BAILIFF *n* sheriff's officer who serves writs and summonses
BAILIFFS > BAILIFF
BAILING > BAIL
BAILIWICK *n* area a person is interested in or operates in
BAILLI *n* magistrate
BAILLIAGE *n* magistrate's area of authority
BAILLIE *variant of* > BAILIE
BAILLIES > BAILLIE
BAILLIS > BAILLI
BAILMENT *n* contractual delivery of goods in trust to a person for a specific purpose
BAILMENTS > BAILMENT
BAILOR *n* person who retains ownership of goods but entrusts possession of them to another under a bailment
BAILORS > BAILOR
BAILOUT *n* instance of helping (a person, organization, etc) out of a predicament
BAILOUTS > BAILOUT
BAILS > BAIL
BAILSMAN *n* one standing bail for another
BAILSMEN > BAILSMAN
BAININ *n* Irish collarless jacket made of white wool
BAININS > BAININ
BAINITE *n* mixture of iron and iron carbide found in incompletely hardened steels, produced when austenite is transformed at temperatures between the pearlite and martensite ranges
BAINITES > BAINITE
BAIRN *n* child
BAIRNISH > BAIRN
BAIRNLIER > BAIRN
BAIRNLIKE > BAIRN
BAIRNLY > BAIRN
BAIRNS > BAIRN
BAISEMAIN *n* kissing of the hand
BAIT *n* piece of food on a hook or in a trap to attract fish or animals ▷ *vb* put a piece of food on or in (a hook or trap)
BAITED > BAIT
BAITER > BAIT
BAITERS > BAIT
BAITFISH *n* small fish used as bait
BAITH *adj* both
BAITING > BAIT
BAITINGS > BAIT
BAITS > BAIT
BAIZA *n* Omani unit of currency
BAIZAS > BAIZA
BAIZE *n* woollen fabric used to cover billiard and card tables ▷ *vb* line or cover with such fabric
BAIZED > BAIZE
BAIZES > BAIZE
BAIZING > BAIZE
BAJADA *n* sloping surface formed from rock deposits
BAJADAS > BAJADA
BAJAN *n* freshman at Aberdeen University
BAJANS > BAJAN
BAJRA *n* Indian millet
BAJRAS > BAJRA
BAJREE *variant of* > BAJRA
BAJREES > BAJREE
BAJRI *variant of* > BAJRA
BAJRIS > BAJRI
BAJU *n* Malay jacket
BAJUS > BAJU
BAKE *vb* cook by dry heat as in an oven ▷ *n* party at which the main dish is baked
BAKEAPPLE *n* cloudberry
BAKEBOARD *n* board for bread-making
BAKED > BAKE
BAKEHOUSE *same as* > BAKERY
BAKELITE *n* tradename for any one of a class of thermosetting resins used as electric insulators and for making plastic ware, telephone receivers, etc
BAKELITES > BAKELITE
BAKEMEAT *n* pie
BAKEMEATS > BAKEMEAT
BAKEN > BAKE
BAKER *n* person whose business is to make or sell bread, cakes, etc
BAKERIES > BAKERY
BAKERS > BAKER
BAKERY *n* place where bread, cakes, etc are baked or sold
BAKES > BAKE
BAKESHOP *n* bakery
BAKESHOPS > BAKESHOP
BAKESTONE *n* flat stone in an oven
BAKEWARE *n* dishes for baking
BAKEWARES > BAKEWARE
BAKHSHISH *same as* > BAKSHEESH
BAKING *n* process of cooking bread, cakes, etc ▷ *adj* (esp of weather) very hot and dry
BAKINGS > BAKING
BAKKIE *n* small truck
BAKKIES > BAKKIE
BAKLAVA *n* rich cake of Middle Eastern origin consisting of thin layers of pastry filled with nuts and honey
BAKLAVAS > BAKLAVA
BAKLAWA *same as* > BAKLAVA
BAKLAWAS > BAKLAWA
BAKRA *n* White person, esp one from Britain ▷ *adj* (of people) White, esp British
BAKRAS > BAKRA
BAKSHEESH *n* (in some Eastern countries) money given as a tip ▷ *vb* give such money to (a person)
BAKSHISH *same as* > BAKSHEESH
BAL *n* balmoral
BALACLAVA *n* close-fitting woollen hood that covers the ears and neck, as originally worn by soldiers in the Crimean War
BALADIN *n* dancer
BALADINE *n* female dancer
BALADINES > BALADINE
BALADINS > BALADIN
BALALAIKA *n* guitar-like musical instrument with a triangular body
BALANCE *n* stability of mind or body ▷ *vb* weigh in a balance
BALANCED *adj* having weight equally distributed
BALANCER *n* person or thing that balances
BALANCERS > BALANCER
BALANCES > BALANCE
BALANCING > BALANCE
BALANITIS *n* inflammation of the glans penis, usually due to infection
BALAS *n* red variety of spinel, used as a gemstone
BALASES > BALAS
BALATA *n* tropical American sapotaceous tree, *Manilkara bidentata*, yielding a latex-like sap
BALATAS > BALATA
BALBOA *n* standard currency unit of Panama, divided into 100 centesimos
BALBOAS > BALBOA
BALCONET *n* small balcony
BALCONETS > BALCONET
BALCONIED > BALCONY
BALCONIES > BALCONY
BALCONY *n* platform on the outside of a building with a rail along the outer edge
BALD *adj* having little or no hair on the scalp ▷ *vb* make bald
BALDACHIN *n* richly ornamented silk and gold brocade
BALDAQUIN *same*

as > BALDACHIN
BALDED > BALD
BALDER > BALD
BALDEST > BALD
BALDFACED *same as* > BALD
BALDHEAD *n* person with a bald head
BALDHEADS > BALDHEAD
BALDICOOT *another name for* > COOT
BALDIER > BALDY
BALDIES > BALDY
BALDIEST > BALDY
BALDING *adj* becoming bald
BALDISH > BALD
BALDLY > BALD
BALDMONEY *another name for* > SPIGNEL
BALDNESS > BALD
BALDPATE *n* person with a bald head
BALDPATED > BALDPATE
BALDPATES > BALDPATE
BALDRIC *n* wide silk sash or leather belt worn over the right shoulder to the left hip for carrying a sword, etc
BALDRICK *same as* > BALDRIC
BALDRICKS > BALDRICK
BALDRICS > BALDRIC
BALDS > BALD
BALDY *adj* bald ▷ *n* bald person
BALE *same as* > BAIL
BALECTION *same as* > BOLECTION
BALED > BALE
BALEEN *n* whalebone
BALEENS > BALEEN
BALEFIRE *n* bonfire
BALEFIRES > BALEFIRE
BALEFUL *adj* vindictive or menacing
BALEFULLY > BALEFUL
BALER > BAIL
BALERS > BAIL
BALES > BALE
BALING > BALE
BALISAUR *n* badger-like animal
BALISAURS > BALISAUR
BALISTA *same as* > BALLISTA
BALISTAE > BALISTA
BALISTAS > BALISTA
BALK *vb* stop short, esp suddenly or unexpectedly ▷ *n* roughly squared heavy timber beam
BALKANISE *variant of* > BALKANIZE
BALKANIZE *vb* divide (a territory) into small warring states
BALKED > BALK
BALKER > BALK
BALKERS > BALK
BALKIER > BALKY
BALKIEST > BALKY
BALKILY > BALKY
BALKINESS > BALKY
BALKING > BALK
BALKINGLY > BALK
BALKINGS > BALK
BALKLINE *n* line delimiting the balk area on a snooker table
BALKLINES > BALKLINE
BALKS > BALK
BALKY *adj* inclined to stop abruptly and unexpectedly
BALL *n* round or nearly round object, esp one used in games ▷ *vb* form into a ball
BALLABILE *n* part of ballet where all dancers perform
BALLABILI > BALLABILE
BALLAD *n* narrative poem or song ▷ *vb* sing or write a ballad
BALLADE *n* verse form consisting of three stanzas and an envoy, all ending with the same line
BALLADED > BALLAD
BALLADEER *n* singer of ballads ▷ *vb* perform as a balladeer
BALLADES > BALLADE
BALLADIC > BALLAD
BALLADIN *same as* > BALADIN
BALLADINE *same as* > BALADINE
BALLADING > BALLAD
BALLADINS > BALLADIN
BALLADIST > BALLAD
BALLADRY *n* ballad poetry or songs
BALLADS > BALLAD
BALLAN *n* species of fish
BALLANS > BALLAN
BALLANT *vb* write a ballad
BALLANTED > BALLANT
BALLANTS > BALLANT
BALLAST *n* substance, such as sand, used to stabilize a ship when it is not carrying cargo ▷ *vb* give stability or weight to
BALLASTED > BALLAST
BALLASTER > BALLAST
BALLASTS > BALLAST
BALLAT *vb* write a ballad
BALLATED > BALLAT
BALLATING > BALLAT
BALLATS > BALLAT
BALLCLAY *n* clay suitable for ceramics
BALLCLAYS > BALLCLAY
BALLCOCK *n* device for regulating the flow of a liquid into a tank, cistern, etc, consisting of a floating ball mounted at one end of an arm and a valve on the other end that opens and closes as the ball falls and rises
BALLCOCKS > BALLCOCK
BALLED > BALL
BALLER *n* ball-game player
BALLERINA *n* female ballet dancer
BALLERINE > BALLERINA
BALLERS > BALLER
BALLET *n* classical style of expressive dancing based on conventional steps
BALLETED > BALLAD
BALLETIC > BALLET
BALLETING > BALLAD
BALLETS > BALLET
BALLGAME *n* any game played with a ball
BALLGAMES > BALLGAME
BALLHAWK *n* skilled baseball player
BALLHAWKS > BALLHAWK
BALLIES > BALLY
BALLING > BALL
BALLINGS > BALL
BALLISTA *n* ancient catapult for hurling stones, etc
BALLISTAE > BALLISTA
BALLISTAS > BALLISTA
BALLISTIC *adj* of or relating to ballistics ▷ *n* the study of the flight of projectiles
BALLIUM *same as* > BAILEY
BALLIUMS > BALLIUM
BALLOCKS *same as* > BOLLOCKS
BALLON *n* light, graceful quality
BALLONET *n* air or gas compartment in a balloon or nonrigid airship, used to control buoyancy and shape
BALLONETS > BALLONET
BALLONNE *n* bouncing step
BALLONNES > BALLONNE
BALLONS > BALLON
BALLOON *n* inflatable rubber bag used as a plaything or decoration ▷ *vb* fly in a balloon
BALLOONED > BALLOON
BALLOONS > BALLOON
BALLOT *n* method of voting ▷ *vb* vote or ask for a vote from
BALLOTED > BALLOT
BALLOTEE > BALLOT
BALLOTEES > BALLOT
BALLOTER > BALLOT
BALLOTERS > BALLOT
BALLOTING > BALLOT
BALLOTINI *n* small glass beads
BALLOTS > BALLOT
BALLOW *n* heavy club
BALLOWS > BALLOW
BALLPARK *n* stadium used for baseball games
BALLPARKS > BALLPARK
BALLPOINT *n* pen with a tiny ball bearing as a writing point
BALLROOM *n* large hall for dancing
BALLROOMS > BALLROOM
BALLS *pl n* testicles
BALLSIER > BALLSY
BALLSIEST > BALLSY
BALLSY *adj* courageous and spirited
BALLUP *n* something botched or muddled
BALLUPS > BALLUP
BALLUTE *n* inflatable balloon parachute
BALLUTES > BALLUTE
BALLY *another word for* > BALLYHOO
BALLYARD *n* baseball ground
BALLYARDS > BALLYARD
BALLYHOO *n* exaggerated fuss ▷ *vb* advertise or publicize by sensational or blatant methods
BALLYHOOS > BALLYHOO
BALLYRAG *same as* > BULLYRAG
BALLYRAGS > BALLYRAG
BALM *n* aromatic substance used for healing and soothing ▷ *vb* apply balm to
BALMACAAN *n* man's knee-length loose flaring overcoat with raglan sleeves
BALMED > BALM
BALMIER > BALMY
BALMIEST > BALMY
BALMILY > BALMY
BALMINESS > BALMY
BALMING > BALM
BALMLIKE > BALM
BALMORAL *n* laced walking shoe
BALMORALS > BALMORAL
BALMS > BALM
BALMY *adj* (of weather) mild and pleasant
BALNEAL *adj* of or relating to baths or bathing
BALNEARY *same as* > BALNEAL
BALONEY *n* foolish talk; nonsense
BALONEYS > BALONEY
BALOO *n* bear
BALOOS > BALOO
BALS > BAL
BALSA *n* very light wood from a tropical American tree
BALSAM *n* type of fragrant balm ▷ *vb* embalm
BALSAMED > BALSAM
BALSAMIC > BALSAM
BALSAMING > BALSAM
BALSAMS > BALSAM
BALSAMY > BALSAM
BALSAS > BALSA
BALSAWOOD *same as* > BALSA
BALTHASAR *same as* > BALTHAZAR
BALTHAZAR *n* wine bottle holding the equivalent of sixteen normal bottles (approximately 12 litres)
BALTI *n* spicy Indian dish served in a metal dish
BALTIS > BALTI
BALU *same as* > BALOO
BALUN *n* device for coupling

two electrical circuit elements, such as an aerial and its feeder cable, where one is balanced and the other is unbalanced
BALUNS > BALUN
BALUS > BALU
BALUSTER *n* set of posts supporting a rail ▷ *adj* (of a shape) swelling at the base and rising in a concave curve to a narrow stem or neck
BALUSTERS > BALUSTER
BALZARINE *n* light fabric
BAM *vb* cheat
BAMBI *n* born-again middle-aged biker: an affluent middle-aged man who rides a powerful motorbike
BAMBINI > BAMBINO
BAMBINO *n* young child, esp an Italian one
BAMBINOS > BAMBINO
BAMBIS > BAMBI
BAMBOO *n* tall treelike tropical grass with hollow stems
BAMBOOS > BAMBOO
BAMBOOZLE *vb* cheat or mislead
BAMMED > BAM
BAMMER > BAM
BAMMERS > BAM
BAMMING > BAM
BAMPOT *n* fool
BAMPOTS > BAMPOT
BAMS > BAM
BAN *vb* prohibit or forbid officially ▷ *n* official prohibition
BANAK *n* tree of the genus *Virola*, of Central America: family *Myristicaceae*
BANAKS > BANAK
BANAL *adj* ordinary and unoriginal
BANALER > BANAL
BANALEST > BANAL
BANALISE > BANAL
BANALISED > BANAL
BANALISES > BANAL
BANALITY > BANAL
BANALIZE > BANAL
BANALIZED > BANAL
BANALIZES > BANAL
BANALLY > BANAL
BANANA *n* yellow crescent-shaped fruit
BANANAS *adj* crazy
BANAUSIAN > BANAUSIC
BANAUSIC *adj* merely mechanical
BANC *n in banc* sitting as a full court
BANCO *n* call made in gambling games
BANCOS > BANCO
BANCS > BANC
BAND *n* group of musicians playing together ▷ *vb* unite
BANDA *n* African thatched hut
BANDAGE *n* piece of material used to cover a wound or wrap an injured limb ▷ *vb* cover with a bandage
BANDAGED > BANDAGE
BANDAGER > BANDAGE
BANDAGERS > BANDAGE
BANDAGES > BANDAGE
BANDAGING > BANDAGE
BANDAID *n* tradename for an adhesive plaster for cut
BANDALORE *n* old-fashioned type of yo-yo
BANDANA *same as* > BANDANNA
BANDANAS > BANDANA
BANDANNA *n* large brightly coloured handkerchief or neckerchief
BANDANNAS > BANDANNA
BANDAR *n* species of monkey
BANDARI *n* Indian English word for female monkey
BANDARIS > BANDARI
BANDARS > BANDAR
BANDAS > BANDA
BANDBOX *n* lightweight usually cylindrical box for hats
BANDBOXES > BANDBOX
BANDBRAKE *n* type of brake
BANDEAU *n* narrow ribbon worn round the head
BANDEAUS > BANDEAU
BANDEAUX > BANDEAU
BANDED > BAND
BANDELET *n* moulding round top of column
BANDELETS > BANDELET
BANDELIER *same as* > BANDOLEER
BANDER > BAND
BANDEROL *same as* > BANDEROLE
BANDEROLE *n* narrow flag usually with forked ends
BANDEROLS > BANDEROL
BANDERS > BAND
BANDH *n* (in India) a general strike
BANDHS > BANDH
BANDICOOT *n* ratlike Australian marsupial
BANDIED > BANDY
BANDIER > BANDY
BANDIES > BANDY
BANDIEST > BANDY
BANDINESS > BANDY
BANDING *n* practice of grouping schoolchildren according to ability to ensure a balanced intake at different levels of ability to secondary school
BANDINGS > BANDING
BANDIT *n* robber, esp a member of an armed gang
BANDITO *n* Mexican bandit
BANDITOS > BANDITO
BANDITRY > BANDIT
BANDITS > BANDIT
BANDITTI > BANDIT
BANDITTIS > BANDIT
BANDMATE *n* fellow member of band
BANDMATES > BANDMATE
BANDOBAST *same as* > BANDOBUST
BANDOBUST *n* (in India and Pakistan) an arrangement
BANDOG *n* ferocious dog
BANDOGS > BANDOG
BANDOLEER *same as* > BANDOLIER
BANDOLEON *same as* > BANDONEON
BANDOLERO *n* highwayman
BANDOLIER *n* shoulder belt for holding cartridges
BANDOLINE *n* glutinous hair dressing, used (esp formerly) to keep the hair in place
BANDONEON *n* type of square concertina, esp used in Argentina
BANDONION *same as* > BANDONEON
BANDOOK *same as* > BUNDOOK
BANDOOKS > BANDOOK
BANDORA *same as* > BANDORE
BANDORAS > BANDORA
BANDORE *n* 16th-century plucked musical instrument resembling a lute but larger and fitted with seven pairs of metal strings
BANDORES > BANDORE
BANDROL *same as* > BANDEROLE
BANDROLS > BANDROL
BANDS > BAND
BANDSAW *n* power saw with continuous blade
BANDSAWS > BANDSAW
BANDSHELL *n* bandstand concave at back
BANDSMAN *n* player in a musical band
BANDSMEN > BANDSMAN
BANDSTAND *n* roofed outdoor platform for a band
BANDSTER *n* binder of wheat sheaves
BANDSTERS > BANDSTER
BANDURA *n* type of lute
BANDURAS > BANDURA
BANDWAGON *n* type of wagon
BANDWIDTH *n* range of frequencies within a given waveband used for a particular transmission
BANDY *adj* having legs curved outwards at the knees ▷ *vb* exchange (words) in a heated manner
BANDYING > BANDY
BANDYINGS > BANDY
BANDYMAN *n* carriage or cart
BANDYMEN > BANDYMAN
BANE *n* person or thing that causes misery or distress ▷ *vb* cause harm or distress to (someone)
BANEBERRY *n* any ranunculaceous plant of the genus *Actaea*, esp *A. spicata*, which has small white flowers and red or white poisonous berries
BANED > BANE
BANEFUL *adj* destructive, poisonous, or fatal
BANEFULLY > BANEFUL
BANES > BANE
BANG *vb* make a short explosive noise
BANGALAY *n* myrtaceous Australian tree, *Eucalyptus botryoides*, valued for its hard red wood
BANGALAYS > BANGALAY
BANGALORE as in *bangalore torpedo* explosive device in a long metal tube, used to blow gaps in barbed-wire barriers
BANGALOW *n* Australian palm, *Archontophoenix cunninghamiana*, native to New South Wales and Queensland
BANGALOWS > BANGALOW
BANGED > BANG
BANGER *n* old decrepit car
BANGERS > BANGER
BANGING > BANG
BANGINGS > BANG
BANGKOK *n* type of straw hat
BANGKOKS > BANGKOK
BANGLE *n* bracelet worn round the arm or the ankle
BANGLED > BANGLE
BANGLES > BANGLE
BANGS > BANG
BANGSRING *same as* > BANXRING
BANGSTER *n* ruffian
BANGSTERS > BANGSTER
BANGTAIL *n* horse's tail cut straight across but not through the bone
BANGTAILS > BANGTAIL
BANI > BAN
BANIA *same as* > BANYAN
BANIAN *same as* > BANYAN
BANIANS > BANIAN
BANIAS > BANIA
BANING > BANE
BANISH *vb* send (someone) into exile
BANISHED > BANISH
BANISHER > BANISH
BANISHERS > BANISH
BANISHES > BANISH
BANISHING > BANISH
BANISTER *same as* > BANNISTER
BANISTERS *pl n* railing supported by posts on a staircase

BANJAX *vb* ruin; destroy
BANJAXED > BANJAX
BANJAXES > BANJAX
BANJAXING > BANJAX
BANJO *n* guitar-like musical instrument with a circular body
BANJOES > BANJO
BANJOIST > BANJO
BANJOISTS > BANJO
BANJOS > BANJO
BANJULELE *n* small banjo
BANK *n* institution offering services such as the safekeeping and lending of money ▷ *vb* deposit (cash or cheques) in a bank
BANKABLE *adj* likely to ensure financial success
BANKBOOK *n* book held by depositors at certain banks, in which the bank enters a record of deposits, withdrawals, and earned interest
BANKBOOKS > BANKBOOK
BANKCARD *n* card guaranteeing payment of cheque
BANKCARDS > BANKCARD
BANKED > BANK
BANKER *n* manager or owner of a bank
BANKERLY > BANKER
BANKERS > BANKER
BANKET *n* gold-bearing conglomerate found in South Africa
BANKETS > BANKET
BANKING > BANK
BANKINGS > BANK
BANKIT *same as* > BANQUETTE
BANKITS > BANKIT
BANKNOTE *n* piece of paper money
BANKNOTES > BANKNOTE
BANKROLL *n* roll of currency notes ▷ *vb* provide the capital for
BANKROLLS > BANKROLL
BANKRUPT *n* person declared by a court to be unable to pay his or her debts ▷ *adj* financially ruined ▷ *vb* make bankrupt
BANKRUPTS > BANKRUPT
BANKS > BANK
BANKSIA *n* Australian evergreen tree or shrub
BANKSIAS > BANKSIA
BANKSIDE *n* riverside
BANKSIDES > BANKSIDE
BANKSMAN *n* crane driver's helper, who signals instructions to the driver for the movement of the crane and its jib
BANKSMEN > BANKSMAN
BANLIEUE *n* suburb of a city
BANLIEUES > BANLIEUE
BANNABLE > BAN
BANNED > BAN
BANNER *n* long strip of cloth displaying a slogan, advertisement, etc ▷ *vb* (of a newspaper headline) to display (a story) prominently ▷ *adj* outstandingly successful
BANNERALL *same as* > BANDEROLE
BANNERED > BANNER
BANNERET *n* small banner
BANNERETS > BANNERET
BANNERING > BANNER
BANNEROL *same as* > BANDEROLE
BANNEROLS > BANNEROL
BANNERS > BANNER
BANNET *n* bonnet
BANNETS > BANNET
BANNING > BAN
BANNISTER *same as* > BANISTERS
BANNOCK *n* round flat cake made from oatmeal or barley
BANNOCKS > BANNOCK
BANNS *pl n* public declaration, esp in a church, of an intended marriage
BANOFFEE *n* filling for a pie, consisting of toffee and banana
BANOFFEES > BANOFFEE
BANOFFI *same as* > BANOFFEE
BANOFFIS > BANOFFI
BANQUET *n* elaborate formal dinner ▷ *vb* hold or take part in a banquet
BANQUETED > BANQUET
BANQUETER > BANQUET
BANQUETS > BANQUET
BANQUETTE *n* upholstered bench
BANS *same as* > BANNS
BANSELA *same as* > BONSELA
BANSELAS > BANSELA
BANSHEE *n* (in Irish folklore) female spirit whose wailing warns of a coming death
BANSHEES > BANSHEE
BANSHIE *same as* > BANSHEE
BANSHIES > BANSHIE
BANT *n* string ▷ *vb* tie with string
BANTAM *n* small breed of chicken
BANTAMS > BANTAM
BANTED > BANT
BANTENG *n* wild ox
BANTENGS > BANTENG
BANTER *vb* tease jokingly ▷ *n* teasing or joking conversation
BANTERED > BANTER
BANTERER > BANTER
BANTERERS > BANTER
BANTERING > BANTER
BANTERS > BANTER
BANTIES > BANTY
BANTING > BANT
BANTINGS > BANT
BANTLING *n* young child
BANTLINGS > BANTLING
BANTS > BANT
BANTU *n* offensive name for a person who speaks a Bantu language
BANTUS > BANTU
BANTY *n* bantam
BANXRING *n* tree-shrew
BANXRINGS > BANXRING
BANYAN *n* Indian tree whose branches grow down into the soil forming additional trunks
BANYANS > BANYAN
BANZAI *interj* patriotic cheer, battle cry, or salutation
BANZAIS > BANZAI
BAOBAB *n* African tree with a thick trunk and angular branches
BAOBABS > BAOBAB
BAP *n* large soft bread roll
BAPS > BAP
BAPTISE *same as* > BAPTIZE
BAPTISED > BAPTISE
BAPTISER > BAPTISE
BAPTISERS > BAPTISE
BAPTISES > BAPTISE
BAPTISIA *n* species of wild flower
BAPTISIAS > BAPTISIA
BAPTISING > BAPTISE
BAPTISM *n* Christian religious ceremony in which a person is immersed in or sprinkled with water as a sign of being cleansed from sin and accepted into the Church
BAPTISMAL > BAPTISM
BAPTISMS > BAPTISM
BAPTIST *n* one who baptizes
BAPTISTRY *n* part of a Christian church in which baptisms are carried out
BAPTISTS > BAPTIST
BAPTIZE *vb* perform baptism on
BAPTIZED > BAPTIZE
BAPTIZER > BAPTIZE
BAPTIZERS > BAPTIZE
BAPTIZES > BAPTIZE
BAPTIZING > BAPTIZE
BAPU *n* spiritual father
BAPUS > BAPU
BAR *n* rigid usually straight length of metal, wood, etc, that is longer than it is wide or thick, used esp as a barrier or as a structural or mechanical part ▷ *vb* fasten or secure with a bar
BARACAN *same as* > BARRACAN
BARACANS > BARACAN
BARACHOIS *n* (in the Atlantic Provinces of Canada) a shallow lagoon formed by a sand bar
BARAGOUIN *n* incomprehensible language
BARASINGA *n* type of deer
BARATHEA *n* fabric made of silk and wool or cotton and rayon, used esp for coats
BARATHEAS > BARATHEA
BARATHRUM *n* abyss
BARAZA *n* place where public meetings are held
BARAZAS > BARAZA
BARB *n* cutting remark ▷ *vb* provide with a barb or barbs
BARBAL *adj* of a beard
BARBARIAN *n* member of a primitive or uncivilized people ▷ *adj* uncivilized or brutal
BARBARIC *adj* cruel or brutal
BARBARISE *same as* > BARBARIZE
BARBARISM *n* condition of being backward or ignorant
BARBARITY *n* state of being barbaric or barbarous
BARBARIZE *vb* make or become barbarous
BARBAROUS *adj* uncivilized
BARBASCO *n* S American plant
BARBASCOS > BARBASCO
BARBASTEL *n* insectivorous forest bat
BARBATE *adj* having tufts of long hairs
BARBATED > BARBATE
BARBE *n* Waldensian missionary
BARBECUE *n* grill on which food is cooked over hot charcoal, usu. outdoors ▷ *vb* cook (food) on a barbecue
BARBECUED > BARBECUE
BARBECUER > BARBECUE
BARBECUES > BARBECUE
BARBED > BARB
BARBEL *n* long thin growth that hangs from the jaws of certain fishes, such as the carp
BARBELL *n* long metal rod to which heavy discs are attached at each end for weightlifting
BARBELLS > BARBELL
BARBELS > BARBEL
BARBEQUE *same as* > BARBECUE
BARBEQUED > BARBEQUE
BARBEQUES > BARBEQUE
BARBER *n* person who cuts men's hair and shaves beards ▷ *vb* cut the hair of
BARBERED > BARBER
BARBERING > BARBER
BARBERRY *n* shrub with orange or red berries
BARBERS > BARBER
BARBES > BARBE

BARBET *n* any small tropical brightly coloured bird of the family *Capitonidae*, having short weak wings and a sharp stout bill with tuftlike feathers at its base: order *Piciformes* (woodpeckers, etc)
BARBETS > BARBET
BARBETTE *n* (formerly) an earthen platform inside a parapet, from which heavy guns could fire over the top
BARBETTES > BARBETTE
BARBICAN *n* walled defence to protect a gate or drawbridge of a fortification
BARBICANS > BARBICAN
BARBICEL *n* any of the minute hooks on the barbules of feathers that interlock with those of adjacent barbules
BARBICELS > BARBICEL
BARBIE *short for* > BARBECUE
BARBIES > BARBIE
BARBING > BARB
BARBITAL *same as* > BARBITONE
BARBITALS > BARBITAL
BARBITONE *n* long-acting barbiturate used medicinally, usually in the form of the sodium salt, as a sedative or hypnotic
BARBLESS > BARB
BARBOLA *n* small models of flowers, etc made from plastic paste
BARBOLAS > BARBOLA
BARBOTINE *n* clay used in making decorated pottery
BARBS > BARB
BARBULE *n* very small barb
BARBULES > BARBULE
BARBUT *n* open-faced helmet
BARBUTS > BARBUT
BARBWIRE *n* barbed wire
BARBWIRES > BARBWIRE
BARBY > BARBECUE
BARCA *n* boat
BARCAROLE *n* Venetian boat song
BARCAS > BARCA
BARCHAN *n* crescent-shaped shifting sand dune, convex on the windward side and steeper and concave on the leeward
BARCHANE *same as* > BARCHAN
BARCHANES > BARCHANE
BARCHANS > BARCHAN
BARD *n* poet ▷ *vb* place a piece of pork fat on
BARDASH *n* kept boy in a homosexual relationship
BARDASHES > BARDASH
BARDE *same as* > BARD
BARDED > BARDE
BARDES > BARDE
BARDIC > BARD
BARDIE *n* type of Australian grub
BARDIER > BARD
BARDIES > BARDIE
BARDIEST > BARD
BARDING > BARD
BARDISM > BARD
BARDISMS > BARD
BARDLING *n* inferior poet
BARDLINGS > BARDLING
BARDO *n* (in Tibetan Buddhism) the state of the soul between its death and its rebirth
BARDOS > BARDO
BARDS > BARD
BARDSHIP > BARD
BARDSHIPS > BARD
BARDY > BARD
BARE *adj* unclothed, naked ▷ *vb* uncover
BAREBACK *adv* (of horse-riding) without a saddle
BAREBOAT *n* boat chartered without crew, provisions, etc
BAREBOATS > BAREBOAT
BAREBONE *n* computer casing containing bare essentials
BAREBONED *adj* short of resources
BAREBONES > BAREBONE
BARED > BARE
BAREFACED *adj* shameless or obvious
BAREFIT > BAREFOOT
BAREFOOT *adv* with the feet uncovered
BAREGE *n* light silky gauze fabric made of wool ▷ *adj* made of such a fabric
BAREGES > BAREGE
BAREGINE *n* curative ingredient in thermal waters
BAREGINES > BAREGINE
BAREHAND *vb* handle with bare hands
BAREHANDS > BAREHAND
BAREHEAD *adv* with head unvovered
BARELY *adv* only just
BARENESS > BARE
BARER > BARE
BARES > BARE
BARESARK *another word for* > BERSERK
BARESARKS > BARESARK
BAREST > BARE
BARF *vb* vomit ▷ *n* act of vomiting
BARFED > BARF
BARFING > BARF
BARFLIES > BARFLY
BARFLY *n* person who frequents bars
BARFS > BARF
BARFUL *adj* presenting difficulties
BARGAIN *n* agreement establishing what each party will give, receive, or perform in a transaction ▷ *vb* negotiate the terms of an agreement
BARGAINED > BARGAIN
BARGAINER > BARGAIN
BARGAINS > BARGAIN
BARGANDER *same as* > BERGANDER
BARGE *n* flat-bottomed boat used to transport freight ▷ *vb* push violently
BARGED > BARGE
BARGEE *n* person in charge of a barge
BARGEES > BARGEE
BARGEESE > BARGOOSE
BARGELLO *n* zigzag tapestry stitch
BARGELLOS > BARGELLO
BARGEMAN *same as* > BARGEE
BARGEMEN > BARGEMAN
BARGEPOLE *n* long pole used to propel a barge
BARGES > BARGE
BARGEST *same as* > BARGHEST
BARGESTS > BARGEST
BARGHEST *n* mythical goblin in the shape of a dog
BARGHESTS > BARGHEST
BARGING > BARGE
BARGOON *Canadian word for* > BARGAIN
BARGOONS > BARGOON
BARGOOSE *n* type of goose; sheldrake
BARGUEST *same as* > BARGHEST
BARGUESTS > BARGUEST
BARHOP *vb* visit several bars in succession
BARHOPPED > BARHOP
BARHOPS > BARHOP
BARIATRIC *adj* of the treatment of obesity
BARIC *adj* of or containing barium
BARILLA *n* impure mixture of sodium carbonate and sodium sulphate obtained from the ashes of certain plants, such as the saltworts
BARILLAS > BARILLA
BARING > BARE
BARISH *adj* quite thinly covered
BARISTA *n* person who makes and sells coffee in a coffee bar
BARISTAS > BARISTA
BARITE *n* colourless or white mineral consisting of barium sulphate in orthorhombic crystalline form, occurring in sedimentary rocks and with sulphide ores: a source of barium.
BARITES > BARITE
BARITONAL > BARITONE
BARITONE *n* (singer with) the second lowest adult male voice ▷ *adj* relating to or denoting a baritone
BARITONES > BARITONE
BARIUM *n* soft white metallic element
BARIUMS > BARIUM
BARK *vb* (of a dog) make its typical loud abrupt cry
BARKAN *same as* > BARCHAN
BARKANS > BARKAN
BARKED > BARK
BARKEEP *n* barkeeper
BARKEEPER *another name (esp US) for* > BARTENDER
BARKEEPS > BARKEEP
BARKEN *vb* become dry with a bark-like outer layer
BARKENED > BARKEN
BARKENING > BARKEN
BARKENS > BARKEN
BARKER *n* person at a fairground who calls loudly to passers-by in order to attract customers
BARKERS > BARKER
BARKHAN *same as* > BARCHAN
BARKHANS > BARKHAN
BARKIER > BARKY
BARKIEST > BARKY
BARKING *adj* mad ▷ *adv* extremely
BARKLESS > BARK
BARKS > BARK
BARKY *adj* having the texture or appearance of bark
BARLEDUC *n* French preserve made of currants
BARLEDUCS > BARLEDUC
BARLESS > BAR
BARLEY *n* tall grasslike plant cultivated for grain ▷ *sentence substitute* cry for truce or respite from the rules of a game
BARLEYS > BARLEY
BARLOW *n* type of strong knife
BARLOWS > BARLOW
BARM *n* yeasty froth on fermenting malt liquors
BARMAID *n* woman who serves in a pub
BARMAIDS > BARMAID
BARMAN *same as* > BARTENDER
BARMBRACK *n* loaf of bread with currants in it
BARMEN > BARMAN
BARMIE *same as* > BARMY
BARMIER > BARMY
BARMIEST > BARMY
BARMINESS > BARMY
BARMKIN *n* protective wall around castle
BARMKINS > BARMKIN
BARMS > BARM
BARMY *adj* insane
BARN *n* large building on a farm used for storing grain ▷ *vb* keep in a barn
BARNACLE *n* shellfish that lives attached to rocks, ship bottoms, etc

BARNACLED > BARNACLE
BARNACLES > BARNACLE
BARNBRACK *same as* > BARMBRACK
BARNED > BARN
BARNET *n* hair
BARNETS > BARNET
BARNEY *n* noisy fight or argument ▷ *vb* argue or quarrel
BARNEYED > BARNEY
BARNEYING > BARNEY
BARNEYS > BARNEY
BARNIER > BARNY
BARNIEST > BARNY
BARNING > BARN
BARNLIKE > BARN
BARNS > BARN
BARNSTORM *vb* tour rural districts putting on shows or making speeches in a political campaign
BARNY *adj* reminiscent of a barn
BARNYARD *n* yard adjoining a barn
BARNYARDS > BARNYARD
BAROCCO *same as* > BAROQUE
BAROCCOS > BAROCCO
BAROCK *same as* > BAROQUE
BAROCKS > BAROCK
BAROGRAM *n* record of atmospheric pressure traced by a barograph or similar instrument
BAROGRAMS > BAROGRAM
BAROGRAPH *n* barometer that automatically keeps a record of changes in atmospheric pressure
BAROLO *n* red Italian wine
BAROLOS > BAROLO
BAROMETER *n* instrument for measuring atmospheric pressure
BAROMETRY > BAROMETER
BAROMETZ *n* fern whose woolly rhizoma resemble a lamb
BARON *n* member of the lowest rank of nobility
BARONAGE *n* barons collectively
BARONAGES > BARONAGE
BARONESS *n* woman holding the rank of baron
BARONET *n* commoner who holds the lowest hereditary British title
BARONETCY *n* rank, position, or patent of a baronet
BARONETS > BARONET
BARONG *n* broad-bladed cleaver-like knife used in the Philippines
BARONGS > BARONG
BARONIAL *adj* of, relating to, or befitting a baron or barons
BARONIES > BARONY
BARONNE *n* baroness
BARONNES > BARONNE
BARONS > BARON
BARONY *n* domain or rank of a baron
BAROPHILE > BAROPHILIC
BAROQUE *n* highly ornate style of art, architecture, or music from the late 16th to the early 18th century ▷ *adj* ornate in style
BAROQUELY > BAROQUE
BAROQUES > BAROQUE
BAROSAUR *n* large dinosaur
BAROSAURS > BAROSAUR
BAROSCOPE *n* any instrument for measuring atmospheric pressure, esp a manometer with one side open to the atmosphere
BAROSTAT *n* device for maintaining constant pressure, such as one used in an aircraft cabin
BAROSTATS > BAROSTAT
BAROUCHE *n* four-wheeled horse-drawn carriage, popular in the 19th century, having a retractable hood over the rear half, seats inside for two couples facing each other, and a driver's seat outside at the front
BAROUCHES > BAROUCHE
BARP *n* hillock or bank of stones
BARPERSON *n* person who serves in a pub: used esp in advertisements
BARPS > BARP
BARQUE *n* sailing ship, esp one with three masts
BARQUES > BARQUE
BARQUETTE *n* boat-shaped pastry shell
BARRA *n* barramundi
BARRABLE > BAR
BARRACAN *n* thick, strong fabric
BARRACANS > BARRACAN
BARRACE *n* record of teams entering a sports contest
BARRACES > BARRACE
BARRACK *vb* criticize loudly or shout against (a team or speaker)
BARRACKED > BARRACK
BARRACKER > BARRACK
BARRACKS *pl n* building used to accommodate military personnel
BARRACOON *n* (formerly) a temporary place of confinement for slaves or convicts, esp those awaiting transportation
BARRACUDA *n* tropical sea fish
BARRAGE *n* continuous delivery of questions, complaints, etc ▷ *vb* attack or confront with a barrage
BARRAGED > BARRAGE
BARRAGES > BARRAGE
BARRAGING > BARRAGE
BARRANCA *n* ravine or precipice
BARRANCAS > BARRANCA
BARRANCO *same as* > BARRANCA
BARRANCOS > BARRANCO
BARRAS > BARRA
BARRAT *n* fraudulent dealings
BARRATER *same as* > BARRATOR
BARRATERS > BARRATER
BARRATOR *n* person guilty of barratry
BARRATORS > BARRATOR
BARRATRY *n* (formerly) the vexatious stirring up of quarrels or bringing of lawsuits
BARRATS > BARRAT
BARRE *n* rail at hip height used for ballet practice ▷ *vb* execute guitar chords by laying the index finger over some or all of the strings so that the pitch of each stopped string is simultaneously raised ▷ *adv* by using the barré
BARRED > BAR
BARREED > BARRE
BARREFULL *same as* > BARFUL
BARREING > BARRE
BARREL *n* cylindrical container with rounded sides and flat ends ▷ *vb* put in a barrel
BARRELAGE > BARREL
BARRELED > BARREL
BARRELFUL *same as* > BARREL
BARRELING > BARREL
BARRELLED > BARREL
BARRELS > BARREL
BARREN *adj* (of a woman or female animal) incapable of producing offspring
BARRENER > BARREN
BARRENEST > BARREN
BARRENLY > BARREN
BARRENS *pl n* (in North America) a stretch of usually level land that is sparsely vegetated or barren
BARRES > BARRE
BARRET *n* small flat cap resembling a biretta
BARRETOR *n* quarrelsome person
BARRETORS > BARRETOR
BARRETRY *same as* > BARRATRY
BARRETS > BARRET
BARRETTE *n* clasp or pin for holding women's hair in place
BARRETTER *same as* > BARRETOR
BARRETTES > BARRETTE
BARRICADE *n* barrier, esp one erected hastily for defence ▷ *vb* erect a barricade across (an entrance)
BARRICADO *same as* > BARRICADE
BARRICO *n* small container for liquids
BARRICOES > BARRICO
BARRICOS > BARRICO
BARRIE *adj* very good
BARRIER *n* anything that prevents access, progress, or union ▷ *vb* create or form a barrier
BARRIERED > BARRIER
BARRIERS > BARRIER
BARRIES > BARRY
BARRIEST > BARRY
BARRING > BAR
BARRINGS > BAR
BARRIO *n* Spanish-speaking quarter in a town or city, esp in the US
BARRIOS > BARRIO
BARRISTER *n* lawyer qualified to plead in a higher court
BARRO *adj* embarrassing
BARROOM *n* room or building where alcoholic drinks are served over a counter
BARROOMS > BARROOM
BARROW *n* wheelbarrow
BARROWFUL *same as* > BARROW
BARROWS > BARROW
BARRULET *n* narrow band across heraldic shield
BARRULETS > BARRULET
BARRY *n* mistake or blunder
BARS > BAR
BARSTOOL *n* high stool in bar
BARSTOOLS > BARSTOOL
BARTEND *vb* serve drinks from a bar
BARTENDED > BARTEND
BARTENDER *n* man who serves in a bar
BARTENDS > BARTEND
BARTER *vb* trade (goods) in exchange for other goods ▷ *n* trade by the exchange of goods
BARTERED > BARTER
BARTERER > BARTER
BARTERERS > BARTER
BARTERING > BARTER
BARTERS > BARTER
BARTISAN *same as* > BARTIZAN
BARTISANS > BARTISAN
BARTIZAN *n* small turret projecting from a wall, parapet, or tower
BARTIZANS > BARTIZAN
BARTON *n* farmyard
BARTONS > BARTON
BARTSIA *n* type of semiparasitic plant
BARTSIAS > BARTSIA
BARWARE *n* glasses, etc

used in a bar
BARWARES > BARWARE
BARWOOD *n* red wood from small African tree
BARWOODS > BARWOOD
BARYE *n* unit of pressure in the cgs system equal to one dyne per square centimetre. 1 barye is equivalent to 1 microbar
BARYES > BARYE
BARYON *n* elementary particle that has a mass greater than or equal to that of the proton
BARYONIC *adj* of or relating to a baryon
BARYONS > BARYON
BARYTA *same as* > BARITE
BARYTAS > BARYTA
BARYTE *same as* > BARYTA
BARYTES > BARYTE
BARYTIC > BARYTA
BARYTON *n* bass viol with sympathetic strings as well as its six main strings
BARYTONE *adj* having the last syllable unaccented ▷ *n* word in which the last syllable is unaccented
BARYTONES > BARYTONE
BARYTONS > BARYTON
BAS > BA
BASAL *adj* of, at, or constituting a base
BASALLY > BASAL
BASALT *n* dark volcanic rock
BASALTES *n* unglazed black stoneware
BASALTIC > BASALT
BASALTINE *n* type of mineral
BASALTS > BASALT
BASAN *n* sheepskin tanned in bark
BASANITE *n* black basaltic rock containing plagioclase, augite, olivine, and nepheline, leucite, or analcite, formerly used as a touchstone
BASANITES > BASANITE
BASANS > BASAN
BASCINET *same as* > BASINET
BASCINETS > BASCINET
BASCULE *n* drawbridge that operates by a counterbalanced weight
BASCULES > BASCULE
BASE *n* bottom or supporting part of anything ▷ *vb* use as a basis (for) ▷ *adj* dishonourable or immoral
BASEBALL *n* team game in which runs are scored by hitting a ball with a bat then running round four bases
BASEBALLS > BASEBALL
BASEBAND *n* transmission technique using a narrow range of frequencies that allows only one message to be telecommunicated at a time
BASEBANDS > BASEBAND
BASEBOARD *n* board functioning as the base of anything
BASEBORN *adj* born of humble parents
BASED > BASE
BASELARD *n* short sword
BASELARDS > BASELARD
BASELESS *adj* not based on fact
BASELINE *n* value or starting point on an imaginary scale with which other things are compared
BASELINER *n* tennis player who plays most of his or her shots from the back of the court
BASELINES > BASELINE
BASELY > BASE
BASEMAN *n* fielder positioned near a base
BASEMEN > BASEMAN
BASEMENT *n* partly or wholly underground storey of a building
BASEMENTS > BASEMENT
BASENESS > BASE
BASENJI *n* small smooth-haired breed of dog of African origin having a tightly curled tail and an inability to bark
BASENJIS > BASENJI
BASEPLATE *n* flat supporting plate or frame
BASER > BASE
BASES > BASIS
BASEST > BASE
BASH *vb* hit violently or forcefully ▷ *n* heavy blow
BASHAW *n* important or pompous person
BASHAWISM > BASHAW
BASHAWS > BASHAW
BASHED > BASH
BASHER > BASH
BASHERS > BASH
BASHES > BASH
BASHFUL *adj* shy or modest
BASHFULLY > BASHFUL
BASHING > BASH
BASHINGS > BASH
BASHLESS *adj* not ashamed
BASHLIK *n* Caucasian hood
BASHLIKS > BASHLIK
BASHLYK *same as* > BASHLIK
BASHLYKS > BASHLYK
BASHO *n* grand tournament in sumo wrestling
BASIC *adj* of or forming a base or basis ▷ *n* fundamental principle, fact, etc
BASICALLY *adv* in a fundamental or elementary manner
BASICITY *n* state of being a base
BASICS > BASIC
BASIDIA > BASIDIUM
BASIDIAL > BASIDIUM
BASIDIUM *n* structure, produced by basidiomycetous fungi after sexual reproduction, in which spores are formed at the tips of projecting slender stalks
BASIFIED > BASIFY
BASIFIER > BASIFY
BASIFIERS > BASIFY
BASIFIES > BASIFY
BASIFIXED *adj* (of an anther) attached to the filament by its base
BASIFUGAL *a less common word for* > ACROPETAL
BASIFY *vb* make basic
BASIFYING > BASIFY
BASIL *n* aromatic herb used in cooking
BASILAR *adj* of or situated at a base
BASILARY *same as* > BASILAR
BASILECT *n* debased dialect
BASILECTS > BASILECT
BASILIC > BASILICA
BASILICA *n* rectangular church with a rounded end and two aisles
BASILICAE > BASILICA
BASILICAL > BASILICA
BASILICAN > BASILICA
BASILICAS > BASILICA
BASILICON *n* healing ointment
BASILISK *n* legendary serpent said to kill by its breath or glance
BASILISKS > BASILISK
BASILS > BASIL
BASIN *n* round open container
BASINAL > BASIN
BASINED > BASIN
BASINET *n* close-fitting medieval helmet of light steel usually with a visor
BASINETS > BASINET
BASINFUL *n* amount a basin will hold
BASINFULS > BASINFUL
BASING > BASE
BASINLIKE > BASIN
BASINS > BASIN
BASION *n* (in anatomy) midpoint on the forward border of the foramen magnum
BASIONS > BASION
BASIPETAL *adj* (of leaves and flowers) produced in order from the apex downwards so that the youngest are at the base
BASIS *n* fundamental principles etc from which something is started or developed
BASK *vb* lie in or be exposed to something, esp pleasant warmth
BASKED > BASK
BASKET *n* container made of interwoven strips of wood or cane
BASKETFUL *n* as much as a basket will hold
BASKETRY *n* art or practice of making baskets
BASKETS > BASKET
BASKING > BASK
BASKS > BASK
BASMATI *n* variety of long-grain rice with slender aromatic grains, used for savoury dishes
BASMATIS > BASMATI
BASNET *same as* > BASINET
BASNETS > BASNET
BASOCHE *n* society of medieval French lawyers who performed comic plays
BASOCHES > BASOCHE
BASON *same as* > BASIN
BASONS > BASON
BASOPHIL *adj* (of cells or cell contents) easily stained by basic dyes ▷ *n* basophil cell, esp a leucocyte
BASOPHILE *same as* > BASOPHIL
BASOPHILS > BASOPHIL
BASQUE *n* tight-fitting bodice for women
BASQUED > BASQUE
BASQUES > BASQUE
BASQUINE *n* tight-fitting bodice
BASQUINES > BASQUINE
BASS *vb* speak or sing in a low pitch
BASSE *same as* > BASS
BASSED > BASS
BASSER > BASS
BASSES > BASS
BASSEST > BASS
BASSET *n* long low smooth-haired breed of hound with short strong legs and long ears ▷ *vb* outcrop
BASSETED > BASSET
BASSETING > BASSET
BASSETS > BASSET
BASSETT *same as* > BASSET
BASSETTED > BASSET
BASSETTS > BASSET
BASSI > BASSO
BASSIER > BASSY
BASSIEST > BASSY
BASSINET *n* wickerwork or wooden cradle or pram, usually hooded
BASSINETS > BASSINET
BASSING > BASS
BASSIST *n* player of a double bass, esp in a jazz band
BASSISTS > BASSIST
BASSLY > BASS
BASSNESS > BASS

BASSO *n* singer with a bass voice
BASSOON *n* low-pitched woodwind instrument
BASSOONS > BASSOON
BASSOS > BASSO
BASSWOOD *n* any of several North American linden trees, esp *Tilia americana*
BASSWOODS > BASSWOOD
BASSY *adj* manifesting strong bass tones
BAST *n* fibrous material obtained from the phloem of jute, hemp, flax, lime, etc, used for making rope, matting, etc
BASTA *interj* enough; stop
BASTARD *n* offensive term for an obnoxious or despicable person ▷ *adj* offensive term for an illegitimate by birth
BASTARDLY > BASTARD
BASTARDRY *n* malicious or cruel behaviour
BASTARDS > BASTARD
BASTARDY *n* condition of being a bastard
BASTE *vb* moisten (meat) during cooking with hot fat
BASTED > BASTE
BASTER > BASTE
BASTERS > BASTE
BASTES > BASTE
BASTI *n* (in India) a slum inhabited by poor people
BASTIDE *n* small isolated house in France
BASTIDES > BASTIDE
BASTILE *same as* > BASTILLE
BASTILES > BASTILE
BASTILLE *n* prison
BASTILLES > BASTILLE
BASTINADE *same as* > BASTINADO
BASTINADO *n* punishment or torture by beating on the soles of the feet with a stick ▷ *vb* beat (a person) in this way
BASTING *n* loose temporary stitches
BASTINGS > BASTING
BASTION *n* projecting part of a fortification
BASTIONED > BASTION
BASTIONS > BASTION
BASTIS > BASTI
BASTLE *n* fortified house
BASTLES > BASTLE
BASTO *n* ace of clubs in certain card games
BASTOS > BASTO
BASTS > BAST
BASUCO *n* cocaine-based drug
BASUCOS > BASUCO
BAT *n* any of various types of club used to hit the ball in certain sports ▷ *vb* strike with or as if with a bat
BATABLE > BAT
BATATA *n* sweet potato
BATATAS > BATATA
BATAVIA *n* variety of lettuce with smooth pale green leaves
BATAVIAS > BATAVIA
BATBOY *n* boy who works at baseball game
BATBOYS > BATBOY
BATCH *n* group of people or things dealt with at the same time ▷ *vb* group (items) for efficient processing
BATCHED > BATCH
BATCHER > BATCH
BATCHERS > BATCH
BATCHES > BATCH
BATCHING > BATCH
BATCHINGS > BATCH
BATE *vb* (of hawks) to jump violently from a perch or the falconer's fist, often hanging from the leash while struggling to escape
BATEAU *n* light flat-bottomed boat used on rivers in Canada and the northern US
BATEAUX > BATEAU
BATED > BATE
BATELESS > BATE
BATELEUR *n* African crested bird of prey, *Terathopius ecaudatus*, with a short tail and long wings: subfamily *Circaetinae*, family *Accipitridae* (hawks, etc)
BATELEURS > BATELEUR
BATEMENT *n* reduction
BATEMENTS > BATEMENT
BATES > BATE
BATFISH *n* any angler of the family *Ogcocephalidae*, having a flattened scaleless body and moving on the sea floor by means of fleshy pectoral and pelvic fins
BATFISHES > BATFISH
BATFOWL *vb* catch birds by temporarily blinding them with light
BATFOWLED > BATFOWL
BATFOWLER > BATFOWL
BATFOWLS > BATFOWL
BATGIRL *n* girl who works at baseball games
BATGIRLS > BATGIRL
BATH *n* large container in which to wash the body ▷ *vb* wash in a bath
BATHCUBE *n* cube of soluble scented material for use in a bath
BATHCUBES > BATHCUBE
BATHE *vb* swim in open water for pleasure
BATHED > BATHE
BATHER > BATHE
BATHERS *pl n* swimming costume
BATHES > BATHE
BATHETIC *adj* containing or displaying bathos
BATHHOUSE *n* building containing baths, esp for public use
BATHING > BATHE
BATHLESS > BATH
BATHMAT *n* mat to stand on after a bath
BATHMATS > BATHMAT
BATHMIC > BATHMISM
BATHMISM *n* growth-force
BATHMISMS > BATHMISM
BATHOLITE *same as* > BATHOLITH
BATHOLITH *n* very large irregular-shaped mass of igneous rock, esp granite, formed from an intrusion of magma at great depth, esp one exposed after erosion of less resistant overlying rocks
BATHORSE *n* officer's packhorse
BATHORSES > BATHORSE
BATHOS *n* sudden ludicrous change in speech or writing from a serious subject to a trivial one
BATHOSES > BATHOS
BATHROBE *n* loose-fitting garment for wear before or after a bath or swimming
BATHROBES > BATHROBE
BATHROOM *n* room with a bath, sink, and usu. a toilet
BATHROOMS > BATHROOM
BATHS > BATH
BATHTUB *n* bath, esp one not permanently fixed
BATHTUBS > BATHTUB
BATHWATER *n* used or unused water in a bathtub
BATHYAL *adj* denoting or relating to an ocean depth of between 200 and 2000 metres (about 100 and 1000 fathoms), corresponding to the continental slope
BATHYBIUS *n* gelatinous substance on seabed
BATHYLITE *same as* > BATHOLITH
BATHYLITH *same as* > BATHOLITH
BATIK *n* process of printing fabric using wax to cover areas not to be dyed ▷ *vb* treat material with this process
BATIKED > BATIK
BATIKING > BATIK
BATIKS > BATIK
BATING > BATE
BATISTE *n* fine plain-weave cotton fabric: used esp for shirts and dresses
BATISTES > BATISTE
BATLER *n* flat piece of wood for beating clothes, etc before washing
BATLERS > BATLER
BATLET *same as* > BATLER
BATLETS > BATLET
BATLIKE > BAT
BATMAN *n* officer's servant in the armed forces
BATMEN > BATMAN
BATOLOGY *n* study of brambles
BATON *n* thin stick used by the conductor of an orchestra ▷ *vb* carry or wave a baton
BATONED > BATON
BATONING > BATON
BATONS > BATON
BATOON *same as* > BATON
BATOONED > BATOON
BATOONING > BATOON
BATOONS > BATOON
BATRACHIA *n* group of amphibians including frogs and toads
BATS > BAT
BATSMAN *n* person who bats or specializes in batting
BATSMEN > BATSMAN
BATSWING *adj* in the form of the wing of a bat
BATSWOMAN > BATSMAN
BATSWOMEN > BATSMAN
BATT *same as* > BAT
BATTA *n* soldier's allowance
BATTALIA *n* arrangement of army prepared for battle
BATTALIAS > BATTALIA
BATTALION *n* army unit consisting of three or more companies
BATTAS > BATTA
BATTEAU *same as* > BATEAU
BATTEAUX > BATTEAU
BATTED > BAT
BATTEL *vb* make fertile
BATTELED > BATTEL
BATTELER > BATTEL
BATTELERS > BATTEL
BATTELING > BATTEL
BATTELLED > BATTEL
BATTELS > BATTEL
BATTEMENT *n* extension of one leg forwards, sideways, or backwards, either once or repeatedly
BATTEN *n* strip of wood fixed to something, esp to hold it in place ▷ *vb* strengthen or fasten with battens
BATTENED > BATTEN
BATTENER > BATTEN
BATTENERS > BATTEN
BATTENING > BATTEN
BATTENS > BATTEN
BATTER *vb* hit repeatedly ▷ *n* mixture of flour, eggs, and milk, used in cooking
BATTERED *adj* subjected to persistent physical violence, esp by a close relative living in the same house
BATTERER *n* person who batters someone

BATTERERS > BATTERER
BATTERIE *n* movement in ballet involving the legs beating together
BATTERIES > BATTERY
BATTERING *n* act or practice of battering someone
BATTERO *n* heavy club
BATTEROS > BATTERO
BATTERS > BATTER
BATTERY *n* device that produces electricity in a torch, radio, etc ▷ *adj* kept in series of cages for intensive rearing
BATTIER > BATTY
BATTIEST > BATTY
BATTIK *same as* > BATIK
BATTIKS > BATTIK
BATTILL *old spelling of* > BATTLE
BATTILLED > BATTILL
BATTILLS > BATTILL
BATTINESS > BATTY
BATTING > BAT
BATTINGS > BAT
BATTLE *n* fight between large armed forces ▷ *vb* struggle
BATTLEBUS *n* coach that transports politicians and their advisers round the country during an election campaign
BATTLED > BATTLE
BATTLER > BATTLE
BATTLERS > BATTLE
BATTLES > BATTLE
BATTLING > BATTLE
BATTOLOGY *n* unnecessary repetition of words
BATTS > BATT
BATTU *adj* (in ballet) involving a beating movement
BATTUE *n* beating of woodland or cover to force game to flee in the direction of hunters
BATTUES > BATTUE
BATTUTA *n* (in music) a beat
BATTUTAS > BATTUTA
BATTY *adj* eccentric or crazy
BATWING *adj* shaped like the wings of a bat, as a black tie, collar, etc
BATWOMAN *n* female servant in any of the armed forces
BATWOMEN > BATWOMAN
BAUBEE *same as* > BAWBEE
BAUBEES > BAUBEE
BAUBLE *n* trinket of little value
BAUBLES > BAUBLE
BAUBLING > BAUBLE
BAUCHLE *vb* shuffle along
BAUCHLED > BAUCHLE
BAUCHLES > BAUCHLE
BAUCHLING > BAUCHLE
BAUD *n* unit used to measure the speed of transmission of electronic data
BAUDEKIN *old variant of* > BALDACHIN
BAUDEKINS > BAUDEKIN
BAUDRIC *same as* > BALDRIC
BAUDRICK *same as* > BALDRIC
BAUDRICKE *same as* > BALDRIC
BAUDRICKS > BAUDRICK
BAUDRICS > BAUDRIC
BAUDRONS *n* name for a cat
BAUDS > BAUD
BAUERA *n* small evergreen Australian shrub
BAUERAS > BAUERA
BAUHINIA *n* any climbing or shrubby leguminous plant of the genus *Bauhinia*, of tropical and warm regions, widely cultivated for ornament
BAUHINIAS > BAUHINIA
BAUK *same as* > BALK
BAUKED > BAUK
BAUKING > BAUK
BAUKS > BAUK
BAULK > BALK
BAULKED > BALK
BAULKER > BALK
BAULKERS > BALK
BAULKIER > BAULKY
BAULKIEST > BAULKY
BAULKILY > BALKY
BAULKING > BALK
BAULKS > BALK
BAULKY *same as* > BALKY
BAUR *n* humorous anecdote; joke
BAURS > BAUR
BAUSOND *adj* (of animal) dappled with white spots
BAUXITE *n* claylike substance that is the chief source of aluminium
BAUXITES > BAUXITE
BAUXITIC > BAUXITE
BAVARDAGE *n* chattering
BAVAROIS *n* cold dessert consisting of a rich custard set with gelatine and flavoured in various ways
BAVIN *n* impure limestone
BAVINS > BAVIN
BAWBEE *n* former Scottish silver coin
BAWBEES > BAWBEE
BAWBLE *same as* > BAUBLE
BAWBLES > BAWBLE
BAWCOCK *n* fine fellow
BAWCOCKS > BAWCOCK
BAWD *n* person who runs a brothel, esp a woman
BAWDIER > BAWDY
BAWDIES > BAWDY
BAWDIEST > BAWDY
BAWDILY > BAWDY
BAWDINESS > BAWDY
BAWDKIN *same as* > BALDACHIN
BAWDKINS > BAWDKIN
BAWDRIC *n* heavy belt to support sword
BAWDRICS > BAWDRIC
BAWDRIES > BAWDRY
BAWDRY *n* obscene talk or language
BAWDS > BAWD
BAWDY *adj* (of writing etc) containing humorous references to sex ▷ *n* obscenity or eroticism, esp in writing or drama
BAWL *vb* shout or weep noisily ▷ *n* loud shout or cry
BAWLED > BAWL
BAWLER > BAWL
BAWLERS > BAWL
BAWLEY *n* small fishing boat
BAWLEYS > BAWLEY
BAWLING > BAWL
BAWLINGS > BAWL
BAWLS > BAWL
BAWN *n* fortified enclosure
BAWNEEN *same as* > BAININ
BAWNEENS > BAWNEEN
BAWNS > BAWN
BAWR *same as* > BAUR
BAWRS > BAWR
BAWSUNT *adj* black and white in colour
BAWTIE *n* name for a dog
BAWTIES > BAWTIE
BAWTY *same as* > BAWTIE
BAXTER *old variant of* > BAKER
BAXTERS > BAXTER
BAY *n* wide semicircular indentation of a shoreline ▷ *vb* howl in deep tones
BAYADEER *same as* > BAYADERE
BAYADEERS > BAYADEER
BAYADERE *n* dancing girl, esp one serving in a Hindu temple ▷ *adj* (of fabric, etc) having horizontal stripes
BAYADERES > BAYADERE
BAYAMO *n* Cuban strong wind
BAYAMOS > BAYAMO
BAYARD *n* bay horse
BAYARDS > BAYARD
BAYBERRY *n* tropical American tree that yields an oil used in making bay rum
BAYE *vb* bathe
BAYED > BAY
BAYES > BAYE
BAYING > BAY
BAYLE *n* barrier
BAYLES > BAYLE
BAYMAN *n* fisherman
BAYMEN > BAYMAN
BAYONET *n* sharp blade that can be fixed to the end of a rifle ▷ *vb* stab with a bayonet
BAYONETED > BAYONET
BAYONETS > BAYONET
BAYOU *n* (in the southern US) a sluggish marshy tributary of a lake or river
BAYOUS > BAYOU
BAYS > BAY
BAYT *same as* > BATE
BAYTED > BAYT
BAYTING > BAYT
BAYTS > BAYT
BAYWOOD *n* light soft wood of a tropical American mahogany tree, *Swietenia macrophylla*, of the bay region of SE Mexico
BAYWOODS > BAYWOOD
BAYYAN *n* Islamic declaration
BAYYANS > BAYYAN
BAZAAR *n* sale in aid of charity
BAZAARS > BAZAAR
BAZAR *same as* > BAZAAR
BAZARS > BAZAR
BAZAZZ *same as* > PIZZAZZ
BAZAZZES > BAZAZZ
BAZILLION *same as* > GAZILLION
BAZOO *a US slang word for* > MOUTH
BAZOOKA *n* portable rocket launcher that fires an armour-piercing projectile
BAZOOKAS > BAZOOKA
BAZOOMS *pl n* woman's breasts
BAZOOS > BAZOO
BAZOUKI *same as* > BOUZOUKI
BAZOUKIS > BAZOUKI
BDELLIUM *n* any of several African or W Asian trees of the burseraceous genus *Commiphora* that yield a gum resin
BDELLIUMS > BDELLIUM
BE *vb* exist or live
BEACH *n* area of sand or pebbles on a shore ▷ *vb* run or haul (a boat) onto a beach
BEACHBALL *n* light ball for playing on beach
BEACHBOY *n* male lifeguard on beach
BEACHBOYS > BEACHBOY
BEACHCOMB *vb* collect objects, seashells, etc on seashore
BEACHED > BEACH
BEACHES > BEACH
BEACHGOER *n* person who goes to the beach
BEACHHEAD *n* beach captured by an attacking army on which troops can be landed
BEACHIER > BEACHY
BEACHIEST > BEACHY
BEACHING > BEACH
BEACHSIDE *adj* situated near a beach
BEACHWEAR *n* clothes suitable for the beach
BEACHY *adj* with gentle sandy slopes
BEACON *n* fire or light on a hill or tower, used as a

warning ▷ *vb* guide or warn
BEACONED > BEACON
BEACONING > BEACON
BEACONS > BEACON
BEAD *n* small piece of plastic, wood, etc, pierced for threading on a string to form a necklace etc ▷ *vb* decorate with beads
BEADBLAST *n* jet of small glass beads blown from a nozzle under air or steam pressure ▷ *vb* clean or treat (a surface) with a beadblast
BEADED > BEAD
BEADER *n* person making things with beads
BEADERS > BEADER
BEADHOUSE *n* chapel
BEADIER > BEADY
BEADIEST > BEADY
BEADILY > BEADY
BEADINESS > BEADY
BEADING *n* strip of moulding used for edging furniture
BEADINGS > BEADING
BEADLE *n* (formerly) a minor parish official who acted as an usher
BEADLEDOM *n* petty officialdom
BEADLES > BEADLE
BEADLIKE > BEAD
BEADMAN *same as* > BEADSMAN
BEADMEN > BEADMAN
BEADROLL *n* list of persons for whom prayers are to be offered
BEADROLLS > BEADROLL
BEADS > BEAD
BEADSMAN *n* person who prays for another's soul, esp one paid or fed for doing so
BEADSMEN > BEADSMAN
BEADWORK *same as* > BEADING
BEADWORKS > BEADWORK
BEADY *adj* small, round, and glittering
BEAGLE *n* small hound with short legs and drooping ears ▷ *vb* hunt with beagles, normally on foot
BEAGLED > BEAGLE
BEAGLER *n* person who hunts with beagles
BEAGLERS > BEAGLER
BEAGLES > BEAGLE
BEAGLING > BEAGLE
BEAGLINGS > BEAGLE
BEAK *n* projecting horny jaws of a bird ▷ *vb* strike with the beak
BEAKED > BEAK
BEAKER *n* large drinking cup
BEAKERS > BEAKER
BEAKIER > BEAK
BEAKIEST > BEAK
BEAKLESS > BEAK
BEAKLIKE > BEAK
BEAKS > BEAK
BEAKY > BEAK
BEAM *n* broad smile ▷ *vb* smile broadly
BEAMED > BEAM
BEAMER *n* full-pitched ball bowled at the batsman's head
BEAMERS > BEAMER
BEAMIER > BEAM
BEAMIEST > BEAM
BEAMILY > BEAM
BEAMINESS > BEAM
BEAMING > BEAM
BEAMINGLY > BEAM
BEAMINGS > BEAM
BEAMISH *adj* smiling
BEAMISHLY > BEAMISH
BEAMLESS > BEAM
BEAMLET *n* small beam
BEAMLETS > BEAMLET
BEAMLIKE > BEAM
BEAMS > BEAM
BEAMY > BEAM
BEAN *n* seed or pod of various plants, eaten as a vegetable or used to make coffee etc ▷ *vb* strike on the head
BEANBAG *n* small cloth bag filled with dried beans and thrown in games
BEANBAGS > BEANBAG
BEANBALL *n* baseball intended to hit batter's head
BEANBALLS > BEANBALL
BEANED > BEAN
BEANERIES > BEANERY
BEANERY *n* cheap restaurant
BEANFEAST *n* any festive or merry occasion
BEANIE *n* close-fitting woollen hat
BEANIES > BEANY
BEANING > BEAN
BEANLIKE > BEAN
BEANO *n* celebration or party
BEANOS > BEANO
BEANPOLE *n* tall thin person
BEANPOLES > BEANPOLE
BEANS > BEAN
BEANSTALK *n* stem of a bean plant
BEANY *same as* > BEANIE
BEAR *vb* support or hold up (something) ▷ *n* any plantigrade mammal of the family *Ursidae*
BEARABLE *adj* endurable
BEARABLY > BEARABLE
BEARBERRY *n* type of shrub
BEARBINE *n* type of bindweed
BEARBINES > BEARBINE
BEARCAT *n* lesser panda
BEARCATS > BEARCAT
BEARD *n* hair growing on the lower parts of a man's face ▷ *vb* oppose boldly
BEARDED > BEARD
BEARDIE *n* another name for bearded loach
BEARDIER > BEARDY
BEARDIES > BEARDIE
BEARDIEST > BEARDY
BEARDING > BEARD
BEARDLESS *adj* without a beard
BEARDS > BEARD
BEARDY *adj* having a beard
BEARE *same as* > BEAR
BEARED > BEAR
BEARER *n* person who carries, presents, or upholds something
BEARERS > BEARER
BEARES > BEARE
BEARGRASS *n* North American plant
BEARHUG *n* wrestling hold in which the arms are locked tightly round an opponent's chest and arms
BEARHUGS > BEARHUG
BEARING > BEAR
BEARINGS > BEAR
BEARISH *adj* like a bear
BEARISHLY > BEARISH
BEARLIKE > BEAR
BEARNAISE *n* rich sauce made from egg yolks, lemon juice or wine vinegar, butter, shallots, herbs, and seasoning
BEARS > BEAR
BEARSKIN *n* tall fur helmet worn by some British soldiers
BEARSKINS > BEARSKIN
BEARWARD *n* bear keeper
BEARWARDS > BEARWARD
BEARWOOD *another name for* > CASCARA
BEARWOODS > BEARWOOD
BEAST *n* large wild animal
BEASTHOOD > BEAST
BEASTIE *n* small animal
BEASTIES > BEASTIE
BEASTILY > BESTIAL
BEASTINGS *same as* > BEESTINGS
BEASTLIER > BEASTLY
BEASTLIKE > BEAST
BEASTLY *adj* unpleasant or disagreeable ▷ *adv* extremely
BEASTOID *n* autonomous robot that can perform some of the tasks of animals
BEASTOIDS > BEASTOID
BEASTS > BEAST
BEAT *vb* strike with or as if with a series of violent blows; dash or pound repeatedly (against) ▷ *n* stroke or blow ▷ *adj* totally exhausted
BEATABLE > BEAT
BEATBOX *n* drum machine
BEATBOXES > BEATBOX
BEATEN > BEAT
BEATER *n* device used for beating
BEATERS > BEATER
BEATH *vb* dry; heat
BEATHED > BEATH
BEATHING > BEATH
BEATHS > BEATH
BEATIER > BEATY
BEATIEST > BEATY
BEATIFIC *adj* displaying great happiness
BEATIFIED > BEATIFY
BEATIFIES > BEATIFY
BEATIFY *vb* declare (a dead person) to be among the blessed in heaven: the first step towards canonization
BEATING > BEAT
BEATINGS > BEAT
BEATITUDE *n* any of the blessings on the poor, meek, etc, in the Sermon on the Mount
BEATLESS > BEAT
BEATNIK *n* young person in the late 1950s who rebelled against conventional attitudes etc
BEATNIKS > BEATNIK
BEATS > BEAT
BEATY *adj* (of music) having a strong rhythm
BEAU *n* boyfriend or admirer
BEAUCOUP *n* large amount
BEAUCOUPS > BEAUCOUP
BEAUFET *same as* > BUFFET
BEAUFETS > BEAUFET
BEAUFFET *same as* > BUFFET
BEAUFFETS > BEAUFFET
BEAUFIN *same as* > BIFFIN
BEAUFINS > BEAUFIN
BEAUISH *adj* vain and showy
BEAUS > BEAU
BEAUT *n* person or thing that is outstanding or distinctive ▷ *adj* good or excellent ▷ *interj* exclamation of joy or pleasure
BEAUTEOUS *adj* beautiful
BEAUTIED > BEAUTY
BEAUTIES > BEAUTY
BEAUTIFUL *adj* very attractive to look at
BEAUTIFY *vb* make beautiful
BEAUTS > BEAUT
BEAUTY *n* combination of all the qualities of a person or thing that delight the senses and mind ▷ *interj* expression of approval or agreement ▷ *vb* make beautiful
BEAUTYING > BEAUTY
BEAUX > BEAU
BEAUXITE *same as* > BAUXITE
BEAUXITES > BEAUXITE
BEAVER *n* amphibious rodent with a big flat tail ▷ *vb* work steadily or

assiduously
BEAVERED > BEAVER
BEAVERIES > BEAVERY
BEAVERING > BEAVER
BEAVERS > BEAVER
BEAVERY *n* place for keeping beavers
BEBEERINE *n* alkaloid, resembling quinine, obtained from the bark of the greenheart and other plants
BEBEERU *n* tropical American tree
BEBEERUS > BEBEERU
BEBLOOD *vb* stain with blood
BEBLOODED > BEBLOOD
BEBLOODS > BEBLOOD
BEBOP *same as* > BOP
BEBOPPED > BEBOP
BEBOPPER > BEBOP
BEBOPPERS > BEBOP
BEBOPPING > BEBOP
BEBOPS > BEBOP
BEBUNG *n* vibrato effect on clavichord
BEBUNGS > BEBUNG
BECALL *vb* use insulting words about someone
BECALLED > BECALL
BECALLING > BECALL
BECALLS > BECALL
BECALM *vb* make calm
BECALMED *adj* (of a sailing ship) motionless through lack of wind
BECALMING > BECALM
BECALMS > BECALM
BECAME > BECOME
BECAP *vb* put cap on
BECAPPED > BECAP
BECAPPING > BECAP
BECAPS > BECAP
BECARPET *vb* lay carpet on
BECARPETS > BECARPET
BECASSE *n* woodcock
BECASSES > BECASSE
BECAUSE *conj* on account of the fact that; on account of being; since
BECCACCIA *n* woodcock
BECCAFICO *n* any of various European songbirds, esp warblers of the genus *Sylvia*, eaten as a delicacy in Italy and other countries
BECHALK *vb* mark with chalk
BECHALKED > BECHALK
BECHALKS > BECHALK
BECHAMEL *n* thick white sauce flavoured with onion and seasoning
BECHAMELS > BECHAMEL
BECHANCE *vb* happen (to)
BECHANCED > BECHANCE
BECHANCES > BECHANCE
BECHARM *vb* delight
BECHARMED > BECHARM
BECHARMS > BECHARM
BECK *n* stream ▷ *vb* attract someone's attention by nodding or gesturing
BECKE *same as* > BEAK
BECKED > BECK
BECKES > BECKE
BECKET *n* clevis forming part of one end of a sheave, used for securing standing lines by means of a thimble
BECKETS > BECKET
BECKING > BECK
BECKON *vb* summon with a gesture ▷ *n* summoning gesture
BECKONED > BECKON
BECKONER > BECKON
BECKONERS > BECKON
BECKONING > BECKON
BECKONS > BECKON
BECKS > BECK
BECLAMOR *vb* clamour excessively
BECLAMORS > BECLAMOR
BECLASP *vb* embrace
BECLASPED > BECLASP
BECLASPS > BECLASP
BECLOAK *vb* dress in cloak
BECLOAKED > BECLOAK
BECLOAKS > BECLOAK
BECLOG *vb* put clogs on
BECLOGGED > BECLOG
BECLOGS > BECLOG
BECLOTHE *vb* put clothes on
BECLOTHED > BECLOTHE
BECLOTHES > BECLOTHE
BECLOUD *vb* cover or obscure with a cloud
BECLOUDED > BECLOUD
BECLOUDS > BECLOUD
BECLOWN *vb* clown around
BECLOWNED > BECLOWN
BECLOWNS > BECLOWN
BECOME *vb* come to be
BECOMES > BECOME
BECOMING *adj* attractive or pleasing ▷ *n* any process of change
BECOMINGS > BECOMING
BECOWARD *vb* make cowardly
BECOWARDS > BECOWARD
BECQUEREL *n* SI unit of activity of a radioactive source
BECRAWL *vb* crawl all over
BECRAWLED > BECRAWL
BECRAWLS > BECRAWL
BECRIME *vb* make someone guilty of a crime
BECRIMED > BECRIME
BECRIMES > BECRIME
BECRIMING > BECRIME
BECROWD *vb* crowd with something
BECROWDED > BECROWD
BECROWDS > BECROWD
BECRUST *vb* cover with crust
BECRUSTED > BECRUST
BECRUSTS > BECRUST
BECUDGEL *vb* arm with cudgel
BECUDGELS > BECUDGEL
BECURL *vb* curl
BECURLED > BECURL
BECURLING > BECURL
BECURLS > BECURL
BECURSE *vb* curse
BECURSED > BECURSE
BECURSES > BECURSE
BECURSING > BECURSE
BECURST > BECURSE
BED *n* piece of furniture on which to sleep ▷ *vb* plant in a bed
BEDABBLE *vb* dabble; moisten
BEDABBLED > BEDABBLE
BEDABBLES > BEDABBLE
BEDAD *interj* by God (oath)
BEDAGGLE *vb* soil by trailing through dirt
BEDAGGLED > BEDAGGLE
BEDAGGLES > BEDAGGLE
BEDAMN *vb* damn
BEDAMNED > BEDAMN
BEDAMNING > BEDAMN
BEDAMNS > BEDAMN
BEDARKEN *vb* make dark
BEDARKENS > BEDARKEN
BEDASH *vb* sprinkle with liquid
BEDASHED > BEDASH
BEDASHES > BEDASH
BEDASHING > BEDASH
BEDAUB *vb* smear with something sticky or dirty
BEDAUBED > BEDAUB
BEDAUBING > BEDAUB
BEDAUBS > BEDAUB
BEDAWIN *same as* > BEDOUIN
BEDAWINS > BEDAWIN
BEDAZE *vb* daze
BEDAZED > BEDAZE
BEDAZES > BEDAZE
BEDAZING > BEDAZE
BEDAZZLE *vb* dazzle or confuse, as with brilliance
BEDAZZLED > BEDAZZLE
BEDAZZLES > BEDAZZLE
BEDBOARD *n* base of bed
BEDBOARDS > BEDBOARD
BEDBUG *n* small blood-sucking wingless insect that infests dirty houses
BEDBUGS > BEDBUG
BEDCHAIR *n* adjustable chair to support invalid in bed
BEDCHAIRS > BEDCHAIR
BEDCOVER *n* cover for bed
BEDCOVERS > BEDCOVER
BEDDABLE *adj* sexually attractive
BEDDED > BED
BEDDER *n* (at some universities) a college servant employed to keep students' rooms in order
BEDDERS > BEDDER
BEDDING > BED
BEDDINGS > BED
BEDE *n* prayer
BEDEAFEN *vb* deafen
BEDEAFENS > BEDEAFEN
BEDECK *vb* cover with decorations
BEDECKED > BEDECK
BEDECKING > BEDECK
BEDECKS > BEDECK
BEDEGUAR *n* growth found on rosebushes
BEDEGUARS > BEDEGUAR
BEDEHOUSE *same as* > BEADHOUSE
BEDEL *archaic spellings of* > BEADLE
BEDELL *same as* > BEADLE
BEDELLS > BEDELL
BEDELS > BEDEL
BEDELSHIP > BEDEL
BEDEMAN *same as* > BEADSMAN
BEDEMEN > BEDEMAN
BEDERAL *same as* > BEDRAL
BEDERALS > BEDERAL
BEDES > BEDE
BEDESMAN *same as* > BEADSMAN
BEDESMEN > BEDESMAN
BEDEVIL *vb* harass, confuse, or torment
BEDEVILED > BEDEVIL
BEDEVILS > BEDEVIL
BEDEW *vb* wet or cover with or as if with drops of dew
BEDEWED > BEDEW
BEDEWING > BEDEW
BEDEWS > BEDEW
BEDFAST *an archaic word for* > BEDRIDDEN
BEDFELLOW *n* temporary associate
BEDFRAME *n* framework of bed
BEDFRAMES > BEDFRAME
BEDGOWN *n* night dress
BEDGOWNS > BEDGOWN
BEDIAPER *vb* put a nappy on
BEDIAPERS > BEDIAPER
BEDIDE > BEDYE
BEDIGHT *vb* array or adorn ▷ *adj* adorned or bedecked
BEDIGHTED > BEDIGHT
BEDIGHTS > BEDIGHT
BEDIM *vb* make dim or obscure
BEDIMMED > BEDIM
BEDIMMING > BEDIM
BEDIMPLE *vb* form dimples in
BEDIMPLED > BEDIMPLE
BEDIMPLES > BEDIMPLE
BEDIMS > BEDIM
BEDIRTIED > BEDIRTY
BEDIRTIES > BEDIRTY
BEDIRTY *vb* make dirty
BEDIZEN *vb* dress or decorate gaudily or tastelessly
BEDIZENED > BEDIZEN
BEDIZENS > BEDIZEN
BEDLAM *n* noisy confused situation
BEDLAMISM > BEDLAM
BEDLAMITE *n* lunatic
BEDLAMP *n* bedside light
BEDLAMPS > BEDLAMP
BEDLAMS > BEDLAM
BEDLESS > BED
BEDLIKE *adj* like a bed

BEDMAKER *n* person who makes beds
BEDMAKERS > BEDMAKER
BEDMATE *n* person who shares a bed
BEDMATES > BEDMATE
BEDOTTED *adj* scattered; strewn
BEDOUIN *n* member of any of the nomadic tribes of Arabs inhabiting the deserts of Arabia, Jordan, and Syria, as well as parts of the Sahara
BEDOUINS > BEDOUIN
BEDPAN *n* shallow bowl used as a toilet by bedridden people
BEDPANS > BEDPAN
BEDPLATE *n* heavy metal platform or frame to which an engine or machine is attached
BEDPLATES > BEDPLATE
BEDPOST *n* vertical support on a bedstead
BEDPOSTS > BEDPOST
BEDQUILT *n* padded bed cover
BEDQUILTS > BEDQUILT
BEDRAGGLE *vb* make (hair, clothing, etc) limp, untidy, or dirty, as with rain or mud
BEDRAIL *n* rail or board along the side of a bed that connects the headboard with the footboard
BEDRAILS > BEDRAIL
BEDRAL *n* minor church official
BEDRALS > BEDRAL
BEDRAPE *vb* adorn
BEDRAPED > BEDRAPE
BEDRAPES > BEDRAPE
BEDRAPING > BEDRAPE
BEDRENCH *vb* drench
BEDRID *same as* > BEDRIDDEN
BEDRIDDEN *adj* confined to bed because of illness or old age
BEDRIGHT *n* rights expected in the marital bed
BEDRIGHTS > BEDRIGHT
BEDRIVEL *vb* drivel around
BEDRIVELS > BEDRIVEL
BEDROCK *n* solid rock beneath the surface soil
BEDROCKS > BEDROCK
BEDROLL *n* portable roll of bedding, such as a sleeping bag, used esp for sleeping in the open
BEDROLLS > BEDROLL
BEDROOM *n* room used for sleeping ▷ *adj* containing references to sex
BEDROOMED *adj* containing specified number of bedrooms
BEDROOMS > BEDROOM
BEDROP *vb* drop on
BEDROPPED > BEDROP
BEDROPS > BEDROP
BEDROPT > BEDROP
BEDRUG *vb* drug excessively
BEDRUGGED > BEDRUG
BEDRUGS > BEDRUG
BEDS > BED
BEDSHEET *n* sheet for bed
BEDSHEETS > BEDSHEET
BEDSIDE *n* area beside a bed ▷ *adj* placed at or near the side of the bed
BEDSIDES > BEDSIDE
BEDSIT *n* furnished sitting room with a bed
BEDSITS > BEDSIT
BEDSITTER *same as* > BEDSIT
BEDSOCKS *n* socks worn in bed
BEDSONIA *n* bacterium causing diseases such as trachoma
BEDSONIAS > BEDSONIA
BEDSORE *n* ulcer on the skin, caused by a lengthy period of lying in bed due to illness
BEDSORES > BEDSORE
BEDSPREAD *n* top cover on a bed
BEDSPRING *vb* spring supporting mattress on bed
BEDSTAND *n* bedside table
BEDSTANDS > BEDSTAND
BEDSTEAD *n* framework of a bed
BEDSTEADS > BEDSTEAD
BEDSTRAW *n* plant with small white or yellow flowers
BEDSTRAWS > BEDSTRAW
BEDTICK *n* case containing stuffing in mattress
BEDTICKS > BEDTICK
BEDTIME *n* time when one usually goes to bed
BEDTIMES > BEDTIME
BEDU *adj* relating to beduins
BEDUCK *vb* duck under water
BEDUCKED > BEDUCK
BEDUCKING > BEDUCK
BEDUCKS > BEDUCK
BEDUIN *variant of* > BEDOUIN
BEDUINS > BEDUIN
BEDUMB *vb* make dumb
BEDUMBED > BEDUMB
BEDUMBING > BEDUMB
BEDUMBS > BEDUMB
BEDUNCE *vb* cause to look or feel foolish
BEDUNCED > BEDUNCE
BEDUNCES > BEDUNCE
BEDUNCING > BEDUNCE
BEDUNG *vb* spread with dung
BEDUNGED > BEDUNG
BEDUNGING > BEDUNG
BEDUNGS > BEDUNG
BEDUST *vb* cover with dust
BEDUSTED > BEDUST
BEDUSTING > BEDUST
BEDUSTS > BEDUST
BEDWARD *adj* towards bed
BEDWARDS *adv* towards bed
BEDWARF *vb* hamper growth of
BEDWARFED > BEDWARF
BEDWARFS > BEDWARF
BEDWARMER *n* metal pan containing hot coals, formerly used to warm a bed
BEDWETTER *n* person who urinates in bed
BEDYDE > BEDYE
BEDYE *vb* dye
BEDYED > BEDYE
BEDYEING > BEDYE
BEDYES > BEDYE
BEE *n* insect that makes wax and honey
BEEBEE *n* air rifle
BEEBEES > BEEBEE
BEEBREAD *n* mixture of pollen and nectar prepared by worker bees and fed to the larvae
BEEBREADS > BEEBREAD
BEECH *n* tree with a smooth greyish bark
BEECHEN > BEECH
BEECHES > BEECH
BEECHIER > BEECH
BEECHIEST > BEECH
BEECHMAST *n* nuts of beech tree
BEECHNUT *n* small brown triangular edible nut of the beech tree
BEECHNUTS > BEECHNUT
BEECHWOOD *n* wood of beech tree
BEECHY > BEECH
BEEDI *n* Indian cigarette
BEEDIES > BEEDI
BEEF *n* flesh of a cow, bull, or ox ▷ *vb* complain
BEEFALO *n* cross between cow and buffalo
BEEFALOES > BEEFALO
BEEFALOS > BEEFALO
BEEFCAKE *n* musclemen as displayed in photographs
BEEFCAKES > BEEFCAKE
BEEFEATER *n* yeoman warder at the Tower of London
BEEFED > BEEF
BEEFIER > BEEFY
BEEFIEST > BEEFY
BEEFILY > BEEFY
BEEFINESS > BEEFY
BEEFING > BEEF
BEEFLESS > BEEF
BEEFS > BEEF
BEEFSTEAK *n* piece of beef that can be grilled, fried, etc, cut from any lean part of the animal
BEEFWOOD *n* any of various trees that produce very hard wood
BEEFWOODS > BEEFWOOD
BEEFY *adj* like beef
BEEGAH *same as* > BIGHA
BEEGAHS > BEEGAH
BEEHIVE *n* structure in which bees live
BEEHIVES > BEEHIVE
BEEKEEPER *n* person who keeps bees for their honey
BEELIKE > BEE
BEELINE *n* most direct route between two places ▷ *adj* make a beeline for (something)
BEELINED > BEELINE
BEELINES > BEELINE
BEELINING > BEELINE
BEEN > BE
BEENAH *n* understanding; insight
BEENAHS > BEENAH
BEENTO *n* person who has resided in Britain, esp during part of his education ▷ *adj* of, relating to, or characteristic of such a person
BEENTOS > BEENTO
BEEP *n* high-pitched sound, like that of a car horn ▷ *vb* (cause to) make this noise
BEEPED > BEEP
BEEPER > BEEP
BEEPERS > BEEP
BEEPING > BEEP
BEEPS > BEEP
BEER *n* alcoholic drink brewed from malt and hops
BEERAGE *n* brewing industry
BEERAGES > BEERAGE
BEERHALL *n* large public room where beer is consumed
BEERHALLS > BEERHALL
BEERIER > BEERY
BEERIEST > BEERY
BEERILY > BEERY
BEERINESS > BEERY
BEERS > BEER
BEERY *adj* smelling or tasting of beer
BEES > BEE
BEESOME *same as* > BISSON
BEESTINGS *n* first milk secreted by the mammary glands of a cow or similar animal immediately after giving birth
BEESWAX *n* wax secreted by bees, used in polishes etc ▷ *vb* polish with such wax
BEESWAXED > BEESWAX
BEESWAXES > BEESWAX
BEESWING *n* light filmy crust of tartar that forms in port and some other wines after long keeping in the bottle
BEESWINGS > BEESWING
BEET *n* plant with an edible root and leaves ▷ *vb*

improve or make better
BEETED > BEET
BEETFLIES > BEETFLY
BEETFLY *n* muscid fly, *Pegomyia hyoscyami*: a common pest of beets and mangel-wurzels
BEETING > BEET
BEETLE *n* insect with a hard wing cover on its back ▷ *adj* overhang or jut ▷ *vb* scuttle or scurry
BEETLED > BEETLE
BEETLER *n* one who operates a beetling machine
BEETLERS > BEETLER
BEETLES > BEETLE
BEETLING > BEETLE
BEETROOT *n* type of beet plant with a dark red root
BEETROOTS > BEETROOT
BEETS > BEET
BEEVES > BEEF
BEEYARD *n* place where bees are kept
BEEYARDS > BEEYARD
BEEZER *n* person or chap ▷ *adj* excellent
BEEZERS > BEEZER
BEFALL *vb* happen to (someone)
BEFALLEN > BEFALL
BEFALLING > BEFALL
BEFALLS > BEFALL
BEFANA *n* Italian gift-bearing good fairy
BEFANAS > BEFANA
BEFELD > BEFALL
BEFELL > BEFALL
BEFFANA *same as* > BEFANA
BEFFANAS > BEFFANA
BEFINGER *vb* mark by handling
BEFINGERS > BEFINGER
BEFINNED *adj* with fins
BEFIT *vb* be appropriate or suitable for
BEFITS > BEFIT
BEFITTED > BEFIT
BEFITTING > BEFIT
BEFLAG *vb* decorate with flags
BEFLAGGED > BEFLAG
BEFLAGS > BEFLAG
BEFLEA *vb* infect with fleas
BEFLEAED > BEFLEA
BEFLEAING > BEFLEA
BEFLEAS > BEFLEA
BEFLECK *vb* fleck
BEFLECKED > BEFLECK
BEFLECKS > BEFLECK
BEFLOWER *vb* decorate with flowers
BEFLOWERS > BEFLOWER
BEFLUM *vb* fool; deceive
BEFLUMMED > BEFLUM
BEFLUMS > BEFLUM
BEFOAM *vb* cover with foam
BEFOAMED > BEFOAM
BEFOAMING > BEFOAM
BEFOAMS > BEFOAM
BEFOG *vb* surround with fog
BEFOGGED > BEFOG
BEFOGGING > BEFOG
BEFOGS > BEFOG
BEFOOL *vb* make a fool of
BEFOOLED > BEFOOL
BEFOOLING > BEFOOL
BEFOOLS > BEFOOL
BEFORE *adv* indicating something earlier in time, in front of, or preferred to ▷ *prep* preceding in space or time
BEFORTUNE *vb* happen to
BEFOUL *vb* make dirty or foul
BEFOULED > BEFOUL
BEFOULER > BEFOUL
BEFOULERS > BEFOUL
BEFOULING > BEFOUL
BEFOULS > BEFOUL
BEFRET *vb* fret about something
BEFRETS > BEFRET
BEFRETTED > BEFRET
BEFRIEND *vb* become friends with
BEFRIENDS > BEFRIEND
BEFRINGE *vb* decorate with fringe
BEFRINGED > BEFRINGE
BEFRINGES > BEFRINGE
BEFUDDLE *vb* confuse, muddle, or perplex
BEFUDDLED > BEFUDDLE
BEFUDDLES > BEFUDDLE
BEG *vb* solicit (money, food, etc), esp in the street
BEGAD *interj* emphatic exclamation
BEGALL *vb* make sore by rubbing
BEGALLED > BEGALL
BEGALLING > BEGALL
BEGALLS > BEGALL
BEGAN > BEGIN
BEGAR *n* compulsory labour
BEGARS > BEGAR
BEGAT > BEGET
BEGAZE *vb* gaze about or around
BEGAZED > BEGAZE
BEGAZES > BEGAZE
BEGAZING > BEGAZE
BEGEM *vb* decorate with gems
BEGEMMED > BEGEM
BEGEMMING > BEGEM
BEGEMS > BEGEM
BEGET *vb* cause or create
BEGETS > BEGET
BEGETTER > BEGET
BEGETTERS > BEGET
BEGETTING > BEGET
BEGGAR *n* person who begs, esp one who lives by begging ▷ *vb* be beyond the resources of
BEGGARDOM > BEGGAR
BEGGARED > BEGGAR
BEGGARIES > BEGGARY
BEGGARING > BEGGAR
BEGGARLY *adj* meanly inadequate
BEGGARS > BEGGAR
BEGGARY *n* extreme poverty or need
BEGGED > BEG
BEGGING > BEG
BEGGINGLY > BEG
BEGGINGS > BEG
BEGHARD *n* member of a Christian brotherhood that was founded in Flanders in the 13th century and followed a life based on that of the Beguines
BEGHARDS > BEGHARD
BEGIFT *vb* give gift or gifts to
BEGIFTED > BEGIFT
BEGIFTING > BEGIFT
BEGIFTS > BEGIFT
BEGILD *vb* gild
BEGILDED > BEGILD
BEGILDING > BEGILD
BEGILDS > BEGILD
BEGILT > BEGILD
BEGIN *vb* start
BEGINNE *same as* > BEGINNING
BEGINNER *n* person who has just started learning to do something
BEGINNERS > BEGINNER
BEGINNES > BEGINNE
BEGINNING *n* start
BEGINS > BEGIN
BEGIRD *vb* surround
BEGIRDED > BEGIRD
BEGIRDING > BEGIRD
BEGIRDLE *vb* surround with girdle
BEGIRDLED > BEGIRDLE
BEGIRDLES > BEGIRDLE
BEGIRDS > BEGIRD
BEGIRT > BEGIRD
BEGLAD *vb* make glad
BEGLADDED > BEGLAD
BEGLADS > BEGLAD
BEGLAMOR *same as* > BEGLAMOUR
BEGLAMORS > BEGLAMOR
BEGLAMOUR *vb* glamourize
BEGLERBEG *n* governor in the Ottoman empire
BEGLOOM *vb* make gloomy
BEGLOOMED > BEGLOOM
BEGLOOMS > BEGLOOM
BEGNAW *vb* gnaw at
BEGNAWED > BEGNAW
BEGNAWING > BEGNAW
BEGNAWS > BEGNAW
BEGO *vb* harrass; beset
BEGOES > BEGO
BEGOGGLED *adj* wearing goggles
BEGOING > BEGO
BEGONE > BEGO
BEGONIA *n* tropical plant with waxy flowers
BEGONIAS > BEGONIA
BEGORAH *same as* > BEGORRA
BEGORED *adj* smear with gore
BEGORRA *interj* emphatic exclamation, regarded as a characteristic utterance of Irishmen
BEGORRAH *same as* > BEGORRA
BEGOT *past participle of* > BEGET
BEGOTTEN *past participle of* > BEGET
BEGRIM *same as* > BEGRIME
BEGRIME *vb* make dirty
BEGRIMED > BEGRIME
BEGRIMES > BEGRIME
BEGRIMING > BEGRIME
BEGRIMMED > BEGRIM
BEGRIMS > BEGRIM
BEGROAN *vb* groan at
BEGROANED > BEGROAN
BEGROANS > BEGROAN
BEGRUDGE *vb* envy (someone) the possession of something
BEGRUDGED > BEGRUDGE
BEGRUDGER > BEGRUDGE
BEGRUDGES > BEGRUDGE
BEGS > BEG
BEGUILE *vb* cheat or mislead
BEGUILED > BEGUILE
BEGUILER > BEGUILE
BEGUILERS > BEGUILE
BEGUILES > BEGUILE
BEGUILING *adj* charming, often in a deceptive way
BEGUIN *another name for* > BEGHARD
BEGUINAGE *n* convent for members of beguine sisterhood
BEGUINE *n* S American dance
BEGUINES > BEGUINE
BEGUINS > BEGUIN
BEGULF *vb* overwhelm
BEGULFED > BEGULF
BEGULFING > BEGULF
BEGULFS > BEGULF
BEGUM *n* Muslim woman of high rank
BEGUMS > BEGUM
BEGUN *past participle of* > BEGIN
BEGUNK *vb* delude; trick
BEGUNKED > BEGUNK
BEGUNKING > BEGUNK
BEGUNKS > BEGUNK
BEHALF *n* interest, part, benefit, or respect
BEHALVES > BEHALF
BEHAPPEN *vb* befall
BEHAPPENS > BEHAPPEN
BEHATTED *adj* wearing a hat
BEHAVE *vb* act or function in a particular way
BEHAVED > BEHAVE
BEHAVER > BEHAVE
BEHAVERS > BEHAVE
BEHAVES > BEHAVE
BEHAVING > BEHAVE
BEHAVIOR *same as* > BEHAVIOUR
BEHAVIORS > BEHAVIOR
BEHAVIOUR *n* manner of behaving
BEHEAD *vb* remove the head

from
BEHEADAL > BEHEAD
BEHEADALS > BEHEAD
BEHEADED > BEHEAD
BEHEADER > BEHEAD
BEHEADERS > BEHEAD
BEHEADING > BEHEAD
BEHEADS > BEHEAD
BEHELD > BEHOLD
BEHEMOTH *n* huge person or thing
BEHEMOTHS > BEHEMOTH
BEHEST *n* order or earnest request
BEHESTS > BEHEST
BEHIGHT *vb* entrust
BEHIGHTS > BEHIGHT
BEHIND *adv* indicating position to the rear, lateness, responsibility, etc ▷ *n* buttocks ▷ *prep* in or to a position further back than ▷ *adj* in a position further back
BEHINDS > BEHIND
BEHOLD *vb* look (at)
BEHOLDEN *adj* indebted or obliged
BEHOLDER > BEHOLD
BEHOLDERS > BEHOLD
BEHOLDING > BEHOLD
BEHOLDS > BEHOLD
BEHOOF *n* advantage or profit
BEHOOFS > BEHOOF
BEHOOVE *same as* > BEHOVE
BEHOOVED > BEHOOVE
BEHOOVES > BEHOOVE
BEHOOVING > BEHOOVE
BEHOTE *same as* > BEHIGHT
BEHOTES > BEHOTE
BEHOTING > BEHOTE
BEHOVE *vb* be necessary or fitting for
BEHOVED > BEHOVE
BEHOVEFUL *adj* useful; of benefit
BEHOVELY *adj* useful
BEHOVES > BEHOVE
BEHOVING > BEHOVE
BEHOWL *vb* howl at
BEHOWLED > BEHOWL
BEHOWLING > BEHOWL
BEHOWLS > BEHOWL
BEIGE *adj* pale brown ▷ *n* very light brown, sometimes with a yellowish tinge, similar to the colour of undyed wool
BEIGEL *same as* > BAGEL
BEIGELS > BEIGEL
BEIGES > BEIGE
BEIGNE *variant of* > BEIGNET
BEIGNES > BEIGNE
BEIGNET *n* square deep-fried pastry served hot and sprinkled with icing sugar
BEIGNETS > BEIGNET
BEIGY > BEIGE
BEIN *adj* financially comfortable
BEING > BE
BEINGLESS > BE
BEINGNESS > BE
BEINGS > BE
BEINKED *adj* daubed with ink
BEINNESS > BEIN
BEJABBERS *same as* > BEJABERS
BEJABERS *interj* by Jesus!
BEJADE *vb* jade; tire
BEJADED > BEJADE
BEJADES > BEJADE
BEJADING > BEJADE
BEJANT *same as* > BAJAN
BEJANTS > BEJANT
BEJEEBERS *same as* > BEJABERS
BEJEEZUS *same as* > BEJESUS
BEJESUIT *vb* convert to Jesuitism
BEJESUITS > BEJESUIT
BEJESUS *interj* exclamation of surprise
BEJEWEL *vb* decorate with or as if with jewels
BEJEWELED > BEJEWEL
BEJEWELS > BEJEWEL
BEJUMBLE *vb* jumble up
BEJUMBLED > BEJUMBLE
BEJUMBLES > BEJUMBLE
BEKAH *n* half shekel
BEKAHS > BEKAH
BEKISS *vb* smother with kisses
BEKISSED > BEKISS
BEKISSES > BEKISS
BEKISSING > BEKISS
BEKNAVE *vb* treat as knave
BEKNAVED > BEKNAVE
BEKNAVES > BEKNAVE
BEKNAVING > BEKNAVE
BEKNIGHT *vb* esteem
BEKNIGHTS > BEKNIGHT
BEKNOT *vb* tie knot or knots in
BEKNOTS > BEKNOT
BEKNOTTED > BEKNOT
BEKNOWN *adj* known about
BEL *n* unit for comparing two power levels or measuring the intensity of a sound, equal to 10 decibels
BELABOR *same as* > BELABOUR
BELABORED > BELABOR
BELABORS > BELABOR
BELABOUR *vb* attack verbally or physically
BELABOURS > BELABOUR
BELACE *vb* decorate with lace
BELACED > BELACE
BELACES > BELACE
BELACING > BELACE
BELADIED > BELADY
BELADIES > BELADY
BELADY *vb* call a lady
BELADYING > BELADY
BELAH *n* Australian casuarina tree, *Casuarina glauca*, yielding a useful timber
BELAHS > BELAH
BELAMIES > BELAMY
BELAMOURE *n* loved one
BELAMY *n* close friend
BELAR *same as* > BELAH
BELARS > BELAR
BELATE *vb* cause to be late
BELATED *adj* late or too late
BELATEDLY > BELATED
BELATES > BELATE
BELATING > BELATE
BELAUD *vb* praise highly
BELAUDED > BELAUD
BELAUDING > BELAUD
BELAUDS > BELAUD
BELAY *vb* secure a line to a pin or cleat ▷ *n* attachment (of a climber) to a mountain by tying the rope off round a rock spike, piton, nut, etc, to safeguard the party in the event of a fall
BELAYED > BELAY
BELAYER > BELAY
BELAYERS > BELAY
BELAYING > BELAY
BELAYS > BELAY
BELCH *vb* expel wind from the stomach noisily through the mouth ▷ *n* act of belching
BELCHED > BELCH
BELCHER > BELCH
BELCHERS > BELCH
BELCHES > BELCH
BELCHING > BELCH
BELDAM *n* old woman, esp an ugly or malicious one
BELDAME *same as* > BELDAM
BELDAMES > BELDAME
BELDAMS > BELDAM
BELEAGUER *vb* trouble persistently
BELEAP *vb* leap over
BELEAPED > BELEAP
BELEAPING > BELEAP
BELEAPS > BELEAP
BELEAPT > BELEAP
BELEE *vb* put on sheltered side
BELEED > BELEE
BELEEING > BELEE
BELEES > BELEE
BELEMNITE *n* any extinct marine cephalopod mollusc of the order *Belemnoidea*, related to the cuttlefish
BELEMNOID *adj* shaped like a dart
BELFRIED *adj* with a belfry
BELFRIES > BELFRY
BELFRY *n* part of a tower where bells are hung
BELGA *n* former Belgian monetary unit worth five francs
BELGARD *n* kind gaze
BELGARDS > BELGARD
BELGAS > BELGA
BELIE *vb* show to be untrue
BELIED > BELIE
BELIEF *n* faith or confidence
BELIEFS > BELIEF
BELIER > BELIE
BELIERS > BELIE
BELIES > BELIE
BELIEVE *vb* accept as true or real
BELIEVED > BELIEVE
BELIEVER > BELIEVE
BELIEVERS > BELIEVE
BELIEVES > BELIEVE
BELIEVING > BELIEVE
BELIKE *adv* perhaps
BELIQUOR *vb* cause to be drunk
BELIQUORS > BELIQUOR
BELITTLE *vb* treat as having little value or importance
BELITTLED > BELITTLE
BELITTLER > BELITTLE
BELITTLES > BELITTLE
BELIVE *adv* speedily
BELL *n* hollow, usu. metal, cup-shaped instrument that emits a ringing sound when struck ▷ *vb* utter (such a cry)
BELLBIND *n* bindweed-type climber
BELLBINDS > BELLBIND
BELLBIRD *n* Australasian bird with bell-like call
BELLBIRDS > BELLBIRD
BELLBOY *n* man or boy employed in a hotel, club, etc, to carry luggage and answer calls for service
BELLBOYS > BELLBOY
BELLCOTE *n* small roofed structure for bell
BELLCOTES > BELLCOTE
BELLE *n* beautiful woman, esp the most attractive woman at a function
BELLED > BELL
BELLEEK *n* kind of thin fragile porcelain with a lustrous glaze
BELLEEKS > BELLEEK
BELLES > BELLE
BELLETER *n* person who makes bells
BELLETERS > BELLETER
BELLHOP *same as* > BELLBOY
BELLHOPS > BELLHOP
BELLIBONE *n* beautiful and good woman
BELLICOSE *adj* warlike and aggressive
BELLIED > BELLY
BELLIES > BELLY
BELLING > BELL
BELLINGS > BELL
BELLMAN *n* man who rings a bell, esp (formerly) a town crier
BELLMEN > BELLMAN
BELLOCK *vb* shout
BELLOCKED > BELLOCK
BELLOCKS > BELLOCK
BELLOW *vb* make a low deep cry like that of a bull ▷ *n* loud deep roar
BELLOWED > BELLOW

BELLOWER > BELLOW
BELLOWERS > BELLOW
BELLOWING > BELLOW
BELLOWS *pl n* instrument for pumping a stream of air into something
BELLPULL *n* handle, rope, or cord pulled to operate a doorbell or servant's bell
BELLPULLS > BELLPULL
BELLPUSH *n* button pressed to operate an electric bell
BELLS > BELL
BELLWORT *n* any plant of the North American liliaceous genus *Uvularia*, having slender bell-shaped yellow flowers
BELLWORTS > BELLWORT
BELLY *n* part of the body of a vertebrate which contains the intestines ▷ *vb* (cause to) swell out
BELLYACHE *n* pain in the abdomen ▷ *vb* complain repeatedly
BELLYBAND *n* strap around the belly of a draught animal, holding the shafts of a vehicle
BELLYFUL *n* more than one can tolerate
BELLYFULS > BELLYFUL
BELLYING > BELLY
BELLYINGS > BELLY
BELLYLIKE > BELLY
BELOMANCY *n* art of divination using arrows
BELON *n* type of oyster
BELONG *vb* be the property of
BELONGED > BELONG
BELONGER *n* native-born Caribbean
BELONGERS > BELONGER
BELONGING *n* secure relationship
BELONGS > BELONG
BELONS > BELON
BELOVE *vb* love
BELOVED *adj* dearly loved ▷ *n* person dearly loved
BELOVEDS > BELOVED
BELOVES > BELOVE
BELOVING > BELOVE
BELOW *adv* at or to a position lower than, under ▷ *prep* at or to a position lower than
BELOWS *same as* > BELLOWS
BELS > BEL
BELT *n* band of cloth, leather, etc, worn usu. around the waist ▷ *vb* fasten with a belt
BELTED > BELT
BELTER *n* outstanding person or event
BELTERS > BELTER
BELTING *n* material used to make a belt or belts ▷ *adj* excellent
BELTINGS > BELTING
BELTLESS > BELT
BELTLINE *n* line separating car's windows from main body
BELTLINES > BELTLINE
BELTMAN *n* (formerly) the member of a beach life-saving team who swam out with a line attached to his belt
BELTMEN > BELTMAN
BELTS > BELT
BELTWAY *n* people and institutions located in the area bounded by the Washington Beltway, taken to be politically and socially out of touch with the rest of America and much given to political intrigue
BELTWAYS > BELTWAY
BELUGA *n* large white sturgeon of the Black and Caspian Seas, from which caviar and isinglass are obtained
BELUGAS > BELUGA
BELVEDERE *n* building designed and situated to look out on pleasant scenery
BELYING > BELIE
BEMA *n* speaker's platform in the assembly in ancient Athens
BEMAD *vb* cause to become mad
BEMADAM *vb* call a person madam
BEMADAMED > BEMADAM
BEMADAMS > BEMADAM
BEMADDED > BEMAD
BEMADDEN *vb* cause to become mad
BEMADDENS > BEMADDEN
BEMADDING > BEMAD
BEMADS > BEMAD
BEMAS > BEMA
BEMATA > BEMA
BEMAUL *vb* maul
BEMAULED > BEMAUL
BEMAULING > BEMAUL
BEMAULS > BEMAUL
BEMAZED *adj* amazed
BEMBEX *n* type of wasp
BEMBEXES > BEMBEX
BEMBIX *same as* > BEMBEX
BEMBIXES > BEMBIX
BEMEAN *a less common word for* > DEMEAN
BEMEANED > BEMEAN
BEMEANING > BEMEAN
BEMEANS > BEMEAN
BEMEANT > BEMEAN
BEMEDAL *vb* decorate with medals
BEMEDALED > BEMEDAL
BEMEDALS > BEMEDAL
BEMETE *vb* measure
BEMETED > BEMETE
BEMETES > BEMETE
BEMETING > BEMETE
BEMINGLE *vb* mingle
BEMINGLED > BEMINGLE
BEMINGLES > BEMINGLE
BEMIRE *vb* soil with or as if with mire
BEMIRED > BEMIRE
BEMIRES > BEMIRE
BEMIRING > BEMIRE
BEMIST *vb* cloud with mist
BEMISTED > BEMIST
BEMISTING > BEMIST
BEMISTS > BEMIST
BEMIX *vb* mix thoroughly
BEMIXED > BEMIX
BEMIXES > BEMIX
BEMIXING > BEMIX
BEMIXT > BEMIX
BEMOAN *vb* express sorrow or dissatisfaction about
BEMOANED > BEMOAN
BEMOANER > BEMOAN
BEMOANERS > BEMOAN
BEMOANING > BEMOAN
BEMOANS > BEMOAN
BEMOCK *vb* mock
BEMOCKED > BEMOCK
BEMOCKING > BEMOCK
BEMOCKS > BEMOCK
BEMOIL *vb* soil with mud
BEMOILED > BEMOIL
BEMOILING > BEMOIL
BEMOILS > BEMOIL
BEMONSTER *vb* treat as monster
BEMOUTH *vb* endow with mouth
BEMOUTHED > BEMOUTH
BEMOUTHS > BEMOUTH
BEMUD *vb* cover with mud
BEMUDDED > BEMUD
BEMUDDING > BEMUD
BEMUDDLE *vb* confound
BEMUDDLED > BEMUDDLE
BEMUDDLES > BEMUDDLE
BEMUDS > BEMUD
BEMUFFLE *vb* muffle up
BEMUFFLED > BEMUFFLE
BEMUFFLES > BEMUFFLE
BEMURMUR *vb* murmur at
BEMURMURS > BEMURMUR
BEMUSE *vb* confuse
BEMUSED *adj* puzzled or confused
BEMUSEDLY > BEMUSED
BEMUSES > BEMUSE
BEMUSING > BEMUSE
BEMUZZLE *vb* put muzzle on
BEMUZZLED > BEMUZZLE
BEMUZZLES > BEMUZZLE
BEN *n* mountain peak ▷ *adv* in ▷ *adj* inner
BENADRYL *n* tradename of an antihistamine drug used in sleeping tablets
BENADRYLS > BENADRYL
BENAME *an archaic word for* > NAME
BENAMED > BENAME
BENAMES > BENAME
BENAMING > BENAME
BENCH *n* long seat ▷ *vb* put a person on a bench
BENCHED > BENCH
BENCHER *n* member of the governing body of one of the Inns of Court, usually a judge or a Queen's Counsel
BENCHERS > BENCHER
BENCHES > BENCH
BENCHIER > BENCHY
BENCHIEST > BENCHY
BENCHING > BENCH
BENCHLAND *n* level ground at foot of mountains
BENCHLESS > BENCH
BENCHMARK *n* criterion by which to measure something ▷ *vb* measure or test against a benchmark
BENCHTOP *adj* for use at bench
BENCHY *adj* (of a hillside) hollowed out in benches
BEND *vb* (cause to) form a curve ▷ *n* curved part
BENDABLE > BEND
BENDAY *vb* (printing) reproduce using Benday technique
BENDAYED > BENDAY
BENDAYING > BENDAY
BENDAYS > BENDAY
BENDED > BEND
BENDEE *same as* > BENDY
BENDEES > BENDEE
BENDER *n* drinking bout
BENDERS > BENDER
BENDIER > BENDY
BENDIEST > BENDY
BENDING > BEND
BENDINGLY > BEND
BENDINGS > BEND
BENDLET *n* narrow diagonal stripe on heraldic shield
BENDLETS > BENDLET
BENDS > BEND
BENDWAYS *same as* > BENDWISE
BENDWISE *adv* diagonally
BENDY *adj* flexible or pliable ▷ *n same as* > OKRA
BENDYS > BENDY
BENE *n* blessing
BENEATH *prep* below ▷ *adv* below
BENEDICK *n* recently-married man
BENEDICKS > BENEDICK
BENEDICT *n* newly married man
BENEDICTS > BENEDICT
BENEDIGHT *adj* blessed
BENEFACT *vb* be benefactor to
BENEFACTS > BENEFACT
BENEFIC *adj* a rare word for beneficent
BENEFICE *n* church office providing its holder with an income ▷ *vb* provide with a benefice
BENEFICED > BENEFICE
BENEFICES > BENEFICE
BENEFIT *n* something that improves or promotes ▷ *vb* do or receive good

BENEFITED > BENEFIT
BENEFITER > BENEFIT
BENEFITS > BENEFIT
BENEMPT *a past participle of* > NAME
BENEMPTED > BENEMPT
BENES > BENE
BENET *vb* trap (something) in a net
BENETS > BENET
BENETTED > BENET
BENETTING > BENET
BENGALINE *n* heavy corded fabric, esp silk with woollen or cotton cord
BENI *n* sesame plant
BENIGHT *vb* shroud in darkness
BENIGHTED *adj* ignorant or uncultured
BENIGHTEN *same as* > BENIGHT
BENIGHTER > BENIGHT
BENIGHTS > BENIGHT
BENIGN *adj* showing kindliness
BENIGNANT *adj* kind or gracious
BENIGNER > BENIGN
BENIGNEST > BENIGN
BENIGNITY *n* kindliness
BENIGNLY > BENIGN
BENIS > BENI
BENISEED *n* sesame
BENISEEDS > BENISEED
BENISON *n* blessing, esp a spoken one
BENISONS > BENISON
BENITIER *n* basin for holy water
BENITIERS > BENITIER
BENJ *another word for* > BHANG
BENJAMIN *same as* > BENZOIN
BENJAMINS > BENJAMIN
BENJES > BENJ
BENNE *another name for* > SESAME
BENNES > BENNE
BENNET *n* Eurasian and N African rosaceous plant, *Geum urbanum*, with yellow flowers
BENNETS > BENNET
BENNI *n* sesame
BENNIES > BENNY
BENNIS > BENNI
BENNY *n* amphetamine tablet, esp benzedrine: a stimulant
BENOMYL *n* fungicide, derived from imidazole, used on cereal and fruit crops: suspected of being carcinogenic
BENOMYLS > BENOMYL
BENS > BEN
BENT *adj* not straight ▷ *n* personal inclination, propensity, or aptitude
BENTGRASS *n* variety of grass
BENTHAL > BENTHOS
BENTHIC > BENTHOS
BENTHOAL > BENTHON
BENTHON *same as* > BENTHOS
BENTHONIC > BENTHOS
BENTHONS > BENTHON
BENTHOS *n* animals and plants living at the bottom of a sea or lake
BENTHOSES > BENTHOS
BENTIER > BENTY
BENTIEST > BENTY
BENTO *n* thin lightweight box divided into compartments, which contain small separate dishes comprising a Japanese meal
BENTONITE *n* valuable clay, formed by the decomposition of volcanic ash, that swells as it absorbs water: used as a filler in the building, paper, and pharmaceutical industries
BENTOS > BENTO
BENTS > BENT
BENTWOOD *n* wood bent in moulds, used mainly for furniture ▷ *adj* made from such wood
BENTWOODS > BENTWOOD
BENTY *adj* covered with bentgrass
BENUMB *vb* make numb or powerless
BENUMBED > BENUMB
BENUMBING > BENUMB
BENUMBS > BENUMB
BENZAL *n* transparent crystalline substance
BENZALS > BENZAL
BENZENE *n* flammable poisonous liquid used as a solvent, insecticide, etc
BENZENES > BENZENE
BENZENOID *adj* similar to benzene
BENZIDIN *same as* > BENZIDINE
BENZIDINE *n* grey or reddish poisonous crystalline powder
BENZIDINS > BENZIDINE
BENZIL *n* yellow compound radical
BENZILS > BENZIL
BENZIN *same as* > BENZINE
BENZINE *n* volatile liquid used as a solvent
BENZINES > BENZINE
BENZINS > BENZIN
BENZOATE *n* any salt or ester of benzoic acid, containing the group C_6H_5COO- or the ion $C_6H_5COO^-$
BENZOATES > BENZOATE
BENZOIC *adj* of, containing, or derived from benzoic acid or benzoin
BENZOIN *n* gum resin containing benzoic acid, obtained from various trees of the genus *Styrax*, esp *S. benzoin* of Java and Sumatra, and used in ointments, perfume, etc
BENZOINS > BENZOIN
BENZOL *n* crude form of benzene, containing toluene, xylene, and other hydrocarbons, obtained from coal tar or coal gas and used as a fuel
BENZOLE *same as* > BENZOL
BENZOLES > BENZOLE
BENZOLINE *n* unpurified benzene
BENZOLS > BENZOL
BENZOYL *n* of, consisting of, or containing the monovalent group C_6H_5CO-
BENZOYLS > BENZOYL
BENZYL *n* of, consisting of, or containing the monovalent group $C_6H_5CH_2-$
BENZYLIC > BENZYL
BENZYLS > BENZYL
BEPAINT *vb* dye; paint
BEPAINTED > BEPAINT
BEPAINTS > BEPAINT
BEPAT *vb* pat
BEPATCHED *adj* mended with or covered in patches
BEPATS > BEPAT
BEPATTED > BEPAT
BEPATTING > BEPAT
BEPEARL *vb* decorate with pearls
BEPEARLED > BEPEARL
BEPEARLS > BEPEARL
BEPELT *vb* pelt energetically
BEPELTED > BEPELT
BEPELTING > BEPELT
BEPELTS > BEPELT
BEPEPPER *vb* shower with small missiles
BEPEPPERS > BEPEPPER
BEPESTER *vb* pester persistently
BEPESTERS > BEPESTER
BEPIMPLE *vb* form pimples on
BEPIMPLED > BEPIMPLE
BEPIMPLES > BEPIMPLE
BEPITIED > BEPITY
BEPITIES > BEPITY
BEPITY *vb* feel great pity for
BEPITYING > BEPITY
BEPLASTER *vb* cover in thick plaster
BEPLUMED *adj* decorated with feathers
BEPOMMEL *vb* beat vigorously
BEPOMMELS > BEPOMMEL
BEPOWDER *vb* cover with powder
BEPOWDERS > BEPOWDER
BEPRAISE *vb* praise highly
BEPRAISED > BEPRAISE
BEPRAISES > BEPRAISE
BEPROSE *vb* (of poetry) reduce to prose
BEPROSED > BEPROSE
BEPROSES > BEPROSE
BEPROSING > BEPROSE
BEPUFF *vb* puff up
BEPUFFED > BEPUFF
BEPUFFING > BEPUFF
BEPUFFS > BEPUFF
BEQUEATH *vb* dispose of (property) as in a will
BEQUEATHS > BEQUEATH
BEQUEST *n* legal gift of money or property by someone who has died
BEQUESTS > BEQUEST
BERAKE *vb* rake thoroughly
BERAKED > BERAKE
BERAKES > BERAKE
BERAKING > BERAKE
BERASCAL *vb* accuse of being rascal
BERASCALS > BERASCAL
BERATE *vb* scold harshly
BERATED > BERATE
BERATES > BERATE
BERATING > BERATE
BERAY *vb* soil; defile
BERAYED > BERAY
BERAYING > BERAY
BERAYS > BERAY
BERBERE *n* hot-tasting Ethiopian paste made from garlic, cayenne pepper, coriander, and other spices, often used in stews
BERBERES > BERBERE
BERBERIN *same as* > BERBERINE
BERBERINE *n* yellow bitter-tasting alkaloid obtained from barberry
BERBERINS > BERBERIN
BERBERIS *n* shrub with red berries
BERBICE as in *berbice chair* large armchair with long arms that can be folded inwards to act as leg rests
BERCEAU *n* arched trellis for climbing plants
BERCEAUX > BERCEAU
BERCEUSE *n* lullaby
BERCEUSES > BERCEUSE
BERDACHE *n* Native American transvestite
BERDACHES > BERDACHE
BERDASH *same as* > BERDACHE
BERDASHES > BERDASH
BERE *n* barley
BEREAVE *vb* deprive (of) something or someone valued, esp through death
BEREAVED *adj* having recently lost a close friend or relative through death
BEREAVEN > BEREAVE
BEREAVER > BEREAVE
BEREAVERS > BEREAVE
BEREAVES > BEREAVE
BEREAVING > BEREAVE
BEREFT *adj* deprived

BERES > BERE
BERET *n* round flat close-fitting brimless cap
BERETS > BERET
BERETTA *n* type of pistol
BERETTAS > BERETTA
BERG *n* iceberg
BERGAMA *n* type of Turkish rug
BERGAMAS > BERGAMA
BERGAMASK *n* person from Bergamo
BERGAMOT *n* small Asian tree, the fruit of which yields an oil used in perfumery
BERGAMOTS > BERGAMOT
BERGANDER *n* species of duck
BERGEN *n* large rucksack with a capacity of over 50 litres
BERGENIA *n* evergreen ground-covering plant
BERGENIAS > BERGENIA
BERGENS > BERGEN
BERGERE *n* type of French armchair
BERGERES > BERGERE
BERGFALL *n* avalanche
BERGFALLS > BERGFALL
BERGHAAN *same as* > BERGMEHL
BERGHAANS > BERGHAAN
BERGMEHL *n* light powdery variety of calcite
BERGMEHLS > BERGMEHL
BERGOMASK *same as* > BERGAMASK
BERGS > BERG
BERGYLT *n* large northern marine food fish
BERGYLTS > BERGYLT
BERHYME *vb* mention in poetry
BERHYMED > BERHYME
BERHYMES > BERHYME
BERHYMING > BERHYME
BERIBERI *n* disease, endemic in E and S Asia, caused by dietary deficiency of thiamine (vitamin B_1). It affects the nerves to the limbs, producing pain, paralysis, and swelling
BERIBERIS > BERIBERI
BERIMBAU *n* Brazilian single-stringed bowed instrument, used to accompany capoeira
BERIMBAUS > BERIMBAU
BERIME *same as* > BERHYME
BERIMED > BERIME
BERIMES > BERIME
BERIMING > BERIME
BERINGED *adj* wearing a ring or rings
BERK *n* stupid person
BERKELIUM *n* radioactive element
BERKO *adj* berserk
BERKS > BERK
BERLEY *n* bait scattered on water to attract fish ▷ *vb* scatter (bait) on water
BERLEYED > BERLEY
BERLEYING > BERLEY
BERLEYS > BERLEY
BERLIN *n* fine wool yarn used for tapestry work, etc
BERLINE *same as* > BERLIN
BERLINES > BERLINE
BERLINS > BERLIN
BERM *n* narrow grass strip between the road and the footpath in a residential area ▷ *vb* create a berm
BERME *same as* > BERM
BERMED > BERM
BERMES > BERME
BERMING > BERM
BERMS > BERM
BERMUDAS *pl n* close-fitting shorts that come down to the knees
BERNICLE *n* barnacle goose: a N European goose that has a black-and-white head and body and grey wings
BERNICLES > BERNICLE
BEROB *vb* rob
BEROBBED > BEROB
BEROBBING > BEROB
BEROBED *adj* wearing a robe
BEROBS > BEROB
BEROUGED *adj* wearing rouge
BERRET *same as* > BERET
BERRETS > BERRET
BERRETTA *same as* > BIRETTA
BERRETTAS > BERRETTA
BERRIED > BERRY
BERRIES > BERRY
BERRIGAN *n* Australian tree, *Pittosporum phylliraeoides*, with hanging branches
BERRIGANS > BERRIGAN
BERRY *n* small soft stoneless fruit ▷ *vb* bear or produce berries
BERRYING > BERRY
BERRYINGS > BERRY
BERRYLESS > BERRY
BERRYLIKE > BERRY
BERSEEM *n* Mediterranean clover, *Trifolium alexandrinum*, grown as a forage crop and to improve the soil in the southwestern US and the Nile valley
BERSEEMS > BERSEEM
BERSERK *adj* frenziedly violent or destructive ▷ *n* member of a class of ancient Norse warriors who worked themselves into a frenzy before battle and fought with insane fury and courage
BERSERKER *same as* > BERSERK
BERSERKLY > BERSERK
BERSERKS > BERSERK
BERTH *n* bunk in a ship or train ▷ *vb* dock (a ship)
BERTHA *n* wide deep capelike collar, often of lace, usually to cover up a low neckline
BERTHAGE *n* place for mooring boats
BERTHAGES > BERTHAGE
BERTHAS > BERTHA
BERTHE *n* type of lace collar
BERTHED > BERTH
BERTHES > BERTHE
BERTHING > BERTH
BERTHS > BERTH
BERYL *n* hard transparent mineral
BERYLINE > BERYL
BERYLLIA *n* beryllium oxide
BERYLLIAS > BERYLLIA
BERYLLIUM *n* toxic silvery-white metallic element
BERYLS > BERYL
BES *variant of* > BETH
BESAINT *vb* give saint status to
BESAINTED > BESAINT
BESAINTS > BESAINT
BESANG > BESING
BESAT > BESIT
BESAW > BESEE
BESCATTER *vb* strew
BESCORCH *vb* scorch badly
BESCOUR *vb* scour thoroughly
BESCOURED > BESCOUR
BESCOURS > BESCOUR
BESCRAWL *vb* cover with scrawls
BESCRAWLS > BESCRAWL
BESCREEN *vb* conceal with screen
BESCREENS > BESCREEN
BESEE *vb* provide for; mind
BESEECH *vb* ask earnestly
BESEECHED > BESEECH
BESEECHER > BESEECH
BESEECHES > BESEECH
BESEEING > BESEE
BESEEKE *same as* > BESEECH
BESEEKES > BESEEKE
BESEEKING > BESEEKE
BESEEM *vb* be suitable for
BESEEMED > BESEEM
BESEEMING > BESEEM
BESEEMLY > BESEEM
BESEEMS > BESEEM
BESEEN > BESEE
BESEES > BESEE
BESES > BES
BESET *vb* trouble or harass constantly
BESETMENT > BESET
BESETS > BESET
BESETTER > BESET
BESETTERS > BESET
BESETTING *adj* tempting, harassing, or assailing
BESHADOW *vb* darken with shadow
BESHADOWS > BESHADOW
BESHAME *vb* cause to feel shame
BESHAMED > BESHAME
BESHAMES > BESHAME
BESHAMING > BESHAME
BESHINE *vb* illuminate
BESHINES > BESHINE
BESHINING > BESHINE
BESHIVER *vb* shatter
BESHIVERS > BESHIVER
BESHONE > BESHINE
BESHOUT *vb* shout about
BESHOUTED > BESHOUT
BESHOUTS > BESHOUT
BESHREW *vb* wish evil on
BESHREWED > BESHREW
BESHREWS > BESHREW
BESHROUD *vb* cover with a shroud
BESHROUDS > BESHROUD
BESIDE *prep* at, by, or to the side of
BESIDES *prep* in addition ▷ *adv* in addition
BESIEGE *vb* surround with military forces
BESIEGED > BESIEGE
BESIEGER > BESIEGE
BESIEGERS > BESIEGE
BESIEGES > BESIEGE
BESIEGING > BESIEGE
BESIGH *vb* sigh for
BESIGHED > BESIGH
BESIGHING > BESIGH
BESIGHS > BESIGH
BESING *vb* sing about joyfully
BESINGING > BESING
BESINGS > BESING
BESIT *vb* suit; fit
BESITS > BESIT
BESITTING > BESIT
BESLAVE *vb* treat as slave
BESLAVED > BESLAVE
BESLAVER *vb* fawn over
BESLAVERS > BESLAVER
BESLAVES > BESLAVE
BESLAVING > BESLAVE
BESLIME *vb* cover with slime
BESLIMED > BESLIME
BESLIMES > BESLIME
BESLIMING > BESLIME
BESLOBBER *vb* slobber over
BESLUBBER *same as* > BESLOBBER
BESMEAR *vb* smear over
BESMEARED > BESMEAR
BESMEARER > BESMEAR
BESMEARS > BESMEAR
BESMILE *vb* smile on
BESMILED > BESMILE
BESMILES > BESMILE
BESMILING > BESMILE
BESMIRCH *vb* tarnish (someone's name or reputation)
BESMOKE *vb* blacken with smoke
BESMOKED > BESMOKE
BESMOKES > BESMOKE
BESMOKING > BESMOKE
BESMOOTH *vb* smooth
BESMOOTHS > BESMOOTH
BESMUDGE *vb* blacken

BESMUDGED > BESMUDGE
BESMUDGES > BESMUDGE
BESMUT *vb* blacken with smut
BESMUTCH *same as* > BESMIRCH
BESMUTS > BESMUT
BESMUTTED > BESMUT
BESNOW *vb* cover with snow
BESNOWED > BESNOW
BESNOWING > BESNOW
BESNOWS > BESNOW
BESOGNIO *n* worthless person
BESOGNIOS > BESOGNIO
BESOIN *n* need
BESOINS > BESOIN
BESOM *n* broom made of twigs ▷ *vb* sweep with a besom
BESOMED > BESOM
BESOMING > BESOM
BESOMS > BESOM
BESONIAN *same as* > BEZONIAN
BESONIANS > BESONIAN
BESOOTHE *vb* soothe
BESOOTHED > BESOOTHE
BESOOTHES > BESOOTHE
BESORT *vb* fit
BESORTED > BESORT
BESORTING > BESORT
BESORTS > BESORT
BESOT *vb* make stupid or muddled
BESOTS > BESOT
BESOTTED *adj* infatuated
BESOTTING > BESOT
BESOUGHT *a past participle of* > BESEECH
BESOULED *adj* having a soul
BESPAKE *same as* > BESPOKE
BESPANGLE *vb* cover or adorn with or as if with spangles
BESPAT > BESPIT
BESPATE > BESPIT
BESPATTER *vb* splash, e.g. with dirty water
BESPEAK *vb* indicate or suggest
BESPEAKS > BESPEAK
BESPECKLE *vb* mark with speckles
BESPED > BESPEED
BESPEED *vb* get on with (doing something)
BESPEEDS > BESPEED
BESPICE *vb* flavour with spices
BESPICED > BESPICE
BESPICES > BESPICE
BESPICING > BESPICE
BESPIT *vb* cover with spittle
BESPITS > BESPIT
BESPOKE *adj* (esp of a suit) made to the customer's specifications
BESPOKEN > BESPEAK
BESPORT *vb* amuse oneself
BESPORTED > BESPORT
BESPORTS > BESPORT
BESPOT *vb* mark with spots
BESPOTS > BESPOT
BESPOTTED > BESPOT
BESPOUSE *vb* marry
BESPOUSED > BESPOUSE
BESPOUSES > BESPOUSE
BESPOUT *vb* speak pretentiously
BESPOUTED > BESPOUT
BESPOUTS > BESPOUT
BESPREAD *vb* cover (a surface) with something
BESPREADS > BESPREAD
BESPRENT *adj* sprinkled over
BEST *adj* most excellent of a particular group etc ▷ *adv* in a manner surpassing all others ▷ *n* utmost effort ▷ *vb* defeat
BESTAD *same as* > BESTEAD
BESTADDE *same as* > BESTEAD
BESTAIN *vb* stain
BESTAINED > BESTAIN
BESTAINS > BESTAIN
BESTAR *vb* decorate with stars
BESTARRED > BESTAR
BESTARS > BESTAR
BESTEAD *vb* serve; assist
BESTEADED > BESTEAD
BESTEADS > BESTEAD
BESTED > BEST
BESTI *Indian English word for* > SHAME
BESTIAL *adj* brutal or savage
BESTIALLY > BESTIAL
BESTIALS > BESTIAL
BESTIARY *n* medieval collection of descriptions of animals
BESTICK *vb* cover with sharp points
BESTICKS > BESTICK
BESTILL *vb* cause to be still
BESTILLED > BESTILL
BESTILLS > BESTILL
BESTING > BEST
BESTIR *vb* cause (oneself) to become active
BESTIRRED > BESTIR
BESTIRS > BESTIR
BESTIS > BESTI
BESTORM *vb* assault
BESTORMED > BESTORM
BESTORMS > BESTORM
BESTOW *vb* present (a gift) or confer (an honour)
BESTOWAL > BESTOW
BESTOWALS > BESTOW
BESTOWED > BESTOW
BESTOWER > BESTOW
BESTOWERS > BESTOW
BESTOWING > BESTOW
BESTOWS > BESTOW
BESTREAK *vb* streak
BESTREAKS > BESTREAK
BESTREW *vb* scatter or lie scattered over (a surface)
BESTREWED > BESTREW
BESTREWN > BESTREW
BESTREWS > BESTREW
BESTRID > BESTRIDE
BESTRIDE *vb* have or put a leg on either side of
BESTRIDES > BESTRIDE
BESTRODE > BESTRIDE
BESTROW *same as* > BESTREW
BESTROWED > BESTROW
BESTROWN > BESTROW
BESTROWS > BESTROW
BESTS > BEST
BESTUCK > BESTICK
BESTUD *vb* set with, or as with studs
BESTUDDED > BESTUD
BESTUDS > BESTUD
BESUITED *adj* wearing a suit
BESUNG > BESING
BESWARM *vb* swarm over
BESWARMED > BESWARM
BESWARMS > BESWARM
BET *n* agreement between two parties that a sum of money or other stake will be paid by the loser to the party who correctly predicts the outcome of an event ▷ *vb* make or place a bet with (a person or persons)
BETA *n* second letter in the Greek alphabet, a consonant, transliterated as *b*
BETACISM *vb* type of speech impediment
BETACISMS > BETACISM
BETAINE *n* sweet-tasting alkaloid that occurs in the sugar beet
BETAINES > BETAINE
BETAKE *vb betake oneself* go
BETAKEN > BETAKE
BETAKES > BETAKE
BETAKING > BETAKE
BETAS > BETA
BETATOPIC *adj* (of atoms) differing in proton number by one, theoretically as a result of emission of a beta particle
BETATRON *n* type of particle accelerator for producing high-energy beams of electrons
BETATRONS > BETATRON
BETATTER *vb* make ragged
BETATTERS > BETATTER
BETAXED *adj* burdened with taxes
BETE *same as* > BEET
BETED > BETE
BETEEM *vb* accord
BETEEME *same as* > BETEEM
BETEEMED > BETEEM
BETEEMES > BETEEME
BETEEMING > BETEEM
BETEEMS > BETEEM
BETEL *n* Asian climbing plant, the leaves and nuts of which can be chewed
BETELNUT *n* seed of the betel palm, chewed with betel leaves and lime by people in S and SE Asia as a digestive stimulant and narcotic
BETELNUTS > BETELNUT
BETELS > BETEL
BETES > BETE
BETH *n* second letter of the Hebrew alphabet transliterated as *b*
BETHANK *vb* thank
BETHANKED > BETHANK
BETHANKIT *n* grace spoken before meal
BETHANKS > BETHANK
BETHEL *n* seaman's chapel
BETHELS > BETHEL
BETHESDA *n* church building of certain Christian denomintaions
BETHESDAS > BETHESDA
BETHINK *vb* cause (oneself) to consider or meditate
BETHINKS > BETHINK
BETHORN *vb* cover with thorns
BETHORNED > BETHORN
BETHORNS > BETHORN
BETHOUGHT > BETHINK
BETHRALL *vb* make slave of
BETHRALLS > BETHRALL
BETHS > BETH
BETHUMB *vb* (of books) wear by handling
BETHUMBED > BETHUMB
BETHUMBS > BETHUMB
BETHUMP *vb* thump hard
BETHUMPED > BETHUMP
BETHUMPS > BETHUMP
BETHWACK *vb* strike hard with flat object
BETHWACKS > BETHWACK
BETID > BETIDE
BETIDE *vb* happen (to)
BETIDED > BETIDE
BETIDES > BETIDE
BETIDING > BETIDE
BETIGHT > BETIDE
BETIME *vb* befall
BETIMED > BETIME
BETIMES > BETIME
BETIMING > BETIME
BETING > BETE
BETISE *n* folly or lack of perception
BETISES > BETISE
BETITLE *vb* give title to
BETITLED > BETITLE
BETITLES > BETITLE
BETITLING > BETITLE
BETOIL *vb* tire through hard work
BETOILED > BETOIL
BETOILING > BETOIL
BETOILS > BETOIL
BETOKEN *vb* indicate or signify
BETOKENED > BETOKEN
BETOKENS > BETOKEN
BETON *n* concrete
BETONIES > BETONY
BETONS > BETON
BETONY *n* North American plant
BETOOK *the past tense of* > BETAKE

BETOSS *vb* toss about
BETOSSED > BETOSS
BETOSSES > BETOSS
BETOSSING > BETOSS
BETRAY *vb* hand over or expose (one's nation, friend, etc) treacherously to an enemy
BETRAYAL > BETRAY
BETRAYALS > BETRAY
BETRAYED > BETRAY
BETRAYER > BETRAY
BETRAYERS > BETRAY
BETRAYING > BETRAY
BETRAYS > BETRAY
BETREAD *vb* tread over
BETREADS > BETREAD
BETRIM *vb* decorate
BETRIMMED > BETRIM
BETRIMS > BETRIM
BETROD > BETREAD
BETRODDEN > BETREAD
BETROTH *vb* promise to marry or to give in marriage
BETROTHAL *n* engagement to be married
BETROTHED *adj* engaged to be married ▷ *n* person to whom one is engaged
BETROTHS > BETROTH
BETS > BET
BETTA *n* fighting fish
BETTAS > BETTA
BETTED > BET
BETTER *adj* more excellent than others ▷ *adv* in a more excellent manner ▷ *pl n* one's superiors ▷ *vb* improve upon
BETTERED > BETTER
BETTERING > BETTER
BETTERS > BETTER
BETTIES > BETTY
BETTING > BET
BETTINGS > BET
BETTONG *n* short-nosed rat kangaroo
BETTONGS > BETTONG
BETTOR *n* person who bets
BETTORS > BETTOR
BETTY *n* type of short crowbar
BETUMBLED *adj* thrown into disorder
BETWEEN *adv* indicating position in the middle, alternatives, etc ▷ *prep* at a point intermediate to two other points in space, time, etc
BETWEENS > BETWEEN
BETWIXT *adv* between
BEUNCLED *adj* having many uncles
BEURRE *n* butter
BEURRES > BEURRE
BEVATRON *n* proton synchrotron at the University of California
BEVATRONS > BEVATRON
BEVEL *n* slanting edge ▷ *vb* slope
BEVELED > BEVEL
BEVELER > BEVEL
BEVELERS > BEVEL
BEVELING > BEVEL
BEVELLED > BEVEL
BEVELLER > BEVEL
BEVELLERS > BEVEL
BEVELLING > BEVEL
BEVELMENT > BEVEL
BEVELS > BEVEL
BEVER *n* snack
BEVERAGE *n* drink
BEVERAGES > BEVERAGE
BEVERS > BEVER
BEVIES > BEVY
BEVOMIT *vb* vomit over
BEVOMITED > BEVOMIT
BEVOMITS > BEVOMIT
BEVOR *n* armour protecting lower part of face
BEVORS > BEVOR
BEVUE *n* careless error
BEVUES > BEVUE
BEVVIED > BEVVY
BEVVIES > BEVVY
BEVVY *n* alcoholic drink ▷ *vb* drink alcohol
BEVVYING > BEVVY
BEVY *n* flock or group
BEWAIL *vb* express great sorrow over
BEWAILED > BEWAIL
BEWAILER > BEWAIL
BEWAILERS > BEWAIL
BEWAILING > BEWAIL
BEWAILS > BEWAIL
BEWARE *vb* be on one's guard (against)
BEWARED > BEWARE
BEWARES > BEWARE
BEWARING > BEWARE
BEWEARIED > BEWEARY
BEWEARIES > BEWEARY
BEWEARY *vb* cause to be weary
BEWEEP *vb* express grief through weeping
BEWEEPING > BEWEEP
BEWEEPS > BEWEEP
BEWENT > BEGO
BEWEPT > BEWEEP
BEWET *vb* make wet
BEWETS > BEWET
BEWETTED > BEWET
BEWETTING > BEWET
BEWHORE *vb* treat as whore
BEWHORED > BEWHORE
BEWHORES > BEWHORE
BEWHORING > BEWHORE
BEWIG *vb* adorn with wig
BEWIGGED > BEWIG
BEWIGGING > BEWIG
BEWIGS > BEWIG
BEWILDER *vb* confuse utterly
BEWILDERS > BEWILDER
BEWINGED *adj* having wings
BEWITCH *vb* attract and fascinate
BEWITCHED > BEWITCH
BEWITCHER > BEWITCH
BEWITCHES > BEWITCH
BEWORM *vb* fill with worms
BEWORMED > BEWORM
BEWORMING > BEWORM
BEWORMS > BEWORM
BEWORRIED > BEWORRY
BEWORRIES > BEWORRY
BEWORRY *vb* beset with worry
BEWRAP *vb* wrap up
BEWRAPPED > BEWRAP
BEWRAPS > BEWRAP
BEWRAPT > BEWRAP
BEWRAY *an obsolete word for* > BETRAY
BEWRAYED > BEWRAY
BEWRAYER > BEWRAY
BEWRAYERS > BEWRAY
BEWRAYING > BEWRAY
BEWRAYS > BEWRAY
BEY *n* (in the Ottoman empire) a title given to senior officers, provincial governors, and certain other officials
BEYLIC *n* province ruled over by bey
BEYLICS > BEYLIC
BEYLIK *same as* > BEYLIC
BEYLIKS > BEYLIK
BEYOND *prep* at or to a point on the other side of ▷ *adv* at or to the far side of something ▷ *n* unknown, esp life after death
BEYONDS > BEYOND
BEYS > BEY
BEZ *n* part of deer's horn
BEZANT *n* medieval Byzantine gold coin
BEZANTS > BEZANT
BEZAZZ *another word for* > PIZZAZZ
BEZAZZES > BEZAZZ
BEZEL *n* sloping edge of a cutting tool
BEZELS > BEZEL
BEZES > BEZ
BEZIL *archaic word for* > ALCOHOLIC
BEZILS > BEZIL
BEZIQUE *n* card game for two or more players
BEZIQUES > BEZIQUE
BEZOAR *n* hard mass, such as a stone or hairball, in the stomach and intestines of animals, esp ruminants, and man: formerly thought to be an antidote to poisons
BEZOARDIC *adj* relating to bezoar
BEZOARS > BEZOAR
BEZONIAN *n* knave or rascal
BEZONIANS > BEZONIAN
BEZZANT *same as* > BEZANT
BEZZANTS > BEZZANT
BEZZLE *vb* drink to excess
BEZZLED > BEZZLE
BEZZLES > BEZZLE
BEZZLING > BEZZLE
BHAGEE *same as* > BHAJI
BHAGEES > BHAGEE
BHAJAN *n* singing of devotional songs and hymns
BHAJANS > BHAJAN
BHAJEE *same as* > BHAJI
BHAJEES > BHAJEE
BHAJI *n* Indian deep-fried savoury of chopped vegetables in spiced batter
BHAJIS > BHAJI
BHAKTA *n* Hindu term for devotee of God
BHAKTAS > BHAKTA
BHAKTI *n* loving devotion to God leading to nirvana
BHAKTIS > BHAKTI
BHANG *n* preparation of Indian hemp used as a narcotic and intoxicant
BHANGRA *n* type of traditional Punjabi folk music combined with elements of Western pop music
BHANGRAS > BHANGRA
BHANGS > BHANG
BHARAL *n* wild Himalayan sheep, *Pseudois nayaur*, with a bluish-grey coat and round backward-curving horns
BHARALS > BHARAL
BHAT *n* currency of Thailand
BHAVAN *n* (in India) a large house or building
BHAVANS > BHAVAN
BHAWAN *same as* > BHAVAN
BHAWANS > BHAWAN
BHEESTIE *same as* > BHEESTY
BHEESTIES > BHEESTY
BHEESTY *same as* > BUISHTI
BHEL *same as* > BAEL
BHELS > BHEL
BHIKHU *n* fully ordained Buddhist monk
BHIKHUS > BHIKHU
BHIKKHUNI *n* fully ordained Buddhist nun
BHINDI *same as* > BINDHI
BHINDIS > BHINDI
BHISHTI *n* (formerly in India) a water-carrier
BHISHTIS > BHISHTI
BHISTEE *same as* > BHISHTI
BHISTEES > BHISTEE
BHISTI *same as* > BHISHTI
BHISTIE *same as* > BHISHTI
BHISTIES > BHISTIE
BHISTIS > BHISTI
BHOOT *same as* > BHUT
BHOOTS > BHOOT
BHUNA *n* Indian sauce
BHUNAS > BHUNA
BHUT *n* Hindu term for type of ghost
BHUTS > BHUT
BI *short for* > BISEXUAL
BIACETYL *adj* liquid with strong odour
BIACETYLS > BIACETYL
BIALI *same as* > BIALY
BIALIES > BIALY
BIALIS > BIALI
BIALY *n* type of bagel
BIALYS > BIALY
BIANNUAL *adj* occurring

twice a year ▷ *n* something that happens biannually
BIANNUALS > BIANNUAL
BIAS *n* mental tendency, esp prejudice ▷ *vb* cause to have a bias ▷ *adj* slanting obliquely ▷ *adv* obliquely
BIASED > BIAS
BIASEDLY > BIAS
BIASES > BIAS
BIASING > BIAS
BIASINGS > BIAS
BIASNESS > BIAS
BIASSED > BIAS
BIASSEDLY > BIAS
BIASSES > BIAS
BIASSING > BIAS
BIATHLETE *n* athlete taking part in biathlon
BIATHLON *n* contest in which skiers with rifles shoot at four targets along a 20-kilometre (12.5-mile) cross-country course
BIATHLONS > BIATHLON
BIAXAL *same as* > BIAXIAL
BIAXIAL *adj* (esp of a crystal) having two axes
BIAXIALLY > BIAXIAL
BIB *same as* > BIBCOCK
BIBACIOUS *adj* tending to drink to excess
BIBASIC *adj* with two bases
BIBATION *n* drinking to excess
BIBATIONS > BIBATION
BIBB *n* wooden support on a mast for the trestletrees
BIBBED > BIB
BIBBER *n* drinker
BIBBERIES > BIBBERY
BIBBERS > BIBBER
BIBBERY *n* drinking to excess
BIBBING > BIB
BIBBLE *n* pebble
BIBBLES > BIBBLE
BIBBS > BIBB
BIBCOCK *n* tap with a nozzle bent downwards
BIBCOCKS > BIBCOCK
BIBELOT *n* attractive or curious trinket
BIBELOTS > BIBELOT
BIBLE *n* any book containing the sacred writings of a religion
BIBLES > BIBLE
BIBLESS > BIB
BIBLICAL *adj* of, occurring in, or referring to the Bible
BIBLICISM *n* bible-learning
BIBLICIST > BIBLICISM
BIBLIKE > BIB
BIBLIOTIC *n* study of books
BIBLIST *same as* > BIBLICIST
BIBLISTS > BIBLIST
BIBS > BIB
BIBULOUS *adj* addicted to alcohol
BICAMERAL *adj* (of a legislature) consisting of two chambers
BICARB *n* bicarbonate of soda
BICARBS > BICARB
BICAUDAL *adj* having two tails
BICCIES > BICCY
BICCY *n* biscuit
BICE *n* medium blue colour
BICENTRIC *adj* having two centres
BICEP *same as* > BICEPS
BICEPS *n* muscle with two origins, esp the muscle that flexes the forearm
BICEPSES > BICEPS
BICES > BICE
BICHORD *adj* having two strings for each note
BICHROME *adj* having two colours
BICIPITAL *adj* having two heads
BICKER *vb* argue over petty matters ▷ *n* petty squabble
BICKERED > BICKER
BICKERER > BICKER
BICKERERS > BICKER
BICKERING > BICKER
BICKERS > BICKER
BICKIE *short for* > BISCUIT
BICKIES > BICKIE
BICOASTAL *adj* relating to both the east and west coasts of the US
BICOLOR *same as* > BICOLOUR
BICOLORED *same as* > BICOLOUR
BICOLORS > BICOLOR
BICOLOUR *adj* two-coloured
BICOLOURS > BICOLOUR
BICONCAVE *adj* (of a lens) having concave faces on both sides
BICONVEX *adj* (of a lens) having convex faces on both sides
BICORN *adj* having two horns or hornlike parts
BICORNATE *same as* > BICORN
BICORNE *same as* > BICORN
BICORNES > BICORNE
BICORNS > BICORN
BICRON *n* billionth part of a metre
BICRONS > BICRON
BICUSPID *adj* having two points ▷ *n* bicuspid tooth
BICUSPIDS > BICUSPID
BICYCLE *n* vehicle with two wheels, one behind the other, pedalled by the rider ▷ *vb* ride a bicycle
BICYCLED > BICYCLE
BICYCLER > BICYCLE
BICYCLERS > BICYCLE
BICYCLES > BICYCLE
BICYCLIC *adj* of, forming, or formed by two circles, cycles, etc
BICYCLING > BICYCLE
BICYCLIST > BICYCLE
BID *vb* offer (an amount) in attempting to buy something, esp in competition with others as at an auction ▷ *n* offer of a specified amount, as at an auction
BIDARKA *n* canoe covered in animal skins, esp sealskin, used by the Inuit of Alaska
BIDARKAS > BIDARKA
BIDARKEE *same as* > BIDARKA
BIDARKEES > BIDARKEE
BIDDABLE *adj* obedient
BIDDABLY > BIDDABLE
BIDDEN > BID
BIDDER > BID
BIDDERS > BID
BIDDIES > BIDDY
BIDDING > BID
BIDDINGS > BID
BIDDY *n* woman, esp an old gossipy one
BIDE *vb* stay or continue
BIDED > BIDE
BIDENT *n* instrument with two prongs
BIDENTAL *n* sacred place where lightning has struck
BIDENTALS > BIDENTAL
BIDENTATE > BIDENT
BIDENTS > BIDENT
BIDER > BIDE
BIDERS > BIDE
BIDES > BIDE
BIDET *n* low basin for washing the genital area
BIDETS > BIDET
BIDI *same as* > BEEDI
BIDING > BIDE
BIDINGS > BIDE
BIDIS > BIDI
BIDON *n* oil drum
BIDONS > BIDON
BIDS > BID
BIELD *n* shelter ▷ *vb* shelter or take shelter
BIELDED > BIELD
BIELDIER > BIELDY
BIELDIEST > BIELDY
BIELDING > BIELD
BIELDS > BIELD
BIELDY *adj* sheltered
BIEN *adv* well
BIENNALE *n* event occurring every two years
BIENNALES > BIENNALE
BIENNIA > BIENNIUM
BIENNIAL *adj* occurring every two years ▷ *n* plant that completes its life cycle in two years
BIENNIALS > BIENNIAL
BIENNIUM *n* period of two years
BIENNIUMS > BIENNIUM
BIER *n* stand on which a corpse or coffin rests before burial
BIERS > BIER
BIESTINGS *same as* > BEESTINGS
BIFACE *n* prehistoric stone tool
BIFACES > BIFACE
BIFACIAL *adj* having two faces or surfaces
BIFARIOUS *adj* having parts arranged in two rows on either side of a central axis
BIFF *n* blow with the fist ▷ *vb* give (someone) such a blow
BIFFED > BIFF
BIFFER *n* someone, such as a sportsperson, who has a reputation for hitting hard
BIFFERS > BIFFER
BIFFIES > BIFFY
BIFFIN *n* variety of red cooking apple
BIFFING > BIFF
BIFFINS > BIFFIN
BIFFO *n* fighting or aggressive behaviour ▷ *adj* aggressive
BIFFOS > BIFFO
BIFFS > BIFF
BIFFY *n* outdoor toilet
BIFID *adj* divided into two by a cleft in the middle
BIFIDITY > BIFID
BIFIDLY > BIFID
BIFILAR *adj* having two parallel threads, as in the suspension of certain measuring instruments
BIFILARLY > BIFILAR
BIFLEX *adj* bent or flexed in two places
BIFOCAL *adj* having two different focuses
BIFOCALED *adj* wearing bifocals
BIFOCALS *pl n* spectacles with lenses permitting near and distant vision
BIFOLD *adj* that can be folded in two places
BIFOLIATE *adj* having only two leaves
BIFORATE *adj* having two openings, pores, or perforations
BIFORKED *adj* two-pronged
BIFORM *adj* having or combining the characteristics of two forms, as a centaur
BIFORMED *same as* > BIFORM
BIFTER *n* cannabis cigarette
BIFTERS > BIFTER
BIFURCATE *vb* fork into two branches ▷ *adj* forked into two branches
BIG *adj* of considerable size, height, number, or capacity ▷ *adv* on a grand

scale ▷ *vb* build
BIGA *n* chariot drawn by two horses
BIGAE > BIGA
BIGAMIES > BIGAMY
BIGAMIST > BIGAMY
BIGAMISTS > BIGAMY
BIGAMOUS > BIGAMY
BIGAMY *n* crime of marrying a person while still legally married to someone else
BIGARADE *n* Seville orange
BIGARADES > BIGARADE
BIGAROON *same as* > BIGARREAU
BIGAROONS > BIGAROON
BIGARREAU *n* any of several heart-shaped varieties of sweet cherry that have firm flesh
BIGEMINAL *adj* double; twinned
BIGEMINY *n* heart complaint
BIGENER *n* hybrid between individuals of different genera
BIGENERIC *adj* (of a hybrid plant) derived from parents of two different genera
BIGENERS > BIGENER
BIGEYE *n* any tropical or subtropical red marine percoid fish of the family *Priacanthidae*, having very large eyes and rough scales
BIGEYES > BIGEYE
BIGFEET > BIGFOOT
BIGFOOT *n* yeti ▷ *vb* throw one's weight around
BIGFOOTED > BIGFOOT
BIGFOOTS > BIGFOOT
BIGG *n* type of barley
BIGGED > BIG
BIGGER > BIG
BIGGEST > BIG
BIGGETY *same as* > BIGGITY
BIGGIE *n* something big or important
BIGGIES > BIGGIE
BIGGIN *n* plain close-fitting cap, often tying under the chin, worn in the Middle Ages and by children in the 17th century
BIGGING > BIG
BIGGINGS > BIG
BIGGINS > BIGGIN
BIGGISH > BIG
BIGGITY *adj* conceited
BIGGON *same as* > BIGGIN
BIGGONS > BIGGON
BIGGS > BIGG
BIGGY *same as* > BIGGIE
BIGHA *n* in India, unit for measuring land
BIGHAS > BIGHA
BIGHEAD *n* conceited person
BIGHEADED > BIGHEAD
BIGHEADS > BIGHEAD
BIGHORN *n* large wild sheep, *Ovis canadensis*, inhabiting mountainous regions in North America and NE Asia: family *Bovidae*, order *Artiodactyla*. The male has massive curved horns, and the species is well adapted for climbing and leaping
BIGHORNS > BIGHORN
BIGHT *n* long curved shoreline ▷ *vb* fasten or bind with a bight
BIGHTED > BIGHT
BIGHTING > BIGHT
BIGHTS > BIGHT
BIGLY > BIG
BIGMOUTH *n* noisy, indiscreet, or boastful person
BIGMOUTHS > BIGMOUTH
BIGNESS > BIG
BIGNESSES > BIG
BIGNONIA *n* any tropical American bignoniaceous climbing shrub of the genus *Bignonia* (or *Doxantha*), cultivated for their trumpet-shaped yellow or reddish flowers
BIGNONIAS > BIGNONIA
BIGOS *n* Polish stew
BIGOSES > BIGOS
BIGOT *n* person who is intolerant, esp regarding religion or race
BIGOTED > BIGOT
BIGOTEDLY > BIGOT
BIGOTRIES > BIGOTRY
BIGOTRY *n* attitudes, behaviour, or way of thinking of a bigot
BIGOTS > BIGOT
BIGS > BIG
BIGSTICK *adj* of or relating to irresistible military strength
BIGTIME *adj* important
BIGUANIDE *n* any of a class of compounds some of which are used in the treatment of certain forms of diabetes
BIGWIG *n* important person
BIGWIGS > BIGWIG
BIHOURLY *adj* occurring every two hours
BIJECTION *n* mathematical function or mapping that is both an injection and a surjection and therefore has an inverse
BIJECTIVE *adj* (of a function, relation, etc) associating two sets in such a way that every member of each set is uniquely paired with a member of the other
BIJOU *adj* (of a house) small but elegant ▷ *n* something small and delicately worked
BIJOUS > BIJOU
BIJOUX > BIJOU
BIJUGATE *adj* (of compound leaves) having two pairs of leaflets
BIJUGOUS *same as* > BIJUGATE
BIJWONER *same as* > BYWONER
BIJWONERS > BIJWONER
BIKE *same as* > BICYCLE
BIKED > BIKE
BIKER *n* person who rides a motorcycle
BIKERS > BIKER
BIKES > BIKE
BIKEWAY *n* cycle lane
BIKEWAYS > BIKEWAY
BIKIE *n* member of a motorcycle gang
BIKIES > BIKIE
BIKING > BIKE
BIKINGS > BIKE
BIKINI *n* woman's brief two-piece swimming costume
BIKINIED > BIKINI
BIKINIS > BIKINI
BIKKIE *slang word for* > BISCUIT
BIKKIES > BIKKIE
BILABIAL *adj* of, relating to, or denoting a speech sound articulated using both lips ▷ *n* bilabial speech sound
BILABIALS > BILABIAL
BILABIATE *adj* divided into two lips
BILANDER *n* small two-masted cargo ship
BILANDERS > BILANDER
BILATERAL *adj* affecting or undertaken by two parties
BILAYER *n* part of cell membrane
BILAYERS > BILAYER
BILBERRY *n* bluish-black edible berry
BILBIES > BILBY
BILBO *n* (formerly) a sword with a marked temper and elasticity
BILBOA *same as* > BILBO
BILBOAS > BILBOA
BILBOES > BILBO
BILBOS > BILBO
BILBY *n* Australian marsupial with long pointed ears and grey fur
BILE *n* bitter yellow fluid secreted by the liver ▷ *vb* Scots word for BOIL
BILECTION *same as* > BOLECTION
BILED > BILE
BILES > BILE
BILESTONE *another name for* > GALLSTONE
BILEVEL *n* hairstyle with two different lengths
BILEVELS > BILEVEL
BILGE *n* nonsense ▷ *vb* (of a vessel) to take in water at the bilge
BILGED > BILGE
BILGES > BILGE
BILGIER > BILGE
BILGIEST > BILGE
BILGING > BILGE
BILGY > BILGE
BILHARZIA *n* disease caused by infestation of the body with blood flukes
BILIAN *n* type of tree used for its wood
BILIANS > BILIAN
BILIARIES > BILIARY
BILIARY *adj* of bile, the ducts that convey bile, or the gall bladder ▷ *n* disease found in dogs
BILIMBI *n* type of fruit-bearing tree
BILIMBING *same as* > BILIMBI
BILIMBIS > BILIMBI
BILINEAR *adj* of or referring to two lines
BILING > BILE
BILINGUAL *adj* involving or using two languages ▷ *n* bilingual person
BILIOUS *adj* sick, nauseous
BILIOUSLY > BILIOUS
BILIRUBIN *n* orange-yellow pigment in the bile
BILITERAL *adj* relating to two letters
BILK *vb* cheat, esp by not paying ▷ *n* swindle or cheat
BILKED > BILK
BILKER > BILK
BILKERS > BILK
BILKING > BILK
BILKS > BILK
BILL *n* n money owed for goods or services supplied ▷ *vb* to send or present an account for payment to (a person)
BILLABLE *adj* that can be charged to a client
BILLABONG *n* stagnant pool in an intermittent stream
BILLBOARD *n* large outdoor board for displaying advertisements
BILLBOOK *n* business record of bills received, paid, etc
BILLBOOKS > BILLBOOK
BILLBUG *n* type of weevil
BILLBUGS > BILLBUG
BILLED > BILL
BILLER *n* stem of a plant
BILLERS > BILLER
BILLET *vb* assign a lodging to (a soldier) ▷ *n* accommodation for a soldier in civil lodgings
BILLETED > BILLET
BILLETEE > BILLET
BILLETEES > BILLET
BILLETER > BILLET

BILLETERS > BILLET
BILLETING > BILLET
BILLETS > BILLET
BILLFISH *n* any of various fishes having elongated jaws, esp any fish of the family *Istiophoridae*, such as the spearfish and marlin
BILLFOLD *n* small folding case, usually of leather, for holding paper money, documents, etc
BILLFOLDS > BILLFOLD
BILLHEAD *n* printed form for making out bills
BILLHEADS > BILLHEAD
BILLHOOK *n* tool with a hooked blade, used for chopping etc
BILLHOOKS > BILLHOOK
BILLIARD *n* (modifier) of or relating to billiards
BILLIARDS *n* game played on a table with balls and a cue
BILLIE *same as* > BILLY
BILLIES > BILLY
BILLING *n* relative importance of a performer or act as reflected in the prominence given in programmes, advertisements, etc
BILLINGS > BILLING
BILLION *n* one thousand million ▷ *determiner* amounting to a billion
BILLIONS > BILLION
BILLIONTH > BILLION
BILLMAN *n* person who uses a billhook
BILLMEN > BILLMAN
BILLON *n* alloy consisting of gold or silver and a base metal, usually copper, used esp for coinage
BILLONS > BILLON
BILLOW *n* large sea wave ▷ *vb* rise up or swell out
BILLOWED > BILLOW
BILLOWIER > BILLOWY
BILLOWING > BILLOW
BILLOWS > BILLOW
BILLOWY *adj* full of or forming billows
BILLS > BILL
BILLY *n* metal can or pot for cooking on a camp fire
BILLYBOY *n* type of river barge
BILLYBOYS > BILLYBOY
BILLYCAN *same as* > BILLY
BILLYCANS > BILLYCAN
BILLYCOCK *n* any of several round-crowned brimmed hats of felt, such as the bowler
BILLYO *n like billyo* phrase used to emphasize or intensify something
BILLYOH *same as* > BILLYO
BILLYOHS > BILLYOH
BILLYOS > BILLYO
BILOBAR *same as* > BILOBATE
BILOBATE *adj* divided into or having two lobes
BILOBATED *same as* > BILOBATE
BILOBED *same as* > BILOBATE
BILOBULAR *adj* having two lobules
BILOCULAR *adj* divided into two chambers or cavities
BILSTED *n* American gum tree
BILSTEDS > BILSTED
BILTONG *n* strips of dried meat
BILTONGS > BILTONG
BIMA *same as* > BEMA
BIMAH *same as* > BEMA
BIMAHS > BIMAH
BIMANAL *same as* > BIMANOUS
BIMANOUS *adj* (of man and the higher primates) having two hands distinct in form and function from the feet
BIMANUAL *adj* using or requiring both hands
BIMAS > BIMA
BIMBASHI *n* Turkish military official
BIMBASHIS > BIMBASHI
BIMBETTE *n* particularly unintelligent bimbo
BIMBETTES > BIMBETTE
BIMBLE as in *bimble box* type of dense Australian tree
BIMBO *n* attractive but empty-headed young person, esp a woman
BIMBOES > BIMBO
BIMBOS > BIMBO
BIMENSAL *adj* occurring every two months
BIMESTER *n* period of two months
BIMESTERS > BIMESTER
BIMETAL *n* material made from two sheets of metal
BIMETALS > BIMETAL
BIMETHYL *another word for* > ETHANE
BIMETHYLS > BIMETHYL
BIMODAL *adj* having two modes
BIMONTHLY *adj* every two months ▷ *adv* every two months ▷ *n* periodical published every two months
BIMORPH *n* assembly of two piezoelectric crystals cemented together so that an applied voltage causes one to expand and the other to contract, converting electrical signals into mechanical energy. Conversely, bending can generate a voltage: used in loudspeakers, gramophone pick-ups, etc
BIMORPHS > BIMORPH
BIN *n* container for rubbish or for storing grain, coal, etc ▷ *vb* put in a rubbish bin
BINAL *adj* twofold
BINARIES > BINARY
BINARISM *n* state of being binary
BINARISMS > BINARISM
BINARY *adj* composed of, relating to, or involving two ▷ *n* something composed of two parts or things
BINATE *adj* occurring in two parts or in pairs
BINATELY > BINATE
BINAURAL *adj* relating to, having, or hearing with both ears
BIND *vb* make secure with or as if with a rope ▷ *n* annoying situation
BINDABLE > BIND
BINDER *n* firm cover for holding loose sheets of paper together
BINDERIES > BINDERY
BINDERS > BINDER
BINDERY *n* bookbindery
BINDHI *same as* > BINDI
BINDHIS > BINDHI
BINDI *n* decorative dot worn in the middle of the forehead, esp by Hindu women
BINDING > BIND
BINDINGLY > BIND
BINDINGS > BIND
BINDIS > BINDI
BINDLE *n* small packet
BINDLES > BINDLE
BINDS > BIND
BINDWEED *n* plant that twines around a support
BINDWEEDS > BINDWEED
BINE *n* climbing or twining stem of any of various plants, such as the woodbine or bindweed
BINER *n* clip used by climbers
BINERS > BINER
BINERVATE *adj* having two nerves
BINES > BINE
BING *n* heap or pile, esp of spoil from a mine
BINGE *n* bout of excessive indulgence, esp in drink ▷ *vb* indulge in a binge (esp of eating or drinking)
BINGED > BINGE
BINGEING > BINGE
BINGER *n* person who is addicted to crack cocaine
BINGERS > BINGER
BINGES > BINGE
BINGHI *n* Australian derogatory slang for an Aboriginal person
BINGHIS > BINGHI
BINGIES > BINGY
BINGING > BINGE
BINGLE *n* minor crash or upset, as in a car or on a surfboard ▷ *vb* layer (hair)
BINGLED > BINGLE
BINGLES > BINGLE
BINGLING > BINGLE
BINGO *n* gambling game in which numbers are called out and covered by the players on their individual cards ▷ *sentence substitute* cry by the winner of a game of bingo
BINGOES > BINGO
BINGOS > BINGO
BINGS > BING
BINGY *Australian slang for* > STOMACH
BINIOU *n* small high-pitched Breton bagpipe
BINIOUS > BINIOU
BINIT *n* (computing) early form of bit
BINITS > BINIT
BINK *n* ledge
BINKS > BINK
BINMAN *another name for* > DUSTMAN
BINMEN > BINMAN
BINNACLE *n* box holding a ship's compass
BINNACLES > BINNACLE
BINNED > BIN
BINNING > BIN
BINOCLE *n* binocular-style telescope
BINOCLES > BINOCLE
BINOCS > BINOCULAR
BINOCULAR *adj* involving both eyes
BINOMIAL *adj* consisting of two terms ▷ *n* mathematical expression consisting of two terms, such as $3x + 2y$
BINOMIALS > BINOMIAL
BINOMINAL *adj* of or denoting the binomial nomenclature ▷ *n* two-part taxonomic name
BINOVULAR *adj* relating to or derived from two different ova
BINS > BIN
BINT *n* derogatory term for a girl
BINTS > BINT
BINTURONG *n* arboreal SE Asian viverrine mammal, *Arctictis binturong*, closely related to the palm civets but larger and having long shaggy black hair
BINUCLEAR *adj* having two nuclei
BIO *short for* > BIOGRAPHY
BIOACTIVE *adj* able to interact with living system
BIOASSAY *n* method of determining the concentration, activity,

or effect of a change to substance by testing its effect on a living organism and comparing this with the activity of an agreed standard ▷ *vb* subject to a bioassay
BIOASSAYS > BIOASSAY
BIOBLAST *same as* > BIOPLAST
BIOBLASTS > BIOBLAST
BIOCENOSE *adj* living together in mutual dependence
BIOCHEMIC *adj* of or relating to chemical compounds, reactions, etc, occurring in living organisms
BIOCHIP *n* small glass or silicon plate containing an array of biochemical molecules or structures, used as a biosensor or in gene sequencing
BIOCHIPS > BIOCHIP
BIOCIDAL > BIOCIDE
BIOCIDE *n* substance used to destroy living things
BIOCIDES > BIOCIDE
BIOCLEAN *adj* free from harmful bacteria
BIOCYCLE *n* cycling of chemicals through the biosphere
BIOCYCLES > BIOCYCLE
BIODATA *n* information regarding an individual's education and work history, esp in the context of a selection process
BIODIESEL *n* biofuel intended for use in diesel engines
BIODOT *n* temperature-sensitive device stuck to the skin in order to monitor stress
BIODOTS > BIODOT
BIOETHIC > BIOETHICS
BIOETHICS *n* study of ethical problems arising from biological research and its applications in such fields as organ transplantation, genetic engineering, or artificial insemination
BIOFACT *n* item of biological information
BIOFACTS > BIOFACT
BIOFILM *n* thin layer of living organisms
BIOFILMS > BIOFILM
BIOFOULER *n* animal that obstructs or pollutes the environment
BIOFUEL *n* gaseous, liquid, or solid substance of biological origin that is used as a fuel
BIOFUELED *adj* running on biofuel
BIOFUELS > BIOFUEL
BIOG *short form of* > BIOGRAPHY
BIOGAS *n* gaseous fuel produced by the fermentation of organic waste
BIOGASES > BIOGAS
BIOGASSES > BIOGAS
BIOGEN *n* hypothetical protein assumed to be the basis of the formation and functioning of body cells and tissues
BIOGENIC *adj* originating from a living organism
BIOGENIES > BIOGENY
BIOGENOUS > BIOGENY
BIOGENS > BIOGEN
BIOGENY *n* principle that a living organism must originate from a parent form similar to itself
BIOGRAPH *vb* write biography of
BIOGRAPHS > BIOGRAPH
BIOGRAPHY *n* account of a person's life by another person
BIOGS > BIOG
BIOHAZARD *n* material of biological origin that is hazardous to humans
BIOHERM *n* mound of material laid down by sedentary marine organisms, esp a coral reef
BIOHERMS > BIOHERM
BIOLOGIC *adj* of or relating to biology ▷ *n* drug, such as a vaccine, that is derived from a living organism
BIOLOGICS > BIOLOGIC
BIOLOGIES > BIOLOGY
BIOLOGISM *n* explaining human behaviour through biology
BIOLOGIST > BIOLOGY
BIOLOGY *n* study of living organisms
BIOLYSES > BIOLYSIS
BIOLYSIS *n* death and dissolution of a living organism
BIOLYTIC > BIOLYSIS
BIOMARKER *n* substance, physiological characteristic, gene, etc that indicates, or may indicate, the presence of disease, a physiological abnormality, or a psychological condition
BIOMASS *n* total number of living organisms in a given area
BIOMASSES > BIOMASS
BIOME *n* major ecological community, extending over a large area and usually characterized by a dominant vegetation
BIOMES > BIOME
BIOMETER *n* device for measuring natural radiation
BIOMETERS > BIOMETER
BIOMETRIC *adj* of any automated system using physiological or behavioural traits as a means of identification.
BIOMETRY *n* analysis of biological data using mathematical and statistical methods, especially for purposes of identification
BIOMINING *n* using plants, etc to collect precious metals for extraction
BIOMORPH *n* form or pattern resembling living thing
BIOMORPHS > BIOMORPH
BIONIC *adj* having a part of the body that is operated electronically
BIONICS *n* study of biological functions in order to develop electronic equipment that operates similarly
BIONOMIC > BIONOMICS
BIONOMICS *a less common name for* > ECOLOGY
BIONOMIES > BIONOMY
BIONOMIST > BIONOMICS
BIONOMY *n* laws of life
BIONT *n* living thing
BIONTIC > BIONT
BIONTS > BIONT
BIOPARENT *n* biological parent
BIOPHILIA *n* innate love for the natural world, supposed to be felt universally by humankind
BIOPHOR *n* hypothetical material particle
BIOPHORE *same as* > BIOPHOR
BIOPHORES > BIOPHORE
BIOPHORS > BIOPHOR
BIOPIC *n* film based on the life of a famous person
BIOPICS > BIOPIC
BIOPIRACY *n* use of wild plants by international companies to develop medicines, without recompensing the countries from which they are taken
BIOPIRATE > BIOPIRACY
BIOPLASM *n* living matter
BIOPLASMS > BIOPLASM
BIOPLAST *n* very small unit of bioplasm
BIOPLASTS > BIOPLAST
BIOPSIC > BIOPSY
BIOPSIED > BIOPSY
BIOPSIES > BIOPSY
BIOPSY *n* examination of tissue from a living body ▷ *vb* perform a biopsy on
BIOPSYING > BIOPSY
BIOPTIC > BIOPSY
BIOREGION *n* area in which climate and environment are consistent
BIORHYTHM *n* complex recurring pattern of physiological states, believed to affect physical, emotional, and mental states
BIOS > BIO
BIOSAFETY *n* precautions taken to control the cultivation and distribution of genetically modified crops and products
BIOSCOPE *n* kind of early film projector
BIOSCOPES > BIOSCOPE
BIOSCOPY *n* examination of a body to determine whether it is alive
BIOSENSOR *n* device used to monitor living systems
BIOSOCIAL *adj* relating to the interaction of biological and social elements
BIOSOLID *n* residue from treated sewage
BIOSOLIDS > BIOSOLID
BIOSPHERE *n* part of the earth's surface and atmosphere inhabited by living things
BIOSTABLE *adj* resistant to the effects of microorganisms
BIOSTATIC *adj* of or relating to the branch of biology that deals with the structure of organisms in relation to their function
BIOSTROME *n* rock layer consisting of a deposit of organic material, such as fossils
BIOTA *n* plant and animal life of a particular region or period
BIOTAS > BIOTA
BIOTECH *n* biotechnology
BIOTECHS > BIOTECH
BIOTERROR *n* use of biological weapons by terrorists
BIOTIC *adj* of or relating to living organisms ▷ *n* living organism
BIOTICAL *same as* > BIOTIC
BIOTICS > BIOTIC
BIOTIN *n* vitamin of the B complex, abundant in egg yolk and liver
BIOTINS > BIOTIN
BIOTITE *n* black or dark green mineral of the mica group
BIOTITES > BIOTITE
BIOTITIC > BIOTITE
BIOTOPE *n* small area, such as the bark of a tree, that supports its own distinctive community

BIOTOPES > BIOTOPE
BIOTOXIN *n* toxic substance produced by a living organism
BIOTOXINS > BIOTOXIN
BIOTRON *n* climate-control chamber
BIOTRONS > BIOTRON
BIOTROPH *n* parasitic organism, esp a fungus
BIOTROPHS > BIOTROPH
BIOTURBED *adj* stirred by organisms
BIOTYPE *n* group of genetically identical plants within a species, produced by apomixis
BIOTYPES > BIOTYPE
BIOTYPIC > BIOTYPE
BIOVULAR *adj* (of twins) from two separate eggs
BIOWEAPON *n* living organism or a toxic product manufactured from it, used to kill or incapacitate
BIPACK *n* obsolete filming process
BIPACKS > BIPACK
BIPAROUS *adj* producing offspring in pairs
BIPARTED *adj* divided into two parts
BIPARTITE *adj* consisting of two parts
BIPARTY *adj* involving two parties
BIPED *n* animal with two feet ▷ *adj* having two feet
BIPEDAL *adj* having two feet
BIPEDALLY > BIPEDAL
BIPEDS > BIPED
BIPHASIC *adj* having two phases
BIPHENYL *n* white or colourless crystalline solid used as a heat-transfer agent
BIPHENYLS > BIPHENYL
BIPINNATE *adj* (of pinnate leaves) having the leaflets themselves divided into smaller leaflets
BIPLANE *n* aeroplane with two sets of wings, one above the other
BIPLANES > BIPLANE
BIPOD *n* two-legged support or stand
BIPODS > BIPOD
BIPOLAR *adj* having two poles
BIPRISM *n* prism having a highly obtuse angle to facilitate beam splitting
BIPRISMS > BIPRISM
BIPYRAMID *n* geometrical form consisting of two pyramids with a common polygonal base
BIRACIAL *adj* for, representing, or including members of two races, esp White and Black
BIRADIAL *adj* showing both bilateral and radial symmetry, as certain sea anemones
BIRADICAL *n* molecule with two centres
BIRAMOSE *same as* > BIRAMOUS
BIRAMOUS *adj* divided into two parts, as the appendages of crustaceans
BIRCH *n* tree with thin peeling bark ▷ *vb* flog with a birch
BIRCHBARK as in *birchbark biting* Native Canadian craft in which designs are bitten onto bark from birch trees
BIRCHED > BIRCH
BIRCHEN > BIRCH
BIRCHES > BIRCH
BIRCHING > BIRCH
BIRD *n* creature with feathers and wings, most types of which can fly ▷ *vb* hunt for birds
BIRDBATH *n* small basin or trough for birds to bathe in, usually in a garden
BIRDBATHS > BIRDBATH
BIRDBRAIN *n* stupid person
BIRDCAGE *n* wire or wicker cage in which captive birds are kept
BIRDCAGES > BIRDCAGE
BIRDCALL *n* characteristic call or song of a bird
BIRDCALLS > BIRDCALL
BIRDDOG *n* dog used or trained to retrieve game birds
BIRDDOGS > BIRDDOG
BIRDED > BIRD
BIRDER *n* birdwatcher
BIRDERS > BIRDER
BIRDFARM *n* place where birds are kept
BIRDFARMS > BIRDFARM
BIRDFEED *n* food for birds
BIRDFEEDS > BIRDFEED
BIRDHOUSE *n* small shelter or box for birds to nest in
BIRDIE *n* score of one stroke under par for a hole ▷ *vb* play (a hole) in one stroke under par
BIRDIED > BIRDIE
BIRDIEING > BIRDIE
BIRDIES > BIRDIE
BIRDING > BIRD
BIRDINGS > BIRD
BIRDLIFE *n* birds collectively
BIRDLIKE > BIRD
BIRDLIME *n* sticky substance smeared on twigs to catch small birds ▷ *vb* smear (twigs) with birdlime to catch (small birds)
BIRDLIMED > BIRDLIME
BIRDLIMES > BIRDLIME
BIRDMAN *n* man concerned with birds, such as a fowler or ornithologist
BIRDMEN > BIRDMAN
BIRDS > BIRD
BIRDSEED *n* mixture of various kinds of seeds for feeding cage birds
BIRDSEEDS > BIRDSEED
BIRDSEYE *n* type of primrose
BIRDSEYES > BIRDSEYE
BIRDSHOT *n* small pellets designed for shooting birds
BIRDSHOTS > BIRDSHOT
BIRDSONG *n* musical call of a bird or birds
BIRDSONGS > BIRDSONG
BIRDWATCH *vb* watch birds
BIRDWING *n* type of butterfly
BIRDWINGS > BIRDWING
BIREME *n* ancient galley having two banks of oars
BIREMES > BIREME
BIRETTA *n* stiff square cap worn by the Catholic clergy
BIRETTAS > BIRETTA
BIRIANI *same as* > BIRYANI
BIRIANIS > BIRIANI
BIRIYANI *same as* > BIRIANI
BIRIYANIS > BIRIYANI
BIRK *n* birch tree ▷ *adj* consisting or made of birch
BIRKEN *adj* relating to the birch tree
BIRKIE *n* spirited or lively person ▷ *adj* lively
BIRKIER > BIRKIE
BIRKIES > BIRKIE
BIRKIEST > BIRKIE
BIRKS > BIRK
BIRL *same as* > BURL
BIRLE *same as* > BURL
BIRLED > BIRL
BIRLER > BIRL
BIRLERS > BIRL
BIRLES > BIRLE
BIRLIEMAN *n* judge dealing with local law
BIRLIEMEN > BIRLIEMAN
BIRLING > BIRL
BIRLINGS > BIRL
BIRLINN *n* small Scottish book
BIRLINNS > BIRLINN
BIRLS > BIRL
BIRO *n* tradename of a kind of ballpoint pen
BIROS > BIRO
BIRR *vb* make or cause to make a whirring sound ▷ *n* whirring sound
BIRRED > BIRR
BIRRETTA *same as* > BIRETTA
BIRRETTAS > BIRRETTA
BIRRING > BIRR
BIRROTCH *n* Ethiopian monetary unit
BIRRS > BIRR
BIRSE *n* bristle
BIRSES > BIRSE
BIRSIER > BIRSY
BIRSIEST > BIRSY
BIRSLE *vb* roast
BIRSLED > BIRSLE
BIRSLES > BIRSLE
BIRSLING > BIRSLE
BIRSY *adj* bristly
BIRTH *n* process of bearing young ▷ *vb* give birth to
BIRTHDAY *n* anniversary of the day of one's birth
BIRTHDAYS > BIRTHDAY
BIRTHDOM *n* birthright
BIRTHDOMS > BIRTHDOM
BIRTHED > BIRTH
BIRTHING > BIRTH
BIRTHINGS > BIRTH
BIRTHMARK *n* blemish on the skin formed before birth
BIRTHNAME *n* name person was born with
BIRTHRATE *n* ratio of live births in a specified area, group, etc, to the population of that area, etc, usually expressed per 1000 population per year
BIRTHROOT *n* any of several North American plants of the genus *Trillium*, esp *T. erectum*, whose tuber-like roots were formerly used by the American Indians as an aid in childbirth: family *Trilliaceae*
BIRTHS > BIRTH
BIRTHWORT *n* any of several climbing plants of the genus *Aristolochia*, esp *A. clematitis* of Europe, once believed to ease childbirth: family *Aristolochiaceae*
BIRYANI *n* any of a variety of Indian dishes made with rice, highly flavoured and coloured with saffron or turmeric, mixed with meat or fish
BIRYANIS > BIRYANI
BIS *adv* twice ▷ *sentence substitute* encore! again!
BISCACHA *same as* > VISCACHA
BISCACHAS > BISCACHA
BISCOTTI > BISCOTTO
BISCOTTO *n* small Italian biscuit
BISCUIT *n* small flat dry sweet or plain cake ▷ *adj* pale brown
BISCUITS > BISCUIT
BISCUITY *adj* reminiscent of biscuit
BISE *n* cold dry northerly wind in Switzerland and the neighbouring parts of France and Italy, usually in the spring

BISECT *vb* divide into two equal parts
BISECTED > BISECT
BISECTING > BISECT
BISECTION > BISECT
BISECTOR *n* straight line or plane that bisects an angle
BISECTORS > BISECTOR
BISECTRIX *n* bisector of the angle between the optic axes of a crystal
BISECTS > BISECT
BISERIAL *adj* in two rows
BISERIATE *adj* (of plant parts, such as petals) arranged in two whorls, cycles, rows, or series
BISERRATE *adj* (of leaf margins, etc) having serrations that are themselves serrate
BISES > BISE
BISEXUAL *adj* sexually attracted to both men and women ▷ *n* bisexual person
BISEXUALS > BISEXUAL
BISH *n* mistake
BISHES > BISH
BISHOP *n* clergyman who governs a diocese ▷ *vb* make a bishop
BISHOPDOM *n* jurisdiction of bishop
BISHOPED > BISHOP
BISHOPESS > BISHOP
BISHOPING > BISHOP
BISHOPRIC *n* diocese or office of a bishop
BISHOPS > BISHOP
BISK *a less common spelling of* > BISQUE
BISKS > BISK
BISMAR *n* type of weighing scale
BISMARS > BISMAR
BISMILLAH *interj* in the name of Allah, a preface to all except one of the surahs of the Koran, used by Muslims as a blessing before eating or some other action
BISMUTH *n* pinkish-white metallic element
BISMUTHAL > BISMUTH
BISMUTHIC *adj* of or containing bismuth in the pentavalent state
BISMUTHS > BISMUTH
BISNAGA *n* type of cactus
BISNAGAS > BISNAGA
BISON *same as* > BUFFALO
BISONS > BISON
BISONTINE *adj* relating to bison
BISQUE *n* thick rich soup made from shellfish
BISQUES > BISQUE
BISSON *adj* blind
BIST *a form of the second person singular of* > BE
BISTABLE *adj* (of an electronic system) having two stable states ▷ *n* bistable system
BISTABLES > BISTABLE
BISTATE *adj* involving two states
BISTER *same as* > BESTIR
BISTERED > BISTER
BISTERS > BISTER
BISTORT *n* Eurasian polygonaceous plant, *Polygonum bistorta*, having leaf stipules fused to form a tube around the stem and a spike of small pink flowers
BISTORTS > BISTORT
BISTOURY *n* long surgical knife with a narrow blade
BISTRE *n* transparent water-soluble brownish-yellow pigment made by boiling the soot of wood, used for pen and wash drawings
BISTRED > BISTRE
BISTRES > BISTRE
BISTRO *n* small restaurant
BISTROIC > BISTRO
BISTROS > BISTRO
BISULCATE *adj* marked by two grooves
BISULFATE *n* bisulphate
BISULFIDE *n* bisulphide
BISULFITE *n* bisulphite
BIT *n* small piece, portion, or quantity
BITABLE > BITE
BITCH *n* female dog, fox, or wolf ▷ *vb* complain or grumble
BITCHED > BITCH
BITCHEN *same as* > BITCHING
BITCHERY *n* spiteful talk
BITCHES > BITCH
BITCHFEST *n* malicious and spiteful discussion of people, events, etc
BITCHIER > BITCHY
BITCHIEST > BITCHY
BITCHILY > BITCHY
BITCHING *adj* wonderful or excellent
BITCHY *adj* spiteful or malicious
BITE *vb* grip, tear, or puncture the skin, as with the teeth or jaws ▷ *n* act of biting
BITEABLE > BITE
BITEPLATE *n* device used by dentists
BITER > BITE
BITERS > BITE
BITES > BITE
BITESIZE *adj* small enough to put in the mouth whole
BITEWING *n* dental x-ray film
BITEWINGS > BITEWING
BITING > BITE
BITINGLY > BITE
BITINGS > BITE
BITLESS *adj* without a bit
BITMAP *n* picture created by colour or shading on a visual display unit ▷ *vb* create a bitmap of
BITMAPPED > BITMAP
BITMAPS > BITMAP
BITO *n* African and Asian tree
BITONAL *adj* consisting of black and white tones
BITOS > BITO
BITOU *bitou bush* type of sprawling woody shrub
BITS > BIT
BITSER *n* mongrel dog
BITSERS > BITSER
BITSIER > BITSY
BITSIEST > BITSY
BITSTOCK *n* handle or stock of a tool into which a drilling bit is fixed
BITSTOCKS > BITSTOCK
BITSTREAM *n* sequence of digital data
BITSY *adj* very small
BITT *n* one of a pair of strong posts on the deck of a ship for securing mooring and other lines ▷ *vb* secure (a line) by means of a bitt
BITTACLE *same as* > BINNACLE
BITTACLES > BITTACLE
BITTE *interj* you're welcome
BITTED > BITT
BITTEN > BITE
BITTER *adj* having a sharp unpleasant taste ▷ *n* beer with a slightly bitter taste ▷ *adv* very ▷ *vb* make or become bitter
BITTERED > BITTER
BITTERER > BITTER
BITTEREST > BITTER
BITTERING > BITTER
BITTERISH > BITTER
BITTERLY > BITTER
BITTERN *n* wading marsh bird with a booming call
BITTERNS > BITTERN
BITTERNUT *n* E North American hickory tree, *Carya cordiformis*, with thin-shelled nuts and bitter kernels
BITTERS *pl n* bitter-tasting spirits flavoured with plant extracts
BITTIE *n* small piece
BITTIER > BITTY
BITTIES > BITTIE
BITTIEST > BITTY
BITTINESS > BITTY
BITTING > BITT
BITTINGS > BITT
BITTOCK *n* small amount
BITTOCKS > BITTOCK
BITTOR *n* bittern
BITTORS > BITTOR
BITTOUR *same as* > BITTOR
BITTOURS > BITTOUR
BITTS > BITT
BITTUR *same as* > BITTOR
BITTURS > BITTUR
BITTY *adj* lacking unity, disjointed
BITUMED *adj* covered with bitumen
BITUMEN *n* black sticky substance obtained from tar or petrol
BITUMENS > BITUMEN
BIUNIQUE *adj* one-to-one correspondence
BIVALENCE *n* semantic principle that there are exactly two truth values, so that every meaningful statement is either true or false
BIVALENCY > BIVALENT
BIVALENT *adj* (of homologous chromosomes) associated together in pairs ▷ *n* structure formed during meiosis consisting of two homologous chromosomes associated together
BIVALENTS > BIVALENT
BIVALVATE *same as* > BIVALVE
BIVALVE *adj* (marine mollusc) with two hinged segments to its shell ▷ *n* sea creature, such as an oyster or mussel, that has a shell consisting of two hinged valves and breathes through gills
BIVALVED > BIVALVE
BIVALVES > BIVALVE
BIVARIANT *same as* > BIVARIATE
BIVARIATE *adj* (of a distribution) involving two random variables, not necessarily independent of one another
BIVIA > BIVIUM
BIVINYL *another word for* > BUTADIENE
BIVINYLS > BIVINYL
BIVIOUS *adj* offering a choice of two different ways
BIVIUM *n* parting of ways
BIVOUAC *n* temporary camp in the open air ▷ *vb* camp in a bivouac
BIVOUACKS > BIVOUAC
BIVOUACS > BIVOUAC
BIVVIED > BIVVY
BIVVIES > BIVVY
BIVVY *n* small tent or shelter ▷ *vb* camp in a bivouac
BIVVYING > BIVVY
BIWEEKLY *adv* every two weeks ▷ *n* periodical published every two weeks
BIYEARLY *adv* every two years
BIZ *n* business

BIZARRE *adj* odd or unusual ▷ *n* bizarre thing
BIZARRELY > BIZARRE
BIZARRES > BIZARRE
BIZARRO *n* bizarre person
BIZARROS > BIZARRO
BIZAZZ *same as* > PIZAZZ
BIZAZZES > BIZAZZ
BIZCACHA *same as* > VISCACHA
BIZCACHAS > BIZCACHA
BIZE *n* dry, cold wind in France
BIZES > BIZE
BIZNAGA *same as* > BISNAGA
BIZNAGAS > BIZNAGA
BIZONAL > BIZONE
BIZONE *n* place comprising two zones
BIZONES > BIZONE
BIZZES > BIZ
BIZZIES > BIZZY
BIZZO *n* empty and irrelevant talk or ideas
BIZZOS > BIZZO
BIZZY *n* policeman
BLAB *vb* reveal (secrets) indiscreetly
BLABBED > BLAB
BLABBER *vb* talk without thinking ▷ *n* person who blabs
BLABBERED > BLABBER
BLABBERS > BLABBER
BLABBING > BLAB
BLABBINGS > BLAB
BLABBY *adj* talking too much; indiscreet
BLABS > BLAB
BLACK *adj* of the darkest colour, like coal ▷ *n* darkest colour ▷ *vb* make black
BLACKBALL *vb* exclude from a group ▷ *n* hard boiled sweet with black-and-white stripes
BLACKBAND *n* type of iron ore
BLACKBIRD *n* common European thrush ▷ *vb* (formerly) to kidnap and sell into slavery
BLACKBODY *n* hypothetical body that would be capable of absorbing all the electromagnetic radiation falling on it
BLACKBOY *n* grass tree
BLACKBOYS > BLACKBOY
BLACKBUCK *n* Indian antelope, *Antilope cervicapra*, the male of which has spiral horns, a dark back, and a white belly
BLACKBUTT *n* Australian eucalyptus tree with hard wood used as timber
BLACKCAP *n* brownish-grey warbler, the male of which has a black crown
BLACKCAPS > BLACKCAP
BLACKCOCK *n* male of the black grouse
BLACKDAMP *n* air that is low in oxygen content and high in carbon dioxide as a result of an explosion in a mine
BLACKED > BLACK
BLACKEN *vb* make or become black
BLACKENED > BLACKEN
BLACKENER > BLACKEN
BLACKENS > BLACKEN
BLACKER > BLACK
BLACKEST > BLACK
BLACKFACE *n* performer made up to imitate a Black person
BLACKFIN *n* type of tuna
BLACKFINS > BLACKFIN
BLACKFISH *n* small dark Australian estuary fish
BLACKFLY *n* black aphid, *Aphis fabae*, that infests beans, sugar beet, and other plants
BLACKGAME *n* large N European grouse
BLACKGUM *n* US tree
BLACKGUMS > BLACKGUM
BLACKHEAD *n* black-tipped plug of fatty matter clogging a skin pore
BLACKING *n* preparation for giving a black finish to shoes, metals, etc
BLACKINGS > BLACKING
BLACKISH > BLACK
BLACKJACK *n* pontoon or a similar card game ▷ *vb* hit with or as if with a kind of truncheon
BLACKLAND *n* dark soil
BLACKLEAD *another name for* > GRAPHITE
BLACKLEG *n* person who continues to work during a strike ▷ *vb* refuse to join a strike
BLACKLEGS > BLACKLEG
BLACKLIST *n* list of people or organizations considered untrustworthy etc ▷ *vb* put on a blacklist
BLACKLY > BLACK
BLACKMAIL *n* act of attempting to extort money by threats ▷ *vb* (attempt to) obtain money by blackmail
BLACKNESS > BLACK
BLACKOUT *n* extinguishing of all light as a precaution against an air attack
BLACKOUTS > BLACKOUT
BLACKPOLL *n* North American warbler, *Dendroica striata*, the male of which has a black-and-white head
BLACKS > BLACK
BLACKTAIL *n* variety of mule deer having a black tail
BLACKTOP *n* bituminous mixture used for paving
BLACKTOPS > BLACKTOP
BLACKWASH *n* wash for colouring a surface black
BLACKWOOD *n* tall Australian acacia tree, *A. melanoxylon*, having small clusters of flowers and curved pods and yielding highly valued black timber
BLAD *same as* > BLAUD
BLADDED > BLAD
BLADDER *n* sac in the body where urine is held
BLADDERED *adj* intoxicated
BLADDERS > BLADDER
BLADDERY > BLADDER
BLADDING > BLAD
BLADE *n* cutting edge of a weapon or tool
BLADED > BLADE
BLADELESS > BLADE
BLADELIKE > BLADE
BLADER *n* person skating with in-line skates
BLADERS > BLADER
BLADES > BLADE
BLADEWORK *n* rowing technique
BLADING *n* act or instance of skating with in-line skates
BLADINGS > BLADING
BLADS > BLAD
BLADY as in *blady grass* coarse leafy Australasian grass
BLAE *adj* bluish-grey
BLAEBERRY *another name for* > BILBERRY
BLAER > BLAE
BLAES *n* hardened clay or shale, esp when crushed and used to form the top layer of a sports pitch: bluish-grey or reddish in colour
BLAEST > BLAE
BLAFF *n* West Indian stew
BLAFFS > BLAFF
BLAG *vb* obtain by wheedling or cadging ▷ *n* robbery, esp with violence
BLAGGED > BLAG
BLAGGER > BLAG
BLAGGERS > BLAG
BLAGGING > BLAG
BLAGGINGS > BLAG
BLAGS > BLAG
BLAGUE *n* pretentious but empty talk
BLAGUER > BLAGUE
BLAGUERS > BLAGUE
BLAGUES > BLAGUE
BLAGUEUR *n* bluffer
BLAGUEURS > BLAGUEUR
BLAH *n* worthless or silly talk ▷ *adj* uninteresting ▷ *vb* talk nonsense or boringly
BLAHED > BLAH
BLAHING > BLAH
BLAHS > BLAH
BLAIN *n* blister, blotch, or sore on the skin
BLAINS > BLAIN
BLAISE *same as* > BLAES
BLAIZE *same as* > BLAES
BLAM *n* representation of the sound of a bullet being fired
BLAMABLE > BLAME
BLAMABLY > BLAME
BLAME *vb* consider (someone) responsible ▷ *n* responsibility for something that is wrong
BLAMEABLE > BLAME
BLAMEABLY > BLAME
BLAMED *euphemistic word for* > DAMNED
BLAMEFUL *adj* deserving blame
BLAMELESS *adj* free from blame
BLAMER > BLAME
BLAMERS > BLAME
BLAMES > BLAME
BLAMING > BLAME
BLAMS > BLAM
BLANCH *vb* become white or pale
BLANCHED > BLANCH
BLANCHER > BLANCH
BLANCHERS > BLANCH
BLANCHES > BLANCH
BLANCHING > BLANCH
BLANCO *n* whitening substance ▷ *vb* whiten (something) with blanco
BLANCOED > BLANCO
BLANCOING > BLANCO
BLANCOS > BLANCO
BLAND *adj* dull and uninteresting ▷ *n* bland thing
BLANDER > BLAND
BLANDEST > BLAND
BLANDISH *vb* persuade by mild flattery
BLANDLY > BLAND
BLANDNESS > BLAND
BLANDS > BLAND
BLANK *adj* not written on ▷ *n* empty space ▷ *vb* cross out, blot, or obscure
BLANKED > BLANK
BLANKER > BLANK
BLANKEST > BLANK
BLANKET *n* large thick cloth used as covering for a bed ▷ *adj* applying to a wide group of people, situations, conditions, etc ▷ *vb* cover as with a blanket
BLANKETED > BLANKET
BLANKETS > BLANKET
BLANKETY *adv* euphemism for any taboo word
BLANKIES > BLANKY
BLANKING > BLANK
BLANKINGS > BLANK
BLANKLY > BLANK
BLANKNESS > BLANK
BLANKS > BLANK
BLANKY *n* comfort blanket
BLANQUET *n* variety of pear

BLANQUETS > BLANQUET
BLARE *vb* sound loudly and harshly ▷ *n* loud harsh noise
BLARED > BLARE
BLARES > BLARE
BLARING > BLARE
BLARNEY *n* flattering talk ▷ *vb* cajole with flattery
BLARNEYED > BLARNEY
BLARNEYS > BLARNEY
BLART *vb* sound loudly and harshly
BLARTED > BLART
BLARTING > BLART
BLARTS > BLART
BLASE *adj* indifferent or bored through familiarity
BLASH *n* splash
BLASHES > BLASH
BLASHIER > BLASHY
BLASHIEST > BLASHY
BLASHY *adj* windy and rainy
BLASPHEME *vb* speak disrespectfully of (God or sacred things)
BLASPHEMY *n* behaviour or language that shows disrespect for God or sacred things
BLAST *n* explosion ▷ *vb* blow up (a rock etc) with explosives ▷ *interj* expression of annoyance
BLASTED *adv* extreme or extremely ▷ *adj* blighted or withered
BLASTEMA *n* mass of undifferentiated animal cells that will develop into an organ or tissue: present at the site of regeneration of a lost part
BLASTEMAL > BLASTEMA
BLASTEMAS > BLASTEMA
BLASTEMIC > BLASTEMA
BLASTER > BLAST
BLASTERS > BLAST
BLASTIE *n* ugly creature
BLASTIER > BLASTY
BLASTIES > BLASTIE
BLASTIEST > BLASTY
BLASTING *n* distortion of sound caused by overloading certain components of a radio system
BLASTINGS > BLASTING
BLASTMENT *n* something that frustrates one's plans
BLASTOFF *n* launching of a rocket
BLASTOFFS > BLASTOFF
BLASTOID *n* extinct echinoderm found in fossil form
BLASTOIDS > BLASTOID
BLASTOMA *n* tumour composed of embryonic tissue that has not yet developed a specialized function
BLASTOMAS > BLASTOMA
BLASTOPOR *n* opening of the archenteron in the gastrula that develops into the anus of some animals
BLASTS > BLAST
BLASTULA *n* early form of an animal embryo that develops from a morula, consisting of a sphere of cells with a central cavity
BLASTULAE > BLASTULA
BLASTULAR > BLASTULA
BLASTULAS > BLASTULA
BLASTY *adj* gusty
BLAT *vb* cry out or bleat like a sheep
BLATANCY > BLATANT
BLATANT *adj* glaringly obvious
BLATANTLY > BLATANT
BLATE *adj* shy; ill at ease
BLATER > BLATE
BLATEST > BLATE
BLATHER *vb* speak foolishly ▷ *n* foolish talk
BLATHERED > BLATHER
BLATHERER > BLATHER
BLATHERS > BLATHER
BLATS > BLAT
BLATT *n* newspaper
BLATTANT *same as* > BLATANT
BLATTED > BLAT
BLATTER *n, vb* prattle
BLATTERED > BLATTER
BLATTERS > BLATTER
BLATTING > BLAT
BLATTS > BLATT
BLAUBOK *n* South African antelope
BLAUBOKS > BLAUBOK
BLAUD *vb* slap
BLAUDED > BLAUD
BLAUDING > BLAUD
BLAUDS > BLAUD
BLAW *vb* blow
BLAWED > BLAW
BLAWING > BLAW
BLAWN > BLAW
BLAWORT *n* harebell
BLAWORTS > BLAWORT
BLAWS > BLAW
BLAY *n* small river fish
BLAYS > BLAY
BLAZE *n* strong fire or flame ▷ *vb* burn or shine brightly
BLAZED > BLAZE
BLAZER *n* lightweight jacket, often in the colours of a school etc
BLAZERED > BLAZER
BLAZERS > BLAZER
BLAZES *pl n* hell
BLAZING > BLAZE
BLAZINGLY > BLAZING
BLAZON *vb* proclaim publicly ▷ *n* coat of arms
BLAZONED > BLAZON
BLAZONER > BLAZON
BLAZONERS > BLAZON
BLAZONING > BLAZON
BLAZONRY *n* art or process of describing heraldic arms in proper form
BLAZONS > BLAZON
BLEACH *vb* make or become white or colourless ▷ *n* bleaching agent
BLEACHED > BLEACH
BLEACHER > BLEACH
BLEACHERS *pl n* tier of seats in a sports stadium, etc, that are unroofed and inexpensive
BLEACHERY *n* place where bleaching is carried out
BLEACHES > BLEACH
BLEACHING > BLEACH
BLEAK *adj* exposed and barren ▷ *n* any slender silvery European cyprinid fish of the genus *Alburnus*, esp *A. lucidus*, occurring in slow-flowing rivers
BLEAKER > BLEAK
BLEAKEST > BLEAK
BLEAKISH > BLEAK
BLEAKLY > BLEAK
BLEAKNESS > BLEAK
BLEAKS > BLEAK
BLEAKY *same as* > BLEAK
BLEAR *vb* make (eyes or sight) dim with or as if with tears ▷ *adj* bleary
BLEARED > BLEAR
BLEARER > BLEAR
BLEAREST > BLEAR
BLEAREYED *adj* with eyes blurred, as with old age or after waking
BLEARIER > BLEARY
BLEARIEST > BLEARY
BLEARILY > BLEARY
BLEARING > BLEAR
BLEARS > BLEAR
BLEARY *adj* with eyes dimmed, as by tears or tiredness
BLEAT *vb* (of a sheep, goat, or calf) utter its plaintive cry ▷ *n* cry of sheep, goats, and calves
BLEATED > BLEAT
BLEATER > BLEAT
BLEATERS > BLEAT
BLEATING > BLEAT
BLEATINGS > BLEAT
BLEATS > BLEAT
BLEB *n* fluid-filled blister on the skin
BLEBBING *n* formation of bleb
BLEBBINGS > BLEB
BLEBBY > BLEB
BLEBS > BLEB
BLED > BLEED
BLEE *n* complexion; hue
BLEED *vb* lose or emit blood
BLEEDER *n* despicable person
BLEEDERS > BLEEDER
BLEEDING > BLEED
BLEEDINGS > BLEED
BLEEDS > BLEED
BLEEP *n* high-pitched signal or beep ▷ *vb* make such a noise
BLEEPED > BLEEP
BLEEPER *n* small portable radio receiver that makes a bleeping signal
BLEEPERS > BLEEPER
BLEEPING > BLEEP
BLEEPS > BLEEP
BLEES > BLEE
BLELLUM *n* babbler; blusterer
BLELLUMS > BLELLUM
BLEMISH *n* defect or stain ▷ *vb* spoil or tarnish
BLEMISHED > BLEMISH
BLEMISHER > BLEMISH
BLEMISHES > BLEMISH
BLENCH *vb* shy away, as in fear
BLENCHED > BLENCH
BLENCHER > BLENCH
BLENCHERS > BLENCH
BLENCHES > BLENCH
BLENCHING > BLENCH
BLEND *vb* mix or mingle (components or ingredients) ▷ *n* mixture
BLENDE *n* mineral consisting mainly of zinc sulphide
BLENDED > BLEND
BLENDER *n* electrical appliance for puréeing vegetables etc
BLENDERS > BLENDER
BLENDES > BLENDE
BLENDING > BLEND
BLENDINGS > BLEND
BLENDS > BLEND
BLENNIES > BLENNY
BLENNIOID *adj* of, relating to, or belonging to the *Blennioidea*, a large suborder of small mainly marine spiny-finned fishes having an elongated body with reduced pelvic fins. The group includes the blennies, butterfish, and gunnel ▷ *n* any fish belonging to the *Blennioidea*
BLENNY *n* small fish with a tapering scaleless body
BLENT *a past participle of* > BLEND
BLERT *n* foolish person
BLERTS > BLERT
BLESBOK *n* antelope, *Damaliscus dorcas* (or *albifrons*), of southern Africa. The coat is a deep reddish-brown with a white blaze between the eyes
BLESBOKS > BLESBOK
BLESBUCK *same as* > BLESBOK
BLESBUCKS > BLESBUCK
BLESS *vb* make holy by means of a religious rite
BLESSED > BLESS
BLESSEDER > BLESS
BLESSEDLY > BLESS
BLESSER > BLESS
BLESSERS > BLESS
BLESSES > BLESS

BLESSING > BLESS
BLESSINGS > BLESS
BLEST > BLESS
BLET *n* state of softness or decay in certain fruits, such as the medlar, brought about by overripening ▷ *vb* go soft
BLETHER *same as* > BLATHER
BLETHERED > BLETHER
BLETHERER > BLETHER
BLETHERS > BLETHER
BLETS > BLET
BLETTED > BLET
BLETTING > BLET
BLEUATRE *adj* blueish
BLEW > BLOW
BLEWART *same as* > BLAWORT
BLEWARTS > BLEWART
BLEWITS *n* edible saprotroph agaricaceous fungus, *Tricholoma saevum*, having a pale brown cap and bluish stalk
BLEWITSES > BLEWITS
BLEY *same as* > BLAY
BLEYS > BLEY
BLIGHT *n* person or thing that spoils or prevents growth ▷ *vb* cause to suffer a blight
BLIGHTED > BLIGHT
BLIGHTER *n* irritating person
BLIGHTERS > BLIGHTER
BLIGHTIES > BLIGHTY
BLIGHTING > BLIGHT
BLIGHTS > BLIGHT
BLIGHTY *n* home country; home leave
BLIKSEM *interj* South African expression of surprise
BLIMBING *same as* > BILIMBI
BLIMBINGS > BLIMBING
BLIMEY *interj* exclamation of surprise or annoyance
BLIMP *n* small airship
BLIMPISH *adj* complacent and reactionary
BLIMPS > BLIMP
BLIMY *same as* > BLIMEY
BLIN *Scots word for* > BLIND
BLIND *adj* unable to see ▷ *vb* deprive of sight ▷ *n* covering for a window
BLINDAGE *n* (esp formerly) a protective screen or structure, as over a trench
BLINDAGES > BLINDAGE
BLINDED > BLIND
BLINDER > BLIND
BLINDERS > BLIND
BLINDEST > BLIND
BLINDFISH *n* any of various small fishes, esp the cavefish, that have rudimentary or functionless eyes and occur in subterranean streams
BLINDFOLD *vb* prevent (a person) from seeing by covering the eyes ▷ *n* piece of cloth used to cover the eyes ▷ *adv* with the eyes covered by a cloth
BLINDGUT *same as* > CAECUM
BLINDGUTS > BLINDGUT
BLINDING *n* sand or grit spread over a road surface to fill up cracks ▷ *adj* making one blind or as if blind
BLINDINGS > BLINDING
BLINDLESS > BLIND
BLINDLY > BLIND
BLINDNESS > BLIND
BLINDS > BLIND
BLINDSIDE *vb* take (someone) by surprise
BLINDWORM *same as* > SLOWWORM
BLING *adj* flashy ▷ *n* ostentatious jewellery
BLINGER > BLING
BLINGEST > BLING
BLINGING *adj* flashy and expensive
BLINGLISH *n* spoken English mixed with Black slang
BLINGS > BLING
BLINI *pl n* Russian pancakes made of buckwheat flour and yeast
BLINIS *same as* > BLINI
BLINK *vb* close and immediately reopen (the eyes) ▷ *n* act of blinking
BLINKARD *n* something that twinkles
BLINKARDS > BLINKARD
BLINKED > BLINK
BLINKER *vb* provide (a horse) with blinkers ▷ *n* flashing light for sending messages, as a warning device, etc, such as a direction indicator on a road vehicle
BLINKERED *adj* considering only a narrow point of view
BLINKERS > BLIND
BLINKING *adv* extreme or extremely
BLINKS > BLINK
BLINNED > BLIN
BLINNING > BLIN
BLINS > BLIN
BLINTZ *n* thin pancake folded over a filling usually of apple, cream cheese, or meat
BLINTZE *same as* > BLINTZ
BLINTZES > BLINTZE
BLINY *same as* > BLINI
BLIP *n* spot of light on a radar screen indicating the position of an object ▷ *vb* produce such a noise
BLIPPED > BLIP
BLIPPING > BLIP
BLIPS > BLIP
BLIPVERT *n* very short television advertisement
BLIPVERTS > BLIPVERT
BLISS *n* perfect happiness ▷ *vb* make or become perfectly happy
BLISSED > BLISS
BLISSES > BLISS
BLISSFUL *adj* serenely joyful or glad
BLISSING > BLISS
BLISSLESS > BLISS
BLIST *archaic form of* > BLESSED
BLISTER *n* small bubble on the skin ▷ *vb* (cause to) have blisters
BLISTERED > BLISTER
BLISTERS > BLISTER
BLISTERY > BLISTER
BLITE *n* type of herb
BLITES > BLITE
BLITHE *adj* casual and indifferent
BLITHEFUL *same as* > BLITHE
BLITHELY > BLITHE
BLITHER *same as* > BLETHER
BLITHERED > BLITHER
BLITHERS > BLITHER
BLITHEST > BLITHE
BLITZ *n* violent and sustained attack by aircraft ▷ *vb* attack suddenly and intensively
BLITZED > BLITZ
BLITZER > BLITZ
BLITZERS > BLITZ
BLITZES > BLITZ
BLITZING > BLITZ
BLIVE *same as* > BELIVE
BLIZZARD *n* blinding storm of wind and snow
BLIZZARDS > BLIZZARD
BLIZZARDY > BLIZZARD
BLOAT *vb* cause to swell, as with liquid or air ▷ *n* abnormal distention of the abdomen in cattle, sheep, etc, caused by accumulation of gas in the stomach
BLOATED *adj* swollen, as with a liquid, air, or wind
BLOATER *n* salted smoked herring
BLOATERS > BLOATER
BLOATING > BLOAT
BLOATINGS > BLOAT
BLOATS > BLOAT
BLOATWARE *n* software with more features than necessary
BLOB *n* soft mass or drop ▷ *vb* put blobs, as of ink or paint, on
BLOBBED > BLOB
BLOBBIER > BLOB
BLOBBIEST > BLOB
BLOBBING > BLOB
BLOBBY > BLOB
BLOBS > BLOB
BLOC *n* people or countries combined by a common interest
BLOCK *n* large solid piece of wood, stone, etc ▷ *vb* obstruct or impede by introducing an obstacle
BLOCKABLE > BLOCK
BLOCKADE *n* sealing off of a place to prevent the passage of goods ▷ *vb* impose a blockade on
BLOCKADED > BLOCKADE
BLOCKADER > BLOCKADE
BLOCKADES > BLOCKADE
BLOCKAGE *n* act of blocking or state of being blocked
BLOCKAGES > BLOCKAGE
BLOCKBUST *vb* (try to) bring about the sale of property at a bargain price by stirring up fears of racial change in an area
BLOCKED *adj* functionally impeded by amphetamine
BLOCKER *n* person or thing that blocks
BLOCKERS > BLOCKER
BLOCKHEAD *n* stupid person
BLOCKHOLE *n* lines marked near stumps on cricket pitch
BLOCKIE *n* owner of a small property, esp a farm
BLOCKIER > BLOCKY
BLOCKIES > BLOCKIE
BLOCKIEST > BLOCKY
BLOCKING *n* interruption of anode current in a valve because of the application of a high negative voltage to the grid
BLOCKINGS > BLOCKING
BLOCKISH *adj* lacking vivacity or imagination
BLOCKS > BLOCK
BLOCKWORK *n* wall-building style
BLOCKY *adj* like a block, esp in shape and solidity
BLOCS > BLOC
BLOG *n* journal written on-line and accessible to users of the internet
BLOGGER > BLOG
BLOGGERS > BLOG
BLOGGING > BLOG
BLOGGINGS > BLOG
BLOGS > BLOG
BLOKE *n* man
BLOKEDOM *n* state of being a bloke
BLOKEDOMS > BLOKEDOM
BLOKEISH *adj* denoting or exhibiting the characteristics believed typical of an ordinary man
BLOKES > BLOKE
BLOKEY *same as* > BLOKEISH
BLOKIER > BLOKEY
BLOKIEST > BLOKEY
BLOKISH *same as* > BLOKEISH
BLONCKET *adj* blue-grey
BLOND *adj* (of men's hair) of a light colour ▷ *n* person, esp a man, having light-

coloured hair and skin
BLONDE *n* fair-haired (person) ▷ *adj* (of hair) fair
BLONDER > BLONDE
BLONDES > BLONDE
BLONDEST > BLONDE
BLONDINE *vb* dye hair blonde
BLONDINED > BLONDINE
BLONDINES > BLONDINE
BLONDING *n* act or an instance of dyeing hair blonde
BLONDINGS > BLONDING
BLONDISH > BLOND
BLONDNESS > BLOND
BLONDS > BLOND
BLOOD *n* red fluid that flows around the body ▷ *vb* initiate (a person) to war or hunting
BLOODBATH *n* massacre
BLOODED *adj* (of horses, cattle, etc) of good breeding
BLOODFIN *n* silvery red-finned South American freshwater fish, *Aphyocharax rubripinnis*: a popular aquarium fish: family *Characidae* (characins)
BLOODFINS > BLOODFIN
BLOODHEAT *n* normal human body temperature
BLOODIED > BLOODY
BLOODIER > BLOODY
BLOODIES > BLOODY
BLOODIEST > BLOODY
BLOODILY > BLOODY
BLOODING > BLOOD
BLOODINGS > BLOOD
BLOODLESS *adj* without blood or bloodshed
BLOODLIKE > BLOOD
BLOODLINE *n* all the members of a family group over generations, esp regarding characteristics common to that group
BLOODLUST *n* desire to see bloodshed
BLOODRED *adj* having a deep red colour
BLOODROOT *n* North American papaveraceous plant, *Sanguinaria canadensis*, having a single whitish flower and a fleshy red root that yields a red dye
BLOODS > BLOOD
BLOODSHED *n* slaughter or killing
BLOODSHOT *adj* (of an eye) inflamed
BLOODWOOD *n* any of several species of Australian eucalyptus that exude a red sap
BLOODWORM *n* red wormlike aquatic larva of the midge, *Chironomus plumosus*, which lives at the bottom of stagnant pools and ditches
BLOODWORT *n* plant with red dye in roots
BLOODY *adj* covered with blood ▷ *adv* extreme or extremely ▷ *vb* stain with blood
BLOODYING > BLOODY
BLOOEY *adj* out of order; faulty
BLOOIE *same as* > BLOOEY
BLOOM *n* blossom on a flowering plant ▷ *vb* (of flowers) open
BLOOMED *adj* (of a lens) coated with a thin film of magnesium fluoride or some other substance to reduce the amount of light lost by reflection
BLOOMER *n* stupid mistake
BLOOMERS *pl n* woman's baggy knickers
BLOOMERY *n* place in which malleable iron is produced directly from iron ore
BLOOMIER > BLOOMY
BLOOMIEST > BLOOMY
BLOOMING *adj* extreme or extremely
BLOOMLESS > BLOOM
BLOOMS > BLOOM
BLOOMY *adj* having a fine whitish coating on the surface, such as on the rind of a cheese
BLOOP *vb* (baseball) hit a ball into air beyond infield
BLOOPED > BLOOP
BLOOPER *n* stupid mistake
BLOOPERS > BLOOPER
BLOOPING > BLOOP
BLOOPS > BLOOP
BLOOSME *same as* > BLOSSOM
BLOOSMED > BLOOSME
BLOOSMES > BLOOSME
BLOOSMING > BLOOSME
BLOQUISTE *n* supporter of autonomy for Quebec
BLORE *n* strong blast of wind
BLORES > BLORE
BLOSSOM *n* flowers of a plant ▷ *vb* (of plants) flower
BLOSSOMED > BLOSSOM
BLOSSOMS > BLOSSOM
BLOSSOMY > BLOSSOM
BLOT *n* spot or stain ▷ *vb* cause a blemish in or on
BLOTCH *n* discoloured area or stain ▷ *vb* become or cause to become marked by such discoloration
BLOTCHED > BLOTCH
BLOTCHES > BLOTCH
BLOTCHIER > BLOTCHY
BLOTCHILY > BLOTCHY
BLOTCHING > BLOTCH
BLOTCHY *adj* covered in or marked by blotches
BLOTLESS > BLOT
BLOTS > BLOT
BLOTTED > BLOT
BLOTTER *n* sheet of blotting paper
BLOTTERS > BLOTTER
BLOTTIER > BLOTTY
BLOTTIEST > BLOTTY
BLOTTING *n* blot analysis
BLOTTINGS > BLOTTING
BLOTTO *adj* extremely drunk
BLOTTY *adj* covered in blots
BLOUBOK *same as* > BLAUBOK
BLOUBOKS > BLOUBOK
BLOUSE *n* woman's shirtlike garment ▷ *vb* hang or cause to hang in full loose folds
BLOUSED > BLOUSE
BLOUSES > BLOUSE
BLOUSIER > BLOUSY
BLOUSIEST > BLOUSY
BLOUSILY > BLOUSY
BLOUSING > BLOUSE
BLOUSON *n* short loose jacket with a tight waist
BLOUSONS > BLOUSON
BLOUSY *adj* loose; blouse-like
BLOVIATE *vb* discourse at length
BLOVIATED > BLOVIATE
BLOVIATES > BLOVIATE
BLOW *vb* (of air, the wind, etc) move ▷ *n* hard hit
BLOWBACK *n* escape to the rear of gases formed during the firing of a weapon or in a boiler, internal-combustion engine, etc
BLOWBACKS > BLOWBACK
BLOWBALL *n* dandelion seed head
BLOWBALLS > BLOWBALL
BLOWBY *n* leakage of gas past the piston of an engine at maximum pressure
BLOWBYS > BLOWBY
BLOWDOWN *n* accident in a nuclear reactor in which a cooling pipe bursts causing the loss of essential coolant ▷ *vb* open a valve in a steam boiler to eject any sediment that has collected
BLOWDOWNS > BLOWDOWN
BLOWED > BLOW
BLOWER *n* mechanical device, such as a fan, that blows
BLOWERS > BLOWER
BLOWFISH *a popular name for* > PUFFER
BLOWFLIES > BLOWFLY
BLOWFLY *n* fly that lays its eggs in meat
BLOWGUN *same as* > BLOWPIPE
BLOWGUNS > BLOWGUN
BLOWHARD *n* boastful person ▷ *adj* blustering or boastful
BLOWHARDS > BLOWHARD
BLOWHOLE *n* nostril of a whale
BLOWHOLES > BLOWHOLE
BLOWIE *n* bluebottle
BLOWIER > BLOWY
BLOWIES > BLOWIE
BLOWIEST > BLOWY
BLOWINESS > BLOWY
BLOWING > BLOW
BLOWJOB *slang term for* > FELLATIO
BLOWJOBS > BLOWJOB
BLOWKART *n* land vehicle with a sail
BLOWKARTS > BLOWKART
BLOWLAMP *another name for* > BLOWTORCH
BLOWLAMPS > BLOWLAMP
BLOWN > BLOW
BLOWOFF *n* discharge of a surplus fluid
BLOWOFFS > BLOWOFF
BLOWOUT *n* sudden loss of air in a tyre
BLOWOUTS > BLOWOUT
BLOWPIPE *n* long tube from which darts etc are shot by blowing
BLOWPIPES > BLOWPIPE
BLOWS > BLOW
BLOWSE *n* large, red-faced woman
BLOWSED *same as* > BLOWSY
BLOWSES > BLOWSE
BLOWSIER > BLOWSY
BLOWSIEST > BLOWSY
BLOWSILY > BLOWSY
BLOWSY *adj* fat, untidy, and red-faced
BLOWTORCH *n* small burner producing a very hot flame
BLOWTUBE *n* tube for blowing air or oxygen into a flame to intensify its heat
BLOWTUBES > BLOWTUBE
BLOWUP *n* fit of temper
BLOWUPS > BLOWUP
BLOWY *adj* windy
BLOWZE *variant of* > BLOWSE
BLOWZED *same as* > BLOWSY
BLOWZES > BLOWZE
BLOWZIER > BLOWZY
BLOWZIEST > BLOWZY
BLOWZILY > BLOWZY
BLOWZY *same as* > BLOWSY
BLUB *a slang word for* > BLUBBER
BLUBBED > BLUB
BLUBBER *n vb* sob without restraint ▷ *adj* swollen or fleshy ▷ *n* fat of whales, seals, etc
BLUBBERED > BLUBBER
BLUBBERER > BLUBBER
BLUBBERS > BLUBBER
BLUBBERY *adj* of, containing, or like blubber
BLUBBING > BLUB
BLUBS > BLUB
BLUCHER *n* high shoe with

laces over the tongue
BLUCHERS > BLUCHER
BLUDE *Scots form of* > BLOOD
BLUDES > BLUDE
BLUDGE *vb* evade work ▷ *n* easy task
BLUDGED > BLUDGE
BLUDGEON *n* short thick club ▷ *vb* hit with a bludgeon
BLUDGEONS > BLUDGEON
BLUDGER *n* person who scrounges
BLUDGERS > BLUDGER
BLUDGES > BLUDGE
BLUDGING > BLUDGE
BLUDIE *Scots form of* > BLOODY
BLUDIER > BLUDIE
BLUDIEST > BLUDIE
BLUDY *same as* > BLUDIE
BLUE *n* colour of a clear unclouded sky ▷ *adj* of the colour blue ▷ *vb* make or become blue
BLUEBACK *n* type of salmon
BLUEBACKS > BLUEBACK
BLUEBALL *n* type of European herb
BLUEBALLS > BLUEBALL
BLUEBEARD *n* any man who murders his wife or wives
BLUEBEAT *n* type of West Indian pop music of the 1960s
BLUEBEATS > BLUEBEAT
BLUEBELL *n* flower with blue bell-shaped flowers
BLUEBELLS > BLUEBELL
BLUEBERRY *n* very small blackish edible fruit that grows on a North American shrub
BLUEBILL *another name for* > SCAUP
BLUEBILLS > BLUEBILL
BLUEBIRD *n* North American songbird with a blue plumage
BLUEBIRDS > BLUEBIRD
BLUEBLOOD *n* royal or aristocratic person
BLUEBOOK *n* (in Britain) a government publication, usually the report of a commission
BLUEBOOKS > BLUEBOOK
BLUEBUCK *same as* > BLAUBOK
BLUEBUCKS > BLUEBUCK
BLUEBUSH *n* any of various blue-grey herbaceous Australian shrubs of the genus *Maireana*
BLUECAP *another name for* > BLUETIT
BLUECAPS > BLUECAP
BLUECOAT *n* person who wears blue uniform
BLUECOATS > BLUECOAT
BLUECURLS *n* North American plant
BLUED > BLUE
BLUEFIN *another name for* > TUNNY
BLUEFINS > BLUEFIN
BLUEFISH *n* bluish marine percoid food and game fish, *Pomatomus saltatrix*, related to the horse mackerel: family *Pomatomidae*
BLUEGILL *n* common North American freshwater sunfish, *Lepomis macrochirus*: an important food and game fish
BLUEGILLS > BLUEGILL
BLUEGOWN *n* in past, pauper, recipient of blue gown on King's birthday
BLUEGOWNS > BLUEGOWN
BLUEGRASS *n* any of several North American bluish-green grasses
BLUEGUM *n* tall fast-growing widely cultivated Australian myrtaceous tree, *Eucalyptus globulus*, having aromatic leaves containing a medicinal oil, bark that peels off in shreds, and hard timber
BLUEGUMS > BLUEGUM
BLUEHEAD *n* type of fish
BLUEHEADS > BLUEHEAD
BLUEING > BLUE
BLUEINGS > BLUE
BLUEISH *same as* > BLUISH
BLUEJACK *n* type of oak tree
BLUEJACKS > BLUEJACK
BLUEJAY *n* common North American jay, *Cyanocitta cristata*, having bright blue plumage with greyish-white underparts
BLUEJAYS > BLUEJAY
BLUEJEANS *n* blue denim jeans
BLUELINE *n* blue-toned photographic proof
BLUELINER *n* machine for making blueprints
BLUELINES > BLUELINE
BLUELY > BLUE
BLUENESS > BLUE
BLUENOSE *n* puritanical or prudish person
BLUENOSED > BLUENOSE
BLUENOSES > BLUENOSE
BLUEPOINT *n* type of small oyster
BLUEPRINT *n* photographic print of a plan ▷ *vb* make a blueprint of (a plan)
BLUER > BLUE
BLUES *pl n* type of music
BLUESHIFT *n* shift in the spectral lines of a stellar spectrum
BLUESIER > BLUES
BLUESIEST > BLUES
BLUESMAN *n* blues musician
BLUESMEN > BLUESMAN
BLUEST > BLUE
BLUESTEM *n* type of tall grass
BLUESTEMS > BLUESTEM
BLUESTONE *n* blue-grey sandstone containing much clay, used for building and paving
BLUESY > BLUES
BLUET *n* North American rubiaceous plant, *Houstonia caerulea*, with small four-petalled blue flowers
BLUETICK *n* fast-running dog
BLUETICKS > BLUETICK
BLUETIT *n* small European bird with a blue crown, wings, and tail and yellow underparts
BLUETITS > BLUETIT
BLUETS > BLUET
BLUETTE *n* short, brilliant piece of music
BLUETTES > BLUETTE
BLUEWEED *n* Eurasian boraginaceous weed, *Echium vulgare*, having blue flowers and pink buds
BLUEWEEDS > BLUEWEED
BLUEWING *n* type of duck
BLUEWINGS > BLUEWING
BLUEWOOD *n* type of Mexican shrub
BLUEWOODS > BLUEWOOD
BLUEY *adj* bluish ▷ *n* informal Australian word meaning blanket
BLUEYS > BLUEY
BLUFF *vb* pretend to be confident in order to influence (someone) ▷ *n* act of bluffing ▷ *adj* good-naturedly frank and hearty
BLUFFABLE > BLUFF
BLUFFED > BLUFF
BLUFFER > BLUFF
BLUFFERS > BLUFF
BLUFFEST > BLUFF
BLUFFING > BLUFF
BLUFFLY > BLUFF
BLUFFNESS > BLUFF
BLUFFS > BLUFF
BLUGGIER > BLUGGY
BLUGGIEST > BLUGGY
BLUGGY *same as* > BLOODY
BLUID *Scots word for* > BLOOD
BLUIDIER > BLUID
BLUIDIEST > BLUID
BLUIDS > BLUID
BLUIDY > BLUID
BLUIER > BLUEY
BLUIEST > BLUEY
BLUING > BLUE
BLUINGS > BLUE
BLUISH *adj* slightly blue
BLUME *Scots word for* > BLOOM
BLUMED > BLUME
BLUMES > BLUME
BLUMING > BLUME
BLUNDER *n* clumsy mistake ▷ *vb* make a blunder
BLUNDERED > BLUNDER
BLUNDERER > BLUNDER
BLUNDERS > BLUNDER
BLUNGE *vb* mix (clay or a similar substance) with water in order to form a suspension for use in ceramics
BLUNGED > BLUNGE
BLUNGER *n* large vat in which the contents, esp clay and water, are mixed by rotating arms
BLUNGERS > BLUNGER
BLUNGES > BLUNGE
BLUNGING > BLUNGE
BLUNK *vb* ruin; botch
BLUNKED > BLUNK
BLUNKER > BLUNK
BLUNKERS > BLUNK
BLUNKING > BLUNK
BLUNKS > BLUNK
BLUNT *adj* not having a sharp edge or point ▷ *vb* make less sharp ▷ *n* cannabis cigarette
BLUNTED > BLUNT
BLUNTER > BLUNT
BLUNTEST > BLUNT
BLUNTHEAD *n* frequent user of marijuana
BLUNTING > BLUNT
BLUNTISH > BLUNT
BLUNTLY > BLUNT
BLUNTNESS > BLUNT
BLUNTS > BLUNT
BLUR *vb* make or become vague or less distinct ▷ *n* something vague, hazy, or indistinct
BLURB *n* promotional description, as on the jacket of a book ▷ *vb* describe or recommend in a blurb
BLURBED > BLURB
BLURBING > BLURB
BLURBIST *n* writer of blurbs
BLURBISTS > BLURBIST
BLURBS > BLURB
BLURRED > BLUR
BLURREDLY > BLUR
BLURRIER > BLUR
BLURRIEST > BLUR
BLURRILY > BLUR
BLURRING > BLUR
BLURRY > BLUR
BLURS > BLUR
BLURT *vb* utter suddenly and involuntarily
BLURTED > BLURT
BLURTER > BLURT
BLURTERS > BLURT
BLURTING > BLURT
BLURTINGS > BLURT
BLURTS > BLURT
BLUSH *vb* become red in the face, esp from embarrassment or shame ▷ *n* reddening of the face
BLUSHED > BLUSH
BLUSHER *n* cosmetic for

giving the cheeks a rosy colour
BLUSHERS > BLUSHER
BLUSHES > BLUSH
BLUSHET *n* modest young woman
BLUSHETS > BLUSHET
BLUSHFUL > BLUSH
BLUSHING > BLUSH
BLUSHINGS > BLUSH
BLUSHLESS > BLUSH
BLUSTER *vb* speak loudly or in a bullying way ▷ *n* empty threats or protests
BLUSTERED > BLUSTER
BLUSTERER > BLUSTER
BLUSTERS > BLUSTER
BLUSTERY > BLUSTER
BLUSTROUS *adj* inclined to bluster
BLUTWURST *n* blood sausage
BLYPE *n* piece of skin peeled off after sunburn
BLYPES > BLYPE
BO *interj, n* exclamation uttered to startle or surprise someone, esp a child in a game
BOA *n* large nonvenomous snake
BOAB *short for* > BAOBAB
BOABS > BOAB
BOAK *same as* > BOKE
BOAKED > BOAK
BOAKING > BOAK
BOAKS > BOAK
BOAR *n* uncastrated male pig
BOARD *n* long flat piece of sawn timber ▷ *vb* go aboard (a train, aeroplane, etc)
BOARDABLE > BOARD
BOARDED > BOARD
BOARDER *n* person who pays rent in return for accommodation in someone else's home
BOARDERS > BOARDER
BOARDING *n* act of embarking on an aircraft, train, ship, etc
BOARDINGS > BOARDING
BOARDLIKE > BOARD
BOARDMAN *n* man who carries a sandwich board
BOARDMEN > BOARDMAN
BOARDROOM *n* room where the board of a company meets
BOARDS > BOARD
BOARDWALK *n* promenade, esp along a beach, usually made of planks
BOARFISH *n* any of various spiny-finned marine teleost fishes of the genera *Capros*, *Antigonia*, etc, related to the dories, having a deep compressed body, a long snout, and large eyes
BOARHOUND *n* dog used to hunt boar
BOARISH *adj* coarse, cruel, or sensual
BOARISHLY > BOARISH
BOARS > BOAR
BOART *same as* > BORT
BOARTS > BOART
BOAS > BOA
BOAST *vb* speak too proudly about one's talents etc ▷ *n* bragging statement
BOASTED > BOAST
BOASTER > BOAST
BOASTERS > BOAST
BOASTFUL *adj* tending to boast
BOASTING > BOAST
BOASTINGS > BOAST
BOASTLESS > BOAST
BOASTS > BOAST
BOAT *n* small vehicle for travelling across water ▷ *vb* travel in a boat
BOATABLE *adj* able to be carried by boat
BOATBILL *n* nocturnal tropical American wading bird, *Cochlearius cochlearius*, similar to the night herons but with a broad flattened bill: family *Ardeidae*, order *Ciconiiformes*
BOATBILLS > BOATBILL
BOATED > BOAT
BOATEL *n* waterside hotel catering for boating people
BOATELS > BOATEL
BOATER *n* flat straw hat
BOATERS > BOATER
BOATFUL > BOAT
BOATFULS > BOAT
BOATHOOK *n* pole with a hook at one end, used aboard a vessel for fending off other vessels or obstacles or for catching a line or mooring buoy
BOATHOOKS > BOATHOOK
BOATHOUSE *n* shelter by the edge of a river, lake, etc, for housing boats
BOATIE *n* boating enthusiast
BOATIES > BOATIE
BOATING *n* rowing, sailing, or cruising in boats as a form of recreation
BOATINGS > BOATING
BOATLIFT *n* evacuation by boat
BOATLIFTS > BOATLIFT
BOATLIKE > BOAT
BOATLOAD *n* amount of cargo or number of people held by a boat or ship
BOATLOADS > BOATLOAD
BOATMAN *n* man who works on, hires out, or repairs boats
BOATMEN > BOATMAN
BOATNECK *n* wide open neck on garment
BOATNECKS > BOATNECK
BOATS > BOAT
BOATSMAN *same as* > BOATMAN
BOATSMEN > BOATSMAN
BOATSWAIN *n* petty officer on a merchant ship or a warrant officer on a warship who is responsible for the maintenance of the ship and its equipment
BOATTAIL *n* type of blackbird
BOATTAILS > BOATTAIL
BOATYARD *n* place where boats are kept, repaired, etc
BOATYARDS > BOATYARD
BOB *vb* move or cause to move up and down repeatedly, as while floating in water ▷ *n* short abrupt movement, as of the head
BOBA *n* type of Chinese tea
BOBAC *same as* > BOBAK
BOBACS > BOBAC
BOBAK *n* type of marmot
BOBAKS > BOBAK
BOBAS > BOBA
BOBBED > BOB
BOBBEJAAN *n* baboon
BOBBER *n* type of float for fishing
BOBBERIES > BOBBERY
BOBBERS > BOBBER
BOBBERY *n* mixed pack of hunting dogs, often not belonging to any of the hound breeds ▷ *adj* noisy or excitable
BOBBIES > BOBBY
BOBBIN *n* reel on which thread is wound
BOBBINET *n* netted fabric of hexagonal mesh, made on a lace machine
BOBBINETS > BOBBINET
BOBBING > BOB
BOBBINS > BOBBIN
BOBBISH > CHEERY
BOBBITT *vb* sever the penis of
BOBBITTED > BOBBITT
BOBBITTS > BOBBITT
BOBBLE *n* small ball of material, usu for decoration ▷ *vb* (of a ball) to bounce erratically because of an uneven playing surface
BOBBLED > BOBBLE
BOBBLES > BOBBLE
BOBBLIER > BOBBLY
BOBBLIEST > BOBBLY
BOBBLING > BOBBLE
BOBBLY *adj* (of fabric) covered in small balls; worn
BOBBY *n* policeman
BOBBYSOCK *n* ankle-length sock worn esp by teenage girls
BOBBYSOX *pl n* bobbysocks
BOBCAT *n* North American feline mammal, *Lynx rufus*, closely related to but smaller than the lynx, having reddish-brown fur with dark spots or stripes, tufted ears, and a short tail
BOBCATS > BOBCAT
BOBECHE *n* candle drip-catcher
BOBECHES > BOBECHE
BOBFLOAT *n* small buoyant float, usually consisting of a quill stuck through a piece of cork
BOBFLOATS > BOBFLOAT
BOBLET *n* two-man bobsleigh
BOBLETS > BOBLET
BOBOL *n* fraud carried out by one or more persons with access to public funds in collusion with someone in a position of authority ▷ *vb* commit a bobol
BOBOLINK *n* American songbird, *Dolichonyx oryzivorus*, the male of which has a white back and black underparts in the breeding season: family *Icteridae* (American orioles)
BOBOLINKS > BOBOLINK
BOBOLLED > BOBOL
BOBOLLING > BOBOL
BOBOLS > BOBOL
BOBOTIE *n* dish of curried mince
BOBOTIES > BOBOTIE
BOBOWLER *n* large moth
BOBOWLERS > BOBOWLER
BOBS > BOB
BOBSLED *same as* > BOBSLEIGH
BOBSLEDS > BOBSLED
BOBSLEIGH *n* sledge for racing down an icy track ▷ *vb* ride on a bobsleigh
BOBSTAY *n* strong stay between a bowsprit and the stem of a vessel for holding down the bowsprit
BOBSTAYS > BOBSTAY
BOBTAIL *n* docked tail ▷ *adj* having the tail cut short ▷ *vb* dock the tail of
BOBTAILED > BOBTAIL
BOBTAILS > BOBTAIL
BOBWEIGHT *n* balance weight
BOBWHEEL *n* poetic device
BOBWHEELS > BOBWHEEL
BOBWHITE *n* brown North American quail, *Colinus virginianus*, the male of which has white markings on the head: a popular game bird
BOBWHITES > BOBWHITE
BOBWIG *n* type of short wig
BOBWIGS > BOBWIG
BOCACCIO *n* edible

American fish
BOCACCIOS > BOCACCIO
BOCAGE *n* wooded countryside characteristic of northern France, with small irregular-shaped fields and many hedges and copses
BOCAGES > BOCAGE
BOCCA *n* mouth
BOCCAS > BOCCA
BOCCE *same as* > BOCCIE
BOCCES > BOCCE
BOCCI *same as* > BOCCIE
BOCCIA *same as* > BOCCIE
BOCCIAS > BOCCIA
BOCCIE *n* Italian version of bowls played on a lawn smaller than a bowling green
BOCCIES > BOCCIE
BOCCIS > BOCCI
BOCHE *n* derogatory slang for a German soldier
BOCHES > BOCHE
BOCK *a variant spelling of* > BOKE
BOCKED > BOCK
BOCKEDY *adj* (of a structure, piece of furniture, etc) unsteady
BOCKING > BOCK
BOCKS > BOCK
BOCONCINI *pl n* small pieces of mozzarella
BOD *n* person
BODACH *n* old man
BODACHS > BODACH
BODACIOUS *adj* impressive or remarkable
BODDLE *same as* > BODLE
BODDLES > BODDLE
BODE *vb* portend or presage
BODED > BODE
BODEFUL *adj* portentous
BODEGA *n* shop in a Spanish-speaking country that sells wine
BODEGAS > BODEGA
BODEGUERO *n* wine seller or grocer
BODEMENT > BODE
BODEMENTS > BODE
BODES > BODE
BODGE *vb* make a mess of
BODGED > BODGE
BODGER *adj* worthless or second-rate
BODGERS > BODGER
BODGES > BODGE
BODGIE *n* unruly or uncouth young man, esp in the 1950s ▷ *adj* inferior
BODGIER > BODGIE
BODGIES > BODGIE
BODGIEST > BODGIE
BODGING > BODGE
BODHRAN *n* shallow one-sided drum popular in Irish and Scottish folk music
BODHRANS > BODHRAN
BODICE *n* upper part of a dress
BODICES > BODICE
BODIED > BODY
BODIES > BODY
BODIKIN *n* little body
BODIKINS > BODIKIN
BODILESS *adj* having no body or substance
BODILY *adj* relating to the body ▷ *adv* by taking hold of the body
BODING > BODE
BODINGLY > BODE
BODINGS > BODE
BODKIN *n* blunt large-eyed needle
BODKINS > BODKIN
BODLE *n* small obsolete Scottish coin
BODLES > BODLE
BODRAG *n* enemy attack
BODRAGS > BODRAG
BODS > BOD
BODY *n* entire physical structure of an animal or human
BODYBOARD *n* surfboard that is shorter and blunter than the standard board and on which the surfer lies rather than stands
BODYCHECK *n* obstruction of another player ▷ *vb* deliver a bodycheck to (an opponent)
BODYGUARD *n* person or group of people employed to protect someone
BODYING > BODY
BODYLINE *n* (in cricket) fast bowling aimed at the batsman's body
BODYLINES > BODYLINE
BODYSHELL *n* external shell of a motor vehicle
BODYSUIT *n* one-piece undergarment for a baby
BODYSUITS > BODYSUIT
BODYSURF *vb* ride a wave by lying on it without a surfboard
BODYSURFS > BODYSURF
BODYWORK *n* outer shell of a motor vehicle
BODYWORKS > BODYWORK
BOEHMITE *n* grey, red, or brown mineral that consists of alumina in rhombic crystalline form and occurs in bauxite
BOEHMITES > BOEHMITE
BOEP *n* South African word for a big belly
BOEPS > BOEP
BOERBUL *n* crossbred mastiff used esp as a watchdog
BOERBULS > BOERBUL
BOEREWORS *n* spiced sausage
BOERTJIE *South African word for* > FRIEND
BOERTJIES > BOERTJIE
BOET *n* brother
BOETS > BOET
BOEUF *boeuf bourgignon* casserole of beef, vegetables, herbs, etc, cooked in red wine
BOFF *n* boffin ▷ *vb* hit
BOFFED > BOFF
BOFFIN *n* scientist or expert
BOFFING > BOFF
BOFFINS > BOFFIN
BOFFO *adj* very good
BOFFOLA *n* great success
BOFFOLAS > BOFFOLA
BOFFOS > BOFFO
BOFFS > BOFF
BOG *n* wet spongy ground ▷ *vb* mire or delay
BOGAN *n* youth who dresses and behaves rebelliously
BOGANS > BOGAN
BOGART *vb* monopolize or keep (something, esp a marijuana cigarette) to oneself selfishly
BOGARTED > BOGART
BOGARTING > BOGART
BOGARTS > BOGART
BOGBEAN *same as* > BUCKBEAN
BOGBEANS > BOGBEAN
BOGEY *n* evil or mischievous spirit ▷ *vb* play (a hole) in one stroke over par
BOGEYED > BOGEY
BOGEYING > BOGEY
BOGEYISM *n* demonization
BOGEYISMS > BOGEYISM
BOGEYMAN *n* frightening person, real or imaginary, used as a threat, esp to children
BOGEYMEN > BOGEYMAN
BOGEYS > BOGEY
BOGGARD *same as* > BOGGART
BOGGARDS > BOGGARD
BOGGART *n* ghost or poltergeist
BOGGARTS > BOGGART
BOGGED > BOG
BOGGER *n* lavatory
BOGGERS > BOGGER
BOGGIER > BOG
BOGGIEST > BOG
BOGGINESS > BOG
BOGGING > BOG
BOGGISH > BOG
BOGGLE *vb* be surprised, confused, or alarmed
BOGGLED > BOGGLE
BOGGLER > BOGGLE
BOGGLERS > BOGGLE
BOGGLES > BOGGLE
BOGGLING > BOGGLE
BOGGY > BOG
BOGIE *same as* > BOGEY
BOGIED > BOGIE
BOGIEING > BOGIE
BOGIES > BOGY
BOGLAND *n* area of wetland
BOGLANDS > BOGLAND
BOGLE *n* rhythmic dance performed to ragga music
BOGLES > BOGLE
BOGMAN *n* body of a person found preserved in a peat bog
BOGMEN > BOGMAN
BOGOAK *n* oak or other wood found preserved in peat bogs; bogwood
BOGOAKS > BOGOAK
BOGONG *n* large nocturnal Australian moth
BOGONGS > BOGONG
BOGS > BOG
BOGUS *adj* not genuine
BOGUSLY > BOGUS
BOGUSNESS > BOGUS
BOGWOOD *same as* > BOGOAK
BOGWOODS > BOGWOOD
BOGY *same as* > BOGEY
BOGYISM *same as* > BOGEYISM
BOGYISMS > BOGYISM
BOGYMAN *same as* > BOGEYMAN
BOGYMEN > BOGYMAN
BOH *same as* > BO
BOHEA *n* black Chinese tea, once regarded as the choicest, but now as an inferior grade
BOHEAS > BOHEA
BOHEMIA *n* area frequented by unconventional (esp creative) people
BOHEMIAN *adj* unconventional in lifestyle or appearance ▷ *n* person, esp an artist or writer, who lives an unconventional life
BOHEMIANS > BOHEMIAN
BOHEMIAS > BOHEMIA
BOHO *short for* > BOHEMIAN
BOHOS > BOHO
BOHRIUM *n* element artificially produced in minute quantities
BOHRIUMS > BOHRIUM
BOHS > BOH
BOHUNK *n* derogatory name for a labourer from east or central Europe
BOHUNKS > BOHUNK
BOI *n* lesbian who dresses like a boy
BOIL *vb* (cause to) change from a liquid to a vapour so quickly that bubbles are formed ▷ *n* state or action of boiling
BOILABLE > BOIL
BOILED > BOIL
BOILER *n* piece of equipment which provides hot water
BOILERIES > BOILERY
BOILERS > BOILER
BOILERY *n* place where water is boiled to extract salt
BOILING *adj* very hot ▷ *n* sweet
BOILINGLY > BOILING
BOILINGS > BOILING
BOILOFF *n* quantity of liquified gases lost in

evaporation
BOILOFFS > BOILOFF
BOILOVER *n* surprising result in a sporting event, esp in a horse race
BOILOVERS > BOILOVER
BOILS > BOIL
BOING *vb* rebound making a noise
BOINGED > BOING
BOINGING > BOING
BOINGS > BOING
BOINK *same as* > BOING
BOINKED > BOINK
BOINKING > BOINK
BOINKS > BOINK
BOIS > BOI
BOISERIE *n* finely crafted wood-carving
BOISERIES > BOISERIE
BOITE *n* artist's portfolio
BOITES > BOITE
BOK *n* S African antelope
BOKE *vb* retch or vomit ▷ *n* retch
BOKED > BOKE
BOKES > BOKE
BOKING > BOKE
BOKO *slang word for* > NOSE
BOKOS > BOKO
BOKS > BOK
BOLA *n* missile used by gauchos and Indians of South America, consisting of two or more heavy balls on a cord. It is hurled at a running quarry, such as an ox or rhea, so as to entangle its legs
BOLAR *adj* relating to clay
BOLAS *same as* > BOLA
BOLASES > BOLAS
BOLD *adj* confident and fearless ▷ *n* boldface
BOLDEN *vb* make bold
BOLDENED > BOLDEN
BOLDENING > BOLDEN
BOLDENS > BOLDEN
BOLDER > BOLD
BOLDEST > BOLD
BOLDFACE *n* weight of type characterized by thick heavy lines ▷ *vb* print in boldface
BOLDFACED > BOLDFACE
BOLDFACES > BOLDFACE
BOLDLY > BOLD
BOLDNESS > BOLD
BOLDS > BOLD
BOLE *n* tree trunk
BOLECTION *n* stepped moulding covering and projecting beyond the joint between two members having surfaces at different levels
BOLERO *n* (music for) traditional Spanish dance
BOLEROS > BOLERO
BOLES > BOLE
BOLETE *n* type of fungus
BOLETES > BOLETE
BOLETI > BOLETUS
BOLETUS *n* any saprotroph basidiomycetous fungus of the genus *Boletus*, having a brownish umbrella-shaped cap with spore-bearing tubes in the underside: family *Boletaceae*. Many species are edible
BOLETUSES > BOLETUS
BOLIDE *n* large exceptionally bright meteor that often explodes
BOLIDES > BOLIDE
BOLINE *n* (in Wicca) a knife, usually sickle-shaped and with a white handle, used for gathering herbs and carving symbols
BOLINES > BOLINE
BOLIVAR *n* standard monetary unit of Venezuela, equal to 100 céntimos
BOLIVARES > BOLIVAR
BOLIVARS > BOLIVAR
BOLIVIA *n* type of woollen fabric
BOLIVIANO *n* (until 1963 and from 1987) the standard monetary unit of Bolivia, equal to 100 centavos
BOLIVIAS > BOLIVIA
BOLIX *same as* > BOLLOCKS
BOLIXED > BOLIX
BOLIXES > BOLIX
BOLIXING > BOLIX
BOLL *n* rounded seed capsule of cotton, flax, etc ▷ *vb* form into a boll
BOLLARD *n* short thick post used to prevent the passage of motor vehicles
BOLLARDS > BOLLARD
BOLLED > BOLL
BOLLEN > BOLL
BOLLETRIE *n* type of W Indian tree
BOLLING > BOLL
BOLLIX *same as* > BOLLOCKS
BOLLIXED > BOLLIX
BOLLIXES > BOLLIX
BOLLIXING > BOLLIX
BOLLOCK *vb* rebuke severely
BOLLOCKED > BOLLOCK
BOLLOCKS *pl n* testicles ▷ *interj* exclamation of annoyance, disbelief, etc ▷ *vb* rebuke severely
BOLLOX *same as* > BOLLOCKS
BOLLOXED > BOLLOX
BOLLOXES > BOLLOX
BOLLOXING > BOLLOX
BOLLS > BOLL
BOLLWORM *n* any of various moth caterpillars that feed on and destroy cotton bolls
BOLLWORMS > BOLLWORM
BOLO *n* large single-edged knife, originating in the Philippines
BOLOGNA *n* type of sausage
BOLOGNAS > BOLOGNA
BOLOGRAPH *n* record made by a bolometer
BOLOMETER *n* sensitive instrument for measuring radiant energy by the increase in the resistance of an electrical conductor
BOLOMETRY > BOLOMETER
BOLONEY *a variant spelling of* > BALONEY
BOLONEYS > BOLONEY
BOLOS > BOLO
BOLSHEVIK *n* any political radical
BOLSHIE *adj* difficult or rebellious ▷ *n* any political radical
BOLSHIER > BOLSHIE
BOLSHIES > BOLSHY
BOLSHIEST > BOLSHIE
BOLSHY *same as* > BOLSHIE
BOLSON *n* desert valley surrounded by mountains, with a shallow lake at the centre
BOLSONS > BOLSON
BOLSTER *vb* support or strengthen ▷ *n* long narrow pillow
BOLSTERED > BOLSTER
BOLSTERER > BOLSTER
BOLSTERS > BOLSTER
BOLT *n* sliding metal bar for fastening a door etc ▷ *vb* run away suddenly
BOLTED > BOLT
BOLTER > BOLT
BOLTERS > BOLT
BOLTHEAD *n* glass receptacle used in chemistry
BOLTHEADS > BOLTHEAD
BOLTHOLE *n* place of escape from danger
BOLTHOLES > BOLTHOLE
BOLTING > BOLT
BOLTINGS > BOLT
BOLTLESS > BOLT
BOLTLIKE > BOLT
BOLTONIA *n* any North American plant of the genus *Boltonia*, having daisy-like flowers with white, violet, or pinkish rays: family *Compositae* (composites)
BOLTONIAS > BOLTONIA
BOLTROPE *n* rope sewn to the foot or luff of a sail to strengthen it
BOLTROPES > BOLTROPE
BOLTS > BOLT
BOLUS *same as* > BOLE
BOLUSES > BOLUS
BOMA *n* enclosure, esp a palisade or fence of thorn bush, set up to protect a camp, herd of animals, etc
BOMAS > BOMA
BOMB *n* container fitted with explosive material ▷ *vb* attack with bombs
BOMBABLE > BOMB
BOMBARD *vb* attack with heavy gunfire or bombs ▷ *n* ancient type of cannon that threw stone balls
BOMBARDE *n* alto wind instrument similar to the oboe or medieval shawm, used mainly in Breton traditional music
BOMBARDED > BOMBARD
BOMBARDER > BOMBARD
BOMBARDES > BOMBARDE
BOMBARDON *n* brass instrument of the tuba type, similar to a sousaphone
BOMBARDS > BOMBARD
BOMBASINE *same as* > BOMBAZINE
BOMBAST *n* pompous language ▷ *vb* speak pompous language
BOMBASTED > BOMBAST
BOMBASTER > BOMBAST
BOMBASTIC > BOMBAST
BOMBASTS > BOMBAST
BOMBAX *n* type of S American tree
BOMBAXES > BOMBAX
BOMBAZINE *n* twill fabric, usually of silk and worsted, formerly worn dyed black for mourning
BOMBE *n* dessert of ice cream lined or filled with custard, cake crumbs, etc ▷ *adj* (of furniture) having a projecting swollen shape
BOMBED > BOMB
BOMBER *n* aircraft that drops bombs
BOMBERS > BOMBER
BOMBES > BOMBE
BOMBESIN *n* hormone found in brain
BOMBESINS > BOMBESIN
BOMBILATE *same as* > BOMBINATE
BOMBINATE *vb* make a buzzing noise
BOMBING > BOMB
BOMBINGS > BOMB
BOMBLET *n* small bomb
BOMBLETS > BOMBLET
BOMBLOAD *n* quantity of bombs carried at one time
BOMBLOADS > BOMBLOAD
BOMBO *n* inferior wine
BOMBORA *n* submerged reef
BOMBORAS > BOMBORA
BOMBOS > BOMBO
BOMBPROOF *adj* able to withstand the impact of a bomb
BOMBS > BOMB
BOMBSHELL *n* shocking or unwelcome surprise
BOMBSIGHT *n* mechanical or electronic device in an aircraft for aiming bombs
BOMBSITE *n* area where the buildings have been destroyed by bombs

BOMBSITES > BOMBSITE
BOMBYCID *n* any moth, including the silkworm moth, of the family *Bombycidae*, most of which occur in Africa and SE Asia ▷ *adj* of, relating to, or belonging to the *Bombycidae*
BOMBYCIDS > BOMBYCID
BOMBYCOID *adj* of or like bombycids
BOMBYX *n* type of moth
BOMBYXES > BOMBYX
BOMMIE *n* outcrop of coral reef
BOMMIES > BOMMIE
BON *adj* good
BONA *n* goods
BONACI *n* type of fish
BONACIS > BONACI
BONAMANI > BONAMANO
BONAMANO *n* gratuity
BONAMIA *n* parasite
BONAMIAS > BONAMIA
BONANZA *n* sudden good luck or wealth
BONANZAS > BONANZA
BONASSUS *same as* > BONASUS
BONASUS *n* European bison
BONASUSES > BONASUS
BONBON *n* sweet
BONBONS > BONBON
BONCE *n* head
BONCES > BONCE
BOND *n* something that binds, fastens or holds together ▷ *vb* bind
BONDABLE > BOND
BONDAGE *n* slavery
BONDAGER > BONDAGE
BONDAGERS > BONDAGE
BONDAGES > BONDAGE
BONDED *adj* consisting of, secured by, or operating under a bond or bonds
BONDER *same as* > BONDSTONE
BONDERS > BONDER
BONDING *n* process by which individuals become emotionally attached to one another
BONDINGS > BONDING
BONDLESS > BOND
BONDMAID *n* unmarried female serf or slave
BONDMAIDS > BONDMAID
BONDMAN *same as* > BONDSMAN
BONDMEN > BONDMAN
BONDS > BOND
BONDSMAN *n* person bound by bond to act as surety for another
BONDSMEN > BONDSMAN
BONDSTONE *n* long stone or brick laid in a wall as a header
BONDUC *n* type of N American tree
BONDUCS > BONDUC
BONDWOMAN *n* female slave
BONDWOMEN > BONDWOMAN
BONE *n* any of the hard parts in the body that form the skeleton ▷ *vb* remove the bones from (meat for cooking etc)
BONEBLACK *n* black residue from the destructive distillation of bones, containing about 10 per cent carbon and 80 per cent calcium phosphate, used as a decolorizing agent and pigment
BONED > BONE
BONEFISH *n* silvery marine clupeoid game fish, *Albula vulpes*, occurring in warm shallow waters: family *Albulidae*
BONEHEAD *n* stupid or obstinate person
BONEHEADS > BONEHEAD
BONELESS > BONE
BONEMEAL *n* product of dried and ground animal bones, used as a fertilizer or in stock feeds
BONEMEALS > BONEMEAL
BONER *n* blunder
BONERS > BONER
BONES > BONE
BONESET *n* any of various North American plants of the genus *Eupatorium*, esp *E. perfoliatum*, which has flat clusters of small white flowers: family *Asteraceae* (composites)
BONESETS > BONESET
BONEY *same as* > BONY
BONEYARD *an informal name for a* > CEMETERY
BONEYARDS > BONEYARD
BONEYER > BONEY
BONEYEST > BONEY
BONFIRE *n* large outdoor fire
BONFIRES > BONFIRE
BONG *n* deep reverberating sound, as of a large bell ▷ *vb* make a deep reverberating sound
BONGED > BONG
BONGING > BONG
BONGO *n* small drum played with the fingers
BONGOES > BONGO
BONGOIST *n* bongo player
BONGOISTS > BONGOIST
BONGOS > BONGO
BONGRACE *n* shade for face
BONGRACES > BONGRACE
BONGS > BONG
BONHAM *n* piglet
BONHAMS > BONHAM
BONHOMIE *n* cheerful friendliness
BONHOMIES > BONHOMIE
BONHOMMIE *same as* > BONHOMIE
BONHOMOUS *adj* exhibiting bonhomie
BONIATO *n* sweet potato
BONIATOS > BONIATO
BONIBELL *same as* > BONNIBELL
BONIBELLS > BONIBELL
BONIE *same as* > BONNY
BONIER > BONY
BONIEST > BONY
BONIFACE *n* pub landlord
BONIFACES > BONIFACE
BONILASSE *n* an attractive young woman
BONINESS > BONY
BONING > BONE
BONINGS > BONE
BONISM *n* doctrine that the world is good, although not the best of all possible worlds
BONISMS > BONISM
BONIST > BONISM
BONISTS > BONISM
BONITA *slang term for* > HEROIN
BONITAS > BONITA
BONITO *n* small tunny-like marine food fish
BONITOES > BONITO
BONITOS > BONITO
BONJOUR *interj* hello
BONK *vb* have sex with
BONKED > BONK
BONKERS *adj* crazy
BONKING > BONK
BONKINGS > BONK
BONKS > BONK
BONNE *n* housemaid or female servant
BONNES > BONNE
BONNET *n* metal cover over a vehicle's engine ▷ *vb* place a bonnet on
BONNETED > BONNET
BONNETING > BONNET
BONNETS > BONNET
BONNIBELL *n* beautiful girl
BONNIE *same as* > BONNY
BONNIER > BONNY
BONNIES > BONNY
BONNIEST > BONNY
BONNILY > BONNY
BONNINESS > BONNY
BONNOCK *n* thick oatmeal cake
BONNOCKS > BONNOCK
BONNY *adj* beautiful ▷ *adv* agreeably or well
BONOBO *n* anthropoid ape, *Pan paniscus*, of central W Africa: similar to the chimpanzee but much smaller and having a black face.
BONOBOS > BONOBO
BONSAI *n* ornamental miniature tree or shrub
BONSAIS > BONSAI
BONSELA *n* small gift of money
BONSELAS > BONSELA
BONSELLA *same as* > BONSELA
BONSELLAS > BONSELLA
BONSOIR *interj* good evening
BONSPELL *same as* > BONSPIEL
BONSPELLS > BONSPIEL
BONSPIEL *n* curling match
BONSPIELS > BONSPIEL
BONTEBOK *n* antelope, *Damaliscus pygargus* (or *dorcas*), of southern Africa, having a deep reddish-brown coat with a white blaze, tail, and rump patch
BONTEBOKS > BONTEBOK
BONUS *n* something given, paid, or received above what is due or expected
BONUSES > BONUS
BONXIE *n* great skua
BONXIES > BONXIE
BONY *adj* having many bones
BONZA *same as* > BONZER
BONZE *n* Chinese or Japanese Buddhist priest or monk
BONZER *adj* excellent
BONZES > BONZE
BOO *interj* shout of disapproval ▷ *vb* shout 'boo' to show disapproval
BOOB *n* foolish mistake ▷ *vb* make a foolish mistake ▷ *adj* of poor quality, similar to that provided in prison
BOOBED > BOOB
BOOBHEAD *n* repeat offender in a prison
BOOBHEADS > BOOBHEAD
BOOBIALLA *n* any of various trees or shrubs of the genus *Myoporum*, esp *M. insulare*
BOOBIE *same as* > BOOBY
BOOBIES > BOOBY
BOOBING > BOOB
BOOBIRD *n* person who boos
BOOBIRDS > BOOBIRD
BOOBISH > BOOBY
BOOBOISIE *n* group of people considered as stupid
BOOBOO *n* blunder
BOOBOOK *n* small spotted Australian brown owl
BOOBOOKS > BOOBOOK
BOOBOOS > BOOBOO
BOOBS > BOOB
BOOBY *n* foolish person
BOOBYISH > BOOBY
BOOBYISM > BOOBY
BOOBYISMS > BOOBY
BOOCOO *same as* > BEAUCOUP
BOOCOOS > BOOCOO
BOODIE *n* type of kangaroo
BOODIED > BOODY
BOODIES > BOODY
BOODLE *n* money or valuables, esp when stolen, counterfeit, or used as a bribe ▷ *vb* give or receive money corruptly or illegally
BOODLED > BOODLE

BOODLER > BOODLE
BOODLERS > BOODLE
BOODLES > BOODLE
BOODLING > BOODLE
BOODY *vb* sulk
BOODYING > BOODY
BOOED > BOO
BOOFHEAD *n* stupid person
BOOFHEADS > BOOFHEAD
BOOFIER > BOOFY
BOOFIEST > BOOFY
BOOFY *adj* muscular and strong but stupid
BOOGER *n* dried mucous from the nose
BOOGERMAN *American form of* > BOGEYMAN
BOOGERMEN > BOOGERMAN
BOOGERS > BOOGER
BOOGEY *same as* > BOOGIE
BOOGEYED > BOOGEY
BOOGEYING > BOOGEY
BOOGEYMAN *same as* > BOGEYMAN
BOOGEYMEN > BOOGEYMAN
BOOGEYS > BOOGEY
BOOGIE *vb* dance to fast pop music ▷ *n* session of dancing to pop music
BOOGIED > BOOGIE
BOOGIEING > BOOGIE
BOOGIEMAN *same as* > BOGEYMAN
BOOGIEMEN > BOOGIEMAN
BOOGIES > BOOGIE
BOOGY *same as* > BOOGIE
BOOGYING > BOOGY
BOOGYMAN *same as* > BOGEYMAN
BOOGYMEN > BOOGYMAN
BOOH *same as* > BOO
BOOHAI *n up the boohai* thoroughly lost
BOOHAIS > BOOHAI
BOOHED > BOOH
BOOHING > BOOH
BOOHOO *vb* sob or pretend to sob noisily ▷ *n* distressed or pretended sobbing
BOOHOOED > BOOHOO
BOOHOOING > BOOHOO
BOOHOOS > BOOHOO
BOOHS > BOOH
BOOING > BOO
BOOJUM *n* American tree
BOOJUMS > BOOJUM
BOOK *n* number of pages bound together between covers ▷ *vb* reserve (a place, passage, etc) in advance
BOOKABLE > BOOK
BOOKCASE *n* piece of furniture containing shelves for books
BOOKCASES > BOOKCASE
BOOKED > BOOK
BOOKEND *n* one of a pair of usually ornamental supports for holding a row of books upright
BOOKENDS > BOOKEND
BOOKER > BOOK
BOOKERS > BOOK
BOOKFUL > BOOK
BOOKFULS > BOOK
BOOKIE *short for* > BOOKMAKER
BOOKIER > BOOKY
BOOKIES > BOOKIE
BOOKIEST > BOOKY
BOOKING *n* reservation, as of a table or seat
BOOKINGS > BOOKING
BOOKISH *adj* fond of reading
BOOKISHLY > BOOKISH
BOOKLAND *n* common land given to private owner
BOOKLANDS > BOOKLAND
BOOKLESS > BOOK
BOOKLET *n* thin book with paper covers
BOOKLETS > BOOKLET
BOOKLICE > BOOKLOUSE
BOOKLIGHT *n* small light that can be clipped onto a book for reading by
BOOKLORE *n* knowledge or beliefs gleaned from books
BOOKLORES > BOOKLORE
BOOKLOUSE *n* wingless insect that feeds on bookbinding paste, etc
BOOKMAKER *n* person whose occupation is taking bets
BOOKMAN *n* learned person
BOOKMARK *n* person whose occupation is taking bets ▷ *vb* identify and store (a website) so that one can return to it quickly and easily
BOOKMARKS > BOOKMARK
BOOKMEN > BOOKMAN
BOOKOO *same as* > BOOCOO
BOOKOOS > BOOKOO
BOOKPLATE *n* label bearing the owner's name and an individual design or coat of arms, pasted into a book
BOOKRACK *n* rack for holding books
BOOKRACKS > BOOKRACK
BOOKREST *n* stand for supporting open book
BOOKRESTS > BOOKREST
BOOKS > BOOK
BOOKSHELF *n* shelf for books
BOOKSHOP *n* shop where books are sold
BOOKSHOPS > BOOKSHOP
BOOKSIE *same as* > BOOKSY
BOOKSIER > BOOKSY
BOOKSIEST > BOOKSY
BOOKSTALL *n* stall or stand where periodicals, newspapers, or books are sold
BOOKSTAND *n* support for open book
BOOKSTORE *same as* > BOOKSHOP
BOOKSY *adj* inclined to be bookish or literary
BOOKWORK *n* academic study
BOOKWORKS > BOOKWORK
BOOKWORM *n* person devoted to reading
BOOKWORMS > BOOKWORM
BOOKY *adj* bookish
BOOL *n* bowling bowl ▷ *vb* play bowls
BOOLED > BOOL
BOOLING > BOOL
BOOLS > BOOL
BOOM *vb* make a loud deep echoing sound ▷ *n* loud deep echoing sound
BOOMBOX *n* portable stereo system
BOOMBOXES > BOOMBOX
BOOMED > BOOM
BOOMER *n* large male kangaroo
BOOMERANG *n* curved wooden missile which can be made to return to the thrower ▷ *vb* (of a plan) recoil unexpectedly
BOOMERS > BOOMER
BOOMIER > BOOMY
BOOMIEST > BOOMY
BOOMING > BOOM
BOOMINGLY > BOOM
BOOMINGS > BOOM
BOOMKIN *n* short boom projecting from the deck of a ship, used to secure the main-brace blocks or to extend the lower edge of the foresail
BOOMKINS > BOOMKIN
BOOMLET *n* small boom in business, birth rate, etc
BOOMLETS > BOOMLET
BOOMS > BOOM
BOOMSLANG *n* large greenish venomous tree-living snake of southern Africa
BOOMTOWN *n* town that is enjoying sudden prosperity or has grown rapidly
BOOMTOWNS > BOOMTOWN
BOOMY *adj* characterized by heavy bass sound
BOON *n* something extremely useful, helpful, or beneficial
BOONDOCK > BOONDOCKS
BOONDOCKS *n* remote rural area
BOONER *n* young working-class person from Canberra
BOONERS > BOONER
BOONG *n* offensive term for a Black person
BOONGA *n* offensive term for a Pacific Islander
BOONGARY *n* tree kangaroo of NE Queensland, Australia
BOONGAS
BOONGS > BOONG
BOONIES *short form of* > BOONDOCKS
BOONLESS > BOON
BOONS > BOON
BOOR *n* rude or insensitive person
BOORD *obsolete spelling of* > BOARD
BOORDE *obsolete spelling of* > BOARD
BOORDES > BOORDE
BOORDS > BOORD
BOORISH *adj* ill-mannered, clumsy, or insensitive
BOORISHLY > BOORISH
BOORKA *same as* > BURKA
BOORKAS > BOORKA
BOORS > BOOR
BOORTREE *same as* > BOURTREE
BOORTREES > BOORTREE
BOOS > BOO
BOOSE *same as* > BOOZE
BOOSED > BOOSE
BOOSES > BOOSE
BOOSHIT *adj* very good
BOOSING > BOOSE
BOOST *n* encouragement or help ▷ *vb* improve
BOOSTED > BOOST
BOOSTER *n* small additional injection of a vaccine
BOOSTERS > BOOSTER
BOOSTING > BOOST
BOOSTS > BOOST
BOOT *n* outer covering for the foot that extends above the ankle ▷ *vb* kick
BOOTABLE > BOOT
BOOTBLACK *another word for* > SHOEBLACK
BOOTED *adj* wearing boots
BOOTEE *n* baby's soft shoe
BOOTEES > BOOTEE
BOOTERIES > BOOTERY
BOOTERY *n* shop where boots and shoes are sold
BOOTH *n* small partly enclosed cubicle
BOOTHOSE *n* stocking worn with boots
BOOTHS > BOOTH
BOOTIE *n* Royal Marine
BOOTIES > BOOTY
BOOTIKIN *n* small boot
BOOTIKINS > BOOTIKIN
BOOTING > BOOT
BOOTJACK *n* device that grips the heel of a boot to enable the foot to be withdrawn easily
BOOTJACKS > BOOTJACK
BOOTLACE *n* strong lace for fastening a boot
BOOTLACES > BOOTLACE
BOOTLAST *n* foot shape placed in boots or shoes to keep their shape
BOOTLASTS > BOOTLAST
BOOTLEG *adj* produced, distributed, or sold illicitly ▷ *vb* make, carry, or sell (illicit goods) ▷ *n* something made or sold illicitly, such as alcohol

during Prohibition in the US
BOOTLEGS > BOOTLEG
BOOTLESS *adj* of little or no use
BOOTLICK *vb* seek favour by servile or ingratiating behaviour towards (someone, esp someone in authority)
BOOTLICKS > BOOTLICK
BOOTMAKER *n* person who makes boots and shoes
BOOTS > BOOT
BOOTSTRAP *n* leather or fabric loop on the back or side of a boot
BOOTY *n* valuable articles obtained as plunder
BOOZE *n* (consume) alcoholic drink ▷ *vb* drink alcohol, esp in excess
BOOZED > BOOZE
BOOZER *n* person who is fond of drinking
BOOZERS > BOOZER
BOOZES > BOOZE
BOOZEY *same as* > BOOZY
BOOZIER > BOOZY
BOOZIEST > BOOZY
BOOZILY > BOOZY
BOOZINESS > BOOZY
BOOZING > BOOZE
BOOZY *adj* inclined to or involving excessive drinking of alcohol
BOP *vb* dance to pop music ▷ *n* form of jazz with complex rhythms and harmonies
BOPEEP *n* quick look; peek
BOPEEPS > BOPEEP
BOPPED > BOP
BOPPER > BOP
BOPPERS > BOP
BOPPING > BOP
BOPS > BOP
BOR *n* neighbour
BORA *n* Aboriginal ceremony
BORACES > BORAX
BORACHIO *n* pig's skin wine carrier
BORACHIOS > BORACHIO
BORACIC *same as* > BORIC
BORACITE *n* white mineral that forms salt deposits of magnesium borate
BORACITES > BORACITE
BORAGE *n* Mediterranean plant with star-shaped blue flowers
BORAGES > BORAGE
BORAK *n* rubbish
BORAKS > BORAK
BORAL *n* type of fine powder
BORALS > BORAL
BORANE *n* any compound of boron and hydrogen, used in the synthesis of other boron compounds and as high-energy fuels
BORANES > BORANE
BORAS > BORA
BORATE *n* salt or ester of boric acid. Salts of boric acid consist of BO_3 and BO_4 units linked together ▷ *vb* treat with borax, boric acid, or borate
BORATED > BORATE
BORATES > BORATE
BORATING > BORATE
BORAX *n* soluble white mineral occurring in alkaline soils and salt deposits
BORAXES > BORAX
BORAZON *n* extremely hard form of boron nitride
BORAZONS > BORAZON
BORD *obsolete spelling of* > BOARD
BORDAR *n* smallholder who held cottage in return for menial work
BORDARS > BORDAR
BORDE *obsolete spelling of* > BOARD
BORDEAUX *adj* any of several wines produced around Bordeaux
BORDEL *same as* > BORDELLO
BORDELLO *n* brothel
BORDELLOS > BORDELLO
BORDELS > BORDEL
BORDER *n* dividing line between political or geographical regions ▷ *vb* provide with a border
BORDEREAU *n* memorandum or invoice prepared for a company by an underwriter, containing a list of reinsured risks
BORDERED > BORDER
BORDERER *n* person who lives in a border area, esp the border between England and Scotland
BORDERERS > BORDERER
BORDERING > BORDER
BORDERS > BORDER
BORDES > BORDE
BORDS > BORD
BORDURE *n* outer edge of a shield, esp when decorated distinctively
BORDURES > BORDURE
BORE *vb* make (someone) weary by being dull
BOREAL *adj* of or relating to the north or the north wind
BOREALIS *aurora borealis* lights seen around the North Pole
BOREAS *n* name for the north wind
BOREASES > BOREAS
BORECOLE *another name for* > KALE
BORECOLES > BORECOLE
BORED > BORE
BOREDOM *n* state of being bored
BOREDOMS > BOREDOM
BOREE *same as* > MYALL
BOREEN *n* country lane or narrow road
BOREENS > BOREEN
BOREES > BOREE
BOREHOLE *n* hole driven into the ground to obtain geological information, release water, etc
BOREHOLES > BOREHOLE
BOREL *adj* unlearned
BORER *n* machine or hand tool for boring holes
BORERS > BORER
BORES > BEAR
BORESCOPE *n* long narrow device for inspection of, e.g. bore
BORESOME *adj* boring
BORGHETTO *n* settlement outside city walls
BORGO *n* small attractive medieval village
BORGOS > BORGO
BORIC *adj* of or containing boron
BORIDE *n* compound in which boron is the most electronegative element, esp a compound of boron and a metal
BORIDES > BORIDE
BORING *n* act or process of making or enlarging a hole ▷ *adj* dull
BORINGLY > BORING
BORINGS > BORING
BORK *vb* dismiss from job unfairly
BORKED > BORK
BORKING > BORK
BORKS > BORK
BORLOTTI as in *borlotti bean* variety of kidney bean
BORM *vb* smear with paint, oil, etc
BORMED > BORM
BORMING > BORM
BORMS > BORM
BORN *adj* possessing certain qualities from birth
BORNA as in *borna disease* viral disease found in mammals, esp horses
BORNE > BEAR
BORNEOL *n* white solid terpene alcohol
BORNEOLS > BORNEOL
BORNITE *n* mineral consisting of a sulphide of copper and iron that tarnishes to purple
BORNITES > BORNITE
BORNITIC > BORNITE
BORNYL as in *bornyl alcohol* white solid alcohol from a Malaysian tree
BORNYLS > BORNYL
BORON *n* element used in hardening steel
BORONIA *n* Australian aromatic flowering shrub
BORONIAS > BORONIA
BORONIC > BORON
BORONS > BORON
BOROUGH *n* town or district with its own council
BOROUGHS > BOROUGH
BORREL *adj* ignorant
BORRELIA *n* type of bacterium
BORRELIAS > BORRELIA
BORRELL *same as* > BORREL
BORROW *vb* obtain (something) temporarily
BORROWED > BORROW
BORROWER > BORROW
BORROWERS > BORROW
BORROWING > BORROW
BORROWS > BORROW
BORS > BORS
BORSCH *same as* > BORSCHT
BORSCHES > BORSCH
BORSCHT *n* Russian soup based on beetroot
BORSCHTS > BORSCHT
BORSHCH *same as* > BORSCHT
BORSHCHES > BORSHCH
BORSHT *same as* > BORSCHT
BORSHTS > BORSHT
BORSIC *n* strong light composite material of boron fibre and silicon carbide used in aviation
BORSICS > BORSIC
BORSTAL *n* (formerly in Britain) prison for young criminals
BORSTALL *same as* > BORSTAL
BORSTALLS > BORSTAL
BORSTALS > BORSTAL
BORT *n* inferior grade of diamond used for cutting and drilling or, in powdered form, as an industrial abrasive
BORTIER > BORT
BORTIEST > BORT
BORTS > BORT
BORTSCH *same as* > BORSCHT
BORTSCHES > BORTSCH
BORTY > BORT
BORTZ *same as* > BORT
BORTZES > BORTZ
BORZOI *n* tall dog with a long silky coat
BORZOIS > BORZOI
BOS > BO
BOSBERAAD *n* meeting in an isolated venue to break a political deadlock
BOSBOK *same as* > BUSHBUCK
BOSBOKS > BOSBOK
BOSCAGE *n* mass of trees and shrubs
BOSCAGES > BOSCAGE
BOSCHBOK *same as* > BUSHBUCK
BOSCHBOKS > BOSCHBOK
BOSCHE *same as* > BOCHE
BOSCHES > BOSCHE
BOSCHVARK *same as* > BUSHPIG
BOSCHVELD *same as* > BUSHVELD

BOSH *n* empty talk, nonsense
BOSHBOK *same as* > BUSHBUCK
BOSHBOKS > BOSHBOK
BOSHES > BOSH
BOSHTA *same as* > BOSHTER
BOSHTER *adj* excellent
BOSHVARK *same as* > BOSCHVARK
BOSHVARKS > BOSHVARK
BOSK *n* small wood of bushes and small trees
BOSKAGE *same as* > BOSCAGE
BOSKAGES > BOSKAGE
BOSKER *adj* excellent
BOSKET *n* clump of small trees or bushes
BOSKETS > BOSKET
BOSKIER > BOSKY
BOSKIEST > BOSKY
BOSKINESS > BOSKY
BOSKS > BOSK
BOSKY *adj* containing or consisting of bushes or thickets
BOSOM *n* chest of a person, esp the female breasts ▷ *adj* very dear ▷ *vb* embrace
BOSOMED > BOSOM
BOSOMIER > BOSOMY
BOSOMIEST > BOSOMY
BOSOMING > BOSOM
BOSOMS > BOSOM
BOSOMY *adj* (of a woman) having large breasts
BOSON *n* any of a group of elementary particles, such as a photon or pion, that has zero or integral spin and obeys the rules of Bose-Einstein statistics
BOSONIC > BOSON
BOSONS > BOSON
BOSQUE *same as* > BOSK
BOSQUES > BOSQUE
BOSQUET *same as* > BOSKET
BOSQUETS > BOSQUET
BOSS *n* raised knob or stud ▷ *vb* employ, supervise, or be in charge of ▷ *adj* excellent
BOSSBOY *n* Black African foreman of a gang of workers
BOSSBOYS > BOSSBOY
BOSSDOM *n* bosses collectively
BOSSDOMS > BOSSDOM
BOSSED > BOSS
BOSSER > BOSS
BOSSES > BOSS
BOSSEST > BOSS
BOSSET *n* either of the rudimentary antlers found in young deer
BOSSETS > BOSSET
BOSSIER > BOSSY
BOSSIES > BOSSY
BOSSIEST > BOSSY
BOSSILY > BOSSY
BOSSINESS > BOSSY
BOSSING *n* act of shaping malleable metal, such as lead cladding, with mallets to fit a surface
BOSSISM *n* domination or the system of domination of political organizations by bosses
BOSSISMS > BOSSISM
BOSSY *same as* > BOSS
BOSTANGI *n* imperial Turkish guard
BOSTANGIS > BOSTANGI
BOSTHOON *n* boor
BOSTHOONS > BOSTHOON
BOSTON *n* card game for four, played with two packs
BOSTONS > BOSTON
BOSTRYX *n* phenomenon in which flowers develop on one side only
BOSTRYXES > BOSTRYX
BOSUN *same as* > BOATSWAIN
BOSUNS > BOSUN
BOT *n* larva of a botfly, which typically develops inside the body of a horse, sheep, or man
BOTA *n* leather container
BOTANIC *same as* > BOTANICAL
BOTANICA *n* botany
BOTANICAL *adj* of or relating to botany or plants ▷ *n* any drug or pesticide that is made from parts of a plant
BOTANICAS > BOTANICA
BOTANICS > BOTANIC
BOTANIES > BOTANY
BOTANISE *same as* > BOTANIZE
BOTANISED > BOTANISE
BOTANISER > BOTANIZE
BOTANISES > BOTANISE
BOTANIST > BOTANY
BOTANISTS > BOTANY
BOTANIZE *vb* collect or study plants
BOTANIZED > BOTANIZE
BOTANIZER > BOTANIZE
BOTANIZES > BOTANIZE
BOTANY *n* study of plants
BOTARGO *n* relish consisting of the roe of mullet or tunny, salted and pressed into rolls
BOTARGOES > BOTARGO
BOTARGOS > BOTARGO
BOTAS > BOTA
BOTCH *vb* spoil through clumsiness ▷ *n* badly done piece of work or repair
BOTCHED > BOTCH
BOTCHEDLY > BOTCH
BOTCHER > BOTCH
BOTCHERS > BOTCH
BOTCHERY *n* instance of botching
BOTCHES > BOTCH
BOTCHIER > BOTCHY
BOTCHIEST > BOTCHY
BOTCHILY > BOTCHY
BOTCHING > BOTCH
BOTCHINGS > BOTCH
BOTCHY *adj* clumsily done or made
BOTEL *same as* > BOATEL
BOTELS > BOTEL
BOTFLIES > BOTFLY
BOTFLY *n* any of various stout-bodied hairy dipterous flies of the families *Oestridae* and *Gasterophilidae*, the larvae of which are parasites of man, sheep, and horses
BOTH *pron* two considered together ▷ *adj* two considered together ▷ *determiner* two
BOTHAN *n* unlicensed drinking house
BOTHANS > BOTHAN
BOTHER *vb* take the time or trouble ▷ *n* trouble, fuss, or difficulty ▷ *interj* exclamation of slight annoyance
BOTHERED > BOTHER
BOTHERING > BOTHER
BOTHERS > BOTHER
BOTHIE *same as* > BOTHY
BOTHIES > BOTHY
BOTHOLE *n* hole made by the larva of the botfly
BOTHOLES > BOTHOLE
BOTHRIA > BOTHRIUM
BOTHRIUM *n* groove-shaped sucker on tapeworm
BOTHRIUMS > BOTHRIUM
BOTHY *n* hut used for temporary shelter
BOTHYMAN *n* man who lives in bothy
BOTHYMEN > BOTHYMAN
BOTNET *n* network of infected computers
BOTNETS > BOTNET
BOTONE *adj* having lobes at the ends
BOTONEE *same as* > BOTONE
BOTONNEE *same as* > BOTONE
BOTRYOID *adj* shaped like a bunch of grapes
BOTRYOSE *same as* > BOTRYOID
BOTRYTIS *n* any of a group of fungi of the genus *Botrytis*, several of which cause plant diseases
BOTS *n* digestive disease of horses and some other animals caused by the presence of botfly larvae in the stomach
BOTT *same as* > BOT
BOTTE *n* thrust or hit
BOTTED > BOT
BOTTEGA *n* workshop; studio
BOTTEGAS > BOTTEGA
BOTTES > BOTTE
BOTTIES > BOTTY
BOTTINE *n* light boot for women or children
BOTTINES > BOTTINE
BOTTING > BOT
BOTTLE *n* container for holding liquids ▷ *vb* put in a bottle
BOTTLED > BOTTLE
BOTTLEFUL > BOTTLE
BOTTLER *n* exceptional person or thing
BOTTLERS > BOTTLER
BOTTLES > BOTTLE
BOTTLING > BOTTLE
BOTTLINGS > BOTTLE
BOTTOM *n* lowest, deepest, or farthest removed part of a thing ▷ *adj* lowest or last ▷ *vb* provide with a bottom
BOTTOMED > BOTTOM
BOTTOMER *n* pit worker
BOTTOMERS > BOTTOMER
BOTTOMING *n* lowest level of foundation material for a road or other structure
BOTTOMRY *n* contract whereby the owner of a ship borrows money to enable the vessel to complete the voyage and pledges the ship as security for the loan
BOTTOMS > BOTTOM
BOTTOMSET as in *bottomset bed* fine sediment deposited at the front of a growing delta
BOTTONY *same as* > BOTONE
BOTTS > BOTT
BOTTY *n* diminutive for bottom
BOTULIN *n* potent toxin produced by the bacterium *Clostridium botulinum* in imperfectly preserved food, etc, causing botulism
BOTULINAL > BOTULIN
BOTULINS > BOTULIN
BOTULINUM *n* botulin-secreting bacterium
BOTULINUS *n* anaerobic bacterium, *Clostridium botulinum*, whose toxins (botulins) cause botulism: family *Bacillaceae*
BOTULISM *n* severe food poisoning
BOTULISMS > BOTULISM
BOUBOU *n* long flowing garment worn by men and women in Mali, Nigeria, Senegal, and some other parts of Africa
BOUBOUS > BOUBOU
BOUCHE *n* notch cut in top corner of shield
BOUCHEE *n* small pastry case filled with a savoury mixture, served hot with cocktails or as an hors d'oeuvre
BOUCHEES > BOUCHEE
BOUCHES > BOUCHE

BOUCLE *n* looped yarn giving a knobbly effect ▷ *adj* of or designating such a yarn or fabric
BOUCLEE *n* support for a cue in billiards formed by doubling the first finger so that its tip is aligned with the thumb at its second joint, to form a loop through which the cue may slide
BOUCLEES > BOUCLEE
BOUCLES > BOUCLE
BOUDERIE *n* sulkiness
BOUDERIES > BOUDERIE
BOUDIN *n* French version of a black pudding
BOUDINS > BOUDIN
BOUDOIR *n* woman's bedroom or private sitting room
BOUDOIRS > BOUDOIR
BOUFFANT *adj* (of a hairstyle) having extra height through backcombing ▷ *n* bouffant hair style
BOUFFANTS > BOUFFANT
BOUFFE *n* type of light or satirical opera common in France during the 19th century
BOUFFES > BOUFFE
BOUGE *vb* move
BOUGED > BOUGE
BOUGES > BOUGE
BOUGET *n* budget
BOUGETS > BOUGET
BOUGH *n* large branch of a tree
BOUGHED > BOUGH
BOUGHLESS > BOUGH
BOUGHPOT *n* container for displaying boughs
BOUGHPOTS > BOUGHPOT
BOUGHS > BOUGH
BOUGHT > BUY
BOUGHTEN *a dialect word for* > BUY
BOUGHTS > BUY
BOUGIE *n* long slender semiflexible cylindrical instrument for inserting into body passages, such as the rectum or urethra, to dilate structures, introduce medication, etc
BOUGIES > BOUGIE
BOUGING > BOUGE
BOUILLI *n* stew
BOUILLIS > BOUILLI
BOUILLON *n* thin clear broth or stock
BOUILLONS > BOUILLON
BOUK *n* bulk; volume
BOUKS > BOUK
BOULDER *n* large rounded rock ▷ *vb* convert into boulders
BOULDERED > BOULDER
BOULDERER > BOULDER
BOULDERS > BOULDER
BOULDERY > BOULDER
BOULE *same as* > BOULLE
BOULES *n* game, popular in France, in which metal bowls are thrown to land as close as possible to a target ball
BOULEVARD *n* wide, usu. tree-lined, street
BOULLE *adj* denoting or relating to a type of marquetry of patterned inlays of brass and tortoiseshell, occasionally with other metals such as pewter, much used on French furniture from the 17th century ▷ *n* something ornamented with such marquetry
BOULLES > BOULLE
BOULT *same as* > BOLT
BOULTED > BOULT
BOULTER > BOLT
BOULTERS > BOLT
BOULTING > BOULT
BOULTINGS > BOULT
BOULTS > BOULT
BOUN *vb* prepare to go out
BOUNCE *vb* (of a ball etc) rebound from an impact ▷ *n* act of rebounding
BOUNCED > BOUNCE
BOUNCER *n* person employed at a disco etc to remove unwanted people
BOUNCERS > BOUNCER
BOUNCES > BOUNCE
BOUNCIER > BOUNCY
BOUNCIEST > BOUNCY
BOUNCILY > BOUNCY
BOUNCING *adj* vigorous and robust
BOUNCY *adj* lively, exuberant, or self-confident
BOUND > BIND
BOUNDABLE > BIND
BOUNDARY *n* dividing line that indicates the farthest limit
BOUNDED *adj* (of a set) having a bound, esp where a measure is defined in terms of which all the elements of the set, or the differences between all pairs of members, are less than some value, or else all its members lie within some other well-defined set
BOUNDEN *adj* morally obligatory
BOUNDER *n* morally reprehensible person
BOUNDERS > BOUNDER
BOUNDING > BIND
BOUNDLESS *adj* unlimited
BOUNDNESS > BIND
BOUNDS *pl n* limit
BOUNED > BOUN
BOUNING > BOUN
BOUNS > BOUN
BOUNTEOUS *adj* giving freely
BOUNTIED > BOUNTY
BOUNTIES > BOUNTY
BOUNTIFUL *adj* plentiful
BOUNTREE *another name for* > BOUNTREE
BOUNTREES > BOUNTREE
BOUNTY *n* generosity
BOUNTYHED *n* generosity
BOUQUET *n* bunch of flowers
BOUQUETS > BOUQUET
BOURASQUE *n* violent storm
BOURBON *n* whiskey made from maize
BOURBONS > BOURBON
BOURD *n* prank
BOURDER *n* prankster
BOURDERS > BOURDER
BOURDON *n* 16-foot organ stop of the stopped diapason type
BOURDONS > BOURDON
BOURDS > BOURD
BOURG *n* French market town, esp one beside a castle
BOURGEOIS *n* middle-class (person) ▷ *adj* characteristic of or comprising the middle class
BOURGEON *same as* > BURGEON
BOURGEONS > BOURGEON
BOURGS > BOURG
BOURKHA *same as* > BURKA
BOURKHAS *same as* > BOURKHA
BOURLAW *same as* > BYRLAW
BOURLAWS > BOURLAW
BOURN *n* (in S Britain) stream
BOURNE *same as* > BOURN
BOURNES > BOURNE
BOURNS > BOURN
BOURREE *n* traditional French dance in fast duple time
BOURREES > BOURREE
BOURRIDE *n* Mediterranean fish soup
BOURRIDES > BOURRIDE
BOURSE *n* stock exchange of continental Europe, esp Paris
BOURSES > BOURSE
BOURSIER *n* stock-exchange worker
BOURSIERS > BOURSIER
BOURSIN *n* tradename of a smooth white creamy cheese, often flavoured with garlic
BOURSINS > BOURSIN
BOURTREE *n* elder tree
BOURTREES > BOURTREE
BOUSE *vb* raise or haul with a tackle
BOUSED > BOUSE
BOUSES > BOUSE
BOUSIER > BOUSY
BOUSIEST > BOUSY
BOUSING > BOUSE
BOUSOUKI *same as* > BOUZOUKI
BOUSOUKIA > BOUSOUKI
BOUSOUKIS > BOUSOUKI
BOUSY *adj* drunken; boozy
BOUT *n* period of activity or illness
BOUTADE *n* outburst
BOUTADES > BOUTADE
BOUTIQUE *n* small clothes shop
BOUTIQUES > BOUTIQUE
BOUTIQUEY *adj* typical of boutiques
BOUTON *n* knob-shaped contact between nerve fibres
BOUTONNE *adj* reserved or inhibited
BOUTONNEE *same as* > BOUTONNE
BOUTONS > BOUTON
BOUTS > BOUT
BOUVARDIA *n* flowering plant
BOUVIER *n* large powerful dog of a Belgian breed, having a rough shaggy coat: used esp for cattle herding and guarding
BOUVIERS > BOUVIER
BOUZOUKI *n* Greek stringed musical instrument
BOUZOUKIA > BOUZOUKI
BOUZOUKIS > BOUZOUKI
BOVATE *n* obsolete measure of land
BOVATES > BOVATE
BOVID *adj* of, relating to, or belonging to the *Bovidae*, a family of ruminant artiodactyl hollow-horned mammals including sheep, goats, cattle, antelopes, and buffalo ▷ *n* any bovid animal
BOVIDS > BOVID
BOVINE *adj* relating to cattle ▷ *n* any animal belonging to the *Bovini*
BOVINELY > BOVINE
BOVINES > BOVINE
BOVINITY > BOVINE
BOVVER *n* rowdiness, esp caused by gangs of teenage youths
BOVVERS > BOVVER
BOW *vb* lower (one's head) or bend (one's knee or body) as a sign of respect or shame ▷ *n* movement made when bowing
BOWAT *n* lamp
BOWATS > BOWAT
BOWBENT *adj* bent; bow-like
BOWED *adj* lowered, bent forward, or curved
BOWEL *n* intestine, esp the large intestine ▷ *vb* remove the bowels
BOWELED > BOWEL
BOWELING > BOWEL
BOWELLED > BOWEL
BOWELLESS > BOWEL

BOWELLING > BOWEL
BOWELS > BOWEL
BOWER *n* shady leafy shelter ▷ *vb* surround as with a bower
BOWERBIRD *n* songbird of Australia and New Guinea, the males of which build bower-like display grounds to attract females
BOWERED > BOWER
BOWERIES > BOWER
BOWERING > BOWER
BOWERS > BOWER
BOWERY > BOWER
BOWES *same as* > BOUGH
BOWET *same as* > BOWAT
BOWETS > BOWET
BOWFIN *n* primitive North American freshwater bony fish, *Amia calva*, with an elongated body and a very long dorsal fin: family *Amiidae*
BOWFINS > BOWFIN
BOWFRONT *adj* having a front that curves outwards
BOWGET *obsolete variant of* > BUDGET
BOWGETS > BOWGET
BOWHEAD *n* large-mouthed arctic whale, *Balaena mysticetus*, that has become rare through overfishing but is now a protected species
BOWHEADS > BOWHEAD
BOWHUNTER *n* person hunting with bow and arrows
BOWIE as in *Bowie knife* type of hunting knife
BOWING *n* technique of using the bow in playing a violin, viola, cello, or related instrument
BOWINGLY > BOWING
BOWINGS > BOWING
BOWKNOT *n* decorative knot usually having two loops and two loose ends
BOWKNOTS > BOWKNOT
BOWL *n* round container with an open top ▷ *vb* roll smoothly along the ground
BOWLDER *same as* > BOULDER
BOWLDERS > BOWLDER
BOWLED > BOWL
BOWLEG > BOWLEGS
BOWLEGGED *adj* having legs that curve outwards like a bow
BOWLEGS
BOWLER *n* player who sends (a ball) towards the batsman
BOWLERS > BOWLER
BOWLESS > BOW
BOWLFUL *same as* > BOWL
BOWLFULS > BOWLFUL
BOWLIKE > BOW
BOWLINE *n* line used to keep the sail taut against the wind
BOWLINES > BOWLINE
BOWLING *n* game in which bowls are rolled at a group of pins
BOWLINGS > BLOW
BOWLLIKE > BOWL
BOWLS *n* game played on a very smooth area of grass in which opponents roll biased wooden bowls as near a small bowl (the jack) as possible
BOWMAN *n* archer
BOWMEN > BOWMAN
BOWNE *same as* > BOUN
BOWNED > BOWNE
BOWNES > BOWNE
BOWNING > BOWNE
BOWPOT *same as* > BOUGHPOT
BOWPOTS > BOWPOT
BOWR *n* muscle
BOWRS > BOWR
BOWS > BOW
BOWSAW *n* saw with a thin blade in a bow-shaped frame
BOWSAWS > BOWSAW
BOWSE *same as* > BOUSE
BOWSED > BOWSE
BOWSER *n* tanker containing fuel for aircraft, military vehicles, etc
BOWSERS > BOWSER
BOWSES > BOWSE
BOWSEY *n* Irish word for mean person
BOWSEYS > BOWSEY
BOWSHOT *n* distance an arrow travels from the bow
BOWSHOTS > BOWSHOT
BOWSIE *n* low-class mean or obstreperous person
BOWSIES > BOWSIE
BOWSING > BOWSE
BOWSPRIT *n* spar projecting from the bow of a sailing ship
BOWSPRITS > BOWSPRIT
BOWSTRING *n* string of an archer's bow
BOWSTRUNG > BOWSTRING
BOWWOW *n* imitation of the bark of a dog ▷ *vb* make a noise like a dog
BOWWOWED > BOWWOW
BOWWOWING > BOWWOW
BOWWOWS > BOWWOW
BOWYANG *n* band worn round trouser leg below knee
BOWYANGS > BOWYANG
BOWYER *n* person who makes or sells archery bows
BOWYERS > BOWYER
BOX *n* container with a firm flat base and sides ▷ *vb* put into a box
BOXBALL *n* street ball game
BOXBALLS > BOXBALL
BOXBERRY *n* fruit of the partridgeberry or wintergreen
BOXBOARD *n* tough paperboard made from wood and wastepaper pulp: used for making boxes, etc
BOXBOARDS > BOXBOARD
BOXCAR *n* closed railway freight van
BOXCARS > BOXCAR
BOXED > BOX
BOXEN > BOX
BOXER *n* person who participates in the sport of boxing
BOXERCISE *n* system of sustained exercises combining boxing movements with aerobic activities
BOXERS > BOXER
BOXES > BOX
BOXFISH *another name for* > TRUNKFISH
BOXFISHES > BOXFISH
BOXFUL > BOX
BOXFULS > BOX
BOXHAUL *vb* bring (a square-rigger) onto a new tack by backwinding the foresails and steering hard round
BOXHAULED > BOXHAUL
BOXHAULS > BOXHAUL
BOXIER > BOXY
BOXIEST > BOXY
BOXILY > BOXY
BOXINESS > BOXY
BOXING *n* sport of fighting with the fists
BOXINGS > BOXING
BOXKEEPER *n* person responsible for theatre boxes
BOXLIKE > BOX
BOXROOM *n* small room in which boxes, cases, etc may be stored
BOXROOMS > BOXROOM
BOXTHORN *n* matrimony vine
BOXTHORNS > BOXTHORN
BOXWALLAH *n* salesman
BOXWOOD *n* hard yellow wood of the box tree, used to make tool handles, etc
BOXWOODS > BOXWOOD
BOXY *adj* squarish or chunky
BOY *n* male child ▷ *vb* act the part of a boy in a play
BOYAR *n* member of an old order of Russian nobility, ranking immediately below the princes: abolished by Peter the Great
BOYARD *same as* > BOYAR
BOYARDS > BOYARD
BOYARISM > BOYAR
BOYARISMS > BOYAR
BOYARS > BOYAR
BOYAU *n* connecting trench
BOYAUX > BOYAU
BOYCHICK *same as* > BOYCHIK
BOYCHICKS > BOYCHICK
BOYCHIK *n* young boy
BOYCHIKS > BOYCHIK
BOYCOTT *vb* refuse to deal with (an organization or country) ▷ *n* instance of boycotting
BOYCOTTED > BOYCOTT
BOYCOTTER > BOYCOTT
BOYCOTTS > BOYCOTT
BOYED > BOY
BOYF *n* boyfriend
BOYFRIEND *n* male friend with whom a person is romantically or sexually involved
BOYFS > BOYF
BOYG *n* troll-like mythical creature
BOYGS > BOYG
BOYHOOD *n* state or time of being a boy
BOYHOODS > BOYHOOD
BOYING > BOY
BOYISH *adj* of or like a boy in looks, behaviour, or character, esp when regarded as attractive or endearing
BOYISHLY > BOYISH
BOYLA *n* Australian Aboriginal word for magician
BOYLAS > BOYLA
BOYO *n* boy or young man: often used in direct address
BOYOS > BOYO
BOYS > BOY
BOYSIER > BOYSY
BOYSIEST > BOYSY
BOYSY *adj* suited to or typical of boys or young men
BOZO *n* man, esp a stupid one
BOZOS > BOZO
BOZZETTI > BOZZETTO
BOZZETTO *n* small sketch of planned work
BRA *same as* > BRASSIERE
BRAAI *vb* grill or roast (meat) over open coals
BRAAIED > BRAAI
BRAAIING > BRAAI
BRAAIS > BRAAI
BRAATA *n* small portion added to a purchase of food by a market vendor, to encourage the customer to return
BRAATAS *same as* > BRAATA
BRAATASES > BRAATAS
BRABBLE *rare word for* > SQUABBLE
BRABBLED > BRABBLE
BRABBLER > BRABBLE
BRABBLERS > BRABBLE
BRABBLES > BRABBLE
BRABBLING > BRABBLE
BRACCATE *adj* (of birds) having feathered legs

BRACCIA > BRACCIO
BRACCIO *n* former unit of measurement; length of man's arm
BRACE *n* object fastened to something to straighten or support it ▷ *vb* steady or prepare (oneself) for something unpleasant
BRACED > BRACE
BRACELET *n* ornamental chain or band for the wrist
BRACELETS *pl n* handcuffs
BRACER *n* person or thing that braces
BRACERO *n* Mexican World War II labourer
BRACEROS > BRACERO
BRACERS > BRACER
BRACES *pl n* pair of straps worn over the shoulders for holding up the trousers
BRACH *n* bitch hound
BRACHAH *n* blessing
BRACHAHS > BRACHAH
BRACHES > BRACH
BRACHET *same as* > BRACH
BRACHETS > BRACHET
BRACHIA > BRACHIUM
BRACHIAL *adj* of or relating to the arm or to an armlike part or structure ▷ *n* brachial part or structure
BRACHIALS > BRACHIAL
BRACHIATE *adj* having widely divergent paired branches ▷ *vb* (of some arboreal apes and monkeys) swing by the arms from one hold to the next
BRACHIUM *n* arm, esp the upper part
BRACHS > BRACH
BRACING *adj* refreshing and invigorating ▷ *n* system of braces used to strengthen or support
BRACINGLY > BRACING
BRACINGS > BRACING
BRACIOLA *n* Italian meat roulade
BRACIOLAS > BRACIOLA
BRACIOLE *same as* > BRACIOLA
BRACIOLES > BRACIOLE
BRACK *same as* > BARMBRACK
BRACKEN *n* large fern
BRACKENS > BRACKEN
BRACKET *n* pair of characters used to enclose a section of writing ▷ *vb* put in brackets
BRACKETED > BRACKET
BRACKETS > BRACKET
BRACKISH *adj* (of water) slightly salty
BRACKS > BRACK
BRACONID *n* type of fly with parasitic larva
BRACONIDS > BRACONID
BRACT *n* leaf at the base of a flower
BRACTEAL > BRACT
BRACTEATE *adj* (of a plant) having bracts ▷ *n* fine decorated dish or plate of precious metal
BRACTED > BRACT
BRACTEOLE *n* secondary bract subtending a flower within an inflorescence
BRACTLESS > BRACT
BRACTLET *variant of* > BRACTEOLE
BRACTLETS > BRACTLET
BRACTS > BRACT
BRAD *n* small tapered nail with a small head
BRADAWL *n* small boring tool
BRADAWLS > BRADAWL
BRADDED > BRAD
BRADDING > BRAD
BRADOON *same as* > BRIDOON
BRADOONS > BRADOON
BRADS > BRAD
BRAE *n* hill or slope
BRAEHEID *n* summit of a hill or slope
BRAEHEIDS > BRAEHEID
BRAES > BRAE
BRAG *vb* speak arrogantly and boastfully ▷ *n* boastful talk or behaviour
BRAGGART *n* person who boasts loudly ▷ *adj* boastful
BRAGGARTS > BRAGGART
BRAGGED > BRAG
BRAGGER > BRAG
BRAGGERS > BRAG
BRAGGEST > BRAG
BRAGGIER > BRAGGY
BRAGGIEST > BRAGGY
BRAGGING > BRAG
BRAGGINGS > BRAG
BRAGGY *adj* boastful
BRAGLY > BRAG
BRAGS > BRAG
BRAHMA *n* heavy breed of domestic fowl with profusely feathered legs and feet
BRAHMAN *n* member of highest Hindu caste
BRAHMANI *n* woman of the highest Hindu caste
BRAHMANIS > BRAHMANI
BRAHMANS > BRAHMAN
BRAHMAS > BRAHMA
BRAHMIN *same as* > BRAHMAN
BRAHMINS > BRAHMIN
BRAID *vb* interweave (hair, thread, etc) ▷ *n* length of hair etc that has been braided ▷ *adj* broad ▷ *adv* broadly
BRAIDE *adj* given to deceit
BRAIDED *adj* (of a river or stream) flowing in several shallow interconnected channels separated by banks of deposited material
BRAIDER > BRAID
BRAIDERS > BRAID
BRAIDEST > BRAID
BRAIDING *n* braids collectively
BRAIDINGS > BRAIDING
BRAIDS > BRAID
BRAIL *n* one of several lines fastened to the leech of a fore-and-aft sail to aid in furling it ▷ *vb* furl (a fore-and-aft sail) using brails
BRAILED > BRAIL
BRAILING > BRAIL
BRAILLE *n* system of writing for the blind consisting of raised dots that can be interpreted by touch ▷ *vb* print or write using this method
BRAILLED > BRAILLE
BRAILLER *n* device for producing text in braille
BRAILLERS > BRAILLER
BRAILLES > BRAILLE
BRAILLING > BRAILLE
BRAILLIST *n* braille transcriber
BRAILS > BRAIL
BRAIN *n* soft mass of nervous tissue in the head ▷ *vb* hit (someone) hard on the head
BRAINBOX *n* skull
BRAINCASE *n* part of cranium that covers brain
BRAINDEAD *adj* having suffered irreversible stoppage of breathing due to brain damage
BRAINED > BRAIN
BRAINFART *n* idea expressed without much previous thought
BRAINIAC *n* highly intelligent person
BRAINIACS > BRAINIAC
BRAINIER > BRAINY
BRAINIEST > BRAINY
BRAINILY > BRAINY
BRAINING > BRAIN
BRAINISH *adj* impulsive
BRAINLESS *adj* stupid
BRAINPAN *n* skull
BRAINPANS > BRAINPAN
BRAINS > BRAIN
BRAINSICK *adj* relating to or caused by insanity
BRAINSTEM *n* stalklike part of the brain consisting of the medulla oblongata, the midbrain, and the pons Varolii
BRAINWASH *vb* cause (a person) to alter his or her beliefs, esp by methods based on isolation, sleeplessness, etc
BRAINWAVE *n* sudden idea
BRAINY *adj* clever
BRAIRD *vb* appear as shoots
BRAIRDED > BRAIRD
BRAIRDING > BRAIRD
BRAIRDS > BRAIRD
BRAISE *vb* cook slowly in a covered pan with a little liquid
BRAISED > BRAISE
BRAISES > BRAISE
BRAISING > BRAISE
BRAIZE *same as* > BRAISE
BRAIZES > BRAIZE
BRAK *n* crossbred dog ▷ *adj* (of water) slightly salty
BRAKE *same as* > BRACKEN
BRAKEAGE > BRAKE
BRAKEAGES > BRAKE
BRAKED > BRAKE
BRAKELESS > BRAKE
BRAKEMAN *n* crew member of a goods or passenger train. His duties include controlling auxiliary braking power and inspecting the train
BRAKEMEN > BRAKEMAN
BRAKES > BRAKE
BRAKESMAN *n* pithead winch operator
BRAKESMEN > BRAKESMAN
BRAKIER > BRAKY
BRAKIEST > BRAKY
BRAKING > BRAKE
BRAKS > BRAK
BRAKY *adj* brambly
BRALESS > BRA
BRAMBLE *n* Scots word for blackberry
BRAMBLED > BRAMBLE
BRAMBLES > BRAMBLE
BRAMBLIER > BRAMBLE
BRAMBLING *n* Eurasian finch, *Fringilla montifringilla*, with a speckled head and back and, in the male, a reddish brown breast and darker wings and tail
BRAMBLY > BRAMBLE
BRAME *n* powerful feeling of emotion
BRAMES > BRAME
BRAN *n* husks of cereal grain
BRANCARD *n* couch on shafts, carried between two horses
BRANCARDS > BRANCARD
BRANCH *n* secondary stem of a tree ▷ *vb* (of stems, roots, etc) divide, then develop in different directions
BRANCHED > BRANCH
BRANCHER *n* young bird learning to fly
BRANCHERS > BRANCHER
BRANCHERY *n* branches
BRANCHES > BRANCH
BRANCHIA *n* gill in aquatic animals
BRANCHIAE > BRANCHIA
BRANCHIAL *adj* of or relating to the gills of an aquatic animal, esp a fish
BRANCHIER > BRANCH
BRANCHING > BRANCH
BRANCHLET *n* small branch
BRANCHY > BRANCH
BRAND *n* particular product

▷ *vb* mark with a brand
BRANDADE *n* French puréed fish dish
BRANDADES > BRANDADE
BRANDED *adj* identifiable as being the product of a particular manufacturer or marketing company
BRANDER > BRAND
BRANDERED > BRAND
BRANDERS > BRAND
BRANDIED > BRANDY
BRANDIES > BRANDY
BRANDING > BRAND
BRANDINGS > BRAND
BRANDISE *n* three-legged metal stand for cooking pots
BRANDISES > BRANDISE
BRANDISH *vb* wave (a weapon etc) in a threatening way ▷ *n* threatening or defiant flourish
BRANDLESS > BRAND
BRANDLING *n* small red earthworm, *Eisenia foetida* (or *Helodrilus foetidus*), found in manure and used as bait by anglers
BRANDRETH *n* framework of bars used for cooking meat over fire
BRANDS > BRAND
BRANDY *n* alcoholic spirit distilled from wine ▷ *vb* give brandy to
BRANDYING > BRANDY
BRANGLE *vb* quarrel noisily
BRANGLED > BRANGLE
BRANGLES > BRANGLE
BRANGLING > BRANGLE
BRANK *vb* walk with swaggering gait
BRANKED > BRANK
BRANKIER > BRANKY
BRANKIEST > BRANKY
BRANKING > BRANK
BRANKS *pl n* (formerly) iron bridle used to restrain scolding women
BRANKY *adj* ostentatious
BRANLE *n* old French country dance performed in a linked circle
BRANLES > BRANLE
BRANNED > BRAN
BRANNER *n* person or machine that treats metal with bran
BRANNERS > BRANNER
BRANNIER > BRANNY
BRANNIEST > BRANNY
BRANNIGAN *n* noisy quarrel
BRANNING > BRAN
BRANNY *adj* having the appearance or texture of bran
BRANS > BRAN
BRANSLE *another word for* > BRANTLE
BRANSLES > BRANSLE
BRANT *n* small goose, *Branta bernicla*, that has a dark grey plumage and short neck and occurs in most northern coastal regions
BRANTAIL *n* singing bird with red tail
BRANTAILS > BRANTAIL
BRANTLE *n* French country dance
BRANTLES > BRANTLE
BRANTS > BRANT
BRAS > BRA
BRASCO *n* lavatory
BRASCOS > BRASCO
BRASERO *n* metal grid for burning coals
BRASEROS > BRASERO
BRASES > BRA
BRASH *adj* offensively loud, showy, or self-confident ▷ *n* loose rubbish, such as broken rock, hedge clippings, etc ▷ *vb* assault
BRASHED > BRASH
BRASHER > BRASH
BRASHES > BRASH
BRASHEST > BRASH
BRASHIER > BRASHY
BRASHIEST > BRASHY
BRASHING > BRASH
BRASHLY > BRASH
BRASHNESS > BRASH
BRASHY *adj* loosely fragmented
BRASIER *same as* > BRAZIER
BRASIERS > BRASIER
BRASIL *same as* > BRAZIL
BRASILEIN *same as* > BRAZILEIN
BRASILIN *same as* > BRAZILIN
BRASILINS > BRASILIN
BRASILS > BRASIL
BRASS *n* alloy of copper and zinc ▷ *vb* make irritated or annoyed
BRASSAGE *n* amount charged by government for making coins
BRASSAGES > BRASSAGE
BRASSARD *n* identifying armband or badge
BRASSARDS > BRASSARD
BRASSART *same as* > BRASSARD
BRASSARTS > BRASSART
BRASSED > BRASS
BRASSERIE *n* restaurant serving drinks and cheap meals
BRASSES > BRASS
BRASSET *same as* > BRASSART
BRASSETS > BRASSET
BRASSICA *n* any plant of the cabbage and turnip family
BRASSICAS > BRASSICA
BRASSIE *n* former name for a club, a No. 2 wood, originally having a brass-plated sole and with a shallower face than a driver to give more loft
BRASSIER > BRASSY
BRASSIERE *n* bra
BRASSIES > BRASSIE
BRASSIEST > BRASSY
BRASSILY > BRASSY
BRASSING > BRASS
BRASSISH > BRASS
BRASSWARE *n* items made of brass
BRASSY *same as* > BRASSIE
BRAST *same as* > BURST
BRASTING > BRAST
BRASTS > BRAST
BRAT *n* unruly child
BRATCHET *n* hunting dog
BRATCHETS > BRATCHET
BRATLING *n* small badly-behaved child
BRATLINGS > BRATLING
BRATPACK *n* group of precocious and successful young actors, writers, etc
BRATPACKS > BRATPACK
BRATS > BRAT
BRATTICE *n* partition of wood or treated cloth used to control ventilation in a mine ▷ *vb* fit with a brattice
BRATTICED > BRATTICE
BRATTICES > BRATTICE
BRATTIER > BRAT
BRATTIEST > BRAT
BRATTISH *same as* > BRATTICE
BRATTLE *vb* make a rattling sound
BRATTLED > BRATTLE
BRATTLES > BRATTLE
BRATTLING > BRATTLE
BRATTY > BRAT
BRATWURST *n* type of small pork sausage
BRAUNCH *old variant of* > BRANCH
BRAUNCHED > BRAUNCH
BRAUNCHES > BRAUNCH
BRAUNITE *n* brown or black mineral
BRAUNITES > BRAUNITE
BRAVA *n* professional assassin
BRAVADO *n* showy display of self-confidence ▷ *vb* behave with bravado
BRAVADOED > BRAVADO
BRAVADOES > BRAVADO
BRAVADOS > BRAVADO
BRAVAS > BRAVA
BRAVE *adj* having or showing courage, resolution, and daring ▷ *n* Native American warrior ▷ *vb* confront with resolution or courage
BRAVED > BRAVE
BRAVELY > BRAVE
BRAVENESS > BRAVE
BRAVER > BRAVE
BRAVERIES > BRAVE
BRAVERS > BRAVE
BRAVERY > BRAVE
BRAVES > BRAVE
BRAVEST > BRAVE
BRAVI > BRAVO
BRAVING > BRAVE
BRAVO *interj* well done! ▷ *n* cry of 'bravo' ▷ *vb* cry or shout 'bravo'
BRAVOED > BRAVO
BRAVOES > BRAVO
BRAVOING > BRAVO
BRAVOS > BRAVO
BRAVURA *n* display of boldness or daring
BRAVURAS > BRAVURA
BRAVURE > BRAVURA
BRAW *adj* fine or excellent, esp in appearance or dress ▷ *pl n* best clothes
BRAWER > BRAW
BRAWEST > BRAW
BRAWL *n* noisy fight ▷ *vb* fight noisily
BRAWLED > BRAWL
BRAWLER > BRAWL
BRAWLERS > BRAWL
BRAWLIE *adj* in good health
BRAWLIER > BRAWLIE
BRAWLIEST > BRAWLIE
BRAWLING > BRAWL
BRAWLINGS > BRAWL
BRAWLS > BRAWL
BRAWLY > BRAW
BRAWN *n* physical strength
BRAWNED > BRAWN
BRAWNIER > BRAWNY
BRAWNIEST > BRAWNY
BRAWNILY > BRAWNY
BRAWNS > BRAWN
BRAWNY *adj* muscular and strong
BRAWS *n* fine apparel
BRAXIES > BRAXY
BRAXY *n* acute and usually fatal bacterial disease of sheep characterized by high fever, coma, and inflammation of the fourth stomach, caused by infection with *Clostridium septicum*
BRAY *vb* (of a donkey) utter its loud harsh sound ▷ *n* donkey's loud harsh sound
BRAYED > BRAY
BRAYER > BRAY
BRAYERS > BRAY
BRAYING > BRAY
BRAYS > BRAY
BRAZA *n* Spanish unit of measurement
BRAZAS > BRAZA
BRAZE *vb* join (two metal surfaces) with brass ▷ *n* high-melting solder or alloy used in brazing
BRAZED > BRAZE
BRAZELESS > BRAZE
BRAZEN *adj* shameless and bold ▷ *vb* face and overcome boldly or shamelessly
BRAZENED > BRAZEN
BRAZENING > BRAZEN
BRAZENLY > BRAZEN
BRAZENRY *adj* audacity

BRAZENS > BRAZEN
BRAZER > BRAZE
BRAZERS > BRAZE
BRAZES > BRAZE
BRAZIER *n* portable container for burning charcoal or coal
BRAZIERS > BRAZIER
BRAZIERY > BRAZIER
BRAZIL *n* red wood obtained from various tropical leguminous trees of the genus *Caesalpinia*, such as *C. echinata* of America: used for cabinetwork
BRAZILEIN *n* red crystalline solid
BRAZILIN *n* pale yellow soluble crystalline solid
BRAZILINS > BRAZILIN
BRAZILS > BRAZIL
BRAZING > BRAZE
BREACH *n* breaking of a promise, obligation, etc ▷ *vb* break (a promise, law, etc)
BREACHED > BREACH
BREACHER > BREACH
BREACHERS > BREACH
BREACHES > BREACH
BREACHING > BREACH
BREAD *n* food made by baking a mixture of flour and water or milk ▷ *vb* cover (food) with breadcrumbs before cooking
BREADBOX *n* airtight container for bread, cakes, etc
BREADED > BREAD
BREADHEAD *n* person solely concerned with money
BREADING > BREAD
BREADLESS > BREAD
BREADLINE *n* queue of people waiting for free food given as charity
BREADNUT *n* moraceous tree, *Brosimum alicastrum*, of Central America and the Caribbean
BREADNUTS > BREADNUT
BREADROOM *n* place where bread is kept on ship
BREADROOT *n* leguminous plant, *Psoralea esculenta*, of central North America, having an edible starchy root
BREADS > BREAD
BREADTH *n* extent of something from side to side
BREADTHS > BREADTH
BREADY *adj* having the appearance or texture of bread
BREAK > BRACKEN
BREAKABLE *adj* capable of being broken ▷ *n* fragile easily broken article
BREAKAGE *n* act or result of breaking
BREAKAGES > BREAKAGE
BREAKAWAY *n* (consisting of) a dissenting group who have left a larger unit ▷ *adj* dissenting ▷ *vb* leave hastily or escape
BREAKBACK *adj* backbreaking; arduous
BREAKBEAT *n* type of electronic dance music
BREAKBONE as in *breakbone fever* dengue
BREAKDOWN *n* act or instance of breaking down
BREAKER *n* large wave
BREAKERS > BREAKER
BREAKEVEN *n* the level of commercial activity at which the total cost and total revenue of a business enterprise are equal
BREAKFAST *n* first meal of the day ▷ *vb* eat breakfast
BREAKING > BRACKEN
BREAKINGS > BRACKEN
BREAKNECK *adj* fast and dangerous
BREAKOFF *n* act or an instance of breaking off or stopping
BREAKOFFS > BREAKOFF
BREAKOUT *n* escape, esp from prison or confinement
BREAKOUTS > BREAKOUT
BREAKS > BRACKEN
BREAKTIME *n* period of rest or recreation, esp at school
BREAKUP *n* separation or disintegration
BREAKUPS > BREAKUP
BREAKWALL *n* breakwater
BREAM *n* any of several Eurasian freshwater cyprinid fishes of the genus *Abramis*, esp *A. brama*, having a deep compressed body covered with silvery scales ▷ *vb* clean debris (from the bottom of a vessel)
BREAMED > BREAM
BREAMING > BREAM
BREAMS > BREAM
BREARE *same as* > BRIER
BREARES > BREARE
BREASKIT *same as* > BRISKET
BREASKITS > BREASKIT
BREAST *n* either of the two soft fleshy milk-secreting glands on a woman's chest ▷ *vb* reach the summit of
BREASTED > BREAST
BREASTFED *adj* fed at mother's breast
BREASTING > BREAST
BREASTPIN *n* brooch worn on the breast, esp to close a garment
BREASTS > BREAST
BREATH *n* taking in and letting out of air during breathing
BREATHE *vb* take in oxygen and give out carbon dioxide
BREATHED *adj* relating to or denoting a speech sound for whose articulation the vocal cords are not made to vibrate
BREATHER *n* short rest
BREATHERS > BREATHER
BREATHES > BREATHE
BREATHFUL > BREATH
BREATHIER > BREATHY
BREATHILY > BREATHY
BREATHING *n* passage of air into and out of the lungs to supply the body with oxygen
BREATHS > BREATH
BREATHY *adj* (of the speaking voice) accompanied by an audible emission of breath
BRECCIA *n* rock consisting of angular fragments embedded in a finer matrix, formed by erosion, impact, volcanic activity, etc
BRECCIAL > BRECCIA
BRECCIAS > BRECCIA
BRECCIATE > BRECCIA
BRECHAM *n* straw horse-collar
BRECHAMS > BRECHAM
BRECHAN *same as* > BRECHAM
BRECHANS > BRECHAN
BRED > BREED
BREDE *archaic spelling of* > BRAID
BREDED > BREDE
BREDES > BREDE
BREDIE *n* meat and vegetable stew
BREDIES > BREDIE
BREDING > BREDE
BREE *n* broth, stock, or juice
BREECH *n* buttocks ▷ *vb* fit (a gun) with a breech
BREECHED > BREECH
BREECHES *pl n* trousers extending to just below the knee
BREECHING *n* strap of a harness that passes behind a horse's haunches
BREED *vb* produce new or improved strains of (domestic animals or plants) ▷ *n* group of animals etc within a species that have certain clearly defined characteristics
BREEDER *n* person who breeds plants or animals
BREEDERS > BREEDER
BREEDING > BREED
BREEDINGS > BREED
BREEDS > BREED
BREEKS *pl n* trousers
BREEM *same as* > BREME
BREENGE *vb* lunge forward ▷ *n* violent movement
BREENGED > BREENGE
BREENGES > BREENGE
BREENGING > BREENGE
BREER *another word for* > BRAIRD
BREERED > BREER
BREERING > BREER
BREERS > BREER
BREES > BREE
BREESE *same as* > BREEZE
BREESES > BREESE
BREEST > BREAST
BREESTS > BREAST
BREEZE *n* gentle wind ▷ *vb* move quickly or casually
BREEZED > BREEZE
BREEZES > BREEZE
BREEZEWAY *n* roofed passageway connecting two buildings, sometimes with the sides enclosed
BREEZIER > BREEZY
BREEZIEST > BREEZY
BREEZILY > BREEZY
BREEZING > BREEZE
BREEZY *adj* windy
BREGMA *n* point on the top of the skull where the coronal and sagittal sutures meet: in infants this corresponds to the anterior fontanelle
BREGMATA > BREGMA
BREGMATE > BREGMA
BREGMATIC > BREGMA
BREHON *n* (formerly) judge in Ireland
BREHONS > BREHON
BREI *vb* speak with a uvular *r*, esp in Afrikaans
BREID *n* bread
BREIDS > BREID
BREIING > BREI
BREINGE *same as* > BREENGE
BREINGED > BREINGE
BREINGES > BREINGE
BREINGING > BREINGE
BREIS > BREI
BREIST *Scot word for* > BREAST
BREISTS > BREIST
BREKKIES > BREKKY
BREKKY *slang word for* > BREAKFAST
BRELOQUE *n* charm attached to watch chain
BRELOQUES > BRELOQUE
BREME *adj* well-known
BREN *n* type of machine gun
BRENNE *vb* burn
BRENNES > BRENNE
BRENNING > BREN
BRENS > BREN
BRENT *n* type of goose ▷ *adj* steep
BRENTER > BRENT
BRENTEST > BRENT
BRENTS > BRENT
BRER *n* brother: usually

prefixed to a name
BRERE *same as* > BRIER
BRERES > BRERE
BRERS > BRER
BRETASCHE *another word for* > BRATTICE
BRETESSE *another word for* > BRATTICE
BRETESSES > BRETESSE
BRETHREN > BROTHER
BRETON *n* hat with an upturned brim and a rounded crown
BRETONS > BRETON
BRETTICE *same as* > BRATTICE
BRETTICED > BRETTICE
BRETTICES > BRETTICE
BREVE *n* accent (˘), placed over a vowel to indicate that it is short or is pronounced in a specified way
BREVES > BREVE
BREVET *n* document entitling a commissioned officer to hold temporarily a higher military rank without the appropriate pay and allowances ▷ *vb* promote by brevet
BREVETCY > BREVET
BREVETE *adj* patented
BREVETED > BREVET
BREVETING > BREVET
BREVETS > BREVET
BREVETTED > BREVET
BREVIARY *n* book of prayers to be recited daily by a Roman Catholic priest
BREVIATE *n* summary
BREVIATES > BREVIATE
BREVIER *n* (formerly) size of printer's type approximately equal to 8 point
BREVIERS > BREVIER
BREVIS *same as* > BREWIS
BREVISES > BREVIS
BREVITIES > BREVITY
BREVITY *n* shortness
BREW *vb* make (beer etc) by steeping, boiling, and fermentation ▷ *n* beverage produced by brewing
BREWAGE *n* product of brewing
BREWAGES > BREWAGE
BREWED > BREW
BREWER > BREW
BREWERIES > BREWERY
BREWERS > BREW
BREWERY *n* place where beer etc is brewed
BREWING *n* quantity of a beverage brewed at one time
BREWINGS > BREWING
BREWIS *n* bread soaked in broth, gravy, etc
BREWISES > BREWIS
BREWPUB *n* pub that incorporates a brewery on its premises
BREWPUBS > BREWPUB
BREWS > BREW
BREWSKI *n* beer
BREWSKIES > BREWSKI
BREWSKIS > BREWSKI
BREWSTER *n* person, particularly a woman, who brews
BREWSTERS > BREWSTER
BREY *same as* > BREI
BREYED > BREY
BREYING > BREY
BREYS > BREY
BRIAR *n* ericaceous shrub, *Erica arborea*, of S Europe, having a hard woody root (briarroot)
BRIARD *n* medium-sized dog of an ancient French sheep-herding breed having a long rough coat of a single colour
BRIARDS > BRIARD
BRIARED > BRIAR
BRIARROOT *n* hard woody root of the briar, used for making tobacco pipes
BRIARS > BRIAR
BRIARWOOD *same as* > BRIARROOT
BRIARY > BRIAR
BRIBABLE > BRIBE
BRIBE *vb* offer or give something to someone to gain favour, influence, etc ▷ *n* something given or offered as a bribe
BRIBEABLE > BRIBE
BRIBED > BRIBE
BRIBEE *n* one who is bribed
BRIBEES > BRIBEE
BRIBER > BRIBE
BRIBERIES > BRIBERY
BRIBERS > BRIBE
BRIBERY *n* process of giving or taking bribes
BRIBES > BRIBE
BRIBING > BRIBE
BRICABRAC *n* miscellaneous small objects, esp furniture and curios, kept because they are ornamental or rare
BRICHT *Scot word for* > BRIGHT
BRICHTER > BRICHT
BRICHTEST > BRICHT
BRICK *n* (rectangular block of) baked clay used in building ▷ *vb* build, enclose, or fill with bricks
BRICKBAT *n* blunt criticism
BRICKBATS > BRICKBAT
BRICKCLAY *n* clay for making bricks
BRICKED > BRICK
BRICKEN *adj* made of brick
BRICKIE *n* bricklayer
BRICKIER > BRICKY
BRICKIES > BRICKIE
BRICKIEST > BRICKY
BRICKING > BRICK
BRICKINGS > BRICK
BRICKKILN *n* kiln for making bricks
BRICKLE *variant of* > BRITTLE
BRICKLES > BRICKLE
BRICKLIKE > BRICK
BRICKS > BRICK
BRICKWALL *same as* > BRICOLE
BRICKWORK *n* structure, such as a wall, built of bricks
BRICKY *same as* > BRICKIE
BRICKYARD *n* place in which bricks are made, stored, or sold
BRICOLAGE *n* jumbled effect produced by the close proximity of buildings from different periods and in different architectural styles
BRICOLE *n* shot in which the cue ball touches a cushion after striking the object ball and before touching another ball
BRICOLES > BRICOLE
BRIDAL *adj* of a bride or a wedding ▷ *n* wedding or wedding feast
BRIDALLY > BRIDAL
BRIDALS > BRIDAL
BRIDE *n* woman who has just been or is about to be married
BRIDECAKE *n* wedding cake
BRIDED > BRIDE
BRIDEMAID *n* old form of bridesmaid
BRIDEMAN *n* bridegroom's attendant
BRIDEMEN > BRIDEMAN
BRIDES > BRIDE
BRIDESMAN *same as* > BRIDEMAN
BRIDESMEN > BRIDESMAN
BRIDEWELL *n* house of correction
BRIDGABLE > BRIDGE
BRIDGE *n* structure for crossing a river etc ▷ *vb* build a bridge over (something)
BRIDGED > BRIDGE
BRIDGES > BRIDGE
BRIDGING *n* one or more timber struts fixed between floor or roof joists to stiffen the construction and distribute the loads
BRIDGINGS > BRIDGING
BRIDIE *n* semicircular pie containing meat and onions
BRIDIES > BRIDIE
BRIDING > BRIDE
BRIDLE *n* headgear for controlling a horse ▷ *vb* show anger or indignation
BRIDLED > BRIDLE
BRIDLER > BRIDLE
BRIDLERS > BRIDLE
BRIDLES > BRIDLE
BRIDLEWAY *n* path for riding horses
BRIDLING > BRIDLE
BRIDOON *n* horse's bit: small snaffle used in double bridles
BRIDOONS > BRIDOON
BRIE *same as* > BREE
BRIEF *adj* short in duration ▷ *n* condensed statement or written synopsis ▷ *vb* give information and instructions to (a person)
BRIEFCASE *n* small flat case for carrying papers, books, etc
BRIEFED > BRIEF
BRIEFER > BRIEF
BRIEFERS > BRIEF
BRIEFEST > BRIEF
BRIEFING *n* meeting at which detailed information or instructions are given, as for military operations, etc
BRIEFINGS > BRIEFING
BRIEFLESS *adj* (said of a barrister) without clients
BRIEFLY > BRIEF
BRIEFNESS > BRIEF
BRIEFS *pl n* men's or women's underpants without legs
BRIER *same as* > BRIAR
BRIERED > BRIER
BRIERIER > BRIER
BRIERIEST > BRIER
BRIERROOT *same as* > BRIARROOT
BRIERS > BRIER
BRIERWOOD *same as* > BRIARROOT
BRIERY > BRIER
BRIES > BRIE
BRIG *n* two-masted square-rigged ship
BRIGADE *n* army unit smaller than a division ▷ *vb* organize into a brigade
BRIGADED > BRIGADE
BRIGADES > BRIGADE
BRIGADIER *n* high-ranking army officer
BRIGADING > BRIGADE
BRIGALOW *n* type of acacia tree
BRIGALOWS > BRIGALOW
BRIGAND *n* bandit
BRIGANDRY > BRIGAND
BRIGANDS > BRIGAND
BRIGHT *adj* emitting or reflecting much light ▷ *adv* brightly
BRIGHTEN *vb* make or become bright or brighter
BRIGHTENS > BRIGHTEN
BRIGHTER > BRIGHT
BRIGHTEST > BRIGHT
BRIGHTISH > BRIGHT
BRIGHTLY > BRIGHT
BRIGHTS *pl n* high beam of the headlights of a motor

vehicle
BRIGS > BRIG
BRIGUE *vb* solicit
BRIGUED > BRIGUE
BRIGUES > BRIGUE
BRIGUING > BRIGUE
BRIGUINGS > BRIGUE
BRIK *n* Tunisian deep-fried spicy pastry filled with fish or meat and sometimes an egg
BRIKS > BRIK
BRILL *n* European food fish, *Scophthalmus rhombus*, a flatfish similar to the turbot but lacking tubercles on the body: family *Bothidae*
BRILLER > BRILL
BRILLEST > BRILL
BRILLIANT *adj* shining with light ▷ *n* popular circular cut for diamonds and other gemstones in the form of two many-faceted pyramids (the top one truncated) joined at their bases
BRILLO *n* tradename for a type of scouring pad impregnated with a detergent
BRILLOS > BRILLO
BRILLS > BRILL
BRIM *n* upper rim of a vessel ▷ *vb* fill or be full to the brim
BRIMFUL *adj* completely filled with
BRIMFULL *same as* > BRIMFUL
BRIMFULLY > BRIMFUL
BRIMING *n* phosphorescence of sea
BRIMINGS > BRIMING
BRIMLESS > BRIM
BRIMMED > BRIM
BRIMMER *n* vessel, such as a glass or bowl, filled to the brim
BRIMMERS > BRIMMER
BRIMMING > BRIM
BRIMS > BRIM
BRIMSTONE *n* sulphur
BRIMSTONY > BRIMSTONE
BRIN *n* thread of silk from silkworm
BRINDED *adj* streaky or patchy
BRINDISI *n* song sung in celebration
BRINDISIS > BRINDISI
BRINDLE *n* brindled animal
BRINDLED *adj* brown or grey streaked with a darker colour
BRINDLES > BRINDLE
BRINE *n* salt water ▷ *vb* soak in or treat with brine
BRINED > BRINE
BRINELESS > BRINE
BRINER > BRINE
BRINERS > BRINE
BRINES > BRINE
BRING *vb* carry, convey, or take to a designated place or person
BRINGDOWN *n* cause to be elated and then suddenly depressed, as from using drugs
BRINGER > BRING
BRINGERS > BRING
BRINGING > BRING
BRINGINGS > BRING
BRINGS > BRING
BRINIER > BRINY
BRINIES > BRINY
BRINIEST > BRINY
BRININESS > BRINY
BRINING > BRINE
BRINISH > BRINE
BRINJAL *n* dark purple tropical fruit, cooked and eaten as a vegetable
BRINJALS > BRINJAL
BRINJARRY *n* grain trader
BRINK *n* edge of a steep place
BRINKMAN *n* one who goes in for brinkmanship
BRINKMEN > BRINKMAN
BRINKS > BRINK
BRINNIES > BRINNY
BRINNY *n* stone, esp when thrown
BRINS > BRIN
BRINY *adj* very salty
BRIO *n* liveliness
BRIOCHE *n* soft roll or loaf made from a very light yeast dough, sometimes mixed with currants
BRIOCHES > BRIOCHE
BRIOLETTE *n* pear-shaped gem cut with long triangular facets
BRIONIES > BRIONY
BRIONY *same as* > BRYONY
BRIOS > BRIO
BRIQUET *same as* > BRIQUETTE
BRIQUETED > BRIQUET
BRIQUETS > BRIQUET
BRIQUETTE *n* block of compressed coal dust ▷ *vb* make into the form of a brick or bricks
BRIS *n* ritual circumcision of male babies, usually at eight days old, regarded as the formal entry of the child to the Jewish community
BRISANCE *n* shattering effect or power of an explosion or explosive
BRISANCES > BRISANCE
BRISANT > BRISANCE
BRISE *n* type of jump
BRISES > BRIS
BRISK *adj* lively and quick ▷ *vb* enliven
BRISKED > BRISK
BRISKEN *vb* make or become more lively or brisk
BRISKENED > BRISKEN
BRISKENS > BRISKEN
BRISKER > BRISK
BRISKEST > BRISK
BRISKET *n* beef from the breast of a cow
BRISKETS > BRISKET
BRISKING > BRISK
BRISKISH > BRISK
BRISKLY > BRISK
BRISKNESS > BRISK
BRISKS > BRISK
BRISKY *another word for* > BRISK
BRISLING *same as* > SPRAT
BRISLINGS > BRISLING
BRISS *same as* > BRIS
BRISSES > BRIS
BRISTLE *n* short stiff hair ▷ *vb* (cause to) stand up like bristles
BRISTLED > BRISTLE
BRISTLES > BRISTLE
BRISTLIER > BRISTLE
BRISTLING > BRISTLE
BRISTLY > BRISTLE
BRISTOL *n bristol board* type of heavy cardboard
BRISTOLS *pl n* woman's breasts
BRISURE *n* mark of cadency in heraldry
BRISURES > BRISURE
BRIT *n* young of a herring, sprat, or similar fish
BRITANNIA *n* coin bearing figure of Britannia
BRITCHES *same as* > BREECHES
BRITH *same as* > BRIS
BRITHS > BRITH
BRITS > BRIT
BRITSCHKA *n* light open carriage
BRITSKA *same as* > BRITZKA
BRITSKAS > BRITSKA
BRITT *n* young herring or sprat
BRITTANIA *variant spelling of* > BRITANNIA
BRITTLE *adj* hard but easily broken ▷ *n* crunchy sweet made with treacle and nuts
BRITTLED > BRITTLE
BRITTLELY > BRITTLE
BRITTLER > BRITTLE
BRITTLES > BRITTLE
BRITTLEST > BRITTLE
BRITTLING > BRITTLE
BRITTLY > BRITTLE
BRITTS > BRITT
BRITZKA *n* long horse-drawn carriage with a folding top over the rear seat and a rear-facing front seat
BRITZKAS > BRITZKA
BRITZSKA *same as* > BRITZKA
BRITZSKAS > BRITZSKAS
BRIZE *same as* > BREEZE
BRIZES > BRIZE
BRO *n* family member
BROACH *vb* introduce (a topic) for discussion ▷ *n* spit for roasting meat
BROACHED > BROACH
BROACHER > BROACH
BROACHERS > BROACH
BROACHES > BROACH
BROACHING > BROACH
BROAD *adj* having great breadth or width ▷ *n* woman
BROADAX *same as* > BROADAXE
BROADAXE *n* broad-bladed axe
BROADAXES > BROADAXE
BROADBAND *n* telecommunication transmission technique using a wide range of frequencies
BROADBEAN *n* variety of bean
BROADBILL *n* any passerine bird of the family *Eurylaimidae*, of tropical Africa and Asia, having bright plumage and a short wide bill
BROADBRIM *n* broad-brimmed hat, esp one worn by the Quakers in the 17th century
BROADCAST *n* programme or announcement on radio or television ▷ *vb* transmit (a programme or announcement) on radio or television ▷ *adj* dispersed over a wide area ▷ *adv* far and wide
BROADEN *vb* make or become broad or broader
BROADENED > BROADEN
BROADENER > BROADEN
BROADENS > BROADEN
BROADER > BROAD
BROADEST > BROAD
BROADISH > BROAD
BROADLEAF *n* any tobacco plant having broad leaves, used esp in making cigars
BROADLINE *n* company dealing in large volumes of cheap products
BROADLOOM *adj* of or designating carpets woven on a wide loom ▷ *n* of or designating carpets or carpeting woven on a wide loom to obviate the need for seams
BROADLY > BROAD
BROADNESS > BROAD
BROADS > BROAD
BROADSIDE *n* strong verbal or written attack ▷ *adv* with a broader side facing an object
BROADTAIL *n* highly valued black wavy fur obtained from the skins of newly born karakul lambs
BROADWAY *n* wide road
BROADWAYS > BROADWAY

BROADWISE *adv* rare form of breadthwise
BROCADE *n* rich fabric woven with a raised design ▷ *vb* weave with such a design
BROCADED > BROCADE
BROCADES > BROCADE
BROCADING > BROCADE
BROCAGE *another word for* > BROKERAGE
BROCAGES > BROCAGE
BROCARD *n* basic principle of civil law
BROCARDS > BROCARD
BROCATEL *n* heavy upholstery brocade
BROCATELS > BROCATEL
BROCCOLI *n* type of cabbage with greenish flower heads
BROCCOLIS > BROCCOLI
BROCH *n* (in Scotland) a circular dry-stone tower large enough to serve as a fortified home
BROCHAN *n* type of thin porridge
BROCHANS > BROCHAN
BROCHE *adj* woven with a raised design, as brocade
BROCHED > BROCHE
BROCHES > BROCHE
BROCHETTE *n* skewer used for holding pieces of meat or vegetables while grilling
BROCHING > BROCHE
BROCHO *same as* > BRACHAH
BROCHOS > BROCHO
BROCHS > BROCH
BROCHURE *n* booklet that contains information about a product or service
BROCHURES > BROCHURE
BROCK *n* badger
BROCKAGE *same as* > BROKERAGE
BROCKAGES > BROCKAGE
BROCKED *adj* having different colours
BROCKET *n* any small deer of the genus *Mazama*, of tropical America, having small unbranched antlers
BROCKETS > BROCKET
BROCKIT *same as* > BROCKED
BROCKRAM *another word for* > BRECCIA
BROCKRAMS > BROCKRAM
BROCKS > BROCK
BROCOLI *same as* > BROCCOLI
BROCOLIS > BROCOLI
BROD *vb* prod
BRODDED > BROD
BRODDING > BROD
BRODDLE *vb* poke or pierce (something)
BRODDLED > BRODDLE
BRODDLES > BRODDLE
BRODDLING > BRODDLE
BRODEKIN *another word for* > BUSKIN
BRODEKINS > BRODEKIN
BRODKIN *same as* > BRODEKIN
BRODKINS > BRODKIN
BRODS > BROD
BROEKIES *pl n* underpants
BROG *n* bradawl
BROGAN *n* heavy laced, usually ankle-high, work boot
BROGANS > BROGAN
BROGGED > BROG
BROGGING > BROG
BROGH *same as* > BROCH
BROGHS > BROGH
BROGS > BROG
BROGUE *n* sturdy walking shoe
BROGUEISH > BROGUE
BROGUERY > BROGUE
BROGUES > BROGUE
BROGUISH > BROGUE
BROIDER *archaic word for* > EMBROIDER
BROIDERED > BROIDER
BROIDERER > BROIDER
BROIDERS > BROIDER
BROIDERY *n* old form of embroidery
BROIL *vb* cook by direct heat under a grill ▷ *n* process of broiling
BROILED > BROIL
BROILER *n* young tender chicken for roasting
BROILERS > BROILER
BROILING > BROIL
BROILS > BROIL
BROKAGE *another word for* > BROKERAGE
BROKAGES > BROKAGE
BROKE *vb* negotiate or deal
BROKED > BROKE
BROKEN > BRACKEN
BROKENLY > BRACKEN
BROKER *n* agent who buys or sells goods, securities, etc ▷ *vb* act as a broker (in)
BROKERAGE *n* commission charged by a broker
BROKERED > BROKER
BROKERIES > BROKERY
BROKERING > BROKER
BROKERS > BROKER
BROKERY *n* work done by broker
BROKES > BROKE
BROKING > BROKE
BROKINGS > BROKE
BROLGA *n* large grey Australian crane with a trumpeting call
BROLGAS > BROLGA
BROLLIES > BROLLY
BROLLY *n* umbrella
BROMAL *n* yellowish oily synthetic liquid formerly used medicinally as a sedative and hypnotic
BROMALS > BROMAL
BROMATE *same as* > BROMINATE
BROMATED > BROMATE
BROMATES > BROMATE
BROMATING > BROMATE
BROME *n* type of grass
BROMELAIN *n* enzyme in pineapples
BROMELIA *n* type of plant
BROMELIAD *n* any plant of the tropical American family *Bromeliaceae*, typically epiphytes with a rosette of fleshy leaves. The family includes the pineapple and Spanish moss
BROMELIAS > BROMELIA
BROMELIN *n* protein-digesting enzyme found in pineapple and extracted for use in treating joint pain and inflammation, hay fever, and various other conditions
BROMELINS > BROMELIN
BROMEOSIN *another name for* > EOSIN
BROMES > BROME
BROMIC *adj* of or containing bromine in the trivalent or pentavalent state
BROMID *same as* > BROMIDE
BROMIDE *n* chemical compound used in medicine and photography
BROMIDES > BROMIDE
BROMIDIC *adj* ordinary
BROMIDS > BROMID
BROMIN *same as* > BROMINE
BROMINATE *vb* treat or react with bromine
BROMINE *n* dark red liquid element that gives off a pungent vapour
BROMINES > BROMINE
BROMINISM *same as* > BROMISM
BROMINS > BROMIN
BROMISE *same as* > BROMIZE
BROMISED > BROMIZE
BROMISES > BROMIZE
BROMISING > BROMIZE
BROMISM *n* poisoning caused by the excessive intake of bromine or compounds containing bromine
BROMISMS > BROMISM
BROMIZE *vb* treat with bromine
BROMIZED > BROMIZE
BROMIZES > BROMIZE
BROMIZING > BROMIZE
BROMMER *n* S African word for bluebottle
BROMMERS > BROMMER
BROMO *n* something that contains bromide
BROMOFORM *n* heavy colourless liquid substance with a sweetish taste
BROMOS > BROMO
BRONC *same as* > BRONCO
BRONCHI > BRONCHUS
BRONCHIA *pl n* bronchial tubes
BRONCHIAL *adj* of the bronchi
BRONCHIUM *n* medium-sized bronchial tube
BRONCHO *same as* > BRONCO
BRONCHOS > BRONCHO
BRONCHUS *n* either of the two branches of the windpipe
BRONCO *n* (in the US) wild or partially tamed pony
BRONCOS > BRONCO
BRONCS > BRONC
BROND *n* old form of brand
BRONDS > BROND
BRONDYRON *n* sword
BRONZE *n* alloy of copper and tin ▷ *adj* made of, or coloured like, bronze ▷ *vb* (esp of the skin) make or become brown
BRONZED > BRONZE
BRONZEN *adj* made of or the colour of bronze
BRONZER *n* cosmetic applied to the skin to simulate a sun tan
BRONZERS > BRONZER
BRONZES > BRONZE
BRONZIER > BRONZE
BRONZIEST > BRONZE
BRONZIFY *vb* cause to become colour of bronze
BRONZING *n* blue pigment producing a metallic lustre when ground into paint media at fairly high concentrations
BRONZINGS > BRONZING
BRONZITE *n* type of orthopyroxene often having a metallic or pearly sheen
BRONZITES > BRONZITE
BRONZY > BRONZE
BROO *n* brow of hill
BROOCH *n* ornament with a pin, worn fastened to clothes ▷ *vb* decorate with a brooch
BROOCHED > BROOCH
BROOCHES > BROOCH
BROOCHING > BROOCH
BROOD *n* number of birds produced at one hatching ▷ *vb* (of a bird) sit on or hatch eggs
BROODED > BROOD
BROODER *n* enclosure or other structure, usually heated, used for rearing young chickens or other fowl
BROODERS > BROODER
BROODIER > BROODY
BROODIEST > BROODY
BROODILY > BROODY
BROODING > BROOD
BROODINGS > BROOD
BROODLESS > BROOD
BROODMARE *n* mare for breeding

BROODS > BROOD
BROODY *adj* moody and sullen
BROOK *n* small stream ▷ *vb* bear or tolerate
BROOKABLE > BROOK
BROOKED > BROOK
BROOKIE *n* brook trout
BROOKIES > BROOKIE
BROOKING > BROOK
BROOKITE *n* reddish-brown to black mineral
BROOKITES > BROOKITE
BROOKLET *n* small brook
BROOKLETS > BROOKLET
BROOKLIKE > BROOK
BROOKLIME *n* either of two blue-flowered scrophulariaceous trailing plants, *Veronica americana* of North America or *V. beccabunga* of Europe and Asia, growing in moist places
BROOKS > BROOK
BROOKWEED *n* either of two white-flowered primulaceous plants, *Samolus valerandi* of Europe or *S. floribundus* of North America, growing in moist places
BROOL *n* low roar
BROOLS > BROOL
BROOM *n* long-handled sweeping brush ▷ *vb* sweep with a broom
BROOMBALL *n* type of ice hockey played with broom
BROOMCORN *n* variety of sorghum, *Sorghum vulgare technicum*, the long stiff flower stalks of which have been used for making brooms
BROOMED > BROOM
BROOMIER > BROOMY
BROOMIEST > BROOMY
BROOMING > BROOM
BROOMRAPE *n* any orobanchaceous plant of the genus *Orobanche*: brownish small-flowered leafless parasites on the roots of other plants, esp on legumes
BROOMS > BROOM
BROOMY *adj* covered with growth of broom
BROOS > BROO
BROOSE *n* race at country wedding
BROOSES > BROOSE
BROS > BRO
BROSE *n* oatmeal or pease porridge, sometimes with butter or fat added
BROSES > BROSE
BROSY *adj* smeared with porridge
BROTH *n* soup, usu. containing vegetables
BROTHEL *n* house where men pay to have sex with prostitutes
BROTHELS > BROTHEL
BROTHER *n* boy or man with the same parents as another person ▷ *interj* exclamation of amazement, disgust, surprise, disappointment, etc ▷ *vb* treat someone like a brother
BROTHERED > BROTHER
BROTHERLY *adj* of or like a brother, esp in showing loyalty and affection ▷ *adv* in a brotherly way
BROTHERS > BROTHER
BROTHS > BROTH
BROTHY *adj* having appearance or texture of broth
BROUGH *same as* > BROCH
BROUGHAM *n* horse-drawn closed carriage with a raised open driver's seat in front
BROUGHAMS > BROUGHAM
BROUGHS > BROUGH
BROUGHT > BRING
BROUGHTA *same as* > BRAATA
BROUGHTAS *same as* > BRAATA
BROUHAHA *n* loud confused noise
BROUHAHAS > BROUHAHA
BROUZE *same as* > BROOSE
BROUZES > BROUZE
BROW *n* part of the face from the eyes to the hairline
BROWALLIA *n* flowering plant
BROWBAND *n* strap of a horse's bridle that goes across the forehead
BROWBANDS > BROWBAND
BROWBEAT *vb* frighten (someone) with threats
BROWBEATS > BROWBEAT
BROWED *adj* having a brow
BROWLESS > BROW
BROWN *n* colour of earth or wood ▷ *adj* (of bread) made from wheatmeal or wholemeal flour ▷ *vb* make or become brown
BROWNED > BROWN
BROWNER > BROWN
BROWNEST > BROWN
BROWNIE *n* small square nutty chocolate cake
BROWNIER > BROWN
BROWNIES > BROWNIE
BROWNIEST > BROWN
BROWNING *n* substance used to darken gravies
BROWNINGS > BROWNING
BROWNISH > BROWN
BROWNNESS > BROWN
BROWNNOSE *vb* be abjectly subservient
BROWNOUT *n* dimming or reduction in the use of electric lights in a city, esp to conserve electric power or as a defensive precaution in wartime
BROWNOUTS > BROWNOUT
BROWNS > BROWN
BROWNY > BROWN
BROWRIDGE *n* ridge of bone over eyes
BROWS > BROW
BROWSABLE > BROWSE
BROWSE *vb* look through (a book or articles for sale) in a casual manner ▷ *n* instance of browsing
BROWSED > BROWSE
BROWSER *n* software package that enables a user to read hypertext, esp on the Internet
BROWSERS > BROWSER
BROWSES > BROWSE
BROWSIER > BROWSE
BROWSIEST > BROWSE
BROWSING > BROWSE
BROWSINGS > BROWSE
BROWST *n* brewing (of ale, tea)
BROWSTS > BROWST
BROWSY > BROWSE
BRR *same as* > BRRR
BRRR *interj* used to suggest shivering
BRU *South African word for* > FRIEND
BRUCELLA *n* type of bacterium
BRUCELLAE > BRUCELLA
BRUCELLAS > BRUCELLA
BRUCHID *n* type of beetle
BRUCHIDS > BRUCHID
BRUCIN *same as* > BRUCINE
BRUCINE *n* bitter poisonous alkaloid resembling strychnine
BRUCINES > BRUCINE
BRUCINS > BRUCIN
BRUCITE *n* white translucent mineral
BRUCITES > BRUCITE
BRUCKLE *adj* brittle
BRUGH *n* large house
BRUGHS > BRUGH
BRUHAHA *same as* > BROUHAHA
BRUHAHAS > BRUHAHA
BRUILZIE *same as* > BRULZIE
BRUILZIES > BRUILZIE
BRUIN *n* name for a bear, used in children's tales, fables, etc
BRUINS > BRUIN
BRUISE *n* discoloured area on the skin caused by an injury ▷ *vb* cause a bruise on
BRUISED > BRUISE
BRUISER *n* strong tough person
BRUISERS > BRUISER
BRUISES > BRUISE
BRUISING *adj* causing bruises, as by a blow ▷ *n* bruise or bruises
BRUISINGS > BRUISING
BRUIT *vb* report ▷ *n* abnormal sound heard within the body during auscultation, esp a heart murmur
BRUITED > BRUIT
BRUITER > BRUIT
BRUITERS > BRUIT
BRUITING > BRUIT
BRUITS > BRUIT
BRULE *n* shortened form of the archaic word for a mixed-race person of Canadian Indian and White (usually French-Canadian) ancestry
BRULES > BRULE
BRULOT *n* coffee-based alcoholic drink, served flaming
BRULOTS > BRULOT
BRULYIE *same as* > BRULYIE
BRULYIES > BRULYIE
BRULZIE *n* noisy dispute
BRULZIES > BRULZIE
BRUMAL *adj* of, characteristic of, or relating to winter
BRUMBIES > BRUMBY
BRUMBY *n* wild horse
BRUME *n* heavy mist or fog
BRUMES > BRUME
BRUMMAGEM *n* something that is cheap and flashy, esp imitation jewellery
BRUMMER *same as* > BROMMER
BRUMMERS > BRUMMER
BRUMOUS > BRUME
BRUNCH *n* breakfast and lunch combined ▷ *vb* eat brunch
BRUNCHED > BRUNCH
BRUNCHER > BRUNCH
BRUNCHERS > BRUNCH
BRUNCHES > BRUNCH
BRUNCHING > BRUNCH
BRUNET *adj* dark brown
BRUNETS > BRUNET
BRUNETTE *n* girl or woman with dark brown hair ▷ *adj* dark brown
BRUNETTES > BRUNETTE
BRUNG > BRING
BRUNIZEM *n* prairie soil
BRUNIZEMS > BRUNIZEM
BRUNT *n* main force or shock of a blow, attack, etc ▷ *vb* suffer the main force or shock of a blow, attack, etc
BRUNTED > BRUNT
BRUNTING > BRUNT
BRUNTS > BRUNT
BRUS > BRU
BRUSH *n* device made of bristles, wires, etc used for cleaning, painting, etc ▷ *vb* clean, scrub, or paint with a brush
BRUSHBACK *n* (baseball) ball intended to hit the batter
BRUSHED *adj* treated with a

brushing process to raise the nap and give a softer and warmer finish
BRUSHER > BRUSH
BRUSHERS > BRUSH
BRUSHES > BRUSH
BRUSHFIRE *n* fire in bushes and scrub
BRUSHIER > BRUSHY
BRUSHIEST > BRUSHY
BRUSHING > BRUSH
BRUSHINGS > BRUSH
BRUSHLAND *n* land characterized by patchy shrubs
BRUSHLESS > BRUSH
BRUSHLIKE > BRUSH
BRUSHMARK *n* indented lines sometimes left by the bristles of a brush on a painted surface
BRUSHOFF *n* an abrupt dismissal or rejection
BRUSHOFFS > BRUSHOFF
BRUSHUP *n* the act or an instance of tidying one's appearance
BRUSHUPS > BRUSHUP
BRUSHWOOD *n* cut or broken-off tree branches and twigs
BRUSHWORK *n* characteristic manner of applying paint with a brush
BRUSHY *adj* like a brush
BRUSK *same as* > BRUSQUE
BRUSKER > BRUSK
BRUSKEST > BRUSK
BRUSQUE *adj* blunt or curt in manner or speech
BRUSQUELY > BRUSQUE
BRUSQUER > BRUSQUE
BRUSQUEST > BRUSQUE
BRUSSEN *adj* bold
BRUST *same as* > BURST
BRUSTING > BRUST
BRUSTS > BRUST
BRUT *adj* (of champagne or sparkling wine) very dry ▷ *n* very dry champagne
BRUTAL *adj* cruel and vicious
BRUTALISE *same as* > BRUTALIZE
BRUTALISM *n* austere architectural style of the 1950s on, characterized by the use of exposed concrete and angular shapes
BRUTALIST > BRUTALISM
BRUTALITY > BRUTAL
BRUTALIZE *vb* make or become brutal
BRUTALLY > BRUTAL
BRUTE *n* brutal person ▷ *adj* wholly instinctive or physical, like an animal
BRUTED > BRUTE
BRUTELIKE > BRUTE
BRUTELY > BRUTE
BRUTENESS > BRUTE
BRUTER *n* diamond cutter
BRUTERS > BRUTER
BRUTES > BRUTE
BRUTIFIED > BRUTIFY
BRUTIFIES > BRUTIFY
BRUTIFY *less common word for* > BRUTALIZE
BRUTING *n* diamond cutting
BRUTINGS > BRUTING
BRUTISH *adj* of or like an animal
BRUTISHLY > BRUTISH
BRUTISM *n* stupidity; vulgarity
BRUTISMS > BRUTISM
BRUTS > BRUT
BRUX *vb* grind one's teeth
BRUXED > BRUX
BRUXES > BRUX
BRUXING > BRUX
BRUXISM *n* habit of grinding the teeth, esp unconsciously
BRUXISMS > BRUXISM
BRYOLOGY *n* branch of botany concerned with the study of bryophytes
BRYONIES > BRYONY
BRYONY *n* wild climbing hedge plant
BRYOPHYTE *n* any plant of the phyla *Bryophyta* (mosses), *Hepatophyta* (liverworts), or *Anthocerophyta* (hornworts), having stems and leaves but lacking true vascular tissue and roots and reproducing by spores
BRYOZOAN *n* any aquatic invertebrate animal of the phylum *Bryozoa*, forming colonies of polyps each having a ciliated feeding organ (lophophore) ▷ *adj* of, relating to, or belonging to the *Bryozoa*
BRYOZOANS > BRYOZOAN
BUAT *same as* > BOWAT
BUATS > BUAT
BUAZE *n* fibrous African plant
BUAZES > BUAZE
BUB *n* youngster
BUBA *another name for* > YAWS
BUBAL *n* any of various antelopes, esp an extinct N African variety of hartebeest
BUBALE *n* large antelope
BUBALES > BUBALE
BUBALINE *adj* (of antelopes) related to or resembling the bubal
BUBALIS *same as* > BUBAL
BUBALISES > BUBALIS
BUBALS > BUBAL
BUBAS > BUBA
BUBBA *n* ordinary American person
BUBBAS > BUBBA
BUBBIES > BUBBY
BUBBLE *n* ball of air in a liquid or solid ▷ *vb* form bubbles
BUBBLED > BUBBLE
BUBBLEGUM *n* type of chewing gum that can be blown into large bubbles
BUBBLER *n* drinking fountain in which the water is forced in a stream from a small vertical nozzle
BUBBLERS > BUBBLER
BUBBLES > BUBBLE
BUBBLIER > BUBBLY
BUBBLIES > BUBBLY
BUBBLIEST > BUBBLY
BUBBLING > BUBBLE
BUBBLY *adj* excited and lively ▷ *n* champagne
BUBBY *n* old word for woman's breast
BUBINGA *n* reddish-brown wood from African tree
BUBINGAS > BUBINGA
BUBKES *n* very small amount
BUBO *n* inflammation and swelling of a lymph node, esp in the armpit or groin
BUBOED > BUBO
BUBOES > BUBO
BUBONIC > BUBO
BUBS > BUB
BUBU *same as* > BOUBOU
BUBUKLE *n* red spot on skin
BUBUKLES > BUBUKLE
BUBUS > BUBU
BUCCAL *adj* of or relating to the cheek
BUCCALLY > BUCCAL
BUCCANEER *n* pirate ▷ *vb* be or act like a buccaneer
BUCCANIER *same as* > BUCCANEER
BUCCINA *n* curved Roman horn
BUCCINAS > BUCCINA
BUCELLAS *n* type of Portuguese white wine
BUCENTAUR *n* state barge of Venice from which the doge and other officials dropped a ring into the sea on Ascension Day to symbolize the ceremonial marriage of the state with the Adriatic
BUCHU *n* any of several S. African rutaceous shrubs of the genus *Barosma*, esp *B. betulina*, whose leaves are used as an antiseptic and diuretic
BUCHUS > BUCHU
BUCK *n* male of the goat, hare, kangaroo, rabbit, and reindeer ▷ *vb* (of a horse etc) jump with legs stiff and back arched
BUCKAROO *n* cowboy
BUCKAROOS > BUCKAROO
BUCKAYRO *same as* > BUCKAROO
BUCKAYROS > BUCKAYRO
BUCKBEAN *n* marsh plant, *Menyanthes trifoliata*, with white or pink flowers: family *Menyanthaceae*
BUCKBEANS > BUCKBEAN
BUCKBOARD *n* open four-wheeled horse-drawn carriage with the seat attached to a flexible board between the front and rear axles
BUCKBRUSH *n* American shrub
BUCKED > BUCK
BUCKEEN *n* (in Ireland) poor young man who aspires to the habits and dress of the wealthy
BUCKEENS > BUCKEEN
BUCKER > BUCK
BUCKEROO *same as* > BUCKAROO
BUCKEROOS > BUCKEROO
BUCKERS > BUCK
BUCKET *vb* open-topped roughly cylindrical container ▷ *vb* rain heavily
BUCKETED > BUCKET
BUCKETFUL *same as* > BUCKET
BUCKETING > BUCKET
BUCKETS > BUCKET
BUCKEYE *n* any of several North American trees of the genus *Aesculus*, esp *A. glabra* (Ohio buckeye), having erect clusters of white or red flowers and prickly fruits: family *Hippocastanaceae*
BUCKEYES > BUCKEYE
BUCKHORN *n* horn from a buck, used for knife handles, etc
BUCKHORNS > BUCKHORN
BUCKHOUND *n* hound, smaller than a staghound, used for hunting the smaller breeds of deer, esp fallow deer
BUCKIE *n* whelk or its shell
BUCKIES > BUCKIE
BUCKING > BUCK
BUCKINGS > BUCK
BUCKISH > BUCK
BUCKISHLY > BUCK
BUCKLE *n* clasp for fastening a belt or strap ▷ *vb* fasten or be fastened with a buckle
BUCKLED > BUCKLE
BUCKLER *n* small round shield worn on the forearm ▷ *vb* defend
BUCKLERED > BUCKLER
BUCKLERS > BUCKLER
BUCKLES > BUCKLE
BUCKLING *another name for* > BLOATER
BUCKLINGS > BUCKLING
BUCKO *n* lively young fellow: often a term of address

BUCKOES > BUCKO
BUCKOS > BUCKO
BUCKRA *n* (used contemptuously by Black people, esp in the US) White man
BUCKRAKE *n* large rake attached to tractor
BUCKRAKES > BUCKRAKE
BUCKRAM *n* cotton or linen cloth stiffened with size, etc, used in lining or stiffening clothes, bookbinding, etc ▷ *vb* stiffen with buckram
BUCKRAMED > BUCKRAM
BUCKRAMS > BUCKRAM
BUCKRAS > BUCKRA
BUCKS > BUCK
BUCKSAW *n* woodcutting saw having its blade set in a frame and tensioned by a turnbuckle across the back of the frame
BUCKSAWS > BUCKSAW
BUCKSHEE *adj* free
BUCKSHEES > BUCKSHEE
BUCKSHISH *n* tip, present or gift
BUCKSHOT *n* large lead pellets used for shooting game
BUCKSHOTS > BUCKSHOT
BUCKSKIN *n* skin of a male deer ▷ *adj* greyish-yellow
BUCKSKINS *pl n* (in the US and Canada) breeches, shoes, or a suit of buckskin
BUCKSOM *same as* > BUXOM
BUCKTAIL *n* in fishing, fly with appearance of minnow
BUCKTAILS > BUCKTAIL
BUCKTEETH > BUCKTOOTH
BUCKTHORN *n* thorny shrub whose berries were formerly used as a purgative
BUCKTOOTH *n* projecting upper front tooth
BUCKU *same as* > BUCHU
BUCKUS > BUCKU
BUCKWHEAT *n* small black grain used for making flour
BUCKYBALL *n* ball-like polyhedral carbon molecule of the type found in buckminsterfullerene and other fullerenes
BUCKYTUBE *n* tube of carbon atoms structurally similar to buckminsterfullerene
BUCOLIC *adj* of the countryside or country life ▷ *n* pastoral poem
BUCOLICAL > BUCOLIC
BUCOLICS > BUCOLIC
BUD *n* swelling on a plant that develops into a leaf or flower ▷ *vb* produce buds
BUDA *n* derogatory Indian English word for an old man
BUDAS > BUDA
BUDDED > BUD
BUDDER > BUD
BUDDERS > BUD
BUDDHA *n* person who has achieved a state of perfect enlightenment
BUDDHAS > BUDDHA
BUDDIED > BUDDY
BUDDIER > BUDDY
BUDDIES > BUDDY
BUDDIEST > BUDDY
BUDDING > BUDDY
BUDDINGS > BUDDY
BUDDLE *n* sloping trough in which ore is washed ▷ *vb* wash (ore) in a buddle
BUDDLED > BUDDLE
BUDDLEIA *n* shrub with long spikes of purple flowers
BUDDLEIAS > BUDDLEIA
BUDDLES > BUDDLE
BUDDLING > BUDDLE
BUDDY *n* friend ▷ *vb* act as a friend to ▷ *adj* friendly
BUDDYING > BUDDY
BUDGE *vb* move slightly ▷ *n* lambskin dressed for the fur to be worn on the outer side
BUDGED > BUDGE
BUDGER > BUDGE
BUDGEREE *adj* good
BUDGERO *same as* > BUDGEROW
BUDGEROS > BUDGERO
BUDGEROW *n* barge use on Ganges
BUDGEROWS > BUDGEROW
BUDGERS > BUDGE
BUDGES > BUDGE
BUDGET *n* financial plan for a period of time ▷ *vb* plan the expenditure of (money or time) ▷ *adj* cheap
BUDGETARY > BUDGET
BUDGETED > BUDGET
BUDGETEER > BUDGET
BUDGETER > BUDGET
BUDGETERS > BUDGET
BUDGETING > BUDGET
BUDGETS > BUDGET
BUDGIE *n* short form of budgerigar
BUDGIES > BUDGIE
BUDGING > BUDGE
BUDI *n* derogatory Indian English word an for old woman
BUDIS > BUDI
BUDLESS > BUD
BUDLIKE > BUD
BUDMASH *same as* > BADMASH
BUDMASHES > BUDMASH
BUDO *n* combat and spirit in martial arts
BUDOS > BUDO
BUDS > BUD
BUDWORM *n* pest that eats tree leaves and buds
BUDWORMS > BUDWORM
BUFF *n* soft flexible undyed leather ▷ *adj* dull yellowish-brown ▷ *vb* clean or polish with soft material
BUFFA > BUFFO
BUFFABLE > BUFF
BUFFALO *n* member of the cattle tribe, *Syncerus caffer*, mostly found in game reserves in southern and eastern Africa and having upward-curving horns ▷ *vb* confuse
BUFFALOED > BUFFALO
BUFFALOES > BUFFALO
BUFFALOS > BUFFALO
BUFFE > BUFFO
BUFFED > BUFF
BUFFEL as in *buffel grass* grass used for pasture in Africa, India, and Australia
BUFFER *same as* > BUFF
BUFFERED > BUFFER
BUFFERING > BUFFER
BUFFERS > BUFFER
BUFFEST > BUFF
BUFFET *n* counter where drinks and snacks are served ▷ *vb* knock against or about
BUFFETED > BUFFET
BUFFETER > BUFFET
BUFFETERS > BUFFET
BUFFETING *n* response of an aircraft structure to buffet, esp an irregular oscillation of the tail
BUFFETS > BUFFET
BUFFI > BUFFO
BUFFIER > BUFFY
BUFFIEST > BUFFY
BUFFING > BUFF
BUFFINGS > BUFFING
BUFFO *n* (in Italian opera of the 18th century) comic part, esp one for a bass
BUFFOON *n* clown or fool
BUFFOONS > BUFFOON
BUFFOS > BUFFO
BUFFS > BUFF
BUFFY *adj* having appearance or texture of buff
BUFO *n* type of toad
BUFOS > BUFO
BUFOTALIN *n* principal poisonous substance in the skin and saliva of the common European toad
BUG *n* insect ▷ *vb* irritate
BUGABOO *n* imaginary source of fear
BUGABOOS > BUGABOO
BUGBANE *n* any of several ranunculaceous plants of the genus *Cimicifuga*, esp *C. foetida* of Europe, whose flowers are reputed to repel insects
BUGBANES > BUGBANE
BUGBEAR *n* thing that causes obsessive anxiety
BUGBEARS > BUGBEAR
BUGEYE *n* oyster-dredging boat
BUGEYES > BUGEYE
BUGGAN *n* evil spirit
BUGGANE *same as* > BUGGAN
BUGGANES > BUGGANE
BUGGANS > BUGGAN
BUGGED > BUG
BUGGER *n* unpleasant or difficult person or thing ▷ *vb* tire ▷ *interj* exclamation of annoyance or disappointment
BUGGERED > BUGGER
BUGGERIES > BUGGERY
BUGGERING > BUGGER
BUGGERS > BUGGER
BUGGERY *n* anal intercourse
BUGGIER > BUGGY
BUGGIES > BUGGY
BUGGIEST > BUGGY
BUGGIN *same as* > BUGGAN
BUGGINESS > BUGGY
BUGGING > BUG
BUGGINGS > BUG
BUGGINS > BUGGIN
BUGGY *n* light horse-drawn carriage having two or four wheels ▷ *adj* infested with bugs
BUGHOUSE *n* offensive name for a mental hospital or asylum ▷ *adj* offensive word for insane
BUGHOUSES > BUGHOUSE
BUGLE *n* instrument like a small trumpet ▷ *vb* play or sound (on) a bugle
BUGLED > BUGLE
BUGLER > BUGLE
BUGLERS > BUGLE
BUGLES > BUGLE
BUGLET *n* small bugle
BUGLETS > BUGLET
BUGLEWEED *same as* > BUGLE
BUGLING > BUGLE
BUGLOSS *n* any of various hairy Eurasian boraginaceous plants of the genera *Anchusa*, *Lycopsis*, and *Echium*, esp *L. arvensis*, having clusters of blue flowers
BUGLOSSES > BUGLOSS
BUGONG *same as* > BOGONG
BUGONGS > BUGONG
BUGOUT *n* act of running away
BUGOUTS > BUGOUT
BUGS > BUG
BUGSEED *n* form of tumbleweed
BUGSEEDS > BUGSEED
BUGSHA *same as* > BUQSHA
BUGSHAS > BUGSHA
BUGWORT *another name for* > BUGBANE
BUGWORTS > BUGWORT
BUHL *same as* > BOULLE
BUHLS > BUHL
BUHLWORK *n* woodwork with decorative inlay
BUHLWORKS > BUHLWORK
BUHR > BURR

BUHRS > BURR
BUHRSTONE *n* hard tough rock containing silica, fossils, and cavities, formerly used as a grindstone
BUHUND *n* type of Norwegian dog
BUHUNDS > BUHUND
BUIBUI *n* piece of black cloth worn as a shawl by Muslim women, esp on the E African coast
BUIBUIS > BUIBUI
BUIK *same as* > BOOK
BUIKS > BUIK
BUILD *vb* make, construct, or form by joining parts or materials ▷ *n* shape of the body
BUILDABLE *adj* suitable for building on
BUILDDOWN *n* planned reduction
BUILDED > BUILD
BUILDER *n* person who constructs houses and other buildings
BUILDERS > BUILDER
BUILDING > BUILD
BUILDINGS > BUILD
BUILDS > BUILD
BUILDUP *n* gradual approach to a climax or critical point
BUILDUPS > BUILDUP
BUILT > BUILD
BUIRDLIER > BUIRDLY
BUIRDLY *adj* well-built
BUIST *vb* brand sheep with identification mark
BUISTED > BUIST
BUISTING > BUIST
BUISTS > BUIST
BUKE *same as* > BOOK
BUKES > BUKE
BUKKAKE *n* type of sexual practice
BUKKAKES > BUKKAKE
BUKSHEE *n* person in charge of paying wages
BUKSHEES > BUKSHEE
BUKSHI *same as* > BUKSHEE
BUKSHIS > BUKSHI
BULB *n* onion-shaped root which grows into a flower or plant ▷ *vb* form into the shape of a bulb
BULBAR *adj* of or relating to a bulb, esp the medulla oblongata
BULBED > BULB
BULBEL *same as* > BULBIL
BULBELS > BULBEL
BULBIL *n* small bulblike organ of vegetative reproduction growing in leaf axils or on flower stalks of plants such as the onion and tiger lily
BULBILS > BULBIL
BULBING > BULB
BULBLET *n* small bulb at base of main bulb
BULBLETS > BULBLET
BULBOSITY > BULBOUS
BULBOUS *adj* round and fat
BULBOUSLY > BULBOUS
BULBS > BULB
BULBUL *n* any songbird of the family *Pycnonotidae* of tropical Africa and Asia, having brown plumage and, in many species, a distinct crest
BULBULS > BULBUL
BULGE *n* swelling on a normally flat surface ▷ *vb* swell outwards
BULGED > BULGE
BULGER > BULGE
BULGERS > BULGE
BULGES > BULGE
BULGHUR *same as* > BULGUR
BULGHURS > BULGHUR
BULGIER > BULGE
BULGIEST > BULGE
BULGINE *same as* > BULLGINE
BULGINES > BULGINE
BULGINESS > BULGE
BULGING > BULGE
BULGINGLY > BULGE
BULGUR *n* kind of dried cracked wheat
BULGURS > BULGUR
BULGY > BULGE
BULIMIA *n* disorder characterized by compulsive overeating followed by vomiting
BULIMIAC > BULIMIA
BULIMIAS > BULIMIA
BULIMIC > BULIMIA
BULIMICS > BULIMIA
BULIMIES > BULIMIA
BULIMUS > BULIMIA
BULIMUSES > BULIMIA
BULIMY > BULIMIA
BULK *n* volume, size, or magnitude of something ▷ *vb* cohere or cause to cohere in a mass
BULKAGE > BULK
BULKAGES > BULK
BULKED > BULK
BULKER *n* ship that carries unpackaged cargo, usually consisting of a single dry commodity, such as coal or grain
BULKERS > BULKER
BULKHEAD *n* partition in a ship or aeroplane
BULKHEADS > BULKHEAD
BULKIER > BULKY
BULKIEST > BULKY
BULKILY > BULKY
BULKINESS > BULKY
BULKING *n* expansion of excavated material to a volume greater than that of the excavation from which it came
BULKS > BULK
BULKY *adj* very large and massive, esp so as to be unwieldy
BULL *adj* any male bovine animal, esp one that is sexually mature
BULLA *n* leaden seal affixed to a papal bull, having a representation of Saints Peter and Paul on one side and the name of the reigning pope on the other
BULLACE *n* small Eurasian rosaceous tree, *Prunus domestica insititia* (or *P. insititia*), of which the damson is the cultivated form
BULLACES > BULLACE
BULLAE > BULLA
BULLARIES > BULLARY
BULLARY *n* boilery for preparing salt
BULLATE *adj* puckered or blistered in appearance
BULLBAR *singular form of* > BULLBARS
BULLBARS *n* large protective metal grille on the front of some vehicles, esp four-wheel-drive vehicles
BULLBAT *another name for* > NIGHTHAWK
BULLBATS > BULLBAT
BULLBRIER *n* prickly Americaan vine
BULLDOG *n* thickset dog with a broad head and a muscular body
BULLDOGS > BULLDOG
BULLDOZE *vb* demolish or flatten with a bulldozer
BULLDOZED > BULLDOZE
BULLDOZER *n* powerful tractor for moving earth
BULLDOZES > BULLDOZE
BULLDUST *n* fine dust
BULLDUSTS > BULLDUST
BULLDYKE *n* mannish lesbian
BULLDYKES > BULLDYKE
BULLED > BULL
BULLER *vb* make bubbling sound
BULLERED > BULLER
BULLERING > BULLER
BULLERS > BULLER
BULLET *n* small piece of metal fired from a gun ▷ *vb* move extremely quickly
BULLETED > BULLET
BULLETIN *n* short official report or announcement ▷ *vb* make known by bulletin
BULLETING > BULLET
BULLETINS > BULLETIN
BULLETRIE *n* W Indian fruit tree
BULLETS > BULLET
BULLFIGHT *n* public show in which a matador kills a bull
BULLFINCH *n* common European songbird
BULLFROG *n* large American frog with a deep croak
BULLFROGS > BULLFROG
BULLGINE *n* steam locomotive
BULLGINES > BULLGINE
BULLHEAD *n* any of various small northern mainly marine scorpaenoid fishes of the family *Cottidae* that have a large head covered with bony plates and spines
BULLHEADS > BULLHEAD
BULLHORN *n* portable loudspeaker having a built-in amplifier and microphone
BULLHORNS > BULLHORN
BULLIED > BULLY
BULLIER > BULLY
BULLIES > BULLY
BULLIEST > BULLY
BULLING > BULL
BULLINGS > BULL
BULLION *n* gold or silver in the form of bars
BULLIONS > BULLION
BULLISH *adj* like a bull
BULLISHLY > BULLISH
BULLNECK *n* enlarged neck
BULLNECKS > BULLNECK
BULLNOSE *n* rounded exterior angle, as where two walls meet
BULLNOSES > BULLNOSE
BULLOCK *n* castrated bull ▷ *vb* work hard and long
BULLOCKED > BULLOCK
BULLOCKS > BULLOCK
BULLOCKY *n* driver of a team of bullocks
BULLOSA *epidermolysis bullosa* type of genetic skin disorder
BULLOUS *adj* blistered
BULLPEN *n* large cell where prisoners are confined together temporarily
BULLPENS > BULLPEN
BULLPOUT *n* type of fish
BULLPOUTS > BULLPOUT
BULLRING *n* arena for staging bullfights
BULLRINGS > BULLRING
BULLRUSH *same as* > BULRUSH
BULLS > BULL
BULLSHAT > BULLSHIT
BULLSHIT *n* exaggerated or foolish talk ▷ *vb* talk bullshit to
BULLSHITS > BULLSHIT
BULLSHOT *n* cocktail of vodka and beef stock
BULLSHOTS > BULLSHOT
BULLSNAKE *n* American burrowing snake
BULLWADDY *n* N Australian tree, *Macropteranthes kekwickii*, growing in dense thickets
BULLWEED *n* knapweed
BULLWEEDS > BULLWEED

BULLWHACK *vb* flog with short whip
BULLWHIP *n* long tapering heavy whip, esp one of plaited rawhide ▷ *vb* whip with a bullwhip
BULLWHIPS > BULLWHIP
BULLY *n* person who hurts, persecutes, or intimidates weaker people ▷ *vb* hurt, intimidate, or persecute (a weaker or smaller person), esp to make him do something ▷ *adj* dashing
BULLYBOY *n* ruffian or tough, esp a hired one
BULLYBOYS > BULLYBOY
BULLYING > BULLY
BULLYISM > BULLY
BULLYISMS > BULLY
BULLYRAG *vb* bully, esp by means of cruel practical jokes
BULLYRAGS > BULLYRAG
BULNBULN *another name for* > LYREBIRD
BULNBULNS > BULNBULN
BULRUSH *n* tall stiff reed
BULRUSHES > BULRUSH
BULRUSHY > BULRUSH
BULSE *n* purse or bag for diamonds
BULSES > BULSE
BULWADDEE > BULLWADDY
BULWADDY > BULLWADDY
BULWARK *n* wall used as a fortification ▷ *vb* defend or fortify with or as if with a bulwark
BULWARKED > BULWARK
BULWARKS > BULWARK
BUM *n* buttocks or anus ▷ *vb* get by begging ▷ *adj* of poor quality
BUMALO *same as* > BUMMALO
BUMALOTI *same as* > BUMMALOTI
BUMALOTIS > BUMALOTI
BUMBAG *n* small bag attached to a belt and worn round the waist
BUMBAGS > BUMBAG
BUMBAZE *vb* confuse; bewilder
BUMBAZED > BUMBAZE
BUMBAZES > BUMBAZE
BUMBAZING > BUMBAZE
BUMBLE *vb* speak, do, or move in a clumsy way ▷ *n* blunder or botch
BUMBLEBEE *n* large hairy bee
BUMBLED > BUMBLE
BUMBLEDOM *n* self-importance in a minor office
BUMBLER > BUMBLE
BUMBLERS > BUMBLE
BUMBLES > BUMBLE
BUMBLING > BUMBLE
BUMBLINGS > BUMBLE
BUMBO *n* drink with gin or rum, nutmeg, lemon juice, etc
BUMBOAT *n* any small boat used for ferrying supplies or goods for sale to a ship at anchor or at a mooring
BUMBOATS > BUMBOAT
BUMBOS > BUMBO
BUMELIA *n* thorny shrub
BUMELIAS > BUMELIA
BUMF *n* official documents or forms
BUMFLUFF *n* soft and fluffy growth of hair on the chin of an adolescent
BUMFLUFFS > BUMFLUFF
BUMFS > BUMF
BUMFUZZLE *vb* confuse
BUMKIN *same as* > BUMPKIN
BUMKINS > BUMKIN
BUMMALO *n* Bombay duck
BUMMALOS > BUMMALO
BUMMALOTI *another word for* > BUMMALO
BUMMAREE *n* dealer at Billingsgate fish market
BUMMAREES > BUMMAREE
BUMMED > BUM
BUMMEL *n* stroll
BUMMELS > STROLL
BUMMER *n* unpleasant or disappointing experience
BUMMERS > BUMMER
BUMMEST > BUM
BUMMING > BUM
BUMMLE *Scots variant of* > BUMBLE
BUMMLED > BUMMLE
BUMMLES > BUMMLE
BUMMLING > BUMMLE
BUMMOCK *n* submerged mass of ice projecting downwards
BUMMOCKS > BUMMOCK
BUMP *vb* knock or strike with a jolt ▷ *n* dull thud from an impact or collision
BUMPED > BUMP
BUMPER *n* bar on the front and back of a vehicle to protect against damage ▷ *adj* unusually large or abundant ▷ *vb* toast with a bumper
BUMPERED > BUMPER
BUMPERING > BUMPER
BUMPERS > BUMPER
BUMPH *same as* > BUMF
BUMPHS > BUMPH
BUMPIER > BUMPY
BUMPIEST > BUMPY
BUMPILY > BUMPY
BUMPINESS > BUMPY
BUMPING > BUMP
BUMPINGS > BUMP
BUMPKIN *n* awkward simple country person
BUMPKINLY > BUMPKIN
BUMPKINS > BUMPKIN
BUMPOLOGY *n* humorous word for phrenology
BUMPS > BUMP
BUMPTIOUS *adj* offensively self-assertive
BUMPY *adj* having an uneven surface
BUMS > BUM
BUMSTERS *pl n* trousers cut so that the top lies just above the cleft of the buttocks
BUMSUCKER *n* toady
BUN *n* small sweet bread roll or cake
BUNA *n* synthetic rubber formed by polymerizing butadiene or by copolymerizing it with such compounds as acrylonitrile or styrene
BUNAS > BUNA
BUNCE *n* windfall; boom ▷ *vb* charge someone too much money
BUNCED > BUNCE
BUNCES > BUNCE
BUNCH *n* number of things growing, fastened, or grouped together ▷ *vb* group or be grouped together in a bunch
BUNCHED > BUNCH
BUNCHES *pl n* hairstyle in which hair is tied into two sections on either side of the head at the back
BUNCHIER > BUNCHY
BUNCHIEST > BUNCHY
BUNCHILY > BUNCHY
BUNCHING > BUNCH
BUNCHINGS > BUNCH
BUNCHY *adj* composed of or resembling bunches
BUNCING > BUNCE
BUNCO *n* swindle, esp one by confidence tricksters ▷ *vb* swindle
BUNCOED > BUNCO
BUNCOING > BUNCO
BUNCOMBE *same as* > BUNKUM
BUNCOMBES > BUNCOMBE
BUNCOS > BUNCO
BUND *n* embankment or German federation ▷ *vb* form into an embankment
BUNDE > BUND
BUNDED > BUND
BUNDH *same as* > BANDH
BUNDHS > BUNDH
BUNDIES > BUNDY
BUNDING > BUND
BUNDIST > BUND
BUNDISTS > BUND
BUNDLE *n* number of things gathered loosely together ▷ *vb* cause to go roughly or unceremoniously
BUNDLED > BUNDLE
BUNDLER > BUNDLE
BUNDLERS > BUNDLE
BUNDLES > BUNDLE
BUNDLING > BUNDLE
BUNDLINGS > BUNDLE
BUNDOBUST *same as* > BANDOBUST
BUNDOOK *n* rifle
BUNDOOKS > BUNDOOK
BUNDS > BUND
BUNDT *n* type of sweet cake
BUNDTS > BUNDT
BUNDU *n* largely uninhabited wild region far from towns
BUNDUS > BUNDU
BUNDWALL *n* concrete or earth wall surrounding a storage tank containing crude oil or its refined product, designed to hold the contents of the tank in the event of a rupture or leak
BUNDWALLS > BUNDWALL
BUNDY *n* time clock at work
BUNFIGHT *n* tea party
BUNFIGHTS > BUNFIGHT
BUNG *n* stopper for a cask etc ▷ *vb* close with a bung
BUNGALOID *n* bungalow-type house
BUNGALOW *n* one-storey house
BUNGALOWS > BUNGALOW
BUNGED > BUNG
BUNGEE *n* strong elastic cable
BUNGEES > BUNGEE
BUNGER *n* firework
BUNGERS > BUNGER
BUNGEY *same as* > BUNGEE
BUNGEYS > BUNGEY
BUNGHOLE *n* hole in a cask or barrel through which liquid can be drained
BUNGHOLES > BUNGHOLE
BUNGIE *same as* > BUNGEE
BUNGIES > BUNGY
BUNGING > BUNG
BUNGLE *vb* spoil through incompetence ▷ *n* blunder or muddle
BUNGLED > BUNGLE
BUNGLER > BUNGLE
BUNGLERS > BUNGLE
BUNGLES > BUNGLE
BUNGLING > BUNGLE
BUNGLINGS > BUNGLE
BUNGS > BUNG
BUNGWALL *n* Australian fern, *Blechnum indicum*, having an edible rhizome
BUNGWALLS > BUNGWALL
BUNGY > BUNGEE
BUNIA *same as* > BUNNIA
BUNIAS > BUNIA
BUNION *n* inflamed swelling on the big toe
BUNIONS > BUNION
BUNJE *same as* > BUNGEE
BUNJEE *same as* > BUNGEE
BUNJEES > BUNJEE
BUNJES > BUNJE
BUNJIE *same as* > BUNGEE
BUNJIES > BUNJIE
BUNJY *same as* > BUNGEE
BUNK *n* narrow shelflike bed ▷ *vb* prepare to sleep
BUNKED > BUNK
BUNKER *n* sand-filled hollow forming an obstacle on a golf course ▷ *vb* drive (the ball) into a bunker

BUNKERED > BUNKER
BUNKERING > BUNKER
BUNKERS > BUNKER
BUNKHOUSE *n* (in the US and Canada) building containing the sleeping quarters of workers on a ranch
BUNKING > BUNK
BUNKMATE *n* person who sleeps in the same quarters as another
BUNKMATES > BUNKMATE
BUNKO *same as* > BUNCO
BUNKOED > BUNKO
BUNKOING > BUNKO
BUNKOS > BUNKO
BUNKS > BUNK
BUNKUM *n* nonsense
BUNKUMS > BUNKUM
BUNN *same as* > BUN
BUNNET *same as* > BONNET
BUNNETS > BUNNET
BUNNIA *n* Hindu shopkeeper
BUNNIAS > BUNNIA
BUNNIES > BUNNY
BUNNS > BUNN
BUNNY *n* child's word for a rabbit
BUNODONT *adj* (of the teeth of certain mammals) having cusps that are separate and rounded
BUNRAKU *n* Japanese form of puppet theatre in which the puppets are usually about four feet high, with moving features as well as limbs and each puppet is manipulated by up to three puppeteers who remain onstage
BUNRAKUS > BUNRAKU
BUNS *pl n* buttocks
BUNSEN as in *bunsen burner* gas burner used in scientific labs
BUNSENS > BUNSEN
BUNT *vb* (of an animal) butt (something) with the head or horns ▷ *n* act or an instance of bunting
BUNTAL *n* straw obtained from leaves of the talipot palm
BUNTALS > BUNTAL
BUNTED > BUNT
BUNTER *n* batter who deliberately taps ball lightly
BUNTERS > BUNTER
BUNTIER > BUNT
BUNTIEST > BUNT
BUNTING *n* decorative flags
BUNTINGS > BUNTING
BUNTLINE *n* one of several lines fastened to the foot of a square sail for hauling it up to the yard when furling
BUNTLINES > BUNTLINE
BUNTS > BUNT
BUNTY > BUNT
BUNYA *n* tall dome-shaped Australian coniferous tree
BUNYAS > BUNYA
BUNYIP *n* legendary monster said to live in swamps and lakes
BUNYIPS > BUNYIP
BUOY *n* floating marker anchored in the sea ▷ *vb* prevent from sinking
BUOYAGE *n* system of buoys
BUOYAGES > BUOYAGE
BUOYANCE *same as* > BUOYANCY
BUOYANCES > BUOYANCE
BUOYANCY *n* ability to float in a liquid or to rise in a fluid
BUOYANT *adj* able to float
BUOYANTLY > BUOYANT
BUOYED > BUOY
BUOYING > BUOY
BUOYS > BUOY
BUPKES *same as* > BUBKES
BUPKUS *same as* > BUBKES
BUPLEVER *n* type of plant
BUPLEVERS > BUPLEVER
BUPPIE *n* affluent young Black person
BUPPIES > BUPPY
BUPPY *variant of* > BUPPY
BUPRESTID *n* any beetle of the mainly tropical family *Buprestidae*, the adults of which are brilliantly coloured and the larvae of which bore into and cause damage to trees, roots, etc ▷ *adj* of, relating to, or belonging to the family *Buprestidae*
BUQSHA *n* former Yemeni coin
BUQSHAS > BUQSHA
BUR > BURR
BURA *same as* > BURAN
BURAN *n* blizzard, with the wind blowing from the north and reaching gale force
BURANS > BURAN
BURAS > BURA
BURB *n* suburb
BURBLE *vb* make a bubbling sound ▷ *n* bubbling or gurgling sound
BURBLED > BURBLE
BURBLER > BURBLE
BURBLERS > BURBLE
BURBLES > BURBLE
BURBLIER > BURBLY
BURBLIEST > BURBLY
BURBLING > BURBLE
BURBLINGS > BURBLE
BURBLY *adj* burbling
BURBOT *n* freshwater fish of the cod family that has barbels around its mouth
BURBOTS > BURBOT
BURBS > BURB
BURD *Scots form of* > BIRD
BURDASH *n* fringed sash worn over coat
BURDASHES > BURDASH
BURDEN *n* heavy load ▷ *vb* put a burden on
BURDENED > BURDEN
BURDENER > BURDEN
BURDENERS > BURDEN
BURDENING > BURDEN
BURDENOUS > BURDEN
BURDENS > BURDEN
BURDIE *Scots form of* > BIRDIE
BURDIES > BURDIE
BURDIZZO *n* surgical instrument used to castrate animals
BURDIZZOS > BURDIZZO
BURDOCK *n* weed with prickly burrs
BURDOCKS > BURDOCK
BURDS > BURD
BUREAU *n* office that provides a service
BUREAUS > BUREAU
BUREAUX > BUREAU
BURET *same as* > BURETTE
BURETS > BURET
BURETTE *n* glass tube for dispensing known volumes of fluids
BURETTES > BURETTE
BURG *n* fortified town
BURGAGE *n* (in England) tenure of land or tenement in a town or city, which originally involved a fixed money rent
BURGAGES > BURGAGE
BURGANET *same as* > BURGONET
BURGANETS > BURGANET
BURGEE *n* triangular or swallow-tailed flag flown from the mast of a merchant ship for identification and from the mast of a yacht to indicate its owner's membership of a particular yacht club
BURGEES > BURGEE
BURGEON *vb* develop or grow rapidly ▷ *n* bud of a plant
BURGEONED > BURGEON
BURGEONS > BURGEON
BURGER *n* hamburger
BURGERS > BURGER
BURGESS *n* (in England) citizen or freeman of a borough
BURGESSES > BURGESS
BURGH *n* Scottish borough
BURGHAL > BURGH
BURGHER *n* citizen
BURGHERS > BURGHER
BURGHS > BURGH
BURGHUL *same as* > BULGUR
BURGHULS > BURGHUL
BURGLAR *n* person who enters a building to commit a crime, esp theft ▷ *vb* burgle
BURGLARED > BURGLAR
BURGLARS > BURGLAR
BURGLARY *n* crime of entering a building as a trespasser to commit theft or another offence
BURGLE *vb* break into (a house, shop, etc)
BURGLED > BURGLE
BURGLES > BURGLE
BURGLING > BURGLE
BURGONET *n* light 16th-century helmet, usually made of steel, with hinged cheekpieces
BURGONETS > BURGONET
BURGOO *n* porridge
BURGOOS > BURGOO
BURGOUT *same as* > BURGOO
BURGOUTS > BURGOUT
BURGRAVE *n* military governor of a German town or castle, esp in the 12th and 13th centuries
BURGRAVES > BURGRAVE
BURGS > BURG
BURGUNDY *adj* dark-purplish red
BURHEL *same as* > BHARAL
BURHELS > BURHEL
BURIAL *n* burying of a dead body
BURIALS > BURIAL
BURIED > BURY
BURIER *n* person or thing that buries
BURIERS > BURIER
BURIES > BURY
BURIN *n* steel chisel used for engraving metal, wood, or marble
BURINIST > BURIN
BURINISTS > BURIN
BURINS > BURIN
BURITI *n* type of palm tree
BURITIS > BURITI
BURK *same as* > BERK
BURKA *same as* > BURQA
BURKAS > BURKA
BURKE *vb* murder in such a way as to leave no marks on the body, usually by suffocation
BURKED > BURKE
BURKER > BURKE
BURKERS > BURKE
BURKES > BURKE
BURKING > BURKE
BURKITE > BURKE
BURKITES > BURKE
BURKS > BURK
BURL *n* small knot or lump in wool ▷ *vb* remove the burls from (cloth)
BURLADERO *n* safe area for bull-fighter in bull ring
BURLAP *n* coarse fabric woven from jute, hemp, or the like
BURLAPS > BURLAP
BURLED > BURL
BURLER > BURL
BURLERS > BURL
BURLESK *same as* > BURLESQUE
BURLESKS > BURLESK
BURLESQUE *n* artistic work

which satirizes a subject by caricature ▷ *adj* of or characteristic of a burlesque ▷ *vb* represent or imitate (a person or thing) in a ludicrous way
BURLETTA *n* type of comic opera
BURLETTAS > BURLETTA
BURLEY *same as* > BERLEY
BURLEYCUE *same as* > BURLESQUE
BURLEYED > BURLEY
BURLEYING > BURLEY
BURLEYS > BURLEY
BURLIER > BURLY
BURLIEST > BURLY
BURLILY > BURLY
BURLINESS > BURLY
BURLING > BURL
BURLS > BURL
BURLY *adj* (of a person) broad and strong
BURN *vb* be or set on fire ▷ *n* injury or mark caused by fire or exposure to heat
BURNABLE > BURN
BURNABLES > BURN
BURNED > BURN
BURNER *n* part of a stove or lamp that produces the flame
BURNERS > BURNER
BURNET *n* type of rose
BURNETS > BURNET
BURNIE *n* sideburn
BURNIES > BURNIE
BURNING > BURN
BURNINGLY > BURN
BURNINGS > BURN
BURNISH *vb* make smooth and shiny by rubbing ▷ *n* shiny finish
BURNISHED > BURNISH
BURNISHER > BURNISH
BURNISHES > BURNISH
BURNOOSE *same as* > BURNOUS
BURNOOSED > BURNOUS
BURNOOSES > BURNOOSE
BURNOUS *n* long circular cloak with a hood, worn esp by Arabs
BURNOUSE *same as* > BURNOUS
BURNOUSED > BURNOUS
BURNOUSES > BURNOUSE
BURNOUT *n* failure of a mechanical device from excessive heating
BURNOUTS > BURNOUT
BURNS > BURN
BURNSIDE *n* land along side of burn
BURNSIDES > BURNSIDE
BURNT > BURN
BUROO *n* government office from which unemployment benefit is distributed
BUROOS > BUROO
BURP *n* belch ▷ *vb* belch
BURPED > BURP
BURPEE *n* type of physical exercise movement
BURPEES > BURPEE
BURPING > BURP
BURPS > BURP
BURQA *n* long enveloping garment worn by Muslim women in public, covering all but the wearer's eyes
BURQAS > BURQA
BURR *n* small power-driven hand-operated rotary file, esp for removing burrs or for machining recesses ▷ *vb* form a rough edge on (a workpiece)
BURRAMYS *n* very rare mountain pigmy possum, *Burramys parvus*, of Australia. It is about the size of a rat and restricted in habitat to very high altitudes, mainly Mt Hotham, Victoria. Until 1966 it was known only as a fossil
BURRAWANG *n* Australian plant with fernlike leaves and an edible nut
BURRED > BURR
BURREL *same as* > BHARAL
BURRELL *variant of* > BHARAL
BURRELLS > BURRELL
BURRELS > BURREL
BURRER *n* person who removes burrs
BURRERS > BURRER
BURRHEL *same as* > BURREL
BURRHELS > BURRHEL
BURRIER > BURRY
BURRIEST > BURRY
BURRING > BURR
BURRITO *n* tortilla folded over a filling of minced beef, chicken, cheese, or beans
BURRITOS > BURRITO
BURRO *n* donkey, esp one used as a pack animal
BURROS > BURRO
BURROW *n* hole dug in the ground by a rabbit etc ▷ *vb* dig holes in the ground
BURROWED > BURROW
BURROWER > BURROW
BURROWERS > BURROW
BURROWING > BURROW
BURROWS > BURROW
BURRS > BURR
BURRSTONE *same as* > BUHRSTONE
BURRY *adj* full of or covered in burs
BURS > BURR
BURSA *n* small fluid-filled sac that reduces friction between movable parts of the body, esp at joints
BURSAE > BURSA
BURSAL > BURSA
BURSAR *n* treasurer of a school, college, or university
BURSARIAL *adj* of, relating to, or paid by a bursar or bursary
BURSARIES > BURSARY
BURSARS > BURSAR
BURSARY *n* scholarship
BURSAS > BURSA
BURSATE > BURSA
BURSE *n* flat case used at Mass as a container for the corporal
BURSEED *n* type of plant
BURSEEDS > BURSEED
BURSERA *adj* of a type of gum tree
BURSES > BURSE
BURSICON *n* hormone, produced by the insect brain, that regulates processes associated with ecdysis, such as darkening of the cuticle
BURSICONS > BURSICON
BURSIFORM *adj* shaped like a pouch or sac
BURSITIS *n* inflammation of a bursa, esp one in the shoulder joint
BURST *vb* break or cause to break open or apart suddenly and noisily, esp from internal pressure ▷ *n* sudden breaking open or apart ▷ *adj* broken apart
BURSTED > BURST
BURSTEN > BURST
BURSTER > BURST
BURSTERS > BURST
BURSTING > BURST
BURSTONE *same as* > BUHRSTONE
BURSTONES > BURSTONE
BURSTS > BURST
BURTHEN *archaic word for* > BURDEN
BURTHENED > BURTHEN
BURTHENS > BURTHEN
BURTON *n* type of hoisting tackle
BURTONS > BURTON
BURWEED *n* any of various plants that bear burs, such as the burdock
BURWEEDS > BURWEED
BURY *vb* place in a grave
BURYING > BURY
BUS *n* large motor vehicle for carrying passengers between stops ▷ *vb* travel by bus
BUSBAR *n* electrical conductor, maintained at a specific voltage and capable of carrying a high current, usually used to make a common connection between several circuits in a system
BUSBARS > BUSBAR
BUSBIES > BUSBY
BUSBOY *n* waiter's assistant
BUSBOYS > BUSBOY
BUSBY *n* tall fur hat worn by some soldiers
BUSED > BUS
BUSERA *n* Ugandan alcoholic drink made from millet: sometimes mixed with honey
BUSERAS > BUSERA
BUSES > BUS
BUSGIRL *n* waiter's assistant
BUSGIRLS > BUSGIRL
BUSH *n* dense woody plant, smaller than a tree ▷ *vb* fit a bush to (a casing or bearing)
BUSHBABY *n* small African tree-living mammal with large eyes
BUSHBUCK *n* small nocturnal spiral-horned antelope, *Tragelaphus scriptus*, of the bush and tropical forest of Africa. Its coat is reddish-brown with a few white markings
BUSHBUCKS > BUSHBUCK
BUSHCRAFT *n* ability and experience in matters concerned with living in the bush
BUSHED *adj* extremely tired
BUSHEL *n* obsolete unit of measure equal to 8 gallons (36.4 litres) ▷ *vb* alter or mend (a garment)
BUSHELED > BUSHEL
BUSHELER > BUSHEL
BUSHELERS > BUSHEL
BUSHELING > BUSHEL
BUSHELLED > BUSHEL
BUSHELLER > BUSHEL
BUSHELMAN > BUSHEL
BUSHELMEN > BUSHEL
BUSHELS > BUSHEL
BUSHER > BUSH
BUSHERS > BUSH
BUSHES > BUSH
BUSHFIRE *n* uncontrolled fire in the bush
BUSHFIRES > BUSHFIRE
BUSHFLIES > BUSHFLY
BUSHFLY *n* any of various small black dipterous flies of Australia, esp *Musca vetustissima*, that breed in faeces and dung: family *Calliphoridae*
BUSHGOAT *n* S African antelope
BUSHGOATS > BUSHGOAT
BUSHIDO *n* feudal code of the Japanese samurai, stressing self-discipline, courage and loyalty
BUSHIDOS > BUSHIDO
BUSHIE *same as* > BUSHY
BUSHIER > BUSHY
BUSHIES > BUSHY
BUSHIEST > BUSHY
BUSHILY > BUSHY
BUSHINESS > BUSHY
BUSHING *same as* > BUSH
BUSHINGS > BUSHING
BUSHLAND *n* land characterized by natural

vegetation
BUSHLANDS > BUSHLAND
BUSHLESS > BUSH
BUSHLIKE > BUSH
BUSHMAN *n* person who lives or travels in the bush
BUSHMEAT *n* meat taken from any animal native to African forests, including species that may be endangered or not usually eaten outside Africa
BUSHMEATS > BUSHMEAT
BUSHMEN > BUSHMAN
BUSHPIG *n* wild pig, *Potamochoerus porcus*, inhabiting forests in tropical Africa and Madagascar. It is brown or black, with pale markings on the face
BUSHPIGS > BUSHPIG
BUSHTIT *n* small grey active North American songbird
BUSHTITS > BUSHTIT
BUSHVELD *n* bushy countryside
BUSHVELDS > BUSHVELD
BUSHWA *n* nonsense
BUSHWAH *same as* > BUSHWA
BUSHWAHS > BUSHWAH
BUSHWALK *vb* hike through bushland
BUSHWALKS > BUSHWALK
BUSHWAS > BUSHWA
BUSHWHACK *vb* ambush
BUSHWOMAN > BUSHMAN
BUSHWOMEN > BUSHMAN
BUSHY *adj* (of hair) thick and shaggy ▷ *n* person who lives in the bush
BUSIED > BUSY
BUSIER > BUSY
BUSIES > BUSY
BUSIEST > BUSY
BUSILY *adv* in a busy manner
BUSINESS *n* purchase and sale of goods and services
BUSINESSY *adj* of, relating to, typical of, or suitable for the world of commercial or industrial business
BUSING > BUS
BUSINGS > BUS
BUSK *vb* act as a busker ▷ *n* strip of whalebone, wood, steel, etc, inserted into the front of a corset to stiffen it
BUSKED > BUSK
BUSKER > BUSK
BUSKERS > BUSK
BUSKET *n* bouquet
BUSKETS > BUSKET
BUSKIN *n* (formerly) sandal-like covering for the foot and leg, reaching the calf and usually laced
BUSKINED *adj* relating to tragedy
BUSKING > BUSK
BUSKINGS > BUSK
BUSKINS > BUSKIN
BUSKS > BUSK
BUSKY *same as* > BOSKY
BUSLOAD *n* number of people bus carries
BUSLOADS > BUSLOAD
BUSMAN *n* person who drives a bus
BUSMEN > BUSMAN
BUSS *archaic or dialect word for* > KISS
BUSSED > BUS
BUSSES > BUS
BUSSING > BUS
BUSSINGS > BUS
BUSSU *n* type of palm tree
BUSSUS > BUSSU
BUST *n* chest of a human being, esp a woman's bosom ▷ *adj* broken ▷ *vb* burst or break
BUSTARD *n* bird with long strong legs, a heavy body, a long neck, and speckled plumage
BUSTARDS > BUSTARD
BUSTED > BUST
BUSTEE *same as* > BASTI
BUSTEES > BUSTEE
BUSTER *n* person or thing destroying something as specified
BUSTERS > BUSTER
BUSTI *same as* > BASTI
BUSTIC *n* type of small American tree
BUSTICATE *vb* break
BUSTICS > BUSTIC
BUSTIER *n* close-fitting strapless women's top
BUSTIERS > BUSTIER
BUSTIEST > BUSTY
BUSTINESS > BUSTY
BUSTING > BUST
BUSTINGS > BUST
BUSTIS > BUSTI
BUSTLE *vb* hurry with a show of activity or energy ▷ *n* energetic and noisy activity
BUSTLED > BUSTLE
BUSTLER > BUSTLE
BUSTLERS > BUSTLE
BUSTLES > BUSTLE
BUSTLINE *n* shape or size of woman's bust
BUSTLINES > BUSTLINE
BUSTLING > BUSTLE
BUSTS > BUST
BUSTY *adj* (of a woman) having a prominent bust
BUSULFAN *n* drug used to treat cancer
BUSULFANS > BUSULFAN
BUSUUTI *n* long garment with short sleeves and a square neckline, worn by Ugandan women, esp in S Uganda
BUSUUTIS > BUSUUTI
BUSY *adj* actively employed ▷ *vb* keep (someone, esp oneself) busy
BUSYBODY *n* meddlesome or nosy person
BUSYING > BUSY
BUSYNESS > BUSY
BUSYWORK *n* unproductive work
BUSYWORKS > BUSYWORK
BUT *prep* except ▷ *adv* only ▷ *n* outer room of a two-roomed cottage: usually the kitchen
BUTADIENE *n* colourless easily liquefiable flammable gas
BUTANE *n* gas used for fuel
BUTANES > BUTANE
BUTANOL *n* colourless substance
BUTANOLS > BUTANOL
BUTANONE *n* colourless soluble flammable liquid used mainly as a solvent for resins
BUTANONES > BUTANONE
BUTCH *adj* markedly or aggressively masculine ▷ *n* lesbian who is noticeably masculine
BUTCHER *n* person who slaughters animals or sells their meat ▷ *vb* kill and prepare (animals) for meat
BUTCHERED > BUTCHER
BUTCHERER > BUTCHER
BUTCHERLY > BUTCHER
BUTCHERS > BUTCHER
BUTCHERY *n* senseless slaughter
BUTCHES > BUTCH
BUTCHEST > BUTCH
BUTCHING > BUTCH
BUTCHINGS > BUTCH
BUTCHNESS > BUTCH
BUTE *n* drug used illegally to dope horses
BUTENE *n* pungent colourless gas
BUTENES > BUTENE
BUTEO *n* type of American hawk
BUTEONINE *adj* of hawks
BUTEOS > BUTEO
BUTES > BUTE
BUTLE *vb* act as butler
BUTLED > BUTLE
BUTLER *n* chief male servant ▷ *vb* act as a butler
BUTLERAGE > BUTLER
BUTLERED > BUTLER
BUTLERIES > BUTLERY
BUTLERING > BUTLER
BUTLERS > BUTLER
BUTLERY *n* butler's room
BUTLES > BUTLE
BUTLING > BUTLE
BUTMENT *same as* > ABUTMENT
BUTMENTS > BUTMENT
BUTS > BUT
BUTSUDAN *n* (in Buddhism) small household altar
BUTSUDANS > BUTSUDAN
BUTT *n* thicker or blunt end of something, such as the end of the stock of a rifle ▷ *vb* strike or push with the head or horns
BUTTALS *n* abuttal
BUTTE *n* isolated steep flat-topped hill
BUTTED > BUTT
BUTTER *n* edible fatty yellow solid made form cream ▷ *vb* put butter on
BUTTERBUR *n* plant of the Eurasian genus *Petasites* with fragrant whitish or purple flowers, woolly stems, and leaves formerly used to wrap butter: family *Asteraceae* (composites)
BUTTERCUP *n* small yellow flower
BUTTERED > BUTTER
BUTTERFAT *n* fatty substance of milk from which butter is made, consisting of a mixture of glycerides, mainly butyrin, olein, and palmitin
BUTTERFLY *n* insect with brightly coloured wings
BUTTERIER > BUTTERY
BUTTERIES > BUTTERY
BUTTERINE *n* artificial butter made partly from milk
BUTTERING > BUTTER
BUTTERNUT *n* walnut tree, *Juglans cinerea* of E North America
BUTTERS > BUTTER
BUTTERY *n* (in some universities) room in which food and drink are sold to students ▷ *adj* containing, like, or coated with butter
BUTTES > BUTTE
BUTTHEAD *n* stupid person
BUTTHEADS > BUTTHEAD
BUTTIES > BUTTY
BUTTING > BUTT
BUTTINSKI *same as* > BUTTINSKY
BUTTINSKY *n* busybody
BUTTLE *vb* act as butler
BUTTLED > BUTTLE
BUTTLES > BUTTLE
BUTTLING > BUTTLE
BUTTOCK *n* either of the two fleshy masses that form the human rump ▷ *vb* perform a kind of wrestling manoeuvre on a person
BUTTOCKED > BUTTOCK
BUTTOCKS > BUTTOCK
BUTTON *n* small disc or knob sewn to clothing, which can be passed through a slit in another piece of fabric to fasten them ▷ *vb* fasten with buttons
BUTTONED > BUTTON
BUTTONER > BUTTON

BUTTONERS > BUTTON
BUTTONING > BUTTON
BUTTONS *n* page boy
BUTTONY > BUTTON
BUTTRESS *n* structure to support a wall ▷ *vb* support with, or as if with, a buttress
BUTTS > BUTT
BUTTSTOCK *n* part of gun
BUTTY *n* sandwich
BUTTYMAN *n* offensive term for a homosexual
BUTTYMEN > BUTTYMAN
BUTUT *n* Gambian monetary unit worth one hundredth of a dalasi
BUTUTS > BUTUT
BUTYL *adj* of or containing any of four isomeric forms of the group C_4H_9– ▷ *n* of, consisting of, or containing any of four isomeric forms of the group C_4H_9–
BUTYLATE *vb* introduce butyl into (compound)
BUTYLATED > BUTYLATE
BUTYLATES > BUTYLATE
BUTYLENE *same as* > BUTENE
BUTYLENES > BUTYLENE
BUTYLS > BUTYL
BUTYRAL *n* type of resin
BUTYRALS > BUTYRAL
BUTYRATE *n* any salt or ester of butyric acid
BUTYRATES > BUTYRATE
BUTYRIC as in *butyric acid* type of acid
BUTYRIN *n* colourless liquid ester or oil found in butter. It is formed from butyric acid and glycerine
BUTYRINS > BUTYRIN
BUTYROUS *adj* butyraceous
BUTYRYL *n* radical of butyric acid
BUTYRYLS > BUTYRYL
BUVETTE *n* roadside café
BUVETTES > BUVETTE
BUXOM *adj* (of a woman) healthily plump and full-bosomed
BUXOMER > BUXOM
BUXOMEST > BUXOM
BUXOMLY > BUXOM
BUXOMNESS > BUXOM
BUY *vb* acquire by paying money for ▷ *n* thing acquired through payment
BUYABLE > BUY
BUYABLES > BUY
BUYBACK *n* repurchase by a company of some or all of its shares from an investor, who acquired them by putting venture capital into the company when it was formed
BUYBACKS > BUYBACK
BUYER *n* customer
BUYERS > BUYER
BUYING > BUY
BUYOFF *n* purchase
BUYOFFS > BUYOFF
BUYOUT *n* purchase of a company, esp by its former management or staff
BUYOUTS > BUYOUT
BUYS > BUY
BUZKASHI *n* game played in Aghanistan, in which opposing teams of horsemen strive for possession of the headless carcass of a goat
BUZKASHIS > BUZKASHI
BUZUKI *same as* > BOUZOUKI
BUZUKIA > BUZUKI
BUZUKIS > BUZUKI
BUZZ *n* rapidly vibrating humming sound ▷ *vb* make a humming sound
BUZZARD *n* bird of prey of the hawk family
BUZZARDS > BUZZARD
BUZZCUT *n* very short haircut
BUZZCUTS > BUZZCUT
BUZZED > BUZZ
BUZZER *n* electronic device that produces a buzzing sound as a signal
BUZZERS > BUZZER
BUZZES > BUZZ
BUZZIER > BUZZY
BUZZIEST > BUZZY
BUZZING > BUZZ
BUZZINGLY > BUZZ
BUZZINGS > BUZZ
BUZZWIG *n* bushy wig
BUZZWIGS > BUZZWIG
BUZZWORD *n* word, often originating in a particular jargon, that becomes a vogue word in the community as a whole or among a particular group
BUZZWORDS > BUZZWORD
BUZZY *adj* making a buzzing sound
BWANA *n* (in E Africa) master, often used as a respectful form of address corresponding to *sir*
BWANAS > BWANA
BWAZI *same as* > BUAZE
BWAZIS > BWAZI
BY *prep* indicating the doer of an action, nearness, movement past, time before or during which, etc ▷ *adv* near ▷ *n* bye
BYCATCH *n* unwanted fish and other sea animals caught in a fishing net along with the desired kind of fish
BYCATCHES > BYCATCH
BYCOKET *n* former Italian high-crowned hat
BYCOKETS > BYCOKET
BYDE *same as* > BIDE
BYDED > BYDE
BYDES > BYDE
BYDING > BYDE
BYE *n* situation where a player or team wins a round by having no opponent ▷ *interj* goodbye ▷ *sentence substitute* goodbye
BYELAW *n* rule made by a local authority for the regulation of its affairs or management of the area it governs
BYELAWS > BYELAW
BYES > BYE
BYGONE *adj* past
BYGONES > BYGONE
BYKE > BICYCLE
BYKED > BICYCLE
BYKES > BICYCLE
BYKING > BICYCLE
BYLANDER *same as* > BILANDER
BYLANDERS > BYLANDER
BYLANE *n* side lane or alley off a road
BYLANES > BYLANE
BYLAW *n* rule made by a local authority
BYLAWS > BYLAW
BYLINE *n* line under the title of a newspaper or magazine article giving the author's name ▷ *vb* give a byline to
BYLINED > BYLINE
BYLINER > BYLINE
BYLINERS > BYLINE
BYLINES > BYLINE
BYLINING > BYLINE
BYLIVE *same as* > BELIVE
BYNAME *n* nickname
BYNAMES > BYNAME
BYNEMPT > BENAME
BYPASS *n* main road built to avoid a city ▷ *vb* go round or avoid
BYPASSED > BYPASS
BYPASSES > BYPASS
BYPASSING > BYPASS
BYPAST > BYPASS
BYPATH *n* little-used path or track, esp in the country
BYPATHS > BYPATH
BYPLACE *n* private place
BYPLACES > BYPLACE
BYPLAY *n* secondary action or talking carried on apart while the main action proceeds, esp in a play
BYPLAYS > BYPLAY
BYPRODUCT *n* secondary product
BYRE *n* shelter for cows
BYREMAN *n* man who works in byre
BYREMEN > BYREMAN
BYRES > BYRE
BYREWOMAN *n* woman who works in byre
BYREWOMEN > BYREWOMAN
BYRL *same as* > BIRL
BYRLADY *interj* short for By Our Lady
BYRLAKIN *interj* By Our Ladykin
BYRLAW *same as* > BYLAW
BYRLAWS > BYRLAW
BYRLED > BYRL
BYRLING > BYRL
BYRLS > BYRL
BYRNIE *n* archaic word for coat of mail
BYRNIES > BYRNIE
BYROAD *n* secondary or side road
BYROADS > BYROAD
BYROOM *n* private room
BYROOMS > BYROOM
BYS > BY
BYSSAL *adj* of mollusc's byssus
BYSSI > BYSSUS
BYSSINE *adj* made from flax
BYSSOID *adj* consisting of fine fibres
BYSSUS *n* mass of strong threads secreted by a sea mussel or similar mollusc that attaches the animal to a hard fixed surface
BYSSUSES > BYSSUS
BYSTANDER *n* person present but not involved
BYSTREET *n* obscure or secondary street
BYSTREETS > BYSTREET
BYTALK *n* trivial conversation
BYTALKS > BYTALK
BYTE *n* group of bits processed as one unit of data
BYTES > BYTE
BYTOWNITE *n* rare mineral
BYWAY *n* minor road
BYWAYS > BYWAY
BYWONER *n* poor tenant-farmer
BYWONERS > BYWONER
BYWORD *n* person or thing regarded as a perfect example of something
BYWORDS > BYWORD
BYWORK *n* work done outside usual working hours
BYWORKS > BYWORK
BYZANT *same as* > BEZANT
BYZANTINE *adj* of, characteristic of, or relating to Byzantium or the Byzantine Empire
BYZANTS > BYZANT

C

CAA *a Scot word for* > CALL
CAAED > CAA
CAAING > CAA
CAAS > CAA
CAATINGA *n* Brazilian semi-arid scrub forest
CAATINGAS > CAATINGA
CAB *n* taxi ▷ *vb* take a taxi
CABA *same as* > CABAS
CABAL *n* small group of political plotters ▷ *vb* form a cabal
CABALA *a variant spelling of* > KABBALAH
CABALAS > CABALA
CABALETTA *n* final section of an aria
CABALETTE > CABALETTA
CABALISM > CABALA
CABALISMS > CABALA
CABALIST > CABALA
CABALISTS > CABALA
CABALLED > CABAL
CABALLER > CABAL
CABALLERO *n* Spanish gentleman
CABALLERS > CABAL
CABALLINE *adj* pertaining to a horse
CABALLING > CABAL
CABALS > CABAL
CABANA *n* tent used as a dressing room by the sea
CABANAS > CABANA
CABARET *n* dancing and singing show in a nightclub
CABARETS > CABARET
CABAS *n* reticule
CABBAGE *n* vegetable with a large head of green leaves ▷ *vb* steal
CABBAGED > CABBAGE
CABBAGES > CABBAGE
CABBAGEY > CABBAGE
CABBAGING > CABBAGE
CABBAGY > CABBAGE
CABBALA *a variant spelling of* > KABBALAH
CABBALAH *same as* > CABBALA
CABBALAHS > CABBALA
CABBALAS > CABBALA
CABBALISM > CABBALA
CABBALIST > CABBALA
CABBED > CAB
CABBIE *n* taxi driver
CABBIES > CABBIE
CABBING > CAB
CABBY *same as* > CABBIE
CABDRIVER *n* taxi-driver
CABER *n* tree trunk tossed in competition at Highland games
CABERNET *n* type of grape, or the red wine made from it
CABERNETS > CABERNET
CABERS > CABER
CABESTRO *n* halter made from horsehair
CABESTROS > CABESTRO
CABEZON *n* large food fish, *Scorpaenichthys marmoratus*, of North American Pacific coastal waters, having greenish flesh: family *Cottidae* (bullheads and sea scorpions)
CABEZONE *same as* > CABEZON
CABEZONES > CABEZON
CABEZONS > CABEZON
CABILDO *n* Spanish municipal council
CABILDOS > CABILDO
CABIN *n* compartment in a ship or aircraft ▷ *vb* confine in a small space
CABINED > CABIN
CABINET *n* piece of furniture with drawers or shelves
CABINETRY *n* cabinetmaking
CABINETS > CABINET
CABINING > CABIN
CABINMATE *n* sharer of cabin
CABINS > CABIN
CABLE *n* strong thick rope; a wire or bundle of wires that conduct electricity ▷ *vb* send (someone) a message by cable
CABLECAST *n* broadcast on cable
CABLED > CABLE
CABLEGRAM *n* message sent by cable
CABLER *n* cable broadcasting company
CABLERS > CABLER
CABLES > CABLE
CABLET *n* small cable, esp a cable-laid rope that has a circumference of less than 25 centimetres (ten inches)
CABLETS > CABLET
CABLEWAY *n* system for moving people or bulk materials in which suspended cars, buckets, etc, run on cables that extend between terminal towers
CABLEWAYS > CABLEWAY
CABLING > CABLE
CABLINGS > CABLE
CABMAN *n* driver of a cab
CABMEN > CABMAN
CABOB *vb* roast on a skewer
CABOBBED > CABOB
CABOBBING > CABOB
CABOBS > CABOB
CABOC *n* type of Scottish cheese
CABOCEER *n* in African history, indigenous representative appointed by his leader to deal with European slave traders
CABOCEERS > CABOCEER
CABOCHED *adj* in heraldry, with the face exposed, but neck concealed
CABOCHON *n* smooth domed gem, polished but unfaceted
CABOCHONS > CABOCHON
CABOCS > CABOC
CABOMBA *n* type of aquatic plant
CABOMBAS > CABOMBA
CABOODLE *n* lot, bunch, or group
CABOODLES > CABOODLE
CABOOSE *n* guard's van on a train
CABOOSES > CABOOSE
CABOSHED *same as* > CABOCHED
CABOTAGE *n* coastal navigation or shipping, esp within the borders of one country
CABOTAGES > CABOTAGE
CABOVER *adj* of or denoting a truck or lorry in which the cab is over the engine
CABRE *adj* heraldic term designating an animal

rearing
CABRESTA *variant of* > CABESTRO
CABRESTAS > CABRESTA
CABRESTO *variant of* > CABESTRO
CABRESTOS > CABRESTO
CABRETTA *n* soft leather obtained from the skins of certain South American or African sheep
CABRETTAS > CABRETTA
CABRIE *n* pronghorn antelope
CABRIES > CABRIE
CABRILLA *n* any of various serranid food fishes, esp *Epinephelus analogus*, occurring in warm seas around Florida and the Caribbean
CABRILLAS > CABRILLA
CABRIO *short for* > CABRIOLET
CABRIOLE *n* type of furniture leg, popular in the first half of the 18th century, in which an upper convex curve descends tapering to a concave curve
CABRIOLES > CABRIOLE
CABRIOLET *n* small horse-drawn carriage with a folding hood
CABRIOS > CABRIO
CABRIT *n* pronghorn antelope
CABRITS > CABRIT
CABS > CAB
CABSTAND *n* taxi-rank
CABSTANDS > CABSTAND
CACA *n* heroin
CACAFOGO *same as* > CACAFUEGO
CACAFOGOS > CACAFUEGO
CACAFUEGO *n* spitfire
CACAO *same as* > COCOA
CACAOS > COCOA
CACAS > CACA
CACHAEMIA *n* poisoned condition of the blood
CACHAEMIC > CACHAEMIA
CACHALOT *n* sperm whale
CACHALOTS > CACHALOT
CACHE *n* hidden store of weapons or treasure ▷ *vb* store in a cache
CACHECTIC > CACHEXIA
CACHED > CACHE
CACHEPOT *n* ornamental container for a flowerpot
CACHEPOTS > CACHEPOT
CACHES > CACHE
CACHET *n* prestige, distinction ▷ *vb* apply a commemorative design to an envelope, as a first-day cover
CACHETED > CACHET
CACHETING > CACHET
CACHETS > CACHET
CACHEXIA *n* generally weakened condition of body or mind resulting from any debilitating chronic disease
CACHEXIAS > CACHEXIA
CACHEXIC > CACHEXIA
CACHEXIES > CACHEXIA
CACHEXY *same as* > CACHEXIA
CACHING > CACHE
CACHOLONG *n* a type of opal
CACHOLOT *same as* > CACHALOT
CACHOLOTS > CACHALOT
CACHOU *same as* > CATECHU
CACHOUS > CATECHU
CACHUCHA *n* graceful Spanish solo dance in triple time
CACHUCHAS > CACHUCHA
CACIQUE *n* American Indian chief in a Spanish-speaking region
CACIQUES > CACIQUE
CACIQUISM *n* (esp in Spanish America) government by local political bosses
CACKIER > CACKY
CACKIEST > CACKY
CACKLE *vb* laugh shrilly ▷ *n* cackling noise
CACKLED > CACKLE
CACKLER > CACKLE
CACKLERS > CACKLE
CACKLES > CACKLE
CACKLING > CACKLE
CACKY *adj* of or like excrement
CACODEMON *n* evil spirit or devil
CACODOXY *n* heterodoxy
CACODYL *n* oily poisonous liquid with a strong garlic smell
CACODYLIC > CACODYL
CACODYLS > CACODYL
CACOEPIES > CACOEPY
CACOEPY *n* bad or mistaken pronunciation
CACOETHES *n* uncontrollable urge or desire, esp for something harmful
CACOETHIC > CACOETHES
CACOGENIC *adj* reducing the quality of a race
CACOLET *n* seat fitted to the back of a mule
CACOLETS > CACOLET
CACOLOGY *n* bad choice of words
CACOMIXL *n* carnivorous mammal
CACOMIXLE *same as* > CACOMIXL
CACOMIXLS > CACOMIXL
CACONYM *n* erroneous name
CACONYMS > CACONYM
CACONYMY > CACONYM
CACOON *n* large seed of the sword-bean
CACOONS > CACOON
CACOPHONY *n* harsh discordant sound
CACOTOPIA *n* dystopia, the opposite of utopia
CACTI > CACTUS
CACTIFORM *adj* cactus-like
CACTOID *adj* resembling a cactus
CACTUS *n* fleshy desert plant with spines but no leaves
CACTUSES > CACTUS
CACUMEN *n* apex
CACUMINA > CACUMEN
CACUMINAL *adj* relating to or denoting a consonant articulated with the tip of the tongue turned back towards the hard palate ▷ *n* consonant articulated in this manner
CAD *n* dishonourable man
CADAGA *n* eucalyptus tree, *E. torelliana*, of tropical and subtropical Australia, having a smooth green trunk
CADAGAS > CADAGA
CADAGI *same as* > CADAGA
CADAGIS > CADAGI
CADASTER *n* official register showing details of ownership, boundaries, and value of real property in a district, made for taxation purposes
CADASTERS > CADASTER
CADASTRAL > CADASTER
CADASTRE *same as* > CADASTER
CADASTRES > CADASTER
CADAVER *n* corpse
CADAVERIC > CADAVER
CADAVERS > CADAVER
CADDICE *same as* > CADDIS
CADDICES > CADDIS
CADDIE *n* person who carries a golfer's clubs ▷ *vb* act as a caddie
CADDIED > CADDIE
CADDIES > CADDIE
CADDIS *n* type of coarse woollen yarn, braid, or fabric
CADDISED *adj* trimmed with a type of ribbon
CADDISES > CADDIS
CADDISFLY *n* small fly
CADDISH > CAD
CADDISHLY > CAD
CADDY *same as* > CADDIE
CADDYING > CADDIE
CADDYSS *same as* > CADDIS
CADDYSSES > CADDIS
CADE *n* juniper tree ▷ *adj* (of a young animal) left by its mother and reared by humans, usually as a pet
CADEAU *n* present
CADEAUX > CADEAU
CADEE *old form of* > CADET
CADEES > CADEE
CADELLE *n* widely distributed beetle, *Tenebroides mauritanicus*, that feeds on flour, grain, and other stored foods: family *Trogositidae*
CADELLES > CADELLE
CADENCE *n* rise and fall in the pitch of the voice ▷ *vb* modulate musically
CADENCED > CADENCE
CADENCES > CADENCE
CADENCIES > CADENCY
CADENCING > CADENCE
CADENCY *same as* > CADENCE
CADENT *adj* having cadence
CADENTIAL > CADENT
CADENZA *n* complex solo passage in a piece of music
CADENZAS > CADENZA
CADES > CADE
CADET *n* young person training for the armed forces or police
CADETS > CADET
CADETSHIP > CADET
CADGE *vb* get (something) by taking advantage of someone's generosity
CADGED > CADGE
CADGER *n* person who cadges
CADGERS > CADGER
CADGES > CADGE
CADGIER > CADGY
CADGIEST > CADGY
CADGING > CADGE
CADGY *adj* cheerful
CADI *n* judge in a Muslim community
CADIE *n* messenger
CADIES > CADIE
CADIS > CADI
CADMIC > CADMIUM
CADMIUM *n* bluish-white metallic element used in alloys
CADMIUMS > CADMIUM
CADRANS *n* instrument used in gemcutting
CADRANSES > CADRANS
CADRE *n* small group of people selected and trained to form the core of a political organization or military unit
CADRES > CADRE
CADS > CAD
CADUAC *n* windfall
CADUACS > CADUAC
CADUCEAN > CADUCEUS
CADUCEI > CADUCEUS
CADUCEUS *n* staff entwined with two serpents and bearing a pair of wings at the top, carried by Hermes (Mercury) as messenger of the gods
CADUCITY *n* perishableness
CADUCOUS *adj* (of parts of a plant or animal) shed during the life of the organism
CAECA > CAECUM
CAECAL > CAECUM
CAECALLY > CAECUM

CAECILIAN *n* any tropical limbless cylindrical amphibian of the order *Apoda* (or *Gymnophiona*), resembling earthworms and inhabiting moist soil
CAECITIS *n* inflammation of the caecum
CAECUM *n* pouch at the beginning of the large intestine
CAEOMA *n* aecium in some rust fungi that has no surrounding membrane
CAEOMAS > CAEOMA
CAERULE *same as* > CERULE
CAERULEAN *same as* > CERULEAN
CAESAR *n* any emperor, autocrat, dictator, or other powerful ruler
CAESAREAN *n* surgical incision through the abdominal and uterine walls in order to deliver a baby
CAESARIAN *variant spelling of* > CAESAREAN
CAESARISM *another word for* > IMPERIALISM
CAESARS > CAESAR
CAESE *interj* Shakespearean interjection
CAESIOUS *adj* having a waxy bluish-grey coating
CAESIUM *n* silvery-white metallic element used in photocells
CAESIUMS > CAESIUM
CAESTUS *same as* > CESTUS
CAESTUSES > CAESTUS
CAESURA *n* pause in a line of verse
CAESURAE > CAESURA
CAESURAL > CAESURA
CAESURAS > CAESURA
CAESURIC > CAESURA
CAFARD *n* feeling of severe depression
CAFARDS > CAFARD
CAFE *n* small or inexpensive restaurant serving light refreshments
CAFES > CAFE
CAFETERIA *n* self-service restaurant
CAFETIERE *n* kind of coffeepot in which boiling water is poured onto ground coffee and a plunger fitted with a metal filter is pressed down, forcing the grounds to the bottom
CAFETORIA *variant of* > CAFETERIA
CAFF *n* café
CAFFEIN *same as* > CAFFEINE
CAFFEINE *n* stimulant found in tea and coffee
CAFFEINES > CAFFEINE
CAFFEINIC *adj* of or containing caffeine
CAFFEINS > CAFFEINE
CAFFEISM *n* addiction to caffeine
CAFFEISMS > CAFFEISM
CAFFILA *n* caravan train
CAFFILAS > CAFFILA
CAFFS > CAFF
CAFILA *same as* > CAFFILA
CAFILAS > CAFILA
CAFTAN *same as* > KAFTAN
CAFTANED *adj* wearing caftan
CAFTANS > CAFTAN
CAG *same as* > CAGOULE
CAGANER *n* figure of a squatting defecating person, a traditional character in Catalan Christmas crèche scenes
CAGANERS > CAGANER
CAGE *n* enclosure of bars or wires, for keeping animals or birds ▷ *vb* confine in a cage
CAGEBIRD *n* bird habitually kept caged
CAGEBIRDS > CAGEBIRD
CAGED > CAGE
CAGEFUL *n* amount which fills a cage to capacity
CAGEFULS > CAGEFUL
CAGELIKE > CAGE
CAGELING *n* bird kept in a cage
CAGELINGS > CAGELING
CAGER *n* basketball player
CAGERS > CAGER
CAGES > CAGE
CAGEWORK *n* something constructed as if from the bars of a cage
CAGEWORKS > CAGEWORK
CAGEY *adj* reluctant to go into details
CAGEYNESS > CAGEY
CAGIER > CAGEY
CAGIEST > CAGEY
CAGILY > CAGEY
CAGINESS > CAGY
CAGING > CAGE
CAGMAG *adj* done shoddily ▷ *vb* chat idly
CAGMAGGED > CAGMAG
CAGMAGS > CAGMAG
CAGOT *n* member of a class of French outcasts
CAGOTS > CAGOT
CAGOUL *same as* > CAGOULE
CAGOULE *n* lightweight hooded waterproof jacket
CAGOULES > CAGOULE
CAGOULS > CAGOUL
CAGS > CAG
CAGY *same as* > CAGEY
CAGYNESS > CAGY
CAHIER *n* notebook
CAHIERS > CAHIER
CAHOOT *n* partnership
CAHOOTS > CAHOOT
CAHOW *n* Bermuda petrel
CAHOWS > CAHOW
CAID *n* Moroccan district administrator
CAIDS > CAID
CAILLACH *same as* > CAILLEACH
CAILLACHS > CAILLACH
CAILLE *n* quail
CAILLEACH *n* old woman
CAILLES > CAILLE
CAILLIACH *same as* > CAILLEACH
CAIMAC *same as* > CAIMACAM
CAIMACAM *n* Turkish governor of a sanjak
CAIMACAMS > CAIMACAM
CAIMACS > CAIMAC
CAIMAN *same as* > CAYMAN
CAIMANS > CAIMAN
CAIN *n* (in Scotland and Ireland) payment in kind, usually farm produce paid as rent
CAINS > CAIN
CAIQUE *n* long narrow light rowing skiff used on the Bosporus
CAIQUES > CAIQUE
CAIRD *n* travelling tinker
CAIRDS > CAIRD
CAIRN *n* mound of stones erected as a memorial or marker
CAIRNED *adj* marked by a cairn
CAIRNGORM *n* yellow or brownish quartz gemstone
CAIRNS > CAIRN
CAIRNY *adj* covered with cairns
CAISSON *same as* > COFFERDAM
CAISSONS > CAISSON
CAITIFF *n* cowardly or base person ▷ *adj* cowardly
CAITIFFS > CAITIFF
CAITIVE *n* captive
CAITIVES > CAITIVE
CAJAPUT *same as* > CAJUPUT
CAJAPUTS > CAJAPUT
CAJEPUT *same as* > CAJUPUT
CAJEPUTS > CAJEPUT
CAJOLE *vb* persuade by flattery
CAJOLED > CAJOLE
CAJOLER > CAJOLE
CAJOLERS > CAJOLE
CAJOLERY > CAJOLE
CAJOLES > CAJOLE
CAJOLING > CAJOLE
CAJON *n* Peruvian wooden box used as a drum
CAJONES > CAJON
CAJUN *n* music of the Cajun people, combining blues and European folk music
CAJUPUT *n* small myrtaceous tree or shrub, *Melaleuca leucadendron*, native to the East Indies and Australia, with whitish flowers and leaves
CAJUPUTS > CAJUPUT
CAKE *n* sweet food baked from a mixture of flour, eggs, etc ▷ *vb* form into a hardened mass or crust
CAKED > CAKE
CAKES > CAKE
CAKEWALK *n* dance based on a march with intricate steps, originally performed by African-Americans with the prize of a cake for the best performers ▷ *vb* perform the cakewalk
CAKEWALKS > CAKEWALK
CAKEY > CAKE
CAKIER > CAKE
CAKIEST > CAKE
CAKINESS > CAKE
CAKING > CAKE
CAKINGS > CAKE
CAKY > CAKE
CALABASH *n* type of large round gourd
CALABAZA *n* variety of squash
CALABAZAS > CALABAZA
CALABOGUS *n* mixed drink containing rum, spruce beer, and molasses
CALABOOSE *n* prison
CALABRESE *n* kind of green sprouting broccoli
CALADIUM *n* any of various tropical plants of the aroid genus *Caladium*, which are widely cultivated as potted plants for their colourful variegated foliage
CALADIUMS > CALADIUM
CALALOO *same as* > CALALU
CALALOOS > CALALOO
CALALU *n* edible leaves of various plants, used as greens or in making thick soups
CALALUS > CALALU
CALAMANCO *n* glossy woollen fabric woven with a checked design that shows on one side only
CALAMAR *n* any member of the squid family
CALAMARI *n* squid cooked for eating, esp cut into rings and fried in batter
CALAMARIS > CALAMARI
CALAMARS > CALAMAR
CALAMARY *variant of* > CALAMARI
CALAMATA *same as* > KALAMATA
CALAMATAS > CALAMATA
CALAMI > CALAMUS
CALAMINE *n* pink powder consisting chiefly of zinc oxide, used in skin lotions and ointments ▷ *vb* apply calamine
CALAMINED > CALAMINE
CALAMINES > CALAMINE
CALAMINT *n* any aromatic Eurasian plant of the genus *Satureja* (or *Calamintha*), having clusters of purple or pink

flowers: family *Lamiaceae* (labiates)
CALAMINTS > CALAMINT
CALAMITE *n* any extinct treelike plant of the genus *Calamites*, of Carboniferous times, related to the horsetails
CALAMITES > CALAMITE
CALAMITY *n* disaster
CALAMUS *n* any tropical Asian palm of the genus *Calamus*, some species of which are a source of rattan and canes
CALANDO *adv* (to be performed) with gradually decreasing tone and speed
CALANDRIA *n* cylindrical vessel through which vertical tubes pass, esp one forming part of an evaporator, heat exchanger, or nuclear reactor
CALANTHE *n* type of orchid
CALANTHES > CALANTHE
CALASH *n* horse-drawn carriage with low wheels and a folding top
CALASHES > CALASH
CALATHEA *n* S American perennial plant, many species of which are grown as greenhouse or house plants for their decorative variegated leaves
CALATHEAS > CALATHEA
CALATHI > CALATHUS
CALATHOS *same as* > CALATHUS
CALATHUS *n* vase-shaped basket represented in ancient Greek art, used as a symbol of fruitfulness
CALAVANCE *n* type of pulse
CALCANEA > CALCANEUS
CALCANEAL > CALCANEUS
CALCANEAN > CALCANEUS
CALCANEI > CALCANEUS
CALCANEUM *same as* > CALCANEUS
CALCANEUS *n* largest tarsal bone, forming the heel in man
CALCAR *n* spur or spurlike process, as on the leg of a bird or the corolla of a flower
CALCARATE > CALCAR
CALCARIA > CALCAR
CALCARINE > CALCAR
CALCARS > CALCAR
CALCEATE *vb* to shoe
CALCEATED > CALCEATE
CALCEATES > CALCEATE
CALCED *adj* wearing shoes
CALCEDONY *n* a microcrystalline often greyish form of quartz with crystals arranged in parallel fibres: a gemstone.
CALCES > CALX
CALCIC *adj* of, containing, or concerned with lime or calcium
CALCICOLE *n* any plant that thrives in lime-rich soils
CALCIFIC *adj* forming or causing to form lime or chalk
CALCIFIED > CALCIFY
CALCIFIES > CALCIFY
CALCIFUGE *n* any plant that thrives in acid soils but not in lime-rich soils
CALCIFY *vb* harden by the depositing of calcium salts
CALCIMINE *n* white or pale tinted wash for walls ▷ *vb* cover with calcimine
CALCINE *vb* oxidize (a substance) by heating
CALCINED > CALCINE
CALCINES > CALCINE
CALCINING > CALCINE
CALCITE *n* colourless or white form of calcium carbonate
CALCITES > CALCITE
CALCITIC > CALCITE
CALCIUM *n* silvery-white metallic element found in bones, teeth, limestone, and chalk
CALCIUMS > CALCIUM
CALCRETE *another name for* > CALICHE
CALCRETES > CALCRETE
CALCSPAR *another name for* > CALCITE
CALCSPARS > CALCSPAR
CALCTUFA *another name for* > TUFA
CALCTUFAS > CALCTUFA
CALCTUFF *another name for* > TUFA
CALCTUFFS > CALCTUFF
CALCULAR *adj* relating to calculus
CALCULARY *adj* relating to stone
CALCULATE *vb* solve or find out by a mathematical procedure or by reasoning
CALCULI > CALCULUS
CALCULOSE *adj* relating to calculi
CALCULOUS *adj* of or suffering from a stonelike accretion of minerals and salts found in ducts or hollow organs of the body
CALCULUS *n* branch of mathematics dealing with infinitesimal changes to a variable number or quantity
CALDARIA > CALDARIUM
CALDARIUM *n* (in ancient Rome) a room for taking hot baths
CALDERA *n* large basin-shaped crater at the top of a volcano, formed by the collapse or explosion of the cone
CALDERAS > CALDERA
CALDRON *same as* > CAULDRON
CALDRONS > CALDRON
CALECHE *a variant of* > CALASH
CALECHES > CALECHE
CALEFIED > CALEFY
CALEFIES > CALEFY
CALEFY *vb* to make warm
CALEFYING > CALEFY
CALEMBOUR *n* pun
CALENDAL > CALENDS
CALENDAR *n* chart showing a year divided up into months, weeks, and days ▷ *vb* enter in a calendar
CALENDARS > CALENDAR
CALENDER *n* machine in which paper or cloth is smoothed by passing it between rollers ▷ *vb* smooth in such a machine
CALENDERS > CALENDER
CALENDRER > CALENDER
CALENDRIC > CALENDAR
CALENDRY *n* place where calendering is carried out
CALENDS *pl n* first day of each month in the ancient Roman calendar
CALENDULA *n* marigold
CALENTURE *n* mild fever of tropical climates, similar in its symptoms to sunstroke
CALESA *n* horse-drawn buggy
CALESAS > CALESA
CALESCENT *adj* increasing in heat
CALF *n* young cow, bull, elephant, whale, or seal
CALFDOZER *n* small bulldozer
CALFLESS > CALF
CALFLICK *another word for* > COWLICK
CALFLICKS > CALFLICK
CALFLIKE > CALF
CALFS > CALF
CALFSKIN *n* fine leather made from the skin of a calf
CALFSKINS > CALFSKIN
CALIATOUR *n* red sandalwood
CALIBER *same as* > CALIBRE
CALIBERED > CALIBER
CALIBERS > CALIBER
CALIBRATE *vb* mark the scale or check the accuracy of (a measuring instrument)
CALIBRE *n* person's ability or worth
CALIBRED > CALIBRE
CALIBRES > CALIBRE
CALICES > CALIX
CALICHE *n* bed of sand or clay in arid regions cemented by calcium carbonate, sodium chloride, and other soluble minerals
CALICHES > CALICHE
CALICLE *same as* > CALYCLE
CALICLES > CALICLE
CALICO *n* white cotton fabric
CALICOES > CALICO
CALICOS > CALICO
CALICULAR > CALYCLE
CALID *adj* warm
CALIDITY > CALID
CALIF *same as* > CALIPH
CALIFATE *same as* > CALIPHATE
CALIFATES > CALIFATE
CALIFONT *n* gas water heater
CALIFONTS > CALIFONT
CALIFS > CALIF
CALIGO *n* speck on the cornea causing poor vision
CALIGOES > CALIGO
CALIGOS > CALIGO
CALIMA *n* Saharan dust-storm
CALIMAS > CALIMA
CALIOLOGY *n* the study of birds' nests
CALIPASH *n* greenish glutinous edible part of the turtle found next to the upper shell, considered a delicacy
CALIPEE *n* yellow glutinous edible part of the turtle found next to the lower shell, considered a delicacy
CALIPEES > CALIPEE
CALIPER *same as* > CALLIPER
CALIPERED > CALLIPER
CALIPERS > CALIPER
CALIPH *n* Muslim ruler
CALIPHAL > CALIPH
CALIPHATE *n* office, jurisdiction, or reign of a caliph
CALIPHS > CALIPH
CALISAYA *n* bark of any of several tropical trees of the rubiaceous genus *Cinchona*, esp *C. calisaya*, from which quinine is extracted
CALISAYAS > CALISAYA
CALIVER *n* type of musket
CALIVERS > CALIVER
CALIX *n* cup
CALK *same as* > CAULK
CALKED > CALK
CALKER > CALK
CALKERS > CALK
CALKIN > CALK
CALKING > CALK
CALKINGS > CALK
CALKINS > CALK
CALKS > CALK
CALL *vb* name ▷ *n* cry, shout
CALLA *n* any southern African plant of the aroid genus *Zantedeschia*, esp *Z. aethiopica*, which has a white funnel-shaped

spathe enclosing a yellow spadix
CALLABLE *adj* (of a security) subject to redemption before maturity
CALLAIDES > CALLAIS
CALLAIS *n* green stone found as beads and ornaments in the late Neolithic and early Bronze Age of W Europe
CALLALOO *n* leafy green vegetable
CALLALOOS > CALLALOO
CALLAN *same as* > CALLANT
CALLANS > CALLAN
CALLANT *n* youth
CALLANTS > CALLANT
CALLAS > CALLA
CALLBACK *n* telephone call made in response to an earlier call
CALLBACKS > CALLBACK
CALLBOARD *n* notice board listing opportunities for performers
CALLBOY *n* person who notifies actors when it is time to go on stage
CALLBOYS > CALLBOY
CALLED > CALL
CALLEE *n* computer function being used
CALLEES > CALLEE
CALLER *n* person or thing that calls, esp a person who makes a brief visit ▷ *adj* (of food, esp fish) fresh
CALLERS > CALLER
CALLET *n* scold
CALLETS > CALLET
CALLID *adj* cunning
CALLIDITY > CALLID
CALLIGRAM *n* poem in which words are positioned so as to create a visual image of the subject on the page
CALLING *n* vocation, profession
CALLINGS > CALLING
CALLIOPE *n* steam organ
CALLIOPES > CALLIOPE
CALLIPASH *same as* > CALIPASH
CALLIPEE *same as* > CALIPEE
CALLIPEES > CALLIPEE
CALLIPER *n* metal splint for supporting the leg ▷ *vb* measure the dimensions of (an object) with callipers
CALLIPERS > CALLIPER
CALLOP *n* edible freshwater fish, *Plectroplites ambiguus*, of Australia, often golden or pale yellow in colour
CALLOPS > CALLOP
CALLOSE *n* carbohydrate, a polymer of glucose, found in plants, esp in the sieve tubes
CALLOSES > CALLOSE
CALLOSITY *same as* > CALLUS
CALLOUS *adj* showing no concern for other people's feelings ▷ *vb* make or become callous
CALLOUSED > CALLOUS
CALLOUSES > CALLOUS
CALLOUSLY > CALLOUS
CALLOW *adj* young and inexperienced ▷ *n* someone young and inexperienced
CALLOWER > CALLOW
CALLOWEST > CALLOW
CALLOWS > CALLOW
CALLS > CALL
CALLUNA *n* type of heather
CALLUNAS > CALLUNA
CALLUS *n* area of thick hardened skin ▷ *vb* produce or cause to produce a callus
CALLUSED > CALLUS
CALLUSES > CALLUS
CALLUSING > CALLUS
CALM *adj* not agitated or excited ▷ *n* peaceful state ▷ *vb* make or become calm
CALMANT *n* sedative
CALMANTS > CALMANT
CALMATIVE *adj* (of a remedy or agent) sedative ▷ *n* sedative remedy or drug
CALMED > CALM
CALMER > CALM
CALMEST > CALM
CALMIER > CALMY
CALMIEST > CALMY
CALMING > CALM
CALMINGLY > CALM
CALMINGS > CALM
CALMLY > CALM
CALMNESS > CALM
CALMS > CALM
CALMSTONE *same as* > CAMSTONE
CALMY *adj* tranquil
CALO *n* military servant
CALOMEL *n* colourless tasteless powder
CALOMELS > CALOMEL
CALORIC *adj* of heat or calories ▷ *n* hypothetical elastic fluid formerly postulated as the embodiment of heat
CALORICS > CALORIC
CALORIE *n* unit of measurement for the energy value of food
CALORIES > CALORIE
CALORIFIC *adj* of calories or heat
CALORISE *same as* > CALORIZE
CALORISED > CALORISE
CALORISES > CALORISE
CALORIST *n* believer in caloric theory
CALORISTS > CALORIST
CALORIZE *vb* coat (a ferrous metal) by spraying with aluminium powder and then heating
CALORIZED > CALORIZE
CALORIZES > CALORIZE
CALORY *same as* > CALORIE
CALOS > CALO
CALOTTE *n* skullcap worn by Roman Catholic clergy
CALOTTES > CALOTTE
CALOTYPE *n* early photographic process invented by W. H. Fox Talbot, in which the image was produced on paper treated with silver iodide and developed by sodium thiosulphite
CALOTYPES > CALOTYPE
CALOYER *n* monk of the Greek Orthodox Church, esp of the Basilian Order
CALOYERS > CALOYER
CALP *n* type of limestone
CALPA *n* Hindu unit of time
CALPAC *n* large black brimless hat made of sheepskin or felt, worn by men in parts of the Near East
CALPACK *same as* > CALPAC
CALPACKS > CALPACK
CALPACS > CALPAC
CALPAIN *n* type of enzyme
CALPAINS > CALPAIN
CALPAS > CALPA
CALPS > CALP
CALQUE *same as* > CAULK
CALQUED > CALQUE
CALQUES > CALQUE
CALQUING > CALQUE
CALTHA *n* marsh marigold
CALTHAS > CALTHA
CALTHROP *same as* > CALTHROP
CALTHROPS > CALTROP
CALTRAP *same as* > CALTROP
CALTRAPS > CALTRAP
CALTROP *n* floating Asian plant
CALTROPS > CALTROP
CALUMBA *n* Mozambiquan root used for medicinal purposes
CALUMBAS > CALUMBA
CALUMET *n* peace pipe
CALUMETS > CALUMET
CALUMNIES > CALUMNY
CALUMNY *n* false or malicious statement
CALUTRON *n* device used for the separation of isotopes
CALUTRONS > CALUTRON
CALVADOS *n* type of apple brandy
CALVARIA *n* top part of the skull of vertebrates
CALVARIAL > CALVARIUM
CALVARIAN > CALVARIUM
CALVARIAS > CALVARIA
CALVARIES > CALVARY
CALVARIUM *same as* > CALVARIA
CALVARY *n* representation of Christ's crucifixion, usually sculptured and in the open air
CALVE *vb* give birth to a calf
CALVED > CALVE
CALVER *vb* prepare fish for cooking
CALVERED > CALVER
CALVERING > CALVER
CALVERS > CALVER
CALVES > CALF
CALVING > CALVE
CALVITIES *n* baldness
CALX *n* powdery metallic oxide formed when an ore or mineral is roasted
CALXES > CALX
CALYCATE > CALYX
CALYCEAL *adj* resembling a calyx
CALYCES > CALYX
CALYCINAL *same as* > CALYCINE
CALYCINE *adj* relating to, belonging to, or resembling a calyx
CALYCLE *n* cup-shaped structure, as in the coral skeleton
CALYCLED > CALYCLE
CALYCLES > CALYCLE
CALYCOID *adj* resembling a calyx
CALYCULAR > CALYCLE
CALYCULE *n* bracts surrounding the base of the calyx
CALYCULES > CALYCULE
CALYCULI > CALYCULUS
CALYCULUS *same as* > CALYCLE
CALYPSO *n* West Indian song with improvised topical lyrics
CALYPSOES > CALYPSO
CALYPSOS > CALYPSO
CALYPTER *n* alula
CALYPTERA *same as* > CALYPTRA
CALYPTERS > CALYPTER
CALYPTRA *n* membranous hood covering the spore-bearing capsule of mosses and liverworts
CALYPTRAS > CALYPTRA
CALYX *n* outer leaves that protect a flower bud
CALYXES > CALYX
CALZONE *n* folded pizza filled with cheese, tomatoes, etc
CALZONES > CALZONE
CALZONI > CALZONE
CAM *n* device that converts a circular motion to a to-and-fro motion ▷ *vb* furnish (a machine) with a cam
CAMA *n* hybrid offspring of a camel and a llama
CAMAIEU *n* cameo
CAMAIEUX > CAMAIEU
CAMAIL *n* neck and shoulders covering of mail worn with and laced to the

basinet
CAMAILED > CAMAIL
CAMAILS > CAMAIL
CAMAN *n* wooden stick used to hit the ball in shinty
CAMANACHD *n* shinty
CAMANS > CAMAN
CAMARILLA *n* group of confidential advisers, esp formerly, to the Spanish kings
CAMARON *n* shrimp
CAMARONS > CAMARON
CAMAS *same as* > CAMASS
CAMASES > CAMAS
CAMASH *same as* > CAMASS
CAMASHES > CAMASH
CAMASS *n* type of North American plant
CAMASSES > CAMASS
CAMBER *n* slight upward curve to the centre of a surface ▷ *vb* form or be formed with a surface that curves upwards to its centre
CAMBERED > CAMBER
CAMBERING > CAMBER
CAMBERS > CAMBER
CAMBIA > CAMBIUM
CAMBIAL > CAMBIUM
CAMBIFORM > CAMBIUM
CAMBISM > CAMBIST
CAMBISMS > CAMBIST
CAMBIST *n* dealer or expert in foreign exchange
CAMBISTRY > CAMBIST
CAMBISTS > CAMBIST
CAMBIUM *n* meristem that increases the girth of stems and roots by producing additional xylem and phloem
CAMBIUMS > CAMBIUM
CAMBOGE *n* type of gum resin
CAMBOGES > CAMBOGE
CAMBOGIA *another name for* > GAMBOGE
CAMBOGIAS > CAMBOGIA
CAMBOOSE *n* cabin built as living quarters for a gang of lumbermen
CAMBOOSES > CAMBOOSE
CAMBREL *a variant of* > GAMBREL
CAMBRELS > CAMBREL
CAMBRIC *n* fine white linen fabric
CAMBRICS > CAMBRIC
CAMCORDER *n* combined portable video camera and recorder
CAME > COME
CAMEL *n* humped mammal that can survive long periods without food or water in desert regions
CAMELBACK *n* type of locomotive
CAMELEER *n* camel-driver
CAMELEERS > CAMELEER
CAMELEON *same as* > CHAMELEON
CAMELEONS > CAMELEON
CAMELHAIR *n* hair of camel
CAMELIA *same as* > CAMELLIA
CAMELIAS > CAMELIA
CAMELID *adj* of or relating to camels ▷ *n* any animal of the camel family
CAMELIDS > CAMELID
CAMELINE *n* material made from camel hair
CAMELINES > CAMELINE
CAMELISH > CAMEL
CAMELLIA *n* evergreen ornamental shrub with white, pink, or red flowers
CAMELLIAS > CAMELLIA
CAMELLIKE > CAMEL
CAMELOID *n* member of the camel family
CAMELOIDS > CAMELOID
CAMELOT *n* supposedly idyllic period or age
CAMELOTS > CAMELOT
CAMELRIES > CAMELRY
CAMELRY *n* troops mounted on camels
CAMELS > CAMEL
CAMEO *n* brooch or ring with a profile head carved in relief ▷ *vb* to appear in a brief role
CAMEOED > CAMEO
CAMEOING > CAMEO
CAMEOS > CAMEO
CAMERA *n* apparatus used for taking photographs or pictures for television or cinema
CAMERAE > CAMERA
CAMERAL *adj* of or relating to a judicial or legislative chamber
CAMERAMAN *n* man who operates a camera for television or cinema
CAMERAMEN > CAMERAMAN
CAMERAS > CAMERA
CAMERATED *adj* vaulted
CAMES obsolete form of > CANVAS
CAMESE *same as* > CAMISE
CAMESES > CAMESE
CAMION *n* lorry, or, esp formerly, a large dray
CAMIONS > CAMION
CAMIS *n* light robe
CAMISA *n* smock
CAMISADE *same as* > CAMISADO
CAMISADES > CAMISADE
CAMISADO *n* (formerly) an attack made under cover of darkness
CAMISADOS > CAMISADO
CAMISAS > CAMISA
CAMISE *n* loose light shirt, smock, or tunic originally worn in the Middle Ages
CAMISES > CAMISE
CAMISIA *n* surplice
CAMISIAS > CAMISIA
CAMISOLE *n* woman's bodice-like garment
CAMISOLES > CAMISOLE
CAMLET *n* tough waterproof cloth
CAMLETS > CAMLET
CAMMED > CAM
CAMMIE *n* webcam award
CAMMIES > CAMMIE
CAMMING > CAM
CAMO short for camouflage
CAMOGIE *n* form of hurling played by women
CAMOGIES > CAMOGIE
CAMOMILE *n* aromatic plant, used to make herbal tea
CAMOMILES > CAMOMILE
CAMOODI *a Caribbean name for* > ANACONDA
CAMOODIS > CAMOODI
CAMORRA *n* secret criminal group
CAMORRAS > CAMORRA
CAMORRIST > CAMORRA
CAMOS > CAMO
CAMOTE *n* type of sweet potato
CAMOTES > CAMOTE
CAMOUFLET *n* type of bomb used in a seige to collapse an enemy's tunnel
CAMP *vb* stay in a camp ▷ *adj* effeminate or homosexual ▷ *adj* (place for) temporary lodgings consisting of tents, huts, or cabins
CAMPAGNA *same as* > CHAMPAIGN
CAMPAGNAS > CAMPAGNA
CAMPAGNE > CAMPAGNA
CAMPAIGN *n* series of coordinated activities designed to achieve a goal ▷ *vb* take part in a campaign
CAMPAIGNS > CAMPAIGN
CAMPANA *n* bell or bell shape
CAMPANAS > CAMPANA
CAMPANERO *n* South American bellbird
CAMPANILE *n* bell tower, usu. one not attached to another building
CAMPANILI > CAMPANILE
CAMPANIST *n* expert on bells
CAMPANULA *n* plant with blue or white bell-shaped flowers
CAMPCRAFT *n* skills required when camping
CAMPEADOR *n* champion; term applied especially to El Cid
CAMPED > CAMP
CAMPER *n* person who lives or temporarily stays in a tent, cabin, etc
CAMPERS > CAMPER
CAMPESINO *n* Latin American rural peasant
CAMPEST > CAMP
CAMPFIRE *n* outdoor fire in a camp, esp one used for cooking or as a focal point for community events
CAMPFIRES > CAMPFIRE
CAMPHANE *n* one of the terpene hydrocarbons
CAMPHANES > CAMPHANE
CAMPHENE *n* colourless crystalline insoluble terpene
CAMPHENES > CAMPHENE
CAMPHINE *n* type of solvent
CAMPHINES > CAMPHINE
CAMPHIRE *an archaic name for* > HENNA
CAMPHIRES > CAMPHIRE
CAMPHOL *another word for* > BORNEOL
CAMPHOLS > CAMPHOL
CAMPHOR *n* aromatic crystalline substance used medicinally and in mothballs
CAMPHORIC > CAMPHOR
CAMPHORS > CAMPHOR
CAMPI > CAMPO
CAMPIER > CAMPY
CAMPIEST > CAMPY
CAMPILY > CAMPY
CAMPINESS > CAMPY
CAMPING > CAMP
CAMPINGS > CAMP
CAMPION *n* red, pink, or white wild flower
CAMPIONS > CAMPION
CAMPLE *vb* to argue
CAMPLED > CAMPLE
CAMPLES > CAMPLE
CAMPLING > CAMPLE
CAMPLY > CAMP
CAMPNESS > CAMP
CAMPO *n* level or undulating savanna country, esp in the uplands of Brazil
CAMPODEID *n* member of the Campodea genus of bristle-tails
CAMPONG *n* in Malaysia, a village
CAMPONGS > CAMPONG
CAMPOREE *n* local meeting or assembly of Scouts
CAMPOREES > CAMPOREE
CAMPOS > CAMPO
CAMPOUT *n* camping trip
CAMPOUTS > CAMPOUT
CAMPS > CAMP
CAMPSHIRT *n* short-sleeved shirt
CAMPSITE *n* area on which holiday makers may pitch a tent
CAMPSITES > CAMPSITE
CAMPSTOOL *n* folding stool
CAMPUS *n* grounds of a university or college ▷ *vb* to restrict a student to campus, as a punishment
CAMPUSED > CAMPUS
CAMPUSES > CAMPUS
CAMPUSING > CAMPUS
CAMPY *adj* effeminate
CAMS > CAM
CAMSHAFT *n* part of an

engine consisting of a rod to which cams are fixed
CAMSHAFTS > CAMSHAFT
CAMSHO *adj* crooked
CAMSHOCH *same as* > CAMSHO
CAMSTAIRY *adj* perverse
CAMSTANE *same as* > CAMSTONE
CAMSTANES > CAMSTONE
CAMSTEARY *same as* > CAMSTAIRY
CAMSTONE *n* a limestome used for whitening stone doorsteps
CAMSTONES > CAMSTONE
CAMUS *n* type of loose robe
CAMUSES > CAMUS
CAMWOOD *n* W African leguminous tree, *Baphia nitida*, whose hard wood was formerly used in making a red dye
CAMWOODS > CAMWOOD
CAN *vb* be able to ▷ *n* metal container for food or liquids
CANADA *n* canada goose
CANADAS > CANADA
CANAIGRE *n* dock, *Rumex hymenosepalus*, of the southern US, the root of which yields a substance used in tanning
CANAIGRES > CANAIGRE
CANAILLE *n* masses or rabble
CANAILLES > CANAILLE
CANAKIN *same as* > CANNIKIN
CANAKINS > CANAKIN
CANAL *n* artificial waterway ▷ *vb* dig a canal through
CANALBOAT *n* boat made for canals
CANALED > CANAL
CANALING > CANAL
CANALISE *same as* > CANALIZE
CANALISED > CANALIZE
CANALISES > CANALIZE
CANALIZE *vb* give direction to
CANALIZED > CANALIZE
CANALIZES > CANALIZE
CANALLED > CANAL
CANALLER *n* canal boat worker
CANALLERS > CANALLER
CANALLING > CANAL
CANALS > CANAL
CANAPE *n* small piece of bread or toast with a savoury topping
CANAPE > CANAPE
CANARD *n* false report
CANARDS > CANARD
CANARIED > CANARY
CANARIES > CANARY
CANARY *n* small yellow songbird often kept as a pet ▷ *vb* perform a dance called the canary
CANARYING > CANARY
CANASTA *n* card game like rummy, played with two packs
CANASTAS > CANASTA
CANASTER *n* coarsely broken dried tobacco leaves
CANASTERS > CANASTER
CANBANK *n* container for receiving cans for recycling
CANBANKS > CANBANK
CANCAN *n* lively high-kicking dance performed by a female group
CANCANS > CANCAN
CANCEL *vb* stop (something that has been arranged) from taking place ▷ *n* new leaf or section of a book replacing a defective one, one containing errors, or one that has been omitted
CANCELED > CANCEL
CANCELEER *vb* (of a hawk) to turn in flight when a stoop fails, in order to re-attempt it
CANCELER > CANCEL
CANCELERS > CANCEL
CANCELIER *a variant of* > CANCELEER
CANCELING > CANCEL
CANCELLED > CANCEL
CANCELLER > CANCEL
CANCELLI *n* any lattice-like structures
CANCELS > CANCEL
CANCER *n* serious disease resulting from a malignant growth or tumour
CANCERATE *vb* to become cancerous
CANCERED *adj* affected by cancer
CANCEROUS > CANCER
CANCERS > CANCER
CANCHA *n* toasted maize
CANCHAS > CANCHA
CANCRINE *adj* crab-like
CANCROID *adj* resembling a cancerous growth ▷ *n* skin cancer, esp one of only moderate malignancy
CANCROIDS > CANCROID
CANDELA *n* unit of luminous intensity
CANDELAS > CANDELA
CANDENT *adj* emitting light as a result of being heated to a high temperature
CANDID *adj* honest and straightforward ▷ *n* unposed photograph
CANDIDA *n* yeastlike parasitic fungus which causes thrush
CANDIDACY > CANDIDATE
CANDIDAL > CANDIDA
CANDIDAS > CANDIDA
CANDIDATE *n* person seeking a job or position
CANDIDER > CANDID
CANDIDEST > CANDID
CANDIDLY > CANDID
CANDIDS > CANDID
CANDIE *n* South Indian unit of weight
CANDIED *adj* coated with sugar
CANDIES > CANDY
CANDLE *n* stick of wax enclosing a wick, which is burned to produce light ▷ *vb* test by holding up to a candle
CANDLED > CANDLE
CANDLELIT *adj* lit by the light of candles
CANDLENUT *n* euphorbiaceous tree, *Aleurites mollucana*, of tropical Asia and Polynesia
CANDLEPIN *n* bowling pin, as used in skittles, tenpin bowling, candlepins, etc
CANDLER > CANDLE
CANDLERS > CANDLE
CANDLES > CANDLE
CANDLING > CANDLE
CANDOCK *n* type of water lily, or horsetail
CANDOCKS > CANDOCK
CANDOR *same as* > CANDOUR
CANDORS > CANDOR
CANDOUR *n* honesty and straightforwardness
CANDOURS > CANDOUR
CANDY *n* sweet or sweets ▷ *vb* make sweet
CANDYGRAM *n* message accompanied by sweets
CANDYING > CANDY
CANDYTUFT *n* garden plant with clusters of white, pink, or purple flowers
CANE *n* stem of the bamboo or similar plant ▷ *vb* beat with a cane
CANEBRAKE *n* thicket of canes
CANED > CANE
CANEFRUIT *n* fruit, like the raspberry, which grows on woody-stemmed plants
CANEH *n* Hebrew unit of length
CANEHS > CANEH
CANELLA *n* fragrant cinnamon-like inner bark of a West Indian tree, *Canella winterana* (family *Canellaceae*) used as a spice and in medicine
CANELLAS > CANELLA
CANELLINI *n* white kidney bean
CANEPHOR *n* sculpted figure carrying a basket on its head
CANEPHORA *same as* > CANEPHOR
CANEPHORE *same as* > CANEPHOR
CANEPHORS > CANEPHOR
CANER > CANE
CANERS > CANE
CANES > CANE
CANESCENT *adj* white or greyish due to the presence of numerous short white hairs
CANEWARE *n* type of unglazed stoneware
CANEWARES > CANEWARE
CANFIELD *n* gambling game adapted from a type of patience
CANFIELDS > CANFIELD
CANFUL *n* amount a can will hold
CANFULS > CANFUL
CANG *same as* > CANGUE
CANGLE *vb* to wrangle
CANGLED > CANGLE
CANGLES > CANGLE
CANGLING > CANGLE
CANGS > CANG
CANGUE *n* (formerly in China) a large wooden collar worn by petty criminals as a punishment
CANGUES > CANGUE
CANICULAR *adj* of or relating to the star Sirius or its rising
CANID *n* animal of the dog family
CANIDS > CANID
CANIER > CANY
CANIEST > CANY
CANIKIN *same as* > CANNIKIN
CANIKINS > CANIKIN
CANINE *adj* of or like a dog ▷ *n* sharp pointed tooth between the incisors and the molars
CANINES > CANINE
CANING *n* beating with a cane as a punishment
CANINGS > CANING
CANINITY > CANINE
CANISTEL *n* Caribbean fruit
CANISTELS > CANISTEL
CANISTER *n* metal container ▷ *vb* to put into canisters
CANISTERS > CANISTER
CANITIES *n* grey hair
CANKER *n* ulceration, ulcerous disease ▷ *vb* infect or become infected with or as if with canker
CANKERED > CANKER
CANKERING > CANKER
CANKEROUS *adj* having cankers
CANKERS > CANKER
CANKERY *adj* like a canker
CANN *vb* direct a ship's steering
CANNA *n* any of various tropical plants constituting the genus *Canna*, having broad leaves and red or yellow showy flowers for which they are cultivated: family *Cannaceae*

CANNABIC > CANNABIS
CANNABIN *n* greenish-black poisonous resin obtained from the Indian hemp plant
CANNABINS > CANNABIN
CANNABIS *n* Asian plant with tough fibres
CANNACH *n* cotton grass
CANNACHS > CANNACH
CANNAE *vb* can not
CANNAS > CANNA
CANNED > CAN
CANNEL *n* type of dull coal
CANNELON *n* type of meat loaf
CANNELONI *pl n* pasta in the shape of tubes, which are usually stuffed
CANNELONS > CANNELON
CANNELS > CANNEL
CANNELURE *n* groove or fluting, esp one around the cylindrical part of a bullet
CANNER *n* person or organization whose job is to can foods
CANNERIES > CANNERY
CANNERS > CANNER
CANNERY *n* factory where food is canned
CANNIBAL *n* person who eats human flesh
CANNIBALS > CANNIBAL
CANNIE *same as* > CANNY
CANNIER > CANNY
CANNIEST > CANNY
CANNIKIN *n* small can, esp one used as a drinking vessel
CANNIKINS > CANNIKIN
CANNILY > CANNY
CANNINESS > CANNY
CANNING > CAN
CANNINGS > CAN
CANNISTER *same as* > CANISTER
CANNOLI *n* Sicilian pudding of pasta shells filled with sweetened ricotta
CANNOLIS > CANNOLI
CANNON *n* gun of large calibre ▷ *vb* to collide (with)
CANNONADE *n* continuous heavy gunfire ▷ *vb* attack (a target) with cannon
CANNONED > CANNON
CANNONEER *n* (formerly) a soldier who served and fired a cannon
CANNONIER *same as* > CANNONEER
CANNONING > CANNON
CANNONRY *n* volley of artillery fire
CANNONS > CANNON
CANNOT *vb* can not
CANNS > CANN
CANNULA *n* narrow tube for insertion into a bodily cavity, as for draining off fluid, introducing medication, etc
CANNULAE > CANNULA
CANNULAR *adj* shaped like a cannula
CANNULAS > CANNULA
CANNULATE *vb* insert a cannula into ▷ *adj* shaped like a cannula
CANNY *adj* shrewd, cautious ▷ *adv* quite
CANOE *n* light narrow open boat propelled by a paddle or paddles ▷ *vb* use a canoe
CANOEABLE > CANOE
CANOED > CANOE
CANOEING > CANOE
CANOEINGS > CANOE
CANOEIST > CANOE
CANOEISTS > CANOE
CANOER > CANOE
CANOERS > CANOE
CANOES > CANOE
CANOEWOOD *n* type of tree
CANOLA *n* cooking oil extracted from a variety of rapeseed developed in Canada
CANOLAS > CANOLA
CANON *n* priest serving in a cathedral
CANONESS *n* woman belonging to any one of several religious orders and living under a rule but not under a vow
CANONIC *same as* > CANONICAL
CANONICAL *adj* conforming with canon law
CANONISE *same as* > CANONIZE
CANONISED > CANONISE
CANONISER > CANONISE
CANONISES > CANONISE
CANONIST *n* specialist in canon law
CANONISTS > CANONIST
CANONIZE *vb* declare (a person) officially to be a saint
CANONIZED > CANONIZE
CANONIZER > CANONIZE
CANONIZES > CANONIZE
CANONRIES > CANONRY
CANONRY *n* office, benefice, or status of a canon
CANONS > CANON
CANOODLE *vb* kiss and cuddle
CANOODLED > CANOODLE
CANOODLER > CANOODLE
CANOODLES > CANOODLE
CANOPIC *adj* of ancient Egyptian vase
CANOPIED > CANOPY
CANOPIES > CANOPY
CANOPY *n* covering above a bed, door, etc ▷ *vb* cover with or as if with a canopy
CANOPYING > CANOPY
CANOROUS *adj* tuneful
CANS > CAN
CANSFUL > CANFUL
CANSO *n* love song
CANSOS > CANSO
CANST *vb* form of CAN used with the pronoun *thou* or its relative form
CANSTICK *n* candlestick
CANSTICKS > CANSTICK
CANT *n* insincere talk ▷ *vb* use cant ▷ *adj* oblique
CANTABANK *n* itinerant singer
CANTABILE *adv* flowing and melodious ▷ *n* piece or passage performed in this way
CANTAL *n* French cheese
CANTALA *n* tropical American plant, *Agave cantala*, similar to the century plant: family *Agavaceae* (agaves)
CANTALAS > CANTALA
CANTALOUP *n* type of melon
CANTALS > CANTAL
CANTAR *variant form of* > KANTAR
CANTARS > CANTAR
CANTATA *n* musical work consisting of arias, duets, and choruses
CANTATAS > CANTATA
CANTATE *n* 98th psalm sung as a nonmetrical hymn
CANTATES > CANTATE
CANTDOG *same as* > CANTHOOK
CANTDOGS > CANTDOG
CANTED > CANT
CANTEEN *n* restaurant attached to a workplace or school
CANTEENS > CANTEEN
CANTER *vb* move at gait between trot and gallop
CANTERED > CANTER
CANTERING > CANTER
CANTERS > CANTER
CANTEST > CANT
CANTHAL > CANTHUS
CANTHARI > CANTHARUS
CANTHARID *n* any beetle of the family *Cantharidae*, having a soft elongated body
CANTHARIS *n* singular of plural noun, cantharides: a diuretic and urogenital stimulant or irritant prepared from the dried bodies of Spanish fly (family *Meloidae*, not *Cantharidae*), once thought to be an aphrodisiac
CANTHARUS *n* large two-handled pottery cup
CANTHI > CANTHUS
CANTHITIS *n* inflammation of canthus
CANTHOOK *n* wooden pole with a hook used for handling logs
CANTHOOKS > CANTHOOK
CANTHUS *n* inner or outer corner or angle of the eye, formed by the natural junction of the eyelids
CANTIC > CANT
CANTICLE *n* short hymn with words from the Bible
CANTICLES > CANTICLE
CANTICO *vb* to dance as part of an act of worship
CANTICOED > CANTICO
CANTICOS > CANTICO
CANTICOY *same as* > CANTICO
CANTICOYS > CANTICOY
CANTICUM *n* canticle
CANTICUMS > CANTICUM
CANTIER > CANTY
CANTIEST > CANTY
CANTILENA *n* smooth flowing style in the writing of vocal music
CANTILY > CANTY
CANTINA *n* bar or wine shop, esp in a Spanish-speaking country
CANTINAS > CANTINA
CANTINESS > CANTY
CANTING > CANT
CANTINGLY > CANT
CANTINGS > CANT
CANTION *n* song
CANTIONS > CANTION
CANTLE *n* back part of a saddle that slopes upwards ▷ *vb* to set up, or stand, on high
CANTLED > CANTLE
CANTLES > CANTLE
CANTLET *n* piece
CANTLETS > CANTLET
CANTLING > CANTLE
CANTO *same as* > CANTUS
CANTON *n* political division of a country, esp Switzerland ▷ *vb* divide into cantons
CANTONAL > CANTON
CANTONED > CANTON
CANTONING > CANTON
CANTONISE *vb* to divide into cantons
CANTONIZE *same as* > CANTONISE
CANTONS > CANTON
CANTOR *n* man employed to lead services in a synagogue
CANTORIAL *adj* of or relating to a precentor
CANTORIS *adj* (in antiphonal music) to be sung by the cantorial side of a choir
CANTORS > CANTOR
CANTOS > CANTO
CANTRAIP *n* witch's spell or charm
CANTRAIPS > CANTRAIP
CANTRAP *same as* > CANTRAIP
CANTRAPS > CANTRAP
CANTRED *n* district comprising a hundred villages

CANTREDS > CANTRED
CANTREF *same as* > CANTRED
CANTREFS > CANTREF
CANTRIP *n* magic spell ▷ *adj* (of an effect) produced by black magic
CANTRIPS > CANTRIP
CANTS > CANT
CANTUS *n* medieval form of church singing
CANTY *adj* lively
CANULA *same as* > CANNULA
CANULAE > CANULA
CANULAR *adj* shaped like a cannula
CANULAS > CANULA
CANULATE *same as* > CANNULATE
CANULATED > CANULATE
CANULATES > CANULATE
CANVAS *n* heavy coarse cloth used for sails and tents, and for oil painting ▷ *vb* to cover with, or be applied to, canvas
CANVASED > CANVAS
CANVASER > CANVAS
CANVASERS > CANVAS
CANVASES > CANVAS
CANVASING > CANVAS
CANVASS *vb* try to get votes or support (from) ▷ *n* canvassing
CANVASSED > CANVASS
CANVASSER > CANVASS
CANVASSES > CANVASS
CANY *adj* cane-like
CANYON *n* deep narrow valley
CANYONEER *n* canyon explorer
CANYONING *n* sport of going down a canyon river by any of various means
CANYONS > CANYON
CANZONA *n* type of 16th- or 17th-century contrapuntal music, usually for keyboard, lute, or instrumental ensemble
CANZONAS > CANZONA
CANZONE *n* Provençal or Italian lyric, often in praise of love or beauty
CANZONES > CANZONE
CANZONET *n* short, cheery, or lively Italian song
CANZONETS > CANZONET
CANZONI > CANZONE
CAP *n* soft close-fitting covering for the head ▷ *vb* cover or top with something
CAPA *n* type of Spanish cloak
CAPABLE *adj* having the ability (for)
CAPABLER > CAPABLE
CAPABLEST > CAPABLE
CAPABLY > CAPABLE
CAPACIOUS *adj* roomy
CAPACITOR *n* device for storing electrical charge
CAPACITY *n* ability to contain, absorb, or hold ▷ *adj* of the maximum amount or number possible
CAPARISON *n* decorated covering for a horse or other animal, esp (formerly) for a warhorse ▷ *vb* put a caparison on
CAPAS > CAPA
CAPE *n* short cloak ▷ *vb* to cut and remove the hide of an animal
CAPED > CAPE
CAPELAN *another word for* > CAPELIN
CAPELANS > CAPELAN
CAPELET *n* small cape
CAPELETS > CAPELET
CAPELIN *n* small marine food fish, *Mallotus villosus*, occurring in northern and Arctic seas: family *Osmeridae* (smelts)
CAPELINE *n* cap-shaped bandage to cover the head or an amputation stump
CAPELINES > CAPELINE
CAPELINS > CAPELIN
CAPELLET *n* wen-like swelling on a horse
CAPELLETS > CAPELLET
CAPELLINE *same as* > CAPELINE
CAPELLINI *n* type of pasta
CAPER *n* high-spirited prank ▷ *vb* skip about
CAPERED > CAPER
CAPERER > CAPER
CAPERERS > CAPER
CAPERING > CAPER
CAPERS *pl n* pickled flower buds of a Mediterranean shrub used in sauces
CAPES > CAPE
CAPESKIN *n* soft leather obtained from the skins of a type of lamb or sheep having hairlike wool ▷ *adj* made of this leather
CAPESKINS > CAPESKIN
CAPEWORK *n* use of the cape by the matador in bullfighting
CAPEWORKS > CAPEWORK
CAPFUL *n* quantity held by a (usually bottle) cap
CAPFULS > CAPFUL
CAPH *n* letter of the Hebrew alphabet
CAPHS > CAPH
CAPI > CAPO
CAPIAS *n* (formerly) a writ directing a sheriff or other officer to arrest a named person
CAPIASES > CAPIAS
CAPILLARY *n* very fine blood vessel ▷ *adj* (of a tube) having a fine bore
CAPING > CAPE
CAPITA > CAPUT
CAPITAL *n* chief city of a country ▷ *adj* involving or punishable by death
CAPITALLY *adv* in an excellent manner
CAPITALS > CAPITAL
CAPITAN *another name for* > HOGFISH
CAPITANI > CAPITANO
CAPITANO *n* chief; captain
CAPITANOS > CAPITANO
CAPITANS > CAPITAN
CAPITATE *adj* shaped like a head, as certain flowers or inflorescences
CAPITATED *adj* having fixed upper limit
CAPITAYN *n* captain
CAPITAYNS > CAPITAYN
CAPITELLA *n* plural form of singular: capitellum, an enlarged knoblike structure at the end of a bone that forms an articulation with another bone
CAPITOL *n* (in America) building housing the state legislature
CAPITOLS > CAPITOL
CAPITULA > CAPITULUM
CAPITULAR *adj* of or associated with a cathedral chapter ▷ *n* member of a cathedral chapter
CAPITULUM *n* racemose inflorescence in the form of a disc of sessile flowers, the youngest at the centre. It occurs in the daisy and related plants
CAPIZ *n* bivalve shell of a mollusc (*Placuna placenta*) found esp in the Philippines and having a smooth translucent shiny interior: used in jewellery, ornaments, lampshades, etc
CAPIZES > CAPIZ
CAPLE *n* horse
CAPLES > CAPLE
CAPLESS > CAP
CAPLET *n* medicinal tablet, usually oval in shape, coated in a soluble substance
CAPLETS > CAPLET
CAPLIN *same as* > CAPELIN
CAPLINS > CAPLIN
CAPMAKER > CAP
CAPMAKERS > CAP
CAPO *n* device fitted across the strings of a guitar or similar instrument so as to raise the pitch
CAPOCCHIA *n* fool
CAPOEIRA *n* combination of martial art and dance, which originated among African slaves in 19th-century Brazil
CAPOEIRAS > CAPOEIRA
CAPON *n* castrated cock fowl fattened for eating
CAPONATA *n* Sicilian antipasto relish
CAPONATAS > CAPONATA
CAPONIER *n* covered passageway built across a ditch as a military defence
CAPONIERE *same as* > CAPONIER
CAPONIERS > CAPONIER
CAPONISE *same as* > CAPONIZE
CAPONISED > CAPONISE
CAPONISES > CAPONISE
CAPONIZE *vb* make (a cock) into a capon
CAPONIZED > CAPONIZE
CAPONIZES > CAPONIZE
CAPONS > CAPON
CAPORAL *n* strong coarse dark tobacco
CAPORALS > CAPORAL
CAPOS > CAPO
CAPOT *n* winning of all the tricks by one player ▷ *vb* score a capot (against)
CAPOTASTO *same as* > CAPO
CAPOTE *n* long cloak or soldier's coat, usually with a hood
CAPOTES > CAPOTE
CAPOTS > CAPOT
CAPOTTED > CAPOT
CAPOTTING > CAPOT
CAPOUCH *same as* > CAPUCHE
CAPOUCHES > CAPOUCHE
CAPPED > CAP
CAPPER > CAP
CAPPERS > CAP
CAPPING > CAP
CAPPINGS > CAP
CAPRATE *n* any salt of capric acid
CAPRATES > CAPRATE
CAPRIC *adj* (of a type of acid) smelling of goats
CAPRICCI > CAPRICCIO
CAPRICCIO *n* lively piece composed freely and without adhering to the rules for any specific musical form
CAPRICE *same as* > CAPRICCIO
CAPRICES > CAPRICE
CAPRID *n* any member of the goat family
CAPRIDS > CAPRID
CAPRIFIED > CAPRIFY
CAPRIFIES > CAPRIFY
CAPRIFIG *n* wild variety of fig, *Ficus carica sylvestris*, of S Europe and SW Asia, used in the caprification of the edible fig
CAPRIFIGS > CAPRIFIG
CAPRIFOIL *variant of* > CAPRIFOLE
CAPRIFOLE *n* honeysuckle
CAPRIFORM *adj* goatlike
CAPRIFY *vb* induce figs to ripen
CAPRINE *adj* of or resembling a goat
CAPRIOLE *n* upward but

not forward leap made by a horse ▷ *vb* perform a capriole
CAPRIOLED > CAPRIOLE
CAPRIOLES > CAPRIOLE
CAPRIS *pl n* women's tight-fitting trousers
CAPROATE *n* any salt of caproic acid
CAPROATES > CAPROATE
CAPROCK *n* layer of rock that overlies a salt dome
CAPROCKS > CAPROCK
CAPROIC as in *caproic acid* oily acid found in milk
CAPRYLATE *n* any salt of caprylic acid
CAPRYLIC *variant of* > CAPRIC
CAPS > CAP
CAPSAICIN *n* colourless crystalline bitter alkaloid
CAPSICIN *n* liquid or resin extracted from capsicum
CAPSICINS > CAPSICIN
CAPSICUM *n* kind of pepper used as a vegetable or as a spice
CAPSICUMS > CAPSICUM
CAPSID *n* outer protein coat of a mature virus
CAPSIDAL > CAPSID
CAPSIDS > CAPSID
CAPSIZAL > CAPSIZE
CAPSIZALS > CAPSIZE
CAPSIZE *vb* (of a boat) overturn accidentally
CAPSIZED > CAPSIZE
CAPSIZES > CAPSIZE
CAPSIZING > CAPSIZE
CAPSOMER *n* one of the units making up a viral capsid
CAPSOMERE *n* any of the protein units that together form the capsid of a virus
CAPSOMERS > CAPSOMER
CAPSTAN *n* rotating cylinder round which a ship's rope is wound
CAPSTANS > CAPSTAN
CAPSTONE *n* one of a set of slabs on the top of a wall, building, etc
CAPSTONES > CAPSTONE
CAPSULAR *adj* relating to a capsule
CAPSULARY *same as* > CAPSULAR
CAPSULATE *adj* within or formed into a capsule
CAPSULE *n* soluble gelatine case containing a dose of medicine ▷ *adj* very concise ▷ *vb* to contain within a capsule
CAPSULED > CAPSULE
CAPSULES > CAPSULE
CAPSULING > CAPSULE
CAPSULISE *same as* > CAPSULIZE
CAPSULIZE *vb* state (information) in a highly condensed form
CAPTAIN *n* commander of a ship or civil aircraft ▷ *vb* be captain of
CAPTAINCY > CAPTAIN
CAPTAINED > CAPTAIN
CAPTAINRY *n* condition or skill of being a captain
CAPTAINS > CAPTAIN
CAPTAN *n* type of fungicide
CAPTANS > CAPTAN
CAPTION *n* title or explanation accompanying an illustration ▷ *vb* provide with a caption
CAPTIONED > CAPTION
CAPTIONS > CAPTION
CAPTIOUS *adj* tending to make trivial criticisms
CAPTIVATE *vb* attract and hold the attention of
CAPTIVE *n* person kept in confinement ▷ *adj* kept in confinement ▷ *vb* to take prisoner
CAPTIVED > CAPTIVE
CAPTIVES > CAPTIVE
CAPTIVING > CAPTIVE
CAPTIVITY *n* state of being kept in confinement
CAPTOPRIL *n* drug used to treat high blood pressure and congestive heart failure
CAPTOR *n* person who captures a person or animal
CAPTORS > CAPTOR
CAPTURE *vb* take by force ▷ *n* capturing
CAPTURED > CAPTURE
CAPTURER > CAPTURE
CAPTURERS > CAPTURE
CAPTURES > CAPTURE
CAPTURING > CAPTURE
CAPUCCIO *n* hood
CAPUCCIOS > CAPUCCIO
CAPUCHE *n* large hood or cowl, esp that worn by Capuchin friars
CAPUCHED *adj* hooded
CAPUCHES > CAPUCHE
CAPUCHIN *n* S American monkey with thick hair on the top of its head
CAPUCHINS > CAPUCHIN
CAPUERA *variant of* > CAPOEIRA
CAPUERAS > CAPUERA
CAPUL *same as* > CAPLE
CAPULS > CAPUL
CAPUT *n* main or most prominent part of an organ or structure
CAPYBARA *n* very large S American rodent
CAPYBARAS > CAPYBARA
CAR *n* motor vehicle designed to carry a small number of people
CARABAO *n* water buffalo
CARABAOS > CARABAO
CARABID *n* any typically dark-coloured beetle of the family *Carabidae*, including the bombardier and other ground beetles. ▷ *adj* of, relating to, or belonging to the *Carabidae*
CARABIDS > CARABID
CARABIN *same as* > CARBINE
CARABINE *same as* > CARBINE
CARABINER *a variant spelling of* > KARABINER
CARABINES > CARABINE
CARABINS > CARABIN
CARACAL *n* lynx with reddish fur, which inhabits deserts of N Africa and S Asia
CARACALS > CARACAL
CARACARA *n* any of various large carrion-eating diurnal birds of prey of the genera *Caracara*, *Polyborus*, etc, of S North, Central, and South America, having long legs and naked faces: family *Falconidae* (falcons)
CARACARAS > CARACARA
CARACK *same as* > CARRACK
CARACKS > CARACK
CARACOL *same as* > CARACOLE
CARACOLE *n* half turn to the right or left ▷ *vb* execute a half turn to the right or left
CARACOLED > CARACOLE
CARACOLER > CARACOLE
CARACOLES > CARACOLE
CARACOLS > CARACOL
CARACT *n* sign or symbol
CARACTS > CARACT
CARACUL *n* black loosely curled fur obtained from the skins of newly born lambs of the karakul sheep
CARACULS > CARACUL
CARAFE *n* glass bottle for serving water or wine
CARAFES > CARAFE
CARAGANA *n* pea tree
CARAGANAS > CARAGANA
CARAGEEN *same as* > CARRAGEEN
CARAGEENS > CARAGEEN
CARAMBA *n* Spanish interjection similar to 'wow!'
CARAMBOLA *n* yellow edible star-shaped fruit that grows on a Brazilian tree
CARAMBOLE *vb* make a carom or carambola (shot in billiards)
CARAMEL *n* chewy sweet made from sugar and milk ▷ *vb* to turn into caramel
CARAMELS > CARAMEL
CARANGID *n* any marine percoid fish of the family *Carangidae*, having a compressed body and deeply forked tail. The group includes the jacks, horse mackerel, pompano, and pilot fish ▷ *adj* of, relating to, or belonging to the *Carangidae*
CARANGIDS > CARANGID
CARANGOID *same as* > CARANGID
CARANNA *n* gumlike substance
CARANNAS > CARANNA
CARAP *n* crabwood
CARAPACE *n* hard upper shell of tortoises and crustaceans
CARAPACED *adj* having carapace
CARAPACES > CARAPACE
CARAPAX *n* carapace
CARAPAXES > CARAPAX
CARAPS > CARAP
CARASSOW *same as* > CURASSOW
CARASSOWS > CARASSOW
CARAT *n* unit of weight of precious stones
CARATE *n* tropical disease
CARATES > CARATE
CARATS > CARAT
CARAUNA *same as* > CARANNA
CARAUNAS > CARAUNA
CARAVAN *n* large enclosed vehicle for living in, designed to be towed by a car or horse ▷ *vb* travel or have a holiday in a caravan
CARAVANCE *same as* > CALAVANCE
CARAVANED > CARAVAN
CARAVANER *n* person who holidays in a caravan
CARAVANS > CARAVAN
CARAVEL *n* two- or three-masted sailing ship, esp one with a broad beam, high poop deck, and lateen rig that was used by the Spanish and Portuguese in the 15th and 16th centuries
CARAVELLE *variant of* > CARAVEL
CARAVELS > CARAVEL
CARAWAY *n* plant whose seeds are used as a spice
CARAWAYS > CARAWAY
CARB *n* carbohydrate
CARBACHOL *n* carbamylcholine, a cholinergic agent
CARBAMATE *n* salt or ester of carbamic acid
CARBAMIC as in *carbamic acid* hypothetical compound known only in carbamate salts
CARBAMIDE *another name for* > UREA
CARBAMINO *adj* relating to the compound produced when carbon dioxide reacts with an amino group
CARBAMOYL *same as* > CARBAMYL
CARBAMYL *n* radical from carbamic acid

CARBAMYLS > CARBAMYL
CARBANION *n* negatively charged organic ion in which most of the negative charge is localized on a carbon atom
CARBARN *n* streetcar depot
CARBARNS > CARBARN
CARBARYL *n* organic compound of the carbamate group
CARBARYLS > CARBARYL
CARBAZOLE *n* colourless insoluble solid obtained from coal tar
CARBEEN *n* Australian eucalyptus tree, *E. tessellaris*, having drooping branches and grey bark
CARBEENS > CARBEEN
CARBENE *n* neutral divalent free radical, such as methylene: CH_2
CARBENES > CARBENE
CARBIDE *n* compound of carbon with a metal
CARBIDES > CARBIDE
CARBIES > CARBY
CARBINE *n* light automatic rifle
CARBINEER *n* (formerly) a soldier equipped with a carbine
CARBINES > CARBINE
CARBINIER *same as* > CARBINEER
CARBINOL *another word for* > CARABINOL
CARBINOLS > CARBINOL
CARBO *n* carbohydrate
CARBOLIC as in *carbolic acid* phenol, when it is used as a disinfectant
CARBOLICS > CARBOLIC
CARBOLISE *same as* > CARBOLIZE
CARBOLIZE *another word for* > PHENOLATE
CARBON *n* nonmetallic element occurring as charcoal, graphite, and diamond, found in all organic matter
CARBONADE *n* stew of beef and onions cooked in beer
CARBONADO *n* piece of meat, fish, etc, scored and grilled ▷ *vb* score and grill (meat, fish, etc)
CARBONARA *n* pasta sauce containing cream, bacon and cheese
CARBONATE *n* salt or ester of carbonic acid ▷ *vb* form or turn into a carbonate
CARBONIC *adj* containing carbon
CARBONISE *same as* > CARBONIZE
CARBONIUM as in *carbonium ion* type of positively charged organic ion
CARBONIZE *vb* turn into carbon as a result of heating
CARBONOUS > CARBON
CARBONS > CARBON
CARBONYL *n* of, consisting of, or containing the divalent group =CO
CARBONYLS > CARBONYL
CARBORA *n* former name for the koala
CARBORAS > CARBORA
CARBOS > CARBO
CARBOXYL as in *carboxyl group* functional group in organic acids
CARBOXYLS > CARBOXYL
CARBOY *n* large bottle with a protective casing
CARBOYED > CARBOY
CARBOYS > CARBOY
CARBS > CARB
CARBUNCLE *n* inflamed boil
CARBURATE *same as* > CARBURET
CARBURET *vb* combine or mix (a gas) with carbon or carbon compounds ▷ *vb* to combine with carbon
CARBURETS > CARBURET
CARBURISE *same as* > CARBONIZE
CARBURIZE *same as* > CARBONIZE
CARBY *n* short for carburettor
CARCAJOU *a North American name for* > WOLVERINE
CARCAJOUS > CARCAJOU
CARCAKE *n* (formerly, in Scotland) a cake traditionally made for Shrove Tuesday
CARCAKES > CARCAKE
CARCANET *n* jewelled collar or necklace
CARCANETS > CARCANET
CARCASE *same as* > CARCASS *vb* to make a carcase of
CARCASED > CARCASE
CARCASES > CARCASE
CARCASING > CARCASE
CARCASS *n* dead body of an animal ▷ *vb* to make a carcass of
CARCASSED > CARCASS
CARCASSES > CARCASS
CARCEL *n* French unit of light
CARCELS > CARCEL
CARCERAL *adj* relating to prison
CARCINOID *n* small serotonin-secreting tumour
CARCINOMA *n* malignant tumour
CARD *n* piece of thick stiff paper or cardboard used for identification, reference, or sending greetings or messages ▷ *vb* comb out fibres of wool or cotton before spinning
CARDAMINE *n* bittercress
CARDAMOM *n* spice obtained from the seeds of a tropical plant
CARDAMOMS > CARDAMOM
CARDAMON *same as* > CARDAMOM
CARDAMONS > CARDAMON
CARDAMUM *same as* > CARDAMOM
CARDAMUMS > CARDAMUM
CARDAN as in *cardan joint* type of universal joint
CARDBOARD *n* thin stiff board made from paper pulp ▷ *adj* without substance
CARDCASE *n* small case for holding business cards
CARDCASES > CARDCASE
CARDECU *n* old French coin (a quarter of a crown)
CARDECUE *same as* > CARDECU
CARDECUES > CARDECUE
CARDECUS > CARDECU
CARDED > CARD
CARDER > CARD
CARDERS > CARD
CARDI *n* cardigan
CARDIA *n* lower oesophageal sphincter
CARDIAC *adj* of the heart ▷ *n* person with a heart disorder
CARDIACAL > CARDIAC
CARDIACS > CARDIAC
CARDIAE > CARDIA
CARDIALGY *n* pain in or near the heart
CARDIAS > CARDIA
CARDIE *short for* > CARDIGAN
CARDIES > CARDIE
CARDIGAN *n* knitted jacket
CARDIGANS > CARDIGAN
CARDINAL *n* any of the high-ranking clergymen of the RC Church who elect the Pope and act as his counsellors ▷ *adj* fundamentally important
CARDINALS > CARDINAL
CARDING > CARD
CARDINGS > CARD
CARDIO *adj* exercising heart
CARDIOID *n* heart-shaped curve generated by a fixed point on a circle as it rolls around another fixed circle of equal radius, *a*. Equation: *r* = *a*(1 – cos _Gphi_), where *r* is the radius vector and _Gphi_ is the polar angle.
CARDIOIDS > CARDIOID
CARDIS > CARDI
CARDITIC > CARDITIS
CARDITIS *n* inflammation of the heart
CARDON *n* variety of cactus
CARDONS > CARDON
CARDOON *n* thistle-like S European plant, *Cynara cardunculus*, closely related to the artichoke, with spiny leaves, purple flowers, and a leafstalk that may be blanched and eaten: family *Asteraceae* (composites)
CARDOONS > CARDOON
CARDPHONE *n* public telephone operated by the insertion of a phonecard instead of coins
CARDPUNCH *n* device for putting data from a CPU onto punched cards
CARDS > CARD
CARDSHARP *n* professional card player who cheats
CARDUUS *n* thistle
CARDUUSES > CARDUUS
CARDY *same as* > CARDIE
CARE *vb* be concerned ▷ *n* careful attention, caution
CARED > CARE
CAREEN *vb* tilt over to one side
CAREENAGE > CAREEN
CAREENED > CAREEN
CAREENER > CAREEN
CAREENERS > CAREEN
CAREENING > CAREEN
CAREENS > CAREEN
CAREER *n* series of jobs in a profession or occupation that a person has through their life ▷ *vb* rush in an uncontrolled way ▷ *adj* having chosen to dedicate his or her life to a particular occupation
CAREERED > CAREER
CAREERER > CAREER
CAREERERS > CAREER
CAREERING > CAREER
CAREERISM > CAREERIST
CAREERIST *n* person who seeks advancement by any possible means
CAREERS > CAREER
CAREFREE *adj* without worry or responsibility
CAREFUL *adj* cautious in attitude or action
CAREFULLY > CAREFUL
CAREGIVER *same as* > CARER
CARELESS *adj* done or acting with insufficient attention
CARELINE *n* telephone service set up by a company or other organization to provide its customers or clients with information about its products or services
CARELINES > CARELINE
CAREME *n* period of Lent
CAREMES > CAREME
CARER *n* person who looks after someone who is ill or old, often a relative
CARERS > CARER
CARES > CARE
CARESS *n* gentle affectionate touch or

embrace ▷ *vb* touch gently and affectionately
CARESSED > CARESS
CARESSER > CARESS
CARESSERS > CARESS
CARESSES > CARESS
CARESSING > CARESS
CARESSIVE *adj* caressing
CARET *n* symbol indicating a place in written or printed matter where something is to be inserted
CARETAKE *vb* to work as a caretaker
CARETAKEN > CARETAKE
CARETAKER *n* person employed to look after a place ▷ *adj* performing the duties of an office temporarily
CARETAKES > CARETAKE
CARETOOK > CARETAKE
CARETS > CARET
CAREWORN *adj* showing signs of worry
CAREX *n* any member of the sedge family
CARFARE *n* fare that a passenger is charged for a ride on a bus, etc
CARFARES > CARFARE
CARFAX *n* place where principal roads or streets intersect, esp a place in a town where four roads meet
CARFAXES > CARFAX
CARFOX *same as* > CARFAX
CARFOXES > CARFOX
CARFUFFLE *a variant spelling of* > KERFUFFLE
CARFUL *n* maximum number of people a car will hold
CARFULS > CARFUL
CARGEESE > CARGOOSE
CARGO *n* goods carried by a ship, aircraft, etc ▷ *vb* to load
CARGOED > CARGO
CARGOES > CARGO
CARGOING > CARGO
CARGOOSE *n* crested grebe
CARGOS > CARGO
CARHOP *n* waiter or waitress at a drive-in restaurant ▷ *vb* work as a carhop
CARHOPPED > CARHOP
CARHOPS > CARHOP
CARIACOU *n* type of deer
CARIACOUS > CARIACOU
CARIAMA *another word for* > SERIEMA
CARIAMAS > CARIAMA
CARIBE *n* piranha
CARIBES > CARIBE
CARIBOU *n* large N American reindeer
CARIBOUS > CARIBOU
CARICES > CAREX
CARIED *adj* (of teeth) decayed
CARIERE *obsolete word for* > CAREER
CARIERES > CARIERE
CARIES *n* tooth decay
CARILLON *n* set of bells played by keyboard or mechanically ▷ *vb* play a carillon
CARILLONS > CARILLON
CARINA *n* keel-like part or ridge, as in the breastbone of birds or the fused lower petals of a leguminous flower
CARINAE > CARINA
CARINAL *adj* keel-like
CARINAS > CARINA
CARINATE *adj* having a keel or ridge
CARINATED *same as* > CARINATE
CARING *adj* feeling or showing care and compassion for other people ▷ *n* practice or profession of providing social or medical care
CARIOCA *n* Brazilian dance similar to the samba
CARIOCAS > CARIOCA
CARIOLE *n* small open two-wheeled horse-drawn vehicle
CARIOLES > CARIOLE
CARIOSE *same as* > CARIOUS
CARIOSITY > CARIOUS
CARIOUS *adj* (of teeth or bone) affected with caries
CARITAS *n* divine love; charity
CARITASES > CARITAS
CARITATES > CARITAS
CARJACK *vb* attack (a car driver) to rob them or to steal the car ▷ *vb* to steal a car, by force, from a person who is present
CARJACKED > CARJACK
CARJACKER > CARJACK
CARJACKS > CARJACK
CARJACOU *variation of* > CARIACOU
CARJACOUS > CARJACOU
CARK *vb* break down
CARKED > CARK
CARKING > CARK
CARKS > CARK
CARL *another word for* > CHURL
CARLE *same as* > CARL
CARLES > CARLE
CARLESS > CAR
CARLIN *same as* > CARLING
CARLINE *same as* > CARLING
CARLINES > CARLINE
CARLING *n* fore-and-aft beam in a vessel, used for supporting the deck, esp around a hatchway or other opening
CARLINGS > CARLING
CARLINS > CARLING
CARLISH *adj* churlish
CARLOAD *n* amount that can be carried by a car
CARLOADS > CARLOAD
CARLOCK *n* type of Russian isinglass
CARLOCKS > CARLOCK
CARLOT *n* boor
CARLOTS > CARLOT
CARLS > CARL
CARMAKER *n* car manufacturing company
CARMAKERS > CARMAKER
CARMAN *n* man who drives a car or cart
CARMELITE *n* member of an order of mendicant friars
CARMEN > CARMAN
CARMINE *adj* vivid red ▷ *n* vivid red colour, sometimes with a purplish tinge
CARMINES > CARMINE
CARN *n* cairn
CARNAGE *n* extensive slaughter of people
CARNAGES > CARNAGE
CARNAHUBA *same as* > CARNAUBA
CARNAL *adj* of a sexual or sensual nature ▷ *vb* act in a carnal manner
CARNALISE *vb* to sensualise
CARNALISM > CARNALISE
CARNALIST > CARNALISE
CARNALITY > CARNAL
CARNALIZE *same as* > CARNALISE
CARNALLED > CARNAL
CARNALLY > CARNAL
CARNALS > CARNAL
CARNAROLI *n* variety of short-grain rice used for risotto
CARNATION *n* cultivated plant with fragrant white, pink, or red flowers
CARNAUBA *n* Brazilian fan palm, *Copernicia cerifera*
CARNAUBAS > CARNAUBA
CARNELIAN *n* reddish-yellow gemstone
CARNEOUS *adj* fleshy
CARNET *n* customs licence permitting motorists to take their cars across certain frontiers
CARNETS > CARNET
CARNEY *same as* > CARNY
CARNEYED > CARNEY
CARNEYING > CARNEY
CARNEYS > CARNEY
CARNIE *same as* > CARNY
CARNIED > CARNY
CARNIER > CARNY
CARNIES > CARNY
CARNIEST > CARNY
CARNIFEX *n* executioner
CARNIFIED > CARNIFY
CARNIFIES > CARNIFY
CARNIFY *vb* (esp of lung tissue, as the result of pneumonia) to be altered so as to resemble skeletal muscle
CARNITINE *n* type of white betaine
CARNIVAL *n* festive period with processions, music, and dancing in the street
CARNIVALS > CARNIVAL
CARNIVORA *n* members of a group of carnivorous mammals
CARNIVORE *n* meat-eating animal
CARNIVORY *n* state of being carnivore
CARNOSAUR *n* meat-eating dinosaur
CARNOSE *adj* fleshy
CARNOSITY *n* fleshy protrusion
CARNOTITE *n* radioactive yellow mineral
CARNS > CARN
CARNY *vb* coax or cajole or act in a wheedling manner ▷ *n* person who works in a carnival ▷ *adj* sly
CARNYING > CARNY
CAROACH *same as* > CAROCHE
CAROACHES > CAROACH
CAROB *n* pod of a Mediterranean tree, used as a chocolate substitute
CAROBS > CAROB
CAROCH *same as* > CAROCHE
CAROCHE *n* stately ceremonial carriage used in the 16th and 17th centuries
CAROCHES > CAROCHE
CAROL *n* joyful Christmas hymn ▷ *vb* sing carols
CAROLED > CAROL
CAROLER > CAROL
CAROLERS > CAROL
CAROLI > CAROLUS
CAROLING > CAROL
CAROLINGS > CAROL
CAROLLED > CAROL
CAROLLER > CAROL
CAROLLERS > CAROL
CAROLLING > CAROL
CAROLS > CAROL
CAROLUS *n* any of several coins struck in the reign of a king called Charles, esp an English gold coin from the reign of Charles I
CAROLUSES > CAROLUS
CAROM *n* shot in which the cue ball is caused to contact one object ball after another ▷ *vb* to carambole
CAROMED > CAROM
CAROMEL *vb* to turn into caramel
CAROMELS > CAROMEL
CAROMING > CAROM
CAROMS > CAROM
CAROTENE *n* any of four orange-red hydrocarbons, found in many plants, converted to vitamin A in the liver

CAROTENES > CAROTENE
CAROTID *n* either of the two arteries supplying blood to the head ▷ *adj* of either of these arteries
CAROTIDAL > CAROTID
CAROTIDS > CAROTID
CAROTIN *same as* > CAROTENE
CAROTINS > CAROTIN
CAROUSAL *n* merry drinking party
CAROUSALS > CAROUSAL
CAROUSE *vb* have a merry drinking party
CAROUSED > CAROUSE
CAROUSEL *n* revolving conveyor belt for luggage or photographic slides
CAROUSELS > CAROUSEL
CAROUSER > CAROUSE
CAROUSERS > CAROUSE
CAROUSES > CAROUSE
CAROUSING > CAROUSE
CARP *n* large freshwater fish ▷ *vb* complain, find fault
CARPACCIO *n* Italian dish of thin slices of raw meat or fish
CARPAL *n* wrist bone
CARPALE *same as* > CARPAL
CARPALES > CARPAL
CARPALIA > CARPAL
CARPALS > CARPAL
CARPARK *n* area or building reserved for parking cars
CARPARKS > CARPARK
CARPED > CARP
CARPEL *n* female reproductive organ of a flowering plant
CARPELS > CARPEL
CARPENTER *n* person who makes or repairs wooden structures ▷ *vb* do the work of a carpenter
CARPENTRY *n* skill or work of a carpenter
CARPER > CARP
CARPERS > CARP
CARPET *n* heavy fabric for covering floors ▷ *vb* cover with a carpet
CARPETBAG *n* travelling bag made of carpeting
CARPETED > CARPET
CARPETING *n* carpet material or carpets in general
CARPETS > CARPET
CARPI > CARPUS
CARPING *adj* tending to make petty complaints ▷ *n* petty complaint
CARPINGLY > CARPING
CARPINGS > CARPING
CARPOLOGY *n* branch of botany concerned with the study of fruits and seeds
CARPOOL *vb* (of a group of people) to share the use of a single car to travel to work or school
CARPOOLED > CARPOOL
CARPOOLER > CARPOOL
CARPOOLS > CARPOOL
CARPORT *n* shelter for a car, consisting of a roof supported by posts
CARPORTS > CARPORT
CARPS > CARP
CARPUS *n* set of eight bones of the wrist
CARR *n* area of bog or fen in which scrub, esp willow, has become established
CARRACK *n* galleon sailed in the Mediterranean as a merchantman in the 15th and 16th centuries
CARRACKS > CARRACK
CARRACT *same as* > CARRACK
CARRACTS > CARRACT
CARRAGEEN *n* edible red seaweed of North America and N Europe
CARRAT *same as* > CARAT
CARRATS > CARRAT
CARRAWAY *same as* > CARAWAY
CARRAWAYS > CARRAWAY
CARRECT *same as* > CARRACK
CARRECTS > CARRECT
CARREFOUR *n* public square, esp one at the intersection of several roads
CARREL *n* small individual study room or private desk, often in a library, where a student or researcher can work undisturbed
CARRELL *same as* > CARREL
CARRELLS > CARRELL
CARRELS > CARREL
CARRIAGE *n* one of the sections of a train for passengers
CARRIAGES > CARRIAGE
CARRICK as in *carrick bend* type of knot
CARRIED > CARRY
CARRIER *n* person or thing that carries something
CARRIERS > CARRIER
CARRIES > CARRY
CARRIOLE *same as* > CARIOLE
CARRIOLES > CARRIOLE
CARRION *n* dead and rotting flesh
CARRIONS > CARRION
CARRITCH *n* catechism
CARROCH *variant of* > CAROCHE
CARROCHES > CAROM
CARROM *same as* > CAROM
CARROMED > CARROM
CARROMING > CARROM
CARROMS > CARROM
CARRON as in *carron oil* ointment of limewater and linseed oil
CARRONADE *n* obsolete naval gun of short barrel and large bore
CARROT *n* long tapering orange root vegetable
CARROTIER > CARROTY
CARROTIN *n* carotene
CARROTINS > CARROTIN
CARROTS > CARROT
CARROTTOP *n* facetious term for a person with red hair
CARROTY *adj* (of hair) reddish-orange
CARROUSEL *a variant spelling of* > CAROUSEL
CARRS > CARR
CARRY *vb* take from one place to another
CARRYALL *n* light four-wheeled horse-drawn carriage usually designed to carry four passengers
CARRYALLS > CARRYALL
CARRYBACK *n* amount carried back in accounting
CARRYCOT *n* light portable bed for a baby, with handles and a hood
CARRYCOTS > CARRYCOT
CARRYING > CARRY
CARRYON *n* fuss or commotion
CARRYONS > CARRYON
CARRYOUT *n* hot cooked food bought in a shop for consumption elsewhere
CARRYOUTS > CARRYOUT
CARRYOVER *n* sum or balance carried forward in accounting
CARRYTALE *n* gossip
CARS > CAR
CARSE *n* riverside area of flat fertile alluvium
CARSES > CARSE
CARSEY *slang word for* > TOILET
CARSEYS > CARSEY
CARSICK *adj* nauseated from riding in a car
CART *n* open two-wheeled horse-drawn vehicle for carrying goods or passengers ▷ *vb* carry, usu. with some effort
CARTA *n* charter
CARTABLE > CART
CARTAGE *n* process or cost of carting
CARTAGES > CARTAGE
CARTAS > CARTA
CARTE *n* fencing position
CARTED > CART
CARTEL *n* association of competing firms formed to fix prices
CARTELISE *same as* > CARTELIZE
CARTELISM > CARTEL
CARTELIST > CARTEL
CARTELIZE *vb* form or be formed into a cartel
CARTELS > CARTEL
CARTER > CART
CARTERS > CART
CARTES > CARTE
CARTFUL *n* amount a cart can hold
CARTFULS > CARTFUL
CARTHORSE *n* large heavily built horse
CARTILAGE *n* strong flexible tissue forming part of the skeleton
CARTING > CART
CARTLOAD *n* amount a cart can hold
CARTLOADS > CARTLOAD
CARTOGRAM *n* map showing statistical information in diagrammatic form
CARTOLOGY *n* theory of mapmaking
CARTON *n* container made of cardboard or waxed paper ▷ *vb* enclose (goods) in a carton
CARTONAGE *n* material from which mummy masks and coffins were made
CARTONED > CARTON
CARTONING > CARTON
CARTONS > CARTON
CARTOON *n* humorous or satirical drawing ▷ *vb* to depict in a cartoon
CARTOONED > CARTOON
CARTOONS > CARTOON
CARTOONY > CARTOON
CARTOP *adj* designed to be transported on top of a vehicle
CARTOPPER *n* anything designed to be transported on top of a vehicle
CARTOUCH *same as* > CARTOUCHE
CARTOUCHE *n* ornamental tablet or panel in the form of a scroll
CARTRIDGE *n* casing containing an explosive charge and bullet for a gun
CARTROAD *n* road for carts to drive on
CARTROADS > CARTROAD
CARTS > CART
CARTULARY *n* collection of charters or records, esp relating to the title to an estate or monastery
CARTWAY *n* way by which carts travel
CARTWAYS > CARTWAY
CARTWHEEL *n* sideways somersault supported by the hands with legs outstretched ▷ *vb* to perform a cartwheel movement
CARUCAGE *n* tax due on a carucate
CARUCAGES > CARUCAGE
CARUCATE *n* area of land an oxen team could plough in a year
CARUCATES > CARUCATE

CARUNCLE *n* fleshy outgrowth on the heads of certain birds, such as a cock's comb
CARUNCLES > CARUNCLE
CARVACROL *n* aromatic phenol found in oregano
CARVE *vb* cut to form an object
CARVED > CARVE
CARVEL *same as* > CARAVEL
CARVELS > CARVEL
CARVEN *an archaic or literary past participle of* > CARVE
CARVER *n* carving knife
CARVERIES > CARVERY
CARVERS > CARVER
CARVERY *n* restaurant where customers pay a set price for unrestricted helpings of carved meat and other food
CARVES > CARVE
CARVIES > CARVY
CARVING *n* figure or design produced by carving stone or wood
CARVINGS > CARVING
CARVY *n* caraway seed
CARWASH *n* drive-through structure containing automated equipment for washing cars
CARWASHES > CARWASH
CARYATIC *same as* > CARYATID
CARYATID *n* supporting column in the shape of a female figure
CARYATIDS > CARYATID
CARYOPSES > CARYOPSIS
CARYOPSIS *n* dry seedlike fruit having the pericarp fused to the seed coat of the single seed: produced by the grasses
CARYOTIN *variant of* > KARYOTIN
CARYOTINS > CARYOTIN
CASA *n* house
CASABA *n* kind of winter muskmelon having a yellow rind and sweet juicy flesh
CASABAS > CASABA
CASAS > CASA
CASAVA *same as* > CASSAVA
CASAVAS > CASAVA
CASBAH *n* citadel of a N African city
CASBAHS > CASBAH
CASCABEL *n* knoblike protrusion on the rear part of the breech of an obsolete muzzle-loading cannon
CASCABELS > CASCABEL
CASCABLE *same as* > CASCABEL
CASCABLES > CASCABLE
CASCADE *n* waterfall ▷ *vb* flow or fall in a cascade
CASCADED > CASCADE
CASCADES > CASCADE
CASCADING > CASCADE
CASCADURA *n* Trinidadian fish
CASCARA *n* bark of a N American shrub, used as a laxative
CASCARAS > CASCARA
CASCHROM *n* wooden hand-plough
CASCHROMS > CASCHROM
CASCO *n* Argentinian homestead
CASCOS > CASCO
CASE *n* instance, example ▷ *vb* inspect (a building) with the intention of burgling it
CASEASE *n* proteolytic enzyme formed by certain bacteria that activates the solution of albumin and casein in milk and cheese
CASEASES > CASEASE
CASEATE *vb* undergo caseation
CASEATED > CASEATE
CASEATES > CASEATE
CASEATING > CASEATE
CASEATION *n* formation of cheese from casein during the coagulation of milk
CASEBOOK *n* book in which records of legal or medical cases are kept
CASEBOOKS > CASEBOOK
CASEBOUND *another word for* > HARDBACK
CASED > CASE
CASEFIED > CASEFY
CASEFIES > CASEFY
CASEFY *vb* make or become similar to cheese
CASEFYING > CASEFY
CASEIC *adj* relating to cheese
CASEIN *n* a phosphoprotein, precipitated from milk by the action of rennin, forming the basis of cheese: used in the manufacture of plastics and adhesives
CASEINATE *n* protein found in milk
CASEINS > CASEIN
CASELOAD *n* number of cases that someone like a doctor or social worker deals with at any one time
CASELOADS > CASELOAD
CASEMAKER *n* in bookbinding, machine that makes stiff covers for hardbacks
CASEMAN *n* in printing, a person who sets and corrects type
CASEMATE *n* armoured compartment in a ship or fortification in which guns are mounted
CASEMATED > CASEMATE
CASEMATES > CASEMATE
CASEMEN > CASEMAN
CASEMENT *n* window that is hinged on one side
CASEMENTS > CASEMENT
CASEOSE *n* peptide produced by the peptic digestion of casein
CASEOSES > CASEOSE
CASEOUS *adj* of or like cheese
CASERN *n* (formerly) a billet or accommodation for soldiers in a town
CASERNE *same as* > CASERN
CASERNES > CASERNE
CASERNS > CASERN
CASES > CASE
CASETTE *variant of* > CASSETTE
CASETTES > CASETTE
CASEWORK *n* social work based on close study of the personal histories and circumstances of individuals and families
CASEWORKS > CASEWORK
CASEWORM *n* caddis worm
CASEWORMS > CASEWORM
CASH *n* banknotes and coins ▷ *adj* of, for, or paid in cash ▷ *vb* obtain cash for
CASHABLE > CASH
CASHAW *n* winter squash
CASHAWS > CASHAW
CASHBACK *n* discount offered in return for immediate payment
CASHBACKS > CASHBACK
CASHBOOK *n* journal in which cash receipts and payments are recorded
CASHBOOKS > CASHBOOK
CASHBOX *n* box for holding cash
CASHBOXES > CASHBOX
CASHED > CASH
CASHES > CASH
CASHEW *n* edible kidney-shaped nut
CASHEWS > CASHEW
CASHIER *n* person responsible for handling cash in a bank, shop, etc ▷ *vb* dismiss with dishonour from the armed forces
CASHIERED > CASHIER
CASHIERER > CASHIER
CASHIERS > CASHIER
CASHING > CASH
CASHLESS *adj* functioning, operated, or performed without using coins or banknotes for money transactions but instead using credit cards or electronic transfer of funds
CASHMERE *n* fine soft wool obtained from goats
CASHMERES > CASHMERE
CASHOO *n* catechu
CASHOOS > CASHOO
CASHPOINT *n* cash dispenser
CASIMERE *same as* > CASSIMERE
CASIMERES > CASIMERE
CASIMIRE *variant of* > CASSIMERE
CASIMIRES > CASIMIRE
CASING *n* protective case, covering
CASINGS > CASING
CASINI > CASINO
CASINO *n* public building or room where gambling games are played
CASINOS > CASINO
CASITA *n* small house
CASITAS > CASITA
CASK *n* barrel used to hold alcoholic drink ▷ *vb* to put into a cask
CASKED > CASK
CASKET *n* small box for valuables ▷ *vb* to put into a casket
CASKETED > CASKET
CASKETING > CASKET
CASKETS > CASKET
CASKING > CASK
CASKS > CASK
CASKSTAND *n* frame on which a cask rests
CASKY *adj* (of wine) having a musty smell due to resting too long in the cask
CASQUE *n* helmet or a helmet-like process or structure, as on the bill of most hornbills
CASQUED > CASQUE
CASQUES > CASQUE
CASSABA *same as* > CASABA
CASSABAS > CASSABA
CASSAREEP *n* juice of the bitter cassava root, boiled down to a syrup and used as a flavouring, esp in West Indian cookery
CASSATA *n* ice cream, originating in Italy, usually containing nuts and candied fruit
CASSATAS > CASSATA
CASSATION *n* (esp in France) annulment, as of a judicial decision by a higher court
CASSAVA *n* starch obtained from the roots of a tropical American plant, used to make tapioca
CASSAVAS > CASSAVA
CASSENA *same as* > CASSINA
CASSENAS > CASSENA
CASSENE *same as* > CASSINA
CASSENES > CASSENE
CASSEROLE *n* covered dish in which food is cooked slowly, usu. in an oven ▷ *vb* cook in a casserole
CASSETTE *n* plastic container for magnetic tape
CASSETTES > CASSETTE
CASSIA *n* tropical plant

whose pods yield a mild laxative
CASSIAS > CASSIA
CASSIMERE *n* woollen suiting cloth of plain or twill weave
CASSINA *n* American tree
CASSINAS > CASSINA
CASSINE *same as* > CASSINA
CASSINES > CASSINE
CASSINGLE *n* cassette single
CASSINO *n* card game for two to four players in which players pair cards from their hands with others exposed on the table
CASSINOS > CASSINO
CASSIS *n* blackcurrant cordial
CASSISES > CASSIS
CASSOCK *n* long tunic, usu. black, worn by priests
CASSOCKED > CASSOCK
CASSOCKS > CASSOCK
CASSONADE *n* raw sugar
CASSONE *n* highly-decorated Italian dowry chest
CASSONES > CASSONE
CASSOULET *n* stew originating from France, made from haricot beans and goose, duck, pork, etc
CASSOWARY *n* large flightless bird of Australia and New Guinea
CASSPIR *n* armoured military vehicle
CASSPIRS > CASSPIR
CAST *n* actors in a play or film collectively ▷ *vb* select (an actor) to play a part in a play or film
CASTABLE *adj* able to be cast
CASTANET > CASTANETS
CASTANETS *pl n* musical instrument, used by Spanish dancers, consisting of curved pieces of hollow wood clicked together in the hand
CASTAWAY *n* shipwrecked person ▷ *adj* shipwrecked or put adrift ▷ *vb* cause (a ship, person, etc) to be shipwrecked or abandoned
CASTAWAYS > CASTAWAY
CASTE *n* any of the hereditary classes into which Hindu society is divided
CASTED *adj* having a caste
CASTEISM *n* belief in, and adherence to, the caste system
CASTEISMS > CASTEISM
CASTELESS *adj* having no caste
CASTELLA > CASTELLUM
CASTELLAN *n* keeper or governor of a castle
CASTELLUM *n* fort
CASTER *n* person or thing that casts
CASTERS > CASTER
CASTES > CASTE
CASTIGATE *vb* reprimand severely
CASTING > CAST
CASTINGS > CAST
CASTLE *n* large fortified building, often built as a ruler's residence ▷ *vb* (in chess) move (the king) two squares laterally on the first rank and place the nearest rook on the square passed over by the king
CASTLED *adj* like a castle in construction
CASTLES > CASTLE
CASTLING > CASTLE
CASTOCK *n* kale stalk
CASTOCKS > CASTOCK
CASTOFF *n* person or thing that has been discarded or abandoned
CASTOFFS > CASTOFF
CASTOR *same as* > CASTER
CASTOREUM *n* oil secreted from the beaver, used as bait by trappers
CASTORIES > CASTORY
CASTORS > CASTOR
CASTORY *n* dye derived from beaver pelts
CASTRAL *adj* relating to camps
CASTRATE *vb* remove the testicles of
CASTRATED > CASTRATE
CASTRATER > CASTRATE
CASTRATES > CASTRATE
CASTRATI > CASTRATO
CASTRATO *n* (in 17th- and 18th-century opera) a male singer whose testicles were removed before puberty, allowing the retention of a soprano or alto voice
CASTRATOR > CASTRATE
CASTRATOS > CASTRATO
CASTS > CAST
CASUAL *adj* careless, nonchalant ▷ *n* occasional worker
CASUALISE *vb* to make (a regular employee) into a casual worker
CASUALISM > CASUALISE
CASUALIZE *same as* > CASUALISE
CASUALLY > CASUAL
CASUALS > CASUAL
CASUALTY *n* person killed or injured in an accident or war
CASUARINA *n* Australian tree with jointed green branches
CASUIST *n* person, esp a theologian, who attempts to resolve moral dilemmas by the application of general rules and the careful distinction of special cases
CASUISTIC > CASUIST
CASUISTRY *n* reasoning that is misleading or oversubtle
CASUISTS > CASUIST
CASUS *n* event
CAT *n* small domesticated furry mammal ▷ *vb* flog with a cat-'o-nine-tails
CATABASES > CATABASIS
CATABASIS *n* descent or downward movement
CATABATIC > CATABASIS
CATABOLIC *adj* of a metabolic process in which complex molecules are broken down into simple ones with the release of energy
CATACLASM *n* breaking down
CATACLYSM *n* violent upheaval
CATACOMB *n* underground burial place, esp the galleries at Rome, consisting of tunnels with vaults or niches leading off them for tombs
CATACOMBS > CATACOMB
CATAFALCO *n* temporary raised platform on which a body lies in state before or during a funeral
CATALASE *n* enzyme that catalyses the decomposition of hydrogen peroxide
CATALASES > CATALASE
CATALATIC *adj* relating to catalase
CATALEPSY *n* trancelike state in which the body is rigid
CATALEXES > CATALEXIS
CATALEXIS *n* the state of lacking a syllable in the last foot of a line of poetry
CATALO *same as* > CATTALO
CATALOES > CATALO
CATALOG *same as* > CATALOGUE
CATALOGED > CATALOGUE
CATALOGER > CATALOGUE
CATALOGIC > CATALOG
CATALOGS > CATALOG
CATALOGUE *n* book containing details of items for sale ▷ *vb* enter (an item) in a catalogue
CATALOS > CATALO
CATALPA *n* tree of N America and Asia with bell-shaped whitish flowers
CATALPAS > CATALPA
CATALYSE *vb* speed up (a chemical reaction) by a catalyst
CATALYSED > CATALYSE
CATALYSER > CATALYSE
CATALYSES > CATALYSIS
CATALYSIS *n* acceleration of a chemical reaction by the action of a catalyst
CATALYST *n* substance that speeds up a chemical reaction without itself changing
CATALYSTS > CATALYST
CATALYTIC *adj* of or relating to catalysis
CATALYZE *same as* > CATALYSE
CATALYZED > CATALYZE
CATALYZER > CATALYZE
CATALYZES > CATALYZE
CATAMARAN *n* boat with twin parallel hulls
CATAMENIA *another word for* > MENSES
CATAMITE *n* boy kept as a homosexual partner
CATAMITES > CATAMITE
CATAMOUNT *n* any of various medium-sized felines, such as the puma or lynx
CATAPAN *n* governor in the Byzantine Empire
CATAPANS > CATAPAN
CATAPHORA *n* use of a word such as a pronoun that has the same reference as a word used subsequently in the same discourse
CATAPHYLL *n* simplified form of plant leaf, such as a scale leaf or cotyledon
CATAPLASM *another name for* > POULTICE
CATAPLEXY *n* sudden temporary paralysis, brought on by severe shock
CATAPULT *n* Y-shaped device with a loop of elastic, used by children for firing stones ▷ *vb* shoot forwards or upwards violently
CATAPULTS > CATAPULT
CATARACT *n* eye disease in which the lens becomes opaque
CATARACTS > CATARACT
CATARHINE *n* having a thin or narrow nose
CATARRH *n* excessive mucus in the nose and throat, during or following a cold
CATARRHAL > CATARRH
CATARRHS > CATARRH
CATASTA *n* platform on which slaves were presented for sale
CATASTAS > CATASTA
CATATONIA *n* form of schizophrenia characterized by stupor, with outbreaks of excitement
CATATONIC > CATATONIA

CATATONY *another word for* > CATATONIA
CATAWBA *n* type of red North American grape
CATAWBAS > CATAWBA
CATBIRD *n* any of several North American songbirds of the family *Mimidae* (mockingbirds), esp *Dumetella carolinensis*, whose call resembles the mewing of a cat
CATBIRDS > CATBIRD
CATBOAT *n* sailing vessel with a single mast, set well forward and often unstayed, and a large sail, usually rigged with a gaff
CATBOATS > CATBOAT
CATBRIER *n* greenbrier
CATBRIERS > CATBRIER
CATCALL *n* derisive whistle or cry ▷ *vb* utter such a call (at)
CATCALLED > CATCALL
CATCALLER > CATCALL
CATCALLS > CATCALL
CATCH *vb* seize, capture ▷ *n* device for fastening a door, window, etc
CATCHABLE > CATCH
CATCHALL *n* something designed to cover a variety of situations
CATCHALLS > CATCHALL
CATCHCRY *n* well-known much-used phrase, perhaps associated with a particular group
CATCHED *rarely used past tense of* > CATCH
CATCHEN *same as* > CATCH
CATCHER *n* person or thing that catches, esp in a game or sport
CATCHERS > CATCHER
CATCHES > CATCH
CATCHFLY *n* any of several caryophyllaceous plants of the genus *Silene* that have sticky calyxes and stems on which insects are sometimes trapped
CATCHIER > CATCHY
CATCHIEST > CATCHY
CATCHING > CATCH
CATCHINGS > CATCH
CATCHMENT *n* structure in which water is collected
CATCHPOLE *n* (in medieval England) a sheriff's officer who arrested debtors
CATCHPOLL *same as* > CATCHPOLE
CATCHT *same as* > CATCHED
CATCHUP *a variant spelling (esp US) of* > KETCHUP
CATCHUPS > CATCHUP
CATCHWEED *n* goosegrass
CATCHWORD *n* well-known and frequently used phrase
CATCHY *adj* (of a tune) pleasant and easily remembered
CATCLAW *n* type of shrub; black bead
CATCLAWS > CATCLAW
CATE *n* delicacy
CATECHIN *n* soluble yellow solid substance found in mahogany wood
CATECHINS > CATECHIN
CATECHISE *same as* > CATECHIZE
CATECHISM *n* instruction on the doctrine of a Christian Church in a series of questions and answers
CATECHIST > CATECHIZE
CATECHIZE *vb* instruct by using a catechism
CATECHOL *n* colourless crystalline phenol found in resins and lignins
CATECHOLS > CATECHOL
CATECHU *n* water-soluble astringent resinous substance obtained from any of certain tropical plants, esp the leguminous tree *Acacia catechu* of S Asia, and used in medicine, tanning, and dyeing
CATECHUS > CATECHU
CATEGORIC *adj* unqualified
CATEGORY *n* class, group
CATELOG *obsolete word for* > CATALOGUE
CATELOGS > CATELOG
CATENA *n* connected series, esp of patristic comments on the Bible
CATENAE > CATENA
CATENANE *n* type of chemical compound in which the molecules have two or more rings that are interlocked like the links of a chain
CATENANES > CATENANE
CATENARY *n* curve assumed by a heavy uniform flexible cord hanging freely from two points. When symmetrical about the *y*-axis and intersecting it at $y = a$, the equation is $y = a \cosh x/a$ ▷ *adj* of, resembling, relating to, or constructed using a catenary or suspended chain
CATENAS > CATENA
CATENATE *vb* arrange or be arranged in a series of chains or rings
CATENATED > CATENATE
CATENATES > CATENATE
CATENOID *n* geometrical surface generated by rotating a catenary about its axis
CATENOIDS > CATENOID
CATER *vb* provide what is needed or wanted, esp food or services
CATERAN *n* (formerly) a member of a band of brigands and marauders in the Scottish highlands
CATERANS > CATERAN
CATERED > CATER
CATERER *n* person whose job is to provide food for social events such as parties and weddings
CATERERS > CATERER
CATERESS *n* female caterer
CATERING *n* supplying of food for a social event
CATERINGS > CATERING
CATERS > CATER
CATERWAUL *n* wail, yowl ▷ *vb* make a yowling noise like a cat
CATES *pl n* choice dainty food
CATFACE *n* deformity of the surface of a tree trunk, caused by fire or disease
CATFACES > CATFACE
CATFACING *n* disorder that affects tomatoes, causing scarring of the fruit
CATFALL *n* line used as a tackle for hoisting an anchor to the cathead
CATFALLS > CATFALL
CATFIGHT *n* fight between two women
CATFIGHTS > CATFIGHT
CATFISH *n* fish with whisker-like barbels round the mouth
CATFISHES > CATFISH
CATGUT *n* strong cord used to string musical instruments and sports rackets
CATGUTS > CATGUT
CATHARISE *vb* to purify
CATHARIZE *same as* > CATHARISE
CATHARSES > CATHARSIS
CATHARSIS *n* relief of strong suppressed emotions
CATHARTIC *adj* causing catharsis ▷ *n* drug that causes catharsis
CATHEAD *n* fitting at the bow of a vessel for securing the anchor when raised
CATHEADS > CATHEAD
CATHECT *vb* to invest mental or emotional energy in
CATHECTED > CATHECT
CATHECTIC *adj* of or relating to cathexis
CATHECTS > CATHECT
CATHEDRA *n* bishop's throne
CATHEDRAE > CATHEDRA
CATHEDRAL *n* principal church of a diocese
CATHEDRAS > CATHEDRA
CATHEPSIN *n* proteolytic enzyme responsible for the autolysis of cells after death
CATHEPTIC > CATHEPSIN
CATHETER *n* tube inserted into a body cavity to drain fluid
CATHETERS > CATHETER
CATHETUS *n* straight line or radius perpendicular to another line or radius
CATHEXES > CATHEXIS
CATHEXIS *n* concentration of psychic energy on a single goal
CATHISMA *n* short hymn used as a response
CATHISMAS > CATHISMA
CATHODAL > CATHODE
CATHODE *n* negative electrode, by which electrons leave a circuit
CATHODES > CATHODE
CATHODIC > CATHODE
CATHOLE *n* hole in a ship through which ropes are passed
CATHOLES > CATHOLE
CATHOLIC *adj* (of tastes or interests) covering a wide range ▷ *n* member of the Roman Catholic Church
CATHOLICS > CATHOLIC
CATHOLYTE *same as* > CATOLYTE
CATHOOD *n* state of being a cat
CATHOODS > CATHOOD
CATHOUSE *a slang word for* > BROTHEL
CATHOUSES > CATHOUSE
CATION *n* positively charged ion
CATIONIC > CATION
CATIONS > CATION
CATJANG *n* tropical shrub
CATJANGS > CATJANG
CATKIN *n* drooping flower spike of certain trees
CATKINATE *adj* like catkin
CATKINS > CATKIN
CATLIKE > CAT
CATLIN *same as* > CATLING
CATLING *n* long double-edged surgical knife for amputations
CATLINGS > CATLING
CATLINS > CATLIN
CATMINT *n* Eurasian plant with scented leaves that attract cats
CATMINTS > CATMINT
CATNAP *vb* doze ▷ *n* short sleep or doze
CATNAPER > CATNAP
CATNAPERS > CATNAP
CATNAPPED > CATNAP
CATNAPPER > CATNAP
CATNAPS > CATNAP
CATNEP *same as* > CATMINT
CATNEPS > CATNEP
CATNIP *same as* > CATMINT
CATNIPS > CATMINT
CATOLYTE *n* part of the electrolyte that surrounds the cathode in an

electrolytic cell
CATOLYTES > CATOLYTE
CATOPTRIC *adj* relating to reflection
CATRIGGED *adj* rigged like a catboat
CATS > CAT
CATSKIN *n* skin and/or fur of a cat
CATSKINS > CATSKIN
CATSPAW *n* person used by another as a tool
CATSPAWS > CATSPAW
CATSUIT *n* one-piece usually close-fitting trouser suit
CATSUITS > CATSUIT
CATSUP *a variant (esp US) of* > KETCHUP
CATSUPS > CATSUP
CATTABU *n* cross between common cattle and zebu
CATTABUS > CATTABU
CATTAIL *n* reed mace
CATTAILS > CATTAIL
CATTALO *n* hardy breed of cattle developed by crossing the American bison with domestic cattle
CATTALOES > CATTALO
CATTALOS > CATTALO
CATTED > CAT
CATTERIES > CATTERY
CATTERY *n* place where cats are bred or looked after
CATTIE *same as* > CATTY
CATTIER > CATTY
CATTIES > CATTY
CATTIEST > CATTY
CATTILY > CATTY
CATTINESS > CATTY
CATTING > CAT
CATTISH > CAT
CATTISHLY > CAT
CATTLE *pl n* domesticated cows and bulls
CATTLEMAN *n* person who breeds, rears, or tends cattle
CATTLEMEN > CATTLEMAN
CATTLEYA *n* any tropical American orchid of the genus *Cattleya*, cultivated for their purplish-pink or white showy flowers
CATTLEYAS > CATTLEYA
CATTY *adj* spiteful ▷ *n* unit of weight, used esp in China, equal to about one and a half pounds or about 0.67 kilogram
CATWALK *n* narrow pathway or platform
CATWALKS > CATWALK
CATWORKS *n* machinery on a drilling platform
CATWORM *n* active carnivorous polychaete worm, *Nephthys hombergi*, that is about 10cm (4in) long, having a pearly sheen to its body: often dug for bait
CATWORMS > CATWORM
CAUCHEMAR *n* nightmare
CAUCUS *n* local committee or faction of a political party ▷ *vb* hold a caucus
CAUCUSED > CAUCUS
CAUCUSES > CAUCUS
CAUCUSING > CAUCUS
CAUCUSSED > CAUCUS
CAUCUSSES > CAUCUS
CAUDA *n* area behind the anus of an animal
CAUDAD *adv* towards the tail or posterior part
CAUDAE > CAUDA
CAUDAL *adj* at or near an animal's tail
CAUDALLY > CAUDAL
CAUDATE *adj* having a tail or a tail-like appendage ▷ *n* lizard-like amphibian
CAUDATED *same as* > CAUDATE
CAUDATES > CAUDATE
CAUDATION > CAUDATE
CAUDEX *n* thickened persistent stem base of some herbaceous perennial plants
CAUDEXES > CAUDEX
CAUDICES > CAUDEX
CAUDICLE *n* stalk to which an orchid's pollen masses are attached
CAUDICLES > CAUDICLE
CAUDILLO *n* (in Spanish-speaking countries) a military or political leader
CAUDILLOS > CAUDILLO
CAUDLE *n* hot spiced wine drink made with gruel, formerly used medicinally ▷ *vb* make such a drink
CAUDLED > CAUDLE
CAUDLES > CAUDLE
CAUDLING > CAUDLE
CAUDRON *Spenserian spelling of* > CAULDRON
CAUDRONS > CAUDRON
CAUF *n* cage for holding live fish in the water
CAUGHT > CATCH
CAUK *n* type of barite
CAUKER *n* one who caulks
CAUKERS > CAUKER
CAUKS > CAUK
CAUL *n* membrane sometimes covering a child's head at birth
CAULD *a Scot word for* > COLD
CAULDER > CAULD
CAULDEST > CAULD
CAULDRIFE *adj* susceptible to cold
CAULDRON *n* large pot used for boiling
CAULDRONS > CAULDRON
CAULDS > CAULD
CAULES > CAULIS
CAULICLE *n* small stalk or stem
CAULICLES > CAULICLE
CAULICULI *n* plural form of singular cauliculus: another word for caulicle
CAULIFORM *adj* resembling a caulis
CAULINARY *another word for* > CAULINE
CAULINE *adj* relating to or growing from a plant stem
CAULIS *n* main stem of a plant
CAULK *vb* fill in (cracks) with paste etc
CAULKED > CAULK
CAULKER > CAULK
CAULKERS > CAULK
CAULKING > CAULK
CAULKINGS > CAULK
CAULKS > CAULK
CAULOME *n* plant's stem structure, considered as a whole
CAULOMES > CAULOME
CAULS > CAUL
CAUM *same as* > CAM
CAUMED > CAUM
CAUMING > CAUM
CAUMS > CAUM
CAUMSTONE *same as* > CAMSTONE
CAUP *n* type of quaich
CAUPS > CAUP
CAUSA *n* reason or cause
CAUSABLE > CAUSE
CAUSAE > CAUSA
CAUSAL *adj* of or being a cause ▷ *n* something that suggests a cause
CAUSALGIA *n* burning sensation along the course of a peripheral nerve together with local changes in the appearance of the skin
CAUSALGIC > CAUSALGIA
CAUSALITY *n* relationship of cause and effect
CAUSALLY > CAUSAL
CAUSALS > CAUSAL
CAUSATION *n* relationship of cause and effect
CAUSATIVE *adj* producing an effect ▷ *n* causative form or class of verbs
CAUSE *n* something that produces a particular effect ▷ *vb* be the cause of
CAUSED > CAUSE
CAUSELESS > CAUSE
CAUSEN *old infinitive of* > CAUSE
CAUSER > CAUSE
CAUSERIE *n* informal talk or conversational piece of writing
CAUSERIES > CAUSERIE
CAUSERS > CAUSE
CAUSES > CAUSE
CAUSEWAY *n* raised path or road across water or marshland
CAUSEWAYS > CAUSEWAY
CAUSEY *n* cobbled street ▷ *vb* cobble
CAUSEYED > CAUSEY
CAUSEYS > CAUSEY
CAUSING > CAUSE
CAUSTIC *adj* capable of burning by chemical action ▷ *n* caustic substance
CAUSTICAL > CAUSTIC
CAUSTICS > CAUSTIC
CAUTEL *n* craftiness
CAUTELOUS > CAUTEL
CAUTELS > CAUTEL
CAUTER *n* cauterising instrument
CAUTERANT *same as* > CAUTERY
CAUTERIES > CAUTERY
CAUTERISE *same as* > CAUTERIZE
CAUTERISM > CAUTERIZE
CAUTERIZE *vb* burn (a wound) with heat or a caustic agent to prevent infection
CAUTERS > CAUTER
CAUTERY *n* coagulation of blood or destruction of body tissue by cauterizing
CAUTION *n* care, esp in the face of danger ▷ *vb* warn, advise
CAUTIONED > CAUTION
CAUTIONER > CAUTION
CAUTIONRY *n* in Scots law, standing surety
CAUTIONS > CAUTION
CAUTIOUS *adj* showing caution
CAUVES > CAUF
CAVA *n* Spanish sparkling wine produced by a method similar to that used for champagne
CAVALCADE *n* procession of people on horseback or in cars
CAVALERO *n* cavalier
CAVALEROS > CAVALERO
CAVALETTI *n* bars supported on low stands used in dressage and horse jumping
CAVALIER *adj* showing haughty disregard ▷ *n* gallant gentleman
CAVALIERS > CAVALIER
CAVALLA *n* any of various tropical carangid fishes, such as *Gnathanodon speciosus* (golden cavalla)
CAVALLAS > CAVALLA
CAVALLIES > CAVALLY
CAVALLY *same as* > CAVALLA
CAVALRIES > CAVALRY
CAVALRY *n* part of the army orig. on horseback, but now often using fast armoured vehicles
CAVAS > CAVA
CAVASS *n* Turkish armed police officer
CAVASSES > CAVASS
CAVATINA *n* solo song resembling a simple aria
CAVATINAS > CAVATINA
CAVATINE > CAVATINA

CAVE *n* hollow in the side of a hill or cliff ▷ *vb* hollow out
CAVEAT *n* warning ▷ *vb* to introduce a caveat
CAVEATED > CAVEAT
CAVEATING > CAVEAT
CAVEATOR *n* person who enters a caveat
CAVEATORS > CAVEATOR
CAVEATS > CAVEAT
CAVED > CAVE
CAVEFISH *n* any of various small freshwater cyprinodont fishes of the genera *Amblyopsis*, *Chologaster*, etc, living in subterranean and other waters in S North America
CAVEL *n* drawing of lots among miners for an easy and profitable place at the coalface
CAVELIKE *adj* resembling a cave
CAVELS > CAVEL
CAVEMAN *n* prehistoric cave dweller
CAVEMEN > CAVEMAN
CAVENDISH *n* tobacco that has been sweetened and pressed into moulds to form bars
CAVER > CAVING
CAVERN *n* large cave ▷ *vb* shut in or as if in a cavern
CAVERNED > CAVERN
CAVERNING > CAVERN
CAVERNOUS *adj* like a cavern in vastness, depth, or hollowness
CAVERNS > CAVERN
CAVERS > CAVING
CAVES > CAVE
CAVESSON *n* kind of hard noseband, used (esp formerly) in breaking a horse in
CAVESSONS > CAVESSON
CAVETTI > CAVETTO
CAVETTO *n* concave moulding, shaped to a quarter circle in cross section
CAVETTOS > CAVETTO
CAVIAR *n* salted sturgeon roe, regarded as a delicacy
CAVIARE *same as* > CAVIAR
CAVIARES > CAVIARE
CAVIARIE *same as* > CAVIAR
CAVIARIES > CAVIARY
CAVIARS > CAVIAR
CAVICORN *adj* (of sheep, goats, etc) having hollow horns as distinct from the solid antlers of deer ▷ *n* sheep, goats, etc with hollow horns as distinct from the solid antlers of deer
CAVICORNS > CAVICORN
CAVIE *n* hen coop
CAVIER *same as* > CAVIAR
CAVIERS > CAVIER
CAVIES > CAVY
CAVIL *vb* make petty objections ▷ *n* petty objection
CAVILED > CAVIL
CAVILER > CAVIL
CAVILERS > CAVIL
CAVILING > CAVIL
CAVILLED > CAVIL
CAVILLER > CAVIL
CAVILLERS > CAVIL
CAVILLING > CAVIL
CAVILS > CAVIL
CAVING *n* sport of exploring caves
CAVINGS > CAVING
CAVITARY *adj* containing cavities
CAVITATE *vb* to form cavities or bubbles
CAVITATED > CAVITATE
CAVITATES > CAVITATE
CAVITIED > CAVITY
CAVITIES > CAVITY
CAVITY *n* hollow space
CAVORT *vb* skip about
CAVORTED > CAVORT
CAVORTER > CAVORT
CAVORTERS > CAVORT
CAVORTING > CAVORT
CAVORTS > CAVORT
CAVY *n* any small South American hystricomorph rodent of the family *Caviidae*, esp any of the genus *Cavia*, having a thickset body and very small tail
CAW *n* cry of a crow, rook, or raven ▷ *vb* make this cry
CAWED > CAW
CAWING > CAW
CAWINGS > CAW
CAWK *same as* > CAUK
CAWKER *n* metal projection on a horse's shoe to prevent slipping
CAWKERS > CAWKER
CAWKS > CAWK
CAWS > CAW
CAXON *n* type of wig
CAXONS > CAXON
CAY *n* low island or bank composed of sand and coral fragments
CAYENNE *n* very hot condiment, bright red in colour, made from dried capsicums
CAYENNED *adj* seasoned with cayenne
CAYENNES > CAYENNE
CAYMAN *n* S American reptile similar to an alligator
CAYMANS > CAYMAN
CAYS > CAY
CAYUSE *n* small American Indian pony used by cowboys
CAYUSES > CAYUSE
CAZ *short for* > CASUAL
CAZIQUE *same as* > CACIQUE
CAZIQUES > CAZIQUE
CEANOTHUS *n* any shrub of the North American rhamnaceous genus *Ceanothus*: grown for their ornamental, often blue, flower clusters
CEAS *same as* > CAESE
CEASE *vb* bring or come to an end
CEASED > CEASE
CEASEFIRE *n* temporary truce
CEASELESS *adj* without stopping
CEASES > CEASE
CEASING > CEASE
CEASINGS > CEASE
CEAZE *obsolete spelling of* > SEIZE
CEAZED > CEAZE
CEAZES > CEAZE
CEAZING > CEAZE
CEBADILLA *same as* > SABADILLA
CEBID *n* any member of the Cebidae family of New World monkeys
CEBIDS > CEBID
CEBOID *same as* > CEBID
CEBOIDS > CEBOID
CECA > CECUM
CECAL > CECUM
CECALLY > CECUM
CECILS *n* fried meatballs
CECITIES > CECITY
CECITIS *n* inflammation of the c(a)ecum
CECITISES > CECITIS
CECITY *n* rare word for blindness
CECROPIA *n* large North American moth
CECROPIAS > CECROPIA
CECUM *same as* > CAECUM
CEDAR *n* evergreen coniferous tree ▷ *adj* made of the wood of a cedar tree
CEDARBIRD *n* type of waxwing
CEDARED *adj* covered with cedars
CEDARN *adj* relating to cedar
CEDARS > CEDAR
CEDARWOOD *n* wood of any of the cedar trees
CEDARY *adj* like cedar
CEDE *vb* surrender (territory or legal rights)
CEDED > CEDE
CEDER > CEDE
CEDERS > CEDE
CEDES > CEDE
CEDI *n* standard monetary unit of Ghana, divided into 100 pesewas
CEDILLA *n* character placed under a *c* in some languages, to show that it is pronounced *s*, not *k*
CEDILLAS > CEDILLA
CEDING > CEDE
CEDIS > CEDI
CEDRATE *n* citron
CEDRATES > CEDRATE
CEDRINE *adj* relating to cedar
CEDULA *n* form of identification in Spanish-speaking countries
CEDULAS > CEDULA
CEE *n* third letter of the alphabet
CEES > CEE
CEIBA *n* any bombacaceous tropical tree of the genus *Ceiba*, such as the silk-cotton tree
CEIBAS > CEIBA
CEIL *vb* line (a ceiling) with plaster, boarding, etc
CEILED > CEIL
CEILER > CEIL
CEILERS > CEIL
CEILI *variant spelling of* > CEILIDH
CEILIDH *n* informal social gathering for singing and dancing, esp in Scotland
CEILIDHS > CEILIDH
CEILING *n* inner upper surface of a room ▷ *vb* make a ceiling
CEILINGED > CEILING
CEILINGS > CEILING
CEILIS > CEILI
CEILS > CEIL
CEINTURE *n* belt
CEINTURES > CEINTURE
CEL *short for* > CELLULOID
CELADON *n* type of porcelain having a greyish-green glaze: mainly Chinese
CELADONS > CELADON
CELANDINE *n* wild plant with yellow flowers
CELEB *n* celebrity
CELEBRANT *n* person who performs a religious ceremony
CELEBRATE *vb* hold festivities to mark (a happy event, anniversary, etc)
CELEBRITY *n* famous person
CELEBS > CELEB
CELERIAC *n* variety of celery with a large turnip-like root
CELERIACS > CELERIAC
CELERIES > CELERY
CELERITY *n* swiftness
CELERY *n* vegetable with long green crisp edible stalks
CELESTA *n* instrument like a small piano in which key operated hammers strike metal plates
CELESTAS > CELESTA
CELESTE *same as* > CELESTA
CELESTES > CELESTE
CELESTIAL *adj* heavenly, divine
CELESTINE *same*

as > CELESTITE
CELESTITE *n* white, red, or blue mineral
CELIAC *same as* > COELIAC
CELIACS > CELIAC
CELIBACY > CELIBATE
CELIBATE *adj* unmarried or abstaining from sex, esp because of a religious vow of chastity ▷ *n* celibate person
CELIBATES > CELIBATE
CELIBATIC *adj* celibate
CELL *n* smallest unit of an organism that is able to function independently
CELLA *n* inner room of a classical temple, esp the room housing the statue of a deity
CELLAE > CELLA
CELLAR *n* underground room for storage ▷ *vb* store in a cellar
CELLARAGE *n* area of a cellar
CELLARED > CELLAR
CELLARER *n* monastic official responsible for food, drink, etc
CELLARERS > CELLARER
CELLARET *n* case, cabinet, or sideboard with compartments for holding wine bottles
CELLARETS > CELLARET
CELLARING > CELLAR
CELLARIST *same as* > CELLARER
CELLARMAN *n* person in charge of a cellar
CELLARMEN > CELLARMAN
CELLAROUS *adj* relating to a cellar
CELLARS > CELLAR
CELLARWAY *n* way into cellar
CELLBLOCK *n* group of prison cells
CELLED *adj* cellular
CELLI > CELLO
CELLING *n* formation of cells
CELLIST > CELLO
CELLISTS > CELLO
CELLMATE *n* person with whom a prisoner shares a prison cell
CELLMATES > CELLMATE
CELLO *n* large low-pitched instrument of the violin family
CELLOIDIN *n* nitrocellulose compound derived from pyroxylin, used in a solution of alcohol and ether for embedding specimens before cutting sections for microscopy
CELLOS > CELLO
CELLOSE *n* a disaccharide obtained by the hydrolysis of cellulose by cellulase.
CELLOSES > CELLOSE
CELLPHONE *n* portable telephone operated by cellular radio
CELLS > CELL
CELLULAR *adj* of or consisting of cells ▷ *n* cellular phone
CELLULARS > CELLULAR
CELLULASE *n* any enzyme that converts cellulose to the disaccharide cellobiose
CELLULE *n* very small cell
CELLULES > CELLULE
CELLULITE *n* fat deposits under the skin alleged to resist dieting
CELLULOID *n* kind of plastic used to make toys and, formerly, photographic film
CELLULOSE *n* main constituent of plant cell walls, used in making paper, plastics, etc
CELLULOUS > CELLULOSE
CELOM *same as* > COELOM
CELOMATA > CELOM
CELOMIC > CELOM
CELOMS > CELOM
CELOSIA *same as* > COCKSCOMB
CELOSIAS > CELOSIA
CELOTEX *n* tradename for a type of insulation board
CELOTEXES > CELOTEX
CELS > CEL
CELSITUDE *n* loftiness
CELT *n* stone or metal axelike instrument with a bevelled edge
CELTS > CELT
CEMBALI > CEMBALO
CEMBALIST > CEMBALO
CEMBALO *n* harpsichord
CEMBALOS > CEMBALO
CEMBRA *n* Swiss pine
CEMBRAS > CEMBRA
CEMENT *n* fine grey powder mixed with water and sand to make mortar or concrete ▷ *vb* join, bind, or cover with cement
CEMENTA > CEMENTUM
CEMENTED > CEMENT
CEMENTER > CEMENT
CEMENTERS > CEMENT
CEMENTING > CEMENT
CEMENTITE *n* hard brittle compound of iron and carbon
CEMENTS > CEMENT
CEMENTUM *n* thin bonelike tissue that covers the dentine in the root of a tooth
CEMENTUMS > CEMENTUM
CEMETERY *n* place where dead people are buried
CEMITARE *obsolete spelling of* > SCIMITAR
CEMITARES > CEMITARE
CENACLE *n* supper room, esp one on an upper floor
CENACLES > CENACLE
CENDRE *adj* ash-blond
CENOBITE *same as* > COENOBITE
CENOBITES > CENOBITE
CENOBITIC > CENOBITE
CENOTAPH *n* monument honouring soldiers who died in a war
CENOTAPHS > CENOTAPH
CENOTE *n* (esp in the Yucatán peninsula) a natural well formed by the collapse of an overlying limestone crust: often used as a sacrificial site by the Mayas
CENOTES > CENOTE
CENOZOIC *adj* of or relating to the most recent geologiacl era, characterized by the development and increase of the mammals
CENS *n* type of annual property rent
CENSE *vb* burn incense near or before (an altar, shrine, etc)
CENSED > CENSE
CENSER *n* container for burning incense
CENSERS > CENSER
CENSES > CENSE
CENSING > CENSE
CENSOR *n* person authorized to examine films, books, etc, to ban or cut anything considered obscene or objectionable ▷ *vb* ban or cut parts of (a film, book, etc)
CENSORED > CENSOR
CENSORIAL > CENSOR
CENSORIAN > CENSOR
CENSORING > CENSOR
CENSORS > CENSOR
CENSUAL > CENSUS
CENSURE *n* severe disapproval ▷ *vb* criticize severely
CENSURED > CENSURE
CENSURER > CENSURE
CENSURERS > CENSURE
CENSURES > CENSURE
CENSURING > CENSURE
CENSUS *n* official count of a population ▷ *vb* to conduct a census
CENSUSED > CENSUS
CENSUSES > CENSUS
CENSUSING > CENSUS
CENT *n* hundredth part of a monetary unit such as the dollar or euro
CENTAGE *n* rate per hundred
CENTAGES > CENTAGE
CENTAI > CENTAS
CENTAL *n* unit of weight equal to 100 pounds (45.3 kilograms)
CENTALS > CENTAL
CENTARE *same as* > CENTIARE
CENTARES > CENTARE
CENTAS *n* monetary unit of Lithuania, worth one hundredth of a litas
CENTAUR *n* mythical creature with the head, arms, and torso of a man, and the lower body and legs of a horse
CENTAUREA *n* any plant of the genus *Centaurea*, which includes the cornflower and knapweed
CENTAURIC *adj* integrating mind and body
CENTAURS > CENTAUR
CENTAURY *n* any Eurasian plant of the genus *Centaurium*, esp *C. erythraea*, having purplish-pink flowers and formerly believed to have medicinal properties: family *Gentianaceae*
CENTAVO *n* monetary unit worth one hundredth of the main unit of currency in Portugal and many Latin American countries
CENTAVOS > CENTAVO
CENTENARY *n* 100th anniversary or its celebration ▷ *adj* of or relating to a period of 100 years
CENTENIER *n* in Jersey, a local police officer
CENTER *same as* > CENTRE
CENTERED > CENTER
CENTERING *same as* > CENTRING
CENTERS > CENTER
CENTESES > CENTESIS
CENTESIMI > CENTESIMO
CENTESIMO *n* former monetary unit of Italy, San Marino, and the Vatican City worth one hundredth of a lira
CENTESIS *n* surgical puncturing of part of the body with a hollow needle, to extract fluid
CENTIARE *n* unit of area equal to one square metre
CENTIARES > CENTIARE
CENTIGRAM *n* one hundredth of a gram
CENTILE *n* one of 99 actual or notional values of a variable dividing its distribution into 100 groups with equal frequencies
CENTILES > CENTILE
CENTIME *n* monetary unit worth one hundredth of a franc
CENTIMES > CENTIME
CENTIMO *n* monetary unit of Costa Rica, Paraguay, Peru, and Venezuela. It is

worth one hundredth of their respective standard currency units
CENTIMOS > CENTIMO
CENTINEL *obsolete variant of* > SENTINEL
CENTINELL *obsolete variant of* > SENTINEL
CENTINELS > CENTINEL
CENTIPEDE *n* small wormlike creature with many legs
CENTNER *n* unit of weight equivalent to 100 pounds (45.3 kilograms)
CENTNERS > CENTNER
CENTO *n* piece of writing, esp a poem, composed of quotations from other authors
CENTOIST *n* one who composes centos
CENTOISTS > CENTOIST
CENTONATE *adj* having many patches
CENTONEL *obsolete variant of* > SENTINEL
CENTONELL *obsolete variant of* > SENTINEL
CENTONELS > CENTONEL
CENTONES > CENTO
CENTONIST *same as* > CENTOIST
CENTOS > CENTO
CENTRA > CENTRUM
CENTRAL *adj* of, at, or forming the centre ▷ *n* workplace serving as a telecommunications facility
CENTRALER > CENTRAL
CENTRALLY > CENTRAL
CENTRALS > CENTRAL
CENTRE *n* middle point or part ▷ *vb* put in the centre of something
CENTRED *adj* mentally and emotionally confident, focused, and well-balanced
CENTREING *same as* > CENTRING
CENTRES > CENTRE
CENTRIC *adj* being central or having a centre
CENTRICAL *same as* > CENTRIC
CENTRIES > CENTRY
CENTRING *n* temporary structure, esp one made of timber, used to support an arch during construction
CENTRINGS > CENTRING
CENTRIOLE *n* either of two rodlike bodies in most animal cells that form the poles of the spindle during mitosis
CENTRISM > CENTRIST
CENTRISMS > CENTRIST
CENTRIST *n* person favouring political moderation
CENTRISTS > CENTRIST
CENTRODE *n* locus produced by plotting course of the instantaneous centre of two bodies in relative motion
CENTRODES > CENTRODE
CENTROID *n* centre of mass of an object of uniform density, esp of a geometric figure
CENTROIDS > CENTROID
CENTRUM *n* main part or body of a vertebra
CENTRUMS > CENTRUM
CENTRY *obsolete variant of* > SENTRY
CENTS > CENT
CENTU *n* Lithuanian money unit
CENTUM *adj* denoting or belonging to the Indo-European languages in which original velar stops (*k*) were not palatalized, namely languages of the Hellenic, Italic, Celtic, Germanic, Anatolian, and Tocharian branches ▷ *n* hundred
CENTUMS > CENTUM
CENTUMVIR *n* one of the Roman judges who sat in civil cases
CENTUPLE *n* one hundredfold
CENTUPLED > CENTUPLE
CENTUPLES > CENTUPLE
CENTURIAL *adj* of or relating to a Roman century
CENTURIES > CENTURY
CENTURION *n* (in ancient Rome) officer commanding 100 men
CENTURY *n* period of 100 years
CEORL *n* freeman of the lowest class in Anglo-Saxon England
CEORLISH > CEORL
CEORLS > CEORL
CEP *another name for* > PORCINO
CEPACEOUS *adj* having an onion-like smell or taste
CEPE *another spelling of* > CEP
CEPES > CEPE
CEPHALAD *adv* towards the head or anterior part
CEPHALATE *adj* possessing a head
CEPHALIC *adj* of or relating to the head ▷ *n* remedy for pains in the head
CEPHALICS > CEPHALIC
CEPHALIN *n* phospholipid, similar to lecithin, that occurs in the nerve tissue and brain
CEPHALINS > CEPHALIN
CEPHALOUS *adj* with a head
CEPHEID *n* type of variable star with a regular cycle of variations in luminosity
CEPHEIDS > CEPHEID
CEPS > CEP
CERACEOUS *adj* waxlike or waxy
CERAMAL *same as* > CERMET
CERAMALS > CERAMAL
CERAMIC *n* hard brittle material made by heating clay to a very high temperature ▷ *adj* made of ceramic
CERAMICS *n* art of producing ceramic objects
CERAMIDE *n* any of a class of biologically important compounds used as moisturizers in skin-care preparations
CERAMIDES > CERAMIDE
CERAMIST > CERAMICS
CERAMISTS > CERAMICS
CERASIN *n* meta-arabinic acid
CERASINS > CERASIN
CERASTES *n* any venomous snake of the genus *Cerastes*, esp the horned viper
CERASTIUM *n* mouse-eared chickweed
CERATE *n* hard ointment or medicated paste consisting of lard or oil mixed with wax or resin
CERATED *adj* (of certain birds, such as the falcon) having a cere
CERATES > CERATE
CERATIN *same as* > KERATIN
CERATINS > CERATIN
CERATITIS *same as* > KERATITIS
CERATODUS *n* any of various extinct lungfish constituting the genus *Ceratodus*, common in Cretaceous and Triassic times
CERATOID *adj* having the shape or texture of animal horn
CERBEREAN *adj* of or resembling Cerberus, the three-headed dog that guarded the entrance to Hades in Greek mythology
CERBERIAN *same as* > CERBEREAN
CERCAL *adj* of or relating to a tail
CERCARIA *n* one of the larval forms of trematode worms. It has a short forked tail and resembles an immature adult
CERCARIAE > CERCARIA
CERCARIAL > CERCARIA
CERCARIAN > CERCARIA
CERCARIAS > CERCARIA
CERCI > CERCUS
CERCIS *n* any tree or shrub of the leguminous genus *Cercis*, which includes the redbud and Judas tree
CERCISES > CERCIS
CERCUS *n* one of a pair of sensory appendages at the tip of the abdomen of some insects and other arthropods
CERE *n* soft waxy swelling, containing the nostrils, at the base of the upper beak of a parrot ▷ *vb* wrap (a corpse) in a cerecloth
CEREAL *n* grass plant with edible grain, such as oat or wheat
CEREALIST *n* expert in cereals
CEREALS > CEREAL
CEREBELLA *n* plural of singular cerebellum: one of the major divisions of the vertebrate brain
CEREBRA > CEREBRUM
CEREBRAL *same as* > CACUMINAL
CEREBRALS > CEREBRAL
CEREBRATE *vb* use the mind
CEREBRIC > CEREBRUM
CEREBROID > CEREBRUM
CEREBRUM *n* main part of the brain
CEREBRUMS > CEREBRUM
CERECLOTH *n* waxed waterproof cloth of a kind formerly used as a shroud
CERED > CERE
CEREMENT *n* any burial clothes
CEREMENTS > CEREMENT
CEREMONY *n* formal act or ritual
CEREOUS *adj* waxlike
CERES > CERE
CERESIN *n* white wax extracted from ozocerite
CERESINE *same as* > CERESIN
CERESINES > CERESINE
CERESINS > CERESIN
CEREUS *n* any tropical American cactus of the genus *Cereus*, esp *C. jamacaru* of N Brazil, which grows to a height of 13 metres (40 feet)
CEREUSES > CEREUS
CERGE *n* large altar candle
CERGES > CERGE
CERIA *n* ceric oxide
CERIAS > CERIA
CERIC *adj* of or containing cerium in the tetravalent state
CERING > CERE
CERIPH *same as* > SERIF
CERIPHS > CERIPH
CERISE *adj* cherry-red ▷ *n* moderate to dark red colour
CERISES > CERISE
CERITE *n* hydrous silicate of cerium

CERITES > CERITE
CERIUM *n* steel-grey metallic element
CERIUMS > CERIUM
CERMET *n* any of several materials consisting of a metal matrix with ceramic particles disseminated through it. They are hard and resistant to high temperatures
CERMETS > CERMET
CERNE *obsolete variant of* > ENCIRCLE
CERNED > CERNE
CERNES > CERNE
CERNING > CERNE
CERNUOUS *adj* (of some flowers or buds) drooping
CERO *n* large spiny-finned food fish, *Scomberomorus regalis*, of warm American coastal regions of the Atlantic: family *Scombridae* (mackerels, tunnies, etc)
CEROGRAPH *n* writing on wax
CEROMANCY *n* divination by interpreting significance of shapes formed when melted wax is dropped into water
CEROON *n* hide-covered bale
CEROONS > CEROON
CEROS > CERO
CEROTIC as in *cerotic acid* white insoluble odourless wax
CEROTYPE *n* process for preparing a printing plate by engraving a wax-coated copper plate and then using this as a mould for an electrotype
CEROTYPES > CEROTYPE
CEROUS *adj* of or containing cerium in the trivalent state
CERRIAL *adj* relating to the cerris
CERRIS *n* Turkey oak
CERRISES > CERRIS
CERT *n* certainty
CERTAIN *adj* positive and confident
CERTAINER > CERTAIN
CERTAINLY *adv* without doubt ▷ *sentence substitute* by all means
CERTAINTY *n* state of being sure
CERTES *adv* with certainty
CERTIFIED > CERTIFY
CERTIFIER > CERTIFY
CERTIFIES > CERTIFY
CERTIFY *vb* confirm, attest to
CERTITUDE *n* confidence, certainty
CERTS > CERT
CERULE *adj* sky-blue
CERULEAN *n* deep blue colour ▷ *n* light shade of blue
CERULEANS > CERULEAN
CERULEIN *n* type of dyestuff
CERULEINS > CERULEIN
CERULEOUS *adj* sky-blue
CERUMEN *n* soft brownish-yellow wax secreted by glands in the auditory canal of the external ear
CERUMENS > CERUMEN
CERUSE *n* white lead
CERUSES > CERUSE
CERUSITE *same as* > CERUSSITE
CERUSITES > CERUSITE
CERUSSITE *n* usually white mineral, found in veins
CERVELAS *n* French garlicky pork sausage
CERVELAT *n* smoked sausage made from pork and beef
CERVELATS > CERVELAT
CERVEZA *n* Spanish word for beer
CERVEZAS > CERVEZA
CERVICAL *adj* of or relating to the neck or cervix
CERVICES > CERVIX
CERVICUM *n* flexible region between the prothorax and head in insects
CERVICUMS > CERVICUM
CERVID *n* any ruminant mammal of the family *Cervidae*, including the deer, characterized by the presence of antlers ▷ *adj* of, relating to, or belonging to the *Cervidae*
CERVIDS > CERVID
CERVINE *adj* resembling or relating to a deer
CERVIX *n* narrow entrance of the womb
CERVIXES > CERVIX
CESAREAN *variant of* > CAESAREAN
CESAREANS > CESAREAN
CESAREVNA *n* wife of a Russian tsar's eldest son
CESARIAN *US variant of* > CAESAREAN
CESARIANS > CESARIAN
CESIOUS *same as* > CAESIOUS
CESIUM *same as* > CAESIUM
CESIUMS > CESIUM
CESPITOSE *adj* growing in dense tufts
CESS *n* any of several special taxes, such as a land tax in Scotland ▷ *vb* tax or assess for taxation
CESSATION *n* ceasing
CESSE *obsolete variant of* > CEASE
CESSED > CESS
CESSER *n* coming to an end of a term interest or annuity
CESSERS > CESSER
CESSES > CESS
CESSING > CESS
CESSION *n* ceding
CESSIONS > CESSION
CESSPIT *same as* > CESSPOOL
CESSPITS > CESSPIT
CESSPOOL *n* covered tank or pit for collecting and storing sewage or waste water
CESSPOOLS > CESSPOOL
CESTA *n* in jai alai, the basket used to throw and catch the pelota
CESTAS > CESTA
CESTI > CESTUS
CESTODE *n* any parasitic flatworm of the class *Cestoda*, which includes the tapeworms
CESTODES > CESTODE
CESTOI > CESTOS
CESTOID *adj* (esp of tapeworms and similar animals) ribbon-like in form ▷ *n* ribbon-like worm
CESTOIDS > CESTOID
CESTOS *same as* > CESTUS
CESTOSES > CESTOS
CESTUI *n* "the one (who)"; legal term, used in certain phrases, to designate a person
CESTUIS > CESTUI
CESTUS *n* girdle of Aphrodite (Venus) decorated to cause amorousness
CESTUSES > CESTUS
CESURA *a variant spelling of* > CAESURA
CESURAE > CESURA
CESURAL > CESURA
CESURAS > CESURA
CESURE *same as* > CAESURA
CESURES > CESURE
CETACEAN *n* fish-shaped sea mammal such as a whale or dolphin ▷ *adj* relating to these mammals
CETACEANS > CETACEAN
CETACEOUS *same as* > CETACEAN
CETANE *n* colourless liquid hydrocarbon, used as a solvent
CETANES > CETANE
CETE *n* group of badgers
CETERACH *n* scale-fern
CETERACHS > CETERACH
CETES > CETE
CETOLOGY *n* branch of zoology concerned with the study of whales (cetaceans)
CETRIMIDE *n* quaternary ammonium compound used as a detergent
CETYL *n* univalent alcohol radical
CETYLS > CETYL
CETYWALL *n* valerian
CETYWALLS > CETYWALL
CEVADILLA *same as* > SABADILLA
CEVAPCICI *n* sausages made with beef and paprika
CEVICHE *n* Peruvian seafood dish
CEVICHES > CEVICHE
CEYLANITE *same as* > CEYLONITE
CEYLONITE *n* pleonaste
CH *variant of* > ICH
CHA *n* tea
CHABAZITE *n* pink, white, or colourless zeolite mineral
CHABLIS *n* dry white French wine
CHABOUK *n* type of whip
CHABOUKS > CHABOUK
CHABUK *same as* > CHABOUK
CHABUKS > CHABUK
CHACE *obsolete variant of* > CHASE
CHACED > CHACE
CHACES > CHACE
CHACHKA *n* cheap trinket
CHACHKAS > CHACHKA
CHACING > CHACE
CHACK *vb* to bite
CHACKED > CHACK
CHACKING > CHACK
CHACKS > CHACK
CHACMA *n* baboon, *Papio* (or *Chaeropithecus*) *ursinus*, having coarse greyish hair and occurring in southern and eastern Africa
CHACMAS > CHACMA
CHACO *same as* > SHAKO
CHACOES > CHACO
CHACONNE *n* musical form consisting of a set of variations on a repeated melodic bass line
CHACONNES > CHACONNE
CHACOS > CHACO
CHAD *n* small pieces removed during the punching of holes in punch cards, printer paper, etc
CHADAR *same as* > CHUDDAR
CHADARIM > CHEDER
CHADARS > CHADAR
CHADDAR *same as* > CHUDDAR
CHADDARS > CHADDAR
CHADDOR *same as* > CHUDDAR
CHADDORS > CHADDOR
CHADLESS *adj* (of a keypunch) not producing chads
CHADO *n* Japanese tea ceremony
CHADOR *same as* > CHUDDAR
CHADORS > CHADOR
CHADOS > CHADO
CHADRI *n* shroud which covers the body from head to foot, usually worn by females in Islamic countries
CHADS > CHAD

CHAEBOL *n* large, usually family-owned, business group in South Korea
CHAEBOLS > CHAEBOL
CHAETA *n* any of the chitinous bristles on the body of such annelids as the earthworm and the lugworm: used in locomotion
CHAETAE > CHAETA
CHAETAL > CHAETA
CHAETODON *n* butterfly fish
CHAETOPOD *n* any annelid worm of the classes *Oligochaeta* or *Polychaeta*
CHAFE *vb* make sore or worn by rubbing
CHAFED > CHAFE
CHAFER *n* large beetle
CHAFERS > CHAFER
CHAFES > CHAFE
CHAFF *n* grain husks ▷ *vb* tease good-naturedly
CHAFFED > CHAFF
CHAFFER *vb* haggle
CHAFFERED > CHAFFER
CHAFFERER > CHAFFER
CHAFFERS > CHAFFER
CHAFFERY *n* bargaining
CHAFFIER > CHAFF
CHAFFIEST > CHAFF
CHAFFINCH *n* small European songbird
CHAFFING > CHAFF
CHAFFINGS > CHAFF
CHAFFRON *same as* > CHAMFRON
CHAFFRONS > CHAFFRON
CHAFFS > CHAFF
CHAFFY > CHAFF
CHAFING > CHAFE
CHAFT *n* jaw
CHAFTS > CHAFT
CHAGAN *n* Mongolian royal or imperial title
CHAGANS > CHAGAN
CHAGRIN *n* annoyance and disappointment ▷ *vb* embarrass and annoy
CHAGRINED > CHAGRIN
CHAGRINS > CHAGRIN
CHAI *n* tea, esp as made in India with added spices
CHAIN *n* flexible length of connected metal links ▷ *vb* restrict or fasten with or as if with a chain
CHAINE *adj* (of a dance turn) producing a full rotation for every two steps taken ▷ *vb* produce a full rotation for every two steps taken
CHAINED > CHAIN
CHAINES > CHAINE
CHAINFALL *n* type of hoist
CHAINING > CHAIN
CHAINLESS *adj* having no chain
CHAINLET *n* small chain
CHAINLETS > CHAINLET
CHAINMAN *n* person who does the chaining in a survey
CHAINMEN > CHAINMAN
CHAINS > CHAIN
CHAINSAW *n* motor-driven saw with teeth linked in a continuous chain ▷ *vb* operate a chainsaw
CHAINSAWS > CHAINSAW
CHAINSHOT *n* cannon shot of two balls joined by a chain
CHAINWORK *n* work linked or looped in the manner of a chain
CHAIR *n* seat with a back, for one person ▷ *vb* preside over (a meeting)
CHAIRDAYS *n* old age
CHAIRED > CHAIR
CHAIRING > CHAIR
CHAIRLIFT *n* series of chairs suspended from a moving cable for carrying people up a slope
CHAIRMAN *n* person in charge of a company's board of directors or a meeting ▷ *vb* to act as chairman of
CHAIRMANS > CHAIRMAN
CHAIRMEN > CHAIRMAN
CHAIRS > CHAIR
CHAIS > CHAI
CHAISE *n* light horse-drawn carriage
CHAISES > CHAISE
CHAKALAKA *n* relish made from tomatoes, onions, and spices
CHAKRA *n* (in yoga) any of the seven major energy centres in the body
CHAKRAS > CHAKRA
CHAL *n* in Romany, person or fellow
CHALAH *same as* > CHALLAH
CHALAHS > CHALAH
CHALAN *vb* (in India) to cause an accused person to appear before a magistrate
CHALANED > CHALAN
CHALANING > CHALAN
CHALANS > CHALAN
CHALAZA *n* one of a pair of spiral threads of albumen holding the yolk of a bird's egg in position
CHALAZAE > CHALAZA
CHALAZAL > CHALAZA
CHALAZAS > CHALAZA
CHALAZIA > CHALAZION
CHALAZION *n* small cyst on the eyelid resulting from chronic inflammation of a meibomian gland
CHALCID *n* any tiny hymenopterous insect of the family *Chalcididae* and related families, whose larvae are parasites of other insects
CHALCIDS > CHALCID
CHALCOGEN *n* any of the elements oxygen, sulphur, selenium, tellurium, or polonium, of group 6A of the periodic table
CHALDER *n* former Scottish dry measure
CHALDERS > CHALDER
CHALDRON *n* unit of capacity equal to 36 bushels. Formerly used in the US for the measurement of solids, being equivalent to 1.268 cubic metres. Used in Britain for both solids and liquids, it is equivalent to 1.309 cubic metres
CHALDRONS > CHALDRON
CHALEH *same as* > CHALLAH
CHALEHS > CHALEH
CHALET *n* kind of Swiss wooden house with a steeply sloping roof
CHALETS > CHALET
CHALICE *n* large goblet
CHALICED *adj* (of plants) having cup-shaped flowers
CHALICES > CHALICE
CHALK *n* soft white rock consisting of calcium carbonate ▷ *vb* draw or mark with chalk
CHALKED > CHALK
CHALKFACE *n* work or art of teaching in a school
CHALKIER > CHALK
CHALKIEST > CHALK
CHALKING > CHALK
CHALKLIKE > CHALK
CHALKPIT *n* quarry for chalk
CHALKPITS > CHALKPIT
CHALKS > CHALK
CHALKY > CHALK
CHALLA *same as* > CHALLAH
CHALLAH *n* bread, usually in the form of a plaited loaf, traditionally eaten by Jews to celebrate the Sabbath
CHALLAHS > CHALLAH
CHALLAN *same as* > CHALAN
CHALLANED > CHALLAN
CHALLANS > CHALLAN
CHALLAS > CHALLA
CHALLENGE *n* demanding or stimulating situation ▷ *vb* issue a challenge to
CHALLIE *same as* > CHALLIS
CHALLIES > CHALLIE
CHALLIS *n* lightweight plain-weave fabric of wool, cotton, etc, usually with a printed design
CHALLISES > CHALLIS
CHALLOT > CHALLAH
CHALLOTH > CHALLAH
CHALLY *same as* > CHALLIS
CHALONE *n* any internal secretion that inhibits a physiological process or function
CHALONES > CHALONE
CHALONIC > CHALONE
CHALOT > CHALAH
CHALOTH > CHALAH
CHALS > CHAL
CHALUMEAU *n* early type of reed instrument, precursor of the clarinet
CHALUPA *n* Mexican dish
CHALUPAS > CHALUPA
CHALUTZ *n* member of an organization of immigrants to Israeli agricultural settlements
CHALUTZES > CHALUTZ
CHALUTZIM > CHALUTZ
CHALYBEAN *adj* (of steel) of superior quality
CHALYBITE *another name for* > SIDERITE
CHAM *an archaic word for* > KHAN
CHAMADE *n* (formerly) a signal by drum or trumpet inviting an enemy to a parley
CHAMADES > CHAMADE
CHAMBER *n* hall used for formal meetings ▷ *vb* act lasciviously
CHAMBERED > CHAMBER
CHAMBERER *n* lascivious person
CHAMBERS *pl n* judge's room for hearing private cases not taken in open court
CHAMBRAY *n* smooth light fabric of cotton, linen, etc, with white weft and a coloured warp
CHAMBRAYS > CHAMBRAY
CHAMBRE *adj* (of wine) at room temperature
CHAMELEON *n* small lizard that changes colour to blend in with its surroundings
CHAMELOT *same as* > CAMLET
CHAMELOTS > CHAMELOT
CHAMETZ *n* leavened food which may not be eaten during Passover
CHAMETZES > CHAMETZ
CHAMFER *same as* > CHASE
CHAMFERED > CHAMFER
CHAMFERER > CHAMFER
CHAMFERS > CHAMFER
CHAMFRAIN *same as* > CHAMFRON
CHAMFRON *n* piece of armour for a horse's head
CHAMFRONS > CHAMFRON
CHAMISA *n* American shrub
CHAMISAL *n* place overgrown with chamiso
CHAMISALS > CHAMISAL
CHAMISAS > CHAMISA
CHAMISE *same as* > CHAMISO
CHAMISES > CHAMISE
CHAMISO *n* fourwing saltbush
CHAMISOS > CHAMISO
CHAMLET *same as* > CAMLET
CHAMLETS > CHAMLET
CHAMMIED > CHAMMY
CHAMMIES > CHAMMY

CHAMMY *same as* > CHAMOIS
CHAMMYING > CHAMMY
CHAMOIS *n* small mountain antelope or a pice of leather from its skin, used for polishing ▷ *vb* polish with a chamois
CHAMOISED > CHAMOIS
CHAMOISES > CHAMOIS
CHAMOIX *same as* > CHAMOIS
CHAMOMILE *same as* > CAMOMILE
CHAMP *vb* chew noisily
CHAMPAC *n* magnoliaceous tree, *Michelia champaca*, of India and the East Indies. Its fragrant yellow flowers yield an oil used in perfumes and its wood is used for furniture
CHAMPACA *same as* > CHAMPAC
CHAMPACAS > CHAMPACA
CHAMPACS > CHAMPAC
CHAMPAGNE *n* sparkling white French wine ▷ *adj* denoting a luxurious lifestyle
CHAMPAIGN *n* expanse of open level or gently undulating country
CHAMPAK *same as* > CHAMPAC
CHAMPAKS > CHAMPAK
CHAMPART *n* granting of land to a person, on condition that a portion of the crops will be given to the seller
CHAMPARTS > CHAMPART
CHAMPED > CHAMP
CHAMPER > CHAMP
CHAMPERS *n* champagne
CHAMPERTY *n* (formerly) an illegal bargain between a party to litigation and an outsider whereby the latter agrees to pay for the action and thereby share in any proceeds recovered
CHAMPING > CHAMP
CHAMPION *n* overall winner of a competition ▷ *vb* support ▷ *adj* excellent ▷ *adv* very well
CHAMPIONS > CHAMPION
CHAMPLEVE *adj* of or relating to a process of enamelling by which grooves are cut into a metal base and filled with enamel colours ▷ *n* object enamelled by this process
CHAMPS > CHAMP
CHAMPY *adj* (of earth) churned up (by cattle, for example)
CHAMS > CHAM
CHANCE *n* likelihood, probability ▷ *vb* risk, hazard
CHANCED > CHANCE
CHANCEFUL > CHANCE
CHANCEL *n* part of a church containing the altar and choir
CHANCELS > CHANCEL
CHANCER *n* unscrupulous or dishonest opportunist who is prepared to try any dubious scheme for making money or furthering his own ends
CHANCERS > CHANCER
CHANCERY *n* Lord Chancellor's court, now a division of the High Court of Justice
CHANCES > CHANCE
CHANCEY *same as* > CHANCY
CHANCIER > CHANCY
CHANCIEST > CHANCY
CHANCILY > CHANCY
CHANCING > CHANCE
CHANCRE *n* small hard growth which is the first sign of syphilis
CHANCRES > CHANCRE
CHANCROID *n* soft venereal ulcer, esp of the male genitals, caused by infection with the bacillus *Haemophilus ducreyi* ▷ *adj* relating to or resembling a chancroid or chancre
CHANCROUS > CHANCRE
CHANCY *adj* uncertain, risky
CHANDELLE *n* abrupt climbing turn almost to the point of stalling, in which an aircraft's momentum is used to increase its rate of climb ▷ *vb* carry out a chandelle
CHANDLER *n* dealer, esp in ships' supplies
CHANDLERS > CHANDLER
CHANDLERY *n* business, warehouse, or merchandise of a chandler
CHANFRON *same as* > CHAMFRON
CHANFRONS > CHANFRON
CHANG *n* loud discordant noise
CHANGA *interj* in Indian English, an expression of approval or agreement
CHANGE *n* becoming different ▷ *vb* make or become different
CHANGED > CHANGE
CHANGEFUL *adj* often changing
CHANGER > CHANGE
CHANGERS > CHANGE
CHANGES > CHANGE
CHANGEUP *n* type of baseball pitch
CHANGEUPS > CHANGEUP
CHANGING > CHANGE
CHANGS > CHANG
CHANK *n* shell of several types of sea conch, used to make bracelets
CHANKS > CHANK
CHANNEL *n* band of broadcasting frequencies ▷ *vb* direct or convey through a channel
CHANNELED > CHANNEL
CHANNELER > CHANNEL
CHANNELS > CHANNEL
CHANNER *n* gravel
CHANNERS > CHANNER
CHANOYO *a variant of* > CHADO
CHANOYOS > CHANOYO
CHANOYU *same as* > CHADO
CHANOYUS > CHADO
CHANSON *n* song
CHANSONS > CHANSON
CHANT *vb* utter or sing (a slogan or psalm) ▷ *n* rhythmic or repetitious slogan
CHANTABLE > CHANT
CHANTAGE *n* blackmail
CHANTAGES > CHANTAGE
CHANTED > CHANT
CHANTER *n* (on bagpipes) pipe on which the melody is played
CHANTERS > CHANTER
CHANTEUSE *n* female singer, esp in a nightclub or cabaret
CHANTEY *the usual US spelling of* > SHANTY
CHANTEYS > CHANTEY
CHANTIE *n* chamber pot
CHANTIES > CHANTY
CHANTILLY as in *chantilly lace* delicate ornamental lace
CHANTING > CHANT
CHANTOR *same as* > CHANTER
CHANTORS > CHANTOR
CHANTRESS *n* female chanter
CHANTRIES > CHANTRY
CHANTRY *n* endowment for the singing of Masses for the soul of the founder or others designated by him
CHANTS > CHANT
CHANTY *same as* > SHANTY
CHANUKIAH *a variant spelling of* > HANUKIAH
CHAO *n* Vietnamese rice porridge
CHAOLOGY *n* study of chaos theory
CHAORDIC *adj* combining elements of chaos and order
CHAOS *n* complete disorder or confusion
CHAOSES > CHAOS
CHAOTIC > CHAOS
CHAP *n* man or boy ▷ *vb* (of the skin) to make or become raw and cracked, esp by exposure to cold
CHAPARRAL *n* (in the southwestern US) a dense growth of shrubs and trees, esp evergreen oaks
CHAPATI *n* (in Indian cookery) flat thin unleavened bread
CHAPATIES > CHAPATI
CHAPATIS > CHAPATI
CHAPATTI *same as* > CHAPATI
CHAPATTIS > CHAPATTI
CHAPBOOK *n* book of popular ballads, stories, etc, formerly sold by chapmen or pedlars
CHAPBOOKS > CHAPBOOK
CHAPE *n* metal tip or trimming for a scabbard
CHAPEAU *n* hat
CHAPEAUS > CHAPEAU
CHAPEAUX > CHAPEAU
CHAPEL *n* place of worship with its own altar, within a church
CHAPELESS > CHAPE
CHAPELRY *n* district legally assigned to and served by an Anglican chapel
CHAPELS > CHAPEL
CHAPERON *n* (esp formerly) an older or married woman who accompanies or supervises a young unmarried woman on social occasions ▷ *vb* act as a chaperon to
CHAPERONE *same as* > CHAPERON
CHAPERONS > CHAPERON
CHAPES > CHAPE
CHAPESS *n* woman
CHAPESSES > CHAPESS
CHAPITER *same as* > CAPITAL
CHAPITERS > CHAPITER
CHAPKA *same as* > CZAPKA
CHAPKAS > CHAPKA
CHAPLAIN *n* clergyman attached to a chapel, military body, or institution
CHAPLAINS > CHAPLAIN
CHAPLESS *adj* lacking a lower jaw
CHAPLET *n* garland for the head ▷ *vb* create a garland
CHAPLETED > CHAPLET
CHAPLETS > CHAPLET
CHAPMAN *n* travelling pedlar
CHAPMEN > CHAPMAN
CHAPPAL *n* one of a pair of sandals, usually of leather, worn in India
CHAPPALS > CHAPPAL
CHAPPATI *same as* > CHAPATI
CHAPPATIS > CHAPPATI
CHAPPED > CHAP
CHAPPESS *same as* > CHAPESS
CHAPPIE *n* man or boy
CHAPPIER > CHAPPY
CHAPPIES > CHAPPIE
CHAPPIEST > CHAPPY
CHAPPING > CHAP
CHAPPY *adj* (of skin) chapped
CHAPRASSI *n* in India, during the British Empire, an office messenger
CHAPS > CHAP
CHAPSTICK *n* cylinder of a

substance for preventing or soothing chapped lips
CHAPT *adj* chapped
CHAPTER *n* division of a book ▷ *vb* divide into chapters
CHAPTERAL > CHAPTER
CHAPTERED > CHAPTER
CHAPTERS > CHAPTER
CHAPTREL *n* capital of a pillar supporting an arch
CHAPTRELS > CHAPTREL
CHAQUETA *n* South American cowboy jacket
CHAQUETAS > CHAQUETA
CHAR *vb* blacken by partial burning ▷ *n* charwoman
CHARA *n* type of green freshwater algae
CHARABANC *n* coach for sightseeing
CHARACID *same as* > CHARACIN
CHARACIDS > CHARACIN
CHARACIN *n* any small carnivorous freshwater cyprinoid fish of the family *Characidae*, of Central and South America and Africa. They are similar to the carps but more brightly coloured
CHARACINS > CHARACIN
CHARACT *n* distinctive mark
CHARACTER *n* combination of qualities distinguishing a person, group, or place
CHARACTS > CHARACT
CHARADE *n* absurd pretence
CHARADES *n* game in which one team acts out each syllable of a word or phrase, which the other team has to guess
CHARANGA *n* type of orchestra used in performing traditional Cuban music
CHARANGAS > CHARANGA
CHARANGO *n* Andean ten-stringed mandolin
CHARANGOS > CHARANGO
CHARAS *another name for* > HASHISH
CHARASES > CHARAS
CHARBROIL *vb* to grill over charcoal
CHARCOAL *n* black substance formed by partially burning wood ▷ *adj* very dark grey ▷ *vb* write, draw, or blacken with charcoal
CHARCOALS > CHARCOAL
CHARCOALY > CHARCOAL
CHARD *n* variety of beet, *Beta vulgaris cicla*, with large succulent leaves and thick stalks, used as a vegetable
CHARDS > CHARD
CHARE *same as* > CHAR
CHARED > CHAR
CHARES > CHAR
CHARET *obsolete variant of* > CHARIOT
CHARETS > CHARET
CHARGE *vb* ask as a price ▷ *n* price charged
CHARGED > CHARGE
CHARGEFUL *adj* expensive
CHARGER *n* device for charging an accumulator
CHARGERS > CHARGER
CHARGES > CHARGE
CHARGING > CHARGE
CHARGRILL *vb* to grill over charcoal
CHARIDEE *n* jocular spelling of charity, as pronounced in a mid-Atlantic accent
CHARIDEES > CHARIDEE
CHARIER > CHARY
CHARIEST > CHARY
CHARILY *adv* cautiously
CHARINESS *n* state of being chary
CHARING > CHAR
CHARIOT *n* two-wheeled horse-drawn vehicle used in ancient times in wars and races ▷ *vb* to ride in a chariot
CHARIOTED > CHARIOT
CHARIOTS > CHARIOT
CHARISM *same as* > CHARISMA
CHARISMA *n* person's power to attract or influence people
CHARISMAS > CHARISMA
CHARISMS > CHARISM
CHARITIES > CHARITY
CHARITY *n* organization that gives help, such as money or food, to those in need
CHARIVARI *n* discordant mock serenade to newlyweds, made with pans, kettles, etc ▷ *vb* make such a serenade
CHARK *vb* to char
CHARKA *same as* > CHARKHA
CHARKAS > CHARKA
CHARKED > CHARK
CHARKHA *n* (in India) a spinning wheel, esp for cotton
CHARKHAS > CHARKHA
CHARKING > CHARK
CHARKS > CHARK
CHARLADY *same as* > CHARWOMAN
CHARLATAN *n* person who claims expertise that he or she does not have
CHARLEY as in *charley horse* muscle stiffness after strenuous exercise
CHARLEYS > CHARLEY
CHARLIE *n* fool
CHARLIER as in *charlier shoe* special light horseshoe
CHARLIES > CHARLIE
CHARLOCK *n* weed with hairy leaves and yellow flowers
CHARLOCKS > CHARLOCK
CHARLOTTE *n* dessert made with fruit and bread or cake crumbs
CHARM *n* attractive quality ▷ *vb* attract, delight
CHARMED *adj* delighted or fascinated
CHARMER *n* attractive person
CHARMERS > CHARMER
CHARMEUSE *n* trademark for a lightweight fabric with a satin-like finish
CHARMFUL *adj* highly charming or enchanting
CHARMING *adj* attractive
CHARMLESS *adj* devoid of charm
CHARMONIA *pl n* elementary particles containing an antiquark and a charm quark
CHARMS > CHARM
CHARNECO *n* type of sweet wine
CHARNECOS > CHARNECO
CHARNEL *adj* ghastly ▷ *n* ghastly thing
CHARNELS > CHARNEL
CHAROSET *n* dish of chopped fruit, nuts and wine, eaten at Passover
CHAROSETH *same as* > CHAROSET
CHAROSETS > CHAROSET
CHARPAI *same as* > CHARPOY
CHARPAIS > CHARPAI
CHARPIE *n* lint pieces used to make surgical dressings
CHARPIES > CHARPIE
CHARPOY *n* bedstead of woven webbing or hemp stretched on a wooden frame on four legs, common in India
CHARPOYS > CHARPOY
CHARQUI *n* meat, esp beef, cut into strips and dried
CHARQUID > CHARQUI
CHARQUIS > CHARQUI
CHARR *same as* > CHAR
CHARRED > CHAR
CHARRIER > CHARRY
CHARRIEST > CHARRY
CHARRING > CHAR
CHARRO *n* Mexican cowboy
CHARROS > CHARRO
CHARRS > CHARR
CHARRY *adj* of or relating to charcoal
CHARS > CHAR
CHART *n* graph, table, or diagram showing information ▷ *vb* plot the course of
CHARTA *n* charter
CHARTABLE > CHART
CHARTAS > CHARTA
CHARTED > CHART
CHARTER *n* document granting or demanding certain rights ▷ *vb* hire by charter
CHARTERED *adj* officially qualified to practise a profession
CHARTERER > CHARTER
CHARTERS > CHARTER
CHARTING > CHART
CHARTISM *n* historical reform movement in Britain
CHARTISMS > CHARTISM
CHARTIST *n* supporter of chartism
CHARTISTS > CHARTIST
CHARTLESS *adj* not mapped
CHARTS > CHART
CHARVER *n* derogatory term for a young woman
CHARVERS > CHARVER
CHARWOMAN *n* woman whose job is to clean other people's homes
CHARWOMEN > CHARWOMAN
CHARY *adj* wary, careful
CHAS > CHA
CHASE *vb* run after quickly in order to catch or drive away ▷ *n* chasing, pursuit
CHASEABLE > CHASE
CHASED > CHASE
CHASEPORT *n* porthole through which a chase gun is fired
CHASER *n* milder drink drunk after another stronger one
CHASERS > CHASER
CHASES > CHASE
CHASING > CHASE
CHASINGS > CHASE
CHASM *n* deep crack in the earth ▷ *vb* create a chasm
CHASMAL > CHASM
CHASMED > CHASM
CHASMIC > CHASM
CHASMIER > CHASMY
CHASMIEST > CHASMY
CHASMS > CHASM
CHASMY *adj* full of chasms
CHASSE *n* one of a series of gliding steps in ballet in which the same foot always leads ▷ *vb* perform either of these steps
CHASSED > CHASSE
CHASSEED > CHASSE
CHASSEING > CHASSE
CHASSEPOT *n* breech-loading bolt-action rifle formerly used by the French Army
CHASSES > CHASSE
CHASSEUR *n* member of a unit specially trained and equipped for swift deployment ▷ *adj* designating or cooked in a sauce consisting of white wine and mushrooms
CHASSEURS > CHASSEUR
CHASSIS *n* frame, wheels, and mechanical parts of a

vehicle
CHASTE *adj* abstaining from sex outside marriage or altogether
CHASTELY > CHASTE
CHASTEN *vb* subdue by criticism
CHASTENED > CHASTEN
CHASTENER > CHASTEN
CHASTENS > CHASTEN
CHASTER > CHASTE
CHASTEST > CHASTE
CHASTISE *vb* scold severely
CHASTISED > CHASTISE
CHASTISER > CHASTISE
CHASTISES > CHASTISE
CHASTITY *n* state of being chaste
CHASUBLE *n* long sleeveless robe worn by a priest when celebrating Mass
CHASUBLES > CHASUBLE
CHAT *n* informal conversation ▷ *vb* have an informal conversation
CHATBOT *n* computer program in the form of a virtual e-mail correspondent that can reply to messages from computer users
CHATBOTS > CHATBOT
CHATCHKA *variant of* > TCHOTCHKE
CHATCHKAS > CHATCHKA
CHATCHKE *same as* > TCHOTCHKE
CHATCHKES > CHATCHKE
CHATEAU *n* French castle
CHATEAUS > CHATEAU
CHATEAUX > CHATEAU
CHATELAIN *same as* > CASTELLAN
CHATLINE *n* telephone service enabling callers to join in general conversation with each other
CHATLINES > CHATLINE
CHATON *n* in jewellery, a stone with a reflective metal foil backing
CHATONS > CHATON
CHATOYANT *adj* having changeable lustre ▷ *n* gemstone with a changeable lustre
CHATROOM *n* site on the Internet where users have group discussions by e-mail
CHATROOMS > CHATROOM
CHATS > CHAT
CHATTA *n* umbrella
CHATTAS > CHATTA
CHATTED > CHAT
CHATTEL *n* item of movable personal property
CHATTELS > CHATTEL
CHATTER *vb* speak quickly and continuously about unimportant things ▷ *n* idle talk
CHATTERED > CHATTER
CHATTERER *same as* > COTINGA
CHATTERS > CHATTER
CHATTERY > CHATTER
CHATTI *n* (in India) an earthenware pot
CHATTIER > CHATTY
CHATTIES > CHATTI
CHATTIEST > CHATTY
CHATTILY > CHATTY
CHATTING > CHAT
CHATTIS > CHATTI
CHATTY *adj* (of a person) fond of friendly, informal conversation
CHAUFE *obsolete variant of* > CHAFE
CHAUFED > CHAUFE
CHAUFER *same as* > CHAUFFER
CHAUFERS > CHAUFER
CHAUFES > CHAUFE
CHAUFF *obsolete variant of* > CHAFE
CHAUFFED > CHAUFF
CHAUFFER *n* small portable heater or stove
CHAUFFERS > CHAUFFER
CHAUFFEUR *n* person employed to drive a car for someone ▷ *vb* act as driver for (someone)
CHAUFFING > CHAUFF
CHAUFFS > CHAUFF
CHAUFING > CHAUFE
CHAUMER *n* chamber
CHAUMERS > CHAUMER
CHAUNCE *archaic variant of* > CHANCE
CHAUNCED > CHAUNCE
CHAUNCES > CHAUNCE
CHAUNCING > CHAUNCE
CHAUNGE *archaic variant of* > CHANGE
CHAUNGED > CHAUNGE
CHAUNGES > CHAUNGE
CHAUNGING > CHAUNGE
CHAUNT *a less common variant of* > CHANT
CHAUNTED > CHAUNT
CHAUNTER > CHAUNT
CHAUNTERS > CHAUNT
CHAUNTING > CHAUNT
CHAUNTRY *same as* > CHANTRY
CHAUNTS > CHAUNT
CHAUSSES *n* tight-fitting medieval garment covering the feet and legs, usually made of chain mail
CHAUSSURE *n* any type of footwear
CHAUVIN *n* chauvinist
CHAUVINS > CHAUVIN
CHAV *n* informal derogatory word for a young working-class person who wears casual sports clothes
CHAVE *vb* old dialect term for "I have"
CHAVENDER *n* chub
CHAVETTE *n* informal derogatory word for a young working-class female who wears casual sports clothes
CHAVETTES > CHAVETTE
CHAVISH > CHAV
CHAVS > CHAV
CHAW *vb* chew (tobacco), esp without swallowing it ▷ *n* something chewed, esp a plug of tobacco
CHAWBACON *n* bumpkin
CHAWDRON *n* entrails
CHAWDRONS > CHAWDRON
CHAWED > CHAW
CHAWER > CHAW
CHAWERS > CHAW
CHAWING > CHAW
CHAWK *n* jackdaw
CHAWKS > CHAWK
CHAWS > CHAW
CHAY *n* plant of the madder family
CHAYA *same as* > CHAY
CHAYAS > CHAYA
CHAYOTE *n* tropical American cucurbitaceous climbing plant, *Sechium edule*, that has edible pear-shaped fruit enclosing a single enormous seed
CHAYOTES > CHAYOTE
CHAYROOT *n* root of the chay plant
CHAYROOTS > CHAYROOT
CHAYS > CHAY
CHAZAN *same as* > CANTOR
CHAZANIM > CHAZAN
CHAZANS > CHAZAN
CHAZZAN *variant of* > CHAZAN
CHAZZANIM > CHAZZAN
CHAZZANS > CHAZZAN
CHAZZEN *same as* > CHAZZAN
CHAZZENIM > CHAZZEN
CHAZZENS > CHAZZEN
CHE *pron* dialectal form meaning "I"
CHEAP *adj* costing relatively little ▷ *adv* at very little cost ▷ *n* bargain ▷ *vb* take the cheapest option
CHEAPED > CHEAP
CHEAPEN *vb* lower the reputation of
CHEAPENED > CHEAPEN
CHEAPENER > CHEAPEN
CHEAPENS > CHEAPEN
CHEAPER > CHEAP
CHEAPEST > CHEAP
CHEAPIE *n* something inexpensive
CHEAPIES > CHEAPIE
CHEAPING > CHEAP
CHEAPISH > CHEAP
CHEAPJACK *n* person who sells cheap and shoddy goods ▷ *adj* shoddy or inferior
CHEAPLY > CHEAP
CHEAPNESS > CHEAP
CHEAPO *n* very cheap and possibly shoddy thing
CHEAPOS > CHEAPO
CHEAPS > CHEAP
CHEAPY *same as* > CHEAPIE
CHEAT *vb* act dishonestly to gain profit or advantage ▷ *n* person who cheats
CHEATABLE > CHEAT
CHEATED > CHEAT
CHEATER > CHEAT
CHEATERS > CHEAT
CHEATERY *n* cheating
CHEATING > CHEAT
CHEATINGS > CHEAT
CHEATS > CHEAT
CHEBEC *n* type of boat
CHEBECS > CHEBEC
CHECHAKO *same as* > CHEECHAKO
CHECHAKOS > CHECHAKO
CHECHAQUO *same as* > CHEECHAKO
CHECHIA *n* Berber skullcap
CHECHIAS > CHECHIA
CHECK *vb* examine or investigate ▷ *n* control designed to ensure accuracy
CHECKABLE > CHECK
CHECKBOOK *n* American word for chequebook
CHECKED > CHECK
CHECKER *same as* > CHEQUER
CHECKERED *same as* > CHEQUERED
CHECKERS *n* game for two players using a checkerboard and 12 checkers each. The object is to jump over and capture the opponent's pieces
CHECKING > CHECK
CHECKLESS *adj* without check or restraint
CHECKLIST *vb* check items, facts, etc, against those in a list used for verification
CHECKMARK *vb* make a mark of approval or verification
CHECKMATE *n* winning position in which an opponent's king is under attack and unable to escape ▷ *vb* place the king of (one's opponent) in checkmate ▷ *interj* call made when placing an opponent's king in checkmate
CHECKOFF *n* procedure where an employer pays the employee's union dues straight from his or her salary
CHECKOFFS > CHECKOFF
CHECKOUT *n* counter in a supermarket, where customers pay
CHECKOUTS > CHECKOUT
CHECKRAIL *another word for* > GUARDRAIL
CHECKREIN *n* bearing rein
CHECKROOM *n* place at a railway station, airport, etc, where luggage may

be left for a small charge with an attendant for safekeeping
CHECKROW *n* row of plants, esp corn, in which the spaces between adjacent plants are equal to those between adjacent rows to facilitate cultivation ▷ *vb* plant in checkrows
CHECKROWS > CHECKROW
CHECKS > CHECK
CHECKSUM *n* digit representing the number of bits of information transmitted, attached to the end of a message, to verify the integrity of data
CHECKSUMS > CHECKSUM
CHECKUP *n* thorough medical examination ▷ *vb* investigate or make an inquiry into (a person's character, evidence, etc), esp when suspicions have been aroused
CHECKUPS > CHECKUP
CHECKY *adj* having squares of alternating tinctures or furs
CHEDDAR *n* type of smooth hard yellow or whitish cheese
CHEDDARS > CHEDDAR
CHEDDARY > CHEDDAR
CHEDDITE *n* explosive made by mixing a powdered chlorate or perchlorate with a fatty substance, such as castor oil
CHEDDITES > CHEDDITE
CHEDER *n* (in Western countries) elementary religious education classes, usually outside normal school hours
CHEDERS > CHEDER
CHEDITE *same as* > CHEDDITE
CHEDITES > CHEDITE
CHEECHAKO *n* local name for a newcomer to Alaska
CHEEK *n* either side of the face below the eye ▷ *vb* speak impudently to
CHEEKBONE *n* bone at the top of the cheek, just below the eye
CHEEKED > CHEEK
CHEEKFUL *n* quantity that can be held in a cheek
CHEEKFULS > CHEEKFUL
CHEEKIER > CHEEKY
CHEEKIEST > CHEEKY
CHEEKILY > CHEEKY
CHEEKING > CHEEK
CHEEKLESS > CHEEK
CHEEKS > CHEEK
CHEEKY *adj* impudent, disrespectful
CHEEP *n* young bird's high-pitched cry ▷ *vb* utter a cheep
CHEEPED > CHEEP
CHEEPER > CHEEP
CHEEPERS > CHEEP
CHEEPING > CHEEP
CHEEPS > CHEEP
CHEER *vb* applaud or encourage with shouts ▷ *n* shout of applause or encouragement
CHEERED > CHEER
CHEERER > CHEER
CHEERERS > CHEER
CHEERFUL *adj* having a happy disposition
CHEERIER > CHEERY
CHEERIEST > CHEERY
CHEERILY > CHEERY
CHEERING > CHEER
CHEERIO *interj* goodbye ▷ *n* small red cocktail sausage ▷ *sentence substitute* farewell greeting
CHEERIOS > CHEERIO
CHEERLEAD *vb* to lead a crowd in formal cheers at sports events
CHEERLED > CHEERLEAD
CHEERLESS *adj* dreary, gloomy
CHEERLY *adv* cheerful or cheerfully
CHEERO *same as* > CHEERIO
CHEEROS > CHEERO
CHEERS *interj* drinking toast ▷ *sentence substitute* drinking toast
CHEERY *adj* cheerful
CHEESE *n* food made from coagulated milk curd ▷ *vb* stop
CHEESED > CHEESE
CHEESES > CHEESE
CHEESEVAT *n* in cheesemaking, vat in which curds are formed and cut
CHEESIER > CHEESY
CHEESIEST > CHEESY
CHEESILY > CHEESY
CHEESING > CHEESE
CHEESY *adj* like cheese
CHEETAH *n* large fast-running spotted African wild cat
CHEETAHS > CHEETAH
CHEEWINK *same as* > CHEWINK
CHEEWINKS > CHEEWINK
CHEF *n* cook in a restaurant ▷ *vb* to work as a chef
CHEFDOM *n* state or condition of being a chef
CHEFDOMS > CHEFDOM
CHEFED > CHEF
CHEFFED > CHEF
CHEFFING > CHEF
CHEFING > CHEF
CHEFS > CHEF
CHEGOE *same as* > CHIGGER
CHEGOES > CHIGGER
CHEILITIS *n* inflammation of the lip(s)
CHEKA *n* secret police set up in Russia in 1917
CHEKAS > CHEKA
CHEKIST *n* member of the cheka
CHEKISTS > CHEKIST
CHELA *n* disciple of a religious teacher
CHELAE > CHELA
CHELAS > CHELA
CHELASHIP > CHELA
CHELATE *n* coordination compound in which a metal atom or ion is bound to a ligand at two or more points on the ligand, so as to form a heterocyclic ring containing a metal atom ▷ *adj* of or possessing chelae ▷ *vb* form a chelate
CHELATED > CHELATE
CHELATES > CHELATE
CHELATING > CHELATE
CHELATION *n* process by which a chelate is formed
CHELATOR > CHELATE
CHELATORS > CHELATE
CHELICERA *n* one of a pair of appendages on the head of spiders and other arachnids: often modified as food-catching claws
CHELIFORM *adj* shaped like a chela
CHELIPED *n* (on a arthropod) either of two legs which each carry a claw
CHELIPEDS > CHELIPED
CHELLUP *n* noise
CHELLUPS > CHELLUP
CHELOID *a variant spelling of* > KELOID
CHELOIDAL > CHELOID
CHELOIDS > CHELOID
CHELONE *n* any plant of the hardy N American genus *Chelone*, grown for its white, rose, or purple flower spikes: family *Scrophulariaceae*
CHELONES > CHELONE
CHELONIAN *n* any reptile of the order *Chelonia*, including the tortoises and turtles, in which most of the body is enclosed in a protective bony capsule ▷ *adj* of, relating to, or belonging to the *Chelonia*
CHELP *vb* (esp of women or children) to chatter or speak out of turn
CHELPED > CHELP
CHELPING > CHELP
CHELPS > CHELP
CHEMIC *vb* to bleach ▷ *n* chemist
CHEMICAL *n* substance used in or resulting from a reaction involving changes to atoms or molecules ▷ *adj* of chemistry or chemicals
CHEMICALS > CHEMICAL
CHEMICKED > CHEMIC
CHEMICS > CHEMIC
CHEMISE *n* woman's loose-fitting slip
CHEMISES > CHEMISE
CHEMISM *n* chemical action
CHEMISMS > CHEMISM
CHEMISORB *vb* take up (a substance) by chemisorption
CHEMIST *n* shop selling medicines and cosmetics
CHEMISTRY *n* science of the composition, properties, and reactions of substances
CHEMISTS > CHEMIST
CHEMITYPE *n* process by which a relief impression is obtained from an engraving
CHEMITYPY > CHEMITYPE
CHEMMIES > CHEMMY
CHEMMY *n* gambling card game
CHEMO *n* short form of chemotherapy
CHEMOKINE *n* type of protein
CHEMOS > CHEMO
CHEMOSORB *same as* > CHEMISORB
CHEMOSTAT *n* apparatus for growing bacterial cultures at a constant rate by controlling the supply of nutrient medium
CHEMPADUK *n* evergreen moraceous tree, *Artocarpus champeden* (or *A. integer*), of Malaysia, similar to the jackfruit
CHEMURGIC > CHEMURGY
CHEMURGY *n* branch of chemistry concerned with the industrial use of organic raw materials, esp materials of agricultural origin
CHENAR *n* oriental plane tree
CHENARS > CHENAR
CHENET *another word for* > GENIP
CHENETS > CHENET
CHENILLE *n* (fabric of) thick tufty yarn
CHENILLES > CHENILLE
CHENIX *n* ancient measure slightly more than a quart
CHENIXES > CHENIX
CHENOPOD *n* any flowering plant of the family *Chenopodiaceae*, which includes the beet, mangel-wurzel, spinach, and goosefoot
CHENOPODS > CHENOPOD
CHEONGSAM *n* straight dress, usually of silk or cotton, with a stand-up collar and a slit in one side of the skirt, worn by Chinese women
CHEQUE *n* written order to

one's bank to pay money from one's account

CHEQUER *n* piece used in Chinese chequers ▷ *vb* make irregular in colour or character

CHEQUERED *adj* marked by varied fortunes

CHEQUERS *n* game of draughts

CHEQUES > CHEQUE

CHEQUING as in *chequing account* (in Canada) account against which cheques can be drawn

CHEQUY *same as* > CHECKY

CHER *adj* dear or expensive

CHERALITE *n* rare phosphate-silicate of Thorium and Calcium

CHERE *feminine variant of* > CHER

CHERIMOYA *n* large tropical fruit with custardlike flesh

CHERISH *vb* cling to (an idea or feeling)

CHERISHED > CHERISH

CHERISHER > CHERISH

CHERISHES > CHERISH

CHERNOZEM *n* black soil, rich in humus and carbonates, in cool or temperate semiarid regions, as the grasslands of Russia

CHEROOT *n* cigar with both ends cut flat

CHEROOTS > CHEROOT

CHERRIED > CHERRY

CHERRIER > CHERRY

CHERRIES > CHERRY

CHERRIEST > CHERRY

CHERRY *n* small red or black fruit with a stone ▷ *adj* deep red ▷ *vb* to cheer

CHERRYING > CHERRY

CHERT *n* microcrystalline form of silica usually occurring as bands or layers of pebbles in sedimentary rock. Formula: SiO_2. Varieties include flint, lyddite (Lydian stone)

CHERTIER > CHERT

CHERTIEST > CHERT

CHERTS > CHERT

CHERTY > CHERT

CHERUB *n* angel, often represented as a winged child

CHERUBIC > CHERUB

CHERUBIM > CHERUB

CHERUBIMS > CHERUB

CHERUBIN *n* cherub ▷ *adj* cherubic

CHERUBINS > CHERUBIN

CHERUBS > CHERUB

CHERUP *same as* > CHIRRUP

CHERUPED > CHERUP

CHERUPING > CHERUP

CHERUPS > CHERUP

CHERVIL *n* aniseed-flavoured herb

CHERVILS > CHERVIL

CHESHIRE *n* breed of American pig

CHESHIRES > CHESHIRE

CHESIL *n* gravel or shingle

CHESILS > CHESIL

CHESNUT *rare variant of* > CHESTNUT

CHESNUTS > CHESNUT

CHESS *n* game for two players with 16 pieces each, played on a chequered board of 64 squares

CHESSEL *n* mould used in cheese-making

CHESSELS > CHESSEL

CHESSES > CHESS

CHESSMAN *n* piece used in chess

CHESSMEN > CHESSMAN

CHEST *n* front of the body, from neck to waist ▷ *vb* to hit with the chest, as with a ball in football

CHESTED > CHEST

CHESTFUL *n* amount a chest will hold

CHESTFULS > CHESTFUL

CHESTIER > CHESTY

CHESTIEST > CHESTY

CHESTILY > CHESTY

CHESTING > CHEST

CHESTNUT *n* reddish-brown edible nut ▷ *adj* (of hair or a horse) reddish-brown

CHESTNUTS > CHESTNUT

CHESTS > CHEST

CHESTY *adj* symptomatic of chest disease

CHETAH *same as* > CHEETAH

CHETAHS > CHETAH

CHETH *same as* > HETH

CHETHS > CHETH

CHETNIK *n* member of a Serbian nationalist paramilitary group

CHETNIKS > CHETNIK

CHETRUM *n* monetary unit in Bhutan

CHETRUMS > CHETRUM

CHEVAL as in *cheval glass* full-length mirror that can swivel

CHEVALET *n* bridge of a stringed musical instrument

CHEVALETS > CHEVALET

CHEVALIER *n* member of the French Legion of Honour

CHEVELURE *n* nebulous part of the tail of a comet

CHEVEN *n* chub

CHEVENS > CHEVEN

CHEVEREL *n* kid or goatskin leather

CHEVERELS > CHEVEREL

CHEVERIL *same as* > CHEVEREL

CHEVERILS > CHEVERIL

CHEVERON *same as* > CHEVRON

CHEVERONS > CHEVERON

CHEVERYE *same as* > CHIEFERY

CHEVERYES > CHEVERYE

CHEVET *n* semicircular or polygonal east end of a church, esp a French Gothic church, often with a number of attached apses

CHEVETS > CHEVET

CHEVIED > CHEVY

CHEVIES > CHEVY

CHEVILLE *n* peg of a stringed musical instrument

CHEVILLES > CHEVILLE

CHEVIN *same as* > CHEVEN

CHEVINS > CHEVIN

CHEVIOT *n* type of British sheep reared for its wool

CHEVIOTS > CHEVIOT

CHEVRE *n* any cheese made from goats' milk

CHEVRES > CHEVRE

CHEVRET *n* type of goats' cheese

CHEVRETS > CHEVRET

CHEVRETTE *n* skin of a young goat

CHEVRON *n* V-shaped pattern, esp on the sleeve of a military uniform to indicate rank ▷ *vb* make a chevron

CHEVRONED > CHEVRON

CHEVRONS > CHEVRON

CHEVRONY *adj* in heraldry, bearing chevrons

CHEVY *same as* > CHIVY

CHEVYING > CHEVY

CHEW *vb* grind (food) between the teeth ▷ *n* act of chewing

CHEWABLE > CHEW

CHEWED > CHEW

CHEWER > CHEW

CHEWERS > CHEW

CHEWET *n* type of meat pie

CHEWETS > CHEWET

CHEWIE *n* chewing gum

CHEWIER > CHEWY

CHEWIES > CHEWY

CHEWIEST > CHEWY

CHEWINESS > CHEWY

CHEWING > CHEW

CHEWINK *n* towhee

CHEWINKS > CHEWINK

CHEWS > CHEW

CHEWY *adj* requiring a lot of chewing ▷ *n* dog's rubber toy

CHEZ *prep* at the home of

CHI *n* 22nd letter of the Greek alphabet, a consonant, transliterated as *ch* or rarely *kh*

CHIA *n* plant of the mint family

CHIACK *vb* tease or banter ▷ *n* good-humoured banter

CHIACKED > CHIACK

CHIACKING > CHIACK

CHIACKS > CHIACK

CHIANTI *n* dry red Italian wine

CHIANTIS > CHIANT

CHIAO *n* Chinese coin equal to one tenth of one yuan

CHIAREZZA *n* (in music) clarity

CHIAREZZE > CHIAREZZA

CHIAS > CHIA

CHIASM *same as* > CHIASMA

CHIASMA *n* cross-shaped connection produced by the crossing over of pairing chromosomes during meiosis

CHIASMAL > CHIASMA

CHIASMAS > CHIASMA

CHIASMATA > CHIASMA

CHIASMI > CHIASMUS

CHIASMIC > CHIASMA

CHIASMS > CHIASMA

CHIASMUS *n* reversal of the order of words in the second of two parallel phrases

CHIASTIC > CHIASMUS

CHIAUS *same as* > CHOUSE

CHIAUSED > CHIAUS

CHIAUSES > CHIAUS

CHIAUSING > CHIAUS

CHIB *vb* in Scots English, stab or slash with a sharp weapon ▷ *n* sharp weapon

CHIBBED > CHIB

CHIBBING > CHIB

CHIBOL *n* spring onion

CHIBOLS > CHIBOL

CHIBOUK *n* Turkish tobacco pipe with an extremely long stem

CHIBOUKS > CHIBOUK

CHIBOUQUE *same as* > CHIBOUK

CHIBS > CHIB

CHIC *adj* stylish, elegant ▷ *n* stylishness, elegance

CHICA *n* Spanish young girl

CHICALOTE *n* poppy, *Argemone platyceras*, of the southwestern US and Mexico with prickly leaves and white or yellow flowers

CHICANA *n* female chicano

CHICANAS > CHICANA

CHICANE *n* obstacle in a motor-racing circuit ▷ *vb* deceive or trick by chicanery

CHICANED > CHICANE

CHICANER > CHICANE

CHICANERS > CHICANE

CHICANERY *n* trickery, deception

CHICANES > CHICANE

CHICANING > CHICANE

CHICANO *n* American citizen of Mexican origin

CHICANOS > CHICANO

CHICAS > CHICA

CHICCORY *a variant spelling of* > CHICORY

CHICER > CHIC

CHICEST > CHIC
CHICH *another word for* > CHICKPEA
CHICHA *n* Andean drink made from fermented maize
CHICHAS > CHICHA
CHICHES > CHICKPEA
CHICHI *adj* affectedly pretty or stylish ▷ *n* quality of being affectedly pretty or stylish
CHICHIER > CHICHI
CHICHIEST > CHICHI
CHICHIS > CHICHI
CHICK *n* baby bird
CHICKADEE *n* small N American songbird
CHICKAREE *n* American red squirrel
CHICKEE *n* opensided, thatched building on stilts
CHICKEES > CHICKEE
CHICKEN *n* domestic fowl ▷ *adj* cowardly ▷ *vb* to lose one's nerve
CHICKENED > CHICKEN
CHICKENS > CHICKEN
CHICKLING *n* small chick
CHICKORY *same as* > CHICORY
CHICKPEA *n* edible yellow pealike seed
CHICKPEAS > CHICKPEA
CHICKS > CHICK
CHICKWEED *n* weed with small white flowers
CHICLE *n* gumlike substance obtained from the sapodilla
CHICLES > CHICLE
CHICLY > CHIC
CHICNESS > CHIC
CHICO *n* spiny chenopodiaceous shrub
CHICON *same as* > CHICORY
CHICONS > CHICON
CHICORIES > CHICORY
CHICORY *n* plant whose leaves are used in salads
CHICOS > CHICO
CHICS > CHIC
CHID > CHIDE
CHIDDEN > CHIDE
CHIDE *vb* rebuke, scold
CHIDED > CHIDE
CHIDER > CHIDE
CHIDERS > CHIDE
CHIDES > CHIDE
CHIDING > CHIDE
CHIDINGLY > CHIDE
CHIDINGS > CHIDE
CHIDLINGS *n* intestines of a pig prepared as a dish
CHIEF *n* head of a group of people ▷ *adj* most important
CHIEFDOM *n* any tribal social group led by a chief
CHIEFDOMS > CHIEFDOM
CHIEFER > CHIEF
CHIEFERY *n* lands belonging to a chief
CHIEFESS *n* female chief
CHIEFEST > CHIEF
CHIEFLESS *adj* lacking a chief
CHIEFLING *n* petty chief
CHIEFLY *adv* especially ▷ *adj* of or relating to a chief or chieftain
CHIEFRIES > CHIEFRY
CHIEFRY *same as* > CHIEFERY
CHIEFS > CHIEF
CHIEFSHIP *n* state of being a chief
CHIEFTAIN *n* leader of a tribe
CHIEL *n* young man
CHIELD *same as* > CHIEL
CHIELDS > CHIEL
CHIELS > CHIEL
CHIFFON *n* fine see-through fabric ▷ *adj* made of chiffon
CHIFFONS > CHIFFON
CHIFFONY > CHIFFON
CHIGETAI *n* variety of the Asiatic wild ass, *Equus hemionus*, of Mongolia
CHIGETAIS > CHIGETAI
CHIGGA *n* informal Australian derogatory word for a young working-class person from Hobart, Tasmania
CHIGGAS > CHIGGA
CHIGGER *n* parasitic larva of any of various free-living mites of the family *Trombidiidae*, which causes intense itching of human skin
CHIGGERS > CHIGGER
CHIGNON *n* knot of hair pinned up at the back of the head ▷ *vb* make a chignon
CHIGNONED > CHIGNON
CHIGNONS > CHIGNON
CHIGOE *same as* > CHIGGER
CHIGOES > CHIGOE
CHIGRE *same as* > CHIGGER
CHIGRES > CHIGRE
CHIHUAHUA *n* tiny short-haired dog
CHIK *n* slatted blind
CHIKARA *n* Indian seven-stringed musical instrument
CHIKARAS > CHIKARA
CHIKHOR *same as* > CHUKAR
CHIKHORS > CHIKHOR
CHIKOR *same as* > CHUKAR
CHIKORS > CHIKOR
CHIKS > CHIK
CHILBLAIN *n* inflammation of the fingers or toes, caused by exposure to cold
CHILD *n* young human being, boy or girl ▷ *vb* to give birth
CHILDBED *n* condition of giving birth to a child
CHILDBEDS > CHILDBED
CHILDCARE *n* care provided for children without homes (or with a seriously disturbed home life) by a local authority
CHILDE *n* young man of noble birth
CHILDED > CHILD
CHILDER *dialect variant of* > CHILDREN
CHILDES > CHILDE
CHILDHOOD *n* time or condition of being a child
CHILDING > CHILD
CHILDISH *adj* immature, silly
CHILDLESS > CHILD
CHILDLIER > CHILD
CHILDLIKE *adj* innocent, trustful
CHILDLY > CHILD
CHILDNESS *n* nature of a child
CHILDREN > CHILD
CHILDS > CHILD
CHILE *a variant spelling of* > CHILLI
CHILES > CHILE
CHILI *same as* > CHILLI
CHILIAD *n* group of one thousand
CHILIADAL > CHILIAD
CHILIADIC > CHILIAD
CHILIADS > CHILIAD
CHILIAGON *n* thousand-sided polygon
CHILIARCH *n* commander of a thousand men
CHILIASM *n* belief in the Second Coming of Christ
CHILIASMS > CHILIASM
CHILIAST > CHILIASM
CHILIASTS > CHILIASM
CHILIDOG *n* hot dog served with chilli sauce
CHILIDOGS > CHILIDOG
CHILIES > CHILI
CHILIOI *n* thousand
CHILIOIS > CHILIOI
CHILIS > CHILI
CHILL *n* feverish cold ▷ *vb* make (something) cool or cold ▷ *adj* unpleasantly cold
CHILLADA *n* spicy Mexican dish made of fried vegetables and pulses
CHILLADAS > CHILLADA
CHILLED > CHILL
CHILLER *n* cooling or refrigerating device
CHILLERS > CHILLER
CHILLEST > CHILL
CHILLI *n* small red or green hot-tasting capsicum pod, used in cooking
CHILLIER > CHILLY
CHILLIES > CHILLI
CHILLIEST > CHILLY
CHILLILY > CHILLY
CHILLING > CHILL
CHILLINGS > CHILL
CHILLIS > CHILLI
CHILLNESS > CHILL
CHILLS > CHILL
CHILLUM *n* short pipe, usually of clay, used esp for smoking cannabis
CHILLUMS > CHILLUM
CHILLY *adj* moderately cold
CHILOPOD *n* any arthropod of the class *Chilopoda*, which includes the centipedes
CHILOPODS > CHILOPOD
CHILTEPIN *n* variety of chilli pepper
CHIMAERA *same as* > CHIMERA
CHIMAERAS > CHIMAERA
CHIMAERIC > CHIMAERA
CHIMAR *same as* > CHIMERE
CHIMARS > CHIMAR
CHIMB *same as* > CHIME
CHIMBLEY *same as* > CHIMNEY
CHIMBLEYS > CHIMBLEY
CHIMBLIES > CHIMBLY
CHIMBLY *same as* > CHIMNEY
CHIMBS > CHIME
CHIME *n* musical ringing sound of a bell or clock ▷ *vb* make a musical ringing sound
CHIMED > CHIME
CHIMER > CHIME
CHIMERA *n* unrealistic hope or idea
CHIMERAS > CHIMERA
CHIMERE *n* sleeveless red or black gown, part of a bishop's formal dress though not a vestment
CHIMERES > CHIMERE
CHIMERIC > CHIMERA
CHIMERID *n* fish of the genus Chimaera
CHIMERIDS > CHIMERID
CHIMERISM *n* medical condition in which a person possesses two genetically distinct sets of cells
CHIMERS > CHIME
CHIMES > CHIME
CHIMING > CHIME
CHIMLA *same as* > CHIMNEY
CHIMLAS > CHIMLA
CHIMLEY *same as* > CHIMNEY
CHIMLEYS > CHIMLEY
CHIMNEY *n* hollow vertical structure for carrying away smoke from a fire ▷ *vb* to climb two vertical, parallel, chimney-like rock faces
CHIMNEYED > CHIMNEY
CHIMNEYS > CHIMNEY
CHIMO *interj* Inuit greeting and toast
CHIMP *n* chimpanzee
CHIMPS > CHIMP
CHIN *n* part of the face below the mouth ▷ *vb* hit someone in the chin
CHINA *n* fine earthenware or porcelain
CHINAMAN *n* in cricket, a

ball bowled by a left-handed bowler to a right-handed batsman that spins from off to leg
CHINAMEN >CHINAMAN
CHINAMPA *n* in Mesoamerican agriculture, an artificially created island used for growing crops
CHINAMPAS >CHINAMPA
CHINAR *same as* >CHINAR
CHINAROOT *n* bristly greenbrier
CHINARS >CHENAR
CHINAS >CHINA
CHINAWARE *n* articles made of china, esp those made for domestic use
CHINBONE *n* front part of the mandible which forms the chin
CHINBONES >CHINBONE
CHINCAPIN *n* dwarf chestnut tree
CHINCH *another name for a* >BEDBUG
CHINCHES >CHINCH
CHINCHIER >CHINCHY
CHINCHY *adj* tightfisted
CHINCOUGH *n* whooping cough
CHINDIT *n* Allied soldier fighting behind the Japanese lines in Burma during World War II
CHINDITS >CHINDIT
CHINE *same as* >CHIME
CHINED >CHINE
CHINES >CHINE
CHINESE *adj* of or relating to China
CHINING >CHINE
CHINK *n* small narrow opening ▷*vb* make a light ringing sound
CHINKAPIN *same as* >CHINCAPIN
CHINKARA *n* Indian gazelle
CHINKARAS >CHINKARA
CHINKED >CHINK
CHINKIE *n* offensive term for a (takeaway) meal of Chinese food
CHINKIER >CHINK
CHINKIES >CHINKIE
CHINKIEST >CHINK
CHINKING >CHINK
CHINKS >CHINK
CHINKY >CHINK
CHINLESS *adj* having a receding chin
CHINNED >CHIN
CHINNING >CHIN
CHINO *n* durable cotton twill cloth
CHINONE *n* benzoquinone
CHINONES >CHINONE
CHINOOK *n* warm dry southwesterly wind blowing down the eastern slopes of the Rocky Mountains
CHINOOKS >CHINOOK
CHINOS *pl n* trousers made of a kind of hard-wearing cotton
CHINOVNIK *n* Russian official or bureaucrat
CHINS >CHIN
CHINSTRAP *n* strap on a helmet which fastens under the chin
CHINTS *obsolete variant of* >CHINTZ
CHINTSES >CHINTS
CHINTZ *n* printed cotton fabric with a glazed finish
CHINTZES >CHINTZ
CHINTZIER >CHINTZY
CHINTZY *adj* of or covered with chintz
CHINWAG *n* chat
CHINWAGS >CHINWAG
CHIP *n* strip of potato, fried in deep fat ▷*vb* break small pieces from
CHIPBOARD *n* thin board made of compressed wood particles
CHIPMUCK *another word for* >CHIPMUCK
CHIPMUCKS >CHIPMUK
CHIPMUNK *n* small squirrel-like N American rodent with a striped back
CHIPMUNKS >CHIPMUNK
CHIPOCHIA *same as* >CAPOCCHIA
CHIPOLATA *n* small sausage
CHIPOTLE *n* dried chilli pepper
CHIPOTLES >CHIPOTLE
CHIPPABLE >CHIP
CHIPPED >CHIP
CHIPPER *vb* chirp or chatter
CHIPPERED >CHIPPER
CHIPPERS >CHIPPER
CHIPPIE *same as* >CHIPPY
CHIPPIER >CHIPPY
CHIPPIES >CHIPPY
CHIPPIEST >CHIPPY
CHIPPING >CHIP
CHIPPINGS >CHIP
CHIPPY *n* fish-and-chip shop ▷*adj* resentful or oversensitive about being perceived as inferior
CHIPS >CHIP
CHIPSET *n* highly integrated circuit on the motherboard of a computer that controls many of its data transfer functions
CHIPSETS >CHIPSET
CHIRAGRA *n* gout occurring in the hands
CHIRAGRAS >CHIRAGRA
CHIRAGRIC >CHIRAGRA
CHIRAL >CHIRALITY
CHIRALITY *n* configuration or handedness (left or right) of an asymmetric, optically active chemical compound
CHIRIMOYA *same as* >CHERIMOYA
CHIRK *vb* to creak, like a door ▷*adj* spritely; high-spirited
CHIRKED >CHIRK
CHIRKER >CHIRK
CHIRKEST >CHIRK
CHIRKING >CHIRK
CHIRKS >CHIRK
CHIRL *vb* to warble
CHIRLED >CHIRL
CHIRLING >CHIRL
CHIRLS >CHIRL
CHIRM *n* chirping of birds ▷*vb* (esp of a bird) to chirp
CHIRMED >CHIRM
CHIRMING >CHIRM
CHIRMS >CHIRM
CHIRO *n* an informal name for chiropractor
CHIROLOGY *n* palmistry
CHIRONOMY *n* art of hand movement in oratory or theatrical performance
CHIROPODY *n* treatment of the feet, esp the treatment of corns, verrucas, etc
CHIROPTER *n* type of bat
CHIROS >CHIRO
CHIRP *vb* (of a bird or insect) make a short high-pitched sound ▷*n* chirping sound
CHIRPED >CHIRP
CHIRPER >CHIRP
CHIRPERS >CHIRP
CHIRPIER >CHIRPY
CHIRPIEST >CHIRPY
CHIRPILY >CHIRPY
CHIRPING >CHIRP
CHIRPS >CHIRP
CHIRPY *adj* lively and cheerful
CHIRR *vb* (esp of certain insects, such as crickets) to make a shrill trilled sound ▷*n* sound of chirring
CHIRRE *same as* >CHIRR
CHIRRED >CHIRR
CHIRREN *n* dialect form of children
CHIRRES >CHIRRE
CHIRRING >CHIRR
CHIRRS >CHIRR
CHIRRUP *vb* (of some birds) to chirp repeatedly ▷*n* chirruping sound
CHIRRUPED >CHIRRUP
CHIRRUPER >CHIRRUP
CHIRRUPS >CHIRRUP
CHIRRUPY >CHIRRUP
CHIRT *vb* to squirt
CHIRTED >CHIRT
CHIRTING >CHIRT
CHIRTS >CHIRT
CHIRU *n* Tibetan antelope, *Pantholops hodgsoni*, having a dense woolly pinkish-brown fleece prized as the source of shahtoosh wool: now close to extinction due to illegal slaughter for its fleece
CHIRUS >CHIRU
CHIS >CHI
CHISEL *n* metal tool with a sharp end for shaping wood or stone ▷*vb* carve or form with a chisel
CHISELED *same as* >CHISELLED
CHISELER >CHISEL
CHISELERS >CHISEL
CHISELING >CHISEL
CHISELLED *adj* finely or sharply formed
CHISELLER *n* person who uses a chisel
CHISELS >CHISEL
CHIT *n* short official note, such as a receipt ▷*vb* to sprout
CHITAL *n* type of deer
CHITALS >CHITAL
CHITCHAT *n* chat, gossip ▷*vb* gossip
CHITCHATS >CHITCHAT
CHITIN *n* tough substance forming the outer layer of the bodies of arthropods
CHITINOID >CHITIN
CHITINOUS >CHITIN
CHITINS >CHITIN
CHITLIN >CHITLINS
CHITLING >CHITLINGS
CHITLINGS *same as* >CHIDLINGS
CHITLINS *same as* >CHITTERLINGS
CHITON *n* (in ancient Greece and Rome) a loose woollen tunic worn knee length by men and full length by women
CHITONS >CHITON
CHITOSAN *n* polysaccharide derived from chitin
CHITOSANS >CHITOSAN
CHITS >CHIT
CHITTED >CHIT
CHITTER *vb* twitter or chirp
CHITTERED >CHITTER
CHITTERS >CHITTER
CHITTIER >CHIT
CHITTIES >CHITTY
CHITTIEST >CHIT
CHITTING >CHIT
CHITTY *same as* >CHIT *adj* childish
CHIV *n* knife ▷*vb* stab (someone)
CHIVALRIC >CHIVALRY
CHIVALRY *n* courteous behaviour, esp by men towards women
CHIVAREE *same as* >CHARIVARI *vb* to perform a chivaree
CHIVAREED >CHIVAREE
CHIVAREES >CHIVAREE
CHIVARI *same as* >CHARIVARI
CHIVARIED >CHIVARI
CHIVARIES >CHIVARI

CHIVE *n* small Eurasian purple-flowered alliaceous plant, *Allium schoenoprasum*, whose long slender hollow leaves are used in cooking to flavour soups, stews, etc ▷ *vb* file or cut off
CHIVED > CHIVE
CHIVES *same as* > CHIVE
CHIVIED > CHIVY
CHIVIES > CHIVY
CHIVING > CHIVE
CHIVS > CHIV
CHIVVED > CHIV
CHIVVIED > CHIVVY
CHIVVIES > CHIVVY
CHIVVING > CHIV
CHIVVY *same as* > CHIVY
CHIVVYING > CHIVVY
CHIVY *vb* harass or nag ▷ *n* hunt
CHIVYING > CHIVY
CHIYOGAMI *n* type of highly decorated Japanese craft paper
CHIZ *n* cheat ▷ *vb* cheat
CHIZZ *same as* > CHIZ
CHIZZED > CHIZ
CHIZZES > CHIZ
CHIZZING > CHIZ
CHLAMYDES > CHLAMYS
CHLAMYDIA *n* any Gram-negative bacteria of the genus *Chlamydia*, responsible for some sexually transmitted diseases
CHLAMYS *n* woollen cloak worn by ancient Greek soldiers
CHLAMYSES > CHLAMYS
CHLOASMA *n* appearance on a person's skin, esp of the face, of patches of darker colour: associated with hormonal changes caused by liver disease or the use of oral contraceptives
CHLOASMAS > CHLOASMA
CHLORACNE *n* disfiguring skin disease that results from contact with or ingestion or inhalation of certain chlorinated aromatic hydrocarbons
CHLORAL *n* colourless oily liquid with a pungent odour, made from chlorine and acetaldehyde and used in preparing chloral hydrate and DDT
CHLORALS > CHLORAL
CHLORATE *n* type of chemical salt
CHLORATES > CHLORATE
CHLORDAN *same as* > CHLORDANE
CHLORDANE *n* white insoluble toxic solid
CHLORDANS > CHLORDAN
CHLORELLA *n* any microscopic unicellular green alga of the genus *Chlorella:* some species are used in the preparation of human food
CHLORIC *adj* of or containing chlorine in the pentavalent state
CHLORID *n* type of chlorine compound
CHLORIDE *n* compound of chlorine and another substance
CHLORIDES > CHLORIDE
CHLORIDIC > CHLORIDE
CHLORIDS > CHLORID
CHLORIN *same as* > CHLORINE
CHLORINE *n* strong-smelling greenish-yellow gaseous element, used to disinfect water
CHLORINES > CHLORINE
CHLORINS > CHLORIN
CHLORITE *n* any of a group of green soft secondary minerals consisting of the hydrated silicates of aluminium, iron, and magnesium in monoclinic crystalline form: common in metamorphic rocks
CHLORITES > CHLORITE
CHLORITIC > CHLORITE
CHLOROSES > CHLOROSIS
CHLOROSIS *n* disorder, formerly common in adolescent girls, characterized by pale greenish-yellow skin, weakness, and palpitation and caused by insufficient iron in the body
CHLOROTIC > CHLOROSIS
CHLOROUS *adj* of or containing chlorine in the trivalent state
CHOANA *n* posterior nasal aperture
CHOANAE > CHOANA
CHOBDAR *n* in India and Nepal, king's macebearer or attendant
CHOBDARS > CHOBDAR
CHOC *short form of* > CHOCOLATE
CHOCCIER > CHOCCY
CHOCCIES > CHOCCY
CHOCCIEST > CHOCCY
CHOCCY *n* chocolate ▷ *adj* made of, tasting of, smelling of, or resembling chocolate
CHOCHO *same as* > CHAYOTE
CHOCHOS > CHOCHO
CHOCK *n* block or wedge used to prevent a heavy object from moving ▷ *vb* secure by a chock ▷ *adv* as closely or tightly as possible
CHOCKED > CHOCK
CHOCKER *adj* full up
CHOCKFUL *adj* filled to capacity
CHOCKFULL *variant of* > CHOCKFUL
CHOCKING > CHOCK
CHOCKO *same as* > CHOCO
CHOCKOS > CHOCKO
CHOCKS > CHOCK
CHOCO *n* member of the Australian army
CHOCOLATE *n* sweet food made from cacao seeds ▷ *adj* dark brown
CHOCOLATY > CHOCOLATE
CHOCOS > CHOCO
CHOCS > CHOC
CHOCTAW *n* turn from the inside edge of one skate to the outside edge of the other or vice versa
CHOCTAWS > CHOCTAW
CHODE > CHIDE
CHOENIX *same as* > CHENIX
CHOENIXES > CHOENIX
CHOG *n* core of a piece of fruit
CHOGS > CHOG
CHOICE *n* choosing ▷ *adj* of high quality
CHOICEFUL *adj* fickle
CHOICELY > CHOICE
CHOICER > CHOICE
CHOICES > CHOICE
CHOICEST > CHOICE
CHOIR *n* organized group of singers, esp in church ▷ *vb* to sing in chorus
CHOIRBOY *n* boy who sings in a church choir
CHOIRBOYS > CHOIRBOY
CHOIRED > CHOIR
CHOIRGIRL *n* girl who sings in a choir
CHOIRING > CHOIR
CHOIRLIKE > CHOIR
CHOIRMAN *n* man who sings in a choir
CHOIRMEN > CHOIRMAN
CHOIRS > CHOIR
CHOKE *vb* hinder or stop the breathing of (a person) by strangling or smothering ▷ *n* device controlling the amount of air that is mixed with the fuel in a petrol engine
CHOKEABLE > CHOKE
CHOKEBORE *n* shotgun bore that becomes narrower towards the muzzle so that the shot is not scattered
CHOKECOIL *n* type of electronic inductor
CHOKED *adj* disappointed or angry
CHOKEDAMP *another word for* > BLACKDAMP
CHOKEHOLD *n* act of holding a person's neck across the windpipe, esp from behind
CHOKER *n* tight-fitting necklace
CHOKERS > CHOKER
CHOKES > CHOKE
CHOKEY *n* a slang word for prison ▷ *adj* involving, caused by, or causing choking
CHOKEYS > CHOKEY
CHOKIDAR *n* in India, a gatekeeper
CHOKIDARS > CHOKIDAR
CHOKIER > CHOKEY
CHOKIES > CHOKEY
CHOKIEST > CHOKEY
CHOKING > CHOKE
CHOKINGLY > CHOKE
CHOKO *n* pear-shaped fruit of a tropical American vine, eaten as a vegetable
CHOKOS > CHOKO
CHOKRA *n* in India, a boy or young man
CHOKRAS > CHOKRA
CHOKRI *n* in India, a girl or young woman
CHOKRIS > CHOKRI
CHOKY *same as* > CHOKEY
CHOLA *n* Hispanic girl
CHOLAEMIA *n* toxic medical condition indicated by the presence of bile in the blood
CHOLAEMIC > CHOLAEMIA
CHOLAS > CHOLA
CHOLATE *n* salt of cholic acid
CHOLATES > CHOLATE
CHOLECYST *n* gall bladder
CHOLELITH *n* gallstone
CHOLEMIA *same as* > CHOLAEMIA
CHOLEMIAS > CHOLEMIA
CHOLENT *n* meal usually consisting of a stew of meat, potatoes, and pulses prepared before the Sabbath on Friday and left to cook until eaten for Sabbath lunch
CHOLENTS > CHOLENT
CHOLER *n* bad temper
CHOLERA *n* serious infectious disease causing severe vomiting and diarrhoea
CHOLERAIC > CHOLERA
CHOLERAS > CHOLERA
CHOLERIC *adj* bad-tempered
CHOLEROID > CHOLERA
CHOLERS > CHOLER
CHOLI *n* short-sleeved bodice, as worn by Indian women
CHOLIAMB *n* imperfect iambic trimeter, with a spondee as the last foot
CHOLIAMBS > CHOLIAMB
CHOLIC as in *cholic acid* crystalline acid found in bile
CHOLINE *n* colourless viscous soluble alkaline substance present in animal tissues, esp as a constituent of lecithin: used as a supplement to the diet of poultry and in medicine for preventing

the accumulation of fat in the liver
CHOLINES > CHOLINE
CHOLIS > CHOLI
CHOLLA *n* any of several spiny cacti of the genus *Opuntia* that grow in the southwestern US and Mexico and have cylindrical stem segments
CHOLLAS > CHOLLA
CHOLLERS *pl n* jowls or cheeks
CHOLO *n* chicano gangster
CHOLOS > CHOLO
CHOLTRIES > CHOLTRY
CHOLTRY *n* caravanserai
CHOMA *same as* > CHOMMIE
CHOMAS > CHOMA
CHOMETZ *same as* > CHAMETZ
CHOMETZES > CHOMETZ
CHOMMIE *n* (in informal South African English) friend
CHOMMIES > CHOMMIE
CHOMP *vb* chew noisily ▷ *n* act or sound of chewing in this manner
CHOMPED > CHOMP
CHOMPER > CHOMP
CHOMPERS > CHOMP
CHOMPING > CHOMP
CHOMPS > CHOMP
CHON *n* North and South Korean monetary unit worth one hundredth of a won
CHONDRAL *adj* of or relating to cartilage
CHONDRE *another word for* > CHONDRULE
CHONDRES > CHONDRE
CHONDRI > CHONDRUS
CHONDRIFY *vb* become or convert into cartilage
CHONDRIN *n* resilient translucent bluish-white substance that forms the matrix of cartilage
CHONDRINS > CHONDRIN
CHONDRITE *n* stony meteorite consisting mainly of silicate minerals in the form of chondrules
CHONDROID *adj* resembling cartilage
CHONDROMA *n* benign cartilaginous growth or neoplasm
CHONDRULE *n* one of the small spherical masses of mainly silicate minerals present in chondrites
CHONDRUS *n* cartilage
CHONS > CHON
CHOOF *vb* go away
CHOOFED > CHOOF
CHOOFING > CHOOF
CHOOFS > CHOOF
CHOOK *n* hen or chicken ▷ *vb* make the sound of a hen of chicken
CHOOKED > CHOOK
CHOOKIE *same as* > CHOOK
CHOOKIES > CHOOK
CHOOKING > CHOOK
CHOOKS > CHOOK
CHOOM *n* Englishman
CHOOMS > CHOOM
CHOOSE *vb* select from a number of alternatives
CHOOSER > CHOOSE
CHOOSERS > CHOOSE
CHOOSES > CHOOSE
CHOOSEY *same as* > CHOOSY
CHOOSIER > CHOOSY
CHOOSIEST > CHOOSY
CHOOSING > CHOOSE
CHOOSY *adj* fussy, hard to please
CHOP *vb* cut with a blow from an axe or knife ▷ *n* cutting or sharp blow
CHOPHOUSE *n* restaurant specializing in steaks, grills, chops, etc
CHOPIN *same as* > CHOPINE
CHOPINE *n* sandal-like shoe on tall wooden or cork bases popular in the 18th century
CHOPINES > CHOPINE
CHOPINS > CHOPIN
CHOPLOGIC *n* person who uses excessively subtle or involved logic
CHOPPED > CHOP
CHOPPER *n* helicopter ▷ *vb* travel by helicopter
CHOPPERED > CHOPPER
CHOPPERS > CHOPPER
CHOPPIER > CHOPPY
CHOPPIEST > CHOPPY
CHOPPILY > CHOPPY
CHOPPING > CHOP
CHOPPINGS > CHOP
CHOPPY *adj* (of the sea) fairly rough
CHOPS > CHOP
CHOPSOCKY *n* genre of martial arts film
CHOPSTICK *n* one of a pair of thin sticks used as eating utensils
CHORAGI > CHORAGUS
CHORAGIC > CHORAGUS
CHORAGUS *n* leader of a chorus
CHORAL *adj* of a choir
CHORALE *n* slow stately hymn tune
CHORALES > CHORALE
CHORALIST *n* singer or composer of chorals
CHORALLY > CHORAL
CHORALS > CHORAL
CHORD *n* straight line joining two points on a curve ▷ *vb* provide (a melodic line) with chords
CHORDA *n* in anatomy, a cord
CHORDAE > CHORDA
CHORDAL > CHORD
CHORDATE *n* any animal that has a long fibrous rod just above the gut to support the body, such as the vertebrates ▷ *adj* of, relating to, or belonging to the *Chordata*
CHORDATES > CHORDATE
CHORDED > CHORD
CHORDEE *n* painful penile erection, a symptom of gonorrhoea
CHORDEES > CHORDEE
CHORDING *n* distribution of chords throughout a piece of harmony
CHORDINGS > CHORDING
CHORDS > CHORD
CHORDWISE *adv* in the direction of an aerofoil chord ▷ *adj* moving in this direction
CHORE *n* routine task ▷ *vb* to carry out chores
CHOREA *n* disorder of the nervous system characterized by uncontrollable brief jerky movements
CHOREAL > CHOREA
CHOREAS > CHOREA
CHOREATIC > CHOREA
CHORED > CHORE
CHOREE *n* trochee
CHOREES > CHOREE
CHOREGI > CHOREGUS
CHOREGIC > CHOREGUS
CHOREGUS *n* in ancient Greece, the producer/ financier of a dramatist's works
CHOREIC > CHOREA
CHOREMAN *n* handyman
CHOREMEN > CHOREMAN
CHOREOID *adj* resembling chorea
CHORES > CHORE
CHOREUS *same as* > CHOREE
CHOREUSES > CHOREUS
CHORIA > CHORION
CHORIAL > CHORION
CHORIAMB *n* metrical foot used in classical verse consisting of four syllables, two short ones between two long ones
CHORIAMBI > CHORIAMB
CHORIAMBS > CHORIAMB
CHORIC *adj* of, like, for, or in the manner of a chorus, esp of singing, dancing, or the speaking of verse
CHORINE *n* chorus girl
CHORINES > CHORINE
CHORING > CHORE
CHORIOID *same as* > CHOROID
CHORIOIDS > CHORIOID
CHORION *n* outer of two membranes that form a sac around the embryonic reptile, bird, or mammal
CHORIONIC > CHORION
CHORIONS > CHORION
CHORISES > CHORISIS
CHORISIS *n* multiplication of leaves etc by branching or splitting
CHORISM > CHORISIS
CHORISMS > CHORISIS
CHORIST *n* choir member
CHORISTER *n* singer in a choir
CHORISTS > CHORIST
CHORIZO *n* kind of highly seasoned pork sausage of Spain or Mexico
CHORIZONT *n* person who challenges the authorship of a work
CHORIZOS > CHORIZO
CHOROID *adj* resembling the chorion, esp in being vascular ▷ *n* brownish vascular membrane of the eyeball between the sclera and the retina
CHOROIDAL > CHOROID
CHOROIDS > CHOROID
CHOROLOGY *n* study of the causal relations between geographical phenomena occurring within a particular region
CHORRIE *n* dilapidated old car
CHORRIES > CHORRIE
CHORTEN *n* Buddhist shrine
CHORTENS > CHORTEN
CHORTLE *vb* chuckle in amusement ▷ *n* amused chuckle
CHORTLED > CHORTLE
CHORTLER > CHORTLE
CHORTLERS > CHORTLE
CHORTLES > CHORTLE
CHORTLING > CHORTLE
CHORUS *n* large choir ▷ *vb* sing or say together
CHORUSED > CHORUS
CHORUSES > CHORUS
CHORUSING > CHORUS
CHORUSSED > CHORUS
CHORUSSES > CHORUS
CHOSE > CHOOSE
CHOSEN > CHOOSE
CHOSES > CHOOSE
CHOTA *adj* (in British Empire Indian usage) small
CHOTT *a variant spelling of* > SHOTT
CHOTTS > CHOTT
CHOU *n* type of cabbage
CHOUGH *n* large black Eurasian and N African bird of the crow family
CHOUGHS > CHOUGH
CHOULTRY *same as* > CHOLTRY
CHOUNTER *same as* > CHUNTER
CHOUNTERS > CHOUNTER
CHOUSE *vb* to cheat
CHOUSED > CHOUSE
CHOUSER > CHOUSE
CHOUSERS > CHOUSE
CHOUSES > CHOUSE
CHOUSH *n* Turkish messenger
CHOUSHES > CHOUSH
CHOUSING > CHOUSE

CHOUT *n* blackmail
CHOUTS > CHOUT
CHOUX > CHOU
CHOW *n* thick-coated dog with a curled tail, orig. from China ▷ *vb* eat
CHOWCHOW *same as* > CHOW
CHOWCHOWS > CHOWCHOW
CHOWDER *n* thick soup containing clams or fish ▷ *vb* to make a chowder of
CHOWDERED > CHOWDER
CHOWDERS > CHOWDER
CHOWED > CHOW
CHOWHOUND *n* person who loves eating
CHOWING > CHOW
CHOWK *n* marketplace or market area
CHOWKIDAR *same as* > CHOKIDAR
CHOWKS > CHOWK
CHOWRI *n* fly-whisk
CHOWRIES > CHOWRI
CHOWRIS > CHOWRI
CHOWRY *same as* > CHOWRI
CHOWS > CHOW
CHOWSE *same as* > CHOUSE
CHOWSED > CHOWSE
CHOWSES > CHOWSE
CHOWSING > CHOWSE
CHOWTIME *n* mealtime
CHOWTIMES > CHOWTIME
CHRESARD *n* amount of water present in the soil that is available to plants
CHRESARDS > CHRESARD
CHRISM *n* consecrated oil used for anointing in some churches
CHRISMA > CHRISMON
CHRISMAL *n* chrism container
CHRISMALS > CHRISMAL
CHRISMON *n* monogram and symbol of Christ's name
CHRISMONS > CHRISMON
CHRISMS > CHRISM
CHRISOM *same as* > CHRISM
CHRISOMS > CHRISOM
CHRISTEN *vb* baptize
CHRISTENS > CHRISTEN
CHRISTIAN *adj* exhibiting kindness or goodness
CHRISTIE *same as* > CHRISTY
CHRISTIES > CHRISTIE
CHRISTOM *same as* > CHRISOM
CHRISTOMS > CHRISTOM
CHRISTY *n* skiing turn for stopping or changing direction quickly
CHROMA *n* attribute of a colour that enables an observer to judge how much chromatic colour it contains irrespective of achromatic colour present
CHROMAKEY *n* (in colour television) a special effect in which a coloured background can be eliminated and a different background substituted
CHROMAS > CHROMA
CHROMATE *n* any salt or ester of chromic acid
CHROMATES > CHROMATE
CHROMATIC *adj* of colour or colours
CHROMATID *n* either of the two strands into which a chromosome divides during mitosis. They separate to form daughter chromosomes at anaphase
CHROMATIN *n* part of the nucleus of a cell that forms the chromosomes and can easily be dyed
CHROME *n* anything plated with chromium ▷ *vb* plate with chromium ▷ *vb* to chromium-plate ▷ *adj* of or having the appearance of chrome
CHROMED > CHROME
CHROMEL *n* nickel-based alloy containing about 10 per cent chromium, used in heating elements
CHROMELS > CHROMEL
CHROMENE *n* chemical compound
CHROMENES > CHROMENE
CHROMES > CHROME
CHROMIC *adj* of or containing chromium in the trivalent state
CHROMIDE *n* any member of the cichlid family of fish
CHROMIDES > CHROMIDE
CHROMIDIA *n* chromatins in cell cytoplasm
CHROMIER > CHROME
CHROMIEST > CHROMY
CHROMING > CHROME
CHROMINGS > CHROME
CHROMISE *same as* > CHROMIZE
CHROMISED > CHROMISE
CHROMISES > CHROMISE
CHROMITE *n* brownish-black mineral which is the only commercial source of chromium
CHROMITES > CHROMITE
CHROMIUM *n* grey metallic element used in steel alloys and for electroplating
CHROMIUMS > CHROMIUM
CHROMIZE *vb* chrome-plate
CHROMIZED > CHROMIZE
CHROMIZES > CHROMIZE
CHROMO *n* picture produced by the process of making coloured prints by lithography
CHROMOGEN *n* compound that forms coloured compounds on oxidation
CHROMOS > CHROMO
CHROMOUS *adj* of or containing chromium in the divalent state
CHROMY > CHROME
CHROMYL *n* of, consisting of, or containing the divalent radical CrO_2
CHROMYLS > CHROMYL
CHRONAXIE *n* minimum time required for excitation of a nerve or muscle when the stimulus is double the minimum (threshold) necessary to elicit a basic response
CHRONAXY *same as* > CHRONAXIE
CHRONIC *adj* (of an illness) lasting a long time ▷ *n* chronically-ill patient
CHRONICAL > CHRONIC
CHRONICLE *n* record of events in order of occurrence ▷ *vb* record in or as if in a chronicle
CHRONICS > CHRONIC
CHRONON *n* unit of time equal to the time that a photon would take to traverse the diameter of an electron: about 10^{-24} seconds
CHRONONS > CHRONON
CHRYSALID *adj* of or relating to a chrysalis
CHRYSALIS *n* insect in the stage between larva and adult, when it is in a cocoon
CHRYSANTH *n* chrysanthemum
CHTHONIAN *adj* of or relating to the underworld
CHTHONIC *same as* > CHTHONIAN
CHUB *n* European freshwater fish of the carp family
CHUBASCO *n* in Mexico, a hurricane
CHUBASCOS > CHUBASCO
CHUBBIER > CHUBBY
CHUBBIEST > CHUBBY
CHUBBILY > CHUBBY
CHUBBY *adj* plump and round
CHUBS > CHUB
CHUCK *vb* throw ▷ *n* cut of beef from the neck to the shoulder
CHUCKED > CHUCK
CHUCKER *n* person who throws something
CHUCKERS > CHUCKER
CHUCKHOLE *n* pothole
CHUCKIE *n* small stone
CHUCKIES > CHUCKIE
CHUCKING > CHUCK
CHUCKLE *vb* laugh softly ▷ *n* soft laugh
CHUCKLED > CHUCKLE
CHUCKLER > CHUCKLE
CHUCKLERS > CHUCKLE
CHUCKLES > CHUCKLE
CHUCKLING > CHUCKLE
CHUCKS > CHUCK
CHUCKY *same as* > CHUCKIE
CHUDDAH *same as* > CHUDDAR
CHUDDAHS > CHUDDAH
CHUDDAR *n* large shawl or veil worn by Muslim or Hindu women that covers them from head to foot
CHUDDARS > CHUDDAR
CHUDDER *same as* > CHUDDAR
CHUDDERS > CHUDDER
CHUDDIES *pl n* underpants
CHUDDY *n* chewing gum
CHUFA *n* sedge, *Cyperus esculentus*, of warm regions of the Old World, with nutlike edible tubers
CHUFAS > CHUFA
CHUFF *vb* (of a steam engine) move while making a puffing sound ▷ *n* puffing sound of or as if of a steam engine ▷ *adj* boorish
CHUFFED *adj* very pleased
CHUFFER > CHUFF
CHUFFEST > CHUFF
CHUFFIER > CHUFFY
CHUFFIEST > CHUFFY
CHUFFING > CHUFF
CHUFFS > CHUFF
CHUFFY *adj* boorish and surly
CHUG *n* short dull sound like the noise of an engine ▷ *vb* operate or move with this sound
CHUGALUG *vb* to gulp down a drink in one go
CHUGALUGS > CHUGALUG
CHUGGED > CHUG
CHUGGER > CHUG
CHUGGERS > CHUG
CHUGGING > CHUG
CHUGS > CHUG
CHUKAR *n* common Indian partridge, *Alectoris chukar* (or *graeca*), having red legs and bill and a black-barred sandy plumage
CHUKARS > CHUKAR
CHUKKA *n* period of play in polo
CHUKKAR *same as* > CHUKKA
CHUKKARS > CHUKKAR
CHUKKAS > CHUKKA
CHUKKER *same as* > CHUKKA
CHUKKERS > CHUKKER
CHUKOR *same as* > CHUKAR
CHUKORS > CHUKOR
CHUM *n* close friend ▷ *vb* be or become an intimate friend (of)
CHUMASH *n* printed book containing one of the Five Books of Moses
CHUMASHES > CHUMASH
CHUMLEY *same as* > CHIMNEY
CHUMLEYS > CHUMLEY
CHUMMAGE *n* formerly, fee paid by a prisoner for sole occupancy of a cell
CHUMMAGES > CHUMMAGE

CHUMMED > CHUM
CHUMMIER > CHUMMY
CHUMMIES > CHUMMY
CHUMMIEST > CHUMMY
CHUMMILY > CHUMMY
CHUMMING > CHUM
CHUMMY *adj* friendly ▷ *n* chum
CHUMP *n* stupid person ▷ *vb* chew noisily
CHUMPED > CHUMP
CHUMPING *n* collecting wood for bonfires on Guy Fawkes Day
CHUMPINGS > CHUMPING
CHUMPS > CHUMP
CHUMS > CHUM
CHUMSHIP *n* friendship
CHUMSHIPS > CHUMSHIP
CHUNDER *vb* vomit ▷ *n* vomit
CHUNDERED > CHUNDER
CHUNDERS > CHUNDER
CHUNK *n* thick solid piece ▷ *vb* to break up into chunks
CHUNKED > CHUNK
CHUNKIER > CHUNKY
CHUNKIEST > CHUNKY
CHUNKILY > CHUNKY
CHUNKING *n* grouping together of a number of items by the mind, after which they can be remembered as a single item, such as a word or a musical phrase
CHUNKINGS > CHUNKING
CHUNKS > CHUNK
CHUNKY *adj* (of a person) broad and heavy
CHUNNEL *n* rail tunnel beneath the English Channel, linking England and France
CHUNNELS > CHUNNEL
CHUNNER *same as* > CHUNTER
CHUNNERED > CHUNNER
CHUNNERS > CHUNNER
CHUNTER *vb* mutter or grumble incessantly in a meaningless fashion
CHUNTERED > CHUNTER
CHUNTERS > CHUNTER
CHUPATI *same as* > CHUPATTI
CHUPATIS > CHUPATI
CHUPATTI *variant spellings of* > CHAPATI
CHUPATTIS > CHUPATTI
CHUPATTY *same as* > CHUPATTI
CHUPPA *variant of* > CHUPPAH
CHUPPAH *n* canopy under which a marriage is performed
CHUPPAHS > CHUPPAH
CHUPPAS > CHUPPA
CHUPRASSY *same as* > CHAPRASSI
CHURCH *n* building for public Christian worship ▷ *vb* bring (someone, esp a woman after childbirth) to church for special ceremonies
CHURCHED > CHURCH
CHURCHES > CHURCH
CHURCHIER > CHURCHY
CHURCHING > CHURCH
CHURCHISM *n* adherence to the principles of an established church
CHURCHLY *adj* appropriate to, associated with, or suggestive of church life and customs
CHURCHMAN *n* clergyman
CHURCHMEN > CHURCHMAN
CHURCHWAY *n* way or road that leads to a church
CHURCHY *adj* like a church, church service, etc
CHURIDAR as in *churidar pyjamas* long tight-fitting trousers, worn by Indian men and women
CHURIDARS > CHURIDAR
CHURINGA *n* sacred amulet of the native Australians
CHURINGAS > CHURINGA
CHURL *n* surly ill-bred person
CHURLISH *adj* surly and rude
CHURLS > CHURL
CHURN *n* machine in which cream is shaken to make butter ▷ *vb* stir (cream) vigorously to make butter
CHURNED > CHURN
CHURNER > CHURN
CHURNERS > CHURN
CHURNING *n* quantity of butter churned at any one time
CHURNINGS > CHURNING
CHURNMILK *n* buttermilk
CHURNS > CHURN
CHURR *same as* > CHIRR
CHURRED > CHURR
CHURRING > CHURR
CHURRO *n* Spanish dough stick snack
CHURROS > CHURRO
CHURRS > CHURR
CHURRUS *n* hemp resin
CHURRUSES > CHURRUS
CHUSE *obsolete variant of* > CHOOSE
CHUSES > CHUSE
CHUSING > CHUSE
CHUT *interj* expression of surprise or annoyance ▷ *vb* make such an expression
CHUTE *n* steep slope down which things may be slid ▷ *vb* to descend by a chute
CHUTED > CHUTE
CHUTES > CHUTE
CHUTING > CHUTE
CHUTIST > CHUTE
CHUTISTS > CHUTE
CHUTNEE *same as* > CHUTNEY
CHUTNEES > CHUTNEE
CHUTNEY *n* pickle made from fruit, vinegar, spices, and sugar
CHUTNEYS > CHUTNEY
CHUTZPA *same as* > CHUTZPAH
CHUTZPAH *n* unashamed self-confidence
CHUTZPAHS > CHUTZPAH
CHUTZPAS > CHUTZPA
CHYACK *same as* > CHIACK
CHYACKED > CHYACK
CHYACKING > CHYACK
CHYACKS > CHYACK
CHYLDE *archaic word for* > CHILD
CHYLE *n* milky fluid formed in the small intestine during digestion
CHYLES > CHYLE
CHYLIFIED > CHYLIFY
CHYLIFIES > CHYLIFY
CHYLIFY *vb* to be turned into chyle
CHYLOUS > CHYLE
CHYLURIA *n* presence of chyle in urine
CHYLURIAS > CHYLURIA
CHYME *n* thick fluid mass of partially digested food that leaves the stomach
CHYMES > CHYME
CHYMIC *same as* > CHEMIC
CHYMICS > CHYMIC
CHYMIFIED > CHYMIFY
CHYMIFIES > CHYMIFY
CHYMIFY *vb* to form into chyme
CHYMIST *same as* > CHEMIST
CHYMISTRY *same as* > CHEMISTRY
CHYMISTS > CHYMIST
CHYMOSIN *another name for* > RENNIN
CHYMOSINS > CHYMOSIN
CHYMOUS > CHYME
CHYND *adj* chined
CHYPRE *n* perfume made from sandalwood
CHYPRES > CHYPRE
CHYTRID *n* variety of fungus
CHYTRIDS > CHYTRID
CIABATTA *n* type of bread made with olive oil
CIABATTAS > CIABATTA
CIABATTE > CIABATTA
CIAO *an informal word for* > HELLO
CIAOS > CIAO
CIBATION *n* feeding
CIBATIONS > CIBATION
CIBOL *same as* > CHIBOL
CIBOLS > CIBOL
CIBORIA > CIBORIUM
CIBORIUM *n* goblet-shaped lidded vessel used to hold consecrated wafers in Holy Communion
CIBOULE *same as* > CHIBOL
CIBOULES > CIBOULE
CICADA *n* large insect that makes a high-pitched drone
CICADAE > CICADA
CICADAS > CICADA
CICALA *same as* > CICADA
CICALAS > CICALA
CICALE > CICALA
CICATRICE *n* scar
CICATRISE *same as* > CICATRIZE
CICATRIX *n* scar
CICATRIZE *vb* (of a wound or defect in tissue) to close or be closed by scar formation
CICELIES > CICELY
CICELY *n* type of plant
CICERO *n* measure for type that is somewhat larger than the pica
CICERONE *n* person who guides and informs sightseers ▷ *vb* to act as a cicerone
CICERONED > CICERONE
CICERONES > CICERONE
CICERONI > CICERONE
CICEROS > CICERO
CICHLID *n* any tropical freshwater percoid fish of the family *Cichlidae*, which includes the mouthbrooders. Cichlids are popular aquarium fishes ▷ *adj* of, relating to, or belonging to the *Cichlidae*
CICHLIDAE *n* cichlids
CICHLIDS > CICHLID
CICHLOID > CICHLID
CICINNUS *n* scorpioid cyme
CICISBEI > CICISBEO
CICISBEO *n* escort or lover of a married woman, esp in 18th-century Italy
CICISBEOS > CICISBEO
CICLATON *n* rich material of silk and gold
CICLATONS > CICLATON
CICLATOUN *same as* > CICLATON
CICOREE *same as* > CHICORY
CICOREES > CICOREE
CICUTA *n* spotted hemlock
CICUTAS > CICUTA
CICUTINE *same as* > CONIINE
CICUTINES > CICUTINE
CID *n* leader
CIDARIS *n* sea urchin
CIDARISES > CIDARIS
CIDE *Shakespearean variant of* > DECIDE
CIDED > CIDE
CIDER *n* alcoholic drink made from fermented apple juice
CIDERKIN *n* weak type of cider
CIDERKINS > CIDERKIN
CIDERS > CIDER
CIDERY > CIDER
CIDES > CIDE
CIDING > CIDE

CIDS > CID
CIEL *same as* > CEIL
CIELED > CIEL
CIELING > CIEL
CIELINGS > CIEL
CIELS > CIEL
CIERGE *same as* > CERGE
CIERGES > CIERGE
CIG *same as* > CIGARETTE
CIGAR *n* roll of cured tobacco leaves for smoking
CIGARET *same as* > CIGARETTE
CIGARETS > CIGARET
CIGARETTE *n* thin roll of shredded tobacco in thin paper, for smoking
CIGARILLO *n* small cigar often only slightly larger than a cigarette
CIGARLIKE > CIGAR
CIGARS > CIGAR
CIGGIE *same as* > CIGARETTE
CIGGIES > CIGGIE
CIGGY *same as* > CIGARETTE
CIGS > CIG
CIGUATERA *n* food poisoning caused by a toxin in seafood
CILANTRO *same as* > CORIANDER
CILANTROS > CILANTRO
CILIA > CILIUM
CILIARY *adj* of or relating to cilia
CILIATE *adj* possessing or relating to cilia ▷ *n* protozoan of the phylum *Ciliophora*
CILIATED > CILIATE
CILIATELY > CILIATE
CILIATES > CILIATE
CILIATION > CILIATE
CILICE *n* haircloth fabric or garment
CILICES > CILICE
CILICIOUS *adj* made of hair
CILIOLATE *adj* covered with minute hairs, as some plants
CILIUM *n* short thread projecting from a cell, whose rhythmic beating causes movement
CILL *a variant spelling (used in the building industry) for* > SILL
CILLS > CILL
CIMAR *same as* > CYMAR
CIMARS > CIMAR
CIMBALOM *n* type of dulcimer, esp of Hungary
CIMBALOMS > CIMBALOM
CIMELIA *n* (especially, ecclesiastical) treasures
CIMEX *n* any of the heteropterous insects of the genus *Cimex*, esp the bedbug
CIMICES > CIMEX
CIMIER *n* crest of a helmet
CIMIERS > CIMIER
CIMINITE *n* type of igneous rock
CIMINITES > CIMINITE
CIMMERIAN *adj* very dark or gloomy
CIMOLITE *n* clayey, whitish mineral
CIMOLITES > CIMOLITE
CINCH *n* easy task ▷ *vb* fasten a girth around (a horse)
CINCHED > CINCH
CINCHES > CINCH
CINCHING > CINCH
CINCHINGS > CINCH
CINCHONA *same as* > CALISAYA
CINCHONAS > CINCHONA
CINCHONIC > CINCHONA
CINCINNUS *same as* > CICINNUS
CINCT *adj* encircled
CINCTURE *n* something, such as a belt or girdle, that goes around another thing ▷ *vb* to encircle
CINCTURED > CINCTURE
CINCTURES > CINCTURE
CINDER *n* piece of material that will not burn, left after burning coal ▷ *vb* burn to cinders
CINDERED > CINDER
CINDERING > CINDER
CINDEROUS > CINDER
CINDERS > CINDER
CINDERY > CINDER
CINE as in *cine camera* camera able to film moving pictures
CINEAST *same as* > CINEASTE
CINEASTE *n* enthusiast for films
CINEASTES > CINEASTE
CINEASTS > CINEAST
CINEMA *n* place for showing films
CINEMAS > CINEMA
CINEMATIC > CINEMA
CINEOL *n* colourless oily liquid with a camphor-like odour and a spicy taste
CINEOLE *same as* > CINEOL
CINEOLES > CINEOLE
CINEOLS > CINEOL
CINEPHILE *n* film enthusiast
CINEPLEX *n* (tradename for) a large cinema complex
CINERAMIC *adj* relating to a cinematic process producing widescreen images
CINERARIA *n* garden plant with daisy-like flowers
CINERARY *adj* of (someone's) ashes
CINERATOR *same as* > CREMATOR
CINEREA *n* grey matter of the brain and nervous system
CINEREAL *adj* ashy
CINEREAS > CINEREA
CINEREOUS *adj* of a greyish colour
CINERIN *n* either of two organic compounds used as insecticides
CINERINS > CINERIN
CINES > CINE
CINGULA > CINGULUM
CINGULAR *adj* ring-shaped
CINGULATE > CINGULUM
CINGULUM *n* girdle-like part, such as the ridge round the base of a tooth or the band of fibres connecting parts of the cerebrum
CINNABAR *n* heavy red mineral containing mercury
CINNABARS > CINNABAR
CINNAMIC > CINNAMON
CINNAMON *n* spice obtained from the bark of an Asian tree
CINNAMONS > CINNAMON
CINNAMONY > CINNAMON
CINNAMYL *n* univalent radical of cinnamic compounds
CINNAMYLS > CINNAMYL
CINQUAIN *n* stanza of five lines
CINQUAINS > CINQUAIN
CINQUE *n* number five in cards, dice, etc
CINQUES > CINQUE
CION *same as* > SCION
CIONS > CION
CIOPPINO *n* Italian rich fish stew
CIOPPINOS > CIOPPINO
CIPHER *n* system of secret writing ▷ *vb* put (a message) into secret writing
CIPHERED > CIPHER
CIPHERER > CIPHER
CIPHERERS > CIPHER
CIPHERING > CIPHER
CIPHERS > CIPHER
CIPHONIES > CIPHONY
CIPHONY *n* ciphered telephony; process of enciphering audio information, producing encrypted speech
CIPOLIN *n* Italian marble with alternating white and green streaks
CIPOLINS > CIPOLIN
CIPOLLINO *same as* > CIPOLIN
CIPPI > CIPPUS
CIPPUS *n* pillar bearing an inscription
CIRCA *prep* approximately, about
CIRCADIAN *adj* of biological processes that occur regularly at 24-hour intervals
CIRCAR *n* in India, part of a province
CIRCARS > CIRCAR
CIRCINATE *adj* (of part of a plant, such as a young fern) coiled so that the tip is at the centre
CIRCITER *prep* around, about
CIRCLE *n* perfectly round geometric figure, line, or shape ▷ *vb* move in a circle (round)
CIRCLED > CIRCLE
CIRCLER > CIRCLE
CIRCLERS > CIRCLE
CIRCLES > CIRCLE
CIRCLET *n* circular ornament worn on the head
CIRCLETS > CIRCLET
CIRCLING > CIRCLE
CIRCLINGS > CIRCLE
CIRCLIP *n* flat spring ring split at one point so that it can be sprung open, passed over a shaft or spindle, and allowed to close into a closely fitting annular recess to form a collar on the shaft. A similar design can be closed to pass into a bore and allowed to spring out into an annular recess to form a shoulder in the bore
CIRCLIPS > CIRCLIP
CIRCS *pl n* circumstances
CIRCUIT *n* complete route or course, esp a circular one ▷ *vb* make or travel in a circuit around (something)
CIRCUITAL > CIRCUIT
CIRCUITED > CIRCUIT
CIRCUITRY *n* electrical circuit(s)
CIRCUITS > CIRCUIT
CIRCUITY *n* (of speech, reasoning, etc) a roundabout or devious quality
CIRCULAR *adj* in the shape of a circle ▷ *n* letter for general distribution
CIRCULARS > CIRCULAR
CIRCULATE *vb* send, go, or pass from place to place or person to person
CIRCUS *n* (performance given by) a travelling company of acrobats, clowns, performing animals, etc
CIRCUSES > CIRCUS
CIRCUSSY > CIRCUS
CIRCUSY > CIRCUS
CIRE *adj* (of fabric) treated with a heat or wax process to make it smooth ▷ *n* such a surface on a fabric
CIRES > CIRE
CIRL *n* bird belonging to the bunting family
CIRLS > CIRL
CIRQUE *n* steep-sided

semicircular hollow found in mountainous areas
CIRQUES > CIRQUE
CIRRATE *adj* bearing or resembling cirri
CIRRHOSED > CIRRHOSIS
CIRRHOSES > CIRRHOSIS
CIRRHOSIS *n* serious liver disease, often caused by drinking too much alcohol
CIRRHOTIC > CIRRHOSIS
CIRRI > CIRRUS
CIRRIFORM *adj* cirrus-like
CIRRIPED *same as* > CIRRIPEDE
CIRRIPEDE *n* any marine crustacean of the subclass *Cirripedia*, including the barnacles, the adults of which are sessile or parasitic ▷ *adj* of, relating to, or belonging to the *Cirripedia*
CIRRIPEDS > CIRRIPED
CIRROSE *same as* > CIRRATE
CIRROUS *same as* > CIRRATE
CIRRUS *n* high wispy cloud
CIRSOID *adj* resembling a varix
CIS *adj* having two groups of atoms on the same side of a double bond
CISALPINE *adj* on this (the southern) side of the Alps, as viewed from Rome
CISCO *n* whitefish, esp the lake herring of cold deep lakes of North America
CISCOES > CISCO
CISCOS > CISCO
CISELEUR *n* person who is expert in ciselure
CISELEURS > CISELEUR
CISELURE *n* art or process of chasing metal
CISELURES > CISELURE
CISLUNAR *adj* of or relating to the space between the earth and the moon
CISPADANE *adj* on this (the southern) side of the River Po, as viewed from Rome
CISPLATIN *n* cytotoxic drug that acts by preventing DNA replication and hence cell division, used in the treatment of tumours, esp of the ovary and testis
CISSIER > CISSY
CISSIES > CISSY
CISSIEST > CISSY
CISSIFIED *another word for* > SISSY
CISSING *n* appearance of pinholes, craters, etc, in paintwork due to poor adhesion of the paint to the surface
CISSINGS > CISSING
CISSOID *n* geometric curve whose two branches meet in a cusp at the origin and are asymptotic to a line parallel to the *y*-axis
CISSOIDS > CISSOID
CISSUS *n* any plant of the climbing genus *Cissus*, some species of which, esp the kangaroo vine (*C. antarctica*) from Australia, are grown as greenhouse or house plants for their shiny green or mottled leaves: family *Vitaceae*
CISSUSES > CISSUS
CISSY *same as* > SISSY
CIST *n* wooden box for holding ritual objects used in ancient Rome and Greece ▷ *vb* make a cist
CISTED > CIST
CISTERN *n* water tank, esp one that holds water for flushing a toilet
CISTERNA *n* sac or partially closed space containing body fluid, esp lymph or cerebrospinal fluid
CISTERNAE > CISTERNA
CISTERNAL > CISTERN
CISTERNS > CISTERN
CISTIC *adj* cist-like
CISTRON *n* section of a chromosome that encodes a single polypeptide chain
CISTRONIC > CISTRON
CISTRONS > CISTRON
CISTS > CIST
CISTUS *n* any plant of the genus *Cistus*
CISTUSES > CISTUS
CISTVAEN *n* pre-Christian stone coffin or burial chamber
CISTVAENS > CISTVAEN
CIT *n* pejorative term for a town dweller
CITABLE > CITE
CITADEL *n* fortress in a city
CITADELS > CITADEL
CITAL *n* court summons
CITALS > CITAL
CITATION *n* commendation for bravery
CITATIONS > CITATION
CITATOR *n* legal publication listing cases and statutes, their history and current status
CITATORS > CITATOR
CITATORY > CITATION
CITE *vb* quote, refer to
CITEABLE > CITE
CITED > CITE
CITER > CITE
CITERS > CITE
CITES > CITE
CITESS *n* female cit
CITESSES > CITESS
CITHARA *n* stringed musical instrument of ancient Greece and elsewhere, similar to the lyre and played with a plectrum
CITHARAS > CITHARA
CITHARIST *n* player of the cithara
CITHER *same as* > CITTERN
CITHERN *same as* > CITTERN
CITHERNS > CITHERN
CITHERS > CITHER
CITHREN *same as* > CITHARA
CITHRENS > CITHREN
CITIED *adj* having cities
CITIES > CITY
CITIFIED > CITIFY
CITIFIES > CITIFY
CITIFY *vb* cause to conform to or adopt the customs, habits, or dress of city people
CITIFYING > CITIFY
CITIGRADE *adj* relating to (fast-moving) wolf spiders
CITING > CITE
CITIZEN *n* native or naturalized member of a state or nation
CITIZENLY > CITIZEN
CITIZENRY *n* citizens collectively
CITIZENS > CITIZEN
CITO *adv* swiftly
CITOLA *n* type of medieval stringed instrument
CITOLAS > CITOLA
CITOLE *a rare word for* > CITTERN
CITOLES > CITOLE
CITRAL *n* yellow volatile liquid with a lemon-like odour, found in oils of lemon grass, orange, and lemon and used in perfumery
CITRALS > CITRAL
CITRANGE *n* type of acidic and aromatic orange
CITRANGES > CITRANGE
CITRATE *n* any salt or ester of citric acid
CITRATED *adj* treated with a citrate
CITRATES > CITRATE
CITREOUS *adj* of a greenish-yellow colour
CITRIC *adj* of or derived from citrus fruits or citric acid
CITRIN *n* vitamin P
CITRINE *n* brownish-yellow variety of quartz: a gemstone
CITRINES > CITRINE
CITRININ *n* a mycotoxin
CITRININS > CITRININ
CITRINS > CITRIN
CITRON *n* lemon-like fruit of a small Asian tree
CITRONS > CITRON
CITROUS *same as* > CITRUS
CITRUS *n* any tree or shrub of the tropical and subtropical rutaceous genus *Citrus*, which includes the orange, lemon, lime, grapefruit, citron, and calamondin ▷ *adj* of, relating to, or belonging to the genus *Citrus* or to the fruits of plants of this genus
CITRUSES > CITRUS
CITRUSSY *adj* having or resembling the taste or colour of a citrus fruit
CITRUSY *same as* > CITRUSSY
CITS > CIT
CITTERN *n* medieval stringed instrument resembling a lute but having wire strings and a flat back
CITTERNS > CITTERN
CITY *n* large or important town
CITYFIED > CITYFY
CITYFIES > CITYFY
CITYFY *same as* > CITIFY
CITYFYING > CITYFY
CITYSCAPE *n* urban landscape
CITYWARD *adv* towards a city
CITYWIDE *adj* occurring throughout a city
CIVE *same as* > CHIVE
CIVES > CIVE
CIVET *n* spotted catlike African mammal
CIVETLIKE > CIVET
CIVETS > CIVET
CIVIC *adj* of a city or citizens
CIVICALLY > CIVIC
CIVICISM *n* principle of civil government
CIVICISMS > CIVICISM
CIVICS *n* study of the rights and responsibilities of citizenship
CIVIE *same as* > CIVVY
CIVIES > CIVIE
CIVIL *adj* relating to the citizens of a state as opposed to the armed forces or the Church
CIVILIAN *adj* not belonging to the armed forces ▷ *n* person who is not a member of the armed forces or police
CIVILIANS > CIVILIAN
CIVILISE *same as* > CIVILIZE
CIVILISED *same as* > CIVILIZED
CIVILISER > CIVILISE
CIVILISES > CIVILISE
CIVILIST *n* civilian
CIVILISTS > CIVILIST
CIVILITY *n* polite or courteous behaviour
CIVILIZE *vb* refine or educate (a person)
CIVILIZED *adj* having a high state of culture and social development
CIVILIZER > CIVILIZE
CIVILIZES > CIVILIZE
CIVILLY > CIVIL
CIVILNESS > CIVIL
CIVISM *n* good citizenship
CIVISMS > CIVISM
CIVVIES > CIVVY

CIVVY *n* civilian
CIZERS *archaic spelling of* > SCISSORS
CLABBER *vb* to cover with mud
CLABBERED > CLABBER
CLABBERS > CLABBER
CLACH *n* stone
CLACHAN *n* small village
CLACHANS > CLACHAN
CLACHS > CLACH
CLACK *n* sound made by two hard objects striking each other ▷ *vb* make this sound
CLACKBOX *n* casing enclosing a clack
CLACKDISH *n* formerly, a dish carried by a beggar
CLACKED > CLACK
CLACKER *n* object that makes a clacking sound
CLACKERS > CLACKER
CLACKING > CLACK
CLACKS > CLACK
CLAD *vb* bond a metal to (another metal), esp to form a protective coat
CLADDAGH *n* Irish ring
CLADDAGHS > CLADDAGH
CLADDED *adj* covered with cladding
CLADDER > CLAD
CLADDERS > CLAD
CLADDIE *another name for* > KORARI
CLADDIES > CLADDIE
CLADDING > CLOTHE
CLADDINGS > CLOTHE
CLADE *n* group of organisms considered as having evolved from a common ancestor
CLADES > CLADE
CLADISM > CLADIST
CLADISMS > CLADIST
CLADIST *n* proponent of cladistics: a method of grouping animals that makes use of lines of descent rather than structural similarities
CLADISTIC > CLADIST
CLADISTS > CLADIST
CLADODE *n* flattened stem resembling and functioning as a leaf, as in butcher's-broom
CLADODES > CLADODE
CLADODIAL > CLADODE
CLADOGRAM *n* treelike diagram illustrating the development of a clade
CLADS > CLAD
CLAES *Scots word for* > CLOTHES
CLAFOUTI *same as* > CLAFOUTIS
CLAFOUTIS *n* French baked pudding
CLAG *n* sticky mud ▷ *vb* stick, as mud
CLAGGED > CLAG
CLAGGIER > CLAGGY
CLAGGIEST > CLAGGY
CLAGGING > CLAG
CLAGGY *adj* stickily clinging, as mud
CLAGS > CLAG
CLAIM *vb* assert as a fact ▷ *n* assertion that something is true
CLAIMABLE > CLAIM
CLAIMANT *n* person who makes a claim
CLAIMANTS > CLAIMANT
CLAIMED > CLAIM
CLAIMER > CLAIM
CLAIMERS > CLAIM
CLAIMING > CLAIM
CLAIMS > CLAIM
CLAM *n* edible shellfish with a hinged shell ▷ *vb* gather clams
CLAMANCY *n* urgency
CLAMANT *adj* noisy
CLAMANTLY > CLAMANT
CLAMBAKE *n* picnic, often by the sea, at which clams, etc, are baked
CLAMBAKES > CLAMBAKE
CLAMBE *old variant of* > CLIMB
CLAMBER *vb* climb awkwardly ▷ *n* climb performed in this manner
CLAMBERED > CLAMBER
CLAMBERER > CLAMBER
CLAMBERS > CLAMBER
CLAME *archaic variant of* > CLAIM
CLAMES > CLAIM
CLAMLIKE > CLAM
CLAMMED > CLAM
CLAMMER *n* person who gathers clams
CLAMMERS > CLAMMER
CLAMMIER > CLAMMY
CLAMMIEST > CLAMMY
CLAMMILY > CLAMMY
CLAMMING > CLAM
CLAMMY *adj* unpleasantly moist and sticky
CLAMOR *same as* > CLAMOUR
CLAMORED > CLAMOR
CLAMORER > CLAMOR
CLAMORERS > CLAMOR
CLAMORING > CLAMOR
CLAMOROUS > CLAMOR
CLAMORS > CLAMOR
CLAMOUR *n* loud protest ▷ *vb* make a loud noise or outcry
CLAMOURED > CLAMOUR
CLAMOURER > CLAMOUR
CLAMOURS > CLAMOUR
CLAMP *n* tool with movable jaws for holding things together tightly ▷ *vb* fasten with a clamp
CLAMPDOWN *n* sudden restrictive measure
CLAMPED > CLAMP
CLAMPER *n* spiked metal frame fastened to the sole of a shoe to prevent slipping on ice ▷ *vb* to tread heavily
CLAMPERED > CLAMPER
CLAMPERS > CLAMPER
CLAMPING > CLAMP
CLAMPS > CLAMP
CLAMS > CLAM
CLAMSHELL *n* dredging bucket that is hinged like the shell of a clam
CLAMWORM *the US name for the* > RAGWORM
CLAMWORMS > CLAMWORM
CLAN *n* group of families with a common ancestor, esp among Scottish Highlanders
CLANG *vb* make a loud ringing metallic sound ▷ *n* ringing metallic sound
CLANGBOX *n* device fitted to a jet-engine to change the direction of thrust
CLANGED > CLANG
CLANGER *n* obvious mistake
CLANGERS > CLANGER
CLANGING > CLANG
CLANGINGS > CLANG
CLANGOR *same as* > CLANGOUR
CLANGORED > CLANGOR
CLANGORS > CLANGOR
CLANGOUR *n* loud continuous clanging sound ▷ *vb* make or produce a loud resonant noise
CLANGOURS > CLANGOUR
CLANGS > CLANG
CLANK *n* harsh metallic sound ▷ *vb* make such a sound
CLANKED > CLANK
CLANKIER > CLANKY
CLANKIEST > CLANKY
CLANKING > CLANK
CLANKINGS > CLANK
CLANKS > CLANK
CLANKY *adj* making clanking sounds
CLANNISH *adj* (of a group) tending to exclude outsiders
CLANS > CLAN
CLANSHIP *n* association of families under the leadership of a chieftain
CLANSHIPS > CLANSHIP
CLANSMAN *n* man belonging to a clan
CLANSMEN > CLANSMAN
CLAP *vb* applaud by hitting the palms of one's hands sharply together ▷ *n* act or sound of clapping
CLAPBOARD *n* long thin timber board with one edge thicker than the other, used esp in the US and Canada in wood-frame construction by lapping each board over the one below ▷ *vb* cover with such boards
CLAPBREAD *n* type of cake made from oatmeal
CLAPDISH *same as* > CLACKDISH
CLAPNET *n* net that can be closed instantly by pulling a string
CLAPNETS > CLAPNET
CLAPPED > CLAP
CLAPPER *n* piece of metal inside a bell, which causes it to sound when struck against the side ▷ *vb* make a sound like a clapper
CLAPPERED > CLAPPER
CLAPPERS > CLAPPER
CLAPPING > CLAP
CLAPPINGS > CLAP
CLAPS > CLAP
CLAPT old inflection > CLAP
CLAPTRAP *n* foolish or pretentious talk
CLAPTRAPS > CLAPTRAP
CLAQUE *n* group of people hired to applaud
CLAQUER *same as* > CLAQUEUR
CLAQUERS > CLAQUER
CLAQUES > CLAQUE
CLAQUEUR *n* member of a claque
CLAQUEURS > CLAQUEUR
CLARAIN *n* one of the four major lithotypes of banded coal
CLARAINS > CLARAIN
CLARENCE *n* closed four-wheeled horse-drawn carriage, having a glass front
CLARENCES > CLARENCE
CLARENDON *n* style of boldface roman type
CLARET *n* dry red wine from Bordeaux ▷ *adj* purplish-red ▷ *vb* to drink claret
CLARETED > CLARET
CLARETING > CLARET
CLARETS > CLARET
CLARIES > CLARY
CLARIFIED > CLARIFY
CLARIFIER > CLARIFY
CLARIFIES > CLARIFY
CLARIFY *vb* make (a matter) clear and unambiguous
CLARINET *n* keyed woodwind instrument with a single reed
CLARINETS > CLARINET
CLARINI > CLARINO
CLARINO *adj* of or relating to a high passage for the trumpet in 18th-century music ▷ *n* high register of the trumpet
CLARINOS > CLARINO
CLARION *n* obsolete high-pitched trumpet ▷ *adj* clear and ringing ▷ *vb* proclaim loudly
CLARIONED > CLARION
CLARIONET *same as* > CLARINET

CLARIONS > CLARION
CLARITIES > CLARITY
CLARITY *n* clearness
CLARKIA *n* any North American onagraceous plant of the genus *Clarkia*: cultivated for their red, purple, or pink flowers
CLARKIAS > CLARKIA
CLARO *n* mild light-coloured cigar
CLAROES > CLARO
CLAROS > CLARO
CLARSACH *n* Celtic harp of Scotland and Ireland
CLARSACHS > CLARSACH
CLART *vb* to dirty
CLARTED > CLART
CLARTHEAD *n* slow-witted or stupid person
CLARTIER > CLARTY
CLARTIEST > CLARTY
CLARTING > CLART
CLARTS *pl n* lumps of mud, esp on shoes
CLARTY *adj* dirty, esp covered in mud
CLARY *n* any of several European plants of the genus *Salvia*, having aromatic leaves and blue flowers: family *Lamiaceae* (labiates)
CLASH *vb* come into conflict ▷ *n* fight, argument
CLASHED > CLASH
CLASHER > CLASH
CLASHERS > CLASH
CLASHES > CLASH
CLASHING > CLASH
CLASHINGS > CLASH
CLASP *n* device for fastening things ▷ *vb* grasp or embrace firmly
CLASPED > CLASP
CLASPER > CLASP
CLASPERS *pl n* paired organ of male insects, used to clasp the female during copulation
CLASPING > CLASP
CLASPINGS > CLASP
CLASPS > CLASP
CLASPT *old inflection of* > CLASP
CLASS *n* group of people sharing a similar social position ▷ *vb* place in a class
CLASSABLE > CLASS
CLASSED > CLASS
CLASSER > CLASS
CLASSERS > CLASS
CLASSES > CLASSIS
CLASSIBLE *adj* able to be classed
CLASSIC *adj* being a typical example of something ▷ *n* author, artist, or work of art of recognized excellence
CLASSICAL *adj* of or in a restrained conservative style
CLASSICO *adj* (of Italian wines) coming from the centre of a specific wine-growing region
CLASSICS *pl n the.* a body of literature regarded as great or lasting, esp that of ancient Greece or Rome
CLASSIER > CLASSY
CLASSIEST > CLASSY
CLASSIFIC *adj* relating to classification
CLASSIFY *vb* divide into groups with similar characteristics
CLASSILY > CLASSY
CLASSING > CLASS
CLASSINGS > CLASS
CLASSIS *n* governing body of elders or pastors
CLASSISM *n* belief that people from certain social or economic classes are superior to others
CLASSISMS > CLASSISM
CLASSIST > CLASSISM
CLASSISTS > CLASSISM
CLASSLESS *adj* not belonging to a class
CLASSMAN *n* graduate of Oxford University with a classed honours degree
CLASSMATE *n* friend or contemporary in the same class of a school
CLASSMEN > CLASSMAN
CLASSON *n* elementary atomic particle
CLASSONS > CLASSON
CLASSROOM *n* room in a school where lessons take place
CLASSWORK *n* school work done in class
CLASSY *adj* stylish and elegant
CLAST *n* fragment of a clastic rock
CLASTIC *adj* (of sedimentary rock, etc) composed of fragments of pre-existing rock that have been transported some distance from their points of origin ▷ *n* clast
CLASTICS > CLASTIC
CLASTS > CLAST
CLAT *n* irksome or troublesome task ▷ *vb* to scrape
CLATCH *vb* to move making a squelching sound
CLATCHED > CLATCH
CLATCHES > CLATCH
CLATCHING > CLATCH
CLATHRATE *adj* resembling a net or lattice ▷ *n* solid compound in which molecules of one substance are physically trapped in the crystal lattice of another
CLATS > CLAT
CLATTED > CLAT
CLATTER *n* (make) a rattling noise ▷ *vb* make a rattling noise, as when hard objects hit each other
CLATTERED > CLATTER
CLATTERER > CLATTER
CLATTERS > CLATTER
CLATTERY > CLATTER
CLATTING > CLAT
CLAUCHT *vb* to seize by force
CLAUCHTED > CLAUCHT
CLAUCHTS > CLAUCHT
CLAUGHT *same as* > CLAUCHT
CLAUGHTED > CLAUGHT
CLAUGHTS > CLAUGHT
CLAUSAL > CLAUSE
CLAUSE *n* section of a legal document
CLAUSES > CLAUSE
CLAUSTRA > CLAUSTRUM
CLAUSTRAL *same as* > CLOISTRAL
CLAUSTRUM *n* thin layer of gret matter in the brain
CLAUSULA *n* type of cadence in polyphony
CLAUSULAE > CLAUSULA
CLAUSULAR > CLAUSE
CLAUT *same as* > CLAT
CLAUTED > CLAUT
CLAUTING > CLAUT
CLAUTS > CLAUT
CLAVATE *adj* shaped like a club with the thicker end uppermost
CLAVATED *same as* > CLAVATE
CLAVATELY > CLAVATE
CLAVATION > CLAVATE
CLAVE *n* one of a pair of hardwood sticks struck together to make a hollow sound, esp to mark the beat of Latin-American dance music
CLAVECIN *n* harpsichord
CLAVECINS > CLAVECIN
CLAVER *vb* talk idly ▷ *n* idle talk
CLAVERED > CLAVER
CLAVERING > CLAVER
CLAVERS > CLAVER
CLAVES > CLAVE
CLAVI > CLAVUS
CLAVICLE *n* either of the two bones connecting the shoulder blades with the upper part of the breastbone
CLAVICLES > CLAVICLE
CLAVICORN *n* any beetle of the group *Clavicornia*, including the ladybirds, characterized by club-shaped antennae ▷ *adj* of, relating to, or belonging to the *Clavicornia*
CLAVICULA *n* clavicle
CLAVIE *n* tar-barrel traditionally set alight in Moray in Scotland on Hogmanay
CLAVIER *n* any keyboard instrument
CLAVIERS > CLAVIER
CLAVIES > CLAVIE
CLAVIFORM *same as* > CLAVATE
CLAVIGER *n* key- or club-bearer
CLAVIGERS > CLAVIGER
CLAVIS *n* key
CLAVULATE *adj* club-shaped
CLAVUS *n* corn on the toe
CLAW *n* sharp hooked nail of a bird or beast ▷ *vb* tear with claws or nails
CLAWBACK *n* recovery of a sum of money
CLAWBACKS > CLAWBACK
CLAWED > CLAW
CLAWER > CLAW
CLAWERS > CLAW
CLAWING > CLAW
CLAWLESS > CLAW
CLAWLIKE *adj* resembling a claw or claws
CLAWS > CLAW
CLAXON *same as* > KLAXON
CLAXONS > CLAXON
CLAY *n* fine-grained earth, soft when moist and hardening when baked, used to make bricks and pottery ▷ *vb* cover or mix with clay
CLAYBANK *n* dull brownish-orange colour
CLAYBANKS > CLAYBANK
CLAYED > CLAY
CLAYEY > CLAY
CLAYIER > CLAY
CLAYIEST > CLAY
CLAYING > CLAY
CLAYISH > CLAY
CLAYLIKE > CLAY
CLAYMORE *n* large two-edged sword formerly used by Scottish Highlanders
CLAYMORES > CLAYMORE
CLAYPAN *n* layer of stiff impervious clay situated just below the surface of the ground, which holds water after heavy rain
CLAYPANS > CLAYPAN
CLAYS > CLAY
CLAYSTONE *n* compact very fine-grained rock consisting of consolidated clay particles
CLAYTONIA *n* any low-growing North American succulent portulacaceous plant of the genus *Claytonia*
CLAYWARE *n* pottery
CLAYWARES > CLAYWARE
CLEAN *adj* free from dirt or impurities ▷ *vb* make (something) free from dirt ▷ *adv* completely
CLEANABLE > CLEAN
CLEANED > CLEAN
CLEANER *n* person or thing that removes dirt

CLEANERS >CLEANER
CLEANEST >CLEAN
CLEANING *n* act of cleaning something
CLEANINGS >CLEANING
CLEANLIER >CLEANLY
CLEANLILY >CLEANLY
CLEANLY *adv* easily or smoothly ▷ *adj* habitually clean or neat
CLEANNESS >CLEAN
CLEANS >CLEAN
CLEANSE *vb* make clean
CLEANSED >CLEANSE
CLEANSER *n* cleansing agent, such as a detergent
CLEANSERS >CLEANSER
CLEANSES >CLEANSE
CLEANSING >CLEANSE
CLEANSKIN *n* unbranded animal
CLEANUP *n* process of cleaning up or eliminating something
CLEANUPS >CLEANUP
CLEAR *adj* free from doubt or confusion ▷ *adv* in a clear or distinct manner ▷ *vb* make or become clear
CLEARABLE >CLEAR
CLEARAGE *n* clearance
CLEARAGES >CLEARAGE
CLEARANCE *n* clearing
CLEARCOLE *n* type of size containing whiting ▷ *vb* paint (a wall) with this size
CLEARCUT *n* act of felling all trees in area
CLEARCUTS >CLEARCUT
CLEARED >CLEAR
CLEARER >CLEAR
CLEARERS >CLEAR
CLEAREST >CLEAR
CLEAREYED *adj* having good judgment
CLEARING *n* treeless area in a wood
CLEARINGS >CLEARING
CLEARLY *adv* in a clear, distinct, or obvious manner
CLEARNESS >CLEAR
CLEARS >CLEAR
CLEARSKIN *same as* >CLEANSKIN
CLEARWAY *n* stretch of road on which motorists may stop in an emergency
CLEARWAYS >CLEARWAY
CLEARWEED *n* plant like nettle
CLEARWING *n* type of moth
CLEAT *n* wedge ▷ *vb* supply or support with a cleat or cleats
CLEATED >CLEAT
CLEATING >CLEAT
CLEATS >CLEAT
CLEAVABLE >CLEAVE
CLEAVAGE *n* space between a woman's breasts, as revealed by a low-cut dress
CLEAVAGES >CLEAVAGE
CLEAVE *vb* split apart ▷ *n* split
CLEAVED >CLEAVE
CLEAVER *n* butcher's heavy knife with a square blade
CLEAVERS *n* plant with small white flowers and sticky fruits
CLEAVES >CLEAVE
CLEAVING >CLEAVE
CLEAVINGS >CLEAVE
CLECHE *adj* (in heraldry) voided so that only a narrow border is visible
CLECK *vb* (of birds) to hatch ▷ *n* piece of gossip
CLECKED >CLECK
CLECKIER >CLECK
CLECKIEST >CLECK
CLECKING >CLECK
CLECKINGS >CLECK
CLECKS >CLECK
CLECKY >CLECK
CLEEK *n* large hook, such as one used to land fish ▷ *vb* to seize
CLEEKED >CLEEK
CLEEKING >CLEEK
CLEEKIT >CLEEK
CLEEKS >CLEEK
CLEEP *same as* >CLEPE
CLEEPED >CLEEP
CLEEPING >CLEEP
CLEEPS >CLEEP
CLEEVE *n* cliff
CLEEVES >CLEEVE
CLEF *n* symbol at the beginning of a stave to show the pitch
CLEFS >CLEF
CLEFT >CLEAVE
CLEFTED >CLEAVE
CLEFTING >CLEAVE
CLEFTS >CLEAVE
CLEG *another name for a* >HORSEFLY
CLEGS >CLEG
CLEIDOIC as in *cleidoic egg* egg of birds and insects
CLEIK *same as* >CLEEK
CLEIKS >CLEEK
CLEITHRAL *adj* covered with a roof
CLEM *vb* be hungry or cause to be hungry
CLEMATIS *n* climbing plant with large colourful flowers
CLEMENCY *n* kind or lenient treatment
CLEMENT *adj* (of weather) mild
CLEMENTLY >CLEMENT
CLEMMED >CLEM
CLEMMING >CLEM
CLEMS >CLEM
CLENCH *vb* close or squeeze (one's teeth or fist) tightly ▷ *n* firm grasp or grip
CLENCHED >CLENCH
CLENCHER >CLENCH
CLENCHERS >CLENCH
CLENCHES >CLENCH
CLENCHING >CLENCH
CLEOME *n* any herbaceous or shrubby plant of the mostly tropical capparidaceous genus *Cleome*, esp *C. spinosa*, cultivated for their clusters of white or purplish flowers with long stamens
CLEOMES >CLEOME
CLEOPATRA *n* yellow butterfly, *Gonepteryx cleopatra*, the male of which has its wings flushed with orange
CLEPE *vb* call by the name of
CLEPED >CLEPE
CLEPES >CLEPE
CLEPING >CLEPE
CLEPSYDRA *n* ancient device for measuring time by the flow of water or mercury through a small aperture
CLEPT >CLEPE
CLERGIES >CLERGY
CLERGY *n* priests and ministers as a group
CLERGYMAN *n* member of the clergy
CLERGYMEN >CLERGYMAN
CLERIC *n* member of the clergy
CLERICAL *adj* of clerks or office work
CLERICALS *pl n* distinctive dress of a clergyman
CLERICATE *n* clerical post
CLERICITY *n* condition of being a clergyman
CLERICS >CLERIC
CLERID *n* beetle that preys on other insects
CLERIDS >CLERID
CLERIHEW *n* form of comic or satiric verse, consisting of two couplets and containing the name of a well-known person
CLERIHEWS >CLERIHEW
CLERISIES >CLERISY
CLERISY *n* learned or educated people
CLERK *n* employee in an office, bank, or court who keeps records, files, and accounts ▷ *vb* work as a clerk
CLERKDOM >CLERK
CLERKDOMS >CLERK
CLERKED >CLERK
CLERKESS *n* female office clerk
CLERKING >CLERK
CLERKISH >CLERK
CLERKLIER >CLERKLY
CLERKLIKE *adj* acting in a scholarly manner
CLERKLING *n* young or inexperienced clerk
CLERKLY *adj* of or like a clerk ▷ *adv* in the manner of a clerk
CLERKS >CLERK
CLERKSHIP >CLERK
CLERUCH *n* settler in a cleruchy
CLERUCHIA *same as* >CLERUCHY
CLERUCHS >CLERUCH
CLERUCHY *n* (in the ancient world) a special type of Athenian colony, in which settlers retained their Athenian citizenship and the community remained a political dependency of Athens
CLEUCH *same as* >CLOUGH
CLEUCHS >CLEUCH
CLEUGH *same as* >CLOUGH
CLEUGHS >CLEUGH
CLEVE *same as* >CLEEVE
CLEVEITE *n* crystalline variety of the mineral uranitite
CLEVEITES >CLEVEITE
CLEVER *adj* intelligent, quick at learning
CLEVERER >CLEVER
CLEVEREST >CLEVER
CLEVERISH >CLEVER
CLEVERLY >CLEVER
CLEVES >CLEEVE
CLEVIS *n* U-shaped component of a shackle for attaching a drawbar to a plough or similar implement
CLEVISES >CLEVIS
CLEW *n* ball of thread, yarn, or twine ▷ *vb* coil or roll into a ball
CLEWED >CLEW
CLEWING >CLEW
CLEWS >CLEW
CLIANTHUS *n* Australian or NZ plant with slender scarlet flowers
CLICHE *n* expression or idea that is no longer effective because of overuse ▷ *vb* use a cliché (in speech or writing)
CLICHED >CLICHE
CLICHEED >CLICHE
CLICHES >CLICHE
CLICK *n* short sharp sound ▷ *vb* make this sound
CLICKABLE *adj* (of a website) having links that can be accessed by clicking a computer mouse
CLICKED >CLICK
CLICKER >CLICK
CLICKERS >CLICK
CLICKET *vb* make a click
CLICKETED >CLICKET
CLICKETS >CLICKET
CLICKING >CLICK
CLICKINGS >CLICK
CLICKLESS >CLICK
CLICKS >CLICK
CLICKWRAP *adj* (of agreement) consented to by user clicking computer button
CLIED >CLY

CLIENT *n* person who uses the services of a professional person or company

CLIENTAGE *same as* > CLIENTELE

CLIENTAL > CLIENT

CLIENTELE *n* clients collectively

CLIENTS > CLIENT

CLIES > CLY

CLIFF *n* steep rock face, esp along the sea shore ▷ *vb* scale a cliff

CLIFFED > CLIFF

CLIFFHANG *vb* (of a serial or film) to end on a note of suspense

CLIFFHUNG > CLIFFHANG

CLIFFIER > CLIFF

CLIFFIEST > CLIFF

CLIFFLIKE > CLIFF

CLIFFS > CLIFF

CLIFFY > CLIFF

CLIFT *same as* > CLIFF

CLIFTED > CLIFF

CLIFTIER > CLIFF

CLIFTIEST > CLIFF

CLIFTS > CLIFF

CLIFTY > CLIFF

CLIMACTIC *adj* consisting of, involving, or causing a climax

CLIMATAL > CLIMATE

CLIMATE *n* typical weather conditions of an area ▷ *vb* acclimatize

CLIMATED > CLIMATE

CLIMATES > CLIMATE

CLIMATIC > CLIMATE

CLIMATING > CLIMATE

CLIMATISE *vb* in Australia, adapt or become accustomed to a new climate or environment

CLIMATIZE *same as* > CLIMATISE

CLIMATURE *n* clime

CLIMAX *n* most intense point of an experience, series of events, or story ▷ *vb* reach a climax

CLIMAXED > CLIMAX

CLIMAXES > CLIMAX

CLIMAXING > CLIMAX

CLIMB *vb* go up, ascend ▷ *n* climbing

CLIMBABLE > CLIMB

CLIMBDOWN *n* act of backing down from opinion

CLIMBED > CLIMB

CLIMBER *n* person or thing that climbs

CLIMBERS > CLIMBER

CLIMBING > CLIMB

CLIMBINGS > CLIMB

CLIMBS > CLIMB

CLIME *n* place or its climate

CLIMES > CLIME

CLINAL > CLINE

CLINALLY > CLINE

CLINAMEN *n* bias

CLINAMENS > CLINAMEN

CLINCH *vb* settle (an argument or agreement) decisively ▷ *n* movement in which one competitor holds on to the other to avoid punches

CLINCHED > CLINCH

CLINCHER *n* something decisive

CLINCHERS > CLINCHER

CLINCHES > CLINCH

CLINCHING > CLINCH

CLINE *n* continuous variation in form between members of a species having a wide variable geographical or ecological range

CLINES > CLINE

CLING *vb* hold tightly or stick closely ▷ *n* tendency of cotton fibres in a sample to stick to each other

CLINGED > CLING

CLINGER > CLING

CLINGERS > CLING

CLINGFILM *n* thin polythene material for wrapping food

CLINGFISH *n* any small marine teleost fish of the family *Gobiesocidae*, having a flattened elongated body with a sucking disc beneath the head for clinging to rocks, etc

CLINGIER > CLING

CLINGIEST > CLING

CLINGING > CLING

CLINGS > CLING

CLINGY > CLING

CLINIC *n* building where outpatients receive medical treatment or advice

CLINICAL *adj* of a clinic

CLINICIAN *n* physician, psychiatrist, etc, who specializes in clinical work as opposed to one engaged in laboratory or experimental studies

CLINICS > CLINIC

CLINIQUE *same as* > CLINIC

CLINIQUES > CLINIC

CLINK *n* (make) a light sharp metallic sound ▷ *vb* make a light sharp metallic sound

CLINKED > CLINK

CLINKER *n* fused coal left over in a fire or furnace ▷ *vb* form clinker during burning

CLINKERED > CLINKER

CLINKERS > CLINKER

CLINKING > CLINK

CLINKS > CLINK

CLINOAXES > CLINOAXIS

CLINOAXIS *n* in a monoclinic crystal, the lateral axis which forms an oblique angle with the vertical axis

CLINOSTAT *n* apparatus for studying tropisms in plants, usually a rotating disc to which the plant is attached so that it receives an equal stimulus on all sides

CLINQUANT *adj* glittering, esp with tinsel ▷ *n* tinsel or imitation gold leaf

CLINT *n* section of a limestone pavement separated from adjacent sections by solution fissures

CLINTONIA *n* any temperate liliaceous plant of the genus *Clintonia*, having white, greenish-yellow, or purplish flowers, broad ribbed leaves, and blue berries

CLINTS > CLINT

CLIP *vb* cut with shears or scissors ▷ *n* short extract of a film

CLIPART *n* large collection of simple drawings stored in a computer

CLIPARTS > CLIPART

CLIPBOARD *n* portable writing board with a clip at the top for holding paper

CLIPE *same as* > CLYPE

CLIPED > CLIPE

CLIPES > CLIPE

CLIPING > CLIPE

CLIPPABLE > CLIP

CLIPPED > CLIP

CLIPPER *n* fast commercial sailing ship

CLIPPERS *pl n* tool for clipping

CLIPPIE *n* bus conductress

CLIPPIES > CLIPPIE

CLIPPING > CLIP

CLIPPINGS > CLIP

CLIPS > CLIP

CLIPSHEAR *n* earwig

CLIPSHEET *n* sheet of paper with text printed on one side only

CLIPT *old inflection of* > CLIP

CLIQUE *n* small exclusive group ▷ *vb* to form a clique

CLIQUED > CLIQUE

CLIQUES > CLIQUE

CLIQUEY *adj* exclusive, confined to a small group

CLIQUIER > CLIQUEY

CLIQUIEST > CLIQUEY

CLIQUING > CLIQUE

CLIQUISH > CLIQUE

CLIQUISM > CLIQUE

CLIQUISMS > CLIQUE

CLIQUY *same as* > CLIQUEY

CLITELLA > CLITELLUM

CLITELLAR > CLITELLUM

CLITELLUM *n* thickened saddle-like region of epidermis in earthworms and leeches whose secretions bind copulating worms together and later form a cocoon around the eggs

CLITHRAL *same as* > CLEITHRAL

CLITIC *adj* (of a word) incapable of being stressed, usually pronounced as if part of the word that follows or precedes it: for example, in French, *me*, *te*, and *le* are clitic pronouns ▷ *n* clitic word

CLITICISE *same as* > CLITICIZE

CLITICIZE *vb* pronounce as part of following or preceding word

CLITICS > CLITIC

CLITORAL > CLITORIS

CLITORIC > CLITORIS

CLITORIS *n* small sexually sensitive organ at the front of the vulva

CLITTER *vb* to stridulate

CLITTERED > CLITTER

CLITTERS > CLITTER

CLIVERS *same as* > CLEAVERS

CLIVIA *n* plant belonging to the Amaryllid family

CLIVIAS > CLIVIA

CLOACA *n* cavity in most animals, except higher mammals, into which the alimentary canal and the genital and urinary ducts open

CLOACAE > CLOACA

CLOACAL > CLOACA

CLOACAS > CLOACA

CLOACINAL > CLOACA

CLOACITIS *n* inflammation of the cloaca in birds, including domestic fowl, and other animals with a common opening of the urinary and gastrointestinal tracts

CLOAK *n* loose sleeveless outer garment ▷ *vb* cover or conceal

CLOAKED > CLOAK

CLOAKING > CLOAK

CLOAKROOM *n* room where coats may be left temporarily

CLOAKS > CLOAK

CLOAM *adj* made of clay or earthenware ▷ *n* clay or earthenware pots, dishes, etc, collectively

CLOAMS > CLOAM

CLOBBER *vb* hit ▷ *n* belongings, esp clothes

CLOBBERED > CLOBBER

CLOBBERS > CLOBBER

CLOCHARD *n* tramp

CLOCHARDS > CLOCHARD

CLOCHE *n* cover to protect young plants

CLOCHES > CLOCHE

CLOCK *n* instrument for showing the time ▷ *vb* record (time) with a stopwatch
CLOCKED > CLOCK
CLOCKER > CLOCK
CLOCKERS > CLOCK
CLOCKING > CLOCK
CLOCKINGS > CLOCK
CLOCKLIKE > CLOCK
CLOCKS > CLOCK
CLOCKWISE *adj* in the direction in which the hands of a clock rotate
CLOCKWORK *n* mechanism similar to the kind in a clock, used in wind-up toys
CLOD *n* lump of earth ▷ *vb* pelt with clods
CLODDED > CLOD
CLODDIER > CLOD
CLODDIEST > CLOD
CLODDING > CLOD
CLODDISH > CLOD
CLODDY > CLOD
CLODLY > CLOD
CLODPATE *n* dull or stupid person
CLODPATED *adj* stupid
CLODPATES > CLODPATE
CLODPOLE *same as* > CLODPATE
CLODPOLES > CLODPOLE
CLODPOLL *same as* > CLODPATE
CLODPOLLS > CLODPOLL
CLODS > CLOD
CLOFF *n* cleft of a tree
CLOFFS > CLOFF
CLOG *vb* obstruct ▷ *n* wooden or wooden-soled shoe
CLOGDANCE *n* dance performed in clogs
CLOGGED > CLOG
CLOGGER *n* clogmaker
CLOGGERS > CLOGGER
CLOGGIER > CLOG
CLOGGIEST > CLOG
CLOGGILY > CLOG
CLOGGING > CLOG
CLOGGY > CLOG
CLOGS > CLOG
CLOISON *n* partition
CLOISONNE *n* design made by filling in a wire outline with coloured enamel ▷ *adj* of, relating to, or made by cloisonné
CLOISONS > CLOISON
CLOISTER *n* covered pillared arcade, usu. in a monastery ▷ *vb* confine or seclude in or as if in a monastery
CLOISTERS > CLOISTER
CLOISTRAL *adj* of, like, or characteristic of a cloister
CLOKE *same as* > CLOAK
CLOKED > CLOKE
CLOKES > CLOKE
CLOKING > CLOKE
CLOMB *a past tense and past participle of* > CLIMB
CLOMP *same as* > CLUMP
CLOMPED > CLOMP
CLOMPING > CLOMP
CLOMPS > CLOMP
CLON *same as* > CLONE
CLONAL > CLONE
CLONALLY > CLONE
CLONE *n* animal or plant produced artificially from the cells of another animal or plant, and identical to the original ▷ *vb* produce as a clone
CLONED > CLONE
CLONER > CLONE
CLONERS > CLONE
CLONES > CLONE
CLONIC > CLONUS
CLONICITY > CLONUS
CLONIDINE *n* antihypertensive drug
CLONING > CLONE
CLONINGS > CLONE
CLONISM *n* series of clonic spasms
CLONISMS > CLONISM
CLONK *vb* make a loud dull thud ▷ *n* loud thud
CLONKED > CLONK
CLONKING > CLONK
CLONKS > CLONK
CLONS > CLON
CLONUS *n* type of convulsion characterized by rapid contraction and relaxation of a muscle
CLONUSES > CLONUS
CLOOP *n* sound made when a cork is drawn from a bottle
CLOOPS > CLOOP
CLOOT *n* hoof
CLOOTS > CLOOT
CLOP *vb* make or move along with a sound as of a horse's hooves striking the ground ▷ *n* sound of this nature
CLOPPED > CLOP
CLOPPING > CLOP
CLOPS > CLOP
CLOQUE *n* fabric with an embossed surface
CLOQUES > CLOQUE
CLOSABLE > CLOSE
CLOSE *vb* shut ▷ *n* end, conclusion ▷ *adj* near ▷ *adv* closely, tightly ▷ *n* passageway leading to a tenement building
CLOSEABLE > CLOSE
CLOSED > CLOSE
CLOSEDOWN *n* closure or stoppage of operations
CLOSEHEAD *n* entrance to a close
CLOSELY > CLOSE
CLOSENESS > CLOSE
CLOSEOUT *n* termination of an account on which the margin is exhausted
CLOSEOUTS > CLOSEOUT
CLOSER > CLOSE
CLOSERS > CLOSE
CLOSES > CLOSE
CLOSEST > CLOSE
CLOSET *n* cupboard ▷ *adj* private, secret ▷ *vb* shut (oneself) away in private
CLOSETED > CLOSET
CLOSETFUL *n* quantity that may be contained in a closet
CLOSETING > CLOSET
CLOSETS > CLOSET
CLOSEUP *n* photo taken close to subject
CLOSEUPS > CLOSEUP
CLOSING > CLOSE
CLOSINGS > CLOSE
CLOSURE *n* closing ▷ *vb* (in a deliberative body) to end (debate) by closure
CLOSURED > CLOSURE
CLOSURES > CLOSURE
CLOSURING > CLOSURE
CLOT *n* soft thick lump formed from liquid ▷ *vb* form soft thick lumps
CLOTBUR *n* burdock
CLOTBURS > CLOTBUR
CLOTE *n* burdock
CLOTES > CLOTE
CLOTH *n* (piece of) woven fabric
CLOTHE *vb* put clothes on
CLOTHED > CLOTHE
CLOTHES *n* garments
CLOTHIER *n* maker or seller of clothes or cloth
CLOTHIERS > CLOTHIER
CLOTHING > CLOTHE
CLOTHINGS > CLOTHE
CLOTHLIKE > CLOTH
CLOTHS > CLOTH
CLOTPOLL *same as* > CLODPOLL
CLOTPOLLS > CLOTPOLL
CLOTS > CLOT
CLOTTED > CLOT
CLOTTER *vb* to clot
CLOTTERED > CLOTTER
CLOTTERS > CLOTTER
CLOTTIER > CLOTTY
CLOTTIEST > CLOTTY
CLOTTING > CLOT
CLOTTINGS > CLOT
CLOTTISH > CLOT
CLOTTY *adj* full of clots
CLOTURE *n* closure in the US Senate ▷ *vb* end (debate) in the US Senate by cloture
CLOTURED > CLOTURE
CLOTURES > CLOTURE
CLOTURING > CLOTURE
CLOU *n* crux; focus
CLOUD *n* mass of condensed water vapour floating in the sky ▷ *vb* become cloudy
CLOUDAGE *n* mass of clouds
CLOUDAGES > CLOUDAGE
CLOUDED > CLOUD
CLOUDIER > CLOUDY
CLOUDIEST > CLOUDY
CLOUDILY > CLOUDY
CLOUDING > CLOUD
CLOUDINGS > CLOUD
CLOUDLAND *n* realm or fantasy or impractical notions
CLOUDLESS > CLOUD
CLOUDLET *n* small cloud
CLOUDLETS > CLOUDLET
CLOUDLIKE > CLOUD
CLOUDS > CLOUD
CLOUDTOWN *n* cloudland
CLOUDY *adj* having a lot of clouds
CLOUGH *n* gorge or narrow ravine
CLOUGHS > CLOUGH
CLOUR *vb* to thump or dent
CLOURED > CLOUR
CLOURING > CLOUR
CLOURS > CLOUR
CLOUS > CLOU
CLOUT *n* hard blow ▷ *vb* hit hard
CLOUTED > CLOUT
CLOUTER > CLOUT
CLOUTERLY *adj* clumsy
CLOUTERS > CLOUT
CLOUTING > CLOUT
CLOUTS > CLOUT
CLOVE *n* tropical evergreen myrtaceous tree
CLOVEN > CLEAVE
CLOVEPINK *n* carnation
CLOVER *n* plant with three-lobed leaves
CLOVERED *adj* covered with clover
CLOVERS > CLOVER
CLOVERY > CLOVER
CLOVES > CLOVE
CLOVIS as in *clovis point* flint projectile dating from the 10th millennium BC
CLOW *n* clove
CLOWDER *n* collective terms for a group of cats
CLOWDERS > CLOWDER
CLOWN *n* comic entertainer in a circus ▷ *vb* behave foolishly
CLOWNED > CLOWN
CLOWNERY > CLOWN
CLOWNING > CLOWN
CLOWNINGS > CLOWN
CLOWNISH > CLOWN
CLOWNS > CLOWN
CLOWS > CLOW
CLOY *vb* make weary or cause weariness through an excess of something initially pleasurable or sweet
CLOYE *vb* to claw
CLOYED > CLOY
CLOYES > CLOYE
CLOYING *adj* sickeningly sweet
CLOYINGLY > CLOYING
CLOYLESS *adj* not cloying
CLOYMENT *n* satiety
CLOYMENTS > CLOYMENT
CLOYS > CLOY
CLOYSOME *adj* cloying
CLOZAPINE *n* drug used to treat mental illness

CLOZE as in *cloze test* test of the ability to understand text
CLOZES > CLOZE
CLUB *n* association of people with common interests ▷ *vb* hit with a club
CLUBABLE *same as* > CLUBBABLE
CLUBBABLE *adj* suitable to be a member of a club
CLUBBED > CLUB
CLUBBER *n* person who regularly frequents nightclubs and similar establishments
CLUBBERS > CLUBBER
CLUBBIER > CLUBBY
CLUBBIEST > CLUBBY
CLUBBILY > CLUBBY
CLUBBING > CLUB
CLUBBINGS > CLUB
CLUBBISH *adj* clubby
CLUBBISM *n* advantage gained through membership of a club or clubs
CLUBBISMS > CLUBBISM
CLUBBIST > CLUBBISM
CLUBBISTS > CLUBBISM
CLUBBY *adj* sociable, esp effusively so
CLUBFACE *n* face of golf club
CLUBFACES > CLUBFACE
CLUBFEET > CLUBFOOT
CLUBFOOT *n* congenital deformity of the foot
CLUBHAND *n* congenital deformity of the hand
CLUBHANDS > CLUBHAND
CLUBHAUL *vb* force (a sailing vessel) onto a new tack, esp in an emergency
CLUBHAULS > CLUBHAUL
CLUBHEAD *n* head of golf club
CLUBHEADS > CLUBHEAD
CLUBHOUSE *n* premises of a sports or other club, esp a golf club
CLUBLAND *n* (in Britain) the area of London around St. James's, which contains most of the famous London clubs
CLUBLANDS > CLUBLAND
CLUBMAN *n* man who is an enthusiastic member of a club or clubs
CLUBMEN > CLUBMAN
CLUBROOM *n* room in which a club meets
CLUBROOMS > CLUBROOM
CLUBROOT *n* disease of cabbages
CLUBROOTS > CLUBROOT
CLUBRUSH *n* any rush of the genus Scirpus
CLUBS > CLUB
CLUBWOMAN *n* woman who is an enthusiastic member of a club or clubs
CLUBWOMEN > CLUBWOMAN
CLUCK *n* low clicking noise made by a hen ▷ *vb* make this noise
CLUCKED > CLUCK
CLUCKIER > CLUCKY
CLUCKIEST > CLUCKY
CLUCKING > CLUCK
CLUCKS > CLUCK
CLUCKY *adj* wishing to have a baby
CLUDGIE *n* toilet
CLUDGIES > CLUDGIE
CLUE *n* something that helps to solve a mystery or puzzle ▷ *vb* help solve a mystery or puzzle
CLUED > CLUE
CLUEING > CLUE
CLUELESS *adj* stupid
CLUES > CLUE
CLUING > CLUE
CLUMBER *n* type of thickset spaniel
CLUMBERS > CLUMBER
CLUMP *n* small group of things or people ▷ *vb* walk heavily
CLUMPED > CLUMP
CLUMPER > CLUMP
CLUMPERS > CLUMP
CLUMPIER > CLUMP
CLUMPIEST > CLUMP
CLUMPING > CLUMP
CLUMPISH > CLUMP
CLUMPLIKE > CLUMP
CLUMPS > CLUMP
CLUMPY > CLUMP
CLUMSIER > CLUMSY
CLUMSIEST > CLUMSY
CLUMSILY > CLUMSY
CLUMSY *adj* lacking skill or physical coordination
CLUNCH *n* hardened clay
CLUNCHES > CLUNCH
CLUNG > CLING
CLUNK *n* dull metallic sound ▷ *vb* make such a sound
CLUNKED > CLUNK
CLUNKER *n* dilapidated old car or other machine
CLUNKERS > CLUNKER
CLUNKIER > CLUNKY
CLUNKIEST > CLUNKY
CLUNKING > CLUNK
CLUNKS > CLUNK
CLUNKY *adj* making a clunking noise
CLUPEID *n* any widely distributed soft-finned teleost fish of the family *Clupeidae*, typically having oily flesh, and including the herrings, sardines, shad, etc ▷ *adj* of, relating to, or belonging to the family *Clupeidae*
CLUPEIDS > CLUPEID
CLUPEOID *adj* of, relating to, or belonging to the *Isospondyli* (or *Clupeiformes*), a large order of soft-finned fishes, including the herrings, salmon, and tarpon ▷ *n* any fish belonging to the order *Isospondyli*
CLUPEOIDS > CLUPEOID
CLUSIA *n* tree of the tropical American genus Clusia
CLUSIAS > CLUSIA
CLUSTER *n* small close group ▷ *vb* gather in clusters
CLUSTERED > CLUSTER
CLUSTERS > CLUSTER
CLUSTERY > CLUSTER
CLUTCH *vb* grasp tightly ▷ *n* device enabling two revolving shafts to be connected and disconnected, esp in a motor vehicle
CLUTCHED > CLUTCH
CLUTCHES > CLUTCH
CLUTCHING > CLUTCH
CLUTCHY *adj* (of a person) tending to cling
CLUTTER *vb* scatter objects about (a place) untidily ▷ *n* untidy mess
CLUTTERED > CLUTTER
CLUTTERS > CLUTTER
CLUTTERY *adj* full of clutter
CLY *vb* to steal or seize
CLYING > CLY
CLYPE *vb* tell tales ▷ *n* person who tells tales
CLYPEAL > CLYPEUS
CLYPEATE > CLYPEUS
CLYPED > CLYPE
CLYPEI > CLYPEUS
CLYPES > CLYPE
CLYPEUS *n* cuticular plate on the head of some insects between the labrum and the frons
CLYPING > CLYPE
CLYSTER *a former name for an* > ENEMA
CLYSTERS > CLYSTER
CNEMIAL > CNEMIS
CNEMIDES > CNEMIS
CNEMIS *n* shin or tibia
CNIDA *n* nematocyst
CNIDAE > CNIDA
CNIDARIAN *n* any invertebrate of the phylum *Cnidaria*, which comprises the coelenterates ▷ *adj* of, relating to, or belonging to the *Cnidaria*
COACH *n* long-distance bus ▷ *vb* train, teach
COACHABLE *adj* capable of being coached
COACHDOG *n* Dalmatian dog
COACHDOGS > COACHDOG
COACHED > COACH
COACHEE *n* person who receives training from a coach, esp in business or office practice
COACHEES > COACHEE
COACHER > COACH
COACHERS > COACH
COACHES > COACH
COACHIES > COACHY
COACHING > COACH
COACHINGS > COACH
COACHLINE *n* decorative line on the bodywork of a vehicle
COACHLOAD *n* quantity that a coach can carry
COACHMAN *n* driver of a horse-drawn coach or carriage
COACHMEN > COACHMAN
COACHWHIP *n* whipsnake
COACHWOOD *n* Australian tree, *Ceratopetalum apetalum*, yielding light aromatic wood used for furniture, turnery, etc
COACHWORK *n* body of a car
COACHY *n* coachman
COACT *vb* to act together
COACTED > COACT
COACTING > COACT
COACTION *n* any relationship between organisms within a community
COACTIONS > COACTION
COACTIVE > COACTION
COACTOR > COACT
COACTORS > COACT
COACTS > COACT
COADAPTED *adj* adapted to one another
COADJUTOR *n* bishop appointed as assistant to a diocesan bishop
COADMIRE *vb* to admire together
COADMIRED > COADMIRE
COADMIRES > COADMIRE
COADMIT *vb* to admit together
COADMITS > COADMIT
COADUNATE *same as* > CONNATE
COAEVAL *n* contemporary
COAEVALS > COAEVAL
COAGENCY *n* joint agency
COAGENT > COAGENCY
COAGENTS > COAGENCY
COAGULA > COAGULUM
COAGULANT *n* substance causing coagulation
COAGULASE *n* any enzyme that causes coagulation of blood
COAGULATE *vb* change from a liquid to a semisolid mass ▷ *n* solid or semisolid substance produced by coagulation
COAGULUM *n* any coagulated mass
COAGULUMS > COAGULUM
COAITA *n* spider monkey
COAITAS > COAITA
COAL *n* black rock consisting mainly of carbon, used as fuel ▷ *vb* take in, or turn into coal
COALA *same as* > KOALA

COALAS > COALA
COALBALL *n* in coal, nodule containing petrified plant or animal remains
COALBALLS > COALBALL
COALBIN *n* bin for holding coal
COALBINS > COALBIN
COALBOX *n* box for holding coal
COALBOXES > COALBOX
COALED > COAL
COALER *n* ship, train, etc, used to carry or supply coal
COALERS > COALER
COALESCE *vb* come together, merge
COALESCED > COALESCE
COALESCES > COALESCE
COALFACE *n* exposed seam of coal in a mine
COALFACES > COALFACE
COALFIELD *n* area with coal under the ground
COALFISH *n* dark-coloured gadoid food fish, *Pollachius virens*, occurring in northern seas
COALHOLE *n* small coal cellar
COALHOLES > COALHOLE
COALHOUSE *n* shed or building for storing coal
COALIER > COAL
COALIEST > COAL
COALIFIED > COALIFY
COALIFIES > COALIFY
COALIFY *vb* to turn into coal
COALING > COAL
COALISE *vb* to form a coalition
COALISED > COALISE
COALISES > COALISE
COALISING > COALISE
COALITION *n* temporary alliance, esp between political parties
COALIZE *same as* > COALISE
COALIZED > COALIZE
COALIZES > COALIZE
COALIZING > COALIZE
COALLESS *adj* without coal
COALMAN *n* man who delivers coal
COALMEN > COALMAN
COALMINE *n* mine from which coal is extracted
COALMINER > COALMINE
COALMINES > COALMINE
COALPIT *n* pit from which coal is extracted
COALPITS > COALPIT
COALS > COAL
COALSACK *n* dark nebula near the constellation Cygnus
COALSACKS > COALSACK
COALSHED *n* shed in which coal is stored
COALSHEDS > COALSHED
COALTAR *n* black tar distilled from coal
COALTARS > COALTAR
COALY > COAL
COALYARD *n* yard in which coal is stored
COALYARDS > COALYARD
COAMING *n* raised frame round a ship's hatchway for keeping out water
COAMINGS > COAMING
COANCHOR *vb* to co-present a TV programme
COANCHORS > COANCHOR
COANNEX *vb* to annex with something else
COANNEXED > COANNEX
COANNEXES > COANNEX
COAPPEAR *vb* to appear jointly
COAPPEARS > COAPPEAR
COAPT *vb* to secure
COAPTED > COAPT
COAPTING > COAPT
COAPTS > COAPT
COARB *n* spiritual successor
COARBS > COARB
COARCTATE *adj* (of a pupa) enclosed in a hard barrel-shaped case (puparium), as in the housefly ▷ *vb* (esp of the aorta) to become narrower
COARSE *adj* rough in texture
COARSELY > COARSE
COARSEN *vb* make or become coarse
COARSENED > COARSEN
COARSENS > COARSEN
COARSER > COARSE
COARSEST > COARSE
COARSISH > COARSE
COASSIST *vb* to assist jointly
COASSISTS > COASSIST
COASSUME *vb* to assume jointly
COASSUMED > COASSUME
COASSUMES > COASSUME
COAST *n* place where the land meets the sea ▷ *vb* move by momentum, without the use of power
COASTAL > COAST
COASTALLY > COAST
COASTED > COAST
COASTER *n* small mat placed under a glass
COASTERS > COASTER
COASTING > COAST
COASTINGS > COAST
COASTLAND *n* land fringing a coast
COASTLINE *n* outline of a coast
COASTS > COAST
COASTWARD *adv* towards the coast
COASTWISE *adv* along the coast
COAT *n* outer garment with long sleeves ▷ *vb* cover with a layer
COATDRESS *n* garment that can be worn as a coat or a dress
COATE *same as* > QUOTE
COATED *adj* covered with an outer layer, film, etc
COATEE *n* short coat, esp for a baby
COATEES > COATEE
COATER *n* machine that applies a coating to something
COATERS > COATER
COATES > COATE
COATI *n* any omnivorous mammal of the genera *Nasua* and *Nasuella*, of Central and South America: family *Procyonidae*, order *Carnivora* (carnivores). They are related to but larger than the raccoons, having a long flexible snout and a brindled coat
COATING *n* covering layer
COATINGS > COATING
COATIS > COATI
COATLESS *adj* without a coat
COATRACK *n* rack for hanging coats on
COATRACKS > COATRACK
COATROOM *n* cloakroom
COATROOMS > COATROOM
COATS > COAT
COATSTAND *n* stand for hanging coats on
COATTAIL *n* long tapering tail at the back of a man's tailored coat
COATTAILS > COATTAIL
COATTEND *vb* to attend jointly
COATTENDS > COATTEND
COATTEST *vb* to attest jointly
COATTESTS > COATTEST
COAUTHOR *n* person who shares the writing of a book, article, etc, with another ▷ *vb* be the joint author of (a book, article, etc)
COAUTHORS > COAUTHOR
COAX *vb* persuade gently
COAXAL *same as* > COAXIAL
COAXED > COAX
COAXER > COAX
COAXERS > COAX
COAXES > COAX
COAXIAL *adj* (of a cable) transmitting by means of two concentric conductors separated by an insulator
COAXIALLY > COAXIAL
COAXING > COAX
COAXINGLY > COAX
COB *n* stalk of an ear of maize ▷ *vb* beat, esp on the buttocks
COBAEA *n* any climbing shrub of the tropical American genus *Cobaea*, esp *C. scandens*, grown for its large trumpet-shaped purple or white flowers: family *Polemoniaceae*
COBAEAS > COBAEA
COBALAMIN *n* vitamin B12
COBALT *n* brittle silvery-white metallic element
COBALTIC *adj* of or containing cobalt, esp in the trivalent state
COBALTINE *same as* > COBALTITE
COBALTITE *n* rare silvery-white mineral
COBALTOUS *adj* of or containing cobalt in the divalent state
COBALTS > COBALT
COBB *same as* > COB
COBBED > COB
COBBER *n* friend
COBBERS > COBBER
COBBIER > COBBY
COBBIEST > COBBY
COBBING > COB
COBBLE *n* cobblestone ▷ *vb* pave (a road) with cobblestones
COBBLED > COBBLE
COBBLER *n* shoe mender
COBBLERS *pl n* nonsense ▷ *interj* exclamation of strong disagreement
COBBLERY *n* shoemaking or shoemending
COBBLES *pl n* coal in small rounded lumps
COBBLING > COBBLE
COBBLINGS > COBBLE
COBBS > COBB
COBBY *adj* short and stocky
COBIA *n* large dark-striped game fish of tropical and subtropical seas
COBIAS > COBIA
COBLE *n* small single-masted flat-bottomed fishing boat
COBLES > COBLE
COBLOAF *n* round loaf of bread
COBLOAVES > COBLOAF
COBNUT *another name for* > HAZELNUT
COBNUTS > COBNUT
COBRA *n* venomous hooded snake of Asia and Africa
COBRAS > COBRA
COBRIC > COBRA
COBRIFORM *adj* cobra-like
COBS > COB
COBURG *n* rounded loaf with a cross cut on the top
COBURGS > COBURG
COBWEB *n* spider's web
COBWEBBED > COBWEB
COBWEBBY > COBWEB
COBWEBS > COBWEB
COBZA *n* Romanian lute
COBZAS > COBZA
COCA *n* dried leaves of a S American shrub which contain cocaine
COCAIN *same as* > COCAINE
COCAINE *n* addictive drug

used as a narcotic and as an anaesthetic
COCAINES > COCAINE
COCAINISE *same as* > COCAINIZE
COCAINISM *n* use of cocaine
COCAINIST *n* cocaine addict
COCAINIZE *vb* anaesthetize with cocaine
COCAINS > COCAIN
COCAPTAIN *vb* to captain jointly
COCAS > COCA
COCCAL > COCCUS
COCCI > COCCUS
COCCIC > COCCUS
COCCID *n* any homopterous insect of the superfamily *Coccoidea*, esp any of the family *Coccidae*, which includes the scale insects
COCCIDIA > COCCIDIUM
COCCIDIUM *n* any parasitic protozoan of the order Coccidia
COCCIDS > COCCID
COCCO *n* taro
COCCOID > COCCUS
COCCOIDAL > COCCUS
COCCOIDS > COCCUS
COCCOLITE *n* variety of pyroxene
COCCOLITH *n* any of the round calcareous plates in chalk formations: formed the outer layer of unicellular plankton
COCCOS > COCCO
COCCOUS > COCCUS
COCCUS *n* any spherical or nearly spherical bacterium, such as a staphylococcus
COCCYGEAL > COCCYX
COCCYGES > COCCYX
COCCYGIAN > COCCYX
COCCYX *n* bone at the base of the spinal column
COCCYXES > COCCYX
COCH *obsolete variant of* > COACH
COCHAIR *vb* to chair jointly
COCHAIRED > COCHAIR
COCHAIRS > COCHAIR
COCHES > COCH
COCHIN *n* large breed of domestic fowl
COCHINEAL *n* red dye obtained from a Mexican insect, used for food colouring
COCHINS > COCHIN
COCHLEA *n* spiral tube in the internal ear, which converts sound vibrations into nerve impulses
COCHLEAE > COCHLEA
COCHLEAR *adj* of or relating to the cochlea ▷ *n* spoonful
COCHLEARE *variant of* > COCHLEAR
COCHLEARS > COCHLEAR
COCHLEAS > COCHLEA
COCHLEATE *adj* shaped like a snail's shell
COCINERA *n* in Mexico, a female cook
COCINERAS > COCINERA
COCK *n* male bird, esp of domestic fowl ▷ *vb* draw back (the hammer of a gun) to firing position
COCKADE *n* feather or rosette worn on a hat as a badge
COCKADED > COCKADE
COCKADES > COCKADE
COCKAMAMY *adj* ridiculous or nonsensical
COCKAPOO *n* cross between a cocker spaniel and a poodle
COCKAPOOS > COCKAPOO
COCKATEEL *same as* > COCKATIEL
COCKATIEL *n* crested Australian parrot with a greyish-brown and yellow plumage
COCKATOO *n* crested parrot of Australia or the East Indies
COCKATOOS > COCKATOO
COCKBILL *vb* to tilt up one end of
COCKBILLS > COCKBILL
COCKBIRD *n* male bird
COCKBIRDS > COCKBIRD
COCKBOAT *n* any small boat
COCKBOATS > COCKBOAT
COCKCROW *n* daybreak
COCKCROWS > COCKCROW
COCKED > COCK
COCKER *n* devotee of cockfighting ▷ *vb* pamper or spoil by indulgence
COCKERED > COCKER
COCKEREL *n* young domestic cock
COCKERELS > COCKEREL
COCKERING > COCKER
COCKERS > COCKER
COCKET *n* document issued by a customs officer
COCKETS > COCKET
COCKEYE *n* eye affected with strabismus or one that squints
COCKEYED *adj* crooked, askew
COCKEYES > COCKEYE
COCKFIGHT *n* fight between two gamecocks fitted with sharp metal spurs
COCKHORSE *n* rocking horse
COCKIER > COCKY
COCKIES > COCKY
COCKIEST > COCKY
COCKILY > COCKY
COCKINESS *n* conceited self-assurance
COCKING > COCK
COCKISH *adj* wanton
COCKLE *n* edible shellfish ▷ *vb* fish for cockles
COCKLEBUR *n* any coarse weed of the genus *Xanthium*, having spiny burs: family *Asteraceae* (composites)
COCKLED > COCKLE
COCKLEERT *a Southwest English dialect variant of* > COCKCROW
COCKLEMAN *n* man who collects cockles
COCKLEMEN > COCKLEMAN
COCKLER *n* person employed to gather cockles
COCKLERS > COCKLER
COCKLES > COCKLE
COCKLIKE *adj* resembling a cock
COCKLING > COCKLE
COCKLOFT *n* small loft, garret, or attic
COCKLOFTS > COCKLOFT
COCKMATCH *n* cockfight
COCKNEY *n* native of London, esp of its East End ▷ *adj* characteristic of cockneys or their dialect
COCKNEYFY *vb* cause (one's speech, manners, etc) to fit the stereotyped idea of a cockney
COCKNEYS > COCKNEY
COCKNIFY *same as* > COCKNEYFY
COCKPIT *n* pilot's compartment in an aircraft
COCKPITS > COCKPIT
COCKROACH *n* beetle-like insect which is a household pest
COCKS > COCK
COCKSCOMB *n* comb of a domestic cock
COCKSFOOT *n* perennial Eurasian grass, *Dactylis glomerata*, cultivated as a pasture grass in North America and South Africa
COCKSHIES > COCKSHY
COCKSHOT *another name for* > COCKSHY
COCKSHOTS > COCKSHOT
COCKSHUT *n* dusk
COCKSHUTS > COCKSHUT
COCKSHY *n* target aimed at in throwing games
COCKSIER > COCKSY
COCKSIEST > COCKSY
COCKSPUR *n* spur on the leg of a cock
COCKSPURS > COCKSPUR
COCKSURE *adj* overconfident, arrogant
COCKSWAIN *same as* > COXSWAIN
COCKSY *adj* cocky
COCKTAIL *n* mixed alcoholic drink
COCKTAILS > COCKTAIL
COCKUP *n* something done badly ▷ *vb* ruin or spoil
COCKUPS > COCKUP
COCKY *adj* conceited and overconfident ▷ *n* farmer whose farm is regarded as small or of little account
COCO *n* coconut palm
COCOA *n* powder made from the seed of the cacao tree
COCOANUT *same as* > COCONUT
COCOANUTS > COCONUT
COCOAS > COCOA
COCOBOLA *n* type of rosewood
COCOBOLAS > COCOBOLA
COCOBOLO *same as* > COCOBOLA
COCOBOLOS > COCOBOLO
COCOMAT *n* mat made from coconut fibre
COCOMATS > COCOMAT
COCONUT *n* large hard fruit of a type of palm tree
COCONUTS > COCONUT
COCOON *n* silky protective covering of a silkworm ▷ *vb* wrap up tightly for protection
COCOONED > COCOON
COCOONERY *n* place where silkworms feed and make cocoons
COCOONING > COCOON
COCOONS > COCOON
COCOPAN *n* (in South Africa) a small wagon running on narrow-gauge railway lines used in mines
COCOPANS > COCOPAN
COCOPLUM *n* tropical shrub, also known as icaco, or its fruit
COCOPLUMS > COCOPLUM
COCOS > COCO
COCOTTE *n* small fireproof dish in which individual portions of food are cooked
COCOTTES > COCOTTE
COCOUNSEL *vb* to counsel jointly
COCOYAM *n* either of two food plants of West Africa, the taro or the yantia, both of which have edible underground stems
COCOYAMS > COCOYAM
COCOZELLE *n* variety of squash
COCREATE *vb* to create jointly
COCREATED > COCREATE
COCREATES > COCREATE
COCREATOR > COCREATE
COCTILE *adj* made by exposing to heat
COCTION *n* boiling
COCTIONS > COCTION
COCULTURE *vb* to culture together
COCURATOR *n* joint curator
COCUSWOOD *n* wood from

the tropical American leguminous tree *Brya ebenus*, used for inlaying, turnery, musical instruments, etc
COD *n* large food fish of the North Atlantic ▷ *adj* having the character of an imitation or parody ▷ *vb* make fun of
CODA *n* final part of a musical composition
CODABLE *adj* capable of being coded
CODAS > CODA
CODDED > COD
CODDER *n* cod fisherman or his boat
CODDERS > CODDER
CODDING > COD
CODDLE *vb* pamper, overprotect ▷ *n* stew made from ham and bacon scraps
CODDLED > CODDLE
CODDLER > CODDLE
CODDLERS > CODDLE
CODDLES > CODDLE
CODDLING > CODDLE
CODE *n* system of letters, symbols, or prearranged signals by which messages can be communicated secretly or briefly ▷ *vb* put into code
CODEBOOK *n* book containing the means to decipher a code
CODEBOOKS > CODEBOOK
CODEBTOR *n* fellow debtor
CODEBTORS > CODEBTOR
CODEC *n* set of equipment that encodes an analogue speech or video signal into digital form for transmission purposes and at the receiving end decodes the digital signal into a form close to its original
CODECS > CODEC
CODED > CODE
CODEIA *n* codeine
CODEIAS > CODEIA
CODEIN *same as* > CODEINE
CODEINA *obsolete variant of* > CODEINE
CODEINAS > CODEINA
CODEINE *n* drug used as a painkiller
CODEINES > CODEINE
CODEINS > CODEIN
CODELESS *adj* lacking a code
CODEN *n* unique six-character code assigned to a publication for identification purposes
CODENAME *same as* > CODEWORD
CODENAMES > CODEWORD
CODENS > CODEN
CODER *n* person or thing that codes
CODERIVE *vb* to derive jointly
CODERIVED > CODERIVE
CODERIVES > CODERIVE
CODERS > CODER
CODES > CODE
CODESIGN *vb* to design jointly
CODESIGNS > CODESIGN
CODETTA *n* short coda
CODETTAS > CODETTA
CODEVELOP *vb* to develop jointly
CODEWORD *n* (esp in military use) a word used to identify a classified plan, operation, etc
CODEWORDS > CODEWORD
CODEX *n* volume of manuscripts of an ancient text
CODFISH *n* cod
CODFISHES > CODFISH
CODGER *n* old man
CODGERS > CODGER
CODICES > CODEX
CODICIL *n* addition to a will
CODICILS > CODICIL
CODIFIED > CODIFY
CODIFIER > CODIFY
CODIFIERS > CODIFY
CODIFIES > CODIFY
CODIFY *vb* organize (rules or procedures) systematically
CODIFYING > CODIFY
CODILLA *n* coarse tow of hemp and flax
CODILLAS > CODILLA
CODILLE *n* in the cardgame ombre, term indicating that the game is won
CODILLES > CODILLE
CODING > CODE
CODINGS > CODE
CODIRECT *vb* to direct jointly
CODIRECTS > CODIRECT
CODIST *n* codifier
CODISTS > CODIST
CODLIN *same as* > CODLING
CODLING *n* young cod
CODLINGS > CODLING
CODLINS > CODLIN
CODOLOGY *n* art or practice of bluffing or deception
CODOMAIN *n* set of values that a function is allowed to take
CODOMAINS > CODOMAIN
CODON *n* unit that consists of three adjacent bases on a DNA molecule and that determines the position of a specific amino acid in a protein molecule during protein synthesis
CODONS > CODON
CODPIECE *n* bag covering the male genitals, attached to the breeches
CODPIECES > CODPIECE
CODRIVE *vb* take alternate turns driving a car with another person
CODRIVEN > CODRIVE
CODRIVER *n* one of two drivers who take turns to drive a car
CODRIVERS > CODRIVER
CODRIVES > CODRIVE
CODRIVING > CODRIVE
CODROVE > CODRIVE
CODS > COD
COED *adj* educating both sexes together ▷ *n* school or college that educates both sexes together
COEDIT *vb* edit (a book, newspaper, etc) jointly
COEDITED > COEDIT
COEDITING > COEDIT
COEDITOR > COEDIT
COEDITORS > COEDIT
COEDITS > COEDIT
COEDS > COED
COEFFECT *n* secondary effect
COEFFECTS > COEFFECT
COEHORN *n* type of small artillery mortar
COEHORNS > COEHORN
COELIAC *adj* of or relating to the abdomen ▷ *n* person who has coeliac disease
COELIACS > COELIAC
COELOM *n* body cavity of many multicellular animals, situated in the mesoderm and containing the digestive tract and other visceral organs
COELOMATA *n* animals possessing a coelom
COELOMATE *adj* possessing a coelom
COELOME *same as* > COELOM
COELOMES > COELOME
COELOMIC > COELOM
COELOMS > COELOM
COELOSTAT *n* astronomical instrument consisting of a plane mirror mounted parallel to the earth's axis and rotated about this axis once every two days so that light from a celestial body, esp the sun, is reflected onto a second mirror, which reflects the beam into a telescope
COEMBODY *vb* to embody jointly
COEMPLOY *vb* to employ together
COEMPLOYS > COEMPLOY
COEMPT *vb* buy up something in its entirety
COEMPTED > COEMPT
COEMPTING > COEMPT
COEMPTION *n* buying up of the complete supply of a commodity
COEMPTS > COEMPT
COENACLE *same as* > CENACLE
COENACLES > COENACLE
COENACT *vb* to enact jointly
COENACTED > COENACT
COENACTS > COENACT
COENAMOR *vb* enamour jointly
COENAMORS > COENAMOR
COENDURE *vb* to endure together
COENDURED > COENDURE
COENDURES > COENDURE
COENOBIA > COENOBIUM
COENOBITE *n* member of a religious order in a monastic community
COENOBIUM *n* monastery or convent
COENOCYTE *n* mass of protoplasm containing many nuclei and enclosed by a cell wall: occurs in many fungi and some algae
COENOSARC *n* system of protoplasmic branches connecting the polyps of colonial organisms such as corals
COENURE *variant form of* > COENURUS
COENURES > COENURE
COENURI > COENURUS
COENURUS *n* encysted larval form of the tapeworm *Multiceps*, containing many encapsulated heads. In sheep it can cause the gid, and when eaten by dogs it develops into several adult forms
COENZYME *n* nonprotein organic molecule that forms a complex with certain enzymes and is essential for their activity
COENZYMES > COENZYME
COEQUAL *n* equal ▷ *adj* of the same size, rank, etc
COEQUALLY > COEQUAL
COEQUALS > COEQUAL
COEQUATE *vb* to equate together
COEQUATED > COEQUATE
COEQUATES > COEQUATE
COERCE *vb* compel, force
COERCED > COERCE
COERCER > COERCE
COERCERS > COERCE
COERCES > COERCE
COERCIBLE > COERCE
COERCIBLY > COERCE
COERCING > COERCE
COERCION *n* act or power of coercing
COERCIONS > COERCION
COERCIVE > COERCE
COERECT *vb* to erect together
COERECTED > COERECT
COERECTS > COERECT
COESITE *n* polymorph of silicon dioxide
COESITES > COESITE
COETERNAL *adj* existing

together eternally
COEVAL *n* contemporary ▷ *adj* contemporary
COEVALITY > COEVAL
COEVALLY > COEVAL
COEVALS > COEVAL
COEVOLVE *vb* to evolve together
COEVOLVED > COEVOLVE
COEVOLVES > COEVOLVE
COEXERT *vb* to exert together
COEXERTED > COEXERT
COEXERTS > COEXERT
COEXIST *vb* exist together, esp peacefully despite differences
COEXISTED > COEXIST
COEXISTS > COEXIST
COEXTEND *vb* extend or cause to extend equally in space or time
COEXTENDS > COEXTEND
COFACTOR *n* number associated with an element in a square matrix, equal to the determinant of the matrix formed by removing the row and column in which the element appears from the given determinant
COFACTORS > COFACTOR
COFEATURE *vb* to feature together
COFF *vb* buy
COFFED > COFF
COFFEE *n* drink made from the roasted and ground seeds of a tropical shrub ▷ *adj* medium-brown
COFFEEPOT *n* pot in which coffee is brewed or served
COFFEES > COFFEE
COFFER *n* chest, esp for storing valuables ▷ *vb* store
COFFERDAM *n* watertight enclosure pumped dry to enable construction work to be done
COFFERED > COFFERDAM
COFFERING > COFFERDAM
COFFERS > COFFERDAM
COFFIN *n* box in which a corpse is buried or cremated ▷ *vb* place in or as in a coffin
COFFINED > COFFIN
COFFING > COFF
COFFINING > COFFIN
COFFINITE *n* uranium-bearing silicate mineral
COFFINS > COFFIN
COFFLE *n* (esp formerly) a line of slaves, beasts, etc, fastened together ▷ *vb* to fasten together in a coffle
COFFLED > COFFLE
COFFLES > COFFLE
COFFLING > COFFLE
COFFRET *n* small coffer
COFFRETS > COFFRET
COFFS > COFF
COFINANCE *vb* to finance jointly
COFOUND *vb* to found jointly
COFOUNDED > COFOUND
COFOUNDER > COFOUND
COFOUNDS > COFOUND
COFT > COFF
COG *n* one of the teeth on the rim of a gearwheel ▷ *vb* roll (cast-steel ingots) to convert them into blooms
COGENCE > COGENT
COGENCES > COGENT
COGENCIES > COGENT
COGENCY > COGENT
COGENER *n* congener
COGENERS > COGENER
COGENT *adj* forcefully convincing
COGENTLY > COGENT
COGGED > COG
COGGER *n* deceiver
COGGERS > COGGER
COGGIE *n* quaich or drinking cup
COGGIES > COGGIE
COGGING > COG
COGGINGS > COG
COGGLE *vb* wobble or rock
COGGLED > COGGLE
COGGLES > COGGLE
COGGLIER > COGGLE
COGGLIEST > COGGLE
COGGLING > COGGLE
COGGLY > COGGLE
COGIE *same as* > COGGIE
COGIES > COGIE
COGITABLE *adj* conceivable
COGITATE *vb* think deeply about
COGITATED > COGITATE
COGITATES > COGITATE
COGITATOR > COGITATE
COGITO *n* philosophical theory that one must exist because one is capable of thought
COGITOS > COGITO
COGNAC *n* French brandy
COGNACS > COGNAC
COGNATE *adj* derived from a common original form ▷ *n* cognate word or language
COGNATELY > COGNATE
COGNATES > COGNATE
COGNATION > COGNATE
COGNISANT *same as* > COGNIZANT
COGNISE *same as* > COGNIZE
COGNISED > COGNISE
COGNISER > COGNISE
COGNISERS > COGNISE
COGNISES > COGNISE
COGNISING > COGNISE
COGNITION *n* act or experience of knowing or acquiring knowledge
COGNITIVE *adj* of or relating to cognition
COGNIZANT *adj* aware
COGNIZE *vb* perceive, become aware of, or know
COGNIZED > COGNIZE
COGNIZER > COGNIZE
COGNIZERS > COGNIZE
COGNIZES > COGNIZE
COGNIZING > COGNIZE
COGNOMEN *n* nickname
COGNOMENS > COGNOMEN
COGNOMINA > COGNOMEN
COGNOSCE *vb* in Scots law, to give judgment upon
COGNOSCED > COGNOSCE
COGNOSCES > COGNOSCE
COGNOVIT *n* in law, a defendant's confession that the case against him is just
COGNOVITS > COGNOVIT
COGON *n* any of the coarse tropical grasses of the genus *Imperata*, esp *I. cylindrica* and *I. exaltata* of the Philippines, which are used for thatching
COGONS > COGON
COGS > COG
COGUE *n* wooden pail or drinking vessel
COGUES > COGUE
COGWAY *n* rack railway
COGWAYS > COGWAY
COGWHEEL *same as* > GEARWHEEL
COGWHEELS > COGWHEEL
COHAB *n* cohabitor
COHABIT *vb* live together as husband and wife without being married
COHABITED > COHABIT
COHABITEE > COHABIT
COHABITER > COHABIT
COHABITOR > COHABIT
COHABITS > COHABIT
COHABS > COHAB
COHEAD *vb* to head jointly
COHEADED > COHEAD
COHEADING > COHEAD
COHEADS > COHEAD
COHEIR *n* person who inherits jointly with others
COHEIRESS > COHEIR
COHEIRS > COHEIR
COHERE *vb* hold or stick together
COHERED > COHERE
COHERENCE *n* logical or natural connection or consistency
COHERENCY *same as* > COHERENCE
COHERENT *adj* logical and consistent
COHERER *n* electrical component formerly used to detect radio waves, consisting of a tube containing loosely packed metal particles. The waves caused the particles to cohere, thereby changing the current through the circuit
COHERERS > COHERER
COHERES > COHERE
COHERING > COHERE
COHERITOR *n* coheir
COHESIBLE *adj* capable of cohesion
COHESION *n* sticking together
COHESIONS > COHESION
COHESIVE *adj* sticking together to form a whole
COHIBIT *vb* to restrain
COHIBITED > COHIBIT
COHIBITS > COHIBIT
COHO *n* Pacific salmon, *Oncorhynchus kisutch*
COHOBATE *vb* redistil (a distillate), esp by allowing it to mingle with the remaining matter
COHOBATED > COHOBATE
COHOBATES > COHOBATE
COHOE *same as* > COHO
COHOES > COHO
COHOG *n* quahog, an edible clam
COHOGS > COHOG
COHOLDER *n* joint holder
COHOLDERS > COHOLDER
COHORN *same as* > COEHORN
COHORNS > COEHORN
COHORT *n* band of associates
COHORTS > COHORT
COHOS > COHO
COHOSH *n* type of N American plant
COHOSHES > COHOSH
COHOST *vb* to host jointly
COHOSTED > COHOST
COHOSTESS *vb* (of a woman) to host jointly
COHOSTING > COHOST
COHOSTS > COHOST
COHOUSING *n* type of housing with some shared facilities
COHUNE *n* tropical American feather palm, *Attalea* (or *Orbignya*) *cohune*, whose large oily nuts yield an oil similar to coconut oil
COHUNES > COHUNE
COHYPONYM *n* word which is one of multiple hyponyms of another word
COIF *vb* arrange the hair of ▷ *n* close-fitting cap worn in the Middle Ages
COIFED *adj* wearing a coif
COIFFE *vb* to coiffure
COIFFED > COIF
COIFFES > COIFFE
COIFFEUR *n* hairdresser
COIFFEURS > COIFFEUR
COIFFEUSE > COIFFEUR
COIFFING > COIF
COIFFURE *n* hairstyle ▷ *vb* dress or arrange (the hair)
COIFFURED > COIFFURE
COIFFURES > COIFFURE
COIFING > COIF
COIFS > COIF
COIGN *variant spelling of* > QUOIN *vb* wedge

COIGNE *same as* >COIGN
COIGNED >COIGN
COIGNES >COIGNE
COIGNING >COIGN
COIGNS >COIGN
COIL *vb* wind in loops ▷ *n* something coiled
COILED >COIL
COILER >COIL
COILERS >COIL
COILING >COIL
COILS >COIL
COIN *n* piece of metal money ▷ *vb* invent (a word or phrase)
COINABLE >COIN
COINAGE *n* coins collectively
COINAGES >COINAGE
COINCIDE *vb* happen at the same time
COINCIDED >COINCIDE
COINCIDES >COINCIDE
COINED >COIN
COINER >COIN
COINERS >COIN
COINFECT *vb* infect at same time as other infection
COINFECTS >COINFECT
COINFER *vb* infer jointly
COINFERS >COINFER
COINHERE *vb* to inhere together
COINHERED >COINHERE
COINHERES >COINHERE
COINING >COIN
COININGS >COIN
COINMATE *n* fellow inmate
COINMATES >COINMATE
COINS >COIN
COINSURE *vb* insure jointly
COINSURED >COINSURE
COINSURER >COINSURE
COINSURES >COINSURE
COINTER *vb* to inter together
COINTERS >COINTER
COINTREAU *n* tradename for a French orange liqueur
COINVENT *vb* to invent jointly
COINVENTS >COINVENT
COIR *n* coconut fibre, used for matting
COIRS >COIR
COISTREL *n* knave
COISTRELS >COISTREL
COISTRIL *same as* >COISTREL
COISTRILS >COISTRIL
COIT *n* buttocks
COITAL >COITUS
COITALLY >COITUS
COITION *same as* >COITUS
COITIONAL >COITION
COITIONS >COITION
COITS >COIT
COITUS *n* sexual intercourse
COITUSES >COITUS
COJOIN *vb* to conjoin
COJOINED >COJOIN
COJOINING >COJOIN
COJOINS >COJOIN
COJONES *pl n* testicles
COKE *n* solid fuel left after gas has been distilled from coal ▷ *vb* become or convert into coke
COKED >COKE
COKEHEAD *n* cocaine addict
COKEHEADS >COKEHEAD
COKELIKE >COKE
COKERNUT *same as* >COCONUT
COKERNUTS >COKERNUT
COKES *n* fool
COKESES >COKES
COKIER >COKY
COKIEST >COKY
COKING >COKE
COKULORIS *n* palette with irregular holes, placed between lighting and camera to prevent glare
COKY *adj* like coke
COL *n* high mountain pass
COLA *n* dark brown fizzy soft drink
COLANDER *n* perforated bowl for straining or rinsing foods
COLANDERS >COLANDER
COLAS >COLA
COLBIES >COLBY
COLBY *n* type of mild-tasting hard cheese
COLBYS >COLBY
COLCANNON *n* dish, originating in Ireland, of potatoes and cabbage or other greens boiled and mashed together
COLCHICA >COLCHICUM
COLCHICUM *n* any Eurasian liliaceous plant of the genus *Colchicum*, such as the autumn crocus
COLCOTHAR *n* finely powdered form of ferric oxide produced by heating ferric sulphate and used as a pigment and as jewellers' rouge
COLD *adj* lacking heat ▷ *n* lack of heat
COLDBLOOD *n* any heavy draught-horse
COLDCOCK *vb* to knock to the ground
COLDCOCKS >COLDCOCK
COLDER >COLD
COLDEST >COLD
COLDHOUSE *n* unheated greenhouse
COLDIE *n* cold can or bottle of beer
COLDIES >COLDIE
COLDISH >COLD
COLDLY >COLD
COLDNESS >COLD
COLDS >COLD
COLE *same as* >CABBAGE
COLEAD *vb* to lead together
COLEADER >COLEAD
COLEADERS >COLEAD
COLEADING >COLEAD
COLEADS >COLEAD
COLECTOMY *n* surgical removal of part or all of the colon
COLED >COLEAD
COLEOPTER *n* aircraft that has an annular wing with the fuselage and engine on the centre line
COLES >COLE
COLESEED *n* common rape or cole
COLESEEDS >COLESEED
COLESLAW *n* salad dish of shredded raw cabbage in a dressing
COLESLAWS >COLESLAW
COLESSEE *n* joint lessee
COLESSEES >COLESSEE
COLESSOR *n* joint lessor
COLESSORS >COLESSOR
COLETIT *n* coal tit
COLETITS >COLETIT
COLEUS *n* any plant of the Old World genus *Coleus*: cultivated for their variegated leaves, typically marked with red, yellow, or white
COLEUSES >COLEUS
COLEWORT >CABBAGE
COLEWORTS >CABBAGE
COLEY *same as* >COALFISH
COLEYS >COLEY
COLIBRI *n* hummingbird
COLIBRIS >COLIBRI
COLIC *n* severe pains in the stomach and bowels
COLICIN *n* bacteriocidal protein
COLICINE *n* antibacterial protein
COLICINES >COLICINE
COLICINS >COLICIN
COLICKIER >COLICKY
COLICKY *adj* relating to or suffering from colic
COLICROOT *n* either of two North American liliaceous plants, *Aletris farinosa* or *A. aurea*, having tubular white or yellow flowers and a bitter root formerly used to relieve colic
COLICS >COLIC
COLICWEED *n* any of several plants of the genera *Dicentra* or *Corydalis*, such as the squirrel corn and Dutchman's-breeches: family *Fumariaceae*
COLIES >COLY
COLIFORM *n* type of bacteria of the intestinal tract
COLIFORMS >COLIFORM
COLIN *n* quail
COLINEAR *same as* >COLLINEAR
COLINS >COLIN
COLIPHAGE *n* bacteriophage
COLISEUM *n* large building, such as a stadium or theatre, used for entertainments, sports, etc
COLISEUMS >COLISEUM
COLISTIN *n* polymyxin antibiotic
COLISTINS >COLISTIN
COLITIC >COLITIS
COLITIS *n* inflammation of the colon
COLITISES >COLITIS
COLL *vb* to embrace
COLLAGE *n* art form in which various materials or objects are glued onto a surface ▷ *vb* to make a collage
COLLAGED >COLLAGE
COLLAGEN *n* protein found in cartilage and bone that yields gelatine when boiled
COLLAGENS >COLLAGEN
COLLAGES >COLLAGE
COLLAGING >COLLAGE
COLLAGIST >COLLAGE
COLLAPSAR *n* collapsed star, either a white dwarf, neutron star, or black hole
COLLAPSE *vb* fall down suddenly ▷ *n* collapsing
COLLAPSED >COLLAPSE
COLLAPSES >COLLAPSE
COLLAR *n* part of a garment round the neck ▷ *vb* seize, arrest
COLLARD *n* variety of the cabbage, *Brassica oleracea acephala*, having a crown of edible leaves
COLLARDS >COLLARD
COLLARED >COLLAR
COLLARET *n* small collar
COLLARETS >COLLARET
COLLARING >COLLAR
COLLARS >COLLAR
COLLATE *vb* gather together, examine, and put in order
COLLATED >COLLATE
COLLATES >COLLATE
COLLATING >COLLATE
COLLATION *n* collating
COLLATIVE *adj* involving collation
COLLATOR *n* person or machine that collates texts or manuscripts
COLLATORS >COLLATOR
COLLEAGUE *n* fellow worker, esp in a profession
COLLECT *vb* gather together ▷ *n* short prayer
COLLECTED *adj* calm and controlled
COLLECTOR *n* person who collects objects as a hobby
COLLECTS >COLLECT
COLLED >COLL
COLLEEN *n* girl
COLLEENS >COLLEEN
COLLEGE *n* place of higher education
COLLEGER *n* member of a college

COLLEGERS > COLLEGER
COLLEGES > COLLEGE
COLLEGIA > COLLEGIUM
COLLEGIAL *adj* of or relating to a college
COLLEGIAN *n* member of a college
COLLEGIUM *n* (in the former Soviet Union) a board in charge of a department
COLLET *n* (in a jewellery setting) a band or coronet-shaped claw that holds an individual stone ▷ *vb* mount in a collet
COLLETED > COLLET
COLLETING > COLLET
COLLETS > COLLET
COLLICULI *n* plural form of singular colliculus: small elevation, as on the surface of the optic lobe of the brain
COLLIDE *vb* crash together violently
COLLIDED > COLLIDE
COLLIDER *n* particle accelerator in which beams of particles are made to collide
COLLIDERS > COLLIDER
COLLIDES > COLLIDE
COLLIDING > COLLIDE
COLLIE *n* silky-haired sheepdog
COLLIED > COLLY
COLLIER *n* coal miner
COLLIERS > COLLIER
COLLIERY *n* coal mine
COLLIES > COLLY
COLLIGATE *vb* connect or link together
COLLIMATE *vb* adjust the line of sight of (an optical instrument)
COLLINEAR *adj* lying on the same straight line
COLLING *n* embrace
COLLINGS > COLLING
COLLINS *n* tall fizzy iced drink made with gin, vodka, rum, etc, mixed with fruit juice, soda water, and sugar
COLLINSES > COLLINS
COLLINSIA *n* North American plant of the scrophulariaceous genus *Collinsia*, having blue, white, or purple flowers
COLLISION *n* violent crash between moving objects
COLLOCATE *vb* (of words) occur together regularly
COLLODION *n* colourless or yellow syrupy liquid that consists of a solution of pyroxylin in ether and alcohol: used in medicine and in the manufacture of photographic plates, lacquers, etc
COLLODIUM *same as* > COLLODION
COLLOGUE *vb* confer confidentially
COLLOGUED > COLLOGUE
COLLOGUES > COLLOGUE
COLLOID *n* suspension of particles in a solution ▷ *adj* of or relating to the gluelike translucent material found in certain degenerating tissues
COLLOIDAL *adj* of, denoting, or having the character of a colloid
COLLOIDS > COLLOID
COLLOP *n* small slice of meat
COLLOPS > COLLOP
COLLOQUE *vb* to converse
COLLOQUED > COLLOQUE
COLLOQUES > COLLOQUE
COLLOQUIA *n* plural form of singular colloquium: informal gathering
COLLOQUY *n* conversation or conference
COLLOTYPE *n* method of lithographic printing from a flat surface of hardened gelatine: used mainly for fine-detail reproduction in monochrome or colour
COLLOTYPY > COLLOTYPE
COLLS > COLL
COLLUDE *vb* act in collusion
COLLUDED > COLLUDE
COLLUDER > COLLUDE
COLLUDERS > COLLUDE
COLLUDES > COLLUDE
COLLUDING > COLLUDE
COLLUSION *n* secret or illegal cooperation
COLLUSIVE > COLLUSION
COLLUVIA > COLLUVIUM
COLLUVIAL > COLLUVIUM
COLLUVIES *n* offscourings
COLLUVIUM *n* mixture of rock fragments from the bases of cliffs
COLLY *n* soot or grime, such as coal dust ▷ *vb* begrime
COLLYING > COLLY
COLLYRIA > COLLYRIUM
COLLYRIUM *a technical name for an* > EYEWASH
COLOBI > COLOBUS
COLOBID > COLOBUS
COLOBOMA *n* structural defect of the eye, esp in the choroid, retina, or iris
COLOBOMAS > COLOBOMA
COLOBUS *n* any leaf-eating arboreal Old World monkey of the genus *Colobus*, of W and central Africa, having a slender body, long silky fur, long tail, and reduced or absent thumbs
COLOBUSES > COLOBUS
COLOCATE *vb* to locate together
COLOCATED > COLOCATE
COLOCATES > COLOCATE
COLOCYNTH *n* cucurbitaceous climbing plant, *Citrullus colocynthis*, of the Mediterranean region and Asia, having bitter-tasting fruit
COLOG *n* logarithm of the reciprocal of a number
COLOGNE *n* mild perfume
COLOGNED > COLOGNE
COLOGNES > COLOGNE
COLOGS > COLOG
COLOMBARD *n* grape used to make wine
COLON *n* punctuation mark (:); Costa Rican monetary unit
COLONE *variant of* > COLON
COLONEL *n* senior commissioned army or air-force officer
COLONELCY > COLONEL
COLONELS > COLONEL
COLONES > COLONE
COLONI > COLONUS
COLONIAL *n* inhabitant of a colony ▷ *adj* of or inhabiting a colony or colonies
COLONIALS > COLONIAL
COLONIC *adj* of or relating to the colon ▷ *n* irrigation of the colon by injecting large amounts of fluid high into the colon
COLONICS > COLONIC
COLONIES > COLONY
COLONISE *same as* > COLONIZE
COLONISED > COLONISE
COLONISER > COLONISE
COLONISES > COLONISE
COLONIST *n* settler in a colony
COLONISTS > COLONIST
COLONITIS *same as* > COLITIS
COLONIZE *vb* make into a colony
COLONIZED > COLONIZE
COLONIZER > COLONIZE
COLONIZES > COLONIZE
COLONNADE *n* row of columns
COLONS > COLON
COLONUS *n* ancient Roman farmer
COLONY *n* group of people who settle in a new country but remain under the rule of their homeland
COLOPHON *n* publisher's symbol on a book
COLOPHONS > COLOPHON
COLOPHONY *another name for* > ROSIN
COLOR *same as* > COLOUR
COLORABLE > COLOR
COLORABLY > COLOR
COLORADO *adj* (of a cigar) of middling colour and strength
COLORANT *n* any substance that imparts colour, such as a pigment, dye, or ink
COLORANTS > COLORANT
COLORBRED *adj* (of animals) bred for their colour
COLORCAST *vb* broadcast in colour
COLORED *US spelling of* > COLOURED
COLOREDS > COLORED
COLORER > COLOR
COLORERS > COLOR
COLORFAST *adj* variant of colourfast: (of a fabric) having a colour that does not run when washed
COLORFUL > COLOR
COLORIFIC *adj* producing, imparting, or relating to colour
COLORING > COLOUR
COLORINGS > COLOUR
COLORISE *same as* > COLOURIZE
COLORISED > COLORISE
COLORISER > COLORISE
COLORISES > COLORISE
COLORISM > COLOR
COLORISMS > COLOR
COLORIST > COLOR
COLORISTS > COLOR
COLORIZE *same as* > COLOURIZE
COLORIZED > COLOURIZE
COLORIZER > COLORIZE
COLORIZES > COLORIZE
COLORLESS > COLOR
COLORMAN *same as* > COLOURMAN
COLORMEN > COLORMAN
COLORS > COLOR
COLORWAY *variant of* > COLOURWAY
COLORWAYS > COLORWAY
COLORY *same as* > COLOURY
COLOSSAL *adj* very large
COLOSSEUM *same as* > COLISEUM
COLOSSI > COLOSSUS
COLOSSUS *n* huge statue
COLOSTOMY *n* operation to form an opening from the colon onto the surface of the body, for emptying the bowel
COLOSTRAL > COLOSTRUM
COLOSTRIC > COLOSTRUM
COLOSTRUM *n* thin milky secretion from the nipples that precedes and follows true lactation. It consists largely of serum and white blood cells
COLOTOMY *n* colonic incision
COLOUR *n* appearance of things as a result of reflecting light ▷ *vb* apply colour to
COLOURANT *same as* > COLORANT
COLOURED *adj* having colour ▷ *n* person who is not white

COLOUREDS > COLOURED
COLOURER > COLOUR
COLOURERS > COLOUR
COLOURFUL *adj* with bright or varied colours
COLOURING *n* application of colour
COLOURISE *same as* > COLOURIZE
COLOURIST *n* person who uses colour, esp an artist
COLOURIZE *vb* add colour electronically to (an old black-and-white film)
COLOURMAN *n* person who deals in paints
COLOURMEN > COLOURMAN
COLOURS > COLOUR
COLOURWAY *n* one of several different combinations of colours in which a given pattern is printed on fabrics, wallpapers, etc
COLOURY *adj* possessing colour
COLPITIS *another name for* > VAGINITIS
COLPOTOMY *n* surgical incision into the wall of the vagina
COLS > COL
COLT *n* young male horse ▷ *vb* to fool
COLTAN *n* metallic ore found esp in the E Congo, consisting of columbite and tantalite and used as a source of tantalum
COLTANS > COLTAN
COLTED > COLT
COLTER *same as* > COULTER
COLTERS > COULTER
COLTING > COLT
COLTISH *adj* inexperienced
COLTISHLY > COLTISH
COLTS > COLT
COLTSFOOT *n* weed with yellow flowers and heart-shaped leaves
COLTWOOD *n* plant mentioned in Spenser's Faerie Queene
COLTWOODS > COLTWOOD
COLUBRIAD *n* epic poem about a snake
COLUBRID *n* any snake of the family *Colubridae*, including many harmless snakes, such as the grass snake and whip snakes, and some venomous types ▷ *adj* of, relating to, or belonging to the *Colubridae*
COLUBRIDS > COLUBRID
COLUBRINE *adj* of or resembling a snake
COLUGO *n* flying lemur
COLUGOS > COLUGO
COLUMBARY *n* dovecote
COLUMBATE *n* niobate
COLUMBIC *another word for* > NIOBIC
COLUMBINE *n* garden flower with five petals ▷ *adj* of, relating to, or resembling a dove
COLUMBITE *n* black mineral occurring in coarse granite
COLUMBIUM *the former name of* > NIOBIUM
COLUMBOUS *another word for* > NIOBOUS
COLUMEL *n* in botany, the central column in a capsule
COLUMELLA *n* central part of the spore-producing body of some fungi and mosses
COLUMELS > COLUMEL
COLUMN *n* pillar ▷ *vb* create a column
COLUMNAL > COLUMN
COLUMNAR > COLUMN
COLUMNEA *n* flowering plant
COLUMNEAS > COLUMNEA
COLUMNED > COLUMN
COLUMNIST *n* journalist who writes a regular feature in a newspaper
COLUMNS > COLUMN
COLURE *n* either of two great circles on the celestial sphere, one of which passes through the celestial poles and the equinoxes and the other through the poles and the solstices
COLURES > COLURE
COLY *n* any of the arboreal birds of the genus *Colius*, family *Coliidae*, and order *Coliiformes*, of southern Africa. They have a soft hairlike plumage, crested head, and very long tail
COLZA *n* oilseed rape, a Eurasian plant with bright yellow flowers
COLZAS > COLZA
COMA *n* state of deep unconsciousness
COMADE > COMAKE
COMAE > COMA
COMAKE *vb* to make together
COMAKER > COMAKE
COMAKERS > COMAKE
COMAKES > COMAKE
COMAKING > COMAKE
COMAL > COMA
COMANAGE *vb* to manage jointly
COMANAGED > COMANAGE
COMANAGER > COMANAGE
COMANAGES > COMANAGE
COMARB *same as* > COARB
COMARBS > COMARB
COMART *n* covenant
COMARTS > COMART
COMAS > COMA
COMATE *adj* having tufts of hair ▷ *n* companion
COMATES > COMATE
COMATIC > COMA
COMATIK *variant of* > KOMATIK
COMATIKS > COMATIK
COMATOSE *adj* in a coma
COMATULA *same as* > COMATULID
COMATULAE > COMATULID
COMATULID *n* any of a group of crinoid echinoderms, including the feather stars, in which the adults are free-swimming
COMB *n* toothed implement for arranging the hair ▷ *vb* use a comb on
COMBAT *vb* fight, struggle ▷ *n* fight or struggle
COMBATANT *n* fighter ▷ *adj* fighting
COMBATED > COMBAT
COMBATER > COMBAT
COMBATERS > COMBAT
COMBATING > COMBAT
COMBATIVE *adj* eager or ready to fight, argue, etc
COMBATS > COMBAT
COMBATTED > COMBAT
COMBE *same as* > COMB
COMBED > COMB
COMBER *n* long curling wave
COMBERS > COMBER
COMBES > COMBE
COMBI *n* combination boiler
COMBIER > COMBY
COMBIES > COMBY
COMBIEST > COMBY
COMBINATE *adj* betrothed
COMBINE *vb* join together ▷ *n* association of people or firms for a common purpose
COMBINED > COMBINE
COMBINEDS > COMBINE
COMBINER > COMBINE
COMBINERS > COMBINE
COMBINES > COMBINE
COMBING > COMB
COMBINGS *pl n* loose hair or fibres removed by combing, esp from animals
COMBINING > COMBINE
COMBIS > COMBI
COMBLE *n* apex; zenith
COMBLES > COMBLE
COMBLESS *adj* without a comb
COMBLIKE *adj* resembling a comb
COMBO *n* small group of jazz musicians
COMBOS > COMBO
COMBRETUM *n* any tree or shrub belonging to the genus Combretum
COMBS > COMB
COMBUST *adj* (of a star or planet) invisible for a period between 24 and 30 days each year due to its proximity to the sun ▷ *vb* burn
COMBUSTED > COMBUST
COMBUSTOR *n* combustion system of a jet engine or ramjet, comprising the combustion chamber, the fuel injection apparatus, and the igniter
COMBUSTS > COMBUST
COMBWISE *adv* in the manner of a comb
COMBY *adj* comb-like ▷ *n* combination boiler
COME *vb* move towards a place, arrive
COMEBACK *n* return to a former position ▷ *vb* return, esp to the memory
COMEBACKS > COMEBACK
COMEDDLE *vb* mix
COMEDDLED > COMEDDLE
COMEDDLES > COMEDDLE
COMEDIAN *n* entertainer who tells jokes
COMEDIANS > COMEDIAN
COMEDIC *adj* of or relating to comedy
COMEDIES > COMEDY
COMEDO *the technical name for* > BLACKHEAD
COMEDONES > COMEDO
COMEDOS > COMEDO
COMEDOWN *n* decline in status ▷ *vb* come to a place regarded as lower
COMEDOWNS > COMEDOWN
COMEDY *n* humorous play, film, or programme
COMELIER > COMELY
COMELIEST > COMELY
COMELILY > COMELY
COMELY *adj* nice-looking
COMEMBER *n* fellow member
COMEMBERS > COMEMBER
COMEOVER *n* person who has come from Britain to the Isle of Man to settle
COMEOVERS > COMEOVER
COMER *n* person who come[s]
COMERS > COMER
COMES > COME
COMET *n* heavenly body with a long luminous tail
COMETARY > COMET
COMETH > COME
COMETHER *n* coaxing; allur[e]
COMETHERS > COMETHER
COMETIC > COMET
COMETS > COMET
COMFIER > COMFY
COMFIEST > COMFY
COMFINESS > COMFY
COMFIT *n* sugar-coated sweet
COMFITS > COMFIT
COMFITURE *n* confiture
COMFORT *n* physical ease or wellbeing ▷ *vb* soothe, console
COMFORTED > COMFORT
COMFORTER *n* person or thing that comforts
COMFORTS > COMFORT
COMFREY *n* tall plant with

bell-shaped flowers
:OMFREYS > COMFREY
:OMFY *adj* comfortable
:OMIC *adj* humorous, funny ▷ *n* comedian
:OMICAL *adj* amusing
:OMICALLY > COMICAL
:OMICE *n* kind of pear
:OMICES > COMICE
:OMICS > COMIC
:OMING > COME
:OMINGLE *same as* > COMMINGLE
:OMINGLED > COMMINGLE
:OMINGLES > COMINGLE
:OMINGS > COME
:OMIQUE *n* comic actor
:OMIQUES > COMIQUE
.OMITADJI *n* Balkan guerrilla fighter
.OMITAL *adj* relating to a count or earl
.OMITATUS *n* leader's retinue
.OMITIA *n* ancient Roman assembly that elected officials and exercised judicial and legislative authority
OMITIAL > COMITIA
.OMITIAS > COMITIA
.OMITIES > COMITY
.OMITY *n* friendly politeness, esp between different countries
OMIX *n* comic books in general
OMM as in *comm badge* small wearable badge-shaped radio transmitter and receiver
OMMA *n* punctuation mark (,)
:OMMAND *vb* order ▷ *n* authoritative instruction that something must be done
OMMANDED > COMMAND
OMMANDER *n* military officer in command of a group or operation
OMMANDO *n* (member of) a military unit trained for swift raids in enemy territory
OMMANDOS > COMMANDO
OMMANDS > COMMAND
OMMAS > COMMA
OMMATA > COMMA
OMMENCE *vb* begin
OMMENCED > COMMENCE
OMMENCER > COMMENCE
OMMENCES > COMMENCE
OMMEND *vb* praise
OMMENDAM *n* temporary holding of an ecclesiastical benefice
OMMENDED > COMMEND
OMMENDER > COMMEND
OMMENDS > COMMEND
OMMENSAL *adj* (of two different species of plant or animal) living in close association, such that one species benefits without harming the other ▷ *n* commensal plant or animal
COMMENT *n* remark ▷ *vb* make a comment
COMMENTED > COMMENT
COMMENTER > COMMENT
COMMENTOR > COMMENT
COMMENTS > COMMENT
COMMER *same as* > COMER
COMMERCE *n* buying and selling, trade ▷ *vb* to trade
COMMERCED > COMMERCE
COMMERCES > COMMERCE
COMMERE *n* female compere
COMMERES > COMMERE
COMMERGE *vb* to merge together
COMMERGED > COMMERGE
COMMERGES > COMMERGE
COMMERS > COMMER
COMMIE *adj* communist
COMMIES > COMMIE
COMMINATE *vb* to anathematise
COMMINGLE *vb* mix or be mixed
COMMINUTE *vb* break (a bone) into several small fragments
COMMIS *n* apprentice waiter or chef ▷ *adj* (of a waiter or chef) apprentice
COMMISSAR *n* (formerly) official responsible for political education in Communist countries
COMMIT *vb* perform (a crime or error)
COMMITS > COMMIT
COMMITTAL *n* act of committing or pledging
COMMITTED > COMMIT
COMMITTEE *n* group of people appointed to perform a specified service or function
COMMITTER > COMMIT
COMMIX *a rare word for* > MIX
COMMIXED > COMMIX
COMMIXES > COMMIX
COMMIXING > COMMIX
COMMIXT > COMMIX
COMMO *short for* > COMMUNIST
COMMODE *n* seat with a hinged flap concealing a chamber pot
COMMODES > COMMODE
COMMODIFY *vb* to make into a commodity
COMMODITY *n* something that can be bought or sold
COMMODO *same as* > COMODO
COMMODORE *n* senior commissioned officer in the navy
COMMON *adj* occurring often ▷ *n* area of grassy land belonging to a community ▷ *vb* sit at table with strangers
COMMONAGE *n* use of something, esp a pasture, in common with others
COMMONED > COMMON
COMMONER *n* person who does not belong to the nobility
COMMONERS > COMMONER
COMMONEST > COMMON
COMMONEY *n* playing marble of a common sort
COMMONEYS > COMMONEY
COMMONING > COMMON
COMMONLY *adv* usually
COMMONS *n* people not of noble birth viewed as forming a political order
COMMORANT *n* resident
COMMOS > COMMO
COMMOT *n* in medieval Wales, a division of land
COMMOTE *same as* > COMMOT
COMMOTES > COMMOTE
COMMOTION *n* noisy disturbance
COMMOTS > COMMOT
COMMOVE *vb* disturb
COMMOVED > COMMOVE
COMMOVES > COMMOVE
COMMOVING > COMMOVE
COMMS *pl n* communications
COMMUNAL *adj* shared
COMMUNARD *n* member of a commune
COMMUNE *n* group of people who live together and share everything ▷ *vb* feel very close (to)
COMMUNED > COMMUNE
COMMUNER > COMMUNE
COMMUNERS > COMMUNE
COMMUNES > COMMUNE
COMMUNING > COMMUNE
COMMUNION *n* sharing of thoughts or feelings
COMMUNISE *same as* > COMMUNIZE
COMMUNISM *n* belief that all property and means of production should be shared by the community
COMMUNIST *n* supporter of any form of communism ▷ *adj* of, characterized by, favouring, or relating to communism
COMMUNITY *n* all the people living in one district
COMMUNIZE *vb* make (property) public
COMMUTATE *vb* reverse the direction of (an electric current)
COMMUTE *vb* travel daily to and from work ▷ *n* journey made by commuting
COMMUTED > COMMUTE
COMMUTER *n* person who commutes to and from work
COMMUTERS > COMMUTER
COMMUTES > COMMUTE
COMMUTING > COMMUTE
COMMUTUAL *adj* mutual
COMMY *same as* > COMMIE
COMODO *adv* (to be performed) at a convenient relaxed speed
COMONOMER *n* monomer that, with another, constitutes a copolymer
COMORBID *adj* (of illness) happening at same time as other illness
COMOSE *another word for* > COMATE
COMOUS *adj* hairy
COMP *n* person who sets and corrects type ▷ *vb* set or correct type
COMPACT *adj* closely packed ▷ *n* small flat case containing a mirror and face powder ▷ *vb* pack closely together
COMPACTED > COMPACT
COMPACTER > COMPACT
COMPACTLY > COMPACT
COMPACTOR *n* machine which compresses waste material for easier disposal
COMPACTS > COMPACT
COMPADRE *n* masculine friend
COMPADRES > COMPADRE
COMPAGE *obsolete form of* > COMPAGES
COMPAGES *n* structure or framework
COMPAND *vb* (of a transmitter signal) to compress before, and expand after, transmission
COMPANDED > COMPAND
COMPANDER *n* system for improving the signal-to-noise ratio of a signal at a transmitter or recorder by first compressing the volume range of the signal and then restoring it to its original amplitude level at the receiving or reproducing apparatus
COMPANDOR *same as* > COMPANDER
COMPANDS > COMPAND
COMPANIED > COMPANY
COMPANIES > COMPANY
COMPANING > COMPANY
COMPANION *n* person who associates with or accompanies someone ▷ *vb* accompany or be a companion to
COMPANY *n* business organization ▷ *vb* associate or keep company with someone
COMPARE *vb* examine (things) and point out the resemblances or differences
COMPARED > COMPARE
COMPARER > COMPARE
COMPARERS > COMPARE

COMPARES > COMPARE
COMPARING > COMPARE
COMPART *vb* to divide into parts
COMPARTED > COMPART
COMPARTS > COMPART
COMPAS *n* rhythm in flamenco
COMPASS *n* instrument for showing direction, with a needle that points north ▷ *vb* encircle or surround
COMPASSED > COMPASS
COMPASSES > COMPASS
COMPAST *adj* rounded
COMPEAR *vb* in Scots law, to appear in court
COMPEARED > COMPEAR
COMPEARS > COMPEAR
COMPED > COMPOSITOR
COMPEER *n* person of equal rank, status, or ability ▷ *vb* to equal
COMPEERED > COMPEER
COMPEERS > COMPEER
COMPEL *vb* force (to be or do)
COMPELLED > COMPEL
COMPELLER > COMPEL
COMPELS > COMPEL
COMPEND *n* compendium
COMPENDIA *n* plural form of singular compendium: book containing a collection of useful hints
COMPENDS > COMPEND
COMPER *n* person who regularly enters competitions in newspapers, magazines, etc, esp competitions offering consumer goods as prizes
COMPERE *n* person who presents a stage, radio, or television show ▷ *vb* be the compere of
COMPERED > COMPERE
COMPERES > COMPERE
COMPERING > COMPERE
COMPERS > COMPER
COMPESCE *vb* to curb
COMPESCED > COMPESCE
COMPESCES > COMPESCE
COMPETE *vb* try to win or achieve (a prize, profit, etc)
COMPETED > COMPETE
COMPETENT *adj* having the skill or knowledge to do something well
COMPETES > COMPETE
COMPETING > COMPETE
COMPILE *vb* collect and arrange (information), esp to make a book
COMPILED > COMPILE
COMPILER *n* person who compiles information
COMPILERS > COMPILER
COMPILES > COMPILE
COMPILING > COMPILE
COMPING > COMP
COMPINGS > COMP
COMPITAL *adj* pertaining to crossroads
COMPLAIN *vb* express resentment or displeasure
COMPLAINS > COMPLAIN
COMPLAINT *n* complaining
COMPLEAT *an archaic spelling of* > COMPLETE
COMPLECT *vb* interweave or entwine
COMPLECTS > COMPLECT
COMPLETE *adj* thorough, absolute ▷ *vb* finish
COMPLETED > COMPLETE
COMPLETER > COMPLETE
COMPLETES > COMPLETE
COMPLEX *adj* made up of parts ▷ *n* whole made up of parts ▷ *vb* to form a complex
COMPLEXED > COMPLEX
COMPLEXER > COMPLEX
COMPLEXES > COMPLEX
COMPLEXLY > COMPLEX
COMPLEXUS *n* complex
COMPLIANT *adj* complying, obliging, or yielding
COMPLICE *n* associate or accomplice
COMPLICES > COMPLICE
COMPLICIT *adj* involved in a crime or questionable act
COMPLIED > COMPLY
COMPLIER > COMPLY
COMPLIERS > COMPLY
COMPLIES > COMPLY
COMPLIN *same as* > COMPLINE
COMPLINE *n* last service of the day in the Roman Catholic Church
COMPLINES > COMPLINE
COMPLINS > COMPLIN
COMPLISH *vb* accomplish
COMPLOT *n* plot or conspiracy ▷ *vb* plot together
COMPLOTS > COMPLOT
COMPLUVIA *n* plural form of singular compluvium: an unroofed space over the atrium in a Roman house, though which rain fell and was collected
COMPLY *vb* act in accordance (with)
COMPLYING > COMPLY
COMPO *n* mixture of materials, such as mortar, plaster, etc ▷ *adj* intended to last for several days
COMPONE *same as* > COMPONY
COMPONENT *adj* (being) part of a whole ▷ *n* constituent part or feature of a whole
COMPONY *adj* made up of alternating metal and colour, colour and fur, or fur and metal
COMPORT *vb* behave (oneself) in a specified way
COMPORTED > COMPORT
COMPORTS > COMPORT
COMPOS > COMPO
COMPOSE *vb* put together
COMPOSED *adj* calm
COMPOSER *n* person who writes music
COMPOSERS > COMPOSER
COMPOSES > COMPOSE
COMPOSING > COMPOSE
COMPOSITE *adj* made up of separate parts ▷ *n* something composed of separate parts ▷ *vb* merge related motions from local branches of (a political party, trade union, etc) so as to produce a manageable number of proposals for discussion at national level
COMPOST *n* decayed plants used as a fertilizer ▷ *vb* make (vegetable matter) into compost
COMPOSTED > COMPOST
COMPOSTER *n* bin or other container used to turn garden waste into compost
COMPOSTS > COMPOST
COMPOSURE *n* calmness
COMPOT *same as* > COMPOTE
COMPOTE *n* fruit stewed with sugar
COMPOTES > COMPOTE
COMPOTIER *n* dish for holding compote
COMPOTS > COMPOT
COMPOUND *adj* (thing, esp chemical) made up of two or more combined parts or elements ▷ *vb* combine or make by combining ▷ *n* fenced enclosure containing buildings
COMPOUNDS > COMPOUND
COMPRADOR *n* (formerly in China and some other Asian countries) a native agent of a foreign enterprise
COMPRESS *vb* squeeze together ▷ *n* pad applied to stop bleeding or cool inflammation
COMPRINT *vb* to print jointly
COMPRINTS > COMPRINT
COMPRISAL > COMPRISE
COMPRISE *vb* be made up of or make up
COMPRISED > COMPRISE
COMPRISES > COMPRISE
COMPRIZE *same as* > COMPRISE
COMPRIZED > COMPRIZE
COMPRIZES > COMPRIZE
COMPS > COMP
COMPT *obsolete variant of* > COUNT
COMPTABLE *n* countable
COMPTED > COMPT
COMPTER *n* formerly, a prison
COMPTERS > COMPT
COMPTIBLE *same as* > COMPTABLE
COMPTING > COUNT
COMPTROLL *obsolete variant of* > CONTROL
COMPTS > COUNT
COMPULSE *vb* to compel
COMPULSED > COMPULSE
COMPULSES > COMPULSE
COMPUTANT *n* calculator
COMPUTE *vb* calculate, esp using a computer ▷ *n* calculation
COMPUTED > COMPUTE
COMPUTER *n* electronic machine that stores and processes data
COMPUTERS > COMPUTER
COMPUTES > COMPUTE
COMPUTING *n* activity of using computers and writing programs for them ▷ *adj* of or relating to computers
COMPUTIST *n* one who computes
COMRADE *n* fellow member of a union or socialist political party
COMRADELY > COMRADE
COMRADERY *n* comradeship
COMRADES > COMRADE
COMS *pl n* one-piece woollen undergarment with longs sleeves and legs
COMSYMP *n* Communist Party sympathizer
COMSYMPS > COMSYMP
COMTE *n* European nobleman
COMTES > COMTE
COMUS *n* wild party
COMUSES > COMUS
CON *vb* deceive, swindle ▷ convict ▷ *prep* with
CONACRE *n* farming land let for a season or for eleven months ▷ *vb* to let conacre
CONACRED > CONACRE
CONACRES > CONACRE
CONACRING > CONACRE
CONARIA > CONARIUM
CONARIAL > CONARIUM
CONARIUM *n* pineal gland
CONATION *n* element in psychological processes that tends towards activity or change and appears as desire, volition and striving
CONATIONS > CONATION
CONATIVE *adj* denoting an aspect of verbs in some languages used to indicate the effort of the agent in performing the activity described by the verb
CONATUS *n* effort or striving of natural impulse
CONCAUSE *n* shared cause
CONCAUSES > CONCAUSE
CONCAVE *adj* curving

inwards ▷ *vb* make concave
CONCAVED > CONCAVE
CONCAVELY > CONCAVE
CONCAVES > CONCAVE
CONCAVING > CONCAVE
CONCAVITY *n* state or quality of being concave
CONCEAL *vb* cover and hide
CONCEALED > CONCEAL
CONCEALER > CONCEAL
CONCEALS > CONCEAL
CONCEDE *vb* admit to be true
CONCEDED > CONCEDE
CONCEDER > CONCEDE
CONCEDERS > CONCEDE
CONCEDES > CONCEDE
CONCEDING > CONCEDE
CONCEDO *interj* I allow; I concede (a point)
CONCEIT *n* too high an opinion of oneself ▷ *vb* like or be able to bear (something, such as food or drink)
CONCEITED *adj* having an excessively high opinion of oneself
CONCEITS > CONCEIT
CONCEITY *adj* full of conceit
CONCEIVE *vb* imagine, think
CONCEIVED > CONCEIVE
CONCEIVER > CONCEIVE
CONCEIVES > CONCEIVE
CONCENT *n* concord, as of sounds, voices, etc
CONCENTER *same as* > CONCENTRE
CONCENTRE *vb* converge or cause to converge on a common centre
CONCENTS > CONCENT
CONCENTUS *n* vocal harmony
CONCEPT *n* abstract or general idea
CONCEPTI > CONCEPTUS
CONCEPTS > CONCEPT
CONCEPTUS *n* any product of conception, including the embryo, foetus and surrounding tissue
CONCERN *n* anxiety, worry ▷ *vb* worry (someone)
CONCERNED *adj* interested, involved
CONCERNS > CONCERN
CONCERT *n* musical entertainment
CONCERTED *adj* done together
CONCERTI > CONCERTO
CONCERTO *n* large-scale composition for a solo instrument and orchestra
CONCERTOS > CONCERTO
CONCERTS > CONCERT
CONCETTI > CONCETTO
CONCETTO *n* conceit, ingenious thought
CONCH *same as* > CONCHA
CONCHA *n* any bodily organ or part resembling a shell in shape, such as the external ear
CONCHAE > CONCHA
CONCHAL > CONCHA
CONCHAS > CONCHA
CONCHATE *adj* shell-shaped
CONCHE *vb* (in chocolate-making) to use a conche (machine which mixes and smooths the chocolate mass)
CONCHED > CONCHE
CONCHES > CONCHE
CONCHIE *n* conscientious objector
CONCHIES > CONCHIE
CONCHING > CONCHE
CONCHITIS *n* inflammation of the outer ear
CONCHO *n* American metal ornament
CONCHOID *n* type of plane curve
CONCHOIDS > CONCHOID
CONCHOS > CONCHO
CONCHS > CONCH
CONCHY *same as* > CONCHIE
CONCIERGE *n* (in France) caretaker in a block of flats
CONCILIAR *adj* of, from, or by means of a council, esp an ecclesiastical one
CONCISE *adj* brief and to the point ▷ *vb* mutilate
CONCISED > CONCISE
CONCISELY > CONCISE
CONCISER > CONCISE
CONCISES > CONCISE
CONCISEST > CONCISE
CONCISING > CONCISE
CONCISION *n* quality of being concise
CONCLAVE *n* secret meeting
CONCLAVES > CONCLAVE
CONCLUDE *vb* decide by reasoning
CONCLUDED > CONCLUDE
CONCLUDER > CONCLUDE
CONCLUDES > CONCLUDE
CONCOCT *vb* make up (a story or plan)
CONCOCTED > CONCOCT
CONCOCTER > CONCOCT
CONCOCTOR > CONCOCT
CONCOCTS > CONCOCT
CONCOLOR *adj* of a single colour
CONCORD *n* state of peaceful agreement, harmony ▷ *vb* to agree
CONCORDAL > CONCORD
CONCORDAT *n* pact or treaty
CONCORDED > CONCORD
CONCORDS > CONCORD
CONCOURS *n* contest
CONCOURSE *n* large open public place where people can gather
CONCREATE *vb* to create at the same time
CONCRETE *n* mixture of cement, sand, stone, and water, used in building ▷ *vb* cover with concrete ▷ *adj* made of concrete
CONCRETED > CONCRETE
CONCRETES > CONCRETE
CONCREW *vb* to grow together
CONCREWED > CONCREW
CONCREWS > CONCREW
CONCUBINE *n* woman living in a man's house but not married to him and kept for his sexual pleasure
CONCUPIES > CONCUPY
CONCUPY *n* concupiscence
CONCUR *vb* agree
CONCURRED > CONCUR
CONCURS > CONCUR
CONCUSS *vb* injure (the brain) by a fall or blow
CONCUSSED > CONCUSS
CONCUSSES > CONCUSS
CONCYCLIC *adj* (of a set of geometric points) lying on a common circle
COND *old inflection of* > CON
CONDEMN *vb* express disapproval of
CONDEMNED > CONDEMN
CONDEMNER > CONDEMN
CONDEMNOR > CONDEMN
CONDEMNS > CONDEMN
CONDENSE *vb* make shorter
CONDENSED *adj* (of printers' type) narrower than usual for a particular height
CONDENSER *same as* > CAPACITOR
CONDENSES > CONDENSE
CONDER *n* person who directs the steering of a vessel
CONDERS > CONDER
CONDIDDLE *vb* to steal
CONDIE *n* culvert; tunnel
CONDIES > CONDIE
CONDIGN *adj* (esp of a punishment) fitting
CONDIGNLY > CONDIGN
CONDIMENT *n* seasoning for food, such as salt or pepper
CONDITION *n* particular state of being ▷ *vb* train or influence to behave in a particular way
CONDO *n* condominium
CONDOES > CONDO
CONDOLE *vb* express sympathy with someone in grief, pain, etc
CONDOLED > CONDOLE
CONDOLENT *adj* expressing sympathy with someone in grief
CONDOLER > CONDOLE
CONDOLERS > CONDOLE
CONDOLES > CONDOLE
CONDOLING > CONDOLE
CONDOM *n* rubber sheath worn on the penis or in the vagina during sexual intercourse to prevent conception or infection
CONDOMS > CONDOM
CONDONE *vb* overlook or forgive (wrongdoing)
CONDONED > CONDONE
CONDONER > CONDONE
CONDONERS > CONDONE
CONDONES > CONDONE
CONDONING > CONDONE
CONDOR *n* large vulture of S America
CONDORES > CONDOR
CONDORS > CONDOR
CONDOS > CONDO
CONDUCE *vb* lead or contribute (to a result)
CONDUCED > CONDUCE
CONDUCER > CONDUCE
CONDUCERS > CONDUCE
CONDUCES > CONDUCE
CONDUCING > CONDUCE
CONDUCIVE *adj* likely to lead (to)
CONDUCT *n* management of an activity ▷ *vb* carry out (a task)
CONDUCTED > CONDUCT
CONDUCTI > CONDUCTUS
CONDUCTOR *n* person who conducts musicians
CONDUCTS > CONDUCT
CONDUCTUS *n* medieval liturgical composition
CONDUIT *n* channel or tube for fluid or cables
CONDUITS > CONDUIT
CONDYLAR > CONDYLE
CONDYLE *n* rounded projection on the articulating end of a bone, such as the ball portion of a ball-and-socket joint
CONDYLES > CONDYLE
CONDYLOID *adj* of or resembling a condyle
CONDYLOMA *n* skin tumour near the anus or genital organs, esp as a result of syphilis
CONE *n* object with a circular base, tapering to a point ▷ *vb* shape like a cone or part of a cone
CONED > CONE
CONELRAD *n* US defence and information system for use in the event of air attack
CONELRADS > CONELRAD
CONENOSE *n* bloodsucking bug of the genus Triatoma
CONENOSES > CONENOSE
CONEPATE *same as* > CONEPATL
CONEPATES > CONEPATE
CONEPATL *n* skunk
CONEPATLS > CONEPATL
CONES > CONE
CONEY *same as* > CONY
CONEYS > CONEY
CONF *n* online forum
CONFAB *n* conversation ▷ *vb* converse
CONFABBED > CONFAB

CONFABS > CONFAB
CONFECT *vb* prepare by combining ingredients
CONFECTED > CONFECT
CONFECTS > CONFECT
CONFER *vb* discuss together
CONFEREE *n* person who takes part in a conference
CONFEREES > CONFEREE
CONFERRAL > CONFER
CONFERRED > CONFER
CONFERREE *same as* > CONFEREE
CONFERRER > CONFER
CONFERS > CONFER
CONFERVA *n* any of various threadlike green algae, esp any of the genus *Tribonema*, typically occurring in fresh water
CONFERVAE > CONFERVA
CONFERVAL > CONFERVA
CONFERVAS > CONFERVA
CONFESS *vb* admit (a fault or crime)
CONFESSED > CONFESS
CONFESSES > CONFESS
CONFESSOR *n* priest who hears confessions
CONFEST *adj* admitted
CONFESTLY *adv* confessedly
CONFETTI *n* small pieces of coloured paper thrown at weddings
CONFETTO *n* sweetmeat
CONFIDANT *n* person confided in
CONFIDE *vb* tell someone (a secret)
CONFIDED > CONFIDE
CONFIDENT *adj* sure, esp of oneself
CONFIDER > CONFIDE
CONFIDERS > CONFIDE
CONFIDES > CONFIDE
CONFIDING *adj* trusting
CONFIGURE *vb* to design or set up
CONFINE *vb* keep within bounds ▷ *n* limit
CONFINED *adj* enclosed or restricted
CONFINER > CONFINE
CONFINERS > CONFINE
CONFINES > CONFINE
CONFINING > CONFINE
CONFIRM *vb* prove to be true
CONFIRMED *adj* firmly established in a habit or condition
CONFIRMEE *n* person to whom a confirmation is made
CONFIRMER > CONFIRM
CONFIRMOR *n* person who makes a confirmation
CONFIRMS > CONFIRM
CONFISEUR *n* confectioner
CONFIT *n* preserve
CONFITEOR *n* Catholic prayer asking for forgiveness
CONFITS > CONFIT
CONFITURE *n* confection, preserve of fruit, etc
CONFIX *vb* to fasten
CONFIXED > CONFIX
CONFIXES > CONFIX
CONFIXING > CONFIX
CONFLATE *vb* combine or blend into a whole
CONFLATED > CONFLATE
CONFLATES > CONFLATE
CONFLICT *n* disagreement ▷ *vb* be incompatible
CONFLICTS > CONFLICT
CONFLUENT *adj* flowing together or merging ▷ *n* stream that flows into another, usually of approximately equal size
CONFLUX *n* merging or folowing togther, especially of rivers
CONFLUXES > CONFLUX
CONFOCAL *adj* having a common focus or common foci
CONFORM *vb* comply with accepted standards or customs
CONFORMAL *adj* (of a transformation) preserving the angles of the depicted surface
CONFORMED > CONFORM
CONFORMER > CONFORM
CONFORMS > CONFORM
CONFOUND *vb* astound, bewilder
CONFOUNDS > CONFOUND
CONFRERE *n* colleague
CONFRERES > CONFRERE
CONFRERIE *n* brotherhood
CONFRONT *vb* come face to face with
CONFRONTE *adj* in heraldry, (of two animals) face to face
CONFRONTS > CONFRONT
CONFS > CONF
CONFUSE *vb* mix up
CONFUSED *adj* lacking a clear understanding of something
CONFUSES > CONFUSE
CONFUSING *adj* causing bewilderment
CONFUSION *n* mistaking one person or thing for another
CONFUTE *vb* prove wrong
CONFUTED > CONFUTE
CONFUTER > CONFUTE
CONFUTERS > CONFUTE
CONFUTES > CONFUTE
CONFUTING > CONFUTE
CONGA *n* dance performed by a number of people in single file ▷ *vb* dance the conga
CONGAED > CONGA
CONGAING > CONGA
CONGAS > CONGA
CONGE *n* permission to depart or dismissal, esp when formal ▷ *vb* to take one's leave
CONGEAL *vb* (of a liquid) become thick and sticky
CONGEALED > CONGEAL
CONGEALER > CONGEAL
CONGEALS > CONGEAL
CONGED > CONGE
CONGEE *same as* > CONGE
CONGEED > CONGEE
CONGEEING > CONGEE
CONGEES > CONGEE
CONGEING > CONGE
CONGENER *n* member of a class, group, or other category, esp any animal of a specified genus
CONGENERS > CONGENER
CONGENIAL *adj* pleasant, agreeable
CONGENIC *adj* (of inbred animal cells) genetically identical except for a single gene locus
CONGER *n* large sea eel
CONGERIES *n* collection of objects or ideas
CONGERS > CONGER
CONGES > CONGE
CONGEST *vb* crowd or become crowded to excess
CONGESTED *adj* crowded to excess
CONGESTS > CONGEST
CONGIARY *n* Roman emperor's gift to the people or soldiers
CONGII > CONGIUS
CONGIUS *n* unit of liquid measure equal to 1 Imperial gallon
CONGLOBE *vb* to gather into a globe or ball
CONGLOBED > CONGLOBE
CONGLOBES > CONGLOBE
CONGO *same as* > CONGOU
CONGOES > CONGOU
CONGOS > CONGO
CONGOU *n* kind of black tea from China
CONGOUS > CONGOU
CONGRATS *sentence substitute* congratulations
CONGREE *vb* to agree
CONGREED > CONGREE
CONGREES > CONGREE
CONGREET *vb* (of two or more people) to greet one another
CONGREETS > CONGREET
CONGRESS *n* formal meeting for discussion
CONGRUE *vb* to agree
CONGRUED > CONGRUE
CONGRUENT *adj* similar, corresponding
CONGRUES > CONGRUE
CONGRUING > CONGRUE
CONGRUITY > CONGRUOUS
CONGRUOUS *adj* appropriate or in keeping
CONI > CONUS
CONIA *same as* > CONIINE
CONIAS > CONIINE
CONIC *adj* having the shape of a cone
CONICAL *adj* cone-shaped
CONICALLY > CONIC
CONICINE *same as* > CONIINE
CONICINES > CONICINE
CONICITY > CONICAL
CONICS *n* branch of geometry concerned with the parabola, ellipse, and hyperbola
CONIDIA > CONIDIUM
CONIDIAL > CONIDIUM
CONIDIAN > CONIDIUM
CONIDIUM *n* asexual spore formed at the tip of a specialized hypha (conidiophore) in fungi such as *Penicillium*
CONIES > CONY
CONIFER *n* cone-bearing tree, such as the fir or pine
CONIFERS > CONIFER
CONIFORM *adj* cone-shaped
CONIINE *n* colourless poisonous soluble liquid alkaloid found in hemlock
CONIINES > CONIINE
CONIMA *n* gum resin from the conium hemlock tree
CONIMAS > CONIMA
CONIN *same as* > CONIINE
CONINE *same as* > CONIINE
CONINES > CONINE
CONING > CONE
CONINS > CONIN
CONIOLOGY *a variant spelling of* > KONIOLOGY
CONIOSES > CONIOSIS
CONIOSIS *n* any disease or condition caused by dust inhalation
CONIUM *n* either of the two N temperate plants of the umbelliferous genus *Conium*, esp hemlock
CONIUMS > CONIUM
CONJECT *vb* to conjecture
CONJECTED > CONJECT
CONJECTS > CONJECT
CONJEE *vb* prepare as, or in a conjee (a gruel of boiled rice and water)
CONJEED > CONJEE
CONJEEING > CONJEE
CONJEES > CONJEE
CONJOIN *vb* join or become joined
CONJOINED > CONJOIN
CONJOINER > CONJOIN
CONJOINS > CONJOIN
CONJOINT *adj* united, joint or associated
CONJUGAL *adj* of marriage
CONJUGANT *n* either of a pair of organisms or gametes undergoing conjugation
CONJUGATE *vb* inflect (a verb) systematically
CONJUNCT *adj* joined ▷ *n* one of the propositions or formulas in a conjunction
CONJUNCTS > CONJUNCT

CONJUNTO *n* style of Mexican music
CONJUNTOS > CONJUNTO
CONJURE *vb* perform tricks that appear to be magic
CONJURED > CONJURE
CONJURER *same as* > CONJUROR
CONJURERS > CONJUROR
CONJURES > CONJURE
CONJURIES > CONJURY
CONJURING *n* performance of tricks that appear to defy natural laws ▷ *adj* denoting or relating to such tricks or entertainment
CONJUROR *n* person who performs magic tricks for people's entertainment
CONJURORS > CONJUROR
CONJURY *n* magic
CONK *n* nose ▷ *vb* strike (someone) on the head or nose
CONKED > CONK
CONKER *n* nut of the horse chestnut
CONKERS *n* game played with conkers tied on strings
CONKIER > CONKY
CONKIEST > CONKY
CONKING > CONK
CONKS > CONK
ONKY *adj* affected by the timber disease, conk
ONN *same as* > CON
ONNATE *adj* existing in a person or thing from birth
ONNATELY > CONNATE
ONNATION *n* joining of similar parts or organs
ONNATURE *n* sharing a common nature or character
ONNE *same as* > CON
ONNECT *vb* join together
ONNECTED *adj* joined or linked together
ONNECTER > CONNECT
ONNECTOR > CONNECT
ONNECTS > CONNECT
ONNED > CON
ONNER *same as* > CONDER
ONNERS > CONNER
ONNES > CONNE
ONNEXION *n* act or state of connecting
ONNEXIVE *adj* connective
ONNING > CON
ONNINGS > CON
ONNIVE *vb* allow (wrongdoing) by ignoring it
ONNIVED > CONNIVE
ONNIVENT *adj* (of parts of plants and animals) touching without being fused, as some petals, insect wings, etc
ONNIVER > CONNIVE
ONNIVERS > CONNIVE
ONNIVERY *n* act of conniving
CONNIVES > CONNIVE
CONNIVING > CONNIVE
CONNOTATE *vb* to connote
CONNOTE *vb* (of a word, phrase, etc) to imply or suggest (associations or ideas) other than the literal meaning
CONNOTED > CONNOTE
CONNOTES > CONNOTE
CONNOTING > CONNOTE
CONNOTIVE *adj* act or state of connecting
CONNS > CONN
CONNUBIAL *adj* of marriage
CONODONT *n* any of various small Palaeozoic toothlike fossils derived from an extinct eel-like marine animal
CONODONTS > CONODONT
CONOID *n* geometric surface formed by rotating a parabola, ellipse, or hyperbola about one axis ▷ *adj* conical, cone-shaped
CONOIDAL *same as* > CONOID
CONOIDIC > CONOID
CONOIDS > CONOID
CONOMINEE *n* joint nominee
CONQUER *vb* defeat
CONQUERED > CONQUER
CONQUERER *variant of* > CONQUEROR
CONQUEROR > CONQUER
CONQUERS > CONQUER
CONQUEST *n* conquering
CONQUESTS > CONQUEST
CONQUIAN *same as* > COONCAN
CONQUIANS > COONCAN
CONS > CON
CONSCIENT *adj* conscious
CONSCIOUS *adj* alert and awake ▷ *n* conscious part of the mind
CONSCRIBE *vb* to enrol compulsorily
CONSCRIPT *n* person enrolled for compulsory military service ▷ *vb* enrol (someone) for compulsory military service
CONSEIL *n* advice
CONSEILS > CONSEIL
CONSENSUS *n* general agreement
CONSENT *n* agreement, permission ▷ *vb* permit, agree to
CONSENTED > CONSENT
CONSENTER > CONSENT
CONSENTS > CONSENT
CONSERVE *vb* protect from harm, decay, or loss ▷ *n* jam containing large pieces of fruit
CONSERVED > CONSERVE
CONSERVER > CONSERVE
CONSERVES > CONSERVE
CONSIDER *vb* regard as
CONSIDERS > CONSIDER
CONSIGN *vb* put somewhere
CONSIGNED > CONSIGN
CONSIGNEE *n* person, agent, organization, etc, to which merchandise is consigned
CONSIGNER *same as* > CONSIGNOR
CONSIGNOR *n* person, enterprise, etc, that consigns goods
CONSIGNS > CONSIGN
CONSIST *vb* be composed (of)
CONSISTED > CONSIST
CONSISTS > CONSIST
CONSOCIES *n* natural community with a single dominant species
CONSOL *n* consolidated annuity, a British government bond
CONSOLATE *vb* to console
CONSOLE *vb* comfort in distress ▷ *n* panel of controls for electronic equipment
CONSOLED > CONSOLE
CONSOLER > CONSOLE
CONSOLERS > CONSOLE
CONSOLES > CONSOLE
CONSOLING > CONSOLE
CONSOLS *pl n* irredeemable British government securities carrying annual interest rates of two and a half or four per cent
CONSOLUTE *adj* (of two or more liquids) mutually soluble in all proportions
CONSOMME *n* thin clear meat soup
CONSOMMES > CONSOMME
CONSONANT *n* speech sound made by partially or completely blocking the breath stream, such as *b* or *f* ▷ *adj* agreeing (with)
CONSONOUS *adj* harmonious
CONSORT *vb* keep company (with) ▷ *n* husband or wife of a monarch
CONSORTED > CONSORT
CONSORTER > CONSORT
CONSORTIA *n* plural form of singular consortium: association of financiers, companies etc
CONSORTS > CONSORT
CONSPIRE *vb* plan a crime together in secret
CONSPIRED > CONSPIRE
CONSPIRER > CONSPIRE
CONSPIRES > CONSPIRE
CONSTABLE *n* police officer of the lowest rank
CONSTANCY *n* quality of having a resolute mind, purpose, or affection
CONSTANT *adj* continuous ▷ *n* unvarying quantity
CONSTANTS > CONSTANT
CONSTATE *vb* to affirm
CONSTATED > CONSTATE
CONSTATES > CONSTATE
CONSTER *obsolete variant of* > CONSTRUE
CONSTERED > CONSTRUE
CONSTERS > CONSTRUE
CONSTRAIN *vb* compel, force
CONSTRICT *vb* make narrower by squeezing
CONSTRUAL *n* act of construing
CONSTRUCT *vb* build or put together ▷ *n* complex idea resulting from the combination of simpler ideas
CONSTRUE *vb* interpret ▷ *n* something that is construed, such as a piece of translation
CONSTRUED > CONSTRUE
CONSTRUER > CONSTRUE
CONSTRUES > CONSTRUE
CONSUL *n* official representing a state in a foreign country
CONSULAGE *n* duty paid by merchants for a consul's protection of their goods while abroad
CONSULAR *n* anyone of consular rank
CONSULARS > CONSULAR
CONSULATE *n* workplace or position of a consul
CONSULS > CONSUL
CONSULT *vb* go to for advice or information
CONSULTA *n* official planning meeting
CONSULTAS > CONSULTA
CONSULTED > CONSULT
CONSULTEE *n* person who is consulted
CONSULTER > CONSULT
CONSULTOR > CONSULT
CONSULTS > CONSULT
CONSUME *vb* eat or drink
CONSUMED > CONSUME
CONSUMER *n* person who buys goods or uses services
CONSUMERS > CONSUMER
CONSUMES > CONSUME
CONSUMING > CONSUME
CONSUMPT *n* quantity used up; consumption
CONSUMPTS > CONSUMPT
CONTACT *n* communicating ▷ *vb* get in touch with ▷ *interj* (formerly) a call made by the pilot to indicate that an aircraft's ignition is switched on and that the engine is ready for starting by swinging the propeller
CONTACTED > CONTACT
CONTACTEE *n* person contacted by aliens
CONTACTOR *n* type of

switch for repeatedly opening and closing an electric circuit. Its operation can be mechanical, electromagnetic, or pneumatic
CONTACTS > CONTACT
CONTADINA *n* female Italian farmer
CONTADINE > CONTADINA
CONTADINI > CONTADINO
CONTADINO *n* Italian farmer
CONTAGIA > CONTAGIUM
CONTAGION *n* passing on of disease by contact
CONTAGIUM *n* specific virus or other direct cause of any infectious disease
CONTAIN *vb* hold or be capable of holding
CONTAINED > CONTAIN
CONTAINER *n* object used to hold or store things in
CONTAINS > CONTAIN
CONTANGO *n* (formerly, on the London Stock Exchange) postponement of payment for and delivery of stock from one account day to the next ▷ *vb* arrange such a postponement of payment (for)
CONTANGOS > CONTANGO
CONTE *n* tale or short story, esp of adventure
CONTECK *n* contention
CONTECKS > CONTECK
CONTEMN *vb* regard with contempt
CONTEMNED > CONTEMN
CONTEMNER > CONTEMN
CONTEMNOR > CONTEMN
CONTEMNS > CONTEMN
CONTEMPER *vb* to modify
CONTEMPO *adj* contemporary
CONTEMPT *n* dislike and disregard
CONTEMPTS > CONTEMPT
CONTEND *vb* deal with
CONTENDED > CONTEND
CONTENDER > CONTEND
CONTENDS > CONTEND
CONTENT *n* meaning or substance of a piece of writing ▷ *adj* satisfied with things as they are ▷ *vb* make (someone) content
CONTENTED *adj* satisfied with one's situation or life
CONTENTLY > CONTENT
CONTENTS > CONTENT
CONTES > CONTE
CONTESSA *n* Italian countess
CONTESSAS > CONTESSA
CONTEST *n* competition or struggle ▷ *vb* dispute, object to
CONTESTED > CONTEST
CONTESTER > CONTEST
CONTESTS > CONTEST
CONTEXT *n* circumstances of an event or fact
CONTEXTS > CONTEXT
CONTICENT *adj* silent
CONTINENT *n* one of the earth's large masses of land ▷ *adj* able to control one's bladder and bowels
CONTINUA > CONTINUUM
CONTINUAL *adj* constant
CONTINUE *vb* (cause to) remain in a condition or place
CONTINUED > CONTINUE
CONTINUER > CONTINUE
CONTINUES > CONTINUE
CONTINUO *n* continuous bass part, usu. played on a keyboard instrument
CONTINUOS > CONTINUO
CONTINUUM *n* continuous series
CONTLINE *n* space between the bilges of stowed casks
CONTLINES > CONTLINE
CONTO *n* former Portuguese monetary unit worth 1000 escudos
CONTORNO *n* in Italy, side dish of salad or vegetables
CONTORNOS > CONTORNO
CONTORT *vb* twist out of shape
CONTORTED *adj* twisted out of shape
CONTORTS > CONTORT
CONTOS > CONTO
CONTOUR *n* outline ▷ *vb* shape so as to form or follow the contour of something
CONTOURED > CONTOUR
CONTOURS > CONTOUR
CONTRA *n* counter-argument
CONTRACT *n* (document setting out) a formal agreement ▷ *vb* make a formal agreement (to do something)
CONTRACTS > CONTRACT
CONTRAIL *n* aeroplane's vapour trail
CONTRAILS > CONTRAIL
CONTRAIR *adj* contrary
CONTRALTI > CONTRALTO
CONTRALTO *n* (singer with) the lowest female voice ▷ *adj* of or denoting a contralto
CONTRARY *n* complete opposite ▷ *adj* opposed, completely different ▷ *adv* in opposition
CONTRAS > CONTRA
CONTRAST *n* obvious difference ▷ *vb* compare in order to show differences
CONTRASTS > CONTRAST
CONTRASTY *adj* (of a photograph or subject) having sharp gradations in tone, esp between light and dark areas
CONTRAT *old form of* > CONTRACT
CONTRATE *adj* (of gears) having teeth set at a right angle to the axis
CONTRATS > CONTRAT
CONTRIST *vb* to make sad
CONTRISTS > CONTRIST
CONTRITE *adj* sorry and apologetic
CONTRIVE *vb* make happen
CONTRIVED *adj* planned or artificial
CONTRIVER > CONTRIVE
CONTRIVES > CONTRIVE
CONTROL *n* power to direct something ▷ *vb* have power over
CONTROLE *adj* officially registered
CONTROLS > CONTROL
CONTROUL *obsolete variant of* > CONTROL
CONTROULS > CONTROUL
CONTUMACY *n* obstinate disobedience
CONTUMELY *n* scornful or insulting treatment
CONTUND *vb* to pummel
CONTUNDED > CONTUND
CONTUNDS > CONTUND
CONTUSE *vb* injure (the body) without breaking the skin
CONTUSED > CONTUSE
CONTUSES > CONTUSE
CONTUSING > CONTUSE
CONTUSION *n* bruise
CONTUSIVE > CONTUSE
CONUNDRUM *n* riddle
CONURBAN *adj* relating to an urban region
CONURBIA *n* conurbations considered collectively
CONURBIAS > CONURBIA
CONURE *n* any of various small American parrots of the genus *Aratinga* and related genera
CONURES > CONURE
CONUS *n* any of several cone-shaped structures, such as the conus medullaris, the lower end of the spinal cord
CONVECT *vb* to circulate hot air by convection
CONVECTED > CONVECT
CONVECTOR *n* heater that gives out hot air
CONVECTS > CONVECT
CONVENE *vb* gather or summon for a formal meeting
CONVENED > CONVENE
CONVENER *n* person who calls a meeting
CONVENERS > CONVENER
CONVENES > CONVENE
CONVENING > CONVENE
CONVENOR *same as* > CONVENER
CONVENORS > CONVENOR
CONVENT *n* building where nuns live ▷ *vb* to summon
CONVENTED > CONVENT
CONVENTS > CONVENT
CONVERGE *vb* meet or join
CONVERGED > CONVERGE
CONVERGES > CONVERGE
CONVERSE *vb* have a conversation ▷ *n* opposite or contrary ▷ *adj* reversed or opposite
CONVERSED > CONVERSE
CONVERSER > CONVERSE
CONVERSES > CONVERSE
CONVERSO *n* medieval Spanish Jew converting to Catholicism
CONVERSOS > CONVERSO
CONVERT *vb* change in form, character, or function ▷ *n* person who has converted to a different belief or religion
CONVERTED > CONVERT
CONVERTER *n* person or thing that converts
CONVERTOR *same as* > CONVERTER
CONVERTS > CONVERT
CONVEX *adj* curving outwards ▷ *vb* make convex
CONVEXED > CONVEX
CONVEXES > CONVEX
CONVEXING > CONVEX
CONVEXITY *n* state or quality of being convex
CONVEXLY > CONVEX
CONVEY *vb* communicate (information)
CONVEYAL *n* act or means of conveying
CONVEYALS > CONVEYAL
CONVEYED > CONVEY
CONVEYER *same as* > CONVEYOR
CONVEYERS > CONVEYER
CONVEYING > CONVEY
CONVEYOR *n* person or thing that conveys
CONVEYORS > CONVEYOR
CONVEYS > CONVEY
CONVICT *vb* declare guilty ▷ *n* person serving a prison sentence ▷ *adj* convicted
CONVICTED > CONVICT
CONVICTS > CONVICT
CONVINCE *vb* persuade by argument or evidence
CONVINCED > CONVINCE
CONVINCER > CONVINCE
CONVINCES > CONVINCE
CONVIVE *vb* to feast together
CONVIVED > CONVIVE
CONVIVES > CONVIVE
CONVIVIAL *adj* sociable, lively
CONVIVING > CONVIVE
CONVO *n* conversation
CONVOCATE *vb* to call

together
ONVOKE *vb* call together
ONVOKED > CONVOKE
ONVOKER > CONVOKE
ONVOKERS > CONVOKE
ONVOKES > CONVOKE
ONVOKING > CONVOKE
ONVOLUTE *vb* form into a twisted, coiled, or rolled shape ▷ *adj* rolled longitudinally upon itself
ONVOLVE *vb* wind or roll together
ONVOLVED > CONVOLVE
ONVOLVES > CONVOLVE
ONVOS > CONVO
ONVOY *n* group of vehicles or ships travelling together ▷ *vb* escort while in transit
ONVOYED > CONVOY
ONVOYING > CONVOY
ONVOYS > CONVOY
ONVULSE *vb* (of part of the body) undergo violent spasms
ONVULSED > CONVULSE
ONVULSES > CONVULSE
ONY *n* rabbit
OO *vb* (of a dove or pigeon) make a soft murmuring sound ▷ *n* sound of cooing ▷ *interj* exclamation of surprise, awe, etc
OOCH *n* slang term for vagina
OOCHES > COOCH
OOCOO *old spelling of* > CUCKOO
OOED > COO
OOEE *interj* call to attract attention ▷ *vb* utter this call ▷ *n* calling distance
OOEED > COOEE
OOEEING > COOEE
OOEES > COOEE
OOER > COO
OOERS > COO
OOEY *same as* > COOEE
OOEYED > COOEY
OOEYING > COOEY
OOEYS > COOEY
OOF *n* simpleton
OOFS > COOF
OOING > COO
OOINGLY > COO
OOINGS > COO
OOK *vb* prepare (food) by heating ▷ *n* person who cooks food
OOKABLE > COOK
OOKBOOK *n* book containing recipes and instructions for cooking
OOKBOOKS > COOKBOOK
OOKED > COOK
OOKER *n* apparatus for cooking heated by gas or electricity
OOKERIES > COOKERY
OOKERS > COOKER
OOKERY *n* art of cooking
OOKEY *same as* > COOKIE
COOKEYS > COOKEY
COOKHOUSE *n* place for cooking, esp a camp kitchen
COOKIE *n* biscuit
COOKIES > COOKIE
COOKING > COOK
COOKINGS > COOK
COOKLESS *adj* devoid of a cook
COOKMAID *n* maid who assists a cook
COOKMAIDS > COOKMAID
COOKOFF *n* cookery competition
COOKOFFS > COOKOFF
COOKOUT *n* party where a meal is cooked and eaten out of doors
COOKOUTS > COOKOUT
COOKROOM *n* room in which food is cooked
COOKROOMS > COOKROOM
COOKS > COOK
COOKSHACK *n* makeshift building in which food is cooked
COOKSHOP *n* shop that sells cookery equipment
COOKSHOPS > COOKSHOP
COOKSTOVE *n* stove for cooking
COOKTOP *n* flat unit for cooking in saucepans or the top part of a stove
COOKTOPS > COOKTOP
COOKWARE *n* cooking utensils
COOKWARES > COOKWARE
COOKY *same as* > COOKIE
COOL *adj* moderately cold ▷ *vb* make or become cool ▷ *n* coolness
COOLABAH *n* Australian myrtaceous tree, *Eucalyptus microtheca*, that grows along rivers and has smooth bark and long narrow leaves
COOLABAHS > COOLABAH
COOLAMON *n* shallow dish of wood or bark, used for carrying water
COOLAMONS > COOLAMON
COOLANT *n* fluid used to cool machinery while it is working
COOLANTS > COOLANT
COOLDOWN *n* gentle stretching exercises after strenuous activity, to allow the heart rate gradually to return to normal
COOLDOWNS > COOLDOWN
COOLED > COOL
COOLER *n* container for making or keeping things cool
COOLERS > COOLER
COOLEST > COOL
COOLHOUSE *n* greenhouse in which a cool temperature is maintained
COOLIBAH *same as* > COOLABAH
COOLIBAHS > COOLIBAH
COOLIBAR *same as* > COOLABAH
COOLIBARS > COOLIBAR
COOLIE *n* unskilled Oriental labourer
COOLIES > COOLIE
COOLING > COOL
COOLINGLY > COOL
COOLISH > COOL
COOLLY > COOL
COOLNESS > COOL
COOLS > COOL
COOLTH *n* coolness
COOLTHS > COOLTH
COOLY *same as* > COOLIE
COOM *n* waste material, such as dust from coal, grease from axles, etc ▷ *vb* to blacken
COOMB *same as* > COMB
COOMBE *same as* > COMB
COOMBES > COOMBE
COOMBS > COOMB
COOMED > COOM
COOMIER > COOMY
COOMIEST > COOMY
COOMING > COOM
COOMS > COOM
COOMY *adj* grimy
COON *n* raccoon
COONCAN *n* card game for two players, similar to rummy
COONCANS > COONCAN
COONDOG *n* dog trained to hunt raccoons
COONDOGS > COONDOG
COONHOUND *n* dog for hunting raccoons
COONS > COON
COONSKIN *n* pelt of a raccoon
COONSKINS > COONSKIN
COONTIE *n* evergreen plant, *Zamia floridana* of S Florida, related to the cycads and having large dark green leathery leaves: family *Zamiaceae*
COONTIES > COONTIE
COONTY *same as* > COONTIE
COOP *n* cage or pen for poultry ▷ *vb* confine in a restricted area
COOPED > COOP
COOPER *n* person who makes or repairs barrels ▷ *vb* make or mend (barrels, casks, etc)
COOPERAGE *n* craft, place of work, or products of a cooper
COOPERATE *vb* work or act together
COOPERED > COOPER
COOPERIES > COOPERY
COOPERING > COOPER
COOPERS > COOPER
COOPERY *same as* > COOPERAGE
COOPING > COOP
COOPS > COOP
COOPT *vb* add (someone) to a group by the agreement of the existing members
COOPTED > COOPT
COOPTING > COOPT
COOPTION > COOPT
COOPTIONS > COOPT
COOPTS > COOPT
COORDINAL *adj* (of animals or plants) belonging to the same order
COORIE *same as* > COURIE
COORIED > COORIE
COORIEING > COORIE
COORIES > COORIE
COOS > COO
COOSEN *same as* > COZEN
COOSENED > COOSEN
COOSENING > COOSEN
COOSENS > COOSEN
COOSER *n* stallion
COOSERS > COOSER
COOSIN *same as* > COZEN
COOSINED > COOSIN
COOSINING > COOSIN
COOSINS > COOSIN
COOST *Scots form of* > CAST
COOT *n* small black water bird
COOTCH *n* hiding place ▷ *vb* hide
COOTCHED > COOTCH
COOTCHES > COOTCH
COOTCHING > COOTCH
COOTER *n* type of freshwater turtle
COOTERS > COOTER
COOTIE *same as* > LOUSE
COOTIES > COOTIE
COOTIKIN *n* gaiter
COOTIKINS > COOTIKIN
COOTS > COOT
COOZE *n* US and Canadian taboo slang word for the female genitals
COOZES > COOZE
COP *same as* > COPPER
COPACETIC *adj* very good
COPAIBA *n* transparent yellowish viscous oleoresin obtained from certain tropical South American trees of the leguminous genus *Copaifera*: used in varnishes and ointments
COPAIBAS > COPAIBA
COPAIVA *same as* > COPAIBA
COPAIVAS > COPAIVA
COPAL *n* resin used in varnishes
COPALM *n* aromatic brown resin obtained from the sweet gum tree
COPALMS > COPALM
COPALS > COPAL
COPARCENY *n* form of joint ownership of property
COPARENT *n* fellow parent
COPARENTS > COPARENT
COPARTNER *n* partner or associate

COPASETIC *same as* > COPACETIC
COPASTOR *n* fellow pastor
COPASTORS > COPASTOR
COPATAINE *adj* (of a hat) high-crowned
COPATRIOT *n* fellow patriot
COPATRON *n* fellow patron
COPATRONS > COPATRON
COPAY *n* amount payable for treatment by person with medical insurance
COPAYMENT *n* fee paid for medical insurance
COPAYS > COPAY
COPE *vb* deal successfully (with) ▷ *n* large ceremonial cloak worn by some Christian priests
COPECK *same as* > KOPECK
COPECKS > COPECK
COPED > COPE
COPEMATE *n* partner
COPEMATES > COPEMATE
COPEN *n* shade of blue
COPENS > COPEN
COPEPOD *n* any minute free-living or parasitic crustacean of the subclass *Copepoda* of marine and fresh waters: an important constituent of plankton ▷ *adj* of, relating to, or belonging to the *Copepoda*
COPEPODS > COPEPOD
COPER *n* horse-dealer ▷ *vb* to smuggle liquor to deep-sea fishermen
COPERED > COPER
COPERING > COPER
COPERS > COPER
COPES > COPE
COPESETIC *same as* > COPACETIC
COPESTONE *same as* > CAPSTONE
COPIED > COPY
COPIER *n* machine that copies
COPIERS > COPIER
COPIES > COPY
COPIHUE *n* Chilean bellflower
COPIHUES > COPIHUE
COPILOT *n* second pilot of an aircraft
COPILOTS > COPILOT
COPING *n* sloping top row of a wall
COPINGS > COPING
COPIOUS *adj* abundant, plentiful
COPIOUSLY > COPIOUS
COPITA *n* tulip-shaped sherry glass
COPITAS > COPITA
COPLANAR *adj* lying in the same plane
COPLOT *vb* plot together
COPLOTS > COPLOT
COPLOTTED > COPLOT
COPOLYMER *n* chemical compound of high molecular weight formed by uniting the molecules of two or more different compounds (monomers)
COPOUT *n* act of avoiding responsibility
COPOUTS > COPOUT
COPPED > COPPER
COPPER *n* soft reddish-brown metal ▷ *adj* reddish-brown ▷ *vb* coat or cover with copper
COPPERAH *same as* > COPRA
COPPERAHS > COPPERAH
COPPERAS *n* ferrous sulphate
COPPERED > COPPER
COPPERING > COPPER
COPPERISH *adj* copper-like
COPPERS > COPPER
COPPERY > COPPER
COPPICE *n* small group of trees growing close together ▷ *vb* trim back (trees or bushes) to form a coppice
COPPICED > COPPICE
COPPICES > COPPICE
COPPICING > COPPICE
COPPIES > COPPY
COPPIN *n* ball of thread
COPPING > COPPER
COPPINS > COPPIN
COPPLE *n* hill rising to a point
COPPLES > COPPLE
COPPRA *same as* > COPRA
COPPRAS > COPPRA
COPPY *n* small wooden stool
COPRA *n* dried oil-yielding kernel of the coconut
COPRAH *same as* > COPRA
COPRAHS > COPRAH
COPRAS > COPRA
COPREMIA *n* poisoning due to chronic constipation
COPREMIAS > COPREMIA
COPREMIC > COPREMIA
COPRESENT *vb* to present jointly
COPRINCE *n* fellow prince
COPRINCES > COPRINCE
COPRODUCE *vb* to produce jointly
COPRODUCT *n* joint product
COPROLITE *n* any of various rounded stony nodules thought to be the fossilized faeces of Palaeozic-Cenozoic vertebrates
COPROLITH *n* hard stony mass of dried faeces
COPROLOGY *n* preoccupation with excrement
COPROSMA *n* any shrub of the Australasian rubiaceous genus *Coprosma*: sometimes planted for ornament
COPROSMAS > COPROSMA
COPROZOIC *adj* (of animals) living in dung
COPS > COPPER
COPSE *same as* > COPPICE *vb* to trim back (trees) to form a copse
COPSED > COPSE
COPSES > COPSE
COPSEWOOD *n* brushwood
COPSHOP *n* police station
COPSHOPS > COPSHOP
COPSIER > COPSY
COPSIEST > COPSY
COPSING > COPSE
COPSY *adj* having copses
COPTER *n* helicopter
COPTERS > COPTER
COPUBLISH *vb* to publish jointly
COPULA *n* verb used to link the subject and complement of a sentence, e.g. *become* in *they become chums*
COPULAE > COPULA
COPULAR > COPULA
COPULAS > COPULA
COPULATE *vb* have sexual intercourse
COPULATED > COPULATE
COPULATES > COPULATE
COPURIFY *vb* to purify together
COPY *n* thing made to look exactly like another ▷ *vb* make a copy of
COPYABLE > COPY
COPYBOOK *n* book of specimens for imitation
COPYBOOKS > COPYBOOK
COPYBOY *n* formerly, in journalism, boy who carried copy and ran errands
COPYBOYS > COPYBOY
COPYCAT *n* person who imitates or copies someone ▷ *vb* to imitate with great attention to detail
COPYCATS > COPYCAT
COPYDESK *n* desk where newspaper copy is edited
COPYDESKS > COPYDESK
COPYEDIT *vb* prepare text for printing by styling, correcting, etc
COPYEDITS > COPYEDIT
COPYGIRL *n* female copyboy
COPYGIRLS > COPYGIRL
COPYGRAPH *n* process for copying type
COPYHOLD *n* tenure less than freehold of land in England evidenced by a copy of the Court roll
COPYHOLDS > COPYHOLD
COPYING > COPY
COPYISM *n* slavish copying
COPYISMS > COPYISM
COPYIST *n* person who makes written copies
COPYISTS > COPYIST
COPYLEFT *n* permission to use something free of charge
COPYLEFTS > COPYLEFT
COPYREAD *vb* subedit
COPYREADS > COPYREAD
COPYRIGHT *n* exclusive legal right to reproduce and control a book, work of art, etc ▷ *vb* take out a copyright on ▷ *adj* protected by copyright
COPYTAKER *n* (esp in a newspaper office) a perso[n] employed to type reports as journalists dictate the[m] over the telephone
COQUET *vb* behave flirtatiously
COQUETRY *n* flirtation
COQUETS > COQUET
COQUETTE *n* woman who flirts
COQUETTED > COQUET
COQUETTES > COQUETTE
COQUILLA *n* type of South American nut
COQUILLAS > COQUILLA
COQUILLE *n* any dish, esp seafood, served in a scallo[p] shell
COQUILLES > COQUILLE
COQUINA *n* soft limestone consisting of shells, coral[s] etc, that occurs in parts o[f] the US
COQUINAS > COQUINA
COQUITO *n* Chilean palm tree, *Jubaea spectabilis*, yielding edible nuts and a syrup
COQUITOS > COQUITO
COR *interj* exclamation of surprise, amazement, or admiration
CORACLE *n* small round boat of wicker covered with skins
CORACLES > CORACLE
CORACOID *n* paired ventra[l] bone of the pectoral girdl[e] in vertebrates
CORACOIDS > CORACOID
CORAGGIO *interj* exhortation to hold one's nerve
CORAGGIOS > CORAGGIO
CORAL *n* hard substance formed from the skeleton[s] of very small sea animals ▷ *adj* orange-pink
CORALLA > CORALLUM
CORALLINE *adj* of, relatin[g] to, or resembling coral ▷ any of various red algae impregnated with calciu[m] carbonate, esp any of the genus *Corallina*
CORALLITE *n* skeleton of a coral polyp
CORALLOID *same as* > CORALLINE
CORALLUM *n* skeleton of a[n] zoophyte
CORALROOT *n* any N temperate leafless orchi[d]

of the genus *Corallorhiza*, with small yellow-green or purple flowers and branched roots resembling coral
CORALS > CORAL
CORALWORT *n* coralroot or toothwort
CORAM *prep* before, in the presence of
CORAMINE *n* drug which is a circulatory stimulant
CORAMINES > CORAMINE
CORANACH *same as* > CORONACH
CORANACHS > CORANACH
CORANTO *same as* > COURANTE
CORANTOES > CORANTO
CORANTOS > CORANTO
CORBAN *n* gift to God
CORBANS > CORBAN
CORBE *obsolete variant of* > CORBEL
CORBEAU *n* blackish green colour
CORBEAUS > CORBEAU
CORBEIL *n* carved ornament in the form of a basket of fruit, flowers, etc
CORBEILLE *same as* > CORBEIL
CORBEILS > CORBEIL
CORBEL *n* stone or timber support sticking out of a wall ▷ *vb* lay (a stone or brick) so that it forms a corbel
CORBELED > CORBEL
CORBELING *n* set of corbels stepped outwards, one above another
CORBELLED > CORBEL
CORBELS > CORBEL
CORBES > CORBE
CORBICULA *n* pollen basket
CORBIE *n* raven or crow
CORBIES > CORBIE
CORBINA *n* type of North American whiting
CORBINAS > CORBINA
CORBY *same as* > CORBIE
CORCASS *n* in Ireland, marshland
CORCASSES > CORCASS
CORD *n* thin rope or thick string ▷ *adj* (of fabric) ribbed ▷ *vb* bind or furnish with a cord or cords
CORDAGE *n* lines and rigging of a vessel
CORDAGES > CORDAGE
CORDATE *adj* heart-shaped
CORDATELY > CORDATE
CORDED *adj* tied or fastened with cord
CORDELLE *vb* to tow
CORDELLED > CORDELLE
CORDELLES > CORDELLE
CORDER > CORD
CORDERS > CORD
CORDGRASS *n* type of coarse grass
CORDIAL *adj* warm and friendly ▷ *n* drink with a fruit base
CORDIALLY > CORDIAL
CORDIALS > CORDIAL
CORDIFORM *adj* heart-shaped
CORDINER *n* shoemaker
CORDINERS > CORDINER
CORDING > CORD
CORDINGS > CORD
CORDITE *n* explosive used in guns and bombs
CORDITES > CORDITE
CORDLESS *adj* (of an electrical appliance) powered by an internal battery, so that there is no cable connecting the appliance itself to the electrical mains
CORDLIKE > CORD
CORDOBA *n* standard monetary unit of Nicaragua, divided into 100 centavos
CORDOBAS > CORDOBA
CORDON *n* chain of police, soldiers, etc, guarding an area ▷ *vb* put or form a cordon (around)
CORDONED > CORDON
CORDONING > CORDON
CORDONNET *n* type of thread
CORDONS > CORDON
CORDOTOMY *n* method of pain relief in which nerves are cut > CHORDOTOMY
CORDOVAN *n* fine leather now made principally from horsehide, isolated from the skin layers above and below it and tanned
CORDOVANS > CORDOVAN
CORDS *pl n* trousers made of corduroy
CORDUROY *n* cotton fabric with a velvety ribbed surface
CORDUROYS *pl n* trousers made of corduroy
CORDWAIN *an archaic name for* > CORDOVAN
CORDWAINS > CORDWAIN
CORDWOOD *n* wood that has been cut into lengths of four feet so that it can be stacked in cords
CORDWOODS > CORDWOOD
CORDYLINE *n* any tree of the genus Cordyline
CORE *n* central part of certain fruits, containing the seeds ▷ *vb* remove the core from
CORED > CORE
COREDEEM *vb* to redeem together
COREDEEMS > COREDEEM
COREGENT *n* joint regent
COREGENTS > COREGENT
COREIGN *vb* to reign jointly
COREIGNS > COREIGN
CORELATE *same as* > CORRELATE
CORELATED > CORELATE
CORELATES > CORELATE
CORELESS > CORE
CORELLA *n* white Australian cockatoo
CORELLAS > CORELLA
COREMIA > COREMIUM
COREMIUM *n* spore-producing organ of certain fungi
COREOPSIS *n* any plant of the genus *Coreopsis*, of America and tropical Africa, cultivated for their yellow, brown, or yellow-and-red daisy-like flowers: family *Asteraceae* (composites)
CORER > CORE
CORERS > CORE
CORES > CORE
COREY *n* slang word for the penis
COREYS > COREY
CORF *n* wagon or basket used formerly in mines
CORFHOUSE *n* shed used for curing salmon and storing nets
CORGI *n* short-legged sturdy dog
CORGIS > CORGI
CORIA > CORIUM
CORIANDER *n* plant grown for its aromatic seeds and leaves
CORIES > CORY
CORING > CORE
CORIOUS *adj* leathery
CORIUM *n* deep inner layer of the skin, beneath the epidermis, containing connective tissue, blood vessels, and fat
CORIUMS > CORIUM
CORIVAL *same as* > CORRIVAL
CORIVALRY > CORIVAL
CORIVALS > CORIVAL
CORIXID *n* type of water bug
CORIXIDS > CORIXID
CORK *n* thick light bark of a Mediterranean oak ▷ *vb* seal with a cork ▷ *adj* made of cork
CORKAGE *n* restaurant's charge for serving wine bought elsewhere
CORKAGES > CORKAGE
CORKBOARD *n* thin slab made of granules of cork, used as a floor or wall finish and as an insulator
CORKBORER *n* tool for cutting a hole in a stopper to insert a glass tube
CORKED *adj* (of wine) spoiled through having a decayed cork
CORKER *n* splendid or outstanding person or thing
CORKERS > CORKER
CORKIER > CORKY
CORKIEST > CORKY
CORKINESS > CORKY
CORKING *adj* excellent
CORKIR *n* lichen from which red or purple dye is made
CORKIRS > CORKIR
CORKLIKE > CORK
CORKS > CORK
CORKSCREW *n* spiral metal tool for pulling corks from bottles ▷ *adj* like a corkscrew in shape ▷ *vb* move in a spiral or zigzag course
CORKTREE *n* type of evergreen oak tree
CORKTREES > CORKTREE
CORKWING *n* greenish or bluish European fish of the wrasse family, *Ctenolabrus melops*
CORKWINGS > CORKWING
CORKWOOD *n* small tree, *Leitneria floridana*, of the southeastern US, having very lightweight porous wood: family *Leitneriaceae*
CORKWOODS > CORKWOOD
CORKY *same as* > CORKED
CORM *n* bulblike underground stem of certain plants
CORMEL *n* new small corm arising from the base of a fully developed one
CORMELS > CORMEL
CORMIDIA > CORMIDIUM
CORMIDIUM *n* iteration of the repeating zooid pattern in a siphosome
CORMLIKE *adj* resembling a corm
CORMOID *adj* like a corm
CORMORANT *n* large dark-coloured long-necked sea bird
CORMOUS > CORM
CORMS > CORM
CORMUS *n* corm
CORMUSES > CORMUS
CORN *n* cereal plant such as wheat or oats ▷ *vb* feed (animals) with corn, esp oats
CORNACRE *same as* > CONACRE
CORNACRES > CORNACRE
CORNAGE *n* rent fixed according to the number of horned cattle pastured
CORNAGES > CORNAGE
CORNBALL *n* person given to mawkish or unsophisticated behaviour
CORNBALLS > CORNBALL
CORNBORER *n* larva of the pyralid moth
CORNBRAID *vb* braid hair in cornrows

CORNBRASH *n* type of limestone which produces good soil for growing corn
CORNBREAD *n* bread made from maize meal
CORNCAKE *n* kind of cornmeal flatbread
CORNCAKES > CORNCAKE
CORNCOB *n* core of an ear of maize, to which the kernels are attached
CORNCOBS > CORNCOB
CORNCRAKE *n* brown Eurasian bird with a harsh cry
CORNCRIB *n* ventilated building for the storage of unhusked maize
CORNCRIBS > CORNCRIB
CORNEA *n* transparent membrane covering the eyeball
CORNEAE > CORNEA
CORNEAL > CORNEA
CORNEAS > CORNEA
CORNED *adj* (esp of beef) cooked and then preserved or pickled in salt or brine, now often canned
CORNEITIS *n* inflammation of cornea
CORNEL *n* any cornaceous plant of the genus *Cornus*, such as the dogwood and dwarf cornel
CORNELIAN *same as* > CARNELIAN
CORNELS > CORNEL
CORNEMUSE *n* French bagpipe
CORNEOUS *adj* horny
CORNER *n* area or angle where two converging lines or surfaces meet ▷ *vb* force into a difficult or inescapable position
CORNERED > CORNER
CORNERING > CORNER
CORNERMAN *n* in baseball, first baseman
CORNERMEN > CORNERMAN
CORNERS > CORNER
CORNET *same as* > CORNETT
CORNETCY *n* commission or rank of a cornet
CORNETIST *n* person who plays the cornet
CORNETS > CORNET
CORNETT *n* musical instrument consisting of a straight or curved tube of wood or ivory having finger holes like a recorder and a cup-shaped mouthpiece like a trumpet
CORNETTI > CORNETTO
CORNETTO *same as* > CORNETT
CORNETTS > CORNETT
CORNFED *adj* fed on corn
CORNFIELD *n* field planted with cereal crops
CORNFLAG *n* gladiolus
CORNFLAGS > CORNFLAG
CORNFLAKE *n* singular form of plural cornflakes: toasted flakes made from cornmeal, sold as a breakfast cereal
CORNFLIES > CORNFLY
CORNFLOUR *n* fine maize flour
CORNFLY *n* small fly whose larvae cause swollen, gouty stems in cereal crops
CORNHUSK *n* outer protective covering of an ear of maize
CORNHUSKS > CORNHUSK
CORNI > CORNO
CORNICE *n* decorative moulding round the top of a wall ▷ *vb* furnish or decorate with or as if with a cornice
CORNICED > CORNICE
CORNICES > CORNICE
CORNICHE *n* coastal road, esp one built into the face of a cliff
CORNICHES > CORNICHE
CORNICHON *n* type of small gherkin
CORNICING > CORNICE
CORNICLE *n* wax-secreting organ on an aphid's abdomen
CORNICLES > CORNICLE
CORNICULA *n* plural form of singular corniculum: small horn
CORNIER > CORNY
CORNIEST > CORNY
CORNIFIC *adj* producing horns
CORNIFIED > CORNIFY
CORNIFIES > CORNIFY
CORNIFORM *adj* horn-shaped
CORNIFY *vb* turn soft tissue hard
CORNILY > CORNY
CORNINESS > CORNY
CORNING > CORN
CORNIST *n* horn-player
CORNISTS > CORNIST
CORNLAND *n* land suitable for growing corn or grain
CORNLANDS > CORNLAND
CORNLOFT *n* loft for storing corn
CORNLOFTS > CORNLOFT
CORNMEAL *n* meal made from maize
CORNMEALS > CORNMEAL
CORNMILL *n* flour mill
CORNMILLS > CORNMILL
CORNMOTH *n* moth whose larvae feed on grain
CORNMOTHS > CORNMOTH
CORNO *n* French horn
CORNOPEAN *n* cornet (the brass musical instrument)
CORNPIPE *n* musical instrument made from a stalk of corn etc
CORNPIPES > CORNPIPE
CORNPONE *n* American corn bread
CORNPONES > CORNPONE
CORNRENT *n* rent paid in corn, rather than money
CORNRENTS > CORNRENT
CORNROW *n* hairstyle in which the hair is plaited in close parallel rows ▷ *vb* style the hair in a cornrow
CORNROWED > CORNROW
CORNROWS > CORNROW
CORNS > CORN
CORNSTALK *n* stalk or stem of corn
CORNSTONE *n* mottled green and red limestone
CORNU *n* part or structure resembling a horn or having a hornlike pattern, such as a cross section of the grey matter of the spinal cord
CORNUA > CORNU
CORNUAL > CORNU
CORNUS *n* any member of the genus Cornus, such as dogwood
CORNUSES > CORNUS
CORNUTE *adj* having or resembling cornua ▷ *vb* to make a cuckold of
CORNUTED *same as* > CORNUTE
CORNUTES > CORNUTE
CORNUTING > CORNUTE
CORNUTO *n* cuckold
CORNUTOS > CORNUTO
CORNWORM *n* cornmoth larva
CORNWORMS > CORNWORM
CORNY *adj* unoriginal or oversentimental
COROCORE *same as* > COROCORO
COROCORES > COROCORE
COROCORO *n* South Asian vessel fitted with outriggers
COROCOROS > COROCORO
CORODIES > CORODY
CORODY *n* (originally) the right of a lord to receive free quarters from his vassal
COROLLA *n* petals of a flower collectively
COROLLARY *n* idea, fact, or proposition which is the natural result of something else ▷ *adj* consequent or resultant
COROLLAS > COROLLA
COROLLATE *adj* having a corolla
COROLLINE *adj* relating to a corolla
CORONA *n* ring of light round the moon or sun
CORONACH *n* dirge or lamentation for the dead
CORONACHS > CORONACH
CORONAE > CORONA
CORONAL *n* circlet for the head ▷ *adj* of or relating to a corona or coronal
CORONALLY > CORONAL
CORONALS > CORONAL
CORONARY *adj* of the arteries surrounding the heart ▷ *n* coronary thrombosis
CORONAS > CORONA
CORONATE *vb* to crown
CORONATED > CORONATE
CORONATES > CORONATE
CORONEL *n* iron head of a tilting spear
CORONELS > CORONEL
CORONER *n* official responsible for the investigation of violent, sudden, or suspicious deaths
CORONERS > CORONER
CORONET *n* small crown
CORONETED *adj* wearing a coronet
CORONETS > CORONET
CORONIS *n* in Greek grammar, symbol placed over a contracted syllable
CORONISES > CORONIS
CORONIUM *n* highly-ionized iron and nickel seen as a green line in the solar coronal spectrum
CORONIUMS > CORONIUM
CORONOID *adj* crown-shaped
COROTATE *vb* to rotate together
COROTATED > COROTATE
COROTATES > COROTATE
COROZO *n* tropical American palm, *Corozo oleifera*, whose seeds yield a useful oil
COROZOS > COROZO
CORPORA > CORPUS
CORPORAL *n* noncommissioned officer in an army ▷ *adj* of the body
CORPORALE *same as* > CORPORAL
CORPORALS > CORPORAL
CORPORAS *n* communion cloth
CORPORATE *adj* of business corporations
CORPOREAL *adj* physical or tangible
CORPORIFY *vb* to embody
CORPOSANT *n* Saint Elmo's fire
CORPS *n* military unit with a specific function
CORPSE *n* dead body ▷ *vb* laugh or cause to laugh involuntarily or inopportunely while on stage
CORPSED > CORPSE
CORPSES > CORPSE
CORPSING > CORPSE
CORPSMAN *n* medical orderly or stretcher-bearer
CORPSMEN > CORPSMAN

CORPULENT *adj* fat or plump
CORPUS *n* collection of writings, esp by a single author
CORPUSCLE *n* red or white blood cell
CORPUSES > CORPUS
CORRADE *vb* (of rivers, streams, etc) to erode (land) by the abrasive action of rock particles
CORRADED > CORRADE
CORRADES > CORRADE
CORRADING > CORRADE
CORRAL *n* enclosure for cattle or horses ▷ *vb* put in a corral
CORRALLED > CORRAL
CORRALS > CORRAL
CORRASION *n* erosion of rocks caused by fragments transported over them by water, wind, or ice
CORRASIVE > CORRASION
CORREA *n* Australian evergreen shrub of the genus *Correa*, with large showy tubular flowers
CORREAS > CORREA
CORRECT *adj* free from error, true ▷ *vb* put right
CORRECTED > CORRECT
CORRECTER > CORRECT
CORRECTLY > CORRECT
CORRECTOR > CORRECT
CORRECTS > CORRECT
CORRELATE *vb* place or be placed in a mutual relationship ▷ *n* either of two things mutually related ▷ *adj* having a mutual, complementary, or reciprocal relationship
CORRIDA *the Spanish word for* > BULLFIGHT
CORRIDAS > CORRIDA
CORRIDOR *n* passage in a building or train
CORRIDORS > CORRIDOR
CORRIE *same as* > CIRQUE
CORRIES > CORRIE
CORRIGENT *n* corrective
CORRIVAL *a rare word for* > RIVAL *vb* to vie
CORRIVALS > CORRIVAL
CORRODANT > CORRODE
CORRODE *vb* eat or be eaten away by chemical action or rust
CORRODED > CORRODE
CORRODENT > CORRODE
CORRODER > CORRODE
CORRODERS > CORRODE
CORRODES > CORRODE
CORRODIES > CORRODY
CORRODING > CORRODE
CORRODY *same as* > CORODY
CORROSION *n* process by which something, esp a metal, is corroded
CORROSIVE *adj* (esp of acids or alkalis) capable of destroying solid materials ▷ *n* corrosive substance, such as a strong acid or alkali
CORRUGATE *vb* fold into alternate grooves and ridges ▷ *adj* folded into furrows and ridges
CORRUPT *adj* open to or involving bribery ▷ *vb* make corrupt
CORRUPTED > CORRUPT
CORRUPTER > CORRUPT
CORRUPTLY > CORRUPT
CORRUPTOR > CORRUPT
CORRUPTS > CORRUPT
CORS > COR
CORSAC *n* fox, *Vulpes corsac*, of central Asia
CORSACS > CORSAC
CORSAGE *n* small bouquet worn on the bodice of a dress
CORSAGES > CORSAGE
CORSAIR *n* pirate
CORSAIRS > CORSAIR
CORSE *n* corpse
CORSELET *n* one-piece undergarment combining a corset and bra
CORSELETS > CORSELET
CORSES > CORSE
CORSET *n* women's close-fitting undergarment worn to shape the torso ▷ *vb* dress or enclose in, or as in, a corset
CORSETED > CORSET
CORSETIER *n* man who makes and fits corsets
CORSETING > CORSET
CORSETRY *n* making of or dealing in corsets
CORSETS > CORSET
CORSEY *n* pavement or pathway
CORSEYS > CORSEY
CORSIVE *n* corrodent
CORSIVES > CORSIVE
CORSLET *same as* > CORSELET
CORSLETED > CORSLET
CORSLETS > CORSLET
CORSNED *n* ordeal whereby an accused person had to eat a morsel of bread; swallowing it freely indicated innocence; choking, guilt
CORSNEDS > CORSNED
CORSO *n* promenade
CORSOS > CORSO
CORTEGE *n* funeral procession
CORTEGES > CORTEGE
CORTEX *n* outer layer of the brain or other internal organ
CORTEXES > CORTEX
CORTICAL > CORTEX
CORTICATE *adj* (of plants, seeds, etc) having a bark, husk, or rind
CORTICES > CORTEX
CORTICOID *n* steroid hormone
CORTICOSE *adj* consisting of or like bark
CORTILE *n* open, internal courtyard
CORTILI > CORTILE
CORTIN *n* adrenal cortex extract containing cortisone and other hormones
CORTINA *n* weblike part of certain mushrooms
CORTINAS > CORTINA
CORTINS > CORTIN
CORTISOL *n* principal glucocorticoid secreted by the adrenal cortex
CORTISOLS > CORTISOL
CORTISONE *n* steroid hormone used to treat various diseases
CORULER *n* joint ruler
CORULERS > CORULER
CORUNDUM *n* hard mineral used as an abrasive
CORUNDUMS > CORUNDUM
CORUSCANT *adj* giving off flashes of light
CORUSCATE *vb* sparkle
CORVEE *n* day's unpaid labour owed by a feudal vassal to his lord
CORVEES > CORVEE
CORVES > CORF
CORVET *same as* > CURVET
CORVETED > CORVET
CORVETING > CORVET
CORVETS > CORVET
CORVETTE *n* lightly armed escort warship ▷ *vb* to participate in social activities with fellow Corvette car enthusiasts
CORVETTED > CORVETTE
CORVETTES > CORVETTE
CORVID *n* any member of the crow family
CORVIDS > CORVID
CORVINA *same as* > CORBINA
CORVINAS > CORVINA
CORVINE *adj* of, relating to, or resembling a crow
CORVUS *n* type of ancient hook
CORVUSES > CORVUS
CORY *n* catfish belonging to the South American Corydoras genus
CORYBANT *n* wild attendant of the goddess Cybele
CORYBANTS > CORYBANT
CORYDALIS *n* any erect or climbing plant of the N temperate genus *Corydalis*, having finely-lobed leaves and spurred yellow or pinkish flowers: family *Fumariaceae*
CORYLUS *n* hazel genus
CORYLUSES > CORYLUS
CORYMB *n* flat-topped flower cluster with the stems growing progressively shorter towards the centre ▷ *vb* be corymb-like
CORYMBED > CORYMB
CORYMBOSE > CORYMB
CORYMBOUS > CORYMB
CORYMBS > CORYMB
CORYPHAEI *n* plural form of singular coryphaeus: leader of the chorus
CORYPHE *n* coryphaeus
CORYPHEE *n* leading dancer of a corps de ballet
CORYPHEES > CORYPHEE
CORYPHENE *n* any fish of the genus Coryphaena
CORYPHES > CORYPHE
CORYZA *n* acute inflammation of the mucous membrane of the nose, with discharge of mucus
CORYZAL > CORYZA
CORYZAS > CORYZA
COS *same as* > COSINE
COSCRIPT *vb* to script jointly
COSCRIPTS > COSCRIPT
COSE *vb* get cosy
COSEC *same as* > COSECANT
COSECANT *n* (in trigonometry) the ratio of the length of the hypotenuse to that of the opposite side in a right-angled triangle
COSECANTS > COSECANT
COSECH *n* hyperbolic cosecant
COSECHS > COSECH
COSECS > COSEC
COSED > COSE
COSEISMAL *adj* of or designating points at which earthquake waves are felt at the same time ▷ *n* such a line on a map
COSEISMIC *same as* > COSEISMAL
COSES > COSE
COSET *n* mathematical set
COSETS > COSET
COSEY *n* tea cosy
COSEYS > COSEY
COSH *n* heavy blunt weapon ▷ *vb* hit with a cosh
COSHED > COSH
COSHER *vb* pamper or coddle
COSHERED > COSHER
COSHERER > COSHER
COSHERERS > COSHER
COSHERIES > COSHERY
COSHERING > COSHER
COSHERS > COSHER
COSHERY *n* Irish chief's right to lodge at his tenants' houses
COSHES > COSH
COSHING > COSH
COSIE *same as* > COSY
COSIED > COSY
COSIER *n* cobbler
COSIERS > COSIER
COSIES > COSY

COSIEST > COSY
COSIGN *vb* to sign jointly
COSIGNED > COSIGN
COSIGNER > COSIGN
COSIGNERS > COSIGN
COSIGNING > COSIGN
COSIGNS > COSIGN
COSILY > COSY
COSINE *n* (in trigonometry) ratio of the length of the adjacent side to that of the hypotenuse in a right-angled triangle
COSINES > COSINE
COSINESS > COSY
COSING > COSE
COSMEA *n* plant of the genus Cosmos
COSMEAS > COSMEA
COSMESES > COSMESIS
COSMESIS *n* aesthetic covering on a prosthesis to make it look more natural
COSMETIC *n* preparation used to improve the appearance of a person's skin ▷ *adj* improving the appearance only
COSMETICS > COSMETIC
COSMIC *adj* of the whole universe
COSMICAL > COSMIC
COSMID *n* segment of DNA
COSMIDS > COSMID
COSMIN *same as* > COSMINE
COSMINE *n* substance resembling dentine, forming the outer layer of cosmoid scales
COSMINES > COSMINE
COSMINS > COSMIN
COSMISM *n* Russian cultural and philosophical movement
COSMISMS > COSMISM
COSMIST > COSMISM
COSMISTS > COSMISM
COSMOCRAT *n* ruler of the world
COSMOGENY *same as* > COSMOGONY
COSMOGONY *n* study of the origin of the universe
COSMOID *adj* (of the scales of coelacanths and lungfish) consisting of two inner bony layers and an outer layer of cosmine
COSMOLINE *n* type of petroleum jelly
COSMOLOGY *n* study of the origin and nature of the universe
COSMONAUT *n* Russian name for an astronaut
COSMORAMA *n* lifelike display, using mirrors and lenses, which shows reflections of various views of parts of the world
COSMOS *n* universe
COSMOSES > COSMOS
COSMOTRON *n* large type of particle accelerator
COSPHERED *adj* sharing the same sphere
COSPONSOR *vb* to sponsor jointly
COSS *another name for* > KOS
COSSACK *n* Slavonic warrior-peasant who served in the Russian cavalry under the tsars
COSSACKS > COSSACK
COSSES > COSS
COSSET *vb* pamper ▷ *n* any pet animal, esp a lamb
COSSETED > COSSET
COSSETING > COSSET
COSSETS > COSSET
COSSIE *n* informal name for a swimming costume
COSSIES > COSSIE
COST *n* amount of money, time, labour, etc, required for something ▷ *vb* have as its cost
COSTA *n* riblike part, such as the midrib of a plant leaf
COSTAE > COSTA
COSTAL *n* strengthening rib of an insect's wing
COSTALGIA *n* pain in the ribs
COSTALLY > COSTAL
COSTALS > COSTAL
COSTAR *n* actor who shares the billing with another ▷ *vb* share the billing with another actor
COSTARD *n* English variety of apple tree
COSTARDS > COSTARD
COSTARRED > COSTAR
COSTARS > COSTAR
COSTATE *adj* having ribs
COSTATED *same as* > COSTATE
COSTE *vb* to draw near
COSTEAN *vb* to mine for lodes
COSTEANED > COSTEAN
COSTEANS > COSTEAN
COSTED > COST
COSTER *n* person who sells fruit, vegetables etc from a barrow
COSTERS > COSTER
COSTES > COSTE
COSTING > COST
COSTIVE *adj* having or causing constipation
COSTIVELY > COSTIVE
COSTLESS > COST
COSTLIER > COSTLY
COSTLIEST > COSTLY
COSTLY *adj* expensive
COSTMARY *n* herbaceous plant, *Chrysanthemum balsamita*, native to Asia. Its fragrant leaves were used as a seasoning and to flavour ale: family *Asteraceae* (composites)
COSTOTOMY *n* surgical incision into a rib
COSTREL *n* flask, usually of earthenware or leather
COSTRELS > COSTREL
COSTS > COST
COSTUME *n* style of dress of a particular place or time, or for a particular activity ▷ *vb* provide with a costume
COSTUMED > COSTUME
COSTUMER *same as* > COSTUMIER
COSTUMERS > COSTUMIER
COSTUMERY *n* collective term for costumes
COSTUMES > COSTUME
COSTUMEY *adj* (stage) costume-like; unrealistic
COSTUMIER *n* maker or seller of costumes
COSTUMING > COSTUME
COSTUS *n* Himalayan herb with an aromatic root
COSTUSES > COSTUS
COSY *adj* warm and snug ▷ *n* cover for keeping things warm ▷ *vb* to make oneself snug and warm
COSYING > COSY
COT *n* baby's bed with high sides ▷ *vb* entangle or become entangled
COTAN *same as* > COTANGENT
COTANGENT *n* (in trigonometry) the ratio of the length of the adjacent side to that of the opposite side in a right-angled triangle
COTANS > COTANGENT
COTE *same as* > COT
COTEAU *n* hillside
COTEAUX > COTEAU
COTED > COT
COTELETTE *n* cutlet
COTELINE *n* kind of muslin
COTELINES > COTELINE
COTENANCY > COTENANT
COTENANT *n* person who holds property jointly or in common with others
COTENANTS > COTENANT
COTERIE *n* exclusive group, clique
COTERIES > COTERIE
COTES > COTE
COTH *n* hyperbolic cotangent
COTHS > COTH
COTHURN *same as* > COTHURNUS
COTHURNAL > COTHURNUS
COTHURNI > COTHURNUS
COTHURNS > COTHURNUS
COTHURNUS *n* buskin worn in ancient Greek tragedy
COTICULAR *adj* relating to whetstones
COTIDAL *adj* (of a line on a tidal chart) joining points at which high tide occurs simultaneously
COTILLION *n* French formation dance of the 18th century
COTILLON *same as* > COTILLION
COTILLONS > COTILLON
COTING > COT
COTINGA *n* any tropical American passerine bird of the family *Cotingidae*, such as the umbrella bird and the cock-of-the-rock, having a broad slightly hooked bill
COTINGAS > COTINGA
COTININE *n* substance used to indicate presence of nicotine
COTININES > COTININE
COTISE *same as* > COTTISE
COTISED > COTISE
COTISES > COTISE
COTISING > COTISE
COTLAND *n* grounds that belong to a cotter
COTLANDS > COTLAND
COTQUEAN *n* coarse woman
COTQUEANS > COTQUEAN
COTRUSTEE *n* fellow trustee
COTS > COT
COTT *same as* > COT
COTTA *n* short form of surplice
COTTABUS *n* ancient Greek game involving throwing wine into a vessel
COTTAE > COTTA
COTTAGE *n* small house in the country ▷ *vb* engage in homosexual activity in a public lavatory
COTTAGED > COTTAGE
COTTAGER *n* person who lives in a cottage
COTTAGERS > COTTAGER
COTTAGES > COTTAGE
COTTAGEY *adj* resembling a cottage
COTTAGING *n* homosexual activity between men in a public lavatory
COTTAR *same as* > COTTER
COTTARS > COTTAR
COTTAS > COTTA
COTTED > COT
COTTER *n* pin or wedge used to secure machine parts ▷ *vb* secure (two parts) with a cotter
COTTERED > COTTER
COTTERING > COTTER
COTTERS > COTTIER
COTTID *n* any fish of the scorpaenoid family *Cottidae*, typically possessing a large head, tapering body, and spiny fins, including the pogge, sea scorpion, bullhead, father lasher, and cottus
COTTIDS > COTTID
COTTIER *same as* > COTTER
COTTIERS > COTTIER
COTTING > COT
COTTISE *n* type of heraldic decoration ▷ *vb* (in heraldry) decorate with a

cottise
COTTISED > COTTISE
COTTISES > COTTISE
COTTISING > COTTISE
COTTOID *adj* resembling a fish of the genus Cottus
COTTON *n* white downy fibre covering the seeds of a tropical plant ▷ *vb* take a liking
COTTONADE *n* coarse fabric of cotton or mixed fibres, used for work clothes, etc
COTTONED > COTTON
COTTONING > COTTON
COTTONS > COTTON
COTTONY > COTTON
COTTOWN *Scots variant of* > COTTON
COTTOWNS > COTTON
COTTS > COTT
COTTUS *n* scorpaenoid fish of the family *Cottidae;* the type genus, having four yellowish knobs on its head
COTTUSES > COTTUS
COTURNIX *n* variety of quail
COTWAL *n* Indian police officer
COTWALS > COTWAL
COTYLAE > COTYLE
COTYLE *n* cuplike cavity
COTYLEDON *n* first leaf of a plant embryo
COTYLES > COTYLE
COTYLOID *adj* shaped like a cup ▷ *n* small bone forming part of the acetabular cavity in some mammals
COTYLOIDS > COTYLOID
COTYPE *n* additional type specimen from the same brood as the original type specimen
COTYPES > COTYPE
COUCAL *n* any ground-living bird of the genus *Centropus*, of Africa, S Asia, and Australia, having long strong legs: family *Cuculidae* (cuckoos)
COUCALS > COUCAL
COUCH *n* piece of upholstered furniture for seating more than one person ▷ *vb* express in a particular way
COUCHANT *adj* in a lying position
COUCHE *adj* in heraldry (of a shield), tilted
COUCHED > COUCH
COUCHEE *n* reception held late at night
COUCHEES > COUCHEE
COUCHER > COUCH
COUCHERS > COUCH
COUCHES > COUCH
COUCHETTE *n* bed converted from seats on a train or ship
COUCHING *n* method of embroidery in which the thread is caught down at intervals by another thread passed through the material from beneath
COUCHINGS > COUCHING
COUDE *adj* (of a reflecting telescope) having plane mirrors positioned to reflect light from the primary mirror along the axis onto a detector
COUGAN *n* drunk and rowdy person
COUGANS > COUGAN
COUGAR *n* puma
COUGARS > COUGAR
COUGH *vb* expel air from the lungs abruptly and noisily ▷ *n* act or sound of coughing
COUGHED > COUGH
COUGHER > COUGH
COUGHERS > COUGH
COUGHING > COUGH
COUGHINGS > COUGH
COUGHS > COUGH
COUGUAR *same as* > COUGAR
COUGUARS > COUGUAR
COULD > CAN
COULDEST *same as* > COULDST
COULDST *vb* form of COULD used with the pronoun *thou* or its relative form
COULEE *n* flow of molten lava
COULEES > COULEE
COULIBIAC *n* Russian fish pie
COULIS *n* thin purée of vegetables or fruit, usually served as a sauce surrounding a dish
COULISSE *n* timber member grooved to take a sliding panel, such as a sluicegate, portcullis, or stage flat
COULISSES > COULISSE
COULOIR *n* deep gully on a mountain side, esp in the French Alps
COULOIRS > COULOIR
COULOMB *n* SI unit of electric charge
COULOMBIC > COULOMB
COULOMBS > COULOMB
COULTER *n* blade at the front of a ploughshare
COULTERS > COULTER
COUMARIC > COUMARIN
COUMARIN *n* white vanilla-scented crystalline ester, used in perfumes and flavourings and as an anticoagulant
COUMARINS > COUMARIN
COUMARONE *n* a colourless insoluble aromatic liquid obtained from coal tar and used in the manufacture of synthetic resins
COUMAROU *n* tonka bean tree, or its seed
COUMAROUS > COUMAROU
COUNCIL *n* group meeting for discussion or consultation ▷ *adj* of or by a council
COUNCILOR *n* member of a council
COUNCILS > COUNCIL
COUNSEL *n* advice or guidance ▷ *vb* give guidance to
COUNSELED > COUNSEL
COUNSELEE *n* one who is counselled
COUNSELOR *n* person who gives counsel
COUNSELS > COUNSEL
COUNT *vb* say numbers in order ▷ *n* counting
COUNTABLE *adj* capable of being counted
COUNTABLY > COUNTABLE
COUNTBACK *n* system of deciding the winner of a tied competition by comparing earlier points or scores
COUNTDOWN *n* counting backwards to zero of the seconds before an event ▷ *vb* count numbers backwards towards zero, esp in timing such a critical operation
COUNTED > COUNT
COUNTER *n* long flat surface in a bank or shop, on which business is transacted ▷ *vb* oppose, retaliate against ▷ *adv* in the opposite direction
COUNTERED > COUNTER
COUNTERS > COUNTER
COUNTESS *n* woman holding the rank of count or earl
COUNTIAN *n* dweller in a given county
COUNTIANS > COUNTIAN
COUNTIES > COUNTY
COUNTING > COUNT
COUNTLESS *adj* too many to count
COUNTLINE *n* (in confectionery marketing) a chocolate-based bar
COUNTRIES > COUNTRY
COUNTROL *obsolete variant of* > CONTROL
COUNTROLS > COUNTROL
COUNTRY *n* nation
COUNTS > COUNT
COUNTSHIP > COUNT
COUNTY *n* (in some countries) division of a country ▷ *adj* upper-class
COUP *n* successful action ▷ *vb* turn or fall over
COUPE *n* sports car with two doors and a sloping fixed roof
COUPED > COUP
COUPEE *n* (in dance) a forward movement on one leg, with the other slightly bent and raised
COUPEES > COUPEE
COUPER *n* dealer
COUPERS > COUPER
COUPES > COUPE
COUPING > COUP
COUPLE *n* two people who are married or romantically involved ▷ *vb* connect, associate
COUPLED > COUPLE
COUPLEDOM *n* state of living as a couple, esp when regarded as being interested in each other to the exclusion of the outside world
COUPLER *n* link or rod transmitting power between two rotating mechanisms or a rotating part and a reciprocating part
COUPLERS > COUPLER
COUPLES > COUPLE
COUPLET *n* two consecutive lines of verse, usu. rhyming and of the same metre
COUPLETS > COUPLET
COUPLING *n* device for connecting things, such as railway carriages
COUPLINGS > COUPLING
COUPON *n* piece of paper entitling the holder to a discount or gift
COUPONING *n* in marketing, distribution or redemption of promotional coupons
COUPONS > COUPON
COUPS > COUP
COUPURE *n* entrenchment made by beseiged forces behind a breach in their defences
COUPURES > COUPURE
COUR *obsolete variant of* > COVER
COURAGE *n* ability to face danger or pain without fear
COURAGES > COURAGE
COURANT *n* courante ▷ *adj* (of an animal) running
COURANTE *n* old dance in quick triple time
COURANTES > COURANTE
COURANTO *same as* > COURANTE
COURANTOS > COURANTO
COURANTS > COURANT
COURB *vb* to bend
COURBARIL *n* tropical American leguminous tree, *Hymenaea courbaril*. Its wood is a useful timber and its gum is a source of copal
COURBED > COURB
COURBETTE *same*

as > CURVET
COURBING > COURB
COURBS > COURB
COURD *obsolete variant of* > COVERED
COURE *obsolete variant of* > COVER
COURED > COURE
COURES > COURE
COURGETTE *n* type of small vegetable marrow
COURIE *vb* nestle or snuggle
COURIED > COURIE
COURIEING > COURIE
COURIER *n* person employed to look after holiday-makers ▷ *vb* send (a parcel, letter, etc) by courier
COURIERS > COURIER
COURIES > COURIE
COURING > COUR
COURLAN *another name for* > LIMPKIN
COURLANS > COURLAN
COURS > COUR
COURSE *n* series of lessons or medical treatment ▷ *vb* (of liquid) run swiftly
COURSED > COURSE
COURSER *n* swift horse
COURSERS > COURSER
COURSES *another word for* > MENSES
COURSING *n* hunting with hounds trained to hunt game by sight
COURSINGS > COURSING
COURT *n* body which decides legal cases ▷ *vb* try to gain the love of
COURTED > COURT
COURTEOUS *adj* polite
COURTER *n* suitor
COURTERS > COURTER
COURTESAN *n* mistress or high-class prostitute
COURTESY *n* politeness, good manners
COURTEZAN *same as* > COURTESAN
COURTIER *n* attendant at a royal court
COURTIERS > COURTIER
COURTING > COURT
COURTINGS > COURT
COURTLET *n* small court
COURTLETS > COURTLET
COURTLIER > COURTLY
COURTLIKE *adj* courtly
COURTLING *n* fawning courtier
COURTLY *adj* ceremoniously polite
COURTROOM *n* room in which the sittings of a law court are held
COURTS > COURT
COURTSHIP *n* courting of an intended spouse or mate
COURTSIDE *n* in sport, area closest to the court
COURTYARD *n* paved space enclosed by buildings or walls
COUSCOUS *n* type of semolina used in North African cookery
COUSIN *n* child of one's uncle or aunt
COUSINAGE *n* kinship
COUSINLY > COUSIN
COUSINRY *n* collective term for cousins
COUSINS > COUSIN
COUTEAU *n* large two-edged knife used formerly as a weapon
COUTEAUX > COUTEAU
COUTER *n* armour designed to protect the elbow
COUTERS > COUTER
COUTH *adj* refined ▷ *n* refinement
COUTHER > COUTH
COUTHEST > COUTH
COUTHIE *adj* sociable
COUTHIER > COUTHIE
COUTHIEST > COUTHIE
COUTHS > COUTH
COUTHY *same as* > COUTHIE
COUTIL *n* type of tightly-woven twill cloth
COUTILLE *same as* > COUTIL
COUTILLES > COUTILLE
COUTILS > COUTIL
COUTURE *n* high-fashion designing and dressmaking ▷ *adj* relating to high fashion design and dress-making
COUTURES > COUTURE
COUTURIER *n* person who designs women's fashion clothes
COUVADE *n* custom in certain cultures of treating the husband of a woman giving birth as if he were bearing the child
COUVADES > COUVADE
COUVERT *another word for* > COVER
COUVERTS > COUVERT
COUZIN *n* South African word for a friend
COUZINS > COUZIN
COVALENCE *same as* > COVALENCY
COVALENCY *n* ability to form a bond in which two atoms share a pair of electrons
COVALENT > COVALENCY
COVARIANT *n* variant that varies leaving certain mathematical relationships it has with another variant (its covariant) unchanged
COVARIATE *n* statistical variable
COVARIED > COVARY
COVARIES > COVARY
COVARY *vb* vary together maintaining a certain mathematical relationship
COVARYING > COVARY
COVE *n* small bay or inlet ▷ *vb* form an architectural cove in
COVED > COVE
COVELET *n* small cove
COVELETS > COVELET
COVELLINE *same as* > COVELLITE
COVELLITE *n* indigo copper (blue sulphide of copper)
COVEN *n* meeting of witches
COVENANT *n* contract ▷ *vb* agree by a covenant
COVENANTS > COVENANT
COVENS > COVEN
COVENT *same as* > CONVENT
COVENTS > COVENT
COVER *vb* place something over, to protect or conceal ▷ *n* anything that covers
COVERABLE > COVER
COVERAGE *n* amount or extent covered
COVERAGES > COVERAGE
COVERALL *n* thing that covers something entirely
COVERALLS > COVERALL
COVERED > COVER
COVERER > COVER
COVERERS > COVER
COVERING *another word for* > COVER
COVERINGS > COVERING
COVERLESS > COVER
COVERLET *n* bed cover
COVERLETS > COVERLET
COVERLID *same as* > COVERLET
COVERLIDS > COVERLID
COVERS > COVER
COVERSED as in *coversed sine* obsolete function in trigonometry
COVERSINE *n* function in trigometry
COVERSLIP *n* very thin piece of glass placed over a specimen on a glass slide
COVERT *adj* concealed, secret ▷ *n* thicket giving shelter to game birds or animals
COVERTLY > COVERT
COVERTS > COVERT
COVERTURE *n* condition or status of a married woman considered as being under the protection and influence of her husband
COVERUP *n* concealment of a mistake, crime, etc
COVERUPS > COVERUP
COVES > COVE
COVET *vb* long to possess (what belongs to someone else)
COVETABLE > COVET
COVETED > COVET
COVETER > COVET
COVETERS > COVET
COVETING > COVET
COVETISE *n* covetousness
COVETISES > COVETISE
COVETOUS *adj* jealously longing to possess something
COVETS > COVET
COVEY *n* small flock of grouse or partridge
COVEYS > COVEY
COVIN *n* conspiracy between two or more persons to act to the detriment or injury of another
COVING *same as* > COVE
COVINGS > COVING
COVINOUS *adj* deceitful
COVINS > COVIN
COVYNE *same as* > COVIN
COVYNES > COVYNE
COW *n* mature female of cattle and of certain other mammals, such as the elephant or seal ▷ *vb* intimidate, subdue
COWAGE *n* tropical climbing leguminous plant, *Stizolobium* (or *Mucuna*) *pruriens*, whose bristly pods cause severe itching and stinging
COWAGES > COWAGE
COWAL *n* shallow lake or swampy depression supporting vegetation
COWALS > COWAL
COWAN *n* drystone waller
COWANS > COWAN
COWARD *n* person who lacks courage ▷ *vb* show (someone) up to be a coward
COWARDED > COWARD
COWARDICE *n* lack of courage
COWARDING > COWARD
COWARDLY *adj* of or characteristic of a coward
COWARDRY *n* cowardice
COWARDS > COWARD
COWBANE *n* any of several N temperate poisonous umbelliferous marsh plants of the genus *Cicuta*, esp *C. virosa*, having clusters of small white flowers
COWBANES > COWBANE
COWBELL *n* bell hung around a cow's neck
COWBELLS > COWBELL
COWBERRY *n* creeping ericaceous evergreen shrub, *Vaccinium vitis-idaea*, of N temperate and arctic regions, with pink or red flowers and edible slightly acid berries
COWBIND *n* any of various bryony plants, esp the white bryony
COWBINDS > COWBIND

COWBIRD *n* any of various American orioles of the genera *Molothrus*, *Tangavius*, etc, esp *M. ater* (common or brown-headed cowbird). They have a dark plumage and short bill
COWBIRDS > COWBIRD
COWBOY *n* (in the US) ranch worker who herds and tends cattle, usu. on horseback ▷ *vb* work or behave as a cowboy
COWBOYED > COWBOY
COWBOYING > COWBOY
COWBOYS > COWBOY
COWED > COW
COWEDLY > COW
COWER *vb* cringe in fear
COWERED > COWER
COWERING > COWER
COWERS > COWER
COWFEEDER *n* dairyman
COWFISH *n* any trunkfish, such as *Lactophrys quadricornis*, having hornlike spines over the eyes
COWFISHES > COWFISH
COWFLAP *n* cow dung
COWFLAPS > COWFLAP
COWFLOP *n* foxglove
COWFLOPS > COWFLOP
COWGIRL *n* female cowboy
COWGIRLS > COWGIRL
COWGRASS *n* red clover
COWHAGE *same as* > COWAGE
COWHAGES > COWHAGE
COWHAND *same as* > COWBOY
COWHANDS > COWBOY
COWHEARD *same as* > COWHERD
COWHEARDS > COWHEARD
COWHEEL *n* heel of a cow, used as cooking ingredient
COWHEELS > COWHEEL
COWHERB *n* European caryophyllaceous plant, *Saponaria vaccaria*, having clusters of pink flowers: a weed in the US
COWHERBS > COWHERB
COWHERD *n* person employed to tend cattle
COWHERDS > COWHERD
COWHIDE *n* hide of a cow ▷ *vb* to lash with a cowhide whip
COWHIDED > COWHIDE
COWHIDES > COWHIDE
COWHIDING > COWHIDE
COWHOUSE *n* byre
COWHOUSES > COWHOUSE
COWIER > COWY
COWIEST > COWY
COWING > COW
COWINNER *n* joint winner
COWINNERS > COWINNER
COWISH *adj* cowardly
COWITCH *another name for* > COWAGE
COWITCHES > COWITCH
COWK *vb* retch or feel nauseated
COWKED > COWK
COWKING > COWK
COWKS > COWK
COWL *same as* > COWLING
COWLED *adj* wearing a cowl
COWLICK *n* tuft of hair over the forehead
COWLICKS > COWLICK
COWLING *n* cover on an engine
COWLINGS > COWLING
COWLS > COWL
COWLSTAFF *n* pole, used by two people, for carrying a vessel
COWMAN *n* man who owns cattle
COWMEN > COWMAN
COWORKER *n* fellow worker
COWORKERS > COWORKER
COWP *same as* > COUP
COWPAT *n* pool of cow dung
COWPATS > COWPAT
COWPEA *n* leguminous tropical climbing plant, *Vigna sinensis*, producing long pods containing edible pealike seeds: grown for animal fodder and sometimes as human food
COWPEAS > COWPEA
COWPED > COWP
COWPIE *n* cowpat
COWPIES > COWPIE
COWPING > COWP
COWPLOP *n* cow dung
COWPLOPS > COWPLOP
COWPOKE *n* cowboy
COWPOKES > COWPOKE
COWPOX *n* disease of cows, the virus of which is used in the smallpox vaccine
COWPOXES > COWPOX
COWPS > COWP
COWRIE *n* brightly-marked sea shell
COWRIES > COWRIE
COWRITE *vb* to write jointly
COWRITER > COWRITE
COWRITERS > COWRITE
COWRITES > COWRITE
COWRITING > COWRITE
COWRITTEN > COWRITE
COWROTE > COWRITE
COWRY *same as* > COWRIE
COWS > COW
COWSHED *n* byre
COWSHEDS > COWSHED
COWSKIN *same as* > COWHIDE
COWSKINS > COWSKIN
COWSLIP *n* small yellow wild European flower
COWSLIPS > COWSLIP
COWTREE *n* South American tree that produces latex
COWTREES > COWTREE
COWY *adj* cowlike
COX *n* coxswain ▷ *vb* act as cox of (a boat)
COXA *n* technical name for the hipbone or hip joint
COXAE > COXA
COXAL > COXA
COXALGIA *n* pain in the hip joint
COXALGIAS > COXALGIA
COXALGIC > COXALGIA
COXALGIES > COXALGIA
COXALGY *same as* > COXALGIA
COXCOMB *same as* > COCKSCOMB
COXCOMBIC > COXCOMB
COXCOMBRY *n* conceited arrogance or foppishness
COXCOMBS > COXCOMB
COXED > COX
COXES > COX
COXIER > COXY
COXIEST > COXY
COXINESS > COXY
COXING > COX
COXITIDES > COXITIS
COXITIS *n* inflammation of the hip joint
COXLESS > COX
COXSWAIN *n* person who steers a rowing boat
COXSWAINS > COXSWAIN
COXY *adj* cocky
COY *adj* affectedly shy or modest ▷ *vb* to caress
COYDOG *n* cross between a coyote and a dog
COYDOGS > COYDOG
COYED > COY
COYER > COY
COYEST > COY
COYING > COY
COYISH > COY
COYISHLY > COY
COYLY > COY
COYNESS > COY
COYNESSES > COY
COYOTE *n* prairie wolf of N America
COYOTES > COYOTE
COYOTILLO *n* thorny poisonous rhamnaceous shrub, *Karwinskia humboldtiana* of Mexico and the southwestern US, the berries of which cause paralysis
COYPOU *same as* > COYPU
COYPOUS > COYPOU
COYPU *n* beaver-like aquatic rodent native to S America, bred for its fur
COYPUS > COYPU
COYS > COY
COYSTREL *same as* > COISTREL
COYSTRELS > COYSTREL
COYSTRIL *same as* > COISTREL
COYSTRILS > COYSTRIL
COZ *n archaic word for* > COUSIN
COZE *vb* to chat
COZED > COZE
COZEN *vb* cheat, trick
COZENAGE > COZEN
COZENAGES > COZEN
COZENED > COZEN
COZENER > COZEN
COZENERS > COZEN
COZENING > COZEN
COZENS > COZEN
COZES > COZE
COZEY *n* tea cosy
COZEYS > COZEY
COZIE *same as* > COZEY
COZIED > COSY
COZIER *n* cobbler
COZIERS > COZIER
COZIES > COZEY
COZIEST > COZY
COZILY > COZY
COZINESS > COZY
COZING > COZE
COZY *same as* > COSY *vb* to make oneself snug and warm
COZYING > COZY
COZZES > COZ
CRAAL *vb* to enclose in a craal (or kraal)
CRAALED > CRAAL
CRAALING > CRAAL
CRAALS > CRAAL
CRAB *n* edible shellfish with ten legs, the first pair modified into pincers
CRABABBLE *n* tree bearing small sour apple-like fruit
CRABBED > CRAB
CRABBEDLY > CRAB
CRABBER *n* crab fisherman
CRABBERS > CRABBER
CRABBIER > CRABBY
CRABBIEST > CRABBY
CRABBILY > CRABBY
CRABBING > CRAB
CRABBY *adj* bad-tempered
CRABEATER *n* species of seal
CRABGRASS *n* type of coarse weedy grass
CRABLIKE *adj* resembling a crab
CRABMEAT *n* edible flesh of a crab
CRABMEATS > CRABMEAT
CRABS > CRAB
CRABSTICK *n* stick, cane, or cudgel made of crabapple wood
CRABWISE *adv* (of motion) sideways
CRABWOOD *n* tropical American meliaceous tree, *Carapa guianensis*
CRABWOODS > CRABWOOD
CRACK *vb* break or split partially ▷ *n* sudden sharp noise ▷ *adj* first-rate, excellent
CRACKA *n* US derogatory word for a poor White person
CRACKAS > CRACKA
CRACKBACK *n* in American football, illegal blocking of an opponent
CRACKDOWN *n* severe disciplinary measures
CRACKED *adj* damaged by cracking ▷ *n* sharp noise
CRACKER *n* thin dry biscuit

CRACKERS *adj* insane
CRACKET *n* low stool, often one with three legs
CRACKETS > CRACKET
CRACKHEAD *n* person addicted to the drug crack
CRACKING *adj* very fast
CRACKINGS > CRACKING
CRACKJAW *adj* difficult to pronounce ▷ *n* word or phrase that is difficult to pronounce
CRACKJAWS > CRACKJAW
CRACKLE *vb* make small sharp popping noises ▷ *n* crackling sound
CRACKLED > CRACKLE
CRACKLES > CRACKLE
CRACKLIER > CRACKLY
CRACKLING *n* crackle
CRACKLY *adj* making a cracking sound
CRACKNEL *n* type of hard plain biscuit
CRACKNELS > CRACKNEL
CRACKPOT *adj* eccentric ▷ *n* eccentric person
CRACKPOTS > CRACKPOT
CRACKS > CRACK
CRACKSMAN *n* burglar, esp a safe-breaker
CRACKSMEN > CRACKSMAN
CRACKUP *n* physical or mental breakdown
CRACKUPS > CRACKUP
CRACKY *adj* full of cracks
CRACOWE *n* medieval shoe with a sharply pointed toe
CRACOWES > CRACOWE
CRADLE *n* baby's bed on rockers ▷ *vb* hold gently as if in a cradle
CRADLED > CRADLE
CRADLER > CRADLE
CRADLERS > CRADLE
CRADLES > CRADLE
CRADLING *n* framework of iron or wood, esp as used in the construction of a ceiling
CRADLINGS > CRADLING
CRAFT *n* occupation requiring skill with the hands ▷ *vb* make skilfully
CRAFTED > CRAFT
CRAFTER *n* person doing craftwork
CRAFTERS > CRAFTER
CRAFTIER > CRAFTY
CRAFTIEST > CRAFTY
CRAFTILY > CRAFTY
CRAFTING > CRAFT
CRAFTLESS *adj* guileless
CRAFTS > CRAFT
CRAFTSMAN *n* skilled worker
CRAFTSMEN > CRAFTSMAN
CRAFTWORK *n* handicraft
CRAFTY *adj* skilled in deception
CRAG *n* steep rugged rock
CRAGFAST *adj* stranded on a crag
CRAGGED *same as* > CRAGGY
CRAGGIER > CRAGGY
CRAGGIEST > CRAGGY
CRAGGILY > CRAGGY
CRAGGY *adj* having many crags
CRAGS > CRAG
CRAGSMAN *n* rock climber
CRAGSMEN > CRAGSMAN
CRAIC *n* Irish word meaning fun
CRAICS > CRAIC
CRAIG *a Scot word for* > CRAG
CRAIGS > CRAIG
CRAKE *n* bird of the rail family, such as the corncrake ▷ *vb* to boast
CRAKED > CRAKE
CRAKES > CRAKE
CRAKING > CRAKE
CRAM *vb* force into too small a space ▷ *n* act or condition of cramming
CRAMBE *n* any plant of the genus Crambe
CRAMBES > CRAMBE
CRAMBO *n* word game in which one team says a rhyme or rhyming line for a word or line given by the other team
CRAMBOES > CRAMBO
CRAMBOS > CRAMBO
CRAME *n* merchant's booth or stall
CRAMES > CRAME
CRAMESIES > CRAMESY
CRAMESY *same as* > CRAMOISY
CRAMMABLE *adj* able to be crammed or filled
CRAMMED > CRAM
CRAMMER *n* person or school that prepares pupils for an examination
CRAMMERS > CRAMMER
CRAMMING > CRAM
CRAMOISIE *same as* > CRAMOISY
CRAMOISY *adj* of a crimson colour ▷ *n* crimson cloth
CRAMP *n* painful muscular contraction ▷ *vb* affect with a cramp
CRAMPBARK *n* guelder rose
CRAMPED *adj* closed in
CRAMPER *n* spiked metal plate used as a brace for the feet in throwing the stone
CRAMPERS > CRAMPER
CRAMPET *n* cramp iron
CRAMPETS > CRAMPET
CRAMPFISH *n* electric ray
CRAMPIER > CRAMPY
CRAMPIEST > CRAMPY
CRAMPING > CRAMP
CRAMPIT *same as* > CRAMPET
CRAMPITS > CRAMPIT
CRAMPON *n* spiked plate strapped to a boot for climbing on ice ▷ *vb* climb using crampons
CRAMPONED > CRAMPON
CRAMPONS > CRAMPON
CRAMPOON *same as* > CRAMPON
CRAMPOONS > CRAMPOON
CRAMPS > CRAMP
CRAMPY *adj* affected with cramp
CRAMS > CRAM
CRAN *n* unit of capacity used for measuring fresh herring, equal to 37.5 gallons
CRANAGE *n* use of a crane
CRANAGES > CRANAGE
CRANBERRY *n* sour edible red berry
CRANCH *vb* to crunch
CRANCHED > CRANCH
CRANCHES > CRANCH
CRANCHING > CRANCH
CRANE *n* machine for lifting and moving heavy weights ▷ *vb* stretch (one's neck) to see something
CRANED > CRANE
CRANEFLY *n* fly with long legs, slender wings, and a narrow body
CRANES > CRANE
CRANIA > CRANIUM
CRANIAL *adj* of or relating to the skull
CRANIALLY > CRANIAL
CRANIATE *adj* having a skull or cranium ▷ *n* vertebrate
CRANIATES > CRANIATE
CRANING > CRANE
CRANIUM *n* skull
CRANIUMS > CRANIUM
CRANK *n* arm projecting at right angles from a shaft, for transmitting or converting motion ▷ *vb* turn with a crank ▷ *adj* (of a sailing vessel) easily keeled over by the wind
CRANKCASE *n* metal case that encloses the crankshaft in an internal-combustion engine
CRANKED > CRANK
CRANKER > CRANK
CRANKEST > CRANK
CRANKIER > CRANK
CRANKIEST > CRANK
CRANKILY > CRANK
CRANKING > CRANK
CRANKISH *adj* somewhat eccentric or bad-tempered
CRANKLE *vb* to bend or wind
CRANKLED > CRANKLE
CRANKLES > CRANKLE
CRANKLING > CRANKLE
CRANKLY *adj* vigorously
CRANKNESS *n* (of a vessel) liability to capsize
CRANKOUS *adj* fretful
CRANKPIN *n* short cylindrical pin in a crankshaft, to which the connecting rod is attached
CRANKPINS > CRANKPIN
CRANKS > CRANK
CRANKY *same as* > CRANK
CRANNIED > CRANNY
CRANNIES > CRANNY
CRANNOG *n* ancient Celtic lake or bog dwelling dating from the late Bronze Age to the 16th century AD, often fortified and used as a refuge
CRANNOGE *same as* > CRANNOG
CRANNOGES > CRANNOGE
CRANNOGS > CRANNOG
CRANNY *n* narrow opening ▷ *vb* to become full of crannies
CRANNYING > CRANNY
CRANREUCH *n* hoarfrost
CRANS > CRAN
CRANTS *n* garland carried in front of a maiden's bier
CRANTSES > CRANTS
CRAP *n* rubbish, nonsense ▷ *vb* defecate
CRAPAUD *n* frog or toad
CRAPAUDS > CRAPAUD
CRAPE *same as* > CREPE
CRAPED > CRAPE
CRAPELIKE > CRAPE
CRAPES > CRAPE
CRAPIER > CRAPE
CRAPIEST > CRAPE
CRAPING > CRAPE
CRAPLE *same as* > GRAPPLE
CRAPLES > CRAPLE
CRAPOLA *n* rubbish
CRAPOLAS > CRAPOLA
CRAPPED > CRAP
CRAPPER *n* toilet
CRAPPERS > CRAPPER
CRAPPIE *n* N American freshwater fish
CRAPPIER > CRAPPY
CRAPPIES > CRAPPIE
CRAPPIEST > CRAPPY
CRAPPING > CRAP
CRAPPY *adj* worthless, lousy
CRAPS > CRAP
CRAPSHOOT *n* dice game
CRAPULENT *adj* given to or resulting from excessive eating or drinking
CRAPULOUS *same as* > CRAPULENT
CRAPY > CRAPE
CRARE *n* type of trading vessel
CRARES > CRARE
CRASES > CRASIS
CRASH *n* collision involving a vehicle or vehicles ▷ *vb* (cause to) collide violently with a vehicle, a stationary object, or the ground ▷ *adj* requiring or using great effort in order to achieve results quickly
CRASHED > CRASH
CRASHER > CRASH
CRASHERS > CRASH
CRASHES > CRASH
CRASHING *adj* extreme

CRASHLAND *n* land an aircraft in an emergency causing damage
CRASHPAD *n* place to sleep or live temporarily
CRASHPADS > CRASHPAD
CRASIS *n* fusion or contraction of two adjacent vowels into one
CRASS *adj* stupid and insensitive
CRASSER > CRASS
CRASSEST > CRASS
CRASSLY > CRASS
CRASSNESS > CRASS
CRATCH *n* rack for holding fodder for cattle, etc
CRATCHES > CRATCH
CRATE *n* large wooden container for packing goods ▷ *vb* put in a crate
CRATED > CRATE
CRATEFUL > CRATE
CRATEFULS > CRATE
CRATER *n* bowl-shaped opening at the top of a volcano *vb* make or form craters
CRATERED > CRATER
CRATERING > CRATER
CRATERLET *n* small crater
CRATEROUS > CRATER
CRATERS > CRATER
CRATES > CRATE
CRATING > CRATE
CRATON *n* stable part of the earth's continental crust or lithosphere that has not been deformed significantly for many millions, even hundreds of millions, of years
CRATONIC > CRATON
CRATONS > CRATON
CRATUR *n the.* whisky or whiskey
CRATURS > CRATUR
CRAUNCH *same as* > CRUNCH
CRAUNCHED > CRAUNCH
CRAUNCHES > CRAUNCH
CRAUNCHY > CRAUNCH
CRAVAT *n* man's scarf worn like a tie ▷ *vb* wear a cravat
CRAVATS > CRAVAT
CRAVATTED > CRAVAT
CRAVE *vb* desire intensely
CRAVED > CRAVE
CRAVEN *adj* cowardly ▷ *n* coward ▷ *vb* to make cowardly
CRAVENED > CRAVEN
CRAVENING > CRAVEN
CRAVENLY > CRAVEN
CRAVENS > CRAVEN
CRAVER > CRAVE
CRAVERS > CRAVE
CRAVES > CRAVE
CRAVING *n* intense desire or longing
CRAVINGS > CRAVING
CRAW *n* pouchlike part of a bird's oesophagus
CRAWDAD *n* crayfish
CRAWDADDY *n* crayfish
CRAWDADS > CRAWDAD
CRAWFISH *same as* > CRAYFISH
CRAWL *vb* move on one's hands and knees ▷ *n* crawling motion or pace
CRAWLED > CRAWL
CRAWLER *n* servile flatterer
CRAWLERS > CRAWLER
CRAWLIER > CRAWLY
CRAWLIEST > CRAWLY
CRAWLING *n* defect in freshly applied paint or varnish characterized by bare patches and ridging
CRAWLINGS > CRAWLING
CRAWLS > CRAWL
CRAWLWAY *n* in a mine, low passageway that can only be negotiated by crawling
CRAWLWAYS > CRAWLWAY
CRAWLY *adj* feeling or causing a sensation like creatures crawling on one's skin
CRAWS > CRAW
CRAY *n* crayfish
CRAYER *same as* > CRARE
CRAYERS > CRAYER
CRAYFISH *n* edible shellfish like a lobster
CRAYON *n* a stick or pencil of coloured wax or clay ▷ *vb* draw or colour with a crayon
CRAYONED > CRAYON
CRAYONER > CRAYON
CRAYONERS > CRAYON
CRAYONING > CRAYON
CRAYONIST > CRAYON
CRAYONS > CRAYON
CRAYS > CRAY
CRAYTHUR *variant of* > CRATUR
CRAYTHURS > CRAYTHUR
CRAZE *n* short-lived fashion or enthusiasm ▷ *vb* make mad
CRAZED *adj* wild and uncontrolled
CRAZES > CRAZE
CRAZIER > CRAZY
CRAZIES > CRAZY
CRAZIEST > CRAZY
CRAZILY > CRAZY
CRAZINESS > CRAZY
CRAZING > CRAZE
CRAZY *adj* ridiculous ▷ *n* crazy person ▷ *n* crazy person
CRAZYWEED *n* locoweed
CREACH *same as* > CREAGH
CREACHS > CREACH
CREAGH *n* foray
CREAGHS > CREAGH
CREAK *n* (make) a harsh squeaking sound ▷ *vb* make or move with a harsh squeaking sound
CREAKED > CREAK
CREAKIER > CREAK
CREAKIEST > CREAK
CREAKILY > CREAK
CREAKING > CREAK
CREAKS > CREAK
CREAKY > CREAK
CREAM *n* fatty part of milk ▷ *adj* yellowish-white ▷ *vb* beat to a creamy consistency
CREAMCUPS *n* Californian papaveraceous plant, *Platystemon californicus*, with small cream-coloured or yellow flowers on long flower stalks
CREAMED > CREAM
CREAMER *n* powdered milk substitute for use in coffee
CREAMERS > CREAMER
CREAMERY *n* place where dairy products are made or sold
CREAMIER > CREAMY
CREAMIEST > CREAMY
CREAMILY > CREAMY
CREAMING > CREAM
CREAMLAID *adj* (of laid paper) cream-coloured and of a ribbed appearance
CREAMLIKE > CREAM
CREAMPUFF *n* puff pastry filled with cream
CREAMS > CREAM
CREAMWARE *n* type of earthenware with a deep cream body developed about 1720 and widely produced
CREAMWOVE *adj* (of wove paper) cream-coloured and even-surfaced
CREAMY *adj* resembling cream in colour, taste, or consistency
CREANCE *n* long light cord used in falconry
CREANCES > CREANCE
CREANT *adj* formative
CREASE *n* line made by folding or pressing ▷ *vb* crush or line
CREASED > CREASE
CREASER > CREASE
CREASERS > CREASE
CREASES > CREASE
CREASIER > CREASE
CREASIEST > CREASE
CREASING > CREASE
CREASOTE *same as* > CREOSOTE
CREASOTED > CREASOTE
CREASOTES > CREASOTE
CREASY > CREASE
CREATABLE > CREATE
CREATE *vb* make, cause to exist
CREATED > CREATE
CREATES > CREATE
CREATIC *adj* relating to flesh or meat
CREATIN *same as* > CREATINE
CREATINE *n* important metabolite involved in many biochemical reactions and present in many types of living cells
CREATINES > CREATINE
CREATING > CREATE
CREATINS > CREATIN
CREATION *n* creating or being created
CREATIONS > CREATION
CREATIVE *adj* imaginative or inventive ▷ *n* person who is creative professionally
CREATIVES > CREATIVE
CREATOR *n* person who creates
CREATORS > CREATOR
CREATRESS > CREATOR
CREATRIX > CREATOR
CREATURAL > CREATURE
CREATURE *n* animal, person, or other being
CREATURES > CREATURE
CRECHE *n* place where small children are looked after while their parents are working, shopping, etc
CRECHES > CRECHE
CRED *n* short for credibility
CREDAL > CREED
CREDENCE *n* belief in the truth or accuracy of a statement
CREDENCES > CREDENCE
CREDENDA > CREDENDUM
CREDENDUM *n* article of faith
CREDENT *adj* believing or believable
CREDENZA *n* type of small sideboard
CREDENZAS > CREDENZA
CREDIBLE *adj* believable
CREDIBLY > CREDIBLE
CREDIT *n* system of allowing customers to receive goods and pay later ▷ *vb* enter as a credit in an account
CREDITED > CREDIT
CREDITING > CREDIT
CREDITOR *n* person to whom money is owed
CREDITORS > CREDITOR
CREDITS *pl n* list of people responsible for the production of a film, programme, or record
CREDO *n* creed
CREDOS > CREDO
CREDS > CRED
CREDULITY *n* willingness to believe something on little evidence
CREDULOUS *adj* too willing to believe
CREE *vb* to soften grain by boiling or soaking
CREED *n* statement or system of (Christian) beliefs or principles
CREEDAL > CREED
CREEDS > CREED
CREEING > CREE
CREEK *n* narrow inlet or bay
CREEKIER > CREEKY

CREEKIEST > CREEKY
CREEKS > CREEK
CREEKY *adj* abounding in creeks
CREEL *n* wicker basket used by anglers ▷ *vb* to fish using creels
CREELED > CREEL
CREELING > CREEL
CREELS > CREEL
CREEP *vb* move quietly and cautiously ▷ *n* creeping movement
CREEPAGE *n* imperceptible movement
CREEPAGES > CREEPAGE
CREEPED > CREEP
CREEPER *n* creeping plant ▷ *vb* train a plant to creep
CREEPERED > CREEPER
CREEPERS > CREEPER
CREEPIE *n* low stool
CREEPIER > CREEPY
CREEPIES > CREEPIE
CREEPIEST > CREEPY
CREEPILY > CREEPY
CREEPING > CREEP
CREEPS > CREEP
CREEPY *adj* causing a feeling of fear or disgust
CREES > CREE
CREESE *a rare spelling of* > KRIS *vb* to stab with a creese (or kris)
CREESED > CREESE
CREESES > CREESE
CREESH *vb* to lubricate
CREESHED > CREESH
CREESHES > CREESH
CREESHIER > CREESHY
CREESHING > CREESH
CREESHY *adj* greasy
CREESING > CREESE
CREM *n* crematorium
CREMAINS *n* cremated remains of a body
CREMANT *adj* (of wine) moderately sparkling
CREMASTER *n* muscle which raises and lowers the scrotum
CREMATE *vb* burn (a corpse) to ash
CREMATED > CREMATE
CREMATES > CREMATE
CREMATING > CREMATE
CREMATION > CREMATE
CREMATOR *n* furnace for cremating corpses
CREMATORS > CREMATOR
CREMATORY *adj* of or relating to cremation or crematoriums
CREME *n* cream ▷ *adj* (of a liqueur) rich and sweet
CREMES > CREME
CREMINI *n* variety of mushroom
CREMINIS > CREMINI
CREMOCARP *n* any fruit, such as anise or fennel, consisting of two united carpels
CREMONA *same as* > CROMORNA
CREMONAS > CREMONA
CREMOR *n* cream
CREMORNE *n* penis
CREMORNES > CREMORNE
CREMORS > CREMOR
CREMOSIN *adj* crimson
CREMS > CREM
CREMSIN *same as* > CREMOSIN
CRENA *n* cleft or notch
CRENAS > CRENA
CRENATE *adj* having a scalloped margin, as certain leaves
CRENATED *same as* > CRENATE
CRENATELY > CRENATE
CRENATION *n* any of the rounded teeth or the notches between them on a crenate structure
CRENATURE *same as* > CRENATION
CRENEL *n* any of a set of openings formed in the top of a wall or parapet and having slanting sides, as in a battlement ▷ *vb* to crenelate
CRENELATE *vb* supply with battlements
CRENELED > CRENEL
CRENELING > CRENEL
CRENELLE *same as* > CRENEL
CRENELLED > CRENEL
CRENELLES > CRENELLE
CRENELS > CRENEL
CRENSHAW *n* variety of melon
CRENSHAWS > CRENSHAW
CRENULATE *adj* having a margin very finely notched with rounded projections, as certain leaves
CREODONT *n* any of a group of extinct Tertiary mammals some of which are thought to have been the ancestors of modern carnivores: order *Carnivora*
CREODONTS > CREODONT
CREOLE *n* language developed from a mixture of languages ▷ *adj* of or relating to a creole
CREOLES > CREOLE
CREOLIAN *n* Creole
CREOLIANS > CREOLIAN
CREOLISE *vb* (of a pidgin language) to become the native language of a speech community
CREOLISED *same as* > CREOLIZED
CREOLISES > CREOLISE
CREOLIST *n* student of creole languages
CREOLISTS > CREOLIST
CREOLIZE *same as* > CREOLISE
CREOLIZED *adj* (of a language) incorporating a considerable range of features from one or more unrelated languages, as the result of contact between language communities
CREOLIZES > CREOLIZE
CREOPHAGY *n* act of eating meat
CREOSOL *n* colourless or pale yellow insoluble oily liquid with a smoky odour and a burning taste
CREOSOLS > CREOSOL
CREOSOTE *n* dark oily liquid made from coal tar and used for preserving wood ▷ *vb* treat with creosote
CREOSOTED > CREOSOTE
CREOSOTES > CREOSOTE
CREOSOTIC > CREOSOTE
CREPANCE *n* injury to a horse's hind leg caused by being struck by the shoe of the other hind foot
CREPANCES > CREPANCE
CREPE *n* fabric or rubber with a crinkled texture ▷ *vb* cover or drape with crepe ▷ *vb* to crimp or frizz
CREPED > CREPE
CREPERIE *n* eating establishment that specializes in pancakes
CREPERIES > CREPERIE
CREPES > CREPE
CREPEY *same as* > CREPY
CREPIER > CREPY
CREPIEST > CREPY
CREPINESS > CREPY
CREPING > CREPE
CREPITANT > CREPITATE
CREPITATE *vb* make a rattling or crackling sound
CREPITUS *n* crackling chest sound heard in pneumonia and other lung diseases
CREPOLINE *n* light silk material used in dressmaking
CREPON *n* thin material made of fine wool and/or silk
CREPONS > CREPON
CREPT > CREEP
CREPUSCLE *n* twilight
CREPY *adj* (esp of the skin) having a dry wrinkled appearance like crepe
CRESCENDI > CRESCENDO
CRESCENDO *n* gradual increase in loudness, esp in music ▷ *adv* gradually getting louder ▷ *vb* increase in loudness or force
CRESCENT *n* (curved shape of) the moon as seen in its first or last quarter ▷ *adj* crescent-shaped
CRESCENTS > CRESCENT
CRESCIVE *adj* increasing
CRESOL *n* aromatic compound derived from phenol, existing in three isomeric forms: found in coal tar and creosote and used in making synthetic resins and as an antiseptic and disinfectant
CRESOLS > CRESOL
CRESS *n* plant with strong-tasting leaves, used in salads
CRESSES > CRESS
CRESSET *n* metal basket mounted on a pole in which oil or pitch was burned for illumination
CRESSETS > CRESSET
CRESSY > CRESS
CREST *n* top of a mountain, hill, or wave ▷ *vb* come to or be at the top of
CRESTA as in *cresta run* high-speed tobogganing down a steep narrow passage of compacted snow and ice
CRESTAL > CREST
CRESTED > CREST
CRESTING *same as* > CREST
CRESTINGS > CREST
CRESTLESS > CREST
CRESTON *n* hogback
CRESTONS > CRESTON
CRESTS > CREST
CRESYL *n* tolyl
CRESYLIC *adj* of, concerned with, or containing creosote or cresol
CRESYLS > CRESYL
CRETIC *n* metrical foot consisting of three syllables, the first long, the second short, and the third long
CRETICS > CRETIC
CRETIN *n* stupid person
CRETINISE *vb* make (someone) a cretin
CRETINISM *n* condition arising from a deficiency of thyroid hormone, present from birth, characterized by dwarfism and mental retardation
CRETINIZE *same as* > CRETINISE
CRETINOID > CRETIN
CRETINOUS > CRETIN
CRETINS > CRETIN
CRETISM *n* lying
CRETISMS > CRETISM
CRETONNE *n* heavy printed cotton fabric used in furnishings
CRETONNES > CRETONNE
CREUTZER *n* former copper and silver coin of Germany or Austria
CREUTZERS > CREUTZER
CREVALLE *n* any fish of the family Carangidae
CREVALLES > CREVALLE
CREVASSE *n* deep open crack in a glacier ▷ *vb*

make a break or fissure in (a dyke, wall, etc)
CREVASSED > CREVASSE
CREVASSES > CREVASSE
CREVETTE *n* shrimp
CREVETTES > CREVETTE
CREVICE *n* narrow crack or gap in rock
CREVICED > CREVICE
CREVICES > CREVICE
CREW *n* people who work on a ship or aircraft ▷ *vb* serve as a crew member (on)
CREWCUT *n* very short haircut
CREWCUTS > CREWCUT
CREWE *n* type of pot
CREWED > CREW
CREWEL *n* fine worsted yarn used in embroidery ▷ *vb* to embroider in crewel
CREWELIST > CREWEL
CREWELLED > CREWEL
CREWELS > CREWEL
CREWES > CREWE
CREWING > CREW
CREWLESS *adj* lacking a crew
CREWMAN *n* member of a ship's crew
CREWMATE *n* colleague on the crew of a boat or ship
CREWMATES > CREWMATE
CREWMEN > CREWMAN
CREWNECK *n* plain round neckline in sweaters
CREWNECKS > CREWNECK
CREWS > CREW
CRIANT *adj* garish
CRIB *n* piece of writing stolen from elsewhere ▷ *vb* copy (someone's work) dishonestly
CRIBBAGE *n* card game for two to four players
CRIBBAGES > CRIBBAGE
CRIBBED > CRIB
CRIBBER > CRIB
CRIBBERS > CRIB
CRIBBING > CRIB
CRIBBINGS > CRIB
CRIBBLE *vb* to sift
CRIBBLED > CRIBBLE
CRIBBLES > CRIBBLE
CRIBBLING > CRIBBLE
CRIBELLA > CRIBELLUM
CRIBELLAR > CRIBELLUM
CRIBELLUM *n* sievelike spinning organ in certain spiders that occurs between the spinnerets
CRIBLE *adj* dotted
CRIBRATE *adj* sievelike
CRIBROSE *adj* pierced with holes
CRIBROUS > CRIBROSE
CRIBS > CRIB
CRIBWORK > CRIB
CRIBWORKS > CRIBWORK
CRICETID *n* any member of the family Cricetidae, such as the hamster and vole
CRICETIDS > CRICETID
CRICK *n* muscle spasm or cramp in the back or neck ▷ *vb* cause a crick in
CRICKED > CRICK
CRICKET *n* outdoor game played with bats, a ball, and wickets by two teams of eleven ▷ *vb* play cricket
CRICKETED > CRICKET
CRICKETER > CRICKET
CRICKETS > CRICKET
CRICKEY *same as* > CRIKEY
CRICKING > CRICK
CRICKS > CRICK
CRICKY *same as* > CRIKEY
CRICOID *adj* of or relating to the ring-shaped lowermost cartilage of the larynx ▷ *n* this cartilage
CRICOIDS > CRICOID
CRIED > CRY
CRIER *n* (formerly) official who made public announcements
CRIERS > CRIER
CRIES > CRY
CRIKEY *interj* expression of surprise
CRIM *short for* > CRIMINAL
CRIME *n* unlawful act ▷ *vb* charge with a crime
CRIMED > CRIME
CRIMEFUL *adj* criminal
CRIMELESS *adj* innocent
CRIMEN *n* crime
CRIMES > CRIME
CRIMEWAVE *n* period of increased criminal activity
CRIMINA > CRIMEN
CRIMINAL *n* person guilty of a crime ▷ *adj* of crime
CRIMINALS > CRIMINAL
CRIMINATE *vb* charge with a crime
CRIMINE *interj* expression of surprise
CRIMING > CRIME
CRIMINI *same as* > CRIMINE
CRIMINIS *n* accomplice in crime
CRIMINOUS *adj* criminal
CRIMINY *interj* cry of surprise
CRIMMER *a variant spelling of* > KRIMMER
CRIMMERS > CRIMMER
CRIMP *vb* fold or press into ridges ▷ *n* act or result of crimping
CRIMPED > CRIMP
CRIMPER > CRIMP
CRIMPERS > CRIMP
CRIMPIER > CRIMP
CRIMPIEST > CRIMP
CRIMPING > CRIMP
CRIMPLE *vb* crumple, wrinkle, or curl
CRIMPLED > CRIMPLE
CRIMPLES > CRIMPLE
CRIMPLING > CRIMPLE
CRIMPS > CRIMP
CRIMPY > CRIMP
CRIMS > CRIM
CRIMSON *adj* deep purplish-red ▷ *n* deep or vivid red colour ▷ *vb* make or become crimson
CRIMSONED > CRIMSON
CRIMSONS > CRIMSON
CRINAL *adj* relating to the hair
CRINATE *adj* having hair
CRINATED *same as* > CRINATE
CRINE *vb* to shrivel
CRINED > CRINE
CRINES > CRINE
CRINGE *vb* flinch in fear ▷ *n* act of cringing
CRINGED > CRINGE
CRINGER > CRINGE
CRINGERS > CRINGE
CRINGES > CRINGE
CRINGING > CRINGE
CRINGINGS > CRINGE
CRINGLE *n* eye at the edge of a sail, usually formed from a thimble or grommet
CRINGLES > CRINGLE
CRINING > CRINE
CRINITE *adj* covered with soft hairs or tufts ▷ *n* sedimentary rock
CRINITES > CRINITE
CRINKLE *n* wrinkle, crease, or fold ▷ *vb* become slightly creased or folded
CRINKLED > CRINKLE
CRINKLES > CRINKLE
CRINKLIER > CRINKLY
CRINKLIES > CRINKLY
CRINKLING > CRINKLE
CRINKLY *adj* wrinkled ▷ *n* old person
CRINOID *n* any primitive echinoderm of the class *Crinoidea*, having delicate feathery arms radiating from a central disc. The group includes the free-swimming feather stars, the sessile sea lilies, and many stemmed fossil forms ▷ *adj* of, relating to, or belonging to the *Crinoidea*
CRINOIDAL > CRINOID
CRINOIDS > CRINOID
CRINOLINE *n* hooped petticoat
CRINOSE *adj* hairy
CRINUM *n* any plant of the mostly tropical amaryllidaceous genus *Crinum*, having straplike leaves and clusters of lily-like flowers
CRINUMS > CRINUM
CRIOLLO *n* native or inhabitant of Latin America of European descent, esp of Spanish descent ▷ *adj* of, relating to, or characteristic of a criollo or criollos
CRIOLLOS > CRIOLLO
CRIOS *n* multicoloured woven woollen belt traditionally worn by men in the Aran Islands
CRIOSES > CRIOS
CRIPE *variant of* > CRIPES
CRIPES *interj* expression of surprise
CRIPPLE *n* offensive word for a person who is lame or disabled ▷ *vb* make lame or disabled
CRIPPLED > CRIPPLE
CRIPPLER > CRIPPLE
CRIPPLERS > CRIPPLE
CRIPPLES > CRIPPLE
CRIPPLING *adj* damaging or injurious
CRIS *variant of* > KRIS
CRISE *n* crisis
CRISES > CRISIS
CRISIC *adj* relating to a crisis
CRISIS *n* crucial stage, turning point
CRISP *adj* fresh and firm ▷ *n* very thin slice of potato fried till crunchy ▷ *vb* make or become crisp
CRISPATE *adj* having a curled or waved appearance
CRISPATED *same as* > CRISPATE
CRISPED *same as* > CRISPATE
CRISPEN *vb* to make crisp
CRISPENED > CRISPEN
CRISPENS > CRISPEN
CRISPER *n* compartment in a refrigerator for storing salads, vegetables, etc, in order to keep them fresh
CRISPERS > CRISPER
CRISPEST > CRISP
CRISPHEAD *n* variety of lettuce
CRISPIER > CRISPY
CRISPIEST > CRISPY
CRISPILY > CRISPY
CRISPIN *n* cobbler
CRISPING > CRISP
CRISPINS > CRISPIN
CRISPLY > CRISP
CRISPNESS > CRISP
CRISPS > CRISP
CRISPY *adj* hard and crunchy
CRISSA > CRISSUM
CRISSAL > CRISSUM
CRISSUM *n* area or feathers surrounding the cloaca of a bird
CRISTA *n* structure resembling a ridge or crest, such as that formed by folding of the inner membrane of a mitochondrion
CRISTAE > CRISTA
CRISTATE *adj* having a crest
CRISTATED *same as* > CRISTATE
CRIT *abbreviation of* > CRITICISM

CRITERIA > CRITERION
CRITERIAL > CRITERION
CRITERION *n* standard of judgment
CRITERIUM *n* type of bicycle race, involving many laps of a short course
CRITH *n* unit of weight for gases
CRITHS > CRITH
CRITIC *n* professional judge of any of the arts
CRITICAL *adj* very important or dangerous
CRITICISE *same as* > CRITICIZE
CRITICISM *n* fault-finding
CRITICIZE *vb* find fault with
CRITICS > CRITIC
CRITIQUE *n* critical essay ▷ *vb* to review critically
CRITIQUED > CRITIQUE
CRITIQUES > CRITIQUE
CRITS > CRIT
CRITTER *a dialect word for* > CREATURE
CRITTERS > CRITTER
CRITTUR *same as* > CRITTER
CRITTURS > CRITTUR
CRIVENS *interj* expression of surprise
CRIVVENS *same as* > CRIVENS
CROAK *vb* (of a frog or crow) give a low hoarse cry ▷ *n* low hoarse sound
CROAKED > CROAK
CROAKER *n* animal, bird, etc, that croaks
CROAKERS > CROAKER
CROAKIER > CROAK
CROAKIEST > CROAK
CROAKILY > CROAK
CROAKING > CROAK
CROAKINGS > CROAK
CROAKS > CROAK
CROAKY > CROAK
CROC *short for* > CROCODILE
CROCEATE *adj* saffron-coloured
CROCEIN *n* any one of a group of red or orange acid azo dyes
CROCEINE *same as* > CROCEIN
CROCEINES > CROCEIN
CROCEINS > CROCEIN
CROCEOUS *adj* saffron-coloured
CROCHE *n* knob at the top of a deer's horn
CROCHES > CROCHE
CROCHET *vb* make by looping and intertwining yarn with a hooked needle ▷ *n* work made in this way
CROCHETED > CROCHET
CROCHETER > CROCHET
CROCHETS > CROCHET
CROCI > CROCUS
CROCINE *adj* relating to the crocus
CROCK *n* earthenware pot or jar ▷ *vb* become or cause to become weak or disabled
CROCKED *adj* injured
CROCKERY *n* dishes
CROCKET *n* carved ornament in the form of a curled leaf or cusp, used in Gothic architecture
CROCKETED > CROCKET
CROCKETS > CROCKET
CROCKING > CROCK
CROCKPOT *n* tradename for a brand of slow cooker
CROCKPOTS > CROCKPOT
CROCKS > CROCK
CROCODILE *n* large amphibious tropical reptile
CROCOITE *n* rare orange secondary mineral
CROCOITES > CROCOITE
CROCOSMIA *n* any plant of the cormous S. African genus *Crocosmia*, including the plant known to gardeners as montbretia: family *Iridaceae*
CROCS > CROC
CROCUS *n* flowering plant
CROCUSES > CROCUS
CROFT *n* small farm worked by one family in Scotland
CROFTER *n* owner or tenant of a small farm, esp in Scotland or northern England
CROFTERS > CROFTER
CROFTING *n* system or occupation of working land in crofts
CROFTINGS > CROFTING
CROFTS > CROFT
CROG *vb* ride on a bicycle as a passenger
CROGGED > CROG
CROGGIES > CROGGY
CROGGING > CROG
CROGGY *n* ride on a bicycle as a passenger
CROGS > CROG
CROISSANT *n* rich flaky crescent-shaped roll
CROJIK *n* triangular sail
CROJIKS > CROJIK
CROKINOLE *n* board game popular in Canada in which players flick wooden discs
CROMACK *same as* > CRUMMOCK
CROMACKS > CROMACK
CROMB *same as* > CROME
CROMBEC *n* any African Old World warbler of the genus *Sylvietta*, having colourful plumage
CROMBECS > CROMBEC
CROMBED > CROMB
CROMBING > CROMB
CROMBS > CROMB
CROME *n* hook ▷ *vb* use a crome
CROMED > CROME
CROMES > CROME
CROMING > CROME
CROMLECH *n* circle of prehistoric standing stones
CROMLECHS > CROMLECH
CROMORNA *n* one of the reed stops in an organ
CROMORNAS > CROMORNA
CROMORNE *variant of* > CROMORNA
CROMORNES > CROMORNE
CRONE *n* witchlike old woman
CRONES > CRONE
CRONET *n* hair which grows over the top of a horse's hoof
CRONETS > CRONET
CRONIES > CRONY
CRONISH > CRONE
CRONK *adj* unfit
CRONKER > CRONK
CRONKEST > CRONK
CRONY *n* close friend
CRONYISM *n* practice of appointing friends to high-level, esp political, posts regardless of their suitability
CRONYISMS > CRONYISM
CROODLE *vb* to nestle close
CROODLED > CROODLE
CROODLES > CROODLE
CROODLING > CROODLE
CROOK *n* dishonest person ▷ *vb* bend or curve
CROOKBACK *a rare word for* > HUNCHBACK
CROOKED *adj* bent or twisted
CROOKEDER > CROOKED
CROOKEDLY > CROOKED
CROOKER > CROOK
CROOKERY *n* illegal or dishonest activity
CROOKEST > CROOK
CROOKING > CROOK
CROOKNECK *n* any type of summer squash
CROOKS > CROOK
CROOL *vb* spoil
CROOLED > CROOL
CROOLING > CROOL
CROOLS > CROOL
CROON *vb* sing, hum, or speak in a soft low tone ▷ *n* soft low singing or humming
CROONED > CROON
CROONER > CROON
CROONERS > CROON
CROONING > CROON
CROONINGS > CROON
CROONS > CROON
CROOVE *n* animal enclosure
CROOVES > CROOVE
CROP *n* cultivated plant ▷ *vb* cut very short
CROPBOUND *n* poultry disease causing a pendulous crop
CROPFUL *n* quantity that can be held in the craw
CROPFULL *adj* satiated
CROPFULS > CROPFUL
CROPLAND *n* land on which crops are grown
CROPLANDS > CROPLAND
CROPLESS *adj* without crops
CROPPED > CROP
CROPPER *n* person who cultivates or harvests a crop
CROPPERS > CROPPER
CROPPIE *same as* > CROPPY
CROPPIES > CROPPY
CROPPING > CROP
CROPPINGS > CROP
CROPPY *n* rebel in the Irish rising of 1798
CROPS > CROP
CROPSICK *adj* sick from excessive food or drink
CROQUANTE *n* crisp nut-filled chocolate or cake
CROQUET *n* game played on a lawn in which balls are hit through hoops ▷ *vb* drive away (another player's ball) by hitting one's own ball when the two are in contact
CROQUETED > CROQUET
CROQUETS > CROQUET
CROQUETTE *n* fried cake of potato, meat, or fish
CROQUIS *n* rough sketch
CRORE *n* (in Indian English) ten million
CRORES > CRORE
CROSIER *n* staff surmounted by a crook or cross, carried by bishops as a symbol of pastoral office ▷ *vb* bear or carry such a cross
CROSIERED > CROSIER
CROSIERS > CROSIER
CROSS *vb* move or go across (something) ▷ *n* structure, symbol, or mark of two intersecting lines ▷ *adj* angry, annoyed
CROSSABLE *adj* capable of being crossed
CROSSARM *n* in mining, horizontal bar on which a drill is mounted
CROSSARMS > CROSSARM
CROSSBAND *vb* to set the grain of layers of wood at right angles to one another
CROSSBAR *n* horizontal bar across goalposts or on a bicycle ▷ *vb* provide with crossbars
CROSSBARS > CROSSBAR
CROSSBEAM *n* beam that spans from one support to another
CROSSBILL *n* finch that has a bill with crossed tips
CROSSBIT > CROSSBITE
CROSSBITE *vb* to trick
CROSSBOW *n* weapon

consisting of a bow fixed across a wooden stock
CROSSBOWS > CROSSBOW
CROSSBRED *adj* bred from two different types of animal or plant ▷ *n* crossbred plant or animal, esp an animal resulting from a cross between two pure breeds
CROSSBUCK *n* US roadsign used at railroad crossings
CROSSCUT *vb* cut across ▷ *adj* cut across ▷ *n* transverse cut or course
CROSSCUTS > CROSSCUT
CROSSE *n* light staff with a triangular frame to which a network is attached, used in playing lacrosse
CROSSED > CROSS
CROSSER > CROSS
CROSSERS > CROSS
CROSSES > CROSS
CROSSEST > CROSS
CROSSETTE *n* in architecture, return in a corner of the architrave of a window or door
CROSSFALL *n* camber of a road
CROSSFIRE *n* gunfire crossing another line of fire
CROSSFISH *n* starfish
CROSSHAIR *n* one of two fine wires that cross in the focal plane of a gunsight or other optical instrument, used to define the line of sight
CROSSHEAD *n* subsection or paragraph heading printed within the body of the text
CROSSING *n* place where a street may be crossed safely
CROSSINGS > CROSSING
CROSSISH > CROSS
CROSSJACK *n* square sail on a ship's mizzenmast
CROSSLET *n* cross having a smaller cross near the end of each arm
CROSSLETS > CROSSLET
CROSSLY > CROSS
CROSSNESS > CROSS
CROSSOVER *n* place at which a crossing is made ▷ *adj* (of music, fashion, art, etc) combining two distinct styles
CROSSROAD *n* road that crosses another road
CROSSRUFF *n* alternate trumping of each other's leads by two partners, or by declarer and dummy ▷ *vb* trump alternately in two hands of a partnership
CROSSTALK *n* rapid or witty talk
CROSSTIE *n* railway sleeper
CROSSTIED *adj* tied with ropes going across
CROSSTIES > CROSSTIE
CROSSTOWN *adj* going across town
CROSSTREE *n* either of a pair of wooden or metal braces on the head of a mast to support the topmast, etc
CROSSWALK *n* place marked where pedestrians may cross a road
CROSSWAY *same as* > CROSSROAD
CROSSWAYS *same as* > CROSSWISE
CROSSWIND *n* wind that blows at right angles to the direction of travel
CROSSWISE *adv* across ▷ *adj* across
CROSSWORD *n* puzzle in which the solver deduces words suggested by clues and writes them into a grid
CROSSWORT *n* herbaceous perennial Eurasian rubiaceous plant, *Galium cruciata*, with pale yellow flowers and whorls of hairy leaves
CROST > CROSS
CROSTINI > CROSTINO
CROSTINIS > CROSTINO
CROSTINO *n* piece of toasted bread served with a savoury topping
CROTAL *n* any of various lichens used in dyeing wool, esp for the manufacture of tweeds
CROTALA > CROTALUM
CROTALINE *adj* relating to rattlesnakes
CROTALISM *n* posoining due to ingestion of plants of the genus Crotalaria
CROTALS > CROTAL
CROTALUM *n* ancient castanet-like percussion instrument
CROTCH *n* part of the body between the tops of the legs ▷ *vb* have crotch (usu of a piece of clothing) removed
CROTCHED > CROTCH
CROTCHES > CROTCH
CROTCHET *n* musical note half the length of a minim
CROTCHETS > CROTCHET
CROTCHETY *adj* bad-tempered
CROTON *n* any shrub or tree of the chiefly tropical euphorbiaceous genus *Croton*, esp *C. tiglium*, the seeds of which yield croton oil
CROTONBUG *n* species of cockroach
CROTONIC as in *crotonic acid* type of colourless acid
CROTONS > CROTON
CROTTLE *same as* > CROTAL
CROTTLES > CROTTLE
CROUCH *vb* bend low with the legs and body close ▷ *n* this position
CROUCHED > CROUCH
CROUCHES > CROUCH
CROUCHING > CROUCH
CROUP *n* throat disease of children, with a cough ▷ *vb* have croup
CROUPADE *n* leap by a horse, pulling the hind legs towards the belly
CROUPADES > CROUPADE
CROUPE *same as* > CROUP
CROUPED > CROUP
CROUPER *obsolete variant of* > CRUPPER
CROUPERS > CROUPER
CROUPES > CROUPE
CROUPIER *n* person who collects bets and pays out winnings at a gambling table in a casino
CROUPIERS > CROUPIER
CROUPIEST > CROUP
CROUPILY > CROUP
CROUPING > CROUP
CROUPON *n* type of highly-polished flexible leather
CROUPONS > CROUPON
CROUPOUS > CROUP
CROUPS > CROUP
CROUPY > CROUP
CROUSE *adj* lively, confident, or saucy
CROUSELY > CROUSE
CROUSTADE *n* pastry case in which food is served
CROUT *n* sauerkraut
CROUTE *n* small round of toasted bread on which a savoury mixture is served
CROUTES > CROUTE
CROUTON *n* small piece of fried or toasted bread served in soup
CROUTONS > CROUTON
CROUTS > CROUT
CROW *n* large black bird with a harsh call ▷ *vb* (of a cock) make a shrill squawking sound
CROWBAR *n* iron bar used as a lever ▷ *vb* use a crowbar to lever (something)
CROWBARS > CROWBAR
CROWBERRY *n* low-growing N temperate evergreen shrub, *Empetrum nigrum*, with small purplish flowers and black berry-like fruit: family *Empetraceae*
CROWBOOT *n* type of Inuit boot made of fur and leather
CROWBOOTS > CROWBOOT
CROWD *n* large group of people or things ▷ *vb* gather together in large numbers
CROWDED > CROWD
CROWDEDLY > CROWD
CROWDER > CROWD
CROWDERS > CROWD
CROWDIE *n* porridge of meal and water
CROWDIES > CROWDIE
CROWDING > CROWD
CROWDS > CROWD
CROWDY *same as* > CROWDIE
CROWEA *n* Australian shrub of the genus *Crowea*, having pink flowers
CROWEAS > CROWEA
CROWED > CROW
CROWER > CROW
CROWERS > CROW
CROWFEET > CROWFOOT
CROWFOOT *n* type of plant
CROWFOOTS > CROWFOOT
CROWING > CROW
CROWINGLY > CROW
CROWN *n* monarch's headdress of gold and jewels ▷ *vb* put a crown on the head of (someone) to proclaim him or her monarch
CROWNED > CROWN
CROWNER *n* promotional label consisting of a shaped printed piece of card or paper attached to a product on display
CROWNERS > CROWNER
CROWNET *n* coronet
CROWNETS > CROWNET
CROWNING *n* stage of labour when the infant's head is passing through the vaginal opening
CROWNINGS > CROWNING
CROWNLAND *n* large administrative division of the former empire of Austria-Hungary
CROWNLESS > CROWN
CROWNLET *n* small crown
CROWNLETS > CROWNLET
CROWNS > CROWN
CROWNWORK *n* manufacture of artificial crowns for teeth
CROWS > CROW
CROWSFEET > CROWSFOOT
CROWSFOOT *n* wrinkle at side of eye
CROWSTEP *n* set of steps to the top of a gable on a building
CROWSTEPS > CROWSTEP
CROZE *n* recess cut at the end of a barrel or cask to receive the head
CROZER *n* machine which cuts grooves in cask staves
CROZERS > CROZER
CROZES > CROZE
CROZIER *same as* > CROSIER
CROZIERS > CROZIER
CROZZLED *adj* blackened or burnt at the edges

CRU *n* (in France) a vineyard, group of vineyards, or wine-producing region
CRUBEEN *n* pig's trotter
CRUBEENS > CRUBEEN
CRUCES > CRUX
CRUCIAL *adj* very important
CRUCIALLY > CRUCIAL
CRUCIAN *n* European cyprinid fish, *Carassius carassius*, with a dark-green back, a golden-yellow undersurface, and reddish dorsal and tail fins: an aquarium fish
CRUCIANS > CRUCIAN
CRUCIATE *adj* shaped or arranged like a cross
CRUCIBLE *n* pot in which metals are melted
CRUCIBLES > CRUCIBLE
CRUCIFER *n* any plant of the family *Brassicaceae* (formerly *Cruciferae*), having a corolla of four petals arranged like a cross and a fruit called a siliqua. The family includes the brassicas, mustard, cress, and wallflower
CRUCIFERS > CRUCIFER
CRUCIFIED > CRUCIFY
CRUCIFIER > CRUCIFY
CRUCIFIES > CRUCIFY
CRUCIFIX *n* model of Christ on the Cross
CRUCIFORM *adj* cross-shaped ▷ *n* geometric curve, shaped like a cross, that has four similar branches asymptotic to two mutually perpendicular pairs of lines. Equation: $x^2y^2 - a^2x^2 - a^2y^2 = 0$, where $x = y = \pm a$ are the four lines.
CRUCIFY *vb* put to death by fastening to a cross
CRUCK *n* one of a pair of curved wooden timbers supporting the end of the roof in certain types of building
CRUCKS > CRUCK
CRUD *n* sticky or encrusted substance ▷ *interj* expression of disgust, disappointment, etc ▷ *vb* cover with a sticky or encrusted substance
CRUDDED > CRUD
CRUDDIER > CRUDDY
CRUDDIEST > CRUDDY
CRUDDING > CRUD
CRUDDLE *vb* to curdle
CRUDDLED > CRUDDLE
CRUDDLES > CRUDDLE
CRUDDLING > CRUDDLE
CRUDDY *adj* dirty or unpleasant
CRUDE *adj* rough and simple ▷ *n* crude oil
CRUDELY > CRUDE
CRUDENESS > CRUDE
CRUDER > CRUDE
CRUDES > CRUDE
CRUDEST > CRUDE
CRUDITES *pl n* selection of raw vegetables often served with a variety of dips before a meal
CRUDITIES > CRUDE
CRUDITY > CRUDE
CRUDS > CRUD
CRUDY *adj* raw
CRUE *obsolete variant of* > CREW
CRUEL *adj* delighting in others' pain
CRUELER > CRUEL
CRUELEST > CRUEL
CRUELLER > CRUEL
CRUELLEST > CRUEL
CRUELLS *same as* > CRUELS
CRUELLY > CRUEL
CRUELNESS > CRUEL
CRUELS *n* disease of cattle and sheep, caused by infection with an *Actinobacillus lignieresii* and characterized by soft tissue lesions, esp of the tongue
CRUELTIES > CRUELTY
CRUELTY *n* deliberate infliction of pain or suffering
CRUES > CREW
CRUET *n* small container for salt, pepper, etc, at table
CRUETS > CRUET
CRUISE *n* sail for pleasure ▷ *vb* sail from place to place for pleasure
CRUISED > CRUISE
CRUISER *n* fast warship
CRUISERS > CRUISER
CRUISES > CRUISE
CRUISEWAY *n* canal used for recreational purposes
CRUISIE *same as* > CRUIZIE
CRUISIES > CRUISIE
CRUISING > CRUISE
CRUISINGS > CRUISE
CRUIVE *n* animal enclosure
CRUIVES > CRUIVE
CRUIZIE *n* oil lamp
CRUIZIES > CRUIZIE
CRULLER *n* light sweet ring-shaped cake, fried in deep fat
CRULLERS > CRULLER
CRUMB *n* small fragment of bread or other dry food ▷ *vb* prepare or cover (food) with breadcrumbs ▷ *adj* (esp of pie crusts) made with a mixture of biscuit crumbs, sugar, etc
CRUMBED > CRUMB
CRUMBER > CRUMB
CRUMBERS > CRUMB
CRUMBIER > CRUMBY
CRUMBIEST > CRUMBY
CRUMBING > CRUMB
CRUMBLE *vb* break into fragments ▷ *n* pudding of stewed fruit with a crumbly topping
CRUMBLED > CRUMBLE
CRUMBLES > CRUMBLE
CRUMBLIER > CRUMBLY
CRUMBLIES *n* elderly people
CRUMBLING > CRUMBLE
CRUMBLY *adj* easily crumbled or crumbling
CRUMBS *interj* expression of dismay or surprise
CRUMBUM *n* rogue
CRUMBUMS > CRUMBUM
CRUMBY *adj* full of crumbs
CRUMEN *n* deer's larmier or tear-pit
CRUMENAL *n* purse
CRUMENALS > CRUMENAL
CRUMENS > CRUMEN
CRUMHORN *n* medieval woodwind instrument of bass pitch, consisting of an almost cylindrical tube curving upwards and blown through a double reed covered by a pierced cap
CRUMHORNS > CRUMHORN
CRUMMACK *same as* > CRUMMOCK
CRUMMACKS > CRUMMACK
CRUMMIE *n* cow with a crumpled horn
CRUMMIER > CRUMMY
CRUMMIES > CRUMMY
CRUMMIEST > CRUMMY
CRUMMOCK *n* stick with a crooked head
CRUMMOCKS > CRUMMOCK
CRUMMY *adj* of poor quality ▷ *n* lorry that carries loggers to work from their camp
CRUMP *vb* thud or explode with a loud dull sound ▷ *n* crunching, thudding, or exploding noise ▷ *adj* crooked
CRUMPED > CRUMP
CRUMPER > CRUMP
CRUMPEST > CRUMP
CRUMPET *n* round soft yeast cake, eaten buttered
CRUMPETS > CRUMPET
CRUMPIER > CRUMPY
CRUMPIEST > CRUMPY
CRUMPING > CRUMP
CRUMPLE *vb* crush, crease ▷ *n* untidy crease or wrinkle
CRUMPLED > CRUMPLE
CRUMPLES > CRUMPLE
CRUMPLIER > CRUMPLE
CRUMPLING > CRUMPLE
CRUMPLY > CRUMPLE
CRUMPS > CRUMP
CRUMPY *adj* crisp
CRUNCH *vb* bite or chew with a noisy crushing sound ▷ *n* crunching sound
CRUNCHED > CRUNCH
CRUNCHER > CRUNCH
CRUNCHERS > CRUNCH
CRUNCHES > CRUNCH
CRUNCHIE *n* derogatory word for an Afrikaner
CRUNCHIER > CRUNCH
CRUNCHIES > CRUNCHIE
CRUNCHILY > CRUNCH
CRUNCHING > CRUNCH
CRUNCHY > CRUNCH
CRUNKLE *Scots variant of* > CRINKLE
CRUNKLED > CRUNKLE
CRUNKLES > CRUNKLE
CRUNKLING > CRUNKLE
CRUNODAL > CRUNODE
CRUNODE *n* point at which two branches of a curve intersect, each branch having a distinct tangent
CRUNODES > CRUNODE
CRUOR *n* blood clot
CRUORES > CRUOR
CRUORS > CRUOR
CRUPPER *n* strap that passes from the back of a saddle under a horse's tail
CRUPPERS > CRUPPER
CRURA > CRUS
CRURAL *adj* of or relating to the leg or thigh
CRUS *n* leg, esp from the knee to the foot
CRUSADE *n* medieval Christian war to recover the Holy Land from the Muslims ▷ *vb* take part in a crusade
CRUSADED > CRUSADE
CRUSADER > CRUSADE
CRUSADERS > CRUSADE
CRUSADES > CRUSADE
CRUSADING > CRUSADE
CRUSADO *n* former gold or silver coin of Portugal bearing on its reverse the figure of a cross
CRUSADOES > CRUSADO
CRUSADOS > CRUSADO
CRUSE *n* small earthenware jug or pot
CRUSES > CRUSE
CRUSET *n* goldsmith's crucible
CRUSETS > CRUSET
CRUSH *vb* compress so as to injure, break, or crumple ▷ *n* dense crowd
CRUSHABLE > CRUSH
CRUSHED > CRUSH
CRUSHER > CRUSH
CRUSHERS > CRUSH
CRUSHES > CRUSH
CRUSHING > CRUSH
CRUSIAN *variant of* > CRUCIAN
CRUSIANS > CRUSIAN
CRUSIE *same as* > CRUIZIE
CRUSIES > CRUSIE
CRUSILY *adj* (in heraldry) strewn with crosses
CRUST *n* hard outer part of something, esp bread ▷ *vb* cover with or form a crust

CRUSTA *n* hard outer layer
CRUSTACEA *n* members of the Crustacea class of arthropods including the lobster
CRUSTAE > CRUSTA
CRUSTAL *adj* of or relating to the earth's crust
CRUSTATE *adj* covered with a crust
CRUSTATED *same as* > CRUSTATE
CRUSTED > CRUST
CRUSTIER > CRUSTY
CRUSTIES > CRUSTY
CRUSTIEST > CRUSTY
CRUSTILY > CRUSTY
CRUSTING > CRUST
CRUSTLESS *adj* lacking a crust
CRUSTOSE *adj* having a crustlike appearance
CRUSTS > CRUST
CRUSTY *adj* having a crust ▷ *n* dirty type of punk or hippy whose lifestyle involves travelling and squatting
CRUSY *same as* > CRUIZIE
CRUTCH *n* long sticklike support with a rest for the armpit, used by a lame person ▷ *vb* support or sustain (a person or thing) as with a crutch
CRUTCHED > CRUTCH
CRUTCHES > CRUTCH
CRUTCHING > CRUTCH
CRUVE *same as* > CRUIVE
CRUVES > CRUVE
CRUX *n* crucial or decisive point
CRUXES > CRUX
CRUZADO *same as* > CRUSADO
CRUZADOES > CRUZADO
CRUZADOS > CRUZADO
CRUZEIRO *n* former monetary unit of Brazil, replaced by the cruzeiro real
CRUZEIROS > CRUZEIRO
CRUZIE *same as* > CRUIZIE
CRUZIES > CRUZIE
CRWTH *n* ancient stringed instrument of Celtic origin similar to the cithara but bowed in later types
CRWTHS > CRWTH
CRY *vb* shed tears ▷ *n* fit of weeping
CRYBABIES > CRYBABY
CRYBABY *n* person, esp a child, who cries too readily
CRYING > CRY
CRYINGLY > CRY
CRYINGS > CRY
CRYOBANK *n* place for storing genetic material at low temperature
CRYOBANKS > CRYOBANK
CRYOCABLE *n* highly conducting electrical cable cooled with a refrigerant such as liquid nitrogen
CRYOGEN *n* substance used to produce low temperatures
CRYOGENIC *adj* of the branch of physics converned with the production of very low temperatures
CRYOGENS > CRYOGEN
CRYOGENY *n* cryogenic science
CRYOLITE *n* white or colourless mineral
CRYOLITES > CRYOLITE
CRYOMETER *n* thermometer for measuring low temperatures
CRYOMETRY > CRYOMETER
CRYONIC > CRYONICS
CRYONICS *n* practice of freezing a human corpse in the hope of restoring it to life in the future
CRYOPHYTE *n* organism, esp an alga or moss, that grows on snow or ice
CRYOPROBE *n* supercooled instrument used in surgery
CRYOSCOPE *n* any instrument used to determine the freezing point of a substance
CRYOSCOPY *n* determination of freezing points, esp for the determination of molecular weights by measuring the lowering of the freezing point of a solvent when a known quantity of solute is added
CRYOSTAT *n* apparatus for maintaining a constant low temperature or a vessel in which a substance is stored at a low temperature
CRYOSTATS > CRYOSTAT
CRYOTRON *n* miniature switch working at the temperature of liquid helium and depending for its action on the production and destruction of superconducting properties in the conductor
CRYOTRONS > CRYOTRON
CRYPT *n* vault under a church, esp one used as a burial place
CRYPTADIA *n* things to be kept hidden
CRYPTAL > CRYPT
CRYPTIC *adj* obscure in meaning, secret
CRYPTICAL *same as* > CRYPTIC
CRYPTO *n* person who is a secret member of an organization or sect
CRYPTOGAM *n* plant that reproduces by spores not seeds
CRYPTON *n* krypton
CRYPTONS > CRYPTON
CRYPTONYM *n* code name
CRYPTOS > CRYPTO
CRYPTS > CRYPT
CRYSTAL *n* (single grain of) a symmetrically shaped solid formed naturally by some substances ▷ *adj* bright and clear
CRYSTALS > CRYSTAL
CSARDAS *n* type of Hungarian folk dance
CSARDASES > CSARDAS
CTENE *n* locomotor organ found in ctenophores (or comb jellies)
CTENES > CTENE
CTENIDIA > CTENIDIUM
CTENIDIUM *n* one of the comblike respiratory gills of molluscs
CTENIFORM *adj* comblike
CTENOID *adj* toothed like a comb, as the scales of perches
CUADRILLA *n* matador's assistants in a bullfight
CUATRO *n* four-stringed guitar
CUATROS > CUATRO
CUB *n* young wild animal such as a bear or fox ▷ *adj* young or inexperienced ▷ *vb* give birth to cubs
CUBAGE *same as* > CUBATURE
CUBAGES > CUBATURE
CUBANE *n* rare octahedral hydrocarbon
CUBANELLE *n* variety of pepper
CUBANES > CUBANE
CUBATURE *n* determination of the cubic contents of something
CUBATURES > CUBATURE
CUBBED > CUB
CUBBIES > CUBBY
CUBBING > CUB
CUBBINGS > CUB
CUBBISH > CUB
CUBBISHLY > CUB
CUBBY *same as* > CUBBYHOLE
CUBBYHOLE *n* small enclosed space or room
CUBE *n* object with six equal square sides ▷ *vb* cut into cubes
CUBEB *n* SE Asian treelike piperaceous woody climbing plant, *Piper cubeba*, with brownish berries
CUBEBS > CUBEB
CUBED > CUBE
CUBER > CUBE
CUBERS > CUBE
CUBES > CUBE
CUBHOOD *n* state of being a cub
CUBHOODS > CUBHOOD
CUBIC *adj* having three dimensions ▷ *n* cubic equation, such as $x^3 + x + 2 = 0$
CUBICA *n* fine shalloon-like fabric
CUBICAL *adj* of or related to volume
CUBICALLY > CUBICAL
CUBICAS > CUBICA
CUBICITY *n* property of being cubelike
CUBICLE *n* enclosed part of a large room, screened for privacy
CUBICLES > CUBICLE
CUBICLY > CUBIC
CUBICS > CUBIC
CUBICULA > CUBICULUM
CUBICULUM *n* underground burial chamber in Imperial Rome, such as those found in the catacombs
CUBIFORM *adj* having the shape of a cube
CUBING > CUBE
CUBISM *n* style of art in which objects are represented by geometrical shapes
CUBISMS > CUBISM
CUBIST > CUBISM
CUBISTIC > CUBISM
CUBISTS > CUBISM
CUBIT *n* old measure of length based on the length of the forearm
CUBITAL *adj* of or relating to the forearm
CUBITI *adj* of elbow
CUBITS > CUBIT
CUBITUS *n* elbow
CUBITUSES > CUBITUS
CUBLESS *adj* having no cubs
CUBOID *adj* shaped like a cube ▷ *n* geometric solid whose six faces are rectangles
CUBOIDAL *same as* > CUBOID
CUBOIDS > CUBOID
CUBS > CUB
CUCKING as in *cucking stool* stool to which suspected witches, etc, were tied and pelted or ducked into water as punishment
CUCKOLD *n* man whose wife has been unfaithful ▷ *vb* be unfaithful to (one's husband)
CUCKOLDED > CUCKOLD
CUCKOLDLY *adj* possessing the qualities of a cuckold
CUCKOLDOM *n* state of being a cuckold
CUCKOLDRY > CUCKOLD
CUCKOLDS > CUCKOLD
CUCKOO *n* migratory bird with a characteristic two-note call, which lays its eggs in the nests of other birds ▷ *adj* insane or foolish ▷ *interj* imitation or representation of

the call of a cuckoo ▷ *vb* repeat over and over
CUCKOOED > CUCKOO
CUCKOOING > CUCKOO
CUCKOOS > CUCKOO
CUCULLATE *adj* shaped like a hood or having a hoodlike part
CUCUMBER *n* long green-skinned fleshy fruit used in salads
CUCUMBERS > CUCUMBER
CUCURBIT *n* any creeping flowering plant of the mainly tropical and subtropical family *Cucurbitaceae*, which includes the pumpkin, cucumber, squashes, and gourds
CUCURBITS > CUCURBIT
CUD *n* partially digested food which a ruminant brings back into its mouth to chew again
CUDBEAR *another name for* > ORCHIL
CUDBEARS > CUDBEAR
CUDDEN *n* young coalfish
CUDDENS > CUDDEN
CUDDIE *same as* > CUDDY
CUDDIES > CUDDY
CUDDIN *same as* > CUDDEN
CUDDINS > CUDDIN
CUDDLE *n* hug ▷ *vb* hold (another person or thing) close or (of two people, etc) to hold each other close, as for affection, comfort, or warmth
CUDDLED > CUDDLE
CUDDLER > CUDDLE
CUDDLERS > CUDDLE
CUDDLES > CUDDLE
CUDDLIER > CUDDLE
CUDDLIEST > CUDDLE
CUDDLING > CUDDLE
CUDDLY > CUDDLE
CUDDY *n* small cabin in a boat
CUDGEL *n* short thick stick used as a weapon ▷ *vb* use a cudgel
CUDGELED > CUDGEL
CUDGELER > CUDGEL
CUDGELERS > CUDGEL
CUDGELING > CUDGEL
CUDGELLED > CUDGEL
CUDGELLER > CUDGEL
CUDGELS > CUDGEL
CUDGERIE *n* large tropical rutaceous tree, *Flindersia schottina*, having light-coloured wood
CUDGERIES > CUDGERIE
CUDS > CUD
CUDWEED *n* any of various temperate woolly plants of the genus *Gnaphalium*, having clusters of whitish or yellow button-like flowers: family *Asteraceae* (composites)
CUDWEEDS > CUDWEED
CUE *n* signal to an actor or musician to begin speaking or playing ▷ *vb* give a cue to
CUED > CUE
CUEING > CUE
CUEIST *n* snooker or billiards player
CUEISTS > CUEIST
CUES > CUE
CUESTA *n* long low ridge with a steep scarp slope and a gentle back slope, formed by the differential erosion of strata of differing hardness
CUESTAS > CUESTA
CUFF *n* end of a sleeve ▷ *vb* hit with an open hand
CUFFED > CUFF
CUFFIN *n* man
CUFFING > CUFF
CUFFINS > CUFFIN
CUFFLE *vb* scuffle
CUFFLED > CUFFLE
CUFFLES > CUFFLE
CUFFLESS *adj* having no cuff(s)
CUFFLING > CUFFLE
CUFFLINK *n* detachable fastener for shirt cuff
CUFFLINKS > CUFFLINK
CUFFO *adv* free of charge
CUFFS > CUFF
CUFFUFFLE *same as* > KERFUFFLE
CUIF *same as* > COOF
CUIFS > CUIF
CUING > CUE
CUIRASS *n* piece of armour, of leather or metal covering the chest and back ▷ *vb* equip with a cuirass
CUIRASSED > CUIRASS
CUIRASSES > CUIRASS
CUISH *same as* > CUISSE
CUISHES > CUISH
CUISINART *n* tradename for a type of food processor
CUISINE *n* style of cooking
CUISINES > CUISINE
CUISINIER *n* cook
CUISSE *n* piece of armour for the thigh
CUISSER *same as* > COOSER
CUISSERS > CUISSER
CUISSES > CUISSE
CUIT *n* ankle
CUITER *vb* to pamper
CUITERED > CUITER
CUITERING > CUITER
CUITERS > CUITER
CUITIKIN *n* gaiter
CUITIKINS > CUITIKIN
CUITS > CUIT
CUITTLE *vb* to wheedle
CUITTLED > CUITTLE
CUITTLES > CUITTLE
CUITTLING > CUITTLE
CUKE *n* cucumber
CUKES > CUKE
CULCH *n* mass of broken stones, shells, and gravel that forms the basis of an oyster bed
CULCHES > CULCH
CULCHIE *n* rough or unsophisticated country-dweller from outside Dublin
CULCHIES > CULCHIE
CULET *n* flat face at the bottom of a gem
CULETS > CULET
CULEX *n* any mosquito of the genus *Culex*, such as *C. pipiens*, the common mosquito
CULEXES > CULEX
CULICES > CULEX
CULICID *n* any dipterous insect of the family *Culicidae*, which comprises the mosquitoes ▷ *adj* of, relating to, or belonging to the *Culicidae*
CULICIDS > CULICID
CULICINE *n* any member of the genus Culex containing mosquitoes
CULICINES > CULICINE
CULINARY *adj* of kitchens or cookery
CULL *vb* choose, gather ▷ *n* culling
CULLAY *n* soapbark tree
CULLAYS > CULLAY
CULLED > CULL
CULLENDER *same as* > COLANDER
CULLER *n* person employed to cull animals
CULLERS > CULLER
CULLET *n* waste glass for melting down to be reused
CULLETS > CULLET
CULLIED > CULLY
CULLIES > CULLY
CULLING > CULL
CULLINGS > CULL
CULLION *n* rascal
CULLIONLY > CULLION
CULLIONS > CULLION
CULLIS *same as* > COULISSE
CULLISES > CULLIS
CULLS > CULL
CULLY *n* pal ▷ *vb* to trick
CULLYING > CULLY
CULLYISM *n* state of being a dupe
CULLYISMS > CULLYISM
CULM *n* coal-mine waste ▷ *vb* to form a culm or grass stem
CULMED > CULM
CULMEN *n* summit
CULMENS > CULMEN
CULMINANT *adj* highest or culminating
CULMINATE *vb* reach the highest point or climax
CULMING > CULM
CULMS > CULM
CULOTTE > CULOTTES
CULOTTES *pl n* women's knee-length trousers cut to look like a skirt
CULPA *n* act of neglect
CULPABLE *adj* deserving blame
CULPABLY > CULPABLE
CULPAE > CULPA
CULPATORY *adj* expressing blame
CULPRIT *n* person guilty of an offence or misdeed
CULPRITS > CULPRIT
CULT *n* specific system of worship ▷ *adj* very popular among a limited group of people
CULTCH *same as* > CULTCH
CULTCHES > CULTCH
CULTER *same as* > COULTER
CULTERS > CULTER
CULTI > CULTUS
CULTIC *adj* of or relating to a religious cult
CULTIER > CULTY
CULTIEST > CULTY
CULTIGEN *n* species of plant that is known only as a cultivated form and did not originate from a wild type
CULTIGENS > CULTIGEN
CULTISH *adj* intended to appeal to a small group of fashionable people
CULTISHLY > CULTISH
CULTISM > CULT
CULTISMS > CULT
CULTIST > CULT
CULTISTS > CULT
CULTIVAR *n* variety of a plant that was produced from a natural species and is maintained by cultivation
CULTIVARS > CULTIVAR
CULTIVATE *vb* prepare (land) to grow crops
CULTLIKE *adj* resembling a cult
CULTRATE *adj* shaped like a knife blade
CULTRATED *same as* > CULTRATE
CULTS > CULT
CULTURAL *adj* of or relating to artistic or social pursuits or events considered to be valuable or enlightened
CULTURATI *n* people interested in cultural activities
CULTURE *n* ideas, customs, and art of a particular society ▷ *vb* grow (bacteria) for study
CULTURED *adj* showing good taste or manners
CULTURES > CULTURE
CULTURING > CULTURE
CULTURIST > CULTURE
CULTUS *another word for* > CULT
CULTUSES > CULTUS
CULTY *same as* > CULTISH
CULVER *an archaic or poetic*

name for > PIGEON
CULVERIN *n* long-range medium to heavy cannon used during the 15th, 16th, and 17th centuries
CULVERINS > CULVERIN
CULVERS > CULVER
CULVERT *n* drain under a road or railway
CULVERTS > CULVERT
CUM *prep* with
CUMACEAN *n* any small malacostracan marine crustacean of the *Cumacea* family, mostly dwelling on the sea bed but sometimes found among the plankton ▷ *adj* of, relating to, or belonging to the *Cumacea*
CUMACEANS > CUMACEAN
CUMARIC > CUMARIN
CUMARIN *same as* > COUMARIN
CUMARINS > CUMARIN
CUMARONE *variant spelling of* > COUMARONE
CUMARONES > CUMARONE
CUMBENT *adj* lying down
CUMBER *vb* obstruct or hinder ▷ *n* hindrance or burden
CUMBERED > CUMBER
CUMBERER > CUMBER
CUMBERERS > CUMBER
CUMBERING > CUMBER
CUMBERS > CUMBER
CUMBIA *n* Colombian style of music
CUMBIAS > CUMBIA
CUMBRANCE *n* burden, obstacle, or hindrance
CUMBROUS *adj* awkward because of size, weight, or height
CUMBUNGI *n* any of various tall Australian marsh plants of the genus *Typha*
CUMBUNGIS > CUMBUNGI
CUMEC *n* unit of volumetric rate of flow
CUMECS > CUMEC
CUMIN *n* sweet-smelling seeds of a Mediterranean plant, used in cooking
CUMINS > CUMIN
CUMMER *n* gossip
CUMMERS > CUMMER
CUMMIN *same as* > CUMIN
CUMMINS > CUMMIN
CUMQUAT *same as* > KUMQUAT
CUMQUATS > CUMQUAT
CUMSHAW *n* (used, esp formerly, by beggars in Chinese ports) a present or tip
CUMSHAWS > CUMSHAW
CUMULATE *vb* accumulate ▷ *adj* heaped up
CUMULATED > CUMULATE
CUMULATES > CUMULATE
CUMULET *n* variety of domestic fancy pigeon, pure white or white with light red markings
CUMULETS > CUMULET
CUMULI > CUMULUS
CUMULOSE *adj* full of heaps
CUMULOUS *adj* resembling or consisting of cumulus clouds
CUMULUS *n* thick white or dark grey cloud
CUNABULA *n* cradle
CUNCTATOR *n* person in habit of being late
CUNDIES > CUNDY
CUNDUM *n* early form of condom
CUNDUMS > CUNDUM
CUNDY *n* sewer
CUNEAL *same as* > CUNEIFORM
CUNEATE *adj* wedge-shaped: cuneate leaves are attached at the narrow end
CUNEATED *same as* > CUNEATE
CUNEATELY > CUNEATE
CUNEATIC *adj* cuneiform
CUNEI > CUNEUS
CUNEIFORM *adj* (written in) an ancient system of writing using wedge-shaped characters ▷ *n* ancient system of writing using wedge-shaped characters
CUNETTE *n* small trench dug in the main ditch of a fortification
CUNETTES > CUNETTE
CUNEUS *n* small wedge-shaped area of the cerebral cortex
CUNIFORM *same as* > CUNIFORM
CUNIFORMS > CUNIFORM
CUNJEVOI *n* plant of tropical Asia and Australia with small flowers, cultivated for its edible rhizome
CUNJEVOIS > CUNJEVOI
CUNNER *n* fish of the wrasse family
CUNNERS > CUNNER
CUNNING *adj* clever at deceiving ▷ *n* cleverness at deceiving
CUNNINGER > CUNNING
CUNNINGLY > CUNNING
CUNNINGS > CUNNING
CUNT *n* taboo word for female genitals
CUNTS > CUNT
CUP *n* small bowl-shaped drinking container with a handle ▷ *vb* form (one's hands) into the shape of a cup
CUPBEARER *n* attendant who fills and serves wine cups, as in a royal household
CUPBOARD *n* piece of furniture or alcove with a door, for storage ▷ *vb* to store in a cupboard
CUPBOARDS > CUPBOARD
CUPCAKE *n* small cake baked in a cup-shaped foil or paper case
CUPCAKES > CUPCAKE
CUPEL *n* refractory pot in which gold or silver is refined ▷ *vb* refine (gold or silver) by means of cupellation
CUPELED > CUPEL
CUPELER > CUPEL
CUPELERS > CUPEL
CUPELING > CUPEL
CUPELLED > CUPEL
CUPELLER > CUPEL
CUPELLERS > CUPEL
CUPELLING > CUPEL
CUPELS > CUPEL
CUPFERRON *n* compound used in chemical analysis
CUPFUL *n* amount a cup will hold
CUPFULS > CUPFUL
CUPGALL *n* gall found on oakleaves
CUPGALLS > CUPGALL
CUPHEAD *n* type of bolt or rivet with a cup-shaped head
CUPHEADS > CUPHEAD
CUPID *n* figure representing the Roman god of love
CUPIDITY *n* greed for money or possessions
CUPIDS > CUPID
CUPLIKE > CUP
CUPMAN *n* drinking companion
CUPMEN > CUPMAN
CUPOLA *n* domed roof or ceiling ▷ *vb* to provide with a cupola
CUPOLAED > CUPOLA
CUPOLAING > CUPOLA
CUPOLAR > CUPOLA
CUPOLAS > CUPOLA
CUPOLATED > CUPOLA
CUPPA *n* cup of tea
CUPPAS > CUPPA
CUPPED > CUP
CUPPER *same as* > CUPPA
CUPPERS > CUPPER
CUPPIER > CUPPY
CUPPIEST > CUPPY
CUPPING > CUP
CUPPINGS > CUP
CUPPY *adj* cup-shaped
CUPREOUS *adj* of copper
CUPRESSUS *n* any tree of the genus *Cupressus*
CUPRIC *adj* of or containing copper in the divalent state
CUPRITE *n* red secondary mineral
CUPRITES > CUPRITE
CUPROUS *adj* of or containing copper in the monovalent state
CUPRUM *an obsolete name for* > COPPER
CUPRUMS > CUPRUM
CUPS > CUP
CUPSFUL > CUPFUL
CUPULA *n* dome-shaped structure, esp the sensory structure within the semicircular canals of the ear
CUPULAE > CUPULA
CUPULAR *same as* > CUPULATE
CUPULATE *adj* shaped like a small cup
CUPULE *n* cup-shaped part or structure, such as the cup around the base of an acorn
CUPULES > CUPULE
CUR *n* mongrel dog
CURABLE *adj* capable of being cured
CURABLY > CURABLE
CURACAO *n* orange-flavoured liqueur
CURACAOS > CURACAO
CURACIES > CURACY
CURACOA *same as* > CURACAO
CURACOAS > CURACOA
CURACY *n* work or position of a curate
CURAGH *same as* > CURRACH
CURAGHS > CURAGH
CURANDERA *n* female faith healer
CURANDERO *n* male faith healer
CURARA *same as* > CURARE
CURARAS > CURARA
CURARE *n* poisonous resin of a S American tree, used as a muscle relaxant in medicine
CURARES > CURARE
CURARI *same as* > CURARE
CURARINE *n* alkaloid extracted from curare, used as a muscle relaxant in surgery
CURARINES > CURARINE
CURARIS > CURARI
CURARISE *same as* > CURARIZE
CURARISED > CURARISE
CURARISES > CURARISE
CURARIZE *vb* paralyse or treat with curare
CURARIZED > CURARIZE
CURARIZES > CURARIZE
CURASSOW *n* gallinaceous ground-nesting bird with long legs and tails and, typically, a distinctive crest of curled feathers
CURASSOWS > CURASSOW
CURAT *n* cuirass
CURATE *n* clergyman who assists a parish priest ▷ *vb* be in charge of (an art exhibition or museum) ▷ *vb* to act as a curator
CURATED > CURATE
CURATES > CURATE
CURATING > CURATE

CURATIVE *n* something able to cure ▷ *adj* able to cure
CURATIVES > CURATIVE
CURATOR *n* person in charge of a museum or art gallery
CURATORS > CURATOR
CURATORY > CURATOR
CURATRIX *n* female curator
CURATS > CURAT
CURB *n* something that restrains ▷ *vb* control, restrain
CURBABLE *adj* capable of being restrained
CURBED > CURB
CURBER > CURB
CURBERS > CURB
CURBING *the US spelling of* > KERBING
CURBINGS > CURBING
CURBLESS *adj* having no restraint
CURBS > CURB
CURBSIDE *n* pavement
CURBSIDES > CURBSIDE
CURBSTONE *the US spelling of* > KERBSTONE
CURCH *n* woman's plain cap or kerchief
CURCHEF *same as* > CURCH
CURCHEFS > CURCHEF
CURCHES > CURCH
CURCULIO *n* type of American weevil
CURCULIOS > CURCULIO
CURCUMA *n* type of tropical Asian tuberous plant
CURCUMAS > CURCUMA
CURCUMIN *n* yellow dye derived from turmeric
CURCUMINE *same as* > CURCUMIN
CURCUMINS > CURCUMIN
CURD *n* coagulated milk, used to make cheese ▷ *vb* turn into or become curd
CURDED > CURD
CURDIER > CURD
CURDIEST > CURD
CURDINESS > CURD
CURDING > CURD
CURDLE *vb* turn into curd, coagulate
CURDLED > CURDLE
CURDLER > CURDLE
CURDLERS > CURDLE
CURDLES > CURDLE
CURDLING > CURDLE
CURDS > CURD
CURDY > CURD
CURE *vb* get rid of (an illness or problem) ▷ *n* (treatment causing) curing of an illness or person
CURED > CURE
CURELESS > CURE
CURER > CURE
CURERS > CURE
CURES > CURE
CURET *same as* > CURETTE
CURETS > CURET
CURETTAGE *n* process of using a curette
CURETTE *n* surgical instrument for scraping tissue from body cavities ▷ *vb* scrape with a curette
CURETTED > CURETTE
CURETTES > CURETTE
CURETTING > CURETTE
CURF *n* type of limestone
CURFEW *n* law ordering people to stay inside their homes after a specific time at night
CURFEWS > CURFEW
CURFS > CURF
CURFUFFLE *vb* make a kerfuffle
CURIA *n* papal court and government of the Roman Catholic Church
CURIAE > CURIA
CURIAL > CURIA
CURIALISM *n* ultramontanism
CURIALIST > CURIALISM
CURIAS > CURIA
CURIE *n* standard unit of radioactivity
CURIES > CURIE
CURIET *n* cuirass
CURIETS > CURIET
CURING > CURE
CURIO *n* rare or unusual object valued as a collector's item
CURIOS > CURIO
CURIOSA *n* curiosities
CURIOSITY *n* eagerness to know or find out
CURIOUS *adj* eager to learn or know
CURIOUSER > CURIOUS
CURIOUSLY > CURIOUS
CURITE *n* oxide of uranium and lead
CURITES > CURITE
CURIUM *n* radioactive element artificially produced from plutonium
CURIUMS > CURIUM
CURL *n* curved piece of hair ▷ *vb* make (hair) into curls or (of hair) grow in curls
CURLED > CURL
CURLER *n* pin or small tube for curling hair
CURLERS > CURLER
CURLEW *n* long-billed wading bird
CURLEWS > CURLEW
CURLI *pl n* curled hairlike processes on the surface of the bacterium *Escherichia coli* by means of which the bacterium adheres to and infects wounds
CURLICUE *n* ornamental curl or twist ▷ *vb* to curl or twist elaborately, as in curlicues
CURLICUED > CURLICUE
CURLICUES > CURLICUE
CURLIER > CURLY
CURLIEST > CURLY
CURLILY > CURLY
CURLINESS > CURLY
CURLING *n* game like bowls, played with heavy stones on ice
CURLINGS > CURLING
CURLPAPER *n* strip of paper used to roll up and set a section of hair, usually wetted, into a curl
CURLS > CURL
CURLY *adj* tending to curl
CURLYCUE *same as* > CURLICUE
CURLYCUES > CURLYCUE
CURN *n* grain (of corn etc)
CURNEY *same as* > CURNY
CURNIER > CURNY
CURNIEST > CURNY
CURNS > CURN
CURNY *adj* granular
CURPEL *same as* > CRUPPER
CURPELS > CURPEL
CURR *vb* to purr
CURRACH *a Scot or Irish name for* > CORACLE
CURRACHS > CURRACH
CURRAGH *same as* > CURRACH
CURRAGHS > CURRAGH
CURRAJONG *same as* > KURRAJONG
CURRAN *n* black bun
CURRANS > CURRAN
CURRANT *n* small dried grape
CURRANTS > CURRANT
CURRANTY > CURRANT
CURRAWONG *n* Australian songbird
CURRED > CURR
CURREJONG *same as* > KURRAJONG
CURRENCY *n* money in use in a particular country
CURRENT *adj* of the immediate present ▷ *n* flow of water or air in one direction
CURRENTLY > CURRENT
CURRENTS > CURRENT
CURRICLE *n* two-wheeled open carriage drawn by two horses side by side
CURRICLES > CURRICLE
CURRICULA *n* plural form of singular curriculum: course of study in one subject at school or college
CURRIE *same as* > CURRY
CURRIED > CURRY
CURRIER *n* person who curries leather
CURRIERS > CURRIER
CURRIERY *n* trade, work, or place of occupation of a currier
CURRIES > CURRY
CURRIJONG *same as* > KURRAJONG
CURRING > CURR
CURRISH *adj* of or like a cur
CURRISHLY > CURRISH
CURRS > CURR
CURRY *n* Indian dish of meat or vegetables in a hot spicy sauce ▷ *vb* prepare (food) with curry powder
CURRYCOMB *n* ridged comb used for grooming horses
CURRYING > CURRY
CURRYINGS > CURRY
CURS > CUR
CURSAL > CURSUS
CURSE *vb* swear (at) ▷ *n* swearword
CURSED > CURSE
CURSEDER > CURSE
CURSEDEST > CURSE
CURSEDLY > CURSE
CURSENARY *same as* > CURSORARY
CURSER > CURSE
CURSERS > CURSE
CURSES > CURSE
CURSI > CURSUS
CURSING > CURSE
CURSINGS > CURSE
CURSITOR *n* clerk in the Court of Chancery
CURSITORS > CURSITOR
CURSITORY > CURSITOR
CURSIVE *n* (handwriting) done with joined letters ▷ *adj* of handwriting or print in which letters are joined in a flowing style
CURSIVELY > CURSIVE
CURSIVES > CURSIVE
CURSOR *n* movable point of light that shows a specific position on a visual display unit
CURSORARY *adj* cursory
CURSORES > CURSOR
CURSORIAL *adj* adapted for running
CURSORILY > CURSORY
CURSORS > CURSOR
CURSORY *adj* quick and superficial
CURST > CURSE
CURSTNESS *n* peevishness
CURSUS *n* Neolithic parallel earthworks
CURT *adj* brief and rather rude
CURTAIL *vb* cut short
CURTAILED > CURTAIL
CURTAILER > CURTAIL
CURTAILS > CURTAIL
CURTAIN *n* piece of cloth hung at a window or opening as a screen ▷ *vb* provide with curtains
CURTAINED > CURTAIN
CURTAINS *pl n* death or ruin
CURTAL *adj* cut short ▷ *n* animal whose tail has been docked
CURTALAX *same as* > CURTALAXE
CURTALAXE *n* cutlass
CURTALS > CURTAL
CURTANA *n* unpointed sword carried before an English sovereign at a

coronation as an emblem of mercy
CURTANAS > CURTANA
CURTATE *adj* shortened
CURTATION > CURTATE
CURTAXE *same as* > CURTALAXE
CURTAXES > CURTAXE
CURTER > CURT
CURTESIES > CURTESY
CURTEST > CURT
CURTESY *n* widower's life interest in his wife's estate
CURTILAGE *n* enclosed area of land adjacent to a dwelling house
CURTLY > CURT
CURTNESS > CURT
CURTSEY *same as* > CURTSY
CURTSEYED > CURTSEY
CURTSEYS > CURTSEY
CURTSIED > CURTSY
CURTSIES > CURTSY
CURTSY *n* woman's gesture of respect made by bending the knees and bowing the head ▷ *vb* make a curtsy
CURTSYING > CURTSY
CURULE *adj* (in ancient Rome) of the highest rank, esp one entitled to use a curule chair
CURVATE *adj* curved
CURVATED *same as* > CURVATE
CURVATION > CURVATE
CURVATIVE *adj* having curved edges
CURVATURE *n* curved shape
CURVE *n* continuously bending line with no straight parts ▷ *vb* form or move in a curve
CURVEBALL *n* in baseball, a ball pitched in a curving path ▷ *vb* pitch a curveball
CURVED > CURVE
CURVEDLY > CURVE
CURVES > CURVE
CURVESOME *adj* curvaceous
CURVET *n* horse's low leap with all four feet off the ground ▷ *vb* make such a leap
CURVETED > CURVET
CURVETING > CURVET
CURVETS > CURVET
CURVETTED > CURVET
CURVEY *same as* > CURVY
CURVIER > CURVE
CURVIEST > CURVE
CURVIFORM *adj* having a curved form
CURVING > CURVE
CURVITAL *adj* relating to curvature
CURVITIES > CURVITY
CURVITY *n* curvedness
CURVY > CURVE
CUSCUS *n* large Australian nocturnal possum
CUSCUSES > CUSCUS
CUSEC *n* unit of flow equal to 1 cubic foot per second
CUSECS > CUSEC
CUSH *n* cushion
CUSHAT *n* wood pigeon
CUSHATS > CUSHAT
CUSHAW *same as* > CASHAW
CUSHAWS > CUSHAW
CUSHES > CUSH
CUSHIE *same as* > CUSHAT
CUSHIER > CUSHY
CUSHIES > CUSHIE
CUSHIEST > CUSHY
CUSHILY > CUSHY
CUSHINESS > CUSHY
CUSHION *n* bag filled with soft material, to make a seat more comfortable ▷ *vb* lessen the effects of
CUSHIONED > CUSHION
CUSHIONET *n* small cushion
CUSHIONS > CUSHION
CUSHIONY > CUSHION
CUSHTY *interj* exclamation of pleasure, agreement, approval, etc
CUSHY *adj* easy
CUSK *n* gadoid food fish, *Brosmius brosme*, of northern coastal waters, having a single long dorsal fin
CUSKS > CUSK
CUSP *n* pointed end, esp on a tooth
CUSPAL > CUSP
CUSPATE *adj* having a cusp or cusps
CUSPATED *same as* > CUSPATE
CUSPED *same as* > CUSPATE
CUSPID *n* tooth having one point
CUSPIDAL *same as* > CUSPIDATE
CUSPIDATE *adj* having a cusp or cusps
CUSPIDES > CUSPIS
CUSPIDOR *another word (esp US) for* > SPITTOON
CUSPIDORE *same as* > CUSPIDOR
CUSPIDORS > CUSPIDOR
CUSPIDS > CUSPID
CUSPIS *n* in anatomy, tapering structure
CUSPS > CUSP
CUSS *n* curse, oath ▷ *vb* swear (at)
CUSSED *adj* obstinate
CUSSEDLY > CUSSED
CUSSER *same as* > COOSER
CUSSERS > CUSSER
CUSSES > CUSS
CUSSING > CUSS
CUSSO *n* tree of the rose family
CUSSOS > CUSSO
CUSSWORD *n* swearword
CUSSWORDS > CUSSWORD
CUSTARD *n* sweet yellow sauce made from milk and eggs
CUSTARDS > CUSTARD
CUSTARDY > CUSTARD
CUSTOCK *same as* > CASTOCK
CUSTOCKS > CUSTOCK
CUSTODE *n* custodian
CUSTODES > CUSTODE
CUSTODIAL > CUSTODY
CUSTODIAN *n* person in charge of a public building
CUSTODIER *n* custodian
CUSTODIES > CUSTODY
CUSTODY *n* protective care
CUSTOM *n* long-established activity or action ▷ *adj* made to the specifications of an individual customer
CUSTOMARY *adj* usual ▷ *n* statement in writing of customary laws and practices
CUSTOMED *adj* accustomed
CUSTOMER *n* person who buys goods or services
CUSTOMERS > CUSTOMER
CUSTOMISE *same as* > CUSTOMIZE
CUSTOMIZE *vb* make (something) according to a customer's individual requirements
CUSTOMS *n* duty charged on imports or exports
CUSTOS *n* superior in the Franciscan religious order
CUSTREL *n* knave
CUSTRELS > CUSTREL
CUSTUMAL *another word for* > CUSTOMARY
CUSTUMALS > CUSTUMAL
CUSTUMARY *n* customary
CUT *vb* open up, penetrate, wound, or divide with a sharp instrument ▷ *n* act of cutting
CUTANEOUS *adj* of the skin
CUTAWAY *adj* (of a drawing or model) having part of the outside omitted to reveal the inside ▷ *n* man's coat cut diagonally from the front waist to the back of the knees
CUTAWAYS > CUTAWAY
CUTBACK *n* decrease or reduction ▷ *vb* shorten by cutting
CUTBACKS > CUTBACK
CUTBANK *n* steep banking at a bend in a river
CUTBANKS > CUTBANK
CUTCH *same as* > CATECHU
CUTCHA *adj* crude
CUTCHERRY *n* (formerly, in India) government offices and law courts collectively
CUTCHERY *same as* > CUTCHERRY
CUTCHES > CUTCH
CUTDOWN *n* decrease
CUTDOWNS > CUTDOWN
CUTE *adj* appealing or attractive
CUTELY > CUTE
CUTENESS > CUTE
CUTER > CUTE
CUTES > CUTIS
CUTESIE *same as* > CUTESY
CUTESIER > CUTESY
CUTESIEST > CUTESY
CUTEST > CUTE
CUTESY *adj* affectedly cute or coy
CUTEY *same as* > CUTIE
CUTEYS > CUTEY
CUTGLASS *adj* (of an accent) upper-class
CUTGRASS *n* any grass of the genus Leersia
CUTICLE *n* skin at the base of a fingernail or toenail
CUTICLES > CUTICLE
CUTICULA *n* cuticle
CUTICULAE > CUTICULA
CUTICULAR > CUTICLE
CUTIE *n* person regarded as appealing or attractive, esp a girl or woman
CUTIES > CUTIE
CUTIKIN *same as* > CUTIKIN
CUTIKINS > CUTIKIN
CUTIN *n* waxy waterproof substance, consisting of derivatives of fatty acids, that is the main constituent of the plant cuticle
CUTINISE *same as* > CUTINIZE
CUTINISED > CUTINISE
CUTINISES > CUTINISE
CUTINIZE *vb* become or cause to become covered or impregnated with cutin
CUTINIZED > CUTINIZE
CUTINIZES > CUTINIZE
CUTINS > CUTIN
CUTIS *a technical name for the* > SKIN
CUTISES > CUTIS
CUTLAS *same as* > CUTLASS
CUTLASES > CUTLAS
CUTLASS *n* curved one-edged sword formerly used by sailors
CUTLASSES > CUTLASS
CUTLER *n* maker of cutlery
CUTLERIES > CUTLERY
CUTLERS > CUTLER
CUTLERY *n* knives, forks, and spoons
CUTLET *n* small piece of meat like a chop
CUTLETS > CUTLET
CUTLINE *n* caption
CUTLINES > CUTLINE
CUTOFF *n* limit or termination
CUTOFFS > CUTOFF
CUTOUT *n* something that has been cut out from something else
CUTOUTS > CUTOUT
CUTOVER *n* transitional period in IT system changeover, during which old and new systems are working concurrently
CUTOVERS > CUTOVER

CUTPURSE *n* pickpocket
CUTPURSES > CUTPURSE
CUTS > CUT
CUTTABLE *adj* capable of being cut
CUTTAGE *n* propagation by using parts taken from growing plants
CUTTAGES > CUTTAGE
CUTTER *n* person or tool that cuts
CUTTERS > CUTTER
CUTTHROAT *n* person who cuts throats
CUTTIER > CUTTY
CUTTIES > CUTTY
CUTTIEST > CUTTY
CUTTING > CUT
CUTTINGLY > CUT
CUTTINGS > CUT
CUTTLE *vb* to whisper
CUTTLED > CUTTLE
CUTTLES > CUTTLE
CUTTLING > CUTTLE
CUTTO *n* large knife
CUTTOE *same as* > CUTTO
CUTTOES > CUTTO
CUTTY *adj* short or cut short ▷ *n* something cut short, such as a spoon or short-stemmed tobacco pipe
CUTUP *n* joker or prankster
CUTUPS > CUTUP
CUTWATER *n* forward part of the stem of a vessel, which cuts through the water
CUTWATERS > CUTWATER
CUTWORK *n* openwork embroidery in which the pattern is cut away from the background
CUTWORKS > CUTWORK
CUTWORM *n* caterpillar of various noctuid moths, esp those of the genus *Argrotis*, which is a pest of young crop plants in North America
CUTWORMS > CUTWORM
CUVEE *n* individual batch or blend of wine
CUVEES > CUVEE
CUVETTE *n* shallow dish or vessel for holding liquid
CUVETTES > CUVETTE
CUZ *n* cousin
CUZZES > CUZ
CWM *same as* > CIRQUE
CWMS > CWM
CWTCH *vb* be snuggled up
CWTCHED > CWTCH
CWTCHES > CWTCH
CWTCHING > CWTCH
CYAN *n* highly saturated green-blue that is the complementary colour of red and forms, with magenta and yellow, a set of primary colours ▷ *adj* of this colour
CYANAMID *same as* > CYANAMIDE
CYANAMIDE *n* white or colourless crystalline soluble weak dibasic acid, which can be hydrolysed to urea
CYANAMIDS > CYANAMID
CYANATE *n* any salt or ester of cyanic acid
CYANATES > CYANATE
CYANIC as in *cyanic acid* colourless poisonous volatile liquid acid
CYANID *same as* > CYANIDE
CYANIDE *n* extremely poisonous chemical compound ▷ *vb* treat with cyanide
CYANIDED > CYANIDE
CYANIDES > CYANIDE
CYANIDING > CYANIDE
CYANIDS > CYANID
CYANIN *same as* > CYANINE
CYANINE *n* blue dye used to extend the sensitivity of photographic emulsions to colours other than blue and ultraviolet
CYANINES > CYANINE
CYANINS > CYANIN
CYANISE *vb* to turn into cyanide
CYANISED > CYANISE
CYANISES > CYANISE
CYANISING > CYANISE
CYANITE *a variant spelling of* > KYANITE
CYANITES > CYANITE
CYANITIC > CYANITE
CYANIZE *same as* > CYANISE
CYANIZED > CYANIZE
CYANIZES > CYANIZE
CYANIZING > CYANIZE
CYANO *adj* containing cyanogen
CYANOGEN *n* poisonous colourless flammable gas
CYANOGENS > CYANOGEN
CYANOSED *adj* affected by cyanosis
CYANOSES > CYANOSIS
CYANOSIS *n* blueness of the skin, caused by a deficiency of oxygen in the blood
CYANOTIC > CYANOSIS
CYANOTYPE *another name for* > BLUEPRINT
CYANS > CYAN
CYANURATE *n* chemical derived from cyanide
CYANURET *n* cyanide
CYANURETS > CYANURET
CYATHI > CYATHUS
CYATHIA > CYATHIUM
CYATHIUM *n* inflorescence of the type found on the poinsettia
CYATHUS *n* ancient measure of wine
CYBER *adj* involving computers
CYBERCAFE *n* café equipped with computer terminals which customers can use to access the internet
CYBERCAST *same as* > WEBCAST
CYBERNATE *vb* control (a manufacturing process) with a servomechanism or (of a process) to be controlled by a servomechanism
CYBERNAUT *n* person using internet
CYBERPET *n* electronic toy that simulates the activities of a pet, requiring the owner to feed, discipline, and entertain it
CYBERPETS > CYBERPET
CYBERPORN *n* pornography on Internet
CYBERPUNK *n* genre of science fiction that features rebellious computer hackers and is set in a dystopian society integrated by computer networks
CYBERSEX *n* exchanging of sexual messages or information via the internet
CYBERWAR *n* information warfare
CYBERWARS > CYBERWAR
CYBORG *n* (in science fiction) a living being whose powers are enhanced by computer implants
CYBORGS > CYBORG
CYBRARIAN *n* person in charge of computer archives
CYBRID *n* cytoplasmic hybrid (hybrid resulting from the fusion of a cytoplast and a whole cell)
CYBRIDS > CYBRID
CYCAD *n* any tropical or subtropical gymnosperm plant of the phylum *Cycadophyta*, having an unbranched stem with fernlike leaves crowded at the top
CYCADEOID *n* (now extinct) plant with a woody stem and tough leaves
CYCADS > CYCAD
CYCAS *n* palm tree of the genus Cycas
CYCASES > CYCAS
CYCASIN *n* glucoside, toxic to mammals, occurring in cycads
CYCASINS > CYCASIN
CYCLAMATE *n* salt or ester of cyclamic acid. Certain of the salts have a very sweet taste and were formerly used as food additives and sugar substitutes
CYCLAMEN *n* plant with red, pink, or white flowers ▷ *adj* of a dark reddish-purple colour
CYCLAMENS > CYCLAMEN
CYCLASE *n* enzyme which acts as a catalyst in the formation of a cyclic compound
CYCLASES > CYCLASE
CYCLE *vb* ride a bicycle ▷ *n* bicycle
CYCLECAR *n* any light car with an engine capacity of 1100cc or less
CYCLECARS > CYCLECAR
CYCLED > CYCLE
CYCLER *same as* > CYCLIST
CYCLERIES > CYCLERY
CYCLERS > CYCLIST
CYCLERY *n* business dealing in bicycles and bicycle accessories
CYCLES > CYCLE
CYCLEWAY *n* path or way designed, and reserved for, cyclists
CYCLEWAYS > CYCLEWAY
CYCLIC *adj* recurring or revolving in cycles
CYCLICAL *same as* > CYCLIC *n* short-term trend, of which reversal is expected
CYCLICALS > CYCLIC
CYCLICISM > CYCLIC
CYCLICITY > CYCLIC
CYCLICLY > CYCLIC
CYCLIN *n* type of protein
CYCLING > CYCLE
CYCLINGS > CYCLE
CYCLINS > CYCLIN
CYCLISE *same as* > CYCLIZE
CYCLISED > CYCLISE
CYCLISES > CYCLISE
CYCLISING > CYCLISE
CYCLIST *n* person who rides a bicycle
CYCLISTS > CYCLIST
CYCLITOL *n* alicyclic compound
CYCLITOLS > CYCLITOL
CYCLIZE *vb* be cyclical
CYCLIZED > CYCLIZE
CYCLIZES > CYCLIZE
CYCLIZINE *n* drug used to relieve the symptoms of motion sickness
CYCLIZING > CYCLIZE
CYCLO *n* type of rickshaw
CYCLOGIRO *n* aircraft lifted and propelled by pivoted blades rotating parallel to roughly horizontal transverse axes
CYCLOID *adj* resembling a circle ▷ *n* curve described by a point on the circumference of a circle as the circle rolls along a straight line
CYCLOIDAL > CYCLOID
CYCLOIDS > CYCLOID
CYCLOLITH *n* stone circle
CYCLONAL > CYCLONE
CYCLONE *n* violent wind

moving round a central area
CYCLONES > CYCLONE
CYCLONIC > CYCLONE
CYCLONITE *n* white crystalline insoluble explosive prepared by the action of nitric acid on hexamethylenetetramine
CYCLOPEAN *adj* of or relating to the Cyclops
CYCLOPES > CYCLOPS
CYCLOPIAN > CYCLOPS
CYCLOPIC > CYCLOPS
CYCLOPS *n* any copepod of the genus *Cyclops*, characterized by having one eye
CYCLORAMA *n* large picture, such as a battle scene, on the interior wall of a cylindrical room, designed to appear in natural perspective to a spectator in the centre
CYCLOS > CYCLO
CYCLOSES > CYCLOSIS
CYCLOSIS *n* circulation of cytoplasm or cell organelles, such as food vacuoles in some protozoans
CYCLOTRON *n* apparatus that accelerates charged particles by means of a strong vertical magnetic field
CYCLUS *n* cycle
CYCLUSES > CYCLUS
CYDER *same as* > CIDER
CYDERS > CYDER
CYESES > CYESIS
CYESIS *the technical name for* > PREGNANCY
CYGNET *n* young swan
CYGNETS > CYGNET
CYLICES > CYLIX
CYLINDER *n* solid or hollow body with straight sides and circular ends
CYLINDERS > CYLINDER
CYLINDRIC *adj* shaped like, or characteristic of a cylinder
CYLIX *a variant of* > KYLIX
CYMA *n* moulding with a double curve, part concave and part convex
CYMAE > CYMA
CYMAGRAPH *same as* > CYMOGRAPH
CYMAR *n* woman's short fur-trimmed jacket, popular in the 17th and 18th centuries
CYMARS > CYMAR
CYMAS > CYMA
CYMATIA > CYMATIUM
CYMATICS *n* theory and practice of a therapy whereby sound waves are directed at the body, with the aim of promoting health
CYMATIUM *n* top moulding of a classical cornice or entablature
CYMBAL *n* percussion instrument consisting of a brass plate which is struck against another or hit with a stick
CYMBALEER > CYMBAL
CYMBALER > CYMBAL
CYMBALERS > CYMBAL
CYMBALIST > CYMBAL
CYMBALO *another name for* > DULCIMER
CYMBALOES > CYMBALO
CYMBALOM *same as* > CIMBALOM
CYMBALOMS > CYMBALOM
CYMBALOS > CYMBALO
CYMBALS > CYMBAL
CYMBIDIA > CYMBIDIUM
CYMBIDIUM *n* any orchid of the genus Cymbidium
CYMBIFORM *adj* shaped like a boat
CYMBLING *same as* > CYMLING
CYMBLINGS > CYMLING
CYME *n* flower cluster which has a single flower on the end of each stem and of which the central flower blooms first
CYMENE *n* colourless insoluble liquid with an aromatic odour that exists in three isomeric forms
CYMENES > CYMENE
CYMES > CYME
CYMLIN *same as* > CYMLING
CYMLING *n* pattypan squash
CYMLINGS > CYMLING
CYMLINS > CYMLIN
CYMOGENE *n* mixture of volatile flammable hydrocarbons, mainly butane, obtained in the distillation of petroleum
CYMOGENES > CYMOGENE
CYMOGRAPH *n* instrument for tracing the outline of an architectural moulding
CYMOID *adj* resembling a cyme or cyma
CYMOL *same as* > CYMENE
CYMOLS > CYMOL
CYMOPHANE *n* yellow or green opalescent variety of chrysoberyl
CYMOSE *adj* having the characteristics of a cyme
CYMOSELY > CYMOSE
CYMOUS *adj* relating to a cyme
CYNANCHE *n* any disease characterised by inflammation and swelling of the throat
CYNANCHES > CYNANCHE
CYNEGETIC *adj* relating to hunting
CYNIC *n* person who believes that people always act selfishly ▷ *adj* of or relating to Sirius, the Dog Star
CYNICAL *adj* believing that people always act selfishly
CYNICALLY > CYNICAL
CYNICISM *n* attitude or beliefs of a cynic
CYNICISMS > CYNICISM
CYNICS > CYNIC
CYNODONT *n* carnivorous mammal-like reptile of the late Permian and Triassic periods, whose specialized teeth were well developed
CYNODONTS > CYNODONT
CYNOMOLGI *n* plural form of singular cynomolgus: type of monkey
CYNOSURAL > CYNOSURE
CYNOSURE *n* centre of attention
CYNOSURES > CYNOSURE
CYPHER *same as* > CIPHER
CYPHERED > CYPHER
CYPHERING > CYPHER
CYPHERS > CYPHER
CYPRES *n* legal doctrine stating that a testator's intentions should be carried out as closely as possible
CYPRESES > CYPRES
CYPRESS *n* evergreen tree with dark green leaves
CYPRESSES > CYPRESS
CYPRIAN *n* prostitute or dancer
CYPRIANS > CYPRIAN
CYPRID *n* cypris
CYPRIDES > CYPRIS
CYPRIDS > CYPRID
CYPRINE *adj* relating to carp
CYPRINID *n* any teleost fish of the mainly freshwater family *Cyprinidae*, typically having toothless jaws and cycloid scales and including such food and game fishes as the carp, tench, roach, rudd, and dace ▷ *adj* of, relating to, or belonging to the *Cyprinidae*
CYPRINIDS > CYPRINID
CYPRINOID *adj* of, relating to, or belonging to the *Cyprinoidea*, a large suborder of teleost fishes including the cyprinids, characins, electric eels, and loaches ▷ *n* any fish belonging to the *Cyprinoidea*
CYPRIS *n* member of the genus Cypris (small bivalve freshwater crustaceans)
CYPRUS *same as* > CYPRESS
CYPRUSES > CYPRUS
CYPSELA *n* dry one-seeded fruit of the daisy and related plants, which resembles an achene but is surrounded by a calyx sheath
CYPSELAE > CYPSELA
CYST *n* (abnormal) sac in the body containing fluid or soft matter
CYSTEIN *same as* > CYSTEINE
CYSTEINE *n* sulphur-containing amino acid
CYSTEINES > CYSTEINE
CYSTEINIC > CYSTEINE
CYSTEINS > CYSTEIN
CYSTIC *adj* of, relating to, or resembling a cyst
CYSTID *n* cystidean
CYSTIDEAN *n* any echinoderm of the class Cystoidea, an extinct order of sea lilies
CYSTIDS > CYSTID
CYSTIFORM *adj* having the form of a cyst
CYSTINE *n* sulphur-containing amino acid
CYSTINES > CYSTINE
CYSTITIS *n* inflammation of the bladder
CYSTOCARP *n* reproductive body in red algae, developed after fertilization and consisting of filaments bearing carpospores
CYSTOCELE *n* hernia of the urinary bladder, esp one protruding into the vagina
CYSTOID *adj* resembling a cyst or bladder ▷ *n* tissue mass, such as a tumour, that resembles a cyst but lacks an outer membrane
CYSTOIDS > CYSTOID
CYSTOLITH *n* knoblike deposit of calcium carbonate in the epidermal cells of such plants as the stinging nettle
CYSTOTOMY *n* surgical incision into the gall bladder or urinary bladder
CYSTS > CYST
CYTASE *n* cellulose-dissolving enzyme
CYTASES > CYTASE
CYTASTER *another word for* > ASTER
CYTASTERS > CYTASTER
CYTE *n* biological cell
CYTES > CYTE
CYTIDINE *n* nucleoside formed by the condensation of cytosine and ribose
CYTIDINES > CYTIDINE
CYTIDYLIC as in *cytidylic acid* nucleotide that is found in DNA
CYTISI > CYTISUS
CYTISINE *n* poisonous alkaloid found in laburnum seeds
CYTISINES > CYTISINE
CYTISUS *n* any plant of the

broom genus, Cytisus
CYTODE *n* mass of protoplasm without a nucleus
CYTODES > CYTODE
CYTOGENY *n* origin and development of plant cells
CYTOID *adj* resembling a cell
CYTOKINE *n* any of various proteins, secreted by cells, that carry signals to neighbouring cells. Cytokines include interferon
CYTOKINES > CYTOKINE
CYTOKININ *n* any of a group of plant hormones that promote cell division and retard ageing in plants
CYTOLOGIC > CYTOLOGY
CYTOLOGY *n* study of plant and animal cells
CYTOLYSES > CYTOLYSIS
CYTOLYSIN *n* substance that can partially or completely destroy animal cells
CYTOLYSIS *n* dissolution of cells, esp by the destruction of their membranes
CYTOLYTIC > CYTOLYSIS
CYTOMETER *n* glass slide used to count and measure blood cells
CYTOMETRY *n* counting of blood cells using a cytometer
CYTON *n* main part of a neuron
CYTONS > CYTON
CYTOPENIA *n* blood disorder where there is a deficiency in the blood cells
CYTOPLASM *n* protoplasm of a cell excluding the nucleus
CYTOPLAST *n* intact cytoplasm of a single cell
CYTOSINE *n* white crystalline pyrimidine occurring in nucleic acids
CYTOSINES > CYTOSINE
CYTOSOL *n* solution of proteins and metabolites inside a biological cell, in which the organelles are suspended
CYTOSOLIC > CYTOSOL
CYTOSOLS > CYTOSOL
CYTOSOME *n* body of a cell excluding its nucleus
CYTOSOMES > CYTOSOME
CYTOTAXES > CYTOTAXIS
CYTOTAXIS *n* movement of cells due to external stimulation
CYTOTOXIC *adj* poisonous to living cells: denoting certain drugs used in the treatment of leukaemia and other cancers
CYTOTOXIN *n* any substance that is poisonous to living cells
CZAPKA *n* leather and felt peaked military helmet of Polish origin
CZAPKAS > CZAPKA
CZAR *same as* > TSAR
CZARDAS *n* Hungarian national dance of alternating slow and fast sections
CZARDASES > CZARDAS
CZARDOM > CZAR
CZARDOMS > CZAR
CZAREVICH *n* son of a czar
CZAREVNA *a variant spelling (esp US) of* > TSAREVNA
CZAREVNAS > CZAREVNA
CZARINA *variant spellings (esp US) of* > TSARINA
CZARINAS > CZARINA
CZARISM *a variant spelling (esp US) of* > TSARISM
CZARISMS > CZARISM
CZARIST > CZARISM
CZARISTS > CZARISM
CZARITSA *n* Russian empress
CZARITSAS > CZARITSA
CZARITZA *same as* > CZARINA
CZARITZAS > CZARINA
CZARS > CZAR

Dd

DA *n* Burmese knife
DAB *vb* pat lightly ▷ *n* small amount of something soft or moist
DABBA *n* in Indian cookery, round metal box used to transport hot food
DABBAS > DABBA
DABBED > DAB
DABBER *n* pad used by printers for applying ink by hand
DABBERS > DABBER
DABBING > DAB
DABBITIES > DABBITY
DABBITY *n* temporary tattoo
DABBLE *vb* be involved in something superficially
DABBLED > DABBLE
DABBLER > DABBLE
DABBLERS > DABBLE
DABBLES > DABBLE
DABBLING > DABBLE
DABBLINGS > DABBLE
DABCHICK *n* any of several small grebes of the genera *Podiceps* and *Podilymbus*, such as *Podiceps ruficollis* of the Old World
DABCHICKS > DABCHICK
DABS > DAB
DABSTER *n* incompetent or amateurish worker
DABSTERS > DABSTER
DACE *n* small European freshwater fish
DACES > DACE
DACHA *n* country cottage in Russia
DACHAS > DACHA
DACHSHUND *n* dog with a long body and short legs
DACITE *n* volcanic rock
DACITES > DACITE
DACK *vb* remove the trousers from (someone) by force
DACKED > DACK
DACKER *vb* walk slowly
DACKERED > DACKER
DACKERING > DACKER
DACKERS > DACKER
DACKING > DACK
DACKS > DACK
DACOIT *n* (in India and Myanmar) a member of a gang of armed robbers
DACOITAGE *n* robbery by armed gang
DACOITIES > DACOITY
DACOITS > DACOIT
DACOITY *n* (in India and Myanmar) robbery by an armed gang
DACQUOISE *n* cake with meringue layers
DACRON *n* US tradename for a synthetic polyester fibre or fabric characterized by lightness and crease resistance
DACRONS > DACRON
DACTYL *n* metrical foot of three syllables, one long followed by two short
DACTYLAR *adj* poetry term
DACTYLI > DACTYLUS
DACTYLIC *same as* > DACTYL
DACTYLICS > DACTYLIC
DACTYLIST *n* poet
DACTYLS > DACTYL
DACTYLUS *n* tip of a squid's tentacular club
DAD *n* father ▷ *vb* act or treat as a father
DADA *n* nihilistic artistic movement of the early 20th century
DADAH *n* illegal drugs
DADAHS > DADAH
DADAISM *same as* > DADA
DADAISMS > DADAISM
DADAIST > DADA
DADAISTIC > DADA
DADAISTS > DADA
DADAS > DADA
DADDED > DAD
DADDIES > DADDY
DADDING > DAD
DADDLE *vb* walk unsteadily
DADDLED > DADDLE
DADDLES > DADDLE
DADDLING > DADDLE
DADDOCK *n* core of a dead tree
DADDOCKS > DADDOCK
DADDY *n* father
DADGUM *mild form of* > DAMNED
DADO *n* lower part of an interior wall, below a rail, decorated differently from the upper part ▷ *vb* provide with a dado
DADOED > DADO
DADOES > DADO
DADOING > DADO
DADOS > DADO
DADS > DAD
DAE *a Scot word for* > DO
DAEDAL *adj* skilful or intricate
DAEDALEAN *same as* > DAEDALIAN
DAEDALIAN *adj* of, relating to, or resembling the work of Daedalus, the Athenian architect and inventor of Greek mythology
DAEDALIC *same as* > DAEDALIAN
DAEING > DAE
DAEMON *same as* > DEMON
DAEMONES > DAEMON
DAEMONIC > DAEMON
DAEMONS > DAEMON
DAES > DAE
DAFF *vb* frolic
DAFFED > DAFF
DAFFIER > DAFFY
DAFFIES > DAFFY
DAFFIEST > DAFFY
DAFFILY > DAFFY
DAFFINESS > DAFFY
DAFFING > DAFF
DAFFINGS > DAFF
DAFFODIL *n* yellow trumpet-shaped flower that blooms in spring ▷ *adj* brilliant yellow
DAFFODILS > DAFFODIL
DAFFS > DAFF
DAFFY *another word for* > DAFT
DAFT *adj* foolish or crazy
DAFTAR *Indian word for* > OFFICE
DAFTARS > DAFTAR
DAFTER > DAFT
DAFTEST > DAFT
DAFTIE *n* foolish person
DAFTIES > DAFTIE
DAFTLY > DAFT
DAFTNESS > DAFT
DAG *n* character ▷ *vb* cut daglocks from sheep
DAGABA *n* shrine for Buddhist relics
DAGABAS > DAGABA
DAGGA *n* cannabis
DAGGAS > DAGGA

DAGGED > DAG
DAGGER > DAG
DAGGERED > DAG
DAGGERING > DAG
DAGGERS > DAG
DAGGIER > DAGGY
DAGGIEST > DAGGY
DAGGING > DAG
DAGGINGS > DAG
DAGGLE *vb* trail through water
DAGGLED > DAGGLE
DAGGLES > DAGGLE
DAGGLING > DAGGLE
DAGGY *adj* amusing
DAGLOCK *n* dung-caked lock of wool around the hindquarters of a sheep
DAGLOCKS > DAGLOCK
DAGO *n* offensive term for a member of a Latin race, esp a Spaniard or Portuguese
DAGOBA *n* dome-shaped shrine containing relics of the Buddha or a Buddhist saint
DAGOBAS > DAGOBA
DAGOES > DAGO
DAGOS > DAGO
DAGS > DAG
DAGWOOD *n* European shrub
DAGWOODS > DAGWOOD
DAH *n* long sound used in combination with the short sound *dit*, in the spoken representation of Morse and other telegraphic codes
DAHABEAH *n* houseboat used on the Nile
DAHABEAHS > DAHABEAH
DAHABEEAH *n* Egyptian houseboat
DAHABIAH *same as* > DAHABEAH
DAHABIAHS > DAHABIAH
DAHABIEH *n* Egyptian houseboat
DAHABIEHS > DAHABIEH
DAHABIYA *n* Egyptian houseboat
DAHABIYAH *n* Egyptian houseboat
DAHABIYAS > DAHABIYA
DAHABIYEH *n* Egyptian houseboat
DAHL *same as* > DHAL
DAHLIA *n* brightly coloured garden flower
DAHLIAS > DAHLIA
DAHLS > DAHL
DAHOON *n* evergreen shrub
DAHOONS > DAHOON
DAHS > DAH
DAIDLE *vb* waddle about
DAIDLED > DAIDLE
DAIDLES > DAIDLE
DAIDLING > DAIDLE
DAIDZEIN *n* type of protein
DAIDZEINS > DAIDZEIN
DAIKER *vb* walk slowly
DAIKERED > DAIKER
DAIKERING > DAIKER
DAIKERS > DAIKER
DAIKON *another name for* > MOOLI
DAIKONS > DAIKON
DAILIES > DAILY
DAILINESS > DAILY
DAILY *adj* occurring every day or every weekday ▷ *adv* every day ▷ *n* daily newspaper
DAILYNESS > DAILY
DAIMEN *adj* occasional
DAIMIO *same as* > DAIMYO
DAIMIOS > DAIMIO
DAIMOKU *n* Nichiren Buddhist chant
DAIMOKUS > DAIMOKU
DAIMON *same as* > DEMON
DAIMONES *pl n* disembodied souls
DAIMONIC > DAIMON
DAIMONS > DAIMON
DAIMYO *n* (in Japan) one of the territorial magnates who dominated much of the country from about the 11th to the 19th century
DAIMYOS > DAIMYO
DAINE *vb* condescend
DAINED > DAINE
DAINES > DAINE
DAINING > DAINE
DAINT *adj* dainty
DAINTIER > DAINTY
DAINTIES > DAINTY
DAINTIEST > DAINTY
DAINTILY > DAINTY
DAINTY *adj* delicate or elegant ▷ *n* small cake or sweet
DAIQUIRI *n* iced drink containing rum, lime juice, and sugar
DAIQUIRIS > DAIQUIRI
DAIRIES > DAIRY
DAIRY *n* place for the processing or sale of milk and its products ▷ *adj* of milk or its products
DAIRYING *n* business of producing, processing, and selling dairy products
DAIRYINGS > DAIRYING
DAIRYMAID *n* (formerly) woman employed to milk cows
DAIRYMAN *n* man employed to look after cows
DAIRYMEN > DAIRYMAN
DAIS *n* raised platform in a hall, used by a speaker
DAISES > DAIS
DAISHIKI *n* upper garment
DAISHIKIS > DAISHIKI
DAISIED > DAISY
DAISIES > DAISY
DAISY *n* small wild flower with a yellow centre and white petals
DAK *n* system of mail delivery or passenger transport by relays of bearers or horses stationed at intervals along a route
DAKER *vb* walk slowly
DAKERED > DAKER
DAKERHEN *n* European bird
DAKERHENS > DAKERHEN
DAKERING > DAKER
DAKERS > DAKER
DAKOIT *same as* > DACOIT
DAKOITI > DAKOIT
DAKOITIES > DAKOIT
DAKOITIS > DAKOIT
DAKOITS > DAKOIT
DAKOITY *n* armed robbery
DAKS *an informal name for* > TROUSERS
DAL *same as* > DECALITRE
DALAPON *n* herbicide
DALAPONS > DALAPON
DALASI *n* standard monetary unit of The Gambia, divided into 100 bututs
DALASIS > DALASI
DALE *n* (esp in N England) valley
DALED *same as* > DALETH
DALEDH *n* letter of Hebrew alphabet
DALEDHS > DALEDH
DALEDS > DALED
DALES > DALE
DALESMAN *n* person living in a dale, esp in the dales of N England
DALESMEN > DALESMAN
DALETH *n* fourth letter of the Hebrew alphabet, transliterated as *d* or, when final, *dh*
DALETHS > DALETH
DALGYTE *another name for* > BILBY
DALGYTES > DALGYTE
DALI *n* type of tree
DALIS > DALI
DALLE > DALLES
DALLES *pl n* stretch of a river between high rock walls, with rapids and dangerous currents
DALLIANCE *n* flirtation
DALLIED > DALLY
DALLIER > DALLY
DALLIERS > DALLY
DALLIES > DALLY
DALLOP *n* semisolid lump
DALLOPS > DALLOP
DALLY *vb* waste time
DALLYING > DALLY
DALMAHOY *n* bushy wig
DALMAHOYS > DALMAHOY
DALMATIAN *n* breed of dog characterized by its striking spotted markings
DALMATIC *n* wide-sleeved tunic-like vestment open at the sides, worn by deacons and bishops
DALMATICS > DALMATIC
DALS > DAL
DALT *n* foster child
DALTON *n* atomic mass unit
DALTONIAN > DALTON
DALTONIC > DALTONISM
DALTONISM *n* colour blindness, esp the confusion of red and green
DALTONS > DALTON
DALTS > DALT
DAM *n* barrier built across a river to create a lake ▷ *vb* build a dam across (a river)
DAMAGE *vb* harm, spoil ▷ *n* harm to a person or thing
DAMAGED > DAMAGE
DAMAGER > DAMAGE
DAMAGERS > DAMAGE
DAMAGES *pl n* money awarded as compensation for injury or loss
DAMAGING > DAMAGE
DAMAN *n* esp the Syrian rock hyrax
DAMANS > DAMAN
DAMAR *same as* > DAMMAR
DAMARS > DAMMAR
DAMASCENE *vb* ornament (metal, esp steel) by etching or by inlaying, usually with gold or silver ▷ *n* design or article produced by this process ▷ *adj* of or relating to this process
DAMASK *n* fabric with a pattern woven into it, used for tablecloths etc ▷ *vb* ornament (metal) by etching or inlaying, usually with gold or silver
DAMASKED > DAMASK
DAMASKEEN *vb* decorate metal
DAMASKIN *vb* decorate metal
DAMASKING > DAMASK
DAMASKINS > DAMASKIN
DAMASKS > DAMASK
DAMASQUIN *vb* decorate metal
DAMASSIN *n* patterned damask
DAMASSINS > DAMASSIN
DAMBOARD *n* draughtboard
DAMBOARDS > DAMBOARD
DAMBROD *n* draughtboard
DAMBRODS > DAMBROD
DAME *n* woman
DAMES > DAME
DAMEWORT *n* sweet-scented perennial plant with mauve or white flowers
DAMEWORTS > DAMEWORT
DAMFOOL *adj* foolish
DAMIANA *n* herbal medicine
DAMIANAS > DAMIANA
DAMMAR *n* any of various resins obtained from SE Asian trees used for varnishes, lacquers, bases for oil paints, etc
DAMMARS > DAMMAR
DAMME *interj* exclamation of surprise
DAMMED > DAM
DAMMER *same as* > DAMMAR
DAMMERS > DAMMER

DAMMING > DAM
DAMMIT *interj* exclamation of surprise
DAMN *interj* exclamation of annoyance ▷ *adj* extreme(ly) ▷ *vb* condemn as bad or worthless
DAMNABLE *adj* annoying
DAMNABLY *adv* in a detestable manner
DAMNATION *interj* exclamation of anger ▷ *n* eternal punishment
DAMNATORY *adj* threatening or occasioning condemnation
DAMNDEST *n* utmost
DAMNDESTS > DAMNDEST
DAMNED *adj* condemned to hell ▷ *adv* extreme or extremely
DAMNEDER > DAMNED
DAMNEDEST *n* utmost
DAMNER *n* person who damns
DAMNERS > DAMNER
DAMNIFIED > DAMNIFY
DAMNIFIES > DAMNIFY
DAMNIFY *vb* cause loss or damage to (a person)
DAMNING > DAMN
DAMNINGLY > DAMN
DAMNS > DAMN
DAMOISEL *same as* > DAMSEL
DAMOISELS > DAMOISEL
DAMOSEL *same as* > DAMSEL
DAMOSELS > DAMOSEL
DAMOZEL *same as* > DAMOISELLE
DAMOZELS > DAMOZEL
DAMP *adj* slightly wet ▷ *n* slight wetness, moisture ▷ *vb* make damp
DAMPED > DAMP
DAMPEN *vb* reduce the intensity of
DAMPENED > DAMPEN
DAMPENER > DAMPEN
DAMPENERS > DAMPEN
DAMPENING > DAMPEN
DAMPENS > DAMPEN
DAMPER *n* movable plate to regulate the draught in a fire
DAMPERS > DAMPER
DAMPEST > DAMP
DAMPIER > DAMPY
DAMPIEST > DAMPY
DAMPING *n* moistening or wetting
DAMPINGS > DAMPING
DAMPISH > DAMP
DAMPLY > DAMP
DAMPNESS > DAMP
DAMPS > DAMP
DAMPY *adj* damp
DAMS > DAM
DAMSEL *n* young woman
DAMSELFLY *n* any insect of the suborder *Zygoptera*, similar to but smaller than dragonflies and usually resting with the wings closed over the back: order *Odonata*
DAMSELS > DAMSEL
DAMSON *n* small blue-black plumlike fruit
DAMSONS > DAMSON
DAN *n* in judo, any of the 10 black-belt grades of proficiency
DANAZOL *n* type of drug
DANAZOLS > DANAZOL
DANCE *vb* move the feet and body rhythmically in time to music ▷ *n* series of steps and movements in time to music
DANCEABLE > DANCE
DANCED > DANCE
DANCEHALL *n* style of dance-oriented reggae
DANCER > DANCE
DANCERS > DANCE
DANCES > DANCE
DANCETTE *another name for* > CHEVRON
DANCETTEE *adj* having a zigzag pattern
DANCETTES > DANCETTE
DANCETTY *adj* having a zigzag pattern
DANCEY *adj* of, relating to, or resembling dance music
DANCIER > DANCEY
DANCIEST > DANCEY
DANCING > DANCE
DANCINGS > DANCE
DANDELION *n* yellow-flowered wild plant
DANDER *n* stroll ▷ *vb* stroll
DANDERED > DANDER
DANDERING > DANDER
DANDERS > DANDER
DANDIACAL *adj* like a dandy
DANDIER > DANDY
DANDIES > DANDY
DANDIEST > DANDY
DANDIFIED > DANDIFY
DANDIFIES > DANDIFY
DANDIFY *vb* dress like or cause to resemble a dandy
DANDILY > DANDY
DANDIPRAT *n* small English coin minted in the 16th century
DANDLE *vb* move (a child) up and down on one's knee
DANDLED > DANDLE
DANDLER > DANDLE
DANDLERS > DANDLE
DANDLES > DANDLE
DANDLING > DANDLE
DANDRIFF *same as* > DANDRUFF
DANDRIFFS > DANDRIFF
DANDRUFF *n* loose scales of dry dead skin shed from the scalp
DANDRUFFS > DANDRUFF
DANDRUFFY > DANDRUFF
DANDY *n* man who is overconcerned with the elegance of his appearance ▷ *adj* very good
DANDYFUNK *n* ship's biscuit
DANDYISH > DANDY
DANDYISM > DANDY
DANDYISMS > DANDY
DANDYPRAT *n* English coin
DANEGELD *n* tax levied in Anglo-Saxon England to provide protection money for, or to finance forces to oppose, Viking invaders
DANEGELDS > DANEGELD
DANEGELT *same as* > DANEGELD
DANEGELTS > DANEGELT
DANELAGH *same as* > DANELAW
DANELAGHS > DANELAGH
DANELAW *n* Danish law and customs of northern, central, and eastern parts of Anglo-Saxon England
DANELAWS > DANELAW
DANEWEED *n* dwarf elder
DANEWEEDS > DANEWEED
DANEWORT *n* dwarf elder
DANEWORTS > DANEWORT
DANG *a euphemistic word for* > DAMN
DANGED > DANG
DANGER *n* possibility of being injured or killed ▷ *vb* in archaic usage, endanger
DANGERED > DANGER
DANGERING > DANGER
DANGEROUS *adj* likely or able to cause injury or harm
DANGERS > DANGER
DANGING > DANG
DANGLE *vb* hang loosely ▷ *n* act of dangling or something that dangles
DANGLED > DANGLE
DANGLER > DANGLE
DANGLERS > DANGLE
DANGLES > DANGLE
DANGLIER > DANGLE
DANGLIEST > DANGLE
DANGLING > DANGLE
DANGLINGS > DANGLE
DANGLY > DANGLE
DANGS > DANG
DANIO *n* any brightly coloured tropical freshwater cyprinid fish of the genus *Danio* and related genera: popular aquarium fishes
DANIOS > DANIO
DANISH *n* sweet pastry
DANISHES > DANISH
DANK *adj* unpleasantly damp and chilly ▷ *n* unpleasant damp and chilliness
DANKER > DANK
DANKEST > DANK
DANKISH > DANK
DANKLY > DANK
DANKNESS > DANK
DANKS > DANK
DANNEBROG *n* Danish flag
DANNIES > DANNY
DANNY *n* hand (used esp when addressing children)
DANS > DAN
DANSEUR *n* male ballet dancer
DANSEURS > DANSEUR
DANSEUSE *n* female ballet dancer
DANSEUSES > DANSEUSE
DANT *vb* intimidate
DANTED > DANT
DANTHONIA *n* any of various grasses of the genus *Danthonia*, of N temperate regions and South America
DANTING > DANT
DANTON *same as* > DAUNTON
DANTONED > DANTON
DANTONING > DANTON
DANTONS > DANTON
DANTS > DANT
DAP *vb* fish with a natural or artificial fly on a floss silk line so that the wind makes the fly bob on and off the surface of the water
DAPHNE *n* any shrub of the Eurasian thymelaeaceous genus *Daphne*, such as the mezereon and spurge laurel: ornamentals with shiny evergreen leaves and clusters of small bell-shaped flowers
DAPHNES > DAPHNE
DAPHNIA *n* any water flea of the genus *Daphnia*, having a rounded body enclosed in a transparent shell and bearing branched swimming antennae
DAPHNIAS > DAPHNIA
DAPHNID *n* water flea
DAPHNIDS > DAPHNID
DAPPED > DAP
DAPPER *adj* (of a man) neat in appearance ▷ *n* fisherman or -woman who uses a bobbing bait
DAPPERER > DAPPER
DAPPEREST > DAPPER
DAPPERLY > DAPPER
DAPPERS > DAPPER
DAPPING > DAP
DAPPLE *vb* mark or become marked with spots or patches of a different colour ▷ *n* mottled or spotted markings ▷ *adj* marked with dapples or spots
DAPPLED > DAPPLE
DAPPLES > DAPPLE
DAPPLING > DAPPLE
DAPS > DAP
DAPSONE *n* antimicrobial drug used to treat leprosy and certain types of dermatitis
DAPSONES > DAPSONE
DAQUIRI *n* rum cocktail
DAQUIRIS > DAQUIRI
DARAF *n* unit of elastance equal to a reciprocal farad
DARAFS > DARAF
DARB *n* something

excellent
DARBAR *n* hall in Sikh temple
DARBARS > DARBAR
DARBIES > HANDCUFFS
DARBS > DARB
DARCIES > DARCY
DARCY *n* unit expressing the permeability coefficient of rock
DARCYS > DARCY
DARE *vb* be courageous enough to try (to do something) ▷ *n* challenge to do something risky
DARED > DARE
DAREDEVIL *n* recklessly bold person ▷ *adj* recklessly bold or daring
DAREFUL *adj* daring
DARER > DARE
DARERS > DARE
DARES > DARE
DARESAY *vb* venture to say
DARG *n* day's work
DARGA *n* Muslim shrine
DARGAH *n* tomb of a Muslim saint
DARGAHS > DARGAH
DARGAS > DARGA
DARGLE *n* wooded hollow
DARGLES > DARGLE
DARGS > DARG
DARI *n* variety of sorghum
DARIC *n* gold coin of ancient Persia
DARICS > DARIC
DARING *adj* willing to take risks ▷ *n* courage to do dangerous things
DARINGLY > DARING
DARINGS > DARING
DARIOLE *n* small cup-shaped mould used for making individual sweet or savoury dishes
DARIOLES > DARIOLE
DARIS > DARI
DARK *adj* having little or no light ▷ *n* absence of light ▷ *vb* in archaic usage, darken
DARKED > DARK
DARKEN *vb* make or become dark or darker
DARKENED > DARKEN
DARKENER > DARKEN
DARKENERS > DARKEN
DARKENING > DARKEN
DARKENS > DARKEN
DARKER > DARK
DARKEST > DARK
DARKEY *same as* > DARKY
DARKEYS > DARKEY
DARKIE *same as* > DARKY
DARKIES > DARKY
DARKING > DARK
DARKISH > DARK
DARKLE *vb* grow dark
DARKLED > DARKLE
DARKLES > DARKLE
DARKLIER > DARK
DARKLIEST > DARK
DARKLING *adj* in the dark or night
DARKLINGS *adv* in darkness
DARKLY > DARK
DARKMANS *n* slang term for night-time
DARKNESS > DARK
DARKROOM *n* darkened room for processing photographic film
DARKROOMS > DARKROOM
DARKS > DARK
DARKSOME *adj* dark or darkish
DARKY *n* offensive word for a Black person
DARLING *n* much-loved person ▷ *adj* much-loved
DARLINGLY > DARLING
DARLINGS > DARLING
DARN *vb* mend (a garment) with a series of interwoven stitches ▷ *n* patch of darned work
DARNATION *mild form of* > DAMNATION
DARNDEST *n* utmost
DARNDESTS > DARNDEST
DARNED *adj* damned
DARNEDER > DARNED
DARNEDEST *a euphemistic word for* > DAMNEDEST
DARNEL *n* weed that grows in grain fields
DARNELS > DARNEL
DARNER > DARN
DARNERS > DARN
DARNING > DARN
DARNINGS > DARN
DARNS > DARN
DAROGHA *n* in India, manager
DAROGHAS > DAROGHA
DARRAIGN *same as* > DERAIGN
DARRAIGNE *vb* clear from guilt
DARRAIGNS > DARRAIGN
DARRAIN *vb* clear of guilt
DARRAINE *vb* clear of guilt
DARRAINED > DARRAINE
DARRAINES > DARRAINE
DARRAINS > DARRAIN
DARRAYN *vb* clear of guilt
DARRAYNED > DARRAYN
DARRAYNS > DARRAYN
DARRE *vb* dare
DARRED > DARRE
DARRES > DARRE
DARRING > DARRE
DARSHAN *n* Hindu blessing
DARSHANS > DARSHAN
DART *n* small narrow pointed missile that is thrown or shot, esp in the game of darts ▷ *vb* move or direct quickly and suddenly
DARTBOARD *n* circular board used as the target in the game of darts
DARTED > DART
DARTER *n* any aquatic bird of the genus *Anhinga* and family *Anhingidae*, of tropical and subtropical inland waters, having a long slender neck and bill: order *Pelecaniformes* (pelicans, cormorants, etc)
DARTERS > DARTER
DARTING > DART
DARTINGLY > DART
DARTLE *vb* move swiftly
DARTLED > DARTLE
DARTLES > DARTLE
DARTLING > DARTLE
DARTRE *n* skin disease
DARTRES > DARTRE
DARTROUS *adj* having a skin disease
DARTS *n* game in which darts are thrown at a dartboard
DARZI *n* tailor in India
DARZIS > DARZI
DAS > DA
DASH *vb* move quickly ▷ *n* sudden quick movement
DASHBOARD *n* instrument panel in a vehicle
DASHED > DASH
DASHEEN *another name for* > TARO
DASHEENS > DASHEEN
DASHEKI *n* upper garment
DASHEKIS > DASHEKI
DASHER *n* one of the boards surrounding an ice-hockey rink
DASHERS > DASHER
DASHES > DASH
DASHI *n* clear stock made from dried fish and kelp
DASHIER > DASHY
DASHIEST > DASHY
DASHIKI *n* large loose-fitting buttonless upper garment worn esp by Blacks in the US, Africa, and the Caribbean
DASHIKIS > DASHIKI
DASHING *adj* stylish and attractive
DASHINGLY > DASHING
DASHIS > DASHI
DASHPOT *n* device for damping vibrations
DASHPOTS > DASHPOT
DASHY *adj* showy
DASSIE *n* type of hoofed rodent-like animal
DASSIES > DASSIE
DASTARD *n* contemptible sneaking coward
DASTARDLY *adj* wicked and cowardly
DASTARDS > DASTARD
DASTARDY *n* cowardice
DASYMETER *n* device for measuring density of gases
DASYPOD *n* armadillo
DASYPODS > DASYPOD
DASYURE *n* small marsupial of Australia, New Guinea, and adjacent islands
DASYURES > DASYURE
DATA *n* information consisting of observations, measurements, or facts
DATABANK *n* store of a large amount of information, esp in a form that can be handled by a computer
DATABANKS > DATABANK
DATABASE *n* store of information in a form that can be easily handled by a computer ▷ *vb* put data into a database
DATABASED > DATABASE
DATABASES > DATABASE
DATABLE > DATE
DATABUS *n* computing term
DATABUSES > DATABUS
DATACARD *n* smart card
DATACARDS > DATACARD
DATACOMMS *n* computing term
DATAFLOW as in *dataflow architecture* means of arranging computer data processing in which operations are governed by the data present and the processing it requires rather than by a prewritten program that awaits data to be processed
DATAGLOVE *n* computing term
DATAL *adj* slow-witted ▷ *n* day labour
DATALLER *n* worker paid by the day
DATALLERS > DATALLER
DATALS > DATAL
DATARIA *n* Roman Catholic office
DATARIAS > DATARIA
DATARIES > DATARY
DATARY *n* head of the dataria, the papal office that assesses candidates for benefices reserved to the Holy See
DATCHA *same as* > DACHA
DATCHAS > DATCHA
DATE *n* specified day of the month ▷ *vb* mark with the date
DATEABLE > DATE
DATEBOOK *n* list of forthcoming events
DATEBOOKS > DATEBOOK
DATED *adj* old-fashioned
DATEDLY > DATED
DATEDNESS > DATED
DATELESS > DATE
DATELINE *n* information about the place and time a story was written, placed at the top of the article
DATELINED > DATELINE
DATELINES > DATELINE
DATER *n* person who dates
DATERS > DATER
DATES > DATE
DATING *n* any of several

techniques, such as radioactive dating, dendrochronology, or varve dating, for establishing the age of rocks, palaeontological or archaeological specimens, etc
DATINGS > DATING
DATIVAL > DATIVE
DATIVE *adj* denoting a case of nouns, pronouns, and adjectives used to express the indirect object ▷ *n* this grammatical case
DATIVELY > DATIVE
DATIVES > DATIVE
DATO *n* chief of any of certain Muslim tribes in the Philippine Islands
DATOLITE *n* colourless mineral
DATOLITES > DATOLITE
DATOS > DATO
DATTO *n* Datsun car
DATTOS > DATTO
DATUM *n* single piece of information in the form of a fact or statistic
DATUMS > DATUM
DATURA *n* any of various chiefly Indian solanaceous plants of the genus *Datura*, such as the moonflower and thorn apple, having large trumpet-shaped flowers, prickly pods, and narcotic properties
DATURAS > DATURA
DATURIC > DATURA
DATURINE *n* poisonous alkaloid
DATURINES > DATURINE
DAUB *vb* smear or spread quickly or clumsily ▷ *n* crude or badly done painting
DAUBE *n* braised meat stew
DAUBED > DAUB
DAUBER > DAUB
DAUBERIES > DAUBERY
DAUBERS > DAUB
DAUBERY *n* act or an instance of daubing
DAUBES > DAUBE
DAUBIER > DAUB
DAUBIEST > DAUB
DAUBING > DAUB
DAUBINGLY > DAUB
DAUBINGS > DAUB
DAUBRIES > DAUBRY
DAUBRY *n* unskilful painting
DAUBS > DAUB
DAUBY > DAUB
DAUD *n* lump or chunk of something ▷ *vb* (in dialect) whack
DAUDED > DAUD
DAUDING > DAUD
DAUDS > DAUD
DAUGHTER *n* female child ▷ *adj* denoting a cell, chromosome, etc produced by the division of one of its own kind
DAUGHTERS > DAUGHTER
DAULT *n* foster child
DAULTS > DAULT
DAUNDER *vb* stroll
DAUNDERED > DAUNDER
DAUNDERS > DAUNDER
DAUNER *vb* stroll
DAUNERED > DAUNER
DAUNERING > DAUNER
DAUNERS > DAUNER
DAUNT *vb* intimidate
DAUNTED > DAUNT
DAUNTER > DAUNT
DAUNTERS > DAUNT
DAUNTING *adj* intimidating or worrying
DAUNTLESS *adj* fearless
DAUNTON *vb* dishearten
DAUNTONED > DAUNTON
DAUNTONS > DAUNTON
DAUNTS > DAUNT
DAUPHIN *n* (formerly) eldest son of the king of France
DAUPHINE *n* wife of a dauphin
DAUPHINES > DAUPHINE
DAUPHINS > DAUPHIN
DAUR *a Scot word for* > DARE
DAURED > DAUR
DAURING > DAUR
DAURS > DAUR
DAUT *vb* fondle
DAUTED > DAUT
DAUTIE *n* darling
DAUTIES > DAUTIE
DAUTING > DAUT
DAUTS > DAUT
DAVEN *vb* pray
DAVENED > DAVEN
DAVENING > DAVEN
DAVENPORT *n* small writing table with drawers
DAVENS > DAVEN
DAVIDIA *n* Chinese shrub
DAVIDIAS > DAVIDIA
DAVIES > DAVY
DAVIT *n* crane, usu. one of a pair, at a ship's side, for lowering and hoisting a lifeboat
DAVITS > DAVIT
DAVY *n* miner's safety lamp
DAW *n* an archaic, dialect, or poetic name for a jackdaw ▷ *vb* old word for dawn
DAWAH *n* practice of educating non-Muslims about the message of Islam
DAWAHS > DAWAH
DAWBAKE *n* foolish or slow-witted person
DAWBAKES > DAWBAKE
DAWBRIES > DAWBRY
DAWBRY *n* unskilful painting
DAWCOCK *n* male jackdaw
DAWCOCKS > DAWCOCK
DAWD *vb* thump
DAWDED > DAWD
DAWDING > DAWD
DAWDLE *vb* walk slowly, lag behind
DAWDLED > DAWDLE
DAWDLER > DAWDLE
DAWDLERS > DAWDLE
DAWDLES > DAWDLE
DAWDLING > DAWDLE
DAWDS > DAWD
DAWED > DAW
DAWEN > DAW
DAWING > DAW
DAWISH > DAW
DAWK *same as* > DAK
DAWKS > DAWK
DAWN *n* daybreak ▷ *vb* begin to grow light
DAWNED > DAWN
DAWNER *vb* stroll
DAWNERED > DAWNER
DAWNERING > DAWNER
DAWNERS > DAWNER
DAWNEY *adj* (of a person) dull or slow
DAWNING > DAWN
DAWNINGS > DAWN
DAWNLIKE > DAWN
DAWNS > DAWN
DAWS > DAW
DAWSONITE *n* mineral
DAWT *vb* fondle
DAWTED > DAWT
DAWTIE *n* darling
DAWTIES > DAWTIE
DAWTING > DAWT
DAWTS > DAWT
DAY *n* period of 24 hours
DAYAN *n* senior rabbi, esp one who sits in a religious court
DAYANIM > DAYAN
DAYANS > DAYAN
DAYBED *n* narrow bed with a head piece and sometimes a foot piece and back, for day use
DAYBEDS > DAYBED
DAYBOOK *n* book in which the transactions of each day are recorded as they occur
DAYBOOKS > DAYBOOK
DAYBOY *n* boy who attends a boarding school daily, but returns home each evening
DAYBOYS > DAYBOY
DAYBREAK *n* time in the morning when light first appears
DAYBREAKS > DAYBREAK
DAYCARE *n* occupation, treatment, or supervision during the working day for people who might be at risk if left on their own, or whose usual carers need daytime relief
DAYCARES > DAYCARE
DAYCENTRE *n* building used for daycare or other welfare services
DAYCH *vb* thatch
DAYCHED > DAYCH
DAYCHES > DAYCH
DAYCHING > DAYCH
DAYDREAM *n* pleasant fantasy indulged in while awake ▷ *vb* indulge in idle fantasy
DAYDREAMS > DAYDREAM
DAYDREAMT > DAYDREAM
DAYDREAMY > DAYDREAM
DAYFLIES > DAYFLY
DAYFLOWER *n* any of various tropical and subtropical plants of the genus *Commelina*, having jointed creeping stems, narrow pointed leaves, and blue or purplish flowers which wilt quickly: family *Commelinaceae*
DAYFLY *another name for* > MAYFLY
DAYGLO *n* fluorescent colours
DAYGLOW *n* fluorescent colours
DAYGLOWS > DAYGLOW
DAYLIGHT *n* light from the sun
DAYLIGHTS *pl n* consciousness or wits
DAYLILIES > DAYLILY
DAYLILY *n* any of various plants having lily-like flowers that typically last only one day before being succeeded by others
DAYLIT > DAYLIGHT
DAYLONG *adv* lasting the entire day
DAYMARE *n* bad dream during the day
DAYMARES > DAYMARE
DAYMARK *n* navigation aid
DAYMARKS > DAYMARK
DAYNT *adj* dainty
DAYROOM *n* communal living room in a residential institution
DAYROOMS > DAYROOM
DAYS *adv* during the day, esp regularly
DAYSACK *n* rucksack
DAYSACKS > DAYSACK
DAYSHELL *n* thistle
DAYSHELLS > DAYSHELL
DAYSIDE *n* side of a planet nearest the sun
DAYSIDES > DAYSIDE
DAYSMAN *n* umpire
DAYSMEN > DAYSMAN
DAYSPRING *a poetic word for* > DAWN
DAYSTAR *a poetic word for* > SUN
DAYSTARS > DAYSTAR
DAYTALE *n* day labour
DAYTALER *n* worker paid by the day
DAYTALERS > DAYTALER
DAYTALES > DAYTALE
DAYTIME *n* time from sunrise to sunset
DAYTIMES > DAYTIME
DAYWORK *n* daytime work
DAYWORKER > DAYWORK

DAYWORKS > DAYWORK
DAZE *vb* stun, by a blow or shock ▷ *n* state of confusion or shock
DAZED > DAZE
DAZEDLY > DAZE
DAZEDNESS > DAZE
DAZER > DAZE
DAZERS > DAZE
DAZES > DAZE
DAZING > DAZE
DAZZLE *vb* impress greatly ▷ *n* bright light that dazzles
DAZZLED > DAZZLE
DAZZLER > DAZZLE
DAZZLERS > DAZZLE
DAZZLES > DAZZLE
DAZZLING > DAZZLE
DAZZLINGS > DAZZLING
DE *prep* of or from
DEACIDIFY *vb* removal acid from
DEACON *n* ordained minister ranking immediately below a priest ▷ *vb* make a deacon of
DEACONED > DEACON
DEACONESS *n* (in the early church and in some modern Churches) a female member of the laity with duties similar to those of a deacon
DEACONING > DEACON
DEACONRY *n* office or status of a deacon
DEACONS > DEACON
DEAD *adj* no longer alive ▷ *n* period during which coldness or darkness is most intense ▷ *adv* extremely ▷ *vb* in archaic usage, die or kill
DEADBEAT *n* lazy useless person
DEADBEATS > DEADBEAT
DEADBOLT *n* bolt operated without a spring
DEADBOLTS > DEADBOLT
DEADBOY *same as* > DEADMAN
DEADBOYS > DEADBOY
DEADED > DEAD
DEADEN *vb* make less intense
DEADENED > DEADEN
DEADENER > DEADEN
DEADENERS > DEADEN
DEADENING > DEADEN
DEADENS > DEADEN
DEADER > DEAD
DEADERS > DEAD
DEADEST > DEAD
DEADEYE *n* either of a pair of disclike wooden blocks, supported by straps in grooves around them, between which a line is rove so as to draw them together to tighten a shroud
DEADEYES > DEADEYE
DEADFALL *n* type of trap, used esp for catching large animals, in which a heavy weight falls to crush the prey
DEADFALLS > DEADFALL
DEADHEAD *n* person who does not pay on a bus, at a game, etc ▷ *vb* cut off withered flowers from (a plant)
DEADHEADS > DEADHEAD
DEADHOUSE *n* mortuary
DEADING > DEAD
DEADLIER > DEADLY
DEADLIEST > DEADLY
DEADLIFT *vb* weightlifting term
DEADLIFTS > DEADLIFT
DEADLIGHT *n* bull's-eye let into the deck or hull of a vessel to admit light to a cabin
DEADLINE *n* time limit ▷ *vb* put a time limit on an action, decision, etc
DEADLINED > DEADLINE
DEADLINES > DEADLINE
DEADLOCK *n* point in a dispute at which no agreement can be reached ▷ *vb* bring or come to a deadlock
DEADLOCKS > DEADLOCK
DEADLY *adj* likely to cause death ▷ *adv* extremely
DEADMAN *n* heavy plate, wall, or block buried in the ground that acts as an anchor for a retaining wall, sheet pile, etc, by a tie connecting the two
DEADMEN > DEADMAN
DEADNESS > DEAD
DEADPAN *adv* showing no emotion or expression ▷ *adj* deliberately emotionless ▷ *n* deadpan expression or manner
DEADPANS > DEADPAN
DEADS > DEAD
DEADSTOCK *n* farm equipment
DEADWOOD *n* dead trees or branches
DEADWOODS > DEADWOOD
DEAERATE *vb* remove air from
DEAERATED > DEAERATE
DEAERATES > DEAERATE
DEAERATOR > DEAERATE
DEAF *adj* unable to hear
DEAFBLIND *adj* unable to hear or see
DEAFEN *vb* make deaf, esp temporarily
DEAFENED > DEAFEN
DEAFENING *n* excessively loud
DEAFENS > DEAFEN
DEAFER > DEAF
DEAFEST > DEAF
DEAFISH > DEAF
DEAFLY > DEAF
DEAFNESS > DEAF
DEAIR *vb* reove air from
DEAIRED > DEAIR
DEAIRING > DEAIR
DEAIRS > DEAIR
DEAL *n* agreement or transaction ▷ *vb* inflict (a blow) on ▷ *adj* of fir or pine
DEALATE *adj* (of ants and other insects) having lost their wings, esp by biting or rubbing them off after mating ▷ *n* insect that has shed its wings
DEALATED *same as* > DEALATE
DEALATES > DEALATE
DEALATION > DEALATE
DEALBATE *adj* bleached
DEALER *n* person whose business involves buying and selling
DEALERS > DEALER
DEALFISH *n* long thin fish
DEALING > DEAL
DEALINGS *pl n* transactions or business relations
DEALS > DEAL
DEALT > DEAL
DEAMINASE *n* enzyme that breaks down amino compounds
DEAMINATE *vb* remove one or more amino groups from (a molecule)
DEAMINISE *same as* > DEAMINATE
DEAMINIZE *same as* > DEAMINATE
DEAN *n* chief administrative official of a college or university faculty ▷ *vb* punish (a student) by sending them to the dean
DEANED > DEAN
DEANER *n* shilling
DEANERIES > DEANERY
DEANERS > DEANER
DEANERY *n* office or residence of a dean
DEANING > DEAN
DEANS > DEAN
DEANSHIP > DEAN
DEANSHIPS > DEAN
DEAR *n* someone regarded with affection ▷ *adj* much-loved
DEARE *vb* harm
DEARED > DEARE
DEARER > DEAR
DEARES > DEARE
DEAREST > DEAR
DEARIE *same as* > DEARY
DEARIES > DEARY
DEARING > DEARE
DEARLING *n* darling
DEARLINGS > DEARLING
DEARLY *adv* very much
DEARN *vb* hide
DEARNESS > DEAR
DEARNFUL *adj* secret
DEARNLY > DEARN
DEARNS > DEARN
DEARS > DEAR
DEARTH *n* inadequate amount, scarcity
DEARTHS > DEARTH
DEARY *n* term of affection: now often sarcastic or facetious
DEASH *vb* remove ash from
DEASHED > DEASH
DEASHES > DEASH
DEASHING > DEASH
DEASIL *adv* in the direction of the apparent course of the sun ▷ *n* motion in this direction
DEASILS > DEASIL
DEASIUL *n* motion towards the sun
DEASIULS > DEASIUL
DEASOIL *n* motion towards the sun
DEASOILS > DEASOIL
DEATH *n* permanent end of life in a person or animal
DEATHBED *n* bed where a person is about to die or has just died
DEATHBEDS > DEATHBED
DEATHBLOW *n* thing or event that destroys hope
DEATHCUP *n* poisonous fungus
DEATHCUPS > DEATHCUP
DEATHFUL *adj* murderous
DEATHIER > DEATH
DEATHIEST > DEATH
DEATHLESS *adj* everlasting because of fine qualities
DEATHLIER > DEATHLY
DEATHLIKE > DEATH
DEATHLY *adv* like death ▷ *adj* resembling death
DEATHS > DEATH
DEATHSMAN *n* executioner
DEATHSMEN > DEATHSMAN
DEATHTRAP *n* building, vehicle, etc, that is considered very unsafe
DEATHWARD *adv* heading towards death
DEATHY > DEATH
DEAVE *vb* deafen
DEAVED > DEAVE
DEAVES > DEAVE
DEAVING > DEAVE
DEAW *n* dew
DEAWIE > DEAW
DEAWS > DEAW
DEAWY > DEAW
DEB *n* debutante
DEBACLE *n* disastrous failure
DEBACLES > DEBACLE
DEBAG *vb* remove the trousers from (someone) by force
DEBAGGED > DEBAG
DEBAGGING > DEBAG
DEBAGS > DEBAG
DEBAR *vb* prevent, bar
DEBARK *vb* remove the bark from (a tree)
DEBARKED > DEBARK

DEBARKER > DEBARK
DEBARKERS > DEBARK
DEBARKING > DEBARK
DEBARKS > DEBARK
DEBARMENT > DEBAR
DEBARRASS *vb* relieve
DEBARRED > DEBAR
DEBARRING > DEBAR
DEBARS > DEBAR
DEBASE *vb* lower in value, quality, or character
DEBASED > DEBASE
DEBASER > DEBASE
DEBASERS > DEBASE
DEBASES > DEBASE
DEBASING > DEBASE
DEBATABLE *adj* not absolutely certain
DEBATABLY > DEBATABLE
DEBATE *n* discussion ▷ *vb* discuss formally
DEBATED > DEBATE
DEBATEFUL *adj* quarrelsome
DEBATER > DEBATE
DEBATERS > DEBATE
DEBATES > DEBATE
DEBATING > DEBATE
DEBAUCH *vb* make (someone) bad or corrupt, esp sexually ▷ *n* instance or period of extreme dissipation
DEBAUCHED > DEBAUCH
DEBAUCHEE *n* man who leads a life of reckless drinking, promiscuity, and self-indulgence
DEBAUCHER > DEBAUCH
DEBAUCHES > DEBAUCH
DEBBIER > DEBBY
DEBBIES > DEBBY
DEBBIEST > DEBBY
DEBBY *n* debutante ▷ *adj* of, or resembling a debutante
DEBE *n* tin
DEBEAK *vb* remove part of the beak of poultry to reduce the risk of such habits as feather-picking or cannibalism
DEBEAKED > DEBEAK
DEBEAKING > DEBEAK
DEBEAKS > DEBEAK
DEBEARD *vb* remove beard from mussel
DEBEARDED > DEBEARD
DEBEARDS > DEBEARD
DEBEL *vb* beat in war
DEBELLED > DEBEL
DEBELLING > DEBEL
DEBELS > DEBEL
DEBENTURE *n* long-term bond bearing fixed interest, issued by a company or a government agency
DEBES > DEBE
DEBILE *adj* lacking strength
DEBILITY *n* weakness, infirmity
DEBIT *n* acknowledgment of a sum owing by entry on the left side of an account ▷ *vb* charge (an account) with a debt
DEBITED > DEBIT
DEBITING > DEBIT
DEBITOR *n* person in debt
DEBITORS > DEBITOR
DEBITS > DEBIT
DEBONAIR *adj* (of a man) charming and refined
DEBONAIRE *adj* sauve and refined
DEBONE *vb* remove bones from
DEBONED > DEBONE
DEBONER > DEBONE
DEBONERS > DEBONE
DEBONES > DEBONE
DEBONING > DEBONE
DEBOSH *vb* debauch
DEBOSHED > DEBOSH
DEBOSHES > DEBOSH
DEBOSHING > DEBOSH
DEBOSS *vb* carve a design into
DEBOSSED > DEBOSS
DEBOSSES > DEBOSS
DEBOSSING > DEBOSS
DEBOUCH *vb* move out from a narrow place to a wider one ▷ *n* outlet or passage, as for the exit of troops
DEBOUCHE *same as* > DEBOUCH
DEBOUCHED > DEBOUCH
DEBOUCHES > DEBOUCH
DEBRIDE *vb* remove dead tissue from
DEBRIDED > DEBRIDE
DEBRIDES > DEBRIDE
DEBRIDING > DEBRIDE
DEBRIEF *vb* receive a report from (a soldier, diplomat, etc) after an event
DEBRIEFED > DEBRIEF
DEBRIEFER > DEBRIEF
DEBRIEFS > DEBRIEF
DEBRIS *n* fragments of something destroyed
DEBRUISE *vb* (in heraldry) overlay or partly cover
DEBRUISED > DEBRUISE
DEBRUISES > DEBRUISE
DEBS > DEB
DEBT *n* something owed, esp money
DEBTED *adj* in debt
DEBTEE *n* person owed a debt
DEBTEES > DEBTEE
DEBTLESS > DEBT
DEBTOR *n* person who owes money
DEBTORS > DEBTOR
DEBTS > DEBT
DEBUD *same as* > DISBUD
DEBUDDED > DEBUD
DEBUDDING > DEBUD
DEBUDS > DEBUD
DEBUG *vb* find and remove defects in (a computer program) ▷ *n* something, esp a computer program, that locates and removes defects in a device, system, etc
DEBUGGED > DEBUG
DEBUGGER > DEBUG
DEBUGGERS > DEBUG
DEBUGGING > DEBUG
DEBUGS > DEBUG
DEBUNK *vb* expose the falseness of
DEBUNKED > DEBUNK
DEBUNKER > DEBUNK
DEBUNKERS > DEBUNK
DEBUNKING > DEBUNK
DEBUNKS > DEBUNK
DEBURR *vb* remove burrs from (a workpiece)
DEBURRED > DEBURR
DEBURRING > DEBURR
DEBURRS > DEBURR
DEBUS *vb* unload (goods) or (esp of troops) to alight from a motor vehicle
DEBUSED > DEBUS
DEBUSES > DEBUS
DEBUSING > DEBUS
DEBUSSED > DEBUS
DEBUSSES > DEBUS
DEBUSSING > DEBUS
DEBUT *n* first public appearance of a performer ▷ *vb* make a debut
DEBUTANT *n* person who is making a first appearance in a particular capacity, such as a sportsperson playing in a first game for a team
DEBUTANTE *n* young upper-class woman being formally presented to society
DEBUTANTS > DEBUTANT
DEBUTED > DEBUT
DEBUTING > DEBUT
DEBUTS > DEBUT
DEBYE *n* unit of electric dipole moment
DEBYES > DEBYE
DECACHORD *n* instrument with ten strings
DECAD *n* ten years
DECADAL > DECADE
DECADE *n* period of ten years
DECADENCE *n* deterioration in morality or culture
DECADENCY *same as* > DECADENCE
DECADENT *adj* characterized by decay or decline, as in being self-indulgent or morally corrupt ▷ *n* decadent person
DECADENTS > DECADENT
DECADES > DECADE
DECADS > DECAD
DECAF *n* decaffeinated coffee ▷ *adj* decaffeinated
DECAFF *n* decaffeinated coffee
DECAFFS > DECAFF
DECAFS > DECAF
DECAGON *n* geometric figure with ten faces
DECAGONAL > DECAGON
DECAGONS > DECAGON
DECAGRAM *n* ten grams
DECAGRAMS > DECAGRAM
DECAHEDRA *n* plural form of singular decahedron: solid figure with ten plane faces
DECAL *vb* transfer (a design) by decalcomania
DECALCIFY *vb* remove calcium or lime from (bones, teeth, etc)
DECALED > DECAL
DECALING > DECAL
DECALITER *same as* > DECALITRE
DECALITRE *n* measure of volume equivalent to 10 litres
DECALLED > DECAL
DECALLING > DECAL
DECALOG *same as* > DECALOGUE
DECALOGS > DECALOG
DECALOGUE *n* Ten Commandments
DECALS > DECAL
DECAMETER *same as* > DECAMETRE
DECAMETRE *n* unit of length equal to ten metres
DECAMP *vb* depart secretly or suddenly
DECAMPED > DECAMP
DECAMPING > DECAMP
DECAMPS > DECAMP
DECANAL *adj* of or relating to a dean or deanery
DECANALLY > DECANAL
DECANE *n* liquid alkane hydrocarbon
DECANES > DECANE
DECANI *adv* be sung by the decanal side of a choir
DECANOIC as in *decanoic acid* white crystalline insoluble carboxylic acid with an unpleasant odour, used in perfumes and for making fruit flavours
DECANT *vb* pour (a liquid) from one container to another
DECANTATE *vb* decant
DECANTED > DECANT
DECANTER *n* stoppered bottle for wine or spirits
DECANTERS > DECANTER
DECANTING > DECANT
DECANTS > DECANT
DECAPOD *n* creature, such as a crab, with five pairs of walking limbs ▷ *adj* of, relating to, or belonging to these creatures
DECAPODAL > DECAPOD
DECAPODAN > DECAPOD
DECAPODS > DECAPOD
DECARB *vb* decoke
DECARBED > DECARB
DECARBING > DECARB

DECARBS > DECARB
DECARE *n* ten ares or 1000 square metres
DECARES > DECARE
DECASTERE *n* ten steres
DECASTICH *n* poem with ten lines
DECASTYLE *n* portico consisting of ten columns
DECATHLON *n* athletic contest with ten events
DECAUDATE *vb* remove the tail from
DECAY *vb* become weaker or more corrupt ▷ *n* process of decaying
DECAYABLE > DECAY
DECAYED > DECAY
DECAYER > DECAY
DECAYERS > DECAY
DECAYING > DECAY
DECAYLESS *adj* immortal
DECAYS > DECAY
DECCIE *n* decoration
DECCIES > DECCIE
DECEASE *n* death
DECEASED *adj* dead ▷ *n* dead person
DECEASES > DECEASE
DECEASING > DECEASE
DECEDENT *n* deceased person
DECEDENTS > DECEDENT
DECEIT *n* behaviour intended to deceive
DECEITFUL *adj* full of deceit
DECEITS > DECEIT
DECEIVE *vb* mislead by lying
DECEIVED > DECEIVE
DECEIVER > DECEIVE
DECEIVERS > DECEIVE
DECEIVES > DECEIVE
DECEIVING > DECEIVE
DECELERON *n* type of aileron
DECEMVIR *n* (in ancient Rome) a member of a board of ten magistrates, esp either of the two commissions established in 451 and 450 BC to revise the laws
DECEMVIRI > DECEMVIR
DECEMVIRS > DECEMVIR
DECENARY *adj* of or relating to a tithing
DECENCIES *pl n* generally accepted standards of good behaviour
DECENCY *n* conformity to the prevailing standards of what is right
DECENNARY *same as* > DECENARY
DECENNIA > DECENNIUM
DECENNIAL *adj* lasting for ten years ▷ *n* tenth anniversary or its celebration
DECENNIUM *a less common word for* > DECADE
DECENT *adj* (of a person) polite and morally acceptable
DECENTER *vb* put out of centre
DECENTERS > DECENTER
DECENTEST > DECENT
DECENTLY > DECENT
DECENTRE *vb* put out of centre
DECENTRED > DECENTRE
DECENTRES > DECENTRE
DECEPTION *n* deceiving
DECEPTIVE *adj* likely or designed to deceive
DECEPTORY *adj* deceiving
DECERN *vb* decree or adjudge
DECERNED > DECERN
DECERNING > DECERN
DECERNS > DECERN
DECERTIFY *vb* withdraw or remove a certificate or certification from (a person, organization, or country)
DECESSION *n* departure
DECHEANCE *n* forfeiting
DECIARE *n* one tenth of an are or 10 square metres
DECIARES > DECIARE
DECIBEL *n* unit for measuring the intensity of sound
DECIBELS > DECIBEL
DECIDABLE *adj* able to be decided
DECIDE *vb* (cause to) reach a decision
DECIDED *adj* unmistakable
DECIDEDLY > DECIDED
DECIDER *n* point, goal, game, etc, that determines who wins a match or championship
DECIDERS > DECIDER
DECIDES > DECIDE
DECIDING > DECIDE
DECIDUA *n* specialized mucous membrane that lines the uterus of some mammals during pregnancy: is shed, with the placenta, at parturition
DECIDUAE > DECIDUA
DECIDUAL > DECIDUA
DECIDUAS > DECIDUA
DECIDUATE > DECIDUA
DECIDUOUS *adj* (of a tree) shedding its leaves annually
DECIGRAM *n* tenth of a gram
DECIGRAMS > DECIGRAM
DECILE *n* one of nine actual or notional values of a variable dividing its distribution into ten groups with equal frequencies: the ninth decile is the value below which 90% of the population lie
DECILES > DECILE
DECILITER *same as* > DECILITRE
DECILITRE *n* measure of volume equivalent to one tenth of a litre
DECILLION *n* (in Britain, France, and Germany) the number represented as one followed by 60 zeros (10^{60})
DECIMAL *n* fraction written in the form of a dot followed by one or more numbers ▷ *adj* relating to or using powers of ten
DECIMALLY > DECIMAL
DECIMALS > DECIMAL
DECIMATE *vb* destroy or kill a large proportion of
DECIMATED > DECIMATE
DECIMATES > DECIMATE
DECIMATOR > DECIMATE
DECIME *n* a former French coin
DECIMES > DECIME
DECIMETER *same as* > DECIMETRE
DECIMETRE *n* unit of length equal to one tenth of a metre
DECIPHER *vb* work out the meaning of (something illegible or in code)
DECIPHERS > DECIPHER
DECISION *n* judgment, conclusion, or resolution
DECISIONS > DECISION
DECISIVE *adj* having a definite influence
DECISORY *adj* deciding
DECISTERE *n* tenth of a stere
DECK *n* area of a ship that forms a floor ▷ dress or decorate
DECKCHAIR *n* folding wooden and canvas chair designed for use outside
DECKED *adj* having a wooden deck or platform
DECKEL *same as* > DECKLE
DECKELS > DECKEL
DECKER > DECK
DECKERS > DECK
DECKHAND *n* seaman assigned various duties, such as mooring and cargo handling, on the deck of a ship
DECKHANDS > DECKHAND
DECKHOUSE *n* houselike cabin on the deck of a ship
DECKING *n* wooden platform in a garden
DECKINGS > DECKING
DECKLE *n* frame used to contain pulp on the mould in the making of handmade paper
DECKLED > DECKLE
DECKLES > DECKLE
DECKO *n* look ▷ *vb* have a look
DECKOED > DECKO
DECKOING > DECKO
DECKOS > DECKO
DECKS > DECK
DECLAIM *vb* speak loudly and dramatically
DECLAIMED > DECLAIM
DECLAIMER > DECLAIM
DECLAIMS > DECLAIM
DECLARANT *n* person who makes a declaration
DECLARE *vb* state firmly and forcefully
DECLARED > DECLARE
DECLARER *n* person who declares
DECLARERS > DECLARER
DECLARES > DECLARE
DECLARING > DECLARE
DECLASS *vb* lower in social status or position
DECLASSE *adj* having lost social standing or status
DECLASSED > DECLASS
DECLASSEE *adj* (of a woman) having lost social standing or status
DECLASSES > DECLASS
DECLAW *vb* remove claws from
DECLAWED > DECLAW
DECLAWING > DECLAW
DECLAWS > DECLAW
DECLINAL *adj* bending down
DECLINANT *adj* heraldry term
DECLINATE *adj* (esp of plant parts) descending from the horizontal in a curve
DECLINE *vb* become smaller, weaker, or less important ▷ *n* gradual weakening or loss
DECLINED > DECLINE
DECLINER > DECLINE
DECLINERS > DECLINE
DECLINES > DECLINE
DECLINING > DECLINE
DECLINIST *n* person believing something is in decline
DECLIVITY *n* downward slope
DECLIVOUS *adj* steep
DECLUTCH *vb* disengage the clutch of a motor vehicle
DECLUTTER *vb* simplify or get rid of mess, disorder, complications, etc
DECO as in *art deco* style of art, jewellery, design, etc
DECOCT *vb* extract the essence from (a substance) by boiling
DECOCTED > DECOCT
DECOCTING > DECOCT
DECOCTION *n* extraction by boiling
DECOCTIVE > DECOCT
DECOCTS > DECOCT
DECOCTURE *n* substance obtained by decoction

DECODE *vb* convert from code into ordinary language
DECODED > DECODE
DECODER > DECODE
DECODERS > DECODE
DECODES > DECODE
DECODING > DECODE
DECOHERER *n* electrical device
DECOKE *same as* > DECARBONIZE
DECOKED > DECOKE
DECOKES > DECOKE
DECOKING > DECOKE
DECOLLATE *vb* separate (continuous stationery, etc) into individual forms
DECOLLETE *adj* (of a woman's garment) low-cut ▷ *n* low-cut neckline
DECOLOR *vb* bleach
DECOLORED > DECOLOR
DECOLORS > DECOLOR
DECOLOUR *vb* deprive of colour, as by bleaching
DECOLOURS > DECOLOUR
DECOMMIT *vb* withdraw from a commitment or agreed course of action
DECOMMITS > DECOMMIT
DECOMPLEX *adj* repeatedly compound
DECOMPOSE *vb* be broken down through chemical or bacterial action
DECONGEST *vb* relieve congestion in
DECONTROL *vb* free of restraints or controls, esp government controls
DECOR *n* style in which a room or house is decorated
DECORATE *vb* make more attractive by adding something ornamental
DECORATED > DECORATE
DECORATES > DECORATE
DECORATOR *n* person whose profession is the painting and wallpapering of buildings
DECOROUS *adj* polite, calm, and sensible in behaviour
DECORS > DECOR
DECORUM *n* polite and socially correct behaviour
DECORUMS > DECORUM
DECOS > DECO
DECOUPAGE *n* art or process of decorating a surface with shapes or illustrations cut from paper, card, etc
DECOUPLE *vb* separate (joined or coupled subsystems) thereby enabling them to exist and operate separately
DECOUPLED > DECOUPLE
DECOUPLER > DECOUPLE
DECOUPLES > DECOUPLE
DECOY *n* person or thing used to lure someone into danger ▷ *vb* lure away by means of a trick
DECOYED > DECOY
DECOYER > DECOY
DECOYERS > DECOY
DECOYING > DECOY
DECOYS > DECOY
DECREASE *vb* make or become less ▷ *n* lessening, reduction
DECREASED > DECREASE
DECREASES > DECREASE
DECREE *n* law made by someone in authority ▷ *vb* order by decree
DECREED > DECREE
DECREEING > DECREE
DECREER > DECREE
DECREERS > DECREE
DECREES > DECREE
DECREET *n* final judgment or sentence of a court
DECREETS > DECREET
DECREMENT *n* act of decreasing
DECREPIT *adj* weakened or worn out by age or long use
DECRETAL *n* papal decree ▷ *adj* of or relating to a decretal or a decree
DECRETALS > DECRETAL
DECRETIST *n* law student
DECRETIVE *adj* of a decree
DECRETORY *adj* of a decree
DECREW *vb* decrease
DECREWED > DECREW
DECREWING > DECREW
DECREWS > DECREW
DECRIAL > DECRY
DECRIALS > DECRY
DECRIED > DECRY
DECRIER > DECRY
DECRIERS > DECRY
DECRIES > DECRY
DECROWN *vb* depose
DECROWNED > DECROWN
DECROWNS > DECROWN
DECRY *vb* express disapproval of
DECRYING > DECRY
DECRYPT *vb* decode (a message) with or without previous knowledge of its key
DECRYPTED > DECRYPT
DECRYPTS > DECRYPT
DECTET *n* ten musicians
DECTETS > DECTET
DECUBITAL > DECUBITUS
DECUBITI > DECUBITUS
DECUBITUS *n* posture adopted when lying down
DECUMAN *n* large wave
DECUMANS > DECUMAN
DECUMBENT *adj* lying down or lying flat
DECUPLE *vb* increase by ten times ▷ *n* amount ten times as large as a given reference ▷ *adj* increasing tenfold
DECUPLED > DECUPLE
DECUPLES > DECUPLE
DECUPLING > DECUPLE
DECURIA *n* group of ten
DECURIAS > DECURIA
DECURIES > DECURY
DECURION *n* local councillor
DECURIONS > DECURION
DECURRENT *adj* extending down the stem, esp (of a leaf) having the base of the blade extending down the stem as two wings
DECURSION *n* state of being decurrent
DECURSIVE *adj* extending downwards
DECURVE *vb* curve downwards
DECURVED *adj* bent or curved downwards
DECURVES > DECURVE
DECURVING > DECURVE
DECURY *n* (in ancient Rome) a body of ten men
DECUSSATE *vb* cross or cause to cross in the form of the letter X ▷ *adj* in the form of the letter X
DEDAL *same as* > DAEDAL
DEDALIAN *adj* of Daedalus
DEDANS *n* open gallery at the server's end of the court
DEDICANT *n* person who dedicates
DEDICANTS > DEDICANT
DEDICATE *vb* commit (oneself or one's time) wholly to a special purpose or cause
DEDICATED *adj* devoted to a particular purpose or cause
DEDICATEE > DEDICATE
DEDICATES > DEDICATE
DEDICATOR > DEDICATE
DEDIMUS *n* legal term
DEDIMUSES > DEDIMUS
DEDUCE *vb* reach (a conclusion) by reasoning from evidence
DEDUCED > DEDUCE
DEDUCES > DEDUCE
DEDUCIBLE > DEDUCE
DEDUCIBLY > DEDUCE
DEDUCING > DEDUCE
DEDUCT *vb* subtract
DEDUCTED > DEDUCT
DEDUCTING > DEDUCT
DEDUCTION *n* deducting
DEDUCTIVE *adj* of or relating to deduction
DEDUCTS > DEDUCT
DEE *a Scot word for* > DIE
DEED *n* something that is done ▷ *vb* convey or transfer (property) by deed ▷ *adj* Scots form of dead
DEEDED > DEED
DEEDER > DEED
DEEDEST > DEED
DEEDFUL *adj* full of exploits
DEEDIER > DEEDY
DEEDIEST > DEEDY
DEEDILY > DEEDY
DEEDING > DEED
DEEDLESS *adj* without exploits
DEEDS > DEED
DEEDY *adj* hard-working
DEEING > DEE
DEEJAY *n* disc jockey ▷ *vb* work or act as a disc jockey
DEEJAYED > DEEJAY
DEEJAYING > DEEJAY
DEEJAYS > DEEJAY
DEEK *vb* look at
DEELY as in *deely boppers* hairband with two bobbing antennae-like attachments
DEEM *vb* consider, judge
DEEMED > DEEM
DEEMING > DEEM
DEEMS > DEEM
DEEMSTER *n* title of one of the two justices in the Isle of Man
DEEMSTERS > DEEMSTER
DEEN *n* din
DEENS > DEEN
DEEP *adj* extending or situated far down, inwards, backwards, or sideways ▷ *n* any deep place on land or under water
DEEPEN *vb* make or become deeper or more intense
DEEPENED > DEEPEN
DEEPENER > DEEPEN
DEEPENERS > DEEPEN
DEEPENING > DEEPEN
DEEPENS > DEEPEN
DEEPER > DEEP
DEEPEST > DEEP
DEEPFELT *adj* sincere
DEEPFROZE *vb* froze in a freezer
DEEPIE *n* 3D film
DEEPIES > DEEPIE
DEEPLY > DEEP
DEEPMOST *adj* deepest
DEEPNESS > DEEP
DEEPS > DEEP
DEEPWATER *adj* seagoing
DEER *n* large wild animal, the male of which has antlers
DEERBERRY *n* huckleberry
DEERE *adj* serious
DEERFLIES > DEERFLY
DEERFLY *n* insect related to the horsefly
DEERGRASS *n* perennial cyperaceous plant, *Trichophorum caespitosum*, that grows in dense tufts in peat bogs of temperate regions
DEERHORN *n* deer's antler
DEERHORNS > DEERHORN
DEERHOUND *n* very large rough-coated breed of dog of the greyhound type
DEERLET *n* ruminant mammal

DEERLETS > DEERLET
DEERLIKE *adj* like a deer
DEERS > DEER
DEERSKIN *n* hide of a deer
DEERSKINS > DEERSKIN
DEERWEED *n* forage plant
DEERWEEDS > DEERWEED
DEERYARD *n* gathering place for deer
DEERYARDS > DEERYARD
DEES > DEE
DEET *n* insect-repellent
DEETS > DEET
DEEV *n* mythical monster
DEEVE *vb* deafen
DEEVED > DEEVE
DEEVES > DEEVE
DEEVING > DEEVE
DEEVS > DEEV
DEEWAN *n* chief of a village in India
DEEWANS > DEEWAN
DEF *adj* very good
DEFACE *vb* deliberately spoil the appearance of
DEFACED > DEFACE
DEFACER > DEFACE
DEFACERS > DEFACE
DEFACES > DEFACE
DEFACING > DEFACE
DEFAECATE *same as* > DEFECATE
DEFALCATE *vb* make wrong use of funds entrusted to one
DEFAME *vb* attack the good reputation of
DEFAMED > DEFAME
DEFAMER > DEFAME
DEFAMERS > DEFAME
DEFAMES > DEFAME
DEFAMING > DEFAME
DEFAMINGS > DEFAME
DEFANG *vb* remove the fangs of
DEFANGED > DEFANG
DEFANGING > DEFANG
DEFANGS > DEFANG
DEFAST *adj* defaced
DEFASTE *adj* defaced
DEFAT *vb* remove fat from
DEFATS > DEFAT
DEFATTED > DEFAT
DEFATTING > DEFAT
DEFAULT *n* failure to do something ▷ *vb* fail to fulfil an obligation
DEFAULTED > DEFAULT
DEFAULTER *n* person who defaults
DEFAULTS > DEFAULT
DEFEAT *vb* win a victory over ▷ *n* defeating
DEFEATED > DEFEAT
DEFEATER > DEFEAT
DEFEATERS > DEFEAT
DEFEATING > DEFEAT
DEFEATISM *n* ready acceptance or expectation of defeat
DEFEATIST > DEFEATISM
DEFEATS > DEFEAT
DEFEATURE *vb* deform
DEFECATE *vb* discharge waste from the body through the anus
DEFECATED > DEFECATE
DEFECATES > DEFECATE
DEFECATOR > DEFECATE
DEFECT *n* imperfection, blemish ▷ *vb* desert one's cause or country to join the opposing forces
DEFECTED > DEFECT
DEFECTING > DEFECT
DEFECTION *n* act or an instance of defecting
DEFECTIVE *adj* imperfect, faulty
DEFECTOR > DEFECT
DEFECTORS > DEFECT
DEFECTS > DEFECT
DEFENCE *n* resistance against attack
DEFENCED > DEFENCE
DEFENCES > DEFENCE
DEFENCING > DEFENCE
DEFEND *vb* protect from harm or danger
DEFENDANT *n* person accused of a crime ▷ *adj* making a defence
DEFENDED > DEFEND
DEFENDER > DEFEND
DEFENDERS > DEFEND
DEFENDING > DEFEND
DEFENDS > DEFEND
DEFENSE *same as* > DEFENCE
DEFENSED > DEFENSE
DEFENSES > DEFENSE
DEFENSING > DEFENSE
DEFENSIVE *adj* intended for defence
DEFER *vb* delay (something) until a future time
DEFERABLE > DEFER
DEFERENCE *n* polite and respectful behaviour
DEFERENT *adj* (esp of a bodily nerve, vessel, or duct) conveying an impulse, fluid, etc, outwards, down, or away ▷ *n* (in the Ptolemaic system) a circle centred on the earth around which the centre of the epicycle was thought to move
DEFERENTS > DEFERENT
DEFERMENT *n* act of deferring or putting off until another time
DEFERRAL *same as* > DEFERMENT
DEFERRALS > DEFERRAL
DEFERRED *adj* withheld over a certain period
DEFERRER > DEFER
DEFERRERS > DEFER
DEFERRING > DEFER
DEFERS > DEFER
DEFFER > DEF
DEFFEST > DEF
DEFFLY *archaic word meaning the same as* > DEFTLY
DEFFO *interj* definitely: an expression of agreement or consent
DEFI *n* challenge
DEFIANCE *n* open resistance or disobedience
DEFIANCES > DEFIANCE
DEFIANT *adj* marked by resistance or bold opposition, as to authority
DEFIANTLY > DEFIANT
DEFICIENT *adj* lacking some essential thing or quality
DEFICIT *n* amount by which a sum of money is too small
DEFICITS > DEFICIT
DEFIED > DEFY
DEFIER > DEFY
DEFIERS > DEFY
DEFIES > DEFY
DEFILADE *n* protection provided by obstacles against enemy crossfire from the rear, or observation ▷ *vb* provide protection for by defilade
DEFILADED > DEFILADE
DEFILADES > DEFILADE
DEFILE *vb* treat (something sacred or important) without respect ▷ *n* narrow valley or pass
DEFILED > DEFILE
DEFILER > DEFILE
DEFILERS > DEFILE
DEFILES > DEFILE
DEFILING > DEFILE
DEFINABLE > DEFINE
DEFINABLY > DEFINE
DEFINE *vb* state precisely the meaning of
DEFINED > DEFINE
DEFINER > DEFINE
DEFINERS > DEFINE
DEFINES > DEFINE
DEFINIENS *n* word or words used to define or give an account of the meaning of another word, as in a dictionary entry
DEFINING > DEFINE
DEFINITE *adj* firm, clear, and precise
DEFIS > DEFI
DEFLATE *vb* (cause to) collapse through the release of air
DEFLATED > DEFLATE
DEFLATER > DEFLATE
DEFLATERS > DEFLATE
DEFLATES > DEFLATE
DEFLATING > DEFLATE
DEFLATION *n* reduction in economic activity resulting in lower output and investment
DEFLATOR > DEFLATE
DEFLATORS > DEFLATE
DEFLEA *vb* remove fleas from
DEFLEAED > DEFLEA
DEFLEAING > DEFLEA
DEFLEAS > DEFLEA
DEFLECT *vb* (cause to) turn aside from a course
DEFLECTED > DEFLECT
DEFLECTOR > DEFLECT
DEFLECTS > DEFLECT
DEFLEX *vb* turn downwards
DEFLEXED > DEFLEX
DEFLEXES > DEFLEX
DEFLEXING > DEFLEX
DEFLEXION *same as* > DEFLECTION
DEFLEXURE *n* act of deflecting
DEFLORATE *vb* deflower
DEFLOWER *vb* deprive (a woman) of her virginity
DEFLOWERS > DEFLOWER
DEFLUENT *adj* running downwards
DEFLUXION *n* discharge
DEFOAM *vb* remove foam from
DEFOAMED > DEFOAM
DEFOAMER > DEFOAM
DEFOAMERS > DEFOAM
DEFOAMING > DEFOAM
DEFOAMS > DEFOAM
DEFOCUS *vb* put out of focus
DEFOCUSED > DEFOCUS
DEFOCUSES > DEFOCUS
DEFOG *vb* clear of vapour
DEFOGGED > DEFOG
DEFOGGER > DEFOG
DEFOGGERS > DEFOG
DEFOGGING > DEFOG
DEFOGS > DEFOG
DEFOLIANT *n* chemical sprayed or dusted onto trees to cause their leaves to fall, esp to remove cover from an enemy in warfare
DEFOLIATE *vb* deprive (a plant) of its leaves ▷ *adj* (of a plant) having shed its leaves
DEFORCE *vb* withhold (property, esp land) wrongfully or by force from the rightful owner
DEFORCED > DEFORCE
DEFORCER > DEFORCE
DEFORCERS > DEFORCE
DEFORCES > DEFORCE
DEFORCING > DEFORCE
DEFOREST *vb* clear of trees
DEFORESTS > DEFOREST
DEFORM *vb* put out of shape or spoil the appearance of
DEFORMED *adj* disfigured or misshapen
DEFORMER > DEFORM
DEFORMERS > DEFORM
DEFORMING > DEFORM
DEFORMITY *n* distortion of a body part
DEFORMS > DEFORM
DEFOUL *vb* defile
DEFOULED > DEFOUL
DEFOULING > DEFOUL
DEFOULS > DEFOUL
DEFRAG *vb* defragment

DEFRAGGED > DEFRAG
DEFRAGGER > DEFRAG
DEFRAGS > DEFRAG
DEFRAUD *vb* cheat out of money, property, etc
DEFRAUDED > DEFRAUD
DEFRAUDER > DEFRAUD
DEFRAUDS > DEFRAUD
DEFRAY *vb* provide money for (costs or expenses)
DEFRAYAL > DEFRAY
DEFRAYALS > DEFRAY
DEFRAYED > DEFRAY
DEFRAYER > DEFRAY
DEFRAYERS > DEFRAY
DEFRAYING > DEFRAY
DEFRAYS > DEFRAY
DEFREEZE *vb* defrost
DEFREEZES > DEFREEZE
DEFROCK *vb* deprive (a priest) of priestly status
DEFROCKED > DEFROCK
DEFROCKS > DEFROCK
DEFROST *vb* make or become free of ice
DEFROSTED > DEFROST
DEFROSTER *n* device by which the de-icing process of a refrigerator is accelerated, usually by circulating the refrigerant without the expansion process
DEFROSTS > DEFROST
DEFROZE > DEFREEZE
DEFROZEN > DEFREEZE
DEFT *adj* quick and skilful in movement
DEFTER > DEFT
DEFTEST > DEFT
DEFTLY > DEFT
DEFTNESS > DEFT
DEFUEL *vb* remove fuel from
DEFUELED > DEFUEL
DEFUELING > DEFUEL
DEFUELLED > DEFUEL
DEFUELS > DEFUEL
DEFUNCT *adj* no longer existing or operative ▷ *n* deceased person
DEFUNCTS > DEFUNCT
DEFUND *vb* stop funds to
DEFUNDED > DEFUND
DEFUNDING > DEFUND
DEFUNDS > DEFUND
DEFUSE *vb* remove the fuse of (an explosive device)
DEFUSED > DEFUSE
DEFUSER > DEFUSE
DEFUSERS > DEFUEL
DEFUSES > DEFUSE
DEFUSING > DEFUSE
DEFUZE *same as* > DEFUSE
DEFUZED > DEFUZE
DEFUZES > DEFUZE
DEFUZING > DEFUZE
DEFY *vb* resist openly and boldly
DEFYING > DEFY
DEG *vb* water (a plant, etc)
DEGAGE *adj* unconstrained in manner
DEGAME *n* tree of South and Central America
DEGAMES > DEGAME
DEGAMI *same as* > DEGAME
DEGAMIS > DEGAMI
DEGARNISH *vb* remove ornament from
DEGAS *vb* remove gas from (a container, vacuum tube, liquid, adsorbent, etc)
DEGASES > DEGAS
DEGASSED > DEGAS
DEGASSER > DEGAS
DEGASSERS > DEGAS
DEGASSES > DEGAS
DEGASSING > DEGAS
DEGAUSS *same as* > DEMAGNETIZE
DEGAUSSED > DEGAUSS
DEGAUSSER > DEGAUSS
DEGAUSSES > DEGAUSS
DEGEARING *n* process in which a company replaces some or all of its fixed-interest loan stock with ordinary shares
DEGENDER *vb* remove reference to gender from
DEGENDERS > DEGENDER
DEGERM *vb* remove germs from
DEGERMED > DEGERM
DEGERMING > DEGERM
DEGERMS > DEGERM
DEGGED > DEG
DEGGING > DEG
DEGLAZE *vb* dilute meat sediments in (a pan) in order to make a sauce or gravy
DEGLAZED > DEGLAZE
DEGLAZES > DEGLAZE
DEGLAZING > DEGLAZE
DEGOUT *n* disgust
DEGOUTS > DEGOUT
DEGRADE *vb* reduce to dishonour or disgrace
DEGRADED > DEGRADE
DEGRADER > DEGRADE
DEGRADERS > DEGRADE
DEGRADES > DEGRADE
DEGRADING *adj* causing humiliation
DEGRAS *n* emulsion used for dressing hides
DEGREASE *vb* remove grease from
DEGREASED > DEGREASE
DEGREASER > DEGREASE
DEGREASES > DEGREASE
DEGREE *n* stage in a scale of relative amount or intensity
DEGREED *adj* having a degree
DEGREES > DEGREE
DEGS > DEG
DEGUM *vb* remove gum from
DEGUMMED > DEGUM
DEGUMMING > DEGUM
DEGUMS > DEGUM
DEGUST *vb* taste, esp with care or relish
DEGUSTATE *same as* > DEGUST
DEGUSTED > DEGUST
DEGUSTING > DEGUST
DEGUSTS > DEGUST
DEHISCE *vb* (of the seed capsules of some plants) to burst open spontaneously
DEHISCED > DEHISCE
DEHISCENT *adj* (of fruits, anthers, etc) opening spontaneously to release seeds or pollen
DEHISCES > DEHISCE
DEHISCING > DEHISCE
DEHORN *vb* remove or prevent the growth of the horns of (cattle, sheep, or goats)
DEHORNED > DEHORN
DEHORNER > DEHORN
DEHORNERS > DEHORN
DEHORNING > DEHORN
DEHORNS > DEHORN
DEHORT *vb* dissuade
DEHORTED > DEHORT
DEHORTER > DEHORT
DEHORTERS > DEHORT
DEHORTING > DEHORT
DEHORTS > DEHORT
DEHYDRATE *vb* remove water from (food) to preserve it
DEI > DEUS
DEICE *vb* to free or be freed of ice
DEICED > DEICE
DEICER > DEICE
DEICERS > DEICE
DEICES > DEICE
DEICIDAL > DEICIDE
DEICIDE *n* act of killing a god
DEICIDES > DEICIDE
DEICING > DEICE
DEICTIC *adj* proving by direct argument
DEICTICS > DEICTIC
DEID *a Scot word for* > DEAD
DEIDER > DEID
DEIDEST > DEID
DEIDS > DEID
DEIF *a Scot word for* > DEAF
DEIFER > DEIF
DEIFEST > DEIF
DEIFIC *adj* making divine or exalting to the position of a god
DEIFICAL *adj* divine
DEIFIED > DEIFY
DEIFIER > DEIFY
DEIFIERS > DEIFY
DEIFIES > DEIFY
DEIFORM *adj* having the form or appearance of a god
DEIFY *vb* treat or worship as a god
DEIFYING > DEIFY
DEIGN *vb* agree (to do something), but as if doing someone a favour
DEIGNED > DEIGN
DEIGNING > DEIGN
DEIGNS > DEIGN
DEIL *a Scot word for* > DEVIL
DEILS > DEIL
DEINDEX *vb* cause to become no longer index-linked
DEINDEXED > DEINDEX
DEINDEXES > DEINDEX
DEINOSAUR *n* dinosaur
DEIONISE *same as* > DEIONIZE
DEIONISED > DEIONISE
DEIONISER > DEIONISE
DEIONISES > DEIONISE
DEIONIZE *vb* to remove ions from (water, etc), esp by ion exchange
DEIONIZED > DEIONIZE
DEIONIZER > DEIONIZE
DEIONIZES > DEIONIZE
DEIPAROUS *adj* giving birth to a god
DEISEAL *n* clockwise motion
DEISEALS > DEISEAL
DEISHEAL *n* clockwise motion
DEISHEALS > DEISHEAL
DEISM *n* belief in God but not in divine revelation
DEISMS > DEISM
DEIST > DEISM
DEISTIC > DEISM
DEISTICAL > DEISM
DEISTS > DEISM
DEITIES > DEITY
DEITY *n* god or goddess
DEIXES > DEIXIS
DEIXIS *n* use or reference of a deictic word
DEIXISES > DEIXIS
DEJECT *vb* have a depressing effect on ▷ *adj* downcast
DEJECTA *pl n* waste products excreted through the anus
DEJECTED *adj* unhappy
DEJECTING > DEJECT
DEJECTION *n* lowness of spirits
DEJECTORY *adj* causing dejection
DEJECTS > DEJECT
DEJEUNE *n* lunch
DEJEUNER *n* lunch
DEJEUNERS > DEJEUNER
DEJEUNES > DEJEUNE
DEKAGRAM *n* ten grams
DEKAGRAMS > DEKAGRAM
DEKALITER *n* ten litres
DEKALITRE *n* ten litres
DEKALOGY *n* series of ten related works
DEKAMETER *n* ten meters
DEKAMETRE *n* ten metres
DEKARE *n* unit of measurement equal to ten ares
DEKARES > DEKARE
DEKE *vb* (in ice hockey or box lacrosse) to draw (a defending player) out of position by faking a shot or movement ▷ *n* such a shot or movement

DEKED > DEKE
DEKEING > DEKE
DEKES > DEKE
DEKING > DEKE
DEKKO *n* look ▷ *vb* have a look
DEKKOED > DEKKO
DEKKOING > DEKKO
DEKKOS > DEKKO
DEL *n* differential operator
DELAINE *n* sheer wool or wool and cotton fabric
DELAINES > DELAINE
DELAPSE *vb* be inherited
DELAPSED > DELAPSE
DELAPSES > DELAPSE
DELAPSING > DELAPSE
DELAPSION *n* falling down
DELATE *vb* (formerly) to bring a charge against
DELATED > DELATE
DELATES > DELATE
DELATING > DELATE
DELATION > DELATE
DELATIONS > DELATE
DELATOR > DELATE
DELATORS > DELATE
DELAY *vb* put off to a later time ▷ *n* act of delaying
DELAYABLE > DELAY
DELAYED > DELAY
DELAYER > DELAY
DELAYERS > DELAY
DELAYING > DELAY
DELAYS > DELAY
DELE *n* sign indicating that typeset matter is to be deleted ▷ *vb* mark (matter to be deleted) with a dele
DELEAD *vb* remove lead from
DELEADED > DELEAD
DELEADING > DELEAD
DELEADS > DELEAD
DELEAVE *vb* separate copies
DELEAVED > DELEAVE
DELEAVES > DELEAVE
DELEAVING > DELEAVE
DELEBLE *adj* able to be deleted
DELECTATE *vb* delight
DELED > DELE
DELEGABLE > DELEGATE
DELEGACY *n* elected standing committee at some British universities
DELEGATE *n* person chosen to represent others, esp at a meeting ▷ *vb* entrust (duties or powers) to someone
DELEGATED > DELEGATE
DELEGATEE > DELEGATE
DELEGATES > DELEGATE
DELEGATOR > DELEGATE
DELEING > DELE
DELENDA *pl n* items for deleting
DELES > DELE
DELETABLE > DELETE
DELETE *vb* remove (something written or printed)
DELETED > DELETE
DELETES > DELETE
DELETING > DELETE
DELETION *n* act of deleting or fact of being deleted
DELETIONS > DELETION
DELETIVE > DELETE
DELETORY > DELETE
DELF *n* kind of earthenware
DELFS > DELF
DELFT *n* tin-glazed earthenware, typically having blue designs on white
DELFTS > DELFT
DELFTWARE *same as* > DELFT
DELI *n* delicatessen
DELIBATE *vb* taste
DELIBATED > DELIBATE
DELIBATES > DELIBATE
DELIBLE *adj* able to be deleted
DELICACY *n* being delicate
DELICATE *adj* fine or subtle in quality or workmanship ▷ *n* delicacy
DELICATES > DELICATE
DELICE *n* delicacy
DELICES > DELICE
DELICIOUS *adj* very appealing to taste or smell
DELICT *n* wrongful act for which the person injured has the right to a civil remedy
DELICTS > DELICT
DELIGHT *n* (source of) great pleasure ▷ *vb* please greatly
DELIGHTED *adj* greatly pleased ▷ *sentence substitute* I should be delighted to!
DELIGHTER > DELIGHT
DELIGHTS > DELIGHT
DELIME *vb* remove lime from
DELIMED > DELIME
DELIMES > DELIME
DELIMING > DELIME
DELIMIT *vb* mark or lay down the limits of
DELIMITED > DELIMIT
DELIMITER > DELIMIT
DELIMITS > DELIMIT
DELINEATE *vb* show by drawing
DELIQUIUM *n* loss of consciousness
DELIRIA > DELIRIUM
DELIRIANT > DELIRIUM
DELIRIOUS *adj* suffering from delirium
DELIRIUM *n* state of excitement and mental confusion, often with hallucinations
DELIRIUMS > DELIRIUM
DELIS > DELI
DELISH *adj* delicious
DELIST *vb* remove from a list
DELISTED > DELIST
DELISTING > DELIST
DELISTS > DELIST
DELIVER *vb* carry (goods etc) to a destination
DELIVERED > DELIVER
DELIVERER > DELIVER
DELIVERLY *adv* quickly
DELIVERS > DELIVER
DELIVERY *n* delivering
DELL *n* small wooded hollow
DELLIES > DELLY
DELLS > DELL
DELLY *n* delicatessen
DELO *an informal word for* > DELEGATE
DELOPE *vb* shoot into the air
DELOPED > DELOPE
DELOPES > DELOPE
DELOPING > DELOPE
DELOS > DELO
DELOUSE *vb* rid (a person or animal) of lice
DELOUSED > DELOUSE
DELOUSER > DELOUSE
DELOUSERS > DELOUSE
DELOUSES > DELOUSE
DELOUSING > DELOUSE
DELPH *n* kind of earthenware
DELPHIC *adj* obscure or ambiguous
DELPHIN *n* fatty substance from dolphin oil
DELPHINIA *n* plural form of singular delphinium: garden plant with blue, white or pink flowers
DELPHS > DELPH
DELS > DEL
DELT *n* deltoid muscle
DELTA *n* fourth letter in the Greek alphabet
DELTAIC > DELTA
DELTAS > DELTA
DELTIC > DELTA
DELTOID *n* thick muscle forming the rounded contour of the outer edge of the shoulder and acting to raise the arm ▷ *adj* shaped like a Greek capital delta
DELTOIDEI *n* deltoid
DELTOIDS > DELTOID
DELTS > DELT
DELUBRUM *n* shrine
DELUBRUMS > DELUBRUM
DELUDABLE > DELUDE
DELUDE *vb* deceive
DELUDED > DELUDE
DELUDER > DELUDE
DELUDERS > DELUDE
DELUDES > DELUDE
DELUDING > DELUDE
DELUGE *n* great flood ▷ *vb* flood
DELUGED > DELUGE
DELUGES > DELUGE
DELUGING > DELUGE
DELUNDUNG *n* spotted mammal
DELUSION *n* mistaken idea or belief
DELUSIONS > DELUSION
DELUSIVE > DELUSION
DELUSORY > DELUSION
DELUSTER *vb* remove the lustre from
DELUSTERS > DELUSTER
DELUXE *adj* rich, elegant, superior, or sumptuous
DELVE *vb* research deeply (for information)
DELVED > DELVE
DELVER > DELVE
DELVERS > DELVE
DELVES > DELVE
DELVING > DELVE
DEMAGOG *same as* > DEMAGOGUE
DEMAGOGED > DEMAGOG
DEMAGOGIC *adj* of, characteristic of, relating to, or resembling a demagogue
DEMAGOGS > DEMAGOG
DEMAGOGUE *n* political agitator who appeals to the prejudice and passions of the mob
DEMAGOGY *n* demagoguery
DEMAIN *n* demesne
DEMAINE *n* demesne
DEMAINES > DEMAINE
DEMAINS > DEMAIN
DEMAN *vb* reduce the workforce of (a plant, industry, etc)
DEMAND *vb* request forcefully ▷ *n* forceful request
DEMANDANT *n* (formerly) the plaintiff in an action relating to real property
DEMANDED > DEMAND
DEMANDER > DEMAND
DEMANDERS > DEMAND
DEMANDING *adj* requiring a lot of time or effort
DEMANDS > DEMAND
DEMANNED > DEMAN
DEMANNING > DEMAN
DEMANS > DEMAN
DEMANTOID *n* bright green variety of andradite garnet
DEMARCATE *vb* mark, fix, or draw the boundaries, limits, etc, of
DEMARCHE *n* move, step, or manoeuvre, esp in diplomatic affairs
DEMARCHES > DEMARCHE
DEMARK *vb* demarcate
DEMARKED > DEMARK
DEMARKET *vb* discourage consumers from buying (a particular product), either because it is faulty or because it could jeopardize the seller's reputation
DEMARKETS > DEMARKET
DEMARKING > DEMARK
DEMARKS > DEMARK
DEMAST *vb* remove the mast from

DEMASTED > DEMAST
DEMASTING > DEMAST
DEMASTS > DEMAST
DEMAYNE *n* demesne
DEMAYNES > DEMAYNE
DEME *n* (in preclassical Greece) the territory inhabited by a tribe
DEMEAN *vb* lower (oneself) in dignity, status, or character
DEMEANE *n* demesne
DEMEANED > DEMEAN
DEMEANES *n* demesne
DEMEANING > DEMEAN
DEMEANOR *same as* > DEMEANOUR
DEMEANORS > DEMEANOR
DEMEANOUR *n* way a person behaves
DEMEANS > DEMEAN
DEMENT *vb* deteriorate mentally, esp because of old age
DEMENTATE *vb* deteriorate mentally
DEMENTED *adj* mad
DEMENTI *n* denial
DEMENTIA *n* state of serious mental deterioration
DEMENTIAL > DEMENTIA
DEMENTIAS > DEMENTIA
DEMENTING > DEMENT
DEMENTIS > DEMENTI
DEMENTS > DEMENT
DEMERARA *n* brown crystallized cane sugar from the Caribbean and nearby countries
DEMERARAN *adj* from Demerara
DEMERARAS > DEMERARA
DEMERGE *vb* separate a company from another with which it was previously merged
DEMERGED > DEMERGE
DEMERGER *n* separation of two or more companies which have previously been merged
DEMERGERS > DEMERGER
DEMERGES > DEMERGE
DEMERGING > DEMERGE
DEMERIT *n* fault, disadvantage ▷ *vb* deserve
DEMERITED > DEMERIT
DEMERITS > DEMERIT
DEMERSAL *adj* living or occurring on the bottom of a sea or a lake
DEMERSE *vb* immerse
DEMERSED > DEMERSE
DEMERSES > DEMERSE
DEMERSING > DEMERSE
DEMERSION > DEMERSE
DEMES > DEME
DEMESNE *n* land surrounding a house
DEMESNES > DEMESNE
DEMETON *n* insecticide
DEMETONS > DEMETON
DEMIC *adj* of population
DEMIES > DEMY
DEMIGOD *n* being who is part mortal, part god
DEMIGODS > DEMIGOD
DEMIJOHN *n* large bottle with a short neck, often encased in wicker
DEMIJOHNS > DEMIJOHN
DEMILUNE *n* outwork in front of a fort, shaped like a crescent moon
DEMILUNES > DEMILUNE
DEMIMONDE *n* (esp in the 19th century) class of women considered to be outside respectable society because of promiscuity
DEMIPIQUE *n* low pique on a saddle
DEMIREP *n* woman of bad repute, esp a prostitute
DEMIREPS > DEMIREP
DEMISABLE > DEMISE
DEMISE *n* eventual failure (of something successful) ▷ *vb* transfer for a limited period
DEMISED > DEMISE
DEMISES > DEMISE
DEMISING > DEMISE
DEMISS *adj* humble
DEMISSION *n* relinquishment of or abdication from an office, responsibility, etc
DEMISSIVE *adj* humble
DEMISSLY > DEMISS
DEMIST *vb* remove condensation from (a windscreen)
DEMISTED > DEMIST
DEMISTER *n* device incorporating a heater and/or blower used in a motor vehicle to free the windscreen of condensation
DEMISTERS > DEMISTER
DEMISTING > DEMIST
DEMISTS > DEMIST
DEMIT *vb* resign (an office, position, etc)
DEMITASSE *n* small cup used to serve coffee, esp after a meal
DEMITS > DEMIT
DEMITTED > DEMIT
DEMITTING > DEMIT
DEMIURGE *n* (in the philosophy of Plato) the creator of the universe
DEMIURGES > DEMIURGE
DEMIURGIC > DEMIURGE
DEMIURGUS *n* demiurge
DEMIVEG *n* person who eats poultry and fish, but no red meat ▷ *adj* denoting a person who eats poultry and fish, but no red meat
DEMIVEGES > DEMIVEG
DEMIVOLT *n* half turn on the hind legs
DEMIVOLTE *same as* > DEMIVOLT
DEMIVOLTS > DEMIVOLT
DEMIWORLD *n* demimonde
DEMO *n* demonstration, organized expression of public opinion ▷ *vb* demonstrate
DEMOB *vb* demobilize ▷ *n* (*as modifier*)
DEMOBBED > DEMOB
DEMOBBING > DEMOB
DEMOBS > DEMOB
DEMOCRACY *n* government by the people or their elected representatives
DEMOCRAT *n* advocate of democracy
DEMOCRATS > DEMOCRAT
DEMOCRATY *n* democracy
DEMODE *adj* out of fashion
DEMODED *adj* out of fashion
DEMOED > DEMO
DEMOING > DEMO
DEMOLISH *vb* knock down or destroy (a building)
DEMOLOGY *n* demography
DEMON *n* evil spirit
DEMONESS *n* female demon
DEMONIAC *adj* appearing to be possessed by a devil ▷ *n* person possessed by an evil spirit or demon
DEMONIACS > DEMONIAC
DEMONIAN *adj* of a demon
DEMONIC *adj* evil
DEMONICAL *adj* demonic
DEMONISE *same as* > DEMONIZE
DEMONISED > DEMONISE
DEMONISES > DEMONISE
DEMONISM *same as* > DEMONOLOGY
DEMONISMS > DEMONISM
DEMONIST > DEMONISM
DEMONISTS > DEMONISM
DEMONIZE *vb* make into a demon
DEMONIZED > DEMONIZE
DEMONIZES > DEMONIZE
DEMONRIES > DEMON
DEMONRY > DEMON
DEMONS > DEMON
DEMOS *n* people of a nation regarded as a political unit
DEMOSES > DEMOS
DEMOTE *vb* reduce in status or rank
DEMOTED > DEMOTE
DEMOTES > DEMOTE
DEMOTIC *adj* of the common people ▷ *n* demotic script of ancient Egypt
DEMOTICS > DEMOTIC
DEMOTING > DEMOTE
DEMOTION > DEMOTE
DEMOTIONS > DEMOTE
DEMOTIST > DEMOTIC
DEMOTISTS > DEMOTIC
DEMOUNT *vb* remove (a motor, gun, etc) from its mounting or setting
DEMOUNTED > DEMOUNT
DEMOUNTS > DEMOUNT
DEMPSTER *same as* > DEEMSTER
DEMPSTERS > DEMPSTER
DEMPT > DEEM
DEMULCENT *adj* soothing ▷ *n* drug or agent that soothes the irritation of inflamed or injured skin surfaces
DEMULSIFY *vb* undergo or cause to undergo a process in which an emulsion is permanently broken down into its constituents
DEMUR *vb* raise objections or show reluctance ▷ *n* act of demurring
DEMURE *adj* quiet, reserved, and rather shy ▷ *vb* archaic for look demure ▷ *n* archaic for demure look
DEMURED > DEMURE
DEMURELY > DEMURE
DEMURER > DEMURE
DEMURES > DEMURE
DEMUREST > DEMURE
DEMURING > DEMURE
DEMURRAGE *n* delaying of a ship, railway wagon, etc, caused by the charterer's failure to load, unload, etc, before the time of scheduled departure
DEMURRAL *n* act of demurring
DEMURRALS > DEMURRAL
DEMURRED > DEMUR
DEMURRER *n* pleading that admits an opponent's point but denies that it is a relevant or valid argument
DEMURRERS > DEMURRER
DEMURRING > DEMUR
DEMURS > DEMUR
DEMY *n* size of printing paper, 17½ by 22½ inches (444.5 × 571.5 mm)
DEMYSHIP > DEMY
DEMYSHIPS > DEMY
DEMYSTIFY *vb* remove the mystery from
DEN *n* home of a wild animal ▷ *vb* live in or as if in a den
DENAR *n* standard monetary unit of Macedonia, divided into 100 deni
DENARI > DENAR
DENARIES > DENARIUS
DENARII > DENARIUS
DENARIUS *n* ancient Roman silver coin, often called a penny in translation
DENARS > DENAR
DENARY *adj* calculated by tens
DENATURE *vb* change the nature of
DENATURED > DENATURE

DENATURES > DENATURE
DENAY *vb* deny
DENAYED > DENAY
DENAYING > DENAY
DENAYS > DENAY
DENAZIFY *vb* free or declare (people, institutions, etc) freed from Nazi influence or ideology
DENDRIMER *n* chemical compound with treelike molecular structure
DENDRITE *n* any of the short branched threadlike extensions of a nerve cell, which conduct impulses towards the cell body
DENDRITES > DENDRITE
DENDRITIC > DENDRITE
DENDROID *adj* freely branching
DENDRON *same as* > DENDRITE
DENDRONS > DENDRON
DENE *n* narrow wooded valley
DENERVATE *vb* deprive (a tissue or organ) of its nerve supply
DENES > DENE
DENET *vb* remove from the Net Book Agreement
DENETS > DENET
DENETTED > DENET
DENETTING > DENET
DENGUE *n* viral disease transmitted by mosquitoes, characterized by headache, fever, pains in the joints, and a rash
DENGUES > DENGUE
DENI *n* monetary unit of the Former Yugoslav Republic of Macedonia, worth one hundredth of a denar
DENIABLE *adj* able to be denied
DENIABLY > DENIABLE
DENIAL *n* statement that something is not true
DENIALS > DENIAL
DENIED > DENY
DENIER *n* unit of weight used to measure the fineness of nylon or silk
DENIERS > DENIER
DENIES > DENY
DENIGRATE *vb* criticize unfairly
DENIM *n* hard-wearing cotton fabric, usu. blue
DENIMED *adj* wearing denim
DENIMS *pl n* jeans or overalls made of denim
DENIS > DENI
DENITRATE *vb* undergo or cause to undergo a process in which a compound loses a nitro or nitrate group, nitrogen dioxide, or nitric acid
DENITRIFY *vb* undergo or cause to undergo loss or removal of nitrogen compounds or nitrogen
DENIZEN *n* inhabitant ▷ *vb* make a denizen
DENIZENED > DENIZEN
DENIZENS > DENIZEN
DENNED > DEN
DENNET *n* carriage for one horse
DENNETS > DENNET
DENNING > DEN
DENOMINAL *adj* formed from a noun
DENOTABLE > DENOTE
DENOTATE *vb* denote
DENOTATED > DENOTATE
DENOTATES > DENOTATE
DENOTE *vb* be a sign of
DENOTED > DENOTE
DENOTES > DENOTE
DENOTING > DENOTE
DENOTIVE > DENOTE
DENOUNCE *vb* speak vehemently against
DENOUNCED > DENOUNCE
DENOUNCER > DENOUNCE
DENOUNCES > DENOUNCE
DENS > DEN
DENSE *adj* closely packed
DENSELY > DENSE
DENSENESS > DENSE
DENSER > DENSE
DENSEST > DENSE
DENSIFIED > DENSIFY
DENSIFIER > DENSIFY
DENSIFIES > DENSIFY
DENSIFY *vb* make or become dense
DENSITIES > DENSITY
DENSITY *n* degree to which something is filled or occupied
DENT *n* hollow in the surface of something, made by hitting it ▷ *vb* make a dent in
DENTAL *adj* of teeth or dentistry ▷ *n* dental consonant
DENTALIA > DENTALIUM
DENTALITY *n* use of teeth in pronouncing words
DENTALIUM *n* any scaphopod mollusc of the genus *Dentalium*
DENTALLY > DENTAL
DENTALS > DENTAL
DENTARIA *n* botanical term
DENTARIAS > DENTARIA
DENTARIES > DENTARY
DENTARY *n* lower jawbone with teeth
DENTATE *adj* having teeth or teethlike notches
DENTATED *adj* having teeth
DENTATELY > DENTATE
DENTATION *n* state or condition of being dentate
DENTED > DENT
DENTEL *n* architectural term
DENTELLE *n* bookbinding term
DENTELLES > DENTELLE
DENTELS > DENTEL
DENTEX *n* large active predatory sparid fish, *Dentex dentex*, of Mediterranean and E Atlantic waters, having long sharp teeth and powerful jaws
DENTEXES > DENTEX
DENTICLE *n* small tooth or toothlike part, such as any of the placoid scales of sharks
DENTICLES > DENTICLE
DENTIFORM *adj* shaped like a tooth
DENTIL *n* one of a set of small square or rectangular blocks evenly spaced to form an ornamental row, usually under a classical cornice on a building, piece of furniture, etc
DENTILED > DENTIL
DENTILS > DENTIL
DENTIN *same as* > DENTINE
DENTINAL > DENTINE
DENTINE *n* hard dense tissue forming the bulk of a tooth
DENTINES > DENTINE
DENTING > DENT
DENTINS > DENTIN
DENTIST *n* person qualified to practise dentistry
DENTISTRY *n* branch of medicine concerned with the teeth and gums
DENTISTS > DENTIST
DENTITION *n* typical arrangement of teeth in a species
DENTOID *adj* resembling a tooth
DENTS > DENT
DENTULOUS *adj* having teeth
DENTURAL > DENTURE
DENTURE *n* false tooth
DENTURES > DENTURE
DENTURIST *n* person who makes dentures
DENUDATE *adj* denuded ▷ *vb* denude
DENUDATED > DENUDATE
DENUDATES > DENUDATE
DENUDE *vb* remove the covering or protection from
DENUDED > DENUDE
DENUDER > DENUDE
DENUDERS > DENUDE
DENUDES > DENUDE
DENUDING > DENUDE
DENY *vb* declare to be untrue
DENYING > DENY
DENYINGLY > DENY
DEODAND *n* (formerly) a thing that had caused a person's death and was forfeited to the crown for a charitable purpose: abolished 1862
DEODANDS > DEODAND
DEODAR *n* Himalayan cedar with drooping branches
DEODARA *same as* > DEODAR
DEODARAS > DEODARA
DEODARS > DEODAR
DEODATE *n* offering to God
DEODATES > DEODATE
DEODORANT *n* substance applied to the body to mask the smell of perspiration
DEODORISE *same as* > DEODORIZE
DEODORIZE *vb* remove or disguise the smell of
DEONTIC *adj* of or relating to such ethical concepts as obligation and permissibility
DEONTICS > DEONTIC
DEORBIT *vb* go out of orbit
DEORBITED > DEORBIT
DEORBITS > DEORBIT
DEOXIDATE *vb* remove oxygen atoms from
DEOXIDISE *same as* > DEOXIDIZE
DEOXIDIZE *vb* remove oxygen atoms from (a compound, molecule, etc)
DEOXY *adj* having less oxygen than a specified related compound
DEPAINT *vb* depict
DEPAINTED > DEPAINT
DEPAINTS > DEPAINT
DEPANNEUR *n* (in Quebec) a convenience store
DEPART *vb* leave
DEPARTED *adj* dead
DEPARTEE > DEPART
DEPARTEES > DEPART
DEPARTER > DEPART
DEPARTERS > DEPART
DEPARTING > DEPART
DEPARTS > DEPART
DEPARTURE *n* act of departing
DEPASTURE *vb* graze or denude by grazing (a pasture, esp a meadow specially grown for the purpose)
DEPECHE *n* message
DEPECHES > DEPECHE
DEPEINCT *vb* paint
DEPEINCTS > DEPEINCT
DEPEND *vb* put trust (in)
DEPENDANT *same as* > DEPENDENT
DEPENDED > DEPEND
DEPENDENT *adj* depending on someone or something ▷ *n* element in a phrase or clause that is not the governor
DEPENDING > DEPEND
DEPENDS > DEPEND
DEPEOPLE *vb* reduce population
DEPEOPLED > DEPEOPLE

DEPEOPLES > DEPEOPLE
DEPERM *vb* demagnetize
DEPERMED > DEPERM
DEPERMING > DEPERM
DEPERMS > DEPERM
DEPICT *vb* produce a picture of
DEPICTED > DEPICT
DEPICTER > DEPICT
DEPICTERS > DEPICT
DEPICTING > DEPICT
DEPICTION > DEPICT
DEPICTIVE > DEPICT
DEPICTOR > DEPICT
DEPICTORS > DEPICT
DEPICTS > DEPICT
DEPICTURE *a less common word for* > DEPICT
DEPILATE *vb* remove the hair from
DEPILATED > DEPILATE
DEPILATES > DEPILATE
DEPILATOR > DEPILATE
DEPLANE *vb* disembark from an aeroplane
DEPLANED > DEPLANE
DEPLANES > DEPLANE
DEPLANING > DEPLANE
DEPLETE *vb* use up
DEPLETED > DEPLETE
DEPLETER > DEPLETE
DEPLETERS > DEPLETE
DEPLETES > DEPLETE
DEPLETING > DEPLETE
DEPLETION > DEPLETE
DEPLETIVE > DEPLETE
DEPLETORY > DEPLETE
DEPLORE *vb* condemn strongly
DEPLORED > DEPLORE
DEPLORER > DEPLORE
DEPLORERS > DEPLORE
DEPLORES > DEPLORE
DEPLORING > DEPLORE
DEPLOY *vb* organize (troops or resources) into a position ready for immediate action
DEPLOYED > DEPLOY
DEPLOYER > DEPLOY
DEPLOYERS > DEPLOY
DEPLOYING > DEPLOY
DEPLOYS > DEPLOY
DEPLUME *vb* deprive of feathers
DEPLUMED > DEPLUME
DEPLUMES > DEPLUME
DEPLUMING > DEPLUME
DEPOLISH *vb* remove the polish from
DEPONE *vb* declare (something) under oath
DEPONED > DEPONE
DEPONENT *n* person who makes a statement on oath ▷ *adj* (of a verb, esp in Latin) having the inflectional endings of a passive verb but the meaning of an active verb
DEPONENTS > DEPONENT
DEPONES > DEPONE
DEPONING > DEPONE
DEPORT *vb* remove forcibly from a country
DEPORTED > DEPORT
DEPORTEE *n* person deported or awaiting deportation
DEPORTEES > DEPORTEE
DEPORTER > DEPORT
DEPORTERS > DEPORT
DEPORTING > DEPORT
DEPORTS > DEPORT
DEPOSABLE > DEPOSE
DEPOSAL *another word for* > DEPOSITION
DEPOSALS > DEPOSAL
DEPOSE *vb* remove from an office or position of power
DEPOSED > DEPOSE
DEPOSER > DEPOSE
DEPOSERS > DEPOSE
DEPOSES > DEPOSE
DEPOSING > DEPOSE
DEPOSIT *vb* put down ▷ *n* sum of money paid into a bank account
DEPOSITED > DEPOSIT
DEPOSITOR *n* person who places or has money on deposit in a bank or similar organization
DEPOSITS > DEPOSIT
DEPOT *n* building where goods or vehicles are kept when not in use ▷ *adj* (of a drug or drug dose) designed for gradual release from the site of an injection so as to act over a long period
DEPOTS > DEPOT
DEPRAVE *vb* make morally bad
DEPRAVED *adj* morally bad
DEPRAVER > DEPRAVE
DEPRAVERS > DEPRAVE
DEPRAVES > DEPRAVE
DEPRAVING > DEPRAVE
DEPRAVITY *n* moral corruption
DEPRECATE *vb* express disapproval of
DEPREDATE *vb* plunder or destroy
DEPREHEND *vb* apprehend
DEPRENYL *n* drug combating effects of ageing
DEPRENYLS > DEPRENYL
DEPRESS *vb* make sad
DEPRESSED *adj* low in spirits
DEPRESSES > DEPRESS
DEPRESSOR *n* person or thing that depresses
DEPRIVAL > DEPRIVE
DEPRIVALS > DEPRIVE
DEPRIVE *vb* prevent from (having or enjoying)
DEPRIVED *adj* lacking adequate living conditions, education, etc
DEPRIVER > DEPRIVE
DEPRIVERS > DEPRIVE
DEPRIVES > DEPRIVE
DEPRIVING > DEPRIVE
DEPROGRAM *same as* > DEPROGRAMME
DEPSIDE *n* any ester formed by the condensation of the carboxyl group of one phenolic carboxylic acid with the hydroxyl group of another, found in plant cells
DEPSIDES > DEPSIDE
DEPTH *n* distance downwards, backwards, or inwards
DEPTHLESS *adj* immeasurably deep
DEPTHS > DEPTH
DEPURANT *same as* > DEPURATIVE
DEPURANTS > DEPURANT
DEPURATE *vb* cleanse or purify or to be cleansed or purified
DEPURATED > DEPURATE
DEPURATES > DEPURATE
DEPURATOR > DEPURATE
DEPUTABLE > DEPUTE
DEPUTE *vb* appoint (someone) to act on one's behalf ▷ *n* deputy
DEPUTED > DEPUTE
DEPUTES > DEPUTE
DEPUTIES > DEPUTY
DEPUTING > DEPUTE
DEPUTISE *same as* > DEPUTIZE
DEPUTISED > DEPUTISE
DEPUTISES > DEPUTISE
DEPUTIZE *vb* act as deputy
DEPUTIZED > DEPUTIZE
DEPUTIZES > DEPUTIZE
DEPUTY *n* person appointed to act on behalf of another
DERACINE *adj* uprooted
DERAIGN *vb* contest (a claim, suit, etc)
DERAIGNED > DERAIGN
DERAIGNS > DERAIGN
DERAIL *vb* cause (a train) to go off the rails ▷ *n* device designed to make rolling stock or locomotives leave the rails to avoid a collision or accident
DERAILED > DERAIL
DERAILER *same as* > DERAIL
DERAILERS > DERAILER
DERAILING > DERAIL
DERAILS > DERAIL
DERANGE *vb* disturb the order or arrangement of
DERANGED > DERANGE
DERANGER > DERANGE
DERANGERS > DERANGE
DERANGES > DERANGE
DERANGING > DERANGE
DERAT *vb* remove rats from
DERATE *vb* assess the value of (some types of property, such as agricultural land) at a lower rate than others for local taxation
DERATED > DERATE
DERATES > DERATE
DERATING > DERATE
DERATINGS > DERATE
DERATION *vb* end rationing of (food, petrol, etc)
DERATIONS > DERATION
DERATS > DERAT
DERATTED > DERAT
DERATTING > DERAT
DERAY *vb* go mad
DERAYED > DERAY
DERAYING > DERAY
DERAYS > DERAY
DERBIES > DERBY
DERBY *n* bowler hat
DERE *vb* injure
DERED > DERE
DERELICT *adj* unused and falling into ruins ▷ *n* social outcast, vagrant
DERELICTS > DERELICT
DEREPRESS *vb* induce operation of gene
DERES > DERE
DERHAM *same as* > DIRHAM
DERHAMS > DERHAM
DERIDE *vb* treat with contempt or ridicule
DERIDED > DERIDE
DERIDER > DERIDE
DERIDERS > DERIDE
DERIDES > DERIDE
DERIDING > DERIDE
DERIG *vb* remove equipment, e.g. from stage set
DERIGGED > DERIG
DERIGGING > DERIG
DERIGS > DERIG
DERING > DERE
DERINGER *same as* > DERRINGER
DERINGERS > DERINGER
DERISIBLE *adj* subject to or deserving of derision
DERISION *n* act of deriding
DERISIONS > DERISION
DERISIVE *adj* mocking, scornful
DERISORY *adj* too small or inadequate to be considered seriously
DERIVABLE > DERIVE
DERIVABLY > DERIVE
DERIVATE *n* derivative
DERIVATES > DERIVATE
DERIVE *vb* take or develop (from)
DERIVED > DERIVE
DERIVER > DERIVE
DERIVERS > DERIVE
DERIVES > DERIVE
DERIVING > DERIVE
DERM *same as* > DERMA
DERMA *n* beef or fowl intestine used as a casing for certain dishes, esp kishke
DERMAL *adj* of or relating to the skin
DERMAS > DERMA
DERMATIC *adj* of skin
DERMATOID *adj* resembling skin

DERMATOME *n* surgical instrument for cutting thin slices of skin, esp for grafting
DERMESTID *n* any beetle of the family *Dermestidae*, whose members are destructive at both larval and adult stages to a wide range of stored organic materials such as wool, fur, feathers, and meat. They include the bacon (*or* larder), cabinet, carpet, leather, and museum beetles
DERMIC > DERMIS
DERMIS *another name for* > CORIUM
DERMISES > DERMIS
DERMOID *adj* of or resembling skin ▷ *n* congenital cystic tumour whose walls are lined with epithelium
DERMOIDS > DERMOID
DERMS > DERM
DERN *n* concealment
DERNFUL *adj* sorrowful
DERNIER *adj* last
DERNLY *adv* sorrowfully
DERNS > DERN
DERO *n* tramp or derelict
DEROGATE *vb* detract from ▷ *adj* debased or degraded
DEROGATED > DEROGATE
DEROGATES > DEROGATE
DEROS > DERO
DERRICK *n* simple crane ▷ *vb* raise or lower the jib of (a crane)
DERRICKED > DERRICK
DERRICKS > DERRICK
DERRIERE > BUTTOCK
DERRIERES > DERRIERE
DERRIES > DERRY
DERRINGER *n* small large-bored pistol
DERRIS *n* any East Indian leguminous woody climbing plant of the genus *Derris*, esp *D. elliptica*, whose roots yield the compound rotenone
DERRISES > DERRIS
DERRO *n* vagrant
DERROS > DERRO
DERRY *n* derelict house, esp one used by tramps, drug addicts, etc
DERTH *same as* > DEARTH
DERTHS > DERTH
DERV *n* diesel oil, when used for road transport
DERVISH *n* member of a Muslim religious order noted for a frenzied whirling dance
DERVISHES > DERVISH
DERVS > DERV
DESALT *same as* > DESALINATE
DESALTED > DESALT
DESALTER > DESALT
DESALTERS > DESALT
DESALTING > DESALT
DESALTS > DESALT
DESAND *vb* remove sand from
DESANDED > DESAND
DESANDING > DESAND
DESANDS > DESAND
DESCALE *vb* remove a hard coating from inside (a kettle or pipe)
DESCALED > DESCALE
DESCALES > DESCALE
DESCALING > DESCALE
DESCANT *n* tune played or sung above a basic melody ▷ *adj* denoting the highest member in a family of musical instruments ▷ *vb* compose or perform a descant (for a piece of music)
DESCANTED > DESCANT
DESCANTER > DESCANT
DESCANTS > DESCANT
DESCEND *vb* move down (a slope etc)
DESCENDED > DESCEND
DESCENDER > DESCEND
DESCENDS > DESCEND
DESCENT *n* descending
DESCENTS > DESCENT
DESCHOOL *vb* separate education from the institution of school and operate through the pupil's life experience as opposed to a set curriculum
DESCHOOLS > DESCHOOL
DESCRIBE *vb* give an account of (something or someone) in words
DESCRIBED > DESCRIBE
DESCRIBER > DESCRIBE
DESCRIBES > DESCRIBE
DESCRIED > DESCRY
DESCRIER > DESCRY
DESCRIERS > DESCRY
DESCRIES > DESCRY
DESCRIVE *vb* describe
DESCRIVED > DESCRIVE
DESCRIVES > DESCRIVE
DESCRY *vb* catch sight of
DESCRYING > DESCRY
DESECRATE *vb* damage or insult (something sacred)
DESELECT *vb* refuse to select (an MP) for re-election
DESELECTS > DESELECT
DESERT *n* region with little or no vegetation because of low rainfall ▷ *vb* abandon (a person or place) without intending to return
DESERTED > DESERT
DESERTER > DESERT
DESERTERS > DESERT
DESERTIC *adj* (of soil) developing in hot climates
DESERTIFY *vb* turn into desert
DESERTING > DESERT
DESERTION *n* act of deserting or abandoning or the state of being deserted or abandoned
DESERTS > DESERT
DESERVE *vb* be entitled to or worthy of
DESERVED > DESERVE
DESERVER > DESERVE
DESERVERS > DESERVE
DESERVES > DESERVE
DESERVING *adj* worthy of help, praise, or reward ▷ *n* merit or demerit
DESEX *same as* > DESEXUALIZE
DESEXED > DESEX
DESEXES > DESEX
DESEXING > DESEX
DESHI *same as* > DESI
DESI *adj* in Indian English, indigenous or local
DESICCANT *adj* desiccating or drying ▷ *n* substance, such as calcium oxide, that absorbs water and is used to remove moisture
DESICCATE *vb* remove most of the water from
DESIGN *vb* work out the structure or form of (something), by making a sketch or plans ▷ *n* preliminary drawing
DESIGNATE *vb* give a name to ▷ *adj* appointed but not yet in office
DESIGNED > DESIGN
DESIGNEE *n* person designated to do something
DESIGNEES > DESIGNEE
DESIGNER *n* person who draws up original sketches or plans from which things are made ▷ *adj* designed by a well-known designer
DESIGNERS > DESIGNER
DESIGNFUL *adj* scheming
DESIGNING *adj* cunning and scheming
DESIGNS > DESIGN
DESILVER *vb* remove silver from
DESILVERS > DESILVER
DESINE *same as* > DESIGN
DESINED > DESINE
DESINENCE *n* ending or termination, esp an inflectional ending of a word
DESINENT > DESINENCE
DESINES > DESINE
DESINING > DESINE
DESIPIENT *adj* foolish
DESIRABLE *adj* worth having ▷ *n* person or thing that is the object of desire
DESIRABLY > DESIRABLE
DESIRE *vb* want very much ▷ *n* wish, longing
DESIRED > DESIRE
DESIRER > DESIRE
DESIRERS > DESIRE
DESIRES > DESIRE
DESIRING > DESIRE
DESIROUS *adj* having a desire for
DESIST *vb* stop (doing something)
DESISTED > DESIST
DESISTING > DESIST
DESISTS > DESIST
DESK *n* piece of furniture with a writing surface and drawers
DESKBOUND *adj* engaged in or involving sedentary work, as at an office desk
DESKFAST *n* breakfast eaten at one's desk at work
DESKFASTS > DESKFAST
DESKILL *vb* mechanize or computerize (a job) thereby reducing the skill required to do it
DESKILLED > DESKILL
DESKILLS > DESKILL
DESKMAN *n* police officer in charge in police station
DESKMEN > DESKMAN
DESKNOTE *n* small computer
DESKNOTES > DESKNOTE
DESKS > DESK
DESKTOP *adj* (of a computer) small enough to use at a desk ▷ *n* denoting a computer system, esp for word processing, that is small enough to use at a desk
DESKTOPS > DESKTOP
DESMAN *n* either of two molelike amphibious mammals
DESMANS > DESMAN
DESMID *n* any freshwater green alga of the mainly unicellular family *Desmidioideae*, typically constricted into two symmetrical halves
DESMIDIAN > DESMID
DESMIDS > DESMID
DESMINE *n* type of mineral
DESMINES > DESMINE
DESMODIUM *n* type of plant
DESMOID *adj* resembling a tendon or ligament ▷ *n* very firm tumour of connective tissue
DESMOIDS > DESMOID
DESMOSOME *n* structure in the cell membranes of adjacent cells that binds them together
DESNOOD *vb* remove the snood of a turkey poult to reduce the risk of cannibalism
DESNOODED > DESNOOD
DESNOODS > DESNOOD
DESOEUVRE *adj* with nothing to do
DESOLATE *adj* uninhabited

and bleak ▷ *vb* deprive of inhabitants
DESOLATED > DESOLATE
DESOLATER > DESOLATE
DESOLATES > DESOLATE
DESOLATOR > DESOLATE
DESORB *vb* change from an adsorbed state on a surface to a gaseous or liquid state
DESORBED > DESORB
DESORBING > DESORB
DESORBS > DESORB
DESOXY *same as* > DEOXY
DESPAIR *n* total loss of hope ▷ *vb* lose hope
DESPAIRED > DESPAIR
DESPAIRER *n* one who despairs
DESPAIRS > DESPAIR
DESPATCH *same as* > DISPATCH
DESPERADO *n* reckless person ready to commit any violent illegal act
DESPERATE *adj* in despair and reckless
DESPIGHT *obsolete form of* > DESPITE
DESPIGHTS > DESPIGHT
DESPISAL > DESPISE
DESPISALS > DESPISE
DESPISE *vb* regard with contempt
DESPISED > DESPISE
DESPISER > DESPISE
DESPISERS > DESPISE
DESPISES > DESPISE
DESPISING > DESPISE
DESPITE *prep* in spite of ▷ *n* contempt ▷ *vb* show contempt for
DESPITED > DESPITE
DESPITES > DESPITE
DESPITING > DESPITE
DESPOIL *vb* plunder
DESPOILED > DESPOIL
DESPOILER > DESPOIL
DESPOILS > DESPOIL
DESPOND *vb* lose heart or hope
DESPONDED > DESPOND
DESPONDS > DESPOND
DESPOT *n* person in power who acts unfairly or cruelly
DESPOTAT *n* despot's domain
DESPOTATE *same as* > DESPOTAT
DESPOTATS > DESPOTAT
DESPOTIC > DESPOT
DESPOTISM *n* unfair or cruel government or behaviour
DESPOTS > DESPOT
DESPUMATE *vb* clarify or purify (a liquid) by skimming a scum from its surface
DESSE *n* desk
DESSERT *n* sweet course served at the end of a meal
DESSERTS > DESSERT
DESSES > DESSE
DESTAIN *vb* remove stain from
DESTAINED > DESTAIN
DESTAINS > DESTAIN
DESTEMPER *same as* > DISTEMPER
DESTINATE *same as* > DESTINE
DESTINE *vb* set apart or appoint (for a certain purpose or person, or to do something)
DESTINED *adj* certain to be or to do something
DESTINES > DESTINE
DESTINIES > DESTINY
DESTINING > DESTINE
DESTINY *n* future marked out for a person or thing
DESTITUTE *adj* having no money or possessions
DESTOCK *vb* (of a retailer) to reduce the amount of stock held or cease to stock certain products
DESTOCKED > DESTOCK
DESTOCKS > DESTOCK
DESTRIER *an archaic word for* > WARHORSE
DESTRIERS > DESTRIER
DESTROY *vb* ruin, demolish
DESTROYED > DESTROY
DESTROYER *n* small heavily armed warship
DESTROYS > DESTROY
DESTRUCT *vb* destroy (one's own missile or rocket) for safety ▷ *n* act of destructing ▷ *adj* designed to be capable of destroying itself or the object, system, or installation containing it
DESTRUCTO *n* person who causes havoc or destruction
DESTRUCTS > DESTRUCT
DESUETUDE *n* condition of not being in use
DESUGAR *vb* remove sugar from
DESUGARED > DESUGAR
DESUGARS > DESUGAR
DESULFUR *same as* > DESULPHUR
DESULFURS > DESULFUR
DESULPHUR *vb* remove sulphur from
DESULTORY *adj* jumping from one thing to another, disconnected
DESYATIN *n* Russian unit of area
DESYATINS > DESYATIN
DESYNE *same as* > DESIGN
DESYNED > DESYNE
DESYNES > DESYNE
DESYNING > DESYNE
DETACH *vb* disengage and separate
DETACHED *adj* (of a house) not joined to another house
DETACHER > DETACH
DETACHERS > DETACH
DETACHES > DETACH
DETACHING > DETACH
DETAIL *n* individual piece of information ▷ *vb* list fully
DETAILED *adj* having many details
DETAILER > DETAIL
DETAILERS > DETAIL
DETAILING > DETAIL
DETAILS > DETAIL
DETAIN *vb* delay (someone)
DETAINED > DETAIN
DETAINEE > DETAIN
DETAINEES > DETAIN
DETAINER *n* wrongful withholding of the property of another person
DETAINERS > DETAINER
DETAINING > DETAIN
DETAINS > DETAIN
DETASSEL *vb* remove top part of corn plant
DETASSELS > DETASSEL
DETECT *vb* notice
DETECTED > DETECT
DETECTER > DETECT
DETECTERS > DETECT
DETECTING > DETECT
DETECTION *n* act of noticing, discovering, or sensing something
DETECTIVE *n* police officer or private agent who investigates crime ▷ *adj* used in or serving for detection
DETECTOR *n* instrument used to find something
DETECTORS > DETECTOR
DETECTS > DETECT
DETENT *n* locking piece of a mechanism, often spring-loaded to check the movement of a wheel in one direction only
DETENTE *n* easing of tension between nations
DETENTES > DETENTE
DETENTION *n* imprisonment
DETENTIST *n* supporter of detente
DETENTS > DETENT
DETENU *n* prisoner
DETENUE *n* female prisoner
DETENUES > DETENUE
DETENUS > DETENU
DETER *vb* discourage (someone) from doing something by instilling fear or doubt
DETERGE *vb* wash or wipe away
DETERGED > DETERGE
DETERGENT *n* chemical substance for washing clothes or dishes ▷ *adj* having cleansing power
DETERGER *n* detergent
DETERGERS > DETERGER
DETERGES > DETERGE
DETERGING > DETERGE
DETERMENT > DETER
DETERMINE *vb* settle (an argument or a question) conclusively
DETERRED > DETER
DETERRENT *n* something that deters ▷ *adj* tending to deter
DETERRER > DETER
DETERRERS > DETERRER
DETERRING > DETER
DETERS > DETER
DETERSION *n* act of cleansing
DETERSIVE *same as* > DETERGENT
DETEST *vb* dislike intensely
DETESTED > DETEST
DETESTER > DETEST
DETESTERS > DETEST
DETESTING > DETEST
DETESTS > DETEST
DETHATCH *vb* remove dead grass from lawn
DETHRONE *vb* remove from a throne or position of power
DETHRONED > DETHRONE
DETHRONER > DETHRONE
DETHRONES > DETHRONE
DETICK *vb* remove ticks from
DETICKED > DETICK
DETICKER > DETICK
DETICKERS > DETICK
DETICKING > DETICK
DETICKS > DETICK
DETINUE *n* action brought by a plaintiff to recover goods wrongfully detained
DETINUES > DETINUE
DETONABLE *adj* that can be detonated
DETONATE *vb* explode
DETONATED > DETONATE
DETONATES > DETONATE
DETONATOR *n* small amount of explosive, or a device, used to set off an explosion
DETORSION > DETORT
DETORT *vb* pervert
DETORTED > DETORT
DETORTING > DETORT
DETORTION > DETORT
DETORTS > DETORT
DETOUR *n* route that is not the most direct one ▷ *vb* deviate or cause to deviate from a direct route or course of action
DETOURED > DETOUR
DETOURING > DETOUR
DETOURS > DETOUR
DETOX *n* treatment to rid the body of poisonous substances ▷ *vb* undergo treatment to rid the body of poisonous substances, esp alcohol and drugs
DETOXED > DETOX
DETOXES > DETOX
DETOXIFY *vb* remove poison from

DETOXING > DETOX
DETRACT *vb* make (something) seem less good
DETRACTED > DETRACT
DETRACTOR > DETRACT
DETRACTS > DETRACT
DETRAIN *vb* leave or cause to leave a railway train, as passengers, etc
DETRAINED > DETRAIN
DETRAINS > DETRAIN
DETRAQUE *n* insane person
DETRAQUEE *n* female insane person
DETRAQUES > DETRAQUE
DETRIMENT *n* disadvantage or damage
DETRITAL > DETRITUS
DETRITION *n* act of rubbing or wearing away by friction
DETRITUS *n* loose mass of stones and silt worn away from rocks
DETRUDE *vb* force down or thrust away or out
DETRUDED > DETRUDE
DETRUDES > DETRUDE
DETRUDING > DETRUDE
DETRUSION > DETRUDE
DETUNE *vb* change pitch of (stringed instrument)
DETUNED > DETUNE
DETUNES > DETUNE
DETUNING > DETUNE
DEUCE *vb* score deuce in tennis ▷ *n* score of forty all
DEUCED *adj* damned
DEUCEDLY > DEUCED
DEUCES > DEUCE
DEUCING > DEUCE
DEUDDARN *n* two-tiered Welsh dresser
DEUDDARNS > DEUDDARN
DEUS *n* god
DEUTERATE *vb* treat or combine with deuterium
DEUTERIC *adj* (of mineral) formed by metasomatic changes
DEUTERIDE *n* compound of deuterium with some other element. It is analogous to a hydride
DEUTERIUM *n* isotope of hydrogen twice as heavy as the normal atom
DEUTERON *n* nucleus of a deuterium atom, consisting of one proton and one neutron
DEUTERONS > DEUTERON
DEUTON *old form of* > DEUTERON
DEUTONS > DEUTON
DEUTZIA *n* shrub with clusters of pink or white flowers
DEUTZIAS > DEUTZIA
DEV *same as* > DEVA
DEVA *n* (in Hinduism and Buddhism) divine being or god
DEVALL *vb* stop
DEVALLED > DEVALL
DEVALLING > DEVALL
DEVALLS > DEVALL
DEVALUATE *same as* > DEVALUE
DEVALUE *vb* reduce the exchange value of (a currency)
DEVALUED > DEVALUE
DEVALUES > DEVALUE
DEVALUING > DEVALUE
DEVAS > DEVA
DEVASTATE *vb* destroy
DEVEIN *vb* remove vein from
DEVEINED > DEVEIN
DEVEINING > DEVEIN
DEVEINS > DEVEIN
DEVEL *same as* > DEVVEL
DEVELED > DEVEL
DEVELING > DEVEL
DEVELLED > DEVEL
DEVELLING > DEVEL
DEVELOP *vb* grow or bring to a later, more elaborate, or more advanced stage
DEVELOPE *old form of* > DEVELOP
DEVELOPED > DEVELOP
DEVELOPER *n* person who develops property
DEVELOPES > DEVELOPE
DEVELOPPE *n* ballet position
DEVELOPS > DEVELOP
DEVELS > DEVEL
DEVERBAL *n* word deriving from verb
DEVERBALS > DEVERBAL
DEVEST *variant spelling of* > DIVEST
DEVESTED > DEVEST
DEVESTING > DEVEST
DEVESTS > DEVEST
DEVIANCE *n* act or state of being deviant
DEVIANCES > DEVIANCE
DEVIANCY *same as* > DEVIANCE
DEVIANT *adj* (person) deviating from what is considered acceptable behaviour ▷ *n* person whose behaviour deviates from what is considered to be acceptable
DEVIANTS > DEVIANT
DEVIATE *vb* differ from others in belief or thought
DEVIATED > DEVIATE
DEVIATES > DEVIATE
DEVIATING > DEVIATE
DEVIATION *n* act or result of deviating
DEVIATIVE *adj* tending to deviate
DEVIATOR > DEVIATE
DEVIATORS > DEVIATE
DEVIATORY > DEVIATE
DEVICE *n* machine or tool used for a specific task
DEVICEFUL *adj* full of devices
DEVICES > DEVICE
DEVIL *n* evil spirit ▷ *vb* prepare (food) with a highly flavoured spiced mixture
DEVILDOM *n* domain of evil spirits
DEVILDOMS > DEVILDOM
DEVILED > DEVIL
DEVILESS *n* female devil
DEVILET *n* young devil
DEVILETS > DEVILET
DEVILFISH *n* manta fish
DEVILING > DEVIL
DEVILINGS > DEVIL
DEVILISH *adj* cruel or unpleasant ▷ *adv* extremely
DEVILISM *n* doctrine of devil
DEVILISMS > DEVILISM
DEVILKIN *n* small devil
DEVILKINS > DEVILKIN
DEVILLED > DEVIL
DEVILLING > DEVIL
DEVILMENT *n* mischievous conduct
DEVILRIES > DEVILRY
DEVILRY *n* mischievousness
DEVILS > DEVIL
DEVILSHIP *n* character of devil
DEVILTRY *same as* > DEVILRY
DEVILWOOD *n* small US tree
DEVIOUS *adj* insincere and dishonest
DEVIOUSLY > DEVIOUS
DEVISABLE *adj* (of property, esp realty) capable of being transferred by will
DEVISAL *n* act of inventing, contriving, or devising
DEVISALS > DEVISAL
DEVISE *vb* work out (something) in one's mind ▷ *n* disposition of property by will
DEVISED > DEVISE
DEVISEE *n* person to whom property, esp realty, is devised by will
DEVISEES > DEVISEE
DEVISER > DEVISE
DEVISERS > DEVISE
DEVISES > DEVISE
DEVISING > DEVISE
DEVISOR *n* person who devises property, esp realty, by will
DEVISORS > DEVISOR
DEVITRIFY *vb* change from a vitreous state to a crystalline state
DEVLING *n* young devil
DEVLINGS > DEVLING
DEVOICE *vb* make (a voiced speech sound) voiceless
DEVOICED > DEVOICE
DEVOICES > DEVOICE
DEVOICING > DEVOICE
DEVOID *adj* completely lacking (in)
DEVOIR *n* duty
DEVOIRS > DEVOIR
DEVOLVE *vb* pass (power or duties) or (of power or duties) be passed to a successor or substitute
DEVOLVED > DEVOLVE
DEVOLVES > DEVOLVE
DEVOLVING > DEVOLVE
DEVON *n* bland processed meat in sausage form, eaten cold in slices
DEVONIAN *adj* of, denoting, or formed in the fourth period of the Palaeozoic era, between the Silurian and Carboniferous periods
DEVONPORT *same as* > DAVENPORT
DEVONS > DEVON
DEVORE *n* velvet fabric with a raised pattern created by disintegrating some of the pile with chemicals
DEVORES > DEVORE
DEVOT *n* devotee
DEVOTE *vb* apply or dedicate to a particular purpose
DEVOTED *adj* showing loyalty or devotion
DEVOTEDLY > DEVOTED
DEVOTEE *n* person who is very enthusiastic about something
DEVOTEES > DEVOTEE
DEVOTES > DEVOTE
DEVOTING > DEVOTE
DEVOTION *n* strong affection for or loyalty to someone or something
DEVOTIONS > DEVOTION
DEVOTS > DEVOT
DEVOUR *vb* eat greedily
DEVOURED > DEVOUR
DEVOURER > DEVOUR
DEVOURERS > DEVOUR
DEVOURING > DEVOUR
DEVOURS > DEVOUR
DEVOUT *adj* deeply religious
DEVOUTER > DEVOUT
DEVOUTEST > DEVOUT
DEVOUTLY > DEVOUT
DEVS > DEV
DEVVEL *vb* strike with blow
DEVVELLED > DEVVEL
DEVVELS > DEVVEL
DEW *n* drops of water that form on the ground at night from vapour in the air ▷ *vb* moisten with or as with dew
DEWAN *n* (formerly in India) the chief minister or finance minister of a state ruled by an Indian prince
DEWANI *n* post of dewan
DEWANIS > DEWANI
DEWANNIES > DEWANNY
DEWANNY *same as* > DEWANI
DEWANS > DEWAN
DEWAR as in *dewar flask*

type of vacuum flask
DEWARS > DEWAR
DEWATER *vb* remove water from
DEWATERED > DEWATER
DEWATERER > DEWATER
DEWATERS > DEWATER
DEWAX *vb* remove wax from
DEWAXED > DEWAX
DEWAXES > DEWAX
DEWAXING > DEWAX
DEWBERRY *n* type of bramble with blue-black fruits
DEWCLAW *n* nonfunctional claw on a dog's leg
DEWCLAWED > DEWCLAW
DEWCLAWS > DEWCLAW
DEWDROP *n* drop of dew
DEWDROPS > DEWDROP
DEWED > DEW
DEWFALL *n* formation of dew
DEWFALLS > DEWFALL
DEWFULL *obsolete form of* > DUE
DEWIER > DEWY
DEWIEST > DEWY
DEWILY > DEWY
DEWINESS > DEWY
DEWING > DEW
DEWITT *vb* kill, esp hang unlawfully
DEWITTED > DEWITT
DEWITTING > DEWITT
DEWITTS > DEWITT
DEWLAP *n* loose fold of skin hanging under the throat in dogs, cattle, etc
DEWLAPPED > DEWLAP
DEWLAPS > DEWLAP
DEWLAPT > DEWLAP
DEWLESS > DEW
DEWOOL *vb* remove wool from
DEWOOLED > DEWOOL
DEWOOLING > DEWOOL
DEWOOLS > DEWOOL
DEWORM *vb* rid of worms
DEWORMED > DEWORM
DEWORMER > DEWORM
DEWORMERS > DEWORM
DEWORMING > DEWORM
DEWORMS > DEWORM
DEWPOINT *n* temperature at which water vapour in the air becomes saturated and water droplets begin to form
DEWPOINTS > DEWPOINT
DEWS > DEW
DEWY *adj* moist with or as with dew
DEX *n* dextroamphetamine
DEXES > DEX
DEXIE *n* pill containing dextroamphetamine
DEXIES > DEXIE
DEXTER *adj* of or on the right side of a shield, etc, from the bearer's point of view ▷ *n* small breed of red or black beef cattle, originally from Ireland
DEXTERITY *n* skill in using one's hands
DEXTEROUS *adj* possessing or done with dexterity
DEXTERS > DEXTER
DEXTRAL *adj* of, relating to, or located on the right side, esp of the body
DEXTRALLY > DEXTRAL
DEXTRAN *n* polysaccharide produced by the action of bacteria on sucrose: used as a substitute for plasma in blood transfusions
DEXTRANS > DEXTRAN
DEXTRIN *n* sticky substance obtained from starch, used as a thickening agent in food
DEXTRINE *same as* > DEXTRIN
DEXTRINES > DEXTRINE
DEXTRINS > DEXTRIN
DEXTRO *adj* dextrorotatory or rotating to the right
DEXTRORSE *adj* (of some climbing plants) growing upwards in a helix from left to right or anticlockwise
DEXTROSE *n* glucose occurring in fruit, honey, and the blood of animals
DEXTROSES > DEXTROSE
DEXTROUS *same as* > DEXTEROUS
DEXY *same as* > DEXIE
DEY *n* title given to commanders or (from 1710) governors of the Janissaries of Algiers (1671–1830)
DEYS > DEY
DEZINC *vb* remove zinc from
DEZINCED > DEZINC
DEZINCING > DEZINC
DEZINCKED > DEZINC
DEZINCS > DEZINC
DHAK *n* tropical Asian leguminous tree, *Butea frondosa*, that has bright red flowers and yields a red resin, used as an astringent
DHAKS > DHAK
DHAL *n* curry made from lentils or beans
DHALS > DHAL
DHAMMA *variant of* > DHARMA
DHAMMAS > DHAMMA
DHANSAK *n* any of a variety of Indian dishes consisting of meat or vegetables braised with water or stock and lentils
DHANSAKS > DHANSAK
DHARMA *n* moral law or behaviour
DHARMAS > DHARMA
DHARMIC > DHARMA
DHARMSALA *n* Indian hostel
DHARNA *n* (in India) a method of obtaining justice, as the payment of a debt, by sitting, fasting, at the door of the person from whom reparation is sought
DHARNAS > DHARNA
DHOBI *n* (in India, Malaya, East Africa, etc, esp formerly) a washerman
DHOBIS > DHOBI
DHOL *n* type of Indian drum
DHOLE *n* fierce canine mammal, *Cuon alpinus*, of the forests of central and SE Asia, having a reddish-brown coat and rounded ears: hunts in packs
DHOLES > DHOLE
DHOLL *same as* > DHAL
DHOLLS > DHOLL
DHOLS > DHOL
DHOOLIES > DHOOLY
DHOOLY *same as* > DOOLIE
DHOORA *same as* > DURRA
DHOORAS > DHOORA
DHOOTI *same as* > DHOTI
DHOOTIE *same as* > DHOTI
DHOOTIES > DHOOTIE
DHOOTIS > DHOOTI
DHOTI *n* long loincloth worn by men in India
DHOTIS > DHOTI
DHOURRA *same as* > DURRA
DHOURRAS > DHOURRA
DHOW *n* Arab sailing ship
DHOWS > DHOW
DHURNA *same as* > DHARNA
DHURNAS > DHURNA
DHURRA *same as* > DURRA
DHURRAS > DHURRA
DHURRIE *same as* > DURRIE
DHURRIES > DHURRIE
DHUTI *same as* > DHOTI
DHUTIS > DHUTI
DI > DEUS
DIABASE *n* altered dolerite
DIABASES > DIABASE
DIABASIC > DIABASE
DIABETES *n* disorder in which an abnormal amount of urine containing an excess of sugar is excreted
DIABETIC *n* person who has diabetes ▷ *adj* of or having diabetes
DIABETICS > DIABETIC
DIABLE *n* type of sauce
DIABLERIE *n* magic or witchcraft connected with devils
DIABLERY *same as* > DIABLERIE
DIABLES > DIABLE
DIABOLIC *adj* of the Devil
DIABOLISE *same as* > DIABOLIZE
DIABOLISM *n* witchcraft, devil worship
DIABOLIST > DIABOLISM
DIABOLIZE *vb* make (someone or something) diabolical
DIABOLO *n* game in which one throws and catches a spinning top on a cord fastened to two sticks held in the hands
DIABOLOGY *n* study of devils
DIABOLOS > DIABOLO
DIACETYL *n* aromatic compound
DIACETYLS > DIACETYL
DIACHRONY *n* change over time
DIACHYLON *n* acid or salt that contains two acidic hydrogen atoms
DIACHYLUM *n* plaster containing glycerin with lead salts
DIACID *n* lead plaster
DIACIDIC *adj* (of a base, such as calcium hydroxide $Ca(OH)_2$) capable of neutralizing two protons with one of its molecules
DIACIDS > DIACID
DIACODION *n* herbal remedy aiding sleep
DIACODIUM *n* syrup of poppies
DIACONAL *adj* of or associated with a deacon or the diaconate
DIACONATE *n* position or period of office of a deacon
DIACRITIC *n* sign above or below a character to indicate phonetic value or stress
DIACT *n* two-rayed
DIACTINAL *adj* having two pointed ends
DIACTINE *adj* two-rayed
DIACTINIC *adj* able to transmit photochemically active radiation
DIADEM *n* crown ▷ *vb* adorn or crown with or as with a diadem
DIADEMED > DIADEM
DIADEMING > DIADEM
DIADEMS > DIADEM
DIADOCHI *pl n* the six Macedonian generals who, after the death of Alexander the Great, fought for control of his empire
DIADOCHY *n* replacement of one element in a crystal by another
DIADROM *n* complete course of pendulum
DIADROMS > DIADROM
DIAERESES > DIAERESIS
DIAERESIS *n* mark (¨) placed over a vowel to show that it is pronounced separately from the preceding one, for example in *Noël*
DIAERETIC > DIAERESIS
DIAGLYPH *n* figure cut into stone
DIAGLYPHS > DIAGLYPH
DIAGNOSE *vb* determine by

diagnosis
DIAGNOSED > DIAGNOSE
DIAGNOSES > DIAGNOSIS
DIAGNOSIS *n* discovery and identification of diseases from the examination of symptoms
DIAGONAL *adj* from corner to corner ▷ *n* diagonal line
DIAGONALS > DIAGONAL
DIAGRAM *n* sketch showing the form or workings of something ▷ *vb* show in or as if in a diagram
DIAGRAMED > DIAGRAM
DIAGRAMS > DIAGRAM
DIAGRAPH *n* device for enlarging or reducing maps, plans, etc
DIAGRAPHS > DIAGRAPH
DIAGRID *n* diagonal structure network
DIAGRIDS > DIAGRID
DIAL *n* face of a clock or watch ▷ *vb* operate the dial or buttons on a telephone in order to contact (a number)
DIALECT *n* form of a language spoken in a particular area
DIALECTAL > DIALECT
DIALECTIC *n* logical debate by question and answer to resolve differences between two views ▷ *adj* of or relating to logical disputation
DIALECTS > DIALECT
DIALED > DIAL
DIALER > DIAL
DIALERS > DIAL
DIALING > DIAL
DIALINGS > DIAL
DIALIST *n* dial-maker
DIALISTS > DIALIST
DIALLAGE *n* green or brownish-black variety of the mineral augite in the form of layers of platelike crystals
DIALLAGES > DIALLAGE
DIALLAGIC > DIALLAGE
DIALLED > DIAL
DIALLEL *n* interbreeding among a group of parents
DIALLER > DIAL
DIALLERS > DIAL
DIALLING > DIAL
DIALLINGS > DIAL
DIALLIST *same as* > DIALIST
DIALLISTS > DIALLIST
DIALOG *same as* > DIALOGUE
DIALOGED > DIALOG
DIALOGER > DIALOG
DIALOGERS > DIALOG
DIALOGIC > DIALOGUE
DIALOGING > DIALOG
DIALOGISE *same as* > DIALOGIZE
DIALOGISM *n* deduction with one premise and a disjunctive conclusion
DIALOGIST *n* person who writes or takes part in a dialogue
DIALOGITE *n* carbonate mineral
DIALOGIZE *vb* carry on a dialogue
DIALOGS > DIALOG
DIALOGUE *n* conversation between two people, esp in a book, film, or play ▷ *vb* put into the form of a dialogue
DIALOGUED > DIALOGUE
DIALOGUER > DIALOGUE
DIALOGUES > DIALOGUE
DIALS > DIAL
DIALYSATE *n* liquid used in dialysis
DIALYSE *vb* separate by dialysis
DIALYSED > DIALYSE
DIALYSER *n* machine that performs dialysis, esp one that removes impurities from the blood of patients with malfunctioning kidneys
DIALYSERS > DIALYSER
DIALYSES > DIALYSIS
DIALYSING > DIALYSE
DIALYSIS *n* filtering of blood through a membrane to remove waste products
DIALYTIC > DIALYSIS
DIALYZATE *same as* > DIALYSATE
DIALYZE *same as* > DIALYSE
DIALYZED > DIALYZE
DIALYZER *same as* > DIALYSER
DIALYZERS > DIALYZER
DIALYZES > DIALYZE
DIALYZING > DIALYZE
DIAMAGNET *n* substance exhibiting diamagnetism
DIAMANTE *adj* decorated with artificial jewels or sequins ▷ *n* fabric so covered
DIAMANTES > DIAMANTE
DIAMETER *n* (length of) a straight line through the centre of a circle or sphere
DIAMETERS > DIAMETER
DIAMETRAL *same as* > DIAMETRIC
DIAMETRIC *adj* of a diameter
DIAMIDE *n* compound containing two amido groups
DIAMIDES > DIAMIDE
DIAMIN *same as* > DIAMIN
DIAMINE *n* any chemical compound containing two amino groups in its molecules
DIAMINES > DIAMINE
DIAMINS > DIAMIN
DIAMOND *n* exceptionally hard, usu. colourless, precious stone ▷ *adj* (of an anniversary) the sixtieth ▷ *vb* stud or decorate with diamonds
DIAMONDED > DIAMOND
DIAMONDS > DIAMOND
DIAMYL *adj* with two amyl groups
DIANDRIES > DIANDRY
DIANDROUS *adj* (of some flowers or flowering plants) having two stamens
DIANDRY *n* practice of having two husbands
DIANODAL *adj* going through a node
DIANOETIC *adj* of or relating to thought, esp to discursive reasoning rather than intuition
DIANOIA *n* perception and experience regarded as lower modes of knowledge
DIANOIAS > DIANOIA
DIANTHUS *n* any Eurasian caryophyllaceous plant of the widely cultivated genus *Dianthus*, such as the carnation, pink, and sweet william
DIAPASE *same as* > DIAPASON
DIAPASES > DIAPASE
DIAPASON *n* either of two stops found throughout the range of a pipe organ
DIAPASONS > DIAPASON
DIAPAUSE *vb* undergo diapause ▷ *n* period of suspended development and growth accompanied by decreased metabolism in insects and some other animals. It is correlated with seasonal changes
DIAPAUSED > DIAPAUSE
DIAPAUSES > DIAPAUSE
DIAPENTE *n* (in classical Greece) the interval of a perfect fifth
DIAPENTES > DIAPENTE
DIAPER *n* nappy ▷ *vb* decorate with a geometric pattern
DIAPERED > DIAPER
DIAPERING > DIAPER
DIAPERS > DIAPER
DIAPHONE *n* set of all realizations of a given phoneme in a language
DIAPHONES > DIAPHONE
DIAPHONIC > DIAPHONY
DIAPHONY *n* style of two-part polyphonic singing
DIAPHRAGM *n* muscular partition that separates the abdominal cavity and chest cavity
DIAPHYSES > DIAPHYSIS
DIAPHYSIS *n* shaft of a long bone
DIAPIR *n* anticlinal fold in which the brittle overlying rock has been pierced by material, such as salt, from beneath
DIAPIRIC > DIAPIR
DIAPIRISM > DIAPIR
DIAPIRS > DIAPIR
DIAPSID *n* reptile with two holes in rear of skull
DIAPSIDS > DIAPSID
DIAPYESES > DIAPYESIS
DIAPYESIS *n* discharge of pus
DIAPYETIC > DIAPYESIS
DIARCH *adj* (of a vascular bundle) having two strands of xylem
DIARCHAL > DIARCHY
DIARCHIC > DIARCHY
DIARCHIES > DIARCHY
DIARCHY *n* government by two states, individuals, etc
DIARIAL > DIARY
DIARIAN > DIARY
DIARIES > DIARY
DIARISE *same as* > DIARIZE
DIARISED > DIARISE
DIARISES > DIARISE
DIARISING > DIARISE
DIARIST *n* person who writes a diary
DIARISTIC > DIARIST
DIARISTS > DIARIST
DIARIZE *vb* record in diary
DIARIZED > DIARIZE
DIARIZES > DIARIZE
DIARIZING > DIARIZE
DIARRHEA *same as* > DIARRHOEA
DIARRHEAL > DIARRHEA
DIARRHEAS > DIARRHEA
DIARRHEIC > DIARRHEA
DIARRHOEA *n* frequent discharge of abnormally liquid faeces
DIARY *n* (book for) a record of daily events, appointments, or observations
DIASCOPE *n* optical projector used to display transparencies
DIASCOPES > DIASCOPE
DIASPORA *n* dispersion or spreading, as of people originally belonging to one nation or having a common culture
DIASPORAS > DIASPORA
DIASPORE *n* white, yellowish, or grey mineral
DIASPORES > DIASPORE
DIASPORIC > DIASPORA
DIASTASE *n* enzyme that converts starch into sugar
DIASTASES > DIASTASIS
DIASTASIC > DIASTASE
DIASTASIS *n* separation of an epiphysis from the long bone to which it is normally attached without fracture of the bone
DIASTATIC > DIASTASIS
DIASTEM *same as* > DIASTEMA

DIASTEMA *n* abnormal space, fissure, or cleft in a bodily organ or part

DIASTEMAS > DIASTEMA

DIASTEMS > DIASTEM

DIASTER *n* stage in cell division at which the chromosomes are in two groups at the poles of the spindle before forming daughter nuclei

DIASTERS > DIASTER

DIASTOLE *n* dilation of the chambers of the heart

DIASTOLES > DIASTOLE

DIASTOLIC > DIASTOLE

DIASTRAL > DIASTER

DIASTYLE *adj* having columns about three diameters apart ▷ *n* diastyle building

DIASTYLES > DIASTYLE

DIATHERMY *n* local heating of the body tissues with an electric current for medical or surgical purposes

DIATHESES > DIATHESIS

DIATHESIS *n* hereditary or acquired susceptibility of the body to one or more diseases

DIATHETIC > DIATHESIS

DIATOM *n* microscopic unicellular alga

DIATOMIC *adj* containing two atoms

DIATOMIST *n* specialist in diatoms

DIATOMITE *n* soft very fine-grained whitish rock consisting of the siliceous remains of diatoms deposited in the ocean or in ponds or lakes. It is used as an absorbent, filtering medium, insulator, filler, etc

DIATOMS > DIATOM

DIATONIC *adj* of a regular major or minor scale

DIATRETUM *n* Roman glass bowl

DIATRIBE *n* bitter critical attack

DIATRIBES > DIATRIBE

DIATRON *n* circuit that uses diodes

DIATRONS > DIATRON

DIATROPIC *adj* relating to a type of response in plants to an external stimulus

DIAXON *n* bipolar cell

DIAXONS > DIAXON

DIAZEPAM *n* chemical compound used as a minor tranquillizer and muscle relaxant and to treat acute epilepsy

DIAZEPAMS > DIAZEPAM

DIAZEUXES > DIAZEUXIS

DIAZEUXIS *n* separation of two tetrachords by interval of a tone

DIAZIN *same as* > DIAZINE

DIAZINE *n* organic compound

DIAZINES > DIAZINE

DIAZINON *n* type of insecticide

DIAZINONS > DIAZINON

DIAZINS > DIAZIN

DIAZO *adj* of, or relating to the reproduction of documents using the bleaching action of ultraviolet radiation on diazonium salts ▷ *n* document produced by this method

DIAZOES > DIAZO

DIAZOLE *n* type of organic compound

DIAZOLES > DIAZOLE

DIAZONIUM *n* type of chemical group

DIAZOS > DIAZO

DIAZOTISE *same as* > DIAZOTIZE

DIAZOTIZE *vb* cause (an aryl amine) to react with nitrous acid to produce a diazonium salt

DIB *vb* fish by allowing the bait to bob and dip on the surface

DIBASIC *adj* (of an acid, such as sulphuric acid, H_2SO_4) containing two acidic hydrogen atoms

DIBBED > DIB

DIBBER *same as* > DIBBLE

DIBBERED > DIBBER

DIBBERING > DIBBER

DIBBERS > DIBBER

DIBBING > DIB

DIBBLE *n* small hand tool used to make holes in the ground for seeds or plants ▷ *vb* make a hole in (the ground) with a dibble

DIBBLED > DIBBLE

DIBBLER > DIBBLE

DIBBLERS > DIBBLE

DIBBLES > DIBBLE

DIBBLING > DIBBLE

DIBBS *n* money

DIBBUK *variant spelling of* > DYBBUK

DIBBUKIM > DIBBUK

DIBBUKKIM > DIBBUK

DIBBUKS > DIBBUK

DIBROMIDE *n* chemical compound that contains two bromine atoms per molecule

DIBS > DIB

DIBUTYL *adj* with two butyl groups

DICACIOUS *adj* teasing

DICACITY *n* playful teasing

DICACODYL *n* oily slightly water-soluble poisonous liquid with garlic-like odour

DICAMBA *n* type of weedkiller

DICAMBAS > DICAMBA

DICAST *n* (in ancient Athens) a juror in the popular courts chosen by lot from a list of citizens

DICASTERY *another word for* > CONGREGATION

DICASTIC > DICAST

DICASTS > DICAST

DICE *n* small cube each of whose sides has a different number of spots (1 to 6), used in games of chance ▷ *vb* cut (food) into small cubes

DICED > DICE

DICENTRA *n* any Asian or North American plant of the genus *Dicentra*, such as bleeding heart and Dutchman's-breeches, having finely divided leaves and ornamental clusters of drooping flowers: family *Fumariaceae*

DICENTRAS > DICENTRA

DICENTRIC *n* abnormal chromosome with two centromeres

DICER > DICE

DICERS > DICE

DICES > DICE

DICEY *adj* dangerous or risky

DICH *interj* archaic expression meaning "may it do"

DICHASIA > DICHASIUM

DICHASIAL > DICHASIUM

DICHASIUM *n* cymose inflorescence in which each branch bearing a flower gives rise to two other flowering branches, as in the stitchwort

DICHOGAMY *n* maturation of male and female parts of a flower at different times, preventing automatic self-pollination

DICHONDRA *n* creeping perennial herb

DICHOPTIC *adj* having the eyes distinctly separate

DICHORD *n* two-stringed musical instrument

DICHORDS > DICHORD

DICHOTIC *adj* relating to or involving the stimulation of each ear simultaneously by different sounds

DICHOTOMY *n* division into two opposed groups or parts

DICHROIC *adj* having or consisting of only two colours

DICHROISM *n* property of a uniaxial crystal, such as tourmaline, of showing a perceptible difference in colour when viewed along two different axes in transmitted white light

DICHROITE *n* grey or violet-blue dichroic material

DICHROMAT *n* person able to distinguish only two colours

DICHROMIC *adj* of or involving only two colours

DICHT *vb* wipe

DICHTED > DICHT

DICHTING > DICHT

DICHTS > DICHT

DICIER > DICEY

DICIEST > DICEY

DICING > DICE

DICINGS > DICE

DICK *n* penis ▷ *vb* penetrate with a penis

DICKED > DICK

DICKENS *n* euphemism for devil

DICKENSES > DICKENS

DICKER *vb* trade (goods) by bargaining ▷ *n* petty bargain or barter

DICKERED > DICKER

DICKERING > DICKER

DICKERS > DICKER

DICKEY *same as* > DICKY

DICKEYS > DICKEY

DICKHEAD *n* stupid or despicable man or boy

DICKHEADS > DICKHEAD

DICKIE *same as* > DICKY

DICKIER > DICKY

DICKIES > DICKY

DICKIEST > DICKY

DICKING > DICK

DICKS > DICK

DICKTIER > DICKTY

DICKTIEST > DICKTY

DICKTY *same as* > DICTY

DICKY *n* false shirt front ▷ *adj* shaky or weak

DICKYBIRD *See* > DICKY

DICLINIES > DICLINOUS

DICLINISM > DICLINOUS

DICLINOUS *adj* (of flowering plants) bearing unisexual flowers

DICLINY > DICLINOUS

DICOT *n* type of flowering plant

DICOTS > DICOT

DICOTYL *n* a type of flowering plant; dicotyledon

DICOTYLS > DICOTYL

DICROTAL *same as* > DICROTIC

DICROTIC *adj* having or relating to a double pulse for each heartbeat

DICROTISM > DICROTIC

DICROTOUS *same as* > DICROTIC

DICT *vb* dictate

DICTA > DICTUM

DICTATE *vb* say aloud for someone else to write down ▷ *n* authoritative command

DICTATED > DICTATE

DICTATES > DICTATE

DICTATING > DICTATE

DICTATION *n* act of dictating words to be

taken down in writing
DICTATOR *n* ruler who has complete power
DICTATORS > DICTATOR
DICTATORY *adj* tending to dictate
DICTATRIX > DICTATOR
DICTATURE *n* dictatorship
DICTED > DICT
DICTIER > DICTY
DICTIEST > DICTY
DICTING > DICT
DICTION *n* manner of pronouncing words and sounds
DICTIONAL > DICTION
DICTIONS > DICTION
DICTS > DICT
DICTUM *n* formal statement
DICTUMS > DICTUM
DICTY *adj* conceited; snobbish
DICTYOGEN *n* plant with net-veined leaves
DICUMAROL *n* anticoagulant drug
DICYCLIC *adj* having the perianth arranged in two whorls
DICYCLIES > DICYCLIC
DICYCLY > DICYCLIC
DID > DO
DIDACT *n* instructive person
DIDACTIC *adj* intended to instruct
DIDACTICS *n* art or science of teaching
DIDACTS > DIDACT
DIDACTYL *adj* having only two toes on each foot ▷ *n* animal with only two toes on each foot
DIDACTYLS > DIDACTYL
DIDAKAI *same as* > DIDICOY
DIDAKAIS > DIDAKAI
DIDAKEI *same as* > DIDICOY
DIDAKEIS > DIDAKEI
DIDAPPER *n* small grebe
DIDAPPERS > DIDAPPER
DIDDER *vb* shake with fear
DIDDERED > DIDDER
DIDDERING > DIDDER
DIDDERS > DIDDER
DIDDICOY *same as* > DIDICOY
DIDDICOYS > DIDDICOY
DIDDIER > DIDDY
DIDDIES > DIDDY
DIDDIEST > DIDDY
DIDDLE *vb* swindle
DIDDLED > DIDDLE
DIDDLER > DIDDLE
DIDDLERS > DIDDLE
DIDDLES > DIDDLE
DIDDLEY *n* worthless amount
DIDDLEYS > DIDDLEY
DIDDLIES > DIDDLY
DIDDLING > DIDDLE
DIDDLY *n* worthless amount
DIDDY *n* female breast or nipple ▷ *adj* of or relating to a diddy
DIDELPHIC *adj* with two genital tubes or ovaries
DIDELPHID *n* marsupial
DIDICOI *same as* > DIDICOY
DIDICOIS > DIDICOI
DIDICOY *n* (in Britain) one of a group of caravan-dwelling roadside people who live like Gypsies but are not true Romanies
DIDICOYS > DIDICOY
DIDIE *same as* > DIDY
DIDIES > DIDY
DIDJERIDU *n* Australian Aboriginal wind instrument
DIDO *n* antic
DIDOES > DIDO
DIDOS > DIDO
DIDRACHM *n* two-drachma piece
DIDRACHMA *same as* > DIDRACHM
DIDRACHMS > DIDRACHM
DIDST *form of the past tense of* > DO
DIDY *n* woman's breast
DIDYMIUM *n* mixture of the metallic rare earths neodymium and praseodymium, once thought to be an element
DIDYMIUMS > DIDYMIUM
DIDYMOUS *adj* in pairs or in two parts
DIDYNAMY *n* (of stamens) being in two unequal pairs
DIE *vb* (of a person, animal, or plant) cease all biological activity permanently ▷ *n* shaped block used to cut or form metal
DIEB *n* N African jackal
DIEBACK *n* disease of trees and shrubs characterized by death of the young shoots, which spreads to the larger branches: caused by injury to the roots or attack by bacteria or fungi ▷ *vb* (of plants) to suffer from dieback
DIEBACKS > DIEBACK
DIEBS > DIEB
DIECIOUS *same as* > DIOECIOUS
DIED > DIE
DIEDRAL *same as* > DIHEDRAL
DIEDRALS > DIEDRAL
DIEDRE *n* large shallow groove or corner in a rock face
DIEDRES > DIEDRE
DIEGESES > DIEGESIS
DIEGESIS *n* utterance of fact
DIEHARD *n* person who resists change or who holds on to an outdated attitude
DIEHARDS > DIEHARD
DIEING > DIE
DIEL *n* 24-hour period
DIELDRIN *n* highly toxic insecticide
DIELDRINS > DIELDRIN
DIELYTRA *n* genus of herbaceous plants
DIELYTRAS > DIELYTRA
DIEMAKER *n* one who makes dies
DIEMAKERS > DIEMAKER
DIENE *n* hydrocarbon that contains two carbon-to-carbon double bonds in its molecules
DIENES > DIENE
DIEOFF *n* process of dying in large numbers
DIEOFFS > DIEOFF
DIERESES > DIERESIS
DIERESIS *same as* > DIAERESIS
DIERETIC > DIERESIS
DIES > DIE
DIESEL *vb* drive diesel-fueled vehicle ▷ *n* diesel engine
DIESELED > DIESEL
DIESELING > DIESEL
DIESELISE *same as* > DIESELIZE
DIESELIZE *vb* be equipped with diesel engine
DIESELS > DIESEL
DIESES > DIESIS
DIESINKER *n* person who engraves dies
DIESIS *n* (in ancient Greek theory) any interval smaller than a whole tone, esp a semitone in the Pythagorean scale
DIESTER *n* synthetic lubricant
DIESTERS > DIESTER
DIESTOCK *n* device holding the dies used to cut an external screw thread
DIESTOCKS > DIESTOCK
DIESTROUS *same as* > DIOESTRUS
DIESTRUM *another word for* > DIESTROUS
DIESTRUMS > DIESTRUM
DIESTRUS *same as* > DIOESTRUS
DIET *n* food that a person or animal regularly eats ▷ *vb* follow a special diet so as to lose weight ▷ *adj* (of food) suitable for a weight-reduction diet
DIETARIAN *n* dieter
DIETARIES > DIETARY
DIETARILY > DIETARY
DIETARY *adj* of or relating to a diet ▷ *n* regulated diet
DIETED > DIET
DIETER > DIET
DIETERS > DIET
DIETETIC *adj* prepared for special dietary requirements
DIETETICS *n* study of diet and nutrition
DIETHER *n* chemical compound
DIETHERS > DIETHER
DIETHYL as in *diethyl ether same as* > ETHER
DIETHYLS > DIETHYL
DIETICIAN *n* person who specializes in dietetics
DIETINE *n* low-ranking diet
DIETINES > DIETINE
DIETING > DIET
DIETINGS > DIET
DIETIST *another word for* > DIETITIAN
DIETISTS > DIETIST
DIETITIAN *same as* > DIETICIAN
DIETS > DIET
DIF *same as* > DIFF
DIFF *shortening of* > DIFFERENCE
DIFFER *vb* be unlike
DIFFERED > DIFFER
DIFFERENT *adj* unlike
DIFFERING > DIFFER
DIFFERS > DIFFER
DIFFICILE *adj* difficult
DIFFICULT *adj* requiring effort or skill to do or understand
DIFFIDENT *adj* lacking self-confidence
DIFFLUENT *adj* flowing; not fixed
DIFFORM *adj* irregular in form
DIFFRACT *vb* cause to undergo diffraction
DIFFRACTS > DIFFRACT
DIFFS > DIFF
DIFFUSE *vb* spread over a wide area ▷ *adj* widely spread
DIFFUSED > DIFFUSE
DIFFUSELY > DIFFUSE
DIFFUSER *n* person or thing that diffuses
DIFFUSERS > DIFFUSER
DIFFUSES > DIFFUSE
DIFFUSING > DIFFUSE
DIFFUSION *n* act of diffusing or the fact of being diffused
DIFFUSIVE *adj* characterized by diffusion
DIFFUSOR *same as* > DIFFUSER
DIFFUSORS > DIFFUSOR
DIFS > DIF
DIG *vb* cut into, break up, and turn over or remove (earth), esp with a spade ▷ *n* digging
DIGAMIES > DIGAMY
DIGAMIST > DIGAMY
DIGAMISTS > DIGAMY
DIGAMMA *n* letter of the Greek alphabet that became obsolete before the classical period of the language.
DIGAMMAS > DIGAMMA

DIGAMOUS > DIGAMY
DIGAMY *n* second marriage contracted after the termination of the first by death or divorce
DIGASTRIC *adj* (of certain muscles) having two fleshy portions joined by a tendon ▷ *n* muscle of the mandible that assists in lowering the lower jaw
DIGENESES > DIGENESIS
DIGENESIS *n* ability to alternate sexual and asexual means of reproduction
DIGENETIC *adj* of or relating to digenesis
DIGERATI *pl n* people who earn large amounts of money through internet-related business
DIGEST *vb* subject to a process of digestion ▷ *n* shortened version of a book, report, or article
DIGESTANT *same as* > DIGESTIVE
DIGESTED > DIGEST
DIGESTER *n* apparatus or vessel, such as an autoclave, in which digestion is carried out
DIGESTERS > DIGESTER
DIGESTIF *n* something, esp a drink, taken as an aid to digestion, either before or after a meal
DIGESTIFS > DIGESTIF
DIGESTING > DIGEST
DIGESTION *n* (body's system for) breaking down food into easily absorbed substances
DIGESTIVE *adj* relating to digestion
DIGESTOR *same as* > DIGESTER
DIGESTORS > DIGESTOR
DIGESTS > DIGEST
DIGGABLE *adj* that can be dug
DIGGED *a past tense of* > DIG
DIGGER *n* machine used for digging
DIGGERS > DIGGER
DIGGING > DIG
DIGGINGS *pl n* material that has been dug out
DIGHT *vb* adorn or equip, as for battle
DIGHTED > DIGHT
DIGHTING > DIGHT
DIGHTS > DIGHT
DIGICAM *n* digital camera
DIGICAMS > DIGICAM
DIGIT *n* finger or toe
DIGITAL *adj* displaying information as numbers rather than with hands and a dial ▷ *n* one of the keys on the manuals of an organ or on a piano, harpsichord, etc
DIGITALIN *n* poisonous amorphous crystalline mixture of glycosides extracted from digitalis leaves and formerly used in treating heart disease.
DIGITALIS *n* drug made from foxglove leaves, used as a heart stimulant
DIGITALLY > DIGITAL
DIGITALS > DIGITAL
DIGITATE *adj* (of leaves) having leaflets in the form of a spread hand
DIGITATED *same as* > DIGITATE
DIGITISE *same as* > DIGITIZE
DIGITISED > DIGITISE
DIGITISER > DIGITIZE
DIGITISES > DIGITISE
DIGITIZE *vb* transcribe (data) into a digital form for processing by a computer
DIGITIZED *adj* recorded or stored in digital form
DIGITIZER > DIGITIZE
DIGITIZES > DIGITIZE
DIGITONIN *n* type of glycoside
DIGITOXIN *same as* > DIGOXIN
DIGITRON *n* type of tube, for displaying information, having a common anode and several cathodes shaped in the form of characters, which can be lit by a glow discharge
DIGITRONS > DIGITRON
DIGITS > DIGIT
DIGITULE *n* any small finger-like process
DIGITULES > DIGITULE
DIGLOSSIA *n* existence in a language of a high, or socially prestigious, and a low, or everyday, form, as German and Swiss German in Switzerland
DIGLOSSIC > DIGLOSSIA
DIGLOT *n* bilingual book
DIGLOTS > DIGLOT
DIGLOTTIC > DIGLOT
DIGLYPH *n* ornament in Doric frieze with two grooves
DIGLYPHS > DIGLYPH
DIGNIFIED *adj* calm, impressive, and worthy of respect
DIGNIFIES > DIGNIFY
DIGNIFY *vb* add distinction to
DIGNITARY *n* person of high official position
DIGNITIES > DIGNITY
DIGNITY *n* serious, calm, and controlled behaviour or manner
DIGONAL *adj* of or relating to a symmetry operation in which the original figure is reconstructed after a 180° turn about an axis
DIGOXIN *n* glycoside extracted from the leaves of the woolly foxglove
DIGOXINS > DIGOXIN
DIGRAPH *n* two letters used to represent a single sound, such as *gh* in *tough*
DIGRAPHIC > DIGRAPH
DIGRAPHS > DIGRAPH
DIGRESS *vb* depart from the main subject in speech or writing
DIGRESSED > DIGRESS
DIGRESSER > DIGRESS
DIGRESSES > DIGRESS
DIGS > DIG
DIGYNIAN *adj* relating to plant class Digynia
DIGYNOUS *another word for* > DIGYNIAN
DIHEDRA > DIHEDRON
DIHEDRAL *adj* having or formed by two intersecting planes ▷ *n* figure formed by two intersecting planes
DIHEDRALS > DIHEDRAL
DIHEDRON *same as* > DIHEDRAL
DIHEDRONS > DIHEDRON
DIHYBRID *n* offspring of two individuals that differ with respect to two pairs of genes
DIHYBRIDS > DIHYBRID
DIHYDRIC *adj* (of an alcohol) containing two hydroxyl groups per molecule
DIKA *n* wild mango
DIKAS > DIKA
DIKAST *same as* > DICAST
DIKASTS > DIKAST
DIKDIK *n* small African antelope
DIKDIKS > DIKDIK
DIKE *same as* > DYKE
DIKED > DIKE
DIKER *n* builder of dikes
DIKERS > DIKER
DIKES > DIKE
DIKEY *adj* (of a lesbian) masculine
DIKIER > DIKEY
DIKIEST > DIKEY
DIKING > DIKE
DIKKOP *n* any of several brownish shore birds of the family *Burhinidae*, esp *Burhinus oedicnemus*, having a large head and eyes: order *Charadriiformes*
DIKKOPS > DIKKOP
DIKTAT *n* dictatorial decree
DIKTATS > DIKTAT
DILATABLE > DILATE
DILATABLY > DILATE
DILATANCY *n* phenomenon caused by the nature of the stacking or fitting together of particles or granules in a heterogeneous system, such as the solidification of certain sols under pressure, and the thixotropy of certain gels
DILATANT *adj* tending to dilate ▷ *n* something, such as a catheter, that causes dilation
DILATANTS > DILATANT
DILATATE *same as* > DILATE
DILATATOR *same as* > DILATOR
DILATE *vb* make or become wider or larger
DILATED > DILATE
DILATER *same as* > DILATOR
DILATERS > DILATER
DILATES > DILATE
DILATING > DILATE
DILATION > DILATE
DILATIONS > DILATE
DILATIVE > DILATE
DILATOR *n* something that dilates an object, esp a surgical instrument for dilating a bodily cavity
DILATORS > DILATOR
DILATORY *adj* tending or intended to waste time
DILDO *n* object used as a substitute for an erect penis
DILDOE *same as* > DILDO
DILDOES > DILDOE
DILDOS > DILDO
DILEMMA *n* situation offering a choice between two equally undesirable alternatives
DILEMMAS > DILEMMA
DILEMMIC > DILEMMA
DILIGENCE *n* steady and careful application
DILIGENT *adj* careful and persevering in carrying out duties
DILL *vb* flavour with dill ▷ *n* sweet-smelling herb
DILLED > DILL
DILLI *n* dilly bag; small bag, esp one made of plaited grass and used for carrying food
DILLIER > DILLY
DILLIES > DILLY
DILLIEST > DILLY
DILLING > DILL
DILLINGS > DILL
DILLIS > DILLI
DILLS > DILL
DILLY *adj* foolish ▷ *n* person or thing that is remarkable
DILTIAZEM *n* drug used to treat angina
DILUENT *adj* causing dilution or serving to dilute ▷ *n* substance used for or causing dilution
DILUENTS > DILUENT

DILUTABLE > DILUTE
DILUTE *vb* make (a liquid) less concentrated, esp by adding water ▷ *adj* (of a liquid) thin and watery
DILUTED > DILUTE
DILUTEE > DILUTE
DILUTEES > DILUTE
DILUTER > DILUTE
DILUTERS > DILUTE
DILUTES > DILUTE
DILUTING > DILUTE
DILUTION *n* act of diluting or state of being diluted
DILUTIONS > DILUTION
DILUTIVE *adj* having effect of decreasing earnings per share
DILUTOR *n* having diluting effect
DILUTORS > DILUTOR
DILUVIA > DILUVIUM
DILUVIAL *adj* of a flood, esp the great Flood described in the Old Testament
DILUVIAN *same as* > DILUVIAL
DILUVION *same as* > DILUVIUM
DILUVIONS > DILUVION
DILUVIUM *n* glacial drift
DILUVIUMS > DILUVIUM
DIM *adj* badly lit ▷ *vb* make or become dim
DIMBLE *n* wooded hollow; dingle
DIMBLES > DIMBLE
DIME *n* coin of the US and Canada, worth ten cents
DIMENSION *n* measurement of the size of something in a particular direction ▷ *vb* shape or cut to specified dimensions
DIMER *n* molecule made up of two identical molecules bonded together
DIMERIC *adj* of a dimer
DIMERISE *same as* > DIMERIZE
DIMERISED > DIMERISE
DIMERISES > DIMERISE
DIMERISM > DIMEROUS
DIMERISMS > DIMEROUS
DIMERIZE *vb* react or cause to react to form a dimer
DIMERIZED > DIMERIZE
DIMERIZES > DIMERIZE
DIMEROUS *adj* consisting of or divided into two segments, as the tarsi of some insects
DIMERS > DIMER
DIMES > DIME
DIMETER *n* line of verse consisting of two metrical feet or a verse written in this metre
DIMETERS > DIMETER
DIMETHYL *n* ethane
DIMETHYLS > DIMETHYL
DIMETRIC *adj* of, relating to, or shaped like a quadrilateral
DIMIDIATE *adj* divided in halves ▷ *vb* halve (two bearings) so that they can be represented on the same shield
DIMINISH *vb* make or become smaller, fewer, or less
DIMISSORY *adj* granting permission to be ordained
DIMITIES > DIMITY
DIMITY *n* light strong cotton fabric with woven stripes or squares
DIMLY > DIM
DIMMABLE *adj* that can be dimmed
DIMMED > DIM
DIMMER > DIM
DIMMERS > DIM
DIMMEST > DIM
DIMMING > DIM
DIMMISH > DIM
DIMNESS > DIM
DIMNESSES > DIM
DIMORPH *n* either of two forms of a substance that exhibits dimorphism
DIMORPHIC > DIMORPHISM
DIMORPHS > DIMORPH
DIMOUT *n* reduction of lighting
DIMOUTS > DIMOUT
DIMP *n* in Northern English dialect, a cigarette butt
DIMPLE *n* small natural dent, esp in the cheeks or chin ▷ *vb* produce dimples by smiling
DIMPLED > DIMPLE
DIMPLES > DIMPLE
DIMPLIER > DIMPLE
DIMPLIEST > DIMPLE
DIMPLING > DIMPLE
DIMPLY > DIMPLE
DIMPS > DIMP
DIMPSIES > DIMPSY
DIMPSY *n* twilight
DIMS > DIM
DIMWIT *n* stupid person
DIMWITS > DIMWIT
DIMWITTED > DIMWIT
DIMYARIAN *adj* with two adductor muscles
DIN *n* loud unpleasant confused noise ▷ *vb* instil (something) into someone by constant repetition
DINAR *n* monetary unit of various Balkan, Middle Eastern, and North African countries
DINARCHY *same as* > DIARCHY
DINARS > DINAR
DINDLE *another word for* > DINNLE
DINDLED > DINDLE
DINDLES > DINDLE
DINDLING > DINDLE
DINE *vb* eat dinner
DINED > DINE
DINER *n* person eating a meal
DINERIC *adj* of or concerned with the interface between immiscible liquids
DINERO *n* money
DINEROS > DINERO
DINERS > DINER
DINES > DINE
DINETTE *n* alcove or small area for use as a dining room
DINETTES > DINETTE
DINFUL *adj* noisy
DING *n* small dent in a vehicle ▷ *vb* ring or cause to ring, esp with tedious repetition
DINGBAT *n* any unnamed object, esp one used as a missile
DINGBATS > DINGBAT
DINGDONG *n* sound of a bell or bells ▷ *vb* make such a sound
DINGE *n* dent ▷ *vb* make a dent in (something)
DINGED > DINGE
DINGER *n* (in baseball) home run
DINGERS > DINGER
DINGES *n* jocular word for something whose name is unknown or forgotten
DINGESES > DINGES
DINGEY *same as* > DINGHY
DINGEYS > DINGEY
DINGHIES > DINGHY
DINGHY *n* small boat, powered by sails, oars, or a motor
DINGIER > DINGY
DINGIES > DINGY
DINGIEST > DINGY
DINGILY > DINGY
DINGINESS > DINGY
DINGING > DINGE
DINGLE *n* small wooded hollow or valley
DINGLES > DINGLE
DINGO *n* Australian wild dog ▷ *vb* act in a cowardly manner
DINGOED > DINGO
DINGOES > DINGO
DINGOING > DINGO
DINGS > DING
DINGUS *same as* > DINGES
DINGUSES > DINGUS
DINGY *adj* lacking light
DINIC *n* remedy for vertigo
DINICS > DINIC
DINING > DINE
DINITRO *adj* containing two nitro groups
DINK *adj* neat or neatly dressed ▷ *vb* carry (a second person) on a horse, bicycle, etc ▷ *n* ball struck delicately
DINKED > DINK
DINKER > DINK
DINKEST > DINK
DINKEY *n* small locomotive
DINKEYS > DINKEY
DINKIE *n* affluent married childless person ▷ *adj* designed for or appealing to dinkies
DINKIER > DINKY
DINKIES > DINKIE
DINKIEST > DINKY
DINKING > DINK
DINKLY *adj* neat
DINKS > DINK
DINKUM *n* truth or genuineness
DINKUMS > DINKUM
DINKY *adj* small and neat
DINMONT *n* neutered sheep
DINMONTS > DINMONT
DINNA *vb* a Scots word for do not
DINNED > DIN
DINNER *vb* dine ▷ *n* main meal of the day, eaten either in the evening or at midday
DINNERED > DINNER
DINNERING > DINNER
DINNERS > DINNER
DINNING > DIN
DINNLE *vb* shake
DINNLED > DINNLE
DINNLES > DINNLE
DINNLING > DINNLE
DINO *n* dinosaur
DINOCERAS *another name for a* > UINTATHERE
DINOMANIA *n* strong interest in dinosaurs
DINOS > DINO
DINOSAUR *n* type of extinct prehistoric reptile, many of which were of gigantic size
DINOSAURS > DINOSAUR
DINOTHERE *n* any extinct late Tertiary elephant-like mammal of the genus *Dinotherium* (or *Deinotherium*), having a down-turned jaw with tusks curving downwards and backwards
DINS > DIN
DINT *variant of* > DENT
DINTED > DINT
DINTING > DINT
DINTLESS > DINT
DINTS > DINT
DIOBOL *n* ancient Greek coin
DIOBOLON *same as* > DIOBOL
DIOBOLONS > DIOBOLON
DIOBOLS > DIOBOL
DIOCESAN *adj* of or relating to a diocese ▷ *n* bishop of a diocese
DIOCESANS > DIOCESAN
DIOCESE *n* district over which a bishop has control
DIOCESES > DIOCESE
DIODE *n* semiconductor device for converting alternating current to

direct current
DIODES > DIODE
DIOECIES > DIOECY
DIOECIOUS *adj* (of plants) having the male and female reproductive organs on separate plants
DIOECISM > DIOECIOUS
DIOECISMS > DIOECIOUS
DIOECY *n* state of being dioecious
DIOESTRUS *n* period in mammal's oestral cycle
DIOICOUS *same as* > DIOECIOUS
DIOL *n* any of a class of alcohols that have two hydroxyl groups in each molecule
DIOLEFIN *n* type of polymer
DIOLEFINS > DIOLEFIN
DIOLS > DIOL
DIONYSIAC *same as* > DIONYSIAN
DIONYSIAN *adj* wild or orgiastic
DIOPSIDE *n* colourless or pale-green pyroxene mineral
DIOPSIDES > DIOPSIDE
DIOPSIDIC > DIOPSIDE
DIOPTASE *n* green glassy mineral
DIOPTASES > DIOPTASE
DIOPTER *same as* > DIOPTRE
DIOPTERS > DIOPTER
DIOPTRAL > DIOPTRE
DIOPTRATE *adj* (of compound eye) divided by transverse line
DIOPTRE *n* unit for measuring the refractive power of a lens
DIOPTRES > DIOPTRE
DIOPTRIC *adj* of or concerned with dioptrics
DIOPTRICS *n* branch of geometrical optics concerned with the formation of images by lenses
DIORAMA *n* miniature three-dimensional scene, in which models of figures are seen against a three-dimensional background
DIORAMAS > DIORAMA
DIORAMIC > DIORAMA
DIORISM *n* definition; clarity
DIORISMS > DIORISM
DIORISTIC > DIORISM
DIORITE *n* dark coarse-grained igneous plutonic rock consisting of plagioclase feldspar and ferromagnesian minerals such as hornblende
DIORITES > DIORITE
DIORITIC > DIORITE
DIOSGENIN *n* yam-based substance used in hormone therapy
DIOTA *n* type of ancient vase
DIOTAS > DIOTA
DIOXAN *n* colourless insoluble toxic liquid made by heating ethanediol with sulphuric acid
DIOXANE *same as* > DIOXAN
DIOXANES > DIOXANE
DIOXANS > DIOXAN
DIOXID *same as* > DIOXIDE
DIOXIDE *n* oxide containing two oxygen atoms per molecule
DIOXIDES > DIOXIDE
DIOXIDS > DIOXID
DIOXIN *n* any of a number of mostly poisonous chemical by-products of the manufacture of certain herbicides and bactericides, esp the extremely toxic 2,3,7,8-tetrachlorodibenzo-para-dioxin
DIOXINS > DIOXIN
DIP *vb* plunge quickly or briefly into a liquid ▷ *n* dipping
DIPCHICK *same as* > DABCHICK
DIPCHICKS > DIPCHICK
DIPEPTIDE *n* compound consisting of two linked amino acids
DIPHASE *adj* of, having, or concerned with two phases
DIPHASIC *same as* > DIPHASE
DIPHENYL *another name for* > BIPHENYL
DIPHENYLS > DIPHENYL
DIPHONE *n* combination of two speech sounds
DIPHONES > DIPHONE
DIPHTHONG *n* union of two vowel sounds in a single compound sound
DIPHYSITE *n* belief in Christ having both divine and human natures
DIPLEGIA *n* paralysis of corresponding parts on both sides of the body
DIPLEGIAS > DIPLEGIA
DIPLEGIC > DIPLEGIA
DIPLEX *adj* (in telecommunications) permitting the transmission of simultaneous signals in both directions
DIPLEXER *n* device that enables the simultaneous transmission of more than one signal
DIPLEXERS > DIPLEXER
DIPLOE *n* spongy bone separating the two layers of compact bone of the skull
DIPLOES > DIPLOE
DIPLOGEN *n* heavy hydrogen
DIPLOGENS > DIPLOGEN
DIPLOIC *adj* relating to diploe
DIPLOID *adj* denoting a cell or organism with pairs of homologous chromosomes ▷ *n* diploid cell or organism
DIPLOIDIC > DIPLOID
DIPLOIDS > DIPLOID
DIPLOIDY > DIPLOID
DIPLOMA *vb* bestow diploma on ▷ *n* qualification awarded by a college on successful completion of a course
DIPLOMACY *n* conduct of the relations between nations by peaceful means
DIPLOMAED > DIPLOMA
DIPLOMAS > DIPLOMA
DIPLOMAT *n* official engaged in diplomacy
DIPLOMATA > DIPLOMA
DIPLOMATE *n* any person who has been granted a diploma, esp a physician certified as a specialist
DIPLOMATS > DIPLOMAT
DIPLON *another name for* > DEUTERON
DIPLONEMA *a less common name for* > DIPLOTENE
DIPLONS > DIPLON
DIPLONT *n* animal or plant that has the diploid number of chromosomes in its somatic cells
DIPLONTIC > DIPLONT
DIPLONTS > DIPLONT
DIPLOPIA *n* visual defect in which a single object is seen in duplicate
DIPLOPIAS > DIPLOPIA
DIPLOPIC > DIPLOPIA
DIPLOPOD *n* any arthropod of the class *Diplopoda*, which includes the millipedes
DIPLOPODS > DIPLOPOD
DIPLOSES > DIPLOSIS
DIPLOSIS *n* doubling of the haploid number of chromosomes that occurs during fusion of gametes to form a diploid zygote
DIPLOTENE *n* fourth stage of the prophase of meiosis, during which the paired homologous chromosomes separate except at the places where genetic exchange has occurred
DIPLOZOA *n* type of parasitic worm
DIPLOZOIC *adj* (of certain animals) bilaterally symmetrical
DIPLOZOON *n* type of parasitic worm
DIPNET *vb* fish using fishing net on pole
DIPNETS > DIPNET
DIPNETTED > DIPNET
DIPNOAN *adj* of, relating to, or belonging to the *Dipnoi*, a subclass of bony fishes comprising the lungfishes ▷ *n* any lungfish
DIPNOANS > DIPNOAN
DIPNOOUS *adj* having lungs and gills
DIPODIC > DIPODY
DIPODIES > DIPODY
DIPODY *n* metrical unit consisting of two feet
DIPOLAR > DIPOLE
DIPOLE *n* two equal but opposite electric charges or magnetic poles separated by a small distance
DIPOLES > DIPOLE
DIPPABLE > DIP
DIPPED > DIP
DIPPER *n* ladle used for dipping
DIPPERFUL *n* amount held by scoop
DIPPERS > DIPPER
DIPPIER > DIPPY
DIPPIEST > DIPPY
DIPPINESS > DIPPY
DIPPING > DIP
DIPPINGS > DIP
DIPPY *adj* odd, eccentric, or crazy
DIPROTIC *adj* having two hydrogen atoms
DIPS > DIP
DIPSADES > DIPSAS
DIPSAS *n* type of snake
DIPSHIT *n* stupid person
DIPSHITS > DIPSHIT
DIPSO *same as* > DIPSOMANIAC
DIPSOS > DIPSO
DIPSTICK *n* notched rod dipped into a container to measure the level of a liquid
DIPSTICKS > DIPSTICK
DIPT > DIP
DIPTERA *n* order of insects with two wings
DIPTERAL *adj* having a double row of columns
DIPTERAN *n* dipterous insect ▷ *adj* having two wings or winglike parts
DIPTERANS > DIPTERAN
DIPTERAS > DIPTERA
DIPTERIST *n* fly expert
DIPTEROI > DIPTEROS
DIPTERON *same as* > DIPTERAN
DIPTERONS > DIPTERON
DIPTEROS *n* Greek building with double columns
DIPTEROUS *adj* having two wings or winglike parts
DIPTYCA *same as* > DIPTYCH
DIPTYCAS > DIPTYCA
DIPTYCH *n* painting on two hinged panels
DIPTYCHS > DIPTYCH

DIQUARK *n* low-energy configuration of two quarks attracted to one another by virtue of having antisymmetric colours and spins
DIQUARKS > DIQUARK
DIQUAT *n* type of herbicide
DIQUATS > DIQUAT
DIRAM *n* money unit of Tajikistan
DIRAMS > DIRAM
DIRDAM *same as* > DIRDUM
DIRDAMS > DIRDAM
DIRDUM *n* tumult
DIRDUMS > DIRDUM
DIRE *adj* disastrous, urgent, or terrible
DIRECT *adj* (of a route) shortest, straight ▷ *adv* in a direct manner ▷ *vb* lead and organize
DIRECTED *adj* (of a number, line, or angle) having either a positive or negative sign to distinguish measurement in one direction or orientation from that in the opposite direction or orientation
DIRECTER > DIRECT
DIRECTEST > DIRECT
DIRECTING > DIRECT
DIRECTION *n* course or line along which a person or thing moves, points, or lies
DIRECTIVE *n* instruction, order ▷ *adj* tending to direct
DIRECTLY *adv* in a direct manner
DIRECTOR *n* person or thing that directs or controls
DIRECTORS > DIRECTOR
DIRECTORY *n* book listing names, addresses, and telephone numbers ▷ *adj* directing
DIRECTRIX *n* fixed reference line, situated on the convex side of a conic section, that is used when defining or calculating its eccentricity
DIRECTS > DIRECT
DIREFUL *same as* > DIRE
DIREFULLY > DIREFUL
DIRELY > DIRE
DIREMPT *vb* separate with force
DIREMPTED > DIREMPT
DIREMPTS > DIREMPT
DIRENESS > DIRE
DIRER > DIRE
DIREST > DIRE
DIRGE *n* slow sad song of mourning
DIRGEFUL > DIRGE
DIRGELIKE > DIRGE
DIRGES > DIRGE
DIRHAM *n* standard monetary unit of Morocco, divided into 100 centimes
DIRHAMS > DIRHAM
DIRHEM *same as* > DIRHAM
DIRHEMS > DIRHEM
DIRIGE *n* dirge
DIRIGENT *adj* directing
DIRIGES > DIRIGE
DIRIGIBLE *adj* able to be steered ▷ *n* airship
DIRIGISM *same as* > DIRIGISME
DIRIGISME *n* control by the state of economic and social matters
DIRIGISMS > DIRIGISM
DIRIGISTE > DIRIGISME
DIRIMENT *adj* (of an impediment to marriage in canon law) totally invalidating
DIRK *n* dagger, formerly worn by Scottish Highlanders ▷ *vb* stab with a dirk
DIRKE *variant of* > DIRK
DIRKED > DIRK
DIRKES > DIRKE
DIRKING > DIRK
DIRKS > DIRK
DIRL *vb* tingle; vibrate
DIRLED > DIRL
DIRLING > DIRL
DIRLS > DIRL
DIRNDL *n* full gathered skirt originating from Tyrolean peasant wear
DIRNDLS > DIRNDL
DIRT *vb* soil ▷ *n* unclean substance, filth
DIRTBAG *n* filthy person
DIRTBAGS > DIRTBAG
DIRTED > DIRT
DIRTIED > DIRTY
DIRTIER > DIRTY
DIRTIES > DIRTY
DIRTIEST > DIRTY
DIRTILY > DIRTY
DIRTINESS > DIRTY
DIRTING > DIRT
DIRTS > DIRT
DIRTY *adj* covered or marked with dirt ▷ *vb* make dirty
DIRTYING > DIRTY
DIS *same as* > DISS
DISA *n* type of orchid
DISABLE *vb* make ineffective, unfit, or incapable
DISABLED *adj* lacking a physical power, such as the ability to walk
DISABLER > DISABLE
DISABLERS > DISABLE
DISABLES > DISABLE
DISABLING > DISABLE
DISABUSAL > DISABUSE
DISABUSE *vb* rid (someone) of a mistaken idea
DISABUSED > DISABUSE
DISABUSES > DISABUSE
DISACCORD *n* lack of agreement or harmony ▷ *vb* be out of agreement
DISADORN *vb* deprive of ornamentation
DISADORNS > DISADORN
DISAFFECT *vb* cause to lose loyalty or affection
DISAFFIRM *vb* deny or contradict (a statement)
DISAGREE *vb* argue or have different opinions
DISAGREED > DISAGREE
DISAGREES > DISAGREE
DISALLIED > DISALLY
DISALLIES > DISALLY
DISALLOW *vb* reject as untrue or invalid
DISALLOWS > DISALLOW
DISALLY *vb* separate
DISANCHOR *vb* raise anchor of
DISANNEX *vb* disunite
DISANNUL *vb* cancel
DISANNULS > DISANNUL
DISANOINT *vb* invalidate anointment of
DISAPPEAR *vb* cease to be visible
DISAPPLY *vb* make (law) invalid
DISARM *vb* deprive of weapons
DISARMED > DISARM
DISARMER > DISARM
DISARMERS > DISARM
DISARMING *adj* removing hostility or suspicion
DISARMS > DISARM
DISARRAY *n* confusion and lack of discipline ▷ *vb* throw into confusion
DISARRAYS > DISARRAY
DISAS > DISA
DISASTER *n* occurrence that causes great distress or destruction
DISASTERS > DISASTER
DISATTIRE *vb* remove clothes from
DISATTUNE *vb* render out of tune
DISAVOUCH *archaic form of* > DISAVOW
DISAVOW *vb* deny connection with or responsibility for
DISAVOWAL > DISAVOW
DISAVOWED > DISAVOW
DISAVOWER > DISAVOW
DISAVOWS > DISAVOW
DISBAND *vb* (cause to) cease to function as a group
DISBANDED > DISBAND
DISBANDS > DISBAND
DISBAR *vb* deprive (a barrister) of the right to practise
DISBARK *same as* > DISEMBARK
DISBARKED > DISBARK
DISBARKS > DISBARK
DISBARRED > DISBAR
DISBARS > DISBAR
DISBELIEF *n* refusal or reluctance to believe
DISBENCH *vb* remove from bench
DISBODIED *adj* disembodied
DISBOSOM *vb* disclose
DISBOSOMS > DISBOSOM
DISBOUND *adj* unbound
DISBOWEL *vb* disembowel
DISBOWELS > DISBOWEL
DISBRANCH *vb* remove or cut a branch or branches from (a tree)
DISBUD *vb* remove superfluous buds, flowers, or shoots from (a plant, esp a fruit tree)
DISBUDDED > DISBUD
DISBUDS > DISBUD
DISBURDEN *vb* remove a load from (a person or animal)
DISBURSAL > DISBURSE
DISBURSE *vb* pay out
DISBURSED > DISBURSE
DISBURSER > DISBURSE
DISBURSES > DISBURSE
DISC *n* flat circular object ▷ *vb* work (land) with a disc harrow
DISCAGE *vb* release from cage
DISCAGED > DISCAGE
DISCAGES > DISCAGE
DISCAGING > DISCAGE
DISCAL *adj* relating to or resembling a disc
DISCALCED *adj* barefooted: used to denote friars and nuns who wear sandals
DISCANDIE *same as* > DISCANDY
DISCANDY *vb* melt; dissolve
DISCANT *same as* > DESCANT
DISCANTED > DISCANT
DISCANTER > DISCANT
DISCANTS > DISCANT
DISCARD *vb* get rid of (something or someone) as useless or undesirable ▷ *n* person or thing that has been cast aside
DISCARDED > DISCARD
DISCARDER > DISCARD
DISCARDS > DISCARD
DISCASE *vb* remove case from
DISCASED > DISCASE
DISCASES > DISCASE
DISCASING > DISCASE
DISCED > DISC
DISCEPT *vb* discuss
DISCEPTED > DISCEPT
DISCEPTS > DISCEPT
DISCERN *vb* see or be aware of (something) clearly
DISCERNED > DISCERN
DISCERNER > DISCERN
DISCERNS > DISCERN
DISCERP *vb* divide
DISCERPED > DISCERP
DISCERPS > DISCERP
DISCHARGE *vb* release, allow to go ▷ *n* substance that comes out from a

place

DISCHURCH *vb* deprive of church membership

DISCI > DISCUS

DISCIDE *vb* split

DISCIDED > DISCIDE

DISCIDES > DISCIDE

DISCIDING > DISCIDE

DISCIFORM *adj* disc-shaped

DISCINCT *adj* loosely dressed, without belt

DISCING > DISC

DISCIPLE *vb* teach ▷ *n* follower of the doctrines of a teacher, esp Jesus Christ

DISCIPLED > DISCIPLE

DISCIPLES > DISCIPLE

DISCLAIM *vb* deny (responsibility for or knowledge of something)

DISCLAIMS > DISCLAIM

DISCLIKE > DISC

DISCLIMAX *n* climax community resulting from the activities of man or domestic animals in climatic and other conditions that would otherwise support a different type of community

DISCLOSE *vb* make known

DISCLOSED > DISCLOSE

DISCLOSER > DISCLOSE

DISCLOSES > DISCLOSE

DISCLOST > DISCLOSE

DISCO *vb* go to a disco ▷ *n* nightclub where people dance to amplified pop records

DISCOBOLI *pl n* discus throwers

DISCOED > DISCO

DISCOER > DISCO

DISCOERS > DISCO

DISCOID *adj* like a disc ▷ *n* disclike object

DISCOIDAL *adj* like a disc

DISCOIDS > DISCOID

DISCOING > DISCO

DISCOLOGY *n* study of gramophone records

DISCOLOR *same as* > DISCOLOUR

DISCOLORS > DISCOLOR

DISCOLOUR *vb* change in colour, fade

DISCOMFIT *vb* make uneasy or confused

DISCOMMON *vb* deprive (land) of the character and status of common, as by enclosure

DISCORD *n* lack of agreement or harmony between people ▷ *vb* disagree

DISCORDED > DISCORD

DISCORDS > DISCORD

DISCOS > DISCO

DISCOUNT *vb* take no account of (something) because it is considered to be unreliable, prejudiced, or irrelevant ▷ *n* deduction from the full price of something

DISCOUNTS > DISCOUNT

DISCOURE *vb* discover

DISCOURED > DISCOURE

DISCOURES > DISCOURE

DISCOURSE *n* conversation ▷ *vb* speak or write (about) at length

DISCOVER *vb* be the first to find or to find out about

DISCOVERS > DISCOVER

DISCOVERT *adj* (of a woman) not under the protection of a husband

DISCOVERY *n* discovering

DISCREDIT *vb* damage the reputation of ▷ *n* damage to someone's reputation

DISCREET *adj* careful to avoid embarrassment, esp by keeping confidences secret

DISCRETE *adj* separate, distinct

DISCRETER > DISCRETE

DISCROWN *vb* deprive of a crown

DISCROWNS > DISCROWN

DISCS > DISC

DISCUMBER *vb* disencumber

DISCURE *old form of* > DISCOVER

DISCURED > DISCURE

DISCURES > DISCURE

DISCURING > DISCURE

DISCURSUS *n* discursive reasoning

DISCUS *n* heavy disc-shaped object thrown in sports competitions

DISCUSES > DISCUS

DISCUSS *vb* consider (something) by talking it over

DISCUSSED > DISCUSS

DISCUSSER > DISCUSS

DISCUSSES > DISCUSS

DISDAIN *n* feeling of superiority and dislike ▷ *vb* refuse with disdain

DISDAINED > DISDAIN

DISDAINS > DISDAIN

DISEASE *vb* make uneasy ▷ *n* illness, sickness

DISEASED *adj* having or affected with disease

DISEASES > DISEASE

DISEASING > DISEASE

DISEDGE *vb* render blunt

DISEDGED > DISEDGE

DISEDGES > DISEDGE

DISEDGING > DISEDGE

DISEMBARK *vb* get off a ship, aircraft, or bus

DISEMBODY *vb* free from the body or from physical form

DISEMPLOY *vb* dismiss from employment

DISENABLE *vb* cause to become incapable

DISENDOW *vb* take away an endowment from

DISENDOWS > DISENDOW

DISENGAGE *vb* release from a connection

DISENROL *vb* remove from register

DISENROLS > DISENROL

DISENTAIL *vb* free (an estate) from entail ▷ *n* act of disentailing

DISENTOMB *vb* disinter

DISESTEEM *vb* think little of ▷ *n* lack of esteem

DISEUR *same as* > DISEUSE

DISEURS > DISEUR

DISEUSE *n* (esp formerly) an actress who presents dramatic recitals, usually sung accompanied by music

DISEUSES > DISEUSE

DISFAME *n* discredit

DISFAMES > DISFAME

DISFAVOR *same as* > DISFAVOUR

DISFAVORS > DISFAVOR

DISFAVOUR *n* disapproval or dislike ▷ *vb* regard or treat with disapproval or dislike

DISFIGURE *vb* spoil the appearance of

DISFLESH *vb* reduce flesh of

DISFLUENT *adj* lacking fluency in speech

DISFOREST *same as* > DEFOREST

DISFORM *vb* change form of

DISFORMED > DISFORM

DISFORMS > DISFORM

DISFROCK *another word for* > UNFROCK

DISFROCKS > DISFROCK

DISGAVEL *vb* deprive of quality of gavelkind

DISGAVELS > DISGAVEL

DISGEST *vb* digest

DISGESTED > DISGEST

DISGESTS > DISGEST

DISGODDED *adj* deprived of religion

DISGORGE *vb* empty out, discharge

DISGORGED > DISGORGE

DISGORGER *n* thin notched metal implement for removing hooks from a fish

DISGORGES > DISGORGE

DISGOWN *vb* remove gown from

DISGOWNED > DISGOWN

DISGOWNS > DISGOWN

DISGRACE *n* condition of shame, loss of reputation, or dishonour ▷ *vb* bring shame upon (oneself or others)

DISGRACED > DISGRACE

DISGRACER > DISGRACE

DISGRACES > DISGRACE

DISGRADE *vb* degrade

DISGRADED > DISGRADE

DISGRADES > DISGRADE

DISGUISE *vb* change the appearance or manner in order to conceal the identity of (someone or something) ▷ *n* mask, costume, or manner that disguises

DISGUISED > DISGUISE

DISGUISER > DISGUISE

DISGUISES > DISGUISE

DISGUST *n* great loathing or distaste ▷ *vb* sicken, fill with loathing

DISGUSTED > DISGUST

DISGUSTS > DISGUST

DISH *n* shallow container used for holding or serving food ▷ *vb* put into a dish

DISHABIT *vb* dislodge

DISHABITS > DISHABIT

DISHABLE *obsolete form of* > DISABLE

DISHABLED > DISHABLE

DISHABLES > DISHABLE

DISHALLOW *vb* make unholy

DISHCLOTH *n* cloth for washing dishes

DISHCLOUT *same as* > DISHCLOTH

DISHDASHA *n* long-sleeved collarless white garment worn by some Muslim men

DISHED *adj* shaped like a dish

DISHELM *vb* remove helmet from

DISHELMED > DISHELM

DISHELMS > DISHELM

DISHERIT *vb* disinherit

DISHERITS > DISHERIT

DISHES > DISH

DISHEVEL *vb* disarrange (the hair or clothes) of (someone)

DISHEVELS > DISHEVEL

DISHFUL *n* the amount that a dish is able to hold

DISHFULS > DISHFUL

DISHIER > DISHY

DISHIEST > DISHY

DISHING > DISH

DISHINGS > DISH

DISHLIKE > DISH

DISHOME *vb* deprive of home

DISHOMED > DISHOME

DISHOMES > DISHOME

DISHOMING > DISHOME

DISHONEST *adj* not honest or fair

DISHONOR *same as* > DISHONOUR

DISHONORS > DISHONOR

DISHONOUR *vb* treat with disrespect ▷ *n* lack of respect

DISHORN *vb* remove horns from

DISHORNED > DISHORN

DISHORNS > DISHORN
DISHORSE *vb* dismount
DISHORSED > DISHORSE
DISHORSES > DISHORSE
DISHOUSE *vb* deprive of home
DISHOUSED > DISHOUSE
DISHOUSES > DISHOUSE
DISHPAN *n* large pan for washing dishes, pots, etc
DISHPANS > DISHPAN
DISHRAG *n* dishcloth
DISHRAGS > DISHRAG
DISHTOWEL *n* towel for drying dishes and kitchen utensils
DISHUMOUR *vb* upset; offend
DISHWARE *n* tableware
DISHWARES > DISHWARE
DISHWATER *n* water in which dishes and kitchen utensils are or have been washed
DISHY *adj* good-looking
DISILLUDE *vb* remove illusions from
DISIMMURE *vb* release
DISINFECT *vb* rid of harmful germs, chemically
DISINFEST *vb* rid of vermin
DISINFORM *vb* give wrong information
DISINHUME *vb* dig up
DISINTER *vb* dig up
DISINTERS > DISINTER
DISINURE *vb* render unaccustomed
DISINURED > DISINURE
DISINURES > DISINURE
DISINVEST *vb* remove investment (from)
DISINVITE *vb* retract invitation to
DISJASKIT *adj* fatigued
DISJECT *vb* break apart
DISJECTED > DISJECT
DISJECTS > DISJECT
DISJOIN *vb* disconnect or become disconnected
DISJOINED > DISJOIN
DISJOINS > DISJOIN
DISJOINT *vb* take apart or come apart at the joints ▷ *adj* (of two sets) having no members in common
DISJOINTS > DISJOINT
DISJUNCT *adj* not united or joined ▷ *n* one of the propositions or formulas in a disjunction
DISJUNCTS > DISJUNCT
DISJUNE *n* breakfast
DISJUNES > DISJUNE
DISK *same as* > DISC
DISKED > DISK
DISKETTE *n* floppy disk
DISKETTES > DISKETTE
DISKING > DISK
DISKLESS > DISK
DISKLIKE > DISK
DISKS > DISK
DISLEAF *vb* remove leaf or leaves from
DISLEAFED > DISLEAF
DISLEAFS > DISLEAF
DISLEAL *archaic form of* > DISLOYAL
DISLEAVE *variant of* > DISLEAF
DISLEAVED > DISLEAVE
DISLEAVES > DISLEAVE
DISLIKE *vb* consider unpleasant or disagreeable ▷ *n* feeling of not liking something or someone
DISLIKED > DISLIKE
DISLIKEN *vb* render dissimilar to
DISLIKENS > DISLIKEN
DISLIKER > DISLIKE
DISLIKERS > DISLIKE
DISLIKES > DISLIKE
DISLIKING > DISLIKE
DISLIMB *vb* remove limbs from
DISLIMBED > DISLIMB
DISLIMBS > DISLIMB
DISLIMN *vb* efface
DISLIMNED > DISLIMN
DISLIMNS > DISLIMN
DISLINK *vb* disunite
DISLINKED > DISLINK
DISLINKS > DISLINK
DISLOAD *vb* unload
DISLOADED > DISLOAD
DISLOADS > DISLOAD
DISLOCATE *vb* displace (a bone or joint) from its normal position
DISLODGE *vb* remove (something) from a previously fixed position
DISLODGED > DISLODGE
DISLODGES > DISLODGE
DISLOIGN *vb* put at a distance
DISLOIGNS > DISLOIGN
DISLOYAL *adj* not loyal, deserting one's allegiance
DISLUSTRE *vb* remove lustre from
DISMAL *adj* gloomy and depressing
DISMALER > DISMAL
DISMALEST > DISMAL
DISMALITY > DISMAL
DISMALLER > DISMAL
DISMALLY > DISMAL
DISMALS *pl n* gloomy state of mind
DISMAN *vb* remove men from
DISMANNED > DISMAN
DISMANS > DISMAN
DISMANTLE *vb* take apart piece by piece
DISMASK *vb* remove mask from
DISMASKED > DISMASK
DISMASKS > DISMASK
DISMAST *vb* break off the mast or masts of (a sailing vessel)
DISMASTED > DISMAST
DISMASTS > DISMAST
DISMAY *vb* fill with alarm or depression ▷ *n* alarm mixed with sadness
DISMAYD > DISMAY
DISMAYED > DISMAY
DISMAYFUL > DISMAY
DISMAYING > DISMAY
DISMAYL *vb* remove a coat of mail from
DISMAYLED > DISMAYL
DISMAYLS > DISMAYL
DISMAYS > DISMAY
DISME *old form of* > DIME
DISMEMBER *vb* remove the limbs of
DISMES > DISME
DISMISS *vb* remove (an employee) from a job ▷ *sentence substitute* order to end an activity or give permission to disperse
DISMISSAL *n* official notice of discharge from employment or service
DISMISSED > DISMISS
DISMISSES > DISMISS
DISMODED *adj* no longer fashionable
DISMOUNT *vb* get off a horse or bicycle ▷ *n* act of dismounting
DISMOUNTS > DISMOUNT
DISNEST *vb* remove from nest
DISNESTED > DISNEST
DISNESTS > DISNEST
DISOBEY *vb* neglect or refuse to obey
DISOBEYED > DISOBEY
DISOBEYER > DISOBEY
DISOBEYS > DISOBEY
DISOBLIGE *vb* disregard the desires of
DISOMIC *adj* having an extra chromosome in the haploid state that is homologous to an existing chromosome in this set
DISOMIES > DISOMIC
DISOMY > DISOMIC
DISORBED *adj* thrown out of orbit
DISORDER *n* state of untidiness and disorganization ▷ *vb* upset the order of
DISORDERS > DISORDER
DISORIENT *same as* > DISORIENTATE
DISOWN *vb* deny any connection with (someone)
DISOWNED > DISOWN
DISOWNER > DISOWN
DISOWNERS > DISOWN
DISOWNING > DISOWN
DISOWNS > DISOWN
DISPACE *vb* move or travel about
DISPACED > DISPACE
DISPACES > DISPACE
DISPACING > DISPACE
DISPARAGE *vb* speak contemptuously of
DISPARATE *adj* completely different ▷ *n* unlike things or people
DISPARITY *n* inequality or difference
DISPARK *vb* release
DISPARKED > DISPARK
DISPARKS > DISPARK
DISPART *vb* separate
DISPARTED > DISPART
DISPARTS > DISPART
DISPATCH *vb* send off to a destination or to perform a task ▷ *n* official communication or report, sent in haste
DISPATHY *obsolete spelling of* > DYSPATHY
DISPAUPER *vb* state that someone is no longer a pauper
DISPEACE *n* absence of peace
DISPEACES > DISPEACE
DISPEL *vb* destroy or remove
DISPELLED > DISPEL
DISPELLER > DISPEL
DISPELS > DISPEL
DISPENCE *same as* > DISPENSE
DISPENCED > DISPENCE
DISPENCES > DISPENCE
DISPEND *vb* spend
DISPENDED > DISPEND
DISPENDS > DISPEND
DISPENSE *vb* distribute in portions
DISPENSED > DISPENSE
DISPENSER *n* device, such as a vending machine, that automatically dispenses a single item or a measured quantity
DISPENSES > DISPENSE
DISPEOPLE *vb* remove inhabitants from
DISPERSAL *n* act of dispersing or the condition of being dispersed
DISPERSE *vb* scatter over a wide area ▷ *adj* of or consisting of the particles in a colloid or suspension
DISPERSED > DISPERSE
DISPERSER > DISPERSE
DISPERSES > DISPERSE
DISPIRIT *vb* make downhearted
DISPIRITS > DISPIRIT
DISPLACE *vb* move from the usual location
DISPLACED > DISPLACE
DISPLACER > DISPLACE
DISPLACES > DISPLACE
DISPLANT *vb* displace
DISPLANTS > DISPLANT
DISPLAY *vb* make visible or noticeable ▷ *n* displaying
DISPLAYED > DISPLAY
DISPLAYER > DISPLAY
DISPLAYS > DISPLAY
DISPLE *vb* punish
DISPLEASE *vb* annoy or

upset
DISPLED > DISPLE
DISPLES > DISPLE
DISPLING > DISPLE
DISPLODE *obsolete word for* > EXPLODE
DISPLODED > DISPLODE
DISPLODES > DISPLODE
DISPLUME *vb* remove feathers from
DISPLUMED > DISPLUME
DISPLUMES > DISPLUME
DISPONDEE *n* (poetry) double foot of two long syllables
DISPONE *vb* transfer ownership
DISPONED > DISPONE
DISPONEE *vb* person whom something is disponed to
DISPONEES > DISPONEE
DISPONER > DISPONE
DISPONERS > DISPONE
DISPONES > DISPONE
DISPONGE *same as* > DISPUNGE
DISPONGED > DISPONGE
DISPONGES > DISPONGE
DISPONING > DISPONE
DISPORT *vb* indulge (oneself) in pleasure ▷ *n* amusement
DISPORTED > DISPORT
DISPORTS > DISPORT
DISPOSAL *n* getting rid of something
DISPOSALS > DISPOSAL
DISPOSE *vb* place in a certain order
DISPOSED *adj* willing or eager
DISPOSER > DISPOSE
DISPOSERS > DISPOSE
DISPOSES > DISPOSE
DISPOSING > DISPOSE
DISPOST *vb* remove from post
DISPOSTED > DISPOST
DISPOSTS > DISPOST
DISPOSURE *a rare word for* > DISPOSAL
DISPRAD *old form of* > DISPREAD
DISPRAISE *vb* express disapproval or condemnation of ▷ *n* disapproval, etc, expressed
DISPREAD *vb* spread out
DISPREADS > DISPREAD
DISPRED *old spelling of* > DISPREAD
DISPREDS > DISPRED
DISPRISON *vb* release from captivity
DISPRIZE *vb* scorn
DISPRIZED > DISPRIZE
DISPRIZES > DISPRIZE
DISPROFIT *n* loss
DISPROOF *n* facts that disprove something
DISPROOFS > DISPROOF
DISPROOVE *vb* disapprove of
DISPROVAL > DISPROVE
DISPROVE *vb* show (an assertion or claim) to be incorrect
DISPROVED > DISPROVE
DISPROVEN > DISPROVE
DISPROVER > DISPROVE
DISPROVES > DISPROVE
DISPUNGE *vb* expunge
DISPUNGED > DISPUNGE
DISPUNGES > DISPUNGE
DISPURSE *another word for* > DISBURSE
DISPURSED > DISPURSE
DISPURSES > DISPURSE
DISPURVEY *vb* strip of equipment, provisions, etc
DISPUTANT *n* person who argues ▷ *adj* engaged in argument
DISPUTE *n* disagreement, argument ▷ *vb* argue about (something)
DISPUTED > DISPUTE
DISPUTER > DISPUTE
DISPUTERS > DISPUTE
DISPUTES > DISPUTE
DISPUTING > DISPUTE
DISQUIET *n* feeling of anxiety ▷ *vb* make (someone) anxious ▷ *adj* uneasy or anxious
DISQUIETS > DISQUIET
DISRANK *vb* demote
DISRANKED > DISRANK
DISRANKS > DISRANK
DISRATE *vb* punish (an officer) by lowering in rank
DISRATED > DISRATE
DISRATES > DISRATE
DISRATING > DISRATE
DISREGARD *vb* give little or no attention to ▷ *n* lack of attention or respect
DISRELISH *vb* have a feeling of aversion for ▷ *n* such a feeling
DISREPAIR *n* condition of being worn out or in poor working order
DISREPUTE *n* loss or lack of good reputation
DISROBE *vb* undress
DISROBED > DISROBE
DISROBER > DISROBE
DISROBERS > DISROBE
DISROBES > DISROBE
DISROBING > DISROBE
DISROOT *vb* uproot
DISROOTED > DISROOT
DISROOTS > DISROOT
DISRUPT *vb* interrupt the progress of
DISRUPTED > DISRUPT
DISRUPTER > DISRUPT
DISRUPTOR > DISRUPT
DISRUPTS > DISRUPT
DISS *vb* treat (a person) with contempt
DISSAVE *vb* spend savings
DISSAVED > DISSAVE
DISSAVES > DISSAVE
DISSAVING > DISSAVE
DISSEAT *vb* unseat
DISSEATED > DISSEAT
DISSEATS > DISSEAT
DISSECT *vb* cut open (a corpse) to examine it
DISSECTED *adj* in the form of narrow lobes or segments
DISSECTOR > DISSECT
DISSECTS > DISSECT
DISSED > DISS
DISSEISE *vb* deprive of seisin
DISSEISED > DISSEISE
DISSEISEE *n* person who is disseised
DISSEISES > DISSEISE
DISSEISIN *n* act of disseising or state of being disseised
DISSEISOR > DISSEISE
DISSEIZE *same as* > DISSEISE
DISSEIZED > DISSEIZE
DISSEIZEE *n* person who is disseized
DISSEIZES > DISSEIZE
DISSEIZIN *same as* > DISSEISIN
DISSEIZOR > DISSEIZE
DISSEMBLE *vb* conceal one's real motives or emotions by pretence
DISSEMBLY *n* dismantling
DISSENSUS *n* disagreement within group
DISSENT *vb* disagree ▷ *n* disagreement
DISSENTED > DISSENT
DISSENTER > DISSENT
DISSENTS > DISSENT
DISSERT *n* give or make a dissertation; dissertate
DISSERTED > DISSERT
DISSERTS > DISSERT
DISSERVE *vb* do a disservice to
DISSERVED > DISSERVE
DISSERVES > DISSERVE
DISSES > DISS
DISSEVER *vb* break off or become broken off
DISSEVERS > DISSEVER
DISSHIVER *vb* break in pieces
DISSIDENT *n* person who disagrees with and criticizes the government ▷ *adj* disagreeing with the government
DISSIGHT *n* eyesore
DISSIGHTS > DISSIGHT
DISSIMILE *n* comparison using contrast
DISSING > DISS
DISSIPATE *vb* waste or squander
DISSOCIAL *same as* > DISSOCIABLE
DISSOLUTE *adj* leading an immoral life
DISSOLVE *vb* (cause to) become liquid ▷ *n* scene filmed or televised by dissolving
DISSOLVED > DISSOLVE
DISSOLVER > DISSOLVE
DISSOLVES > DISSOLVE
DISSONANT *adj* discordant
DISSUADE *vb* deter (someone) by persuasion from doing something
DISSUADED > DISSUADE
DISSUADER > DISSUADE
DISSUADES > DISSUADE
DISSUNDER *vb* separate
DISTAFF *n* rod on which wool etc is wound for spinning
DISTAFFS > DISTAFF
DISTAIN *vb* stain; tarnish
DISTAINED > DISTAIN
DISTAINS > DISTAIN
DISTAL *adj* (of a muscle, bone, limb, etc) situated farthest from the centre, median line, or point of attachment or origin
DISTALLY > DISTAL
DISTANCE *n* space between two points
DISTANCED > DISTANCE
DISTANCES > DISTANCE
DISTANT *adj* far apart
DISTANTLY > DISTANT
DISTASTE *n* dislike, disgust
DISTASTED > DISTASTE
DISTASTES > DISTASTE
DISTAVES > DISTAFF
DISTEMPER *n* highly contagious viral disease of dogs ▷ *vb* paint with distemper
DISTEND *vb* (of part of the body) swell
DISTENDED > DISTEND
DISTENDER > DISTEND
DISTENDS > DISTEND
DISTENT *adj* bloated; swollen
DISTHENE *n* bluish-green mineral
DISTHENES > DISTHENE
DISTHRONE *vb* remove from throne
DISTICH *n* unit of two verse lines
DISTICHAL > DISTICH
DISTICHS > DISTICH
DISTIL *vb* subject to or obtain by distillation
DISTILL *same as* > DISTIL
DISTILLED > DISTIL
DISTILLER *n* person or company that makes strong alcoholic drink, esp whisky
DISTILLS > DISTILL
DISTILS > DISTIL
DISTINCT *adj* not the same
DISTINGUE *adj* distinguished or noble
DISTOME *n* parasitic flatworm
DISTOMES > DISTOME
DISTORT *vb* misrepresent (the truth or facts)
DISTORTED > DISTORT

DISTORTER > DISTORT
DISTORTS > DISTORT
DISTRACT *vb* draw the attention of (a person) away from something
DISTRACTS > DISTRACT
DISTRAIL *n* trail made by aircraft flying through cloud
DISTRAILS > DISTRAIL
DISTRAIN *vb* seize (personal property) to enforce payment of a debt
DISTRAINS > DISTRAIN
DISTRAINT *n* act or process of distraining
DISTRAIT *adj* absent-minded or preoccupied
DISTRAITE *feminine form of* > DISTRAIT
DISTRESS *n* extreme unhappiness ▷ *vb* upset badly
DISTRICT *n* area of land regarded as an administrative or geographical unit ▷ *vb* divide into districts
DISTRICTS > DISTRICT
DISTRIX *n* splitting of the ends of hairs
DISTRIXES > DISTRIX
DISTRUST *vb* regard as untrustworthy ▷ *n* feeling of suspicion or doubt
DISTRUSTS > DISTRUST
DISTUNE *vb* cause to be out of tune
DISTUNED > DISTUNE
DISTUNES > DISTUNE
DISTUNING > DISTUNE
DISTURB *vb* intrude on
DISTURBED *adj* emotionally upset or maladjusted
DISTURBER > DISTURB
DISTURBS > DISTURB
DISTYLE *n* temple with two columns
DISTYLES > DISTYLE
DISULFATE *n* chemical compound containing two sulfate ions
DISULFID *same as* > DISULFIDE
DISULFIDE *n* compound of a base with two atoms of sulfur
DISULFIDS > DISULFID
DISUNION > DISUNITE
DISUNIONS > DISUNITE
DISUNITE *vb* cause disagreement among
DISUNITED > DISUNITE
DISUNITER > DISUNITE
DISUNITES > DISUNITE
DISUNITY *n* dissension or disagreement
DISUSAGE *n* disuse
DISUSAGES > DISUSAGE
DISUSE *vb* stop using ▷ *n* state of being no longer used
DISUSED *adj* no longer used
DISUSES > DISUSE
DISUSING > DISUSE
DISVALUE *vb* belittle
DISVALUED > DISVALUE
DISVALUES > DISVALUE
DISVOUCH *vb* dissociate oneself from
DISYOKE *vb* unyoke
DISYOKED > DISYOKE
DISYOKES > DISYOKE
DISYOKING > DISYOKE
DIT *vb* stop something happening ▷ *n* short sound used, in combination with the long sound *dah*, in the spoken representation of Morse and other telegraphic codes
DITA *n* apocynaceous shrub, *Alstonia scholaris*, of tropical Africa and Asia, having large shiny whorled leaves and medicinal bark
DITAL *n* key for raising pitch of lute string
DITALS > DITAL
DITAS > DITA
DITCH *n* narrow channel dug in the earth for drainage or irrigation ▷ *vb* abandon
DITCHED > DITCH
DITCHER > DITCH
DITCHERS > DITCH
DITCHES > DITCH
DITCHING > DITCH
DITCHLESS > DITCH
DITE *vb* set down in writing
DITED > DITE
DITES > DITE
DITHECAL *adj* having two thecae
DITHECOUS *another word for* > DITHECAL
DITHEISM *n* belief in two equal gods
DITHEISMS > DITHEISM
DITHEIST > DITHEISM
DITHEISTS > DITHEISM
DITHELETE *n* one believing that Christ had two wills
DITHELISM *n* belief that Christ had two wills
DITHER *vb* be uncertain or indecisive ▷ *n* state of indecision or agitation
DITHERED > DITHER
DITHERER > DITHER
DITHERERS > DITHER
DITHERIER > DITHER
DITHERING > DITHER
DITHERS > DITHER
DITHERY > DITHER
DITHIOL *n* chemical compound
DITHYRAMB *n* (in ancient Greece) a passionate choral hymn in honour of Dionysus
DITING > DITE
DITOKOUS *adj* producing two eggs
DITONE *n* interval of two tones
DITONES > DITONE
DITROCHEE *n* double metrical foot
DITS > DIT
DITSIER > DITSY
DITSIEST > DITSY
DITSINESS > DITSY
DITSY *same as* > DITZY
DITT *same as* > DIT
DITTANDER *n* plant, *Lepidium latifolium*, of coastal regions of Europe, N Africa, and SW Asia, with clusters of small white flowers: family *Brassicaceae* (crucifers)
DITTANIES > DITTANY
DITTANY *n* aromatic Cretan plant, *Origanum dictamnus*, with pink drooping flowers: formerly credited with great medicinal properties: family *Lamiaceae* (labiates)
DITTAY *n* accusation; charge
DITTAYS > DITTAY
DITTED > DIT
DITTIED > DITTY
DITTIES > DITTY
DITTING > DIT
DITTIT > DIT
DITTO *n* same ▷ *adv* in the same way ▷ *sentence substitute* used to avoid repeating or to confirm agreement with an immediately preceding sentence ▷ *vb* copy
DITTOED > DITTO
DITTOING > DITTO
DITTOLOGY *n* interpretation in two ways
DITTOS > DITTO
DITTS > DITT
DITTY *vb* set to music ▷ *n* short simple poem or song
DITTYING > DITTY
DITZ *n* silly scatterbrained person
DITZES > DITZ
DITZIER > DITZY
DITZIEST > DITZY
DITZINESS > DITZY
DITZY *adj* silly and scatterbrained
DIURESES > DIURESIS
DIURESIS *n* excretion of an unusually large quantity of urine
DIURETIC *n* drug that increases the flow of urine ▷ *adj* acting to increase the flow of urine
DIURETICS > DIURETIC
DIURNAL *adj* happening during the day or daily ▷ *n* service book containing all the canonical hours except matins
DIURNALLY > DIURNAL
DIURNALS > DIURNAL
DIURON *n* type of herbicide
DIURONS > DIURON
DIUTURNAL *adj* long-lasting
DIV *n* stupid or foolish person
DIVA *n* distinguished female singer
DIVAGATE *vb* digress or wander
DIVAGATED > DIVAGATE
DIVAGATES > DIVAGATE
DIVALENCE > DIVALENT
DIVALENCY > DIVALENT
DIVALENT *n* element that can unite with two atoms ▷ *adj* having two valencies or a valency of two
DIVALENTS > DIVALENT
DIVAN *n* low backless bed
DIVANS > DIVAN
DIVAS > DIVA
DIVE *vb* plunge headfirst into water ▷ *n* diving
DIVEBOMB *vb* bomb while making steep dives
DIVEBOMBS > DIVEBOMB
DIVED > DIVE
DIVELLENT *adj* separating
DIVER *n* person who works or explores underwater
DIVERGE *vb* separate and go in different directions
DIVERGED > DIVERGE
DIVERGENT *adj* diverging or causing divergence
DIVERGES > DIVERGE
DIVERGING > DIVERGE
DIVERS *adj* various ▷ *determiner* various
DIVERSE *vb* turn away ▷ *adj* having variety, assorted
DIVERSED > DIVERSE
DIVERSELY > DIVERSE
DIVERSES > DIVERSE
DIVERSIFY *vb* create different forms of
DIVERSING > DIVERSE
DIVERSION *n* official detour used by traffic when a main route is closed
DIVERSITY *n* quality of being different or varied
DIVERSLY > DIVERS
DIVERT *vb* change the direction of
DIVERTED > DIVERT
DIVERTER > DIVERT
DIVERTERS > DIVERT
DIVERTING > DIVERT
DIVERTIVE > DIVERT
DIVERTS > DIVERT
DIVES > DIVE
DIVEST *vb* strip (of clothes)
DIVESTED > DIVEST
DIVESTING > DIVEST
DIVESTS > DIVEST
DIVESTURE > DIVEST
DIVI *alternative spelling of* > DIVVY
DIVIDABLE > DIVIDE
DIVIDANT *adj* distinct

DIVIDE *vb* separate into parts ▷ *n* division, split
DIVIDED *adj* split
DIVIDEDLY > DIVIDED
DIVIDEND *n* sum of money representing part of the profit made, paid by a company to its shareholders
DIVIDENDS > DIVIDEND
DIVIDER *n* screen used to divide a room into separate areas
DIVIDERS *pl n* compasses with two pointed arms, used for measuring or dividing lines
DIVIDES > DIVIDE
DIVIDING > DIVIDE
DIVIDINGS > DIVIDE
DIVIDIVI *n* tropical tree
DIVIDIVIS > DIVIDIVI
DIVIDUAL *adj* divisible
DIVIDUOUS *adj* divided
DIVINABLE > DIVINE
DIVINATOR *n* diviner
DIVINE *adj* of God or a god ▷ *vb* discover (something) by intuition or guessing ▷ *n* priest who is learned in theology
DIVINED > DIVINE
DIVINELY > DIVINE
DIVINER > DIVINE
DIVINERS > DIVINE
DIVINES > DIVINE
DIVINEST > DIVINE
DIVING > DIVE
DIVINGS > DIVE
DIVINIFY *vb* give divine status to
DIVINING > DIVINE
DIVINISE *same as* > DIVINIZE
DIVINISED > DIVINISE
DIVINISES > DIVINISE
DIVINITY *n* study of religion
DIVINIZE *vb* make divine
DIVINIZED > DIVINIZE
DIVINIZES > DIVINIZE
DIVIS > DIVI
DIVISIBLE *adj* capable of being divided
DIVISIBLY > DIVISIBLE
DIVISIM *adv* separately
DIVISION *n* dividing, sharing out
DIVISIONS > DIVISION
DIVISIVE *adj* tending to cause disagreement
DIVISOR *n* number to be divided into another number
DIVISORS > DIVISOR
DIVORCE *n* legal ending of a marriage ▷ *vb* legally end one's marriage (to)
DIVORCED > DIVORCE
DIVORCEE *n* person who is divorced
DIVORCEES > DIVORCEE
DIVORCER > DIVORCE
DIVORCERS > DIVORCE
DIVORCES > DIVORCE
DIVORCING > DIVORCE
DIVORCIVE > DIVORCE
DIVOT *n* small piece of turf
DIVOTS > DIVOT
DIVS > DIV
DIVULGATE *vb* make publicly known
DIVULGE *vb* make known, disclose
DIVULGED > DIVULGE
DIVULGER > DIVULGE
DIVULGERS > DIVULGE
DIVULGES > DIVULGE
DIVULGING > DIVULGE
DIVULSE *vb* tear apart
DIVULSED > DIVULSE
DIVULSES > DIVULSE
DIVULSING > DIVULSE
DIVULSION *n* tearing or pulling apart
DIVULSIVE > DIVULSION
DIVVIED > DIVVY
DIVVIES > DIVVY
DIVVY *vb* divide and share ▷ *n* stupid person
DIVVYING > DIVVY
DIWAN *same as* > DEWAN
DIWANS > DIWAN
DIXI *interj* I have spoken
DIXIE *n* large metal pot for cooking, brewing tea, etc
DIXIES > DIXIE
DIXIT *n* statement
DIXITS > DIXIT
DIXY *same as* > DIXIE
DIZAIN *n* ten-line poem
DIZAINS > DIZAIN
DIZEN *archaic word for* > BEDIZEN
DIZENED > DIZEN
DIZENING > DIZEN
DIZENMENT > DIZEN
DIZENS > DIZEN
DIZYGOTIC *adj* developed from two separately fertilized eggs
DIZYGOUS *another word for* > DIZYGOTIC
DIZZARD *n* dunce
DIZZARDS > DIZZARD
DIZZIED > DIZZY
DIZZIER > DIZZY
DIZZIES > DIZZY
DIZZIEST > DIZZY
DIZZILY > DIZZY
DIZZINESS > DIZZY
DIZZY *adj* having or causing a whirling sensation ▷ *vb* make dizzy
DIZZYING > DIZZY
DJEBEL *a variant spelling of* > JEBEL
DJEBELS > DJEBEL
DJELLABA *n* kind of loose cloak with a hood, worn by men esp in North Africa and the Middle East
DJELLABAH *same as* > DJELLABA
DJELLABAS > DJELLABA
DJEMBE *n* W African drum played by beating with the hand
DJEMBES > DJEMBE
DJIBBAH *same as* > JUBBAH
DJIBBAHS > DJIBBAH
DJIN *same as same as* > JINN
DJINN > DJINNI
DJINNI *same as* > JINNI
DJINNS > DJINN
DJINNY *same as same as* > JINNI
DJINS > DJIN
DO *vb* perform or complete (a deed or action) ▷ *n* party, celebration
DOAB *n* alluvial land between two converging rivers, esp the area between the Ganges and Jumna in N India
DOABLE *adj* capable of being done
DOABS > DOAB
DOAT *same as* > DOTE
DOATED > DOAT
DOATER > DOAT
DOATERS > DOAT
DOATING > DOAT
DOATINGS > DOAT
DOATS > DOAT
DOB as in *dob in* inform against or report
DOBBED > DOB
DOBBER *n* informant or traitor
DOBBERS > DOBBER
DOBBIE *same as* > DOBBY
DOBBIES > DOBBY
DOBBIN *n* name for a horse, esp a workhorse, often used in children's tales, etc
DOBBING > DOB
DOBBINS > DOBBIN
DOBBY *n* attachment to a loom, used in weaving small figures
DOBCHICK *same as* > DABCHICK
DOBCHICKS > DOBCHICK
DOBHASH *n* interpreter
DOBHASHES > DOBHASH
DOBIE *n* cannabis
DOBIES > DOBIE
DOBLA *n* medieval Spanish gold coin, probably worth 20 maravedis
DOBLAS > DOBLA
DOBLON *a variant spelling of* > DOUBLOON
DOBLONES > DOBLON
DOBLONS > DOBLON
DOBRA *n* standard monetary unit of São Tomé e Principe, divided into 100 cêntimos
DOBRAS > DOBRA
DOBRO *n* tradename for a type of acoustic guitar having a metal resonator built into the body
DOBROS > DOBRO
DOBS > DOB
DOBSON *n* larva of dobsonfly
DOBSONFLY *n* large N American insect
DOBSONS > DOBSON
DOBY *same as* > DOBIE
DOC *same as* > DOCTOR
DOCENT *n* voluntary worker who acts as a guide in a museum, art gallery, etc
DOCENTS > DOCENT
DOCETIC *adj* believer in docetism: a heresy that the humanity of Christ was apparent rather than real
DOCHMIAC > DOCHMIUS
DOCHMII > DOCHMIUS
DOCHMIUS *n* five-syllable foot
DOCHT > DOW
DOCIBLE *adj* easily tamed
DOCILE *adj* (of a person or animal) easily controlled
DOCILELY > DOCILE
DOCILER > DOCILE
DOCILEST > DOCILE
DOCILITY > DOCILE
DOCIMASY *n* close examination
DOCK *n* enclosed area of water where ships are loaded, unloaded, or repaired ▷ *vb* bring or be brought into dock
DOCKAGE *n* charge levied upon a vessel for using a dock
DOCKAGES > DOCKAGE
DOCKED > DOCK
DOCKEN *n* something of no value or importance
DOCKENS > DOCKEN
DOCKER *n* person employed to load and unload ships
DOCKERS > DOCKER
DOCKET *n* label on a package or other delivery, stating contents, delivery instructions, etc ▷ *vb* fix a docket to (a package or other delivery)
DOCKETED > DOCKET
DOCKETING > DOCKET
DOCKETS > DOCKET
DOCKHAND *n* dock labourer
DOCKHANDS > DOCKHAND
DOCKING > DOCK
DOCKINGS > DOCK
DOCKISE *same as* > DOCKIZE
DOCKISED > DOCKISE
DOCKISES > DOCKISE
DOCKISING > DOCKISE
DOCKIZE *vb* convert into docks
DOCKIZED > DOCKIZE
DOCKIZES > DOCKIZE
DOCKIZING > DOCKIZE
DOCKLAND *n* area around the docks
DOCKLANDS > DOCKLAND
DOCKS > DOCK
DOCKSIDE *n* area next to dock
DOCKSIDES > DOCKSIDE
DOCKYARD *n* place where ships are built or repaired
DOCKYARDS > DOCKYARD
DOCO *short*

for > DOCUMENTARY
DOCOS > DOCO
DOCQUET *same as* > DOCKET
DOCQUETED > DOCQUET
DOCQUETS > DOCQUET
DOCS > DOC
DOCTOR *n* person licensed to practise medicine ▷ *vb* alter in order to deceive
DOCTORAL > DOCTOR
DOCTORAND *n* student working towards doctorate
DOCTORATE *n* highest academic degree in any field of knowledge
DOCTORED > DOCTOR
DOCTORESS *n* female doctor
DOCTORIAL > DOCTOR
DOCTORING > DOCTOR
DOCTORLY > DOCTOR
DOCTORS > DOCTOR
DOCTRESS *same as* > DOCTORESS
DOCTRINAL > DOCTRINE
DOCTRINE *n* body of teachings of a religious, political, or philosophical group
DOCTRINES > DOCTRINE
DOCUDRAMA *n* film or television programme based on true events, presented in a dramatized form
DOCUMENT *n* piece of paper providing an official record of something ▷ *vb* record or report (something) in detail
DOCUMENTS > DOCUMENT
DOD *vb* clip
DODDARD *adj* archaic word for missing branches; rotten
DODDED > DOD
DODDER *vb* move unsteadily ▷ *n* any rootless parasitic plant of the convolvulaceous genus *Cuscuta*, lacking chlorophyll and having slender twining stems with suckers for drawing nourishment from the host plant, scalelike leaves, and whitish flowers
DODDERED > DODDER
DODDERER > DODDER
DODDERERS > DODDER
DODDERIER > DODDER
DODDERING *adj* shaky, feeble, or infirm, esp from old age
DODDERS > DODDER
DODDERY > DODDER
DODDIER > DODDY
DODDIES > DODDY
DODDIEST > DODDY
DODDING > DOD
DODDIPOLL *same as* > DODDYPOLL
DODDLE *n* something easily accomplished
DODDLES > DODDLE
DODDY *n* bad mood ▷ *adj* sulky
DODDYPOLL *n* dunce
DODECAGON *n* geometric figure with twelve sides
DODGE *vb* avoid (a blow, being seen, etc) by moving suddenly ▷ *n* cunning or deceitful trick
DODGEBALL *n* game in which the players form a circle and try to hit opponents in the circle with a large ball
DODGED > DODGE
DODGEM *n* bumper car
DODGEMS > DODGEM
DODGER *n* person who evades a responsibility or duty
DODGERIES > DODGERY
DODGERS > DODGER
DODGERY *n* deception
DODGES > DODGE
DODGIER > DODGY
DODGIEST > DODGY
DODGINESS > DODGY
DODGING > DODGE
DODGINGS > DODGE
DODGY *adj* dangerous, risky
DODKIN *n* coin of little value
DODKINS > DODKIN
DODMAN *n* snail
DODMANS > DODMAN
DODO *n* large flightless extinct bird
DODOES > DODO
DODOISM > DODO
DODOISMS > DODO
DODOS > DODO
DODS > DOD
DOE *n* female deer, hare, or rabbit
DOEK *n* square of cloth worn on the head by women
DOEKS > DOEK
DOEN > DO
DOER *n* active or energetic person
DOERS > DOER
DOES > DO
DOESKIN *n* skin of a deer, lamb, or sheep
DOESKINS > DOESKIN
DOEST > DO
DOETH > DO
DOF *informal South African word for* > STUPID
DOFF *vb* take off or lift (one's hat) in polite greeting
DOFFED > DOFF
DOFFER > DOFF
DOFFERS > DOFF
DOFFING > DOFF
DOFFS > DOFF
DOG *n* domesticated four-legged mammal of many different breeds ▷ *vb* follow (someone) closely
DOGARESSA *n* wife of doge
DOGATE *n* office of doge
DOGATES > DOGATE
DOGBANE *n* any of several North American apocynaceous plants of the genus *Apocynum*, esp *A. androsaemifolium*, having bell-shaped white or pink flowers: thought to be poisonous to dogs
DOGBANES > DOGBANE
DOGBERRY *n* any of certain plants that have berry-like fruits, such as the European dogwood or the bearberry
DOGBOLT *n* bolt on cannon
DOGBOLTS > DOGBOLT
DOGCART *n* light horse-drawn two-wheeled cart
DOGCARTS > DOGCART
DOGDAYS *pl n* hot period of the summer reckoned in ancient times from the heliacal rising of Sirius (the Dog Star)
DOGDOM *n* world of dogs
DOGDOMS > DOGDOM
DOGE *n* (formerly) chief magistrate of Venice or Genoa
DOGEAR *vb* fold down the corner of (a page) ▷ *n* folded-down corner of a page
DOGEARED > DOGEAR
DOGEARING > DOGEAR
DOGEARS > DOGEAR
DOGEATE *n* office of doge
DOGEATES > DOGEATE
DOGEDOM *n* domain of doge
DOGEDOMS > DOGEDOM
DOGES > DOGE
DOGESHIP > DOGE
DOGESHIPS > DOGE
DOGEY *same as* > DOGIE
DOGEYS > DOGEY
DOGFACE *n* WW2 US soldier
DOGFACES > DOGFACE
DOGFIGHT *vb* fight in confused way ▷ *n* close-quarters combat between fighter aircraft
DOGFIGHTS > DOGFIGHT
DOGFISH *n* small shark
DOGFISHES > DOGFISH
DOGFOUGHT > DOGFIGHT
DOGFOX *n* male fox
DOGFOXES > DOGFOX
DOGGED > DOG
DOGGEDER > DOG
DOGGEDEST > DOG
DOGGEDLY > DOG
DOGGER *n* Dutch fishing vessel with two masts
DOGGEREL *n* poorly written poetry, usu. comic
DOGGERELS > DOGGEREL
DOGGERIES > DOGGERY
DOGGERMAN *n* sailor on dogger
DOGGERMEN > DOGGERMAN
DOGGERS > DOGGER
DOGGERY *n* surly behaviour
DOGGESS *n* female dog
DOGGESSES > DOGGESS
DOGGIE *same as* > DOGGY
DOGGIER > DOGGY
DOGGIES > DOGGY
DOGGIEST > DOGGY
DOGGINESS > DOGGY
DOGGING > DOG
DOGGINGS > DOG
DOGGISH *adj* of or like a dog
DOGGISHLY > DOGGISH
DOGGO *adv* in hiding and keeping quiet
DOGGONE *interj* exclamation of annoyance, disappointment, etc ▷ *vb* damn ▷ *adj* damnedest
DOGGONED > DOGGONE
DOGGONER > DOGGONE
DOGGONES > DOGGONE
DOGGONEST > DOGGONE
DOGGONING > DOGGONE
DOGGREL *same as* > DOGGEREL
DOGGRELS > DOGGREL
DOGGY *n* child's word for a dog ▷ *adj* of or like a dog
DOGHANGED *same as* > HANGDOG
DOGHOLE *n* squalid dwelling place
DOGHOLES > DOGHOLE
DOGHOUSE *n* kennel
DOGHOUSES > DOGHOUSE
DOGIE *n* motherless calf
DOGIES > DOGY
DOGLEG *n* sharp bend ▷ *vb* go off at an angle ▷ *adj* of or with the shape of a dogleg
DOGLEGGED > DOGLEG
DOGLEGS > DOGLEG
DOGLIKE > DOG
DOGMA *n* doctrine or system of doctrines proclaimed by authority as true
DOGMAN *n* person who directs the operation of a crane whilst riding on an object being lifted by it
DOGMAS > DOGMA
DOGMATA > DOGMA
DOGMATIC *adj* habitually stating one's opinions forcefully or arrogantly
DOGMATICS *n* study of religious dogmas and doctrines
DOGMATISE *same as* > DOGMATIZE
DOGMATISM > DOGMATIZE
DOGMATIST *n* dogmatic person
DOGMATIZE *vb* say or state (something) in a dogmatic manner
DOGMATORY > DOGMA
DOGMEN > DOGMAN
DOGNAP *vb* carry off and hold (a dog), usually for ransom
DOGNAPED > DOGNAP
DOGNAPER > DOGNAP

DOGNAPERS > DOGNAP
DOGNAPING > DOGNAP
DOGNAPPED > DOGNAP
DOGNAPPER > DOGNAP
DOGNAPS > DOGNAP
DOGROBBER *n* army cook
DOGS > DOG
DOGSBODY *n* person who carries out boring tasks for others ▷ *vb* act as a dogsbody
DOGSHIP *n* condition of being a dog
DOGSHIPS > DOGSHIP
DOGSHORES *n* pieces of wood to prop up boat
DOGSKIN *n* leather from dog's skin
DOGSKINS > DOGSKIN
DOGSLED *n* sleigh drawn by dogs
DOGSLEDS > DOGSLED
DOGSLEEP *n* feigned sleep
DOGSLEEPS > DOGSLEEP
DOGTEETH > DOGTOOTH
DOGTOOTH *n* carved ornament in the form of four leaflike projections radiating from a raised centre, used in England in the 13th century
DOGTOWN *n* community of prairie dogs
DOGTOWNS > DOGTOWN
DOGTROT *n* gently paced trot
DOGTROTS > DOGTROT
DOGVANE *n* light windvane consisting of a feather or a piece of cloth or yarn mounted on the side of a vessel
DOGVANES > DOGVANE
DOGWATCH *n* either of two watches aboard ship, from four to six pm or from six to eight pm
DOGWOOD *n* any of various cornaceous trees or shrubs of the genus *Cornus*, esp *C. sanguinea*, a European shrub with clusters of small white flowers and black berries: the shoots are red in winter
DOGWOODS > DOGWOOD
DOGY *same as* > DOGIE
DOH *n* in tonic sol-fa, first degree of any major scale ▷ *interj* exclamation of annoyance when something goes wrong
DOHS > DOH
DOHYO *n* sumo wrestling ring
DOHYOS > DOHYO
DOILED *same as* > DOILT
DOILIES > DOILY
DOILT *adj* foolish
DOILTER > DOILT
DOILTEST > DOILT
DOILY *n* decorative lacy paper mat, laid on a plate
DOING > DO
DOINGS *pl n* deeds or actions
DOIT *n* former small copper coin of the Netherlands
DOITED *adj* foolish or childish, as from senility
DOITIT *same as* > DOITED
DOITKIN *same as* > DOIT
DOITKINS > DOITKIN
DOITS > DOIT
DOJO *n* room or hall for the practice of martial arts
DOJOS > DOJO
DOL *n* unit of pain intensity, as measured by dolorimetry
DOLABRATE *adj* shaped like a hatchet or axe head
DOLCE *n* dessert ▷ *adv* (to be performed) gently and sweetly
DOLCES > DOLCE
DOLCETTO *n* variety of grape for making wine
DOLCETTOS > DOLCETTO
DOLCI > DOLCE
DOLDRUMS *pl n* depressed state of mind
DOLE *n* money received from the state while unemployed ▷ *vb* distribute in small quantities
DOLED > DOLE
DOLEFUL *adj* dreary, unhappy
DOLEFULLY > DOLEFUL
DOLENT *adj* sad
DOLENTE *adv* (to be performed) in a sorrowful manner
DOLERITE *n* dark basic intrusive igneous rock consisting of plagioclase feldspar and a pyroxene, such as augite
DOLERITES > DOLERITE
DOLERITIC > DOLERITE
DOLES > DOLE
DOLESOME *same as* > DOLEFUL
DOLIA > DOLIUM
DOLICHOS *n* tropical vines
DOLICHURI *n* poetic term
DOLINA *same as* > DOLINE
DOLINAS > DOLINA
DOLINE *n* shallow usually funnel-shaped depression of the ground surface formed by solution in limestone regions
DOLINES > DOLINE
DOLING > DOLE
DOLIUM *n* genus of molluscs
DOLL *n* small model of a human being, used as a toy ▷ *vb* as in *doll up* dress up
DOLLAR *n* standard monetary unit of many countries
DOLLARED *adj* flagged with a dollar sign
DOLLARISE *same as* > DOLLARIZE
DOLLARIZE *vb* replace a country's currency with US dollar
DOLLARS > DOLLAR
DOLLDOM > DOLL
DOLLDOMS > DOLL
DOLLED > DOLL
DOLLHOOD > DOLL
DOLLHOODS > DOLL
DOLLHOUSE *n* toy house in which dolls and miniature furniture can be put
DOLLIED > DOLLY
DOLLIER *n* person who operates a dolly
DOLLIERS > DOLLIER
DOLLIES > DOLLY
DOLLINESS > DOLLY
DOLLING > DOLL
DOLLISH > DOLL
DOLLISHLY > DOLL
DOLLOP *n* lump (of food) ▷ *vb* serve out (food)
DOLLOPED > DOLLOP
DOLLOPING > DOLLOP
DOLLOPS > DOLLOP
DOLLS > DOLL
DOLLY *adj* attractive and unintelligent ▷ *n* wheeled support on which a camera may be mounted; shaped block of lead used to hammer dents out of sheet metal ▷ *vb* wheel (a camera) backwards or forwards on a dolly
DOLLYBIRD *n* pretty and fashionable young woman
DOLLYING > DOLLY
DOLMA *n* vine leaf stuffed with a filling of meat and rice
DOLMADES > DOLMA
DOLMAN *n* long Turkish outer robe
DOLMANS > DOLMAN
DOLMAS > DOLMA
DOLMEN *n* prehistoric monument consisting of a horizontal stone supported by vertical stones
DOLMENIC > DOLMEN
DOLMENS > DOLMEN
DOLOMITE *n* mineral consisting of calcium magnesium carbonate
DOLOMITES > DOLOMITE
DOLOMITIC > DOLOMITE
DOLOR *same as* > DOLOUR
DOLORIFIC *adj* causing pain or sadness
DOLOROSO *adv* (to be performed) in a sorrowful manner
DOLOROUS *adj* sad, mournful
DOLORS > DOLOR
DOLOS *n* knucklebone of a sheep, buck, etc, used esp by diviners
DOLOSSE > DOLOS
DOLOSTONE *n* rock composed of the mineral dolomite
DOLOUR *n* grief or sorrow
DOLOURS > DOLOUR
DOLPHIN *n* sea mammal of the whale family, with a beaklike snout
DOLPHINET *n* female dolphin
DOLPHINS > DOLPHIN
DOLS > DOL
DOLT *n* stupid person
DOLTISH > DOLT
DOLTISHLY > DOLT
DOLTS > DOLT
DOM *n* title given to Benedictine, Carthusian, and Cistercian monks and to certain of the canons regular
DOMAIN *n* field of knowledge or activity
DOMAINAL > DOMAIN
DOMAINE *n* French estate where wine is made
DOMAINES > DOMAINE
DOMAINS > DOMAIN
DOMAL *adj* of a house
DOMANIAL > DOMAIN
DOMATIA > DOMATIUM
DOMATIUM *n* plant cavity inhabited by commensal insects or mites or, occasionally, microorganisms
DOME *n* rounded roof built on a circular base ▷ *vb* cover with or as if with a dome
DOMED > DOME
DOMELIKE > DOME
DOMES > DOME
DOMESDAY *same as* > DOOMSDAY
DOMESDAYS > DOMESDAY
DOMESTIC *adj* of one's own country or a specific country ▷ *n* person whose job is to do housework in someone else's house
DOMESTICS > DOMESTIC
DOMETT *n* wool and cotton cloth
DOMETTS > DOMETT
DOMIC *adj* dome-shaped
DOMICAL > DOME
DOMICALLY > DOME
DOMICIL *same as* > DOMICILE
DOMICILE *n* place where one lives ▷ *vb* establish or be established in a dwelling place
DOMICILED > DOMICILE
DOMICILES > DOMICILE
DOMICILS > DOMICIL
DOMIER > DOMY
DOMIEST > DOMY
DOMINANCE *n* control
DOMINANCY > DOMINANCE
DOMINANT *adj* having authority or influence ▷ *n* dominant allele or character

DOMINANTS > DOMINANT
DOMINATE *vb* control or govern
DOMINATED > DOMINATE
DOMINATES > DOMINATE
DOMINATOR > DOMINATE
DOMINE *n* clergyman
DOMINEE *n* minister of the Dutch Reformed Church
DOMINEER *vb* act with arrogance or tyranny
DOMINEERS > DOMINEER
DOMINEES > DOMINEE
DOMINES > DOMINE
DOMING > DOME
DOMINICAL *adj* of, relating to, or emanating from Jesus Christ as Lord
DOMINICK *n* breed of chicken
DOMINICKS > DOMINICK
DOMINIE *n* minister or clergyman: also used as a term of address
DOMINIES > DOMINIE
DOMINION *same as* > DOMINIUM
DOMINIONS > DOMINION
DOMINIQUE *n* type of chicken
DOMINIUM *n* ownership or right to possession of property, esp realty
DOMINIUMS > DOMINIUM
DOMINO *n* small rectangular block marked with dots, used in dominoes
DOMINOES *n* game in which dominoes with matching halves are laid together
DOMINOS > DOMINO
DOMS > DOM
DOMY *adj* having a dome or domes
DON *vb* put on (clothing) ▷ *n* member of the teaching staff at a university or college
DONA *n* Spanish lady
DONAH *n* woman
DONAHS > DONAH
DONARIES > DONARY
DONARY *n* thing given for holy use
DONAS > DONA
DONATARY *n* recipient
DONATE *vb* give, esp to a charity or organization
DONATED > DONATE
DONATES > DONATE
DONATING > DONATE
DONATION *n* donating
DONATIONS > DONATION
DONATISM *n* doctrine and beliefs relating to a schismatic heretical Christian sect originating in N Africa in 311 AD
DONATISMS > DONATISM
DONATIVE *n* gift or donation ▷ *adj* of or like a donation
DONATIVES > DONATIVE
DONATOR > DONATE
DONATORS > DONATE
DONATORY *n* recipient
DONDER *vb* beat (someone) up ▷ *n* wretch
DONDERED > DONDER
DONDERING > DONDER
DONDERS > DONDER
DONE > DO
DONEE *n* person who receives a gift
DONEES > DONEE
DONENESS *n* extent to which something is cooked
DONER as in *doner kebab* grilled meat and salad served in pitta bread with chilli sauce
DONG *n* deep reverberating sound of a large bell ▷ *vb* (of a bell) to make a deep reverberating sound
DONGA *n* steep-sided gully created by soil erosion
DONGAS > DONGA
DONGED > DONG
DONGING > DONG
DONGLE *n* electronic device that accompanies a software item to prevent the unauthorized copying of programs
DONGLES > DONGLE
DONGOLA *n* leather tanned using a particular method
DONGOLAS > DONGOLA
DONGS > DONG
DONING *n* act of giving blood
DONINGS > DONING
DONJON *n* heavily fortified central tower of a castle
DONJONS > DONJON
DONKEY *n* long-eared member of the horse family
DONKEYS > DONKEY
DONKO *n* tearoom or cafeteria in a factory, wharf area, etc
DONKOS > DONKO
DONNA *n* Italian lady
DONNARD *same as* > DONNERT
DONNART *same as* > DONNERT
DONNAS > DONNA
DONNAT *n* lazy person
DONNATS > DONNAT
DONNE *same as* > DONNEE
DONNED > DON
DONNEE *n* subject or theme
DONNEES > DONNEE
DONNERD *adj* stupid
DONNERED *same as* > DONNERT
DONNERT *adj* stunned
DONNES > DONNE
DONNICKER *n* toilet
DONNIES > DONNY
DONNIKER *same as* > DONNICKER
DONNIKERS > DONNIKER
DONNING > DON
DONNISH *adj* serious and academic
DONNISHLY > DONNISH
DONNISM *n* loftiness
DONNISMS > DONNISM
DONNOT *n* lazy person
DONNOTS > DONNOT
DONNY *same as* > DANNY
DONOR *n* person who gives blood or organs for use in the treatment of another person
DONORS > DONOR
DONORSHIP > DONOR
DONS > DON
DONSHIP *n* state or condition of being a don
DONSHIPS > DONSHIP
DONSIE *adj* rather unwell
DONSIER > DONSIE
DONSIEST > DONSIE
DONSY *same as* > DONSIE
DONUT *same as* > DOUGHNUT
DONUTS > DONUT
DONUTTED > DONUT
DONUTTING > DONUT
DONZEL *n* man of high birth
DONZELS > DONZEL
DOO *a Scot word for* > DOVE
DOOB *n* cannabis cigarette
DOOBIE *same as* > DOOB
DOOBIES > DOOBIE
DOOBS > DOOB
DOOCED as in *get dooced* be dismissed on account of indiscretions written in a blog or on a website
DOOCOT *n* dovecote
DOOCOTS > DOOCOT
DOODAD *same as* > DOODAH
DOODADS > DOODAD
DOODAH *n* unnamed thing, esp an object the name of which is unknown or uncertain
DOODAHS > DOODAH
DOODIES > DOODY
DOODLE *vb* scribble or draw aimlessly ▷ *n* shape or picture drawn aimlessly
DOODLEBUG *n* diviner's rod
DOODLED > DOODLE
DOODLER > DOODLE
DOODLERS > DOODLE
DOODLES > DOODLE
DOODLING > DOODLE
DOODOO *n* excrement
DOODOOS > DOODOO
DOODY *same as* > DOODOO
DOOFER *n* thingamajig
DOOFERS > DOOFER
DOOFUS *n* slow-witted or stupid person
DOOFUSES > DOOFUS
DOOHICKEY *another name for* > DOODAH
DOOK *n* wooden plug driven into a wall to hold a nail, screw, etc ▷ *vb* dip or plunge
DOOKED > DOOK
DOOKET *n* dovecote
DOOKETS > DOOKET
DOOKING > DOOK
DOOKS > DOOK
DOOL *n* boundary marker
DOOLALLY *adj* out of one's mind
DOOLAN *n* Roman Catholic
DOOLANS > DOOLAN
DOOLE *same as* > DOOL
DOOLEE *same as* > DOOLIE
DOOLEES > DOOLEE
DOOLES > DOOLE
DOOLIE *n* enclosed couch on poles for carrying passengers
DOOLIES > DOOLIE
DOOLS > DOOL
DOOLY *same as* > DOOLIE
DOOM *n* death or a terrible fate ▷ *vb* destine or condemn to death or a terrible fate
DOOMED > DOOM
DOOMFUL > DOOM
DOOMFULLY > DOOM
DOOMIER > DOOMY
DOOMIEST > DOOMY
DOOMILY > DOOMY
DOOMING > DOOM
DOOMS > DOOM
DOOMSAYER *n* pessimist
DOOMSDAY *n* day on which the Last Judgment will occur
DOOMSDAYS > DOOMSDAY
DOOMSMAN *n* pessimist
DOOMSMEN > DOOMSMAN
DOOMSTER *n* person habitually given to predictions of impending disaster or doom
DOOMSTERS > DOOMSTER
DOOMWATCH *n* surveillance of the environment to warn of and prevent harm to it from human factors such as pollution or overpopulation
DOOMY *adj* despondent or pessimistic
DOON *same as* > DOWN
DOONA *n* large quilt used as a bed cover in place of the top sheet and blankets
DOONAS > DOONA
DOOR *n* hinged or sliding panel for closing the entrance to a building, room, etc
DOORBELL *n* device for visitors to announce presence at a door
DOORBELLS > DOORBELL
DOORCASE *same as* > DOORFRAME
DOORCASES > DOORCASE
DOORFRAME *n* frame that supports a door
DOORJAMB *n* vertical post forming one side of a door frame
DOORJAMBS > DOORJAMB
DOORKNOB *n* knob for opening and closing a door
DOORKNOBS > DOORKNOB
DOORKNOCK *n* fund-raising

campaign for charity conducted by seeking donations from door to door
DOORLESS > DOOR
DOORMAN *n* man employed to be on duty at the entrance to a large public building
DOORMAT *n* mat for wiping dirt from shoes before going indoors
DOORMATS > DOORMAT
DOORMEN > DOORMAN
DOORN *n* thorn
DOORNAIL as in *dead as a doornail* dead beyond any doubt
DOORNAILS > DOORNAIL
DOORNS > DOORN
DOORPLATE *n* name-plate on door
DOORPOST *same as* > DOORJAMB
DOORPOSTS > DOORPOST
DOORS > DOOR
DOORSILL *n* horizontal member of wood, stone, etc, forming the bottom of a doorframe
DOORSILLS > DOORSILL
DOORSMAN *n* doorkeeper
DOORSMEN > DOORSMAN
DOORSTEP *n* step in front of a door
DOORSTEPS > DOORSTEP
DOORSTONE *n* stone of threshold
DOORSTOP *n* heavy object or one fixed to the floor, which prevents a door from closing or from striking a wall
DOORSTOPS > DOORSTOP
DOORWAY *n* opening into a building or room
DOORWAYS > DOORWAY
DOORWOMAN *n* female doorman
DOORWOMEN > DOORWOMAN
DOORYARD *n* yard in front of the front or back door of a house
DOORYARDS > DOORYARD
DOOS > DOO
DOOSRA *n* in cricket, a delivery, bowled by an off-spinner, that turns the opposite way from an off-break
DOOSRAS > DOOSRA
DOOWOP *n* style of singing in harmony
DOOWOPS > DOOWOP
DOOZER *same as* > DOOZY
DOOZERS > DOOZER
DOOZIE *same as* > DOOZY
DOOZIES > DOOZIE
DOOZY *n* something excellent
DOP *vb* curtsy ▷ *n* tot or small drink, usually alcoholic ▷ *vb* fail to reach the required standard in (an examination, course, etc)
DOPA *n* precursor to dopamine
DOPAMINE *n* chemical found in the brain that acts as a neurotransmitter
DOPAMINES > DOPAMINE
DOPANT *n* element or compound used to dope a semiconductor
DOPANTS > DOPANT
DOPAS > DOPA
DOPATTA *n* headscarf
DOPATTAS > DOPATTA
DOPE *n* illegal drug, usu. cannabis ▷ *vb* give a drug to, esp in order to improve performance in a race ▷ *adj* excellent
DOPED > DOPE
DOPEHEAD *n* habitual drug user
DOPEHEADS > DOPEHEAD
DOPER *n* person who administers dope
DOPERS > DOPER
DOPES > DOPE
DOPESHEET *n* document giving information on horse races
DOPESTER *n* person who makes predictions, esp in sport or politics
DOPESTERS > DOPESTER
DOPEY *adj* half-asleep, drowsy
DOPEYNESS > DOPEY
DOPIAZA *n* Indian meat or fish dish cooked in onion sauce
DOPIAZAS > DOPIAZA
DOPIER > DOPY
DOPIEST > DOPY
DOPILY > DOPEY
DOPINESS > DOPEY
DOPING > DOPE
DOPINGS > DOPE
DOPPED > DOP
DOPPER *n* member of an Afrikaner church that practises a stict Calvinism
DOPPERS > DOPPER
DOPPIE *n* cartridge case
DOPPIES > DOPPIE
DOPPING > DOP
DOPPINGS > DOP
DOPPIO *n* double measure, esp of espresso coffee
DOPPIOS > DOPPIO
DOPS > DOP
DOPY *same as* > DOPEY
DOR *n* any European dung beetle of the genus *Geotrupes* and related genera, esp *G. stercorarius*, having a droning flight
DORAD *n* South American river fish
DORADO *n* large marine percoid fish
DORADOS > DORADO
DORADS > DORAD
DORB *same as* > DORBA
DORBA *n* stupid, inept, or clumsy person
DORBAS > DORBA
DORBEETLE *same as* > DOR
DORBS > DORB
DORBUG *n* type of beetle
DORBUGS > DORBUG
DORE *n* walleye fish
DOREE *n* type of fish
DOREES > DOREE
DORHAWK *n* nightjar
DORHAWKS > DORHAWK
DORIC *adj* rustic
DORIDOID *n* shell-less mollusc
DORIDOIDS > DORIDOID
DORIES > DORY
DORIS *n* woman
DORISE *same as* > DORIZE
DORISED > DORISE
DORISES > DORISE
DORISING > DORISE
DORIZE *vb* become Doric
DORIZED > DORIZE
DORIZES > DORIZE
DORIZING > DORIZE
DORK *n* stupid person
DORKIER > DORK
DORKIEST > DORK
DORKINESS > DORK
DORKS > DORK
DORKY > DORK
DORLACH *n* quiver of arrows
DORLACHS > DORLACH
DORM *same as* > DORMITORY
DORMANCY > DORMANT
DORMANT *n* supporting beam ▷ *adj* temporarily quiet, inactive, or not being used
DORMANTS > DORMANT
DORMER *n* window that sticks out from a sloping roof
DORMERED *adj* having dormer windows
DORMERS > DORMER
DORMICE > DORMOUSE
DORMIE *adj* (of a player or side) as many holes ahead of an opponent as there are still to play
DORMIENT *adj* dormant
DORMIN *n* hormone found in plants
DORMINS > DORMIN
DORMITION *n* Mary's assumption to heaven
DORMITIVE *adj* sleep-inducing
DORMITORY *n* large room, esp at a school, containing several beds ▷ *adj* (of a town or suburb) having many inhabitants who travel to work in a nearby city
DORMOUSE *n* small mouselike rodent with a furry tail
DORMS > DORM
DORMY *same as* > DORMIE
DORNECK *same as* > DORNICK
DORNECKS > DORNECK
DORNICK *n* heavy damask cloth, formerly used for vestments, curtains, etc
DORNICKS > DORNICK
DORNOCK *n* type of coarse fabric
DORNOCKS > DORNOCK
DORONICUM *n* any plant of the Eurasian and N African genus *Doronicum*, such as leopard's-bane, having yellow daisy-like flower heads: family *Asteraceae* (composites)
DORP *n* small town
DORPER *n* breed of sheep
DORPERS > DORPER
DORPS > DORP
DORR *same as* > DOR
DORRED > DOR
DORRING > DOR
DORRS > DORR
DORS > DOR
DORSA > DORSUM
DORSAD *adj* towards the back or dorsal aspect
DORSAL *adj* of or on the back ▷ *n* dorsal fin
DORSALLY > DORSAL
DORSALS > DORSAL
DORSE *n* type of small fish
DORSEL *another word for* > DOSSAL
DORSELS > DORSEL
DORSER *n* hanging tapestry
DORSERS > DORSER
DORSES > DORSE
DORSIFLEX *adj* bending towards the back
DORSUM *n* the back
DORT *vb* sulk
DORTED > DORT
DORTER *n* dormitory
DORTERS > DORTER
DORTIER > DORTY
DORTIEST > DORTY
DORTINESS > DORTY
DORTING > DORT
DORTOUR *same as* > DORTER
DORTOURS > DORTOUR
DORTS > DORT
DORTY *adj* haughty, or sullen
DORY *n* spiny-finned edible sea fish
DOS > DO
DOSAGE *same as* > DOSE
DOSAGES > DOSAGE
DOSE *n* specific quantity of a medicine taken at one time ▷ *vb* give a dose to
DOSED > DOSE
DOSEH *n* former Egyptian religious ceremony
DOSEHS > DOSEH
DOSEMETER *same as* > DOSIMETER
DOSER > DOSE
DOSERS > DOSE
DOSES > DOSE
DOSH *n* money
DOSHES > DOSH
DOSIMETER *n* instrument for measuring the dose of

X-rays or other radiation absorbed by matter or the intensity of a source of radiation
DOSIMETRY > DOSIMETER
DOSING > DOSE
DOSIOLOGY *n* study of doses
DOSOLOGY *same as* > DOSIOLOGY
DOSS *vb* sleep, esp in a dosshouse ▷ *n* bed, esp in a dosshouse
DOSSAL *n* ornamental hanging, placed at the back of an altar or at the sides of a chancel
DOSSALS > DOSSAL
DOSSED > DOSS
DOSSEL *same as* > DOSSAL
DOSSELS > DOSSEL
DOSSER *n* bag or basket for carrying objects on the back
DOSSERET *n* stone above column supporting an arch
DOSSERETS > DOSSERET
DOSSERS > DOSSER
DOSSES > DOSS
DOSSHOUSE *n* cheap lodging house for homeless people
DOSSIER *n* collection of documents about a subject or person
DOSSIERS > DOSSIER
DOSSIL *n* lint for dressing wound
DOSSILS > DOSSIL
DOSSING > DOSS
DOST *a singular form of the present tense (indicative mood) of* > DO
DOT *n* small round mark ▷ *vb* mark with a dot
DOTAGE *n* weakness as a result of old age
DOTAGES > DOTAGE
DOTAL > DOT
DOTANT *another word for* > DOTARD
DOTANTS > DOTANT
DOTARD *n* person who is feeble-minded through old age
DOTARDLY > DOTARD
DOTARDS > DOTARD
DOTATION *n* act of giving a dowry
DOTATIONS > DOTATION
DOTCOM *n* company that does most of its business on the Internet
DOTCOMMER *n* person who carries out business on the internet
DOTCOMS > DOTCOM
DOTE *vb* love to an excessive or foolish degree
DOTED > DOTE
DOTER > DOTE
DOTERS > DOTE
DOTES > DOTE
DOTH *a singular form of the present tense of* > DO
DOTIER > DOTY
DOTIEST > DOTY
DOTING > DOTE
DOTINGLY > DOTE
DOTINGS > DOTE
DOTISH *adj* foolish
DOTS > DOT
DOTTED > DOT
DOTTEL *same as* > DOTTLE
DOTTELS > DOTTEL
DOTTER > DOT
DOTTEREL *n* rare kind of plover
DOTTERELS > DOTTEREL
DOTTERS > DOT
DOTTIER > DOTTY
DOTTIEST > DOTTY
DOTTILY > DOTTY
DOTTINESS > DOTTY
DOTTING > DOT
DOTTLE *n* tobacco left in a pipe after smoking ▷ *adj* relating to dottle
DOTTLED *adj* foolish
DOTTLER > DOTTLE
DOTTLES > DOTTLE
DOTTLEST > DOTTLE
DOTTREL *same as* > DOTTEREL
DOTTRELS > DOTTREL
DOTTY *adj* rather eccentric
DOTY *adj* (of wood) rotten
DOUANE *n* customs house
DOUANES > DOUANE
DOUANIER *n* customs officer
DOUANIERS > DOUANIER
DOUAR *same as* > DUAR
DOUARS > DOUAR
DOUBLE *adj* as much again in number, amount, size, etc ▷ *adv* twice over ▷ *n* twice the number, amount, size, etc ▷ *vb* make or become twice as much or as many
DOUBLED > DOUBLE
DOUBLER > DOUBLE
DOUBLERS > DOUBLE
DOUBLES *n* game between two pairs of players
DOUBLET *n* man's close-fitting jacket, with or without sleeves
DOUBLETON *n* original holding of two cards only in a suit
DOUBLETS > DOUBLET
DOUBLING > DOUBLE
DOUBLINGS > DOUBLE
DOUBLOON *n* former Spanish gold coin
DOUBLOONS > DOUBLOON
DOUBLURE *n* decorative lining of vellum or leather, etc, on the inside of a book cover
DOUBLURES > DOUBLURE
DOUBLY *adv* in a greater degree, quantity, or measure
DOUBT *n* uncertainty about the truth, facts, or existence of something ▷ *vb* question the truth of
DOUBTABLE > DOUBT
DOUBTABLY > DOUBT
DOUBTED > DOUBT
DOUBTER > DOUBT
DOUBTERS > DOUBT
DOUBTFUL *adj* unlikely ▷ *n* person who is undecided or uncertain about an issue
DOUBTFULS > DOUBTFUL
DOUBTING > DOUBT
DOUBTINGS > DOUBT
DOUBTLESS *adv* probably or certainly ▷ *adj* certain
DOUBTS > DOUBT
DOUC *n* Old World monkey, *Pygathrix nemaeus*, of SE Asia, with a bright yellow face surrounded by tufts of reddish-brown fur, a white tail, and white hindquarters: one of the langurs
DOUCE *adj* quiet
DOUCELY > DOUCE
DOUCENESS > DOUCE
DOUCEPERE *same as* > DOUZEPER
DOUCER > DOUCE
DOUCEST > DOUCE
DOUCET *n* former flute-like instrument
DOUCETS > DOUCET
DOUCEUR *n* gratuity, tip, or bribe
DOUCEURS > DOUCEUR
DOUCHE *n* (instrument for applying) a stream of water directed onto or into the body for cleansing or medical purposes ▷ *vb* cleanse or treat by means of a douche
DOUCHEBAG *n* despicable person
DOUCHED > DOUCHE
DOUCHES > DOUCHE
DOUCHING > DOUCHE
DOUCINE *n* type of moulding for cornice
DOUCINES > DOUCINE
DOUCS > DOUC
DOUGH *n* thick mixture of flour and water or milk, used for making bread etc
DOUGHBOY *n* infantryman, esp in World War I
DOUGHBOYS > DOUGHBOY
DOUGHFACE *n* Northern Democrat who sided with the South in the American Civil War
DOUGHIER > DOUGHY
DOUGHIEST > DOUGHY
DOUGHLIKE > DOUGH
DOUGHNUT *n* small cake of sweetened dough fried in deep fat ▷ *vb* (of Members of Parliament) to surround (a speaker) during the televising of Parliament to give the impression that the chamber is crowded or the speaker is well supported
DOUGHNUTS > DOUGHNUT
DOUGHS > DOUGH
DOUGHT > DOW
DOUGHTIER > DOUGHTY
DOUGHTILY > DOUGHTY
DOUGHTY *adj* brave and determined
DOUGHY *adj* resembling dough in consistency, colour, etc
DOUK *same as* > DOOK
DOUKED > DOUK
DOUKING > DOUK
DOUKS > DOUK
DOULA *n* woman who is trained to provide support to women and their families during pregnancy, childbirth, and the period of time following the birth
DOULAS > DOULA
DOULEIA *same as* > DULIA
DOULEIAS > DOULEIA
DOUM as in *doum palm* variety of palm tree
DOUMA *same as* > DUMA
DOUMAS > DOUMA
DOUMS > DOUM
DOUN *same as* > DOWN
DOUP *n* bottom
DOUPIONI *n* type of fabric
DOUPIONIS > DOUPIONI
DOUPPIONI *n* type of silk yarn
DOUPS > DOUP
DOUR *adj* sullen and unfriendly
DOURA *same as* > DURRA
DOURAH *same as* > DURRA
DOURAHS > DOURAH
DOURAS > DOURA
DOURER > DOUR
DOUREST > DOUR
DOURINE *n* infectious venereal disease of horses characterized by swollen glands, inflamed genitals, and paralysis of the hindquarters, caused by the protozoan *Trypanosom equiperdum* contracted during copulation
DOURINES > DOURINE
DOURLY > DOUR
DOURNESS > DOUR
DOUSE *vb* drench with water or other liquid ▷ *n* immersion
DOUSED > DOUSE
DOUSER > DOUSE
DOUSERS > DOUSE
DOUSES > DOUSE
DOUSING > DOUSE
DOUT *vb* extinguish
DOUTED > DOUT
DOUTER > DOUT
DOUTERS > DOUT
DOUTING > DOUT
DOUTS > DOUT
DOUX *adj* sweet

DOUZEPER *n* distinguished person
DOUZEPERS > DOUZEPER
DOVE *vb* be semi-conscious ▷ *n* bird with a heavy body, small head, and short legs
DOVECOT *same as* > DOVECOTE
DOVECOTE *n* structure for housing pigeons
DOVECOTES > DOVECOTE
DOVECOTS > DOVECOT
DOVED > DOVE
DOVEISH *adj* dovelike
DOVEKEY *same as* > DOVEKIE
DOVEKEYS > DOVEKEY
DOVEKIE *n* small short-billed auk
DOVEKIES > DOVEKIE
DOVELET *n* small dove
DOVELETS > DOVELET
DOVELIKE > DOVE
DOVEN *vb* pray
DOVENED > DOVEN
DOVENING > DOVEN
DOVENS > DOVEN
DOVER *vb* doze ▷ *n* doze
DOVERED > DOVER
DOVERING > DOVER
DOVERS > DOVER
DOVES > DOVE
DOVETAIL *n* joint containing wedge-shaped tenons ▷ *vb* fit together neatly
DOVETAILS > DOVETAIL
DOVIE *Scots word for* > STUPID
DOVIER > DOVIE
DOVIEST > DOVIE
DOVING > DOVE
DOVISH > DOVE
DOW *vb* archaic word meaning be of worth
DOWABLE *adj* capable of being endowed
DOWAGER *n* widow possessing property or a title obtained from her husband
DOWAGERS > DOWAGER
DOWAR *same as* > DUAR
DOWARS > DOWAR
DOWD *n* woman who wears unfashionable clothes
DOWDIER > DOWDY
DOWDIES > DOWDY
DOWDIEST > DOWDY
DOWDILY > DOWDY
DOWDINESS > DOWDY
DOWDS > DOWD
DOWDY *adj* dull and old-fashioned ▷ *n* dowdy woman
DOWDYISH > DOWDY
DOWDYISM > DOWD
DOWDYISMS > DOWD
DOWED > DOW
DOWEL *n* wooden or metal peg that fits into two corresponding holes to join two adjacent parts ▷ *vb* join pieces of wood using dowels
DOWELED > DOWEL
DOWELING *n* joining of two pieces of wood using dowels
DOWELLED > DOWEL
DOWELLING *same as* > DOWELING
DOWELS > DOWEL
DOWER *n* life interest in a part of her husband's estate allotted to a widow by law ▷ *vb* endow
DOWERED > DOWER
DOWERIES > DOWERY
DOWERING > DOWER
DOWERLESS > DOWER
DOWERS > DOWER
DOWERY *same as* > DOWRY
DOWF *adj* dull; listless
DOWFNESS > DOWF
DOWIE *adj* dull and dreary
DOWIER > DOWIE
DOWIEST > DOWIE
DOWING > DOW
DOWITCHER *n* either of two snipelike shore birds, *Limnodromus griseus* or *L. scolopaceus*, of arctic and subarctic North America: family *Scolopacidae* (sandpipers, etc), order *Charadriiformes*
DOWL *n* fluff
DOWLAS *n* coarse fabric
DOWLASES > DOWLAS
DOWLE *same as* > DOWL
DOWLES > DOWLE
DOWLIER > DOWLY
DOWLIEST > DOWLY
DOWLNE *obsolete form of* > DOWN
DOWLNES > DOWLNE
DOWLNEY > DOWLNE
DOWLS > DOWL
DOWLY *adj* dull
DOWN *adv* indicating movement to or position in a lower place ▷ *adj* depressed, unhappy ▷ *vb* drink quickly ▷ *n* soft fine feathers
DOWNA *obsolete Scots form of* > CANNOT
DOWNBEAT *adj* gloomy ▷ *n* first beat of a bar
DOWNBEATS > DOWNBEAT
DOWNBOW *n* (in music) a downward stroke of the bow across the strings
DOWNBOWS > DOWNBOW
DOWNBURST *n* very high-speed downward movement of turbulent air in a limited area for a short time. Near the ground it spreads out from its centre with high horizontal velocities
DOWNCAST *adj* sad, dejected ▷ *n* ventilation shaft
DOWNCASTS > DOWNCAST
DOWNCOME *same as* > DOWNCOMER
DOWNCOMER *n* pipe that connects a cistern to a WC, wash basin, etc
DOWNCOMES > DOWNCOME
DOWNCOURT *adj* in far end a of court
DOWNDRAFT *n* downward air current
DOWNED > DOWN
DOWNER *n* barbiturate, tranquillizer, or narcotic
DOWNERS > DOWNER
DOWNFALL *same as* > DEADFALL
DOWNFALLS > DOWNFALL
DOWNFIELD *adj* at far end of field
DOWNFLOW *n* something that flows down
DOWNFLOWS > DOWNFLOW
DOWNFORCE *n* force produced by air resistance plus gravity that increases the stability of an aircraft or motor vehicle by pressing it downwards
DOWNGRADE *vb* reduce in importance or value
DOWNHAUL *n* line for hauling down a sail or for increasing the tension at its luff
DOWNHAULS > DOWNHAUL
DOWNHILL *adj* going or sloping down ▷ *adv* towards the bottom of a hill ▷ *n* downward slope
DOWNHILLS > DOWNHILL
DOWNHOLE *adj* (in the oil industry) denoting any piece of equipment that is used in the well itself
DOWNIER > DOWNY
DOWNIEST > DOWNY
DOWNINESS > DOWNY
DOWNING > DOWN
DOWNLAND *same as* > DOWNS
DOWNLANDS > DOWNLAND
DOWNLESS > DOWN
DOWNLIGHT *n* lamp shining downwards
DOWNLIKE > DOWN
DOWNLINK *n* satellite transmission channel
DOWNLINKS > DOWNLINK
DOWNLOAD *vb* transfer (data) from the memory of one computer to that of another, especially over the Internet ▷ *n* file transferred in such a way
DOWNLOADS > DOWNLOAD
DOWNMOST *adj* lowest
DOWNPIPE *n* pipe for carrying rainwater from a roof gutter to the ground or to a drain
DOWNPIPES > DOWNPIPE
DOWNPLAY *vb* play down
DOWNPLAYS > DOWNPLAY
DOWNPOUR *n* heavy fall of rain
DOWNPOURS > DOWNPOUR
DOWNRANGE *adv* in the direction of the intended flight path of a rocket or missile
DOWNRIGHT *adv* extreme(ly) ▷ *adj* absolute
DOWNRIVER *adv* in direction of current
DOWNRUSH *n* instance of rushing down
DOWNS *pl n* low grassy hills, esp in S England
DOWNSCALE *vb* reduce in scale
DOWNSHIFT *vb* reduce work hours
DOWNSIDE *n* disadvantageous aspect of a situation
DOWNSIDES > DOWNSIDE
DOWNSIZE *vb* reduce the number of people employed by (a company)
DOWNSIZED > DOWNSIZE
DOWNSIZES > DOWNSIZE
DOWNSLIDE *n* downward trend
DOWNSLOPE *adv* towards the bottom of a slope
DOWNSPIN *n* sudden downturn
DOWNSPINS > DOWNSPIN
DOWNSPOUT *same as* > DOWNPIPE
DOWNSTAGE *adj* or at the front part of the stage ▷ *adv* at or towards the front of the stage ▷ *n* front half of the stage
DOWNSTAIR *adj* situated on lower floor
DOWNSTATE *adj* in, or relating to the part of the state away from large cities, esp the southern part ▷ *adv* towards the southern part of a state ▷ *n* southern part of a state
DOWNSWING *n* statistical downward trend in business activity, the death rate, etc
DOWNTHROW *n* state of throwing down or being thrown down
DOWNTICK *n* small decrease
DOWNTICKS > DOWNTICK
DOWNTIME *n* time during which a computer or other machine is not working
DOWNTIMES > DOWNTIME
DOWNTOWN *n* central or lower part of a city, esp the main commercial area ▷ *adv* towards, to, or into this area ▷ *adj* of, relating to, or situated in the downtown area
DOWNTOWNS > DOWNTOWN
DOWNTREND *n* downward trend
DOWNTROD *same as* > DOWNTRODDEN
DOWNTURN *n* drop in the success of an economy or a

business
DOWNTURNS > DOWNTURN
DOWNWARD *same as* > DOWNWARDS
DOWNWARDS *adv* from a higher to a lower level, condition, or position
DOWNWASH *n* downward deflection of an airflow, esp one caused by an aircraft wing
DOWNWIND *adj* in the same direction towards which the wind is blowing
DOWNY *adj* covered with soft fine hair or feathers
DOWNZONE *vb* reduce density of housing in area
DOWNZONED > DOWNZONE
DOWNZONES > DOWNZONE
DOWP *same as* > DOUP
DOWPS > DOWP
DOWRIES > DOWRY
DOWRY *n* property brought by a woman to her husband at marriage
DOWS > DOW
DOWSABEL *obsolete word for* > SWEETHEART
DOWSABELS > DOWSABEL
DOWSE *same as* > DOUSE
DOWSED > DOWSE
DOWSER > DOWSE
DOWSERS > DOWSE
DOWSES > DOWSE
DOWSET *same as* > DOUCET
DOWSETS > DOWSET
DOWSING > DOWSE
DOWT *n* cigarette butt
DOWTS > DOWT
DOXASTIC *adj* of or relating to belief
DOXIE *same as* > DOXY
DOXIES > DOXY
DOXOLOGY *n* short hymn of praise to God
DOXY *n* opinion or doctrine, esp concerning religious matters
DOY *n* beloved person: used esp as an endearment
DOYEN *n* senior member of a group, profession, or society
DOYENNE > DOYEN
DOYENNES > DOYEN
DOYENS > DOYEN
DOYLEY *same as* > DOILY
DOYLEYS > DOYLEY
DOYLIES > DOYLY
DOYLY *same as* > DOILY
DOYS > DOY
DOZE *vb* sleep lightly or briefly ▷ *n* short sleep
DOZED *adj* (of timber or rubber) rotten or decayed
DOZEN *vb* stun
DOZENED > DOZEN
DOZENING > DOZEN
DOZENS > DOZEN
DOZENTH > DOZEN
DOZENTHS > DOZEN
DOZER > DOZE
DOZERS > DOZE
DOZES > DOZE
DOZIER > DOZY
DOZIEST > DOZY
DOZILY > DOZY
DOZINESS > DOZY
DOZING > DOZE
DOZINGS > DOZE
DOZY *adj* feeling sleepy
DRAB *adj* dull and dreary ▷ *n* light olive-brown colour ▷ *vb* consort with prostitutes
DRABBED > DRAB
DRABBER *n* one who frequents low women
DRABBERS > DRABBER
DRABBEST > DRAB
DRABBET *n* yellowish-brown fabric of coarse linen
DRABBETS > DRABBET
DRABBIER > DRABBY
DRABBIEST > DRABBY
DRABBING > DRAB
DRABBISH *adj* promiscuous
DRABBLE *vb* make or become wet or dirty
DRABBLED > DRABBLE
DRABBLER *n* part fixed to bottom of sail
DRABBLERS > DRABBLER
DRABBLES > DRABBLE
DRABBLING > DRABBLE
DRABBY *adj* promiscuous
DRABETTE *n* type of rough linen fabric
DRABETTES > DRABETTE
DRABLER *same as* > DRABBLE
DRABLERS > DRABLER
DRABLY > DRAB
DRABNESS > DRAB
DRABS > DRAB
DRAC *same as* > DRACK
DRACAENA *n* any tropical plant of the genus *Dracaena*: some species are cultivated as house plants for their decorative foliage: family *Agavaceae*
DRACAENAS > DRACAENA
DRACENA *same as* > DRACAENA
DRACENAS > DRACENA
DRACHM *same as* > DRAM
DRACHMA *n* former monetary unit of Greece
DRACHMAE > DRACHMA
DRACHMAI > DRACHMA
DRACHMAS > DRACHMA
DRACHMS > DRACHM
DRACK *adj* (esp of a woman) unattractive
DRACO as in *draco lizard* flying lizard
DRACONE *n* large flexible cylindrical container towed by a ship, used for transporting liquids
DRACONES > DRACONE
DRACONIAN *adj* severe, harsh
DRACONIC *same as* > DRACONIAN
DRACONISM > DRACONIAN
DRACONTIC *same as* > DRACONIC
DRAD > DREAD
DRAFF *n* residue of husks after fermentation of the grain used in brewing, used as a food for cattle
DRAFFIER > DRAFF
DRAFFIEST > DRAFF
DRAFFISH *adj* worthless
DRAFFS > DRAFF
DRAFFY > DRAFF
DRAFT *same as* > DRAUGHT
DRAFTABLE > DRAFT
DRAFTED > DRAFT
DRAFTEE *n* conscript
DRAFTEES > DRAFTEE
DRAFTER > DRAFT
DRAFTERS > DRAFT
DRAFTIER > DRAFTY
DRAFTIEST > DRAFTY
DRAFTILY > DRAFTY
DRAFTING > DRAFT
DRAFTINGS > DRAFT
DRAFTS > DRAFT
DRAFTSMAN *same as* > DRAUGHTSMAN
DRAFTSMEN > DRAFTSMAN
DRAFTY *same as* > DRAUGHTY
DRAG *vb* pull with force, esp along the ground ▷ *n* person or thing that slows up progress
DRAGEE *n* sweet made of a nut, fruit, etc, coated with a hard sugar icing
DRAGEES > DRAGEE
DRAGGED > DRAG
DRAGGER > DRAG
DRAGGERS > DRAG
DRAGGIER > DRAGGY
DRAGGIEST > DRAGGY
DRAGGING > DRAG
DRAGGLE *vb* make or become wet or dirty by trailing on the ground
DRAGGLED > DRAGGLE
DRAGGLES > DRAGGLE
DRAGGLING > DRAGGLE
DRAGGY *adj* slow or boring
DRAGHOUND *n* hound used to follow an artificial trail of scent in a drag hunt
DRAGLINE *same as* > DRAGROPE
DRAGLINES > DRAGLINE
DRAGNET *n* net used to scour the bottom of a pond or river to search for something
DRAGNETS > DRAGNET
DRAGOMAN *n* (in some Middle Eastern countries) professional interpreter or guide
DRAGOMANS > DRAGOMAN
DRAGOMEN > DRAGOMAN
DRAGON *n* mythical fire-breathing monster like a huge lizard
DRAGONESS > DRAGON
DRAGONET *n* any small spiny-finned fish of the family *Callionymidae*, having a flat head and a slender tapering brightly coloured body and living at the bottom of shallow seas
DRAGONETS > DRAGONET
DRAGONFLY *n* brightly coloured insect with a long slender body and two pairs of wings
DRAGONISE *same as* > DRAGONIZE
DRAGONISH > DRAGON
DRAGONISM *n* vigilance
DRAGONIZE *vb* turn into dragon
DRAGONNE *adj* dragonlike
DRAGONS > DRAGON
DRAGOON *n* heavily armed cavalryman ▷ *vb* coerce, force
DRAGOONED > DRAGOON
DRAGOONS > DRAGOON
DRAGROPE *n* rope used to drag military equipment, esp artillery
DRAGROPES > DRAGROPE
DRAGS > DRAG
DRAGSMAN *n* carriage driver
DRAGSMEN > DRAGSMAN
DRAGSTER *n* car specially built or modified for drag racing
DRAGSTERS > DRAGSTER
DRAGSTRIP *n* track for drag racing
DRAIL *n* weighted hook used in trolling ▷ *vb* fish with a drail
DRAILED > DRAIL
DRAILING > DRAIL
DRAILS > DRAIL
DRAIN *n* pipe or channel that carries off water or sewage ▷ *vb* draw off or remove liquid from
DRAINABLE > DRAIN
DRAINAGE *n* system of drains
DRAINAGES > DRAINAGE
DRAINED > DRAIN
DRAINER *n* person or thing that drains
DRAINERS > DRAINER
DRAINING > DRAIN
DRAINPIPE > DOWNPIPE
DRAINS > DRAIN
DRAISENE *same as* > DRAISINE
DRAISENES > DRAISENE
DRAISINE *n* light rail vehicle
DRAISINES > DRAISINE
DRAKE *n* male duck
DRAKES > DRAKE
DRAM *n* small amount of a strong alcoholic drink, esp whisky ▷ *vb* drink a dram
DRAMA *n* serious play for theatre, television, or radio
DRAMADIES > DRAMEDY
DRAMADY *same as* > DRAMEDY
DRAMAS > DRAMA

DRAMATIC *adj* of or like drama
DRAMATICS *n* art of acting or producing plays
DRAMATISE *same as* > DRAMATIZE
DRAMATIST *n* person who writes plays
DRAMATIZE *vb* rewrite (a book) in the form of a play
DRAMATURG *n* literary adviser at a theatre
DRAMEDIES > DRAMEDY
DRAMEDY *n* television or film drama in which there are important elements of comedy
DRAMMACH *n* oatmeal mixed with cold water
DRAMMACHS > DRAMMACH
DRAMMED > DRAM
DRAMMING > DRAM
DRAMMOCK *same as* > DRAMMACH
DRAMMOCKS > DRAMMOCK
DRAMS > DRAM
DRAMSHOP *n* bar
DRAMSHOPS > DRAMSHOP
DRANGWAY *n* narrow lane
DRANGWAYS > DRANGWAY
DRANK > DRINK
DRANT *vb* drone
DRANTED > DRANT
DRANTING > DRANT
DRANTS > DRANT
DRAP *a Scot word for* > DROP
DRAPABLE > DRAPE
DRAPE *vb* cover with material, usu. in folds ▷ *n* piece of cloth hung at a window or opening as a screen
DRAPEABLE > DRAPE
DRAPED > DRAPE
DRAPER *n* person who sells fabrics and sewing materials
DRAPERIED > DRAPERY
DRAPERIES > DRAPERY
DRAPERS > DRAPER
DRAPERY *n* fabric or clothing arranged and draped
DRAPES *pl n* material hung at an opening or window to shut out light or to provide privacy
DRAPET *n* cloth
DRAPETS > DRAPET
DRAPEY *adj* hanging in loose folds
DRAPIER *n* draper
DRAPIERS > DRAPIER
DRAPING > DRAPE
DRAPPED > DRAP
DRAPPIE *n* little drop, esp a small amount of spirits
DRAPPIES > DRAPPIE
DRAPPING > DRAP
DRAPPY *n* drop (of liquid)
DRAPS > DRAP
DRASTIC *n* strong purgative ▷ *adj* strong and severe
DRASTICS > DRASTIC
DRAT *interj* exclamation of annoyance ▷ *vb* curse
DRATCHELL *n* low woman
DRATS > DRAT
DRATTED *adj* wretched
DRATTING > DRAT
DRAUGHT *vb* make preliminary plan ▷ *n* current of cold air, esp in an enclosed space ▷ *adj* (of an animal) used for pulling heavy loads
DRAUGHTED > DRAUGHT
DRAUGHTER > DRAUGHT
DRAUGHTS *n* game for two players using a draughtboard and 12 draughtsmen each
DRAUGHTY *adj* exposed to draughts of air
DRAUNT *same as* > DRANT
DRAUNTED > DRAUNT
DRAUNTING > DRAUNT
DRAUNTS > DRAUNT
DRAVE *archaic past of* > DRIVE
DRAW *vb* sketch (a figure, picture, etc) with a pencil or pen ▷ *n* raffle or lottery
DRAWABLE > DRAW
DRAWBACK *n* disadvantage ▷ *vb* move backwards
DRAWBACKS > DRAWBACK
DRAWBAR *n* strong metal bar on a tractor, locomotive, etc, bearing a hook or link and pin to attach a trailer, wagon, etc
DRAWBARS > DRAWBAR
DRAWBORE *n* hole bored through tenon
DRAWBORES > DRAWBORE
DRAWDOWN *n* decrease
DRAWDOWNS > DRAWDOWN
DRAWEE *n* person or organization on which a cheque or other order for payment is drawn
DRAWEES > DRAWEE
DRAWER *n* sliding box-shaped part of a piece of furniture, used for storage
DRAWERFUL *n* amount contained in drawer
DRAWERS *pl n* undergarment worn on the lower part of the body
DRAWING > DRAW
DRAWINGS > DRAW
DRAWKNIFE *n* woodcutting tool with two handles at right angles to the blade, used to shave wood
DRAWL *vb* speak slowly, with long vowel sounds ▷ *n* drawling manner of speech
DRAWLED > DRAWL
DRAWLER > DRAWL
DRAWLERS > DRAWL
DRAWLIER > DRAWL
DRAWLIEST > DRAWL
DRAWLING > DRAWL
DRAWLS > DRAWL
DRAWLY > DRAWL
DRAWN > DRAW
DRAWNWORK *n* type of ornamental needlework
DRAWPLATE *n* plate used to reduce the diameter of wire by drawing it through conical holes
DRAWS > DRAW
DRAWSHAVE *same as* > DRAWKNIFE
DRAWTUBE *n* tube, such as one of the component tubes of a telescope, fitting coaxially within another tube through which it can slide
DRAWTUBES > DRAWTUBE
DRAY *vb* pull using cart ▷ *n* low cart used for carrying heavy loads
DRAYAGE *n* act of transporting something a short distance by lorry or other vehicle
DRAYAGES > DRAYAGE
DRAYED > DRAY
DRAYHORSE *n* large powerful horse used for drawing a dray
DRAYING > DRAY
DRAYMAN *n* driver of a dray
DRAYMEN > DRAYMAN
DRAYS > DRAY
DRAZEL *n* low woman
DRAZELS > DRAZEL
DREAD *vb* anticipate with apprehension or fear ▷ *n* great fear ▷ *adj* awesome
DREADED > DREAD
DREADER > DREAD
DREADERS > DREAD
DREADFUL *n* cheap, often lurid or sensational book or magazine ▷ *adj* very disagreeable or shocking
DREADFULS > DREADFUL
DREADING > DREAD
DREADLESS > DREAD
DREADLOCK *n* Rastafarian hair braid
DREADLY > DREAD
DREADS > DREAD
DREAM *n* imagined series of events experienced in the mind while asleep ▷ *vb* see imaginary pictures in the mind while asleep ▷ *adj* ideal
DREAMBOAT *n* exceptionally attractive person or thing, esp a person of the opposite sex
DREAMED > DREAM
DREAMER *n* person who dreams habitually
DREAMERS > DREAMER
DREAMERY *n* dream world
DREAMFUL > DREAM
DREAMHOLE *n* light-admitting hole in a tower
DREAMIER > DREAMY
DREAMIEST > DREAMY
DREAMILY > DREAMY
DREAMING > DREAM
DREAMINGS > DREAM
DREAMLAND *n* ideal land existing in dreams or in the imagination
DREAMLESS > DREAM
DREAMLIKE > DREAM
DREAMS > DREAM
DREAMT > DREAM
DREAMTIME *n* time when the world was new and fresh
DREAMY *adj* vague or impractical
DREAR *same as* > DREARY
DREARE *obsolete form of* > DREAR
DREARER > DREAR
DREARES > DREARE
DREAREST > DREAR
DREARIER > DREARY
DREARIES > DREARY
DREARIEST > DREARY
DREARILY > DREARY
DREARING *n* sorrow
DREARINGS > DREARING
DREARS > DREAR
DREARY *adj* dull, boring ▷ *n* a dreary thing or person
DRECK *n* rubbish
DRECKIER > DRECK
DRECKIEST > DRECK
DRECKS > DRECK
DRECKSILL *n* doorstep
DRECKY > DRECK
DREDGE *vb* clear or search (a river bed or harbour) by removing silt or mud ▷ *n* machine used to scoop or suck up silt or mud from a river bed or harbour
DREDGED > DREDGE
DREDGER *same as* > DREDGE
DREDGERS > DREDGER
DREDGES > DREDGE
DREDGING > DREDGE
DREDGINGS > DREDGE
DREE *vb* endure
DREED > DREE
DREEING > DREE
DREES > DREE
DREG *n* small quantity
DREGGIER > DREGGY
DREGGIEST > DREGGY
DREGGISH *adj* foul
DREGGY *adj* like or full of dregs
DREGS *pl n* solid particles that settle at the bottom of some liquids
DREICH *adj* dreary
DREICHER > DREICH
DREICHEST > DREICH
DREIDEL *n* spinning top
DREIDELS > DREIDEL
DREIDL *same as* > DREIDEL
DREIDLS > DREIDL
DREIGH *same as* > DREICH
DREK *same as* > DRECK
DREKS > DREK
DRENCH *vb* make completely wet ▷ *n* act or an instance of drenching

DRENCHED > DRENCH
DRENCHER > DRENCH
DRENCHERS > DRENCH
DRENCHES > DRENCH
DRENCHING > DRENCH
DRENT > DRENCH
DREPANID *n* any moth of the superfamily *Drepanoidae* (family *Drepanidae*): it comprises the hook-tip moths
DREPANIDS > DREPANID
DREPANIUM *n* type of flower cluster
DRERE *obsolete form of* > DREAR
DRERES > DRERE
DRERIHEAD *n* obsolete word for dreary
DRESS *n* one-piece garment for a woman or girl, consisting of a skirt and bodice and sometimes sleeves ▷ *vb* put clothes on ▷ *adj* suitable for a formal occasion
DRESSAGE *n* training of a horse to perform manoeuvres in response to the rider's body signals
DRESSAGES > DRESSAGE
DRESSED > DRESS
DRESSER *n* piece of furniture with shelves and with cupboards, for storing or displaying dishes
DRESSERS > DRESSER
DRESSES > DRESS
DRESSIER > DRESSY
DRESSIEST > DRESSY
DRESSILY > DRESSY
DRESSING *n* sauce for salad
DRESSINGS *pl n* dressed stonework, mouldings, and carved ornaments used to form quoins, keystones, sills, and similar features
DRESSMADE > DRESSMAKE
DRESSMAKE *vb* make clothes
DRESSY *adj* (of clothes) elegant
DREST > DRESS
DREVILL *n* offensive person
DREVILLS > DREVILL
DREW > DRAW
DREY *n* squirrel's nest
DREYS > DREY
DRIB *vb* flow in drops
DRIBBED > DRIB
DRIBBER > DRIB
DRIBBERS > DRIB
DRIBBING > DRIB
DRIBBLE *vb* (allow to) flow in drops ▷ *n* small quantity of liquid falling in drops
DRIBBLED > DRIBBLE
DRIBBLER > DRIBBLE
DRIBBLERS > DRIBBLE
DRIBBLES > DRIBBLE
DRIBBLET *same as* > DRIBLET
DRIBBLETS > DRIBBLET
DRIBBLIER > DRIBBLE
DRIBBLING > DRIBBLE
DRIBBLY > DRIBBLE
DRIBLET *n* small amount
DRIBLETS > DRIBLET
DRIBS > DRIB
DRICE *n* pellets of frozen carbon dioxide
DRICES > DRICE
DRICKSIE *same as* > DRUXY
DRICKSIER > DRICKSIE
DRIED > DRY
DRIEGH *adj* tedious
DRIER > DRY
DRIERS > DRY
DRIES > DRY
DRIEST > DRY
DRIFT *vb* be carried along by currents of air or water ▷ *n* something piled up by the wind or current, such as a snowdrift
DRIFTAGE *n* act of drifting
DRIFTAGES > DRIFTAGE
DRIFTED > DRIFT
DRIFTER *n* person who moves aimlessly from place to place or job to job
DRIFTERS > DRIFTER
DRIFTIER > DRIFT
DRIFTIEST > DRIFT
DRIFTING > DRIFT
DRIFTLESS > DRIFT
DRIFTPIN *same as* > DRIFT
DRIFTPINS > DRIFTPIN
DRIFTS > DRIFT
DRIFTWOOD *n* wood floating on or washed ashore by the sea
DRIFTY > DRIFT
DRILL *n* tool or machine for boring holes ▷ *vb* bore a hole in (something) with or as if with a drill
DRILLABLE > DRILL
DRILLED > DRILL
DRILLER > DRILL
DRILLERS > DRILL
DRILLING > DRILL
DRILLINGS > DRILL
DRILLS > DRILL
DRILLSHIP *n* floating drilling platform
DRILY *adv* in a dry manner
DRINK *vb* swallow (a liquid) ▷ *n* (portion of) a liquid suitable for drinking
DRINKABLE > DRINK
DRINKABLY > DRINK
DRINKER *n* person who drinks, esp a person who drinks alcohol habitually
DRINKERS > DRINKER
DRINKING > DRINK
DRINKINGS > DRINK
DRINKS > DRINK
DRIP *vb* (let) fall in drops ▷ *n* falling of drops of liquid
DRIPLESS > DRIP
DRIPPED > DRIP
DRIPPER > DRIP
DRIPPERS > DRIP
DRIPPIER > DRIPPY
DRIPPIEST > DRIPPY
DRIPPILY > DRIPPY
DRIPPING > DRIP
DRIPPINGS > DRIP
DRIPPY *adj* mawkish, insipid, or inane
DRIPS > DRIP
DRIPSTONE *n* form of calcium carbonate existing in stalactites or stalagmites
DRIPT > DRIP
DRISHEEN *n* pudding made of sheep's intestines filled with meal and sheep's blood
DRISHEENS > DRISHEEN
DRIVABLE > DRIVE
DRIVE *vb* guide the movement of (a vehicle) ▷ *n* journey by car, van, etc
DRIVEABLE > DRIVE
DRIVEL *n* foolish talk ▷ *vb* speak foolishly
DRIVELED > DRIVEL
DRIVELER > DRIVEL
DRIVELERS > DRIVEL
DRIVELINE *n* transmission line from engine to wheels of vehicle
DRIVELING > DRIVEL
DRIVELLED > DRIVEL
DRIVELLER > DRIVEL
DRIVELS > DRIVEL
DRIVEN > DRIVE
DRIVER *n* person who drives a vehicle
DRIVERS > DRIVER
DRIVES > DRIVE
DRIVEWAY *n* path for vehicles connecting a building to a public road
DRIVEWAYS > DRIVEWAY
DRIVING > DRIVE
DRIVINGLY > DRIVE
DRIVINGS > DRIVE
DRIZZLE *n* very light rain ▷ *vb* rain lightly
DRIZZLED > DRIZZLE
DRIZZLES > DRIZZLE
DRIZZLIER > DRIZZLE
DRIZZLING > DRIZZLE
DRIZZLY > DRIZZLE
DROGER *n* W Indian boat
DROGERS > DROGER
DROGHER *same as* > DROGER
DROGHERS > DROGHER
DROGUE *n* any funnel-like device, esp one of canvas, used as a sea anchor
DROGUES > DROGUE
DROGUET *n* woollen fabric
DROGUETS > DROGUET
DROICH *n* dwarf
DROICHIER > DROICHY
DROICHS > DROICH
DROICHY *adj* dwarfish
DROID *same as* > ANDROID
DROIDS > DROID
DROIL *vb* carry out boring menial work
DROILED > DROIL
DROILING > DROIL
DROILS > DROIL
DROIT *n* legal or moral right or claim
DROITS > DROIT
DROLE *adj* amusing ▷ *n* scoundrel
DROLER > DROLE
DROLES > DROLE
DROLEST > DROLE
DROLL *vb* speak wittily ▷ *adj* quaintly amusing
DROLLED > DROLL
DROLLER > DROLL
DROLLERY *n* humour
DROLLEST > DROLL
DROLLING > DROLL
DROLLINGS > DROLL
DROLLISH *adj* somewhat droll
DROLLNESS > DROLL
DROLLS > DROLL
DROLLY > DROLL
DROME *n* informal word for > AERODROME
DROMEDARE *obsolete form of* > DROMEDARY
DROMEDARY *n* camel with a single hump
DROMES > DROME
DROMIC *adj* relating to running track
DROMICAL *same as* > DROMIC
DROMOI > DROMOS
DROMON *same as* > DROMOND
DROMOND *n* large swift sailing vessel of the 12th to 15th centuries
DROMONDS > DROMOND
DROMONS > DROMON
DROMOS *n* Greek passageway
DRONE *n* male bee ▷ *vb* make a monotonous low dull sound
DRONED > DRONE
DRONER > DRONE
DRONERS > DRONE
DRONES > DRONE
DRONGO *n* tropical songbird with a glossy black plumage, a forked tail, and a stout bill
DRONGOES > DRONGO
DRONGOS > DRONGO
DRONIER > DRONY
DRONIEST > DRONY
DRONING > DRONE
DRONINGLY > DRONE
DRONISH > DRONE
DRONISHLY > DRONE
DRONKLAP *n* South African word for a drunkard
DRONKLAPS > DRONKLAP
DRONY *adj* monotonous
DROOB *n* pathetic person
DROOBS > DROOB
DROOG *n* ruffian
DROOGISH > DROOG
DROOGS > DROOG
DROOK *same as* > DROUK
DROOKED > DROOK
DROOKING > DROOK

DROOKINGS > DROOK
DROOKIT *same as* > DROUKIT
DROOKS > DROOK
DROOL *vb* show excessive enthusiasm (for)
DROOLED > DROOL
DROOLIER > DROOLY
DROOLIEST > DROOLY
DROOLING > DROOL
DROOLS > DROOL
DROOLY *adj* tending to drool
DROOME *obsolete form of* > DRUM
DROOMES > DRUM
DROOP *vb* hang downwards loosely ▷ *n* act or state of drooping
DROOPED > DROOP
DROOPIER > DROOPY
DROOPIEST > DROOPY
DROOPILY > DROOPY
DROOPING > DROOP
DROOPS > DROOP
DROOPY *adj* hanging or sagging downwards
DROP *vb* (allow to) fall vertically ▷ *n* small quantity of liquid forming a round shape
DROPCLOTH *n* cloth spread on floor to catch drips while painting
DROPFLIES > DROPFLY
DROPFLY *n* (angling) artificial fly
DROPFORGE *vb* forge metal between two dies
DROPHEAD as in *drophead coupe* two-door car with a folding roof and sloping back
DROPHEADS > DROPHEAD
DROPKICK *n* (in certain ball games) a kick in which the ball is first dropped then kicked as it bounces from the ground
DROPKICKS > DROPKICK
DROPLET *n* very small drop of liquid
DROPLETS > DROPLET
DROPLIGHT *n* electric light that may be raised or lowered by means of a pulley or other mechanism
DROPOUT *n* person who rejects conventional society ▷ *vb* abandon or withdraw (from an institution or group)
DROPOUTS > DROPOUT
DROPPABLE > DROP
DROPPED > DROP
DROPPER *n* small tube with a rubber part at one end for drawing up and dispensing drops of liquid
DROPPERS > DROPPER
DROPPING > DROP
DROPPINGS *pl n* faeces of certain animals, such as rabbits or birds
DROPPLE *n* trickle
DROPPLES > DROPPLE
DROPS > DROP
DROPSHOT *n* (in tennis) shot in which a softly returned ball just clears the net before falling abruptly
DROPSHOTS > DROPSHOT
DROPSICAL > DROPSY
DROPSIED > DROPSY
DROPSIES > DROPSY
DROPSONDE *n* radiosonde dropped by parachute
DROPSTONE *n* calcium carbonate in stalactites
DROPSY *n* illness in which watery fluid collects in the body
DROPT > DROP
DROPWISE *adv* in form of a drop
DROPWORT *See also* > MEADOWSWEET
DROPWORTS > DROPWORT
DROSERA *n* insectivorous plant
DROSERAS > DROSERA
DROSHKIES > DROSHKY
DROSHKY *n* open four-wheeled horse-drawn passenger carriage, formerly used in Russia
DROSKIES > DROSKY
DROSKY *same as* > DROSHKY
DROSS *n* scum formed on the surfaces of molten metals
DROSSES > DROSS
DROSSIER > DROSS
DROSSIEST > DROSS
DROSSY > DROSS
DROSTDIES > DROSTDY
DROSTDY *n* office of landdrost
DROSTDYS > DROSTDY
DROUGHT *n* prolonged shortage of rainfall
DROUGHTS > DROUGHT
DROUGHTY > DROUGHT
DROUK *vb* drench
DROUKED > DROUK
DROUKING > DROUK
DROUKINGS > DROUK
DROUKIT *adj* drenched
DROUKS > DROUK
DROUTH *same as* > DROUGHT
DROUTHIER > DROUTHY
DROUTHS > DROUTH
DROUTHY *adj* thirsty or dry
DROVE > DRIVE
DROVED > DRIVE
DROVER *n* person who drives sheep or cattle
DROVERS > DROVER
DROVES > DRIVE
DROVING > DRIVE
DROVINGS > DRIVE
DROW *n* sea fog
DROWN *vb* die or kill by immersion in liquid
DROWND *dialect form of* > DROWN
DROWNDED > DROWND
DROWNDING > DROWND
DROWNDS > DROWND
DROWNED > DROWN
DROWNER > DROWN
DROWNERS > DROWN
DROWNING > DROWN
DROWNINGS > DROWN
DROWNS > DROWN
DROWS > DROW
DROWSE *vb* be sleepy, dull, or sluggish ▷ *n* state of being drowsy
DROWSED > DROWSE
DROWSES > DROWSE
DROWSIER > DROWSY
DROWSIEST > DROWSY
DROWSIHED *adj* old form of drowsy
DROWSILY > DROWSY
DROWSING > DROWSE
DROWSY *adj* feeling sleepy
DRUB *vb* beat as with a stick ▷ *n* blow, as from a stick
DRUBBED > DRUB
DRUBBER > DRUB
DRUBBERS > DRUB
DRUBBING > DRUB
DRUBBINGS > DRUB
DRUBS > DRUB
DRUCKEN *adj* drunken
DRUDGE *n* person who works hard at uninteresting tasks ▷ *vb* work at such tasks
DRUDGED > DRUDGE
DRUDGER > DRUDGE
DRUDGERS > DRUDGE
DRUDGERY *n* uninteresting work that must be done
DRUDGES > DRUDGE
DRUDGING > DRUDGE
DRUDGISM > DRUDGE
DRUDGISMS > DRUDGE
DRUG *n* substance used in the treatment or prevention of disease ▷ *vb* give a drug to (a person or animal) to cause sleepiness or unconsciousness
DRUGGED > DRUG
DRUGGER *n* druggist
DRUGGERS > DRUGGER
DRUGGET *n* coarse fabric used as a protective floor-covering, etc
DRUGGETS > DRUGGET
DRUGGIE *n* drug addict
DRUGGIER > DRUG
DRUGGIES > DRUGGIE
DRUGGIEST > DRUG
DRUGGING > DRUG
DRUGGIST *n* pharmacist
DRUGGISTS > DRUGGIST
DRUGGY > DRUG
DRUGLORD *n* criminal who controls the distribution and sale of large quantities of illegal drugs
DRUGLORDS > DRUGLORD
DRUGMAKER *n* manufacturer of drugs
DRUGS > DRUG
DRUGSTORE *n* pharmacy where a wide range of goods are available
DRUID *n* member of an ancient order of priests in Gaul, Britain, and Ireland in the pre-Christian era
DRUIDESS > DRUID
DRUIDIC > DRUID
DRUIDICAL > DRUID
DRUIDISM > DRUID
DRUIDISMS > DRUID
DRUIDRIES > DRUID
DRUIDRY > DRUID
DRUIDS > DRUID
DRUM *n* percussion instrument sounded by striking a membrane stretched across the opening of a hollow cylinder ▷ *vb* play (music) on a drum
DRUMBEAT *n* sound made by beating a drum
DRUMBEATS > DRUMBEAT
DRUMBLE *vb* be inactive
DRUMBLED > DRUMBLE
DRUMBLES > DRUMBLE
DRUMBLING > DRUMBLE
DRUMFIRE *n* heavy, rapid, and continuous gunfire, the sound of which resembles rapid drumbeats
DRUMFIRES > DRUMFIRE
DRUMFISH *n* one of several types of fish that make a drumming sound
DRUMHEAD *n* part of a drum that is struck
DRUMHEADS > DRUMHEAD
DRUMLIER > DRUMLY
DRUMLIEST > DRUMLY
DRUMLIKE > DRUM
DRUMLIN *n* streamlined mound of glacial drift, rounded or elongated in the direction of the original flow of ice
DRUMLINS > DRUMLIN
DRUMLY *adj* dismal; dreary
DRUMMED > DRUM
DRUMMER *n* person who plays a drum or drums
DRUMMERS > DRUMMER
DRUMMIES > DRUMMY
DRUMMING > DRUM
DRUMMOCK *same as* > DRAMMOCK
DRUMMOCKS > DRUMMOCK
DRUMMY *n* (in South Africa) drum majorette
DRUMROLL *n* continued repeated sound of drum
DRUMROLLS > DRUMROLL
DRUMS > DRUM
DRUMSTICK *n* stick used for playing a drum
DRUNK > DRINK
DRUNKARD *n* person who frequently gets drunk
DRUNKARDS > DRUNKARD
DRUNKEN *adj* drunk or frequently drunk
DRUNKENLY > DRUNKEN
DRUNKER > DRINK

DRUNKEST > DRINK
DRUNKS > DRINK
DRUPE *n* fleshy fruit with a stone, such as the peach or cherry
DRUPEL *same as* > DRUPELET
DRUPELET *n* small drupe, usually one of a number forming a compound fruit
DRUPELETS > DRUPELET
DRUPELS > DRUPEL
DRUPES > DRUPE
DRUSE *n* aggregate of small crystals within a cavity, esp those lining a cavity in a rock or mineral
DRUSES > DRUSE
DRUSIER > DRUSY
DRUSIEST > DRUSY
DRUSY *adj* made of tiny crystals
DRUTHERS *n* preference
DRUXIER > DRUXY
DRUXIEST > DRUXY
DRUXY *adj* (of wood) having decayed white spots
DRY *adj* lacking moisture ▷ *vb* make or become dry
DRYABLE > DRY
DRYAD *n* wood nymph
DRYADES > DRYAD
DRYADIC > DRYAD
DRYADS > DRYAD
DRYASDUST *adj* boringly bookish
DRYBEAT *vb* beat severely
DRYBEATEN > DRYBEAT
DRYBEATS > DRYBEAT
DRYER > DRY
DRYERS > DRY
DRYEST > DRY
DRYING > DRY
DRYINGS > DRY
DRYISH *adj* fairly dry
DRYLAND *adj* of an arid area
DRYLOT *n* livestock enclosure
DRYLOTS > DRYLOT
DRYLY *same as* > DRILY
DRYMOUTH *n* condition of insufficient saliva
DRYMOUTHS > DRYMOUTH
DRYNESS > DRY
DRYNESSES > DRY
DRYPOINT *n* copper engraving technique using a hard steel needle
DRYPOINTS > DRYPOINT
DRYS > DRY
DRYSALTER *n* dealer in certain chemical products, such as dyestuffs and gums, and in dried, tinned, or salted foods and edible oils
DRYSTONE *adj* (of a wall) made without mortar
DRYWALL *n* wall built without mortar ▷ *vb* build a wall without mortar
DRYWALLED > DRYWALL
DRYWALLS > DRYWALL
DRYWELL *n* type of sewage disposal system
DRYWELLS > DRYWELL
DSO *same as* > ZHO
DSOBO *same as* > ZOBO
DSOBOS > DSOBO
DSOMO *same as* > ZHOMO
DSOMOS > DSOMO
DSOS > DSO
DUAD *a rare word for* > PAIR
DUADS > DUAD
DUAL *adj* having two parts, functions, or aspects ▷ *n* dual number ▷ *vb* make (a road) into a dual carriageway
DUALIN *n* explosive substance
DUALINS > DUALIN
DUALISE *same as* > DUALIZE
DUALISED > DUALISE
DUALISES > DUALISE
DUALISING > DUALISE
DUALISM *n* state of having or being believed to have two distinct parts or aspects
DUALISMS > DUALISM
DUALIST > DUALISM
DUALISTIC > DUALISM
DUALISTS > DUALISM
DUALITIES > DUALITY
DUALITY *n* state or quality of being two or in two parts
DUALIZE *vb* cause to have two parts
DUALIZED > DUALIZE
DUALIZES > DUALIZE
DUALIZING > DUALIZE
DUALLED > DUAL
DUALLING > DUAL
DUALLY > DUAL
DUALS > DUAL
DUAN *n* poem
DUANS > DUAN
DUAR *n* Arab camp
DUARCHIES > DUARCHY
DUARCHY *same as* > DIARCHY
DUARS > DUAR
DUATHLON *n* athletic contest in which each athlete competes in running and cycling events
DUATHLONS > DUATHLON
DUB *vb* give (a person or place) a name or nickname ▷ *n* style of reggae record production involving exaggeration of instrumental parts, echo, etc
DUBBED > DUB
DUBBER > DUB
DUBBERS > DUB
DUBBIN *n* thick grease applied to leather to soften and waterproof it
DUBBING > DUB
DUBBINGS > DUB
DUBBINS > DUBBIN
DUBBO *adj* stupid ▷ *n* stupid person
DUBBOS > DUBBO
DUBIETIES > DUBIETY
DUBIETY *n* state of being doubtful
DUBIOSITY *same as* > DUBIETY
DUBIOUS *adj* feeling or causing doubt
DUBIOUSLY > DUBIOUS
DUBITABLE *adj* open to doubt
DUBITABLY > DUBITABLE
DUBITANCY > DUBITATE
DUBITATE *vb* doubt
DUBITATED > DUBITATE
DUBITATES > DUBITATE
DUBNIUM *n* element produced in minute quantities by bombarding plutonium with high-energy neon ions
DUBNIUMS > DUBNIUM
DUBONNET *n* dark purplish-red colour
DUBONNETS > DUBONNET
DUBS > DUB
DUCAL *adj* of a duke
DUCALLY > DUCAL
DUCAT *n* former European gold or silver coin
DUCATOON *n* former silver coin
DUCATOONS > DUCATOON
DUCATS > DUCAT
DUCDAME *interj* Shakespearean nonsense word
DUCE *n* leader
DUCES > DUCE
DUCHESS *n* woman who holds the rank of duke ▷ *vb* overwhelm with flattering attention
DUCHESSE *n* type of satin
DUCHESSED > DUCHESS
DUCHESSES > DUCHESS
DUCHIES > DUCHY
DUCHY *n* territory of a duke or duchess
DUCI > DUCE
DUCK *n* water bird with short legs, webbed feet, and a broad blunt bill ▷ *vb* move (the head or body) quickly downwards, to avoid being seen or to dodge a blow
DUCKBILL *n* duckbilled platypus
DUCKBILLS > DUCKBILL
DUCKBOARD *n* board or boards laid so as to form a floor or path over wet or muddy ground
DUCKED > DUCK
DUCKER > DUCK
DUCKERS > DUCK
DUCKFOOT as in *duckfoot quote* chevron-shaped quotation mark
DUCKIE *same as* > DUCKY
DUCKIER > DUCKY
DUCKIES > DUCKY
DUCKIEST > DUCKY
DUCKING > DUCK
DUCKINGS > DUCK
DUCKLING *n* baby duck
DUCKLINGS > DUCKLING
DUCKMOLE *another word for* > DUCKBILL
DUCKMOLES > DUCKMOLE
DUCKPIN *n* short bowling pin
DUCKPINS > DUCKPIN
DUCKS > DUCK
DUCKSHOVE *vb* evade responsibility
DUCKTAIL *n* Teddy boy's hairstyle
DUCKTAILS > DUCKTAIL
DUCKWALK *vb* walk in a squatting posture
DUCKWALKS > DUCKWALK
DUCKWEED *n* any of various small stemless aquatic plants of the family *Lemnaceae*, esp any of the genus *Lemna*, that have rounded leaves and occur floating on still water in temperate regions
DUCKWEEDS > DUCKWEED
DUCKY *n* darling or dear: used as a term of endearment among women, but now often used in imitation of the supposed usage of homosexual men ▷ *adj* delightful
DUCT *vb* convey via a duct ▷ *n* tube, pipe, or channel through which liquid or gas is conveyed
DUCTAL > DUCT
DUCTED > DUCT
DUCTILE *adj* (of a metal) able to be shaped into sheets or wires
DUCTILELY > DUCTILE
DUCTILITY > DUCTILE
DUCTING > DUCT
DUCTINGS > DUCT
DUCTLESS > DUCT
DUCTS > DUCT
DUCTULE *n* small duct
DUCTULES > DUCTULE
DUCTWORK *n* system of ducts
DUCTWORKS > DUCTWORK
DUD *n* ineffectual person or thing ▷ *adj* bad or useless
DUDDER *n* door-to-door salesman
DUDDERIES > DUDDERY
DUDDERS > DUDDER
DUDDERY *n* place where old clothes are sold
DUDDIE *adj* ragged
DUDDIER > DUDDIE
DUDDIEST > DUDDIE
DUDDY *same as* > DUDDIE
DUDE *vb* dress fashionably ▷ *n* man
DUDED > DUDE
DUDEEN *n* clay pipe with a short stem
DUDEENS > DUDEEN
DUDES > DUDE
DUDGEON *n* anger or resentment

DUDGEONS > DUDGEON
DUDHEEN *n* type of pipe
DUDHEENS > DUDHEEN
DUDING > DUDE
DUDISH > DUDE
DUDISHLY > DUDE
DUDISM *n* being a dude
DUDISMS > DUDISM
DUDS > DUD
DUE *vb* supply with ▷ *adj* expected or scheduled to be present or arrive ▷ *n* something that is owed or required ▷ *adv* directly or exactly
DUECENTO *n* thirteenth century (in Italian art)
DUECENTOS > DUECENTO
DUED > DUE
DUEFUL *adj* proper
DUEL *n* formal fight with deadly weapons between two people, to settle a quarrel ▷ *vb* fight in a duel
DUELED > DUEL
DUELER > DUEL
DUELERS > DUEL
DUELING > DUEL
DUELIST > DUEL
DUELISTS > DUEL
DUELLED > DUEL
DUELLER > DUEL
DUELLERS > DUEL
DUELLI > DUELLO
DUELLING > DUEL
DUELLINGS > DUEL
DUELLIST > DUEL
DUELLISTS > DUEL
DUELLO *n* art of duelling
DUELLOS > DUELLO
DUELS > DUEL
DUELSOME *adj* given to duelling
DUENDE *n* Spanish goblin
DUENDES > DUENDE
DUENESS > DUE
DUENESSES > DUE
DUENNA *n* (esp in Spain) elderly woman acting as chaperone to a young woman
DUENNAS > DUENNA
DUES *pl n* membership fees paid to a club or organization
DUET *n* piece of music for two performers ▷ *vb* perform a duet
DUETED > DUET
DUETING > DUET
DUETS > DUET
DUETT *same as* > DUET
DUETTED > DUET
DUETTI > DUETTO
DUETTING > DUET
DUETTINO *n* simple duet
DUETTINOS > DUETTINO
DUETTIST > DUET
DUETTISTS > DUET
DUETTO *same as* > DUET
DUETTOS > DUETTO
DUETTS > DUETT
DUFF *adj* broken or useless ▷ *vb* change the appearance of or give a false appearance to (old or stolen goods) ▷ *n* rump or buttocks
DUFFED > DUFF
DUFFEL *n* heavy woollen cloth with a thick nap
DUFFELS > DUFFEL
DUFFER *n* dull or incompetent person
DUFFERDOM *n* condition of being a duffer
DUFFERISM *same as* > DUFFERDOM
DUFFERS > DUFFER
DUFFEST > DUFF
DUFFING > DUFF
DUFFINGS > DUFF
DUFFLE *same as* > DUFFEL
DUFFLES > DUFFLE
DUFFS > DUFF
DUFUS *same as* > DOOFUS
DUFUSES > DUFUS
DUG > DIG
DUGITE *n* medium-sized Australian venomous snake
DUGITES > DUGITE
DUGONG *n* whalelike mammal of tropical waters
DUGONGS > DUGONG
DUGOUT *n* (at a sports ground) covered bench where managers and substitutes sit
DUGOUTS > DUGOUT
DUGS > DIG
DUH *interj* ironic response to a question or statement, implying that the speaker is stupid or that the reply is obvious
DUHKHA *same as* > DUKKHA
DUHKHAS > DUHKHA
DUI > DUO
DUIKER *n* small African antelope
DUIKERBOK *same as* > DUIKER
DUIKERS > DUIKER
DUING > DUE
DUIT *n* former Dutch coin
DUITS > DUIT
DUKA *n* shop
DUKAS > DUKA
DUKE *vb* fight with fists ▷ *n* nobleman of the highest rank
DUKED > DUKE
DUKEDOM *n* title, rank, or position of a duke
DUKEDOMS > DUKEDOM
DUKELING *n* low-ranking duke
DUKELINGS > DUKELING
DUKERIES > DUKERY
DUKERY *n* duke's domain
DUKES *pl n* fists
DUKESHIP > DUKE
DUKESHIPS > DUKE
DUKING > DUKE
DUKKA *n* mix of ground roast nuts and spices, originating in Egypt, and used for sprinkling on meat or as a dip
DUKKAH *same as* > DUKKA
DUKKAHS > DUKKAH
DUKKAS > DUKKA
DUKKHA *n* (in Theravada Buddhism) the belief that all things are suffering, due to the desire to seek permanence or recognise the self when neither exist: one of the three basic characteristics of existence
DUKKHAS > DUKKHA
DULCAMARA *n* orange-fruited vine
DULCET *adj* (of a sound) soothing or pleasant ▷ *n* soft organ stop
DULCETLY > DULCET
DULCETS > DULCET
DULCIAN *n* precursor to the bassoon
DULCIANA *n* sweet-toned organ stop, controlling metal pipes of narrow scale
DULCIANAS > DULCIANA
DULCIANS > DULCIAN
DULCIFIED > DULCIFY
DULCIFIES > DULCIFY
DULCIFY *vb* make pleasant or agreeable
DULCIMER *n* tuned percussion instrument consisting of a set of strings stretched over a sounding board and struck with hammers
DULCIMERS > DULCIMER
DULCIMORE *former name for* > DULCIMER
DULCINEA *n* man's sweetheart
DULCINEAS > DULCINEA
DULCITE *n* sweet substance
DULCITES > DULCITE
DULCITOL *another word for* > DULCITE
DULCITOLS > DULCITOL
DULCITUDE *n* sweetness
DULCOSE *another word for* > DULCITE
DULCOSES > DULCOSE
DULE *n* suffering; misery
DULES > DULE
DULIA *n* veneration accorded to saints in the Roman Catholic and Eastern Churches, as contrasted with hyperdulia and latria
DULIAS > DULIA
DULL *adj* not interesting ▷ *vb* make or become dull
DULLARD *n* dull or stupid person
DULLARDS > DULLARD
DULLED > DULL
DULLER > DULL
DULLEST > DULL
DULLIER > DULL
DULLIEST > DULL
DULLING > DULL
DULLISH > DULL
DULLISHLY > DULL
DULLNESS > DULL
DULLS > DULL
DULLY > DULL
DULNESS > DULL
DULNESSES > DULL
DULOCRACY *n* rule by slaves
DULOSES > DULOSIS
DULOSIS *n* practice of some ants, in which one species forces members of a different species to do the work of the colony
DULOTIC > DULOSIS
DULSE *n* seaweed with large red edible fronds
DULSES > DULSE
DULY *adv* in a proper manner
DUMA *n* elective legislative assembly established by Tsar Nicholas II in 1905: overthrown by the Bolsheviks in 1917
DUMAIST *n* member of duma
DUMAISTS > DUMAIST
DUMAS > DUMA
DUMB *vb* silence ▷ *adj* lacking the power to speak
DUMBBELL *n* short bar with a heavy ball or disc at each end, used for physical exercise
DUMBBELLS > DUMBBELL
DUMBCANE *n* West Indian aroid plant
DUMBCANES > DUMBCANE
DUMBED > DUMB
DUMBER > DUMB
DUMBEST > DUMB
DUMBFOUND *vb* strike dumb with astonishment
DUMBHEAD *n* dunce
DUMBHEADS > DUMBHEAD
DUMBING > DUMB
DUMBLY > DUMB
DUMBNESS > DUMB
DUMBO *n* slow-witted unintelligent person
DUMBOS > DUMBO
DUMBS > DUMB
DUMBSHIT *n* taboo slang word for a stupid person
DUMBSHITS > DUMBSHIT
DUMDUM *n* soft-nosed bullet that expands on impact and causes serious wounds
DUMDUMS > DUMDUM
DUMELA *sentence substitute* hello
DUMFOUND *same as* > DUMBFOUND
DUMFOUNDS > DUMFOUND
DUMKA *n* Slavonic lyrical song
DUMKY > DUMKA
DUMMERER *n* person who pretends to be dumb

DUMMERERS > DUMMERER
DUMMIED > DUMMY
DUMMIER > DUMMY
DUMMIES > DUMMY
DUMMIEST > DUMMY
DUMMINESS > DUMMY
DUMMKOPF *n* stupid person
DUMMKOPFS > DUMMKOPF
DUMMY *adj* sham ▷ *n* figure representing the human form, used for displaying clothes etc ▷ *adj* imitation, substitute ▷ *vb* prepare a dummy of (a proposed book, page, etc)
DUMMYING > DUMMY
DUMOSE *adj* bushlike
DUMOSITY > DUMOSE
DUMOUS *same as* > DUMOSE
DUMP *vb* drop or let fall in a careless manner ▷ *n* place where waste materials are left
DUMPBIN *n* free-standing unit in a bookshop in which a particular publisher's books are displayed
DUMPBINS > DUMPBIN
DUMPCART *n* cart for dumping without handling
DUMPCARTS > DUMPCART
DUMPED > DUMP
DUMPER > DUMP
DUMPERS > DUMP
DUMPIER > DUMPY
DUMPIES > DUMPY
DUMPIEST > DUMPY
DUMPILY > DUMPY
DUMPINESS > DUMPY
DUMPING > DUMP
DUMPINGS > DUMP
DUMPISH *same as* > DUMPY
DUMPISHLY > DUMPISH
DUMPLE *vb* form into dumpling shape
DUMPLED > DUMPLE
DUMPLES > DUMPLE
DUMPLING *n* small ball of dough cooked and served with stew
DUMPLINGS > DUMPLING
DUMPS *pl n* state of melancholy or depression
DUMPSITE *n* location of dump
DUMPSITES > DUMPSITE
DUMPSTER *n* refuse skip
DUMPSTERS > DUMPSTER
DUMPTRUCK *n* lorry with a tipping container
DUMPY *n* dumpy person ▷ *adj* short and plump
DUN *adj* brownish-grey ▷ *vb* demand payment from (a debtor) ▷ *n* demand for payment
DUNAM *n* unit of area measurement
DUNAMS > DUNAM
DUNCE *n* person who is stupid or slow to learn
DUNCEDOM > DUNCE
DUNCEDOMS > DUNCE
DUNCELIKE > DUNCE
DUNCERIES > DUNCERY
DUNCERY *n* duncelike behaviour
DUNCES > DUNCE
DUNCH *vb* push against gently
DUNCHED > DUNCH
DUNCHES > DUNCH
DUNCHING > DUNCH
DUNCICAL *adj* duncelike
DUNCISH *adj* duncelike
DUNCISHLY > DUNCE
DUNDER *n* cane juice lees
DUNDERS > DUNDER
DUNE *n* mound or ridge of drifted sand
DUNELAND *n* land characterized by dunes
DUNELANDS > DUNELAND
DUNELIKE > DUNE
DUNES > DUNE
DUNG *n* faeces from animals such as cattle ▷ *vb* cover (ground) with manure
DUNGAREE *n* coarse cotton fabric used chiefly for work clothes, etc
DUNGAREED *adj* wearing dungarees
DUNGAREES > DUNGAREE
DUNGED > DUNG
DUNGEON *vb* hold captive in dungeon ▷ *n* underground prison cell
DUNGEONED > DUNGEON
DUNGEONER *n* jailer
DUNGEONS > DUNGEON
DUNGER *n* old decrepit car
DUNGERS > DUNGER
DUNGHILL *n* heap of dung
DUNGHILLS > DUNGHILL
DUNGIER > DUNG
DUNGIEST > DUNG
DUNGING > DUNG
DUNGMERE *n* cesspool
DUNGMERES > DUNGMERE
DUNGS > DUNG
DUNGY > DUNG
DUNITE *n* ultrabasic igneous rock consisting mainly of olivine
DUNITES > DUNITE
DUNITIC > DUNITE
DUNK *vb* dip (a biscuit or bread) in a drink or soup before eating it
DUNKED > DUNK
DUNKER > DUNK
DUNKERS > DUNK
DUNKING > DUNK
DUNKS > DUNK
DUNLIN *n* small sandpiper with a brown back found in northern regions
DUNLINS > DUNLIN
DUNNAGE *n* loose material used for packing cargo
DUNNAGES > DUNNAGE
DUNNAKIN *n* lavatory
DUNNAKINS > DUNNAKIN
DUNNART *n* mouselike insectivorous marsupial of the genus *Sminthopsis* of Australia and New Guinea
DUNNARTS > DUNNART
DUNNED > DUN
DUNNER > DUN
DUNNESS > DUN
DUNNESSES > DUN
DUNNEST > DUN
DUNNIER > DUNNY
DUNNIES > DUNNY
DUNNIEST > DUNNY
DUNNING > DUN
DUNNINGS > DUN
DUNNISH > DUN
DUNNITE *n* explosive containing ammonium picrate
DUNNITES > DUNNITE
DUNNO *vb* slang for don't know
DUNNOCK *n* hedge sparrow
DUNNOCKS > DUNNOCK
DUNNY *n* in Australia, toilet ▷ *adj* relating to dunny
DUNS > DUN
DUNSH *same as* > DUNCH
DUNSHED > DUNSH
DUNSHES > DUNSH
DUNSHING > DUNSH
DUNT *n* blow ▷ *vb* strike or hit
DUNTED > DUNT
DUNTING > DUNT
DUNTS > DUNT
DUO *same as* > DUET
DUOBINARY *adj* denoting a communications system for coding digital data in which three data bands are used, 0, +1, −1
DUODECIMO *n* book size resulting from folding a sheet of paper into twelve leaves
DUODENA > DUODENUM
DUODENAL > DUODENUM
DUODENARY *adj* of or relating to the number 12
DUODENUM *n* first part of the small intestine, just below the stomach
DUODENUMS > DUODENUM
DUOLOG *same as* > DUOLOGUE
DUOLOGS > DUOLOG
DUOLOGUE *n* (in drama) conversation between only two speakers
DUOLOGUES > DUOLOGUE
DUOMI > DUOMO
DUOMO *n* cathedral in Italy
DUOMOS > DUOMO
DUOPOLIES > DUOPOLY
DUOPOLY *n* situation in which control of a commodity or service in a particular market is vested in just two producers or suppliers
DUOPSONY *n* two rival buyers controlling sellers
DUOS > DUO
DUOTONE *n* process for producing halftone illustrations using two shades of a single colour or black and a colour
DUOTONES > DUOTONE
DUP *vb* open
DUPABLE > DUPE
DUPATTA *n* scarf worn in India
DUPATTAS > DUPATTA
DUPE *vb* deceive or cheat ▷ *n* person who is easily deceived
DUPED > DUPE
DUPER > DUPE
DUPERIES > DUPE
DUPERS > DUPE
DUPERY > DUPE
DUPES > DUPE
DUPING > DUPE
DUPION *n* silk fabric made from the threads of double cocoons
DUPIONS > DUPION
DUPLE *adj* having two beats in a bar
DUPLET *n* pair of electrons shared between two atoms in a covalent bond
DUPLETS > DUPLET
DUPLEX *vb* duplicate ▷ *n* apartment on two floors ▷ *adj* having two parts
DUPLEXED > DUPLEX
DUPLEXER *n* telecommunications system
DUPLEXERS > DUPLEXER
DUPLEXES > DUPLEX
DUPLEXING > DUPLEX
DUPLEXITY > DUPLEX
DUPLICAND *n* feu duty doubled
DUPLICATE *adj* copied exactly from an original ▷ *n* exact copy ▷ *vb* make an exact copy of
DUPLICITY *n* deceitful behaviour
DUPLIED > DUPLY
DUPLIES > DUPLY
DUPLY *vb* give a second reply
DUPLYING > DUPLY
DUPONDII > DUPONDIUS
DUPONDIUS *n* brass coin of ancient Rome worth half a sesterce
DUPPED > DUP
DUPPIES > DUPPY
DUPPING > DUP
DUPPY *n* spirit or ghost
DUPS > DUP
DURA *same as* > DURRA
DURABLE *adj* long-lasting
DURABLES *pl n* goods that require infrequent replacement
DURABLY > DURABLE
DURAL *n* alloy of aluminium and copper
DURALS > DURAL
DURALUMIN *n* light and strong aluminium alloy containing copper,

silicon, magnesium, and manganese
DURAMEN *another name for* > HEARTWOOD
DURAMENS > DURAMEN
DURANCE *n* imprisonment
DURANCES > DURANCE
DURANT *n* tough, leathery cloth
DURANTS > DURANT
DURAS > DURA
DURATION *n* length of time that something lasts
DURATIONS > DURATION
DURATIVE *adj* denoting an aspect of verbs that includes the imperfective and the progressive ▷ *n* durative aspect of a verb
DURATIVES > DURATIVE
DURBAR *n* (formerly) the court of a native ruler or a governor in India
DURBARS > DURBAR
DURDUM *same as* > DIRDUM
DURDUMS > DURDUM
DURE *vb* endure
DURED > DURE
DUREFUL *adj* lasting
DURES > DURE
DURESS *n* compulsion by use of force or threats
DURESSE *same as* > DURESS
DURESSES > DURESS
DURGAH *same as* > DARGAH
DURGAHS > DURGAH
DURGAN *n* dwarf
DURGANS > DURGAN
DURGIER > DURGY
DURGIEST > DURGY
DURGY *adj* dwarflike
DURIAN *n* SE Asian bombacaceous tree, *Durio zibethinus*, having very large oval fruits with a hard spiny rind containing seeds surrounded by edible evil-smelling aril
DURIANS > DURIAN
DURICRUST *another name for* > CALICHE
DURING *prep* throughout or within the limit of (a period of time)
DURION *same as* > DURIAN
DURIONS > DURION
DURMAST *n* large Eurasian oak tree, *Quercus petraea*, with lobed leaves and sessile acorns
DURMASTS > DURMAST
DURN *vb* variant of > DARN
DURNDEST *same as* > DARNEDEST
DURNED > DURN
DURNEDER > DURN
DURNEDEST > DURN
DURNING > DURN
DURNS > DURN
DURO *n* silver peso of Spain or Spanish America
DUROC *n* breed of pig
DUROCS > DUROC
DUROMETER *n* instrument for measuring hardness
DUROS > DURO
DUROY *n* coarse woollen fabric
DUROYS > DUROY
DURR *same as* > DURRA
DURRA *n* Old World variety of sorghum, *Sorghum vulgare durra*, with erect hairy flower spikes and round seeds: cultivated for grain and fodder
DURRAS > DURRA
DURRIE *n* cotton carpet made in India, often in rectangular pieces fringed at the ends: sometimes used as a sofa cover, wall hanging, etc
DURRIES > DURRY
DURRS > DURR
DURRY *n* cigarette
DURST *a past tense of* > DARE
DURUKULI *n* S American monkey
DURUKULIS > DURUKULI
DURUM *n* variety of wheat, *Triticum durum*, with a high gluten content, cultivated mainly in the Mediterranean region, and used chiefly to make pastas
DURUMS > DURUM
DURZI *n* Indian tailor
DURZIS > DURZI
DUSH *vb* strike hard
DUSHED > DUSH
DUSHES > DUSH
DUSHING > DUSH
DUSK *n* time just before nightfall, when it is almost dark ▷ *adj* shady ▷ *vb* make or become dark
DUSKED > DUSK
DUSKEN *vb* grow dark
DUSKENED > DUSKEN
DUSKENING > DUSKEN
DUSKENS > DUSKEN
DUSKER > DUSK
DUSKEST > DUSK
DUSKIER > DUSKY
DUSKIEST > DUSKY
DUSKILY > DUSKY
DUSKINESS > DUSKY
DUSKING > DUSK
DUSKISH > DUSK
DUSKISHLY > DUSK
DUSKLY > DUSK
DUSKNESS > DUSK
DUSKS > DUSK
DUSKY *adj* dark in colour
DUST *n* small dry particles of earth, sand, or dirt ▷ *vb* remove dust from (furniture) by wiping
DUSTBIN *n* large container for household rubbish
DUSTBINS > DUSTBIN
DUSTCART *n* truck for collecting household rubbish
DUSTCARTS > DUSTCART
DUSTCOVER *same as* > DUSTSHEET
DUSTED > DUST
DUSTER *n* cloth used for dusting
DUSTERS > DUSTER
DUSTHEAP *n* accumulation of refuse
DUSTHEAPS > DUSTHEAP
DUSTIER > DUSTY
DUSTIEST > DUSTY
DUSTILY > DUSTY
DUSTINESS > DUSTY
DUSTING > DUST
DUSTINGS > DUST
DUSTLESS > DUST
DUSTLIKE > DUST
DUSTMAN *n* man whose job is to collect household rubbish
DUSTMEN > DUSTMAN
DUSTOFF *n* casualty evacuation helicopter
DUSTOFFS > DUSTOFF
DUSTPAN *n* short-handled shovel into which dust is swept from floors
DUSTPANS > DUSTPAN
DUSTPROOF *adj* repelling dust
DUSTRAG *n* cloth for dusting
DUSTRAGS > DUSTRAG
DUSTS > DUST
DUSTSHEET *n* large cloth cover to protect furniture from dust
DUSTSTORM *n* storm with whirling column of dust
DUSTUP *n* quarrel, fight, or argument
DUSTUPS > DUSTUP
DUSTY *adj* covered with dust
DUTCH *n* wife
DUTCHES > DUTCH
DUTCHMAN *n* piece of wood, metal, etc, used to repair or patch faulty workmanship
DUTCHMEN > DUTCHMAN
DUTEOUS *adj* dutiful or obedient
DUTEOUSLY > DUTEOUS
DUTIABLE *adj* (of goods) requiring payment of duty
DUTIED *adj* liable for duty
DUTIES > DUTY
DUTIFUL *adj* doing what is expected
DUTIFULLY > DUTIFUL
DUTY *n* work or a task performed as part of one's job
DUUMVIR *n* one of two coequal magistrates or officers
DUUMVIRAL > DUUMVIR
DUUMVIRI > DUUMVIR
DUUMVIRS > DUUMVIR
DUVET *same as* > DOONA
DUVETINE *same as* > DUVETYN
DUVETINES > DUVETINE
DUVETS > DUVET
DUVETYN *n* soft napped velvety fabric of cotton, silk, wool, or rayon
DUVETYNE *same as* > DUVETYN
DUVETYNES > DUVETYNE
DUVETYNS > DUVETYN
DUX *n* (in Scottish and certain other schools) the top pupil in a class or school
DUXELLES *n* paste of mushrooms and onions
DUXES > DUX
DUYKER *same as* > DUIKER
DUYKERS > DUYKER
DVANDVA *n* class of compound words consisting of two elements having a coordinate relationship as if connected by *and*
DVANDVAS > DVANDVA
DVORNIK *n* Russian doorkeeper
DVORNIKS > DVORNIK
DWAAL *n* state of absent-mindedness
DWAALS > DWAAL
DWALE *n* deadly nightshade
DWALES > DWALE
DWALM *vb* faint
DWALMED > DWALM
DWALMING > DWALM
DWALMS > DWALM
DWAM *n* stupor or daydream ▷ *vb* faint or fall ill
DWAMMED > DWAM
DWAMMING > DWAM
DWAMS > DWAM
DWANG *n* short piece of wood inserted in a timber-framed wall
DWANGS > DWANG
DWARF *adj* undersized ▷ *n* person who is smaller than average ▷ *adj* (of an animal or plant) much smaller than the usual size for the species ▷ *vb* cause (someone or something) to seem small by being much larger
DWARFED > DWARF
DWARFER > DWARF
DWARFEST > DWARF
DWARFING > DWARF
DWARFISH > DWARF
DWARFISM *n* condition of being a dwarf
DWARFISMS > DWARFISM
DWARFLIKE > DWARF
DWARFNESS > DWARF
DWARFS > DWARF
DWARVES > DWARF
DWAUM *same as* > DWAM
DWAUMED > DWAUM
DWAUMING > DWAUM
DWAUMS > DWAUM
DWEEB *n* stupid or uninteresting person
DWEEBIER > DWEEBY
DWEEBIEST > DWEEBY
DWEEBISH > DWEEB

DWEEBS > DWEEB
DWEEBY *adj* like or typical of a dweeb
DWELL *vb* live, reside ▷ *n* regular pause in the operation of a machine
DWELLED > DWELL
DWELLER > DWELL
DWELLERS > DWELL
DWELLING > DWELL
DWELLINGS > DWELL
DWELLS > DWELL
DWELT > DWELL
DWILE *n* floor cloth
DWILES > DWILE
DWINDLE *vb* grow less in size, strength, or number
DWINDLED > DWINDLE
DWINDLES > DWINDLE
DWINDLING > DWINDLE
DWINE *vb* languish
DWINED > DWINE
DWINES > DWINE
DWINING > DWINE
DYABLE > DYE
DYAD *n* operator that is the unspecified product of two vectors. It can operate on a vector to produce either a scalar or vector product
DYADIC *adj* of or relating to a dyad ▷ *n* sum of a particular number of dyads
DYADICS > DYADIC
DYADS > DYAD
DYARCHAL > DIARCHY
DYARCHIC > DYARCHY
DYARCHIES > DYARCHY
DYARCHY *same as* > DIARCHY
DYBBUK *n* (in the folklore of the cabala) the soul of a dead sinner that has transmigrated into the body of a living person
DYBBUKIM > DYBBUK
DYBBUKKIM > DYBBUK
DYBBUKS > DYBBUK
DYE *n* colouring substance ▷ *vb* colour (hair or fabric) by applying a dye
DYEABLE > DYE
DYED > DYE
DYEING > DYE
DYEINGS > DYE
DYELINE *same as* > DIAZO
DYELINES > DYELINE
DYER > DYE
DYERS > DYE
DYES > DYE
DYESTER *n* dyer
DYESTERS > DYESTER
DYESTUFF *n* substance that can be used as a dye or from which a dye can be obtained
DYESTUFFS > DYESTUFF
DYEWEED *n* plant that produces dye
DYEWEEDS > DYEWEED
DYEWOOD *n* any wood, such as brazil, from which dyes and pigments can be obtained
DYEWOODS > DYEWOOD
DYING > DIE
DYINGLY > DIE
DYINGNESS > DIE
DYINGS > DIE
DYKE *n* wall built to prevent flooding ▷ *vb* embankment or wall built to confine a river to a particular course
DYKED > DYKE
DYKES > DYKE
DYKEY *same as* > DIKEY
DYKIER > DYKEY
DYKIEST > DYKEY
DYKING > DYKE
DYNAMETER *n* instrument for determining the magnifying power of telescopes
DYNAMIC *adj* full of energy, ambition, and new ideas ▷ *n* energetic or driving force
DYNAMICAL *same as* > DYNAMIC
DYNAMICS *n* branch of mechanics concerned with the forces that change or produce the motions of bodies
DYNAMISE *same as* > DYNAMIZE
DYNAMISED > DYNAMISE
DYNAMISES > DYNAMISE
DYNAMISM *n* great energy and enthusiasm
DYNAMISMS > DYNAMISM
DYNAMIST > DYNAMISM
DYNAMISTS > DYNAMISM
DYNAMITE *n* explosive made of nitroglycerine ▷ *vb* blow (something) up with dynamite
DYNAMITED > DYNAMITE
DYNAMITER > DYNAMITE
DYNAMITES > DYNAMITE
DYNAMITIC > DYNAMITE
DYNAMIZE *vb* cause to be dynamic
DYNAMIZED > DYNAMIZE
DYNAMIZES > DYNAMIZE
DYNAMO *n* device for converting mechanical energy into electrical energy
DYNAMOS > DYNAMO
DYNAMOTOR *n* electrical machine having a single magnetic field and two independent armature windings of which one acts as a motor and the other a generator: used to convert direct current from a battery into alternating current
DYNAST *n* hereditary ruler
DYNASTIC > DYNASTY
DYNASTIES > DYNASTY
DYNASTS > DYNAST
DYNASTY *n* sequence of hereditary rulers
DYNATRON as in *dynatron oscillator* type of oscillator
DYNATRONS > DYNATRON
DYNE *n* cgs unit of force
DYNEIN *n* class of proteins
DYNEINS > DYNEIN
DYNEL *n* trade name for synthetic fibre
DYNELS > DYNEL
DYNES > DYNE
DYNODE *n* electrode onto which a beam of electrons can fall, causing the emission of a greater number of electrons by secondary emission. They are used in photomultipliers to amplify the signal
DYNODES > DYNODE
DYNORPHIN *n* drug used to treat cocaine addiction
DYSBINDIN *n* gene associated with schizophrenia
DYSCHROA *n* discolouration of skin
DYSCHROAS > DYSCHROA
DYSCHROIA *same as* > DYSCHROA
DYSCRASIA *n* any abnormal physiological condition, esp of the blood
DYSCRASIC > DYSCRASIA
DYSCRATIC > DYSCRASIA
DYSENTERY *n* infection of the intestine causing severe diarrhoea
DYSGENIC *adj* of, relating to, or contributing to a degeneration or deterioration in the fitness and quality of a race or strain
DYSGENICS *n* study of factors capable of reducing the quality of a race or strain, esp the human race
DYSLALIA *n* defective speech characteristic of those affected by aphasia
DYSLALIAS > DYSLALIA
DYSLECTIC > DYSLEXIA
DYSLEXIA *n* disorder causing impaired ability to read
DYSLEXIAS > DYSLEXIA
DYSLEXIC > DYSLEXIA
DYSLEXICS > DYSLEXIA
DYSLOGIES > DYSLOGY
DYSLOGY *n* uncomplimentary remarks
DYSMELIA *n* condition of missing or stunted limbs
DYSMELIAS > DYSMELIA
DYSMELIC > DYSMELIA
DYSODIL *n* yellow or green mineral
DYSODILE *same as* > DYSODIL
DYSODILES > DYSODILE
DYSODILS > DYSODIL
DYSODYLE *same as* > DYSODIL
DYSODYLES > DYSODYLE
DYSPATHY *n* dislike
DYSPEPSIA *n* indigestion
DYSPEPSY *same as* > DYSPEPSIA
DYSPEPTIC *adj* relating to or suffering from dyspepsia ▷ *n* person suffering from dyspepsia
DYSPHAGIA *n* difficulty in swallowing, caused by obstruction or spasm of the oesophagus
DYSPHAGIC > DYSPHAGIA
DYSPHAGY *same as* > DYSPHAGIA
DYSPHASIA *n* disorder of language caused by a brain lesion
DYSPHASIC > DYSPHASIA
DYSPHONIA *n* any impairment in the ability to speak normally, as from spasm or strain of the vocal cords
DYSPHONIC > DYSPHONIA
DYSPHORIA *n* feeling of being ill at ease
DYSPHORIC > DYSPHORIA
DYSPLASIA *n* abnormal development of an organ or part of the body, including congenital absence
DYSPNEA *same as* > DYSPNOEA
DYSPNEAL > DYSPNEA
DYSPNEAS > DYSPNEA
DYSPNEIC > DYSPNEA
DYSPNOEA *n* difficulty in breathing or in catching the breath
DYSPNOEAL > DYSPNOEA
DYSPNOEAS > DYSPNOEA
DYSPNOEIC > DYSPNOEA
DYSPNOIC > DYSPNOEA
DYSPRAXIA *n* impairment in the control of the motor system
DYSTAXIA *n* lack of muscular coordination resulting in shaky limb movements and unsteady gait
DYSTAXIAS > DYSTAXIA
DYSTECTIC *adj* difficult to fuse together
DYSTHESIA *n* unpleasant skin sensation
DYSTHETIC > DYSTHESIA
DYSTHYMIA *n* characteristics of the neurotic and introverted, including anxiety, depression, and compulsive behaviour
DYSTHYMIC > DYSTHYMIA
DYSTOCIA *n* abnormal, slow, or difficult childbirth, usually because of disordered or ineffective contractions of the uterus
DYSTOCIAL > DYSTOCIA
DYSTOCIAS > DYSTOCIA

DYSTONIA *n* neurological disorder, caused by disease of the basal ganglia, in which the muscles of the trunk, shoulders, and neck go into spasm, so that the head and limbs are held in unnatural positions
DYSTONIAS > DYSTONIA
DYSTONIC > DYSTONIA
DYSTOPIA *n* imaginary place where everything is as bad as it can be
DYSTOPIAN > DYSTOPIA
DYSTOPIAS > DYSTOPIA
DYSTROPHY *n* any of various bodily disorders, characterized by wasting of tissues
DYSURIA *n* difficult or painful urination
DYSURIAS > DYSURIA
DYSURIC > DYSURIA
DYSURIES > DYSURY
DYSURY *same as* > DYSURIA
DYTISCID *n* any carnivorous aquatic beetle of the family *Dytiscidae*, having large flattened back legs used for swimming ▷ *adj* of, relating to, or belonging to the *Dytiscidae*
DYTISCIDS > DYTISCID
DYVOUR *n* debtor
DYVOURIES > DYVOURY
DYVOURS > DYVOUR
DYVOURY *n* bankruptcy
DZEREN *n* Chinese yellow antelope
DZERENS > DZEREN
DZHO *same as* > ZHO
DZHOS > DZHO
DZIGGETAI *a variant of* > CHIGETAI
DZO *a variant spelling of* > ZO
DZOS > ZO

Ee

EA *n* river
EACH *pron* every (one) taken separately ▷ *determiner* every (one) of two or more considered individually ▷ *adv* for, to, or from each one
EACHWHERE *adv* everywhere
EADISH *n* aftermath
EADISHES > EADISH
EAGER *adj* showing or feeling great desire, keen ▷ *n* eagre
EAGERER > EAGER
EAGEREST > EAGER
EAGERLY > EAGER
EAGERNESS > EAGER
EAGERS > EAGER
EAGLE *n* bird of prey ▷ *vb* in golf, score two strokes under par for a hole
EAGLED > EAGLE
EAGLES > EAGLE
EAGLET *n* young eagle
EAGLETS > EAGLET
EAGLEWOOD *n* Asian thymelaeaceous tree with fragrant wood that yields a resin used as a perfume
EAGLING > EAGLE
EAGRE *n* tidal bore, esp of the Humber or Severn estuaries
EAGRES > EAGRE
EALDORMAN *n* official of Anglo-Saxon England, appointed by the king, who was responsible for law, order, and justice in his shire and for leading his local fyrd in battle
EALDORMEN > EALDORMAN
EALE *n* beast in Roman legend
EALES > EALE
EAN *vb* give birth
EANED > EAN
EANING > EAN
EANLING *n* newborn lamb
EANLINGS > EANLING
EANS > EAN
EAR *n* organ of hearing, esp the external part of it ▷ *vb* (of cereal plants) to develop such parts
EARACHE *n* pain in the ear
EARACHES > EARACHE
EARBALL *n* (in acupressure) a small ball kept in position in the ear and pressed when needed to relieve stress
EARBALLS > EARBALL
EARBASH *vb* talk incessantly
EARBASHED > EARBASH
EARBASHER > EARBASH
EARBASHES > EARBASH
EARBOB *n* earring
EARBOBS > EARBOB
EARBUD *n* small earphone
EARBUDS > EARBUD
EARCON *n* sound representing object or event
EARCONS > EARCON
EARD *vb* bury
EARDED > EARD
EARDING > EARD
EARDROP *n* pendant earring
EARDROPS *pl n* liquid medication for inserting into the external ear
EARDRUM *n* thin piece of skin inside the ear which enables one to hear sounds
EARDRUMS > EARDRUM
EARDS > EARD
EARED *adj* having an ear or ears
EARFLAP *n* either of two pieces of fabric or fur attached to a cap, which can be let down to keep the ears warm
EARFLAPS > EARFLAP
EARFUL *n* scolding or telling-off
EARFULS > EARFUL
EARING *n* line fastened to a corner of a sail for reefing
EARINGS > EARING
EARL *n* British nobleman ranking next below a marquess
EARLAP *same as* > EARFLAP
EARLAPS > EARLAP
EARLDOM *n* rank, title, or dignity of an earl or countess
EARLDOMS > EARLDOM
EARLESS > EAR
EARLIER > EARLY
EARLIES > EARLY
EARLIEST > EARLY
EARLIKE > EAR
EARLINESS > EARLY
EARLOBE *n* fleshy lower part of the outer ear
EARLOBES > EARLOBE
EARLOCK *n* curl of hair close to ear
EARLOCKS > EARLOCK
EARLS > EARL
EARLSHIP *n* title or position of earl
EARLSHIPS > EARLSHIP
EARLY *adv* before the expected or usual time ▷ *adj* occurring or arriving before the correct or expected time ▷ *n* something which is early
EARLYWOOD *n* light wood made by tree in spring
EARMARK *vb* set (something) aside for a specific purpose ▷ *n* distinguishing mark
EARMARKED > EARMARK
EARMARKS > EARMARK
EARMUFF *n* one of a pair of pads of fur or cloth, joined by a headband, for keeping the ears warm
EARMUFFS > EARMUFF
EARN *vb* obtain by work or merit
EARNED > EARN
EARNER > EARN
EARNERS > EARN
EARNEST *adj* serious and sincere ▷ *n* part payment given in advance, esp to confirm a contract
EARNESTLY > EARNEST
EARNESTS > EARNEST
EARNING > EARN
EARNINGS *pl n* money earned
EARNS > EARN
EARPHONE *n* receiver for a radio etc, held to or put in the ear
EARPHONES > EARPHONE
EARPICK *n* instrument for removing ear wax
EARPICKS > EARPICK
EARPIECE *n* earphone in a telephone receiver

EARPIECES > EARPIECE
EARPLUG *n* piece of soft material placed in the ear to keep out water or noise
EARPLUGS > EARPLUG
EARRING *n* ornament for the lobe of the ear
EARRINGED *adj* wearing earrings
EARRINGS > EARRING
EARS > EAR
EARSHOT *n* hearing range
EARSHOTS > EARSHOT
EARST *adv* first; previously
EARSTONE *n* calcium carbonate crystal in the ear
EARSTONES > EARSTONE
EARTH *n* planet that we live on ▷ *vb* connect (a circuit) to earth
EARTHBORN *adj* of earthly origin
EARTHED > EARTH
EARTHEN *adj* made of baked clay or earth
EARTHFALL *n* landslide
EARTHFAST *adj* method of building
EARTHFLAX *n* type of asbestos
EARTHIER > EARTHY
EARTHIEST > EARTHY
EARTHILY > EARTHY
EARTHING > EARTH
EARTHLIER > EARTHLY
EARTHLIES > EARTHLY
EARTHLIKE > EARTH
EARTHLING *n* (esp in poetry or science fiction) an inhabitant of the earth
EARTHLY *adj* conceivable or possible ▷ *n* a chance
EARTHMAN *n* (esp in science fiction) an inhabitant or native of the earth
EARTHMEN > EARTHMAN
EARTHNUT *n* perennial umbelliferous plant of Europe and Asia, with edible dark brown tubers
EARTHNUTS > EARTHNUT
EARTHPEA *n* peanut; groundnut
EARTHPEAS > EARTHPEA
EARTHRISE *n* rising of the earth above the lunar horizon, as seen from a spacecraft emerging from the lunar farside
EARTHS > EARTH
EARTHSET *n* setting of the earth below the lunar horizon, as seen from a spacecraft emerging from the lunar farside
EARTHSETS > EARTHSET
EARTHSTAR *n* any of various basidiomycetous saprotrophic woodland fungi of the genus *Geastrum*, whose brown onion-shaped reproductive body splits into a star shape to release the spores
EARTHWARD *adv* towards the earth
EARTHWAX *n* ozocerite
EARTHWOLF *n* aardvark
EARTHWORK *n* fortification made of earth
EARTHWORM *n* worm which burrows in the soil
EARTHY *adj* coarse or crude
EARWAX *nontechnical name for* > CERUMEN
EARWAXES > EARWAX
EARWIG *n* small insect with a pincer-like tail ▷ *vb* eavesdrop
EARWIGGED > EARWIG
EARWIGGY > EARWIG
EARWIGS > EARWIG
EARWORM *n* irritatingly catchy tune
EARWORMS > EARWORM
EAS > EA
EASE *n* freedom from difficulty, discomfort, or worry ▷ *vb* give bodily or mental ease to
EASED > EASE
EASEFUL *adj* characterized by or bringing ease
EASEFULLY > EASEFUL
EASEL *n* frame to support an artist's canvas or a blackboard
EASELED *adj* mounted on easel
EASELESS > EASE
EASELS > EASEL
EASEMENT *n* right enjoyed by a landowner of making limited use of his neighbour's land, as by crossing it to reach his own property
EASEMENTS > EASEMENT
EASER > EASE
EASERS > EASE
EASES > EASE
EASIED > EASY
EASIER > EASY
EASIES > EASY
EASIEST > EASY
EASILY *adv* without difficulty
EASINESS *n* quality or condition of being easy to accomplish, do, obtain, etc
EASING > EASE
EASLE *n* hot ash
EASLES > EASLE
EASSEL *adv* easterly
EASSIL *adv* easterly
EAST *n* (direction towards) the part of the horizon where the sun rises ▷ *adj* in the east ▷ *adv* in, to, or towards the east ▷ *vb* move or turn east
EASTBOUND *adj* going towards the east
EASTED > EAST
EASTER *n* most important festival of the Christian Church, commemorating the Resurrection of Christ
EASTERLY *adj* of or in the east ▷ *adv* towards the east ▷ *n* wind from the east
EASTERN *adj* situated in or towards the east
EASTERNER *n* person from the east of a country or area
EASTERS > EASTER
EASTING *n* net distance eastwards made by a vessel moving towards the east
EASTINGS > EASTING
EASTLAND *n* land to east
EASTLANDS > EASTLAND
EASTLIN *adj* easterly
EASTLING *adj* easterly
EASTLINGS *adv* eastward
EASTLINS *adv* eastward
EASTMOST *adj* furthest east
EASTS > EAST
EASTWARD *same as* > EASTWARDS
EASTWARDS *adv* towards the east
EASY *adj* not needing much work or effort ▷ *vb* stop rowing
EASYGOING *adj* relaxed in manner
EASYING > EASY
EAT *vb* take (food) into the mouth and swallow it
EATABLE *adj* fit or suitable for eating
EATABLES *pl n* food
EATAGE *n* grazing rights
EATAGES > EATAGE
EATCHE *n* adze
EATCHES > EATCHE
EATEN > EAT
EATER > EAT
EATERIE *same as* > EATERY
EATERIES > EATERY
EATERS > EAT
EATERY *n* restaurant or eating house
EATH *adj* easy
EATHE *same as* > EATH
EATHLY > EATH
EATING > EAT
EATINGS > EAT
EATS > EAT
EAU *same as* > EA
EAUS > EAU
EAUX > EAU
EAVE *vb* form eaves
EAVED > EAVE
EAVES *pl n* overhanging edges of a roof
EAVESDRIP *n* water dropping from eaves
EAVESDROP *vb* listen secretly to a private conversation
EAVING > EAVE
EBAUCHE *n* rough sketch
EBAUCHES > EBAUCHE
EBAYER *n* any person who buys or sells using the internet auction site, eBay
EBAYERS > EBAYER
EBAYING *n* buying or selling using the internet auction site eBay
EBAYINGS > EBAYING
EBB *vb* (of tide water) flow back ▷ *n* flowing back of the tide
EBBED > EBB
EBBET *n* type of newt
EBBETS > EBBET
EBBING > EBB
EBBLESS > EBB
EBBS > EBB
EBBTIDE *n* ebbing tide
EBBTIDES > EBBTIDE
EBENEZER *n* chapel
EBENEZERS > EBENEZER
EBENISTE *n* cabinetmaker
EBENISTES > EBENISTE
EBIONISE *same as* > EBIONIZE
EBIONISED > EBIONISE
EBIONISES > EBIONISE
EBIONISM *n* doctrine that the poor shall be saved
EBIONISMS > EBIONISM
EBIONITIC > EBIONISM
EBIONIZE *vb* preach ebionism
EBIONIZED > EBIONIZE
EBIONIZES > EBIONIZE
EBON *poetic word for* > EBONY
EBONICS *n* dialect used by African-Americans
EBONIES > EBONY
EBONISE *same as* > EBONIZE
EBONISED > EBONISE
EBONISES > EBONISE
EBONISING > EBONISE
EBONIST *n* carver of ebony
EBONISTS > EBONIST
EBONITE *another name for* > VULCANITE
EBONITES > EBONITE
EBONIZE *vb* stain or otherwise finish in imitation of ebony
EBONIZED > EBONIZE
EBONIZES > EBONIZE
EBONIZING > EBONIZE
EBONS > EBON
EBONY *n* hard black wood ▷ *adj* deep black
EBOOK *n* book in electronic form
EBOOKS > EBOOK
EBRIATE *adj* drunk
EBRIATED > EBRIATE
EBRIETIES > EBRIETY
EBRIETY *n* drunkenness
EBRILLADE *n* jerk on rein, when horse refuses to turn
EBRIOSE *adj* drunk
EBRIOSITY > EBRIOSE
EBULLIENT *adj* full of enthusiasm or excitement
EBURNEAN *adj* made of ivory
EBURNEOUS *adj* like ivory
ECAD *n* organism whose form has been affected by its environment

ECADS > ECAD
ECARINATE *adj* having no carina or keel
ECARTE *n* card game for two, played with 32 cards and king high
ECARTES > ECARTE
ECAUDATE *adj* tailless
ECBOLE *n* digression
ECBOLES > ECBOLE
ECBOLIC *adj* hastening labour or abortion ▷ *n* drug or agent that hastens labour or abortion
ECBOLICS > ECBOLIC
ECCE *interj* behold
ECCENTRIC *adj* odd or unconventional ▷ *n* eccentric person
ECCLESIA *n* (in formal Church usage) a congregation
ECCLESIAE > ECCLESIA
ECCLESIAL *adj* ecclesiastical
ECCO *interj* look there
ECCRINE *adj* of or denoting glands that secrete externally, esp the numerous sweat glands on the human body
ECCRISES > ECCRISIS
ECCRISIS *n* excrement
ECCRITIC *n* purgative
ECCRITICS > ECCRITIC
ECDEMIC *adj* not indigenous or endemic
ECDYSES > ECDYSIS
ECDYSIAL > ECDYSIS
ECDYSIAST *facetious word for* > STRIPPER
ECDYSIS *n* periodic shedding of the cuticle in insects and other arthropods or the outer epidermal layer in reptiles
ECDYSON > ECDYSONE
ECDYSONE *n* hormone secreted by the prothoracic gland of insects that controls ecdysis and stimulates metamorphosis
ECDYSONES > ECDYSONE
ECDYSONS > ECDYSON
ECESIC > ECESIS
ECESIS *n* establishment of a plant in a new environment
ECESISES > ECESIS
ECH *same as* > ECHE
ECHAPPE *n* leap in ballet
ECHAPPES > ECHAPPE
ECHARD *n* water that is present in the soil but cannot be absorbed or otherwise utilized by plants
ECHARDS > ECHARD
ECHE *vb* eke out
ECHED > ECHE
ECHELLE *n* ladder; scale
ECHELLES > ECHELLE
ECHELON *n* level of power or responsibility ▷ *vb* assemble in echelon
ECHELONED > ECHELON
ECHELONS > ECHELON
ECHES > ECHE
ECHEVERIA *n* any of various tropical American crassulaceous plants of the genus *Echeveria*, cultivated for their colourful foliage
ECHIDNA *n* Australian spiny egg-laying mammal
ECHIDNAE > ECHIDNA
ECHIDNAS > ECHIDNA
ECHIDNINE *n* snake poison
ECHINACEA *n* either of the two N American plants of the genus *Echinacea*, having flower heads with purple rays and black centres: family *Compositae* (composites)
ECHINATE *adj* covered with spines, bristles, or bristle-like outgrowths
ECHINATED *same as* > ECHINATE
ECHING > ECHE
ECHINI > ECHINUS
ECHINOID *n* any of the echinoderms constituting the class *Echinoidea*, typically having a rigid ovoid body. The class includes the sea urchins and sand dollars ▷ *adj* of or belonging to this class
ECHINOIDS > ECHINOID
ECHINUS *n* ovolo moulding between the shaft and the abacus of a Doric column
ECHINUSES > ECHINUS
ECHIUM *n* any plant of the Eurasian and African genus *Echium*
ECHIUMS > ECHIUM
ECHIUROID *n* marine worm
ECHO *n* repetition of sounds by reflection of sound waves off a surface ▷ *vb* repeat or be repeated as an echo
ECHOED > ECHO
ECHOER > ECHO
ECHOERS > ECHO
ECHOES > ECHO
ECHOEY > ECHO
ECHOGRAM *n* record made by echography
ECHOGRAMS > ECHOGRAM
ECHOIC *adj* characteristic of or resembling an echo
ECHOING > ECHO
ECHOISE *same as* > ECHOIZE
ECHOISED > ECHOISE
ECHOISES > ECHOISE
ECHOISING > ECHOISE
ECHOISM *n* onomatopoeia as a source of word formation
ECHOISMS > ECHOISM
ECHOIST > ECHOISM
ECHOISTS > ECHOISM
ECHOIZE *vb* repeat like echo
ECHOIZED > ECHOIZE
ECHOIZES > ECHOIZE
ECHOIZING > ECHOIZE
ECHOLALIA *n* tendency to repeat mechanically words just spoken by another person: can occur in cases of brain damage, mental retardation, and schizophrenia
ECHOLALIC > ECHOLALIA
ECHOLESS > ECHO
ECHOS > ECHO
ECHOVIRUS *n* any of a group of viruses that can cause symptoms of mild meningitis, the common cold, or infections of the intestinal and respiratory tracts
ECHT *adj* real
ECLAIR *n* finger-shaped pastry filled with cream and covered with chocolate
ECLAIRS > ECLAIR
ECLAMPSIA *n* serious condition that can develop towards the end of a pregnancy, causing high blood pressure, swelling, and convulsions
ECLAMPSY *same as* > ECLAMPSIA
ECLAMPTIC > ECLAMPSIA
ECLAT *n* brilliant success
ECLATS > ECLAT
ECLECTIC *adj* selecting from various styles, ideas, or sources ▷ *n* person who takes an eclectic approach
ECLECTICS > ECLECTIC
ECLIPSE *n* temporary obscuring of one star or planet by another ▷ *vb* surpass or outclass
ECLIPSED > ECLIPSE
ECLIPSER > ECLIPSE
ECLIPSERS > ECLIPSE
ECLIPSES > ECLIPSIS
ECLIPSING > ECLIPSE
ECLIPSIS *same as* > ELLIPSIS
ECLIPTIC *n* apparent path of the sun ▷ *adj* of or relating to an eclipse
ECLIPTICS > ECLIPTIC
ECLOGITE *n* rare coarse-grained basic rock consisting principally of garnet and pyroxene. Quartz, feldspar, etc, may also be present. It is thought to originate by metamorphism or igneous crystallization at extremely high pressure
ECLOGITES > ECLOGITE
ECLOGUE *n* pastoral or idyllic poem, usually in the form of a conversation or soliloquy
ECLOGUES > ECLOGUE
ECLOSE *vb* emerge
ECLOSED > ECLOSE
ECLOSES > ECLOSE
ECLOSING > ECLOSE
ECLOSION *n* emergence of an insect larva from the egg or an adult from the pupal case
ECLOSIONS > ECLOSION
ECO *n* ecology activist
ECOCIDAL > ECOCIDE
ECOCIDE *n* total destruction of an area of the natural environment, esp by human agency
ECOCIDES > ECOCIDE
ECOD *same as* > EGAD
ECOFREAK *n* environmentalist
ECOFREAKS > ECOFREAK
ECOLOGIC > ECOLOGY
ECOLOGIES > ECOLOGY
ECOLOGIST > ECOLOGY
ECOLOGY *n* study of the relationships between living things and their environment
ECOMMERCE *n* business transactions conducted on the internet
ECONOBOX *n* fuel efficient utility vehicle
ECONOMIC *adj* of economics
ECONOMICS *n* social science concerned with the production and consumption of goods and services
ECONOMIES > ECONOMY
ECONOMISE *same as* > ECONOMIZE
ECONOMISM *n* political theory that regards economics as the main factor in society, ignoring or reducing to simplistic economic terms other factors such as culture, nationality, etc
ECONOMIST *n* specialist in economics
ECONOMIZE *vb* reduce expense or waste
ECONOMY *n* system of interrelationship of money, industry, and employment in a country ▷ *adj* denoting a class of air travel that is cheaper than first-class
ECONUT *n* environmentalist
ECONUTS > ECONUT
ECOPHOBIA *n* fear of home
ECORCHE *n* anatomical figure without the skin, so that the muscular structure is visible
ECORCHES > ECORCHE
ECOREGION *n* area defined by its environmental conditions, esp climate, landforms, and soil characteristics

ECOS > ECO
ECOSPHERE *n* planetary ecosystem, consisting of all living organisms and their environment
ECOSSAISE *n* lively dance in two-four time
ECOSTATE *adj* with no ribs or nerves
ECOSYSTEM *n* system involving interactions between a community and its environment
ECOTAGE *n* sabotage for ecological motives
ECOTAGES > ECOTAGE
ECOTONAL > ECOTONE
ECOTONE *n* zone between two major ecological communities
ECOTONES > ECOTONE
ECOTOUR *n* holiday taking care not to damage environment
ECOTOURS > ECOTOUR
ECOTOXIC *adj* harmful to animals, plants or the environment
ECOTYPE *n* group of organisms within a species that is adapted to particular environmental conditions and therefore exhibits behavioural, structural, or physiological differences from other members of the species
ECOTYPES > ECOTYPE
ECOTYPIC > ECOTYPE
ECRASEUR *n* surgical device consisting of a heavy wire loop placed around a part to be removed and tightened until it cuts through
ECRASEURS > ECRASEUR
ECRITOIRE *n* writing desk with compartments and drawers
ECRU *adj* pale creamy-brown ▷ *n* greyish-yellow to a light greyish colour
ECRUS > ECRU
ECSTASES > ECSTASIS
ECSTASIED > ECSTASY
ECSTASIES > ECSTASY
ECSTASIS *same as* > ECSTASY
ECSTASISE *same as* > ECSTASIZE
ECSTASIZE *vb* make or become ecstatic
ECSTASY *n* state of intense delight
ECSTATIC *adj* in a trancelike state of great rapture or delight ▷ *n* person who has periods of intense trancelike joy
ECSTATICS *pl n* fits of delight or rapture
ECTASES > ECTASIS
ECTASIA *n* distension or dilation of a duct, vessel, or hollow viscus
ECTASIAS > ECTASIA
ECTASIS *same as* > ECTASIA
ECTATIC > ECTASIA
ECTHYMA *n* local inflammation of the skin characterized by flat ulcerating pustules
ECTHYMAS > ECTHYMA
ECTHYMATA > ECTHYMA
ECTOBLAST *same as* > EPIBLAST
ECTOCRINE *n* substance that is released by an organism into the external environment and influences the development, behaviour, etc, of members of the same or different species
ECTODERM *n* outer germ layer of an animal embryo, which gives rise to epidermis and nervous tissue
ECTODERMS > ECTODERM
ECTOGENIC *adj* capable of developing outside the host
ECTOGENY *n* (of bacteria, etc) development outside the host
ECTOMERE *n* any of the blastomeres that later develop into ectoderm
ECTOMERES > ECTOMERE
ECTOMERIC > ECTOMERE
ECTOMORPH *n* person with a thin body build: said to be correlated with cerebrotonia
ECTOPHYTE *n* parasitic plant that lives on the surface of its host
ECTOPIA *n* congenital displacement or abnormal positioning of an organ or part
ECTOPIAS > ECTOPIA
ECTOPIC > ECTOPIA
ECTOPIES > ECTOPY
ECTOPLASM *n* substance that supposedly is emitted from the body of a medium during a trance
ECTOPROCT *another word for* > BRYOZOAN
ECTOPY *same as* > ECTOPIA
ECTOSARC *n* ectoplasm of an amoeba or any other protozoan
ECTOSARCS > ECTOSARC
ECTOTHERM *n* animal whose body temperature is determined by ambient temperature
ECTOZOA > ECTOZOON
ECTOZOAN *same as* > ECTOZOON
ECTOZOANS > ECTOZOAN
ECTOZOIC > ECTOZOON
ECTOZOON *n* parasitic organism that lives on the outside of its host
ECTROPIC > ECTROPION
ECTROPION *n* condition in which the eyelid turns over exposing some of the inner lid
ECTROPIUM *same as* > ECTROPION
ECTYPAL > ECTYPE
ECTYPE *n* copy as distinguished from a prototype
ECTYPES > ECTYPE
ECU *n* any of various former French gold or silver coins
ECUELLE *n* covered soup bowl with handles
ECUELLES > ECUELLE
ECUMENIC *adj* tending to promote unity among Churches
ECUMENICS > ECUMENIC
ECUMENISM *n* aim of unity among Christian churches throughout the world
ECUMENIST > ECUMENISM
ECURIE *n* team of motor-racing cars
ECURIES > ECURIE
ECUS > ECU
ECZEMA *n* skin disease causing intense itching
ECZEMAS > ECZEMA
ED *n* editor
EDACIOUS *adj* devoted to eating
EDACITIES > EDACIOUS
EDACITY > EDACIOUS
EDAPHIC *adj* of or relating to the physical and chemical conditions of the soil, esp in relation to the plant and animal life it supports
EDDIED > EDDY
EDDIES > EDDY
EDDISH *n* pasture grass
EDDISHES > EDDISH
EDDO *same as* > TARO
EDDOES > EDDO
EDDY *n* circular movement of air, water, etc ▷ *vb* move with a circular motion
EDDYING > EDDY
EDELWEISS *n* alpine plant with white flowers
EDEMA *same as* > OEDEMA
EDEMAS > EDEMA
EDEMATA > EDEMA
EDEMATOSE > EDEMA
EDEMATOUS > EDEMA
EDENIC *adj* delightful, like the Garden of Eden
EDENTAL *adj* having few or no teeth
EDENTATE *n* mammal with few or no teeth, such as an armadillo or a sloth ▷ *adj* denoting such a mammal
EDENTATES > EDENTATE
EDGE *n* border or line where something ends or begins ▷ *vb* provide an edge or border for
EDGEBONE *n* aitchbone
EDGEBONES > EDGEBONE
EDGED > EDGE
EDGELESS > EDGE
EDGER > EDGE
EDGERS > EDGE
EDGES > EDGE
EDGEWAYS *adv* with the edge forwards or uppermost
EDGEWISE *same as* > EDGEWAYS
EDGIER > EDGY
EDGIEST > EDGY
EDGILY > EDGY
EDGINESS > EDGY
EDGING *n* anything placed along an edge to finish it ▷ *adj* relating to or used for making an edge
EDGINGS > EDGING
EDGY *adj* nervous or irritable
EDH *n* character of the runic alphabet used to represent the voiced dental fricative as in *then, mother, bathe*
EDHS > EDH
EDIBILITY > EDIBLE
EDIBLE *adj* fit to be eaten
EDIBLES *pl n* articles fit to eat
EDICT *n* order issued by an authority
EDICTAL > EDICT
EDICTALLY > EDICT
EDICTS > EDICT
EDIFICE *n* large building
EDIFICES > EDIFICE
EDIFICIAL > EDIFICE
EDIFIED > EDIFY
EDIFIER > EDIFY
EDIFIERS > EDIFY
EDIFIES > EDIFY
EDIFY *vb* improve morally by instruction
EDIFYING > EDIFY
EDILE *variant spelling of* > AEDILE
EDILES > EDILE
EDIT *vb* prepare (a book, film, etc) for publication or broadcast ▷ *n* act of editing
EDITABLE > EDIT
EDITED > EDIT
EDITING > EDIT
EDITINGS > EDIT
EDITION *n* number of copies of a new publication printed at one time ▷ *vb* produce multiple copies of (an original work of art)
EDITIONS > EDITION
EDITOR *n* person who edits
EDITORIAL *n* newspaper article stating the opinion of the editor ▷ *adj* of editing or editors
EDITORS > EDITOR
EDITRESS *n* female editor
EDITRICES > EDITRIX
EDITRIX *n* female editor

EDITRIXES > EDITRIX
EDITS > EDIT
EDS > ED
EDUCABLE *adj* capable of being trained or educated ▷ *n* mentally retarded person who is capable of being educated
EDUCABLES > EDUCABLE
EDUCATE *vb* teach
EDUCATED *adj* having an education, esp a good one
EDUCATES > EDUCATE
EDUCATING > EDUCATE
EDUCATION *n* process of acquiring knowledge and understanding
EDUCATIVE *adj* educating
EDUCATOR *n* person who educates
EDUCATORS > EDUCATOR
EDUCATORY *adj* educative or educational
EDUCE *vb* evolve or develop, esp from a latent or potential state
EDUCED > EDUCE
EDUCEMENT > EDUCE
EDUCES > EDUCE
EDUCIBLE > EDUCE
EDUCING > EDUCE
EDUCT *n* substance separated from another substance without chemical change
EDUCTION *n* something educed
EDUCTIONS > EDUCTION
EDUCTIVE > EDUCE
EDUCTOR > EDUCE
EDUCTORS > EDUCE
EDUCTS > EDUCT
EDUSKUNTA *n* Finnish parliament
EE *Scots word for* > EYE
EECH *same as* > ECHE
EECHED > EECH
EECHES > EECH
EECHING > EECH
EEJIT *Scots and Irish word for* > IDIOT
EEJITS > EEJIT
EEK *interj* indicating shock or fright
EEL *n* snakelike fish
EELFARE *n* young eel
EELFARES > EELFARE
EELGRASS *n* any of several perennial submerged marine plants of the genus *Zostera*, esp *Z. marina*, having grasslike leaves: family *Zosteraceae*
EELIER > EEL
EELIEST > EEL
EELLIKE *adj* resembling an eel
EELPOUT *n* marine eel-like blennioid fish
EELPOUTS > EELPOUT
EELS > EEL
EELWORM *n* any of various nematode worms, esp the wheatworm and the vinegar eel
EELWORMS > EELWORM
EELWRACK *n* grasslike plant growing in seawater
EELWRACKS > EELWRACK
EELY > EEL
EEN > EE
EERIE *adj* uncannily frightening or disturbing
EERIER > EERIE
EERIEST > EERIE
EERILY > EERIE
EERINESS > EERIE
EERY *same as* > EERIE
EEVEN *n* evening
EEVENS > EEVEN
EEVN *n* evening
EEVNING *n* evening
EEVNINGS > EEVNING
EEVNS > EEVN
EF *n* sixth letter of Roman alphabet
EFF *vb* say the word 'fuck'
EFFABLE *adj* capable of being expressed in words
EFFACE *vb* remove by rubbing
EFFACED > EFFACE
EFFACER > EFFACE
EFFACERS > EFFACE
EFFACES > EFFACE
EFFACING > EFFACE
EFFECT *n* change or result caused by someone or something ▷ *vb* cause to happen, accomplish
EFFECTED > EFFECT
EFFECTER > EFFECT
EFFECTERS > EFFECT
EFFECTING > EFFECT
EFFECTIVE *adj* producing a desired result ▷ *n* serviceman who is equipped and prepared for action
EFFECTOR *n* nerve ending that terminates in a muscle or gland and provides neural stimulation causing contraction or secretion
EFFECTORS > EFFECTOR
EFFECTS *pl n* personal belongings
EFFECTUAL *adj* producing the intended result
EFFED > EFF
EFFEIR *vb* suit
EFFEIRED > EFFEIR
EFFEIRING > EFFEIR
EFFEIRS > EFFEIR
EFFENDI *n* (in the Ottoman Empire) a title of respect used to address men of learning or social standing
EFFENDIS > EFFENDI
EFFERE *same as* > EFFEIR
EFFERED > EFFERE
EFFERENCE > EFFERENT
EFFERENT *adj* carrying or conducting outwards from a part or an organ of the body, esp from the brain or spinal cord ▷ *n* nerve that carries impulses outwards from the brain or spinal cord
EFFERENTS > EFFERENT
EFFERES > EFFERE
EFFERING > EFFERE
EFFETE *adj* powerless, feeble
EFFETELY > EFFETE
EFFICACY *n* quality of being successful in producing an intended result
EFFICIENT *adj* functioning effectively with little waste of effort
EFFIERCE *vb* archaic word meaning make fierce
EFFIERCED > EFFIERCE
EFFIERCES > EFFIERCE
EFFIGIAL > EFFIGY
EFFIGIES > EFFIGY
EFFIGY *n* image or likeness of a person
EFFING > EFF
EFFINGS > EFF
EFFLUENCE *n* act or process of flowing out
EFFLUENT *n* liquid discharged as waste ▷ *adj* flowing out or forth
EFFLUENTS > EFFLUENT
EFFLUVIA > EFFLUVIUM
EFFLUVIAL > EFFLUVIUM
EFFLUVIUM *n* unpleasant smell, as of decaying matter or gaseous waste
EFFLUX *same as* > EFFLUENCE
EFFLUXES > EFFLUX
EFFLUXION *same as* > EFFLUX
EFFORCE *vb* force
EFFORCED > EFFORCE
EFFORCES > EFFORCE
EFFORCING > EFFORCE
EFFORT *n* physical or mental exertion
EFFORTFUL > EFFORT
EFFORTS > EFFORT
EFFRAIDE *same as* > AFRAID
EFFRAY *same as* > AFFRAY
EFFRAYS > EFFRAY
EFFS > EFF
EFFULGE *vb* radiate
EFFULGED > EFFULGE
EFFULGENT *adj* radiant
EFFULGES > EFFULGE
EFFULGING > EFFULGE
EFFUSE *vb* pour or flow out ▷ *adj* (esp of an inflorescence) spreading out loosely
EFFUSED > EFFUSE
EFFUSES > EFFUSE
EFFUSING > EFFUSE
EFFUSION *n* unrestrained outburst
EFFUSIONS > EFFUSION
EFFUSIVE *adj* openly emotional, demonstrative
EFS > EF
EFT *n* dialect or archaic name for a newt ▷ *adv* again
EFTEST *adj* nearest at hand
EFTS > EFT
EFTSOON > EFTSOONS
EFTSOONS *adv* soon afterwards
EGAD *n* mild oath or expression of surprise
EGADS > EGAD
EGAL *adj* equal
EGALITE *n* equality
EGALITES > EGALITY
EGALITIES > EGALITY
EGALITY *n* equality
EGALLY > EGAL
EGAREMENT *n* confusion
EGENCE *n* need
EGENCES > EGENCE
EGENCIES > EGENCY
EGENCY *same as* > EGENCE
EGER *same as* > EAGRE
EGERS > EGER
EGEST *vb* excrete (waste material)
EGESTA *pl n* anything egested, as waste material from the body
EGESTED > EGEST
EGESTING > EGEST
EGESTION > EGEST
EGESTIONS > EGEST
EGESTIVE > EGEST
EGESTS > EGEST
EGG *n* oval or round object laid by the females of birds and other creatures, containing a developing embryo ▷ *vb* urge or incite, esp to daring or foolish acts
EGGAR *same as* > EGGER
EGGARS > EGGAR
EGGBEATER *n* kitchen utensil for beating eggs, whipping cream, etc
EGGCUP *n* cup for holding a boiled egg
EGGCUPS > EGGCUP
EGGED > EGG
EGGER *n* any of various widely distributed moths having brown bodies and wings
EGGERIES > EGGERY
EGGERS > EGGER
EGGERY *n* place where eggs are laid
EGGFRUIT *n* fruit of eggplant
EGGFRUITS > EGGFRUIT
EGGHEAD *n* intellectual person
EGGHEADED > EGGHEAD
EGGHEADS > EGGHEAD
EGGIER > EGGY
EGGIEST > EGGY
EGGING > EGG
EGGLER *n* egg dealer: sometimes itinerant
EGGLERS > EGGLER
EGGLESS > EGG
EGGMASS *n* intelligentsia
EGGMASSES > EGGMASS
EGGNOG *n* drink made of

raw eggs, milk, sugar, spice, and brandy or rum
EGGNOGS > EGGNOG
EGGPLANT *n* dark purple tropical fruit, cooked and eaten as a vegetable
EGGPLANTS > EGGPLANT
EGGS > EGG
EGGSHELL *n* hard covering round the egg of a bird or animal ▷ *adj* (of paint) having a very slight sheen
EGGSHELLS > EGGSHELL
EGGWASH *n* beaten egg for brushing on pastry
EGGWASHES > EGGWASH
EGGWHISK *same as* > EGGBEATER
EGGWHISKS > EGGWHISK
EGGY *adj* soaked in or tasting of egg
EGIS *rare spelling of* > AEGIS
EGISES > EGIS
EGLANTINE *n* Eurasian rose
EGLATERE *archaic name for* > EGLANTINE
EGLATERES > EGLATERE
EGLOMISE *n* gilding
EGMA *mispronunciation of* > ENIGMA
EGMAS > EGMA
EGO *n* conscious mind of an individual
EGOISM *n* excessive concern for one's own interests
EGOISMS > EGOISM
EGOIST *n* person who is preoccupied with his own interests
EGOISTIC > EGOIST
EGOISTS > EGOIST
EGOITIES > EGOITY
EGOITY *n* essence of the ego
EGOLESS *adj* without an ego
EGOMANIA *n* obsessive concern with fulfilling one's own needs and desires, regardless of the effect on other people
EGOMANIAC > EGOMANIA
EGOMANIAS > EGOMANIA
EGOS > EGO
EGOTHEISM *n* making god of oneself
EGOTISE *same as* > EGOTIZE
EGOTISED > EGOTISE
EGOTISES > EGOTISE
EGOTISING > EGOTISE
EGOTISM *n* concern only for one's own interests and feelings
EGOTISMS > EGOTISM
EGOTIST *n* conceited boastful person
EGOTISTIC > EGOTIST
EGOTISTS > EGOTIST
EGOTIZE *vb* talk or write in self-important way
EGOTIZED > EGOTIZE
EGOTIZES > EGOTIZE
EGOTIZING > EGOTIZE
EGREGIOUS *adj* outstandingly bad
EGRESS *same as* > EMERSION
EGRESSED > EGRESS
EGRESSES > EGRESS
EGRESSING > EGRESS
EGRESSION *same as* > EGRESS
EGRET *n* lesser white heron
EGRETS > EGRET
EGYPTIAN *n* type of typeface
EGYPTIANS > EGYPTIAN
EH *interj* exclamation of surprise or inquiry, or to seek confirmation of a statement or question ▷ *vb* say 'eh'
EHED > EH
EHING > EH
EHS > EH
EIDE *adj* enhanced integrated drive electronics
EIDENT *adj* diligent
EIDER *n* Arctic duck
EIDERDOWN *n* quilt (orig. stuffed with eider feathers)
EIDERS > EIDER
EIDETIC *adj* (of visual, or sometimes auditory, images) exceptionally vivid and allowing detailed recall of something previously perceived ▷ *n* person with eidetic ability
EIDETICS > EIDETIC
EIDOGRAPH *n* device for copying drawings
EIDOLA > EIDOLON
EIDOLIC > EIDOLON
EIDOLON *n* unsubstantial image
EIDOLONS > EIDOLON
EIDOS *n* intellectual character of a culture or a social group
EIGENMODE *n* characteristic vibration pattern
EIGENTONE *n* characteristic acoustic resonance frequency of a system
EIGHT *n* one more than seven ▷ *adj* amounting to eight
EIGHTBALL *n* black ball in pool
EIGHTEEN *n* eight and ten ▷ *adj* amounting to eighteen ▷ *determiner* amounting to eighteen
EIGHTEENS > EIGHTEEN
EIGHTFOIL *n* eight leaved flower shape in heraldry
EIGHTFOLD *adj* having eight times as many or as much ▷ *adv* by eight times as many or as much
EIGHTFOOT *adj* measuring eight feet
EIGHTH *n* (of) number eight in a series ▷ *adj* coming after the seventh and before the ninth in numbering or counting order, position, time, etc ▷ *adv* after the seventh person, position, event, etc
EIGHTHLY *same as* > EIGHTH
EIGHTHS > EIGHTH
EIGHTIES > EIGHTY
EIGHTIETH *n* one of 80 approximately equal parts of something
EIGHTS > EIGHT
EIGHTSMAN *n* member of an eight-man team
EIGHTSMEN > EIGHTSMAN
EIGHTSOME *n* group of eight people
EIGHTVO *another word for* > OCTAVO
EIGHTVOS > EIGHTVO
EIGHTY *n* eight times ten ▷ *adj* amounting to eighty ▷ *determiner* amounting to eighty
EIGNE *adj* firstborn
EIK *variant form of* > EKE
EIKED > EIK
EIKING > EIK
EIKON *variant spelling of* > ICON
EIKONES > EIKON
EIKONS > EIKON
EIKS > EIK
EILD *n* old age
EILDING *n* fuel
EILDINGS > EILDING
EILDS > EILD
EINA *interj* exclamation of pain
EINE *pl n* eyes
EINKORN *n* variety of wheat of Greece and SW Asia
EINKORNS > EINKORN
EINSTEIN *n* scientific genius
EINSTEINS > EINSTEIN
EIRACK *n* young hen
EIRACKS > EIRACK
EIRENIC *variant spelling of* > IRENIC
EIRENICAL *same as* > IRENIC
EIRENICON *n* proposition that attempts to harmonize conflicting viewpoints
EISEGESES > EISEGESIS
EISEGESIS *n* interpretation of a text, esp a biblical text, using one's own ideas
EISEL *n* vinegar
EISELL *same as* > EISEL
EISELLS > EISELL
EISELS > EISEL
EISH *interj* South African exclamation expressive of surprise, agreement, disapproval, etc
EISWEIN *n* wine made from grapes frozen on the vine
EISWEINS > EISWEIN
EITHER *pron* one or the other (of two) ▷ *adv* likewise ▷ *determiner* one or the other (of two)
EJACULATE *vb* eject (semen)
EJECT *vb* force out, expel
EJECTA *pl n* matter thrown out of a crater by an erupting volcano or during a meteorite impact
EJECTABLE > EJECT
EJECTED > EJECT
EJECTING > EJECT
EJECTION > EJECT
EJECTIONS > EJECT
EJECTIVE *adj* relating to or causing ejection ▷ *n* ejective consonant
EJECTIVES > EJECTIVE
EJECTMENT *n* (formerly) an action brought by a wrongfully dispossessed owner seeking to recover possession of his land
EJECTOR *n* person or thing that ejects
EJECTORS > EJECTOR
EJECTS > EJECT
EKE *vb* increase, enlarge, or lengthen
EKED > EKE
EKES > EKE
EKING > EKE
EKISTIC > EKISTICS
EKISTICAL > EKISTICS
EKISTICS *n* science or study of human settlements
EKKA *n* type of one-horse carriage
EKKAS > EKKA
EKLOGITE *same as* > ECLOGITE
EKLOGITES > EKLOGITE
EKPHRASES > EKPHRASIS
EKPHRASIS *n* description of a visual work of art
EKPWELE *n* former monetary unit of Equatorial Guinea
EKPWELES > EKPWELE
EKTEXINE *n* in pollen and spores, the outer of the two layers that make up the exine
EKTEXINES > EKTEXINE
EKUELE *same as* > EKPWELE
EL *n* American elevated railway
ELABORATE *adj* with a lot of fine detail ▷ *vb* expand upon
ELAEOLITE *n* nephelite
ELAIN *same as* > TRIOLEIN
ELAINS > ELAIN
ELAIOSOME *n* oil-rich body on seeds or fruits that attracts ants, which act as dispersal agents
ELAN *n* style and vigour
ELANCE *vb* throw a lance

ELANCED > ELANCE
ELANCES > ELANCE
ELANCING > ELANCE
ELAND *n* large antelope of southern Africa
ELANDS > ELAND
ELANET *n* bird of prey
ELANETS > ELANET
ELANS > ELAN
ELAPHINE *adj* of or like a red deer
ELAPID *n* any venomous snake of the mostly tropical family *Elapidae*
ELAPIDS > ELAPID
ELAPINE *adj* of or like an elapid
ELAPSE *vb* (of time) pass by
ELAPSED > ELAPSE
ELAPSES > ELAPSE
ELAPSING > ELAPSE
ELASTANCE *n* reciprocal of capacitance
ELASTANE *n* synthetic fibre that is able to return to its original shape after being stretched
ELASTANES > ELASTANE
ELASTASE *n* enzyme that digests elastin
ELASTASES > ELASTASE
ELASTIC *adj* resuming normal shape after distortion ▷ *n* tape or fabric containing interwoven strands of flexible rubber
ELASTICS > ELASTIC
ELASTIN *n* fibrous scleroprotein constituting the major part of elastic tissue, such as the walls of arteries
ELASTINS > ELASTIN
ELASTOMER *n* any material, such as natural or synthetic rubber, that is able to resume its original shape when a deforming force is removed
ELATE *vb* fill with high spirits, exhilaration, pride or optimism
ELATED ▷ *adj* extremely happy and excited
ELATEDLY > ELATED
ELATER *n* elaterid beetle
ELATERID *n* any of the beetles constituting the widely distributed family *Elateridae* (click beetles)
ELATERIDS > ELATERID
ELATERIN *n* white crystalline substance found in elaterium, used as a purgative
ELATERINS > ELATERIN
ELATERITE *n* dark brown naturally occurring bitumen resembling rubber
ELATERIUM *n* greenish sediment prepared from the juice of the squirting cucumber, used as a purgative
ELATERS > ELATER
ELATES > ELATE
ELATING > ELATE
ELATION *n* feeling of great happiness and excitement
ELATIONS > ELATION
ELATIVE *adj* (in the grammar of Finnish and other languages) denoting a case of nouns expressing a relation of motion or direction, usually translated by the English prepositions *out of* or *away from* ▷ *n* elative case
ELATIVES > ELATIVE
ELBOW *n* joint between the upper arm and the forearm ▷ *vb* shove or strike with the elbow
ELBOWED > ELBOW
ELBOWING > ELBOW
ELBOWROOM *n* sufficient scope to move or function
ELBOWS > ELBOW
ELCHEE *n* ambassador
ELCHEES > ELCHEE
ELCHI *same as* > ELCHEE
ELCHIS > ELCHI
ELD *n* old age
ELDER *adj* older ▷ *n* older person
ELDERCARE *n* care of elderly
ELDERLIES > ELDERLY
ELDERLY *adj* (fairly) old
ELDERS > ELDER
ELDERSHIP > ELDER
ELDEST *adj* oldest
ELDIN *n* fuel
ELDING *same as* > ELDIN
ELDINGS > ELDING
ELDINS > ELDIN
ELDORADO *n* place of great riches or fabulous opportunity
ELDORADOS > ELDORADO
ELDRESS *n* woman elder
ELDRESSES > ELDRESS
ELDRICH *same as* > ELDRITCH
ELDRITCH *adj* weird, uncanny
ELDS > ELD
ELECT *vb* choose by voting ▷ *adj* appointed but not yet in office
ELECTABLE > ELECT
ELECTED > ELECT
ELECTEE *n* someone who is elected
ELECTEES > ELECTEE
ELECTING > ELECT
ELECTION *n* choosing of representatives by voting
ELECTIONS > ELECTION
ELECTIVE *adj* chosen by election ▷ *n* optional course or hospital placement undertaken by a medical student
ELECTIVES > ELECTIVE
ELECTOR *n* someone who has the right to vote in an election
ELECTORAL *adj* of or relating to elections
ELECTORS > ELECTOR
ELECTRESS *n* female elector
ELECTRET *n* permanently polarized dielectric material
ELECTRETS > ELECTRET
ELECTRIC *adj* produced by, transmitting, or powered by electricity ▷ *n* electric train, car, etc
ELECTRICS > ELECTRIC
ELECTRIFY *vb* adapt for operation by electric power
ELECTRISE *same as* > ELECTRIZE
ELECTRIZE *vb* electrify
ELECTRO *vb* (in printing) make a metallic copy of a page
ELECTRODE *n* conductor through which an electric current enters or leaves a battery, vacuum tube, etc
ELECTROED > ELECTRO
ELECTRON *n* elementary particle in all atoms that has a negative electrical charge
ELECTRONS > ELECTRON
ELECTROS > ELECTRO
ELECTRUM *n* alloy of gold (55–88 per cent) and silver used for jewellery and ornaments
ELECTRUMS > ELECTRUM
ELECTS > ELECT
ELECTUARY *n* paste taken orally, containing a drug mixed with syrup or honey
ELEDOISIN *n* substance extracted from the salivary glands of a small octopus for medical applications
ELEGANCE *n* dignified grace in appearance, movement, or behaviour
ELEGANCES > ELEGANCE
ELEGANCY *same as* > ELEGANCE
ELEGANT *adj* pleasing or graceful in dress, style, or design
ELEGANTLY > ELEGANT
ELEGIAC *adj* mournful or plaintive ▷ *n* elegiac couplet or stanza
ELEGIACAL > ELEGIAC
ELEGIACS > ELEGIAC
ELEGIAST *n* writer of elegies
ELEGIASTS > ELEGIAST
ELEGIES > ELEGY
ELEGISE *same as* > ELEGIZE
ELEGISED > ELEGISE
ELEGISES > ELEGISE
ELEGISING > ELEGISE
ELEGIST > ELEGIZE
ELEGISTS > ELEGIZE
ELEGIT *n* writ delivering debtor's property to plaintiff
ELEGITS > ELEGIT
ELEGIZE *vb* compose an elegy or elegies (in memory of)
ELEGIZED > ELEGIZE
ELEGIZES > ELEGIZE
ELEGIZING > ELEGIZE
ELEGY *n* mournful poem, esp a lament for the dead
ELEMENT *n* component part
ELEMENTAL *adj* of primitive natural forces or passions ▷ *n* spirit or force that is said to appear in physical form
ELEMENTS > ELEMENT
ELEMI *n* any of various fragrant resins obtained from tropical trees, esp trees of the family *Burseraceae*: used in making varnishes, ointments, inks, etc
ELEMIS > ELEMI
ELENCH *n* refutation in logic
ELENCHI > ELENCHUS
ELENCHIC > ELENCHUS
ELENCHS > ELENCH
ELENCHTIC *same as* > ELENCTIC
ELENCHUS *n* refutation of an argument by proving the contrary of its conclusion, esp syllogistically
ELENCTIC *adj* refuting an argument by proving the falsehood of its conclusion
ELEOPTENE *n* liquid part of a volatile oil
ELEPHANT *n* huge four-footed thick-skinned animal with ivory tusks and a long trunk
ELEPHANTS *adj* in Australia, a slang word for drunk
ELEUTHERI *pl n* secret society
ELEVATE *vb* raise in rank or status
ELEVATED *adj* higher than normal ▷ *n* railway that runs on an elevated structure
ELEVATEDS > ELEVATED
ELEVATES > ELEVATE
ELEVATING > ELEVATE
ELEVATION *n* raising
ELEVATOR *n* lift for carrying people
ELEVATORS > ELEVATOR
ELEVATORY > ELEVATE
ELEVEN *n* one more than ten ▷ *adj* amounting to eleven ▷ *determiner* amounting to eleven
ELEVENS > ELEVEN
ELEVENSES *n* mid-morning snack

ELEVENTH *n* (of) number eleven in a series ▷ *adj* coming after the tenth in numbering or counting order, position, time, etc
ELEVENTHS > ELEVENTH
ELEVON *n* aircraft control surface that combines the functions of an elevator and aileron, usually fitted to tailless or delta-wing aircraft
ELEVONS > ELEVON
ELF *n* (in folklore) small mischievous fairy ▷ *vb* entangle (esp hair)
ELFED > ELF
ELFHOOD > ELF
ELFHOODS > ELF
ELFIN *adj* small and delicate ▷ *n* young elf
ELFING > ELF
ELFINS > ELFIN
ELFISH *adj* of, relating to, or like an elf or elves ▷ *n* supposed language of elves
ELFISHLY > ELFISH
ELFLAND *another name for* > FAIRYLAND
ELFLANDS > ELFLAND
ELFLIKE > ELF
ELFLOCK *n* lock of hair, fancifully regarded as having been tangled by the elves
ELFLOCKS > ELFLOCK
ELFS > ELF
ELHI *adj* informal word for or relating to elementary high school
ELIAD *n* glance
ELIADS > ELIAD
ELICHE *n* pasta in the form of spirals
ELICHES > ELICHE
ELICIT *vb* bring about (a response or reaction)
ELICITED > ELICIT
ELICITING > ELICIT
ELICITOR > ELICIT
ELICITORS > ELICIT
ELICITS > ELICIT
ELIDE *vb* omit (a vowel or syllable) from a spoken word
ELIDED > ELIDE
ELIDES > ELIDE
ELIDIBLE > ELIDE
ELIDING > ELIDE
ELIGIBLE *adj* meeting the requirements or qualifications needed ▷ *n* eligible person or thing
ELIGIBLES > ELIGIBLE
ELIGIBLY > ELIGIBLE
ELIMINANT > ELIMINATE
ELIMINATE *vb* get rid of
ELINT *n* electronic intelligence
ELINTS > ELINT
ELISION *n* omission of a syllable or vowel from a spoken word
ELISIONS > ELISION
ELITE *n* most powerful, rich, or gifted members of a group ▷ *adj* of, relating to, or suitable for an elite
ELITES > ELITE
ELITISM *n* belief that society should be governed by a small group of superior people
ELITISMS > ELITISM
ELITIST > ELITISM
ELITISTS > ELITISM
ELIXIR *n* imaginary liquid that can prolong life or turn base metals into gold
ELIXIRS > ELIXIR
ELK *n* large deer of N Europe and Asia
ELKHOUND *n* powerful breed of dog of the spitz type with a thick grey coat and tightly curled tail
ELKHOUNDS > ELKHOUND
ELKS > ELK
ELL *n* obsolete unit of length equal to approximately 45 inches
ELLAGIC *adj* of an acid derived from gallnuts
ELLIPSE *n* oval shape
ELLIPSES > ELLIPSIS
ELLIPSIS *n* omission of letters or words in a sentence
ELLIPSOID *n* surface whose plane sections are ellipses or circles
ELLIPTIC *adj* relating to or having the shape of an ellipse
ELLOPS *same as* > ELOPS
ELLOPSES > ELLOPS
ELLS > ELL
ELLWAND *n* stick for measuring lengths
ELLWANDS > ELLWAND
ELM *n* tree with serrated leaves
ELMEN *adj* of or relating to elm trees
ELMIER > ELMY
ELMIEST > ELMY
ELMS > ELM
ELMWOOD *n* wood from an elm tree
ELMWOODS > ELMWOOD
ELMY *adj* of or relating to elm trees
ELOCUTE *vb* speak as if practising elocution
ELOCUTED > ELOCUTE
ELOCUTES > ELOCUTE
ELOCUTING > ELOCUTE
ELOCUTION *n* art of speaking clearly in public
ELOCUTORY > ELOCUTION
ELODEA *n* type of American plant
ELODEAS > ELODEA
ELOGE *same as* > EULOGY
ELOGES > ELOGE
ELOGIES > ELOGY
ELOGIST > ELOGY
ELOGISTS > ELOGY
ELOGIUM *same as* > EULOGY
ELOGIUMS > ELOGIUM
ELOGY *same as* > EULOGY
ELOIGN *vb* remove (oneself, one's property, etc) to a distant place
ELOIGNED > ELOIGN
ELOIGNER > ELOIGN
ELOIGNERS > ELOIGN
ELOIGNING > ELOIGN
ELOIGNS > ELOIGN
ELOIN *same as* > ELOIGN
ELOINED > ELOIN
ELOINER > ELOIGN
ELOINERS > ELOIGN
ELOINING > ELOIN
ELOINMENT > ELOIGN
ELOINS > ELOIN
ELONGATE *vb* make or become longer ▷ *adj* long and narrow
ELONGATED > ELONGATE
ELONGATES > ELONGATE
ELOPE *vb* (of two people) run away secretly to get married
ELOPED > ELOPE
ELOPEMENT > ELOPE
ELOPER > ELOPE
ELOPERS > ELOPE
ELOPES > ELOPE
ELOPING > ELOPE
ELOPS *n* type of fish
ELOPSES > ELOPS
ELOQUENCE *n* fluent powerful use of language
ELOQUENT *adj* (of speech or writing) fluent and persuasive
ELPEE *n* LP, long-playing record
ELPEES > ELPEE
ELS > EL
ELSE *adv* in addition or more
ELSEWHERE *adv* in or to another place
ELSEWISE *adv* otherwise
ELSHIN *n* cobbler's awl
ELSHINS > ELSHIN
ELSIN *variant of* > ELSHIN
ELSINS > ELSIN
ELT *n* young female pig
ELTCHI *variant of* > ELCHEE
ELTCHIS > ELTCHI
ELTS > ELT
ELUANT *same as* > ELUENT
ELUANTS > ELUANT
ELUATE *n* solution of adsorbed material in the eluent obtained during the process of elution
ELUATES > ELUATE
ELUCIDATE *vb* make (something difficult) clear
ELUDE *vb* escape from by cleverness or quickness
ELUDED > ELUDE
ELUDER > ELUDE
ELUDERS > ELUDE
ELUDES > ELUDE
ELUDIBLE *adj* able to be eluded
ELUDING > ELUDE
ELUENT *n* solvent used for eluting
ELUENTS > ELUENT
ELUSION > ELUDE
ELUSIONS > ELUDE
ELUSIVE *adj* difficult to catch or remember
ELUSIVELY > ELUSIVE
ELUSORY *adj* avoiding the issue
ELUTE *vb* wash out (a substance) by the action of a solvent, as in chromatography
ELUTED > ELUTE
ELUTES > ELUTE
ELUTING > ELUTE
ELUTION > ELUTE
ELUTIONS > ELUTE
ELUTOR > ELUTE
ELUTORS > ELUTE
ELUTRIATE *vb* purify or separate (a substance or mixture) by washing and straining or decanting
ELUVIA > ELUVIUM
ELUVIAL > ELUVIUM
ELUVIATE *vb* remove material suspended in water in a layer of soil by the action of rainfall
ELUVIATED > ELUVIATE
ELUVIATES > ELUVIATE
ELUVIUM *n* mass of sand, silt, etc: a product of the erosion of rocks that has remained in its place of origin
ELUVIUMS > ELUVIUM
ELVAN *n* type of rock
ELVANITE *variant of* > ELVAN
ELVANITES > ELVANITE
ELVANS > ELVAN
ELVER *n* young eel
ELVERS > ELVER
ELVES > ELF
ELVISH *same as* > ELFISH
ELVISHLY > ELVISH
ELYSIAN *adj* delightful, blissful
ELYTRA > ELYTRUM
ELYTRAL > ELYTRON
ELYTROID > ELYTRON
ELYTRON *n* either of the horny front wings of beetles and some other insects, which cover and protect the hind wings
ELYTROUS > ELYTRON
ELYTRUM *same as* > ELYTRON
EM *n* square of a body of any size of type, used as a unit of measurement
EMACIATE *vb* become or cause to become abnormally thin
EMACIATED *adj* abnormally thin
EMACIATES > EMACIATE
EMACS *n* powerful computer program used for creating and editing

text
EMACSEN > EMACS
EMAIL *n* electronic mail ▷ *vb* send a message by electronic mail
EMAILED > EMAIL
EMAILING > EMAIL
EMAILS > EMAIL
EMANANT > EMANATE
EMANATE *vb* issue, proceed from a source
EMANATED > EMANATE
EMANATES > EMANATE
EMANATING > EMANATE
EMANATION *n* act or instance of emanating
EMANATIST > EMANATE
EMANATIVE > EMANATE
EMANATOR > EMANATE
EMANATORS > EMANATE
EMANATORY > EMANATE
EMBACE *variant of* > EMBASE
EMBACED > EMBACE
EMBACES > EMBACE
EMBACING > EMBACE
EMBAIL *vb* enclose in a circle
EMBAILED > EMBAIL
EMBAILING > EMBAIL
EMBAILS > EMBAIL
EMBALE *vb* bind
EMBALED > EMBALE
EMBALES > EMBALE
EMBALING > EMBALE
EMBALL *vb* enclose in a circle
EMBALLED > EMBALL
EMBALLING > EMBALL
EMBALLS > EMBALL
EMBALM *vb* preserve (a corpse) from decay by the use of chemicals etc
EMBALMED > EMBALM
EMBALMER > EMBALM
EMBALMERS > EMBALM
EMBALMING > EMBALM
EMBALMS > EMBALM
EMBANK *vb* protect, enclose, or confine (a waterway, road, etc) with an embankment
EMBANKED > EMBANK
EMBANKER > EMBANK
EMBANKERS > EMBANK
EMBANKING > EMBANK
EMBANKS > EMBANK
EMBAR *vb* close in with bars
EMBARGO *n* order by a government prohibiting trade with a country ▷ *vb* put an embargo on
EMBARGOED > EMBARGO
EMBARGOES > EMBARGO
EMBARK *vb* board a ship or aircraft
EMBARKED > EMBARK
EMBARKING > EMBARK
EMBARKS > EMBARK
EMBARRASS *vb* cause to feel self-conscious or ashamed
EMBARRED > EMBAR
EMBARRING > EMBAR
EMBARS > EMBAR
EMBASE *vb* degrade or debase
EMBASED > EMBASE
EMBASES > EMBASE
EMBASING > EMBASE
EMBASSADE *n* embassy
EMBASSAGE *n* work of an embassy
EMBASSIES > EMBASSY
EMBASSY *n* offices or official residence of an ambassador
EMBASTE > EMBASE
EMBATHE *vb* bathe with water
EMBATHED > EMBATHE
EMBATHES > EMBATHE
EMBATHING > EMBATHE
EMBATTLE *vb* deploy (troops) for battle
EMBATTLED *adj* having a lot of difficulties
EMBATTLES > EMBATTLE
EMBAY *vb* form into a bay
EMBAYED > EMBAY
EMBAYING > EMBAY
EMBAYLD > EMBAIL
EMBAYMENT *n* shape resembling a bay
EMBAYS > EMBAY
EMBED *vb* fix firmly in something solid ▷ *n* journalist accompanying an active military unit
EMBEDDED > EMBED
EMBEDDING *n* practice of assigning or being assigned a journalist to accompany an active military unit
EMBEDMENT > EMBED
EMBEDS > EMBED
EMBELLISH *vb* decorate
EMBER *n* glowing piece of wood or coal in a dying fire
EMBERS > EMBER
EMBEZZLE *vb* steal money that has been entrusted to one
EMBEZZLED > EMBEZZLE
EMBEZZLER > EMBEZZLE
EMBEZZLES > EMBEZZLE
EMBITTER *vb* make (a person) resentful or bitter
EMBITTERS > EMBITTER
EMBLAZE *vb* cause to light up
EMBLAZED > EMBLAZE
EMBLAZER > EMBLAZE
EMBLAZERS > EMBLAZE
EMBLAZES > EMBLAZE
EMBLAZING > EMBLAZE
EMBLAZON *vb* decorate with bright colours
EMBLAZONS > EMBLAZON
EMBLEM *n* object or design that symbolizes a quality, type, or group ▷ *vb* represent or signify
EMBLEMA *n* mosaic decoration
EMBLEMATA > EMBLEMA
EMBLEMED > EMBLEM
EMBLEMING > EMBLEM
EMBLEMISE *same as* > EMBLEMIZE
EMBLEMIZE *vb* function as an emblem of
EMBLEMS > EMBLEM
EMBLIC *n* type of Indian tree
EMBLICS > EMBLIC
EMBLOOM *vb* adorn with blooms
EMBLOOMED > EMBLOOM
EMBLOOMS > EMBLOOM
EMBLOSSOM *vb* adorn with blossom
EMBODIED > EMBODY
EMBODIER > EMBODY
EMBODIERS > EMBODY
EMBODIES > EMBODY
EMBODY *vb* be an example or expression of
EMBODYING > EMBODY
EMBOG *vb* sink down into a bog
EMBOGGED > EMBOG
EMBOGGING > EMBOG
EMBOGS > EMBOG
EMBOGUE *vb* go out through a narrow channel or passage
EMBOGUED > EMBOGUE
EMBOGUES > EMBOGUE
EMBOGUING > EMBOGUE
EMBOIL *vb* enrage or be enraged
EMBOILED > EMBOIL
EMBOILING > EMBOIL
EMBOILS > EMBOIL
EMBOLDEN *vb* encourage (someone)
EMBOLDENS > EMBOLDEN
EMBOLI > EMBOLUS
EMBOLIC *adj* of or relating to an embolus or embolism
EMBOLIES > EMBOLY
EMBOLISE *same as* > EMBOLIZE
EMBOLISED > EMBOLISE
EMBOLISES > EMBOLISE
EMBOLISM *n* blocking of a blood vessel by a blood clot or air bubble
EMBOLISMS > EMBOLISM
EMBOLIZE *vb* cause embolism in (a blood vessel)
EMBOLIZED > EMBOLIZE
EMBOLIZES > EMBOLIZE
EMBOLUS *n* material, such as a blood clot, that blocks a blood vessel
EMBOLUSES > EMBOLUS
EMBOLY *n* infolding of the outer layer of cells of an organism or part of an organism so as to form a pocket in the surface
EMBORDER *vb* edge or border
EMBORDERS > EMBORDER
EMBOSCATA *n* sudden attack or raid
EMBOSK *vb* hide or cover
EMBOSKED > EMBOSK
EMBOSKING > EMBOSK
EMBOSKS > EMBOSK
EMBOSOM *vb* enclose or envelop, esp protectively
EMBOSOMED > EMBOSOM
EMBOSOMS > EMBOSOM
EMBOSS *vb* mould or carve a decoration on (a surface) so that it stands out from the surface
EMBOSSED *adj* (of a design or pattern) standing out from a surface
EMBOSSER > EMBOSS
EMBOSSERS > EMBOSS
EMBOSSES > EMBOSS
EMBOSSING > EMBOSS
EMBOST > EMBOSS
EMBOUND *vb* surround or encircle
EMBOUNDED > EMBOUND
EMBOUNDS > EMBOUND
EMBOW *vb* design or create (a structure) in the form of an arch or vault
EMBOWED > EMBOW
EMBOWEL *vb* bury or embed deeply
EMBOWELED > EMBOWEL
EMBOWELS > EMBOWEL
EMBOWER *vb* enclose in or as in a bower
EMBOWERED > EMBOWER
EMBOWERS > EMBOWER
EMBOWING > EMBOW
EMBOWMENT > EMBOW
EMBOWS > EMBOW
EMBOX *vb* put in a box
EMBOXED > EMBOX
EMBOXES > EMBOX
EMBOXING > EMBOX
EMBRACE *vb* clasp in the arms, hug ▷ *n* act of embracing
EMBRACED > EMBRACE
EMBRACEOR *n* person guilty of embracery
EMBRACER > EMBRACE
EMBRACERS > EMBRACE
EMBRACERY *n* offence of attempting by corrupt means to influence a jury or juror, as by bribery or threats
EMBRACES > EMBRACE
EMBRACING > EMBRACE
EMBRACIVE > EMBRACE
EMBRAID *vb* braid or interweave
EMBRAIDED > EMBRAID
EMBRAIDS > EMBRAID
EMBRANGLE *vb* confuse or entangle
EMBRASOR *n* one who embraces
EMBRASORS > EMBRASOR
EMBRASURE *n* door or window having splayed sides so that the opening is larger on the inside
EMBRAVE *vb* adorn or decorate
EMBRAVED > EMBRAVE
EMBRAVES > EMBRAVE
EMBRAVING > EMBRAVE

EMBRAZURE *variant of* > EMBRASURE
EMBREAD *vb* braid
EMBREADED > EMBREAD
EMBREADS > EMBREAD
EMBREATHE *vb* breathe in air
EMBRITTLE *vb* become brittle
EMBROCATE *vb* apply a liniment or lotion to (a part of the body)
EMBROGLIO *same as* > IMBROGLIO
EMBROIDER *vb* decorate with needlework
EMBROIL *vb* involve (a person) in problems
EMBROILED > EMBROIL
EMBROILER > EMBROIL
EMBROILS > EMBROIL
EMBROWN *vb* make or become brown
EMBROWNED > EMBROWN
EMBROWNS > EMBROWN
EMBRUE *variant spelling of* > IMBRUE
EMBRUED > EMBRUE
EMBRUES > EMBRUE
EMBRUING > EMBRUE
EMBRUTE *variant of* > IMBRUTE
EMBRUTED > EMBRUTE
EMBRUTES > EMBRUTE
EMBRUTING > EMBRUTE
EMBRYO *n* unborn creature in the early stages of development
EMBRYOID > EMBRYO
EMBRYOIDS > EMBRYO
EMBRYON *variant of* > EMBRYO
EMBRYONAL *same as* > EMBRYONIC
EMBRYONIC *adj* at an early stage
EMBRYONS > EMBRYON
EMBRYOS > EMBRYO
EMBRYOTIC *variant of* > EMBRYONIC
EMBUS *vb* cause (troops) to board or (of troops) to board a transport vehicle
EMBUSED > EMBUS
EMBUSES > EMBUS
EMBUSIED > EMBUSY
EMBUSIES > EMBUSY
EMBUSING > EMBUS
EMBUSQUE *n* man who avoids military conscription by obtaining a government job
EMBUSQUES > EMBUSQUE
EMBUSSED > EMBUS
EMBUSSES > EMBUS
EMBUSSING > EMBUS
EMBUSY *vb* keep occupied
EMBUSYING > EMBUSY
EMCEE *n* master of ceremonies ▷ *vb* act as master of ceremonies (for or at)
EMCEED > EMCEE
EMCEEING > EMCEE
EMCEES > EMCEE
EMDASH *n* long dash in punctuation
EMDASHES > EMDASH
EME *n* uncle
EMEER *variant of* > EMIR
EMEERATE *variant of* > EMIRATE
EMEERATES > EMEERATE
EMEERS > EMEER
EMEND *vb* remove errors from
EMENDABLE > EMEND
EMENDALS *pl n* funds put aside for repairs
EMENDATE *vb* make corrections
EMENDATED > EMENDATE
EMENDATES > EMENDATE
EMENDATOR *n* one who emends a text
EMENDED > EMEND
EMENDER > EMEND
EMENDERS > EMEND
EMENDING > EMEND
EMENDS > EMEND
EMERALD *n* bright green precious stone ▷ *adj* bright green
EMERALDS > EMERALD
EMERAUDE *archaic variant of* > EMERALD
EMERAUDES > EMERAUDE
EMERGE *vb* come into view
EMERGED > EMERGE
EMERGENCE *n* act or process of emerging
EMERGENCY *n* sudden unforeseen occurrence needing immediate action
EMERGENT *adj* coming into being or notice ▷ *n* aquatic plant with stem and leaves above the water
EMERGENTS > EMERGENT
EMERGES > EMERGE
EMERGING > EMERGE
EMERIED > EMERY
EMERIES > EMERY
EMERITA *adj* retired, but retaining an honorary title ▷ *n* woman who is retired, but retains an honorary title
EMERITAE > EMERITA
EMERITAS > EMERITA
EMERITI > EMERITUS
EMERITUS *adj* retired, but retaining an honorary title ▷ *n* man who is retired, but retains an honorary title
EMEROD *n* haemorrhoid
EMERODS > EMEROD
EMEROID *variant of* > EMEROD
EMEROIDS > EMEROID
EMERSED *adj* (of the leaves or stems of aquatic plants) protruding above the surface of the water
EMERSION *n* act or an instance of emerging
EMERSIONS > EMERSION
EMERY *n* hard mineral used for smoothing and polishing ▷ *vb* apply emery to
EMERYING > EMERY
EMES > EME
EMESES > EMESIS
EMESIS *technical name for* > VOMITING
EMETIC *n* substance that causes vomiting ▷ *adj* causing vomiting
EMETICAL *same as* > EMETIC
EMETICS > EMETIC
EMETIN *same as* > EMETINE
EMETINE *n* white bitter poisonous alkaloid
EMETINES > EMETINE
EMETINS > EMETIN
EMEU *variant of* > EMU
EMEUS > EMEU
EMEUTE *n* uprising or rebellion
EMEUTES > EMEUTE
EMIC *adj* of or relating to a significant linguistic unit
EMICANT > EMICATE
EMICATE *vb* twinkle
EMICATED > EMICATE
EMICATES > EMICATE
EMICATING > EMICATE
EMICATION > EMICATE
EMICTION *n* passing of urine
EMICTIONS > EMICTION
EMICTORY > EMICTION
EMIGRANT *n* person who leaves one place or country, esp a native country, to settle in another
EMIGRANTS > EMIGRANT
EMIGRATE *vb* go and settle in another country
EMIGRATED > EMIGRATE
EMIGRATES > EMIGRATE
EMIGRE *n* someone who has left his native country for political reasons
EMIGRES > EMIGRE
EMINENCE *n* position of superiority or fame
EMINENCES > EMINENCE
EMINENCY *same as* > EMINENCE
EMINENT *adj* distinguished, well-known
EMINENTLY > EMINENT
EMIR *n* Muslim ruler
EMIRATE *n* emir's country
EMIRATES > EMIRATE
EMIRS > EMIR
EMISSARY *n* agent sent on a mission by a government ▷ *adj* (of veins) draining blood from sinuses in the dura mater to veins outside the skull
EMISSILE *adj* able to be emitted
EMISSION *n* act of giving out heat, light, a smell, etc
EMISSIONS > EMISSION
EMISSIVE > EMISSION
EMIT *vb* give out
EMITS > EMIT
EMITTANCE > EMIT
EMITTED > EMIT
EMITTER *n* person or thing that emits
EMITTERS > EMITTER
EMITTING > EMIT
EMLETS as in *blood-drop emlets* Chilean plant with red-spotted yellow flowers
EMMA *n* former communications code for the letter A
EMMARBLE *vb* decorate with marble
EMMARBLED > EMMARBLE
EMMARBLES > EMMARBLE
EMMAS > EMMA
EMMER *n* variety of wheat grown in mountainous parts of Europe
EMMERS > EMMER
EMMESH *variant of* > ENMESH
EMMESHED > EMMESH
EMMESHES > EMMESH
EMMESHING > EMMESH
EMMET *n* tourist or holiday-maker
EMMETROPE *n* person whose vision is normal
EMMETS > EMMET
EMMEW *vb* restrict
EMMEWED > EMMEW
EMMEWING > EMMEW
EMMEWS > EMMEW
EMMOVE *vb* cause emotion in
EMMOVED > EMMOVE
EMMOVES > EMMOVE
EMMOVING > EMMOVE
EMMY *n* (in the US) one of the gold-plated statuettes awarded annually for outstanding television performances and productions
EMMYS > EMMY
EMO *n* type of music combining hard rock with emotional lyrics
EMODIN *n* type of chemical compound
EMODINS > EMODIN
EMOLLIATE *vb* make soft or smooth
EMOLLIENT *adj* softening, soothing ▷ *n* substance which softens or soothes the skin
EMOLUMENT *n* fees or wages from employment
EMONG *variant of* > AMONG
EMONGES *variant of* > AMONG
EMONGEST *variant of* > AMONGST
EMONGST *variant of* > AMONGST
EMOS > EMO
EMOTE *vb* display exaggerated emotion, as if acting
EMOTED > EMOTE
EMOTER > EMOTE

EMOTERS > EMOTE
EMOTES > EMOTE
EMOTICON *n* any of several combinations of symbols used in electronic mail and text messaging to indicate the state of mind of the writer, such as :-) to express happiness
EMOTICONS > EMOTICON
EMOTING > EMOTE
EMOTION *n* strong feeling
EMOTIONAL *adj* readily affected by or appealing to the emotions
EMOTIONS > EMOTION
EMOTIVE *adj* tending to arouse emotion
EMOTIVELY > EMOTIVE
EMOTIVISM *n* theory that moral utterances do not have a truth value but express the feelings of the speaker, so that *murder is wrong* is equivalent to *down with murder*
EMOTIVITY > EMOTIVE
EMOVE *vb* cause to feel emotion
EMOVED > EMOVE
EMOVES > EMOVE
EMOVING > EMOVE
EMPACKET *vb* wrap up
EMPACKETS > EMPACKET
EMPAESTIC *adj* embossed
EMPAIRE *variant of* > IMPAIR
EMPAIRED > EMPAIRE
EMPAIRES > EMPAIRE
EMPAIRING > EMPAIRE
EMPALE *less common spelling of* > IMPALE
EMPALED > EMPALE
EMPALER > EMPALE
EMPALERS > EMPALE
EMPALES > EMPALE
EMPALING > EMPALE
EMPANADA *n* Spanish meat-filled pastry
EMPANADAS > EMPANADA
EMPANEL *vb* enter on a list (names of persons to be summoned for jury service)
EMPANELED > EMPANEL
EMPANELS > EMPANEL
EMPANOPLY *vb* put armour on
EMPARE *variant of* > IMPAIR
EMPARED > EMPARE
EMPARES > EMPARE
EMPARING > EMPARE
EMPARL *variant of* > IMPARL
EMPARLED > EMPARL
EMPARLING > EMPARL
EMPARLS > EMPARL
EMPART *variant of* > IMPART
EMPARTED > EMPART
EMPARTING > EMPART
EMPARTS > EMPART
EMPATHIC *adj* of or relating to empathy
EMPATHIES > EMPATHY
EMPATHISE *same as* > EMPATHIZE
EMPATHIST > EMPATHY
EMPATHIZE *vb* sense and understand someone else's feelings as if they were one's own
EMPATHY *n* ability to understand someone else's feelings as if they were one's own
EMPATRON *vb* treat in the manner of a patron
EMPATRONS > EMPATRON
EMPAYRE *variant of* > IMPAIR
EMPAYRED > EMPAYRE
EMPAYRES > EMPAYRE
EMPAYRING > EMPAYRE
EMPEACH *variant of* > IMPEACH
EMPEACHED > EMPEACH
EMPEACHES > EMPEACH
EMPENNAGE *n* rear part of an aircraft, comprising the fin, rudder, and tailplane
EMPEOPLE *vb* bring people into
EMPEOPLED > EMPEOPLE
EMPEOPLES > EMPEOPLE
EMPERCE *variant of* > EMPIERCE
EMPERCED > EMPERCE
EMPERCES > EMPERCE
EMPERCING > EMPERCE
EMPERIES > EMPERY
EMPERISE *variant of* > EMPERIZE
EMPERISED > EMPERISE
EMPERISES > EMPERISE
EMPERISH *vb* damage or harm
EMPERIZE *vb* act like an emperor
EMPERIZED > EMPERIZE
EMPERIZES > EMPERIZE
EMPEROR *n* ruler of an empire
EMPERORS > EMPEROR
EMPERY *n* dominion or power
EMPHASES > EMPHASIS
EMPHASIS *n* special importance or significance
EMPHASISE *same as* > EMPHASIZE
EMPHASIZE *vb* give emphasis or prominence to
EMPHATIC *adj* showing emphasis ▷ *n* emphatic consonant, as used in Arabic
EMPHATICS > EMPHATIC
EMPHLYSES > EMPHLYSIS
EMPHLYSIS *n* outbreak of blisters on the body
EMPHYSEMA *n* condition in which the air sacs of the lungs are grossly enlarged, causing breathlessness
EMPIERCE *vb* pierce or cut
EMPIERCED > EMPIERCE
EMPIERCES > EMPIERCE
EMPIGHT *adj* attached or positioned
EMPIRE *n* group of territories under the rule of one state or person
EMPIRES > EMPIRE
EMPIRIC *n* person who relies on empirical methods
EMPIRICAL *adj* relying on experiment or experience, not on theory ▷ *n* posterior probability of an event derived on the basis of its observed frequency in a sample
EMPIRICS > EMPIRIC
EMPLACE *vb* put in place or position
EMPLACED > EMPLACE
EMPLACES > EMPLACE
EMPLACING > EMPLACE
EMPLANE *vb* board or put on board an aeroplane
EMPLANED > EMPLANE
EMPLANES > EMPLANE
EMPLANING > EMPLANE
EMPLASTER *vb* cover with plaster
EMPLASTIC *adj* sticky
EMPLEACH *variant of* > IMPLEACH
EMPLECTON *n* type of masonry filled with rubbish
EMPLECTUM *variant of* > EMPLECTON
EMPLONGE *variant of* > IMPLUNGE
EMPLONGED > EMPLONGE
EMPLONGES > EMPLONGE
EMPLOY *vb* engage or make use of the services of (a person) in return for money ▷ *n* state of being employed
EMPLOYE *same as* > EMPLOYEE
EMPLOYED > EMPLOY
EMPLOYEE *n* person who is hired to work for someone in return for payment
EMPLOYEES > EMPLOYEE
EMPLOYER *n* person or organization that employs someone
EMPLOYERS > EMPLOYER
EMPLOYES > EMPLOYE
EMPLOYING > EMPLOY
EMPLOYS > EMPLOY
EMPLUME *vb* put a plume on
EMPLUMED > EMPLUME
EMPLUMES > EMPLUME
EMPLUMING > EMPLUME
EMPOISON *vb* embitter or corrupt
EMPOISONS > EMPOISON
EMPOLDER *variant spelling of* > IMPOLDER
EMPOLDERS > EMPOLDER
EMPORIA > EMPORIUM
EMPORIUM *n* large general shop
EMPORIUMS > EMPORIUM
EMPOWER *vb* enable, authorize
EMPOWERED > EMPOWER
EMPOWERS > EMPOWER
EMPRESS *n* woman who rules an empire
EMPRESSE *adj* keen; zealous
EMPRESSES > EMPRESS
EMPRISE *n* chivalrous or daring enterprise
EMPRISES > EMPRISE
EMPRIZE *variant of* > EMPRISE
EMPRIZES > EMPRIZE
EMPT *vb* empty
EMPTED > EMPT
EMPTIABLE > EMPTY
EMPTIED > EMPTY
EMPTIER > EMPTY
EMPTIERS > EMPTY
EMPTIES > EMPTY
EMPTIEST > EMPTY
EMPTILY > EMPTY
EMPTINESS > EMPTY
EMPTING > EMPT
EMPTINGS *variant of* > EMPTINS
EMPTINS *pl n* liquid leavening agent made from potatoes
EMPTION *n* process of buying something
EMPTIONAL > EMPTION
EMPTIONS > EMPTION
EMPTS > EMPT
EMPTY *adj* containing nothing ▷ *vb* make or become empty ▷ *n* empty container, esp a bottle
EMPTYING > EMPTY
EMPTYINGS > EMPTY
EMPTYSES > EMPTYSIS
EMPTYSIS *n* act of spitting up blood
EMPURPLE *vb* make or become purple
EMPURPLED > EMPURPLE
EMPURPLES > EMPURPLE
EMPUSA *n* goblin in Greek mythology
EMPUSAS > EMPUSA
EMPUSE *variant of* > EMPUSA
EMPUSES > EMPUSE
EMPYEMA *n* collection of pus in a body cavity, esp in the chest
EMPYEMAS > EMPYEMA
EMPYEMATA > EMPYEMA
EMPYEMIC > EMPYEMA
EMPYESES > EMPYESIS
EMPYESIS *n* pus-filled boil on the skin
EMPYREAL *variant of* > EMPYREAN
EMPYREAN *n* heavens or sky ▷ *adj* of or relating to the sky or the heavens
EMPYREANS > EMPYREAN
EMPYREUMA *n* smell and taste associated with burning vegetable and animal matter
EMS > EM
EMU *n* large Australian flightless bird with long

legs
EMULATE *vb* attempt to equal or surpass by imitating
EMULATED > EMULATE
EMULATES > EMULATE
EMULATING > EMULATE
EMULATION *n* act of emulating or imitating
EMULATIVE > EMULATE
EMULATOR > EMULATE
EMULATORS > EMULATE
EMULE *variant of* > EMULATE
EMULED > EMULE
EMULES > EMULE
EMULGE *vb* remove liquid from
EMULGED > EMULGE
EMULGENCE > EMULGE
EMULGENT > EMULGE
EMULGES > EMULGE
EMULGING > EMULGE
EMULING > EMULE
EMULOUS *adj* desiring or aiming to equal or surpass another
EMULOUSLY > EMULOUS
EMULSIBLE > EMULSIFY
EMULSIFY *vb* (of two liquids) join together
EMULSIN *n* enzyme that is found in almonds
EMULSINS > EMULSIN
EMULSION *n* light-sensitive coating on photographic film ▷ *vb* paint with emulsion paint
EMULSIONS > EMULSION
EMULSIVE > EMULSION
EMULSOID *n* sol with a liquid disperse phase
EMULSOIDS > EMULSOID
EMULSOR *n* device that emulsifies
EMULSORS > EMULSOR
EMUNCTION > EMUNCTORY
EMUNCTORY *adj* of or relating to a bodily organ or duct having an excretory function ▷ *n* excretory organ or duct, such as a skin pore
EMUNGE *vb* clean or clear out
EMUNGED > EMUNGE
EMUNGES > EMUNGE
EMUNGING > EMUNGE
EMURE *variant of* > IMMURE
EMURED > EMURE
EMURES > EMURE
EMURING > EMURE
EMUS > EMU
EMYD *n* freshwater tortoise or terrapin
EMYDE *same as* > EMYD
EMYDES > EMYDE
EMYDS > EMYD
EMYS *n* freshwater tortoise or terrapin
EN *n* unit of measurement, half the width of an em
ENABLE *vb* provide (a person) with the means, opportunity, or authority (to do something)
ENABLED > ENABLE
ENABLER > ENABLE
ENABLERS > ENABLE
ENABLES > ENABLE
ENABLING > ENABLE
ENACT *vb* establish by law
ENACTABLE > ENACT
ENACTED > ENACT
ENACTING > ENACT
ENACTION > ENACT
ENACTIONS > ENACT
ENACTIVE > ENACT
ENACTMENT > ENACT
ENACTOR > ENACT
ENACTORS > ENACT
ENACTORY > ENACT
ENACTS > ENACT
ENACTURE > ENACT
ENACTURES > ENACT
ENALAPRIL *n* ACE inhibitor used to treat high blood pressure and congestive heart failure
ENALLAGE *n* act of using one grammatical form in the place of another
ENALLAGES > ENALLAGE
ENAMEL *n* glasslike coating applied to metal etc to preserve the surface ▷ *vb* cover with enamel
ENAMELED > ENAMEL
ENAMELER > ENAMEL
ENAMELERS > ENAMEL
ENAMELING > ENAMEL
ENAMELIST > ENAMEL
ENAMELLED > ENAMEL
ENAMELLER > ENAMEL
ENAMELS > ENAMEL
ENAMINE *n* type of unsaturated compound
ENAMINES > ENAMINE
ENAMOR *same as* > ENAMOUR
ENAMORADO *n* beloved one, lover
ENAMORED *same as* > ENAMOURED
ENAMORING > ENAMOR
ENAMORS > ENAMOR
ENAMOUR *vb* inspire with love
ENAMOURED *adj* inspired with love
ENAMOURS > ENAMOUR
ENARCH *variant of* > INARCH
ENARCHED > ENARCH
ENARCHES > ENARCH
ENARCHING > ENARCH
ENARM *vb* provide with arms
ENARMED > ENARM
ENARMING > ENARM
ENARMS > ENARM
ENATE *adj* growing out or outwards ▷ *n* relative on the mother's side
ENATES > ENATE
ENATIC *adj* related on one's mother's side
ENATION > ENATE
ENATIONS > ENATE
ENAUNTER *conj* in case that
ENCAENIA *n* festival of dedication or commemoration
ENCAENIAS > ENCAENIA
ENCAGE *vb* confine in or as in a cage
ENCAGED > ENCAGE
ENCAGES > ENCAGE
ENCAGING > ENCAGE
ENCALM *vb* becalm, settle
ENCALMED > ENCALM
ENCALMING > ENCALM
ENCALMS > ENCALM
ENCAMP *vb* set up in a camp
ENCAMPED > ENCAMP
ENCAMPING > ENCAMP
ENCAMPS > ENCAMP
ENCANTHIS *n* tumour of the eye
ENCAPSULE *vb* enclose or be enclosed in or as if in a capsule
ENCARPUS *n* decoration of fruit or flowers on a frieze
ENCASE *vb* enclose or cover completely
ENCASED > ENCASE
ENCASES > ENCASE
ENCASH *vb* exchange (a cheque) for cash
ENCASHED > ENCASH
ENCASHES > ENCASH
ENCASHING > ENCASH
ENCASING > ENCASE
ENCASTRE *adj* (of a beam) fixed at the ends
ENCAUSTIC *adj* decorated by any process involving burning in colours, esp by inlaying coloured clays and baking or by fusing wax colours to the surface ▷ *n* process of burning in colours
ENCAVE *variant of* > INCAVE
ENCAVED > ENCAVE
ENCAVES > ENCAVE
ENCAVING > ENCAVE
ENCEINTE *n* boundary wall enclosing a defended area
ENCEINTES > ENCEINTE
ENCEPHALA *n* brains
ENCHAFE *vb* heat up
ENCHAFED > ENCHAFE
ENCHAFES > ENCHAFE
ENCHAFING > ENCHAFE
ENCHAIN *vb* bind with chains
ENCHAINED > ENCHAIN
ENCHAINS > ENCHAIN
ENCHANT *vb* delight and fascinate
ENCHANTED > ENCHANT
ENCHANTER > ENCHANT
ENCHANTS > ENCHANT
ENCHARGE *vb* give into the custody of
ENCHARGED > ENCHARGE
ENCHARGES > ENCHARGE
ENCHARM *vb* enchant
ENCHARMED > ENCHARM
ENCHARMS > ENCHARM
ENCHASE *less common word for* > CHASE
ENCHASED > ENCHASE
ENCHASER > ENCHASE
ENCHASERS > ENCHASE
ENCHASES > ENCHASE
ENCHASING > ENCHASE
ENCHEASON *n* reason
ENCHEER *vb* cheer up
ENCHEERED > ENCHEER
ENCHEERS > ENCHEER
ENCHILADA *n* Mexican dish of a tortilla filled with meat, served with chilli sauce
ENCHORIAL *adj* of or used in a particular country: used esp of the popular (demotic) writing of the ancient Egyptians
ENCHORIC *same as* > ENCHORIAL
ENCIERRO *n* Spanish bull run
ENCIERROS > ENCIERRO
ENCINA *n* type of oak
ENCINAL > ENCINA
ENCINAS > ENCINA
ENCIPHER *vb* convert (a message, document, etc) from plain text into code or cipher
ENCIPHERS > ENCIPHER
ENCIRCLE *vb* form a circle around
ENCIRCLED > ENCIRCLE
ENCIRCLES > ENCIRCLE
ENCLASP *vb* clasp
ENCLASPED > ENCLASP
ENCLASPS > ENCLASP
ENCLAVE *n* part of a country entirely surrounded by foreign territory ▷ *vb* hold in an enclave
ENCLAVED > ENCLAVE
ENCLAVES > ENCLAVE
ENCLAVING > ENCLAVE
ENCLISES > ENCLISIS
ENCLISIS *n* state of being enclitic
ENCLITIC *adj* denoting or relating to a monosyllabic word or form that is treated as a suffix of the preceding word, as Latin *-que* in *populusque* ▷ *n* enclitic word or linguistic form
ENCLITICS > ENCLITIC
ENCLOSE *vb* surround completely
ENCLOSED > ENCLOSE
ENCLOSER > ENCLOSE
ENCLOSERS > ENCLOSE
ENCLOSES > ENCLOSE
ENCLOSING > ENCLOSE
ENCLOSURE *n* area of land enclosed by a fence, wall, or hedge
ENCLOTHE *vb* clothe
ENCLOTHED > ENCLOTHE
ENCLOTHES > ENCLOTHE
ENCLOUD *vb* hide with clouds
ENCLOUDED > ENCLOUD
ENCLOUDS > ENCLOUD

ENCODABLE > ENCODE
ENCODE *vb* convert (a message) into code
ENCODED > ENCODE
ENCODER > ENCODE
ENCODERS > ENCODE
ENCODES > ENCODE
ENCODING > ENCODE
ENCOLOUR *vb* give a colour to
ENCOLOURS > ENCOLOUR
ENCOLPION *n* religious symbol worn on the breast
ENCOLPIUM *variant of* > ENCOLPION
ENCOLURE *n* mane of a horse
ENCOLURES > ENCOLURE
ENCOMIA > ENCOMIUM
ENCOMIAST *n* person who speaks or writes an encomium
ENCOMION *variant of* > ENCOMIUM
ENCOMIUM *n* formal expression of praise
ENCOMIUMS > ENCOMIUM
ENCOMPASS *vb* surround
ENCORE *interj* again, once more ▷ *n* extra performance due to enthusiastic demand ▷ *vb* demand an extra or repeated performance of (a work, piece of music, etc) by (a performer)
ENCORED > ENCORE
ENCORES > ENCORE
ENCORING > ENCORE
ENCOUNTER *vb* meet unexpectedly ▷ *n* unexpected meeting
ENCOURAGE *vb* inspire with confidence
ENCRADLE *vb* put in a cradle
ENCRADLED > ENCRADLE
ENCRADLES > ENCRADLE
ENCRATIES > ENCRATY
ENCRATY *n* control of one's desires, actions, etc
ENCREASE *variant form of* > INCREASE
ENCREASED > ENCREASE
ENCREASES > ENCREASE
ENCRIMSON *vb* make crimson
ENCRINAL > ENCRINITE
ENCRINIC > ENCRINITE
ENCRINITE *n* sedimentary rock formed almost exclusively from the skeletal plates of crinoids
ENCROACH *vb* intrude gradually on a person's rights or land
ENCRUST *vb* cover with a layer of something
ENCRUSTED > ENCRUST
ENCRUSTS > ENCRUST
ENCRYPT *vb* put (a message) into code
ENCRYPTED > ENCRYPT
ENCRYPTS > ENCRYPT
ENCUMBER *vb* hinder or impede
ENCUMBERS > ENCUMBER
ENCURTAIN *vb* cover or surround with curtains
ENCYCLIC *n* letter sent by the Pope to all bishops
ENCYCLICS > ENCYCLIC
ENCYST *vb* enclose or become enclosed by a cyst, thick membrane, or shell
ENCYSTED > ENCYST
ENCYSTING > ENCYST
ENCYSTS > ENCYST
END *n* furthest point or part ▷ *vb* bring or come to a finish
ENDAMAGE *vb* cause injury to
ENDAMAGED > ENDAMAGE
ENDAMAGES > ENDAMAGE
ENDAMEBA *same as* > ENDAMOEBA
ENDAMEBAE > ENDAMEBA
ENDAMEBAS > ENDAMEBA
ENDAMEBIC > ENDAMEBA
ENDAMOEBA *same as* > ENTAMOEBA
ENDANGER *vb* put in danger
ENDANGERS > ENDANGER
ENDARCH *adj* (of a xylem strand) having the first-formed xylem internal to that formed later
ENDARCHY *n* state of being endarch
ENDART *variant of* > INDART
ENDARTED > ENDART
ENDARTING > ENDART
ENDARTS > ENDART
ENDASH *n* short dash in punctuation
ENDASHES > ENDASH
ENDBRAIN *n* part of the brain
ENDBRAINS > ENDBRAIN
ENDEAR *vb* cause to be liked
ENDEARED > ENDEAR
ENDEARING *adj* giving rise to love or esteem
ENDEARS > ENDEAR
ENDEAVOR *same as* > ENDEAVOUR
ENDEAVORS > ENDEAVOR
ENDEAVOUR *vb* try ▷ *n* effort
ENDECAGON *n* figure with eleven sides
ENDED > END
ENDEICTIC > ENDEIXIS
ENDEIXES > ENDEIXIS
ENDEIXIS *n* sign or mark
ENDEMIAL *same as* > ENDEMIC
ENDEMIC *adj* present within a localized area or peculiar to a particular group of people ▷ *n* endemic disease or plant
ENDEMICAL *adj* endemic
ENDEMICS > ENDEMIC
ENDEMISM > ENDEMIC
ENDEMISMS > ENDEMIC
ENDENIZEN *vb* make a denizen
ENDER > END
ENDERMIC *adj* (of a medicine) acting by absorption through the skin
ENDERON *variant of* > ANDIRON
ENDERONS > ENDERON
ENDERS > END
ENDEW *variant of* > ENDUE
ENDEWED > ENDEW
ENDEWING > ENDEW
ENDEWS > ENDEW
ENDEXINE *n* inner layer of an exine
ENDEXINES > ENDEXINE
ENDGAME *n* closing stage of a game of chess, in which only a few pieces are left on the board
ENDGAMES > ENDGAME
ENDING *n* last part or conclusion of something
ENDINGS > ENDING
ENDIRON *variant of* > ANDIRON
ENDIRONS > ENDIRON
ENDITE *variant of* > INDICT
ENDITED > ENDITE
ENDITES > ENDITE
ENDITING > ENDITE
ENDIVE *n* curly-leaved plant used in salads
ENDIVES > ENDIVE
ENDLANG *variant of* > ENDLONG
ENDLEAF *n* endpaper in a book
ENDLEAFS > ENDLEAF
ENDLEAVES > ENDLEAF
ENDLESS *adj* having no end
ENDLESSLY > ENDLESS
ENDLONG *adv* lengthways or on end
ENDMOST *adj* nearest the end
ENDNOTE *n* note at the end of a section of writing
ENDNOTES > ENDNOTE
ENDOBLAST *less common name for* > ENDODERM
ENDOCARP *n* inner, usually woody, layer of the pericarp of a fruit, such as the stone of a peach or cherry
ENDOCARPS > ENDOCARP
ENDOCAST *n* cast made of the inside of a cranial cavity to show the size and shape of a brain
ENDOCASTS > ENDOCAST
ENDOCRINE *adj* relating to the glands which secrete hormones directly into the bloodstream ▷ *n* endocrine gland
ENDOCYTIC *adj* involving absorption of cells
ENDODERM *n* inner germ layer of an animal embryo, which gives rise to the lining of the digestive and respiratory tracts
ENDODERMS > ENDODERM
ENDODYNE *same as* > AUTODYNE
ENDOERGIC *adj* (of a nuclear reaction) occurring with absorption of energy, as opposed to *exoergic*
ENDOGAMIC > ENDOGAMY
ENDOGAMY *n* marriage within one's own tribe or similar unit
ENDOGEN *n* plant that increases in size by internal growth
ENDOGENIC > ENDOGEN
ENDOGENS > ENDOGEN
ENDOGENY *n* development by internal growth
ENDOLYMPH *n* fluid that fills the membranous labyrinth of the internal ear
ENDOMIXES > ENDOMIXIS
ENDOMIXIS *n* reorganization of certain nuclei with some protozoa
ENDOMORPH *n* person with a fat and heavy body build: said to be correlated with viscerotonia
ENDOPHAGY *n* cannibalism within the same group or tribe
ENDOPHYTE *n* fungus, or occasionally an alga or other organism, that lives within a plant
ENDOPLASM *n* inner cytoplasm in some cells, esp protozoa, which is more granular and fluid than the outer cytoplasm
ENDOPOD *n* inner branch of a two-branched crustacean
ENDOPODS > ENDOPOD
ENDOPROCT *n* small animal living in water
ENDORPHIN *n* chemical occurring in the brain, which has a similar effect to morphine
ENDORSE *vb* give approval to
ENDORSED > ENDORSE
ENDORSEE *n* person in whose favour a negotiable instrument is endorsed
ENDORSEES > ENDORSEE
ENDORSER > ENDORSE
ENDORSERS > ENDORSE
ENDORSES > ENDORSE
ENDORSING > ENDORSE
ENDORSIVE > ENDORSE
ENDORSOR > ENDORSE
ENDORSORS > ENDORSE
ENDOSARC *same as* > ENDOPLASM
ENDOSARCS > ENDOSARC
ENDOSCOPE *n* long slender medical instrument used for examining the interior of hollow organs including

the lung, stomach, bladder and bowel
ENDOSCOPY > ENDOSCOPE
ENDOSMOS *same as* > ENDOSMOSE
ENDOSMOSE *n* osmosis in which water enters a cell or organism from the surrounding solution
ENDOSOME *n* sac within a biological cell
ENDOSOMES > ENDOSOME
ENDOSPERM *n* tissue within the seed of a flowering plant that surrounds and nourishes the developing embryo
ENDOSPORE *n* small asexual spore produced by some bacteria and algae
ENDOSS *vb* endorse
ENDOSSED > ENDOSS
ENDOSSES > ENDOSS
ENDOSSING > ENDOSS
ENDOSTEA > ENDOSTEUM
ENDOSTEAL > ENDOSTEUM
ENDOSTEUM *n* highly vascular membrane lining the marrow cavity of long bones, such as the femur and humerus
ENDOSTYLE *n* groove or fold in the pharynx of various chordates
ENDOTHERM *n* animal with warm blood
ENDOTOXIC > ENDOTOXIN
ENDOTOXIN *n* toxin contained within the protoplasm of an organism, esp a bacterium, and liberated only at death
ENDOW *vb* provide permanent income for
ENDOWED > ENDOW
ENDOWER > ENDOW
ENDOWERS > ENDOW
ENDOWING > ENDOW
ENDOWMENT *n* money given to an institution, such as a hospital
ENDOWS > ENDOW
ENDOZOA > ENDOZOON
ENDOZOIC *adj* (of a plant) living within an animal
ENDOZOON *variant of* > ENTOZOON
ENDPAPER *n* either of two leaves at the front and back of a book pasted to the inside of the cover
ENDPAPERS > ENDPAPER
ENDPLATE *n* any usually flat platelike structure at the end of something
ENDPLATES > ENDPLATE
ENDPLAY *n* way of playing the last few tricks in a hand so that an opponent is forced to make a particular lead ▷ *vb* force (an opponent) to make a particular lead near the end of a hand
ENDPLAYED > ENDPLAY
ENDPLAYS > ENDPLAY
ENDPOINT *n* point at which anything is complete
ENDPOINTS > ENDPOINT
ENDRIN *n* type of insecticide
ENDRINS > ENDRIN
ENDS > END
ENDSHIP *n* small village
ENDSHIPS > ENDSHIP
ENDUE *vb* invest or provide, as with some quality or trait
ENDUED > ENDUE
ENDUES > ENDUE
ENDUING > ENDUE
ENDUNGEON *vb* put in a dungeon
ENDURABLE > ENDURE
ENDURABLY > ENDURE
ENDURANCE *n* act or power of enduring
ENDURE *vb* bear (hardship) patiently
ENDURED > ENDURE
ENDURER > ENDURE
ENDURERS > ENDURE
ENDURES > ENDURE
ENDURING *adj* long-lasting
ENDURO *n* long-distance race for vehicles, intended to test endurance
ENDUROS > ENDURO
ENDWAYS *adv* having the end forwards or upwards ▷ *adj* vertical or upright
ENDWISE *same as* > ENDWAYS
ENDYSES > ENDYSIS
ENDYSIS *n* formation of new layers of integument after ecdysis
ENE *variant of* > EVEN
ENEMA *n* medicine injected into the rectum to empty the bowels
ENEMAS > ENEMA
ENEMATA > ENEMA
ENEMIES > ENEMY
ENEMY *n* hostile person or nation, opponent ▷ *adj* of or belonging to an enemy
ENERGETIC *adj* having or showing energy and enthusiasm
ENERGIC > ENERGY
ENERGID *n* nucleus and the cytoplasm associated with it in a syncytium
ENERGIDS > ENERGID
ENERGIES > ENERGY
ENERGISE *same as* > ENERGIZE
ENERGISED > ENERGISE
ENERGISER > ENERGISE
ENERGISES > ENERGISE
ENERGIZE *vb* give vigour to
ENERGIZED > ENERGIZE
ENERGIZER > ENERGIZE
ENERGIZES > ENERGIZE
ENERGUMEN *n* person thought to be possessed by an evil spirit
ENERGY *n* capacity for intense activity
ENERVATE *vb* deprive of strength or vitality ▷ *adj* deprived of strength or vitality
ENERVATED > ENERVATE
ENERVATES > ENERVATE
ENERVATOR > ENERVATE
ENERVE *vb* enervate
ENERVED > ENERVE
ENERVES > ENERVE
ENERVING > ENERVE
ENES > ENE
ENEW *vb* force a bird into water
ENEWED > ENEW
ENEWING > ENEW
ENEWS > ENEW
ENFACE *vb* write, print, or stamp (something) on the face of (a document)
ENFACED > ENFACE
ENFACES > ENFACE
ENFACING > ENFACE
ENFANT *n* French child
ENFANTS > ENFANT
ENFEEBLE *vb* weaken
ENFEEBLED > ENFEEBLE
ENFEEBLER > ENFEEBLE
ENFEEBLES > ENFEEBLE
ENFELON *vb* infuriate
ENFELONED > ENFELON
ENFELONS > ENFELON
ENFEOFF *vb* invest (a person) with possession of a freehold estate in land
ENFEOFFED > ENFEOFF
ENFEOFFS > ENFEOFF
ENFESTED *adj* made bitter
ENFETTER *vb* fetter
ENFETTERS > ENFETTER
ENFEVER *vb* make feverish
ENFEVERED > ENFEVER
ENFEVERS > ENFEVER
ENFIERCE *vb* make ferocious
ENFIERCED > ENFIERCE
ENFIERCES > ENFIERCE
ENFILADE *n* burst of gunfire sweeping from end to end along a line of troops ▷ *vb* attack with an enfilade
ENFILADED > ENFILADE
ENFILADES > ENFILADE
ENFILED *adj* passed through
ENFIRE *vb* set alight
ENFIRED > ENFIRE
ENFIRES > ENFIRE
ENFIRING > ENFIRE
ENFIX *variant of* > INFIX
ENFIXED > ENFIX
ENFIXES > ENFIX
ENFIXING > ENFIX
ENFLAME *variant of* > INFLAME
ENFLAMED > ENFLAME
ENFLAMES > ENFLAME
ENFLAMING > ENFLAME
ENFLESH *vb* make flesh
ENFLESHED > ENFLESH
ENFLESHES > ENFLESH
ENFLOWER *vb* put flowers on
ENFLOWERS > ENFLOWER
ENFOLD *vb* cover by wrapping something around
ENFOLDED > ENFOLD
ENFOLDER > ENFOLD
ENFOLDERS > ENFOLD
ENFOLDING > ENFOLD
ENFOLDS > ENFOLD
ENFORCE *vb* impose obedience (to a law etc)
ENFORCED > ENFORCE
ENFORCER > ENFORCE
ENFORCERS > ENFORCE
ENFORCES > ENFORCE
ENFORCING > ENFORCE
ENFOREST *vb* make into a forest
ENFORESTS > ENFOREST
ENFORM *variant of* > INFORM
ENFORMED > ENFORM
ENFORMING > ENFORM
ENFORMS > ENFORM
ENFRAME *vb* put inside a frame
ENFRAMED > ENFRAME
ENFRAMES > ENFRAME
ENFRAMING > ENFRAME
ENFREE *vb* release, make free
ENFREED > ENFREE
ENFREEDOM *variant of* > ENFREE
ENFREEING > ENFREE
ENFREES > ENFREE
ENFREEZE *vb* freeze
ENFREEZES > ENFREEZE
ENFROSEN > ENFREEZE
ENFROZE > ENFREEZE
ENFROZEN > ENFREEZE
ENG *another name for* > AGMA
ENGAGE *vb* take part, participate ▷ *adj* (of a writer or artist, esp a man) morally or politically committed to some ideology
ENGAGED *adj* pledged to be married
ENGAGEDLY > ENGAGED
ENGAGEE *adj* (of a female writer or artist) morally or politically committed to some ideology
ENGAGER > ENGAGE
ENGAGERS > ENGAGE
ENGAGES > ENGAGE
ENGAGING *adj* charming
ENGAOL *vb* put into gaol
ENGAOLED > ENGAOL
ENGAOLING > ENGAOL
ENGAOLS > ENGAOL
ENGARLAND *vb* cover with garlands
ENGENDER *vb* produce, cause to occur
ENGENDERS > ENGENDER
ENGENDURE > ENGENDER
ENGILD *vb* cover with or as if with gold
ENGILDED > ENGILD

ENGILDING > ENGILD
ENGILDS > ENGILD
ENGILT > ENGILD
ENGINE *n* any machine which converts energy into mechanical work ▷ *vb* put an engine in
ENGINED > ENGINE
ENGINEER *n* person trained in any branch of engineering ▷ *vb* plan in a clever manner
ENGINEERS > ENGINEER
ENGINER > ENGINE
ENGINERS > ENGINE
ENGINERY *n* collection or assembly of engines
ENGINES > ENGINE
ENGINING > ENGINE
ENGINOUS *adj* ingenious or clever
ENGIRD *vb* surround
ENGIRDED > ENGIRD
ENGIRDING > ENGIRD
ENGIRDLE *variant of* > ENGIRD
ENGIRDLED > ENGIRDLE
ENGIRDLES > ENGIRDLE
ENGIRDS > ENGIRD
ENGIRT > ENGIRD
ENGISCOPE *variant of* > ENGYSCOPE
ENGLACIAL *adj* embedded in, carried by, or running through a glacier
ENGLISH *vb* put a spinning movement on a billiard ball
ENGLISHED > ENGLISH
ENGLISHES > ENGLISH
ENGLOBE *vb* surround as if in a globe
ENGLOBED > ENGLOBE
ENGLOBES > ENGLOBE
ENGLOBING > ENGLOBE
ENGLOOM *vb* make dull or dismal
ENGLOOMED > ENGLOOM
ENGLOOMS > ENGLOOM
ENGLUT *vb* devour ravenously
ENGLUTS > ENGLUT
ENGLUTTED > ENGLUT
ENGOBE *n* liquid put on pottery before glazing
ENGOBES > ENGOBE
ENGORE *vb* pierce or wound
ENGORED > ENGORE
ENGORES > ENGORE
ENGORGE *vb* clog with blood
ENGORGED > ENGORGE
ENGORGES > ENGORGE
ENGORGING > ENGORGE
ENGORING > ENGORE
ENGOULED *adj* (in heraldry) with ends coming from the mouths of animals
ENGOUMENT *n* obsessive liking
ENGRACE *vb* give grace to
ENGRACED > ENGRACE
ENGRACES > ENGRACE
ENGRACING > ENGRACE
ENGRAFF *variant of* > ENGRAFT
ENGRAFFED > ENGRAFF
ENGRAFFS > ENGRAFF
ENGRAFT *vb* graft (a shoot, bud, etc) onto a stock
ENGRAFTED > ENGRAFT
ENGRAFTS > ENGRAFT
ENGRAIL *vb* decorate or mark (the edge of) (a coin) with small carved notches
ENGRAILED > ENGRAIL
ENGRAILS > ENGRAIL
ENGRAIN *variant spelling of* > INGRAIN
ENGRAINED > ENGRAIN
ENGRAINER > ENGRAIN
ENGRAINS > ENGRAIN
ENGRAM *n* physical basis of an individual memory in the brain
ENGRAMMA *variant of* > ENGRAM
ENGRAMMAS > ENGRAMMA
ENGRAMME *variant of* > ENGRAM
ENGRAMMES > ENGRAMME
ENGRAMMIC > ENGRAM
ENGRAMS > ENGRAM
ENGRASP *vb* grasp or seize
ENGRASPED > ENGRASP
ENGRASPS > ENGRASP
ENGRAVE *vb* carve (a design) onto a hard surface
ENGRAVED > ENGRAVE
ENGRAVEN > ENGRAVE
ENGRAVER > ENGRAVE
ENGRAVERS > ENGRAVE
ENGRAVERY > ENGRAVE
ENGRAVES > ENGRAVE
ENGRAVING *n* print made from an engraved plate
ENGRENAGE *n* act of putting into gear
ENGRIEVE *vb* grieve
ENGRIEVED > ENGRIEVE
ENGRIEVES > ENGRIEVE
ENGROOVE *vb* put a groove in
ENGROOVED > ENGROOVE
ENGROOVES > ENGROOVE
ENGROSS *vb* occupy the attention of (a person) completely
ENGROSSED > ENGROSS
ENGROSSER > ENGROSS
ENGROSSES > ENGROSS
ENGS > ENG
ENGUARD *vb* protect or defend
ENGUARDED > ENGUARD
ENGUARDS > ENGUARD
ENGULF *vb* cover or surround completely
ENGULFED > ENGULF
ENGULFING > ENGULF
ENGULFS > ENGULF
ENGULPH *variant of* > ENGULF
ENGULPHED > ENGULPH
ENGULPHS > ENGULPH
ENGYSCOPE *n* microscope
ENHALO *vb* surround with or as if with a halo
ENHALOED > ENHALO
ENHALOES > ENHALO
ENHALOING > ENHALO
ENHALOS > ENHALO
ENHANCE *vb* increase in quality, value, or attractiveness
ENHANCED > ENHANCE
ENHANCER > ENHANCE
ENHANCERS > ENHANCE
ENHANCES > ENHANCE
ENHANCING > ENHANCE
ENHANCIVE > ENHANCE
ENHEARSE *variant of* > INHEARSE
ENHEARSED > ENHEARSE
ENHEARSES > ENHEARSE
ENHEARTEN *vb* give heart to, encourage
ENHUNGER *vb* cause to be hungry
ENHUNGERS > ENHUNGER
ENHYDRITE *n* type of mineral
ENHYDROS *n* piece of chalcedony that contains water
ENHYDROUS > ENHYDROS
ENIAC *n* early type of computer built in the 1940s
ENIACS > ENIAC
ENIGMA *n* puzzling thing or person
ENIGMAS > ENIGMA
ENIGMATA > ENIGMA
ENIGMATIC > ENIGMA
ENISLE *vb* put on or make into an island
ENISLED > ENISLE
ENISLES > ENISLE
ENISLING > ENISLE
ENJAMB *vb* (of a line of verse) run over into the next line
ENJAMBED > ENJAMB
ENJAMBING > ENJAMB
ENJAMBS > ENJAMB
ENJOIN *vb* order (someone) to do something
ENJOINDER *n* order
ENJOINED > ENJOIN
ENJOINER > ENJOIN
ENJOINERS > ENJOIN
ENJOINING > ENJOIN
ENJOINS > ENJOIN
ENJOY *vb* take joy in
ENJOYABLE > ENJOY
ENJOYABLY > ENJOY
ENJOYED > ENJOY
ENJOYER > ENJOY
ENJOYERS > ENJOY
ENJOYING > ENJOY
ENJOYMENT *n* act or condition of receiving pleasure from something
ENJOYS > ENJOY
ENKERNEL *vb* put inside a kernel
ENKERNELS > ENKERNEL
ENKINDLE *vb* set on fire
ENKINDLED > ENKINDLE
ENKINDLER > ENKINDLE
ENKINDLES > ENKINDLE
ENLACE *vb* bind or encircle with or as with laces
ENLACED > ENLACE
ENLACES > ENLACE
ENLACING > ENLACE
ENLARD *vb* put lard on
ENLARDED > ENLARD
ENLARDING > ENLARD
ENLARDS > ENLARD
ENLARGE *vb* make or grow larger
ENLARGED > ENLARGE
ENLARGEN *variant of* > ENLARGE
ENLARGENS > ENLARGEN
ENLARGER *n* optical instrument for making enlarged photographic prints in which a negative is brightly illuminated and its enlarged image is focused onto a sheet of sensitized paper
ENLARGERS > ENLARGER
ENLARGES > ENLARGE
ENLARGING > ENLARGE
ENLEVE *adj* having been abducted
ENLIGHT *vb* light up
ENLIGHTED > ENLIGHT
ENLIGHTEN *vb* give information to
ENLIGHTS > ENLIGHT
ENLINK *vb* link together
ENLINKED > ENLINK
ENLINKING > ENLINK
ENLINKS > ENLINK
ENLIST *vb* enter the armed forces
ENLISTED > ENLIST
ENLISTEE > ENLIST
ENLISTEES > ENLIST
ENLISTER > ENLIST
ENLISTERS > ENLIST
ENLISTING > ENLIST
ENLISTS > ENLIST
ENLIT > ENLIGHT
ENLIVEN *vb* make lively or cheerful
ENLIVENED > ENLIVEN
ENLIVENER > ENLIVEN
ENLIVENS > ENLIVEN
ENLOCK *vb* lock or secure
ENLOCKED > ENLOCK
ENLOCKING > ENLOCK
ENLOCKS > ENLOCK
ENLUMINE *vb* illuminate
ENLUMINED > ENLUMINE
ENLUMINES > ENLUMINE
ENMESH *vb* catch or involve in or as if in a net or snare
ENMESHED > ENMESH
ENMESHES > ENMESH
ENMESHING > ENMESH
ENMEW *variant of* > EMMEW
ENMEWED > ENMEW
ENMEWING > ENMEW
ENMEWS > ENMEW
ENMITIES > ENMITY
ENMITY *n* ill will, hatred
ENMOSSED *adj* having a covering of moss
ENMOVE *variant*

of > EMMOVE
ENMOVED > ENMOVE
ENMOVES > ENMOVE
ENMOVING > ENMOVE
ENNAGE *n* total number of ens in a piece of matter to be set in type
ENNAGES > ENNAGE
ENNEAD *n* group or series of nine
ENNEADIC > ENNEAD
ENNEADS > ENNEAD
ENNEAGON *another name for* > NONAGON
ENNEAGONS > ENNEAGON
ENNOBLE *vb* make noble, elevate
ENNOBLED > ENNOBLE
ENNOBLER > ENNOBLE
ENNOBLERS > ENNOBLE
ENNOBLES > ENNOBLE
ENNOBLING > ENNOBLE
ENNOG *n* back alley
ENNOGS > ENNOG
ENNUI *n* boredom, dissatisfaction ▷ *vb* bore
ENNUIED > ENNUI
ENNUIS > ENNUI
ENNUYE *adj* bored
ENNUYED > ENNUI
ENNUYEE *same as* > ENNUYE
ENNUYING > ENNUI
ENODAL *adj* having no nodes
ENOKI *variant of* > ENOKITAKE
ENOKIDAKE *variant of* > ENOKITAKE
ENOKIS > ENOKI
ENOKITAKE *n* Japanese mushroom
ENOL *n* any organic compound containing the group -CH:CO-, often existing in chemical equilibrium with the corresponding keto form
ENOLASE *n* type of enzyme
ENOLASES > ENOLASE
ENOLIC > ENOL
ENOLOGIES > ENOLOGY
ENOLOGIST *n* wine expert
ENOLOGY *usual US spelling of* > OENOLOGY
ENOLS > ENOL
ENOMOTIES > ENOMOTY
ENOMOTY *n* division of the Spartan army in ancient Greece
ENOPHILE *n* lover of wine
ENOPHILES > ENOPHILE
ENORM *variant of* > ENORMOUS
ENORMITY *n* great wickedness
ENORMOUS *adj* very big, vast
ENOSES > ENOSIS
ENOSIS *n* union of Greece and Cyprus
ENOSISES > ENOSIS
ENOUGH *adj* as much or as many as necessary ▷ *n* sufficient quantity ▷ *adv* sufficiently
ENOUGHS > ENOUGH
ENOUNCE *vb* enunciate
ENOUNCED > ENOUNCE
ENOUNCES > ENOUNCE
ENOUNCING > ENOUNCE
ENOW *archaic word for* > ENOUGH
ENOWS > ENOW
ENPLANE *vb* board an aircraft
ENPLANED > ENPLANE
ENPLANES > ENPLANE
ENPLANING > ENPLANE
ENPRINT *n* standard photographic print produced from a negative
ENPRINTS > ENPRINT
ENQUIRE *same as* > INQUIRE
ENQUIRED > ENQUIRE
ENQUIRER > ENQUIRE
ENQUIRERS > ENQUIRE
ENQUIRES > ENQUIRE
ENQUIRIES > ENQUIRE
ENQUIRING > ENQUIRE
ENQUIRY > ENQUIRE
ENRACE *vb* bring in a race of people
ENRACED > ENRACE
ENRACES > ENRACE
ENRACING > ENRACE
ENRAGE *vb* make extremely angry
ENRAGED > ENRAGE
ENRAGEDLY > ENRAGE
ENRAGES > ENRAGE
ENRAGING > ENRAGE
ENRANCKLE *vb* upset, make irate
ENRANGE *vb* arrange, organize
ENRANGED > ENRANGE
ENRANGES > ENRANGE
ENRANGING > ENRANGE
ENRANK *vb* put in a row
ENRANKED > ENRANK
ENRANKING > ENRANK
ENRANKS > ENRANK
ENRAPT > ENRAPTURE
ENRAPTURE *vb* fill with delight
ENRAUNGE *variant of* > ENRANGE
ENRAUNGED > ENRAUNGE
ENRAUNGES > ENRAUNGE
ENRAVISH *vb* enchant
ENRHEUM *vb* pass a cold on to
ENRHEUMED > ENRHEUM
ENRHEUMS > ENRHEUM
ENRICH *vb* improve in quality
ENRICHED > ENRICH
ENRICHER > ENRICH
ENRICHERS > ENRICH
ENRICHES > ENRICH
ENRICHING > ENRICH
ENRIDGED *adj* ridged
ENRING *vb* put a ring round
ENRINGED > ENRING
ENRINGING > ENRING
ENRINGS > ENRING
ENRIVEN *adj* ripped
ENROBE *vb* dress in or as if in a robe
ENROBED > ENROBE
ENROBER > ENROBE
ENROBERS > ENROBE
ENROBES > ENROBE
ENROBING > ENROBE
ENROL *vb* (cause to) become a member
ENROLL *same as* > ENROL
ENROLLED > ENROLL
ENROLLEE > ENROL
ENROLLEES > ENROL
ENROLLER > ENROL
ENROLLERS > ENROL
ENROLLING > ENROLL
ENROLLS > ENROLL
ENROLMENT *n* act of enrolling or state of being enrolled
ENROLS > ENROL
ENROOT *vb* establish (plants) by fixing their roots in the earth
ENROOTED > ENROOT
ENROOTING > ENROOT
ENROOTS > ENROOT
ENROUGH *vb* roughen
ENROUGHED > ENROUGH
ENROUGHS > ENROUGH
ENROUND *vb* encircle
ENROUNDED > ENROUND
ENROUNDS > ENROUND
ENS *n* being or existence in the most general abstract sense
ENSAMPLE *n* example ▷ *vb* make an example
ENSAMPLED > ENSAMPLE
ENSAMPLES > ENSAMPLE
ENSATE *adj* shaped like a sword
ENSCONCE *vb* settle firmly or comfortably
ENSCONCED > ENSCONCE
ENSCONCES > ENSCONCE
ENSCROLL *variant of* > INSCROLL
ENSCROLLS > ENSCROLL
ENSEAL *vb* seal up
ENSEALED > ENSEAL
ENSEALING > ENSEAL
ENSEALS > ENSEAL
ENSEAM *vb* put a seam on
ENSEAMED > ENSEAM
ENSEAMING > ENSEAM
ENSEAMS > ENSEAM
ENSEAR *vb* dry
ENSEARED > ENSEAR
ENSEARING > ENSEAR
ENSEARS > ENSEAR
ENSEMBLE *n* all the parts of something taken together ▷ *adv* all together or at once ▷ *adj* (of a film or play) involving several separate but often interrelated story lines
ENSEMBLES > ENSEMBLE
ENSERF *vb* enslave
ENSERFED > ENSERF
ENSERFING > ENSERF
ENSERFS > ENSERF
ENSEW *variant of* > ENSUE
ENSEWED > ENSEW
ENSEWING > ENSEW
ENSEWS > ENSEW
ENSHEATH *variant of* > INSHEATHE
ENSHEATHE *variant of* > INSHEATHE
ENSHEATHS > ENSHEATH
ENSHELL *variant of* > INSHELL
ENSHELLED > ENSHELL
ENSHELLS > ENSHELL
ENSHELTER *vb* shelter
ENSHIELD *vb* protect
ENSHIELDS > ENSHIELD
ENSHRINE *vb* cherish or treasure
ENSHRINED > ENSHRINE
ENSHRINEE > ENSHRINE
ENSHRINES > ENSHRINE
ENSHROUD *vb* cover or hide as with a shroud
ENSHROUDS > ENSHROUD
ENSIFORM *adj* shaped like a sword blade
ENSIGN *n* naval flag ▷ *vb* mark with a sign
ENSIGNCY > ENSIGN
ENSIGNED > ENSIGN
ENSIGNING > ENSIGN
ENSIGNS > ENSIGN
ENSILAGE *n* process of ensiling green fodder ▷ *vb* make into silage
ENSILAGED > ENSILAGE
ENSILAGES > ENSILAGE
ENSILE *vb* store and preserve (green fodder) in an enclosed pit or silo
ENSILED > ENSILE
ENSILES > ENSILE
ENSILING > ENSILE
ENSKIED > ENSKY
ENSKIES > ENSKY
ENSKY *vb* put in the sky
ENSKYED > ENSKY
ENSKYING > ENSKY
ENSLAVE *vb* make a slave of (someone)
ENSLAVED > ENSLAVE
ENSLAVER > ENSLAVE
ENSLAVERS > ENSLAVE
ENSLAVES > ENSLAVE
ENSLAVING > ENSLAVE
ENSNARE *vb* catch in or as if in a snare
ENSNARED > ENSNARE
ENSNARER > ENSNARE
ENSNARERS > ENSNARE
ENSNARES > ENSNARE
ENSNARING > ENSNARE
ENSNARL *vb* become tangled in
ENSNARLED > ENSNARL
ENSNARLS > ENSNARL
ENSORCEL *vb* enchant
ENSORCELL *variant of* > ENSORCEL
ENSORCELS > ENSORCEL
ENSOUL *vb* endow with a soul
ENSOULED > ENSOUL
ENSOULING > ENSOUL
ENSOULS > ENSOUL
ENSPHERE *vb* enclose in or as if in a sphere

ENSPHERED > ENSPHERE
ENSPHERES > ENSPHERE
ENSTAMP *vb* imprint with a stamp
ENSTAMPED > ENSTAMP
ENSTAMPS > ENSTAMP
ENSTATITE *n* grey, green, yellow, or brown pyroxene mineral consisting of magnesium silicate in orthorhombic crystalline form
ENSTEEP *vb* soak in water
ENSTEEPED > ENSTEEP
ENSTEEPS > ENSTEEP
ENSTYLE *vb* give a name to
ENSTYLED > ENSTYLE
ENSTYLES > ENSTYLE
ENSTYLING > ENSTYLE
ENSUE *vb* come next, result
ENSUED > ENSUE
ENSUES > ENSUE
ENSUING *adj* following subsequently or in order
ENSURE *vb* make certain or sure
ENSURED > ENSURE
ENSURER > ENSURE
ENSURERS > ENSURE
ENSURES > ENSURE
ENSURING > ENSURE
ENSWATHE *vb* bind or wrap
ENSWATHED > ENSWATHE
ENSWATHES > ENSWATHE
ENSWEEP *vb* sweep across
ENSWEEPS > ENSWEEP
ENSWEPT > ENSWEEP
ENTAIL *vb* bring about or impose inevitably ▷ *n* restriction imposed by entailing an estate
ENTAILED > ENTAIL
ENTAILER > ENTAIL
ENTAILERS > ENTAIL
ENTAILING > ENTAIL
ENTAILS > ENTAIL
ENTAME *vb* make tame
ENTAMEBA *same as* > ENTAMOEBA
ENTAMEBAE > ENTAMEBA
ENTAMEBAS > ENTAMEBA
ENTAMED > ENTAME
ENTAMES > ENTAME
ENTAMING > ENTAME
ENTAMOEBA *n* parasitic amoeba that lives in the intestines of man and causes amoebic dysentery
ENTANGLE *vb* catch or involve in or as if in a tangle
ENTANGLED > ENTANGLE
ENTANGLER > ENTANGLE
ENTANGLES > ENTANGLE
ENTASES > ENTASIS
ENTASIA *same as* > ENTASIS
ENTASIAS > ENTASIA
ENTASIS *n* slightly convex curve given to the shaft of a column, pier, or similar structure, to correct the illusion of concavity produced by a straight shaft
ENTASTIC *adj* (of a disease) characterized by spasms
ENTAYLE *variant of* > ENTAIL
ENTAYLED > ENTAYLE
ENTAYLES > ENTAYLE
ENTAYLING > ENTAYLE
ENTELECHY *n* (in the philosophy of Aristotle) actuality as opposed to potentiality
ENTELLUS *n* langur of S Asia
ENTENDER *vb* make more tender
ENTENDERS > ENTENDER
ENTENTE *n* friendly understanding between nations
ENTENTES > ENTENTE
ENTER *vb* come or go in
ENTERA > ENTERON
ENTERABLE > ENTER
ENTERAL *same as* > ENTERIC
ENTERALLY > ENTERIC
ENTERATE *adj* with an intestine separate from the outer wall of the body
ENTERED > ENTER
ENTERER > ENTER
ENTERERS > ENTER
ENTERIC *adj* intestinal ▷ *n* infectious disease of the intestines
ENTERICS > ENTERIC
ENTERING > ENTER
ENTERINGS > ENTER
ENTERITIS *n* inflammation of the intestine, causing diarrhoea
ENTERON *n* alimentary canal, esp of an embryo or a coelenterate
ENTERONS > ENTERON
ENTERS > ENTER
ENTERTAIN *vb* amuse
ENTERTAKE *vb* entertain
ENTERTOOK > ENTERTAKE
ENTETE *adj* obsessed
ENTETEE *variant of* > ENTETE
ENTHALPY *n* thermodynamic property of a system equal to the sum of its internal energy and the product of its pressure and volume
ENTHETIC *adj* (esp of infectious diseases) introduced into the body from without
ENTHRAL *vb* hold the attention of
ENTHRALL *same as* > ENTHRAL
ENTHRALLS > ENTHRALL
ENTHRALS > ENTHRAL
ENTHRONE *vb* place (someone) on a throne
ENTHRONED > ENTHRONE
ENTHRONES > ENTHRONE
ENTHUSE *vb* (cause to) show enthusiasm
ENTHUSED > ENTHUSE
ENTHUSES > ENTHUSE
ENTHUSING > ENTHUSE
ENTHYMEME *n* incomplete syllogism, in which one or more premises are unexpressed as their truth is considered to be self-evident
ENTIA > ENS
ENTICE *vb* attract by exciting hope or desire, tempt
ENTICED > ENTICE
ENTICER > ENTICE
ENTICERS > ENTICE
ENTICES > ENTICE
ENTICING > ENTICE
ENTICINGS > ENTICE
ENTIRE *adj* including every detail, part, or aspect of something ▷ *n* state of being entire
ENTIRELY *adv* without reservation or exception
ENTIRES > ENTIRE
ENTIRETY *n* state of being entire or whole
ENTITIES > ENTITY
ENTITLE *vb* give a right to
ENTITLED > ENTITLE
ENTITLES > ENTITLE
ENTITLING > ENTITLE
ENTITY *n* separate distinct thing
ENTOBLAST *less common name for* > ENDODERM
ENTODERM *same as* > ENDODERM
ENTODERMS > ENTODERM
ENTOIL *archaic word for* > ENSNARE
ENTOILED > ENTOIL
ENTOILING > ENTOIL
ENTOILS > ENTOIL
ENTOMB *vb* place (a corpse) in a tomb
ENTOMBED > ENTOMB
ENTOMBING > ENTOMB
ENTOMBS > ENTOMB
ENTOMIC *adj* denoting or relating to insects
ENTOPHYTE *variant of* > ENDOPHYTE
ENTOPIC *adj* situated in its normal place or position
ENTOPROCT *n* type of marine animal
ENTOPTIC *adj* (of visual sensation) resulting from structures within the eye itself
ENTOPTICS *n* study of entoptic visions
ENTOTIC *adj* of or relating to the inner ear
ENTOURAGE *n* group of people who assist an important person
ENTOZOA > ENTOZOON
ENTOZOAL > ENTOZOON
ENTOZOAN *same as* > ENTOZOON
ENTOZOANS > ENTOZOAN
ENTOZOIC *adj* of or relating to an entozoon
ENTOZOON *n* internal parasite
ENTRAIL *vb* twist or entangle
ENTRAILED > ENTRAIL
ENTRAILS *pl n* intestines
ENTRAIN *vb* board or put aboard a train
ENTRAINED > ENTRAIN
ENTRAINER > ENTRAIN
ENTRAINS > ENTRAIN
ENTRALL *variant of* > ENTRAILS
ENTRALLES *variant of* > ENTRAILS
ENTRAMMEL *vb* hamper or obstruct by entangling
ENTRANCE *n* way into a place ▷ *vb* delight ▷ *adj* necessary in order to enter something
ENTRANCED > ENTRANCE
ENTRANCES > ENTRANCE
ENTRANT *n* person who enters a university, contest, etc
ENTRANTS > ENTRANT
ENTRAP *vb* trick into difficulty etc
ENTRAPPED > ENTRAP
ENTRAPPER > ENTRAP
ENTRAPS > ENTRAP
ENTREAT *vb* ask earnestly
ENTREATED > ENTREAT
ENTREATS > ENTREAT
ENTREATY *n* earnest request
ENTRECHAT *n* leap in ballet during which the dancer repeatedly crosses his feet or beats them together
ENTRECOTE *n* beefsteak cut from between the ribs
ENTREE *n* dish served before a main course
ENTREES > ENTREE
ENTREMES *variant of* > ENTREMETS
ENTREMETS *n* dessert
ENTRENCH *vb* establish firmly
ENTREPOT *n* warehouse for commercial goods
ENTREPOTS > ENTREPOT
ENTRESOL *another name for* > MEZZANINE
ENTRESOLS > ENTRESOL
ENTREZ *interj* enter
ENTRIES > ENTRY
ENTRISM *variant of* > ENTRYISM
ENTRISMS > ENTRISM
ENTRIST > ENTRYISM
ENTRISTS > ENTRYISM
ENTROLD *adj* surrounded
ENTROPIC > ENTROPY
ENTROPIES > ENTROPY
ENTROPION *n* turning inwards of the edge of the eyelid
ENTROPIUM *variant of* > ENTROPION
ENTROPY *n* lack of

organization
ENTRUST *vb* put into the care or protection of
ENTRUSTED > ENTRUST
ENTRUSTS > ENTRUST
ENTRY *n* entrance ▷ *adj* necessary in order to enter something
ENTRYISM *n* policy or practice of members of a particular political group joining an existing political party with the intention of changing its principles and policies, instead of forming a new party
ENTRYISMS > ENTRYISM
ENTRYIST > ENTRYISM
ENTRYISTS > ENTRYISM
ENTRYWAY *n* entrance passage
ENTRYWAYS > ENTRYWAY
ENTWINE *vb* twist together or around
ENTWINED > ENTWINE
ENTWINES > ENTWINE
ENTWINING > ENTWINE
ENTWIST *vb* twist together or around
ENTWISTED > ENTWIST
ENTWISTS > ENTWIST
ENUCLEATE *vb* remove the nucleus from (a cell) ▷ *adj* (of cells) deprived of their nuclei
ENUF *common intentional literary misspelling of* > ENOUGH
ENUMERATE *vb* name one by one
ENUNCIATE *vb* pronounce clearly
ENURE *variant spelling of* > INURE
ENURED > ENURE
ENUREMENT > ENURE
ENURES > ENURE
ENURESES > ENURESIS
ENURESIS *n* involuntary discharge of urine, esp during sleep
ENURETIC > ENURESIS
ENURETICS > ENURESIS
ENURING > ENURE
ENVASSAL *vb* make a vassal of
ENVASSALS > ENVASSAL
ENVAULT *vb* enclose in a vault; entomb
ENVAULTED > ENVAULT
ENVAULTS > ENVAULT
ENVEIGLE *same as* > INVEIGLE
ENVEIGLED > ENVEIGLE
ENVEIGLES > ENVEIGLE
ENVELOP *vb* wrap up, enclose
ENVELOPE *n* folded gummed paper cover for a letter
ENVELOPED > ENVELOP
ENVELOPER > ENVELOP
ENVELOPES > ENVELOPE
ENVELOPS > ENVELOP
ENVENOM *vb* fill or impregnate with venom
ENVENOMED > ENVENOM
ENVENOMS > ENVENOM
ENVERMEIL *vb* dye vermilion
ENVIABLE *adj* arousing envy, fortunate
ENVIABLY > ENVIABLE
ENVIED > ENVY
ENVIER > ENVY
ENVIERS > ENVY
ENVIES > ENVY
ENVIOUS *adj* full of envy
ENVIOUSLY > ENVIOUS
ENVIRO *n* environmentalist
ENVIRON *vb* encircle or surround
ENVIRONED > ENVIRON
ENVIRONS *pl n* surrounding area, esp of a town
ENVIROS > ENVIRO
ENVISAGE *vb* conceive of as a possibility
ENVISAGED > ENVISAGE
ENVISAGES > ENVISAGE
ENVISION *vb* conceive of as a possibility, esp in the future
ENVISIONS > ENVISION
ENVOI *same as* > ENVOY
ENVOIS > ENVOI
ENVOY *n* messenger
ENVOYS > ENVOY
ENVOYSHIP > ENVOY
ENVY *n* feeling of discontent aroused by another's good fortune ▷ *vb* grudge (another's good fortune, success, or qualities)
ENVYING > ENVY
ENVYINGLY > ENVY
ENVYINGS > ENVY
ENWALL *vb* wall in
ENWALLED > ENWALL
ENWALLING > ENWALL
ENWALLOW *vb* sink or plunge
ENWALLOWS > ENWALLOW
ENWALLS > ENWALL
ENWHEEL *archaic word for* > ENCIRCLE
ENWHEELED > ENWHEEL
ENWHEELS > ENWHEEL
ENWIND *vb* wind or coil around
ENWINDING > ENWIND
ENWINDS > ENWIND
ENWOMB *vb* enclose in or as if in a womb
ENWOMBED > ENWOMB
ENWOMBING > ENWOMB
ENWOMBS > ENWOMB
ENWOUND > ENWIND
ENWRAP *vb* wrap or cover up
ENWRAPPED > ENWRAP
ENWRAPS > ENWRAP
ENWREATH *vb* surround or encircle with or as with a wreath or wreaths
ENWREATHE *same as* > ENWREATH
ENWREATHS > ENWREATH
ENZIAN *n* gentian violet
ENZIANS > ENZIAN
ENZONE *vb* enclose in a zone
ENZONED > ENZONE
ENZONES > ENZONE
ENZONING > ENZONE
ENZOOTIC *adj* (of diseases) affecting animals within a limited region ▷ *n* enzootic disease
ENZOOTICS > ENZOOTIC
ENZYM *same as* > ENZYME
ENZYMATIC > ENZYME
ENZYME *n* any of a group of complex proteins that act as catalysts in specific biochemical reactions
ENZYMES > ENZYME
ENZYMIC > ENZYME
ENZYMS > ENZYM
EOAN *adj* of or relating to the dawn
EOBIONT *n* hypothetical chemical precursor of a living cell
EOBIONTS > EOBIONT
EOCENE *adj* of, denoting, or formed in the second epoch of the Tertiary period
EOHIPPUS *n* earliest horse: an extinct Eocene dog-sized animal of the genus with four-toed forelegs, three-toed hindlegs, and teeth specialized for browsing
EOLIAN *adj* of or relating to the wind
EOLIENNE *n* type of fine cloth
EOLIENNES > EOLIENNE
EOLIPILE *variant of* > AEOLIPILE
EOLIPILES > EOLIPILE
EOLITH *n* stone, usually crudely broken, used as a primitive tool in Eolithic times
EOLITHIC > EOLITH
EOLITHS > EOLITH
EOLOPILE *variant of* > AEOLIPILE
EOLOPILES > EOLOPILE
EON *n* longest division of geological time, comprising two or more eras
EONIAN *adj* of or relating to an eon
EONISM *n* adoption of female dress and behaviour by a male
EONISMS > EONISM
EONS > EON
EORL *n* Anglo-Saxon nobleman
EORLS > EORL
EOSIN *n* red crystalline water-insoluble derivative of fluorescein
EOSINE *same as* > EOSIN
EOSINES > EOSINE
EOSINIC > EOSIN
EOSINS > EOSIN
EOTHEN *adv* from the East
EPACRID *n* type of heath-like plant
EPACRIDS > EPACRID
EPACRIS *n* genus of the epacrids
EPACRISES > EPACRIS
EPACT *n* difference in time, about 11 days, between the solar year and the lunar year
EPACTS > EPACT
EPAENETIC *adj* eulogistic
EPAGOGE *n* inductive reasoning
EPAGOGES > EPAGOGE
EPAGOGIC > EPAGOGE
EPANODOS *n* return to main theme after a digression
EPARCH *n* bishop or metropolitan in charge of an eparchy
EPARCHATE *same as* > EPARCHY
EPARCHIAL > EPARCHY
EPARCHIES > EPARCHY
EPARCHS > EPARCH
EPARCHY *n* diocese of the Eastern Christian Church
EPATANT *adj* startling or shocking, esp through being unconventional
EPAULE *n* shoulder of a fortification
EPAULES > EPAULE
EPAULET *same as* > EPAULETTE
EPAULETS > EPAULET
EPAULETTE *n* shoulder ornament on a uniform
EPAXIAL *adj* above the axis
EPAZOTE *n* type of herb
EPAZOTES > EPAZOTE
EPEDAPHIC *adj* of or relating to atmospheric conditions
EPEE *n* straight-bladed sword used in fencing
EPEEIST *n* one who uses or specializes in using an epee
EPEEISTS > EPEEIST
EPEES > EPEE
EPEIRA *same as* > EPEIRID
EPEIRAS > EPEIRA
EPEIRIC *adj* in, of, or relating to a continent
EPEIRID *n* type of spider
EPEIRIDS > EPEIRID
EPENDYMA *n* membrane lining the ventricles of the brain and the central canal of the spinal cord
EPENDYMAL > EPENDYMA
EPENDYMAS > EPENDYMA
EPEOLATRY *n* worship of words
EPERDU *adj* distracted
EPERDUE *adj* distracted
EPERGNE *n* ornamental centrepiece for a table: a stand with holders for

sweetmeats, fruit, flowers, etc
EPERGNES > EPERGNE
EPHA *same as* > EPHAH
EPHAH *n* Hebrew unit of dry measure equal to approximately one bushel or about 33 litres
EPHAHS > EPHAH
EPHAS > EPHA
EPHEBE *n* (in ancient Greece) youth about to enter full citizenship, esp one undergoing military training
EPHEBES > EPHEBE
EPHEBI > EPHEBE
EPHEBIC > EPHEBE
EPHEBOI > EPHEBOS
EPHEBOS *same as* > EPHEBE
EPHEBUS *same as* > EPHEBE
EPHEDRA *n* gymnosperm shrub of warm regions of America and Eurasia
EPHEDRAS > EPHEDRA
EPHEDRIN *same as* > EPHEDRINE
EPHEDRINE *n* alkaloid used for treatment of asthma and hay fever
EPHEDRINS > EPHEDRIN
EPHELIDES > EPHELIS
EPHELIS *n* freckle
EPHEMERA *n* something transitory or short-lived
EPHEMERAE > EPHEMERA
EPHEMERAL *adj* short-lived ▷ *n* short-lived organism, such as the mayfly
EPHEMERAS > EPHEMERA
EPHEMERID *n* mayfly
EPHEMERIS *n* table giving the future positions of a planet, comet, or satellite
EPHEMERON > EPHEMERA
EPHIALTES *n* incubus
EPHOD *n* embroidered vestment believed to resemble an apron with shoulder straps, worn by priests in ancient Israel
EPHODS > EPHOD
EPHOR *n* (in ancient Greece) one of a board of senior magistrates in any of several Dorian states, esp the five Spartan ephors, who were elected by the vote of all full citizens and who wielded effective power
EPHORAL > EPHOR
EPHORALTY > EPHOR
EPHORATE > EPHOR
EPHORATES > EPHOR
EPHORI > EPHOR
EPHORS > EPHOR
EPIBIOSES > EPIBIOSIS
EPIBIOSIS *n* any relationship between two organisms in which one grows on the other but is not parasitic on it
EPIBIOTIC > EPIBIOSIS
EPIBLAST *n* outermost layer of an embryo, which becomes the ectoderm at gastrulation
EPIBLASTS > EPIBLAST
EPIBLEM *n* outermost cell layer of a root
EPIBLEMS > EPIBLEM
EPIBOLIC > EPIBOLY
EPIBOLIES > EPIBOLY
EPIBOLY *n* process that occurs during gastrulation in vertebrates, in which cells on one side of the blastula grow over and surround the remaining cells and yolk and eventually form the ectoderm
EPIC *n* long poem, book, or film about heroic events or actions ▷ *adj* very impressive or ambitious
EPICAL > EPIC
EPICALLY > EPIC
EPICALYX *n* series of small sepal-like bracts forming an outer calyx beneath the true calyx in some flowers
EPICANTHI *n* folds of skin extending vertically over the inner angles of the eyes
EPICARDIA *n* layers of pericardia in direct contact with the heart
EPICARP *n* outermost layer of the pericarp of fruits: forms the skin of a peach or grape
EPICARPS > EPICARP
EPICEDE *same as* > EPICEDIUM
EPICEDES > EPICEDE
EPICEDIA > EPICEDIUM
EPICEDIAL > EPICEDIUM
EPICEDIAN > EPICEDIUM
EPICEDIUM *n* funeral ode
EPICENE *adj* having the characteristics of both sexes; hermaphroditic ▷ *n* epicene person or creature
EPICENES > EPICENE
EPICENISM > EPICENE
EPICENTER *same as* > EPICENTRE
EPICENTRA *n* epicentres
EPICENTRE *n* point on the earth's surface immediately above the origin of an earthquake
EPICIER *n* grocer
EPICIERS > EPICIER
EPICISM *n* style or trope characteristic of epics
EPICISMS > EPIC
EPICIST *n* writer of epics
EPICISTS > EPIC
EPICLESES > EPICLESIS
EPICLESIS *n* invocation of the Holy Spirit to consecrate the bread and wine of the Eucharist
EPICLIKE *adj* resembling or reminiscent of an epic
EPICOTYL *n* part of an embryo plant stem above the cotyledons but beneath the terminal bud
EPICOTYLS > EPICOTYL
EPICRANIA *n* tissue covering the cranium
EPICRISES > EPICRISIS
EPICRISIS *n* secondary crisis occurring in the course of a disease
EPICRITIC *adj* (of certain nerve fibres of the skin) serving to perceive and distinguish fine variations of temperature or touch
EPICS > EPIC
EPICURE *n* person who enjoys good food and drink
EPICUREAN *adj* devoted to sensual pleasures, esp food and drink ▷ *n* epicure
EPICURES > EPICURE
EPICURISE *same as* > EPICURIZE
EPICURISM > EPICURE
EPICURIZE *vb* act as an epicure
EPICYCLE *n* (in the Ptolemaic system) a small circle, around which a planet was thought to revolve
EPICYCLES > EPICYCLE
EPICYCLIC > EPICYCLE
EPIDEMIC *n* widespread occurrence of a disease ▷ *adj* (esp of a disease) affecting many people in an area
EPIDEMICS > EPIDEMIC
EPIDERM *same as* > EPIDERMIS
EPIDERMAL > EPIDERMIS
EPIDERMIC > EPIDERMIS
EPIDERMIS *n* outer layer of the skin
EPIDERMS > EPIDERM
EPIDICTIC *adj* designed to display something, esp the skill of the speaker in rhetoric
EPIDOSITE *n* rock formed of quartz and epidote
EPIDOTE *n* green mineral consisting of hydrated calcium iron aluminium silicate in monoclinic crystalline form: common in metamorphic rocks
EPIDOTES > EPIDOTE
EPIDOTIC > EPIDOTE
EPIDURAL *n* spinal anaesthetic injected to relieve pain during childbirth ▷ *adj* on or over the outermost membrane covering the brain and spinal cord
EPIDURALS > EPIDURAL
EPIFAUNA *n* animals that live on the surface of the seabed
EPIFAUNAE > EPIFAUNA
EPIFAUNAL > EPIFAUNA
EPIFAUNAS > EPIFAUNA
EPIFOCAL *adj* situated or occurring at an epicentre
EPIGAEAL *same as* > EPIGEAL
EPIGAEAN *same as* > EPIGEAL
EPIGAEOUS *same as* > EPIGEAL
EPIGAMIC *adj* attractive to the opposite sex
EPIGEAL *adj* of or relating to seed germination in which the cotyledons appear above the ground because of the growth of the hypocotyl
EPIGEAN *same as* > EPIGEAL
EPIGEIC *same as* > EPIGEAL
EPIGENE *adj* formed or taking place at or near the surface of the earth
EPIGENIC *adj* pertaining to the theory of the gradual development of the embryo
EPIGENIST *n* one who studies or espouses the theory of the gradual development of the embryo
EPIGENOUS *adj* growing on the surface, esp the upper surface, of an organism or part
EPIGEOUS *same as* > EPIGEAL
EPIGON *same as* > EPIGONE
EPIGONE *n* inferior follower or imitator
EPIGONES > EPIGONE
EPIGONI > EPIGONE
EPIGONIC > EPIGONE
EPIGONISM > EPIGONE
EPIGONOUS > EPIGONE
EPIGONS > EPIGON
EPIGONUS *same as* > EPIGONE
EPIGRAM *n* short witty remark or poem
EPIGRAMS > EPIGRAM
EPIGRAPH *n* quotation at the start of a book
EPIGRAPHS > EPIGRAPH
EPIGRAPHY *n* study of ancient inscriptions
EPIGYNIES > EPIGYNOUS
EPIGYNOUS *adj* (of flowers) having the receptacle enclosing and fused with the gynoecium so that the other floral parts arise above it
EPIGYNY > EPIGYNOUS
EPILATE *vb* remove hair from
EPILATED > EPILATE
EPILATES > EPILATE
EPILATING > EPILATE
EPILATION > EPILATE
EPILATOR *n* electrical appliance consisting of a metal spiral head that rotates at high speed,

plucking unwanted hair
EPILATORS > EPILATOR
EPILEPSY *n* disorder of the nervous system causing loss of consciousness and sometimes convulsions
EPILEPTIC *adj* of or having epilepsy ▷ *n* person who has epilepsy
EPILIMNIA *n* upper layers of water in lakes
EPILITHIC *adj* (of plants) growing on the surface of rock
EPILOBIUM *n* willow-herb
EPILOG *same as* > EPILOGUE
EPILOGIC > EPILOGUE
EPILOGISE *same as* > EPILOGIZE
EPILOGIST > EPILOGUE
EPILOGIZE *vb* write or deliver epilogues
EPILOGS > EPILOG
EPILOGUE *n* short speech or poem at the end of a literary work, esp a play
EPILOGUED *adj* followed by an epilogue
EPILOGUES > EPILOGUE
EPIMER *n* isomer
EPIMERASE *n* enzyme that interconverts epimers
EPIMERE *n* dorsal part of the mesoderm of a vertebrate embryo, consisting of a series of segments
EPIMERES > EPIMERE
EPIMERIC > EPIMERISM
EPIMERISM *n* optical isomerism in which isomers can form about asymmetric atoms within the molecule
EPIMERS > EPIMER
EPIMYSIA > EPIMYSIUM
EPIMYSIUM *n* sheath of connective tissue that encloses a skeletal muscle
EPINAOI > EPINAOS
EPINAOS *n* rear vestibule
EPINASTIC > EPINASTY
EPINASTY *n* increased growth of the upper surface of a plant part, such as a leaf, resulting in a downward bending of the part
EPINEURAL *adj* outside a nerve trunk
EPINEURIA *n* sheaths of connective tissue around bundles of nerve fibres
EPINICIAN > EPINICION
EPINICION *n* victory song
EPINIKIAN > EPINICION
EPINIKION *same as* > EPINICION
EPINOSIC *adj* unhealthy
EPIPHANIC > EPIPHANY
EPIPHANY *n* moment of great or sudden revelation
EPIPHRAGM *n* disc of calcium phosphate and mucilage secreted by snails over the aperture of their shells before hibernation
EPIPHYSES > EPIPHYSIS
EPIPHYSIS *n* end of a long bone, initially separated from the shaft (diaphysis) by a section of cartilage that eventually ossifies so that the two portions fuse together
EPIPHYTAL > EPIPHYTE
EPIPHYTE *n* plant that grows on another plant but is not parasitic on it
EPIPHYTES > EPIPHYTE
EPIPHYTIC > EPIPHYTE
EPIPLOIC > EPIPLOON
EPIPLOON *n* greater omentum
EPIPLOONS > EPIPLOON
EPIPOLIC > EPIPOLISM
EPIPOLISM *n* fluorescence
EPIROGENY *n* formation and submergence of continents by broad, relatively slow, displacements of the earth's crust
EPIRRHEMA *n* address in Greek comedy
EPISCIA *n* creeping plant
EPISCIAS > EPISCIA
EPISCOPAL *adj* of or governed by bishops
EPISCOPE *n* optical device that projects an enlarged image of an opaque object, such as a printed page or photographic print, onto a screen by means of reflected light
EPISCOPES > EPISCOPE
EPISCOPY *n* area overseen
EPISEMON *n* emblem
EPISEMONS > EPISEMON
EPISODAL *same as* > EPISODIC
EPISODE *n* incident in a series of incidents
EPISODES > EPISODE
EPISODIAL *same as* > EPISODIC
EPISODIC *adj* occurring at irregular intervals
EPISOMAL > EPISOME
EPISOME *n* unit of genetic material (DNA) in bacteria, such as a plasmid, that can either replicate independently or can be integrated into the host chromosome
EPISOMES > EPISOME
EPISPERM *n* protective outer layer of certain seeds
EPISPERMS > EPISPERM
EPISPORE *n* outer layer of certain spores
EPISPORES > EPISPORE
EPISTASES > EPISTASIS
EPISTASIS *n* scum on the surface of a liquid, esp on an old specimen of urine
EPISTASY *same as* > EPISTASIS
EPISTATIC > EPISTASIS
EPISTAXES > EPISTAXIS
EPISTAXIS *technical name for* > NOSEBLEED
EPISTEMIC *adj* of or relating to knowledge or epistemology
EPISTERNA *n* parts of the sternums of mammals
EPISTLE *n* letter, esp of an apostle ▷ *vb* preface
EPISTLED > EPISTLE
EPISTLER *n* writer of an epistle or epistles
EPISTLERS > EPISTLER
EPISTLES > EPISTLE
EPISTLING > EPISTLE
EPISTOLER *same as* > EPISTLER
EPISTOLET *n* short letter
EPISTOLIC > EPISTLE
EPISTOME *n* area between the mouth and antennae of crustaceans
EPISTOMES > EPISTOME
EPISTYLE *n* lowest part of an entablature that bears on the columns
EPISTYLES > EPISTYLE
EPITAPH *n* commemorative inscription on a tomb ▷ *vb* compose an epitaph
EPITAPHED > EPITAPH
EPITAPHER > EPITAPH
EPITAPHIC > EPITAPH
EPITAPHS > EPITAPH
EPITASES > EPITASIS
EPITASIS *n* (in classical drama) part of a play in which the main action develops
EPITAXES > EPITAXIS
EPITAXIAL > EPITAXY
EPITAXIC > EPITAXY
EPITAXIES > EPITAXY
EPITAXIS *same as* > EPITAXY
EPITAXY *n* growth of a thin layer on the surface of a crystal so that the layer has the same structure as the underlying crystal
EPITHECA *n* outer and older layer of the cell wall of a diatom
EPITHECAE > EPITHECA
EPITHELIA *n* animal tissues consisting of one or more layers of closely packed cells covering the external and internal surfaces of the body
EPITHEM *n* external topical application
EPITHEMA > EPITHEM
EPITHEMS > EPITHEM
EPITHESES > EPITHESIS
EPITHESIS *n* addition of a letter to the end of a word, so that its sense does not change
EPITHET *n* descriptive word or name ▷ *vb* name
EPITHETED > EPITHET
EPITHETIC > EPITHET
EPITHETON *same as* > EPITHET
EPITHETS > EPITHET
EPITOME *n* typical example
EPITOMES > EPITOME
EPITOMIC > EPITOME
EPITOMISE *same as* > EPITOMIZE
EPITOMIST > EPITOMIZE
EPITOMIZE *vb* be the epitome of
EPITONIC *adj* undergoing too great a strain
EPITOPE *n* site on an antigen at which a specific antibody becomes attached
EPITOPES > EPITOPE
EPITRITE *n* metrical foot with three long syllables and one short one
EPITRITES > EPITRITE
EPIZEUXES > EPIZEUXIS
EPIZEUXIS *n* deliberate repetition of a word
EPIZOA > EPIZOON
EPIZOAN *same as* > EPIZOON
EPIZOANS > EPIZOAN
EPIZOIC *adj* (of an animal or plant) growing or living on the exterior of a living animal
EPIZOISM > EPIZOIC
EPIZOISMS > EPIZOIC
EPIZOITE *n* organism that lives on an animal but is not parasitic on it
EPIZOITES > EPIZOITE
EPIZOON *n* animal, such as a parasite, that lives on the body of another animal
EPIZOOTIC *adj* (of a disease) suddenly and temporarily affecting a large number of animals over a large area ▷ *n* epizootic disease
EPIZOOTY *n* animal disease
EPOCH *n* period of notable events
EPOCHA *same as* > EPOCH
EPOCHAL > EPOCH
EPOCHALLY > EPOCH
EPOCHAS > EPOCHA
EPOCHS > EPOCH
EPODE *n* part of a lyric ode that follows the strophe and the antistrophe
EPODES > EPODE
EPODIC > EPODE
EPONYM *n* name, esp a place name, derived from the name of a real or mythical person, as for example *Constantinople* from *Constantine I*
EPONYMIC > EPONYM
EPONYMIES > EPONYMY
EPONYMOUS *adj* after whom a book, play, etc is named

EPONYMS > EPONYM
EPONYMY *n* derivation of names of places, etc, from those of persons
EPOPEE *n* epic poem
EPOPEES > EPOPEE
EPOPOEIA *same as* > EPOPEE
EPOPOEIAS > EPOPOEIA
EPOPT *n* one initiated into mysteries
EPOPTS > EPOPT
EPOS *n* body of poetry in which the tradition of a people is conveyed, esp a group of poems concerned with a common epic theme
EPOSES > EPOS
EPOXIDE *n* compound containing an oxygen atom joined to two different groups that are themselves joined to other groups
EPOXIDES > EPOXIDE
EPOXIDISE *same as* > EPOXIDIZE
EPOXIDIZE *vb* form an epoxide
EPOXIED > EPOXY
EPOXIES > EPOXY
EPOXY *adj* of or containing an oxygen atom joined to two different groups that are themselves joined to other groups ▷ *n* epoxy resin ▷ *vb* glue with epoxy resin
EPOXYED > EPOXY
EPOXYING > EPOXY
EPRIS *adj* enamoured
EPRISE *feminine form of* > EPRIS
EPROM *n* type of computer memory
EPROMS > EPROM
EPSILON *n* fifth letter of the Greek alphabet, a short vowel, transliterated as *e*
EPSILONIC *adj* of or relating to an arbitrary small quantity
EPSILONS > EPSILON
EPSOMITE *n* sulphate of magnesium
EPSOMITES > EPSOMITE
EPUISE *adj* exhausted
EPUISEE *feminine form of* > EPUISE
EPULARY *adj* of or relating to feasting
EPULATION *n* feasting
EPULIDES > EPULIS
EPULIS *n* swelling of the gum, usually as a result of fibrous hyperplasia
EPULISES > EPULIS
EPULOTIC *n* scarring
EPULOTICS > EPULOTIC
EPURATE *vb* purify
EPURATED > EPURATE
EPURATES > EPURATE
EPURATING > EPURATE
EPURATION > EPURATE
EPYLLIA > EPYLLION
EPYLLION *n* miniature epic
EPYLLIONS > EPYLLION
EQUABLE *adj* even-tempered
EQUABLY > EQUABLE
EQUAL *adj* identical in size, quantity, degree, etc ▷ *n* person or thing equal to another ▷ *vb* be equal to
EQUALED > EQUAL
EQUALI *pl n* pieces for a group of instruments of the same kind
EQUALING > EQUAL
EQUALISE *same as* > EQUALIZE
EQUALISED > EQUALISE
EQUALISER *same as* > EQUALIZER
EQUALISES > EQUALISE
EQUALITY *n* state of being equal
EQUALIZE *vb* make or become equal
EQUALIZED > EQUALIZE
EQUALIZER *n* person or thing that equalizes, esp a device to counterbalance opposing forces
EQUALIZES > EQUALIZE
EQUALLED > EQUAL
EQUALLING > EQUAL
EQUALLY > EQUAL
EQUALNESS *n* equality
EQUALS > EQUAL
EQUANT *n* circle in which a planet was formerly believed to move
EQUANTS > EQUANT
EQUATABLE > EQUATE
EQUATE *vb* make or regard as equivalent
EQUATED > EQUATE
EQUATES > EQUATE
EQUATING > EQUATE
EQUATION *n* mathematical statement that two expressions are equal
EQUATIONS > EQUATION
EQUATOR *n* imaginary circle round the earth, equidistant from the poles
EQUATORS > EQUATOR
EQUERRIES > EQUERRY
EQUERRY *n* officer who acts as an attendant to a member of a royal family
EQUID *n* any animal of the horse family
EQUIDS > EQUID
EQUIMOLAL *adj* having an equal number of moles
EQUIMOLAR *same as* > EQUIMOLAL
EQUINAL *same as* > EQUINE
EQUINE *adj* of or like a horse ▷ *n* any animal of the horse family
EQUINELY > EQUINE
EQUINES > EQUINE
EQUINIA *n* glanders
EQUINIAS > EQUINIA
EQUINITY *n* horse-like nature
EQUINOX *n* time of year when day and night are of equal length
EQUINOXES > EQUINOX
EQUIP *vb* provide with supplies, components, etc
EQUIPAGE *n* horse-drawn carriage, esp one elegantly equipped and attended by liveried footmen ▷ *vb* equip
EQUIPAGED > EQUIPAGE
EQUIPAGES > EQUIPAGE
EQUIPE *n* (esp in motor racing) team
EQUIPES > EQUIPE
EQUIPMENT *n* set of tools or devices used for a particular purpose
EQUIPOISE *n* perfect balance ▷ *vb* offset or balance in weight or force
EQUIPPED > EQUIP
EQUIPPER > EQUIP
EQUIPPERS > EQUIP
EQUIPPING > EQUIP
EQUIPS > EQUIP
EQUISETA > EQUISETUM
EQUISETIC > EQUISETUM
EQUISETUM *n* tracheophyte plant of the genus *Equisetum*
EQUITABLE *adj* fair and reasonable
EQUITABLY > EQUITABLE
EQUITANT *adj* (of a leaf) having the base folded around the stem so that it overlaps the leaf above and opposite
EQUITES *pl n* cavalry
EQUITIES > EQUITY
EQUITY *n* fairness
EQUIVALVE *adj* equipped with identical valves
EQUIVOCAL *adj* ambiguous
EQUIVOKE *same as* > EQUIVOQUE
EQUIVOKES > EQUIVOKE
EQUIVOQUE *n* play on words
ER *interj* sound made when hesitating in speech
ERA *n* period of time considered as distinctive
ERADIATE *less common word for* > RADIATE
ERADIATED > ERADIATE
ERADIATES > ERADIATE
ERADICANT > ERADICATE
ERADICATE *vb* destroy completely
ERAS > ERA
ERASABLE > ERASE
ERASE *vb* destroy all traces of
ERASED > ERASE
ERASEMENT > ERASE
ERASER *n* object for erasing something written
ERASERS > ERASER
ERASES > ERASE
ERASING > ERASE
ERASION *n* act of erasing
ERASIONS > ERASION
ERASURE *n* erasing
ERASURES > ERASURE
ERATHEM *n* stratum of rocks representing a specific geological era
ERATHEMS > ERATHEM
ERBIA *n* oxide of erbium
ERBIAS > ERBIA
ERBIUM *n* metallic element of the lanthanide series
ERBIUMS > ERBIUM
ERE *prep* before ▷ *vb* plough
ERECT *vb* build ▷ *adj* upright
ERECTABLE > ERECT
ERECTED > ERECT
ERECTER *same as* > ERECTOR
ERECTERS > ERECTER
ERECTILE *adj* capable of becoming erect from sexual excitement
ERECTING > ERECT
ERECTION *n* act of erecting or the state of being erected
ERECTIONS > ERECTION
ERECTIVE *adj* producing erections
ERECTLY > ERECT
ERECTNESS > ERECT
ERECTOR *n* any muscle that raises a part or makes it erect
ERECTORS > ERECTOR
ERECTS > ERECT
ERED > ERE
ERELONG *adv* before long
EREMIC *adj* of or relating to deserts
EREMITAL > EREMITE
EREMITE *n* Christian hermit
EREMITES > EREMITE
EREMITIC > EREMITE
EREMITISH > EREMITE
EREMITISM > EREMITE
EREMURI > EREMURUS
EREMURUS *n* type of herb
ERENOW *adv* long before the present
EREPSIN *n* mixture of proteolytic enzymes secreted by the small intestine
EREPSINS > EREPSIN
ERES > ERE
ERETHIC > ERETHISM
ERETHISM *n* abnormally high degree of irritability or sensitivity in any part of the body
ERETHISMS > ERETHISM
ERETHITIC > ERETHISM
EREV *n* day before
EREVS > EREV
EREWHILE *adv* short time ago
EREWHILES *same as* > EREWHILE
ERF *n* plot of land, usually urban, marked off for

building purposes
ERG *same as* > ERGOMETER
ERGASTIC *adj* consisting of the non-living by-products of protoplasmic activity
ERGATANER *n* wingless male ant
ERGATE *n* worker ant
ERGATES > ERGATE
ERGATIVE *adj* denoting a type of verb that takes the same noun as either direct object or as subject, with equivalent meaning. Thus, "fuse" is an ergative verb: "He fused the lights" and "The lights fused" have equivalent meaning ▷ *n* ergative verb
ERGATIVES > ERGATIVE
ERGATOID > ERGATE
ERGO *same as* > ERGOMETER
ERGODIC *adj* of or relating to the probability that any state will recur
ERGOGENIC *adj* giving energy
ERGOGRAM *n* tracing produced by an ergograph
ERGOGRAMS > ERGOGRAM
ERGOGRAPH *n* instrument that measures and records the amount of work a muscle does during contraction, its rate of fatigue, etc
ERGOMANIA *n* excessive desire to work
ERGOMETER *n* dynamometer
ERGOMETRY *n* measurement of work done
ERGON *n* work
ERGONOMIC *adj* designed to minimize effort
ERGONS > ERGON
ERGOS > ERGO
ERGOT *n* fungal disease of cereal
ERGOTIC > ERGOT
ERGOTISE *same as* > ERGOTIZE
ERGOTISED > ERGOTISE
ERGOTISES > ERGOTISE
ERGOTISM *n* ergot poisoning, producing either burning pains and eventually gangrene in the limbs or itching skin and convulsions
ERGOTISMS > ERGOTISM
ERGOTIZE *vb* inflict ergotism upon
ERGOTIZED > ERGOTIZE
ERGOTIZES > ERGOTIZE
ERGOTS > ERGOT
ERGS > ERG
ERIACH *same as* > ERIC
ERIACHS > ERIACH
ERIC *n* (in old Irish law) fine paid by a murderer to the family of his victim
ERICA *n* genus of plants including heathers
ERICAS > ERICA
ERICK *same as* > ERIC
ERICKS > ERICK
ERICOID *adj* (of leaves) small and tough, resembling those of heather
ERICS > ERIC
ERIGERON *n* any plant of the genus *Erigeron*
ERIGERONS > ERIGERON
ERING > ERE
ERINGO *same as* > ERYNGO
ERINGOES > ERINGO
ERINGOS > ERINGO
ERINITE *n* arsenate of copper
ERINITES > ERINITE
ERINUS *n* any plant of the scrophulariaceous genus *Erinus*
ERINUSES > ERINUS
ERIOMETER *n* device for measuring the diameters of minute particles or fibres
ERIONITE *n* common form of zeolite
ERIONITES > ERIONITE
ERIOPHYID *n* type of mite
ERISTIC *adj* of, relating, or given to controversy or logical disputation, esp for its own sake ▷ *n* person who engages in logical disputes
ERISTICAL *same as* > ERISTIC
ERISTICS > ERISTIC
ERK *n* aircraftman or naval rating
ERKS > ERK
ERLANG *n* unit of traffic intensity in a telephone system equal to the intensity for a specific period when the average number of simultaneous calls is unity
ERLANGS > ERLANG
ERLKING *n* malevolent spirit who carries off children
ERLKINGS > ERLKING
ERMELIN *n* ermine
ERMELINS > ERMELIN
ERMINE *n* stoat in northern regions, where it has a white winter coat with a black-tipped tail
ERMINED *adj* clad in the fur of the ermine
ERMINES > ERMINE
ERN *archaic variant of* > EARN
ERNE *n* fish-eating (European) sea eagle
ERNED > ERN
ERNES > ERNE
ERNING > ERN
ERNS > ERN
ERODABLE > ERODE
ERODE *vb* wear away
ERODED > ERODE
ERODENT > ERODE
ERODENTS > ERODE
ERODES > ERODE
ERODIBLE > ERODE
ERODING > ERODE
ERODIUM *n* type of geranium
ERODIUMS > ERODIUM
EROGENIC *same as* > EROGENOUS
EROGENOUS *adj* sensitive to sexual stimulation
EROS *n* lust
EROSE *adj* jagged or uneven, as though gnawed or bitten
EROSELY > EROSE
EROSES > EROS
EROSIBLE *adj* able to be eroded
EROSION *n* wearing away of rocks or soil by the action of water, ice, or wind
EROSIONAL > EROSION
EROSIONS > EROSION
EROSIVE > EROSION
EROSIVITY > EROSION
EROSTRATE *adj* without a beak
EROTEMA *n* rhetorical question
EROTEMAS > EROTEMA
EROTEME *same as* > EROTEMA
EROTEMES > EROTEME
EROTESES > EROTESIS
EROTESIS *same as* > EROTEMA
EROTETIC *adj* pertaining to a rhetorical question
EROTIC *adj* relating to sexual pleasure or desire ▷ *n* person who has strong sexual desires or is especially responsive to sexual stimulation
EROTICA *n* sexual literature or art
EROTICAL *adj* erotic
EROTICISE *same as* > EROTICIZE
EROTICISM *n* erotic quality or nature
EROTICIST > EROTICISM
EROTICIZE *vb* regard or present in a sexual way
EROTICS > EROTIC
EROTISE *same as* > EROTIZE
EROTISED > EROTISE
EROTISES > EROTISE
EROTISING > EROTISE
EROTISM *same as* > EROTICISM
EROTISMS > EROTISM
EROTIZE *vb* make erotic
EROTIZED > EROTIZE
EROTIZES > EROTIZE
EROTIZING > EROTIZE
EROTOLOGY *n* study of erotic stimuli and sexual behaviour
ERR *vb* make a mistake
ERRABLE *adj* capable of making a mistake
ERRANCIES > ERRANCY
ERRANCY *n* state or an instance of erring or a tendency to err
ERRAND *n* short trip to do something for someone
ERRANDS > ERRAND
ERRANT *adj* behaving in a manner considered to be unacceptable ▷ *n* knight-errant
ERRANTLY > ERRANT
ERRANTRY *n* way of life of a knight errant
ERRANTS > ERRANT
ERRATA > ERRATUM
ERRATAS *informal variant of* > ERRATA
ERRATIC *adj* irregular or unpredictable ▷ *n* rock that has been transported by glacial action
ERRATICAL *adj* erratic
ERRATICS > ERRATIC
ERRATUM *n* error in writing or printing
ERRED > ERR
ERRHINE *adj* causing nasal secretion ▷ *n* errhine drug or agent
ERRHINES > ERRHINE
ERRING > ERR
ERRINGLY > ERR
ERRINGS > ERR
ERRONEOUS *adj* incorrect, mistaken
ERROR *n* mistake, inaccuracy, or misjudgment
ERRORIST *n* one who makes errors
ERRORISTS > ERRORIST
ERRORLESS > ERROR
ERRORS > ERROR
ERRS > ERR
ERS *same as* > ERVIL
ERSATZ *adj* made in imitation ▷ *n* ersatz substance or article
ERSATZES > ERSATZ
ERSES > ERS
ERST *adv* long ago
ERSTWHILE *adj* former ▷ *adv* formerly
ERUCIC as in *erucic acid* crystalline fatty acid derived from rapeseed, mustard seed and wallflower seed
ERUCIFORM *adj* resembling a caterpillar
ERUCT *vb* belch
ERUCTATE *same as* > ERUCT
ERUCTATED > ERUCTATE
ERUCTATES > ERUCTATE
ERUCTED > ERUCT
ERUCTING > ERUCT
ERUCTS > ERUCT
ERUDITE *adj* having great academic knowledge ▷ *n* erudite person
ERUDITELY > ERUDITE
ERUDITES > ERUDITE

ERUDITION > ERUDITE
ERUGO *n* verdigris
ERUGOS > ERUGO
ERUMPENT *adj* bursting out or (esp of plant parts) developing as though bursting through an overlying structure
ERUPT *vb* eject (steam, water, or volcanic material) violently
ERUPTED > ERUPT
ERUPTIBLE > ERUPT
ERUPTING > ERUPT
ERUPTION > ERUPT
ERUPTIONS > ERUPT
ERUPTIVE *adj* erupting or tending to erupt ▷ *n* type of volcanic rock
ERUPTIVES > ERUPTIVE
ERUPTS > ERUPT
ERUV *n* area, circumscribed by a symbolic line, within which certain activities forbidden to Orthodox Jews on the Sabbath are permitted
ERUVIM > ERUV
ERUVIN > ERUV
ERUVS > ERUV
ERVALENTA *n* health food made from lentil and barley flour
ERVEN > ERF
ERVIL *n* type of vetch
ERVILS > ERVIL
ERYNGIUM *n* any plant of the temperate and subtropical perennial umbelliferous genus *Eryngium*
ERYNGIUMS > ERYNGIUM
ERYNGO *n* any umbelliferous plant of the genus *Eryngium*
ERYNGOES > ERYNGO
ERYNGOS > ERYNGO
ERYTHEMA *n* patchy inflammation of the skin
ERYTHEMAL > ERYTHEMA
ERYTHEMAS > ERYTHEMA
ERYTHEMIC > ERYTHEMA
ERYTHRINA *n* tropical tree with red flowers
ERYTHRISM *n* abnormal red coloration, as in plumage or hair
ERYTHRITE *n* sweet crystalline compound extacted from certain algae and lichens
ERYTHROID *adj* red or reddish
ERYTHRON *n* red blood cells and their related tissues
ERYTHRONS > ERYTHRON
ES *n* letter S
ESCALADE *n* assault by the use of ladders, esp on a fortification ▷ *vb* gain access to (a place) by the use of ladders
ESCALADED > ESCALADE
ESCALADER > ESCALADE
ESCALADES > ESCALADE
ESCALADO *n* escalade
ESCALATE *vb* increase in extent or intensity
ESCALATED > ESCALATE
ESCALATES > ESCALATE
ESCALATOR *n* moving staircase
ESCALIER *n* staircase
ESCALIERS > ESCALIER
ESCALLOP *another word for* > SCALLOP
ESCALLOPS > ESCALLOP
ESCALOP *another word for* > SCALLOP
ESCALOPE *n* thin slice of meat, esp veal
ESCALOPED > ESCALOP
ESCALOPES > ESCALOPE
ESCALOPS > ESCALOP
ESCAPABLE > ESCAPE
ESCAPADE *n* mischievous adventure
ESCAPADES > ESCAPADE
ESCAPADO *n* escaped criminal
ESCAPE *vb* get free (of) ▷ *n* act of escaping
ESCAPED > ESCAPE
ESCAPEE *n* person who has escaped
ESCAPEES > ESCAPEE
ESCAPER > ESCAPE
ESCAPERS > ESCAPE
ESCAPES > ESCAPE
ESCAPING > ESCAPE
ESCAPISM *n* taking refuge in fantasy to avoid unpleasant reality
ESCAPISMS > ESCAPISM
ESCAPIST > ESCAPISM
ESCAPISTS > ESCAPISM
ESCAR *same as* > ESKER
ESCARGOT *n* variety of edible snail, usually eaten with a sauce made of melted butter and garlic
ESCARGOTS > ESCARGOT
ESCAROLE *n* variety of endive with broad leaves, used in salads
ESCAROLES > ESCAROLE
ESCARP *n* inner side of the ditch separating besiegers and besieged ▷ *vb* make into a slope
ESCARPED > ESCARP
ESCARPING > ESCARP
ESCARPS > ESCARP
ESCARS > ESCAR
ESCHALOT *another name for a* > SHALLOT
ESCHALOTS > ESCHALOT
ESCHAR *n* dry scab or slough, esp one following a burn or cauterization of the skin
ESCHARS > ESCHAR
ESCHEAT *n* private possessions that become state property in the absence of an heir ▷ *vb* attain such property
ESCHEATED > ESCHEAT
ESCHEATOR > ESCHEAT
ESCHEATS > ESCHEAT
ESCHEW *vb* abstain from, avoid
ESCHEWAL > ESCHEW
ESCHEWALS > ESCHEW
ESCHEWED > ESCHEW
ESCHEWER > ESCHEW
ESCHEWERS > ESCHEW
ESCHEWING > ESCHEW
ESCHEWS > ESCHEW
ESCLANDRE *n* scandal or notoriety
ESCOLAR *n* slender spiny-finned fish
ESCOLARS > ESCOLAR
ESCOPETTE *n* carbine
ESCORT *n* people or vehicles accompanying another person for protection or as an honour ▷ *vb* act as an escort to
ESCORTAGE > ESCORT
ESCORTED > ESCORT
ESCORTING > ESCORT
ESCORTS > ESCORT
ESCOT *vb* maintain
ESCOTED > ESCOT
ESCOTING > ESCOT
ESCOTS > ESCOT
ESCOTTED > ESCOT
ESCOTTING > ESCOT
ESCRIBANO *n* clerk
ESCRIBE *vb* draw (a circle) so that it is tangential to one side of a triangle and to the other two sides produced
ESCRIBED > ESCRIBE
ESCRIBES > ESCRIBE
ESCRIBING > ESCRIBE
ESCROC *n* conman
ESCROCS > ESCROC
ESCROL *same as* > ESCROLL
ESCROLL *n* scroll
ESCROLLS > ESCROLL
ESCROLS > ESCROL
ESCROW *n* money, goods, or a written document, such as a contract bond, delivered to a third party and held by him pending fulfilment of some condition ▷ *vb* place (money, a document, etc) in escrow
ESCROWED > ESCROW
ESCROWING > ESCROW
ESCROWS > ESCROW
ESCUAGE *(in medieval Europe) another word for* > SCUTAGE
ESCUAGES > ESCUAGE
ESCUDO *n* former monetary unit of Portugal
ESCUDOS > ESCUDO
ESCULENT *adj* edible ▷ *n* any edible substance
ESCULENTS > ESCULENT
ESEMPLASY *n* unification
ESERINE *n* crystalline alkaloid
ESERINES > ESERINE
ESES > ES
ESILE *n* vinegar
ESILES > ESILE
ESKAR *same as* > ESKER
ESKARS > ESKAR
ESKER *n* long winding ridge of gravel, sand, etc, originally deposited by a meltwater stream running under a glacier
ESKERS > ESKER
ESKIES > ESKY
ESKY *n* portable insulated container for keeping food and drink cool
ESLOIN *same as* > ELOIGN
ESLOINED > ESLOIN
ESLOINING > ESLOIN
ESLOINS > ESLOIN
ESLOYNE *same as* > ELOIGN
ESLOYNED > ESLOYNE
ESLOYNES > ESLOYNE
ESLOYNING > ESLOYNE
ESNE *n* household slave
ESNECIES > ESNECY
ESNECY *n* right of the eldest daughter to make the first choice when dividing inheritance
ESNES > ESNE
ESOPHAGI > ESOPHAGUS
ESOPHAGUS *n* part of the alimentary canal between the pharynx and the stomach
ESOTERIC *adj* understood by only a small number of people with special knowledge
ESOTERICA *pl n* esoteric things
ESOTERIES > ESOTERIC
ESOTERISM > ESOTERIC
ESOTERY > ESOTERIC
ESOTROPIA *n* condition in which eye turns inwards
ESOTROPIC > ESOTROPIA
ESPADA *n* sword
ESPADAS > ESPADA
ESPAGNOLE *n* tomato and sherry sauce
ESPALIER *n* shrub or fruit tree trained to grow flat ▷ *vb* train (a plant) on an espalier
ESPALIERS > ESPALIER
ESPANOL *n* Spanish person
ESPANOLES > ESPANOL
ESPARTO *n* grass of S Europe and N Africa used for making rope etc
ESPARTOS > ESPARTO
ESPECIAL *adj* special
ESPERANCE *n* hope or expectation
ESPIAL *n* act or fact of being seen or discovered
ESPIALS > ESPIAL
ESPIED > ESPY
ESPIEGLE *adj* playful
ESPIER > ESPY
ESPIERS > ESPY
ESPIES > ESPY
ESPIONAGE *n* spying
ESPLANADE *n* wide open road used as a public

promenade
ESPOUSAL *n* adoption or support
ESPOUSALS > ESPOUSAL
ESPOUSE *vb* adopt or give support to (a cause etc)
ESPOUSED > ESPOUSE
ESPOUSER > ESPOUSE
ESPOUSERS > ESPOUSE
ESPOUSES > ESPOUSE
ESPOUSING > ESPOUSE
ESPRESSO *n* strong coffee made by forcing steam or boiling water through ground coffee beans
ESPRESSOS > ESPRESSO
ESPRIT *n* spirit, liveliness, or wit
ESPRITS > ESPRIT
ESPUMOSO *n* sparkling wine
ESPUMOSOS > ESPUMOSO
ESPY *vb* catch sight of
ESPYING > ESPY
ESQUIRE *n* courtesy title placed after a man's name ▷ *vb* escort
ESQUIRED > ESQUIRE
ESQUIRES > ESQUIRE
ESQUIRESS *feminine form of* > ESQUIRE
ESQUIRING > ESQUIRE
ESQUISSE *n* sketch
ESQUISSES > ESQUISSE
ESS *n* letter S
ESSAY *n* short literary composition ▷ *vb* attempt
ESSAYED > ESSAY
ESSAYER > ESSAY
ESSAYERS > ESSAY
ESSAYETTE *n* short essay
ESSAYING > ESSAY
ESSAYISH > ESSAY
ESSAYIST *n* person who writes essays
ESSAYISTS > ESSAYIST
ESSAYS > ESSAY
ESSE *n* existence
ESSENCE *n* most important feature of a thing which determines its identity
ESSENCES > ESSENCE
ESSENTIAL *adj* vitally important ▷ *n* something fundamental or indispensable
ESSES > ESS
ESSIVE *n* grammatical case
ESSIVES > ESSIVE
ESSOIN *n* excuse
ESSOINER > ESSOIN
ESSOINERS > ESSOIN
ESSOINS > ESSOIN
ESSONITE *variant spelling of* > HESSONITE
ESSONITES > ESSONITE
ESSOYNE *same as* > ESSOIN
ESSOYNES > ESSOYNE
EST *n* treatment intended to help people towards psychological growth, in which they spend many hours in large groups, deprived of food and water and hectored by stewards
ESTABLISH *vb* set up on a permanent basis
ESTACADE *n* defensive arrangement of stakes
ESTACADES > ESTACADE
ESTAFETTE *n* mounted courier
ESTAMINET *n* small café, bar, or bistro, esp a shabby one
ESTANCIA *n* (in Spanish America) a large estate or cattle ranch
ESTANCIAS > ESTANCIA
ESTATE *n* landed property ▷ *vb* provide with an estate
ESTATED > ESTATE
ESTATES > ESTATE
ESTATING > ESTATE
ESTEEM *n* high regard ▷ *vb* think highly of
ESTEEMED > ESTEEM
ESTEEMING > ESTEEM
ESTEEMS > ESTEEM
ESTER *n* compound produced by the reaction between an acid and an alcohol
ESTERASE *n* any of a group of enzymes that hydrolyse esters into alcohols and acids
ESTERASES > ESTERASE
ESTERIFY *vb* change or cause to change into an ester
ESTERS > ESTER
ESTHESES > ESTHESIS
ESTHESIA *US spelling of* > AESTHESIA
ESTHESIAS > ESTHESIA
ESTHESIS *n* esthesia
ESTHETE *US spelling of* > AESTHETE
ESTHETES > ESTHETE
ESTHETIC > ESTHETE
ESTHETICS > ESTHETE
ESTIMABLE *adj* worthy of respect
ESTIMABLY > ESTIMABLE
ESTIMATE *vb* calculate roughly ▷ *n* approximate calculation
ESTIMATED > ESTIMATE
ESTIMATES > ESTIMATE
ESTIMATOR *n* person or thing that estimates
ESTIVAL *usual US spelling of* > AESTIVAL
ESTIVATE *usual US spelling of* > AESTIVATE
ESTIVATED > ESTIVATE
ESTIVATES > ESTIVATE
ESTIVATOR > ESTIVATE
ESTOC *n* short stabbing sword
ESTOCS > ESTOC
ESTOILE *n* heraldic star with wavy points
ESTOILES > ESTOILE
ESTOP *vb* preclude by estoppel
ESTOPPAGE > ESTOP
ESTOPPED > ESTOP
ESTOPPEL *n* rule of evidence whereby a person is precluded from denying the truth of a statement of facts he has previously asserted
ESTOPPELS > ESTOPPEL
ESTOPPING > ESTOP
ESTOPS > ESTOP
ESTOVER *same as* > ESTOVERS
ESTOVERS *pl n* right allowed by law to tenants of land to cut timber, esp for fuel and repairs
ESTRADE *n* dais or raised platform
ESTRADES > ESTRADE
ESTRADIOL *n* most potent estrogenic hormone secreted by the mammalian ovary
ESTRAGON *another name for* > TARRAGON
ESTRAGONS > ESTRAGON
ESTRAL *US spelling of* > OESTRAL
ESTRANGE *vb* separate and live apart from (one's spouse)
ESTRANGED *adj* no longer living with one's spouse
ESTRANGER > ESTRANGE
ESTRANGES > ESTRANGE
ESTRAPADE *n* attempt by a horse to throw its rider
ESTRAY *n* stray domestic animal of unknown ownership ▷ *vb* stray
ESTRAYED > ESTRAY
ESTRAYING > ESTRAY
ESTRAYS > ESTRAY
ESTREAT *n* true copy of or extract from a court record ▷ *vb* enforce (a recognizance that has been forfeited) by sending an extract of the court record to the proper authority
ESTREATED > ESTREAT
ESTREATS > ESTREAT
ESTREPE *vb* lay waste
ESTREPED > ESTREPE
ESTREPES > ESTREPE
ESTREPING > ESTREPE
ESTRICH *n* ostrich
ESTRICHES > ESTRICH
ESTRIDGE *n* ostrich
ESTRIDGES > ESTRIDGE
ESTRILDID *n* weaver finch
ESTRIN *US spelling of* > OESTRIN
ESTRINS > ESTRIN
ESTRIOL *usual US spelling of* > OESTRIOL
ESTRIOLS > ESTRIOL
ESTRO *n* poetic inspiration
ESTROGEN *usual US spelling of* > OESTROGEN
ESTROGENS > ESTROGEN
ESTRONE *usual US spelling of* > OESTRONE
ESTRONES > ESTRONE
ESTROS > ESTRO
ESTROUS > ESTRUS
ESTRUAL > ESTRUS
ESTRUM *usual US spelling of* > OESTRUM
ESTRUMS > ESTRUM
ESTRUS *usual US spelling of* > OESTRUS
ESTRUSES > ESTRUS
ESTS > EST
ESTUARIAL > ESTUARY
ESTUARIAN > ESTUARY
ESTUARIES > ESTUARY
ESTUARINE *adj* formed or deposited in an estuary
ESTUARY *n* mouth of a river
ESURIENCE > ESURIENT
ESURIENCY > ESURIENT
ESURIENT *adj* greedy
ET *dialect past tense of* > EAT
ETA *n* seventh letter in the Greek alphabet, a long vowel sound
ETACISM *n* pronunciation of eta as a long vowel sound
ETACISMS > ETACISM
ETAERIO *n* aggregate fruit, as one consisting of drupes (raspberry) or achenes (traveller's joy)
ETAERIOS > ETAERIO
ETAGE *n* floor in a multi-storey building
ETAGERE *n* stand with open shelves for displaying ornaments, etc
ETAGERES > ETAGERE
ETAGES > ETAGE
ETALAGE *n* display
ETALAGES > ETALAGE
ETALON *n* device used in spectroscopy to measure wavelengths by interference effects produced by multiple reflections between parallel half-silvered glass or quartz plates
ETALONS > ETALON
ETAMIN *same as* > ETAMINE
ETAMINE *n* cotton or worsted fabric of loose weave, used for clothing, curtains, etc
ETAMINES > ETAMINE
ETAMINS > ETAMIN
ETAPE *n* public storehouse
ETAPES > ETAPE
ETAS > ETA
ETAT *n* state
ETATISM *same as* > ETATISME
ETATISME *n* authoritarian control by the state
ETATISMES > ETATISME
ETATISMS > ETATISM
ETATIST > ETATISME
ETATISTE > ETATISME
ETATISTES > ETATISME
ETATS > ETAT

ETCETERA *n* number of other items
ETCETERAS *pl n* miscellaneous extra things or people
ETCH *vb* wear away or cut the surface of (metal, glass, etc) with acid
ETCHANT *n* any acid or corrosive used for etching
ETCHANTS > ETCHANT
ETCHED > ETCH
ETCHER > ETCH
ETCHERS > ETCH
ETCHES > ETCH
ETCHING *n* picture printed from an etched metal plate
ETCHINGS > ETCHING
ETEN *n* giant
ETENS > ETEN
ETERNAL *adj* without beginning or end ▷ *n* eternal thing
ETERNALLY > ETERNAL
ETERNALS > ETERNAL
ETERNE *archaic or poetic word for* > ETERNAL
ETERNISE *same as* > ETERNIZE
ETERNISED > ETERNISE
ETERNISES > ETERNISE
ETERNITY *n* infinite time
ETERNIZE *vb* make eternal
ETERNIZED > ETERNIZE
ETERNIZES > ETERNIZE
ETESIAN *adj* (of NW winds) recurring annually in the summer in the E Mediterranean ▷ *n* etesian wind
ETESIANS > ETESIAN
ETH *same as* > EDH
ETHAL *n* cetyl alcohol
ETHALS > ETHAL
ETHANAL *n* colourless volatile pungent liquid
ETHANALS > ETHANAL
ETHANE *n* odourless flammable gas obtained from natural gas and petroleum
ETHANES > ETHANE
ETHANOATE *same as* > ACETATE
ETHANOIC as in *ethanoic acid* acetic acid
ETHANOL *same as* > ALCOHOL
ETHANOLS > ETHANOL
ETHANOYL *n* substance consisting of or containing the monovalent group CH_3CO-
ETHANOYLS > ETHANOYL
ETHE *adj* easy
ETHENE *same as* > ETHYLENE
ETHENES > ETHENE
ETHEPHON *n* synthetic plant-growth regulator
ETHEPHONS > ETHEPHON
ETHER *n* colourless sweet-smelling liquid used as an anaesthetic
ETHERCAP *n* spider
ETHERCAPS > ETHERCAP
ETHEREAL *adj* extremely delicate
ETHEREOUS *same as* > ETHEREAL
ETHERIAL *same as* > ETHEREAL
ETHERIC > ETHER
ETHERICAL > ETHER
ETHERIFY *vb* change (a compound, such as an alcohol) into an ether
ETHERION *n* gas formerly believed to exist in air
ETHERIONS > ETHERION
ETHERISE *same as* > ETHERIZE
ETHERISED > ETHERISE
ETHERISER > ETHERISE
ETHERISES > ETHERISE
ETHERISH > ETHER
ETHERISM *n* addiction to ether
ETHERISMS > ETHERISM
ETHERIST > ETHERISM
ETHERISTS > ETHERISM
ETHERIZE *vb* subject (a person) to the anaesthetic influence of ether fumes
ETHERIZED > ETHERIZE
ETHERIZER > ETHERIZE
ETHERIZES > ETHERIZE
ETHERS > ETHER
ETHIC *n* moral principle
ETHICAL *adj* of or based on a system of moral beliefs about right and wrong ▷ *n* drug available only by prescription
ETHICALLY > ETHICAL
ETHICALS > ETHICAL
ETHICIAN > ETHICS
ETHICIANS > ETHICS
ETHICISE *same as* > ETHICIZE
ETHICISED > ETHICISE
ETHICISES > ETHICISE
ETHICISM > ETHICS
ETHICISMS > ETHICS
ETHICIST > ETHICS
ETHICISTS > ETHICS
ETHICIZE *vb* make or consider as ethical
ETHICIZED > ETHICIZE
ETHICIZES > ETHICIZE
ETHICS *n* code of behaviour
ETHINYL *same as* > ETHYNYL
ETHINYLS > ETHINYL
ETHION *n* type of pesticide
ETHIONINE *n* type of amino acid
ETHIONS > ETHION
ETHIOPS *n* dark-coloured chemical compound
ETHIOPSES > ETHIOPS
ETHMOID *adj* denoting or relating to a bone of the skull that forms part of the eye socket and the nasal cavity ▷ *n* ethmoid bone
ETHMOIDAL *same as* > ETHMOID
ETHMOIDS > ETHMOID
ETHNARCH *n* ruler of a people or province, as in parts of the Roman and Byzantine Empires
ETHNARCHS > ETHNARCH
ETHNARCHY > ETHNARCH
ETHNIC *adj* relating to a people or group that shares a culture, religion, or language ▷ *n* member of an ethnic group, esp a minority group
ETHNICAL *same as* > ETHNIC
ETHNICISM *n* paganism
ETHNICITY > ETHNIC
ETHNICS > ETHNIC
ETHNOCIDE *n* extermination of a race
ETHNOGENY *n* branch of ethnology that deals with the origin of races or peoples
ETHNOLOGY *n* study of human races
ETHNONYM *n* name of ethnic group
ETHNONYMS > ETHNONYM
ETHNOS *n* ethnic group
ETHNOSES > ETHNOS
ETHOGRAM *n* description of animal's behaviour
ETHOGRAMS > ETHOGRAM
ETHOLOGIC > ETHOLOGY
ETHOLOGY *n* study of the behaviour of animals in their normal environment
ETHONONE *another name for* > KETENE
ETHONONES > ETHONONE
ETHOS *n* distinctive spirit and attitudes of a people, culture, etc
ETHOSES > ETHOS
ETHOXIDE *n* any of a class of saltlike compounds
ETHOXIDES > ETHOXIDE
ETHOXIES > ETHOXY
ETHOXY > ETHOXYL
ETHOXYL *n* univalent radical
ETHOXYLS > ETHOXYL
ETHS > ETH
ETHYL *adj* type of chemical hydrocarbon group
ETHYLATE *same as* > ETHOXIDE
ETHYLATED > ETHYLATE
ETHYLATES > ETHYLATE
ETHYLENE *n* poisonous gas used as an anaesthetic and as fuel
ETHYLENES > ETHYLENE
ETHYLENIC > ETHYLENE
ETHYLIC > ETHYL
ETHYLS > ETHYL
ETHYNE *another name for* > ACETYLENE
ETHYNES > ETHYNE
ETHYNYL *n* univalent radical
ETHYNYLS > ETHYNYL
ETIC *adj* (in linguistics) of or relating to items analyzed without consideration of their structural function
ETIOLATE *vb* become pale and weak
ETIOLATED > ETIOLATE
ETIOLATES > ETIOLATE
ETIOLIN *n* yellow pigment
ETIOLINS > ETIOLIN
ETIOLOGIC > ETIOLOGY
ETIOLOGY *n* study of the causes of diseases
ETIQUETTE *n* conventional code of conduct
ETNA *n* container used to heat liquids
ETNAS > ETNA
ETOILE *n* star
ETOILES > ETOILE
ETOUFFEE *n* spicy Cajun stew
ETOUFFEES > ETOUFFEE
ETOURDI *adj* foolish
ETOURDIE *feminine form of* > ETOURDI
ETRANGER *n* foreigner
ETRANGERE *feminine form of* > ETRANGER
ETRANGERS > ETRANGER
ETRENNE *n* New Year's gift
ETRENNES > ETRENNE
ETRIER *n* short portable ladder or set of webbing loops that can be attached to a karabiner or fifi hook
ETRIERS > ETRIER
ETTERCAP *n* spider
ETTERCAPS > ETTERCAP
ETTIN *n* giant
ETTINS > ETTIN
ETTLE *vb* intend
ETTLED > ETTLE
ETTLES > ETTLE
ETTLING > ETTLE
ETUDE *n* short musical composition for a solo instrument, esp intended as a technical exercise
ETUDES > ETUDE
ETUI *n* small usually ornamented case for holding needles, cosmetics, or other small articles
ETUIS > ETUI
ETWEE *same as* > ETUI
ETWEES > ETUI
ETYMA > ETYMON
ETYMIC > ETYMON
ETYMOLOGY *n* study of the sources and development of words
ETYMON *n* form of a word or morpheme, usually the earliest recorded form or a reconstructed form, from which another word or morpheme is derived: *the etymon of English "ewe" is Indo-European "owi"*
ETYMONS > ETYMON
ETYPIC *n* unable to conform to type
ETYPICAL *same as* > ETYPIC
EUCAIN *same as* > EUCAINE

EUCAINE *n* crystalline optically active substance formerly used as a local anaesthetic
EUCAINES > EUCAINE
EUCAINS > EUCAIN
EUCALYPT *n* myrtaceous tree
EUCALYPTI *n* eucalypts
EUCALYPTS > EUCALYPT
EUCARYON *same as* > EUKARYOTE
EUCARYONS > EUCARYON
EUCARYOT *same as* > EUKARYOTE
EUCARYOTE *same as* > EUKARYOTE
EUCARYOTS > EUCARYOT
EUCHARIS *n* any amaryllidaceous plant of the South American genus *Eucharis*, cultivated for their large white fragrant flowers
EUCHLORIC > EUCHLORIN
EUCHLORIN *n* explosive gaseous mixture of chlorine and chlorine dioxide
EUCHOLOGY *n* prayer formulary
EUCHRE *n* US and Canadian card game similar to écarté for two to four players, using a poker pack with joker ▷ *vb* prevent (a player) from making his contracted tricks
EUCHRED > EUCHRE
EUCHRES > EUCHRE
EUCHRING > EUCHRE
EUCLASE *n* brittle green gem
EUCLASES > EUCLASE
EUCLIDEAN *adj* of or relating to Euclid (Greek mathematician of Alexandria, 3rd century BC), esp his system of geometry
EUCLIDIAN *same as* > EUCLIDEAN
EUCRITE *n* type of stony meteorite
EUCRITES > EUCRITE
EUCRITIC > EUCRITE
EUCRYPHIA *n* any tree or shrub of the mostly evergreen genus *Eucryphia*, native to Australia and S America, having leaves of a dark lustrous green and white flowers: family *Eucryphiaceae*
EUCYCLIC *adj* (of plants) having the same number of leaves in each whorl
EUDAEMON *same as* > EUDEMON
EUDAEMONS > EUDAEMON
EUDAEMONY *same as* > EUDEMONIA
EUDAIMON *same as* > EUDAEMON
EUDAIMONS > EUDAIMON
EUDEMON *n* benevolent spirit or demon
EUDEMONIA *n* happiness, esp (in the philosophy of Aristotle) that resulting from a rational active life
EUDEMONIC > EUDEMONIA
EUDEMONS > EUDEMON
EUDIALYTE *n* brownish-red mineral
EUGARIE *another name for* > PIPI
EUGARIES > EUGARIE
EUGE *interj* well done!
EUGENIA *n* plant of the clove family
EUGENIAS > EUGENIA
EUGENIC > EUGENICS
EUGENICAL > EUGENICS
EUGENICS *n* study of methods of improving the human race
EUGENISM > EUGENICS
EUGENISMS > EUGENICS
EUGENIST > EUGENICS
EUGENISTS > EUGENICS
EUGENOL *n* colourless or pale yellow oily liquid substance with a spicy taste and an odour of cloves, used in perfumery
EUGENOLS > EUGENOL
EUGH *archaic form of* > YEW
EUGHEN *archaic form of* > YEW
EUGHS > EUGH
EUGLENA *n* any freshwater unicellular organism of the genus *Euglena*, moving by means of flagella and typically having holophytic nutrition. It has been variously regarded as an alga or a protozoan but is now usually classified as a protoctist (phylum *Euglenophyta*)
EUGLENAS > EUGLENA
EUGLENID *same as* > EUGLENA
EUGLENIDS > EUGLENID
EUGLENOID > EUGLENA
EUK *vb* itch
EUKARYON *same as* > EUKARYOTE
EUKARYONS > EUKARYON
EUKARYOT *same as* > EUKARYOTE
EUKARYOTE *n* any member of the *Eukarya*, a domain of organisms having cells each with a distinct nucleus within which the genetic material is contained
EUKARYOTS > EUKARYOT
EUKED > EUK
EUKING > EUK
EUKS > EUK
EULACHAN *same as* > EULACHON
EULACHANS > EULACHAN
EULACHON *n* salmonoid food fish
EULACHONS > EULACHON
EULOGIA *n* blessed bread distributed to members of the congregation after the liturgy, esp to those who have not communed
EULOGIAE > EULOGIA
EULOGIAS > EULOGIA
EULOGIES > EULOGY
EULOGISE *same as* > EULOGIZE
EULOGISED > EULOGISE
EULOGISER > EULOGISE
EULOGISES > EULOGISE
EULOGIST > EULOGIZE
EULOGISTS > EULOGIZE
EULOGIUM *same as* > EULOGY
EULOGIUMS > EULOGIUM
EULOGIZE *vb* praise (a person or thing) highly in speech or writing
EULOGIZED > EULOGIZE
EULOGIZER > EULOGIZE
EULOGIZES > EULOGIZE
EULOGY *n* speech or writing in praise of a person
EUMELANIN *n* dark melanin
EUMERISM *n* collection of similar parts
EUMERISMS > EUMERISM
EUMONG *same as* > EUMUNG
EUMONGS > EUMONG
EUMUNG *n* any of various Australian acacias
EUMUNGS > EUMUNG
EUNUCH *n* castrated man, esp (formerly) a guard in a harem
EUNUCHISE *same as* > EUNUCHIZE
EUNUCHISM > EUNUCH
EUNUCHIZE *vb* castrate
EUNUCHOID *n* one suffering from deficient sexual development
EUNUCHS > EUNUCH
EUOI *n* cry of Bacchic frenzy
EUONYMIN *n* extract derived from the bark of the eunonymus
EUONYMINS > EUONYMIN
EUONYMUS *n* any tree or shrub of the N temperate genus *Euonymus*
EUOUAE *n* cry of Bacchic frenzy
EUOUAES > EUOUAE
EUPAD *n* antiseptic powder
EUPADS > EUPAD
EUPATRID *n* (in ancient Greece) hereditary noble or landowner
EUPATRIDS > EUPATRID
EUPEPSIA *n* good digestion
EUPEPSIAS > EUPEPSIA
EUPEPSIES > EUPEPSY
EUPEPSY *same as* > EUPEPSIA
EUPEPTIC > EUPEPSIA
EUPHAUSID *n* small pelagic shrimplike crustacean
EUPHEMISE *same as* > EUPHEMIZE
EUPHEMISM *n* inoffensive word or phrase substituted for one considered offensive or upsetting
EUPHEMIST > EUPHEMISM
EUPHEMIZE *vb* speak in euphemisms or refer to by means of a euphemism
EUPHENIC *n* of or pertaining to biological improvement
EUPHENICS *n* science of biological improvement
EUPHOBIA *n* fear of good news
EUPHOBIAS > EUPHOBIA
EUPHON *n* glass harmonica
EUPHONIA *same as* > EUPHONY
EUPHONIAS > EUPHONIA
EUPHONIC *adj* denoting or relating to euphony
EUPHONIES > EUPHONY
EUPHONISE *same as* > EUPHONIZE
EUPHONISM *n* use of pleasant-sounding words
EUPHONIUM *n* brass musical instrument, tenor tuba
EUPHONIZE *vb* make pleasant to hear
EUPHONS > EUPHON
EUPHONY *n* pleasing sound
EUPHORBIA *n* any plant of the genus *Euphorbia*
EUPHORIA *n* sense of elation
EUPHORIAS > EUPHORIA
EUPHORIC > EUPHORIA
EUPHORIES > EUPHORY
EUPHORY *same as* > EUPHORIA
EUPHOTIC *adj* denoting or relating to the uppermost part of a sea or lake down to about 100 metres depth, which receives enough light to enable photosynthesis to take place
EUPHRASY *same as* > EYEBRIGHT
EUPHROE *n* wooden block with holes through which the lines of a crowfoot are rove
EUPHROES > EUPHROE
EUPHUISE *same as* > EUPHUIZE
EUPHUISED > EUPHUISE
EUPHUISES > EUPHUISE
EUPHUISM *n* artificial prose style of the Elizabethan period, marked by extreme use of antithesis, alliteration, and extended similes and allusions
EUPHUISMS > EUPHUISM
EUPHUIST > EUPHUISM
EUPHUISTS > EUPHUISM
EUPHUIZE *vb* write in euphuism
EUPHUIZED > EUPHUIZE

EUPHUIZES > EUPHUIZE
EUPLASTIC *adj* healing quickly and well
EUPLOID *adj* having chromosomes present in an exact multiple of the haploid number ▷ *n* euploid cell or individual
EUPLOIDS > EUPLOID
EUPLOIDY > EUPLOID
EUPNEA *same as* > EUPNOEA
EUPNEAS > EUPNEA
EUPNEIC > EUPNOEA
EUPNOEA *n* normal relaxed breathing
EUPNOEAS > EUPNOEA
EUPNOEIC > EUPNOEA
EUREKA *n* exclamation of triumph at finding something
EUREKAS > EUREKA
EURHYTHMY *n* rhythmic movement
EURIPI > EURIPUS
EURIPUS *n* strait or channel with a strong current or tide
EURIPUSES > EURIPUS
EURO *n* unit of the single currency of the European Union
EUROBOND *n* bond issued in a eurocurrency
EUROBONDS > EUROBOND
EUROCRAT *n* member, esp a senior member, of the administration of the European Union
EUROCRATS > EUROCRAT
EUROCREEP *n* gradual introduction of the euro into use in Britain
EUROKIES > EUROKY
EUROKOUS > EUROKY
EUROKY *n* ability of an organism to live under different conditions
EURONOTE *n* form of euro-commercial paper consisting of short-term negotiable bearer notes
EURONOTES > EURONOTE
EUROPHILE *n* person who admires Europe, Europeans, or the European Union
EUROPIUM *n* silvery-white element of the lanthanide series
EUROPIUMS > EUROPIUM
EUROS > EURO
EURYBATH *n* organism that can live at different depths underwater
EURYBATHS > EURYBATH
EURYOKIES > EURYOKY
EURYOKOUS > EURYOKY
EURYOKY *same as* > EUROKY
EURYTHERM *n* organism that can tolerate widely differing temperatures
EURYTHMIC *adj* having a pleasing and harmonious rhythm, order, or structure
EURYTHMY > EURYTHMICS
EURYTOPIC *adj* (of a species) able to tolerate a wide range of environments
EUSOCIAL *adj* using division of labour
EUSOL *n* solution of eupad in water
EUSOLS > EUSOL
EUSTACIES > EUSTATIC
EUSTACY > EUSTATIC
EUSTASIES > EUSTATIC
EUSTASY > EUSTATIC
EUSTATIC *adj* denoting or relating to worldwide changes in sea level, caused by the melting of ice sheets, movements of the ocean floor, sedimentation, etc
EUSTELE *n* central cylinder of a seed plant
EUSTELES > EUSTELE
EUSTYLE *n* building with columns optimally spaced
EUSTYLES > EUSTYLE
EUTAXIA *n* condition of being easily melted
EUTAXIAS > EUTAXIA
EUTAXIES > EUTAXY
EUTAXITE *n* banded volcanic rock
EUTAXITES > EUTAXITE
EUTAXITIC > EUTAXITE
EUTAXY *n* good order
EUTECTIC *adj* (of a mixture of substances, esp an alloy) having the lowest freezing point of all possible mixtures of the substances ▷ *n* eutectic mixture
EUTECTICS > EUTECTIC
EUTECTOID *n* mixture of substances similar to a eutectic, but forming two or three constituents from a solid instead of from a melt ▷ *adj* concerned with or suitable for eutectoid mixtures
EUTEXIA *same as* > EUTAXIA
EUTEXIAS > EUTEXIA
EUTHANASY *n* the act of killing someone painlessly
EUTHANISE *same as* > EUTHANIZE
EUTHANIZE *vb* put (someone, esp one suffering from a terminal illness) to death painlessly
EUTHENICS *n* study of the control of the environment, esp with a view to improving the health and living standards of the human race
EUTHENIST > EUTHENICS
EUTHERIAN *adj* of, relating to, or belonging to the *Eutheria*, a subclass of mammals all of which have a placenta and reach an advanced state of development before birth ▷ *n* any eutherian mammal
EUTHYMIA *n* pleasant state of mind
EUTHYMIAS > EUTHYMIA
EUTHYROID *n* condition of having thyroid glands that function normally
EUTRAPELY *n* conversational skill
EUTROPHIC *adj* (of lakes and similar habitats) rich in organic and mineral nutrients and supporting an abundant plant life, which in the process of decaying depletes the oxygen supply for animal life
EUTROPHY > EUTROPHIC
EUTROPIC > EUTROPY
EUTROPIES > EUTROPY
EUTROPOUS > EUTROPY
EUTROPY *n* regular variation of the crystalline structure of a series of compounds according to atomic number
EUXENITE *n* rare brownish-black mineral containing erbium, cerium, uranium, columbium, and yttrium
EUXENITES > EUXENITE
EVACUANT *adj* serving to promote excretion, esp of the bowels ▷ *n* evacuant agent
EVACUANTS > EVACUANT
EVACUATE *vb* send (someone) away from a place of danger
EVACUATED > EVACUATE
EVACUATES > EVACUATE
EVACUATOR > EVACUATE
EVACUEE *n* person evacuated from a place of danger, esp in wartime
EVACUEES > EVACUEE
EVADABLE > EVADE
EVADE *vb* get away from or avoid
EVADED > EVADE
EVADER > EVADE
EVADERS > EVADE
EVADES > EVADE
EVADIBLE > EVADE
EVADING > EVADE
EVADINGLY > EVADE
EVAGATION *n* digression
EVAGINATE *vb* turn (an organ or part) inside out
EVALUABLE > EVALUATE
EVALUATE *vb* find or judge the value of
EVALUATED > EVALUATE
EVALUATES > EVALUATE
EVALUATOR > EVALUATE
EVANESCE *vb* fade gradually from sight
EVANESCED > EVANESCE
EVANESCES > EVANESCE
EVANGEL *n* gospel of Christianity
EVANGELIC *adj* of, based upon, or following from the gospels
EVANGELS > EVANGEL
EVANGELY *n* gospel
EVANISH *poetic word for* > VANISH
EVANISHED > EVANISH
EVANISHES > EVANISH
EVANITION > EVANISH
EVAPORATE *vb* change from a liquid or solid to a vapour
EVAPORITE *n* any sedimentary rock, such as rock salt, gypsum, or anhydrite, formed by evaporation of former sea or salt-water lakes
EVASIBLE > EVASION
EVASION *n* act of evading something, esp a duty or responsibility, by cunning or illegal means
EVASIONAL > EVASION
EVASIONS > EVASION
EVASIVE *adj* not straightforward
EVASIVELY > EVASIVE
EVE *n* evening or day before some special event
EVECTION *n* irregularity in the moon's motion caused by perturbations of the sun and planets
EVECTIONS > EVECTION
EVEJAR *n* nightjar
EVEJARS > EVEJAR
EVEN *adj* flat or smooth ▷ *adv* equally ▷ *vb* make even ▷ *n* eve
EVENED > EVEN
EVENEMENT *n* event
EVENER > EVEN
EVENERS > EVEN
EVENEST > EVEN
EVENFALL *n* early evening
EVENFALLS > EVENFALL
EVENING *n* end of the day or early part of the night ▷ *adj* of or in the evening
EVENINGS *adv* in the evening, esp regularly
EVENLY > EVEN
EVENNESS > EVEN
EVENS *adv* (of a bet) winning the same as the amount staked if successful
EVENSONG *n* evening prayer
EVENSONGS > EVENSONG
EVENT *n* anything that takes place ▷ *vb* take part or ride (a horse) in eventing
EVENTED > EVENT
EVENTER > EVENTING
EVENTERS > EVENTING
EVENTFUL *adj* full of exciting incidents
EVENTIDE *n* evening
EVENTIDES > EVENTIDE
EVENTING *n* riding competitions, usu.

involving cross-country, jumping, and dressage
VENTINGS > EVENTING
VENTISE *same as* > EVENTIZE
VENTISED > EVENTISE
VENTISES > EVENTISE
VENTIZE *vb* arrange an occasion so that it is seen as being a special event
VENTIZED > EVENTIZE
VENTIZES > EVENTIZE
VENTLESS > EVENT
VENTRATE *vb* open the belly of
VENTS > EVENT
VENTUAL *adj* ultimate
VENTUATE *vb* result ultimately (in)
VER *adv* at any time
VERGLADE *n* large area of submerged marshland
VERGREEN *adj* (tree or shrub) having leaves throughout the year ▷ *n* evergreen tree or shrub
VERMORE *adv* for all time to come
VERNET *n* hypothetical form of internet that is continuously accessible using a wide variety of devices
VERNETS > EVERNET
VERSIBLE > EVERT
VERSION > EVERT
VERSIONS > EVERT
VERT *vb* turn (an eyelid, the intestines, or some other bodily part) outwards or inside out
VERTED > EVERT
VERTING > EVERT
VERTOR *n* any muscle that turns a part outwards
VERTORS > EVERTOR
VERTS > EVERT
VERWHERE *adv* to or in all parts or places
VERWHICH *dialect version of* > WHICHEVER
VERY *adj* each without exception
VERYBODY *pron* every person
VERYDAY *adj* usual or ordinary ▷ *n* ordinary day
VERYDAYS > EVERYDAY
VERYMAN *n* ordinary person; common man
VERYMEN > EVERYMAN
VERYONE *pron* every person
VERYWAY *adv* in every way
VERYWHEN *adv* to or in all parts or places
VES > EVE
VET *n* eft
VETS > EVET
VHOE *interj* cry of Bacchic frenzy
VICT *vb* legally expel (someone) from his or her home
EVICTED > EVICT
EVICTEE > EVICT
EVICTEES > EVICT
EVICTING > EVICT
EVICTION > EVICT
EVICTIONS > EVICT
EVICTOR > EVICT
EVICTORS > EVICT
EVICTS > EVICT
EVIDENCE *n* ground for belief ▷ *vb* demonstrate, prove
EVIDENCED > EVIDENCE
EVIDENCES > EVIDENCE
EVIDENT *adj* easily seen or understood ▷ *n* item of evidence
EVIDENTLY *adv* without question
EVIDENTS > EVIDENT
EVIL *n* wickedness ▷ *adj* harmful ▷ *adv* in an evil manner
EVILDOER *n* wicked person
EVILDOERS > EVILDOER
EVILDOING > EVILDOER
EVILER > EVIL
EVILEST > EVIL
EVILLER > EVIL
EVILLEST > EVIL
EVILLY > EVIL
EVILNESS > EVIL
EVILS > EVIL
EVINCE *vb* make evident
EVINCED > EVINCE
EVINCES > EVINCE
EVINCIBLE > EVINCE
EVINCIBLY > EVINCE
EVINCING > EVINCE
EVINCIVE > EVINCE
EVIRATE *vb* castrate
EVIRATED > EVIRATE
EVIRATES > EVIRATE
EVIRATING > EVIRATE
EVITABLE *adj* able to be avoided
EVITATE *archaic word for* > AVOID
EVITATED > EVITATE
EVITATES > EVITATE
EVITATING > EVITATE
EVITATION > EVITATE
EVITE *archaic word for* > AVOID
EVITED > EVITE
EVITERNAL *adj* eternal
EVITES > EVITE
EVITING > EVITE
EVO *informal word for* > EVENING
EVOCABLE > EVOKE
EVOCATE *vb* evoke
EVOCATED > EVOCATE
EVOCATES > EVOCATE
EVOCATING > EVOCATE
EVOCATION *n* act of evoking
EVOCATIVE *adj* tending or serving to evoke
EVOCATOR *n* person or thing that evokes
EVOCATORS > EVOCATOR
EVOCATORY *adj* evocative
EVOE *interj* cry of Bacchic frenzy
EVOHE *interj* cry of Bacchic frenzy
EVOKE *vb* call or summon up (a memory, feeling, etc)
EVOKED > EVOKE
EVOKER > EVOKE
EVOKERS > EVOKE
EVOKES > EVOKE
EVOKING > EVOKE
EVOLUE *n* (in the African former colonies of Belgium and France) African person educated according to European principles
EVOLUES > EVOLUE
EVOLUTE *n* geometric curve that describes the locus of the centres of curvature of another curve ▷ *adj* having the margins rolled outwards ▷ *vb* evolve
EVOLUTED > EVOLUTE
EVOLUTES > EVOLUTE
EVOLUTING > EVOLUTE
EVOLUTION *n* gradual change in the characteristics of living things over successive generations, esp to a more complex form
EVOLUTIVE *adj* relating to, tending to, or promoting evolution
EVOLVABLE > EVOLVE
EVOLVE *vb* develop gradually
EVOLVED > EVOLVE
EVOLVENT *adj* evolving
EVOLVER > EVOLVE
EVOLVERS > EVOLVE
EVOLVES > EVOLVE
EVOLVING > EVOLVE
EVONYMUS *same as* > EUONYMUS
EVOS > EVO
EVOVAE *n* cry of Bacchic frenzy
EVOVAES > EVOVAE
EVULGATE *vb* make public
EVULGATED > EVULGATE
EVULGATES > EVULGATE
EVULSE *vb* extract by force
EVULSED > EVULSE
EVULSES > EVULSE
EVULSING > EVULSE
EVULSION *n* act of extracting by force
EVULSIONS > EVULSION
EVZONE *n* soldier in an elite Greek infantry regiment
EVZONES > EVZONE
EWE *n* female sheep
EWER *n* large jug with a wide mouth
EWERS > EWER
EWES > EWE
EWEST *Scots word for* > NEAR
EWFTES *Spenserian plural of* > EFT
EWGHEN *archaic form of* > YEW
EWHOW *interj* expression of pity or regret
EWK *vb* itch
EWKED > EWK
EWKING > EWK
EWKS > EWK
EWT *archaic form of* > NEWT
EWTS > EWT
EX *prep* not including ▷ *vb* cross out or delete
EXABYTE *n* very large unit of computer memory
EXABYTES > EXABYTE
EXACT *adj* correct and complete in every detail ▷ *vb* demand (payment or obedience)
EXACTA *n* horse-racing bet in which the first and second horses must be named in the correct order
EXACTABLE > EXACT
EXACTAS > EXACTA
EXACTED > EXACT
EXACTER > EXACT
EXACTERS > EXACT
EXACTEST > EXACT
EXACTING *adj* making rigorous or excessive demands
EXACTION *n* act of obtaining or demanding money as a right
EXACTIONS > EXACTION
EXACTLY *adv* precisely, in every respect ▷ *interj* just so! precisely!
EXACTMENT *n* condition of being exact
EXACTNESS > EXACT
EXACTOR > EXACT
EXACTORS > EXACT
EXACTRESS > EXACT
EXACTS > EXACT
EXACUM *n* any plant of the annual or perennial tropical genus *Exacum*; some are grown as greenhouse biennials for their bluish-purple platter-shaped flowers: family *Gentianaceae*
EXACUMS > EXACUM
EXAHERTZ *n* very large unit of frequency
EXALT *vb* praise highly
EXALTED *adj* high or elevated in rank, position, dignity, etc
EXALTEDLY > EXALTED
EXALTER > EXALT
EXALTERS > EXALT
EXALTING > EXALT
EXALTS > EXALT
EXAM *n* examination
EXAMEN *n* examination of conscience, usually made daily by Jesuits and others
EXAMENS > EXAMEN
EXAMINANT *n* examiner
EXAMINATE *n* examinee
EXAMINE *vb* look at closely
EXAMINED > EXAMINE
EXAMINEE *n* person who sits an exam
EXAMINEES > EXAMINEE

EXAMINER > EXAMINE
EXAMINERS > EXAMINE
EXAMINES > EXAMINE
EXAMINING > EXAMINE
EXAMPLAR *archaic form of* > EXEMPLAR
EXAMPLARS > EXAMPLAR
EXAMPLE *n* specimen typical of its group
EXAMPLED > EXAMPLE
EXAMPLES > EXAMPLE
EXAMPLING > EXAMPLE
EXAMS > EXAM
EXANIMATE *adj* lacking life
EXANTHEM *same as* > EXANTHEMA
EXANTHEMA *n* skin eruption or rash occurring as a symptom in a disease such as measles or scarlet fever
EXANTHEMS > EXANTHEM
EXAPTED *adj* biologically adapted
EXAPTIVE *adj* involving biological adaptation
EXARATE *adj* (of the pupa of such insects as ants and bees) having legs, wings, antennae, etc, free and movable
EXARATION *n* writing
EXARCH *n* head of certain autonomous Orthodox Christian Churches, such as that of Bulgaria and Cyprus ▷ *adj* (of a xylem strand) having the first-formed xylem external to that formed later
EXARCHAL > EXARCH
EXARCHATE *n* office, rank, or jurisdiction of an exarch
EXARCHIES > EXARCHY
EXARCHIST *n* supporter of an exarch
EXARCHS > EXARCH
EXARCHY *same as* > EXARCHATE
EXCAMB *vb* exchange
EXCAMBED > EXCAMB
EXCAMBING > EXCAMB
EXCAMBION *n* exchange, esp of land
EXCAMBIUM *same as* > EXCAMBION
EXCAMBS > EXCAMB
EXCARNATE *vb* remove flesh from
EXCAUDATE *adj* having no tail or tail-like process
EXCAVATE *vb* unearth buried objects from (a piece of land) methodically to learn about the past
EXCAVATED > EXCAVATE
EXCAVATES > EXCAVATE
EXCAVATOR *n* large machine used for digging
EXCEED *vb* be greater than
EXCEEDED > EXCEED
EXCEEDER > EXCEED
EXCEEDERS > EXCEED
EXCEEDING *adj* very great
EXCEEDS > EXCEED
EXCEL *vb* be superior to
EXCELLED > EXCEL
EXCELLENT *adj* exceptionally good
EXCELLING > EXCEL
EXCELS > EXCEL
EXCELSIOR *n* excellent: used as a motto and as a trademark for various products, esp in the US for fine wood shavings used for packing breakable objects
EXCENTRIC *same as* > ECCENTRIC
EXCEPT *prep* other than, not including ▷ *vb* leave out; omit; exclude
EXCEPTANT *n* person taking exception
EXCEPTED > EXCEPT
EXCEPTING *prep* except
EXCEPTION *n* excepting
EXCEPTIVE *adj* relating to or forming an exception
EXCEPTOR > EXCEPT
EXCEPTORS > EXCEPT
EXCEPTS > EXCEPT
EXCERPT *n* passage taken from a book, speech, etc ▷ *vb* take a passage from a book, speech, etc
EXCERPTA > EXCERPTUM
EXCERPTED > EXCERPT
EXCERPTER > EXCERPT
EXCERPTOR > EXCERPT
EXCERPTS > EXCERPT
EXCERPTUM *n* excerpt
EXCESS *n* state or act of exceeding the permitted limits ▷ *vb* make (a position) redundant
EXCESSED > EXCESS
EXCESSES > EXCESS
EXCESSING > EXCESS
EXCESSIVE *adj* exceeding the normal or permitted extents or limits
EXCHANGE *vb* give or receive (something) in return for something else ▷ *n* act of exchanging
EXCHANGED > EXCHANGE
EXCHANGER *n* person or thing that exchanges
EXCHANGES > EXCHANGE
EXCHEAT *same as* > ESCHEAT
EXCHEATS > EXCHEAT
EXCHEQUER *n* (in Britain and certain other countries) accounting department of the Treasury, responsible for receiving and issuing funds
EXCIDE *vb* cut out
EXCIDED > EXCIDE
EXCIDES > EXCIDE
EXCIDING > EXCIDE
EXCIMER *n* excited dimer formed by the association of excited and unexcited molecules, which would remain dissociated in the ground state
EXCIMERS > EXCIMER
EXCIPIENT *n* substance, such as sugar or gum, used to prepare a drug or drugs in a form suitable for administration
EXCIPLE *n* part of a lichen
EXCIPLES > EXCIPLE
EXCISABLE > EXCISE
EXCISE *n* tax on goods produced for the home market ▷ *vb* cut out or away
EXCISED > EXCISE
EXCISEMAN *n* (formerly) a government agent who collected excise and prevented smuggling
EXCISEMEN > EXCISEMAN
EXCISES > EXCISE
EXCISING > EXCISE
EXCISION > EXCISE
EXCISIONS > EXCISE
EXCITABLE *adj* easily excited
EXCITABLY > EXCITABLE
EXCITANCY *n* ability to excite
EXCITANT *adj* able to excite or stimulate ▷ *n* something, such as a drug or other agent, able to excite
EXCITANTS > EXCITANT
EXCITE *vb* arouse to strong emotion
EXCITED *adj* emotionally aroused, esp to pleasure or agitation
EXCITEDLY > EXCITED
EXCITER *n* person or thing that excites
EXCITERS > EXCITER
EXCITES > EXCITE
EXCITING *adj* causing excitement
EXCITON *n* mobile neutral entity in a crystalline solid consisting of an excited electron bound to the hole produced by its excitation
EXCITONIC > EXCITON
EXCITONS > EXCITON
EXCITOR *n* nerve that, when stimulated, causes increased activity in the organ or part it supplies
EXCITORS > EXCITOR
EXCLAIM *vb* speak suddenly, cry out
EXCLAIMED > EXCLAIM
EXCLAIMER > EXCLAIM
EXCLAIMS > EXCLAIM
EXCLAVE *n* part of a country entirely surrounded by foreign territory: viewed from the position of the home country
EXCLAVES > EXCLAVE
EXCLOSURE *n* area of land, esp in a forest, fenced round to keep out unwanted animals
EXCLUDE *vb* keep out, leave out
EXCLUDED > EXCLUDE
EXCLUDEE > EXCLUDE
EXCLUDEES > EXCLUDE
EXCLUDER > EXCLUDE
EXCLUDERS > EXCLUDE
EXCLUDES > EXCLUDE
EXCLUDING *prep* excepting
EXCLUSION *n* act or an instance of excluding or the state of being excluded
EXCLUSIVE *adj* excluding everything else ▷ *n* story reported in only one newspaper
EXCLUSORY > EXCLUDE
EXCORIATE *vb* censure severely
EXCREMENT *n* waste matter discharged from the body
EXCRETA *n* excrement
EXCRETAL > EXCRETA
EXCRETE *vb* discharge (waste matter) from the body
EXCRETED > EXCRETE
EXCRETER > EXCRETE
EXCRETERS > EXCRETE
EXCRETES > EXCRETE
EXCRETING > EXCRETE
EXCRETION > EXCRETE
EXCRETIVE > EXCRETE
EXCRETORY > EXCRETE
EXCUBANT *adj* keeping guard
EXCUDIT *sentence substitute* (named person) made this
EXCULPATE *vb* free from blame or guilt
EXCURRENT *adj* having an outward flow, as certain pores in sponges, ducts, etc
EXCURSE *vb* wander
EXCURSED > EXCURSE
EXCURSES > EXCURSE
EXCURSING > EXCURSE
EXCURSION *n* short journey, esp for pleasure
EXCURSIVE *adj* tending to digress
EXCURSUS *n* incidental digression from the main topic under discussion or from the main story in a narrative
EXCUSABLE > EXCUSE
EXCUSABLY > EXCUSE
EXCUSAL > EXCUSE
EXCUSALS > EXCUSE
EXCUSE *n* explanation offered to justify (a fault etc) ▷ *vb* put forward a reason or justification for (a fault etc)
EXCUSED > EXCUSE
EXCUSER > EXCUSE
EXCUSERS > EXCUSE
EXCUSES > EXCUSE
EXCUSING > EXCUSE
EXCUSIVE *adj* excusing
EXEAT *n* leave of absence

from school or some other institution
EXEATS > EXEAT
EXEC *n* executive
EXECRABLE *adj* of very poor quality
EXECRABLY > EXECRABLE
EXECRATE *vb* feel and express loathing and hatred of (someone or something)
EXECRATED > EXECRATE
EXECRATES > EXECRATE
EXECRATOR > EXECRATE
EXECS > EXEC
EXECUTANT *n* performer, esp of musical works
EXECUTARY *n* person whose job comprises tasks appropriate to a middle-management executive as well as those traditionally carried out by a secretary
EXECUTE *vb* put (a condemned person) to death
EXECUTED > EXECUTE
EXECUTER > EXECUTE
EXECUTERS > EXECUTE
EXECUTES > EXECUTE
EXECUTING > EXECUTE
EXECUTION *n* act of executing
EXECUTIVE *n* person or group in an administrative position ▷ *adj* having the function of carrying out plans, orders, laws, etc
EXECUTOR *n* person appointed to perform the instructions of a will
EXECUTORS > EXECUTOR
EXECUTORY *adj* (of a law, agreement, etc) coming into operation at a future date
EXECUTRIX *n* female executor
EXECUTRY *n* condition of being an executor
EXED > EX
EXEDRA *n* building, room, portico, or apse containing a continuous bench, used in ancient Greece and Rome for holding discussions
EXEDRAE > EXEDRA
EXEEM *same as* > EXEME
EXEEMED > EXEEM
EXEEMING > EXEEM
EXEEMS > EXEEM
EXEGESES > EXEGESIS
EXEGESIS *n* explanation of a text, esp of the Bible
EXEGETE *n* person who practises exegesis
EXEGETES > EXEGETE
EXEGETIC *adj* of or relating to exegesis
EXEGETICS *n* scientific study of exegesis and exegetical methods
EXEGETIST *same as* > EXEGETE
EXEME *vb* set free
EXEMED > EXEME
EXEMES > EXEME
EXEMING > EXEME
EXEMPLA > EXEMPLUM
EXEMPLAR *n* person or thing to be copied, model
EXEMPLARS > EXEMPLAR
EXEMPLARY *adj* being a good example
EXEMPLE *same as* > EXAMPLE
EXEMPLES > EXEMPLE
EXEMPLIFY *vb* show an example of
EXEMPLUM *n* anecdote that supports a moral point or sustains an argument, used esp in medieval sermons
EXEMPT *adj* not subject to an obligation etc ▷ *vb* release from an obligation etc ▷ *n* person who is exempt from an obligation, tax, etc
EXEMPTED > EXEMPT
EXEMPTING > EXEMPT
EXEMPTION > EXEMPT
EXEMPTIVE > EXEMPT
EXEMPTS > EXEMPT
EXEQUATUR *n* official authorization issued by a host country to a consular agent, permitting him to perform his official duties
EXEQUIAL > EXEQUY
EXEQUIES > EXEQUY
EXEQUY *n* funeral rite
EXERCISE *n* activity to train the body or mind ▷ *vb* make use of
EXERCISED > EXERCISE
EXERCISER *n* device with springs or elasticated cords for muscular exercise
EXERCISES > EXERCISE
EXERCYCLE *n* exercise bicycle
EXERGONIC *adj* (of a biochemical reaction) producing energy and therefore occurring spontaneously
EXERGUAL > EXERGUE
EXERGUE *n* space on the reverse of a coin or medal below the central design, often containing the date, place of minting, etc
EXERGUES > EXERGUE
EXERT *vb* use (influence, authority, etc) forcefully or effectively
EXERTED > EXERT
EXERTING > EXERT
EXERTION > EXERT
EXERTIONS > EXERT
EXERTIVE > EXERT
EXERTS > EXERT
EXES > EX
EXEUNT *vb* (they) go out
EXFOLIANT *n* cosmetic removing dead skin
EXFOLIATE *vb* peel in scales or layers
EXHALABLE > EXHALE
EXHALANT *adj* emitting a vapour or liquid ▷ *n* organ or vessel that emits a vapour or liquid
EXHALANTS > EXHALANT
EXHALE *vb* breathe out
EXHALED > EXHALE
EXHALENT *same as* > EXHALANT
EXHALENTS > EXHALENT
EXHALES > EXHALE
EXHALING > EXHALE
EXHAUST *vb* tire out ▷ *n* gases ejected from an engine as waste products
EXHAUSTED > EXHAUST
EXHAUSTER > EXHAUST
EXHAUSTS > EXHAUST
EXHEDRA *same as* > EXEDRA
EXHEDRAE > EXHEDRA
EXHIBIT *vb* display to the public ▷ *n* object exhibited to the public
EXHIBITED > EXHIBIT
EXHIBITER > EXHIBIT
EXHIBITOR *n* person or thing that exhibits
EXHIBITS > EXHIBIT
EXHORT *vb* urge earnestly
EXHORTED > EXHORT
EXHORTER > EXHORT
EXHORTERS > EXHORT
EXHORTING > EXHORT
EXHORTS > EXHORT
EXHUMATE *same as* > EXHUME
EXHUMATED > EXHUMATE
EXHUMATES > EXHUMATE
EXHUME *vb* dig up (something buried, esp a corpse)
EXHUMED > EXHUME
EXHUMER > EXHUME
EXHUMERS > EXHUME
EXHUMES > EXHUME
EXHUMING > EXHUME
EXIES *n* hysterics
EXIGEANT *adj* exacting
EXIGEANTE *same as* > EXIGEANT
EXIGENCE *same as* > EXIGENCY
EXIGENCES > EXIGENCE
EXIGENCY *n* urgent demand or need
EXIGENT *adj* urgent ▷ *n* emergency
EXIGENTLY > EXIGENT
EXIGENTS > EXIGENT
EXIGIBLE *adj* liable to be exacted or required
EXIGUITY > EXIGUOUS
EXIGUOUS *adj* scanty or meagre
EXILABLE > EXILE
EXILE *n* prolonged, usu. enforced, absence from one's country ▷ *vb* expel from one's country
EXILED > EXILE
EXILEMENT *same as* > EXILE
EXILER > EXILE
EXILERS > EXILE
EXILES > EXILE
EXILIAN > EXILE
EXILIC > EXILE
EXILING > EXILE
EXILITIES > EXILITY
EXILITY *n* poverty or meagreness
EXIMIOUS *adj* select and distinguished
EXINE *n* outermost coat of a pollen grain or a spore
EXINES > EXINE
EXING > EX
EXIST *vb* have being or reality
EXISTED > EXIST
EXISTENCE *n* fact or state of being real, live, or actual
EXISTENT *adj* in existence ▷ *n* person or a thing that exists
EXISTENTS > EXISTENT
EXISTING > EXIST
EXISTS > EXIST
EXIT *n* way out ▷ *vb* go out
EXITANCE *n* measure of the ability of a surface to emit radiation
EXITANCES > EXITANCE
EXITED > EXIT
EXITING > EXIT
EXITLESS > EXIT
EXITS > EXIT
EXO *informal word for* > EXCELLENT
EXOCARP *same as* > EPICARP
EXOCARPS > EXOCARP
EXOCRINE *adj* relating to a gland, such as the sweat gland, that secretes externally through a duct ▷ *n* exocrine gland
EXOCRINES > EXOCRINE
EXOCYCLIC *adj* (of a sea urchin) having the anus situated outside the apical disc
EXOCYTIC *adj* outside biological cell
EXOCYTOSE *vb* secrete substance from within cell
EXODE *n* exodus
EXODERM *same as* > ECTODERM
EXODERMAL > EXODERM
EXODERMIS *same as* > ECTODERM
EXODERMS > EXODERM
EXODES > EXODE
EXODIC > EXODE
EXODIST > EXODUS
EXODISTS > EXODUS
EXODOI > EXODOS
EXODONTIA *n* branch of dental surgery concerned with the extraction of teeth
EXODOS *n* processional song performed at the end of a play

EXODUS *n* departure of a large number of people
EXODUSES > EXODUS
EXOENZYME *n* extracellular enzyme
EXOERGIC *adj* (of a nuclear reaction) occurring with evolution of energy
EXOGAMIC > EXOGAMY
EXOGAMIES > EXOGAMY
EXOGAMOUS > EXOGAMY
EXOGAMY *n* custom or an act of marrying a person belonging to another tribe, clan, or similar social unit
EXOGEN *n* plant with a stem that develops through the growth of new layers on its outside
EXOGENISM > EXOGENOUS
EXOGENOUS *adj* having an external origin
EXOGENS > EXOGEN
EXOMION *same as* > EXOMIS
EXOMIONS > EXOMION
EXOMIS *n* sleeveless jacket
EXOMISES > EXOMIS
EXON *n* one of the four officers who command the Yeomen of the Guard
EXONERATE *vb* free from blame or a criminal charge
EXONIC > EXON
EXONS > EXON
EXONUMIA *n* objects of interest to numismatists that are not coins, such as medals and tokens
EXONUMIST *n* collector of medals and tokens
EXONYM *n* name given to a place by foreigners
EXONYMS > EXONYM
EXOPHAGY *n* (among cannibals) custom of eating only members of other tribes
EXOPHORIC *adj* denoting or relating to a pronoun such as "I" or "you", the meaning of which is determined by reference outside the discourse rather than by a preceding or following expression
EXOPLANET *n* planet that orbits a star in a solar system other than that of Earth
EXOPLASM *another name for* > ECTOPLASM
EXOPLASMS > EXOPLASM
EXOPOD *same as* > EXOPODITE
EXOPODITE *n* outer projection on the hind legs of some crustaceans
EXOPODS > EXOPOD
EXORABLE *adj* able to be persuaded or moved by pleading
EXORATION *n* plea
EXORCISE *same as* > EXORCIZE
EXORCISED > EXORCISE
EXORCISER > EXORCISE
EXORCISES > EXORCISE
EXORCISM > EXORCIZE
EXORCISMS > EXORCIZE
EXORCIST > EXORCIZE
EXORCISTS > EXORCIZE
EXORCIZE *vb* expel (evil spirits) by prayers and religious rites
EXORCIZED > EXORCIZE
EXORCIZER > EXORCIZE
EXORCIZES > EXORCIZE
EXORDIA > EXORDIUM
EXORDIAL > EXORDIUM
EXORDIUM *n* introductory part or beginning, esp of an oration or discourse
EXORDIUMS > EXORDIUM
EXOSMIC > EXOSMOSIS
EXOSMOSE *same as* > EXOSMOSIS
EXOSMOSES > EXOSMOSIS
EXOSMOSIS *n* osmosis in which water flows from a cell or organism into the surrounding solution
EXOSMOTIC > EXOSMOSIS
EXOSPHERE *n* outermost layer of the earth's atmosphere
EXOSPORAL > EXOSPORE
EXOSPORE *n* outer layer of the spores of some algae and fungi
EXOSPORES > EXOSPORE
EXOSPORIA *n* exospores
EXOSTOSES > EXOSTOSIS
EXOSTOSIS *n* abnormal bony outgrowth from the surface of a bone
EXOTERIC *adj* intelligible to or intended for more than a select or initiated minority
EXOTIC *adj* having a strange allure or beauty ▷ *n* non-native plant
EXOTICA *pl n* (collection of) exotic objects
EXOTICISM > EXOTIC
EXOTICIST > EXOTIC
EXOTICS > EXOTIC
EXOTISM > EXOTIC
EXOTISMS > EXOTIC
EXOTOXIC > EXOTOXIN
EXOTOXIN *n* toxin produced by a microorganism and secreted into the surrounding medium
EXOTOXINS > EXOTOXIN
EXOTROPIA *n* condition in which eye turns outwards
EXOTROPIC > EXOTROPIA
EXPAND *vb* make or become larger
EXPANDED *adj* (of printer's type) wider than usual for a particular height
EXPANDER *n* device for exercising and developing the muscles of the body
EXPANDERS > EXPANDER
EXPANDING > EXPAND
EXPANDOR *same as* > EXPANDER
EXPANDORS > EXPANDOR
EXPANDS > EXPAND
EXPANSE *n* uninterrupted wide area
EXPANSES > EXPANSE
EXPANSILE *adj* able to expand or cause expansion
EXPANSION *n* act of expanding
EXPANSIVE *adj* wide or extensive
EXPAT *n* short for
EXPATIATE *vb* speak or write at great length (on)
EXPATS > EXPAT
EXPECT *vb* regard as probable
EXPECTANT *adj* expecting or hopeful ▷ *n* person who expects something
EXPECTED > EXPECT
EXPECTER *n* person who expects
EXPECTERS > EXPECTER
EXPECTING *adj* pregnant
EXPECTS > EXPECT
EXPEDIENT *n* something that achieves a particular purpose ▷ *adj* suitable to the circumstances, appropriate
EXPEDITE *vb* hasten the progress of ▷ *adj* unimpeded or prompt
EXPEDITED > EXPEDITE
EXPEDITER *n* person who expedites something, esp a person employed in an industry to ensure that work on each job progresses efficiently
EXPEDITES > EXPEDITE
EXPEDITOR *same as* > EXPEDITER
EXPEL *vb* drive out with force
EXPELLANT *adj* forcing out or having the capacity to force out ▷ *n* medicine used to expel undesirable substances or organisms from the body, esp worms from the digestive tract
EXPELLED > EXPEL
EXPELLEE > EXPEL
EXPELLEES > EXPEL
EXPELLENT *same as* > EXPELLANT
EXPELLER > EXPEL
EXPELLERS *pl n* residue remaining after an oilseed has been crushed to expel the oil, used for animal fodder
EXPELLING > EXPEL
EXPELS > EXPEL
EXPEND *vb* spend, use up
EXPENDED > EXPEND
EXPENDER > EXPEND
EXPENDERS > EXPEND
EXPENDING > EXPEND
EXPENDS > EXPEND
EXPENSE *n* cost
EXPENSED > EXPENSE
EXPENSES > EXPENSE
EXPENSING > EXPENSE
EXPENSIVE *adj* high-priced
EXPERT *n* person with extensive skill or knowledge in a particular field ▷ *adj* skilful or knowledgeable ▷ *vb* experience
EXPERTED > EXPERT
EXPERTING > EXPERT
EXPERTISE *same as* > EXPERTIZE
EXPERTISM > EXPERTIZE
EXPERTIZE *vb* act as an expert or give an expert opinion (on)
EXPERTLY > EXPERT
EXPERTS > EXPERT
EXPIABLE *adj* capable of being expiated or atoned for
EXPIATE *vb* make amends for
EXPIATED > EXPIATE
EXPIATES > EXPIATE
EXPIATING > EXPIATE
EXPIATION *n* act, process, or a means of expiating
EXPIATOR > EXPIATE
EXPIATORS > EXPIATE
EXPIATORY *adj* capable of making expiation
EXPIRABLE > EXPIRE
EXPIRANT *n* one who expires
EXPIRANTS > EXPIRANT
EXPIRE *vb* finish or run out
EXPIRED > EXPIRE
EXPIRER > EXPIRE
EXPIRERS > EXPIRE
EXPIRES > EXPIRE
EXPIRIES > EXPIRY
EXPIRING > EXPIRE
EXPIRY *n* end, esp of a contract period
EXPISCATE *vb* find; fish out
EXPLAIN *vb* make clear and intelligible
EXPLAINED > EXPLAIN
EXPLAINER > EXPLAIN
EXPLAINS > EXPLAIN
EXPLANT *vb* transfer (living tissue) from its natural site to a new site or to a culture medium ▷ *n* piece of tissue treated in this way
EXPLANTED > EXPLANT
EXPLANTS > EXPLANT
EXPLETIVE *n* swearword ▷ *adj* expressing no particular meaning, esp when filling out a line of verse
EXPLETORY *adj* expletive
EXPLICATE *vb* explain
EXPLICIT *adj* precisely and clearly expressed ▷ *n* word used to indicate the end of a book

EXPLICITS > EXPLICIT
EXPLODE *vb* burst with great violence, blow up
EXPLODED > EXPLODE
EXPLODER > EXPLODE
EXPLODERS > EXPLODE
EXPLODES > EXPLODE
EXPLODING > EXPLODE
EXPLOIT *vb* take advantage of for one's own purposes ▷ *n* notable feat or deed
EXPLOITED > EXPLOIT
EXPLOITER > EXPLOIT
EXPLOITS > EXPLOIT
EXPLORE *vb* investigate
EXPLORED > EXPLORE
EXPLORER > EXPLORE
EXPLORERS > EXPLORE
EXPLORES > EXPLORE
EXPLORING > EXPLORE
EXPLOSION *n* exploding
EXPLOSIVE *adj* tending to explode ▷ *n* substance that causes explosions
EXPO *n* exposition, large public exhibition
EXPONENT *n* person who advocates an idea, cause, etc ▷ *adj* offering a declaration, explanation, or interpretation
EXPONENTS > EXPONENT
EXPONIBLE *adj* able to be explained
EXPORT *n* selling or shipping of goods to a foreign country ▷ *vb* sell or ship (goods) to a foreign country
EXPORTED > EXPORT
EXPORTER > EXPORT
EXPORTERS > EXPORT
EXPORTING > EXPORT
EXPORTS > EXPORT
EXPOS > EXPO
EXPOSABLE > EXPOSE
EXPOSAL > EXPOSE
EXPOSALS > EXPOSE
EXPOSE *vb* uncover or reveal ▷ *n* bringing of a crime, scandal, etc to public notice
EXPOSED *adj* not concealed
EXPOSER > EXPOSE
EXPOSERS > EXPOSE
EXPOSES > EXPOSE
EXPOSING > EXPOSE
EXPOSIT *vb* state
EXPOSITED > EXPOSIT
EXPOSITOR *n* person who expounds
EXPOSITS > EXPOSIT
EXPOSTURE *n* exposure
EXPOSURE *n* exposing
EXPOSURES > EXPOSURE
EXPOUND *vb* explain in detail
EXPOUNDED > EXPOUND
EXPOUNDER > EXPOUND
EXPOUNDS > EXPOUND
EXPRESS *vb* put into words ▷ *adj* explicitly stated ▷ *n* fast train or bus stopping at only a few stations ▷ *adv* by express delivery
EXPRESSED > EXPRESS
EXPRESSER > EXPRESS
EXPRESSES > EXPRESS
EXPRESSLY *adv* definitely
EXPRESSO *variant of* > ESPRESSO
EXPRESSOS > EXPRESSO
EXPUGN *vb* storm
EXPUGNED > EXPUGN
EXPUGNING > EXPUGN
EXPUGNS > EXPUGN
EXPULSE *vb* expel
EXPULSED > EXPULSE
EXPULSES > EXPULSE
EXPULSING > EXPULSE
EXPULSION *n* act of expelling or the fact of being expelled
EXPULSIVE *adj* tending or serving to expel
EXPUNCT *vb* expunge
EXPUNCTED > EXPUNCT
EXPUNCTS > EXPUNCT
EXPUNGE *vb* delete, erase, blot out
EXPUNGED > EXPUNGE
EXPUNGER > EXPUNGE
EXPUNGERS > EXPUNGE
EXPUNGES > EXPUNGE
EXPUNGING > EXPUNGE
EXPURGATE *vb* remove objectionable parts from (a book etc)
EXPURGE *vb* purge
EXPURGED > EXPURGE
EXPURGES > EXPURGE
EXPURGING > EXPURGE
EXQUISITE *adj* of extreme beauty or delicacy ▷ *n* dandy
EXSCIND *vb* cut off or out
EXSCINDED > EXSCIND
EXSCINDS > EXSCIND
EXSECANT *n* trigonometric function
EXSECANTS > EXSECANT
EXSECT *vb* cut out
EXSECTED > EXSECT
EXSECTING > EXSECT
EXSECTION > EXSECT
EXSECTS > EXSECT
EXSERT *vb* thrust out ▷ *adj* protruded, stretched out, or (esp of stamens) projecting beyond the corolla of a flower
EXSERTED > EXSERT
EXSERTILE > EXSERT
EXSERTING > EXSERT
EXSERTION > EXSERT
EXSERTS > EXSERT
EXSICCANT > EXSICCATE
EXSICCATE *vb* dry up
EXSTROPHY *n* congenital eversion of a hollow organ, esp the urinary bladder
EXSUCCOUS *adj* without sap or juice
EXTANT *adj* still existing
EXTASIES > EXTASY
EXTASY *same as* > ECSTASY
EXTATIC *same as* > ECSTATIC
EXTEMPORE *adj* without planning or preparation ▷ *adv* without planning or preparation
EXTEND *vb* draw out or be drawn out, stretch
EXTENDANT *adj* (in heraldry) with wings spread
EXTENDED *same as* > EXPANDED
EXTENDER *n* person or thing that extends
EXTENDERS > EXTENDER
EXTENDING > EXTEND
EXTENDS > EXTEND
EXTENSE *adj* extensive
EXTENSILE *adj* capable of being extended
EXTENSION *n* room or rooms added to an existing building ▷ *adj* denoting something that can be extended or that extends another object
EXTENSITY *n* that part of sensory perception relating to the spatial aspect of objects
EXTENSIVE *adj* having a large extent, widespread
EXTENSOR *n* muscle that extends a part of the body
EXTENSORS > EXTENSOR
EXTENT *n* range over which something extends, area
EXTENTS > EXTENT
EXTENUATE *vb* make (an offence or fault) less blameworthy
EXTERIOR *n* part or surface on the outside ▷ *adj* of, on, or coming from the outside
EXTERIORS > EXTERIOR
EXTERMINE *vb* exterminate
EXTERN *n* person, such as a physician at a hospital, who has an official connection with an institution but does not reside in it
EXTERNAL *adj* of, situated on, or coming from the outside ▷ *n* external circumstance or aspect, esp one that is superficial or inessential
EXTERNALS > EXTERNAL
EXTERNAT *n* day school
EXTERNATS > EXTERNAT
EXTERNE *same as* > EXTERN
EXTERNES > EXTERNE
EXTERNS > EXTERN
EXTINCT *adj* having died out ▷ *vb* extinguish
EXTINCTED > EXTINCT
EXTINCTS > EXTINCT
EXTINE *same as* > EXINE
EXTINES > EXTINE
EXTIRP *vb* extirpate
EXTIRPATE *vb* destroy utterly
EXTIRPED > EXTIRP
EXTIRPING > EXTIRP
EXTIRPS > EXTIRP
EXTOL *vb* praise highly
EXTOLD *archaic past participle of* > EXTOL
EXTOLL *same as* > EXTOL
EXTOLLED > EXTOLL
EXTOLLER > EXTOL
EXTOLLERS > EXTOL
EXTOLLING > EXTOLL
EXTOLLS > EXTOLL
EXTOLMENT > EXTOL
EXTOLS > EXTOL
EXTORSIVE *adj* intended or tending to extort
EXTORT *vb* get (something) by force or threats
EXTORTED > EXTORT
EXTORTER > EXTORT
EXTORTERS > EXTORT
EXTORTING > EXTORT
EXTORTION *n* act of securing money, favours, etc by intimidation or violence
EXTORTIVE > EXTORT
EXTORTS > EXTORT
EXTRA *adj* more than is usual, expected or needed ▷ *n* additional person or thing ▷ *adv* unusually or exceptionally
EXTRABOLD *n* very bold typeface
EXTRACT *vb* pull out by force ▷ *n* something extracted, such as a passage from a book etc
EXTRACTED > EXTRACT
EXTRACTOR *n* person or thing that extracts
EXTRACTS > EXTRACT
EXTRADITE *vb* send (an accused person) back to his or her own country for trial
EXTRADOS *n* outer curve or surface of an arch or vault
EXTRAIT *n* extracts
EXTRAITS > EXTRAIT
EXTRALITY *n* diplomatic immunity
EXTRANET *n* intranet that is modified to allow outsiders access to it, esp one belonging to a business that allows access to customers
EXTRANETS > EXTRANET
EXTRAPOSE *vb* move (a word or words) to the end of a clause or sentence
EXTRAS > EXTRA
EXTRAUGHT *old past participle of* > EXTRACT
EXTRAVERT *same as* > EXTROVERT
EXTREAT *n* extraction
EXTREATS > EXTREAT
EXTREMA > EXTREMUM
EXTREMAL *n* clause in a recursive definition that specifies that no items other than those

generated by the stated rules fall within the definition, as in *1 is an integer, if n is an integer so is n+1, and nothing else is*
EXTREMALS > EXTREMAL
EXTREME *adj* of a high or the highest degree or intensity ▷ *n* either of the two limits of a scale or range
EXTREMELY > EXTREME
EXTREMER > EXTREME
EXTREMES > EXTREME
EXTREMEST > EXTREME
EXTREMISM > EXTREMIST
EXTREMIST *n* person who favours immoderate methods ▷ *adj* holding extreme opinions
EXTREMITY *n* farthest point
EXTREMUM *n* extreme point
EXTRICATE *vb* free from complication or difficulty
EXTRINSIC *adj* not contained or included within
EXTRORSAL *same as* > EXTRORSE
EXTRORSE *adj* turned or opening outwards or away from the axis
EXTROVERT *adj* lively and outgoing ▷ *n* extrovert person
EXTRUDE *vb* squeeze or force out
EXTRUDED > EXTRUDE
EXTRUDER > EXTRUDE
EXTRUDERS > EXTRUDE
EXTRUDES > EXTRUDE
EXTRUDING > EXTRUDE
EXTRUSION *n* act or process of extruding
EXTRUSIVE *adj* tending to extrude
EXTRUSORY > EXTRUDE
EXTUBATE *vb* remove tube from hollow organ
EXTUBATED > EXTUBATE
EXTUBATES > EXTUBATE
EXUBERANT *adj* high-spirited
EXUBERATE *vb* be exuberant
EXUDATE *same as* > EXUDATION
EXUDATES > EXUDATE
EXUDATION *n* act of exuding or oozing out
EXUDATIVE > EXUDATION
EXUDE *vb* (of a liquid or smell) seep or flow out slowly and steadily
EXUDED > EXUDE
EXUDES > EXUDE
EXUDING > EXUDE
EXUL *n* exile
EXULS > EXUL
EXULT *vb* be joyful or jubilant
EXULTANCE > EXULTANT
EXULTANCY > EXULTANT
EXULTANT *adj* elated or jubilant, esp because of triumph or success
EXULTED > EXULT
EXULTING > EXULT
EXULTS > EXULT
EXURB *n* residential area beyond suburbs
EXURBAN > EXURBIA
EXURBIA *n* region outside the suburbs of a city, consisting of residential areas that are occupied predominantly by rich commuters
EXURBIAS > EXURBIA
EXURBS > EXURB
EXUVIA *n* cast-off exoskeleton of animal
EXUVIAE > EXUVIA
EXUVIAL > EXUVIA
EXUVIATE *vb* shed (a skin or similar outer covering)
EXUVIATED > EXUVIATE
EXUVIATES > EXUVIATE
EXUVIUM *n* cast-off exoskeleton of animal
EYALET *n* province of Ottoman Empire
EYALETS > EYALET
EYAS *n* nestling hawk or falcon, esp one reared for training in falconry
EYASES > EYAS
EYASS *same as* > EYAS
EYASSES > EYASS
EYE *n* organ of sight ▷ *vb* look at carefully or warily
EYEABLE *adj* pleasant to look at
EYEBALL *n* ball-shaped part of the eye ▷ *vb* eye
EYEBALLED > EYEBALL
EYEBALLS > EYEBALL
EYEBANK *n* place in which corneas are stored for use in corneal grafts
EYEBANKS > EYEBANK
EYEBAR *n* bar with flattened ends with holes for connecting pins
EYEBARS > EYEBAR
EYEBATH *same as* > EYECUP
EYEBATHS > EYEBATH
EYEBEAM *n* glance
EYEBEAMS > EYEBEAM
EYEBLACK *another name for* > MASCARA
EYEBLACKS > EYEBLACK
EYEBLINK *n* very small amount of time
EYEBLINKS > EYEBLINK
EYEBOLT *n* threaded bolt, the head of which is formed into a ring or eye for lifting, pulling, or securing
EYEBOLTS > EYEBOLT
EYEBRIGHT *n* any scrophulariaceous annual plant of the genus *Euphrasia*, esp *E. nemorosa*, having small white-and-purple two-lipped flowers: formerly used in the treatment of eye disorders
EYEBROW *n* line of hair on the bony ridge above the eye ▷ *vb* equip with artificial eyebrows
EYEBROWED > EYEBROW
EYEBROWS > EYEBROW
EYECUP *same as* > EYEBATH
EYECUPS > EYECUP
EYED > EYE
EYEDNESS > EYE
EYEDROPS *n* medicine applied to the eyes in drops
EYEFOLD *n* fold of skin above eye
EYEFOLDS > EYEFOLD
EYEFUL *n* view
EYEFULS > EYEFUL
EYEGLASS *n* lens for aiding defective vision
EYEHOLE *n* hole through which something, such as a rope, hook, or bar, is passed
EYEHOLES > EYEHOLE
EYEHOOK *n* hook attached to a ring at the extremity of a rope or chain
EYEHOOKS > EYEHOOK
EYEING > EYE
EYELASH *n* short hair that grows out from the eyelid
EYELASHES > EYELASH
EYELESS > EYE
EYELET *n* small hole for a lace or cord to be passed through ▷ *vb* supply with an eyelet or eyelets
EYELETED > EYELET
EYELETEER *n* small bodkin or other pointed tool for making eyelet holes
EYELETING > EYELET
EYELETS > EYELET
EYELETTED > EYELET
EYELEVEL *adj* level with a person's eyes
EYELIAD *same as* > OEILLADE
EYELIADS > EYELIAD
EYELID *n* fold of skin that covers the eye when it is closed
EYELIDS > EYELID
EYELIFT *n* cosmetic surgery for eyes
EYELIFTS > EYELIFT
EYELIKE > EYE
EYELINER *n* cosmetic used to outline the eyes
EYELINERS > EYELINER
EYEN *pl n* eyes
EYEOPENER *n* something surprising
EYEPIECE *n* lens in a microscope, telescope, etc, into which the person using it looks
EYEPIECES > EYEPIECE
EYEPOINT *n* position of a lens at which the sharpest image is obtained
EYEPOINTS > EYEPOINT
EYEPOPPER *n* something that excites the eye
EYER *n* someone who eyes
EYERS > EYER
EYES > EYE
EYESHADE *n* opaque or tinted translucent visor, worn on the head like a cap to protect the eyes from glare
EYESHADES > EYESHADE
EYESHADOW *n* coloured cosmetic put around the eyes so as to enhance their colour or shape
EYESHINE *n* reflection of light from animal eye at night
EYESHINES > EYESHINE
EYESHOT *n* range of vision
EYESHOTS > EYESHOT
EYESIGHT *n* ability to see
EYESIGHTS > EYESIGHT
EYESOME *adj* attractive
EYESORE *n* ugly object
EYESORES > EYESORE
EYESPOT *n* small area of light-sensitive pigment in some protozoans, algae, and other simple organisms
EYESPOTS > EYESPOT
EYESTALK *n* movable stalk bearing a compound eye at its tip: occurs in crustaceans and some molluscs
EYESTALKS > EYESTALK
EYESTONE *n* device for removing foreign body from eye
EYESTONES > EYESTONE
EYESTRAIN *n* fatigue or irritation of the eyes, caused by tiredness or a failure to wear glasses
EYESTRING *n* tendon holding eye in place
EYETEETH > EYETOOTH
EYETOOTH *n* either of the two canine teeth in the upper jaw
EYEWASH *n* nonsense
EYEWASHES > EYEWASH
EYEWATER *n* lotion for the eyes
EYEWATERS > EYEWATER
EYEWEAR *n* spectacles; glasses
EYEWINK *n* wink of the eye; instant
EYEWINKS > EYEWINK
EYING > EYE
EYLIAD *same as* > OEILLADE
EYLIADS > EYLIAD
EYNE *poetic plural of* > EYE
EYOT *n* island
EYOTS > EYOT
EYRA *n* reddish-brown variety of the jaguarondi
EYRAS > EYRA
EYRE *n* any of the circuit courts held in each shire

from 1176 until the late 13th century
EYRES > EYRE
EYRIE *n* nest of an eagle
EYRIES > EYRIE
EYRIR *n* Icelandic monetary unit worth one hundredth of a krona
EYRY *same as* > EYRIE

Ff

FA *same as* > FAH
FAA *Scot word for* > FALL
FAAN > FAA
FAAS > FAA
FAB *adj* excellent ▷ *n* excellent thing
FABACEOUS *less common term for* > LEGUMINOUS
FABBER > FAB
FABBEST > FAB
FABLE *n* story with a moral ▷ *vb* relate or tell (fables)
FABLED *adj* made famous in legend
FABLER > FABLE
FABLERS > FABLE
FABLES > FABLE
FABLIAU *n* comic usually ribald verse tale, of a kind popular in France in the 12th and 13th centuries
FABLIAUX > FABLIAU
FABLING > FABLE
FABLINGS > FABLE
FABRIC *n* knitted or woven cloth
FABRICANT *n* manufacturer
FABRICATE *vb* make up (a story or lie)
FABRICKED *adj* built
FABRICS > FABRIC
FABS > FAB
FABULAR *adj* relating to fables
FABULATE *vb* make up fables
FABULATED > FABULATE
FABULATES > FABULATE
FABULATOR > FABULATE
FABULISE *vb* make up fables
FABULISED > FABULISE
FABULISES > FABULISE
FABULIST *n* person who invents or recounts fables
FABULISTS > FABULIST
FABULIZE *vb* make up fables
FABULIZED > FABULIZE
FABULIZES > FABULIZE
FABULOUS *adj* excellent
FABURDEN *n* early form of counterpoint
FABURDENS > FABURDEN
FACADE *n* front of a building
FACADES > FACADE
FACE *n* front of the head ▷ *vb* look or turn towards
FACEABLE > FACE
FACEBAR *n* wrestling hold in which a wrestler stretches the skin on his opponent's face backwards
FACEBARS > FACEBAR
FACECLOTH *n* small piece of cloth used to wash the face and hands
FACED > FACE
FACEDOWN *vb* confront and force (someone or something) to back down
FACEDOWNS > FACEDOWN
FACELESS *adj* impersonal, anonymous
FACELIFT *n* cosmetic surgery for the face
FACELIFTS > FACELIFT
FACEMAIL *n* computer program which uses an electronically generated face to deliver messages on screen
FACEMAILS > FACEMAIL
FACEMAN *n* miner who works at the coalface
FACEMASK *n* protective mask for the face
FACEMASKS > FACEMASK
FACEMEN > FACEMAN
FACEPLATE *n* perforated circular metal plate that can be attached to the headstock of a lathe in order to hold flat or irregularly shaped workpieces
FACEPRINT *n* digitally recorded representation of a person's face that can be used for security purposes because it is as individual as a fingerprint
FACER *n* difficulty or problem
FACERS > FACER
FACES > FACE
FACET *n* aspect ▷ *vb* cut facets in (a gemstone)
FACETE *adj* witty and humorous
FACETED > FACET
FACETELY > FACETE
FACETIAE *pl n* humorous or witty sayings
FACETING > FACET
FACETIOUS *adj* funny or trying to be funny, esp at inappropriate times
FACETS > FACET
FACETTED > FACET
FACETTING > FACET
FACEUP *adj* with the face or surface exposed
FACIA *same as* > FASCIA
FACIAE > FACIA
FACIAL *adj* of or relating to the face ▷ *n* beauty treatment for the face
FACIALLY > FACIAL
FACIALS > FACIAL
FACIAS > FACIA
FACIEND *n* multiplicand
FACIENDS > FACIEND
FACIES *n* general form and appearance of an individual or a group of plants or animals
FACILE *adj* (of a remark, argument, etc) superficial and showing lack of real thought
FACILELY > FACILE
FACILITY *n* skill
FACING *n* lining or covering for decoration or reinforcement
FACINGS > FACING
FACONNE *adj* denoting a fabric with the design woven in ▷ *n* such a fabric
FACONNES > FACONNE
FACSIMILE *n* exact copy ▷ *vb* make an exact copy of
FACT *n* event or thing known to have happened or existed
FACTFUL > FACT
FACTICE *n* soft rubbery material made by reacting sulphur or sulphur chloride with vegetable oil
FACTICES > FACTICE
FACTICITY *n* philosophical process
FACTION *n* (dissenting) minority group within a larger body
FACTIONAL > FACTION
FACTIONS > FACTION

FACTIOUS *adj* of or producing factions
FACTIS *variant of* > FACTICE
FACTISES > FACTIS
FACTITIVE *adj* denoting a verb taking a direct object as well as a noun in apposition, as for example *elect* in *They elected John president*, where *John* is the direct object and *president* is the complement
FACTIVE *adj* (of a linguistic context) giving rise to the presupposition that a sentence occurring in that context is true, as *John regrets that Mary did not attend*
FACTOID *n* piece of unreliable information believed to be true because of the way it is presented or repeated in print
FACTOIDAL > FACTOID
FACTOIDS > FACTOID
FACTOR *n* element contributing to a result ▷ *vb* engage in the business of a factor
FACTORAGE *n* commission payable to a factor
FACTORED > FACTOR
FACTORIAL *n* product of all the integers from one to a given number ▷ *adj* of factorials or factors
FACTORIES > FACTORY
FACTORING *n* business of a factor
FACTORISE *same as* > FACTORIZE
FACTORIZE *vb* calculate the factors of (a number)
FACTORS > FACTOR
FACTORY *n* building where goods are manufactured
FACTOTUM *n* person employed to do all sorts of work
FACTOTUMS > FACTOTUM
FACTS > FACT
FACTSHEET *n* printed sheet containing information relating to items covered in a television or radio programme
FACTUAL *adj* concerning facts rather than opinions or theories
FACTUALLY > FACTUAL
FACTUM *n* something done, deed
FACTUMS > FACTUM
FACTURE *n* construction
FACTURES > FACTURE
FACULA *n* any of the bright areas on the sun's surface, usually appearing just before a sunspot and subject to the same 11-year cycle
FACULAE > FACULA
FACULAR > FACULA
FACULTIES > FACULTY
FACULTY *n* physical or mental ability
FACUNDITY *n* eloquence, fluency of speech
FAD *n* short-lived fashion
FADABLE > FADE
FADAISE *n* silly remark
FADAISES > FADAISE
FADDIER > FADDY
FADDIEST > FADDY
FADDINESS *n* excessive fussiness
FADDISH > FAD
FADDISHLY > FAD
FADDISM > FAD
FADDISMS > FAD
FADDIST > FAD
FADDISTS > FAD
FADDLE *vb* mess around, toy with
FADDLED > FADDLE
FADDLES > FADDLE
FADDLING > FADDLE
FADDY *adj* unreasonably fussy, particularly about food
FADE *vb* (cause to) lose brightness, colour, or strength ▷ *n* act or an instance of fading
FADEAWAY *n* fading to the point of disappearance
FADEAWAYS > FADEAWAY
FADED > FADE
FADEDLY > FADE
FADEDNESS > FADE
FADEIN *n* gradual appearance of image on film
FADEINS > FADEIN
FADELESS *adj* not subject to fading
FADEOUT *n* gradual disappearance of image on film
FADEOUTS > FADEOUT
FADER > FADE
FADERS > FADE
FADES > FADE
FADEUR *n* blandness, insipidness
FADEURS > FADEUR
FADGE *vb* agree ▷ *n* package of wool in a wool-bale that weighs less than 100 kilograms
FADGED > FADGE
FADGES > FADGE
FADGING > FADGE
FADIER > FADY
FADIEST > FADY
FADING *n* variation in the strength of received radio signals due to variations in the conditions of the transmission medium
FADINGS > FADING
FADLIKE > FAD
FADO *n* type of melancholy Portuguese folk song
FADOMETER *n* instrument used to determine the resistance to fading of a pigment or dye
FADOS > FADO
FADS > FAD
FADY *adj* faded
FAE *Scot word for* > FROM
FAECAL *adj* of, relating to, or consisting of faeces
FAECES *pl n* waste matter discharged from the anus
FAENA *n* matador's final series of passes with sword and cape before the kill
FAENAS > FAENA
FAERIE *n* land of fairies
FAERIES > FAERY
FAERY *same as* > FAERIE
FAFF *vb* dither or fuss
FAFFED > FAFF
FAFFING > FAFF
FAFFS > FAFF
FAG *same as* > FAGGOT
FAGACEOUS *adj* of, relating to, or belonging to the *Fagaceae*, a family of trees, including beech, oak, and chestnut, whose fruit is partly or wholly enclosed in a husk (cupule)
FAGGED > FAG
FAGGERIES > FAGGERY
FAGGERY *n* offensive term for homosexuality
FAGGIER > FAG
FAGGIEST > FAG
FAGGING > FAG
FAGGINGS > FAG
FAGGOT *n* ball of chopped liver, herbs, and bread ▷ *vb* collect into a bundle or bundles
FAGGOTED > FAGGOT
FAGGOTING *n* decorative needlework done by tying vertical threads together in bundles
FAGGOTRY *n* offensive term for homosexuality
FAGGOTS > FAGGOT
FAGGOTY > FAGGOT
FAGGY > FAG
FAGIN *n* criminal
FAGINS > FAGIN
FAGOT *same as* > FAGGOT
FAGOTED > FAGOT
FAGOTER > FAGOT
FAGOTERS > FAGOT
FAGOTING *same as* > FAGGOTING
FAGOTINGS > FAGOTING
FAGOTS > FAGOT
FAGOTTI > FAGOTTO
FAGOTTIST *n* bassoon player
FAGOTTO *n* bassoon
FAGS > FAG
FAH *n* (in tonic sol-fa) fourth degree of any major scale
FAHLBAND *n* thin bed of schistose rock impregnated with metallic sulphides
FAHLBANDS > FAHLBAND
FAHLERZ *n* copper ore
FAHLERZES > FAHLERZ
FAHLORE *n* copper ore
FAHLORES > FAHLORE
FAHS > FAH
FAIBLE *variant of* > FOIBLE
FAIBLES > FAIBLE
FAIENCE *n* tin-glazed earthenware
FAIENCES > FAIENCE
FAIK *vb* grasp
FAIKED > FAIK
FAIKES > FAIK
FAIKING > FAIK
FAIKS > FAIK
FAIL *vb* be unsuccessful ▷ *n* instance of not passing an exam or test
FAILED > FAIL
FAILING *n* weak point ▷ *prep* in the absence of
FAILINGLY > FAILING
FAILINGS > FAILING
FAILLE *n* soft light ribbed fabric of silk, rayon, or taffeta
FAILLES > FAILLE
FAILS > FAIL
FAILURE *n* act or instance of failing
FAILURES > FAILURE
FAIN *adv* gladly ▷ *adj* willing or eager
FAINE *variant of* > FAIN
FAINEANCE > FAINEANT
FAINEANCY > FAINEANT
FAINEANT *n* lazy person ▷ *adj* indolent
FAINEANTS > FAINEANT
FAINED > FAIN
FAINER > FAIN
FAINES > FAINE
FAINEST > FAIN
FAINING > FAIN
FAINITES *interj* cry for truce or respite from the rules of a game
FAINLY > FAIN
FAINNE *n* small ring-shaped metal badge worn by advocates of the Irish language
FAINNES > FAINNE
FAINNESS > FAIN
FAINS *same as* > FAINITES
FAINT *adj* lacking clarity, brightness, or volume ▷ *vb* lose consciousness temporarily ▷ *n* temporary loss of consciousness
FAINTED > FAINT
FAINTER > FAINT
FAINTERS > FAINT
FAINTEST > FAINT
FAINTIER > FAINTY
FAINTIEST > FAINTY
FAINTING > FAINT
FAINTINGS > FAINT
FAINTISH > FAINT
FAINTLY > FAINT
FAINTNESS > FAINT
FAINTS > FAINT
FAINTY > FAINT

FAIR *adj* unbiased and reasonable ▷ *adv* fairly ▷ *n* travelling entertainment with sideshows, rides, and amusements ▷ *vb* join together so as to form a smooth or regular shape or surface
FAIRED > FAIR
FAIRER > FAIR
FAIREST > FAIR
FAIRFACED *adj* (of brickwork) having a neat smooth unplastered surface
FAIRGOER *n* person attending fair
FAIRGOERS > FAIRGOER
FAIRIES > FAIRY
FAIRILY > FAIRY
FAIRING *n* curved metal structure fitted round part of a car, aircraft, etc to reduce drag
FAIRINGS > FAIRING
FAIRISH *adj* moderately good, well, etc
FAIRISHLY > FAIRISH
FAIRLEAD *n* block or ring through which a line is rove to keep it clear of obstructions, prevent chafing, or maintain it at an angle
FAIRLEADS > FAIRLEAD
FAIRLY *adv* moderately
FAIRNESS > FAIR
FAIRS > FAIR
FAIRWAY *n* smooth area between the tee and the green
FAIRWAYS > FAIRWAY
FAIRY *n* imaginary small creature with magic powers
FAIRYDOM > FAIRY
FAIRYDOMS > FAIRY
FAIRYHOOD > FAIRY
FAIRYISM > FAIRY
FAIRYISMS > FAIRY
FAIRYLAND *n* imaginary place where fairies live
FAIRYLIKE > FAIRY
FAIRYTALE *n* story about fairies or other mythical or magical beings, esp one of traditional origin told to children
FAITH *n* strong belief, esp without proof
FAITHCURE *n* healing through prayer
FAITHED *adj* having faith or a faith
FAITHER *Scot word for* > FATHER
FAITHERS > FAITHER
FAITHFUL *adj* loyal
FAITHFULS > FAITHFUL
FAITHING *n* practising a faith
FAITHLESS *adj* disloyal or dishonest
FAITHS > FAITH
FAITOR *n* traitor, impostor
FAITORS > FAITOR
FAITOUR *n* impostor
FAITOURS > FAITOUR
FAIX *n* faith
FAJITA > FAJITAS
FAJITAS *pl n* Mexican dish of soft tortillas wrapped around fried strips of meat or vegetables
FAKE *vb* cause something not genuine to appear real or more valuable by fraud ▷ *n* person, thing, or act that is not genuine ▷ *adj* not genuine
FAKED > FAKE
FAKEER *same as* > FAKIR
FAKEERS > FAKEER
FAKEMENT *n* something false, counterfeit
FAKEMENTS > FAKEMENT
FAKER > FAKE
FAKERIES > FAKE
FAKERS > FAKE
FAKERY > FAKE
FAKES > FAKE
FAKEY *n* skateboarding term
FAKING > FAKE
FAKIR *n* Muslim who spurns worldly possessions
FAKIRISM > FAKIR
FAKIRISMS > FAKIR
FAKIRS > FAKIR
FALAFEL *n* ball or cake of ground spiced chickpeas, deep-fried and often served with pitta bread
FALAFELS > FALAFEL
FALAJ *n* water channel
FALANGISM > FALANGIST
FALANGIST *n* member of the Fascist movement founded in Spain in 1933
FALBALA *n* gathered flounce, frill, or ruffle
FALBALAS > FALBALA
FALCADE *n* movement of a horse
FALCADES > FALCADE
FALCATE *adj* shaped like a sickle
FALCATED > FALCATE
FALCATION > FALCATE
FALCES > FALX
FALCHION *n* short and slightly curved medieval sword broader towards the point
FALCHIONS > FALCHION
FALCIFORM *same as* > FALCATE
FALCON *n* small bird of prey
FALCONER *n* person who breeds or trains hawks or who follows the sport of falconry
FALCONERS > FALCONER
FALCONET *n* any of various small falcons, esp any of the Asiatic genus *Microhierax*
FALCONETS > FALCONET
FALCONINE *adj* of, relating to, or resembling a falcon
FALCONOID *n* chemical thought to resist cancer
FALCONRY *n* art of training falcons
FALCONS > FALCON
FALCULA *n* sharp curved claw, esp of a bird
FALCULAE > FALCULA
FALCULAS > FALCULA
FALCULATE > FALCULA
FALDAGE *n* feudal right
FALDAGES > FALDAGE
FALDERAL *n* showy but worthless trifle
FALDERALS > FALDERAL
FALDEROL *same as* > FALDERAL
FALDEROLS > FALDEROL
FALDETTA *n* Maltese woman's garment with a stiffened hood
FALDETTAS > FALDETTA
FALDSTOOL *n* backless seat, sometimes capable of being folded, used by bishops and certain other prelates
FALL *vb* drop from a higher to a lower place through the force of gravity ▷ *n* falling
FALLACIES > FALLACY
FALLACY *n* false belief
FALLAL *n* showy ornament, trinket, or article of dress
FALLALERY > FALLAL
FALLALS > FALLAL
FALLAWAY *n* friendship that has been withdrawn
FALLAWAYS > FALLAWAY
FALLBACK *n* something that recedes or retreats
FALLBACKS > FALLBACK
FALLBOARD *n* cover for piano keyboard
FALLEN > FALL
FALLER *n* any device that falls or operates machinery by falling, as in a spinning machine
FALLERS > FALLER
FALLFISH *n* large North American freshwater cyprinid fish, *Semotilus corporalis*, resembling the chub
FALLIBLE *adj* (of a person) liable to make mistakes
FALLIBLY > FALLIBLE
FALLING > FALL
FALLINGS > FALL
FALLOFF *n* decline or drop
FALLOFFS > FALLOFF
FALLOUT *n* radioactive particles spread as a result of a nuclear explosion ▷ *vb* disagree and quarrel ▷ *sentence substitute* order to leave a parade or disciplinary formation
FALLOUTS > FALLOUT
FALLOW *adj* (of land) ploughed but left unseeded to regain fertility ▷ *n* land treated in this way ▷ *vb* leave (land) unseeded after ploughing and harrowing it
FALLOWED > FALLOW
FALLOWER > FALLOW
FALLOWEST > FALLOW
FALLOWING > FALLOW
FALLOWS > FALLOW
FALLS > FALL
FALSE *adj* not true or correct ▷ *adv* in a false or dishonest manner ▷ *vb* falsify
FALSED > FALSE
FALSEFACE *n* mask
FALSEHOOD *n* quality of being untrue
FALSELY > FALSE
FALSENESS > FALSE
FALSER > FALSE
FALSERS *n* colloquial term for false teeth
FALSES > FALSE
FALSEST > FALSE
FALSETTO *n* voice pitched higher than one's natural range
FALSETTOS > FALSETTO
FALSEWORK *n* framework supporting something under construction
FALSIE *n* pad used to enlarge breast shape
FALSIES > FALSIE
FALSIFIED > FALSIFY
FALSIFIER > FALSIFY
FALSIFIES > FALSIFY
FALSIFY *vb* alter fraudulently
FALSING > FALSE
FALSISH > FALSE
FALSISM > FALSE
FALSISMS > FALSE
FALSITIES > FALSITY
FALSITY *n* state of being false
FALTBOAT *n* collapsible boat made of waterproof material stretched over a light framework
FALTBOATS > FALTBOAT
FALTER *vb* be hesitant, weak, or unsure ▷ *n* uncertainty or hesitancy in speech or action
FALTERED > FALTER
FALTERER > FALTER
FALTERERS > FALTER
FALTERING > FALTER
FALTERS > FALTER
FALX *n* sickle-shaped anatomical structure
FAME *n* state of being widely known or recognized ▷ *vb* make known or famous
FAMED > FAME

FAMELESS > FAME
FAMES > FAME
FAMILIAL *adj* of or relating to the family
FAMILIAR *adj* well-known ▷ *n* demon supposed to attend a witch
FAMILIARS *n* attendant demons
FAMILIES > FAMILY
FAMILISM *n* practice of a mystical Christian religious sect of the 16th and 17th centuries based upon love
FAMILISMS > FAMILISM
FAMILLE *n* type of Chinese porcelain
FAMILLES > FAMILLE
FAMILY *n* group of parents and their children ▷ *adj* suitable for parents and children together
FAMINE *n* severe shortage of food
FAMINES > FAMINE
FAMING > FAME
FAMISH *vb* be or make very hungry or weak
FAMISHED *adj* very hungry
FAMISHES > FAMISH
FAMISHING > FAMISH
FAMOUS *adj* very well-known ▷ *vb* make famous
FAMOUSED > FAMOUS
FAMOUSES > FAMOUS
FAMOUSING > FAMOUS
FAMOUSLY *adv* excellently
FAMULI > FAMULUS
FAMULUS *n* (formerly) the attendant of a sorcerer or scholar
FAMULUSES > FAMULUS
FAN *n* hand-held or mechanical object used to create a current of air for ventilation or cooling ▷ *vb* blow or cool with a fan
FANAL *n* lighthouse
FANALS > FANAL
FANATIC *n* person who is excessively enthusiastic about something ▷ *adj* excessively enthusiastic
FANATICAL *adj* surpassing what is normal or accepted in enthusiasm for or belief in something
FANATICS > FANATIC
FANBASE *n* body of admirers of a particular pop singer, sports team, etc
FANBASES > FANBASE
FANCIABLE *adj* sexually attractive
FANCIED *adj* imaginary
FANCIER *n* person who is interested in and often breeds plants or animals
FANCIERS > FANCIER
FANCIES > FANCY
FANCIEST > FANCY
FANCIFIED > FANCIFY
FANCIFIES > FANCIFY
FANCIFUL *adj* not based on fact
FANCIFY *vb* make more beautiful
FANCILESS > FANCY
FANCILY > FANCY
FANCINESS > FANCY
FANCY *adj* elaborate, not plain ▷ *n* sudden irrational liking or desire ▷ *vb* be sexually attracted to
FANCYING > FANCY
FANCYWORK *n* ornamental needlework
FAND *vb* try
FANDANGLE *n* elaborate ornament
FANDANGO *n* lively Spanish dance
FANDANGOS > FANDANGO
FANDED > FAND
FANDING > FAND
FANDOM *n* collectively, the fans of a sport, pastime or person
FANDOMS > FANDOM
FANDS > FAND
FANE *n* temple or shrine
FANEGA *n* Spanish unit of measurement
FANEGADA *n* Spanish unit of land area
FANEGADAS > FANEGADA
FANEGAS > FANEGA
FANES > FANE
FANFARADE *n* fanfare
FANFARE *n* short loud tune played on brass instruments ▷ *vb* perform a fanfare
FANFARED > FANFARE
FANFARES > FANFARE
FANFARING > FANFARE
FANFARON *n* braggart
FANFARONA *n* gold chain
FANFARONS > FANFARON
FANFIC *n* fiction written around previously established characters invented by other authors
FANFICS > FANFIC
FANFOLD *vb* fold (paper) like a fan
FANFOLDED > FANFOLD
FANFOLDS > FANFOLD
FANG *n* snake's tooth which injects poison ▷ *vb* seize
FANGA *same as* > FANEGA
FANGAS > FANGA
FANGED > FANG
FANGING > FANG
FANGLE *vb* fashion
FANGLED > FANGLE
FANGLES > FANGLE
FANGLESS > FANG
FANGLIKE > FANG
FANGLING > FANGLE
FANGO *n* mud from thermal springs in Italy, used in the treatment of rheumatic disease
FANGOS > FANGO
FANGS > FANG
FANION *n* small flag used by surveyors to mark stations
FANIONS > FANION
FANJET *same as* > TURBOFAN
FANJETS > FANJET
FANK *n* sheep pen
FANKLE *vb* entangle ▷ *n* tangle
FANKLED > FANKLE
FANKLES > FANKLE
FANKLING > FANKLE
FANKS > FANK
FANLIGHT *n* semicircular window over a door or window
FANLIGHTS > FANLIGHT
FANLIKE > FAN
FANNED > FAN
FANNEL *n* ecclesiastical vestment
FANNELL *variant of* > FANNEL
FANNELLS > FANNELL
FANNELS > FANNEL
FANNER > FAN
FANNERS > FAN
FANNIES > FANNY
FANNING > FAN
FANNINGS > FAN
FANNY *n* taboo word for female genitals
FANO *same as* > FANON
FANON *n* collar-shaped vestment worn by the pope when celebrating mass
FANONS > FANON
FANOS > FANO
FANS > FAN
FANTAD *n* nervous, agitated state
FANTADS > FANTAD
FANTAIL *n* small New Zealand bird with a tail like a fan
FANTAILED *adj* having a tail like a fan
FANTAILS > FANTAIL
FANTASIA *n* musical composition of an improvised nature
FANTASIAS > FANTASIA
FANTASIE *same as* > FANTASY
FANTASIED > FANTASY
FANTASIES > FANTASY
FANTASISE *same as* > FANTASIZE
FANTASIST *n* person who indulges in fantasies
FANTASIZE *vb* indulge in daydreams
FANTASM *archaic spelling of* > PHANTASM
FANTASMAL > FANTASM
FANTASMIC > FANTASM
FANTASMS > FANTASM
FANTASQUE *n* fantasy
FANTAST *n* dreamer or visionary
FANTASTIC *adj* very good ▷ *n* person who dresses or behaves eccentrically
FANTASTRY *n* condition of being fantastic
FANTASTS > FANTAST
FANTASY *n* far-fetched notion ▷ *adj* of a competition in which a participant selects players for an imaginary, ideal team and points are awarded according to the actual performances of the chosen players ▷ *vb* fantasize
FANTEEG *n* nervous, agitated state
FANTEEGS > FANTEEG
FANTIGUE *variant of* > FANTEEG
FANTIGUES > FANTIGUE
FANTOD *n* crotchety or faddish behaviour
FANTODS > FANTOD
FANTOM *archaic spelling of* > PHANTOM
FANTOMS > FANTOM
FANTOOSH *adj* pretentious
FANUM *n* temple
FANUMS > FANUM
FANWISE *adj* like a fan
FANWORT *n* aquatic plant
FANWORTS > FANWORT
FANZINE *n* magazine produced by fans of a specific interest, soccer club, etc, for fellow fans
FANZINES > FANZINE
FAP *adj* drunk
FAQIR *same as* > FAKIR
FAQIRS > FAQIR
FAQUIR *variant of* > FAQIR
FAQUIRS > FAQUIR
FAR *adv* at, to, or from a great distance ▷ *adj* remote in space or time ▷ *vb* go far
FARAD *n* unit of electrical capacitance
FARADAIC *same as* > FARADIC
FARADAY *n* quantity of electricity, used in electrochemical calculations
FARADAYS > FARADAY
FARADIC *adj* of or concerned with an intermittent asymmetric alternating current such as that induced in the secondary winding of an induction coil
FARADISE *same as* > FARADIZE
FARADISED > FARADISE
FARADISER > FARADISE
FARADISES > FARADISE
FARADISM *n* therapeutic use of faradic currents
FARADISMS > FARADISM
FARADIZE *vb* treat (an organ or part) with faradic currents
FARADIZED > FARADIZE

FARADIZER > FARADIZE
FARADIZES > FARADIZE
FARADS > FARAD
FARAND *n* manner, fashion
FARANDINE *n* silk and wool cloth
FARANDOLE *n* lively dance in six-eight or four-four time from Provence
FARAWAY *adj* very distant
FARAWAYS *same as* > FARAWAY
FARCE *n* boisterous comedy ▷ *vb* enliven (a speech, etc) with jokes
FARCED > FARCE
FARCEMEAT > FORCEMEAT
FARCER *same as* > FARCEUR
FARCERS > FARCER
FARCES > FARCE
FARCEUR *n* writer of or performer in farces
FARCEURS > FARCEUR
FARCEUSE *n* female farceur
FARCEUSES > FARCEUSE
FARCI *adj* (of food) stuffed
FARCICAL *adj* ludicrous
FARCIE *same as* > FARCI
FARCIED *adj* afflicted with farcy
FARCIES > FARCY
FARCIFIED > FARCIFY
FARCIFIES > FARCIFY
FARCIFY *vb* turn into a farce
FARCIN *n* equine disease
FARCING > FARCE
FARCINGS > FARCE
FARCINS > FARCIN
FARCY *n* form of glanders in which lymph vessels near the skin become thickened, with skin lesions and abscess-forming nodules, caused by a bacterium, *Burkholderia mallei*
FARD *n* paint for the face, esp white paint ▷ *vb* paint (the face) with fard
FARDAGE *n* material laid beneath or between cargo
FARDAGES > FARDAGE
FARDED > FARD
FARDEL *n* bundle or burden
FARDELS > FARDEL
FARDEN *n* farthing
FARDENS > FARDEN
FARDING > FARD
FARDINGS > FARD
FARDS > FARD
FARE *n* charge for a passenger's journey ▷ *vb* get on (as specified)
FAREBOX *n* box where money for bus fares is placed
FAREBOXES > FAREBOX
FARED > FARE
FARER > FARE
FARERS > FARE
FARES > FARE
FAREWELL *interj* goodbye ▷ *n* act of saying goodbye and leaving ▷ *vb* say goodbye ▷ *adj* parting or closing ▷ *sentence substitute* goodbye
FAREWELLS > FAREWELL
FARFAL *same as* > FELAFEL
FARFALLE *n* pasta in bow shapes
FARFALS > FARFAL
FARFEL *same as* > FELAFEL
FARFELS *same as* > FARFEL
FARFET *adj* far-fetched
FARINA *n* flour or meal made from any kind of cereal grain
FARINAS > FARINA
FARING > FARE
FARINHA *n* cassava meal
FARINHAS > FARINHA
FARINOSE *adj* similar to or yielding farina
FARL *n* thin cake of oatmeal, often triangular in shape
FARLE *same as* > FARL
FARLES > FARLE
FARLS > FARL
FARM *n* area of land for growing crops or rearing livestock ▷ *vb* cultivate (land)
FARMABLE > FARM
FARMED *adj* (of fish or game) reared on a farm rather than caught in the wild
FARMER *n* person who owns or runs a farm
FARMERESS *n* female farmer
FARMERIES > FARMERY
FARMERS > FARMER
FARMERY *n* farm buildings
FARMHAND *n* person who is hired to work on a farm
FARMHANDS > FARMHAND
FARMHOUSE *n* house attached to a farm
FARMING *n* business or skill of agriculture
FARMINGS > FARMING
FARMLAND *n* land that is used for or suitable for farming
FARMLANDS > FARMLAND
FARMOST > FAR
FARMS > FARM
FARMSTEAD *n* farm and its buildings
FARMWIFE *n* woman who works on a farm
FARMWIVES > FARMWIFE
FARMWORK *n* tasks carried out on a farm
FARMWORKS > FARMWORK
FARMYARD *n* small area of land enclosed by or around the farm buildings
FARMYARDS > FARMYARD
FARNARKEL *vb* spend time or act in a careless or inconsequential manner
FARNESOL *n* colourless aromatic sesquiterpene alcohol found in many essential oils and used in the form of its derivatives in perfumery
FARNESOLS > FARNESOL
FARNESS > FAR
FARNESSES > FAR
FARO *n* gambling game in which players bet against the dealer on what cards he will turn up
FAROLITO *n* votive candle
FAROLITOS > FAROLITO
FAROS > FARO
FAROUCHE *adj* sullen or shy
FARRAGO *n* jumbled mixture of things
FARRAGOES > FARRAGO
FARRAGOS > FARRAGO
FARRAND *variant of* > FARAND
FARRANT *variant of* > FARAND
FARRED > FAR
FARREN *n* allotted ground
FARRENS > FARREN
FARRIER *n* person who shoes horses
FARRIERS > FARRIER
FARRIERY *n* art, work, or establishment of a farrier
FARRING > FAR
FARROW *n* litter of piglets ▷ *vb* (of a sow) give birth ▷ *adj* (of a cow) not calving in a given year
FARROWED > FARROW
FARROWING > FARROW
FARROWS > FARROW
FARRUCA *n* flamenco dance performed by men
FARRUCAS > FARRUCA
FARS > FAR
FARSE *vb* insert into
FARSED > FARSE
FARSEEING *adj* having shrewd judgment
FARSES > FARSE
FARSIDE *n* part of the Moon facing away from the Earth
FARSIDES > FARSIDE
FARSING > FARSE
FART *n* emission of gas from the anus ▷ *vb* emit gas from the anus
FARTED > FART
FARTHEL *same as* > FARL
FARTHELS > FARTHEL
FARTHER > FAR
FARTHEST > FAR
FARTHING *n* former British coin equivalent to a quarter of a penny
FARTHINGS > FARTHING
FARTING > FART
FARTLEK *n* in sport, another name for interval training
FARTLEKS > FARTLEK
FARTS > FART
FAS > FA
FASCES *pl n* (in ancient Rome) a bundle of rods containing an axe with its blade pointing out
FASCI > FASCIO
FASCIA *n* outer surface of a dashboard
FASCIAE > FASCIA
FASCIAL > FASCIA
FASCIAS > FASCIA
FASCIATE *adj* (of stems and branches) abnormally flattened due to coalescence
FASCIATED *same as* > FASCIATE
FASCICLE *same as* > FASCICULE
FASCICLED *adj* in instalments
FASCICLES > FASCICLE
FASCICULE *n* one part of a printed work that is published in instalments
FASCICULI > FASCICULE
FASCIITIS *n* inflammation of the fascia of a muscle
FASCINATE *vb* attract and interest strongly
FASCINE *n* bundle of long sticks used for filling in ditches and in the construction of embankments, roads, fortifications, etc
FASCINES > FASCINE
FASCIO *n* political group
FASCIOLA *n* band
FASCIOLAS > FASCIOLA
FASCIOLE *n* band
FASCIOLES > FASCIOLE
FASCIS > FASCI
FASCISM *n* right-wing totalitarian political system characterized by state control and extreme nationalism
FASCISMI > FASCISMO
FASCISMO *Italian word for* > FASCISM
FASCISMS > FASCISM
FASCIST *n* adherent or practitioner of fascism ▷ *adj* characteristic of or relating to fascism
FASCISTA *Italian word for* > FASCIST
FASCISTI > FASCISTA
FASCISTIC > FASCIST
FASCISTS > FASCIST
FASCITIS *same as* > FASCIITIS
FASH *n* worry ▷ *vb* trouble
FASHED > FASH
FASHERIES > FASHERY
FASHERY *n* difficulty, trouble
FASHES > FASH
FASHING > FASH
FASHION *n* style in clothes, hairstyle, etc, popular at a particular time ▷ *vb* form or make into a particular shape
FASHIONED > FASHION

FASHIONER > FASHION
FASHIONS > FASHION
FASHIONY *adj* of or relating to fashion
FASHIOUS *adj* troublesome
FAST *adj* (capable of) acting or moving quickly ▷ *adv* quickly ▷ *vb* go without food, esp for religious reasons ▷ *n* period of fasting
FASTBACK *n* car having a back that forms one continuous slope from roof to rear
FASTBACKS > FASTBACK
FASTBALL *n* ball pitched at the pitcher's top speed
FASTBALLS > FASTBALL
FASTED > FAST
FASTEN *vb* make or become firmly fixed or joined
FASTENED > FASTEN
FASTENER > FASTEN
FASTENERS > FASTEN
FASTENING *n* something that fastens something, such as a clasp or lock
FASTENS > FASTEN
FASTER > FAST
FASTERS > FAST
FASTEST > FAST
FASTI *n* in ancient Rome, days when business could legally be carried out
FASTIE *n* deceitful act
FASTIES > FASTIE
FASTIGIUM *n* highest point
FASTING > FAST
FASTINGS > FAST
FASTISH > FAST
FASTLY > FAST
FASTNESS *n* fortress, safe place
FASTS > FAST
FASTUOUS *adj* arrogant
FAT *adj* having excess flesh on the body ▷ *n* extra flesh on the body
FATAL *adj* causing death or ruin
FATALISM *n* belief that all events are predetermined and people are powerless to change their destinies
FATALISMS > FATALISM
FATALIST > FATALISM
FATALISTS > FATALISM
FATALITY *n* death caused by an accident or disaster
FATALLY *adv* resulting in death or disaster
FATALNESS > FATAL
FATBACK *n* fat, usually salted, from the upper part of a side of pork
FATBACKS > FATBACK
FATBIRD *n* nocturnal bird
FATBIRDS > FATBIRD
FATE *n* power supposed to predetermine events ▷ *vb* predetermine
FATED *adj* destined
FATEFUL *adj* having important, usu disastrous, consequences
FATEFULLY > FATEFUL
FATES > FATE
FATHEAD *n* stupid person
FATHEADED *adj* stupid
FATHEADS > FATHEAD
FATHER *n* male parent ▷ *vb* be the father of (offspring)
FATHERED > FATHER
FATHERING > FATHER
FATHERLY *adj* kind or protective, like a father
FATHERS > FATHER
FATHOM *n* unit of length, used in navigation, equal to six feet (1.83 metres) ▷ *vb* understand
FATHOMED > FATHOM
FATHOMER > FATHOM
FATHOMERS > FATHOM
FATHOMING > FATHOM
FATHOMS > FATHOM
FATIDIC *adj* prophetic
FATIDICAL *same as* > FATIDIC
FATIGABLE > FATIGUE
FATIGATE *vb* fatigue
FATIGATED > FATIGATE
FATIGATES > FATIGATE
FATIGUE *n* extreme physical or mental tiredness ▷ *vb* tire out
FATIGUED > FATIGUE
FATIGUES > FATIGUE
FATIGUING > FATIGUE
FATING > FATE
FATISCENT > FATISCENCE
FATLESS > FAT
FATLIKE > FAT
FATLING *n* young farm animal fattened for killing
FATLINGS > FATLING
FATLY > FAT
FATNESS > FAT
FATNESSES > FAT
FATS > FAT
FATSIA *n* any shrub of the araliaceous genus *Fatsia*, esp *F. japonica*, with large deeply palmate leaves and umbels of white flowers
FATSIAS > FATSIA
FATSO *n* fat person: used as an insulting or disparaging term of address
FATSOES > FATSO
FATSOS > FATSO
FATSTOCK *n* livestock fattened and ready for market
FATSTOCKS > FATSTOCK
FATTED > FAT
FATTEN *vb* (cause to) become fat
FATTENED > FATTEN
FATTENER > FATTEN
FATTENERS > FATTEN
FATTENING > FATTEN
FATTENS > FATTEN
FATTER > FAT
FATTEST > FAT
FATTIER > FATTY
FATTIES > FATTY
FATTIEST > FATTY
FATTILY > FATTY
FATTINESS > FATTY
FATTING > FAT
FATTISH > FAT
FATTISM *n* discrimination on the basis of weight, esp prejudice against those considered to be overweight
FATTISMS > FATTISM
FATTIST > FATTISM
FATTISTS > FATTISM
FATTRELS *n* ends of ribbon
FATTY *adj* containing fat ▷ *n* fat person
FATUITIES > FATUITY
FATUITOUS > FATUITY
FATUITY *n* foolish thoughtlessness
FATUOUS *adj* foolish
FATUOUSLY > FATUOUS
FATWA *n* religious decree issued by a Muslim leader ▷ *vb* issue a fatwa
FATWAED > FATWA
FATWAH *same as* > FATWA
FATWAHED > FATWAH
FATWAHING > FATWAH
FATWAHS > FATWAH
FATWAING > FATWA
FATWAS > FATWA
FATWOOD *n* wood used for kindling
FATWOODS > FATWOOD
FAUBOURG *n* suburb or quarter, esp of a French city
FAUBOURGS > FAUBOURG
FAUCAL *adj* of or relating to the fauces
FAUCALS > FAUCAL
FAUCES *n* area between the cavity of the mouth and the pharynx, including the surrounding tissues
FAUCET *n* tap
FAUCETS > FAUCET
FAUCHION *n* short sword
FAUCHIONS > FAUCHION
FAUCHON *variant of* > FAUCHION
FAUCHONS > FAUCHON
FAUCIAL *same as* > FAUCAL
FAUGH *interj* exclamation of disgust, scorn, etc
FAULCHION *variant of* > FAUCHION
FAULD *n* piece of armour
FAULDS > FAULD
FAULT *n* responsibility for something wrong ▷ *vb* criticize or blame
FAULTED > FAULT
FAULTFUL > FAULT
FAULTIER > FAULTY
FAULTIEST > FAULTY
FAULTILY > FAULTY
FAULTING > FAULT
FAULTLESS *adj* without fault
FAULTS > FAULT
FAULTY *adj* badly designed or not working properly
FAUN *n* (in Roman legend) creature with a human face and torso and a goat's horns and legs
FAUNA *n* animals of a given place or time
FAUNAE > FAUNA
FAUNAL > FAUNA
FAUNALLY > FAUNA
FAUNAS > FAUNA
FAUNIST > FAUNA
FAUNISTIC > FAUNA
FAUNISTS > FAUNA
FAUNLIKE > FAUN
FAUNS > FAUN
FAUNULA *n* fauna of a small single environment
FAUNULAE > FAUNULA
FAUNULE *same as* > FAUNULA
FAUNULES > FAUNULE
FAUR *Scot word for* > FAR
FAURD *adj* favoured
FAURER > FAUR
FAUREST > FAUR
FAUSTIAN *adj* of or relating to Faust, esp reminiscent of his bargain with the devil
FAUT *Scot word for* > FAULT
FAUTED > FAUT
FAUTEUIL *n* armchair, the sides of which are not upholstered
FAUTEUILS > FAUTEUIL
FAUTING > FAUT
FAUTOR *n* patron
FAUTORS > FAUTOR
FAUTS > FAUT
FAUVE *adj* of the style of the Fauve art movement
FAUVES > FAUVE
FAUVETTE *n* singing bird, warbler
FAUVETTES > FAUVETTE
FAUVISM > FAUVE
FAUVISMS > FAUVISM
FAUVIST *n* artist following the Fauve style of painting
FAUVISTS > FAUVIST
FAUX *adj* false
FAVA *n* type of bean
FAVAS > FAVA
FAVE *short for* > FAVOURITE
FAVEL *n* dun-coloured horse
FAVELA *n* (in Brazil) a shanty or shantytown
FAVELAS > FAVELA
FAVELL *variant of* > FAVEL
FAVELLA *n* group of spores
FAVELLAS > FAVELLA
FAVEOLATE *adj* pitted with cell-like cavities
FAVER > FAVE
FAVES > FAVE
FAVEST > FAVE
FAVISM *n* type of anaemia
FAVISMS > FAVISM
FAVONIAN *adj* of or relating to the west wind
FAVOR *same as* > FAVOUR
FAVORABLE *same as* > FAVOURABLE

FAVORABLY > FAVOURABLE
FAVORED > FAVOR
FAVORER > FAVOUR
FAVORERS > FAVOUR
FAVORING > FAVOR
FAVORITE *same as* > FAVOURITE
FAVORITES > FAVORITE
FAVORLESS > FAVOR
FAVORS *same as* > FAVOURS
FAVOSE *same as* > FAVEOLATE
FAVOUR *n* approving attitude ▷ *vb* prefer
FAVOURED > FAVOUR
FAVOURER > FAVOUR
FAVOURERS > FAVOUR
FAVOURING > FAVOUR
FAVOURITE *adj* most liked ▷ *n* preferred person or thing
FAVOURS *pl n* sexual intimacy, as when consented to by a woman
FAVOUS *adj* resembling honeycomb
FAVRILE *n* type of iridescent glass
FAVRILES > FAVRILE
FAVUS *n* infectious fungal skin disease of man and some domestic animals, characterized by formation of a honeycomb-like mass of roundish dry cup-shaped crusts
FAVUSES > FAVUS
FAW *n* gypsy
FAWN *n* young deer ▷ *adj* light yellowish-brown ▷ *vb* seek attention from (someone) by insincere flattery
FAWNED > FAWN
FAWNER > FAWN
FAWNERS > FAWN
FAWNIER > FAWNY
FAWNIEST > FAWNY
FAWNING > FAWN
FAWNINGLY > FAWN
FAWNINGS > FAWN
FAWNLIKE > FAWN
FAWNS > FAWN
FAWNY *adj* of a fawn colour
FAWS > FAW
FAX *n* electronic system for sending facsimiles of documents by telephone ▷ *vb* send (a document) by this system
FAXED > FAX
FAXES > FAX
FAXING > FAX
FAY *n* fairy or sprite ▷ *adj* of or resembling a fay ▷ *vb* fit or be fitted closely or tightly
FAYALITE *n* rare brown or black mineral
FAYALITES > FAYALITE
FAYED > FAY
FAYENCE *variant of* > FAIENCE
FAYENCES > FAYENCE
FAYER > FAY
FAYEST > FAY
FAYING > FAY
FAYNE *vb* pretend
FAYNED > FAYNE
FAYNES > FAYNE
FAYNING > FAYNE
FAYRE *pseudo-archaic spelling of* > FAIR
FAYRES > FAYRE
FAYS > FAY
FAZE *vb* disconcert or fluster
FAZED *adj* worried or disconcerted
FAZENDA *n* large estate or ranch
FAZENDAS > FAZENDA
FAZES > FAZE
FAZING > FAZE
FE *same as* > FEE
FEAGUE *vb* whip or beat
FEAGUED > FEAGUE
FEAGUES > FEAGUE
FEAGUING > FEAGUE
FEAL *vb* conceal
FEALED > FEAL
FEALING > FEAL
FEALS > FEAL
FEALTIES > FEALTY
FEALTY *n* (in feudal society) subordinate's loyalty to his ruler or lord
FEAR *n* distress or alarm caused by impending danger or pain ▷ *vb* be afraid of (something or someone)
FEARE *n* companion, spouse
FEARED > FEAR
FEARER > FEAR
FEARERS > FEAR
FEARES > FEARE
FEARFUL *adj* feeling fear
FEARFULLY *adv* in a fearful manner
FEARING > FEAR
FEARLESS > FEAR
FEARS > FEAR
FEARSOME *adj* terrifying
FEASANCE *n* performance of an act
FEASANCES > FEASANCE
FEASE *vb* perform an act
FEASED > FEASE
FEASES > FEASE
FEASIBLE *adj* able to be done, possible
FEASIBLY > FEASIBLE
FEASING > FEASE
FEAST *n* lavish meal ▷ *vb* eat a feast
FEASTED > FEAST
FEASTER > FEAST
FEASTERS > FEAST
FEASTFUL *adj* festive
FEASTING > FEAST
FEASTINGS > FEAST
FEASTLESS > FEAST
FEASTS > FEAST
FEAT *n* remarkable, skilful, or daring action
FEATED > FEAT
FEATEOUS *adj* neat
FEATER > FEAT
FEATEST > FEAT
FEATHER *n* one of the barbed shafts forming the plumage of birds ▷ *vb* fit or cover with feathers
FEATHERED > FEATHER
FEATHERS > FEATHER
FEATHERY > FEATHER
FEATING > FEAT
FEATLIER > FEAT
FEATLIEST > FEAT
FEATLY > FEAT
FEATOUS *variant of* > FEATEOUS
FEATS > FEAT
FEATUOUS *variant of* > FEATEOUS
FEATURE *n* part of the face, such as the eyes ▷ *vb* have as a feature or be a feature in
FEATURED *adj* having features as specified
FEATURELY *adj* handsome
FEATURES > FEATURE
FEATURING > FEATURE
FEAZE *same as* > FEEZE
FEAZED > FEAZE
FEAZES > FEAZE
FEAZING > FEAZE
FEBLESSE *n* feebleness
FEBLESSES > FEBLESSE
FEBRICITY *n* condition of having a fever
FEBRICULA *n* slight transient fever
FEBRICULE *variant of* > FEBRICULA
FEBRIFIC *adj* causing or having a fever
FEBRIFUGE *n* any drug or agent for reducing fever ▷ *adj* serving to reduce fever
FEBRILE *adj* very active and nervous
FEBRILITY > FEBRILE
FECAL *same as* > FAECAL
FECES *same as* > FAECES
FECHT *Scot word for* > FIGHT
FECHTER > FECHT
FECHTERS > FECHT
FECHTING > FECHT
FECHTS > FECHT
FECIAL *adj* heraldic
FECIALS > FECIAL
FECIT (he or she) made it: used formerly on works of art next to the artist's name
FECK *n* worth
FECKIN *same as* > FECKING
FECKING *adj* slang word for absolute
FECKLESS *adj* ineffectual or irresponsible
FECKLY > FECK
FECKS > FECK
FECULA *n* starch obtained by washing the crushed parts of plants, such as the potato
FECULAE > FECULA
FECULAS > FECULA
FECULENCE > FECULENT
FECULENCY > FECULENT
FECULENT *adj* filthy, scummy, muddy, or foul
FECUND *adj* fertile
FECUNDATE *vb* make fruitful
FECUNDITY *n* fertility
FED *n* FBI agent
FEDARIE *n* accomplice
FEDARIES > FEDARIE
FEDAYEE *n* (in Arab states) a commando, esp one fighting against Israel
FEDAYEEN > FEDAYEE
FEDELINI *n* type of pasta
FEDELINIS > FEDELINI
FEDERACY *n* alliance
FEDERAL *adj* of a system in which power is divided between one central government and several regional governments ▷ *n* supporter of federal union or federation
FEDERALLY > FEDERAL
FEDERALS > FEDERAL
FEDERARIE *variant of* > FEDARIE
FEDERARY *variant of* > FEDARIE
FEDERATE *vb* unite in a federation ▷ *adj* federal
FEDERATED > FEDERATE
FEDERATES > FEDERATE
FEDERATOR > FEDERATE
FEDEX *vb* send by FedEx
FEDEXED > FEDEX
FEDEXES > FEDEX
FEDEXING > FEDEX
FEDORA *n* man's soft hat with a brim
FEDORAS > FEDORA
FEDS > FEE
FEE *n* charge paid to be allowed to do something ▷ *vb* pay a fee to
FEEB *n* contemptible person
FEEBLE *adj* lacking physical or mental power ▷ *vb* make feeble
FEEBLED > FEEBLE
FEEBLER > FEEBLE
FEEBLES > FEEBLE
FEEBLEST > FEEBLE
FEEBLING > FEEBLE
FEEBLISH > FEEBLE
FEEBLY > FEEBLE
FEEBS > FEEB
FEED *vb* give food to ▷ *n* act of feeding
FEEDABLE > FEE
FEEDBACK *n* information received in response to something done ▷ *adv* return (part of the output of a system) to its input
FEEDBACKS > FEEDBACK
FEEDBAG *n* any bag in which feed for livestock is

sacked
FEEDBAGS > FEEDBAG
FEEDBOX trough, manger
FEEDBOXES > FEEDBOX
FEEDER *n* baby's bib
FEEDERS > FEEDER
FEEDGRAIN *n* cereal grown to feed livestock
FEEDHOLE *n* small hole through which cable etc is inserted
FEEDHOLES > FEEDHOLE
FEEDING > FEED
FEEDINGS > FEED
FEEDLOT *n* area or building where livestock are fattened rapidly for market
FEEDLOTS > FEEDLOT
FEEDS > FEED
FEEDSTOCK *n* main raw material used in the manufacture of a product
FEEDSTUFF *n* any material used as a food, esp for animals
FEEDWATER *n* water, previously purified to prevent scale deposit or corrosion, that is fed to boilers for steam generation
FEEDYARD *n* place where cattle are kept and fed
FEEDYARDS > FEEDYARD
FEEING > FEE
FEEL *vb* have a physical or emotional sensation of ▷ *n* act of feeling
FEELBAD *n* something inducing depression
FEELBADS > FEELBAD
FEELER *n* organ of touch in some animals
FEELERS > FEELER
FEELESS > FEE
FEELGOOD *adj* causing or characterized by a feeling of self-satisfaction
FEELGOODS > FEELGOOD
FEELING > FEEL
FEELINGLY > FEEL
FEELINGS > FEEL
FEELS > FEEL
FEEN *n* in Irish dialect, an informal word for 'man'
FEENS > FEEN
FEER *vb* make a furrow
FEERED > FEER
FEERIE *n* fairyland
FEERIES > FEERIE
FEERIN *n* furrow
FEERING > FEER
FEERINGS > FEER
FEERINS > FEERIN
FEERS > FEER
FEES > FEE
FEESE *vb* perturb
FEESED > FEESE
FEESES > FEESE
FEESING > FEESE
FEET > FOOT
FEETFIRST *adv* with the feet coming first
FEETLESS > FOOT
FEEZE *vb* beat ▷ *n* rush
FEEZED > FEEZE
FEEZES > FEEZE
FEEZING > FEEZE
FEG *same as* > FIG
FEGARIES > FEGARY
FEGARY *variant of* > VAGARY
FEGS > FEG
FEH *n* Hebrew coin
FEHM *n* medieval German court
FEHME > FEHM
FEHMIC > FEHM
FEHS > FEH
FEIGN *vb* pretend
FEIGNED > FEIGN
FEIGNEDLY > FEIGN
FEIGNER > FEIGN
FEIGNERS > FEIGN
FEIGNING > FEIGN
FEIGNINGS > FEIGN
FEIGNS > FEIGN
FEIJOA *n* evergreen myrtaceous shrub of S America
FEIJOAS > FEIJOA
FEINT *n* sham attack or blow meant to distract an opponent ▷ *vb* make a feint ▷ *adj* printing term meaning ruled with faint lines
FEINTED > FEINT
FEINTER > FEINT
FEINTEST > FEINT
FEINTING > FEINT
FEINTS *pl n* leavings of the second distillation of Scotch malt whisky
FEIRIE *adj* nimble
FEIS *n* Irish music and dance festival
FEISEANNA > FEIS
FEIST *n* small aggressive dog
FEISTIER > FEISTY
FEISTIEST > FEISTY
FEISTILY > FEISTY
FEISTS > FEIST
FEISTY *adj* showing courage or spirit
FELAFEL *same as* > FALAFEL
FELAFELS > FELAFEL
FELDGRAU *n* ordinary German soldier (from uniform colour)
FELDGRAUS > FELDGRAU
FELDSCHAR *same as* > FELDSHER
FELDSCHER *same as* > FELDSHER
FELDSHER *n* (in Russia) a medical doctor's assistant
FELDSHERS > FELDSHER
FELDSPAR *n* hard mineral that is the main constituent of igneous rocks
FELDSPARS > FELDSPAR
FELDSPATH *variant of* > FELDSPAR
FELICIA *n* type of African herb
FELICIAS > FELICIA
FELICIFIC *adj* making or tending to make happy
FELICITER > FELICITY
FELICITY *n* happiness
FELID *n* any animal belonging to the family *Felidae*; a cat
FELIDS > FELID
FELINE *adj* of cats ▷ *n* member of the cat family
FELINELY > FELINE
FELINES > FELINE
FELINITY > FELINE
FELL *vb* cut or knock down ▷ *adj* cruel or deadly
FELLA *nonstandard variant of* > FELLOW
FELLABLE > FALL
FELLAH *n* peasant in Arab countries
FELLAHEEN > FELLAH
FELLAHIN > FELLAH
FELLAHS > FELLAH
FELLAS > FELLA
FELLATE *vb* perform fellatio on (a person)
FELLATED > FELLATE
FELLATES > FELLATE
FELLATING > FELLATE
FELLATIO *n* sexual activity in which the penis is stimulated by the partner's mouth
FELLATION *same as* > FELLATIO
FELLATIOS > FELLATIO
FELLATOR > FELLATIO
FELLATORS > FELLATIO
FELLATRIX > FELLATIO
FELLED > FELL
FELLER *n* person or thing that fells
FELLERS > FELLER
FELLEST > FELL
FELLIES > FELLY
FELLING > FELL
FELLNESS > FELL
FELLOE *n* (segment of) the rim of a wheel
FELLOES > FELLOE
FELLOW *n* man or boy ▷ *adj* in the same group or condition
FELLOWED > FELLOW
FELLOWING > FELLOW
FELLOWLY *adj* friendly, companionable
FELLOWMAN *n* companion
FELLOWMEN > FELLOWMAN
FELLOWS > FELLOW
FELLS > FELL
FELLY *same as* > FELLOE
FELON *n* (formerly) person guilty of a felony ▷ *adj* evil
FELONIES > FELONY
FELONIOUS *adj* of, involving, or constituting a felony
FELONOUS *adj* wicked
FELONRIES > FELONRY
FELONRY *n* felons collectively
FELONS > FELON
FELONY *n* serious crime
FELSIC *adj* relating to igneous rock
FELSITE *n* any fine-grained igneous rock consisting essentially of quartz and feldspar
FELSITES > FELSITE
FELSITIC > FELSITE
FELSPAR *same as* > FELDSPAR
FELSPARS > FELSPAR
FELSTONE *same as* > FELSITE
FELSTONES > FELSTONE
FELT *n* matted fabric ▷ *vb* become matted
FELTED > FELT
FELTER *vb* mat together
FELTERED > FELTER
FELTERING > FELTER
FELTERS > FELTER
FELTIER > FELT
FELTIEST > FELT
FELTING *n* felted material
FELTINGS > FELTING
FELTLIKE > FEEL
FELTS > FELT
FELTY > FELT
FELUCCA *n* narrow lateen-rigged vessel of the Mediterranean
FELUCCAS > FELUCCA
FELWORT *n* biennial gentianaceous plant, *Gentianella amarella*, of Europe and SW China, having purple flowers and rosettes of leaves
FELWORTS > FELWORT
FEM *n* passive homosexual
FEMAL *adj* effeminate ▷ *n* effeminate person
FEMALE *adj* of the sex which bears offspring ▷ *n* female person or animal
FEMALES > FEMALE
FEMALITY > FEMALE
FEMALS > FEMAL
FEME *n* woman or wife
FEMERALL *n* ventilator or smoke outlet on a roof
FEMERALLS > FEMERALL
FEMES > FEME
FEMETARY *variant of* > FUMITORY
FEMINACY *n* feminine character
FEMINAL *adj* feminine, female
FEMINAZI *n* militant feminist
FEMINAZIS > FEMINAZI
FEMINEITY *n* quality of being feminine
FEMINIE *n* women collectively
FEMININE *adj* having qualities traditionally regarded as suitable for, or typical of, women ▷ *n* short for feminine noun
FEMININES > FEMININE
FEMINISE *same as* > FEMINIZE
FEMINISED > FEMINISE

FEMINISES > FEMINISE
FEMINISM *n* advocacy of equal rights for women
FEMINISMS > FEMINISM
FEMINIST *n* person who advocates equal rights for women ▷ *adj* of, relating to, or advocating feminism
FEMINISTS > FEMINIST
FEMINITY > FEMINAL
FEMINIZE *vb* make or become feminine
FEMINIZED > FEMINIZE
FEMINIZES > FEMINIZE
FEMITER *variant of* > FUMITORY
FEMITERS > FEMITER
FEMME *n* woman or wife
FEMMES > FEMME
FEMMIER > FEMMY
FEMMIEST > FEMMY
FEMMY *adj* markedly or exaggeratedly feminine in appearance, manner, etc
FEMORA > FEMUR
FEMORAL *adj* of the thigh
FEMS > FEM
FEMUR *n* thighbone
FEMURS > FEMUR
FEN *n* low-lying flat marshy land
FENAGLE *variant of* > FINAGLE
FENAGLED > FENAGLE
FENAGLES > FENAGLE
FENAGLING > FENAGLE
FENCE *n* barrier of posts linked by wire or wood, enclosing an area ▷ *vb* enclose with or as if with a fence
FENCED > FENCE
FENCELESS > FENCE
FENCELIKE > FENCE
FENCER *n* person who fights with a sword, esp one who practises the art of fencing
FENCEROW *n* uncultivated land flanking a fence
FENCEROWS > FENCEROW
FENCERS > FENCER
FENCES > FENCE
FENCIBLE *n* (formerly) a person who undertook military service in immediate defence of his homeland only
FENCIBLES > FENCIBLE
FENCING *n* sport of fighting with swords
FENCINGS > FENCING
FEND *vb* give support (to someone, esp oneself) ▷ *n* shift or effort
FENDED > FEND
FENDER *n* low metal frame in front of a fireplace
FENDERED *adj* having a fender
FENDERS > FENDER
FENDIER > FENDY
FENDIEST > FENDY
FENDING > FEND
FENDS > FEND
FENDY *adj* thrifty
FENESTRA *n* small opening in or between bones, esp one of the openings between the middle and inner ears
FENESTRAE > FENESTRA
FENESTRAL > FENESTRA
FENESTRAS > FENESTRA
FENI *n* Goan alcoholic drink
FENIS > FENI
FENITAR *variant of* > FUMITORY
FENITARS > FENITAR
FENKS *n* whale blubber
FENLAND > FEN
FENLANDS > FEN
FENMAN > FEN
FENMEN > FEN
FENNEC *n* very small nocturnal fox, *Fennecus zerda*, inhabiting deserts of N Africa and Arabia, having pale fur and enormous ears
FENNECS > FENNEC
FENNEL *n* fragrant plant whose seeds, leaves, and root are used in cookery
FENNELS > FENNEL
FENNIER > FENNY
FENNIES > FENNY
FENNIEST > FENNY
FENNISH > FEN
FENNY *adj* boggy or marshy ▷ *n* feni
FENS > FEN
FENT *n* piece of waste fabric
FENTANYL *n* narcotic drug used in medicine to relieve pain
FENTANYLS > FENTANYL
FENTHION *n* type of pesticide
FENTHIONS > FENTHION
FENTS > FENT
FENUGREEK *n* Mediterranean plant grown for its heavily scented seeds
FENURON *n* type of herbicide
FENURONS > FENURON
FEOD *same as* > FEUD
FEODAL > FEOD
FEODARIES > FEOD
FEODARY > FEOD
FEODS > FEOD
FEOFF *same as* > FIEF
FEOFFED > FEOFF
FEOFFEE *n* (in feudal society) a vassal granted a fief by his lord
FEOFFEES > FEOFFEE
FEOFFER > FEOFF
FEOFFERS > FEOFF
FEOFFING > FEOFF
FEOFFMENT *n* (in medieval Europe) a lord's act of granting a fief to his man
FEOFFOR > FEOFF
FEOFFORS > FEOFF
FEOFFS > FEOFF
FER *same as* > FAR
FERACIOUS *adj* fruitful
FERACITY > FERACIOUS
FERAL *adj* wild ▷ *n* person who displays such tendencies and appearance
FERALISED *same as* > FERALIZED
FERALIZED *adj* once domesticated, but now wild
FERALS > FERAL
FERBAM *n* black slightly water-soluble fluffy powder used as a fungicide
FERBAMS > FERBAM
FERE *n* companion ▷ *adj* fierce
FERER > FERE
FERES > FERE
FEREST > FERE
FERETORY *n* shrine, usually portable, for a saint's relics
FERIA *n* weekday, other than Saturday, on which no feast occurs
FERIAE > FERIA
FERIAL *adj* of or relating to a feria
FERIAS > FERIA
FERINE *same as* > FERAL
FERITIES > FERAL
FERITY > FERAL
FERLIE *same as* > FERLY
FERLIED > FERLY
FERLIER > FERLY
FERLIES > FERLY
FERLIEST > FERLY
FERLY *adj* wonderful ▷ *n* wonder ▷ *vb* wonder
FERLYING > FERLY
FERM *variant of* > FARM
FERMATA *another word for* > PAUSE
FERMATAS > FERMATA
FERMATE > FERMATA
FERMENT *n* any agent that causes fermentation ▷ *vb* (cause to) undergo fermentation
FERMENTED > FERMENT
FERMENTER > FERMENT
FERMENTOR > FERMENT
FERMENTS > FERMENT
FERMI *n* unit of length used in nuclear physics equal to 10^{-15} metre
FERMION *n* any of a group of elementary particles, such as a nucleon, that has half-integral spin and obeys Fermi-Dirac statistics
FERMIONIC > FERMION
FERMIONS > FERMION
FERMIS > FERMI
FERMIUM *n* element artificially produced by neutron bombardment of plutonium
FERMIUMS > FERMIUM
FERMS > FERM
FERN *n* flowerless plant with fine fronds
FERNBIRD *n* small brown and white New Zealand swamp bird, *Bowdleria punctata*, with a fernlike tail
FERNBIRDS > FERNBIRD
FERNERIES > FERNERY
FERNERY *n* place where ferns are grown
FERNIER > FERN
FERNIEST > FERN
FERNING *n* production of a fern-like pattern
FERNINGS > FERNING
FERNINST *same as* > FORNENST
FERNLESS > FERN
FERNLIKE > FERN
FERNS > FERN
FERNSHAW *n* fern thicket
FERNSHAWS > FERNSHAW
FERNTICLE *variant of* > FERNTICKLE
FERNY > FERN
FEROCIOUS *adj* savagely fierce or cruel
FEROCITY > FEROCIOUS
FERRATE *n* type of salt
FERRATES > FERRATE
FERREL *variant of* > FERRULE
FERRELED > FERREL
FERRELING > FERREL
FERRELLED > FERREL
FERRELS > FERREL
FERREOUS *adj* containing or resembling iron
FERRET *n* tamed polecat used to catch rabbits or rats ▷ *vb* hunt with ferrets
FERRETED > FERRET
FERRETER > FERRET
FERRETERS > FERRET
FERRETING > FERRET
FERRETS > FERRET
FERRETY > FERRET
FERRIAGE *n* transportation by ferry
FERRIAGES > FERRIAGE
FERRIC *adj* of or containing iron
FERRIED > FERRY
FERRIES > FERRY
FERRITE *n* any of a group of ferromagnetic highly resistive ceramic compounds
FERRITES > FERRITE
FERRITIC > FERRITE
FERRITIN *n* protein that contains iron and plays a part in the storage of iron in the body. It occurs in the liver and spleen
FERRITINS > FERRITIN
FERROCENE *n* reddish-orange insoluble crystalline compound
FERROTYPE *n* photographic print produced directly in a

camera by exposing a sheet of iron or tin coated with a sensitized enamel
FERROUS *adj* of or containing iron in the divalent state
FERRUGO *n* disease affecting plants
FERRUGOS > FERRUGO
FERRULE *n* metal cap to strengthen the end of a stick ▷ *vb* equip (a stick, etc) with a ferrule
FERRULED > FERRULE
FERRULES > FERRULE
FERRULING > FERRULE
FERRUM *Latin word for* > IRON
FERRUMS > FERRUM
FERRY *n* boat for transporting people and vehicles ▷ *vb* carry by ferry
FERRYBOAT *same as* > FERRY
FERRYING > FERRY
FERRYMAN *n* someone who provides a ferry service
FERRYMEN > FERRYMAN
FERTIGATE *vb* fertilize and irrigate at the same time
FERTILE *adj* capable of producing young, crops, or vegetation
FERTILELY > FERTILE
FERTILER > FERTILE
FERTILEST > FERTILE
FERTILISE *same as* > FERTILIZE
FERTILITY *n* ability to produce offspring, esp abundantly
FERTILIZE *vb* provide (an animal or plant) with sperm or pollen to bring about fertilization
FERULA *n* any large umbelliferous plant of the Mediterranean genus *Ferula*, having thick stems and dissected leaves: cultivated as the source of several strongly-scented gum resins, such as galbanum
FERULAE > FERULA
FERULAS > FERULA
FERULE *same as* > FERRULE
FERULED > FERULE
FERULES > FERULE
FERULING > FERULE
FERVENCY *another word for* > FERVOUR
FERVENT *adj* intensely passionate and sincere
FERVENTER > FERVENT
FERVENTLY > FERVENT
FERVID *same as* > FERVENT
FERVIDER > FERVID
FERVIDEST > FERVID
FERVIDITY > FERVID
FERVIDLY > FERVID
FERVOR *same as* > FERVOUR
FERVOROUS > FERVOUR
FERVORS > FERVOR
FERVOUR *n* intensity of feeling
FERVOURS > FERVOUR
FES > FE
FESCUE *n* pasture and lawn grass with stiff narrow leaves
FESCUES > FESCUE
FESS *same as* > FESSE
FESSE *n* ordinary consisting of a horizontal band across a shield, conventionally occupying a third of its length and being wider than a bar
FESSED > FESS
FESSES > FESSE
FESSING > FESS
FESSWISE *adv* in heraldry, with a horizontal band across the shield
FEST *n* event at which the emphasis is on a particular activity
FESTA *n* festival
FESTAL *adj* festive ▷ *n* festivity
FESTALLY > FESTAL
FESTALS > FESTAL
FESTAS > FESTA
FESTER *vb* grow worse and increasingly hostile ▷ *n* small ulcer or sore containing pus
FESTERED > FESTER
FESTERING > FESTER
FESTERS > FESTER
FESTIER > FESTY
FESTIEST > FESTY
FESTILOGY *n* treatise about church festivals
FESTINATE *vb* hurry
FESTIVAL *n* organized series of special events or performances
FESTIVALS > FESTIVAL
FESTIVE *adj* of or like a celebration
FESTIVELY > FESTIVE
FESTIVITY *n* happy celebration
FESTIVOUS > FESTIVE
FESTOLOGY *variant of* > FESTILOGY
FESTOON *vb* hang decorations in loops ▷ *n* decorative chain of flowers or ribbons suspended in loops
FESTOONED > FESTOON
FESTOONS > FESTOON
FESTS > FEST
FESTY *adj* dirty
FET *vb* fetch
FETA *n* white salty Greek cheese
FETAL *adj* of, relating to, or resembling a fetus
FETAS > FETA
FETATION *n* state of pregnancy
FETATIONS > FETATION
FETCH *vb* go after and bring back ▷ *n* ghost or apparition of a living person
FETCHED > FETCH
FETCHER *n* person or animal that fetches
FETCHERS > FETCHER
FETCHES > FETCH
FETCHING *adj* attractive
FETE *n* gala, bazaar, etc, usu held outdoors ▷ *vb* honour or entertain regally
FETED > FETE
FETERITA *n* type of sorghum
FETERITAS > FETERITA
FETES > FETE
FETIAL *n* (in ancient Rome) any of the 20 priestly heralds involved in declarations of war and in peace negotiations ▷ *adj* of or relating to the fetiales
FETIALES > FETIAL
FETIALIS *n* priest in ancient Rome
FETIALS > FETIAL
FETICH *same as* > FETISH
FETICHE *variant of* > FETICH
FETICHES > FETICH
FETICHISE *variant of* > FETICHIZE
FETICHISM *same as* > FETISHISM
FETICHIST > FETISHISM
FETICHIZE *vb* be excessively or irrationally devoted to an object, activity, etc
FETICIDAL > FETICIDE
FETICIDE *n* destruction of a fetus in the uterus
FETICIDES > FETICIDE
FETID *adj* stinking
FETIDER > FETID
FETIDEST > FETID
FETIDITY > FETID
FETIDLY > FETID
FETIDNESS > FETID
FETING > FETE
FETISH *n* form of behaviour in which sexual pleasure is derived from looking at or handling an inanimate object
FETISHES > FETISH
FETISHISE *same as* > FETISHIZE
FETISHISM *n* condition in which the handling of an inanimate object or a specific part of the body other than the sexual organs is a source of sexual satisfaction
FETISHIST > FETISHISM
FETISHIZE *vb* be excessively or irrationally devoted to (an object, activity, etc)
FETLOCK *n* projection behind and above a horse's hoof
FETLOCKED *adj* having fetlocks
FETLOCKS > FETLOCK
FETOLOGY *n* branch of medicine concerned with the fetus in the uterus
FETOR *n* offensive stale or putrid odour
FETORS > FETOR
FETOSCOPE *n* fibreoptic instrument that can be passed through the abdomen of a pregnant woman to enable examination of the fetus and withdrawal of blood for sampling in prenatal diagnosis
FETOSCOPY > FETOSCOPE
FETS > FET
FETT *variant of* > FET
FETTA *variant of* > FETA
FETTAS > FETTA
FETTED > FET
FETTER *n* chain or shackle for the foot ▷ *vb* restrict
FETTERED > FETTER
FETTERER > FETTER
FETTERERS > FETTER
FETTERING > FETTER
FETTERS > FETTER
FETTING > FET
FETTLE *same as* > FETTLING
FETTLED > FETTLE
FETTLER *n* person employed to maintain railway tracks
FETTLERS > FETTLER
FETTLES > FETTLE
FETTLING *n* refractory material used to line the hearth of puddling furnaces
FETTLINGS > FETTLING
FETTS > FETT
FETTUCINE *n* type of pasta in the form of narrow ribbons
FETTUCINI *same as* > FETTUCINE
FETUS *n* embryo of a mammal in the later stages of development
FETUSES > FETUS
FETWA *variant of* > FATWA
FETWAS > FETWA
FEU *n* (in Scotland) right of use of land in return for a fixed annual payment
FEUAR *n* tenant of a feu
FEUARS > FEUAR
FEUD *n* long bitter hostility between two people or groups ▷ *vb* carry on a feud
FEUDAL *adj* of or like feudalism
FEUDALISE *same as* > FEUDALIZE
FEUDALISM *n* medieval system in which people held land from a lord, and in return worked and fought for him
FEUDALIST > FEUDALISM
FEUDALITY *n* state or

quality of being feudal
FEUDALIZE *vb* make feudal
FEUDALLY > FEUDAL
FEUDARIES > FEUDARY
FEUDARY *n* holder of land through feudal right
FEUDATORY *n* person holding a fief ▷ *adj* relating to or characteristic of the relationship between lord and vassal
FEUDED > FEUD
FEUDING > FEUD
FEUDINGS > FEUD
FEUDIST *n* person who takes part in a feud or quarrel
FEUDISTS > FEUDIST
FEUDS > FEUD
FEUED > FEU
FEUILLETE *n* puff pastry
FEUING > FEU
FEUS > FEU
FEUTRE *vb* place in a resting position
FEUTRED > FEUTRE
FEUTRES > FEUTRE
FEUTRING > FEUTRE
FEVER *n* (illness causing) high body temperature ▷ *vb* affect with or as if with fever
FEVERED > FEVER
FEVERFEW *n* bushy European strong-scented perennial plant, *Tanacetum parthenium*, with white flower heads, formerly used medicinally: family *Asteraceae* (composites)
FEVERFEWS > FEVERFEW
FEVERING > FEVER
FEVERISH *adj* suffering from fever
FEVERLESS > FEVER
FEVEROUS *same as* > FEVERISH
FEVERROOT *n* American wild plant
FEVERS > FEVER
FEVERWEED *n* plant thought to be medicinal
FEVERWORT *n* any of several plants considered to have medicinal properties, such as horse gentian and boneset
FEW *adj* not many
FEWER > FEW
FEWEST > FEW
FEWMET *variant of* > FUMET
FEWMETS > FEWMET
FEWNESS > FEW
FEWNESSES > FEW
FEWTER *variant of* > FEUTRE
FEWTERED > FEUTRE
FEWTERING > FEUTRE
FEWTERS > FEUTRE
FEWTRILS *n* trifles, trivia
FEY *adj* whimsically strange ▷ *vb* clean out
FEYED > FEY
FEYER > FEY
FEYEST > FEY
FEYING > FEY
FEYLY > FEY
FEYNESS > FEY
FEYNESSES > FEY
FEYS > FEY
FEZ *n* brimless tasselled cap, orig. from Turkey
FEZES > FEZ
FEZZED *adj* wearing a fez
FEZZES > FEZ
FEZZY > FEZ
FIACRE *n* small four-wheeled horse-drawn carriage, usually with a folding roof
FIACRES > FIACRE
FIANCE *n* man engaged to be married
FIANCEE *n* woman who is engaged to be married
FIANCEES > FIANCEE
FIANCES > FIANCE
FIAR *n* property owner
FIARS *n* legally fixed price of corn
FIASCHI > FIASCO
FIASCO *n* ridiculous or humiliating failure
FIASCOES > FIASCO
FIASCOS > FIASCO
FIAT *n* arbitrary order ▷ *vb* issue a fiat
FIATED > FIAT
FIATING > FIAT
FIATS > FIAT
FIAUNT *n* fiat
FIAUNTS > FIAUNT
FIB *n* trivial lie ▷ *vb* tell a lie
FIBBED > FIB
FIBBER > FIB
FIBBERIES > FIB
FIBBERS > FIB
FIBBERY > FIB
FIBBING > FIB
FIBER *same as* > FIBRE
FIBERED > FIBRE
FIBERFILL *same as* > FIBREFILL
FIBERISE *same as* > FIBERIZE
FIBERISED > FIBERISE
FIBERISES > FIBERISE
FIBERIZE *vb* break into fibres
FIBERIZED > FIBERIZE
FIBERIZES > FIBERIZE
FIBERLESS > FIBRE
FIBERLIKE > FIBER
FIBERS > FIBER
FIBRANNE *n* synthetic fabric
FIBRANNES > FIBRANNE
FIBRE *n* thread that can be spun into yarn
FIBRED > FIBRE
FIBREFILL *n* synthetic fibre used as a filling for pillows, quilted materials, etc
FIBRELESS > FIBRE
FIBRES > FIBRE
FIBRIFORM *adj* having the form of a fibre or fibres
FIBRIL *n* small fibre
FIBRILAR > FIBRIL
FIBRILLA *same as* > FIBRIL
FIBRILLAE > FIBRILLA
FIBRILLAR > FIBRIL
FIBRILLIN *n* kind of protein
FIBRILS > FIBRIL
FIBRIN *n* white insoluble elastic protein formed when blood clots
FIBRINOID > FIBRIN
FIBRINOUS *adj* of, containing, or resembling fibrin
FIBRINS > FIBRIN
FIBRO *n* mixture of cement and asbestos fibre, used in sheets for building
FIBROCYTE *n* type of fibroblast
FIBROID *adj* (of structures or tissues) containing or resembling fibres ▷ *n* benign tumour composed of fibrous connective tissue
FIBROIDS > FIBROID
FIBROIN *n* tough elastic protein that is the principal component of spiders' webs and raw silk
FIBROINS > FIBROIN
FIBROLINE *n* type of yarn
FIBROLITE *n* trademark name for a type of building board containing asbestos and cement
FIBROMA *n* benign tumour derived from fibrous connective tissue
FIBROMAS > FIBROMA
FIBROMATA > FIBROMA
FIBROS > FIBRO
FIBROSE *vb* become fibrous
FIBROSED > FIBROSE
FIBROSES > FIBROSE
FIBROSING > FIBROSE
FIBROSIS *n* formation of an abnormal amount of fibrous tissue
FIBROTIC > FIBROSIS
FIBROUS *adj* consisting of, containing, or resembling fibres
FIBROUSLY > FIBROUS
FIBS > FIB
FIBSTER *n* fibber
FIBSTERS > FIBSTER
FIBULA *n* slender outer bone of the lower leg
FIBULAE > FIBULA
FIBULAR > FIBULA
FIBULAS > FIBULA
FICE *n* small aggressive dog
FICES > FICE
FICHE *n* sheet of film for storing publications in miniaturized form
FICHES > FICHE
FICHU *n* woman's shawl or scarf of some light material, worn esp in the 18th century
FICHUS > FICHU
FICIN *n* enzyme
FICINS > FICIN
FICKLE *adj* changeable, inconstant ▷ *vb* puzzle
FICKLED > FICKLE
FICKLER > FICKLE
FICKLES > FICKLE
FICKLEST > FICKLE
FICKLING > FICKLE
FICKLY > FICKLE
FICO *n* worthless trifle
FICOES > FICO
FICOS > FICO
FICTILE *adj* moulded or capable of being moulded from clay
FICTION *n* literary works of the imagination, such as novels
FICTIONAL > FICTION
FICTIONS > FICTION
FICTIVE *adj* of, relating to, or able to create fiction
FICTIVELY > FICTIVE
FICTOR *n* sculptor
FICTORS > FICTOR
FICUS *n* any plant of the genus *Ficus*, which includes the edible fig and several greenhouse and house plants
FICUSES > FICUS
FID *n* spike for separating strands of rope in splicing
FIDDIOUS *vb* treat someone as Coriolanus, in the eponymous play, dealt with Aufidius
FIDDLE *n* violin ▷ *vb* play the violin
FIDDLED > FIDDLE
FIDDLER *n* person who plays the fiddle
FIDDLERS > FIDDLER
FIDDLES > FIDDLE
FIDDLEY *n* vertical space above a vessel's engine room extending into its stack
FIDDLEYS > FIDDLEY
FIDDLIER > FIDDLY
FIDDLIEST > FIDDLY
FIDDLING *adj* trivial
FIDDLY *adj* awkward to do or use
FIDEISM *n* theological doctrine that religious truth is a matter of faith and cannot be established by reason
FIDEISMS > FIDEISM
FIDEIST > FIDEISM
FIDEISTIC > FIDEISM
FIDEISTS > FIDEISM
FIDELISMO *n* belief in, adherence to, or advocacy of the principles of Fidel Castro, the Cuban Communist statesman (born 1927)

FIDELISTA *n* advocate of fidelism; a fidelist
FIDELITY *n* faithfulness
FIDGE *obsolete word for* > FIDGET
FIDGED > FIDGE
FIDGES > FIDGE
FIDGET *vb* move about restlessly ▷ *n* person who fidgets
FIDGETED > FIDGET
FIDGETER > FIDGET
FIDGETERS > FIDGET
FIDGETIER > FIDGET
FIDGETING > FIDGET
FIDGETS > FIDGET
FIDGETY > FIDGET
FIDGING > FIDGE
FIDIBUS *n* spill for lighting a candle or pipe
FIDIBUSES > FIDIBUS
FIDO *n* generic term for a dog
FIDOS > FIDO
FIDS > FID
FIDUCIAL *adj* used as a standard of reference or measurement
FIDUCIARY *n* person bound to act for someone else's benefit, as a trustee ▷ *adj* of a trust or trustee
FIE *interj* exclamation of disapproval
FIEF *n* land granted by a lord in return for war service
FIEFDOM *n* (in Feudal Europe) the property owned by a lord
FIEFDOMS > FIEFDOM
FIEFS > FIEF
FIELD *n* piece of land, usu enclosed with a fence or hedge, and used for pasture or growing crops ▷ *vb* stop, catch, or return (the ball) as a fielder
FIELDED > FIELD
FIELDER *n* (in certain sports) player whose task is to field the ball
FIELDERS > FIELDER
FIELDFARE *n* type of large Old World thrush
FIELDING > FIELD
FIELDINGS > FIELD
FIELDMICE *pl n* nocturnal mice
FIELDS > FIELD
FIELDSMAN *n* fielder
FIELDSMEN > FIELDSMAN
FIELDVOLE *n* small rodent
FIELDWARD *adv* towards a field or fields
FIELDWORK *n* investigation made in the field as opposed to the classroom or the laboratory
FIEND *n* evil spirit
FIENDISH *adj* of or like a fiend
FIENDLIKE > FIEND
FIENDS > FIEND
FIENT *n* fiend
FIENTS > FIENT
FIER *same as* > FERE
FIERCE *adj* wild or aggressive
FIERCELY > FIERCE
FIERCER > FIERCE
FIERCEST > FIERCE
FIERE > FERE
FIERES > FERE
FIERIER > FIERY
FIERIEST > FIERY
FIERILY > FIERY
FIERINESS > FIERY
FIERS > FIER
FIERY *adj* consisting of or like fire
FIEST > FIE
FIESTA *n* religious festival, carnival
FIESTAS > FIESTA
FIFE *n* small high-pitched flute ▷ *vb* play (music) on a fife
FIFED > FIFE
FIFER > FIFE
FIFERS > FIFE
FIFES > FIFE
FIFI *n* type of mountaineering hook
FIFING > FIFE
FIFTEEN *n* five and ten ▷ *adj* amounting to fifteen ▷ *determiner* amounting to fifteen
FIFTEENER *n* fifteen-syllable line of poetry
FIFTEENS > FIFTEEN
FIFTEENTH *adj* coming after the fourteenth in order, position, time, etc. Often written: 15th ▷ *n* one of 15 equal or nearly equal parts of something
FIFTH *n* (of) number five in a series ▷ *adj* of or being number five in a series ▷ *adv* after the fourth person, position, event, etc
FIFTHLY *same as* > FIFTH
FIFTHS > FIFTH
FIFTIES > FIFTY
FIFTIETH *adj* being the ordinal number of *fifty* in order, position, time, etc. Often written: 50th ▷ *n* one of 50 equal or approximately equal parts of something
FIFTIETHS > FIFTIETH
FIFTY *n* five times ten ▷ *adj* amounting to fifty ▷ *determiner* amounting to fifty
FIFTYISH > FIFTY
FIG *n* soft pear-shaped fruit ▷ *vb* dress (up) or rig (out)
FIGEATER *n* large beetle
FIGEATERS > FIGEATER
FIGGED > FIG
FIGGERIES > FIGGERY
FIGGERY *n* adornment, ornament
FIGGING > FIG
FIGHT *vb* struggle (against) in battle or physical combat ▷ *n* aggressive conflict between two (groups of) people
FIGHTABLE > FIGHT
FIGHTBACK *n* act or campaign of resistance
FIGHTER *n* boxer
FIGHTERS > FIGHTER
FIGHTING > FIGHT
FIGHTINGS > FIGHT
FIGHTS > FIGHT
FIGJAM *n* very conceited person
FIGJAMS > FIGJAM
FIGMENT *n* fantastic notion, invention, or fabrication
FIGMENTS > FIGMENT
FIGO *variant of* > FICO
FIGOS > FIGO
FIGS > FIG
FIGULINE *adj* of or resembling clay ▷ *n* article made of clay
FIGULINES > FIGULINE
FIGURABLE > FIGURE
FIGURAL *adj* composed of or relating to human or animal figures
FIGURALLY > FIGURAL
FIGURANT *n* ballet dancer who does group work but no solo roles
FIGURANTE *n* female figurant
FIGURANTS > FIGURANT
FIGURATE *adj* exhibiting or produced by figuration
FIGURE *n* numerical symbol ▷ *vb* calculate (sums or amounts)
FIGURED *adj* decorated with a design
FIGUREDLY > FIGURED
FIGURER > FIGURE
FIGURERS > FIGURE
FIGURES > FIGURE
FIGURINE *n* statuette
FIGURINES > FIGURINE
FIGURING > FIGURE
FIGURIST *n* user of numbers
FIGURISTS > FIGURIST
FIGWORT *n* any scrophulariaceous plant of the N temperate genus *Scrophularia*, having square stems and small brown or greenish flowers
FIGWORTS > FIGWORT
FIKE *vb* fidget
FIKED > FIKE
FIKERIES > FIKERY
FIKERY *n* fuss
FIKES > FIKE
FIKIER > FIKY
FIKIEST > FIKY
FIKING > FIKE
FIKISH *adj* fussy
FIKY *adj* fussy
FIL *same as* > FILS
FILA > FILUM
FILABEG *variant of* > FILIBEG
FILABEGS > FILABEG
FILACEOUS *adj* made of threads
FILACER *n* formerly, English legal officer
FILACERS > FILACER
FILAGREE *same as* > FILIGREE
FILAGREED > FILAGREE
FILAGREES > FILAGREE
FILAMENT *n* fine wire in a light bulb that gives out light
FILAMENTS > FILAMENT
FILANDER *n* species of kangaroo
FILANDERS > FILANDER
FILAR *adj* of thread
FILAREE *n* type of storksbill, a weed
FILAREES > FILAREE
FILARIA *n* any parasitic nematode worm of the family *Filariidae*, living in the blood and tissues of vertebrates and transmitted by insects: the cause of filariasis
FILARIAE > FILARIA
FILARIAL > FILARIA
FILARIAN > FILARIA
FILARIAS > FILARIA
FILARIID *adj* of or relating to a family of threadlike roundworms
FILARIIDS > FILARIID
FILASSE *n* vegetable fibre such as jute
FILASSES > FILASSE
FILATORY *n* machine for making threads
FILATURE *n* act or process of spinning silk, etc, into threads
FILATURES > FILATURE
FILAZER *variant of* > FILACER
FILAZERS > FILAZER
FILBERD *variant of* > FILBERT
FILBERDS > FILBERD
FILBERT *n* hazelnut
FILBERTS > FILBERT
FILCH *vb* steal (small amounts)
FILCHED > FILCH
FILCHER > FILCH
FILCHERS > FILCH
FILCHES > FILCH
FILCHING > FILCH
FILCHINGS > FILCH
FILE *n* box or folder used to keep documents in order ▷ *vb* place (a document) in a file
FILEABLE > FILE
FILECARD *n* type of brush with sharp steel bristles, used for cleaning the teeth of a file
FILECARDS > FILECARD

FILED > FILE
FILEFISH *n* any tropical triggerfish, such as *Alutera scripta*, having a narrow compressed body and a very long dorsal spine
FILEMOT *n* type of brown colour
FILEMOTS > FILEMOT
FILENAME *n* arrangement of characters that enables a computer system to permit the user to have access to a particular file
FILENAMES > FILENAME
FILER > FILE
FILERS > FILE
FILES > FILE
FILET *variant of* > FILLET
FILETED > FILET
FILETING > FILET
FILETS > FILET
FILFOT *variant of* > FYLFOT
FILFOTS > FILFOT
FILIAL *adj* of or befitting a son or daughter
FILIALLY > FILIAL
FILIATE *vb* fix judicially the paternity of (a child, esp one born out of wedlock)
FILIATED > FILIATE
FILIATES > FILIATE
FILIATING > FILIATE
FILIATION *n* line of descent
FILIBEG *n* kilt worn by Scottish Highlanders
FILIBEGS > FILIBEG
FILICIDAL > FILICIDE
FILICIDE *n* act of killing one's own son or daughter
FILICIDES > FILICIDE
FILIFORM *adj* having the form of a thread
FILIGRAIN *n* filigree
FILIGRANE *variant of* > FILIGRAIN
FILIGREE *n* delicate ornamental work of gold or silver wire ▷ *adj* made of filigree ▷ *vb* decorate with or as if with filigree
FILIGREED > FILIGREE
FILIGREES > FILIGREE
FILING > FILE
FILINGS *pl n* shavings removed by a file
FILIOQUE *n* theological term found in the Nicene Creed
FILIOQUES > FILIOQUE
FILISTER *same as* > FILLISTER
FILISTERS > FILISTER
FILL *vb* make or become full
FILLABLE > FILL
FILLAGREE *same as* > FILIGREE
FILLE *n* girl
FILLED > FILL
FILLER *n* substance that fills a gap or increases bulk
FILLERS > FILLER
FILLES > FILLE
FILLESTER *same as* > FILLISTER
FILLET *n* boneless piece of meat or fish ▷ *vb* remove the bones from
FILLETED > FILLET
FILLETING > FILLET
FILLETS > FILLET
FILLIBEG *same as* > FILIBEG
FILLIBEGS > FILLIBEG
FILLIES > FILLY
FILLING *n* substance that fills a gap or cavity, esp in a tooth ▷ *adj* (of food) substantial and satisfying
FILLINGS > FILLING
FILLIP *n* something that adds stimulation or enjoyment ▷ *vb* stimulate or excite
FILLIPED > FILLIP
FILLIPEEN *n* philopoena
FILLIPING > FILLIP
FILLIPS > FILLIP
FILLISTER *n* adjustable plane for cutting rabbets, grooves, etc
FILLO *variant of* > FILO
FILLOS > FILLO
FILLS > FILL
FILLY *n* young female horse
FILM *n* sequence of images projected on a screen, creating the illusion of movement ▷ *vb* photograph with a movie or video camera ▷ *adj* connected with films or the cinema
FILMABLE > FILM
FILMCARD *n* cinema loyalty card
FILMCARDS > FILMCARD
FILMDOM *n* cinema industry
FILMDOMS > FILMDOM
FILMED > FILM
FILMER *n* film-maker
FILMERS > FILMER
FILMGOER *n* person who goes regularly to the cinema
FILMGOERS > FILMGOER
FILMGOING > FILMGOER
FILMI *adj* in Indian English, of or relating to the Indian film industry or Indian films
FILMIC *adj* of or suggestive of films or the cinema
FILMIER > FILMY
FILMIEST > FILMY
FILMILY > FILMY
FILMINESS > FILMY
FILMING > FILM
FILMIS > FILMI
FILMISH > FILM
FILMLAND *n* cinema industry
FILMLANDS > FILMLAND
FILMLESS > FILM
FILMLIKE > FILM
FILMMAKER *n* person who makes films
FILMS > FILM
FILMSET *vb* set (type matter) by filmsetting
FILMSETS > FILMSET
FILMSTRIP *n* strip of film composed of different images projected separately as slides
FILMY *adj* very thin, delicate
FILO *n* type of flaky Greek pastry in very thin sheets
FILOPLUME *n* any of the hairlike feathers that lack vanes and occur between the contour feathers
FILOPODIA *n* plural form of singular filopodium: ectoplasmic pseudopodium
FILOS > FILO
FILOSE *adj* resembling or possessing a thread or threadlike process
FILOSELLE *n* soft silk thread, used esp for embroidery
FILOVIRUS *n* any member of a family of viruses that includes the agents responsible for Ebola virus disease and Marburg disease
FILS *n* fractional monetary unit of Bahrain, Iraq, Jordan, and Kuwait, worth one thousandth of a dinar
FILTER *n* material or device permitting fluid to pass but retaining solid particles ▷ *vb* remove impurities from (a substance) with a filter
FILTERED > FILTER
FILTERER > FILTER
FILTERERS > FILTER
FILTERING > FILTER
FILTERS > FILTER
FILTH *n* disgusting dirt
FILTHIER > FILTHY
FILTHIEST > FILTHY
FILTHILY > FILTHY
FILTHS > FILTH
FILTHY *adj* characterized by or full of filth ▷ *adv* extremely
FILTRABLE *adj* capable of being filtered
FILTRATE *n* filtered gas or liquid ▷ *vb* remove impurities with a filter
FILTRATED > FILTRATE
FILTRATES > FILTRATE
FILUM *n* any threadlike structure or part
FIMBLE *n* male plant of the hemp, which matures before the female plant
FIMBLES > FIMBLE
FIMBRIA *n* fringe or fringelike margin or border, esp at the opening of the Fallopian tubes
FIMBRIAE > FIMBRIA
FIMBRIAL > FIMBRIA
FIMBRIATE *adj* having a fringed margin, as some petals, antennae, etc
FIN *n* any of the firm appendages that are the organs of locomotion and balance in fishes and some other aquatic mammals ▷ *vb* provide with fins
FINABLE *adj* liable to a fine
FINAGLE *vb* get or achieve by craftiness or trickery
FINAGLED > FINAGLE
FINAGLER > FINAGLE
FINAGLERS > FINAGLE
FINAGLES > FINAGLE
FINAGLING > FINAGLE
FINAL *adj* at the end ▷ *n* deciding contest between winners of previous rounds in a competition
FINALE *n* concluding part of a dramatic performance or musical work
FINALES > FINALE
FINALIS *n* musical finishing note
FINALISE *same as* > FINALIZE
FINALISED > FINALISE
FINALISER > FINALISE
FINALISES > FINALISE
FINALISM *n* doctrine that final causes determine the course of all events
FINALISMS > FINALISM
FINALIST *n* competitor in a final
FINALISTS > FINALIST
FINALITY *n* condition or quality of being final or settled
FINALIZE *vb* put into final form
FINALIZED > FINALIZE
FINALIZER > FINALIZE
FINALIZES > FINALIZE
FINALLY *adv* after a long delay
FINALS *pl n* deciding part of a competition
FINANCE *vb* provide or obtain funds for ▷ *n* system of money, credit, and investment
FINANCED > FINANCE
FINANCES > FINANCE
FINANCIAL *adj* of or relating to finance, finances, or people who manage money
FINANCIER *n* person involved in large-scale financial business
FINANCING > FINANCE
FINBACK *another name for* > RORQUAL
FINBACKS > FINBACK
FINCA *n* Spanish villa
FINCAS > FINCA

FINCH *n* small songbird with a short strong beak
FINCHED *adj* with streaks or spots on the back
FINCHES > FINCH
FIND *vb* discover by chance ▷ *n* person or thing found, esp when valuable
FINDABLE > FIND
FINDER *n* small telescope fitted to a larger one
FINDERS > FINDER
FINDING > FIND
FINDINGS > FIND
FINDRAM *variant of* > FINNAN
FINDRAMS > FINDRAM
FINDS > FIND
FINE *adj* very good ▷ *n* payment imposed as a penalty ▷ *vb* impose a fine on
FINEABLE *same as* > FINABLE
FINED > FINE
FINEER *variant of* > VENEER
FINEERED > FINEER
FINEERING > FINEER
FINEERS > FINEER
FINEISH > FINE
FINELESS > FINE
FINELY *adv* into small pieces
FINENESS *n* state or quality of being fine
FINER > FINE
FINERIES > FINERY
FINERS > FINE
FINERY *n* showy clothing
FINES > FINE
FINESPUN *adj* spun or drawn out to a fine thread
FINESSE *n* delicate skill ▷ *vb* bring about with finesse
FINESSED > FINESSE
FINESSER > FINESSE
FINESSERS > FINESSE
FINESSES > FINESSE
FINESSING > FINESSE
FINEST > FINE
FINFISH *n* fish with fins, as opposed to shellfish
FINFISHES > FINFISH
FINFOOT *n* any aquatic bird of the tropical and subtropical family *Heliornithidae*, having broadly lobed toes, a long slender head and neck, and pale brown plumage: order *Gruiformes* (cranes, rails etc)
FINFOOTS > FINFOOT
FINGAN *variant of* > FINJAN
FINGANS > FINGAN
FINGER *n* one of the four long jointed parts of the hand ▷ *vb* touch or handle with the fingers
FINGERED *adj* marked or dirtied by handling
FINGERER > FINGER
FINGERERS > FINGER
FINGERING *n* technique of using the fingers in playing a musical instrument
FINGERS > FINGER
FINGERTIP *n* end joint or tip of a finger
FINI *n* end; finish
FINIAL *n* ornament at the apex of a gable or spire
FINIALED *adj* having a finial or finials
FINIALS > FINIAL
FINICAL *another word for* > FINICKY
FINICALLY > FINICAL
FINICKETY *adj* fussy or tricky
FINICKIER > FINICKY
FINICKIN *variant of* > FINICKY
FINICKING *same as* > FINICKY
FINICKY *adj* excessively particular, fussy
FINIKIN *variant of* > FINICKY
FINIKING *variant of* > FINICKY
FINING *n* process of removing undissolved gas bubbles from molten glass
FININGS > FINING
FINIS > FINI
FINISES > FINIS
FINISH *vb* bring to an end, stop ▷ *n* end, last part
FINISHED *adj* perfected
FINISHER *n* craftsman who carries out the final tasks in a manufacturing process
FINISHERS > FINISHER
FINISHES > FINISH
FINISHING *n* act or skill of goal scoring
FINITE *adj* having limits in space, time, or size
FINITELY > FINITE
FINITES > FINITE
FINITISM *n* view that only those entities may be admitted to mathematics that can be constructed in a finite number of steps, and only those propositions entertained whose truth can be proved in a finite number of steps
FINITISMS > FINITISM
FINITO *adj* finished
FINITUDE > FINITE
FINITUDES > FINITE
FINJAN *n* small, handleless coffee cup
FINJANS > FINJAN
FINK *n* strikebreaker ▷ *vb* inform (on someone), as to the police
FINKED > FINK
FINKING > FINK
FINKS > FINK
FINLESS > FIN
FINLIKE > FIN
FINMARK *n* monetary unit of Finland
FINMARKS > FINMARK
FINNAC *variant of* > FINNOCK
FINNACK *variant of* > FINNOCK
FINNACKS > FINNACK
FINNACS > FINNAC
FINNAN *n* smoked haddock
FINNANS > FINNAN
FINNED > FIN
FINNER *another name for* > RORQUAL
FINNERS > FINNER
FINNESKO *n* reindeer-skin boot
FINNICKY *variant of* > FINICKY
FINNIER > FINNY
FINNIEST > FINNY
FINNING > FIN
FINNMARK *n* Finnish monetary unit
FINNMARKS > FINNMARK
FINNOCHIO *variant of* > FINOCCHIO
FINNOCK *n* young sea trout on its first return to fresh water
FINNOCKS > FINNOCK
FINNSKO *variant of* > FINNESKO
FINNY *adj* relating to or containing many fishes
FINO *n* very dry sherry
FINOCCHIO *n* variety of fennel, *Foeniculum vulgare dulce*, with thickened stalks that resemble celery and are eaten as a vegetable, esp in S Europe
FINOCHIO *same as* > FINOCCHIO
FINOCHIOS > FINOCHIO
FINOS > FINO
FINS > FIN
FINSKO *variant of* > FINNESKO
FIORATURA *same as* > FIORITURA
FIORD *same as* > FJORD
FIORDS > FIORD
FIORIN *n* temperate perennial grass, *Agrostis stolonifera*
FIORINS > FIORIN
FIORITURA *n* embellishment, esp ornamentation added by the performer
FIORITURE > FIORITURA
FIPPENCE *n* fivepence
FIPPENCES > FIPPENCE
FIPPLE *n* wooden plug forming a flue in the end of a pipe, as the mouthpiece of a recorder
FIPPLES > FIPPLE
FIQUE *n* hemp
FIQUES > FIQUE
FIR *n* pyramid-shaped tree with needle-like leaves and erect cones
FIRE *n* state of combustion producing heat, flames, and smoke ▷ *vb* operate (a weapon) so that a bullet or missile is released
FIREABLE > FIRE
FIREARM *n* rifle, pistol, or shotgun
FIREARMED *adj* carrying firearm
FIREARMS > FIREARM
FIREBACK *n* ornamental iron slab against the back wall of a hearth
FIREBACKS > FIREBACK
FIREBALL *n* ball of fire at the centre of an explosion
FIREBALLS > FIREBALL
FIREBASE *n* artillery base from which heavy fire is directed at the enemy
FIREBASES > FIREBASE
FIREBIRD *n* any of various songbirds having a bright red plumage, esp the Baltimore oriole
FIREBIRDS > FIREBIRD
FIREBOARD *n* mantelpiece
FIREBOAT *n* motor vessel with fire-fighting apparatus
FIREBOATS > FIREBOAT
FIREBOMB *n* bomb that is designed to cause fires
FIREBOMBS > FIREBOMB
FIREBOX *n* furnace chamber of a boiler in a steam locomotive
FIREBOXES > FIREBOX
FIREBRAND *n* person who causes unrest
FIREBRAT *n* small primitive wingless insect, *Thermobia domestica*, that occurs in warm buildings, feeding on starchy food scraps, fabric, etc: order *Thysanura* (bristletails)
FIREBRATS > FIREBRAT
FIREBREAK *n* strip of cleared land to stop the advance of a fire
FIREBRICK *n* heat-resistant brick used for lining furnaces, fireplaces, etc
FIREBUG *n* person who deliberately sets fire to property
FIREBUGS > FIREBUG
FIREBUSH as in *Chilean firebush* South American shrub with scarlet flowers
FIRECLAY *n* heat-resistant clay used in the making of firebricks, furnace linings, etc
FIRECLAYS > FIRECLAY
FIRECREST *n* small European warbler, *Regulus ignicapillus*, having a crown striped with yellow, black, and white
FIRED > FIRE

FIREDAMP *n* explosive gas, composed mainly of methane, formed in mines
FIREDAMPS > FIREDAMP
FIREDOG *n* either of a pair of decorative metal stands used to support logs in an open fire
FIREDOGS > FIREDOG
FIREDRAKE *n* fire-breathing dragon
FIREFANG *vb* become overheated through decomposition
FIREFANGS > FIREFANG
FIREFIGHT *n* brief small-scale engagement between opposing military ground forces using short-range light weapons
FIREFLIES > FIREFLY
FIREFLOAT *n* boat used for firefighting
FIREFLOOD *n* method of extracting oil from a well by burning some of the oil to increase the rate of flow
FIREFLY *n* beetle that glows in the dark
FIREGUARD *same as* > FIREBREAK
FIREHALL *n* US and Canadian word for fire station
FIREHALLS > FIREHALL
FIREHOUSE *n* firestation
FIRELESS > FIRE
FIRELIGHT *n* light from a fire
FIRELIT *adj* lit by firelight
FIRELOCK *n* obsolete type of gunlock with a priming mechanism ignited by sparks
FIRELOCKS > FIRELOCK
FIREMAN *n* man whose job is to put out fires and rescue people endangered by them
FIREMANIC > FIREMAN
FIREMARK *n* plaque indicating that a building is insured
FIREMARKS > FIREMARK
FIREMEN > FIREMAN
FIREPAN *n* metal container for a fire in a room
FIREPANS > FIREPAN
FIREPINK *n* wildflower belonging to the pink family
FIREPINKS > FIREPINK
FIREPLACE *n* recess in a room for a fire
FIREPLUG *n* US and New Zealand name for a fire hydrant
FIREPLUGS > FIREPLUG
FIREPOT *n* Chinese fondue-like cooking pot
FIREPOTS > FIREPOT
FIREPOWER *n* amount of fire that may be delivered by a unit or weapon
FIREPROOF *adj* capable of resisting damage by fire ▷ *vb* make resistant to fire
FIRER > FIRE
FIREROOM *n* stokehold
FIREROOMS > FIREROOM
FIRERS > FIRE
FIRES > FIRE
FIRESHIP *n* vessel loaded with flammable materials, ignited, and directed among enemy warships to set them alight
FIRESHIPS > FIRESHIP
FIRESIDE *n* hearth
FIRESIDES > FIRESIDE
FIRESTONE *n* sandstone that withstands intense heat, esp one used for lining kilns, furnaces, etc
FIRESTORM *n* uncontrollable blaze sustained by violent winds that are drawn into the column of rising hot air over the burning area: often the result of heavy bombing
FIRETHORN *n* any rosaceous evergreen spiny shrub of the genus *Pyracantha*, of SE Europe and Asia, having bright red or orange fruits: cultivated for ornament
FIRETRAP *n* building that would burn easily or one without fire escapes
FIRETRAPS > FIRETRAP
FIRETRUCK *n* fire engine
FIREWALL *n* appliance that prevents unauthorized access to a computer network from the internet
FIREWALLS > FIREWALL
FIREWATER *n* any alcoholic spirit
FIREWEED *n* any of various plants that appear as first vegetation in burnt-over areas, esp rosebay willowherb
FIREWEEDS > FIREWEED
FIREWOMAN *n* female firefighter
FIREWOMEN > FIREWOMAN
FIREWOOD *n* wood for burning
FIREWOODS > FIREWOOD
FIREWORK *n* device containing chemicals that is ignited to produce spectacular explosions and coloured sparks
FIREWORKS *pl n* show in which fireworks are let off
FIREWORM *n* cranberry worm
FIREWORMS > FIREWORM
FIRIE *n* in Australian English, informal word for a firefighter
FIRIES > FIRIE
FIRING *n* discharge of a firearm
FIRINGS > FIRING
FIRK *vb* beat
FIRKED > FIRK
FIRKIN *n* small wooden barrel or similar container
FIRKING > FIRK
FIRKINS > FIRKIN
FIRKS > FIRK
FIRLOT *n* unit of measurement for grain
FIRLOTS > FIRLOT
FIRM *adj* not soft or yielding ▷ *adv* in an unyielding manner ▷ *vb* make or become firm ▷ *n* business company
FIRMAMENT *n* sky or the heavens
FIRMAN *n* edict of an Oriental sovereign
FIRMANS > FIRMAN
FIRMED > FIRM
FIRMER > FIRM
FIRMERS > FIRM
FIRMEST > FIRM
FIRMING > FIRM
FIRMLESS *adj* unstable
FIRMLY > FIRM
FIRMNESS > FIRM
FIRMS > FIRM
FIRMWARE *n* fixed form of software programmed into a read-only memory
FIRMWARES > FIRMWARE
FIRN *another name for* > NEVE
FIRNS > FIRN
FIRRIER > FIRRY
FIRRIEST > FIRRY
FIRRING *n* wooden battens used in building construction
FIRRINGS > FIRRING
FIRRY *adj* of, relating to, or made from fir trees
FIRS > FIR
FIRST *adj* earliest in time or order ▷ *n* person or thing coming before all others ▷ *adv* before anything else
FIRSTBORN *adj* eldest of the children in a family ▷ *n* eldest child in a family
FIRSTHAND *adj* from the original source
FIRSTLING *n* first, esp the first offspring
FIRSTLY *adv* coming before other points, questions, etc
FIRSTNESS > FIRST
FIRSTS *pl n* saleable goods of the highest quality
FIRTH *n* narrow inlet of the sea, esp in Scotland
FIRTHS > FIRTH
FISC *n* state or royal treasury
FISCAL *adj* of government finances, esp taxes ▷ *n* (in some countries) a public prosecutor
FISCALIST > FISCAL
FISCALLY > FISCAL
FISCALS > FISCAL
FISCS > FISC
FISGIG *variant of* > FISHGIG
FISGIGS > FISGIG
FISH *n* cold-blooded vertebrate with gills, that lives in water ▷ *vb* try to catch fish
FISHABLE > FISH
FISHBALL *n* fried ball of flaked fish and mashed potato
FISHBALLS > FISHBALL
FISHBOLT *n* bolt used for fastening a fishplate to a rail
FISHBOLTS > FISHBOLT
FISHBONE *n* bone of a fish
FISHBONES > FISHBONE
FISHBOWL *n* goldfish bowl
FISHBOWLS > FISHBOWL
FISHCAKE *n* mixture of flaked fish and mashed potatoes formed into a flat circular shape
FISHCAKES > FISHCAKE
FISHED > FISH
FISHER *n* fisherman
FISHERIES > FISHERY
FISHERMAN *n* person who catches fish for a living or for pleasure
FISHERMEN > FISHERMAN
FISHERS > FISHER
FISHERY *n* area of the sea used for fishing
FISHES > FISH
FISHEYE *n* in photography, a lens of small focal length, having a highly curved protruding front element, that covers an angle of view of almost 180°
FISHEYES > FISHEYE
FISHFUL *adj* teeming with fish
FISHGIG *n* pole with barbed prongs for impaling fish
FISHGIGS > FISHGIG
FISHHOOK *n* sharp hook used in angling, esp one with a barb
FISHHOOKS > FISHHOOK
FISHIER > FISHY
FISHIEST > FISHY
FISHIFIED > FISHIFY
FISHIFIES > FISHIFY
FISHIFY *vb* change into fish
FISHILY > FISHY
FISHINESS > FISHY
FISHING *n* job or pastime of catching fish
FISHINGS > FISHING
FISHKILL *n* mass killing of fish by pollution
FISHKILLS > FISHKILL
FISHLESS > FISH
FISHLIKE > FISH
FISHLINE *n* line used on a

fishing-rod
FISHLINES > FISHLINE
FISHMEAL *n* ground dried fish used as feed for farm animals or as a fertilizer
FISHMEALS > FISHMEAL
FISHNET *n* open mesh fabric resembling netting
FISHNETS > FISHNET
FISHPLATE *n* metal plate holding rails together
FISHPOLE *n* boom arm for a microphone
FISHPOLES > FISHPOLE
FISHPOND > FISH
FISHPONDS > FISH
FISHSKIN *n* skin of a fish
FISHSKINS > FISHSKIN
FISHTAIL *n* nozzle having a long narrow slot at the top, placed over a Bunsen burner to produce a thin fanlike flame ▷ *vb* slow an aeroplane by moving the tail from side to side
FISHTAILS > FISHTAIL
FISHWAY *n* fish ladder
FISHWAYS > FISHWAY
FISHWIFE *n* coarse scolding woman
FISHWIVES > FISHWIFE
FISHWORM *n* worm used as fishing bait
FISHWORMS > FISHWORM
FISHY *adj* of or like fish
FISHYBACK *n* goods supply chain involving container transfer from lorry to ship
FISK *vb* frisk
FISKED > FISK
FISKING > FISK
FISKS > FISK
FISNOMIE *n* physiognomy
FISNOMIES > FISNOMIE
FISSATE > FISSILE
FISSILE *adj* capable of undergoing nuclear fission
FISSILITY > FISSILE
FISSION *n* splitting
FISSIONAL > FISSION
FISSIONED *adj* split or broken into parts
FISSIONS > FISSION
FISSIPED *adj* having toes that are separated from one another, as dogs, cats, bears, and similar carnivores ▷ *n* fissiped animal
FISSIPEDE > FISSIPED
FISSIPEDS > FISSIPED
FISSIVE > FISSILE
FISSLE *vb* rustle
FISSLED > FISSLE
FISSLES > FISSLE
FISSLING > FISSLE
FISSURAL > FISSURE
FISSURE *n* long narrow cleft or crack ▷ *vb* crack or split apart
FISSURED > FISSURE
FISSURES > FISSURE
FISSURING > FISSURE
FIST *n* clenched hand ▷ *vb* hit with the fist
FISTED > FIST
FISTFIGHT *n* fight using bare fists
FISTFUL *n* quantity that can be held in a fist or hand
FISTFULS > FISTFUL
FISTIANA *n* world of boxing
FISTIC *adj* of or relating to fisticuffs or boxing
FISTICAL > FISTIC
FISTICUFF > FISTICUFFS
FISTIER > FIST
FISTIEST > FIST
FISTING > FIST
FISTMELE *n* measure of the width of a hand and the extended thumb, used to calculate the approximate height of the string of a braced bow
FISTMELES > FISTMELE
FISTNOTE *n* note in printed text preceded by the fist symbol
FISTNOTES > FISTNOTE
FISTS > FIST
FISTULA *n* long narrow ulcer
FISTULAE > FISTULA
FISTULAR *same as* > FISTULOUS
FISTULAS > FISTULA
FISTULATE *same as* > FISTULOUS
FISTULOSE *variant of* > FISTULOUS
FISTULOUS *adj* containing, relating to, or resembling a fistula
FISTY > FIST
FIT *vb* be appropriate or suitable for ▷ *adj* appropriate ▷ *n* way in which something fits
FITCH *n* fur of the polecat or ferret
FITCHE *adj* pointed
FITCHEE *variant of* > FITCHE
FITCHES > FITCH
FITCHET *same as* > FITCH
FITCHETS > FITCHET
FITCHEW *archaic name for* > POLECAT
FITCHEWS > FITCHEW
FITCHY *variant of* > FITCHE
FITFUL *adj* occurring in irregular spells
FITFULLY > FITFUL
FITLIER > FITLY
FITLIEST > FITLY
FITLY *adv* in a proper manner or place or at a proper time
FITMENT *n* accessory attached to a machine
FITMENTS > FITMENT
FITNA *n* state of trouble or chaos
FITNAS > FITNA
FITNESS *n* state of being fit
FITNESSES > FITNESS
FITS > FIT
FITT *n* song
FITTABLE > FIT
FITTE *variant of* > FITT
FITTED > FIT
FITTER > FIT
FITTERS > FIT
FITTES > FITTE
FITTEST > FIT
FITTING > FIT
FITTINGLY > FIT
FITTINGS > FIT
FITTS > FITT
FIVE *n* one more than four ▷ *adj* amounting to five ▷ *determiner* amounting to five
FIVEFOLD *adj* having five times as many or as much ▷ *adv* by five times as many or as much
FIVEPENCE *n* five-penny coin
FIVEPENNY *adj* (of a nail) one and three-quarters of an inch in length
FIVEPIN > FIVEPINS
FIVEPINS *n* bowling game played esp in Canada
FIVER *n* five-pound note
FIVERS > FIVER
FIVES *n* ball game resembling squash but played with bats or the hands
FIX *vb* make or become firm, stable, or secure ▷ *n* difficult situation
FIXABLE > FIX
FIXATE *vb* become or cause to become fixed
FIXATED > FIXATE
FIXATES > FIXATE
FIXATIF *variant of* > FIXATIVE
FIXATIFS > FIXATIF
FIXATING > FIXATE
FIXATION *n* obsessive interest in something
FIXATIONS > FIXATION
FIXATIVE *n* liquid used to preserve or hold things in place ▷ *adj* serving or tending to fix
FIXATIVES > FIXATIVE
FIXATURE *n* something that holds an object in place
FIXATURES > FIXATURE
FIXED *adj* attached or placed so as to be immovable
FIXEDLY > FIXED
FIXEDNESS > FIXED
FIXER *n* solution used to make a photographic image permanent
FIXERS > FIXER
FIXES > FIX
FIXING *n* means of attaching one thing to another, as a pipe to a wall, slate to a roof, etc
FIXINGS *pl n* apparatus or equipment
FIXIT *n* solution to a complex problem
FIXITIES > FIXITY
FIXITY *n* state or quality of a person's gaze, attitude, or concentration not changing or weakening
FIXIVE > FIX
FIXT *adj* fixed
FIXTURE *n* permanently fitted piece of household equipment
FIXTURES > FIXTURE
FIXURE *n* firmness
FIXURES > FIXURE
FIZ *variant of* > FIZZ
FIZGIG *same as* > FISHGIG
FIZGIGS > FIZGIG
FIZZ *vb* make a hissing or bubbling noise ▷ *n* hissing or bubbling noise
FIZZED > FIZZ
FIZZEN *variant of* > FOISON
FIZZENS > FIZZEN
FIZZER *n* anything that fizzes
FIZZERS > FIZZER
FIZZES > FIZZ
FIZZGIG *variant of* > FISHGIG
FIZZGIGS > FIZZGIG
FIZZIER > FIZZ
FIZZIEST > FIZZ
FIZZINESS > FIZZ
FIZZING > FIZZ
FIZZINGS > FIZZ
FIZZLE *vb* make a weak hissing or bubbling sound ▷ *n* hissing or bubbling sound
FIZZLED > FIZZLE
FIZZLES > FIZZLE
FIZZLING > FIZZLE
FIZZY > FIZZ
FJELD *n* high rocky plateau with little vegetation in Scandinavian countries
FJELDS > FJELD
FJORD *n* long narrow inlet of the sea between cliffs, esp in Norway
FJORDIC > FJORD
FJORDS > FJORD
FLAB *n* unsightly body fat
FLABBIER > FLABBY
FLABBIEST > FLABBY
FLABBILY > FLABBY
FLABBY *adj* having flabby flesh
FLABELLA > FLABELLUM
FLABELLUM *n* fan-shaped organ or part, such as the tip of the proboscis of a honeybee
FLABS > FLAB
FLACCID *adj* soft and limp
FLACCIDER > FLACCID
FLACCIDLY > FLACCID
FLACK *vb* flutter
FLACKED > FLACK
FLACKER *vb* flutter like a bird
FLACKERED > FLACKER
FLACKERS > FLACKER

FLACKERY > FLACK
FLACKET *n* flagon
FLACKETS > FLACKET
FLACKING > FLACK
FLACKS > FLACK
FLACON *n* small stoppered bottle or flask, such as one used for perfume
FLACONS > FLACON
FLAFF *vb* flap
FLAFFED > FLAFF
FLAFFER *vb* flutter
FLAFFERED > FLAFFER
FLAFFERS > FLAFFER
FLAFFING > FLAFF
FLAFFS > FLAFF
FLAG *n* piece of cloth attached to a pole as an emblem or signal ▷ *vb* mark with a flag or sticker
FLAGELLA > FLAGELLUM
FLAGELLAR > FLAGELLUM
FLAGELLIN *n* structural protein of bacterial flagella
FLAGELLUM *n* whiplike outgrowth from a cell that acts as an organ of movement
FLAGEOLET *n* small instrument like a recorder
FLAGGED > FLAG
FLAGGER > FLAG
FLAGGERS > FLAG
FLAGGIER > FLAGGY
FLAGGIEST > FLAGGY
FLAGGING > FLAG
FLAGGINGS > FLAG
FLAGGY *adj* drooping
FLAGITATE *vb* importune
FLAGLESS > FLAG
FLAGMAN *n* person who has charge of, carries, or signals with a flag, esp a railway employee
FLAGMEN > FLAGMAN
FLAGON *n* wide bottle for wine or cider
FLAGONS > FLAGON
FLAGPOLE *n* pole for a flag
FLAGPOLES > FLAGPOLE
FLAGRANCE > FLAGRANT
FLAGRANCY > FLAGRANT
FLAGRANT *adj* openly outrageous
FLAGS > FLAG
FLAGSHIP *n* admiral's ship
FLAGSHIPS > FLAGSHIP
FLAGSTAFF *same as* > FLAGPOLE
FLAGSTICK *n* in golf, pole used to indicate position of hole
FLAGSTONE *n* flat slab of hard stone for paving
FLAIL *vb* wave about wildly ▷ *n* tool formerly used for threshing grain by hand
FLAILED > FLAIL
FLAILING > FLAIL
FLAILS > FLAIL
FLAIR *n* natural ability
FLAIRS > FLAIR
FLAK *n* anti-aircraft fire
FLAKE *n* small thin piece, esp chipped off something ▷ *vb* peel off in flakes
FLAKED > FLAKE
FLAKER > FLAKE
FLAKERS > FLAKE
FLAKES > FLAKE
FLAKEY *same as* > FLAKY
FLAKIER > FLAKY
FLAKIES *n* dandruff
FLAKIEST > FLAKY
FLAKILY > FLAKY
FLAKINESS > FLAKY
FLAKING > FLAKE
FLAKS > FLAK
FLAKY *adj* like or made of flakes
FLAM *n* falsehood, deception, or sham ▷ *vb* cheat or deceive
FLAMBE *vb* cook or serve (food) in flaming brandy ▷ *adj* (of food, such as steak or pancakes) served in flaming brandy
FLAMBEAU *n* burning torch, as used in night processions
FLAMBEAUS > FLAMBEAU
FLAMBEAUX > FLAMBEAU
FLAMBEE *same as* > FLAMBE
FLAMBEED > FLAMBEE
FLAMBEES > FLAMBEE
FLAMBEING > FLAMBE
FLAMBES > FLAMBE
FLAME *n* luminous burning gas coming from burning material ▷ *vb* burn brightly
FLAMED > FLAME
FLAMELESS > FLAME
FLAMELET > FLAME
FLAMELETS > FLAME
FLAMELIKE > FLAME
FLAMEN *n* (in ancient Rome) any of 15 priests who each served a particular deity
FLAMENCO *n* rhythmical Spanish dance accompanied by a guitar and vocalist
FLAMENCOS > FLAMENCO
FLAMENS > FLAMEN
FLAMEOUT *n* failure of an aircraft jet engine in flight due to extinction of the flame ▷ *vb* (of a jet engine) to fail in flight or to cause (a jet engine) to fail in flight
FLAMEOUTS > FLAMEOUT
FLAMER > FLAME
FLAMERS > FLAME
FLAMES > FLAME
FLAMFEW *n* fantastic trifle
FLAMFEWS > FLAMFEW
FLAMIER > FLAME
FLAMIEST > FLAME
FLAMINES > FLAMEN
FLAMING *adj* burning with flames ▷ *adv* extremely
FLAMINGLY > FLAMING
FLAMINGO *n* large pink wading bird with a long neck and legs
FLAMINGOS > FLAMINGO
FLAMM *variant of* > FLAM
FLAMMABLE *adj* easily set on fire
FLAMMED > FLAM
FLAMMING > FLAM
FLAMMS > FLAMM
FLAMMULE *n* small flame
FLAMMULES > FLAMMULE
FLAMS > FLAM
FLAMY > FLAME
FLAN *n* open sweet or savoury tart
FLANCARD *n* armour covering a horse's flank
FLANCARDS > FLANCARD
FLANCH *variant of* > FLAUNCH
FLANCHED > FLANCH
FLANCHES > FLANCH
FLANCHING > FLANCH
FLANERIE *n* aimless strolling or lounging
FLANERIES > FLANERIE
FLANES *n* arrows
FLANEUR *n* idler or loafer
FLANEURS > FLANEUR
FLANGE *n* projecting rim or collar ▷ *vb* attach or provide (a component) with a flange
FLANGED > FLANGE
FLANGER > FLANGE
FLANGERS > FLANGE
FLANGES > FLANGE
FLANGING > FLANGE
FLANK *n* part of the side between the hips and ribs ▷ *vb* be at or move along the side of
FLANKED > FLANK
FLANKEN *n* cut of beef
FLANKER *n* one of a detachment of soldiers detailed to guard the flanks, esp of a formation
FLANKERED > FLANKER
FLANKERS > FLANKER
FLANKING > FLANK
FLANKS > FLANK
FLANNEL *n* small piece of cloth for washing the face ▷ *vb* talk evasively
FLANNELED > FLANNEL
FLANNELET *n* cotton imitation of flannel
FLANNELLY > FLANNEL
FLANNELS > FLANNEL
FLANNEN *adj* made of flannel
FLANNENS > FLANNEN
FLANS > FLAN
FLAP *vb* move back and forwards or up and down ▷ *n* action or sound of flapping
FLAPERON *n* control flap on aircraft wing
FLAPERONS > FLAPERON
FLAPJACK *n* chewy biscuit made with oats
FLAPJACKS > FLAPJACK
FLAPLESS > FLAP
FLAPPABLE > FLAP
FLAPPED > FLAP
FLAPPER *n* (in the 1920s) a lively young woman who dressed and behaved unconventionally
FLAPPERS > FLAPPER
FLAPPIER > FLAPPY
FLAPPIEST > FLAPPY
FLAPPING > FLAP
FLAPPINGS > FLAP
FLAPPY *adj* loose
FLAPS > FLAP
FLAPTRACK *n* component in an aircraft wing
FLARE *vb* blaze with a sudden unsteady flame ▷ *n* sudden unsteady flame
FLAREBACK *n* flame in the breech of a gun when fired
FLARED > FLARE
FLARES *pl n* trousers with legs that widen below the knee
FLAREUP *n* outbreak of something
FLAREUPS > FLAREUP
FLARIER > FLARE
FLARIEST > FLARE
FLARING > FLARE
FLARINGLY > FLARE
FLARY > FLARE
FLASER *n* type of sedimentary structure in rock
FLASERS > FLASER
FLASH *n* sudden burst of light or flame ▷ *adj* vulgarly showy ▷ *vb* (cause to) burst into flame
FLASHBACK *n* scene in a book, play, or film, that shows earlier events ▷ *vb* return in a novel, film, etc, to a past event
FLASHBULB *n* small light bulb that produces a bright flash of light
FLASHCARD *n* card shown briefly as a memory test
FLASHCUBE *n* in photography, a cube with a bulb that is attached to a camera
FLASHED > FLASH
FLASHER *n* man who exposes himself indecently
FLASHERS > FLASHER
FLASHES > FLASH
FLASHEST > FLASH
FLASHGUN *n* type of electronic flash, attachable to or sometimes incorporated in a camera, that emits a very brief flash of light when the shutter is open
FLASHGUNS > FLASHGUN
FLASHIER > FLASHY
FLASHIEST > FLASHY
FLASHILY > FLASHY
FLASHING *n* watertight

material used to cover joins in a roof
FLASHINGS > FLASHING
FLASHLAMP *n* electric lamp producing a flash of intense light
FLASHOVER *n* electric discharge over or around the surface of an insulator
FLASHTUBE *n* tube used in a flashlamp
FLASHY *adj* showy in a vulgar way
FLASK *n* flat bottle for carrying alcoholic drink in the pocket
FLASKET *n* long shallow basket
FLASKETS > FLASKET
FLASKS > FLASK
FLAT *adj* level and horizontal ⊳ *adv* in or into a flat position ⊳ *n* flat surface ⊳ *vb* live in a flat
FLATBACK *n* flat-backed ornament, designed for viewing from front
FLATBACKS > FLATBACK
FLATBED *n* printing machine on which the type forme is carried on a flat bed under a revolving paper-bearing cylinder
FLATBEDS > FLATBED
FLATBOAT *n* flat-bottomed boat for transporting goods on a canal
FLATBOATS > FLATBOAT
FLATBREAD *n* type of thin unleavened bread
FLATCAP *n* Elizabethan man's hat with a narrow down-turned brim
FLATCAPS > FLATCAP
FLATCAR *n* flatbed
FLATCARS > FLATCAR
FLATETTE *n* very small flat
FLATETTES > FLATETTE
FLATFEET > FLATFOOT
FLATFISH *n* sea fish, such as the sole, which has a flat body
FLATFOOT *n* condition in which the entire sole of the foot is able to touch the ground because of flattening of the instep arch
FLATFOOTS > FLATFOOT
FLATHEAD *n* common Australian flatfish
FLATHEADS > FLATHEAD
FLATIRON *n* (formerly) an iron for pressing clothes that was heated by being placed on a stove
FLATIRONS > FLATIRON
FLATLAND *n* land notable for its levelness
FLATLANDS > FLATLAND
FLATLET *n* small flat
FLATLETS > FLATLET
FLATLINE *vb* die or be so near death that the display of one's vital signs on medical monitoring equipment shows a flat line rather than peaks and troughs
FLATLINED > FLATLINE
FLATLINER > FLATLINE
FLATLINES > FLATLINE
FLATLING *adv* in a flat or prostrate position ⊳ *adj* with the flat side, as of a sword
FLATLINGS *same as* > FLATLING
FLATLONG *adv* prostrate
FLATLY > FLAT
FLATMATE *n* person with whom one shares a flat
FLATMATES > FLATMATE
FLATNESS > FLAT
FLATPACK *n* (of a piece of furniture, equipment, or other construction) supplied in pieces packed into a flat box for assembly by the buyer
FLATPACKS > FLATPACK
FLATS > FLAT
FLATSHARE *n* state of living in a flat where each occupant shares the facilities and expenses ⊳ *vb* live in a flat with other people who are not relatives
FLATTED > FLAT
FLATTEN *vb* make or become flat or flatter
FLATTENED > FLATTEN
FLATTENER > FLATTEN
FLATTENS > FLATTEN
FLATTER *vb* praise insincerely
FLATTERED > FLATTER
FLATTERER > FLATTER
FLATTERS > FLATTER
FLATTERY *n* excessive or insincere praise
FLATTEST > FLAT
FLATTIE *n* flat tyre
FLATTIES > FLATTIE
FLATTING > FLAT
FLATTINGS > FLAT
FLATTISH *adj* somewhat flat
FLATTOP *n* informal name for an aircraft carrier
FLATTOPS > FLATTOP
FLATTY *n* flat shoe
FLATULENT *adj* suffering from or caused by too much gas in the intestines
FLATUOUS > FLATUS
FLATUS *n* gas generated in the alimentary canal
FLATUSES > FLATUS
FLATWARE *n* cutlery
FLATWARES > FLATWARE
FLATWASH *n* laundry that can be ironed mechanically
FLATWAYS *adv* with the flat or broad side down or in contact with another surface
FLATWISE *same as* > FLATWAYS
FLATWORK *n* laundry that can be ironed mechanically
FLATWORKS > FLATWORK
FLATWORM *n* worm, such as a tapeworm, with a flattened body
FLATWORMS > FLATWORM
FLAUGHT *vb* flutter
FLAUGHTED > FLAUGHT
FLAUGHTER *vb* cut peat
FLAUGHTS > FLAUGHT
FLAUNCH *n* cement or mortar slope around a chimney top, manhole, etc, to throw off water ⊳ *vb* cause to slope in this manner
FLAUNCHED > FLAUNCH
FLAUNCHES > FLAUNCH
FLAUNE *variant of* > FLAM
FLAUNES > FLAUNE
FLAUNT *vb* display (oneself or one's possessions) arrogantly ⊳ *n* act of flaunting
FLAUNTED > FLAUNT
FLAUNTER > FLAUNT
FLAUNTERS > FLAUNT
FLAUNTIER > FLAUNTY
FLAUNTILY > FLAUNTY
FLAUNTING > FLAUNT
FLAUNTS > FLAUNT
FLAUNTY *adj* characterized by or inclined to ostentatious display or flaunting
FLAUTA *n* tortilla rolled around a filling
FLAUTAS > FLAUTA
FLAUTIST *n* flute player
FLAUTISTS > FLAUTIST
FLAVANOL *n* type of flavonoid
FLAVANOLS > FLAVANOL
FLAVANONE *n* flavone-derived compound
FLAVIN *n* heterocyclic ketone
FLAVINE *same as* > FLAVIN
FLAVINES > FLAVINE
FLAVINS > FLAVIN
FLAVONE *n* crystalline compound occurring in plants
FLAVONES > FLAVONE
FLAVONOID *n* any of a group of organic compounds that occur as pigments in fruit and flowers
FLAVONOL *n* flavonoid that occurs in red wine and is said to offer protection against heart disease
FLAVONOLS > FLAVONOL
FLAVOR *same as* > FLAVOUR
FLAVORED > FLAVOR
FLAVORER > FLAVOR
FLAVORERS > FLAVOR
FLAVORFUL *same as* > FLAVOURFUL
FLAVORING *same as* > FLAVORING
FLAVORIST *n* blender of ingredients, to create or enhance flavours
FLAVOROUS *adj* having flavour
FLAVORS > FLAVOR
FLAVORY *adj* flavoursome
FLAVOUR *n* distinctive taste ⊳ *vb* give flavour to
FLAVOURED > FLAVOUR
FLAVOURER > FLAVOUR
FLAVOURS > FLAVOUR
FLAVOURY *adj* flavoursome
FLAW *n* imperfection or blemish ⊳ *vb* make or become blemished, defective, or imperfect
FLAWED > FLAW
FLAWIER > FLAW
FLAWIEST > FLAW
FLAWING > FLAW
FLAWLESS > FLAW
FLAWN *variant of* > FLAM
FLAWNS > FLAWN
FLAWS > FLAW
FLAWY > FLAW
FLAX *n* plant grown for its stem fibres and seeds
FLAXEN *adj* (of hair) pale yellow
FLAXES > FLAX
FLAXIER > FLAXY
FLAXIEST > FLAXY
FLAXSEED *n* seed of the flax plant, which yields linseed oil
FLAXSEEDS > FLAXSEED
FLAXY *same as* > FLAXEN
FLAY *same as* > FLEY
FLAYED > FLAY
FLAYER > FLAY
FLAYERS > FLAY
FLAYING > FLAY
FLAYS > FLAY
FLAYSOME *adj* frightening
FLEA *n* small wingless jumping bloodsucking insect
FLEABAG *n* dirty or unkempt person, esp a woman
FLEABAGS > FLEABAG
FLEABANE as in *Canadian fleabane*
FLEABANES > FLEABANE
FLEABITE *n* bite of a flea
FLEABITES > FLEABITE
FLEAM *n* lancet used for letting blood
FLEAMS > FLEAM
FLEAPIT *n* shabby cinema or theatre
FLEAPITS > FLEAPIT
FLEAS > FLEA
FLEASOME > FLEA
FLEAWORT *n* any of various plants of the genus *Senecio*, esp *S. integrifolius*, a European species with yellow daisy-like flowers and rosettes of downy

leaves: family *Asteraceae* (composites)
FLEAWORTS > FLEAWORT
FLECHE *n* slender spire, esp over the intersection of the nave and transept ridges of a church roof
FLECHES > FLECHE
FLECHETTE *n* steel dart or missile dropped from an aircraft, as in World War I
FLECK *n* small mark, streak, or speck ▷ *vb* speckle
FLECKED > FLECK
FLECKER *same as* > FLECK
FLECKERED > FLECKER
FLECKERS > FLECKER
FLECKING > FLECK
FLECKLESS > FLECK
FLECKS > FLECK
FLECKY > FLECK
FLECTION *n* act of bending or the state of being bent
FLECTIONS > FLECTION
FLED > FLEE
FLEDGE *vb* feed and care for (a young bird) until it is able to fly
FLEDGED > FLEDGE
FLEDGES > FLEDGE
FLEDGIER > FLEDGY
FLEDGIEST > FLEDGY
FLEDGING > FLEDGE
FLEDGLING *n* young bird ▷ *adj* new or inexperienced
FLEDGY *adj* feathery or feathered
FLEE *vb* run away (from)
FLEECE *n* sheep's coat of wool ▷ *vb* defraud or overcharge
FLEECED > FLEECE
FLEECER > FLEECE
FLEECERS > FLEECE
FLEECES > FLEECE
FLEECH *vb* flatter
FLEECHED > FLEECH
FLEECHES > FLEECH
FLEECHING > FLEECH
FLEECIE *n* person who collects fleeces after shearing and prepares them for baling
FLEECIER > FLEECY
FLEECIES > FLEECIE
FLEECIEST > FLEECY
FLEECILY > FLEECY
FLEECING > FLEECE
FLEECY *adj* made of or like fleece ▷ *n* person who collects fleeces after shearing and prepares them for baling
FLEEIN > FLEE
FLEEING > FLEE
FLEER *vb* grin or laugh at ▷ *n* derisory glance or grin
FLEERED > FLEER
FLEERER > FLEER
FLEERERS > FLEER
FLEERING > FLEER
FLEERINGS > FLEER
FLEERS > FLEER
FLEES > FLEE
FLEET *n* number of warships organized as a unit ▷ *adj* swift in movement ▷ *vb* move rapidly
FLEETED > FLEET
FLEETER > FLEET
FLEETEST > FLEET
FLEETING *adj* rapid and soon passing
FLEETLY > FLEET
FLEETNESS > FLEET
FLEETS > FLEET
FLEG *vb* scare
FLEGGED > FLEG
FLEGGING > FLEG
FLEGS > FLEG
FLEHMEN *vb* (of mammal) grimace
FLEHMENED > FLEHMEN
FLEHMENS > FLEHMEN
FLEISHIG *same as* > FLEISHIK
FLEISHIK *adj* (of food) containing or derived from meat or meat products and therefore to be prepared and eaten separately from dairy foods
FLEME *vb* drive out
FLEMES > FLEME
FLEMING *n* native or inhabitant of Flanders or a Flemish-speaking Belgian
FLEMISH *vb* stow (a rope) in a Flemish coil
FLEMISHED > FLEMISH
FLEMISHES > FLEMISH
FLEMIT > FLEME
FLENCH *same as* > FLENSE
FLENCHED > FLENCH
FLENCHER > FLENCH
FLENCHERS > FLENCH
FLENCHES > FLENCH
FLENCHING > FLENCH
FLENSE *vb* strip (a whale, seal, etc) of (its blubber or skin)
FLENSED > FLENSE
FLENSER > FLENSE
FLENSERS > FLENSE
FLENSES > FLENSE
FLENSING > FLENSE
FLESH *n* soft part of a human or animal body
FLESHED > FLESH
FLESHER *n* person or machine that fleshes hides or skins
FLESHERS > FLESHER
FLESHES > FLESH
FLESHHOOD incarnation
FLESHIER > FLESHY
FLESHIEST > FLESHY
FLESHILY > FLESHY
FLESHING > FLESH
FLESHINGS *pl n* flesh-coloured tights
FLESHLESS > FLESH
FLESHLIER > FLESHLY
FLESHLING *n* voluptuary
FLESHLY *adj* carnal
FLESHMENT *n* act of fleshing
FLESHPOT *n* pot in which meat is cooked
FLESHPOTS *pl n* places, such as brothels and strip clubs, where sexual desires are catered to
FLESHWORM *n* flesh-eating worm
FLESHY *adj* plump
FLETCH *same as* > FLEDGE
FLETCHED > FLETCH
FLETCHER *n* person who makes arrows
FLETCHERS > FLETCHER
FLETCHES > FLETCH
FLETCHING > FLETCH
FLETTON *n* type of brick
FLETTONS > FLETTON
FLEURET *same as* > FLEURETTE
FLEURETS > FLEURET
FLEURETTE *n* ornament resembling a flower
FLEURON *n* decorative piece of pastry
FLEURONS > FLEURON
FLEURY *same as* > FLORY
FLEW > FLY
FLEWED *adj* having large flews
FLEWS *pl n* fleshy hanging upper lip of a bloodhound or similar dog
FLEX *n* flexible insulated electric cable ▷ *vb* bend
FLEXAGON *n* hexagon made from a single pliable strip of triangles
FLEXAGONS > FLEXAGON
FLEXED > FLEX
FLEXES > FLEX
FLEXIBLE *adj* easily bent
FLEXIBLY > FLEXIBLE
FLEXILE *same as* > FLEXIBLE
FLEXING > FLEX
FLEXION *n* act of bending a joint or limb
FLEXIONAL > FLEXION
FLEXIONS > FLEXION
FLEXITIME *n* system permitting variation in starting and finishing times of work
FLEXO *n, adj, adv* flexography
FLEXOR *n* any muscle whose contraction serves to bend a joint or limb
FLEXORS > FLEXOR
FLEXOS > FLEXO
FLEXTIME *same as* > FLEXITIME
FLEXTIMER > FLEXTIME
FLEXTIMES > FLEXTIME
FLEXUOSE *same as* > FLEXUOUS
FLEXUOUS *adj* full of bends or curves
FLEXURAL > FLEXURE
FLEXURE *n* act of flexing or the state of being flexed
FLEXURES > FLEXURE
FLEY *vb* be afraid or cause to be afraid
FLEYED > FLEY
FLEYING > FLEY
FLEYS > FLEY
FLIBBERT *n* small piece or bit
FLIBBERTS > FLIBBERT
FLIC *n* French police office[r]
FLICHTER *vb* flutter
FLICHTERS > FLICHTER
FLICK *vb* touch or move with the finger or hand in a quick movement ▷ *n* tap or quick stroke
FLICKABLE > FLICK
FLICKED > FLICK
FLICKER *vb* shine unsteadily or intermittently ▷ *n* unsteady brief light
FLICKERED > FLICKER
FLICKERS > FLICKER
FLICKERY > FLICKER
FLICKING > FLICK
FLICKS > FLICK
FLICS > FLIC
FLIED > FLY
FLIER > FLY
FLIERS > FLY
FLIES > FLY
FLIEST > FLY
FLIGHT *n* journey by air ▷ *vb* cause (a ball, dart, etc) to float slowly or deceptively towards its target
FLIGHTED > FLIGHT
FLIGHTIER > FLIGHTY
FLIGHTILY > FLIGHTY
FLIGHTING > FLIGHT
FLIGHTS > FLIGHT
FLIGHTY *adj* frivolous and fickle
FLIM *n* five-pound note
FLIMFLAM *n* nonsense ▷ *vb* deceive
FLIMFLAMS > FLIMFLAM
FLIMP *vb* steal
FLIMPED > FLIMP
FLIMPING > FLIMP
FLIMPS > FLIMP
FLIMS > FLIM
FLIMSIER > FLIMSY
FLIMSIES > FLIMSY
FLIMSIEST > FLIMSY
FLIMSILY > FLIMSY
FLIMSY *adj* not strong or substantial ▷ *n* thin paper used for making carbon copies of a letter, etc
FLINCH *same as* > FLENSE
FLINCHED > FLINCH
FLINCHER > FLINCH
FLINCHERS > FLINCH
FLINCHES > FLINCH
FLINCHING > FLINCH
FLINDER *n* fragment
FLINDERS > FLINDER
FLING *vb* throw, send, or move forcefully or hurriedly ▷ *n* spell of self-indulgent enjoyment
FLINGER > FLING
FLINGERS > FLING

FLINGING > FLING
FLINGS > FLING
FLINKITE *n* anhydrous phosphate
FLINKITES > FLINKITE
FLINT *n* hard grey stone ▷ *vb* fit or provide with a flint
FLINTED > FLINT
FLINTHEAD *n* American wading bird
FLINTIER > FLINTY
FLINTIEST > FLINTY
FLINTIFY *vb* turn to flint
FLINTILY > FLINTY
FLINTING > FLINT
FLINTLIKE > FLINT
FLINTLOCK *n* obsolete gun in which the powder was lit by a spark from a flint
FLINTS > FLINT
FLINTY *adj* cruel
FLIP *vb* throw (something small or light) carelessly ▷ *n* snap or tap ▷ *adj* flippant
FLIPBOOK *n* book of drawings made to seem animated by flipping pages
FLIPBOOKS > FLIPBOOK
FLIPFLOP *n* rubber sandal
FLIPFLOPS > FLIPFLOP
FLIPPANCY > FLIPPANT
FLIPPANT *adj* treating serious things lightly
FLIPPED > FLIP
FLIPPER *n* limb of a sea animal adapted for swimming
FLIPPERS > FLIPPER
FLIPPEST > FLIP
FLIPPING > FLIP
FLIPPY *adj* (of clothes) tending to move to and fro as the wearer walks
FLIPS > FLIP
FLIR *n* forward looking infrared radar
FLIRS > FLIR
FLIRT *vb* behave as if sexually attracted to someone ▷ *n* person who flirts
FLIRTED > FLIRT
FLIRTER > FLIRT
FLIRTERS > FLIRT
FLIRTIER > FLIRT
FLIRTIEST > FLIRT
FLIRTING > FLIRT
FLIRTINGS > FLIRT
FLIRTISH > FLIRT
FLIRTS > FLIRT
FLIRTY > FLIRT
FLISK *vb* skip
FLISKED > FLISK
FLISKIER > FLISK
FLISKIEST > FLISK
FLISKING > FLISK
FLISKS > FLISK
FLISKY > FLISK
FLIT *vb* move lightly and rapidly ▷ *n* act of flitting
FLITCH *n* side of pork salted and cured ▷ *vb* cut (a tree trunk) into flitches
FLITCHED > FLITCH
FLITCHES > FLITCH
FLITCHING > FLITCH
FLITE *vb* scold or rail at ▷ *n* dispute or scolding
FLITED > FLITE
FLITES > FLITE
FLITING > FLITE
FLITS > FLIT
FLITT *adj* fleet
FLITTED > FLIT
FLITTER > FLIT
FLITTERED > FLIT
FLITTERN *n* bark of young oak tree
FLITTERNS > FLITTERN
FLITTERS > FLIT
FLITTING > FLIT
FLITTINGS > FLIT
FLIVVER *n* old, cheap, or battered car
FLIVVERS > FLIVVER
FLIX *n* fur ▷ *vb* have fur
FLIXED > FLIX
FLIXES > FLIX
FLIXING > FLIX
FLOAT *vb* rest on the surface of a liquid ▷ *n* light object used to help someone or something float
FLOATABLE > FLOAT
FLOATAGE *same as* > FLOTAGE
FLOATAGES > FLOATAGE
FLOATANT *n* substance used in fly-fishing, to help dry flies to float
FLOATANTS > FLOATANT
FLOATCUT as in *floatcut file* file with rows of parallel teeth
FLOATED > FLOAT
FLOATEL *same as* > FLOTEL
FLOATELS > FLOATEL
FLOATER *n* person or thing that floats
FLOATERS > FLOATER
FLOATIER > FLOATY
FLOATIEST > FLOATY
FLOATING *adj* moving about, changing
FLOATINGS > FLOATING
FLOATS *pl n* footlights
FLOATY *adj* filmy and light
FLOC *same as* > FLOCK
FLOCCED > FLOC
FLOCCI > FLOCCUS
FLOCCING > FLOC
FLOCCOSE *adj* consisting of or covered with woolly tufts or hairs
FLOCCULAR > FLOCCUS
FLOCCULE *n* small aggregate of flocculent material
FLOCCULES > FLOCCULE
FLOCCULI > FLOCCULUS
FLOCCULUS *same as* > FLOCCULE
FLOCCUS *n* downy or woolly covering, as on the young of certain birds ▷ *adj* (of a cloud) having the appearance of woolly tufts at odd intervals in its structure
FLOCK *n* number of animals of one kind together ▷ *vb* gather in a crowd ▷ *adj* (of wallpaper) with a velvety raised pattern
FLOCKED > FLOCK
FLOCKIER > FLOCK
FLOCKIEST > FLOCK
FLOCKING > FLOCK
FLOCKINGS > FLOCK
FLOCKLESS > FLOCK
FLOCKS > FLOCK
FLOCKY > FLOCK
FLOCS > FLOC
FLOE *n* sheet of floating ice
FLOES > FLOE
FLOG *vb* beat with a whip or stick
FLOGGABLE > FLOG
FLOGGED > FLOG
FLOGGER > FLOG
FLOGGERS > FLOG
FLOGGING > FLOG
FLOGGINGS > FLOG
FLOGS > FLOG
FLOKATI *n* Greek hand-woven shaggy woollen rug
FLOKATIS > FLOKATI
FLONG *n* material, usually pulped paper or cardboard, used for making moulds in stereotyping
FLONGS > FLONG
FLOOD *n* overflow of water onto a normally dry area ▷ *vb* cover or become covered with water
FLOODABLE > FLOOD
FLOODED > FLOOD
FLOODER > FLOOD
FLOODERS > FLOOD
FLOODGATE *n* gate used to control the flow of water
FLOODING *n* submerging of land under water, esp due to heavy rain, a lake or river overflowing, etc
FLOODINGS > FLOODING
FLOODLESS > FLOOD
FLOODLIT *adj* illuminated with a floodlight
FLOODMARK *n* high-water mark
FLOODS > FLOOD
FLOODTIDE *n* rising tide
FLOODWALL *n* wall built as a defence against floods
FLOODWAY *n* conduit for floodwater
FLOODWAYS > FLOODWAY
FLOOEY *adj* awry
FLOOIE *same as* > FLOOEY
FLOOR *n* lower surface of a room ▷ *vb* knock down
FLOORAGE *n* area of floor
FLOORAGES > FLOORAGE
FLOORED > FLOOR
FLOORER *n* coup de grâce
FLOORERS > FLOORER
FLOORHEAD *n* upper side of a floor timber
FLOORING > FLOOR
FLOORINGS > FLOOR
FLOORLESS > FLOOR
FLOORS > FLOOR
FLOORSHOW *n* entertainment on floor of nightclub
FLOOSIE *same as* > FLOOZY
FLOOSIES > FLOOSIE
FLOOSY *variant of* > FLOOSIE
FLOOZIE *same as* > FLOOZY
FLOOZIES > FLOOZY
FLOOZY *n* disreputable woman
FLOP *vb* bend, fall, or collapse loosely or carelessly ▷ *n* failure
FLOPHOUSE *n* cheap lodging house, esp one used by tramps
FLOPOVER *n* TV visual effect of page being turned
FLOPOVERS > FLOPOVER
FLOPPED > FLOP
FLOPPER > FLOP
FLOPPERS > FLOP
FLOPPIER > FLOPPY
FLOPPIES > FLOPPY
FLOPPIEST > FLOPPY
FLOPPILY > FLOPPY
FLOPPING > FLOP
FLOPPY *adj* hanging downwards, loose ▷ *n* floppy disk
FLOPS > FLOP
FLOPTICAL *n* type of floppy disk
FLOR *n* yeast formed on the surface of sherry after fermentation
FLORA *n* plants of a given place or time
FLORAE > FLORA
FLORAL *adj* consisting of or decorated with flowers ▷ *n* class of perfume
FLORALLY > FLORAL
FLORALS > FLORAL
FLORAS > FLORA
FLOREANT > FLOREAT
FLOREAT *vb* may (a person, institution, etc) flourish
FLOREATED *same as* > FLORIATED
FLORENCE *n* type of fennel
FLORENCES > FLORENCE
FLORET *n* small flower forming part of a composite flower head
FLORETS > FLORET
FLORIATED *adj* having ornamentation based on flowers and leaves
FLORICANE *n* fruiting stem of plant
FLORID *adj* with a red or flushed complexion
FLORIDEAN *n* member of the red seaweed family
FLORIDER > FLORID
FLORIDEST > FLORID
FLORIDITY > FLORID

FLORIDLY > FLORID
FLORIER > FLORY
FLORIEST > FLORY
FLORIFORM *adj* flower-shaped
FLORIGEN *n* hypothetical plant hormone that induces flowering, thought to be synthesized in the leaves as a photoperiodic response and transmitted to the flower buds
FLORIGENS > FLORIGEN
FLORIN *n* former British and Australian coin
FLORINS > FLORIN
FLORIST *n* seller of flowers
FLORISTIC *adj* of or relating to flowers or a flora
FLORISTRY > FLORIST
FLORISTS > FLORIST
FLORS > FLOR
FLORUIT *vb* (he or she) flourished: used to indicate the period when a historical figure, whose birth and death dates are unknown, was most active
FLORULA *n* flora of a small single environment
FLORULAE > FLORULA
FLORULE *same as* > FLORULA
FLORULES > FLORULE
FLORY *adj* containing a fleur-de-lys
FLOSCULAR > FLOSCULE
FLOSCULE *n* floret
FLOSCULES > FLOSCULE
FLOSH hopper-shaped box
FLOSHES > FLOSH
FLOSS *n* fine silky fibres ▷ *vb* clean (between the teeth) with dental floss
FLOSSED > FLOSS
FLOSSER > FLOSS
FLOSSERS > FLOSS
FLOSSES > FLOSS
FLOSSIE *variant of* > FLOSSY
FLOSSIER > FLOSSY
FLOSSIES > FLOSSY
FLOSSIEST > FLOSSY
FLOSSILY > FLOSSY
FLOSSING > FLOSS
FLOSSINGS > FLOSS
FLOSSY *adj* consisting of or resembling floss ▷ *n* floozy
FLOTA *n* formerly, Spanish commercial fleet
FLOTAGE *n* act or state of floating
FLOTAGES > FLOTAGE
FLOTANT *adj* in heraldry, flying in the air
FLOTAS > FLOTA
FLOTATION *n* launching or financing of a business enterprise
FLOTE *n* aquatic perennial grass
FLOTEL *n* (in the oil industry) an oil rig or boat used as accommodation for workers in off-shore oil fields
FLOTELS > FLOTEL
FLOTES > FLOTE
FLOTILLA *n* small fleet or fleet of small ships
FLOTILLAS > FLOTILLA
FLOTSAM *n* floating wreckage
FLOTSAMS > FLOTSAM
FLOUNCE *vb* go with emphatic movements ▷ *n* flouncing movement
FLOUNCED > FLOUNCE
FLOUNCES > FLOUNCE
FLOUNCIER > FLOUNCE
FLOUNCING *n* material, such as lace or embroidered fabric, used for making flounces
FLOUNCY > FLOUNCE
FLOUNDER *vb* move with difficulty, as in mud ▷ *n* edible flatfish
FLOUNDERS > FLOUNDER
FLOUR *n* powder made by grinding grain, esp wheat ▷ *vb* sprinkle with flour
FLOURED > FLOUR
FLOURIER > FLOUR
FLOURIEST > FLOUR
FLOURING > FLOUR
FLOURISH *vb* be active, successful, or widespread ▷ *n* dramatic waving motion
FLOURISHY > FLOURISH
FLOURLESS > FLOUR
FLOURS > FLOUR
FLOURY > FLOUR
FLOUSE *vb* splash
FLOUSED > FLOUSE
FLOUSES > FLOUSE
FLOUSH *variant of* > FLOUSE
FLOUSHED > FLOUSH
FLOUSHES > FLOUSH
FLOUSHING > FLOUSH
FLOUSING > FLOUSE
FLOUT *vb* deliberately disobey (a rule, law, etc)
FLOUTED > FLOUT
FLOUTER > FLOUT
FLOUTERS > FLOUT
FLOUTING > FLOUT
FLOUTS > FLOUT
FLOW *vb* (of liquid) move in a stream ▷ *n* act, rate, or manner of flowing
FLOWAGE *n* act of flowing or overflowing or the state of having overflowed
FLOWAGES > FLOWAGE
FLOWCHART *n* diagrammatic representation of the sequence of operations or equipment in an industrial process, computer program, etc
FLOWED > FLOW
FLOWER *n* part of a plant that produces seeds ▷ *vb* produce flowers, bloom
FLOWERAGE *n* mass of flowers
FLOWERBED *n* piece of ground for growing flowers
FLOWERED *adj* decorated with a floral design
FLOWERER *n* plant that flowers at a specified time or in a specified way
FLOWERERS > FLOWERER
FLOWERET *another name for* > FLORET
FLOWERETS > FLOWERET
FLOWERFUL *adj* having plentiful flowers
FLOWERIER > FLOWERY
FLOWERILY > FLOWERY
FLOWERING *adj* (of certain species of plants) capable of producing conspicuous flowers
FLOWERPOT *n* pot in which plants are grown
FLOWERS > FLOWER
FLOWERY *adj* decorated with a floral design
FLOWING > FLOW
FLOWINGLY > FLOW
FLOWMETER *n* instrument that measures the rate of flow of a liquid or gas within a pipe or tube
FLOWN > FLY
FLOWS > FLOW
FLOWSTONE *n* type of speleothem
FLU *n* any of various viral infections, esp a respiratory or intestinal infection
FLUATE *n* fluoride
FLUATES > FLUATE
FLUB *vb* bungle
FLUBBED > FLUB
FLUBBER > FLUB
FLUBBERS > FLUB
FLUBBING > FLUB
FLUBDUB *n* bunkum
FLUBDUBS > FLUBDUB
FLUBS > FLUB
FLUCTUANT *adj* inclined to vary or fluctuate
FLUCTUATE *vb* change frequently and erratically
FLUE *n* passage or pipe for smoke or hot air
FLUED *adj* having a flue
FLUELLEN *n* type of plant
FLUELLENS > FLUELLEN
FLUELLIN *same as* > FLUELLEN
FLUELLINS > FLUELLIN
FLUENCE > FLUENCY
FLUENCES > FLUENCY
FLUENCIES > FLUENCY
FLUENCY *n* quality of being fluent, esp facility in speech or writing
FLUENT *adj* able to speak or write with ease ▷ *n* variable quantity in fluxions
FLUENTLY > FLUENT
FLUENTS > FLUENT
FLUERIC *adj* of or relating to fluidics
FLUERICS *pl n* fluidics
FLUES > FLUE
FLUEWORK *n* collectively, organ stops
FLUEWORKS > FLUEWORK
FLUEY *adj* involved in, caused by, or like influenza
FLUFF *n* soft fibres ▷ *vb* make or become soft and puffy
FLUFFED > FLUFF
FLUFFER *n* person employed on a pornographic film set to ensure that male actors are kept aroused
FLUFFERS *n* fluffer
FLUFFIER > FLUFFY
FLUFFIEST > FLUFFY
FLUFFILY > FLUFFY
FLUFFING > FLUFF
FLUFFS > FLUFF
FLUFFY *adj* of, resembling, or covered with fluff
FLUGEL *n* grand piano or harpsichord
FLUGELMAN *variant of* > FUGLEMAN
FLUGELMEN > FLUGELMAN
FLUGELS > FLUGEL
FLUID *n* substance able to flow and change its shape ▷ *adj* able to flow or change shape easily
FLUIDAL > FLUID
FLUIDALLY > FLUID
FLUIDIC > FLUIDICS
FLUIDICS *n* study and use of systems in which the flow of fluids in tubes simulates the flow of electricity in conductors. Such systems are used in place of electronics in certain applications, such as the control of apparatus
FLUIDIFY *vb* make fluid
FLUIDISE *same as* > FLUIDIZE
FLUIDISED > FLUIDISE
FLUIDISER > FLUIDISE
FLUIDISES > FLUIDISE
FLUIDITY *n* state of being fluid
FLUIDIZE *vb* make fluid, esp to make (solids) fluid by pulverizing them so that they can be transported in a stream of gas as if they were liquids
FLUIDIZED > FLUIDIZE
FLUIDIZER > FLUIDIZE
FLUIDIZES > FLUIDIZE
FLUIDLIKE > FLUID
FLUIDLY > FLUID
FLUIDNESS > FLUID
FLUIDRAM *n* British imperial measure
FLUIDRAMS > FLUIDRAM
FLUIDS > FLUID
FLUIER > FLUEY

FLUIEST > FLUEY
FLUISH > FLU
FLUKE *n* accidental stroke of luck ▷ *vb* gain, make, or hit by a fluke
FLUKED > FLUKE
FLUKES > FLUKE
FLUKEY *same as* > FLUKY
FLUKIER > FLUKY
FLUKIEST > FLUKY
FLUKILY > FLUKY
FLUKINESS > FLUKY
FLUKING > FLUKE
FLUKY *adj* done or gained by an accident, esp a lucky one
FLUME *n* narrow sloping channel for water ▷ *vb* transport (logs) in a flume
FLUMED > FLUME
FLUMES > FLUME
FLUMING > FLUME
FLUMMERY *n* silly or trivial talk
FLUMMOX *vb* puzzle or confuse
FLUMMOXED > FLUMMOX
FLUMMOXES > FLUMMOX
FLUMP *vb* move or fall heavily
FLUMPED > FLUMP
FLUMPING > FLUMP
FLUMPS > FLUMP
FLUNG > FLING
FLUNK *vb* fail ▷ *n* low grade below the pass standard
FLUNKED > FLUNK
FLUNKER > FLUNK
FLUNKERS > FLUNK
FLUNKEY *same as* > FLUNKY
FLUNKEYS > FLUNKEY
FLUNKIE *same as* > FLUNKY
FLUNKIES > FLUNKY
FLUNKING > FLUNK
FLUNKS > FLUNK
FLUNKY *n* servile person
FLUNKYISM > FLUNKY
FLUOR > FLUORSPAR
FLUORENE *n* white insoluble crystalline solid
FLUORENES > FLUORENE
FLUORESCE *vb* exhibit fluorescence
FLUORIC *adj* of, concerned with, or produced from fluorine or fluorspar
FLUORID *same as* > FLUORIDE
FLUORIDE *n* compound containing fluorine
FLUORIDES > FLUORIDE
FLUORIDS > FLUORID
FLUORIN *same as* > FLUORINE
FLUORINE *n* toxic yellow gas: most reactive of all the elements
FLUORINES > FLUORINE
FLUORINS > FLUORIN
FLUORITE *same as* > FLUORSPAR
FLUORITES > FLUORITE
FLUOROSES > FLUOROSIS
FLUOROSIS *n* fluoride poisoning, due to ingestion of too much fluoride in drinking water over a long period or to ingestion of pesticides containing fluoride salts. Chronic fluorosis results in mottling of the teeth of children
FLUOROTIC > FLUOROSIS
FLUORS > FLUOR
FLUORSPAR *n* white or colourless mineral, consisting of calcium fluoride in crystalline form: the chief ore of fluorine
FLURR *vb* scatter
FLURRED > FLURR
FLURRIED > FLURRY
FLURRIES > FLURRY
FLURRING > FLURR
FLURRS > FLURR
FLURRY *n* sudden commotion ▷ *vb* confuse
FLURRYING > FLURRY
FLUS > FLU
FLUSH *vb* blush or cause to blush ▷ *n* blush ▷ *adj* level with the surrounding surface ▷ *adv* so as to be level
FLUSHABLE > FLUSH
FLUSHED > FLUSH
FLUSHER > FLUSH
FLUSHERS > FLUSH
FLUSHES > FLUSH
FLUSHEST > FLUSH
FLUSHIER > FLUSHY
FLUSHIEST > FLUSHY
FLUSHING *n* extra feeding given to ewes before mating to increase the lambing percentage
FLUSHINGS > FLUSHING
FLUSHNESS > FLUSH
FLUSHWORK *n* decorative treatment of the surface of an outside wall with flints split to show their smooth black surface, combined with dressed stone to form patterns such as tracery or initials
FLUSHY *adj* ruddy
FLUSTER *vb* make nervous or upset ▷ *n* nervous or upset state
FLUSTERED > FLUSTER
FLUSTERS > FLUSTER
FLUSTERY > FLUSTER
FLUSTRATE *vb* fluster
FLUTE *n* wind instrument consisting of a tube with sound holes and a mouth hole in the side ▷ *vb* utter in a high-pitched tone
FLUTED *adj* having decorative grooves
FLUTELIKE > FLUTE
FLUTER *n* craftsman who makes flutes or fluting
FLUTERS > FLUTER
FLUTES > FLUTE
FLUTEY > FLUTE
FLUTIER > FLUTE
FLUTIEST > FLUTE
FLUTINA *n* type of accordion
FLUTINAS > FLUTINA
FLUTING *n* design of decorative grooves
FLUTINGS > FLUTING
FLUTIST *same as* > FLAUTIST
FLUTISTS > FLUTIST
FLUTTER *vb* wave rapidly ▷ *n* flapping movement
FLUTTERED > FLUTTER
FLUTTERER > FLUTTER
FLUTTERS > FLUTTER
FLUTTERY *adj* flapping rapidly
FLUTY > FLUTE
FLUVIAL *adj* of rivers
FLUVIATIC > FLUVIAL
FLUX *n* constant change or instability ▷ *vb* make or become fluid
FLUXED > FLUX
FLUXES > FLUX
FLUXGATE *n* type of magnetometer
FLUXGATES > FLUXGATE
FLUXING > FLUX
FLUXION *n* rate of change of a function, especially the instantaneous velocity of a moving body
FLUXIONAL > FLUXION
FLUXIONS > FLUXION
FLUXIVE > FLUX
FLUXMETER *n* any instrument for measuring magnetic flux, usually by measuring the charge that flows through a coil when the flux changes
FLUYT *n* Dutch sailing ship
FLUYTS > FLUYT
FLY *vb* move through the air on wings or in an aircraft ▷ *n* fastening at the front of trousers ▷ *adj* sharp and cunning
FLYABLE > FLY
FLYAWAY *adj* (of hair) very fine and soft ▷ *n* person who is frivolous or flighty
FLYAWAYS > FLYAWAY
FLYBACK *n* fast return of the spot on a cathode-ray tube after completion of each trace
FLYBACKS > FLYBACK
FLYBANE *n* type of campion
FLYBANES > FLYBANE
FLYBELT *n* strip of tsetse-infested land
FLYBELTS > FLYBELT
FLYBLEW > FLYBLOW
FLYBLOW *vb* contaminate, esp with the eggs or larvae of the blowfly ▷ *n* egg or young larva of a blowfly, deposited on meat, paper, etc
FLYBLOWN *adj* covered with blowfly eggs
FLYBLOWS > FLYBLOW
FLYBOAT *n* any small swift boat
FLYBOATS > FLYBOAT
FLYBOOK *n* small case or wallet used by anglers for storing artificial flies
FLYBOOKS > FLYBOOK
FLYBOY *n* air force pilot
FLYBOYS > FLYBOY
FLYBRIDGE *n* highest navigational bridge on a ship
FLYBY *n* flight past a particular position or target, esp the close approach of a spacecraft to a planet or satellite for investigation of conditions
FLYBYS > FLYBY
FLYER > FLY
FLYERS > FLY
FLYEST > FLY
FLYHAND *n* device for transferring printed sheets from the press to a flat pile
FLYHANDS > FLYHAND
FLYING > FLY
FLYINGS > FLY
FLYLEAF *n* blank leaf at the beginning or end of a book
FLYLEAVES > FLYLEAF
FLYLESS > FLY
FLYMAKER *n* person who makes fishing flies
FLYMAKERS > FLYMAKER
FLYMAN *n* stagehand who operates the scenery, curtains, etc, in the flies
FLYMEN > FLYMAN
FLYOFF *n* total volume of water transferred from the earth to the atmosphere
FLYOFFS > FLYOFF
FLYOVER *n* road passing over another by a bridge
FLYOVERS > FLYOVER
FLYPAPER *n* paper with a sticky poisonous coating, used to kill flies
FLYPAPERS > FLYPAPER
FLYPAST *n* ceremonial flight of aircraft over a given area
FLYPASTS > FLYPAST
FLYPE *vb* fold back
FLYPED > FLYPE
FLYPES > FLYPE
FLYPING > FLYPE
FLYPITCH *n* area for unlicensed stalls at markets
FLYRODDER *n* angler using artificial fly
FLYSCH *n* marine sedimentary facies consisting of a sequence of sandstones, conglomerates, marls, shales, and clays that were formed by erosion during a period of mountain

building and subsequently deformed as the mountain building continued
FLYSCHES > FLYSCH
FLYSCREEN *n* wire-mesh screen over a window to prevent flies from entering a room
FLYSHEET *n* part of tent
FLYSHEETS > FLYSHEET
FLYSPECK *n* small speck of the excrement of a fly ▷ *vb* mark with flyspecks
FLYSPECKS > FLYSPECK
FLYSTRIKE *n* infestation of wounded sheep by blowflies or maggots
FLYTE *same as* > FLITE
FLYTED > FLYTE
FLYTES > FLYTE
FLYTIER *n* person who makes his own fishing flies
FLYTIERS > FLYTIER
FLYTING > FLYTE
FLYTINGS > FLYTE
FLYTRAP *n* any of various insectivorous plants, esp Venus's flytrap
FLYTRAPS > FLYTRAP
FLYWAY *n* usual route used by birds when migrating
FLYWAYS > FLYWAY
FLYWEIGHT *n* boxer weighing up to 112lb (professional) or 51kg (amateur)
FLYWHEEL *n* heavy wheel regulating the speed of a machine
FLYWHEELS > FLYWHEEL
FOAL *n* young of a horse or related animal ▷ *vb* give birth to a foal
FOALED > FOAL
FOALFOOT *n* coltsfoot
FOALFOOTS > FOALFOOT
FOALING > FOAL
FOALS > FOAL
FOAM *n* mass of small bubbles on a liquid ▷ *vb* produce foam
FOAMABLE > FOAM
FOAMED > FOAM
FOAMER *n* (possibly obsessive) enthusiast
FOAMERS > FOAMER
FOAMIER > FOAMY
FOAMIEST > FOAMY
FOAMILY > FOAMY
FOAMINESS > FOAMY
FOAMING > FOAM
FOAMINGLY > FOAM
FOAMINGS > FOAM
FOAMLESS > FOAM
FOAMLIKE > FOAM
FOAMS > FOAM
FOAMY *adj* of, resembling, consisting of, or covered with foam
FOB *n* short watch chain ▷ *vb* cheat
FOBBED > FOB
FOBBING > FOB
FOBS > FOB
FOCACCIA *n* flat Italian bread made with olive oil and yeast
FOCACCIAS > FOCACCIA
FOCAL *adj* of or at a focus
FOCALISE > FOCUS
FOCALISED > FOCUS
FOCALISES > FOCUS
FOCALIZE *less common word for* > FOCUS
FOCALIZED > FOCALIZE
FOCALIZES > FOCALIZE
FOCALLY > FOCAL
FOCI > FOCUS
FOCIMETER *n* photographic focusing device
FOCOMETER *n* instrument for measuring the focal length of a lens
FOCUS *n* point at which light or sound waves converge ▷ *vb* bring or come into focus
FOCUSABLE > FOCUS
FOCUSED > FOCUS
FOCUSER > FOCUS
FOCUSERS > FOCUS
FOCUSES > FOCUS
FOCUSING > FOCUS
FOCUSINGS > FOCUS
FOCUSLESS > FOCUS
FOCUSSED > FOCUS
FOCUSSES > FOCUS
FOCUSSING > FOCUS
FODDER *n* feed for livestock ▷ *vb* supply (livestock) with fodder
FODDERED > FODDER
FODDERER > FODDER
FODDERERS > FODDER
FODDERING > FODDER
FODDERS > FODDER
FODGEL *adj* buxom
FOE *n* enemy, opponent
FOEDARIE *variant of* > FEDARIE
FOEDARIES > FOEDARIE
FOEDERATI > FOEDERATUS
FOEHN *same as* > FOHN
FOEHNS > FOEHN
FOEMAN *n* enemy in war
FOEMEN > FOEMAN
FOEN > FOE
FOES > FOE
FOETAL *same as* > FETAL
FOETATION *same as* > FETATION
FOETICIDE *same as* > FETICIDE
FOETID *same as* > FETID
FOETIDER > FOETID
FOETIDEST > FOETID
FOETIDLY > FOETID
FOETOR *same as* > FETOR
FOETORS > FOETOR
FOETUS *same as* > FETUS
FOETUSES > FOETUS
FOG *n* mass of condensed water vapour in the lower air, often greatly reducing visibility ▷ *vb* cover with steam
FOGASH *n* type of Hungarian pike perch
FOGASHES > FOGASH
FOGBOUND *adj* prevented from operating by fog
FOGBOW *n* faint arc of light sometimes seen in a fog bank
FOGBOWS > FOGBOW
FOGDOG *n* whitish spot sometimes seen in fog near the horizon
FOGDOGS > FOGDOG
FOGEY *n* old-fashioned person
FOGEYDOM > FOGEY
FOGEYDOMS > FOGEY
FOGEYISH > FOGEY
FOGEYISM > FOGEY
FOGEYISMS > FOGEY
FOGEYS > FOGEY
FOGFRUIT *n* wildflower of the verbena family
FOGFRUITS > FOGFRUIT
FOGGAGE *n* grass grown for winter grazing
FOGGAGES > FOGGAGE
FOGGED > FOG
FOGGER *n* device that generates a fog
FOGGERS > FOGGER
FOGGIER > FOG
FOGGIEST > FOG
FOGGILY > FOG
FOGGINESS > FOG
FOGGING > FOG
FOGGY > FOG
FOGHORN *n* large horn sounded to warn ships in fog
FOGHORNS > FOGHORN
FOGIE *variant of* > FOGEY
FOGIES > FOGIE
FOGLE *n* silk handkerchief
FOGLES > FOGLE
FOGLESS > FOG
FOGMAN *n* person in charge of railway fog-signals
FOGMEN > FOGMAN
FOGRAM *n* fogey
FOGRAMITE > FOGRAM
FOGRAMITY > FOGRAM
FOGRAMS > FOGRAM
FOGS > FOG
FOGY *same as* > FOGEY
FOGYDOM > FOGY
FOGYDOMS > FOGY
FOGYISH > FOGY
FOGYISM > FOGY
FOGYISMS > FOGY
FOH *interj* expression of disgust
FOHN *n* warm dry wind blowing down the northern slopes of the Alps
FOHNS > FOHN
FOHS > FOH
FOIBLE *n* minor weakness or slight peculiarity
FOIBLES > FOIBLE
FOID *same as* > FELDSPATHOID
FOIDS > FOID
FOIL *vb* ruin (someone's plan) ▷ *n* metal in a thin sheet, esp for wrapping food
FOILABLE > FOIL
FOILBORNE *adj* moving by means of hydrofoils
FOILED > FOIL
FOILING > FOIL
FOILINGS > FOIL
FOILS > FOIL
FOILSMAN *n* person who uses or specializes in using a foil
FOILSMEN > FOILSMAN
FOIN *n* thrust or lunge with a weapon ▷ *vb* thrust with a weapon
FOINED > FOIN
FOINING > FOIN
FOININGLY > FOIN
FOINS > FOIN
FOISON *n* plentiful supply or yield
FOISONS > FOISON
FOIST *vb* force or impose on
FOISTED > FOIST
FOISTER > FOIST
FOISTERS > FOIST
FOISTING > FOIST
FOISTS > FOIST
FOLACIN *n* folic acid
FOLACINS > FOLACIN
FOLATE *n* folic acid
FOLATES > FOLIC
FOLD *vb* bend so that one part covers another ▷ *n* folded piece or part
FOLDABLE > FOLD
FOLDAWAY *adj* (of a bed) able to be folded and put away when not in use
FOLDAWAYS > FOLDAWAY
FOLDBACK *n* (in multitrack recording) a process for returning a signal to a performer instantly
FOLDBACKS > FOLDBACK
FOLDBOAT *another name for* > FALTBOAT
FOLDBOATS > FOLDBOAT
FOLDED > FOLD
FOLDER *n* piece of folded cardboard for holding loose papers
FOLDEROL *same as* > FALDERAL
FOLDEROLS > FOLDEROL
FOLDERS > FOLDER
FOLDING > FOLD
FOLDINGS > FOLDING
FOLDOUT *another name for* > GATEFOLD
FOLDOUTS > FOLDOUT
FOLDS > FOLD
FOLDUP *n* something that folds up
FOLDUPS > FOLDUP
FOLEY *n* footsteps editor
FOLEYS > FOLEY
FOLIA > FOLIUM
FOLIAGE *n* leaves
FOLIAGED *adj* having foliage
FOLIAGES > FOLIAGE

FOLIAR *adj* of or relating to a leaf or leaves
FOLIATE *adj* relating to, possessing, or resembling leaves ▷ *vb* ornament with foliage or with leaf forms such as foils
FOLIATED *adj* ornamented with or made up of foliage or foils
FOLIATES > FOLIATE
FOLIATING > FOLIATE
FOLIATION *n* process of producing leaves
FOLIATURE > FOLIATION
FOLIC as in *folic acid*, any of a group of vitamins of the B complex, including pteroylglutamic acid and its derivatives: used in the treatment of megaloblastic anaemia
FOLIE *n* madness
FOLIES > FOLIE
FOLIO *n* sheet of paper folded in half to make two leaves of a book ▷ *adj* of or made in the largest book size, common esp in early centuries of European printing ▷ *vb* number the leaves of (a book) consecutively
FOLIOED > FOLIO
FOLIOING > FOLIO
FOLIOLATE *adj* possessing or relating to leaflets
FOLIOLE *n* part of a compound leaf
FOLIOLES > FOLIOLE
FOLIOLOSE > FOLIOLE
FOLIOS > FOLIO
FOLIOSE *another word for* > FOLIACEOUS
FOLIOUS *adj* foliose
FOLIUM *n* plane geometrical curve consisting of a loop whose two ends, intersecting at a node, are asymptotic to the same line. Standard equation: $x^3 + y^3 = 3axy$ where $x=y+a$ is the equation of the line
FOLIUMS > FOLIUM
FOLK *n* people in general ▷ *adj* originating from or traditional to the common people of a country
FOLKIE *n* devotee of folk music ▷ *adj* of or relating to folk music
FOLKIER > FOLKIE
FOLKIES > FOLKIE
FOLKIEST > FOLKIE
FOLKISH > FOLK
FOLKLAND *n* former type of land tenure
FOLKLANDS > FOLKLAND
FOLKLIFE *n* traditional customs, arts, crafts, and other forms of cultural expression of a people
FOLKLIKE > FOLK
FOLKLIVES > FOLKLIFE
FOLKLORE *n* traditional beliefs and stories of a people
FOLKLORES > FOLKLORE
FOLKLORIC > FOLKLORE
FOLKMOOT *n* (in early medieval England) an assembly of the people of a district, town, or shire
FOLKMOOTS > FOLKMOOT
FOLKMOT *same as* > FOLKMOOT
FOLKMOTE *same as* > FOLKMOOT
FOLKMOTES > FOLKMOTE
FOLKMOTS > FOLKMOT
FOLKS > FOLK
FOLKSIER > FOLKSY
FOLKSIEST > FOLKSY
FOLKSILY > FOLKSY
FOLKSONG *n* traditional song
FOLKSONGS > FOLKSONG
FOLKSY *adj* simple and unpretentious
FOLKTALE *n* tale or legend originating among a people and typically becoming part of an oral tradition
FOLKTALES > FOLKTALE
FOLKWAY *singular form of* > FOLKWAYS
FOLKWAYS *pl n* traditional and customary ways of living
FOLKY *same as* > FOLKIE
FOLLES > FOLLIS
FOLLICLE *n* small cavity in the body, esp one from which a hair grows
FOLLICLES > FOLLICLE
FOLLIED > FOLLY
FOLLIES > FOLLY
FOLLIS *n* Roman coin
FOLLOW *vb* go or come after
FOLLOWED > FOLLOW
FOLLOWER *n* disciple or supporter
FOLLOWERS > FOLLOWER
FOLLOWING *adj* about to be mentioned ▷ *n* group of supporters ▷ *prep* as a result of
FOLLOWS > FOLLOW
FOLLOWUP *n* further action
FOLLOWUPS > FOLLOWUP
FOLLY *n* foolishness ▷ *vb* behave foolishly
FOLLYING > FOLLY
FOMENT *vb* encourage or stir up (trouble)
FOMENTED > FOMENT
FOMENTER > FOMENT
FOMENTERS > FOMENT
FOMENTING > FOMENT
FOMENTS > FOMENT
FOMES *n* any material, such as bedding or clothing, that may harbour pathogens and therefore convey disease
FOMITE > FOMES
FOMITES > FOMES
FON *vb* compel
FOND *adj* tender, loving ▷ *n* background of a design, as in lace ▷ *vb* dote
FONDA *n* Spanish hotel
FONDANT *n* (sweet made from) flavoured paste of sugar and water ▷ *adj* (of a colour) soft
FONDANTS > FONDANT
FONDAS > FONDA
FONDED > FOND
FONDER > FOND
FONDEST > FOND
FONDING > FOND
FONDLE *vb* caress
FONDLED > FONDLE
FONDLER > FONDLE
FONDLERS > FONDLE
FONDLES > FONDLE
FONDLING > FONDLE
FONDLINGS > FONDLE
FONDLY > FOND
FONDNESS > FOND
FONDS > FOND
FONDU *n* ballet movement, lowering the body by bending the leg(s)
FONDUE *n* Swiss dish of a hot melted cheese sauce into which pieces of bread are dipped ▷ *vb* cook and serve (food) as a fondue
FONDUED > FONDUE
FONDUEING > FONDUE
FONDUES > FONDUE
FONDUING > FONDUE
FONDUS > FONDU
FONE *variant of* > FOE
FONLY *adv* foolishly
FONNED > FON
FONNING > FON
FONS > FON
FONT *n* bowl in a church for baptismal water
FONTAL > FONT
FONTANEL *same as* > FONTANELLE
FONTANELS > FONTANEL
FONTANGE *n* type of tall headdress
FONTANGES > FONTANGE
FONTICULI > FONTICULUS
FONTINA *n* semihard, pale yellow, mild Italian cheese made from cow's milk
FONTINAS > FONTINA
FONTLET > FONT
FONTLETS > FONT
FONTS > FONT
FOOBAR *same as* > FUBAR
FOOD *n* what one eats; solid nourishment
FOODFUL *adj* supplying abundant food
FOODIE *n* gourmet
FOODIES > FOODIE
FOODISM *n* enthusiasm for and interest in the preparation and consumption of good food
FOODISMS > FOODISM
FOODLESS > FOOD
FOODS > FOOD
FOODSTUFF *n* substance used as food
FOODWAYS *pl n* customs and traditions relating to food and its preparation
FOODY *same as* > FOODIE
FOOFARAW *n* vulgar ornamentation
FOOFARAWS > FOOFARAW
FOOL *n* person lacking sense or judgment ▷ *vb* deceive (someone)
FOOLED > FOOL
FOOLERIES > FOOLERY
FOOLERY *n* foolish behaviour
FOOLFISH *n* orange filefish or winter flounder
FOOLHARDY *adj* recklessly adventurous
FOOLING > FOOL
FOOLINGS > FOOL
FOOLISH *adj* unwise, silly, or absurd
FOOLISHER > FOOLISH
FOOLISHLY > FOOLISH
FOOLPROOF *adj* unable to fail
FOOLS > FOOL
FOOLSCAP *n* size of paper, 34.3 x 43.2 centimetres
FOOLSCAPS > FOOLSCAP
FOOSBALL *n* US and Canadian name for table football
FOOSBALLS > FOOSBALL
FOOT *n* part of the leg below the ankle ▷ *vb* kick
FOOTAGE *n* amount of film used
FOOTAGES > FOOTAGE
FOOTBAG *n* sport of keeping small round object off the ground by kicking it
FOOTBAGS > FOOTBAG
FOOTBALL *n* game played by two teams of eleven players kicking a ball in an attempt to score goals
FOOTBALLS > FOOTBALL
FOOTBAR *n* any bar designed as a footrest or to be operated by the foot
FOOTBARS > FOOTBAR
FOOTBATH *n* vessel for bathing the feet
FOOTBATHS > FOOTBATH
FOOTBOARD *n* treadle or foot-operated lever on a machine
FOOTBOY *n* boy servant
FOOTBOYS > FOOTBOY
FOOTCLOTH *obsolete word for* > CAPARISON
FOOTED > FOOT
FOOTER *n* person who goes on foot ▷ *vb* potter
FOOTERED > FOOTER
FOOTERING > FOOTER
FOOTERS > FOOTER
FOOTFALL *n* sound of a footstep
FOOTFALLS > FOOTFALL

FOOTFAULT *n* fault that occurs when the server fails to keep both feet behind the baseline until he/she has served
FOOTGEAR *another name for* > FOOTWEAR
FOOTGEARS > FOOTGEAR
FOOTHILL *n* lower slope of a mountain or a relatively low hill at the foot of a mountain
FOOTHILLS > FOOTHILL
FOOTHOLD *n* secure position from which progress may be made
FOOTHOLDS > FOOTHOLD
FOOTIE *same as* > FOOTY
FOOTIER > FOOTY
FOOTIES > FOOTIE
FOOTIEST > FOOTY
FOOTING *n* basis or foundation
FOOTINGS > FOOTING
FOOTLE *vb* loiter aimlessly ▷ *n* foolishness
FOOTLED > FOOTLE
FOOTLER > FOOTLE
FOOTLERS > FOOTLE
FOOTLES > FOOTLE
FOOTLESS > FOOT
FOOTLIGHT *n* light illuminating the front of a stage
FOOTLIKE > FOOT
FOOTLING *adj* trivial ▷ *n* trifle
FOOTLINGS > FOOTLING
FOOTLOOSE *adj* free from ties
FOOTMAN *n* male servant in uniform
FOOTMARK *n* mark or trace of mud, wetness, etc, left by a person's foot on a surface
FOOTMARKS > FOOTMARK
FOOTMEN > FOOTMAN
FOOTMUFF *n* muff used to keep the feet warm
FOOTMUFFS > FOOTMUFF
FOOTNOTE *n* note printed at the foot of a page ▷ *vb* supply (a page, book, etc) with footnotes
FOOTNOTED > FOOTNOTE
FOOTNOTES > FOOTNOTE
FOOTPACE *n* normal or walking pace
FOOTPACES > FOOTPACE
FOOTPAD *n* highwayman, on foot rather than horseback
FOOTPADS > FOOTPAD
FOOTPAGE *n* errand-boy
FOOTPAGES > FOOTPAGE
FOOTPATH *n* narrow path for walkers only
FOOTPATHS > FOOTPATH
FOOTPLATE *n* platform in the cab of a locomotive for the driver
FOOTPOST *n* post delivered on foot
FOOTPOSTS > FOOTPOST
FOOTPRINT *n* mark left by a foot
FOOTRA *variant of* > FOUTRA
FOOTRACE *n* race run on foot
FOOTRACES > FOOTRACE
FOOTRAS > FOOTRA
FOOTREST *n* something that provides a support for the feet, such as a low stool, rail, etc
FOOTRESTS > FOOTREST
FOOTROPE *n* part of a boltrope to which the foot of a sail is stitched
FOOTROPES > FOOTROPE
FOOTROT *n* contagious fungal disease of the feet of sheep
FOOTROTS > FOOTROT
FOOTRULE *n* rigid measure, one foot in length
FOOTRULES > FOOTRULE
FOOTS *pl n* sediment that accumulates at the bottom of a vessel containing any of certain liquids, such as vegetable oil or varnish
FOOTSIE *n* flirtation involving the touching together of feet
FOOTSIES > FOOTSIE
FOOTSLOG *vb* march
FOOTSLOGS > FOOTSLOG
FOOTSORE *adj* having sore or tired feet, esp from much walking
FOOTSTALK *n* small supporting stalk in animals and plants
FOOTSTALL *n* pedestal, plinth, or base of a column, pier, or statue
FOOTSTEP *n* step in walking
FOOTSTEPS > FOOTSTEP
FOOTSTOCK *another name for* > TAILSTOCK
FOOTSTONE *n* memorial stone at the foot of a grave
FOOTSTOOL *n* low stool used to rest the feet on while sitting
FOOTSY *variant of* > FOOTSIE
FOOTWALL *n* rocks on the lower side of an inclined fault plane or mineral vein
FOOTWALLS > FOOTWALL
FOOTWAY *n* way or path for pedestrians, such as a raised walk along the edge of a bridge
FOOTWAYS > FOOTWAY
FOOTWEAR *n* anything worn to cover the feet
FOOTWEARS > FOOTWEAR
FOOTWEARY *adj* tired from walking
FOOTWELL *n* part of a car in which the foot pedals are located
FOOTWELLS > FOOTWELL
FOOTWORK *n* skilful use of the feet, as in sport or dancing
FOOTWORKS > FOOTWORK
FOOTWORN *adj* footsore
FOOTY *n* football ▷ *adj* mean
FOOZLE *vb* bungle (a shot) ▷ *n* bungled shot
FOOZLED > FOOZLE
FOOZLER > FOOZLE
FOOZLERS > FOOZLE
FOOZLES > FOOZLE
FOOZLING > FOOZLE
FOOZLINGS > FOOZLE
FOP *n* man excessively concerned with fashion ▷ *vb* act like a fop
FOPLING *n* vain affected dandy
FOPLINGS > FOPLING
FOPPED > FOP
FOPPERIES > FOPPERY
FOPPERY *n* clothes, affectations, obsessions, etc, of or befitting a fop
FOPPING > FOP
FOPPISH > FOP
FOPPISHLY > FOP
FOPS > FOP
FOR *prep* indicating a person intended to benefit from or receive something, span of time or distance, person or thing represented by someone, etc
FORA > FORUM
FORAGE *vb* search about (for) ▷ *n* food for cattle or horses
FORAGED > FORAGE
FORAGER > FORAGE
FORAGERS > FORAGE
FORAGES > FORAGE
FORAGING > FORAGE
FORAM *same as* > FORAMINIFER
FORAMEN *n* natural hole, esp one in a bone through which nerves pass
FORAMENS > FORAMEN
FORAMINA > FORAMEN
FORAMINAL > FORAMEN
FORAMS > FORAM
FORANE as in *vicar forane*, in the Roman Catholic church, vicar or priest appointed to act in a certain area of the diocese
FORASMUCH *conj* since
FORAY *n* brief raid or attack ▷ *vb* raid or ravage (a town, district, etc)
FORAYED > FORAY
FORAYER > FORAY
FORAYERS > FORAY
FORAYING > FORAY
FORAYS > FORAY
FORB *n* any herbaceous plant that is not a grass
FORBAD > FORBID
FORBADE > FORBID
FORBARE > FORBEAR
FORBEAR *vb* cease or refrain (from doing something)
FORBEARER > FORBEAR
FORBEARS > FORBEAR
FORBID *vb* prohibit, refuse to allow
FORBIDAL > FORBID
FORBIDALS > FORBIDAL
FORBIDDAL *n* prohibition
FORBIDDEN *adj* not permitted by order or law
FORBIDDER > FORBID
FORBIDS > FORBID
FORBODE *vb* obsolete word meaning forbid ▷ *n* obsolete word meaning forbidding
FORBODED > FORBODE
FORBODES > FORBODE
FORBODING > FORBODE
FORBORE *past tense of* > FORBEAR
FORBORNE > FORBEAR
FORBS > FORB
FORBY *adv* besides
FORBYE *same as* > FORBY
FORCAT *n* convict or galley slave
FORCATS > FORCAT
FORCE *n* strength or power ▷ *vb* compel, make (someone) do something
FORCEABLE > FORCE
FORCED *adj* compulsory
FORCEDLY > FORCED
FORCEFUL *adj* emphatic and confident
FORCELESS > FORCE
FORCEMEAT *n* mixture of chopped ingredients used for stuffing
FORCEPS *pl n* surgical pincers
FORCEPSES > FORCEPS
FORCER > FORCE
FORCERS > FORCE
FORCES > FORCE
FORCIBLE *adj* involving physical force or violence
FORCIBLY > FORCIBLE
FORCING > FORCE
FORCINGLY > FORCE
FORCIPATE > FORCEPS
FORCIPES > FORCEPS
FORD *n* shallow place where a river may be crossed ▷ *vb* cross (a river) at a ford
FORDABLE > FORD
FORDED > FORD
FORDID > FORDO
FORDING > FORD
FORDLESS > FORD
FORDO *vb* destroy
FORDOES > FORDO
FORDOING > FORDO
FORDONE > FORDO
FORDS > FORD
FORE *adj* in, at, or towards the front ▷ *n* front part ▷ *interj* golfer's shouted warning to a person in the path of a ball
FOREANENT *prep* opposite
FOREARM *n* arm from the

wrist to the elbow ▷ *vb* prepare beforehand

FOREARMED > FOREARM

FOREARMS > FOREARM

FOREBAY *n* reservoir or canal

FOREBAYS > FOREBAY

FOREBEAR *n* ancestor

FOREBEARS > FOREBEAR

FOREBITT *n* post at a ship's foremast for securing cables

FOREBITTS > FOREBITT

FOREBODE *vb* warn of or indicate (an event, result, etc) in advance

FOREBODED > FOREBODE

FOREBODER > FOREBODE

FOREBODES > FOREBODE

FOREBODY *n* part of a ship forward of the foremast

FOREBOOM *n* boom of a foremast

FOREBOOMS > FOREBOOM

FOREBRAIN *nontechnical name for* > PROSENCEPHALON

FOREBY *variant of* > FORBY

FOREBYE *variant of* > FORBY

FORECABIN *n* forward cabin on a vessel

FORECAR *n* three-wheeled passenger vehicle attached to a motorcycle

FORECARS > FORECAR

FORECAST *vb* predict (weather, events, etc) ▷ *n* prediction

FORECASTS > FORECAST

FORECHECK *vb* in ice-hockey, to try to gain control of the puck while at opponents' end of rink

FORECLOSE *vb* take possession of (property bought with borrowed money which has not been repaid)

FORECLOTH *n* cloth hung over the front of something, especially an altar

FORECOURT *n* courtyard or open space in front of a building

FOREDATE *vb* antedate

FOREDATED > FOREDATE

FOREDATES > FOREDATE

FOREDECK *n* deck between the bridge and the forecastle

FOREDECKS > FOREDECK

FOREDID > FOREDO

FOREDO *same as* > FORDO

FOREDOES > FOREDO

FOREDOING > FOREDO

FOREDONE > FOREDO

FOREDOOM *vb* doom or condemn beforehand

FOREDOOMS > FOREDOOM

FOREFACE *n* muzzle of an animal

FOREFACES > FOREFACE

FOREFEEL *vb* have a premonition of

FOREFEELS > FOREFEEL

FOREFEET > FOREFOOT

FOREFELT > FOREFEEL

FOREFEND *same as* > FORFEND

FOREFENDS > FOREFEND

FOREFOOT *n* either of the front feet of an animal

FOREFRONT *n* most active or prominent position

FOREGLEAM *n* early or premonitory inkling or indication

FOREGO *same as* > FORGO

FOREGOER > FOREGO

FOREGOERS > FOREGO

FOREGOES > FOREGO

FOREGOING *adj* going before, preceding

FOREGONE *adj* gone or completed

FOREGUT *n* anterior part of the digestive tract of vertebrates, between the buccal cavity and the bile duct

FOREGUTS > FOREGUT

FOREHAND *n* stroke played with the palm of the hand facing forward ▷ *adj* (of a stroke) made so that the racket is held with the wrist facing the direction of play ▷ *adv* with a forehand stroke ▷ *vb* play (a shot) forehand

FOREHANDS > FOREHAND

FOREHEAD *n* part of the face above the eyebrows

FOREHEADS > FOREHEAD

FOREHENT *vb* seize in advance

FOREHENTS > FOREHENT

FOREHOCK *n* foreleg cut of bacon or pork

FOREHOCKS > FOREHOCK

FOREHOOF *n* front hoof

FOREHOOFS > FOREHOOF

FOREIGN *adj* not of, or in, one's own country

FOREIGNER *n* person from a foreign country

FOREIGNLY > FOREIGN

FOREJUDGE *same as* > FORJUDGE

FOREKING *n* previous king

FOREKINGS > FOREKING

FOREKNEW > FOREKNOW

FOREKNOW *vb* know in advance

FOREKNOWN > FOREKNOW

FOREKNOWS > FOREKNOW

FOREL *n* type of parchment

FORELADY *n* forewoman of a jury

FORELAID > FORELAY

FORELAIN > FORELIE

FORELAND *n* headland, cape, or coastal promontory

FORELANDS > FORELAND

FORELAY *archaic word for* > AMBUSH

FORELAYS > FORELAY

FORELEG *n* either of the front legs of an animal

FORELEGS > FORELEG

FORELEND *vb* give up

FORELENDS > FORELEND

FORELENT > FORELEND

FORELIE *vb* lie in front of

FORELIES > FORELIE

FORELIFT *vb* lift up in front

FORELIFTS > FORELIFT

FORELIMB *n* either of the front or anterior limbs of a four-limbed vertebrate: a foreleg, flipper, or wing

FORELIMBS > FORELIMB

FORELOCK *n* lock of hair over the forehead ▷ *vb* secure (a bolt) by means of a forelock

FORELOCKS > FORELOCK

FORELS > FOREL

FORELYING > FORELIE

FOREMAN *n* person in charge of a group of workers

FOREMAST *n* mast nearest the bow of a ship

FOREMASTS > FOREMAST

FOREMEAN *vb* intend in advance

FOREMEANS > FOREMEAN

FOREMEANT > FOREMEAN

FOREMEN > FOREMAN

FOREMILK *n* first milk drawn from a cow's udder prior to milking

FOREMILKS > FOREMILK

FOREMOST *adv* first in time, place, or importance ▷ *adj* first in time, place, or importance

FORENAME *n* first name

FORENAMED *adj* named or mentioned previously

FORENAMES > FORENAME

FORENIGHT *n* evening

FORENOON *n* morning

FORENOONS > FORENOON

FORENSIC *adj* used in or connected with courts of law

FORENSICS *n* art or study of formal debating

FOREPART *n* first or front part in place, order, or time

FOREPARTS > FOREPART

FOREPAST *adj* bygone

FOREPAW *n* either of the front feet of a land mammal that does not have hooves

FOREPAWS > FOREPAW

FOREPEAK *n* interior part of a vessel that is furthest forward

FOREPEAKS > FOREPEAK

FOREPLAN *vb* plan in advance

FOREPLANS > FOREPLAN

FOREPLAY *n* sexual stimulation before intercourse

FOREPLAYS > FOREPLAY

FOREPOINT *vb* predetermine or indicate in advance

FORERAN > FORERUN

FORERANK *n* first rank

FORERANKS > FORERANK

FOREREACH *vb* keep moving under momentum without engine or sails

FOREREAD *vb* foretell

FOREREADS > FOREREAD

FORERUN *vb* serve as a herald for

FORERUNS > FORERUN

FORES > FORE

FORESAID *less common word for* > AFORESAID

FORESAIL *n* main sail on the foremast of a ship

FORESAILS > FORESAIL

FORESAW > FORESEE

FORESAY *vb* foretell

FORESAYS > FORESAY

FORESEE *vb* see or know beforehand

FORESEEN > FORESEE

FORESEER > FORESEE

FORESEERS > FORESEE

FORESEES > FORESEE

FORESHANK *n* top of the front leg of an animal

FORESHEET *n* sheet of a foresail

FORESHEW *variant of* > FORESHOW

FORESHEWN > FORESHEW

FORESHEWS > FORESHEW

FORESHIP *n* fore part of a ship

FORESHIPS > FORESHIP

FORESHOCK *n* relatively small earthquake heralding the arrival of a much larger one. Some large earthquakes are preceded by a series of foreshocks

FORESHORE *n* part of the shore between high- and low-tide marks

FORESHOW *vb* indicate in advance

FORESHOWN > FORESHOW

FORESHOWS > FORESHOW

FORESIDE *n* front or upper side or part

FORESIDES > FORESIDE

FORESIGHT *n* ability to anticipate and provide for future needs

FORESKIN *n* fold of skin covering the tip of the penis

FORESKINS > FORESKIN

FORESKIRT *n* front skirt of a garment (as opposed to the train)

FORESLACK *variant of* > FORSLACK

FORESLOW *variant of* > FORSLOW

FORESLOWS > FORESLOW

FORESPAKE > FORESPEAK

FORESPEAK *vb* predict

FORESPEND *variant of* > FORSPEND
FORESPENT > FORESPEND
FORESPOKE > FORESPEAK
FOREST *n* large area with a thick growth of trees ▷ *vb* create a forest (in)
FORESTAGE *n* part of a stage in front of the curtain
FORESTAIR *n* external stair
FORESTAL > FOREST
FORESTALL *vb* prevent or guard against in advance
FORESTAY *n* adjustable stay leading from the truck of the foremast to the deck, stem, or bowsprit, for controlling the motion or bending of the mast
FORESTAYS > FORESTAY
FORESTEAL > FOREST
FORESTED > FOREST
FORESTER *n* person skilled in forestry
FORESTERS > FORESTER
FORESTIAL > FOREST
FORESTINE > FOREST
FORESTING > FOREST
FORESTRY *n* science of planting and caring for trees
FORESTS > FOREST
FORESWEAR *vb* forgo
FORESWORE > FORESWEAR
FORESWORN > FORESWEAR
FORETASTE *n* early limited experience of something to come ▷ *vb* have a foretaste of
FORETEACH *vb* teach beforehand
FORETEETH > FORETOOTH
FORETELL *vb* tell or indicate beforehand
FORETELLS > FORETELL
FORETHINK *vb* have prescience
FORETIME *n* time already gone
FORETIMES > FORETIME
FORETOKEN *n* sign of a future event ▷ *vb* foreshadow
FORETOLD > FORETELL
FORETOOTH *another word for an* > INCISOR
FORETOP *n* platform at the top of the foremast
FORETOPS > FORETOP
FOREVER *adv* without end
FOREVERS > FOREVER
FOREWARD *n* vanguard
FOREWARDS > FOREWARD
FOREWARN *vb* warn beforehand
FOREWARNS > FOREWARN
FOREWEIGH *vb* assess in advance
FOREWENT *past tense of* > FOREGO
FOREWIND *n* favourable wind
FOREWINDS > FOREWIND
FOREWING *n* either wing of the anterior pair of an insect's two pairs of wings
FOREWINGS > FOREWING
FOREWOMAN *n* woman in charge of a group of workers
FOREWOMEN > FOREWOMAN
FOREWORD *n* introduction to a book
FOREWORDS > FOREWORD
FOREWORN *same as* > FORWORN
FOREX *n* foreign exchange
FOREXES > FOREX
FOREYARD *n* yard for supporting the foresail of a square-rigger
FOREYARDS > FOREYARD
FORFAIR *vb* perish
FORFAIRED > FORFAIR
FORFAIRN *adj* worn out
FORFAIRS > FORFAIR
FORFAITER > FORFAITING
FORFAULT *variant of* > FORFEIT
FORFAULTS > FORFAULT
FORFEIT *n* thing lost or given up as a penalty for a fault or mistake ▷ *vb* lose as a forfeit ▷ *adj* lost as a forfeit
FORFEITED > FORFEIT
FORFEITER > FORFEIT
FORFEITS > FORFEIT
FORFEND *vb* protect or secure
FORFENDED > FORFEND
FORFENDS > FORFEND
FORFEX *n* pair of pincers, esp the paired terminal appendages of an earwig
FORFEXES > FORFEX
FORFICATE *adj* (esp of the tails of certain birds) deeply forked
FORFOCHEN *Scots word for* > EXHAUSTED
FORGAT *past tense of* > FORGET
FORGATHER *vb* gather together
FORGAVE > FORGIVE
FORGE *n* place where metal is worked, smithy ▷ *vb* make a fraudulent imitation of (something)
FORGEABLE > FORGE
FORGED > FORGE
FORGEMAN > FORGE
FORGEMEN > FORGE
FORGER > FORGE
FORGERIES > FORGERY
FORGERS > FORGE
FORGERY *n* illegal copy of something
FORGES > FORGE
FORGET *vb* fail to remember
FORGETFUL *adj* tending to forget
FORGETIVE *adj* imaginative and inventive
FORGETS > FORGET
FORGETTER > FORGET
FORGING *n* process of producing a metal component by hammering
FORGINGS > FORGING
FORGIVE *vb* cease to blame or hold resentment against, pardon
FORGIVEN > FORGIVE
FORGIVER > FORGIVE
FORGIVERS > FORGIVE
FORGIVES > FORGIVE
FORGIVING *adj* willing to forgive
FORGO *vb* do without or give up
FORGOER > FORGO
FORGOERS > FORGO
FORGOES > FORGO
FORGOING > FORGO
FORGONE > FORGO
FORGOT *past tense of* > FORGET
FORGOTTEN *past participle of* > FORGET
FORHAILE *vb* distress
FORHAILED > FORHAILE
FORHAILES > FORHAILE
FORHENT *variant of* > FOREHENT
FORHENTS > FORHENT
FORHOO *vb* forsake
FORHOOED > FORHOO
FORHOOIE *variant of* > FORHOO
FORHOOIED > FORHOOIE
FORHOOIES > FORHOOIE
FORHOOING > FORHOO
FORHOOS > FORHOO
FORHOW *variant of* > FORHOO
FORHOWED > FORHOW
FORHOWING > FORHOW
FORHOWS > FORHOW
FORINSEC *adj* foreign
FORINT *n* standard monetary unit of Hungary, divided into 100 fillér
FORINTS > FORINT
FORJASKIT *adj* exhausted
FORJESKIT *variant of* > FORJASKIT
FORJUDGE *vb* deprive of a right by the judgment of a court
FORJUDGED > FORJUDGE
FORJUDGES > FORJUDGE
FORK *n* tool for eating food, with prongs and a handle ▷ *vb* pick up, dig, etc with a fork
FORKBALL *n* method of pitching in baseball
FORKBALLS > FORKBALL
FORKED *adj* having a fork or forklike parts
FORKEDLY > FORKED
FORKER > FORK
FORKERS > FORK
FORKFUL > FORK
FORKFULS > FORK
FORKHEAD *n* forked head of a rod
FORKHEADS > FORKHEAD
FORKIER > FORKY
FORKIEST > FORKY
FORKINESS > FORKY
FORKING > FORK
FORKLESS > FORK
FORKLIFT *n* vehicle having two power-operated horizontal prongs that can be raised and lowered for loading, transporting, and unloading goods, esp goods that are stacked on wooden pallets
FORKLIFTS > FORKLIFT
FORKLIKE > FORK
FORKS > FORK
FORKSFUL > FORK
FORKTAIL *n* bird belonging to the flycatcher family
FORKTAILS > FORKTAIL
FORKY *adj* forked
FORLANA *n* Venetian dance
FORLANAS > FORLANA
FORLEND *variant of* > FORELEND
FORLENDS > FORLEND
FORLENT > FORLEND
FORLESE *vb* lose
FORLESES > FORLESE
FORLESING > FORLESE
FORLORE > FORLESE
FORLORN *adj* lonely and unhappy ▷ *n* forsaken person
FORLORNER > FORLORN
FORLORNLY > FORLORN
FORLORNS > FORLORN
FORM *n* shape or appearance ▷ *vb* give a (particular) shape to or take a (particular) shape
FORMABLE > FORM
FORMABLY > FORM
FORMAL *adj* of or characterized by established conventions of ceremony and behaviour
FORMALIN *n* solution of formaldehyde in water, used as a disinfectant or a preservative for biological specimens
FORMALINS > FORMALIN
FORMALISE *same as* > FORMALIZE
FORMALISM *n* concern with outward appearances and structure at the expense of content
FORMALIST > FORMALISM
FORMALITY *n* requirement of custom or etiquette
FORMALIZE *vb* make official or formal
FORMALLY > FORMAL
FORMALS > FORMAL
FORMAMIDE *n* amide derived from formic acid
FORMANT *n* any of several frequency ranges within which the partials of a sound, esp a vowel sound, are at their strongest, thus imparting to the sound its own special quality, tone colour, or timbre

FORMANTS > FORMANT
FORMAT *n* size and shape of a publication ▷ *vb* arrange in a format
FORMATE *n* any salt or ester of formic acid containing the ion $HCOO^-$ or the group HCOO–
FORMATED > FORMAT
FORMATES > FORMATE
FORMATING > FORMAT
FORMATION *n* forming
FORMATIVE *adj* of or relating to development ▷ *n* inflectional or derivational affix
FORMATS > FORMAT
FORMATTED > FORMAT
FORMATTER > FORMAT
FORME *n* type matter, blocks, etc, assembled in a chase and ready for printing
FORMED > FORM
FORMEE *n* type of heraldic cross
FORMER *adj* of an earlier time, previous ▷ *n* person or thing that forms or shapes
FORMERLY *adv* in the past
FORMERS > FORMER
FORMES > FORME
FORMFUL *adj* imaginative
FORMIATE *variant of* > FORMATE
FORMIATES > FORMIATE
FORMIC *adj* of, relating to, or derived from ants
FORMICA *n* tradename for any of various laminated plastic sheets, containing melamine, used esp for heat-resistant surfaces that can be easily cleaned
FORMICANT *adj* low-tension (of pulse)
FORMICARY *n* ant hill
FORMICAS > FORMICA
FORMICATE *vb* crawl around like ants
FORMING > FORM
FORMINGS > FORM
FORMLESS *adj* without a definite shape or form
FORMOL *same as* > FORMALIN
FORMOLS > FORMOL
FORMS > FORM
FORMULA *n* group of numbers, letters, or symbols expressing a scientific or mathematical rule
FORMULAE > FORMULA
FORMULAIC > FORMULA
FORMULAR *adj* of or relating to formulas
FORMULARY *n* book of prescribed formulas ▷ *adj* of, relating to, or of the nature of a formula
FORMULAS > FORMULA
FORMULATE *vb* plan or describe precisely and clearly
FORMULISE *vb* express in a formula
FORMULISM *n* adherence to or belief in formulas
FORMULIST > FORMULISM
FORMULIZE *variant of* > FORMULISE
FORMWORK *n* arrangement of wooden boards, bolts, etc, used to shape reinforced concrete while it is setting
FORMWORKS > FORMWORK
FORMYL *n* of, consisting of, or containing the monovalent group HCO-
FORMYLS > FORMYL
FORNENST *prep* situated against or facing towards
FORNENT *variant of* > FORNENST
FORNICAL > FORNIX
FORNICATE *vb* have sexual intercourse without being married ▷ *adj* arched or hoodlike in form
FORNICES > FORNIX
FORNIX *n* any archlike structure, esp the arched band of white fibres at the base of the brain
FORPET *n* quarter of a peck (measure)
FORPETS > FORPET
FORPINE *vb* waste away
FORPINED > FORPINE
FORPINES > FORPINE
FORPINING > FORPINE
FORPIT *variant of* > FORPET
FORPITS > FORPIT
FORRAD *adv* forward
FORRADER > FORRAD
FORRARDER *adv* further forward
FORRAY *archaic variant of* > FORAY
FORRAYED > FORRAY
FORRAYING > FORRAY
FORRAYS > FORRAY
FORREN *adj* foreign
FORRIT *adv* forward(s)
FORSAID > FORSAY
FORSAKE *vb* withdraw support or friendship from
FORSAKEN *adj* completely deserted or helpless
FORSAKER > FORSAKE
FORSAKERS > FORSAKE
FORSAKES > FORSAKE
FORSAKING > FORSAKE
FORSAY *vb* renounce
FORSAYING > FORSAY
FORSAYS > FORSAY
FORSLACK *vb* be neglectful
FORSLACKS > FORSLACK
FORSLOE *variant of* > FORSLOW
FORSLOED > FORSLOE
FORSLOES > FORSLOE
FORSLOW *vb* hinder
FORSLOWED > FORSLOW
FORSLOWS > FORSLOW
FORSOOK *past tense of* > FORSAKE
FORSOOTH *adv* indeed
FORSPEAK *vb* bewitch
FORSPEAKS > FORSPEAK
FORSPEND *vb* exhaust
FORSPENDS > FORSPEND
FORSPENT > FORSPEND
FORSPOKE > FORSPEAK
FORSPOKEN > FORSPEAK
FORSWATT *adj* sweat-covered
FORSWEAR *vb* renounce or reject
FORSWEARS > FORSWEAR
FORSWINK *vb* exhaust through toil
FORSWINKS > FORSWINK
FORSWONCK *variant of* > FORSWUNK
FORSWORE > FORSWEAR
FORSWORN *past participle of* > FORSWEAR
FORSWUNK *adj* overworked
FORSYTHIA *n* shrub with yellow flowers in spring
FORT *n* fortified building or place ▷ *vb* fortify
FORTALICE *n* small fort or outwork of a fortification
FORTE *n* thing at which a person excels ▷ *adv* loudly
FORTED > FORT
FORTES > FORTIS
FORTH *adv* forwards, out, or away ▷ *prep* out of
FORTHCAME > FORTHCOME
FORTHCOME *vb* come forth
FORTHINK *vb* regret
FORTHINKS > FORTHINK
FORTHWITH *adv* at once
FORTHY *adv* therefore
FORTIES > FORTY
FORTIETH *adj* being the ordinal number of *forty* in numbering or counting order, position, time, etc. Often written: 40th ▷ *n* one of 40 approximately equal parts of something
FORTIETHS > FORTIETH
FORTIFIED > FORTIFY
FORTIFIER > FORTIFY
FORTIFIES > FORTIFY
FORTIFY *vb* make (a place) defensible, as by building walls
FORTILAGE *n* small fort
FORTING > FORT
FORTIS *adj* (of a consonant) articulated with considerable muscular tension of the speech organs or with a great deal of breath pressure or plosion ▷ *n* consonant, such as English *p* or *f*, pronounced with considerable muscular force or breath pressure
FORTITUDE *n* courage in adversity or pain
FORTLET > FORT
FORTLETS > FORT
FORTNIGHT *n* two weeks
FORTRESS *n* large fort or fortified town ▷ *vb* protect with or as if with a fortress
FORTS > FORT
FORTUITY *n* chance or accidental occurrence
FORTUNATE *adj* having good luck
FORTUNE *n* luck, esp when favourable ▷ *vb* befall
FORTUNED > FORTUNE
FORTUNES > FORTUNE
FORTUNING > FORTUNE
FORTUNISE *same as* > FORTUNIZE
FORTUNIZE *vb* make happy
FORTY *n* four times ten ▷ *adj* amounting to forty ▷ *determiner* amounting to forty
FORTYISH > FORTY
FORUM *n* meeting or medium for open discussion or debate
FORUMS > FORUM
FORWANDER *vb* wander far
FORWARD *same as* > FORWARDS
FORWARDED > FORWARD
FORWARDER *n* person or thing that forwards
FORWARDLY > FORWARD
FORWARDS *adv* towards or at a place further ahead in space or time
FORWARN *archaic word for* > FORBID
FORWARNED > FORWARN
FORWARNS > FORWARN
FORWASTE *vb* lay waste
FORWASTED > FORWASTE
FORWASTES > FORWASTE
FORWEARY *vb* exhaust
FORWENT *past tense of* > FORGO
FORWHY *adv* for what reason
FORWORN *adj* weary
FORZA *n* force
FORZANDI > FORZANDO
FORZANDO *another word for* > SFORZANDO
FORZANDOS > FORZANDO
FORZAS > FORZA
FORZATI > FORZATO
FORZATO *variant of* > FORZANDO
FORZATOS > FORZATO
FOSCARNET *n* drug used to treat AIDS
FOSS *same as* > FOSSE
FOSSA *n* anatomical depression, trench, or hollow area
FOSSAE > FOSSA
FOSSAS > FOSSA
FOSSATE *adj* having cavities or depressions
FOSSE *n* ditch or moat, esp one dug as a fortification
FOSSED *adj* having a ditch or moat
FOSSES > FOSSE

FOSSETTE *n* small depression or fossa, as in a bone
FOSSETTES > FOSSETTE
FOSSICK *vb* search, esp for gold or precious stones
FOSSICKED > FOSSICK
FOSSICKER > FOSSICK
FOSSICKS > FOSSICK
FOSSIL *n* hardened remains of a prehistoric animal or plant preserved in rock ▷ *adj* of, like, or being a fossil
FOSSILISE *same as* > FOSSILIZE
FOSSILIZE *vb* turn into a fossil
FOSSILS > FOSSIL
FOSSOR *n* grave digger
FOSSORIAL *adj* (of the forelimbs and skeleton of burrowing animals) adapted for digging
FOSSORS > FOSSOR
FOSSULA *n* small fossa
FOSSULAE > FOSSULA
FOSSULATE *adj* hollowed
FOSTER *vb* promote the growth or development of ▷ *adj* of or involved in fostering a child
FOSTERAGE *n* act of caring for or bringing up a foster child
FOSTERED > FOSTER
FOSTERER > FOSTER
FOSTERERS > FOSTER
FOSTERING > FOSTER
FOSTERS > FOSTER
FOSTRESS *n* female fosterer
FOTHER *vb* stop a leak in a ship's hull
FOTHERED > FOTHER
FOTHERING > FOTHER
FOTHERS > FOTHER
FOU *adj* full ▷ *n* bushel
FOUAT *n* succulent pink-flowered plant
FOUATS > FOUAT
FOUD *n* sheriff in Orkney and Shetland
FOUDRIE *n* foud's district or office
FOUDRIES > FOUDRIE
FOUDS > FOUD
FOUER > FOU
FOUEST > FOU
FOUET *n* archaic word for a whip
FOUETS > FOUET
FOUETTE *n* step in ballet in which the dancer stands on one foot and makes a whiplike movement with the other
FOUETTES > FOUETTE
FOUGADE *n* booby-trapped pit or type of mine
FOUGADES > FOUGADE
FOUGASSE *n* type of bread made with olive oil
FOUGASSES > FOUGASSE
FOUGHT > FIGHT
FOUGHTEN > FIGHT
FOUGHTIER > FOUGHTY
FOUGHTY *adj* musty
FOUL *adj* loathsome or offensive ▷ *n* violation of the rules ▷ *vb* make dirty or polluted
FOULARD *n* soft light fabric of plain-weave or twill-weave silk or rayon, usually with a printed design
FOULARDS > FOULARD
FOULBROOD *n* disease of honeybees
FOULDER *vb* flash like lightning
FOULDERED > FOULDER
FOULDERS > FOULDER
FOULE *n* type of woollen cloth
FOULED > FOUL
FOULER > FOUL
FOULES > FOULE
FOULEST > FOUL
FOULIE *n* bad mood
FOULIES > FOULIE
FOULING > FOUL
FOULINGS > FOUL
FOULLY > FOUL
FOULMART *n* polecat
FOULMARTS > FOULMART
FOULNESS *n* state or quality of being foul
FOULS > FOUL
FOUMART *former name for the* > POLECAT
FOUMARTS > FOUMART
FOUND *vb* set up or establish (an institution, etc)
FOUNDED > FOUND
FOUNDER *vb* break down or fail ▷ *n* person who establishes an institution, company, society, etc
FOUNDERED > FOUNDER
FOUNDERS > FOUNDER
FOUNDING > FOUND
FOUNDINGS > FOUND
FOUNDLING *n* abandoned baby
FOUNDRESS > FOUNDER
FOUNDRIES > FOUNDRY
FOUNDRY *n* place where metal is melted and cast
FOUNDS > FOUND
FOUNT *same as* > FONT
FOUNTAIN *n* jet of water
FOUNTAINS > FOUNTAIN
FOUNTFUL *adj* full of springs
FOUNTS > FOUNT
FOUR *n* one more than three ▷ *adj* amounting to four ▷ *determiner* amounting to four
FOURBALL *n* in golf, match for two pairs in which each player uses his own ball, the better score of each pair being counted at every hole
FOURBALLS > FOURBALL
FOURCHEE *n* type of heraldic cross
FOUREYED *adj* wearing spectacles
FOURFOLD *adj* having four times as many or as much ▷ *adv* by four times as many or as much
FOURGON *n* long covered wagon, used mainly for carrying baggage, supplies, etc
FOURGONS > FOURGON
FOURPENCE *n* former English silver coin then worth four pennies
FOURPENNY *adj* blow, esp with the fist
FOURPLEX *n* building that contains four separate dwellings
FOURS > FOUR
FOURSCORE *adj* eighty
FOURSES *n* snack eaten at four o'clock
FOURSOME *n* group of four people
FOURSOMES > FOURSOME
FOURTEEN *n* four and ten ▷ *adj* amounting to fourteen ▷ *determiner* amounting to fourteen
FOURTEENS > FOURTEEN
FOURTH *n* (of) number four in a series ▷ *adj* of or being number four in a series ▷ *adv* after the third person, position, event, etc
FOURTHLY > FOURTH
FOURTHS > FOURTH
FOUS > FOU
FOUSSA *n* Madagascan civet-like animal
FOUSSAS > FOUSSA
FOUSTIER > FOUSTY
FOUSTIEST > FOUSTY
FOUSTY *archaic variant of* > FUSTY
FOUTER *same as* > FOOTER
FOUTERED > FOUTER
FOUTERING > FOUTER
FOUTERS > FOUTER
FOUTH *n* abundance
FOUTHS > FOUTH
FOUTRA *n* fig; expression of contempt
FOUTRAS > FOUTRA
FOUTRE *vb* footer
FOUTRED > FOUTRE
FOUTRES > FOUTRE
FOUTRING > FOUTRE
FOVEA *n* any small pit or depression in the surface of a bodily organ or part
FOVEAE > FOVEA
FOVEAL > FOVEA
FOVEAS > FOVEA
FOVEATE > FOVEA
FOVEATED > FOVEA
FOVEIFORM *adj* shaped like small pit
FOVEOLA *n* small fovea
FOVEOLAE > FOVEOLA
FOVEOLAR > FOVEOLA
FOVEOLAS > FOVEOLA
FOVEOLATE > FOVEOLA
FOVEOLE *same as* > FOVEOLA
FOVEOLES > FOVEOLE
FOVEOLET *same as* > FOVEOLA
FOVEOLETS > FOVEOLET
FOWL *n* domestic cock or hen ▷ *vb* hunt or snare wild birds
FOWLED > FOWL
FOWLER > FOWLING
FOWLERS > FOWLING
FOWLING *n* shooting or trapping of birds for sport or as a livelihood
FOWLINGS > FOWLING
FOWLPOX *n* viral infection of poultry and other birds
FOWLPOXES > FOWLPOX
FOWLS > FOWL
FOWTH *variant of* > FOUTH
FOWTHS > FOWTH
FOX *n* reddish-brown bushy-tailed animal of the dog family ▷ *vb* perplex or deceive
FOXBERRY *n* lingonberry
FOXED > FOX
FOXES > FOX
FOXFIRE *n* luminescent glow emitted by certain fungi on rotting wood
FOXFIRES > FOXFIRE
FOXFISH *n* type of shark
FOXFISHES > FOXFISH
FOXGLOVE *n* tall plant with purple or white flowers
FOXGLOVES > FOXGLOVE
FOXHOLE *n* small pit dug for protection
FOXHOLES > FOXHOLE
FOXHOUND *n* dog bred for hunting foxes
FOXHOUNDS > FOXHOUND
FOXHUNT *n* hunting of foxes with hounds ▷ *vb* hunt foxes with hounds
FOXHUNTED > FOXHUNT
FOXHUNTER > FOXHUNT
FOXHUNTS > FOXHUNT
FOXIE *n* fox terrier
FOXIER > FOXY
FOXIES > FOXIE
FOXIEST > FOXY
FOXILY > FOXY
FOXINESS > FOXY
FOXING *n* piece of leather used to reinforce or trim part of the upper of a shoe
FOXINGS > FOXING
FOXLIKE > FOX
FOXSHARK *n* thresher shark
FOXSHARKS > FOXSHARK
FOXSHIP *n* cunning
FOXSHIPS > FOXSHIP
FOXSKIN *adj* made from the skin of a fox ▷ *n* skin of a fox
FOXSKINS > FOXSKIN
FOXTAIL *n* any grass of the genus *Alopecurus*, esp *A. pratensis*, of Europe, Asia,

and South America, having soft cylindrical spikes of flowers: cultivated as a pasture grass
'OXTAILS > FOXTAIL
'OXTROT *n* ballroom dance with slow and quick steps ▷ *vb* perform this dance
'OXTROTS > FOXTROT
'OXY *adj* of or like a fox, esp in craftiness
'OY *n* loyalty
'OYBOAT *n* small rowing boat
'OYBOATS > FOYBOAT
'OYER *n* entrance hall in a theatre, cinema, or hotel
'OYERS > FOYER
'OYLE *variant of* > FOIL
'OYLED > FOYLE
'OYLES > FOYLE
'OYLING > FOYLE
'OYNE *variant of* > FOIN
'OYNED > FOYNE
'OYNES > FOYNE
'OYNING > FOYNE
'OYS > FOY
'OZIER > FOZY
'OZIEST > FOZY
'OZINESS > FOZY
'OZY *adj* spongy
'RA *n* brother: a title given to an Italian monk or friar
'RAB *vb* nag
'RABBED > FRAB
'RABBING > FRAB
'RABBIT *adj* peevish
'RABJOUS *adj* splendid
'RABS > FRAB
'RACAS *n* noisy quarrel
'RACASES > FRACAS
'RACK *adj* bold
'RACKING *n* method of releasing oil or gas from rock
'RACKINGS > FRACKING
'RACT *vb* break
'RACTAL *n* figure or surface generated by successive subdivisions of a simpler polygon or polyhedron, according to some iterative process ▷ *adj* of, relating to, or involving such a process
'RACTALS > FRACTAL
'RACTED > FRACT
'RACTI > FRACTUS
'RACTING > FRACT
'RACTION *n* numerical quantity that is not a whole number ▷ *vb* divide
RACTIONS > FRACTION
RACTIOUS *adj* easily upset and angered
'RACTS > FRACT
RACTUR *variant of* > FRAKTUR
RACTURAL > FRACTURE
'RACTURE *n* breaking, esp of a bone ▷ *vb* break
'RACTURED > FRACTURE
'RACTURER > FRACTURE
RACTURES > FRACTURE
FRACTURS > FRACTUR
FRACTUS *n* ragged-shaped cloud formation
FRAE *Scot word for* > FROM
FRAENA > FRAENUM
FRAENUM *n* fold of membrane or skin, such as the fold beneath the tongue, that supports an organ
FRAENUMS > FRAENUM
FRAG *vb* kill or wound (a fellow soldier or superior officer) deliberately with an explosive device
FRAGGED > FRAG
FRAGGING > FRAG
FRAGGINGS > FRAG
FRAGILE *adj* easily broken or damaged
FRAGILELY > FRAGILE
FRAGILER > FRAGILE
FRAGILEST > FRAGILE
FRAGILITY > FRAGILE
FRAGMENT *n* piece broken off ▷ *vb* break into pieces
FRAGMENTS > FRAGMENT
FRAGOR *n* sudden sound
FRAGORS > FRAGOR
FRAGRANCE *n* pleasant smell
FRAGRANCY *same as* > FRAGRANCE
FRAGRANT *adj* sweet-smelling
FRAGS > FRAG
FRAICHEUR *n* freshness
FRAIL *adj* physically weak ▷ *n* rush basket for figs or raisins
FRAILER > FRAIL
FRAILEST > FRAIL
FRAILISH > FRAIL
FRAILLY > FRAIL
FRAILNESS > FRAIL
FRAILS > FRAIL
FRAILTEE *variant of* > FRAILTY
FRAILTEES > FRAILTEE
FRAILTIES > FRAILTY
FRAILTY *n* physical or moral weakness
FRAIM *n* stranger
FRAIMS > FRAIM
FRAISE *n* neck ruff worn during the 16th century ▷ *vb* provide a rampart with a palisade
FRAISED > FRAISE
FRAISES > FRAISE
FRAISING > FRAISE
FRAKTUR *n* style of typeface, formerly used in German typesetting for many printed works
FRAKTURS > FRAKTUR
FRAMABLE > FRAME
FRAMBESIA *same as* > FRAMBOESIA
FRAMBOISE *n* brandy distilled from raspberries in the Alsace-Lorraine region
FRAME *n* structure giving shape or support ▷ *vb* put together, construct
FRAMEABLE > FRAME
FRAMED > FRAME
FRAMELESS > FRAME
FRAMER > FRAME
FRAMERS > FRAME
FRAMES > FRAME
FRAMEWORK *n* supporting structure
FRAMING *n* frame, framework, or system of frames
FRAMINGS > FRAMING
FRAMPAL *same as* > FRAMPOLD
FRAMPLER *n* quarrelsome person
FRAMPLERS > FRAMPLER
FRAMPOLD *adj* peevish
FRANC *n* monetary unit of Switzerland, various African countries, and formerly of France and Belgium
FRANCHISE *n* right to vote ▷ *vb* grant (a person, firm, etc) a franchise
FRANCISE *same as* > FRANCIZE
FRANCISED > FRANCISE
FRANCISES > FRANCISE
FRANCIUM *n* radioactive metallic element
FRANCIUMS > FRANCIUM
FRANCIZE *vb* make French
FRANCIZED > FRANCIZE
FRANCIZES > FRANCIZE
FRANCO *adj* post-free
FRANCOLIN *n* any African or Asian partridge of the genus *Francolinus*
FRANCS > FRANC
FRANGER *n* condom
FRANGERS > FRANGER
FRANGIBLE *adj* breakable or fragile
FRANGLAIS *n* informal French containing a high proportion of words of English origin
FRANION *n* lover, paramour
FRANIONS > FRANION
FRANK *adj* honest and straightforward in speech or attitude ▷ *n* official mark on a letter permitting delivery ▷ *vb* put such a mark on (a letter)
FRANKABLE > FRANK
FRANKED > FRANK
FRANKER > FRANK
FRANKERS > FRANK
FRANKEST > FRANK
FRANKFORT *same as* > FRANKFURT
FRANKFURT *n* light brown smoked sausage
FRANKING > FRANK
FRANKLIN *n* (in 14th- and 15th-century England) a substantial landholder of free but not noble birth
FRANKLINS > FRANKLIN
FRANKLY *adv* in truth
FRANKNESS > FRANK
FRANKS > FRANK
FRANSERIA *n* American shrub
FRANTIC *adj* distracted with rage, grief, joy, etc
FRANTICLY > FRANTIC
FRANZIER > FRANZY
FRANZIEST > FRANZY
FRANZY *adj* irritable
FRAP *vb* lash down or together
FRAPE *adj* tightly bound
FRAPPANT *adj* striking, vivid
FRAPPE *adj* (of drinks) chilled ▷ *n* drink consisting of a liqueur, etc, poured over crushed ice
FRAPPED > FRAP
FRAPPEE > FRAPPE
FRAPPES > FRAPPE
FRAPPING > FRAP
FRAPS > FRAP
FRAS > FRA
FRASCATI *n* dry or semisweet white wine from the Lazio region of Italy
FRASCATIS > FRASCATI
FRASS *n* excrement or other refuse left by insects and insect larvae
FRASSES > FRASS
FRAT *n* member of a fraternity
FRATCH *n* quarrel ▷ *vb* quarrel
FRATCHES > FRATCH
FRATCHETY *same as* > FRATCHY
FRATCHIER > FRATCHY
FRATCHING > FRATCH
FRATCHY *adj* quarrelsome
FRATE *n* friar
FRATER *n* mendicant friar or a lay brother in a monastery or priory
FRATERIES > FRATER
FRATERNAL *adj* of a brother, brotherly
FRATERS > FRATER
FRATERY > FRATER
FRATI > FRATE
FRATRIES > FRATER
FRATRY > FRATER
FRATS > FRAT
FRAU *n* married German woman
FRAUD *n* (criminal) deception, swindle
FRAUDFUL > FRAUD
FRAUDS > FRAUD
FRAUDSMAN *n* practitioner of criminal fraud
FRAUDSMEN > FRAUDSMAN
FRAUDSTER *n* person who commits a fraud
FRAUGHAN *Irish word for* > WHORTLEBERRY
FRAUGHANS > FRAUGHAN
FRAUGHT *adj* tense or

anxious ▷ *vb* archaic word for load ▷ *n* archaic word for freight
FRAUGHTED > FRAUGHT
FRAUGHTER > FRAUGHT
FRAUGHTS > FRAUGHT
FRAULEIN *n* unmarried German woman
FRAULEINS > FRAULEIN
FRAUS > FRAU
FRAUTAGE *variant of* > FRAUGHTAGE
FRAUTAGES > FRAUTAGE
FRAWZEY *n* celebration
FRAWZEYS > FRAWZEY
FRAY *n* noisy quarrel or conflict ▷ *vb* make or become ragged at the edge
FRAYED > FRAY
FRAYING > FRAY
FRAYINGS > FRAY
FRAYS > FRAY
FRAZIL *n* small pieces of ice that form in water moving turbulently enough to prevent the formation of a sheet of ice
FRAZILS > FRAZIL
FRAZZLE *n* exhausted state ▷ *vb* tire out
FRAZZLED > FRAZZLE
FRAZZLES > FRAZZLE
FRAZZLING > FRAZZLE
FREAK *n* abnormal person or thing ▷ *adj* abnormal ▷ *vb* streak with colour
FREAKED > FREAK
FREAKERY as in *control freakery* obsessive need to be in control of events
FREAKFUL *variant of* > FREAKISH
FREAKIER > FREAKY
FREAKIEST > FREAKY
FREAKILY > FREAKY
FREAKING > FREAK
FREAKISH *adj* of, related to, or characteristic of a freak
FREAKOUT *n* heightened emotional state
FREAKOUTS > FREAKOUT
FREAKS > FREAK
FREAKY *adj* weird, peculiar
FRECKLE *n* small brown spot on the skin ▷ *vb* mark or become marked with freckles
FRECKLED > FRECKLE
FRECKLES > FRECKLE
FRECKLIER > FRECKLE
FRECKLING > FRECKLE
FRECKLY > FRECKLE
FREDAINE *n* escapade
FREDAINES > FREDAINE
FREE *adj* able to act at will, not compelled or restrained ▷ *vb* release, liberate
FREEBASE *n* cocaine that has been refined by heating it in ether or some other solvent ▷ *vb* refine (cocaine) in this way
FREEBASED > FREEBASE
FREEBASER > FREEBASE
FREEBASES > FREEBASE
FREEBEE *variant of* > FREEBIE
FREEBEES > FREEBEE
FREEBIE *n* something provided without charge ▷ *adj* without charge
FREEBIES > FREEBIE
FREEBOARD *n* space or distance between the deck of a vessel and the water line
FREEBOOT *vb* act as a freebooter
FREEBOOTS > FREEBOOT
FREEBOOTY > FREEBOOT
FREEBORN *adj* not born in slavery
FREED > FREE
FREEDMAN *n* man freed from slavery
FREEDMEN > FREEDMAN
FREEDOM *n* being free
FREEDOMS > FREEDOM
FREEFORM *n* irregular flowing shape, often used in industrial or fabric design ▷ *adj* freely flowing, spontaneous
FREEGAN *n* person who avoids buying consumer goods, recycling discarded goods instead
FREEGANS > FREEGAN
FREEHAND *adj* drawn without guiding instruments
FREEHOLD *n* tenure of land for life without restrictions ▷ *adj* of or held by freehold
FREEHOLDS > FREEHOLD
FREEING > FREE
FREELANCE *n* (of) a self-employed person doing specific pieces of work for various employers ▷ *vb* work as a freelance ▷ *adv* of or as a freelance
FREELOAD *vb* act as a freeloader
FREELOADS > FREELOAD
FREELY > FREE
FREEMAN *n* person who has been given the freedom of a city
FREEMASON *n* member of a guild of itinerant skilled stonemasons, who had a system of secret signs and passwords with which they recognized each other
FREEMEN > FREEMAN
FREENESS > FREE
FREEPHONE *n* system of telephone use in which the cost of calls in response to an advertisement is borne by the advertiser
FREER *n* liberator
FREERS > FREER
FREES > FREE
FREESHEET *n* newspaper that is distributed free, paid for by its advertisers
FREESIA *n* plant with fragrant tubular flowers
FREESIAS > FREESIA
FREEST > FREE
FREESTONE *n* any fine-grained stone, esp sandstone or limestone, that can be cut and worked in any direction without breaking
FREESTYLE *n* competition, such as in swimming, in which each participant may use a style of his or her choice
FREET *n* omen or superstition
FREETIER > FREETY
FREETIEST > FREETY
FREETS > FREET
FREETY *adj* superstitious
FREEWARE *n* computer software that may be distributed and used without payment
FREEWARES > FREEWARE
FREEWAY *n* motorway
FREEWAYS > FREEWAY
FREEWHEEL *vb* travel downhill on a bicycle without pedalling ▷ *n* device in the rear hub of a bicycle wheel that permits it to rotate freely while the pedals are stationary
FREEWILL *n* apparent human ability to make choices that are not externally determined
FREEWOMAN *n* woman who is free or at liberty
FREEWOMEN > FREEWOMAN
FREEWRITE *vb* write freely without stopping or thinking
FREEWROTE > FREEWRITE
FREEZABLE > FREEZE
FREEZE *vb* change from a liquid to a solid by the reduction of temperature, as water to ice ▷ *n* period of very cold weather
FREEZER *n* insulated cabinet for cold-storage of perishable foods
FREEZERS > FREEZER
FREEZES > FREEZE
FREEZING > FREEZE
FREEZINGS > FREEZE
FREIGHT *n* commercial transport of goods ▷ *vb* send by freight
FREIGHTED > FREIGHT
FREIGHTER *n* ship or aircraft for transporting goods
FREIGHTS > FREIGHT
FREIT *variant of* > FREET
FREITIER > FREITY
FREITIEST > FREITY
FREITS > FREIT
FREITY *adj* superstitious
FREMD *adj* alien or strange
FREMDS > FREMD
FREMIT *same as* > FREMD
FREMITS > FREMIT
FREMITUS *n* vibration felt by the hand when placed on a part of the body, esp the chest, when the patient is speaking or coughing
FRENA > FRENUM
FRENCH *vb* (of food) cut into thin strips
FRENCHED > FRENCH
FRENCHES > FRENCH
FRENCHIFY *vb* make or become French in appearance, behaviour, etc
FRENCHING > FRENCH
FRENETIC *adj* uncontrolled, excited ▷ *n* madman
FRENETICS > FRENETIC
FRENNE *variant of* > FREMD
FRENULA > FRENULUM
FRENULAR > FRENULUM
FRENULUM *n* strong bristle or group of bristles on the hind wing of some moths and other insects, by which the forewing and hind wing are united during flight
FRENULUMS > FRENULUM
FRENUM *same as* > FRAENUM
FRENUMS > FRENUM
FRENZICAL > FRENZY
FRENZIED *adj* filled with or as if with frenzy
FRENZIES > FRENZY
FRENZILY > FRENZY
FRENZY *n* violent mental derangement ▷ *vb* make frantic
FRENZYING > FRENZY
FREON *n* trademark term meaning any of a group of chemically unreactive chlorofluorocarbons used as aerosol propellants, refrigerants, and solvents
FREONS > FREON
FREQUENCE *same as* > FREQUENCY
FREQUENCY *n* rate of occurrence
FREQUENT *adj* happening often ▷ *vb* visit habitually
FREQUENTS > FREQUENT
FRERE *n* friar
FRERES > FRERE
FRESCADE *n* shady place or cool walk
FRESCADES > FRESCADE
FRESCO *n* watercolour painting done on wet plaster on a wall ▷ *vb* paint a fresco
FRESCOED > FRESCO
FRESCOER > FRESCO
FRESCOERS > FRESCO
FRESCOES > FRESCO
FRESCOING > FRESCO

FRESCOIST > FRESCO
FRESCOS > FRESCO
FRESH *adj* newly made, acquired, etc ▷ *adv* recently ▷ *vb* freshen
FRESHED > FRESH
FRESHEN *vb* make or become fresh or fresher
FRESHENED > FRESHEN
FRESHENER > FRESHEN
FRESHENS > FRESHEN
FRESHER *n* first-year student
FRESHERS > FRESHER
FRESHES > FRESH
FRESHEST > FRESH
FRESHET *n* sudden overflowing of a river
FRESHETS > FRESHET
FRESHIE *n* in Indian English, new immigrant to the UK from the Asian subcontinent
FRESHIES > FRESHIE
FRESHING > FRESH
FRESHISH > FRESH
FRESHLY > FRESH
FRESHMAN *same as* > FRESHER
FRESHMEN > FRESHMAN
FRESHNESS > FRESH
FRESNEL *n* unit of frequency equivalent to 10^{12} hertz
FRESNELS > FRESNEL
FRET *vb* be worried ▷ *n* worried state
FRETBOARD *n* fingerboard with frets on a stringed musical instrument
FRETFUL *adj* irritable
FRETFULLY > FRETFUL
FRETLESS > FRET
FRETS > FRET
FRETSAW *n* fine saw with a narrow blade, used for fretwork
FRETSAWS > FRETSAW
FRETSOME *adj* vexing
FRETTED > FRET
FRETTER > FRET
FRETTERS > FRET
FRETTIER > FRETTY
FRETTIEST > FRETTY
FRETTING > FRET
FRETTINGS > FRET
FRETTY *adj* decorated with frets
FRETWORK *n* decorative carving in wood
FRETWORKS > FRETWORK
FRIABLE *adj* easily crumbled
FRIAND *n* small almond cake
FRIANDE *variant of* > FRIAND
FRIANDES > FRIANDE
FRIANDS > FRIAND
FRIAR *n* member of a male Roman Catholic religious order
FRIARBIRD *n* any of various Australian honeyeaters of the genus *Philemon*, having a naked head
FRIARIES > FRIARY
FRIARLY > FRIAR
FRIARS > FRIAR
FRIARY *n* house of friars
FRIB *n* short heavy-conditioned piece of wool removed from a fleece during classing
FRIBBLE *vb* fritter away ▷ *n* wasteful or frivolous person or action ▷ *adj* frivolous
FRIBBLED > FRIBBLE
FRIBBLER > FRIBBLE
FRIBBLERS > FRIBBLE
FRIBBLES > FRIBBLE
FRIBBLING > FRIBBLE
FRIBBLISH *adj* trifling
FRIBS > FRIB
FRICADEL *variant of* > FRIKKADEL
FRICADELS > FRICADEL
FRICANDO *same as* > FRICANDEAU
FRICASSEE *n* stewed meat served in a thick white sauce ▷ *vb* prepare (meat) as a fricassee
FRICATIVE *n* consonant produced by friction of the breath through a partially open mouth, such as (f) or (z) ▷ *adj* relating to or being a fricative
FRICHT *vb* frighten
FRICHTED > FRICHT
FRICHTING > FRICHT
FRICHTS > FRICHT
FRICKING *adj* slang word for absolute
FRICTION *n* resistance met with by a body moving over another
FRICTIONS > FRICTION
FRIDGE *n* apparatus in which food and drinks are kept cool ▷ *vb* archaic word for chafe
FRIDGED > FRIDGE
FRIDGES > FRIDGE
FRIDGING > FRIDGE
FRIED > FRY
FRIEDCAKE *n* type of doughnut
FRIEND *n* person whom one knows well and likes ▷ *vb* befriend
FRIENDED > FRIEND
FRIENDING > FRIEND
FRIENDLY *adj* showing or expressing liking ▷ *n* match played for its own sake and not as part of a competition
FRIENDS > FRIEND
FRIER *same as* > FRYER
FRIERS > FRIER
FRIES > FRY
FRIEZE *n* ornamental band on a wall ▷ *vb* give a nap to (cloth)
FRIEZED > FRIEZE
FRIEZES > FRIEZE
FRIEZING > FRIEZE
FRIG *vb* taboo word meaning masturbate ▷ *n* fridge
FRIGATE *n* medium-sized fast warship
FRIGATES > FRIGATE
FRIGATOON *n* Venetian sailing ship
FRIGES > FRIG
FRIGGED > FRIG
FRIGGER > FRIG
FRIGGERS > FRIG
FRIGGING > FRIG
FRIGGINGS > FRIG
FRIGHT *n* sudden fear or alarm
FRIGHTED > FRIGHT
FRIGHTEN *vb* scare or terrify
FRIGHTENS > FRIGHTEN
FRIGHTFUL *adj* horrifying
FRIGHTING > FRIGHT
FRIGHTS > FRIGHT
FRIGID *adj* (of a woman) sexually unresponsive
FRIGIDER > FRIGID
FRIGIDEST > FRIGID
FRIGIDITY > FRIGID
FRIGIDLY > FRIGID
FRIGOT *variant of* > FRIGATE
FRIGOTS > FRIGOT
FRIGS > FRIG
FRIJOL *n* variety of bean, esp of the French bean, extensively cultivated for food in Mexico
FRIJOLE *variant of* > FRIJOL
FRIJOLES > FRIJOL
FRIKKADEL *n* South African meatball
FRILL *n* gathered strip of fabric attached at one edge ▷ *vb* adorn or fit with a frill or frills
FRILLED > FRILL
FRILLER > FRILL
FRILLERS > FRILL
FRILLIER > FRILLY
FRILLIES *pl n* flimsy women's underwear
FRILLIEST > FRILLY
FRILLING > FRILL
FRILLINGS > FRILL
FRILLS > FRILL
FRILLY *adj* with a frill or frills
FRINGE *n* hair cut short and hanging over the forehead ▷ *vb* decorate with a fringe ▷ *adj* (of theatre) unofficial or unconventional
FRINGED > FRINGE
FRINGES > FRINGE
FRINGIER > FRINGY
FRINGIEST > FRINGY
FRINGING > FRINGE
FRINGY *adj* having a fringe
FRIPON *n* rogue
FRIPONS > FRIPON
FRIPPER *n* dealer in old clothes
FRIPPERER *same as* > FRIPPER
FRIPPERS > FRIPPER
FRIPPERY *n* useless ornamentation
FRIPPET *n* frivolous or flamboyant young woman
FRIPPETS > FRIPPET
FRIS *n* frieze
FRISBEE *n* tradename of a light plastic disc, thrown with a spinning motion for recreation or in competition
FRISBEES > FRISBEE
FRISE *n* fabric with a long normally uncut nap used for upholstery and rugs
FRISEE *n* endive
FRISEES > FRISEE
FRISES > FRIS
FRISETTE *n* curly or frizzed fringe, often an artificial hairpiece, worn by women on the forehead
FRISETTES > FRISETTE
FRISEUR *n* hairdresser
FRISEURS > FRISEUR
FRISK *vb* move or leap playfully ▷ *n* playful movement
FRISKA *n* in Hungarian music, the fast movement of a piece
FRISKAS > FRISKA
FRISKED > FRISK
FRISKER > FRISK
FRISKERS > FRISK
FRISKET *n* light rectangular frame, attached to the tympan of a hand printing press, that carries a parchment sheet to protect the nonprinting areas
FRISKETS > FRISKET
FRISKFUL > FRISK
FRISKIER > FRISKY
FRISKIEST > FRISKY
FRISKILY > FRISKY
FRISKING > FRISK
FRISKINGS > FRISK
FRISKS > FRISK
FRISKY *adj* lively or high-spirited
FRISSON *n* shiver of fear or excitement
FRISSONS > FRISSON
FRIST *archaic word for* > POSTPONE
FRISTED > FRIST
FRISTING > FRIST
FRISTS > FRIST
FRISURE *n* styling the hair into curls
FRISURES > FRISURE
FRIT *n* basic materials, partially or wholly fused, for making glass, glazes for pottery, enamel, etc ▷ *vb* fuse (materials) in making frit
FRITES *pl n* chipped potatoes

FRITFLIES > FRITFLY
FRITFLY *n* small black dipterous fly, *Oscinella frit*, whose larvae are destructive to barley, wheat, rye, oats, etc
FRITH *same as* > FIRTH
FRITHBORH *n* type of pledge
FRITHS > FRITH
FRITS > FRIT
FRITT *same as* > FRIT
FRITTATA *n* Italian dish made with eggs and chopped vegetables or meat, resembling a flat thick omelette
FRITTATAS > FRITTATA
FRITTED > FRIT
FRITTER *n* piece of food fried in batter ▷ *vb* waste or squander
FRITTERED > FRITTER
FRITTERER > FRITTER
FRITTERS > FRITTER
FRITTING > FRIT
FRITTS > FRITY
FRITURE *archaic word for* > FRITTER
FRITURES > FRITURE
FRITZ *n* derogatory term for a German soldier
FRITZES > FRITZ
FRIVOL *vb* behave frivolously
FRIVOLED > FRIVOL
FRIVOLER > FRIVOL
FRIVOLERS > FRIVOL
FRIVOLING > FRIVOL
FRIVOLITY > FRIVOLOUS
FRIVOLLED > FRIVOL
FRIVOLLER > FRIVOL
FRIVOLOUS *adj* not serious or sensible
FRIVOLS > FRIVOL
FRIZ *variant of* > FRIZZ
FRIZE *n* coarse woollen fabric ▷ *vb* freeze
FRIZED > FRIZE
FRIZER *n* person who gives nap to cloth
FRIZERS > FRIZER
FRIZES > FRIZE
FRIZETTE *same as* > FRISETTE
FRIZETTES > FRIZETTE
FRIZING > FRIZE
FRIZZ *vb* form (hair) into stiff wiry curls ▷ *n* hair that has been frizzed
FRIZZANTE *adj* (of wine) slightly effervescent
FRIZZED > FRIZZ
FRIZZER > FRIZZ
FRIZZERS > FRIZZ
FRIZZES > FRIZZ
FRIZZIER > FRIZZY
FRIZZIES *n* condition of having frizzy hair
FRIZZIEST > FRIZZY
FRIZZILY > FRIZZY
FRIZZING > FRIZZ
FRIZZLE *vb* cook or heat until crisp and shrivelled ▷ *n* tight curl
FRIZZLED > FRIZZLE
FRIZZLER > FRIZZLE
FRIZZLERS > FRIZZLE
FRIZZLES > FRIZZLE
FRIZZLIER > FRIZZLE
FRIZZLING > FRIZZLE
FRIZZLY > FRIZZLE
FRIZZY *adj* (of the hair) in tight crisp wiry curls
FRO *adv* away ▷ *n* afro
FROCK *n* dress ▷ *vb* invest (a person) with the office or status of a cleric
FROCKED > FROCK
FROCKING *n* coarse material suitable for making frocks or work clothes
FROCKINGS > FROCKING
FROCKLESS > FROCK
FROCKS > FROCK
FROE *n* cutting tool with handle and blade at right angles, used for stripping young trees, etc
FROES > FROE
FROG *n* smooth-skinned tailless amphibian with long back legs used for jumping
FROGBIT *n* floating aquatic Eurasian plant
FROGBITS > FROGBIT
FROGEYE *n* plant disease
FROGEYED *adj* affected by frogeye
FROGEYES > FROGEYE
FROGFISH *n* any angler (fish) of the family *Antennariidae*, in which the body is covered with fleshy processes, including a fleshy lure on top of the head
FROGGED *adj* decorated with frogging
FROGGERY *n* place where frogs are kept
FROGGIER > FROGGY
FROGGIEST > FROGGY
FROGGING *n* decorative fastening of looped braid on a coat
FROGGINGS > FROGGING
FROGGY *adj* like a frog
FROGLET *n* young frog
FROGLETS > FROGLET
FROGLIKE > FROG
FROGLING *n* young frog
FROGLINGS > FROGLING
FROGMAN *n* swimmer with a rubber suit and breathing equipment for working underwater
FROGMARCH *vb* force (a resisting person) to move by holding his arms ▷ *n* method of carrying a resisting person in which each limb is held and the victim is face downwards
FROGMEN > FROGMAN
FROGMOUTH *n* any nocturnal insectivorous bird of the genera *Podargus* and *Batrachostomus*, of SE Asia and Australia, similar to the nightjars: family *Podargidae*, order *Caprimulgiformes*
FROGS > FROG
FROGSPAWN *n* jelly-like substance containing frog's eggs
FROIDEUR *n* coldness
FROIDEURS > FROIDEUR
FROING as in *toing and froing* going back and forth
FROINGS > FROING
FROISE *n* kind of pancake
FROISES > FROISE
FROLIC *vb* run and play in a lively way ▷ *n* lively and merry behaviour ▷ *adj* full of merriment or fun
FROLICKED > FROLIC
FROLICKER > FROLIC
FROLICKY *same as* > FROLICSOME
FROLICS > FROLIC
FROM *prep* indicating the point of departure, source, distance, cause, change of state, etc
FROMAGE as in *fromage frais* low-fat soft cheese
FROMAGES > FROMAGE
FROMENTY *same as* > FRUMENTY
FROND *n* long leaf or leaflike part of a fern, palm, or seaweed
FRONDAGE *n* fronds collectively
FRONDAGES > FRONDAGE
FRONDED *adj* having fronds
FRONDENT *adj* leafy
FRONDEUR 17th-century French rebel
FRONDEURS > FRONDEUR
FRONDLESS > FROND
FRONDOSE *adj* leafy or like a leaf
FRONDOUS *adj* leafy or like a leaf
FRONDS > FROND
FRONS *n* anterior cuticular plate on the head of some insects, in front of the clypeus
FRONT *n* fore part ▷ *adj* of or at the front ▷ *vb* face (onto)
FRONTAGE *n* facade of a building
FRONTAGER *n* owner of a building or land on the front of a street
FRONTAGES > FRONTAGE
FRONTAL *adj* of, at, or in the front ▷ *n* decorative hanging for the front of an altar
FRONTALLY > FRONTAL
FRONTALS > FRONTAL
FRONTED > FRONT
FRONTENIS *n* racket used in Basque ball game
FRONTER > FRONT
FRONTES > FRONS
FRONTIER *n* area of a country bordering on another
FRONTIERS > FRONTIER
FRONTING > FRONT
FRONTLESS > FRONT
FRONTLET *n* small decorative loop worn on a woman's forehead, projecting from under her headdress, in the 15th century
FRONTLETS > FRONTLET
FRONTLINE *adj* of, relating to, or suitable for the front line of a military formation
FRONTLIST *n* list of books about to be published
FRONTMAN *n* nominal leader of an organization, etc, who lacks real power or authority, esp one who lends respectability to some nefarious activity
FRONTMEN > FRONTMAN
FRONTON *n* wall against which pelota or jai alai is played
FRONTONS > FRONTON
FRONTOON *variant of* > FRONTON
FRONTOONS > FRONTOON
FRONTPAGE *adj* on or suitable for the front page of a newspaper
FRONTS > FRONT
FRONTWARD *same as* > FRONTWARDS
FRONTWAYS *adv* with the front forward
FRONTWISE *variant of* > FRONTWAYS
FRORE *adj* very cold or frosty
FROREN *variant of* > FRORE
FRORN *variant of* > FRORE
FRORNE *variant of* > FRORE
FRORY *adj* frozen
FROS > FRO
FROSH *n* freshman
FROSHES > FROSH
FROST *n* white frozen dew or mist ▷ *vb* become covered with frost
FROSTBIT > FROSTBITE
FROSTBITE *n* destruction of tissue, esp of the fingers or ears, by cold ▷ *vb* affect with frostbite
FROSTED *adj* (of glass) having a rough surface to make it opaque ▷ *n* type of ice cream dish
FROSTEDS > FROSTED
FROSTFISH *n* American fish appearing in frosty weather
FROSTIER > FROSTY
FROSTIEST > FROSTY
FROSTILY > FROSTY

FROSTING *n* sugar icing
FROSTINGS > FROSTING
FROSTLESS > FROST
FROSTLIKE > FROST
FROSTLINE *n* depth to which ground freezes in winter
FROSTNIP *n* milder form of frostbite
FROSTNIPS > FROSTNIP
FROSTS > FROST
FROSTWORK *n* patterns made by frost on glass, metal, etc
FROSTY *adj* characterized or covered by frost
FROTH *n* mass of small bubbles ▷ *vb* foam
FROTHED > FROTH
FROTHER > FROTH
FROTHERS > FROTH
FROTHERY *n* anything insubstantial, like froth
FROTHIER > FROTH
FROTHIEST > FROTH
FROTHILY > FROTH
FROTHING > FROTH
FROTHLESS > FROTH
FROTHS > FROTH
FROTHY > FROTH
FROTTAGE *n* act or process of taking a rubbing from a rough surface, such as wood, for a work of art
FROTTAGES > FROTTAGE
FROTTEUR *n* person who rubs against another person's body for a sexual thrill
FROTTEURS > FROTTEUR
FROUFROU *n* swishing sound, as made by a long silk dress
FROUFROUS > FROUFROU
FROUGHIER > FROUGHY
FROUGHY *adj* rancid
FROUNCE *vb* wrinkle
FROUNCED > FROUNCE
FROUNCES > FROUNCE
FROUNCING > FROUNCE
FROUZIER > FROUZY
FROUZIEST > FROUZY
FROUZILY > FROUZY
FROUZY *same as* > FROWZY
FROW *same as* > FROE
FROWARD *adj* obstinate
FROWARDLY > FROWARD
FROWARDS > FROWARD
FROWIE *variant of* > FROUGHY
FROWIER > FROWIE
FROWIEST > FROWIE
FROWN *vb* wrinkle one's brows in worry, anger, or thought ▷ *n* frowning expression
FROWNED > FROWN
FROWNER > FROWN
FROWNERS > FROWN
FROWNING > FROWN
FROWNS > FROWN
FROWS > FROW
FROWSIER > FROWSY
FROWSIEST > FROWSY
FROWST *n* hot and stale atmosphere ▷ *vb* abandon oneself to such an atmosphere
FROWSTED > FROWST
FROWSTER > FROWST
FROWSTERS > FROWST
FROWSTIER > FROWSTY
FROWSTING > FROWST
FROWSTS > FROWST
FROWSTY *adj* stale or musty
FROWSY *same as* > FROWZY
FROWY *variant of* > FROUGHY
FROWZIER > FROWZY
FROWZIEST > FROWZY
FROWZILY > FROWZY
FROWZY *adj* dirty or unkempt
FROŻE > FREEZE
FROZEN > FREEZE
FROZENLY > FREEZE
FRUCTAN *n* type of polymer of fructose, present in certain fruits
FRUCTANS > FRUCTAN
FRUCTED *adj* fruit-bearing
FRUCTIFY *vb* (cause to) bear fruit
FRUCTIVE *adj* fruitful
FRUCTOSE *n* crystalline sugar occurring in many fruits
FRUCTOSES > FRUCTOSE
FRUCTUARY *n* archaic word for a person who enjoys the fruits of something
FRUCTUATE *vb* bear fruit
FRUCTUOUS *adj* productive or fruitful
FRUG *vb* perform the frug, a 1960s dance
FRUGAL *adj* thrifty, sparing
FRUGALIST > FRUGAL
FRUGALITY > FRUGAL
FRUGALLY > FRUGAL
FRUGGED > FRUG
FRUGGING > FRUG
FRUGIVORE > FRUGIVOROUS
FRUGS > FRUG
FRUICT *obsolete variant of* > FRUIT
FRUICTS > FRUICT
FRUIT *n* part of a plant containing seeds, esp if edible ▷ *vb* bear fruit
FRUITAGE *n* process, state, or season of producing fruit
FRUITAGES > FRUITAGE
FRUITCAKE *n* cake containing dried fruit
FRUITED > FRUIT
FRUITER *n* fruit grower
FRUITERER *n* person who sells fruit
FRUITERS > FRUITER
FRUITERY *n* fruitage
FRUITFUL *adj* useful or productive
FRUITIER > FRUITY
FRUITIEST > FRUITY
FRUITILY > FRUITY
FRUITING > FRUIT
FRUITINGS > FRUIT
FRUITION *n* fulfilment of something worked for or desired
FRUITIONS > FRUITION
FRUITIVE *adj* enjoying
FRUITLESS *adj* useless or unproductive
FRUITLET *n* small fruit
FRUITLETS > FRUITLET
FRUITLIKE > FRUIT
FRUITS > FRUIT
FRUITWOOD *n* wood of a fruit tree
FRUITY *adj* of or like fruit
FRUMENTY *n* kind of porridge made from hulled wheat boiled with milk, sweetened, and spiced
FRUMP *n* dowdy woman ▷ *vb* mock or taunt
FRUMPED > FRUMP
FRUMPIER > FRUMPY
FRUMPIEST > FRUMPY
FRUMPILY > FRUMPY
FRUMPING > FRUMP
FRUMPISH *same as* > FRUMPY
FRUMPLE *vb* wrinkle or crumple
FRUMPLED > FRUMPLE
FRUMPLES > FRUMPLE
FRUMPLING > FRUMPLE
FRUMPS > FRUMP
FRUMPY *adj* (of a woman, clothes, etc) dowdy, drab, or unattractive
FRUSEMIDE *n* diuretic used to relieve oedema, for example caused by heart or kidney disease
FRUSH *vb* break into pieces
FRUSHED > FRUSH
FRUSHES > FRUSH
FRUSHING > FRUSH
FRUST *n* fragment
FRUSTA > FRUSTUM
FRUSTRATE *vb* upset or anger ▷ *adj* frustrated or thwarted
FRUSTS > FRUST
FRUSTULE *n* hard siliceous cell wall of a diatom
FRUSTULES > FRUSTULE
FRUSTUM *n* part of a cone or pyramid contained between the base and a plane parallel to the base that intersects the solid
FRUSTUMS > FRUSTUM
FRUTEX *n* shrub
FRUTICES > FRUTEX
FRUTICOSE *same as* > FRUTESCENT
FRUTIFIED > FRUTIFY
FRUTIFIES > FRUTIFY
FRUTIFY *vb* malapropism for notify; used for comic effect by Shakespeare
FRY *vb* cook or be cooked in fat or oil ▷ *n* dish of fried food
FRYABLE > FRY
FRYBREAD *n* Native American fried bread
FRYBREADS > FRYBREAD
FRYER *n* person or thing that fries
FRYERS > FRYER
FRYING > FRY
FRYINGS > FRY
FRYPAN *n* long-handled shallow pan used for frying
FRYPANS > FRYPAN
FUB *vb* cheat
FUBAR *adj* irreparably damaged or bungled
FUBBED > FUB
FUBBERIES > FUBBERY
FUBBERY *n* cheating
FUBBIER > FUBBY
FUBBIEST > FUBBY
FUBBING > FUB
FUBBY *adj* chubby
FUBS > FUB
FUBSIER > FUBSY
FUBSIEST > FUBSY
FUBSY *adj* short and stout
FUCHSIA *n* ornamental shrub with hanging flowers
FUCHSIAS > FUCHSIA
FUCHSIN *n* greenish crystalline substance
FUCHSINE *same as* > FUCHSIN
FUCHSINES > FUCHSINE
FUCHSINS > FUCHSIN
FUCHSITE *n* form of mica
FUCHSITES > FUCHSITE
FUCI > FUCUS
FUCK *vb* taboo word meaning to have sexual intercourse (with) ▷ *n* taboo word for an act of sexual intercourse
FUCKED > FUCK
FUCKER *n* taboo word for a despicable or obnoxious person
FUCKERS > FUCKER
FUCKING > FUCK
FUCKINGS > FUCK
FUCKOFF *n* taboo word for an annoying or unpleasant person
FUCKOFFS > FUCKOFF
FUCKS > FUCK
FUCKUP *vb* taboo word meaning to damage or bungle ▷ *n* taboo word meaning an act or an instance of bungling
FUCKUPS > FUCKUP
FUCKWIT *n* taboo word for a fool or idiot
FUCKWITS > FUCKWIT
FUCOID *adj* of, relating to, or resembling seaweeds of the genus *Fucus* ▷ *n* any seaweed of the genus *Fucus*
FUCOIDAL *adj* of, relating to, or resembling seaweeds of the genus *Fucus* ▷ *n* any seaweed of the genus *Fucus*
FUCOIDS > FUCOID
FUCOSE *n* aldose
FUCOSES > FUCOSE

FUCOUS *same as* > FUCOIDAL
FUCUS *n* any seaweed of the genus *Fucus*, common in the intertidal regions of many shores and typically having greenish-brown slimy fronds
FUCUSED *adj* archaic word meaning made up with cosmetics
FUCUSES > FUCUS
FUD *n* rabbit's tail
FUDDIES > FUDDY
FUDDLE *vb* cause to be intoxicated or confused ▷ *n* confused state
FUDDLED > FUDDLE
FUDDLER > FUDDLE
FUDDLERS > FUDDLE
FUDDLES > FUDDLE
FUDDLING > FUDDLE
FUDDLINGS > FUDDLE
FUDDY *n* old-fashioned person
FUDGE *n* soft caramel-like sweet ▷ *vb* make (an issue) less clear deliberately ▷ *interj* mild exclamation of annoyance
FUDGED > FUDGE
FUDGES > FUDGE
FUDGING > FUDGE
FUDS > FUD
FUEHRER *n* leader: applied esp to Adolf Hitler
FUEHRERS > FUEHRER
FUEL *n* substance burned or treated to produce heat or power ▷ *vb* provide with fuel
FUELED > FUEL
FUELER > FUEL
FUELERS > FUEL
FUELING > FUEL
FUELLED > FUEL
FUELLER > FUEL
FUELLERS > FUEL
FUELLING > FUEL
FUELS > FUEL
FUELWOOD *n* any wood used as a fuel
FUELWOODS > FUELWOOD
FUERO *n* Spanish code of laws
FUEROS > FUERO
FUFF *vb* puff
FUFFED > FUFF
FUFFIER > FUFFY
FUFFIEST > FUFFY
FUFFING > FUFF
FUFFS > FUFF
FUFFY *adj* puffy
FUG *n* hot stale atmosphere ▷ *vb* sit in a fug
FUGACIOUS *adj* passing quickly away
FUGACITY *n* property of a gas that expresses its tendency to escape or expand
FUGAL *adj* of, relating to, or in the style of a fugue
FUGALLY > FUGAL
FUGATO *adj* in the manner or style of a fugue ▷ *n* movement, section, or piece in this style
FUGATOS > FUGATO
FUGGED > FUG
FUGGIER > FUG
FUGGIEST > FUG
FUGGILY > FUG
FUGGING > FUG
FUGGY > FUG
FUGHETTA *n* short fugue
FUGHETTAS > FUGHETTA
FUGIE *n* runaway
FUGIES > FUGIE
FUGIO *n* former US copper coin worth one dollar, the first authorized by Congress (1787)
FUGIOS > FUGIO
FUGITIVE *n* person who flees, esp from arrest or pursuit ▷ *adj* fleeing
FUGITIVES > FUGITIVE
FUGLE *vb* act as a fugleman
FUGLED > FUGLE
FUGLEMAN *n* (formerly) a soldier used as an example for those learning drill
FUGLEMEN > FUGLEMAN
FUGLES > FUGLE
FUGLIER > FUGLY
FUGLIEST > FUGLY
FUGLING > FUGLE
FUGLY *adj* offensive word for very ugly
FUGS > FUG
FUGU *n* puffer fish
FUGUE *n* musical composition in which a theme is repeated in different parts ▷ *vb* be in a dreamlike, altered state of consciousness
FUGUED > FUGUE
FUGUELIKE > FUGUE
FUGUES > FUGUE
FUGUING > FUGUE
FUGUIST *n* composer of fugues
FUGUISTS > FUGUIST
FUGUS > FUGU
FUHRER *same as* > FUEHRER
FUHRERS > FUHRER
FUJI *n* type of African music
FUJIS > FUJI
FULCRA > FULCRUM
FULCRATE > FULCRUM
FULCRUM *n* pivot about which a lever turns
FULCRUMS > FULCRUM
FULFIL *vb* bring about the achievement of (a desire or promise)
FULFILL *same as* > FULFIL
FULFILLED > FULFILL
FULFILLER > FULFIL
FULFILLS > FULFILL
FULFILS > FULFIL
FULGENCY > FULGENT
FULGENT *adj* shining brilliantly
FULGENTLY > FULGENT
FULGID *same as* > FULGENT
FULGOR *n* brilliance
FULGOROUS > FULGOR
FULGORS > FULGOR
FULGOUR *variant of* > FULGOR
FULGOURS > FULGOUR
FULGURAL > FULGURATE
FULGURANT > FULGURATE
FULGURATE *vb* flash like lightning
FULGURITE *n* tube of glassy mineral matter found in sand and rock, formed by the action of lightning
FULGUROUS *adj* flashing like or resembling lightning
FULHAM *n* loaded die
FULHAMS > FULHAM
FULL *adj* containing as much or as many as possible ▷ *adv* completely ▷ *vb* clean, shrink, and press cloth
FULLAGE *n* price charged for fulling cloth
FULLAGES > FULLAGE
FULLAM *variant of* > FULHAM
FULLAMS > FULLAM
FULLAN *variant of* > FULHAM
FULLANS > FULLAN
FULLBACK *n* defensive player
FULLBACKS > FULLBACK
FULLBLOOD *n* person of unmixed race
FULLED > FULL
FULLER *n* person who fulls cloth for his living ▷ *vb* forge (a groove) or caulk (a riveted joint) with a fuller
FULLERED > FULLER
FULLERENE *n* any of various carbon molecules with a polyhedral structure similar to that of buckminsterfullerene, such as C_{70}, C_{76}, and C_{84}
FULLERIDE *n* compound of a fullerene in which atoms are trapped inside the cage of carbon atoms
FULLERIES > FULLERY
FULLERING > FULLER
FULLERITE *n* crystalline form of a fullerene
FULLERS > FULLER
FULLERY *n* place where fulling is carried out
FULLEST > FULL
FULLFACE *n* in printing, a letter that takes up full body size
FULLFACES > FULLFACE
FULLING > FULL
FULLISH > FULL
FULLNESS > FULL
FULLS > FULL
FULLY *adv* greatest degree or extent
FULMAR *n* Arctic sea bird
FULMARS > FULMAR
FULMINANT *adj* sudden and violent
FULMINATE *vb* criticize or denounce angrily ▷ *n* any salt or ester of fulminic acid, esp the mercury salt, which is used as a detonator
FULMINE *vb* fulminate
FULMINED > FULMINE
FULMINES > FULMINE
FULMINIC as in *fulminic acid*, unstable volatile acid known only in solution and in the form of its salts and esters
FULMINING > FULMINE
FULMINOUS *adj* harshly critical
FULNESS > FULL
FULNESSES > FULL
FULSOME *adj* distastefully excessive or insincere
FULSOMELY > FULSOME
FULSOMER > FULSOME
FULSOMEST > FULSOME
FULVID *variant of* > FULVOUS
FULVOUS *adj* of a dull brownish-yellow colour
FUM *n* phoenix, in Chinese mythology
FUMADO *n* salted, smoked fish
FUMADOES > FUMADO
FUMADOS > FUMADO
FUMAGE *n* hearth money
FUMAGES > FUMAGE
FUMARASE *n* enzyme
FUMARASES > FUMARASE
FUMARATE *n* salt of fumaric acid
FUMARATES > FUMARATE
FUMARIC as in *fumaric acid*, colourless crystalline acid with a fruity taste, found in some plants and manufactured from benzene
FUMAROLE *n* vent in or near a volcano from which hot gases, esp steam, are emitted
FUMAROLES > FUMAROLE
FUMAROLIC > FUMAROLE
FUMATORIA > FUMATORIUM
FUMATORY *same as* > FUMATORIUM
FUMBLE *vb* handle awkwardly ▷ *n* act of fumbling
FUMBLED > FUMBLE
FUMBLER > FUMBLE
FUMBLERS > FUMBLE
FUMBLES > FUMBLE
FUMBLING > FUMBLE
FUME *vb* be very angry ▷ *pl n* pungent smoke or vapour
FUMED *adj* (of wood, esp oak) having a dark colour and distinctive grain from exposure to ammonia fumes
FUMELESS > FUME
FUMELIKE > FUME
FUMER > FUME

FUMEROLE *variant of* > FUMAROLE
FUMEROLES > FUMEROLE
FUMERS > FUME
FUMES > FUME
FUMET *n* strong-flavoured liquor from cooking fish, meat, or game: used to flavour sauces
FUMETS > FUMET
FUMETTE *variant of* > FUMET
FUMETTES > FUMETTE
FUMETTI > FUMETTO
FUMETTO *n* speech balloon in a comic or cartoon
FUMIER > FUME
FUMIEST > FUME
FUMIGANT *n* substance used for fumigating
FUMIGANTS > FUMIGANT
FUMIGATE *vb* disinfect with fumes
FUMIGATED > FUMIGATE
FUMIGATES > FUMIGATE
FUMIGATOR > FUMIGATE
FUMING > FUME
FUMINGLY > FUME
FUMITORY *n* any plant of the chiefly European genus *Fumaria*, esp *F. officinalis*, having spurred flowers and formerly used medicinally: family *Fumariaceae*
FUMOSITY > FUME
FUMOUS > FUME
FUMS > FUM
FUMULI > FUMULUS
FUMULUS *n* smokelike cloud
FUMY > FUME
FUN *n* enjoyment or amusement ▷ *vb* trick
FUNBOARD *n* type of surfboard
FUNBOARDS > FUNBOARD
FUNCTION *n* purpose something exists for ▷ *vb* operate or work
FUNCTIONS > FUNCTION
FUNCTOR *n* performer of a function
FUNCTORS > FUNCTOR
FUND *n* stock of money for a special purpose ▷ *vb* provide money to
FUNDABLE > FUND
FUNDAMENT *n* buttocks
FUNDED > FUND
FUNDER > FUND
FUNDERS > FUND
FUNDI *n* expert or boffin
FUNDIC > FUNDUS
FUNDIE *n* fundamentalist Christian
FUNDIES > FUNDIE
FUNDING > FUND
FUNDINGS > FUND
FUNDIS > FUNDI
FUNDLESS > FUND
FUNDRAISE *vb* raise money for a cause
FUNDS *pl n* money that is readily available
FUNDUS *n* base of an organ or the part farthest away from its opening
FUNDY *n* fundamentalist
FUNEBRAL *variant of* > FUNEBRIAL
FUNEBRE *adj* funereal or mournful
FUNEBRIAL *same as* > FUNEREAL
FUNERAL *n* ceremony of burying or cremating a dead person
FUNERALS > FUNERAL
FUNERARY *adj* of or for a funeral
FUNEREAL *adj* gloomy or sombre
FUNEST *adj* lamentable
FUNFAIR *n* entertainment with machines to ride on and stalls
FUNFAIRS > FUNFAIR
FUNFEST *n* enjoyable time
FUNFESTS > FUNFEST
FUNG *same as* > FUNK
FUNGAL *adj* of, derived from, or caused by a fungus or fungi ▷ *n* fungus or fungal infection
FUNGALS > FUNGAL
FUNGI > FUNGUS
FUNGIBLE *n* moveable perishable goods of a sort that may be estimated by number or weight, such as grain, wine, etc ▷ *adj* having the nature or quality of fungibles
FUNGIBLES > FUNGIBLE
FUNGIC > FUNGUS
FUNGICIDE *n* substance that destroys fungi
FUNGIFORM *adj* shaped like a mushroom or similar fungus
FUNGISTAT *n* substance that inhibits the growth of fungi
FUNGO *n* in baseball, act of tossing and hitting the ball ▷ *vb* toss and hit a ball
FUNGOES > FUNGO
FUNGOID *adj* resembling a fungus
FUNGOIDAL > FUNGOID
FUNGOIDS > FUNGOID
FUNGOSITY > FUNGOUS
FUNGOUS *adj* appearing suddenly and spreading quickly like a fungus
FUNGS > FUNG
FUNGUS *n* plant without leaves, flowers, or roots, such as a mushroom or mould
FUNGUSES > FUNGUS
FUNHOUSE *n* amusing place at fairground
FUNHOUSES > FUNHOUSE
FUNICLE *n* stalk that attaches an ovule or seed to the wall of the ovary
FUNICLES > FUNICLE
FUNICULAR *n* cable railway on a mountainside or cliff ▷ *adj* relating to or operated by a rope, cable, etc
FUNICULI > FUNICULUS
FUNICULUS *same as* > FUNICLE
FUNK *n* style of dance music with a strong beat ▷ *vb* avoid (doing something) through fear
FUNKED > FUNK
FUNKER > FUNK
FUNKERS > FUNK
FUNKHOLE *n* dugout
FUNKHOLES > FUNKHOLE
FUNKIA *n* hosta
FUNKIAS > FUNKIA
FUNKIER > FUNKY
FUNKIEST > FUNKY
FUNKILY > FUNKY
FUNKINESS > FUNKY
FUNKING > FUNK
FUNKS > FUNK
FUNKSTER *n* performer or fan of funk music
FUNKSTERS > FUNKSTER
FUNKY *adj* (of music) having a strong beat
FUNNED > FUN
FUNNEL *n* cone-shaped tube for pouring liquids into a narrow opening ▷ *vb* (cause to) move through or as if through a funnel
FUNNELED > FUNNEL
FUNNELING > FUNNEL
FUNNELLED > FUNNEL
FUNNELS > FUNNEL
FUNNER > FUN
FUNNEST > FUN
FUNNIER > FUNNY
FUNNIES *pl n* comic strips in a newspaper
FUNNIEST > FUNNY
FUNNILY > FUNNY
FUNNINESS > FUNNY
FUNNING > FUN
FUNNY *adj* comical, humorous ▷ *n* joke or witticism
FUNNYMAN *n* comedian
FUNNYMEN > FUNNYMAN
FUNPLEX *n* large amusement centre
FUNPLEXES > FUNPLEX
FUNS > FUN
FUNSTER *n* funnyman
FUNSTERS > FUNSTER
FUR *n* soft hair of a mammal ▷ *vb* cover or become covered with fur
FURACIOUS *adj* thievish
FURACITY > FURACIOUS
FURAL *n* furfural
FURALS > FURAL
FURAN *n* colourless flammable toxic liquid heterocyclic compound
FURANE *variant of* > FURAN
FURANES > FURANE
FURANOSE *n* simple sugar containing a furan ring
FURANOSES > FURANOSE
FURANS > FURAN
FURBEARER *n* mammal hunted for its pelt or fur
FURBELOW *n* flounce, ruffle, or other ornamental trim ▷ *vb* put a furbelow on (a garment)
FURBELOWS > FURBELOW
FURBISH *vb* smarten up
FURBISHED > FURBISH
FURBISHER > FURBISH
FURBISHES > FURBISH
FURCA *n* any forklike structure, esp in insects
FURCAE > FURCA
FURCAL > FURCA
FURCATE *vb* divide into two parts ▷ *adj* forked, branching
FURCATED > FURCATE
FURCATELY > FURCATE
FURCATES > FURCATE
FURCATING > FURCATE
FURCATION > FURCATE
FURCRAEA *n* plant belonging to the Agave family
FURCRAEAS > FURCRAEA
FURCULA *n* any forklike part or organ, esp the fused clavicles (wishbone) of birds
FURCULAE > FURCULA
FURCULAR > FURCULA
FURCULUM *same as* > FURCULA
FURDER *same as* > FURTHER
FUREUR *n* rage or anger
FUREURS > FUREUR
FURFAIR *variant of* > FURFUR
FURFAIRS > FURFAIR
FURFUR *n* scurf or scaling of the skin
FURFURAL *n* colourless liquid used as a solvent
FURFURALS > FURFURAL
FURFURAN *same as* > FURAN
FURFURANS > FURFURAN
FURFURES > FURFUR
FURFUROL *variant of* > FURFURAL
FURFUROLE *variant of* > FURFURAL
FURFUROLS > FURFUROL
FURFUROUS > FURFUR
FURFURS > FURFUR
FURIBUND *adj* furious
FURIES > FURY
FURIOSITY > FURIOUS
FURIOSO *adv* in a frantically rushing manner ▷ *n* passage or piece to be performed in this way
FURIOSOS > FURIOSO
FURIOUS *adj* very angry
FURIOUSLY > FURIOUS
FURKID *n* companion animal
FURKIDS > FURKID
FURL *vb* roll up and fasten (a sail, umbrella, or flag) ▷ *n* act or an instance of

furling
FURLABLE > FURL
FURLANA *variant of* > FORLANA
FURLANAS > FURLANA
FURLED > FURL
FURLER > FURL
FURLERS > FURL
FURLESS > FUR
FURLING > FURL
FURLONG *n* unit of length equal to 220 yards (201.168 metres)
FURLONGS > FURLONG
FURLOUGH *n* leave of absence ▷ *vb* grant a furlough to
FURLOUGHS > FURLOUGH
FURLS > FURL
FURMENTY *same as* > FRUMENTY
FURMETIES > FURMETY
FURMETY *same as* > FRUMENTY
FURMITIES > FURMITY
FURMITY *same as* > FRUMENTY
FURNACE *n* enclosed chamber containing a very hot fire ▷ *vb* burn in a furnace
FURNACED > FURNACE
FURNACES > FURNACE
FURNACING > FURNACE
FURNIMENT *n* furniture
FURNISH *vb* provide (a house or room) with furniture
FURNISHED > FURNISH
FURNISHER > FURNISH
FURNISHES > FURNISH
FURNITURE *n* large movable articles such as chairs and wardrobes
FUROL *variant of* > FURFURAL
FUROLE *variant of* > FURFURAL
FUROLES > FUROLE
FUROLS > FUROL
FUROR *same as* > FURORE
FURORE *n* very excited or angry reaction
FURORES > FURORE
FURORS > FUROR
FURPHIES > FURPHY
FURPHY *n* rumour or fictitious story
FURR *vb* furrow
FURRED *same as* > FURRY
FURRIER *n* dealer in furs
FURRIERS > FURRIER
FURRIERY *n* occupation of a furrier
FURRIES > FURRY
FURRIEST > FURRY
FURRILY > FURRY
FURRINER *n* dialect rendering of foreigner
FURRINERS > FURRINER
FURRINESS > FURRY
FURRING > FUR
FURRINGS > FUR
FURROW *n* trench made by a plough ▷ *vb* make or become wrinkled
FURROWED > FURROW
FURROWER > FURROW
FURROWERS > FURROW
FURROWING > FURROW
FURROWS > FURROW
FURROWY > FURROW
FURRS > FURR
FURRY *adj* like or covered with fur or something furlike ▷ *n* child's fur-covered toy animal
FURS > FUR
FURTH *adv* out
FURTHER *adv* in addition ▷ *adj* more distant ▷ *vb* promote
FURTHERED > FURTHER
FURTHERER > FUTHER
FURTHERS > FURTHER
FURTHEST *adv* to the greatest degree ▷ *adj* most distant
FURTIVE *adj* sly and secretive
FURTIVELY > FURTIVE
FURUNCLE *technical name for* > BOIL
FURUNCLES > FURUNCLE
FURY *n* wild anger
FURZE *n* gorse
FURZES > FURZE
FURZIER > FURZE
FURZIEST > FURZE
FURZY > FURZE
FUSAIN *n* fine charcoal pencil or stick made from the spindle tree
FUSAINS > FUSAIN
FUSARIA > FUSARIUM
FUSARIUM *n* type of fungus
FUSAROL *variant of* > FUSAROLE
FUSAROLE *n* type of architectural moulding
FUSAROLES > FUSAROLE
FUSAROLS > FUSAROL
FUSC *adj* dark or dark-brown
FUSCOUS *adj* of a brownish-grey colour
FUSE *n* cord containing an explosive for detonating a bomb ▷ *vb* (cause to) fail as a result of a blown fuse
FUSED > FUSE
FUSEE *n* (in early clocks and watches) a spirally grooved spindle, functioning as an equalizing force on the unwinding of the mainspring
FUSEES > FUSEE
FUSEL *n* mixture of amyl alcohols, propanol, and butanol: a by-product in the distillation of fermented liquors used as a source of amyl alcohols
FUSELAGE *n* body of an aircraft
FUSELAGES > FUSELAGE
FUSELESS > FUSE
FUSELIKE > FUSE
FUSELS > FUSEL
FUSES > FUSE
FUSHION *n* spirit
FUSHIONS > FUSHION
FUSIBLE *adj* capable of being melted
FUSIBLY > FUSIBLE
FUSIFORM *adj* elongated and tapering at both ends
FUSIL *n* light flintlock musket
FUSILE *adj* easily melted
FUSILEER *same as* > FUSILIER
FUSILEERS > FUSILEER
FUSILIER *n* soldier of certain regiments
FUSILIERS > FUSILIER
FUSILLADE *n* continuous discharge of firearms ▷ *vb* attack with a fusillade
FUSILLI *n* spiral-shaped pasta
FUSILLIS > FUSILLI
FUSILS > FUSIL
FUSING > FUSE
FUSION *n* melting ▷ *adj* of a style of cooking that combines traditional Western techniques and ingredients with those used in Eastern cuisine
FUSIONAL > FUSION
FUSIONISM *n* favouring of coalitions among political groups
FUSIONIST > FUSIONISM
FUSIONS > FUSION
FUSS *n* needless activity or worry ▷ *vb* make a fuss
FUSSED > FUSS
FUSSER > FUSS
FUSSERS > FUSS
FUSSES > FUSS
FUSSIER > FUSSY
FUSSIEST > FUSSY
FUSSILY > FUSSY
FUSSINESS > FUSSY
FUSSING > FUSS
FUSSPOT *n* person who is difficult to please and complains often
FUSSPOTS > FUSSPOT
FUSSY *adj* inclined to fuss
FUST *vb* become mouldy
FUSTED > FUST
FUSTET *n* wood of the Venetian sumach shrub
FUSTETS > FUSTET
FUSTIAN *n* (formerly) a hard-wearing fabric of cotton mixed with flax or wool ▷ *adj* cheap
FUSTIANS > FUSTIAN
FUSTIC *n* large tropical American moraceous tree, *Chlorophora tinctoria*
FUSTICS > FUSTIC
FUSTIER > FUSTY
FUSTIEST > FUSTY
FUSTIGATE *vb* beat
FUSTILUGS *n* fat person
FUSTILY > FUSTY
FUSTINESS > FUSTY
FUSTING > FUST
FUSTOC *variant of* > FUSTIC
FUSTOCS > FUSTOC
FUSTS > FUST
FUSTY *adj* stale-smelling
FUSULINID *n* any of various extinct foraminifers
FUSUMA *n* Japanese sliding door
FUTCHEL *n* timber support in a carriage
FUTCHELS > FUTCHEL
FUTHARC *same as* > FUTHARK
FUTHARCS > FUTHARC
FUTHARK *n* phonetic alphabet consisting of runes
FUTHARKS > FUTHARK
FUTHORC *same as* > FUTHARK
FUTHORCS > FUTHORC
FUTHORK *same as* > FUTHARK
FUTHORKS > FUTHORK
FUTILE *adj* unsuccessful or useless
FUTILELY > FUTILE
FUTILER > FUTILE
FUTILEST > FUTILE
FUTILITY *n* lack of effectiveness or success
FUTON *n* Japanese-style bed
FUTONS > FUTON
FUTSAL *n* form of association football, played indoors with five players on each side
FUTSALS > FUTSAL
FUTTOCK *n* one of the ribs in the frame of a wooden vessel
FUTTOCKS > FUTTOCK
FUTURAL *adj* relating to the future
FUTURE *n* time to come ▷ *adj* yet to come or be
FUTURES *pl n* commodities bought or sold at an agreed price for delivery at a specified future date
FUTURISM *n* early 20th-century artistic movement making use of the characteristics of the machine age
FUTURISMS > FUTURISM
FUTURIST > FUTURISM
FUTURISTS > FUTURISM
FUTURITY *n* future
FUTZ *vb* fritter time away
FUTZED > FUTZ
FUTZES > FUTZ
FUTZING > FUTZ
FUZE *same as* > FUSE
FUZED > FUZE
FUZEE *same as* > FUSEE
FUZEES > FUZEE
FUZES > FUZE
FUZIL *variant of* > FUSIL
FUZILS > FUZIL
FUZING > FUZE
FUZZ *n* mass of fine or curly hairs or fibres ▷ *vb* make or become fuzzy

FUZZED > FUZZ
FUZZES > FUZZ
FUZZIER > FUZZY
FUZZIEST > FUZZY
FUZZILY > FUZZY
FUZZINESS > FUZZY
FUZZING > FUZZ
FUZZLE *vb* make drunk
FUZZLED > FUZZLE
FUZZLES > FUZZLE
FUZZLING > FUZZLE
FUZZTONE *n* device distorting electric guitar sound
FUZZTONES > FUZZTONE
FUZZY *adj* of, like, or covered with fuzz
FY *variant of* > FIE
FYCE *variant of* > FICE
FYCES > FYCE
FYKE *n* fish trap consisting of a net suspended over a series of hoops, laid horizontally in the water ▷ *vb* catch fish in this manner
FYKED > FYKE
FYKES > FYKE
FYKING > FYKE
FYLE *variant of* > FILE
FYLES > FYLE
FYLFOT *rare word for* > SWASTIKA
FYLFOTS > FYLFOT
FYNBOS *n* area of low-growing, evergreen vegetation
FYNBOSES > FYNBOS
FYRD *n* local militia of an Anglo-Saxon shire, in which all freemen had to serve
FYRDS > FYRD
FYTTE *n* song
FYTTES > FYTTE

Gg

GAB *vb* talk or chatter ▷ *n* hook or open notch in a rod or lever that drops over the spindle of a valve to form a temporary connection for operating the valve
GABARDINE *n* strong twill cloth used esp for raincoats
GABBARD *same as* > GABBART
GABBARDS > GABBARD
GABBART *n* Scottish sailing barge
GABBARTS > GABBART
GABBED > GAB
GABBER > GAB
GABBERS > GAB
GABBIER > GABBY
GABBIEST > GABBY
GABBINESS > GABBY
GABBING > GAB
GABBLE *vb* speak rapidly and indistinctly ▷ *n* rapid indistinct speech
GABBLED > GABBLE
GABBLER > GABBLE
GABBLERS > GABBLE
GABBLES > GABBLE
GABBLING > GABBLE
GABBLINGS > GABBLE
GABBRO *n* dark coarse-grained basic plutonic igneous rock consisting of plagioclase feldspar, pyroxene, and often olivine
GABBROIC > GABBRO
GABBROID *adj* gabbro-like
GABBROS > GABBRO
GABBY *adj* talkative
GABELLE *n* salt tax levied until 1790
GABELLED > GABELLE
GABELLER *n* person who collects the gabelle
GABELLERS > GABELLER
GABELLES > GABELLE
GABERDINE *same as* > GABARDINE
GABFEST *n* prolonged gossiping or conversation
GABFESTS > GABFEST
GABIES > GABY
GABION *n* cylindrical metal container filled with stones, used in the construction of underwater foundations
GABIONADE *n* row of gabions submerged in a waterway, stream, river, etc, to control the flow of water
GABIONAGE *n* structure composed of gabions
GABIONED > GABION
GABIONS > GABION
GABLE *n* triangular upper part of a wall between sloping roofs
GABLED > GABLE
GABLELIKE > GABLE
GABLES > GABLE
GABLET *n* small gable
GABLETS > GABLET
GABLING > GABLE
GABNASH *n* chatter
GABNASHES > GABNASH
GABOON *n* dark mahogany-like wood from a western and central African burseraceous tree, *Aucoumea klaineana*, used in plywood, for furniture, and as a veneer
GABOONS > GABOON
GABS > GAB
GABY *n* simpleton
GAD *vb* go about in search of pleasure ▷ *n* carefree adventure (esp in the phrase **on** *or* **upon the gad**)
GADABOUT *n* pleasure-seeker
GADABOUTS > GADABOUT
GADARENE *adj* headlong
GADDED > GAD
GADDER > GAD
GADDERS > GAD
GADDI *n* cushion on an Indian prince's throne
GADDING > GAD
GADDIS > GADDI
GADE *same as* > GAD
GADES > GADE
GADFLIES > GADFLY
GADFLY *n* fly that bites cattle
GADGE *n* man
GADGES > GADGE
GADGET *n* small mechanical device or appliance
GADGETEER *n* person who delights in gadgetry
GADGETRY *n* gadgets
GADGETS > GADGET
GADGETY > GADGET
GADGIE *n* fellow
GADGIES > GADGIE
GADI *n* Indian throne
GADID *n* any marine teleost fish of the family *Gadidae*, which includes the cod, haddock, whiting, and pollack ▷ *adj* of, relating to, or belonging to the *Gadidae*
GADIDS > GADID
GADIS > GADI
GADJE *same as* > GADGIE
GADJES > GADJE
GADJO variant of > GORGIO
GADLING *n* vagabond
GADLINGS > GADLING
GADOID *adj* of the cod family of marine fishes ▷ *n* gadoid fish
GADOIDS > GADOID
GADOLINIC *adj* relating to gadolinium, a silvery white metallic element
GADROON *n* moulding composed of a series of convex flutes and curves joined to form a decorative pattern, used esp as an edge to silver articles
GADROONED > GADROON
GADROONS > GADROON
GADS > GAD
GADSMAN *n* person who uses a gad when driving animals
GADSMEN > GADSMAN
GADSO *n* archaic expression of surprise
GADSOS > GADSO
GADWALL *n* duck, *Anas strepera*, related to the mallard
GADWALLS > GADWALL
GADZOOKS *interj* mild oath
GAE *Scot word for* > GO
GAED > GAE
GAEING > GAE
GAELICISE *vb* adapt to conform to Gaelic spelling and pronunciation
GAELICISM > GAELICISE
GAELICIZE *same as* > GAELICISE

GAEN > GAE
GAES > GAE
GAFF *n* stick with an iron hook for landing large fish ▷ *vb* hook or land (a fish) with a gaff
GAFFE *n* social blunder
GAFFED > GAFF
GAFFER *n* foreman or boss
GAFFERS > GAFFER
GAFFES > GAFFE
GAFFING > GAFF
GAFFINGS > GAFF
GAFFS > GAFF
GAFFSAIL *n* quadrilateral fore-and-aft sail on a sailing vessel
GAFFSAILS > GAFFSAIL
GAG *vb* choke or retch ▷ *n* cloth etc put into or tied across the mouth
GAGA *adj* senile
GAGAKU *n* type of traditional Japanese music
GAGAKUS > GAGAKU
GAGE *vb* gauge ▷ *n* (formerly) a glove or other object thrown down to indicate a challenge to fight
GAGEABLE > GAGE
GAGEABLY > GAGE
GAGED > GAGE
GAGER *same as* > GAUGER
GAGERS > GAGER
GAGES > GAGE
GAGGED > GAG
GAGGER *n* person or thing that gags
GAGGERIES > GAGGERY
GAGGERS > GAGGER
GAGGERY *n* practice of telling jokes
GAGGING > GAG
GAGGLE *n* disorderly crowd ▷ *vb* (of geese) to cackle
GAGGLED > GAGGLE
GAGGLES > GAGGLE
GAGGLING > GAGGLE
GAGGLINGS > GAGGLE
GAGING > GAGE
GAGMAN *n* person who writes gags for a comedian
GAGMEN > GAGMAN
GAGS > GAG
GAGSTER *n* standup comedian
GAGSTERS > GAGSTER
GAHNITE *n* dark green mineral of the spinel group consisting of zinc aluminium oxide
GAHNITES > GAHNITE
GAID *same as* > GAD
GAIDS > GAID
GAIETIES > GAIETY
GAIETY *n* cheerfulness
GAIJIN *n* (in Japan) a foreigner
GAILLARD *same as* > GALLIARD
GAILLARDE *same as* > GAILLARD
GAILY *adv* merrily
GAIN *vb* acquire or obtain ▷ *n* profit or advantage ▷ *adj* straight or near
GAINABLE > GAIN
GAINED > GAIN
GAINER *n* person or thing that gains
GAINERS > GAINER
GAINEST > GAIN
GAINFUL *adj* useful or profitable
GAINFULLY > GAINFUL
GAINING > GAIN
GAININGS *pl n* profits or earnings
GAINLESS > GAIN
GAINLIER > GAINLY
GAINLIEST > GAINLY
GAINLY *adj* graceful or well-formed ▷ *adv* conveniently or suitably
GAINS *pl n* profits or winnings
GAINSAID > GAINSAY
GAINSAY *vb* deny or contradict
GAINSAYER > GAINSAY
GAINSAYS > GAINSAY
GAINST *short for* > AGAINST
GAIR *n* strip of green grass on a hillside
GAIRFOWL *same as* > GAREFOWL
GAIRFOWLS > GAIRFOWL
GAIRS > GAIR
GAIT *n* manner of walking ▷ *vb* teach (a horse) a particular gait
GAITED > GAIT
GAITER *n* cloth or leather covering for the lower leg
GAITERS > GAITER
GAITING > GAIT
GAITS > GAIT
GAITT *Scots word for* > GATE
GAITTS > GAITT
GAJO *same as* > GORGIO
GAJOS > GAJO
GAL *n* girl
GALA *n* festival
GALABEA *same as* > DJELLABA
GALABEAH *same as* > DJELLABA
GALABEAHS > GALABEAH
GALABEAS > GALABEA
GALABIA *same as* > DJELLABA
GALABIAH *same as* > DJELLABA
GALABIAHS > GALABIAH
GALABIAS > GALABIA
GALABIEH *same as* > DJELLABA
GALABIEHS > GALABIEH
GALABIYA *same as* > DJELLABA
GALABIYAH *same as* > DJELLABA
GALABIYAS > GALABIYA
GALACTIC *adj* of the Galaxy or other galaxies
GALACTOSE *n* white water-soluble monosaccharide found in lactose
GALAGE *same as* > GALOSH
GALAGES > GALAGE
GALAGO *another name for* > BUSHBABY
GALAGOS > GALAGO
GALAH *n* Australian cockatoo, *Kakatoe roseicapilla*, having grey wings, back, and crest and a pink body
GALAHS > GALAH
GALANGA *same as* > GALINGALE
GALANGAL *same as* > GALINGALE
GALANGALS > GALANGAL
GALANGAS > GALANGAL
GALANT *n* 18th-century style of music characterized by homophony and elaborate ornamentation
GALANTINE *n* cold dish of meat or poultry, which is boned, cooked, stuffed, then pressed into a neat shape and glazed
GALANTY as in *galanty show* pantomime shadow play, esp one in miniature using figures cut from paper
GALAPAGO *n* tortoise
GALAPAGOS > GALAPAGO
GALAS > GALA
GALATEA *n* strong twill-weave cotton fabric, striped or plain, for clothing
GALATEAS > GALATEA
GALAVANT *same as* > GALLIVANT
GALAVANTS > GALAVANT
GALAX *n* coltsfoot
GALAXES > GALAX
GALAXIES > GALAXY
GALAXY *n* system of stars
GALBANUM *n* bitter aromatic gum resin extracted from any of several Asian umbelliferous plants of the genus *Ferula*, esp *F. galbaniflua*, and used in incense and medicinally as a counterirritant
GALBANUMS > GALBANUM
GALDRAGON *old Scots word for a* > SORCERESS
GALE *n* strong wind
GALEA *n* part or organ shaped like a helmet or hood, such as the petals of certain flowers
GALEAE > GALEA
GALEAS > GALEA
GALEATE > GALEA
GALEATED > GALEA
GALEIFORM > GALEA
GALENA *n* soft bluish-grey mineral consisting of lead sulphide: the chief source of lead
GALENAS > GALENA
GALENGALE *same as* > GALINGALE
GALENIC > GALENA
GALENICAL *n* any drug prepared from plant or animal tissue, esp vegetables, rather than being chemically synthesized ▷ *adj* denoting or belonging to this group of drugs
GALENITE *same as* > GALENA
GALENITES > GALENITE
GALENOID *adj* pertaining to galena
GALERE *n* group of people having a common interest, esp a coterie of undesirable people
GALERES > GALERE
GALES > GALE
GALETTE *n* type of savoury pancake
GALETTES > GALETTE
GALILEE *n* porch or chapel at the entrance to some medieval churches and cathedrals in England
GALILEES > GALILEE
GALINGALE *n* European cyperaceous plant, *Cyperus longus*, with rough-edged leaves, reddish spikelets of flowers, and aromatic roots
GALIONGEE *n* sailor
GALIOT *n* small swift galley formerly sailed on the Mediterranean
GALIOTS > GALIOT
GALIPOT *n* resin obtained from several species of pine
GALIPOTS > GALIPOT
GALIVANT *same as* > GALLIVANT
GALIVANTS > GALIVANT
GALL *n* impudence ▷ *vb* annoy
GALLABEA *same as* > DJELLABA
GALLABEAH *same as* > DJELLABA
GALLABEAS > GALLABEA
GALLABIA *same as* > DJELLABA
GALLABIAH *same as* > DJELLABA
GALLABIAS > GALLABIA
GALLABIEH *same as* > DJELLABA
GALLABIYA *same as* > DJELLABA
GALLAMINE *n* muscle relaxant used in anaesthesia
GALLANT *adj* brave and noble ▷ *n* young man who tried to impress women with his fashionable clothes or daring acts ▷ *vb* court or flirt (with)
GALLANTED > GALLANT
GALLANTER > GALLANT
GALLANTLY > GALLANT

GALLANTRY *n* showy, attentive treatment of women
GALLANTS > GALLANT
GALLATE *n* salt of gallic acid
GALLATES > GALLATE
GALLEASS *n* three-masted lateen-rigged galley used as a warship in the Mediterranean from the 15th to the 18th centuries
GALLED > GALL
GALLEIN *n* type of dyestuff
GALLEINS > GALLEIN
GALLEON *n* large three-masted sailing ship of the 15th–17th centuries
GALLEONS > GALLEON
GALLERIA *n* central court through several storeys of a shopping centre or department store onto which shops or departments open at each level
GALLERIAS > GALLERIA
GALLERIED *adj* having a gallery or galleries
GALLERIES > GALLERY
GALLERIST *n* person who owns or runs an art gallery
GALLERY *n* room or building for displaying works of art ▷ *vb* tunnel; form an underground gallery
GALLET *vb* (in roofing) use small pieces of slate mixed with mortar to support an upper slate
GALLETA *n* low-growing, coarse grass
GALLETAS > GALLETA
GALLETED > GALLET
GALLETING > GALLET
GALLETS > GALLET
GALLEY *n* kitchen of a ship or aircraft
GALLEYS > GALLEY
GALLFLIES > GALLFLY
GALLFLY *n* any of several small insects that produce galls in plant tissues, such as the gall wasp and gall midge
GALLIARD *n* spirited dance in triple time for two persons, popular in the 16th and 17th centuries ▷ *adj* lively
GALLIARDS > GALLIARD
GALLIASS *same as* > GALLEASS
GALLIC *adj* of or containing gallium in the trivalent state
GALLICA *n* variety of rose
GALLICAN *adj* of or relating to a movement favouring the restriction of papal control and greatern autonomy for the French church
GALLICAS > GORGIO
GALLICISE *same as* > GALLICIZE
GALLICISM *n* word or idiom borrowed from French
GALLICIZE *vb* make or become French in attitude, language, etc
GALLIED > GALLY
GALLIES > GALLY
GALLINAZO *n* black vulture
GALLING *adj* annoying or bitterly humiliating
GALLINGLY > GALLING
GALLINULE *n* moorhen
GALLIOT *same as* > GALIOT
GALLIOTS > GALLIOT
GALLIPOT *same as* > GALIPOT
GALLIPOTS > GALLIPOT
GALLISE *vb* add water and sugar to unfermented grape juice to increase the quantity of wine produced
GALLISED > GALLISE
GALLISES > GALLISE
GALLISING > GALLISE
GALLISISE *vb* gallise
GALLISIZE *same as* > GALLISE
GALLIUM *n* soft grey metallic element used in semiconductors
GALLIUMS > GALLIUM
GALLIVANT *vb* go about in search of pleasure
GALLIVAT *n* Oriental armed vessel
GALLIVATS > GALLIVAT
GALLIWASP *n* any lizard of the Central American genus *Diploglossus*, esp *D. monotropis* of the Caribbean: family *Anguidae*
GALLIZE *same as* > GALLISE
GALLIZED > GALLIZE
GALLIZES > GALLIZE
GALLIZING > GALLIZE
GALLNUT *n* type of plant gall that resembles a nut
GALLNUTS > GALLNUT
GALLOCK *adj* left-handed
GALLON *n* liquid measure of eight pints, equal to 4.55 litres
GALLONAGE *n* capacity measured in gallons
GALLONS > GALLON
GALLOON *n* narrow band of cord, embroidery, silver or gold braid, etc, used on clothes and furniture
GALLOONED > GALLOON
GALLOONS > GALLOON
GALLOOT *same as* > GALLOOT
GALLOOTS > GALOOT
GALLOP *n* horse's fastest pace ▷ *vb* go or ride at a gallop
GALLOPADE *n* gallop ▷ *vb* perform a gallopade
GALLOPED > GALLOP
GALLOPER > GALLOP
GALLOPERS > GALLOP
GALLOPING *adj* progressing at or as if at a gallop
GALLOPS > GALLOP
GALLOUS *adj* of or containing gallium in the divalent state
GALLOW *vb* frighten
GALLOWED > GALLOW
GALLOWING > GALLOW
GALLOWS *n* wooden structure used for hanging criminals
GALLOWSES > GALLOWS
GALLS > GALL
GALLSTONE *n* hard mass formed in the gall bladder or its ducts
GALLUMPH *same as* > GALUMPH
GALLUMPHS > GALLUMPH
GALLUS *adj* bold ▷ *n* suspender for trousers
GALLUSED *adj* held up by galluses
GALLUSES > GALLUS
GALLY *vb* frighten
GALLYING > GALLY
GALOCHE *same as* > GALOSH
GALOCHED > GALOCHE
GALOCHES > GALOCHE
GALOCHING > GALOCHE
GALOOT *n* clumsy or uncouth person
GALOOTS > GALOOT
GALOP *n* 19th-century dance in quick duple time ▷ *vb* dance a galop
GALOPADE > GALOP
GALOPADES > GALOP
GALOPED > GALOP
GALOPIN *n* boy who ran errands for a cook
GALOPING > GALOP
GALOPINS > GALOPIN
GALOPPED > GALOP
GALOPPING > GALOP
GALOPS > GALOP
GALORE *adv* in abundance ▷ *adj* in abundance ▷ *n* abundance
GALORES > GALORE
GALOSH *n* waterproof overshoe ▷ *vb* cover with galoshes
GALOSHE *same as* > GALOSH
GALOSHED > GALOSH
GALOSHES > GALOSH
GALOSHING > GALOSH
GALOWSES *Shakespearean plural for* > GALLOWS
GALRAVAGE *same as* > GILRAVAGE
GALS > GAL
GALTONIA *n* any plant of the bulbous genus *Galtonia*, esp *G. candicans*, with lanceolate leaves, drooping racemes of waxy white flowers, and a fragrant scent: family *Liliaceae*
GALTONIAS > GALTONIA
GALUMPH *vb* leap or move about clumsily
GALUMPHED > GALUMPH
GALUMPHER > GALUMPH
GALUMPHS > GALUMPH
GALUT *same as* > GALUTH
GALUTH *n* exile of Jews from Palestine
GALUTHS > GALUTH
GALUTS > GALUT
GALVANIC *adj* of or producing an electric current generated by chemical means
GALVANISE *same as* > GALVANIZE
GALVANISM *n* electricity, esp when produced by chemical means as in a cell or battery
GALVANIST > GALVANISM
GALVANIZE *vb* stimulate into action ▷ *n* galvanized iron, usually in the form of corrugated sheets as used in roofing
GALVO *n* instrument for measuring electric current
GALVOS > GALVO
GALYAC *same as* > GALYAK
GALYACS > GALYAC
GALYAK *n* smooth glossy fur obtained from the skins of newborn or premature lambs and kids
GALYAKS > GALYAK
GAM *n* school of whales ▷ *vb* (of whales) form a school
GAMA *n* tall perennial grass
GAMAHUCHE *derogatory term vb* practise cunnilingus or fellatio on ▷ *n* cunnilingus or fellatio
GAMARUCHE *same as* > GAMAHUCHE
GAMAS > GAMA
GAMASH *n* type of gaiter
GAMASHES > GAMASH
GAMAY *n* red grape variety, or the wine made from it
GAMAYS > GAMAY
GAMB *n* in heraldry, the whole foreleg of a beast
GAMBA *n* second-largest member of the viol family
GAMBADE *same as* > GAMBADO
GAMBADES > GAMBADE
GAMBADO *n* leap or gambol; caper ▷ *vb* perform a gambado
GAMBADOED > GAMBADO
GAMBADOES > GAMBADO
GAMBADOS > GAMBADO
GAMBAS > GAMBA
GAMBE *same as* > GAMB
GAMBES > GAMBE
GAMBESON *n* quilted and padded or stuffed leather or cloth garment worn under mail in the Middle Ages and later as a doublet by men and women
GAMBESONS > GAMBESON
GAMBET *n* tattler

GAMBETS > GAMBET
GAMBETTA *n* redshank
GAMBETTAS > GAMBETTA
GAMBIA *same as* > GAMBIER
GAMBIAS > GAMBIA
GAMBIER *n* astringent resinous substance obtained from a rubiaceous tropical Asian woody climbing plant, *Uncaria gambir* (or *U. gambier*)
GAMBIERS > GAMBIER
GAMBIR *same as* > GAMBIER
GAMBIRS > GAMBIR
GAMBIST *n* person who plays the (viola da) gamba
GAMBISTS > GAMBIST
GAMBIT *n* opening line or move intended to secure an advantage ▷ *vb* sacrifice a chess piece, in opening, to gain a better position
GAMBITED > GAMBIT
GAMBITING > GAMBIT
GAMBITS > GAMBIT
GAMBLE *vb* play games of chance to win money ▷ *n* risky undertaking
GAMBLED > GAMBLE
GAMBLER > GAMBLE
GAMBLERS > GAMBLE
GAMBLES > GAMBLE
GAMBLING > GAMBLE
GAMBLINGS > GAMBLE
GAMBO *n* farm cart
GAMBOGE *n* gum resin used as a yellow pigment and purgative
GAMBOGES > GAMBOGE
GAMBOGIAN > GAMBOGE
GAMBOGIC > GAMBOGE
GAMBOL *vb* jump about playfully, frolic ▷ *n* frolic
GAMBOLED > GAMBOL
GAMBOLING > GAMBOL
GAMBOLLED > GAMBOL
GAMBOLS > GAMBOL
GAMBOS > GAMBO
GAMBREL *n* hock of a horse or similar animal
GAMBRELS > GAMBREL
GAMBROON *n* type of linen cloth
GAMBROONS > GAMBROON
GAMBS > GAMB
GAMBUSIA *n* small fish that feeds on mosquito larvae
GAMBUSIAS > GAMBUSIA
GAME *n* amusement or pastime ▷ *vb* gamble ▷ *adj* brave
GAMECOCK *n* cock bred and trained for fighting
GAMECOCKS > GAMECOCK
GAMED > GAME
GAMELAN *n* type of percussion orchestra common in the East Indies
GAMELANS > GAMELAN
GAMELIKE > GAME
GAMELY *adv* in a brave or sporting manner
GAMENESS *n* courage or bravery
GAMEPLAY *n* plot of a computer or video game or the way that it is played
GAMEPLAYS > GAMEPLAY
GAMER *n* person who plays computer games
GAMERS > GAMER
GAMES > GAME
GAMESIER > GAMESY
GAMESIEST > GAMESY
GAMESMAN *n* one who practises gamesmanship: the art of winning by cunning practices without actually cheating
GAMESMEN > GAMESMAN
GAMESOME *adj* full of merriment
GAMEST > GAME
GAMESTER *n* gambler
GAMESTERS > GAMESTER
GAMESY *adj* sporty
GAMETAL > GAMETE
GAMETE *n* reproductive cell
GAMETES > GAMETE
GAMETIC > GAMETE
GAMEY *adj* having the smell or flavour of game
GAMIC *adj* (esp of reproduction) requiring the fusion of gametes
GAMIER > GAMEY
GAMIEST > GAMEY
GAMILY > GAMEY
GAMIN *n* street urchin
GAMINE *n* slim boyish young woman
GAMINERIE *n* impish behaviour
GAMINES > GAMINE
GAMINESS > GAMEY
GAMING *n* gambling
GAMINGS > GAMING
GAMINS > GAMIN
GAMMA *n* third letter of the Greek alphabet
GAMMADIA > GAMMADION
GAMMADION *n* decorative figure composed of a number of Greek capital gammas, esp radiating from a centre, as in a swastika
GAMMAS > GAMMA
GAMMAT *n* derogatory term for a Cape Coloured person
GAMMATIA > GAMMATION
GAMMATION *same as* > GAMMADION
GAMMATS > GAMMAT
GAMME *n* musical scale
GAMMED > GAM
GAMMER *n* dialect word for an old woman: now chiefly humorous or contemptuous
GAMMERS > GAMMER
GAMMES > GAMME
GAMMIER > GAMMY
GAMMIEST > GAMMY
GAMMING > GAM
GAMMOCK *vb* clown around
GAMMOCKED > GAMMOCK
GAMMOCKS > GAMMOCK
GAMMON *n* cured or smoked ham ▷ *vb* score a double victory in backgammon over
GAMMONED > GAMMON
GAMMONER > GAMMON
GAMMONERS > GAMMON
GAMMONING > GAMMON
GAMMONS > GAMMON
GAMMY *adj* (of the leg) lame
GAMODEME *n* isolated breeding population
GAMODEMES > GAMODEME
GAMONE *n* any chemical substance secreted by a gamete that attracts another gamete during sexual reproduction
GAMONES > GAMONE
GAMP *n* umbrella
GAMPISH *adj* bulging
GAMPS > GAMP
GAMS > GAM
GAMUT *n* whole range or scale (of music, emotions, etc)
GAMUTS > GAMUT
GAMY *same as* > GAMEY
GAMYNESS > GAMY
GAN *vb* go
GANACHE *n* rich icing or filling made of chocolate and cream
GANACHES > GANACHE
GANCH *vb* impale
GANCHED > GANCH
GANCHES > GANCH
GANCHING > GANCH
GANDER *n* male goose ▷ *vb* look
GANDERED > GANDER
GANDERING > GANDER
GANDERISM > GANDER
GANDERS > GANDER
GANDY *adj* as in *gandy dancer* railway track maintenance worker
GANE > GANGUE
GANEF *n* unscrupulous opportunist who stoops to sharp practice
GANEFS > GANEF
GANEV *same as* > GANEF
GANEVS > GANEV
GANG *n* (criminal) group ▷ *vb* become or act as a gang
GANGBANG *n* sexual intercourse between one woman and several men one after the other, esp against her will ▷ *vb* force (a woman) to take part in a gangbang
GANGBANGS > GANGBANG
GANGBOARD *n* gangway
GANGED > GANG
GANGER *n* foreman of a gang of labourers
GANGERS > GANGER
GANGING > GANG
GANGINGS > GANG
GANGLAND *n* criminal underworld
GANGLANDS > GANGLAND
GANGLIA > GANGLION
GANGLIAL > GANGLION
GANGLIAR > GANGLION
GANGLIATE *vb* form a ganglion
GANGLIER > GANGLY
GANGLIEST > GANGLY
GANGLING *adj* lanky and awkward
GANGLION *n* group of nerve cells
GANGLIONS > GANGLION
GANGLY *same as* > GANGLING
GANGPLANK *n* portable bridge for boarding or leaving a ship
GANGPLOW *n* plough designed to produce parallel furrows
GANGPLOWS > GANGPLOW
GANGREL *n* wandering beggar
GANGRELS > GANGREL
GANGRENE *n* decay of body tissue as a result of disease or injury ▷ *vb* become or cause to become affected with gangrene
GANGRENED > GANGRENE
GANGRENES > GANGRENE
GANGS > GANG
GANGSHAG *vb* participate in group sex with
GANGSHAGS > GANGSHAG
GANGSMAN *n* foreman
GANGSMEN > GANGSMAN
GANGSTA *n* member of a street gang
GANGSTAS > GANGSTA
GANGSTER *n* member of a criminal gang
GANGSTERS > GANGSTER
GANGUE *n* valueless material in an ore
GANGUES > GANGUE
GANGWAY *same as* > GANGPLANK
GANGWAYS > GANGWAY
GANISTER *n* highly refractory siliceous sedimentary rock occurring beneath coal seams: used for lining furnaces
GANISTERS > GANISTER
GANJA *n* highly potent form of cannabis, usually used for smoking
GANJAH *same as* > GANJA
GANJAHS > GANJAH
GANJAS > GANJA
GANNED > GAN
GANNET *n* large sea bird
GANNETRY *n* gannets' breeding-place
GANNETS > GANNET
GANNING > GAN
GANNISTER *same as* > GANISTER
GANOF *same as* > GANEF
GANOFS > GANOF

GANOID *adj* (of the scales of certain fishes) consisting of an inner bony layer covered with an enamel-like substance ▷ *n* ganoid fish
GANOIDS > GANOID
GANOIN *n* substance of which the outer layer of fish scales is composed
GANOINE *same as* > GANOIN
GANOINES > GANOINE
GANOINS > GANOIN
GANS > GAN
GANSEY *n* jersey or pullover
GANSEYS > GANSEY
GANT *vb* yawn
GANTED > GANT
GANTELOPE *same as* > GAUNTLET
GANTING > GANT
GANTLET *n* section of a railway where two tracks overlap ▷ *vb* make railway tracks form a gantlet
GANTLETED > GANTLET
GANTLETS > GANTLET
GANTLINE *n* line rove through a sheave for hoisting men or gear
GANTLINES > GANTLINE
GANTLOPE *same as* > GAUNTLET
GANTLOPES > GANTLOPE
GANTRIES > GANTRY
GANTRY *n* structure supporting something such as a crane or rocket
GANTS > GANT
GANYMEDE *n* catamite
GANYMEDES > GANYMEDE
GAOL *same as* > JAIL
GAOLBIRD *n* person who is or has been confined to gaol, esp repeatedly
GAOLBIRDS > GAOLBIRD
GAOLBREAK *n* escape from gaol
GAOLED > GAOL
GAOLER > GAOL
GAOLERESS *n* female gaoler
GAOLERS > GAOL
GAOLING > GAOL
GAOLLESS > GAOL
GAOLS > GAOL
GAP *n* break or opening
GAPE *vb* stare in wonder ▷ *n* act of gaping
GAPED > GAPE
GAPER *n* person or thing that gapes
GAPERS > GAPER
GAPES *n* disease of young domestic fowl, characterized by gaping or gasping for breath and caused by gapeworms
GAPESEED *n* person who stares, mouth agape, at something
GAPESEEDS > GAPESEED
GAPEWORM *n* parasitic nematode worm, *Syngamus trachea*, that lives in the trachea of birds
GAPEWORMS > GAPEWORM
GAPING *adj* wide open ▷ *n* state of having a gaping mouth
GAPINGLY > GAPING
GAPINGS > GAPING
GAPLESS > GAP
GAPO *n* forest near a river, regularly flooded in the rainy season
GAPOS > GAPO
GAPOSIS *n* gap between closed fastenings on a garment
GAPOSISES > GAPOSIS
GAPPED > GAP
GAPPER *n* in British English, person taking a year out between school and further education
GAPPERS > GAPPER
GAPPIER > GAP
GAPPIEST > GAP
GAPPING > GAP
GAPPY > GAP
GAPS > GAP
GAPY > GAPES
GAR *same as* > GARPIKE
GARAGE *n* building used to house cars ▷ *vb* put or keep a car in a garage
GARAGED > GARAGE
GARAGEMAN *n* car mechanic
GARAGEMEN > GARAGEMAN
GARAGES > GARAGE
GARAGING *n* accommodation for housing a motor vehicle
GARAGINGS > GARAGING
GARAGIST *n* person who runs a garage
GARAGISTE *n* small-scale wine-maker
GARAGISTS > GARAGIST
GARB *n* clothes ▷ *vb* clothe
GARBAGE *n* rubbish
GARBAGES > GARBAGE
GARBAGEY > GARBAGE
GARBAGY > GARBAGE
GARBANZO *another name for* > CHICKPEA
GARBANZOS > GARBANZO
GARBE *n* in heraldry, a wheat-sheaf
GARBED > GARB
GARBES > GARBE
GARBING > GARB
GARBLE *vb* jumble (a story, quotation, etc), esp unintentionally ▷ *n* act of garbling
GARBLED *adj* (of a story etc) jumbled and confused
GARBLER > GARBLE
GARBLERS > GARBLE
GARBLES > GARBLE
GARBLESS > GARB
GARBLING > GARBLE
GARBLINGS > GARBLE
GARBO *n* dustman
GARBOARD *n* bottommost plank of a vessel's hull
GARBOARDS > GARBOARD
GARBOIL *n* confusion or disturbance
GARBOILS > GARBOIL
GARBOLOGY *n* study of the contents of domestic dustbins to analyse the consumption patterns of households
GARBOS > GARBO
GARBS > GARB
GARBURE *n* thick soup from Bearn in France
GARBURES > GARBURE
GARCINIA *n* tropical tree
GARCINIAS > GARCINIA
GARCON *n* waiter
GARCONS > GARCON
GARDA *n* member of the police force of the Republic of Ireland
GARDAI > GARDA
GARDANT *same as* > GUARDANT
GARDANTS > GUARDANT
GARDEN *n* piece of land for growing flowers, fruit, or vegetables ▷ *vb* cultivate a garden
GARDENED > GARDEN
GARDENER *n* person who works in or takes care of a garden as an occupation or pastime
GARDENERS > GARDENER
GARDENFUL *n* quantity that will fill a garden
GARDENIA *n* large fragrant white waxy flower
GARDENIAS > GARDENIA
GARDENING *n* planning and cultivation of a garden
GARDENS > GARDEN
GARDEROBE *n* wardrobe or the contents of a wardrobe
GARDYLOO *n* act of throwing slops from a window
GARDYLOOS > GARDYLOO
GARE *n* filth
GAREFOWL *n* great auk
GAREFOWLS > GAREFOWL
GARFISH *same as* > GARPIKE
GARFISHES > GARFISH
GARGANEY *n* small Eurasian duck, closely related to the mallard
GARGANEYS > GARGANEY
GARGANTUA *n* monster in Japanese film
GARGARISE *vb* gargle
GARGARISM *n* gargle
GARGARIZE *same as* > GARGARISE
GARGET *n* inflammation of the mammary gland of domestic animals, esp cattle
GARGETS > GARGET
GARGETY > GARGET
GARGLE *vb* wash the throat with (a liquid) by breathing out slowly through the liquid ▷ *n* liquid used for gargling
GARGLED > GARGLE
GARGLER > GARGLE
GARGLERS > GARGLE
GARGLES > GARGLE
GARGLING > GARGLE
GARGOYLE *n* waterspout carved in the form of a grotesque face, esp on a church ▷ *vb* provide with gargoyles
GARGOYLED > GARGOYLE
GARGOYLES > GARGOYLE
GARI *n* thinly sliced pickled ginger, often served with sushi
GARIAL *same as* > GAVIAL
GARIALS > GARIAL
GARIBALDI *n* woman's loose blouse with long sleeves popular in the 1860s, copied from the red flannel shirt worn by Garibaldi's soldiers
GARIGUE *n* open shrubby vegetation of dry Mediterranean regions, consisting of spiny or aromatic dwarf shrubs interspersed with colourful ephemeral species
GARIGUES > GARIGUE
GARIS > GARI
GARISH *adj* crudely bright or colourful ▷ *vb* heal
GARISHED > GARISH
GARISHES > GARISH
GARISHING > GARISH
GARISHLY > GARISH
GARJAN *same as* > GURJUN
GARJANS > GARJAN
GARLAND *n* wreath of flowers worn or hung as a decoration ▷ *vb* decorate with garlands
GARLANDED > GARLAND
GARLANDRY *n* collective term for garlands
GARLANDS > GARLAND
GARLIC *n* pungent bulb of a plant of the onion family, used in cooking
GARLICKED *adj* flavoured with garlic
GARLICKY *adj* containing or resembling the taste or odour of garlic
GARLICS > GARLIC
GARMENT *n* article of clothing ▷ *vb* cover or clothe
GARMENTED > GARMENT
GARMENTS > GARMENT
GARNER *vb* collect or store ▷ *n* place for storage or safekeeping
GARNERED > GARNER
GARNERING > GARNER
GARNERS > GARNER
GARNET *n* red semiprecious stone
GARNETS > GARNET
GARNI *adj* garnished
GARNISH *vb* decorate (food

▷ *n* decoration for food
GARNISHED > GARNISH
GARNISHEE *n* person upon whom a notice of warning has been served ▷ *vb* attach (a debt or other property) by a notice of warning
GARNISHER > GARNISH
GARNISHES > GARNISH
GARNISHRY *n* decoration
GARNITURE *n* decoration or embellishment
GAROTE *same as* > GARROTTE
GAROTED > GAROTE
GAROTES > GAROTE
GAROTING > GAROTE
GAROTTE *same as* > GARROTTE
GAROTTED > GAROTTE
GAROTTER > GAROTTE
GAROTTERS > GAROTTE
GAROTTES > GAROTTE
GAROTTING > GAROTTE
GAROUPA *in Chinese and SE Asian cookery, another name for* > GROPER
GAROUPAS > GAROUPA
GARPIKE *n* any primitive freshwater elongated bony fish of the genus *Lepisosteus*, of North and Central America, having very long toothed jaws and a body covering of thick scales
GARPIKES > GARPIKE
GARRAN *same as* > GARRON
GARRANS > GARRAN
GARRE *vb* compel
GARRED > GAR
GARRES > GARRE
GARRET *n* attic in a house
GARRETED *adj* living in a garret
GARRETEER *n* person who lives in a garret
GARRETS > GARRET
GARRIGUE *same as* > GARIGUE
GARRIGUES > GARRIGUE
GARRING > GAR
GARRISON *n* troops stationed in a town or fort ▷ *vb* station troops in
GARRISONS > GARRISON
GARRON *n* small sturdy pony bred and used chiefly in Scotland and Ireland
GARRONS > GARRON
GARROT *n* goldeneye duck
GARROTE *same as* > GARROTTE
GARROTED > GARROTE
GARROTER > GARROTE
GARROTERS > GARROTE
GARROTES > GARROTE
GARROTING > GARROTE
GARROTS > GARROT
GARROTTE *n* Spanish method of execution by strangling ▷ *vb* kill by this method
GARROTTED > GARROTTE
GARROTTER > GARROTTE
GARROTTES > GARROTTE
GARRULITY > GARRULOUS
GARRULOUS *adj* talkative
GARRYA *n* any ornamental catkin-bearing evergreen shrub of the North American genus *Garrya*: family *Garryaceae*
GARRYAS > GARRYA
GARRYOWEN *n* (in rugby union) high kick forwards followed by a charge to the place where the ball lands
GARS > GAR
GART *vb* compel
GARTER *n* band worn round the leg to hold up a sock or stocking ▷ *vb* secure with a garter
GARTERED > GARTER
GARTERING > GARTER
GARTERS > GARTER
GARTH *n* courtyard surrounded by a cloister
GARTHS > GARTH
GARUDA *n* Hindu god
GARUDAS > GARUDA
GARUM *n* fermented fish sauce
GARUMS > GARUM
GARVEY *n* small flat-bottomed yacht
GARVEYS > GARVEY
GARVIE *n* sprat
GARVIES > GARVIE
GARVOCK *n* sprat
GARVOCKS > GARVOCK
GAS *n* airlike substance that is not liquid or solid ▷ *vb* poison or render unconscious with gas
GASAHOL *n* mixture of petrol and alcohol used as fuel
GASAHOLS > GASAHOL
GASALIER *same as* > GASOLIER
GASALIERS > GASALIER
GASBAG *n* person who talks too much ▷ *vb* talk in a voluble way, esp about unimportant matters
GASBAGGED > GASBAG
GASBAGS > GASBAG
GASCON *n* boaster
GASCONADE *n* boastful talk, bragging, or bluster ▷ *vb* boast, brag, or bluster
GASCONISM > GASCON
GASCONS > GASCON
GASEITIES > GASEITY
GASEITY *n* state of being gaseous
GASELIER *same as* > GASOLIER
GASELIERS > GASELIER
GASEOUS *adj* of or like gas
GASES > GAS
GASFIELD *n* area in which natural gas is found underground
GASFIELDS > GASFIELD
GASH *vb* make a long deep cut in ▷ *n* long deep cut ▷ *adj* surplus to requirements ▷ *adj* witty
GASHED > GASH
GASHER > GASH
GASHES > GASH
GASHEST > GASH
GASHFUL *adj* full of gashes
GASHING > GASH
GASHLY *adv* wittily
GASHOLDER *n* large tank for storing gas
GASHOUSE *n* gasworks
GASHOUSES > GASHOUSE
GASIFIED > GASIFY
GASIFIER > GASIFY
GASIFIERS > GASIFY
GASIFIES > GASIFY
GASIFORM *adj* in a gaseous form
GASIFY *vb* change into a gas
GASIFYING > GASIFY
GASKET *n* piece of rubber etc placed between the faces of a metal joint to act as a seal
GASKETS > GASKET
GASKIN *n* lower part of a horse's thigh, between the hock and the stifle
GASKING *same as* > GASKET
GASKINGS > GASKING
GASKINS > GASKIN
GASLESS > GAS
GASLIGHT *n* lamp in which light is produced by burning gas
GASLIGHTS > GASLIGHT
GASLIT *adj* lit by gas
GASMAN *n* man employed to read household gas meters and install or repair gas fittings, etc
GASMEN > GASMAN
GASOGENE *n* siphon bottle
GASOGENES > GASOGENE
GASOHOL *n* mixture of 80% or 90% petrol with 20% or 10% ethyl alcohol, for use as a fuel in internal-combustion engines
GASOHOLS > GASOHOL
GASOLENE *same as* > GASOLINE
GASOLENES > GASOLENE
GASOLIER *n* branched hanging fitting for gaslights
GASOLIERS > GASOLIER
GASOLINE *n* petrol
GASOLINES > GASOLINE
GASOLINIC > GASOLINE
GASOMETER *same as* > GASHOLDER
GASOMETRY *n* measurement of quantities of gases
GASP *vb* draw in breath sharply or with difficulty ▷ *n* convulsive intake of breath
GASPED > GASP
GASPER *n* person who gasps
GASPEREAU *another name for* > ALEWIFE
GASPERS > GASPER
GASPIER > GASP
GASPIEST > GASP
GASPINESS > GASP
GASPING > GASP
GASPINGLY > GASP
GASPINGS > GASP
GASPS > GASP
GASPY > GASP
GASSED > GAS
GASSER *n* drilling or well that yields natural gas
GASSERS > GASSER
GASSES > GAS
GASSIER > GASSY
GASSIEST > GASSY
GASSILY > GASSY
GASSINESS > GASSY
GASSING > GAS
GASSINGS > GAS
GASSY *adj* filled with gas
GAST *vb* frighten
GASTED > GAST
GASTER > GAST
GASTERS > GAST
GASTFULL *adj* dismal
GASTIGHT *adj* not allowing gas to enter or escape
GASTING > GAST
GASTNESS *n* dread
GASTNESSE *same as* > GASTNESS
GASTRAEA *n* hypothetical primeval form posited by Haeckel
GASTRAEAS > GASTRAEA
GASTRAEUM *n* underside of the body
GASTRAL *adj* relating to the stomach
GASTREA *same as* > GASTRAEA
GASTREAS > GASTREAS
GASTRIC *adj* of the stomach
GASTRIN *n* polypeptide hormone secreted by the stomach: stimulates secretion of gastric juice
GASTRINS > GASTRIN
GASTRITIC > GASTRITIS
GASTRITIS *n* inflammation of the stomach lining
GASTROPOD *n* mollusc, such as a snail, with a single flattened muscular foot ▷ *adj* of, relating to, or belonging to the *Gastropoda*
GASTRULA *n* saclike animal embryo consisting of three layers of cells (see ECTODERM, MESODERM, and ENDODERM) surrounding a central cavity (archenteron) with a small opening (blastopore) to the exterior
GASTRULAE > GASTRULA

GASTRULAR > GASTRULA
GASTRULAS > GASTRULA
GASTS > GAST
GASWORKS *n* plant where coal gas is made
GAT *n* pistol or revolver
GATE *n* movable barrier, usu hinged, in a wall or fence ▷ *vb* provide with a gate or gates
GATEAU *n* rich elaborate cake
GATEAUS > GATEAU
GATEAUX > GATEAU
GATECRASH *vb* gain entry to (a party, concert, etc) without invitation or payment
GATED > GATE
GATEFOLD *n* oversize page in a book or magazine that is folded in
GATEFOLDS > GATEFOLD
GATEHOUSE *n* building at or above a gateway
GATELEG *adj* (of a table) with one or two drop leaves that are supported when in use by a hinged leg swung out from the frame
GATELESS > GATE
GATELIKE > GATE
GATEMAN *n* gatekeeper
GATEMEN > GATEMAN
GATEPOST *n* post on which a gate is hung
GATEPOSTS > GATEPOST
GATER *variant of* > GATOR
GATERS > GATER
GATES > GATE
GATEWAY *n* entrance with a gate
GATEWAYS > GATEWAY
GATH *n* (in Indian music) second section of a raga
GATHER *vb* assemble ▷ *n* act of gathering
GATHERED > GATHER
GATHERER > GATHER
GATHERERS > GATHER
GATHERING *n* assembly
GATHERS > GATHER
GATHS > GATH
GATING > GATE
GATINGS > GATE
GATOR *shortened form of* > ALLIGATOR
GATORS > GATOR
GATS > GAT
GATVOL *adj* in South African English, fed up
GAU *n* district set up by the Nazi Party during the Third Reich
GAUCHE *adj* socially awkward
GAUCHELY > GAUCHE
GAUCHER > GAUCHE
GAUCHERIE *n* quality of being gauche
GAUCHESCO *adj* relating to the folk traditions of the gauchos
GAUCHEST > GAUCHE
GAUCHO *n* S American cowboy
GAUCHOS > GAUCHO
GAUCIE *variant of* > GAUCY
GAUCIER > GAUCY
GAUCIEST > GAUCY
GAUCY *adj* plump or jolly
GAUD *n* article of cheap finery ▷ *vb* decorate gaudily
GAUDEAMUS *n* first word of a traditional graduation song, hence the song itself
GAUDED > GAUD
GAUDERIES > GAUDERY
GAUDERY *n* cheap finery or display
GAUDGIE *same as* > GADGIE
GAUDGIES > GADGIE
GAUDIER > GAUDY
GAUDIES > GAUDY
GAUDIEST > GAUDY
GAUDILY > GAUDY
GAUDINESS > GAUDY
GAUDING > GAUD
GAUDS > GAUD
GAUDY *adj* vulgarly bright or colourful ▷ *n* celebratory festival or feast held at some schools and colleges
GAUFER *n* wafer
GAUFERS > GAUFER
GAUFFER *same as* > GOFFER
GAUFFERED > GAUFFER
GAUFFERS > GAUFFER
GAUFRE *same as* > GAUFER
GAUFRES > GAUFRE
GAUGE *vb* estimate or judge ▷ *n* measuring instrument ▷ *adj* (of a pressure measurement) measured on a pressure gauge that registers zero at atmospheric pressure
GAUGEABLE > GAUGE
GAUGEABLY > GAUGE
GAUGED > GAUGE
GAUGER *n* person or thing that gauges
GAUGERS > GAUGER
GAUGES > GAUGE
GAUGING > GAUGE
GAUGINGS > GAUGE
GAUJE *same as* > GADGIE
GAUJES > GAUJE
GAULEITER *n* person in a position of authority who behaves in an overbearing authoritarian manner
GAULT *n* stiff compact clay or thick heavy clayey soil
GAULTER *n* person who digs gault
GAULTERS > GAULTER
GAULTS > GAULT
GAUM *vb* understand
GAUMED > GAUM
GAUMIER > GAUMY
GAUMIEST > GAUMY
GAUMING > GAUM
GAUMLESS *variant spelling of* > GORMLESS
GAUMS > GAUM
GAUMY *adj* clogged
GAUN > GO
GAUNCH *same as* > GANCH
GAUNCHED > GAUNCH
GAUNCHES > GAUNCH
GAUNCHING > GAUNCH
GAUNT *adj* lean and haggard ▷ *vb* yawn
GAUNTED > GAUNT
GAUNTER > GAUNT
GAUNTEST > GAUNT
GAUNTING > GAUNT
GAUNTLET *n* heavy glove with a long cuff ▷ *vb* run (or cause to run) the gauntlet
GAUNTLETS > GAUNTLET
GAUNTLY > GAUNT
GAUNTNESS > GAUNT
GAUNTREE *same as* > GANTRY
GAUNTREES > GAUNTREE
GAUNTRIES > GAUNTRY
GAUNTRY *same as* > GANTRY
GAUNTS > GAUNT
GAUP *same as* > GAWP
GAUPED > GAUP
GAUPER > GAUP
GAUPERS > GAUP
GAUPING > GAUP
GAUPS > GAUP
GAUPUS *same as* > GAWPUS
GAUPUSES > GAUPUS
GAUR *n* large wild member of the cattle tribe, *Bos gaurus*, inhabiting mountainous regions of S Asia
GAURS > GAUR
GAUS > GAU
GAUSS *n* cgs unit of magnetic flux density
GAUSSES > GAUSS
GAUSSIAN *adj* of or relating to the principles established by Karl Friedrich Gauss, the German mathematician
GAUZE *n* transparent loosely-woven fabric, often used for surgical dressings
GAUZELIKE > GAUZE
GAUZES > GAUZE
GAUZIER > GAUZY
GAUZIEST > GAUZY
GAUZILY > GAUZY
GAUZINESS > GAUZY
GAUZY *adj* resembling gauze
GAVAGE *n* forced feeding by means of a tube inserted into the stomach through the mouth
GAVAGES > GAVAGE
GAVE > GIVE
GAVEL *n* small hammer banged on a table by a judge, auctioneer, or chairman to call for attention ▷ *vb* use a gavel to restore order
GAVELED > GAVEL
GAVELING > GAVEL
GAVELKIND *n* former system of land tenure peculiar to Kent based on the payment of rent to the lord instead of the performance of services by the tenant
GAVELLED > GAVEL
GAVELLING > GAVEL
GAVELMAN *n* gavelkind tenant
GAVELMEN > GAVELMAN
GAVELOCK *n* iron crowbar
GAVELOCKS > GAVELOCK
GAVELS > GAVEL
GAVIAL as in *false gavial* small crocodile
GAVIALOID *adj* of or like gavials
GAVIALS > GAVIAL
GAVOT *same as* > GAVOTTE
GAVOTS > GAVOT
GAVOTTE *n* old formal dance ▷ *vb* dance a gavotte
GAVOTTED > GAVOTTE
GAVOTTES > GAVOTTE
GAVOTTING > GAVOTTE
GAWCIER > GAWCY
GAWCIEST > GAWCY
GAWCY *same as* > GAUCY
GAWD *same as* > GAUD
GAWDS > GAWD
GAWK *vb* stare stupidly ▷ *n* clumsy awkward person
GAWKED > GAWK
GAWKER > GAWK
GAWKERS > GAWK
GAWKIER > GAWKY
GAWKIES > GAWKY
GAWKIEST > GAWKY
GAWKIHOOD *n* state of being gawky
GAWKILY > GAWKY
GAWKINESS > GAWKY
GAWKING > GAWK
GAWKISH *same as* > GAWKY
GAWKISHLY > GAWKY
GAWKS > GAWK
GAWKY *adj* clumsy or awkward ▷ *n* simpleton
GAWP *vb* stare stupidly
GAWPED > GAWP
GAWPER > GAWP
GAWPERS > GAWP
GAWPING > GAWP
GAWPS > GAWP
GAWPUS *n* silly person
GAWPUSES > GAWPUS
GAWSIE *same as* > GAUCY
GAWSIER > GAWSIE
GAWSIEST > GAWSIE
GAWSY *same as* > GAUCY
GAY *adj* homosexual ▷ *n* homosexual
GAYAL *n* ox of India and Myanmar, *Bibos frontalis*, possibly a semidomesticated variety of gaur, black or brown with white stockings
GAYALS > GAYAL
GAYDAR *n* supposed ability of a homosexual person to determine whether

or not another person is homosexual
GAYDARS > GAYDAR
GAYER > GAY
GAYEST > GAY
GAYETIES > GAYETY
GAYETY *same as* > GAIETY
GAYLY > GAY
GAYNESS > GAY
GAYNESSES > GAY
GAYS > GAY
GAYSOME *adj* full of merriment
GAYWINGS *n* flowering wintergreen
GAZABO *n* fellow or companion
GAZABOES > GAZABO
GAZABOS > GAZABO
GAZAL *same as* > GHAZAL
GAZALS > GAZAL
GAZANIA *n* any plant of the S African genus *Gazania*, grown for their rayed flowers in variegated colours
GAZANIAS > GAZANIA
GAZAR *n* type of silk cloth
GAZARS > GAZAR
GAZE *vb* look fixedly ▷ *n* fixed look
GAZEBO *n* summerhouse with a good view
GAZEBOES > GAZEBO
GAZEBOS > GAZEBO
GAZED > GAZE
GAZEFUL *adj* gazing
GAZEHOUND *n* hound such as a greyhound that hunts by sight rather than by scent
GAZELLE *n* small graceful antelope
GAZELLES > GAZELLE
GAZEMENT *n* view
GAZEMENTS > GAZEMENT
GAZER > GAZE
GAZERS > GAZE
GAZES > GAZE
GAZETTE *n* official publication containing announcements ▷ *vb* announce or report (facts or an event) in a gazette
GAZETTED > GAZETTE
GAZETTEER *n* (part of) a book that lists and describes places ▷ *vb* list in a gazetteer
GAZETTES > GAZETTE
GAZETTING > GAZETTE
GAZIER > GAZY
GAZIEST > GAZY
GAZILLION *n* in informal English, an extremely large but unspecified number, quantity, or amount
GAZING > GAZE
GAZINGS > GAZE
GAZOGENE *same as* > GASOGENE
GAZOGENES > GAZOGENE
GAZON *n* sod used to cover a parapet in a fortification
GAZONS > GAZON
GAZOO *n* kazoo
GAZOOKA *same as* > GAZOO
GAZOOKAS > GAZOOKA
GAZOON *same as* > GAZON
GAZOONS > GAZOON
GAZOOS > GAZOO
GAZPACHO *n* Spanish soup made from tomatoes, peppers, etc, and served cold
GAZPACHOS > GAZPACHO
GAZUMP *vb* raise the price of a property after verbally agreeing it with (a prospective buyer) ▷ *n* act or an instance of gazumping
GAZUMPED > GAZUMP
GAZUMPER > GAZUMP
GAZUMPERS > GAZUMP
GAZUMPING > GAZUMP
GAZUMPS > GAZUMP
GAZUNDER *vb* reduce an offer on a property immediately before exchanging contracts having earlier agreed a higher price with the seller ▷ *n* act or instance of gazundering
GAZUNDERS > GAZUNDER
GAZY *adj* prone to gazing
GEAL *vb* congeal
GEALED > GEAL
GEALING > GEAL
GEALOUS *Spenserian spelling of* > JEALOUS
GEALOUSY *Spenserian spelling of* > JEALOUSY
GEALS > GEAL
GEAN *n* white-flowered rosaceous tree, *Prunus avium*, of Europe, W Asia, and N Africa, the ancestor of the cultivated sweet cherries
GEANS > GEAN
GEAR *n* set of toothed wheels connecting with another or with a rack to change the direction or speed of transmitted motion ▷ *vb* prepare or organize for something
GEARBOX *n* case enclosing a set of gears in a motor vehicle
GEARBOXES > GEARBOX
GEARCASE *n* protective casing for gears
GEARCASES > GEARCASE
GEARE *Spenserian spelling of* > JEER
GEARED > GEAR
GEARES > GEARE
GEARHEAD *n* part in engine gear system
GEARHEADS > GEARHEAD
GEARING *n* system of gears designed to transmit motion
GEARINGS > GEARING
GEARLESS > GEAR
GEARS > GEAR
GEARSHIFT *n* lever used to move gearwheels relative to each other, esp in a motor vehicle
GEARWHEEL *n* one of the toothed wheels in the gears of a motor vehicle
GEASON *adj* wonderful
GEAT *n* in casting, the channel through which molten metal runs into a mould
GEATS > GEAT
GEBUR *n* tenant farmer
GEBURS > GEBUR
GECK *vb* beguile
GECKED > GECK
GECKING > GECK
GECKO *n* small tropical lizard
GECKOES > GECKO
GECKOS > GECKO
GECKS > GECK
GED *Scots word for* > PIKE
GEDACT *n* flutelike stopped metal diapason organ pipe
GEDACTS > GEDACT
GEDDIT *interj* exclamation meaning *do you understand it?*
GEDECKT *same as* > GEDACT
GEDECKTS > GEDECKT
GEDS > GED
GEE *interj* mild exclamation of surprise, admiration, etc ▷ *vb* move (an animal, esp a horse) ahead
GEEBAG *n* in Irish slang, a disagreeable woman
GEEBAGS > GEEBAG
GEEBUNG *n* Australian tree or shrub with an edible but tasteless fruit
GEEBUNGS > GEEBUNG
GEECHEE *n* Black person from the southern states of the US
GEECHEES > GEECHEE
GEED > GEE
GEEGAW *same as* > GEWGAW
GEEGAWS > GEEGAW
GEEING > GEE
GEEK *n* boring, unattractive person
GEEKDOM > GEEK
GEEKDOMS > GEEK
GEEKED *adj* highly excited
GEEKIER > GEEK
GEEKIEST > GEEK
GEEKINESS > GEEK
GEEKS > GEEK
GEEKSPEAK *n* slang word for jargon used by geeks, esp computer enthusiasts
GEEKY > GEEK
GEELBEK *n* edible marine fish
GEELBEKS > GEELBEK
GEEP *n* cross between a goat and a sheep
GEEPOUND *another name for* > SLUG
GEEPOUNDS > SLUG
GEEPS > GEEP
GEES > GEE
GEESE > GOOSE
GEEST *n* area of sandy heathland in N Germany and adjacent areas
GEESTS > GEEST
GEEZ *interj* expression of surprise
GEEZAH *variant spelling of* > GEEZER
GEEZAHS > GEEZAH
GEEZER *n* man
GEEZERS > GEEZER
GEFILTE as in *gefilte fish* dish of fish stuffed with various ingredients
GEFUFFLE *same as* > KERFUFFLE
GEFUFFLED > GEFUFFLE
GEFUFFLES > GEFUFFLE
GEFULLTE as in *gefullte fish* dish of fish stuffed with various ingredients
GEGGIE *Scottish, esp Glaswegian, slang word for the* > MOUTH
GEGGIES > GEGGIE
GEHLENITE *n* green mineral consisting of calcium aluminium silicate in tetragonal crystalline form
GEISHA *n* (in Japan) professional female companion for men
GEISHAS > GEISHA
GEIST *n* spirit
GEISTS > GEIST
GEIT *n* border on clothing
GEITS > GEIT
GEL *n* jelly-like substance, esp one used to secure a hairstyle ▷ *vb* form a gel
GELABLE *adj* capable of forming a gel
GELADA *n* NE African baboon, *Theropithecus gelada*, with dark brown hair forming a mane over the shoulders, a bare red chest, and a ridge muzzle: family *Cercopithecidae*
GELADAS > GELADA
GELANDE as in *gelande jump* jump made in downhill skiing
GELANT *same as* > GELLANT
GELANTS > GELANT
GELASTIC *adj* relating to laughter
GELATE *vb* form a gel
GELATED > GELATE
GELATES > GELATE
GELATI *n* layered dessert of frozen custard and ice cream
GELATIN *same as* > GELATINE
GELATINE *n* substance made by boiling animal bones
GELATINES > GELATINE
GELATING > GELATE

GELATINS > GELATIN
GELATION *n* act or process of freezing a liquid
GELATIONS > GELATION
GELATIS > GELATI
GELATO *n* Italian frozen dessert, similar to ice cream
GELATOS > GELATO
GELCAP *n* dose of medicine enclosed in a soluble case of gelatine
GELCAPS > GELCAP
GELD *vb* castrate ▷ *n* tax on land levied in late Anglo-Saxon and Norman England
GELDED > GELD
GELDER > GELD
GELDERS > GELD
GELDING > GELD
GELDINGS > GELD
GELDS > GELD
GELEE *n* jelly
GELEES > GELEE
GELID *adj* very cold, icy, or frosty
GELIDER > GELID
GELIDEST > GELID
GELIDITY > GELID
GELIDLY > GELID
GELIDNESS > GELID
GELIGNITE *n* type of dynamite used for blasting
GELLANT *n* compound that forms a solid structure
GELLANTS > GELLANT
GELLED > GEL
GELLIES > GELLY
GELLING > GEL
GELLY *same as* > GELIGNITE
GELOSIES > GELOSY
GELOSY *Spenserian spelling of* > JEALOUSY
GELS > GEL
GELSEMIA > GELSEMIUM
GELSEMINE *n* alkaloid obtained from gelsemium
GELSEMIUM *n* any climbing shrub of the loganiaceous genus *Gelsemium*, of SE Asia and North America, esp the yellow jasmine, having fragrant yellow flowers
GELT > GELD
GELTS > GELD
GEM *n* precious stone or jewel ▷ *vb* set or ornament with gems
GEMATRIA *n* numerology of the Hebrew language and alphabet
GEMATRIAS > GEMATRIA
GEMCLIP *n* paperclip
GEMCLIPS > GEMCLIP
GEMEL *n* in heraldry, parallel bars
GEMELS > GEMEL
GEMFISH *n* Australian food fish with a delicate flavour
GEMFISHES > GEMFISH
GEMINAL *adj* occurring in pairs
GEMINALLY > GEMINAL
GEMINATE *adj* combined in pairs ▷ *vb* arrange or be arranged in pairs
GEMINATED > GEMINATE
GEMINATES > GEMINATE
GEMINI *n* expression of surprise
GEMINIES > GEMINY
GEMINOUS *adj* in pairs
GEMINY *n* pair
GEMLIKE > GEM
GEMMA *n* small asexual reproductive structure in liverworts, mosses, etc, that becomes detached from the parent and develops into a new individual
GEMMAE > GEMMA
GEMMAN *dialect form of* > GENTLEMAN
GEMMATE *adj* (of some plants and animals) having or reproducing by gemmae ▷ *vb* produce or reproduce by gemmae
GEMMATED > GEMMATE
GEMMATES > GEMMATE
GEMMATING > GEMMATE
GEMMATION > GEMMATE
GEMMATIVE *adj* relating to gemmation
GEMMED > GEM
GEMMEN > GEMMAN
GEMMEOUS *adj* gem-like
GEMMERIES > GEMMERY
GEMMERY *n* gems collectively
GEMMIER > GEM
GEMMIEST > GEM
GEMMILY > GEM
GEMMINESS > GEM
GEMMING > GEM
GEMMOLOGY *same as* > GEMOLOGY
GEMMULE *n* cell or mass of cells produced asexually by sponges and developing into a new individual
GEMMULES > GEMMULE
GEMMY > GEM
GEMOLOGY *n* branch of mineralogy that is concerned with gems and gemstones
GEMONY *same as* > JIMINY
GEMOT *n* (in Anglo-Saxon England) a legal or administrative assembly of a community, such as a shire or hundred
GEMOTE *same as* > GEMOT
GEMOTES > GEMOTE
GEMOTS > GEMOT
GEMS > GEM
GEMSBOK *same as* > ORYX
GEMSBOKS > GEMSBOK
GEMSBUCK > ORYX
GEMSBUCKS > GEMSBUCK
GEMSHORN *n* type of medieval flute
GEMSHORNS > GEMSHORN
GEMSTONE *n* precious or semiprecious stone, esp one which has been cut and polished
GEMSTONES > GEMSTONE
GEMUTLICH *adj* having a feeling or atmosphere of warmth and friendliness
GEN *n* information ▷ *vb* gain information
GENA *n* cheek
GENAL > GENA
GENAPPE *n* smooth worsted yarn used for braid, etc
GENAPPES > GENAPPE
GENAS > GENA
GENDARME *n* member of the French police force
GENDARMES > GENDARME
GENDER *n* state of being male or female ▷ *vb* have sex
GENDERED > GENDER
GENDERING > GENDER
GENDERISE *same as* > GENDERIZE
GENDERIZE *vb* make distinctions according to gender in or among
GENDERS > GENDER
GENE *n* part of a cell which determines inherited characteristics
GENEALOGY *n* (study of) the history and descent of a family or families
GENERA > GENUS
GENERABLE *adj* able to be generated
GENERAL *adj* common or widespread ▷ *n* very senior army officer ▷ *vb* act as a general
GENERALCY *n* rank of general
GENERALE *singular form of* > GENERALIA
GENERALIA *n* generalities
GENERALLY *adv* usually
GENERALS > GENERAL
GENERANT *n* something that generates
GENERANTS > GENERANT
GENERATE *vb* produce or bring into being
GENERATED > GENERATE
GENERATES > GENERATE
GENERATOR *n* machine for converting mechanical energy into electrical energy
GENERIC *adj* of a class, group, or genus ▷ *n* drug, food product, etc that does not have a trademark
GENERICAL *same as* > GENERIC
GENERICS > GENERIC
GENEROUS *adj* free in giving
GENES > GENE
GENESES > GENESIS
GENESIS *n* beginning or origin
GENET *n* any agile catlike viverrine mammal of the genus *Genetta*, inhabiting wooded regions of Africa and S Europe, having an elongated head, thick spotted or blotched fur, and a very long tail
GENETIC *adj* of genes or genetics
GENETICAL *same as* > GENETIC
GENETICS *n* study of heredity and variation in organisms
GENETRIX *n* female progenitor
GENETS > GENET
GENETTE *same as* > GENET
GENETTES > GENETTE
GENEVA *n* gin
GENEVAS > GENEVA
GENIAL *adj* cheerful and friendly
GENIALISE *vb* make genial
GENIALITY > GENIAL
GENIALIZE *same as* > GENIALISE
GENIALLY > GENIAL
GENIC *adj* of or relating to a gene or genes
GENICALLY > GENIC
GENICULAR *adj* of or relating to the knee
GENIE *n* (in fairy tales) servant who appears by magic and grants wishes
GENIES > GENIE
GENII > GENIUS
GENIP *same as* > GENIPAP
GENIPAP *n* evergreen Caribbean rubiaceous tree, *Genipa americana*, with reddish-brown edible orange-like fruits
GENIPAPS > GENIPAP
GENIPS > GENIP
GENISTA *n* any member of the broom family
GENISTAS > GENISTA
GENISTEIN *n* substance found in plants, thought to fight cancer
GENITAL *adj* of the sexual organs or reproduction
GENITALIA *same as* > GENITALS
GENITALIC > GENITALIA
GENITALLY > GENITAL
GENITALS *pl n* external sexual organs
GENITIVAL > GENITIVE
GENITIVE *n* grammatical case indicating possession or association ▷ *adj* denoting a case of nouns, pronouns, and adjectives in inflected languages used to indicate a relation of ownership or association, usually translated by English *of*
GENITIVES > GENITIVE
GENITOR *n* biological father as distinguished from the pater or legal

father
GENITORS > GENITOR
GENITRIX *same as* > GENETRIX
GENITURE *n* birth
GENITURES > GENITURE
GENIUS *n* (person with) exceptional ability in a particular field
GENIUSES > GENIUS
GENIZAH *n* repository (usually in a synagogue) for books and other sacred objects which can no longer be used but which may not be destroyed
GENIZAHS > GENIZAH
GENLOCK *n* generator locking device
GENLOCKS > GENLOCK
GENNAKER *n* type of sail for boats
GENNAKERS > GENNAKER
GENNED > GEN
GENNEL *same as* > GINNEL
GENNELS > GENNEL
GENNET *n* female donkey or ass
GENNETS > GENNET
GENNIES > GENNY
GENNING > GEN
GENNY *same as* > GENOA
GENOA *n* large triangular jib sail, often with a foot that extends as far aft as the clew of the mainsail
GENOAS > GENOA
GENOCIDAL > GENOCIDE
GENOCIDE *n* murder of a race of people
GENOCIDES > GENOCIDE
GENOGRAM *n* expanded family tree
GENOGRAMS > GENOGRAM
GENOISE *n* rich sponge cake
GENOISES > GENOISE
GENOM *same as* > GENOME
GENOME *n* full complement of genetic material within an organism
GENOMES > GENOME
GENOMIC > GENOME
GENOMICS *n* branch of molecular genetics concerned with the study of genomes
GENOMS > GENOM
GENOTYPE *n* genetic constitution of an organism
GENOTYPES > GENOTYPE
GENOTYPIC > GENOTYPE
GENRE *n* style of literary, musical, or artistic work
GENRES > GENRE
GENRO *n* group of highly respected elder statesmen in late 19th- and early 20th-century Japan
GENROS > GENRO
GENS *n* (in ancient Rome) any of a group of aristocratic families, having a common name and claiming descent from a common ancestor in the male line
GENSENG *same as* > GINSENG
GENSENGS > GENSENG
GENT *n* gentleman
GENTEEL *adj* affectedly proper and polite
GENTEELER > GENTEEL
GENTEELLY > GENTEEL
GENTES > GENS
GENTIAN *n* mountain plant with deep blue flowers
GENTIANS > GENTIAN
GENTIER > GENTY
GENTIEST > GENTY
GENTIL *adj* gentle
GENTILE *n* non-Jewish (person) ▷ *adj* denoting an adjective or proper noun used to designate a place or the inhabitants of a place, as *Spanish* and *Spaniard*
GENTILES > GENTILE
GENTILIC *adj* tribal
GENTILISE *vb* live like a gentile
GENTILISH *adj* heathenish
GENTILISM *n* heathenism
GENTILITY *n* noble birth or ancestry
GENTILIZE *same as* > GENTILISE
GENTLE *adj* mild or kindly ▷ *vb* tame or subdue (a horse) ▷ *n* maggot, esp when used as bait in fishing
GENTLED > GENTLE
GENTLEMAN *n* polite well-bred man
GENTLEMEN > GENTLEMAN
GENTLER > GENTLE
GENTLES > GENTLE
GENTLEST > GENTLE
GENTLING > GENTLE
GENTLY > GENTLE
GENTOO *n* grey-backed penguin
GENTOOS > GENTOO
GENTRICE *n* high birth
GENTRICES > GENTRICE
GENTRIES > GENTRY
GENTRIFY *vb* change the character of a neighbourhood by restoring property or introducing amenities that appeal to the middle classes
GENTRY *n* informal, often derogatory term for people just below the nobility in social rank
GENTS *n* men's public toilet
GENTY *adj* neat
GENU *n* any knee-like bend in a structure or part
GENUA > GENU
GENUFLECT *vb* bend the knee as a sign of reverence or deference
GENUINE *adj* not fake, authentic
GENUINELY > GENUINE
GENUS *n* group into which a family of animals or plants is divided
GENUSES > GENUS
GEO *n* (esp in Shetland) a small fjord or gully
GEOBOTANY *n* study of plants in relation to their geological habitat
GEOCARPIC > GEOCARPY
GEOCARPY *n* ripening of fruits below ground, as occurs in the peanut
GEOCORONA *n* outer layer of earth's atmosphere
GEODE *n* cavity, usually lined with crystals, within a rock mass or nodule
GEODES > GEODE
GEODESIC *adj* of the geometry of curved surfaces ▷ *n* shortest line between two points on a curve
GEODESICS > GEODESIC
GEODESIES > GEODESY
GEODESIST > GEODESY
GEODESY *n* study of the shape and size of the earth
GEODETIC *same as* > GEODESIC
GEODETICS *same as* > GEODETIC
GEODIC > GEODE
GEODUCK *n* king clam
GEODUCKS > GEODUCK
GEOFACT *n* rock shaped by natural forces, as opposed to a manmade artefact
GEOFACTS > GEOFACT
GEOGENIES > GEOGENY
GEOGENY *same as* > GEOGONY
GEOGNOSES > GEOGNOSY
GEOGNOSIS *same as* > GEOGNOSY
GEOGNOST > GEOGNOSY
GEOGNOSTS > GEOGNOSY
GEOGNOSY *n* study of the origin and distribution of minerals and rocks in the earth's crust: superseded generally by the term GEOLOGY
GEOGONIC > GEOGONY
GEOGONIES > GEOGONY
GEOGONY *n* science of the earth's formation
GEOGRAPHY *n* study of the earth's physical features, climate, population, etc
GEOID *n* hypothetical surface that corresponds to mean sea level and extends at the same level under the continents
GEOIDAL > GEOID
GEOIDS > GEOID
GEOLATRY *n* worship of the earth
GEOLOGER > GEOLOGY
GEOLOGERS > GEOLOGY
GEOLOGIAN > GEOLOGY
GEOLOGIC > GEOLOGY
GEOLOGIES > GEOLOGY
GEOLOGISE *same as* > GEOLOGIZE
GEOLOGIST > GEOLOGY
GEOLOGIZE *vb* study the geological features of (an area)
GEOLOGY *n* study of the earth's origin, structure, and composition
GEOMANCER > GEOMANCY
GEOMANCY *n* prophecy from the pattern made when a handful of earth is cast down or dots are drawn at random and connected with lines
GEOMANT *n* geomancer
GEOMANTIC > GEOMANCY
GEOMANTS > GEOMANT
GEOMETER *n* person who is practised in or who studies geometry
GEOMETERS > GEOMETER
GEOMETRIC *adj* of geometry
GEOMETRID *n* any moth of the family *Geometridae*, the larvae of which are called measuring worms, inchworms, or loopers ▷ *adj* of, relating to, or belonging to the *Geometridae*
GEOMETRY *n* branch of mathematics dealing with points, lines, curves, and surfaces
GEOMYOID *adj* relating to burrowing rodents of the genus Geomys
GEOPHAGIA *same as* > GEOPHAGY
GEOPHAGY *n* practice of eating earth, clay, chalk, etc, found in some primitive tribes
GEOPHILIC *adj* soil-loving
GEOPHONE *n* device for recording seismic movement
GEOPHONES > GEOPHONE
GEOPHYTE *n* perennial plant that propagates by means of buds below the soil surface
GEOPHYTES > GEOPHYTE
GEOPHYTIC > GEOPHYTE
GEOPONIC *adj* of or relating to agriculture, esp as a science
GEOPONICS *n* science of agriculture
GEOPROBE *n* probing device used for sampling soil
GEOPROBES > GEOPROBE
GEORGETTE *n* fine silky fabric
GEORGIC *adj* agricultural ▷ *n* poem about rural or agricultural life

GEORGICAL *same as* > GEORGIC
GEORGICS > GEORGIC
GEOS > GEO
GEOSPHERE *another name for* > LITHOSPHERE
GEOSTATIC *adj* denoting or relating to the pressure exerted by a mass of rock or a similar substance
GEOTACTIC > GEOTAXIS
GEOTAXES > GEOTAXIS
GEOTAXIS *n* movement of an organism in response to the stimulus of gravity
GEOTHERM *n* line or surface within or on the earth connecting points of equal temperature
GEOTHERMS > GEOTHERM
GEOTROPIC *adj* of geotropism: the response of a plant to the stimulus of gravity
GERAH *n* ancient Hebrew unit of weight
GERAHS > GERAH
GERANIAL *n* *cis-* isomer of citral
GERANIALS > GERANIAL
GERANIOL *n* colourless or pale yellow terpine alcohol with an odour of roses, found in many essential oils: used in perfumery
GERANIOLS > GERANIOL
GERANIUM *n* cultivated plant with red, pink, or white flowers
GERANIUMS > GERANIUM
GERARDIA *n* any plant of the genus Gerardia
GERARDIAS > GERARDIA
GERBE *same as* > GARBE
GERBERA *n* any plant of the perennial genus *Gerbera*, esp the Barberton daisy from S. Africa, *G. jamesonii*, grown, usually as a greenhouse plant, for its large brightly coloured daisy-like flowers: family *Asteraceae*
GERBERAS > GERBERA
GERBES > GARBE
GERBIL *n* burrowing desert rodent of Asia and Africa
GERBILLE *same as* > GERBIL
GERBILLES > GERBILLE
GERBILS > GERBIL
GERE *Spenserian spelling of* > GEAR
GERENT *n* person who rules or manages
GERENTS > GERENT
GERENUK *n* slender E African antelope, *Litocranius walleri*, with a long thin neck and backward-curving horns
GERENUKS > GERENUK
GERES > GEAR
GERFALCON *same as* > GYRFALCON
GERIATRIC *n* derogatory term for old person ▷ *adj* of geriatrics or old people
GERLE *Spenserian spelling of* > GIRL
GERLES > GERLE
GERM *n* microbe, esp one causing disease ▷ *vb* sprout
GERMAIN *same as* > GERMEN
GERMAINE *same as* > GERMEN
GERMAINES > GERMAINE
GERMAINS > GERMAIN
GERMAN *n* dance consisting of complicated figures and changes of partners ▷ *adj* having the same parents as oneself
GERMANDER *n* any of several plants of the genus *Teucrium*
GERMANE *adj* relevant
GERMANELY > GERMANE
GERMANIC *adj* of or containing germanium in the tetravalent state
GERMANISE *same as* > GERMANIZE
GERMANITE *n* mineral consisting of a complex copper arsenic sulphide containing germanium, gallium, iron, zinc, and lead: an ore of germanium and gallium
GERMANIUM *n* brittle grey element that is a semiconductor
GERMANIZE *vb* adopt or cause to adopt German customs, speech, institutions, etc
GERMANOUS *adj* of or containing germanium in the divalent state
GERMANS > GERMAN
GERMED > GERM
GERMEN *n* mass of undifferentiated cells that gives rise to the germ cells
GERMENS > GERMEN
GERMFREE > GERM
GERMICIDE *n* substance that kills germs
GERMIER > GERMY
GERMIEST > GERMY
GERMIN *same as* > GERMEN
GERMINA > GERMEN
GERMINAL *adj* of or in the earliest stage of development
GERMINANT *adj* in the process of germinating
GERMINATE *vb* (cause to) sprout or begin to grow
GERMINESS > GERMY
GERMING > GERM
GERMINS > GERMIN
GERMLIKE > GERM
GERMPLASM *n* plant genetic material
GERMPROOF *adj* protected against the penetration of germs
GERMS > GERM
GERMY *adj* full of germs
GERNE *vb* grin
GERNED > GERNE
GERNES > GERNE
GERNING > GERNE
GERONIMO *interj* shout given by US paratroopers as they jump into battle
GERONTIC *adj* of or relating to the senescence of an organism
GEROPIGA *n* grape syrup used to sweeten inferior port wines
GEROPIGAS > GEROPIGA
GERT *adv* in dialect, great or very big
GERTCHA *interj* get out of here!
GERUND *n* noun formed from a verb
GERUNDIAL > GERUND
GERUNDIVE *n* (in Latin grammar) an adjective formed from a verb, expressing the desirability of the activity denoted by the verb ▷ *adj* of or relating to the gerund or gerundive
GERUNDS > GERUND
GESNERIA *n* any plant of the mostly tuberous-rooted S. American genus *Gesneria*, grown as a greenhouse plant for its large leaves and showy tubular flowers in a range of bright colours: family *Gesneriaceae*
GESNERIAD > GESNERIA
GESNERIAS > GESNERIA
GESSAMINE *another word for* > JASMINE
GESSE *Spenserian spelling of* > GUESS
GESSED > GESS
GESSES > GESS
GESSING > GESS
GESSO *n* plaster used for painting or in sculpture ▷ *vb* apply gesso to
GESSOED > GESSO
GESSOES > GESSO
GEST *n* notable deed or exploit
GESTALT *n* perceptual pattern or structure possessing qualities as a whole that cannot be described merely as a sum of its parts
GESTALTEN > GESTALT
GESTALTS > GESTALT
GESTANT *adj* laden
GESTAPO *n* any secret state police organization
GESTAPOS > GESTAPO
GESTATE *vb* carry (developing young) in the uterus during pregnancy
GESTATED > GESTATE
GESTATES > GESTATE
GESTATING > GESTATE
GESTATION *n* (period of) carrying of young in the womb between conception and birth
GESTATIVE > GESTATION
GESTATORY > GESTATION
GESTE *same as* > GEST
GESTES > GESTE
GESTIC *adj* consisting of gestures
GESTICAL > GESTIC
GESTS > GEST
GESTURAL > GESTURE
GESTURE *n* movement to convey meaning ▷ *vb* gesticulate
GESTURED > GESTURE
GESTURER > GESTURE
GESTURERS > GESTURE
GESTURES > GESTURE
GESTURING > GESTURE
GET *vb* obtain or receive
GETA *n* type of Japanese wooden sandal
GETABLE > GET
GETAS > GETA
GETATABLE *adj* accessible
GETAWAY *n* used in escape
GETAWAYS > GETAWAY
GETS > GET
GETTABLE > GET
GETTER *n* person or thing that gets ▷ *vb* remove (a gas) by the action of a getter
GETTERED > GETTER
GETTERING > GETTER
GETTERS > GETTER
GETTING > GET
GETTINGS > GET
GETUP *n* outfit
GETUPS > GETUP
GEUM *n* any herbaceous plant of the rosaceous genus *Geum*, having compound leaves and red, orange, or white flowers
GEUMS > GEUM
GEWGAW *n* showy but valueless trinket ▷ *adj* showy and valueless
GEWGAWED *adj* decorated gaudily
GEWGAWS > GEWGAW
GEY *adv* extremely ▷ *adj* gallant
GEYAN *adv* somewhat
GEYER > GEY
GEYEST > GEY
GEYSER *n* spring that discharges steam and hot water
GEYSERITE *n* mineral form of hydrated silica resembling opal, deposited from the waters of geysers and hot springs
GEYSERS > GEYSER
GHARIAL *same as* > GAVIAL
GHARIALS > GHARIAL
GHARRI *same as* > GHARRY
GHARRIES > GHARRY

GHARRIS > GHARRI
GHARRY *n* (in India) horse-drawn vehicle available for hire
GHAST *vb* terrify
GHASTED > GHAST
GHASTFUL *adj* dismal
GHASTING > GHAST
GHASTLIER > GHASTLY
GHASTLY *adj* unpleasant ▷ *adv* unhealthily
GHASTNESS *n* dread
GHASTS > GHAST
GHAT *n* (in India) steps leading down to a river
GHATS > GHAT
GHAUT *n* small cleft in a hill through which a rivulet runs down to the sea
GHAUTS > GHAUT
GHAZAL *n* Arabic love poem
GHAZALS > GHAZAL
GHAZEL *same as* > GHAZAL
GHAZELS > GHAZEL
GHAZI *n* Muslim fighter against infidels
GHAZIES > GHAZI
GHAZIS > GHAZI
GHEE *n* (in Indian cookery) clarified butter
GHEES > GHEE
GHERAO *n* form of industrial action in India in which workers imprison their employers on the premises until their demands are met ▷ *vb* trap an employer in his office, to indicate the workforce's discontent
GHERAOED > GHERAO
GHERAOES > GHERAO
GHERAOING > GHERAO
GHERAOS > GHERAO
GHERKIN *n* small pickled cucumber
GHERKINS > GHERKIN
GHESSE *Spenserian spelling of* > GUESS
GHESSED > GHESS
GHESSES > GHESS
GHESSING > GHESS
GHEST > GHESS
GHETTO *n* slum area inhabited by a deprived minority ▷ *vb* ghettoize
GHETTOED > GHETTO
GHETTOES > GHETTO
GHETTOING > GHETTO
GHETTOISE *same as* > GHETTOIZE
GHETTOIZE *vb* confine (someone or something) to a particular area or category
GHETTOS > GHETTO
GHI *same as* > GHEE
GHIBLI *n* fiercely hot wind of North Africa
GHIBLIS > GHIBLI
GHILGAI *same as* > GILGAI
GHILGAIS > GHILGAI
GHILLIE *n* type of tongueless shoe with lacing up the instep, originally worn by the Scots ▷ *vb* act as a g(h)illie
GHILLIED > GHILLIE
GHILLIES > GHILLIE
GHILLYING > GHILLIE
GHIS > GHI
GHOST *n* disembodied spirit of a dead person ▷ *vb* ghostwrite
GHOSTED > GHOST
GHOSTIER > GHOSTY
GHOSTIEST > GHOSTY
GHOSTING > GHOST
GHOSTINGS > GHOST
GHOSTLIER > GHOSTLY
GHOSTLIKE > GHOST
GHOSTLY *adj* frightening in appearance or effect
GHOSTS > GHOST
GHOSTY *adj* pertaining to ghosts
GHOUL *n* person with morbid interests
GHOULIE *n* goblin
GHOULIES > GHOULIE
GHOULISH *adj* of or relating to ghouls
GHOULS > GHOUL
GHYLL *same as* > GILL
GHYLLS > GHYLL
GI *n* loose-fitting white suit worn in judo, karate, and other martial arts
GIAMBEUX *n* jambeaux; leg armour
GIANT *n* mythical being of superhuman size ▷ *adj* huge
GIANTESS *same as* > GIANT
GIANTHOOD *n* condition of being a giant
GIANTISM *same as* > GIGANTISM
GIANTISMS > GIANTISM
GIANTLIER > GIANTLY
GIANTLIKE > GIANT
GIANTLY *adj* giantlike
GIANTRIES > GIANTRY
GIANTRY *n* collective term for giants
GIANTS > GIANT
GIANTSHIP *n* style of address for a giant
GIAOUR *n* derogatory term for a non-Muslim, esp a Christian, used esp by the Turks
GIAOURS > GIAOUR
GIARDIA *n* species of parasite
GIARDIAS > GIARDIA
GIB *n* metal wedge, pad, or thrust bearing, esp a brass plate let into a steam engine crosshead ▷ *vb* fasten or supply with a gib
GIBBED > GIB
GIBBER *vb* speak or utter rapidly and unintelligibly ▷ *n* boulder
GIBBERED > GIBBER
GIBBERING > GIBBER
GIBBERISH *n* rapid unintelligible talk
GIBBERS > GIBBER
GIBBET *n* gallows for displaying executed criminals ▷ *vb* put to death by hanging on a gibbet
GIBBETED > GIBBET
GIBBETING > GIBBET
GIBBETS > GIBBET
GIBBETTED > GIBBET
GIBBING > GIB
GIBBON *n* agile tree-dwelling ape of S Asia
GIBBONS > GIBBON
GIBBOSE *same as* > GIBBOUS
GIBBOSITY *n* state of being gibbous
GIBBOUS *adj* (of the moon) more than half but less than fully illuminated
GIBBOUSLY > GIBBOUS
GIBBSITE *n* mineral consisting of hydrated aluminium oxide
GIBBSITES > GIBBSITE
GIBE *vb* make jeering or scoffing remarks (at) ▷ *n* derisive or provoking remark
GIBED > GIBE
GIBEL *n* Prussian carp
GIBELS > GIBEL
GIBER > GIBE
GIBERS > GIBE
GIBES > GIBE
GIBING > GIBE
GIBINGLY > GIBE
GIBLET > GIBLETS
GIBLETS *pl n* gizzard, liver, heart, and neck of a fowl
GIBLI *same as* > GHIBLI
GIBLIS > GIBLI
GIBS > GIB
GIBSON *n* martini garnished with onion
GIBSONS > GIBSON
GIBUS *n* collapsible top hat operated by a spring
GIBUSES > GIBUS
GID *n* disease of sheep characterized by an unsteady gait and staggering, caused by infestation of the brain with tapeworms (*Taenia caenuris*)
GIDDAP *interj* exclamation used to make a horse go faster
GIDDAY *interj* expression of greeting
GIDDIED > GIDDY
GIDDIER > GIDDY
GIDDIES > GIDDY
GIDDIEST > GIDDY
GIDDILY > GIDDY
GIDDINESS > GIDDY
GIDDUP *same as* > GIDDYUP
GIDDY *adj* having or causing a feeling of dizziness ▷ *vb* make giddy
GIDDYAP *same as* > GIDDYUP
GIDDYING > GIDDY
GIDDYUP *interj* exclamation used to make a horse go faster
GIDGEE *n* small acacia trees, which at times emit an unpleasant smell
GIDGEES > GIDGEE
GIDJEE *same as* > GIDGEE
GIDJEES > GIDJEE
GIDS > GID
GIE *Scot word for* > GIVE
GIED > GIVE
GIEING > GIVE
GIEN > GIVE
GIES > GIVE
GIF *obsolete word for* > IF
GIFT *n* present ▷ *vb* make a present of
GIFTABLE *adj* suitable as gift ▷ *n* something suitable as gift
GIFTABLES > GIFTABLE
GIFTED *adj* talented
GIFTEDLY > GIFTED
GIFTEE *n* person given a gift
GIFTEES > GIFTEE
GIFTING > GIFT
GIFTLESS > GIFT
GIFTS > GIFT
GIFTSHOP *n* shop selling articles suitable for gifts
GIFTSHOPS > GIFTSHOP
GIFTWARE *n* anything that may be given as a present
GIFTWARES > GIFTWARE
GIFTWRAP *vb* wrap (a gift) in decorative wrapping paper
GIFTWRAPS > GIFTWRAP
GIG *n* single performance by pop or jazz musicians ▷ *vb* play a gig or gigs
GIGA *same as* > GIGUE
GIGABIT *n* unit of information in computing
GIGABITS > GIGABIT
GIGABYTE *n* one thousand and twenty-four megabytes
GIGABYTES > GIGABYTE
GIGACYCLE *same as* > GIGAHERTZ
GIGAFLOP *n* measure of processing speed, consisting of a thousand million floating-point operations a second
GIGAFLOPS > GIGAFLOP
GIGAHERTZ *n* unit of frequency equal to 10^9 hertz.
GIGANTEAN *adj* gigantic
GIGANTIC *adj* enormous
GIGANTISM *n* excessive growth of the entire body, caused by overproduction of growth hormone by the pituitary gland during childhood or adolescence
GIGAS > GIGA
GIGATON *n* unit of explosive force
GIGATONS > GIGATON
GIGAWATT *n* unit of power

equal to 1 billion watts
GIGAWATTS > GIGAWATT
GIGGED > GIG
GIGGING > GIG
GIGGIT *vb* move quickly
GIGGITED > GIGGIT
GIGGITING > GIGGIT
GIGGITS > GIGGIT
GIGGLE *vb* laugh nervously or foolishly ▷ *n* such a laugh
GIGGLED > GIGGLE
GIGGLER > GIGGLE
GIGGLERS > GIGGLE
GIGGLES > GIGGLE
GIGGLIER > GIGGLE
GIGGLIEST > GIGGLE
GIGGLING > GIGGLE
GIGGLINGS > GIGGLE
GIGGLY > GIGGLE
GIGHE > GIGA
GIGLET *n* flighty girl
GIGLETS > GIGLET
GIGLOT *same as* > GIGLET
GIGLOTS > GIGLOT
GIGMAN *n* one who places great importance on respectability
GIGMANITY > GIGMAN
GIGMEN > GIGMAN
GIGOLO *n* man paid by an older woman to be her escort or lover
GIGOLOS > GIGOLO
GIGOT *n* leg of lamb or mutton
GIGOTS > GIGOT
GIGS > GIG
GIGUE *n* piece of music, usually in six-eight time and often fugal, incorporated into the classical suite
GIGUES > GIGUE
GILA *n* large venomous brightly coloured lizard
GILAS > GILA
GILBERT *n* unit of magnetomotive force
GILBERTS > GILBERT
GILCUP *same as* > GILTCUP
GILCUPS > GILCUP
GILD *vb* put a thin layer of gold on
GILDED > GILD
GILDEN *adj* gilded
GILDER > GILD
GILDERS > GILD
GILDHALL *same as* > GUILDHALL
GILDHALLS > GILDHALL
GILDING > GILD
GILDINGS > GILD
GILDS > GILD
GILDSMAN > GILD
GILDSMEN > GILD
GILET *n* waist- or hip-length garment, usually sleeveless, fastening up the front
GILETS > GILET
GILGAI *n* natural water hole
GILGAIS > GILGAI
GILGIE *n* type of freshwater crayfish
GILGIES > GILGIE
GILL *n* radiating structure beneath the cap of a mushroom ▷ *vb* catch (fish) or (of fish) to be caught in a gill net
GILLAROO *n* type of brown trout
GILLAROOS > GILLAROO
GILLED > GILL
GILLER > GILL
GILLERS > GILL
GILLET *n* mare
GILLETS > GILLET
GILLFLIRT *n* flirtatious woman
GILLIE *n* (in Scotland) attendant for hunting or fishing ▷ *vb* act as a gillie
GILLIED > GILLIE
GILLIES > GILLY
GILLING > GILL
GILLION *n* (no longer in technical use) one thousand million
GILLIONS > GILLION
GILLNET *n* net designed to catch fish by the gills ▷ *vb* fish using a gillnet
GILLNETS > GILLNET
GILLS *pl n* breathing organs in fish and other water creatures
GILLY *vb* act as a gillie
GILLYING > GILLY
GILLYVOR *n* type of carnation
GILLYVORS > GILLYVOR
GILPEY *n* mischievous, frolicsome boy or girl
GILPEYS > GILPEY
GILPIES > GILPIE
GILPY *same as* > GILPEY
GILRAVAGE *vb* make merry, especially to excess
GILSONITE *n* very pure form of asphalt found in Utah and Colorado
GILT > GILD
GILTCUP *n* buttercup
GILTCUPS > GILTCUP
GILTHEAD *n* sparid fish, *Sparus aurata*, of Mediterranean and European Atlantic waters, having a gold-coloured band between the eyes
GILTHEADS > GILTHEAD
GILTS > GILD
GILTWOOD *adj* made of wood and gilded
GIMBAL *vb* support on gimbals
GIMBALED > GIMBAL
GIMBALING > GIMBAL
GIMBALLED > GIMBAL
GIMBALS *pl n* set of pivoted rings which allow nautical instruments to remain horizontal at sea
GIMCRACK *adj* showy but cheap ▷ *n* cheap showy trifle or gadget
GIMCRACKS > GIMCRACK
GIMEL *n* third letter of the Hebrew alphabet
GIMELS > GIMEL
GIMLET *n* small tool with a screwlike tip for boring holes in wood ▷ *adj* penetrating or piercing ▷ *vb* make holes in (wood) using a gimlet
GIMLETED > GIMLET
GIMLETING > GIMLET
GIMLETS > GIMLET
GIMMAL *n* ring composed of interlocking rings ▷ *vb* provide with gimmals
GIMMALLED > GIMMAL
GIMMALS > GIMMAL
GIMME *interj* give me! ▷ *n* short putt that one is excused by one's opponent from playing because it is considered too easy to miss
GIMMER *n* year-old ewe
GIMMERS > GIMMER
GIMMES > GIMME
GIMMICK *n* something designed to attract attention or publicity ▷ *vb* make gimmicky
GIMMICKED > GIMMICK
GIMMICKRY > GIMMICK
GIMMICKS > GIMMICK
GIMMICKY > GIMMICK
GIMMIE *n* in golf, an easy putt conceded to one's opponent
GIMMIES > GIMMIE
GIMMOR *n* mechanical device
GIMMORS > GIMMOR
GIMP *n* tapelike trimming of silk, wool, or cotton, often stiffened with wire ▷ *vb* derogatory term for limp
GIMPED > GIMP
GIMPIER > GIMPY
GIMPIEST > GIMPY
GIMPING > GIMP
GIMPS > GIMP
GIMPY *same as* > GAMMY
GIN *n* spirit flavoured with juniper berries ▷ *vb* free (cotton) of seeds with a gin; begin
GING *n* child's catapult
GINGAL *n* type of musket mounted on a swivel
GINGALL *same as* > GINGAL
GINGALLS > GINGALL
GINGALS > GINGAL
GINGE *n* person with ginger hair
GINGELEY *same as* > GINGILI
GINGELEYS > GINGELEY
GINGELI *same as* > GINGILI
GINGELIES > GINGELY
GINGELIS > GINGELI
GINGELLI *same as* > GINGILI
GINGELLIS > GINGILI
GINGELLY *same as* > GINGILI
GINGELY *same as* > GINGILI
GINGER *n* root of a tropical plant, used as a spice ▷ *adj* light reddish-brown ▷ *vb* add the spice ginger to (a dish)
GINGERADE *n* fizzy drink flavoured with ginger
GINGERED > GINGER
GINGERING > GINGER
GINGERLY *adv* cautiously ▷ *adj* cautious
GINGEROUS *adj* reddish
GINGERS > GINGER
GINGERY *adj* like or tasting of ginger
GINGES > GINGE
GINGHAM *n* cotton cloth, usu checked or striped
GINGHAMS > GINGHAM
GINGILI *n* oil obtained from sesame seeds
GINGILIS > GINGILI
GINGILLI *same as* > GINGILI
GINGILLIS > GINGILLI
GINGIVA *same as* > GUM
GINGIVAE > GINGIVA
GINGIVAL > GINGIVA
GINGKO *same as* > GINKGO
GINGKOES > GINGKO
GINGKOS > GINGKO
GINGLE *same as* > JINGLE
GINGLES > GINGLE
GINGLYMI > GINGLYMUS
GINGLYMUS *n* hinge joint
GINGS > GING
GINHOUSE *n* building where cotton is ginned
GINHOUSES > GINHOUSE
GINK *n* man or boy, esp one considered to be odd
GINKGO *n* ornamental Chinese tree
GINKGOES > GINKGO
GINKGOS > GINKGO
GINKS > GINK
GINN *same as* > JINN
GINNED > GIN
GINNEL *n* narrow passageway between buildings
GINNELS > GINNEL
GINNER > GIN
GINNERIES > GINHOUSE
GINNERS > GIN
GINNERY *another word for* > GINHOUSE
GINNIER > GINNY
GINNIEST > GINNY
GINNING > GIN
GINNINGS > GIN
GINNY *adj* relating to the spirit gin
GINORMOUS *adj* very large
GINS > GIN
GINSENG *n* (root of) a plant believed to have tonic and energy-giving properties
GINSENGS > GINSENG
GINSHOP *n* tavern
GINSHOPS > GINSHOP
GINZO *n* disparaging term for person of Italian descent

GINZOES > GINZO
GIO *same as* > GEO
GIOCOSO *adv* (of music) to be expressed joyfully or playfully
GIOS > GIO
GIP *same as* > GYP
GIPON *another word for* > JUPON
GIPONS > GIPON
GIPPED > GIP
GIPPER > GIP
GIPPERS > GIP
GIPPIES > GIPPY
GIPPING > GIP
GIPPO *same as* > GIPPY
GIPPOES > GIPPO
GIPPOS > GIPPO
GIPPY *n* starling
GIPS > GIP
GIPSEN *obsolete word for* > GYPSY
GIPSENS > GIPSEN
GIPSIED > GIPSY
GIPSIES > GIPSY
GIPSY *n* member of a nomadic people scattered throughout Europe and North America ▷ *vb* live like a gypsy
GIPSYDOM > GIPSY
GIPSYDOMS > GIPSY
GIPSYHOOD > GIPSY
GIPSYING > GIPSY
GIPSYISH > GIPSY
GIPSYWORT *n* hairy Eurasian plant, *Lycopus europaeus*, having two-lipped white flowers with purple dots on the lower lip: family *Lamiaceae* (labiates)
GIRAFFE *n* African ruminant mammal with a spotted yellow skin and long neck and legs
GIRAFFES > GIRAFFE
GIRAFFID *adj* giraffe-like
GIRAFFINE *adj* relating to a giraffe
GIRAFFISH > GIRAFFE
GIRAFFOID *adj* giraffe-like
GIRANDOLA *same as* > GIRANDOLE
GIRANDOLE *n* ornamental branched wall candleholder, usually incorporating a mirror
GIRASOL *n* type of opal that has a red or pink glow in bright light
GIRASOLE *same as* > GIRASOL
GIRASOLES > GIRASOLE
GIRASOLS > GIRASOL
GIRD *vb* put a belt round ▷ *n* blow or stroke
GIRDED > GIRD
GIRDER *n* large metal beam
GIRDERS > GIRDER
GIRDING > GIRD
GIRDINGLY > GIRD
GIRDINGS > GIRD
GIRDLE *n* woman's elastic corset ▷ *vb* surround or encircle
GIRDLED > GIRDLE
GIRDLER *n* person or thing that girdles
GIRDLERS > GIRDLER
GIRDLES > GIRDLE
GIRDLING > GIRDLE
GIRDS > GIRD
GIRKIN *same as* > GHERKIN
GIRKINS > GIRKIN
GIRL *n* female child
GIRLHOOD *n* state or time of being a girl
GIRLHOODS > GIRLHOOD
GIRLIE *adj* (of a magazine, calendar, etc) featuring pictures of naked or scantily clad women ▷ *n* little girl
GIRLIER > GIRLY
GIRLIES > GIRLIE
GIRLIEST > GIRLY
GIRLISH *adj* of or like a girl in looks, behaviour, innocence, etc
GIRLISHLY > GIRLISH
GIRLOND *obsolete word for* > GARLAND
GIRLONDS > GIRLOND
GIRLS > GIRL
GIRLY *same as* > GIRLIE
GIRN *vb* snarl
GIRNED > GIRN
GIRNEL *n* large chest for storing meal
GIRNELS > GIRNEL
GIRNER > GIRN
GIRNERS > GIRN
GIRNIE *adj* peevish
GIRNIER > GIRNIE
GIRNIEST > GIRNIE
GIRNING > GIRN
GIRNS > GIRN
GIRO *n* (in some countries) system of transferring money within a post office or bank directly from one account to another
GIROLLE *another word for* > CHANTERELLE
GIROLLES > GIROLLE
GIRON *n* charge consisting of the lower half of a diagonally divided quarter, usually in the top left corner of the shield
GIRONIC > GIRON
GIRONNY *adj* divided into segments from the fesse point
GIRONS > GIRON
GIROS > GIRO
GIROSOL *same as* > GIRASOL
GIROSOLS > GIROSOL
GIRR *same as* > GIRD
GIRRS > GIRR
GIRSH *n* currency unit of Saudi Arabia
GIRSHES > GIRSH
GIRT *vb* gird; bind
GIRTED > GIRD
GIRTH *n* measurement round something ▷ *vb* fasten a girth on (a horse)
GIRTHED > GIRTH
GIRTHING > GIRTH
GIRTHLINE *same as* > GIRTLINE
GIRTHS > GIRTH
GIRTING > GIRD
GIRTLINE *n* gantline
GIRTLINES > GIRTLINE
GIRTS > GIRT
GIS > GI
GISARME *n* long-shafted battle-axe with a sharp point on the back of the axe head
GISARMES > GISARME
GISM *n* semen
GISMO *same as* > GIZMO
GISMOLOGY *same as* > GIZMOLOGY
GISMOS > GISMO
GISMS > GISM
GIST *n* substance or main point of a matter
GISTS > GIST
GIT *n* contemptible person ▷ *vb* dialect version of get
GITANA *n* female gypsy
GITANAS > GITANA
GITANO *n* male gypsy
GITANOS > GITANO
GITE *n* self-catering holiday cottage for let in France
GITES > GITE
GITS > GIT
GITTARONE *n* acoustic bass guitar
GITTED > GIT
GITTERN *n* obsolete medieval stringed instrument resembling the guitar ▷ *vb* play the gittern
GITTERNED > GITTERN
GITTERNS > GITTERN
GITTIN *n* Jewish divorce
GITTING > GIT
GIUST *same as* > JOUST
GIUSTED > GIUST
GIUSTING > GIUST
GIUSTO *adv* be observed strictly
GIUSTS > GIUST
GIVABLE > GIVE
GIVE *vb* present (something) to another person ▷ *n* resilience or elasticity
GIVEABLE > GIVE
GIVEAWAY *n* something that reveals hidden feelings or intentions ▷ *adj* very cheap or free
GIVEAWAYS > GIVEAWAY
GIVEBACK *n* reduction in wages in return for some other benefit, in time of recession
GIVEBACKS > GIVEBACK
GIVED *same as* > GYVED
GIVEN *n* assumed fact
GIVENNESS *n* condition of being given
GIVENS > GIVEN
GIVER > GIVE
GIVERS > GIVE
GIVES > GIVE
GIVING > GIVE
GIVINGS > GIVE
GIZMO *n* device
GIZMOLOGY *n* study of gadgets
GIZMOS > GIZMO
GIZZ *n* wig
GIZZARD *n* part of a bird's stomach
GIZZARDS > GIZZARD
GIZZEN *vb* (of wood) to warp
GIZZENED > GIZZEN
GIZZENING > GIZZEN
GIZZENS > GIZZEN
GIZZES > GIZZ
GJETOST *n* type of Norwegian cheese
GJETOSTS > GJETOST
GJU *n* type of violin used in Shetland
GJUS > GJU
GLABELLA *n* smooth elevation of the frontal bone just above the bridge of the nose: a reference point in physical anthropology or craniometry
GLABELLAE > GLABELLA
GLABELLAR > GLABELLA
GLABRATE *same as* > GLABROUS
GLABROUS *adj* without hair or a similar growth
GLACE *adj* preserved in a thick sugary syrup ▷ *vb* ice or candy (cakes, fruits, etc)
GLACEED > GLACE
GLACEING > GLACE
GLACES > GLACE
GLACIAL *adj* of ice or glaciers ▷ *n* ice age
GLACIALLY > GLACIAL
GLACIALS > GLACIAL
GLACIATE *vb* cover or become covered with glaciers or masses of ice
GLACIATED > GLACIATE
GLACIATES > GLACIATE
GLACIER *n* slow-moving mass of ice formed by accumulated snow
GLACIERED *adj* having a glacier or glaciers
GLACIERS > GLACIER
GLACIS *n* slight incline
GLACISES > GLACIS
GLAD *adj* pleased and happy ▷ *vb* become glad ▷ *n* gladiolus
GLADDED > GLAD
GLADDEN *vb* make glad
GLADDENED > GLADDEN
GLADDENER > GLADDEN
GLADDENS > GLADDEN
GLADDER > GLAD
GLADDEST > GLAD
GLADDIE *same as* > GLAD

GLADDIES > GLADDIE
GLADDING > GLAD
GLADDON *n* stinking iris
GLADDONS > GLADDON
GLADE *n* open space in a forest
GLADELIKE > GLADE
GLADES > GLADE
GLADFUL *adj* full of gladness
GLADIATE *adj* shaped like a sword
GLADIATOR *n* (in ancient Rome) man trained to fight in arenas to provide entertainment
GLADIER > GLADE
GLADIEST > GLADE
GLADIOLA *same as* > GLADIOLUS
GLADIOLAR > GLADIOLUS
GLADIOLAS > GLADIOLA
GLADIOLE *same as* > GLADIOLUS
GLADIOLES > GLADIOLE
GLADIOLI > GLADIOLUS
GLADIOLUS *n* garden plant with sword-shaped leaves
GLADIUS *n* short sword used by Roman legionaries
GLADIUSES > GLADIUS
GLADLIER > GLAD
GLADLIEST > GLAD
GLADLY > GLAD
GLADNESS > GLAD
GLADS > GLAD
GLADSOME *adj* joyous or cheerful
GLADSOMER > GLADSOME
GLADSTONE *n* light four-wheeled horse-drawn vehicle
GLADWRAP *n* in New Zealand English, thin film for wrapping food ▷ *vb* cover with gladwrap
GLADWRAPS > GLADWRAP
GLADY > GLADE
GLAIK *n* prank
GLAIKET *same as* > GLAIKIT
GLAIKIT *adj* foolish
GLAIKS > GLAIK
GLAIR *n* white of egg, esp when used as a size, glaze, or adhesive, usually in bookbinding ▷ *vb* apply glair to (something)
GLAIRE *same as* > GLAIR
GLAIRED > GLAIR
GLAIREOUS > GLAIR
GLAIRES > GLAIRE
GLAIRIER > GLAIR
GLAIRIEST > GLAIR
GLAIRIN *n* viscous deposit found in some mineral waters
GLAIRING > GLAIR
GLAIRINS > GLAIRIN
GLAIRS > GLAIR
GLAIRY > GLAIR
GLAIVE *archaic word for* > SWORD
GLAIVED *adj* armed with a sword
GLAIVES > GLAIVE
GLAM *n* magical illusion
GLAMOR *same as* > GLAMOUR
GLAMORED > GLAMOR
GLAMORING > GLAMOR
GLAMORISE *same as* > GLAMORIZE
GLAMORIZE *vb* cause to be or seem glamorous
GLAMOROUS *adj* alluring
GLAMORS > GLAMOR
GLAMOUR *n* alluring charm or fascination ▷ *vb* bewitch
GLAMOURED > GLAMOUR > GLAMOUROUSNESS
GLAMOURS > GLAMOUR
GLAMS > GLAM
GLANCE *vb* look rapidly or briefly ▷ *n* brief look
GLANCED > GLANCE
GLANCER *n* log or pole used to protect standing trees from damage
GLANCERS > GLANCER
GLANCES > GLANCE
GLANCING > GLANCE
GLANCINGS > GLANCE
GLAND *n* organ that produces and secretes substances in the body
GLANDERED > GLANDERS
GLANDERS *n* highly infectious bacterial disease of horses, sometimes transmitted to man, caused by *Actinobacillus mallei* and characterized by inflammation and ulceration of the mucous membranes of the air passages, skin, and lymph glands
GLANDES > GLANS
GLANDLESS > GLAND
GLANDLIKE > GLAND
GLANDS > GLAND
GLANDULAR *adj* of or affecting a gland or glands
GLANDULE *n* small gland
GLANDULES > GLANDULE
GLANS *n* any small rounded body or glandlike mass, such as the head of the penis
GLARE *vb* stare angrily ▷ *n* angry stare ▷ *adj* smooth and glassy
GLAREAL *adj* (of a plant) growing in cultivated land
GLARED > GLARE
GLARELESS > GLARE
GLAREOUS *adj* resembling the white of an egg
GLARES > GLARE
GLARIER > GLARE
GLARIEST > GLARE
GLARINESS > GLARE
GLARING *adj* conspicuous
GLARINGLY > GLARING
GLARY > GLARE
GLASNOST *n* policy of openness and accountability, esp, formerly, in the USSR
GLASNOSTS > GLASNOST
GLASS *n* hard brittle, usu transparent substance consisting of metal silicates or similar compounds ▷ *vb* cover with, enclose in, or fit with glass
GLASSED > GLASS
GLASSEN *adj* glassy
GLASSES *pl n* pair of lenses for correcting faulty vision, in a frame that rests on the nose and hooks behind the ears
GLASSFUL *n* amount held by a full glass
GLASSFULS > GLASSFUL
GLASSIE *same as* > GLASSY
GLASSIER > GLASSY
GLASSIES > GLASSY
GLASSIEST > GLASSY
GLASSIFY *vb* turn into glass
GLASSILY > GLASSY
GLASSINE *n* glazed translucent paper used for book jackets
GLASSINES > GLASSINE
GLASSING > GLASS
GLASSLESS > GLASS
GLASSLIKE > GLASS
GLASSMAN *n* man whose work is making or selling glassware
GLASSMEN > GLASSMAN
GLASSWARE *n* articles made of glass
GLASSWORK *n* production of glassware
GLASSWORM *n* larva of gnat
GLASSWORT *n* any plant of the chenopodiaceous genus *Salicornia*, of salt marshes, having fleshy stems and scalelike leaves: formerly used as a source of soda for glass-making
GLASSY *adj* like glass ▷ *n* glass marble
GLAUCOMA *n* eye disease
GLAUCOMAS > GLAUCOMA
GLAUCOUS *adj* covered with a bluish waxy or powdery bloom
GLAUM *vb* snatch
GLAUMED > GLAUM
GLAUMING > GLAUM
GLAUMS > GLAUM
GLAUR *n* mud or mire
GLAURIER > GLAUR
GLAURIEST > GLAUR
GLAURS > GLAUR
GLAURY > GLAUR
GLAZE *vb* fit or cover with glass ▷ *n* transparent coating
GLAZED > GLAZE
GLAZEN *adj* glazed
GLAZER > GLAZE
GLAZERS > GLAZE
GLAZES > GLAZE
GLAZIER *n* person who fits windows with glass
GLAZIERS > GLAZIER
GLAZIERY > GLAZIER
GLAZIEST > GLAZE
GLAZILY > GLAZE
GLAZINESS > GLAZE
GLAZING *n* surface of a glazed object
GLAZINGS > GLAZING
GLAZY > GLAZE
GLEAM *n* small beam or glow of light ▷ *vb* emit a gleam
GLEAMED > GLEAM
GLEAMER *n* mirror used to cheat in card games
GLEAMERS > GLEAMER
GLEAMIER > GLEAM
GLEAMIEST > GLEAM
GLEAMING > GLEAM
GLEAMINGS > GLEAM
GLEAMS > GLEAM
GLEAMY > GLEAM
GLEAN *vb* gather (facts etc) bit by bit
GLEANABLE > GLEAN
GLEANED > GLEAN
GLEANER > GLEAN
GLEANERS > GLEAN
GLEANING > GLEAN
GLEANINGS *pl n* pieces of information that have been gleaned
GLEANS > GLEAN
GLEAVE *same as* > SWORD
GLEAVES > GLEAVE
GLEBA *n* mass of spores
GLEBAE > GLEBA
GLEBE *n* land granted to a member of the clergy as part of his or her benefice
GLEBELESS > GLEBE
GLEBES > GLEBE
GLEBOUS *adj* gleby
GLEBY *adj* relating to a glebe
GLED *n* kite
GLEDE *same as* > GLED
GLEDES > GLEDE
GLEDGE *vb* glance sideways
GLEDGED > GLEDGE
GLEDGES > GLEDGE
GLEDGING > GLEDGE
GLEDS > GLED
GLEE *n* triumph and delight ▷ *vb* be full of glee
GLEED *n* burning ember or hot coal
GLEEDS > GLEED
GLEEFUL *adj* merry or joyful, esp over someone else's mistake or misfortune
GLEEFULLY > GLEEFUL
GLEEING > GLEE
GLEEK *vb* jeer
GLEEKED > GLEEK
GLEEKING > GLEEK
GLEEKS > GLEEK
GLEEMAN *n* minstrel
GLEEMEN > GLEEMAN
GLEENIE *n* guinea fowl
GLEENIES > GLEENIE

GLEES > GLEE
GLEESOME *adj* full of glee
GLEET *n* inflammation of the urethra with a slight discharge of thin pus and mucus: a stage of chronic gonorrhoea ▷ *vb* discharge gleet
GLEETED > GLEET
GLEETIER > GLEET
GLEETIEST > GLEET
GLEETING > GLEET
GLEETS > GLEET
GLEETY > GLEET
GLEG *adj* quick
GLEGGER > GLEG
GLEGGEST > GLEG
GLEGLY > GLEG
GLEGNESS > GLEG
GLEI *same as* > GLEY
GLEIS > GLEI
GLEN *n* deep narrow valley, esp in Scotland
GLENGARRY *n* brimless Scottish cap with a crease down the crown
GLENLIKE > GLEN
GLENOID *adj* resembling or having a shallow cavity ▷ *n* shallow cavity
GLENOIDAL > GLENOID
GLENOIDS > GLENOID
GLENS > GLEN
GLENT *same as* > GLINT
GLENTED > GLENT
GLENTING > GLENT
GLENTS > GLENT
GLEY *n* bluish-grey compact sticky soil occurring in certain humid regions ▷ *vb* squint
GLEYED > GLEY
GLEYING > GLEY
GLEYINGS > GLEY
GLEYS > GLEY
GLIA *n* delicate web of connective tissue that surrounds and supports nerve cells
GLIADIN *n* protein of cereals, esp wheat, with a high proline content: forms a sticky mass with water that binds flour into dough
GLIADINE *same as* > GLIADIN
GLIADINES > GLIADINE
GLIADINS > GLIADIN
GLIAL > GLIA
GLIAS > GLIA
GLIB *adj* fluent but insincere or superficial ▷ *vb* castrate
GLIBBED > GLIB
GLIBBER > GLIB
GLIBBERY *adj* slippery
GLIBBEST > GLIB
GLIBBING > GLIB
GLIBLY > GLIB
GLIBNESS > GLIB
GLIBS > GLIB
GLID *adj* moving smoothly and easily
GLIDDER > GLID
GLIDDERY *adj* slippery
GLIDDEST > GLID
GLIDE *vb* move easily and smoothly ▷ *n* smooth easy movement
GLIDED > GLIDE
GLIDEPATH *n* path followed by aircraft coming in to land
GLIDER *n* flying phalanger
GLIDERS > GLIDER
GLIDES > GLIDE
GLIDING *n* sport of flying gliders
GLIDINGLY > GLIDE
GLIDINGS > GLIDING
GLIFF *vb* slap
GLIFFING > GLIFF
GLIFFINGS > GLIFF
GLIFFS > GLIFF
GLIFT *n* moment
GLIFTS > GLIFT
GLIKE *same as* > GLEEK
GLIKES > GLIKE
GLIM *n* light or lamp
GLIME *vb* glance sideways
GLIMED > GLIME
GLIMES > GLIME
GLIMING > GLIME
GLIMMER *vb* shine faintly, flicker ▷ *n* faint gleam
GLIMMERED > GLIMMER
GLIMMERS > GLIMMER
GLIMMERY > GLIMMER
GLIMPSE *n* brief or incomplete view ▷ *vb* catch a glimpse of
GLIMPSED > GLIMPSE
GLIMPSER > GLIMPSE
GLIMPSERS > GLIMPSE
GLIMPSES > GLIMPSE
GLIMPSING > GLIMPSE
GLIMS > GLIM
GLINT *vb* gleam brightly ▷ *n* bright gleam
GLINTED > GLINT
GLINTIER > GLINT
GLINTIEST > GLINT
GLINTING > GLINT
GLINTS > GLINT
GLINTY > GLINT
GLIOMA *n* tumour of the brain and spinal cord, composed of neuroglia cells and fibres
GLIOMAS > GLIOMA
GLIOMATA > GLIOMA
GLIOSES > GLIOSIS
GLIOSIS *n* process leading to scarring in the central nervous system
GLISK *n* glimpse
GLISKS > GLISK
GLISSADE *n* gliding step in ballet ▷ *vb* perform a glissade
GLISSADED > GLISSADE
GLISSADER > GLISSADE
GLISSADES > GLISSADE
GLISSANDI > GLISSANDO
GLISSANDO *n* slide between two notes in which all intermediate notes are played
GLISTEN *vb* gleam by reflecting light ▷ *n* gleam or gloss
GLISTENED > GLISTEN
GLISTENS > GLISTEN
GLISTER *archaic word for* > GLITTER
GLISTERED > GLISTER
GLISTERS > GLISTER
GLIT *n* slimy matter
GLITCH *n* small problem that stops something from working properly
GLITCHES > GLITCH
GLITCHIER > GLITCH
GLITCHY > GLITCH
GLITS > GLIT
GLITTER *vb* shine with bright flashes ▷ *n* sparkle or brilliance
GLITTERED > GLITTER
GLITTERS > GLITTER
GLITTERY > GLITTER
GLITZ *n* ostentatious showiness ▷ *vb* make something more attractive
GLITZED > GLITZ
GLITZES > GLITZ
GLITZIER > GLITZY
GLITZIEST > GLITZY
GLITZILY > GLITZY
GLITZING > GLITZ
GLITZY *adj* showily attractive
GLOAM *n* dusk
GLOAMING *n* twilight
GLOAMINGS > GLOAMING
GLOAMS > GLOAM
GLOAT *vb* regard one's own good fortune or the misfortune of others with smug or malicious pleasure ▷ *n* act of gloating
GLOATED > GLOAT
GLOATER > GLOAT
GLOATERS > GLOAT
GLOATING > GLOAT
GLOATS > GLOAT
GLOB *n* rounded mass of thick fluid
GLOBAL *adj* worldwide
GLOBALISE *same as* > GLOBALIZE
GLOBALISM *n* policy which is worldwide in scope
GLOBALIST > GLOBALISM
GLOBALIZE *vb* put (something) into effect worldwide
GLOBALLY > GLOBAL
GLOBATE *adj* shaped like a globe
GLOBATED *same as* > GLOBATE
GLOBBIER > GLOBBY
GLOBBIEST > GLOBBY
GLOBBY *adj* thick and lumpy
GLOBE *n* sphere with a map of the earth on it ▷ *vb* form or cause to form into a globe
GLOBED > GLOBE
GLOBEFISH *another name for* > PUFFER
GLOBELIKE > GLOBE
GLOBES > GLOBE
GLOBESITY *n* informal word for obesity seen as a worldwide social problem
GLOBETROT *vb* regularly travel internationally
GLOBI > GLOBUS
GLOBIN *n* protein component of the pigments myoglobin and haemoglobin
GLOBING > GLOBE
GLOBINS > GLOBIN
GLOBOID *adj* shaped approximately like a globe ▷ *n* globoid body, such as any of those occurring in certain plant granules
GLOBOIDS > GLOBOID
GLOBOSE *adj* spherical or approximately spherical ▷ *n* globose object
GLOBOSELY > GLOBOSE
GLOBOSES > GLOBOSE
GLOBOSITY > GLOBOSE
GLOBOUS *same as* > GLOBOSE
GLOBS > GLOB
GLOBULAR *adj* shaped like a globe or globule ▷ *n* globular star cluster
GLOBULARS > GLOBULAR
GLOBULE *n* small round drop
GLOBULES > GLOBULE
GLOBULET *n* small globule
GLOBULETS > GLOBULET
GLOBULIN *n* simple protein found in living tissue
GLOBULINS > GLOBULIN
GLOBULITE *n* spherical form of crystallite
GLOBULOUS *same as* > GLOBULAR
GLOBUS *n* any spherelike structure
GLOBY *adj* round
GLOCHID *n* barbed spine on a plant
GLOCHIDIA *n, plural form of singular* glochidium, a barbed hair on some plants
GLOCHIDS > GLOCHID
GLODE > GLIDE
GLOGG *n* hot alcoholic mixed drink, originally from Sweden, consisting of sweetened brandy, red wine, bitters or other flavourings, and blanched almonds
GLOGGS > GLOGG
GLOIRE *n* glory
GLOIRES > GLOIRE
GLOM *vb* attach oneself to or associate oneself with
GLOMERA > GLOMUS
GLOMERATE *adj* gathered into a compact rounded mass ▷ *vb* wind into a ball

GLOMERULE *n* cymose inflorescence in the form of a ball-like cluster of flowers
GLOMERULI *n, plural of singular* glomerulus: a knot of blood vessels in the kidney
GLOMMED > GLOM
GLOMMING > GLOM
GLOMS > GLOM
GLOMUS *n* small anastomosis in an artery or vein
GLONOIN *n* nitroglycerin
GLONOINS > GLONOIN
GLOOM *n* melancholy or depression ▷ *vb* look sullen or depressed
GLOOMED > GLOOM
GLOOMFUL > GLOOM
GLOOMIER > GLOOMY
GLOOMIEST > GLOOMY
GLOOMILY > GLOOMY
GLOOMING > GLOOM
GLOOMINGS > GLOOM
GLOOMLESS > GLOOM
GLOOMS > GLOOM
GLOOMY *adj* despairing or sad
GLOOP *vb* cover with a viscous substance
GLOOPED > GLOOP
GLOOPIER > GLOOP
GLOOPIEST > GLOOP
GLOOPING > GLOOP
GLOOPS > GLOOP
GLOOPY > GLOOP
GLOP *vb* cover with a viscous substance
GLOPPED > GLOP
GLOPPIER > GLOP
GLOPPIEST > GLOP
GLOPPING > GLOP
GLOPPY > GLOP
GLOPS > GLOP
GLORIA *n* silk, wool, cotton, or nylon fabric used esp for umbrellas
GLORIAS > GLORIA
GLORIED > GLORY
GLORIES > GLORY
GLORIFIED > GLORIFY
GLORIFIER > GLORIFY
GLORIFIES > GLORIFY
GLORIFY *vb* make (something) seem more worthy than it is
GLORIOLE *another name for a* > HALO
GLORIOLES > GLORIOLE
GLORIOSA *n* bulbous African tropical plant
GLORIOSAS > GLORIOSA
GLORIOUS *adj* brilliantly beautiful
GLORY *n* praise or honour ▷ *vb* triumph or exalt
GLORYING > GLORY
GLOSS *n* surface shine or lustre ▷ *vb* make glossy
GLOSSA *n* paired tonguelike lobe in the labium of an insect
GLOSSAE > GLOSSA
GLOSSAL > GLOSSA
GLOSSARY *n* list of special or technical words with definitions
GLOSSAS > GLOSSA
GLOSSATOR *n* writer of glosses and commentaries, esp (in the Middle Ages) an interpreter of Roman and Canon Law
GLOSSED > GLOSS
GLOSSEME *n* smallest meaningful unit of a language, such as stress, form, etc
GLOSSEMES > GLOSSEME
GLOSSER > GLOSS
GLOSSERS > GLOSS
GLOSSES > GLOSS
GLOSSIER > GLOSSY
GLOSSIES > GLOSSY
GLOSSIEST > GLOSSY
GLOSSILY > GLOSSY
GLOSSINA *n* tsetse fly
GLOSSINAS > GLOSSINA
GLOSSING > GLOSS
GLOSSIST *same as* > GLOSSATOR
GLOSSISTS > GLOSSIST
GLOSSITIC > GLOSSITIS
GLOSSITIS *n* inflammation of the tongue
GLOSSLESS > GLOSS
GLOSSY *adj* smooth and shiny ▷ *n* expensively produced magazine
GLOST *n* lead glaze used for pottery
GLOSTS > GLOST
GLOTTAL *adj* of the glottis
GLOTTIC *adj* of or relating to the tongue or the glottis
GLOTTIDES > GLOTTIS
GLOTTIS *n* vocal cords and the space between them
GLOTTISES > GLOTTIS
GLOUT *vb* look sullen
GLOUTED > GLOUT
GLOUTING > GLOUT
GLOUTS > GLOUT
GLOVE *n* covering for the hand with individual sheaths for each finger and the thumb
GLOVED > GLOVE
GLOVELESS > GLOVE
GLOVER *n* person who makes or sells gloves
GLOVERS > GLOVER
GLOVES > GLOVE
GLOVING > GLOVE
GLOVINGS > GLOVE
GLOW *vb* emit light and heat without flames ▷ *n* glowing light
GLOWED > GLOW
GLOWER *n* scowl ▷ *vb* stare angrily
GLOWERED > GLOWER
GLOWERING > GLOWER
GLOWERS > GLOWER
GLOWFLIES > GLOWFLY
GLOWFLY *n* firefly
GLOWING *adj* full of praise
GLOWINGLY > GLOWING
GLOWLAMP *n* small light consisting of two or more electrodes in an inert gas
GLOWLAMPS > GLOWLAMP
GLOWS > GLOW
GLOWSTICK *n* plastic tube containing a luminescent material, waved or held aloft esp at gigs, raves, etc
GLOWWORM *n* European beetle, the females and larvae of which bear luminescent organs producing a greenish light
GLOWWORMS > GLOWWORM
GLOXINIA *n* tropical plant with large bell-shaped flowers
GLOXINIAS > GLOXINIA
GLOZE *vb* explain away ▷ *n* flattery or deceit
GLOZED > GLOZE
GLOZES > GLOZE
GLOZING > GLOZE
GLOZINGS > GLOZE
GLUCAGON *n* polypeptide hormone, produced in the pancreas by the islets of Langerhans, that stimulates the release of glucose into the blood
GLUCAGONS > GLUCAGON
GLUCAN *n* any polysaccharide consisting of a polymer of glucose, such as cellulose or starch
GLUCANS > GLUCAN
GLUCINA *n* oxide of glucinum
GLUCINAS > GLUCINA
GLUCINIC > GLUCINIUM
GLUCINIUM *former name of* > BERYLLIUM
GLUCINUM *same as* > GLUCINIUM
GLUCINUMS > GLUCINUM
GLUCONATE *n* compound formed when a mineral is bound to gluconic acid
GLUCOSE *n* kind of sugar found in fruit
GLUCOSES > GLUCOSE
GLUCOSIC > GLUCOSE
GLUCOSIDE *n* any of a large group of glycosides that yield glucose on hydrolysis
GLUE *n* natural or synthetic sticky substance used as an adhesive ▷ *vb* fasten with glue
GLUED > GLUE
GLUEING > GLUE
GLUELIKE > GLUE
GLUEPOT *n* container for holding glue
GLUEPOTS > GLUEPOT
GLUER > GLUE
GLUERS > GLUE
GLUES > GLUE
GLUEY > GLUE
GLUEYNESS > GLUE
GLUG *n* word representing a gurgling sound, as of liquid being poured from a bottle or swallowed ▷ *vb* drink noisily, taking big gulps
GLUGGABLE *adj* (of wine) easy and pleasant to drink
GLUGGED > GLUG
GLUGGING > GLUG
GLUGS > GLUG
GLUHWEIN *n* mulled wine
GLUHWEINS > GLUHWEIN
GLUIER > GLUE
GLUIEST > GLUE
GLUILY > GLUE
GLUINESS > GLUE
GLUING > GLUE
GLUISH > GLUE
GLUM *adj* sullen or gloomy
GLUME *n* one of a pair of dry membranous bracts at the base of the spikelet of grasses
GLUMELIKE > GLUME
GLUMELLA *n* palea
GLUMELLAS > GLUMELLA
GLUMES > GLUME
GLUMLY > GLUM
GLUMMER > GLUM
GLUMMEST > GLUM
GLUMNESS > GLUM
GLUMPIER > GLUMPY
GLUMPIEST > GLUMPY
GLUMPILY > GLUMPY
GLUMPISH > GLUMPY
GLUMPS *n* state of sulking
GLUMPY *adj* sullen
GLUMS *n* gloomy feelings
GLUNCH *vb* look sullen
GLUNCHED > GLUNCH
GLUNCHES > GLUNCH
GLUNCHING > GLUNCH
GLUON *n* hypothetical particle believed to be exchanged between quarks in order to bind them together to form particles
GLUONS > GLUON
GLURGE *n* stories, often sent by email, that are supposed to be true and uplifting, but which are often fabricated and sentimental
GLURGES > GLURGE
GLUT *n* excessive supply ▷ *vb* oversupply
GLUTAEAL > GLUTAEUS
GLUTAEI > GLUTAEUS
GLUTAEUS *same as* > GLUTEUS
GLUTAMATE *n* any salt of glutamic acid, esp its sodium salt
GLUTAMIC as in *glutamic acid* nonessential amino acid that plays a part in nitrogen metabolism
GLUTAMINE *n* nonessential amino acid occurring in proteins: plays an

important role in protein metabolism
GLUTE *n same as* > GLUTEUS
GLUTEAL > GLUTEUS
GLUTEI > GLUTEUS
GLUTELIN *n* any of a group of water-insoluble plant proteins found in cereals. They are precipitated by alcohol and are not coagulated by heat
GLUTELINS > GLUTELIN
GLUTEN *n* protein found in cereal grain
GLUTENIN *n* type of protein
GLUTENINS > GLUTENIN
GLUTENOUS > GLUTEN
GLUTENS > GLUTEN
GLUTES > GLUTE
GLUTEUS *n* any of the three muscles of the buttock
GLUTINOUS *adj* sticky or gluey
GLUTS > GLUT
GLUTTED > GLUT
GLUTTING > GLUT
GLUTTON *n* greedy person
GLUTTONS > GLUTTON
GLUTTONY *n* practice of eating too much
GLYCAEMIA *n* presence of glucose in blood
GLYCAEMIC > GLYCAEMIA
GLYCAN *n* polysaccharide
GLYCANS > GLYCAN
GLYCEMIA *US spelling of* > GLYCAEMIA
GLYCEMIAS > GLYCEMIA
GLYCEMIC > GLYCEMIA
GLYCERIA *n* manna grass
GLYCERIAS > GLYCERIA
GLYCERIC *adj* of, containing, or derived from glycerol
GLYCERIDE *n* any fatty-acid ester of glycerol
GLYCERIN *same as* > GLYCEROL
GLYCERINE *same as* > GLYCEROL
GLYCERINS > GLYCERIN
GLYCEROL *n* colourless odourless syrupy liquid obtained from animal and vegetable fats, used as a solvent, antifreeze, and sweetener, and in explosives
GLYCEROLS > GLYCEROL
GLYCERYL *n* (something) derived from glycerol by replacing or removing one or more of its hydroxyl groups
GLYCERYLS > GLYCERYL
GLYCIN *same as* > GLYCINE
GLYCINE *n* nonessential amino acid occurring in most proteins
GLYCINES > GLYCINE
GLYCINS > GLYCIN
GLYCOCOLL *n* glycine
GLYCOGEN *n* starchlike carbohydrate stored in the liver and muscles of humans and animals
GLYCOGENS > GLYCOGEN
GLYCOL *n* another name (not in technical usage) for or a diol
GLYCOLIC > GLYCOL
GLYCOLLIC > GLYCOL
GLYCOLS > GLYCOL
GLYCONIC *n* verse consisting of a spondee, choriamb and pyrrhic
GLYCONICS > GLYCONIC
GLYCOSE *n* any of various monosaccharides
GLYCOSES > GLYCOSE
GLYCOSIDE *n* any of a group of substances, such as digitoxin, derived from monosaccharides by replacing the hydroxyl group by another group
GLYCOSYL *n* glucose-derived radical
GLYCOSYLS > GLYCOSYL
GLYCYL *n* radical of glycine
GLYCYLS > GLYCYL
GLYPH *n* carved channel or groove, esp a vertical one as used on a Doric frieze
GLYPHIC > GLYPH
GLYPHS > GLYPH
GLYPTAL *n* alkyd resin obtained from polyhydric alcohols and polybasic organic acids or their anhydrides
GLYPTALS > GLYPTAL
GLYPTIC *adj* of or relating to engraving or carving, esp on precious stones
GLYPTICS *n* art of engraving precious stones
GMELINITE *n* zeolitic mineral
GNAMMA *variant of* > NAMMA
GNAR *same as* > GNARL
GNARL *n* any knotty protuberance or swelling on a tree ▷ *vb* knot or cause to knot
GNARLED *adj* rough, twisted, and knobbly
GNARLIER > GNARLY
GNARLIEST > GNARLY
GNARLING > GNARL
GNARLS > GNARL
GNARLY *adj* good
GNARR *same as* > GNARL
GNARRED > GNAR
GNARRING > GNAR
GNARRS > GNARR
GNARS > GNAR
GNASH *vb* grind (the teeth) together in anger or pain ▷ *n* act of gnashing the teeth
GNASHED > GNASH
GNASHER *n* tooth
GNASHERS *pl n* teeth, esp false ones
GNASHES > GNASH
GNASHING > GNASH
GNAT *n* small biting two-winged fly
GNATHAL *same as* > GNATHIC
GNATHIC *adj* of or relating to the jaw
GNATHION *n* lowest point of the midline of the lower jaw: a reference point in craniometry
GNATHIONS > GNATHION
GNATHITE *n* appendage of an arthropod that is specialized for grasping or chewing
GNATHITES > GNATHITE
GNATHONIC *adj* deceitfully flattering
GNATLIKE > GNAT
GNATLING *n* small gnat
GNATLINGS > GNATLING
GNATS > GNAT
GNATTIER > GNATTY
GNATTIEST > GNATTY
GNATTY *adj* infested with gnats
GNAW *vb* bite or chew steadily ▷ *n* act or an instance of gnawing
GNAWABLE > GNAW
GNAWED > GNAW
GNAWER > GNAW
GNAWERS > GNAW
GNAWING > GNAW
GNAWINGLY > GNAW
GNAWINGS > GNAW
GNAWN > GNAW
GNAWS > GNAW
GNEISS *n* coarse-grained metamorphic rock
GNEISSES > GNEISS
GNEISSIC > GNEISS
GNEISSOID > GNEISS
GNEISSOSE > GNEISS
GNOCCHI *n* dumplings made of pieces of semolina pasta, or sometimes potato, used to garnish soup or served alone with sauce
GNOCCHIS > GNOCCHI
GNOMAE > GNOME
GNOME *n* imaginary creature like a little old man
GNOMELIKE > GNOME
GNOMES > GNOME
GNOMIC *adj* of pithy sayings
GNOMICAL *same as* > GNOMIC
GNOMISH > GNOME
GNOMIST *n* writer of pithy sayings
GNOMISTS > GNOMIST
GNOMON *n* stationary arm that projects the shadow on a sundial
GNOMONIC > GNOMON
GNOMONICS > GNOMON
GNOMONS > GNOMON
GNOSES > GNOSIS
GNOSIS *n* supposedly revealed knowledge of various spiritual truths, esp that said to have been possessed by ancient Gnostics
GNOSTIC *adj* of, relating to, or possessing knowledge, esp esoteric spiritual knowledge ▷ *n* one who knows
GNOSTICAL *same as* > GNOSTIC
GNOSTICS > GNOSTIC
GNOW *n* Australian wild bird
GNOWS > GNOW
GNU *n* ox-like S African antelope
GNUS > GNU
GO *vb* move to or from a place ▷ *n* attempt
GOA *n* gazelle, *Procapra picticaudata*, inhabiting the plains of the Tibetan plateau, having a brownish-grey coat and backward-curving horns
GOAD *vb* provoke (someone) to take some kind of action, usu in anger ▷ *n* spur or provocation
GOADED > GOAD
GOADING > GOAD
GOADLIKE > GOAD
GOADS > GOAD
GOADSMAN *n* person who uses a goad
GOADSMEN > GOADSMAN
GOADSTER *n* goadsman
GOADSTERS > GOADSTER
GOAF *n* waste left in old mine workings
GOAFS > GOAF
GOAL *n* posts through which the ball or puck has to be propelled to score ▷ *vb* in rugby, to convert a try into a goal
GOALBALL *n* game played by two teams who compete to score goals by throwing a ball that emits audible sound when in motion. Players, who may be blind or sighted, are blindfolded during play
GOALBALLS > GOALBALL
GOALED > GOAL
GOALIE *n* goalkeeper
GOALIES > GOALIE
GOALING > GOAL
GOALLESS > GOAL
GOALMOUTH *n* area in front of the goal
GOALPOST *n* one of the two posts marking the limit of a goal
GOALPOSTS > GOALPOST
GOALS > GOAL
GOALWARD *adv* towards a goal
GOANNA *n* large Australian lizard
GOANNAS > GOANNA
GOARY *variant spelling of* > GORY
GOAS > GOA
GOAT *n* sure-footed ruminant animal with

horns
GOATEE *n* pointed tuft-like beard
GOATEED > GOATEE
GOATEES > GOATEE
GOATFISH *n* red mullet
GOATHERD *n* person who looks after a herd of goats
GOATHERDS > GOATHERD
GOATIER > GOAT
GOATIEST > GOAT
GOATISH *adj* of, like, or relating to a goat
GOATISHLY > GOATISH
GOATLIKE > GOAT
GOATLING *n* young goat
GOATLINGS > GOATLING
GOATS > GOAT
GOATSKIN *n* leather made from the skin of a goat
GOATSKINS > GOATSKIN
GOATWEED *n* plant of the genus Capraria
GOATWEEDS > GOATWEED
GOATY > GOAT
GOB *n* lump of a soft substance ▷ *vb* spit
GOBAN *n* board on which go is played
GOBANG *n* Japanese board-game
GOBANGS > GOBANG
GOBANS > GOBAN
GOBBED > GOB
GOBBELINE *same as* > GOBLIN
GOBBET *n* lump, esp of food
GOBBETS > GOBBET
GOBBI > GOBBO
GOBBIER > GOBBY
GOBBIEST > GOBBY
GOBBING > GOB
GOBBLE *vb* eat hastily and greedily ▷ *n* rapid gurgling cry of the male turkey ▷ *interj* imitation of this sound
GOBBLED > GOBBLE
GOBBLER *n* turkey
GOBBLERS > GOBBLER
GOBBLES > GOBBLE
GOBBLING > GOBBLE
GOBBO *n* hunchback
GOBBY *adj* loudmouthed and offensive
GOBIES > GOBY
GOBIID *n* member of the genus Gobius
GOBIIDS > GOBIID
GOBIOID *adj* of or relating to the *Gobioidea*, a suborder of spiny-finned teleost fishes that includes gobies and mudskippers (family *Gobiidae*) and sleepers (family *Eleotridae*) ▷ *n* any gobioid fish
GOBIOIDS > GOBIOID
GOBLET *n* drinking cup without handles
GOBLETS > GOBLET
GOBLIN *n* (in folklore) small malevolent creature
GOBLINS > GOBLIN
GOBO *n* shield placed around a microphone to exclude unwanted sounds
GOBOES > GOBO
GOBONEE *same as* > GOBONY
GOBONY *adj* in heraldry, composed of a row of small, alternately-coloured, squares
GOBOS > GOBO
GOBS > GOB
GOBSHITE *n* stupid person
GOBSHITES > GOBSHITE
GOBURRA *n* kookaburra
GOBURRAS > GOBURRA
GOBY *n* small spiny-finned fish
GOD *n* spirit or being worshipped as having supernatural power ▷ *vb* deify
GODCHILD *n* child for whom a person stands as godparent
GODDAM *vb* damn
GODDAMMED > GODDAM
GODDAMN *interj* oath expressing anger, surprise, etc ▷ *adj* extremely ▷ *vb* damn
GODDAMNED > GODDAMN
GODDAMNS > GODDAMN
GODDAMS > GODDAM
GODDED > GOD
GODDEN *n* evening greeting
GODDENS > GODDEN
GODDESS *n* female divinity
GODDESSES > GODDESS
GODDING > GOD
GODET *n* triangular piece of material inserted into a garment, such as into a skirt to create a flare
GODETIA *n* plant with showy flowers
GODETIAS > GODETIA
GODETS > GODET
GODFATHER *n* male godparent ▷ *vb* be a godfather to
GODHEAD *n* essential nature and condition of being a god
GODHEADS > GODHEAD
GODHOOD *n* state of being divine
GODHOODS > GODHOOD
GODLESS *adj* wicked or unprincipled
GODLESSLY > GODLESS
GODLIER > GODLY
GODLIEST > GODLY
GODLIKE *adj* resembling or befitting a god or God
GODLILY > GODLY
GODLINESS > GODLY
GODLING *n* little god
GODLINGS > GODLING
GODLY *adj* devout or pious
GODMOTHER *n* female godparent
GODOWN *n* (in East Asia and India) warehouse
GODOWNS > GODOWN
GODPARENT *n* person who promises at a child's baptism to bring the child up as a Christian
GODROON *same as* > GADROON
GODROONED > GODROON
GODROONS > GODROON
GODS > GOD
GODSEND *n* something unexpected but welcome
GODSENDS > GODSEND
GODSHIP *n* divinity
GODSHIPS > GODSHIP
GODSLOT *n* time in a television or radio schedule traditionally reserved for religious broadcasts
GODSLOTS > GODSLOT
GODSO *same as* > GADSO
GODSON *n* male godchild
GODSONS > GODSON
GODSOS > GODSO
GODSPEED *n* expression of one's good wishes for a person's success and safety
GODSPEEDS > GODSPEED
GODSQUAD *n* informal, sometimes derogatory term for any group of evangelical Christians, members of which are regarded as intrusive and exuberantly pious
GODSQUADS > GODSQUAD
GODWARD *adv* towards God
GODWARDS *same as* > GODWARD
GODWIT *n* shore bird with long legs and an upturned bill
GODWITS > GODWIT
GOE *same as* > GO
GOEL *n* in Jewish law, blood-avenger
GOELS > GOEL
GOER *n* person who attends something regularly
GOERS > GOER
GOES > GO
GOETHITE *n* black, brown, or yellow mineral consisting of hydrated iron oxide in the form of orthorhombic crystals or fibrous masses
GOETHITES > GOETHITE
GOETIC > GOETY
GOETIES > GOETY
GOETY *n* witchcraft
GOEY *adj* go-ahead
GOFER *n* employee or assistant whose duties include menial tasks such as running errands
GOFERS > GOFER
GOFF *obsolete variant of* > GOLF
GOFFED > GOFF
GOFFER *vb* press pleats into (a frill) ▷ *n* ornamental frill made by pressing pleats
GOFFERED > GOFFER
GOFFERING > GOFFER
GOFFERS > GOFFER
GOFFING > GOFF
GOFFS > GOFF
GOGGA *n* any small insect
GOGGAS > GOGGA
GOGGLE *vb* (of the eyes) bulge ▷ *n* fixed or bulging stare
GOGGLEBOX *n* television set
GOGGLED > GOGGLE
GOGGLER *n* big-eyed scad
GOGGLERS > GOGGLER
GOGGLES > GOGGLE
GOGGLIER > GOGGLE
GOGGLIEST > GOGGLE
GOGGLING > GOGGLE
GOGGLINGS > GOGGLE
GOGGLY > GOGGLE
GOGLET *n* long-necked water-cooling vessel of porous earthenware, used esp in India
GOGLETS > GOGLET
GOGO *n* disco
GOGOS > GOGO
GOHONZON *n* (in Nichiren Buddhism) paper scroll to which devotional chanting is directed
GOHONZONS > GOHONZON
GOIER > GOEY
GOIEST > GOEY
GOING > GO
GOINGS > GO
GOITER *same as* > GOITRE
GOITERED > GOITER
GOITERS > GOITER
GOITRE *n* swelling of the thyroid gland in the neck
GOITRED > GOITRE
GOITRES > GOITRE
GOITROGEN *n* substance that induces the formation of a goitre
GOITROUS > GOITRE
GOLCONDA *n* source of wealth or riches, esp a mine
GOLCONDAS > GOLCONDA
GOLD *n* yellow precious metal ▷ *adj* made of gold
GOLDARN *euphemistic variant of* > GODDAMN
GOLDARNS > GODDAMN
GOLDBRICK *vb* swindle
GOLDBUG *n* American beetle with a bright metallic lustre
GOLDBUGS > GOLDBUG
GOLDCREST *n* small bird with a yellow crown
GOLDEN *adj* made of gold ▷ *vb* gild
GOLDENED > GOLDEN
GOLDENER > GOLDEN
GOLDENEST > GOLDEN
GOLDENEYE *n* either of two black-and-white diving ducks, *Bucephala clangula* or *B. islandica*, of northern regions
GOLDENING > GOLDEN

GOLDENLY > GOLDEN
GOLDENROD *n* tall plant with spikes of small yellow flowers
GOLDENS > GOLDEN
GOLDER > GOLD
GOLDEST > GOLD
GOLDEYE *n* North American clupeoid fish, *Hiodon alosoides*, with yellowish eyes, silvery sides, and a dark blue back: family *Hiodontidae* (mooneyes)
GOLDEYES > GOLDEYE
GOLDFIELD *n* area in which there are gold deposits
GOLDFINCH *n* kind of finch, the male of which has yellow-and-black wings
GOLDFINNY *same as* > GOLDSINNY
GOLDFISH *n* orange fish kept in ponds or aquariums
GOLDIER > GOLDY
GOLDIEST > GOLDY
GOLDISH > GOLD
GOLDLESS > GOLD
GOLDMINER *n* miner who works in a gold mine
GOLDS > GOLD
GOLDSINNY *n* any of various small European wrasses, esp the brightly coloured *Ctenolabrus rupestris*
GOLDSIZE *n* adhesive used to fix gold leaf to a surface
GOLDSIZES > GOLDSIZE
GOLDSMITH *n* dealer in or maker of gold articles
GOLDSPINK *n* goldfinch
GOLDSTICK *n* colonel in the Life Guards who carries out ceremonial duties
GOLDSTONE *another name for* > AVENTURINE
GOLDTAIL as in *goldtail moth* European moth with white wings and a soft white furry body with a yellow tail tuft
GOLDTONE *adj* gold-coloured
GOLDURN *variant of* > GODDAMN
GOLDURNS > GOLDURN
GOLDY *adj* gold-like
GOLE *obsolete spelling of* > GOAL
GOLEM *n* (in Jewish legend) artificially created human being brought to life by supernatural means
GOLEMS > GOLEM
GOLES > GOLE
GOLF *n* outdoor game in which a ball is struck with clubs into a series of holes ▷ *vb* play golf
GOLFED > GOLF
GOLFER *n* person who plays golf
GOLFERS > GOLFER
GOLFIANA *n* golfing collectibles
GOLFIANAS > GOLFIANA
GOLFING > GOLF
GOLFINGS > GOLF
GOLFS > GOLF
GOLGOTHA *n* place of burial
GOLGOTHAS > GOLGOTHA
GOLIARD *n* one of a number of wandering scholars in 12th- and 13th-century Europe famed for their riotous behaviour, intemperance, and composition of satirical and ribald Latin verse
GOLIARDIC > GOLIARD
GOLIARDS > GOLIARD
GOLIARDY > GOLIARD
GOLIAS *vb* behave outrageously
GOLIASED > GOLIAS
GOLIASES > GOLIAS
GOLIASING > GOLIAS
GOLIATH *n* giant
GOLIATHS > GOLIATH
GOLLAN *n* yellow flower
GOLLAND *same as* > GOLLAN
GOLLANDS > GOLLAND
GOLLANS > GOLLAN
GOLLAR *same as* > GOLLER
GOLLARED > GOLLAR
GOLLARING > GOLLAR
GOLLARS > GOLLAR
GOLLER *vb* roar
GOLLERED > GOLLER
GOLLERING > GOLLER
GOLLERS > GOLLER
GOLLIED > GOLLY
GOLLIES > GOLLY
GOLLIWOG *n* soft black-faced doll
GOLLIWOGG *same as* > GOLLIWOG
GOLLIWOGS > GOLLIWOG
GOLLOP *vb* eat or drink (something) quickly or greedily
GOLLOPED > GOLLOP
GOLLOPER > GOLLOP
GOLLOPERS > GOLLOP
GOLLOPING > GOLLOP
GOLLOPS > GOLLOP
GOLLY *interj* exclamation of mild surprise ▷ *n* short for GOLLIWOG: used chiefly by children ▷ *vb* spit
GOLLYING > GOLLY
GOLLYWOG *same as* > GOLLIWOG
GOLLYWOGS > GOLLYWOG
GOLOMYNKA *n* oily fish found only in Lake Baikal
GOLOSH *same as* > GALOSH
GOLOSHE *same as* > GALOSH
GOLOSHED > GOLOSH
GOLOSHES > GOLOSH
GOLOSHING > GOLOSH
GOLOSHOES > GOLOSH
GOLP *same as* > GOLPE
GOLPE *n* in heraldry, a purple circle
GOLPES > GOLPE
GOLPS > GOLP
GOMBEEN *n* usury
GOMBEENS > GOMBEEN
GOMBO *same as* > GUMBO
GOMBOS > GOMBO
GOMBRO *same as* > GUMBO
GOMBROON *n* Persian and Chinese pottery and porcelain wares
GOMBROONS > GOMBROON
GOMBROS > GOMBRO
GOMER *n* unwanted hospital patient
GOMERAL *same as* > GOMERIL
GOMERALS > GOMERAL
GOMEREL *same as* > GOMERIL
GOMERELS > GOMEREL
GOMERIL *n* slow-witted or stupid person
GOMERILS > GOMERIL
GOMERS > GOMER
GOMOKU *another word for* > GOBANG
GOMOKUS > GOMOKU
GOMPA *n* Tibetan monastery
GOMPAS > GOMPA
GOMPHOSES > GOMPHOSIS
GOMPHOSIS *n* form of immovable articulation in which a peglike part fits into a cavity, as in the setting of a tooth in its socket
GOMUTI *n* East Indian feather palm, *Arenga pinnata*, whose sweet sap is a source of sugar
GOMUTIS > GOMUTI
GOMUTO *same as* > GOMUTI
GOMUTOS > GOMUTO
GON *n* geometrical grade
GONAD *n* organ producing reproductive cells, such as a testicle or ovary
GONADAL > GONAD
GONADIAL > GONAD
GONADIC > GONAD
GONADS > GONAD
GONDELAY *same as* > GONDOLA
GONDELAYS > GONDELAY
GONDOLA *n* long narrow boat used in Venice
GONDOLAS > GONDOLA
GONDOLIER *n* person who propels a gondola
GONE > GO
GONEF *same as* > GANEF
GONEFS > GONEF
GONENESS *n* faintness from hunger
GONER *n* person or thing beyond help or recovery
GONERS > GONER
GONFALON *n* banner hanging from a crossbar, used esp by certain medieval Italian republics or in ecclesiastical processions
GONFALONS > GONFALON
GONFANON *same as* > GONFALON
GONFANONS > GONFANON
GONG *n* rimmed metal disc that produces a note when struck ▷ *vb* sound a gong
GONGED > GONG
GONGING > GONG
GONGLIKE > GONG
GONGS > GONG
GONGSTER *n* person who strikes a gong
GONGSTERS > GONGSTER
GONGYO *n* (in Nichiren Buddhism) ceremony, performed twice a day, involving reciting parts of the Lotus Sutra and chanting the Daimoku to the Gohonzon
GONGYOS > GONGYO
GONIA > GONION
GONIATITE *n* any extinct cephalopod mollusc of the genus *Goniatites* and related genera, similar to ammonites
GONIDIA > GONIDIUM
GONIDIAL > GONIDIUM
GONIDIC > GONIDIUM
GONIDIUM *n* green algal cell in the thallus of a lichen
GONIF *same as* > GANEF
GONIFF *same as* > GANEF
GONIFFS > GONIFF
GONIFS > GANIF
GONION *n* point or apex of the angle of the lower jaw
GONIUM *n* immature reproductive cell
GONK *n* stuffed toy, often used as a mascot
GONKS > GONK
GONNA *vb* going to
GONOCOCCI *n, plural of singular* gonococcus: bacterium that causes gonorrhea
GONOCYTE *n* oocyte or spermatocyte
GONOCYTES > GONOCYTE
GONODUCT *n* duct leading from a gonad to the exterior, through which gametes pass
GONODUCTS > GONODUCT
GONOF *same as* > GANEF
GONOFS > GANOF
GONOPH *same as* > GANEF
GONOPHORE *n* polyp in certain coelenterates that bears gonads
GONOPHS > GONOPH
GONOPOD *n* either member of a pair of appendages that are the external reproductive organs of insects and some other arthropods
GONOPODS > GONOPOD
GONOPORE *n* external pore in insects, earthworms, etc, through which the gametes are extruded
GONOPORES > GONOPORE
GONORRHEA *n* infectious venereal disease

GONOSOME *n* individuals, collectively, in a colonial animal that are involved with reproduction
GONOSOMES > GONOSOME
GONS > GON
GONYS *n* lower outline of a bird's bill
GONYSES > GONYS
GONZO *adj* wild or crazy
GOO *n* sticky substance
GOOBER *another name for* > PEANUT
GOOBERS > GOOBER
GOOBIES > GOOBY
GOOBY *n* spittle
GOOD *adj* giving pleasure ▷ *n* benefit
GOODBY *same as* > GOODBYE
GOODBYE *n* expression used on parting ▷ *interj* expression used on parting ▷ *sentence substitute* farewell: a conventional expression used at leave-taking or parting with people and at the loss or rejection of things or ideas
GOODBYES > GOODBYE
GOODBYS > GOODBY
GOODFACED *adj* with a handsome face
GOODIE *same as* > GOODY
GOODIER > GOODY
GOODIES > GOODY
GOODIEST > GOODY
GOODINESS > GOODY
GOODISH > GOOD
GOODLIER > GOODLY
GOODLIEST > GOODLY
GOODLY *adj* considerable
GOODMAN *n* husband
GOODMEN > GOODMAN
GOODNESS *n* quality of being good ▷ *interj* exclamation of surprise
GOODNIGHT *n* conventional expression of farewell used in the evening or at night
GOODS > GOOD
GOODSIRE *n* grandfather
GOODSIRES > GOODSIRE
GOODTIME *adj* wildly seeking pleasure
GOODWIFE *n* mistress of a household
GOODWILL *n* kindly feeling
GOODWILLS > GOODWILL
GOODWIVES > GOODWIFE
GOODY *n* hero in a book or film ▷ *interj* child's exclamation of pleasure ▷ *adj* smug and sanctimonious
GOODYEAR *n* euphemistic term for the Devil
GOODYEARS > GOODYEAR
GOOEY *adj* sticky and soft
GOOEYNESS > GOOEY
GOOF *n* mistake ▷ *vb* make a mistake
GOOFBALL *n* barbiturate sleeping pill
GOOFBALLS > GOOFBALL
GOOFED > GOOF
GOOFIER > GOOFY
GOOFIEST > GOOFY
GOOFILY > GOOFY
GOOFINESS > GOOFY
GOOFING > GOOF
GOOFS > GOOF
GOOFY *adj* silly or ridiculous
GOOG *n* egg
GOOGLE *vb* search for (something) on the internet using a search engine
GOOGLED > GOOGLE
GOOGLES > GOOGLE
GOOGLIES > GOOGLY
GOOGLING > GOOGLE
GOOGLY *n* ball that spins unexpectedly from off to leg on the bounce
GOOGOL *n* number represented as one followed by 100 zeros (10^{100})
GOOGOLS > GOOGOL
GOOGS > GOOG
GOOIER > GOOEY
GOOIEST > GOOEY
GOOILY > GOOEY
GOOK *n* derogatory word for a person from a Far Eastern country
GOOKS > GOOK
GOOKY *adj* sticky and messy
GOOL *n* corn marigold
GOOLD *Scots word for* > GOLD
GOOLDS > GOOLD
GOOLEY *same as* > GOOLIE
GOOLEYS > GOOLEY
GOOLIE *n* testicle
GOOLIES > GOOLIE
GOOLS > GOOL
GOOLY *same as* > GOOLIE
GOOMBAH *n* patron or mentor
GOOMBAHS > GOOMBAH
GOOMBAY *n* Bahamian soft drink
GOOMBAYS > GOOMBAY
GOON *n* stupid person
GOONDA *n* (in India) habitual criminal
GOONDAS > GOONDA
GOONEY *n* albatross
GOONEYS > GOONEY
GOONIE *Scots word for a* > GOWN
GOONIER > GOON
GOONIES > GOONIE
GOONIEST > GOON
GOONS > GOON
GOONY > GOON
GOOP *n* rude or ill-mannered person
GOOPIER > GOOP
GOOPIEST > GOOP
GOOPS > GOOP
GOOPY > GOOP
GOOR *same as* > GUR
GOORAL *same as* > GORAL
GOORALS > GOORAL
GOORIE *See* > KURI
GOORIES > GOORIE
GOOROO *same as* > GURU
GOOROOS > GOOROO
GOORS > GOOR
GOORY > GOOR
GOOS > GOO
GOOSANDER *n* type of duck
GOOSE *n* web-footed bird like a large duck ▷ *vb* prod (someone) playfully in the bottom
GOOSED > GOOSE
GOOSEFISH *another name for* > MONKFISH
GOOSEFOOT *n* any typically weedy chenopodiaceous plant of the genus *Chenopodium*, having small greenish flowers and leaves shaped like a goose's foot
GOOSEGOB > GOOSEBERRY
GOOSEGOBS > GOOSEBERRY
GOOSEGOG *dialect or informal word for* > GOOSEGOG
GOOSEGOGS > GOOSEBERRY
GOOSEHERD *n* person who herds geese
GOOSENECK *n* pivot between the forward end of a boom and a mast, to allow the boom to swing freely
GOOSERIES > GOOSERY
GOOSERY *n* place for keeping geese
GOOSES > GOOSE
GOOSEY *same as* > GOOSY
GOOSEYS > GOOSEY
GOOSIER > GOOSY
GOOSIES > GOOSY
GOOSIEST > GOOSY
GOOSINESS > GOOSY
GOOSING > GOOSE
GOOSY *adj* of or like a goose
GOPAK *n* spectacular high-leaping Russian peasant dance for men
GOPAKS > GOPAK
GOPHER *n* American burrowing rodent ▷ *vb* burrow
GOPHERED > GOPHER
GOPHERING > GOPHER
GOPHERS > GOPHER
GOPIK *n* money unit of Azerbaijan
GOPURA *n* gateway tower of an Indian temple
GOPURAM *same as* > GOPURA
GOPURAMS > GOPURA
GOPURAS > GOPURA
GOR *interj* God!
GORA *n* (in informal Indian English) White or fair-skinned male
GORAL *n* small goat antelope, *Naemorhedus goral*, inhabiting mountainous regions of S Asia. It has a yellowish-grey and black coat and small conical horns
GORALS > GORAL
GORAMIES > GORAMY
GORAMY *same as* > GOURAMI
GORAS > GORA
GORBELLY *n* large belly
GORBLIMEY *interj* exclamation of surprise or annoyance
GORBLIMY *same as* > GORBLIMEY
GORCOCK *n* male of the red grouse
GORCOCKS > GORCOCK
GORCROW *n* carrion crow
GORCROWS > GORCROW
GORDITA *n* small thick tortilla
GORDITAS > GORDITA
GORE *n* blood from a wound ▷ *vb* pierce with horns
GORED > GORE
GOREHOUND *n* enthusiast of gory horror films
GORES > GORE
GORGE *n* deep narrow valley ▷ *vb* eat greedily
GORGEABLE > GORGE
GORGED > GORGE
GORGEDLY > GORGE
GORGEOUS *adj* strikingly beautiful or attractive
GORGER > GORGE
GORGERIN *another name for* > NECKING
GORGERINS > GORGERIN
GORGERS > GORGE
GORGES > GORGE
GORGET *n* collar-like piece of armour worn to protect the throat
GORGETED > GORGET
GORGETS > GORGET
GORGIA *n* improvised sung passage
GORGIAS > GORGIA
GORGING > GORGE
GORGIO *n* word used by gypsies for a non-gypsy
GORGIOS > GORGIO
GORGON *n* terrifying or repulsive woman
GORGONEIA *n* plural of gorgoneion: representation of a Gorgon's head
GORGONIAN *n* any coral of the order *Gorgonacea*, having a horny or calcareous branching skeleton: includes the sea fans and red corals ▷ *adj* of, relating to, or belonging to the *Gorgonacea*
GORGONISE *vb* turn to stone
GORGONIZE *same as* > GORGONISE
GORGONS > GORGON
GORHEN *n* female red grouse
GORHENS > GORHEN
GORI *n* in informal Indian English, a White or fair-skinned female
GORIER > GORY

GORIEST > GORY
GORILLA *n* largest of the apes, found in Africa
GORILLAS > GORILLA
GORILLIAN > GORILLA
GORILLINE > GORILLA
GORILLOID > GORILLA
GORILY > GORY
GORINESS > GORY
GORING > GORE
GORINGS > GORE
GORIS > GORI
GORM *n* foolish person ▷ *vb* understand
GORMAND *same as* > GOURMAND
GORMANDS > GOURMAND
GORMED > GORM
GORMIER > GORMY
GORMIEST > GORMY
GORMING > GORM
GORMLESS *adj* stupid
GORMS > GORM
GORMY *adj* gormless
GORP *same as* > GAWP
GORPED > GAWP
GORPING > GAWP
GORPS > GAWP
GORSE *n* prickly yellow-flowered shrub
GORSEDD *n* meeting of bards and druids held daily before an eisteddfod
GORSEDDS > GORSEDD
GORSES > GORSE
GORSIER > GORSE
GORSIEST > GORSE
GORSOON *n* young boy
GORSOONS > GORSOON
GORSY > GORSE
GORY *adj* horrific or bloodthirsty
GOS > GO
GOSH *interj* exclamation of mild surprise or wonder
GOSHAWK *n* large hawk
GOSHAWKS > GOSHAWK
GOSHT *n* Indian meat dish
GOSHTS > GOSHT
GOSLARITE *n* hydrated zinc sulphate
GOSLET *n* pygmy goose
GOSLETS > GOSLET
GOSLING *n* young goose
GOSLINGS > GOSLING
GOSPEL *n* any of the first four books of the New Testament ▷ *adj* denoting a kind of religious music originating in the churches of the Black people in the Southern US ▷ *vb* teach the gospel
GOSPELER *same as* > GOSPELLER
GOSPELERS > GOSPELER
GOSPELISE *vb* evangelise
GOSPELIZE *same as* > GOSPELISE
GOSPELLED > GOSPEL
GOSPELLER *n* person who reads or chants the Gospel in a religious service
GOSPELLY > GOSPEL
GOSPELS > GOSPEL
GOSPODA > GOSPODIN
GOSPODAR *n* hospodar
GOSPODARS > GOSPODAR
GOSPODIN *n* Russian title of address, often indicating respect, equivalent to *sir* when used alone or to *Mr* when before a name
GOSPORT *n* aeroplane communication device
GOSPORTS > GOSPORT
GOSS *vb* spit
GOSSAMER *n* very fine fabric
GOSSAMERS > GOSSAMER
GOSSAMERY > GOSSAMER
GOSSAN *n* oxidised portion of a mineral vein in rock
GOSSANS > GOSSAN
GOSSE *variant of* > GORSE
GOSSED > GOSS
GOSSES > GOSSE
GOSSIB *n* gossip
GOSSIBS > GOSSIB
GOSSING > GOSS
GOSSIP *n* idle talk, esp about other people ▷ *vb* engage in gossip
GOSSIPED > GOSSIP
GOSSIPER > GOSSIP
GOSSIPERS > GOSSIP
GOSSIPING > GOSSIP
GOSSIPPED > GOSSIP
GOSSIPPER > GOSSIP
GOSSIPRY *n* idle talk
GOSSIPS > GOSSIP
GOSSIPY > GOSSIP
GOSSOON *n* boy, esp a servant boy
GOSSOONS > GOSSOON
GOSSYPINE *adj* cottony
GOSSYPOL *n* toxic crystalline pigment that is a constituent of cottonseed oil
GOSSYPOLS > GOSSYPOL
GOSTER *vb* laugh uncontrollably
GOSTERED > GOSTER
GOSTERING > GOSTER
GOSTERS > GOSTER
GOT > GET
GOTCHA as in *gotcha lizard* Australian name for a crocodile
GOTCHAS > GOTCHA
GOTH *n* aficionado of Goth music and fashion
GOTHIC *adj* of or relating to a literary style characterized by gloom, the grotesque, and the supernatural ▷ *n* family of heavy script typefaces
GOTHICISE *same as* > GOTHICIZE
GOTHICISM > GOTHIC
GOTHICIZE *vb* make gothic in style
GOTHICS > GOTHIC
GOTHITE *same as* > GOETHITE
GOTHITES > GOTHITE
GOTHS > GOTH
GOTTA *vb* got to
GOTTEN *past participle of* > GET
GOUACHE *n* (painting using) watercolours mixed with glue
GOUACHES > GOUACHE
GOUGE *vb* scoop or force out ▷ *n* hole or groove
GOUGED > GOUGE
GOUGER *n* person or tool that gouges
GOUGERE *n* choux pastry flavoured with cheese
GOUGERES > GOUGERE
GOUGERS > GOUGER
GOUGES > GOUGE
GOUGING > GOUGE
GOUJEERS *same as* > GOODYEAR
GOUJON *n* small strip of fish or chicken, coated in breadcrumbs and deep-fried
GOUJONS > GOUJON
GOUK *same as* > GOWK
GOUKS > GOUK
GOULASH *n* rich stew seasoned with paprika
GOULASHES > GOULASH
GOURA *n* large, crested ground pigeon found in New Guinea
GOURAMI *n* large SE Asian labyrinth fish, *Osphronemus goramy*, used for food and (when young) as an aquarium fish
GOURAMIES > GOURAMI
GOURAMIS > GOURAMI
GOURAS > GOURA
GOURD *n* fleshy fruit of a climbing plant
GOURDE *n* standard monetary unit of Haiti, divided into 100 centimes
GOURDES > GOURDE
GOURDIER > GOURDY
GOURDIEST > GOURDY
GOURDLIKE > GOURD
GOURDS > GOURD
GOURDY *adj* (of horses) swollen-legged
GOURMAND *n* person who is very keen on food and drink
GOURMANDS > GOURMAND
GOURMET *n* connoisseur of food and drink
GOURMETS > GOURMET
GOUSTIER > GOUSTY
GOUSTIEST > GOUSTY
GOUSTROUS *adj* stormy
GOUSTY *adj* dismal
GOUT *n* disease causing inflammation of the joints
GOUTFLIES > GOUTFLY
GOUTFLY *n* fly whose larvae infect crops
GOUTIER > GOUT
GOUTIEST > GOUT
GOUTILY > GOUT
GOUTINESS > GOUT
GOUTS > GOUT
GOUTTE *n* in heraldry, charge shaped like a drop of liquid
GOUTTES > GOUTTE
GOUTWEED *n* widely naturalized Eurasian umbelliferous plant, *Aegopodium podagraria*, with white flowers and creeping underground stems
GOUTWEEDS > GOUTWEED
GOUTWORT *n* bishop's weed
GOUTWORTS > GOUTWORT
GOUTY > GOUT
GOV *n* boss
GOVERN *vb* rule, direct, or control
> GOVERNABLENESS
GOVERNALL *n* government
GOVERNED > GOVERN
GOVERNESS *n* woman teacher in a private household ▷ *vb* act as a governess
GOVERNING > GOVERN
GOVERNOR *n* official governing a province or state
GOVERNORS > GOVERNOR
GOVERNS > GOVERN
GOVS > GOV
GOWAN *n* any of various yellow or white flowers growing in fields, esp the common daisy
GOWANED > GOWAN
GOWANS > GOWAN
GOWANY > GOWAN
GOWD *Scots word for* > GOWD
GOWDER > GOWD
GOWDEST > GOWD
GOWDS > GOWD
GOWDSPINK *n* goldfinch
GOWF *vb* strike
GOWFED > GOWF
GOWFER > GOWF
GOWFERS > GOWF
GOWFING > GOWF
GOWFS > GOWF
GOWK *n* stupid person
GOWKS > GOWK
GOWL *n* substance often found in the corner of the eyes after sleep ▷ *vb* howl
GOWLAN *same as* > GOLLAN
GOWLAND *same as* > GOLLAN
GOWLANDS > GOWLAND
GOWLANS > GOWLAN
GOWLED > GOWL
GOWLING > GOWL
GOWLS > GOWL
GOWN *n* woman's long formal dress ▷ *vb* supply with or dress in a gown
GOWNBOY *n* foundationer schoolboy who wears a gown
GOWNBOYS > GOWNBOY
GOWNED > GOWN
GOWNING > GOWN
GOWNMAN *n* professional person, such as a lawyer, who wears a gown

GOWNMEN > GOWNMAN
GOWNS > GOWN
GOWNSMAN *same as* > GOWNMAN
GOWNSMEN > GOWNSMAN
GOWPEN *n* pair of cupped hands
GOWPENFUL *n* amount that can be contained in cupped hands
GOWPENS > GOWPEN
GOX *n* gaseous oxygen
GOXES > GOX
GOY *n* Jewish word for a non-Jew
GOYIM > GOY
GOYISCH > GOY
GOYISH > GOY
GOYS > GOY
GOZZAN *same as* > GOSSAN
GOZZANS > GOZZAN
GRAAL *n* holy grail
GRAALS > GRAAL
GRAB *vb* grasp suddenly, snatch ▷ *n* sudden snatch
GRABBABLE > GRAB
GRABBED > GRAB
GRABBER > GRAB
GRABBERS > GRAB
GRABBIER > GRABBY
GRABBIEST > GRABBY
GRABBING > GRAB
GRABBLE *vb* scratch or feel about with the hands
GRABBLED > GRABBLE
GRABBLER > GRABBLE
GRABBLERS > GRABBLE
GRABBLES > GRABBLE
GRABBLING > GRABBLE
GRABBY *adj* greedy or selfish
GRABEN *n* elongated trough of land produced by subsidence of the earth's crust between two faults
GRABENS > GRABEN
GRABS > GRAB
GRACE *n* beauty and elegance ▷ *vb* honour
GRACED > GRACE
GRACEFUL *adj* having beauty of movement, style, or form
GRACELESS *adj* lacking elegance
GRACES > GRACE
GRACILE *adj* gracefully thin or slender
GRACILES > GRACILIS
GRACILIS *n* thin muscle on the inner thigh
GRACILITY > GRACILE
GRACING > GRACE
GRACIOSO *n* clown in Spanish comedy
GRACIOSOS > GRACIOSO
GRACIOUS *adj* kind and courteous ▷ *interj* expression of mild surprise or wonder ▷ *interj* expression of surprise
GRACKLE *n* any American songbird of the genera *Quiscalus* and *Cassidix*, having a dark iridescent plumage: family *Icteridae* (American orioles)
GRACKLES > GRACKLE
GRAD *n* graduate
GRADABLE *adj* capable of being graded ▷ *n* word of this kind
GRADABLES > GRADABLE
GRADATE *vb* change or cause to change imperceptibly, as from one colour, tone, or degree to another
GRADATED > GRADATE
GRADATES > GRADATE
GRADATIM *adv* step by step
GRADATING > GRADATE
GRADATION *n* (stage in) a series of degrees or steps
GRADATORY *adj* moving step by step
GRADDAN *vb* dress corn
GRADDANED > GRADDAN
GRADDANS > GRADDAN
GRADE *n* place on a scale of quality, rank, or size ▷ *vb* arrange in grades
GRADED > GRADE
GRADELESS > GRADE
GRADELIER > GRADELY
GRADELY *adj* fine
GRADER *n* person or thing that grades
GRADERS > GRADER
GRADES > GRADE
GRADIENT *n* (degree of) slope ▷ *adj* sloping uniformly
GRADIENTS > GRADIENT
GRADIN *n* ledge above or behind an altar on which candles, a cross, or other ornaments stand
GRADINE *same as* > GRADIN
GRADINES > GRADINE
GRADING > GRADE
GRADINI > GRADINO
GRADINO *n* step above an altar
GRADINS > GRADIN
GRADS > GRAD
GRADUAL *adj* occurring, developing, or moving in small stages ▷ *n* antiphon or group of several antiphons, usually from the Psalms, sung or recited immediately after the epistle at Mass
GRADUALLY > GRADUAL
GRADUALS > GRADUAL
GRADUAND *n* person who is about to graduate
GRADUANDS > GRADUAND
GRADUATE *vb* receive a degree or diploma ▷ *n* holder of a degree
GRADUATED > GRADUATE
GRADUATES > GRADUATE
GRADUATOR > GRADUATE
GRADUS *n* book of études or other musical exercises arranged in order of increasing difficulty
GRADUSES > GRADUS
GRAECISE *same as* > GRAECIZE
GRAECISED > GRAECISE
GRAECISES > GRAECISE
GRAECIZE *vb* make or become like the ancient Greeks
GRAECIZED > GRAECIZE
GRAECIZES > GRAECIZE
GRAFF *same as* > GRAFT
GRAFFED > GRAFF
GRAFFING > GRAFF
GRAFFITI *pl n* words or drawings scribbled or sprayed on walls etc
GRAFFITIS > GRAFFITI
GRAFFITO *n* instance of graffiti
GRAFFS > GRAFF
GRAFT *n* surgical transplant of skin or tissue ▷ *vb* transplant (living tissue) surgically
GRAFTAGE *n* in horticulture, the art of grafting
GRAFTAGES > GRAFTAGE
GRAFTED > GRAFT
GRAFTER > GRAFT
GRAFTERS > GRAFT
GRAFTING > GRAFT
GRAFTINGS > GRAFT
GRAFTS > GRAFT
GRAHAM *n* made of graham flour
GRAHAMS > GRAHAM
GRAIL *n* any desired ambition or goal
GRAILE *same as* > GRAIL
GRAILES > GRAILE
GRAILS > GRAIL
GRAIN *n* seedlike fruit of a cereal plant ▷ *vb* paint in imitation of the grain of wood or leather
GRAINAGE *n* duty paid on grain
GRAINAGES > GRAINAGE
GRAINE *n* eggs of the silkworm
GRAINED > GRAIN
GRAINER > GRAIN
GRAINERS > GRAIN
GRAINES > GRAINE
GRAINIER > GRAINY
GRAINIEST > GRAINY
GRAINING *n* pattern or texture of the grain of wood, leather, etc
GRAININGS > GRAINING
GRAINLESS > GRAIN
GRAINS > GRAIN
GRAINY *adj* resembling, full of, or composed of grain
GRAIP *n* long-handled gardening fork
GRAIPS > GRAIP
GRAITH *vb* clothe
GRAITHED > GRAITH
GRAITHING > GRAITH
GRAITHLY > GRAITH
GRAITHS > GRAITH
GRAKLE *same as* > GRACKLE
GRAKLES > GRAKLE
GRALLOCH *n* entrails of a deer ▷ *vb* disembowel (a deer killed in a hunt)
GRALLOCHS > GRALLOCH
GRAM *n* metric unit of mass equal to one thousandth of a kilogram
GRAMA *n* any of various grasses of the genus *Bouteloua*, of W North America and South America: often used as pasture grasses
GRAMARIES > GRAMARY
GRAMARY *same as* > GRAMARYE
GRAMARYE *n* magic, necromancy, or occult learning
GRAMARYES > GRAMARYE
GRAMAS > GRAMA
GRAMASH *n* type of gaiter
GRAMASHES > GRAMASH
GRAME *n* sorrow
GRAMERCY *interj* many thanks
GRAMES > GRAME
GRAMMA *n* pasture grass of the South American plains
GRAMMAGE *n* weight of paper expressed as grams per square metre
GRAMMAGES > GRAMMAGE
GRAMMAR *n* branch of linguistics dealing with the form, function, and order of words
GRAMMARS > GRAMMAR
GRAMMAS > GRAMMA
GRAMMATIC *adj* of or relating to grammar
GRAMME *same as* > GRAME
GRAMMES > GRAM
GRAMOCHE *same as* > GRAMASH
GRAMOCHES > GRAMOCHE
GRAMP *n* grandfather
GRAMPA *variant of* > GRANDPA
GRAMPAS > GRAMPA
GRAMPS > GRAMP
GRAMPUS *n* dolphin-like mammal
GRAMPUSES > GRAMPUS
GRAMS > GRAM
GRAN *n* grandmother
GRANA > GRANUM
GRANARIES > GRANARY
GRANARY *n* storehouse for grain
GRAND *adj* large or impressive, imposing ▷ *n* thousand pounds or dollars
GRANDAD *n* grandfather
GRANDADDY *same as* > GRANDAD
GRANDADS > GRANDAD
GRANDAM *archaic word for* > GRANDMOTHER
GRANDAME *same as* > GRANDAM

GRANDAMES > GRANDAME
GRANDAMS > GRANDAM
GRANDAUNT *n* great-aunt
GRANDBABY *n* very young grandchild
GRANDDAD *same as* > GRANDDAD
GRANDDADS > GRANDAD
GRANDDAM *same as* > GRANDAM
GRANDDAMS > GRANDDAM
GRANDE *feminine form of* > GRAND
GRANDEE *n* Spanish nobleman of the highest rank
GRANDEES > GRANDEE
GRANDER > GRAND
GRANDEST > GRAND
GRANDEUR *n* magnificence
GRANDEURS > GRANDEUR
GRANDIOSE *adj* imposing
GRANDIOSO *adv* (to be played) in a grand manner
GRANDKID *n* grandchild
GRANDKIDS > GRANDKID
GRANDLY > GRAND
GRANDMA *n* grandmother
GRANDMAMA *same as* > GRANDMA
GRANDMAS > GRANDMA
GRANDNESS > GRAND
GRANDPA *n* grandfather
GRANDPAPA *same as* > GRANDPA
GRANDPAS > GRANDPA
GRANDS > GRAND
GRANDSIR *same as* > GRANDSIRE
GRANDSIRE *n* grandfather
GRANDSIRS > GRANDSIR
GRANDSON *n* male grandchild
GRANDSONS > GRANDSON
GRANFER *n* grandfather
GRANFERS > GRANFER
GRANGE *n* country house with farm buildings
GRANGER *n* keeper or member of a grange
GRANGERS > GRANGER
GRANGES > GRANGE
GRANITA *n* Italian iced drink
GRANITAS > GRANITA
GRANITE *n* very hard igneous rock often used in building
GRANITES > GRANITE
GRANITIC > GRANITE
GRANITISE *vb* form granite
GRANITITE *n* any granite with a high content of biotite
GRANITIZE *same as* > GRANITISE
GRANITOID > GRANITE
GRANIVORE *n* animal that feeds on seeds and grain
GRANNAM *n* old woman
GRANNAMS > GRANNAM
GRANNIE *vb* defeat (in a game or contest) so that one's opponent does not score a single point
GRANNIED > GRANNY
GRANNIES *pl n* Granny Smith apples
GRANNOM *n* widespread caddis fly, *Brachycentrus subnubilus*, the larvae of which attach their cases to vegetation under running water and are esteemed as a bait by anglers
GRANNOMS > GRANNOM
GRANNY *n* grandmother ▷ *vb* defeat (in a game or contest) so that one's opponent does not score a single point
GRANNYING > GRANNY
GRANNYISH *adj* typical of or suitable for an elderly woman
GRANOLA *n* muesli-like breakfast cereal
GRANOLAS > GRANOLA
GRANOLITH *n* paving material consisting of a mixture of cement and crushed granite or granite chippings
GRANS > GRAN
GRANT *vb* consent to fulfil (a request) ▷ *n* sum of money provided by a government for a specific purpose, such as education
GRANTABLE > GRANT
GRANTED > GRANT
GRANTEE *n* person to whom a grant is made
GRANTEES > GRANTEE
GRANTER > GRANT
GRANTERS > GRANT
GRANTING > GRANT
GRANTOR *n* person who makes a grant
GRANTORS > GRANTOR
GRANTS > GRANT
GRANTSMAN *n* student who specializes in obtaining grants
GRANTSMEN > GRANTSMAN
GRANULAR *adj* of or like grains
GRANULARY *adj* granular
GRANULATE *vb* make into grains
GRANULE *n* small grain
GRANULES > GRANULE
GRANULITE *n* granular foliated metamorphic rock in which the minerals form a mosaic of equal-sized granules
GRANULOMA *n* tumour composed of granulation tissue produced in response to chronic infection, inflammation, a foreign body, or to unknown causes
GRANULOSE *less common word for* > GRANULAR
GRANULOUS *adj* consisting of grains or granules
GRANUM *n* membrane layers in a chloroplast
GRAPE *n* small juicy green or purple berry, eaten raw or used to produce wine, raisins, currants, or sultanas ▷ *vb* grope
GRAPED > GRAPE
GRAPELESS > GRAPE
GRAPELIKE > GRAPE
GRAPERIES > GRAPERY
GRAPERY *n* building where grapes are grown
GRAPES *n* abnormal growth, resembling a bunch of grapes, on the fetlock of a horse
GRAPESEED *n* seed of the grape
GRAPESHOT *n* bullets which scatter when fired
GRAPETREE *n* sea grape, a shrubby plant resembling a grapevine
GRAPEVINE *n* grape-bearing vine
GRAPEY > GRAPE
GRAPH *n* drawing showing the relation of different numbers or quantities plotted against a set of axes ▷ *vb* draw or represent in a graph
GRAPHED > GRAPH
GRAPHEME *n* one of a set of orthographic symbols (letters or combinations of letters) in a given language that serve to distinguish one word from another and usually correspond to or represent phonemes, e.g. the *f* in *fun*, the *ph* in *phantom*, and the *gh* in *laugh*
GRAPHEMES > GRAPHEME
GRAPHEMIC > GRAPHEME
GRAPHIC *adj* vividly descriptive
GRAPHICAL *same as* > GRAPHIC
GRAPHICLY > GRAPHIC
GRAPHICS *pl n* diagrams, graphs, etc, esp as used on a television programme or computer screen
GRAPHING > GRAPH
GRAPHITE *n* soft black form of carbon, used in pencil leads
GRAPHITES > GRAPHITE
GRAPHITIC > GRAPHITE
GRAPHIUM *n* stylus (for writing)
GRAPHIUMS > GRAPHIUM
GRAPHS > GRAPH
GRAPIER > GRAPE
GRAPIEST > GRAPE
GRAPINESS > GRAPE
GRAPING > GRAPE
GRAPLE *same as* > GRAPPLE
GRAPLES > GRAPLE
GRAPLIN *same as* > GRAPNEL
GRAPLINE *same as* > GRAPNEL
GRAPLINES > GRAPLINE
GRAPLINS > GRAPLIN
GRAPNEL *n* device with several hooks, used to grasp or secure things
GRAPNELS > GRAPNEL
GRAPPA *n* spirit distilled from the fermented remains of grapes after pressing
GRAPPAS > GRAPPA
GRAPPLE *vb* try to cope with (something difficult) ▷ *n* grapnel
GRAPPLED > GRAPPLE
GRAPPLER > GRAPPLE
GRAPPLERS > GRAPPLE
GRAPPLES > GRAPPLE
GRAPPLING *n* act of gripping or seizing, as in wrestling
GRAPY > GRAPE
GRASP *vb* grip something firmly ▷ *n* grip or clasp
GRASPABLE > GRASP
GRASPED > GRASP
GRASPER > GRASP
GRASPERS > GRASP
GRASPING *adj* greedy or avaricious
GRASPLESS *adj* relaxed
GRASPS > GRASP
GRASS *n* common type of plant with jointed stems and long narrow leaves, including cereals and bamboo ▷ *vb* cover with grass
GRASSED > GRASS
GRASSER *n* police informant
GRASSERS > GRASSER
GRASSES > GRASS
GRASSHOOK *another name for* > SICKLE
GRASSIER > GRASSY
GRASSIEST > GRASSY
GRASSILY > GRASSY
GRASSING > GRASS
GRASSINGS > GRASS
GRASSLAND *n* land covered with grass
GRASSLESS > GRASS
GRASSLIKE > GRASS
GRASSPLOT *n* plot of ground overgrown with grass
GRASSQUIT *n* any tropical American finch of the genus *Tiaris* and related genera, such as *T. olivacea* (**yellow-faced grassquit**)
GRASSROOT *adj* relating to the ordinary people, especially as part of the electorate
GRASSUM *n* in Scots law, lump sum paid when taking up a lease
GRASSUMS > GRASSUM
GRASSY *adj* covered with, containing, or resembling

grass
GRASTE *archaic past participle of* > GRACE
GRAT > GREET
GRATE *vb* rub into small bits on a rough surface ▷ *n* framework of metal bars for holding fuel in a fireplace
GRATED > GRATE
GRATEFUL *adj* feeling or showing gratitude
GRATELESS > GRATE
GRATER *n* tool with a sharp surface for grating food
GRATERS > GRATER
GRATES > GRATE
GRATICULE *n* grid of intersecting lines, esp of latitude and longitude on which a map is drawn
GRATIFIED > GRATIFY
GRATIFIER > GRATIFY
GRATIFIES > GRATIFY
GRATIFY *vb* satisfy or please ▷ *adj* giving one satisfaction or pleasure
GRATIN *n* crust of browned breadcrumbs
GRATINATE *vb* cook until the juice is absorbed and the surface crisps
GRATINE *adj* cooked au gratin
GRATINEE *vb* cook au gratin
GRATINEED > GRATINEE
GRATINEES > GRATINEE
GRATING *adj* harsh or rasping ▷ *n* framework of metal bars covering an opening
GRATINGLY > GRATING
GRATINGS > GRATING
GRATINS > GRATIN
GRATIS *adj* free, for nothing
GRATITUDE *n* feeling of being thankful for a favour or gift
GRATTOIR *n* scraper made of flint
GRATTOIRS > GRATTOIR
GRATUITY *n* money given for services rendered, tip
GRATULANT > GRATULATE
GRATULATE *vb* greet joyously
GRAUNCH *vb* crush or destroy
GRAUNCHED > GRAUNCH
GRAUNCHER > GRAUNCH
GRAUNCHES > GRAUNCH
GRAUPEL *n* soft hail or snow pellets
GRAUPELS > GRAUPEL
GRAV *n* unit of acceleration equal to the standard acceleration of free fall
GRAVADLAX *same as* > GRAVLAX
GRAVAMEN *n* that part of an accusation weighing most heavily against an accused
GRAVAMENS > GRAVAMEN
GRAVAMINA > GRAVAMEN
GRAVE *n* hole for burying a corpse ▷ *adj* causing concern ▷ *vb* cut, carve, sculpt, or engrave ▷ *adv* to be performed in a solemn manner
GRAVED > GRAVE
GRAVEL *n* mixture of small stones and coarse sand ▷ *vb* cover with gravel
GRAVELED > GRAVEL
GRAVELESS > GRAVE
GRAVELIKE > GRAVE
GRAVELING > GRAVEL
GRAVELISH > GRAVEL
GRAVELLED > GRAVEL
GRAVELLY *adj* covered with gravel
GRAVELS > GRAVEL
GRAVELY > GRAVE
GRAVEN > GRAVE
GRAVENESS > GRAVE
GRAVER *n* any of various engraving, chasing, or sculpting tools, such as a burin
GRAVERS > GRAVER
GRAVES > GRAVE
GRAVESIDE *n* area surrounding a grave
GRAVESITE *n* site of grave
GRAVEST > GRAVE
GRAVEWARD *adj* moving towards grave
GRAVEYARD *n* cemetery
GRAVID *adj* pregnant
GRAVIDA *n* pregnant woman
GRAVIDAE > GRAVIDA
GRAVIDAS > GRAVIDA
GRAVIDITY > GRAVID
GRAVIDLY > GRAVID
GRAVIES > GRAVY
GRAVING > GRAVE
GRAVINGS > GRAVE
> GRAVIPERCEPTION
GRAVIS *adj* as in *myasthenia gravis* chronic muscle-weakening disease
GRAVITAS *n* seriousness or solemnity
GRAVITATE *vb* be influenced or drawn towards
GRAVITIES > GRAVITY
GRAVITINO *n* hypothetical subatomic particle
GRAVITON *n* postulated quantum of gravitational energy
GRAVITONS > GRAVITON
GRAVITY *n* force of attraction of one object for another, esp of objects to the earth
GRAVLAKS *same as* > GRAVLAX
GRAVLAX *n* dry-cured salmon, marinated in salt, sugar, and spices, as served in Scandinavia
GRAVLAXES > GRAVLAX
GRAVS > GRAV
GRAVURE *n* method of intaglio printing using a plate with many small etched recesses
GRAVURES > GRAVURE
GRAVY *n* juices from meat in cooking
GRAY *same as* > GREY
GRAYBACK *same as* > GREYBACK
GRAYBACKS > GRAYBACK
GRAYBEARD *same as* > GREYBEARD
GRAYED > GRAY
GRAYER > GRAY
GRAYEST > GRAY
GRAYFISH *n* dogfish
GRAYFLIES > GRAYFLY
GRAYFLY *n* trumpet fly
GRAYHOUND *US spelling of* > GREYHOUND
GRAYING > GRAY
GRAYISH > GRAY
GRAYLAG *same as* > GREYLAG
GRAYLAGS > GRAYLAG
GRAYLE *n* holy grail
GRAYLES > GRAYLE
GRAYLING *n* fish of the salmon family
GRAYLINGS > GRAYLING
GRAYLY > GRAY
GRAYMAIL *n* tactic to avoid prosecution in espionage case by threatening to expose state secrets during trial
GRAYMAILS > GRAYMAIL
GRAYNESS > GREY
GRAYOUT *n* in aeronautics, impairment of vision due to lack of oxygen
GRAYOUTS > GRAYOUT
GRAYS > GRAY
GRAYSCALE *adj* in shades of grey
GRAYWACKE *same as* > GREYWACKE
GRAYWATER *n* water that has been used
GRAZABLE > GRAZE
GRAZE *vb* feed on grass ▷ *n* slight scratch or scrape
GRAZEABLE > GRAZE
GRAZED > GRAZE
GRAZER > GRAZE
GRAZERS > GRAZE
GRAZES > GRAZE
GRAZIER *n* person who feeds cattle for market
GRAZIERS > GRAZIER
GRAZING *n* land on which grass for livestock is grown
GRAZINGLY > GRAZE
GRAZINGS > GRAZING
GRAZIOSO *adv* (of music) to be played gracefully
GREASE *n* soft melted animal fat ▷ *vb* apply grease to
GREASED > GREASE
GREASER *n* mechanic, esp of motor vehicles
GREASERS > GREASER
GREASES > GREASE
GREASIER > GREASY
GREASIES > GREASY
GREASIEST > GREASY
GREASILY > GREASY
GREASING > GREASE
GREASY *adj* covered with or containing grease ▷ *n* shearer
GREAT *adj* large in size or number ▷ *n* distinguished person
GREATCOAT *n* heavy overcoat
GREATEN *vb* make or become great
GREATENED > GREATEN
GREATENS > GREATEN
GREATER > GREAT
GREATEST *n* most outstanding individual in a given field
GREATESTS > GREATEST
GREATLY > GREAT
GREATNESS > GREAT
GREATS > GREAT
GREAVE *n* piece of armour for the shin ▷ *vb* grieve
GREAVED > GREAVE
GREAVES *pl n* residue left after the rendering of tallow
GREAVING > GREAVE
GREBE *n* diving water bird
GREBES > GREBE
GRECE *n* flight of steps
GRECES > GRECE
GRECIAN *same as* > GRECE
GRECIANS > GRECIAN
GRECISE *same as* > GRAECIZE
GRECISED > GRECISE
GRECISES > GRECISE
GRECISING > GRECISE
GRECIZE *same as* > GRAECIZE
GRECIZED > GRECIZE
GRECIZES > GRECIZE
GRECIZING > GRECIZE
GRECQUE *n* ornament of Greek origin
GRECQUES > GRECQUE
GREE *n* superiority or victory ▷ *vb* come or cause to come to agreement or harmony
GREEBO *n* unkempt or dirty-looking young man
GREEBOES > GREEBO
GREECE *same as* > GRECE
GREECES > GREECE
GREED *n* excessive desire for food, wealth, etc
GREEDIER > GREEDY
GREEDIEST > GREEDY
GREEDILY > GREEDY
GREEDLESS > GREED
GREEDS > GREED
GREEDSOME same as > GREEDY
GREEDY *adj* having an excessive desire for something, such as food or money

GREEGREE *same as* > GRIGRI
GREEGREES > GREEGREE
GREEING > GREE
GREEK *vb* represent text as grey lines on a computer screen
GREEKED > GREEK
GREEKING > GREEK
GREEKINGS > GREEK
GREEN *adj* of a colour between blue and yellow ▷ *n* colour between blue and yellow ▷ *vb* make or become green
GREENBACK *n* inconvertible legal-tender US currency note originally issued during the Civil War in 1862
GREENBELT *n* zone of farmland, parks, and open country surrounding a town or city
GREENBONE *another name for* > BUTTERFISH
GREENBUG *n* common name for Schizaphis graminum
GREENBUGS > GREENBUG
GREENED > GREEN
GREENER *n* recent immigrant
GREENERS > GREENER
GREENERY *n* vegetation
GREENEST > GREEN
GREENFLY *n* green aphid, a common garden pest
GREENGAGE *n* sweet green plum
GREENHAND *n* greenhorn
GREENHEAD *n* male mallard
GREENHORN *n* novice
GREENIE *n* conservationist
GREENIER > GREEN
GREENIES > GREENIE
GREENIEST > GREEN
GREENING *n* process of making or becoming more aware of environmental considerations
GREENINGS > GREENING
GREENISH > GREEN
GREENLET *n* vireo, esp one of the genus *Hylophilus*
GREENLETS > GREENLET
GREENLING *n* any scorpaenoid food fish of the family *Hexagrammidae* of the North Pacific Ocean
GREENLIT *adj* given permission to proceed
GREENLY > GREEN
GREENMAIL *n* practice of a company buying sufficient shares in another company to threaten takeover and making a quick profit as a result of the threatened company buying back its shares at a higher price ▷ *vb* carry out the practice of greenmail
GREENNESS > GREEN
GREENROOM *n* backstage room in a theatre where performers rest or receive visitors
GREENS > GREEN
GREENSAND *n* olive-green sandstone consisting mainly of quartz and glauconite
GREENSICK *adj* suffering from greensickness: same as chlorosis
GREENSOME *n* match for two pairs in which each of the four players tees off and after selecting the better drive the partners of each pair play that ball alternately
GREENTH *n* greenness
GREENTHS > GREENTH
GREENWASH *n* superficial or insincere display of concern for the environment that is shown by an organization ▷ *vb* adopt a 'greenwash' policy
GREENWAY *n* linear open space, with pedestrian and cycle paths
GREENWAYS > GREENWAY
GREENWEED *n* woodwaxen
GREENWING *n* teal
GREENWOOD *n* forest or wood when the leaves are green
GREENY > GREEN
GREES > GREE
GREESE *same as* > GRECE
GREESES > GREESE
GREESING > GREESE
GREESINGS > GREESE
GREET *vb* meet with expressions of welcome ▷ *n* weeping
GREETE *same as* > GREET
GREETED > GREET
GREETER *n* person who greets people at the entrance of a shop, restaurant, casino, etc
GREETERS > GREETER
GREETES > GREETE
GREETING *n* act or words of welcoming on meeting
GREETINGS > GREETING
GREETS > GREET
GREFFIER *n* registrar
GREFFIERS > GREFFIER
GREGALE *n* northeasterly wind occurring in the Mediterranean
GREGALES > GREGALE
GREGARIAN *adj* gregarious
GREGARINE *n* any parasitic protozoan of the order *Gregarinida*, typically occurring in the digestive tract and body cavity of other invertebrates: phylum *Apicomplexa* (sporozoans) ▷ *adj* of, relating to, or belonging to the *Gregarinida*
GREGATIM *adv* in flocks or crowds
GREGE *vb* make heavy
GREGO *n* short, thick jacket
GREGOS > GREGO
GREIGE *adj* (of a fabric or material) not yet dyed ▷ *n* unbleached or undyed cloth or yarn
GREIGES > GREIGE
GREIN *vb* desire fervently
GREINED > GREIN
GREINING > GREIN
GREINS > GREIN
GREISEN *n* light-coloured metamorphic rock consisting mainly of quartz, white mica, and topaz formed by the pneumatolysis of granite
GREISENS > GREISEN
GREISLY *same as* > GRISLY
GREMIAL *n* cloth spread upon the lap of a bishop when seated during Mass
GREMIALS > GREMIAL
GREMLIN *n* imaginary being blamed for mechanical malfunctions
GREMLINS > GREMLIN
GREMMIE *n* young surfer
GREMMIES > GREMMIE
GREMMY *same as* > GREMMIE
GREMOLATA *n* garnish of finely chopped parsley, garlic and lemon
GREN *same as* > GRIN
GRENADE *n* small bomb thrown by hand or fired from a rifle
GRENADES > GRENADE
GRENADIER *n* soldier of a regiment formerly trained to throw grenades
GRENADINE *n* syrup made from pomegranates
GRENNED > GREN
GRENNING > GREN
GRENS > GREN
GRENZ as in *grenz rays* X-rays of long wavelength produced in a device when electrons are accelerated through 25 kilovolts or less
GRESE *same as* > GRECE
GRESES > GRESE
GRESSING *same as* > GRECE
GRESSINGS > GRESSING
GREVE *same as* > GREAVE
GREVES > GREVE
GREVILLEA *n* any of various Australian evergreen trees and shrubs
GREW *vb* shudder
GREWED > GROW
GREWHOUND *n* greyhound
GREWING > GROW
GREWS > GROW
GREWSOME *archaic or US spelling of* > GRUESOME
GREWSOMER > GREWSOME
GREX *n* group of plants that has arisen from the same hybrid parent group
GREXES > GREX
GREY *adj* of a colour between black and white ▷ *n* grey colour ▷ *vb* become or make grey
GREYBACK *n* any of various animals having a grey back, such as the grey whale and the hooded crow
GREYBACKS > GREYBACK
GREYBEARD *n* old man, esp a sage
GREYED > GREY
GREYER > GREY
GREYEST > GREY
GREYHEN *n* female of the black grouse
GREYHENS > GREYHEN
GREYHOUND *n* swift slender dog used in racing
GREYING > GREY
GREYINGS > GREY
GREYISH > GREY
GREYLAG *n* large grey goose
GREYLAGS > GREYLAG
GREYLIST *vb* hold (someone) in suspicion, without actually excluding him or her from a particular activity
GREYLISTS > GREYLIST
GREYLY > GREY
GREYNESS > GREY
GREYS > GREY
GREYSTONE *n* type of grey rock
GREYWACKE *n* any dark sandstone or grit having a matrix of clay minerals
GRIBBLE *n* any small marine isopod crustacean of the genus *Limnoria*, which bores into and damages wharves and other submerged wooden structures
GRIBBLES > GRIBBLE
GRICE *vb* (of a railway enthusiast) to collect objects or visit places connected with trains and railways ▷ *n* object collected or place visited by a railway enthusiast
GRICER > GRICE
GRICERS > GRICE
GRICES > GRICE
GRICING > GRICE
GRICINGS > GRICE
GRID *n* network of horizontal and vertical lines, bars, etc
GRIDDED > GRID
GRIDDER *n* American football player
GRIDDERS > GRIDDER
GRIDDLE *n* flat iron plate for cooking ▷ *vb* cook (food) on a griddle
GRIDDLED > GRIDDLE
GRIDDLES > GRIDDLE
GRIDDLING > GRIDDLE
GRIDE *vb* grate or scrape harshly ▷ *n* harsh or

piercing sound
GRIDED > GRIDE
GRIDELIN *n* greyish violet colour
GRIDELINS > GRIDELIN
GRIDES > GRIDE
GRIDING > GRIDE
GRIDIRON *n* frame of metal bars for grilling food ▷ *vb* cover with parallel lines
GRIDIRONS > GRIDIRON
GRIDLOCK *n* situation where traffic is not moving ▷ *vb* (of traffic) to obstruct (an area)
GRIDLOCKS > GRIDLOCK
GRIDS > GRID
GRIECE *same as* > GRECE
GRIECED > GRIECE
GRIECES > GRIECE
GRIEF *n* deep sadness
GRIEFER *n* online game player who intentionally spoils the game for other players
GRIEFERS > GRIEFER
GRIEFFUL *adj* stricken with grief
GRIEFLESS > GRIEF
GRIEFS > GRIEF
GRIESIE *same as* > GRISY
GRIESLY *same as* > GRISY
GRIESY *same as* > GRISY
GRIEVANCE *n* real or imaginary cause for complaint
GRIEVANT *n* any person with a grievance
GRIEVANTS > GRIEVANT
GRIEVE *vb* (cause to) feel grief ▷ *n* farm manager or overseer
GRIEVED > GRIEVE
GRIEVER > GRIEVE
GRIEVERS > GRIEVE
GRIEVES > GRIEVE
GRIEVING > GRIEVE
GRIEVINGS > GRIEVE
GRIEVOUS *adj* very severe or painful
GRIFF *n* information
GRIFFE *n* carved ornament at the base of a column, often in the form of a claw
GRIFFES > GRIFFE
GRIFFIN *n* mythical monster with an eagle's head and wings and a lion's body
GRIFFINS > GRIFFIN
GRIFFON *same as* > GRIFFIN
GRIFFONS > GRIFFON
GRIFFS > GRIFF
GRIFT *vb* swindle
GRIFTED > GRIFT
GRIFTER > GRIFT
GRIFTERS > GRIFT
GRIFTING > GRIFT
GRIFTS > GRIFT
GRIG *n* lively person ▷ *vb* fish for grigs
GRIGGED > GRIG
GRIGGING > GRIG
GRIGRI *n* African talisman, amulet, or charm
GRIGRIS > GRIGRI
GRIGS > GRIG
GRIKE *n* solution fissure, a vertical crack about 0.5 m wide formed by the dissolving of limestone by water, that divides an exposed limestone surface into sections or clints
GRIKES > GRIKE
GRILL *n* device on a cooker that radiates heat downwards ▷ *vb* cook under a grill
GRILLADE *n* grilled food
GRILLADES > GRILLADE
GRILLAGE *n* arrangement of beams and crossbeams used as a foundation on soft ground
GRILLAGES > GRILLAGE
GRILLE *n* grating over an opening
GRILLED *adj* cooked on a grill or gridiron
GRILLER > GRILL
GRILLERS > GRILL
GRILLERY *n* place where food is grilled
GRILLES > GRILLE
GRILLING > GRILL
GRILLINGS > GRILL
GRILLION *n* extremely large but unspecified number, quantity, or amount ▷ *determiner* amounting to a grillion
GRILLIONS > GRILLION
GRILLROOM *n* restaurant serving grilled foods
GRILLS > GRILL
GRILLWORK *same as* > GRILL
GRILSE *n* salmon on its first return from the sea to fresh water
GRILSES > GRILSE
GRIM *adj* stern
GRIMACE *n* ugly or distorted facial expression of pain, disgust, etc ▷ *vb* make a grimace
GRIMACED > GRIMACE
GRIMACER > GRIMACE
GRIMACERS > GRIMACE
GRIMACES > GRIMACE
GRIMACING > GRIMACE
GRIMALKIN *n* old cat, esp an old female cat
GRIME *n* ingrained dirt ▷ *vb* make very dirty
GRIMED > GRIME
GRIMES > GRIME
GRIMIER > GRIME
GRIMIEST > GRIME
GRIMILY > GRIME
GRIMINESS > GRIME
GRIMING > GRIME
GRIMLY > GRIM
GRIMMER > GRIM
GRIMMEST > GRIM
GRIMNESS > GRIM
GRIMOIRE *n* textbook of sorcery and magic
GRIMOIRES > GRIMOIRE
GRIMY > GRIME
GRIN *vb* smile broadly, showing the teeth ▷ *n* broad smile
GRINCH *n* person whose lack of enthusiasm or bad temper has a depressing effect on others
GRINCHES > GRINCH
GRIND *vb* crush or rub to a powder ▷ *n* hard work
GRINDED *obsolete past participle of* > GRIND
GRINDELIA *n* any coarse plant of the American genus *Grindelia*, having yellow daisy-like flower heads: family *Asteraceae* (composites)
GRINDER *n* device for grinding substances
GRINDERS > GRINDER
GRINDERY *n* place in which tools and cutlery are sharpened
GRINDING > GRIND
GRINDINGS > GRIND
GRINDS > GRIND
GRINGA *n* female gringo
GRINGAS > GRINGA
GRINGO *n* person from an English-speaking country: used as a derogatory term by Latin Americans
GRINGOS > GRINGO
GRINNED > GRIN
GRINNER > GRIN
GRINNERS > GRIN
GRINNING > GRIN
GRINS > GRIN
GRIOT *n* (in Western Africa) member of a caste responsible for maintaining an oral record of tribal history in the form of music, poetry, and storytelling
GRIOTS > GRIOT
GRIP *n* firm hold or grasp ▷ *vb* grasp or hold tightly
GRIPE *vb* complain persistently ▷ *n* complaint
GRIPED > GRIPE
GRIPER > GRIPE
GRIPERS > GRIPE
GRIPES > GRIPE
GRIPEY *adj* causing gripes
GRIPIER > GRIPEY
GRIPIEST > GRIPEY
GRIPING > GRIPE
GRIPINGLY > GRIPE
GRIPLE *same as* > GRIPPLE
GRIPMAN *n* cable-car operator
GRIPMEN > GRIPMAN
GRIPPE *former name for* > INFLUENZA
GRIPPED > GRIP
GRIPPER > GRIP
GRIPPERS > GRIP
GRIPPES > GRIPPE
GRIPPIER > GRIPPY
GRIPPIEST > GRIPPY
GRIPPING > GRIP
GRIPPLE *adj* greedy ▷ *n* hook
GRIPPLES > GRIPPLE
GRIPPY *adj* having grip
GRIPS > GRIP
GRIPSACK *n* travel bag
GRIPSACKS > GRIPSACK
GRIPT *archaic variant of* > GRIPPED
GRIPTAPE *n* rough tape for sticking to a surface to provide a greater grip
GRIPTAPES > GRIPTAPE
GRIPY *same as* > GRIPEY
GRIS *same as* > GRECE
GRISAILLE *n* technique of monochrome painting in shades of grey, as in an oil painting or a wall decoration, imitating the effect of relief
GRISE *vb* shudder
GRISED > GRISE
GRISELY *same as* > GRISLY
GRISEOUS *adj* streaked or mixed with grey
GRISES > GRISE
GRISETTE *n* (esp formerly) a French working-class girl, esp a pretty or flirtatious one
GRISETTES > GRISETTE
GRISGRIS *same as* > GRIGRI
GRISING > GRISE
GRISKIN *n* lean part of a loin of pork
GRISKINS > GRISKIN
GRISLED *another word for* > GRIZZLED
GRISLIER > GRISLY
GRISLIES > GRISLY
GRISLIEST > GRISLY
GRISLY *adj* horrifying or ghastly ▷ *n* large American bear
GRISON *n* either of two musteline mammals, *Grison* (or *Galictis*) *cuja* or *G. vittata*, of Central and South America, having a greyish back and black face and underparts
GRISONS > GRISON
GRISSINI *pl n* thin crisp breadsticks
GRIST *n* grain for grinding
GRISTER *n* device for grinding grain
GRISTERS > GRISTER
GRISTLE *n* tough stringy animal tissue found in meat
GRISTLES > GRISTLE
GRISTLIER > GRISTLE
GRISTLY > GRISTLE
GRISTMILL *n* mill, esp one equipped with large grinding stones for grinding grain
GRISTS > GRIST
GRISY *adj* grim
GRIT *n* rough particles

of sand ▷ *vb* spread grit on (an icy road etc) ▷ *adj* great
GRITH *n* security, peace, or protection, guaranteed either in a certain place, such as a church, or for a period of time
GRITHS > GRITH
GRITLESS > GRIT
GRITS > GRIT
GRITSTONE *same as* > GRIT
GRITTED > GRIT
GRITTER *n* vehicle that spreads grit on the roads in icy weather
GRITTERS > GRITTER
GRITTEST > GRIT
GRITTIER > GRITTY
GRITTIEST > GRITTY
GRITTILY > GRITTY
GRITTING > GRIT
GRITTY *adj* courageous and tough
GRIVATION *n* (in navigation) grid variation
GRIVET *n* E African variety of a common guenon monkey, *Cercopithecus aethiops*, having long white tufts of hair on either side of the face
GRIVETS > GRIVET
GRIZE *same as* > GRECE
GRIZES > GRIZE
GRIZZLE *vb* whine or complain ▷ *n* grey colour
GRIZZLED *adj* grey-haired
GRIZZLER > GRIZZLE
GRIZZLERS > GRIZZLE
GRIZZLES > GRIZZLE
GRIZZLIER > GRIZZLY
GRIZZLIES > GRIZZLY
GRIZZLING > GRIZZLE
GRIZZLY *n* large American bear ▷ *adj* somewhat grey
GROAN *n* deep sound of grief or pain ▷ *vb* utter a groan
GROANED > GROAN
GROANER *n* person or thing that groans
GROANERS > GROANER
GROANFUL *adj* sad
GROANING > GROAN
GROANINGS > GROAN
GROANS > GROAN
GROAT *n* fourpenny piece
GROATS *pl n* hulled and crushed grain of various cereals
GROCER *n* shopkeeper selling foodstuffs
GROCERIES *pl n* food and other household supplies
GROCERS > GROCER
GROCERY *n* business or premises of a grocer
GROCKLE *n* tourist, esp one from the Midlands or the North of England
GROCKLES > GROCKLE
GRODIER > GRODY
GRODIEST > GRODY
GRODY *adj* unpleasant
GROG *n* spirit, usu rum, and water ▷ *vb* drink grog
GROGGED > GROG
GROGGERY *n* grogshop
GROGGIER > GROGGY
GROGGIEST > GROGGY
GROGGILY > GROGGY
GROGGING > GROG
GROGGY *adj* faint, shaky, or dizzy
GROGRAM *n* coarse fabric of silk, wool, or silk mixed with wool or mohair, often stiffened with gum, formerly used for clothing
GROGRAMS > GROGRAM
GROGS > GROG
GROGSHOP *n* drinking place, esp one of disreputable character
GROGSHOPS > GROGSHOP
GROIN *n* place where the legs join the abdomen ▷ *vb* provide or construct with groins
GROINED > GROIN
GROINING > GROIN
GROININGS > GROIN
GROINS > GROIN
GROK *vb* understand completely and intuitively
GROKKED > GROK
GROKKING > GROK
GROKS > GROK
GROMA *n* Roman surveying instrument
GROMAS > GROMA
GROMET *same as* > GROMMET
GROMETS > GROMET
GROMMET *n* ring or eyelet
GROMMETED *adj* having grommets
GROMMETS > GROMMET
GROMWELL *n* any of various hairy plants of the boraginaceous genus *Lithospermum*, esp *L. officinale*, having small greenish-white, yellow, or blue flowers, and smooth nutlike fruits
GROMWELLS > GROMWELL
GRONE *obsolete word for* > GROAN
GRONED > GRONE
GRONEFULL *same as* > GROANFUL
GRONES > GRONE
GRONING > GRONE
GROOF *n* face, or front of the body
GROOFS > GROOF
GROOLIER > GROOLY
GROOLIEST > GROOLY
GROOLY *adj* gruesome
GROOM *n* person who looks after horses ▷ *vb* make or keep one's clothes and appearance neat and tidy
GROOMED > GROOM
GROOMER > GROOM
GROOMERS > GROOM
GROOMING > GROOM
GROOMINGS > GROOM
GROOMS > GROOM
GROOMSMAN *n* man who attends the bridegroom at a wedding, usually the best man
GROOMSMEN > GROOMSMAN
GROOVE *n* long narrow channel in a surface
GROOVED > GROOVE
GROOVER *n* device that makes grooves
GROOVERS > GROOVER
GROOVES > GROOVE
GROOVIER > GROOVY
GROOVIEST > GROOVY
GROOVING > GROOVE
GROOVY *adj* attractive or exciting
GROPE *vb* feel about or search uncertainly ▷ *n* instance of groping
GROPED > GROPE
GROPER *n* any large marine serranid fish of the genus *Epinephelus* and related genera, of warm and tropical seas
GROPERS > GROPER
GROPES > GROPE
GROPING > GROPE
GROPINGLY > GROPE
GROSBEAK *n* finch with a large powerful bill
GROSBEAKS > GROSBEAK
GROSCHEN *n* former Austrian monetary unit worth one hundredth of a schilling
GROSCHENS > GROSCHEN
GROSER *n* gooseberry
GROSERS > GROSER
GROSERT *another word for* > GROSER
GROSERTS > GROSERT
GROSET *another word for* > GROSER
GROSETS > GROSET
GROSGRAIN *n* heavy ribbed silk or rayon fabric
GROSS *adj* flagrant ▷ *n* twelve dozen ▷ *vb* make as total revenue before deductions ▷ *interj* exclamation indicating disgust
GROSSART *another word for* > GROSER
GROSSARTS > GROSSART
GROSSED > GROSS
GROSSER > GROSS
GROSSERS > GROSS
GROSSES > GROSS
GROSSEST > GROSS
GROSSING > GROSS
GROSSLY > GROSS
GROSSNESS > GROSS
GROSSULAR *n* type of garnet
GROSZ *n* Polish monetary unit worth one hundredth of a zloty
GROSZE > GROSZ
GROSZY > GROSZ
GROT *n* rubbish
GROTESQUE *adj* strangely distorted ▷ *n* grotesque person or thing
GROTS > GROT
GROTTIER > GROTTY
GROTTIEST > GROTTY
GROTTO *n* small picturesque cave
GROTTOED *adj* having grotto
GROTTOES > GROTTO
GROTTOS > GROTTO
GROTTY *adj* nasty or in bad condition
GROUCH *vb* grumble or complain ▷ *n* person who is always complaining
GROUCHED > GROUCH
GROUCHES > GROUCH
GROUCHIER > GROUCHY
GROUCHILY > GROUCHY
GROUCHING > GROUCH
GROUCHY *adj* bad-tempered
GROUF *same as* > GROOF
GROUFS > GROUF
GROUGH *n* natural channel or fissure in a peat moor
GROUGHS > GROUGH
GROUND *n* surface of the earth ▷ *adj* on or of the ground ▷ *vb* base or establish
GROUNDAGE *n* fee levied on a vessel entering a port or anchored off a shore
GROUNDED *adj* sensible and down-to-earth
GROUNDEN *obsolete variant of* > GROUND
GROUNDER *n* (in baseball) ball that travels along the ground
GROUNDERS > GROUNDER
GROUNDHOG *another name for* > WOODCHUCK
GROUNDING *n* basic knowledge of a subject
GROUNDMAN *n* groundsman
GROUNDMEN > GROUNDMAN
GROUNDNUT *n* peanut
GROUNDOUT *n* (in baseball) being put out after hitting a grounder that is fielded and thrown to first base
GROUNDS > GROUND
GROUNDSEL *n* yellow-flowered weed
GROUP *n* number of people or things regarded as a unit ▷ *vb* place or form into a group
GROUPABLE > GROUP
GROUPAGE *n* gathering people or objects into a group or groups
GROUPAGES > GROUPAGE
GROUPED > GROUP
GROUPER *n* large edible sea fish
GROUPERS > GROUPER
GROUPIE *n* ardent fan of a celebrity or of a sport or activity
GROUPIES > GROUPIE

GROUPING *n* set of people or organizations who act or work together to achieve a shared aim
GROUPINGS > GROUPING
GROUPIST *n* follower of a group
GROUPISTS > GROUPIST
GROUPLET *n* small group
GROUPLETS > GROUPLET
GROUPOID *n* magma
GROUPOIDS > GROUPOID
GROUPS > GROUP
GROUPWARE *n* software that enables computers within a group or organization to work together, allowing users to exchange electronic-mail messages, access shared files and databases, use video conferencing, etc
GROUPY *same as* > GROUPIE
GROUSE *n* stocky game bird ▷ *vb* grumble or complain ▷ *adj* fine or excellent ▷ *adj* excellent
GROUSED > GROUSE
GROUSER > GROUSE
GROUSERS > GROUSE
GROUSES > GROUSE
GROUSEST > GROUSE
GROUSING > GROUSE
GROUT *n* thin mortar ▷ *vb* fill up with grout
GROUTED > GROUT
GROUTER > GROUT
GROUTERS > GROUT
GROUTIER > GROUTY
GROUTIEST > GROUTY
GROUTING > GROUT
GROUTINGS > GROUT
GROUTS *pl n* sediment or grounds, as from making coffee
GROUTY *adj* sullen or surly
GROVE *n* small group of trees
GROVED > GROVE
GROVEL *vb* behave humbly in order to win a superior's favour
GROVELED > GROVEL
GROVELER > GROVEL
GROVELERS > GROVEL
GROVELESS > GROVE
GROVELING > GROVEL
GROVELLED > GROVEL
GROVELLER > GROVEL
GROVELS > GROVEL
GROVES > GROVE
GROVET *n* wrestling hold in which a wrestler in a kneeling position grips the head of his kneeling opponent with one arm and forces his shoulders down with the other
GROVETS > GROVET
GROW *vb* develop physically
GROWABLE *adj* able to be cultivated
GROWER *n* person who grows plants
GROWERS > GROWER
GROWING > GROW
GROWINGLY > GROW
GROWINGS > GROW
GROWL *vb* make a low rumbling sound ▷ *n* growling sound
GROWLED > GROWL
GROWLER *n* person, animal, or thing that growls
GROWLERS > GROWLER
GROWLERY *n* place to retreat to, alone, when ill-humoured
GROWLIER > GROWL
GROWLIEST > GROWL
GROWLING > GROWL
GROWLINGS > GROWL
GROWLS > GROWL
GROWLY > GROWL
GROWN > GROW
GROWNUP *n* adult
GROWNUPS > GROWNUP
GROWS > GROW
GROWTH *n* growing ▷ *adj* of or relating to growth
GROWTHIER > GROWTHY
GROWTHIST *n* advocate of the importance of economic growth
GROWTHS > GROWTH
GROWTHY *adj* rapid-growing
GROYNE *n* wall built out from the shore to control erosion
GROYNES > GROYNE
GROZING as in *grozing iron* iron for smoothing joints between lead pipes
GRUB *n* legless insect larva ▷ *vb* search carefully for something by digging or by moving things about
GRUBBED > GRUB
GRUBBER *n* person who grubs
GRUBBERS > GRUBBER
GRUBBIER > GRUBBY
GRUBBIEST > GRUBBY
GRUBBILY > GRUBBY
GRUBBING > GRUB
GRUBBLE *same as* > GRABBLE
GRUBBLED > GRUBBLE
GRUBBLES > GRUBBLE
GRUBBLING > GRUBBLE
GRUBBY *adj* dirty
GRUBS > GRUB
GRUBSTAKE *n* supplies provided for a prospector on the condition that the donor has a stake in any finds ▷ *vb* furnish with such supplies
GRUBWORM *another word for* > GRUB
GRUBWORMS > GRUBWORM
GRUDGE *vb* be unwilling to give or allow ▷ *n* resentment ▷ *adj* planned or carried out in order to settle a grudge
GRUDGED > GRUDGE
GRUDGEFUL *adj* envious
GRUDGER > GRUDGE
GRUDGERS > GRUDGE
GRUDGES > GRUDGE
GRUDGING > GRUDGE
GRUDGINGS > GRUDGE
GRUE *n* shiver or shudder ▷ *vb* shiver or shudder
GRUED > GRUE
GRUEING > GRUE
GRUEL *n* thin porridge ▷ *vb* subject to exhausting experiences
GRUELED > GRUEL
GRUELER > GRUEL
GRUELERS > GRUEL
GRUELING *same as* > GRUELLING
GRUELINGS > GRUELING
GRUELLED > GRUEL
GRUELLER > GRUEL
GRUELLERS > GRUEL
GRUELLING *adj* exhausting or severe ▷ *n* severe experience, esp punishment
GRUELS > GRUEL
GRUES > GRUE
GRUESOME *adj* causing horror and disgust
GRUESOMER > GRUESOME
GRUFE *same as* > GROOF
GRUFES > GRUFE
GRUFF *adj* rough or surly in manner or voice ▷ *vb* talk gruffly
GRUFFED > GRUFF
GRUFFER > GRUFF
GRUFFEST > GRUFF
GRUFFIER > GRUFFY
GRUFFIEST > GRUFFY
GRUFFILY > GRUFFY
GRUFFING > GRUFF
GRUFFISH > GRUFF
GRUFFLY > GRUFF
GRUFFNESS > GRUFF
GRUFFS > GRUFF
GRUFFY *adj* gruff
GRUFTED *adj* dirty
GRUGRU *n* any of several tropical American palms, esp *Acrocomia sclerocarpa*, which has a spiny trunk and leaves and edible nuts
GRUGRUS > GRUGRU
GRUIFORM *adj* relating to an order of birds, including cranes and bustards
GRUING > GRUE
GRUM *adj* surly
GRUMBLE *vb* complain ▷ *n* complaint
GRUMBLED > GRUMBLE
GRUMBLER > GRUMBLE
GRUMBLERS > GRUMBLE
GRUMBLES > GRUMBLE
GRUMBLIER > GRUMBLE
GRUMBLING > GRUMBLE
GRUMBLY > GRUMBLE
GRUME *n* clot
GRUMES > GRUME
GRUMLY > GRUM
GRUMMER > GRUM
GRUMMEST > GRUM
GRUMMET *same as* > GROMMET
GRUMMETED *adj* having grummets
GRUMMETS > GRUMMET
GRUMNESS > GRUM
GRUMOSE *same as* > GRUMOUS
GRUMOUS *adj* (esp of plant parts) consisting of granular tissue
GRUMP *n* surly or bad-tempered person ▷ *vb* complain or grumble
GRUMPED > GRUMP
GRUMPH *vb* grunt
GRUMPHED > GRUMPH
GRUMPHIE *n* pig
GRUMPHIES > GRUMPHIE
GRUMPHING > GRUMPH
GRUMPHS > GRUMPH
GRUMPHY *same as* > GRUMPHIE
GRUMPIER > GRUMPY
GRUMPIEST > GRUMPY
GRUMPILY > GRUMPY
GRUMPING > GRUMP
GRUMPISH *same as* > GRUMPY
GRUMPS > GRUMP
GRUMPY *adj* bad-tempered
GRUNDIES *pl n* men's underpants
GRUNGE *n* style of rock music with a fuzzy guitar sound
GRUNGER *n* fan of grunge music
GRUNGERS > GRUNGER
GRUNGES > GRUNGE
GRUNGIER > GRUNGY
GRUNGIEST > GRUNGY
GRUNGY *adj* squalid or seedy
GRUNION *n* Californian marine teleost fish, *Leuresthes tenuis*, that spawns on beaches: family *Atherinidae* (silversides)
GRUNIONS > GRUNION
GRUNT *vb* make a low short gruff sound, like a pig ▷ *n* pig's sound
GRUNTED > GRUNT
GRUNTER *n* person or animal that grunts, esp a pig
GRUNTERS > GRUNTER
GRUNTING > GRUNT
GRUNTINGS > GRUNT
GRUNTLE *vb* grunt or groan
GRUNTLED > GRUNTLE
GRUNTLES > GRUNTLE
GRUNTLING > GRUNTLE
GRUNTS > GRUNT
GRUPPETTI > GRUPPETTO
GRUPPETTO *n* turn
GRUSHIE *adj* healthy and strong
GRUTCH *vb* grudge
GRUTCHED > GRUTCH
GRUTCHES > GRUTCH
GRUTCHING > GRUTCH
GRUTTEN > GREET
GRUYERE *n* hard flat whole milk cheese with holes
GRUYERES > GRUYERE

GRYCE *same as* > GRICE
GRYCES > GRYCE
GRYDE *same as* > GRYDE
GRYDED > GRYDE
GRYDES > GRYDE
GRYDING > GRYDE
GRYESY *adj* grey
GRYFON *same as* > GRIFFIN
GRYFONS > GRYFON
GRYKE *same as* > GRIKE
GRYKES > GRYKE
GRYPE *same as* > GRIPE
GRYPES > GRIPE
GRYPHON *same as* > GRIFFIN
GRYPHONS > GRYPHON
GRYPT *archaic form of* > GRIPPED
GRYSBOK *n* either of two small antelopes, *Raphicerus melanotis* or *R. sharpei*, of central and southern Africa, having small straight horns
GRYSBOKS > GRYSBOK
GRYSELY *same as* > GRISLY
GRYSIE *same as* > GRISY
GU *same as* > GJU
GUACAMOLE *n* spread of mashed avocado, tomato pulp, mayonnaise, and seasoning
GUACHARO *another name for* > OILBIRD
GUACHAROS > GUACHARO
GUACO *n* any of several tropical American plants whose leaves are used as an antidote to snakebite
GUACOS > GUACO
GUAIAC *same as* > GUAIACUM
GUAIACOL *n* yellowish oily creosote-like liquid extracted from guaiacum resin and hardwood tar, used medicinally as an expectorant
GUAIACOLS > GUAIACOL
GUAIACS > GUAIACUM
GUAIACUM *n* any tropical American evergreen tree of the zygophyllaceous genus *Guaiacum*, such as the lignum vitae
GUAIACUMS > GUAIACUM
GUAIOCUM *same as* > GUAIACUM
GUAIOCUMS > GUAIOCUM
GUAN *n* any gallinaceous bird of the genera *Penelope*, *Pipile*, etc, of Central and South America
GUANA *another word for* > IGUANA
GUANABANA *n* tropical tree or its fruit
GUANACO *n* S American animal related to the llama
GUANACOS > GUANACO
GUANAS > GUANA
GUANASE *n* enzyme that converts guanine to xanthine by removal of an amino group
GUANASES > GUANASE
GUANAY *n* type of cormorant
GUANAYS > GUANAY
GUANAZOLO *n* form of guanine
GUANGO *n* rain tree
GUANGOS > GUANGO
GUANIDIN *same as* > GUANIDINE
GUANIDINE *n* strongly alkaline crystalline substance, soluble in water and found in plant and animal tissues
GUANIDINS > GUANIDIN
GUANIN *same as* > GUANINE
GUANINE *n* white almost insoluble compound: one of the purine bases in nucleic acids
GUANINES > GUANINE
GUANINS > GUANINE
GUANO *n* dried sea-bird manure, used as fertilizer
GUANOS > GUANO
GUANOSINE *n* nucleoside consisting of guanine and ribose
GUANS > GUAN
GUANXI *n* Chinese social concept based on the exchange of favours
GUANXIS > GUANXI
GUANYLIC as in *guanylic acid* nucleotide consisting of guanine, ribose or deoxyribose, and a phosphate group
GUAR *n* leguminous Indian plant, *Cyamopsis tetragonolobus*, grown as a fodder crop and for the gum obtained from its seeds
GUARANA *n* type of shrub native to Venezuela
GUARANAS > GUARANA
GUARANI *n* standard monetary unit of Paraguay, divided into 100 céntimos
GUARANIES > GUARANI
GUARANIS > GUARANI
GUARANTEE *n* formal assurance, esp in writing, that a product will meet certain standards ▷ *vb* give a guarantee
GUARANTOR *n* person who gives or is bound by a guarantee
GUARANTY *n* pledge of responsibility for fulfilling another person's obligations in case of default
GUARD *vb* watch over to protect or to prevent escape ▷ *n* person or group that guards
GUARDABLE > GUARD
GUARDAGE *n* state of being in the care of a guardian
GUARDAGES > GUARDAGE
GUARDANT *adj* (of a beast) shown full face ▷ *n* guardian
GUARDANTS > GUARDANT
GUARDDOG *n* dog trained to protect premises
GUARDDOGS > GUARDDOG
GUARDED *adj* cautious or noncommittal
GUARDEDLY > GUARDED
GUARDEE *n* guardsman, esp considered as representing smartness and dash
GUARDEES > GUARDEE
GUARDER > GUARD
GUARDERS > GUARD
GUARDIAN *n* keeper or protector ▷ *adj* protecting or safeguarding
GUARDIANS > GUARDIAN
GUARDING > GUARD
GUARDLESS > GUARD
GUARDLIKE > GUARD
GUARDRAIL *n* railing at the side of a staircase, road, etc, as a safety barrier
GUARDROOM *n* room used by guards
GUARDS > GUARD
GUARDSHIP *n* warship responsible for the safety of other ships in its company
GUARDSMAN *n* member of the Guards
GUARDSMEN > GUARDSMAN
GUARISH *vb* heal
GUARISHED > GUARISH
GUARISHES > GUARISH
GUARS > GUAR
GUAVA *n* yellow-skinned tropical American fruit
GUAVAS > GUAVA
GUAYABERA *n* type of embroidered men's shirt
GUAYULE *n* bushy shrub, *Parthenium argentatum*, of the southwestern US: family *Asteraceae* (composites)
GUAYULES > GUAYULE
GUB *n* white man
GUBBAH *same as* > GUB
GUBBAHS > GUBBAH
GUBBINS *n* object of little or no value
GUBBINSES > GUBBINS
GUBERNIYA *n* territorial division of imperial Russia
GUBS > GUB
GUCK *n* slimy matter
GUCKIER > GUCKY
GUCKIEST > GUCKY
GUCKS > GUCK
GUCKY *adj* slimy and mucky
GUDDLE *vb* catch (fish) by groping with the hands under the banks or stones of a stream ▷ *n* muddle
GUDDLED > GUDDLE
GUDDLES > GUDDLE
GUDDLING > GUDDLE
GUDE *Scots word for* > GOOD
GUDEMAN *n* male householder
GUDEMEN > GUDEMAN
GUDES *n* goods
GUDESIRE *n* grandfather
GUDESIRES > GUDESIRE
GUDEWIFE *n* female householder
GUDEWIVES > GUDEWIFE
GUDGEON *n* small freshwater fish ▷ *vb* trick or cheat
GUDGEONED > GUDGEON
GUDGEONS > GUDGEON
GUE *same as* > GJU
GUENON *n* any slender agile Old World monkey of the genus *Cercopithecus*, inhabiting wooded regions of Africa and having long hind limbs and tail and long hair surrounding the face
GUENONS > GUENON
GUERDON *n* reward or payment ▷ *vb* give a guerdon to
GUERDONED > GUERDON
GUERDONER > GUERDON
GUERDONS > GUERDON
GUEREZA *n* handsome colobus monkey of the mountain forests of Ethiopia
GUEREZAS > GUEREZA
GUERIDON *n* small ornately-carved table
GUERIDONS > GUERIDON
GUERILLA *same as* > GUERRILLA
GUERILLAS > GUERILLA
GUERITE *n* turret used by a sentry
GUERITES > GUERITE
GUERNSEY *n* seaman's knitted woolen sweater
GUERNSEYS > GUERNSEY
GUERRILLA *n* member of an unofficial armed force fighting regular forces
GUES > GUE
GUESS *vb* estimate or draw a conclusion without proper knowledge ▷ *n* estimate or conclusion reached by guessing
GUESSABLE > GUESS
GUESSED > GUESS
GUESSER > GUESS
GUESSERS > GUESS
GUESSES > GUESS
GUESSING > GUESS
GUESSINGS > GUESS
GUESSWORK *n* process or results of guessing
GUEST *n* person entertained at another's house or at another's expense ▷ *vb* appear as a visiting player or performer
GUESTED > GUEST
GUESTEN *vb* stay as a guest in someone's house

GUESTENED > GUESTEN
GUESTENS > GUESTEN
GUESTING > GUEST
GUESTS > GUEST
GUESTWISE *adv* as, or in the manner of, a guest
GUFF *n* nonsense
GUFFAW *n* crude noisy laugh ▷ *vb* laugh in this way
GUFFAWED > GUFFAW
GUFFAWING > GUFFAW
GUFFAWS > GUFFAW
GUFFIE *Scots word for* > PIG
GUFFIES > GUFFIE
GUFFS > GUFF
GUGA *n* gannet chick
GUGAS > GUGA
GUGGLE *vb* drink making a gurgling sound
GUGGLED > GUGGLE
GUGGLES > GUGGLE
GUGGLING > GUGGLE
GUGLET *same as* > GOGLET
GUGLETS > GUGLET
GUICHET *n* grating, hatch, or small opening in a wall, esp a ticket-office window
GUICHETS > GUICHET
GUID *Scot word for* > GOOD
GUIDABLE > GUIDE
GUIDAGE *n* guidance
GUIDAGES > GUIDAGE
GUIDANCE *n* leadership, instruction, or advice
GUIDANCES > GUIDANCE
GUIDE *n* person who conducts tour expeditions ▷ *vb* act as a guide for
GUIDEBOOK *n* handbook with information for visitors to a place
GUIDED > GUIDE
GUIDELESS > GUIDE
GUIDELINE *n* set principle for doing something
GUIDEPOST *n* sign on a post by a road indicating directions
GUIDER > GUIDE
GUIDERS > GUIDE
GUIDES > GUIDE
GUIDESHIP *n* supervision
GUIDEWAY *n* track controlling the motion of something
GUIDEWAYS > GUIDEWAY
GUIDEWORD *n* word at top of dictionary page indicating first entry on page
GUIDING > GUIDE
GUIDINGS > GUIDE
GUIDON *n* small pennant, used as a marker or standard, esp by cavalry regiments
GUIDONS > GUIDON
GUIDS *n* possessions
GUILD *n* organization or club
GUILDER *n* former monetary unit of the Netherlands
GUILDERS > GUILDER
GUILDHALL *n* hall where members of a guild meet
GUILDRIES > GUILDRY
GUILDRY *n* in Scotland, corporation of merchants in a burgh
GUILDS > GUILD
GUILDSHIP *n* condition of being a member of a guild
GUILDSMAN *n* man who is a member of a guild
GUILDSMEN > GUILDSMAN
GUILE *n* cunning or deceit ▷ *vb* deceive
GUILED > GUILE
GUILEFUL > GUILE
GUILELESS *adj* free from guile
GUILER *n* deceiver
GUILERS > GUILER
GUILES > GUILE
GUILING > GUILE
GUILLEMET *n* (in printing) a duckfoot quote
GUILLEMOT *n* black-and-white diving sea bird of N hemisphere
GUILLOCHE *n* ornamental band or border with a repeating pattern of two or more interwoven wavy lines, as in architecture ▷ *vb* decorate with guilloches
GUILT *n* fact or state of having done wrong
GUILTIER > GUILTY
GUILTIEST > GUILTY
GUILTILY > GUILTY
GUILTLESS *adj* innocent
GUILTS > GUILT
GUILTY *adj* responsible for an offence or misdeed
GUIMBARD *n* Jew's harp
GUIMBARDS > GUIMBARD
GUIMP *same as* > GUIMPE
GUIMPE *n* short blouse with sleeves worn under a pinafore dress ▷ *vb* make with gimp
GUIMPED > GUIMPE
GUIMPES > GUIMPE
GUIMPING > GUIMPE
GUIMPS > GUIMP
GUINEA *n* former British monetary unit worth 21 shillings (1.05 pounds)
GUINEAS > GUINEA
GUIPURE *n* heavy lace that has its pattern connected by threads, rather than supported on a net mesh
GUIPURES > GUIPURE
GUIRO *n* percussion instrument made from a hollow gourd
GUIROS > GUIRO
GUISARD *n* guiser
GUISARDS > GUISARD
GUISE *n* false appearance ▷ *vb* disguise or be disguised in fancy dress
GUISED > GUISE
GUISER *n* mummer, esp at Christmas or Halloween revels
GUISERS > GUISER
GUISES > GUISE
GUISING > GUISE
GUISINGS > GUISE
GUITAR *n* stringed instrument with a flat back and a long neck, played by plucking or strumming
GUITARIST > GUITAR
GUITARS > GUITAR
GUITGUIT *n* bird belonging to the family Coerebidae
GUITGUITS > GUITGUIT
GUIZER *same as* > GUISER
GUIZERS > GUIZER
GUL *n* design used in oriental carpets
GULA *n* gluttony
GULAG *n* forced-labour camp
GULAGS > GULAG
GULAR *adj* of, relating to, or situated in the throat or oesophagus
GULAS > GULA
GULCH *n* deep narrow valley ▷ *vb* swallow fast
GULCHED > GULCH
GULCHES > GULCH
GULCHING > GULCH
GULDEN *same as* > GUILDER
GULDENS > GULDEN
GULE *Scots word for* > MARIGOLD
GULES *n* red in heraldry
GULF *n* large deep bay ▷ *vb* swallow up
GULFED > GULF
GULFIER > GULF
GULFIEST > GULF
GULFING > GULF
GULFLIKE > GULF
GULFS > GULF
GULFWEED *n* any brown seaweed of the genus *Sargassum*
GULFWEEDS > GULFWEED
GULFY > GULF
GULL *n* long-winged sea bird ▷ *vb* cheat or deceive
GULLABLE *same as* > GULLIBLE
GULLABLY > GULLABLE
GULLED > GULL
GULLER *n* deceiver
GULLERIES > GULLERY
GULLERS > GULLER
GULLERY *n* breeding-place for gulls
GULLET *n* muscular tube through which food passes from the mouth to the stomach
GULLETS > GULLET
GULLEY *same as* > GULLY
GULLEYED > GULLEY
GULLEYING > GULLEY
GULLEYS > GULLEY
GULLIBLE *adj* easily tricked
GULLIBLY > GULLIBLE
GULLIED > GULLY
GULLIES > GULLY
GULLING > GULL
GULLISH *adj* stupid
GULLS > GULL
GULLWING *adj* (of vehicle door) opening upwards
GULLY *n* channel cut by running water ▷ *vb* make (channels) in (the ground, sand, etc)
GULLYING > GULLY
GULOSITY *n* greed or gluttony
GULP *vb* swallow hastily ▷ *n* gulping
GULPED > GULP
GULPER > GULP
GULPERS > GULP
GULPH *archaic word for* > GULF
GULPHS > GULPH
GULPIER > GULP
GULPIEST > GULP
GULPING > GULP
GULPINGLY > GULP
GULPS > GULP
GULPY > GULP
GULS > GUL
GULY *adj* relating to gules
GUM *n* firm flesh in which the teeth are set ▷ *vb* stick with gum
GUMBALL *n* round piece of chewing gum
GUMBALLS > GUMBALL
GUMBO *n* mucilaginous pods of okra
GUMBOIL *n* abscess on the gum
GUMBOILS > GUMBOIL
GUMBOOT *n* rubber boot
GUMBOOTS *pl n* Wellington boots
GUMBOS > GUMBO
GUMBOTIL *n* sticky clay formed by the weathering of glacial drift
GUMBOTILS > GUMBOTIL
GUMDROP *n* hard jelly-like sweet
GUMDROPS > GUMDROP
GUMLANDS *pl n* infertile land from which the original kauri bush has been removed or burnt producing only kauri gum
GUMLESS > GUM
GUMLIKE > GUM
GUMLINE *n* line where gums meet teeth
GUMLINES > GUMLINE
GUMMA *n* rubbery tumour characteristic of advanced syphilis, occurring esp on the skin, liver, brain or heart
GUMMAS > GUMMA
GUMMATA > GUMMA
GUMMATOUS > GUMMA
GUMMED > GUM
GUMMER *n* punch-cutting tool
GUMMERS > GUMMER
GUMMIER > GUMMY

GUMMIES > GUMMY

GUMMIEST > GUMMY

GUMMILY > GUMMY

GUMMINESS > GUMMY

GUMMING > GUM

GUMMINGS > GUM

GUMMITE *n* orange or yellowish amorphous secondary mineral consisting of hydrated uranium oxides

GUMMITES > GUMMITE

GUMMOSE *same as* > GUMMOUS

GUMMOSES > GUMMOSE

GUMMOSIS *n* abnormal production of excessive gum in certain trees, esp fruit trees, as a result of wounding, infection, adverse weather conditions, severe pruning, etc

GUMMOSITY > GUMMOUS

GUMMOUS *adj* resembling or consisting of gum

GUMMY *adj* toothless ▷ *n* small crustacean-eating shark, *Mustelus antarcticus*, with bony ridges resembling gums in its mouth

GUMNUT *n* hardened seed container of the gumtree

GUMNUTS > GUMNUT

GUMP *vb* guddle

GUMPED > GUMP

GUMPHION *n* funeral banner

GUMPHIONS > GUMPHION

GUMPING > GUMP

GUMPS > GUMP

GUMPTION *n* resourcefulness

GUMPTIONS > GUMPTION

GUMPTIOUS > GUMPTION

GUMS > GUM

GUMSHIELD *n* plate or strip of soft waxy substance used by boxers to protect the teeth and gums

GUMSHOE *n* waterproof overshoe ▷ *vb* act stealthily

GUMSHOED > GUMSHOE

GUMSHOES > GUMSHOE

GUMSUCKER *n* native-born Australian

GUMTREE *n* any of various trees that yield gum, such as the eucalyptus, sweet gum, and sour gum

GUMTREES > GUMTREE

GUMWEED *n* any of several American yellow-flowered plants that have sticky flower heads

GUMWEEDS > GUMWEED

GUMWOOD *same as* > GUMTREE

GUMWOODS > GUMWOOD

GUN *n* weapon with a metal tube from which missiles are fired by explosion ▷ *vb* cause (an engine) to run at high speed

GUNBOAT *n* small warship

GUNBOATS > GUNBOAT

GUNCOTTON *n* form of cellulose nitrate used as an explosive

GUNDIES > GUNDY

GUNDOG *n* dog trained to work with a hunter or gamekeeper

GUNDOGS > GUNDOG

GUNDY *n* toffee

GUNFIGHT *n* fight between persons using firearms ▷ *vb* fight with guns

GUNFIGHTS > GUNFIGHT

GUNFIRE *n* repeated firing of guns

GUNFIRES > GUNFIRE

GUNFLINT *n* piece of flint in a flintlock's hammer used to strike the spark that ignites the charge

GUNFLINTS > GUNFLINT

GUNFOUGHT > GUNFIGHT

GUNG *adj* as in *gung ho* extremely or excessively enthusiastic about something

GUNGE *n* sticky unpleasant substance ▷ *vb* block or encrust with gunge

GUNGED > GUNGE

GUNGES > GUNGE

GUNGIER > GUNGE

GUNGIEST > GUNGE

GUNGING > GUNGE

GUNGY > GUNGE

GUNHOUSE *n* on a warship, an armoured rotatable enclosure for guns

GUNHOUSES > GUNHOUSE

GUNITE *n* cement-sand mortar that is sprayed onto formwork, walls, or rock by a compressed air ejector giving a very dense strong concrete layer: used to repair reinforced concrete, to line tunnel walls or mine airways, etc

GUNITES > GUNITE

GUNK *n* slimy or filthy substance

GUNKHOLE *vb* make a series of short boat excursions

GUNKHOLED > GUNKHOLE

GUNKHOLES > GUNKHOLE

GUNKIER > GUNK

GUNKIEST > GUNK

GUNKS > GUNK

GUNKY > GUNK

GUNLAYER *n* person who aims a ship's gun

GUNLAYERS > GUNLAYER

GUNLESS > GUN

GUNLOCK *n* mechanism in some firearms that causes the charge to be exploded

GUNLOCKS > GUNLOCK

GUNMAKER *n* person who makes guns

GUNMAKERS > GUNMAKER

GUNMAN *n* armed criminal

GUNMEN > GUNMAN

GUNMETAL *n* alloy of copper, tin, and zinc ▷ *adj* dark grey

GUNMETALS > GUNMETAL

GUNNAGE *n* number of guns carried by a warship

GUNNAGES > GUNNAGE

GUNNED > GUN

GUNNEL *same as* > GUNWALE

GUNNELS > GUNNEL

GUNNEN > GUN

GUNNER *n* artillery soldier

GUNNERA *n* any herbaceous perennial plant of the genus *Gunnera*, found throughout the S hemisphere and cultivated for its large leaves

GUNNERAS > GUNNERA

GUNNERIES > GUNNERY

GUNNERS > GUNNER

GUNNERY *n* use or science of large guns

GUNNIES > GUNNY

GUNNING > GUN

GUNNINGS > GUN

GUNNY *n* strong coarse fabric used for sacks

GUNNYBAG *same as* > GUNNYSACK

GUNNYBAGS > GUNNYBAG

GUNNYSACK *n* sack made from gunny

GUNPAPER *n* cellulose nitrate explosive made by treating paper with nitric acid

GUNPAPERS > GUNPAPER

GUNPLAY *n* use of firearms, as by criminals

GUNPLAYS > GUNPLAY

GUNPOINT *n* muzzle of a gun

GUNPOINTS > GUNPOINT

GUNPORT *n* porthole, or other, opening for a gun

GUNPORTS > GUNPORT

GUNPOWDER *n* explosive mixture of potassium nitrate, sulphur, and charcoal

GUNROOM *n* (esp in the Royal Navy) the mess allocated to subordinate or junior officers

GUNROOMS > GUNROOM

GUNRUNNER *n* person who smuggles guns and ammunition

GUNS > GUN

GUNSEL *n* catamite

GUNSELS > GUNSEL

GUNSHIP *n* ship or helicopter armed with heavy guns

GUNSHIPS > GUNSHIP

GUNSHOT *n* shot or range of a gun

GUNSHOTS > GUNSHOT

GUNSMITH *n* person who manufactures or repairs firearms, esp portable guns

GUNSMITHS > GUNSMITH

GUNSTICK *n* ramrod

GUNSTICKS > GUNSTICK

GUNSTOCK *n* wooden handle to which the barrel of a rifle is attached

GUNSTOCKS > GUNSTOCK

GUNSTONE *n* cannonball

GUNSTONES > GUNSTONE

GUNTER *n* type of gaffing in which the gaff is hoisted parallel to the mast

GUNTERS > GUNTER

GUNWALE *n* top of a ship's side

GUNWALES > GUNWALE

GUNYAH *n* hut or shelter in the bush

GUNYAHS > GUNYAH

GUP *n* gossip

GUPPIES > GUPPY

GUPPY *n* small colourful aquarium fish

GUPS > GUP

GUR *n* unrefined cane sugar

GURAMI *same as* > GOURAMI

GURAMIS > GURAMI

GURDWARA *n* Sikh place of worship

GURDWARAS > GURDWARA

GURGE *vb* swallow up

GURGED > GURGE

GURGES > GURGE

GURGING > GURGE

GURGLE *n* bubbling noise ▷ *vb* (of water) to make low bubbling noises when flowing

GURGLED > GURGLE

GURGLES > GURGLE

GURGLET *same as* > GOGLET

GURGLETS > GURGLET

GURGLING > GURGLE

GURGOYLE *same as* > GARGOYLE

GURGOYLES > GURGOYLE

GURJUN *n* any of several S or SE Asian dipterocarpaceous trees of the genus *Dipterocarpus* that yield a resin

GURJUNS > GURJUN

GURL *vb* snarl

GURLED > GURL

GURLET *n* type of pickaxe

GURLETS > GURLET

GURLIER > GURLY

GURLIEST > GURLY

GURLING > GURL

GURLS > GURL

GURLY *adj* stormy

GURN *variant spelling of* > GIRN

GURNARD *n* spiny armour-headed sea fish

GURNARDS > GURNARD

GURNED > GURN

GURNET *same as* > GURNARD

GURNETS > GURNARD

GURNEY *n* wheeled stretcher for transporting hospital patients

GURNEYS > GURNEY

GURNING > GURN

GURNS > GURN
GURRAH *n* type of coarse muslin
GURRAHS > GURRAH
GURRIER *n* low-class tough ill-mannered person
GURRIERS > GURRIER
GURRIES > GURRY
GURRY *n* dog-fight
GURS > GUR
GURSH *n* unit of currency in Saudi Arabia
GURSHES > GURSH
GURU *n* Hindu or Sikh religious teacher or leader
GURUDOM *n* state of being a guru
GURUDOMS > GURUDOM
GURUISM > GURU
GURUISMS > GURU
GURUS > GURU
GURUSHIP > GURU
GURUSHIPS > GURU
GUS > GU
GUSH *vb* flow out suddenly and profusely ▷ *n* sudden copious flow
GUSHED > GUSH
GUSHER *n* spurting oil well
GUSHERS > GUSHER
GUSHES > GUSH
GUSHIER > GUSHY
GUSHIEST > GUSHY
GUSHILY > GUSHY
GUSHINESS > GUSHY
GUSHING > GUSH
GUSHINGLY > GUSH
GUSHY *adj* displaying excessive admiration or sentimentality
GUSLA *n* Balkan single-stringed musical instrument
GUSLAR *n* player of the gusla
GUSLARS > GUSLAR
GUSLAS > GUSLA
GUSLE *same as* > GUSLA
GUSLES > GUSLE
GUSLI *n* Russian harp-like musical instrument
GUSLIS > GUSLI
GUSSET *n* piece of material sewn into a garment to strengthen it ▷ *vb* put a gusset in (a garment)
GUSSETED > GUSSET
GUSSETING > GUSSET
GUSSETS > GUSSET
GUSSIE *n* young pig
GUSSIED > GUSSY
GUSSIES > GUSSY
GUSSY *vb* dress elaborately
GUSSYING > GUSSY
GUST *n* sudden blast of wind ▷ *vb* blow in gusts
GUSTABLE *n* anything that can be tasted
GUSTABLES > GUSTABLE
GUSTATION *n* act of tasting or the faculty of taste
GUSTATIVE > GUSTATION
GUSTATORY > GUSTATION
GUSTED > GUST
GUSTFUL *adj* tasty
GUSTIE *adj* tasty
GUSTIER > GUSTY
GUSTIEST > GUSTY
GUSTILY > GUSTY
GUSTINESS > GUSTY
GUSTING > GUST
GUSTLESS *adj* tasteless
GUSTO *n* enjoyment or zest
GUSTOES > GUSTO
GUSTOS > GUSTO
GUSTS > GUST
GUSTY *adj* blowing or occurring in gusts or characterized by blustery weather
GUT *n* intestine ▷ *vb* remove the guts from ▷ *adj* basic or instinctive
GUTBUCKET *n* highly emotional style of jazz playing
GUTCHER *n* grandfather
GUTCHERS > GUTCHER
GUTFUL *n* bellyful
GUTFULS > GUTFUL
GUTLESS *adj* cowardly
GUTLIKE > GUT
GUTROT *n* diarrhoea
GUTROTS > GUTROT
GUTS > GUT *vb* devour greedily
GUTSED > GUTS
GUTSER as in *come a gutser* fall heavily to the ground
GUTSERS > GUTSER
GUTSES > GUTS
GUTSFUL *n* bellyful
GUTSFULS > GUTSFUL
GUTSIER > GUTSY
GUTSIEST > GUTSY
GUTSILY > GUTSY
GUTSINESS > GUTSY
GUTSING > GUTS
GUTSY *adj* courageous
GUTTA *n* one of a set of small drop-like ornaments, esp as used on the architrave of a Doric entablature ▷ *n* rubber substance obtained from the coagulated latex of the guttapercha tree
GUTTAE > GUTTA
GUTTAS > GUTTA
GUTTATE *adj* (esp of plants) covered with small drops or drop-like markings, esp oil glands ▷ *vb* exude droplets of liquid
GUTTATED *same as* > GUTTATE
GUTTATES > GUTTATE
GUTTATING > GUTTATE
GUTTATION > GUTTATE
GUTTED > GUT
GUTTER *n* shallow channel for carrying away water from a roof or roadside ▷ *vb* (of a candle) burn unsteadily, with wax running down the sides
GUTTERED > GUTTER
GUTTERING *n* material for gutters
GUTTERS > GUTTER
GUTTERY > GUTTER
GUTTIER > GUTTY
GUTTIES > GUTTY
GUTTIEST > GUTTY
GUTTING > GUT
GUTTLE *vb* eat greedily
GUTTLED > GUTTLE
GUTTLER > GUTTLE
GUTTLERS > GUTTLE
GUTTLES > GUTTLE
GUTTLING > GUTTLE
GUTTURAL *adj* (of a sound) produced at the back of the throat ▷ *n* guttural consonant > GUTTURALISATION > GUTTURALIZATION
GUTTURALS > GUTTURAL
GUTTY *n* urchin or delinquent ▷ *adj* courageous
GUTZER *n* bad fall
GUTZERS > GUTZER
GUV *informal name for* > GOVERNOR
GUVS > GUV
GUY *n* man or boy ▷ *vb* make fun of
GUYED > GUY
GUYING > GUY
GUYLE *same as* > GUILE
GUYLED > GUYLE
GUYLER > GUYLE
GUYLERS > GUYLE
GUYLES > GUYLE
GUYLINE *n* guy rope
GUYLINES > GUYLINE
GUYLING > GUYLE
GUYOT *n* flat-topped submarine mountain, common in the Pacific Ocean, usually an extinct volcano whose summit did not reach above the sea surface
GUYOTS > GUYOT
GUYS > GUY
GUYSE *same as* > GUISE
GUYSES > GUYSE
GUZZLE *vb* eat or drink greedily
GUZZLED > GUZZLE
GUZZLER *n* person or thing that guzzles
GUZZLERS > GUZZLER
GUZZLES > GUZZLE
GUZZLING > GUZZLE
GWEDUC *same as* > GEODUCK
GWEDUCK *same as* > GEODUCK
GWEDUCKS > GWEDUCK
GWEDUCS > GWEDUCK
GWINE *dialect form of* > GOING
GWINIAD *n* powan
GWINIADS > GWINIAD
GWYNIAD *n* freshwater white fish, *Coregonus pennantii*, occurring in Lake Bala in Wales: related to the powan
GWYNIADS > GWYNIAD
GYAL *same as* > GAYAL
GYALS > GYAL
GYBE *vb* (of a fore-and-aft sail) swing suddenly from one side to the other ▷ *n* instance of gybing
GYBED > GYBE
GYBES > GYBE
GYBING > GYBE
GYELD *n* guild
GYELDS > GYELD
GYLDEN *adj* golden
GYM *n* gymnasium
GYMBAL *same as* > GIMBAL
GYMBALS > GYMBAL
GYMKHANA *n* horse-riding competition
GYMKHANAS > GYMKHANA
GYMMAL *same as* > GIMMAL
GYMMALS > GYMMAL
GYMNASIA > GYMNASIUM
GYMNASIAL > GYMNASIUM
GYMNASIC > GYMNASIUM
GYMNASIEN > GYMNASIUM
GYMNASIUM *n* large room with equipment for physical training
GYMNAST *n* expert in gymnastics
GYMNASTIC *adj* of, relating to, like, or involving gymnastics
GYMNASTS > GYMNAST
GYMNIC *adj* gymnastic
GYMNOSOPH *n* adherent of gymnosophy: belief that food and clothing are detrimental to purity of thought
GYMP *same as* > GIMP
GYMPED > GYMP
GYMPIE *n* tall tree with stinging hairs on its leaves
GYMPIES > GYMPIE
GYMPING > GYMP
GYMPS > GYMP
GYMS > GYM
GYMSLIP *n* tunic or pinafore formerly worn by schoolgirls
GYMSLIPS > GYMSLIP
GYNAE *adj* gynaecological ▷ *n* gynaecology
GYNAECEA > GYNAECIUM
GYNAECEUM *same as* > GYNAECIA
GYNAECIA > GYNAECIUM
GYNAECIUM *same as* > GYNOECIUM
GYNAECOID *adj* resembling relating to, or like a woman
GYNAES > GYNAE
GYNANDRY *n* hermaphroditism
GYNARCHIC > GYNARCHY
GYNARCHY *n* government by women
GYNECIA > GYNECIUM
GYNECIC *adj* relating to the female sex
GYNECIUM *same as* > GYNOECIUM
GYNECOID *same as* > GYNAECOID

GYNIATRY *n* gynaecology: medicine concerned with diseases in women
GYNIE *n* gynaecology
GYNIES > GYNIE
GYNNEY *n* guinea hen
GYNNEYS > GYNNEY
GYNNIES > GYNNY
GYNNY *same as* > GYNNEY
GYNOCRACY *n* government by women
GYNOECIA > GYNOECIUM
GYNOECIUM *n* carpels of a flowering plant collectively
GYNOPHOBE *n* person who hates or fears women
GYNOPHORE *n* stalk in some plants that bears the gynoecium above the level of the other flower parts
GYNY *n* gynaecology
GYOZA *n* Japanese fried dumpling
GYOZAS > GYOZA
GYP *vb* swindle, cheat, or defraud ▷ *n* act of cheating
GYPLURE *n* synthetic version of the gypsy moth sex pheromone
GYPLURES > GYPLURE
GYPPED > GYP
GYPPER > GYP
GYPPERS > GYP
GYPPIE *same as* > GIPPY
GYPPIES > GYPPY
GYPPING > GYP
GYPPO *n* derogatory term for a gypsy
GYPPOS > GYPPO
GYPPY *same as* > GIPPY
GYPS > GYP
GYPSEIAN *adj* relating to gypsies
GYPSEOUS > GYPSUM
GYPSIED > GYPSY
GYPSIES > GYPSY
GYPSTER *n* swindler
GYPSTERS > GYPSTER
GYPSUM *n* chalklike mineral used to make plaster of Paris
GYPSUMS > GYPSUM
GYPSY *n* member of a nomadic people scattered throughout Europe and North America ▷ *vb* live like a gypsy
GYPSYDOM > GYPSY
GYPSYDOMS > GYPSYDOM
GYPSYHOOD > GYPSY
GYPSYING > GYPSY
GYPSYISH > GYPSY
GYPSYISM *n* state of being a gypsy
GYPSYISMS > GYPSYISM
GYPSYWORT *n* type of Eurasian herb with white flowers
GYRAL *adj* having a circular, spiral, or rotating motion
GYRALLY > GYRAL
GYRANT *adj* gyrating
GYRASE *n* topoisomerase enzyme
GYRASES > GYRASE
GYRATE *vb* rotate or spiral about a point or axis ▷ *adj* curved or coiled into a circle
GYRATED > GYRATE
GYRATES > GYRATE
GYRATING > GYRATE
GYRATION *n* act or process of gyrating
GYRATIONS > GYRATION
GYRATOR *n* electronic circuit that inverts the impedance
GYRATORS > GYRATOR
GYRATORY > GYRATE
GYRE *n* circular or spiral movement or path ▷ *vb* whirl
GYRED > GYRE
GYRENE *n* nickname for a member of the US Marine Corps
GYRENES > GYRENE
GYRES > GYRE
GYRFALCON *n* very large rare falcon of northern regions
GYRI > GYRUS
GYRING > GYRE
GYRO *n* gyrocompass: nonmagnmetic compass that uses a motor-driven gyroscope to indicate true north
GYROCAR *n* two-wheeled car
GYROCARS > GYROCAR
GYRODYNE *n* aircraft that uses a powered rotor to take off and manoeuvre, but uses autorotation when cruising
GYRODYNES > GYRODYNE
GYROIDAL *adj* spiral
GYROLITE *n* silicate
GYROLITES > GYROLITE
GYROMANCY *n* divination by spinning in a circle, then falling on any of various letters that have been written on the ground
GYRON *same as* > GIRON
GYRONIC > GYRON
GYRONNY *same as* > GIRONNY
GYRONS > GYRON
GYROPILOT *n* type of automatic pilot
GYROPLANE *another name for* > AUTOGIRO
GYROS > GYRO
GYROSCOPE *n* disc rotating on an axis that can turn in any direction, so the disc maintains the same position regardless of the movement of the surrounding structure
GYROSE *adj* marked with sinuous lines
GYROSTAT *same as* > GYROSCOPE
GYROSTATS > GYROSTAT
GYROUS *adj* gyrose
GYROVAGUE *n* peripatetic monk
GYRUS *another name for* > CONVOLUTION
GYRUSES > GYRUS
GYTE *n* goat
GYTES > GYTE
GYTRASH *n* spirit that haunts lonely roads
GYTRASHES > GYTRASH
GYTTJA *n* sediment on lake bottom
GYTTJAS > GYTTJA
GYVE *vb* shackle or fetter ▷ *n* fetters
GYVED > GYVE
GYVES > GYVE
GYVING > GYVE

Hh

HA *interj* exclamation expressing triumph, surprise, or scorn
HAAF *n* deep-sea fishing ground off the Shetland and Orkney Islands
HAAFS > HAAF
HAANEPOOT *same as* > HANEPOOT
HAAR *n* cold sea mist or fog off the North Sea
HAARS > HAAR
HABANERA *n* slow Cuban dance in duple time
HABANERAS > HABANERA
HABANERO *n* variety of chilli pepper
HABANEROS > HABANERO
HABDABS *n* highly nervous state
HABDALAH *n* prayer at end of Jewish sabbath
HABDALAHS > HABDALAH
HABERDINE *n* dried cod
HABERGEON *n* light sleeveless coat of mail worn in the 14th century under the plated hauberk
HABILABLE *adj* able to wear clothes
HABILE *adj* skilful
HABIT *n* established way of behaving ▷ *vb* clothe
HABITABLE *adj* fit to be lived in
HABITABLY > HABITABLE
HABITAN *same as* > HABITANT
HABITANS > HABITAN
HABITANT *n* early French settler in Canada or Louisiana or a descendant of one, esp a farmer
HABITANTS > HABITANT
HABITAT *n* natural home of an animal or plant
HABITATS > HABITAT
HABITED *adj* dressed in a habit
HABITING > HABIT
HABITS > HABIT
HABITUAL *adj* done regularly and repeatedly ▷ *n* person with a habit
HABITUALS > HABITUAL
HABITUATE *vb* accustom
HABITUDE *n* habit or tendency
HABITUDES > HABITUDE
HABITUE *n* frequent visitor to a place
HABITUES > HABITUE
HABITUS *n* general physical state, esp with regard to susceptibility to disease
HABLE *old form of* > ABLE
HABOOB *n* sandstorm
HABOOBS > HABOOB
HABU *n* large venomous snake
HABUS > HABU
HACEK *n* pronunciation symbol in Slavonic language
HACEKS > HACEK
HACENDADO *n* owner of hacienda
HACHIS *n* hash
HACHURE *n* shading of short lines drawn on a map to indicate the degree of steepness of a hill ▷ *vb* mark or show by hachures
HACHURED > HACHURE
HACHURES > HACHURE
HACHURING > HACHURE
HACIENDA *n* ranch or large estate in Latin America
HACIENDAS > HACIENDA
HACK *vb* cut or chop violently ▷ *n* (inferior) writer or journalist ▷ *adj* unoriginal or of a low standard
HACKABLE > HACK
HACKAMORE *n* rope or rawhide halter used for unbroken foals
HACKBERRY *n* American tree or shrub with edible cherry-like fruits
HACKBOLT *n* shearwater
HACKBOLTS > HACKBOLT
HACKBUT *another word for* > ARQUEBUS
HACKBUTS > HACKBUT
HACKED > HACK
HACKEE *n* chipmunk
HACKEES > HACKEE
HACKER *n* computer enthusiast, esp one who breaks into the computer system of a company or government
HACKERIES > HACKERY
HACKERS > HACKER
HACKERY *n* journalism
HACKETTE *n* informal, derogatory term for female journalist
HACKETTES > HACKETTE
HACKIE *n* US word meaning cab driver
HACKIES > HACKIE
HACKING > HACK
HACKINGS > HACK
HACKLE *same as* > HECKLE
HACKLED > HACKLE
HACKLER > HACKLE
HACKLERS > HACKLE
HACKLES *pl n* hairs on the back of the neck and the back of a dog, cat, etc, which rise when the animal is angry or afraid
HACKLET *n* kittiwake
HACKLETS > HACKLET
HACKLIER > HACKLY
HACKLIEST > HACKLY
HACKLING > HACKLE
HACKLY *adj* rough or jagged
HACKMAN *n* taxi driver
HACKMEN > HACKMAN
HACKNEY *n* taxi ▷ *vb* make commonplace and banal by too frequent use
HACKNEYED *adj* (of a word or phrase) unoriginal and overused
HACKNEYS > HACKNEY
HACKS > HACK
HACKSAW *n* small saw for cutting metal ▷ *vb* cut with a hacksaw
HACKSAWED > HACKSAW
HACKSAWN > HACKSAW
HACKSAWS > HACKSAW
HACKWORK *n* dull repetitive work
HACKWORKS > HACKWORK
HACQUETON *n* padded jacket worn under chain mail
HAD *vb* Scots form of hold
HADAL *adj* of, relating to, or constituting very deep zones of the oceans
HADARIM > HEDER
HADAWAY *sentence substitute* exclamation urging the hearer to refrain from delay in the execution of

a task

HADDEN > HAVE

HADDEST *same as* > HADST

HADDIE *n* finnan haddock

HADDIES > HADDIE

HADDING > HAVE

HADDOCK *n* edible sea fish of N Atlantic

HADDOCKS > HADDOCK

HADE *n* angle made to the vertical by the plane of a fault or vein ▷ *vb* incline from the vertical

HADED > HADE

HADEDAH *n* large grey-green S African ibis

HADEDAHS > HADEDAH

HADES > HADE

HADING > HADE

HADITH *n* body of tradition and legend about Mohammed and his followers, used as a basis of Islamic law

HADITHS > HADITH

HADJ *same as* > HAJJ

HADJEE *same as* > HADJI

HADJEES > HADJEE

HADJES > HADJ

HADJI *same as* > HAJJI

HADJIS > HADJI

HADROME *n* part of xylem

HADROMES > HADROME

HADRON *n* any elementary particle capable of taking part in a strong nuclear interaction and therefore excluding leptons and photons

HADRONIC > HADRON

HADRONS > HADRON

HADROSAUR *n* any one of a large group of duck-billed partly aquatic bipedal dinosaurs

HADS > HAVE

HADST *singular form of the past tense (indicative mood) of* > HAVE

HAE *Scot variant of* > HAVE

HAECCEITY *n* property that uniquely identifies an object

HAED > HAE

HAEING > HAE

HAEM *n* complex red organic pigment containing ferrous iron, present in haemoglobin

> HAEMAGGLUTINATE

> HAEMAGGLUTINATE

> HAEMAGGLUTINATE

HAEMAL *adj* of the blood

HAEMATAL *same as* > HAEMAL

HAEMATEIN *n* dark purple water-insoluble crystalline substance obtained from logwood and used as an indicator and biological stain

HAEMATIC *n* agent that stimulates the production of red blood cells

HAEMATICS > HAEMATIC

HAEMATIN *n* dark bluish or brownish pigment containing iron in the ferric state, obtained by the oxidation of haem

HAEMATINS > HAEMATIN

HAEMATITE *same as* > HEMATITE

HAEMATOID *adj* resembling blood

HAEMATOMA *n* tumour of clotted or partially clotted blood

HAEMIC *same as* > HAEMATIC

HAEMIN *n* haematin chloride

HAEMINS > HAEMIN

HAEMOCOEL *n* body cavity of many invertebrates, including arthropods and molluscs, developed from part of the blood system

HAEMOCYTE *n* any blood cell, esp a red blood cell

> HAEMOFLAGELLATE

HAEMOID *same as* > HAEMATOID

HAEMONIES > HAEMONY

HAEMONY *n* plant mentioned in Milton's poetry

HAEMOSTAT *n* surgical instrument that stops bleeding by compression of a blood vessel

HAEMS > HAEM

HAEN > HAE

HAEREDES > HAERES

HAEREMAI *interj* Māori expression of welcome

HAERES *same as* > HERES

HAES > HAE

HAET *n* whit

HAETS > HAET

HAFF *n* lagoon

HAFFET *n* side of head

HAFFETS > HAFFET

HAFFIT *same as* > HAFFET

HAFFITS > HAFFIT

HAFFLIN *same as* > HALFLING

HAFFLINS > HAFFLIN

HAFFS > HAFF

HAFIZ *n* title for a person who knows the Koran by heart

HAFIZES > HAFIZ

HAFNIUM *n* metallic element found in zirconium ores

HAFNIUMS > HAFNIUM

HAFT *n* handle of an axe, knife, or dagger ▷ *vb* provide with a haft

HAFTARA *same as* > HAFTARAH

HAFTARAH *n* (in Judaism) short reading from the Prophets which follows the reading from the Torah on Sabbaths and festivals

HAFTARAHS > HAFTARAH

HAFTARAS > HAFTARA

HAFTAROT > HAFTARAH

HAFTAROTH > HAFTARAH

HAFTED > HAFT

HAFTER > HAFT

HAFTERS > HAFT

HAFTING > HAFT

HAFTORAH *same as* > HAFTARAH

HAFTORAHS > HAFTORAH

HAFTOROS > HAFTORAH

HAFTOROT > HAFTORAH

HAFTOROTH > HAFTORAH

HAFTS > HAFT

HAG *n* ugly old woman ▷ *vb* hack

HAGADIC > HAGGAD

HAGADIST *same as* > HAGGADIST

HAGADISTS > HAGADIST

HAGBERRY *same as* > HACKBERRY

HAGBOLT *same as* > HACKBOLT

HAGBOLTS > HAGBOLT

HAGBORN *adj* born of witch

HAGBUSH *same as* > ARQUEBUS

HAGBUSHES > HAGBUSH

HAGBUT > HAGBUT

HAGBUTEER > HAGBUT

HAGBUTS > HAGBUT

HAGBUTTER > HAGBUT

HAGDEN *same as* > HACKBOLT

HAGDENS > HAGDEN

HAGDON *same as* > HACKBOLT

HAGDONS > HAGDON

HAGDOWN *same as* > HACKBOLT

HAGDOWNS > HAGDOWN

HAGFISH *n* any of various primitive eel-like marine vertebrates

HAGFISHES > HAGFISH

HAGG *n* boggy place

HAGGADA *same as* > HAGGADAH

HAGGADAH *n* book containing the order of service of the traditional Jewish Passover meal

HAGGADAHS > HAGGADAH

HAGGADAS > HAGGADA

HAGGADIC > HAGGADAH

HAGGADIST *n* writer of Aggadoth

HAGGADOT > HAGGADAH

HAGGADOTH > HAGGADAH

HAGGARD *adj* looking tired and ill ▷ *n* hawk that has reached maturity before being caught

HAGGARDLY > HAGGARD

HAGGARDS > HAGGARD

HAGGED > HAG

HAGGING > HAG

HAGGIS *n* Scottish dish made from sheep's offal, oatmeal, suet, and seasonings, boiled in a bag made from the sheep's stomach

HAGGISES > HAGGIS

HAGGISH > HAG

HAGGISHLY > HAG

HAGGLE *vb* bargain or wrangle over a price

HAGGLED > HAGGLE

HAGGLER > HAGGLE

HAGGLERS > HAGGLE

HAGGLES > HAGGLE

HAGGLING > HAGGLE

HAGGS > HAGG

HAGIARCHY *n* government by saints, holy men, or men in holy orders

HAGIOLOGY *n* literature about the lives and legends of saints

HAGLET *same as* > HACKLET

HAGLETS > HAGLET

HAGLIKE > HAG

HAGRIDDEN > HAGRIDE

HAGRIDE *vb* torment or obsess

HAGRIDER > HAGRIDE

HAGRIDERS > HAGRIDE

HAGRIDES > HAGRIDE

HAGRIDING > HAGRIDE

HAGRODE > HAGRIDE

HAGS > HAG

HAH *same as* > HA

HAHA *n* wall or other boundary marker that is set in a ditch so as not to interrupt the landscape

HAHAS > HAHA

HAHNIUM *n* transuranic element artificially produced from californium

HAHNIUMS > HAHNIUM

HAHS > HAH

HAICK *same as* > HAIK

HAICKS > HAICK

HAIDUK *n* rural brigand

HAIDUKS > HAIDUK

HAIK *n* Arab's outer garment of cotton, wool, or silk, for the head and body

HAIKA > HAIK

HAIKAI *same as* > HAIKU

HAIKS > HAIK

HAIKU *n* Japanese verse form in 17 syllables

HAIKUS > HAIKU

HAIL *n* (shower of) small pellets of ice ▷ *vb* fall as or like hail ▷ *sentence substitute* exclamation of greeting

HAILED > HAIL

HAILER > HAIL

HAILERS > HAIL

HAILIER > HAIL

HAILIEST > HAIL

HAILING > HAIL

HAILS > HAIL

HAILSHOT *n* small scattering shot

HAILSHOTS > HAILSHOT

HAILSTONE *n* pellet of hail

HAILSTORM *n* storm during which hail falls

HAILY > HAIL

HAIMISH *same as* > HEIMISH

HAIN *vb* Scots word meaning save

HAINCH *Scots form*

of > HAUNCH
HAINCHED > HAINCH
HAINCHES > HAINCH
HAINCHING > HAINCH
HAINED > HAIN
HAINING > HAIN
HAININGS > HAIN
HAINS > HAIN
HAINT *same as* > HAUNT
HAINTS > HAINT
HAIQUE *same as* > HAIK
HAIQUES > HAIK
HAIR *n* threadlike growth on the skin ▷ *vb* provide with hair
HAIRBALL *n* compact mass of hair that forms in the stomach of cats, calves, etc, as a result of licking and swallowing the fur, and causes vomiting, coughing, bloat, weight loss, and depression
HAIRBALLS > HAIRBALL
HAIRBAND *n* band worn around head to control hair
HAIRBANDS > HAIRBAND
HAIRBELL *same as* > HAREBELL
HAIRBELLS > HAIRBELL
HAIRBRUSH *n* brush for grooming the hair
HAIRCAP *n* type of moss
HAIRCAPS > HAIRCAP
HAIRCLOTH *n* cloth woven from horsehair, used in upholstery
HAIRCUT *n* act or an instance of cutting the hair
HAIRCUTS > HAIRCUT
HAIRDO *n* hairstyle
HAIRDOS > HAIRDO
HAIRDRIER *same as* > HAIRDRYER
HAIRDRYER *n* hand-held electric device that blows out hot air and is used to dry and, sometimes, assist in styling the hair, as in blow-drying
HAIRED *adj* with hair
HAIRGRIP *n* small bent clasp used to fasten the hair
HAIRGRIPS > HAIRGRIP
HAIRIER > HAIRY
HAIRIEST > HAIRY
HAIRIF *another name for* > CLEAVERS
HAIRIFS > HAIRIF
HAIRINESS > HAIRY
HAIRING > HAIR
HAIRLESS *adj* having little or no hair
HAIRLIKE > HAIR
HAIRLINE *n* edge of hair at the top of the forehead ▷ *adj* very fine or narrow
HAIRLINES > HAIRLINE
HAIRLOCK *n* lock of hair
HAIRLOCKS > HAIRLOCK
HAIRNET *n* any of several kinds of light netting worn over the hair to keep it in place
HAIRNETS > HAIRNET
HAIRPIECE *n* section of false hair added to a person's real hair
HAIRPIN *n* U-shaped wire used to hold the hair in place
HAIRPINS > HAIRPIN
HAIRS > HAIR
HAIRSPRAY *n* fixative solution sprayed onto the hair to keep a hairstyle in shape
HAIRST *Scots form of* > HARVEST
HAIRSTED > HAIRST
HAIRSTING > HAIRST
HAIRSTS > HAIRST
HAIRSTYLE *n* cut and arrangement of a person's hair
HAIRTAIL *n* any of various marine spiny-finned fish having a long whiplike scaleless body and long sharp teeth
HAIRTAILS > HAIRTAIL
HAIRWORK *n* thing made from hair
HAIRWORKS > HAIRWORK
HAIRWORM *n* any of various hairlike nematode worms
HAIRWORMS > HAIRWORM
HAIRY *adj* covered with hair
HAIRYBACK *n* offensive word for an Afrikaner
HAITH *interj* Scots oath
HAJ *same as* > HADJ
HAJES > HAJ
HAJI *same as* > HAJJI
HAJIS > HAJI
HAJJ *n* pilgrimage a Muslim makes to Mecca
HAJJAH *n* Muslim woman who has made a pilgrimage to Mecca
HAJJAHS > HAJJAH
HAJJES > HAJJ
HAJJI *n* Muslim who has made a pilgrimage to Mecca
HAJJIS > HAJJI
HAKA *n* ceremonial Māori dance with chanting
HAKAM *n* text written by a rabbi
HAKAMS > HAKAM
HAKARI *n* Māori ritual feast
HAKAS > HAKA
HAKE *n* edible sea fish of N hemisphere
HAKEA *n* Australian tree or shrub with hard woody fruit
HAKEAS > HAKEA
HAKEEM *same as* > HAKIM
HAKEEMS > HAKEEM
HAKES > HAKE
HAKIM *n* Muslim judge, ruler, or administrator
HAKIMS > HAKIM
HAKU *in New Zealand English, same as* > KINGFISH
HAKUS > HAKU
HALACHA *n* Jewish religious law
HALACHAS > HALACHA
HALACHIC > HALACHA
HALACHIST > HALACHA
HALACHOT > HALACHA
HALACHOTH > HALACHA
HALAKAH *same as* > HALACHA
HALAKAHS > HALAKAH
HALAKHA *same as* > HALACHA
HALAKHAH *same as* > HALACHA
HALAKHAHS > HALAKHAH
HALAKHAS > HALAKHA
HALAKHIC > HALAKHAH
HALAKHIST > HALAKHAH
HALAKHOT > HALAKHA
HALAKHOTH > HALAKHAH
HALAKIC > HALAKHA
HALAKIST > HALAKHA
HALAKISTS > HALAKHA
HALAKOTH > HALAKHA
HALAL *n* meat from animals slaughtered according to Muslim law ▷ *adj* of or relating to such meat ▷ *vb* kill (animals) in this way
HALALA *n* money unit in Saudi Arabia
HALALAH *same as* > HALALA
HALALAHS > HALALAH
HALALAS > HALALA
HALALLED > HALAL
HALALLING > HALAL
HALALS > HALAL
HALATION *n* fogging usually seen as a bright ring surrounding a source of light: caused by reflection from the back of the film
HALATIONS > HALATION
HALAVAH *same as* > HALVAH
HALAVAHS > HALAVAH
HALAZONE *n* type of disinfectant
HALAZONES > HALAZONE
HALBERD *n* spear with an axe blade
HALBERDS > HALBERD
HALBERT *same as* > HALBERD
HALBERTS > HALBERT
HALCYON *adj* peaceful and happy ▷ *n* (in Greek mythology) fabulous bird associated with the winter solstice
HALCYONIC *adj* peaceful and happy
HALCYONS > HALCYON
HALE *adj* healthy, robust ▷ *vb* pull or drag
HALED > HALE
HALENESS > HALE
HALER *same as* > HELLER
HALERS > HALER
HALERU > HALER
HALES > HALE
HALEST > HALE
HALF *n* either of two equal parts ▷ *adj* denoting one of two equal parts ▷ *adv* to the extent of half
HALFA *n* African grass
HALFAS > HALFA
HALFBACK *n* player positioned immediately behind the forwards
HALFBACKS > HALFBACK
HALFBEAK *n* type of fish with an elongated body, a short upper jaw, and a long protruding lower jaw
HALFBEAKS > HALFBEAK
HALFEN > HALF
HALFLIFE *n* time taken for half of the atoms in a radioactive material to undergo decay
HALFLIN *same as* > HALFLING
HALFLING *n* person only half-grown
HALFLINGS > HALFLING
HALFLINS > HALFLIN
HALFLIVES > HALFLIFE
HALFNESS > HALF
HALFPACE *n* landing on staircase
HALFPACES > HALFPACE
HALFPENCE > HALFPENNY
HALFPENNY *n* former British coin worth half an old penny
HALFPIPE *n* U-shaped object used in skateboarding stunts
HALFPIPES > HALFPIPE
HALFS > HALF
HALFTIME *n* rest period between the two halves of a game
HALFTIMES > HALFTIME
HALFTONE *n* illustration showing lights and shadows by means of very small dots ▷ *adj* relating to, used in, or made by halftone
HALFTONES > HALFTONE
HALFTRACK *n* vehicle with caterpillar tracks and wheels
HALFWAY *adj* at or to half the distance
HALFWIT *n* foolish or stupid person
HALFWITS > HALFWIT
HALIBUT *n* large edible flatfish of N Atlantic
HALIBUTS > HALIBUT
HALICORE *n* dugong
HALICORES > HALICORE
HALID *same as* > HALIDE
HALIDE *n* binary compound containing a halogen atom or ion in combination with a more electropositive element
HALIDES > HALIDE
HALIDOM *n* holy place or thing
HALIDOME *same as* > HALIDOM

HALIDOMES > HALIDOME
HALIDOMS > HALIDOM
HALIDS > HALID
HALIEUTIC *adj* of fishing
HALIMOT *n* court held by lord
HALIMOTE *same as* > HALIMOT
HALIMOTES > HALIMOTE
HALIMOTS > HALIMOT
HALING > HALE
HALIOTIS *n* type of shellfish
HALITE *n* colourless or white mineral sometimes tinted by impurities, found in beds as an evaporite
HALITES > HALITE
HALITOSES > HALITOSIS
HALITOSIS *n* unpleasant-smelling breath
HALITOTIC > HALITUS
HALITOUS > HALITUS
HALITUS *n* vapour
HALITUSES > HALITUS
HALL *n* entrance passage
HALLAH *variant spelling of* > CHALLAH
HALLAHS > HALLAH
HALLAL *same as* > HALAL
HALLALI *n* bugle call
HALLALIS > HALLALI
HALLALLED > HALLAL
HALLALOO *same as* > HALLOO
HALLALOOS > HALLALOO
HALLALS > HALLAL
HALLAN *n* partition in cottage
HALLANS > HALLAN
HALLEL *n* (in Judaism) section of the liturgy consisting of Psalms 113–18, read during the morning service on festivals, Chanukah, and Rosh Chodesh
HALLELS > HALLEL
HALLIAN *same as* > HALLION
HALLIANS > HALLIAN
HALLIARD *same as* > HALYARD
HALLIARDS > HALLIARD
HALLING *n* Norwegian country dance
HALLINGS > HALLING
HALLION *n* lout
HALLIONS > HALLION
HALLMARK *n* typical feature ▷ *vb* stamp with a hallmark
HALLMARKS > HALLMARK
HALLO *same as* > HALLOO
HALLOA *same as* > HALLOO
HALLOAED > HALLOA
HALLOAING > HALLOA
HALLOAS > HALLOA
HALLOED > HALLO
HALLOES > HALLO
HALLOING > HALLO
HALLOO *interj* shout used to call hounds at a hunt ▷ *sentence substitute* shout to attract attention, esp to call hounds at a hunt ▷ *n* shout of "halloo" ▷ *vb* shout (something) to (someone)
HALLOOED > HALLOO
HALLOOING > HALLOO
HALLOOS > HALLOO
HALLOS > HALLO
HALLOT > HALLAH
HALLOTH *same as* > CHALLAH
HALLOUMI *n* salty white sheep's cheese from Greece or Turkey, usually eaten grilled
HALLOUMIS > HALLOUMI
HALLOW *vb* consecrate or set apart as being holy
HALLOWED *adj* regarded as holy
HALLOWER > HALLOW
HALLOWERS > HALLOW
HALLOWING > HALLOW
HALLOWS > HALLOW
HALLS > HALL
HALLSTAND *n* piece of furniture on which are hung coats, hats, etc
HALLUCAL > HALLUX
HALLUCES > HALLUX
HALLUX *n* first digit on the hind foot of a mammal, bird, reptile, or amphibian
HALLWAY *n* entrance area
HALLWAYS > HALLWAY
HALLYON *same as* > HALLION
HALLYONS > HALLYON
HALM *same as* > HAULM
HALMA *n* board game in which players attempt to transfer their pieces from their own to their opponents' bases
HALMAS > HALMA
HALMS > HALM
HALO *n* ring of light round the head of a sacred figure ▷ *vb* surround with a halo
HALOBIONT *n* plant or animal that lives in a salty environment such as the sea
HALOCLINE *n* gradient in salinity of sea
HALOED > HALO
HALOES > HALO
HALOGEN *n* any of a group of nonmetallic elements including chlorine and iodine
HALOGENS > HALOGEN
HALOGETON *n* herbaceous plant
HALOID *adj* resembling or derived from a halogen ▷ *n* compound containing halogen atoms in its molecules
HALOIDS > HALOID
HALOING > HALO
HALOLIKE > HALO
HALON *n* any of a class of chemical compounds derived from hydrocarbons by replacing one or more hydrogen atoms by bromine atoms and other hydrogen atoms by other halogen atoms (chlorine, fluorine, or iodine). Halons are stable compounds that are used in fire extinguishers, although they may contribute to depletion of the ozone layer
HALONS > HALON
HALOPHILE *n* organism that thrives in an extremely salty environment, such as the Dead Sea
HALOPHILY *n* ability to live in salty environment
HALOPHOBE *n* plant unable to live in salty soil
HALOPHYTE *n* plant that grows in very salty soil, as in a salt marsh
HALOS > HALO
HALOSERE *n* plant community that originates and develops in conditions of high salinity
HALOSERES > HALOSERE
HALOTHANE *n* colourless volatile slightly soluble liquid with an odour resembling that of chloroform
HALOUMI *same as* > HALLOUMI
HALOUMIS > HALOUMI
HALSE *vb* embrace
HALSED > HALSE
HALSER > HALSE
HALSERS > HALSE
HALSES > HALSE
HALSING > HALSE
HALT *vb* come or bring to a stop ▷ *n* temporary stop ▷ *adj* lame
HALTED > HALT
HALTER *n* strap round a horse's head with a rope to lead it with ▷ *vb* put a halter on (a horse)
HALTERE *n* one of a pair of short projections in dipterous insects that are modified hind wings, used for maintaining equilibrium during flight
HALTERED > HALTER
HALTERES > HALTERE
HALTERING > HALTER
HALTERS > HALTER
HALTING > HALT
HALTINGLY > HALT
HALTINGS > HALT
HALTLESS > HALT
HALTS > HALT
HALUTZ *variant spelling of* > CHALUTZ
HALUTZIM > HALUTZ
HALVA *same as* > HALVAH
HALVAH *n* Eastern Mediterranean, Middle Eastern, or Indian sweetmeat made of honey and containing sesame seeds, nuts, rose water, saffron, etc
HALVAHS > HALVAH
HALVAS > HALVA
HALVE *vb* divide in half
HALVED > HALVE
HALVER > HALVE
HALVERS > HALVE
HALVES > HALVE
HALVING > HALVE
HALYARD *n* rope for raising a ship's sail or flag
HALYARDS > HALYARD
HAM *n* smoked or salted meat from a pig's thigh ▷ *vb* overact
HAMADA *n* rocky plateau in desert
HAMADAS > HAMADA
HAMADRYAD *n* one of a class of nymphs, each of which inhabits a tree and dies with it
HAMADRYAS *n* type of baboon
HAMAL *n* (in Middle Eastern countries) a porter, bearer, or servant
HAMALS > HAMAL
HAMAMELIS *n* any of several trees or shrubs native to E Asia and North America and cultivated as ornamentals
HAMARTIA *n* flaw in character which leads to the downfall of the protagonist in a tragedy
HAMARTIAS > HAMARTIA
HAMATE *adj* hook-shaped ▷ *n* small bone in the wrist
HAMATES > HAMATE
HAMAUL *same as* > HAMAL
HAMAULS > HAMAUL
HAMBA *interj* usually offensive term for go away
HAMBLE *vb* mutilate
HAMBLED > HAMBLE
HAMBLES > HAMBLE
HAMBLING > HAMBLE
HAMBONE *vb* strike body to provide percussion
HAMBONED > HAMBONE
HAMBONES > HAMBONE
HAMBONING > HAMBONE
HAMBURG *same as* > HAMBURGER
HAMBURGER *n* minced beef shaped into a flat disc, cooked and usually served in a bread roll
HAMBURGS > HAMBURG
HAME *n* either of the two curved bars holding the traces of the harness, attached to the collar of a draught animal
HAMED > HAME
HAMES > HAME
HAMEWITH *adv* Scots word meaning homewards
HAMFATTER *n* inferior actor

or musician
HAMING > HAME
HAMLET *n* small village
HAMLETS > HAMLET
HAMMADA *same as* > HAMADA
HAMMADAS > HAMMADA
HAMMAL *same as* > HAMAL
HAMMALS > HAMMAL
HAMMAM *n* bathing establishment, such as a Turkish bath
HAMMAMS > HAMMAM
HAMMED > HAM
HAMMER *n* tool with a heavy metal head and a wooden handle, used to drive in nails etc ▷ *vb* hit (as if) with a hammer
HAMMERED > HAMMER
HAMMERER > HAMMER
HAMMERERS > HAMMER
HAMMERING > HAMMER
HAMMERKOP *n* shark with hammer-shaped head
HAMMERMAN *n* person working with hammer
HAMMERMEN > HAMMERMAN
HAMMERS > HAMMER
HAMMERTOE *n* condition in which the toe is permanently bent at the joint
HAMMIER > HAMMY
HAMMIEST > HAMMY
HAMMILY > HAMMY
HAMMINESS > HAMMY
HAMMING > HAM
HAMMOCK *same as* > HUMMOCK
HAMMOCKS > HAMMOCK
HAMMY *adj* (of an actor) overacting or tending to overact
HAMOSE *adj* shaped like hook
HAMOUS *same as* > HAMOSE
HAMPER *vb* make it difficult for (someone or something) to move or progress ▷ *n* large basket with a lid
HAMPERED > HAMPER
HAMPERER > HAMPER
HAMPERERS > HAMPER
HAMPERING > HAMPER
HAMPERS > HAMPER
HAMPSTER *same as* > HAMSTER
HAMPSTERS > HAMPSTER
HAMS > HAM
HAMSTER *n* small rodent with a short tail and cheek pouches
HAMSTERS > HAMSTER
HAMSTRING *n* tendon at the back of the knee ▷ *vb* make it difficult for (someone) to take any action
HAMSTRUNG > HAMSTRING
HAMULAR > HAMULUS
HAMULATE > HAMULUS
HAMULI > HAMULUS
HAMULOSE > HAMULUS
HAMULOUS > HAMULUS
HAMULUS *n* hook or hooklike process at the end of some bones or between the fore and hind wings of a bee or similar insect
HAMZA *n* sign used in Arabic to represent the glottal stop
HAMZAH *same as* > HAMZA
HAMZAHS > HAMZAH
HAMZAS > HAMZA
HAN *archaic inflected form of* > HAVE
HANAP *n* medieval drinking cup
HANAPER *n* small wickerwork basket, often used to hold official papers
HANAPERS > HANAPER
HANAPS > HANAP
HANCE *same as* > HAUNCH
HANCES > HANCE
HANCH *vb* try to bite
HANCHED > HANCH
HANCHES > HANCH
HANCHING > HANCH
HAND *n* part of the body at the end of the arm, consisting of a palm, four fingers, and a thumb ▷ *vb* pass, give
HANDAX *n* small axe held in one hand
HANDAXES > HANDAX
HANDBAG *n* woman's small bag for carrying personal articles in
HANDBAGS *pl n* incident in which people, esp sportsmen, fight or threaten to fight, but without real intent to inflict harm
HANDBALL *n* game in which two teams of seven players try to throw a ball into their opponent's goal ▷ *vb* pass (the ball) with a blow of the fist
HANDBALLS > HANDBALL
HANDBELL *n* bell rung by hand, esp one of a tuned set used in musical performance
HANDBELLS > HANDBELL
HANDBILL *n* small printed notice
HANDBILLS > HANDBILL
HANDBLOWN *adj* (of glass) made by hand
HANDBOOK *n* small reference or instruction book
HANDBOOKS > HANDBOOK
HANDBRAKE *n* brake in a motor vehicle operated by a hand lever
HANDCAR *n* small railway vehicle propelled by hand-pumped mechanism
HANDCARS > HANDCAR
HANDCART *n* simple cart pushed or pulled by hand, used for transporting goods
HANDCARTS > HANDCART
HANDCLAP *n* act of clapping hands
HANDCLAPS > HANDCLAP
HANDCLASP *another word for* > HANDSHAKE
HANDCRAFT *same as* > HANDICRAFT
HANDCUFF *n* one of a linked pair of metal rings designed to be locked round a prisoner's wrists by the police ▷ *vb* put handcuffs on
HANDCUFFS > HANDCUFF
HANDED > HAND
HANDER > HAND
HANDERS > HAND
HANDFAST *n* agreement, esp of marriage, confirmed by a handshake ▷ *vb* betroth or marry (two persons or another person) by joining the hands
HANDFASTS > HANDFAST
HANDFED > HANDFEED
HANDFEED *vb* feed (a person or an animal) by hand
HANDFEEDS > HANDFEED
HANDFUL *n* amount that can be held in the hand
HANDFULS > HANDFUL
HANDGRIP *n* covering, usually of towelling or rubber, that makes the handle of a racket or club easier to hold
HANDGRIPS > HANDGRIP
HANDGUN *n* firearm that can be held, carried, and fired with one hand, such as a pistol
HANDGUNS > HANDGUN
HANDHELD *adj* held in position by the hand ▷ *n* computer that can be held in the hand
HANDHELDS > HANDHELD
HANDHOLD *n* object, crevice, etc, that can be used as a grip or support, as in climbing
HANDHOLDS > HANDHOLD
HANDICAP *n* physical or mental disability ▷ *vb* make it difficult for (someone) to do something
HANDICAPS > HANDICAP
HANDIER > HANDY
HANDIEST > HANDY
HANDILY *adv* in a handy way or manner
HANDINESS > HANDY
HANDING > HAND
HANDISM *n* discrimination against people on the grounds of whether they are left-handed or right-handed
HANDISMS > HANDISM
HANDIWORK *n* result of someone's work or activity
HANDJAR *n* Persian dagger
HANDJARS > HANDJAR
HANDLE *n* part of an object that is held so that it can be used ▷ *vb* hold, feel, or move with the hands
HANDLEBAR as in *handlebar moustache:* bushy extended moustache with curled ends that resembles the handlebars of a bicycle
HANDLED > HANDLE
HANDLER *n* person who controls an animal
HANDLERS > HANDLER
HANDLES > HANDLE
HANDLESS > HAND
HANDLIKE > HAND
HANDLING *n* act or an instance of picking up, turning over, or touching something
HANDLINGS > HANDLING
HANDLIST *n* rough list
HANDLISTS > HANDLIST
HANDLOOM *n* weaving device operated by hand
HANDLOOMS > HANDLOOM
HANDMADE *adj* made by hand, not by machine
HANDMAID *n* person or thing that serves as a useful but subordinate purpose
HANDMAIDS > HANDMAID
HANDOFF *n* (in rugby) act of warding off an opposing player with the open hand
HANDOFFS > HANDOFF
HANDOUT *n* clothing, food, or money given to a needy person
HANDOUTS > HANDOUT
HANDOVER *n* transfer or surrender
HANDOVERS > HANDOVER
HANDPHONE *n* in SE Asian English, mobile phone
HANDPICK *vb* choose or select with great care, as for a special job or purpose
HANDPICKS > HANDPICK
HANDPLAY *n* fighting with fists
HANDPLAYS > HANDPLAY
HANDPRESS *n* printing press operated by hand
HANDPRINT *n* print of hand
HANDRAIL *n* rail alongside a stairway, to provide support
HANDRAILS > HANDRAIL
HANDROLL *n* large dried-seaweed cone filled with cold rice and other ingredients
HANDROLLS > HANDROLL
HANDS > HAND
HANDSAW *n* any saw for use in one hand only
HANDSAWS > HANDSAW
HANDSEL *n* gift for good

luck at the beginning of a new year, new venture, etc ▷ *vb* give a handsel to (a person)
ANDSELED > HANDSEL
ANDSELS > HANDSEL
ANDSET *n* telephone mouthpiece and earpiece in a single unit
ANDSETS > HANDSET
ANDSEWN *adj* sewn by hand
ANDSFUL > HANDFUL
ANDSHAKE *n* act of grasping and shaking a person's hand, such as in greeting or when agreeing on a deal
ANDSOME *adj* (esp of a man) good-looking ▷ *n* term of endearment for a beloved person
ANDSOMER > HANDSOME
ANDSPIKE *n* bar or length of pipe used as a lever
ANDSTAFF *n* staff held in hand
ANDSTAMP *vb* stamp by hand
ANDSTAND *n* act of supporting the body on the hands in an upside-down position
ANDSTURN *n* slightest amount of work
ANDTOWEL *n* towel for drying hands
ANDWHEEL *n* wheel operated by hand
ANDWORK *n* work done by hand rather than by machine
ANDWORKS > HANDWORK
ANDWOVEN *adj* woven by hand
ANDWRIT > HANDWRITE
ANDWRITE *vb* write by hand
ANDWROTE > HANDWRITE
ANDY *adj* convenient, useful
ANDYMAN *n* man who is good at making or repairing things
ANDYMEN > HANDYMAN
ANDYWORK *same as* > HANDIWORK
ANEPOOT *n* variety of muscat grape
ANEPOOTS > HANEPOOT
ANG *vb* attach or be attached at the top with the lower part free
ANGABLE *adj* suitable for hanging
ANGAR *n* large shed for storing aircraft ▷ *vb* put in a hangar
ANGARED > HANGAR
ANGARING > HANGAR
ANGARS > HANGAR
ANGBIRD *n* any bird, esp the Baltimore oriole, that builds a hanging nest
HANGBIRDS > HANGBIRD
HANGDOG *adj* guilty, ashamed ▷ *n* furtive or sneaky person
HANGDOGS > HANGDOG
HANGED > HANG
HANGER *n* curved piece of wood, wire, or plastic, with a hook, for hanging up clothes
HANGERS > HANGER
HANGFIRE *n* failure to fire
HANGFIRES > HANGFIRE
HANGI *n* Māori oven consisting of a hole in the ground filled with hot stones
HANGING > HANG
HANGINGS > HANG
HANGIS > HANGI
HANGMAN *n* man who executes people by hanging
HANGMEN > HANGMAN
HANGNAIL *n* piece of skin partly torn away from the base or side of a fingernail
HANGNAILS > HANGNAIL
HANGNEST *same as* > HANGBIRD
HANGNESTS > HANGNEST
HANGOUT *n* place where one lives or that one frequently visits
HANGOUTS > HANGOUT
HANGOVER *n* headache and nausea as a result of drinking too much alcohol
HANGOVERS > HANGOVER
HANGS > HANG
HANGTAG *n* attached label
HANGTAGS > HANGTAG
HANGUL *n* Korean language
HANGUP *n* emotional or psychological preoccupation or problem
HANGUPS > HANGUP
HANIWA *n* Japanese funeral offering
HANJAR *same as* > HANDJAR
HANJARS > HANJAR
HANK *n* coil, esp of yarn ▷ *vb* attach (a sail) to a stay by hanks
HANKED > HANK
HANKER *vb* desire intensely
HANKERED > HANKER
HANKERER > HANKER
HANKERERS > HANKER
HANKERING > HANKER
HANKERS > HANKER
HANKIE *same as* > HANKY
HANKIES > HANKY
HANKING > HANK
HANKS > HANK
HANKY *n* handkerchief
HANSA *same as* > HANSE
HANSAS > HANSA
HANSE *n* medieval guild of merchants
HANSEATIC > HANSA
HANSEL *same as* > HANDSEL
HANSELED > HANSEL
HANSELING > HANSEL
HANSELLED > HANSEL
HANSELS > HANSEL
HANSES > HANSE
HANSOM *n* formerly, a two-wheeled one-horse carriage with a fixed hood
HANSOMS > HANSOM
HANT *same as* > HAUNT
HANTED > HANT
HANTING > HANT
HANTLE *n* good deal
HANTLES > HANTLE
HANTS > HANT
HANUKIAH *n* candelabrum having nine branches that is lit during the festival of Hanukkah
HANUKIAHS > HANUKIAH
HANUMAN *n* type of monkey
HANUMANS > HANUMAN
HAO *n* monetary unit of Vietnam, worth one tenth of a dông
HAOLE *n* Hawaiian word for white person
HAOLES > HAOLE
HAOMA *n* type of ritual drink
HAOMAS > HAOMA
HAP *n* luck ▷ *vb* cover up
HAPAX *n* word that only appears in once in a work of literature, or in a body of work by a particular author
HAPAXES > HAPAX
HAPHAZARD *adj* not organized or planned ▷ *n* chance
HAPHTARA *same as* > HAFTARAH
HAPHTARAH *same as* > HAFTARAH
HAPHTARAS > HAPHTARA
HAPHTAROT > HAPHTARA
HAPKIDO *n* Korean martial art
HAPKIDOS > HAPKIDO
HAPLESS *adj* unlucky
HAPLESSLY > HAPLESS
HAPLITE *variant of* > APLITE
HAPLITES > HAPLITE
HAPLITIC > HAPLITE
HAPLOID *adj* denoting a cell or organism with unpaired chromosomes ▷ *n* haploid cell or organism
HAPLOIDIC *adj* denoting a cell or organism with unpaired chromosomes
HAPLOIDS > HAPLOID
HAPLOIDY > HAPLOID
HAPLOLOGY *n* omission of a repeated occurrence of a sound or syllable in fluent speech
HAPLONT *n* organism, esp a plant, that has the haploid number of chromosomes in its somatic cells
HAPLONTIC > HAPLONT
HAPLONTS > HAPLONT
HAPLOPIA *n* normal single vision
HAPLOPIAS > HAPLOPIA
HAPLOSES > HAPLOSIS
HAPLOSIS *n* production of a haploid number of chromosomes during meiosis
HAPLOTYPE *n* collection of genetic markers usually inherited together
HAPLY *archaic word for* > PERHAPS
HAPPED > HAP
HAPPEN *vb* take place, occur
HAPPENED > HAPPEN
HAPPENING *n* event, occurrence ▷ *adj* fashionable and up-to-the-minute
HAPPENS > HAPPEN
HAPPIED > HAPPY
HAPPIER > HAPPY
HAPPIES > HAPPY
HAPPIEST > HAPPY
HAPPILY > HAPPY
HAPPINESS > HAPPY
HAPPING > HAP
HAPPY *adj* feeling or causing joy ▷ *vb* make happy
HAPPYING > HAPPY
HAPS > HAP
HAPTEN *n* incomplete antigen that can stimulate antibody production only when it is chemically combined with a particular protein
HAPTENE *same as* > HAPTEN
HAPTENES > HAPTENE
HAPTENIC > HAPTENE
HAPTENS > HAPTEN
HAPTERON *n* cell or group of cells that occurs in certain plants, esp seaweeds, and attaches the plant to its substratum
HAPTERONS > HAPTERON
HAPTIC *adj* relating to or based on the sense of touch
HAPTICAL *same as* > HAPTIC
HAPTICS *n* science of sense of touch
HAPU *n* subtribe
HAPUKA *another name for* > GROPER
HAPUKAS > HAPUKA
HAPUKU *same as* > HAPUKA
HAPUKUS > HAPUKU
HAPUS > HAPU
HAQUETON *same as* > HACQUETON
HAQUETONS > HAQUETON
HARAKEKE *in New Zealand English, another name for* > FLAX
HARAKEKES > HARAKEKE
HARAM *n* anything that is forbidden by Islamic law
HARAMBEE *n* work chant used on the E African coast ▷ *interj* cry of harambee
HARAMBEES > HARAMBEE
HARAMDA *same as* > HARAMZADA

HARAMDAS > HARAMDA
HARAMDI *same as* > HARAMZADI
HARAMDIS > HARAMDI
HARAMS > HARAM
HARAMZADA *n* in Indian English, slang word for an illegitimate male
HARAMZADI *n* in Indian English, slang word for an illegitimate female
HARANGUE *vb* address angrily or forcefully ▷ *n* angry or forceful speech
HARANGUED > HARANGUE
HARANGUER > HARANGUE
HARANGUES > HARANGUE
HARASS *vb* annoy or trouble constantly
HARASSED > HARASS
HARASSER > HARASS
HARASSERS > HARASS
HARASSES > HARASS
HARASSING > HARASS
HARBINGER *n* someone or something that announces the approach of something ▷ *vb* announce the approach or arrival of
HARBOR *same as* > HARBOUR
HARBORAGE *same as* > HARBOURAGE
HARBORED > HARBOR
HARBORER > HARBOR
HARBORERS > HARBOR
HARBORFUL *n* amount a harbour can hold
HARBORING > HARBOR
HARBOROUS *adj* hospitable
HARBORS > HARBOR
HARBOUR *n* sheltered port ▷ *vb* maintain secretly in the mind
HARBOURED > HARBOUR
HARBOURER > HARBOUR
HARBOURS > HARBOUR
HARD *adj* firm, solid, or rigid ▷ *adv* with great energy or effort
HARDASS *n* tough person
HARDASSES > HARDASS
HARDBACK *n* book with a stiff cover ▷ *adj* of or denoting a hardback
HARDBACKS > HARDBACK
HARDBAG *n* rigid container on motorcycle
HARDBAGS > HARDBAG
HARDBAKE *n* almond toffee
HARDBAKES > HARDBAKE
HARDBALL as in *play hardball* act in a ruthless or uncompromising way
HARDBALLS > HARDBALL
HARDBEAM *same as* > HORNBEAM
HARDBEAMS > HARDBEAM
HARDBOARD *n* thin stiff board made of compressed sawdust and wood chips
HARDBOOT *n* type of skiing boot
HARDBOOTS > HARDBOOT
HARDBOUND *same as* > HARDBACK
HARDCASE *n* tough person
HARDCORE *n* style of rock music with short fast songs and little melody
HARDCORES > HARDCORE
HARDCOURT *adj* (of tennis) played on hard surface
HARDCOVER *same as* > HARDBACK
HARDEDGE *n* style of painting in which vividly coloured subjects are clearly delineated ▷ *adj* of, relating to, or denoting this style of painting
HARDEDGES > HARDEDGE
HARDEN *vb* make or become hard ▷ *n* rough fabric made from hards
HARDENED *adj* toughened by experience
HARDENER *n* person or thing that hardens
HARDENERS > HARDENER
HARDENING *n* act or process of becoming or making hard
HARDENS > HARDEN
HARDER > HARD
HARDEST > HARD
HARDFACE *n* uncompromising person
HARDFACES > HARDFACE
HARDGOODS *same as* > HARDWARE
HARDGRASS *n* coarse grass
HARDHACK *n* woody North American rosaceous plant with downy leaves and clusters of small pink or white flowers
HARDHACKS > HARDHACK
HARDHAT *n* hat made of a hard material for protection, worn esp by construction workers, equestrians, etc ▷ *adj* (in US English) characteristic of the presumed conservative attitudes and prejudices typified by construction workers
HARDHATS > HARDHAT
HARDHEAD *same as* > HARDHEADS
HARDHEADS *n* thistle-like plant
HARDIER > HARDY
HARDIES > HARDY
HARDIEST > HARDY
HARDIHEAD *same as* > HARDIHOOD
HARDIHOOD *n* courage or daring
HARDILY *adv* in a hardy manner
HARDIMENT *same as* > HARDIHOOD
HARDINESS *n* condition or quality of being hardy, robust, or bold
HARDISH > HARD
HARDLINE *adj* uncompromising
HARDLINER > HARDLINE
HARDLY *adv* scarcely or not at all
HARDMAN *n* tough, ruthless, or violent man
HARDMEN > HARDMAN
HARDNESS *n* quality or condition of being hard
HARDNOSE *n* tough person
HARDNOSED *adj* tough, shrewd, and practical
HARDNOSES > HARDNOSE
HARDOKE *n* burdock
HARDOKES > HARDOKE
HARDPACK *n* rigid backpack
HARDPACKS > HARDPACK
HARDPAN *n* hard impervious layer of clay below the soil, resistant to drainage and root growth
HARDPANS > HARDPAN
HARDPARTS *n* skeleton
HARDROCK *adj* (of mining) concerned with extracting minerals other than coal, usually from solid rock ▷ *n* tough uncompromising man
HARDROCKS > HARDROCK
HARDS *pl n* coarse fibres and other refuse from flax and hemp
HARDSET *adj* in difficulties
HARDSHELL *adj* having a shell or carapace that is thick, heavy, or hard
HARDSHIP *n* suffering
HARDSHIPS > HARDSHIP
HARDSTAND *n* hard surface on which vehicles may be parked
HARDTACK *n* kind of hard saltless biscuit, formerly eaten by sailors
HARDTACKS > HARDTACK
HARDTOP *n* car equipped with a metal or plastic roof that is sometimes detachable
HARDTOPS > HARDTOP
HARDWARE *n* metal tools or implements
HARDWARES > HARDWARE
HARDWIRE *vb* instal permanently in computer
HARDWIRED *adj* (of a circuit or instruction) permanently wired into a computer, replacing separate software
HARDWIRES > HARDWIRE
HARDWOOD *n* wood of a broad-leaved tree such as oak or ash
HARDWOODS > HARDWOOD
HARDY *adj* able to stand difficult conditions ▷ *n* any blacksmith's tool made with a square shank so that it can be lodged in a square hole in an anvil
HARE *n* animal like a large rabbit, with longer ears and legs ▷ *vb* run (away) quickly
HAREBELL *n* blue bell-shaped flower
HAREBELLS > HAREBELL
HARED > HARE
HAREEM *same as* > HAREM
HAREEMS > HAREEM
HARELD *n* long-tailed duck
HARELDS > HARELD
HARELIKE > HARE
HARELIP *n* slight split in the upper lip
HARELIPS > HARELIP
HAREM *n* (apartments of) a Muslim man's wives and concubines
HAREMS > HAREM
HARES > HARE
HARESTAIL *n* species of cotton grass
HAREWOOD *n* sycamore wood that has been stained for use in furniture making
HAREWOODS > HAREWOOD
HARIANA *n* Indian breed of cattle
HARIANAS > HARIANA
HARICOT *n* variety of French bean with light-coloured edible seeds, which can be dried and stored
HARICOTS > HARICOT
HARIGALDS *pl n* intestines
HARIGALS *same as* > HARIGALDS
HARIJAN *n* member of an Indian caste once considered untouchable
HARIJANS > HARIJAN
HARIM *same as* > HAREM
HARIMS > HARIM
HARING > HARE
HARIOLATE *vb* practise divination
HARIRA *n* Moroccan soup made from a variety of vegetables with lentils, chickpeas, and coriander
HARIRAS > HARIRA
HARISH *adj* like hare
HARISSA *n* hot paste made from chilli peppers, tomatoes, spices, and olive oil
HARISSAS > HARISSA
HARK *vb* listen
HARKED > HARK
HARKEN *same as* > HEARKEN
HARKENED > HARKEN
HARKENER > HARKEN
HARKENERS > HARKEN
HARKENING > HARKEN
HARKENS > HARKEN
HARKING > HARK
HARKS > HARK
HARL *same as* > HERL
HARLED > HARL
HARLEQUIN *n* stock comic character with a diamond patterned costume and

mask ▷ *adj* in many colours
HARLING > HARL
HARLINGS > HARL
HARLOT *n* prostitute ▷ *adj* of or like a harlot
HARLOTRY > HARLOT
HARLOTS > HARLOT
HARLS > HARL
HARM *vb* injure physically, mentally, or morally ▷ *n* physical, mental, or moral injury
HARMALA *n* African plant
HARMALAS > HARMALA
HARMALIN *n* chemical derived from harmala
HARMALINE *same as* > HARMALIN
HARMALINS > HARMALIN
HARMAN *n* constable
HARMANS > HARMAN
HARMATTAN *n* dry dusty wind from the Sahara blowing towards the W African coast, esp from November to March
HARMDOING *n* doing of harm
HARMED > HARM
HARMEL *same as* > HARMALA
HARMELS > HARMEL
HARMER > HARM
HARMERS > HARM
HARMFUL *adj* causing or tending to cause harm, esp to a person's health
HARMFULLY > HARMFUL
HARMIN *same as* > HARMALIN
HARMINE *same as* > HARMALIN
HARMINES > HARMINE
HARMING > HARM
HARMINS > HARMIN
HARMLESS *adj* safe to use, touch, or be near
HARMONIC *adj* of harmony ▷ *n* overtone of a musical note produced when that note is played, but not usually heard as a separate note
HARMONICA *n* small wind instrument played by sucking and blowing
HARMONICS *n* science of musical sounds
HARMONIES > HARMONY
HARMONISE *same as* > HARMONIZE
HARMONIST *n* person skilled in the art and techniques of harmony
HARMONIUM *n* keyboard instrument like a small organ
HARMONIZE *vb* sing or play in harmony
HARMONY *n* peaceful agreement and cooperation
HARMOST *n* Spartan governor
HARMOSTS > HARMOST
HARMOSTY *n* office of a harmost
HARMOTOME *n* mineral of the zeolite group
HARMS > HARM
HARN *n* coarse linen
HARNESS *n* arrangement of straps for attaching a horse to a cart or plough ▷ *vb* put a harness on
HARNESSED > HARNESS
HARNESSER > HARNESS
HARNESSES > HARNESS
HARNS > HARN
HARO *interj* cry meaning alas
HAROS > HARO
HAROSET *n* Jewish dish eaten at Passover
HAROSETH *same as* > HAROSET
HAROSETHS > HAROSETH
HAROSETS > HAROSET
HARP *n* large triangular stringed instrument played with the fingers ▷ *vb* play the harp
HARPED > HARP
HARPER > HARP
HARPERS > HARP
HARPIES > HARPY
HARPIN *n* type of protein
HARPING > HARP
HARPINGS *pl n* wooden members used for strengthening the bow of a vessel
HARPINS *same as* > HARPINGS
HARPIST > HARP
HARPISTS > HARP
HARPOON *n* barbed spear attached to a rope used for hunting whales ▷ *vb* spear with a harpoon
HARPOONED > HARPOON
HARPOONER > HARPOON
HARPOONS > HARPOON
HARPS > HARP
HARPY *n* nasty or bad-tempered woman
HARPYLIKE > HARPY
HARQUEBUS *variant of* > ARQUEBUS
HARRIDAN *n* nagging or vicious woman
HARRIDANS > HARRIDAN
HARRIED > HARRY
HARRIER *n* cross-country runner
HARRIERS > HARRIER
HARRIES > HARRY
HARROW *n* implement used to break up lumps of soil ▷ *vb* draw a harrow over
HARROWED > HARROW
HARROWER > HARROW
HARROWERS > HARROW
HARROWING > HARROW
HARROWS > HARROW
HARRUMPH *vb* clear or make the noise of clearing the throat
HARRUMPHS > HARRUMPH
HARRY *vb* keep asking (someone) to do something, pester
HARRYING > HARRY
HARSH *adj* severe and difficult to cope with
HARSHEN *vb* make harsh
HARSHENED > HARSHEN
HARSHENS > HARSHEN
HARSHER > HARSH
HARSHEST > HARSH
HARSHLY > HARSH
HARSHNESS > HARSH
HARSLET *same as* > HASLET
HARSLETS > HARSLET
HART *n* adult male deer
HARTAL *n* (in India) the act of closing shops or suspending work, esp in political protest
HARTALS > HARTAL
HARTBEES *same as* > HARTBEEST
HARTBEEST *n* African antelope
HARTELY *archaic spelling of* > HEARTILY
HARTEN *same as* > HEARTEN
HARTENED > HARTEN
HARTENING > HARTEN
HARTENS > HARTEN
HARTLESSE *same as* > HEARTLESS
HARTS > HART
HARTSHORN *n* sal volatile
HARUMPH *same as* > HARRUMPH
HARUMPHED > HARUMPH
HARUMPHS > HARUMPH
HARUSPEX *n* (in ancient Rome) a priest who practised divination, esp by examining the entrails of animals
HARUSPICY > HARUSPEX
HARVEST *n* (season for) the gathering of crops ▷ *vb* gather (a ripened crop)
HARVESTED > HARVEST
HARVESTER *n* harvesting machine, esp a combine harvester
HARVESTS > HARVEST
HAS > HAVE
HASBIAN *n* former lesbian who has become heterosexual or bisexual
HASBIANS > HASBIAN
HASH *n* dish of diced cooked meat and vegetables reheated ▷ *vb* chop into small pieces
HASHED > HASH
HASHEESH *same as* > HASHISH
HASHES > HASH
HASHHEAD *n* regular marijuana user
HASHHEADS > HASHHEAD
HASHIER > HASH
HASHIEST > HASH
HASHING > HASH
HASHISH *n* drug made from the cannabis plant, smoked for its intoxicating effects
HASHISHES > HASHISH
HASHMARK *n* character (#)
HASHMARKS > HASHMARK
HASHY > HASH
HASK *n* archaic name for a basket for transporting fish
HASKS > HASK
HASLET *n* loaf of cooked minced pig's offal, eaten cold
HASLETS > HASLET
HASP *n* clasp that fits over a staple and is secured by a bolt or padlock, used as a fastening ▷ *vb* secure (a door, window, etc) with a hasp
HASPED > HASP
HASPING > HASP
HASPS > HASP
HASSAR *n* South American catfish
HASSARS > HASSAR
HASSEL *variant of* > HASSLE
HASSELS > HASSEL
HASSIUM *n* element synthetically produced in small quantities by high-energy ion bombardment
HASSIUMS > HASSIUM
HASSLE *n* trouble, bother ▷ *vb* bother or annoy
HASSLED > HASSLE
HASSLES > HASSLE
HASSLING > HASSLE
HASSOCK *n* cushion for kneeling on in church
HASSOCKS > HASSOCK
HASSOCKY > HASSOCK
HAST *singular form of the present tense (indicative mood) of* > HAVE
HASTA *Spanish for* > UNTIL
HASTATE *adj* (of a leaf) having a pointed tip and two outward-pointing lobes at the base
HASTATED *same as* > HASTATE
HASTATELY > HASTATE
HASTE *n* (excessive) quickness ▷ *vb* hasten
HASTED > HASTE
HASTEFUL > HASTE
HASTEN *vb* (cause to) hurry
HASTENED > HASTEN
HASTENER > HASTEN
HASTENERS > HASTEN
HASTENING > HASTEN
HASTENS > HASTEN
HASTES > HASTE
HASTIER > HASTY
HASTIEST > HASTY
HASTILY > HASTY
HASTINESS > HASTY
HASTING > HASTE
HASTINGS > HASTE
HASTY *adj* (too) quick
HAT *n* covering for the head, often with a brim

▷ *vb* supply (a person) with a hat or put a hat on (someone)
HATABLE > HATE
HATBAND *n* band or ribbon around the base of the crown of a hat
HATBANDS > HATBAND
HATBOX *n* box or case for a hat or hats
HATBOXES > HATBOX
HATBRUSH *n* brush for hats
HATCH *vb* (cause to) emerge from an egg ▷ *n* hinged door covering an opening in a floor or wall
HATCHABLE > HATCH
HATCHBACK *n* car with a lifting door at the back
HATCHECK *n* cloakroom
HATCHECKS > HATCHECK
HATCHED > HATCH
HATCHEL *same as* > HECKLE
HATCHELED > HATCHEL
HATCHELS > HATCHEL
HATCHER > HATCH
HATCHERS > HATCH
HATCHERY *n* place where eggs are hatched under artificial conditions
HATCHES > HATCH
HATCHET *n* small axe
HATCHETS > HATCHET
HATCHETY *adj* like a hatchet
HATCHING > HATCH
HATCHINGS > HATCH
HATCHLING *n* young animal that has newly hatched from an egg
HATCHMENT *n* diamond-shaped tablet displaying the coat of arms of a dead person
HATCHWAY *n* opening in the deck of a ship
HATCHWAYS > HATCHWAY
HATE *vb* dislike intensely ▷ *n* intense dislike
HATEABLE > HATE
HATED > HATE
HATEFUL *adj* causing or deserving hate
HATEFULLY > HATEFUL
HATELESS > HATE
HATER > HATE
HATERENT *same as* > HATRED
HATERENTS > HATERENT
HATERS > HATE
HATES > HATE
HATFUL *n* amount a hat will hold
HATFULS > HATFUL
HATGUARD *n* string to keep a hat from blowing off
HATGUARDS > HATGUARD
HATH *form of the present tense (indicative mood) of* > HAVE
HATHA as in *hatha yoga* form of yoga
HATING > HATE
HATLESS > HAT
HATLIKE > HAT
HATMAKER *n* maker of hats
HATMAKERS > HATMAKER
HATPEG *n* peg to hang hat on
HATPEGS > HATPEG
HATPIN *n* sturdy pin used to secure a woman's hat to her hair, often having a decorative head
HATPINS > HATPIN
HATRACK *n* rack for hanging hats on
HATRACKS > HATRACK
HATRED *n* intense dislike
HATREDS > HATRED
HATS > HAT
HATSFUL > HATFUL
HATSTAND *n* frame or pole equipped with hooks or arms for hanging up hats, coats, etc
HATSTANDS > HATSTAND
HATTED > HAT
HATTER *n* person who makes and sells hats ▷ *vb* annoy
HATTERED > HATTER
HATTERIA *n* species of reptile
HATTERIAS > HATTERIA
HATTERING > HATTER
HATTERS > HATTER
HATTING > HAT
HATTINGS > HAT
HATTOCK *n* small hat
HATTOCKS > HATTOCK
HAUBERK *n* long sleeveless coat of mail
HAUBERKS > HAUBERK
HAUBOIS *same as* > HAUTBOY
HAUD *Scot word for* > HOLD
HAUDEN > HAUD
HAUDING > HAUD
HAUDS > HAUD
HAUF *Scot word for* > HALF
HAUFS > HAUF
HAUGH *n* low-lying often alluvial riverside meadow
HAUGHS > HAUGH
HAUGHT *same as* > HAUGHTY
HAUGHTIER > HAUGHTY
HAUGHTILY > HAUGHTY
HAUGHTY *adj* proud, arrogant
HAUL *vb* pull or drag with effort ▷ *n* hauling
HAULAGE *n* (charge for) transporting goods
HAULAGES > HAULAGE
HAULD *Scots word for* > HOLD
HAULDS > HAULD
HAULED > HAUL
HAULER *same as* > HAULIER
HAULERS > HAULER
HAULIER *n* firm or person that transports goods by road
HAULIERS > HAULIER
HAULING > HAUL
HAULM *n* stalks of beans, peas, or potatoes collectively
HAULMIER > HAULMY
HAULMIEST > HAULMY
HAULMS > HAULM
HAULMY *adj* having haulms
HAULS > HAUL
HAULST *same as* > HALSE
HAULT *same as* > HAUGHTY
HAULYARD *same as* > HALYARD
HAULYARDS > HAULYARD
HAUNCH *n* human hip or fleshy hindquarter of an animal ▷ *vb* in archaic usage, cause (an animal) to come down on its haunches
HAUNCHED > HAUNCH
HAUNCHES > HAUNCH
HAUNCHING > HAUNCH
HAUNT *vb* visit in the form of a ghost ▷ *n* place visited frequently
HAUNTED *adj* frequented by ghosts
HAUNTER > HAUNT
HAUNTERS > HAUNT
HAUNTING *adj* memorably beautiful or sad
HAUNTINGS > HAUNT
HAUNTS > HAUNT
HAURIANT *adj* rising
HAURIENT *same as* > HAURIANT
HAUSE *same as* > HALSE
HAUSED > HAUSE
HAUSEN *n* variety of sturgeon
HAUSENS > HAUSEN
HAUSES > HAUSE
HAUSFRAU *n* German housewife
HAUSFRAUS > HAUSFRAU
HAUSING > HAUSE
HAUSTELLA *n* pl of haustellum: tip of the proboscis of an insect
HAUSTORIA *n* pl of haustorium: organ of a parasitic plant that absorbs food and water from host tissues
HAUT *same as* > HAUGHTY
HAUTBOIS *same as* > HAUTBOY
HAUTBOY *n* oboe
HAUTBOYS > HAUTBOY
HAUTE *adj* French word meaning high
HAUTEUR *n* haughtiness
HAUTEURS > HAUTEUR
HAUYNE *n* blue mineral containing calcium
HAUYNES > HAUYNE
HAVARTI *n* Danish cheese
HAVARTIS > HAVARTI
HAVDALAH *n* ceremony marking the end of the sabbath or of a festival, including the blessings over wine, candles, and spices
HAVDALAHS > HAVDALAH
HAVDOLOH *same as* > HAVDALAH
HAVDOLOHS > HAVDOLOH
HAVE *vb* possess, hold
HAVELOCK *n* light-coloured cover for a service cap with a flap extending over the back of the neck to protect the head and neck from the sun
HAVELOCKS > HAVELOCK
HAVEN *n* place of safety ▷ *vb* secure or shelter in or as if in a haven
HAVENED > HAVEN
HAVENING > HAVEN
HAVENLESS > HAVEN
HAVENS > HAVEN
HAVEOUR *same as* > HAVIOR
HAVEOURS > HAVEOUR
HAVER *vb* talk nonsense ▷ *n* nonsense
HAVERED > HAVER
HAVEREL *n* fool
HAVERELS > HAVEREL
HAVERING > HAVER
HAVERINGS > HAVER
HAVERS > HAVER
HAVERSACK *n* canvas bag carried on the back or shoulder
HAVERSINE *n* half the value of the versed sine
HAVES > HAVE
HAVILDAR *n* noncommissioned officer in the Indian army, equivalent in rank to sergeant
HAVILDARS > HAVILDAR
HAVING > HAVE
HAVINGS > HAVE
HAVIOR *same as* > HAVIOUR
HAVIORS > HAVIOR
HAVIOUR *n* possession
HAVIOURS > HAVIOUR
HAVOC *n* disorder and confusion ▷ *vb* lay waste
HAVOCKED > HAVOC
HAVOCKER > HAVOC
HAVOCKERS > HAVOC
HAVOCKING > HAVOC
HAVOCS > HAVOC
HAW *n* hawthorn berry ▷ *vb* make an inarticulate utterance
HAWALA *n* Middle Eastern system of money transfer
HAWALAS > HAWALA
HAWBUCK *n* bumpkin
HAWBUCKS > HAWBUCK
HAWED > HAW
HAWFINCH *n* European finch with a stout bill and brown plumage with black-and-white wings
HAWING > HAW
HAWK *n* bird of prey with a short hooked bill and very good eyesight ▷ *vb* offer (goods) for sale in the street or door-to-door
HAWKBELL *n* bell fitted to a hawk's leg
HAWKBELLS > HAWKBELL
HAWKBILL *same as* > HAWKSBILL
HAWKBILLS > HAWKBILL

HAWKBIT *n* any of three perennial plants with yellow dandelion-like flowers
HAWKBITS > HAWKBIT
HAWKED > HAWK
HAWKER *n* person who travels from place to place selling goods
HAWKERS > HAWKER
HAWKEY *same as* > HOCKEY
HAWKEYED *adj* having extremely keen sight
HAWKEYS > HAWKEY
HAWKIE *n* cow with white stripe on face
HAWKIES > HAWKIE
HAWKING *another name for* > FALCONRY
HAWKINGS > HAWKING
HAWKISH *adj* favouring the use or display of force rather than diplomacy to achieve foreign policy goals
HAWKISHLY > HAWKISH
HAWKIT *adj* having a white streak
HAWKLIKE > HAWK
HAWKMOTH *n* powerful narrow-winged moth with the ability to hover over flowers when feeding from the nectar
HAWKMOTHS > HAWKMOTH
HAWKNOSE *n* hooked nose
HAWKNOSES > HAWKNOSE
HAWKS > HAWK
HAWKSBILL *n* type of turtle
HAWKSHAW *n* private detective
HAWKSHAWS > HAWKSHAW
HAWKWEED *n* hairy plant with clusters of dandelion-like flowers
HAWKWEEDS > HAWKWEED
HAWM *vb* be idle and relaxed
HAWMED > HAWM
HAWMING > HAWM
HAWMS > HAWM
HAWS > HAW
HAWSE *vb* of boats, pitch violently when at anchor
HAWSED > HAWSE
HAWSEHOLE *n* one of the holes in the upper part of the bows of a vessel through which the anchor ropes pass
HAWSEPIPE *n* strong metal pipe through which an anchor rope passes
HAWSER *n* large rope used on a ship
HAWSERS > HAWSER
HAWSES > HAWSE
HAWSING > HAWSE
HAWTHORN *n* thorny shrub or tree
HAWTHORNS > HAWTHORN
HAWTHORNY > HAWTHORN
HAY *n* grass cut and dried as fodder ▷ *vb* cut, dry, and store (grass, clover, etc) as fodder
HAYBAND *n* rope made by twisting hay together
HAYBANDS > HAYBAND
HAYBOX *n* airtight box full of hay or other insulating material used to keep partially cooked food warm and allow cooking by retained heat
HAYBOXES > HAYBOX
HAYCOCK *n* small cone-shaped pile of hay left in the field until dry enough to carry to the rick or barn
HAYCOCKS > HAYCOCK
HAYED > HAY
HAYER *n* person who makes hay
HAYERS > HAYER
HAYEY > HAY
HAYFIELD *n* field of hay
HAYFIELDS > HAYFIELD
HAYFORK *n* long-handled fork with two long curved prongs, used for moving or turning hay
HAYFORKS > HAYFORK
HAYING > HAY
HAYINGS > HAY
HAYLAGE *n* type of hay for animal fodder
HAYLAGES > HAYLAGE
HAYLE *n* welfare
HAYLES > HAYLE
HAYLOFT *n* loft for storing hay
HAYLOFTS > HAYLOFT
HAYMAKER *n* person who helps to cut, turn, toss, spread, or carry hay
HAYMAKERS > HAYMAKER
HAYMAKING > HAYMAKER
HAYMOW *n* part of a barn where hay is stored
HAYMOWS > HAYMOW
HAYRACK *n* rack for holding hay for feeding to animals
HAYRACKS > HAYRACK
HAYRICK *same as* > HAYSTACK
HAYRICKS > HAYRICK
HAYRIDE *n* pleasure trip in hay wagon
HAYRIDES > HAYRIDE
HAYS > HAY
HAYSEED *n* seeds or fragments of grass or straw
HAYSEEDS > HAYSEED
HAYSEL *n* season for making hay
HAYSELS > HAYSEL
HAYSTACK *n* large pile of stored hay
HAYSTACKS > HAYSTACK
HAYWARD *n* parish officer in charge of enclosures and fences
HAYWARDS > HAYWARD
HAYWIRE *adj* (of things) not functioning properly ▷ *n* wire for binding hay
HAYWIRES > HAYWIRE
HAZAN *same as* > CANTOR
HAZANIM > HAZAN
HAZANS > HAZAN
HAZARD *n* something that could be dangerous ▷ *vb* put in danger
HAZARDED > HAZARD
HAZARDER > HAZARD
HAZARDERS > HAZARD
HAZARDING > HAZARD
HAZARDIZE *same as* > HAZARD
HAZARDOUS *adj* involving great risk
HAZARDRY *n* taking of risks
HAZARDS > HAZARD
HAZE *n* mist, often caused by heat ▷ *vb* make or become hazy
HAZED > HAZE
HAZEL *n* small tree producing edible nuts ▷ *adj* (of eyes) greenish-brown
HAZELHEN *n* type of grouse
HAZELHENS > HAZELHEN
HAZELLY > HAZEL
HAZELNUT *n* nut of a hazel shrub, which has a smooth shiny hard shell
HAZELNUTS > HAZELNUT
HAZELS > HAZEL
HAZER > HAZE
HAZERS > HAZE
HAZES > HAZE
HAZIER > HAZY
HAZIEST > HAZY
HAZILY > HAZY
HAZINESS > HAZY
HAZING > HAZE
HAZINGS > HAZE
HAZMAT *n* hazardous material
HAZMATS > HAZMAT
HAZY *adj* not clear, misty
HAZZAN *same as* > CANTOR
HAZZANIM > HAZZAN
HAZZANS > HAZZAN
HE *pron* male person or animal ▷ *n* male person or animal ▷ *interj* expression of amusement or derision
HEAD *n* upper or front part of the body, containing the sense organs and the brain ▷ *adj* chief, principal ▷ *vb* be at the top or front of
HEADACHE *n* continuous pain in the head
HEADACHES > HEADACHE
HEADACHEY *same as* > HEADACHY
HEADACHY *adj* suffering from, caused by, or likely to cause a headache
HEADAGE *n* payment to farmer based on number of animals kept
HEADAGES > HEADAGE
HEADBAND *n* ribbon or band worn around the head
HEADBANDS > HEADBAND
HEADBANG *vb* nod one's head violently to the beat of loud rock music
HEADBANGS > HEADBANG
HEADBOARD *n* vertical board at the top end of a bed
HEADCASE *n* insane person
HEADCASES > HEADCASE
HEADCHAIR *n* chair with support for the head
HEADCLOTH *n* kerchief worn on the head
HEADCOUNT *n* count of number of people present
HEADDRESS *n* decorative head covering
HEADED *adj* having a head or heads
HEADEND *n* facility from which cable television is transmitted
HEADENDS > HEADEND
HEADER *n* striking a ball with the head
HEADERS > HEADER
HEADFAST *n* mooring rope at the bows of a ship
HEADFASTS > HEADFAST
HEADFIRST *adv* with the head foremost
HEADFISH *same as* > SUNFISH
HEADFRAME *n* structure supporting winding machinery at mine
HEADFUCK *n* taboo slang for experience that is wildly exciting or impressive
HEADFUCKS > HEADFUCK
HEADFUL *n* amount head will hold
HEADFULS > HEADFUL
HEADGATE *n* a gate that is used to control the flow of water at the upper end of a lock or conduit
HEADGATES > HEADGATE
HEADGEAR *n* hats collectively
HEADGEARS > HEADGEAR
HEADGUARD *n* padded helmet worn to protect the head in contact sports
HEADHUNT *vb* recruit employee from another company
HEADHUNTS > HEADHUNT
HEADIER > HEADY
HEADIEST > HEADY
HEADILY > HEADY
HEADINESS > HEADY
HEADING *same as* > HEAD
HEADINGS > HEADING
HEADLAMP *same as* > HEADLIGHT
HEADLAMPS > HEADLAMP
HEADLAND *n* area of land jutting out into the sea
HEADLANDS > HEADLAND
HEADLEASE *n* main lease often subdivided
HEADLESS *adj* without a head
HEADLIGHT *n* powerful light on the front of a

vehicle
HEADLIKE > HEAD
HEADLINE *n* title at the top of a newspaper article, esp on the front page
HEADLINED > HEADLINE
HEADLINER *n* performer given prominent billing
HEADLINES > HEADLINE
HEADLOCK *n* wrestling hold in which a wrestler locks his opponent's head between the crook of his elbow and the side of his body
HEADLOCKS > HEADLOCK
HEADLONG *adj* with the head first ▷ *adv* with the head foremost
HEADMAN *n* chief or leader
HEADMARK *n* characteristic
HEADMARKS > HEADMARK
HEADMEN > HEADMAN
HEADMOST *less common word for* > FOREMOST
HEADNOTE *n* note at book chapter head
HEADNOTES > HEADNOTE
HEADPEACE *archaic form of* > HEADPIECE
HEADPHONE *n* small loudspeaker held against the ear
HEADPIECE *n* decorative band at the top of a page, chapter, etc
HEADPIN *another word for* > KINGPIN
HEADPINS > HEADPIN
HEADRACE *n* channel that carries water to a water wheel, turbine, etc
HEADRACES > HEADRACE
HEADRAIL *n* end of the table from which play is started, nearest the baulkline
HEADRAILS > HEADRAIL
HEADREACH *n* distance made to windward while tacking ▷ *vb* gain distance over (another boat) when tacking
HEADREST *n* support for the head, as on a dentist's chair or car seat
HEADRESTS > HEADREST
HEADRIG *n* edge of ploughed field
HEADRIGS > HEADRIG
HEADRING *n* African head decoration
HEADRINGS > HEADRING
HEADROOM *n* space below a roof or bridge which allows an object to pass or stay underneath it without touching it
HEADROOMS > HEADROOM
HEADROPE *n* rope round an animal's head
HEADROPES > HEADROPE
HEADS *adv* with the side of a coin which has a portrait of a head on it uppermost
HEADSAIL *n* any sail set forward of the foremast
HEADSAILS > HEADSAIL
HEADSCARF *n* scarf for the head, often worn tied under the chin
HEADSET *n* pair of headphones, esp with a microphone attached
HEADSETS > HEADSET
HEADSHAKE *n* gesture of shaking head
HEADSHIP *n* position or state of being a leader, esp the head teacher of a school
HEADSHIPS > HEADSHIP
HEADSHOT *n* photo of person's head
HEADSHOTS > HEADSHOT
HEADSMAN *n* (formerly) an executioner who beheaded condemned persons
HEADSMEN > HEADSMAN
HEADSPACE *n* space between bolt and cartridge in a rifle
HEADSTALL *n* part of a bridle that fits round a horse's head
HEADSTAND *n* act or an instance of balancing on the head, usually with the hands as support
HEADSTAY *n* rope from mast to bow on ship
HEADSTAYS > HEADSTAY
HEADSTICK *n* piece of wood formerly used in typesetting
HEADSTOCK *n* part of a machine that supports and transmits the drive to the chuck
HEADSTONE *n* memorial stone on a grave
HEADWARD *same as* > HEADWARDS
HEADWARDS *adv* backwards beyond the original source
HEADWATER *n* highest part of river
HEADWAY *same as* > HEADROOM
HEADWAYS > HEADWAY
HEADWIND *n* wind blowing against the course of an aircraft or ship
HEADWINDS > HEADWIND
HEADWORD *n* key word placed at the beginning of a line, paragraph, etc, as in a dictionary entry
HEADWORDS > HEADWORD
HEADWORK *n* mental work
HEADWORKS > HEADWORK
HEADY *adj* intoxicating or exciting
HEAL *vb* make or become well
HEALABLE > HEAL
HEALD *same as* > HEDDLE
HEALDED > HEALD
HEALDING > HEALD
HEALDS > HEALD
HEALED > HEAL
HEALEE *n* person who is being healed
HEALEES > HEALEE
HEALER > HEAL
HEALERS > HEAL
HEALING > HEAL
HEALINGLY > HEAL
HEALINGS > HEAL
HEALS > HEAL
HEALSOME *Scots word for* > WHOLESOME
HEALTH *n* normal (good) condition of someone's body ▷ *interj* exclamation wishing someone good health as part of a toast
HEALTHFUL *same as* > HEALTHY
HEALTHIER > HEALTHY
HEALTHILY > HEALTHY
HEALTHISM *n* lifestyle that prioritizes health and fitness over anything else
HEALTHS > HEALTH
HEALTHY *adj* having good health
HEAME *old form of* > HOME
HEAP *n* pile of things one on top of another ▷ *vb* gather into a pile
HEAPED > HEAP
HEAPER > HEAP
HEAPERS > HEAP
HEAPIER > HEAPY
HEAPIEST > HEAPY
HEAPING *adj* (of a spoonful) heaped
HEAPS > HEAP
HEAPSTEAD *n* buildings at mine
HEAPY *adj* having many heaps
HEAR *vb* perceive (a sound) by ear
HEARABLE > HEAR
HEARD *same as* > HERD
HEARDS > HERD
HEARE *old form of* > HAIR
HEARER > HEAR
HEARERS > HEAR
HEARES > HEARE
HEARIE *old form of* > HAIRY
HEARING > HEAR
HEARINGS > HEAR
HEARKEN *vb* listen
HEARKENED > HEARKEN
HEARKENER > HEARKEN
HEARKENS > HEARKEN
HEARS > HEAR
HEARSAY *n* gossip, rumour
HEARSAYS > HEARSAY
HEARSE *n* funeral car used to carry a coffin ▷ *vb* put in hearse
HEARSED > HEARSE
HEARSES > HEARSE
HEARSIER > HEARSY
HEARSIEST > HEARSY
HEARSING > HEARSE
HEARSY *adj* like a hearse
HEART *n* organ that pumps blood round the body ▷ *vb* (of vegetables) form a heart
HEARTACHE *n* intense anguish
HEARTBEAT *n* one complet[e] pulsation of the heart
HEARTBURN *n* burning sensation in the chest caused by indigestion
HEARTED > HEART
HEARTEN *vb* encourage, make cheerful
HEARTENED > HEARTEN
HEARTENER > HEARTEN
HEARTENS > HEARTEN
HEARTFELT *adj* felt sincerely or strongly
HEARTFREE *adj* not in love
HEARTH *n* floor of a fireplace
HEARTHRUG *n* rug laid before fireplace
HEARTHS > HEARTH
HEARTIER > HEARTY
HEARTIES > HEARTY
HEARTIEST > HEARTY
HEARTIKIN *n* little heart
HEARTILY *adv* thoroughly or vigorously
HEARTING > HEART
HEARTLAND *n* central region of a country or continent
HEARTLESS *adj* cruel, unkind
HEARTLET *n* little heart
HEARTLETS > HEART
HEARTLING *n* little heart
HEARTLY *adv* vigorously
HEARTPEA *same as* > HEARTSEED
HEARTPEAS > HEARTPEA
HEARTS *n* card game in which players must avoid winning tricks containing hearts or the queen of spades
HEARTSEED *n* type of vine
HEARTSICK *adj* deeply dejected or despondent
HEARTSOME *adj* cheering o[r] encouraging
HEARTSORE *adj* greatly distressed
HEARTWOOD *n* central core of dark hard wood in tree trunks
HEARTWORM *n* parasitic nematode worm that lives in the heart and bloodstream of vertebrates
HEARTY *adj* substantial, nourishing ▷ *n* comrade, esp a sailor
HEAST *same as* > HEST
HEASTE *same as* > HEST
HEASTES > HEASTE
HEASTS > HEAST
HEAT *vb* make or become hot ▷ *n* state of being hot
HEATABLE > HEAT

HEATED *adj* angry and excited
HEATEDLY > HEATED
HEATER *n* device for supplying heat
HEATERS > HEATER
HEATH *n* area of open uncultivated land
HEATHBIRD *n* black grouse
HEATHCOCK *same as* > BLACKCOCK
HEATHEN *n* (of) a person who does not believe in an established religion ▷ *adj* of or relating to heathen peoples
HEATHENRY > HEATHEN
HEATHENS > HEATHEN
HEATHER *n* low-growing plant with small purple, pinkish, or white flowers, growing on heaths and mountains ▷ *adj* of a heather colour
HEATHERED > HEATHER
HEATHERS > HEATHER
HEATHERY > HEATHER
HEATHFOWL *Compare* > MOORFOWL
HEATHIER > HEATH
HEATHIEST > HEATH
HEATHLAND *n* area of heath
HEATHLESS > HEATH
HEATHLIKE > HEATH
HEATHS > HEATH
HEATHY > HEATH
HEATING *n* device or system for supplying heat, esp central heating, to a building
HEATINGS > HEATING
HEATLESS > HEAT
HEATPROOF > HEAT
HEATS > HEAT
HEATSPOT *n* spot on skin produced by heat
HEATSPOTS > HEATSPOT
HEAUME *n* (in the 12th and 13th centuries) a large helmet reaching and supported by the shoulders
HEAUMES > HEAUME
HEAVE *vb* lift with effort ▷ *n* heaving
HEAVED > HEAVE
HEAVEN *n* place believed to be the home of God, where good people go when they die
HEAVENLY *adj* of or like heaven
HEAVENS > HEAVEN
HEAVER > HEAVE
HEAVERS > HEAVE
HEAVES > HEAVE
HEAVIER > HEAVY
HEAVIES > HEAVY
HEAVIEST > HEAVY
HEAVILY > HEAVY
HEAVINESS > HEAVY
HEAVING > HEAVE
HEAVINGS > HEAVE
HEAVY *adj* of great weight
HEAVYSET *adj* stockily built
HEBDOMAD *n* number seven or a group of seven
HEBDOMADS > HEBDOMAD
HEBE *n* any of various flowering shrubs
HEBEN *old form of* > EBONY
HEBENON *n* source of poison
HEBENONS > HEBENON
HEBENS > HEBEN
HEBES > HEBE
HEBETANT *adj* causing dullness
HEBETATE *adj* (of plant parts) having a blunt or soft point ▷ *vb* make or become blunted
HEBETATED > HEBETATE
HEBETATES > HEBETATE
HEBETIC *adj* of or relating to puberty
HEBETUDE *n* mental dullness or lethargy
HEBETUDES > HEBETUDE
HEBONA *same as* > HEBENON
HEBONAS > HEBONA
HEBRAISE *same as* > HEBRAIZE
HEBRAISED > HEBRAISE
HEBRAISES > HEBRAISE
HEBRAIZE *vb* become or cause to become Hebrew or Hebraic
HEBRAIZED > HEBRAIZE
HEBRAIZES > HEBRAIZE
HECATOMB *n* (in ancient Greece or Rome) any great public sacrifice and feast, originally one in which 100 oxen were sacrificed
HECATOMBS > HECATOMB
HECH *interj* expression of surprise
HECHT *same as* > HIGHT
HECHTING > HECHT
HECHTS > HECHT
HECK *interj* mild exclamation of surprise, irritation, etc ▷ *n* frame for obstructing the passage of fish in a river
HECKLE *vb* interrupt (a public speaker) with comments, questions, or taunts ▷ *n* instrument for combing flax or hemp
HECKLED > HECKLE
HECKLER > HECKLE
HECKLERS > HECKLE
HECKLES > HECKLE
HECKLING > HECKLE
HECKLINGS > HECKLE
HECKS > HECK
HECOGENIN *n* plant chemical used in drugs
HECTARE *n* one hundred ares or 10 000 square metres (2.471 acres)
HECTARES > HECTARE
HECTIC *adj* rushed or busy ▷ *n* hectic fever or flush
HECTICAL *same as* > HECTIC
HECTICLY > HECTIC
HECTICS > HECTIC
HECTOGRAM *n* one hundred grams. 1 hectogram is equivalent to 3.527 ounces.
HECTOR *vb* bully ▷ *n* blustering bully
HECTORED > HECTOR
HECTORER > HECTOR
HECTORERS > HECTOR
HECTORING > HECTOR
HECTORISM > HECTOR
HECTORLY > HECTOR
HECTORS > HECTOR
HEDDLE *n* one of a set of frames of vertical wires on a loom, each wire having an eye through which a warp thread can be passed ▷ *vb* pass thread through heddle
HEDDLED > HEDDLE
HEDDLES > HEDDLE
HEDDLING > HEDDLE
HEDER *variant spelling of* > CHEDER
HEDERA *See* > IVY
HEDERAL > HEDERA
HEDERAS > HEDERA
HEDERATED *adj* honoured with crown of ivy
HEDERS > HEDER
HEDGE *n* row of bushes forming a barrier or boundary ▷ *vb* be evasive or noncommittal
HEDGEBILL *n* tool for pruning a hedge
HEDGED > HEDGE
HEDGEHOG *n* small mammal with a protective covering of spines
HEDGEHOGS > HEDGEHOG
HEDGEHOP *vb* (of an aircraft) to fly close to the ground, as in crop spraying
HEDGEHOPS > HEDGEHOP
HEDGEPIG *same as* > HEDGEHOG
HEDGEPIGS > HEDGEPIG
HEDGER > HEDGE
HEDGEROW *n* bushes forming a hedge
HEDGEROWS > HEDGEROW
HEDGERS > HEDGE
HEDGES > HEDGE
HEDGIER > HEDGE
HEDGIEST > HEDGE
HEDGING > HEDGE
HEDGINGLY > HEDGE
HEDGINGS > HEDGE
HEDGY > HEDGE
HEDONIC > HEDONISM
HEDONICS *n* branch of psychology concerned with the study of pleasant and unpleasant sensations
HEDONISM *n* doctrine that pleasure is the most important thing in life
HEDONISMS > HEDONISM
HEDONIST > HEDONISM
HEDONISTS > HEDONISM
HEDYPHANE *n* variety of lead ore
HEED *n* careful attention ▷ *vb* pay careful attention to
HEEDED > HEED
HEEDER > HEED
HEEDERS > HEED
HEEDFUL > HEED
HEEDFULLY > HEED
HEEDINESS > HEED
HEEDING > HEED
HEEDLESS *adj* taking no notice
HEEDS > HEED
HEEDY > HEED
HEEHAW *interj* representation of the braying sound of a donkey ▷ *vb* make braying sound
HEEHAWED > HEEHAW
HEEHAWING > HEEHAW
HEEHAWS > HEEHAW
HEEL *n* back part of the foot ▷ *vb* repair the heel of (a shoe)
HEELBALL *n* mixture of beeswax and lampblack used by shoemakers
HEELBALLS > HEELBALL
HEELED > HEEL
HEELER *n* dog that herds cattle by biting at their heels
HEELERS > HEELER
HEELING > HEEL
HEELINGS > HEEL
HEELLESS > HEEL
HEELPIECE *n* piece of a shoe, stocking, etc, designed to fit the heel
HEELPLATE *n* reinforcing piece of metal
HEELPOST *n* post for carrying the hinges of a door or gate
HEELPOSTS > HEELPOST
HEELS > HEEL
HEELTAP *n* layer of leather, etc, in the heel of a shoe
HEELTAPS > HEELTAP
HEEZE *Scots word for* > HOIST
HEEZED > HEEZE
HEEZES > HEEZE
HEEZIE *n* act of lifting
HEEZIES > HEEZIE
HEEZING > HEEZE
HEFT *vb* assess the weight of (something) by lifting ▷ *n* weight
HEFTE *same as* > HEAVE
HEFTED > HEFT
HEFTER > HEFT
HEFTERS > HEFT
HEFTIER > HEFTY
HEFTIEST > HEFTY
HEFTILY > HEFTY
HEFTINESS > HEFTY
HEFTING > HEFT
HEFTS > HEFT
HEFTY *adj* large, heavy, or strong
HEGARI *n* African sorghum
HEGARIS > HEGARI
HEGEMON *n* person in authority
HEGEMONIC > HEGEMONY

HEGEMONS > HEGEMON
HEGEMONY *n* political domination
HEGIRA *n* emigration escape or flight
HEGIRAS > HEGIRA
HEGUMEN *n* head of a monastery of the Eastern Church
HEGUMENE *n* head of Greek nunnery
HEGUMENES > HEGUMENE
HEGUMENOI > HEGUMENOS
HEGUMENOS *same as* > HEGUMEN
HEGUMENS > HEGUMEN
HEGUMENY *n* office of hegumen
HEH *interj* exclamation of surprise or inquiry
HEHS > HEH
HEID *Scot word for* > HEAD
HEIDS > HEID
HEIFER *n* young cow
HEIFERS > HEIFER
HEIGH *same as* > HEY
HEIGHT *n* distance from base to top
HEIGHTEN *vb* make or become higher or more intense
HEIGHTENS > HEIGHTEN
HEIGHTH *obsolete form of* > HEIGHT
HEIGHTHS > HEIGHTH
HEIGHTISM *n* discrimination based on people's heights
HEIGHTS > HEIGHT
HEIL *vb* give a German greeting
HEILED > HEIL
HEILING > HEIL
HEILS > HEIL
HEIMISH *adj* comfortable
HEINIE *n* buttocks
HEINIES > HEINIE
HEINOUS *adj* evil and shocking
HEINOUSLY > HEINOUS
HEIR *n* person entitled to inherit property or rank ▷ *vb* inherit
HEIRDOM *n* succession by right of blood
HEIRDOMS > HEIRDOM
HEIRED > HEIR
HEIRESS *n* woman who inherits or expects to inherit great wealth
HEIRESSES > HEIRESS
HEIRING > HEIR
HEIRLESS > HEIR
HEIRLOOM *n* object that has belonged to a family for generations
HEIRLOOMS > HEIRLOOM
HEIRS > HEIR
HEIRSHIP *n* state or condition of being an heir
HEIRSHIPS > HEIRSHIP
HEISHI *n* Native American shell jewellery
HEIST *n* robbery ▷ *vb* steal or burgle
HEISTED > HEIST
HEISTER > HEIST
HEISTERS > HEIST
HEISTING > HEIST
HEISTS > HEIST
HEITIKI *n* Māori neck ornament of greenstone
HEITIKIS > HEITIKI
HEJAB *same as* > HIJAB
HEJABS > HEJAB
HEJIRA *same as* > HEGIRA
HEJIRAS > HEJIRA
HEJRA *same as* > HEGIRA
HEJRAS > HEJRA
HEKETARA *n* small shrub that has flowers with white petals and yellow centres
HEKETARAS > HEKETARA
HEKTARE *same as* > HECTARE
HEKTARES > HEKTARE
HEKTOGRAM *same as* > HECTOGRAM
HELCOID *adj* having ulcers
HELD > HOLD
HELE as in *hele in* dialect expression meaning insert (cuttings, shoots, etc) into soil before planting to keep them moist
HELED > HELE
HELENIUM *n* plant with daisy-like yellow or variegated flowers
HELENIUMS > HELENIUM
HELES > HELE
HELIAC *same as* > HELIACAL
HELIACAL as in *heliacal rising* rising of a celestial object at approximately the same time as the rising of the sun
HELIAST *n* ancient Greek juror
HELIASTS > HELIAST
HELIBORNE *adj* carried in helicopter
HELIBUS *n* helicopter carrying passengers
HELIBUSES > HELIBUS
HELICAL *adj* spiral
HELICALLY > HELICAL
HELICES > HELIX
HELICITY *n* projection of the spin of an elementary particle on the direction of propagation
HELICLINE *n* spiral-shaped ramp
HELICOID *adj* shaped like a spiral ▷ *n* any surface resembling that of a screw thread
HELICOIDS > HELICOID
HELICON *n* bass tuba made to coil over the shoulder of a band musician
HELICONIA *n* tropical flowering plant
HELICONS > HELICON
HELICOPT *vb* transport using a helicopter
HELICOPTS > HELICOPT
HELICTITE *n* twisted stalactite
HELIDECK *n* landing deck for helicopters on ships, oil platforms, etc
HELIDECKS > HELIDECK
HELIDROME *n* small airport for helicopters
HELILIFT *vb* transport by helicopter
HELILIFTS > HELILIFT
HELIMAN *n* helicopter pilot
HELIMEN > HELIMAN
HELING > HELE
HELIO *n* instrument for sending messages in Morse code by reflecting the sun's rays
HELIODOR *n* clear yellow form of beryl used as a gemstone
HELIODORS > HELIODOR
HELIOGRAM *n* message sent by reflecting the sun's rays in a mirror
HELIOLOGY *n* study of sun
HELIOS > HELIO
HELIOSES > HELIOSIS
HELIOSIS *n* bad effect of overexposure to the sun
HELIOSTAT *n* astronomical instrument used to reflect the light of the sun in a constant direction
HELIOTYPE *n* printing process in which an impression is taken in ink from a gelatine surface that has been exposed under a negative and prepared for printing
HELIOTYPY *same as* > HELIOTYPE
HELIOZOAN *n* type of protozoan, typically having a siliceous shell and stiff radiating cytoplasmic projections
HELIOZOIC > HELIOZOAN
HELIPAD *n* place for helicopters to land and take off
HELIPADS > HELIPAD
HELIPILOT *n* helicopter pilot
HELIPORT *n* airport for helicopters
HELIPORTS > HELIPORT
HELISTOP *n* landing place for helicopter
HELISTOPS > HELISTOP
HELIUM *n* very light colourless odourless gas
HELIUMS > HELIUM
HELIX *n* spiral
HELIXES > HELIX
HELL *n* place believed to be where wicked people go when they die ▷ *vb* act wildly
HELLBENT *adj* intent
HELLBOX *n* (in printing) container for broken type
HELLBOXES > HELLBOX
HELLBROTH *n* evil concoction
HELLCAT *n* spiteful fierce-tempered woman
HELLCATS > HELLCAT
HELLDIVER *n* small greyish-brown North American grebe
HELLEBORE *n* plant with white flowers that bloom in winter
HELLED > HELL
HELLENISE *same as* > HELLENIZE
HELLENIZE *vb* make or become like the ancient Greeks
HELLER *n* monetary unit of the Czech Republic and Slovakia
HELLERI *n* Central American fish
HELLERIES > HELLERY
HELLERIS > HELLERI
HELLERS > HELLER
HELLERY *n* wild or mischievous behaviour
HELLFIRE *n* torment of hell, imagined as eternal fire
HELLFIRES > HELLFIRE
HELLHOLE *n* unpleasant or evil place
HELLHOLES > HELLHOLE
HELLHOUND *n* hound of hell
HELLICAT *n* evil creature
HELLICATS > HELLICAT
HELLIER *n* slater
HELLIERS > HELLIER
HELLING > HELL
HELLION *n* rough or rowdy person, esp a child
HELLIONS > HELLION
HELLISH *adj* very unpleasant ▷ *adv* (intensifier)
HELLISHLY > HELLISH
HELLKITE *n* bird of prey from hell
HELLKITES > HELLKITE
HELLO *interj* expression of greeting or surprise ▷ *n* act of saying 'hello' ▷ *sentence substitute* expression of greeting used on meeting a person or at the start of a telephone call ▷ *vb* say hello
HELLOED > HELLO
HELLOES > HELLO
HELLOING > HELLO
HELLOS > HELLO
HELLOVA *same as* > HELLUVA
HELLS > HELL
HELLUVA *adj* (intensifier)
HELLWARD *adj* towards hell
HELLWARDS *adv* towards hell
HELM *n* tiller or wheel for steering a ship ▷ *vb* direct or steer
HELMED > HELM
HELMER *n* film director

HELMERS > HELMER
HELMET *n* hard hat worn for protection
HELMETED > HELMET
HELMETING *n* wearing or provision of a helmet
HELMETS > HELMET
HELMING > HELM
HELMINTH *n* any parasitic worm, esp a nematode or fluke
HELMINTHS > HELMINTH
HELMLESS > HELM
HELMS > HELM
HELMSMAN *n* person at the helm who steers the ship
HELMSMEN > HELMSMAN
HELO *n* helicopter
HELOPHYTE *n* any perennial marsh plant that bears its overwintering buds in the mud below the surface
HELOS > HELO
HELOT *n* serf or slave
HELOTAGE *same as* > HELOTISM
HELOTAGES > HELOTAGE
HELOTISM *n* condition or quality of being a helot
HELOTISMS > HELOTISM
HELOTRIES > HELOTRY
HELOTRY *n* serfdom or slavery
HELOTS > HELOT
HELP *vb* make something easier, better, or quicker for (someone) ▷ *n* assistance or support
HELPABLE > HELP
HELPDESK *n* place where advice is given by telephone
HELPDESKS > HELPDESK
HELPED > HELP
HELPER > HELP
HELPERS > HELP
HELPFUL *adj* giving help
HELPFULLY > HELPFUL
HELPING *n* single portion of food
HELPINGS > HELPING
HELPLESS *adj* weak or incapable
HELPLINE *n* telephone line set aside for callers to contact an organization for help with a problem
HELPLINES > HELPLINE
HELPMATE *n* companion and helper, esp a husband or wife
HELPMATES > HELPMATE
HELPMEET *less common word for* > HELPMATE
HELPMEETS > HELPMEET
HELPS > HELP
HELVE *n* handle of a hand tool such as an axe or pick ▷ *vb* fit a helve to (a tool)
HELVED > HELVE
HELVES > HELVE
HELVETIUM *same as* > ASTATINE
HELVING > HELVE
HEM *n* bottom edge of a garment, folded under and stitched down ▷ *vb* provide with a hem > HEMAGGLUTINATE
HEMAGOG *same as* > HEMAGOGUE
HEMAGOGS > HEMAGOGUE
HEMAGOGUE *n* haemagogue: drug that promotes the flow of blood
HEMAL *same as* > HAEMAL
HEMATAL *same as* > HEMAL
HEMATEIN *same as* > HAEMATEIN
HEMATEINS > HEMATEIN
HEMATIC *same as* > HAEMATIC
HEMATICS > HEMATIC
HEMATIN *same as* > HAEMATIN
HEMATINE *n* red dye
HEMATINES > HEMATINE
HEMATINIC *same as* > HAEMATIC
HEMATINS > HEMATIN
HEMATITE *n* red, grey, or black mineral
HEMATITES > HEMATITE
HEMATITIC > HEMATITE
HEMATOID *same as* > HAEMATOID
HEMATOMA *same as* > HAEMATOMA
HEMATOMAS > HEMATOMA
HEMATOSES > HEMATOSIS
HEMATOSIS *n* haematosis: oxygenation of venous blood in the lungs
HEMATOZOA *n plural of* hematozoon: protozoan that is parasitic in the blood
HEMATURIA *same as* > HAEMATURIA
HEMATURIC > HEMATURIA
HEME *same as* > HAEM
HEMELYTRA *n plural of* hemelytron: forewing of plant bugs
HEMES > HEME
HEMIALGIA *n* pain limited to one side of the body
HEMIC > HAEMATIC
HEMICYCLE *n* semicircular structure, room, arena, wall, etc
HEMIHEDRY *n* state of crystal having certain kind of symmetry
HEMIN *same as* > HAEMIN
HEMINA *n* old liquid measure
HEMINAS > HEMINA
HEMINS > HEMIN
HEMIOLA *n* rhythmic device involving the superimposition of, for example, two notes in the time of three
HEMIOLAS > HEMIOLA
HEMIOLIA *same as* > HEMIOLA
HEMIOLIAS > HEMIOLIA
HEMIOLIC > HEMIOLA
HEMIONE *same as* > HEMIONUS
HEMIONES > HEMIONE
HEMIONUS *n* Asian wild ass
HEMIOPIA *n* defective vision seeing only halves of things
HEMIOPIAS > HEMIOPIA
HEMIOPIC > HEMIOPIA
HEMIOPSIA *same as* > HEMIOPIA
HEMIPOD *same as* > HEMIPODE
HEMIPODE *n* button quail
HEMIPODES > HEMIPODE
HEMIPODS > HEMIPOD
HEMIPTER *n* insect with beaklike mouthparts
HEMIPTERS > HEMIPTER
HEMISPACE *n* area in brain
HEMISTICH *n* half line of verse
HEMITROPE *another name for* > TWIN
HEMITROPY *n* state of being a twin
HEMLINE *n* level to which the hem of a skirt hangs
HEMLINES > HEMLINE
HEMLOCK *n* poison made from a plant with spotted stems and small white flowers
HEMLOCKS > HEMLOCK
HEMMED > HEM
HEMMER *n* attachment on a sewing machine for hemming
HEMMERS > HEMMER
HEMMING > HEM
HEMOCOEL *same as* > HAEMOCOEL
HEMOCOELS > HEMOCOEL
HEMOCYTE *same as* > HAEMOCYTE
HEMOCYTES > HEMOCYTE
HEMOID *same as* > HAEMATOID
HEMOLYMPH *n* blood-like fluid in invertebrates
HEMOLYSE *vb* break down so that haemoglobulin is released
HEMOLYSED > HEMOLYSE
HEMOLYSES > HEMOLYSIS
HEMOLYSIN *n* haemolysin: substance that breaks down red blood cells
HEMOLYSIS *n* haemolysis: disintegration of red blood cells
HEMOLYTIC > HEMOLYSIS
HEMOLYZE *vb* undergo or make undergo hemolysis
HEMOLYZED > HEMOLYZE
HEMOLYZES > HEMOLYZE
HEMOPHILE *n* haemophile: person with haemophilia
HEMOSTAT *same as* > HAEMOSTAT
HEMOSTATS > HEMOSTAT
HEMOTOXIC > HEMOTOXIN
HEMOTOXIN *n* substance that destroys red blood cells
HEMP *n* Asian plant with tough fibres
HEMPEN > HEMP
HEMPIE *variant of* > HEMPY
HEMPIER > HEMPY
HEMPIES > HEMPY
HEMPIEST > HEMPY
HEMPLIKE > HEMP
HEMPS > HEMP
HEMPSEED *n* seed of hemp
HEMPSEEDS > HEMPSEED
HEMPWEED *n* climbing weed
HEMPWEEDS > HEMPWEED
HEMPY *adj* of or like hemp ▷ *n* rogue
HEMS > HEM
HEMSTITCH *n* decorative edging stitch, usually for a hem, in which the cross threads are stitched in groups ▷ *vb* decorate (a hem, etc) with hemstitches
HEN *n* female domestic fowl ▷ *vb* lose one's courage
HENBANE *n* poisonous plant with sticky hairy leaves
HENBANES > HENBANE
HENBIT *n* European plant with small dark red flowers
HENBITS > HENBIT
HENCE *adv* from this time ▷ *interj* begone! away!
HENCHMAN *n* person employed by someone powerful to carry out orders
HENCHMEN > HENCHMAN
HENCOOP *n* cage for poultry
HENCOOPS > HENCOOP
HEND *vb* seize
HENDED > HEND
HENDIADYS *n* rhetorical device by which two nouns joined by a conjunction are used instead of a noun and modifier
HENDING > HEND
HENDS > HEND
HENEQUEN *n* agave plant native to Yucatán
HENEQUENS > HENEQUEN
HENEQUIN *same as* > HENEQUEN
HENEQUINS > HENEQUIN
HENGE *n* circular monument, often containing a circle of stones, dating from the Neolithic and Bronze Ages
HENGES > HENGE
HENHOUSE *n* coop for hens
HENHOUSES > HENHOUSE
HENIQUEN *same as* > HENEQUEN
HENIQUENS > HENIQUEN
HENIQUIN *same as* > HENIQUEN
HENIQUINS > HENIQUIN
HENLEY *n* type of sweater
HENLEYS > HENLEY

HENLIKE > HEN
HENNA *n* reddish dye made from a shrub or tree ▷ *vb* dye (the hair) with henna
HENNAED > HENNA
HENNAING > HENNA
HENNAS > HENNA
HENNED > HEN
HENNER *n* challenge
HENNERIES > HENNERY
HENNERS > HENNER
HENNERY *n* place or farm for keeping poultry
HENNIER > HENNY
HENNIES > HENNY
HENNIEST > HENNY
HENNIN *n* former women's hat
HENNING > HEN
HENNINS > HENNIN
HENNISH > HEN
HENNISHLY > HEN
HENNY *adj* like hen ▷ *n* cock that looks like hen
HENOTIC *adj* acting to reconcile
HENPECK *vb* (of a woman) to harass or torment (a man, esp her husband) by persistent nagging
HENPECKED *adj* (of a man) dominated by his wife
HENPECKS > HENPECK
HENRIES > HENRY
HENRY *n* unit of electrical inductance
HENRYS > HENRY
HENS > HEN
HENT *vb* seize ▷ *n* anything that has been grasped, esp by the mind
HENTED > HENT
HENTING > HENT
HENTS > HENT
HEP *same as* > HIP
HEPAR *n* compound containing sulphur
HEPARIN *n* polysaccharide, containing sulphate groups, present in most body tissues: an anticoagulant used in the treatment of thrombosis
HEPARINS > HEPARIN
HEPARS > HEPAR
HEPATIC *adj* of the liver ▷ *n* any of various drugs for use in treating diseases of the liver
HEPATICA *n* woodland plant with white, mauve, or pink flowers
HEPATICAE > HEPATICA
HEPATICAL *same as* > HEPATIC
HEPATICAS > HEPATICA
HEPATICS > HEPATIC
HEPATISE *same as* > HEPATIZE
HEPATISED > HEPATISE
HEPATISES > HEPATISE
HEPATITE *n* mineral containing sulphur
HEPATITES > HEPATITE
HEPATITIS *n* inflammation of the liver
HEPATIZE *vb* turn into liver
HEPATIZED > HEPATIZE
HEPATIZES > HEPATIZE
HEPATOMA *n* cancer of liver
HEPATOMAS > HEPATOMA
HEPCAT *n* person who is hep, esp a player or admirer of jazz and swing in the 1940s
HEPCATS > HEPCAT
HEPPER > HEP
HEPPEST > HEP
HEPS > HEP
HEPSTER *same as* > HIPSTER
HEPSTERS > HEPSTER
HEPT *archaic spelling of* > HEAPED
HEPTAD *n* group or series of seven
HEPTADS > HEPTAD
HEPTAGLOT *n* book in seven languages
HEPTAGON *n* geometric figure with seven sides
HEPTAGONS > HEPTAGON
HEPTANE *n* alkane found in petroleum and used as an anaesthetic
HEPTANES > HEPTANE
HEPTAPODY *n* verse with seven beats in rhythm
HEPTARCH > HEPTARCHY
HEPTARCHS > HEPTARCHY
HEPTARCHY *n* government by seven rulers
HEPTOSE *n* any monosaccharide that has seven carbon atoms per molecule
HEPTOSES > HEPTOSE
HER *pron* refers to a female person or animal or anything personified as feminine when the object of a sentence or clause ▷ *adj* belonging to her ▷ *determiner* of, belonging to, or associated with her
HERALD *n* person who announces important news ▷ *vb* signal the approach of
HERALDED > HERALD
HERALDIC *adj* of or relating to heraldry
HERALDING > HERALD
HERALDIST > HERALDRY
HERALDRY *n* study of coats of arms and family trees
HERALDS > HERALD
HERB *n* plant used for flavouring in cookery, and in medicine
HERBAGE *n* herbaceous plants collectively, esp those on which animals graze
HERBAGED *adj* with grass growing on it
HERBAGES > HERBAGE
HERBAL *adj* of or relating to herbs, usually culinary or medicinal herbs ▷ *n* book describing and listing the properties of plants
HERBALISM *n* use of herbal medicine
HERBALIST *n* person who grows or specializes in the use of medicinal herbs
HERBALS > HERBAL
HERBAR *same as* > HERBARY
HERBARIA > HERBARIUM
HERBARIAL > HERBARIUM
HERBARIAN *same as* > HERBALIST
HERBARIES > HERBARY
HERBARIUM *n* collection of dried plants that are mounted and classified systematically
HERBARS > HERBAR
HERBARY *n* herb garden
HERBED *adj* flavoured with herbs
HERBELET *same as* > HERBLET
HERBELETS > HERBELET
HERBICIDE *n* chemical used to destroy plants, esp weeds
HERBIER > HERBY
HERBIEST > HERBY
HERBIST *same as* > HERBALIST
HERBISTS > HERBIST
HERBIVORA *n* animals that eat grass
HERBIVORE *n* animal that eats only plants
HERBIVORY > HERBIVORE
HERBLESS > HERB
HERBLET *n* little herb
HERBLETS > HERBLET
HERBLIKE > HERB
HERBOLOGY *n* use or study of herbal medicine
HERBORISE *same as* > HERBORIZE
HERBORIST *same as* > HERBALIST
HERBORIZE *vb* collect herbs
HERBOSE *same as* > HERBOUS
HERBOUS *adj* with abundance of herbs
HERBS > HERB
HERBY *adj* abounding in herbs
HERCOGAMY *n* prevention of flower pollination
HERCULEAN *adj* requiring great strength or effort
HERCULES as in *hercules beetle* very large tropical American beetle
HERCYNITE *n* mineral containing iron
HERD *n* group of animals feeding and living together ▷ *vb* collect into a herd
HERDBOY *n* boy who looks after herd
HERDBOYS > HERDBOY
HERDED > HERD
HERDEN *n* type of coarse cloth
HERDENS > HERDEN
HERDER *same as* > HERDSMAN
HERDERS > HERDER
HERDESS *n* female herder
HERDESSES > HERDESS
HERDIC *n* small horse-drawn carriage with a rear entrance and side seats
HERDICS > HERDIC
HERDING > HERD
HERDLIKE > HERD
HERDMAN *same as* > HERDSMAN
HERDMEN > HERDMAN
HERDS > HERD
HERDSMAN *n* man who looks after a herd of animals
HERDSMEN > HERDSMAN
HERDWICK *n* hardy breed of sheep
HERDWICKS > HERDWICK
HERE *adv* in, at, or to this place or point
HEREABOUT *same as* > HEREABOUTS
HEREAFTER *adv* after this point or time ▷ *n* life after death
HEREAT *adv* because of this
HEREAWAY *same as* > HEREABOUT
HEREAWAYS *dialect form of* > HERE
HEREBY *adv* by means of or as a result of this
HEREDES > HERES
HEREDITY *n* passing on of characteristics from one generation to another
HEREFROM *adv* from here
HEREIN *adv* in this place, matter, or document
HEREINTO *adv* into this place, circumstance, etc
HERENESS *n* state of being here
HEREOF *adv* of or concerning this
HEREON *archaic word for* > HEREUPON
HERES *n* heir
HERESIES > HERESY
HERESY *n* opinion contrary to accepted opinion or belief
HERETIC *n* person who holds unorthodox opinions
HERETICAL > HERETIC
HERETICS > HERETIC
HERETO *adv* this place, matter, or document
HERETRIX *n* in Scots law, female inheritor
HEREUNDER *adv* (in documents, etc) below this
HEREUNTO *archaic word for* > HERETO
HEREUPON *adv* following

immediately after this
EREWITH *adv* with this
ERIED > HERY
ERIES > HERY
ERIOT *n* (in medieval England) a death duty paid by villeins and free tenants to their lord, often consisting of the dead man's best beast or chattel
ERIOTS > HERIOT
ERISSE *adj* with bristles
ERISSON *n* spiked beam used as fortification
ERISSONS > HERISSON
ERITABLE *adj* capable of being inherited
ERITABLY > HERITABLE
ERITAGE *n* something inherited
ERITAGES > HERITAGE
ERITOR *n* person who inherits
ERITORS > HERITOR
ERITRESS > HERITOR
ERITRIX > HERITOR
ERKOGAMY *same as* > HERCOGAMY
ERL *n* barb or barbs of a feather, used to dress fishing flies
ERLING *n* Scots word for a type of fish
ERLINGS > HERL
ERLS > HERL
ERM *n* (in ancient Greece) a stone head of Hermes surmounting a square stone pillar
ERMA *same as* > HERM
ERMAE > HERMA
ERMAEAN *adj* type of statue
ERMAI > HERMA
ERMANDAD *n* organization of middle classes in Spain
ERMETIC *adj* sealed so as to be airtight
ERMETICS *n* alchemy
ERMETISM *n* belief in pagan mystical knowledge
ERMETIST > HERMETISM
ERMIT *n* person living in solitude, esp for religious reasons
ERMITAGE *n* home of a hermit
ERMITESS *n* female hermit
ERMITIC > HERMIT
ERMITISM *n* act of living as hermit
ERMITRY *n* life as hermit
ERMITS > HERMIT
ERMS > HERM
ERN *archaic or dialect word for* > HERON
ERNIA *n* protrusion of an organ or part through the lining of the surrounding body cavity
ERNIAE > HERNIA
ERNIAL > HERNIA
ERNIAS > HERNIA
HERNIATE *n* form hernia
HERNIATED > HERNIA
HERNIATES > HERNIATE
HERNS > HERN
HERNSHAW *same as* > HERONSHAW
HERNSHAWS > HERNSHAW
HERO *n* principal character in a film, book, etc
HEROE *variant of* > HERO
HEROES > HERO
HEROIC *adj* courageous
HEROICAL *same as* > HEROIC
HEROICISE *same as* > HEROICIZE
HEROICIZE *same as* > HEROIZE
HEROICLY > HEROIC
HEROICS *pl n* extravagant behaviour
HEROIN *n* highly addictive drug derived from morphine
HEROINE *n* principal female character in a novel, play, etc
HEROINES > HEROINE
HEROINISM *n* addiction to heroin
HEROINS > HEROIN
HEROISE *same as* > HEROIZE
HEROISED > HEROISE
HEROISES > HEROISE
HEROISING > HEROISE
HEROISM *n* great courage and bravery
HEROISMS > HEROISM
HEROIZE *vb* make into hero
HEROIZED > HEROIZE
HEROIZES > HEROIZE
HEROIZING > HEROIZE
HERON *n* long-legged wading bird
HERONRIES > HERONRY
HERONRY *n* colony of breeding herons
HERONS > HERON
HERONSEW *same as* > HERONSHAW
HERONSEWS > HERONSEW
HERONSHAW *n* young heron
HEROON *n* temple or monument dedicated to hero
HEROONS > HEROON
HEROS > HERO
HEROSHIP > HERO
HEROSHIPS > HERO
HERPES *n* any of several inflammatory skin diseases, including shingles and cold sores
HERPESES > HERPES
HERPETIC *adj* of or relating to any of the herpes diseases ▷ *n* person suffering from any of the herpes diseases
HERPETICS > HERPETIC
HERPETOID *adj* like reptile
HERPTILE *adj* denoting, relating to, or characterizing both reptiles and amphibians
HERRIED > HERRY
HERRIES > HERRY
HERRIMENT *n* act of plundering
HERRING *n* important food fish of northern seas
HERRINGER *n* person or boat catching herring
HERRINGS > HERRING
HERRY *vb* harry
HERRYING > HERRY
HERRYMENT *same as* > HERRIMENT
HERS *pron* something belonging to her
HERSALL *n* rehearsal
HERSALLS > HERSALL
HERSE *n* harrow
HERSED *adj* arranged like a harrow
HERSELF *pron* feminine singular reflexive form
HERSES > HERSE
HERSHIP *n* act of plundering
HERSHIPS > HERSHIP
HERSTORY *n* history from a female point of view or as it relates to women
HERTZ *n* unit of frequency
HERTZES > HERTZ
HERY *vb* praise
HERYE *same as* > HERY
HERYED > HERYE
HERYES > HERYE
HERYING > HERY
HES > HE
HESITANCE > HESITANT
HESITANCY > HESITANT
HESITANT *adj* undecided or wavering
HESITATE *vb* be slow or uncertain in doing something
HESITATED > HESITATE
HESITATER > HESITATE
HESITATES > HESITATE
HESITATOR > HESITATE
HESP *same as* > HASP
HESPED > HESP
HESPERID *n* species of butterfly
HESPERIDS > HESPERID
HESPING > HESP
HESPS > HESP
HESSIAN *n* coarse jute fabric
HESSIANS > HESSIAN
HESSITE *n* black or grey metallic mineral consisting of silver telluride in cubic crystalline form
HESSITES > HESSITE
HESSONITE *n* orange-brown variety of grossularite garnet
HEST *archaic word for* > BEHEST
HESTERNAL *adj* belonging to yesterday
HESTS > HEST
HET *n* short for heterosexual ▷ *past tense and past participle of* heat ▷ *adj* Scot word for hot
HETAERA *n* (esp in ancient Greece) a female prostitute, esp an educated courtesan
HETAERAE > HETAERA
HETAERAS > HETAERA
HETAERIC > HETAERA
HETAERISM *n* state of being a concubine
HETAERIST > HETAERISM
HETAIRA *same as* > HETAERA
HETAIRAI > HETAIRA
HETAIRAS > HETAIRA
HETAIRIA *n* society
HETAIRIAS > HETAIRIA
HETAIRIC > HETAERA
HETAIRISM *same as* > HETAERISM
HETAIRIST > HETAERISM
HETE *same as* > HIGHT
HETERO *short for* > HETEROSEXUAL
HETERODOX *adj* differing from accepted doctrines or beliefs
HETERONYM *n* one of two or more words pronounced differently but spelt alike
HETEROPOD *n* marine invertebrate with a foot for swimming
HETEROS > HETERO
HETEROSES > HETEROSIS
HETEROSIS *n* increased size, strength, etc, of a hybrid as compared to either of its parents
HETEROTIC > HETEROSIS
HETES > HETE
HETH *n* eighth letter of the Hebrew alphabet
HETHER *same as* > HITHER
HETHS > HETH
HETING > HETE
HETMAN *another word for* > ATAMAN
HETMANATE > HETMAN
HETMANS > HETMAN
HETS > HET
HEUCH *Scots word for* > CRAG
HEUCHERA *n* N American plant with heart-shaped leaves and mostly red flowers
HEUCHERAS > HEUCHERA
HEUCHS > HEUCH
HEUGH *same as* > HEUCH
HEUGHS > HEUGH
HEUREKA *same as* > EUREKA
HEUREKAS > HEUREKA
HEURETIC *same as* > HEURISTIC
HEURETICS *n* use of logic
HEURISM *n* use of logic
HEURISMS > HEURISM
HEURISTIC *adj* involving learning by investigation ▷ *n* science of heuristic procedure
HEVEA *n* rubber-producing South American tree
HEVEAS > HEVEA

HEW *vb* cut with an axe
HEWABLE > HEW
HEWED > HEW
HEWER > HEW
HEWERS > HEW
HEWGH *interj* sound made to imitate the flight of an arrow
HEWING > HEW
HEWINGS > HEW
HEWN > HEW
HEWS > HEW
HEX *adj* of or relating to hexadecimal notation ▷ *n* evil spell ▷ *vb* bewitch
HEXACHORD *n* (in medieval musical theory) any of three diatonic scales based upon C, F, and G, each consisting of six notes, from which solmization was developed
HEXACT *n* part of a sponge with six rays
HEXACTS > HEXACT
HEXAD *n* group or series of six
HEXADE *same as* > HEXAD
HEXADES > HEXADE
HEXADIC > HEXAD
HEXADS > HEXAD
HEXAFOIL *n* pattern with six lobes
HEXAFOILS > HEXAFOIL
HEXAGLOT *n* book in six languages
HEXAGON *n* geometrical figure with six sides
HEXAGONAL *adj* having six sides and six angles
HEXAGONS > HEXAGON
HEXAGRAM *n* star formed by extending the sides of a regular hexagon to meet at six points
HEXAGRAMS > HEXAGRAM
HEXAHEDRA *n* plural of hexahedron: solid figure with six plane faces
HEXAMERAL *adj* arranged in six groups
HEXAMETER *n* verse line consisting of six metrical feet
HEXAMINE *n* type of fuel produced in small solid blocks or tablets for use in miniature camping stoves
HEXAMINES > HEXAMINE
HEXANE *n* liquid alkane existing in five isomeric forms that are found in petroleum and used as solvents
HEXANES > HEXANE
HEXANOIC as in *hexanoic acid* insoluble oily carboxylic acid found in coconut and palm oils and in milk
HEXAPLA *n* edition of the Old Testament compiled by Origen, containing six versions of the text
HEXAPLAR > HEXAPLA
HEXAPLAS > HEXAPLA
HEXAPLOID *adj* with six times the normal number of chromosomes
HEXAPOD *n* six-footed arthropod
HEXAPODIC > HEXAPODY
HEXAPODS > HEXAPOD
HEXAPODY *n* verse measure consisting of six metrical feet
HEXARCH *adj* (of plant) with six veins
HEXARCHY *n* alliance of six states
HEXASTICH *n* poem, stanza, or strophe that consists of six lines
HEXASTYLE *n* portico or façade with six columns ▷ *adj* having six columns
HEXED > HEX
HEXENE *same as* > HEXYLENE
HEXENES > HEXENE
HEXER > HEX
HEXEREI *n* witchcraft
HEXEREIS > HEXEREI
HEXERS > HEX
HEXES > HEX
HEXING > HEX
HEXINGS > HEX
HEXONE *n* colourless insoluble liquid ketone used as a solvent for organic compounds
HEXONES > HEXONE
HEXOSAN *n* any of a group of polysaccharides that yield hexose on hydrolysis
HEXOSANS > HEXOSAN
HEXOSE *n* monosaccharide, such as glucose, that contains six carbon atoms per molecule
HEXOSES > HEXOSE
HEXYL *adj* of, consisting of, or containing the group of atoms C_6H_{13}, esp the isomeric form of this group, $CH_3(CH_2)_4CH_2$-
HEXYLENE *n* chemical compound similar to ethylene
HEXYLENES > HEXYLENE
HEXYLIC > HEXYL
HEXYLS > HEXYL
HEY *interj* expression of surprise or for catching attention ▷ *vb* perform a country dance
HEYDAY *n* time of greatest success, prime
HEYDAYS > HEYDAY
HEYDEY *variant of* > HEYDAY
HEYDEYS > HEYDEY
HEYDUCK *same as* > HAIDUK
HEYDUCKS > HEYDUCK
HEYED > HEY
HEYING > HEY
HEYS > HEY
HI *interj* hello
HIANT *adj* gaping
HIATAL > HIATUS
HIATUS *n* pause or interruption in continuity
HIATUSES > HIATUS
HIBACHI *n* portable brazier for heating and cooking food
HIBACHIS > HIBACHI
HIBAKUSHA *n* survivor of either of the atomic-bomb attacks on Hiroshima and Nagasaki in 1945
HIBERNAL *adj* of or occurring in winter
HIBERNATE *vb* (of an animal) pass the winter as if in a deep sleep
HIBERNISE > HIBERNIZE
HIBERNIZE *vb* make Irish
HIBISCUS *n* tropical plant with large brightly coloured flowers
HIC *interj* representation of the sound of a hiccup
HICATEE *same as* > HICCATEE
HICATEES > HICATEE
HICCATEE *n* tortoise of West Indies
HICCATEES > HICCATEE
HICCOUGH *same as* > HICCUP
HICCOUGHS > HICCOUGH
HICCUP *n* spasm of the breathing organs with a sharp coughlike sound ▷ *vb* make a hiccup
HICCUPED > HICCUP
HICCUPING > HICCUP
HICCUPPED > HICCUP
HICCUPS > HICCUP
HICCUPY > HICCUP
HICK *n* unsophisticated country person
HICKEY *n* object or gadget: used as a name when the correct name is forgotten, etc
HICKEYS > HICKEY
HICKIE *same as* > HICKEY
HICKIES > HICKIE
HICKISH > HICK
HICKORIES > HICKORY
HICKORY *n* N American nut-bearing tree
HICKS > HICK
HICKWALL *n* green woodpecker
HICKWALLS > HICKWALL
HICKYMAL *n* titmouse
HICKYMALS > HICKYMAL
HID > HIDE
HIDABLE > HIDE
HIDAGE *n* former tax on land
HIDAGES > HIDAGE
HIDALGA *n* Spanish noblewoman
HIDALGAS > HIDALGA
HIDALGO *n* member of the lower nobility in Spain
HIDALGOS > HIDALGO
HIDDEN > HIDE
HIDDENITE *n* green transparent variety of the mineral spodumene, used as a gemstone
HIDDENLY > HIDE
HIDDER *n* young ram
HIDDERS > HIDDER
HIDE *vb* put (oneself or an object) somewhere difficult to see or find ▷ *n* place of concealment, esp for a bird-watcher
HIDEAWAY *n* private place
HIDEAWAYS > HIDEAWAY
HIDEBOUND *adj* unwilling to accept new ideas
HIDED > HIDE
HIDELESS > HIDE
HIDEOSITY > HIDEOUS
HIDEOUS *adj* ugly, revolting
HIDEOUSLY > HIDEOUS
HIDEOUT *n* hiding place, esp a remote place used by outlaws, etc; hideaway
HIDEOUTS > HIDEOUT
HIDER > HIDE
HIDERS > HIDE
HIDES > HIDE
HIDING > HIDE
HIDINGS > HIDE
HIDLING *n* hiding place
HIDLINGS *adv* in secret
HIDLINS *same as* > HIDLINGS
HIDROSES > HIDROSIS
HIDROSIS *n* any skin disease affecting the sweat glands
HIDROTIC > HIDROSIS
HIDROTICS > HIDROSIS
HIE *vb* hurry
HIED > HIE
HIEING > HIE
HIELAMAN *n* Australian Aboriginal shield
HIELAMANS > HIELAMAN
HIELAND *adj* characteristic of Highlanders, esp alluding to their supposed gullibility or foolishness in towns or cities
HIEMAL *less common word for* > HIBERNAL
HIEMS *n* winter
HIERACIUM *n* plant of hawkweed family
HIERARCH *n* person in a position of high-priestly authority
HIERARCHS > HIERARCH
HIERARCHY *n* system of people or things arranged in a graded order
HIERATIC *adj* of or relating to priests ▷ *n* hieratic script of ancient Egypt
HIERATICA *n* type of papyrus
HIEROCRAT *n* person who believes in government by religious leaders
HIERODULE *n* (in ancient Greece) a temple slave, esp a sacral prostitute
HIEROGRAM *n* sacred symbol
HIEROLOGY *n* sacred

literature
IERURGY *n* performance of religious drama or music
IES > HIE
IFALUTIN *adj* pompous or pretentious
IGGLE *less common word for* > HAGGLE
IGGLED > HIGGLE
IGGLER > HIGGLE
IGGLERS > HIGGLE
IGGLES > HIGGLE
IGGLING > HIGGLE
IGGLINGS > HIGGLE
IGH *adj* being a relatively great distance from top to bottom; tall ▷ *adv* at or to a height ▷ *n* a high place or level ▷ *vb* hie
IGHBALL *n* tall drink of whiskey with soda water or ginger ale and ice ▷ *vb* move at great speed
IGHBALLS > HIGHBALL
IGHBORN *adj* of noble or aristocratic birth
IGHBOY *n* tall chest of-drawers in two sections, the lower section being a lowboy
IGHBOYS > HIGHBOY
IGHBRED *adj* of noble breeding
IGHBROW *often disparaging n* intellectual and serious person ▷ *adj* concerned with serious, intellectual subjects
IGHBROWS > HIGHBROW
IGHBUSH *adj* (of bush) growing tall
IGHCHAIR *n* long-legged chair with a tray attached, used by a very young child at mealtimes
IGHED > HIGH
IGHER *n* advanced level of the Scottish Certificate of Education ▷ *vb* raise up
IGHERED > HIGHER
IGHERING > HIGHER
IGHERS > HIGHER
IGHEST > HIGH
IGHFLIER *same as* > HIGHFLYER
IGHFLYER *n* person who is extreme in aims, ambition, etc
IGHING > HIGH
IGHISH > HIGH
IGHJACK *same as* > HIJACK
IGHJACKS > HIGHJACK
IGHLAND *n* relatively high ground
IGHLANDS > HIGHLAND
IGHLIFE *n* style of music combining West African elements with US jazz forms, found esp in the cities of West Africa
IGHLIFES > HIGHLIFE
IGHLIGHT *n* outstanding part or feature ▷ *vb* give emphasis to
HIGHLY *adv* extremely
HIGHMAN *n* dice weighted to make it fall in particular way
HIGHMEN > HIGHMAN
HIGHMOST *adj* highest
HIGHNESS *n* condition of being high or lofty
HIGHRISE *n* tall building
HIGHRISES > HIGHRISE
HIGHROAD *n* main road
HIGHROADS > HIGHROAD
HIGHS > HIGH
HIGHSPOT *n* highlight
HIGHSPOTS > HIGHSPOT
HIGHT *vb* archaic word for name or call
HIGHTAIL *vb* go or move in a great hurry
HIGHTAILS > HIGHTAIL
HIGHTED > HIGHT
HIGHTH *old form of* > HEIGHT
HIGHTHS > HIGHTH
HIGHTING *n* oath
HIGHTOP *n* top of ship's mast
HIGHTOPS > HIGHTOP
HIGHTS > HIGHT
HIGHVELD *n* high-altitude grassland region of E South Africa
HIGHVELDS > HIGHVELD
HIGHWAY *n* main road
HIGHWAYS > HIGHWAY
HIJAB *n* covering for the head and face, worn by Muslim women
HIJABS > HIJAB
HIJACK *vb* seize control of (an aircraft or other vehicle) while travelling ▷ *n* instance of hijacking
HIJACKED > HIJACK
HIJACKER > HIJACK
HIJACKERS > HIJACK
HIJACKING > HIJACK
HIJACKS > HIJACK
HIJINKS *n* lively enjoyment
HIJRA *same as* > HIJRAH
HIJRAH *same as* > HEGIRA
HIJRAHS > HIJRAH
HIJRAS > HIJRA
HIKE *n* long walk in the country, esp for pleasure ▷ *vb* go for a long walk
HIKED > HIKE
HIKER > HIKE
HIKERS > HIKE
HIKES > HIKE
HIKING > HIKE
HIKOI *n* walk or march, esp a Māori protest march ▷ *vb* take part in such a march
HIKOIED > HIKOI
HIKOIING > HIKOI
HIKOIS > HIKOI
HILA > HILUM
HILAR > HILUS
HILARIOUS *adj* very funny
HILARITY *n* mirth and merriment
HILCH *vb* hobble
HILCHED > HILCH
HILCHES > HILCH
HILCHING > HILCH
HILD *same as* > HOLD
HILDING *n* coward
HILDINGS > HILDING
HILI > HILUS
HILL *n* raised part of the earth's surface, less high than a mountain ▷ *vb* form into a hill or mound
HILLBILLY *n* usually disparaging term for an unsophisticated country person
HILLCREST *n* crest of hill
HILLED > HILL
HILLER > HILL
HILLERS > HILL
HILLFOLK *n* people living in the hills
HILLFORT *n* hilltop fortified with ramparts and ditches, dating from the second millennium BC
HILLFORTS > HILLFORT
HILLIER > HILL
HILLIEST > HILL
HILLINESS > HILL
HILLING > HILL
HILLMEN *same as* > HILLFOLK
HILLO *same as* > HELLO
HILLOA *same as* > HALLOA
HILLOAED > HILLOA
HILLOAING > HILLOA
HILLOAS > HILLOA
HILLOCK *n* small hill
HILLOCKED > HILLOCK
HILLOCKS > HILLOCK
HILLOCKY > HILLOCK
HILLOED > HILLO
HILLOES > HILLO
HILLOING > HILLO
HILLOS > HILLO
HILLS > HILL
HILLSIDE *n* side of a hill
HILLSIDES > HILLSIDE
HILLSLOPE *same as* > HILLSIDE
HILLTOP *n* top of hill
HILLTOPS > HILLTOP
HILLY > HILL
HILT *n* handle of a sword or knife ▷ *vb* supply with a hilt
HILTED > HILT
HILTING > HILT
HILTLESS > HILT
HILTS > HILT
HILUM *n* scar on a seed marking its point of attachment to the seed vessel
HILUS *rare word for* > HILUM
HIM *pron* refers to a male person or animal when the object of a sentence or clause ▷ *n* male person
HIMATIA > HIMATION
HIMATION *n* (in ancient Greece) a cloak draped around the body
HIMATIONS > HIMATION
HIMBO *n* slang, usually derogarory term for an attractive but empty-headed man
HIMBOS > HIMBO
HIMS > HIM
HIMSELF *pron* masculine singular reflexive form
HIN *n* Hebrew unit of capacity equal to about 12 pints or 3.5 litres
HINAHINA *same as* > MAHOE
HINAU *n* New Zealand tree
HIND *adj* situated at the back ▷ *n* female deer
HINDBERRY *n* raspberry
HINDBRAIN *nontechnical name for* > RHOMBENCEPHALON: part of the brain comprising the cerbellum, pons and medulla oblongata
HINDER *vb* get in the way of ▷ *adj* situated at the back
HINDERED > HINDER
HINDERER > HINDER
HINDERERS > HINDER
HINDERING > HINDER
HINDERS > HINDER
HINDFEET > HINDFOOT
HINDFOOT *n* back foot
HINDGUT *n* part of the vertebrate digestive tract comprising the colon and rectum
HINDGUTS > HINDGUT
HINDHEAD *n* back of head
HINDHEADS > HINDHEAD
HINDLEG *n* back leg
HINDLEGS > HINDLEG
HINDMOST > HIND
HINDRANCE *n* obstruction or snag
HINDS > HIND
HINDSHANK *n* meat from animal's hind leg
HINDSIGHT *n* ability to understand, after something has happened, what should have been done
HINDWARD *adj* at back
HINDWING *n* back wing
HINDWINGS > HINDWING
HING *n* asafoetida
HINGE *n* device for holding together two parts so that one can swing freely ▷ *vb* depend (on)
HINGED > HINGE
HINGELESS > HINGE
HINGELIKE > HINGE
HINGER *n* tool for making hinges
HINGERS > HINGER
HINGES > HINGE
HINGING > HINGE
HINGS > HING
HINKIER > HINKY
HINKIEST > HINKY
HINKY *adj* strange
HINNIED > HINNY

HINNIES > HINNY
HINNY *n* offspring of a male horse and a female donkey ▷ *vb* whinny
HINNYING > HINNY
HINS > HIN
HINT *n* indirect suggestion ▷ *vb* suggest indirectly
HINTED > HINT
HINTER > HINT
HINTERS > HINT
HINTING > HINT
HINTINGLY > HINT
HINTINGS > HINT
HINTS > HINT
HIOI *n* New Zealand plant of the mint family
HIOIS > HIOI
HIP *n* either side of the body between the pelvis and the thigh ▷ *adj* aware of or following the latest trends ▷ *interj* exclamation used to introduce cheers
HIPBONE *n* either of the two bones that form the sides of the pelvis
HIPBONES > HIPBONE
HIPHUGGER *adj* (of trousers) having a low waist
HIPLESS > HIP
HIPLIKE > HIP
HIPLINE *n* widest part of a person's hips
HIPLINES > HIPLINE
HIPLY > HIP
HIPNESS > HIP
HIPNESSES > HIP
HIPPARCH *n* (in ancient Greece) a cavalry commander
HIPPARCHS > HIPPARCH
HIPPED *adj* having a hip or hips
HIPPEN *n* baby's nappy
HIPPENS > HIPPEN
HIPPER > HIP
HIPPEST > HIP
HIPPIATRY *n* treatment of disease in horses
HIPPIC *adj* of horses
HIPPIE *same as* > HIPPY
HIPPIEDOM > HIPPIE
HIPPIEISH > HIPPIE
HIPPIER > HIPPY
HIPPIES > HIPPY
HIPPIEST > HIPPY
HIPPIN *same as* > HIPPEN
HIPPINESS > HIPPY
HIPPING *same as* > HIPPEN
HIPPINGS > HIPPING
HIPPINS > HIPPIN
HIPPISH *adj* in low spirits
HIPPO *n* hippopotamus
HIPPOCRAS *n* old English drink of wine flavoured with spices
HIPPODAME *n* sea horse
HIPPOLOGY *n* study of horses
HIPPOS > HIPPO
HIPPURIC as in *hippuric acid* crystalline solid excreted in the urine of mammals
HIPPURITE *n* type of fossil
HIPPUS *n* spasm of eye
HIPPUSES > HIPPUS
HIPPY *n* (esp in the 1960s) person whose behaviour and dress imply a rejection of conventional values ▷ *adj* having large hips
HIPPYDOM > HIPPY
HIPPYDOMS > HIPPY
HIPS > HIP
HIPSHOT *adj* having a dislocated hip
HIPSTER *n* enthusiast of modern jazz
HIPSTERS *pl n* trousers cut so that the top encircles the hips
HIPT > HIP
HIRABLE > HIRE
HIRAGANA *n* one of the Japanese systems of syllabic writing based on Chinese cursive ideograms. The more widely used of the two current systems, it is employed in newspapers and general literature
HIRAGANAS > HIRAGANA
HIRAGE *n* fee for hiring
HIRAGES > HIRAGE
HIRCINE *adj* of or like a goat, esp in smell
HIRCOSITY *n* quality of being like a goat
HIRE *vb* pay to have temporary use of ▷ *n* hiring
HIREABLE > HIRE
HIREAGE *same as* > HIRAGE
HIREAGES > HIREAGE
HIRED > HIRE
HIREE *n* hired person
HIREES > HIREE
HIRELING *n* derogatory term for a person who works only for wages
HIRELINGS > HIRELING
HIRER > HIRE
HIRERS > HIRE
HIRES > HIRE
HIRING > HIRE
HIRINGS > HIRE
HIRLING *n* Scots word for a type of fish
HIRLINGS > HIRLING
HIRPLE *vb* limp ▷ *n* limping gait
HIRPLED > HIRPLE
HIRPLES > HIRPLE
HIRPLING > HIRPLE
HIRRIENT *n* trilled sound
HIRRIENTS > HIRRIENT
HIRSEL *vb* sort into groups
HIRSELED > HIRSEL
HIRSELING > HIRSEL
HIRSELLED > HIRSEL
HIRSELS > HIRSEL
HIRSLE *vb* wriggle or fidget
HIRSLED > HIRSLE
HIRSLES > HIRSLE
HIRSLING > HIRSLE
HIRSTIE *adj* dry
HIRSUTE *adj* hairy
HIRSUTISM > HIRSUTE
HIRUDIN *n* anticoagulant extracted from the mouth glands of leeches
HIRUDINS > HIRUDIN
HIRUNDINE *adj* of or resembling a swallow
HIS *adj* belonging to him
HISH *same as* > HISS
HISHED > HISH
HISHES > HISH
HISHING > HISH
HISN *dialect form of* > HIS
HISPANISM *n* Spanish turn of phrase
HISPID *adj* covered with stiff hairs or bristles
HISPIDITY > HISPID
HISS *n* sound like that of a long *s* (as an expression of contempt) ▷ *vb* utter a hiss ▷ *interj* exclamation of derision or disapproval
HISSED > HISS
HISSELF *dialect form of* > HIMSELF
HISSER > HISS
HISSERS > HISS
HISSES > HISS
HISSIER > HISSY
HISSIES > HISSY
HISSIEST > HISSY
HISSING > HISS
HISSINGLY > HISS
HISSINGS > HISS
HISSY *n* temper tantrum ▷ *adj* sound similar to a hiss
HIST *interj* exclamation used to attract attention or as a warning to be silent ▷ *vb* make hist sound
HISTAMIN *variant of* > HISTAMINE
HISTAMINE *n* substance released by the body tissues in allergic reactions
HISTAMINS > HISTAMIN
HISTED > HIST
HISTIDIN *variant of* > HISTIDINE
HISTIDINE *n* nonessential amino acid that occurs in most proteins: a precursor of histamine
HISTIDINS > HISTIDIN
HISTIE *same as* > HIRSTIE
HISTING > HIST
HISTIOID *same as* > HISTOID
HISTOGEN *n* (formerly) any of three layers in an apical meristem that were thought to give rise to the different parts of the plant: the apical meristem is now regarded as comprising two layers
HISTOGENS > HISTOGEN
HISTOGENY > HISTOGEN
HISTOGRAM *n* statistical graph in which the frequency of values is represented by vertical bars of varying heights and widths
HISTOID *adj* (esp of a tumour)
HISTOLOGY *n* study of the tissues of an animal or plant
HISTONE *n* any of a group of basic proteins present in cell nuclei and implicated in the spatial organization of DNA
HISTONES > HISTONE
HISTORIAN *n* writer of history
HISTORIC *adj* famous or significant in history
HISTORIED *adj* recorded in history
HISTORIES > HISTORY
HISTORIFY *vb* make part of history
HISTORISM *n* idea that history influences present
HISTORY *n* (record or account of) past events and developments
HISTRIO *n* actor
HISTRION *same as* > HISTRIO
HISTRIONS > HISTRION
HISTRIOS > HISTRIO
HISTS > HIST
HIT *vb* strike, touch forcefully ▷ *n* hitting
HITCH *n* minor problem ▷ *vb* obtain (a lift) by hitchhiking
HITCHED > HITCH
HITCHER > HITCH
HITCHERS > HITCH
HITCHES > HITCH
HITCHHIKE *vb* travel by obtaining free lifts
HITCHIER > HITCH
HITCHIEST > HITCH
HITCHILY > HITCH
HITCHING > HITCH
HITCHY > HITCH
HITHE *n* small harbour
HITHER *adv* or towards this place ▷ *vb* come
HITHERED > HITHER
HITHERING > HITHER
HITHERS > HITHER
HITHERTO *adv* until this time
HITHES > HITHE
HITLESS > HIT
HITMAN *n* professional killer
HITMEN > HITMAN
HITS > HIT
HITTABLE > HIT
HITTER *n* boxer who has a hard punch rather than skill or finesse
HITTERS > HITTER
HITTING > HIT
HIVE *n* structure in which

social bees live and rear their young ▷ *vb* cause (bees) to collect or (of bees) to collect inside a hive
HIVED > HIVE
HIVELESS > HIVE
HIVELIKE > HIVE
HIVER *n* person who keeps beehives
HIVERS > HIVER
HIVES *n* allergic reaction in which itchy red or whitish patches appear on the skin
HIVEWARD *adj* towards hive
HIVEWARDS *adv* towards hive
HIVING > HIVE
HIYA *sentence substitute* informal term of greeting
HIZEN *n* type of Japanese porcelain
HIZENS > HIZEN
HIZZ *same as* > HISS
HIZZED > HIZZ
HIZZES > HIZZ
HIZZING > HIZZ
HIZZONER *n* nickname for mayor
HIZZONERS > HIZZONER
HM *interj* sound made to express hesitation or doubt
HMM *same as* > HM
HO *n* derogatory term for a woman ▷ *interj* imitation or representation of the sound of a deep laugh ▷ *vb* halt
HOA *same as* > HO
HOACTZIN *same as* > HOATZIN
HOACTZINS > HOACTZIN
HOAED > HOA
HOAGIE *n* sandwich made with long bread roll
HOAGIES > HOAGIE
HOAGY *same as* > HOAGIE
HOAING > HOA
HOAR *adj* covered with hoarfrost ▷ *vb* make hoary
HOARD *n* store hidden away for future use ▷ *vb* save or store
HOARDED > HOARD
HOARDER > HOARD
HOARDERS > HOARD
HOARDING *n* large board for displaying advertisements
HOARDINGS > HOARDING
HOARDS > HOARD
HOARED > HOAR
HOARFROST *n* white ground frost
HOARHEAD *n* person with white hair
HOARHEADS > HOARHEAD
HOARHOUND *same as* > HOREHOUND
HOARIER > HOARY
HOARIEST > HOARY
HOARILY > HOARY
HOARINESS > HOARY
HOARING > HOAR
HOARS > HOAR
HOARSE *adj* (of a voice) rough and unclear
HOARSELY > HOARSE
HOARSEN *vb* make or become hoarse
HOARSENED > HOARSEN
HOARSENS > HOARSEN
HOARSER > HOARSE
HOARSEST > HOARSE
HOARY *adj* grey or white(-haired)
HOAS > HOA
HOAST *n* cough ▷ *vb* cough
HOASTED > HOAST
HOASTING > HOAST
HOASTMAN *n* shipper of coal
HOASTMEN > HOASTMAN
HOASTS > HOAST
HOATCHING *adj* infested
HOATZIN *n* South American bird with a brownish plumage and very small crested head
HOATZINES > HOATZIN
HOATZINS > HOATZIN
HOAX *n* deception or trick ▷ *vb* deceive or play a trick upon
HOAXED > HOAX
HOAXER > HOAX
HOAXERS > HOAX
HOAXES > HOAX
HOAXING > HOAX
HOB *n* flat top part of a cooker, or a separate flat surface, containing gas or electric rings for cooking on ▷ *vb* cut or form with a hob
HOBBED > HOB
HOBBER *n* machine used in making gears
HOBBERS > HOBBER
HOBBIES > HOBBY
HOBBING > HOB
HOBBISH *adj* like a clown
HOBBIT *n* one of an imaginary race of half-size people living in holes
HOBBITRY > HOBBIT
HOBBITS > HOBBIT
HOBBLE *vb* walk lamely ▷ *n* strap, rope, etc, used to hobble a horse
HOBBLED > HOBBLE
HOBBLER > HOBBLE
HOBBLERS > HOBBLE
HOBBLES > HOBBLE
HOBBLING > HOBBLE
HOBBLINGS > HOBBLE
HOBBY *n* activity pursued in one's spare time
HOBBYISM > HOBBY
HOBBYISMS > HOBBY
HOBBYIST > HOBBY
HOBBYISTS > HOBBY
HOBBYLESS > HOBBY
HOBDAY *vb* alleviate (a breathing problem in certain horses) by the surgical operation of removing soft tissue ventricles to pull back the vocal fold
HOBDAYED > HOBDAY
HOBDAYING > HOBDAY
HOBDAYS > HOBDAY
HOBGOBLIN *n* mischievous goblin
HOBJOB *vb* do odd jobs
HOBJOBBED > HOBJOB
HOBJOBBER > HOBJOB
HOBJOBS > HOBJOB
HOBLIKE > HOB
HOBNAIL *n* short nail with a large head for protecting the soles of heavy footwear ▷ *vb* provide with hobnails
HOBNAILED > HOBNAIL
HOBNAILS > HOBNAIL
HOBNOB *vb* be on friendly terms (with)
HOBNOBBED > HOBNOB
HOBNOBBER > HOBNOB
HOBNOBBY > HOBNOB
HOBNOBS > HOBNOB
HOBO *n* tramp or vagrant ▷ *vb* live as hobo
HOBODOM > HOBO
HOBODOMS > HOBO
HOBOED > HOBO
HOBOES > HOBO
HOBOING > HOBO
HOBOISM > HOBO
HOBOISMS > HOBO
HOBOS > HOBO
HOBS > HOB
HOC *adj* Latin for this
HOCK *n* joint in the back leg of an animal such as a horse that corresponds to the human ankle ▷ *vb* pawn
HOCKED > HOCK
HOCKER > HOCK
HOCKERS > HOCK
HOCKEY *n* team game played on a field with a ball and curved sticks
HOCKEYS > HOCKEY
HOCKING > HOCK
HOCKLE *vb* spit
HOCKLED > HOCKLE
HOCKLES > HOCKLE
HOCKLING > HOCKLE
HOCKS > HOCK
HOCKSHOP *n* pawnshop
HOCKSHOPS > HOCKSHOP
HOCUS *vb* take in
HOCUSED > HOCUS
HOCUSES > HOCUS
HOCUSING > HOCUS
HOCUSSED > HOCUS
HOCUSSES > HOCUS
HOCUSSING > HOCUS
HOD *n* open wooden box attached to a pole, for carrying bricks or mortar ▷ *vb* bob up and down
HODAD *n* person who pretends to be a surfer
HODADDIES > HODADDY
HODADDY *same as* > HODAD
HODADS > HODAD
HODDED > HOD
HODDEN *n* coarse homespun cloth produced in Scotland: hodden grey is made by mixing black and white wools
HODDENS > HODDEN
HODDIN *same as* > HODDEN
HODDING > HOD
HODDINS > HODDIN
HODDLE *vb* waddle
HODDLED > HODDLE
HODDLES > HODDLE
HODDLING > HODDLE
HODIERNAL *adj* of the present day
HODJA *n* respectful Turkish form of address
HODJAS > HODJA
HODMAN *n* hod carrier
HODMANDOD *n* snail
HODMEN > HODMAN
HODOGRAPH *n* curve of which the radius vector represents the velocity of a moving particle
HODOMETER *another name for* > ODOMETER
HODOMETRY > HODOMETER
HODOSCOPE *n* any device for tracing the path of a charged particle, esp a particle found in cosmic rays
HODS > HOD
HOE *n* long-handled tool used for loosening soil or weeding ▷ *vb* scrape or weed with a hoe
HOECAKE *n* maize cake
HOECAKES > HOECAKE
HOED > HOE
HOEDOWN *n* boisterous square dance
HOEDOWNS > HOEDOWN
HOEING > HOE
HOELIKE > HOE
HOER > HOE
HOERS > HOE
HOES > HOE
HOG *n* castrated male pig ▷ *vb* take more than one's share of
HOGAN *n* wooden dwelling covered with earth, typical of the Navaho Indians of N America
HOGANS > HOGAN
HOGBACK *n* narrow ridge that consists of steeply inclined rock strata
HOGBACKS > HOGBACK
HOGEN *n* strong alcoholic drink
HOGENS > HOGEN
HOGFISH *n* type of fish
HOGFISHES > HOGFISH
HOGG *same as* > HOG
HOGGED > HOG
HOGGER > HOG
HOGGEREL *n* year-old sheep
HOGGERELS > HOGGEREL
HOGGERIES > HOGGERY
HOGGERS > HOG
HOGGERY *n* hogs collectively

HOGGET *n* sheep up to the age of one year that has yet to be sheared
HOGGETS > HOGGET
HOGGIN *n* finely sifted gravel containing enough clay binder for it to be used in its natural form for making paths or roads
HOGGING *same as* > HOGGIN
HOGGINGS > HOGGING
HOGGINS > HOGGIN
HOGGISH *adj* selfish, gluttonous, or dirty
HOGGISHLY > HOGGISH
HOGGS > HOGG
HOGH *n* ridge of land
HOGHOOD *n* condition of being hog
HOGHOODS > HOGHOOD
HOGHS > HOGH
HOGLIKE > HOG
HOGMANAY *n* New Year's Eve
HOGMANAYS > HOGMANAY
HOGMANE *n* short stiff mane
HOGMANES > HOGMANE
HOGMENAY *variant of* > HOGMANAY
HOGMENAYS > HOGMENAY
HOGNOSE as in *hognose snake* puff adder
HOGNOSED as in *hognosed skunk* any of several American skunks having a broad snoutlike nose
HOGNOSES > HOGNOSE
HOGNUT *another name for* > PIGNUT
HOGNUTS > HOGNUT
HOGS > HOG
HOGSHEAD *n* large cask
HOGSHEADS > HOGSHEAD
HOGTIE *vb* tie together the legs or the arms and legs of
HOGTIED > HOGTIE
HOGTIEING > HOGTIE
HOGTIES > HOGTIE
HOGTYING > HOGTIE
HOGWARD *n* person looking after hogs
HOGWARDS > HOGWARD
HOGWASH *n* nonsense
HOGWASHES > HOGWASH
HOGWEED *n* any of several coarse weedy umbelliferous plants, esp cow parsnip
HOGWEEDS > HOGWEED
HOH *same as* > HO
HOHA *n* nuisance
HOHED > HOH
HOHING > HOH
HOHS > HOH
HOI *same as* > HOY
HOICK *vb* raise abruptly and sharply
HOICKED > HOICK
HOICKING > HOICK
HOICKS *interj* cry used to encourage hounds to hunt ▷ *vb* shout hoicks
HOICKSED > HOICKS
HOICKSES > HOICKS
HOICKSING > HOICKS
HOIDEN *same as* > HOYDEN
HOIDENED > HOIDEN
HOIDENING > HOIDEN
HOIDENISH > HOIDEN
HOIDENS > HOIDEN
HOIK *same as* > HOICK
HOIKED > HOIK
HOIKING > HOIK
HOIKS > HOIK
HOING > HO
HOISE *same as* > HOIST
HOISED > HOISE
HOISES > HOISE
HOISIN *n* Chinese sweet spicy reddish-brown sauce made from soya beans, sugar, vinegar, and garlic
HOISING > HOISE
HOISINS > HOISIN
HOIST *vb* raise or lift up ▷ *n* device for lifting things
HOISTED > HOIST
HOISTER > HOIST
HOISTERS > HOIST
HOISTING > HOIST
HOISTINGS > HOIST
HOISTMAN *n* person operating a hoist
HOISTMEN > HOISTMAN
HOISTS > HOIST
HOISTWAY *n* shaft for a hoist
HOISTWAYS > HOISTWAY
HOKA *n* red cod
HOKE *vb* overplay (a part, etc)
HOKED > HOKE
HOKES > HOKE
HOKEY *adj* corny
HOKEYNESS > HOKEY
HOKI *n* fish of New Zealand waters
HOKIER > HOKEY
HOKIEST > HOKEY
HOKILY > HOKEY
HOKINESS > HOKEY
HOKING > HOKE
HOKIS > HOKI
HOKKU *same as* > HAIKU
HOKONUI *n* illicit whisky
HOKONUIS > HOKONUI
HOKUM *n* rubbish, nonsense
HOKUMS > HOKUM
HOKYPOKY *n* trickery
HOLANDRIC *adj* relating to Y-chromosomal genes
HOLARCHY *n* system composed of interacting holons
HOLARD *n* amount of water contained in soil
HOLARDS > HOLARD
HOLD *vb* keep or support in or with the hands or arms ▷ *n* act or way of holding
HOLDABLE > HOLD
HOLDALL *n* large strong travelling bag
HOLDALLS > HOLDALL
HOLDBACK *n* strap of the harness joining the breeching to the shaft, so that the horse can hold back the vehicle
HOLDBACKS > HOLDBACK
HOLDDOWN *n* control function in a computer
HOLDDOWNS > HOLDDOWN
HOLDEN *past participle of* > HOLD
HOLDER *n* person or thing that holds
HOLDERBAT *n* part of pipe used as fastening
HOLDERS > HOLDER
HOLDFAST *n* act of gripping strongly
HOLDFASTS > HOLDFAST
HOLDING > HOLD
HOLDINGS > HOLD
HOLDOUT *n* (in US English) person, country, organization, etc, that continues to resist or refuses to change
HOLDOUTS > HOLDOUT
HOLDOVER *n* (in US and Canadian English) elected official who continues in office after his term has expired
HOLDOVERS > HOLDOVER
HOLDS > HOLD
HOLDUP *n* robbery, esp an armed one
HOLDUPS > HOLDUP
HOLE *n* area hollowed out in a solid ▷ *vb* make holes in
HOLED > HOLE
HOLELESS > HOLE
HOLES > HOLE
HOLESOM *same as* > HOLESOME
HOLESOME *same as* > WHOLESOME
HOLEY *adj* full of holes
HOLEYER > HOLEY
HOLEYEST > HOLEY
HOLIBUT *same as* > HALIBUT
HOLIBUTS > HOLIBUT
HOLIDAY *n* time spent away from home for rest or recreation ▷ *vb* spend a holiday
HOLIDAYED > HOLIDAY
HOLIDAYER > HOLIDAY
HOLIDAYS > HOLIDAY
HOLIER > HOLY
HOLIES > HOLY
HOLIEST > HOLY
HOLILY *adv* in a holy, devout, or sacred manner
HOLINESS *n* state of being holy
HOLING > HOLE
HOLINGS > HOLE
HOLISM *n* view that a whole is greater than the sum of its parts
HOLISMS > HOLISM
HOLIST > HOLISM
HOLISTIC *adj* considering the complete person, physically and mentally, in the treatment of an illness
HOLISTS > HOLISM
HOLK *vb* dig
HOLKED > HOLK
HOLKING > HOLK
HOLKS > HOLK
HOLLA *same as* > HOLLO
HOLLAED > HOLLA
HOLLAING > HOLLA
HOLLAND *n* coarse linen cloth, used esp for furnishing
HOLLANDS > HOLLAND
HOLLAS > HOLLA
HOLLER *n* shout, yell ▷ *vb* shout or yell
HOLLERED > HOLLER
HOLLERING > HOLLER
HOLLERS > HOLLER
HOLLIDAM *same as* > HALIDOM
HOLLIDAMS > HOLLIDAM
HOLLIES > HOLLY
HOLLO *interj* cry for attention, or of encouragement ▷ *vb* shout
HOLLOA *same as* > HOLLO
HOLLOAED > HOLLOA
HOLLOAING > HOLLOA
HOLLOAS > HOLLOA
HOLLOED > HOLLO
HOLLOES > HOLLO
HOLLOING > HOLLO
HOLLOO *same as* > HALLOO
HOLLOOED > HOLLOO
HOLLOOING > HOLLOO
HOLLOOS > HOLLOO
HOLLOS > HOLLO
HOLLOW *adj* having a hole or space inside ▷ *n* cavity or space ▷ *vb* form a hollow in
HOLLOWARE *n* hollow utensils such as cups
HOLLOWED > HOLLOW
HOLLOWER > HOLLOW
HOLLOWEST > HOLLOW
HOLLOWING > HOLLOW
HOLLOWLY > HOLLOW
HOLLOWS > HOLLOW
HOLLY *n* evergreen tree with prickly leaves and red berries
HOLLYHOCK *n* tall garden plant with spikes of colourful flowers
HOLM *n* island in a river, lake, or estuary
HOLMIA *n* oxide of holmium
HOLMIAS > HOLMIA
HOLMIC *adj* of or containing holmium
HOLMIUM *n* silver-white metallic element, the compounds of which are highly magnetic
HOLMIUMS > HOLMIUM
HOLMS > HOLM
HOLOCAUST *n* destruction or loss of life on a massive scale
HOLOCENE *adj* of, denoting or formed in the second and most recent epoch of the Quaternary period, which began 10 000

years ago at the end of the Pleistocene

HOLOCRINE *adj* (of the secretion of glands) characterized by disintegration of the entire glandular cell in releasing its product, as in sebaceous glands

HOLOGAMY *n* condition of having gametes like ordinary cells

HOLOGRAM *n* three-dimensional photographic image

HOLOGRAMS > HOLOGRAM

HOLOGRAPH *n* document handwritten by the author

HOLOGYNIC *adj* passed down through females

HOLOGYNY *n* inheritance of genetic traits through females only

HOLOHEDRA *n* geometrical forms with particular symmetry

HOLON *n* autonomous self-reliant unit, esp in manufacturing

HOLONIC > HOLON

HOLONS > HOLON

HOLOPHOTE *n* device for directing light from lighthouse

HOLOPHYTE *n* plant capable of synthesizing food from inorganic molecules

HOLOPTIC *adj* with eyes meeting at the front

HOLOTYPE *n* original specimen from which a description of a new species is made

HOLOTYPES > HOLOTYPE

HOLOTYPIC > HOLOTYPE

HOLOZOIC *adj* (of animals) obtaining nourishment by feeding on plants or other animals

HOLP *past tense of* > HELP

HOLPEN *past participle of* > HELP

HOLS *pl n* holidays

HOLSTEIN *n* breed of cattle

HOLSTEINS > HOLSTEIN

HOLSTER *n* leather case for a pistol, hung from a belt ▷ *vb* return (a pistol) to its holster

HOLSTERED > HOLSTER

HOLSTERS > HOLSTER

HOLT *n* otter's lair

HOLTS > HOLT

HOLY *adj* of God or a god

HOLYDAM *same as* > HALIDOM

HOLYDAME *same as* > HALIDOM

HOLYDAMES > HOLYDAME

HOLYDAMS > HOLYDAM

HOLYDAY *n* day on which a religious festival is observed

HOLYDAYS > HOLYDAY

HOLYSTONE *n* soft sandstone used for scrubbing the decks of a vessel ▷ *vb* scrub (a vessel's decks) with a holystone

HOLYTIDE *n* time for special religious observance

HOLYTIDES > HOLYTIDE

HOM *n* sacred plant of the Parsees and ancient Persians

HOMA *same as* > HOM

HOMAGE *n* show of respect or honour towards someone or something ▷ *vb* render homage to

HOMAGED > HOMAGE

HOMAGER > HOMAGE

HOMAGERS > HOMAGE

HOMAGES > HOMAGE

HOMAGING > HOMAGE

HOMALOID *n* geometrical plane

HOMALOIDS > HOMALOID

HOMAS > HOMA

HOMBRE *slang word for* > MAN

HOMBRES > HOMBRE

HOMBURG *n* man's soft felt hat with a dented crown and a stiff upturned brim

HOMBURGS > HOMBURG

HOME *n* place where one lives ▷ *adj* of one's home, birthplace, or native country ▷ *adv* to or at home ▷ *vb* direct towards (a point or target)

HOMEBIRTH *n* act of giving birth to a child in one's own home

HOMEBODY *n* person whose life and interests are centred on the home

HOMEBOUND *adj* heading for home

HOMEBOY *n* close friend

HOMEBOYS > HOMEBOY

HOMEBRED *adj* raised or bred at home ▷ *n* animal bred at home

HOMEBREDS > HOMEBRED

HOMEBREW *n* home-made beer

HOMEBREWS > HOMEBREW

HOMEBUILT *adj* built at home

HOMEBUYER *n* person buying a home

HOMECOMER *n* person coming home

HOMECRAFT *n* skills used in the home

HOMED > HOME

HOMEFELT *adj* felt personally

HOMEGIRL > HOMEBOY

HOMEGIRLS > HOMEBOY

HOMEGROWN *adj* (esp of fruit and vegetables) produced in one's own country, district, estate, or garden

HOMELAND *n* country from which a person's ancestors came

HOMELANDS > HOMELAND

HOMELESS *adj* having nowhere to live ▷ *pl n* people who have nowhere to live

HOMELIER > HOMELY

HOMELIEST > HOMELY

HOMELIKE > HOME

HOMELILY > HOMELY

HOMELY *adj* simple, ordinary, and comfortable

HOMELYN *n* species of ray

HOMELYNS > HOMELYN

HOMEMADE *adj* (esp of cakes, jam, and other foods) made at home or on the premises, esp of high-quality ingredients

HOMEMAKER *n* person, esp a housewife, who manages a home

HOMEOBOX *adj* of genes that regulate cell development

HOMEOMERY *n* condition of being made up of similar parts

HOMEOPATH *n* person who treats disease by the use of small amounts of a drug that produces symptoms like those of the disease being treated

HOMEOSES > HOMEOSIS

HOMEOSIS *n* process of one part coming to resemble another

HOMEOTIC > HOMEOSIS

HOMEOWNER *n* person who owns the home in which he or she lives

HOMEPAGE *n* main page of website

HOMEPAGES > HOMEPAGE

HOMEPLACE *n* person's home

HOMEPORT *n* port where vessel is registered

HOMEPORTS > HOMEPORT

HOMER *n* homing pigeon ▷ *vb* score a home run in baseball

HOMERED > HOMER

HOMERIC *adj* grand or heroic

HOMERING > HOMER

HOMEROOM *n* common room at school

HOMEROOMS > HOMEROOM

HOMERS > HOMER

HOMES > HOME

HOMESICK *adj* sad because missing one's home and family

HOMESITE *n* site for building house

HOMESITES > HOMESITE

HOMESPUN *adj* (of philosophies or opinions) plain and unsophisticated ▷ *n* cloth made at home or made of yarn spun at home

HOMESPUNS > HOMESPUN

HOMESTALL *same as* > HOMESTEAD

HOMESTAND *n* series of games played at a team's home ground

HOMESTAY *n* period spent living as a guest in someone's home

HOMESTAYS > HOMESTAY

HOMESTEAD *n* farmhouse plus the adjoining land

HOMETOWN *n* town where one lives or was born

HOMETOWNS > HOMETOWN

HOMEWARD *adj* going home ▷ *adv* towards home

HOMEWARDS *adv* towards home

HOMEWARE *n* crockery, furniture, and furnishings with which a house, room, etc, is furnished

HOMEWARES > HOMEWARE

HOMEWORK *n* school work done at home

HOMEWORKS > HOMEWORK

HOMEY *same as* > HOMY

HOMEYNESS > HOMEY

HOMEYS > HOMEY

HOMICIDAL *adj* of, involving, or characterized by homicide

HOMICIDE *n* killing of a human being

HOMICIDES > HOMICIDE

HOMIE *short for* > HOMEBOY

HOMIER > HOMY

HOMIES > HOMIE

HOMIEST > HOMY

HOMILETIC *adj* of or relating to a homily or sermon

HOMILIES > HOMILY

HOMILIST > HOMILY

HOMILISTS > HOMILY

HOMILY *n* speech telling people how they should behave

HOMINES > HOMO

HOMINESS > HOMY

HOMING *adj* denoting the ability to return home after travelling great distances ▷ *n* relating to the ability to return home after travelling great distances

HOMINGS > HOMING

HOMINIAN *same as* > HOMINID

HOMINIANS > HOMINIAN

HOMINID *n* man or any extinct forerunner of man ▷ *adj* of or belonging to this family

HOMINIDS > HOMINID

HOMINIES > HOMINY

HOMININE *adj* characteristic of humans

HOMINISE *same as* > HOMINIZE

HOMINISED > HOMINISE

HOMINISES > HOMINISE

HOMINIZE *vb* make

suitable for humans
HOMINIZED > HOMINIZE
HOMINIZES > HOMINIZE
HOMINOID *n* manlike animal ▷ *adj* of or like man
HOMINOIDS > HOMINOID
HOMINY *n* coarsely ground maize prepared as a food by boiling in milk or water
HOMME *French word for* > MAN
HOMMES > HOMME
HOMMOCK *same as* > HUMMOCK
HOMMOCKS > HOMMOCK
HOMMOS *same as* > HUMMUS
HOMMOSES > HOMMOS
HOMO *n* homogenized milk
HOMOCERCY *n* condition in fish of having a symmetrical tail
HOMODONT *adj* (of most nonmammalian vertebrates) having teeth that are all of the same type
HOMODYNE *adj* of strengthened radio waves
HOMOEOBOX *same as* > HOMEOBOX
HOMOEOSES > HOMOEOSIS
HOMOEOSIS *n* condition of controlling a system from within
HOMOEOTIC > HOMOEOSIS
HOMOGAMIC > HOMOGAMY
HOMOGAMY *n* condition in which all the flowers of an inflorescence are either of the same sex or hermaphrodite
HOMOGENY *n* similarity in structure of individuals or parts because of common ancestry
HOMOGONY *n* condition in a plant of having stamens and styles of the same length in all the flowers
HOMOGRAFT *n* tissue graft obtained from an organism of the same species as the recipient
HOMOGRAPH *n* word spelt the same as another, but with a different meaning
HOMOLOG *same as* > HOMOLOGUE
HOMOLOGIC *adj* having a related or similar position, structure, etc
HOMOLOGS > HOMOLOG
HOMOLOGUE *n* homologous part or organ
HOMOLOGY *n* condition of being homologous
HOMOLYSES > HOMOLYSIS
HOMOLYSIS *n* dissociation of a molecule into two neutral fragments
HOMOLYTIC > HOMOLYSIS
HOMOMORPH *n* thing same in form as something else
HOMONYM *n* word spelt or pronounced the same as another, but with a different meaning
HOMONYMIC > HOMONYM
HOMONYMS > HOMONYM
HOMONYMY > HOMONYMITY
HOMOPHILE *n* rare word for homosexual: person who is sexually attracted to members of the same sex
HOMOPHOBE *n* person who has an intense hatred of homosexuality
HOMOPHONE *n* word pronounced the same as another, but with a different meaning or spelling
HOMOPHONY *n* linguistic phenomenon whereby words of different origins become identical in pronunciation
HOMOPHYLY *n* resemblance due to common ancestry
HOMOPLASY *n* state of being derived from an individual of the same species as the recipient
HOMOPOLAR *adj* of uniform charge
HOMOS > HOMO
HOMOSEX *n* sexual activity between homosexuals
HOMOSEXES > HOMOSEX
HOMOSPORY *n* state of producing spores of one kind only
HOMOSTYLY *n* (in flowers) existence of styles of only one length
HOMOTAXES > HOMOTAXIS
HOMOTAXIC > HOMOTAXIS
HOMOTAXIS *n* similarity of composition and arrangement in rock strata of different ages or in different regions
HOMOTONIC *adj* of same tone
HOMOTONY > HOMOTONIC
HOMOTYPAL *adj* of normal type
HOMOTYPE *n* something with same structure as something else
HOMOTYPES > HOMOTYPE
HOMOTYPIC *same as* > HOMOTYPAL
HOMOTYPY > HOMOTYPE
HOMOUSIAN *adj* believing God the Son and God the Father to be of the same essence
HOMS > HOM
HOMUNCLE *n* homunculus
HOMUNCLES > HOMUNCLE
HOMUNCULE *n* homunculus
HOMUNCULI *n* plural of homunculus: miniature man
HOMY *adj* like a home
HON *short for* > HONEY
HONAN *n* silk fabric of rough weave
HONANS > HONAN
HONCHO *n* person in charge ▷ *vb* supervise or be in charge of
HONCHOED > HONCHO
HONCHOING > HONCHO
HONCHOS > HONCHO
HOND *old form of* > HAND
HONDA *n* loop through which rope is threaded to make a lasso
HONDAS > HONDA
HONDLE *vb* negotiate on price
HONDLED > HONDLE
HONDLES > HONDLE
HONDLING > HONDLE
HONDS > HOND
HONE *vb* sharpen ▷ *n* fine whetstone used for sharpening edged tools and knives
HONED > HONE
HONER > HONE
HONERS > HONE
HONES > HONE
HONEST *adj* truthful and moral
HONESTER > HONEST
HONESTEST > HONEST
HONESTIES > HONESTY
HONESTLY *adv* in an honest manner ▷ *interj* expression of disgust, surprise, etc
HONESTY *n* quality of being honest
HONEWORT *n* European plant that has clusters of small white flowers
HONEWORTS > HONEWORT
HONEY *n* sweet edible sticky substance made by bees from nectar; term of endearment ▷ *vb* sweeten with or as if with honey
HONEYBEE *n* bee widely domesticated as a source of honey and beeswax
HONEYBEES > HONEYBEE
HONEYBUN *n* term of endearment
HONEYBUNS > HONEYBUN
HONEYCOMB *n* waxy structure of six-sided cells in which honey is stored by bees in a beehive ▷ *vb* pierce or fill with holes, cavities, etc
HONEYDEW *n* sugary substance excreted by aphids and similar insects
HONEYDEWS > HONEYDEW
HONEYED > HONEY
HONEYEDLY > HONEY
HONEYFUL *adj* full of honey
HONEYING > HONEY
HONEYLESS > HONEY
HONEYMOON *n* holiday taken by a newly married couple ▷ *vb* take a honeymoon
HONEYPOT *n* container for honey
HONEYPOTS > HONEYPOT
HONEYS > HONEY
HONEYTRAP *n* scheme in which a victim is lured into a compromising sexual situation that provides the opportunity for blackmail
HONG *n* (in China) a factory, warehouse, etc ▷ *vb* archaic form of hang
HONGI *n* Māori greeting in which people touch noses ▷ *vb* touch noses
HONGIED > HONGI
HONGIES > HONGI
HONGIING > HONGI
HONGING > HONG
HONGIS > HONGI
HONGS > HONG
HONIED > HONEY
HONIEDLY > HONEY
HONING > HONE
HONK *n* sound made by a car horn ▷ *vb* (cause to) make this sound
HONKED > HONK
HONKER *n* person or thing that honks
HONKERS > HONKER
HONKEY *same as* > HONKY
HONKEYS > HONKEY
HONKIE *same as* > HONKY
HONKIES > HONKY
HONKING > HONK
HONKS > HONK
HONKY *n* derogatory slang for White man or White men collectively
HONOR *same as* > HONOUR
HONORABLE *adj* possessing high principles
HONORABLY > HONOURABLE
HONORAND *n* person being honoured
HONORANDS > HONORAND
HONORARIA *n* fee pain for a nominally free service
HONORARY *adj* held or given only as an honour
HONORED > HONOR
HONOREE *same as* > HONORAND
HONOREES > HONOREE
HONORER > HONOUR
HONORERS > HONOUR
HONORIFIC *adj* showing respect
HONORING > HONOR
HONORLESS > HONOUR
HONORS *same as* > HONOURS
HONOUR *n* sense of honesty and fairness ▷ *vb* give praise and attention to
HONOURED > HONOUR
HONOURER > HONOUR
HONOURERS > HONOUR
HONOURING > HONOUR
HONOURS > HONOUR
HONS > HON
HOO *pron* she
HOOCH *n* alcoholic drink, esp illicitly distilled spirits
HOOCHES > HOOCH
HOOCHIE *n* immoral

woman
HOOCHIES > HOOCHIE
HOOD *n* head covering, often attached to a coat or jacket ▷ *vb* cover with or as if with a hood
HOODED *adj* (of a garment) having a hood
HOODIA *n* any of several southern African succulent plants whose sap has appetite-suppressing properties
HOODIAS > HOODIA
HOODIE *n* hooded sweatshirt
HOODIER > HOOD
HOODIES > HOODIE
HOODIEST > HOOD
HOODING > HOOD
HOODLESS > HOOD
HOODLIKE > HOOD
HOODLUM *n* violent criminal, gangster
HOODLUMS > HOODLUM
HOODMAN *n* blindfolded person in blindman's buff
HOODMEN > HOODMAN
HOODMOLD *n* moulding over door or window
HOODMOLDS > HOODMOLD
HOODOO *n* (cause of) bad luck ▷ *vb* bring bad luck to
HOODOOED > HOODOO
HOODOOING > HOODOO
HOODOOISM > HOODOO
HOODOOS > HOODOO
HOODS > HOOD
HOODWINK *vb* trick, deceive
HOODWINKS > HOODWINK
HOODY > HOOD
HOOEY *n* nonsense ▷ *interj* nonsense
HOOEYS > HOOEY
HOOF *n* horny covering of the foot of a horse, deer, etc ▷ *vb* kick or trample with the hooves
HOOFBEAT *n* sound made by hoof on the ground
HOOFBEATS > HOOFBEAT
HOOFBOUND *adj* (of a horse) having dry contracted hooves, with resultant pain and lameness
HOOFED *adj* having a hoof or hoofs
HOOFER *n* professional dancer
HOOFERS > HOOFER
HOOFING > HOOF
HOOFLESS > HOOF
HOOFLIKE > HOOF
HOOFPRINT *n* mark made by hoof on ground
HOOFROT *n* disease of hoof
HOOFROTS > HOOFROT
HOOFS > HOOF
HOOK *n* curved piece of metal, plastic, etc, used to hang, hold, or pull something ▷ *vb* fasten or catch (as if) with a hook
HOOKA *same as* > HOOKAH
HOOKAH *n* oriental pipe in which smoke is drawn through water and a long tube
HOOKAHS > HOOKAH
HOOKAS > HOOKA
HOOKCHECK *n* in ice hockey, act of hooking an opposing player
HOOKED *adj* bent like a hook
HOOKER *n* prostitute
HOOKERS > HOOKER
HOOKEY *same as* > HOOKY
HOOKEYS > HOOKEY
HOOKIER > HOOKY
HOOKIES > HOOKY
HOOKIEST > HOOKY
HOOKING > HOOK
HOOKLESS > HOOK
HOOKLET *n* little hook
HOOKLETS > HOOKLET
HOOKLIKE > HOOK
HOOKNOSE *n* nose with a pronounced outward and downward curve
HOOKNOSED > HOOKNOSE
HOOKNOSES > HOOKNOSE
HOOKS > HOOK
HOOKUP *n* contact of an aircraft in flight with the refuelling hose of a tanker aircraft
HOOKUPS > HOOKUP
HOOKWORM *n* blood-sucking worm with hooked mouthparts
HOOKWORMS > HOOKWORM
HOOKY *n* truancy, usually from school (esp in the phrase play hooky) ▷ *adj* hooklike
HOOLACHAN *n* Highland reel
HOOLEY *n* lively party
HOOLEYS > HOOLEY
HOOLICAN *same as* > HOOLACHAN
HOOLICANS > HOOLICAN
HOOLIE *same as* > HOOLEY
HOOLIER > HOOLY
HOOLIES > HOOLIE
HOOLIEST > HOOLY
HOOLIGAN *n* rowdy young person
HOOLIGANS > HOOLIGAN
HOOLOCK *n* Indian gibbon
HOOLOCKS > HOOLOCK
HOOLY *adj* careful or gentle
HOON *n* loutish youth who drives irresponsibly ▷ *vb* drive irresponsibly
HOONS > HOON
HOOP *n* rigid circular band, used esp as a child's toy or for animals to jump through in the circus ▷ *vb* surround with or as if with a hoop
HOOPED > HOOP
HOOPER *rare word for* > COOPER
HOOPERS > HOOPER
HOOPING > HOOP
HOOPLA *n* fairground game in which hoops are thrown over objects in an attempt to win them
HOOPLAS > HOOPLA
HOOPLESS > HOOP
HOOPLIKE > HOOP
HOOPOE *n* bird with a pinkish-brown plumage and a fanlike crest
HOOPOES > HOOPOE
HOOPOO *same as* > HOOPOE
HOOPOOS > HOOPOO
HOOPS > HOOP
HOOPSKIRT *n* skirt stiffened by hoops
HOOPSTER *n* basketball player
HOOPSTERS > HOOPSTER
HOORAH *same as* > HURRAH
HOORAHED > HOORAH
HOORAHING > HOORAH
HOORAHS > HOORAH
HOORAY *same as* > HURRAH
HOORAYED > HOORAY
HOORAYING > HOORAY
HOORAYS > HOORAY
HOORD *same as* > HOARD
HOORDS > HOORD
HOOROO *same as* > HURRAH
HOOSEGOW *slang word for* > JAIL
HOOSEGOWS > HOOSEGOW
HOOSGOW > JAIL
HOOSGOWS > JAIL
HOOSH *vb* shoo away
HOOSHED > HOOSH
HOOSHES > HOOSH
HOOSHING > HOOSH
HOOT *n* sound of a car horn ▷ *vb* sound (a car horn) ▷ *interj* exclamation of impatience or dissatisfaction: a supposed Scotticism
HOOTCH *same as* > HOOCH
HOOTCHES > HOOTCH
HOOTED > HOOT
HOOTER *n* device that hoots
HOOTERS > HOOTER
HOOTIER > HOOT
HOOTIEST > HOOT
HOOTING > HOOT
HOOTNANNY *n* informal performance by folk singers
HOOTS *same as* > HOOT
HOOTY > HOOT
HOOVE *same as* > HEAVE
HOOVED > HOOVE
HOOVEN > HOOVE
HOOVER *vb* vacuum-clean (a carpet, furniture, etc)
HOOVERED > HOOVER
HOOVERING > HOOVER
HOOVERS > HOOVER
HOOVES > HOOF
HOOVING > HOOVE
HOP *vb* jump on one foot ▷ *n* instance of hopping
HOPBIND *n* stalk of the hop
HOPBINDS > HOPBIND
HOPBINE *same as* > HOPBIND
HOPBINES > HOPBINE
HOPDOG *n* species of caterpillar
HOPDOGS > HOPDOG
HOPE *vb* want (something) to happen or be true ▷ *n* expectation of something desired
HOPED > HOPE
HOPEFUL *adj* having, expressing, or inspiring hope ▷ *n* person considered to be on the brink of success
HOPEFULLY *adv* in a hopeful manner
HOPEFULS > HOPEFUL
HOPELESS *adj* having or offering no hope
HOPER > HOPE
HOPERS > HOPE
HOPES > HOPE
HOPHEAD *n* heroin or opium addict
HOPHEADS > HOPHEAD
HOPING > HOPE
HOPINGLY > HOPE
HOPLITE *n* (in ancient Greece) a heavily armed infantryman
HOPLITES > HOPLITE
HOPLITIC > HOPLITE
HOPLOLOGY *n* study of weapons or armour
HOPPED > HOP
HOPPER *n* container for storing substances such as grain or sand
HOPPERCAR *same as* > HOPPER
HOPPERS > HOPPER
HOPPIER > HOPPY
HOPPIEST > HOPPY
HOPPING > HOP
HOPPINGS > HOP
HOPPLE *same as* > HOBBLE
HOPPLED > HOPPLE
HOPPLER > HOPPLE
HOPPLERS > HOPPLE
HOPPLES > HOPPLE
HOPPLING > HOPPLE
HOPPY *adj* tasting of hops
HOPS > HOP
HOPSACK *n* roughly woven fabric of wool, cotton, etc, used for clothing
HOPSACKS > HOPSACK
HOPSCOTCH *n* children's game of hopping in a pattern drawn on the ground
HOPTOAD *n* toad
HOPTOADS > HOPTOAD
HORA *n* traditional Israeli or Romanian circle dance
HORAH *same as* > HORA
HORAHS > HORAH
HORAL *less common word for* > HOURLY
HORARY *adj* relating to the hours
HORAS > HORA
HORDE *n* large crowd ▷ *vb* form, move in, or live in a horde
HORDED > HORDE

HORDEIN *n* simple protein, rich in proline, that occurs in barley
HORDEINS > HORDEIN
HORDEOLA > HORDEOLUM
HORDEOLUM *n* (in medicine) stye
HORDES > HORDE
HORDING > HORDE
HORDOCK *same as* > HARDOKE
HORDOCKS > HORDOCK
HORE *same as* > HOAR
HOREHOUND *n* plant that produces a bitter juice formerly used as a cough medicine
HORI *derogatory term* *n* Māori ▷ *adj* of or relating to the Māori
HORIATIKI *n* traditional Greek salad consisting of tomatoes, cucumber, onion, olives, and feta cheese
HORIS > HORI
HORIZON *n* apparent line that divides the earth and the sky
HORIZONAL > HORIZON
HORIZONS > HORIZON
HORKEY *same as* > HOCKEY
HORKEYS > HORKEY
HORLICKS as in *make a horlicks* make a mistake or a mess
HORME *n* (in the psychology of C. G. Jung) fundamental vital energy
HORMES > HORME
HORMIC > HORME
HORMONAL > HORMONE
HORMONE *n* substance secreted by certain glands which stimulates certain organs of the body
HORMONES > HORMONE
HORMONIC > HORMONE
HORN *n* one of a pair of bony growths sticking out of the heads of cattle, sheep, etc ▷ *vb* provide with a horn or horns
HORNBAG *n* in Australian slang, a promiscuous woman
HORNBAGS > HORNBAG
HORNBEAK *n* garfish
HORNBEAKS > HORNBEAK
HORNBEAM *n* tree with smooth grey bark
HORNBEAMS > HORNBEAM
HORNBILL *n* bird with a bony growth on its large beak
HORNBILLS > HORNBILL
HORNBOOK *n* page bearing a religious text or the alphabet, held in a frame with a thin window of flattened cattle horn over it
HORNBOOKS > HORNBOOK
HORNBUG *n* stag beetle
HORNBUGS > HORNBUG
HORNED *adj* having a horn, horns, or hornlike parts
HORNER *n* dealer in horn
HORNERS > HORNER
HORNET *n* large wasp with a severe sting
HORNETS > HORNET
HORNFELS *n* hard compact fine-grained metamorphic rock formed by the action of heat from a magmatic intrusion on neighbouring sedimentary rocks
HORNFUL *n* amount a horn will hold
HORNFULS > HORNFUL
HORNGELD *n* feudal rent based on number of cattle
HORNGELDS > HORNGELD
HORNIER > HORNY
HORNIEST > HORNY
HORNILY > HORNY
HORNINESS > HORNY
HORNING > HORN
HORNINGS > HORN
HORNISH *adj* like horn
HORNIST *n* horn player
HORNISTS > HORNIST
HORNITO *n* small vent in volcano
HORNITOS > HORNITO
HORNLESS > HORN
HORNLET *n* small horn
HORNLETS > HORNLET
HORNLIKE > HORN
HORNPIPE *n* (music for) a solo dance, traditionally performed by sailors
HORNPIPES > HORNPIPE
HORNPOUT *n* catfish
HORNPOUTS > HORNPOUT
HORNS > HORN
HORNSTONE *same as* > HORNFELS
HORNTAIL *n* wasplike insect
HORNTAILS > HORNTAIL
HORNWORK *n* bastion in fortifications
HORNWORKS > HORNWORK
HORNWORM *n* caterpillar of hawk moth
HORNWORMS > HORNWORM
HORNWORT *n* aquatic plant
HORNWORTS > HORNWORT
HORNWRACK *n* yellowish bryozoan or sea mat sometimes found on beaches after a storm
HORNY *adj* of or like horn
HORNYHEAD *n* species of fish
HORNYWINK *n* lapwing
HOROEKA *n* New Zealand tree
HOROKAKA *n* low-growing New Zealand plant with fleshy leaves and pink or white flowers
HOROLOGE *rare word for* > TIMEPIECE
HOROLOGER *same as* > HOROLOGIST
HOROLOGES > HOROLOGE
HOROLOGIA *n* plural of horologium: clocktower
HOROLOGIC > HOROLOGY
HOROLOGY *n* art of making clocks and watches or of measuring time
HOROMETRY *n* measurement of time
HOROPITO *n* New Zealand plant
HOROPITOS > HOROPITO
HOROPTER *n* locus of all points in space that stimulate points on each eye that yield the same visual direction as each other
HOROPTERS > HOROPTER
HOROSCOPE *n* prediction of a person's future based on the positions of the planets, sun, and moon at his or her birth
HOROSCOPY *n* casting and interpretation of horoscopes
HORRENT *adj* bristling
HORRIBLE *adj* disagreeable, unpleasant ▷ *n* horrible thing
HORRIBLES > HORRIBLE
HORRIBLY *adv* in a horrible manner
HORRID *adj* disagreeable, unpleasant
HORRIDER > HORRID
HORRIDEST > HORRID
HORRIDLY > HORRID
HORRIFIC *adj* causing horror
HORRIFIED *adj* terrified
HORRIFIES > HORRIFY
HORRIFY *vb* cause to feel horror or shock
HORROR *n* (thing or person causing) terror or hatred ▷ *adj* having a frightening subject, usually concerned with the supernatural
HORRORS *pl n* fit of depression or anxiety ▷ *interj* expression of dismay, sometimes facetious
HORS as in *hors d'oeuvre* appetizer
HORSE *n* large animal with hooves, a mane, and a tail, used for riding and pulling carts etc ▷ *vb* provide with a horse
HORSEBACK *n* horse's back
HORSEBEAN *n* broad bean
HORSEBOX *n* trailer used for transporting horses
HORSECAR *n* streetcar drawn by horses
HORSECARS > HORSECAR
HORSED > HORSE
HORSEFLY *n* large bloodsucking fly
HORSEHAIR *n* hair from the tail or mane of a horse
HORSEHIDE *n* hide of a horse
HORSELESS > HORSE
HORSELIKE > HORSE
HORSEMAN *n* person skilled in riding
HORSEMEAT *n* flesh of the horse used as food
HORSEMEN > HORSEMAN
HORSEMINT *n* European mint plant
HORSEPLAY *n* rough or rowdy play
HORSEPOND *n* pond where horses drink
HORSEPOX *n* viral infection of horses
HORSERACE *n* race for horses
HORSES > HORSE
HORSESHIT *n* rubbish
HORSESHOD > HORSESHOE
HORSESHOE *n* protective U shaped piece of iron nailed to a horse's hoof, regarded as a symbol of good luck ▷ *vb* fit with a horseshoe
HORSETAIL *n* plant with small dark toothlike leave
HORSEWAY *n* road for horse
HORSEWAYS > HORSEWAY
HORSEWEED *n* US name for Canadian fleabane
HORSEWHIP *n* whip with a long thong, used for managing horses ▷ *vb* beat (a person or animal) with such a whip
HORSEY *adj* very keen on horses
HORSIER > HORSY
HORSIEST > HORSY
HORSILY > HORSEY
HORSINESS > HORSEY
HORSING > HORSE
HORSINGS > HORSE
HORSON *same as* > WHORESON
HORSONS > HORSON
HORST *n* ridge of land that has been forced upwards between two parallel faults
HORSTE *variant of* > HORST
HORSTES > HORSTE
HORSTS > HORST
HORSY *same as* > HORSEY
HORTATION > HORTATORY
HORTATIVE *same as* > HORTATORY
HORTATORY *adj* encouraging
HOS > HO
HOSANNA *interj* exclamatio of praise to God ▷ *n* act of crying "hosanna" ▷ *vb* cry hosanna
HOSANNAED > HOSANNA
HOSANNAH *same as* > HOSANNA
HOSANNAHS > HOSANNAH
HOSANNAS > HOSANNA
HOSE *n* flexible pipe for conveying liquid ▷ *vb*

water with a hose
HOSED > HOSE
HOSEL *n* socket in head of golf club
HOSELIKE > HOSE
HOSELS > HOSEL
HOSEMAN *n* fireman in charge of hose
HOSEMEN > HOSEMAN
HOSEN > HOSE
HOSEPIPE *n* hose
HOSEPIPES > HOSEPIPE
HOSER *n* person who swindles or deceives others
HOSERS > HOSER
HOSES > HOSE
HOSEY *vb* claim possession
HOSEYED > HOSEY
HOSEYING > HOSEY
HOSEYS > HOSEY
HOSIER *n* person who sells stockings, etc
HOSIERIES > HOSIERY
HOSIERS > HOSIER
HOSIERY *n* stockings, socks, and tights collectively
HOSING > HOSE
HOSPICE *n* nursing home for the terminally ill
HOSPICES > HOSPICE
HOSPITAGE *n* behaviour of guest
HOSPITAL *n* place where people who are ill are looked after and treated
HOSPITALE *n* lodging
HOSPITALS > HOSPITAL
HOSPITIA > HOSPITIUM
HOSPITIUM *same as* > HOSPICE
HOSPODAR *n* (formerly) the governor or prince of Moldavia or Wallachia under Ottoman rule
HOSPODARS > HOSPODAR
HOSS *n* horse
HOSSES > HOSS
HOST *n* person who entertains guests, esp in his own home ▷ *vb* be the host of
HOSTA *n* ornamental plant
HOSTAGE *n* person who is illegally held prisoner until certain demands are met by other people
HOSTAGES > HOSTAGE
HOSTAS > HOSTA
HOSTED > HOST
HOSTEL *n* building providing accommodation at a low cost for a specific group of people such as students, travellers, homeless people, etc ▷ *vb* stay in hostels
HOSTELED > HOSTEL
HOSTELER *same as* > HOSTELLER
HOSTELERS > HOSTELER
HOSTELING > HOSTEL
HOSTELLED > HOSTEL
HOSTELLER *n* person who stays at youth hostels
HOSTELRY *n* inn, pub
HOSTELS > HOSTEL
HOSTESS *n* woman who receives and entertains guests, esp in her own house ▷ *vb* act as hostess
HOSTESSED > HOSTESS
HOSTESSES > HOSTESS
HOSTIE *n* informal Australian word for an air hostess
HOSTIES > HOSTIE
HOSTILE *adj* unfriendly ▷ *n* hostile person
HOSTILELY > HOSTILE
HOSTILES > HOSTILE
HOSTILITY *n* unfriendly and aggressive feelings or behaviour
HOSTING > HOST
HOSTINGS > HOST
HOSTLER *another name (esp Brit) for* > OSTLER
HOSTLERS > HOSTLER
HOSTLESSE *adj* inhospitable
HOSTLY > HOST
HOSTRIES > HOSTRY
HOSTRY *n* lodging
HOSTS > HOST
HOT *adj* having a high temperature
HOTBED *n* any place encouraging a particular activity
HOTBEDS > HOTBED
HOTBLOOD *n* type of horse
HOTBLOODS > HOTBLOOD
HOTBOX *n* closed room where marijuana is smoked
HOTBOXES > HOTBOX
HOTCAKE *n* pancake
HOTCAKES > HOTCAKE
HOTCH *vb* jog
HOTCHED > HOTCH
HOTCHES > HOTCH
HOTCHING > HOTCH
HOTCHPOT *n* collecting of property so that it may be redistributed in equal shares, esp on the intestacy of a parent who has given property to his children in his lifetime
HOTCHPOTS > HOTCHPOT
HOTDOG *vb* perform a series of manoeuvres in skiing, surfing, etc, esp in a showy manner
HOTDOGGED > HOTDOG
HOTDOGGER > HOTDOG
HOTDOGS > HOTDOG
HOTE > HIGHT
HOTEL *n* commercial establishment providing lodging and meals
HOTELDOM *n* hotel business
HOTELDOMS > HOTELDOM
HOTELIER *n* owner or manager of a hotel
HOTELIERS > HOTELIER
HOTELMAN *n* hotel owner
HOTELMEN > HOTELMAN
HOTELS > HOTEL
HOTEN > HIGHT
HOTFOOT *adv* quickly and eagerly ▷ *vb* move quickly
HOTFOOTED > HOTFOOT
HOTFOOTS > HOTFOOT
HOTHEAD *n* excitable or fiery person
HOTHEADED *adj* impetuous, rash, or hot-tempered
HOTHEADS > HOTHEAD
HOTHOUSE *n* greenhouse
HOTHOUSED *adj* taught intensively
HOTHOUSES > HOTHOUSE
HOTLINE *n* direct telephone link for emergency use
HOTLINES > HOTLINE
HOTLINK *n* area on website connecting to another site
HOTLINKS > HOTLINK
HOTLY > HOT
HOTNESS > HOT
HOTNESSES > HOT
HOTPLATE *n* heated metal surface on an electric cooker
HOTPLATES > HOTPLATE
HOTPOT *n* casserole of meat and vegetables, topped with potatoes
HOTPOTS > HOTPOT
HOTPRESS *vb* subject (paper, cloth, etc) to heat and pressure to give it a smooth surface or extract oil
HOTROD *n* car with an engine that has been radically modified to produce increased power
HOTRODS > HOTROD
HOTS as in *the hots* feeling of lust
HOTSHOT *n* important person or expert, esp when showy
HOTSHOTS > HOTSHOT
HOTSPOT *n* place where wireless broadband services are provided through a wireless local area network
HOTSPOTS > HOTSPOT
HOTSPUR *n* impetuous or fiery person
HOTSPURS > HOTSPUR
HOTTED > HOT
HOTTENTOT as in *hottentot fig* perennial plant with fleshy leaves, showy yellow or purple flowers, and edible fruits
HOTTER *vb* simmer
HOTTERED > HOTTIER
HOTTERING > HOTTER
HOTTERS > HOTTER
HOTTEST > HOT
HOTTIE *n* sexually attractive person
HOTTIES > HOTTIE
HOTTING *n* practice of stealing fast cars and putting on a show of skilful but dangerous driving
HOTTINGS > HOTTING
HOTTISH *adj* fairly hot
HOTTY *same as* > HOTTIE
HOUDAH *same as* > HOWDAH
HOUDAHS > HOUDAH
HOUDAN *n* breed of light domestic fowl originally from France, with a distinctive full crest
HOUDANS > HOUDAN
HOUF *same as* > HOWF
HOUFED > HOUF
HOUFF *same as* > HOWF
HOUFFED > HOUFF
HOUFFING > HOUFF
HOUFFS > HOUFF
HOUFING > HOUF
HOUFS > HOUF
HOUGH *n* in Scotland, a cut of meat corresponding to shin ▷ *vb* hamstring (cattle, horses, etc)
HOUGHED > HOUGH
HOUGHING > HOUGH
HOUGHS > HOUGH
HOUHERE *n* small evergreen New Zealand tree
HOUMMOS *same as* > HUMMUS
HOUMMOSES > HOUMMOS
HOUMOUS > HUMMUS
HOUMOUSES > HOUMOUS
HOUMUS *same as* > HUMMUS
HOUMUSES > HOUMUS
HOUND *n* hunting dog ▷ *vb* pursue relentlessly
HOUNDED > HOUND
HOUNDER > HOUND
HOUNDERS > HOUND
HOUNDFISH *n* name given to various small sharks or dogfish
HOUNDING > HOUND
HOUNDS > HOUND
HOUNGAN *n* voodoo priest
HOUNGANS > HOUNGAN
HOUR *n* twenty-fourth part of a day, sixty minutes
HOURGLASS *n* device with two glass compartments, containing a quantity of sand that takes an hour to trickle from the top section to the bottom one
HOURI *n* any of the nymphs of paradise
HOURIS > HOURI
HOURLIES > HOURLY
HOURLONG *adj* lasting an hour
HOURLY *adv* (happening) every hour ▷ *adj* of, occurring, or done once every hour ▷ *n* something that is done by the hour; someone who is paid by the hour
HOURPLATE *n* dial of clock
HOURS *pl n* indefinite time
HOUSE *n* building used

as a home ▷ *vb* give accommodation to ▷ *adj* (of wine) sold in a restaurant at a lower price than wines on the wine list
HOUSEBOAT *n* stationary boat used as a home
HOUSEBOY *n* male domestic servant
HOUSEBOYS > HOUSEBOY
HOUSECARL *n* (in medieval Europe) a household warrior of Danish kings and noblemen
HOUSECOAT *n* woman's long loose coat-shaped garment for wearing at home
HOUSED > HOUSE
HOUSEFLY *n* common fly often found in houses
HOUSEFUL *n* full amount or number that can be accommodated in a particular house
HOUSEFULS > HOUSEFUL
HOUSEHOLD *n* all the people living in a house ▷ *adj* relating to the running of a household
HOUSEKEEP *vb* run household
HOUSEKEPT > HOUSEKEEP
HOUSEL *vb* give the Eucharist to (someone)
HOUSELED > HOUSEL
HOUSELEEK *n* plant that has a rosette of succulent leaves and pinkish flowers and grows on walls
HOUSELESS > HOUSE
HOUSELINE *n* tarred marline
HOUSELING > HOUSEL
HOUSELLED > HOUSEL
HOUSELS > HOUSEL
HOUSEMAID *n* female servant employed to do housework
HOUSEMAN *n* junior hospital doctor
HOUSEMATE *n* person who is not part of the same family, but with whom one shares a house
HOUSEMEN > HOUSEMAN
HOUSER > HOUSE
HOUSEROOM *n* room for storage or lodging
HOUSERS > HOUSE
HOUSES > HOUSE
HOUSESAT > HOUSESIT
HOUSESIT *vb* live in and look after a house during the absence of its owner or owners
HOUSESITS > HOUSESIT
HOUSETOP *n* rooftop
HOUSETOPS > HOUSETOP
HOUSEWIFE *n* woman who runs her own household and does not have a job
HOUSEWORK *n* work of running a home, such as cleaning, cooking, and shopping
HOUSEY *adj* of or like house music
HOUSIER > HOUSEY
HOUSIEST > HOUSEY
HOUSING *n* (providing of) houses
HOUSINGS > HOUSING
HOUSLING *adj* of sacrament
HOUSTONIA *n* small North American plant with blue, white or purple flowers
HOUT *same as* > HOOT
HOUTED > HOUT
HOUTING *n* type of fish that lives in salt water but spawns in freshwater lakes and is valued for its edible flesh
HOUTINGS > HOUTING
HOUTS > HOUT
HOVE > HEAVE
HOVEA *n* Australian plant with purple flowers
HOVEAS > HOVEA
HOVED > HEAVE
HOVEL *n* small dirty house or hut ▷ *vb* shelter or be sheltered in a hovel
HOVELED > HOVEL
HOVELING > HOVEL
HOVELLED > HOVEL
HOVELLER *n* man working on boat
HOVELLERS > HOVELLER
HOVELLING > HOVEL
HOVELS > HOVEL
HOVEN > HEAVE
HOVER *vb* (of a bird etc) remain suspended in one place in the air ▷ *n* act of hovering
HOVERED > HOVER
HOVERER > HOVER
HOVERERS > HOVER
HOVERFLY *n* hovering wasp-like fly
HOVERING > HOVER
HOVERPORT *n* port for hovercraft
HOVERS > HOVER
HOVES > HEAVE
HOVING > HEAVE
HOW *adv* in what way, by what means ▷ *n* the way a thing is done ▷ *sentence substitute* greeting supposed to be or have been used by American Indians and often used humorously
HOWBE *same as* > HOWBEIT
HOWBEIT *adv* in archaic usage, however
HOWDAH *n* canopied seat on an elephant's back
HOWDAHS > HOWDAH
HOWDIE *n* midwife
HOWDIED > HOWDY
HOWDIES > HOWDY
HOWDY *vb* greet someone
HOWDYING > HOWDY
HOWE *n* depression in the earth's surface, such as a basin or valley
HOWES > HOWE
HOWEVER *adv* nevertheless
HOWF *n* haunt, esp a public house ▷ *vb* visit place frequently
HOWFED > HOWF
HOWFF *vb* visit place frequently
HOWFFED > HOWFF
HOWFFING > HOWFF
HOWFFS > HOWFF
HOWFING > HOWF
HOWFS > HOWF
HOWITZER *n* large gun firing shells at a steep angle
HOWITZERS > HOWITZER
HOWK *vb* dig (out or up)
HOWKED > HOWK
HOWKER > HOWK
HOWKERS > HOWK
HOWKING > HOWK
HOWKS > HOWK
HOWL *n* loud wailing cry ▷ *vb* utter a howl
HOWLBACK *same as* > HOWLROUND
HOWLBACKS > HOWLBACK
HOWLED > HOWL
HOWLER *n* stupid mistake
HOWLERS > HOWLER
HOWLET *another word for* > OWL
HOWLETS > HOWLET
HOWLING *adj* great
HOWLINGLY > HOWL
HOWLINGS > HOWL
HOWLROUND *n* condition, resulting in a howling noise, when sound from a loudspeaker is fed back into the microphone of a public-address or recording system
HOWLS > HOWL
HOWRE *same as* > HOUR
HOWRES > HOWRE
HOWS > HOW
HOWSO *same as* > HOWSOEVER
HOWSOEVER *less common word for* > HOWEVER
HOWTOWDIE *n* Scottish dish of boiled chicken with poached eggs and spinach
HOWZAT > HOW
HOWZIT *informal word for* > HELLO
HOX *vb* hamstring
HOXED > HOX
HOXES > HOX
HOXING > HOX
HOY *interj* cry used to attract someone's attention ▷ *n* freight barge ▷ *vb* drive animal with cry
HOYA *n* any of various E Asian or Australian plants
HOYAS > HOYA
HOYDEN *n* wild or boisterous girl ▷ *vb* behave like a hoyden
HOYDENED > HOYDEN
HOYDENING > HOYDEN
HOYDENISH > HOYDEN
HOYDENISM > HOYDEN
HOYDENS > HOYDEN
HOYED > HOY
HOYING > HOY
HOYLE *n* archer's mark use as a target
HOYLES > HOYLE
HOYS > HOY
HRYVNA *n* standard monetary unit of Ukraine divided into 100 kopiykas
HRYVNAS > HRYVNA
HRYVNIA *n* money unit of Ukraine
HRYVNIAS > HRYVNIA
HRYVNYA *same as* > HRYVNA
HRYVNYAS > HRYVNYA
HUANACO *same as* > GUANAC
HUANACOS > HUANACO
HUAQUERO *n* Central American tomb robber
HUAQUEROS > HUAQUERO
HUARACHE *n* Mexican sandal
HUARACHES > HUARACHE
HUARACHO *same as* > HUARACHE
HUARACHOS > HUARACHO
HUB *n* centre of a wheel, through which the axle passes
HUBBIES > HUBBY
HUBBLY *adj* having an irregular surface
HUBBUB *n* confused noise c many voices
HUBBUBOO *same as* > HUBBUB
HUBBUBOOS > HUBBUBOO
HUBBUBS > HUBBUB
HUBBY *n* husband
HUBCAP *n* metal disc that fits on to and protects the hub of a wheel, esp on a ca
HUBCAPS > HUBCAP
HUBRIS *n* pride, arrogance
HUBRISES > HUBRIS
HUBRISTIC > HUBRIS
HUBS > HUB
HUCK *same as* > HUCKABACK
HUCKABACK *n* coarse absorbent linen or cotton fabric used for towels and informal shirts, etc
HUCKERY *adj* ugly
HUCKLE *n* hip or haunch
HUCKLES > HUCKLE
HUCKS > HUCK
HUCKSTER *n* person using aggressive methods of selling ▷ *vb* peddle
HUCKSTERS > HUCKSTER
HUCKSTERY > HUCKSTER
HUDDEN > HAUD
HUDDLE *vb* hunch (oneself) through cold or fear ▷ *n* small group
HUDDLED > HUDDLE
HUDDLER > HUDDLE
HUDDLERS > HUDDLE

HUDDLES > HUDDLE
HUDDLING > HUDDLE
HUDDUP *interj* get up
HUDNA *n* truce or ceasefire for a fixed duration
HUDNAS > HUDNA
HUDUD *n* set of laws and punishments specified by Allah in the Koran
HUDUDS > HUDUD
HUE *n* colour, shade
HUED *adj* having a hue or colour as specified
HUELESS > HUE
HUER *n* pilchard fisherman
HUERS > HUER
HUES > HUE
HUFF *n* passing mood of anger or resentment ▷ *vb* blow or puff heavily
HUFFED > HUFF
HUFFER > HUFFING
HUFFERS > HUFFING
HUFFIER > HUFF
HUFFIEST > HUFF
HUFFILY > HUFF
HUFFINESS > HUFF
HUFFING *n* practice of inhaling toxic fumes from glue and other household products for their intoxicating effects
HUFFINGS > HUFFING
HUFFISH > HUFF
HUFFISHLY > HUFF
HUFFKIN *n* type of muffin
HUFFKINS > HUFFKIN
HUFFS > HUFF
HUFFY > HUFF
HUG *vb* clasp tightly in the arms, usu with affection ▷ *n* tight or fond embrace
HUGE *adj* very big
HUGELY *adv* very much
HUGENESS > HUGE
HUGEOUS *same as* > HUGE
HUGEOUSLY > HUGEOUS
HUGER > HUGE
HUGEST > HUGE
HUGGABLE > HUG
HUGGED > HUG
HUGGER > HUG
HUGGERS > HUG
HUGGIER > HUGGY
HUGGIEST > HUGGY
HUGGING > HUG
HUGGY *adj* sensitive and caring
HUGS > HUG
HUGY *same as* > HUGE
HUH *interj* exclamation of derision, bewilderment, or inquiry
HUHU *n* type of hairy New Zealand beetle
HUHUS > HUHU
HUI *n* meeting of Māori people
HUIA *n* extinct bird of New Zealand, prized by early Māoris for its distinctive tail feathers
HUIAS > HUIA
HUIC *interj* in hunting, a call to hounds
HUIPIL *n* Mayan woman's blouse
HUIPILES > HUIPIL
HUIPILS > HUIPIL
HUIS > HUI
HUISACHE *n* American tree
HUISACHES > HUISACHE
HUISSIER *n* doorkeeper
HUISSIERS > HUISSIER
HUITAIN *n* verse of eighteen lines
HUITAINS > HUITAIN
HULA *n* swaying Hawaiian dance
HULAS > HULA
HULE *same as* > ULE
HULES > HULE
HULK *n* body of an abandoned ship ▷ *vb* move clumsily
HULKED > HULK
HULKIER > HULKY
HULKIEST > HULKY
HULKING *adj* bulky, unwieldy
HULKS > HULK
HULKY *same as* > HULKING
HULL *n* main body of a boat ▷ *vb* remove the hulls from
HULLED > HULL
HULLER > HULL
HULLERS > HULL
HULLIER > HULLY
HULLIEST > HULLY
HULLING > HULL
HULLO *same as* > HELLO
HULLOA *same as* > HALLOA
HULLOAED > HULLOA
HULLOAING > HULLOA
HULLOAS > HULLOA
HULLOED > HULLO
HULLOES > HULLO
HULLOING > HULLO
HULLOO *same as* > HALLOO
HULLOOED > HULLOO
HULLOOING > HULLOO
HULLOOS > HULLOO
HULLOS > HULLO
HULLS > HULL
HULLY *adj* having husks
HUM *vb* make a low continuous vibrating sound ▷ *n* humming sound
HUMA *n* mythical bird
HUMAN *adj* of or typical of people ▷ *n* human being
HUMANE *adj* kind or merciful
HUMANELY > HUMANE
HUMANER > HUMANE
HUMANEST > HUMANE
HUMANHOOD *n* state of being human
HUMANISE *same as* > HUMANIZE
HUMANISED > HUMANISE
HUMANISER > HUMANISE
HUMANISES > HUMANISE
HUMANISM *n* belief in human effort rather than religion
HUMANISMS > HUMANISM
HUMANIST > HUMANISM
HUMANISTS > HUMANISM > HUMANITARIANIST
HUMANITY *n* human race
HUMANIZE *vb* make human or humane
HUMANIZED > HUMANIZE
HUMANIZER > HUMANIZE
HUMANIZES > HUMANIZE
HUMANKIND *n* human race
HUMANLIKE > HUMAN
HUMANLY *adv* by human powers or means
HUMANNESS > HUMAN
HUMANOID *adj* resembling a human being in appearance ▷ *n* (in science fiction) a robot or creature resembling a human being
HUMANOIDS > HUMANOID
HUMANS > HUMAN
HUMAS > HUMA
HUMATE *n* decomposed plants used as fertilizer
HUMATES > HUMATE
HUMBLE *adj* conscious of one's failings ▷ *vb* cause to feel humble, humiliate
HUMBLEBEE *another name for the* > BUMBLEBEE
HUMBLED > HUMBLE
HUMBLER > HUMBLE
HUMBLERS > HUMBLE
HUMBLES > HUMBLE
HUMBLESSE *n* quality of being humble
HUMBLEST > HUMBLE
HUMBLING > HUMBLE
HUMBLINGS > HUMBLE
HUMBLY > HUMBLE
HUMBUCKER *n* twin-coil guitar pick-up
HUMBUG *n* hard striped peppermint sweet ▷ *vb* cheat or deceive (someone)
HUMBUGGED > HUMBUG
HUMBUGGER > HUMBUG
HUMBUGS > HUMBUG
HUMBUZZ *n* type of beetle
HUMBUZZES > HUMBUZZ
HUMDINGER *n* excellent person or thing
HUMDRUM *adj* ordinary, dull ▷ *n* monotonous routine, task, or person
HUMDRUMS > HUMDRUM
HUMECT *vb* make moist
HUMECTANT *adj* producing moisture ▷ *n* substance added to another substance to keep it moist
HUMECTATE *vb* produce moisture
HUMECTED > HUMECT
HUMECTING > HUMECT
HUMECTIVE > HUMECT
HUMECTS > HUMECT
HUMEFIED > HUMEFY
HUMEFIES > HUMEFY
HUMEFY *same as* > HUMIFY
HUMEFYING > HUMEFY
HUMERAL *adj* of or relating to the humerus ▷ *n* silk shawl worn by a priest at High Mass; humeral veil
HUMERALS > HUMERAL
HUMERI > HUMERUS
HUMERUS *n* bone from the shoulder to the elbow
HUMF *same as* > HUMPH
HUMFED > HUMF
HUMFING > HUMF
HUMFS > HUMF
HUMHUM *n* Indian cotton cloth
HUMHUMS > HUMHUM
HUMIC *adj* of, relating to, derived from, or resembling humus
HUMICOLE *n* any plant that thrives on humus
HUMICOLES > HUMICOLE
HUMID *adj* damp and hot
HUMIDER > HUMID
HUMIDEST > HUMID
HUMIDEX *n* system of measuring discomfort showing the combined effect of humidity and temperature
HUMIDEXES > HUMIDEX
HUMIDICES > HUMIDEX
HUMIDIFY *vb* make the air in (a room) more humid or damp
HUMIDITY *n* dampness
HUMIDLY > HUMID
HUMIDNESS > HUMID
HUMIDOR *n* humid place or container for storing cigars, tobacco, etc
HUMIDORS > HUMIDOR
HUMIFIED > HUMIFY
HUMIFIES > HUMIFY
HUMIFY *vb* convert or be converted into humus
HUMIFYING > HUMIFY
HUMILIANT *adj* humiliating
HUMILIATE *vb* lower the dignity or hurt the pride of
HUMILITY *n* quality of being humble
HUMINT *n* human intelligence
HUMINTS > HUMINT
HUMITE *n* mineral containing magnesium
HUMITES > HUMITE
HUMITURE *n* measure of both humidity and temperature
HUMITURES > HUMITURE
HUMLIE *n* hornless cow
HUMLIES > HUMLIE
HUMMABLE > HUM
HUMMAUM *same as* > HAMMAM
HUMMAUMS > HUMMAUM
HUMMED > HUM
HUMMEL *adj* (of cattle) hornless ▷ *vb* remove horns from
HUMMELLED > HUMMEL
HUMMELLER > HUMMEL
HUMMELS > HUMMEL
HUMMER > HUM
HUMMERS > HUM

HUMMING > HUM
HUMMINGS > HUM
HUMMOCK *n* very small hill ▷ *vb* form into a hummock or hummocks
HUMMOCKED > HUMMOCK
HUMMOCKS > HUMMOCK
HUMMOCKY > HUMMOCK
HUMMUM *same as* > HAMMAM
HUMMUMS > HUMMUM
HUMMUS *n* creamy dip originating in the Middle East, made from puréed chickpeas
HUMMUSES > HUMMUS
HUMOGEN *n* type of fertilizer
HUMOGENS > HUMOGEN
HUMONGOUS *same as* > HUMUNGOUS
HUMOR *same as* > HUMOUR
HUMORAL *adj* denoting or relating to a type of immunity caused by free antibodies circulating in the blood
HUMORALLY > HUMORAL
HUMORED > HUMOR
HUMORESK *n* humorous musical composition
HUMORESKS > HUMORESK
HUMORFUL > HUMOR
HUMORING > HUMOR
HUMORIST *n* writer or entertainer who uses humour in his or her work
HUMORISTS > HUMORIST
HUMORLESS > HUMOR
HUMOROUS *adj* amusing, esp in a witty or clever way
HUMORS > HUMOR
HUMORSOME *same as* > HUMOURSOME
HUMOUR *n* ability to say or perceive things that are amusing ▷ *vb* be kind and indulgent to
HUMOURED > HUMOUR
HUMOURFUL > HUMOUR
HUMOURING > HUMOUR
HUMOURS > HUMOUR
HUMOUS *same as* > HUMUS
HUMP *n* raised piece of ground ▷ *vb* carry or heave
HUMPBACK *same as* > HUNCHBACK
HUMPBACKS > HUMPBACK
HUMPED > HUMP
HUMPEN *n* old German drinking glass
HUMPENS > HUMPEN
HUMPER > HUMP
HUMPERS > HUMP
HUMPH *interj* exclamation of annoyance or scepticism ▷ *vb* exclaim humph
HUMPHED > HUMPH
HUMPHING > HUMPH
HUMPHS > HUMPH
HUMPIER > HUMPY
HUMPIES > HUMPY
HUMPIEST > HUMPY
HUMPINESS > HUMPY
HUMPING > HUMP
HUMPLESS > HUMP
HUMPLIKE > HUMP
HUMPS > HUMP
HUMPTIES > HUMPTY
HUMPTY *n* low padded seat
HUMPY *adj* full of humps ▷ *n* primitive hut
HUMS > HUM
HUMSTRUM *n* medieval musical instrument
HUMSTRUMS > HUMSTRUM
HUMUNGOUS *adj* very large
HUMUS *n* decomposing vegetable and animal mould in the soil
HUMUSES > HUMUS
HUMUSY > HUMUS
HUMVEE *n* military vehicle
HUMVEES > HUMVEE
HUN *n* member of any of several Asiatic nomadic peoples speaking Mongoloid or Turkic languages
HUNCH *n* feeling or suspicion not based on facts ▷ *vb* draw (one's shoulders) up or together
HUNCHBACK *n* person with an abnormal curvature of the spine
HUNCHED > HUNCH
HUNCHES > HUNCH
HUNCHING > HUNCH
HUNDRED *n* ten times ten ▷ *adj* amounting to a hundred
HUNDREDER *n* inhabitant of a hundred
HUNDREDOR *same as* > HUNDREDER
HUNDREDS > HUNDRED
HUNDREDTH *adj* being the ordinal number of 100 in numbering or counting order, position, time, etc ▷ *n* one of 100 approximately equal parts of something
HUNG > HANG
HUNGAN *same as* > HOUNGAN
HUNGANS > HUNGAN
HUNGER *n* discomfort or weakness from lack of food ▷ *vb* want very much
HUNGERED > HUNGER
HUNGERFUL *adj* hungry
HUNGERING > HUNGER
HUNGERLY *adj* hungry
HUNGERS > HUNGER
HUNGOVER *adj* suffering from hangover
HUNGRIER > HUNGRY
HUNGRIEST > HUNGRY
HUNGRILY > HUNGRY
HUNGRY *adj* desiring food
HUNH *same as* > HUH
HUNK *n* large piece
HUNKER *vb* squat
HUNKERED > HUNKER
HUNKERING > HUNKER
HUNKERS *pl n* haunches
HUNKEY *n* person of Hungarian descent
HUNKEYS > HUNKEY
HUNKIE *same as* > HUNKEY
HUNKIER > HUNKY
HUNKIES > HUNKY
HUNKIEST > HUNKY
HUNKS *n* crotchety old person
HUNKSES > HUNKS
HUNKY *adj* excellent
HUNS > HUN
HUNT *vb* seek out and kill (wild animals) for food or sport ▷ *n* hunting
HUNTABLE > HUNT
HUNTAWAY *n* sheepdog trained to drive sheep by barking
HUNTAWAYS > HUNTAWAY
HUNTED *adj* harassed and worn
HUNTEDLY > HUNT
HUNTER *n* person or animal that hunts wild animals for food or sport
HUNTERS > HUNTER
HUNTING *n* pursuit and killing or capture of game and wild animals, regarded as a sport
HUNTINGS > HUNTING
HUNTRESS *same as* > HUNTER
HUNTS > HUNT
HUNTSMAN *n* man who hunts wild animals, esp foxes
HUNTSMEN > HUNTSMAN
HUP *vb* cry hup to get a horse to move
HUPIRO *in New Zealand English, same as* > STINKWOOD
HUPPAH *variant spelling of* > CHUPPAH
HUPPAHS > HUPPAH
HUPPED > HUP
HUPPING > HUP
HUPS > HUP
HURCHEON *same as* > URCHIN
HURCHEONS > HURCHEON
HURDEN *same as* > HARDEN
HURDENS > HURDEN
HURDIES *pl n* buttocks or haunches
HURDLE *n* light barrier for jumping over in some races ▷ *vb* jump over (something)
HURDLED > HURDLE
HURDLER > HURDLE
HURDLERS > HURDLE
HURDLES > HURDLE
HURDLING > HURDLE
HURDLINGS > HURDLE
HURDS *same as* > HARDS
HURL *vb* throw or utter forcefully ▷ *n* act or an instance of hurling
HURLBAT *same as* > WHIRLBAT
HURLBATS > HURLBAT
HURLED > HURL
HURLER > HURL
HURLERS > HURL
HURLEY *n* another word for HURLING (the game)
HURLEYS > HURLEY
HURLIES > HURLY
HURLING *n* Irish game like hockey
HURLINGS > HURLING
HURLS > HURL
HURLY *n* wheeled barrow
HURRA *same as* > HURRAH
HURRAED > HURRA
HURRAH *interj* exclamation of joy or applause ▷ *n* cheer of joy or victory ▷ *vb* shout "hurrah"
HURRAHED > HURRAH
HURRAHING > HURRAH
HURRAHS > HURRAH
HURRAING > HURRA
HURRAS > HURRA
HURRAY *same as* > HURRAH
HURRAYED > HURRAY
HURRAYING > HURRAY
HURRAYS > HURRAY
HURRICANE *n* very strong, often destructive, wind or storm
HURRICANO *same as* > HURRICANE
HURRIED *adj* done quickly or too quickly
HURRIEDLY > HURRIED
HURRIER > HURRY
HURRIERS > HURRY
HURRIES > HURRY
HURRY *vb* (cause to) move or act very quickly ▷ *n* doing something quickly or the need to do something quickly
HURRYING > HURRY
HURRYINGS > HURRY
HURST *n* wood
HURSTS > HURST
HURT *vb* cause physical or mental pain to ▷ *n* physical or mental pain ▷ *adj* injured or pained
HURTER > HURT
HURTERS > HURT
HURTFUL *adj* unkind
HURTFULLY > HURTFUL
HURTING > HURT
HURTLE *vb* move quickly or violently
HURTLED > HURTLE
HURTLES > HURTLE
HURTLESS *adj* uninjured
HURTLING > HURTLE
HURTS > HURT
HUSBAND *n* woman's partner in marriage ▷ *vb* use economically
HUSBANDED > HUSBAND
HUSBANDER > HUSBAND
HUSBANDLY > HUSBAND
HUSBANDRY *n* farming
HUSBANDS > HUSBAND
HUSH *vb* make or be silent ▷ *n* stillness or silence ▷ *interj* plea or demand for silence
HUSHABIED > HUSHABY
HUSHABIES > HUSHABY

HUSHABY *interj* used in quietening a baby or child to sleep ▷ *n* lullaby ▷ *vb* quieten to sleep

HUSHED > HUSH

HUSHEDLY > HUSH

HUSHER *same as* > USHER

HUSHERED > HUSHER

HUSHERING > HUSHER

HUSHERS > HUSHER

HUSHES > HUSH

HUSHFUL *adj* quiet

HUSHIER > HUSHY

HUSHIEST > HUSHY

HUSHING > HUSH

HUSHPUPPY *n* snack of deep-fried dough

HUSHY *adj* secret

HUSK *n* outer covering of certain seeds and fruits ▷ *vb* remove the husk from

HUSKED > HUSK

HUSKER > HUSK

HUSKERS > HUSK

HUSKIER > HUSKY

HUSKIES > HUSKY

HUSKIEST > HUSKY

HUSKILY > HUSKY

HUSKINESS > HUSKY

HUSKING > HUSK

HUSKINGS > HUSK

HUSKLIKE > HUSK

HUSKS > HUSK

HUSKY *adj* slightly hoarse ▷ *n* Arctic sledge dog with thick hair and a curled tail

HUSO *n* sturgeon

HUSOS > HUSO

HUSS *n* flesh of the European dogfish, when used as food

HUSSAR *n* lightly armed cavalry soldier

HUSSARS > HUSSAR

HUSSES > HUSS

HUSSIES > HUSSY

HUSSIF *n* sewing kit

HUSSIFS > HUSSIF

HUSSY *n* immodest or promiscuous woman

HUSTINGS *pl n* political campaigns and speeches before an election

HUSTLE *vb* push about, jostle ▷ *n* lively activity or bustle

HUSTLED > HUSTLE

HUSTLER > HUSTLE

HUSTLERS > HUSTLE

HUSTLES > HUSTLE

HUSTLING > HUSTLE

HUSTLINGS > HUSTLE

HUSWIFE *same as* > HOUSEWIFE

HUSWIFES > HUSWIFE

HUSWIVES > HUSWIFE

HUT *n* small house, shelter, or shed

HUTCH *n* cage for pet rabbits etc ▷ *vb* store or keep in or as if in a hutch

HUTCHED > HUTCH

HUTCHES > HUTCH

HUTCHIE *n* groundsheet draped over an upright stick, used as a temporary shelter

HUTCHIES > HUTCHIE

HUTCHING > HUTCH

HUTIA *n* rodent of West Indies

HUTIAS > HUTIA

HUTLIKE > HUT

HUTMENT *n* number or group of huts

HUTMENTS > HUTMENT

HUTS > HUT

HUTTED > HUT

HUTTING > HUT

HUTTINGS > HUT

HUTZPA *same as* > HUTZPAH

HUTZPAH *variant spelling of* > CHUTZPAH

HUTZPAHS > HUTZPAH

HUTZPAS > HUTZPA

HUZOOR *n* person of rank in India

HUZOORS > HUZOOR

HUZZA *same as* > HUZZAH

HUZZAED > HUZZA

HUZZAH *archaic word for* > HURRAH

HUZZAHED > HUZZAH

HUZZAHING > HUZZAH

HUZZAHS > HUZZAH

HUZZAING > HUZZA

HUZZAS > HUZZA

HUZZIES > HUZZY

HUZZY *same as* > HUSSY

HWAN *another name for* > WON

HWYL *n* emotional fervour, as in the recitation of poetry

HWYLS > HWYL

HYACINE *same as* > HYACINTH

HYACINES > HYACINE

HYACINTH *n* sweet-smelling spring flower that grows from a bulb

HYACINTHS > HYACINTH

HYAENA *same as* > HYENA

HYAENAS > HYAENA

HYAENIC > HYAENA

HYALIN *n* glassy translucent substance, such as occurs in certain degenerative skin conditions or in hyaline cartilage

HYALINE *adj* clear and translucent, with no fibres or granules ▷ *n* glassy transparent surface

HYALINES > HYALINE

HYALINISE *same as* > HYALINIZE

HYALINIZE *vb* give a glassy consistency to

HYALINS > HYALIN

HYALITE *n* clear and colourless variety of opal in globular form

HYALITES > HYALITE

HYALOGEN *n* insoluble substance in body structures

HYALOGENS > HYALOGEN

HYALOID *adj* clear and transparent ▷ *n* delicate transparent membrane enclosing the vitreous humour of the eye

HYALOIDS > HYALOID

HYALONEMA *n* species of sponge

HYBRID *n* offspring of two plants or animals of different species ▷ *adj* of mixed origin

HYBRIDISE *same as* > HYBRIDIZE

HYBRIDISM > HYBRID

HYBRIDIST > HYBRID

HYBRIDITY > HYBRID

HYBRIDIZE *vb* produce or cause (species) to produce hybrids

HYBRIDOMA *n* hybrid cell formed by the fusion of two different types of cell, esp one capable of producing antibodies, but of limited lifespan, fused with an immortal tumour cell

HYBRIDOUS > HYBRID

HYBRIDS > HYBRID

HYBRIS *same as* > HUBRIS

HYBRISES > HYBRIS

HYBRISTIC > HYBRIS

HYDANTOIN *n* colourless odourless crystalline compound present in beet molasses and used in the manufacture of pharmaceuticals and synthetic resins

HYDATHODE *n* pore in plants, esp on the leaves, specialized for excreting water

HYDATID *n* cyst containing tapeworm larvae

HYDATIDS > HYDATID

HYDATOID *adj* watery

HYDRA *n* mythical many-headed water serpent

HYDRACID *n* acid, such as hydrochloric acid, that does not contain oxygen

HYDRACIDS > HYDRACID

HYDRAE > HYDRA

HYDRAEMIA *n* wateriness of blood

HYDRAGOG *n* drug that removes water

HYDRAGOGS > HYDRAGOG

HYDRANGEA *n* ornamental shrub with clusters of pink, blue, or white flowers

HYDRANT *n* outlet from a water main with a nozzle for a hose

HYDRANTH *n* polyp in a colony of hydrozoan coelenterates that is specialized for feeding rather than reproduction

HYDRANTHS > HYDRANTH

HYDRANTS > HYDRANT

HYDRAS > HYDRA

HYDRASE *n* enzyme that removes water

HYDRASES > HYDRASE

HYDRASTIS *n* any of various Japanese and E North American plants, such as goldenseal, having showy foliage and ornamental red fruits

HYDRATE *n* chemical compound of water with another substance ▷ *vb* treat or impregnate with water

HYDRATED *adj* (of a compound) chemically bonded to water molecules

HYDRATES > HYDRATE

HYDRATING > HYDRATE

HYDRATION > HYDRATE

HYDRATOR > HYDRATE

HYDRATORS > HYDRATE

HYDRAULIC *adj* operated by pressure forced through a pipe by a liquid such as water or oil

HYDRAZIDE *n* any of a class of chemical compounds that result when hydrogen in hydrazine or any of its derivatives is replaced by an acid radical

HYDRAZINE *n* colourless basic liquid made from sodium hypochlorite and ammonia: a strong reducing agent, used chiefly as a rocket fuel

HYDRAZOIC as in *hydrazoic acid* colourless highly explosive liquid

HYDREMIA *same as* > HYDRAEMIA

HYDREMIAS > HYDREMIA

HYDRIA *n* (in ancient Greece and Rome) a large water jar

HYDRIAE > HYDRIA

HYDRIC *adj* of or containing hydrogen

HYDRID *same as* > HYDROID

HYDRIDE *n* compound of hydrogen with another element

HYDRIDES > HYDRIDE

HYDRIDS > HYDRID

HYDRILLA *n* aquatic plant used as an oxygenator in aquaria and pools

HYDRILLAS > HYDRILLA

HYDRIODIC as in *hydriodic acid* colourless or pale yellow aqueous solution of hydrogen iodide: a strong acid

HYDRO *n* hotel offering facilities for hydropathy ▷ *adj* electricity as supplied to a residence, business, etc

HYDROCAST *n* gathering of

water samples for analysis
HYDROCELE *n* abnormal collection of fluid in any saclike space, esp around the testicles
HYDROFOIL *n* fast light boat with its hull raised out of the water on one or more pairs of fins
HYDROGEL *n* gel in which the liquid constituent is water
HYDROGELS > HYDROGEL
HYDROGEN *n* light flammable colourless gas that combines with oxygen to form water > HYDROGENISATION > HYDROGENIZATION
HYDROGENS > HYDROGEN
HYDROID *adj* of or relating to an order of colonial hydrozoan coelenterates that have the polyp phase dominant ▷ *n* hydroid colony or individual
HYDROIDS > HYDROID
HYDROLASE *n* enzyme, such as an esterase, that controls hydrolysis
HYDROLOGY *n* study of the distribution, conservation, and use of the water of the earth and its atmosphere
HYDROLYSE *vb* subject to or undergo hydrolysis
HYDROLYTE *n* substance subjected to hydrolysis
HYDROLYZE *same as* > HYDROLYSE
HYDROMA *same as* > HYGROMA
HYDROMAS > HYDROMA
HYDROMATA > HYDROMA
HYDROMEL *n* another word for MEAD (the drink)
HYDROMELS > HYDROMEL
HYDRONAUT *n* person trained to operate deep submergence vessels
HYDRONIC *adj* using hot water in heating system
HYDRONIUM as in *hydronium ion* positive ion, formed by the attachment of a proton to a water molecule: occurs in solutions of acids and behaves like a hydrogen ion
HYDROPATH > HYDROPATHY
HYDROPIC > HYDROPSY
HYDROPS *n* anaemia in a fetus
HYDROPSES > HYDROPS
HYDROPSY *same as* > DROPSY
HYDROPTIC > HYDROPSY
HYDROPULT *n* type of water pump
HYDROS > HYDRO
HYDROSERE *n* sere that begins in an aquatic environment
HYDROSKI *n* hydrofoil used on some seaplanes to provide extra lift when taking off
HYDROSKIS > HYDROSKI
HYDROSOL *n* sol that has water as its liquid phase
HYDROSOLS > HYDROSOL
HYDROSOMA *same as* > HYDROSOME
HYDROSOME *n* body of a colonial hydrozoan
HYDROSTAT *n* device that detects the presence of water as a prevention against drying out, overflow, etc, esp one used as a warning in a steam boiler
HYDROUS *adj* containing water
HYDROVANE *n* vane on a seaplane conferring stability on water (a sponson) or facilitating take-off (a hydrofoil)
HYDROXIDE *n* compound containing a hydroxyl group or ion
HYDROXY *adj* (of a chemical compound) containing one or more hydroxyl groups
HYDROXYL *adj* of or containing the monovalent group –OH or the ion OH^- ▷ *n* of, consisting of, or containing the monovalent group -OH or the ion OH^-
HYDROXYLS > HYDROXYL
HYDROZOA > HYDROZOON
HYDROZOAN *n* any colonial or solitary coelenterate of the class *Hydrozoa*, which includes the hydra, Portuguese man-of-war, and the sertularians ▷ *adj* of, relating to, or belonging to the *Hydrozoa*
HYDROZOON *same as* > HYDROZOAN
HYDYNE *n* type of rocket fuel
HYDYNES > HYDYNE
HYE *same as* > HIE
HYED > HYE
HYEING > HYE
HYEN *same as* > HYENA
HYENA *n* scavenging doglike mammal of Africa and S Asia
HYENAS > HYENA
HYENIC > HYENA
HYENINE *adj* of hyenas
HYENOID *adj* of or like hyenas
HYENS > HYEN
HYES > HYE
HYETAL *adj* of or relating to rain, rainfall, or rainy regions
HYETOLOGY *n* study of rainfall
HYGEIST *same as* > HYGIENIST
HYGEISTS > HYGEIST
HYGIEIST *same as* > HYGIENIST
HYGIEISTS > HYGIEIST
HYGIENE *n* principles and practice of health and cleanliness
HYGIENES > HYGIENE
HYGIENIC *adj* promoting health or cleanliness
HYGIENICS *same as* > HYGIENE
HYGIENIST *n* person skilled in the practice of hygiene
HYGRISTOR *n* electronic component the resistance of which varies with humidity
HYGRODEIK *n* type of thermometer
HYGROLOGY *n* study of humidity of air
HYGROMA *n* swelling in the soft tissue that occurs over a joint, usually caused by repeated injury
HYGROMAS > HYGROMA
HYGROMATA > HYGROMA
HYGROPHIL *adj* moisture-loving
HYGROSTAT *same as* > HUMIDISTAT
HYING > HIE
HYKE *same as* > HAIK
HYKES > HYKE
HYLA *n* type of tropical American tree frog
HYLAS > HYLA
HYLDING *same as* > HILDING
HYLDINGS > HYLDING
HYLE *n* wood
HYLEG *n* dominant planet when someone is born
HYLEGS > HYLEG
HYLES > HYLE
HYLIC *adj* solid
HYLICISM *n* materialism
HYLICISMS > HYLICISM
HYLICIST > HYLICISM
HYLICISTS > HYLICISM
HYLISM *same as* > HYLICISM
HYLISMS > HYLISM
HYLIST > HYLISM
HYLISTS > HYLISM
HYLOBATE *n* gibbon
HYLOBATES > HYLOBATE
HYLOIST *n* materialist
HYLOISTS > HYLOIST
HYLOPHYTE *n* plant that grows in woods
HYLOZOIC > HYLOZOISM
HYLOZOISM *n* philosophical doctrine that life is one of the properties of matter
HYLOZOIST > HYLOZOISM
HYMEN *n* membrane partly covering the opening of a girl's vagina, which breaks before puberty or at the first occurrence of sexual intercourse
HYMENAEAL *same as* > HYMENEAL
HYMENAEAN > HYMEN
HYMENAL > HYMEN
HYMENEAL *adj* of or relating to marriage ▷ *n* wedding song or poem
HYMENEALS > HYMENEAL
HYMENEAN > HYMEN
HYMENIA > HYMENIUM
HYMENIAL > HYMENIUM
HYMENIUM *n* (in basidiomycetous and ascomycetous fungi) a layer of cells some of which produce the spores
HYMENIUMS > HYMENIUM
HYMENS > HYMEN
HYMN *n* Christian song of praise sung to God or a saint ▷ *vb* express (praises, thanks, etc) by singing hymns
HYMNAL *n* book of hymns ▷ *adj* of, relating to, or characteristic of hymns
HYMNALS > HYMNAL
HYMNARIES > HYMNARY
HYMNARY *same as* > HYMNAL
HYMNBOOK *n* book containing the words and music of hymns
HYMNBOOKS > HYMNBOOK
HYMNED > HYMN
HYMNIC > HYMN
HYMNING > HYMN
HYMNIST *n* person who composes hymns
HYMNISTS > HYMNIST
HYMNLESS > HYMN
HYMNLIKE > HYMN
HYMNODIES > HYMNODY
HYMNODIST *same as* > HYMNIST
HYMNODY *n* composition or singing of hymns
HYMNOLOGY *same as* > HYMNODY
HYMNS > HYMN
HYNDE *same as* > HIND
HYNDES > HYNDE
HYOID *adj* of or relating to the hyoid bone ▷ *n* horseshoe-shaped bone that lies at the base of the tongue and above the thyroid cartilage
HYOIDAL *adj* of or relating to the hyoid bone
HYOIDEAN *same as* > HYOIDAL
HYOIDS > HYOID
HYOSCINE *another name for* > SCOPOLAMINE
HYOSCINES > HYOSCINE
HYP *same as* > HYPOTENUSE
HYPALGIA *n* reduced ability to feel pain
HYPALGIAS > HYPALGIA
HYPALLAGE *n* figure of speech in which the natural relations of two words in a statement are interchanged, as in *the fire*

spread the wind

HYPANTHIA *n* plural of hypanthium: cup-shaped receptacle of perigynous or epigynous flowers

HYPATE *n* string of lyre

HYPATES > HYPATE

HYPE *n* intensive or exaggerated publicity or sales promotion ▷ *vb* promote (a product) using intensive or exaggerated publicity

HYPED > HYPE

HYPER > HYPE

HYPERACID *adj* having excess acidity

HYPERARID *adj* extremely dry

HYPERBOLA *n* curve produced when a cone is cut by a plane at a steeper angle to its base than its side

HYPERBOLE *n* deliberate exaggeration for effect

HYPERCUBE *n* figure in a space of four or more dimensions having all its sides equal and all its angles right angles

HYPEREMIA *n* excessive blood in an organ or part

HYPEREMIC > HYPEREMIA

HYPERFINE as in *hyperfine structure* splitting of a spectral line of an atom or molecule into two or more closely spaced components as a result of interaction of the electrons with the magnetic moments of the nuclei

HYPERGAMY *n* custom that forbids a woman to marry a man of lower social status

HYPERGOL *n* type of fuel

HYPERGOLS > HYPERGOL

HYPERICUM *n* herbaceous plant or shrub

HYPERLINK *n* link from a hypertext file that gives users instant access to related material in another file ▷ *vb* link (files) in this way

HYPERMART *n* very large supermarket

HYPERNOVA *n* exploding star that produces even more energy and light than a supernova

HYPERNYM *n* superordinate

HYPERNYMS > HYPERNYM

HYPERNYMY > HYPERNYM

HYPERON *n* any baryon that is not a nucleon

HYPERONS > HYPERON

HYPEROPE *n* person with hyperopia

HYPEROPES > HYPEROPE

HYPEROPIA *n* inability to see near objects clearly because the images received by the eye are focused behind the retina

HYPEROPIC > HYPEROPIA

HYPERPNEA *n* increase in breathing rate

HYPERPURE *adj* extremely pure

HYPERREAL *adj* involving or characterized by particularly realistic graphic representation ▷ *n* that which constitutes hyperreality

HYPERS > HYPE

HYPERTEXT *n* computer software and hardware that allows users to store and view text and move between related items easily

HYPES > HYPE

HYPESTER *n* person or organization that gives an idea or product intense publicity in order to promote it

HYPESTERS > HYPESTER

HYPETHRAL *adj* having no roof

HYPHA *n* any of the filaments that constitute the body (mycelium) of a fungus

HYPHAE > HYPHA

HYPHAL > HYPHA

HYPHEMIA *n* bleeding inside eye

HYPHEMIAS > HYPHEMIA

HYPHEN *n* punctuation mark (-) indicating that two words or syllables are connected ▷ *vb* hyphenate

HYPHENATE *vb* separate (words) with a hyphen

HYPHENED > HYPHEN

HYPHENIC > HYPHEN

HYPHENING > HYPHEN

HYPHENISE *same as* > HYPHENIZE

HYPHENISM > HYPHEN

HYPHENIZE *same as* > HYPHENATE

HYPHENS > HYPHEN

HYPING > HYPE

HYPINOSES > HYPINOSIS

HYPINOSIS *n* protein deficiency in blood

HYPNIC *n* sleeping drug

HYPNICS > HYPNIC

HYPNOGENY *n* hypnosis

HYPNOID *adj* of or relating to a state resembling sleep or hypnosis

HYPNOIDAL *same as* > HYPNOID

HYPNOLOGY *n* study of sleep and hypnosis

HYPNONE *n* sleeping drug

HYPNONES > HYPNONE

HYPNOSES > HYPNOSIS

HYPNOSIS *n* artificially induced state of relaxation in which the mind is more than usually receptive to suggestion

HYPNOTEE *n* person being hypnotized

HYPNOTEES > HYPNOTEE

HYPNOTIC *adj* of or (as if) producing hypnosis ▷ *n* drug that induces sleep

HYPNOTICS > HYPNOTIC

HYPNOTISE *same as* > HYPNOTIZE

HYPNOTISM *n* inducing hypnosis in someone

HYPNOTIST *n* person skilled in the theory and practice of hypnosis

HYPNOTIZE *vb* induce hypnosis in (a person)

HYPNOTOID *adj* like hypnosis

HYPNUM *n* species of moss

HYPNUMS > HYPNUM

HYPO *vb* inject with a hypodermic syringe

HYPOACID *adj* abnormally acidic

HYPOBARIC *adj* below normal pressure

HYPOBLAST *n* inner layer of an embryo at an early stage of development that becomes the endoderm at gastrulation

HYPOBOLE *n* act of anticipating objection

HYPOBOLES > HYPOBOLE

HYPOCAUST *n* ancient Roman heating system in which hot air circulated under the floor and between double walls

HYPOCIST *n* type of juice

HYPOCISTS > HYPOCIST

HYPOCOTYL *n* part of an embryo plant between the cotyledons and the radicle

HYPOCRISY *n* (instance of) pretence of having standards or beliefs that are contrary to one's real character or actual behaviour

HYPOCRITE *n* person who pretends to be what he or she is not

HYPODERM *n* layer of thick-walled tissue in some plants

HYPODERMA *n* layer of skin tissue

HYPODERMS > HYPODERM

HYPOED > HYPO

HYPOGAEA > HYPOGAEUM

HYPOGAEAL > HYPOGAEUM

HYPOGAEAN > HYPOGAEUM

HYPOGAEUM *same as* > HYPOGEUM

HYPOGEA > HYPOGEUM

HYPOGEAL *adj* occurring or living below the surface of the ground

HYPOGEAN > HYPOGEUM

HYPOGENE *adj* formed, taking place, or originating beneath the surface of the earth

HYPOGENIC > HYPOGENE

HYPOGEOUS *same as* > HYPOGEAL

HYPOGEUM *n* underground vault, esp one used for burials

HYPOGYNY *adj* having the gynoecium above the other floral parts

HYPOID as in *hypoid gear* gear having a tooth form generated by a hypocycloidal curve; used extensively in motor vehicle transmissions to withstand a high surface loading

HYPOING > HYPO

HYPOMANIA *n* abnormal condition of extreme excitement, milder than mania but characterized by great optimism and overactivity and often by reckless spending of money

HYPOMANIC > HYPOMANIA

HYPOMORPH *n* mutant gene

HYPONASTY *n* increased growth of the lower surface of a plant part, resulting in an upward bending of the part

HYPONEA *same as* > HYPOPNEA

HYPONEAS > HYPONEA

HYPONOIA *n* underlying meaning

HYPONOIAS > HYPONOIA

HYPONYM *n* word whose meaning is included in that of another word

HYPONYMS > HYPONYM

HYPONYMY > HYPONYM

HYPOPHYGE *another name for* > APOPHYGE

HYPOPLOID *adj* having or designating a chromosome number that is less than a multiple of the haploid number

HYPOPNEA *same as* > HYPOPNOEA

HYPOPNEAS > HYPOPNEA

HYPOPNEIC > HYPOPNEA

HYPOPNOEA *n* abnormally shallow breathing, usually accompanied by a decrease in the breathing rate

HYPOPYON *n* pus in eye

HYPOPYONS > HYPOPYON

HYPOS > HYPO

HYPOSTOME *n* invertebrate body part

HYPOSTYLE *adj* having a roof supported by columns ▷ *n* building constructed in this way

HYPOTAXES > HYPOTAXIS

HYPOTAXIS *n* subordination of one clause to another by a conjunction
HYPOTHEC *n* charge on property in favour of a creditor
HYPOTHECA *n* inner and younger layer of the cell wall of a diatom
HYPOTHECS > HYPOTHEC
HYPOTONIA *n* state of being hypnotized
HYPOTONIC *adj* (of muscles) lacking normal tone or tension
HYPOXEMIA *n* lack of oxygen in blood
HYPOXEMIC > HYPOXEMIA
HYPOXIA *n* deficiency in the amount of oxygen delivered to the body tissues
HYPOXIAS > HYPOXIA
HYPOXIC > HYPOXIA
HYPPED > HYP
HYPPING > HYP
HYPS > HYP
HYPURAL *adj* below the tail
HYRACES > HYRAX
HYRACOID *adj* of, relating to, or belonging to the mammalian order *Hyracoidea*, which contains the hyraxes ▷ *n* hyrax
HYRACOIDS > HYRACOID
HYRAX *n* type of hoofed rodent-like animal of Africa and Asia
HYRAXES > HYRAX
HYSON *n* Chinese green tea
HYSONS > HYSON
HYSSOP *n* sweet-smelling herb used in folk medicine
HYSSOPS > HYSSOP
HYSTERIA *n* state of uncontrolled excitement, anger, or panic
HYSTERIAS > HYSTERIA
HYSTERIC *adj* of or suggesting hysteria
HYSTERICS *pl n* attack of hysteria
HYSTEROID *adj* resembling hysteria
HYTE *adj* insane
HYTHE *same as* > HITHE
HYTHES > HYTHE

Ii

IAMB *n* metrical foot of two syllables, a short one followed by a long one
IAMBI > IAMBUS
IAMBIC *adj* written in metrical units of one short and one long syllable ▷ *n* iambic foot, line, or stanza
IAMBICS > IAMBIC
IAMBIST *n* one who writes iambs
IAMBISTS > IAMBIST
IAMBS > IAMB
IAMBUS *same as* > IAMB
IAMBUSES > IAMBUS
IANTHINE *adj* violet
IATRIC *adj* relating to medicine or physicians
IATRICAL *same as* > IATRIC
IATROGENY *n* disease caused by medical intervention
IBERIS *n* plant with white or purple flowers
IBERISES > IBERIS
IBEX *n* wild goat with large backward-curving horns
IBEXES > IBEX
IBICES > IBEX
IBIDEM *adv* in the same place
IBIS *n* large wading bird with long legs
IBISES > IBIS
IBOGAINE *n* dopamine blocker
IBOGAINES > IBOGAINE
IBUPROFEN *n* drug that relieves pain and reduces inflammation
ICE *n* water in the solid state, formed by freezing liquid water ▷ *vb* form or cause to form ice
ICEBALL *n* ball of ice
ICEBALLS > ICEBALL
ICEBERG *n* large floating mass of ice
ICEBERGS > ICEBERG
ICEBLINK *n* yellowish-white reflected glare in the sky over an ice field
ICEBLINKS > ICEBLINK
ICEBOAT *n* boat that breaks up bodies of ice in water
ICEBOATER > ICEBOAT
ICEBOATS > ICEBOAT
ICEBOUND *adj* covered or made immobile by ice
ICEBOX *n* refrigerator
ICEBOXES > ICEBOX
ICECAP *n* mass of ice permanently covering an area
ICECAPPED *adj* having an icecap
ICECAPS > ICECAP
ICED *adj* covered with icing
ICEFALL *n* very steep part of a glacier that has deep crevasses and resembles a frozen waterfall
ICEFALLS > ICEFALL
ICEFIELD *n* very large flat expanse of ice floating in the sea; large ice floe
ICEFIELDS > ICEFIELD
ICEHOUSE *n* building for storing ice
ICEHOUSES > ICEHOUSE
ICEKHANA *n* motor race on a frozen lake
ICEKHANAS > ICEKHANA
ICELESS > ICE
ICELIKE > ICE
ICEMAKER *n* device for making ice
ICEMAKERS > ICEMAKER
ICEMAN *n* person who sells or delivers ice
ICEMEN > ICEMAN
ICEPACK *n* bag or folded cloth containing ice, applied to a part of the body, esp the head, to cool, reduce swelling, etc
ICEPACKS > ICEPACK
ICER *n* person who ices cakes
ICERS > ICER
ICES > ICE
ICESTONE *n* cryolite
ICESTONES > ICESTONE
ICEWINE *n* dessert wine made from grapes that have frozen before being harvested
ICEWINES > ICEWINE
ICH *archaic form of* > EKE
ICHABOD *interj* the glory has departed
ICHED > ICH
ICHES > ICH
ICHING > ICH
ICHNEUMON *n* greyish-brown mongoose
ICHNITE *n* trace fossil
ICHNITES > ICHNITE
ICHNOLITE *same as* > ICHNITE
ICHNOLOGY *n* study of trace fossils
ICHOR *n* fluid said to flow in the veins of the gods
ICHOROUS > ICHOR
ICHORS > ICHOR
ICHS > ICH
ICHTHIC *same as* > ICHTHYIC
ICHTHYIC *adj* of, relating to, or characteristic of fishes
ICHTHYOID *adj* resembling a fish ▷ *n* fishlike vertebrate
ICHTHYS *n* early Christian emblem
ICHTHYSES > ICHTHYS
ICICLE *n* tapering spike of ice hanging where water has dripped
ICICLED *adj* covered with icicles
ICICLES > ICICLE
ICIER > ICY
ICIEST > ICY
ICILY *adv* in an icy or reserved manner
ICINESS *n* condition of being icy or very cold
ICINESSES > ICINESS
ICING *n* mixture of sugar and water etc, used to cover and decorate cakes
ICINGS > ICING
ICK *interj* expression of disgust
ICKER *n* ear of corn
ICKERS > ICKER
ICKIER > ICKY
ICKIEST > ICKY
ICKILY > ICKY
ICKINESS > ICKY
ICKLE *ironically childish word for* > LITTLE
ICKLER > ICKLE
ICKLEST > ICKLE
ICKY *adj* sticky
ICON *n* picture of Christ or another religious figure, regarded as holy in the

Orthodox Church
ICONES > ICON
ICONIC *adj* relating to, resembling, or having the character of an icon
ICONICAL *same as* > ICONIC
ICONICITY > ICONIC
ICONIFIED > ICONIFY
ICONIFIES > ICONIFY
ICONIFY *vb* render as an icon
ICONISE *same as* > ICONIZE
ICONISED > ICONISE
ICONISES > ICONISE
ICONISING > ICONISE
ICONIZE *vb* render as an icon
ICONIZED > ICONIZE
ICONIZES > ICONIZE
ICONIZING > ICONIZE
ICONOLOGY *n* study or field of art history concerning icons
ICONOSTAS *same as* > ICONOSTASIS
ICONS > ICON
ICTAL > ICTUS
ICTERIC > ICTERUS
ICTERICAL > ICTERUS
ICTERICS > ICTERUS
ICTERID *n* bird of the oriole family
ICTERIDS > ICTERID
ICTERINE > ICTERID
ICTERUS *n* yellowing of plant leaves, caused by excessive cold or moisture
ICTERUSES > ICTERUS
ICTIC > ICTUS
ICTUS *n* metrical or rhythmic stress in verse feet, as contrasted with the stress accent on words
ICTUSES > ICTUS
ICY *adj* very cold
ID *n* mind's instinctive unconscious energies
IDANT *n* chromosome
IDANTS > IDANT
IDE *n* silver orfe fish
IDEA *n* plan or thought formed in the mind ▷ *vb* have or form an idea
IDEAED > IDEA
IDEAL *adj* most suitable ▷ *n* conception of something that is perfect
IDEALESS > IDEA
IDEALISE *same as* > IDEALIZE
IDEALISED > IDEALISE
IDEALISER > IDEALISE
IDEALISES > IDEALISE
IDEALISM *n* tendency to seek perfection in everything
IDEALISMS > IDEALISM
IDEALIST > IDEALISM
IDEALISTS > IDEALISM
IDEALITY > IDEAL
IDEALIZE *vb* regard or portray as perfect or nearly perfect
IDEALIZED > IDEALIZE
IDEALIZER > IDEALIZE
IDEALIZES > IDEALIZE
IDEALLESS > IDEAL
IDEALLY > IDEAL
IDEALNESS > IDEAL
IDEALOGUE *corruption of* > IDEOLOGUE
IDEALOGY *corruption of* > IDEOLOGY
IDEALS > IDEAL
IDEAS > IDEA
IDEATA > IDEATUM
IDEATE *vb* form or have an idea of
IDEATED > IDEATE
IDEATES > IDEATE
IDEATING > IDEATE
IDEATION > IDEATE
IDEATIONS > IDEATE
IDEATIVE > IDEATE
IDEATUM *n* objective reality with which human ideas are supposed to correspond
IDEE *n* idea
IDEES > IDEE
IDEM *adj* same: used to refer to an article, chapter, or book already quoted
IDENT *n* short visual image employed between television programmes that works as a logo to locate the viewer to the channel
IDENTIC *adj* (esp of opinions expressed by two or more governments) having the same wording or intention regarding another power
IDENTICAL *adj* exactly the same
IDENTIFY *vb* prove or recognize as being a certain person or thing
IDENTIKIT *n* trademark name for a set of transparencies of various typical facial characteristics that can be superimposed on one another to build up a picture of a person sought by the police
IDENTITY *n* state of being a specified person or thing
IDENTS > IDENT
IDEOGRAM *n* character or symbol that directly represents a concept or thing, rather than the sounds that form its name
IDEOGRAMS > IDEOGRAM
IDEOGRAPH *same as* > IDEOGRAM
IDEOLOGIC > IDEOLOGY
IDEOLOGUE *same as* > IDEOLOGIST
IDEOLOGY *n* body of ideas and beliefs of a group, nation, etc
IDEOMOTOR *adj* designating automatic muscular movements stimulated by ideas
IDEOPHONE *n* sound that represents a complete idea
IDES *n* (in the Ancient Roman calendar) the 15th of March, May, July, or October, or the 13th of other months
IDIOBLAST *n* plant cell that differs from those around it in the same tissue
IDIOCIES > IDIOCY
IDIOCY *n* utter stupidity
IDIOGRAM *another name for* > KARYOGRAM
IDIOGRAMS > IDIOGRAM
IDIOGRAPH *n* trademark
IDIOLECT *n* variety or form of a language used by an individual
IDIOLECTS > IDIOLECT
IDIOM *n* group of words which when used together have a different meaning from the words individually
IDIOMATIC > IDIOM
IDIOMS > IDIOM
IDIOPATHY *n* any disease of unknown cause
IDIOPHONE *n* percussion instrument, such as a cymbal or xylophone, made of naturally sonorous material
IDIOPLASM *n* germ plasm
IDIOT *n* foolish or stupid person
IDIOTCIES > IDIOTCY
IDIOTCY *same as* > IDIOCY
IDIOTIC *adj* of or resembling an idiot
IDIOTICAL *same as* > IDIOTIC
IDIOTICON *n* dictionary of dialect
IDIOTISH *same as* > IDIOTIC
IDIOTISM *archaic word for* > IDIOCY
IDIOTISMS > IDIOTISM
IDIOTS > IDIOT
IDIOTYPE *n* unique part of antibody
IDIOTYPES > IDIOTYPE
IDIOTYPIC > IDIOTYPE
IDLE *adj* not doing anything ▷ *vb* spend (time) doing very little
IDLED > IDLE
IDLEHOOD > IDLE
IDLEHOODS > IDLE
IDLENESS > IDLE
IDLER *n* person who idles
IDLERS > IDLER
IDLES > IDLE
IDLESSE > IDLE
IDLESSES > IDLE
IDLEST > IDLE
IDLING > IDLE
IDLY > IDLE
IDOCRASE *n* green, brown, or yellow mineral
IDOCRASES > IDOCRASE
IDOL *n* object of excessive devotion
IDOLA > IDOLUM
IDOLATER > IDOLATRY
IDOLATERS > IDOLATRY
IDOLATOR > IDOLATRY
IDOLATORS > IDOLATRY
IDOLATRY *n* worship of idols
IDOLISE *same as* > IDOLIZE
IDOLISED > IDOLISE
IDOLISER > IDOLISE
IDOLISERS > IDOLISE
IDOLISES > IDOLISE
IDOLISING > IDOLISE
IDOLISM > IDOLIZE
IDOLISMS > IDOL
IDOLIST > IDOLIZE
IDOLISTS > IDOLIZE
IDOLIZE *vb* love or admire excessively
IDOLIZED > IDOLIZE
IDOLIZER > IDOLIZE
IDOLIZERS > IDOLIZE
IDOLIZES > IDOLIZE
IDOLIZING > IDOLIZE
IDOLS > IDOL
IDOLUM *n* mental picture
IDONEITY > IDONEOUS
IDONEOUS *adj* appropriate
IDS > ID
IDYL *same as* > IDYLL
IDYLIST *same as* > IDYLLIST
IDYLISTS > IDYLIST
IDYLL *n* scene or time of great peace and happines
IDYLLIAN *same as* > IDYLLI
IDYLLIC *adj* of or relating to an idyll
IDYLLIST *n* writer of idylls
IDYLLISTS > IDYLLIST
IDYLLS > IDYLL
IDYLS > IDYL
IF *n* uncertainty or doubt
IFF *n* military system using radar transmissions to which equipment carried by friendly forces automatically responds with a precoded signal
IFFIER > IFFY
IFFIEST > IFFY
IFFINESS > IFFY
IFFY *adj* doubtful, uncertain
IFS > IF
IFTAR *n* meal eaten by Muslims to break their fast after sunset every day during Ramadan
IFTARS > IFTAR
IGAD *same as* > EGAD
IGAPO *n* flooded forest
IGAPOS > IGAPO
IGARAPE *n* canoe route
IGARAPES > IGARAPE
IGG *vb* antagonize
IGGED > IGG
IGGING > IGG
IGGS > IGG
IGLOO *n* dome-shaped Inuit house made of snow and ice

GLOOS > IGLOO
GLU *same as* > IGLOO
GLUS > IGLU
GNARO *n* ignoramus
GNAROES > IGNARO
GNAROS > IGNARO
GNATIA *n* dried seed
GNATIAS > IGNATIA
GNEOUS *adj* (of rock) formed as molten rock cools and hardens
GNESCENT *adj* giving off sparks when struck, as a flint ▷ *n* ignescent substance
GNIFIED > IGNIFY
GNIFIES > IGNIFY
GNIFY *vb* turn into fire
GNIFYING > IGNIFY
GNITABLE > IGNITE
GNITE *vb* catch fire or set fire to
GNITED > IGNITE
GNITER *n* person or thing that ignites
GNITERS > IGNITER
GNITES > IGNITE
GNITIBLE > IGNITE
GNITING > IGNITE
GNITION *n* system that ignites the fuel-and-air mixture to start an engine
GNITIONS > IGNITION
GNITOR *same as* > IGNITER
GNITORS > IGNITER
GNITRON *n* mercury-arc rectifier controlled by a subsidiary electrode
GNITRONS > IGNITRON
GNOBLE *adj* dishonourable
GNOBLER > IGNOBLE
GNOBLEST > IGNOBLE
GNOBLY > IGNOBLE
GNOMIES > IGNOMY
GNOMINY *n* humiliating disgrace
GNOMY *Shakespearean variant of* > IGNOMINY
GNORABLE > IGNORE
GNORAMI > IGNORAMUS
GNORAMUS *n* ignorant person
GNORANCE *n* lack of knowledge or education
GNORANT *adj* lacking knowledge ▷ *n* ignorant person
GNORANTS > IGNORANT
GNORE *vb* refuse to notice, disregard deliberately ▷ *n* disregard
GNORED > IGNORE
GNORER > IGNORE
GNORERS > IGNORE
GNORES > IGNORE
GNORING > IGNORE
GUANA *n* large tropical American lizard
GUANAS > IGUANA
GUANIAN > IGUANA
GUANIANS > IGUANA
GUANID *same as* > IGUANA
GUANIDS > IGUANID
GUANODON *n* massive herbivorous long-tailed bipedal dinosaur
IHRAM *n* customary white robes worn by Muslim pilgrims to Mecca, symbolizing a sacred or consecrated state
IHRAMS > IHRAM
IJTIHAD *n* effort of a Muslim scholar to derive a legal ruling from the Koran
IJTIHADS > IJTIHAD
IKAN *n* (in Malaysia) fish used esp in names of cooked dishes
IKANS > IKAN
IKAT *n* method of creating patterns in fabric by tie-dyeing the yarn before weaving
IKATS > IKAT
IKEBANA *n* Japanese art of flower arrangement
IKEBANAS > IKEBANA
IKON *same as* > ICON
IKONS > IKON
ILEA > ILEUM
ILEAC *adj* of or relating to the ileum
ILEAL *same as* > ILEAC
ILEITIDES > ILEITIS
ILEITIS *n* inflammation of the ileum
ILEITISES > ILEITIS
ILEOSTOMY *n* surgical formation of a permanent opening through the abdominal wall into the ileum
ILEUM *n* lowest part of the small intestine
ILEUS *n* obstruction of the intestine, esp the ileum, by mechanical occlusion or as the result of distension of the bowel following loss of muscular action
ILEUSES > ILEUS
ILEX *n* any of a genus of trees or shrubs that includes holly
ILEXES > ILEX
ILIA > ILIUM
ILIAC *adj* of or relating to the ilium
ILIACUS *n* iliac
ILIACUSES > ILIACUS
ILIAD *n* epic poem
ILIADS > ILIAD
ILIAL > ILIUM
ILICES > ILEX
ILIUM *n* uppermost and widest of the three sections of the hipbone
ILK *n* type ▷ *determiner* each
ILKA *same as* > ILK
ILKADAY *n* every day
ILKADAYS > ILKADAY
ILKS > ILK
ILL *adj* not in good health ▷ *n* evil, harm ▷ *adv* badly
ILLAPSE *vb* slide in
ILLAPSED > ILLAPSE
ILLAPSES > ILLAPSE
ILLAPSING > ILLAPSE
ILLATION *rare word for* > INFERENCE
ILLATIONS > ILLATION
ILLATIVE *adj* of or relating to illation ▷ *n* illative case
ILLATIVES > ILLATIVE
ILLEGAL *adj* against the law ▷ *n* person who has entered or attempted to enter a country illegally
ILLEGALLY > ILLEGAL
ILLEGALS > ILLEGAL
ILLEGIBLE *adj* unable to be read or deciphered
ILLEGIBLY > ILLEGIBLE
ILLER > ILL
ILLEST > ILL
ILLIAD *n* wink
ILLIADS > ILLIAD
ILLIBERAL *adj* narrow-minded, intolerant
ILLICIT *adj* illegal
ILLICITLY > ILLICIT
ILLIMITED *adj* infinite
ILLINIUM *n* type of radioactive element
ILLINIUMS > ILLINIUM
ILLIPE *n* Asian tree
ILLIPES > ILLIPE
ILLIQUID *adj* (of an asset) not easily convertible into cash
ILLISION *n* act of striking against
ILLISIONS > ILLISION
ILLITE *n* clay mineral of the mica group, found in shales and mudstones
ILLITES > ILLITE
ILLITIC > ILLITE
ILLNESS *n* disease or indisposition
ILLNESSES > ILLNESS
ILLOGIC *n* reasoning characterized by lack of logic
ILLOGICAL *adj* unreasonable
ILLOGICS > ILLOGIC
ILLS > ILL
ILLTH *n* condition of poverty or misery
ILLTHS > ILLTH
ILLUDE *vb* trick or deceive
ILLUDED > ILLUDE
ILLUDES > ILLUDE
ILLUDING > ILLUDE
ILLUME *vb* illuminate
ILLUMED > ILLUME
ILLUMES > ILLUME
ILLUMINE *vb* throw light in or into
ILLUMINED > ILLUMINE
ILLUMINER *n* illuminator
ILLUMINES > ILLUMINE
ILLUMING > ILLUME
ILLUPI *same as* > ILLIPE
ILLUPIS > ILLUPI
ILLUSION *n* deceptive appearance or belief
ILLUSIONS > ILLUSION
ILLUSIVE *same as* > ILLUSORY
ILLUSORY *adj* seeming to be true, but actually false
ILLUVIA > ILLUVIUM
ILLUVIAL > ILLUVIUM
ILLUVIATE *vb* deposit illuvium
ILLUVIUM *n* material, which includes colloids and mineral salts, that is washed down from one layer of soil to a lower layer
ILLUVIUMS > ILLUVIUM
ILLY *adv* badly
ILMENITE *n* black mineral found in igneous rocks as layered deposits and in veins
ILMENITES > ILMENITE
IMAGE *n* mental picture of someone or something ▷ *vb* picture in the mind
IMAGEABLE > IMAGE
IMAGED > IMAGE
IMAGELESS > IMAGE
IMAGER *n* device that produces images
IMAGERIES > IMAGERY
IMAGERS > IMAGER
IMAGERY *n* images collectively, esp in the arts
IMAGES > IMAGE
IMAGINAL *adj* of, relating to, or resembling an imago
IMAGINARY *adj* existing only in the imagination
IMAGINE *vb* form a mental image of ▷ *sentence substitute* exclamation of surprise
IMAGINED > IMAGINE
IMAGINER > IMAGINE
IMAGINERS > IMAGINE
IMAGINES > IMAGO
IMAGING > IMAGE
IMAGINGS > IMAGE
IMAGINING > IMAGINE
IMAGINIST *n* imaginative person
IMAGISM *n* poetic movement in England and America between 1912 and 1917
IMAGISMS > IMAGISM
IMAGIST > IMAGISM
IMAGISTIC > IMAGISM
IMAGISTS > IMAGISM
IMAGO *n* sexually mature adult insect
IMAGOES > IMAGO
IMAGOS > IMAGO
IMAM *n* leader of prayers in a mosque
IMAMATE *n* region or territory governed by an imam
IMAMATES > IMAMATE
IMAMS > IMAM
IMARET *n* (in Turkey) a hospice for pilgrims or travellers
IMARETS > IMARET
IMARI *n* Japanese porcelain
IMARIS > IMARI

IMAUM *same as* > IMAM
IMAUMS > IMAUM
IMBALANCE *n* lack of balance or proportion
IMBALM *same as* > EMBALM
IMBALMED > IMBALM
IMBALMER > IMBALM
IMBALMERS > IMBALM
IMBALMING > IMBALM
IMBALMS > IMBALM
IMBAR *vb* bar in
IMBARK *vb* cover in bark
IMBARKED > IMBARK
IMBARKING > IMBARK
IMBARKS > IMBARK
IMBARRED > IMBAR
IMBARRING > IMBAR
IMBARS > IMBAR
IMBASE *vb* degrade
IMBASED > IMBASE
IMBASES > IMBASE
IMBASING > IMBASE
IMBATHE *vb* bathe
IMBATHED > IMBATHE
IMBATHES > IMBATHE
IMBATHING > IMBATHE
IMBECILE *n* stupid person ▷ *adj* stupid or senseless
IMBECILES > IMBECILE
IMBECILIC > IMBECILE
IMBED *same as* > EMBED
IMBEDDED > IMBED
IMBEDDING > IMBED
IMBEDS > IMBED
IMBIBE *vb* drink (alcoholic drinks)
IMBIBED > IMBIBE
IMBIBER > IMBIBE
IMBIBERS > IMBIBE
IMBIBES > IMBIBE
IMBIBING > IMBIBE
IMBITTER *same as* > EMBITTER
IMBITTERS > IMBITTER
IMBIZO *n* meeting, esp a gathering of the Zulu people called by the king or a traditional leader
IMBIZOS > IMBIZO
IMBLAZE *vb* depict heraldically
IMBLAZED > IMBLAZE
IMBLAZES > IMBLAZE
IMBLAZING > IMBLAZE
IMBODIED > IMBODY
IMBODIES > IMBODY
IMBODY *same as* > EMBODY
IMBODYING > IMBODY
IMBOLDEN *same as* > EMBOLDEN
IMBOLDENS > IMBOLDEN
IMBORDER *vb* enclose in a border
IMBORDERS > IMBORDER
IMBOSK *vb* conceal
IMBOSKED > IMBOSK
IMBOSKING > IMBOSK
IMBOSKS > IMBOSK
IMBOSOM *vb* hold in one's heart
IMBOSOMED > IMBOSOM
IMBOSOMS > IMBOSOM
IMBOSS *same as* > EMBOSS
IMBOSSED > IMBOSS
IMBOSSES > IMBOSS
IMBOSSING > IMBOSS
IMBOWER *vb* enclose in a bower
IMBOWERED > IMBOWER
IMBOWERS > IMBOWER
IMBRANGLE *vb* entangle
IMBRAST *Spenserian past participle of* > EMBRACE
IMBREX *n* curved tile
IMBRICATE *adj* having tiles or slates that overlap ▷ *vb* decorate with a repeating pattern resembling scales or overlapping tiles
IMBRICES > IMBREX
IMBROGLIO *n* confusing and complicated situation
IMBROWN *vb* make brown
IMBROWNED > IMBROWN
IMBROWNS > IMBROWN
IMBRUE *vb* stain, esp with blood
IMBRUED > IMBRUE
IMBRUES > IMBRUE
IMBRUING > IMBRUE
IMBRUTE *vb* reduce to a bestial state
IMBRUTED > IMBRUTE
IMBRUTES > IMBRUTE
IMBRUTING > IMBRUTE
IMBUE *vb* fill or inspire with (ideals or principles)
IMBUED > IMBUE
IMBUEMENT > IMBUE
IMBUES > IMBUE
IMBUING > IMBUE
IMBURSE *vb* pay
IMBURSED > IMBURSE
IMBURSES > IMBURSE
IMBURSING > IMBURSE
IMID *n* immunomodulatory drug
IMIDAZOLE *n* white crystalline basic heterocyclic compound
IMIDE *n* any of a class of organic compounds
IMIDES > IMIDE
IMIDIC > IMIDE
IMIDO > IMIDE
IMIDS > IMID
IMINAZOLE *same as* > IMIDAZOLE
IMINE *n* any of a class of organic compounds
IMINES > IMINE
IMINO > IMINE
IMINOUREA *another name for* > GUANIDINE
IMITABLE > IMITATE
IMITANCY *n* tendency to imitate
IMITANT *same as* > IMITATION
IMITANTS > IMITANT
IMITATE *vb* take as a model
IMITATED > IMITATE
IMITATES > IMITATE
IMITATING > IMITATE
IMITATION *n* copy of an original ▷ *adj* made to look like a material of superior quality
IMITATIVE *adj* imitating or tending to copy
IMITATOR > IMITATE
IMITATORS > IMITATE
IMMANACLE *vb* fetter
IMMANE *adj* monstrous
IMMANELY > IMMANE
IMMANENCE > IMMANENT
IMMANENCY > IMMANENT
IMMANENT *adj* present within and throughout something
IMMANITY > IMMANE
IMMANTLE *vb* cover with a mantle
IMMANTLED > IMMANTLE
IMMANTLES > IMMANTLE
IMMASK *vb* disguise
IMMASKED > IMMASK
IMMASKING > IMMASK
IMMASKS > IMMASK
IMMATURE *n* young animal ▷ *adj* not fully developed
IMMATURES > IMMATURE
IMMEDIACY > IMMEDIATE
IMMEDIATE *adj* occurring at once
IMMENSE *adj* extremely large
IMMENSELY > IMMENSE
IMMENSER > IMMENSE
IMMENSEST > IMMENSE
IMMENSITY *n* state or quality of being immense
IMMERGE *archaic word for* > IMMERSE
IMMERGED > IMMERGE
IMMERGES > IMMERGE
IMMERGING > IMMERGE
IMMERSE *vb* involve deeply, engross
IMMERSED *adj* sunk or submerged
IMMERSER > IMMERSE
IMMERSERS > IMMERSE
IMMERSES > IMMERSE
IMMERSING > IMMERSE
IMMERSION *n* form of baptism in which part or the whole of a person's body is submerged in the water
IMMERSIVE *adj* providing information or stimulation for a number of senses, not only sight and sound
IMMESH *variant of* > ENMESH
IMMESHED > IMMESH
IMMESHES > IMMESH
IMMESHING > IMMESH
IMMEW *vb* confine
IMMEWED > IMMEW
IMMEWING > IMMEW
IMMEWS > IMMEW
IMMIES > IMMY
IMMIGRANT *n* person who comes to a foreign country in order to settle there
IMMIGRATE *vb* come to a place or country of which one is not a native in order to settle there
IMMINENCE > IMMINENT
IMMINENCY > IMMINENT
IMMINENT *adj* about to happen
IMMINGLE *vb* blend or mix together
IMMINGLED > IMMINGLE
IMMINGLES > IMMINGLE
IMMINUTE *adj* reduced
IMMISSION *n* insertion
IMMIT *vb* insert
IMMITS > IMMIT
IMMITTED > IMMIT
IMMITTING > IMMIT
IMMIX *vb* mix in
IMMIXED > IMMIX
IMMIXES > IMMIX
IMMIXING > IMMIX
IMMIXTURE > IMMIX
IMMOBILE *adj* not moving
IMMODEST *adj* behaving in an indecent or improper manner
IMMODESTY > IMMODEST
IMMOLATE *vb* kill as a sacrifice
IMMOLATED > IMMOLATE
IMMOLATES > IMMOLATE
IMMOLATOR > IMMOLATE
IMMOMENT *adj* of no value
IMMORAL *adj* morally wrong, corrupt
IMMORALLY > IMMORAL
IMMORTAL *adj* living foreve ▷ *n* person whose fame will last for all time
IMMORTALS > IMMORTAL
IMMOTILE *adj* (esp of living organisms or their parts) not capable of moving spontaneously and independently.
IMMOVABLE *adj* unable to be moved
IMMOVABLY > IMMOVABLE
IMMUNE *adj* protected against a specific disease ▷ *n* immune person or animal
IMMUNES > IMMUNE
IMMUNISE *same as* > IMMUNIZE
IMMUNISED > IMMUNISE
IMMUNISER > IMMUNISE
IMMUNISES > IMMUNISE
IMMUNITY *n* ability to resis disease
IMMUNIZE *vb* make immune to a disease
IMMUNIZED > IMMUNIZE
IMMUNIZER > IMMUNIZE
IMMUNIZES > IMMUNIZE
IMMUNOGEN *n* any substance that evokes an immune response
IMMURE *vb* imprison
IMMURED > IMMURE
IMMURES > IMMURE
IMMURING > IMMURE
IMMUTABLE *adj* unchangeable
IMMUTABLY > IMMUTABLE
IMMY *n* image-orthicon camera
IMP *n* (in folklore)

mischievous small creature with magical powers ▷ *vb* insert (new feathers) into the stumps of broken feathers in order to repair the wing of a hawk or falcon
MPACABLE *adj* incapable of being placated or pacified
MPACT *n* strong effect ▷ *vb* have a strong effect on
MPACTED > IMPACT
MPACTER > IMPACT
MPACTERS > IMPACT
MPACTFUL > IMPACT
MPACTING > IMPACT
MPACTION > IMPACT
MPACTITE *n* glassy rock formed in a meteor collision
MPACTIVE *adj* of or relating to a physical impact
MPACTOR > IMPACT
MPACTORS > IMPACT
MPACTS > IMPACT
MPAINT *vb* paint
MPAINTED > IMPAINT
MPAINTS > IMPAINT
MPAIR *vb* weaken or damage
MPAIRED > IMPAIR
MPAIRER > IMPAIR
MPAIRERS > IMPAIR
MPAIRING > IMPAIR
MPAIRS > IMPAIR
MPALA *n* southern African antelope
MPALAS > IMPALA
MPALE *vb* pierce with a sharp object
MPALED > IMPALE
MPALER > IMPALE
MPALERS > IMPALE
MPALES > IMPALE
MPALING > IMPALE
MPANATE *adj* embodied in bread
MPANEL *variant spelling (esp US) of* > EMPANEL
MPANELED > IMPANEL
MPANELS > IMPANEL
MPANNEL *same as* > IMPANEL
MPANNELS > IMPANNEL
MPARITY *less common word for* > DISPARITY
MPARK *vb* make into a park
MPARKED > IMPARK
MPARKING > IMPARK
MPARKS > IMPARK
MPARL *vb* parley
MPARLED > IMPARL
MPARLING > IMPARL
MPARLS > IMPARL
MPART *vb* communicate (information)
MPARTED > IMPART
MPARTER > IMPART
MPARTERS > IMPART
MPARTIAL *adj* not favouring one side or the other
IMPARTING > IMPART
IMPARTS > IMPART
IMPASSE *n* situation in which progress is impossible
IMPASSES > IMPASSE
IMPASSION *vb* arouse the passions of
IMPASSIVE *adj* showing no emotion, calm
IMPASTE *vb* apply paint thickly to
IMPASTED > IMPASTE
IMPASTES > IMPASTE
IMPASTING > IMPASTE
IMPASTO *n* technique of applying paint thickly, so that brush marks are evident ▷ *vb* apply impasto
IMPASTOED > IMPASTO
IMPASTOS > IMPASTO
IMPATIENS *n* plant such as balsam, touch-me-not, busy Lizzie, and policeman's helmet
IMPATIENT *adj* irritable at any delay or difficulty
IMPAVE *vb* set in a pavement
IMPAVED > IMPAVE
IMPAVES > IMPAVE
IMPAVID *adj* fearless
IMPAVIDLY > IMPAVID
IMPAVING > IMPAVE
IMPAWN *vb* pawn
IMPAWNED > IMPAWN
IMPAWNING > IMPAWN
IMPAWNS > IMPAWN
IMPEACH *vb* charge with a serious crime against the state
IMPEACHED > IMPEACH
IMPEACHER > IMPEACH
IMPEACHES > IMPEACH
IMPEARL *vb* adorn with pearls
IMPEARLED > IMPEARL
IMPEARLS > IMPEARL
IMPECCANT *adj* not sinning
IMPED > IMP
IMPEDANCE *n* measure of the opposition to the flow of an alternating current
IMPEDE *vb* hinder in action or progress
IMPEDED > IMPEDE
IMPEDER > IMPEDE
IMPEDERS > IMPEDE
IMPEDES > IMPEDE
IMPEDING > IMPEDE
IMPEDOR *n* component, such as an inductor or resistor, that offers impedance
IMPEDORS > IMPEDOR
IMPEL *vb* push or force (someone) to do something
IMPELLED > IMPEL
IMPELLENT > IMPEL
IMPELLER *n* vaned rotating disc of a centrifugal pump, compressor, etc
IMPELLERS > IMPELLER
IMPELLING > IMPEL
IMPELLOR *same as* > IMPELLER
IMPELLORS > IMPELLOR
IMPELS > IMPEL
IMPEND *vb* (esp of something threatening) to be about to happen
IMPENDED > IMPEND
IMPENDENT > IMPEND
IMPENDING > IMPEND
IMPENDS > IMPEND
IMPENNATE *adj* (of birds) lacking true functional wings or feathers
IMPERATOR *n* (in imperial Rome) a title of the emperor
IMPERFECT *adj* having faults or mistakes ▷ *n* imperfect tense
IMPERIA > IMPERIUM
IMPERIAL *adj* of or like an empire or emperor ▷ *n* wine bottle holding the equivalent of eight normal bottles
IMPERIALS > IMPERIAL
IMPERIL *vb* put in danger
IMPERILED > IMPERIL
IMPERILS > IMPERIL
IMPERIOUS *adj* proud and domineering
IMPERIUM *n* (in ancient Rome) the supreme power, held esp by consuls and emperors, to command and administer in military, judicial, and civil affairs
IMPERIUMS > IMPERIUM
IMPETICOS *vb* put in a pocket
IMPETIGO *n* contagious skin disease
IMPETIGOS > IMPETIGO
IMPETRATE *vb* supplicate or entreat for, esp by prayer
IMPETUOUS *adj* done or acting without thought, rash
IMPETUS *n* incentive, impulse
IMPETUSES > IMPETUS
IMPHEE *n* African sugar cane
IMPHEES > IMPHEE
IMPI *n* group of Zulu warriors
IMPIES > IMPI
IMPIETIES > IMPIETY
IMPIETY *n* lack of respect or religious reverence
IMPING > IMP
IMPINGE *vb* affect or restrict
IMPINGED > IMPINGE
IMPINGENT > IMPINGE
IMPINGER > IMPINGE
IMPINGERS > IMPINGE
IMPINGES > IMPINGE
IMPINGING > IMPINGE
IMPINGS > IMP
IMPIOUS *adj* showing a lack of respect or reverence
IMPIOUSLY > IMPIOUS
IMPIS > IMPI
IMPISH *adj* mischievous
IMPISHLY > IMPISH
IMPLANT *n* something put into someone's body, usu. by surgical operation ▷ *vb* put (something) into someone's body, usu. by surgical operation
IMPLANTED > IMPLANT
IMPLANTER > IMPLANT
IMPLANTS > IMPLANT
IMPLATE *vb* sheathe
IMPLATED > IMPLATE
IMPLATES > IMPLATE
IMPLATING > IMPLATE
IMPLEACH *vb* intertwine
IMPLEAD *vb* sue or prosecute
IMPLEADED > IMPLEAD
IMPLEADER > IMPLEAD
IMPLEADS > IMPLEAD
IMPLED > IMPLEAD
IMPLEDGE *vb* pledge
IMPLEDGED > IMPLEDGE
IMPLEDGES > IMPLEDGE
IMPLEMENT *vb* carry out (instructions etc) ▷ *n* tool, instrument
IMPLETE *vb* fill
IMPLETED > IMPLETE
IMPLETES > IMPLETE
IMPLETING > IMPLETE
IMPLETION > IMPLETE
IMPLEX *n* part of an arthropod
IMPLEXES > IMPLEX
IMPLEXION *n* complication
IMPLICATE *vb* show to be involved, esp in a crime
IMPLICIT *adj* expressed indirectly
IMPLICITY > IMPLICIT
IMPLIED *adj* hinted at or suggested
IMPLIEDLY > IMPLIED
IMPLIES > IMPLY
IMPLODE *vb* collapse inwards
IMPLODED > IMPLODE
IMPLODENT *n* sound of an implosion
IMPLODES > IMPLODE
IMPLODING > IMPLODE
IMPLORE *vb* beg earnestly
IMPLORED > IMPLORE
IMPLORER > IMPLORE
IMPLORERS > IMPLORE
IMPLORES > IMPLORE
IMPLORING > IMPLORE
IMPLOSION *n* act or process of imploding
IMPLOSIVE *n* consonant pronounced in a particular way
IMPLUNGE *vb* submerge
IMPLUNGED > IMPLUNGE
IMPLUNGES > IMPLUNGE
IMPLUVIA > IMPLUVIUM
IMPLUVIUM *n* rain-filled water tank
IMPLY *vb* indicate by

hinting, suggest
IMPLYING > IMPLY
IMPOCKET *vb* put in a pocket
IMPOCKETS > IMPOCKET
IMPOLDER *vb* make into a polder
IMPOLDERS > IMPOLDER
IMPOLICY *n* act or an instance of being unjudicious or impolitic
IMPOLITE *adj* showing bad manners
IMPOLITER > IMPOLITE
IMPOLITIC *adj* unwise or inadvisable
IMPONE *vb* impose
IMPONED > IMPONE
IMPONENT *n* person who imposes a duty, etc
IMPONENTS > IMPONENT
IMPONES > IMPONE
IMPONING > IMPONE
IMPOROUS *adj* not porous
IMPORT *vb* bring in (goods) from another country ▷ *n* something imported
IMPORTANT *adj* of great significance or value
IMPORTED > IMPORT
IMPORTER > IMPORT
IMPORTERS > IMPORT
IMPORTING > IMPORT
IMPORTS > IMPORT
IMPORTUNE *vb* harass with persistent requests
IMPOSABLE > IMPOSE
IMPOSE *vb* force the acceptance of
IMPOSED > IMPOSE
IMPOSER > IMPOSE
IMPOSERS > IMPOSE
IMPOSES > IMPOSE
IMPOSING *adj* grand, impressive
IMPOST *n* tax, esp a customs duty ▷ *vb* classify (imported goods) according to the duty payable on them
IMPOSTED > IMPOST
IMPOSTER > IMPOST
IMPOSTERS > IMPOST
IMPOSTING > IMPOST
IMPOSTOR *n* person who cheats or swindles by pretending to be someone else
IMPOSTORS > IMPOSTOR
IMPOSTS > IMPOST
IMPOSTUME *archaic word for* > ABSCESS
IMPOSTURE *n* deception, esp by pretending to be someone else
IMPOT *n* slang term for the act of imposing
IMPOTENCE > IMPOTENT
IMPOTENCY > IMPOTENT
IMPOTENT *n* one who is impotent ▷ *adj* powerless
IMPOTENTS > IMPOTENT
IMPOTS > IMPOT
IMPOUND *vb* take legal possession of, confiscate
IMPOUNDED > IMPOUND
IMPOUNDER > IMPOUND
IMPOUNDS > IMPOUND
IMPOWER *less common spelling of* > EMPOWER
IMPOWERED > IMPOWER
IMPOWERS > IMPOWER
IMPRECATE *vb* swear, curse, or blaspheme
IMPRECISE *adj* inexact or inaccurate
IMPREGN *vb* impregnate
IMPREGNED > IMPREGN
IMPREGNS > IMPREGN
IMPRESA *n* heraldic device
IMPRESARI *n* impresarios
IMPRESAS > IMPRESA
IMPRESE *same as* > IMPRESA
IMPRESES > IMPRESE
IMPRESS *vb* affect strongly, usu. favourably ▷ *n* impressing
IMPRESSE *n* heraldic device
IMPRESSED > IMPRESS
IMPRESSER > IMPRESS
IMPRESSES > IMPRESS
IMPREST *n* fund of cash from which a department or other unit pays incidental expenses, topped up periodically from central funds
IMPRESTS > IMPREST
IMPRIMIS *adv* in the first place
IMPRINT *n* mark made by printing or stamping ▷ *vb* produce (a mark) by printing or stamping
IMPRINTED > IMPRINT
IMPRINTER > IMPRINT
IMPRINTS > IMPRINT
IMPRISON *vb* put in prison
IMPRISONS > IMPRISON
IMPROBITY *n* dishonesty or wickedness
IMPROMPTU *adj* without planning or preparation ▷ *adv* in a spontaneous or improvised way ▷ *n* short piece of instrumental music resembling improvisation
IMPROPER *adj* indecent
IMPROV *n* improvisational comedy
IMPROVE *vb* make or become better
IMPROVED > IMPROVE
IMPROVER > IMPROVE
IMPROVERS > IMPROVE
IMPROVES > IMPROVE
IMPROVING > IMPROVE
IMPROVISE *vb* make use of whatever materials are available
IMPROVS > IMPROV
IMPRUDENT *adj* not sensible or wise
IMPS > IMP
IMPSONITE *n* asphaltite compound
IMPUDENCE *n* quality of being impudent
IMPUDENCY *same as* > IMPUDENCE
IMPUDENT *adj* cheeky, disrespectful
IMPUGN *vb* challenge the truth or validity of
IMPUGNED > IMPUGN
IMPUGNER > IMPUGN
IMPUGNERS > IMPUGN
IMPUGNING > IMPUGN
IMPUGNS > IMPUGN
IMPULSE *vb* give an impulse to ▷ *n* sudden urge to do something
IMPULSED > IMPULSE
IMPULSES > IMPULSE
IMPULSING > IMPULSE
IMPULSION *n* act of impelling or the state of being impelled
IMPULSIVE *adj* acting or done without careful consideration
IMPUNDULU *n* mythical bird associated with witchcraft, frequently manifested as the secretary bird
IMPUNITY *n* exemption or immunity from punishment or recrimination
IMPURE *adj* having dirty or unwanted substances mixed in
IMPURELY > IMPURE
IMPURER > IMPURE
IMPUREST > IMPURE
IMPURITY *n* impure element or thing
IMPURPLE *vb* colour purple
IMPURPLED > IMPURPLE
IMPURPLES > IMPURPLE
IMPUTABLE *adj* capable of being imputed
IMPUTABLY > IMPUTABLE
IMPUTE *vb* attribute responsibility to
IMPUTED > IMPUTE
IMPUTER > IMPUTE
IMPUTERS > IMPUTE
IMPUTES > IMPUTE
IMPUTING > IMPUTE
IMSHI *interj* go away!
IMSHY *same as* > IMSHI
IN *prep* indicating position inside, state or situation, etc ▷ *adv* indicating position inside, entry into, etc ▷ *adj* fashionable ▷ *n* way of approaching or befriending a person
INABILITY *n* lack of means or skill to do something
INACTION *n* act of doing nothing
INACTIONS > INACTION
INACTIVE *adj* idle
INAIDABLE *adj* beyond help
INAMORATA *n* woman with whom one is in love
INAMORATO *n* man with whom one is in love
INANE *adj* senseless, silly ▷ *n* something that is inane
INANELY > INANE
INANENESS > INANE
INANER > INANE
INANES > INANE
INANEST > INANE
INANGA *n* common type of New Zealand grass tree
INANGAS > INANGA
INANIMATE *adj* not living
INANITIES > INANITY
INANITION *n* exhaustion or weakness, as from lack of food
INANITY *n* lack of intelligence or imagination
INAPT *adj* not apt or fitting
INAPTLY > INAPT
INAPTNESS > INAPT
INARABLE *adj* not arable
INARCH *vb* graft (a plant) by uniting stock and scion while both are still growing independently
INARCHED > INARCH
INARCHES > INARCH
INARCHING > INARCH
INARM *vb* embrace
INARMED > INARM
INARMING > INARM
INARMS > INARM
INASMUCH as in *inasmuch as*, in view of the fact that
INAUDIBLE *adj* not loud enough to be heard
INAUDIBLY > INAUDIBLE
INAUGURAL *adj* of or for an inauguration ▷ *n* speech made at an inauguration
INAURATE *adj* gilded
INBEING *n* existence in something else
INBEINGS > INBEING
INBENT *adj* bent inwards
INBOARD *adj* (of a boat's engine) inside the hull ▷ *adv* within the sides of or towards the centre of a vessel or aircraft
INBOARDS *same as* > INBOARD
INBORN *adj* existing from birth, natural
INBOUND *vb* pass into the playing area from outside it ▷ *adj* coming in
INBOUNDED > INBOUND
INBOUNDS > INBOUND
INBREAK *n* breaking in
INBREAKS > INBREAK
INBREATHE *vb* infuse or imbue
INBRED *n* inbred person or animal ▷ *adj* produced as a result of inbreeding
INBREDS > INBRED
INBREED *vb* breed from closely related individuals
INBREEDER > INBREED

INBREEDS > INBREED

INBRING *vb* bring in

INBRINGS > INBRING

INBROUGHT > INBRING

INBUILT *adj* present from the start

INBURNING *adj* burning within

INBURST *n* irruption

INBURSTS > INBURST

INBY *adv* into the house or an inner room ▷ *adj* located near or nearest to the house

INBYE *adv* near the house

INCAGE *vb* confine in or as in a cage

INCAGED > INCAGE

INCAGES > INCAGE

INCAGING > INCAGE

INCANT *vb* chant (a spell)

INCANTED > INCANT

INCANTING > INCANT

INCANTS > INCANT

INCAPABLE *adj* unable (to do something)

INCAPABLY > INCAPABLE

INCARNATE *adj* in human form ▷ *vb* give a bodily or concrete form to

INCASE *variant spelling of* > ENCASE

INCASED > INCASE

INCASES > INCASE

INCASING > INCASE

INCAUTION *n* act of not being cautious

INCAVE *vb* hide

INCAVED > INCAVE

INCAVES > INCAVE

INCAVI > INCAVO

INCAVING > INCAVE

INCAVO *n* incised part of a carving

INCEDE *vb* advance

INCEDED > INCEDE

INCEDES > INCEDE

INCEDING > INCEDE

INCENSE *vb* make very angry ▷ *n* substance that gives off a sweet perfume when burned

INCENSED > INCENSE

INCENSER *n* incense burner

INCENSERS > INCENSER

INCENSES > INCENSE

INCENSING > INCENSE

INCENSOR *n* incense burner

INCENSORS > INCENSOR

INCENSORY *less common name for* > CENSER

INCENT *vb* provide incentive

INCENTED > INCENT

INCENTER *same as* > INCENTRE

INCENTERS > INCENTER

INCENTING > INCENT

INCENTIVE *n* something that encourages effort or action ▷ *adj* encouraging greater effort

INCENTRE *n* centre of an inscribed circle

INCENTRES > INCENTRE

INCENTS > INCENT

INCEPT *vb* (of organisms) to ingest (food) ▷ *n* rudimentary organ

INCEPTED > INCEPT

INCEPTING > INCEPT

INCEPTION *n* beginning

INCEPTIVE *adj* beginning ▷ *n* type of verb

INCEPTOR > INCEPT

INCEPTORS > INCEPT

INCEPTS > INCEPT

INCERTAIN *archaic form of* > UNCERTAIN

INCESSANT *adj* never stopping

INCEST *n* sexual intercourse between two people too closely related to marry

INCESTS > INCEST

INCH *n* unit of length equal to one twelfth of a foot or 2.54 centimetres ▷ *vb* move slowly and gradually

INCHASE *same as* > ENCHASE

INCHASED > INCHASE

INCHASES > INCHASE

INCHASING > INCHASE

INCHED > INCH

INCHER *n* something measuring given amount of inches

INCHERS > INCHER

INCHES > INCH

INCHING > INCH

INCHMEAL *adv* gradually

INCHOATE *adj* just begun and not yet properly developed ▷ *vb* begin

INCHOATED > INCHOATE

INCHOATES > INCHOATE

INCHPIN *n* cervine sweetbread

INCHPINS > INCHPIN

INCHWORM *n* larva of a type of moth

INCHWORMS > INCHWORM

INCIDENCE *n* extent or frequency of occurrence

INCIDENT *n* something that happens ▷ *adj* related (to) or dependent (on)

INCIDENTS > INCIDENT

INCIPIENT *adj* just starting to appear or happen

INCIPIT *n* Latin introductory phrase

INCIPITS > INCIPIT

INCISAL *adj* relating to the cutting edge of incisors and cuspids

INCISE *vb* cut into with a sharp tool

INCISED > INCISE

INCISES > INCISE

INCISING > INCISE

INCISION *n* cut, esp one made during a surgical operation

INCISIONS > INCISION

INCISIVE *adj* direct and forceful

INCISOR *n* front tooth, used for biting into food

INCISORS > INCISOR

INCISORY > INCISOR

INCISURAL > INCISURE

INCISURE *n* incision or notch in an organ or part

INCISURES > INCISURE

INCITABLE > INCITE

INCITANT *n* something that incites

INCITANTS > INCITANT

INCITE *vb* stir up, provoke

INCITED > INCITE

INCITER > INCITE

INCITERS > INCITE

INCITES > INCITE

INCITING > INCITE

INCIVIL *archaic form of* > UNCIVIL

INCIVISM *n* neglect of a citizen's duties

INCIVISMS > INCIVISM

INCLASP *vb* clasp

INCLASPED > INCLASP

INCLASPS > INCLASP

INCLE *same as* > INKLE

INCLEMENT *adj* (of weather) stormy or severe

INCLES > INCLE

INCLINE *vb* lean, slope ▷ *n* slope

INCLINED *adj* having a disposition

INCLINER > INCLINE

INCLINERS > INCLINE

INCLINES > INCLINE

INCLINING > INCLINE

INCLIP *vb* embrace

INCLIPPED > INCLIP

INCLIPS > INCLIP

INCLOSE *less common spelling of* > ENCLOSE

INCLOSED > INCLOSE

INCLOSER > INCLOSE

INCLOSERS > INCLOSE

INCLOSES > INCLOSE

INCLOSING > INCLOSE

INCLOSURE > INCLOSE

INCLUDE *vb* have as part of the whole

INCLUDED *adj* (of the stamens or pistils of a flower) not protruding beyond the corolla

INCLUDES > INCLUDE

INCLUDING > INCLUDE

INCLUSION *n* including or being included

INCLUSIVE *adj* including everything (specified)

INCOG *n* incognito

INCOGNITA *n* female who is in disguise or unknown

INCOGNITO *adv* having adopted a false identity ▷ *n* false identity ▷ *adj* under an assumed name or appearance

INCOGS > INCOG

INCOME *n* amount of money earned from work, investments, etc

INCOMER *n* person who comes to live in a place in which he or she was not born

INCOMERS > INCOMER

INCOMES > INCOME

INCOMING *adj* coming in ▷ *n* act of coming in

INCOMINGS > INCOMING

INCOMMODE *vb* cause inconvenience to

INCOMPACT *adj* not compact

INCONDITE *adj* poorly constructed or composed

INCONIE *adj* fine or delicate

INCONNU *n* whitefish of Arctic waters

INCONNUE *n* unknown woman

INCONNUES > INCONNUE

INCONNUS > INCONNU

INCONY *adj* fine or delicate

INCORPSE *vb* incorporate

INCORPSED > INCORPSE

INCORPSES > INCORPSE

INCORRECT *adj* wrong

INCORRUPT *adj* free from corruption

INCREASE *vb* make or become greater in size, number, etc ▷ *n* rise in number, size, etc

INCREASED > INCREASE

INCREASER > INCREASE

INCREASES > INCREASE

INCREATE *adj* (esp of gods) never having been created

INCREMATE *vb* cremate

INCREMENT *n* increase in money or value, esp a regular salary increase

INCRETION *n* direct secretion into the bloodstream, esp of a hormone from an endocrine gland

INCRETORY > INCRETION

INCROSS *n* plant or animal produced by continued inbreeding ▷ *vb* inbreed or produce by inbreeding

INCROSSED > INCROSS

INCROSSES > INCROSS

INCRUST *same as* > ENCRUST

INCRUSTED > INCRUST

INCRUSTS > INCRUST

INCUBATE *vb* (of a bird) hatch (eggs) by sitting on them

INCUBATED > INCUBATE

INCUBATES > INCUBATE

INCUBATOR *n* heated enclosed apparatus for rearing premature babies

INCUBI > INCUBUS

INCUBOUS *adj* (of a liverwort) having the leaves arranged so that the upper margin of each leaf lies above the lower margin of the next leaf

along
INCUBUS *n* (in folklore) demon believed to have sex with sleeping women
INCUBUSES > INCUBUS
INCUDAL > INCUS
INCUDATE > INCUS
INCUDES > INCUS
INCULCATE *vb* fix in someone's mind by constant repetition
INCULPATE *vb* cause (someone) to be blamed for a crime
INCULT *adj* (of land) uncultivated
INCUMBENT *n* person who holds a particular office or position ▷ *adj* morally binding as a duty
INCUMBER *less common spelling of* > ENCUMBER
INCUMBERS > INCUMBER
INCUNABLE *n* early printed book
INCUR *vb* cause (something unpleasant) to happen
INCURABLE *adj* not able to be cured ▷ *n* person with an incurable disease
INCURABLY > INCURABLE
INCURIOUS *adj* showing no curiosity or interest
INCURRED > INCUR
INCURRENT *adj* (of anatomical ducts, tubes, channels, etc) having an inward flow
INCURRING > INCUR
INCURS > INCUR
INCURSION *n* sudden brief invasion
INCURSIVE > INCURSION
INCURVATE *vb* curve or cause to curve inwards ▷ *adj* curved inwards
INCURVE *vb* curve or cause to curve inwards
INCURVED > INCURVE
INCURVES > INCURVE
INCURVING > INCURVE
INCURVITY > INCURVE
INCUS *n* central of the three small bones in the middle ear of mammals
INCUSE *n* design stamped or hammered onto a coin ▷ *vb* impress (a design) in a coin or to impress (a coin) with a design by hammering or stamping ▷ *adj* stamped or hammered onto a coin
INCUSED > INCUSE
INCUSES > INCUSE
INCUSING > INCUSE
INCUT *adj* cut or etched in
INDABA *n* (among native peoples of southern Africa) a meeting to discuss a serious topic
INDABAS > INDABA
INDAGATE *vb* investigate
INDAGATED > INDAGATE
INDAGATES > INDAGATE
INDAGATOR > INDAGATE
INDAMIN *same as* > INDAMINE
INDAMINE *n* organic base used in the production of the dye safranine
INDAMINES > INDAMINE
INDAMINS > INDAMIN
INDART *vb* dart in
INDARTED > INDART
INDARTING > INDART
INDARTS > INDART
INDEBTED *adj* owing gratitude for help or favours
INDECENCY *n* state or quality of being indecent
INDECENT *adj* morally or sexually offensive
INDECORUM *n* indecorous behaviour or speech
INDEED *adv* really, certainly ▷ *interj* expression of indignation or surprise
INDELIBLE *adj* impossible to erase or remove
INDELIBLY > INDELIBLE
INDEMNIFY *vb* secure against loss, damage, or liability
INDEMNITY *n* insurance against loss or damage
INDENE *n* colourless liquid hydrocarbon extracted from petroleum and coal tar and used in making synthetic resins
INDENES > INDENE
INDENT *vb* make a dent in
INDENTED > INDENT
INDENTER > INDENT
INDENTERS > INDENT
INDENTING > INDENT
INDENTION *n* space between a margin and the start of the line of text
INDENTOR > INDENT
INDENTORS > INDENT
INDENTS > INDENT
INDENTURE *n* contract, esp one binding an apprentice to his or her employer ▷ *vb* bind (an apprentice) by indenture
INDEVOUT *adj* not devout
INDEW *same as* > INDUE
INDEWED > INDEW
INDEWING > INDEW
INDEWS > INDEW
INDEX *n* alphabetical list of names or subjects dealt with in a book ▷ *vb* provide (a book) with an index
INDEXABLE > INDEX
INDEXAL > INDEX
INDEXED > INDEX
INDEXER > INDEX
INDEXERS > INDEX
INDEXES > INDEX
INDEXICAL *adj* arranged as or relating to an index or indexes ▷ *n* term whose reference depends on the context of utterance, such as *I*, *you*, *here*, *now*, or *tomorrow*
INDEXING > INDEX
INDEXINGS > INDEX
INDEXLESS > INDEX
INDICAN *n* compound secreted in the urine, usually in the form of its potassium salt
INDICANS > INDICAN
INDICANT *n* something that indicates
INDICANTS > INDICANT
INDICATE *vb* be a sign or symptom of
INDICATED > INDICATE
INDICATES > INDICATE
INDICATOR *n* something acting as a sign or indication
INDICES *plural of* > INDEX
INDICIA > INDICIUM
INDICIAL > INDICIUM
INDICIAS > INDICIUM
INDICIUM *n* notice
INDICIUMS > INDICIUM
INDICT *vb* formally charge with a crime
INDICTED > INDICT
INDICTEE > INDICT
INDICTEES > INDICT
INDICTER > INDICT
INDICTERS > INDICT
INDICTING > INDICT
INDICTION *n* recurring fiscal period of 15 years, often used as a unit for dating events
INDICTOR > INDICT
INDICTORS > INDICT
INDICTS > INDICT
INDIE *adj* (of rock music) released by an independent record company ▷ *n* independent record company
INDIES > INDIE
INDIGEN *same as* > INDIGENE
INDIGENCE > INDIGENT
INDIGENCY > INDIGENT
INDIGENE *n* indigenous person, animal, or thing
INDIGENES > INDIGENE
INDIGENS > INDIGEN
INDIGENT *adj* extremely poor ▷ *n* impoverished person
INDIGENTS > INDIGENT
INDIGEST *n* undigested mass
INDIGESTS > INDIGEST
INDIGN *adj* undeserving
INDIGNANT *adj* feeling or showing indignation
INDIGNIFY *vb* treat in a humiliating manner
INDIGNITY *n* embarrassing or humiliating treatment
INDIGNLY > INDIGN
INDIGO *adj* deep violet-blue ▷ *n* dye of this colour
INDIGOES > INDIGO
INDIGOID *adj* of, concerned with, or resembling indigo or its blue colour ▷ *n* any of a number of synthetic dyes or pigments related in chemical structure to indigo
INDIGOIDS > INDIGOID
INDIGOS > INDIGO
INDIGOTIC > INDIGO
INDIGOTIN *same as* > INDIGO
INDINAVIR *n* drug used to treat AIDS
INDIRECT *adj* done or caused by someone or something else
INDIRUBIN *n* isomer of indigotin
INDISPOSE *vb* make unwilling or opposed
INDITE *vb* write
INDITED > INDITE
INDITER > INDITE
INDITERS > INDITE
INDITES > INDITE
INDITING > INDITE
INDIUM *n* soft silvery-white metallic element
INDIUMS > INDIUM
INDIVIDUA *pl n* indivisible entities
INDOCIBLE *same as* > INDOCILE
INDOCILE *adj* difficult to discipline or instruct
INDOL *same as* > INDOLE
INDOLE *n* white or yellowish crystalline heterocyclic compound extracted from coal tar and used in perfumery, medicine, and as a flavouring agent
INDOLENCE > INDOLENT
INDOLENCY > INDOLENT
INDOLENT *adj* lazy
INDOLES > INDOLE
INDOLS > INDOL
INDOOR *adj* inside a building
INDOORS *adj* inside or into a building
INDORSE *variant spelling of* > ENDORSE
INDORSED > INDORSE
INDORSEE > INDORSE
INDORSEES > INDORSE
INDORSER > INDORSE
INDORSERS > INDORSE
INDORSES > INDORSE
INDORSING > INDORSE
INDORSOR > INDORSE
INDORSORS > INDORSE
INDOW *archaic variant of* > INDOW
INDOWED > INDOW
INDOWING > INDOW
INDOWS > INDOW
INDOXYL *n* yellow water-soluble crystalline

compound occurring in woad as its glucoside and in urine as its ester
NDOXYLS > INDOXYL
NDRAFT *same as* > INDRAUGHT
NDRAFTS > INDRAFT
NDRAUGHT *n* act of drawing or pulling in
NDRAWN *adj* drawn or pulled in
NDRENCH *vb* submerge
NDRI *same as* > INDRIS
NDRIS *n* large Madagascan arboreal lemuroid primate
NDRISES > INDRIS
NDUBIOUS *adj* certain
NDUCE *vb* persuade or influence
NDUCED > INDUCE
NDUCER > INDUCE
NDUCERS > INDUCE
NDUCES > INDUCE
NDUCIAE *n* time limit for a defendant to appear in court
NDUCIBLE > INDUCE
NDUCING > INDUCE
NDUCT *vb* formally install (someone, esp a clergyman) in office
NDUCTED > INDUCT
NDUCTEE *n* military conscript
NDUCTEES > INDUCTEE
NDUCTILE *adj* not ductile, pliant, or yielding
NDUCTING > INDUCT
NDUCTION > INDUCT
NDUCTIVE *adj* of or using induction
NDUCTOR *n* device designed to create inductance in an electrical circuit
NDUCTORS > INDUCTOR
NDUCTS > INDUCT
NDUE *variant spelling of* > ENDUE
NDUED > INDUE
NDUES > INDUE
NDUING > INDUE
NDULGE *vb* allow oneself pleasure
NDULGED > INDULGE
NDULGENT *adj* kind or lenient, often to excess
NDULGER > INDULGE
NDULGERS > INDULGE
NDULGES > INDULGE
NDULGING > INDULGE
NDULIN *same as* > INDULINE
NDULINE *n* any of a class of blue dyes obtained from aniline and aminoazobenzene
NDULINES > INDULINE
NDULINS > INDULIN
NDULT *n* faculty granted by the Holy See allowing a specific deviation from the Church's common law
INDULTS > INDULT
INDUMENTA *pl n* outer coverings of feather, fur, etc
INDUNA *n* (in South Africa) a Black African overseer in a factory, mine, etc
INDUNAS > INDUNA
INDURATE *vb* make or become hard or callous ▷ *adj* hardened, callous, or unfeeling
INDURATED > INDURATE
INDURATES > INDURATE
INDUSIA > INDUSIUM
INDUSIAL > INDUSIUM
INDUSIATE *adj* covered in indusia
INDUSIUM *n* membranous outgrowth on the undersurface of fern leaves that covers and protects the developing sporangia
INDUSTRY *n* manufacture of goods
INDUVIAE *pl n* withered leaves
INDUVIAL > INDUVIAE
INDUVIATE > INDUVIAE
INDWELL *vb* (of a spirit, principle, etc) to inhabit
INDWELLER > INDWELL
INDWELLS > INDWELL
INDWELT > INDWELL
INEARTH *poetic word for* > BURY
INEARTHED > INEARTH
INEARTHS > INEARTH
INEBRIANT *adj* causing intoxication, esp drunkenness ▷ *n* something that inebriates
INEBRIATE *adj* (person who is) habitually drunk ▷ *n* person who is habitually drunk ▷ *vb* make drunk
INEBRIETY > INEBRIATE
INEBRIOUS *adj* drunk
INEDIBLE *adj* not fit to be eaten
INEDIBLY > INEDIBLE
INEDITA *pl n* unpublished writings
INEDITED *adj* not edited
INEFFABLE *adj* too great for words
INEFFABLY > INEFFABLE
INELASTIC *adj* not elastic
INELEGANT *adj* lacking elegance or refinement
INEPT *adj* clumsy, lacking skill
INEPTER > INEPT
INEPTEST > INEPT
INEPTLY > INEPT
INEPTNESS > INEPT
INEQUABLE *adj* unfair
INEQUITY *n* injustice or unfairness
INERM *adj* without thorns
INERMOUS *same as* > INERM
INERRABLE *adj* not liable to error ▷ *n* person or thing that is incapable of error
INERRABLY > INERRABLE
INERRANCY > INERRABLE
INERRANT *same as* > INERRABLE
INERT *n* inert thing ▷ *adj* without the power of motion or resistance
INERTER > INERT
INERTEST > INERT
INERTIA *n* feeling of unwillingness to do anything
INERTIAE > INERTIA
INERTIAL > INERTIA
INERTIAS > INERTIA
INERTLY > INERT
INERTNESS > INERT
INERTS > INERT
INERUDITE *adj* not erudite
INESSIVE *n* grammatical case in Finnish
INESSIVES > INESSIVE
INEXACT *adj* not exact or accurate
INEXACTLY > INEXACT
INEXPERT *n* unskilled person ▷ *adj* lacking skill
INEXPERTS > INEXPERT
INFALL *vb* move towards a black hole, etc, under the influence of gravity
INFALLING > INFALL
INFALLS > INFALL
INFAME *vb* defame
INFAMED > INFAME
INFAMES > INFAME
INFAMIES > INFAMY
INFAMING > INFAME
INFAMISE *same as* > INFAMIZE
INFAMISED > INFAMISE
INFAMISES > INFAMISE
INFAMIZE *vb* make infamous
INFAMIZED > INFAMIZE
INFAMIZES > INFAMIZE
INFAMOUS *adj* well-known for something bad
INFAMY *n* state of being infamous
INFANCIES > INFANCY
INFANCY *n* early childhood
INFANT *n* very young child ▷ *adj* of, relating to, or designed for young children
INFANTA *n* (formerly) daughter of a king of Spain or Portugal
INFANTAS > INFANTA
INFANTE *n* (formerly) any son of a king of Spain or Portugal, except the heir to the throne
INFANTES > INFANTE
INFANTILE *adj* childish
INFANTINE *adj* infantile
INFANTRY *n* soldiers who fight on foot
INFANTS > INFANT
INFARCT *n* localized area of dead tissue (necrosis) resulting from obstruction of the blood supply to that part, esp by an embolus ▷ *vb* obstruct the blood supply to part of a body
INFARCTED > INFARCT
INFARCTS > INFARCT
INFARE *vb* enter
INFARES > INFARE
INFATUATE *vb* inspire or fill with an intense and unreasoning passion ▷ *n* person who is infatuated
INFAUNA *n* animals that live in ocean and river beds
INFAUNAE > INFAUNA
INFAUNAL > INFAUNA
INFAUNAS > INFAUNA
INFAUST *adj* unlucky
INFECT *vb* affect with a disease ▷ *adj* contaminated or polluted with or as if with a disease
INFECTANT *n* something that infects
INFECTED > INFECT
INFECTER > INFECT
INFECTERS > INFECT
INFECTING > INFECT
INFECTION *n* infectious disease
INFECTIVE *adj* capable of causing infection
INFECTOR > INFECT
INFECTORS > INFECT
INFECTS > INFECT
INFECUND *less common word for* > INFERTILE
INFEFT *vb* give possession of heritable property
INFEFTED > INFEFT
INFEFTING > INFEFT
INFEFTS > INFEFT
INFELT *adj* heartfelt
INFEOFF *same as* > ENFEOFF
INFEOFFED > INFEOFF
INFEOFFS > INFEOFF
INFER *vb* work out from evidence
INFERABLE > INFER
INFERABLY > INFER
INFERE *adv* together
INFERENCE *n* act or process of reaching a conclusion by reasoning from evidence
INFERIAE *pl n* offerings made to the spirits of the dead
INFERIBLE > INFER
INFERIOR *adj* lower in quality, position, or status ▷ *n* person of lower position or status
INFERIORS > INFERIOR
INFERNAL *adj* of hell
INFERNO *n* intense raging fire
INFERNOS > INFERNO
INFERRED > INFER
INFERRER > INFER
INFERRERS > INFER
INFERRING > INFER
INFERS > INFER

INFERTILE *adj* unable to produce offspring
INFEST *vb* inhabit or overrun in unpleasantly large numbers
INFESTANT *n* parasite
INFESTED > INFEST
INFESTER > INFEST
INFESTERS > INFEST
INFESTING > INFEST
INFESTS > INFEST
INFICETE *adj* not witty
INFIDEL *n* person with no religion ▷ *adj* of unbelievers or unbelief
INFIDELIC > INFIDEL
INFIDELS > INFIDEL
INFIELD *n* area of the field near the pitch
INFIELDER *n* player positioned in the infield
INFIELDS > INFIELD
INFIGHT *vb* box at close quarters
INFIGHTER > INFIGHT
INFIGHTS > INFIGHT
INFILL *vb* fill in ▷ *n* act of filling or closing gaps, etc, in something, such as a row of buildings
INFILLED > INFILL
INFILLING > INFILL
INFILLS > INFILL
INFIMA > INFIMUM
INFIMUM *n* greatest lower bound
INFIMUMS > INFIMUM
INFINITE *adj* without any limit or end ▷ *n* something without any limit or end
INFINITES > INFINITE
INFINITY *n* endless space, time, or number
INFIRM *vb* make infirm ▷ *adj* physically or mentally weak
INFIRMARY *n* hospital
INFIRMED > INFIRM
INFIRMER > INFIRM
INFIRMEST > INFIRM
INFIRMING > INFIRM
INFIRMITY *n* state of being infirm
INFIRMLY > INFIRM
INFIRMS > INFIRM
INFIX *vb* fix firmly in ▷ *n* affix inserted into the middle of a word
INFIXED > INFIX
INFIXES > INFIX
INFIXING > INFIX
INFIXION > INFIX
INFIXIONS > INFIX
INFLAME *vb* make angry or excited
INFLAMED > INFLAME
INFLAMER > INFLAME
INFLAMERS > INFLAME
INFLAMES > INFLAME
INFLAMING > INFLAME
INFLATE *vb* expand by filling with air or gas
INFLATED > INFLATE
INFLATER > INFLATE
INFLATERS > INFLATE
INFLATES > INFLATE
INFLATING > INFLATE
INFLATION *n* inflating
INFLATIVE *adj* causing inflation
INFLATOR > INFLATE
INFLATORS > INFLATE
INFLATUS *n* act of breathing in
INFLECT *vb* change (the voice) in tone or pitch
INFLECTED > INFLECT
INFLECTOR > INFLECT
INFLECTS > INFLECT
INFLEXED *adj* curved or bent inwards and downwards towards the axis
INFLEXION *n* modulation of the voice
INFLEXURE *same as* > INFLEXION
INFLICT *vb* impose (something unpleasant) on
INFLICTED > INFLICT
INFLICTER > INFLICT
INFLICTOR > INFLICT
INFLICTS > INFLICT
INFLIGHT *adj* provided during flight in an aircraft
INFLOW *n* something, such as liquid or gas, that flows in ▷ *vb* flow in
INFLOWING > INFLOW
INFLOWS > INFLOW
INFLUENCE *n* effect of one person or thing on another ▷ *vb* have an effect on
INFLUENT *adj* flowing in ▷ *n* something flowing in, esp a tributary
INFLUENTS > INFLUENT
INFLUENZA *n* contagious viral disease causing headaches, muscle pains, and fever
INFLUX *n* arrival or entry of many people or things
INFLUXES > INFLUX
INFLUXION *same as* > INFLUX
INFO *n* information
INFOBAHN *same as* > INTERNET
INFOBAHNS > INFOBAHN
INFOLD *variant spelling of* > ENFOLD
INFOLDED > INFOLD
INFOLDER > INFOLD
INFOLDERS > INFOLD
INFOLDING > INFOLD
INFOLDS > INFOLD
INFOMANIA *n* obsessive devotion to gathering information
INFORCE *same as* > ENFORCE
INFORCED > INFORCE
INFORCES > INFORCE
INFORCING > INFORCE
INFORM *vb* tell ▷ *adj* without shape
INFORMAL *adj* relaxed and friendly
INFORMANT *n* person who gives information
INFORMED > INFORM
INFORMER *n* person who informs to the police
INFORMERS > INFORMER
INFORMING > INFORM
INFORMS > INFORM
INFORTUNE *n* misfortune
INFOS > INFO
INFOUGHT > INFIGHT
INFRA *adv* (esp in textual annotation) below
INFRACT *vb* violate or break (a law, an agreement, etc)
INFRACTED > INFRACT
INFRACTOR > INFRACT
INFRACTS > INFRACT
INFRARED *adj* of or using rays below the red end of the visible spectrum ▷ *n* infrared part of the spectrum
INFRAREDS > INFRARED
INFRINGE *vb* break (a law or agreement)
INFRINGED > INFRINGE
INFRINGER > INFRINGE
INFRINGES > INFRINGE
INFRUGAL *adj* wasteful
INFULA *singular of* > INFULAE
INFULAE *pl n* two ribbons hanging from the back of a bishop's mitre
INFURIATE *vb* make very angry ▷ *adj* furious
INFUSCATE *adj* (esp of the wings of an insect) tinged with brown
INFUSE *vb* fill (with an emotion or quality)
INFUSED > INFUSE
INFUSER *n* any device used to make an infusion, esp a tea maker
INFUSERS > INFUSER
INFUSES > INFUSE
INFUSIBLE *adj* unable to be fused or melted
INFUSING > INFUSE
INFUSION *n* infusing
INFUSIONS > INFUSION
INFUSIVE > INFUSION
INFUSORIA *pl n* tiny water-dwelling animals
INFUSORY *adj* containing infusoria
INGAN *Scots word for* > ONION
INGANS > INGAN
INGATE *n* entrance
INGATES > INGATE
INGATHER *vb* gather together or in (a harvest)
INGATHERS > INGATHER
INGENER *Shakespearean form of* > ENGINEER
INGENERS > INGENER
INGENIOUS *adj* showing cleverness and originality
INGENIUM *n* genius
INGENIUMS > INGENIUM
INGENU *n* artless or inexperienced boy or young man
INGENUE *n* artless or inexperienced girl or young woman
INGENUES > INGENUE
INGENUITY *n* cleverness a[t] inventing things
INGENUOUS *adj* unsophisticated and trusting
INGENUS > INGENU
INGEST *vb* take (food or liquid) into the body
INGESTA *pl n* nourishmen[t] taken into the body through the mouth
INGESTED > INGEST
INGESTING > INGEST
INGESTION > INGEST
INGESTIVE > INGEST
INGESTS > INGEST
INGINE *n* genius
INGINES > INGINE
INGLE *n* fire in a room or a fireplace
INGLENEUK *same as* > INGLENOOK
INGLENOOK *n* corner by a fireplace
INGLES > INGLE
INGLOBE *vb* shape as a sphere
INGLOBED > INGLOBE
INGLOBES > INGLOBE
INGLOBING > INGLOBE
INGLUVIAL > INGLUVIES
INGLUVIES *n* bird's craw
INGO *vb* reveal
INGOES > INGO
INGOING > INGO
INGOINGS > INGO
INGOT *n* oblong block of cast metal ▷ *vb* shape (metal) into ingots
INGOTED > INGOT
INGOTING > INGOT
INGOTS > INGOT
INGRAFT *variant spelling of* > ENGRAFT
INGRAFTED > INGRAFT
INGRAFTS > INGRAFT
INGRAIN *vb* impress deep[ly] on the mind or nature ▷ *adj* (of carpets) made of dyed yarn or of fibre that is dyed before being spun into yarn ▷ *n* carpet mad[e] from ingrained yarn
INGRAINED > INGRAIN
INGRAINS > INGRAIN
INGRAM *adj* ignorant
INGRATE *n* ungrateful person ▷ *adj* ungrateful
INGRATELY > INGRATE
INGRATES > INGRATE
INGRESS *n* entrance
INGRESSES > INGRESS
INGROOVE *vb* cut a groove into

NGROOVED > INGROOVE
NGROOVES > INGROOVE
NGROSS *archaic form of* > ENGROSS
NGROSSED > INGROSS
NGROSSES > INGROSS
NGROUND *adj* sunk into ground
NGROUP *n* highly cohesive and relatively closed social group
NGROUPS > INGROUP
NGROWING *adj* (of a toenail) growing abnormally into the flesh
NGROWN *adj* (esp of a toenail) grown abnormally into the flesh
NGROWTH *n* act of growing inwards
NGROWTHS > INGROWTH
NGRUM *adj* ignorant
NGUINAL *adj* of or relating to the groin
NGULF *variant spelling of* > ENGULF
NGULFED > INGULF
NGULFING > INGULF
NGULFS > INGULF
NGULPH *archaic form of* > ENGULF
NGULPHED > INGULPH
NGULPHS > INGULPH
NHABIT *vb* live in
NHABITED > INHABIT
NHABITER *n* inhabitant
NHABITOR *n* inhabitant
NHABITS > INHABIT
NHALANT *n* medical preparation inhaled to help breathing problems ▷ *adj* inhaled for its soothing or therapeutic effect
NHALANTS > INHALANT
NHALATOR *n* device for converting drugs into a fine spray for inhaling
NHALE *vb* breathe in (air, smoke, etc)
NHALED > INHALE
NHALER *n* container for an inhalant
NHALERS > INHALER
NHALES > INHALE
NHALING > INHALE
NHARMONY *n* discord
NHAUL *n* line for hauling in a sail
NHAULER > INHAUL
NHAULERS > INHAULER
NHAULS > INHAUL
NHAUST *vb* drink in
NHAUSTED > INHAUST
NHAUSTS > INHAUST
NHEARSE *vb* bury
NHEARSED > INHEARSE
NHEARSES > INHEARSE
NHERCE *same as* > INHEARSE
NHERCED > INHERCE
NHERCES > INHERCE
NHERCING > INHERCE
NHERE *vb* be an inseparable part (of)
INHERED > INHERE
INHERENCE *n* state or condition of being inherent
INHERENCY *same as* > INHERENCE
INHERENT *adj* existing as an inseparable part
INHERES > INHERE
INHERING > INHERE
INHERIT *vb* receive (money etc) from someone who has died
INHERITED > INHERIT
INHERITOR > INHERIT
INHERITS > INHERIT
INHESION *less common word for* > INHERENCE
INHESIONS > INHESION
INHIBIN *n* peptide hormone
INHIBINS > INHIBIN
INHIBIT *vb* restrain (an impulse or desire)
INHIBITED > INHIBIT
INHIBITER *same as* > INHIBITOR
INHIBITOR *n* person or thing that inhibits
INHIBITS > INHIBIT
INHOLDER *n* inhabitant
INHOLDERS > INHOLDER
INHOLDING *n* privately owned land inside a federal reserve
INHOOP *vb* confine
INHOOPED > INHOOP
INHOOPING > INHOOP
INHOOPS > INHOOP
INHUMAN *adj* cruel or brutal
INHUMANE *same as* > INHUMAN
INHUMANLY > INHUMAN
INHUMATE *vb* bury
INHUMATED > INHUMATE
INHUMATES > INHUMATE
INHUME *vb* inter
INHUMED > INHUME
INHUMER > INHUME
INHUMERS > INHUME
INHUMES > INHUME
INHUMING > INHUME
INIA > INION
INIMICAL *adj* unfavourable or hostile
INION *n* most prominent point at the back of the head, used as a point of measurement in craniometry
INIONS > INION
INIQUITY *n* injustice or wickedness
INISLE *vb* put on or make into an island
INISLED > INISLE
INISLES > INISLE
INISLING > INISLE
INITIAL *adj* first, at the beginning ▷ *n* first letter, esp of a person's name ▷ *vb* sign with one's initials
INITIALED > INITIAL
INITIALER > INITIAL
INITIALLY > INITIAL
INITIALS > INITIAL
INITIATE *vb* begin or set going ▷ *n* recently initiated person ▷ *adj* initiated
INITIATED > INITIATE
INITIATES > INITIATE
INITIATOR *n* person or thing that initiates
INJECT *vb* put (a fluid) into the body with a syringe
INJECTANT *n* injected substance
INJECTED > INJECT
INJECTING > INJECT
INJECTION *n* fluid injected into the body, esp for medicinal purposes
INJECTIVE > INJECTION
INJECTOR > INJECT
INJECTORS > INJECT
INJECTS > INJECT
INJELLIED > INJELLY
INJELLIES > INJELLY
INJELLY *vb* place in jelly
INJERA *n* white Ethiopian flatbread, similar to a crepe
INJERAS > INJERA
INJOINT *vb* join
INJOINTED > INJOINT
INJOINTS > INJOINT
INJUNCT *vb* issue a legal injunction against (a person)
INJUNCTED > INJUNCT
INJUNCTS > INJUNCT
INJURABLE > INJURE
INJURE *vb* hurt physically or mentally
INJURED > INJURE
INJURER > INJURE
INJURERS > INJURE
INJURES > INJURE
INJURIES > INJURY
INJURING > INJURE
INJURIOUS *adj* causing harm
INJURY *n* physical hurt
INJUSTICE *n* unfairness
INK *n* coloured liquid used for writing or printing ▷ *vb* mark in ink (something already marked in pencil)
INKBERRY *n* North American holly tree
INKBLOT *n* abstract patch of ink, one of ten commonly used in the Rorschach test
INKBLOTS > INKBLOT
INKED > INK
INKER > INK
INKERS > INK
INKHOLDER *same as* > INKHORN
INKHORN *n* (formerly) a small portable container for ink, usually made from horn
INKHORNS > INKHORN
INKIER > INKY
INKIEST > INKY
INKINESS > INKY
INKING > INK
INKJET *n* method of printing streams of electrically charged ink
INKLE *n* kind of linen tape used for trimmings
INKLED *adj* trimmed with inkle
INKLES > INKLE
INKLESS > INK
INKLIKE > INK
INKLING *n* slight idea or suspicion
INKLINGS > INKLING
INKPOT *n* ink-bottle
INKPOTS > INKPOT
INKS > INK
INKSPOT *n* ink stain
INKSPOTS > INKSPOT
INKSTAND *n* stand or tray for holding writing tools and containers for ink
INKSTANDS > INKSTAND
INKSTONE *n* stone used in making ink
INKSTONES > INKSTONE
INKWELL *n* small container for ink, often fitted into the surface of a desk
INKWELLS > INKWELL
INKWOOD *n* type of tree
INKWOODS > INKWOOD
INKY *adj* dark or black
INLACE *variant spelling of* > ENLACE
INLACED > INLACE
INLACES > INLACE
INLACING > INLACE
INLAID > INLAY
INLAND *adv* in or towards the interior of a country, away from the sea ▷ *adj* of or in the interior of a country or region, away from a sea or border ▷ *n* interior of a country or region
INLANDER > INLAND
INLANDERS > INLAND
INLANDS > INLAND
INLAY *n* inlaid substance or pattern ▷ *vb* decorate (an article, esp of furniture) by inserting pieces of wood, ivory, or metal so that the surfaces are smooth and flat
INLAYER > INLAY
INLAYERS > INLAY
INLAYING > INLAY
INLAYINGS > INLAY
INLAYS > INLAY
INLET *n* narrow strip of water extending from the sea into the land ▷ *vb* insert or inlay
INLETS > INLET
INLETTING > INLET
INLIER *n* outcrop of rocks that is entirely surrounded by younger rocks
INLIERS > INLIER

INLOCK *vb* lock up
INLOCKED > INLOCK
INLOCKING > INLOCK
INLOCKS > INLOCK
INLY *adv* inwardly
INLYING *adj* situated within or inside
INMATE *n* person living in an institution such as a prison
INMATES > INMATE
INMESH *variant spelling of* > ENMESH
INMESHED > INMESH
INMESHES > INMESH
INMESHING > INMESH
INMIGRANT *adj* coming in from another area of the same country ▷ *n* inmigrant person or animal
INMOST *adj* innermost
INN *n* pub or small hotel, esp in the country ▷ *vb* stay at an inn
INNAGE *n* measurement from bottom of container to surface of liquid
INNAGES > INNAGE
INNARDS *pl n* internal organs
INNATE *adj* being part of someone's nature, inborn
INNATELY > INNATE
INNATIVE *adj* native
INNED > INN
INNER *adj* happening or located inside ▷ *n* red innermost ring on a target
INNERLY > INNER
INNERMOST *adj* furthest inside
INNERNESS > INNER
INNERS > INNER
INNERSOLE *same as* > INSOLE
INNERVATE *vb* supply nerves to (a bodily organ or part)
INNERVE *vb* supply with nervous energy
INNERVED > INNERVE
INNERVES > INNERVE
INNERVING > INNERVE
INNERWEAR *n* underwear
INNING *n* division of the game consisting of a turn at batting and a turn in the field for each side
INNINGS > INNING
INNKEEPER *n* owner or manager of an inn
INNLESS *adj* without inns
INNOCENCE *n* quality or state of being innocent
INNOCENCY *same as* > INNOCENCE
INNOCENT *adj* not guilty of a crime ▷ *n* innocent person, esp a child
INNOCENTS > INNOCENT
INNOCUITY > INNOCUOUS
INNOCUOUS *adj* not harmful
INNOVATE *vb* introduce new ideas or methods
INNOVATED > INNOVATE
INNOVATES > INNOVATE
INNOVATOR > INNOVATE
INNOXIOUS *adj* not noxious
INNS > INN
INNUENDO *n* (remark making) an indirect reference to something rude or unpleasant
INNUENDOS > INNUENDO
INNYARD *n* courtyard of an inn
INNYARDS > INNYARD
INOCULA > INOCULUM
INOCULANT *same as* > INOCULUM
INOCULATE *vb* protect against disease by injecting with a vaccine
INOCULUM *n* substance used in giving an inoculation
INOCULUMS > INOCULUM
INODOROUS *adj* odourless
INOPINATE *adj* unexpected
INORB *vb* enclose in or as if in an orb
INORBED > INORB
INORBING > INORB
INORBS > INORB
INORGANIC *adj* not having the characteristics of living organisms
INORNATE *adj* simple
INOSINE *n* type of molecule making up cell
INOSINES > INOSINE
INOSITE *same as* > INOSITOL
INOSITES > INOSITE
INOSITOL *n* cyclic alcohol
INOSITOLS > INOSITOL
INOTROPIC *adj* affecting or controlling the contraction of muscles, esp those of the heart
INPATIENT *n* patient who stays in a hospital for treatment
INPAYMENT *n* money paid into a bank account
INPHASE *adj* in the same phase
INPOUR *vb* pour in
INPOURED > INPOUR
INPOURING > INPOUR
INPOURS > INPOUR
INPUT *n* resources put into a project etc ▷ *vb* enter (data) in a computer
INPUTS > INPUT
INPUTTED > INPUT
INPUTTER > INPUT
INPUTTERS > INPUT
INPUTTING > INPUT
INQILAB *n* (in India, Pakistan, etc) revolution
INQILABS > INQILAB
INQUERE *Spenserian form of* > INQUIRE
INQUERED > INQUERE
INQUERES > INQUERE
INQUERING > INQUERE
INQUEST *n* official inquiry into a sudden death
INQUESTS > INQUEST
INQUIET *vb* disturb
INQUIETED > INQUIET
INQUIETLY > INQUIET
INQUIETS > INQUIET
INQUILINE *n* animal that lives in close association with another animal without harming it ▷ *adj* of or living as an inquiline
INQUINATE *vb* corrupt
INQUIRE *vb* seek information or ask (about)
INQUIRED > INQUIRE
INQUIRER > INQUIRE
INQUIRERS > INQUIRE
INQUIRES > INQUIRE
INQUIRIES > INQUIRY
INQUIRING > INQUIRE
INQUIRY *n* question
INQUORATE *adj* without enough people present to make a quorum
INRO *n* Japanese seal-box
INROAD *n* invasion or hostile attack
INROADS > INROAD
INRUN *n* slope down which ski jumpers ski
INRUNS > INRUN
INRUSH *n* sudden and overwhelming inward flow ▷ *vb* flow or rush suddenly and overwhelmingly
INRUSHES > INRUSH
INRUSHING > INRUSH
INS > IN
INSANE *adj* mentally ill
INSANELY > INSANE
INSANER > INSANE
INSANEST > INSANE
INSANIE *n* insanity
INSANIES > INSANIE
INSANITY *n* state of being insane
INSATIATE *adj* not able to be satisfied
INSATIETY *n* insatiability
INSCAPE *n* essential inner nature of a person, an object, etc
INSCAPES > INSCAPE
INSCIENCE *n* ignorance
INSCIENT *adj* ignorant
INSCONCE *vb* fortify
INSCONCED > INSCONCE
INSCONCES > INSCONCE
INSCRIBE *vb* write or carve words on
INSCRIBED > INSCRIBE
INSCRIBER > INSCRIBE
INSCRIBES > INSCRIBE
INSCROLL *vb* write on a scroll
INSCROLLS > INSCROLL
INSCULP *vb* engrave
INSCULPED > INSCULP
INSCULPS > INSCULP
INSCULPT *adj* engraved
INSEAM *vb* contain
INSEAMED > INSEAM
INSEAMING > INSEAM
INSEAMS > INSEAM
INSECT *n* small animal with six legs and usu. wings, such as an ant or fl
INSECTAN > INSECT
INSECTARY *n* place where insects are kept
INSECTEAN > INSECT
INSECTILE > INSECT
INSECTION *n* incision
INSECTS > INSECT
INSECURE *adj* anxious, not confident
INSEEM *vb* cover with grease
INSEEMED > INSEEM
INSEEMING > INSEEM
INSEEMS > INSEEM
INSELBERG *n* isolated rocky hill rising abruptly from a flat plain
INSENSATE *adj* without sensation, unconscious
INSERT *vb* put inside or include ▷ *n* something inserted
INSERTED *adj* (of a muscle) attached to the bone that it moves
INSERTER > INSERT
INSERTERS > INSERT
INSERTING > INSERT
INSERTION *n* act of inserting
INSERTS > INSERT
INSET *n* small picture inserted within a larger one ▷ *vb* place in or within ▷ *adj* decorated with something inserted
INSETS > INSET
INSETTED > INSET
INSETTER > INSET
INSETTERS > INSET
INSETTING > INSET
INSHALLAH *sentence substitute* if Allah wills it
INSHEATH *vb* sheathe
INSHEATHE *vb* sheathe
INSHEATHS > INSHEATH
INSHELL *vb* retreat, as into a shell
INSHELLED > INSHELL
INSHELLS > INSHELL
INSHELTER *vb* put in a shelter
INSHIP *vb* travel or send by ship
INSHIPPED > INSHIP
INSHIPS > INSHIP
INSHORE *adj* close to the shore ▷ *adv* towards the shore
INSHRINE *variant spelling of* > ENSHRINE
INSHRINED > INSHRINE
INSHRINES > INSHRINE
INSIDE *prep* in or to the interior of ▷ *adj* on or of the inside ▷ *adv* on, in, or to the inside, indoors ▷ *n* inner side, surface, or part
INSIDER *n* member of a

group who has privileged knowledge about it
NSIDERS > INSIDER
NSIDES > INSIDE
NSIDIOUS *adj* subtle or unseen but dangerous
NSIGHT *n* deep understanding
NSIGHTS > INSIGHT
NSIGNE *same as* > INSIGNIA
NSIGNIA *n* badge or emblem of honour or office
NSIGNIAS > INSIGNIA
NSINCERE *adj* showing false feelings, not genuine
NSINEW *vb* connect or strengthen, as with sinews
NSINEWED > INSINEW
NSINEWS > INSINEW
NSINUATE *vb* suggest indirectly
NSIPID *adj* lacking interest, spirit, or flavour
NSIPIDLY > INSIPID
NSIPIENT *adj* lacking wisdom
NSIST *vb* demand or state firmly
NSISTED > INSIST
NSISTENT *adj* making persistent demands
NSISTER > INSIST
NSISTERS > INSIST
NSISTING > INSIST
NSISTS > INSIST
NSNARE *less common spelling of* > ENSNARE
NSNARED > INSNARE
NSNARER > INSNARE
NSNARERS > INSNARE
NSNARES > INSNARE
NSNARING > INSNARE
NSOFAR *adv* to the extent
NSOLATE *vb* expose to sunlight, as for bleaching
NSOLATED > INSOLATE
NSOLATES > INSOLATE
NSOLE *n* inner sole of a shoe or boot
NSOLENCE > INSOLENT
NSOLENT *n* insolent person ▷ *adj* rude and disrespectful
NSOLENTS > INSOLENT
NSOLES > INSOLE
NSOLUBLE *adj* incapable of being solved
NSOLUBLY > INSOLUBLE
NSOLVENT *adj* unable to pay one's debts ▷ *n* person who is insolvent
NSOMNIA *n* inability to sleep
NSOMNIAC *adj* exhibiting or causing insomnia ▷ *n* person experiencing insomnia
NSOMNIAS > INSOMNIA
NSOMUCH *adv* such an extent
NSOOTH *adv* indeed
NSOUL *variant of* > ENSOUL
INSOULED > INSOUL
INSOULING > INSOUL
INSOULS > INSOUL
INSPAN *vb* harness (animals) to (a vehicle)
INSPANNED > INSPAN
INSPANS > INSPAN
INSPECT *vb* check closely or officially
INSPECTED > INSPECT
INSPECTOR *n* person who inspects
INSPECTS > INSPECT
INSPHERE *variant spelling of* > ENSPHERE
INSPHERED > INSPHERE
INSPHERES > INSPHERE
INSPIRE *vb* fill with enthusiasm, stimulate
INSPIRED *adj* brilliantly creative
INSPIRER > INSPIRE
INSPIRERS > INSPIRE
INSPIRES > INSPIRE
INSPIRING > INSPIRE
INSPIRIT *vb* fill with vigour
INSPIRITS > INSPIRIT
INSTABLE *less common word for* > UNSTABLE
INSTAL *same as* > INSTALL
INSTALL *vb* put in and prepare (equipment) for use
INSTALLED > INSTALL
INSTALLER > INSTALL
INSTALLS > INSTALL
INSTALS > INSTAL
INSTANCE *n* particular example ▷ *vb* mention as an example
INSTANCED > INSTANCE
INSTANCES > INSTANCE
INSTANCY *n* quality of being urgent or imminent
INSTANT *n* very brief time ▷ *adj* happening at once
INSTANTER *adv* without delay
INSTANTLY *adv* immediately
INSTANTS > INSTANT
INSTAR *vb* decorate with stars ▷ *n* stage in the development of an insect between any two moults
INSTARRED > INSTAR
INSTARS > INSTAR
INSTATE *vb* place in a position or office
INSTATED > INSTATE
INSTATES > INSTATE
INSTATING > INSTATE
INSTEAD *adv* as a replacement or substitute
INSTEP *n* part of the foot forming the arch between the ankle and toes
INSTEPS > INSTEP
INSTIGATE *vb* cause to happen
INSTIL *vb* introduce (an idea etc) gradually into someone's mind
INSTILL *same as* > INSTIL
INSTILLED > INSTILL
INSTILLER > INSTIL
INSTILLS > INSTILL
INSTILS > INSTIL
INSTINCT *n* inborn tendency to behave in a certain way ▷ *adj* animated or impelled (by)
INSTINCTS > INSTINCT
INSTITUTE *n* organization set up for a specific purpose, esp research or teaching ▷ *vb* start or establish
INSTRESS *vb* create or sustain
INSTROKE *n* inward stroke
INSTROKES > INSTROKE
INSTRUCT *vb* order to do something
INSTRUCTS > INSTRUCT
INSUCKEN *adj* of a sucken
INSULA *n* pyramid-shaped area of the brain within each cerebral hemisphere beneath parts of the frontal and temporal lobes
INSULAE > INSULA
INSULANT *same as* > INSULATION
INSULANTS > INSULANT
INSULAR *adj* not open to new ideas, narrow-minded ▷ *n* islander
INSULARLY > INSULAR
INSULARS > INSULAR
INSULAS > INSULA
INSULATE *vb* prevent or reduce the transfer of electricity, heat, or sound by surrounding or lining with a nonconducting material
INSULATED > INSULATE
INSULATES > INSULATE
INSULATOR *n* any material or device that insulates
INSULIN *n* hormone produced in the pancreas that controls the amount of sugar in the blood
INSULINS > INSULIN
INSULSE *adj* stupid
INSULSITY *n* stupidity
INSULT *vb* behave rudely to, offend ▷ *n* insulting remark or action
INSULTANT *adj* insulting
INSULTED > INSULT
INSULTER > INSULT
INSULTERS > INSULT
INSULTING > INSULT
INSULTS > INSULT
INSURABLE > INSURE
INSURANCE *n* agreement by which one makes regular payments to a company who pay an agreed sum if damage, loss, or death occurs
INSURANT *n* holder of an insurance policy
INSURANTS > INSURANT
INSURE *vb* protect by insurance
INSURED *adj* covered by insurance ▷ *n* person, persons, or organization covered by an insurance policy
INSUREDS > INSURED
INSURER *n* person or company that sells insurance
INSURERS > INSURER
INSURES > INSURE
INSURGENT *adj* in revolt against an established authority ▷ *n* person who takes part in a rebellion
INSURING > INSURE
INSWATHE *vb* bind or wrap
INSWATHED > INSWATHE
INSWATHES > INSWATHE
INSWEPT *adj* narrowed towards the front
INSWING *n* movement of a bowled ball from off to leg through the air
INSWINGER *n* ball bowled so as to move from off to leg through the air
INSWINGS > INSWING
INTACT *adj* not changed or damaged in any way
INTACTLY > INTACT
INTAGLI > INTAGLIO
INTAGLIO *n* (gem carved with) an engraved design
INTAGLIOS > INTAGLIO
INTAKE *n* amount or number taken in
INTAKES > INTAKE
INTARSIA *n* decorative or pictorial mosaic of inlaid wood or sometimes ivory of a style developed in the Italian Renaissance and used esp on wooden wall panels
INTARSIAS > INTARSIA
INTEGER *n* positive or negative whole number or zero
INTEGERS > INTEGER
INTEGRAL *adj* being an essential part of a whole ▷ *n* sum of a large number of very small quantities
INTEGRALS > INTEGRAL
INTEGRAND *n* mathematical function to be integrated
INTEGRANT *adj* part of a whole ▷ *n* integrant thing or part
INTEGRATE *vb* combine into a whole ▷ *adj* made up of parts
INTEGRITY *n* quality of having high moral principles
INTEL *n* US military intelligence
INTELLECT *n* power of thinking and reasoning
INTELS > INTEL

INTENABLE *adj* untenable
INTEND *vb* propose or plan (to do something)
INTENDANT *n* provincial or colonial official of France, Spain, or Portugal
INTENDED *adj* planned or future ▷ *n* person whom one is to marry
INTENDEDS > INTENDED
INTENDER > INTEND
INTENDERS > INTEND
INTENDING > INTEND
INTENDS > INTEND
INTENIBLE *adj* incapable of holding
INTENSATE *vb* intensify
INTENSE *adj* of great strength or degree
INTENSELY > INTENSE
INTENSER > INTENSE
INTENSEST > INTENSE
INTENSIFY *vb* make or become more intense
INTENSION *n* set of characteristics or properties by which the referent or referents of a given word are determined
INTENSITY *n* state or quality of being intense
INTENSIVE *adj* using or needing concentrated effort or resources ▷ *n* intensifier or intensive pronoun or grammatical construction
INTENT *n* intention ▷ *adj* paying close attention
INTENTION *n* something intended
INTENTIVE *adj* intent
INTENTLY > INTENT
INTENTS > INTENT
INTER *vb* bury (a corpse)
INTERACT *vb* act on or in close relation with each other
INTERACTS > INTERACT
INTERAGE *adj* between different ages
INTERARCH *vb* have intersecting arches
INTERBANK *adj* conducted between or involving two or more banks
INTERBED *vb* lie between strata of different minerals
INTERBEDS > INTERBED
INTERBRED *adj* having been bred within a single family or strain so as to produce particular characteristics
INTERCEDE *vb* try to end a dispute between two people or groups
INTERCELL *adj* occurring between cells
INTERCEPT *vb* seize or stop in transit ▷ *n* point at which two figures intersect
INTERCITY *adj* (in Britain) denoting a fast train or passenger rail service, esp between main towns
INTERCLAN *adj* occurring between clans
INTERCLUB *adj* of, relating to, or conducted between two or more clubs
INTERCOM *n* internal communication system with loudspeakers
INTERCOMS > INTERCOM
INTERCROP *n* crop grown between the rows of another crop ▷ *vb* grow (one crop) between the rows of (another)
INTERCUT *another word for* > CROSSCUT
INTERCUTS > INTERCUT
INTERDASH *vb* dash between
INTERDEAL *vb* intrigue or plot
INTERDICT *n* official prohibition or restraint ▷ *vb* prohibit or forbid
INTERDINE *vb* eat together
INTERESS *vb* interest
INTERESSE *vb* interest
INTEREST *n* desire to know or hear more about something ▷ *vb* arouse the interest of
INTERESTS > INTEREST
INTERFACE *n* area where two things interact or link ▷ *vb* connect or be connected with by interface
INTERFERE *vb* try to influence other people's affairs where one is not involved or wanted
INTERFILE *vb* place (one or more items) among other items in a file or arrangement
INTERFIRM *adj* occurring between companies
INTERFLOW *vb* flow together
INTERFOLD *vb* fold together
INTERFUSE *vb* mix or become mixed
INTERGANG *adj* occurring between gangs
INTERGREW > INTERGROW
INTERGROW *vb* grow among
INTERIM *adj* temporary, provisional, or intervening ▷ *n* intervening time ▷ *adv* meantime
INTERIMS > INTERIM
INTERIOR *n* inside ▷ *adj* inside, inner
INTERIORS > INTERIOR
INTERJECT *vb* make (a remark) suddenly or as an interruption
INTERJOIN *vb* join together
INTERKNIT *vb* knit together
INTERKNOT *vb* knot together
INTERLACE *vb* join together as if by weaving
INTERLAID > INTERLAY
INTERLAP *less common word for* > OVERLAP
INTERLAPS > INTERLAP
INTERLARD *vb* insert in or occur throughout
INTERLAY *vb* insert (layers) between ▷ *n* material, such as paper, placed between a printing plate and its base
INTERLAYS > INTERLAY
INTERLEAF *n* extra leaf which is inserted
INTERLEND *vb* lend between libraries
INTERLENT > INTERLEND
INTERLINE *vb* write or print (matter) between the lines of (a text or book)
INTERLINK *vb* connect together
INTERLOAN *n* loan between one library and another
INTERLOCK *vb* join firmly together ▷ *n* device used to prevent a mechanism from operating independently or unsafely ▷ *adj* (of fabric) closely knitted
INTERLOOP *vb* loop together
INTERLOPE *vb* intrude
INTERLUDE *n* short rest or break in an activity or event
INTERMALE *adj* occurring between males
INTERMAT *n* patch of seabed devoid of vegetation
INTERMATS > INTERMAT
INTERMENT *n* burial
INTERMESH *vb* net together
INTERMIT *vb* suspend (activity) or (of activity) to be suspended temporarily or at intervals
INTERMITS > INTERMIT
INTERMIX *vb* mix together
INTERMONT *adj* located between mountains
INTERMURE *vb* wall in
INTERN *vb* imprison, esp during a war ▷ *n* trainee doctor in a hospital
INTERNAL *adj* of or on the inside ▷ *n* medical examination of the vagina, uterus, or rectum
INTERNALS > INTERNAL
INTERNE *same as* > INTERN
INTERNED > INTERN
INTERNEE *n* person who is interned
INTERNEES > INTERNEE
INTERNES > INTERNE
INTERNET *n* worldwide computer network
INTERNETS > INTERNET
INTERNING > INTERN
INTERNIST *n* physician who specializes in intern. medicine
INTERNODE *n* part of a plant stem between two nodes
INTERNS > INTERN
INTERPAGE *vb* print (matter) on intervening pages
INTERPLAY *n* action and reaction of two things upon each other
INTERPLED *adj* having instituted a particular type of proceedings
INTERPONE *vb* interpose
INTERPOSE *vb* insert between or among thing
INTERPRET *vb* explain the meaning of
INTERRACE *adj* between races
INTERRAIL *vb* travel on a international rail pass
INTERRED > INTER
INTERREX *n* person who governs during an interregnum
INTERRING > INTER
INTERROW *adj* occurring between rows
INTERRUPT *vb* break into (a conversation etc) ▷ *n* signal to initiate the stopping of the running o one computer program i order to run another
INTERS > INTER
INTERSECT *vb* (of roads) meet and cross
INTERSERT *vb* insert between
INTERSEX *n* condition of having characteristics intermediate between those of a male and a female
INTERTERM *adj* occurring between terms
INTERTEXT *adj* text seen a modifying another text i literary theory
INTERTIE *n* short roofing timber
INTERTIES > INTERTIE
INTERTILL *vb* cultivate between rows of crops
INTERUNIT *adj* occurring between units
INTERVAL *n* time betwee two particular moments or events
INTERVALE *dialect form of* > INTERVAL
INTERVALS > INTERVAL
INTERVEIN *vb* intersect
INTERVENE *vb* involve oneself in a situation, esp to prevent conflict

INTERVIEW *n* formal discussion, esp between a job-seeker and an employer ▷ *vb* conduct an interview with
INTERWAR *adj* of or happening in the period between World War I and World War II
INTERWIND *vb* wind together
INTERWORK *same as* > INTERWEAVE
INTERWOVE *adj* having been woven together
INTERZONE *n* area between two occupied zones
INTESTACY > INTESTATE
INTESTATE *adj* not having made a will ▷ *n* person who dies without having made a will
INTESTINE *n* lower part of the alimentary canal between the stomach and the anus
INTHRAL *archaic form of* > ENTHRAL
INTHRALL *archaic form of* > ENTHRAL
INTHRALLS > INTHRALL
INTHRALS > INTHRAL
INTHRONE *archaic form of* > ENTHRONE
INTHRONED > INTHRONE
INTHRONES > INTHRONE
INTI *n* former monetary unit of Peru
INTIFADA *n* Palestinian uprising against Israel in the West Bank and Gaza Strip
INTIFADAH *same as* > INTIFADA
INTIFADAS > INTIFADA
INTIFADEH *same as* > INTIFADA
INTIL *Scot form of* > INTO
INTIMA *n* innermost layer of an organ or part, esp of a blood vessel
INTIMACY *n* close or warm friendship
INTIMAE > INTIMA
INTIMAL > INTIMA
INTIMAS > INTIMA
INTIMATE *adj* having a close personal relationship ▷ *n* close friend ▷ *vb* hint at or suggest
INTIMATED > INTIMATE
INTIMATER > INTIMATE
INTIMATES > INTIMATE
INTIME *adj* intimate
INTIMISM *n* school of impressionist painting
INTIMISMS > INTIMISM
INTIMIST > INTIMISM
INTIMISTE > INTIMISM
INTIMISTS > INTIMISM
INTIMITY *n* intimacy
INTINE *n* inner wall of a pollen grain or a spore
INTINES > INTINE
INTIRE *archaic form of* > ENTIRE
INTIS > INTI
INTITLE *archaic form of* > ENTITLE
INTITLED > INTITLE
INTITLES > INTITLE
INTITLING > INTITLE
INTITULE *vb* (in Britain) to entitle (an act of parliament)
INTITULED > INTITULE
INTITULES > INTITULE
INTO *prep* indicating motion towards the centre, result of a change, division, etc
INTOED *adj* having inward-turning toes
INTOMB *same as* > ENTOMB
INTOMBED > INTOMB
INTOMBING > INTOMB
INTOMBS > INTOMB
INTONACO *n* wet plaster surface on which frescoes are painted
INTONACOS > INTONACO
INTONATE *vb* pronounce or articulate (continuous connected speech) with a characteristic rise and fall of the voice
INTONATED > INTONATE
INTONATES > INTONATE
INTONATOR > INTONATE
INTONE *vb* speak or recite in an unvarying tone of voice
INTONED > INTONE
INTONER > INTONE
INTONERS > INTONE
INTONES > INTONE
INTONING > INTONE
INTONINGS > INTONE
INTORSION *n* spiral twisting in plant stems or other parts
INTORT *vb* twist inward
INTORTED > INTORT
INTORTING > INTORT
INTORTION > INTORT
INTORTS > INTORT
INTOWN *adj* infield
INTRA *prep* within
INTRACITY *same as* > INTERCITY
INTRADA *n* prelude
INTRADAS > INTRADA
INTRADAY *adj* occurring within one day
INTRADOS *n* inner curve or surface of an arch or vault
INTRANET *n* internal network that makes use of Internet technology
INTRANETS > INTRANET
INTRANT *n* one who enters
INTRANTS > INTRANT
INTREAT *archaic spelling of* > ENTREAT
INTREATED > INTREAT
INTREATS > INTREAT
INTRENCH *less common spelling of* > ENTRENCH
INTREPID *adj* fearless, bold
INTRICACY > INTRICATE
INTRICATE *adj* involved or complicated
INTRIGANT *n* person who intrigues
INTRIGUE *vb* make interested or curious ▷ *n* secret plotting
INTRIGUED > INTRIGUE
INTRIGUER > INTRIGUE
INTRIGUES > INTRIGUE
INTRINCE *adj* intricate
INTRINSIC *adj* essential to the basic nature of something
INTRO *n* introduction
INTRODUCE *vb* present (someone) by name (to another person)
INTROFIED > INTROFY
INTROFIES > INTROFY
INTROFY *vb* increase the wetting properties
INTROIT *n* short prayer said or sung as the celebrant is entering the sanctuary to celebrate Mass
INTROITAL > INTROIT
INTROITS > INTROIT
INTROITUS *n* entrance to a body cavity
INTROJECT *vb* (esp of a child) to incorporate ideas of others, or (in fantasy) of objects
INTROLD *variant of* > ENTROLD
INTROMIT *vb* enter or insert or allow to enter or be inserted
INTROMITS > INTROMIT
INTRON *n* stretch of DNA that interrupts a gene and does not contribute to the specification of a protein
INTRONS > INTRON
INTRORSE *adj* turned inwards or towards the axis
INTROS > INTRO
INTROVERT *n* person concerned more with his or her thoughts and feelings than with the outside world ▷ *adj* shy and quiet ▷ *vb* turn (a hollow organ or part) inside out
INTRUDE *vb* come in or join in without being invited
INTRUDED > INTRUDE
INTRUDER *n* person who enters a place without permission
INTRUDERS > INTRUDER
INTRUDES > INTRUDE
INTRUDING > INTRUDE
INTRUSION *n* act of intruding
INTRUSIVE *adj* characterized by intrusion or tending to intrude
INTRUST *same as* > ENTRUST
INTRUSTED > INTRUST
INTRUSTS > INTRUST
INTUBATE *vb* insert a tube or cannula into (a hollow organ)
INTUBATED > INTUBATE
INTUBATES > INTUBATE
INTUIT *vb* know or discover by intuition
INTUITED > INTUIT
INTUITING > INTUIT
INTUITION *n* instinctive knowledge or insight without conscious reasoning
INTUITIVE *adj* of, possessing, or resulting from intuition
INTUITS > INTUIT
INTUMESCE *vb* swell or become swollen
INTURN *n* inward turn
INTURNED *adj* turned inward
INTURNS > INTURN
INTUSE *n* contusion
INTUSES > INTUSE
INTWINE *less common spelling of* > ENTWINE
INTWINED > INTWINE
INTWINES > INTWINE
INTWINING > INTWINE
INTWIST *vb* twist together
INTWISTED > INTWIST
INTWISTS > INTWIST
INUKSHUIT > INUKSHUK
INUKSHUK *n* stone used by Inuit people to mark a location
INUKSHUKS > INUKSHUK
INULA *n* plant of the elecampane genus
INULAS > INULA
INULASE *n* enzyme that hydrolyses inulin to fructose
INULASES > INULASE
INULIN *n* fructose polysaccharide present in the tubers and rhizomes of some plants
INULINS > INULIN
INUMBRATE *vb* shade
INUNCTION *n* application of an ointment to the skin, esp by rubbing
INUNDANT > INUNDATE
INUNDATE *vb* flood
INUNDATED > INUNDATE
INUNDATES > INUNDATE
INUNDATOR > INUNDATE
INURBANE *adj* not urbane
INURE *vb* cause to accept or become hardened to
INURED > INURE
INUREMENT > INURE
INURES > INURE
INURING > INURE
INURN *vb* place (esp cremated ashes) in an urn
INURNED > INURN
INURNING > INURN
INURNMENT > INURN

INURNS > INURN
INUSITATE *adj* out of use
INUST *adj* burnt in
INUSTION > INUST
INUSTIONS > INUST
INUTILE *adj* useless
INUTILELY > INUTILE
INUTILITY > INUTILE
INVADABLE > INVADE
INVADE *vb* enter (a country) by military force
INVADED > INVADE
INVADER > INVADE
INVADERS > INVADE
INVADES > INVADE
INVADING > INVADE
INVALID *n* disabled or chronically ill person ▷ *vb* dismiss from active service because of illness or injury ▷ *adj* having no legal force
INVALIDED > INVALID
INVALIDLY > INVALID
INVALIDS > INVALID
INVAR *n* alloy made from iron and nickel
INVARIANT *n* entity, quantity, etc, that is unaltered by a particular transformation of coordinates
INVARS > INVAR
INVASION *n* invading
INVASIONS > INVASION
INVASIVE *adj* of or relating to an invasion, intrusion, etc
INVEAGLE *archaic form of* > INVEIGLE
INVEAGLED > INVEAGLE
INVEAGLES > INVEAGLE
INVECKED *same as* > INVECTED
INVECTED *adj* bordered with small convex curves
INVECTIVE *n* abusive speech or writing ▷ *adj* characterized by or using abusive language, bitter sarcasm, etc
INVEIGH *vb* criticize strongly
INVEIGHED > INVEIGH
INVEIGHER > INVEIGH
INVEIGHS > INVEIGH
INVEIGLE *vb* coax by cunning or trickery
INVEIGLED > INVEIGLE
INVEIGLER > INVEIGLE
INVEIGLES > INVEIGLE
INVENIT (he or she) designed it: used formerly on objects such as pocket watches next to the designer's name
INVENT *vb* think up or create (something new)
INVENTED > INVENT
INVENTER *same as* > INVENTOR
INVENTERS > INVENTER
INVENTING > INVENT
INVENTION *n* something invented
INVENTIVE *adj* creative and resourceful
INVENTOR *n* person who invents, esp as a profession
INVENTORS > INVENTOR
INVENTORY *n* detailed list of goods or furnishings ▷ *vb* make a list of
INVENTS > INVENT
INVERITY *n* untruth
INVERNESS *n* type of cape
INVERSE *vb* make something opposite or contrary in effect ▷ *adj* reversed in effect, sequence, direction, etc ▷ *n* exact opposite
INVERSED > INVERSE
INVERSELY > INVERSE
INVERSES > INVERSE
INVERSING > INVERSE
INVERSION *n* act of inverting or state of being inverted
INVERSIVE > INVERSION
INVERT *vb* turn upside down or inside out ▷ *n* homosexual
INVERTASE *n* enzyme, occurring in the intestinal juice of animals and in yeasts
INVERTED > INVERT
INVERTER *n* any device for converting a direct current into an alternating current
INVERTERS > INVERTER
INVERTIN *same as* > INVERTASE
INVERTING > INVERT
INVERTINS > INVERTIN
INVERTOR *same as* > INVERTER
INVERTORS > INVERTOR
INVERTS > INVERT
INVEST *vb* spend (money, time, etc) on something with the expectation of profit
INVESTED > INVEST
INVESTING > INVEST
INVESTOR > INVEST
INVESTORS > INVEST
INVESTS > INVEST
INVEXED *adj* concave
INVIABLE *adj* not viable, esp financially
INVIABLY > INVIABLE
INVIDIOUS *adj* likely to cause resentment
INVIOLACY > INVIOLATE
INVIOLATE *adj* unharmed, unaffected
INVIOUS *adj* without paths or roads
INVIRILE *adj* unmanly
INVISCID *adj* not viscid
INVISIBLE *adj* not able to be seen ▷ *n* invisible item of trade
INVISIBLY > INVISIBLE
INVITAL *adj* not vital
INVITE *vb* request the company of ▷ *n* invitation
INVITED > INVITE
INVITEE *n* one who is invited
INVITEES > INVITEE
INVITER > INVITE
INVITERS > INVITE
INVITES > INVITE
INVITING *adj* tempting, attractive ▷ *n* old word for invitation
INVITINGS > INVITING
INVOCABLE > INVOKE
INVOCATE *archaic word for* > INVOKE
INVOCATED > INVOCATE
INVOCATES > INVOCATE
INVOCATOR > INVOCATE
INVOICE *n* (present with) a bill for goods or services supplied ▷ *vb* present (a customer) with an invoice
INVOICED > INVOICE
INVOICES > INVOICE
INVOICING > INVOICE
INVOKE *vb* put (a law or penalty) into operation
INVOKED > INVOKE
INVOKER > INVOKE
INVOKERS > INVOKE
INVOKES > INVOKE
INVOKING > INVOKE
INVOLUCEL *n* ring of bracts at the base of the florets of a compound umbel
INVOLUCRA *n* involucres
INVOLUCRE *n* ring of bracts at the base of an inflorescence in such plants as the composites
INVOLUTE *adj* complex, intricate, or involved ▷ *n* curve described by the free end of a thread as it is wound around another curve on the same plane ▷ *vb* become involute
INVOLUTED > INVOLUTE
INVOLUTES > INVOLUTE
INVOLVE *vb* include as a necessary part
INVOLVED > INVOLVE
INVOLVER > INVOLVE
INVOLVERS > INVOLVE
INVOLVES > INVOLVE
INVOLVING > INVOLVE
INWALL *vb* surround with a wall
INWALLED > INWALL
INWALLING > INWALL
INWALLS > INWALL
INWARD *adj* directed towards the middle ▷ *adv* towards the inside or middle ▷ *n* inward part
INWARDLY *adv* within the private thoughts or feelings
INWARDS *adv* towards the inside or middle of something
INWEAVE *vb* weave together into or as if into a design, fabric, etc
INWEAVED > INWEAVE
INWEAVES > INWEAVE
INWEAVING > INWEAVE
INWICK *vb* perform a curling stroke in which the stone bounces off another stone
INWICKED > INWICK
INWICKING > INWICK
INWICKS > INWICK
INWIND *vb* wind or coil around
INWINDING > INWIND
INWINDS > INWIND
INWIT *n* conscience
INWITH *adv* within
INWITS > INWIT
INWORK *vb* work in
INWORKED > INWORK
INWORKING > INWORK
INWORKS > INWORK
INWORN *adj* worn in
INWOUND > INWIND
INWOVE > INWEAVE
INWOVEN > INWEAVE
INWRAP *less common spelling of* > ENWRAP
INWRAPPED > INWRAP
INWRAPS > INWRAP
INWREATHE *same as* > ENWREATHE
INWROUGHT *adj* worked or woven into material, esp decoratively
INYALA *n* antelope
INYALAS > INYALA
IO *n* type of moth
IODATE *same as* > IODIZE
IODATED > IODATE
IODATES > IODATE
IODATING > IODATE
IODATION > IODATE
IODATIONS > IODATE
IODIC *adj* of or containing iodine
IODID *same as* > IODIDE
IODIDE *n* compound containing an iodine atom, such as methyl iodide
IODIDES > IODIDE
IODIDS > IODID
IODIN *same as* > IODINE
IODINATE *vb* cause to combine with iodine
IODINATED > IODINATE
IODINATES > IODINATE
IODINE *n* bluish-black element used in medicine and photography
IODINES > IODINE
IODINS > IODIN
IODISE *same as* > IODIZE
IODISED > IODISE
IODISER > IODISE
IODISERS > IODISE
IODISES > IODISE
IODISING > IODISE
IODISM *n* poisoning induced by ingestion of iodine or its compounds
IODISMS > IODISM
IODIZE *vb* treat with iodine
IODIZED > IODIZE

IODIZER > IODIZE
IODIZERS > IODIZE
IODIZES > IODIZE
IODIZING > IODIZE
IODOFORM *n* yellow crystalline insoluble volatile solid
IODOFORMS > IODOFORM
IODOMETRY *n* procedure used in volumetric analysis for determining the quantity of substance present that contains iodine
IODOPHILE *adj* taking an intense iodine stain
IODOPHOR *n* substance in which iodine is combined with an agent that renders it soluble
IODOPHORS > IODOPHOR
IODOPSIN *n* violet light-sensitive pigment in the cones of the retina of the eye that is responsible for colour vision
IODOPSINS > IODOPSIN
IODOUS *adj* of or containing iodine, esp in the trivalent state
IODURET *n* iodide
IODURETS > IODURET
IODYRITE *n* silver iodide
IODYRITES > IODYRITE
IOLITE *n* grey or violet-blue dichroic mineral
IOLITES > IOLITE
ION *n* electrically charged atom
IONIC *adj* of or in the form of ions
IONICITY *n* ionic character
IONICS *pl n* study of ions
IONISABLE > IONISE
IONISE *same as* > IONIZE
IONISED > IONISE
IONISER *same as* > IONIZER
IONISERS > IONISER
IONISES > IONISE
IONISING > IONISE
IONIUM *n* naturally occurring radioisotope of thorium
IONIUMS > IONIUM
IONIZABLE > IONIZE
IONIZE *vb* change into ions
IONIZED > IONIZE
IONIZER *n* person or thing that ionizes, esp an electrical device used within a room to refresh its atmosphere by restoring negative ions
IONIZERS > IONIZER
IONIZES > IONIZE
IONIZING > IONIZE
IONOGEN *n* compound that exists as ions when dissolved
IONOGENIC *adj* forming ions
IONOGENS > IONOGEN
IONOMER *n* thermoplastic with ionic bonding between polymer chains
IONOMERS > IONOMER
IONONE *n* yellowish liquid mixture of two isomers with an odour of violets
IONONES > IONONE
IONOPAUSE *n* transitional zone in the atmosphere between the ionosphere and the exosphere
IONOPHORE *n* chemical compound capable of forming a complex with an ion and transporting it through a biological membrane
IONOSONDE *n* instrument measuring ionization
IONOTROPY *n* reversible interconversion of a pair of organic isomers as a result of the migration of an ionic part of the molecule
IONS > ION
IOS > IO
IOTA *n* ninth letter in the Greek alphabet
IOTACISM *n* pronunciation tendency in Modern Greek
IOTACISMS > IOTACISM
IOTAS > IOTA
IPECAC *n* type of S American shrub
IPECACS > IPECAC
IPOMOEA *n* tropical or subtropical convolvulaceous plant
IPOMOEAS > IPOMOEA
IPPON *n* winning point awarded in a judo or karate competition
IPPONS > IPPON
IPRINDOLE *n* antidepressant
IRACUND *adj* easily angered
IRADE *n* written edict of a Muslim ruler
IRADES > IRADE
IRASCIBLE *adj* easily angered
IRASCIBLY > IRASCIBLE
IRATE *adj* very angry
IRATELY > IRATE
IRATENESS > IRATE
IRATER > IRATE
IRATEST > IRATE
IRE *vb* anger ▷ *n* anger
IRED > IRE
IREFUL > IRE
IREFULLY > IRE
IRELESS > IRE
IRENIC *adj* tending to conciliate or promote peace
IRENICAL *same as* > IRENIC
IRENICISM > IRENICS
IRENICON *variant spelling of* > EIRENICON
IRENICONS > IRENICON
IRENICS *n* that branch of theology that is concerned with unity between Christian sects and denominations
IRENOLOGY *n* study of peace
IRES > IRE
IRID *n* type of iris
IRIDAL > IRID
IRIDEAL > IRID
IRIDES > IRIS
IRIDIAL > IRID
IRIDIAN > IRID
IRIDIC *adj* of or containing iridium, esp in the tetravalent state
IRIDISE *vb* make iridescent
IRIDISED > IRIDISE
IRIDISES > IRIDISE
IRIDISING > IRIDISE
IRIDIUM *n* very hard corrosion-resistant metal
IRIDIUMS > IRIDIUM
IRIDIZE *vb* make iridescent
IRIDIZED > IRIDIZE
IRIDIZES > IRIDIZE
IRIDIZING > IRIDIZE
IRIDOCYTE *n* cell in the skin of fish that gives them iridescence
IRIDOLOGY *n* technique used in complementary medicine to diagnose illness by studying a patient's eyes
IRIDOTOMY *n* surgical incision into the iris, esp to create an artificial pupil
IRIDS > IRID
IRING > IRE
IRIS *n* coloured circular membrane of the eye containing the pupil ▷ *vb* display iridescence
IRISATE *vb* make iridescent
IRISATED > IRISATE
IRISATES > IRISATE
IRISATING > IRISATE
IRISATION > IRISATE
IRISCOPE *n* instrument that displays the prismatic colours
IRISCOPES > IRISCOPE
IRISED > IRIS
IRISES > IRIS
IRISING > IRIS
IRITIC > IRITIS
IRITIS *n* inflammation of the iris of the eye
IRITISES > IRITIS
IRK *vb* irritate, annoy
IRKED > IRK
IRKING > IRK
IRKS > IRK
IRKSOME *adj* irritating, annoying
IRKSOMELY > IRKSOME
IROKO *n* tropical African hardwood tree
IROKOS > IROKO
IRON *n* strong silvery-white metallic element, widely used for structural and engineering purposes ▷ *adj* made of iron ▷ *vb* smooth (clothes or fabric) with an iron
IRONBARK *n* Australian eucalyptus with hard rough bark
IRONBARKS > IRONBARK
IRONBOUND *adj* bound with iron
IRONCLAD *adj* covered or protected with iron ▷ *n* large wooden 19th-century warship with armoured plating
IRONCLADS > IRONCLAD
IRONE *n* fragrant liquid
IRONED > IRON
IRONER > IRON
IRONERS > IRON
IRONES > IRONE
IRONIC *adj* using irony
IRONICAL *same as* > IRONIC
IRONIER > IRONY
IRONIES > IRONY
IRONIEST > IRONY
IRONING *n* clothes to be ironed
IRONINGS > IRONING
IRONISE *same as* > IRONIZE
IRONISED > IRONISE
IRONISES > IRONISE
IRONISING > IRONISE
IRONIST > IRONIZE
IRONISTS > IRONIZE
IRONIZE *vb* use or indulge in irony
IRONIZED > IRONIZE
IRONIZES > IRONIZE
IRONIZING > IRONIZE
IRONLESS > IRON
IRONLIKE > IRON
IRONMAN *n* very strong man
IRONMEN > IRONMAN
IRONNESS > IRON
IRONS > IRON
IRONSIDE *n* person with great stamina or resistance
IRONSIDES > IRONSIDE
IRONSMITH *adj* blacksmith
IRONSTONE *n* rock consisting mainly of iron ore
IRONWARE *n* domestic articles made of iron
IRONWARES > IRONWARE
IRONWEED *n* plant with purplish leaves
IRONWEEDS > IRONWEED
IRONWOMAN *n* very strong woman
IRONWOMEN > IRONWOMAN
IRONWOOD *n* any of various trees, such as hornbeam, with exceptionally hard wood
IRONWOODS > IRONWOOD
IRONWORK *n* work done in iron, esp decorative work
IRONWORKS *n* building in which iron is smelted, cast, or wrought
IRONY *n* mildly sarcastic use of words to imply the

opposite of what is said ▷ *adj* of, resembling, or containing iron
IRRADIANT *adj* radiating light
IRRADIATE *vb* subject to or treat with radiation
IRREAL *adj* unreal
IRREALITY *n* unreality
IRREDENTA *variant of* > IRRIDENTA
IRREGULAR *adj* not regular or even ▷ *n* soldier not in a regular army
IRRELATED *adj* irrelevant
IRRIDENTA *n* region that is ethnically or historically tied to one country, but which is ruled by another
IRRIGABLE > IRRIGATE
IRRIGABLY > IRRIGATE
IRRIGATE *vb* supply (land) with water by artificial channels or pipes
IRRIGATED > IRRIGATE
IRRIGATES > IRRIGATE
IRRIGATOR > IRRIGATE
IRRIGUOUS *adj* well-watered
IRRISION *n* mockery
IRRISIONS > IRRISION
IRRISORY *adj* mocking
IRRITABLE *adj* easily annoyed
IRRITABLY > IRRITABLE
IRRITANCY > IRRITANT
IRRITANT *adj* causing irritation ▷ *n* something that annoys or irritates
IRRITANTS > IRRITANT
IRRITATE *vb* annoy, anger
IRRITATED > IRRITATE
IRRITATES > IRRITATE
IRRITATOR > IRRITATE
IRRUPT *vb* enter forcibly or suddenly
IRRUPTED > IRRUPT
IRRUPTING > IRRUPT
IRRUPTION > IRRUPT
IRRUPTIVE *adj* irrupting or tending to irrupt
IRRUPTS > IRRUPT
IS *third person singular present tense of* > BE
ISABEL *n* brown yellow colour
ISABELLA *same as* > ISABEL
ISABELLAS > ISABELLA
ISABELS > ISABEL
ISAGOGE *n* academic introduction to a specialized subject field or area of research
ISAGOGES > ISAGOGE
ISAGOGIC > ISAGOGICS
ISAGOGICS *n* introductory studies, esp in the history of the Bible
ISALLOBAR *n* line on a map connecting places with equal pressure changes
ISARITHM *n* line on a map connecting places with the same population density
ISARITHMS > ISARITHM
ISATIN *n* yellowish-red crystalline compound soluble in hot water, used for the preparation of vat dyes
ISATINE *same as* > ISATIN
ISATINES > ISATINE
ISATINIC > ISATIN
ISATINS > ISATIN
ISBA *n* log hut
ISBAS > ISBA
ISCHAEMIA *n* inadequate supply of blood to an organ or part, as from an obstructed blood flow
ISCHAEMIC > ISCHAEMIA
ISCHEMIA *same as* > ISCHAEMIA
ISCHEMIAS > ISCHEMIA
ISCHEMIC > ISCHAEMIA
ISCHIA > ISCHIUM
ISCHIADIC > ISCHIUM
ISCHIAL > ISCHIUM
ISCHIATIC > ISCHIUM
ISCHIUM *n* one of the three sections of the hipbone, situated below the ilium
ISCHURIA *n* retention of urine
ISCHURIAS > ISCHURIA
ISEIKONIA *n* seeing of same image in both eyes
ISEIKONIC > ISEIKONIA
ISENERGIC *adj* of equal energy
ISH *n* issue
ISHES > ISH
ISINGLASS *n* kind of gelatine obtained from some freshwater fish
ISIT *sentence substitute* expression used to seek confirmation of something or show one is listening
ISLAND *n* piece of land surrounded by water ▷ *vb* cause to become an island
ISLANDED > ISLAND
ISLANDER *n* person who lives on an island
ISLANDERS > ISLANDER
ISLANDING > ISLAND
ISLANDS > ISLAND
ISLE *vb* make an isle of ▷ *n* island
ISLED > ISLE
ISLELESS *adj* without islands
ISLEMAN *n* islander
ISLEMEN > ISLEMAN
ISLES > ISLE
ISLESMAN *same as* > ISLEMAN
ISLESMEN > ISLESMAN
ISLET *n* small island
ISLETED *adj* having islets
ISLETS > ISLET
ISLING > ISLE
ISLOMANIA *n* obsessional enthusiasm or partiality for islands
ISM *n* doctrine, system, or practice
ISMATIC *adj* following fashionable doctrines
ISMATICAL *same as* > ISMATIC
ISMS > ISM
ISNA *vb* is not
ISNAE *same as* > ISNA
ISO *n* short segment of film that can be replayed easily
ISOAMYL as in *isoamyl acetate*, colourless volatile compound used as a solvent for cellulose lacquers and as a flavouring
ISOAMYLS > ISOAMYL
ISOBAR *n* line on a map connecting places of equal atmospheric pressure
ISOBARE *same as* > ISOBAR
ISOBARES > ISOBARE
ISOBARIC *adj* having equal atmospheric pressure
ISOBARISM > ISOBAR
ISOBARS > ISOBAR
ISOBASE *n* line connecting points of equal land upheaval
ISOBASES > ISOBASE
ISOBATH *n* line on a map connecting points of equal underwater depth
ISOBATHIC > ISOBATH
ISOBATHS > ISOBATH
ISOBRONT *n* line connecting points of simultaneous storm development
ISOBRONTS > ISOBRONT
ISOBUTANE *n* form of butane
ISOBUTENE *n* isomer of butene
ISOBUTYL as in *methyl isobutyl ketone* colourless insoluble liquid ketone used as a solvent for organic compounds
ISOBUTYLS > ISOBUTYL
ISOCHASM *n* line connecting points of equal aurorae frequency
ISOCHASMS > ISOCHASM
ISOCHEIM *n* line on a map connecting places with the same mean winter temperature
ISOCHEIMS > ISOCHEIM
ISOCHIMAL > ISOCHIME
ISOCHIME *same as* > ISOCHEIM
ISOCHIMES > ISOCHIME
ISOCHOR *n* line on a graph showing the variation of the temperature of a fluid with its pressure, when the volume is kept constant
ISOCHORE *same as* > ISOCHOR
ISOCHORES > ISOCHORE
ISOCHORIC > ISOCHOR
ISOCHORS > ISOCHOR
ISOCHRON *n* line on an isotope ratio diagram denoting a suite of rock or mineral samples all formed at the same time
ISOCHRONE *n* line on a ma[p] or diagram connecting places from which it take[s] the same time to travel to a certain point
ISOCHRONS > ISOCHRON
ISOCLINAL *adj* sloping in the same direction and at the same angle ▷ *n* imaginary line connectin[g] points on the earth's surface having equal angles of dip
ISOCLINE *same as* > ISOCLINAL
ISOCLINES > ISOCLINE
ISOCLINIC *same as* > ISOCLINAL
ISOCRACY *n* form of government in which all people have equal powers
ISOCRATIC > ISOCRACY
ISOCRYMAL *same as* > ISOCRYME
ISOCRYME *n* line connecting points of equ[al] winter temperature
ISOCRYMES > ISOCRYME
ISOCYANIC as in *isocyanic acid*, hypothetical acid known only in the form of its compounds
ISOCYCLIC *adj* containin[g] a closed ring of atoms of the same kind, esp carbo[n] atoms
ISODICA > ISODICON
ISODICON *n* short anthem
ISODOMA > ISODOMON
ISODOMON *n* masonry formed of uniform blocks with courses are of equal height
ISODOMONS > ISODOMON
ISODOMOUS > ISODOMON
ISODOMUM *same as* > ISODOMON
ISODONT *n* animal in whic[h] the teeth are of similar siz[e]
ISODONTAL *same as* > ISONDONT
ISODONTS > ISODONT
ISODOSE *n* dose of radiation applied to a part of the body in radiotherapy that is equa[l] to the dose applied to a different part
ISODOSES > ISODOSE
ISOENZYME *same as* > ISOZYME
ISOETES *n* quillwort
ISOFORM *n* protein simila[r] in function but not form t[o] another
ISOFORMS > ISOFORM
ISOGAMETE *n* gamete tha[t] is similar in size and form

to the one with which it unites in fertilization

ISOGAMIC > ISOGAMY

ISOGAMIES > ISOGAMY

ISOGAMOUS > ISOGAMY

ISOGAMY *n* (in some algae and fungi) sexual fusion of gametes of similar size and form

ISOGENEIC *same as* > ISOGENIC

ISOGENIC *same as* > ISOGENOUS

ISOGENIES > ISOGENOUS

ISOGENOUS *adj* of similar origin, as parts derived from the same embryonic tissue

ISOGENY > ISOGENOUS

ISOGLOSS *n* line drawn on a map around the area in which a linguistic feature is to be found, such as a particular pronunciation of a given word

ISOGON *n* equiangular polygon

ISOGONAL *same as* > ISOGONIC

ISOGONALS > ISOGONAL

ISOGONE *same as* > ISOGONIC

ISOGONES > ISOGONE

ISOGONIC *adj* having, making, or involving equal angles ▷ *n* imaginary line connecting points on the earth's surface having equal magnetic declination

ISOGONICS > ISOGONIC

ISOGONIES > ISOGONIC

ISOGONS > ISOGON

ISOGONY > ISOGONIC

ISOGRAFT *vb* grafting tissue from a donor genetically identical to the recipient

ISOGRAFTS > ISOGRAFT

ISOGRAM *same as* > ISOPLETH

ISOGRAMS > ISOGRAM

ISOGRAPH *n* line connecting points of the same linguistic usage

ISOGRAPHS > ISOGRAPH

ISOGRIV *n* line connecting points of equal angular difference between magnetic north and grid north

ISOGRIVS > ISOGRIV

ISOHEL *n* line on a map connecting places with an equal period of sunshine

ISOHELS > ISOHEL

ISOHYDRIC *adj* having the same acidity or hydrogen-ion concentration

ISOHYET *n* line on a map connecting places having equal rainfall

ISOHYETAL > ISOHYET

ISOHYETS > ISOHYET

ISOKONT *same as* > ISOKONTAN

ISOKONTAN *n* alga whose zoophores have equal cilia

ISOKONTS > ISOKONT

ISOLABLE > ISOLATE

ISOLATE *vb* place apart or alone ▷ *n* isolated person or group

ISOLATED > ISOLATE

ISOLATES > ISOLATE

ISOLATING > ISOLATE

ISOLATION > ISOLATE

ISOLATIVE *adj* concerned with isolation

ISOLATOR > ISOLATE

ISOLATORS > ISOLATE

ISOLEAD *n* line on a ballistic graph

ISOLEADS > ISOLEAD

ISOLEX *n* isogloss marking off the area in which a particular item of vocabulary is found

ISOLEXES > ISOLEX

ISOLINE *same as* > ISOPLETH

ISOLINES > ISOLINE

ISOLOG > ISOLOGOUS

ISOLOGOUS *adj* (of two or more organic compounds) having a similar structure but containing different atoms of the same valency

ISOLOGS > ISOLOGOUS

ISOLOGUE > ISOLOGOUS

ISOLOGUES > ISOLOGOUS

ISOMER *n* substance whose molecules contain the same atoms as another but in a different arrangement

ISOMERASE *n* any enzyme that catalyses the conversion of one isomeric form of a compound to another

ISOMERE *same as* > ISOMER

ISOMERES > ISOMERE

ISOMERIC > ISOMER

ISOMERISE *same as* > ISOMERIZE

ISOMERISM *n* existence of two or more compounds having the same molecular formula but a different arrangement of atoms within the molecule

ISOMERIZE *vb* change or cause to change from one isomer to another

ISOMEROUS *adj* having an equal number of parts or markings

ISOMERS > ISOMER

ISOMETRIC *adj* relating to muscular contraction without shortening of the muscle ▷ *n* drawing made in this way

ISOMETRY *n* rigid motion of a plane or space such that the distance between any two points before and after this motion is unaltered

ISOMORPH *n* substance or organism that exhibits isomorphism

ISOMORPHS > ISOMORPH

ISONIAZID *n* soluble colourless crystalline compound used to treat tuberculosis

ISONOME *n* line on a chart connecting points of equal abundance values of a plant species sampled in different sections of an area

ISONOMES > ISONOME

ISONOMIC > ISONOMY

ISONOMIES > ISONOMY

ISONOMOUS > ISONOMY

ISONOMY *n* equality before the law of the citizens of a state

ISOOCTANE *n* colourless liquid alkane hydrocarbon produced from petroleum and used in standardizing petrol

ISOPACH *n* line on a map connecting points below which a particular rock stratum has the same thickness

ISOPACHS > ISOPACH

ISOPHONE *n* isogloss marking off an area in which a particular feature of pronunciation is found

ISOPHONES > ISOPHONE

ISOPHOTAL > ISOPHOTE

ISOPHOTE *n* line on a diagram or image of a galaxy, nebula, or other celestial object joining points of equal surface brightness

ISOPHOTES > ISOPHOTE

ISOPLETH *n* line on a map connecting places registering the same amount or ratio of some geographical or meteorological phenomenon or phenomena

ISOPLETHS > ISOPLETH

ISOPOD *n* type of crustacean including woodlice and pill bugs ▷ *adj* of this type of crustacean

ISOPODAN > ISOPOD

ISOPODANS > ISOPOD

ISOPODOUS > ISOPOD

ISOPODS > ISOPOD

ISOPOLITY *n* equality of political rights

ISOPRENE *n* colourless volatile liquid with a penetrating odour

ISOPRENES > ISOPRENE

ISOPROPYL *n* group of atoms

ISOPYCNAL *n* line on a map connecting points of equal atmospheric density

ISOPYCNIC *same as* > ISOPYCNAL

ISOS > ISO

ISOSCELES *adj* (of a triangle) having two sides of equal length

ISOSMOTIC *same as* > ISOTONIC

ISOSPIN *n* internal quantum number used in the classification of elementary particles

ISOSPINS > ISOSPIN

ISOSPORY *n* condition of having spores of only one kind

ISOSTACY *n* state of balance in earth's crust

ISOSTASY *n* state of balance, or equilibrium, which sections of the earth's lithosphere are thought ultimately to achieve when the vertical forces upon them remain unchanged

ISOSTATIC > ISOSTASY

ISOSTERIC *adj* (of two different molecules) having the same number of atoms and the same number and configuration of valency electrons

ISOTACH *n* line on a map connecting points of equal wind speed

ISOTACHS > ISOTACH

ISOTACTIC *adj* (of a stereospecific polymer) having identical steric configurations of the groups on each asymmetric carbon atom on the chain

ISOTHERAL > ISOTHERE

ISOTHERE *n* line on a map linking places with the same mean summer temperature

ISOTHERES > ISOTHERE

ISOTHERM *n* line on a map connecting points of equal temperature

ISOTHERMS > ISOTHERM

ISOTONE *n* one of two or more atoms of different atomic number that contain the same number of neutrons

ISOTONES > ISOTONE

ISOTONIC *adj* (of two or more muscles) having equal tension

ISOTOPE *n* one of two or more atoms with the same number of protons in the nucleus but a different number of neutrons

ISOTOPES > ISOTOPE

ISOTOPIC > ISOTOPE

ISOTOPIES > ISOTOPE

ISOTOPY > ISOTOPE

ISOTRON *n* device for separating small quantities of isotopes by ionizing them and separating the ions by a mass spectrometer
ISOTRONS > ISOTRON
ISOTROPIC *adj* having uniform physical properties, such as elasticity or conduction in all directions
ISOTROPY > ISOTROPIC
ISOTYPE *n* presentation of statistical information in a row of diagrams
ISOTYPES > ISOTYPE
ISOTYPIC > ISOTYPE
ISOZYME *n* any of a set of structural variants of an enzyme occurring in different tissues in a single species
ISOZYMES > ISOZYME
ISOZYMIC > ISOZYME
ISPAGHULA *n* dietary fibre derived the seed husks and used as a thickener or stabilizer in the food industry
ISSEI *n* first-generation Japanese immigrant
ISSEIS > ISSEI
ISSUABLE *adj* capable of issuing or being issued
ISSUABLY > ISSUABLE
ISSUANCE *n* act of issuing
ISSUANCES > ISSUANCE
ISSUANT *adj* emerging or issuing
ISSUE *n* topic of interest or discussion ▷ *vb* make (a statement etc) publicly
ISSUED > ISSUE
ISSUELESS > ISSUE
ISSUER > ISSUE
ISSUERS > ISSUE
ISSUES > ISSUE
ISSUING > ISSUE
ISTANA *n* (in Malaysia) a royal palace
ISTANAS > ISTANA
ISTHMI > ISTHMUS
ISTHMIAN *n* inhabitant of an isthmus ▷ *adj* relating to or situated in an isthmus
ISTHMIANS > ISTHMIAN
ISTHMIC > ISTHMUS
ISTHMOID > ISTHMUS
ISTHMUS *n* narrow strip of land connecting two areas of land
ISTHMUSES > ISTHMUS
ISTLE *n* fibre obtained from various tropical American agave and yucca trees used in making carpets, cord, etc
ISTLES > ISTLE
IT *pron* refers to a nonhuman, animal, plant, or inanimate object ▷ *n* player whose turn it is to catch the others in children's games
ITA *n* type of palm
ITACISM *n* pronunciation of the Greek letter eta as in Modern Greek
ITACISMS > ITACISM
ITACONIC as in *itaconic acid*, white colourless crystalline carboxylic acid
ITALIC *adj* (of printing type) sloping to the right ▷ *n* style of printing type modelled on this, chiefly used to indicate emphasis, a foreign word, etc
ITALICISE *same as* > ITALICIZE
ITALICIZE *vb* put in italics
ITALICS > ITALIC
ITAS > ITA
ITCH *n* skin irritation causing a desire to scratch ▷ *vb* have an itch
ITCHED > ITCH
ITCHES > ITCH
ITCHIER > ITCH
ITCHIEST > ITCH
ITCHILY > ITCH
ITCHINESS > ITCH
ITCHING > ITCH
ITCHINGS > ITCH
ITCHWEED *n* white hellebore
ITCHWEEDS > ITCHWEED
ITCHY > ITCH
ITEM *n* single thing in a list or collection ▷ *adv* likewise ▷ *vb* itemize
ITEMED > ITEM
ITEMING > ITEM
ITEMISE *same as* > ITEMIZE
ITEMISED > ITEMISE
ITEMISER > ITEMISE
ITEMISERS > ITEMISE
ITEMISES > ITEMISE
ITEMISING > ITEMISE
ITEMIZE *vb* make a list of
ITEMIZED > ITEMIZE
ITEMIZER > ITEMIZE
ITEMIZERS > ITEMIZE
ITEMIZES > ITEMIZE
ITEMIZING > ITEMIZE
ITEMS > ITEM
ITERANCE > ITERATE
ITERANCES > ITERATE
ITERANT > ITERATE
ITERATE *vb* repeat
ITERATED > ITERATE
ITERATES > ITERATE
ITERATING > ITERATE
ITERATION > ITERATE
ITERATIVE *adj* repetitious or frequent
ITERUM *adv* again
ITHER *Scot word for* > OTHER
ITINERACY *same as* > ITINERANCY
ITINERANT *adj* travelling from place to place ▷ *n* itinerant worker or other person
ITINERARY *n* detailed plan of a journey ▷ *adj* of or relating to travel or routes of travel
ITINERATE *vb* travel from place to place
ITS *pron* belonging to it ▷ *adj* of or belonging to it
ITSELF *pron* reflexive form of *it*
IURE *adv* by law
IVIED *adj* covered with ivy
IVIES > IVY
IVORIED > IVORY
IVORIES *pl n* keys of a piano
IVORIST *n* worker in ivory
IVORISTS > IVORIST
IVORY *n* hard white bony substance forming the tusks of elephants ▷ *adj* yellowish-white
IVORYBILL *n* large American woodpecker
IVORYLIKE > IVORY
IVORYWOOD *n* yellowish-white wood of an Australian tree, used for engraving, inlaying, and turnery
IVRESSE *n* drunkenness
IVRESSES > IVRESSE
IVY *n* evergreen climbing plant
IVYLIKE > IVY
IWI *n* Māori tribe
IWIS *archaic word for* > CERTAINLY
IXIA *n* southern African plant of the iris family with showy ornamental funnel-shaped flowers
IXIAS > IXIA
IXODIASES > IXODIASIS
IXODIASIS *n* disease transmitted by ticks
IXODID *n* hard-bodied tick
IXODIDS > IXODID
IXORA *n* flowering shrub
IXORAS > IXORA
IXTLE *same as* > ISTLE
IXTLES > IXTLE
IZAR *n* long garment worn by Muslim women
IZARD *n* type of goat-antelope
IZARDS > IZARD
IZARS > IZAR
IZVESTIA *n* news
IZVESTIAS > IZVESTIA
IZVESTIYA *same as* > IZVESTIA
IZZARD *n* letter Z
IZZARDS > IZZARD
IZZAT *n* honour or prestige
IZZATS > IZZAT

A *interj* yes ▷ *sentence substitute* yes
AAP *n* S African offensive word for a simpleton or country bumpkin
AAPS > JAAP
AB *vb* poke sharply ▷ *n* quick punch or poke
ABBED > JAB
ABBER *vb* talk rapidly or incoherently ▷ *n* rapid or incoherent talk
ABBERED > JABBER
ABBERER > JABBER
ABBERERS > JABBER
ABBERING > JABBER
ABBERS > JABBER
ABBING > JAB
ABBINGLY > JAB
ABBLE *vb* ripple
ABBLED > JABBLE
ABBLES > JABBLE
ABBLING > JABBLE
ABERS *interj* Irish exclamation
ABIRU *n* large white-and-black Australian stork
ABIRUS > JABIRU
ABORANDI *n* any of several tropical American rutaceous shrubs
ABOT *n* frill or ruffle on the front of a blouse or shirt
ABOTS > JABOT
ABS > JAB
ACAL *n* Mexican daub hut
ACALES > JACAL
ACALS > JACAL
ACAMAR *n* tropical American bird with an iridescent plumage
ACAMARS > JACAMAR
ACANA *n* long-legged long-toed bird of tropical and subtropical marshy regions
JACANAS > JACANA
JACARANDA *n* tropical tree with sweet-smelling wood
JACARE *another name for* > CAYMAN
JACARES > JACARE
JACCHUS *n* small monkey
JACCHUSES > JACCHUS
JACENT *adj* lying
JACINTH *another name for* > HYACINTH
JACINTHE *n* hyacinth
JACINTHES > JACINTHE
JACINTHS > JACINTH
JACK *n* device for raising a motor vehicle or other heavy object ▷ *vb* lift or push (an object) with a jack
JACKAL *n* doglike wild animal of Africa and Asia ▷ *vb* behave like a jackal
JACKALLED > JACKAL
JACKALS > JACKAL
JACKAROO *same as* > JACKEROO
JACKAROOS > JACKAROO
JACKASS *n* fool
JACKASSES > JACKASS
JACKBOOT *n* high military boot ▷ *vb* oppress
JACKBOOTS > JACKBOOT
JACKDAW *n* black-and-grey Eurasian bird of the crow family
JACKDAWS > JACKDAW
JACKED > JACK
JACKEEN *n* slick self-assertive lower-class Dubliner
JACKEENS > JACKEEN
JACKER *n* labourer
JACKEROO *n* young male management trainee on a sheep or cattle station ▷ *vb* work as a jackeroo
JACKEROOS > JACKEROO
JACKERS > JACKER
JACKET *n* short coat ▷ *vb* put a jacket on (someone or something)
JACKETED > JACKET
JACKETING > JACKET
JACKETS > JACKET
JACKFISH *n* small pike fish
JACKFRUIT *n* tropical Asian tree
JACKIES > JACKY
JACKING > JACK
JACKINGS > JACK
JACKKNIFE *vb* (of an articulated truck) go out of control so that the trailer swings round at a sharp angle to the cab ▷ *n* large clasp knife
JACKLEG *n* unskilled worker
JACKLEGS > JACKLEG
JACKLIGHT > JACK
JACKMAN *n* retainer
JACKMEN > JACKMAN
JACKPLANE *n* large woodworking plane
JACKPOT *n* largest prize that may be won in a game
JACKPOTS > JACKPOT
JACKROLL *vb* gang-rape
JACKROLLS > JACKROLL
JACKS *n* game in which metal, bone, or plastic pieces are thrown and then picked up between throws of a small ball
JACKSCREW *n* lifting device
JACKSHAFT *n* short length of shafting that transmits power from an engine or motor to a machine
JACKSIE *n* buttocks or anus
JACKSIES > JACKSIE
JACKSMELT *n* food fish of the North Pacific
JACKSMITH *n* smith who makes jacks
JACKSNIPE *n* small Eurasian short-billed snipe
JACKSTAY *n* metal rod, wire rope, or wooden batten to which an edge of a sail is fastened along a yard
JACKSTAYS > JACKSTAY
JACKSTONE > JACK
JACKSTRAW *n* straw mannequin
JACKSY *same as* > JACKSIE
JACKY *n* offensive word for a native Australian
JACOBIN *n* variety of fancy pigeon with a hood of feathers swept up over and around the head
JACOBINS > JACOBIN
JACOBUS *n* English gold coin minted in the reign of James I
JACOBUSES > JACOBUS
JACONET *n* light cotton fabric used for clothing, bandages, etc
JACONETS > JACONET
JACQUARD *n* fabric in which the design is incorporated into the weave instead of

being printed or dyed on
JACQUARDS >JACQUARD
JACQUERIE *n* peasant rising or revolt
JACTATION *n* act of boasting
JACULATE *vb* hurl
JACULATED >JACULATE
JACULATES >JACULATE
JACULATOR >JACULATE
JACUZZI *n* bath or pool equipped with a system of underwater jets
JACUZZIS >JACUZZI
JADE *n* ornamental semiprecious stone, usu dark green ▷ *adj* bluish-green ▷ *vb* exhaust or make exhausted from work or use
JADED *adj* tired and unenthusiastic
JADEDLY >JADED
JADEDNESS >JADED
JADEITE *n* usually green or white mineral, found in igneous and metamorphic rocks
JADEITES >JADEITE
JADELIKE >JADE
JADERIES >JADERY
JADERY *n* shrewishness
JADES >JADE
JADING >JADE
JADISH >JADE
JADISHLY >JADE
JADITIC >JADE
JAEGER *n* marksman in certain units of the German or Austrian armies
JAEGERS >JAEGER
JAFA *n* offensive name for a person from Auckland
JAFAS >JAFA
JAG *n* period of uncontrolled indulgence in an activity ▷ *vb* cut unevenly
JAGA *n* guard ▷ *vb* guard or watch
JAGAED >JAGA
JAGAING >JAGA
JAGAS >JAGA
JAGER *same as* >JAEGER
JAGERS >JAGER
JAGG *same as* >JAG
JAGGARIES >JAGGARY
JAGGARY *same as* >JAGGERY
JAGGED >JAG
JAGGEDER >JAG
JAGGEDEST >JAG
JAGGEDLY >JAG
JAGGER *n* pedlar
JAGGERIES >JAGGERY
JAGGERS >JAGGER
JAGGERY *n* coarse brown sugar made in the East Indies from the sap of the date palm
JAGGHERY *same as* >JAGGERY
JAGGIER >JAGGY
JAGGIES >JAGGY
JAGGIEST >JAGGY
JAGGING >JAG
JAGGS >JAGG
JAGGY *adj* prickly ▷ *n* jagged computer image
JAGHIR *n* Indian regional governance
JAGHIRDAR *n* Indian regional governor
JAGHIRE *n* Indian regional governance
JAGHIRES >JAGHIRE
JAGHIRS >JAGHIR
JAGIR *n* Indian regional governance
JAGIRS >JAGIR
JAGLESS >JAG
JAGRA *n* Hindu festival
JAGRAS >JAGRA
JAGS >JAG
JAGUAR *n* large S American spotted cat
JAGUARS >JAGUAR
JAI *n* victory (to)
JAIL *n* prison ▷ *vb* send to prison
JAILABLE >JAIL
JAILBAIT *n* young woman, or young women collectively, considered sexually attractive but below the age of consent
JAILBIRD *n* person who has often been in prison
JAILBIRDS >JAILBIRD
JAILBREAK *n* escape from jail
JAILED >JAIL
JAILER *n* person in charge of a jail
JAILERESS >JAILER
JAILERS >JAILER
JAILHOUSE *n* jail
JAILING >JAIL
JAILLESS >JAIL
JAILOR *same as* >JAILER
JAILORESS >JAILOR
JAILORS >JAILOR
JAILS >JAIL
JAIS >JAI
JAK >JACK
JAKE *adj* slang word meaning all right
JAKES *n* human excrement
JAKESES >JAKES
JAKEY *n* derogatory Scots word for a homeless alcoholic
JAKEYS >JAKEY
JAKFRUIT *same as* >JACKFRUIT
JAKFRUITS >JAKFRUIT
JAKS >JACK
JAL as in *Ganga jal* sacred water from the Ganges
JALAP *n* Mexican convolvulaceous plant
JALAPENO *n* very hot type of green chilli pepper, used esp in Mexican cookery
JALAPENOS >JALAPENO
JALAPIC >JALAP
JALAPIN *n* purgative resin
JALAPINS >JALAPIN
JALAPS >JALAP
JALOP *same as* >JALAP
JALOPIES >JALOPY
JALOPPIES >JALOPPY
JALOPPY *same as* >JALOPY
JALOPS >JALOP
JALOPY *n* old car
JALOUSE *vb* suspect
JALOUSED >JALOUSE
JALOUSES >JALOUSE
JALOUSIE *n* window blind or shutter constructed from angled slats of wood, plastic, etc
JALOUSIED >JALOUSIE
JALOUSIES >JALOUSIE
JALOUSING >JALOUSE
JAM *vb* pack tightly into a place ▷ *n* fruit preserve or hold-up of traffic
JAMADAR *n* Indian army officer
JAMADARS >JAMADAR
JAMB *n* side post of a door or window frame ▷ *vb* climb up a crack in rock
JAMBALAYA *n* Creole dish made of shrimps, ham, rice, onions, etc
JAMBART *same as* >GREAVE
JAMBARTS >JAMBART
JAMBE *same as* >JAMB
JAMBEAU *another word for* >GREAVE
JAMBEAUX >JAMBEAU
JAMBED >JAMB
JAMBEE *n* light cane
JAMBEES >JAMBEE
JAMBER *same as* >GREAVE
JAMBERS >JAMBER
JAMBES >JAMBE
JAMBEUX >JAMBEAU
JAMBIER *n* greave
JAMBIERS >JAMBIER
JAMBING >JAMB
JAMBIYA *n* curved dagger
JAMBIYAH *same as* >JAMBIYA
JAMBIYAHS >JAMBIYAH
JAMBIYAS >JAMBIYA
JAMBO *sentence substitute* E African salutation
JAMBOK *same as* >SJAMBOK
JAMBOKKED >JAMBOK
JAMBOKS >JAMBOK
JAMBOLAN *n* Asian tree
JAMBOLANA *same as* >JAMBOLAN
JAMBOLANS >JAMBOLAN
JAMBONE *n* type of play in the card game euchre
JAMBONES >JAMBONE
JAMBOOL *same as* >JAMBOLAN
JAMBOOLS >JAMBOOL
JAMBOREE *n* large gathering or celebration
JAMBOREES >JAMBOREE
JAMBOS >JAMBO
JAMBS >JAMB
JAMBU *same as* >JAMBOLAN
JAMBUL *same as* >JAMBOLAN
JAMBULS >JAMBUL
JAMBUS >JAMBU
JAMDANI *n* patterned muslin
JAMDANIS >JAMDANI
JAMES *n* jemmy
JAMESES >JAMES
JAMJAR *n* container for preserves
JAMJARS >JAMJAR
JAMLIKE >JAM
JAMMABLE >JAM
JAMMED >JAM
JAMMER >JAM
JAMMERS >JAM
JAMMIER >JAMMY
JAMMIES *informal word for* >PYJAMAS
JAMMIEST >JAMMY
JAMMING >JAM
JAMMY *adj* lucky
JAMPACKED *adj* very crowded
JAMPAN *n* type of sedan chair used in India
JAMPANEE *n* jampan bearer
JAMPANEES >JAMPANEE
JAMPANI *same as* >JAMPANEE
JAMPANIS >JAMPANI
JAMPANS >JAMPAN
JAMPOT *n* container for preserves
JAMPOTS >JAMPOT
JAMS >JAM
JANDAL *n* sandal with a strap between the toes
JANDALS >JANDAL
JANE *n* girl or woman
JANES >JANE
JANGLE *vb* (cause to) make a harsh ringing noise ▷ *n* harsh ringing noise
JANGLED >JANGLE
JANGLER >JANGLE
JANGLERS >JANGLE
JANGLES >JANGLE
JANGLIER >JANGLY
JANGLIEST >JANGLY
JANGLING >JANGLE
JANGLINGS >JANGLE
JANGLY *adj* making a jangling sound
JANIFORM *adj* with two faces
JANISARY *same as* >JANISSARY
JANISSARY *n* infantryman in the Turkish army, originally a member of the sovereign's personal guard, from the 14th to the early 19th century
JANITOR *n* caretaker of a school or other building
JANITORS >JANITOR
JANITRESS >JANITOR
JANITRIX >JANITOR
JANIZAR *same as* >JANISSARY
JANIZARS >JANIZAR
JANIZARY *same as* >JANISSARY
JANKER *n* device for transporting logs
JANKERS >JANKER
JANN *n* lesser jinn

JANNIES >JANNY
JANNOCK *same as* >JONNOCK
JANNOCKS >JANNOCK
JANNS >JANN
JANNY *n* janitor
JANSKY *n* unit of flux density used predominantly in radio and infrared astronomy
JANSKYS >JANSKY
JANTEE *archaic version of* >JAUNTY
JANTIER >JANTY
JANTIES >JANTY
JANTIEST >JANTY
JANTY *n* petty officer ▷ *adj* (in archaic usage) jaunty
JAP *vb* splash
JAPAN *n* very hard varnish, usu black ▷ *vb* cover with this varnish ▷ *adj* relating to or varnished with japan
JAPANISE *same as* >JAPANIZE
JAPANISED >JAPANISE
JAPANISES >JAPANISE
JAPANIZE *vb* make Japanese
JAPANIZED >JAPANIZE
JAPANIZES >JAPANIZE
JAPANNED >JAPAN
JAPANNER >JAPAN
JAPANNERS >JAPAN
JAPANNING >JAPAN
JAPANS >JAPAN
JAPE *n* joke or prank ▷ *vb* joke or jest (about)
JAPED >JAPE
JAPER >JAPE
JAPERIES >JAPE
JAPERS >JAPE
JAPERY >JAPE
JAPES >JAPE
JAPING >JAPE
JAPINGLY >JAPE
JAPINGS >JAPE
JAPONICA *n* shrub with red flowers
JAPONICAS >JAPONICA
JAPPED >JAP
JAPPING >JAP
JAPS >JAP
JAR *n* wide-mouthed container, usu round and made of glass ▷ *vb* have a disturbing or unpleasant effect
JARARACA *n* South American snake
JARARACAS >JARARACA
JARARAKA *same as* >JARARACA
JARARAKAS >JARARAKA
JARFUL *same as* >JAR
JARFULS >JARFUL
JARGON *n* specialized technical language of a particular subject ▷ *vb* use or speak in jargon
JARGONED >JARGON
JARGONEER *n* user of jargon
JARGONEL *n* pear
JARGONELS >JARGONEL
JARGONING >JARGON
JARGONISE *same as* >JARGONIZE
JARGONISH >JARGON
JARGONIST >JARGON
JARGONIZE *vb* render into jargon
JARGONS >JARGON
JARGONY >JARGON
JARGOON *same as* >JARGON
JARGOONS >JARGOON
JARHEAD *n* US Marine
JARHEADS >JARHEAD
JARINA *n* South American palm tree
JARINAS >JARINA
JARK *n* seal or pass
JARKMAN *n* forger of passes or licences
JARKMEN >JARKMAN
JARKS >JARK
JARL *n* Scandinavian chieftain or noble
JARLDOM >JARL
JARLDOMS >JARL
JARLS >JARL
JARLSBERG *n* Norwegian cheese
JAROOL *n* Indian tree
JAROOLS >JAROOL
JAROSITE *n* yellow to brown mineral
JAROSITES >JAROSITE
JAROVISE *same as* >JAROVIZE
JAROVISED >JAROVISE
JAROVISES >JAROVISE
JAROVIZE *vb* vernalize
JAROVIZED >JAROVIZE
JAROVIZES >JAROVIZE
JARP *vb* strike or smash, esp to break the shell of (an egg) at Easter
JARPED >JARP
JARPING >JARP
JARPS >JARP
JARRAH *n* Australian eucalypt yielding valuable timber
JARRAHS >JARRAH
JARRED >JAR
JARRING >JAR
JARRINGLY >JAR
JARRINGS >JAR
JARS >JAR
JARSFUL >JARFUL
JARTA *n* heart
JARTAS >JARTA
JARUL *variant of* >JAROOL
JARULS >JARUL
JARVEY *n* hackney coachman
JARVEYS >JARVEY
JARVIE *same as* >JARVEY
JARVIES >JARVIE
JASEY *n* wig
JASEYS >JASEY
JASIES >JASEY
JASMIN *same as* >JASMINE
JASMINE *n* shrub with sweet-smelling yellow or white flowers
JASMINES >JASMINE
JASMINS >JASMIN
JASP *another word for* >JASPER
JASPE *adj* resembling jasper ▷ *n* subtly striped woven fabric
JASPER *n* red, yellow, dark green, or brown variety of quartz
JASPERISE *same as* >JASPERIZE
JASPERIZE *vb* turn into jasper
JASPEROUS >JASPER
JASPERS >JASPER
JASPERY >JASPER
JASPES >JASPE
JASPIDEAN >JASPER
JASPILITE *n* rock like jasper
JASPIS *archaic word for* >JASPER
JASPISES >JASPIS
JASPS >JASP
JASS *obsolete variant of* >JAZZ
JASSES >JASS
JASSID *n* leafhopper
JASSIDS >JASSID
JASY *n* wig
JATAKA *n* text describing the birth of Buddha
JATAKAS >JATAKA
JATO *n* jet-assisted takeoff
JATOS >JATO
JAUK *vb* dawdle
JAUKED >JAUK
JAUKING >JAUK
JAUKS >JAUK
JAUNCE *vb* prance
JAUNCED >JAUNCE
JAUNCES >JAUNCE
JAUNCING >JAUNCE
JAUNDICE *n* disease marked by yellowness of the skin ▷ *vb* distort (the judgment, etc) adversely
JAUNDICED >JAUNDICE
JAUNDICES >JAUNDICE
JAUNSE *same as* >JAUNCE
JAUNSED >JAUNSE
JAUNSES >JAUNSE
JAUNSING >JAUNSE
JAUNT *n* short journey for pleasure ▷ *vb* make such a journey
JAUNTED >JAUNT
JAUNTEE *old spelling of* >JAUNTY
JAUNTIE *old spelling of* >JAUNTY
JAUNTIER >JAUNTY
JAUNTIES >JAUNTY
JAUNTIEST >JAUNTY
JAUNTILY >JAUNTY
JAUNTING >JAUNT
JAUNTS >JAUNT
JAUNTY *adj* sprightly and cheerful ▷ *n* master-at-arms on a naval ship
JAUP *same as* >JARP
JAUPED >JAUP
JAUPING >JAUP
JAUPS >JAUP
JAVA *n* coffee or a variety of it
JAVAS >JAVA
JAVEL as in *javel water* aqueous solution containing sodium hypochlorite and some sodium chloride, used as a bleach and disinfectant
JAVELIN *n* light spear thrown in sports competitions ▷ *vb* spear with a javelin
JAVELINA *n* collared peccary
JAVELINAS >JAVELINA
JAVELINED >JAVELIN
JAVELINS >JAVELIN
JAVELS >JAVEL
JAW *n* one of the bones in which the teeth are set ▷ *vb* talk lengthily
JAWAN *n* (in India) a soldier
JAWANS >JAWAN
JAWARI *n* variety of sorghum
JAWARIS >JAWARI
JAWBATION *n* scolding
JAWBONE *n* lower jaw of a person or animal ▷ *vb* try to persuade or bring pressure to bear (on) by virtue of one's high office or position, esp in urging compliance with official policy
JAWBONED >JAWBONE
JAWBONER >JAWBONE
JAWBONERS >JAWBONE
JAWBONES >JAWBONE
JAWBONING >JAWBONE
JAWBOX *n* metal sink
JAWBOXES >JAWBOX
JAWED >JAW
JAWFALL *n* depression
JAWFALLS >JAWFALL
JAWHOLE *n* cesspit
JAWHOLES >JAWHOLE
JAWING >JAW
JAWINGS >JAW
JAWLESS >JAW
JAWLIKE >JAW
JAWLINE *n* outline of the jaw
JAWLINES >JAWLINE
JAWS >JAW
JAXIE *same as* >JACKSIE
JAXIES >JAXIE
JAXY *same as* >JACKSIE
JAY *n* bird with a pinkish body and blue-and-black wings
JAYBIRD *n* jay
JAYBIRDS >JAYBIRD
JAYGEE *n* lieutenant junior grade in the US army
JAYGEES >JAYGEE
JAYHAWKER *n* Unionist guerrilla in US Civil War
JAYS >JAY
JAYVEE *n* junior varsity sports team
JAYVEES >JAYVEE
JAYWALK *vb* cross or walk in a street recklessly or illegally

JAYWALKED > JAYWALK
JAYWALKER > JAYWALK
JAYWALKS > JAYWALK
JAZERANT *n* coat of metal plates sewn onto cloth
JAZERANTS > JAZERANT
JAZIES > JAZY
JAZY *n* wig
JAZZ *n* kind of music with an exciting rhythm, usu involving improvisation ▷ *vb* play or dance to jazz music
JAZZBO *n* jazz musician or fan
JAZZBOS > JAZZBO
JAZZED > JAZZ
JAZZER > JAZZ
JAZZERS > JAZZ
JAZZES > JAZZ
JAZZIER > JAZZY
JAZZIEST > JAZZY
JAZZILY > JAZZY
JAZZINESS > JAZZY
JAZZING > JAZZ
JAZZLIKE > JAZZ
JAZZMAN > JAZZ
JAZZMEN > JAZZ
JAZZY *adj* flashy or showy
JEALOUS *adj* fearful of losing a partner or possession to a rival
JEALOUSE *vb* be jealous of
JEALOUSED > JEALOUSE
JEALOUSES > JEALOUSE
JEALOUSLY > JEALOUS
JEALOUSY *n* state of or an instance of feeling jealous
JEAN *n* tough twill-weave cotton fabric used for hard-wearing trousers, overalls, etc
JEANED *adj* wearing jeans
JEANETTE *n* light jean cloth
JEANETTES > JEANETTE
JEANS *pl n* casual denim trousers
JEAT *n* jet
JEATS > JEAT
JEBEL *n* hill or mountain in an Arab country
JEBELS > JEBEL
JEDI *n* person claiming to live according to a philosophy based on that of the fictional Jedi, from the *Star Wars* films
JEDIS > JEDI
JEE *variant of* > GEE
JEED > JEE
JEEING > JEE
JEEL *vb* make into jelly
JEELED > JEEL
JEELIE *same as* > JEELY
JEELIED > JEELY
JEELIEING > JEELIE
JEELIES > JEELY
JEELING > JEEL
JEELS > JEEL
JEELY *n* jelly ▷ *vb* make into jelly
JEELYING > JEELY
JEEP *n* small military four-wheel drive road vehicle ▷ *vb* travel in a jeep
JEEPED > JEEP
JEEPERS *interj* mild exclamation of surprise
JEEPING > JEEP
JEEPNEY *n* Filipino bus converted from a jeep
JEEPNEYS > JEEPNEY
JEEPS > JEEP
JEER *vb* scoff or deride ▷ *n* cry of derision
JEERED > JEER
JEERER > JEER
JEERERS > JEER
JEERING > JEER
JEERINGLY > JEER
JEERINGS > JEER
JEERS > JEER
JEES > JEE
JEEZ *interj* expression of surprise or irritation
JEFE *n* (in Spanish-speaking countries) a military or political leader
JEFES > JEFE
JEFF *vb* downsize or close down (an organization)
JEFFED > JEFF
JEFFING > JEFF
JEFFS > JEFF
JEHAD *same as* > JIHAD
JEHADI *same as* > JIHADI
JEHADIS > JEHADI
JEHADISM *same as* > JIHADISM
JEHADISMS > JEHADISM
JEHADIST > JEHADISM
JEHADISTS > JEHADISM
JEHADS > JEHAD
JEHU *n* fast driver
JEHUS > JEHU
JEJUNA > JEJUNUM
JEJUNAL > JEJUNUM
JEJUNE *adj* simple or naive
JEJUNELY > JEJUNE
JEJUNITY > JEJUNE
JEJUNUM *n* part of the small intestine between the duodenum and the ileum
JELAB *same as* > JELLABA
JELABS > JELAB
JELL *vb* form into a jelly-like substance
JELLABA *n* loose robe with a hood, worn by some Arab men
JELLABAH *same as* > JELLABA
JELLABAHS > JELLABAH
JELLABAS > JELLABA
JELLED > JELL
JELLIED > JELLY
JELLIES > JELLY
JELLIFIED > JELLIFY
JELLIFIES > JELLIFY
JELLIFY *vb* make into or become jelly
JELLING > JELL
JELLO *n* (in US English) fruit-flavoured clear dessert set with gelatine
JELLOS > JELLO
JELLS > JELL
JELLY *n* fruit-flavoured clear dessert set with gelatine ▷ *vb* jellify
JELLYBEAN *n* bean-shaped sweet with a brightly coloured coating around a gelatinous filling
JELLYFISH *n* small jelly-like sea animal
JELLYING > JELLY
JELLYLIKE > JELLY
JELLYROLL *n* type of cake
JELUTONG *n* Malaysian tree
JELUTONGS > JELUTONG
JEMADAR *n* native junior officer belonging to a locally raised regiment serving as mercenaries in India, esp with the British Army (until 1947)
JEMADARS > JEMADAR
JEMBE *n* hoe
JEMBES > JEMBE
JEMIDAR *same as* > JEMADAR
JEMIDARS > JEMIDAR
JEMIMA *n* boot with elastic sides
JEMIMAS > JEMIMA
JEMMIED > JEMMY
JEMMIER > JEMMY
JEMMIES > JEMMY
JEMMIEST > JEMMY
JEMMINESS > JEMMY
JEMMY *n* short steel crowbar used by burglars ▷ *vb* prise (something) open with a jemmy ▷ *adj* neat
JEMMYING > JEMMY
JENNET *n* female donkey or ass
JENNETING *n* early-season apple
JENNETS > JENNET
JENNIES > JENNY
JENNY *same as* > JENNET
JEOFAIL *n* oversight in legal pleading
JEOFAILS > JEOFAIL
JEON *n* Korean pancake
JEOPARD *vb* put in jeopardy
JEOPARDED > JEOPARD
JEOPARDER > JEOPARD
JEOPARDS > JEOPARD
JEOPARDY *n* danger ▷ *vb* put in jeopardy
JEQUERITY *same as* > JEQUIRITY
JEQUIRITY *n* seed of the Indian liquorice
JERBIL *variant spelling of* > GERBIL
JERBILS > JERBIL
JERBOA *n* small mouselike rodent with long hind legs
JERBOAS > JERBOA
JEREED *same as* > JERID
JEREEDS > JEREED
JEREMIAD *n* long mournful complaint
JEREMIADS > JEREMIAD
JEREPIGO *n* sweet fortified wine similar to port
JEREPIGOS > JEREPIGO
JERFALCON *variant of* > GYRFALCON
JERID *n* wooden javelin used in Muslim countries in military displays on horseback
JERIDS > JERID
JERK *vb* move or throw abruptly ▷ *n* sharp or abruptly stopped movement
JERKED > JERK
JERKER > JERK
JERKERS > JERK
JERKIER > JERKY
JERKIES > JERKY
JERKIEST > JERKY
JERKILY > JERKY
JERKIN *n* sleeveless jacket
JERKINESS > JERKY
JERKING > JERK
JERKINGLY > JERK
JERKINGS > JERK
JERKINS > JERKIN
JERKS > JERK
JERKWATER *adj* inferior and insignificant
JERKY *adj* characterized by jerks ▷ *n* type of cured meat
JEROBOAM *n* wine bottle holding the equivalent of four normal bottles (approximately 104 ounces)
JEROBOAMS > JEROBOAM
JERQUE *vb* search for contraband
JERQUED > JERQUE
JERQUER > JERQUE
JERQUERS > JERQUE
JERQUES > JERQUE
JERQUING > JERQUE
JERQUINGS > JERQUE
JERREED *variant spelling of* > JERID
JERREEDS > JERREED
JERRICAN *n* five-gallon fuel can
JERRICANS > JERRICAN
JERRID *n* blunt javelin
JERRIDS > JERRID
JERRIES > JERRY
JERRY *short for* > JEROBOAM
JERRYCAN *n* flat-sided can used for storing or transporting liquids, esp motor fuel
JERRYCANS > JERRYCAN
JERSEY *n* knitted jumper ▷ *vb* pull an ice-hockey player's jersey over his or her head
JERSEYED > JERSEY
JERSEYING > JERSEY
JERSEYS > JERSEY
JESS *n* short leather strap, one end of which is permanently attached to the leg of a hawk or falcon while the other can be attached to a leash ▷ *vb* put jesses on (a hawk or falcon)
JESSAMIES > JESSAMY

JESSAMINE *same as* >JASMINE
JESSAMY *n* fop
JESSANT *adj* emerging
JESSE *same as* >JESS
JESSED >JESS
JESSERANT *n* coat of metal plates sewn onto cloth
JESSES >JESS
JESSIE *n* effeminate, weak, or cowardly boy or man
JESSIES >JESSIE
JESSING >JESS
JEST *vb* joke ▷ *n* something done or said for amusement
JESTBOOK *n* book of amusing stories
JESTBOOKS >JESTBOOK
JESTED >JEST
JESTEE *n* person about whom a joke is made
JESTEES >JESTEE
JESTER *n* professional clown at court
JESTERS >JESTER
JESTFUL >JEST
JESTING >JEST
JESTINGLY >JEST
JESTINGS >JEST
JESTS >JEST
JESUIT *n* offensive term for a person given to subtle and equivocating arguments
JESUITIC >JESUIT
JESUITISM >JESUIT
JESUITRY >JESUIT
JESUITS >JESUIT
JESUS *n* French paper size
JET *n* aircraft driven by jet propulsion ▷ *vb* fly by jet aircraft
JETBEAD *n* ornamental shrub
JETBEADS >JETBEAD
JETE *n* step in which the dancer springs from one leg and lands on the other
JETES >JETE
JETFOIL *n* type of hydrofoil that is propelled by water jets
JETFOILS >JETFOIL
JETLAG *n* tiredness caused by crossing timezones in jet flight
JETLAGS >JETLAG
JETLIKE >JET
JETLINER *n* commercial airliner powered by jet engines
JETLINERS >JETLINER
JETON *n* gambling chip
JETONS >JETON
JETPLANE *n* aircraft powered by one or more jet engines
JETPLANES >JETPLANE
JETPORT *n* airport for jet planes
JETPORTS >JETPORT
JETS >JET
JETSAM *n* goods thrown overboard to lighten a ship
JETSAMS >JETSAM
JETSOM *same as* >JETSAM
JETSOMS >JETSOM
JETSON *archaic form of* >JETSAM
JETSONS >JETSON
JETSTREAM *n* narrow belt of high-altitude winds moving east at high speeds
JETTATURA *n* evil eye
JETTED >JET
JETTIED >JETTY
JETTIER >JETTY
JETTIES >JETTY
JETTIEST >JETTY
JETTINESS >JETTY
JETTING >JET
JETTISON *vb* abandon
JETTISONS >JETTISON
JETTON *n* counter or token, esp a chip used in such gambling games as roulette
JETTONS >JETTON
JETTY *n* small pier ▷ *adj* of or resembling jet, esp in colour or polish ▷ *vb* equip with a cantilevered floor
JETTYING >JETTY
JETWAY *n* tradename of a mobile elevated gangway connecting an aircraft to a departure gate, allowing passengers to board and disembark
JETWAYS >JETWAY
JEU *n* game
JEUNE *adj* young
JEUX >JEU
JEW *vb* obsolete offensive word for haggle ▷ *n* obsolete offensive word for a haggler
JEWED >JEW
JEWEL *n* precious or semiprecious stone ▷ *vb* fit or decorate with a jewel or jewels
JEWELED >JEWEL
JEWELER *same as* >JEWELLER
JEWELERS >JEWELER
JEWELFISH *n* beautifully coloured fish popular in aquaria
JEWELING >JEWEL
JEWELLED >JEWEL
JEWELLER *n* dealer in jewels
JEWELLERS >JEWELLER
JEWELLERY *n* objects decorated with precious stones
JEWELLIKE >JEWEL
JEWELLING >JEWEL
JEWELRIES >JEWELRY
JEWELRY *same as* >JEWELLERY
JEWELS >JEWEL
JEWELWEED *n* small bushy plant
JEWFISH *n* freshwater catfish
JEWFISHES >JEWFISH
JEWIE *n* jewfish
JEWIES >JEWIE
JEWING >JEW
JEWS >JEW
JEZAIL *n* Afghan musket
JEZAILS >JEZAIL
JEZEBEL *n* shameless or scheming woman
JEZEBELS >JEZEBEL
JHALA *n* Indian musical style
JHALAS >JHALA
JHATKA *n* slaughter of animals for food according to Sikh law
JHATKAS >JHATKA
JIAO *n* Chinese currency unit
JIAOS >JIAO
JIB *same as* >JIBE
JIBB *same as* >JIBE
JIBBAH *same as* >JUBBAH
JIBBAHS >JIBBAH
JIBBED >JIBB
JIBBER *variant of* >GIBBER
JIBBERED >JIBBER
JIBBERING >JIBBER
JIBBERS >JIBBER
JIBBING >JIBB
JIBBINGS >JIBB
JIBBONS *pl n* spring onions
JIBBOOM *n* spar forming an extension of the bowsprit
JIBBOOMS >JIBBOOM
JIBBS >JIBB
JIBE *vb* taunt or jeer ▷ *n* insulting or taunting remark
JIBED >JIBE
JIBER >JIBE
JIBERS >JIBE
JIBES >JIBE
JIBING >JIBE
JIBINGLY >JIBE
JIBS >JIB
JICAMA *n* pale brown turnip with crisp sweet flesh, originating in Mexico
JICAMAS >JICAMA
JICKAJOG *vb* engage in sexual intercourse
JICKAJOGS >JICKAJOG
JIFF *same as* >JIFFY
JIFFIES >JIFFY
JIFFS >JIFF
JIFFY *n* very short period of time
JIG *n* type of lively dance ▷ *vb* dance a jig
JIGABOO *n* offensive term for a Black person
JIGABOOS >JIGABOO
JIGAJIG *vb* engage in sexual intercourse
JIGAJIGS >JIGAJIG
JIGAJOG *variant of* >JIGAJIG
JIGAJOGS >JIGAJOG
JIGAMAREE *n* thing
JIGGED >JIG
JIGGER *n* small whisky glass ▷ *vb* interfere or alter
JIGGERED >JIGGER
JIGGERING >JIGGER
JIGGERS >JIGGER
JIGGIER >JIGGY
JIGGIEST >JIGGY
JIGGING >JIG
JIGGINGS >JIG
JIGGISH >JIG
JIGGLE *vb* move up and down with short jerky movements ▷ *n* short jerky motion
JIGGLED >JIGGLE
JIGGLES >JIGGLE
JIGGLIER >JIGGLE
JIGGLIEST >JIGGLE
JIGGLING >JIGGLE
JIGGLY >JIGGLE
JIGGUMBOB *n* thing
JIGGY *adj* resembling a jig
JIGJIG *variant of* >JIGAJIG
JIGJIGGED >JIGJIG
JIGJIGS >JIGJIG
JIGLIKE >JIG
JIGOT *same as* >GIGOT
JIGOTS >JIGOT
JIGS >JIG
JIGSAW *n* picture cut into interlocking pieces, which the user tries to fit together again ▷ *vb* cut with a jigsaw
JIGSAWED >JIGSAW
JIGSAWING >JIGSAW
JIGSAWN >JIGSAW
JIGSAWS >JIGSAW
JIHAD *n* Islamic holy war against unbelievers
JIHADI *n* person who takes part in a jihad
JIHADIS >JIHADI
JIHADISM *n* Islamic fundamentalist movement that favours the pursuit of jihads in defence of the Islamic faith
JIHADISMS >JIHADISM
JIHADIST >JIHADISM
JIHADISTS >JIHADISM
JIHADS >JIHAD
JILBAB *n* long robe worn by Muslim women
JILBABS >JILBAB
JILGIE *n* freshwater crayfish
JILGIES >JILGIE
JILL *variant spelling of* >GILL
JILLAROO *n* female jackeroo
JILLAROOS >JILLAROO
JILLET *n* wanton woman
JILLETS >JILLET
JILLFLIRT *same as* >JILLET
JILLION *n* extremely large number or amount
JILLIONS >JILLION
JILLIONTH >JILLION
JILLS >JILL
JILT *vb* leave or reject (one's lover) ▷ *n* woman

who jilts a lover
JILTED > JILT
JILTER > JILT
JILTERS > JILT
JILTING > JILT
JILTS > JILT
JIMCRACK *same as* > GIMCRACK
JIMCRACKS > JIMCRACK
JIMINY *interj* expression of surprise
JIMJAM > JIMJAMS
JIMJAMS *pl n* state of nervous tension, excitement, or anxiety
JIMMIE *same as* > JIMMY
JIMMIED > JIMMY
JIMMIES > JIMMY
JIMMINY *interj* expression of surprise
JIMMY *same as* > JEMMY
JIMMYING > JIMMY
JIMP *adj* handsome
JIMPER > JIMP
JIMPEST > JIMP
JIMPIER > JIMPY
JIMPIEST > JIMPY
JIMPLY *adv* neatly
JIMPNESS > JIMP
JIMPY *adj* neat and tidy
JIMSON as in *jimson weed* type of poisonous plant with white flowers and shiny fruits
JIN *n* Chinese unit of weight
JINGAL *n* swivel-mounted gun
JINGALL *same as* > JINGAL
JINGALLS > JINGALL
JINGALS > JINGAL
JINGBANG *n* entirety of something
JINGBANGS > JINGBANG
JINGKO *same as* > GINGKO
JINGKOES > JINGKO
JINGLE *n* catchy verse or song used in a radio or television advert ▷ *vb* (cause to) make a gentle ringing sound
JINGLED > JINGLE
JINGLER > JINGLE
JINGLERS > JINGLE
JINGLES > JINGLE
JINGLET *n* sleigh-bell clapper
JINGLETS > JINGLET
JINGLIER > JINGLE
JINGLIEST > JINGLE
JINGLING > JINGLE
JINGLY > JINGLE
JINGO *n* loud and bellicose patriot; chauvinism
JINGOES > JINGO
JINGOISH > JINGO
JINGOISM *n* aggressive nationalism
JINGOISMS > JINGOISM
JINGOIST > JINGOISM
JINGOISTS > JINGOISM
JINJILI *n* type of sesame
JINJILIS > JINJILI
JINK *vb* move quickly or jerkily in order to dodge someone ▷ *n* jinking movement
JINKED > JINK
JINKER *n* vehicle for transporting timber, consisting of a tractor and two sets of wheels for supporting the logs
JINKERS > JINKER
JINKING > JINK
JINKS > JINK
JINN > JINNI
JINNE *interj* South African exclamation expressing surprise, admiration, shock, etc
JINNEE *same as* > JINNI
JINNI *n* spirit in Muslim mythology
JINNIS > JINNI
JINNS > JINNI
JINRIKSHA *same as* > RICKSHAW
JINS > JIN
JINX *n* person or thing bringing bad luck ▷ *vb* be or put a jinx on
JINXED > JINX
JINXES > JINX
JINXING > JINX
JIPIJAPA *n* palmlike Central and South American plant whose fanlike leaves are bleached for making panama hats
JIPIJAPAS > JIPIJAPA
JIPYAPA *same as* > JIPIJAPA
JIPYAPAS > JIPYAPA
JIRBLE *vb* pour carelessly
JIRBLED > JIRBLE
JIRBLES > JIRBLE
JIRBLING > JIRBLE
JIRD *n* gerbil
JIRDS > JIRD
JIRGA *n* Afghan council
JIRGAS > JIRGA
JIRKINET *n* bodice
JIRKINETS > JIRKINET
JIRRE *same as* > JINNE
JISM *slang word for* > SEMEN
JISMS > JISM
JISSOM *slang word for* > SEMEN
JISSOMS > JISSOM
JITNEY *n* small bus that carries passengers for a low price, originally five cents
JITNEYS > JITNEY
JITTER *vb* be anxious or nervous
JITTERBUG *n* fast jerky American dance that was popular in the 1940s ▷ *vb* dance the jitterbug
JITTERED > JITTER
JITTERIER > JITTERY
JITTERING > JITTER
JITTERS > JITTER
JITTERY *adj* nervous
JIUJITSU *variant spelling of* > JUJITSU
JIUJITSUS > JIUJITSU
JIUJUTSU *same as* > JUJITSU
JIUJUTSUS > JIUJUTSU
JIVE *n* lively dance of the 1940s and '50s ▷ *vb* dance the jive
JIVEASS *adj* misleading or phoney
JIVED > JIVE
JIVER > JIVE
JIVERS > JIVE
JIVES > JIVE
JIVEY > JIVE
JIVIER > JIVE
JIVIEST > JIVE
JIVING > JIVE
JIVY > JIVE
JIZ *n* wig
JIZZ *n* term for the total combination of characteristics that serve to identify a particular species of bird or plant
JIZZES > JIZZ
JNANA *n* type of yoga
JNANAS > JNANA
JO *n* Scots word for sweetheart
JOANNA *n* piano
JOANNAS > JOANNA
JOANNES *same as* > JOHANNES
JOANNESES > JOANNES
JOB *n* occupation or paid employment ▷ *vb* work at casual jobs
JOBATION *n* scolding
JOBATIONS > JOBATION
JOBBED > JOB
JOBBER *n* person who jobs
JOBBERIES > JOBBERY
JOBBERS > JOBBER
JOBBERY *n* practice of making private profit out of a public office
JOBBIE *n* piece of excrement
JOBBIES > JOBBIE
JOBBING *adj* doing individual jobs for payment ▷ *n* act of seeking work
JOBBINGS > JOBBING
JOBCENTRE *n* office where unemployed people can find out about job vacancies
JOBE *vb* scold
JOBED > JOBE
JOBERNOWL *n* stupid person
JOBES > JOBE
JOBHOLDER *n* person who has a job
JOBING > JOBE
JOBLESS *pl n* unemployed people ▷ *adj* unemployed
JOBNAME *n* title of position
JOBNAMES > JOBNAME
JOBS > JOB
JOBSEEKER *n* person looking for employment
JOBSHARE *n* arrangement in which two or more people divide the duties and payment for one position between them, working at different times
JOBSHARES > JOBSHARE
JOBSWORTH *n* person in a position of minor authority who invokes the letter of the law in order to avoid any action requiring initiative, cooperation, etc
JOCK *n* athlete
JOCKETTE *n* female athlete
JOCKETTES > JOCKETTE
JOCKEY *n* person who rides horses in races, esp as a profession or for hire ▷ *vb* ride (a horse) in a race
JOCKEYED > JOCKEY
JOCKEYING > JOCKEY
JOCKEYISH > JOCKEY
JOCKEYISM *n* skills and practices of jockeys
JOCKEYS > JOCKEY
JOCKNEY *n* Scots dialect influenced by cockney speech patterns
JOCKNEYS > JOCKNEY
JOCKO *n* chimpanzee
JOCKOS > JOCKO
JOCKS > JOCK
JOCKSTRAP *n* belt with a pouch to support the genitals, worn by male athletes
JOCKTELEG *n* clasp knife
JOCO *adj* relaxed
JOCOSE *adj* playful or humorous
JOCOSELY > JOCOSE
JOCOSITY > JOCOSE
JOCULAR *adj* fond of joking
JOCULARLY > JOCULAR
JOCULATOR *n* joker
JOCUND *adj* merry or cheerful
JOCUNDITY > JOCUND
JOCUNDLY > JOCUND
JODEL *same as* > YODEL
JODELLED > JODEL
JODELLING > JODEL
JODELS > JODEL
JODHPUR as in *jodphur boots* ankle-length leather riding boots
JODHPURS *pl n* riding breeches, loose-fitting around the hips and tight-fitting from the thighs to the ankles
JOE *same as* > JO
JOES > JOE
JOEY *n* young kangaroo
JOEYS > JOEY
JOG *vb* run at a gentle pace esp for exercise ▷ *n* slow run
JOGGED > JOG
JOGGER *n* person who runs at a jog trot over some distance for exercise, usually regularly
JOGGERS > JOGGER
JOGGING > JOG
JOGGINGS > JOG

OGGLE *vb* shake or move jerkily ▷ *n* act of joggling
OGGLED > JOGGLE
OGGLER > JOGGLE
OGGLERS > JOGGLE
OGGLES > JOGGLE
OGGLING > JOGGLE
OGPANTS *pl n* trousers worn for jogging
OGS > JOG
OGTROT *n* easy bouncy gait, esp of a horse, midway between a walk and a trot
OGTROTS > JOGTROT
OHANNES *n* Portuguese gold coin minted in the early 18th century
OHN *n* toilet
OHNBOAT *n* small flat-bottomed boat
OHNBOATS > JOHNBOAT
OHNNIE *same as* > JOHNNY
OHNNIES > JOHNNY
OHNNY *n* chap
OHNS > JOHN
OHNSON *slang word for* > PENIS
OHNSONS > JOHNSON
OIN *vb* become a member (of) ▷ *n* place where two things are joined
OINABLE > JOIN
OINDER *n* act of joining, esp in legal contexts
OINDERS > JOINDER
OINED > JOIN
OINER *n* maker of finished woodwork
OINERIES > JOINERY
OINERS > JOINER
OINERY *n* joiner's work
OINING > JOIN
OININGS > JOIN
OINS > JOIN
OINT *adj* shared by two or more ▷ *n* place where bones meet but can move ▷ *vb* divide meat into joints
OINTED *adj* having a joint or joints
OINTEDLY > JOINTED
OINTER *n* tool for pointing mortar joints, as in brickwork
OINTERS > JOINTER
OINTING > JOINT
OINTLESS > JOINT
OINTLY > JOINT
OINTNESS > JOINT
OINTRESS *n* woman entitled to a jointure
OINTS > JOINT
OINTURE *n* provision made by a husband for his wife by settling property upon her at marriage for her use after his death
OINTURED > JOINTURE
OINTURES > JOINTURE
OINTWEED *n* American wild plant
OINTWORM *n* larva of chalcid flies which form galls on the stems of cereal plants
JOIST *n* horizontal beam that helps support a floor or ceiling ▷ *vb* construct (a floor, roof, etc) with joists
JOISTED > JOIST
JOISTING > JOIST
JOISTS > JOIST
JOJOBA *n* shrub of SW North America whose seeds yield oil used in cosmetics
JOJOBAS > JOJOBA
JOKE *n* thing said or done to cause laughter ▷ *vb* make jokes
JOKED > JOKE
JOKER *n* person who jokes
JOKERS > JOKER
JOKES > JOKE
JOKESMITH *n* comedian
JOKESOME > JOKE
JOKESTER *n* person who makes jokes
JOKESTERS > JOKESTER
JOKEY *adj* intended as a joke
JOKIER > JOKEY
JOKIEST > JOKEY
JOKILY > JOKE
JOKINESS > JOKE
JOKING > JOKE
JOKINGLY > JOKE
JOKOL *Shetland word for* > YES
JOKY *same as* > JOKEY
JOL *n* party ▷ *vb* have a good time
JOLE *vb* knock
JOLED > JOLE
JOLES > JOLE
JOLING > JOLE
JOLL *variant of* > JOLE
JOLLED > JOL
JOLLEY *same as* > JOLLY
JOLLEYER > JOLLEY
JOLLEYERS > JOLLEY
JOLLEYING > JOLLEY
JOLLEYS > JOLLEY
JOLLIED > JOLLY
JOLLIER *n* joker
JOLLIERS > JOLLIER
JOLLIES > JOLLY
JOLLIEST > JOLLY
JOLLIFIED > JOLLIFY
JOLLIFIES > JOLLIFY
JOLLIFY *vb* be or cause to be jolly
JOLLILY > JOLLY
JOLLIMENT > JOLLY
JOLLINESS > JOLLY
JOLLING > JOL
JOLLITIES > JOLLITY
JOLLITY *n* condition of being jolly
JOLLOP *n* cream or unguent
JOLLOPS > JOLLOP
JOLLS > JOLL
JOLLY *adj* full of good humour ▷ *adv* extremely ▷ *vb* try to make or keep (someone) cheerful ▷ *n* festivity or celebration
JOLLYBOAT *n* small boat used as a utility tender for a vessel
JOLLYER > JOLLY
JOLLYERS > JOLLY
JOLLYHEAD *same as* > JOLLITY
JOLLYING > JOLLY
JOLLYINGS > JOLLY
JOLS > JOL
JOLT *n* unpleasant surprise or shock ▷ *vb* surprise or shock
JOLTED > JOLT
JOLTER > JOLT
JOLTERS > JOLT
JOLTHEAD *n* fool
JOLTHEADS > JOLTHEAD
JOLTIER > JOLT
JOLTIEST > JOLT
JOLTILY > JOLT
JOLTING > JOLT
JOLTINGLY > JOLT
JOLTS > JOLT
JOLTY > JOLT
JOMO *same as* > ZO
JOMON *n* particular era in Japanese history
JOMOS > JOMO
JONCANOE *n* Jamaican ceremony
JONCANOES > JONCANOE
JONES *vb* desire
JONESED > JONES
JONESES > JONES
JONESING > JONES
JONG *n* friend, often used in direct address
JONGLEUR *n* (in medieval France) an itinerant minstrel
JONGLEURS > JONGLEUR
JONNOCK *adj* genuine ▷ *adv* honestly
JONNYCAKE *n* type of flat bread
JONQUIL *n* fragrant narcissus
JONQUILS > JONQUIL
JONTIES > JONTY
JONTY *n* petty officer
JOOK *vb* poke or puncture (the skin) ▷ *n* jab or the resulting wound
JOOKED > JOOK
JOOKERIES > JOOKERY
JOOKERY *n* mischief
JOOKING > JOOK
JOOKS > JOOK
JOR *n* movement in Indian music
JORAM *same as* > JORUM
JORAMS > JORAM
JORDAN *n* chamber pot
JORDANS > JORDAN
JORDELOO *same as* > GARDYLOO
JORDELOOS > JORDELOO
JORS > JOR
JORUM *n* large drinking bowl or vessel or its contents
JORUMS > JORUM
JOSEPH *n* woman's floor-length riding coat with a small cape, worn esp in the 18th century
JOSEPHS > JOSEPH
JOSH *vb* tease ▷ *n* teasing or bantering joke
JOSHED > JOSH
JOSHER > JOSH
JOSHERS > JOSH
JOSHES > JOSH
JOSHING > JOSH
JOSHINGLY > JOSH
JOSKIN *n* bumpkin
JOSKINS > JOSKIN
JOSS *n* Chinese deity worshipped in the form of an idol
JOSSER *n* simpleton
JOSSERS > JOSSER
JOSSES > JOSS
JOSTLE *vb* knock or push against ▷ *n* act of jostling
JOSTLED > JOSTLE
JOSTLER > JOSTLE
JOSTLERS > JOSTLE
JOSTLES > JOSTLE
JOSTLING > JOSTLE
JOSTLINGS > JOSTLE
JOT *vb* write briefly ▷ *n* very small amount
JOTA *n* Spanish dance with castanets in fast triple time, usually to a guitar and voice accompaniment
JOTAS > JOTA
JOTS > JOT
JOTTED > JOT
JOTTER *n* notebook
JOTTERS > JOTTER
JOTTING > JOT
JOTTINGS > JOT
JOTTY > JOT
JOTUN *n* giant
JOTUNN *same as* > JOTUN
JOTUNNS > JOTUNN
JOTUNS > JOTUN
JOUAL *n* nonstandard variety of Canadian French
JOUALS > JOUAL
JOUGS *pl n* iron ring, fastened by a chain to a wall, post, or tree, in which an offender was held by the neck
JOUISANCE *n* joy
JOUK *vb* duck or dodge ▷ *n* sudden evasive movement
JOUKED > JOUK
JOUKERIES > JOUKERY
JOUKERY *same as* > JOOKERY
JOUKING > JOUK
JOUKS > JOUK
JOULE *n* unit of work or energy ▷ *vb* knock
JOULED > JOULE
JOULES > JOULE
JOULING > JOULE
JOUNCE *vb* shake or jolt or cause to shake or jolt ▷ *n* jolting movement
JOUNCED > JOUNCE

JOUNCES > JOUNCE

JOUNCIER > JOUNCE

JOUNCIEST > JOUNCE

JOUNCING > JOUNCE

JOUNCY > JOUNCE

JOUR *n* day

JOURNAL *n* daily newspaper or magazine ▷ *vb* record in a journal

JOURNALED > JOURNAL

JOURNALS > JOURNAL

JOURNEY *n* act or process of travelling from one place to another ▷ *vb* travel

JOURNEYED > JOURNEY

JOURNEYER > JOURNEY

JOURNEYS > JOURNEY

JOURNO *n* journalist

JOURNOS > JOURNO

JOURS > JOUR

JOUST *n* combat with lances between two mounted knights ▷ *vb* fight on horseback using lances

JOUSTED > JOUST

JOUSTER > JOUST

JOUSTERS > JOUST

JOUSTING > JOUST

JOUSTS > JOUST

JOVIAL *adj* happy and cheerful

JOVIALITY > JOVIAL

JOVIALLY > JOVIAL

JOVIALTY *same as* > JOVIAL

JOW *vb* ring (a bell)

JOWAR *n* variety of sorghum

JOWARI *same as* > JOWAR

JOWARIS > JOWAR

JOWARS > JOWAR

JOWED > JOW

JOWING > JOW

JOWL *n* lower jaw ▷ *vb* knock

JOWLED > JOWL

JOWLER *n* dog with prominent jowls

JOWLERS > JOWLER

JOWLIER > JOWL

JOWLIEST > JOWL

JOWLINESS > JOWL

JOWLING > JOWL

JOWLS > JOWL

JOWLY > JOWL

JOWS > JOW

JOY *n* feeling of great delight or pleasure ▷ *vb* feel joy

JOYANCE *n* joyous feeling or festivity

JOYANCES > JOYANCE

JOYED > JOY

JOYFUL *adj* feeling or bringing great joy

JOYFULLER > JOYFUL

JOYFULLY > JOYFUL

JOYING > JOY

JOYLESS *adj* feeling or bringing no joy

JOYLESSLY > JOYLESS

JOYOUS *adj* extremely happy and enthusiastic

JOYOUSLY > JOYOUS

JOYPOP *vb* take addictive drugs occasionally without becoming addicted

JOYPOPPED > JOYPOP

JOYPOPPER > JOYPOP

JOYPOPS > JOYPOP

JOYRIDDEN > JOYRIDE

JOYRIDE *n* drive in a car one has stolen ▷ *vb* take such a ride

JOYRIDER > JOYRIDE

JOYRIDERS > JOYRIDE

JOYRIDES > JOYRIDE

JOYRIDING > JOYRIDE

JOYRODE > JOYRIDE

JOYS > JOY

JOYSTICK *n* control device for an aircraft or computer

JOYSTICKS > JOYSTICK

JUBA *n* lively African-American dance developed in the southern US

JUBAS > JUBA

JUBATE *adj* possessing a mane

JUBBAH *n* long loose outer garment with wide sleeves, worn by Muslim men and women, esp in India

JUBBAHS > JUBBAH

JUBE *n* gallery or loft over the rood screen in a church or cathedral

JUBES > JUBE

JUBHAH *same as* > JUBBAH

JUBHAHS > JUBHAH

JUBILANCE > JUBILANT

JUBILANCY > JUBILANT

JUBILANT *adj* feeling or expressing great joy

JUBILATE *vb* have or express great joy

JUBILATED > JUBILATE

JUBILATES > JUBILATE

JUBILE *same as* > JUBILEE

JUBILEE *n* special anniversary, esp 25th or 50th

JUBILEES > JUBILEE

JUBILES > JUBILE

JUCO *n* junior college in America

JUCOS > JUCO

JUD *n* large block of coal

JUDAS *n* peephole or a very small window in a door

JUDASES > JUDAS

JUDDER *vb* vibrate violently ▷ *n* violent vibration

JUDDERED > JUDDER

JUDDERING > JUDDER

JUDDERS > JUDDER

JUDGE *n* public official who tries cases and passes sentence in a court of law ▷ *vb* act as a judge

JUDGEABLE > JUDGE

JUDGED > JUDGE

JUDGELESS > JUDGE

JUDGELIKE > JUDGE

JUDGEMENT *same as* > JUDGMENT

JUDGER > JUDGE

JUDGERS > JUDGE

JUDGES > JUDGE

JUDGESHIP *n* position, office, or function of a judge

JUDGING > JUDGE

JUDGINGLY > JUDGE

JUDGMATIC *adj* judicious

JUDGMENT *n* opinion reached after careful thought

JUDGMENTS > JUDGMENT

JUDICABLE *adj* capable of being judged, esp in a court of law

JUDICATOR *n* person who acts as a judge

JUDICIAL *adj* of or by a court or judge

JUDICIARY *n* system of courts and judges ▷ *adj* of or relating to courts of law, judgment, or judges

JUDICIOUS *adj* well-judged and sensible

JUDIES > JUDY

JUDO *n* sport in which two opponents try to throw each other to the ground

JUDOGI *n* white two-piece cotton costume worn during judo contests

JUDOGIS > JUDOGI

JUDOIST > JUDO

JUDOISTS > JUDO

JUDOKA *n* competitor or expert in judo

JUDOKAS > JUDOKA

JUDOS > JUDO

JUDS > JUD

JUDY *n* woman

JUG *n* container for liquids, with a handle and small spout ▷ *vb* stew or boil (meat, esp hare) in an earthenware container

JUGA > JUGUM

JUGAL *adj* of or relating to the zygomatic bone ▷ *n* cheekbone

JUGALS > JUGAL

JUGATE *adj* (esp of compound leaves) having parts arranged in pairs

JUGFUL *same as* > JUG

JUGFULS > JUGFUL

JUGGED > JUG

JUGGING > JUG

JUGGINGS > JUG

JUGGINS *n* silly person

JUGGINSES > JUGGINS

JUGGLE *vb* throw and catch (several objects) so that most are in the air at the same time ▷ *n* act of juggling

JUGGLED > JUGGLE

JUGGLER *n* person who juggles, esp a professional entertainer

JUGGLERS > JUGGLER

JUGGLERY > JUGGLE

JUGGLES > JUGGLE

JUGGLING > JUGGLE

JUGGLINGS > JUGGLE

JUGHEAD *n* clumsy person

JUGHEADS > JUGHEAD

JUGLET *n* small jug

JUGLETS > JUGLET

JUGS > JUG

JUGSFUL > JUGFUL

JUGULA > JUGULUM

JUGULAR *n* one of three large veins of the neck tha return blood from the hea to the heart

JUGULARS > JUGULAR

JUGULATE *vb* check (a disease) by extreme measures or remedies

JUGULATED > JUGULATE

JUGULATES > JUGULATE

JUGULUM *n* lower throat

JUGUM *n* small process at the base of each forewing in certain insects by whic the forewings are united to the hindwings during flight

JUGUMS > JUGUM

JUICE *n* liquid part of vegetables, fruit, or meat ▷ *vb* extract juice from fruits and vegetables

JUICED > JUICE

JUICEHEAD *n* alcoholic

JUICELESS > JUICE

JUICER *n* kitchen appliance, usually operated by electricity, fo extracting juice from frui and vegetables

JUICERS > JUICER

JUICES > JUICE

JUICIER > JUICY

JUICIEST > JUICY

JUICILY > JUICY

JUICINESS > JUICY

JUICING > JUICE

JUICY *adj* full of juice

JUJITSU *n* Japanese art of wrestling and self-defenc

JUJITSUS > JUJITSU

JUJU *n* W African magic charm or fetish

JUJUBE *n* chewy sweet made of flavoured gelatin

JUJUBES > JUJUBE

JUJUISM > JUJU

JUJUISMS > JUJU

JUJUIST > JUJU

JUJUISTS > JUJU

JUJUS > JUJU

JUJUTSU *same as* > JUJITSU

JUJUTSUS > JUJUTSU

JUKE *vb* dance or play dance music

JUKEBOX *n* coin-operated machine on which record CDs, or videos can be played

JUKEBOXES > JUKEBOX

JUKED > JUKE

JUKES > JUKE

JUKING > JUKE

JUKSKEI *n* game in which a peg is thrown over a fixe distance at a stake fixed

into the ground
UKSKEIS >JUKE
UKU *n* Japanese martial art
UKUS >JUKU
ULEP *n* sweet alcoholic drink
ULEPS >JULEP
ULIENNE *adj* (of vegetables or meat) cut into thin shreds ▷ *n* clear soup containing thinly shredded vegetables ▷ *vb* cut into thin pieces
ULIENNED >JULIENNE
ULIENNES >JULIENNE
UMAR *n* clamp with a handle that can move freely up a rope on which it is clipped but locks when downward pressure is applied ▷ *vb* climb (up a fixed rope) using jumars
UMARED >JUMAR
UMARING >JUMAR
UMARRED >JUMAR
UMARRING >JUMAR
UMARS >JUMAR
UMART *n* mythical offspring of a bull and a mare
UMARTS >JUMART
UMBAL *same as* >JUMBLE
UMBALS >JUMBAL
UMBIE *n* Caribbean ghost
UMBIES >JUMBIE
UMBLE *n* confused heap or state ▷ *vb* mix in a disordered way
UMBLED >JUMBLE
UMBLER >JUMBLE
UMBLERS >JUMBLE
UMBLES >JUMBLE
UMBLIER >JUMBLE
UMBLIEST >JUMBLE
UMBLING >JUMBLE
UMBLY >JUMBLE
UMBO *adj* very large ▷ *n* large jet airliner
UMBOISE *same as* >JUMBOIZE
UMBOISED >JUMBOISE
UMBOISES >JUMBOISE
UMBOIZE *vb* extend (a ship, esp a tanker) by cutting out the middle part and inserting a new larger part between the original bow and stern
UMBOIZED >JUMBOIZE
UMBOIZES >JUMBOIZE
UMBOS >JUMBO
UMBUCK *n* sheep
UMBUCKS >JUMBUCK
UMBY *n* Caribbean ghost
UMELLE *n* paired objects
UMELLES >JUMELLE
UMP *vb* leap or spring into the air using the leg muscles ▷ *n* act of jumping
UMPABLE >JUMP
UMPED >JUMP
UMPER *n* sweater or pullover
JUMPERS >JUMPER
JUMPIER >JUMPY
JUMPIEST >JUMPY
JUMPILY >JUMPY
JUMPINESS >JUMPY
JUMPING >JUMP
JUMPINGLY >JUMP
JUMPINGS >JUMP
JUMPOFF *n* extra round in a showjumping contest when two or more horses are equal first, the fastest round deciding the winner
JUMPOFFS >JUMPOFF
JUMPS >JUMP
JUMPSUIT *n* one-piece garment of combined trousers and jacket or shirt
JUMPSUITS >JUMPSUIT
JUMPY *adj* nervous
JUN *variant of* >CHON
JUNCATE *same as* >JUNKET
JUNCATES >JUNCATE
JUNCO *n* North American bunting
JUNCOES >JUNCO
JUNCOS >JUNCO
JUNCTION *n* place where routes, railway lines, or roads meet
JUNCTIONS >JUNCTION
JUNCTURAL >JUNCTURE
JUNCTURE *n* point in time, esp a critical one
JUNCTURES >JUNCTURE
JUNCUS *n* type of rush
JUNCUSES >JUNCUS
JUNEATING *n* early-season apple
JUNGLE *n* tropical forest of dense tangled vegetation
JUNGLED *adj* covered with jungle
JUNGLEGYM *n* climbing frame for children
JUNGLES >JUNGLE
JUNGLI *n* uncultured person
JUNGLIER >JUNGLE
JUNGLIEST >JUNGLE
JUNGLIS >JUNGLI
JUNGLIST *n* jungle-music enthusiast
JUNGLISTS >JUNGLIST
JUNGLY >JUNGLE
JUNIOR *adj* of lower standing ▷ *n* junior person
JUNIORATE *n* preparatory course for candidates for religious orders
JUNIORITY *n* condition of being junior
JUNIORS >JUNIOR
JUNIPER *n* evergreen shrub with purple berries
JUNIPERS >JUNIPER
JUNK *n* discarded or useless objects ▷ *vb* discard as junk
JUNKANOO *n* Bahamian ceremony
JUNKANOOS >JUNKANOO
JUNKED >JUNK
JUNKER *n* (formerly) young German nobleman
JUNKERS >JUNKER
JUNKET *n* excursion by public officials paid for from public funds ▷ *vb* (of a public official, committee, etc) to go on a junket
JUNKETED >JUNKET
JUNKETEER >JUNKET
JUNKETER >JUNKET
JUNKETERS >JUNKET
JUNKETING >JUNKET
JUNKETS >JUNKET
JUNKETTED >JUNKET
JUNKETTER >JUNKET
JUNKIE *n* drug addict
JUNKIER >JUNKY
JUNKIES >JUNKY
JUNKIEST >JUNKY
JUNKINESS >JUNKY
JUNKING >JUNK
JUNKMAN *n* man who buys and sells discarded clothing, furniture, etc
JUNKMEN >JUNKMAN
JUNKS >JUNK
JUNKY *n* drug addict ▷ *adj* of low quality
JUNKYARD *n* place where junk is stored or collected for sale
JUNKYARDS >JUNKYARD
JUNTA *n* group of military officers holding power in a country, esp after a coup
JUNTAS >JUNTA
JUNTO *same as* >JUNTA
JUNTOS >JUNTO
JUPATI *n* type of palm tree
JUPATIS >JUPATI
JUPE *n* sleeveless jacket
JUPES >JUPE
JUPON *n* short close-fitting sleeveless padded garment, used in the late 14th and early 15th centuries with armour
JUPONS >JUPON
JURA >JUS
JURAL *adj* of or relating to law or to the administration of justice
JURALLY >JURAL
JURANT *n* person taking oath
JURANTS >JURANT
JURASSIC *adj* of, denoting, or formed in the second period of the Mesozoic era, between the Triassic and Cretaceous periods, lasting for 55 million years during which dinosaurs and ammonites flourished
JURAT *n* statement at the foot of an affidavit, naming the parties, stating when, where, and before whom it was sworn, etc
JURATORY *adj* of, relating to, or expressed in an oath
JURATS >JURAT
JURE *adv* by legal right
JUREL *n* edible fish found in warm American Atlantic waters
JURELS >JUREL
JURIDIC *same as* >JURIDICAL
JURIDICAL *adj* of law or the administration of justice
JURIED >JURY
JURIES >JURY
JURIST *n* expert in law
JURISTIC *adj* of or relating to jurists
JURISTS >JURIST
JUROR *n* member of a jury
JURORS >JUROR
JURY *n* group of people sworn to deliver a verdict in a court of law ▷ *adj* makeshift ▷ *vb* evaluate by jury
JURYING >JURY
JURYLESS >JURY
JURYMAN *n* member of a jury, esp a man
JURYMAST *n* replacement mast
JURYMASTS >JURYMAST
JURYMEN >JURYMAN
JURYWOMAN *n* female member of a jury
JURYWOMEN >JURYWOMAN
JUS *n* right, power, or authority
JUSSIVE *n* mood of verbs used for giving orders; imperative
JUSSIVES >JUSSIVE
JUST *adv* very recently ▷ *adj* fair or impartial in action or judgment ▷ *vb* joust
JUSTED >JUST
JUSTER >JUST
JUSTERS >JUST
JUSTEST >JUST
JUSTICE *n* quality of being just
JUSTICER *n* magistrate
JUSTICERS >JUSTICER
JUSTICES >JUSTICE
JUSTICIAR *n* chief political and legal officer from the time of William I to that of Henry III, who deputized for the king in his absence and presided over the kings' courts
JUSTIFIED >JUSTIFY
JUSTIFIER >JUSTIFY
JUSTIFIES >JUSTIFY
JUSTIFY *vb* prove right or reasonable
JUSTING >JOUST
JUSTLE *less common word for* >JOSTLE
JUSTLED >JUSTLE
JUSTLES >JUSTLE
JUSTLING >JUSTLE
JUSTLY >JUST

JUSTNESS > JUST
JUSTS *same as* > JOUST
JUT *vb* project or stick out ▷ *n* something that juts out
JUTE *n* plant fibre, used for rope, canvas, etc
JUTELIKE > JUTE
JUTES > JUTE
JUTS > JUT
JUTTED > JUT
JUTTIED > JUTTY
JUTTIES > JUTTY
JUTTING > JUT
JUTTINGLY > JUT
JUTTY *vb* project beyond
JUTTYING > JUTTY
JUVE *same as* > JUVENILE
JUVENAL *variant spelling (esp US) of* > JUVENILE
JUVENALS > JUVENAL
JUVENILE *adj* young ▷ *n* young person or child
JUVENILES > JUVENILE
JUVENILIA *pl n* works produced in an author's youth
JUVES > JUVE
JUXTAPOSE *vb* put side by side
JYMOLD *n* ring made of two interlocking rings
JYMOLDS > JYMOLD
JYNX *n* woodpecker
JYNXES > JYNX

Kk

KA *n* (in ancient Egypt) attendant spirit supposedly dwelling as a vital force in a man or statue ▷ *vb* (in archaic usage) help
KAAL *adj* naked
KAAMA *n* large African antelope with lyre-shaped horns
KAAMAS > KAAMA
KAAS *n* Dutch cabinet or wardrobe
KAB *variant spelling of* > CAB
KABAB *same as* > KEBAB
KABABBED > KABAB
KABABBING > KABAB
KABABS > KABAB
KABADDI *n* game in which players try to touch opposing players but avoid being captured by them
KABADDIS > KABADDI
KABAKA *n* any of the former rulers of the Baganda people of S Uganda
KABAKAS > KABAKA
KABALA *same as* > KABBALAH
KABALAS > KABALA
KABALISM > KABALA
KABALISMS > KABALA
KABALIST > KABALA
KABALISTS > KABALA
KABAR *archaic form of* > CABER
KABARS > KABAR
KABAYA *n* tunic
KABAYAS > KABAYA
KABBALA *same as* > KABBALAH
KABBALAH *n* ancient Jewish mystical tradition
KABBALAHS > KABBALAH
KABBALAS > KABBALA
KABBALISM > KABBALAH
KABBALIST > KABBALAH
KABELE *same as* > KEBELE
KABELES > KABELE
KABELJOU *n* large fish that is an important food fish of South African waters
KABELJOUS > KABELJOU
KABELJOUW *same as* > KABELJOU
KABIKI *n* fruit tree found in India
KABIKIS > KABIKI
KABOB *same as* > KEBAB
KABOBBED > KABOB
KABOBBING > KABOB
KABOBS > KABOB
KABS > KAB
KABUKI *n* form of Japanese drama based on popular legends and characterized by elaborate costumes, stylized acting, and the use of male actors for all roles
KABUKIS > KABUKI
KACCHA *same as* > KACHA
KACCHAS > KACCHA
KACHA *n* short trousers traditionally worn by Sikhs as a symbol of their religious and cultural loyalty
KACHAHRI *n* Indian courthouse
KACHAHRIS > KACHAHRI
KACHAS > KACHA
KACHCHA *same as* > KACHA
KACHCHAS > KACHCHA
KACHERA *same as* > KACHA
KACHERAS > KACHERA
KACHERI *same as* > KACHAHRI
KACHERIS > KACHERI
KACHINA *n* any of the supernatural beings believed by the Hopi Indians to be the ancestors of living humans
KACHINAS > KACHINA
KADAITCHA *n* (in certain Central Australian Aboriginal tribes) man with the mission of avenging the death of a tribesman
KADDISH *n* ancient Jewish liturgical prayer
KADDISHES > KADDISH
KADDISHIM > KADDISH
KADE *same as* > KED
KADES > KADE
KADI *variant spelling of* > CADI
KADIS > KADI
KAE *n* dialect word for jackdaw or jay ▷ *vb* (in archaic usage) help
KAED > KAE
KAEING > KAE
KAES > KAE
KAF *n* letter of the Hebrew alphabet
KAFFIR *n* Southern African variety of sorghum, cultivated in dry regions for its grain and as fodder
KAFFIRS > KAFFIR
KAFFIYAH *same as* > KAFFIYEH
KAFFIYAHS > KAFFIYAH
KAFFIYEH *same as* > KEFFIYEH
KAFFIYEHS > KAFFIYEH
KAFILA *n* caravan
KAFILAS > KAFILA
KAFIR *same as* > KAFFIR
KAFIRS > KAFIR
KAFS > KAF
KAFTAN *n* long loose Eastern garment
KAFTANS > KAFTAN
KAGO *n* Japanese sedan chair
KAGOOL *variant spelling of* > CAGOULE
KAGOOLS > KAGOOL
KAGOS > KAGO
KAGOUL *variant spelling of* > CAGOULE
KAGOULE *same as* > KAGOUL
KAGOULES > KAGOULE
KAGOULS > KAGOUL
KAGU *n* crested nocturnal bird of New Caledonia with a red bill and greyish plumage
KAGUS > KAGU
KAHAL *n* Jewish community
KAHALS > KAHAL
KAHAWAI *n* food and game fish of New Zealand
KAHAWAIS > KAHAWAI
KAHIKATEA *n* tall New Zealand coniferous tree
KAHIKATOA *n* tall New Zealand coniferous tree
KAHUNA *n* Hawaiian priest, shaman, or expert
KAHUNAS > KAHUNA
KAI *n* food
KAIAK *same as* > KAYAK
KAIAKED > KAIAK
KAIAKING > KAIAK
KAIAKS > KAIAK
KAID *n* North African chieftan or leader
KAIDS > KAID

KAIE *archaic form of* > KEY
KAIES > KAIE
KAIF *same as* > KIF
KAIFS > KAIF
KAIK *same as* > KAINGA
KAIKA *same as* > KAINGA
KAIKAI *n* food
KAIKAIS > KAIKAI
KAIKAS > KAIKA
KAIKAWAKA *n* small pyramid-shaped New Zealand conifer
KAIKOMAKO *n* small New Zealand tree with white flowers and black fruit
KAIKS > KAIK
KAIL *same as* > KALE
KAILS > KAIL
KAILYAIRD *same as* > KALEYARD
KAILYARD *same as* > KALEYARD
KAILYARDS > KAILYARD
KAIM *same as* > KAME
KAIMAKAM *n* Turkish governor
KAIMAKAMS > KAIMAKAM
KAIMS > KAIM
KAIN *variant spelling of* > CAIN
KAING > KA
KAINGA *n* (in New Zealand) a Māori village or small settlement
KAINGAS > KAINGA
KAINIT *same as* > KAINITE
KAINITE *n* white mineral consisting of potassium chloride and magnesium sulphate: a fertilizer and source of potassium salts
KAINITES > KAINITE
KAINITS > KAINIT
KAINS > KAIN
KAIROMONE *n* substance secreted by animal
KAIS > KAI
KAISER *n* German or Austro-Hungarian emperor
KAISERDOM > KAISER
KAISERIN *n* empress
KAISERINS > KAISERIN
KAISERISM > KAISER
KAISERS > KAISER
KAIZEN *n* philosophy of continuous improvement of working practices that underlies total quality management and just-in-time business techniques
KAIZENS > KAIZEN
KAJAWAH *n* type of seat or panier used on a camel
KAJAWAHS > KAJAWAH
KAJEPUT *n* variety of Australian melaleuca
KAJEPUTS > KAJEPUT
KAK *n* South African slang word for faeces
KAKA *n* parrot of New Zealand
KAKAPO *n* ground-living nocturnal New Zealand parrot that resembles an owl
KAKAPOS > KAKAPO
KAKARIKI *n* green-feathered New Zealand parrot
KAKAS > KAKA
KAKEMONO *n* Japanese paper or silk wall hanging, usually long and narrow, with a picture or inscription on it and a roller at the bottom
KAKEMONOS > KAKEMONO
KAKI *n* Asian persimmon tree
KAKIEMON *n* type of 17th century Japanese porcelain
KAKIEMONS > KAKIEMON
KAKIS > KAKI
KAKODYL *variant spelling of* > CACODYL
KAKODYLS > KAKODYL
KAKS > KAK
KALAM *n* discussion and debate, especially relating to Islamic theology
KALAMATA as in *kalamata olive* aubergine-coloured Greek olive
KALAMATAS > KALAMATA
KALAMDAN *n* Persian box in which to keep pens
KALAMDANS > KALAMDAN
KALAMKARI *n* Indian cloth printing and printed Indian cloth
KALAMS > KALAM
KALANCHOE *n* tropical succulent plant having small brightly coloured flowers and dark shiny leaves
KALE *n* cabbage with crinkled leaves
KALENDAR *variant form of* > CALENDAR
KALENDARS > KALENDAR
KALENDS *same as* > CALENDS
KALES > KALE
KALEWIFE *n* Scots word for a female vegetable or cabbage seller
KALEWIVES > KALEWIFE
KALEYARD *n* vegetable garden
KALEYARDS > KALEYARD
KALI *another name for* > SALTWORT
KALIAN *another name for* > HOOKAH
KALIANS > KALIAN
KALIF *variant spelling of* > CALIPH
KALIFATE *same as* > CALIPHATE
KALIFATES > KALIFATE
KALIFS > KALIF
KALIMBA *n* musical instrument
KALIMBAS > KALIMBA
KALINITE *n* alum
KALINITES > KALINITE
KALIPH *variant spelling of* > CALIPH
KALIPHATE *same as* > CALIPHATE
KALIPHS > KALIPH
KALIS > KALI
KALIUM *n* Latin for potassium
KALIUMS > KALIUM
KALLIDIN *n* type of peptide
KALLIDINS > KALLIDIN
KALLITYPE *n* old printing process
KALMIA *n* N American evergreen ericaceous shrub with showy clusters of white or pink flowers
KALMIAS > KALMIA
KALONG *n* fruit bat
KALONGS > KALONG
KALOTYPE *variant spelling of* > CALOTYPE
KALOTYPES > KALOTYPE
KALPA *n* (in Hindu cosmology) period in which the universe experiences a cycle of creation and destruction
KALPAC *same as* > CALPAC
KALPACS > KALPAC
KALPAK *variant spelling of* > CALPAC
KALPAKS > KALPAK
KALPAS > KALPA
KALPIS *n* Greek water jar
KALPISES > KALPIS
KALSOMINE *variant of* > CALCIMINE
KALUMPIT *n* type of Filipino fruit tree or its fruit
KALUMPITS > KALUMPIT
KALYPTRA *n* Greek veil
KALYPTRAS > KALYPTRA
KAM *Shakespearean word for* > CROOKED
KAMA *n* large African antelope with lyre-shaped horns
KAMAAINA *n* Hawaiian local
KAMAAINAS > KAMAAINA
KAMACITE *n* alloy of iron and nickel, occurring in meteorites
KAMACITES > KAMACITE
KAMAHI *n* tall New Zealand hardwood tree with pinkish flowers
KAMALA *n* East Indian tree
KAMALAS > KAMALA
KAMAS > KAMA
KAME *n* irregular mound or ridge of gravel, sand, etc, deposited by water derived from melting glaciers
KAMEES > KAMEEZ
KAMEESES > KAMEES
KAMEEZ *n* long tunic worn in the Indian subcontinent, often with shalwar
KAMEEZES > KAMEEZ
KAMELA *same as* > KAMALA
KAMELAS > KAMELA
KAMERAD *interj* shout of surrender ▷ *vb* surrender
KAMERADED > KAMERAD
KAMERADS > KAMERAD
KAMES > KAME
KAMI *n* divine being or spiritual force in Shinto
KAMICHI *n* South American bird
KAMICHIS > KAMICHI
KAMIK *n* traditional Inuit boot made of caribou hide or sealskin
KAMIKAZE *n* (in World War II) Japanese pilot who performed a suicide mission ▷ *adj* (of an action) undertaken in the knowledge that it will kill or injure the person performing it
KAMIKAZES > KAMIKAZE
KAMIKS > KAMIK
KAMILA *same as* > KAMALA
KAMILAS > KAMILA
KAMIS *same as* > KAMEEZ
KAMISES > KAMIS
KAMME *same as* > KAM
KAMOKAMO *n* kind of marrow found in New Zealand
KAMPONG *n* (in Malaysia) village
KAMPONGS > KAMPONG
KAMSEEN *same as* > KHAMSIN
KAMSEENS > KAMSEEN
KAMSIN *same as* > KAMSEEN
KAMSINS > KAMSIN
KANA *n* Japanese syllabary, which consists of two written varieties
KANAE *n* grey mullet
KANAKA *n* Australian word for any native of the South Pacific islands, esp (formerly) one abducted to work in Australia
KANAKAS > KANAKA
KANAMYCIN *n* type of antibiotic
KANAS > KANA
KANBAN *n* just-in-time manufacturing process in which the movements of materials through a process are recorded on specially designed cards
KANBANS > KANBAN
KANDIES > KANDY
KANDY *same as* > CANDIE
KANE *n* Hawaiian man or boy
KANEH *n* 6-cubit Hebrew measure
KANEHS > KANEH
KANES > KANE
KANG *n* Chinese heatable platform used for sleeping and sitting on
KANGA *n* piece of gaily decorated thin cotton cloth used as a garment by women in E Africa
KANGAROO *n* Australian

marsupial which moves by jumping with its powerful hind legs ▷ *vb* (of a car) move forward or to cause (a car) to move forward with short sudden jerks, as a result of improper use of the clutch
KANGAROOS > KANGAROO
KANGAS > KANGA
KANGHA *n* comb traditionally worn by Sikhs as a symbol of their religious and cultural loyalty
KANGHAS > KANGHA
KANGS > KANG
KANJI *n* Japanese writing system using characters mainly derived from Chinese ideograms
KANJIS > KANJI
KANS *n* Indian wild sugar cane
KANSES > KANS
KANT *archaic spelling of* > CANT
KANTAR *n* unit of weight used in E Mediterranean countries, equivalent to 100 pounds or 45 kilograms but varying from place to place
KANTARS > KANTAR
KANTED > KANT
KANTELA *same as* > KANTELE
KANTELAS > KANTELA
KANTELE *n* Finnish stringed instrument
KANTELES > KANTELE
KANTEN *same as* > AGAR
KANTENS > KANTEN
KANTHA *n* Bengali embroidered quilt
KANTHAS > KANTHA
KANTIKOY *vb* dance ceremonially
KANTIKOYS > KANTIKOY
KANTING > KANT
KANTS > KANT
KANUKA *n* New Zealand myrtaceous tree
KANZU *n* long garment, usually white, with long sleeves, worn by E African men
KANZUS > KANZU
KAOLIANG *n* any of various E Asian varieties of sorghum
KAOLIANGS > KAOLIANG
KAOLIN *n* fine white clay used to make porcelain and in some medicines
KAOLINE *same as* > KAOLIN
KAOLINES > KAOLINE
KAOLINIC > KAOLIN
KAOLINISE *same as* > KAOLINIZE
KAOLINITE *n* white or grey clay mineral consisting of hydrated aluminium silicate in triclinic crystalline form, the main constituent of kaolin
KAOLINIZE *vb* change into kaolin
KAOLINS > KAOLIN
KAON *n* meson that has a positive or negative charge and a rest mass of about 966 electron masses, or no charge and a rest mass of 974 electron masses
KAONIC > KAON
KAONS > KAON
KAPA *n* Hawaiian cloth made from beaten mulberry bark
KAPAS > KAPA
KAPH *n* 11th letter of the Hebrew alphabet
KAPHS > KAPH
KAPOK *n* fluffy fibre from a tropical tree, used to stuff cushions etc
KAPOKS > KAPOK
KAPPA *n* tenth letter in the Greek alphabet
KAPPAS > KAPPA
KAPUKA *same as* > BROADLEAF
KAPUT *adj* ruined or broken
KAPUTT *same as* > KAPUT
KARA *n* steel bangle traditionally worn by Sikhs as a symbol of their religious and cultural loyalty
KARABINER *n* metal clip with a spring for attaching to a piton, belay, etc
KARAISM *n* beliefs and doctrines of a Jewish sect rejecting Rabbinism
KARAISMS > KARAISM
KARAIT *same as* > KRAIT
KARAITS > KRAIT
KARAKA *n* New Zealand tree
KARAKAS > KARAKA
KARAKIA *n* prayer
KARAKIAS > KARAKIA
KARAKUL *n* sheep of central Asia, the lambs of which have soft curled dark hair
KARAKULS > KARAKUL
KARAMU *n* small New Zealand tree with glossy leaves and orange fruit
KARAMUS > KARAMU
KARANGA *n* call or chant of welcome, sung by a female elder ▷ *vb* perform a karanga
KARANGAED > KARANGA
KARANGAS > KARANGA
KARAOKE *n* form of entertainment in which people sing over a prerecorded backing tape
KARAOKES > KARAOKE
KARAS > KARA
KARAT *n* measure of the proportion of gold in an alloy, expressed as the number of parts of gold in 24 parts of the alloy
KARATE *n* Japanese system of unarmed combat using blows with the feet, hands, elbows, and legs
KARATEIST *same as* > KARATEKA
KARATEKA *n* competitor or expert in karate
KARATEKAS > KARATEKA
KARATES > KARATE
KARATS > KARAT
KAREAREA *n* New Zealand falcon
KARENGO *n* edible type of Pacific seaweed
KARENGOS > KARENGO
KARITE *n* shea tree
KARITES > KARITE
KARK *variant spelling of* > CARK
KARKED > KARK
KARKING > KARK
KARKS > KARK
KARMA *n* person's actions affecting his or her fate in the next reincarnation
KARMAS > KARMA
KARMIC > KARMA
KARN *old word for* > CAIRN
KARNS > KARN
KARO *n* small New Zealand tree or shrub with sweet-smelling brown flowers
KAROO *n* high arid plateau
KAROOS > KAROO
KARORO *n* large seagull with black feathers on its back
KAROROS > KARORO
KAROSHI *n* (in Japan) death caused by overwork
KAROSHIS > KAROSHI
KAROSS *n* blanket made of animal skins sewn together
KAROSSES > KAROSS
KARRI *n* Australian eucalypt
KARRIS > KARRI
KARROO *same as* > KAROO
KARROOS > KARROO
KARSEY *variant spelling of* > KHAZI
KARSEYS > KARSEY
KARSIES > KARSY
KARST *n* denoting the characteristic scenery of a limestone region, including underground streams, gorges, etc
KARSTIC > KARST
KARSTIFY *vb* become karstic
KARSTS > KARST
KARSY *variant spelling of* > KHAZI
KART *n* light low-framed vehicle with small wheels and engine used for recreational racing
KARTER > KART
KARTERS > KART
KARTING > KART
KARTINGS > KART
KARTS > KART
KARYOGAMY *n* fusion of two gametic nuclei during fertilization
KARYOGRAM *n* diagram or photograph of the chromosomes of a cell, arranged in homologous pairs and in a numbered sequence
KARYOLOGY *n* study of cell nuclei, esp with reference to the number and shape of the chromosomes
KARYON *n* nucleus of a cell
KARYONS > KARYON
KARYOSOME *n* any of the dense aggregates of chromatin in the nucleus of a cell
KARYOTIN *less common word for* > CHROMATIN
KARYOTINS > KARYOTIN
KARYOTYPE *n* appearance of the chromosomes in a somatic cell of an individual or species, with reference to their number, size, shape, etc ▷ *vb* determine the karyotype of (a cell)
KARZIES > KARZY
KARZY *variant spelling of* > KHAZI
KAS > KA
KASBAH *n* citadel of any of various North African cities
KASBAHS > KASBAH
KASHA *n* dish originating in Eastern Europe, consisting of boiled or baked buckwheat
KASHAS > KASHA
KASHER *vb* make fit for use
KASHERED > KASHER
KASHERING > KASHER
KASHERS > KASHER
KASHMIR *variant spelling of* > CASHMERE
KASHMIRS > KASHMIR
KASHRUS *same as* > KASHRUTH
KASHRUSES > KASHRUS
KASHRUT *same as* > KASHRUTH
KASHRUTH *n* condition of being fit for ritual use in general
KASHRUTHS > KASHRUTH
KASHRUTS > KASHRUT
KASME *interj* (in Indian English) I swear
KAT *same as* > KHAT
KATA *n* exercise consisting of a sequence of the specific movements of a martial art, used in training and designed to show skill in technique
KATABASES > KATABASIS
KATABASIS *n* retreat of the Greek mercenaries of Cyrus the Younger, after

his death at Cunaxa, from the Euphrates to the Black Sea in 401–400 BC under the leadership of Xenophon
KATABATIC *adj* (of winds) blowing downhill through having become denser with cooling, esp at night when heat is lost from the earth's surface
KATABOLIC *same as* > CATABOLIC
KATAKANA *n* one of the two systems of syllabic writing employed for the representation of Japanese, based on Chinese ideograms. It is used mainly for foreign or foreign-derived words
KATAKANAS > KATAKANA
KATANA *n* Japanese samurai sword
KATANAS > KATANA
KATAS > KATA
KATCHINA *variant spelling of* > KACHINA
KATCHINAS > KATCHINA
KATCINA *variant spelling of* > KACHINA
KATCINAS > KATCINA
KATHAK *n* form of N Indian classical dancing that tells a story
KATHAKALI *n* form of dance drama of S India using mime and based on Hindu literature
KATHAKS > KATHAK
KATHARSES > KATHARSIS
KATHARSIS *variant spelling of* > CATHARSIS
KATHODAL > KATHODE
KATHODE *variant spelling of* > CATHODE
KATHODES > KATHODE
KATHODIC > KATHODE
KATI *variant spelling of* > CATTY
KATION *variant spelling of* > CATION
KATIONS > KATION
KATIPO *n* small poisonous New Zealand spider
KATIPOS > KATIPO
KATIS > KATI
KATORGA *n* labour camp in Imperial Russia or the Soviet Union
KATORGAS > KATORGA
KATS > KAT
KATSURA *n* Asian tree
KATSURAS > KATSURA
KATTI *variant spelling of* > CATTY
KATTIS > KATTI
KATYDID *n* large green grasshopper of N America
KATYDIDS > KATYDID
KAUGH *same as* > KIAUGH
KAUGHS > KAUGH
KAUMATUA *n* senior member of a tribe
KAUMATUAS > KAUMATUA
KAUPAPA *n* strategy, policy, or cause
KAUPAPAS > KAUPAPA
KAURI *n* large NZ conifer that yields valuable timber and resin
KAURIES > KAURY
KAURIS > KAURI
KAURU *n* edible stem of the cabbage tree
KAURY *variant spelling of* > KAURI
KAVA *n* Polynesian shrub
KAVAKAVA *same as* > KAVA
KAVAKAVAS > KAVAKAVA
KAVAS > KAVA
KAVASS *n* armed Turkish constable
KAVASSES > KAVASS
KAW *variant spelling of* > CAW
KAWA *n* protocol or etiquette, particularly in a Māori tribal meeting place
KAWAKAWA *n* aromatic shrub or small tree of New Zealand
KAWAKAWAS > KAWAKAWA
KAWAS > KAWA
KAWAU *n* New Zealand name for black shag
KAWED > KAW
KAWING > KAW
KAWS > KAW
KAY *n* name of the letter K
KAYAK *n* Inuit canoe made of sealskins stretched over a frame ▷ *vb* travel by kayak
KAYAKED > KAYAK
KAYAKER > KAYAK
KAYAKERS > KAYAK
KAYAKING > KAYAK
KAYAKINGS > KAYAK
KAYAKS > KAYAK
KAYLE *n* one of a set of ninepins
KAYLES *pl n* ninepins
KAYLIED *adj* (in British slang) intoxicated or drunk
KAYO *another term for* > KNOCKOUT
KAYOED > KAYO
KAYOES > KAYO
KAYOING > KAYO
KAYOINGS > KAYO
KAYOS > KAYO
KAYS > KAY
KAZACHKI *same as* > KAZACHOK
KAZACHOK *n* Russian folk dance in which the performer executes high kicks from a squatting position
KAZATSKI *same as* > KAZACHOK
KAZATSKY *same as* > KAZACHOK
KAZATZKA *same as* > KAZACHOK
KAZATZKAS > KAZACHOK
KAZI *variant spelling of* > KHAZI
KAZILLION *same as* > GAZILLION
KAZIS > KAZI
KAZOO *n* cigar-shaped metal musical instrument that produces a buzzing sound when the player hums into it
KAZOOS > KAZOO
KBAR *n* kilobar
KBARS > KBAR
KEA *n* large brownish-green parrot of NZ
KEAS > KEA
KEASAR *archaic variant of* > KAISER
KEASARS > KEASAR
KEAVIE *n* archaic or dialect word for a type of crab
KEAVIES > KEAVIE
KEB *vb* Scots word meaning miscarry or reject a lamb
KEBAB *n* dish of small pieces of meat grilled on skewers ▷ *vb* skewer
KEBABBED > KEBAB
KEBABBING > KEBAB
KEBABS > KEBAB
KEBAR *n* Scots word for beam or rafter
KEBARS > KEBAR
KEBBED > KEB
KEBBIE *n* Scots word for shepherd's crook
KEBBIES > KEBBIE
KEBBING > KEB
KEBBOCK *n* Scots word for a cheese
KEBBOCKS > CHEESE
KEBBUCK *same as* > KEBBOCK
KEBBUCKS > KEBBUCK
KEBELE *n* Ethiopian local council
KEBELES > KEBELE
KEBLAH *same as* > KIBLAH
KEBLAHS > KEBLAH
KEBOB *same as* > KEBAB
KEBOBBED > KEBOB
KEBOBBING > KEBOB
KEBOBS > KEBOB
KEBS > KEB
KECK *vb* retch or feel nausea
KECKED > KECK
KECKING > KECK
KECKLE *Scots variant of* > CACKLE
KECKLED > KECKLE
KECKLES > KECKLE
KECKLING > KECKLE
KECKLINGS > KECKLE
KECKS *pl n* trousers
KECKSES > KECKS
KECKSIES > KECKSY
KECKSY *n* dialect word meaning hollow plant stalk
KED as in *sheep ked* sheep tick
KEDDAH *same as* > KHEDA
KEDDAHS > KEDDAH
KEDGE *vb* move (a ship) along by hauling in on the cable of a light anchor ▷ *n* light anchor used for kedging
KEDGED > KEDGE
KEDGER *n* small anchor
KEDGEREE *n* dish of fish with rice and eggs
KEDGEREES > KEDGEREE
KEDGERS > KEDGER
KEDGES > KEDGE
KEDGIER > KEDGY
KEDGIEST > KEDGY
KEDGING > KEDGE
KEDGY *adj* dialect word for happy or lively
KEDS > KED
KEECH *n* old word for lump of fat
KEECHES > KEECH
KEEF *same as* > KIF
KEEFS > KEEF
KEEK *Scot word for* > PEEP
KEEKED > KEEK
KEEKER > KEEK
KEEKERS > KEEK
KEEKING > KEEK
KEEKS > KEEK
KEEL *n* main lengthways timber or steel support along the base of a ship ▷ *vb* mark with this stain
KEELAGE *n* fee charged by certain ports to allow a ship to dock
KEELAGES > KEELAGE
KEELBOAT *n* river boat with a shallow draught and a keel, used for freight and moved by towing, punting, or rowing
KEELBOATS > KEELBOAT
KEELED > KEEL
KEELER *n* bargeman
KEELERS > KEELER
KEELHALE *same as* > KEELHAUL
KEELHALED > KEELHALE
KEELHALES > KEELHALE
KEELHAUL *vb* reprimand (someone) harshly
KEELHAULS > KEELHAUL
KEELIE *n* kestrel
KEELIES > KEELIE
KEELING > KEEL
KEELINGS > KEEL
KEELIVINE *Scots word for* > PENCIL
KEELLESS > KEEL
KEELMAN *n* bargeman
KEELMEN > KEELMAN
KEELS > KEEL
KEELSON *n* lengthways beam fastened to the keel of a ship for strength
KEELSONS > KEELSON
KEELYVINE *same as* > KEELIVINE
KEEN *adj* eager or enthusiastic ▷ *vb* wail over the dead ▷ *n* lament for the dead
KEENED > KEEN
KEENER > KEEN
KEENERS > KEEN
KEENEST > KEEN

EENING > KEEN
EENINGS > KEEN
EENLY > KEEN
EENNESS > KEEN
EENO *same as* > KENO
EENOS > KEENO
EENS > KEEN
EEP *vb* have or retain possession of ▷ *n* cost of food and everyday expenses
EEPABLE > KEEP
EEPER *n* person who looks after animals in a zoo
EEPERS > KEEPER
EEPING > KEEP
EEPINGS > KEEP
EEPNET *n* cylindrical net strung on wire hoops and sealed at one end, suspended in water by anglers to keep alive the fish they have caught
EEPNETS > KEEPNET
EEPS > KEEP
EEPSAKE *n* gift treasured for the sake of the giver
EEPSAKES > KEEPSAKE
EEPSAKY > KEEPSAKE
EESHOND *n* breed of dog of the spitz type with a shaggy greyish coat and tightly curled tail, originating in Holland
EESHONDS > KEESHOND
EESTER *same as* > KEISTER
EESTERS > KEESTER
EET *short for* > PARAKEET
EETS > KEET
EEVE *n* tub or vat
EEVES > KEEVE
EF *same as* > KIF
EFFEL *dialect word for* > HORSE
EFFELS > KEFFEL
EFFIYAH *same as* > KAFFIYEH
EFFIYAHS > KEFFIYAH
EFFIYEH *n* cotton headdress worn by Arabs
EFFIYEHS > KEFFIYEH
EFIR *n* effervescent drink of the Caucasus made from fermented milk
EFIRS > KEFIR
EFS > KEF
EFTEDES *n* Greek dish of meatballs cooked with herbs and onions
EFUFFLE *same as* > KERFUFFLE
EFUFFLED > KEFUFFLE
EFUFFLES > KEFUFFLE
EG *n* small metal beer barrel ▷ *vb* put in kegs
EGELER *same as* > KEGLER
EGELERS > KEGELER
EGGED > KEG
EGGER > KEG
EGGERS > KEG
EGGING > KEG
EGLER *n* participant in a game of tenpin bowling
EGLERS > KEGLER
KEGLING *n* bowling
KEGLINGS > KEGLING
KEGS > KEG
KEHUA *n* ghost or spirit
KEHUAS > KEHUA
KEIGHT > KETCH
KEIR *same as* > KIER
KEIRETSU *n* group of Japanese businesses
KEIRETSUS > KEIRETSU
KEIRS > KEIR
KEISTER *n* rump
KEISTERS > KEISTER
KEITLOA *n* southern African black two-horned rhinoceros
KEITLOAS > KEITLOA
KEKENO *n* New Zealand fur seal
KEKERENGU *n* Māori bug
KEKS *same as* > KECKS
KEKSYE *same as* > KEX
KEKSYES > KEKSYE
KELEP *n* large ant found in Central and South America
KELEPS > KELEP
KELIM *same as* > KILIM
KELIMS > KELIM
KELL *dialect word for* > HAIRNET
KELLAUT *same as* > KHILAT
KELLAUTS > KELLAUT
KELLIES > KELLY
KELLS > KELL
KELLY *n* part of a drill system
KELOID *n* hard smooth pinkish raised growth of scar tissue at the site of an injury, tending to occur more frequently in dark-skinned races
KELOIDAL > KELOID
KELOIDS > KELOID
KELP *n* large brown seaweed ▷ *vb* burn seaweed to make a type of ash used as a source for iodine and potash
KELPED > KELP
KELPER *n* Falkland Islander
KELPERS > KELPER
KELPIE *n* Australian sheepdog with a smooth coat and upright ears
KELPIES > KELPY
KELPING > KELP
KELPS > KELP
KELPY *same as* > KELPIE
KELSON *same as* > KEELSON
KELSONS > KELSON
KELT *n* salmon that has recently spawned
KELTER *same as* > KILTER
KELTERS > KELTER
KELTIE *variant spelling of* > KELTY
KELTIES > KELTY
KELTS > KELT
KELTY *n* old Scots word for an extra drink imposed on someone not thought to be drinking enough
KELVIN *n* SI unit of temperature
KELVINS > KELVIN
KEMB *old word for* > COMB
KEMBED > KEMB
KEMBING > KEMB
KEMBLA *n* small change
KEMBLAS > KEMBLA
KEMBO *same as* > KIMBO
KEMBOED > KEMBO
KEMBOING > KEMBO
KEMBOS > KEMBO
KEMBS > KEMB
KEMP *n* coarse hair or strand of hair, esp one in a fleece that resists dyeing ▷ *vb* dialect word meaning to compete or try to come first
KEMPED > KEMP
KEMPER > KEMP
KEMPERS > KEMP
KEMPIER > KEMPY
KEMPIEST > KEMPY
KEMPING > KEMP
KEMPINGS > KEMP
KEMPLE *n* variable Scottish measure for hay or straw
KEMPLES > KEMPLE
KEMPS > KEMP
KEMPT *adj* (of hair) tidy
KEMPY > KEMP
KEN *vb* know ▷ *n* range of knowledge or perception
KENAF *another name for* > AMBARY
KENAFS > KENAF
KENCH *n* bin for salting and preserving fish
KENCHES > KENCH
KENDO *n* Japanese sport of fencing using wooden staves
KENDOS > KENDO
KENNED > KEN
KENNEL *n* hutlike shelter for a dog ▷ *vb* put or go into a kennel
KENNELED > KENNEL
KENNELING > KENNEL
KENNELLED > KENNEL
KENNELS > KENNEL
KENNER > KEN
KENNERS > KEN
KENNET *n* old word for a small hunting dog
KENNETS > KENNET
KENNETT *vb* spoil or destroy ruthlessly
KENNETTED > KENNETT
KENNETTS > KENNETT
KENNING > KEN
KENNINGS > KEN
KENO *n* game of chance similar to bingo
KENOS > KENO
KENOSES > KENOSIS
KENOSIS *n* Christ's voluntary renunciation of certain divine attributes, in order to identify himself with mankind
KENOSISES > KENOSIS
KENOTIC > KENOSIS
KENOTRON *n* signal-amplifying device
KENOTRONS > KENOTRON
KENS > KEN
KENSPECK *adj* Scots for easily seen or recognized
KENT *dialect word for* > PUNT
KENTE *n* brightly coloured handwoven cloth of Ghana, usually with some gold thread
KENTED > KENT
KENTES > KENTE
KENTIA *n* plant name formerly used to include palms now allotted to several different genera
KENTIAS > KENTIA
KENTING > KENT
KENTLEDGE *n* scrap metal used as ballast in a vessel
KENTS > KENT
KEP *vb* catch
KEPHALIC *variant spelling of* > CEPHALIC
KEPHALICS > KEPHALIC
KEPHALIN *same as* > CEPHALIN
KEPHALINS > KEPHALIN
KEPHIR *same as* > KEFIR
KEPHIRS > KEPHIR
KEPI *n* French military cap with a flat top and a horizontal peak
KEPIS > KEPI
KEPPED > KEP
KEPPEN > KEP
KEPPING > KEP
KEPPIT > KEP
KEPS > KEP
KEPT > KEEP
KERAMIC *rare variant of* > CERAMIC
KERAMICS *rare variant of* > CERAMICS
KERATIN *n* fibrous protein found in the hair and nails
KERATINS > KERATIN
KERATITIS *n* inflammation of the cornea
KERATOID *adj* resembling horn
KERATOMA *n* horny growth on the skin
KERATOMAS > KERATOMA
KERATOSE *adj* (esp of certain sponges) having a horny skeleton
KERATOSES > KERATOSIS
KERATOSIC > KERATOSE
KERATOSIS *n* any skin condition marked by a horny growth, such as a wart
KERATOTIC > KERATOSIS
KERB *n* edging to a footpath ▷ *vb* provide with or enclose with a kerb
KERBAYA *n* blouse worn by Malay women
KERBAYAS > KERBAYA
KERBED > KERB
KERBING *n* material used for a kerb

KERBINGS > KERBING
KERBS > KERB
KERBSIDE *n* edge of a pavement where it drops to the level of the road
KERBSIDES > KERBSIDE
KERBSTONE *n* one of a series of stones that form a kerb
KERCHIEF *n* piece of cloth worn over the head or round the neck
KERCHIEFS > KERCHIEF
KERCHOO *interj* atishoo
KEREL *n* chap or fellow
KERELS > KEREL
KERERU *n* New Zealand pigeon
KERF *n* cut made by a saw, an axe, etc ▷ *vb* cut
KERFED > KERF
KERFING > KERF
KERFLOOEY *adv* into state of destruction or malfunction
KERFS > KERF
KERFUFFLE *n* commotion or disorder ▷ *vb* put into disorder or disarray
KERKIER > KERKY
KERKIEST > KERKY
KERKY *adj* stupid
KERMA *n* quotient of the sum of the initial kinetic energies of all the charged particles liberated by indirectly ionizing radiation in a volume element of a material divided by the mass of the volume element
KERMAS > KERMA
KERMES *n* dried bodies of female scale insects, used as a red dyestuff
KERMESITE *n* red antimony
KERMESS *same as* > KERMIS
KERMESSE *same as* > KERMIS
KERMESSES > KERMESSE
KERMIS *n* (formerly, esp in Holland and Northern Germany) annual country festival or carnival
KERMISES > KERMIS
KERN *n* part of the character on a piece of printer's type that projects beyond the body ▷ *vb* furnish (a typeface) with a kern
KERNE *same as* > KERN
KERNED > KERNE
KERNEL *n* seed of a nut, cereal, or fruit stone ▷ *vb* form kernels
KERNELED > KERNEL
KERNELING > KERNEL
KERNELLED > KERNEL
KERNELLY *adj* with or like kernels
KERNELS > KERNEL
KERNES > KERNE
KERNING *n* adjustment of space between the letters of words to improve the appearance of text matter
KERNINGS > KERNING
KERNISH *adj* of, belonging to, or resembling an armed foot soldier or peasant
KERNITE *n* light soft colourless or white mineral consisting of a hydrated sodium borate in monoclinic crystalline form: an important source of borax and other boron compounds
KERNITES > KERNITE
KERNS > KERN
KERO *short for* > KEROSENE
KEROGEN *n* solid organic material found in some rocks, such as oil shales, that produces hydrocarbons similar to petroleum when heated
KEROGENS > KEROGEN
KEROS > KERO
KEROSENE *n* liquid mixture distilled from petroleum and used as a fuel or solvent
KEROSENES > KEROSENE
KEROSINE *same as* > KEROSENE
KEROSINES > KEROSINE
KERPLUNK *vb* land noisily
KERPLUNKS > KERPLUNK
KERRIA *n* type of shrub with yellow flowers
KERRIAS > KERRIA
KERRIES > KERRY
KERRY *n* breed of dairy cattle
KERSEY *n* smooth woollen cloth used for overcoats, etc
KERSEYS > KERSEY
KERVE *dialect word for* > CARVE
KERVED > KERVE
KERVES > KERVE
KERVING > KERVE
KERYGMA *n* essential news of Jesus, as preached by the early Christians to elicit faith rather than to educate or instruct
KERYGMAS > KERYGMA
KERYGMATA > KERYGMA
KESAR *old variant of* > KAISER
KESARS > KESAR
KESH *n* beard and uncut hair, covered by the turban, traditionally worn by Sikhs as a symbol of their religious and cultural loyalty
KESHES > KESH
KEST *old form of* > CAST
KESTING > KEST
KESTREL *n* type of small falcon
KESTRELS > KESTREL
KESTS > KEST
KET *n* dialect word for carrion
KETA *n* type of salmon
KETAMINE *n* drug, chemically related to PCP, that is used in medicine as a general anaesthetic, being administered by injection
KETAMINES > KETAMINE
KETAS > KETA
KETCH *n* two-masted sailing vessel ▷ *vb* (in archaic usage) catch
KETCHES > KETCH
KETCHING > KETCH
KETCHUP *n* thick cold sauce, usu made of tomatoes
KETCHUPS > KETCHUP
KETE *n* basket woven from flax
KETENE *n* colourless irritating toxic gas used as an acetylating agent in organic synthesis
KETENES > KETENE
KETMIA as in *bladder ketmia* plant with pale yellow flowers and a bladder-like calyx
KETMIAS > KETMIA
KETO as in *keto form* form of tautomeric compounds when they are ketones rather than enol
KETOGENIC *adj* forming or able to stimulate the production of ketone bodies
KETOL *n* nitrogenous substance
KETOLS > KETOL
KETONE *n* type of organic solvent
KETONEMIA *n* excess of ketone bodies in the blood
KETONES > KETONE
KETONIC > KETONE
KETONURIA *n* presence of ketone bodies in the urine
KETOSE *n* any monosaccharide that contains a ketone group
KETOSES > KETOSIS
KETOSIS *n* high concentration of ketone bodies in the blood
KETOTIC > KETOSIS
KETOXIME *n* oxime formed by reaction between hydroxylamine and a ketone
KETOXIMES > KETOXIME
KETS > KET
KETTLE *n* container with a spout and handle used for boiling water
KETTLEFUL > KETTLE
KETTLES > KETTLE
KETUBAH *n* contract that states the obligations within Jewish marriage
KETUBAHS > KETUBAH
KETUBOT > KETUBAH
KETUBOTH > KETUBAH
KEVEL *n* strong bitt or bollard for securing heavy hawsers
KEVELS > KEVEL
KEVIL *old variant of* > KEVE
KEVILS > KEVIL
KEWL *nonstandard variant spelling of* > COOL
KEWLER > KEWL
KEWLEST > KEWL
KEWPIE as in *kewpie doll* (i US and Canadian English) brightly coloured doll, commonly given as a priz at carnival
KEWPIES > KEWPIE
KEX *n* any of several large hollow-stemmed umbelliferous plants, suc as cow parsnip and chervi
KEXES > KEX
KEY *n* device for operating a lock by moving a bolt ▷ *adj* of great importance ▷ *vb* enter (text) using a keyboard
KEYBOARD *n* set of keys on a piano, computer, etc ▷ *vb* enter (text) using a keyboard
KEYBOARDS > KEYBOARD
KEYBUGLE *n* bugle with keys
KEYBUGLES > KEYBUGLE
KEYBUTTON *n* on a keyboard, an object whic when pressed, causes the letter, number, or symbol shown on it to be printed in a document
KEYCARD *n* card with an electronic strip or code or it that allows it to open a corresponding keycard-operated door
KEYCARDS > KEYCARD
KEYED > KEY
KEYHOLE *n* opening for inserting a key into a lock
KEYHOLES > KEYHOLE
KEYING > KEY
KEYINGS > KEY
KEYLESS > KEY
KEYLINE *n* outline image of something on artwork or plans to show where it is to be placed
KEYLINES > KEYLINE
KEYLOGGER *n* device or software application use for covertly recording and monitoring keystrokes made on a remote computer
KEYNOTE *adj* central or dominating ▷ *n* dominant idea of a speec etc ▷ *vb* deliver a keynot address to (a political convention, etc)
KEYNOTED > KEYNOTE
KEYNOTER *n* person delivering a keynote address

YNOTERS > KEYNOTER
YNOTES > KEYNOTE
YNOTING > KEYNOTE
YPAD *n* small panel vith a set of buttons or operating a Teletext system, electronic alculator, etc
YPADS > KEYPAD
YPAL *n* person with whom one regularly exchanges emails for fun
YPALS > KEYPAL
YPUNCH *n* device naving a keyboard that s operated manually o transfer data onto ounched cards, paper tape, etc ▷ *vb* transfer (data) onto punched cards, paper ape, etc, by using a key ounch
YRING *n* split ring lesigned for holding keys
YS *interj* children's cry for ruce or respite from the ules of a game
YSET *n* set of computer eys used for a particular ourpose
YSETS > KEYSET
YSTER *same as* > KEISTER
YSTERS > KEYSTER
YSTONE *n* most mportant part of a process, organization, etc ▷ *vb* project or provide with a distorted image
YSTONED > KEYSTONE
YSTONES > KEYSTONE
YSTROKE *n* single operation of the nechanism of a ypewriter or keyboard-operated typesetting machine by the action of a key ▷ *vb* enter or cause o be recorded by pressing a key
YWAY *n* longitudinal slot cut into a component to accept a key that engages with a similar slot on a mating component to prevent relative motion of he two components
YWAYS > KEYWAY
YWORD *n* word or phrase hat a computer will search for in order to ocate the information or ile that the computer user has requested
YWORDS > KEYWORD
OTLA *n* (in South African English) meeting place for village assemblies, court cases, and meetings of village leaders
OTLAS > KGOTLA
ADDAR *n* cotton cloth of plain weave, produced in ndia
ADDARS > KHADDAR
KHADI *same as* > KHADDAR
KHADIS > KHADI
KHAF *n* letter of the Hebrew alphabet
KHAFS > KHAF
KHAKI *adj* dull yellowish-brown ▷ *n* hard-wearing fabric of this colour used for military uniforms
KHAKILIKE > KHAKI
KHAKIS > KHAKI
KHALAT *same as* > KHILAT
KHALATS > KHALAT
KHALIF *variant spelling of* > CALIPH
KHALIFA *same as* > CALIPH
KHALIFAH *same as* > CALIPH
KHALIFAHS > KHALIFAH
KHALIFAS > KHALIFA
KHALIFAT *same as* > CALIPHATE
KHALIFATE *same as* > CALIPHATE
KHALIFATS > KHALIFAT
KHALIFS > KHALIF
KHAMSEEN *same as* > KHAMSIN
KHAMSEENS > KHAMSEEN
KHAMSIN *n* hot southerly wind blowing from about March to May, esp in Egypt
KHAMSINS > KHAMSIN
KHAN *n* title of respect in Afghanistan and central Asia
KHANATE *n* territory ruled by a khan
KHANATES > KHANATE
KHANDA *n* double-edged sword that appears as the emblem on the Sikh flag and is used in the Amrit ceremony to stir the amrit
KHANDAS > KHANDA
KHANGA *same as* > KANGA
KHANGAS > KHANGA
KHANJAR *n* type of dagger
KHANJARS > KHANJAR
KHANS > KHAN
KHANSAMA *same as* > KHANSAMAH
KHANSAMAH *n* Indian cook or other male servant
KHANSAMAS > KHANSAMA
KHANUM *feminine form of* > KHAN
KHANUMS > KHANUM
KHAPH *n* letter of the Hebrew alphabet
KHAPHS > KHAPH
KHARIF *n* (in Pakistan, India, etc) crop that is harvested at the beginning of winter
KHARIFS > KHARIF
KHAT *n* white-flowered evergreen shrub of Africa and Arabia whose leaves have narcotic properties
KHATS > KHAT
KHAYA *n* type of African tree
KHAYAL *n* kind of Indian classical vocal music
KHAYALS > KHAYAL
KHAYAS > KHAYA
KHAZEN *same as* > CHAZAN
KHAZENIM > KHAZEN
KHAZENS > KHAZEN
KHAZI *n* lavatory
KHAZIS > KHAZI
KHEDA *n* (in India, Myanmar, etc) enclosure into which wild elephants are driven to be captured
KHEDAH *same as* > KHEDA
KHEDAHS > KHEDAH
KHEDAS > KHEDA
KHEDIVA *n* khedive's wife
KHEDIVAL > KHEDIVE
KHEDIVAS > KHEDIVA
KHEDIVATE > KHEDIVE
KHEDIVE *n* viceroy of Egypt under Ottoman suzerainty
KHEDIVES > KHEDIVE
KHEDIVIAL > KHEDIVE
KHET *n* Thai district
KHETH *same as* > HETH
KHETHS > KHETH
KHETS > KHET
KHI *n* letter of the Greek alphabet
KHILAFAT *same as* > CALIPHATE
KHILAFATS > KHILAFAT
KHILAT *n* (in the Middle East) robe or other gift given to someone by a superior as a mark of honour
KHILATS > KHILAT
KHILIM *same as* > KILIM
KHILIMS > KHILIM
KHIRKAH *n* dervish's woollen or cotton outer garment
KHIRKAHS > KHIRKAH
KHIS > KHI
KHODJA *same as* > KHOJA
KHODJAS > KHODJA
KHOJA *n* teacher in a Muslim school
KHOJAS > KHOJA
KHOR *n* watercourse
KHORS > KHOR
KHOTBAH *same as* > KHUTBAH
KHOTBAHS > KHOTBAH
KHOTBEH *same as* > KHUTBAH
KHOTBEHS > KHOTBEH
KHOUM *n* Mauritanian monetary unit
KHOUMS > KHOUM
KHUD *n* Indian ravine
KHUDS > KHUD
KHURTA *same as* > KURTA
KHURTAS > KHURTA
KHUSKHUS *n* aromatic perennial Indian grass whose roots are woven into mats, fans, and baskets
KHUTBAH *n* sermon in a Mosque, especially on a Friday
KHUTBAHS > KHUTBAH
KI *n* Japanese martial art
KIAAT *n* tropical African leguminous tree
KIAATS > KIAAT
KIANG *n* variety of wild ass that occurs in Tibet and surrounding regions
KIANGS > KIANG
KIAUGH *n* (in Scots) anxiety
KIAUGHS > KIAUGH
KIBBE *n* Middle Eastern dish made with minced meat and bulgur
KIBBEH *same as* > KIBBE
KIBBEHS > KIBBEH
KIBBES > KIBBE
KIBBI *same as* > KIBBE
KIBBIS > KIBBI
KIBBITZ *same as* > KIBITZ
KIBBITZED > KIBBITZ
KIBBITZER > KIBBITZ
KIBBITZES > KIBBITZ
KIBBLE *n* bucket used in wells or in mining for hoisting ▷ *vb* grind into small pieces
KIBBLED > KIBBLE
KIBBLES > KIBBLE
KIBBLING > KIBBLE
KIBBUTZ *n* communal farm or factory in Israel
KIBBUTZIM > KIBBUTZ
KIBE *n* chilblain, esp an ulcerated one on the heel
KIBEI *n* someone of Japanese ancestry born in the US and educated in Japan
KIBEIS > KIBEI
KIBES > KIBE
KIBITKA *n* (in Russia) covered sledge or wagon
KIBITKAS > KIBITKA
KIBITZ *vb* interfere or offer unwanted advice, esp as a spectator at a card game
KIBITZED > KIBITZ
KIBITZER > KIBITZ
KIBITZERS > KIBITZ
KIBITZES > KIBITZ
KIBITZING > KIBITZ
KIBLA *same as* > KIBLAH
KIBLAH *n* direction of Mecca, to which Muslims turn in prayer, indicated in mosques by a niche (mihrab) in the wall
KIBLAHS > KIBLAH
KIBLAS > KIBLA
KIBOSH *vb* put a stop to
KIBOSHED > KIBOSH
KIBOSHES > KIBOSH
KIBOSHING > KIBOSH
KICK *vb* drive, push, or strike with the foot ▷ *n* thrust or blow with the foot
KICKABLE > KICK
KICKABOUT *n* informal game of soccer
KICKBACK *n* money paid illegally for favours done ▷ *vb* have a strong reaction
KICKBACKS > KICKBACK
KICKBALL *n* children's ball

game or the large ball used in it
KICKBALLS > KICKBALL
KICKBOARD *n* type of float held on to by a swimmer when practising leg strokes
KICKBOX *vb* box with hands and feet
KICKBOXED > KICKBOX
KICKBOXER *n* someone who practises kickboxing, a martial art that resembles boxing but in which kicks are permitted
KICKBOXES > KICKBOX
KICKDOWN *n* method of changing gear in a car with automatic transmission, by fully depressing the accelerator
KICKDOWNS > KICKDOWN
KICKED > KICK
KICKER *n* person or thing that kicks
KICKERS > KICKER
KICKIER > KICKY
KICKIEST > KICKY
KICKING > KICK
KICKOFF *n* kick from the centre of the field that starts a game of football
KICKOFFS > KICKOFF
KICKS > KICK
KICKSHAW *n* valueless trinket
KICKSHAWS *same as* > KICKSHAW
KICKSTAND *n* short metal bar on a motorcycle, which when kicked into a vertical position holds the cycle upright when stationary
KICKSTART *vb* start by kicking pedal
KICKUP *n* fuss
KICKUPS > KICKUP
KICKY *adj* excitingly unusual and different
KID *n* child ▷ *vb* tease or deceive (someone) ▷ *adj* younger
KIDDED > KID
KIDDER > KID
KIDDERS > KID
KIDDIE *same as* > KIDDY
KIDDIED > KIDDY
KIDDIER *n* old word for a market trader
KIDDIERS > KIDDIER
KIDDIES > KIDDY
KIDDING > KID
KIDDINGLY > KID
KIDDISH > KID
KIDDLE *n* device, esp a barrier constructed of nets and stakes, for catching fish in a river or in the sea
KIDDLES > KIDDLE
KIDDO *n* very informal term of address for a young person
KIDDOES > KIDDO
KIDDOS > KIDDO
KIDDUSH *n* (in Judaism) special blessing said before a meal on sabbaths and festivals
KIDDUSHES > KIDDUSH
KIDDY *n* affectionate word for a child ▷ *vb* tease or deceive
KIDDYING > KIDDY
KIDDYWINK *n* humorous word for a child
KIDEL *same as* > KIDDLE
KIDELS > KIDEL
KIDGE *dialect word for* > LIVELY
KIDGIE *adj* dialect word for friendly and welcoming
KIDGIER > KIDGIE
KIDGIEST > KIDGIE
KIDGLOVE *adj* overdelicate or overrefined
KIDLET *n* humorous word for small child
KIDLETS > KIDLET
KIDLIKE > KID
KIDLING *n* young kid
KIDLINGS > KIDLING
KIDNAP *vb* seize and hold (a person) to ransom
KIDNAPED > KIDNAP
KIDNAPEE > KIDNAP
KIDNAPEES > KIDNAP
KIDNAPER > KIDNAP
KIDNAPERS > KIDNAP
KIDNAPING > KIDNAP
KIDNAPPED > KIDNAP
KIDNAPPEE > KIDNAP
KIDNAPPER > KIDNAP
KIDNAPS > KIDNAP
KIDNEY *n* either of the pair of organs that filter waste products from the blood to produce urine
KIDNEYS > KIDNEY
KIDOLOGY *n* practice of bluffing or deception in order to gain a psychological advantage over someone
KIDS > KID
KIDSKIN *n* soft smooth leather made from the hide of a young goat
KIDSKINS > KIDSKIN
KIDSTAKES *pl n* pretence
KIDULT *n* adult who is interested in forms of entertainment such as computer games, television programmes, etc that are intended for children ▷ *adj* aimed at or suitable for kidults, or both children and adults
KIDULTS > KIDULT
KIDVID *n* informal word for children's video or television
KIDVIDS > KIDVID
KIEF *same as* > KIF
KIEFS > KIEF
KIEKIE *n* climbing bush plant of New Zealand
KIEKIES > KIEKIE
KIELBASA *n* Polish sausage
KIELBASAS > KIELBASA
KIELBASI *same as* > KIELBASA
KIELBASY *same as* > KIELBASA
KIER *n* vat in which cloth is bleached
KIERIE *n* South African cudgel
KIERIES > KIERIE
KIERS > KIER
KIESELGUR *n* type of mineral
KIESERITE *n* white mineral consisting of hydrated magnesium sulphate
KIESTER *same as* > KEISTER
KIESTERS > KIESTER
KIEVE *same as* > KEEVE
KIEVES > KIEVE
KIF *n* any drug or agent that when smoked is capable of producing a euphoric condition
KIFF *adj* South African slang for excellent
KIFS > KIF
KIGHT *n* archaic spelling of kite, the bird of prey
KIGHTS > KIGHT
KIKE *n* offensive word for a Jewish person
KIKES > KIKE
KIKOI *n* piece of cotton cloth with coloured bands, worn wrapped around the body
KIKOIS > KIKOI
KIKUMON *n* chrysanthemum emblem of the imperial family of Japan
KIKUMONS > KIKUMON
KIKUYU *n* type of grass
KIKUYUS > KIKUYU
KILD *old spelling of* > KILLED
KILDERKIN *n* obsolete unit of liquid capacity equal to 16 or 18 Imperial gallons or of dry capacity equal to 16 or 18 wine gallons
KILERG *n* 1000 ergs
KILERGS > KILERG
KILEY *same as* > KYLIE
KILEYS > KILEY
KILIM *n* pileless woven rug of intricate design made in the Middle East
KILIMS > KILIM
KILL *vb* cause the death of ▷ *n* act of killing
KILLABLE > KILL
KILLADAR *n* fort commander or governor
KILLADARS > KILLADAR
KILLAS *n* Cornish clay slate
KILLASES > KILLAS
KILLCOW *n* important person
KILLCOWS > KILLCOW
KILLCROP *n* ever-hungry baby, thought to be a fairy changeling
KILLCROPS > KILLCROP
KILLDEE *same as* > KILLDEER
KILLDEER *n* large brown-and-white North American plover with a noisy cry
KILLDEERS > KILLDEER
KILLDEES > KILLDEE
KILLED > KILL
KILLER *n* person or anima that kills, esp habitually
KILLERS > KILLER
KILLICK *n* small anchor, esp one made of a heavy stone
KILLICKS > KILLICK
KILLIE *same as* > KILLIFIS
KILLIES > KILLIE
KILLIFISH *n* any of various chiefly American minnow-like fishes
KILLING *adj* very tiring ▷ sudden financial success
KILLINGLY > KILLING
KILLINGS > KILLING
KILLJOY *n* person who spoils others' pleasure
KILLJOYS > KILLJOY
KILLOCK *same as* > KILLICK
KILLOCKS > KILLOCK
KILLOGIE *n* sheltered place in front of a kiln
KILLOGIES > KILLOGIE
KILLS > KILL
KILLUT *same as* > KHILAT
KILLUTS > KILLUT
KILN *n* oven for baking, drying, or processing pottery, bricks, etc ▷ *vb* fire or process in a kiln
KILNED > KILN
KILNING > KILN
KILNS > KILN
KILO *n* code word for the letter *k*
KILOBAR *n* 1000 bars
KILOBARS > KILOBAR
KILOBASE *n* unit of measurement for DNA ar RNA equal to 1000 base pairs
KILOBASES > KILOBASE
KILOBAUD *n* 1000 baud
KILOBAUDS > KILOBAUD
KILOBIT *n* 1024 bits
KILOBITS > KILOBIT
KILOBYTE *n* 1024 units of information
KILOBYTES > KILOBYTE
KILOCURIE *n* unit of thousand curies
KILOCYCLE *n* short for kilocycle per second: a former unit of frequency equal to 1 kilohertz
KILOGAUSS *n* 1000 gauss
KILOGRAM *n* one thousan grams
KILOGRAMS > KILOGRAM
KILOGRAY *n* 1000 gray
KILOGRAYS > KILOGRAY
KILOHERTZ *n* one

thousand hertz
ILOJOULE *n* 1000 joules
ILOLITER *US spelling of* > KILOLITRE
ILOLITRE *n* 1000 litres
ILOMETER *same as* > KILOMETRE
ILOMETRE *n* one thousand metres
ILOMOLE *n* 1000 moles
ILOMOLES > KILOMOLE
ILORAD *n* 1000 rads
ILORADS > KILORAD
ILOS > KILO
ILOTON *n* one thousand tons
ILOTONS > KILOTON
ILOVOLT *n* one thousand volts
ILOVOLTS > KILOVOLT
ILOWATT *n* one thousand watts
ILOWATTS > KILOWATT
ILP *dialect form of* > KELP
ILPS > KILP
ILT *n* knee-length pleated tartan skirt-like garment worn orig. by Scottish Highlanders ▷ *vb* put pleats in (cloth)
ILTED > KILT
ILTER *n* working order or alignment
ILTERS > KILTER
ILTIE *n* someone wearing a kilt
ILTIES > KILTIE
ILTING > KILT
ILTINGS > KILT
ILTLIKE > KILT
ILTS > KILT
ILTY *same as* > KILTIE
IMBO *vb* place akimbo
IMBOED > KIMBO
IMBOING > KIMBO
IMBOS > KIMBO
IMCHEE *same as* > KIMCHI
IMCHEES > KIMCHEE
IMCHI *n* Korean dish made from fermented cabbage or other vegetables, garlic, and chillies
IMCHIS > KIMCHI
IMMER *same as* > CUMMER
IMMERS > KIMMER
IMONO *n* loose wide-sleeved Japanese robe, fastened with a sash
IMONOED > KIMONO
IMONOS > KIMONO
IN *n* person's relatives collectively ▷ *adj* related by blood
INA *n* standard monetary unit of Papua New Guinea, divided into 100 toea
INAKINA *same as* > QUININE
INAKINAS > KINAKINA
INARA *n* African candle holder
INARAS > KINARA
INAS > KINA
KINASE *n* any enzyme that can convert an inactive zymogen to the corresponding enzyme
KINASES > KINASE
KINCHIN *old slang word for* > CHILD
KINCHINS > KINCHIN
KINCOB *n* fine silk fabric embroidered with threads of gold or silver, of a kind made in India
KINCOBS > KINCOB
KIND *adj* considerate, friendly, and helpful ▷ *n* class or group with common characteristics ▷ *vb* old word for beget or father
KINDA *adv* very informal shortening of kind of
KINDED > KIND
KINDER *adj* more kind ▷ *n* kindergarten or nursery school
KINDERS > KIND
KINDEST > KIND
KINDIE *same as* > KINDY
KINDIES > KINDY
KINDING > KIND
KINDLE *vb* set (a fire) alight
KINDLED > KINDLE
KINDLER > KINDLE
KINDLERS > KINDLE
KINDLES > KINDLE
KINDLESS *adj* heartless
KINDLIER > KINDLY
KINDLIEST > KINDLY
KINDLILY > KINDLY
KINDLING *n* dry wood or straw for starting fires
KINDLINGS > KINDLING
KINDLY *adj* having a warm-hearted nature ▷ *adv* in a considerate way
KINDNESS *n* quality of being kind
KINDRED *adj* having similar qualities ▷ *n* blood relationship
KINDREDS > KINDRED
KINDS > KIND
KINDY *n* kindergarten
KINE *pl n* cows or cattle ▷ *n* Japanese pestle
KINEMA *same as* > CINEMA
KINEMAS > KINEMA
KINEMATIC *adj* of or relating to the study of the motion of bodies without reference to mass or force
KINES *n* > KINE
KINESCOPE *n* US name for a television tube ▷ *vb* record on film
KINESES > KINESIS
KINESIC *adj* of or relating to kinesics
KINESICS *n* study of the role of body movements, such as winking, shrugging, etc, in communication
KINESIS *n* nondirectional movement of an organism or cell in response to a stimulus, the rate of movement being dependent on the strength of the stimulus
KINETIC *adj* relating to or caused by motion
KINETICAL *same as* > KINETIC
KINETICS *n* branch of mechanics concerned with the study of bodies in motion
KINETIN *n* plant hormone
KINETINS > KINETIN
KINFOLK *another word for* > KINSFOLK
KINFOLKS > KINFOLK
KING *n* male ruler of a monarchy ▷ *vb* make king
KINGBIRD *n* any of several large American flycatchers
KINGBIRDS > KINGBIRD
KINGBOLT *n* pivot bolt that connects the body of a horse-drawn carriage to the front axle and provides the steering joint
KINGBOLTS > KINGBOLT
KINGCRAFT *n* art of ruling as a king, esp by diplomacy and cunning
KINGCUP *n* yellow-flowered plant
KINGCUPS > KINGCUP
KINGDOM *n* state ruled by a king or queen
KINGDOMED *adj* old word for with a kingdom
KINGDOMS > KINGDOM
KINGED > KING
KINGFISH *n* food and game fish occurring in warm American Atlantic coastal waters
KINGHOOD > KING
KINGHOODS > KING
KINGING > KING
KINGKLIP *n* edible eel-like marine fish of S Africa
KINGKLIPS > KINGKLIP
KINGLE *n* Scots word for a type of hard rock
KINGLES > KINGLE
KINGLESS > KING
KINGLET *n* king of a small or insignificant territory
KINGLETS > KINGLET
KINGLIER > KINGLY
KINGLIEST > KINGLY
KINGLIKE > KING
KINGLING *n* minor king
KINGLINGS > KINGLING
KINGLY *adj* appropriate to a king ▷ *adv* in a manner appropriate to a king
KINGMAKER *n* person who has control over appointments to positions of authority
KINGPIN *n* most important person in an organization
KINGPINS > KINGPIN
KINGPOST *n* vertical post connecting the apex of a triangular roof truss to the tie beam
KINGPOSTS > KINGPOST
KINGS > KING
KINGSHIP *n* position or authority of a king
KINGSHIPS > KINGSHIP
KINGSIDE *n* (in chess) side of the board on which a particular king is at the start of a game as opposed to the side the queen is on
KINGSIDES > KINGSIDE
KINGSNAKE *n* North American snake
KINGWOOD *n* hard fine-grained violet-tinted wood of a Brazilian leguminous tree
KINGWOODS > KINGWOOD
KININ *n* any of a group of polypeptides in the blood that cause dilation of the blood vessels and make smooth muscles contract
KININS > KININ
KINK *n* twist or bend in rope, wire, hair, etc ▷ *vb* form or cause to form a kink
KINKAJOU *n* arboreal fruit-eating mammal of Central and South America, with a long prehensile tail
KINKAJOUS > KINKAJOU
KINKED > KINK
KINKIER > KINKY
KINKIEST > KINKY
KINKILY > KINKY
KINKINESS > KINKY
KINKING > KINK
KINKLE *n* little kink
KINKLES > KINKLE
KINKS > KINK
KINKY *adj* given to unusual sexual practices
KINLESS *adj* without any relatives
KINO *same as* > KENO
KINONE *n* benzoquinone, a yellow crystalline water-soluble ketone used in the production of dyestuffs
KINONES > KINONE
KINOS > KINO
KINRED *old form of* > KINDRED
KINREDS > KINRED
KINS > KIN
KINSFOLK *pl n* one's family or relatives
KINSFOLKS > KINSFOLK
KINSHIP *n* blood relationship
KINSHIPS > KINSHIP
KINSMAN *n* relative
KINSMEN > KINSMAN
KINSWOMAN > KINSMAN
KINSWOMEN > KINSMAN
KIORE *n* small brown rat native to New Zealand
KIOSK *n* small booth

selling drinks, cigarettes, newspapers, etc
KIOSKS > KIOSK
KIP *vb* sleep ▷ *n* sleep or slumber
KIPE *n* dialect word for a basket for catching fish
KIPES > KIPE
KIPP *uncommon variant of* > KIP
KIPPA *n* skullcap worn by orthodox male Jews at all times and by others for prayer, esp a crocheted one worn by those with a specifically religious Zionist affiliation
KIPPAGE *n* Scots word for a state of anger or excitement
KIPPAGES > KIPPAGE
KIPPAS > KIPPA
KIPPED > KIP
KIPPEN > KEP
KIPPER *n* cleaned, salted, and smoked herring ▷ *vb* cure (a herring) by salting and smoking it
KIPPERED *adj* (of fish, esp herring) having been cleaned, salted, and smoked
KIPPERER > KIPPER
KIPPERERS > KIPPER
KIPPERING > KIPPER
KIPPERS > KIPPER
KIPPING > KIP
KIPPS > KIPP
KIPS > KIP
KIPSKIN *same as* > KIP
KIPSKINS > KIPSKIN
KIR *n* drink made from dry white wine and cassis
KIRBEH *n* leather bottle
KIRBEHS > KIRBEH
KIRBIGRIP *n* hairgrip
KIRBY as in *kirby grip* hairgrip consisting of a piece of wire bent back on itself and partly bent into ridges
KIRIGAMI *n* art, originally Japanese, of folding and cutting paper into decorative shapes
KIRIGAMIS > KIRIGAMI
KIRIMON *n* Japanese imperial crest
KIRIMONS > KIRIMON
KIRK *Scot word for* > CHURCH
KIRKED > KIRK
KIRKING > KIRK
KIRKINGS > KIRK
KIRKMAN *n* member or strong upholder of the Kirk
KIRKMEN > KIRKMAN
KIRKS > KIRK
KIRKTON *n* village or town with a parish church
KIRKTONS > KIRKTON
KIRKWARD *adv* towards the church
KIRKYAIRD *same as* > KIRKYARD
KIRKYARD *n* churchyard
KIRKYARDS > KIRKYARD
KIRMESS *same as* > KERMIS
KIRMESSES > KIRMESS
KIRN *dialect word for* > CHURN
KIRNED > KIRN
KIRNING > KIRN
KIRNS > KIRN
KIRPAN *n* short sword traditionally carried by Sikhs as a symbol of their religious and cultural loyalty
KIRPANS > KIRPAN
KIRRI *n* Hottentot stick
KIRRIS > KIRRI
KIRS > KIR
KIRSCH *n* cherry brandy
KIRSCHES > KIRSCH
KIRTAN *n* devotional singing, usually accompanied by musical instruments
KIRTANS > KIRTAN
KIRTLE *n* woman's skirt or dress ▷ *vb* dress with a kirtle
KIRTLED > KIRTLE
KIRTLES > KIRTLE
KIS > KI
KISAN *n* peasant or farmer
KISANS > KISAN
KISH *n* graphite formed on the surface of molten iron that contains a large amount of carbon
KISHES > KISH
KISHKA *same as* > KISHKE
KISHKAS > KISHKA
KISHKE *n* beef or fowl intestine or skin stuffed with flour, onion, etc, and boiled and roasted
KISHKES > KISHKE
KISMAT *same as* > KISMET
KISMATS > KISMAT
KISMET *n* fate or destiny
KISMETIC > KISMET
KISMETS > KISMET
KISS *vb* touch with the lips in affection or greeting ▷ *n* touch with the lips
KISSABLE > KISS
KISSABLY > KISS
KISSAGRAM *n* greetings service in which a messenger kisses the person celebrating
KISSED > KISS
KISSEL *n* Russian dessert of sweetened fruit purée thickened with arrowroot
KISSELS > KISSEL
KISSER *n* mouth or face
KISSERS > KISSER
KISSES > KISS
KISSING > KISS
KISSOGRAM *same as* > KISSAGRAM
KISSY *adj* showing exaggerated affection, esp by frequent touching or kissing
KIST *n* large wooden chest ▷ *vb* place in a coffin
KISTED > KIST
KISTFUL > KIST
KISTFULS > KIST
KISTING > KIST
KISTS > KIST
KISTVAEN *n* stone tomb
KISTVAENS > KISTVAEN
KIT *n* outfit or equipment for a specific purpose ▷ *vb* fit or provide
KITBAG *n* bag for a soldier's or traveller's belongings
KITBAGS > KITBAG
KITCHEN *n* room used for cooking ▷ *vb* (in archaic usage) provide with food
KITCHENED > KITCHEN
KITCHENER *n* someone employed in kitchen work
KITCHENET *n* small kitchen or part of another room equipped for use as a kitchen
KITCHENS > KITCHEN
KITE *n* light frame covered with a thin material flown on a string in the wind ▷ *vb* soar and glide
KITED > KITE
KITELIKE > KITE
KITENGE *n* thick cotton cloth
KITENGES > KITENGE
KITER > KITE
KITERS > KITE
KITES > KITE
KITH *n* one's friends and acquaintances
KITHARA *variant of* > CITHARA
KITHARAS > KITHARA
KITHE *same as* > KYTHE
KITHED > KITHE
KITHES > KITHE
KITHING > KITHE
KITHS > KITH
KITING > KITE
KITINGS > KITE
KITLING *dialect word for* > KITTEN
KITLINGS > KITLING
KITS > KIT
KITSCH *n* art or literature with popular sentimental appeal ▷ *n* object or art that is tawdry, vulgarized, oversentimental or pretentious
KITSCHES > KITSCH
KITSCHIER > KITSCH
KITSCHIFY *vb* make kitsch
KITSCHILY > KITSCH
KITSCHY > KITSCH
KITSET *n* New Zealand word for a piece of furniture supplied in pieces for the purchaser to assemble
KITSETS > KITSET
KITTED > KIT
KITTEL *n* white garment worn for certain Jewish rituals or burial
KITTELS > KITTEL
KITTEN *n* young cat ▷ *vb* (of cats) give birth
KITTENED > KITTEN
KITTENING > KITTEN
KITTENISH *adj* lively and flirtatious
KITTENS > KITTEN
KITTENY > KITTEN
KITTIES > KITTY
KITTING > KIT
KITTIWAKE *n* type of seagull
KITTLE *adj* capricious and unpredictable ▷ *vb* be troublesome or puzzling to (someone)
KITTLED > KITTLE
KITTLER > KITTLE
KITTLES > KITTLE
KITTLEST > KITTLE
KITTLIER > KITTLY
KITTLIEST > KITTLY
KITTLING > KITTLE
KITTLY *Scots word for* > TICKLISH
KITTUL *n* type of palm from which jaggery sugar comes
KITTULS > KITTUL
KITTY *n* communal fund
KIVA *n* large underground or partly underground room in a Pueblo Indian village, used chiefly for religious ceremonies
KIVAS > KIVA
KIWI *n* New Zealand flightless bird with a long beak and no tail
KIWIFRUIT *n* edible oval fruit of the kiwi plant
KIWIS > KIWI
KLANG *n* (in music) kind of tone
KLANGS > KLANG
KLAP *vb* slap or spank
KLAPPED > KLAP
KLAPPING > KLAP
KLAPS > KLAP
KLATCH *n* gathering, especially over coffee
KLATCHES > KLATCH
KLATSCH *same as* > KLATCH
KLATSCHES > KLATSCH
KLAVERN *n* local Ku Klux Klan group
KLAVERNS > KLAVERN
KLAVIER *same as* > CLAVIER
KLAVIERS > KLAVIER
KLAXON *n* loud horn used on emergency vehicles as warning signal ▷ *vb* hoot with a klaxon
KLAXONED > KLAXON
KLAXONING > KLAXON
KLAXONS > KLAXON
KLEAGLE *n* person with a particular rank in the Ku Klux Klan
KLEAGLES > KLEAGLE
KLEENEX *n* tradename for a kind of soft paper tissue

used esp as a handkerchief
.EENEXES > KLEENEX
.ENDUSIC *adj* disease-resistant
.EPHT *n* any of the Greeks who fled to the mountains after the 15th-century Turkish conquest of Greece and whose descendants survived as brigands into the 19th century
.EPHTIC > KLEPHT
.EPHTISM > KLEPHT
.EPHTS > KLEPHT
.EPTO *n* compulsive thief
.EPTOS > KLEPTO
.EZMER *n* Jewish folk musician, usually a member of a small band
.EZMERS > KLEZMER
.EZMORIM > KLEZMER
.ICK *n* kilometre
.ICKS > KLICK
.IEG as in *klieg light* intense carbon-arc light used for illumination in producing films
.IK *US military slang word for* > KILOMETRE
.IKS > KLIK
.INKER *n* type of brick used in paving
.INKERS > KLINKER
.INOSTAT *n* rotating and tilting plant holder for studying and experimenting with plant growth
.IPDAS *n* rock hyrax
.IPDASES > KLIPDAS
.ISTER *n* type of ski dressing for improving grip on snow
.ISTERS > KLISTER
.ONDIKE *n* rich source of something ▷ *vb* transfer (bulk loads of fish) to factory ships at sea for processing
.ONDIKED > KLONDIKE
.ONDIKER *same as* > KLONDYKER
.ONDIKES > KLONDIKE
.ONDYKE *n* rich source of something ▷ *vb* transfer bulk loads of fish) to factory ships at sea for processing
.ONDYKED > KLONDYKE
.ONDYKER *n* East European factory ship
.ONDYKES > KLONDYKE
.ONG *n* type of canal in Thailand
.ONGS > KLONG
.OOCH *same as* > KLOOCHMAN
.OOCHES > KLOOCH
.OOCHMAN *n* North American Indian woman
.OOCHMEN > KLOOCHMAN
.OOF *n* mountain pass or gorge
.OOFS > KLOOF
KLOOTCH *same as* > KLOOCHMAN
KLOOTCHES > KLOOTCH
KLUDGE *n* untidy solution involving a variety of cobbled-together elements ▷ *vb* cobble something together
KLUDGED > KLUDGE
KLUDGES > KLUDGE
KLUDGEY > KLUDGE
KLUDGIER > KLUDGE
KLUDGIEST > KLUDGE
KLUDGING > KLUDGE
KLUDGY > KLUDGE
KLUGE *same as* > KLUDGE
KLUGED > KLUGE
KLUGES > KLUGE
KLUGING > KLUGE
KLUTZ *n* clumsy or stupid person
KLUTZES > KLUTZ
KLUTZIER > KLUTZ
KLUTZIEST > KLUTZ
KLUTZY > KLUTZ
KLYSTRON *n* electron tube for the amplification or generation of microwaves by means of velocity modulation
KLYSTRONS > KLYSTRON
KNACK *n* skilful way of doing something ▷ *vb* dialect word for crack or snap
KNACKED *adj* broken or worn out
KNACKER *n* buyer of old horses for killing ▷ *vb* exhaust
KNACKERED *adj* extremely tired
KNACKERS > KNACKER
KNACKERY *n* slaughterhouse for horses
KNACKIER > KNACKY
KNACKIEST > KNACKY
KNACKING > KNACK
KNACKISH *adj* old word meaning cunning or artful
KNACKS > KNACK
KNACKY *adj* old or dialect word for cunning or artful
KNAG *n* knot in wood
KNAGGIER > KNAGGY
KNAGGIEST > KNAGGY
KNAGGY *adj* knotty
KNAGS > KNAG
KNAIDEL *same as* > KNEIDEL
KNAIDLACH > KNAIDEL
KNAP *n* crest of a hill ▷ *vb* hit, hammer, or chip
KNAPPED > KNAP
KNAPPER > KNAP
KNAPPERS > KNAP
KNAPPING > KNAP
KNAPPLE *old word for* > NIBBLE
KNAPPLED > KNAPPLE
KNAPPLES > KNAPPLE
KNAPPLING > KNAPPLE
KNAPS > KNAP
KNAPSACK *n* soldier's or traveller's bag worn strapped on the back
KNAPSACKS > KNAPSACK
KNAPWEED *n* plant with purplish thistle-like flowers
KNAPWEEDS > KNAPWEED
KNAR *old spelling of* > GNAR
KNARL *old spelling of* > GNARL
KNARLS > KNARL
KNARLY *same as* > GNARLY
KNARRED > KNAR
KNARRING > KNAR
KNARRY > KNAR
KNARS > KNAR
KNAUR *variant form of* > KNUR
KNAURS > KNAUR
KNAVE *n* jack at cards
KNAVERIES > KNAVERY
KNAVERY *n* dishonest behaviour
KNAVES > KNAVE
KNAVESHIP *n* old Scottish legal term for the small proportion of milled grain due to the person doing the milling
KNAVISH > KNAVE
KNAVISHLY > KNAVE
KNAWE *same as* > KNAWEL
KNAWEL *n* any of several Old World caryophyllaceous plants of the genus *Scleranthus*, having heads of minute petal-less flowers
KNAWELS > KNAWEL
KNAWES > KNAWE
KNEAD *vb* work (dough) into a smooth mixture with the hands
KNEADABLE > KNEAD
KNEADED > KNEAD
KNEADER > KNEAD
KNEADERS > KNEAD
KNEADING > KNEAD
KNEADS > KNEAD
KNEE *n* joint between thigh and lower leg ▷ *vb* strike or push with the knee
KNEECAP *nontechnical name for* > PATELLA
KNEECAPS > KNEECAP
KNEED > KNEE
KNEEHOLE *n* space for the knees, esp under a desk
KNEEHOLES > KNEEHOLE
KNEEING > KNEE
KNEEJERK *adj* (of a reply or reaction) automatic and predictable
KNEEL *vb* fall or rest on one's knees ▷ *n* act or position of kneeling
KNEELED > KNEEL
KNEELER > KNEEL
KNEELERS > KNEEL
KNEELING > KNEEL
KNEELS > KNEEL
KNEEPAD *n* any of several types of protective covering for the knees
KNEEPADS > KNEEPAD
KNEEPAN *another word for* > PATELLA
KNEEPANS > KNEEPAN
KNEEPIECE *n* knee-shaped piece of timber in ship
KNEES > KNEE
KNEESIES *n* flirtatious touching of knees under table
KNEESOCK *n* type of sock that comes up to the knee
KNEESOCKS > KNEESOCK
KNEIDEL *n* (in Jewish cookery) small dumpling, usually served in chicken soup
KNEIDLACH > KNEIDEL
KNELL *n* sound of a bell, esp at a funeral or death ▷ *vb* ring a knell
KNELLED > KNELL
KNELLING > KNELL
KNELLS > KNELL
KNELT > KNEEL
KNESSET *n* parliament or assembly
KNESSETS > KNESSET
KNEVELL *vb* old Scots word meaning beat
KNEVELLED > KNEVELL
KNEVELLS > KNEVELL
KNEW > KNOW
KNICKER *n* woman's or girl's undergarment covering the lower trunk and having legs or legholes
KNICKERED > KNICKER
KNICKERS *pl n* woman's or girl's undergarment covering the lower trunk and having legs or legholes
KNICKS *pl n* knickers
KNIFE *n* cutting tool or weapon consisting of a sharp-edged blade with a handle ▷ *vb* cut or stab with a knife
KNIFED > KNIFE
KNIFELESS > KNIFE
KNIFELIKE > KNIFE
KNIFEMAN *n* man who is armed with a knife
KNIFEMEN > KNIFEMAN
KNIFER > KNIFE
KNIFEREST *n* support on which a carving knife or carving fork is placed at the table
KNIFERS > KNIFE
KNIFES > KNIFE
KNIFING > KNIFE
KNIFINGS > KNIFE
KNIGHT *n* man who has been given a knighthood ▷ *vb* award a knighthood to
KNIGHTAGE *n* group of knights or knights collectively
KNIGHTED > KNIGHT
KNIGHTING > KNIGHT
KNIGHTLY *adj* of, resembling, or appropriate for a knight
KNIGHTS > KNIGHT

KNIPHOFIA *n* any of several perennial southern African flowering plants
KNISH *n* piece of dough stuffed with potato, meat, or some other filling and baked or fried
KNISHES > KNISH
KNIT *vb* make (a garment) by interlocking a series of loops in wool or other yarn ▷ *n* fabric made by knitting
KNITCH *dialect word for* > BUNDLE
KNITCHES > KNITCH
KNITS > KNIT
KNITTABLE > KNIT
KNITTED > KNIT
KNITTER > KNIT
KNITTERS > KNIT
KNITTING > KNIT
KNITTINGS > KNIT
KNITTLE *n* old word for string or cord
KNITTLES > KNITTLE
KNITWEAR *n* knitted clothes, such as sweaters
KNITWEARS > KNITWEAR
KNIVE *rare variant of* > KNIFE
KNIVED > KNIVE
KNIVES > KNIFE
KNIVING > KNIVE
KNOB *n* rounded projection, such as a switch on a radio ▷ *vb* supply with knobs
KNOBBED > KNOB
KNOBBER *n* two-year-old male deer
KNOBBERS > KNOBBER
KNOBBIER > KNOB
KNOBBIEST > KNOB
KNOBBING > KNOB
KNOBBLE *n* small knob ▷ *vb* dialect word meaning strike
KNOBBLED *same as* > KNOBBLY
KNOBBLES > KNOBBLE
KNOBBLIER > KNOBBLY
KNOBBLING > KNOBBLE
KNOBBLY *adj* covered with small bumps
KNOBBY > KNOB
KNOBHEAD *n* stupid person
KNOBHEADS > KNOBHEAD
KNOBLIKE > KNOB
KNOBS > KNOB
KNOBSTICK *n* stick with a round knob at the end, used as a club or missile by South African tribesmen
KNOCK *vb* give a blow or push to ▷ *n* blow or rap
KNOCKDOWN *adj* (of a price) very low
KNOCKED > KNOCK
KNOCKER *n* metal fitting for knocking on a door
KNOCKERS > KNOCKER
KNOCKING > KNOCK
KNOCKINGS > KNOCK
KNOCKLESS > KNOCK
KNOCKOFF *n* informal word for a cheap, often illegal, copy of something
KNOCKOFFS > KNOCKOFF
KNOCKOUT *n* blow that renders an opponent unconscious ▷ *vb* render (someone) unconscious
KNOCKOUTS > KNOCKOUT
KNOCKS > KNOCK
KNOLL *n* small rounded hill ▷ *vb* (in archaic or dialect usage) knell
KNOLLED > KNOLL
KNOLLER > KNOLL
KNOLLERS > KNOLL
KNOLLING > KNOLL
KNOLLS > KNOLL
KNOLLY > KNOLL
KNOP *n* knob, esp an ornamental one
KNOPPED > KNOP
KNOPS > KNOP
KNOSP *n* budlike architectural feature
KNOSPS > KNOSP
KNOT *n* fastening made by looping and pulling tight strands of string, cord, or rope ▷ *vb* tie with or into a knot
KNOTGRASS *n* polygonaceous weedy plant whose small green flowers produce numerous seeds
KNOTHOLE *n* hole in a piece of wood where a knot has been
KNOTHOLES > KNOTHOLE
KNOTLESS > KNOT
KNOTLIKE > KNOT
KNOTS > KNOT
KNOTTED > KNOT
KNOTTER > KNOT
KNOTTERS > KNOT
KNOTTIER > KNOTTY
KNOTTIEST > KNOTTY
KNOTTILY > KNOTTY
KNOTTING > KNOT
KNOTTINGS > KNOT
KNOTTY *adj* full of knots
KNOTWEED *n* any of several polygonaceous plants of the genus *Polygonum*, having small flowers and jointed stems
KNOTWEEDS > KNOTWEED
KNOTWORK *n* ornamentation consisting of a mass of intertwined and knotted cords
KNOTWORKS > KNOTWORK
KNOUT *n* stout whip used formerly in Russia as an instrument of punishment ▷ *vb* whip
KNOUTED > KNOUT
KNOUTING > KNOUT
KNOUTS > KNOUT
KNOW *vb* be or feel certain of the truth of (information etc)
KNOWABLE > KNOW
KNOWE *same as* > KNOLL
KNOWER > KNOW
KNOWERS > KNOW
KNOWES > KNOWE
KNOWHOW *n* ingenuity, knack, or skill
KNOWHOWS > KNOWHOW
KNOWING > KNOW
KNOWINGER > KNOW
KNOWINGLY > KNOW
KNOWINGS > KNOW
KNOWLEDGE *n* facts, feelings or experiences known by a person or group of people ▷ *vb* (in archaic usage) acknowledge
KNOWN > KNOW
KNOWNS > KNOW
KNOWS > KNOW
KNUB *dialect word for* > KNOB
KNUBBIER > KNUB
KNUBBIEST > KNUB
KNUBBLE *vb* dialect word for beat or pound using one's fists
KNUBBLED > KNUBBLE
KNUBBLES > KNUBBLE
KNUBBLIER > KNUBBLY
KNUBBLING > KNUBBLE
KNUBBLY *adj* having small lumps or protuberances
KNUBBY *adj* knub
KNUBS > KNUB
KNUCKLE *n* bone at the finger joint
KNUCKLED > KNUCKLE
KNUCKLER *n* type of throw in baseball
KNUCKLERS > KNUCKLER
KNUCKLES > KNUCKLE
KNUCKLIER > KNUCKLE
KNUCKLING > KNUCKLE
KNUCKLY > KNUCKLE
KNUR *n* knot or protuberance in a tree trunk or in wood
KNURL *n* small ridge, often one of a series ▷ *vb* impress with a series of fine ridges or serrations
KNURLED > KNURL
KNURLIER > KNURLY
KNURLIEST > KNURLY
KNURLING > KNURL
KNURLINGS > KNURL
KNURLS > KNURL
KNURLY *rare word for* > GNARLED
KNURR *same as* > KNUR
KNURRS > KNURR
KNURS > KNUR
KNUT *n* dandy
KNUTS > KNUT
KO *n* (in New Zealand) traditional digging tool
KOA *n* Hawaiian leguminous tree
KOALA *n* tree-dwelling Australian marsupial with dense grey fur
KOALAS > KOALA
KOAN *n* (in Zen Buddhism) problem or riddle that admits no logical solution
KOANS > KOAN
KOAP *n* (in Papua New Guinean slang) sexual intercourse
KOAPS > KOAP
KOAS > KOA
KOB *n* any of several waterbuck-like species o African antelope
KOBAN *n* old oval-shaped Japanese gold coin
KOBANG *same as* > KOBAN
KOBANGS > KOBANG
KOBANS > KOBAN
KOBO *n* Nigerian monetar unit, worth one hundred of a naira
KOBOLD *n* mischievous household sprite
KOBOLDS > KOBOLD
KOBOS > KOBO
KOBS > KOB
KOCHIA *n* any of several plants whose foliage turr dark red in late summer
KOCHIAS > KOCHIA
KOEKOEA *n* long-tailed cuckoo of New Zealand
KOEL *n* any of several parasitic cuckoos of S anc SE Asia and Australia
KOELS > KOEL
KOFF *n* Dutch masted merchant vessel
KOFFS > KOFF
KOFTA *n* Indian dish of seasoned minced meat shaped into small balls ar cooked
KOFTAS > KOFTA
KOFTGAR *n* (in India) person skilled in the art c inlaying steel with gold
KOFTGARI *n* ornamental Indian metalwork
KOFTGARIS > KOFTGARI
KOFTGARS > KOFTGAR
KOFTWORK *same as* > KOFTGARI
KOFTWORKS > KOFTWORK
KOHA *n* gift or donation, e of cash
KOHAS > KOHA
KOHEKOHE *n* New Zealand tree with large glossy leaves and reddish wood
KOHL *n* cosmetic powder used to darken the edges of the eyelids
KOHLRABI *n* type of cabbage with an edible stem
KOHLRABIS > KOHLRABI
KOHLS > KOHL
KOI *n* any of various ornamental forms of the common carp
KOINE *n* common langua among speakers of different languages
KOINES > KOINE
KOIS > KOI
KOJI *n* Japanese steamed rice
KOJIS > KOJI

OKAKO *n* dark grey long-tailed wattled crow of New Zealand
OKAKOS > KOKAKO
OKANEE *n* freshwater salmon of lakes and rivers in W North America
OKANEES > KOKANEE
OKER *n* Guyanese sluice
OKERS > KOKER
OKIRI *n* rough-skinned New Zealand triggerfish, *Parika scaber*
OKOBEH *adj* (of certain fruit) having a rough skin
OKOPU *n* any of several small freshwater fish of New Zealand
OKOWAI *n* type of clay used in decoration because of its red colour
OKOWAIS > KOKOWAI
OKRA *n* type of wood
OKRAS > KOKRA
OKUM *n* tropical tree
OKUMS > KOKUM
OLA as in *kola nut* caffeine-containing seed used in medicine and soft drinks
OLACKY *n* sweet bun with a fruit, jam, or nut filling
OLAS > KOLA
OLBASI *same as* > KOLBASSI
OLBASIS > KOLBASI
OLBASSI *n* type of sausage
OLBASSIS > KOLBASSI
OLHOZ *same as* > KOLKHOZ
OLHOZES > KOLHOZ
OLHOZY *same as* > KOLKHOZ
OLINSKI *same as* > KOLINSKY
OLINSKY *n* Asian mink
OLKHOS *same as* > KOLKHOZ
OLKHOSES > KOLKHOS
OLKHOSY > KOLKHOS
OLKHOZ *n* (formerly) collective farm in the Soviet Union
OLKHOZES > KOLKHOZ
OLKHOZY > KOLKHOZ
OLKOZ *same as* > KOLKHOZ
OLKOZES > KOLKOZ
OLKOZY > KOLKOZ
OLO *n* Serbian folk dance in which a circle of people dance slowly around one or more dancers in the centre
OLOS > KOLO
OMATIK *n* sledge with wooden runners and crossbars bound with animal hides
OMATIKS > KOMATIK
OMBU *n* dark brown seaweed, the leaves of which are dried and used esp in Japanese cookery
OMBUS > KOMBU
KOMISSAR *same as* > COMMISSAR
KOMISSARS > KOMISSAR
KOMITAJI *n* rebel or revolutionary
KOMITAJIS > KOMITAJI
KOMONDOR *n* large powerful dog of an ancient Hungarian breed, originally used for sheep herding
KOMONDORS > KOMONDOR
KON *old word for* > KNOW
KONAKI *same as* > KONEKE
KONBU *same as* > KOMBU
KONBUS > KONBU
KOND > KON
KONDO *n* (in Uganda) thief or armed robber
KONDOS > KONDO
KONEKE *n* farm vehicle with runners in front and wheels at the rear
KONFYT *n* South African fruit preserve
KONFYTS > KONFYT
KONGONI *n* E African hartbeest, *Alcelaphus buselaphus*
KONIMETER *n* device for measuring airborne dust concentration in which samples are obtained by sucking the air through a hole and allowing it to pass over a glass plate coated with grease on which the particles collect
KONINI *n* edible dark purple berry of the kotukutuku or tree fuchsia
KONIOLOGY *n* study of atmospheric dust and its effects
KONISCOPE *n* device for detecting and measuring dust in the air
KONK *same as* > CONK
KONKED > KONK
KONKING > KONK
KONKS > KONK
KONNING > KON
KONS > KON
KOODOO *same as* > KUDU
KOODOOS > KOODOO
KOOK *n* eccentric person ▷ *vb* dialect word for vanish
KOOKED > KOOK
KOOKIE *same as* > KOOKY
KOOKIER > KOOKY
KOOKIEST > KOOKY
KOOKINESS > KOOKY
KOOKING > KOOK
KOOKS > KOOK
KOOKY *adj* crazy, eccentric, or foolish
KOOLAH *old form of* > KOALA
KOOLAHS > KOOLAH
KOORI *n* Australian Aborigine
KOORIES > KOORI
KOORIS > KOORI
KOP *n* prominent isolated hill or mountain in southern Africa
KOPASETIC *same as* > COPACETIC
KOPECK *n* former Russian monetary unit, one hundredth of a rouble
KOPECKS > KOPECK
KOPEK *same as* > KOPECK
KOPEKS > KOPEK
KOPH *n* 19th letter in the Hebrew alphabet
KOPHS > KOPH
KOPIYKA *n* monetary unit of Ukraine, worth one hundredth of a hryvna
KOPIYKAS > KOPIYKA
KOPJE *n* small hill
KOPJES > KOPJE
KOPPA *n* consonantal letter in the Greek alphabet pronounced like kappa (K) with the point of articulation further back in the throat
KOPPAS > KOPPA
KOPPIE *same as* > KOPJE
KOPPIES > KOPPIE
KOPS > KOP
KOR *n* ancient Hebrew unit of capacity
KORA *n* West African instrument with twenty-one strings, combining features of the harp and the lute
KORAI > KORE
KORARI *n* native New Zealand flax plant, *Phormium tenax*
KORAS > KORA
KORAT as in *korat cat* rare blue-grey breed of cat with brilliant green eyes
KORATS > KORAT
KORE *n* ancient Greek statue of a young woman wearing clothes
KORERO *n* talk or discussion ▷ *vb* speak or converse
KOREROED > KORERO
KOREROING > KORERO
KOREROS > KORERO
KORES > KORE
KORFBALL *n* game similar to basketball, in which each team consists of six men and six women
KORFBALLS > KORFBALL
KORIMAKO *another name for* > BELLBIRD
KORKIR *n* variety of lichen used in dyeing
KORKIRS > KORKIR
KORMA *n* type of mild Indian dish consisting of meat or vegetables cooked in water, yoghurt, or cream
KORMAS > KORMA
KORO *n* elderly Māori man
KOROMIKO *n* flowering New Zealand shrub, *Hebe salicifolia*
KORORA *n* small New Zealand penguin
KORORAS > KORORA
KOROWAI *n* decorative woven cloak worn by a Māori chief
KORS > KOR
KORU *n* stylized curved pattern used esp in carving
KORUN > KORUNA
KORUNA *n* standard monetary unit of the Czech Republic and Slovakia, divided into 100 hellers
KORUNAS > KORUNA
KORUNY > KORUNA
KORUS > KORU
KOS *n* Indian unit of distance having different values in different localities
KOSES > KOS
KOSHER *adj* conforming to Jewish religious law, esp (of food) to Jewish dietary law ▷ *n* kosher food ▷ *vb* prepare in accordance with Jewish dietary rules
KOSHERED > KOSHER
KOSHERING > KOSHER
KOSHERS > KOSHER
KOSMOS *variant form of* > COSMOS
KOSMOSES > KOSMOS
KOSS *same as* > KOS
KOSSES > KOSS
KOTARE *n* small greenish-blue kingfisher found in New Zealand, Australia, and some Pacific islands to the north
KOTCH *vb* South African slang for vomit
KOTCHED > KOTCH
KOTCHES > KOTCH
KOTCHING > KOTCH
KOTO *n* Japanese stringed instrument, consisting of a rectangular wooden body over which are stretched silk strings, which are plucked with plectrums or a nail-like device
KOTOS > KOTO
KOTOW *same as* > KOWTOW
KOTOWED > KOTOW
KOTOWER > KOTOW
KOTOWERS > KOTOW
KOTOWING > KOTOW
KOTOWS > KOTOW
KOTTABOS > COTTABUS
KOTUKU *n* white heron with brilliant white plumage, black legs and yellow eyes and bill
KOTWAL *n* senior police officer or magistrate in an Indian town
KOTWALS > KOTWAL
KOULAN *same as* > KULAN
KOULANS > KOULAN
KOUMIS *same as* > KUMISS
KOUMISES > KOUMIS

KOUMISS *same as* > KUMISS
KOUMISSES > KOUMISS
KOUMYS *same as* > KUMISS
KOUMYSES > KOUMYS
KOUMYSS *same as* > KUMISS
KOUMYSSES > KOUMYSS
KOUPREY *n* large wild SE Asian ox
KOUPREYS > KOUPREY
KOURA *n* New Zealand freshwater crayfish
KOURBASH *same as* > KURBASH
KOUROI > KOUROS
KOUROS *n* ancient Greek statue of a young man
KOUSKOUS *same as* > COUSCOUS
KOUSSO *n* Abyssinian tree whose flowers have useful antiparasitic properties
KOUSSOS > KOUSSO
KOW *old variant of* > COW
KOWHAI *n* New Zealand tree with clusters of yellow flowers
KOWHAIS > KOWHAI
KOWS > KOW
KOWTOW *vb* be servile (towards) ▷ *n* act of kowtowing
KOWTOWED > KOWTOW
KOWTOWER > KOWTOW
KOWTOWERS > KOWTOW
KOWTOWING > KOWTOW
KOWTOWS > KOWTOW
KRAAL *n* S African village surrounded by a strong fence ▷ *adj* denoting or relating to the tribal aspects of the Black African way of life ▷ *vb* enclose (livestock) in a kraal
KRAALED > KRAAL
KRAALING > KRAAL
KRAALS > KRAAL
KRAB *same as* > KARABINER
KRABS > KRAB
KRAFT *n* strong wrapping paper, made from pulp processed with a sulphate solution
KRAFTS > KRAFT
KRAIT *n* any nonaggressive brightly coloured venomous elapid snake of the genus *Bungarus*, of S and SE Asia
KRAITS > KRAIT
KRAKEN *n* legendary sea monster
KRAKENS > KRAKEN
KRAKOWIAK *n* Polish dance
KRAMERIA *another name for* > RHATANY
KRAMERIAS > KRAMERIA
KRANG *n* dead whale from which the blubber has been removed
KRANGS > KRANG
KRANS *n* sheer rock face
KRANSES > KRANS
KRANTZ *same as* > KRANS
KRANTZES > KRANTZ
KRANZ *same as* > KRANS
KRANZES > KRANS
KRATER *same as* > CRATER
KRATERS > KRATER
KRAUT *n* sauerkraut
KRAUTS > KRAUT
KREASOTE *same as* > CREOSOTE
KREASOTED > KREASOTE
KREASOTES > KREASOTE
KREATINE *same as* > CREATINE
KREATINES > KREATINE
KREEP *n* lunar substance that is high in potassium, rare earth elements, and phosphorus
KREEPS > KREEP
KREESE *same as* > KRIS
KREESED > KREESE
KREESES > KREESE
KREESING > KREESE
KREMLIN *n* citadel of any Russian city
KREMLINS > KREMLIN
KRENG *same as* > KRANG
KRENGS > KRENG
KREOSOTE *same as* > CREOSOTE
KREOSOTED > KREOSOTE
KREOSOTES > KREOSOTE
KREPLACH *pl n* small filled dough casings usually served in soup
KREPLECH *same as* > KREPLACH
KREUTZER *n* any of various former copper and silver coins of Germany or Austria
KREUTZERS > KREUTZER
KREUZER *same as* > KREUTZER
KREUZERS > KREUZER
KREWE *n* club taking part in New Orleans carnival parade
KREWES > KREWE
KRILL *n* small shrimplike sea creature
KRILLS > KRILL
KRIMMER *n* tightly curled light grey fur obtained from the skins of lambs from the Crimean region
KRIMMERS > KRIMMER
KRIS *n* Malayan and Indonesian stabbing or slashing knife with a scalloped edge ▷ *vb* stab or slash with a kris
KRISED > KRIS
KRISES > KRIS
KRISING > KRIS
KROMESKY *n* croquette consisting of a piece of bacon wrapped round minced meat or fish
KRONA *n* standard monetary unit of Sweden
KRONE *n* standard monetary unit of Norway and Denmark
KRONEN > KRONE
KRONER > KRONE
KRONOR > KRONA
KRONUR > KRONA
KROON *n* standard monetary unit of Estonia, divided into 100 senti
KROONI > KROON
KROONS > KROON
KRUBI *n* aroid plant with an unpleasant smell
KRUBIS > KRUBI
KRUBUT *same as* > KRUBI
KRUBUTS > KRUBUT
KRULLER *variant spelling of* > CRULLER
KRULLERS > KRULLER
KRUMHORN *variant spelling of* > CRUMHORN
KRUMHORNS > KRUMHORN
KRUMKAKE *n* Scandinavian biscuit
KRUMKAKES > KRUMKAKE
KRUMMHOLZ *n* zone of stunted wind-blown trees growing at high altitudes just above the timberline on tropical mountains
KRUMMHORN *variant spelling of* > CRUMHORN
KRYOLITE *variant spelling of* > CRYOLITE
KRYOLITES > KRYOLITE
KRYOLITH *same as* > CRYOLITE
KRYOLITHS > KRYOLITH
KRYOMETER *same as* > CRYOMETER
KRYPSES > KRYPSIS
KRYPSIS *n* idea that Christ made secret use of his divine attributes
KRYPTON *n* colourless gas present in the atmosphere and used in fluorescent lights
KRYPTONS > KRYPTON
KRYTRON *n* type of fast electronic gas-discharge switch, used as a trigger in nuclear weapons
KRYTRONS > KRYTRON
KSAR *old form of* > TSAR
KSARS > KSAR
KUCHCHA *same as* > KACHA
KUCHEN *n* breadlike cake containing apple, nuts, and sugar, originating from Germany
KUCHENS > KUCHEN
KUDLIK *n* Inuit soapstone seal-oil lamp
KUDLIKS > KUDLIK
KUDO *variant of* > KUDOS
KUDOS *n* fame or credit
KUDOSES > KUDOS
KUDU *n* African antelope with spiral horns
KUDUS > KUDU
KUDZU *n* hairy leguminous climbing plant of China and Japan, with trifoliate leaves and purple fragrant flowers
KUDZUS > KUDZU
KUE *n* name of the letter Q
KUEH *n* (in Malaysia) any cake of Malay, Chinese, or Indian origin
KUES > KUE
KUFI *n* cap for Muslim ma[n]
KUFIS > KUFI
KUFIYAH *same as* > KEFFIYEH
KUFIYAHS > KUFIYAH
KUGEL *n* baked pudding in traditional Jewish cookin[g]
KUGELS > KUGEL
KUIA *n* Māori female elder or elderly woman
KUIAS > KUIA
KUKRI *n* heavy, curved knif[e] used by Gurkhas
KUKRIS > KUKRI
KUKU *n* mussel
KUKUS > KUKU
KULA *n* ceremonial gift exchange practised among a group of islanders in the W Pacific, used to establish relation[s] between islands
KULAK *n* (formerly) property-owning Russian peasant
KULAKI > KULAK
KULAKS > KULAK
KULAN *n* Asiatic wild ass of the Russian steppes, probably a variety of kiang or onager
KULANS > KULAN
KULAS > KULA
KULFI *n* Indian dessert made by freezing milk which has been concentrated by boiling away some of the water in it, and flavoured with nuts and cardamom seeds
KULFIS > KULFI
KULTUR *n* German civilization
KULTURS > KULTUR
KUMARA *n* tropical root vegetable with yellow flesh
KUMARAHOU *n* New Zealand shrub
KUMARAS > KUMARA
KUMARI *n* (in Indian English) maiden
KUMARIS > KUMARI
KUMBALOI *pl n* worry beads
KUMERA *same as* > KUMARA
KUMERAS > KUMERA
KUMIKUMI *same as* > KAMOKAMO
KUMISS *n* drink made from fermented mare's or other milk, drunk by certain Asian tribes, esp in Russia or used for dietetic and medicinal purposes
KUMISSES > KUMISS
KUMITE *n* freestyle sparring or fighting
KUMITES > KUMITE

JMMEL *n* German liqueur flavoured with aniseed and cumin
JMMELS > KUMMEL
JMQUAT *n* citrus fruit resembling a tiny orange
JMQUATS > KUMQUAT
JMYS *same as* > KUMISS
JMYSES > KUMYS
JNA *n* standard monetary unit of Croatia, divided into 100 lipa
JNDALINI *n* (in yoga) life force that resides at the base of the spine
JNE > KUNA
JNJOOS *adj* (in Indian English) mean or stingy
JNKAR *n* type of limestone
JNKARS > KUNKAR
JNKUR *same as* > KUNKAR
JNKURS > KUNKUR
JNZITE *n* pink-coloured transparent variety of the mineral spodumene: a gemstone
JNZITES > KUNZITE
JRBASH *vb* whip with a hide whip
JRBASHED > KURBASH
JRBASHES > KURBASH
JRFUFFLE *same as* > KERFUFFLE
JRGAN *n* Russian burial mound
JRGANS > KURGAN
JRI *n* mongrel dog
JRIS > KURI
JRRAJONG *n* Australian tree or shrub with tough fibrous bark
JRRE *old variant of* > CUR
JRRES > KURRE
JRSAAL *n* public room at a health resort
JRSAALS > KURSAAL
JRTA *n* long loose garment like a shirt without a collar worn in India
JRTAS > KURTA
JRTOSES > KURTOSIS
JRTOSIS *n* measure of the concentration of a distribution around its mean
JRU *n* degenerative disease of the nervous system, restricted to certain tribes in New Guinea, marked by loss of muscular control and thought to be caused by a slow virus
JRUS > KURU
JRVEY *vb* (in old South African English) transport goods by ox cart
JRVEYED > KURVEY
JRVEYING > KURVEY
JRVEYOR > KURVEY
JRVEYORS > KURVEY
JRVEYS > KURVEY
JSSO *variant spelling of* > KOUSSO
KUSSOS > KUSSO
KUTA *n* (in Indian English) male dog
KUTAS > KUTA
KUTCH *same as* > CATECHU
KUTCHA *adj* makeshift or not solid
KUTCHES > KUTCH
KUTI *n* (in Indian English) female dog or bitch
KUTIS > KUTI
KUTU *n* body louse
KUTUS > KUTU
KUVASZ *n* breed of dog from Hungary
KUVASZOK > KUVASZ
KUZU *same as* > KUDZU
KUZUS > KUZU
KVAS *same as* > KVASS
KVASES > KVAS
KVASS *n* alcoholic drink of low strength made in Russia and E Europe from cereals and stale bread
KVASSES > KVASS
KVELL *vb* US word meaning be happy
KVELLED > KVELL
KVELLING > KVELL
KVELLS > KVELL
KVETCH *vb* complain or grumble
KVETCHED > KVETCH
KVETCHER > KVETCH
KVETCHERS > KVETCH
KVETCHES > KVETCH
KVETCHIER > KVETCHY
KVETCHILY > KVETCHY
KVETCHING > KVETCH
KVETCHY *adj* tending to grumble or complain
KWACHA *n* standard monetary unit of Zambia, divided into 100 ngwee
KWACHAS > KWACHA
KWAITO *n* type of South African pop music with lyrics spoken over an instrumental backing usually consisting of slowed-down house music layered with African percussion and melodies
KWAITOS > KWAITO
KWANZA *n* standard monetary unit of Angola, divided into 100 lwei
KWANZAS > KWANZA
KWELA *n* type of pop music popular among the Black communities of South Africa
KWELAS > KWELA
KY *pl n* Scots word for cows
KYACK *n* type of panier
KYACKS > KYACK
KYAK *same as* > KAYAK
KYAKS > KYAK
KYANG *same as* > KIANG
KYANGS > KYANG
KYANISE *same as* > KYANIZE
KYANISED > KYANISE
KYANISES > KYANISE
KYANISING > KYANISE
KYANITE *n* grey, green, or blue mineral consisting of aluminium silicate in triclinic crystalline form
KYANITES > KYANITE
KYANITIC > KYANITE
KYANIZE *vb* treat (timber) with corrosive sublimate to make it resistant to decay
KYANIZED > KYANIZE
KYANIZES > KYANIZE
KYANIZING > KYANIZE
KYAR *same as* > COIR
KYARS > KYAR
KYAT *n* standard monetary unit of Myanmar, divided into 100 pyas
KYATS > KYAT
KYBO *n* temporary lavatory constructed for use when camping
KYBOS > KYBO
KYBOSH *same as* > KIBOSH
KYBOSHED > KYBOSH
KYBOSHES > KYBOSH
KYBOSHING > KYBOSH
KYDST > KYTHE
KYE *n* Korean fundraising meeting
KYES > KYE
KYLE *n* narrow strait or channel
KYLES > KYLE
KYLICES > KYLIX
KYLIE *n* boomerang that is flat on one side and convex on the other
KYLIES > KYLIE
KYLIKES > KYLIX
KYLIN *n* (in Chinese art) mythical animal of composite form
KYLINS > KYLIN
KYLIX *n* shallow two-handled drinking vessel used in ancient Greece
KYLLOSES > KYLLOSIS
KYLLOSIS *n* club foot
KYLOE *n* breed of small long-horned long-haired beef cattle from NW Scotland
KYLOES > KYLOE
KYMOGRAM *n* image or other visual record created by a kymograph
KYMOGRAMS > KYMOGRAM
KYMOGRAPH *n* rotatable drum for holding paper on which a tracking stylus continuously records variations in blood pressure, respiratory movements, etc
KYND *old variant of* > KIND
KYNDE *old variant of* > KIND
KYNDED > KYND
KYNDES > KYNDE
KYNDING > KYND
KYNDS > KYND
KYNE *pl n* archaic word for cows
KYOGEN *n* type of Japanese drama
KYOGENS > KYOGEN
KYPE *n* hook on the lower jaw of a mature male salmon
KYPES > KYPE
KYPHOSES > KYPHOSIS
KYPHOSIS *n* backward curvature of the thoracic spine
KYPHOTIC > KYPHOSIS
KYRIE *n* type of prayer
KYRIELLE *n* verse form of French origin characterized by repeated lines or words
KYRIELLES > KYRIELLE
KYRIES > KYRIE
KYTE *n* belly
KYTES > KYTE
KYTHE *vb* appear
KYTHED > KYTHE
KYTHES > KYTHE
KYTHING > KYTHE
KYU *n* (in judo) one of the five student grades for inexperienced competitors
KYUS > KYU

Ll

LA *n* exclamation of surprise or emphasis
LAAGER *n* (in Africa) a camp defended by a circular formation of wagons ▷ *vb* form (wagons) into a laager
LAAGERED > LAAGER
LAAGERING > LAAGER
LAAGERS > LAAGER
LAARI *same as* > LARI
LAARIS > LAARI
LAB *n* laboratory
LABARA > LABARUM
LABARUM *n* standard or banner carried in Christian religious processions
LABARUMS > LABARUM
LABDA *same as* > LAMBDA
LABDACISM *n* excessive use or idiosyncratic pronunciation of (l)
LABDANUM *n* dark resinous juice obtained from various rockroses
LABDANUMS > LABDANUM
LABDAS > LABDA
LABEL *n* piece of card or other material fixed to an object to show its ownership, destination, etc ▷ *vb* give a label to
LABELABLE > LABEL
LABELED > LABEL
LABELER > LABEL
LABELERS > LABEL
LABELING > LABEL
LABELLA > LABELLUM
LABELLATE > LABELLUM
LABELLED > LABEL
LABELLER > LABEL
LABELLERS > LABEL
LABELLING > LABEL
LABELLIST *n* person who wears only clothes with fashionable brand names
LABELLOID > LABELLUM
LABELLUM *n* lip-like part of certain plants
LABELS > LABEL
LABIA > LABIUM
LABIAL *adj* of the lips ▷ *n* speech sound that involves the lips
LABIALISE *same as* > LABIALIZE
LABIALISM > LABIALIZE
LABIALITY > LABIAL
LABIALIZE *vb* pronounce with articulation involving rounded lips
LABIALLY > LABIAL
LABIALS > LABIAL
LABIATE *n* any of a family of plants with square stems, aromatic leaves, and a two-lipped flower, such as mint or thyme ▷ *adj* of this family
LABIATED *adj* having a lip
LABIATES > LABIATE
LABILE *adj* (of a compound) prone to chemical change
LABILITY > LABILE
LABIS *n* cochlear
LABISES > LABIS
LABIUM *n* lip or liplike structure
LABLAB *n* twining leguminous plant
LABLABS > LABLAB
LABOR *same as* > LABOUR
LABORED *same as* > LABOURED
LABOREDLY > LABOURED
LABORER *same as* > LABOURER
LABORERS > LABORER
LABORING > LABOR
LABORIOUS *adj* involving great prolonged effort
LABORISM *same as* > LABOURISM
LABORISMS > LABORISM
LABORIST *same as* > LABOURIST
LABORISTS > LABORIST
LABORITE *n* adherent of the Labour party
LABORITES > LABORITE
LABORS > LABOR
LABOUR *n* physical work or exertion ▷ *vb* work hard
LABOURED *adj* uttered or done with difficulty
LABOURER *n* person who labours, esp someone doing manual work for wages
LABOURERS > LABOURER
LABOURING > LABOUR
LABOURISM *n* dominance of the working classes
LABOURIST *n* person who supports workers' rights
LABOURS > LABOUR
LABRA > LABRUM
LABRADOR *n* large retriever dog with a usu gold or black coat
LABRADORS > LABRADOR
LABRET *n* piece of bone, shell, etc
LABRETS > LABRET
LABRID *same as* > LABROID
LABRIDS > LABRID
LABROID *n* type of fish ▷ *adj* of or relating to such fish
LABROIDS > LABROID
LABROSE *adj* thick-lipped
LABRUM *n* lip or liplike part
LABRUMS > LABRUM
LABRUSCA *n* grape variety
LABRYS *n* type of axe
LABRYSES > LABRYS
LABS > LAB
LABURNUM *n* ornamental tree with yellow hanging flowers
LABURNUMS > LABURNUM
LABYRINTH *n* complicated network of passages
LAC *same as* > LAKH
LACCOLITE *same as* > LACCOLITH
LACCOLITH *n* dome-shaped body of igneous rock between two layers of older sedimentary rock
LACE *n* delicate loosely woven decorative fabric ▷ *vb* fasten with shoelaces, cords, etc
LACEBARK *n* small evergreen tree
LACEBARKS > LACEBARK
LACED > LACE
LACELESS > LACE
LACELIKE > LACE
LACER > LACE
LACERABLE > LACERATE
LACERANT *adj* painfully distressing
LACERATE *vb* tear (flesh) ▷ *adj* having edges that are jagged or torn
LACERATED > LACERATE
LACERATES > LACERATE
LACERS > LACE
LACERTIAN *n* type of

reptile
ACERTID *n* type of lizard
ACERTIDS > LACERTID
ACERTINE *adj* relating to lacertid
ACES > LACE
ACET *n* braidwork
ACETS > LACET
ACEWING *n* any of various neuropterous insects
ACEWINGS > LACEWING
ACEWOOD *n* wood of sycamore tree
ACEWOODS > LACEWOOD
ACEWORK *n* work made from lace
ACEWORKS > LACEWORK
ACEY *same as* > LACY
ACHES *n* negligence or unreasonable delay in pursuing a legal remedy
ACHESES > LACHES
ACHRYMAL *same as* > LACRIMAL
ACIER > LACY
ACIEST > LACY
ACILY > LACY
ACINESS > LACY
ACING > LACE
ACINGS > LACE
ACINIA *n* narrow fringe on petal
ACINIAE > LACINIA
ACINIATE *adj* jagged
ACK *n* shortage or absence of something needed or wanted ▷ *vb* need or be short of (something)
ACKADAY *another word for* > ALAS
ACKED > LACK
ACKER *variant spelling of* > LACQUER
ACKERED > LACKER
ACKERING > LACKER
ACKERS > LACKER
ACKEY *n* servile follower ▷ *vb* act as a lackey (to)
ACKEYED > LACKEY
ACKEYING > LACKEY
ACKEYS > LACKEY
ACKING > LACK
ACKLAND *n* fool
ACKLANDS > LACKLAND
ACKS > LACK
ACMUS *n* old form of litmus
ACMUSES > LACMUS
ACONIC *adj* using only a few words, terse
ACONICAL *same as* > LACONIC
ACONISM *n* economy of expression
ACONISMS > LACONISM
ACQUER *n* hard varnish for wood or metal ▷ *vb* apply lacquer to
ACQUERED > LACQUER
ACQUERER > LACQUER
ACQUERS > LACQUER
ACQUEY *same as* > LACKEY
ACQUEYED > LACQUEY
ACQUEYS > LACQUEY
ACRIMAL *adj* of tears or the glands which produce them ▷ *n* bone near tear gland
LACRIMALS > LACRIMAL
LACRIMOSO *adj* tearful
LACROSSE *n* sport in which teams catch and throw a ball using long sticks with a pouched net at the end, in an attempt to score goals
LACROSSES > LACROSSE
LACRYMAL *same as* > LACRIMAL
LACRYMALS > LACRYMAL
LACS > LAC
LACTAM *n* any of a group of inner amides
LACTAMS > LACTAM
LACTARIAN *n* vegetarian who eats dairy products
LACTARY *adj* relating to milk
LACTASE *n* any of a group of enzymes that hydrolyse lactose to glucose and galactose
LACTASES > LACTASE
LACTATE *vb* (of mammals) to secrete milk ▷ *n* ester or salt of lactic acid
LACTATED > LACTATE
LACTATES > LACTATE
LACTATING > LACTATE
LACTATION *n* secretion of milk by female mammals to feed young
LACTEAL *adj* of or like milk ▷ *n* any of the lymphatic vessels that convey chyle from the small intestine to the blood
LACTEALLY > LACTEAL
LACTEALS > LACTEAL
LACTEAN *another word for* > LACTEOUS
LACTEOUS *adj* milky
LACTIC *adj* of or derived from milk > LACTIFEROUS
LACTIFIC *adj* yielding milk
LACTONE *n* any of a class of organic compounds
LACTONES > LACTONE
LACTONIC > LACTONE
LACTOSE *n* white crystalline sugar found in milk
LACTOSES > LACTOSE
LACUNA *n* gap or missing part, esp in a document or series
LACUNAE > LACUNA
LACUNAL > LACUNA
LACUNAR *n* ceiling, soffit, or vault having coffers ▷ *adj* of, relating to, or containing a lacuna or lacunas
LACUNARIA > LACUNAR
LACUNARS > LACUNAR
LACUNARY > LACUNA
LACUNAS > LACUNA
LACUNATE > LACUNA
LACUNE *n* hiatus
LACUNES > LACUNE
LACUNOSE > LACUNA
LACY *adj* fine, like lace
LAD *n* boy or young man
LADANUM *same as* > LABDANUM
LADANUMS > LADANUM
LADDER *n* frame of two poles connected by horizontal steps used for climbing ▷ *vb* have or cause to have such a line of undone stitches
LADDERED > LADDER
LADDERING > LADDER
LADDERS > LADDER
LADDERY > LADDER
LADDIE *n* familiar term for a male, esp a young man
LADDIES > LADDIE
LADDISH *adj* informal word for behaving in a macho or immature manner
LADE *vb* put cargo on board (a ship) or (of a ship) to take on cargo ▷ *n* watercourse, esp a millstream
LADED > LADE
LADEN *adj* loaded ▷ *vb* load with cargo
LADENED > LADEN
LADENING > LADEN
LADENS > LADEN
LADER > LADE
LADERS > LADE
LADES > LADE
LADETTE *n* young woman whose social behaviour is similar to that of male adolescents or young men
LADETTES > LADETTE
LADHOOD > LAD
LADHOODS > LAD
LADIES *n* women's public toilet
LADIFIED > LADIFY
LADIFIES > LADIFY
LADIFY *same as* > LADYFY
LADIFYING > LADIFY
LADING > LADE
LADINGS > LADE
LADINO *n* Italian variety of white clover
LADINOS > LADINO
LADLE *n* spoon with a long handle and a large bowl, used for serving soup etc ▷ *vb* serve out
LADLED > LADLE
LADLEFUL > LADLE
LADLEFULS > LADLE
LADLER *n* person who serves with a ladle
LADLERS > LADLER
LADLES > LADLE
LADLING > LADLE
LADRON *same as* > LADRONE
LADRONE *n* thief
LADRONES > LADRONE
LADRONS > LADRON
LADS > LAD
LADY *n* woman regarded as having characteristics of good breeding or high rank ▷ *adj* female
LADYBIRD *n* small red beetle with black spots
LADYBIRDS > LADYBIRD
LADYBOY *n* transvestite or transsexual, esp one from the Far East
LADYBOYS > LADYBOY
LADYBUG *same as* > LADYBIRD
LADYBUGS > LADYBUG
LADYCOW *another word for* > LADYBIRD
LADYCOWS > LADYCOW
LADYFIED > LADYFY
LADYFIES > LADYFY
LADYFISH *n* type of game fish
LADYFLIES > LADYFLY
LADYFLY *another word for* > LADYBIRD
LADYFY *vb* make a lady of (someone)
LADYFYING > LADYFY
LADYHOOD > LADY
LADYHOODS > LADY
LADYISH > LADY
LADYISM > LADY
LADYISMS > LADY
LADYKIN *n* endearing form of lady
LADYKINS > LADYKIN
LADYLIKE *adj* polite and dignified
LADYLOVE *n* beloved woman
LADYLOVES > LADYLOVE
LADYPALM *n* small palm, grown indoors
LADYPALMS > LADYPALM
LADYSHIP *n* title of a peeress
LADYSHIPS > LADYSHIP
LAER *another word for* > LAAGER
LAERED > LAER
LAERING > LAER
LAERS > LAER
LAESIE *old form of* > LAZY
LAETARE *n* fourth Sunday of Lent
LAETARES > LAETARE
LAETRILE *n* drug used to treat cancer
LAETRILES > LAETRILE
LAEVIGATE *same as* > LEVIGATE
LAEVO *adj* on the left
LAEVULIN *n* polysaccharide occurring in the tubers of certain helianthus plants
LAEVULINS > LAEVULIN
LAEVULOSE *n* fructose
LAG *vb* go too slowly, fall behind ▷ *n* delay between events
LAGAN *n* goods or wreckage on the sea bed, sometimes attached to a buoy to permit recovery
LAGANS > LAGAN

LAGENA *n* bottle with a narrow neck
LAGENAS > LAGENA
LAGEND *same as* > LAGAN
LAGENDS > LAGEND
LAGER *n* light-bodied beer ▷ *vb* ferment into lager
LAGERED > LAGER
LAGERING > LAGER
LAGERS > LAGER
LAGGARD *n* person who lags behind ▷ *adj* sluggish, slow, or dawdling
LAGGARDLY > LAGGARD
LAGGARDS > LAGGARD
LAGGED > LAG
LAGGEN *n* spar of a barrel
LAGGENS > LAGGEN
LAGGER *n* person who lags pipes
LAGGERS > LAGGER
LAGGIN *same as* > LAGGEN
LAGGING > LAG
LAGGINGLY > LAG
LAGGINGS > LAG
LAGGINS > LAGGIN
LAGNAPPE *same as* > LAGNIAPPE
LAGNAPPES > LAGNAPPE
LAGNIAPPE *n* small gift, esp one given to a customer who makes a purchase
LAGOMORPH *n* any placental mammal of the order *Lagomorpha*
LAGOON *n* body of water cut off from the open sea by coral reefs or sand bars
LAGOONAL > LAGOON
LAGOONS > LAGOON
LAGRIMOSO *adj* mournful
LAGS > LAG
LAGUNA *n* lagoon
LAGUNAS > LAGUNA
LAGUNE *same as* > LAGOON
LAGUNES > LAGUNE
LAH *n* (in tonic sol-fa) sixth degree of any major scale
LAHAR *n* landslide of volcanic debris and water
LAHARS > LAHAR
LAHS > LAH
LAIC *adj* laical ▷ *n* layman
LAICAL *adj* secular
LAICALLY > LAIC
LAICH *n* low-lying piece of land
LAICHS > LAICH
LAICISE *same as* > LAICIZE
LAICISED > LAICISE
LAICISES > LAICISE
LAICISING > LAICISE
LAICISM > LAIC
LAICISMS > LAIC
LAICITIES > LAICITY
LAICITY *n* state of being laical
LAICIZE *vb* withdraw clerical or ecclesiastical character or status from (an institution, building, etc)
LAICIZED > LAICIZE
LAICIZES > LAICIZE
LAICIZING > LAICIZE
LAICS > LAIC
LAID *Scots form of* > LOAD
LAIDED > LAID
LAIDING > LAID
LAIDLY *adj* very ugly
LAIDS > LAID
LAIGH *adj* low-lying ▷ *n* area of low-lying ground
LAIGHER > LAIGH
LAIGHEST > LAIGH
LAIGHS > LAIGH
LAIK *vb* play (a game, etc)
LAIKA *n* type of small dog
LAIKAS > LAIKA
LAIKED > LAIK
LAIKER > LAIK
LAIKERS > LAIK
LAIKING > LAIK
LAIKS > LAIK
LAIN > LIE
LAIPSE *vb* beat soundly
LAIPSED > LAIPSE
LAIPSES > LAIPSE
LAIPSING > LAIPSE
LAIR *n* resting place of an animal ▷ *vb* (esp of a wild animal) to retreat to or rest in a lair
LAIRAGE *n* accommodation for farm animals, esp at docks or markets
LAIRAGES > LAIRAGE
LAIRD *n* Scottish landowner
LAIRDLY *adj* pertaining to laird or lairds
LAIRDS > LAIRD
LAIRDSHIP *n* state of being laird
LAIRED > LAIR
LAIRIER > LAIRY
LAIRIEST > LAIRY
LAIRING > LAIR
LAIRISE *same as* > LAIRIZE
LAIRISED > LAIRISE
LAIRISES > LAIRISE
LAIRISING > LAIRISE
LAIRIZE *vb* show off
LAIRIZED > LAIRIZE
LAIRIZES > LAIRIZE
LAIRIZING > LAIRIZE
LAIRS > LAIR
LAIRY *adj* gaudy or flashy
LAISSE *n* type of rhyme scheme
LAISSES > LAISSE
LAITANCE *n* white film forming on drying concrete
LAITANCES > LAITANCE
LAITH *Scots form of* > LOATH
LAITHLY *same as* > LAIDLY
LAITIES > LAITY
LAITY *n* people who are not members of the clergy
LAKE *n* expanse of water entirely surrounded by land ▷ *vb* take time away from work
LAKEBED *n* bed of lake
LAKEBEDS > LAKEBED
LAKED > LAKE
LAKEFRONT *n* area at edge of lake
LAKELAND *n* countryside with a lot of lakes
LAKELANDS > LAKELAND
LAKELET *n* small lake
LAKELETS > LAKELET
LAKELIKE > LAKE
LAKEPORT *n* port on lake
LAKEPORTS > LAKEPORT
LAKER *n* cargo vessel used on lakes
LAKERS > LAKER
LAKES > LAKE
LAKESHORE *n* area at edge of lake
LAKESIDE *n* area at edge of lake
LAKESIDES > LAKESIDE
LAKH *n* (in India) 100 000, esp referring to this sum of rupees
LAKHS > LAKH
LAKIER > LAKY
LAKIEST > LAKY
LAKIN *short form of* > LADYKIN
LAKING > LAKE
LAKINGS > LAKE
LAKINS > LAKIN
LAKISH *adj* similar to poetry of Lake poets
LAKSA *n* (in Malaysia) a dish of Chinese origin consisting of rice noodles served in curry or hot soup
LAKSAS > LAKSA
LAKY *adj* of the reddish colour of the pigment lake
LALANG *n* coarse weedy Malaysian grass
LALANGS > LALANG
LALDIE *n* great gusto
LALDIES > LALDIE
LALDY *same as* > LALDIE
LALIQUE *n* type of ornamental glass
LALIQUES > LALIQUE
LALL *vb* make imperfect 'l' or 'r' sounds
LALLAN *n* literary version of the English spoken in Lowland Scotland
LALLAND *same as* > LALLAN
LALLANDS > LALLAND
LALLANS > LALLAN
LALLATION *n* defect of speech consisting of the pronunciation of 'r' as 'l'
LALLED > LALL
LALLING > LALL
LALLINGS > LALL
LALLS > LALL
LALLYGAG *vb* loiter aimlessly
LALLYGAGS > LALLYGAG
LAM *vb* attack vigorously
LAMA *n* Buddhist priest in Tibet or Mongolia
LAMAISTIC *adj* relating to the Mahayana form of Buddhism
LAMANTIN *another word for* > MANATEE
LAMANTINS > LAMANTIN
LAMAS > LAMA
LAMASERAI *same as* > LAMASERY
LAMASERY *n* monastery of lamas
LAMB *n* young sheep ▷ *vb* (of sheep) give birth to a lamb or lambs
LAMBADA *n* erotic Brazilian dance
LAMBADAS > LAMBADA
LAMBAST *vb* beat or thrash
LAMBASTE *same as* > LAMBAST
LAMBASTED > LAMBAST
LAMBASTES > LAMBASTE
LAMBASTS > LAMBAST
LAMBDA *n* 11th letter of the Greek alphabet
LAMBDAS > LAMBDA
LAMBDOID *adj* having the shape of the Greek letter lambda
LAMBED > LAMB
LAMBENCY > LAMBENT
LAMBENT *adj* (of a flame) flickering softly
LAMBENTLY > LAMBENT
LAMBER *n* person that attends to lambing ewes
LAMBERS > LAMBER
LAMBERT *n* cgs unit of illumination, equal to 1 lumen per square centimetre
LAMBERTS > LAMBERT
LAMBIE *same as* > LAMBKIN
LAMBIER > LAMBY
LAMBIES > LAMBIE
LAMBIEST > LAMBY
LAMBING *n* birth of lambs at the end of winter
LAMBINGS > LAMBING
LAMBITIVE *n* medicine taken by licking
LAMBKILL *n* N American dwarf shrub
LAMBKILLS > LAMBKILL
LAMBKIN *n* small or young lamb
LAMBKINS > LAMBKIN
LAMBLIKE > LAMB
LAMBLING *n* small lamb
LAMBLINGS > LAMBLING
LAMBOYS *n* skirt-like piece of armour made from metal strips
LAMBRUSCO *n* Italian sparkling wine
LAMBS > LAMB
LAMBSKIN *n* skin of a lamb usually with the wool still on, used to make coats, slippers, etc
LAMBSKINS > LAMBSKIN
LAMBY *adj* lamb-like
LAME *adj* having an injured or disabled leg or foot ▷ *vb* make lame ▷ *n* fabric interwoven with gold or silver threads
LAMEBRAIN *n* stupid or

slow-witted person
AMED *n* 12th letter in the Hebrew alphabet
AMEDH *same as* > LAMED
AMEDHS > LAMEDH
AMEDS > LAMED
AMELLA *n* thin layer, plate, or membrane, esp any of the calcified layers of which bone is formed
AMELLAE > LAMELLA
AMELLAR > LAMELLA
AMELLAS > LAMELLA
AMELLATE > LAMELLA
AMELLOID *another word for* > LAMELLA
AMELLOSE > LAMELLA
AMELY > LAME
AMENESS > LAME
AMENT *vb* feel or express sorrow (for) ▷ *n* passionate expression of grief
AMENTED *adj* grieved for
AMENTER > LAMENT
AMENTERS > LAMENT
AMENTING > LAMENT
AMENTS > LAMENT
AMER > LAME
AMES > LAME
AMEST > LAME
AMETER *Scots form of* > LAMIGER
AMETERS > LAMETER
AMIA *n* one of a class of female monsters depicted with a snake's body and a woman's head and breasts
AMIAE > LAMIA
AMIAS > LAMIA
AMIGER *n* disabled person
AMIGERS > LAMIGER
AMINA *n* thin plate, esp of bone or mineral
AMINABLE > LAMINATE
AMINAE > LAMINA
AMINAL *n* consonant articulated with blade of tongue
AMINALS > LAMINAL
AMINAR > LAMINA
AMINARIA *n* any brown seaweed of the genus *Laminaria*
AMINARIN *n* carbohydrate, consisting of repeated glucose units, that is the main storage product of brown algae
AMINARY > LAMINA
AMINAS > LAMINA
AMINATE *vb* make (a sheet of material) by sticking together thin sheets ▷ *n* laminated sheet ▷ *adj* composed of lamina
AMINATED *adj* composed of many layers stuck together
AMINATES > LAMINATE
AMINATOR > LAMINATE
AMING > LAME
AMINGTON *n* sponge cake coated with a sweet coating
LAMININ *n* type of protein
LAMININS > LAMININ
LAMINITIS *n* (in animals with hooves) inflammation of the tissue to which the hoof is attached
LAMINOSE > LAMINA
LAMINOUS > LAMINA
LAMISH *adj* rather lame
LAMISTER *n* fugitive
LAMISTERS > LAMISTER
LAMITER *same as* > LAMETER
LAMITERS > LAMITER
LAMMED > LAM
LAMMER *Scots word for* > AMBER
LAMMERS > LAMMER
LAMMIE *same as* > LAMMY
LAMMIES > LAMMY
LAMMIGER *same as* > LAMIGER
LAMMIGERS > LAMIGER
LAMMING > LAM
LAMMINGS > LAM
LAMMY *n* thick woollen jumper
LAMP *n* device which produces light from electricity, oil, or gas ▷ *vb* go quickly with long steps
LAMPAD *n* candlestick
LAMPADARY *n* person who lights the lamps in an Orthodox Greek Church
LAMPADIST *n* prize-winner in race run by young men with torches
LAMPADS > LAMPAD
LAMPAS *n* swelling of the mucous membrane of the hard palate of horses
LAMPASES > LAMPAS
LAMPASSE *same as* > LAMPAS
LAMPASSES > LAMPASSE
LAMPBLACK *n* fine black soot used as a pigment in paint and ink
LAMPED > LAMP
LAMPER *n* lamprey
LAMPERN *n* migratory European lamprey
LAMPERNS > LAMPERN
LAMPERS > LAMPER
LAMPERSES > LAMPERS
LAMPHOLE *n* hole in ground for lowering lamp into sewer
LAMPHOLES > LAMPHOLE
LAMPING > LAMP
LAMPINGS > LAMP
LAMPION *n* oil-burning lamp
LAMPIONS > LAMPION
LAMPLIGHT *n* light produced by lamp
LAMPOON *n* humorous satire ridiculing someone ▷ *vb* satirize or ridicule
LAMPOONED > LAMPOON
LAMPOONER > LAMPOON
LAMPOONS > LAMPOON
LAMPPOST *n* post supporting a lamp in the street
LAMPPOSTS > LAMPPOST
LAMPREY *n* eel-like fish with a round sucking mouth
LAMPREYS > LAMPREY
LAMPS > LAMP
LAMPSHADE *n* shade used to reduce light shed by light bulb
LAMPSHELL *n* brachiopod
LAMPUKA *same as* > LAMPUKI
LAMPUKAS > LAMPUKA
LAMPUKI *n* type of fish
LAMPUKIS > LAMPUKI
LAMPYRID *n* firefly
LAMPYRIDS > LAMPYRID
LAMS > LAM
LAMSTER *n* fugitive
LAMSTERS > LAMSTER
LANA *n* wood from genipap tree
LANAI *Hawaiian word for* > VERANDA
LANAIS > LANAI
LANAS > LANA
LANATE *adj* having or consisting of a woolly covering of hairs
LANATED *same as* > LANATE
LANCE *n* long spear used by a mounted soldier ▷ *vb* pierce (a boil or abscess) with a lancet
LANCED > LANCE
LANCEGAY *n* kind of ancient spear
LANCEGAYS > LANCEGAY
LANCEJACK *n* lance corporal
LANCELET *n* any of several marine animals of the genus *Branchiostoma*
LANCELETS > LANCELET
LANCEOLAR *adj* narrow and tapering to a point at each end
LANCER *n* formerly, cavalry soldier armed with a lance
LANCERS *n* quadrille for eight or sixteen couples
LANCES > LANCE
LANCET *n* pointed two-edged surgical knife
LANCETED *adj* having one or more lancet arches or windows
LANCETS > LANCET
LANCEWOOD *n* New Zealand tree with slender leaves
LANCH *obsolete form of* > LAUNCH
LANCHED > LANCH
LANCHES > LANCH
LANCHING > LANCH
LANCIERS *pl n* type of dance
LANCIFORM *adj* in the form of a lance
LANCINATE *adj* (esp of pain) sharp or cutting
LANCING > LANCE
LAND *n* solid part of the earth's surface ▷ *vb* come or bring to earth after a flight, jump, or fall
LANDAMMAN *n* chairman of the governing council in some Swiss cantons
LANDAU *n* four-wheeled carriage with two folding hoods
LANDAULET *n* small landau
LANDAUS > LANDAU
LANDBOARD *n* narrow board, with wheels larger than those on a skateboard, usually ridden while standing
LANDDAMNE *vb* Shakespearian word for make (a person's life) unbearable
LANDDROS *n* sheriff
LANDDROST *n* South African magistrate
LANDE *n* type of moorland in SW France
LANDED *adj* possessing or consisting of lands
LANDER *n* spacecraft designed to land on a planet or other body
LANDERS > LANDER
LANDES > LANDE
LANDFALL *n* ship's first landing after a voyage
LANDFALLS > LANDFALL
LANDFILL *n* disposing of rubbish by covering it with earth
LANDFILLS > LANDFILL
LANDFORCE *n* body of people trained for land warfare
LANDFORM *n* any natural feature of the earth's surface, such as valleys and mountains
LANDFORMS > LANDFORM
LANDGRAB *n* sudden attempt to establish ownership of or copyright on something in advance of competitors
LANDGRABS > LANDGRAB
LANDGRAVE *n* (from the 13th century to 1806) a count who ruled over a specified territory
LANDING *n* floor area at the top of a flight of stairs
LANDINGS > LANDING
LANDLADY *n* woman who owns and leases property
LANDLER *n* Austrian country dance in which couples spin and clap
LANDLERS > LANDLER
LANDLESS > LAND
LANDLINE *n* telecommunications cable laid over land
LANDLINES > LANDLINE
LANDLOPER *n* vagabond or vagrant
LANDLORD *n* person who

rents out land, houses, etc
LANDLORDS > LANDLORD
LANDMAN *n* person who lives and works on land
LANDMARK *n* prominent object in or feature of a landscape
LANDMARKS > LANDMARK
LANDMASS *n* large continuous area of land
LANDMEN > LANDMAN
LANDOWNER *n* person who owns land
LANDRACE *n* white very long-bodied lop-eared breed of pork pig
LANDRACES > LANDRACE
LANDRAIL *n* type of bird
LANDRAILS > LANDRAIL
LANDS *pl n* holdings in land
LANDSCAPE *n* extensive piece of inland scenery seen from one place ▷ *vb* improve natural features of (a piece of land) ▷ *adj* (of a publication or an illustration in a publication) of greater width than height
LANDSHARK *n* person who makes inordinate profits by buying and selling land
LANDSIDE *n* part of an airport farthest from the aircraft
LANDSIDES > LANDSIDE
LANDSKIP *another word for* > LANDSCAPE
LANDSKIPS > LANDSKIP
LANDSLEIT > LANDSMAN
LANDSLID > LANDSLIDE
LANDSLIDE *vb* cause land or rock to fall from hillside
LANDSLIP *same as* > LANDSLIDE
LANDSLIPS > LANDSLIP
LANDSMAN *n* person who works or lives on land, as distinguished from a seaman
LANDSMEN > LANDSMAN
LANDWARD *same as* > LANDWARDS
LANDWARDS *adv* towards land
LANDWIND *n* wind that comes from the land
LANDWINDS > LANDWIND
LANE *n* narrow road
LANELY *Scots form of* > LONELY
LANES > LANE
LANEWAY *n* lane
LANEWAYS > LANEWAY
LANG *Scot word for* > LONG
LANGAHA *n* type of Madagascan snake
LANGAHAS > LANGAHA
LANGAR *n* dining hall in a gurdwara
LANGARS > LANGAR
LANGER *informal Irish word for* > PENIS
LANGERED *adj* drunk
LANGERS > LANGER
LANGEST > LANG
LANGLAUF *n* cross-country skiing
LANGLAUFS > LANGLAUF
LANGLEY *n* unit of solar radiation
LANGLEYS > LANGLEY
LANGOUSTE *n* spiny lobster
LANGRAGE *n* shot consisting of scrap iron packed into a case, formerly used in naval warfare
LANGRAGES > LANGRAGE
LANGREL *same as* > LANGRAGE
LANGRELS > LANGREL
LANGRIDGE *same as* > LANGRAGE
LANGSHAN *n* breed of chicken
LANGSHANS > LANGSHAN
LANGSPEL *n* type of Scandinavian stringed instrument
LANGSPELS > LANGSPEL
LANGSPIEL *same as* > LANGSPEL
LANGSYNE *adv* long ago ▷ *n* times long past, esp those fondly remembered
LANGSYNES > LANGSYNE
LANGUAGE *n* system of sounds, symbols, etc for communicating thought ▷ *vb* express in language
LANGUAGED > LANGUAGE
LANGUAGES > LANGUAGE
LANGUE *n* language considered as an abstract system or a social institution
LANGUED *adj* having a tongue
LANGUES > LANGUE
LANGUET *n* anything resembling a tongue in shape or function
LANGUETS > LANGUET
LANGUETTE *same as* > LANGUET
LANGUID *adj* lacking energy or enthusiasm
LANGUIDLY > LANGUID
LANGUISH *vb* suffer neglect or hardship
LANGUOR *n* state of dreamy relaxation
LANGUORS > LANGUOR
LANGUR *n* any of various agile arboreal Old World monkeys of the genus *Presbytis*
LANGURS > LANGUR
LANIARD *same as* > LANYARD
LANIARDS > LANIARD
LANIARIES > LANIARY
LANIARY *adj* (esp of canine teeth) adapted for tearing ▷ *n* tooth adapted for tearing
LANITAL *n* fibre used in production of synthetic wool
LANITALS > LANITAL
LANK *adj* (of hair) straight and limp ▷ *vb* become or cause to become lank
LANKED > LANK
LANKER > LANK
LANKEST > LANK
LANKIER > LANKY
LANKIEST > LANKY
LANKILY > LANKY
LANKINESS > LANKY
LANKING > LANK
LANKLY > LANK
LANKNESS > LANK
LANKS > LANK
LANKY *adj* ungracefully tall and thin
LANNER *n* large falcon of Mediterranean regions, N Africa, and S Asia
LANNERET *n* male or tercel of the lanner falcon
LANNERETS > LANNERET
LANNERS > LANNER
LANOLATED > LANOLIN
LANOLIN *n* grease from sheep's wool used in ointments etc
LANOLINE *same as* > LANOLIN
LANOLINES > LANOLINE
LANOLINS > LANOLIN
LANOSE *same as* > LANATE
LANOSITY > LANOSE
LANT *n* stale urine
LANTANA *n* shrub with orange or yellow flowers, considered a weed in Australia
LANTANAS > LANTANA
LANTERLOO *n* old card game
LANTERN *n* light in a transparent protective case ▷ *vb* supply with lantern
LANTERNED > LANTERN
LANTERNS > LANTERN
LANTHANON *n* one of a group of chemical elements
LANTHANUM *n* silvery-white metallic element
LANTHORN *archaic word for* > LANTERN
LANTHORNS > LANTHORN
LANTS > LANT
LANTSKIP *another word for* > LANDSCAPE
LANTSKIPS > LANTSKIP
> LANUGO
LANUGO *n* layer of fine hairs, esp the covering of the human fetus before birth
LANUGOS > LANUGO
LANX *n* dish; plate
LANYARD *n* cord worn round the neck to hold a knife or whistle
LANYARDS > LANYARD
LAODICEAN *adj* indifferent, esp in religious matters ▷ *n* person having a lukewarm attitude towards religious matter
LAOGAI *n* forced labour camp in China
LAOGAIS > LAOGAI
LAP *n* part between the waist and knees of a person when sitting ▷ *vb* overtake an opponent so as to be one or more circuits ahead
LAPBOARD *n* flat board tha can be used on the lap as a makeshift table or desk
LAPBOARDS > LAPBOARD
LAPDOG *n* small pet dog
LAPDOGS > LAPDOG
LAPEL *n* part of the front o a coat or jacket folded bac towards the shoulders
LAPELED > LAPEL
LAPELLED > LAPEL
LAPELS > LAPEL
LAPFUL *same as* > LAP
LAPFULS > LAPFUL
LAPHELD *adj* (esp of a personal computer) small enough to be used on one lap
LAPIDARY *adj* of or relatin to stones ▷ *n* person who cuts, polishes, sets, or deals in gemstones
LAPIDATE *vb* pelt with stones
LAPIDATED > LAPIDATE
LAPIDATES > LAPIDATE
LAPIDEOUS *adj* having appearance or texture of stone
LAPIDES > LAPIS
LAPIDIFIC *adj* transforming into stone
LAPIDIFY *vb* change into stone
LAPIDIST *n* cutter and engraver of precious stones
LAPIDISTS > LAPIDIST
LAPILLI > LAPILLUS
LAPILLUS *n* small piece of lava thrown from a volcano
LAPIN *n* castrated rabbit
LAPINS > LAPIN
LAPIS as in *lapis lazuli* brilliant blue mineral usec as a gemstone
LAPISES > LAPIS
LAPJE *same as* > LAPPIE
LAPJES > LAPJE
LAPPED > LAP
LAPPEL *same as* > LAPEL
LAPPELS > LAPPEL
LAPPER *n* one that laps ▷ *vb* curdle
LAPPERED > LAPPER
LAPPERING > LAPPER
LAPPERS > LAPPER
LAPPET *n* small hanging flap or piece of lace
LAPPETED > LAPPET
LAPPETS > LAPPET
LAPPIE *n* rag

APPIES > LAPPIE
APPING > LAP
APPINGS > LAP
APS > LAP
APSABLE > LAPSE
APSANG *n* smoky-tasting Chinese tea
APSANGS > LAPSANG
APSE *n* temporary drop in a standard, esp through forgetfulness or carelessness ▷ *vb* drop in standard
APSED > LAPSE
APSER > LAPSE
APSERS > LAPSE
APSES > LAPSE
APSIBLE > LAPSE
APSING > LAPSE
APSTONE *n* device used by a cobbler on which leather is beaten
APSTONES > LAPSTONE
APSTRAKE *n* clinker-built boat
APSTREAK *same as* > LAPSTRAKE
APSUS *n* lapse or error
APTOP *adj* small enough to fit on a user's lap ▷ *n* computer small enough to fit on a user's lap
APTOPS > LAPTOP
APTRAY *n* tray with a cushioned underside, designed to rest in a person's lap while supporting reading material, etc
APTRAYS > LAPTRAY
APWING *n* plover with a tuft of feathers on the head
APWINGS > LAPWING
APWORK *n* work with lapping edges
APWORKS > LAPWORK
AQUEARIA *n* ceiling made of panels
AR *n* boy or young man
ARBOARD *n* port (side of a ship)
ARBOARDS > LARBOARD
ARCENER > LARCENY
ARCENERS > LARCENY
ARCENIES > LARCENY
ARCENIST > LARCENY
ARCENOUS > LARCENY
ARCENY *n* theft
ARCH *n* deciduous coniferous tree
ARCHEN *adj* of larch
ARCHES > LARCH
ARD *n* soft white fat obtained from a pig ▷ *vb* insert strips of bacon in (meat) before cooking
ARDALITE *n* type of mineral
ARDED > LARD
ARDER *n* storeroom for food
ARDERER *n* person in charge of larder
ARDERERS > LARDERER
LARDERS > LARDER
LARDIER > LARDY
LARDIEST > LARDY
LARDING > LARD
LARDLIKE > LARD
LARDON *n* strip or cube of fat or bacon used in larding meat
LARDONS > LARDON
LARDOON *same as* > LARDON
LARDOONS > LARDOON
LARDS > LARD
LARDY *adj* fat
LARE *another word for* > LORE
LAREE *n* Asian fish-hook formerly used as currency
LAREES > LAREE
LARES > LARE
LARGANDO *adv* (music) growing slower and more marked
LARGE *adj* great in size, number, or extent ▷ *n* formerly, musical note of particular length
LARGELY *adv* principally
LARGEN *another word for* > ENLARGE
LARGENED > LARGEN
LARGENESS > LARGE
LARGENING > LARGEN
LARGENS > LARGEN
LARGER > LARGE
LARGES > LARGE
LARGESS *same as* > LARGESSE
LARGESSE *n* generous giving, esp of money
LARGESSES > LARGESSE
LARGEST > LARGE
LARGHETTO *adv* be performed moderately slowly ▷ *n* piece or passage to be performed in this way
LARGISH *adj* fairly large
LARGITION *n* act of being generous
LARGO *adv* in a slow and dignified manner ▷ *n* piece or passage to be performed in a slow and stately manner
LARGOS > LARGO
LARI *n* standard monetary unit of Georgia, divided into 100 tetri
LARIAT *n* lasso ▷ *vb* tether with lariat
LARIATED > LARIAT
LARIATING > LARIAT
LARIATS > LARIAT
LARINE *adj* of, relating to, or resembling a gull
LARIS > LARI
LARK *n* small brown songbird, skylark ▷ *vb* have a good time by frolicking
LARKED > LARK
LARKER > LARK
LARKERS > LARK
LARKIER > LARKY
LARKIEST > LARKY
LARKINESS > LARKY
LARKING > LARK
LARKISH > LARK
LARKS > LARK
LARKSOME *adj* mischievous
LARKSPUR *n* plant with spikes of blue, pink, or white flowers with spurs
LARKSPURS > LARKSPUR
LARKY *adj* frolicsome or mischievous
LARMIER *n* pouch under lower eyelid of deer
LARMIERS > LARMIER
LARN *vb* learn
LARNAKES > LARNAX
LARNAX *n* coffin made of terracotta
LARNED > LARN
LARNEY *n* white person ▷ *adj* (of clothes) smart
LARNEYS > LARNEY
LARNIER > LARNEY
LARNIEST > LARNEY
LARNING > LARN
LARNS > LARN
LAROID *adj* relating to Larus genus of gull family
LARRIGAN *n* knee-high oiled leather moccasin boot worn by trappers, etc
LARRIGANS > LARRIGAN
LARRIKIN *n* mischievous or unruly person
LARRIKINS > LARRIKIN
LARRUP *vb* beat or flog
LARRUPED > LARRUP
LARRUPER > LARRUP
LARRUPERS > LARRUP
LARRUPING > LARRUP
LARRUPPED > LARRUP
LARRUPS > LARRUP
LARS > LAR
LARUM *archaic word for* > ALARM
LARUMS > LARUM
LARVA *n* insect in an immature stage, often resembling a worm
LARVAE > LARVA
LARVAL > LARVA
LARVAS > LARVA
LARVATE *adj* masked; concealed
LARVATED *same as* > LARVATE
LARVICIDE *n* chemical used for killing larvae
LARVIFORM *adj* in the form of a larva
LARVIKITE *n* type of mineral
LARYNGAL *adj* laryngeal ▷ *n* sound articulated in the larynx
LARYNGALS > LARYNGAL
LARYNGEAL *adj* of or relating to the larynx
LARYNGES > LARYNX
LARYNX *n* part of the throat containing the vocal cords
LARYNXES > LARYNX
LAS > LA
LASAGNA *same as* > LASAGNE
LASAGNAS > LASAGNA
LASAGNE *n* pasta in wide flat sheets
LASAGNES > LASAGNE
LASCAR *n* East Indian seaman
LASCARS > LASCAR
LASE *vb* (of a substance, such as carbon dioxide or ruby) to be capable of acting as a laser
LASED > LASE
LASER *n* device that produces a very narrow intense beam of light, used for cutting very hard materials and in surgery etc
LASERDISC *n* disk similar in size to a long-playing record, on which data is stored in pits in a similar way to data storage on a compact disk
LASERDISK *same as* > LASERDISC
LASERS > LASER
LASERWORT *n* type of plant
LASES > LASE
LASH *n* eyelash ▷ *vb* hit with a whip
LASHED > LASH
LASHER > LASH
LASHERS > LASH
LASHES > LASH
LASHING > LASH
LASHINGLY > LASH
LASHINGS *pl n* great amount of
LASHINS *variant of* > LASHINGS
LASHKAR *n* troop of Indian men with weapons
LASHKARS > LASHKAR
LASING > LASE
LASINGS > LASE
LASKET *n* loop at the foot of a sail onto which an extra sail may be fastened
LASKETS > LASKET
LASQUE *n* flat-cut diamond
LASQUES > LASQUE
LASS *n* girl
LASSES > LASS
LASSI *n* cold drink made with yoghurt or buttermilk and flavoured with sugar, salt, or a mild spice
LASSIE *n* little lass
LASSIES > LASSIE
LASSIS > LASSI
LASSITUDE *n* physical or mental weariness
LASSLORN *adj* abandoned by a young girl
LASSO *n* rope with a noose for catching cattle and horses ▷ *vb* catch with a lasso
LASSOCK *another word for* > LASS
LASSOCKS > LASSOCK
LASSOED > LASSO

LASSOER > LASSO
LASSOERS > LASSO
LASSOES > LASSO
LASSOING > LASSO
LASSOS > LASSO
LASSU *n* slow part of csárdás folk dance
LASSUS > LASSU
LAST *adv* coming at the end or after all others ▷ *adj* only remaining ▷ *n* last person or thing ▷ *vb* continue
LASTAGE *n* space for storing goods in ship
LASTAGES > LASTAGE
LASTBORN *n* last child to be born
LASTBORNS > LASTBORN
LASTED > LAST
LASTER > LAST
LASTERS > LAST
LASTING *adj* existing or remaining effective for a long time ▷ *n* strong durable closely woven fabric used for shoe uppers, etc
LASTINGLY > LASTING
LASTINGS > LASTING
LASTLY *adv* at the end or at the last point
LASTS > LAST
LAT *n* former coin of Latvia
LATAH *n* psychological condition in which a traumatized individual becomes anxious and suggestible
LATAHS > LATAH
LATAKIA *n* type of Turkish tobacco
LATAKIAS > LATAKIA
LATCH *n* fastening for a door with a bar and lever ▷ *vb* fasten with a latch
LATCHED > LATCH
LATCHES > LATCH
LATCHET *n* shoe fastening, such as a thong or lace
LATCHETS > LATCHET
LATCHING > LATCH
LATCHKEY *n* key for an outside door or gate, esp one that lifts a latch
LATCHKEYS > LATCHKEY
LATE *adj* after the normal or expected time ▷ *adv* after the normal or expected time
LATECOMER *n* person or thing that comes late
LATED *archaic word for* > BELATED
LATEEN *adj* denoting a rig with a triangular sail bent to a yard hoisted to the head of a low mast
LATEENER *n* lateen-rigged ship
LATEENERS > LATEEN
LATEENS > LATEEN
LATELY *adv* in recent times
LATEN *vb* become or cause to become late
LATENCE > LATENT
LATENCES > LATENCE
LATENCIES > LATENT
LATENCY > LATENT
LATENED > LATEN
LATENESS > LATE
LATENING > LATEN
LATENS > LATEN
LATENT *adj* hidden and not yet developed ▷ *n* fingerprint that is not visible to the eye
LATENTLY > LATENT
LATENTS > LATENT
LATER *adv* afterwards
LATERA > LATUS
LATERAD *adv* towards the side
LATERAL *adj* of or relating to the side or sides ▷ *n* lateral object, part, passage, or movement ▷ *vb* pass laterally
LATERALED > LATERAL
LATERALLY > LATERAL
LATERALS > LATERAL
LATERBORN *adj* born later
LATERISE *same as* > LATERIZE
LATERISED > LATERISE
LATERISES > LATERISE
LATERITE *n* any of a group of deposits consisting of residual insoluble ferric and aluminium oxides
LATERITES > LATERITE
LATERITIC > LATERITE
LATERIZE *vb* develop into a laterite
LATERIZED > LATERIZE
LATERIZES > LATERIZE
LATESCENT *n* becoming latent
LATEST *n* the most recent news, fashion, etc
LATESTS > LATEST
LATEWAKE *n* vigil held over corpse
LATEWAKES > LATEWAKE
LATEWOOD *n* wood formed later in tree's growing season
LATEWOODS > LATEWOOD
LATEX *n* milky fluid found in some plants, esp the rubber tree, used in making rubber
LATEXES > LATEX
LATH *n* thin strip of wood used to support plaster, tiles, etc ▷ *vb* attach laths to (a ceiling, roof, floor, etc)
LATHE *n* machine for turning wood or metal while it is being shaped ▷ *vb* shape, bore, or cut a screw thread in or on (a workpiece) on a lathe
LATHED > LATHE
LATHEE *same as* > LATHI
LATHEES > LATHEE
LATHEN *adj* covered with laths
LATHER *n* froth of soap and water ▷ *vb* make frothy
LATHERED > LATHER
LATHERER > LATHER
LATHERERS > LATHER
LATHERIER > LATHER
LATHERING > LATHER
LATHERS > LATHER
LATHERY > LATHER
LATHES > LATHE
LATHI *n* long heavy wooden stick used as a weapon in India, esp by the police
LATHIER > LATHY
LATHIEST > LATHY
LATHING > LATHE
LATHINGS > LATHE
LATHIS > LATHI
LATHLIKE > LATH
LATHS > LATH
LATHWORK *n* work made of laths
LATHWORKS > LATHWORK
LATHY *adj* resembling a lath, esp in being tall and thin
LATHYRISM *n* neurological disease often resulting in weakness and paralysis of the legs
LATHYRUS *n* genus of climbing plant
LATI > LATUS
LATICES > LATEX
LATICIFER *n* cell or group of cells in a plant that contains latex
LATICLAVE *n* broad stripe on Roman senator's tunic
LATIFONDI *pl n* large agricultural estates in ancient Rome
LATIGO *n* strap on horse's saddle
LATIGOES > LATIGO
LATIGOS > LATIGO
LATILLA *n* stick making up part of ceiling
LATILLAS > LATILLA
LATIMERIA *n* any coelacanth fish of the genus *Latimeria*
LATINA *n* female inhabitant of the US who is of Latin American origin
LATINAS > LATINA
LATINISE *same as* > LATINIZE
LATINISED > LATINISE
LATINISES > LATINISE
LATINITY *n* facility in the use of Latin
LATINIZE *vb* translate into Latin
LATINIZED > LATINIZE
LATINIZES > LATINIZE
LATINO *n* male inhabitant of the US who is of Latin American origin
LATINOS > LATINO
LATISH *adv* rather late ▷ *adj* rather late
LATITANCY > LATITANT
LATITANT *adj* concealed
LATITAT *n* writ presuming that person accused was hiding
LATITATS > LATITAT
LATITUDE *n* angular distance measured in degrees N or S of the equator
LATITUDES > LATITUDE
LATKE *n* crispy Jewish pancake
LATKES > LATKE
LATOSOL *n* type of deep, well-drained soil
LATOSOLIC > LATOSOL
LATOSOLS > LATOSOL
LATRANT *adj* barking
LATRATION *n* instance of barking
LATRIA *n* adoration that may be offered to God alone
LATRIAS > LATRIA
LATRINE *n* toilet in a barracks or camp
LATRINES > LATRINE
LATROCINY *n* banditry
LATRON *n* bandit
LATRONS > LATRON
LATS > LAT
LATTE *n* coffee made with hot milk
LATTEN *n* metal or alloy, esp brass, made in thin sheets
LATTENS > LATTEN
LATTER *adj* second of two
LATTERLY *adv* recently
LATTES > LATTE
LATTICE *n* framework of intersecting strips of wood, metal, etc ▷ *vb* make, adorn, or supply with a lattice
LATTICED > LATTICE
LATTICES > LATTICE
LATTICING > LATTICE
LATTICINI > LATTICINO
LATTICINO *n* type of Italian glass
LATTIN *n* brass alloy beaten into a thin sheet
LATTINS > LATTIN
LATU *n* type of seaweed
LATUS as in *latus rectum* (in geometry) chord that passes through the focus of a conic and is perpendicular to the major axis
LAUAN *n* type of wood used in furniture-making
LAUANS > LAUAN
LAUCH *Scots form of* > LAUGH
LAUCHING > LAUCH
LAUCHS > LAUCH
LAUD *vb* praise or glorify ▷ *n* praise or glorification
LAUDABLE *adj* praiseworthy
LAUDABLY > LAUDABLE
LAUDANUM *n* opium-based

sedative
LAUDANUMS > LAUDANUM
LAUDATION *formal word for* > PRAISE
LAUDATIVE *same as* > LAUDATORY
LAUDATOR *n* one who praises highly
LAUDATORS > LAUDATOR
LAUDATORY *adj* praising or glorifying
LAUDED > LAUD
LAUDER > LAUD
LAUDERS > LAUD
LAUDING > LAUD
LAUDS *n* traditional morning prayer of the Western Church, constituting with matins the first of the seven canonical hours
LAUF *n* run in bobsleighing
LAUFS > LAUF
LAUGH *vb* make inarticulate sounds with the voice expressing amusement, merriment, or scorn ▷ *n* act or instance of laughing
LAUGHABLE *adj* ridiculously inadequate
LAUGHABLY > LAUGHABLE
LAUGHED > LAUGH
LAUGHER > LAUGH
LAUGHERS > LAUGH
LAUGHFUL > LAUGH
LAUGHIER > LAUGHY
LAUGHIEST > LAUGHY
LAUGHING > LAUGH
LAUGHINGS > LAUGH
LAUGHLINE *n* funny line in dialogue
LAUGHS > LAUGH
LAUGHSOME *adj* causing laughter
LAUGHTER *n* sound or action of laughing
LAUGHTERS > LAUGHTER
LAUGHY *adj* tending to laugh a lot
LAUNCE *old form of* > LANCE
LAUNCED > LAUNCE
LAUNCES > LAUNCE
LAUNCH *vb* put (a ship or boat) into the water, esp for the first time ▷ *n* launching
LAUNCHED > LAUNCH
LAUNCHER *n* any installation, vehicle, or other device for launching rockets, missiles, or other projectiles
LAUNCHERS > LAUNCHER
LAUNCHES > LAUNCH
LAUNCHING > LAUNCH
LAUNCHPAD *n* platform from which a spacecraft is launched
LAUNCING > LAUNCE
LAUND *n* open grassy space
LAUNDER *vb* wash and iron (clothes and linen) ▷ *n* water trough, esp one used for washing ore in mining
LAUNDERED > LAUNDER
LAUNDERER > LAUNDER
LAUNDERS > LAUNDER
LAUNDRESS *n* woman who launders clothes, sheets, etc, for a living
LAUNDRIES > LAUNDRY
LAUNDRY *n* clothes etc for washing or which have recently been washed
LAUNDS > LAUND
LAURA *n* group of monastic cells
LAURAE > LAURA
LAURAS > LAURA
LAUREATE *adj* crowned with laurel leaves as a sign of honour ▷ *n* person honoured with an award for art or science ▷ *vb* crown with laurel
LAUREATED > LAUREATE
LAUREATES > LAUREATE
LAUREL *n* glossy-leaved shrub, bay tree ▷ *vb* crown with laurel
LAURELED > LAUREL
LAURELING > LAUREL
LAURELLED > LAUREL
LAURELS > LAUREL
LAURIC as in *lauric acid* dodecanoic acid
LAURYL as in *lauryl alcohol* crystalline solid used to make detergents
LAURYLS > LAURYL
LAUWINE *n* avalanche
LAUWINES > LAUWINE
LAV *short for* > LAVATORY
LAVA *n* molten rock thrown out by volcanoes, which hardens as it cools
LAVABO *n* ritual washing of the celebrant's hands after the offertory at Mass
LAVABOES > LAVABO
LAVABOS > LAVABO
LAVAFORM *n* in form of lava
LAVAGE *n* washing out of a hollow organ by flushing with water
LAVAGES > LAVAGE
LAVALAVA *n* draped skirtlike garment worn by Polynesians
LAVALAVAS > LAVALAVA
LAVALIER *n* decorative pendant worn on chain
LAVALIERE *same as* > LAVALIER
LAVALIERS > LAVALIER
LAVALIKE > LAVA
LAVAS > LAVA
LAVASH *n* Armenian flat bread
LAVASHES > LAVASH
LAVATERA *n* any plant of the genus *Lavatera*, closely resembling mallow
LAVATERAS > LAVATERA
LAVATION *n* act or process of washing
LAVATIONS > LAVATION
LAVATORY *n* toilet
LAVE *archaic word for* > WASH
LAVED > LAVE
LAVEER *vb* (in sailing) tack
LAVEERED > LAVEER
LAVEERING > LAVEER
LAVEERS > LAVEER
LAVEMENT *n* washing with injections of water
LAVEMENTS > LAVEMENT
LAVENDER *n* shrub with fragrant flowers ▷ *adj* bluish-purple
LAVENDERS > LAVENDER
LAVER *n* large basin of water used by priests for ritual ablutions
LAVEROCK *Scot and northern English dialect word for* > SKYLARK
LAVEROCKS > LAVEROCK
LAVERS > LAVER
LAVES > LAVE
LAVING > LAVE
LAVISH *adj* great in quantity or richness ▷ *vb* give or spend generously
LAVISHED > LAVISH
LAVISHER > LAVISH
LAVISHERS > LAVISH
LAVISHES > LAVISH
LAVISHEST > LAVISH
LAVISHING > LAVISH
LAVISHLY > LAVISH
LAVOLT *same as* > LAVOLTA
LAVOLTA *n* Italian dance of the 16th and 17th centuries ▷ *vb* dance the lavolta
LAVOLTAED > LAVOLTA
LAVOLTAS > LAVOLTA
LAVOLTED > LAVOLT
LAVOLTING > LAVOLT
LAVOLTS > LAVOLT
LAVRA *same as* > LAURA
LAVRAS > LAVRA
LAVROCK *same as* > LAVEROCK
LAVROCKS > LAVROCK
LAVS > LAV
LAW *n* rule binding on a community ▷ *vb* prosecute ▷ *adj* (in archaic usage) low
LAWBOOK *n* book on subject of law
LAWBOOKS > LAWBOOK
LAWED > LAW
LAWER > LAW
LAWEST > LAW
LAWFUL *adj* allowed by law
LAWFULLY > LAWFUL
LAWGIVER *n* giver of a code of laws
LAWGIVERS > LAWGIVER
LAWGIVING > LAWGIVER
LAWIN *n* bill or reckoning
LAWINE *n* avalanche
LAWINES > LAWINE
LAWING *same as* > LAWIN
LAWINGS > LAWING
LAWINS > LAWIN
LAWK *interj* used to show surprise
LAWKS *same as* > LAWK
LAWLAND *same as* > LOWLAND
LAWLANDS > LAWLAND
LAWLESS *adj* breaking the law, esp in a violent way
LAWLESSLY > LAWLESS
LAWLIKE > LAW
LAWMAKER *same as* > LAWGIVER
LAWMAKERS > LAWMAKER
LAWMAKING *n* process of legislating
LAWMAN *n* officer of the law, such as a policeman or sheriff
LAWMEN > LAWMAN
LAWMONGER *n* inferior lawyer
LAWN *n* area of tended and mown grass
LAWNIER > LAWN
LAWNIEST > LAWN
LAWNMOWER *n* machine for cutting grass on lawns
LAWNS > LAWN
LAWNY > LAWN
LAWS > LAW
LAWSUIT *n* court case brought by one person or group against another
LAWSUITS > LAWSUIT
LAWYER *n* professionally qualified legal expert ▷ *vb* act as lawyer
LAWYERED > LAWYER
LAWYERING > LAWYER
LAWYERLY > LAWYER
LAWYERS > LAWYER
LAX *adj* not strict ▷ *n* laxative
LAXATION *n* act of making lax or the state of being lax
LAXATIONS > LAXATION
LAXATIVE *adj* (medicine) inducing the emptying of the bowels ▷ *n* medicine that induces the emptying of the bowels
LAXATIVES > LAXATIVE
LAXATOR *n* muscle that loosens body part
LAXATORS > LAXATOR
LAXER > LAX
LAXES > LAX
LAXEST > LAX
LAXISM > LAXIST
LAXISMS > LAXIST
LAXIST *n* lenient or tolerant person
LAXISTS > LAXIST
LAXITIES > LAX
LAXITY > LAX
LAXLY > LAX
LAXNESS > LAX
LAXNESSES > LAX
LAY > LIE
LAYABOUT *n* lazy person ▷ *vb* hit out with violent and repeated blows in all directions
LAYABOUTS > LAYABOUT
LAYAWAY *n* merchandise reserved for future delivery

LAYAWAYS > LAYAWAY
LAYBACK *n* technique for climbing cracks by pulling on one side of the crack with the hands and pressing on the other with the feet ▷ *vb* in climbing, use layback technique
LAYBACKED > LAYBACK
LAYBACKS > LAYBACK
LAYDEEZ *pl n* jocular spelling of ladies, as pronounced in a mid-Atlantic accent
LAYED > LAY
LAYER *n* single thickness of some substance, as a cover or coating on a surface ▷ *vb* form a layer
LAYERAGE *n* covering stem or branch with soil to encourage new roots
LAYERAGES > LAYERAGE
LAYERED > LAYER
LAYERING *n* method of propagation that induces a shoot or branch to take root while it is still attached to the parent plant
LAYERINGS > LAYERING
LAYERS > LAYER
LAYETTE *n* clothes for a newborn baby
LAYETTES > LAYETTE
LAYIN *n* basketball score made by dropping ball into basket
LAYING > LAY
LAYINGS > LAY
LAYINS > LAYIN
LAYLOCK *old form of* > LILAC
LAYLOCKS > LAYLOCK
LAYMAN *n* person who is not a member of the clergy
LAYMEN > LAYMAN
LAYOFF *n* act of suspending employees
LAYOFFS > LAYOFF
LAYOUT *n* arrangement, esp of matter for printing or of a building
LAYOUTS > LAYOUT
LAYOVER *n* break in a journey
LAYOVERS > LAYOVER
LAYPEOPLE > LAYPERSON
LAYPERSON *n* person who is not a member of the clergy
LAYS > LIE
LAYSHAFT *n* auxiliary shaft in a gearbox
LAYSHAFTS > LAYSHAFT
LAYSTALL *n* place where waste is deposited
LAYSTALLS > LAYSTALL
LAYTIME *n* time allowed for loading cargo
LAYTIMES > LAYTIME
LAYUP *n* period of incapacity through illness
LAYUPS > LAYUP
LAYWOMAN *n* woman who is not a member of the clergy
LAYWOMEN > LAYWOMAN
LAZAR *archaic word for* > LEPER
LAZARET *same as* > LAZARETTO
LAZARETS > LAZARET
LAZARETTE *same as* > LAZARETTO
LAZARETTO *n* small locker at the stern of a boat or a storeroom between decks of a ship
LAZARS > LAZAR
LAZE *vb* be idle or lazy ▷ *n* time spent lazing
LAZED > LAZE
LAZES > LAZE
LAZIED > LAZY
LAZIER > LAZY
LAZIES > LAZY
LAZIEST > LAZY
LAZILY > LAZY
LAZINESS > LAZY
LAZING > LAZE
LAZO *another word for* > LASSO
LAZOED > LAZO
LAZOES > LAZO
LAZOING > LAZO
LAZOS > LAZO
LAZULI *n* lapis lazuli
LAZULIS > LAZULI
LAZULITE *n* blue mineral, consisting of hydrated magnesium iron phosphate, occurring in metamorphic rocks
LAZULITES > LAZULITE
LAZURITE *n* rare blue mineral consisting of a sodium-calcium-aluminium silicate
LAZURITES > LAZURITE
LAZY *vb* laze ▷ *adj* not inclined to work or exert oneself
LAZYBONES *n* lazy person
LAZYING > LAZY
LAZYISH > LAZY
LAZZARONE *n* Italian street beggar
LAZZARONI > LAZZARONE
LAZZI > LAZZO
LAZZO *n* comic routine in the commedia dell'arte
LEA *n* meadow
LEACH *vb* remove or be removed from a substance by a liquid passing through it ▷ *n* act or process of leaching
LEACHABLE > LEACH
LEACHATE *n* water that carries salts dissolved out of materials through which it has percolated
LEACHATES > LEACHATE
LEACHED > LEACH
LEACHER > LEACH
LEACHERS > LEACH
LEACHES > LEACH
LEACHIER > LEACHY
LEACHIEST > LEACHY
LEACHING > LEACH
LEACHINGS > LEACH
LEACHOUR *old form of* > LECHER
LEACHOURS > LEACHOUR
LEACHY *adj* porous
LEAD *vb* guide or conduct ▷ *n* first or most prominent place ▷ *adj* acting as a leader or lead
LEADED *adj* (of windows) made from many small panes of glass held together by lead strips
LEADEN *adj* heavy or sluggish ▷ *vb* become or cause to become leaden
LEADENED > LEADEN
LEADENING > LEADEN
LEADENLY > LEADEN
LEADENS > LEADEN
LEADER *n* person who leads
LEADERENE *n* strong female leader
LEADERS > LEADER
LEADIER > LEADY
LEADIEST > LEADY
LEADING > LEAD
LEADINGLY > LEAD
LEADINGS > LEAD
LEADLESS *adj* without lead
LEADMAN *n* man who leads
LEADMEN > LEADMAN
LEADOFF *n* initial move or action
LEADOFFS > LEADOFF
LEADPLANT *n* N American shrub
LEADS > LEAD
LEADSCREW *n* threaded rod in a lathe
LEADSMAN *n* sailor who takes soundings with a lead line
LEADSMEN > LEADSMAN
LEADWORK *n* maintenance work involving lead pipes, etc
LEADWORKS > LEADWORK
LEADWORT *n* any shrub of the plumbaginaceous genus *Plumbago*
LEADWORTS > LEADWORT
LEADY *adj* like lead
LEAF *n* flat usu green blade attached to the stem of a plant ▷ *vb* turn (pages) cursorily
LEAFAGE *n* leaves of plants
LEAFAGES > LEAFAGE
LEAFBUD *n* bud producing leaves rather than flowers
LEAFBUDS > LEAFBUD
LEAFED > LEAF
LEAFERIES > LEAFERY
LEAFERY *n* foliage
LEAFIER > LEAFY
LEAFIEST > LEAFY
LEAFINESS > LEAFY
LEAFING > LEAF
LEAFLESS > LEAF
LEAFLET *n* sheet of printed matter for distribution ▷ *vb* distribute leaflets (to)
LEAFLETED > LEAFLET
LEAFLETER > LEAFLET
LEAFLETS > LEAFLET
LEAFLIKE > LEAF
LEAFS > LEAF
LEAFSTALK *n* stalk attaching a leaf to a stem or branch
LEAFWORM *n* cotton plant pest
LEAFWORMS > LEAFWORM
LEAFY *adj* covered with leaves
LEAGUE *n* association promoting the interests of its members
LEAGUED > LEAGUE
LEAGUER *vb* harass; beset ▷ *n* encampment, esp of besiegers
LEAGUERED > LEAGUER
LEAGUERS > LEAGUER
LEAGUES > LEAGUE
LEAGUING > LEAGUE
LEAK *n* hole or defect that allows the escape or entrance of liquid, gas, radiation, etc ▷ *vb* let liquid etc in or out
LEAKAGE *n* act or instance of leaking
LEAKAGES > LEAKAGE
LEAKED > LEAK
LEAKER > LEAK
LEAKERS > LEAK
LEAKIER > LEAKY
LEAKIEST > LEAKY
LEAKILY > LEAKY
LEAKINESS > LEAKY
LEAKING > LEAK
LEAKLESS > LEAK
LEAKPROOF *adj* not likely to leak
LEAKS > LEAK
LEAKY *adj* leaking or tending to leak
LEAL *adj* loyal
LEALER > LEAL
LEALEST > LEAL
LEALLY > LEAL
LEALTIES > LEAL
LEALTY > LEAL
LEAM *vb* shine
LEAMED > LEAM
LEAMING > LEAM
LEAMS > LEAM
LEAN *vb* rest (against) ▷ *adj* thin but healthy-looking ▷ *n* lean part of meat
LEANED > LEAN
LEANER > LEAN
LEANERS > LEAN
LEANEST > LEAN
LEANING > LEAN
LEANINGS > LEAN
LEANLY > LEAN
LEANNESS > LEAN
LEANS > LEAN
LEANT > LEAN
LEANY *old form of* > LEAN
LEAP *vb* make a sudden powerful jump ▷ *n* sudden powerful jump
LEAPED > LEAP

LEAPER > LEAP
LEAPEROUS *old form of* > LEPROUS
LEAPERS > LEAP
LEAPFROG *n* game in which a player vaults over another bending down ▷ *vb* play leapfrog
LEAPFROGS > LEAPFROG
LEAPING > LEAP
LEAPOROUS *old form of* > LEPROUS
LEAPROUS *old form of* > LEPROUS
LEAPS > LEAP
LEAPT > LEAP
LEAR *vb* instruct
LEARE *same as* > LEAR
LEARED > LEAR
LEARES > LEARE
LEARIER > LEARY
LEARIEST > LEARY
LEARINESS > LEARY
LEARING > LEAR
LEARN *vb* gain skill or knowledge by study, practice, or teaching
LEARNABLE > LEARN
LEARNED > LEARN
LEARNEDLY > LEARN
LEARNER *n* someone who is learning something
LEARNERS > LEARNER
LEARNING > LEARN
LEARNINGS > LEARN
LEARNS > LEARN
LEARNT > LEARN
LEARS > LEAR
LEARY *same as* > LEERY
LEAS > LEA
LEASABLE > LEASE
LEASE *n* contract by which land or property is rented for a stated time by the owner to a tenant ▷ *vb* let or rent by lease
LEASEBACK *n* property transaction in which the buyer leases the property to the seller
LEASED > LEASE
LEASEHOLD *adj* (land or property) held on lease ▷ *n* land or property held under a lease
LEASER > LEASE
LEASERS > LEASE
LEASES > LEASE
LEASH *n* lead for a dog ▷ *vb* control by a leash
LEASHED > LEASH
LEASHES > LEASH
LEASHING > LEASH
LEASING > LEASE
LEASINGS > LEASE
LEASOW *vb* pasture
LEASOWE *same as* > LEASOW
LEASOWED > LEASOW
LEASOWES > LEASOWE
LEASOWING > LEASOW
LEASOWS > LEASOW
LEAST *n* smallest amount ▷ *adj* smallest ▷ *n* smallest one ▷ *adv* in the smallest degree
LEASTS > LEAST
LEASTWAYS *adv* at least
LEASTWISE *same as* > LEASTWAYS
LEASURE *old form of* > LEISURE
LEASURES > LEASURE
LEAT *n* trench or ditch that conveys water to a mill wheel
LEATHER *n* material made from specially treated animal skins ▷ *adj* made of leather ▷ *vb* beat or thrash
LEATHERED > LEATHER
LEATHERN *adj* made of or resembling leather
LEATHERS > LEATHER
LEATHERY *adj* like leather, tough
LEATS > LEAT
LEAVE *vb* go away from ▷ *n* permission to be absent from work or duty
LEAVED *adj* with leaves
LEAVEN *n* substance that causes dough to rise ▷ *vb* raise with leaven
LEAVENED > LEAVEN
LEAVENING > LEAVEN
LEAVENOUS *adj* containing leaven
LEAVENS > LEAVEN
LEAVER > LEAVE
LEAVERS > LEAVE
LEAVES > LEAF
LEAVIER > LEAVY
LEAVIEST > LEAVY
LEAVING > LEAVE
LEAVINGS *pl n* something remaining, such as refuse
LEAVY *same as* > LEAFY
LEAZE *same as* > LEASE
LEAZES > LEAZE
LEBBEK *n* type of timber tree
LEBBEKS > LEBBEK
LEBEN *n* semiliquid food made from curdled milk in N Africa and the Levant
LEBENS > LEBEN
LEBKUCHEN *n* biscuit, originating from Germany, usually containing honey, spices, etc
LECANORA *n* type of lichen
LECANORAS > LECANORA
LECCIES > LECCY
LECCY *n* electricity
LECH *vb* behave lecherously (towards) ▷ *n* lecherous act or indulgence
LECHAIM *interj* drinking toast ▷ *n* small drink with which to toast something or someone
LECHAIMS > LECHAIM
LECHAYIM *same as* > LECHAIM
LECHAYIMS > LECHAYIM
LECHED > LECH
LECHER *n* man who has or shows excessive sexual desire ▷ *vb* behave lecherously
LECHERED > LECHER
LECHERIES > LECHERY
LECHERING > LECHER
LECHEROUS *adj* (of a man) having or showing excessive sexual desire
LECHERS > LECHER
LECHERY *n* unrestrained and promiscuous sexuality
LECHES > LECH
LECHING > LECH
LECHWE *n* African antelope
LECHWES > LECHWE
LECITHIN *n* yellow-brown compound found in plant and animal tissues
LECITHINS > LECITHIN
LECTERN *n* sloping reading desk, esp in a church
LECTERNS > LECTERN
LECTIN *n* type of protein possessing high affinity for a specific sugar
LECTINS > LECTIN
LECTION *n* variant reading of a passage in a particular copy or edition of a text
LECTIONS > LECTION
LECTOR *n* lecturer or reader in certain universities
LECTORATE > LECTOR
LECTORS > LECTOR
LECTOTYPE *n* specimen designated by author after the publication of a species name
LECTRESS *n* female reader
LECTURE *n* informative talk to an audience on a subject ▷ *vb* give a talk
LECTURED > LECTURE
LECTURER *n* person who lectures, esp in a university or college
LECTURERS > LECTURER
LECTURES > LECTURE
LECTURING > LECTURE
LECTURN *old form of* > LECTERN
LECTURNS > LECTURN
LECYTHI > LECYTHUS
LECYTHIS *n* genus of very tall trees
LECYTHUS *n* (in ancient Greece) a vase with a narrow neck
LED > LEAD
LEDDEN *n* language; speech
LEDDENS > LEDDEN
LEDGE *n* narrow shelf sticking out from a wall
LEDGED > LEDGE
LEDGER *n* book of debit and credit accounts of a firm ▷ *vb* fish using a wire trace that allows the bait to float freely while the weight sinks
LEDGERED > LEDGER
LEDGERING > LEDGER
LEDGERS > LEDGER
LEDGES > LEDGE
LEDGIER > LEDGE
LEDGIEST > LEDGE
LEDGY > LEDGE
LEDUM *n* evergreen shrub
LEDUMS > LEDUM
LEE *n* sheltered side ▷ *vb* (Scots) lie
LEEAR *Scots form of* > LIAR
LEEARS > LEEAR
LEEBOARD *n* one of two paddle-like boards that can be lowered along the lee side of a vessel to reduce sideways drift
LEEBOARDS > LEEBOARD
LEECH *n* species of bloodsucking worm ▷ *vb* use leeches to suck the blood of
LEECHDOM *n* remedy
LEECHDOMS > LEECHDOM
LEECHED > LEECH
LEECHEE *same as* > LITCHI
LEECHEES > LEECHEE
LEECHES > LEECH
LEECHING > LEECH
LEECHLIKE > LEECH
LEED > LEE
LEEING > LEE
LEEK *n* vegetable of the onion family with a long bulb and thick stem
LEEKS > LEEK
LEEP *vb* boil; scald
LEEPED > LEEP
LEEPING > LEEP
LEEPS > LEEP
LEER *vb* look or grin at in a sneering or suggestive manner ▷ *n* sneering or suggestive look or grin
LEERED > LEER
LEERIER > LEERY
LEERIEST > LEERY
LEERILY > LEERY
LEERINESS > LEERY
LEERING > LEER
LEERINGLY > LEER
LEERINGS > LEER
LEERS > LEER
LEERY *adj* suspicious or wary (of)
LEES *pl n* sediment of wine
LEESE *old form of* > LOOSE
LEESES > LEESE
LEESING > LEESE
LEET *n* list of candidates for an office
LEETLE *form of* > LITTLE
LEETS > LEET
LEEWARD *n* lee side ▷ *adv* towards this side ▷ *adj* of, in, or moving in the direction towards which the wind blows
LEEWARDLY > LEEWARD
LEEWARDS *adv* towards the lee side
LEEWAY *n* room for free movement within limits
LEEWAYS > LEEWAY
LEFT *adj* on the opposite side from right ▷ *n* left

side
LEFTE *old past tense of* > LIFT
LEFTER > LEFT
LEFTEST > LEFT
LEFTIE *same as* > LEFTY
LEFTIES > LEFTY
LEFTISH > LEFT
LEFTISM > LEFTIST
LEFTISMS > LEFTIST
LEFTIST *adj* (person) of the political left ▷ *n* person who supports the political left
LEFTISTS > LEFTIST
LEFTMOST > LEFT
LEFTMOSTS > LEFT
LEFTOVER *n* unused portion of food or material ▷ *adj* left as an unused portion
LEFTOVERS > LEFTOVER
LEFTS > LEFT
LEFTWARD *same as* > LEFTWARDS
LEFTWARDS *adv* towards or on the left
LEFTWING *adj* of or relating to the leftist faction of a party, etc
LEFTY *n* left-winger
LEG *n* one of the limbs on which a person or animal walks, runs, or stands
LEGACIES > LEGACY
LEGACY *n* thing left in a will
LEGAL *adj* established or permitted by law ▷ *n* legal expert
LEGALESE *n* conventional language in which legal documents are written
LEGALESES > LEGALESE
LEGALISE *same as* > LEGALIZE
LEGALISED > LEGALISE
LEGALISER > LEGALISE
LEGALISES > LEGALISE
LEGALISM *n* strict adherence to the letter of the law
LEGALISMS > LEGALISM
LEGALIST > LEGALISM
LEGALISTS > LEGALISM
LEGALITY *n* state or quality of being legal or lawful
LEGALIZE *vb* make legal
LEGALIZED > LEGALIZE
LEGALIZER > LEGALIZE
LEGALIZES > LEGALIZE
LEGALLY > LEGAL
LEGALS > LEGAL
LEGATARY *n* legatee
LEGATE *n* messenger or representative, esp from the Pope ▷ *vb* leave as legacy
LEGATED > LEGATE
LEGATEE *n* recipient of a legacy
LEGATEES > LEGATEE
LEGATES > LEGATE
LEGATINE > LEGATE
LEGATING > LEGATE
LEGATION *n* diplomatic minister and his staff
LEGATIONS > LEGATION
LEGATO *adv* (piece to be played) smoothly ▷ *n* style of playing with no gaps between notes
LEGATOR *n* person who gives a legacy or makes a bequest
LEGATORS > LEGATOR
LEGATOS > LEGATO
LEGEND *n* traditional story or myth
LEGENDARY *adj* famous
LEGENDISE *same as* > LEGENDIZE
LEGENDIST *n* writer of legends
LEGENDIZE *vb* make into legend
LEGENDRY > LEGEND
LEGENDS > LEGEND
LEGER *variant of* > LEDGER
LEGERING > LEGER
LEGERINGS > LEGER
LEGERITY *n* agility
LEGERS > LEGER
LEGES > LEX
LEGGE *vb* lighten or lessen
LEGGED > LEG
LEGGER *n* man who moves barge through tunnel using legs
LEGGERS > LEGGER
LEGGES > LEGGE
LEGGIER > LEGGY
LEGGIERO *adj* light; delicate
LEGGIEST > LEGGY
LEGGIN *same as* > LEGGING
LEGGINESS > LEGGY
LEGGING *n* extra outer covering for the lower leg
LEGGINGED > LEGGING
LEGGINGS > LEGGING
LEGGINS > LEGGIN
LEGGISM *n* blacklegging
LEGGISMS > LEGGISM
LEGGY *adj* having long legs
LEGHORN *n* type of Italian wheat straw that is woven into hats
LEGHORNS > LEGHORN
LEGIBLE *adj* easily read
LEGIBLY > LEGIBLE
LEGION *n* large military force ▷ *adj* very large or numerous
LEGIONARY *adj* of or relating to a legion ▷ *n* soldier belonging to a legion
LEGIONED *adj* arranged in legions
LEGIONS > LEGION
LEGISLATE *vb* make laws
LEGIST *n* person versed in the law
LEGISTS > LEGIST
LEGIT *n* legitimate or professionally respectable drama ▷ *adj* legitimate
LEGITIM *n* amount of inheritance due to children from father
LEGITIMS > LEGITIM
LEGITS > LEGIT
LEGLAN *same as* > LEGLIN
LEGLANS > LEGLAN
LEGLEN *same as* > LEGLIN
LEGLENS > LEGLEN
LEGLESS *adj* without legs
LEGLET *n* jewellery worn around the leg
LEGLETS > LEGLET
LEGLIKE > LEG
LEGLIN *n* milk-pail
LEGLINS > LEGLIN
LEGMAN *n* newsman who reports on news stories from the scene of action or original source
LEGMEN > LEGMAN
LEGONG *n* Indonesian dance
LEGONGS > LEGONG
LEGROOM *n* space to move one's legs comfortably, as in a car
LEGROOMS > LEGROOM
LEGS > LEG
LEGUAAN *n* large S African lizard
LEGUAANS > LEGUAAN
LEGUME *n* pod of a plant of the pea or bean family
LEGUMES > LEGUME
LEGUMIN *n* protein obtained mainly from the seeds of leguminous plants
LEGUMINS > LEGUMIN
LEGWARMER *n* one of a pair of garments resembling stockings without feet
LEGWEAR *n* clothing worn on the legs
LEGWEARS > LEGWEAR
LEGWORK *n* work that involves travelling on foot or as if on foot
LEGWORKS > LEGWORK
LEHAIM *same as* > LECHAIM
LEHAIMS > LEHAIM
LEHAYIM *same as* > LEHAIM
LEHAYIMS > LEHAYIM
LEHR *n* long tunnel-shaped oven used for annealing glass
LEHRJAHRE *n* apprenticeship
LEHRS > LEHR
LEHUA *n* flower of Hawaii
LEHUAS > LEHUA
LEI > LEU
LEIDGER *same as* > LEDGER
LEIDGERS > LEIDGER
LEIGER *same as* > LEDGER
LEIGERS > LEIGER
LEIOMYOMA *same as* > FIBROID
LEIPOA *n* Australian bird
LEIPOAS > LEIPOA
LEIR *same as* > LEAR
LEIRED > LEIR
LEIRING > LEIR
LEIRS > LEIR
LEIS > LEU
LEISH *adj* agile
LEISHER > LEISH
LEISHEST > LEISH
LEISLER *n* small bat
LEISLERS > LEISLER
LEISTER *n* spear with three or more prongs for spearing fish, esp salmon ▷ *vb* spear (a fish) with a leister
LEISTERED > LEISTER
LEISTERS > LEISTER
LEISURE *n* time for relaxation or hobbies ▷ *vb* have leisure
LEISURED > LEISURE
LEISURELY *adj* deliberate unhurried ▷ *adv* slowly
LEISURES > LEISURE
LEISURING > LEISURE
LEITMOTIF *n* recurring theme associated with a person, situation, or thought
LEITMOTIV *same as* > LEITMOTIF
LEK *n* area where birds gather for sexual display and courtship ▷ *vb* (of birds) gather at lek
LEKE *old form of* > LEAK
LEKGOTLA *n* meeting place for village assemblies, court cases, and meetings of village leaders
LEKGOTLAS > LEKGOTLA
LEKKED > LEK
LEKKER *adj* attractive or nice
LEKKING > LEK
LEKKINGS > LEK
LEKS > LEK
LEKU > LEK
LEKVAR *n* prune or apricot pie filling
LEKVARS > LEKVAR
LEKYTHI > LEKYTHOS
LEKYTHOI > LEKYTHOS
LEKYTHOS *n* Greek flask
LEKYTHUS *same as* > LEKYTHOS
LEMAN *n* beloved
LEMANS > LEMAN
LEME *same as* > LEAM
LEMED > LEME
LEMEL *n* metal filings
LEMELS > LEMEL
LEMES > LEME
LEMING > LEME
LEMMA *n* subsidiary proposition, proved for use in the proof of another proposition
LEMMAS > LEMMA
LEMMATA > LEMMA
LEMMATISE *same as* > LEMMATIZE
LEMMATIZE *vb* group together the inflected forms of (a word) for analysis as a single item
LEMMING *n* rodent of arctic regions, reputed to run

into the sea and drown during mass migrations
EMMINGS > LEMMING
EMNISCAL *adj* relating to a type of closed plane curve
EMNISCI > LEMNISCUS
EMNISCUS *technical name for* > FILLET
EMON *n* yellow oval fruit that grows on trees ▷ *adj* pale-yellow ▷ *vb* flavour with lemon
EMONADE *n* lemon-flavoured soft drink, often fizzy
EMONADES > LEMONADE
EMONED > LEMON
EMONFISH *n* type of game fish
EMONIER > LEMONY
EMONIEST > LEMONY
EMONING > LEMON
EMONISH > LEMON
EMONLIKE > LEMON
EMONS > LEMON
EMONWOOD *n* small tree of New Zealand
EMONY *adj* having or resembling the taste or colour of a lemon
EMPIRA *n* standard monetary unit of Honduras, divided into 100 centavos
EMPIRAS > LEMPIRA
EMUR *n* nocturnal animal like a small monkey, found in Madagascar
EMURES *pl n* spirits of the dead
EMURIAN *same as* > LEMUROID
EMURIANS > LEMURIAN
EMURINE *same as* > LEMUROID
EMURINES > LEMURINE
EMURLIKE > LEMUR
EMUROID *adj* of, relating to, or belonging to the superfamily which includes the lemurs and indrises ▷ *n* animal that resembles or is closely related to a lemur
EMUROIDS > LEMUROID
EMURS > LEMUR
END *vb* give the temporary use of
ENDABLE > LEND
ENDER > LEND
ENDERS > LEND
ENDING > LEND
ENDINGS > LEND
ENDS > LEND
ENES > LENIS
ENG *vb* linger ▷ *adj* long
ENGED > LENG
ENGER > LENG
ENGEST > LENG
ENGING > LENG
ENGS > LENG
ENGTH *n* extent or measurement from end to end
LENGTHEN *vb* make or become longer
LENGTHENS > LENGTHEN
LENGTHFUL > LENGTH
LENGTHIER > LENGTHY
LENGTHILY > LENGTHY
LENGTHMAN *n* person whose job it is to maintain a particular length of road or railway line
LENGTHMEN > LENGTHMAN
LENGTHS > LENGTH
LENGTHY *adj* very long or tiresome
LENIENCE > LENIENT
LENIENCES > LENIENT
LENIENCY > LENIENT
LENIENT *adj* tolerant, not strict or severe ▷ *n* lenient person
LENIENTLY > LENIENT
LENIENTS > LENIENT
LENIFIED > LENIFY
LENIFIES > LENIFY
LENIFY *vb* make lenient
LENIFYING > LENIFY
LENIS *adj* (of a consonant) pronounced with little muscular tension ▷ *n* consonant pronounced like this
LENITE *vb* undergo lenition
LENITED > LENITE
LENITES > LENITE
LENITIES > LENITY
LENITING > LENITE
LENITION *n* weakening of consonant sound
LENITIONS > LENITION
LENITIVE *adj* soothing or alleviating of pain or distress ▷ *n* lenitive drug
LENITIVES > LENITIVE
LENITY *n* mercy or clemency
LENO *n* (in textiles) a weave in which the warp yarns are twisted together in pairs between the weft or filling yarns
LENOS > LENO
LENS *n* piece of glass or similar material with one or both sides curved, used to bring together or spread light rays in cameras, spectacles, telescopes, etc
LENSE *same as* > LENS
LENSED *adj* incorporating a lens
LENSES > LENS
LENSING *n* materials which colour and diffuse light
LENSLESS > LENS
LENSMAN *n* camera operator
LENSMEN > LENSMAN
LENT > LEND
LENTANDO *adv* slowing down
LENTEN *adj* of or relating to Lent
LENTI > LENTO
LENTIC *adj* of, relating to, or inhabiting still water
LENTICEL *n* any of numerous pores in the stem of a woody plant
LENTICELS > LENTICEL
LENTICLE *n* lens-shaped layer of mineral or rock embedded in a matrix of different constitution
LENTICLES > LENTICLE
LENTICULE *n* small lentil
LENTIFORM *adj* shaped like a biconvex lens
LENTIGO *technical name for a* > FRECKLE
LENTIL *n* edible seed of a leguminous Asian plant
LENTILS > LENTIL
LENTISK *n* mastic tree
LENTISKS > LENTISK
LENTO *adv* slowly ▷ *n* movement or passage performed slowly
LENTOID *adj* lentiform ▷ *n* lentiform object
LENTOIDS > LENTOID
LENTOR *n* lethargy
LENTORS > LENTOR
LENTOS > LENTO
LENTOUS *adj* lethargic
LENVOY *another word for* > ENVOY
LENVOYS > LENVOY
LEONE *n* standard monetary unit of Sierra Leone, divided into 100 cents
LEONES > LEONE
LEONINE *adj* like a lion
LEOPARD *n* large spotted carnivorous animal of the cat family
LEOPARDS > LEOPARD
LEOTARD *n* tight-fitting garment covering the upper body, worn for dancing or exercise
LEOTARDED *adj* wearing a leotard
LEOTARDS > LEOTARD
LEP *dialect word for* > LEAP
LEPER *n* person suffering from leprosy
LEPERS > LEPER
LEPID *adj* amusing
LEPIDOTE *adj* covered with scales, scaly leaves, or spots ▷ *n* lepidote person, creature, or thing
LEPIDOTES > LEPIDOTE
LEPORID *adj* of, relating to, or belonging to the family of mammals that includes rabbits and hares ▷ *n* any animal belonging to this family
LEPORIDAE > LEPORID
LEPORIDS > LEPORID
LEPORINE *adj* of, relating to, or resembling a hare
LEPPED > LEP
LEPPING > LEP
LEPRA *n* leprosy
LEPRAS > LEPRA
LEPROSE *adj* having or denoting a whitish scurfy surface
LEPROSERY *n* hospital for leprosy sufferers
LEPROSIES > LEPROSY
LEPROSITY *n* state of being leprous
LEPROSY *n* disease attacking the nerves and skin, resulting in loss of feeling in the affected parts
LEPROTIC *adj* relating to leprosy
LEPROUS *adj* having leprosy
LEPROUSLY > LEPROUS
LEPS > LEP
LEPT > LEAP
LEPTA > LEPTON
LEPTIN *n* protein, produced by fat cells in the body, that acts on the brain to regulate the amount of additional fat laid down in the body
LEPTINS > LEPTIN
LEPTOME *n* tissue of plant conducting food
LEPTOMES > LEPTOME
LEPTON *n* any of a group of elementary particles with weak interactions
LEPTONIC > LEPTON
LEPTONS > LEPTON
LEPTOPHOS *n* type of pesticide
LEPTOSOME *n* person with a small bodily frame and a slender physique
LEPTOTENE *n* (in reproduction) early stage in cell division
LEQUEAR *same as* > LACUNAR
LEQUEARS > LEQUEAR
LERE *same as* > LEAR
LERED > LERE
LERES > LERE
LERING > LERE
LERNAEAN *adj* relating to Lerna
LERNEAN *same as* > LERNAEAN
LERP *n* crystallized honeydew
LERPS > LERP
LES *short form of* > LESBIAN
LESBIAN *n* homosexual woman ▷ *adj* of homosexual women
LESBIANS > LESBIAN
LESBIC *adj* relating to lesbians
LESBO *n* lesbian
LESBOS > LESBO
LESES > LES
LESION *n* structural change in an organ of the body caused by illness or injury ▷ *vb* cause lesions
LESIONED > LESION

LESIONING > LESION
LESIONS > LESION
LESPEDEZA *n* bush clover
LESS *n* smaller amount ▷ *adj* smaller in extent, degree, or duration ▷ *pron* smaller part or quantity ▷ *adv* smaller extent or degree ▷ *prep* after deducting, minus
LESSEE *n* person to whom a lease is granted
LESSEES > LESSEE
LESSEN *vb* make or become smaller or not as much
LESSENED > LESSEN
LESSENING > LESSEN
LESSENS > LESSEN
LESSER *adj* not as great in quantity, size, or worth
LESSES > LESS
LESSON *n* class or single period of instruction in a subject ▷ *vb* censure or punish
LESSONED > LESSON
LESSONING > LESSON
LESSONS > LESSON
LESSOR *n* person who grants a lease of property
LESSORS > LESSOR
LEST *conj* so as to prevent any possibility that ▷ *vb* listen
LESTED > LEST
LESTING > LEST
LESTS > LEST
LET *n* act of letting property ▷ *vb* obstruct
LETCH *same as* > LECH
LETCHED > LETCH
LETCHES > LETCH
LETCHING > LETCH
LETCHINGS > LETCH
LETDOWN *n* disappointment
LETDOWNS > LETDOWN
LETHAL *adj* deadly ▷ *n* weapon, etc capable of causing death
LETHALITY > LETHAL
LETHALLY > LETHAL
LETHALS > LETHAL
LETHARGIC > LETHARGY
LETHARGY *n* sluggishness or dullness
LETHE *n* forgetfulness
LETHEAN > LETHE
LETHEE *n* life-blood
LETHEES > LETHEE
LETHES > LETHE
LETHIED *adj* forgetful
LETS > LET
LETTABLE > LET
LETTED > LET
LETTER *n* written message, usu sent by post ▷ *vb* inscribe letters on
LETTERBOX *n* slot through which letters are delivered into a building
LETTERED *adj* learned
LETTERER > LETTER
LETTERERS > LETTER
LETTERING *n* act, art, or technique of inscribing letters on to something
LETTERMAN *n* successful college sportsman
LETTERMEN > LETTERMAN
LETTERN *another word for* > LECTERN
LETTERNS > LETTERN
LETTERS *pl n* literary knowledge or ability
LETTERSET *n* method of rotary printing in which ink is transferred from raised surfaces to paper via a rubber-covered cylinder
LETTING > LET
LETTINGS > LET
LETTRE *n* letter
LETTRES > LETTRE
LETTUCE *n* plant with large green leaves used in salads
LETTUCES > LETTUCE
LETUP *n* lessening or abatement
LETUPS > LETUP
LEU *n* standard monetary unit of Romania and Moldova, divided into 100 bani
LEUCAEMIA *same as* > LEUKAEMIA
LEUCAEMIC > LEUCAEMIA
LEUCEMIA *same as* > LEUKAEMIA
LEUCEMIAS > LEUCEMIA
LEUCEMIC > LEUCEMIA
LEUCH > LAUCH
LEUCHEN > LAUCH
LEUCIN *same as* > LEUCINE
LEUCINE *n* essential amino acid found in many proteins
LEUCINES > LEUCINE
LEUCINS > LEUCIN
LEUCITE *n* grey or white mineral consisting of potassium aluminium silicate
LEUCITES > LEUCITE
LEUCITIC > LEUCITE
LEUCO as in *leuco base* colourless compound formed by reducing a dye
LEUCOCYTE *n* white blood cell
LEUCOMA *n* white opaque scar of the cornea
LEUCOMAS > LEUCOMA
LEUCOSIN *n* albumin in cereal grains
LEUCOSINS > LEUCOSIN
LEUCOTOME *n* needle used in leucotomy
LEUCOTOMY *n* surgical operation of cutting some of the nerve fibres in the frontal lobes of the brain
LEUD *Scots word for* > BREADTH
LEUDES > LEUD
LEUDS > LEUD
LEUGH > LAUCH
LEUGHEN > LAUCH
LEUKAEMIA *n* disease caused by uncontrolled overproduction of white blood cells
LEUKEMIA *same as* > LEUKAEMIA
LEUKEMIAS > LEUKEMIA
LEUKEMIC > LEUKEMIA
LEUKEMICS > LEUKEMIA
LEUKEMOID *adj* resembling leukaemia
LEUKOCYTE *same as* > LEUCOCYTE
LEUKOMA *same as* > LEUCOMA
LEUKOMAS > LEUKOMA
LEUKON *n* white blood cell count
LEUKONS > LEUKON
LEUKOSES > LEUKOSIS
LEUKOSIS *n* abnormal growth of white blood cells
LEUKOTIC > LEUKOSIS
LEUKOTOMY *n* lobotomy
LEV *n* standard monetary unit of Bulgaria, divided into 100 stotinki
LEVA > LEV
LEVANT *n* type of leather made from the skins of goats, sheep, or seals ▷ *vb* bolt or abscond, esp to avoid paying debts
LEVANTED > LEVANT
LEVANTER *n* easterly wind in the W Mediterranean area, esp in the late summer
LEVANTERS > LEVANTER
LEVANTINE *n* cloth of twilled silk
LEVANTING > LEVANT
LEVANTS > LEVANT
LEVATOR *n* any of various muscles that raise a part of the body
LEVATORES > LEVATOR
LEVATORS > LEVATOR
LEVE *adj* darling ▷ *adv* gladly
LEVEE *n* natural or artificial river embankment ▷ *vb* go to the reception of
LEVEED > LEVEE
LEVEEING > LEVEE
LEVEES > LEVEE
LEVEL *adj* horizontal ▷ *vb* make even or horizontal ▷ *n* horizontal line or surface
LEVELED > LEVEL
LEVELER *same as* > LEVELLER
LEVELERS > LEVELER
LEVELING > LEVEL
LEVELLED > LEVEL
LEVELLER *n* person or thing that levels
LEVELLERS > LEVELLER
LEVELLEST > LEVEL
LEVELLING > LEVEL
LEVELLY > LEVEL
LEVELNESS > LEVEL
LEVELS > LEVEL
LEVER *n* handle used to operate machinery ▷ *vb* prise or move with a lever
LEVERAGE *n* action or power of a lever ▷ *vb* borrow capital required
LEVERAGED > LEVERAGE
LEVERAGES > LEVERAGE
LEVERED > LEVER
LEVERET *n* young hare
LEVERETS > LEVERET
LEVERING > LEVER
LEVERS > LEVER
LEVIABLE *adj* (of taxes, tariffs, etc) liable to be levied
LEVIATHAN *n* sea monster
LEVIED > LEVY
LEVIER > LEVY
LEVIERS > LEVY
LEVIES > LEVY
LEVIGABLE > LEVIGATE
LEVIGATE *vb* grind into a fine powder or a smooth paste ▷ *adj* having a smooth polished surface
LEVIGATED > LEVIGATE
LEVIGATES > LEVIGATE
LEVIGATOR > LEVIGATE
LEVIN *archaic word for* > LIGHTNING
LEVINS > LEVIN
LEVIRATE *n* practice, required by Old Testament law, of marrying the widow of one's brother
LEVIRATES > LEVIRATE
LEVIRATIC > LEVIRATE
LEVIS *n* jeans
LEVITATE *vb* rise or cause to rise into the air
LEVITATED > LEVITATE
LEVITATES > LEVITATE
LEVITATOR > LEVITATE
LEVITE *n* Christian clergyman
LEVITES > LEVITE
LEVITIC > LEVITE
LEVITICAL > LEVITE
LEVITIES > LEVITY
LEVITY *n* inclination to make a joke of serious matters
LEVO *adj* anticlockwise
LEVODOPA *n* substance occurring naturally in the bopy and used to treat Parkinson's disease
LEVODOPAS > LEVODOPA
LEVOGYRE *n* counterclockwise spiral
LEVULIN *n* substance obtained from certain bulbs
LEVULINS > LEVULIN
LEVULOSE *n* fructose
LEVULOSES > LEVULOSE
LEVY *vb* impose and collect (a tax) ▷ *n* imposition or collection of taxes
LEVYING > LEVY
LEW *adj* tepid

EWD *adj* lustful or indecent
EWDER > LEWD
EWDEST > LEWD
EWDLY > LEWD
EWDNESS > LEWD
EWDSBIES > LEWDSBY
EWDSBY *another word for* > LEWDSTER
EWDSTER *n* lewd person
EWDSTERS > LEWDSTER
EWIS *n* lifting device for heavy stone or concrete blocks
EWISES > LEWIS
EWISIA *n* type of herb
EWISIAS > LEWISIA
EWISITE *n* colourless oily poisonous liquid
EWISITES > LEWISITE
EWISSON *same as* > LEWIS
EWISSONS > LEWISSON
EX *n* system or body of laws
EXEME *n* minimal meaningful unit of language, the meaning of which cannot be understood from that of its component morphemes
EXEMES > LEXEME
EXEMIC > LEXEME
EXES > LEX
EXICA > LEXICON
EXICAL *adj* relating to the vocabulary of a language
EXICALLY > LEXICAL
EXICON *n* dictionary
EXICONS > LEXICON
EXIGRAM *n* figure or symbol that represents a word
EXIGRAMS > LEXIGRAM
EXIS *n* totality of vocabulary items in a language, including all forms having lexical meaning or grammatical function
EXISES > LEXIS
EY *n* land temporarily under grass
EYLANDI *same as* > LEYLANDII
EYLANDII *n* type of fast-growing cypress tree
EYLANDIS > LEYLANDI
EYS > LEY
EZ *short form of* > LESBIAN
EZES > LEZ
EZZ *short form of* > LESBIAN
EZZA *same as* > LEZZIE
EZZAS > LEZZA
EZZES > LEZZ
EZZIE *n* lesbian
EZZIES > LEZZIE
EZZY *short form of* > LESBIAN
I *n* Chinese measurement of distance
IABILITY *n* hindrance or disadvantage
IABLE *adj* legally obliged or responsible
IAISE *vb* establish and maintain communication (with)
LIAISED > LIAISE
LIAISES > LIAISE
LIAISING > LIAISE
LIAISON *n* communication and contact between groups
LIAISONS > LIAISON
LIANA *n* climbing plant in tropical forests
LIANAS > LIANA
LIANE *same as* > LIANA
LIANES > LIANE
LIANG *n* Chinese unit of weight
LIANGS > LIANG
LIANOID > LIANA
LIAR *n* person who tells lies
LIARD *adj* grey ▷ *n* former small coin of various European countries
LIARDS > LIARD
LIARS > LIAR
LIART *Scots form of* > LIARD
LIAS *n* lowest series of rocks of the Jurassic system
LIASES > LIAS
LIATRIS *n* type of North American plant with small white flowers
LIATRISES > LIATRIS
LIB *n* informal, sometimes derogatory word for liberation ▷ *vb* geld
LIBANT *adj* touching lightly
LIBATE *vb* offer as gift to the gods
LIBATED > LIBATE
LIBATES > LIBATE
LIBATING > LIBATE
LIBATION *n* drink poured as an offering to the gods
LIBATIONS > LIBATION
LIBATORY > LIBATE
LIBBARD *another word for* > LEOPARD
LIBBARDS > LIBBARD
LIBBED > LIB
LIBBER *n* liberationist
LIBBERS > LIBBER
LIBBING > LIB
LIBECCHIO *same as* > LIBECCIO
LIBECCIO *n* strong westerly or southwesterly wind blowing onto the W coast of Corsica
LIBECCIOS > LIBECCIO
LIBEL *n* published statement falsely damaging a person's reputation ▷ *vb* falsely damage the reputation of (someone)
LIBELANT *same as* > LIBELLANT
LIBELANTS > LIBELANT
LIBELED > LIBEL
LIBELEE *same as* > LIBELLEE
LIBELEES > LIBELEE
LIBELER > LIBEL
LIBELERS > LIBEL
LIBELING > LIBEL
LIBELINGS > LIBEL
LIBELIST > LIBEL
LIBELISTS > LIBEL
LIBELLANT *n* party who brings an action in the ecclesiastical courts by presenting a libel
LIBELLED > LIBEL
LIBELLEE *n* person against whom a libel has been filed in an ecclesiastical court
LIBELLEES > LIBELLEE
LIBELLER > LIBEL
LIBELLERS > LIBEL
LIBELLING > LIBEL
LIBELLOUS > LIBEL
LIBELOUS > LIBEL
LIBELS > LIBEL
LIBER *n* tome or book
LIBERAL *adj* having social and political views that favour progress and reform ▷ *n* person who has liberal ideas or opinions
LIBERALLY > LIBERAL
LIBERALS > LIBERAL
LIBERATE *vb* set free
LIBERATED *adj* not bound by traditional sexual and social roles
LIBERATES > LIBERATE
LIBERATOR > LIBERATE
LIBERO *another name for* > SWEEPER
LIBEROS > LIBERO
LIBERS > LIBER
LIBERTIES > LIBERTY
LIBERTINE *n* morally dissolute person ▷ *adj* promiscuous and unscrupulous
LIBERTY *n* freedom
LIBIDINAL > LIBIDO
LIBIDO *n* psychic energy
LIBIDOS > LIBIDO
LIBKEN *n* lodging
LIBKENS > LIBKEN
LIBLAB *n* 19th century British liberal
LIBLABS > LIBLAB
LIBRA *n* ancient Roman unit of weight corresponding to 1 pound, but equal to about 12 ounces
LIBRAE > LIBRA
LIBRAIRE *n* bookseller
LIBRAIRES > LIBRAIRE
LIBRAIRIE *n* bookshop
LIBRARIAN *n* keeper of or worker in a library
LIBRARIES > LIBRARY
LIBRARY *n* room or building where books are kept
LIBRAS > LIBRA
LIBRATE *vb* oscillate or waver
LIBRATED > LIBRATE
LIBRATES > LIBRATE
LIBRATING > LIBRATE
LIBRATION *n* act or an instance of oscillating
LIBRATORY > LIBRATE
LIBRETTI > LIBRETTO
LIBRETTO *n* words of an opera
LIBRETTOS > LIBRETTO
LIBRI > LIBER
LIBRIFORM *adj* (of a fibre of woody tissue) elongated and having a pitted thickened cell wall
LIBS > LIB
LICE > LOUSE
LICENCE *n* document giving official permission to do something ▷ *vb* (in the US) give permission to
LICENCED > LICENCE
LICENCEE *same as* > LICENSEE
LICENCEES > LICENCEE
LICENCER > LICENCE
LICENCERS > LICENCE
LICENCES > LICENCE
LICENCING > LICENCE
LICENSE *vb* grant or give a licence for
LICENSED > LICENSE
LICENSEE *n* holder of a licence, esp to sell alcohol
LICENSEES > LICENSEE
LICENSER > LICENSE
LICENSERS > LICENSE
LICENSES > LICENSE
LICENSING > LICENSE
LICENSOR > LICENSE
LICENSORS > LICENSE
LICENSURE *n* act of conferring licence
LICENTE *adj* permitted; allowed
LICH *n* dead body
LICHANOS *n* note played using forefinger
LICHEE *same as* > LITCHI
LICHEES > LICHEE
LICHEN *n* small flowerless plant forming a crust on rocks, trees, etc ▷ *vb* cover with lichen
LICHENED > LICHEN
LICHENIN *n* complex polysaccharide occurring in certain species of moss
LICHENING > LICHEN
LICHENINS > LICHENIN
LICHENISM *n* type of fungus
LICHENIST *n* person who studies lichens
LICHENOID > LICHEN
LICHENOSE > LICHEN
LICHENOUS > LICHEN
LICHENS > LICHEN
LICHES > LICH
LICHGATE *n* roofed gate to a churchyard
LICHGATES > LICHGATE
LICHI *same as* > LITCHI
LICHIS > LICHI
LICHT *Scot word for* > LIGHT
LICHTED > LICHT
LICHTER > LICHT
LICHTEST > LICHT

LICHTING > LICHT
LICHTLIED > LICHTLY
LICHTLIES > LICHTLY
LICHTLY *vb* treat discourteously
LICHTS > LICHT
LICHWAKE *n* night vigil over a dead body
LICHWAKES > LICHWAKE
LICHWAY *n* path used to carry coffin into church
LICHWAYS > LICHWAY
LICIT *adj* lawful, permitted
LICITLY > LICIT
LICITNESS > LICIT
LICK *vb* pass the tongue over ▷ *n* licking
LICKED > LICK
LICKER > LICK
LICKERISH *adj* lecherous or lustful
LICKERS > LICK
LICKING *n* beating
LICKINGS > LICKING
LICKPENNY *n* something that uses up large amounts of money
LICKS > LICK
LICKSPIT *n* flattering or servile person
LICKSPITS > LICKSPIT
LICORICE *same as* > LIQUORICE
LICORICES > LICORICE
LICTOR *n* one of a group of ancient Roman officials
LICTORIAN > LICTOR
LICTORS > LICTOR
LID *n* movable cover
LIDAR *n* radar-type instrument
LIDARS > LIDAR
LIDDED > LID
LIDDING *n* lids
LIDGER *variant form of* > LEDGER
LIDGERS > LEDGER
LIDLESS *adj* having no lid or top
LIDO *n* open-air centre for swimming and water sports
LIDOCAINE *n* powerful local anaesthetic administered by injection
LIDOS > LIDO
LIDS > LID
LIE *vb* make a deliberately false statement ▷ *n* deliberate falsehood
LIED *n* setting for solo voice and piano of a poem
LIEDER > LIED
LIEF *adv* gladly ▷ *adj* ready ▷ *n* beloved person
LIEFER > LIEF
LIEFEST > LIEF
LIEFLY > LIEF
LIEFS > LIEF
LIEGE *adj* bound to give or receive feudal service ▷ *n* lord
LIEGEDOM > LIEGE
LIEGEDOMS > LIEGE
LIEGELESS > LIEGE
LIEGEMAN *n* (formerly) the subject of a sovereign or feudal lord
LIEGEMEN > LIEGEMAN
LIEGER *same as* > LEDGER
LIEGERS > LIEGER
LIEGES > LIEGE
LIEN *n* right to hold another's property until a debt is paid
LIENABLE *adj* that can be subject of a lien
LIENAL *adj* of or relating to the spleen
LIENS > LIEN
LIENTERIC > LIENTERY
LIENTERY *n* passage of undigested food in the faeces
LIER *n* person who lies down
LIERNE *n* short secondary rib that connects the intersections of the primary ribs, esp as used in Gothic vaulting
LIERNES > LIERNE
LIERS > LIER
LIES > LIE
LIEU *n* stead
LIEUS > LIEU
LIEVE *same as* > LEVE
LIEVER > LIEVE
LIEVEST > LIEVE
LIFE *n* state of living beings, characterized by growth, reproduction, and response to stimuli
LIFEBELT *n* ring filled with air, used to keep a person afloat when in danger of drowning
LIFEBELTS > LIFEBELT
LIFEBLOOD *n* blood vital to life
LIFEBOAT *n* boat used for rescuing people at sea
LIFEBOATS > LIFEBOAT
LIFEBUOY *n* any of various kinds of buoyant device for keeping people afloat
LIFEBUOYS > LIFEBUOY
LIFECARE *n* care of person's health and welfare
LIFECARES > LIFECARE
LIFEFUL *adj* full of life
LIFEGUARD *n* person who saves people from drowning ▷ *vb* work as lifeguard
LIFEHOLD *adj* (of land) held while one is alive
LIFELESS *adj* dead
LIFELIKE *adj* closely resembling or representing life
LIFELINE *n* means of contact or support
LIFELINES > LIFELINE
LIFELONG *adj* lasting all of a person's life
LIFER *n* prisoner sentenced to imprisonment for life
LIFERS > LIFER
LIFES as in *still lifes* paintings or drawings of inanimate objects
LIFESAVER *n* saver of a person's life
LIFESOME *adj* full of life
LIFESPAN *n* period of time during which a person or animal may be expected to live
LIFESPANS > LIFESPAN
LIFESTYLE *n* particular attitudes, habits, etc ▷ *adj* suggestive of a fashionable or desirable lifestyle
LIFETIME *n* length of time a person is alive
LIFETIMES > LIFETIME
LIFEWAY *n* way of life
LIFEWAYS > LIFEWAY
LIFEWORK *n* work to which a person has devoted their life
LIFEWORKS > LIFEWORK
LIFEWORLD *n* way individual experiences world
LIFT *vb* move upwards in position, status, volume, etc ▷ *n* cage raised and lowered in a vertical shaft to transport people or goods
LIFTABLE > LIFT
LIFTBACK *n* hatchback
LIFTBACKS > LIFTBACK
LIFTBOY *n* person who operates a lift, esp in large public or commercial buildings and hotels
LIFTBOYS > LIFTBOY
LIFTED > LIFT
LIFTER > LIFT
LIFTERS > LIFT
LIFTGATE *n* rear opening of hatchback
LIFTGATES > LIFTGATE
LIFTING > LIFT
LIFTMAN *same as* > LIFTBOY
LIFTMEN > LIFTMAN
LIFTOFF *n* moment a rocket leaves the ground ▷ *vb* (of a rocket) to leave its launch pad
LIFTOFFS > LIFTOFF
LIFTS > LIFT
LIFULL *obsolete form of* > LIFEFUL
LIG *n* (esp in the media) a function with free entertainment and refreshments ▷ *vb* attend such a function
LIGAMENT *n* band of tissue joining bones
LIGAMENTS > LIGAMENT
LIGAN *same as* > LAGAN
LIGAND *n* atom, molecule, radical, or ion forming a complex with a central atom
LIGANDS > LIGAND
LIGANS > LIGAN
LIGASE *n* any of a class of enzymes
LIGASES > LIGASE
LIGATE *vb* tie up or constrict (something) with a ligature
LIGATED > LIGATE
LIGATES > LIGATE
LIGATING > LIGATE
LIGATION > LIGATE
LIGATIONS > LIGATE
LIGATIVE > LIGATE
LIGATURE *n* link, bond, or tie ▷ *vb* bind with a ligature
LIGATURED > LIGATURE
LIGATURES > LIGATURE
LIGER *n* hybrid offspring of a female tiger and a male lion
LIGERS > LIGER
LIGGE *obsolete form of* > LIE
LIGGED > LIG
LIGGEN > LIG
LIGGER > LIG
LIGGERS > LIG
LIGGES > LIGGE
LIGGING > LIG
LIGGINGS > LIG
LIGHT *n* electromagnetic radiation by which things are visible ▷ *adj* bright ▷ *vb* ignite ▷ *adv* with little equipment or luggage
LIGHTBULB *n* glass bulb containing gas that emits light when a current is passed through it
LIGHTED > LIGHT
LIGHTEN *vb* make less dark
LIGHTENED > LIGHTEN
LIGHTENER > LIGHTEN
LIGHTENS > LIGHTEN
LIGHTER *n* device for lighting cigarettes etc ▷ *vb* convey in a type of flat-bottomed barge
LIGHTERED > LIGHTER
LIGHTERS > LIGHTER
LIGHTEST > LIGHT
LIGHTFACE *n* weight of type in printing
LIGHTFAST *adj* (of a dye) unaffected by light
LIGHTFUL *adj* full of light
LIGHTING > LIGHT
LIGHTINGS > LIGHT
LIGHTISH > LIGHT
LIGHTLESS > LIGHT
LIGHTLIED > LIGHTLY
LIGHTLIES > LIGHTLY
LIGHTLY *adv* in a light way ▷ *vb* belittle
LIGHTNESS *n* quality of being light
LIGHTNING *n* visible discharge of electricity in the atmosphere ▷ *adj* fast and sudden

IGHTS > LIGHT
IGHTSHIP *n* moored ship used as a lighthouse
IGHTSOME *adj* lighthearted
IGHTWAVE *n* wave of light
IGHTWOOD *n* Australian acacia
IGNAGE *another word for* > LINEAGE
IGNAGES > LIGNAGE
IGNALOES *another name for* > EAGLEWOOD
IGNAN *n* beneficial substance found in plants
IGNANS > LIGNAN
IGNE *n* unit of measurement
IGNEOUS *adj* of or like wood
IGNES > LIGNE
IGNICOLE *adj* growing or living in wood
IGNIFIED > LIGNIFY
IGNIFIES > LIGNIFY
IGNIFORM *adj* having the appearance of wood
IGNIFY *vb* make or become woody as a result of the deposition of lignin in the cell walls
IGNIN *n* complex polymer occurring in certain plant cell walls making the plant rigid
IGNINS > LIGNIN
IGNITE *n* woody textured rock used as fuel
IGNITES > LIGNITE
IGNITIC > LIGNITE
IGNOSE *n* explosive compound
IGNOSES > LIGNOSE
IGNUM *n* wood
IGNUMS > LIGNUM
IGROIN *n* volatile fraction of petroleum that is used as a solvent
IGROINE *same as* > LIGROIN
IGROINES > LIGROINE
IGROINS > LIGROIN
IGS > LIG
IGULA *same as* > LIGULE
IGULAE > LIGULA
IGULAR > LIGULA
IGULAS > LIGULA
IGULATE *adj* having the shape of a strap
IGULATED *same as* > LIGULATE
IGULE *n* membranous outgrowth at the junction between the leaf blade and sheath in many grasses and sedges
IGULES > LIGULE
IGULOID > LIGULA
IGURE *n* any of the 12 precious stones used in the breastplates of high priests
IGURES > LIGURE
IKABLE *adj* easy to like
LIKE *adj* similar ▷ *vb* find enjoyable ▷ *n* favourable feeling, desire, or preference
LIKEABLE *same as* > LIKABLE
LIKED > LIKE
LIKELIER > LIKELY
LIKELIEST > LIKELY
LIKELY *adj* tending or inclined ▷ *adv* probably
LIKEN *vb* compare
LIKENED > LIKEN
LIKENESS *n* resemblance
LIKENING > LIKEN
LIKENS > LIKEN
LIKER > LIKE
LIKERS > LIKE
LIKES > LIKE
LIKEST > LIKE
LIKEWAKE *same as* > LYKEWAKE
LIKEWAKES > LIKEWAKE
LIKEWALK *same as* > LYKEWAKE
LIKEWALKS > LIKEWALK
LIKEWISE *adv* similarly
LIKIN *n* historically, Chinese tax
LIKING *n* fondness
LIKINGS > LIKING
LIKINS > LIKIN
LIKUTA *n* (formerly) a coin used in Zaïre
LILAC *n* shrub with pale mauve or white flowers ▷ *adj* light-purple
LILACS > LILAC
LILANGENI *n* standard monetary unit of Swaziland, divided into 100 cents
LILIED *adj* decorated with lilies
LILIES > LILY
LILL *obsolete form of* > LOLL
LILLED > LILL
LILLING > LILL
LILLIPUT *adj* tiny ▷ *n* tiny person or being
LILLIPUTS > LILLIPUTIAN
LILLS > LILL
LILO *n* trademark for a type of inflatable plastic mattress
LILOS > LILO
LILT *n* pleasing musical quality in speaking ▷ *vb* speak with a lilt
LILTED > LILT
LILTING > LILT
LILTINGLY > LILT
LILTS > LILT
LILY *n* plant which grows from a bulb and has large, often white, flowers
LILYLIKE *adj* resembling a lily
LIMA *n* type of edible bean
LIMACEL *n* small shell inside some kinds of slug
LIMACELS > LIMACEL
LIMACEOUS *adj* relating to the slug
LIMACES > LIMAX
LIMACINE *adj* of, or relating to slugs, esp those of the genus *Limax*
LIMACON *n* heart-shaped curve
LIMACONS > LIMACON
LIMAIL *same as* > LEMEL
LIMAILS > LIMAIL
LIMAN *n* lagoon
LIMANS > LIMAN
LIMAS > LIMA
LIMATION *n* polishing
LIMATIONS > LIMATION
LIMAX *n* slug
LIMB *n* arm, leg, or wing ▷ *vb* dismember
LIMBA *n* type of African tree
LIMBAS > LIMBA
LIMBATE *adj* having an edge or border of a different colour from the rest
LIMBEC *obsolete form of* > ALEMBIC
LIMBECK *obsolete form of* > ALEMBIC
LIMBECKS > LIMBECK
LIMBECS > LIMBEC
LIMBED > LIMB
LIMBER *vb* loosen stiff muscles by exercising ▷ *adj* pliant or supple ▷ *n* part of a gun carriage, consisting of an axle, pole, and two wheels
LIMBERED > LIMBER
LIMBERER > LIMBER
LIMBEREST > LIMBER
LIMBERING > LIMBER
LIMBERLY > LIMBER
LIMBERS > LIMBER
LIMBI > LIMBUS
LIMBIC > LIMBUS
LIMBIER > LIMBY
LIMBIEST > LIMBY
LIMBING > LIMB
LIMBLESS > LIMB
LIMBMEAL *adv* piece by piece
LIMBO *n* supposed region intermediate between Heaven and Hell for the unbaptized
LIMBOS > LIMBO
LIMBOUS *adj* with overlapping edges
LIMBS > LIMB
LIMBUS *n* border
LIMBUSES > LIMBUS
LIMBY *adj* with long legs, stem, branches, etc
LIME *n* calcium compound used as a fertilizer or in making cement ▷ *vb* spread a calcium compound upon (land) ▷ *adj* having the flavour of lime fruit
LIMEADE *n* drink made from sweetened lime juice and plain or carbonated water
LIMEADES > LIMEADE
LIMED > LIME
LIMEKILN *n* kiln in which calcium carbonate is burned to produce quicklime
LIMEKILNS > LIMEKILN
LIMELESS > LIME
LIMELIGHT *n* glare of publicity ▷ *vb* illuminate with limelight
LIMELIT > LIMELIGHT
LIMEN *another term for* > THRESHOLD
LIMENS > LIMEN
LIMEPIT *n* pit containing lime in which hides are placed to remove the hair
LIMEPITS > LIMEPIT
LIMERICK *n* humorous verse of five lines
LIMERICKS > LIMERICK
LIMES *n* fortified boundary of the Roman Empire
LIMESCALE *n* flaky deposit left in containers such as kettles by the action of heat on water containing calcium salts
LIMESTONE *n* sedimentary rock used in building
LIMEWASH *n* mixture of lime and water used to whitewash walls, ceilings, etc
LIMEWATER *n* clear colourless solution of calcium hydroxide in water
LIMEY *n* British person ▷ *adj* British
LIMEYS > LIMEY
LIMIER > LIMY
LIMIEST > LIMY
LIMINA > LIMEN
LIMINAL *adj* relating to the point (or threshold) beyond which a sensation becomes too faint to be experienced
LIMINESS > LIMY
LIMING > LIME
LIMINGS > LIME
LIMIT *n* ultimate extent, degree, or amount of something ▷ *vb* restrict or confine
LIMITABLE > LIMIT
LIMITARY *adj* of, involving, or serving as a limit
LIMITED *adj* having a limit ▷ *n* limited train, bus, etc
LIMITEDLY > LIMITED
LIMITEDS > LIMITED
LIMITER *n* electronic circuit that produces an output signal whose positive or negative amplitude, or both, is limited to some predetermined value above which the peaks become flattened
LIMITERS > LIMITER
LIMITES > LIMES

LIMITING > LIMIT
LIMITINGS > LIMIT
LIMITLESS > LIMIT
LIMITS > LIMIT
LIMMA *n* semitone
LIMMAS > LIMMA
LIMMER *n* scoundrel
LIMMERS > LIMMER
LIMN *vb* represent in drawing or painting
LIMNAEID *n* type of snail
LIMNAEIDS > LIMNAEID
LIMNED > LIMN
LIMNER > LIMN
LIMNERS > LIMN
LIMNETIC *adj* of, relating to, or inhabiting the open water of lakes down to the depth of light penetration
LIMNIC *adj* relating to lakes
LIMNING > LIMN
LIMNOLOGY *n* study of bodies of fresh water with reference to their plant and animal life, physical properties, geographical features, etc
LIMNS > LIMN
LIMO *short for* > LIMOUSINE
LIMONENE *n* liquid optically active terpene with a lemon-like odour
LIMONENES > LIMONENE
LIMONITE *n* common brown, black, or yellow amorphous secondary mineral
LIMONITES > LIMONITE
LIMONITIC > LIMONITE
LIMOS > LIMO
LIMOSES > LIMOSIS
LIMOSIS *n* excessive hunger
LIMOUS *adj* muddy
LIMOUSINE *n* large luxurious car
LIMP *vb* walk with an uneven step ▷ *n* limping walk ▷ *adj* without firmness or stiffness
LIMPA *n* type of rye bread
LIMPAS > LIMPA
LIMPED > LIMP
LIMPER > LIMP
LIMPERS > LIMP
LIMPEST > LIMP
LIMPET *n* shellfish which sticks tightly to rocks ▷ *adj* denoting certain weapons that are magnetically attached to their targets and resist removal
LIMPETS > LIMPET
LIMPID *adj* clear or transparent
LIMPIDITY > LIMPID
LIMPIDLY > LIMPID
LIMPING > LIMP
LIMPINGLY > LIMP
LIMPINGS > LIMP
LIMPKIN *n* rail-like wading bird
LIMPKINS > LIMPKIN
LIMPLY > LIMP
LIMPNESS > LIMP
LIMPS > LIMP
LIMPSEY *same as* > LIMPSY
LIMPSIER > LIMPSY
LIMPSIEST > LIMPSY
LIMPSY *adj* limp
LIMULI > LIMULUS
LIMULOID *n* type of crab
LIMULOIDS > LIMULOID
LIMULUS *n* any horseshoe crab of the genus *Limulus*
LIMULUSES > LIMULUS
LIMY *adj* of, like, or smeared with birdlime
LIN *vb* cease
LINABLE > LINE
LINAC *n* linear accelerator
LINACS > LINAC
LINAGE *n* number of lines in written or printed matter
LINAGES > LINAGE
LINALOL *same as* > LINALOOL
LINALOLS > LINALOL
LINALOOL *n* optically active colourless fragrant liquid
LINALOOLS > LINALOOL
LINCH *n* ledge
LINCHES > LINCH
LINCHET *another word for* > LINCH
LINCHETS > LINCHET
LINCHPIN *n* pin to hold a wheel on its axle
LINCHPINS > LINCHPIN
LINCRUSTA *n* type of wallpaper having a hard embossed surface
LINCTURE *n* medicine taken by licking
LINCTURES > LINCTURE
LINCTUS *n* syrupy cough medicine
LINCTUSES > LINCTUS
LIND *variant of* > LINDEN
LINDANE *n* white poisonous crystalline powder
LINDANES > LINDANE
LINDEN *n* large tree with heart-shaped leaves and fragrant yellowish flowers
LINDENS > LINDEN
LINDIES > LINDY
LINDS > LIND
LINDWORM *n* wingless serpent-like dragon
LINDWORMS > LINDWORM
LINDY *n* lively dance
LINE *n* long narrow mark ▷ *vb* mark with lines
LINEABLE > LINE
LINEAGE *n* descent from an ancestor
LINEAGES > LINEAGE
LINEAL *adj* in direct line of descent
LINEALITY > LINEAL
LINEALLY > LINEAL
LINEAMENT *n* facial feature
LINEAR *adj* of or in lines
LINEARISE *same as* > LINEARIZE
LINEARITY > LINEAR
LINEARIZE *vb* make linear
LINEARLY > LINEAR
LINEATE *adj* marked with lines
LINEATED *same as* > LINEATE
LINEATION *n* act of marking with lines
LINEBRED *adj* having an ancestor that is common to sire and dam
LINECUT *n* method of relief printing
LINECUTS > LINECUT
LINED > LINE
LINELIKE > LINE
LINEMAN *same as* > LINESMAN
LINEMEN > LINEMAN
LINEN *n* cloth or thread made from flax
LINENS > LINEN
LINENY > LINEN
LINEOLATE *adj* marked with very fine parallel lines
LINER *n* large passenger ship or aircraft
LINERLESS > LINER
LINERS > LINER
LINES > LINE
LINESMAN *n* (in some sports) an official who helps the referee or umpire
LINESMEN > LINESMAN
LINEUP *n* row or arrangement of people or things
LINEUPS > LINEUP
LINEY > LINE
LING *n* slender food fish
LINGA *same as* > LINGAM
LINGAM *n* (in Sanskrit grammar) the masculine gender
LINGAMS > LINGAM
LINGAS > LINGA
LINGBERRY *same as* > COWBERRY
LINGCOD *n* any scorpaenoid food fish of the family *Ophiodontidae*
LINGCODS > LINGCOD
LINGEL *n* strong shoemaker's thread
LINGELS > LINGEL
LINGER *vb* delay or prolong departure
LINGERED > LINGER
LINGERER > LINGER
LINGERERS > LINGER
LINGERIE *n* women's underwear or nightwear
LINGERIES > LINGERIE
LINGERING > LINGER
LINGERS > LINGER
LINGIER > LINGY
LINGIEST > LINGY
LINGLE *same as* > LINGEL
LINGLES > LINGLE
LINGO *n* foreign or unfamiliar language or jargon
LINGOES > LINGO
LINGOT *n* ingot
LINGOTS > LINGOT
LINGS > LING
LINGSTER *n* person able tc communicate with aliens
LINGSTERS > LINGSTER
LINGUA *n* any tongue-like structure
LINGUAE > LINGUA
LINGUAL *adj* of the tongue ▷ *n* lingual consonant, such as Scots (r)
LINGUALLY > LINGUAL
LINGUALS > LINGUAL
LINGUAS > LINGUA
LINGUICA *n* Portuguese sausage
LINGUICAS > LINGUICA
LINGUINE *n* kind of pasta in the shape of thin flat strands
LINGUINES > LINGUINE
LINGUINI *same as* > LINGUINE
LINGUINIS > LINGUINI
LINGUISA *same as* > LINGUICA
LINGUISAS > LINGUISA
LINGUIST *n* person skilled in foreign languages
LINGUISTS > LINGUIST
LINGULA *n* small tongue
LINGULAE > LINGULA
LINGULAR > LINGULA
LINGULAS > LINGULA
LINGULATE *adj* shaped like a tongue
LINGY *adj* heather-covered
LINHAY *n* farm building with an open front
LINHAYS > LINHAY
LINIER > LINE
LINIEST > LINE
LINIMENT *n* medicated liquid rubbed on the skin to relieve pain or stiffness
LINIMENTS > LINIMENT
LININ *n* network of viscou material in the nucleus of a cell that connects the chromatin granules
LINING *n* layer of cloth attached to the inside of a garment etc
LININGS > LINING
LININS > LININ
LINISH *vb* polish metal
LINISHED > LINISH
LINISHER > LINISH
LINISHERS > LINISH
LINISHES > LINISH
LINISHING > LINISH
LINK *n* any of the rings forming a chain ▷ *vb* connect with or as if with links
LINKABLE > LINK
LINKAGE *n* act of linking o the state of being linked
LINKAGES > LINKAGE
LINKBOY *n* (formerly) a bo who carried a torch for pedestrians in dark street

LINKBOYS > LINKBOY
LINKED > LINK
LINKER *n* person or thing that links
LINKERS > LINKER
LINKING > LINK
LINKMAN *same as* > LINKBOY
LINKMEN > LINKMAN
LINKS > LINK
LINKSLAND *n* land near sea used for golf
LINKSMAN *same as* > LINKBOY
LINKSMEN > LINKSMAN
LINKSTER *n* interpreter
LINKSTERS > LINKSTER
LINKUP *n* establishing of a connection or union between objects, groups, organizations, etc
LINKUPS > LINKUP
LINKWORK *n* something made up of links
LINKWORKS > LINKWORK
LINKY *adj* (of countryside) consisting of links
LINN *n* waterfall or a pool at the foot of it
LINNED > LIN
LINNET *n* songbird of the finch family
LINNETS > LINNET
LINNEY *same as* > LINHAY
LINNEYS > LINNEY
LINNIES > LINNY
LINNING > LIN
LINNS > LINN
LINNY *same as* > LINHAY
LINO *same as* > LINOLEUM
LINOCUT *n* design cut in relief in linoleum mounted on a block of wood
LINOCUTS > LINOCUT
LINOLEATE *n* ester or salt of linoleic acid
LINOLEIC as in *linoleic acid* colourless oily essential fatty acid found in linseed
LINOLENIC as in *linolenic acid* colourless unsaturated essential fatty acid
LINOLEUM *n* type of floor covering
LINOLEUMS > LINOLEUM
LINOS > LINO
LINOTYPE *n* line of metal type produced by machine ▷ *vb* set as line of type
LINOTYPED > LINOTYPE
LINOTYPER > LINOTYPE
LINOTYPES > LINOTYPE
LINS > LIN
LINSANG *n* any of several forest-dwelling viverrine mammals
LINSANGS > LINSANG
LINSEED *n* seed of the flax plant
LINSEEDS > LINSEED
LINSEY *n* type of cloth
LINSEYS > LINSEY
LINSTOCK *n* long staff holding a lighted match, formerly used to fire a cannon
LINSTOCKS > LINSTOCK
LINT *n* soft material for dressing a wound
LINTED *adj* having lint
LINTEL *n* horizontal beam at the top of a door or window
LINTELLED *adj* having a lintel
LINTELS > LINTEL
LINTER *n* machine for stripping the short fibres of ginned cotton seeds
LINTERS > LINTER
LINTIE *Scot word for* > LINNET
LINTIER > LINT
LINTIES > LINTIE
LINTIEST > LINT
LINTING *n* process of making lint
LINTLESS > LINT
LINTOL *same as* > LINTEL
LINTOLS > LINTEL
LINTS > LINT
LINTSEED *same as* > LINSEED
LINTSEEDS > LINTSEED
LINTSTOCK *same as* > LINSTOCK
LINTWHITE *n* linnet
LINTY > LINT
LINUM *n* any plant of the annual or perennial genus *Linum*
LINUMS > LINUM
LINURON *n* type of herbicide
LINURONS > LINURON
LINUX *n* nonproprietary computer operating system suitable for use on personal computers
LINUXES > LINUX
LINY > LINE
LION *n* large animal of the cat family, the male of which has a shaggy mane
LIONCEL *n* (heraldry) small lion
LIONCELLE *same as* > LIONCEL
LIONCELS > LIONCEL
LIONEL *same as* > LIONCEL
LIONELS > LIONEL
LIONESS *n* female lion
LIONESSES > LIONESS
LIONET *n* young lion
LIONETS > LIONET
LIONFISH *n* any of various scorpion fishes of the Pacific
> LIONHEARTEDNESS
LIONISE *same as* > LIONIZE
LIONISED > LIONISE
LIONISER > LIONISE
LIONISERS > LIONISE
LIONISES > LIONISE
LIONISING > LIONISE
LIONISM *n* lion-like appearance of leprosy
LIONISMS > LIONISM
LIONIZE *vb* treat as a celebrity
LIONIZED > LIONIZE
LIONIZER > LIONIZE
LIONIZERS > LIONIZE
LIONIZES > LIONIZE
LIONIZING > LIONIZE
LIONLIKE > LION
LIONLY > LION
LIONS > LION
LIP *n* either of the fleshy edges of the mouth ▷ *vb* touch with the lips
LIPA *n* monetary unit of Croatia worth one hundredth of a kuna
LIPAEMIA *n* abnormally large amount of fat in the blood
LIPARITE *n* type of igneous rock
LIPARITES > LIPARITE
LIPASE *n* any of a group of enzymes that digest fat
LIPASES > LIPASE
LIPE *n* lurch
LIPECTOMY *n* surgical operation to remove fat
LIPEMIA *same as* > LIPAEMIA
LIPEMIAS > LIPEMIA
LIPID *n* any of a group of organic compounds including fats, oils, waxes, and sterols
LIPIDE *same as* > LIPID
LIPIDES > LIPIDE
LIPIDIC > LIPID
LIPIDS > LIPID
LIPIN *n* family of nuclear proteins
LIPINS > LIPIN
LIPLESS > LIP
LIPLIKE > LIP
LIPO *n* liposuction
LIPOCYTE *n* fat-storing cell
LIPOCYTES > LIPOCYTE
LIPOGRAM *n* piece of writing in which all words containing a particular letter have been deliberately omitted
LIPOGRAMS > LIPOGRAM
LIPOIC as in *lipoic acid* sulphur-containing fatty acid
LIPOID *n* fatlike substance, such as wax
LIPOIDAL > LIPOID
LIPOIDS > LIPOID
LIPOLITIC *same as* > LIPOLYTIC
LIPOLYSES > LIPOLYSIS
LIPOLYSIS *n* hydrolysis of fats resulting in the production of carboxylic acids and glycerol
LIPOLYTIC *adj* fat-burning
LIPOMA *n* benign tumour composed of fatty tissue
LIPOMAS > LIPOMA
LIPOMATA > LIPOMA
LIPOPLAST *n* small particle in plant cytoplasm, esp that of seeds, in which fat is stored
LIPOS > LIPO
LIPOSOMAL > LIPOSOME
LIPOSOME *n* particle formed by lipids
LIPOSOMES > LIPOSOME
LIPOSUCK *vb* subject to liposuction
LIPOSUCKS > LIPOSUCK
LIPOTROPY *n* breaking down of fat in body
LIPPED > LIP
LIPPEN *vb* trust
LIPPENED > LIPPEN
LIPPENING > LIPPEN
LIPPENS > LIPPEN
LIPPER *Scots word for* > RIPPLE
LIPPERED > LIPPER
LIPPERING > LIPPER
LIPPERS > LIPPER
LIPPIE *variant of* > LIPPY
LIPPIER > LIPPY
LIPPIES > LIPPIE
LIPPIEST > LIPPY
LIPPINESS > LIPPY
LIPPING > LIP
LIPPINGS > LIP
LIPPITUDE *n* state of having bleary eyes
LIPPY *adj* insolent or cheeky ▷ *n* lipstick
LIPREAD *vb* follow what someone says by watching their lips
LIPREADER > LIPREAD
LIPREADS > LIPREAD
LIPS > LIP
LIPSTICK *n* cosmetic in stick form, for colouring the lips ▷ *vb* put lipstick on
LIPSTICKS > LIPSTICK
LIPURIA *n* presence of fat in the urine
LIPURIAS > LIPURIA
LIQUABLE *adj* that can be melted
LIQUATE *vb* separate one component of (an alloy, impure metal, or ore) by heating so that the more fusible part melts
LIQUATED > LIQUATE
LIQUATES > LIQUATE
LIQUATING > LIQUATE
LIQUATION > LIQUATE
LIQUEFIED > LIQUEFY
LIQUEFIER > LIQUEFY
LIQUEFIES > LIQUEFY
LIQUEFY *vb* make or become liquid
LIQUESCE *vb* become liquid
LIQUESCED > LIQUESCE
LIQUESCES > LIQUESCE
LIQUEUR *n* flavoured and sweetened alcoholic spirit ▷ *vb* flavour with liqueur
LIQUEURED > LIQUEUR
LIQUEURS > LIQUEUR
LIQUID *n* substance in a physical state which can change shape but not size

▷ *adj* of or being a liquid
LIQUIDATE *vb* pay (a debt)
LIQUIDISE *same as* > LIQUIDIZE
LIQUIDITY *n* state of being able to meet financial obligations
LIQUIDIZE *vb* make or become liquid
LIQUIDLY > LIQUID
LIQUIDS > LIQUID
LIQUIDUS *n* line on graph above which a substance is in liquid form
LIQUIFIED > LIQUIFY
LIQUIFIES > LIQUIFY
LIQUIFY *same as* > LIQUEFY
LIQUOR *n* alcoholic drink, esp spirits ▷ *vb* steep (malt) in warm water to form wort in brewing
LIQUORED > LIQUOR
LIQUORICE *n* black substance used in medicine and as a sweet
LIQUORING > LIQUOR
LIQUORISH *same as* > LICKERISH
LIQUORS > LIQUOR
LIRA *n* monetary unit of Turkey, Malta, and formerly of Italy
LIRAS > LIRA
LIRE > LIRA
LIRI > LIRA
LIRIOPE *n* grasslike plant
LIRIOPES > LIRIOPE
LIRIPIPE *n* tip of a graduate's hood
LIRIPIPES > LIRIPIPE
LIRIPOOP *same as* > LIRIPIPE
LIRIPOOPS > LIRIPOOP
LIRK *vb* wrinkle
LIRKED > LIRK
LIRKING > LIRK
LIRKS > LIRK
LIROT > LIRA
LIROTH > LIRA
LIS *n* fleur-de-lis
LISENTE > SENTE
LISK *Yorkshire dialect for* > GROIN
LISKS > LISK
LISLE *n* strong fine cotton thread or fabric
LISLES > LISLE
LISP *n* speech defect in which *s* and *z* are pronounced *th* ▷ *vb* speak or utter with a lisp
LISPED > LISP
LISPER > LISP
LISPERS > LISP
LISPING > LISP
LISPINGLY > LISP
LISPINGS > LISP
LISPOUND *n* unit of weight
LISPOUNDS > LISPOUND
LISPS > LISP
LISPUND *same as* > LISPOUND
LISPUNDS > LISPUND
LISSES > LIS
LISSOM *adj* supple, agile
LISSOME *same as* > LISSOM
LISSOMELY > LISSOM
LISSOMLY > LISSOM
LIST *n* item-by-item record of names or things, usu written one below another ▷ *vb* make a list of
LISTABLE > LIST
LISTED > LIST
LISTEE *n* person on list
LISTEES > LISTEE
LISTEL *another name for* > FILLET
LISTELS > LISTEL
LISTEN *vb* concentrate on hearing something
LISTENED > LISTEN
LISTENER > LISTEN
LISTENERS > LISTEN
LISTENING > LISTEN
LISTENS > LISTEN
LISTER *n* plough with a double mouldboard designed to throw soil to either side of a central furrow
LISTERIA *n* any rodlike Gram-positive bacterium of the genus *Listeria*
LISTERIAL > LISTERIA
LISTERIAS > LISTERIA
LISTERS > LISTER
LISTETH > LIST
LISTFUL *adj* paying attention
LISTING *n* list or an entry in a list
LISTINGS > LISTING
LISTLESS *adj* lacking interest or energy
LISTS *pl n* field of combat in a tournament
LISTSERV *n* service on the internet that provides an electronic mailing to subscribers with similar interests
LISTSERVS > LISTSERV
LIT *n* archaic word for dye or colouring
LITAI > LITAS
LITANIES > LITANY
LITANY *n* prayer with responses from the congregation
LITAS *n* standard monetary unit of Lithuania, divided into 100 centai
LITCHI *n* Chinese sapindaceous tree cultivated for its round edible fruits
LITCHIS > LITCHI
LITE *same as* > LIGHT
LITED > LIGHT
LITENESS > LITE
LITER *same as* > LITRE
LITERACY *n* ability to read and write
LITERAL *adj* according to the explicit meaning of a word or text, not figurative ▷ *n* misprint or misspelling in a text
LITERALLY *adv* in a literal manner
LITERALS > LITERAL
LITERARY *adj* of or knowledgeable about literature
LITERATE *adj* able to read and write ▷ *n* literate person
LITERATES > LITERATE
LITERATI *pl n* literary people
LITERATIM *adv* letter for letter
LITERATO > LITERATI
LITERATOR *n* professional writer
LITERATUS > LITERATI
LITEROSE *adj* affectedly literary
LITERS > LITER
LITES > LITE
LITH *n* limb or joint
LITHARGE *n* lead monoxide
LITHARGES > LITHARGE
LITHATE *n* salt of uric acid
LITHATES > LITHATE
LITHE *adj* flexible or supple, pliant ▷ *vb* listen
LITHED > LITHE
LITHELY > LITHE
LITHEMIA *n* gout
LITHEMIAS > LITHEMIA
LITHEMIC > LITHEMIA
LITHENESS > LITHE
LITHER > LITHE
LITHERLY *adj* crafty; cunning
LITHES > LITHE
LITHESOME *less common word for* > LISSOM
LITHEST > LITHE
LITHIA *n* lithium present in mineral waters as lithium salts
LITHIAS > LITHIA
LITHIASES > LITHIASIS
LITHIASIS *n* formation of a calculus
LITHIC *adj* of, relating to, or composed of stone
LITHIFIED > LITHIFY
LITHIFIES > LITHIFY
LITHIFY *vb* turn into rock
LITHING > LITHE
LITHISTID *n* type of sponge
LITHITE *n* part of cell with sensory element
LITHITES > LITHITE
LITHIUM *n* chemical element, the lightest known metal
LITHIUMS > LITHIUM
LITHO *n* lithography ▷ *vb* print using lithography
LITHOCYST *n* sac containing otoliths
LITHOED > LITHO
LITHOID *adj* resembling stone or rock
LITHOIDAL *same as* > LITHOID
LITHOING > LITHO
LITHOLOGY *n* physical characteristics of a rock
LITHOPONE *n* white pigment consisting of a mixture of zinc sulphide, zinc oxide, and barium sulphate
LITHOPS *n* fleshy-leaved plant
LITHOS > LITHO
LITHOSOL *n* type of azonal soil consisting chiefly of unweathered or partly weathered rock fragments
LITHOSOLS > LITHOSOL
LITHOTOME *n* instrument used in lithotomy operation
LITHOTOMY *n* surgical removal of a calculus, esp one in the urinary bladder
LITHS > LITH
LITIGABLE *adj* that may be the subject of litigation
LITIGANT *n* person involved in a lawsuit ▷ *adj* engaged in litigation
LITIGANTS > LITIGANT
LITIGATE *vb* bring or contest a law suit
LITIGATED > LITIGATE
LITIGATES > LITIGATE
LITIGATOR > LITIGATE
LITIGIOUS *adj* frequently going to law
LITING > LITE
LITMUS *n* blue dye turned red by acids and restored to blue by alkalis
LITMUSES > LITMUS
LITORAL *same as* > LITTORAL
LITOTES *n* ironical understatement used for effect
LITOTIC > LITOTES
LITRE *n* unit of liquid measure equal to 1000 cubic centimetres or 1.76 pints
LITRES > LITRE
LITS > LIT
LITTEN *adj* lighted
LITTER *n* untidy rubbish dropped in public places ▷ *vb* strew with litter
LITTERBAG *n* bag for putting rubbish in
LITTERBUG *n* person who tends to drop rubbish in public places
LITTERED > LITTER
LITTERER *n* one who litters
LITTERERS > LITTERER
LITTERING > LITTER
LITTERS > LITTER
LITTERY *adj* covered in litter
LITTLE *adj* small or smaller than average ▷ *adv* not a lot ▷ *n* small amount, extent, or duration
LITTLER > LITTLE

ITTLES > LITTLE
ITTLEST > LITTLE
ITTLIE *n* young child
ITTLIES > LITTLIE
ITTLIN *same as* > LITTLING
ITTLING *n* child
ITTLINGS > LITTLING
ITTLINS > LITTLIN
ITTLISH *adj* rather small
ITTORAL *adj* of or by the seashore ▷ *n* coastal district
ITTORALS > LITTORAL
ITU > LITAS
ITURGIC > LITURGY
ITURGICS *n* study of liturgies
ITURGIES > LITURGY
ITURGISM > LITURGIST
ITURGIST *n* student or composer of liturgical forms
ITURGY *n* prescribed form of public worship
ITUUS *n* type of curved trumpet
ITUUSES > LITUUS
IVABLE *adj* tolerable or pleasant to live (with)
IVE *vb* be alive ▷ *adj* living, alive ▷ *adv* in the form of a live performance
IVEABLE *same as* > LIVABLE
IVED > LIVE
IVEDO *n* reddish discoloured patch on the skin
IVEDOS > LIVEDO
IVELIER > LIVELY
IVELIEST > LIVELY
IVELILY > LIVELY
IVELOD *n* livelihood
IVELODS > LIVELOD
IVELONG *adj* long or seemingly long
IVELONGS > LIVELONG
IVELOOD *n* livelihood
IVELOODS > LIVELOOD
IVELY *adj* full of life or vigour
IVEN *vb* make or become lively
IVENED > LIVEN
IVENER > LIVEN
IVENERS > LIVEN
IVENESS *n* state of being alive
IVENING > LIVEN
IVENS > LIVEN
IVER *n* person who lives in a specified way
IVERED *adj* having liver
IVERIED *adj* wearing livery
IVERIES > LIVERY
IVERING *n* process of liquid becoming lumpy
IVERISH *adj* having a disorder of the liver
IVERLEAF *n* woodland plant
IVERLESS > LIVER
IVERS > LIVER
IVERWORT *n* plant resembling seaweed or leafy moss
LIVERY *n* distinctive dress, esp of a servant or servants ▷ *adj* of or resembling liver
LIVERYMAN *n* member of a livery company
LIVERYMEN > LIVERYMAN
LIVES > LIFE
LIVEST > LIVE
LIVESTOCK *n* farm animals
LIVETRAP *n* box constructed to trap an animal without injuring it
LIVETRAPS > LIVETRAP
LIVEWARE *n* programmers, systems analysts, operating staff, and other personnel working in a computer system
LIVEWARES > LIVEWARE
LIVEYER *n* (in Newfoundland) a full-time resident
LIVEYERE *same as* > LIVEYER
LIVEYERES > LIVEYERE
LIVEYERS > LIVEYER
LIVID *adj* angry or furious
LIVIDER > LIVID
LIVIDEST > LIVID
LIVIDITY *n* state of being livid
LIVIDLY > LIVID
LIVIDNESS > LIVID
LIVIER *same as* > LIVEYER
LIVIERS > LIVIER
LIVING *adj* possessing life, not dead or inanimate ▷ *n* condition of being alive
LIVINGLY > LIVING
LIVINGS > LIVING
LIVOR *another word for* > LIVIDITY
LIVORS > LIVOR
LIVRAISON *n* one of the numbers of a book published in parts
LIVRE *n* former French unit of money of account, equal to 1 pound of silver
LIVRES > LIVRE
LIVYER *same as* > LIVEYER
LIVYERS > LIVYER
LIXIVIA > LIXIVIUM
LIXIVIAL > LIXIVIATE
LIXIVIATE *less common word for* > LEACH
LIXIVIOUS > LIXIVIUM
LIXIVIUM *n* alkaline solution obtained by leaching wood ash with water
LIXIVIUMS > LIXIVIUM
LIZARD *n* four-footed reptile with a long body and tail
LIZARDS > LIZARD
LIZZIE as in *busy lizzie* plant with pink, white, or red flowers
LIZZIES > LIZZIE
LLAMA *n* woolly animal of the camel family used as a beast of burden in S America
LLAMAS > LLAMA
LLANERO *n* native of llanos
LLANEROS > LLANERO
LLANO *n* extensive grassy treeless plain, esp in South America
LLANOS > LLANO
LO *interj* look!
LOACH *n* carplike freshwater fish
LOACHES > LOACH
LOAD *n* burden or weight ▷ *vb* put a load on or into
LOADED *adj* (of a question) containing a hidden trap or implication
LOADEN *vb* load
LOADENED > LOADEN
LOADENING > LOADEN
LOADENS > LOADEN
LOADER *n* person who loads a gun or other firearm
LOADERS > LOADER
LOADING *n* load or burden
LOADINGS > LOADING
LOADS *pl n* lots or a lot
LOADSPACE *n* area in a motor vehicle where a load can be carried
LOADSTAR *same as* > LODESTAR
LOADSTARS > LOADSTAR
LOADSTONE *same as* > LODESTONE
LOAF *n* shaped mass of baked bread ▷ *vb* idle, loiter
LOAFED > LOAF
LOAFER *n* person who avoids work
LOAFERISH > LOAFER
LOAFERS > LOAFER
LOAFING > LOAF
LOAFINGS > LOAF
LOAFS > LOAF
LOAM *n* fertile soil ▷ *vb* cover, treat, or fill with loam
LOAMED > LOAM
LOAMIER > LOAM
LOAMIEST > LOAM
LOAMINESS > LOAM
LOAMING > LOAM
LOAMLESS > LOAM
LOAMS > LOAM
LOAMY > LOAM
LOAN *n* money lent at interest ▷ *vb* lend
LOANABLE > LOAN
LOANBACK *n* facility by which an individual can borrow from his or her pension fund ▷ *vb* make use of this facility
LOANBACKS > LOANBACK
LOANED > LOAN
LOANER > LOAN
LOANERS > LOAN
LOANING > LOAN
LOANINGS > LOANING
LOANS > LOAN
LOANSHIFT *n* adaptation of word from one language by another
LOANWORD *n* word adopted from one language into another
LOANWORDS > LOANWORD
LOAST > LOOSE
LOATH *adj* unwilling or reluctant (to)
LOATHE *vb* hate, be disgusted by
LOATHED > LOATHE
LOATHER > LOATHE
LOATHERS > LOATHE
LOATHES > LOATHE
LOATHEST > LOATH
LOATHFUL *adj* causing loathing
LOATHING *n* strong disgust
LOATHINGS > LOATHING
LOATHLY *adv* with reluctance
LOATHNESS > LOATH
LOATHSOME *adj* causing loathing
LOATHY *obsolete form of* > LOATHSOME
LOAVE *vb* make into the form of a loaf
LOAVED > LOAVE
LOAVES > LOAF
LOAVING > LOAVE
LOB *n* ball struck or thrown in a high arc ▷ *vb* strike or throw (a ball) in a high arc
LOBAR *adj* of or affecting a lobe
LOBATE *adj* with or like lobes
LOBATED *same as* > LOBATE
LOBATELY > LOBATE
LOBATION *n* division into lobes
LOBATIONS > LOBATION
LOBBED > LOB
LOBBER *n* one who lobs
LOBBERS > LOBBER
LOBBIED > LOBBY
LOBBIES > LOBBY
LOBBING > LOB
LOBBY *n* corridor into which rooms open ▷ *vb* try to influence (legislators) in the formulation of policy
LOBBYER > LOBBY
LOBBYERS > LOBBY
LOBBYGOW *n* errand boy
LOBBYGOWS > LOBBYGOW
LOBBYING > LOBBY
LOBBYINGS > LOBBY
LOBBYISM > LOBBYIST
LOBBYISMS > LOBBYIST
LOBBYIST *n* person who lobbies on behalf of a particular interest
LOBBYISTS > LOBBYIST
LOBE *n* rounded projection
LOBECTOMY *n* surgical removal of a lobe from any organ or gland in the body
LOBED > LOBE
LOBEFIN *n* type of fish
LOBEFINS > LOBEFIN
LOBELET *n* small lobe

LOBELETS > LOBELET
LOBELIA *n* garden plant with blue, red, or white flowers
LOBELIAS > LOBELIA
LOBELINE *n* crystalline alkaloid extracted from the seeds of the Indian tobacco plant
LOBELINES > LOBELINE
LOBES > LOBE
LOBI > LOBUS
LOBING *n* formation of lobes
LOBINGS > LOBING
LOBIPED *adj* with lobed toes
LOBLOLLY *n* southern US pine tree
LOBO *n* timber wolf
LOBOLA *n* (in African custom) price paid by a bridegroom's family to his bride's family
LOBOLAS > LOBOLA
LOBOLO *same as* > LOBOLA
LOBOLOS > LOBOLO
LOBOS > LOBO
LOBOSE *another word for* > LOBATE
LOBOTOMY *n* surgical incision into a lobe of the brain to treat mental disorders
LOBS > LOB
LOBSCOUSE *n* sailor's stew of meat, vegetables, and hardtack
LOBSTER *n* shellfish with a long tail and claws, which turns red when boiled ▷ *vb* fish for lobsters
LOBSTERED > LOBSTER
LOBSTERER *n* person who catches lobsters
LOBSTERS > LOBSTER
LOBSTICK *n* tree used as landmark
LOBSTICKS > LOBSTICK
LOBULAR > LOBULE
LOBULARLY > LOBULE
LOBULATE > LOBULE
LOBULATED > LOBULE
LOBULE *n* small lobe or a subdivision of a lobe
LOBULES > LOBULE
LOBULI > LOBULUS
LOBULOSE > LOBULE
LOBULUS *n* small lobe
LOBUS *n* lobe
LOBWORM *same as* > LUGWORM
LOBWORMS > LOBWORM
LOCA > LOCUS
LOCAL *adj* of or existing in a particular place ▷ *n* person belonging to a particular district
LOCALE *n* scene of an event
LOCALES > LOCALE
LOCALISE *same as* > LOCALIZE
LOCALISED > LOCALISE
LOCALISER > LOCALISE
LOCALISES > LOCALISE
LOCALISM *n* pronunciation, phrase, etc, peculiar to a particular locality
LOCALISMS > LOCALISM
LOCALIST > LOCALISM
LOCALISTS > LOCALISM
LOCALITE *n* resident of an area
LOCALITES > LOCALITE
LOCALITY *n* neighbourhood or area
LOCALIZE *vb* restrict to a particular place
LOCALIZED > LOCALIZE
LOCALIZER > LOCALIZE
LOCALIZES > LOCALIZE
LOCALLY *adv* within a particular area or place
LOCALNESS > LOCAL
LOCALS > LOCAL
LOCATABLE > LOCATE
LOCATE *vb* discover the whereabouts of
LOCATED > LOCATE
LOCATER > LOCATE
LOCATERS > LOCATE
LOCATES > LOCATE
LOCATING > LOCATE
LOCATION *n* site or position
LOCATIONS > LOCATION
LOCATIVE *adj* (of a word or phrase) indicating place or direction ▷ *n* locative case
LOCATIVES > LOCATIVE
LOCATOR *n* part of index that indicates where to look for information
LOCATORS > LOCATOR
LOCELLATE *adj* split into secondary cells
LOCH *n* lake
LOCHAN *n* small inland loch
LOCHANS > LOCHAN
LOCHIA *n* vaginal discharge of cellular debris, mucus, and blood following childbirth
LOCHIAL > LOCHIA
LOCHS > LOCH
LOCI > LOCUS
LOCK *n* appliance for fastening a door, case, etc ▷ *vb* fasten or become fastened securely
LOCKABLE > LOCK
LOCKAGE *n* system of locks in a canal
LOCKAGES > LOCKAGE
LOCKAWAY *n* investment intended to be held for a relatively long time
LOCKAWAYS > LOCKAWAY
LOCKBOX *n* system of collecting funds from companies by banks
LOCKBOXES > LOCKBOX
LOCKDOWN *n* device used to secure equipment, etc
LOCKDOWNS > LOCKDOWN
LOCKED > LOCK
LOCKER *n* small cupboard with a lock
LOCKERS > LOCKER
LOCKET *n* small hinged pendant for a portrait etc
LOCKETS > LOCKET
LOCKFAST *adj* securely fastened with a lock
LOCKFUL *n* sufficient to fill a canal lock
LOCKFULS > LOCKFUL
LOCKHOUSE *n* house of lock-keeper
LOCKING > LOCK
LOCKINGS > LOCK
LOCKJAW *n* tetanus
LOCKJAWS > LOCKJAW
LOCKMAKER *n* maker of locks
LOCKMAN *n* lock-keeper
LOCKMEN > LOCKMAN
LOCKNUT *n* supplementary nut screwed down upon a primary nut to prevent it from shaking loose
LOCKNUTS > LOCKNUT
LOCKOUT *n* closing of a workplace by an employer to force workers to accept terms
LOCKOUTS > LOCKOUT
LOCKPICK *another word for* > PICKLOCK
LOCKPICKS > LOCKPICK
LOCKRAM *n* type of linen cloth
LOCKRAMS > LOCKRAM
LOCKS > LOCK
LOCKSET *n* hardware used to lock door
LOCKSETS > LOCKSET
LOCKSMAN *same as* > LOCKMAN
LOCKSMEN > LOCKSMAN
LOCKSMITH *n* person who makes and mends locks
LOCKSTEP *n* method of marching in step as closely as possible
LOCKSTEPS > LOCKSTEP
LOCKUP *n* prison
LOCKUPS > LOCKUP
LOCO *n* locomotive ▷ *adj* insane ▷ *vb* poison with locoweed
LOCOED > LOCO
LOCOES > LOCO
LOCOFOCO *n* match
LOCOFOCOS > LOCOFOCO
LOCOING > LOCO
LOCOISM *n* disease of cattle, sheep, and horses caused by eating locoweed
LOCOISMS > LOCOISM
LOCOMAN *n* railwayman, esp an engine-driver
LOCOMEN > LOCOMAN
LOCOMOTE *vb* move from one place to another
LOCOMOTED > LOCOMOTE
LOCOMOTES > LOCOMOTE
LOCOMOTOR *adj* of or relating to locomotion
LOCOPLANT *another word for* > LOCOWEED
LOCOS > LOCO
LOCOWEED *n* any of several perennial leguminous plants
LOCOWEEDS > LOCOWEED
LOCULAR *adj* divided into compartments by septa
LOCULATE *same as* > LOCULAR
LOCULATED *same as* > LOCULATE
LOCULE *n* any of the chambers of an ovary or anther
LOCULED *adj* having locule
LOCULES > LOCULE
LOCULI > LOCULUS
LOCULUS *same as* > LOCULE
LOCUM *n* temporary stand-in for a doctor or clergyman
LOCUMS > LOCUM
LOCUPLETE *adj* well-stored
LOCUS *n* area or place where something happens
LOCUST *n* destructive insect that flies in swarms and eats crops ▷ *vb* ravage, as locusts
LOCUSTA *n* flower cluster unit in grasses
LOCUSTAE > LOCUSTA
LOCUSTAL > LOCUSTA
LOCUSTED > LOCUST
LOCUSTING > LOCUST
LOCUSTS > LOCUST
LOCUTION *n* manner or style of speech
LOCUTIONS > LOCUTION
LOCUTORY *adj* room intended for conversation
LOD *n* type of logarithm
LODE *n* vein of ore
LODEN *n* thick heavy waterproof woollen cloth with a short pile, used to make garments, esp coats
LODENS > LODEN
LODES > LODE
LODESMAN *n* pilot
LODESMEN > LODESMAN
LODESTAR *n* star used in navigation or astronomy as a point of reference
LODESTARS > LODESTAR
LODESTONE *n* magnetic iron ore
LODGE *n* gatekeeper's house ▷ *vb* live in another's house at a fixed charge
LODGEABLE > LODGE
LODGED > LODGE
LODGEMENT *same as* > LODGMENT
LODGEPOLE *n* type of pine tree
LODGER *n* person who pays rent in return for accommodation in someone else's home
LODGERS > LODGER
LODGES > LODGE

LODGING *n* temporary residence
LODGINGS *pl n* rented room or rooms in which to live, esp in another person's house
LODGMENT *n* act of lodging or the state of being lodged
LODGMENTS > LODGMENT
LODICULA *n* delicate scale in grass
LODICULAE > LODICULA
LODICULE *n* any of two or three minute scales at the base of the ovary in grass flowers that represent the corolla
LODICULES > LODICULE
LODS > LOD
LOERIE *same as* > LOURIE
LOERIES > LOERIE
LOESS *n* fine-grained soil, found mainly in river valleys, originally deposited by the wind
LOESSAL > LOESS
LOESSES > LOESS
LOESSIAL > LOESS
LOFT *n* space between the top storey and roof of a building ▷ *vb* strike, throw, or kick (a ball) high into the air
LOFTED > LOFT
LOFTER *n* type of golf club
LOFTERS > LOFTER
LOFTIER > LOFTY
LOFTIEST > LOFTY
LOFTILY > LOFTY
LOFTINESS > LOFTY
LOFTING > LOFT
LOFTLESS > LOFT
LOFTLIKE > LOFT
LOFTS > LOFT
LOFTSMAN *n* person who reproduces in actual size a draughtsman's design for a ship or an aircraft
LOFTSMEN > LOFTSMAN
LOFTY *adj* of great height
LOG *n* portion of a felled tree stripped of branches ▷ *vb* saw logs from a tree
LOGAN *another name for* > BOGAN
LOGANIA *n* type of Australian plant
LOGANIAS > LOGANIA
LOGANS > LOGAN
LOGAOEDIC *adj* of or relating to verse in which mixed metres are combined within a single line to give the effect of prose ▷ *n* line or verse of this kind
LOGARITHM *n* one of a series of arithmetical functions used to make certain calculations easier
LOGBOARD *n* board used for logging a ship's records
LOGBOARDS > LOGBOARD
LOGBOOK *n* book recording the details about a car or a ship's journeys
LOGBOOKS > LOGBOOK
LOGE *n* small enclosure or box in a theatre or opera house
LOGES > LOGE
LOGGAT *n* small piece of wood
LOGGATS > LOGGAT
LOGGED > LOG
LOGGER *n* tractor or crane for handling logs
LOGGERS > LOGGER
LOGGETS *n* old-fashioned game played with sticks
LOGGIA *n* covered gallery at the side of a building
LOGGIAS > LOGGIA
LOGGIE > LOGGIA
LOGGIER > LOGGY
LOGGIEST > LOGGY
LOGGING > LOG
LOGGINGS > LOG
LOGGISH > LOG
LOGGY *adj* slow, sluggish, or listless
LOGIA > LOGION
LOGIC *n* philosophy of reasoning
LOGICAL *adj* of logic
LOGICALLY > LOGICAL
LOGICIAN *n* person who specializes in or is skilled at logic
LOGICIANS > LOGICIAN
LOGICISE *same as* > LOGICIZE
LOGICISED > LOGICISE
LOGICISES > LOGICISE
LOGICISM *n* philosophical theory that all of mathematics can be deduced from logic
LOGICISMS > LOGICISM
LOGICIST > LOGICISM
LOGICISTS > LOGICISM
LOGICIZE *vb* present reasons for or against
LOGICIZED > LOGICIZE
LOGICIZES > LOGICIZE
LOGICLESS > LOGIC
LOGICS > LOGIC
LOGIE *n* fire-place of a kiln
LOGIER > LOGY
LOGIES > LOGIE
LOGIEST > LOGY
LOGILY > LOGY
LOGIN *n* process by which a computer user logs on
LOGINESS > LOGY
LOGINS > LOGIN
LOGION *n* saying of Christ regarded as authentic
LOGIONS > LOGION
LOGISTIC *n* uninterpreted calculus or system of symbolic logic ▷ *adj* (of a curve) having a particular form of equation
LOGISTICS *n* detailed planning and organization of a large, esp military, operation
LOGJAM *n* blockage caused by the crowding together of a number of logs floating in a river ▷ *vb* cause a logjam
LOGJAMMED > LOGJAM
LOGJAMS > LOGJAM
LOGJUICE *n* poor quality port wine
LOGJUICES > LOGJUICE
LOGLINE *n* synopsis of screenplay
LOGLINES > LOGLINE
LOGLOG *n* logarithm of a logarithm (in equations, etc)
LOGLOGS > LOGLOG
LOGNORMAL *adj* (maths) having a natural logarithm with normal distribution
LOGO *same as* > LOGOTYPE
LOGOFF *n* process by which a computer user logs out
LOGOFFS > LOGOFF
LOGOGRAM *n* single symbol representing an entire morpheme, word, or phrase
LOGOGRAMS > LOGOGRAM
LOGOGRAPH *same as* > LOGOGRAM
LOGOGRIPH *n* word puzzle, esp one based on recombination of the letters of a word
LOGOI > LOGOS
LOGOMACH *n* one who argues over words
LOGOMACHS > LOGOMACH
LOGOMACHY *n* argument about words or the meaning of words
LOGON *variant of* > LOGIN
LOGONS > LOGON
LOGOPEDIC *adj* of or relating to speech therapy
LOGOPHILE *n* one who loves words
LOGORRHEA *n* excessive or uncontrollable talkativeness
LOGOS *n* reason or the rational principle expressed in words and things, argument, or justification
LOGOTHETE *n* officer of Byzantine empire
LOGOTYPE *n* piece of type with several uncombined characters cast on it
LOGOTYPES > LOGOTYPE
LOGOTYPY > LOGOTYPE
LOGOUT *variant of* > LOGOFF
LOGOUTS > LOGOUT
LOGROLL *vb* use logrolling in order to procure the passage of (legislation)
LOGROLLED > LOGROLL
LOGROLLER > LOGROLL
LOGROLLS > LOGROLL
LOGS > LOG
LOGWAY *another name for* > GANGWAY
LOGWAYS > LOGWAY
LOGWOOD *n* leguminous tree of the Caribbean and Central America
LOGWOODS > LOGWOOD
LOGY *adj* dull or listless
LOHAN *another word for* > ARHAT
LOHANS > LOHAN
LOID *vb* open (a lock) using a celluloid strip
LOIDED > LOID
LOIDING > LOID
LOIDS > LOID
LOIN *n* part of the body between the ribs and the hips
LOINCLOTH *n* piece of cloth covering the loins only
LOINS *pl n* hips and the inner surface of the legs where they join the body
LOIPE *n* cross-country skiing track
LOIPEN > LOIPE
LOIR *n* large dormouse
LOIRS > LOIR
LOITER *vb* stand or wait aimlessly or idly
LOITERED > LOITER
LOITERER > LOITER
LOITERERS > LOITER
LOITERING > LOITER
LOITERS > LOITER
LOKE *n* track
LOKES > LOKE
LOKSHEN *pl n* noodles
LOLIGO *n* type of squid
LOLIGOS > LOLIGO
LOLIUM *n* type of grass
LOLIUMS > LOLIUM
LOLL *vb* lounge lazily ▷ *n* act or instance of lolling
LOLLED > LOLL
LOLLER > LOLL
LOLLERS > LOLL
LOLLIES > LOLLY
LOLLING > LOLL
LOLLINGLY > LOLL
LOLLIPOP *n* boiled sweet on a small wooden stick
LOLLIPOPS > LOLLIPOP
LOLLOP *vb* move clumsily
LOLLOPED > LOLLOP
LOLLOPING > LOLLOP
LOLLOPS > LOLLOP
LOLLOPY > LOLLOP
LOLLS > LOLL
LOLLY *n* lollipop or ice lolly
LOLLYGAG *same as* > LALLYGAG
LOLLYGAGS > LOLLYGAG
LOLLYPOP *same as* > LOLLIPOP
LOLLYPOPS > LOLLYPOP
LOLOG *same as* > LOGLOG
LOLOGS > LOLOG
LOMA *n* lobe
LOMAS > LOMA
LOMATA > LOMA
LOME *vb* cover with lome
LOMED > LOME
LOMEIN *n* Chinese dish

LOMEINS > LOMEIN
LOMENT *n* pod of certain leguminous plants
LOMENTA > LOMENTUM
LOMENTS > LOMENT
LOMENTUM *same as* > LOMENT
LOMENTUMS > LOMENTUM
LOMES > LOME
LOMING > LOME
LOMPISH *another word for* > LUMPISH
LONE *adj* solitary
LONELIER > LONELY
LONELIEST > LONELY
LONELILY > LONELY
LONELY *adj* sad because alone
LONENESS > LONE
LONER *n* person who prefers to be alone
LONERS > LONER
LONESOME *adj* lonely ▷ *n* own
LONESOMES > LONESOME
LONG *adj* having length, esp great length, in space or time ▷ *adv* for a certain time ▷ *vb* have a strong desire (for)
LONGA *n* long note
LONGAEVAL *adj* long-lived
LONGAN *n* sapindaceous tree of tropical and subtropical Asia
LONGANS > LONGAN
LONGAS > LONGA
LONGBOARD *n* type of surfboard
LONGBOAT *n* largest boat carried on a ship
LONGBOATS > LONGBOAT
LONGBOW *n* large powerful bow
LONGBOWS > LONGBOW
LONGCASE as in *longcase clock* grandfather clock
LONGCLOTH *n* fine plain-weave cotton cloth made in long strips
LONGE *n* rope used in training a horse ▷ *vb* train using a longe
LONGED > LONG
LONGEING > LONGE
LONGER *n* line of barrels on a ship
LONGERON *n* main longitudinal structural member of an aircraft
LONGERONS > LONGERON
LONGERS > LONGER
LONGES > LONGE
LONGEST > LONG
LONGEVAL *another word for* > LONGAEVAL
LONGEVITY *n* long life
LONGEVOUS > LONGEVITY
LONGHAIR *n* cat with long hair
LONGHAIRS > LONGHAIR
LONGHAND *n* ordinary writing, not shorthand or typing
LONGHANDS > LONGHAND
LONGHEAD *n* person with long head
LONGHEADS > LONGHEAD
LONGHORN *n* British breed of beef cattle with long curved horns
LONGHORNS > LONGHORN
LONGHOUSE *n* long communal dwelling of Native American peoples
LONGICORN *n* any beetle of the family *Cerambycidae* ▷ *adj* having or designating long antennae
LONGIES *n* long johns
LONGING *n* yearning ▷ *adj* having or showing desire
LONGINGLY > LONGING
LONGINGS > LONGING
LONGISH *adj* rather long
LONGITUDE *n* distance east or west from a standard meridian
LONGJUMP *n* jumping contest decided by length
LONGJUMPS > LONGJUMP
LONGLEAF *n* North American pine tree
LONGLINE *n* (tennis) straight stroke played down court
LONGLINES > LONGLINE
LONGLY > LONG
LONGNECK *n* US, Canadian and Australian word for a 330-ml beer bottle with a long narrow neck
LONGNECKS > LONGNECK
LONGNESS > LONG
LONGS *pl n* full-length trousers
LONGSHIP *n* narrow open boat with oars and a square sail, used by the Vikings
LONGSHIPS > LONGSHIP
LONGSHORE *adj* situated on, relating to, or along the shore
LONGSOME *adj* slow; boring
LONGSPUR *n* any of various Arctic and North American buntings
LONGSPURS > LONGSPUR
LONGTIME *adj* of long standing
LONGUEUR *n* period of boredom or dullness
LONGUEURS > LONGUEUR
LONGWALL *n* long face in coal mine
LONGWALLS > LONGWALL
LONGWAYS *adv* lengthways
LONGWISE *same as* > LONGWAYS
LONICERA *n* honeysuckle
LONICERAS > LONICERA
LOO *n* informal word meaning lavatory ▷ *vb* Scots word meaning love
LOOBIER > LOOBY
LOOBIES > LOOBY
LOOBIEST > LOOBY
LOOBILY > LOOBY
LOOBY *adj* foolish ▷ *n* foolish or stupid person
LOOED > LOO
LOOEY *n* lieutenant
LOOEYS > LOOEY
LOOF *n* part of ship's side
LOOFA *same as* > LOOFAH
LOOFAH *n* sponge made from the dried pod of a gourd
LOOFAHS > LOOFAH
LOOFAS > LOOFA
LOOFFUL *n* handful
LOOFFULS > LOOFFUL
LOOFS > LOOF
LOOIE *same as* > LOOEY
LOOIES > LOOIE
LOOING > LOO
LOOK *vb* direct the eyes or attention (towards) ▷ *n* instance of looking
LOOKALIKE *n* person who is the double of another
LOOKDOWN *n* way paper appears when looked at under reflected light
LOOKDOWNS > LOOKDOWN
LOOKED > LOOK
LOOKER *n* person who looks
LOOKERS > LOOKER
LOOKING > LOOK
LOOKISM *n* discrimination against a person on the grounds of physical appearance
LOOKISMS > LOOKISM
LOOKIST > LOOKISM
LOOKISTS > LOOKISM
LOOKOUT *n* act of watching for danger or for an opportunity ▷ *vb* be careful
LOOKOUTS > LOOKOUT
LOOKOVER *n* inspection, esp a brief one
LOOKOVERS > LOOKOVER
LOOKS > LOOK
LOOKSISM *same as* > LOOKISM
LOOKSISMS > LOOKSISM
LOOKUP *n* act of looking up information, esp on the internet
LOOKUPS > LOOKUP
LOOM *n* machine for weaving cloth ▷ *vb* appear dimly
LOOMED > LOOM
LOOMING > LOOM
LOOMS > LOOM
LOON *n* diving bird
LOONEY *same as* > LOONY
LOONEYS > LOONY
LOONIE *n* Canadian dollar coin with a loon bird on one of its faces
LOONIER > LOONY
LOONIES > LOONY
LOONIEST > LOONY
LOONILY > LOONY
LOONINESS > LOONY
LOONING *n* cry of the loon
LOONINGS > LOONING
LOONS > LOON
LOONY *adj* foolish or insane ▷ *n* foolish or insane person
LOOP *n* rounded shape made by a curved line or rope crossing itself ▷ *vb* form or fasten with a loop
LOOPED > LOOP
LOOPER *n* person or thing that loops or makes loops
LOOPERS > LOOPER
LOOPHOLE *n* means of evading a rule without breaking it ▷ *vb* provide with loopholes
LOOPHOLED > LOOPHOLE
LOOPHOLES > LOOPHOLE
LOOPIER > LOOPY
LOOPIEST > LOOPY
LOOPILY > LOOPY
LOOPINESS > LOOPY
LOOPING > LOOP
LOOPINGS > LOOP
LOOPS > LOOP
LOOPY *adj* slightly mad or crazy
LOOR > LIEF
LOORD *obsolete word for* > LOUT
LOORDS > LOORD
LOOS > LOO
LOOSE *adj* not tight, fastened, fixed, or tense ▷ *adv* in a loose manner ▷ *vb* free
LOOSEBOX *n* enclosed stall with a door in which an animal can be kept
LOOSED > LOOSE
LOOSELY > LOOSE
LOOSEN *vb* make loose
LOOSENED > LOOSEN
LOOSENER > LOOSEN
LOOSENERS > LOOSEN
LOOSENESS > LOOSE
LOOSENING > LOOSEN
LOOSENS > LOOSEN
LOOSER > LOOSE
LOOSES > LOOSE
LOOSEST > LOOSE
LOOSIE *n* informal word fo loose forward
LOOSIES *pl n* cigarettes sold individually
LOOSING *n* celebration of one's 21st birthday
LOOSINGS > LOOSING
LOOT *vb* pillage ▷ *n* goods stolen during pillaging
LOOTED > LOOT
LOOTEN *Scots past form of* > LET
LOOTER > LOOT
LOOTERS > LOOT
LOOTING > LOOT
LOOTINGS > LOOT
LOOTS > LOOT
LOOVES > LOOF
LOP *vb* cut away (twigs and branches) ▷ *n* part or parts lopped off, as from a tree

LOPE *vb* run with long easy strides ▷ *n* loping stride
LOPED > LOPE
LOPER > LOPE
LOPERS > LOPE
LOPES > LOPE
LOPGRASS *n* smooth-bladed grass
LOPHODONT *adj* (of teeth) having elongated ridges
LOPING > LOPE
LOPOLITH *n* saucer- or lens-shaped body of intrusive igneous rock
LOPOLITHS > LOPOLITH
LOPPED > LOP
LOPPER *n* tool for lopping ▷ *vb* curdle
LOPPERED > LOPPER
LOPPERING > LOPPER
LOPPERS > LOPPER
LOPPIER > LOPPY
LOPPIES > LOPPY
LOPPIEST > LOPPY
LOPPING > LOP
LOPPINGS > LOP
LOPPY *adj* floppy ▷ *n* man employed to do maintenance tasks on a ranch
LOPS > LOP
LOPSIDED *adj* greater in height, weight, or size on one side
LOPSTICK *variant of* > LOBSTICK
LOPSTICKS > LOPSTICK
LOQUACITY *n* tendency to talk a great deal
LOQUAT *n* ornamental evergreen rosaceous tree
LOQUATS > LOQUAT
LOQUITUR *n* stage direction meaning *he* or *she speaks*
LOR *interj* exclamation of surprise or dismay
LORAL *adj* of part of side of bird's head
LORAN *n* radio navigation system operating over long distances
LORANS > LORAN
LORATE *adj* like a strap
LORAZEPAM *n* type of tranquillizer
LORCHA *n* junk-rigged vessel
LORCHAS > LORCHA
LORD *n* person with power over others, such as a monarch or master ▷ *vb* act in a superior manner
LORDED > LORD
LORDING *n* gentleman
LORDINGS > LORDING
LORDKIN *n* little lord
LORDKINS > LORDKIN
LORDLESS > LORD
LORDLIER > LORDLY
LORDLIEST > LORDLY
LORDLIKE > LORD
LORDLING *n* young lord
LORDLINGS > LORDLING
LORDLY *adj* imperious, proud ▷ *adv* in the manner of a lord
LORDOMA *same as* > LORDOSIS
LORDOMAS > LORDOMA
LORDOSES > LORDOSIS
LORDOSIS *n* forward curvature of the lumbar spine
LORDOTIC > LORDOSIS
LORDS > LORD
LORDSHIP *n* position or authority of a lord
LORDSHIPS > LORDSHIP
LORDY *interj* exclamation of surprise or dismay
LORE *n* body of traditions on a subject
LOREAL *adj* concerning or relating to lore
LOREL *another word for* > LOSEL
LORELS > LOREL
LORES > LORE
LORETTE *n* concubine
LORETTES > LORETTE
LORGNETTE *n* pair of spectacles mounted on a long handle
LORGNON *n* monocle or pair of spectacles
LORGNONS > LORGNON
LORIC > LORICA
LORICA *n* hard outer covering of rotifers, ciliate protozoans, and similar organisms
LORICAE > LORICA
LORICATE > LORICA
LORICATED > LORICA
LORICATES > LORICA
LORICS > LORICA
LORIES > LORY
LORIKEET *n* small brightly coloured Australian parrot
LORIKEETS > LORIKEET
LORIMER *n* (formerly) a person who made bits, spurs, and other small metal objects
LORIMERS > LORIMER
LORINER *same as* > LORIMER
LORINERS > LORINER
LORING *n* teaching
LORINGS > LORING
LORIOT *n* golden oriole (bird)
LORIOTS > LORIOT
LORIS *n* any of several omnivorous nocturnal slow-moving prosimian primates
LORISES > LORIS
LORN *adj* forsaken or wretched
LORNNESS > LORN
LORRELL *obsolete word for* > LOSEL
LORRELLS > LORRELL
LORRIES > LORRY
LORRY *n* large vehicle for transporting loads by road
LORY *n* any of various small brightly coloured parrots of Australia and Indonesia
LOS *n* approval
LOSABLE > LOOSE
LOSE *vb* part with or come to be without
LOSED > LOSE
LOSEL *n* worthless person ▷ *adj* (of a person) worthless, useless, or wasteful
LOSELS > LOSEL
LOSEN > LOOSE
LOSER *n* person or thing that loses
LOSERS > LOSER
LOSES > LOOSE
LOSH *interj* lord
LOSING > LOSE
LOSINGLY > LOSE
LOSINGS *pl n* losses, esp money lost in gambling
LOSLYF *n* South African slang for a promiscuous female
LOSLYFS > LOSLYF
LOSS *n* losing
LOSSES > LOSS
LOSSIER > LOSSY
LOSSIEST > LOSSY
LOSSLESS > LOSS
LOSSMAKER *n* organization, industry, or enterprise that consistently fails to make a profit
LOSSY *adj* (of a dielectric material, transmission line, etc) designed to have a high attenuation
LOST *adj* missing
LOSTNESS > LOST
LOT *pron* great number ▷ *n* collection of people or things ▷ *vb* draw lots for
LOTA *n* globular water container, usually of brass, used in India, Myanmar, etc
LOTAH *same as* > LOTA
LOTAHS > LOTAH
LOTAS > LOTA
LOTE *another word for* > LOTUS
LOTES > LOTE
LOTH *same as* > LOATH
LOTHARIO *n* rake, libertine, or seducer
LOTHARIOS > LOTHARIO
LOTHEFULL *obsolete form of* > LOATHFUL
LOTHER > LOTH
LOTHEST > LOTH
LOTHFULL *obsolete form of* > LOATHFUL
LOTHNESS > LOTH
LOTHSOME *same as* > LOATHSOME
LOTI *n* standard monetary unit of Lesotho, divided into 100 lisente
LOTIC *adj* of, relating to, or designating natural communities living in rapidly flowing water
LOTION *n* medical or cosmetic liquid for use on the skin
LOTIONS > LOTION
LOTO *same as* > LOTTO
LOTOS *same as* > LOTUS
LOTOSES > LOTOS
LOTS > LOT
LOTTE *n* type of fish
LOTTED > LOT
LOTTER *n* someone who works an allotment
LOTTERIES > LOTTERY
LOTTERS > LOTTER
LOTTERY *n* method of raising money by selling tickets that win prizes by chance
LOTTES > LOTTE
LOTTING > LOT
LOTTO *n* game of chance like bingo
LOTTOS > LOTTO
LOTUS *n* legendary plant whose fruit induces forgetfulness
LOTUSES > LOTUS
LOTUSLAND *n* idyllic place of contentment
LOU *Scot word for* > LOVE
LOUCHE *adj* shifty or disreputable
LOUCHELY > LOUCHE
LOUD *adj* relatively great in volume
LOUDEN *vb* make or become louder
LOUDENED > LOUDEN
LOUDENING > LOUDEN
LOUDENS > LOUDEN
LOUDER > LOUD
LOUDEST > LOUD
LOUDISH *adj* fairly loud
LOUDLIER > LOUD
LOUDLIEST > LOUD
LOUDLY > LOUD
LOUDMOUTH *n* person who talks too much, esp in a boastful or indiscreet way
LOUDNESS > LOUD
LOUED > LOU
LOUGH *n* loch
LOUGHS > LOUGH
LOUIE *same as* > LOOEY
LOUIES > LOUIE
LOUING > LOU
LOUIS *n* former French gold coin
LOUMA *n* weekly market in rural areas of developing countries
LOUMAS > LOUMA
LOUN *same as* > LOWN
LOUND > LOUN
LOUNDED > LOUND
LOUNDER *vb* beat severely
LOUNDERED > LOUNDER
LOUNDERS > LOUNDER
LOUNDING > LOUND
LOUNDS > LOUND
LOUNED > LOUN
LOUNGE *n* living room in a private house ▷ *vb* sit, lie, or stand in a relaxed

manner
LOUNGED > LOUNGE
LOUNGER *n* comfortable sometimes adjustable couch or extending chair designed for someone to relax on
LOUNGERS > LOUNGER
LOUNGES > LOUNGE
LOUNGING > LOUNGE
LOUNGINGS > LOUNGE
LOUNGY *adj* casual; relaxed
LOUNING > LOUN
LOUNS > LOUN
LOUP *Scot word for* > LEAP
LOUPE *n* magnifying glass used by jewellers, horologists, etc
LOUPED > LOUP
LOUPEN > LOUP
LOUPES > LOUPE
LOUPING > LOUP
LOUPIT > LOUP
LOUPS > LOUP
LOUR *vb* (esp of the sky, weather, etc) to be overcast, dark, and menacing ▷ *n* menacing scowl or appearance
LOURE *n* slow, former French dance
LOURED > LOUR
LOURES > LOURE
LOURIE *n* type of African bird with either crimson or grey plumage
LOURIER > LOURY
LOURIES > LOURIE
LOURIEST > LOURY
LOURING > LOUR
LOURINGLY > LOUR
LOURINGS > LOUR
LOURS > LOUR
LOURY *adj* sombre
LOUS > LOU
LOUSE *n* wingless parasitic insect ▷ *vb* ruin or spoil
LOUSED > LOUSE
LOUSER *n* mean nasty person
LOUSERS > LOUSER
LOUSES > LOUSE
LOUSEWORT *n* any of various N temperate scrophulariaceous plants
LOUSIER > LOUSY
LOUSIEST > LOUSY
LOUSILY > LOUSY
LOUSINESS > LOUSY
LOUSING > LOUSE
LOUSY *adj* mean or unpleasant
LOUT *n* crude, oafish, or aggressive person ▷ *vb* bow or stoop
LOUTED > LOUT
LOUTING > LOUT
LOUTISH *adj* characteristic of a lout
LOUTISHLY > LOUTISH
LOUTS > LOUT
LOUVAR *n* large silvery whalelike scombroid fish
LOUVARS > LOUVAR
LOUVER *same as* > LOUVRE
LOUVERED *same as* > LOUVRED
LOUVERS > LOUVER
LOUVRE *n* one of a set of parallel slats slanted to admit air but not rain
LOUVRED *adj* (of a window, door, etc) having louvres
LOUVRES > LOUVRE
LOVABLE *adj* attracting or deserving affection
LOVABLY > LOVABLE
LOVAGE *n* European plant used for flavouring food
LOVAGES > LOVAGE
LOVAT *n* yellowish-green or bluish-green mixture, esp in tweeds or woollens
LOVATS > LOVAT
LOVE *vb* have a great affection for ▷ *n* great affection
LOVEABLE *same as* > LOVABLE
LOVEABLY > LOEVABLE
LOVEBIRD *n* small parrot
LOVEBIRDS > LOVEBIRD
LOVEBITE *n* temporary red mark left on a person's skin by someone biting or sucking it
LOVEBITES > LOVEBITE
LOVEBUG *n* small US flying insect
LOVEBUGS > LOVEBUG
LOVED > LOVE
LOVEFEST *n* event when people talk about loving one another
LOVEFESTS > LOVEFEST
LOVELESS *adj* without love
LOVELIER > LOVELY
LOVELIES > LOVELY
LOVELIEST > LOVELY
LOVELIGHT *n* brightness of eyes of one in love
LOVELILY > LOVELY
LOVELOCK *n* long lock of hair worn on the forehead
LOVELOCKS > LOVELOCK
LOVELORN *adj* miserable because of unhappiness in love
LOVELY *adj* very attractive ▷ *n* attractive woman
LOVEMAKER *n* one involved in lovemaking
LOVER *n* person having a sexual relationship outside marriage
LOVERED *adj* having a lover
LOVERLESS > LOVER
LOVERLY *adj* loverlike
LOVERS > LOVER
LOVES > LOVE
LOVESEAT *n* armchair for two people
LOVESEATS > LOVESEAT
LOVESICK *adj* pining or languishing because of love
LOVESOME *adj* full of love
LOVEVINE *n* leafless parasitic vine
LOVEVINES > LOVEVINE
LOVEY *another word for* > LOVE
LOVEYS > LOVEY
LOVIES > LOVEY
LOVING *adj* affectionate, tender
LOVINGLY > LOVING
LOVINGS > LOVING
LOW *adj* not tall, high, or elevated ▷ *adv* in or to a low position, level, or degree ▷ *n* low position, level, or degree ▷ *vb* moo
LOWAN *n* type of Australian bird
LOWANS > LOWAN
LOWBALL *vb* deliberately under-charge
LOWBALLED > LOWBALL
LOWBALLS > LOWBALL
LOWBORN *adj* of ignoble or common parentage
LOWBOY *n* table fitted with drawers
LOWBOYS > LOWBOY
LOWBRED *same as* > LOWBORN
LOWBROW *disparaging term adj* with nonintellectual tastes and interests ▷ *n* person with uncultivated or nonintellectual tastes
LOWBROWED > LOWBROW
LOWBROWS > LOWBROW
LOWDOWN *n* inside information
LOWDOWNS > LOWDOWN
LOWE *variant of* > LOW
LOWED > LOW
LOWER *adj* below one or more other things ▷ *vb* cause or allow to move down
LOWERABLE > LOWER
LOWERCASE *n* small letters ▷ *adj* non-capitalized
LOWERED > LOWER
LOWERIER > LOWERY
LOWERIEST > LOWERY
LOWERING > LOWER
LOWERINGS > LOWER
LOWERMOST *adj* lowest
LOWERS > LOWER
LOWERY *adj* sombre
LOWES > LOWE
LOWEST > LOW
LOWING > LOW
LOWINGS > LOW
LOWISH > LOW
LOWLAND *n* low-lying country ▷ *adj* of a lowland or lowlands
LOWLANDER > LOWLAND
LOWLANDS > LOWLAND
LOWLIER > LOWLY
LOWLIEST > LOWLY
LOWLIFE *n* member or members of the underworld
LOWLIFER > LOWLIFE
LOWLIFERS > LOWLIFE
LOWLIFES > LOWLIFE
LOWLIGHT *n* unenjoyable or unpleasant part of an event
LOWLIGHTS > LOWLIGHT
LOWLIHEAD *n* state of being humble
LOWLILY > LOWLY
LOWLINESS > LOWLY
LOWLIVES > LOWLIFE
LOWLY *adj* modest, humble ▷ *adv* in a low or lowly manner
LOWN *vb* calm
LOWND *same as* > LOWN
LOWNDED > LOWND
LOWNDING > LOWND
LOWNDS > LOWND
LOWNE *same as* > LOON
LOWNED > LOWN
LOWNES > LOWNE
LOWNESS > LOW
LOWNESSES > LOW
LOWNING > LOWN
LOWNS > LOWN
LOWP *same as* > LOUP
LOWPED > LOWP
LOWPING > LOWP
LOWPS > LOWP
LOWRIDER *n* car with body close to ground
LOWRIDERS > LOWRIDER
LOWRIE *another name for same as* > LORY
LOWRIES > LOWRY
LOWRY *another name for* > LORY
LOWS > LOW
LOWSE *vb* release or loose ▷ *adj* loose
LOWSED > LOWSE
LOWSENING *same as* > LOOSING
LOWSER > LOWSE
LOWSES > LOWSE
LOWSEST > LOWSE
LOWSING > LOWSE
LOWSIT > LOWSE
LOWT *same as* > LOUT
LOWTED > LOWT
LOWTING > LOWT
LOWTS > LOWT
LOWVELD *n* low ground in S Africa
LOWVELDS > LOWVELD
LOX *vb* load fuel tanks of spacecraft with liquid oxygen ▷ *n* kind of smoked salmon
LOXED > LOX
LOXES > LOX
LOXING > LOX
LOXODROME *n* line on globe crossing all meridians at same angle
LOXODROMY *n* technique of navigating using rhumb lines
LOXYGEN *n* liquid oxygen
LOXYGENS > LOXYGEN
LOY *n* narrow spade with a single footrest
LOYAL *adj* faithful to one's friends, country, or government

LOYALER > LOYAL
LOYALEST > LOYAL
LOYALISM > LOYALIST
LOYALISMS > LOYALIST
LOYALIST *n* patriotic supporter of the sovereign or government
LOYALISTS > LOYALIST
LOYALLER > LOYAL
LOYALLEST > LOYAL
LOYALLY > LOYAL
LOYALNESS > LOYAL
LOYALTIES > LOYALTY
LOYALTY *n* quality of being loyal
LOYS > LOY
LOZELL *obsolete form of* > LOSEL
LOZELLS > LOZELL
LOZEN *n* window pane
LOZENGE *n* medicated tablet held in the mouth until it dissolves
LOZENGED *adj* decorated with lozenges
LOZENGES > LOZENGE
LOZENGY *adj* divided by diagonal lines to form a lattice
LOZENS > LOZEN
LUACH *n* calendar that shows the dates of festivals and, usually, the times of start and finish of the Sabbath
LUAU *n* feast of Hawaiian food
LUAUS > LUAU
LUBBARD *same as* > LUBBER
LUBBARDS > LUBBARD
LUBBER *n* big, awkward, or stupid person
LUBBERLY > LUBBER
LUBBERS > LUBBER
LUBE *n* lubricating oil ▷ *vb* lubricate with oil
LUBED > LUBE
LUBES > LUBE
LUBFISH *n* type of fish
LUBFISHES > LUBFISH
LUBING > LUBE
LUBRA *n* Aboriginal woman
LUBRAS > LUBRA
LUBRIC *adj* slippery
LUBRICAL *same as* > LUBRIC
LUBRICANT *n* lubricating substance, such as oil ▷ *adj* serving to lubricate
LUBRICATE *vb* oil or grease to lessen friction
LUBRICITY *n* lewdness or salaciousness
LUBRICOUS *adj* lewd or lascivious
LUCARNE *n* type of dormer window
LUCARNES > LUCARNE
LUCE *another name for* > PIKE
LUCENCE > LUCENT
LUCENCES > LUCENT
LUCENCIES > LUCENT
LUCENCY > LUCENT
LUCENT *adj* brilliant, shining, or translucent
LUCENTLY > LUCENT
LUCERN *same as* > LUCERNE
LUCERNE *n* alfalfa
LUCERNES > LUCERNE
LUCERNS > LUCERN
LUCES > LUCE
LUCHOT *pl n* engraved tablets of stone
LUCHOTH *same as* > LUCHOT
LUCID *adj* clear and easily understood
LUCIDER > LUCID
LUCIDEST > LUCID
LUCIDITY > LUCID
LUCIDLY > LUCID
LUCIDNESS > LUCID
LUCIFER *n* friction match
LUCIFERIN *n* substance occurring in bioluminescent organisms, such as glow-worms and fireflies
LUCIFERS > LUCIFER
LUCIGEN *n* lamp burning oil mixed with hot air
LUCIGENS > LUCIGEN
LUCITE *n* brand name of a type of transparent acrylic-based plastic
LUCITES > LUCITE
LUCK *n* fortune, good or bad ▷ *vb* have good fortune
LUCKED > LUCK
LUCKEN *adj* shut
LUCKIE *same as* > LUCKY
LUCKIER > LUCKY
LUCKIES > LUCKIE
LUCKIEST > LUCKY
LUCKILY > LUCKY
LUCKINESS > LUCKY
LUCKING > LUCK
LUCKLESS *adj* having bad luck
LUCKPENNY *n* coin kept for luck
LUCKS > LUCK
LUCKY *adj* having or bringing good luck ▷ *n* old woman
LUCRATIVE *adj* very profitable
LUCRE *n* money or wealth
LUCRES > LUCRE
LUCTATION *n* effort; struggle
LUCUBRATE *vb* write or study, esp at night
LUCULENT *adj* easily understood
LUCUMA *n* type of S American tree
LUCUMAS > LUCUMA
LUCUMO *n* Etruscan king
LUCUMONES > LUCUMO
LUCUMOS > LUCUMO
LUD *n* lord ▷ *interj* exclamation of dismay or surprise
LUDE *n* slang word for drug for relieving anxiety
LUDERICK *n* Australian fish, usu black or dark brown in colour
LUDERICKS > LUDERICK
LUDES > LUDE
LUDIC *adj* playful
LUDICALLY > LUDIC
LUDICROUS *adj* absurd or ridiculous
LUDO *n* game played with dice and counters on a board
LUDOS > LUDO
LUDS > LUD
LUDSHIP > LUD
LUDSHIPS > LUD
LUES *n* any venereal disease
LUETIC > LUES
LUETICS > LUES
LUFF *vb* sail (a ship) towards the wind ▷ *n* leading edge of a fore-and-aft sail
LUFFA *same as* > LOOFAH
LUFFAS > LUFFA
LUFFED > LUFF
LUFFING > LUFF
LUFFS > LUFF
LUG *vb* carry or drag with great effort ▷ *n* projection serving as a handle
LUGE *n* racing toboggan on which riders lie on their backs, descending feet first ▷ *vb* ride on a luge
LUGED > LUGE
LUGEING > LUGE
LUGEINGS > LUGE
LUGER *n* tradename for a type of German automatic pistol
LUGERS > LUGER
LUGES > LUGE
LUGGABLE *n* unwieldy portable computer
LUGGABLES > LUGGABLE
LUGGAGE *n* suitcases, bags, etc
LUGGAGES > LUGGAGE
LUGGED > LUG
LUGGER *n* small working boat with an oblong sail
LUGGERS > LUGGER
LUGGIE *n* wooden bowl with handles
LUGGIES > LUGGIE
LUGGING > LUG
LUGHOLE *informal word for* > EAR
LUGHOLES > LUGHOLE
LUGING > LUGE
LUGINGS > LUGE
LUGS > LUG
LUGSAIL *n* four-sided sail bent and hoisted on a yard
LUGSAILS > LUGSAIL
LUGWORM *n* large worm used as bait
LUGWORMS > LUGWORM
LUIT *Scots past form of* > LET
LUITEN > LET
LUKE *variant of* > LUKEWARM
LUKEWARM *adj* moderately warm, tepid
LULIBUB *obsolete form of* > LOLLIPOP
LULIBUBS > LULIBUB
LULL *vb* soothe (someone) by soft sounds or motions ▷ *n* brief time of quiet in a storm etc
LULLABIED > LULLABY
LULLABIES > LULLABY
LULLABY *n* quiet song to send a child to sleep ▷ *vb* quiet or soothe with or as if with a lullaby
LULLED > LULL
LULLER > LULL
LULLERS > LULL
LULLING > LULL
LULLS > LULL
LULU *n* person or thing considered to be outstanding in size, appearance, etc
LULUS > LULU
LUM *n* chimney
LUMA *n* black and white element of TV signal
LUMAS > LUMA
LUMBAGO *n* pain in the lower back
LUMBAGOS > LUMBAGO
LUMBANG *n* type of tree
LUMBANGS > LUMBANG
LUMBAR *adj* of the part of the body between the lowest ribs and the hipbones ▷ *n* old-fashioned kind of ship
LUMBARS > LUMBAR
LUMBER *n* unwanted disused household articles ▷ *vb* burden with something unpleasant
LUMBERED > LUMBER
LUMBERER > LUMBER
LUMBERERS > LUMBER
LUMBERING *n* business or trade of cutting, transporting, preparing, or selling timber ▷ *adj* awkward in movement
LUMBERLY *adj* heavy; clumsy
LUMBERMAN *n* person whose work involves felling trees
LUMBERMEN > LUMBERMAN
LUMBERS > LUMBER
LUMBRICAL *adj* relating to any of the the four wormlike muscles in the hand or foot
LUMBRICI > LUMBRICUS
LUMBRICUS *n* type of worm
LUMEN *n* derived SI unit of luminous flux
LUMENAL > LUMEN
LUMENS > LUMEN
LUMINA > LUMEN
LUMINAIRE *n* light fixture
LUMINAL > LUMEN
LUMINANCE *n* state or quality of radiating or reflecting light
LUMINANT *n* something used to give light
LUMINANTS > LUMINANT

LUMINARIA *n* type of candle
LUMINARY *n* famous person ▷ *adj* of, involving, or characterized by light or enlightenment
LUMINE *vb* illuminate
LUMINED > LUMINE
LUMINES > LUMINE
LUMINESCE *vb* exhibit luminescence
LUMINING > LUMINE
LUMINISM *n* US artistic movement
LUMINISMS > LUMINISM
LUMINIST > LUMINISM
LUMINISTS > LUMINISM
LUMINOUS *adj* reflecting or giving off light
LUMME *interj* exclamation of surprise or dismay
LUMMIER > LUMMY
LUMMIEST > LUMMY
LUMMOX *n* clumsy or stupid person
LUMMOXES > LUMMOX
LUMMY *interj* exclamation of surprise ▷ *adj* excellent
LUMP *n* shapeless piece or mass ▷ *vb* consider as a single group
LUMPED > LUMP
LUMPEN *adj* stupid or unthinking ▷ *n* member of underclass
LUMPENLY > LUMPEN
LUMPENS > LUMPEN
LUMPER *n* stevedore
LUMPERS > LUMPER
LUMPFISH *n* North Atlantic scorpaenoid fish
LUMPIER > LUMPY
LUMPIEST > LUMPY
LUMPILY > LUMPY
LUMPINESS > LUMPY
LUMPING > LUMP
LUMPINGLY > LUMP
LUMPISH *adj* stupid or clumsy
LUMPISHLY > LUMPISH
LUMPKIN *n* lout
LUMPKINS > LUMPKIN
LUMPS > LUMP
LUMPY *adj* full of or having lumps
LUMS > LUM
LUNA *n* type of large American moth
LUNACIES > LUNACY
LUNACY *n* foolishness
LUNANAUT *same as* > LUNARNAUT
LUNANAUTS > LUNANAUT
LUNAR *adj* relating to the moon ▷ *n* lunar distance
LUNARIAN *n* inhabitant of the moon
LUNARIANS > LUNARIAN
LUNARIES > LUNARY
LUNARIST *n* one believing the moon influences weather
LUNARISTS > LUNARIST
LUNARNAUT *n* astronaut who travels to moon
LUNARS > LUNAR
LUNARY *n* moonwort herb
LUNAS > LUNA
LUNATE *adj* shaped like a crescent ▷ *n* crescent-shaped bone forming part of the wrist
LUNATED *variant of* > LUNATE
LUNATELY > LUNATE
LUNATES > LUNATE
LUNATIC *adj* foolish and irresponsible ▷ *n* foolish or annoying person
LUNATICAL *variant of* > LUNATIC
LUNATICS > LUNATIC
LUNATION *See* > MONTH
LUNATIONS > LUNATION
LUNCH *n* meal taken in the middle of the day ▷ *vb* eat lunch
LUNCHBOX *n* container for carrying a packed lunch
LUNCHED > LUNCH
LUNCHEON *n* formal lunch
LUNCHEONS > LUNCHEON
LUNCHER > LUNCH
LUNCHERS > LUNCH
LUNCHES > LUNCH
LUNCHING > LUNCH
LUNCHMEAT *n* mixture of meat and cereal
LUNCHROOM *n* room where lunch is served or people may eat lunches they bring
LUNCHTIME *n* time at which lunch is usually eaten
LUNE *same as* > LUNETTE
LUNES > LUNE
LUNET *n* small moon or satellite
LUNETS > LUNET
LUNETTE *n* anything that is shaped like a crescent
LUNETTES > LUNETTE
LUNG *n* organ that allows an animal or bird to breathe air
LUNGAN *same as* > LONGAN
LUNGANS > LUNGAN
LUNGE *n* sudden forward motion ▷ *vb* move with or make a lunge
LUNGED > LUNGE
LUNGEE *same as* > LUNGI
LUNGEES > LUNGEE
LUNGEING > LUNGE
LUNGER > LUNGE
LUNGERS > LUNGE
LUNGES > LUNGE
LUNGFISH *n* freshwater bony fish with an air-breathing lung
LUNGFUL > LUNG
LUNGFULS > LUNG
LUNGI *n* long piece of cotton cloth worn as a loincloth, sash, or turban by Indian men or as a skirt
LUNGIE *n* guillemot
LUNGIES > LUNGIE
LUNGING > LUNGE
LUNGIS > LUNGI
LUNGS > LUNG
LUNGWORM *n* any parasitic nematode worm of the family *Metastrongylidae*
LUNGWORMS > LUNGWORM
LUNGWORT *n* any of several Eurasian plants of the boraginaceous genus *Pulmonaria*
LUNGWORTS > LUNGWORT
LUNGYI *same as* > LUNGI
LUNGYIS > LUNGYI
LUNIER > LUNY
LUNIES > LUNY
LUNIEST > LUNY
LUNINESS > LUNY
LUNISOLAR *adj* resulting from or based on the combined gravitational attraction of the sun and moon
LUNITIDAL *adj* of or relating to tidal phenomena as produced by the moon
LUNK *n* awkward, heavy, or stupid person
LUNKER *n* very large fish, esp bass
LUNKERS > LUNKER
LUNKHEAD *n* stupid person
LUNKHEADS > LUNKHEAD
LUNKS > LUNK
LUNT *vb* produce smoke
LUNTED > LUNT
LUNTING > LUNT
LUNTS > LUNT
LUNULA *n* white crescent-shaped area at the base of the human fingernail
LUNULAE > LUNULA
LUNULAR *same as* > LUNULATE
LUNULATE *adj* having markings shaped like crescents
LUNULATED *same as* > LUNULATE
LUNULE *same as* > LUNULA
LUNULES > LUNULE
LUNY *same as* > LOONY
LUNYIE *same as* > LUNGIE
LUNYIES > LUNYIE
LUPANAR *n* brothel
LUPANARS > LUPANAR
LUPIN *n* garden plant with tall spikes of flowers
LUPINE *adj* like a wolf ▷ *n* lupin
LUPINES > LUPINE
LUPINS > LUPIN
LUPOUS *adj* relating to lupus
LUPPEN > SCOTS PAST FORM OF > LEAP
LUPULIN *n* resinous powder extracted from the female flowers of the hop plant
LUPULINE *adj* relating to lupulin
LUPULINIC *same as* > LUPULINE
LUPULINS > LUPULIN
LUPUS *n* ulcerous skin disease
LUPUSES > LUPUS
LUR *n* large bronze musical horn found in Danish peat bogs
LURCH *vb* tilt or lean suddenly to one side ▷ *n* lurching movement
LURCHED > LURCH
LURCHER *n* crossbred dog trained to hunt silently
LURCHERS > LURCHER
LURCHES > LURCH
LURCHING > LURCH
LURDAN *n* stupid or dull person ▷ *adj* dull or stupid
LURDANE *same as* > LURDAN
LURDANES > LURDANE
LURDANS > LURDAN
LURDEN *same as* > LURDAN
LURDENS > LURDEN
LURE *vb* tempt or attract by the promise of reward ▷ *n* person or thing that lures
LURED > LURE
LURER > LURE
LURERS > LURE
LURES > LURE
LUREX *n* thin glittery thread
LUREXES > LUREX
LURGI *same as* > LURGY
LURGIES > LURGY
LURGIS > LURGI
LURGY *n* any undetermined illness
LURID *adj* vivid in shocking detail, sensational
LURIDER > LURID
LURIDEST > LURID
LURIDLY > LURID
LURIDNESS > LURID
LURING > LURE
LURINGLY > LURE
LURK *vb* lie hidden or move stealthily, esp for sinister purposes
LURKED > LURK
LURKER > LURK
LURKERS > LURK
LURKING *adj* lingering but almost unacknowledged
LURKINGLY > LURKING
LURKINGS > LURKING
LURKS > LURK
LURRIES > LURRY
LURRY *n* confused jumble
LURS > LUR
LURVE *n* love
LURVES > LURVE
LUSCIOUS *adj* extremely pleasurable to taste or smell
LUSER *n* user of a computer system, as considered by a systems administator or other member of a technical support team
LUSERS > LUSER
LUSH *adj* (of grass etc) growing thickly and

healthily ▷ *n* alcoholic ▷ *vb* drink (alcohol) to excess
LUSHED > LUSH
LUSHER *adj* more lush ▷ *n* drunkard
LUSHERS > LUSHER
LUSHES > LUSH
LUSHEST > LUSH
LUSHIER > LUSHY
LUSHIEST > LUSHY
LUSHING > LUSH
LUSHLY > LUSH
LUSHNESS > LUSH
LUSHY *adj* slightly intoxicated
LUSK *vb* lounge around
LUSKED > LUSK
LUSKING > LUSK
LUSKISH *adj* lazy
LUSKS > LUSK
LUST *n* strong sexual desire ▷ *vb* have passionate desire (for)
LUSTED > LUST
LUSTER *same as* > LUSTRE
LUSTERED > LUSTER
LUSTERING > LUSTER
LUSTERS > LUSTER
LUSTFUL *adj* driven by lust
LUSTFULLY > LUSTFUL
LUSTICK *obsolete word for* > LUSTY
LUSTIER > LUSTY
LUSTIEST > LUSTY
LUSTIHEAD *n* vigour
LUSTIHOOD *n* vigour
LUSTILY > LUSTY
LUSTINESS > LUSTY
LUSTING > LUST
LUSTIQUE *obsolete word for* > LUSTY
LUSTLESS > LUST
LUSTRA > LUSTRUM
LUSTRAL *adj* of or relating to a ceremony of purification
LUSTRATE *vb* purify by means of religious rituals or ceremonies
LUSTRATED > LUSTRATE
LUSTRATES > LUSTRATE
LUSTRE *n* gloss, sheen ▷ *vb* make, be, or become lustrous
LUSTRED > LUSTRE
LUSTRES > LUSTRE
LUSTRINE *same as* > LUSTRING
LUSTRINES > LUSTRINE
LUSTRING *n* glossy silk cloth, formerly used for clothing, upholstery, etc
LUSTRINGS > LUSTRING
LUSTROUS > LUSTRE
LUSTRUM *n* period of five years
LUSTRUMS > LUSTRUM
LUSTS > LUST
LUSTY *adj* vigorous, healthy
LUSUS *n* freak, mutant, or monster
LUSUSES > LUSUS
LUTANIST *same as* > LUTENIST
LUTANISTS > LUTANIST
LUTE *n* ancient guitar-like musical instrument with a body shaped like a half pear ▷ *vb* seal (a joint or surface) with a mixture of cement and clay
LUTEA *adj* yellow
LUTEAL *adj* relating to or characterized by the development of the corpus luteum
LUTECIUM *same as* > LUTETIUM
LUTECIUMS > LUTECIUM
LUTED > LUTE
LUTEFISK *n* Scandinavian fish dish
LUTEFISKS > LUTEFISK
LUTEIN *n* xanthophyll pigment that has a light-absorbing function in photosynthesis
LUTEINISE *same as* > LUTEINIZE
LUTEINIZE *vb* develop into part of corpus luteum
LUTEINS > LUTEIN
LUTENIST *n* person who plays the lute
LUTENISTS > LUTENIST
LUTEOLIN *n* yellow crystalline compound found in many plants
LUTEOLINS > LUTEOLIN
LUTEOLOUS > LUTEOLIN
LUTEOUS *adj* of a light to moderate greenish-yellow colour
LUTER *n* lute player
LUTERS > LUTER
LUTES > LUTE
LUTESCENT *adj* yellowish in colour
LUTETIUM *n* silvery-white metallic element
LUTETIUMS > LUTETIUM
LUTEUM *adj* yellow
LUTFISK *same as* > LUTEFISK
LUTFISKS > LUTFISK
LUTHERN *another name for* > DORMER
LUTHERNS > LUTHERN
LUTHIER *n* lute-maker
LUTHIERS > LUTHIER
LUTING *n* mixture of cement and clay
LUTINGS > LUTING
LUTIST *same as* > LUTENIST
LUTISTS > LUTIST
LUTITE *another name for* > PELITE
LUTITES > LUTITE
LUTTEN > LOOT
LUTZ *n* jump in which the skater takes off from the back outside edge of one skate, makes one, two, or three turns in the air, and lands on the back outside edge of the other skate
LUTZES > LUTZ
LUV *n* love
LUVS > LOVE
LUVVIE *n* person who is involved in acting or the theatre
LUVVIES > LUVVY
LUVVY *same as* > LUVVIE
LUX *n* unit of illumination
LUXATE *vb* put (a shoulder, knee, etc) out of joint
LUXATED > LUXATE
LUXATES > LUXATE
LUXATING > LUXATE
LUXATION > LUXATE
LUXATIONS > LUXATE
LUXE as in *de luxe* rich, elegant, or sumptuous
LUXES > LUXE
LUXMETER *n* device for measuring light
LUXMETERS > LUXMETER
LUXURIANT *adj* rich and abundant
LUXURIATE *vb* take self-indulgent pleasure (in)
LUXURIES > LUXURY
LUXURIOUS *adj* full of luxury, sumptuous
LUXURIST *n* lover of luxury
LUXURISTS > LUXURIST
LUXURY *n* enjoyment of rich, very comfortable living ▷ *adj* of or providing luxury
LUZ *n* supposedly indestructible bone of the human body
LUZERN *n* alfalfa
LUZERNS > LUZERN
LUZZES > LUZ
LWEI *n* Angolan monetary unit
LWEIS > LWEI
LYAM *n* leash
LYAMS > LYAM
LYARD *same as* > LIARD
LYART *same as* > LIARD
LYASE *n* any enzyme that catalyses the separation of two parts of a molecule
LYASES > LYASE
LYCEA > LYCEUM
LYCEE *n* secondary school
LYCEES > LYCEE
LYCEUM *n* public building for events such as concerts and lectures
LYCEUMS > LYCEUM
LYCH *same as* > LICH
LYCHEE *same as* > LITCHI
LYCHEES > LYCHEE
LYCHES > LYCH
LYCHGATE *same as* > LICHGATE
LYCHGATES > LYCHGATE
LYCHNIS *n* any caryophyllaceous plant of the genus *Lychnis*
LYCHNISES > LYCHNIS
LYCOPENE *n* red pigment
LYCOPENES > LYCOPENE
LYCOPOD *n* type of moss
LYCOPODS > LYCOPOD
LYCRA *n* tradename for a type of synthetic elastic fabric and fibre used for tight-fitting garments, such as swimming costumes
LYCRAS > LYCRA
LYDDITE *n* explosive consisting chiefly of fused picric acid
LYDDITES > LYDDITE
LYE *n* caustic solution obtained by leaching wood ash
LYES > LYE
LYFULL *obsolete form of* > LIFEFUL
LYING > LIE
LYINGLY > LIE
LYINGS > LIE
LYKEWAKE *n* watch held over a dead person, often with festivities
LYKEWAKES > LYKEWAKE
LYKEWALK *variant of* > LYKEWAKE
LYKEWALKS > LYKEWALK
LYM *obsolete form of* > LYAM
LYME as in *lyme grass* type of perennial dune grass
LYMES > LYME
LYMITER *same as* > LIMITER
LYMITERS > LIMITER
LYMPH *n* colourless bodily fluid consisting mainly of white blood cells
LYMPHAD *n* ancient rowing boat
LYMPHADS > LYMPHAD
LYMPHATIC *adj* of, relating to, or containing lymph ▷ *n* lymphatic vessel
LYMPHOID *adj* of or resembling lymph, or relating to the lymphatic system
LYMPHOMA *n* any form of cancer of the lymph nodes
LYMPHOMAS > LYMPHOMA
LYMPHS *n* lymph
LYMS > LYM
LYNAGE *obsolete form of* > LINEAGE
LYNAGES > LYNAGE
LYNCEAN *adj* of or resembling a lynx
LYNCH *vb* put to death without a trial
LYNCHED > LYNCH
LYNCHER > LYNCH
LYNCHERS > LYNCH
LYNCHES > LYNCH
LYNCHET *n* terrace or ridge formed in prehistoric or medieval times by ploughing a hillside
LYNCHETS > LYNCHET
LYNCHING > LYNCH
LYNCHINGS > LYNCH
LYNCHPIN *same as* > LINCHPIN
LYNCHPINS > LYNCHPIN
LYNE *n* flax
LYNES > LYNE
LYNX *n* animal of the cat

family with tufted ears and a short tail
LYNXES > LYNX
LYNXLIKE > LYNX
LYOLYSES > LYOLYSIS
LYOLYSIS *n* formation of an acid and a base from the interaction of a salt with a solvent
LYOMEROUS *adj* relating to Lyomeri fish
LYONNAISE *adj* (of food) cooked or garnished with onions, usually fried
LYOPHIL *same as* > LYOPHILIC
LYOPHILE *same as* > LYOPHILIC
LYOPHILED *adj* lyophiliized
LYOPHILIC *adj* (of a colloid) having a dispersed phase with a high affinity for the continuous phase
LYOPHOBE *same as* > LYOPHOBIC
LYOPHOBIC *adj* (of a colloid) having a dispersed phase with little or no affinity for the continuous phase
LYRA as in *lyra viol* lutelike musical instrument of the 16th and 17th centuries
LYRATE *adj* shaped like a lyre
LYRATED *same as* > LYRATE
LYRATELY > LYRATE
LYRE *n* ancient musical instrument like a U-shaped harp
LYREBIRD *n* Australian bird, the male of which spreads its tail into the shape of a lyre
LYREBIRDS > LYREBIRD
LYRES > LYRE
LYRIC *adj* (of poetry) expressing personal emotion in songlike style ▷ *n* short poem in a songlike style
LYRICAL *same as* > LYRIC
LYRICALLY > LYRIC
LYRICISE *same as* > LYRICIZE
LYRICISED > LYRICISE
LYRICISES > LYRICISE
LYRICISM *n* quality or style of lyric poetry
LYRICISMS > LYRICISM
LYRICIST *n* person who writes the words of songs or musicals
LYRICISTS > LYRICIST
LYRICIZE *vb* write lyrics
LYRICIZED > LYRICIZE
LYRICIZES > LYRICIZE
LYRICON *n* wind synthesizer
LYRICONS > LYRICON
LYRICS > LYRIC
LYRIFORM *adj* lyre-shaped
LYRISM *n* art or technique of playing the lyre
LYRISMS > LYRISM
LYRIST *same as* > LYRICIST
LYRISTS > LYRIST
LYSATE *n* material formed by lysis
LYSATES > LYSATE
LYSE *vb* undergo or cause to undergo lysis
LYSED > LYSE
LYSERGIC as in *lysergic acid* crystalline compound used in medical research
LYSERGIDE *n* LSD
LYSES > LYSIS
LYSIGENIC *adj* caused by breaking down of cells
LYSIMETER *n* instrument for determining solubility, esp the amount of water-soluble matter in soil
LYSIN *n* any of a group of antibodies that cause dissolution of cells against which they are directed
LYSINE *n* essential amino acid that occurs in proteins
LYSINES > LYSINE
LYSING > LYSE
LYSINS > LYSIN
LYSIS *n* destruction or dissolution of cells by the action of a particular lysin
LYSOGEN *n* lysis-inducing agent
LYSOGENIC > LYSOGEN
LYSOGENS > LYSOGEN
LYSOGENY > LYSOGEN
LYSOL *n* tradename for a solution used as an antiseptic and disinfectant
LYSOLS > LYSOL
LYSOSOMAL > LYSOSOME
LYSOSOME *n* any of numerous small particles that are present in the cytoplasm of most cells
LYSOSOMES > LYSOSOME
LYSOZYME *n* enzyme occurring in tears, certain body tissues, and egg white
LYSOZYMES > LYSOZYME
LYSSA *less common word for* > RABIES
LYSSAS > LYSSA
LYTE *vb* dismount
LYTED > LYTE
LYTES > LYTE
LYTHE *n* type of fish
LYTHES > LYTHE
LYTIC *adj* relating to, causing, or resulting from lysis
LYTICALLY > LYTIC
LYTING > LYTE
LYTTA *n* rodlike mass of cartilage beneath the tongue in the dog and other carnivores
LYTTAE > LYTTA
LYTTAS > LYTTA

Mm

MA *n* mother
MAA *vb* (of goats) bleat
MAAED > MAA
MAAING > MAA
MAAR *n* coneless volcanic crater that has been formed by a single explosion
MAARE > MAAR
MAARS > MAAR
MAAS *n* thick soured milk
MAATJES *n* pickled herring
MABE *n* type of pearl
MABELA *n* ground kaffir corn used for making porridge
MABELAS > MABELAS
MABES > MABE
MAC *n* macintosh
MACABER *same as* > MACABRE
MACABRE *adj* strange and horrible, gruesome
MACABRELY > MACABRE
MACACO *n* any of various lemurs, esp *Lemur macaco*, the males of which are usually black and the females brown
MACACOS > MACACO
MACADAM *n* road surface of pressed layers of small broken stones
MACADAMIA *n* Australian tree with edible nuts
MACADAMS > MACADAM
MACAHUBA *n* South American palm tree
MACAHUBAS > MACAHUBA
MACALLUM *n* ice cream with raspberry sauce
MACALLUMS > MACALLUM
MACAQUE *n* monkey of Asia and Africa with cheek pouches and either a short tail or no tail
MACAQUES > MACAQUE
MACARISE *vb* congratulate
MACARISED > MACARISE
MACARISES > MACARISE
MACARISM *n* blessing
MACARISMS > MACARISM
MACARIZE *same as* > MACARISE
MACARIZED > MACARIZE
MACARIZES > MACARIZE
MACARONI *n* pasta in short tube shapes
MACARONIC *adj* (of verse) characterized by a mixture of vernacular words jumbled together with Latin words or Latinized words or with words from one or more other foreign languages ▷ *n* macaronic verse
MACARONIS > MACARONI
MACAROON *n* small biscuit or cake made with ground almonds
MACAROONS > MACAROON
MACASSAR *n* oily preparation formerly put on the hair to make it smooth and shiny
MACASSARS > MACASSAR
MACAW *n* large tropical American parrot
MACAWS > MACAW
MACCABAW *same as* > MACCABOY
MACCABAWS > MACCABAW
MACCABOY *n* dark rose-scented snuff
MACCABOYS > MACCABOY
MACCARONI *same as* > MACARONI
MACCHIA *n* thicket in Italy
MACCHIATO *n* espresso coffee served with a dash of hot or cold milk
MACCHIE > MACCHIA
MACCOBOY *same as* > MACCABOY
MACCOBOYS > MACCOBOY
MACE *n* club, usually having a spiked metal head, used esp in the Middle Ages ▷ *vb* use a mace
MACED > MACE
MACEDOINE *n* hot or cold mixture of diced vegetables
MACER *n* macebearer, esp (in Scotland) an official who acts as usher in a court of law
MACERAL *n* any of the organic units that constitute coal: equivalent to any of the mineral constituents of a rock
MACERALS > MACERAL
MACERATE *vb* soften by soaking
MACERATED > MACERATE
MACERATER > MACERATE
MACERATES > MACERATE
MACERATOR > MACERATE
MACERS > MACER
MACES > MACE
MACH *n* ratio of the speed of a body in a particular medium to the speed of sound in that medium
MACHAIR *n* (in the western Highlands of Scotland) a strip of sandy, grassy, often lime-rich land just above the high-water mark at a sandy shore: used as grazing or arable land
MACHAIRS > MACHAIR
MACHAN *n* (in India) a raised platform used in tiger hunting
MACHANS > MACHAN
MACHE *n* papier-mâché
MACHER *n* important or influential person: often used ironically
MACHERS > MACHER
MACHES > MACHE
MACHETE *n* broad heavy knife used for cutting or as a weapon
MACHETES > MACHETE
MACHI as in *machi chips* in Indian English, fish and chips
MACHINATE *vb* contrive, plan, or devise (schemes, plots, etc)
MACHINE *n* apparatus, usu. powered by electricity, designed to perform a particular task ▷ *vb* make or produce by machine
MACHINED > MACHINE
MACHINERY *n* machines or machine parts collectively
MACHINES > MACHINE
MACHINING > MACHINE
MACHINIST *n* person who operates a machine
MACHISMO *n* exaggerated or strong masculinity
MACHISMOS > MACHISMO
MACHMETER *n* instrument for measuring the Mach number of an aircraft in flight

MACHO *adj* strongly or exaggeratedly masculine ▷ *n* strong or exaggerated masculinity
MACHOISM > MACHO
MACHOISMS > MACHO
MACHOS > MACHO
MACHREE *n* Irish form of address meaning my dear
MACHREES > MACHREE
MACHS > MACH
MACHZOR *n* Jewish prayer book containing prescribed holiday rituals
MACHZORIM > MACHZOR
MACHZORS > MACHZOR
MACING > MACE
MACINTOSH *n* waterproof raincoat
MACK *same as* > MAC
MACKEREL *n* edible sea fish
MACKERELS > MACKEREL
MACKINAW *n* thick short double-breasted plaid coat
MACKINAWS > MACKINAW
MACKLE *n* double or blurred impression caused by shifting paper or type ▷ *vb* mend hurriedly or in a makeshift way
MACKLED > MACKLE
MACKLES > MACKLE
MACKLING > MACKLE
MACKS > MACK
MACLE *n* crystal consisting of two parts
MACLED > MACLE
MACLES > MACLE
MACON *n* red or white wine from the Mâcon area, heavier than the other burgundies
MACONS > MACON
MACOYA *n* South American tree
MACOYAS > MACOYA
MACRAME *n* ornamental work of knotted cord
MACRAMES > MACRAME
MACRAMI *same as* > MACRAME
MACRAMIS > MACRAMI
MACRO *n* close-up lens
MACROBIAN *adj* long-lived
MACROCODE *n* computer instruction that triggers many other instructions
MACROCOPY *n* enlargement of printed material for easier reading
MACROCOSM *n* universe
MACROCYST *n* unusually large cyst
MACROCYTE *n* abnormally large red blood cell
MACRODOME *n* dome shape in crystal structure
MACRODONT *adj* having large teeth
MACROGLIA *n* one of the two types of non-nervous tissue (glia) found in the central nervous system: includes astrocytes
MACROLOGY *n* verbose but meaningless talk
MACROMERE *n* any of the large yolk-filled cells formed by unequal cleavage of a fertilized ovum
MACROMOLE *n* large chemistry mole
MACRON *n* mark placed over a letter to represent a long vowel
MACRONS > MACRON
MACROPOD *n* member of kangaroo family
MACROPODS > MACROPOD
MACROPSIA *n* condition of seeing everything in the field of view as larger than it really is, which can occur in diseases of the retina or in some brain disorders
MACROS > MACRO
MACROTOUS *adj* having large ears
MACRURAL > MACRURAN
MACRURAN *n* any decapod crustacean of the group (formerly suborder) *Macrura*, which includes the lobsters, prawns, and crayfish ▷ *adj* of, relating to, or belonging to the *Macrura*
MACRURANS > MACRURAN
MACRUROID > MACRURAN
MACRUROUS > MACRURAN
MACS > MAC
MACTATION *n* sacrificial killing
MACULA *n* small spot or area of distinct colour, such as a freckle
MACULAE > MACULA
MACULAR > MACULA
MACULAS > MACULA
MACULATE *vb* spot, stain, or pollute ▷ *adj* spotted or polluted
MACULATED > MACULATE
MACULATES > MACULATE
MACULE *same as* > MACKLE
MACULED > MACULE
MACULES > MACULE
MACULING > MACULE
MACULOSE *adj* having spots
MACUMBA *n* religious cult in Brazil that combines Christian and voodoo elements
MACUMBAS > MACUMBA
MAD *adj* mentally deranged, insane ▷ *vb* make mad
MADAFU *n* coconut milk
MADAFUS > MADAFU
MADAM *n* polite term of address for a woman ▷ *vb* call someone madam
MADAME *n* French title equivalent to *Mrs*
MADAMED > MADAM
MADAMES > MADAME
MADAMING > MADAM
MADAMS > MADAM
MADAROSES > MADAROSIS
MADAROSIS *n* abnormal loss of eyebrows or eyelashes
MADBRAIN *adj* insane
MADCAP *adj* foolish or reckless ▷ *n* impulsive or reckless person
MADCAPS > MADCAP
MADDED > MAD
MADDEN *vb* infuriate or irritate
MADDENED > MADDEN
MADDENING *adj* serving to send mad
MADDENS > MADDEN
MADDER *n* type of rose
MADDERS > MADAM
MADDEST > MAD
MADDING > MAD
MADDINGLY > MAD
MADDISH > MAD
MADDOCK *same as* > MATTOCK
MADDOCKS > MADDOCK
MADE > MAKE
MADEFIED > MADEFY
MADEFIES > MADEFY
MADEFY *vb* make moist
MADEFYING > MADEFY
MADEIRA *n* kind of rich sponge cake
MADEIRAS > MADEIRA
MADELEINE *n* small fancy sponge cake
MADERISE *vb* become reddish
MADERISED > MADERISE
MADERISES > MADERISE
MADERIZE *same as* > MADERISE
MADERIZED > MADERIZE
MADERIZES > MADERIZE
MADGE *n* type of hammer
MADGES > MADGE
MADHOUSE *n* place filled with uproar or confusion
MADHOUSES > MADHOUSE
MADID *adj* wet
MADISON *n* type of cycle relay race
MADISONS > MADISON
MADLING *n* insane person
MADLINGS > MADLING
MADLY *adv* with great speed and energy
MADMAN *n* person who is insane
MADMEN > MADMAN
MADNESS *n* insanity
MADNESSES > MADNESS
MADONNA *n* picture or statue of the Virgin Mary
MADONNAS > MADONNA
MADOQUA *n* Ethiopian antelope
MADOQUAS > MADOQUA
MADRAS *n* medium-hot curry
MADRASA *same as* > MADRASAH
MADRASAH *n* educational institution, particularly for Islamic religious instruction
MADRASAHS > MADRASAH
MADRASAS > MADRASA
MADRASES > MADRAS
MADRASSA *same as* > MADRASAH
MADRASSAH *same as* > MADRASAH
MADRASSAS > MADRASSA
MADRE *Spanish word for* > MOTHER
MADREPORE *n* any coral of the genus *Madrepora*, many of which occur in tropical seas and form large coral reefs: order *Zoantharia*
MADRES > MADRE
MADRIGAL *n* 16th–17th-century part song for unaccompanied voices
MADRIGALS > MADRIGAL
MADRILENE *n* cold consommé flavoured with tomato juice
MADRONA *n* ericaceous North American evergreen tree or shrub, *Arbutus menziesii*, with white flowers and red berry-like fruits
MADRONAS > MADRONA
MADRONE *same as* > MADRONA
MADRONES > MADRONE
MADRONO *same as* > MADRONA
MADRONOS > MADRONO
MADS > MAD
MADTOM *n* species of catfish
MADTOMS > MADTOM
MADURO *adj* (of cigars) dark and strong ▷ *n* cigar of this type
MADUROS > MADURO
MADWOMAN *n* woman who is insane, esp one who behaves violently
MADWOMEN > MADWOMAN
MADWORT *n* low-growing Eurasian boraginaceous plant, *Asperugo procumbens*, with small blue flowers
MADWORTS > MADWORT
MADZOON *same as* > MATZOON
MADZOONS > MADZOON
MAE as in *mae west* inflatable life jacket, esp as issued to the US armed forces for emergency use
MAELID *n* mythical spirit of apple
MAELIDS > MAELID
MAELSTROM *n* great whirlpool
MAENAD *n* female disciple of Dionysus, the Greek god of wine
MAENADES > MAENAD
MAENADIC > MAENAD
MAENADISM > MAENAD
MAENADS > MAENAD
MAES > MAE
MAESTOSO *adv* be performed majestically

▷ *n* piece or passage directed to be played in this way
MAESTOSOS > MAESTOSO
MAESTRI > MAESTRO
MAESTRO *n* outstanding musician or conductor
MAESTROS > MAESTRO
MAFFIA *same as* > MAFIA
MAFFIAS > MAFFIA
MAFFICK *vb* celebrate extravagantly and publicly
MAFFICKED > MAFFICK
MAFFICKER > MAFFICK
MAFFICKS > MAFFICK
MAFFLED *adj* baffled
MAFFLIN *n* half-witted person
MAFFLING *same as* > MAFFLIN
MAFFLINGS > MAFFLING
MAFFLINS > MAFFLIN
MAFIA *n* international secret organization founded in Sicily, probably in opposition to tyranny. It developed into a criminal organization and in the late 19th century was carried to the US by Italian immigrants
MAFIAS > MAFIA
MAFIC *n* collective term for minerals present in igneous rock
MAFICS > MAFIC
MAFIOSI > MAFIOSO
MAFIOSO *n* member of the Mafia
MAFIOSOS > MAFIOSO
MAFTED *adj* suffering under oppressive heat
MAFTIR *n* final section of the weekly Torah reading
MAFTIRS > MAFTIR
MAG *vb* talk ▷ *n* talk
MAGAININ *n* any of a series of related substances with antibacterial properties, derived from the skins of frogs
MAGAININS > MAGAININ
MAGALOG *same as* > MAGALOGUE
MAGALOGS > MAGALOG
MAGALOGUE *n* combination of a magazine and a catalogue
MAGAZINE *n* periodical publication with articles by different writers
MAGAZINES > MAGAZINE
MAGDALEN *n* reformed prostitute
MAGDALENE *same as* > MAGDALEN
MAGDALENS > MAGDALEN
MAGE *archaic word for* > MAGICIAN
MAGENTA *adj* deep purplish-red ▷ *n* deep purplish red that is the complementary colour of green and, with yellow and cyan, forms a set of primary colours
MAGENTAS > MAGENTA
MAGES > MAGE
MAGESHIP > MAGE
MAGESHIPS > MAGE
MAGG *same as* > MAG
MAGGED > MAG
MAGGIE *n* magpie
MAGGIES > MAGGIE
MAGGING > MAG
MAGGOT *n* larva of an insect
MAGGOTIER > MAGGOTY
MAGGOTS > MAGGOT
MAGGOTY *adj* relating to, resembling, or ridden with maggots
MAGGS > MAGG
MAGI > MAGUS
MAGIAN > MAGUS
MAGIANISM > MAGUS
MAGIANS > MAGUS
MAGIC *n* supposed art of invoking supernatural powers to influence events ▷ *vb* to transform or produce by or as if by magic ▷ *adj* of, using, or like magic
MAGICAL > MAGIC
MAGICALLY > MAGIC
MAGICIAN *n* conjuror
MAGICIANS > MAGICIAN
MAGICKED > MAGIC
MAGICKING > MAGIC
MAGICS > MAGIC
MAGILP *same as* > MEGILP
MAGILPS > MAGILP
MAGISM > MAGUS
MAGISMS > MAGUS
MAGISTER *n* person entitled to teach in medieval university
MAGISTERS > MAGISTER
MAGISTERY *n* agency or substance, such as the philosopher's stone, believed to transmute other substances
MAGISTRAL *adj* of, relating to, or characteristic of a master ▷ *n* fortification in a determining position
MAGLEV *n* type of high-speed train that runs on magnets supported by a magnetic field generated around the track
MAGLEVS > MAGLEV
MAGMA *n* molten rock inside the earth's crust
MAGMAS > MAGMA
MAGMATA > MAGMA
MAGMATIC > MAGMA
MAGMATISM > MAGMA
MAGNALIUM *n* alloy of magnesium and aluminium
MAGNATE *n* influential or wealthy person, esp in industry
MAGNATES > MAGNATE
MAGNES *n* magnetic iron ore
MAGNESES > MAGNES
MAGNESIA *n* white tasteless substance used as an antacid and a laxative
MAGNESIAL > MAGNESIA
MAGNESIAN > MAGNESIA
MAGNESIAS > MAGNESIA
MAGNESIC > MAGNESIA
MAGNESITE *n* white, colourless, or lightly tinted mineral
MAGNESIUM *n* silvery-white metallic element
MAGNET *n* piece of iron or steel capable of attracting iron and pointing north when suspended
MAGNETAR *n* type of neutron star that has a very intense magnetic field, over 1000 times greater than that of a pulsar
MAGNETARS > MAGNETAR
MAGNETIC *adj* having the properties of a magnet
MAGNETICS *n* branch of physics concerned with magnetism
MAGNETISE *same as* > MAGNETIZE
MAGNETISM *n* magnetic property
MAGNETIST > MAGNETISM
MAGNETITE *n* black magnetizable mineral that is an important source of iron
MAGNETIZE *vb* make into a magnet
MAGNETO *n* apparatus for ignition in an internal-combustion engine
MAGNETON *n* unit of magnetic moment
MAGNETONS > MAGNETON
MAGNETOS > MAGNETO
MAGNETRON *n* electronic valve used with a magnetic field to generate microwave oscillations, used. esp in radar
MAGNETS > MAGNET
MAGNIFIC *adj* magnificent, grandiose, or pompous
MAGNIFICO *n* magnate
MAGNIFIED > MAGNIFY
MAGNIFIER > MAGNIFY
MAGNIFIES > MAGNIFY
MAGNIFY *vb* increase in apparent size, as with a lens
MAGNITUDE *n* relative importance or size
MAGNOLIA *n* shrub or tree with showy white or pink flowers
MAGNOLIAS > MAGNOLIA
MAGNON *n* short for Cro-Magnon
MAGNONS > MAGNON
MAGNOX *n* alloy composed mainly of magnesium, used in fuel elements of some nuclear reactors
MAGNOXES > MAGNOX
MAGNUM *n* large wine bottle holding about 1.5 litres
MAGNUMS > MAGNUM
MAGNUS as in *magnus hitch* knot similar to a clove hitch but having one more turn
MAGOT *n* Chinese or Japanese figurine in a crouching position, usually grotesque
MAGOTS > MAGOT
MAGPIE *n* black-and-white bird
MAGPIES > MAGPIE
MAGS > MAG
MAGSMAN *n* raconteur
MAGSMEN > MAGSMAN
MAGUEY *n* any of various tropical American agave plants of the genera *Agave* or *Furcraea*, esp one that yields a fibre or is used in making an alcoholic beverage
MAGUEYS > MAGUEY
MAGUS *n* Zoroastrian priest of the ancient Medes and Persians
MAGYAR *adj* of or relating to a style of sleeve cut in one piece with the bodice
MAHARAJA *same as* > MAHARAJAH
MAHARAJAH *n* former title of some Indian princes
MAHARAJAS > MAHARAJA
MAHARANEE *same as* > MAHARANI
MAHARANI *n* wife of a maharaja
MAHARANIS > MAHARANI
MAHARISHI *n* Hindu religious teacher or mystic
MAHATMA *n* person revered for holiness and wisdom
MAHATMAS > MAHATMA
MAHEWU *n* (in South Africa) fermented liquid mealie-meal porridge, used as a stimulant, esp by Black Africans
MAHEWUS > MAHEWU
MAHIMAHI *n* Pacific fish
MAHIMAHIS > MAHIMAHI
MAHJONG *n* game of Chinese origin, usually played by four people, in which tiles bearing various designs are drawn and discarded until one player has an entire hand of winning combinations
MAHJONGG *same as* > MAHJONG
MAHJONGGS > MAHJONGG
MAHJONGS > MAHJONG
MAHLSTICK *same as* > MAULSTICK
MAHMAL *n* litter used in Muslim ceremony

MAHMALS > MAHMAL
MAHOE *n* New Zealand tree
MAHOES > MAHOE
MAHOGANY *n* hard reddish-brown wood of several tropical trees ▷ *adj* reddish-brown
MAHONIA *n* any evergreen berberidaceous shrub of the Asian and American genus *Mahonia*, esp *M. aquifolium*: cultivated for their ornamental spiny divided leaves and clusters of small yellow flowers
MAHONIAS > MAHONIA
MAHOUT *n* (in India and the East Indies) elephant driver or keeper
MAHOUTS > MAHOUT
MAHSEER *n* any of various large freshwater Indian cyprinid fishes, such as *Barbus tor*
MAHSEERS > MAHSEER
MAHSIR *same as* > MAHSEER
MAHSIRS > MAHSIR
MAHUA *n* Indian tree
MAHUANG *n* herbal medicine from shrub
MAHUANGS > MAHUANG
MAHUAS > MAHUA
MAHWA *same as* > MAHUA
MAHWAS > MAHWA
MAHZOR *same as* > MACHZOR
MAHZORIM > MAHZOR
MAHZORS > MAHZOR
MAIASAUR *same as* > MAIASAURA
MAIASAURA *n* species of dinosaur
MAIASAURS > MAIASAUR
MAID *n* female servant ▷ *vb* work as maid
MAIDAN *n* (in Pakistan, India, etc) an open space used for meetings, sports, etc
MAIDANS > MAIDAN
MAIDED > MAID
MAIDEN *n* young unmarried woman ▷ *adj* unmarried
MAIDENISH > MAIDEN
MAIDENLY *adj* modest
MAIDENS > MAIDEN
MAIDHOOD > MAID
MAIDHOODS > MAID
MAIDING > MAID
MAIDISH > MAID
MAIDISM *n* pellagra
MAIDISMS > MAIDISM
MAIDLESS > MAID
MAIDS > MAID
MAIEUTIC *adj* of or relating to the Socratic method of eliciting knowledge by a series of questions and answers
MAIEUTICS *n* Socratic method
MAIGRE *adj* not containing flesh, and so permissible as food on days of religious abstinence ▷ *n* species of fish
MAIGRES > MAIGRE
MAIHEM *same as* > MAYHEM
MAIHEMS > MAIHEM
MAIK *n* old halfpenny
MAIKO *n* apprentice geisha
MAIKOS > MAIKO
MAIKS > MAIK
MAIL *n* letters and packages transported and delivered by the post office ▷ *vb* send by mail
MAILABLE > MAIL
MAILBAG *n* large bag for transporting or delivering mail
MAILBAGS > MAILBAG
MAILBOX *n* box into which letters and parcels are delivered
MAILBOXES > MAILBOX
MAILCAR *same as* > MAILCOACH
MAILCARS > MAILCAR
MAILCOACH *n* railway coach specially constructed for the transportation of mail
MAILE *n* halfpenny
MAILED > MAIL
MAILER *n* person who addresses or mails letters, etc
MAILERS > MAILER
MAILES > MAILE
MAILGRAM *n* telegram
MAILGRAMS > MAILGRAM
MAILING > MAIL
MAILINGS > MAILING
MAILL *n* Scots word meaning rent
MAILLESS > MAIL
MAILLOT *n* tights worn for ballet, gymnastics, etc
MAILLOTS > MAILLOT
MAILLS > MAILL
MAILMAN *n* postman
MAILMEN > MAILMAN
MAILMERGE *n* computer program for sending mass mailings
MAILPOUCH *same as* > MAILBAG
MAILROOM *n* room where mail to and from building is dealt with
MAILROOMS > MAILROOM
MAILS > MAIL
MAILSACK *same as* > MAILBAG
MAILSACKS > MAILSACK
MAILSHOT *n* posting of advertising material to many selected people at once
MAILSHOTS > MAILSHOT
MAILVAN *n* vehicle used to transport post
MAILVANS > MAILVAN
MAIM *vb* cripple or mutilate ▷ *n* injury or defect
MAIMED > MAIM
MAIMER > MAIM
MAIMERS > MAIM
MAIMING > MAIM
MAIMINGS > MAIM
MAIMS > MAIM
MAIN *adj* chief or principal ▷ *n* principal pipe or line carrying water, gas, or electricity ▷ *vb* lower sails
MAINBOOM spar for mainsail
MAINBOOMS > MAINBOOM
MAINBRACE *n* brace attached to the mainyard
MAINDOOR *n* door from street into house
MAINDOORS > MAINDOOR
MAINED > MAIN
MAINER > MAIN
MAINEST > MAIN
MAINFRAME *adj* denoting a high-speed general-purpose computer ▷ *n* high-speed general-purpose computer, with a large store capacity
MAINING > MAIN
MAINLAND *n* stretch of land which forms the main part of a country
MAINLANDS > MAINLAND
MAINLINE *n* the trunk route between two points, usually fed by branch lines ▷ *vb* to inject a drug into a vein ▷ *adj* having an important position, esp having responsibility for the main areas of activity
MAINLINED > MAINLINE
MAINLINER > MAINLINE
MAINLINES > MAINLINE
MAINLY *adv* for the most part, chiefly
MAINMAST *n* chief mast of a ship
MAINMASTS > MAINMAST
MAINOR *n* act of doing something
MAINORS > MAINOR
MAINOUR *same as* > MAINOR
MAINOURS > MAINOUR
MAINPRISE *n* former legal surety
MAINS > MAIN
MAINSAIL *n* largest sail on a mainmast
MAINSAILS > MAINSAIL
MAINSHEET *n* line used to control the angle of the mainsail to the wind
MAINSTAY *n* chief support
MAINSTAYS > MAINSTAY
MAINTAIN *vb* continue or keep in existence
MAINTAINS > MAINTAIN
MAINTOP *n* top or platform at the head of the mainmast
MAINTOPS > MAINTOP
MAINYARD *n* yard for a square mainsail
MAINYARDS > MAINYARD
MAIOLICA *same as* > MAJOLICA
MAIOLICAS > MAIOLICA
MAIR *Scots form of* > MORE
MAIRE *n* New Zealand tree
MAIREHAU *n* small aromatic shrub of New Zealand
MAIREHAUS > MAIREHAU
MAIRES > MAIRE
MAIRS > MAIR
MAISE *n* measure of herring
MAISES > MAISE
MAIST *Scot word for* > MOST
MAISTER *Scots word for* > MASTER
MAISTERED > MAISTER
MAISTERS > MAISTER
MAISTRIES > MAISTER
MAISTRING > MAISTER
MAISTRY > MAISTER
MAISTS > MAIST
MAIZE *n* type of corn with spikes of yellow grains
MAIZES > MAIZE
MAJAGUA *same as* > MAHOE
MAJAGUAS > MAJAGUA
MAJESTIC *adj* beautiful, dignified, and impressive
MAJESTIES > MAJESTY
MAJESTY *n* stateliness or grandeur
MAJLIS *n* (in various N African and Middle Eastern countries) an assembly; council
MAJLISES > MAJLIS
MAJOLICA *n* type of ornamented Italian pottery
MAJOLICAS > MAJOLICA
MAJOR *adj* greater in number, quality, or extent ▷ *n* middle-ranking army officer ▷ *vb* do one's principal study in (a particular subject)
MAJORAT *n* estate, the right to which is that of the first born child of a family
MAJORATS > MAJORAT
MAJORDOMO *n* chief steward or butler of a great household
MAJORED > MAJOR
MAJORETTE *n* one of a group of girls who practise formation marching and baton twirling
MAJORING > MAJOR
MAJORITY *n* greater number
MAJORLY *adv* very
MAJORS > MAJOR
MAJORSHIP > MAJOR
MAJUSCULE *n* large letter, either capital or uncial, used in printing or writing ▷ *adj* relating to, printed, or written in such letters
MAK *Scot word for* > MAKE
MAKABLE > MAKE
MAKAR *same as* > MAKER
MAKARS > MAKAR
MAKE *vb* create, construct, or establish ▷ *n* brand, type, or style
MAKEABLE > MAKE
MAKEBATE *n* troublemaker

MAKEBATES > MAKEBATE
MAKEFAST *n* strong support to which a vessel is secured
MAKEFASTS > MAKEFAST
MAKELESS > MAKE
MAKEOVER *vb* to transfer the title or possession of (property, etc) ▷ *n* a series of alterations, including beauty treatments and new clothes, intended to make a noticeable improvement in a person's appearance
MAKEOVERS > MAKEOVER
MAKER *n* person or company that makes something
MAKEREADY *n* process of preparing the forme and the cylinder or platen packing to achieve the correct impression all over the forme
MAKERS > MAKER
MAKES > MAKE
MAKESHIFT *adj* serving as a temporary substitute ▷ *n* something serving in this capacity
MAKEUP *n* cosmetics, such as powder, lipstick, etc, applied to the face to improve its appearance ▷ *vb* devise, construct, or compose, sometimes with the intent to deceive
MAKEUPS > MAKEUP
MAKI *n* in Japanese cuisine, rice and other ingredients wrapped in a short seaweed roll
MAKIMONO *n* Japanese scroll
MAKIMONOS > MAKIMONO
MAKING > MAKE
MAKINGS *pl n* potentials, qualities, or materials
MAKIS > MAKI
MAKO *n* powerful shark of the Atlantic and Pacific Oceans
MAKOS > MAKO
MAKS > MAK
MAKUTA *plural of* > LIKUTA
MAKUTU *n* Polynesian witchcraft ▷ *vb* cast a spell on
MAKUTUED > MAKUTU
MAKUTUING > MAKUTU
MAKUTUS > MAKUTU
MAL *n* illness
MALA *n* string of beads or knots, used in praying and meditating
MALACCA *n* stem of the rattan palm
MALACCAS > MALACCA
MALACHITE *n* green mineral
MALACIA *n* pathological softening of an organ or tissue, such as bone
MALACIAS > MALACIA
MALADIES > MALADY
MALADROIT *adj* clumsy or awkward
MALADY *n* disease or illness
MALAGUENA *n* Spanish dance similar to the fandango
MALAISE *n* something wrong which affects a section of society or area of activity
MALAISES > MALAISE
MALAM *same as* > MALLAM
MALAMS > MALAM
MALAMUTE *n* Alaskan sled dog of the spitz type, having a dense usually greyish coat
MALAMUTES > MALAMUTE
MALANDER *same as* > MALANDERS
MALANDERS *pl n* disease of horses characterized by an eczematous inflammation behind the knee
MALANGA *same as* > COCOYAM
MALANGAS > MALANGA
MALAPERT *adj* saucy or impudent ▷ *n* saucy or impudent person
MALAPERTS > MALAPERT
MALAPROP *n* a word unintentionally confused with one of similar sound, esp when creating a ridiculous effect, as in *I am not under the affluence of alcohol*
MALAPROPS > MALAPROP
MALAR *n* cheekbone ▷ *adj* of or relating to the cheek or cheekbone
MALARIA *n* infectious disease caused by the bite of some mosquitoes
MALARIAL > MALARIA
MALARIAN > MALARIA
MALARIAS > MALARIA
MALARIOUS > MALARIA
MALARKEY *n* nonsense or rubbish
MALARKEYS > MALARKEY
MALARKIES > MALARKY
MALARKY *same as* > MALARKEY
MALAROMA *n* bad smell
MALAROMAS > MALAROMA
MALARS > MALAR
MALAS > MALA
MALATE *n* any salt or ester of malic acid
MALATES > MALATE
MALATHION *n* yellow organophosphorus insecticide used as a dust or mist for the control of house flies and garden pests
MALAX *vb* soften
MALAXAGE > MALAX
MALAXAGES > MALAX
MALAXATE *same as* > MALAX
MALAXATED > MALAXATE
MALAXATES > MALAXATE
MALAXATOR *n* machine for kneading or grinding
MALAXED > MALAX
MALAXES > MALAX
MALAXING > MALAX
MALE *adj* of the sex which can fertilize female reproductive cells ▷ *n* male person or animal
MALEATE *n* any salt or ester of maleic acid
MALEATES > MALEATE
MALEDICT *vb* utter a curse against ▷ *adj* cursed or detestable
MALEDICTS > MALEDICT
MALEFFECT *n* bad effect
MALEFIC *adj* causing evil
MALEFICE *n* wicked deed
MALEFICES > MALEFICE
MALEIC as in *maleic acid* colourless soluble crystalline substance used to synthesize other compounds
MALEMIUT *same as* > MALAMUTE
MALEMIUTS > MALEMIUT
MALEMUTE *same as* > MALAMUTE
MALEMUTES > MALEMUTE
MALENESS > MALE
MALENGINE *n* wicked plan
MALES > MALE
MALFED *adj* having malfunctioned
MALFORMED *adj* deformed
MALGRADO *prep* in spite of
MALGRE *same as* > MAUGRE
MALGRED > MALGRE
MALGRES > MALGRE
MALGRING > MALGRE
MALI *n* member of an Indian caste
MALIBU as in *malibu board* lightweight surfboard
MALIC as in *malic acid* colourless crystalline compound occurring in apples and other fruit
MALICE *n* desire to cause harm to others ▷ *vb* wish harm to
MALICED > MALICE
MALICES > MALICE
MALICHO *n* mischief
MALICHOS > MALICHO
MALICING > MALICE
MALICIOUS *adj* characterized by malice
MALIGN *vb* slander or defame ▷ *adj* evil in influence or effect
MALIGNANT *adj* seeking to harm others
MALIGNED > MALIGN
MALIGNER > MALIGN
MALIGNERS > MALIGN
MALIGNING > MALIGN
MALIGNITY *n* evil disposition
MALIGNLY > MALIGN
MALIGNS > MALIGN
MALIHINI *n* (in Hawaii) a foreigner or stranger
MALIHINIS > MALIHINI
MALIK *n* person of authority in India
MALIKS > MALIK
MALINE *n* stiff net
MALINES > MALINE
MALINGER *vb* feign illness to avoid work
MALINGERS > MALINGER
MALINGERY > MALINGER
MALIS > MALI
MALISM *n* belief that evil dominates world
MALISMS > MALISM
MALISON *archaic or poetic word for* > CURSE
MALISONS > MALISON
MALIST > MALISM
MALKIN *archaic or dialect name for a* > CAT
MALKINS > MALKIN
MALL *n* street or shopping area closed to vehicles ▷ *vb* maul
MALLAM *n* (in Islamic W Africa) a man learned in Koranic studies
MALLAMS > MALLAM
MALLANDER *same as* > MALANDERS
MALLARD *n* wild duck
MALLARDS > MALLARD
MALLEABLE *adj* capable of being hammered or pressed into shape
MALLEABLY > MALLEABLE
MALLEATE *vb* hammer
MALLEATED > MALLEATE
MALLEATES > MALLEATE
MALLECHO *same as* > MALICHO
MALLECHOS > MALLECHO
MALLED > MALL
MALLEE *n* low-growing eucalypt in dry regions
MALLEES > MALLEE
MALLEI > MALLEUS
MALLEMUCK *n* any of various sea birds, such as the albatross, fulmar, or shearwater
MALLENDER *same as* > MALANDERS
MALLEOLAR > MALLEOLUS
MALLEOLI > MALLEOLUS
MALLEOLUS *n* either of two rounded bony projections of the tibia and fibula on the sides of each ankle joint
MALLET *n* (wooden) hammer
MALLETS > MALLET
MALLEUS *n* outermost and largest of the three small bones in the middle ear of mammals
MALLEUSES > MALLEUS
MALLING > MALL
MALLINGS > MALL
MALLOW *n* plant with pink or purple flowers

MALLOWS > MALLOW
MALLS > MALL
MALM *n* soft greyish limestone that crumbles easily
MALMAG *n* Asian monkey
MALMAGS > MALMAG
MALMIER > MALMY
MALMIEST > MALMY
MALMS > MALM
MALMSEY *n* sweet Madeira wine
MALMSEYS > MALMSEY
MALMSTONE *same as* > MALM
MALMY *adj* looking like malm
MALODOR *same as* > MALODOUR
MALODORS > MALODOR
MALODOUR *n* unpleasant smell
MALODOURS > MALODOUR
MALONATE *n* salt of malonic acid
MALONATES > MALONATE
MALONIC as in *malonic acid* colourless crystalline compound occurring in sugar beet
MALOTI *plural of* > LOTI
MALPIGHIA *n* tropical shrub
MALPOSED *adj* in abnormal position
MALS > MAL
MALSTICK *same as* > MAULSTICK
MALSTICKS > MALSTICK
MALT *n* grain, such as barley, prepared for use in making beer or whisky ▷ *vb* make into or make with malt
MALTALENT *n* evil intention
MALTASE *n* enzyme that hydrolyses maltose and similar glucosides to glucose
MALTASES > MALTASE
MALTED > MALT
MALTEDS > MALT
MALTHA *n* any of various naturally occurring mixtures of hydrocarbons, such as ozocerite
MALTHAS > MALTHA
MALTIER > MALTY
MALTIEST > MALTY
MALTINESS > MALTY
MALTING *n* building in which malt is made or stored
MALTINGS > MALTING
MALTMAN *same as* > MALTSTER
MALTMEN > MALTMAN
MALTOL *n* food additive
MALTOLS > MALTOL
MALTOSE *n* sugar formed by the action of enzymes on starch
MALTOSES > MALTOSE
MALTREAT *vb* treat badly
MALTREATS > MALTREAT
MALTS > MALT
MALTSTER *n* person who makes or deals in malt
MALTSTERS > MALTSTER
MALTWORM *n* heavy drinker
MALTWORMS > MALTWORM
MALTY *adj* of, like, or containing malt
MALVA *n* mallow plant
MALVAS > MALVA
MALVASIA *n* type of grape used to make malmsey
MALVASIAN > MALVASIA
MALVASIAS > MALVASIA
MALVESIE *same as* > MALMSEY
MALVESIES > MALVESIE
MALVOISIE *n* amber dessert wine made in France, similar to malmsey
MALWA *n* Ugandan drink brewed from millet
MALWARE *n* computer program designed to cause damage or disruption to a system
MALWARES > MALWARE
MALWAS > MALWA
MAM *same as* > MOTHER
MAMA *n* mother
MAMAGUY *vb* deceive or tease, either in jest or by deceitful flattery ▷ *n* instance of such deception or flattery
MAMAGUYED > MAMAGUY
MAMAGUYS > MAMAGUY
MAMAKAU *same as* > MAMAKU
MAMAKO *same as* > MAMAKU
MAMAKU *n* tall edible New Zealand tree fern
MAMALIGA *same as* > POLENTA
MAMALIGAS > MAMALIGA
MAMAS > MAMA
MAMBA *n* deadly S African snake
MAMBAS > MAMBA
MAMBO *n* Latin American dance resembling the rumba ▷ *vb* perform this dance
MAMBOED > MAMBO
MAMBOES > MAMBO
MAMBOING > MAMBO
MAMBOS > MAMBO
MAMEE *same as* > MAMEY
MAMEES > MAMEE
MAMELON *n* small rounded hillock
MAMELONS > MAMELON
MAMELUCO *n* Brazilian of mixed European and South American descent
MAMELUCOS > MAMELUCO
MAMELUKE *n* member of a military class, originally of Turkish slaves, ruling in Egypt from about 1250 to 1517 and remaining powerful until crushed in 1811
MAMELUKES > MAMELUKE
MAMEY *n* tropical tree
MAMEYES > MAMEY
MAMEYS > MAMEY
MAMIE *n* tropical tree
MAMIES > MAMIE
MAMILLA *n* nipple or teat
MAMILLAE > MAMILLA
MAMILLAR *adj* of breast
MAMILLARY > MAMILLA
MAMILLATE *adj* having nipples or nipple-like protuberances
MAMLUK *same as* > MAMELUKE
MAMLUKS > MAMLUK
MAMMA *n* buxom and voluptuous woman
MAMMAE > MAMMA
MAMMAL *n* animal of the type that suckles its young
MAMMALIAN > MAMMAL
MAMMALITY > MAMMAL
MAMMALOGY *n* branch of zoology concerned with the study of mammals
MAMMALS > MAMMAL
MAMMARY *adj* of the breasts or milk-producing glands
MAMMAS > MAMMA
MAMMATE *adj* having breasts
MAMMATI > MAMMATUS
MAMMATUS *n* breast-shaped cloud
MAMMEE *same as* > MAMEY
MAMMEES > MAMMEE
MAMMER *vb* hesitate
MAMMERED > MAMMER
MAMMERING > MAMMER
MAMMERS > MAMMER
MAMMET *same as* > MAUMET
MAMMETRY *n* worship of idols
MAMMETS > MAMMET
MAMMEY *same as* > MAMEY
MAMMEYS > MAMMEY
MAMMIE *same as* > MAMMY
MAMMIES > MAMMY
MAMMIFER *same as* > MAMMAL
MAMMIFERS > MAMMIFER
MAMMIFORM *adj* in form of breast
MAMMILLA *same as* > MAMILLA
MAMMILLAE > MAMMILLA
MAMMITIS *same as* > MASTITIS
MAMMOCK *n* fragment ▷ *vb* tear or shred
MAMMOCKED > MAMMOCK
MAMMOCKS > MAMMOCK
MAMMOGRAM *n* xray to examine the breasts in early detection of cancer
MAMMON *n* wealth regarded as a source of evil
MAMMONISH > MAMMON
MAMMONISM > MAMMON
MAMMONIST > MAMMON
MAMMONITE > MAMMON
MAMMONS > MAMMON
MAMMOTH *n* extinct elephant-like mammal ▷ *adj* colossal
MAMMOTHS > MAMMOTH
MAMMY *n* Black woman employed as a nurse or servant to a White family
MAMPARA *n* foolish person, idiot
MAMPARAS > MAMPARA
MAMPOER *n* home-distilled brandy made from peaches, prickly pears, etc
MAMPOERS > MAMPOER
MAMS > MAM
MAMSELLE *n* mademoiselle
MAMSELLES > MAMSELLE
MAMZER *n* child of an incestuous or adulterous union
MAMZERIM > MAMZER
MAMZERS > MAMZER
MAN *n* adult male ▷ *vb* supply with sufficient people for operation or defence
MANA *n* authority, influence
MANACLE *vb* handcuff or fetter ▷ *n* metal ring or chain put round the wrists or ankles, used to restrict the movements of a prisoner or convict
MANACLED > MANACLE
MANACLES > MANACLE
MANACLING > MANACLE
MANAGE *vb* succeed in doing
MANAGED > MANAGE
MANAGER *n* person in charge of a business, institution, actor, sports team, etc
MANAGERS > MANAGER
MANAGES > MANAGE
MANAGING *adj* having administrative control or authority
MANAIA *n* common figure in Māori carving consisting of a human body and a bird-like head
MANAKIN *same as* > MANIKIN
MANAKINS > MANAKIN
MANANA *n* tomorrow ▷ *adv* tomorrow
MANANAS > MANANA
MANAS > MANA
MANAT *n* standard monetary unit of Azerbaijan, divided into 100 gopik
MANATEE *n* large tropical plant-eating aquatic mammal
MANATEES > MANATEE
MANATI *same as* > MANATEE
MANATIS > MANATI
MANATOID > MANATEE
MANATS > MANAT
MANATU *n* large flowering deciduous New Zealand tree
MANAWA *in New Zealand, same as* > MANGROVE
MANAWAS > MANAWA
MANCALA *n* African and Asian board game

ANCALAS > MANCALA
ANCANDO *adv* musical direction meaning fading away
ANCHE *n* long sleeve
ANCHES > MANCHE
ANCHET *n* type of bread
ANCHETS > MANCHET
ANCIPATE *vb* make legal transfer in ancient Rome
ANCIPLE *n* steward who buys provisions, esp in a college, Inn of Court, or monastery
ANCIPLES > MANCIPLE
ANCUS *n* former English coin
ANCUSES > MANCUS
AND > MAN
ANDALA *n* circular design symbolizing the universe
ANDALAS > MANDALA
ANDALIC > MANDALA
ANDAMUS *n* formerly a writ from, now an order of, a superior court commanding an inferior tribunal, public official, corporation, etc, to carry out a public duty
ANDARIN *n* high-ranking government official
ANDARINE *same as* > MANDARIN
ANDARINS > MANDARIN
ANDATARY *same as* > MANDATORY
ANDATE *n* official or authoritative command ▷ *vb* give authority to
ANDATED > MANDATE
ANDATES > MANDATE
ANDATING > MANDATE
ANDATOR > MANDATE
ANDATORS > MANDATE
ANDATORY *adj* compulsory ▷ *n* person or state holding a mandate
ANDI *n* (in India) a big market
ANDIBLE *n* lower jawbone or jawlike part
ANDIBLES > MANDIBLE
ANDILION *same as* > MANDYLION
ANDIOC *same as* > MANIOC
ANDIOCA *same as* > MANIOC
ANDIOCAS > MANDIOCA
ANDIOCCA *same as* > MANIOC
ANDIOCS > MANDIOC
ANDIR *n* Hindu or Jain temple
ANDIRA *same as* > MANDIR
ANDIRAS > MANDIRA
ANDIRS > MANDIR
ANDIS > MANDI
ANDOLA *n* early type of mandolin
ANDOLAS > MANDOLA
ANDOLIN *n* musical instrument with four pairs of strings
ANDOLINE *same as* > MANDOLIN
MANDOLINS > MANDOLIN
MANDOM *n* mankind
MANDOMS > MANDOM
MANDORA *n* ancestor of mandolin
MANDORAS > MANDORA
MANDORLA *n* (in painting, sculpture, etc) an almond-shaped area of light, usually surrounding the resurrected Christ or the Virgin at the Assumption
MANDORLAS > MANDORLA
MANDRAKE *n* plant with a forked root, formerly used as a narcotic
MANDRAKES > MANDRAKE
MANDREL *n* shaft on which work is held in a lathe
MANDRELS > MANDREL
MANDRIL *same as* > MANDREL
MANDRILL *n* large blue-faced baboon
MANDRILLS > MANDRILL
MANDRILS > MANDRIL
MANDUCATE *vb* eat or chew
MANDYLION *n* loose garment formerly worn over armour
MANE *n* long hair on the neck of a horse, lion, etc
MANED > MANE
MANEGE *n* art of training horses and riders ▷ *vb* train horse
MANEGED > MANEGE
MANEGES > MANEGE
MANEGING > MANEGE
MANEH *same as* > MINA
MANEHS > MANEH
MANELESS > MANE
MANENT > MANET
MANES *pl n* spirits of the dead, often revered as minor deities
MANET *vb* theatre direction, remain on stage
MANEUVER *same as* > MANOEUVRE
MANEUVERS > MANEUVER
MANFUL *adj* determined and brave
MANFULLY > MANFUL
MANG *vb* speak
MANGA *n* type of Japanese comic book with an adult theme
MANGABEY *n* any of several large agile arboreal Old World monkeys of the genus *Cercocebus*, of central Africa, having long limbs and tail and white upper eyelids
MANGABEYS > MANGABEY
MANGABIES > MANGABY
MANGABY *same as* > MANGABEY
MANGAL *n* Turkish brazier
MANGALS > MANGAL
MANGANATE *n* salt of manganic acid
MANGANESE *n* brittle greyish-white metallic element
MANGANIC *adj* of or containing manganese in the trivalent state
MANGANIN *n* copper-based alloy
MANGANINS > MANGANIN
MANGANITE *n* blackish mineral
MANGANOUS *adj* of or containing manganese in the divalent state
MANGAS > MANGA
MANGE *n* skin disease of domestic animals
MANGEAO *n* small New Zealand tree with glossy leaves
MANGED *adj* having mange
MANGEL *n* Eurasian variety of the beet plant, *Beta vulgaris*, cultivated as a cattle food, having a large yellowish root
MANGELS > MANGEL
MANGER *n* eating trough in a stable or barn
MANGERS > MANGER
MANGES > MANGE
MANGETOUT *n* variety of pea with an edible pod
MANGEY *same as* > MANGY
MANGIER > MANGY
MANGIEST > MANGY
MANGILY > MANGY
MANGINESS > MANGY
MANGING > MANG
MANGLE *vb* destroy by crushing and twisting ▷ *n* machine with rollers for squeezing water from washed clothes
MANGLED > MANGLE
MANGLER > MANGLE
MANGLERS > MANGLE
MANGLES > MANGLE
MANGLING > MANGLE
MANGO *n* tropical fruit with sweet juicy yellow flesh
MANGOES > MANGO
MANGOLD *n* type of root vegetable
MANGOLDS > MANGOLD
MANGONEL *n* war engine for hurling stones
MANGONELS > MANGONEL
MANGOS > MANGO
MANGOSTAN *n* East Indian tree with thick leathery leaves and edible fruit
MANGOUSTE *same as* > MONGOOSE
MANGROVE *n* tropical tree with exposed roots, which grows beside water
MANGROVES > MANGROVE
MANGS > MANG
MANGULATE *vb* bend or twist out of shape
MANGY *adj* having mange
MANHANDLE *vb* treat roughly
MANHATTAN *n* mixed drink consisting of four parts whisky, one part vermouth, and a dash of bitters
MANHOLE *n* hole with a cover, through which a person can enter a drain or sewer
MANHOLES > MANHOLE
MANHOOD *n* state or quality of being a man or being manly
MANHOODS > MANHOOD
MANHUNT *n* organized search, usu. by police, for a wanted man or a fugitive
MANHUNTER > MANHUNT
MANHUNTS > MANHUNT
MANI *n* place to pray
MANIA *n* extreme enthusiasm
MANIAC *n* mad person
MANIACAL *adj* affected with or characteristic of mania
MANIACS > MANIAC
MANIAS > MANIA
MANIC *adj* extremely excited or energetic ▷ *n* person afflicted with mania
MANICALLY > MANIC
MANICOTTI *pl n* large tubular noodles, usually stuffed with ricotta cheese and baked in a tomato sauce
MANICS > MANIC
MANICURE *n* cosmetic care of the fingernails and hands ▷ *vb* care for (the fingernails and hands) in this way
MANICURED > MANICURE
MANICURES > MANICURE
MANIES > MANY
MANIFEST *adj* easily noticed, obvious ▷ *vb* show plainly ▷ *n* list of cargo or passengers for customs
MANIFESTO *n* declaration of policy as issued by a political party ▷ *vb* issued manifesto
MANIFESTS > MANIFEST
MANIFOLD *adj* numerous and varied ▷ *n* pipe with several outlets, esp in an internal-combustion engine ▷ *vb* duplicate (a page, book, etc)
MANIFOLDS > MANIFOLD
MANIFORM *adj* like hand
MANIHOC *variation of* > MANIOC
MANIHOCS > MANIHOC
MANIHOT *n* tropical American plant
MANIHOTS > MANIHOT
MANIKIN *n* little man or dwarf
MANIKINS > MANIKIN
MANILA *n* strong brown

paper used for envelopes
MANILAS > MANILA
MANILLA *n* early currency in W Africa in the form of a small bracelet
MANILLAS > MANILLA
MANILLE *n* (in ombre and quadrille) the second best trump
MANILLES > MANILLE
MANIOC *same as* > CASSAVA
MANIOCA *same as* > MANIOC
MANIOCAS > MANIOCA
MANIOCS > MANIOC
MANIPLE *n* (in ancient Rome) a unit of 120 to 200 foot soldiers
MANIPLES > MANIPLE
MANIPLIES *same as* > MANYPLIES
MANIPULAR *adj* of or relating to an ancient Roman maniple
MANIS *n* pangolin
MANITO *same as* > MANITOU
MANITOS > MANITO
MANITOU *n* (among the Algonquian Indians) a deified spirit or force
MANITOUS > MANITOU
MANITU *same as* > MANITOU
MANITUS > MANITU
MANJACK *n* single individual
MANJACKS > MANJACK
MANKIER > MANKY
MANKIEST > MANKY
MANKIND *n* human beings collectively
MANKINDS > MANKIND
MANKY *adj* worthless, rotten, or in bad taste
MANLESS > MAN
MANLIER > MANLY
MANLIEST > MANLY
MANLIKE *adj* resembling or befitting a man
MANLIKELY > MANLIKE
MANLILY > MANLY
MANLINESS > MANLY
MANLY *adj* (possessing qualities) appropriate to a man
MANMADE *adj* made or produced by man
MANNA *n* miraculous food which sustained the Israelites in the wilderness
MANNAN *n* drug derived from mannose
MANNANS > MANNAN
MANNAS > MANNA
MANNED > MAN
MANNEQUIN *n* woman who models clothes at a fashion show
MANNER *n* way a thing happens or is done
MANNERED *adj* affected
MANNERISM *n* person's distinctive habit or trait
MANNERIST > MANNERISM
MANNERLY *adj* having good manners, polite ▷ *adv* with good manners
MANNERS *pl n* person's social conduct viewed in the light of whether it is regarded as polite or acceptable or not
MANNIKIN *same as* > MANIKIN
MANNIKINS > MANNIKIN
MANNING > MAN
MANNISH *adj* (of a woman) like a man
MANNISHLY > MANNISH
MANNITE *same as* > MANNITOL
MANNITES > MANNITE
MANNITIC > MANNITOL
MANNITOL *n* white crystalline water-soluble sweet-tasting alcohol
MANNITOLS > MANNITOL
MANNOSE *n* hexose sugar
MANNOSES > MANNOSE
MANO *n* stone for grinding grain
MANOAO *n* New Zealand shrub
MANOAOS > MANOAO
MANOEUVRE *n* skilful movement ▷ *vb* manipulate or contrive skilfully or cunningly
MANOMETER *n* instrument for comparing pressures
MANOMETRY > MANOMETER
MANOR *n* large country house and its lands
MANORIAL > MANOR
MANORS > MANOR
MANOS > MANO
MANOSCOPY *n* measurement of the densities of gases
MANPACK *n* load carried by one person
MANPACKS > MANPACK
MANPOWER *n* available number of workers
MANPOWERS > MANPOWER
MANQUE *adj* would-be
MANRED *n* homage
MANREDS > MANRED
MANRENT *same as* > MANRED
MANRENTS > MANRENT
MANRIDER *n* train carrying miners in coal mine
MANRIDERS > MANRIDER
MANRIDING *adj* carrying people rather than goods
MANROPE *n* rope railing
MANROPES > MANROPE
MANS > MAN
MANSARD *n* roof with two slopes on both sides and both ends, the lower slopes being steeper than the upper
MANSARDED *adj* having mansard roof
MANSARDS > MANSARD
MANSE *n* house provided for a minister in some religious denominations
MANSES > MANSE
MANSHIFT *n* work done by one person in one shift
MANSHIFTS > MANSHIFT
MANSION *n* large house
MANSIONS > MANSION
MANSLAYER *n* person who kills man
MANSONRY *n* mansions collectively
MANSUETE *adj* gentle
MANSWORN *adj* perjured
MANTA *n* any large ray (fish) of the family *Mobulidae*, having very wide winglike pectoral fins and feeding on plankton
MANTAS > MANTA
MANTEAU *n* cloak or mantle
MANTEAUS > MANTEAU
MANTEAUX > MANTEAU
MANTEEL *n* cloak
MANTEELS > MANTEEL
MANTEL *n* structure round a fireplace ▷ *vb* construct a mantel
MANTELET *n* woman's short mantle, often lace-trimmed, worn in the mid-19th century
MANTELETS > MANTELET
MANTELS > MANTEL
MANTES > MANTIS
MANTIC *adj* of or relating to divination and prophecy
MANTICORA *same as* > MANTICORE
MANTICORE *n* mythical monster with body of lion and human head
MANTID *same as* > MANTIS
MANTIDS > MANTID
MANTIES > MANTY
MANTILLA *n* (in Spain) a lace scarf covering a woman's head and shoulders
MANTILLAS > MANTILLA
MANTIS *n* carnivorous insect like a grasshopper
MANTISES > MANTIS
MANTISSA *n* part of a common logarithm consisting of the decimal point and the figures following it
MANTISSAS > MANTISSA
MANTLE *same as* > MANTEL
MANTLED > MANTLE
MANTLES > MANTLE
MANTLET *same as* > MANTELET
MANTLETS > MANTLET
MANTLING *n* drapery or scrollwork around a shield
MANTLINGS > MANTLING
MANTO *same as* > MANTEAU
MANTOES > MANTO
MANTOS > MANTO
MANTRA *n* any sacred word or syllable used as an object of concentration
MANTRAM *same as* > MANTRA
MANTRAMS > MANTRAM
MANTRAP *n* snare for catching people, esp trespassers
MANTRAPS > MANTRAP
MANTRAS > MANTRA
MANTRIC > MANTRA
MANTUA *n* loose gown of the 17th and 18th centuries worn open in front to show the underskirt
MANTUAS > MANTUA
MANTY *Scots variant of* > MANTUA
MANUAL *adj* of or done with the hands ▷ *n* handbook
MANUALLY > MANUAL
MANUALS > MANUAL
MANUARY *same as* > MANUAL
MANUBRIA > MANUBRIUM
MANUBRIAL > MANUBRIUM
MANUBRIUM *n* any handle-shaped part, esp the upper part of the sternum
MANUHIRI *n* visitor to a Māori marae
MANUHIRIS > MANUHIRI
MANUKA *n* New Zealand tree with strong elastic wood and aromatic leaves
MANUKAS > MANUKA
MANUL *n* Asian wildcat
MANULS > MANUL
MANUMEA *n* pigeon of Samoa
MANUMEAS > MANUMEA
MANUMIT *vb* free from slavery
MANUMITS > MANUMIT
MANURANCE *n* cultivation of land
MANURE *n* animal excrement used as a fertilizer ▷ *vb* fertilize (land) with this
MANURED > MANURE
MANURER > MANURE
MANURERS > MANURE
MANURES > MANURE
MANURIAL > MANURE
MANURING > MANURE
MANURINGS > MANURE
MANUS *n* wrist and hand
MANWARD *adv* towards humankind
MANWARDS *same as* > MANWARD
MANWISE *adv* in human way
MANY *adj* numerous ▷ *n* large number
MANYATA *same as* > MANYATTA
MANYATAS > MANYATA
MANYATTA *n* settlement of Masai people
MANYATTAS > MANYATTA
MANYFOLD *adj* many in number
MANYPLIES *n* third component of the stomach of ruminants
MANZANITA *n* Californian plant
MANZELLO *n* instrument like saxophone
MANZELLOS > MANZELLO

OMAO *n* fish of New
ealand seas
ORMOR *same*
s > MORMAOR
ORMORS > MAORMOR
P *n* representation of
he earth's surface or
ome part of it, showing
eographical features ▷ *vb*
nake a map of
PAU *n* small New Zealand
ree with reddish bark,
romatic leaves, and dark
erries
PLE *n* tree with broad
eaves, a variety of which
ields sugar
PLELIKE > MAPLE
PLES > MAPLE
PLESS > MAP
PLIKE > MAP
PMAKER *n* person who
raws maps
PMAKERS > MAPMAKER
PMAKING > MAPMAKER
PPABLE > MAP
PPED > MAP
PPEMOND *n* map of world
PPER > MAP
PPERIES > MAPPERY
PPERS > MAP
PPERY *n* making of maps
PPING > MAP
PPINGS > MAP
PPIST > MAP
PPISTS > MAP
PS > MAP
PSTICK *same*
s > MOPSTICK
PSTICKS > MAPSTICK
PWISE *adv* like map
QUETTE *n* sculptor's
mall preliminary model
r sketch
QUETTES > MAQUETTE
QUI *n* Chilean shrub
QUILA *n* US-owned
actory in Mexico
QUILAS > MAQUILA
QUIS *n* French
nderground movement
hat fought against the
erman occupying forces
n World War II
QUISARD *n* member of
rench maquis
R *vb* spoil or impair ▷ *n*
isfiguring mark
RA *n* harelike South
merican rodent,
olichotis patagonum,
nhabiting the pampas of
rgentina: family *Caviidae*
avies)
RABI *n* kind of music
opular in S African
ownships in the 1930s
RABIS > MARABI
RABOU *n* large black-and-
hite African stork
RABOUS > MARABOU
RABOUT *n* Muslim holy
an or hermit of North
frica

MARABOUTS > MARABOUT
MARABUNTA *n* any of several social wasps
MARACA *n* shaken percussion instrument made from a gourd containing dried seeds etc
MARACAS > MARACA
MARAE *n* enclosed space in front of a Māori meeting house
MARAES > MARAE
MARAGING as in *maraging steel* strong low-carbon steel containing nickel and small amounts of titanium, aluminium, and niobium, produced by transforming to a martensitic structure and heating at 500°C
MARAGINGS > MARAGING
MARAH *n* bitterness
MARAHS > MARAH
MARANATHA *n* member of Christian sect
MARANTA *n* any plant of the tropical American rhizomatous genus *Maranta*, some species of which are grown as pot plants for their showy leaves in variegated shades of green: family *Marantaceae*
MARANTAS > MARANTA
MARARI *n* eel-like blennoid food fish
MARARIS > MARARI
MARAS > MARA
MARASCA *n* European cherry tree, *Prunus cerasus marasca*, with red acid-tasting fruit from which maraschino is made
MARASCAS > MARASCA
MARASMIC > MARASMUS
MARASMOID > MARASMUS
MARASMUS *n* general emaciation and wasting, esp of infants, thought to be associated with severe malnutrition or impaired utilization of nutrients
MARATHON *n* long-distance race of 26 miles 385 yards (42.195 kilometres) ▷ *adj* of or relating to a race on foot of 26 miles 385 yards (42.195 kilometres)
MARATHONS > MARATHON
MARAUD *vb* wander or raid in search of plunder
MARAUDED > MARAUD
MARAUDER > MARAUD
MARAUDERS > MARAUD
MARAUDING *adj* wandering or raiding in search of plunder
MARAUDS > MARAUD
MARAVEDI *n* any of various Spanish coins of copper or gold
MARAVEDIS > MARAVEDI

MARBELISE *same as* > MARBLEIZE
MARBELIZE *same as* > MARBLEIZE
MARBLE *n* kind of limestone with a mottled appearance, which can be highly polished ▷ *vb* mottle with variegated streaks in imitation of marble
MARBLED > MARBLE
MARBLEISE *same as* > MARBLEIZE
MARBLEIZE *vb* give a marble-like appearance to
MARBLER > MARBLE
MARBLERS > MARBLE
MARBLES *n* game in which marble balls are rolled at one another
MARBLIER > MARBLE
MARBLIEST > MARBLE
MARBLING *n* mottled effect or pattern resembling marble
MARBLINGS > MARBLING
MARBLY > MARBLE
MARC *n* remains of grapes or other fruit that have been pressed for wine-making
MARCASITE *n* crystals of iron pyrites, used in jewellery
MARCATO *adj* (of notes) heavily accented ▷ *adv* with each note heavily accented
MARCATOS > MARCATO
MARCEL *n* hairstyle characterized by repeated regular waves, popular in the 1920s ▷ *vb* make such waves in (the hair) with special hot irons
MARCELLA *n* type of fabric
MARCELLAS > MARCELLA
MARCELLED > MARCEL
MARCELLER > MARCEL
MARCELS > MARCEL
MARCH *vb* walk with a military step ▷ *n* action of marching
MARCHED > MARCH
MARCHEN *n* German story
MARCHER *n* person who marches
MARCHERS > MARCHER
MARCHES > MARCH
MARCHESA *n* (in Italy) the wife or widow of a marchese
MARCHESAS > MARCHESA
MARCHESE *n* (in Italy) a nobleman ranking below a prince and above a count
MARCHESES > MARCHESE
MARCHESI > MARCHESE
MARCHING > MARCH
MARCHLAND *n* border land
MARCHLIKE *adj* like march in rhythm
MARCHMAN *n* person living on border

MARCHMEN > MARCHMAN
MARCHPANE *same as* > MARZIPAN
MARCONI *vb* communicate by wireless
MARCONIED > MARCONI
MARCONIS > MARCONI
MARCS > MARC
MARD > MAR
MARDIED > MARDY
MARDIER > MARDY
MARDIES > MARDY
MARDIEST > MARDY
MARDY *adj* (of a child) spoilt ▷ *vb* behave in mardy way
MARDYING > MARDY
MARE *n* female horse or zebra
MAREMMA *n* marshy unhealthy region near the shore, esp in Italy
MAREMMAS > MAREMMA
MAREMME > MAREMMA
MARENGO *adj* browned in oil and cooked with tomatoes, mushrooms, garlic, wine, etc
MARES > MARE
MARESCHAL *same as* > MARSHAL
MARG *short for* > MARGARINE
MARGARIC *adj* of or resembling pearl
MARGARIN *n* ester of margaric acid
MARGARINE *n* butter substitute made from animal or vegetable fats
MARGARINS > MARGARIN
MARGARITA *n* mixed drink consisting of tequila and lemon juice
MARGARITE *n* pink pearly micaceous mineral
MARGAY *n* feline mammal, *Felis wiedi*, of Central and South America, having a dark-striped coat
MARGAYS > MARGAY
MARGE *n* margarine
MARGENT *same as* > MARGIN
MARGENTED > MARGENT
MARGENTS > MARGENT
MARGES > MARGE
MARGIN *n* edge or border ▷ *vb* provide with a margin
MARGINAL *adj* insignificant, unimportant ▷ *n* marginal constituency
MARGINALS > MARGINAL
MARGINATE *vb* provide with a margin or margins ▷ *adj* having a margin of a distinct colour or form
MARGINED > MARGIN
MARGINING > MARGIN
MARGINS > MARGIN
MARGOSA *n* Indian tree
MARGOSAS > MARGOSA
MARGRAVE *n* (formerly) a German nobleman ranking above a count

MARGRAVES > MARGRAVE
MARGS > MARG
MARIA > MARE
MARIACHI *n* small ensemble of street musicians in Mexico
MARIACHIS > MARIACHI
MARIALITE *n* silicate mineral
MARID *n* spirit in Muslim mythology
MARIDS > MARID
MARIES > MARY
MARIGOLD *n* plant with yellow or orange flowers
MARIGOLDS > MARIGOLD
MARIGRAM *n* graphic record of the tide levels at a particular coastal station
MARIGRAMS > MARIGRAM
MARIGRAPH *n* gauge for recording the levels of the tides
MARIHUANA *same as* > MARIJUANA
MARIJUANA *n* dried flowers and leaves of the cannabis plant, used as a drug, esp in cigarettes
MARIMBA *n* Latin American percussion instrument resembling a xylophone
MARIMBAS > MARIMBA
MARIMBIST > MARIMBA
MARINA *n* harbour for yachts and other pleasure boats
MARINADE *n* seasoned liquid in which fish or meat is soaked before cooking
MARINADED > MARINADE
MARINADES > MARINADE
MARINARA *n* Italian pasta sauce
MARINARAS > MARINARA
MARINAS > MARINA
MARINATE *vb* soak in marinade
MARINATED > MARINATE
MARINATES > MARINATE
MARINE *adj* of the sea or shipping ▷ *n* (esp in Britain and the US) soldier trained for land and sea combat
MARINER *n* sailor
MARINERA *n* folk dance of Peru
MARINERAS > MARINERA
MARINERS > MARINER
MARINES > MARINE
MARINIERE *adj* served in white wine and onion sauce
MARIPOSA *n* any of several liliaceous plants of the genus *Calochortus*, of the southwestern US and Mexico, having brightly coloured tulip-like flowers
MARIPOSAS > MARIPOSA
MARISCHAL *Scots variant of* > MARSHAL
MARISH *n* marsh
MARISHES > MARISH
MARITAGE *n* right of a lord to choose the spouses of his wards
MARITAGES > MARITAGE
MARITAL *adj* relating to marriage
MARITALLY > MARITAL
MARITIME *adj* relating to shipping
MARJORAM *n* aromatic herb used for seasoning food and in salads
MARJORAMS > MARJORAM
MARK *n* line, dot, scar, etc visible on a surface ▷ *vb* make a mark on
MARKA *n* unit of currency introduced as an interim currency in Bosnia-Herzegovina
MARKAS > MARKA
MARKDOWN *n* price reduction ▷ *vb* reduce in price
MARKDOWNS > MARKDOWN
MARKED *adj* noticeable
MARKEDLY > MARKED
MARKER *n* object used to show the position of something
MARKERS > MARKER
MARKET *n* assembly or place for buying and selling ▷ *vb* offer or produce for sale
MARKETED > MARKET
MARKETEER *n* supporter of the European Union and of Britain's membership of it
MARKETER > MARKET
MARKETERS > MARKET
MARKETING *n* part of a business that controls the way that goods or services are sold
MARKETS > MARKET
MARKHOOR *same as* > MARKHOR
MARKHOORS > MARKHOOR
MARKHOR *n* large wild Himalayan goat, *Capra falconeri*, with a reddish-brown coat and large spiralled horns
MARKHORS > MARKHOR
MARKING *n* arrangement of colours on an animal or plant
MARKINGS > MARKING
MARKKA *n* former standard monetary unit of Finland, divided into 100 penniä
MARKKAA > MARKKA
MARKKAS > MARKKA
MARKMAN *n* person owning land
MARKMEN > MARKMAN
MARKS > MARK
MARKSMAN *n* person skilled at shooting
MARKSMEN > MARKSMAN
MARKUP *n* percentage or amount added to the cost of a commodity to provide the seller with a profit and to cover overheads, costs, etc ▷ *vb* increase the price of
MARKUPS > MARKUP
MARL *n* soil formed of clay and lime, used as fertilizer ▷ *vb* fertilize (land) with marl
MARLE *same as* > MARVEL
MARLED > MARL
MARLES > MARLE
MARLIER > MARLY
MARLIEST > MARLY
MARLIN *same as* > MARLINE
MARLINE *n* light rope, usually tarred, made of two strands laid left-handed
MARLINES > MARLINE
MARLING *same as* > MARLINE
MARLINGS > MARLING
MARLINS > MARLIN
MARLITE *n* type of marl that contains clay and calcium carbonate and is resistant to the decomposing action of air
MARLITES > MARLITE
MARLITIC > MARLITE
MARLS > MARL
MARLSTONE *same as* > MARLITE
MARLY *adj* marl-like
MARM *same as* > MADAM
MARMALADE *n* jam made from citrus fruits ▷ *adj* (of cats) streaked orange or yellow and brown
MARMALISE *vb* beat soundly or defeat utterly
MARMALIZE *same as* > MARMALISE
MARMARISE *same as* > MARMARIZE
MARMARIZE *vb* turn to marble
MARMELISE *same as* > MARMELIZE
MARMELIZE *vb* beat soundly
MARMITE *n* large cooking pot
MARMITES > MARMITE
MARMOREAL *adj* of or like marble
MARMOREAN *same as* > MARMOREAL
MARMOSE *n* South American opossum
MARMOSES > MARMOSE
MARMOSET *n* small bushy-tailed monkey
MARMOSETS > MARMOSET
MARMOT *n* burrowing rodent
MARMOTS > MARMOT
MARMS > MARM
MAROCAIN *n* fabric of ribbed crepe
MAROCAINS > MAROCAIN
MARON *n* freshwater crustacean
MARONS > MARON
MAROON *adj* reddish-purp[le] ▷ *vb* abandon ashore, es[p] on an island ▷ *n* explodi[ng] firework or flare used as a warning signal
MAROONED > MAROON
MAROONER > MAROON
MAROONERS > MAROON
MAROONING > MAROON
MAROONS > MAROON
MAROQUIN *n* morocco leather
MAROQUINS > MAROQUIN
MAROR *n* Jewish ceremoni[al] dish of bitter herbs
MARORS > MAROR
MARPLOT *n* person interfering with plot
MARPLOTS > MARPLOT
MARQUE *n* brand of produ[ct] esp of a car
MARQUEE *n* large tent use[d] for a party or exhibition
MARQUEES > MARQUEE
MARQUES > MARQUE
MARQUESS *n* nobleman of the rank below a duke
MARQUETRY *n* ornamenta[l] inlaid work of wood
MARQUIS *n* (in some European countries) nobleman of the rank above a count
MARQUISE *same as* > MARQUEE
MARQUISES > MARQUISE
MARRAM as in *marram gras[s]* any of several grasses of the genus that grow on sandy shores and can withstand drying
MARRAMS > MARRAM
MARRANO *n* Spanish or Portuguese Jew of the late Middle Ages who wa[s] converted to Christianit[y] esp one forcibly converte[d] but secretly adhering to Judaism
MARRANOS > MARRANO
MARRED > MAR
MARRELS *same as* > MERIL[S]
MARRER > MAR
MARRERS > MAR
MARRI *n* species of eucalyptus, *Eucalyptus calophylla*, of Western Australia, widely cultivated for its coloure[d] flowers
MARRIAGE *n* state of bein[g] married
MARRIAGES > MARRIAGE
MARRIED > MARRY
MARRIEDS *pl n* married people
MARRIER > MARRY
MARRIERS > MARRY
MARRIES > MARRY
MARRING > MAR
MARRIS > MARRI
MARRON *n* large edible sweet chestnut

RRONS > MARRON
RROW *n* fatty substance nside bones ▷ *vb* be nate to
RROWED > MARROW
RROWFAT *n* variety of arge pea
RROWING > MARROW
RROWISH > MARROW
RROWS > MARROW
RROWSKY *n* spoonerism
RROWY > MARROW
RRUM *same as* > MARRAM
RRUMS > MARRUM
RRY *vb* take as a usband or wife ▷ *interj* xclamation of surprise or nger
RRYING > MARRY
RRYINGS > MARRY
RS > MAR
RSALA *n* dark sweet essert wine made in icily
RSALAS > MARSALA
RSE *same as* > MASTER
RSEILLE *n* strong otton fabric with a aised pattern, used for edspreads, etc
RSES > MARSE
RSH *n* low-lying wet land
RSHAL *n* officer of the ighest rank ▷ *vb* arrange n order
RSHALCY > MARSHAL
RSHALED > MARSHAL
RSHALER > MARSHAL
RSHALL *n* shortened orm of Marshall Plan, rogramme of US conomic aid for the econstruction of post-Vorld War II Europe 948–52)
RSHALLS > MARSHALL
RSHALS > MARSHAL
RSHBUCK *n* antelope f the central African wamplands, *Strepsiceros pekei*, with spreading oofs adapted to boggy round
RSHES > MARSH
RSHIER > MARSHY
RSHIEST > MARSHY
RSHLAND *n* land onsisting of marshes
RSHLIKE > MARSH
RSHWORT *n* prostrate reeping aquatic perennial mbelliferous plant of he genus *Apium*, esp *A. nundatum*, having small vhite flowers: related to vild celery
RSHY *adj* of, involving, or ke a marsh
RSPORT *n* spoilsport
RSPORTS > MARSPORT
RSQUAKE *n* Martian quivalent of earthquake
RSUPIA > MARSUPIUM
RSUPIAL *n* animal that carries its young in a pouch, such as a kangaroo ▷ *adj* of or like a marsupial
MARSUPIAN > MARSUPIAL
MARSUPIUM *n* external pouch in most female marsupials within which the newly born offspring are suckled and complete their development
MART *n* market ▷ *vb* sell or trade
MARTAGON *n* Eurasian lily plant, *Lilium martagon*, cultivated for its mottled purplish-red flowers with reflexed petals
MARTAGONS > MARTAGON
MARTED > MART
MARTEL *n* hammer-shaped weapon ▷ *vb* use such a weapon
MARTELLED > MARTEL
MARTELLO *n* small circular tower for coastal defence, formerly much used in Europe
MARTELLOS > MARTELLO
MARTELS > MARTEL
MARTEN *n* weasel-like animal
MARTENS > MARTEN
MARTEXT *n* preacher who makes many mistakes
MARTEXTS > MARTEXT
MARTIAL *adj* of war, warlike
MARTIALLY > MARTIAL
MARTIAN *n* inhabitant of Mars
MARTIANS > MARTIAN
MARTIN *n* bird with a slightly forked tail
MARTINET *n* person who maintains strict discipline
MARTINETS > MARTINET
MARTING > MART
MARTINGAL *n* strap of a horse's harness
MARTINI *n* cocktail of vermouth and gin
MARTINIS > MARTINI
MARTINS > MARTIN
MARTLET *n* footless bird often found in coats of arms, standing for either a martin or a swallow
MARTLETS > MARTLET
MARTS > MART
MARTYR *n* person who dies or suffers for his or her beliefs ▷ *vb* make a martyr of
MARTYRDOM *n* sufferings or death of a martyr
MARTYRED > MARTYR
MARTYRIA > MARTYRIUM
MARTYRIES > MARTYRY
MARTYRING > MARTYR
MARTYRISE > MARTYR
MARTYRIUM *same as* > MARTYRY
MARTYRIZE > MARTYR
MARTYRLY > MARTYR
MARTYRS > MARTYR
MARTYRY *n* shrine or chapel erected in honour of a martyr
MARVEL *vb* be filled with wonder ▷ *n* wonderful thing
MARVELED > MARVEL
MARVELING > MARVEL
MARVELLED > MARVEL
MARVELOUS *adj* causing great wonder
MARVELS > MARVEL
MARVER *vb* roll molten glass on slab
MARVERED > MARVER
MARVERING > MARVER
MARVERS > MARVER
MARVY *shortened form of* > MARVELOUS
MARXISANT *adj* sympathetic to Marxism
MARY *shortened form of* > MARYJANE
MARYBUD *n* bud of marigold
MARYBUDS > MARYBUD
MARYJANE *n* slang for marijuana
MARYJANES > MARYJANE
MARZIPAN *n* paste of ground almonds, sugar, and egg whites ▷ *modifier* of or relating to the stratum of middle managers in a financial institution or other business
MARZIPANS > MARZIPAN
MAS > MA
MASA *n* Mexican maize dough
MASALA *n* mixture of spices ground into a paste ▷ *adj* spicy
MASALAS > MASALA
MASAS > MASA
MASCARA *n* cosmetic for darkening the eyelashes
MASCARAED *adj* wearing mascara
MASCARAS > MASCARA
MASCARON *n* in architecture, a face carved in stone or metal
MASCARONS *n* grotesque face used as decoration
MASCLE *n* charge consisting of a lozenge with a lozenge-shaped hole in the middle
MASCLED > MASCLE
MASCLES > MASCLE
MASCON *n* any of several lunar regions of high gravity
MASCONS > MASCON
MASCOT *n* person, animal, or thing supposed to bring good luck
MASCOTS > MASCOT
MASCULINE *adj* relating to males
MASCULIST *n* advocate of rights of men
MASCULY > MASCLE
MASE *vb* function as maser
MASED > MASE
MASER *n* device for amplifying microwaves
MASERS > MASER
MASES > MASE
MASH *n* soft pulpy mass ▷ *vb* crush into a soft mass
MASHALLAH *interj* what Allah wishes
MASHED > MASH
MASHER > MASH
MASHERS > MASH
MASHES > MASH
MASHGIACH *n* person who ensures adherence to kosher rules
MASHGIAH *same as* > MASHGIACH
MASHGIHIM > MASHGIACH
MASHIACH *n* messiah
MASHIACHS > MASHIACH
MASHIE *n* (formerly) a club, corresponding to the modern No. 5 or No. 6 iron, used for approach shots
MASHIER > MASHY
MASHIES > MASHIE
MASHIEST > MASHY
MASHING > MASH
MASHINGS > MASH
MASHLAM *same as* > MASLIN
MASHLAMS > MASHLAM
MASHLIM *same as* > MASLIN
MASHLIMS > MASHLIM
MASHLIN *same as* > MASLIN
MASHLINS > MASHLIN
MASHLOCH *same as* > MASLIN
MASHLOCHS > MASHLOCH
MASHLUM *same as* > MASLIN
MASHLUMS > MASHLUM
MASHMAN *n* brewery worker
MASHMEN > MASHMAN
MASHUA *n* South American plant
MASHUAS > MASHUA
MASHUP *n* piece of recorded or live music in which a producer or DJ blends together two or more tracks, often of contrasting genres
MASHUPS > MASHUP
MASHY *adj* like mash
MASING > MASE
MASJID *same as* > MOSQUE
MASJIDS > MASJID
MASK *n* covering for the face, as a disguise or protection ▷ *vb* cover with a mask
MASKABLE > MASK
MASKED *adj* disguised or covered by or as if by a mask
MASKEG *n* North American bog
MASKEGS > MASKEG
MASKER *n* person who wears a mask or takes part in a masque
MASKERS > MASKER
MASKING *n* act or practice of masking

MASKINGS > MASKING
MASKLIKE > MASK
MASKS > MASK
MASLIN *n* mixture of wheat, rye or other grain
MASLINS > MASLIN
MASOCHISM *n* condition in which (sexual) pleasure is obtained from feeling pain or from being humiliated
MASOCHIST > MASOCHISM
MASON *n* person who works with stone ▷ *vb* construct or strengthen with masonry
MASONED > MASON
MASONIC *adj* of, characteristic of, or relating to Freemasons or Freemasonry
MASONING > MASON
MASONITE *n* tradename for a kind of dark brown hardboard used for partitions, lining, etc
MASONITES > MASONITE
MASONRIED *adj* built of masonry
MASONRIES > MASONRY
MASONRY *n* stonework
MASONS > MASON
MASOOLAH *n* Indian boat used in surf
MASOOLAHS > MASOOLAH
MASQUE *n* 16th–17th-century form of dramatic entertainment
MASQUER *same as* > MASKER
MASQUERS > MASQUER
MASQUES > MASQUE
MASS *n* coherent body of matter ▷ *adj* large-scale ▷ *vb* form into a mass
MASSA *old fashioned variant of* > MASTER
MASSACRE *n* indiscriminate killing of large numbers of people ▷ *vb* kill in large numbers
MASSACRED > MASSACRE
MASSACRER > MASSACRE
MASSACRES > MASSACRE
MASSAGE *n* rubbing and kneading of parts of the body to reduce pain or stiffness ▷ *vb* give a massage to
MASSAGED > MASSAGE
MASSAGER > MASSAGE
MASSAGERS > MASSAGE
MASSAGES > MASSAGE
MASSAGING > MASSAGE
MASSAGIST > MASSAGE
MASSAS > MASSA
MASSCULT *n* culture of masses
MASSCULTS > MASSCULT
MASSE *n* stroke made by hitting the cue ball off centre with the cue held nearly vertically, esp so as to make the ball move in a curve around another ball before hitting the object ball
MASSED > MASS
MASSEDLY > MASS
MASSES *pl n* body of common people
MASSETER *n* muscle of the cheek used in moving the jaw, esp in chewing
MASSETERS > MASSETER
MASSEUR *n* person who gives massages
MASSEURS > MASSEUR
MASSEUSE *n* woman who gives massages, esp as a profession
MASSEUSES > MASSEUSE
MASSICOT *n* yellow earthy secondary mineral
MASSICOTS > MASSICOT
MASSIER > MASSY
MASSIEST > MASSY
MASSIF *n* connected group of mountains
MASSIFS > MASSIF
MASSINESS > MASSY
MASSING > MASS
MASSIVE *adj* large and heavy ▷ *n* group of friends or associates
MASSIVELY > MASSIVE
MASSLESS > MASS
MASSOOLA *same as* > MASOOLAH
MASSOOLAS > MASSOOLA
MASSY *literary word for* > MASSIVE
MASSYMORE *n* underground prison
MAST *n* tall pole for supporting something, esp a ship's sails
MASTABA *n* mud-brick superstructure above tombs in ancient Egypt
MASTABAH *same as* > MASTABA
MASTABAHS > MASTABAH
MASTABAS > MASTABA
MASTED > MAST
MASTER *n* person in control, such as an employer or an owner of slaves or animals ▷ *adj* overall or controlling ▷ *vb* acquire knowledge of or skill in ▷ *modifier* overall or controlling
MASTERATE *n* status of master
MASTERDOM > MASTER
MASTERED > MASTER
MASTERFUL *adj* domineering
MASTERIES > MASTERY
MASTERING > MASTER
MASTERLY *adj* showing great skill
MASTERS > MASTER
MASTERY *n* expertise
MASTFUL > MAST
MASTHEAD *n* head of a mast ▷ *vb* send (a sailor) to the masthead as a punishment
MASTHEADS > MASTHEAD
MASTHOUSE *n* place for storing masts
MASTIC *n* gum obtained from certain trees
MASTICATE *vb* chew
MASTICH *same as* > MASTIC
MASTICHE *same as* > MASTIC
MASTICHES > MASTICHE
MASTICHS > MASTICH
MASTICOT *same as* > MASSICOT
MASTICOTS > MASTICOT
MASTICS > MASTIC
MASTIER > MAST
MASTIEST > MAST
MASTIFF *n* large dog
MASTIFFS > MASTIFF
MASTING > MAST
MASTITIC > MASTITIS
MASTITIS *n* inflammation of a breast or udder
MASTIX *n* type of gum
MASTIXES > MASTIX
MASTLESS > MAST
MASTLIKE > MAST
MASTODON *n* extinct elephant-like mammal
MASTODONS > MASTODON
MASTODONT > MASTODON
MASTOID *n* projection of the bone behind the ear ▷ *adj* shaped like a nipple or breast
MASTOIDAL > MASTOID
MASTOIDS > MASTOID
MASTOPEXY *n* cosmetic surgery of breasts
MASTS > MAST
MASTY > MAST
MASU *n* Japanese salmon
MASULA *same as* > MASOOLAH
MASULAS > MASULA
MASURIUM *n* silver-grey metallic element
MASURIUMS > MASURIUM
MASUS > MASU
MAT *n* piece of fabric used as a floor covering or to protect a surface ▷ *vb* tangle or become tangled into a dense mass ▷ *adj* having a dull, lustreless, or roughened surface
MATACHIN *n* dancer with sword
MATACHINA *n* feamale matachin
MATACHINI > MATACHIN
MATADOR *n* man who kills the bull in bullfights
MATADORA *n* female matador
MATADORAS > MATADORA
MATADORE *n* form of dominoes game
MATADORES > MATADORE
MATADORS > MATADOR
MATAGOURI *n* thorny bush of New Zealand, *Discaria toumatou*, that forms thickets in open country
MATAI *n* New Zealand tree, the wood of which is used for timber for building
MATAIS > MATAI
MATAMATA *(in Malaysia) a former name for* > POLICE
MATAMATAS > MATAMATA
MATAMBALA > TAMBALA
MATATA *same as* > FERNBI
MATCH *n* contest in a game or sport ▷ *vb* be exactly like, equal to, or in harmony with
MATCHABLE > MATCH
MATCHBOOK *n* number of carboard matches attached in folder
MATCHBOX *n* small box fo
holding matches
MATCHED > MATCH
MATCHER > MATCH
MATCHERS > MATCH
MATCHES > MATCH
MATCHET *same as* > MACHETE
MATCHETS > MATCHET
MATCHING > MATCH
MATCHLESS *adj* unequall
MATCHLOCK *n* obsolete ty
of gunlock igniting the powder by means of a slo
match
MATCHMADE > MATCHMAK
MATCHMAKE *vb* bring suitable people togethe
for marriage
MATCHMARK *n* mark made on mating components of an engine, machine, etc, to ensure that the components are assembled in the correct relative positions ▷ *vb* stamp (an object) with matchmarks
MATCHUP *n* sports match
MATCHUPS > MATCHUP
MATCHWOOD *n* small splinters
MATE *n* friend ▷ *vb* pair (animals) or (of animals) be paired for reproducti
MATED > MATE
MATELASSE *adj* (in textile
having a raised design, a
quilting
MATELESS > MATE
MATELOT *n* sailor
MATELOTE *n* fish served with a sauce of wine, onions, seasonings, and fish stock
MATELOTES > MATELOTE
MATELOTS > MATELOT
MATELOTTE *same as* > MATELOTE
MATER *n* mother: often used facetiously
MATERIAL *n* substance of which a thing is made ▷ *adj* of matter or substance
MATERIALS *pl n* equipme
necessary for a particula
activity
MATERIEL *n* materials

nd equipment of an rganization, esp of a nilitary force
TERIELS > MATERIEL
TERNAL *adj* of a mother
TERNITY *n* motherhood *adj* of or for pregnant women
TERS > MATER
TES > MATE
TESHIP *n* comradeship f friends, usually male, iewed as an institution
TESHIPS > MATESHIP
TEY *adj* friendly or ntimate ▷ *n* friend or ellow: usually used in irect address
TEYNESS > MATEY
TEYS > MATEY
TFELON *n* knapweed
TFELONS > MATFELON
TGRASS *n* widespread erennial European grass vith dense tufts of bristly eaves, characteristic of eaty moors
TH *same as* > MATHS
THESES > MATHESIS
THESIS *n* learning or visdom
THS *same as* > MATH
TICO *n* Peruvian shrub
TICOS > MATICO
TIER > MATY
TIES > MATY
TIEST > MATY
TILDA *n* bushman's wag
TILDAS > MATILDA
TILY > MATY
TIN *adj* of or relating to natins
TINAL *same as* > MATIN
TINEE *n* afternoon erformance in a theatre r cinema
TINEES > MATINEE
TINESS > MATY
TING > MATE
TINGS > MATE
TINS *pl n* early morning ervice in various hristian Churches
TIPO *n* New Zealand hrub
TIPOS > MATIPO
TJES *same as* > MAATJES
TLESS > MAT
TLO *same as* > MATELOT
TLOS > MATLO
TLOW *same as* > MATELOT
TLOWS > MATLOW
TOKE *n* (in Uganda) the esh of bananas, boiled nd mashed as a food
TOKES > MATOKE
TOOKE *same as* > MATOKE
TOOKES > MATOOKE
TRASS *n* long-necked lass flask, used for istilling, dissolving ubstances, etc
TRASSES > MATRASS
MATRES > MATER
MATRIARCH *n* female head of a tribe or family
MATRIC *n* matriculation
MATRICE *same as* > MATRIX
MATRICES > MATRIX
MATRICIDE *n* crime of killing one's mother
MATRICS > MATRIC
MATRICULA *n* register
MATRILINY *n* attention to descent of kinship through the female line
MATRIMONY *n* marriage
MATRIX *n* substance or situation in which something originates, takes form, or is enclosed
MATRIXES > MATRIX
MATRON *n* staid or dignified married woman
MATRONAGE *n* state of being a matron
MATRONAL > MATRON
MATRONISE *same as* > MATRONIZE
MATRONIZE *vb* make matronly
MATRONLY *adj* (of a woman) middle-aged and plump
MATRONS > MATRON
MATROSS *n* gunner's assitant
MATROSSES > MATROSS
MATS > MAT
MATSAH *same as* > MATZO
MATSAHS > MATSAH
MATSURI *n* Japanese religious ceremony
MATSURIS > MATSURI
MATSUTAKE *n* Japanese mushroom
MATT *adj* dull, not shiny
MATTAMORE *n* subterranean storehouse or dwelling
MATTE *same as* > MATT
MATTED > MAT
MATTEDLY > MAT
MATTER *n* substance of which something is made ▷ *vb* be of importance
MATTERED > MATTER
MATTERFUL > MATTER
MATTERING > MATTER
MATTERS > MATTER
MATTERY *adj* discharging pus
MATTES > MATTE
MATTIE *n* young herring
MATTIES > MATTIE
MATTIFIED > MATTIFY
MATTIFIES > MATTIFY
MATTIFY *vb* make (the skin of the face) less oily or shiny using cosmetics
MATTIN *same as* > MATIN
MATTING > MAT
MATTINGS > MAT
MATTINS *same as* > MATINS
MATTOCK *n* large pick with one of its blade ends flattened for loosening soil
MATTOCKS > MATTOCK
MATTOID *n* person displaying eccentric behaviour and mental characteristics that approach the psychotic
MATTOIDS > MATTOID
MATTRASS *same as* > MATRASS
MATTRESS *n* large stuffed flat case, often with springs, used on or as a bed
MATTS > MATT
MATURABLE > MATURE
MATURATE *vb* mature or bring to maturity
MATURATED > MATURATE
MATURATES > MATURATE
MATURE *adj* fully developed or grown-up ▷ *vb* make or become mature
MATURED > MATURE
MATURELY > MATURE
MATURER > MATURE
MATURERS > MATURE
MATURES > MATURE
MATUREST > MATURE
MATURING > MATURE
MATURITY *n* state of being mature
MATUTINAL *adj* of, occurring in, or during the morning
MATUTINE *same as* > MATUTINAL
MATWEED *n* grass found on moors
MATWEEDS > MATWEED
MATY *same as* > MATEY
MATZA *same as* > MATZO
MATZAH *same as* > MATZO
MATZAHS > MATZAH
MATZAS > MATZA
MATZO *n* large very thin biscuit of unleavened bread, traditionally eaten by Jews during Passover
MATZOH *same as* > MATZO
MATZOHS > MATZOH
MATZOON *n* fermented milk product similar to yogurt
MATZOONS > MATZOON
MATZOS > MATZO
MATZOT > MATZO
MATZOTH > MATZOH
MAUBIES > MAUBY
MAUBY *n* (in the E Caribbean) a bittersweet drink made from the bark of a rhamnaceous tree
MAUD *n* shawl or rug of grey wool plaid formerly worn in Scotland
MAUDLIN *adj* foolishly or tearfully sentimental
MAUDLINLY > MAUDLIN
MAUDS > MAUD
MAUGER *same as* > MAUGRE
MAUGRE *prep* in spite of ▷ *vb* behave spitefully towards
MAUGRED > MAUGRE
MAUGRES > MAUGRE
MAUGRING > MAUGRE
MAUL *vb* handle roughly ▷ *n* loose scrum
MAULED > MAUL
MAULER > MAUL
MAULERS *pl n* hands
MAULGRE *same as* > MAUGRE
MAULGRED > MAULGRE
MAULGRES > MAULGRE
MAULGRING > MAULGRE
MAULING > MAUL
MAULS > MAUL
MAULSTICK *n* long stick used by artists to steady the hand holding the brush
MAULVI *n* expert in Islamic law
MAULVIS > MAULVI
MAUMET *n* false god
MAUMETRY > MAUMET
MAUMETS > MAUMET
MAUN *dialect word for* > MUST
MAUND *n* unit of weight used in Asia, esp India, having different values in different localities. A common value in India is 82 pounds or 37 kilograms ▷ *vb* beg
MAUNDED > MAUND
MAUNDER *vb* talk or act aimlessly or idly
MAUNDERED > MAUNDER
MAUNDERER > MAUNDER
MAUNDERS > MAUNDER
MAUNDIES > MAUNDY
MAUNDING > MAUND
MAUNDS > MAUND
MAUNDY *n* ceremonial washing of the feet of poor persons in commemoration of Jesus' washing of his disciples' feet (John 13:4–34) re-enacted in some churches on Maundy Thursday
MAUNGIER > MAUNGY
MAUNGIEST > MAUNGY
MAUNGY *adj* (esp of a child) sulky, bad-tempered, or peevish
MAUNNA *vb* Scots term meaning must not
MAURI *n* soul
MAURIS > MAURI
MAUSOLEA > MAUSOLEUM
MAUSOLEAN > MAUSOLEUM
MAUSOLEUM *n* stately tomb
MAUT *same as* > MAHOUT
MAUTHER *n* girl
MAUTHERS > MAUTHER
MAUTS > MAUT
MAUVAIS *adj* bad
MAUVAISE *feminine form of* > MAUVAIS
MAUVE *adj* pale purple ▷ *n* any of various pale to moderate pinkish-purple or bluish-purple colours
MAUVEIN *same as* > MAUVEINE
MAUVEINE *same as* > MAUVE
MAUVEINES > MAUVEINE
MAUVEINS > MAUVEIN
MAUVER > MAUVE
MAUVES > MAUVE
MAUVEST > MAUVE

MAUVIN *same as* > MAUVEINE
MAUVINE *same as* > MAUVEINE
MAUVINES > MAUVINE
MAUVINS > MAUVIN
MAVEN *n* expert or connoisseur
MAVENS > MAVEN
MAVERICK *adj* independent and unorthodox (person) ▷ *n* person of independent or unorthodox views ▷ *vb* take illegally
MAVERICKS > MAVERICK
MAVIE *n* type of thrush
MAVIES > MAVIE
MAVIN *same as* > MAVEN
MAVINS > MAVIN
MAVIS *n* song thrush
MAVISES > MAVIS
MAVOURNIN *n* Irish form of address meaning my darling
MAW *n* animal's mouth, throat, or stomach ▷ *vb* eat or bite
MAWBOUND *adj* (of cattle) constipated
MAWED > MAW
MAWGER *adj* (of persons or animals) thin or lean
MAWING > MAW
MAWK *n* maggot
MAWKIER > MAWK
MAWKIEST > MAWK
MAWKIN *n* slovenly woman
MAWKINS > MAWKIN
MAWKISH *adj* foolishly sentimental
MAWKISHLY > MAWKISH
MAWKS > MAWK
MAWKY > MAWK
MAWMET *same as* > MAUMET
MAWMETRY > MAWMET
MAWMETS > MAWMET
MAWN *n* dialect word for a quantity
MAWPUS *same as* > MOPUS
MAWPUSES > MAWPUS
MAWR *same as* > MAUTHER
MAWRS > MAWR
MAWS > MAW
MAWSEED *n* poppy seed
MAWSEEDS > MAWSEED
MAWTHER *same as* > MAUTHER
MAWTHERS > MAWTHER
MAX *vb* reach the full extent
MAXED > MAX
MAXES > MAX
MAXI *adj* (of a garment) very long ▷ *n* type of large racing yacht
MAXICOAT *n* long coat
MAXICOATS > MAXICOAT
MAXILLA *n* upper jawbone of a vertebrate
MAXILLAE > MAXILLA
MAXILLAR > MAXILLA
MAXILLARY > MAXILLA
MAXILLAS > MAXILLA
MAXILLULA *n* jaw in crustacean
MAXIM *n* general truth or principle
MAXIMA > MAXIMUM
MAXIMAL *adj* maximum ▷ *n* maximum
MAXIMALLY > MAXIMAL
MAXIMALS > MAXIMAL
MAXIMIN *n* highest of a set of minimum values
MAXIMINS > MAXIMIN
MAXIMISE *same as* > MAXIMIZE
MAXIMISED > MAXIMISE
MAXIMISER > MAXIMIZE
MAXIMISES > MAXIMISE
MAXIMIST > MAXIM
MAXIMISTS > MAXIM
MAXIMITE *n* type of explosive
MAXIMITES > MAXIMITE
MAXIMIZE *vb* increase to a maximum
MAXIMIZED > MAXIMIZE
MAXIMIZER > MAXIMIZE
MAXIMIZES > MAXIMIZE
MAXIMS > MAXIM
MAXIMUM *n* greatest possible (amount or number) ▷ *adj* of, being, or showing a maximum or maximums
MAXIMUMLY > MAXIMUM
MAXIMUMS > MAXIMUM
MAXIMUS *n* method rung on twelve bells
MAXIMUSES > MAXIMUS
MAXING > MAX
MAXIS > MAXI
MAXIXE *n* Brazilian dance in duple time, a precursor of the tango
MAXIXES > MAXIXE
MAXWELL *n* cgs unit of magnetic flux
MAXWELLS > MAXWELL
MAY *vb* used as an auxiliary to express possibility, permission, opportunity, etc ▷ *vb* gather may
MAYA *n* illusion, esp the material world of the senses regarded as illusory
MAYAN > MAYA
MAYAPPLE *n* American plant
MAYAPPLES > MAYAPPLE
MAYAS > MAYA
MAYBE *adv* perhaps, possibly ▷ *sentence substitute* possibly
MAYBES > MAYBE
MAYBIRD *n* American songbird
MAYBIRDS > MAYBIRD
MAYBUSH *n* flowering shrub
MAYBUSHES > MAYBUSH
MAYDAY *n* international radiotelephone distress signal
MAYDAYS > MAYDAY
MAYED > MAY
MAYEST *same as* > MAYST
MAYFLIES > MAYFLY
MAYFLOWER *n* any of various plants that bloom in May
MAYFLY *n* short-lived aquatic insect
MAYHAP *archaic word for* > PERHAPS
MAYHAPPEN *same as* > MAYHAP
MAYHEM *n* violent destruction or confusion
MAYHEMS > MAYHEM
MAYING > MAY
MAYINGS > MAYING
MAYO *n* mayonnaise
MAYOR *n* head of a municipality
MAYORAL > MAYOR
MAYORALTY *n* (term of) office of a mayor
MAYORESS *n* mayor's wife
MAYORS > MAYOR
MAYORSHIP > MAYOR
MAYOS > MAYO
MAYPOLE *n* pole set up for dancing round on the first day of May to celebrate spring
MAYPOLES > MAYPOLE
MAYPOP *n* American wild flower
MAYPOPS > MAYPOP
MAYS > MAY
MAYST *singular form of the present tense of* > MAY
MAYSTER *same as* > MASTER
MAYSTERS > MAYSTER
MAYVIN *same as* > MAVEN
MAYVINS > MAYVIN
MAYWEED *n* widespread Eurasian weedy plant, having evil-smelling leaves and daisy-like flower heads
MAYWEEDS > MAYWEED
MAZAEDIA > MAZAEDIUM
MAZAEDIUM *n* part of lichen
MAZARD *same as* > MAZER
MAZARDS > MAZARD
MAZARINE *n* blue colour
MAZARINES > MAZARINE
MAZE *n* complex network of paths or lines designed to puzzle
MAZED > MAZE
MAZEDLY *adv* in bewildered way
MAZEDNESS *n* bewilderment
MAZEFUL > MAZE
MAZELIKE > MAZE
MAZELTOV *interj* congratulations
MAZEMENT > MAZE
MAZEMENTS > MAZE
MAZER *n* large hardwood drinking bowl
MAZERS > MAZER
MAZES > MAZE
MAZEY *adj* dizzy
MAZHBI *n* low-caste Sikh
MAZHBIS > MAZHBI
MAZIER > MAZY
MAZIEST > MAZY
MAZILY > MAZY
MAZINESS > MAZY
MAZING > MAZE
MAZOURKA *same as* > MAZURKA
MAZOURKAS > MAZOURKA
MAZOUT *same as* > MAZUT
MAZOUTS > MAZOUT
MAZUMA *n* money
MAZUMAS > MAZUMA
MAZURKA *n* lively Polish dance
MAZURKAS > MAZURKA
MAZUT *n* residue left afte[r] distillation of petrol
MAZUTS > MAZUT
MAZY *adj* of or like a maze
MAZZARD *same as* > MAZA[RD]
MAZZARDS > MAZZARD
MBAQANGA *n* style of Blac[k] popular music of urban South Africa
MBAQANGAS > MBAQANGA
MBIRA *n* African musical instrument consisting of tuned metal strips attached to a resonatin[g] box, which are plucked with the thumbs
MBIRAS > MBIRA
ME *n* (in tonic sol-fa) thir[d] degree of any major scale ▷ *pron* refers to th[e] speaker or writer
MEACOCK *n* timid person
MEACOCKS > MEACOCK
MEAD *n* alcoholic drink made from honey
MEADOW *n* piece of grassland
MEADOWS > MEADOW
MEADOWY > MEADOW
MEADS > MEAD
MEAGER *same as* > MEAGR[E]
MEAGERLY > MEAGRE
MEAGRE *adj* scanty or insufficient ▷ *n* Mediterranean fish
MEAGRELY > MEAGRE
MEAGRER > MEAGRE
MEAGRES > MEAGRE
MEAGREST > MEAGRE
MEAL *n* occasion when f[ood] is served and eaten ▷ *vb* cover with meal
MEALED > MEAL
MEALER *n* person eating but not lodging at boarding house
MEALERS > MEALER
MEALIE *n* maize
MEALIER > MEALY
MEALIES *South African wo[rd] for* > MAIZE
MEALIEST > MEALY
MEALINESS > MEALY
MEALING > MEAL
MEALLESS > MEAL
MEALS > MEAL
MEALTIME *n* time for me[als]
MEALTIMES > MEALTIME
MEALWORM *n* larva of various beetles of the genus *Tenebrio*, esp *T. molitor*, feeding on meal flour, and similar stored

foods: family *Tenebrionidae*
ALWORMS > MEALWORM
ALY *adj* resembling meal
ALYBUG *n* plant-eating homopterous insect
ALYBUGS > MEALYBUG
AN *vb* intend to convey or express ▷ *adj* miserly, ungenerous, or petty ▷ *n* middle point between two extremes
ANDER *vb* follow a winding course ▷ *n* winding course
ANDERED > MEANDER
ANDERER > MEANDER
ANDERS > MEANDER
ANDRIAN > MEANDER
ANDROUS > MEANDER
ANE *vb* moan
ANED > MEANE
ANER > MEAN
ANERS > MEAN
ANES > MEANE
ANEST > MEAN
ANIE *n* unkind or miserly person
ANIES > MEANY
ANING *n* what something means
ANINGLY > MEAN
ANINGS > MEANING
ANLY > MEAN
ANNESS > MEAN
ANS > MEAN
ANT > MEAN
ANTIME *n* intervening period ▷ *adv* meanwhile
ANTIMES > MEANTIME
ANWHILE *adv* during the intervening period
ANY *same as* > MEANIE
ARE *same as* > MERE
ARES > MEARE
ARING *adj* forming boundary
ASE *vb* assuage
ASED > MEASE
ASES > MEASE
ASING > MEASE
ASLE *vb* infect with measles
ASLED *adj* (of cattle, sheep, or pigs) infested with tapeworm larvae
ASLES *n* infectious disease producing red spots
ASLIER > MEASLY
ASLIEST > MEASLY
ASLING > MEASLE
ASLY *adj* meagre
ASURE *n* size or quantity ▷ *vb* determine the size or quantity of
ASURED *adj* slow and steady
ASURER > MEASURE
ASURERS > MEASURE
ASURES *pl n* rock strata that contain a particular type of deposit
ASURING *adj* used to measure quantities, esp in cooking
MEAT *n* animal flesh as food
MEATAL > MEATUS
MEATAXE *n* meat cleaver
MEATAXES > MEATAXE
MEATBALL *n* minced beef, shaped into a ball before cooking
MEATBALLS > MEATBALL
MEATED *adj* fattened
MEATH *same as* > MEAD
MEATHE *same as* > MEAD
MEATHEAD *n* stupid person
MEATHEADS > MEATHEAD
MEATHES > MEATHE
MEATHS > MEATH
MEATIER > MEATY
MEATIEST > MEATY
MEATILY > MEATY
MEATINESS > MEATY
MEATLESS > MEAT
MEATLOAF *n* chopped meat served in loaf-shaped mass
MEATMAN *n* meat seller
MEATMEN > MEATMAN
MEATS > MEAT
MEATSPACE *n* real physical world, as contrasted with the world of cyberspace
MEATUS *n* natural opening or channel, such as the canal leading from the outer ear to the eardrum
MEATUSES > MEATUS
MEATY *adj* (tasting) of or like meat
MEAWES *same as* > MEWS
MEAZEL *same as* > MESEL
MEAZELS > MEAZEL
MEBOS *n* South African dried apricots
MEBOSES > MEBOS
MECCA *n* place that attracts many visitors
MECCAS > MECCA
MECHANIC *n* person skilled in repairing or operating machinery
MECHANICS *n* scientific study of motion and force
MECHANISE *same as* > MECHANIZE
MECHANISM *n* way a machine works
MECHANIST *same as* > MECHANIC
MECHANIZE *vb* equip with machinery
MECHITZA *n* screen in synagogue separating men and women
MECHITZAS > MECHITZA
MECHITZOT > MECHITZA
MECK *same as* > MAIK
MECKS > MECK
MECLIZINE *n* drug used to treat motion sickness
MECONATE *n* salt of meconic acid
MECONATES > MECONATE
MECONIC *adj* derived from poppies
MECONIN *n* substance found in opium
MECONINS > MECONIN
MECONIUM *n* dark green mucoid material that forms the first faeces of a newborn infant
MECONIUMS > MECONIUM
MED *n* doctor
MEDACCA *n* Japanese freshwater fish
MEDACCAS > MEDACCA
MEDAILLON *n* small round thin piece of food
MEDAKA *same as* > MEDACCA
MEDAKAS > MEDAKA
MEDAL *n* piece of metal with an inscription etc, given as a reward or memento ▷ *vb* honour with a medal
MEDALED > MEDAL
MEDALET *n* small medal
MEDALETS > MEDALET
MEDALING > MEDAL
MEDALIST *same as* > MEDALLIST
MEDALISTS > MEDALIST
MEDALLED > MEDAL
MEDALLIC > MEDAL
MEDALLING > MEDAL
MEDALLION *n* disc-shaped ornament worn on a chain round the neck
MEDALLIST *n* winner of a medal
MEDALS > MEDAL
MEDCINAL *same as* > MEDICINAL
MEDDLE *vb* interfere annoyingly
MEDDLED > MEDDLE
MEDDLER > MEDDLE
MEDDLERS > MEDDLE
MEDDLES > MEDDLE
MEDDLING > MEDDLE
MEDDLINGS > MEDDLE
MEDEVAC *n* evacuation of casualties from forward areas to the nearest hospital or base ▷ *vb* transport (a wounded or sick person) to hospital by medevac
MEDEVACED > MEDEVAC
MEDEVACS > MEDEVAC
MEDFLIES > MEDFLY
MEDFLY *n* Mediterranean fruit fly
MEDIA > MEDIUM
MEDIACIES > MEDIACY
MEDIACY *n* quality or state of being mediate
MEDIAD *adj* situated near the median line or plane of an organism
MEDIAE > MEDIUM
MEDIAEVAL *adj* of, relating to, or in the style of the Middle Ages ▷ *n* person living in medieval times
MEDIAL *adj* of or in the middle ▷ *n* speech sound between being fortis and lenis
MEDIALLY > MEDIAL
MEDIALS > MEDIAL
MEDIAN *n* middle (point or line) ▷ *adj* of, relating to, situated in, or directed towards the middle
MEDIANLY > MEDIAN
MEDIANS > MEDIAN
MEDIANT *n* third degree of a major or minor scale
MEDIANTS > MEDIANT
MEDIAS > MEDIUM
MEDIATE *vb* intervene in a dispute to bring about agreement ▷ *adj* occurring as a result of or dependent upon mediation
MEDIATED > MEDIATE
MEDIATELY > MEDIATE
MEDIATES > MEDIATE
MEDIATING > MEDIATE
MEDIATION *n* act of mediating
MEDIATISE *same as* > MEDIATIZE
MEDIATIVE > MEDIATE
MEDIATIZE *vb* annex (a state) to another state, allowing the former ruler to retain his title and some authority
MEDIATOR > MEDIATE
MEDIATORS > MEDIATE
MEDIATORY > MEDIATE
MEDIATRIX *n* female mediator
MEDIC *n* doctor or medical student
MEDICABLE *adj* potentially able to be treated or cured medically
MEDICABLY > MEDICABLE
MEDICAID *n* health assistance programme financed by federal, state, and local taxes to help pay hospital and medical costs for persons of low income
MEDICAIDS > MEDICAID
MEDICAL *adj* of the science of medicine ▷ *n* medical examination
MEDICALLY > MEDICAL
MEDICALS > MEDICAL
MEDICANT *n* medicinal substance
MEDICANTS > MEDICANT
MEDICARE *n* (in the US) a federally sponsored health insurance programme for persons of 65 or older
MEDICARES > MEDICARE
MEDICATE *vb* treat with a medicinal substance
MEDICATED *adj* (of a patient) having been treated with a medicine or drug
MEDICATES > MEDICATE
MEDICIDE *n* suicide assisted by doctor
MEDICIDES > MEDICIDE
MEDICINAL *adj* having therapeutic properties ▷ *n*

medicinal substance
MEDICINE *n* substance used to treat disease ▷ *vb* treat with medicine
MEDICINED > MEDICINE
MEDICINER *n* physician
MEDICINES > MEDICINE
MEDICK *n* any small leguminous plant of the genus *Medicago*, such as black medick or sickle medick, having yellow or purple flowers and trifoliate leaves
MEDICKS > MEDICK
MEDICO *n* doctor or medical student
MEDICOS > MEDICO
MEDICS > MEDIC
MEDIEVAL *adj* of the Middle Ages ▷ *n* person living in medieval times
MEDIEVALS > MEDIEVAL
MEDIGAP *n* private health insurance
MEDIGAPS > MEDIGAP
MEDII > MEDIUS
MEDINA *n* ancient quarter of any of various North African cities
MEDINAS > MEDINA
MEDIOCRE *adj* average in quality
MEDITATE *vb* reflect deeply, esp on spiritual matters
MEDITATED > MEDITATE
MEDITATES > MEDITATE
MEDITATOR > MEDITATE
MEDIUM *adj* midway between extremes, average ▷ *n* middle state, degree, or condition
MEDIUMS *pl n* medium-dated gilt-edged securities
MEDIUS *n* middle finger
MEDIUSES > MEDIUS
MEDIVAC *variant spelling of* > MEDEVAC
MEDIVACED > MEDIVAC
MEDIVACS > MEDIVAC
MEDLAR *n* apple-like fruit of a small tree, eaten when it begins to decay
MEDLARS > MEDLAR
MEDLE *same as* > MEDDLE
MEDLED > MEDLE
MEDLES > MEDLE
MEDLEY *n* miscellaneous mixture ▷ *adj* of, being, or relating to a mixture or variety
MEDLEYS > MEDLEY
MEDLING > MEDLE
MEDRESE *same as* > MADRASAH
MEDRESES > MEDRESE
MEDRESSEH *same as* > MADRASAH
MEDS > MED
MEDULLA *n* marrow, pith, or inner tissue
MEDULLAE > MEDULLA
MEDULLAR > MEDULLA
MEDULLARY > MEDULLA
MEDULLAS > MEDULLA
MEDULLATE *adj* having medulla
MEDUSA *n* jellyfish
MEDUSAE > MEDUSA
MEDUSAL > MEDUSA
MEDUSAN > MEDUSA
MEDUSANS > MEDUSA
MEDUSAS > MEDUSA
MEDUSOID *same as* > MEDUSA
MEDUSOIDS > MEDUSOID
MEE *n* Malaysian noodle dish
MEED *n* recompense
MEEDS > MEED
MEEK *adj* submissive or humble
MEEKEN *vb* make meek
MEEKENED > MEEKEN
MEEKENING > MEEKEN
MEEKENS > MEEKEN
MEEKER > MEEK
MEEKEST > MEEK
MEEKLY > MEEK
MEEKNESS > MEEK
MEEMIE *n* hysterical person
MEEMIES > MEEMIE
MEER *same as* > MERE
MEERCAT *same as* > MEERKAT
MEERCATS > MEERCAT
MEERED > MEER
MEERING > MEER
MEERKAT *n* S African mongoose
MEERKATS > MEERKAT
MEERS > MEER
MEES > MEE
MEET *vb* come together (with) ▷ *n* meeting, esp a sports meeting ▷ *adj* fit or suitable
MEETER > MEET
MEETERS > MEET
MEETEST > MEET
MEETING > MEET
MEETINGS > MEET
MEETLY > MEET
MEETNESS *n* properness
MEETS > MEET
MEFF *dialect word for* > TRAMP
MEFFS > MEFF
MEG *short for* > MEGABYTE
MEGA *adj* extremely good, great, or successful
MEGABAR *n* unit of million bars
MEGABARS > MEGABAR
MEGABIT *n* one million bits
MEGABITS > MEGABIT
MEGABUCK *n* million dollars
MEGABUCKS > MEGABUCK
MEGABYTE *n* 2S2So or 1 048 576 bytes
MEGABYTES > MEGABYTE
MEGACITY *n* city with over 10 million inhabitants
MEGACURIE *n* unit of million curies
MEGACYCLE *same as* > MEGAHERTZ
MEGADEAL *n* very good deal
MEGADEALS > MEGADEAL
MEGADEATH *n* death of a million people, esp in a nuclear war or attack
MEGADOSE *n* very large dose, as of a medicine, vitamin, etc
MEGADOSES > MEGADOSE
MEGADYNE *n* unit of million dynes
MEGADYNES > MEGADYNE
MEGAFARAD *n* unit of million farads
MEGAFAUNA *n* component of the fauna of a region or period that comprises the larger terrestrial animals
MEGAFLOP *n* measure of processing speed, consisting of a million floating-point operations a second
MEGAFLOPS > MEGAFLOP
MEGAFLORA *n* plants large enough to be seen by naked eye
MEGAFOG *n* amplified fog signal
MEGAFOGS > MEGAFOG
MEGAGAUSS *n* unit of million gauss
MEGAHERTZ *n* one million hertz
MEGAHIT *n* great success
MEGAHITS > MEGAHIT
MEGAJOULE *n* unit of million joules
MEGALITH *n* great stone, esp as part of a prehistoric monument
MEGALITHS > MEGALITH
MEGALITRE *n* one million litres
MEGALOPIC *adj* having large eyes
MEGALOPS *n* crab in larval stage
MEGAPHONE *n* cone-shaped instrument used to amplify the voice ▷ *vb* speak through megaphone
MEGAPHYLL *n* relatively large type of leaf produced by ferns and seed plants
MEGAPIXEL *n* one million pixels
MEGAPLEX *n* cinema complex containing a large number of separate screens, and usually a restaurant or bar
MEGAPOD *same as* > MEGAPODE
MEGAPODE *n* bird of Australia, New Guinea, and adjacent islands
MEGAPODES > MEGAPODE
MEGAPODS > MEGAPOD
MEGARA > MEGARON
MEGARAD *n* unit of million rads
MEGARADS > MEGARAD
MEGARON *n* tripartite rectangular room containing a central hearth surrounded by fou pillars, found in Bronze Age Greece and Asia Min
MEGARONS > MEGARON
MEGASCOPE *n* type of ima projector
MEGASPORE *n* larger of the two types of spore produced by some spore-bearing plants, which develops into the female gametophyte
MEGASS *another name for* > BAGASSE
MEGASSE *same as* > MEGAS
MEGASSES > MEGASS
MEGASTAR *n* very well-known personality in the entertainment business
MEGASTARS > MEGASTAR
MEGASTORE *n* very large store
MEGATHERE *n* any of various gigantic extinct American sloths of the genus *Megatherium* and related genera, common late Cenozoic times
MEGATON *n* explosive pow equal to that of one milli tons of TNT
MEGATONIC > MEGATON
MEGATONS > MEGATON
MEGAVOLT *n* one million volts
MEGAVOLTS > MEGAVOLT
MEGAWATT *n* one million watts
MEGAWATTS > MEGAWATT
MEGILLA *same as* > MEGILLAH
MEGILLAH *n* scroll of the Book of Esther, read on th festival of Purim
MEGILLAHS > MEGILLAH
MEGILLAS > MEGILLA
MEGILLOTH > MEGILLAH
MEGILP *n* oil-painting medium of linseed oil mixed with mastic varni or turpentine
MEGILPH *same as* > MEGILP
MEGILPHS > MEGILPH
MEGILPS > MEGILP
MEGOHM *n* one million ohms.
MEGOHMS > MEGOHM
MEGRIM *n* caprice
MEGRIMS *n* fit of depressi
MEGS > MEG
MEHNDI *n* (esp in India) the practice of painting designs on the hands, fee etc using henna
MEHNDIS > MEHNDI
MEIBOMIAN as in *meibomi gland* any of the small sebaceous glands in the eyelid, beneath the conjunctiva
MEIKLE *adj* Scots word meaning large
MEIN *Scots word for* > MOA

INED > MEIN
INEY *same as* > MEINY
INEYS > MEINEY
INIE *same as* > MEINY
INIES > MEINY
INING > MEIN
INS > MEIN
INT *same as* > MING
INY *n* retinue or ousehold
IOCYTE *n* cell that ivides by meiosis to roduce four haploid spores
IOCYTES > MEIOCYTE
IOFAUNA *n* component of the fauna of a sea or lake ed comprising small (but ot microscopic) animals, uch as tiny worms and rustaceans
IONITE *n* mineral ontaining silica
IONITES > MEIONITE
IOSES > MEIOSIS
IOSIS *n* type of ell division in which eproductive cells are roduced, each containing alf the chromosome umber of the parent ucleus
IOSPORE *n* haploid spore
IOTIC > MEIOSIS
ISHI *n* business card in apan
ISHIS > MEISHI
ISTER *n* person who xcels at a particular ctivity
ISTERS > MEISTER
ITH *n* landmark
ITHS > MEITH
JLIS *same as* > MAJLIS
JLISES > MEJLIS
KKA *same as* > MECCA
KKAS > MEKKA
KOMETER *n* device for neasuring distance
L *n* pure form of oney formerly used in harmaceutical products
LA *n* Asian cultural or eligious fair or festival
LALEUCA *n* Australian hrub or tree with a white runk and black branches
LAMDIM > MELAMED
LAMED *n* Hebrew teacher
LAMINE *n* colourless rystalline compound sed in making synthetic esins
LAMINES > MELAMINE
LAMPODE *n* poisonous lant
LANGE *n* mixture
LANGES > MELANGE
LANIAN *n* freshwater nollusc
LANIC *adj* relating to nelanism or melanosis ▷ *n* darker form of creature
LANICS > MELANIC
MELANIN *n* dark pigment found in the hair, skin, and eyes of humans and animals
MELANINS > MELANIN
MELANISE *same as* > MELANIZE
MELANISED > MELANISE
MELANISES > MELANISE
MELANISM *same as* > MELANOSIS
MELANISMS > MELANISM
MELANIST > MELANISM
MELANISTS > MELANISM
MELANITE *n* black variety of andradite garnet
MELANITES > MELANITE
MELANITIC > MELANITE
MELANIZE *vb* turn into melanin
MELANIZED > MELANIZE
MELANIZES > MELANIZE
MELANO *n* person with abnormally dark skin
MELANOID *adj* resembling melanin ▷ *n* dark substance formed in skin
MELANOIDS > MELANOID
MELANOMA *n* tumour composed of dark-coloured cells, occurring in some skin cancers
MELANOMAS > MELANOMA
MELANOS > MELANO
MELANOSES > MELANOSIS
MELANOSIS *n* skin condition characterized by excessive deposits of melanin
MELANOTIC > MELANOSIS
MELANOUS *adj* having a dark complexion and black hair
MELANURIA *n* presence of melanin in urine
MELANURIC > MELANURIA
MELAPHYRE *n* type of weathered amygdaloidal basalt or andesite
MELAS > MELA
MELASTOME *n* tropical flowering plant
MELATONIN *n* hormone-like secretion of the pineal gland, causing skin colour changes in some animals and thought to be involved in reproductive function
MELD *vb* merge or blend ▷ *n* act of melding
MELDED > MELD
MELDER > MELD
MELDERS > MELD
MELDING > MELD
MELDS > MELD
MELEE *n* noisy confused fight or crowd
MELEES > MELEE
MELENA *n* excrement or vomit stained by blood
MELENAS > MELENA
MELIC *adj* (of poetry, esp ancient Greek lyric poems) intended to be sung ▷ *n* tpye of grass
MELICK *n* either of two pale green perennial grasses
MELICKS > MELICK
MELICS > MELIC
MELIK *same as* > MALIK
MELIKS > MELIK
MELILITE *n* mineral containing calcium
MELILITES > MELILITE
MELILOT *n* any leguminous plant of the Old World genus *Melilotus*, having narrow clusters of small white or yellow fragrant flowers
MELILOTS > MELILOT
MELINITE *n* high explosive made from picric acid
MELINITES > MELINITE
MELIORATE *vb* improve
MELIORISM *n* notion that the world can be improved by human effort
MELIORIST > MELIORISM
MELIORITY *n* improved state
MELISMA *n* expressive vocal phrase or passage consisting of several notes sung to one syllable
MELISMAS > MELISMA
MELISMATA > MELISMA
MELL *vb* mix
MELLAY *same as* > MELEE
MELLAYS > MELLAY
MELLED > MELL
MELLIFIC *adj* forming or producing honey
MELLING > MELL
MELLITE *n* soft yellow mineral
MELLITES > MELLITE
MELLITIC > MELLITE
MELLOTRON *n* musical synthesizer
MELLOW *adj* soft, not harsh ▷ *vb* make or become mellow
MELLOWED > MELLOW
MELLOWER > MELLOW
MELLOWEST > MELLOW
MELLOWING > MELLOW
MELLOWLY > MELLOW
MELLOWS > MELLOW
MELLOWY *same as* > MELLOW
MELLS > MELL
MELOCOTON *n* variety of peach
MELODEON *n* small accordion
MELODEONS > MELODEON
MELODIA *same as* > MELODICA
MELODIAS > MELODIA
MELODIC *adj* of melody
MELODICA *n* type of flute
MELODICAS > MELODICA
MELODICS *n* study of melody
MELODIES > MELODY
MELODION *same as* > MELODEON
MELODIONS > MELODION
MELODIOUS *adj* pleasing to the ear
MELODISE *same as* > MELODIZE
MELODISED > MELODISE
MELODISER > MELODISE
MELODISES > MELODISE
MELODIST *n* composer of melodies
MELODISTS > MELODIST
MELODIZE *vb* provide with a melody
MELODIZED > MELODIZE
MELODIZER > MELODIZE
MELODIZES > MELODIZE
MELODRAMA *n* play full of extravagant action and emotion
MELODRAME *same as* > MELODRAMA
MELODY *n* series of musical notes which make a tune
MELOID *n* any long-legged beetle of the family *Meloidae*, which includes the blister beetles and oil beetles ▷ *adj* of, relating to, or belonging to the *Meloidae*
MELOIDS > MELOID
MELOMANIA *n* great enthusiasm for music
MELOMANIC > MELOMANIA
MELON *n* large round juicy fruit with a hard rind
MELONGENE *n* aubergine
MELONS > MELON
MELPHALAN *n* drug used to treat leukaemia
MELS > MEL
MELT *vb* (cause to) become liquid by heat ▷ *n* act or process of melting
MELTABLE > MELT
MELTAGE *n* process or result of melting or the amount melted
MELTAGES > MELTAGE
MELTDOWN *n* (in a nuclear reactor) melting of the fuel rods, with the possible release of radiation
MELTDOWNS > MELTDOWN
MELTED > MELT
MELTEMI *n* northerly wind in the northeast Mediterranean
MELTEMIS > MELTEMI
MELTER > MELT
MELTERS > MELT
MELTIER > MELTY
MELTIEST > MELTY
MELTING > MELT
MELTINGLY > MELT
MELTINGS > MELT
MELTITH *n* meal
MELTITHS > MELTITH
MELTON *n* heavy smooth woollen fabric with a short nap, used esp for overcoats
MELTONS > MELTON
MELTS > MELT
MELTWATER *n* melted snow or ice
MELTY *adj* tending to melt

MELUNGEON *n* any of a dark-skinned group of people of the Appalachians in E Tennessee, of mixed Indian, White, and Black ancestry
MEM *n* 13th letter in the Hebrew alphabet, transliterated as *m*
MEMBER *n* individual making up a body or society ▷ *adj* (of a country or group) belonging to an organization or alliance
MEMBERED *adj* having members
MEMBERS > MEMBER
MEMBRAL *adj* of limbs
MEMBRANAL > MEMBRANE
MEMBRANE *n* thin flexible tissue in a plant or animal body
MEMBRANED *adj* having membrane
MEMBRANES > MEMBRANE
MEME *n* idea or element of social behaviour passed on through generations in a culture, esp by imitation
MEMENTO *n* thing serving to remind, souvenir
MEMENTOES > MEMENTO
MEMENTOS > MEMENTO
MEMES > MEME
MEMETICS *n* study of gentic transmission of culture
MEMO *n* memorandum
MEMOIR *n* biography or historical account based on personal knowledge
MEMOIRISM *n* writing of memoirs
MEMOIRIST > MEMOIRISM
MEMOIRS *pl n* collection of reminiscences about a period or series of events, written from personal experience
MEMORABLE *adj* worth remembering, noteworthy
MEMORABLY > MEMORABLE
MEMORANDA *n* plural of memorandum: written statement of communications
MEMORIAL *n* something serving to commemorate a person or thing ▷ *adj* serving as a memorial
MEMORIALS > MEMORIAL
MEMORIES > MEMORY
MEMORISE *same as* > MEMORIZE
MEMORISED > MEMORISE
MEMORISER > MEMORIZE
MEMORISES > MEMORISE
MEMORITER *adv* from memory
MEMORIZE *vb* commit to memory
MEMORIZED > MEMORIZE
MEMORIZER > MEMORIZE
MEMORIZES > MEMORIZE
MEMORY *n* ability to remember
MEMOS > MEMO
MEMS > MEM
MEMSAHIB *n* (formerly, in India) term of respect used for a European married woman
MEMSAHIBS > MEMSAHIB
MEN > MAN
MENACE *n* threat ▷ *vb* threaten, endanger
MENACED > MENACE
MENACER > MENACE
MENACERS > MENACE
MENACES > MENACE
MENACING > MENACE
MENAD *same as* > MAENAD
MENADIONE *n* yellow crystalline compound
MENADS > MENAD
MENAGE *old form of* > MANAGE
MENAGED > MENAGE
MENAGERIE *n* collection of wild animals for exhibition
MENAGES > MENAGE
MENAGING > MENAGE
MENARCHE *n* first occurrence of menstruation in a woman's life
MENARCHES > MENARCHE
MENAZON *n* type of insecticide
MENAZONS > MENAZON
MEND *vb* repair or patch ▷ *n* mended area
MENDABLE > MEND
MENDACITY *n* (tendency to) untruthfulness
MENDED > MEND
MENDER > MEND
MENDERS > MEND
MENDICANT *adj* begging ▷ *n* beggar
MENDICITY > MENDICANT
MENDIGO *n* Spanish beggar or vagrant
MENDIGOS > MENDIGO
MENDING *n* something to be mended, esp clothes
MENDINGS > MENDING
MENDS > MEND
MENE *Scots form of* > MOAN
MENED > MENE
MENEER *n* South African title of address equivalent to *sir* when used alone or *Mr* when placed before a name
MENEERS > MENEER
MENES > MENE
MENFOLK *pl n* men collectively, esp the men of a particular family
MENFOLKS *same as* > MENFOLK
MENG *vb* mix
MENGE *same as* > MENG
MENGED > MENG
MENGES > MENGE
MENGING > MENG
MENGS > MENG
MENHADEN *n* marine North American fish, *Brevoortia tyrannus*: source of fishmeal, fertilizer, and oil: family *Clupeidae* (herrings, etc)
MENHADENS > MENHADEN
MENHIR *n* single upright prehistoric stone
MENHIRS > MENHIR
MENIAL *adj* involving boring work of low status ▷ *n* person with a menial job
MENIALLY > MENIAL
MENIALS > MENIAL
MENILITE *n* liver opal
MENILITES > MENILITE
MENING > MENE
MENINGEAL > MENINX
MENINGES > MENINX
MENINX *n* one of three membranes that envelop the brain and spinal cord
MENISCAL > MENISCUS
MENISCATE > MENISCUS
MENISCI > MENISCUS
MENISCOID > MENISCUS
MENISCUS *n* curved surface of a liquid
MENO *adv* (esp preceding a dynamic or tempo marking) to be played less quickly, less softly, etc
MENOLOGY *n* ecclesiastical calendar of the months
MENOMINEE *n* whitefish, found in N America and Siberia
MENOMINI *same as* > MENOMINEE
MENOMINIS > MENOMINI
MENOPAUSE *n* time when a woman's menstrual cycle ceases
MENOPOLIS *n* informal word for an area with a high proportion of single men
MENOPOME *n* American salamander
MENOPOMES > MENOPOME
MENORAH *n* seven-branched candelabrum used as an emblem of Judaism
MENORAHS > MENORAH
MENORRHEA *n* normal bleeding in menstruation
MENSA *n* faint constellation in the S hemisphere lying between Hydrus and Volans and containing part of the Large Magellanic Cloud
MENSAE *n* star of the mensa constellation
MENSAL *adj* monthly
MENSAS > MENSA
MENSCH *n* decent person
MENSCHEN > MENSCH
MENSCHES > MENSCH
MENSCHY > MENSCH
MENSE *vb* grace
MENSED > MENSE
MENSEFUL *adj* gracious
MENSELESS *adj* graceless
MENSES *n* menstruation
MENSH *vb* mention
MENSHED > MENSH
MENSHEN *n* Chinese door god
MENSHES > MENSH
MENSHING > MENSH
MENSING > MENSE
MENSTRUA > MENSTRUUM
MENSTRUAL *adj* of or relating to menstruation
MENSTRUUM *n* solvent, esp one used in the preparation of a drug
MENSUAL *same as* > MENSA
MENSURAL *adj* of or involving measure
MENSWEAR *n* clothing for men
MENSWEARS > MENSWEAR
MENT *same as* > MING
MENTA > MENTUM
MENTAL *adj* of, in, or done by the mind
MENTALESE *n* picturing of concepts in mind without words
MENTALISM *n* doctrine that mind is the fundamental reality and that objects of knowledge exist only as aspects of the subject's consciousness
MENTALIST > MENTALISM
MENTALITY *n* way of thinking
MENTALLY > MENTAL
MENTATION *n* process or result of mental activity
MENTEE *n* person trained by mentor
MENTEES > MENTEE
MENTHENE *n* liquid obtained from menthol
MENTHENES > MENTHENE
MENTHOL *n* organic compound found in peppermint, used medicinally
MENTHOLS > MENTHOL
MENTICIDE *n* destruction of person's mental independence
MENTION *vb* refer to briefly ▷ *n* brief reference to a person or thing
MENTIONED > MENTION
MENTIONER > MENTION
MENTIONS > MENTION
MENTO *n* Jamaican song
MENTOR *n* adviser or guide ▷ *vb* act as a mentor to (someone) ▷ *vb* act as mentor for
MENTORED > MENTOR
MENTORIAL > MENTOR
MENTORING *n* (in business) the practice of assigning a junior member of staff to the care of a more

xperienced person who ssists him in his career
NTORS > MENTOR
NTOS > MENTO
NTUM *n* chin
NU *n* list of dishes to be erved, or from which to rder
NUDO *n* Mexican soup
NUDOS > MENUDO
NUISIER *n* joiner
NUS > MENU
NYIE *same as* > MEINIE
NYIES > MENYIE
OU *same as* > MEOW
OUED > MEOU
OUING > MEOU
OUS > MEOU
OW *vb* (of a cat) to make characteristic crying ound ▷ *interj* imitation f this sound
OWED > MEOW
OWING > MEOW
OWS > MEOW
PACRINE *n* drug formerly idely used to treat nalaria
PHITIC *adj* poisonous
PHITIS *n* foul-smelling ischarge
PHITISM *n* poisoning
RANTI *n* wood from any f several Malaysian trees f the dipterocarpaceous enus *Shorea*
RANTIS > MERANTI
RBROMIN *n* green idescent crystalline ompound
RC *n* mercenary
RCAPTAN *another name not in technical usage)* or > THIOL
RCAPTO *adj* of a articular chemical group
RCAT *Scots word* r > MARKET
RCATS > MERCAT
RCENARY *adj* influenced y greed ▷ *n* hired soldier
RCER *n* dealer in textile abrics and fine cloth
RCERIES > MERCER
RCERISE *same* s > MERCERIZE
RCERIZE *vb* treat otton yarn) with an lkali to increase its trength and reception to ye and impart a lustrous ilky appearance
RCERS > MERCER
RCERY > MERCER
RCES > MERC
RCH *n* merchandise
RCHANT *n* person ngaged in trade, holesale trader ▷ *adj* f ships involved in ommercial trade or their rews ▷ *vb* conduct trade n
RCHANTS > MERCHANT

MERCHES > MERCH
MERCHET *n* (in feudal England) a fine paid by a tenant, esp a villein, to his lord for allowing the marriage of his daughter
MERCHETS > MERCHET
MERCHILD *n* mythical creature with upper body of child and lower body of fish
MERCIABLE *adj* merciful
MERCIES > MERCY
MERCIFIDE > MERCIFY
MERCIFIED > MERCIFY
MERCIFIES > MERCIFY
MERCIFUL *adj* compassionate
MERCIFY *vb* show mercy to
MERCILESS *adj* without mercy
MERCS > MERC
MERCURATE *vb* treat or mix with mercury
MERCURIAL *adj* lively, changeable ▷ *n* any salt of mercury for use as a medicine
MERCURIC *adj* of or containing mercury in the divalent state
MERCURIES > MERCURY
MERCURISE *same as* > MERCURATE
MERCURIZE *same as* > MERCURISE
MERCUROUS *adj* of or containing mercury in the monovalent state
MERCURY *n* silvery liquid metal
MERCY *n* compassionate treatment of an offender or enemy who is in one's power
MERDE *French word for* > EXCREMENT
MERDES > MERDE
MERE *adj* nothing more than ▷ *n* lake ▷ *vb* old form of survey
MERED *adj* forming a boundary
MEREL *same as* > MERIL
MERELL *same as* > MERIL
MERELLS *same as* > MERILS
MERELS > MERILS
MERELY *adv* only
MERENGUE *n* type of lively dance music originating in the Dominican Republic, which combines African and Spanish elements
MERENGUES > MERENGUE
MEREOLOGY *n* formal study of the logical properties of the relation of part and whole
MERER > MERE
MERES > MERE
MERESMAN *n* man who decides on boundaries
MERESMEN > MERESMAN
MEREST > MERE

MERESTONE *n* stone marking boundary
MERFOLK *n* mermaids and mermen
MERFOLKS > MERFOLK
MERGANSER *n* large crested diving duck
MERGE *vb* combine or blend
MERGED > MERGE
MERGEE *n* business taken over by merger
MERGEES > MERGEE
MERGENCE > MERGE
MERGENCES > MERGE
MERGER *n* combination of business firms into one
MERGERS > MERGER
MERGES > MERGE
MERGING > MERGE
MERGINGS > MERGE
MERI *n* Māori war club
MERICARP *n* part of plant fruit
MERICARPS > MERICARP
MERIDIAN *n* imaginary circle of the earth passing through both poles ▷ *adj* along or relating to a meridian
MERIDIANS > MERIDIAN
MERIL *n* counter used in merils
MERILS *n* old board game
MERIMAKE *n* merrymaking
MERIMAKES > MERIMAKE
MERING > MERE
MERINGS > MERING
MERINGUE *n* baked mixture of egg whites and sugar
MERINGUES > MERINGUE
MERINO *n* breed of sheep with fine soft wool
MERINOS > MERINO
MERIS > MERI
MERISES > MERISIS
MERISIS *n* growth by division of cells
MERISM *n* duplication of biological parts
MERISMS > MERISM
MERISTEM *n* plant tissue responsible for growth, whose cells divide and differentiate to form the tissues and organs of the plant
MERISTEMS > MERISTEM
MERISTIC *adj* of or relating to the number of organs or parts in an animal or plant body
MERIT *n* excellence or worth ▷ *vb* deserve
MERITED > MERIT
MERITING > MERIT
MERITLESS > MERIT
MERITS > MERIT
MERK *n* old Scots coin
MERKIN *n* artificial hairpiece for the pudendum
MERKINS > MERKIN
MERKS > MERK
MERL *same as* > MERLE

MERLE *adj* (of a dog, esp a collie) having a bluish-grey coat with speckles or streaks of black
MERLES > MERLE
MERLIN *n* small falcon
MERLING *n* whiting
MERLINGS > MERLING
MERLINS > MERLIN
MERLON *n* solid upright section in a crenellated battlement
MERLONS > MERLON
MERLOT *n* black grape grown in France and now throughout the wine-producing world, used, often in a blend, for making wine
MERLOTS > MERLOT
MERLS > MERL
MERMAID *n* imaginary sea creature with the upper part of a woman and the lower part of a fish
MERMAIDEN *same as* > MERMAID
MERMAIDS > MERMAID
MERMAN *n* male counterpart of the mermaid
MERMEN > MERMAN
MEROCRINE *adj* (of the secretion of glands) characterized by formation of the product without undergoing disintegration
MEROGONY *n* development of embryo from part of ovum
MEROISTIC *adj* producing yolk and ova
MEROME *same as* > MEROSOME
MEROMES > MEROME
MERONYM *n* part of something used to refer to the whole, such as *faces* meaning *people*, as in *they've seen a lot of faces come and go*
MERONYMS > MERONYM
MERONYMY > MERONYM
MEROPIA *n* partial blindness
MEROPIAS > MEROPIA
MEROPIC > MEROPIA
MEROPIDAN *n* bird of bee-eater family
MEROSOME *n* segment in body of worm
MEROSOMES > MEROSOME
MEROZOITE *n* any of the cells formed by fission of a schizont during the life cycle of sporozoan protozoans, such as the malaria parasite
MERPEOPLE *same as* > MERFOLK
MERRIER > MERRY
MERRIES > MERRY
MERRIEST > MERRY
MERRILY > MERRY

MERRIMENT *n* gaiety, fun, or mirth
MERRINESS > MERRY
MERRY *adj* cheerful or jolly ▷ *n* gean
MERRYMAN *n* jester
MERRYMEN > MERRYMAN
MERSALYL *n* salt of sodium
MERSALYLS > MERSALYL
MERSE *n* low level ground by a river or shore, often alluvial and fertile
MERSES > MERSE
MERSION *n* dipping in water
MERSIONS > MERSION
MERYCISM *n* rumination
MERYCISMS > MERYCISM
MES > ME
MESA *n* flat-topped hill found in arid regions
MESAIL *n* visor
MESAILS > MESAIL
MESAL *same as* > MESIAL
MESALLY > MESAL
MESARAIC *adj* of mesentery
MESARCH *adj* (of a xylem strand) having the first-formed xylem surrounded by that formed later, as in fern stems
MESAS > MESA
MESCAL *n* spineless globe-shaped cactus of Mexico and the SW of the USA
MESCALIN *same as* > MESCALINE
MESCALINE *n* hallucinogenic drug obtained from the tops of mescals
MESCALINS > MESCALIN
MESCALISM *n* addiction to mescal
MESCALS > MESCAL
MESCLUM *same as* > MESCLUN
MESCLUMS > MESCLUM
MESCLUN *n* type of green salad
MESCLUNS > MESCLUN
MESDAMES > MADAM
MESE *n* middle string on lyre
MESEEMED > MESEEMS
MESEEMETH *same as* > MESEEMS
MESEEMS *vb* it seems to me
MESEL *n* leper
MESELED *adj* afflicted by leprosy
MESELS > MESEL
MESENTERA > MESENTERON
MESENTERY *n* double layer of peritoneum that is attached to the back wall of the abdominal cavity and supports most of the small intestine
MESES > MESE
MESETA *n* plateau in Spain
MESETAS > MESETA
MESH *n* network or net ▷ *vb* (of gear teeth) engage ▷ *adj* made from mesh
MESHED > MESH
MESHES > MESH
MESHIER > MESH
MESHIEST > MESH
MESHING > MESH
MESHINGS > MESH
MESHUGA *adj* crazy
MESHUGAAS *n* madness
MESHUGAH *same as* > MESHUGA
MESHUGAS *adj* crazy
MESHUGGA *same as* > MESHUGA
MESHUGGAH *same as* > MESHUGA
MESHUGGE *same as* > MESHUGA
MESHWORK *n* network
MESHWORKS > MESHWORK
MESHY > MESH
MESIAD *adj* relating to or situated at the middle or centre
MESIAL *another word for* > MEDIAL
MESIALLY > MESIAL
MESIAN *same as* > MESIAL
MESIC > MESON
MESICALLY > MESON
MESMERIC *adj* holding (someone) as if spellbound
MESMERISE *same as* > MESMERIZE
MESMERISM *n* hypnotic state induced by the operator's imposition of his will on that of the patient
MESMERIST > MESMERISM
MESMERIZE *vb* hold spellbound
MESNALTY *n* lands of a mesne lord
MESNE *adj* in Law, intermediate or intervening: used esp of any assignment of property before the last
MESNES > MESNE
MESOBLAST *another name for* > MESODERM
MESOCARP *n* middle layer of the pericarp of a fruit, such as the flesh of a peach
MESOCARPS > MESOCARP
MESOCRANY *n* medium skull breadth
MESODERM *n* middle germ layer of an animal embryo, giving rise to muscle, blood, bone, connective tissue, etc
MESODERMS > MESODERM
MESOGLEA *n* gelatinous material between the outer and inner cellular layers of jellyfish and other coelenterates
MESOGLEAL > MESOGLEA
MESOGLEAS > MESOGLEA
MESOGLOEA *same as* > MESOGLEA
MESOLITE *n* type of mineral
MESOLITES > MESOLITE
MESOMERE *n* cell in fertilized ovum
MESOMERES > MESOMERE
MESOMORPH *n* person with a muscular body build: said to be correlated with somatotonia
MESON *n* elementary atomic particle
MESONIC > MESON
MESONS > MESON
MESOPAUSE *n* zone of minimum temperature between the mesosphere and the thermosphere
MESOPHILE *n* ideal growth temperature of 20-45 degrees
MESOPHYL *same as* > MESOPHYLL
MESOPHYLL *n* soft chlorophyll-containing tissue of a leaf between the upper and lower layers of epidermis: involved in photosynthesis
MESOPHYLS > MESOPHYL
MESOPHYTE *n* any plant that grows in surroundings receiving an average supply of water
MESOSCALE *adj* of weather phenomena of medium duration
MESOSOME *n* part of bacterial cell
MESOSOMES > MESOSOME
MESOTRON *same as* > MESON
MESOTRONS > MESOTRON
MESOZOAN *n* type of parasite
MESOZOANS > MESOZOAN
MESOZOIC *adj* of, denoting, or relating to an era of geological time
MESPRISE *same as* > MISPRISE
MESPRISES > MESPRISE
MESPRIZE *same as* > MISPRISE
MESPRIZES > MESPRIZE
MESQUIN *adj* mean
MESQUINE *same as* > MESQUIN
MESQUIT *same as* > MESQUITE
MESQUITE *n* small tree whose sugary pods are used as animal fodder
MESQUITES > MESQUITE
MESQUITS > MESQUIT
MESS *n* untidy or dirty confusion ▷ *vb* muddle or dirty
MESSAGE *n* communication sent ▷ *vb* send as a message
MESSAGED > MESSAGE
MESSAGES > MESSAGE
MESSAGING *n* sending and receving of messages
MESSALINE *n* light lustrous twilled-silk fabric
MESSAN *Scots word for* > DC
MESSANS > MESSAN
MESSED > MESS
MESSENGER *n* bearer of a message ▷ *vb* send by messenger
MESSES > MESS
MESSIAH *n* exceptional o hoped for liberator of a country or people
MESSIAHS > MESSIAH
MESSIANIC *adj* of or relating to the Messiah, his awaited deliverance the Jews, or the new age peace expected to follow this
MESSIAS *same as* > MESSI
MESSIASES > MESSIAS
MESSIER > MESSY
MESSIEST > MESSY
MESSIEURS > MONSIEUR
MESSILY > MESSY
MESSINESS > MESSY
MESSING > MESS
MESSMAN *n* sailor workin in ship's mess
MESSMATE *n* person with whom one shares meals a mess, esp in the army
MESSMATES > MESSMATE
MESSMEN > MESSMAN
MESSUAGE *n* dwelling house together with its outbuildings, curtilage, and the adjacent land appropriated to its use
MESSUAGES > MESSUAGE
MESSY *adj* dirty, confused or untidy
MESTEE *same as* > MUSTEE
MESTEES > MESTEE
MESTER *n* master: used as term of address for a ma who is the head of a hou
MESTERS > MESTER
MESTESO *n* Spanish musi genre
MESTESOES > MESTESO
MESTESOS > MESTESO
MESTINO *n* person of mix race
MESTINOES > MESTINO
MESTINOS > MESTINO
MESTIZA > MESTIZO
MESTIZAS > MESTIZO
MESTIZO *n* person of mixed parentage, esp th offspring of a Spanish American and an Americ Indian
MESTIZOES > MESTIZO
MESTIZOS > MESTIZO
MESTO *adj* sad
MESTOM *same as* > MESTOM
MESTOME *n* conducting tissue associated with parenchyma
MESTOMES > MESTOME
MESTOMS > MESTOM
MESTRANOL *n* synthetic oestrogen
MET *n* measuring stick
META *n* indicating chang

lteration, or alternation

TABASES > METABASIS

TABASIS *n* change

TABATIC > METABASIS

TABOLIC *adj* of or related o the sum total of the :hemical processes that occurs in living organisms, esulting in growth, production of energy, elimination of waste naterial, etc

TABOLY *n* ability of some ells, esp protozoans, to alter their shape

TACARPI *n* skeleton of the hand between the vrist and the fingers

TAGE *n* official neasuring of weight or ontents

TAGENIC *adj* of or elating to the production vithin the life cycle of an organism of alternating sexual and sexual eproductive forms

TAGES > METAGE

TAIRIE *n* area of land on which farmer pays rent n kind

TAIRIES > METAIRIE

TAL *n* chemical element, uch as iron or copper, that s malleable and capable of conducting heat and electricity ▷ *adj* made of metal ▷ *vb* fit or cover vith metal

TALED > METAL

TALHEAD *n* fan of heavy netal music

TALING > METAL

TALISE *same* s > METALLIZE

TALISED > METALISE

TALISES > METALISE

TALIST *same* s > METALLIST

TALISTS > METALIST

TALIZE *same* s > METALLIZE

TALIZED > METALIZE

TALIZES > METALIZE

TALLED > METAL

TALLIC *adj* of or onsisting of metal ▷ *n* omething metallic

TALLICS > METALLIC

TALLIKE > METAL

TALLINE *adj* of, esembling, or relating to netals

TALLING > METAL

TALLISE *same* s > METALLIZE

TALLIST *n* person who vorks with metals

TALLIZE *vb* make netallic or to coat or treat vith metal

TALLOID *n* nonmetallic lement, such as arsenic r silicon, that has some of the properties of a metal ▷ *adj* of or being a metalloid

METALLY *adj* like metal

METALMARK *n* variety of butterfly

METALS > METAL

METALWARE *n* items made of metal

METALWORK *n* craft of making objects from metal

METAMALE *n* sterile male organism, esp a fruit fly (*Drosophila*) that has one X chromosome and three sets of autosomes

METAMALES > METAMALE

METAMER *n* any of two or more isomeric compounds exhibiting metamerism

METAMERAL > METAMERE

METAMERE *n* one of the similar body segments into which earthworms, crayfish, and similar animals are divided longitudinally

METAMERES > METAMERE

METAMERIC *adj* divided into or consisting of metameres

METAMERS > METAMER

METAMICT *adj* of or denoting the amorphous state of a substance that has lost its crystalline structure as a result of the radioactivity of uranium or thorium within it

METANOIA *n* repentance

METANOIAS > METANOIA

METAPELET *n* foster mother

METAPHASE *n* second stage of mitosis during which the condensed chromosomes attach to the centre of the spindle

METAPHOR *n* figure of speech in which a term is applied to something it does not literally denote in order to imply a resemblance

METAPHORS > METAPHOR

METAPLASM *n* nonliving constituents, such as starch and pigment granules, of the cytoplasm of a cell

METAPLOT > METAPELET

METARCHON *n* nontoxic substance, such as a chemical to mask pheromones, that reduces the persistence of a pest

METASOMA *n* posterior part of an arachnid's abdomen (opisthosoma) that never carries appendages

METASOMAS > METASOMA

METATAG *n* element of HTML describing the contents of a web page and used by search engines to index pages by subject

METATAGS > METATAG

METATARSI *pl n* skeleton of human foot between toes and tarsus

METATE *n* stone for grinding grain on

METATES > METATE

METAXYLEM *n* xylem tissue that consists of rigid thick-walled cells and occurs in parts of the plant that have finished growing

METAYAGE *n* farming in which rent is paid in kind

METAYAGES > METAYAGE

METAYER *n* farmer who pays rent in kind

METAYERS > METAYER

METAZOA > METAZOAN

METAZOAL > METAZOAN

METAZOAN *n* any animal having a body composed of many cells: includes all animals except sponges and protozoans ▷ *adj* of the metazoans

METAZOANS > METAZOAN

METAZOIC *adj* of, relating to, or belonging to the *Metazoa*

METAZOON *same as* > METAZOAN

METCAST *n* weather forecast

METCASTS > METCAST

METE *vb* deal out as punishment ▷ *n* (to) measure

METED > METE

METEOR *n* small fast-moving heavenly body, visible as a streak of incandescence if it enters the earth's atmosphere

METEORIC *adj* of a meteor

METEORISM *another name for* > TYMPANITES

METEORIST *n* person who studies meteors

METEORITE *n* meteor that has fallen to earth

METEOROID *n* any of the small celestial bodies that are thought to orbit the sun. When they enter the earth's atmosphere, they become visible as meteors

METEOROUS > METEOR

METEORS > METEOR

METEPA *n* type of pesticide

METEPAS > METEPA

METER *same as* > METRE

METERAGE *n* act of measuring

METERAGES > METERAGE

METERED > METER

METERING > METER

METERS > METER

METES > METE

METESTICK *n* measuring rod

METESTRUS *n* period in the oestrous cycle following oestrus, characterized by lack of sexual activity

METEWAND *same as* > METESTICK

METEWANDS > METEWAND

METEYARD *same as* > METESTICK

METEYARDS > METEYARD

METFORMIN *n* drug used to treat diabetes

METH *n* variety of amphetamine

METHADON *same as* > METHADONE

METHADONE *n* drug similar to morphine, sometimes prescribed as a heroin substitute

METHADONS > METHADON

METHANAL *n* colourless poisonous irritating gas with a pungent characteristic odour, made by the oxidation of methanol and used as formalin and in the manufacture of synthetic resins

METHANALS > METHANAL

METHANE *n* colourless inflammable gas

METHANES > METHANE

METHANOIC as in *methanoic acid* systematic name for formic acid

METHANOL *n* colourless poisonous liquid used as a solvent and fuel

METHANOLS > METHANOL

METHEGLIN *n* (esp formerly) spiced or medicated mead

METHINK *same as* > METHINKS

METHINKS *vb* it seems to me

METHO *n* methylated spirits

METHOD *n* way or manner

METHODIC > METHOD

METHODISE *same as* > METHODIZE

METHODISM *n* system and practices of the Methodist Church, developed by the English preacher John Wesley (1703–91) and his followers

METHODIST > METHODISM

METHODIZE *vb* organize according to a method

METHODS > METHOD

METHOS > METHO

METHOUGHT > METHINKS

METHOXIDE *n* saltlike compound in which the hydrogen atom in the hydroxyl group of methanol has been replaced by a metal atom, usually an alkali metal atom as in sodium methoxide, $NaOCH_3$

METHOXY *n* steroid drug

METHOXYL *n* chemical compound of methyl and hydroxyl

METHS *n* methylated spirits

METHYL *n* compound containing a saturated hydrocarbon group of atoms

METHYLAL *n* colourless volatile flammable liquid

METHYLALS > METHYLAL

METHYLASE *n* enzyme

METHYLATE *vb* mix with methanol

METHYLENE *adj* of, consisting of, or containing the divalent group of atoms $=CH_2$

METHYLIC > METHYL

METHYLS > METHYL

METHYSES > METHYSIS

METHYSIS *n* drunkenness

METHYSTIC *adj* intoxicating

METIC *n* (in ancient Greece) an alien having some rights of citizenship in the city in which he lives

METICAIS > METICAL

METICAL *n* money unit in Mozambique

METICALS > METICAL

METICS > METIC

METIER *n* profession or trade

METIERS > METIER

METIF *n* person of mixed race

METIFS > METIF

METING > METE

METIS *n* person of mixed parentage

METISSE > METIS

METISSES > METIS

METOL *n* colourless soluble organic substance used, in the form of its sulphate, as a photographic developer

METOLS > METOL

METONYM *n* word used in a metonymy. For example *the bottle* is a metonym for *alcoholic drink*

METONYMIC > METONYMY

METONYMS > METONYM

METONYMY *n* figure of speech in which one thing is replaced by another associated with it, such as 'the Crown' for 'the queen'

METOPAE > METOPE

METOPE *n* square space between two triglyphs in a Doric frieze

METOPES > METOPE

METOPIC *adj* of or relating to the forehead

METOPISM *n* congenital disfigurement of forehead

METOPISMS > METOPISM

METOPON *n* painkilling drug

METOPONS > METOPON

METOPRYL *n* type of anaesthetic

METOPRYLS > METOPRYL

METRALGIA *n* pain in the uterus

METRAZOL *n* drug used to improve blood circulation

METRAZOLS > METRAZOL

METRE *n* basic unit of length equal to about 1.094 yards (100 centimetres) ▷ *vb* express in poetry

METRED > METRE

METRES > METRE

METRIC *adj* of the decimal system of weights and measures based on the metre

METRICAL *adj* of measurement

METRICATE *vb* convert a measuring system or instrument to metric units

METRICIAN *n* writer of metrical verse

METRICISE *vb* study metre of poetry

METRICISM > METRICISE

METRICIST *same as* > METRICIAN

METRICIZE *same as* > METRICISE

METRICS *n* art of using poetic metre

METRIFIED > METRIFY

METRIFIER > METRIFY

METRIFIES > METRIFY

METRIFY *vb* render into poetic metre

METRING > METRE

METRIST *n* person skilled in the use of poetic metre

METRISTS > METRIST

METRITIS *n* inflammation of the uterus

METRO *n* underground railway system, esp in Paris

METROLOGY *n* science of weights and measures

METRONOME *n* instrument which marks musical time by means of a ticking pendulum

METROPLEX *n* large urban area

METROS > METRO

METS > MET

METTLE *n* courage or spirit

METTLED *adj* spirited, courageous, or valiant

METTLES > METTLE

METUMP *n* band for carrying a load or burden

METUMPS > METUMP

MEU *another name for* > SPIGNEL

MEUNIERE *adj* (of fish) dredged with flour, fried in butter, and served with butter, lemon juice, and parsley

MEUS > MEU

MEUSE *n* gap (in fence, wall etc) through which an animal passed ▷ *vb* go through this gap

MEUSED > MEUSE

MEUSES > MEUSE

MEUSING > MEUSE

MEVE *same as* > MOVE

MEVED > MEVE

MEVES > MEVE

MEVING > MEVE

MEVROU *n* South African title of address equivalent to *Mrs* when placed before a surname or *madam* when used alone

MEVROUS > MEVROU

MEW *n* cry of a cat ▷ *vb* utter this cry

MEWED > MEW

MEWING > MEW

MEWL *vb* (esp of a baby) to cry weakly ▷ *n* weak or whimpering cry

MEWLED > MEWL

MEWLER > MEWL

MEWLERS > MEWL

MEWLING > MEWL

MEWLS > MEWL

MEWS *same as* > MEUSE

MEWSED > MEWS

MEWSES > MEWS

MEWSING > MEWS

MEYNT > MING

MEZAIL *same as* > MESAIL

MEZAILS > MEZAIL

MEZCAL *variant spelling of* > MESCAL

MEZCALINE *variant spelling of* > MESCALINE

MEZCALS > MEZCAL

MEZE *n* type of hors d'oeuvre eaten esp with an apéritif or other drink in Greece and the Near East

MEZEREON *same as* > MEZEREUM

MEZEREONS > MEZEREON

MEZEREUM *n* dried bark of certain shrubs of the genus *Daphne*, esp mezereon, formerly used as a vesicant and to treat arthritis

MEZEREUMS > MEZEREUM

MEZES > MEZE

MEZQUIT *same as* > MESQUITE

MEZQUITE *same as* > MESQUITE

MEZQUITES > MEZQUITE

MEZQUITS > MEZQUIT

MEZUZA *same as* > MEZUZAH

MEZUZAH *n* piece of parchment inscribed with biblical passages and fixed to the doorpost of the rooms of a Jewish house

MEZUZAHS > MEZUZAH

MEZUZAS > MEZUZA

MEZUZOT > MEZUZAH

MEZUZOTH > MEZUZAH

MEZZ *same as* > MEZZANIN

MEZZALUNA *n* half-moon shaped kitchen chopper

MEZZANINE *n* intermedia storey, esp between the ground and first floor ▷ *adj* of or relating to an intermediate stage in a financial process

MEZZE *same as* > MEZE

MEZZES > MEZZE

MEZZO *adv* moderately

MEZZOS > MEZZO

MEZZOTINT *n* method of engraving by scraping th roughened surface of a metal plate ▷ *vb* engrav (a copper plate) in this fashion

MGANGA *n* witch doctor

MGANGAS > MGANGA

MHO *former name for* > SIEMENS

MHORR *n* African gazelle

MHORRS > MHORR

MHOS > MHO

MI *n* (in tonic sol-fa) the third degree of any majo scale

MIAOU *same as* > MEOW

MIAOUED > MIAOU

MIAOUING > MIAOU

MIAOUS > MIAOU

MIAOW *same as* > MEOW

MIAOWED > MIAOW

MIAOWING > MIAOW

MIAOWS > MIAOW

MIASM *same as* > MIASMA

MIASMA *n* unwholesome foreboding atmosphere

MIASMAL > MIASMA

MIASMAS > MIASMA

MIASMATA > MIASMA

MIASMATIC > MIASMA

MIASMIC > MIASMA

MIASMOUS > MIASMA

MIASMS > MIASM

MIAUL *same as* > MEOW

MIAULED > MIAUL

MIAULING > MIAUL

MIAULS > MIAUL

MIB *n* marble used in games

MIBS > MIB

MIC *n* microphone

MICA *n* glasslike mineral used as an electrical insulator

MICACEOUS > MICA

MICAS > MICA

MICATE *vb* add mica to

MICATED > MICATE

MICATES > MICATE

MICATING > MICATE

MICAWBER *n* person who idles and trusts to fortu

MICAWBERS > MICAWBER

MICE > MOUSE

MICELL *same as* > MICELL

MICELLA *same as* > MICEL

MICELLAE > MICELLA

MICELLAR > MICELLE

MICELLAS > MICELLA

MICELLE *n* charged

ggregate of molecules of
olloidal size in a solution
CELLES > MICELLE
CELLS > MICELL
CH *same as* > MITCH
CHE *same as* > MICH
CHED > MICH
CHER > MICH
CHERS > MICH
CHES > MICH
CHIGAN *US name*
or > NEWMARKET
CHIGANS > MICHIGAN
CHING > MICH
CHINGS > MICH
CHT *n* Scots word for
night
CHTS > MICHT
CK *n* derogatory term for
n Irish person
CKEY *n* young bull,
sp one that is wild and
nbranded ▷ *vb* drug
erson's drink
CKEYED > MICKEY
CKEYING > MICKEY
CKEYS > MICKEY
CKIES > MICKY
CKLE *adj* large or
bundant ▷ *adv* much ▷ *n*
reat amount
CKLER > MICKLE
CKLES > MICKLE
CKLEST > MICKLE
CKS > MICK
CKY *same as* > MICKEY
CO *n* marmoset
COS > MICO
CRA > MICRON
CRIFIED > MICRIFY
CRIFIES > MICRIFY
CRIFY *vb* make very
mall
CRO *n* small computer
CROBAR *n* millionth of
ar of pressure
CROBARS > MICROBAR
CROBE *n* minute
rganism, esp one causing
isease
CROBEAM *n* X-ray
nachine with narrow
ocussed beam
CROBES > MICROBE
CROBIAL > MICROBE
CROBIAN > MICROBE
CROBIC > MICROBE
CROBREW *n* beer made in
mall brewery
CROBUS *n* small bus
CROCAP *adj* (of
nvestments) involving
ery small amount of
apital
CROCAR *n* small car
CROCARD *n* card
ontaining microprint
CROCARS > MICROCAR
CROCHIP *n* small wafer
f silicon containing
lectronic circuits ▷ *vb*
mplant (an animal) with
microchip tag linked
o a national computer
network for purposes of identification
MICROCODE *n* set of computer instructions
MICROCOPY *n* greatly reduced photographic copy of a printed page, drawing, etc, on microfilm or microfiche
MICROCOSM *n* miniature representation of something
MICROCYTE *n* unusually small red blood cell
MICRODONT *adj* having unusually small teeth
MICRODOT *n* photographic copy of a document reduced to pinhead size
MICRODOTS > MICRODOT
MICROFILM *n* miniaturized recording of books or documents on a roll of film ▷ *vb* photograph a page or document on microfilm
MICROFORM *n* method of storing symbolic information by using photographic reduction techniques, such as microfilm, microfiche, etc
MICROGLIA *n* one of the two types of non-nervous tissue (glia) found in the central nervous system, having macrophage activity
MICROGRAM *n* photograph or drawing of an object as viewed through a microscope
MICROHM *n* millionth of ohm
MICROHMS > MICROHM
MICROINCH *n* millionth of inch
MICROJET *n* light jet-propelled aircraft
MICROJETS > MICROJET
MICROLITE *n* small private aircraft carrying no more than two people, with an empty weight of not more than 150 kg and a wing area not less than 10 square metres: used in pleasure flying and racing
MICROLITH *n* small Mesolithic flint tool which was made from a blade and formed part of hafted tools
MICROLOAN *n* very small loan
MICROLOGY *n* study of microscopic things
MICROLUX *n* millionth of a lux
MICROMERE *n* any of the small cells formed by unequal cleavage of a fertilized ovum
MICROMESH *n* very fine mesh
MICROMHO *n* millionth of mho
MICROMHOS > MICROMHO
MICROMINI *n* very short skirt
MICROMOLE *n* millionth of mole
MICRON *n* unit of length equal to 10^{-6} metre
MICRONISE *same as* > MICRONIZE
MICRONIZE *vb* break down to very small particles
MICRONS > MICRON
MICROPORE *n* very small pore
MICROPSIA *n* defect of vision in which objects appear to be smaller than they appear to a person with normal vision
MICROPUMP *n* small pump inserted in skin to automatically deliver medicine
MICROPYLE *n* small opening in the integuments of a plant ovule through which the male gametes pass
MICROS > MICRO
MICROSITE *n* website that is intended for a specific limited purpose and is often temporary
MICROSOME *n* any of the small particles consisting of ribosomes and fragments of attached endoplasmic reticulum that can be isolated from cells by centrifugal action
MICROTOME *n* instrument used for cutting thin sections, esp of biological material, for microscopical examination
MICROTOMY *n* cutting of sections with a microtome
MICROTONE *n* any musical interval smaller than a semitone
MICROVOLT *n* millionth of volt
MICROWATT *n* millionth of watt
MICROWAVE *n* electromagnetic wave with a wavelength of a few centimetres, used in radar and cooking ▷ *vb* cook in a microwave oven
MICROWIRE *n* very fine wire
MICRURGY *n* manipulation and examination of single cells under a microscope
MICS > MIC
MICTION *n* urination
MICTIONS > MICTION
MICTURATE *vb* urinate
MID *adj* intermediate, middle ▷ *n* middle ▷ *prep* amid
MIDAIR *n* some point above ground level, in the air
MIDAIRS > MIDAIR
MIDBRAIN *n* part of the brain that develops from the middle portion of the embryonic neural tube
MIDBRAINS > MIDBRAIN
MIDCAP *adj* (of investments) involving very small amount
MIDCOURSE *adj* in middle of course
MIDCULT *n* middlebrow culture
MIDCULTS > MIDCULT
MIDDAY *n* noon
MIDDAYS > MIDDAY
MIDDEN *n* dunghill or rubbish heap
MIDDENS > MIDDEN
MIDDEST *adj* in middle
MIDDIE *n* glass or bottle containing 285ml of beer
MIDDIES > MIDDY
MIDDLE *adj* equidistant from two extremes ▷ *n* middle point or part ▷ *vb* place in the middle
MIDDLED > MIDDLE
MIDDLEMAN *n* trader who buys from the producer and sells to the consumer
MIDDLEMEN > MIDDLEMAN
MIDDLER *n* pupil in middle years at school
MIDDLERS > MIDDLER
MIDDLES > MIDDLE
MIDDLING *adj* mediocre ▷ *adv* moderately
MIDDLINGS *pl n* poorer or coarser part of flour or other products
MIDDORSAL *adj* in middle or back
MIDDY *n* middle-sized glass of beer
MIDFIELD *n* area between the two opposing defences
MIDFIELDS > MIDFIELD
MIDGE *n* small mosquito-like insect
MIDGES > MIDGE
MIDGET *n* very small person or thing ▷ *adj* much smaller than normal
MIDGETS > MIDGET
MIDGIE *n* informal word for a small winged biting insect such as the midge or sandfly
MIDGIES > MIDGIE
MIDGUT *n* middle part of the digestive tract of vertebrates, including the small intestine
MIDGUTS > MIDGUT
MIDGY > MIDGE
MIDI *adj* (of a skirt, coat, etc) reaching to below the knee or midcalf
MIDINETTE *n* Parisian seamstress or salesgirl in a clothes shop

MIDIRON *n* club, usually a No. 5, 6, or 7 iron, used for medium-length approach shots
MIDIRONS > MIDIRON
MIDIS > MIDI
MIDISKIRT *n* skirt of medium length
MIDLAND *n* middle part of a country
MIDLANDS > MIDLAND
MIDLEG *n* middle of leg
MIDLEGS > MIDLEG
MIDLIFE as in *midlife crisis* crisis that may be experienced in middle age involving frustration, panic, and feelings of pointlessness, sometimes resulting in radical and often ill-advised changes of lifestyle
MIDLIFER *n* middle-aged person
MIDLIFERS > MIDLIFER
MIDLINE *n* line at middle of something
MIDLINES > MIDLINE
MIDLIST *n* books in publisher's range that sell reasonably well
MIDLISTS > MIDLIST
MIDLIVES > MIDLIFE
MIDMONTH *n* middle of month
MIDMONTHS > MIDMONTH
MIDMOST *adv* in the middle or midst
MIDMOSTS > MIDMOST
MIDNIGHT *n* twelve o'clock at night
MIDNIGHTS > MIDNIGHT
MIDNOON *n* noon
MIDNOONS > MIDNOON
MIDPOINT *n* point on a line equally distant from either end
MIDPOINTS > MIDPOINT
MIDRANGE *n* part of loudspeaker
MIDRANGES > MIDRANGE
MIDRASH *n* homily on a scriptural passage derived by traditional Jewish exegetical methods and consisting usually of embellishment of the scriptural narrative
MIDRASHIC > MIDRASH
MIDRASHIM > MIDRASH
MIDRASHOT > MIDRASH
MIDRIB *n* main vein of a leaf, running down the centre of the blade
MIDRIBS > MIDRIB
MIDRIFF *n* middle part of the body
MIDRIFFS > MIDRIFF
MIDS > MID
MIDSHIP *adj* in, of, or relating to the middle of a vessel ▷ *n* middle of a vessel
MIDSHIPS *See* > AMIDSHIPS
MIDSIZE *adj* medium-sized
MIDSIZED *same as* > MIDSIZE
MIDSOLE *n* layer between the inner and the outer sole of a shoe, contoured for absorbing shock
MIDSOLES > MIDSOLE
MIDSPACE *n* area in middle of space
MIDSPACES > MIDSPACE
MIDST *See* > AMID
MIDSTORY *n* level of forest trees between smallest and tallest
MIDSTREAM *n* middle of a stream or river ▷ *adj* in or towards the middle of a stream or river
MIDSTS > MIDST
MIDSUMMER *n* middle of summer
MIDTERM *n* middle of a term in a school, university, etc
MIDTERMS > MIDTERM
MIDTOWN *n* centre of a town
MIDTOWNS > MIDTOWN
MIDWATCH *n* naval watch period beginning at midnight
MIDWAY *adv* halfway ▷ *adj* in or at the middle of the distance ▷ *n* place in a fair, carnival, etc, where sideshows are located
MIDWAYS > MIDWAY
MIDWEEK *n* middle of the week
MIDWEEKLY > MIDWEEK
MIDWEEKS > MIDWEEK
MIDWIFE *n* trained person who assists at childbirth ▷ *vb* act as midwife
MIDWIFED > MIDWIFE
MIDWIFERY *n* art or practice of a midwife
MIDWIFES > MIDWIFE
MIDWIFING > MIDWIFE
MIDWINTER *n* middle or depth of winter
MIDWIVE *vb* act as midwife
MIDWIVED > MIDWIVE
MIDWIVES > MIDWIFE
MIDWIVING > MIDWIVE
MIDYEAR *n* middle of the year
MIDYEARS > MIDYEAR
MIELIE *same as* > MEALIE
MIELIES > MIELIE
MIEN *n* person's bearing, demeanour, or appearance
MIENS > MIEN
MIEVE *same as* > MOVE
MIEVED > MIEVE
MIEVES > MIEVE
MIEVING > MIEVE
MIFF *vb* take offence or offend ▷ *n* petulant mood
MIFFED > MIFF
MIFFIER > MIFFY
MIFFIEST > MIFFY
MIFFILY > MIFFY
MIFFINESS > MIFFY
MIFFING > MIFF
MIFFS > MIFF
MIFFY *adj* easily upset
MIFTY *same as* > MIFFY
MIG *n* marble used in games
MIGG *same as* > MIG
MIGGLE *n* US word for playing marble
MIGGLES > MIGGLE
MIGGS > MIGG
MIGHT > MAY
MIGHTEST > MAY
MIGHTFUL *same as* > MIGHTY
MIGHTIER > MIGHTY
MIGHTIEST > MIGHTY
MIGHTILY *adv* great extent, amount, or degree
MIGHTS > MAY
MIGHTST > MAY
MIGHTY *adj* powerful ▷ *adv* very
MIGMATITE *n* composite rock body containing two types of rock (esp igneous and metamorphic rock) that have interacted with each other but are nevertheless still distinguishable
MIGNON *adj* small and pretty ▷ *n* tender boneless cut of meat
MIGNONNE > MIGNON
MIGNONS > MIGNON
MIGRAINE *n* severe headache, often with nausea and visual disturbances
MIGRAINES > MIGRAINE
MIGRANT *n* person or animal that moves from one place to another ▷ *adj* moving from one place to another
MIGRANTS > MIGRANT
MIGRATE *vb* move from one place to settle in another
MIGRATED > MIGRATE
MIGRATES > MIGRATE
MIGRATING > MIGRATE
MIGRATION *n* act or an instance of migrating
MIGRATOR > MIGRATE
MIGRATORS > MIGRATE
MIGRATORY *adj* (of an animal) migrating every year
MIGS > MIG
MIHA *n* young fern frond which has not yet opened
MIHI *n* Māori ceremonial greeting ▷ *vb* greet
MIHIED > MIHI
MIHIING > MIHI
MIHIS > MIHI
MIHRAB *n* niche in a mosque showing the direction of Mecca
MIHRABS > MIHRAB
MIJNHEER *same as* > MYNHEER
MIJNHEERS > MIJNHEER
MIKADO *n* Japanese emperor
MIKADOS > MIKADO
MIKE *n* microphone
MIKED > MIKE
MIKES > MIKE
MIKING > MIKE
MIKRA > MIKRON
MIKRON *same as* > MICRON
MIKRONS > MIKRON
MIKVAH *n* pool used esp by women for ritual purification after their monthly period
MIKVAHS > MIKVAH
MIKVEH *same as* > MIKVAH
MIKVEHS > MIKVEH
MIKVOS > MIKVEH
MIKVOT > MIKVEH
MIKVOTH > MIKVAH
MIL *n* unit of length equa to one thousandth of an inch
MILADI *same as* > MILADY
MILADIES > MILADY
MILADIS > MILADI
MILADY *n* (formerly) a continental title for an English gentlewoman
MILAGE *same as* > MILEAGE
MILAGES > MILAGE
MILCH *adj* (of a cow) givin milk
MILCHIG *same as* > MILCH
MILCHIK *adj* containing or used in the preparatio of milk products and so not to be used with meat products
MILD *adj* not strongly flavoured ▷ *n* dark beer flavoured with fewer hop than bitter ▷ *vb* become gentle
MILDED > MILD
MILDEN *vb* make or beco mild or milder
MILDENED > MILDEN
MILDENING > MILDEN
MILDENS > MILDEN
MILDER > MILD
MILDEST > MILD
MILDEW *same as* > MOULD
MILDEWED > MILDEW
MILDEWING > MILDEW
MILDEWS > MILDEW
MILDEWY > MILDEW
MILDING > MILD
MILDLY > MILD
MILDNESS > MILD
MILDS > MILD
MILE *n* unit of length equ to 1760 yards or 1.609 kilometres
MILEAGE *n* distance travelled in miles
MILEAGES > MILEAGE
MILEPOST *n* signpost tha shows the distance in miles to or from a place
MILEPOSTS > MILEPOST
MILER *n* athlete, horse, e that specializes in races one mile
MILERS > MILER
MILES > MILE

LESIAN *n* Irishman
LESIMO *n* Spanish word meaning thousandth
LESIMOS > MILESIMO
LESTONE *same as* > MILEPOST
LFOIL *same as* > YARROW
LFOILS > MILFOIL
LIA > MILIUM
LIARIA *n* acute itching eruption of the skin, caused by blockage of the sweat glands
LIARIAL > MILIARIA
LIARIAS > MILIARIA
LIARY *adj* resembling or relating to millet seeds
LIEU *n* environment or surroundings
LIEUS > MILIEU
LIEUX > MILIEU
LITANCE > MILITANT
LITANCY > MILITANT
LITANT *adj* aggressive or vigorous in support of a cause ▷ *n* militant person
LITANTS > MILITANT
LITAR *same as* > MILITARY
LITARIA *pl n* items of military interest, such as weapons, uniforms, medals, etc, esp from the past
LITARY *adj* of or for soldiers, armies, or war ▷ *n* armed services
LITATE *vb* have a strong influence or effect
LITATED > MILITATE
LITATES > MILITATE
LITIA *n* military force of trained citizens for use in emergency only
LITIAS > MILITIA
LIUM *n* pimple
LK *n* white fluid produced by female mammals to feed their young ▷ *vb* draw milk from
LKED > MILK
LKEN *adj* of or like milk
LKER *n* cow, goat, etc, that yields milk, esp of a specified quality or amount
LKERS > MILKER
LKFISH *n* large silvery tropical clupeoid food and game fish, *Chanos chanos*: family *Chanidae*
LKIER > MILKY
LKIEST > MILKY
LKILY > MILKY
LKINESS > MILKY
LKING > MILK
LKINGS > MILKING
LKLESS > MILK
LKLIKE > MILK
LKMAID *n* (esp in former times) woman who milks cows
LKMAIDS > MILKMAID
LKMAN *n* man who delivers milk to people's houses
MILKMEN > MILKMAN
MILKO *informal name for* > MILKMAN
MILKOS > MILKO
MILKS > MILK
MILKSHAKE *n* drink of flavoured milk
MILKSHED *n* area where milk is produced
MILKSHEDS > MILKSHED
MILKSOP *n* feeble man
MILKSOPPY > MILKSOP
MILKSOPS > MILKSOP
MILKTOAST *n* meek, submissive, or timid person
MILKWEED *same as* > MONARCH
MILKWEEDS > MILKWEED
MILKWOOD *n* tree producing latex
MILKWOODS > MILKWOOD
MILKWORT *n* any of several plants of the genus *Polygala*, having small blue, pink, or white flowers with two petal-like sepals: family *Polygalaceae*. They were formerly believed to increase milk production in cows
MILKWORTS > MILKWORT
MILKY *adj* of or like milk
MILL *n* factory ▷ *vb* grind, press, or process in or as if in a mill
MILLABLE > MILL
MILLAGE *adj* American tax rate calculated in thousandths per dollar
MILLAGES > MILLAGE
MILLBOARD *n* strong pasteboard, used esp in book covers
MILLCAKE *n* food for livestock
MILLCAKES > MILLCAKE
MILLDAM *n* dam built in a stream to raise the water level sufficiently for it to turn a millwheel
MILLDAMS > MILLDAM
MILLE *French word for* > THOUSAND
MILLED *adj* crushed or ground in a mill
MILLENARY *adj* of or relating to a thousand or to a thousand years ▷ *n* adherent of millenarianism
MILLENNIA *n* plural of millennium: period or cycle of one thousand years
MILLEPED *same as* > MILLEPEDE
MILLEPEDE *same as* > MILLIPEDE
MILLEPEDS > MILLEPED
MILLEPORE *n* any tropical colonial coral-like medusoid hydrozoan of the order *Milleporina*, esp of the genus *Millepora*, having a calcareous skeleton
MILLER *n* person who works in a mill
MILLERITE *n* yellow mineral consisting of nickel sulphide
MILLERS > MILLER
MILLES > MILLE
MILLET *n* type of cereal grass
MILLETS > MILLET
MILLHOUSE *n* house attached to mill
MILLIARD *n* one thousand millions
MILLIARDS > MILLIARD
MILLIARE *n* ancient Roman unit of distance
MILLIARES > MILLIARE
MILLIARY *adj* relating to or marking a distance equal to an ancient Roman mile of a thousand paces
MILLIBAR *n* unit of atmospheric pressure
MILLIBARS > MILLIBAR
MILLIE *n* derogatory name for a young working-class woman
MILLIEME *n* Tunisian monetary unit worth one thousandth of a dinar
MILLIEMES > MILLIEME
MILLIER *n* metric weight of million grams
MILLIERS > MILLIER
MILLIES > MILLIE
MILLIGAL *n* unit of gravity
MILLIGALS > MILLIGAL
MILLIGRAM *n* thousandth part of a gram
MILLILUX *n* thousandth of lux
MILLIME *same as* > MILLIEME
MILLIMES > MILLIME
MILLIMHO *n* thousandth of mho
MILLIMHOS > MILLIMHO
MILLIMOLE *n* thousandth of mole
MILLINE *n* measurement of advertising space
MILLINER *n* maker or seller of women's hats
MILLINERS > MILLINER
MILLINERY *n* hats, trimmings, etc, sold by a milliner
MILLINES > MILLINE
MILLING *n* act or process of grinding, cutting, pressing, or crushing in a mill
MILLINGS > MILLING
MILLIOHM *n* thousandth of ohm
MILLIOHMS > MILLIOHM
MILLION *n* one thousand thousands
MILLIONS > MILLION
MILLIONTH *n* one of 1 000 000 approximately equal parts of something ▷ *adj* being the ordinal number of 1 000 000 in numbering or counting order, etc
MILLIPED *same as* > MILLIPEDE
MILLIPEDE *n* small animal with a jointed body and many pairs of legs
MILLIPEDS > MILLIPED
MILLIREM *n* unit of radiation
MILLIREMS > MILLIREM
MILLIVOLT *n* thousandth of volt
MILLIWATT *n* thousandth of watt
MILLOCRAT *n* member of a government of millowners
MILLPOND *n* pool which provides water to turn a millwheel
MILLPONDS > MILLPOND
MILLRACE *n* current of water that turns a millwheel
MILLRACES > MILLRACE
MILLRIND *n* iron support fitted across an upper millstone
MILLRINDS > MILLRIND
MILLRUN *same as* > MILLRACE
MILLRUNS > MILLRUN
MILLS > MILL
MILLSCALE *n* scale on metal being heated
MILLSTONE *n* flat circular stone for grinding corn
MILLTAIL *n* channel carrying water away from mill
MILLTAILS > MILLTAIL
MILLWHEEL *n* waterwheel that drives a mill
MILLWORK *n* work done in a mill
MILLWORKS > MILLWORK
MILNEB *n* type of pesticide
MILNEBS > MILNEB
MILO *n* any of various early-growing cultivated varieties of sorghum with heads of yellow or pinkish seeds resembling millet
MILOMETER *n* device that records the number of miles that a bicycle or motor vehicle has travelled
MILOR *same as* > MILORD
MILORD *n* (formerly) a continental title used for an English gentleman
MILORDS > MILORD
MILORS > MILOR
MILOS > MILO
MILPA *n* form of subsistence agriculture in Mexico
MILPAS > MILPA
MILREIS *n* former monetary unit of Portugal

and Brazil, divided into 1000 reis
MILS > MIL
MILSEY *n* milk strainer
MILSEYS > MILSEY
MILT *n* sperm of fish ▷ *vb* fertilize (the roe of a female fish) with milt, esp artificially
MILTED > MILT
MILTER *n* male fish that is mature and ready to breed
MILTERS > MILTER
MILTIER > MILTY
MILTIEST > MILTY
MILTING > MILT
MILTONIA *n* tropical American orchid
MILTONIAS > MILTONIA
MILTS > MILT
MILTY *adj* full of milt
MILTZ *same as* > MILT
MILTZES > MILTZ
MILVINE *adj* of kites and related birds
MIM *adj* prim, modest, or demure
MIMBAR *n* pulpit in mosque
MIMBARS > MIMBAR
MIME *n* acting without the use of words ▷ *vb* act in mime
MIMED > MIME
MIMEO *vb* mimeograph
MIMEOED > MIMEO
MIMEOING > MIMEO
MIMEOS > MIMEO
MIMER > MIME
MIMERS > MIME
MIMES > MIME
MIMESES > MIMESIS
MIMESIS *n* imitative representation of nature or human behaviour
MIMESISES > MIMESIS
MIMESTER > MIME
MIMESTERS > MIME
MIMETIC *adj* imitating or representing something
MIMETICAL > MIMETIC
MIMETITE *n* rare secondary mineral
MIMETITES > MIMETITE
MIMIC *vb* imitate (a person or manner), esp for satirical effect ▷ *n* person or animal that is good at mimicking ▷ *adj* of, relating to, or using mimicry
MIMICAL > MIMIC
MIMICKED > MIMIC
MIMICKER > MIMIC
MIMICKERS > MIMIC
MIMICKING > MIMIC
MIMICRIES > MIMICRY
MIMICRY *n* act or art of copying or imitating closely
MIMICS > MIMIC
MIMING > MIME
MIMMER > MIM
MIMMEST > MIM
MIMMICK *same as* > MINNICK
MIMMICKED > MIMMICK
MIMMICKS > MIMMICK
MIMOSA *n* shrub with fluffy yellow flowers and sensitive leaves
MIMOSAS > MIMOSA
MIMSEY *same as* > MIMSY
MIMSIER > MIMSY
MIMSIEST > MIMSY
MIMSY *adj* prim, underwhelming, and ineffectual
MIMULUS *n* plants cultivated for their yellow or red flowers
MIMULUSES > MIMULUS
MINA *n* ancient unit of weight and money, used in Asia Minor, equal to one sixtieth of a talent
MINABLE > MINE
MINACIOUS *adj* threatening
MINACITY > MINACIOUS
MINAE > MINA
MINAR *n* tower
MINARET *n* tall slender tower of a mosque
MINARETED > MINARET
MINARETS > MINARET
MINARS > MINAR
MINAS > MINA
MINATORY *adj* threatening or menacing
MINBAR *same as* > MIMBAR
MINBARS > MINBAR
MINCE *vb* cut or grind into very small pieces ▷ *n* minced meat
MINCED > MINCE
MINCEMEAT *n* sweet mixture of dried fruit and spices
MINCER *n* machine for mincing meat
MINCERS > MINCER
MINCES > MINCE
MINCEUR *adj* (of food) low-fat
MINCIER > MINCY
MINCIEST > MINCY
MINCING *adj* affected in manner
MINCINGLY > MINCING
MINCINGS > MINCING
MINCY *adj* effeminate
MIND *n* thinking faculties ▷ *vb* take offence at
MINDED *adj* having an inclination as specified
MINDER *n* aide or bodyguard
MINDERS > MINDER
MINDFUCK *n* taboo term for deliberate infliction of psychological damage
MINDFUCKS > MINDFUCK
MINDFUL *adj* heedful
MINDFULLY > MINDFUL
MINDING > MIND
MINDINGS > MIND
MINDLESS *adj* stupid
MINDS > MIND
MINDSET *n* ideas and attitudes with which a person approaches a situation, esp when these are seen as being difficult to alter
MINDSETS > MINDSET
MINDSHARE *n* level of awareness in the minds of consumers that a particular product commands
MINE *pron* belonging to me ▷ *n* deep hole for digging out coal, ores, etc ▷ *vb* dig for minerals
MINEABLE > MINE
MINED > MINE
MINEFIELD *n* area of land or water containing mines
MINELAYER *n* warship or aircraft for carrying and laying mines
MINEOLA *same as* > MINNEOLA
MINEOLAS > MINEOLA
MINER *n* person who works in a mine
MINERAL *n* naturally occurring inorganic substance, such as metal ▷ *adj* of, containing, or like minerals
MINERALS > MINERAL
MINERS > MINER
MINES > MINE
MINESHAFT *n* vertical entrance into mine
MINESTONE *n* ore
MINETTE *n* type of rock
MINETTES > MINETTE
MINEVER *same as* > MINIVER
MINEVERS > MINEVER
MING *vb* mix
MINGE *n* taboo word fore female genitals
MINGED > MING
MINGER *n* unattractive person
MINGERS > MINGER
MINGES > MINGE
MINGIER > MINGY
MINGIEST > MINGY
MINGIN *same as* > MINGING
MINGINESS > MINGY
MINGING *adj* unattractive or unpleasant
MINGLE *vb* mix or blend
MINGLED > MINGLE
MINGLER > MINGLE
MINGLERS > MINGLE
MINGLES > MINGLE
MINGLING > MINGLE
MINGLINGS > MINGLE
MINGS > MING
MINGY *adj* miserly
MINI *same as* > MINIDRESS
MINIATE *vb* paint with minium
MINIATED > MINIATE
MINIATES > MINIATE
MINIATING > MINIATE
MINIATION > MINIATE
MINIATURE *n* small portrait, model, or copy ▷ *adj* small-scale ▷ *vb* reproduce in miniature
MINIBAR *n* selection of drinks and confectionery provided in a hotel room
MINIBARS > MINIBAR
MINIBIKE *n* light motorcycle
MINIBIKER > MINIBIKE
MINIBIKES > MINIBIKE
MINIBREAK *n* short holid[a]
MINIBUS *n* small bus
MINIBUSES > MINIBUS
MINICAB *n* ordinary car used as a taxi
MINICABS > MINICAB
MINICAM *n* portable television camera
MINICAMP *n* period spent together in isolation by sports team
MINICAMPS > MINICAMP
MINICAMS > MINICAM
MINICAR *n* small car
MINICARS > MINICAR
MINICOM *n* device used by deaf and hard-of-hearing people, allowing typed telephone messages to b[e] sent and received
MINICOMS > MINICOM
MINIDISC *n* small recordable compact disc
MINIDISCS > MINIDISC
MINIDISH *n* small parabolic aerial for reception or transmissio[n] to a communications satellite
MINIDISK *same as* > MINIDISC
MINIDISKS > MINIDISK
MINIDRESS *n* very short dress, at least four inches above the knee
MINIER > MINY
MINIEST > MINY
MINIFIED > MINIFY
MINIFIES > MINIFY
MINIFY *vb* minimize or lessen the size or importance of (something)
MINIFYING > MINIFY
MINIKIN *n* small, dainty, or affected person or thi[ng] ▷ *adj* dainty, prim, or affected
MINIKINS > MINIKIN
MINILAB *n* equipment fo[r] processing photographi[c] film
MINILABS > MINILAB
MINIM *n* note half the length of a semibreve ▷ [adj] very small
MINIMA > MINIMUM
MINIMAL *adj* minimum ▷ [n] small surfboard
MINIMALLY > MINIMAL
MINIMALS > MINIMAL
MINIMAX *n* lowest of a set of maximum values ▷ *vb* make maximum as low a[s]

ossible
NIMAXED > MINIMAX
NIMAXES > MINIMAX
NIMENT *same*
S > MUNIMENT
NIMENTS > MINIMENT
NIMILL *n* small mill
NIMILLS > MINIMILL
NIMISE *same*
S > MINIMIZE
NIMISED > MINIMISE
NIMISER > MINIMIZE
NIMISES > MINIMISE
NIMISM *n* desire to educe to minimum
NIMISMS > MINIMISM
NIMIST > MINIMISM
NIMISTS > MINIMISM
NIMIZE *vb* reduce to a ninimum
NIMIZED > MINIMIZE
NIMIZER > MINIMIZE
NIMIZES > MINIMIZE
NIMOTO *n* reduced-size eplica motorcycle used for acing
NIMOTOS > MINIMOTO
NIMS > MINIM
NIMUM *n* least possible amount or number) ▷ *adj* of, being, or showing a ninimum or minimums
NIMUMS > MINIMUM
NIMUS *adj* youngest: sometimes used after the urname of a schoolboy naving elder brothers at he same school
NIMUSES > MINIMUS
NING *n* act, process, or ndustry of extracting coal or ores from the earth
NINGS > MINING
NION *n* servile assistant ▷ *adj* dainty, pretty, or elegant
NIONS > MINION
NIPARK *n* small park
NIPARKS > MINIPARK
NIPILL *n* low-dose oral contraceptive containing progestogen only
NIPILLS > MINIPILL
NIRUGBY *n* version of ugby with fewer players
NIS > MINI
NISCULE *same*
S > MINUSCULE
NISH *vb* diminish
NISHED > MINISH
NISHES > MINISH
NISHING > MINISH
NISKI *n* short ski
NISKIRT *n* very short kirt
NISKIS > MINISKI
NISTATE *n* small ndependent state
NISTER *n* head of a overnment department ▷ *vb* attend to the needs of
NISTERS > MINISTER
NISTRY *n* profession or duties of a clergyman

MINITOWER *n* computer in small vertical cabinet
MINITRACK *n* satellite tracking system
MINIUM *n* bright red poisonous insoluble oxide of lead usually obtained as a powder by heating litharge in air
MINIUMS > MINIUM
MINIVAN *n* small van, esp one with seats in the back for carrying passengers
MINIVANS > MINIVAN
MINIVER *n* white fur, used in ceremonial costumes
MINIVERS > MINIVER
MINIVET *n* any brightly coloured tropical Asian cuckoo shrike of the genus *Pericrocotus*
MINIVETS > MINIVET
MINK *n* stoatlike animal
MINKE as in *minke whale* type of small whalebone whale or rorqual
MINKES > MINKE
MINKS > MINK
MINNEOLA *n* juicy citrus fruit that is a cross between a tangerine and a grapefruit
MINNEOLAS > MINNEOLA
MINNICK *vb* behave in fussy way
MINNICKED > MINNICK
MINNICKS > MINNICK
MINNIE *n* mother
MINNIES > MINNIE
MINNOCK *same as* > MINNICK
MINNOCKED > MINNOCK
MINNOCKS > MINNOCK
MINNOW *n* small freshwater fish
MINNOWS > MINNOW
MINNY *same as* > MINNIE
MINO *same as* > MYNAH
MINOR *adj* lesser ▷ *n* person regarded legally as a child ▷ *vb* take a minor
MINORCA *n* breed of light domestic fowl with glossy white, black, or blue plumage
MINORCAS > MINORCA
MINORED > MINOR
MINORING > MINOR
MINORITY *n* lesser number
MINORS > MINOR
MINORSHIP > MINOR
MINOS > MINO
MINOXIDIL *n* drug used to counter baldness
MINSHUKU *n* guesthouse in Japan
MINSHUKUS > MINSHUKU
MINSTER *n* cathedral or large church
MINSTERS > MINSTER
MINSTREL *n* medieval singer or musician
MINSTRELS > MINSTREL
MINT *n* plant with aromatic leaves used for seasoning and flavouring ▷ *vb* make (coins)
MINTAGE *n* process of minting
MINTAGES > MINTAGE
MINTED > MINT
MINTER > MINT
MINTERS > MINT
MINTIER > MINT
MINTIEST > MINT
MINTING > MINT
MINTS > MINT
MINTY > MINT
MINUEND *n* number from which another number is to be subtracted
MINUENDS > MINUEND
MINUET *n* stately dance
MINUETS > MINUET
MINUS *adj* indicating subtraction ▷ *n* sign (-) denoting subtraction or a number less than zero ▷ *prep* reduced by the subtraction of
MINUSCULE *adj* very small ▷ *n* lower-case letter
MINUSES > MINUS
MINUTE *n* 60th part of an hour or degree ▷ *vb* record in the minutes ▷ *adj* very small
MINUTED > MINUTE
MINUTELY *adv* in great detail ▷ *adj* occurring every minute
MINUTEMAN *n* (in the War of American Independence) colonial militiaman who promised to be ready to fight at one minute's notice
MINUTEMEN > MINUTEMAN
MINUTER > MINUTE
MINUTES *pl n* official record of the proceedings of a meeting or conference
MINUTEST > MINUTE
MINUTIA *singular noun of* > MINUTIAE
MINUTIAE *pl n* trifling or precise details
MINUTIAL > MINUTIAE
MINUTING > MINUTE
MINUTIOSE > MINUTIAE
MINX *n* bold or flirtatious girl
MINXES > MINX
MINXISH > MINX
MINY *adj* of or like mines
MINYAN *n* number of persons required by Jewish law to be present for a religious service, namely, at least ten males over thirteen years of age
MINYANIM > MINYAN
MINYANS > MINYAN
MIOCENE *adj* of, denoting, or formed in the fourth epoch of the Tertiary period, between the Oligocene and Pliocene epochs, which lasted for 19 million years
MIOMBO *n* (in E Africa) a dry wooded area with sparse deciduous growth
MIOMBOS > MIOMBO
MIOSES > MIOSIS
MIOSIS *n* excessive contraction of the pupil of the eye, as in response to drugs
MIOTIC > MIOSIS
MIOTICS > MIOSIS
MIPS *n* million instructions per second: a unit used to express the speed of a computer's central processing unit
MIQUELET *n* type of lock on old firearm
MIQUELETS > MIQUELET
MIR *n* peasant commune in prerevolutionary Russia
MIRABELLE *n* small sweet yellow-orange fruit that is a variety of greengage
MIRABILIA *n* wonders
MIRABILIS *n* tropical American plant
MIRABLE *adj* wonderful
MIRACIDIA *n* plural form of singular miracidium: flat ciliated larva of flukes that hatches from the egg and gives rise asexually to other larval forms
MIRACLE *n* wonderful supernatural event
MIRACLES > MIRACLE
MIRADOR *n* window, balcony, or turret
MIRADORS > MIRADOR
MIRAGE *n* optical illusion, esp one caused by hot air
MIRAGES > MIRAGE
MIRANDIZE *vb* (in USA) inform arrested person of rights
MIRBANE *n* substance used in perfumes
MIRBANES > MIRBANE
MIRCHI *Indian English word for* > HOT
MIRE *n* swampy ground ▷ *vb* sink or be stuck in a mire
MIRED > MIRE
MIREPOIX *n* mixture of sautéed root vegetables used as a base for braising meat or for various sauces
MIRES > MIRE
MIREX *n* type of insecticide
MIREXES > MIREX
MIRI > MIR
MIRIER > MIRE
MIRIEST > MIRE
MIRIFIC *adj* achieving wonderful things
MIRIFICAL *same as* > MIRIFIC
MIRIN *n* Japanese rice wine
MIRINESS > MIRE
MIRING > MIRE
MIRINS > MIRIN

MIRITI *n* South American palm
MIRITIS > MIRITI
MIRK *same as* > MURK
MIRKER > MIRK
MIRKEST > MIRK
MIRKIER > MIRK
MIRKIEST > MURKY
MIRKILY > MIRK
MIRKINESS > MIRK
MIRKS > MIRK
MIRKY > MIRK
MIRLIER > MIRLY
MIRLIEST > MIRLY
MIRLIGOES *n* dizzy feeling
MIRLITON *another name (chiefly US) for* > CHAYOTE
MIRLITONS > MIRLITON
MIRLY *same as* > MARLY
MIRO *n* tall New Zealand tree
MIROMIRO *n* small New Zealand bird
MIRROR *n* coated glass surface for reflecting images ▷ *vb* reflect in or as if in a mirror
MIRRORED > MIRROR
MIRRORING > MIRROR
MIRRORS > MIRROR
MIRS > MIR
MIRTH *n* laughter, merriment, or gaiety
MIRTHFUL > MIRTH
MIRTHLESS > MIRTH
MIRTHS > MIRTH
MIRV *n* missile that has several warheads, each one being directed to different enemy targets ▷ *vb* arm with mirvs
MIRVED > MIRV
MIRVING > MIRV
MIRVS > MIRV
MIRY > MIRE
MIRZA *n* title of respect placed before the surname of an official, scholar, or other distinguished man
MIRZAS > MIRZA
MIS > MI
MISACT *vb* act wrongly
MISACTED > MISACT
MISACTING > MISACT
MISACTS > MISACT
MISADAPT *vb* adapt badly
MISADAPTS > MISADAPT
MISADD *vb* add badly
MISADDED > MISADD
MISADDING > MISADD
MISADDS > MISADD
MISADJUST *vb* adjust wrongly
MISADVICE *n* bad advice
MISADVISE *vb* give bad advice to
MISAGENT *n* bad agent
MISAGENTS > MISAGENT
MISAIM *vb* aim badly
MISAIMED > MISAIM
MISAIMING > MISAIM
MISAIMS > MISAIM
MISALIGN *vb* align badly
MISALIGNS > MISALIGN
MISALLEGE *vb* allege wrongly
MISALLIED > MISALLY
MISALLIES > MISALLY
MISALLOT *vb* allot wrongly
MISALLOTS > MISALLOT
MISALLY *vb* form unsuitable alliance
MISALTER *vb* alter wrongly
MISALTERS > MISALTER
MISANDRY *n* hatred of men
MISAPPLY *vb* use something for a purpose for which it is not intended or is not suited
MISARRAY *n* disarray
MISARRAYS > MISARRAY
MISASSAY *vb* assay wrongly
MISASSAYS > MISASSAY
MISASSIGN *vb* assign wrongly
MISATE > MISEAT
MISATONE *vb* atone wrongly
MISATONED > MISATONE
MISATONES > MISATONE
MISAUNTER *n* misadventure
MISAVER *vb* claim wrongly
MISAVERS > MISAVER
MISAVISED *adj* badly advised
MISAWARD *vb* award wrongly
MISAWARDS > MISAWARD
MISBECAME > MISBECOME
MISBECOME *vb* be unbecoming to or unsuitable for
MISBEGAN > MISBEGIN
MISBEGIN *vb* begin badly
MISBEGINS > MISBEGIN
MISBEGOT *adj* illegitimate
MISBEGUN > MISBEGIN
MISBEHAVE *vb* behave badly
MISBELIEF *n* false or unorthodox belief
MISBESEEM *vb* be unsuitable for
MISBESTOW *vb* bestow wrongly
MISBIAS *vb* prejudice wrongly
MISBIASED > MISBIAS
MISBIASES > MISBIAS
MISBILL *vb* present inaccurate bill
MISBILLED > MISBILL
MISBILLS > MISBILL
MISBIND *vb* bind wrongly
MISBINDS > MISBIND
MISBIRTH *n* abortion
MISBIRTHS > MISBIRTH
MISBORN *adj* abortive
MISBOUND > MISBIND
MISBRAND *vb* put misleading label on
MISBRANDS > MISBRAND
MISBUILD *vb* build badly
MISBUILDS > MISBUILD
MISBUILT > MISBUILD
MISBUTTON *vb* button wrongly
MISCALL *vb* call by the wrong name
MISCALLED > MISCALL
MISCALLER > MISCALL
MISCALLS > MISCALL
MISCARRY *vb* have a miscarriage
MISCAST *vb* cast (a role or actor) in (a play or film) inappropriately
MISCASTS > MISCAST
MISCEGEN *n* person of mixed race
MISCEGENE *same as* > MISCEGEN
MISCEGENS > MISCEGEN
MISCEGINE *same as* > MISCEGEN
MISCH as in *misch metal* alloy of cerium and other rare earth metals, used esp as a flint in cigarette lighters
MISCHANCE *n* unlucky event
MISCHANCY *adj* unlucky
MISCHARGE *vb* charge wrongly
MISCHIEF *n* annoying but not malicious behaviour
MISCHIEFS > MISCHIEF
MISCHOICE *n* bad choice
MISCHOOSE *vb* make bad choice
MISCHOSE > MISCHOOSE
MISCHOSEN > MISCHOOSE
MISCIBLE *adj* able to be mixed
MISCITE *vb* cite wrongly
MISCITED > MISCITE
MISCITES > MISCITE
MISCITING > MISCITE
MISCLAIM *vb* claim wrongly
MISCLAIMS > MISCLAIM
MISCLASS *adj* class badly
MISCODE *vb* code wrongly
MISCODED > MISCODE
MISCODES > MISCODE
MISCODING > MISCODE
MISCOIN *vb* coin wrongly
MISCOINED > MISCOIN
MISCOINS > MISCOIN
MISCOLOR *same as* > MISCOLOUR
MISCOLORS > MISCOLOR
MISCOLOUR *vb* give wrong colour to
MISCOOK *vb* cook badly
MISCOOKED > MISCOOK
MISCOOKS > MISCOOK
MISCOPIED > MISCOPY
MISCOPIES > MISCOPY
MISCOPY *vb* copy badly
MISCOUNT *vb* count or calculate incorrectly ▷ *n* false count or calculation
MISCOUNTS > MISCOUNT
MISCREANT *n* wrongdoer ▷ *adj* evil or villainous
MISCREATE *vb* create (something) badly or incorrectly ▷ *adj* badly or unnaturally formed or made
MISCREDIT *vb* disbelieve
MISCREED *n* false creed
MISCREEDS > MISCREED
MISCUE *n* faulty stroke in which the cue tip slips off the cue ball or misses it altogether ▷ *vb* make a miscue
MISCUED > MISCUE
MISCUEING > MISCUE
MISCUES > MISCUE
MISCUING > MISCUE
MISCUT *n* cut wrongly
MISCUTS > MISCUT
MISDATE *vb* date (a letter, event, etc) wrongly
MISDATED > MISDATE
MISDATES > MISDATE
MISDATING > MISDATE
MISDEAL *vb* deal out cards incorrectly ▷ *n* faulty de
MISDEALER > MISDEAL
MISDEALS > MISDEAL
MISDEALT > MISDEAL
MISDEED *n* wrongful act
MISDEEDS > MISDEED
MISDEEM *vb* form bad opinion of
MISDEEMED > MISDEEM
MISDEEMS > MISDEEM
MISDEFINE *vb* define bad
MISDEMEAN *rare word for* > MISBEHAVE
MISDEMPT > MISDEEM
MISDESERT *n* quality of being undeserving
MISDIAL *vb* dial telephon number incorrectly
MISDIALED > MISDIAL
MISDIALS > MISDIAL
MISDID > MISDO
MISDIET *n* wrong diet
MISDIETS > MISDIET
MISDIGHT *adj* done badly
MISDIRECT *vb* give (someone) wrong directions or instruction
MISDIVIDE *vb* divide wrongly
MISDO *vb* do badly or wrongly
MISDOER > MISDO
MISDOERS > MISDO
MISDOES > MISDO
MISDOING > MISDO
MISDOINGS > MISDO
MISDONE *adj* done badly
MISDONNE *same as* > MISDONE
MISDOUBT *archaic word for* > DOUBT
MISDOUBTS > MISDOUBT
MISDRAW *vb* draw poorly
MISDRAWN > MISDRAW
MISDRAWS > MISDRAW
MISDREAD *n* fear of approaching evil
MISDREADS > MISDREAD
MISDREW > MISDRAW
MISDRIVE *vb* drive badly
MISDRIVEN > MISDRIVE
MISDRIVES > MISDRIVE

:SDROVE > MISDRIVE
:SE *n* issue in the obsolete writ of right
'SEASE *n* unease
:SEASES > MISEASE
SEAT *vb* eat unhealthy ood
SEATEN > MISEAT
:SEATING > MISEAT
'SEATS > MISEAT
:SEDIT *vb* edit badly
SEDITED > MISEDIT
SEDITS > MISEDIT
SEMPLOY *vb* employ badly
'SENROL *vb* enrol wrongly
SENROLL *same*
ɪs > MISENROL
:SENROLS > MISENROL
'SENTER *vb* enter wrongly
'SENTERS > MISENTER
SENTRY *n* wrong or nistaken entry
SER *n* person who hoards money and hates pending it
SERABLE *adj* very inhappy, wretched ▷ *n* wretched person
'SERABLY > MISERABLE
'SERE *n* call in solo whist and other card games declaring a hand that will vin no tricks
SERERE *n* type of psalm
SERERES > MISERERE
SERES > MISERE
SERIES > MISERY
SERLIER > MISERLY
SERLY *adj* of or esembling a miser
SERS > MISER
SERY *n* great unhappiness
SES > MISE
SESTEEM *n* lack of espect
SEVENT *n* mishap
SEVENTS > MISEVENT
SFAITH *n* distrust
SFAITHS > MISFAITH
SFALL *vb* happen as piece of bad luck
SFALLEN > MISFALL
SFALLS > MISFALL
SFALNE > MISFALL
SFARE *vb* get on badly
SFARED > MISFARE
SFARES > MISFARE
SFARING > MISFARE
SFEASOR *n* someone who carries out the improper performance of an act that is lawful in itself
SFED > MISFEED
SFEED *vb* feed wrongly
SFEEDS > MISFEED
SFEIGN *vb* feign with evil motive
SFEIGNS > MISFEIGN
SFELL > MISFALL
SFIELD *vb* fail to field properly
MISFIELDS > MISFIELD
MISFILE *vb* file (papers, records, etc) wrongly
MISFILED > MISFILE
MISFILES > MISFILE
MISFILING > MISFILE
MISFIRE *vb* (of a firearm or engine) fail to fire correctly ▷ *n* act or an instance of misfiring
MISFIRED > MISFIRE
MISFIRES > MISFIRE
MISFIRING > MISFIRE
MISFIT *n* person not suited to his or her social environment ▷ *vb* fail to fit or be fitted
MISFITS > MISFIT
MISFITTED > MISFIT
MISFOCUS *n* wrong or poor focus
MISFORM *vb* form badly
MISFORMED > MISFORM
MISFORMS > MISFORM
MISFRAME *vb* frame wrongly
MISFRAMED > MISFRAME
MISFRAMES > MISFRAME
MISGAUGE *vb* gauge badly
MISGAUGED > MISGAUGE
MISGAUGES > MISGAUGE
MISGAVE > MISGIVE
MISGIVE *vb* make or be apprehensive or suspicious
MISGIVEN > MISGIVE
MISGIVES > MISGIVE
MISGIVING *n* feeling of fear or doubt
MISGO *vb* go wrong way
MISGOES > MISGO
MISGOING > MISGO
MISGONE > MISGO
MISGOTTEN *adj* obtained dishonestly
MISGOVERN *vb* govern badly
MISGRADE *vb* grade wrongly
MISGRADED > MISGRADE
MISGRADES > MISGRADE
MISGRAFF *adj* badly done
MISGRAFT *vb* graft wrongly
MISGRAFTS > MISGRAFT
MISGREW > MISGROW
MISGROW *vb* grow in unsuitable way
MISGROWN > MISGROW
MISGROWS > MISGROW
MISGROWTH > MISGROW
MISGUESS *vb* guess wrongly
MISGUGGLE *vb* handle incompetently
MISGUIDE *vb* guide or direct wrongly or badly
MISGUIDED *adj* mistaken or unwise
MISGUIDER > MISGUIDE
MISGUIDES > MISGUIDE
MISHANDLE *vb* handle badly or inefficiently
MISHANTER *n* misfortune
MISHAP *n* minor accident ▷ *vb* happen as bad luck
MISHAPPED > MISHAP
MISHAPPEN *vb* happen as bad luck
MISHAPS > MISHAP
MISHAPT *same as* > MISSHAPEN
MISHEAR *vb* hear (what someone says) wrongly
MISHEARD > MISHEAR
MISHEARS > MISHEAR
MISHEGAAS *same as* > MESHUGAAS
MISHEGOSS *same as* > MESHUGAAS
MISHIT *n* faulty shot, kick, or stroke ▷ *vb* hit or kick a ball with a faulty stroke
MISHITS > MISHIT
MISHMASH *n* confused collection or mixture
MISHMEE *n* root of Asian plant
MISHMEES > MISHMEE
MISHMI *n* evergreen perennial plant
MISHMIS > MISHMI
MISHMOSH *same as* > MISHMASH
MISINFER *vb* infer wrongly
MISINFERS > MISINFER
MISINFORM *vb* give incorrect information to
MISINTEND *vb* intend to harm
MISINTER *vb* bury wrongly
MISINTERS > MISINTER
MISJOIN *vb* join badly
MISJOINED > MISJOIN
MISJOINS > MISJOIN
MISJUDGE *vb* judge wrongly or unfairly
MISJUDGED > MISJUDGE
MISJUDGER > MISJUDGE
MISJUDGES > MISJUDGE
MISKAL *n* unit of weight in Iran
MISKALS > MISKAL
MISKEEP *vb* keep wrongly
MISKEEPS > MISKEEP
MISKEN *vb* be unaware of
MISKENNED > MISKEN
MISKENS > MISKEN
MISKENT > MISKEN
MISKEPT > MISKEEP
MISKEY *vb* key wrongly
MISKEYED > MISKEY
MISKEYING > MISKEY
MISKEYS > MISKEY
MISKICK *vb* fail to kick properly
MISKICKED > MISKICK
MISKICKS > MISKICK
MISKNEW *vb* > MISKNOW
MISKNOW have wrong idea about
MISKNOWN > MISKNOW
MISKNOWS > MISKNOW
MISLABEL *vb* label badly
MISLABELS > MISLABEL
MISLABOR *vb* labour wrongly
MISLABORS > MISLABOR
MISLAID > MISLAY
MISLAIN > MISLAY
MISLAY *vb* lose (something) temporarily
MISLAYER > MISLAY
MISLAYERS > MISLAY
MISLAYING > MISLAY
MISLAYS > MISLAY
MISLEAD *vb* give false or confusing information to
MISLEADER > MISLEAD
MISLEADS > MISLEAD
MISLEARED *adj* badly brought up
MISLEARN *vb* learn wrongly
MISLEARNS > MISLEARN
MISLEARNT > MISLEARN
MISLED > MISLEAD
MISLEEKE *same as* > MISLIKE
MISLEEKED > MISLEEKE
MISLEEKES > MISLEEKE
MISLETOE *same as* > MISTLETOE
MISLETOES > MISLETOE
MISLIE *vb* lie wrongly
MISLIES > MISLIE
MISLIGHT *vb* use light to lead astray
MISLIGHTS > MISLIGHT
MISLIKE *vb* dislike ▷ *n* dislike or aversion
MISLIKED > MISLIKE
MISLIKER > MISLIKE
MISLIKERS > MISLIKE
MISLIKES > MISLIKE
MISLIKING > MISLIKE
MISLIPPEN *vb* distrust
MISLIT > MISLIGHT
MISLIVE *vb* live wickedly
MISLIVED > MISLIVE
MISLIVES > MISLIVE
MISLIVING > MISLIVE
MISLOCATE *vb* put in wrong place
MISLODGE *vb* lodge wrongly
MISLODGED > MISLODGE
MISLODGES > MISLODGE
MISLUCK *vb* have bad luck
MISLUCKED > MISLUCK
MISLUCKS > MISLUCK
MISLYING > MISLIE
MISMADE > MISMAKE
MISMAKE *vb* make badly
MISMAKES > MISMAKE
MISMAKING > MISMAKE
MISMANAGE *vb* organize or run (something) badly
MISMARK *vb* mark wrongly
MISMARKED > MISMARK
MISMARKS > MISMARK
MISMARRY *vb* make unsuitable marriage
MISMATCH *vb* form an unsuitable partner, opponent, or set ▷ *n* unsuitable match
MISMATE *vb* mate wrongly
MISMATED > MISMATE
MISMATES > MISMATE
MISMATING > MISMATE
MISMEET *vb* fail to meet
MISMEETS > MISMEET
MISMET > MISMEET

MISMETRE *vb* fail to follow metre of poem
MISMETRED > MISMETRE
MISMETRES > MISMETRE
MISMOVE *vb* move badly
MISMOVED > MISMOVE
MISMOVES > MISMOVE
MISMOVING > MISMOVE
MISNAME *vb* name badly
MISNAMED > MISNAME
MISNAMES > MISNAME
MISNAMING > MISNAME
MISNOMER *n* incorrect or unsuitable name ▷ *vb* apply misnomer to
MISNOMERS > MISNOMER
MISNUMBER *vb* number wrongly
MISO *n* thick brown salty paste made from soya beans, used to flavour savoury dishes, esp soups
MISOCLERE *adj* hostile to clergy
MISOGAMIC > MISOGAMY
MISOGAMY *n* hatred of marriage
MISOGYNIC > MISOGYNY
MISOGYNY *n* hatred of women
MISOLOGY *n* hatred of reasoning or reasoned argument
MISONEISM *n* hatred of anything new
MISONEIST > MISONEISM
MISORDER *vb* order badly
MISORDERS > MISORDER
MISORIENT *vb* orient incorrectly
MISOS > MISO
MISPAGE *vb* page wrongly
MISPAGED > MISPAGE
MISPAGES > MISPAGE
MISPAGING > MISPAGE
MISPAINT *vb* paint badly or wrongly
MISPAINTS > MISPAINT
MISPARSE *vb* parse wrongly
MISPARSED > MISPARSE
MISPARSES > MISPARSE
MISPART *vb* part wrongly
MISPARTED > MISPART
MISPARTS > MISPART
MISPATCH *vb* patch wrongly
MISPEN *vb* write wrongly
MISPENNED > MISPEN
MISPENS > MISPEN
MISPHRASE *vb* phrase badly
MISPICKEL *n* white or grey metallic mineral consisting of a sulphide of iron and arsenic that forms monoclinic crystals with an orthorhombic shape: an ore of arsenic
MISPLACE *vb* mislay
MISPLACED *adj* (of an emotion or action) directed towards a person or thing that does not deserve it
MISPLACES > MISPLACE
MISPLAN *vb* plan badly or wrongly
MISPLANS > MISPLAN
MISPLANT *vb* plant badly or wrongly
MISPLANTS > MISPLANT
MISPLAY *vb* play badly or wrongly in games or sports ▷ *n* wrong or unskilful play
MISPLAYED > MISPLAY
MISPLAYS > MISPLAY
MISPLEAD *vb* plead incorrectly
MISPLEADS > MISPLEAD
MISPLEASE *vb* displease
MISPLED > MISPLEAD
MISPOINT *vb* punctuate badly
MISPOINTS > MISPOINT
MISPOISE *n* lack of poise ▷ *vb* lack poise
MISPOISED > MISPOISE
MISPOISES > MISPOISE
MISPRAISE *vb* fail to praise properly
MISPRICE *vb* give wrong price to
MISPRICED > MISPRICE
MISPRICES > MISPRICE
MISPRINT *n* printing error ▷ *vb* print a letter incorrectly
MISPRINTS > MISPRINT
MISPRISE *same as* > MISPRIZE
MISPRISED > MISPRISE
MISPRISER > MISPRISE
MISPRISES > MISPRISE
MISPRIZE *vb* fail to appreciate the value of
MISPRIZED > MISPRIZE
MISPRIZER > MISPRIZE
MISPRIZES > MISPRIZE
MISPROUD *adj* undeservedly proud
MISQUOTE *vb* quote inaccurately
MISQUOTED > MISQUOTE
MISQUOTER > MISQUOTE
MISQUOTES > MISQUOTE
MISRAISE *vb* raise wrongly or excessively
MISRAISED > MISRAISE
MISRAISES > MISRAISE
MISRATE *vb* rate wrongly
MISRATED > MISRATE
MISRATES > MISRATE
MISRATING > MISRATE
MISREAD *vb* misinterpret (a situation etc)
MISREADS > MISREAD
MISRECKON *vb* reckon wrongly
MISRECORD *vb* record wrongly
MISREFER *vb* refer wrongly
MISREFERS > MISREFER
MISREGARD *n* lack of attention
MISRELATE *vb* relate badly
MISRELIED > MISRELY
MISRELIES > MISRELY
MISRELY *vb* rely wrongly
MISRENDER *vb* render wrongly
MISREPORT *vb* report falsely or inaccurately ▷ *n* inaccurate or false report
MISRHYMED *adj* badly rhymed
MISROUTE *vb* send wrong way
MISROUTED > MISROUTE
MISROUTES > MISROUTE
MISRULE *vb* govern inefficiently or unjustly ▷ *n* inefficient or unjust government
MISRULED > MISRULE
MISRULES > MISRULE
MISRULING > MISRULE
MISS *vb* fail to notice, hear, hit, reach, find, or catch ▷ *n* fact or instance of missing
MISSA *n* Roman Catholic mass
MISSABLE > MISS
MISSAE > MISSA
MISSAID > MISSAY
MISSAL *n* book containing the prayers and rites of the Mass
MISSALS > MISSAL
MISSAW > MISSEE
MISSAY *vb* say wrongly
MISSAYING > MISSAY
MISSAYS > MISSAY
MISSEAT *vb* seat wrongly
MISSEATED > MISSEAT
MISSEATS > MISSEAT
MISSED > MISS
MISSEE *vb* see wrongly
MISSEEING > MISSEE
MISSEEM *vb* be unsuitable for
MISSEEMED > MISSEEM
MISSEEMS > MISSEEM
MISSEEN > MISSEE
MISSEES > MISSEE
MISSEL as in *missel thrush* large European thrush with a brown back and spotted breast, noted for feeding on mistletoe berries
MISSELS > MISSEL
MISSEND *vb* send wrongly
MISSENDS > MISSEND
MISSENSE *n* type of genetic mutation
MISSENSES > MISSENSE
MISSENT > MISSEND
MISSES > MISS
MISSET *vb* set wrongly
MISSETS > MISSET
MISSHAPE *vb* shape badly ▷ *n* something that is badly shaped
MISSHAPED > MISSHAPE
MISSHAPEN *adj* badly shaped, deformed
MISSHAPER > MISSHAPE
MISSHAPES > MISSHAPE
MISSHOD *adj* badly shod
MISSHOOD *n* state of being unmarried woman
MISSHOODS > MISSHOOD
MISSIER > MISSY
MISSIES > MISSY
MISSIEST > MISSY
MISSILE *n* rocket with an exploding warhead, used as a weapon
MISSILEER *n* serviceman or servicewoman who is responsible for firing missiles
MISSILERY *n* missiles collectively
MISSILES > MISSILE
MISSILRY *same as* > MISSILERY
MISSING *adj* lost or absent
MISSINGLY > MISSING
MISSION *n* specific task or duty ▷ *vb* direct a mission to or establish a mission in (a given region)
MISSIONAL *adj* emphasizing preaching of gospel
MISSIONED > MISSION
MISSIONER *n* person heading a parochial mission in a Christian country
MISSIONS > MISSION
MISSIS *same as* > MISSUS
MISSISES > MISSIS
MISSISH *adj* like schoolgirl
MISSIVE *n* letter ▷ *adj* sent or intended to be sent
MISSIVES > MISSIVE
MISSORT *vb* sort wrongly
MISSORTED > MISSORT
MISSORTS > MISSORT
MISSOUND *vb* sound wrongly
MISSOUNDS > MISSOUND
MISSOUT *n* someone who has been overlooked
MISSOUTS > MISSOUT
MISSPACE *vb* space out wrongly
MISSPACED > MISSPACE
MISSPACES > MISSPACE
MISSPEAK *vb* speak wrongly
MISSPEAKS > MISSPEAK
MISSPELL *vb* spell (a word) wrongly
MISSPELLS > MISSPELL
MISSPELT > MISSPELL
MISSPEND *vb* waste or spend unwisely
MISSPENDS > MISSPEND
MISSPENT > MISSPEND
MISSPOKE > MISSPEAK
MISSPOKEN > MISSPEAK
MISSTAMP *vb* stamp badly
MISSTAMPS > MISSTAMP
MISSTART *vb* start wrongly
MISSTARTS > MISSTART
MISSTATE *vb* state incorrectly
MISSTATED > MISSTATE
MISSTATES > MISSTATE
MISSTEER *vb* steer badly
MISSTEERS > MISSTEER

:SSTEP *n* false step ▷ *vb* ake false step
:SSTEPS > MISSTEP
SSTOP *vb* stop wrongly
:SSTOPS > MISSTOP
SSTRIKE *vb* fail to strike roperly
.SSTRUCK > MISSTRIKE
:SSTYLE *vb* call by wrong ame
'SSTYLED > MISSTYLE
.SSTYLES > MISSTYLE
:SSUIT *vb* be unsuitable or
'SSUITED > MISSUIT
.SSUITS > MISSUIT
:SSUS *n* one's wife or he wife of the person ddressed or referred to
.SSUSES > MISSUS
'SSY *n* affectionate or disparaging form of ddress to a girl ▷ *adj* nissish
'ST *n* thin fog ▷ *vb* cover or be covered with mist
:STAKE *n* error or blunder ▷ *vb* misunderstand
'STAKEN *adj* wrong in udgment or opinion
:STAKER > MISTAKE
STAKERS > MISTAKE
'STAKES > MISTAKE
STAKING > MISTAKE
STAL *n* cow shed
STALS > MISTAL
STAUGHT > MISTEACH
STBOW *same as* > FOGBOW
STBOWS > MISTBOW
STEACH *vb* teach badly
'STED > MIST
STELL *vb* tell wrongly
'STELLS > MISTELL
STEMPER *vb* make disordered
STEND *vb* tend wrongly
'STENDED > MISTEND
STENDS > MISTEND
STER *n* informal form of ddress for a man ▷ *vb* call someone) mister
STERED > MISTER
STERIES > MISTERY
STERING > MISTER
STERM *vb* term badly
STERMED > MISTERM
'STERMS > MISTERM
STERS > MISTER
'STERY *same as* > MYSTERY
STEUK *Scots variant* of > MISTOOK
STFUL > MIST
'STHINK *vb* have poor opinion of
STHINKS > MISTHINK
STHREW > MISTHROW
STHROW *vb* fail to throw properly
STHROWN > MISTHROW
STHROWS > MISTHROW
STICO *n* small Mediterranean sailing hip
STICOS > MISTICO
MISTIER > MISTY
MISTIEST > MISTY
MISTIGRIS *n* joker or a blank card used as a wild card in a variety of draw poker
MISTILY > MISTY
MISTIME *vb* do (something) at the wrong time
MISTIMED > MISTIME
MISTIMES > MISTIME
MISTIMING > MISTIME
MISTINESS > MISTY
MISTING *n* application of a fake suntan by spray
MISTINGS > MISTING
MISTITLE *vb* name badly
MISTITLED > MISTITLE
MISTITLES > MISTITLE
MISTLE *same as* > MIZZLE
MISTLED > MISTLE
MISTLES > MISTLE
MISTLETOE *n* evergreen plant with white berries growing as a parasite on trees
MISTLING > MISTLE
MISTOLD > MISTELL
MISTOOK *past tense of* > MISTAKE
MISTOUCH *vb* fail to touch properly
MISTRACE *vb* trace wrongly
MISTRACED > MISTRACE
MISTRACES > MISTRACE
MISTRAIN *vb* train wrongly
MISTRAINS > MISTRAIN
MISTRAL *n* strong dry northerly wind of S France
MISTRALS > MISTRAL
MISTREAT *vb* treat (a person or animal) badly
MISTREATS > MISTREAT
MISTRESS *n* woman who has a continuing sexual relationship with a married man ▷ *vb* make into mistress
MISTRIAL *n* trial made void because of some error
MISTRIALS > MISTRIAL
MISTRUST *vb* have doubts or suspicions about ▷ *n* lack of trust
MISTRUSTS > MISTRUST
MISTRUTH *n* something untrue
MISTRUTHS > MISTRUTH
MISTRYST *vb* fail to keep appointment with
MISTRYSTS > MISTRYST
MISTS > MIST
MISTUNE *vb* fail to tune properly
MISTUNED > MISTUNE
MISTUNES > MISTUNE
MISTUNING > MISTUNE
MISTUTOR *vb* instruct badly
MISTUTORS > MISTUTOR
MISTY *adj* full of mist
MISTYPE *vb* type badly
MISTYPED > MISTYPE
MISTYPES > MISTYPE
MISTYPING > MISTYPE
MISUNION *n* wrong or bad union
MISUNIONS > MISUNION
MISUSAGE > MISUSE
MISUSAGES > MISUSE
MISUSE *n* incorrect, improper, or careless use ▷ *vb* use wrongly
MISUSED > MISUSE
MISUSER *n* abuse of some right, privilege, office, etc, such as one that may lead to its forfeiture
MISUSERS > MISUSER
MISUSES > MISUSE
MISUSING > MISUSE
MISUST > MISUSE
MISVALUE *vb* value badly
MISVALUED > MISVALUE
MISVALUES > MISVALUE
MISWEEN *vb* assess wrongly
MISWEENED > MISWEEN
MISWEENS > MISWEEN
MISWEND *vb* become lost
MISWENDS > MISWEND
MISWENT > MISWEND
MISWORD *vb* word badly
MISWORDED > MISWORD
MISWORDS > MISWORD
MISWRIT > MISWRITE
MISWRITE *vb* write badly
MISWRITES > MISWRITE
MISWROTE > MISWRITE
MISYOKE *vb* join wrongly
MISYOKED > MISYOKE
MISYOKES > MISYOKE
MISYOKING > MISYOKE
MITCH *vb* play truant from school
MITCHED > MITCH
MITCHES > MITCH
MITCHING > MITCH
MITE *n* very small spider-like animal
MITER *same as* > MITRE
MITERED > MITER
MITERER > MITER
MITERERS > MITER
MITERING > MITER
MITERS > MITER
MITERWORT *same as* > MITREWORT
MITES > MITE
MITHER *vb* fuss over or moan about something
MITHERED > MITHER
MITHERING > MITHER
MITHERS > MITHER
MITICIDAL > MITICIDE
MITICIDE *n* any drug or agent that destroys mites
MITICIDES > MITICIDE
MITIER > MITY
MITIEST > MITY
MITIGABLE > MITIGATE
MITIGANT *adj* acting to mitigate
MITIGATE *vb* make less severe
MITIGATED > MITIGATE
MITIGATES > MITIGATE
MITIGATOR > MITIGATE
MITIS *n* malleable iron, fluid enough for casting, made by adding a small amount of aluminium to wrought iron
MITISES > MITIS
MITOGEN *n* any agent that induces mitosis
MITOGENIC > MITOGEN
MITOGENS > MITOGEN
MITOMYCIN *n*
MITOSES > MITOSIS
MITOSIS *n* type of cell division in which the nucleus divides into two nuclei which each contain the same number of chromosomes as the original nucleus
MITOTIC > MITOSIS
MITRAILLE *n* hail of bullets
MITRAL *adj* of or like a mitre
MITRE *n* bishop's pointed headdress ▷ *vb* join with a mitre joint
MITRED > MITRE
MITRES > MITRE
MITREWORT *n* any of several Asian and North American saxifragaceous plants of the genus *Mitella*, having clusters of small white flowers and capsules resembling a bishop's mitre
MITRIFORM *adj* shaped like mitre
MITRING > MITRE
MITSVAH *same as* > MITZVAH
MITSVAHS > MITSVAH
MITSVOTH > MITSVAH
MITT *same as* > MITTEN
MITTEN *n* glove with one section for the thumb and one for the four fingers together
MITTENED *adj* wearing mittens
MITTENS > MITTEN
MITTIMUS *n* warrant of commitment to prison or a command to a jailer directing him to hold someone in prison
MITTS > MITT
MITUMBA *n* used clothes imported for sale in African countries
MITUMBAS > MITUMBA
MITY *adj* having mites
MITZVAH *n* commandment or precept, esp one found in the Bible
MITZVAHS > MITZVAH
MITZVOTH > MITZVAH
MIURUS *n* type of rhythm in poetry
MIURUSES > MIURUS
MIX *vb* combine or blend into one mass ▷ *n* mixture
MIXABLE > MIX
MIXDOWN *n* (in sound recording) the transfer of a multitrack master mix to two-track stereo tape

MIXDOWNS > MIXDOWN
MIXED *adj* formed or blended together by mixing
MIXEDLY > MIXED
MIXEDNESS > MIXED
MIXEN *n* dunghill
MIXENS > MIXEN
MIXER *n* kitchen appliance used for mixing foods
MIXERS > MIXER
MIXES > MIX
MIXIBLE > MIX
MIXIER > MIX
MIXIEST > MIX
MIXING > MIX
MIXMASTER *n* disc jockey
MIXOLOGY *n* art of mixing cocktails
MIXT > MIX
MIXTE *adj* of or denoting a type of bicycle frame, usually for women, in which angled twin lateral tubes run back to the rear axle
MIXTION *n* amber-based mixture used in making gold leaf
MIXTIONS > MIXTION
MIXTURE *n* something mixed
MIXTURES > MIXTURE
MIXUP *vb* confuse or confound ▷ *n* something that is mixed up
MIXUPS > MIXUP
MIXY *adj* mixed
MIZ *shortened form of* > MISERY
MIZEN *same as* > MIZZEN
MIZENMAST *n* (on a yawl, ketch, or dandy) the after mast
MIZENS > MIZEN
MIZMAZE *n* maze
MIZMAZES > MIZMAZE
MIZUNA *n* Japanese variety of lettuce having crisp green leaves
MIZUNAS > MIZUNA
MIZZ *same as* > MIZ
MIZZEN *n* sail set on a mizzenmast ▷ *adj* of or relating to any kind of gear used with a mizzenmast
MIZZENS > MIZZEN
MIZZES > MIZ
MIZZLE *vb* decamp
MIZZLED > MIZZLE
MIZZLES > MIZZLE
MIZZLIER > MIZZLE
MIZZLIEST > MIZZLE
MIZZLING > MIZZLE
MIZZLINGS > MIZZLE
MIZZLY > MIZZLE
MIZZONITE *n* mineral containing sodium
MIZZY as in *mizzy maze* dialect expression meaning state of confusion
MM *interj* expression of enjoyment of taste or smell
MNA *same as* > MINA
MNAS > MNA
MNEME *n* ability to retain memory
MNEMES > MNEME
MNEMIC > MNEME
MNEMON *n* unit of memory
MNEMONIC *adj* intended to help the memory ▷ *n* something, for instance a verse, intended to help the memory
MNEMONICS *n* art or practice of improving or of aiding the memory
MNEMONIST > MNEMONICS
MNEMONS > MNEMON
MO *n* moment
MOA *n* large extinct flightless New Zealand bird
MOAI *n* any of the gigantic carved stone figures found on Easter Island (Rapa Nui)
MOAN *n* low cry of pain ▷ *vb* make or utter with a moan
MOANED > MOAN
MOANER > MOAN
MOANERS > MOAN
MOANFUL > MOAN
MOANFULLY > MOAN
MOANING > MOAN
MOANINGLY > MOAN
MOANS > MOAN
MOAS > MOA
MOAT *n* deep wide ditch, esp round a castle ▷ *vb* surround with or as if with a moat
MOATED > MOAT
MOATING > MOAT
MOATLIKE > MOAT
MOATS > MOAT
MOB *n* disorderly crowd ▷ *vb* surround in a mob to acclaim or attack
MOBBED > MOB
MOBBER > MOB
MOBBERS > MOB
MOBBIE *same as* > MOBBY
MOBBIES > MOBBY
MOBBING > MOB
MOBBINGS > MOB
MOBBISH > MOB
MOBBISHLY > MOB
MOBBISM *n* behaviour as mob
MOBBISMS > MOBBISM
MOBBLE *same as* > MOBLE
MOBBLED > MOBBLE
MOBBLES > MOBBLE
MOBBLING > MOBBLE
MOBBY *n* West Indian drink
MOBCAP *n* woman's 18th-century cotton cap with a pouched crown
MOBCAPS > MOBCAP
MOBE *n* mobile phone
MOBES > MOBE
MOBIE *n* mobile phone
MOBIES > MOBY
MOBILE *adj* able to move ▷ *n* hanging structure designed to move in air currents
MOBILES > MOBILE
MOBILISE *same as* > MOBILIZE
MOBILISED > MOBILISE
MOBILISER > MOBILISE
MOBILISES > MOBILISE
MOBILITY *n* ability to move physically
MOBILIZE *vb* (of the armed services) prepare for active service
MOBILIZED > MOBILIZE
MOBILIZER > MOBILIZE
MOBILIZES > MOBILIZE
MOBLE *vb* muffle
MOBLED > MOBLE
MOBLES > MOBLE
MOBLING > MOBLE
MOBLOG *n* chronicle, which may be shared with others, of someone's thoughts and experiences recorded in the form of mobile phone calls, text messages, and photographs
MOBLOGGER > MOBLOG
MOBLOGS > MOBLOG
MOBOCRACY *n* rule or domination by a mob
MOBOCRAT > MOBOCRACY
MOBOCRATS > MOBOCRACY
MOBS > MOB
MOBSMAN *n* person in mob
MOBSMEN > MOBSMAN
MOBSTER *n* member of a criminal organization
MOBSTERS > MOBSTER
MOBY *n* mobile phone
MOC *shortening of* > MOCCASIN
MOCASSIN *same as* > MOCCASIN
MOCASSINS > MOCASSIN
MOCCASIN *n* soft leather shoe
MOCCASINS > MOCCASIN
MOCCIES *pl n* informal Australian word for moccasins
MOCH *n* spell of humid weather
MOCHA *n* kind of strong dark coffee
MOCHAS > MOCHA
MOCHELL *same as* > MUCH
MOCHELLS > MOCHELL
MOCHIE *adj* damp or humid
MOCHIER > MOCHIE
MOCHIEST > MOCHIE
MOCHILA *n* South American shoulder bag
MOCHILAS > MOCHILA
MOCHINESS > MOCHIE
MOCHS > MOCH
MOCHY *same as* > MOCHIE
MOCK *vb* make fun of ▷ *adj* sham or imitation ▷ *n* act of mocking
MOCKABLE > MOCK
MOCKADO *n* imitation velvet
MOCKADOES > MOCKADO
MOCKAGE *same as* > MOCKERY
MOCKAGES > MOCKAGE
MOCKED > MOCK
MOCKER > MOCK
MOCKERIES > MOCKERY
MOCKERNUT *n* species of smooth-barked hickory, *Carya tomentosa*, with fragrant foliage that turr bright yellow in autumn
MOCKERS > MOCK
MOCKERY *n* derision
MOCKING > MOCK
MOCKINGLY > MOCK
MOCKINGS > MOCK
MOCKNEY *n* person who affects a cockney accent ▷ *adj* denoting an affect cockney accent or a pers who has one
MOCKNEYS > MOCKNEY
MOCKS > MOCK
MOCKTAIL *n* cocktail without alcohol
MOCKTAILS > MOCKTAIL
MOCKUP *n* working full-scale model of a machin apparatus, etc, for testir research, etc
MOCKUPS > MOCKUP
MOCOCK *n* Native America birchbark container
MOCOCKS > MOCOCK
MOCS > MOC
MOCUCK *same as* > MOCOCI
MOCUCKS > MOCUCK
MOCUDDUM *same as* > MUQADDAM
MOCUDDUMS > MOCUDDUM
MOD *n* member of a group young people, orig. in th mid-1960s, who were ve clothes-conscious and rode motor scooters
MODAL *adj* of or relating to mode or manner ▷ *n* modal word
MODALISM *n* type of Christian doctrine
MODALISMS > MODALISM
MODALIST > MODALISM
MODALISTS > MODALISM
MODALITY *n* condition of being modal
MODALLY > MODAL
MODALS > MODAL
MODE *n* method or manne
MODEL *n* (miniature) representation ▷ *adj* excellent or perfect ▷ *vb* make a model of
MODELED > MODEL
MODELER > MODEL
MODELERS > MODEL
MODELING *same as* > MODELLING
MODELINGS > MODELING
MODELIST *n* person who constructs models
MODELISTS > MODELIST
MODELLED > MODEL
MODELLER > MODEL
MODELLERS > MODEL
MODELLI > MODELLO

DELLING *n* act or an nstance of making a nodel
DELLO *n* artist's oreliminary sketch or nodel
DELLOS > MODELLO
DELS > MODEL
DEM *n* device for connecting two computers by a telephone ine ▷ *vb* send or receive by modem
DEMED > MODEM
DEMING > MODEM
DEMS > MODEM
DENA *n* popular variety of domestic fancy pigeon originating in Modena
DENAS > MODENA
DER *n* intermediate layer n humus
DERATE *adj* not extreme ▷ *n* person of moderate views ▷ *vb* make or become less violent or extreme
DERATED > MODERATE
DERATES > MODERATE
DERATO *adv* at a moderate speed ▷ *n* moderato piece
DERATOR *n* (Presbyterian Church) minister appointed to preside over a Church court, general assembly, etc
DERATOS > MODERATO
DERN *adj* of present or recent times ▷ *n* contemporary person
DERNE *adj* of or relating o the style of architecture and design, prevalent n Europe and the US in he late 1920s and 1930s, ypified by the use of traight lines, tubular chromed steel frames, contrasting inlaid woods, etc
DERNER > MODERN
DERNES *n* being modern
DERNEST > MODERN
DERNISE *same* s > MODERNIZE
DERNISM *n* (support of) modern tendencies, houghts, or styles
DERNIST > MODERNISM
DERNITY *n* quality or tate of being modern
DERNIZE *vb* bring up to late
DERNLY > MODERN
DERNS > MODERN
DERS > MODER
DES > MODE
DEST *adj* not vain or boastful
DESTER > MODEST
DESTEST > MODEST
DESTIES > MODESTY
DESTLY > MODEST
MODESTY *n* quality or condition of being modest
MODGE *vb* do shoddily
MODGED > MODGE
MODGES > MODGE
MODGING > MODGE
MODI > MODUS
MODICA > MODICUM
MODICUM *n* small quantity
MODICUMS > MODICUM
MODIFIED > MODIFY
MODIFIER *n* word that qualifies the sense of another
MODIFIERS > MODIFIER
MODIFIES > MODIFY
MODIFY *vb* change slightly
MODIFYING > MODIFY
MODII > MODIUS
MODILLION *n* one of a set of ornamental brackets under a cornice, esp as used in the Corinthian order
MODIOLAR > MODIOLUS
MODIOLI > MODIOLUS
MODIOLUS *n* central bony pillar of the cochlea
MODISH *adj* in fashion
MODISHLY > MODISH
MODIST *n* follower of fashion
MODISTE *n* fashionable dressmaker or milliner
MODISTES > MODISTE
MODISTS > MODIST
MODIUS *n* ancient Roman quantity measure
MODIWORT *Scots variant of* > MOULDWARP
MODIWORTS > MODIWORT
MODS > MOD
MODULAR *adj* of, consisting of, or resembling a module or modulus ▷ *n* thing comprised of modules
MODULARLY > MODULAR
MODULARS > MODULAR
MODULATE *vb* vary in tone
MODULATED > MODULATE
MODULATES > MODULATE
MODULATOR > MODULATE
MODULE *n* self-contained unit, section, or component with a specific function
MODULES > MODULE
MODULI > MODULUS
MODULO *adv* with reference to modulus
MODULUS *n* coefficient expressing a specified property, for instance elasticity, of a specified substance
MODUS *n* way of doing something
MOE *same as* > MORE
MOELLON *n* rubble
MOELLONS > MOELLON
MOER *n* in South Africa, slang word for the womb ▷ *vb* in South Africa, attack (someone or something) violently
MOERED > MOER
MOERING > MOER
MOERS > MOER
MOES > MOE
MOFETTE *n* opening in a region of nearly extinct volcanic activity, through which carbon dioxide, nitrogen, and other gases pass
MOFETTES > MOFETTE
MOFFETTE *same as* > MOFETTE
MOFFETTES > MOFFETTE
MOFFIE *n* homosexual ▷ *adj* homosexual
MOFFIES > MOFFIE
MOFO *n* offensive term, a shortened form of motherfucker
MOFOS > MOFO
MOFUSSIL *n* provincial area in India
MOFUSSILS > MOFUSSIL
MOG *vb* go away
MOGGAN *n* stocking without foot
MOGGANS > MOGGAN
MOGGED > MOG
MOGGIE *same as* > MOGGY
MOGGIES > MOGGY
MOGGING > MOG
MOGGY *n* cat
MOGHUL *same as* > MOGUL
MOGHULS > MOGHUL
MOGS > MOG
MOGUL *n* important or powerful person
MOGULED *adj* having moguls
MOGULS > MOGUL
MOHAIR *n* fine hair of the Angora goat
MOHAIRS > MOHAIR
MOHALIM *same as* > MOHELIM
MOHAWK *n* half turn from either edge of either skate to the corresponding edge of the other skate
MOHAWKS > MOHAWK
MOHEL *n* man qualified to conduct circumcisions
MOHELIM > MOHEL
MOHELS > MOHEL
MOHICAN *n* punk hairstyle
MOHICANS > MOHICAN
MOHR *same as* > MHORR
MOHRS > MOHR
MOHUA *n* small New Zealand bird with a yellow head and breast
MOHUR *n* former Indian gold coin worth 15 rupees
MOHURS > MOHUR
MOI > ME
MOIDER *same as* > MOITHER
MOIDERED > MOIDER
MOIDERING > MOIDER
MOIDERS > MOIDER
MOIDORE *n* former Portuguese gold coin
MOIDORES > MOIDORE
MOIETIES > MOIETY
MOIETY *n* half
MOIL *vb* moisten or soil or become moist, soiled, etc ▷ *n* toil
MOILED > MOIL
MOILER > MOIL
MOILERS > MOIL
MOILING > MOIL
MOILINGLY > MOIL
MOILS > MOIL
MOINEAU *n* small fortification
MOINEAUS > MOINEAU
MOIRA *n* fate
MOIRAI > MOIRA
MOIRE *adj* having a watered or wavelike pattern ▷ *n* any fabric that has such a pattern
MOIRES > MOIRE
MOISER *n* informer
MOISERS > MOISER
MOIST *adj* slightly wet ▷ *vb* moisten
MOISTED > MOIST
MOISTEN *vb* make or become moist
MOISTENED > MOISTEN
MOISTENER > MOISTEN
MOISTENS > MOISTEN
MOISTER > MOIST
MOISTEST > MOIST
MOISTFUL *adj* full of moisture
MOISTIFY *vb* moisten
MOISTING > MOIST
MOISTLY > MOIST
MOISTNESS > MOIST
MOISTS > MOIST
MOISTURE *n* liquid diffused as vapour or condensed in drops
MOISTURES > MOISTURE
MOIT *same as* > MOTE
MOITHER *vb* bother or bewilder
MOITHERED > MOITHER
MOITHERS > MOITHER
MOITS > MOIT
MOJARRA *n* tropical American sea fish
MOJARRAS > MOJARRA
MOJO *n* charm or magic spell
MOJOES > MOJO
MOJOS > MOJO
MOKADDAM *same as* > MUQADDAM
MOKADDAMS > MOKADDAM
MOKE *n* donkey
MOKES > MOKE
MOKI *n* either of two edible sea fish of New Zealand, the blue cod (*Percis colias*) or the bastard trumpeter (*Latridopsis ciliaris*)
MOKIHI *n* Māori raft
MOKIS > MOKI
MOKO *n* Māori tattoo or tattoo pattern
MOKOMOKO *n* type of skink found in New Zealand
MOKOPUNA *n* grandchild or

young person
MOKOPUNAS > MOKOPUNA
MOKORO *n* (in Botswana) the traditional dugout canoe of the people of the Okavango Delta
MOKOROS > MOKORO
MOKOS > MOKO
MOKSHA *n* freedom from the endless cycle of transmigration into a state of bliss
MOKSHAS > MOKSHA
MOL *same as* > MOLE
MOLA *another name for* > SUNFISH
MOLAL *adj* of or consisting of a solution containing one mole of solute per thousand grams of solvent
MOLALITY *n* (not in technical usage) a measure of concentration equal to the number of moles of solute in a thousand grams of solvent
MOLAR *n* large back tooth used for grinding ▷ *adj* of any of these teeth
MOLARITY *n* concentration
MOLARS > MOLAR
MOLAS > MOLA
MOLASSE *n* soft sediment produced by the erosion of mountain ranges after the final phase of mountain building
MOLASSES *n* dark syrup, a by-product of sugar refining
MOLD *same as* > MOULD
MOLDABLE > MOLD
MOLDAVITE *n* green tektite found in the Czech Republic, thought to be the product of an ancient meteorite impact in Germany
MOLDBOARD *n* curved blade of a plough
MOLDED > MOLD
MOLDER *same as* > MOULDER
MOLDERED > MOLDER
MOLDERING > MOLDER
MOLDERS > MOLDER
MOLDIER > MOLDY
MOLDIEST > MOLDY
MOLDINESS > MOLDY
MOLDING *same as* > MOULDING
MOLDINGS > MOLDING
MOLDS > MOLD
MOLDWARP *same as* > MOULDWARP
MOLDWARPS > MOLDWARP
MOLDY *same as* > MOULDY
MOLE *n* small dark raised spot on the skin
MOLECAST *n* molehill
MOLECASTS > MOLECAST
MOLECULAR *adj* of or relating to molecules
MOLECULE *n* simplest freely existing chemical unit, composed of two or more atoms
MOLECULES > MOLECULE
MOLEHILL *n* small mound of earth thrown up by a burrowing mole
MOLEHILLS > MOLEHILL
MOLEHUNT *n* hunt for moles
MOLEHUNTS > MOLEHUNT
MOLERAT *n* any burrowing molelike African rodent of the famil
MOLERATS > MOLERAT
MOLES > MOLE
MOLESKIN *n* dark grey dense velvety pelt of a mole, used as a fur
MOLESKINS *pl n* clothing of moleskin
MOLEST *vb* interfere with sexually
MOLESTED > MOLEST
MOLESTER > MOLEST
MOLESTERS > MOLEST
MOLESTFUL *adj* molesting
MOLESTING > MOLEST
MOLESTS > MOLEST
MOLIES > MOLY
MOLIMEN *n* effort needed to perform bodily function
MOLIMENS > MOLIMEN
MOLINE *adj* (of a cross) having arms of equal length, forked and curved back at the ends ▷ *n* moline cross
MOLINES > MOLINE
MOLINET *n* stick for whipping chocolate
MOLINETS > MOLINET
MOLL *n* gangster's female accomplice
MOLLA *same as* > MOLLAH
MOLLAH *same as* > MULLAH
MOLLAHS > MOLLAH
MOLLAS > MOLLA
MOLLIE *same as* > MOLLY
MOLLIES > MOLLY
MOLLIFIED > MOLLIFY
MOLLIFIER > MOLLIFY
MOLLIFIES > MOLLIFY
MOLLIFY *vb* pacify or soothe
MOLLITIES *n* softness
MOLLS > MOLL
MOLLUSC *n* soft-bodied, usu. hard-shelled, animal, such as a snail or oyster
MOLLUSCA *n* molluscs collectively
MOLLUSCAN > MOLLUSC
MOLLUSCS > MOLLUSC
MOLLUSCUM *n* viral skin infection
MOLLUSK *same as* > MOLLUSC
MOLLUSKAN > MOLLUSK
MOLLUSKS > MOLLUSK
MOLLY *n* any brightly coloured tropical or subtropical American freshwater cyprinodont fish of the genus *Mollienisia*
MOLLYHAWK *n* juvenile of the southern black-backed gull (*Larus dominicanus*)
MOLLYMAWK *informal name for* > MALLEMUCK
MOLOCH *n* spiny Australian desert-living lizard, *Moloch horridus*, that feeds on ants: family *Agamidae* (agamas)
MOLOCHISE *vb* sacrifice to deity
MOLOCHIZE *same as* > MOLOCHISE
MOLOCHS > MOLOCH
MOLOSSI > MOLOSSUS
MOLOSSUS *n* division of metre in poetry
MOLS > MOL
MOLT *same as* > MOULT
MOLTED > MOLT
MOLTEN > MELT
MOLTENLY > MELT
MOLTER > MOLT
MOLTERS > MOLT
MOLTING > MOLT
MOLTO *adv* very
MOLTS > MOLT
MOLY *n* magic herb given by Hermes to Odysseus to nullify the spells of Circe
MOLYBDATE *n* salt or ester of a molybdic acid
MOLYBDIC *adj* of or containing molybdenum in the trivalent or hexavalent state
MOLYBDOUS *adj* of or containing molybdenum, esp in a low valence state
MOM *same as* > MOTHER
MOME *n* fool
MOMENT *n* short space of time
MOMENTA > MOMENTUM
MOMENTANY *same as* > MOMENTARY
MOMENTARY *adj* lasting only a moment
MOMENTLY *same as* > MOMENT
MOMENTO *same as* > MEMENTO
MOMENTOES > MOMENTO
MOMENTOS > MOMENTO
MOMENTOUS *adj* of great significance
MOMENTS > MOMENT
MOMENTUM *n* impetus to go forward, develop, or get stronger
MOMENTUMS > MOMENTUM
MOMES > MOME
MOMI *same as* > MOM
MOMISM *n* excessive domination of a child by his or her mother
MOMISMS > MOMISM
MOMMA *same as* > MAMMA
MOMMAS > MOMMA
MOMMET *same as* > MAMMET
MOMMETS > MOMMET
MOMMIES > MOMMY
MOMMY *same as* > MOM
MOMS > MOM
MOMSER *same as* > MOMZER
MOMSERS > MOMSER
MOMUS *n* person who ridicules
MOMUSES > MOMUS
MOMZER *same as* > MAMZER
MOMZERIM > MOMZER
MOMZERS > MOMZER
MON *dialect variant of* > MAN
MONA *n* W African guenon monkey, *Cercopithecus mona*, with dark fur on the back and white or yellow underparts
MONACHAL *less common word for* > MONASTIC
MONACHISM > MONACHAL
MONACHIST > MONACHAL
MONACID *same as* > MONOACID
MONACIDIC *same as* > MONACID
MONACIDS > MONACID
MONACT *adj* (of sponge) with single-spiked structures in skeleton
MONACTINE > MONACT
MONAD *n* any fundamental singular metaphysical entity
MONADAL > MONAD
MONADES > MONAS
MONADIC *adj* being or relating to a monad
MONADICAL > MONAD
MONADISM *n* (esp in the writings of Gottfried Leibnitz, the German rationalist philosopher and mathematician (1646–1716)) the philosophical doctrine that monads are the ultimate units of reality
MONADISMS > MONADISM
MONADNOCK *n* residual hill that consists of hard rock in an otherwise eroded area
MONADS > MONAD
MONAL *n* any of several S Asian pheasants of the genus *Lophophorus*, the males of which have a brilliantly coloured plumage
MONALS > MONAL
MONANDRY *n* preference of only one male sexual partner over a period of time
MONARCH *n* sovereign ruler of a state
MONARCHAL > MONARCH
MONARCHIC > MONARCH
MONARCHS > MONARCH
MONARCHY *n* government by or a state ruled by a sovereign
MONARDA *n* any mintlike North American plant of the genus *Monarda*: family *Lamiaceae* (labiates)
MONARDAS > MONARDA
MONAS *same as* > MONAD
MONASES > MONAS

NASTERY *n* residence of a community of monks
NASTIC *adj* of monks, nuns, or monasteries ▷ *n* person who is committed to this way of life, esp a monk
NASTICS > MONASTIC
NATOMIC *adj* consisting of single atoms
NAUL *same as* > MONAL
NAULS > MONAUL
NAURAL *adj* relating to, having, or hearing with only one ear
NAXIAL *another word for* > UNIAXIAL
NAXON *n* type of sponge
NAXONIC > MONAXON
NAXONS > MONAXON
NAZITE *n* yellow to reddish-brown mineral consisting of a phosphate of thorium, cerium, and lanthanum in monoclinic crystalline form
NAZITES > MONAZITE
NDAIN *n* man who moves in fashionable society ▷ *adj* characteristic of fashionable society
NDAINE *n* woman who moves in fashionable society ▷ *adj* characteristic of fashionable society
NDAINES > MONDAINE
NDAINS > MONDAIN
NDE *n* French word meaning world or society
NDES > MONDE
NDIAL *adj* of or involving the whole world
NDO *n* Buddhist questioning technique
NDOS > MONDO
NECIAN *same as* > MONECIOUS
NECIOUS *adj* (of some flowering plants) having the male and female reproductive organs in separate flowers on the same plant
NELLIN *n* sweet protein
NELLINS > MONELLIN
NEME *less common word for* > MORPHEME
NEMES > MONEME
NER *n* hypothetical simple organism
NERA > MONER
NERAN *n* type of bacterium
NERANS > MONERAN
NERGISM *n* Christian doctrine on spiritual regeneration
NERON *same as* > MONER
NETARY *adj* of money or currency
NETH *same as* > MONTH
NETHS > MONETH
NETISE *same as* > MONETIZE
MONETISED > MONETISE
MONETISES > MONETISE
MONETIZE *vb* establish as the legal tender of a country
MONETIZED > MONETIZE
MONETIZES > MONETIZE
MONEY *n* medium of exchange, coins or banknotes
MONEYBAG *n* bag for money
MONEYBAGS *n* very rich person
MONEYED *adj* rich
MONEYER *n* person who coins money
MONEYERS > MONEYER
MONEYLESS > MONEY
MONEYMAN *n* person supplying money
MONEYMEN > MONEY
MONEYS > MONEY
MONEYWORT *n* European and North American creeping primulaceous plant, *Lysimachia nummularia*, with round leaves and yellow flowers
MONG *n* stupid or foolish person
MONGCORN *same as* > MASLIN
MONGCORNS > MONGCORN
MONGED *adj* under the influence of drugs
MONGEESE > MONGOOSE
MONGER *n* trader or dealer ▷ *vb* deal in
MONGERED > MONGER
MONGERIES > MONGER
MONGERING > MONGER
MONGERS > MONGER
MONGERY > MONGER
MONGO *same as* > MUNGO
MONGOE *same as* > MONGO
MONGOES > MONGOE
MONGOL *adj* offensive word for a person affected by Down's syndrome
MONGOLIAN *adj* offensive term meaning affected by Down's syndrome
MONGOLISM > MONGOL
MONGOLOID *adj* offensive term meaning characterized by Down's syndrome ▷ *n* offensive word for a person affected by Down's syndrome
MONGOLS > MONGOL
MONGOOSE *n* stoatlike mammal of Asia and Africa that kills snakes
MONGOOSES > MONGOOSE
MONGOS > MONGO
MONGREL *n* animal, esp a dog, of mixed breed ▷ *adj* of mixed breed or origin
MONGRELLY > MONGREL
MONGRELS > MONGREL
MONGS > MONG
MONGST *short for* > AMONGST
MONIAL *n* mullion
MONIALS > MONIAL
MONICKER *same as* > MONIKER
MONICKERS > MONICKER
MONIE *Scots word for* > MANY
MONIED *same as* > MONEYED
MONIES > MONEY
MONIKER *n* person's name or nickname
MONIKERS > MONIKER
MONILIA *n* type of fungus
MONILIAL *adj* denoting a thrush infection, caused by the fungus *Candida* (formerly *Monilia*) *albicans*
MONILIAS > MONILIA
MONIMENT *same as* > MONUMENT
MONIMENTS > MONIMENT
MONIPLIES *same as* > MANYPLIES
MONISH *same as* > ADMONISH
MONISHED > MONISH
MONISHES > MONISH
MONISHING > MONISH
MONISM *n* doctrine that reality consists of only one basic substance or element, such as mind or matter
MONISMS > MONISM
MONIST > MONISM
MONISTIC > MONISM
MONISTS > MONISM
MONITION *n* warning or caution
MONITIONS > MONITION
MONITIVE *adj* reproving
MONITOR *n* person or device that checks, controls, warns, or keeps a record of something ▷ *vb* watch and check on
MONITORED > MONITOR
MONITORS > MONITOR
MONITORY *adj* acting as or giving a warning ▷ *n* letter containing a monition
MONITRESS > MONITOR
MONK *n* member of an all-male religious community bound by vows
MONKERIES > MONKERY
MONKERY *n* derogatory word for monastic life or practices
MONKEY *n* long-tailed primate ▷ *vb* meddle or fool
MONKEYED > MONKEY
MONKEYING > MONKEY
MONKEYISH > MONKEY
MONKEYISM *n* practice of behaving like monkey
MONKEYPOD *n* Central American tree
MONKEYPOT *n* any of various tropical trees of the genus *Lecythis*: family *Lecythidaceae*
MONKEYS > MONKEY
MONKFISH *n* any of various fish of the genus *Lophius*
MONKHOOD *n* condition of being a monk
MONKHOODS > MONKHOOD
MONKISH *adj* of, relating to, or resembling a monk or monks
MONKISHLY > MONKISH
MONKS > MONK
MONKSHOOD *n* poisonous plant with hooded flowers
MONO *n* monophonic sound
MONOACID *adj* a base which is capable of reacting with only one molecule of a monobasic acid
MONOACIDS > MONOACID
MONOAMINE *n* substance, such as adrenaline, noradrenaline, or serotonin, that contains a single amine group
MONOAO *n* New Zealand plant with rigid leaves
MONOBASIC *adj* (of an acid, such as hydrogen chloride) having only one replaceable hydrogen atom per molecule
MONOBROW *n* appearance of a single eyebrow as a result of the eyebrows joining above a person's nose
MONOBROWS > MONOBROW
MONOCARP *n* plant that is monocarpic
MONOCARPS > MONOCARP
MONOCEROS *n* faint constellation on the celestial equator crossed by the Milky Way and lying close to Orion and Canis Major
MONOCHORD *n* instrument employed in acoustic analysis or investigation, consisting usually of one string stretched over a resonator of wood
MONOCLE *n* eyeglass for one eye only
MONOCLED > MONOCLE
MONOCLES > MONOCLE
MONOCLINE *n* fold in stratified rocks in which the strata are inclined in the same direction from the horizontal
MONOCOQUE *n* vehicle body moulded from a single piece of material with no separate load-bearing parts ▷ *adj* of or relating to the design characteristic of a monocoque
MONOCOT *n* any flowering plant of the class *Monocotyledonae*, having a single embryonic seed leaf, leaves with parallel veins, and flowers with parts in threes: includes grasses, lilies, palms, and orchids
MONOCOTS > MONOCOT

MONOCOTYL *same as* > MONOCOT
MONOCRACY *n* government by one person
MONOCRAT > MONOCRACY
MONOCRATS > MONOCRACY
MONOCULAR *adj* having or for one eye only ▷ *n* device for use with one eye, such as a field glass
MONOCYCLE *another name for* > UNICYCLE
MONOCYTE *n* large phagocytic leucocyte with a spherical nucleus and clear cytoplasm
MONOCYTES > MONOCYTE
MONOCYTIC > MONOCYTE
MONODIC > MONODY
MONODICAL > MONODY
MONODIES > MONODY
MONODIST > MONODY
MONODISTS > MONODY
MONODONT *adj* (of certain animals, esp the male narwhal) having a single tooth throughout life
MONODRAMA *n* play or other dramatic piece for a single performer
MONODY *n* (in Greek tragedy) an ode sung by a single actor
MONOECIES > MONOECY
MONOECISM *n* being both male and female
MONOECY *same as* > MONOECISM
MONOESTER *n* type of ester
MONOFIL *n* synthetic thread or yarn composed of a single strand rather than twisted fibres
MONOFILS > MONOFIL
MONOFUEL *n* single type of fuel
MONOFUELS > MONOFUEL
MONOGAMIC > MONOGAMY
MONOGAMY *n* custom of being married to one person at a time
MONOGENIC *adj* of or relating to an inherited character difference that is controlled by a single gene
MONOGENY *n* the hypothetical descent of all organisms from a single cell or organism
MONOGERM *adj* containing single seed
MONOGLOT *n* person speaking only one language
MONOGLOTS > MONOGLOT
MONOGONY *n* asexual reproduction
MONOGRAM *n* design of combined letters, esp a person's initials ▷ *vb* decorate (clothing, stationery, etc) with a monogram
MONOGRAMS > MONOGRAM
MONOGRAPH *n* book or paper on a single subject ▷ *vb* write a monograph on
MONOGYNY *n* custom of having only one female sexual partner over a period of time
MONOHULL *n* sailing vessel with a single hull
MONOHULLS > MONOHULL
MONOICOUS *adj* (of some flowering plants) having the male and female reproductive organs in separate flowers on the same plant
MONOKINE *n* type of protein
MONOKINES > MONOKINE
MONOKINI *n* bottom half of bikini
MONOKINIS > MONOKINI
MONOLATER > MONOLATRY
MONOLATRY *n* exclusive worship of one god without excluding the existence of others
MONOLAYER *n* single layer of atoms or molecules adsorbed on a surface
MONOLITH *n* large upright block of stone
MONOLITHS > MONOLITH
MONOLOG *same as* > MONOLOGUE
MONOLOGIC > MONOLOGUE
MONOLOGS > MONOLOG
MONOLOGUE *n* long speech by one person
MONOLOGY > MONOLOGUE
MONOMACHY *n* combat between two individuals
MONOMANIA *n* obsession with one thing
MONOMARK *n* series of letters or figures to identify goods, personal articles, etc
MONOMARKS > MONOMARK
MONOMER *n* compound whose molecules can join together to form a polymer
MONOMERIC > MONOMER
MONOMERS > MONOMER
MONOMETER *n* line of verse consisting of one metrical foot
MONOMIAL *n* expression consisting of a single term, such as $5ax$ ▷ *adj* consisting of a single algebraic term
MONOMIALS > MONOMIAL
MONOMODE *adj* denoting or relating to a type of optical fibre with a core less than 10 micrometres in diameter
MONONYM *n* person who is famous enough to be known only by one name, usually the first name
MONONYMS > MONONYM
MONOPHAGY *n* feeding on only one type of food
MONOPHASE *adj* having single alternating electric current
MONOPHONY > MONO
MONOPHYLY *n* group of ancestor and all descendants
MONOPITCH *adj* (of roof) having only one slope
MONOPLANE *n* aeroplane with one pair of wings
MONOPLOID *less common word for* > HAPLOID
MONOPOD *same as* > MONOPODE
MONOPODE *n* member of a legendary one-legged race of Africa
MONOPODES > MONOPODE
MONOPODIA *n* plural of monopodium: the main axis of growth in the pine tree and similar plants: the main stem, which elongates from the tip and gives rise to lateral branches
MONOPODS > MONOPOD
MONOPODY *n* single-foot measure in poetry
MONOPOLE *n* magnetic pole considered in isolation
MONOPOLES > MONOPOLE
MONOPOLY *n* exclusive possession of or right to do something
MONOPSONY *n* situation in which the entire market demand for a product or service consists of only one buyer
MONOPTERA *n* plural of monopteron: circular classical building, esp a temple, that has a single ring of columns surrounding it
MONOPTOTE *n* word with only one form
MONOPULSE *n* radar transmitting single pulse only
MONORAIL *n* single-rail railway
MONORAILS > MONORAIL
MONORCHID *adj* having only one testicle ▷ *n* animal or person with only one testicle
MONORHINE *adj* having single nostril
MONORHYME *n* poem in which all lines rhyme
MONOS > MONO
MONOSEMY *n* fact of having only a single meaning
MONOSES > MONOSIS
MONOSIES > MONOSY
MONOSIS *n* abnormal separation
MONOSKI *n* wide ski on which the skier stands with both feet
MONOSKIER > MONOSKI
MONOSKIS > MONOSKI
MONOSOME *n* unpaired chromosome, esp an X-chromosome in an otherwise diploid cell
MONOSOMES > MONOSOME
MONOSOMIC > MONOSOME
MONOSOMY *n* condition with missing pair of chromosomes
MONOSTELE *n* type of plar tissue
MONOSTELY > MONOSTELE
MONOSTICH *n* poem of a single line
MONOSTOME *adj* having only one mouth, pore, or similar opening
MONOSTYLE *adj* having single shaft
MONOSY *same as* > MONOS
MONOTINT *n* black-and-white photograph or transparency
MONOTINTS > MONOTINT
MONOTONE *n* unvaried pit in speech or sound ▷ *adj* unvarying ▷ *vb* speak in monotone
MONOTONED > MONOTONE
MONOTONES > MONOTONE
MONOTONIC *same as* > MONOTONE
MONOTONY *n* wearisome routine, dullness
MONOTREME *n* any mamm of the primitive order *Monotremata*, of Australia and New Guinea: egg-laying toothless animals with a single opening (cloaca) for the passage c eggs or sperm, faeces, an urine. The group contain only the echidnas and th platypus
MONOTROCH *n* wheelbarro
MONOTYPE *n* single print made from a metal or gla plate on which a picture has been painted
MONOTYPES > MONOTYPE
MONOTYPIC *adj* (of a genu or species) consisting of only one type of animal c plant
MONOVULAR *adj* of single ovum
MONOXIDE *n* oxide that contains one oxygen ato per molecule
MONOXIDES > MONOXIDE
MONOXYLON *n* canoe mad from one log
MONS > MON
MONSIEUR *n* French title of address equivalent to *sir* or *Mr*
MONSIGNOR *n* ecclesiastic title attached to certain offices or distinctions usually bestowed by the Pope
MONSOON *n* seasonal wind

f SE Asia
NSOONAL > MONSOON
NSOONS > MONSOON
NSTER *n* imaginary, usu. rightening, beast ▷ *adj* uge ▷ *vb* criticize (a erson or group) severely
NSTERA *n* any plant f the tropical climbing enus *Monstera*, some pecies of which are grown s greenhouse or pot lants for their unusual eathery perforated leaves: amily *Araceae*. *M. deliciosa* s the Swiss cheese plant
NSTERAS > MONSTERA
NSTERED > MONSTER
NSTERS > MONSTER
NSTROUS *adj* unnatural r ugly
NTADALE *n* breed of heep
NTAGE *n* (making of) a icture composed from ieces of others ▷ *vb* nake as montage
NTAGED > MONTAGE
NTAGES > MONTAGE
NTAGING > MONTAGE
NTAN as in *montan wax* ard wax obtained from ignite and peat used in olishes and candles
NTANE *n* area of nountain dominated by egetation ▷ *adj* of or nhabiting mountainous egions
NTANES > MONTANE
NTANT *n* vertical part in voodwork
NTANTO *n* rising blow
NTANTOS > MONTANTO
NTANTS > MONTANT
NTARIA *n* Brazilian anoe
NTARIAS > MONTARIA
NTE *n* gambling card ame of Spanish origin
NTEITH *n* large rnamental bowl, usually f silver, for cooling vineglasses, which are uspended from the otched rim
NTEITHS > MONTEITH
NTEM *n* former money-aising practice at Eton chool
NTEMS > MONTEM
NTERO *n* round cap with flap at the back worn by unters, esp in Spain in the 7th and 18th centuries
NTEROS > MONTERO
NTES > MONTE
NTH *n* one of the twelve livisions of the calendar ear
NTHLIES > MONTHLY
NTHLING *n* month-old hild
NTHLONG *adj* lasting all month
MONTHLY *adj* happening or payable once a month ▷ *adv* once a month ▷ *n* monthly magazine
MONTHS > MONTH
MONTICLE *same as* > MONTICULE
MONTICLES > MONTICLE
MONTICULE *n* small hill or mound, such as a secondary volcanic cone
MONTIES > MONTY
MONTRE *n* pipes of organ
MONTRES > MONTRE
MONTURE *n* mount or frame
MONTURES > MONTURE
MONTY *n* complete form of something
MONUMENT *n* something, esp a building or statue, that commemorates something
MONUMENTS > MONUMENT
MONURON *n* type of weedkiller
MONURONS > MONURON
MONY *Scot word for* > MANY
MONYPLIES *same as* > MANYPLIES
MONZONITE *n* coarse-grained plutonic igneous rock consisting of equal amounts of plagioclase and orthoclase feldspar, with ferromagnesian minerals
MOO *n* long deep cry of a cow ▷ *vb* make this noise ▷ *interj* instance or imitation of this sound
MOOCH *vb* loiter about aimlessly
MOOCHED > MOOCH
MOOCHER > MOOCH
MOOCHERS > MOOCH
MOOCHES > MOOCH
MOOCHING > MOOCH
MOOD *n* temporary (gloomy) state of mind
MOODIED > MOODY
MOODIER > MOODY
MOODIES > MOODY
MOODIEST > MOODY
MOODILY > MOODY
MOODINESS > MOODY
MOODS > MOOD
MOODY *adj* sullen or gloomy ▷ *vb* flatter
MOODYING > MOODY
MOOED > MOO
MOOI *adj* pleasing or nice
MOOING > MOO
MOOK *n* person regarded with contempt, esp a stupid person
MOOKS > MOOK
MOOKTAR *same as* > MUKHTAR
MOOKTARS > MOOKTAR
MOOL *same as* > MOULD
MOOLA *same as* > MOOLAH
MOOLAH *slang word for* > MONEY
MOOLAHS > MOOLAH
MOOLAS > MOOLA
MOOLED > MOOL
MOOLEY *same as* > MOOLY
MOOLEYS > MOOLEY
MOOLI *n* type of large white radish
MOOLIES > MOOLY
MOOLING > MOOL
MOOLIS > MOOLI
MOOLOO *n* person from the Waikato
MOOLOOS > MOOLOO
MOOLS > MOOL
MOOLVI *same as* > MOOLVIE
MOOLVIE *n* (esp in India) a Muslim doctor of the law, teacher, or learned man also used as a title of respect
MOOLVIES > MOOLVIE
MOOLVIS > MOOLVI
MOOLY *same as* > MULEY
MOON *n* natural satellite of the earth ▷ *vb* be idle in a listless or dreamy way
MOONBEAM *n* ray of moonlight
MOONBEAMS > MOONBEAM
MOONBLIND *adj* (in horses), having a disorder which causes inflammation of the eyes and sometimes blindness
MOONBOW *n* rainbow made by moonlight
MOONBOWS > MOONBOW
MOONCALF *n* born fool
MOONCHILD *n* someone who is born under the Cancer star sign
MOONDUST *n* dust on surface of moon
MOONDUSTS > MOONDUST
MOONED *adj* decorated with a moon
MOONER > MOON
MOONERS > MOON
MOONEYE *n* any of several North American large-eyed freshwater clupeoid fishes of the family *Hiodontidae*, esp *Hiodon tergisus*
MOONEYES > MOONEYE
MOONFACE *n* big round face ▷ *vb* have a moon face
MOONFACED > MOONFACE
MOONFACES > MOONFACE
MOONFISH *n* any of several deep-bodied silvery carangid fishes, occurring in warm and tropical American coastal waters
MOONIER > MOONY
MOONIES > MOONY
MOONIEST > MOONY
MOONILY > MOONY
MOONINESS > MOONY
MOONING > MOON
MOONISH > MOON
MOONISHLY > MOON
MOONLESS > MOON
MOONLET *n* small moon
MOONLETS > MOONLET
MOONLIGHT *n* light from the moon ▷ *adj* illuminated by the moon ▷ *vb* work at a secondary job, esp illegally
MOONLIKE > MOON
MOONLIT *adj* illuminated by the moon
MOONPHASE *n* phase of moon
MOONPORT *n* place from which flights leave for moon
MOONPORTS > MOONPORT
MOONQUAKE *n* light tremor of the moon, detected on the moon's surface
MOONRAKER *n* small square sail set above a skysail
MOONRISE *n* moment when the moon appears above the horizon
MOONRISES > MOONRISE
MOONROCK *n* rock from moon
MOONROCKS > MOONROCK
MOONROOF *same as* > SUNROOF
MOONROOFS > MOONROOF
MOONS > MOON
MOONSAIL *n* small sail high on mast
MOONSAILS > MOONSAIL
MOONSCAPE *n* surface of the moon or a picture or model of it
MOONSEED *n* any menispermaceous climbing plant of the genus *Menispermum* and related genera, having red or black fruits with crescent-shaped or ring-shaped seeds
MOONSEEDS > MOONSEED
MOONSET *n* moment when the moon disappears below the horizon
MOONSETS > MOONSET
MOONSHEE *same as* > MUNSHI
MOONSHEES > MOONSHEE
MOONSHINE *same as* > MOONLIGHT
MOONSHINY > MOONSHINE
MOONSHOT *n* launching of a spacecraft to the moon
MOONSHOTS > MOONSHOT
MOONSTONE *n* translucent semiprecious stone
MOONWALK *n* instance of walking on moon
MOONWALKS > MOONWALK
MOONWARD *adj* towards moon
MOONWARDS *adv* towards moon
MOONWORT *n* any of various ferns of the genus *Botrychium*, esp *B. lunaria*, which has crescent-shaped leaflets
MOONWORTS > MOONWORT

MOONY *adj* dreamy or listless ▷ *n* crazy or foolish person
MOOP *same as* > MOUP
MOOPED > MOOP
MOOPING > MOOP
MOOPS > MOOP
MOOR *n* tract of open uncultivated ground covered with grass and heather ▷ *vb* secure (a ship) with ropes etc
MOORAGE *n* place for mooring a vessel
MOORAGES > MOORAGE
MOORBURN *n* practice of burning off old growth on a heather moor to encourage new growth for grazing
MOORBURNS > MOORBURN
MOORCOCK *n* male of the red grouse
MOORCOCKS > MOORCOCK
MOORED > MOOR
MOORFOWL *n* red grouse
MOORFOWLS > MOORFOWL
MOORHEN *n* small black water bird
MOORHENS > MOORHEN
MOORIER > MOOR
MOORIEST > MOOR
MOORILL *n* disease of cattle on moors
MOORILLS > MOORILL
MOORING *n* place for mooring a ship
MOORINGS *pl n* ropes and anchors used in mooring a vessel
MOORISH *adj* of or relating to the Moor people of North Africa
MOORLAND *n* area of moor
MOORLANDS > MOORLAND
MOORLOG *n* rotted wood below surface of moor
MOORLOGS > MOOR
MOORMAN *n* person living on moor
MOORMEN > MOORMAN
MOORS > MOOR
MOORVA *same as* > MURVA
MOORVAS > MOORVA
MOORWORT *n* low-growing pink-flowered shrub that grows in peaty bogs
MOORWORTS > MOORWORT
MOORY > MOOR
MOOS > MOO
MOOSE *n* large N American deer
MOOSEBIRD *n* North American jay
MOOSEWOOD *n* North American tree
MOOSEYARD *n* place where moose spend winter
MOOT *adj* debatable ▷ *vb* bring up for discussion ▷ *n* (in Anglo-Saxon England) a local administrative assembly
MOOTABLE > MOOT
MOOTED > MOOT
MOOTER > MOOT
MOOTERS > MOOT
MOOTEST > MOOT
MOOTING > MOOT
MOOTINGS > MOOT
MOOTMAN *n* person taking part in moot
MOOTMEN > MOOTMAN
MOOTNESS > MOOT
MOOTS > MOOT
MOOVE *same as* > MOVE
MOOVED > MOOVE
MOOVES > MOOVE
MOOVING > MOOVE
MOP *n* long stick with twists of cotton or a sponge on the end, used for cleaning ▷ *vb* clean or soak up with or as if with a mop
MOPANE *same as* > MOPANI
MOPANES > MOPANE
MOPANI *n* leguminous tree, *Colophospermum* (or *Copaifera*) *mopane*, native to southern Africa, that is highly resistant to drought and produces very hard wood
MOPANIS > MOPANI
MOPBOARD *n* wooden border fixed round the base of an interior wall
MOPBOARDS > MOPBOARD
MOPE *vb* be gloomy and apathetic ▷ *n* gloomy person
MOPED *n* light motorized cycle
MOPEDS > MOPED
MOPEHAWK *same as* > MOPOKE
MOPEHAWKS > MOPEHAWK
MOPER > MOPE
MOPERIES > MOPERY
MOPERS > MOPE
MOPERY *n* gloominess
MOPES *pl n the.* low spirits
MOPEY > MOPE
MOPHEAD *n* person with shaggy hair
MOPHEADS > MOPHEAD
MOPIER > MOPE
MOPIEST > MOPE
MOPINESS > MOPE
MOPING > MOPE
MOPINGLY > MOPE
MOPISH > MOPE
MOPISHLY > MOPE
MOPOKE *n* species of owl
MOPOKES > MOPOKE
MOPPED > MOP
MOPPER > MOP
MOPPERS > MOP
MOPPET *same as* > POPPET
MOPPETS > MOPPET
MOPPIER > MOPPY
MOPPIEST > MOPPY
MOPPING > MOP
MOPPY *adj* drunk
MOPS > MOP
MOPSIES > MOPSY
MOPSTICK *n* mop handle
MOPSTICKS > MOPSTICK
MOPSY *n* untidy or dowdy person
MOPUS *n* person who mopes
MOPUSES > MOPUS
MOPY > MOPE
MOQUETTE *n* thick velvety fabric used for carpets and upholstery
MOQUETTES > MOQUETTE
MOR *n* layer of acidic humus formed in cool moist areas where decomposition is slow
MORA *n* quantity of a short syllable in verse
MORACEOUS *adj* of, relating to, or belonging to the *Moraceae*, mostly tropical and subtropical family of trees and shrubs, including fig, mulberry, breadfruit, and hop, many of which have latex in the stems and heads enclosed in a fleshy receptacle
MORAE > MORA
MORAINAL > MORAINE
MORAINE *n* accumulated mass of debris deposited by a glacier
MORAINES > MORAINE
MORAINIC > MORAINE
MORAL *adj* concerned with right and wrong conduct ▷ *n* lesson to be obtained from a story or event ▷ *vb* moralize
MORALE *n* degree of confidence or hope of a person or group
MORALES > MORALE
MORALISE *same as* > MORALIZE
MORALISED > MORALISE
MORALISER > MORALIZE
MORALISES > MORALISE
MORALISM *n* habit or practice of moralizing
MORALISMS > MORALISM
MORALIST *n* person with a strong sense of right and wrong
MORALISTS > MORALIST
MORALITY *n* good moral conduct
MORALIZE *vb* make moral pronouncements
MORALIZED > MORALIZE
MORALIZER > MORALIZE
MORALIZES > MORALIZE
MORALL *same as* > MURAL
MORALLED > MORALL
MORALLER > MORAL
MORALLERS > MORAL
MORALLING > MORALL
MORALLS > MORALL
MORALLY > MORAL
MORALS > MORAL
MORAS > MORA
MORASS *n* marsh
MORASSES > MORASS
MORASSY > MORASS
MORAT *n* drink containing mulberry juice
MORATORIA *n* plural form of singular moratorium: legally authorized postponement of the fulfilment of an obligati[on]
MORATORY > MORATORIA
MORATS > MORAT
MORAY *n* large voracious [eel]
MORAYS > MORAY
MORBID *adj* unduly interested in death or unpleasant events
MORBIDER > MORBID
MORBIDEST > MORBID
MORBIDITY *n* state of bei[ng] morbid
MORBIDLY > MORBID
MORBIFIC *adj* causing disease
MORBILLI *same as* > MEASLES
MORBUS *n* disease
MORBUSES > MORBUS
MORCEAU *n* fragment or morsel
MORCEAUX > MORCEAU
MORCHA *n* (in India) a hostile demonstration against the government
MORCHAS > MORCHA
MORDACITY *n* quality of sarcasm
MORDANCY > MORDANT
MORDANT *adj* sarcastic or scathing ▷ *n* substance used to fix dyes ▷ *vb* tre[at] (a fabric, yarn, etc) with mordant
MORDANTED > MORDANT
MORDANTLY > MORDANT
MORDANTS > MORDANT
MORDENT *n* melodic ornament consisting of the rapid alternation of a note with a note one degree lower than it
MORDENTS > MORDENT
MORE *adj* greater in amou[nt] or degree ▷ *adv* greater extent ▷ *pron* greater or additional amount or number
MOREEN *n* heavy, usually watered, fabric of wool [or] wool and cotton, used e[sp] in furnishing
MOREENS > MOREEN
MOREISH *adj* (of food) causing a desire for mor[e]
MOREL *n* edible mushroo[m] with a pitted cap
MORELLE *n* nightshade
MORELLES > MORELLE
MORELLO *n* variety of sma[ll] very dark sour cherry
MORELLOS > MORELLO
MORELS > MOREL
MORENDO *adv* (in music) dying away
MORENESS > MORE
MOREOVER *adv* in additio[n] to what has already bee[n] said
MOREPORK *same*

S > MOPOKE
REPORKS > MOREPORK
RES *pl n* customs and conventions embodying the fundamental values of a community
RESQUE *adj* (esp of decoration and architecture) of Moorish style ▷ *n* Moorish design or decoration
RESQUES > MORESQUE
RGAN *n* American breed of small compact saddle horse
RGANITE *n* pink variety of beryl, used as a gemstone
RGANS > MORGAN
RGAY *n* small dogfish
RGAYS > MORGAY
RGEN *n* South African unit of area, equal to about two acres or 0.8 hectare
RGENS > MORGEN
RGUE *same as* > MORTUARY
RGUES > MORGUE
RIA *n* folly
RIAS > MORIA
RIBUND *adj* without force or vitality
RICHE *same as* > MIRITI
RICHES > MORICHE
RION *n* 16th-century helmet with a brim and wide comb
RIONS > MORION
RISCO *n* a morris dance
RISCOES > MORISCO
RISCOS > MORISCO
RISH *same as* > MOREISH
RKIN *n* animal dying in accident
RKINS > MORKIN
RLING *n* sheep killed by disease
RLINGS > MORLING
RMAOR *n* former high-ranking Scottish nobleman
RMAORS > MORMAOR
RN *n* morning
RNAY *adj* served with a cheese sauce
RNAYS > MORNAY
RNE *same as* > MOURN
RNED > MORNE
RNES > MORNE
RNING *n* part of the day before noon
RNINGS > MORNING
RNS > MORN
ROCCO *n* goatskin leather
ROCCOS > MOROCCO
RON *n* foolish or stupid person
RONIC > MORON
RONISM > MORON
RONISMS > MORON
RONITY > MORON
RONS > MORON
ROSE *adj* sullen or moody

MOROSELY > MOROSE
MOROSER > MOROSE
MOROSEST > MOROSE
MOROSITY > MOROSE
MORPH *n* phonological representation of a morpheme ▷ *vb* undergo or cause to undergo morphing
MORPHEAN *adj* of or relating to Morpheus, the god of sleep and dreams
MORPHED > MORPH
MORPHEME *n* speech element having a meaning or grammatical function that cannot be subdivided into further such elements
MORPHEMES > MORPHEME
MORPHEMIC > MORPHEME
MORPHETIC *same as* > MORPHEAN
MORPHEW *n* blemish on skin
MORPHEWS > MORPHEW
MORPHIA *same as* > MORPHINE
MORPHIAS > MORPHIA
MORPHIC as in *morphic resonance* idea that, through a telepathic effect or sympathetic vibration, an event or act can lead to similar events or acts in the future or an idea conceived in one mind can then arise in another
MORPHIN *variant form of* > MORPHINE
MORPHINE *n* drug extracted from opium, used as an anaesthetic and sedative
MORPHINES > MORPHINE
MORPHING *n* computer technique used for graphics and in films, in which one image is gradually transformed into another image without individual changes being noticeable in the process
MORPHINGS > MORPHING
MORPHINIC > MORPHINE
MORPHINS > MORPHINE
MORPHO *n* type of butterfly
MORPHOGEN *n* chemical in body that influences growth
MORPHOS > MORPHO
MORPHOSES > MORPHOSIS
MORPHOSIS *n* development in an organism or its parts characterized by structural change
MORPHOTIC > MORPHOSIS
MORPHS > MORPH
MORRA *same as* > MORA
MORRAS > MORRA
MORRELL *n* tall eucalyptus, *Eucalyptus longicornis*, of SW Australia, having pointed buds
MORRELLS > MORRELL
MORRHUA *n* cod

MORRHUAS > MORRHUA
MORRICE *same as* > MORRIS
MORRICES > MORRICE
MORRION *same as* > MORION
MORRIONS > MORRION
MORRIS *vb* perform morris dance
MORRISED > MORRIS
MORRISES > MORRIS
MORRISING > MORRIS
MORRO *n* rounded hill or promontory
MORROS > MORRO
MORROW *n* next day
MORROWS > MORROW
MORS > MOR
MORSAL > MORSURE
MORSE *n* clasp or fastening on a cope
MORSEL *n* small piece, esp of food ▷ *vb* divide into morsels
MORSELED > MORSEL
MORSELING > MORSEL
MORSELLED > MORSEL
MORSELS > MORSEL
MORSES > MORSE
MORSURE *n* bite
MORSURES > MORSURE
MORT *n* call blown on a hunting horn to signify the death of the animal hunted
MORTAL *adj* subject to death ▷ *n* human being
MORTALISE *same as* > MORTALIZE
MORTALITY *n* state of being mortal
MORTALIZE *vb* make mortal
MORTALLY > MORTAL
MORTALS > MORTAL
MORTAR *n* small cannon with a short range ▷ *vb* fire on with mortars
MORTARED > MORTAR
MORTARING > MORTAR
MORTARMAN *n* person firing mortar
MORTARMEN > MORTAR
MORTARS > MORTAR
MORTARY *adj* of or like mortar
MORTBELL *n* bell rung for funeral
MORTBELLS > MORTBELL
MORTCLOTH *n* cloth spread over coffin
MORTGAGE *n* conditional pledging of property, esp a house, as security for the repayment of a loan ▷ *vb* pledge (property) as security thus ▷ *adj* of or relating to a mortgage
MORTGAGED > MORTGAGE
MORTGAGEE *n* creditor in a mortgage
MORTGAGER *same as* > MORTGAGOR
MORTGAGES > MORTGAGE
MORTGAGOR *n* debtor in a mortgage

MORTICE *same as* > MORTISE
MORTICED > MORTICE
MORTICER > MORTICE
MORTICERS > MORTICE
MORTICES > MORTICE
MORTICIAN *n* undertaker
MORTICING > MORTICE
MORTIFIC *adj* causing death
MORTIFIED > MORTIFY
MORTIFIER > MORTIFY
MORTIFIES > MORTIFY
MORTIFY *vb* humiliate
MORTISE *n* slot or recess, usually rectangular, cut into a piece of wood, stone, etc, to receive a matching projection (tenon) of another piece, or a mortise lock ▷ *vb* cut a slot or recess in (a piece of wood, stone, etc)
MORTISED > MORTISE
MORTISER > MORTISE
MORTISERS > MORTISE
MORTISES > MORTISE
MORTISING > MORTISE
MORTLING *n* corpse
MORTLINGS > MORTLING
MORTMAIN *n* state or condition of lands, buildings, etc, held inalienably, as by an ecclesiastical or other corporation
MORTMAINS > MORTMAIN
MORTS > MORT
MORTSAFE *n* heavy iron cage or grille placed over the grave of a newly deceased person during the 19th century in order to deter body snatchers
MORTSAFES > MORTSAFE
MORTUARY *n* building where corpses are kept before burial or cremation ▷ *adj* of or relating to death or burial
MORULA *n* solid ball of cells resulting from cleavage of a fertilized ovum
MORULAE > MORULA
MORULAR > MORULA
MORULAS > MORULA
MORWONG *n* food fish of Australasian coastal waters belonging to the *Cheilodactylidae* family
MORWONGS > MORWONG
MORYAH *interj* exclamation of annoyance, disbelief, etc
MOS > MO
MOSAIC *n* design or decoration using small pieces of coloured stone or glass
MOSAICISM *n* occurrence of different types of tissue side by side
MOSAICIST > MOSAIC
MOSAICKED *adj* arranged in mosaic form

MOSAICS > MOSAIC
MOSASAUR *n* any of various extinct Cretaceous giant marine lizards of the genus *Mosasaurus* and related genera, typically having paddle-like limbs
MOSASAURI > MOSASAUR
MOSASAURS > MOSASAUR
MOSCHATE *n* odour like musk
MOSCHATEL *n* small N temperate plant, *Adoxa moschatellina*, with greenish-white musk-scented flowers on top of the stem, arranged as four pointing sideways at right angles to each other and one facing upwards: family *Adoxaceae*
MOSE *vb* have glanders
MOSED > MOSE
MOSELLE *n* German white wine from the Moselle valley
MOSELLES > MOSELLE
MOSES > MOSE
MOSEY *vb* walk in a leisurely manner
MOSEYED > MOSEY
MOSEYING > MOSEY
MOSEYS > MOSEY
MOSH *n* type of dance, performed to loud rock music, in which people throw themselves about in a frantic and violent manner ▷ *vb* dance in this manner
MOSHAV *n* cooperative settlement in Israel, consisting of a number of small farms
MOSHAVIM > MOSHAV
MOSHED > MOSH
MOSHER > MOSH
MOSHERS > MOSH
MOSHES > MOSH
MOSHING > MOSH
MOSHINGS > MOSH
MOSHPIT *n* area at a rock-music concert, usually in front of the stage, where members of the audience dance in a frantic and violent manner
MOSHPITS > MOSHPIT
MOSING > MOSE
MOSK *same as* > MOSQUE
MOSKONFYT *n* South African grape syrup
MOSKS > MOSK
MOSLINGS *n* shavings from animal skin being prepared
MOSQUE *n* Muslim temple
MOSQUES > MOSQUE
MOSQUITO *n* blood-sucking flying insect
MOSQUITOS > MOSQUITO
MOSS *n* small flowerless plant growing in masses on moist surfaces ▷ *vb* gather moss
MOSSBACK *n* old turtle, shellfish, etc, that has a growth of algae on its back
MOSSBACKS > MOSSBACK
MOSSED > MOSS
MOSSER > MOSS
MOSSERS > MOSS
MOSSES > MOSS
MOSSGROWN *adj* covered in moss
MOSSIE *n* common sparrow
MOSSIER > MOSS
MOSSIES > MOSSIE
MOSSIEST > MOSS
MOSSINESS > MOSS
MOSSING > MOSS
MOSSLAND *n* land covered in peat
MOSSLANDS > MOSSLAND
MOSSLIKE > MOSS
MOSSO *adv* to be performed with rapidity
MOSSPLANT *n* individual plant in moss
MOSSY > MOSS
MOST *n* greatest number or degree ▷ *adj* greatest in number or degree ▷ *adv* in the greatest degree
MOSTE > MOTE
MOSTEST > MOST
MOSTESTS > MOST
MOSTLY *adv* for the most part, generally
MOSTS > MOST
MOSTWHAT *adv* mostly
MOT *n* girl or young woman, esp one's girlfriend
MOTE *n* tiny speck ▷ *vb* may or might
MOTED *adj* containing motes
MOTEL *n* roadside hotel for motorists
MOTELIER *n* person running motel
MOTELIERS > MOTELIER
MOTELS > MOTEL
MOTEN > MOTE
MOTES > MOTE
MOTET *n* short sacred choral song
MOTETS > MOTET
MOTETT *same as* > MOTET
MOTETTIST > MOTET
MOTETTS > MOTET
MOTEY *adj* containing motes
MOTH *n* nocturnal insect like a butterfly
MOTHBALL *n* small ball of camphor or naphthalene used to repel moths from stored clothes ▷ *vb* store (something operational) for future use
MOTHBALLS > MOTHBALL
MOTHED *adj* damaged by moths
MOTHER *n* female parent ▷ *adj* native or inborn ▷ *vb* look after as a mother
MOTHERED > MOTHER
MOTHERESE *n* simplified and repetitive type of speech, with exaggerated intonation and rhythm, often used by adults when speaking to babies
MOTHERING > MOTHER
MOTHERLY *adj* of or resembling a mother, esp in warmth, or protectiveness
MOTHERS > MOTHER
MOTHERY > MOTHER
MOTHIER > MOTHY
MOTHIEST > MOTHY
MOTHLIKE > MOTH
MOTHPROOF *adj* (esp of clothes) chemically treated so as to repel clothes moths ▷ *vb* make mothproof
MOTHS > MOTH
MOTHY *adj* ragged
MOTI *n* derogatory Indian English word for a fat woman or girl
MOTIER > MOTEY
MOTIEST > MOTEY
MOTIF *n* (recurring) theme or design
MOTIFIC *adj* causing motion
MOTIFS > MOTIF
MOTILE *adj* capable of independent movement ▷ *n* person whose mental imagery strongly reflects movement, esp his own
MOTILES > MOTILE
MOTILITY > MOTILE
MOTION *n* process, action, or way of moving ▷ *vb* direct (someone) by gesture
MOTIONAL > MOTION
MOTIONED > MOTION
MOTIONER > MOTION
MOTIONERS > MOTION
MOTIONING > MOTION
MOTIONIST *n* person proposing many motions
MOTIONS > MOTION
MOTIS > MOTI
MOTIVATE *vb* give incentive to
MOTIVATED > MOTIVATE
MOTIVATES > MOTIVATE
MOTIVATOR > MOTIVATE
MOTIVE *n* reason for a course of action ▷ *adj* causing motion ▷ *vb* motivate
MOTIVED > MOTIVE
MOTIVES > MOTIVE
MOTIVIC *adj* of musical motif
MOTIVING > MOTIVE
MOTIVITY *n* power of moving or of initiating motion
MOTLEY *adj* miscellaneous ▷ *n* costume of a jester
MOTLEYER > MOTLEY
MOTLEYEST > MOTLEY
MOTLEYS > MOTLEY
MOTLIER > MOTLEY
MOTLIEST > MOTLEY
MOTMOT *n* any tropical American bird of the family *Momotidae*, having a long tail and blue and brownish-green plumage order *Coraciiformes* (kingfishers, etc)
MOTMOTS > MOTMOT
MOTOCROSS *n* motorcycle race over a rough course
MOTOR *n* engine, esp of a vehicle ▷ *vb* travel by car ▷ *adj* of or relating to cars and other vehicles powered by petrol or diesel engines
MOTORABLE *adj* (of a road) suitable for use by motor vehicles
MOTORAIL *n* transport of cars by train
MOTORAILS > MOTORAIL
MOTORBIKE *n* motorcycle
MOTORBOAT *n* any boat powered by a motor
MOTORBUS *n* bus driven by an internal-combustion engine
MOTORCADE *n* procession of cars carrying important people
MOTORCAR *n* self-propelled electric railway car
MOTORCARS > MOTORCAR
MOTORDOM *n* world of motor cars
MOTORDOMS > MOTORDOM
MOTORED > MOTOR
MOTORHOME *n* large motor vehicle with living quarters behind the driver's compartment
MOTORIAL > MOTOR
MOTORIC > MOTOR
MOTORING > MOTOR
MOTORINGS > MOTOR
MOTORISE *same as* > MOTORIZE
MOTORISED > MOTORISE
MOTORISES > MOTORISE
MOTORIST *n* driver of a car
MOTORISTS > MOTORIST
MOTORIUM *n* area of nervous system involved in movement
MOTORIUMS > MOTORIUM
MOTORIZE *vb* equip with motor
MOTORIZED > MOTORIZE
MOTORIZES > MOTORIZE
MOTORLESS > MOTOR
MOTORMAN *n* driver of an electric train
MOTORMEN > MOTORMAN
MOTORS > MOTOR
MOTORSHIP *n* ship with motor
MOTORWAY *n* main road for fast-moving traffic
MOTORWAYS > MOTORWAY

TORY > MOTOR
TOSCAFI > MOTOSCAFO
TOSCAFO *n* motorboat
TS > MOT
TSER *n* large sum of money, esp a gambling win
TSERS > MOTSER
TT *n* clump of trees
TTE *n* mound on which a castle was built
TTES > MOTTE
TTIER > MOTTY
TTIES > MOTTY
TTIEST > MOTTY
TTLE *vb* colour with streaks or blotches of different shades ▷ *n* mottled appearance, as of the surface of marble
TTLED > MOTTLE
TTLER *n* paintbrush for mottled effects
TTLERS > MOTTLER
TTLES > MOTTLE
TTLING > MOTTLE
TTLINGS > MOTTLE
TTO *n* saying expressing an ideal or rule of conduct
TTOED *adj* having motto
TTOES > MOTTO
TTOS > MOTTO
TTS > MOTT
TTY *n* target at which coins are aimed in pitch-and-toss ▷ *adj* containing motes
TU *n* derogatory Indian English word for a fat man or boy
TUCA *n* Brazilian fly
TUCAS > MOTUCA
TUS > MOTU
TZA *same as* > MOTSER
TZAS > MOTZA
U *Scots word for* > MOUTH
UCH *same as* > MOOCH
UCHARD *n* police informer
UCHARDS > MOUCHARD
UCHED > MOUCH
UCHER > MOUCH
UCHERS > MOUCH
UCHES > MOUCH
UCHING > MOUCH
UCHOIR *n* handkerchief
UCHOIRS > MOUCHOIR
UDIWART *same as* > MOULDWARP
UDIWORT *same as* > MOULDWARP
UE *n* disdainful or pouting look
UES > MOUE
UFFLON *same as* > MOUFLON
UFFLONS > MOUFFLON
UFLON *n* wild short-fleeced mountain sheep, *Ovis musimon*, of Corsica and Sardinia
UFLONS > MOUFLON
UGHT > MOTE
UILLE *adj* palatalized, as in the sounds represented by Spanish *ll* or *ñ*
MOUJIK *same as* > MUZHIK
MOUJIKS > MOUJIK
MOULAGE *n* mould making
MOULAGES > MOULAGE
MOULD *n* hollow container in which metal etc is cast ▷ *vb* shape
MOULDABLE > MOULD
MOULDED > MOULD
MOULDER *vb* decay into dust ▷ *n* person who moulds or makes moulds
MOULDERED > MOULDER
MOULDERS > MOULDER
MOULDIER > MOULDY
MOULDIEST > MOULDY
MOULDING *n* moulded ornamental edging
MOULDINGS > MOULDING
MOULDS > MOULD
MOULDWARP *archaic or dialect name for a* > MOLE
MOULDY *adj* stale or musty
MOULIN *n* vertical shaft in a glacier, maintained by a constant descending stream of water and debris
MOULINET *n* device for bending crossbow
MOULINETS > MOULINET
MOULINS > MOULIN
MOULS *Scots word for* > MOULD
MOULT *vb* shed feathers, hair, or skin to make way for new growth ▷ *n* process of moulting
MOULTED > MOULT
MOULTEN *adj* having moulted
MOULTER > MOULT
MOULTERS > MOULT
MOULTING > MOULT
MOULTINGS > MOULT
MOULTS > MOULT
MOUND *n* heap, esp of earth or stones ▷ *vb* gather into a mound
MOUNDBIRD *n* Australian bird laying eggs in mounds
MOUNDED > MOUND
MOUNDING > MOUND
MOUNDS > MOUND
MOUNSEER *same as* > MONSIEUR
MOUNSEERS > MOUNSEER
MOUNT *vb* climb or ascend ▷ *n* backing or support on which something is fixed
MOUNTABLE > MOUNT
MOUNTAIN *n* hill of great size ▷ *adj* of, found on, or for use on a mountain or mountains
MOUNTAINS > MOUNTAIN
MOUNTAINY > MOUNTAIN
MOUNTANT *n* adhesive for mounting pictures
MOUNTANTS > MOUNTANT
MOUNTED *adj* riding horses
MOUNTER > MOUNT
MOUNTERS > MOUNT
MOUNTING *same as* > MOUNT
MOUNTINGS > MOUNTING
MOUNTS > MOUNT
MOUP *n* nibble
MOUPED > MOUP
MOUPING > MOUP
MOUPS > MOUP
MOURN *vb* feel or express sorrow for (a dead person or lost thing)
MOURNED > MOURN
MOURNER *n* person attending a funeral
MOURNERS > MOURNER
MOURNFUL *adj* sad or dismal
MOURNING *n* grieving ▷ *adj* of or relating to mourning
MOURNINGS > MOURNING
MOURNIVAL *n* card game
MOURNS > MOURN
MOUS > MOU
MOUSAKA *same as* > MOUSSAKA
MOUSAKAS > MOUSAKA
MOUSE *n* small long-tailed rodent ▷ *vb* stalk and catch mice
MOUSEBIRD *another name for* > COLY
MOUSED > MOUSE
MOUSEKIN *n* little mouse
MOUSEKINS > MOUSEKIN
MOUSELIKE > MOUSE
MOUSEMAT *n* piece of material on which a computer mouse is moved
MOUSEMATS > MOUSEMAT
MOUSEOVER *n* on a web page, any item that changes or pops up when the pointer of a mouse moves over it
MOUSEPAD *n* pad for computer mouse
MOUSEPADS > MOUSEPAD
MOUSER *n* cat used to catch mice
MOUSERIES > MOUSERY
MOUSERS > MOUSER
MOUSERY *n* place infested with mice
MOUSES > MOUSE
MOUSETAIL *n* any of various N temperate ranunculaceous plants of the genus *Myosurus*, esp *M. minimus*, with tail-like flower spikes
MOUSETRAP *n* spring-loaded trap for killing mice
MOUSEY *same as* > MOUSY
MOUSIE *n* little mouse
MOUSIER > MOUSY
MOUSIES > MOUSIE
MOUSIEST > MOUSY
MOUSILY > MOUSY
MOUSINESS > MOUSY
MOUSING *n* lashing, shackle, etc, for closing off a hook to prevent a load from slipping off
MOUSINGS > MOUSING
MOUSLE *vb* handle roughly
MOUSLED > MOUSLE
MOUSLES > MOUSLE
MOUSLING > MOUSLE
MOUSME *n* Japanese girl
MOUSMEE *same as* > MOUSME
MOUSMEES > MOUSMEE
MOUSMES > MOUSME
MOUSSAKA *n* dish made with meat, aubergines, and tomatoes, topped with cheese sauce
MOUSSAKAS > MOUSSAKA
MOUSSE *n* dish of flavoured cream whipped and set ▷ *vb* apply mousse to
MOUSSED > MOUSSE
MOUSSES > MOUSSE
MOUSSING > MOUSSE
MOUST *same as* > MUST
MOUSTACHE *n* hair on the upper lip
MOUSTED > MOUST
MOUSTING > MOUST
MOUSTS > MOUST
MOUSY *adj* like a mouse, esp in hair colour
MOUTAN *n* variety of peony
MOUTANS > MOUTAN
MOUTER *same as* > MULTURE
MOUTERED > MOUTER
MOUTERER > MOUTER
MOUTERERS > MOUTER
MOUTERING > MOUTER
MOUTERS > MOUTER
MOUTH *n* opening in the head for eating and issuing sounds ▷ *vb* form (words) with the lips without speaking
MOUTHABLE *adj* able to be recited
MOUTHED > MOUTH
MOUTHER > MOUTH
MOUTHERS > MOUTH
MOUTHFEEL *n* texture of a substance as it is perceived in the mouth
MOUTHFUL *n* amount of food or drink put into the mouth at any one time when eating or drinking
MOUTHFULS > MOUTHFUL
MOUTHIER > MOUTHY
MOUTHIEST > MOUTHY
MOUTHILY > MOUTHY
MOUTHING > MOUTH
MOUTHLESS > MOUTH
MOUTHLIKE > MOUTH
MOUTHPART *n* any of the paired appendages in arthropods that surround the mouth and are specialized for feeding
MOUTHS > MOUTH
MOUTHWASH *n* medicated liquid for gargling and cleansing the mouth
MOUTHY *adj* bombastic
MOUTON *n* sheepskin processed to resemble the fur of another animal, esp beaver or seal
MOUTONNEE *n* rounded by action of glacier
MOUTONS > MOUTON

MOVABLE *adj* able to be moved or rearranged ▷ *n* movable article, esp a piece of furniture
MOVABLES > MOVABLE
MOVABLY > MOVABLE
MOVE *vb* change in place or position ▷ *n* moving
MOVEABLE *same as* > MOVABLE
MOVEABLES > MOVEABLE
MOVEABLY > MOVEABLE
MOVED > MOVE
MOVELESS *adj* immobile
MOVEMENT *n* action or process of moving
MOVEMENTS > MOVEMENT
MOVER *n* person or animal that moves in a particular way
MOVERS > MOVER
MOVES > MOVE
MOVIE *n* cinema film
MOVIEDOM *n* world of cinema
MOVIEDOMS > MOVIEDOM
MOVIEGOER *n* person who goes to cinema
MOVIELAND *same as* > MOVIEDOM
MOVIEOKE *n* entertainment in which people act out well-known scenes from movies that are silently playing in the background
MOVIEOKES > MOVIEOKE
MOVIEOLA *same as* > MOVIOLA
MOVIEOLAS > MOVIEOLA
MOVIES > MOVIE
MOVING *adj* arousing or touching the emotions
MOVINGLY > MOVING
MOVIOLA *n* viewing machine used in cutting and editing film
MOVIOLAS > MOVIOLA
MOW *vb* cut (grass or crops) ▷ *n* part of a barn where hay, straw, etc, is stored
MOWA *same as* > MAHUA
MOWAS > MOWA
MOWBURN *vb* heat up in mow
MOWBURNED > MOWBURN
MOWBURNS > MOWBURN
MOWBURNT *adj* (of hay, straw, etc) damaged by overheating in a mow
MOWDIE *Scot words for* > MOLE
MOWDIES > MOWDIE
MOWED > MOW
MOWER > MOW
MOWERS > MOW
MOWING > MOW
MOWINGS > MOW
MOWN > MOW
MOWRA *same as* > MAHUA
MOWRAS > MOWRA
MOWS > MOW
MOXA *n* downy material obtained from various plants and used in Oriental medicine by being burned on the skin as a cauterizing agent or counterirritant for the skin
MOXAS > MOXA
MOXIE *n* courage, nerve, or vigour
MOXIES > MOXIE
MOY *n* coin
MOYA *n* mud emitted from a volcano
MOYAS > MOYA
MOYGASHEL *n* type of linen
MOYITIES > MOIETY
MOYITY *same as* > MOIETY
MOYL *same as* > MOYLE
MOYLE *vb* toil
MOYLED > MOYLE
MOYLES > MOYLE
MOYLING > MOYLE
MOYLS > MOYL
MOYS > MOY
MOZ *n* hex ▷ *vb* jinx someone or something
MOZE *vb* give nap to
MOZED > MOZE
MOZES > MOZ
MOZETTA *same as* > MOZZETTA
MOZETTAS > MOZETTA
MOZETTE > MOZETTA
MOZING > MOZE
MOZO *n* porter in southwest USA
MOZOS > MOZO
MOZZ *same as* > MOZ
MOZZES > MOZZ
MOZZETTA *n* short hooded cape worn by the pope, cardinals, etc
MOZZETTAS > MOZZETTA
MOZZETTE > MOZZETTA
MOZZIE *same as* > MOSSIE
MOZZIES > MOZZIE
MOZZLE *n* luck
MOZZLES > MOZZLE
MPRET *n* former Albanian ruler
MPRETS > MPRET
MRIDAMGAM *same as* > MRIDANG
MRIDANG *n* drum used in Indian music
MRIDANGA *same as* > MRIDANG
MRIDANGAM *same as* > MRIDANG
MRIDANGAS > MRIDANGA
MRIDANGS > MRIDANG
MU *n* 12th letter in the Greek alphabet, a consonant, transliterated as *m*
MUCATE *n* salt of mucic acid
MUCATES > MUCATE
MUCH *adj* large amount or degree of ▷ *n* large amount or degree ▷ *adv* great degree
MUCHACHO *n* young man
MUCHACHOS > MUCHACHO
MUCHEL *same as* > MUCH
MUCHELL *same as* > MUCH
MUCHELLS > MUCHELL
MUCHELS > MUCHEL
MUCHES > MUCH
MUCHLY > MUCH
MUCHNESS *n* magnitude
MUCHO *adv* Spanish for very
MUCIC as in *mucic acid* colourless crystalline solid carboxylic acid found in milk sugar and used in the manufacture of pyrrole
MUCID *adj* mouldy, musty, or slimy
MUCIDITY > MUCID
MUCIDNESS > MUCID
MUCIGEN *n* substance present in mucous cells that is converted into mucin
MUCIGENS > MUCIGEN
MUCILAGE *n* gum or glue
MUCILAGES > MUCILAGE
MUCIN *n* any of a group of nitrogenous mucoproteins occurring in saliva, skin, tendon, etc, that produce a very viscous solution in water
MUCINOGEN *n* substance forming mucin
MUCINOID *adj* of or like mucin
MUCINOUS > MUCIN
MUCINS > MUCIN
MUCK *n* dirt, filth
MUCKAMUCK *n* food ▷ *vb* consume food
MUCKED > MUCK
MUCKENDER *n* handkerchief
MUCKER *n* person who shifts broken rock or waste ▷ *vb* hoard
MUCKERED > MUCKER
MUCKERING > MUCKER
MUCKERISH > MUCKER
MUCKERS > MUCKER
MUCKHEAP *n* dunghill
MUCKHEAPS > MUCKHEAP
MUCKIER > MUCKY
MUCKIEST > MUCKY
MUCKILY > MUCKY
MUCKINESS > MUCKY
MUCKING > MUCK
MUCKLE *same as* > MICKLE
MUCKLES > MUCKLE
MUCKLUCK *same as* > MUKLUK
MUCKLUCKS > MUCKLUCK
MUCKRAKE *n* agricultural rake for spreading manure ▷ *vb* seek out and expose scandal, esp concerning public figures
MUCKRAKED > MUCKRAKE
MUCKRAKER > MUCKRAKE
MUCKRAKES > MUCKRAKE
MUCKS > MUCK
MUCKSWEAT *n* profuse sweat
MUCKWORM *n* any larva or worm that lives in mud
MUCKWORMS > MUCKWORM
MUCKY *adj* dirty or muddy
MUCLUC *same as* > MUKLUK
MUCLUCS > MUCLUC
MUCOID *adj* of the nature of or resembling mucin ▷ *n* substance like mucin
MUCOIDAL *same as* > MUCOID
MUCOIDS > MUCOID
MUCOLYTIC *adj* breaking down mucus
MUCOR *n* any fungus belonging to the genus *Mucor*, which comprises many common moulds
MUCORS > MUCOR
MUCOSA *n* mucous membrane: mucus-secreting membrane that lines body cavities or passages that are open to the external environment
MUCOSAE > MUCOSA
MUCOSAL > MUCOSA
MUCOSAS > MUCOSA
MUCOSE *same as* > MUCOUS
MUCOSITY > MUCOUS
MUCOUS *adj* of, resembling or secreting mucus
MUCRO *n* short pointed projection from certain parts or organs, as from the tip of a leaf
MUCRONATE *adj* terminating in a sharp point
MUCRONES > MUCRO
MUCROS > MUCRO
MUCULENT *adj* like mucus
MUCUS *n* slimy secretion of the mucous membranes
MUCUSES > MUCUS
MUD *n* wet soft earth ▷ *vb* cover in mud
MUDBATH *n* medicinal bath in heated mud
MUDBATHS > MUDBATH
MUDBUG *n* crayfish
MUDBUGS > MUDBUG
MUDCAP *vb* use explosive charge in blasting
MUDCAPPED > MUDCAP
MUDCAPS > MUDCAP
MUDCAT *n* any of several large North American catfish living in muddy rivers, esp in the Mississippi valley
MUDCATS > MUDCAT
MUDDED > MUD
MUDDER *n* horse that runs well in mud
MUDDERS > MUDDER
MUDDIED > MUDDY
MUDDIER > MUDDY
MUDDIES > MUDDY
MUDDIEST > MUDDY
MUDDILY > MUDDY
MUDDINESS > MUDDY
MUDDING > MUD
MUDDLE *vb* confuse ▷ *n* state of confusion
MUDDLED > MUDDLE
MUDDLER *n* person who muddles or muddles through
MUDDLERS > MUDDLER
MUDDLES > MUDDLE

JDDLING > MUDDLE
JDDLY > MUDDLE
JDDY *adj* covered or filled with mud ▷ *vb* make muddy
JDDYING > MUDDY
JDEJAR *n* Spanish Moor, esp one permitted to stay in Spain after the Christian reconquest ▷ *adj* of or relating to a style of architecture orginated by Mudéjares
JDEJARES > MUDEJAR
JDEYE *n* larva of the dragonfly, commonly used as a fishing bait
JDEYES > MUDEYE
JDFISH *n* any of various fishes, such as the bowfin and cichlids, that live at or frequent the muddy bottoms of rivers, lakes, etc
JDFISHES > MUDFISH
JDFLAP *n* flap above wheel to deflect mud
JDFLAPS > MUDFLAP
JDFLAT *n* tract of low muddy land, esp near an estuary, that is covered at high tide and exposed at low tide
JDFLATS > MUDFLAT
JDFLOW *n* flow of soil or fine-grained sediment mixed with water down a steep unstable slope
JDFLOWS > MUDFLOW
JDGE *vb* speak vaguely
JDGED > MUDGE
JDGER > MUDGE
JDGERS > MUDGE
JDGES > MUDGE
JDGING > MUDGE
JDGUARD *n* cover over a wheel to prevent mud or water being thrown up by it
JDGUARDS > MUDGUARD
JDHEN *n* water bird living in muddy place
JDHENS > MUDHEN
JDHOLE *n* hole with mud at bottom
JDHOLES > MUDHOLE
JDHOOK *n* anchor
JDHOOKS > MUDHOOK
JDIR *n* local governor
JDIRIA *n* province of mudir
JDIRIAS > MUDIRIA
JDIRIEH *same as* > MUDIRIA
JDIRIEHS > MUDIRIEH
JDIRS > MUDIR
JDLARK *n* street urchin ▷ *vb* play in mud
JDLARKED > MUDLARK
JDLARKS > MUDLARK
JDLOGGER *n* person checking mud for traces of oil
JDPACK *n* cosmetic paste applied to the face to improve the complexion
MUDPACKS > MUDPACK
MUDPUPPY *n* aquatic North American salamander of the genus with red feathery external gills and other persistent larval features
MUDRA *n* any of various ritual hand movements in Hindu religious dancing
MUDRAS > MUDRA
MUDROCK *n* type of sedimentary rock
MUDROCKS > MUDROCK
MUDROOM *n* room where muddy shoes may be left
MUDROOMS > MUDROOM
MUDS > MUD
MUDSCOW *n* boat for travelling over mudflats
MUDSCOWS > MUDSCOW
MUDSILL *n* support for building at or below ground
MUDSILLS > MUDSILL
MUDSLIDE *n* landslide of mud
MUDSLIDES > MUDSLIDE
MUDSTONE *n* dark grey clay rock similar to shale but with the lamination less well developed
MUDSTONES > MUDSTONE
MUDWORT *n* plant growing in mud
MUDWORTS > MUDWORT
MUEDDIN *same as* > MUEZZIN
MUEDDINS > MUEDDIN
MUENSTER *n* whitish-yellow semihard whole milk cheese, often flavoured with caraway or aniseed
MUENSTERS > MUENSTER
MUESLI *n* mixture of grain, nuts, and dried fruit, eaten with milk
MUESLIS > MUESLI
MUEZZIN *n* official who summons Muslims to prayer
MUEZZINS > MUEZZIN
MUFF *n* tube-shaped covering to keep the hands warm ▷ *vb* bungle (an action)
MUFFED > MUFF
MUFFIN *n* light round flat yeast cake
MUFFINEER *n* muffin dish
MUFFING > MUFF
MUFFINS > MUFFIN
MUFFISH > MUFF
MUFFLE *vb* wrap up for warmth or to deaden sound ▷ *n* something that muffles
MUFFLED > MUFFLE
MUFFLER *n* scarf
MUFFLERED *adj* with muffler
MUFFLERS > MUFFLER
MUFFLES > MUFFLE
MUFFLING > MUFFLE
MUFFS > MUFF
MUFLON *same as* > MOUFFLON
MUFLONS > MUFLON
MUFTI *n* civilian clothes worn by a person who usually wears a uniform
MUFTIS > MUFTI
MUG *n* large drinking cup ▷ *vb* attack in order to rob
MUGEARITE *n* crystalline rock
MUGFUL *same as* > MUG
MUGFULS > MUGFUL
MUGG *same as* > MUG
MUGGA *n* Australian eucalyptus tree with dark bark and pink flowers, *Eucalyptus sideroxylon*
MUGGAR *same as* > MUGGER
MUGGARS > MUGGAR
MUGGAS > MUGGA
MUGGED > MUG
MUGGEE *n* mugged person
MUGGEES > MUGGEE
MUGGER *n* person who commits robbery with violence, esp in the street
MUGGERS > MUGGER
MUGGIER > MUGGY
MUGGIEST > MUGGY
MUGGILY > MUGGY
MUGGINESS > MUGGY
MUGGING > MUG
MUGGINGS > MUG
MUGGINS *n* stupid or gullible person
MUGGINSES > MUGGINS
MUGGISH *same as* > MUGGY
MUGGS > MUG
MUGGUR *same as* > MUGGER
MUGGURS > MUGGUR
MUGGY *adj* (of weather) damp and stifling
MUGHAL *same as* > MOGUL
MUGHALS > MUGHAL
MUGS > MUG
MUGSHOT *n* police photograph of person's face
MUGSHOTS > MUGSHOT
MUGWORT *n* N temperate perennial herbaceous plant, *Artemisia vulgaris*, with aromatic leaves and clusters of small greenish-white flowers: family *Asteraceae* (composites)
MUGWORTS > MUGWORT
MUGWUMP *n* neutral or independent person, esp in politics
MUGWUMPS > MUGWUMP
MUHLIES > MUHLY
MUHLY *n* American grass
MUID *n* former French measure of capacity
MUIDS > MUID
MUIL *same as* > MULE
MUILS > MUIL
MUIR *Scots word for* > MOOR
MUIRBURN *same as* > MOORBURN
MUIRBURNS > MUIRBURN
MUIRS > MUIR
MUIST *same as* > MUST
MUISTED > MUIST
MUISTING > MUIST
MUISTS > MUIST
MUJAHEDIN *n* Muslim guerrilla
MUJAHIDIN *same as* > MUJAHEDIN
MUJIK *same as* > MUZHIK
MUJIKS > MUJIK
MUKHTAR *n* lawyer in India
MUKHTARS > MUKHTAR
MUKLUK *n* soft boot, usually of sealskin, worn in the American Arctic
MUKLUKS > MUKLUK
MUKTUK *n* thin outer skin of the beluga, used as food
MUKTUKS > MUKTUK
MULATTA *n* female mulatto
MULATTAS > MULATTA
MULATTO *n* child of one Black and one White parent ▷ *adj* of a light brown colour
MULATTOES > MULATTO
MULATTOS > MULATTO
MULBERRY *n* tree whose leaves are used to feed silkworms ▷ *adj* dark purple
MULCH *n* mixture of wet straw, leaves, etc, used to protect the roots of plants ▷ *vb* cover (land) with mulch
MULCHED > MULCH
MULCHES > MULCH
MULCHING > MULCH
MULCT *vb* cheat or defraud ▷ *n* fine or penalty
MULCTED > MULCT
MULCTING > MULCT
MULCTS > MULCT
MULE *n* offspring of a horse and a donkey ▷ *vb* strike coin with different die on each side
MULED > MULE
MULES *vb* surgically remove folds of skin from a sheep
MULESED > MULES
MULESES > MULES
MULESING > MULES
MULETA *n* small cape attached to a stick used by the matador during the final stages of a bullfight
MULETAS > MULETA
MULETEER *n* mule driver
MULETEERS > MULETEER
MULEY *adj* (of cattle) having no horns ▷ *n* any hornless cow
MULEYS > MULEY
MULGA *n* Australian acacia shrub growing in desert regions
MULGAS > MULGA
MULING > MULE
MULISH *adj* obstinate

MULISHLY > MULISH
MULL *vb* think (over) or ponder ▷ *n* promontory or headland
MULLA *same as* > MULLAH
MULLAH *n* Muslim scholar, teacher, or religious leader
MULLAHISM *n* rule by mullahs
MULLAHS > MULLAH
MULLARKY *same as* > MALARKEY
MULLAS > MULLA
MULLED > MULL
MULLEIN *n* type of European plant
MULLEINS > MULLEIN
MULLEN *same as* > MULLEIN
MULLENS > MULLEN
MULLER *n* flat heavy implement of stone or iron used to grind material against a slab of stone
MULLERED *adj* drunk
MULLERS > MULLER
MULLET *n* edible sea fish
MULLETS > MULLET
MULLEY *same as* > MULEY
MULLEYS > MULLEY
MULLIGAN *n* stew made from odds and ends of food
MULLIGANS > MULLIGAN
MULLING > MULL
MULLION *n* vertical dividing bar in a window ▷ *vb* furnish (a window, screen, etc) with mullions
MULLIONED > MULLION
MULLIONS > MULLION
MULLITE *n* colourless mineral
MULLITES > MULLITE
MULLOCK *n* waste material from a mine
MULLOCKS > MULLOCK
MULLOCKY > MULLOCK
MULLOWAY *n* large Australian sea fish, valued for sport and food
MULLOWAYS > MULLOWAY
MULLS > MULL
MULMUL *n* muslin
MULMULL *same as* > MULMUL
MULMULLS > MULMULL
MULMULS > MULMUL
MULSE *n* drink containing honey
MULSES > MULSE
MULSH *same as* > MULCH
MULSHED > MULSH
MULSHES > MULSH
MULSHING > MULSH
MULTEITY *n* manifoldness
MULTIAGE *adj* involving different age groups
MULTIATOM *adj* involving many atoms
MULTIBAND *adj* involving more than one waveband
MULTIBANK *adj* involving more than one bank
MULTICAR *adj* involving several cars
MULTICAST *n* broadcast from one source simultaneously to several receivers on a network
MULTICELL *adj* involving many cells
MULTICIDE *n* mass murder
MULTICITY *adj* involving more than one city
MULTICOPY *adj* involving many copies
MULTIDAY *adj* involving more than one day
MULTIDISC *adj* involving more than one disc
MULTIDRUG *adj* involving more than one drug
MULTIFID *adj* having or divided into many lobes or similar segments
MULTIFIL *n* fibre made up of many filaments
MULTIFILS > MULTIFIL
MULTIFOIL *n* ornamental design having a large number of foils
MULTIFOLD *adj* many times doubled
MULTIFORM *adj* having many shapes or forms
MULTIGERM *adj* (of plants) having the ability to multiply germinate
MULTIGRID *adj* involving several grids
MULTIGYM *n* exercise apparatus incorporating a variety of weights, used for toning the muscles
MULTIGYMS > MULTIGYM
MULTIHUED *adj* having many colours
MULTIHULL *n* sailing vessel with two or more hulls
MULTIJET *adj* involving more than one jet
MULTILANE *adj* having several lanes
MULTILINE *adj* involving several lines
MULTILOBE *adj* having more than one lobe
MULTIMODE *adj* involving several modes
MULTIPACK *n* form of packaging of foodstuffs, etc, that contains several units and is offered at a price below that of the equivalent number of units
MULTIPAGE *adj* involving many pages
MULTIPARA *n* woman who has given birth to more than one viable fetus or living child
MULTIPART *adj* involving many parts
MULTIPATH *adj* relating to television or radio signals that travel by more than one route from a transmitter and arrive at slightly different times, causing ghost images or audio distortion
MULTIPED *adj* having many feet ▷ *n* insect or animal having many feet
MULTIPEDE *same as* > MULTIPED
MULTIPEDS > MULTIPED
MULTIPION *adj* involving many pions
MULTIPLE *adj* having many parts ▷ *n* quantity which contains another an exact number of times
MULTIPLES > MULTIPLE
MULTIPLET *n* set of closely spaced lines in a spectrum, resulting from small differences between the energy levels of atoms or molecules
MULTIPLEX *n* purpose-built complex containing several cinemas and usu. restaurants and bars ▷ *adj* having many elements, complex ▷ *vb* send (messages or signals) or (of messages or signals) be sent by multiplex
MULTIPLY *vb* increase in number or degree
MULTIPOLE *adj* involving more than one pole
MULTIPORT *adj* involving more than one port
MULTIROLE *adj* having a number of roles, functions, etc
MULTIROOM *adj* having many rooms
MULTISITE *adj* involving more than one site
MULTISIZE *adj* involving more than size
MULTISTEP *adj* involving several steps
MULTITASK *vb* work at several different tasks simultaneously
MULTITON *adj* weighing several tons
MULTITONE *adj* involving more than one tone
MULTITUDE *n* great number
MULTIUNIT *adj* involving more than one unit
MULTIUSE *adj* suitable for more than one use
MULTIUSER > MULTIUSE
MULTIWALL *adj* involving several layers
MULTIYEAR *adj* involving more than one year
MULTUM *n* substance used in brewing
MULTUMS > MULTUM
MULTURE *n* fee formerly paid to a miller for grinding grain ▷ *vb* take multure
MULTURED > MULTURE
MULTURER > MULTURE
MULTURERS > MULTURE
MULTURES > MULTURE
MULTURING > MULTURE
MUM *n* mother ▷ *vb* act in a mummer's play
MUMBLE *vb* speak indistinctly, mutter ▷ *n* indistinct utterance
MUMBLED > MUMBLE
MUMBLER > MUMBLE
MUMBLERS > MUMBLE
MUMBLES > MUMBLE
MUMBLING > MUMBLE
MUMBLINGS > MUMBLE
MUMBLY > MUMBLE
MUMCHANCE *adj* silent
MUMM *same as* > MUM
MUMMED > MUM
MUMMER *n* actor in a traditional English folk play or mime
MUMMERIES > MUMMERY
MUMMERS > MUMMER
MUMMERY *n* performance by mummers
MUMMIA *n* mummified flesh used as medicine
MUMMIAS > MUMMIA
MUMMICHOG *n* small American fish
MUMMIED > MUMMY
MUMMIES > MUMMY
MUMMIFIED > MUMMIFY
MUMMIFIES > MUMMIFY
MUMMIFORM *adj* like mummy
MUMMIFY *vb* preserve the body of (a human or animal) as a mummy
MUMMING > MUM
MUMMINGS > MUM
MUMMOCK *same as* > MAMMOCK
MUMMOCKS > MUMMOCK
MUMMS > MUMM
MUMMY *n* body embalmed and wrapped for burial in ancient Egypt ▷ *vb* mummify
MUMMYING > MUMMY
MUMP *vb* be silent
MUMPED > MUMP
MUMPER > MUMP
MUMPERS > MUMP
MUMPING > MUMP
MUMPISH > MUMPS
MUMPISHLY > MUMPS
MUMPS *n* infectious disease with swelling in the glands of the neck
MUMPSIMUS *n* opinion held obstinately
MUMS > MUM
MUMSIER > MUMSY
MUMSIEST > MUMSY
MUMSY *adj* out of fashion
MUMU *n* oven in Papua New Guinea
MUMUS > MUMU
MUN *same as* > MAUN
MUNCH *vb* chew noisily and steadily
MUNCHABLE > MUNCH
MUNCHED > MUNCH

UNCHER > MUNCH
UNCHERS > MUNCH
UNCHES > MUNCH
UNCHIES *pl n* *the*. craving for food, induced by alcohol or drugs
UNCHING > MUNCH
UNCHKIN *n* undersized person or a child, esp an appealing one
UNCHKINS > MUNCHKIN
UNDANE *adj* everyday
UNDANELY > MUNDANE
UNDANER > MUNDANE
UNDANEST > MUNDANE
UNDANITY > MUNDANE
UNDIC *n* iron pyrites
UNDICS > MUNDIC
UNDIFIED > MUNDIFY
UNDIFIES > MUNDIFY
UNDIFY *vb* cleanse
UNDUNGO *n* tripe in Spain
UNDUNGOS > MUNDUNGO
UNDUNGUS *n* smelly tobacco
UNG *vb* process (computer data)
UNGA *n* army canteen
UNGAS > MUNGA
UNGCORN *n* maslin
UNGCORNS > MUNGCORN
UNGED > MUNG
UNGING > MUNG
UNGO *n* cheap felted fabric made from waste wool
UNGOES > MUNGO
UNGOOSE *same as* > MONGOOSE
UNGOOSES > MUNGOOSE
UNGOS > MUNGO
UNGS > MUNG
UNI *n* municipal radio broadcast
UNICIPAL *adj* relating to a city or town
UNIFIED > MUNIFY
UNIFIES > MUNIFY
UNIFY *vb* fortify
UNIFYING > MUNIFY
UNIMENT *n* means of defence
UNIMENTS *pl n* title deeds or similar documents
UNIS > MUNI
UNITE *vb* strengthen
UNITED > MUNITE
UNITES > MUNITE
UNITING > MUNITE
UNITION *vb* supply with munitions
UNITIONS *pl n* military stores
UNNION *archaic word for* > MULLION
UNNIONS > MUNNION
UNS > MUN
UNSHI *n* secretary in India
UNSHIS > MUNSHI
UNSTER *variant of* > MUENSTER
UNSTERS > MUNSTER
UNT *n* derogatory word for a Black African
UNTER *n* unattractive person
MUNTERS > MUNTER
MUNTIN *n* supporting or strengthening bar for a glass window, door, etc
MUNTING *same as* > MUNTIN
MUNTINGS > MUNTING
MUNTINS > MUNTIN
MUNTJAC *n* any small Asian deer of the genus *Muntiacus*, typically having a chestnut-brown coat, small antlers, and a barklike cry
MUNTJACS > MUNTJAC
MUNTJAK *same as* > MUNTJAC
MUNTJAKS > MUNTJAK
MUNTRIE *n* Australian shrub with green-red edible berries
MUNTRIES > MUNTRIE
MUNTS > MUNT
MUNTU *same as* > MUNT
MUNTUS > MUNTU
MUON *n* positive or negative elementary particle with a mass 207 times that of an electron
MUONIC > MUON
MUONIUM *n* form of hydrogen
MUONIUMS > MUONIUM
MUONS > MUON
MUPPET *n* stupid person
MUPPETS > MUPPET
MUQADDAM *n* person of authority in India
MUQADDAMS > MUQADDAM
MURA *n* group of people living together in Japanese countryside
MURAENA *n* moray eel
MURAENAS > MURAENA
MURAENID *n* eel of moray family
MURAENIDS > MURAENID
MURAGE *n* tax levied for the construction or maintenance of town walls
MURAGES > MURAGE
MURAL *n* painting on a wall ▷ *adj* of or relating to a wall
MURALED *same as* > MURALLED
MURALIST > MURAL
MURALISTS > MURAL
MURALLED *adj* decorated with mural
MURALS > MURAL
MURAS > MURA
MURDABAD *vb* down with
MURDER *n* unlawful intentional killing of a human being ▷ *vb* kill in this way
MURDERED > MURDER
MURDEREE *n* murder victim
MURDEREES > MURDEREE
MURDERER > MURDER
MURDERERS > MURDER
MURDERESS > MURDER
MURDERING > MURDER
MURDEROUS *adj* intending, capable of, or guilty of murder
MURDERS > MURDER
MURE *archaic or literary word for* > IMMURE
MURED > MURE
MUREIN *n* polymer found in cells
MUREINS > MUREIN
MURENA *same as* > MURAENA
MURENAS > MURENA
MURES > MURE
MUREX *n* any of various spiny-shelled marine gastropods of the genus *Murex* and related genera: formerly used as a source of the dye Tyrian purple
MUREXES > MUREX
MURGEON *vb* grimace at
MURGEONED > MURGEON
MURGEONS > MURGEON
MURIATE *obsolete name for a* > CHLORIDE
MURIATED > MURIATE
MURIATES > MURIATE
MURIATIC as in *muriatic acid* former name for a strong acid used in many industrial processes
MURICATE *adj* having a surface roughened by numerous short points
MURICATED *same as* > MURICATE
MURICES > MUREX
MURID *n* animal of mouse family
MURIDS > MURID
MURIFORM *adj* like mouse
MURINE *adj* of, relating to, or belonging to the *Muridae*, an Old World family of rodents, typically having long hairless tails: includes rats and mice ▷ *n* any animal belonging to the *Muridae*
MURINES > MURINE
MURING > MURE
MURK *n* thick darkness ▷ *adj* dark or gloomy
MURKER > MURK
MURKEST > MURK
MURKIER > MURKY
MURKIEST > MURKY
MURKILY > MURKY
MURKINESS > MURKY
MURKISH > MURK
MURKLY > MURK
MURKS > MURK
MURKSOME > MURK
MURKY *adj* dark or gloomy
MURL *vb* crumble
MURLAIN *n* type of basket
MURLAINS > MURLAIN
MURLAN *same as* > MURLAIN
MURLANS > MURLAN
MURLED > MURL
MURLIER > MURL
MURLIEST > MURL
MURLIN *same as* > MURLAIN
MURLING > MURL
MURLINS > MURLIN
MURLS > MURL
MURLY > MURL
MURMUR *vb* speak or say in a quiet indistinct way ▷ *n* continuous low indistinct sound
MURMURED > MURMUR
MURMURER > MURMUR
MURMURERS > MURMUR
MURMURING > MURMUR
MURMUROUS > MURMUR
MURMURS > MURMUR
MURPHIES > MURPHY
MURPHY *dialect or informal word for* > POTATO
MURR *n* former name for a cold
MURRA *same as* > MURRHINE
MURRAGH *n* type of large caddis fly
MURRAGHS > MURRAGH
MURRAIN *n* cattle plague
MURRAINED > MURRAIN
MURRAINS > MURRAIN
MURRAM *n* type of gravel
MURRAMS > MURRAM
MURRAS > MURRA
MURRAY *n* large Australian freshwater fish
MURRAYS > MURRAY
MURRE *n* any guillemot of the genus *Uria*
MURREE *n* native Australian
MURREES > MURREE
MURRELET *n* any of several small diving birds of the genus *Brachyramphus* and related genera, similar and related to the auks: family *Alcidae*, order *Charadriiformes*
MURRELETS > MURRELET
MURREN *same as* > MURRAIN
MURRENS > MURREN
MURRES > MURRE
MURREY *adj* mulberry colour
MURREYS > MURREY
MURRHA *same as* > MURRA
MURRHAS > MURRHA
MURRHINE *adj* of or relating to an unknown substance used in ancient Rome to make vases, cups, etc ▷ *n* substance so used
MURRI *same as* > MURREE
MURRIES > MURRY
MURRIN *same as* > MURRAIN
MURRINE *same as* > MURRHINE
MURRINS > MURRIN
MURRION *same as* > MURRAIN
MURRIONS > MURRION
MURRIS > MURRI
MURRS > MURR
MURRY *same as* > MORAY
MURTHER *same as* > MURDER
MURTHERED > MURTHER
MURTHERER > MURTHER
MURTHERS > MURTHER
MURTI *n* image of a deity, which itself is considered divine once consecrated

MURTIS > MURTI
MURVA *n* type of hemp
MURVAS > MURVA
MUS > MU
MUSACEOUS *adj* of, relating to, a family of tropical flowering plants with large leaves and clusters of elongated berry fruits: includes the banana, edible plantain, and Manila hemp
MUSANG *n* catlike aninal of Malaysia
MUSANGS > MUSANG
MUSAR *n* rabbinic literature concerned with ethics, right conduct, etc
MUSARS > MUSAR
MUSCA *n* small constellation in the S hemisphere lying between the Southern Cross and Chamaeleon
MUSCADEL *same as* > MUSCATEL
MUSCADELS > MUSCADEL
MUSCADET *n* white grape, grown esp in the Loire valley, used for making wine
MUSCADETS > MUSCADET
MUSCADIN *n* Parisian dandy
MUSCADINE *n* woody climbing vitaceous plant, *Vitis rotundifolia*, of the southeastern US
MUSCADINS > MUSCADIN
MUSCAE > MUSCA
MUSCARINE *n* poisonous alkaloid occurring in certain mushrooms
MUSCAT *same as* > MUSCATEL
MUSCATEL *n* rich sweet wine made from muscat grapes
MUSCATELS > MUSCATEL
MUSCATS > MUSCAT
MUSCAVADO *same as* > MUSCOVADO
MUSCID *n* any fly of the dipterous family *Muscidae*, including the housefly and tsetse fly ▷ *adj* of, relating to, or belonging to the *Muscidae*
MUSCIDS > MUSCID
MUSCLE *n* tissue in the body which produces movement by contracting ▷ *vb* force one's way (in)
MUSCLED > MUSCLE
MUSCLEMAN *n* man with highly developed muscles
MUSCLEMEN > MUSCLEMAN
MUSCLES > MUSCLE
MUSCLIER > MUSCLE
MUSCLIEST > MUSCLE
MUSCLING > MUSCLE
MUSCLINGS > MUSCLE
MUSCLY > MUSCLE
MUSCOID *adj* of family of plants
MUSCOLOGY *n* branch of botany
MUSCONE *same as* > MUSKONE
MUSCONES > MUSCONE
MUSCOSE *adj* like moss
MUSCOVADO *n* raw sugar obtained from the juice of sugar cane by evaporating the molasses
MUSCOVITE *n* pale brown, or green, or colourless mineral of the mica group
MUSCULAR *adj* with well-developed muscles
MUSCULOUS *adj* muscular
MUSE *vb* ponder quietly ▷ *n* state of abstraction
MUSED > MUSE
MUSEFUL > MUSE
MUSEFULLY > MUSE
MUSEOLOGY *n* science of museum organization
MUSER > MUSE
MUSERS > MUSE
MUSES > MUSE
MUSET *same as* > MUSIT
MUSETS > MUSET
MUSETTE *n* type of bagpipe with a bellows popular in France during the 17th and 18th centuries
MUSETTES > MUSETTE
MUSEUM *n* building where natural, artistic, historical, or scientific objects are exhibited and preserved
MUSEUMS > MUSEUM
MUSH *n* soft pulpy mass ▷ *interj* order to dogs in a sled team to start up or go faster ▷ *vb* travel by or drive a dogsled
MUSHA *interj* Irish exclamation of surprise
MUSHED > MUSH
MUSHER > MUSH
MUSHERS > MUSH
MUSHES > MUSH
MUSHIER > MUSHY
MUSHIEST > MUSHY
MUSHILY > MUSHY
MUSHINESS > MUSHY
MUSHING > MUSH
MUSHMOUTH *n* person speaking indistinctly
MUSHROOM *n* edible fungus with a stem and cap ▷ *vb* grow rapidly
MUSHROOMS > MUSHROOM
MUSHY *adj* soft and pulpy
MUSIC *n* art form using a melodious and harmonious combination of notes ▷ *vb* play music
MUSICAL *adj* of or like music ▷ *n* play or film with songs and dancing
MUSICALE *n* party or social evening with a musical programme
MUSICALES > MUSICALE
MUSICALLY > MUSICAL
MUSICALS > MUSICAL
MUSICIAN *n* person who plays or composes music, esp as a profession
MUSICIANS > MUSICIAN
MUSICK *same as* > MUSIC
MUSICKED > MUSIC
MUSICKER > MUSIC
MUSICKERS > MUSIC
MUSICKING > MUSIC
MUSICKS > MUSICK
MUSICLESS > MUSIC
MUSICS > MUSIC
MUSIMON *same as* > MOUFFLON
MUSIMONS > MUSIMON
MUSING > MUSE
MUSINGLY > MUSE
MUSINGS > MUSE
MUSIT *n* gap in fence
MUSITS > MUSIT
MUSIVE *adj* mosaic
MUSJID *same as* > MASJID
MUSJIDS > MUSJID
MUSK *n* scent obtained from a gland of the musk deer or produced synthetically ▷ *vb* perfume with musk
MUSKED > MUSK
MUSKEG *n* area of undrained boggy land
MUSKEGS > MUSKEG
MUSKET *n* long-barrelled gun
MUSKETEER *n* (formerly) a soldier armed with a musket
MUSKETOON *n* small musket
MUSKETRY *n* (use of) muskets
MUSKETS > MUSKET
MUSKIE *n* large North American freshwater game fish,
MUSKIER > MUSKIE
MUSKIES > MUSKIE
MUSKIEST > MUSKIE
MUSKILY > MUSKY
MUSKINESS > MUSKY
MUSKING > MUSK
MUSKIT *same as* > MESQUITE
MUSKITS > MUSKIT
MUSKLE *same as* > MUSSEL
MUSKLES > MUSKLE
MUSKMELON *n* any of several varieties of melon, such as the cantaloupe and honeydew
MUSKONE *n* substance in musk
MUSKONES > MUSKONE
MUSKOX *n* large Canadian mammal
MUSKOXEN > MUSKOX
MUSKRAT *n* N American beaver-like rodent
MUSKRATS > MUSKRAT
MUSKROOT *same as* > MOSCHATEL
MUSKROOTS > MUSKROOT
MUSKS > MUSK
MUSKY *same as* > MUSKIE
MUSLIN *n* fine cotton fabric
MUSLINED *adj* wearing muslin
MUSLINET *n* coarse muslin
MUSLINETS > MUSLINET
MUSLINS > MUSLIN
MUSMON *same as* > MUSIMON
MUSMONS > MUSMON
MUSO *n* musician, esp a pop musician, regarded as being overconcerned with technique rather than musical content or expression
MUSOS > MUSO
MUSPIKE *n* Canadian freshwater fish
MUSPIKES > MUSPIKE
MUSQUASH *same as* > MUSKRAT
MUSROL *n* part of bridle
MUSROLS > MUSROL
MUSS *vb* make untidy ▷ *n* state of disorder
MUSSE *same as* > MUSS
MUSSED > MUSS
MUSSEL *n* edible shellfish with a dark hinged shell
MUSSELLED *adj* poisoned through eating bad mussels
MUSSELS > MUSSEL
MUSSES > MUSS
MUSSIER > MUSSY
MUSSIEST > MUSSY
MUSSILY > MUSSY
MUSSINESS > MUSSY
MUSSING > MUSS
MUSSITATE *vb* mutter
MUSSY *adj* untidy or disordered
MUST *vb* used as an auxiliary to express obligation, certainty, or resolution ▷ *n* essential or necessary thing ▷ *vb* powder
MUSTACHE *same as* > MOUSTACHE
MUSTACHED > MUSTACHE
MUSTACHES > MUSTACHE
MUSTACHIO *n* moustache, esp a bushy or elaborate one
MUSTANG *n* wild horse of SW USA
MUSTANGS > MUSTANG
MUSTARD *n* paste made from the powdered seeds of a plant, used as a condiment ▷ *adj* brownish-yellow
MUSTARDS > MUSTARD
MUSTARDY > MUSTARD
MUSTED > MUST
MUSTEE *n* offspring of a White and a quadroon
MUSTEES > MUSTEE
MUSTELID *n* member of weasel family
MUSTELIDS > MUSTELID
MUSTELINE *adj* of, relating to, or belonging to the *Mustelidae*, family of typically predatory mammals including weasels, ferrets, minks,

polecats, badgers, skunks, and otters: order *Carnivora* (carnivores) ▷ *n* any musteline animal
JSTER *vb* summon up (strength, energy, or support) ▷ *n* assembly of military personnel
JSTERED > MUSTER
JSTERER > MUSTER
JSTERERS > MUSTER
JSTERING > MUSTER
JSTERS > MUSTER
JSTH *n* state of frenzied sexual excitement in the males of certain large mammals, esp elephants, associated with discharge from a gland between the ear and eye
JSTHS > MUSTH
JSTIER > MUSTY
JSTIEST > MUSTY
JSTILY > MUSTY
JSTINESS > MUSTY
JSTING > MUST
JSTS > MUST
JSTY *adj* smelling mouldy and stale
JT *another word for* > EM
JTABLE *adj* liable to change
JTABLY > MUTABLE
JTAGEN *n* any substance that can induce genetic mutation
JTAGENIC > MUTAGEN
JTAGENS > MUTAGEN
JTANDA > MUTANDUM
JTANDUM *n* something to be changed
JTANT *n* mutated animal, plant, etc ▷ *adj* of or resulting from mutation
JTANTS > MUTANT
JTASE *n* type of enzyme
JTASES > MUTASE
JTATE *vb* (cause to) undergo mutation
JTATED > MUTATE
JTATES > MUTATE
JTATING > MUTATE
JTATION *same as* > MUTANT
JTATIONS > MUTATION
JTATIVE > MUTATE
JTATORY *adj* subject to change
JTCH *n* close-fitting linen cap formerly worn by women and children in Scotland ▷ *vb* cadge
JTCHED > MUTCH
JTCHES > MUTCH
JTCHING > MUTCH
JTCHKIN *n* Scottish unit of liquid measure equal to slightly less than one pint
JTCHKINS > MUTCHKIN
JTE *adj* silent ▷ *n* person who is unable to speak ▷ *vb* reduce the volume or soften the tone of a musical instrument by means of a mute or soft pedal
MUTED *adj* (of sound or colour) softened
MUTEDLY > MUTED
MUTELY > MUTE
MUTENESS > MUTE
MUTER > MUTE
MUTES > MUTE
MUTEST > MUTE
MUTHA *n* taboo slang word derived from motherfucker
MUTHAS > MUTHA
MUTI *n* medicine, esp herbal medicine
MUTICATE *same as* > MUTICOUS
MUTICOUS *adj* lacking an awn, spine, or point
MUTILATE *vb* deprive of a limb or other part
MUTILATED > MUTILATE
MUTILATES > MUTILATE
MUTILATOR > MUTILATE
MUTINE *vb* mutiny
MUTINED > MUTINE
MUTINEER *n* person who mutinies
MUTINEERS > MUTINEER
MUTINES > MUTINE
MUTING > MUTE
MUTINIED > MUTINY
MUTINIES > MUTINY
MUTINING > MUTINE
MUTINOUS *adj* openly rebellious
MUTINY *n* rebellion against authority, esp by soldiers or sailors ▷ *vb* commit mutiny
MUTINYING > MUTINY
MUTIS > MUTI
MUTISM *n* state of being mute
MUTISMS > MUTISM
MUTON *n* part of gene
MUTONS > MUTON
MUTOSCOPE *n* early form of cine camera
MUTS > MUT
MUTT *n* mongrel dog
MUTTER *vb* utter or speak indistinctly ▷ *n* muttered sound or grumble
MUTTERED > MUTTER
MUTTERER > MUTTER
MUTTERERS > MUTTER
MUTTERING > MUTTER
MUTTERS > MUTTER
MUTTON *n* flesh of sheep, used as food
MUTTONS > MUTTON
MUTTONY > MUTTON
MUTTS > MUTT
MUTUAL *adj* felt or expressed by each of two people about the other ▷ *n* mutual company
MUTUALISE *same as* > MUTUALIZE
MUTUALISM *another name for* > SYMBIOSIS
MUTUALIST > MUTUALISM
MUTUALITY > MUTUAL
MUTUALIZE *vb* make or become mutual
MUTUALLY > MUTUAL
MUTUALS > MUTUAL
MUTUCA *same as* > MOTUCA
MUTUCAS > MUTUCA
MUTUEL *n* system of betting in which those who have bet on the winners of a race share in the total amount wagered less a percentage for the management
MUTUELS > MUTUEL
MUTULAR > MUTULE
MUTULE *n* one of a set of flat blocks below the corona of a Doric cornice
MUTULES > MUTULE
MUTUUM *n* contract for loan of goods
MUTUUMS > MUTUUM
MUUMUU *n* loose brightly-coloured dress worn by women in Hawaii
MUUMUUS > MUUMUU
MUX *vb* spoil
MUXED > MUX
MUXES > MUX
MUXING > MUX
MUZAKY *adj* having a bland sound
MUZHIK *n* Russian peasant, esp under the tsars
MUZHIKS > MUZHIK
MUZJIK *same as* > MUZHIK
MUZJIKS > MUZJIK
MUZZ *vb* make (something) muzzy
MUZZED > MUZZ
MUZZES > MUZZ
MUZZIER > MUZZY
MUZZIEST > MUZZY
MUZZILY > MUZZY
MUZZINESS > MUZZY
MUZZING > MUZZ
MUZZLE *n* animal's mouth and nose ▷ *vb* prevent from being heard or noticed
MUZZLED > MUZZLE
MUZZLER > MUZZLE
MUZZLERS > MUZZLE
MUZZLES > MUZZLE
MUZZLING > MUZZLE
MUZZY *adj* confused or muddled
MVULE *n* tropical African tree
MVULES > MVULE
MWALIMU *n* teacher
MWALIMUS > MWALIMU
MY *adj* belonging to me ▷ *interj* exclamation of surprise or awe ▷ *determiner* of, belonging to, or associated with the speaker or writer (me)
MYAL > MYALISM
MYALGIA *n* pain in a muscle or a group of muscles
MYALGIAS > MYALGIA
MYALGIC > MYALGIA
MYALISM *n* kind of witchcraft, similar to obi, practised esp in the Caribbean
MYALISMS > MYALISM
MYALIST > MYALISM
MYALISTS > MYALISM
MYALL *n* Australian acacia with hard scented wood
MYALLS > MYALL
MYASES > MYASIS
MYASIS *same as* > MYIASIS
MYC *n* oncogene that aids the growth of tumorous cells
MYCELE *n* microscopic spike-like structure in mucus
MYCELES > MYCELE
MYCELIA > MYCELIUM
MYCELIAL > MYCELIUM
MYCELIAN > MYCELIUM
MYCELIUM *n* mass forming the body of a fungus
MYCELLA *n* blue-veined Danish cream cheese, less strongly flavoured than Danish blue
MYCELLAS > MYCELLA
MYCELOID > MYCELIUM
MYCETES *n* fungus
MYCETOMA *n* chronic fungal infection, esp of the foot, characterized by swelling, usually resulting from a wound
MYCETOMAS > MYCETOMA
MYCOBIONT *n* fungal constituent of a lichen
MYCOFLORA *n* all fungus growing in particular place
MYCOLOGIC > MYCOLOGY
MYCOLOGY *n* study of fungi
MYCOPHAGY *n* eating of mushrooms
MYCOPHILE *n* person who likes eating mushrooms
MYCORHIZA *n* association of a fungus and a plant in which the fungus lives within or on the outside of the plant's roots forming a symbiotic or parasitic relationship
MYCOSES > MYCOSIS
MYCOSIS *n* any infection or disease caused by fungus
MYCOTIC > MYCOSIS
MYCOTOXIN *n* any of various toxic substances produced by fungi some of which may affect food and others of which are alleged to have been used in warfare
MYCOVIRUS *n* virus attacking fungi
MYCS > MYC
MYDRIASES > MYDRIASIS
MYDRIASIS *n* abnormal dilation of the pupil of the eye, produced by drugs, coma, etc

MYDRIATIC *adj* relating to or causing mydriasis ▷ *n* mydriatic drug
MYELIN *n* white tissue forming an insulating sheath around certain nerve fibres
MYELINE *same as* > MYELIN
MYELINES > MYELINE
MYELINIC > MYELIN
MYELINS > MYELIN
MYELITIS *n* inflammation of the spinal cord or of the bone marrow
MYELOCYTE *n* immature granulocyte, normally occurring in the bone marrow but detected in the blood in certain diseases
MYELOGRAM *n* X-ray of the spinal cord, after injection with a radio-opaque medium
MYELOID *adj* of or relating to the spinal cord or the bone marrow
MYELOMA *n* tumour of the bone marrow
MYELOMAS > MYELOMA
MYELOMATA > MYELOMA
MYELON *n* spinal cord
MYELONS > MYELON
MYGALE *n* large American spider
MYGALES > MYGALE
MYIASES > MYIASIS
MYIASIS *n* infestation of the body by the larvae of flies
MYIOPHILY *same as* > MYOPHILY
MYLAR *n* tradename for a kind of strong polyester film
MYLARS > MYLAR
MYLODON *n* prehistoric giant sloth
MYLODONS > MYLODON
MYLODONT *same as* > MYLODON
MYLODONTS > MYLODONT
MYLOHYOID *n* muscle in neck
MYLONITE *n* fine-grained metamorphic rock, often showing banding and micaceous fracture, formed by the crushing, grinding, or rolling of the original structure
MYLONITES > MYLONITE
MYLONITIC > MYLONITE
MYNA *same as* > MYNAH
MYNAH *n* tropical Asian starling which can mimic human speech
MYNAHS > MYNAH
MYNAS > MYNA
MYNHEER *n* Dutch title of addres
MYNHEERS > MYNHEER
MYOBLAST *n* cell from which muscle develops
MYOBLASTS > MYOBLAST
MYOCARDIA *pl n* muscular tissues of the heart
MYOCLONIC > MYOCLONUS
MYOCLONUS *n* sudden involuntary muscle contraction
MYOFIBRIL *n* type of cell in muscle
MYOGEN *n* albumin found in muscle
MYOGENIC *adj* originating in or forming muscle tissue
MYOGENS > MYOGEN
MYOGLOBIN *n* protein that is the main oxygen-carrier of muscle
MYOGRAM *n* tracings of muscular contractions
MYOGRAMS > MYOGRAM
MYOGRAPH *n* instrument for recording tracings of muscular contractions
MYOGRAPHS > MYOGRAPH
MYOGRAPHY > MYOGRAPH
MYOID *adj* like muscle
MYOLOGIC > MYOLOGY
MYOLOGIES > MYOLOGY
MYOLOGIST > MYOLOGY
MYOLOGY *n* branch of medical science concerned with the structure and diseases of muscles
MYOMA *n* benign tumour composed of muscle tissue
MYOMANCY *n* divination through observing mice
MYOMANTIC > MYOMANCY
MYOMAS > MYOMA
MYOMATA > MYOMA
MYOMATOUS > MYOMA
MYONEURAL *adj* involving muscle and nerve
MYOPATHIC > MYOPATHY
MYOPATHY *n* any disease affecting muscles or muscle tissue
MYOPE *n* any person afflicted with myopia
MYOPES > MYOPE
MYOPHILY *n* pollination of plants by flies
MYOPIA *n* short-sightedness
MYOPIAS > MYOPIA
MYOPIC *n* shortsighted person
MYOPICS > MYOPIC
MYOPIES > MYOPY
MYOPS *same as* > MYOPE
MYOPSES > MYOPS
MYOPY *same as* > MYOPIA
MYOSCOPE *n* electrical instrument for stimulating muscles
MYOSCOPES > MYOSCOPE
MYOSES > MYOSIS
MYOSIN *n* chief protein of muscle that interacts with actin to form actomyosin during muscle contraction
MYOSINS > MYOSIN
MYOSIS *same as* > MIOSIS
MYOSITIS *n* inflammation of muscle
MYOSOTE *same as* > MYOSOTIS
MYOSOTES > MYOSOTE
MYOSOTIS *n* any plant of the boraginaceous genus *Myosotis*
MYOTIC > MIOSIS
MYOTICS > MIOSIS
MYOTOME *n* any segment of embryonic mesoderm that develops into skeletal muscle in the adult
MYOTOMES > MYOTOME
MYOTONIA *n* lack of muscle tone, frequently including muscle spasm or rigidity
MYOTONIAS > MYOTONIA
MYOTONIC > MYOTONIA
MYOTUBE *n* cylindrical cell in muscle
MYOTUBES > MYOTUBE
MYRBANE *same as* > MIRBANE
MYRBANES > MYRBANE
MYRIAD *adj* innumerable ▷ *n* large indefinite number
MYRIADS > MYRIAD
MYRIADTH > MYRIAD
MYRIADTHS > MYRIAD
MYRIAPOD *n* invertebrate with a long segmented body and many legs, such as a centipede ▷ *adj* of, relating to, or belonging to the *Myriapoda*
MYRIAPODS > MYRIAPOD
MYRICA *n* dried root bark of the wax myrtle, used as a tonic and to treat diarrhoea
MYRICAS > MYRICA
MYRINGA *n* eardrum
MYRINGAS > MYRINGA
MYRIOPOD *same as* > MYRIAPOD
MYRIOPODS > MYRIOPOD
MYRIORAMA *n* picture made up of different parts
MYRISTIC *adj* of nutmeg plant family
MYRMECOID *adj* like ant
MYRMIDON *n* follower or henchman
MYRMIDONS > MYRMIDON
MYROBALAN *n* dried plumlike fruit of various tropical trees of the genus *Terminalia*, used in dyeing, tanning, ink, and medicine
MYRRH *n* aromatic gum used in perfume, incense, and medicine
MYRRHIC > MYRRH
MYRRHINE > MURRA
MYRRHOL *n* oil of myrrh
MYRRHOLS > MYRRHOL
MYRRHS > MYRRH
MYRTLE *n* flowering evergreen shrub
MYRTLES > MYRTLE
MYSELF *pron* reflexive form of *I* or *me*
MYSID *n* small shrimplike crustacean
MYSIDS > MYSID
MYSOST *n* Norwegian cheese
MYSOSTS > MYSOST
MYSTAGOG *n* person instructing others in religious mysteries
MYSTAGOGS > MYSTAGOG
MYSTAGOGY *n* instruction of those who are preparin for initiation into the mysteries
MYSTERIES > MYSTERY
MYSTERY *n* strange or inexplicable event or phenomenon
MYSTIC *n* person who seeks spiritual knowledg ▷ *adj* mystical
MYSTICAL *adj* having a spiritual or religious significance beyond human understanding
MYSTICETE *n* species of whale
MYSTICISM *n* belief in or experience of a reality beyond normal human understanding or experience
MYSTICLY > MYSTIC
MYSTICS > MYSTIC
MYSTIFIED > MYSTIFY
MYSTIFIER > MYSTIFY
MYSTIFIES > MYSTIFY
MYSTIFY *vb* bewilder or puzzle
MYSTIQUE *n* aura of mystery or power
MYSTIQUES > MYSTIQUE
MYTH *n* tale with supernatural characters, usu. of how the world an mankind began
MYTHI > MYTHUS
MYTHIC *same as* > MYTHICA
MYTHICAL *adj* of or relatin to myth
MYTHICISE *same as* > MYTHICIZE
MYTHICISM *n* theory that explains miracles as myt
MYTHICIST > MYTHICIZE
MYTHICIZE *vb* make into treat as a myth
MYTHIER > MYTHY
MYTHIEST > MYTHY
MYTHISE *same as* > MYTHIZ
MYTHISED > MYTHISE
MYTHISES > MYTHISE
MYTHISING > MYTHISE
MYTHISM *same as* > MYTHICISM
MYTHISMS > MYTHISM
MYTHIST > MYTHISM
MYTHISTS > MYTHISM
MYTHIZE *same as* > MYTHICIZE
MYTHIZED > MYTHIZE
MYTHIZES > MYTHIZE
MYTHIZING > MYTHIZE
MYTHMAKER *n* person who

creates myth
/THOI > MYTHOS
/THOLOGY *n* myths collectively
/THOMANE *n* obsession with lying, exaggerating, or relating incredible imaginary adventures as if they had really happened
/THOPEIC *adj* of myths
/THOPOET *n* poet writing on mythical theme
/THOS *n* complex of beliefs, values, attitudes, etc, characteristic of a specific group or society
/THS > MYTH
/THUS *same as* > MYTHOS
/THY *adj* of or like myth
/TILOID *adj* like mussel
/XAMEBA *same as* > MYXAMOEBA
/XAMEBAE > MYXAMEBA
/XAMEBAS > MYXAMEBA
/XAMOEBA *n* cell produced by spore
/XEDEMA *same as* > MYXOEDEMA
/XEDEMAS > MYXEDEMA
/XEDEMIC > MYXOEDEMA
/XO *n* infectious and usually fatal viral disease of rabbits characterized by swelling of the mucous membranes and formation of skin tumours
/XOCYTE *n* cell in mucous tissue
/XOCYTES > MYXOCYTE
/XOEDEMA *n* disease caused by an underactive thyroid gland, characterized by puffy eyes, face, and hands, and mental sluggishness
/XOID *adj* containing mucus
/XOMA *n* tumour composed of mucous connective tissue, usually situated in subcutaneous tissue
/XOMAS > MYXOMA
/XOMATA > MYXOMA
/XOS > MYXO
/XOVIRAL > MYXOVIRUS
/XOVIRUS *n* any of a group of viruses that cause influenza, mumps, and certain other diseases
:EE *n* old person ▷ *adj* advanced in years
:EES > MZEE
:UNGU *n* White person
:UNGUS > MZUNGU

Nn

NA *same as* > NAE
NAAM *same as* > NAM
NAAMS > NAAM
NAAN *n* slightly leavened flat Indian bread
NAANS > NAAN
NAARTJE *same as* > NAARTJIE
NAARTJES > NAARTJE
NAARTJIE *n* tangerine
NAARTJIES > NAARTJIE
NAB *vb* arrest (someone)
NABBED > NAB
NABBER *n* thief
NABBERS > NABBER
NABBING > NAB
NABE *n* Japanese hotpot
NABES > NABE
NABIS *n* Parisian art movement
NABK *n* edible berry
NABKS > NABK
NABLA *another name for* > DEL
NABLAS > NABLA
NABOB *same as* > NAWAB
NABOBERY > NABOB
NABOBESS *n* rich, powerful, or important woman
NABOBISH > NABOB
NABOBISM > NABOB
NABOBISMS > NABOB
NABOBS > NABOB
NABS > NAB
NACARAT *n* red-orange colour
NACARATS > NACARAT
NACELLE *n* streamlined enclosure on an aircraft, esp one housing an engine
NACELLES > NACELLE
NACH *n* Indian dance
NACHAS *n* pleasure
NACHE *n* rump
NACHES *same as* > NACHAS
NACHO *n* snack of a piece of tortilla topped with cheese, peppers, etc
NACHOS > NACHO
NACHTMAAL *same as* > NAGMAAL
NACKET *n* light lunch, snack
NACKETS > NACKET
NACRE *n* mother of pearl
NACRED > NACRE
NACREOUS *adj* relating to or consisting of mother-of-pearl
NACRES > NACRE
NACRITE *n* mineral
NACRITES > NACRITE
NACROUS > NACRE
NADA *n* nothing
NADAS > NADA
NADIR *n* point in the sky opposite the zenith
NADIRAL > NADIR
NADIRS > NADIR
NADORS *n* thirst brought on by excessive consumption of alcohol
NADS *pl n* testicles
NAE *Scot word for* > NO
NAEBODIES > NAEBODY
NAEBODY *Scots variant of* > NOBODY
NAETHING *Scots variant of* > NOTHING
NAETHINGS > NAETHING
NAEVE *n* birthmark
NAEVES > NAEVUS
NAEVI > NAEVUS
NAEVOID > NAEVUS
NAEVUS *n* birthmark or mole
NAFF *adj* lacking quality or taste ▷ *vb* go away
NAFFED > NAFF
NAFFER > NAFF
NAFFEST > NAFF
NAFFING > NAFF
NAFFLY > NAFF
NAFFNESS > NAFF
NAFFS > NAFF
NAG *vb* scold or find fault constantly ▷ *n* person who nags
NAGA *n* cobra
NAGANA *n* disease of all domesticated animals of central and southern Africa
NAGANAS > NAGANA
NAGAPIE *n* bushbaby
NAGAPIES > NAGAPIE
NAGARI *n* set of scripts used as the writing systems for several languages of India
NAGARIS > NAGARI
NAGAS > NAGA
NAGGED > NAG
NAGGER > NAG
NAGGERS > NAG
NAGGIER > NAG
NAGGIEST > NAG
NAGGING > NAG
NAGGINGLY > NAG
NAGGY > NAG
NAGMAAL *n* Communion
NAGMAALS > NAGMAAL
NAGOR *another name for* > REEDBUCK
NAGORS > NAGOR
NAGS > NAG
NAH *same as* > NO
NAHAL *n* agricultural settlement run by an Israeli military youth organization
NAHALS > NAHAL
NAIAD *n* nymph living in a lake or river
NAIADES > NAIAD
NAIADS > NAIAD
NAIANT *adj* swimming
NAIF *less common word for* > NAIVE
NAIFER > NAIF
NAIFEST > NAIF
NAIFLY > NAIVE
NAIFNESS > NAIVE
NAIFS > NAIF
NAIK *n* chief
NAIKS > NAIK
NAIL *n* pointed piece of metal with a head, hit with a hammer to join two objects together ▷ *v* attach (something) with nails
NAILBITER *n* person who bites his or her nails
NAILBRUSH *n* small stiff-bristled brush for cleanin the fingernails
NAILED > NAIL
NAILER > NAIL
NAILERIES > NAILERY
NAILERS > NAIL
NAILERY *n* nail factory
NAILFILE *n* small metal file used to shape and smooth the nails
NAILFILES > NAILFILE
NAILFOLD *n* skin at base c fingernail
NAILFOLDS > NAILFOLD
NAILHEAD *n* decorative device, as on tooled leather, resembling the round head of a nail
NAILHEADS > NAILHEAD

AILING > NAIL
AILINGS > NAIL
AILLESS > NAIL
AILS > NAIL
AILSET *n* punch for driving the head of a nail below the surrounding surface
AILSETS > NAILSET
AIN *adj* own
AINSELL *n* own self
AINSELLS > NAINSELL
AINSOOK *n* light soft plain-weave cotton fabric, used esp for babies' wear
AINSOOKS > NAINSOOK
AIRA *n* standard monetary unit of Nigeria, divided into 100 kobo
AIRAS > NAIRA
AIRU *n* Non-Accelerating Inflation Rate of Unemployment
AIRUS > NAIRU
AISSANCE *French for* > BIRTH
AISSANT *adj* (of a beast) having only the forepart shown above a horizontal division of a shield
AIVE *adj* innocent and gullible ▷ *n* person who is naive, esp in artistic style
AIVELY > NAIVE
AIVENESS > NAIVE
AIVER > NAIVE
AIVES > NAIVE
AIVEST > NAIVE
AIVETE *variant of* > NAIVETY
AIVETES > NAIVETE
AIVETIES > NAIVETY
AIVETY *n* state or quality of being naive
AIVIST > NAIVE
AKED *adj* without clothes
AKEDER > NAKED
AKEDEST > NAKED
AKEDLY > NAKED
AKEDNESS > NAKED
AKER *n* one of a pair of small kettledrums used in medieval music
AKERS > NAKER
AKFA *n* standard currency unit of Eritrea
AKFAS > NAKFA
ALA *n* ravine
ALAS > NALA
ALED *n* type of insecticide
ALEDS > NALED
ALLA *n* ravine
ALLAH *same as* > NALLA
ALLAHS > NALLAH
ALLAS > NALLA
ALOXONE *n* chemical substance that counteracts the effects of opiates by binding to opiate receptors on cells
ALOXONES > NALOXONE
M *n* distraint
MABLE > NAME
MASKAR *n* salutation used in India
NAMASKARS > NAMASKAR
NAMASTE *n* Indian greeting
NAMASTES > NAMASTE
NAMAYCUSH *n* North American freshwater fish
NAME *n* word by which a person or thing is known ▷ *vb* give a name to
NAMEABLE > NAME
NAMECHECK *vb* mention (someone) by name ▷ *n* mention of someone's name, for example on a radio programme
NAMED > NAME
NAMELESS *adj* without a name
NAMELY *adv* that is to say
NAMEPLATE *n* small sign on or by a door giving the occupant's name and, sometimes, profession
NAMER > NAME
NAMERS > NAME
NAMES > NAME
NAMESAKE *n* person with the same name as another
NAMESAKES > NAMESAKE
NAMETAG *n* identification badge
NAMETAGS > NAMETAG
NAMETAPE *n* narrow cloth tape bearing the owner's name and attached to an article
NAMETAPES > NAMETAPE
NAMING > NAME
NAMINGS > NAME
NAMMA as in *namma hole* Australian word for a natural well in rock
NAMS > NAM
NAMU *n* black New Zealand sandfly
NAN *n* grandmother
NANA *same as* > NAN
NANAS > NANA
NANCE *n* homosexual man
NANCES > NANCE
NANCIES > NANCY
NANCIFIED *adj* effeminate
NANCY *n* effeminate or homosexual boy or man
NANDIN *n* type of shrub
NANDINA *n* type of shrub
NANDINAS > NANDINA
NANDINE *n* African palm civet
NANDINES > NANDINE
NANDINS > NANDIN
NANDOO > NANDU
NANDOOS > NANDOO
NANDU *n* type of ostrich
NANDUS > NANDU
NANE *Scot word for* > NONE
NANISM *n* dwarfism
NANISMS > NANISM
NANKEEN *n* hard-wearing buff-coloured cotton fabric
NANKEENS > NANKEEN
NANKIN *same as* > NANKEEN
NANKINS > NANKIN
NANNA *same as* > NAN
NANNAS > NANNA
NANNIE *same as* > NANNY
NANNIED > NANNY
NANNIES > NANNY
NANNY *n* woman whose job is looking after young children ▷ *vb* be too protective towards
NANNYGAI *n* edible sea fish of Australia which is red in colour and has large prominent eyes
NANNYGAIS > NANNYGAI
NANNYING > NANNY
NANNYISH > NANNY
NANOBE *n* microbe that is smaller than the smallest known bacterium
NANOBES > NANOBE
NANODOT *n* microscopic cluster of several hundred nickel atoms used to store large amounts of data in a computer chip
NANODOTS > NANODOT
NANOGRAM *n* unit of measurement
NANOGRAMS > NANOGRAM
NANOMETER *same as* > NANOMETRE
NANOMETRE *n* one thousand-millionth of a metre
NANOOK *n* polar bear
NANOOKS > NANOOK
NANOSCALE *adj* on very small scale
NANOTECH *n* technology of very small objects
NANOTECHS > NANOTECH
NANOTESLA *n* unit of measurement
NANOTUBE *n* cylindrical molecule of carbon
NANOTUBES > NANOTUBE
NANOWATT *n* unit of measurement
NANOWATTS > NANOWATT
NANOWORLD *n* world at a microscopic level, as dealt with by nanotechnology
NANS > NAN
NANUA *same as* > MOKI
NAOI > NAOS
NAOS *n* ancient classical temple
NAOSES > NAOS
NAP *n* short sleep ▷ *vb* have a short sleep
NAPA *n* type of leather
NAPALM *n* highly inflammable jellied petrol, used in bombs ▷ *vb* attack (people or places) with napalm
NAPALMED > NAPALM
NAPALMING > NAPALM
NAPALMS > NAPALM
NAPAS > NAPA
NAPE *n* back of the neck ▷ *vb* attack with napalm
NAPED > NAPE
NAPERIES > NAPERY
NAPERY *n* household linen, esp table linen
NAPES > NAPE
NAPHTHA *n* liquid mixture distilled from coal tar or petroleum, used as a solvent and in petrol
NAPHTHAS > NAPHTHA
NAPHTHENE *n* any of a class of cycloalkanes found in petroleum
NAPHTHOL *n* white crystalline solid used in dyes
NAPHTHOLS > NAPHTHOL
NAPHTHOUS > NAPHTHA
NAPHTHYL *n* of, consisting of, or containing either of two forms of the monovalent group $C_{10}H_7$–
NAPHTHYLS > NAPHTHYL
NAPHTOL *same as* > NAPHTHOL
NAPHTOLS > NAPHTOL
NAPIFORM *adj* shaped like a turnip
NAPING > NAPE
NAPKIN *same as* > NAPPY
NAPKINS > NAPKIN
NAPLESS *adj* threadbare
NAPOLEON *n* former French gold coin worth 20 francs
NAPOLEONS > NAPOLEON
NAPOO *vb* kill
NAPOOED > NAPOO
NAPOOING > NAPOO
NAPOOS > NAPOO
NAPPA *n* soft leather, used in gloves and clothes, made from sheepskin, lambskin, or kid
NAPPAS > NAPPA
NAPPE *n* large sheet or mass of rock that has been thrust from its original position by earth movements
NAPPED > NAP
NAPPER *n* person or thing that raises the nap on cloth
NAPPERS > NAPPER
NAPPES > NAPPE
NAPPIE *same as* > NAPPY
NAPPIER > NAPPY
NAPPIES > NAPPY
NAPPIEST > NAPPY
NAPPINESS > NAPPY
NAPPING > NAP
NAPPY *n* piece of absorbent material fastened round a baby's lower torso to absorb urine and faeces ▷ *adj* having a nap
NAPRON *same as* > APRON
NAPRONS > NAPRON
NAPROXEN *n* pain-killing drug
NAPROXENS > NAPROXEN
NAPS > NAP
NARAS *same as* > NARRAS
NARASES > NARAS
NARC *n* narcotics agent
NARCEEN *same*

as > NARCEINE
NARCEENS > NARCEEN
NARCEIN *same as* > NARCEINE
NARCEINE *n* narcotic alkaloid that occurs in opium
NARCEINES > NARCEINE
NARCEINS > NARCEIN
NARCISM *n* exceptional admiration for oneself
NARCISMS > NARCISM
NARCISSI > NARCISSUS
NARCISSUS *n* yellow, orange, or white flower related to the daffodil
NARCIST *same as* > NARCISSIST
NARCISTIC *adj* excessively admiring of oneself
NARCISTS > NARCIST
NARCO *n* officer working in the area of anti-drug operations
NARCOMA *n* coma caused by intake of narcotic drugs
NARCOMAS > NARCOMA
NARCOMATA > NARCOMA
NARCOS *n* drug smugglers
NARCOSE *same as* > NARCOSIS
NARCOSES > NARCOSIS
NARCOSIS *n* effect of a narcotic
NARCOTIC *adj* of a drug, such as morphine or opium, which produces numbness and drowsiness, used medicinally but addictive ▷ *n* such a drug
NARCOTICS > NARCOTIC
NARCOTINE *n* type of drug
NARCOTISE *same as* > NARCOTIZE
NARCOTISM *n* stupor or addiction induced by narcotic drugs
NARCOTIST *n* person affected by narcotics
NARCOTIZE *vb* place under the influence of a narcotic drug
NARCS > NARC
NARD *n* any of several plants whose aromatic roots were formerly used in medicine ▷ *vb* anoint with nard oil
NARDED > NARD
NARDINE > NARD
NARDING > NARD
NARDOO *n* any of certain cloverlike ferns which grow in swampy areas
NARDOOS > NARDOO
NARDS > NARD
NARE *n* nostril
NARES *pl n* nostrils
NARGHILE *another name for* > HOOKAH
NARGHILES > NARGHILE
NARGHILLY *same as* > NARGHILE
NARGHILY *same as* > NARGHILE
NARGILE *same as* > NARGHILE
NARGILEH *same as* > NARGHILE
NARGILEHS > NARGILEH
NARGILES > NARGILE
NARGILIES > NARGILE
NARGILY *same as* > NARGHILE
NARIAL *adj* of or relating to the nares
NARIC > NARE
NARICORN *n* bird's nostril
NARICORNS > NARICORN
NARINE *same as* > NARIAL
NARIS > NARES
NARK *vb* annoy ▷ *n* informer or spy
NARKED > NARK
NARKIER > NARKY
NARKIEST > NARKY
NARKING > NARK
NARKS > NARK
NARKY *adj* irritable or complaining
NARQUOIS *adj* malicious
NARRAS *n* type of shrub
NARRASES > NARRAS
NARRATE *vb* tell (a story)
NARRATED > NARRATE
NARRATER *same as* > NARRATOR
NARRATERS > NARRATER
NARRATES > NARRATE
NARRATING > NARRATE
NARRATION *n* narrating
NARRATIVE *n* account, story ▷ *adj* telling a story
NARRATOR *n* person who tells a story or gives an account of something
NARRATORS > NARRATOR
NARRATORY > NARRATIVE
NARRE *adj* nearer
NARROW *adj* small in breadth in comparison to length ▷ *vb* make or become narrow
NARROWED > NARROW
NARROWER > NARROW
NARROWEST > NARROW
NARROWING > NARROW
NARROWISH > NARROW
NARROWLY > NARROW
NARROWS *pl n* narrow part of a strait, river, or current
NARTHEX *n* portico at the west end of a basilica or church
NARTHEXES > NARTHEX
NARTJIE *same as* > NAARTJIE
NARTJIES > NARTJIE
NARWAL *same as* > NARWHAL
NARWALS > NARWAL
NARWHAL *n* arctic whale with a long spiral tusk
NARWHALE *same as* > NARWHAL
NARWHALES > NARWHALE
NARWHALS > NARWHAL
NARY *adv* not
NAS *obsolete contraction of* has not
NASAL *adj* of the nose ▷ *n* nasal speech sound, such as English *m*, *n*, or *ng*
NASALISE *same as* > NASALIZE
NASALISED > NASALISE
NASALISES > NASALISE
NASALISM *n* nasal pronunciation
NASALISMS > NASALISM
NASALITY > NASAL
NASALIZE *vb* pronounce nasally
NASALIZED > NASALIZE
NASALIZES > NASALIZE
NASALLY > NASAL
NASALS > NASAL
NASARD *n* organ stop
NASARDS > NASARD
NASCENCE > NASCENT
NASCENCES > NASCENT
NASCENCY > NASCENT
NASCENT *adj* starting to grow or develop
NASEBERRY *another name for* > SAPODILLA
NASHGAB *n* chatter
NASHGABS > NASHGAB
NASHI *n* fruit of the Japanese pear
NASHIS > NASHI
NASIAL > NASION
NASION *n* craniometric point where the top of the nose meets the ridge of the forehead
NASIONS > NASION
NASSELLA as in *nassella tussock* type of tussock grass
NASTALIK *n* type of script
NASTALIKS > NASTALIK
NASTIC *adj* (of movement of plants) independent of the direction of the external stimulus
NASTIER > NASTY
NASTIES > NASTY
NASTIEST > NASTY
NASTILY > NASTY
NASTINESS > NASTY
NASTY *adj* unpleasant ▷ *n* something unpleasant
NASUTE *n* type of termite
NASUTES > NASUTE
NAT *n* supporter of nationalism
NATAL *adj* of or relating to birth
NATALITY *n* birth rate in a given place
NATANT *adj* (of aquatic plants) floating on the water
NATANTLY *adv* in a floating manner
NATATION *n* swimming
NATATIONS > NATATION
NATATORIA *pl n* indoor swimming pools
NATATORY *adj* of or relating to swimming
NATCH *sentence substitute* naturally ▷ *n* notch
NATCHES > NATCH
NATES *pl n* buttocks
NATHELESS *prep* notwithstanding
NATHEMO *same as* > NATHEMORE
NATHEMORE *adv* nevermor
NATHLESS *same as* > NATHELESS
NATIFORM *adj* resembling buttocks
NATION *n* people of one or more cultures or races organized as a single stat
NATIONAL *adj* of or servin a nation as a whole ▷ *n* citizen of a nation
NATIONALS > NATIONAL
NATIONS > NATION
NATIVE *adj* relating to a place where a person was born ▷ *n* person born in a specified place
NATIVELY > NATIVE
NATIVES > NATIVE
NATIVISM *n* policy of favouring the natives of a country over the immigrants
NATIVISMS > NATIVISM
NATIVIST > NATIVISM
NATIVISTS > NATIVISM
NATIVITY *n* birth or origi
NATRIUM *obsolete name for* > SODIUM
NATRIUMS > NATRIUM
NATROLITE *n* colourless, white, or yellow zeolite mineral
NATRON *n* whitish or yello mineral
NATRONS > NATRON
NATS > NAT
NATTER *vb* talk idly or chatter ▷ *n* long idle cha
NATTERED > NATTER
NATTERER > NATTER
NATTERERS > NATTER
NATTERING > NATTER
NATTERS > NATTER
NATTERY *adj* irritable
NATTIER > NATTY
NATTIEST > NATTY
NATTILY > NATTY
NATTINESS > NATTY
NATTY *adj* smart and spru
NATURA *n* nature
NATURAE > NATURA
NATURAL *adj* normal or to be expected ▷ *n* person with an inborn talent or skill
NATURALLY > NATURAL
NATURALS > NATURAL
NATURE *n* whole system of the existence, forces, and events of the physica world that are not controlled by human beings
NATURED *adj* having a certain disposition
NATURES > NATURE

ATURING *adj* creative
ATURISM *n* nudism
ATURISMS > NATURISM
ATURIST > NATURISM
ATURISTS > NATURISM
AUCH *same as* > NAUTCH
AUCHES > NAUCH
AUGAHYDE *n* type of vinyl-coated fabric
AUGHT *n* nothing ▷ *adv* not at all
AUGHTIER > NAUGHTY
AUGHTIES > NAUGHTY
AUGHTILY > NAUGHTY
AUGHTS > NAUGHT
AUGHTY *adj* disobedient or mischievous ▷ *n* act of sexual intercourse
AUMACHIA *n* mock sea fight performed as an entertainment
AUMACHY *same as* > NAUMACHIA
AUNT *n* aunt
AUNTS > NAUNT
AUPLIAL > NAUPLIUS
AUPLII > NAUPLIUS
AUPLIOID > NAUPLIUS
AUPLIUS *n* larva of many crustaceans
AUSEA *n* feeling of being about to vomit
AUSEANT *n* substance inducing nausea
AUSEANTS > NAUSEANT
AUSEAS > NAUSEA
AUSEATE *vb* make (someone) feel sick
AUSEATED > NAUSEATE
AUSEATES > NAUSEATE
AUSEOUS *adj* as if about to vomit
AUTCH *n* intricate traditional Indian dance performed by professional dancing girls
AUTCHES > NAUTCH
AUTIC *same as* > NAUTICAL
AUTICAL *adj* of the sea or ships
AUTICS > NAUTIC
AUTILI > NAUTILUS
AUTILOID *n* type of mollusc ▷ *adj* of this type of mollusc
AUTILUS *n* shellfish with many tentacles
AVAID *n* navigational aid
AVAIDS > NAVAID
AVAL *adj* of or relating to a navy or ships
AVALISM *n* domination of naval interests
AVALISMS > NAVALISM
AVALLY > NAVAL
AVAR *n* system of air navigation
AVARCH *n* admiral
AVARCHS > NAVARCH
AVARCHY *n* navarch's term of office
AVARHO *n* aircraft navigation system
AVARHOS > NAVARHO
NAVARIN *n* stew of mutton or lamb with root vegetables
NAVARINS > NAVARIN
NAVARS > NAVAR
NAVE *n* long central part of a church
NAVEL *n* hollow in the middle of the abdomen where the umbilical cord was attached
NAVELS > NAVEL
NAVELWORT *another name for* > PENNYWORT
NAVES > NAVE
NAVETTE *n* gem cut
NAVETTES > NAVETTE
NAVEW *another name for* > TURNIP
NAVEWS > NAVEW
NAVICERT *n* certificate specifying the contents of a neutral ship's cargo
NAVICERTS > NAVICERT
NAVICULA *n* incense holder
NAVICULAR *adj* shaped like a boat ▷ *n* small boat-shaped bone of the wrist or foot
NAVICULAS > NAVICULA
NAVIES > NAVY
NAVIGABLE *adj* wide, deep, or safe enough to be sailed through
NAVIGABLY > NAVIGABLE
NAVIGATE *vb* direct or plot the path or position of a ship, aircraft, or car
NAVIGATED > NAVIGATE
NAVIGATES > NAVIGATE
NAVIGATOR *n* person who is skilled in or performs navigation, esp on a ship or aircraft
NAVVIED > NAVVY
NAVVIES > NAVVY
NAVVY *n* labourer employed on a road or a building site ▷ *vb* work as a navvy
NAVVYING > NAVVY
NAVY *n* branch of a country's armed services comprising warships with their crews and organization ▷ *adj* navy-blue
NAW *same as* > NO
NAWAB *n* (formerly) a Muslim ruler or powerful landowner in India
NAWABS > NAWAB
NAY *interj* no ▷ *n* person who votes against a motion ▷ *adv* used for emphasis ▷ *sentence substitute* no
NAYS > NAY
NAYSAID > NAYSAY
NAYSAY *vb* say no
NAYSAYER *n* refuser
NAYSAYERS > NAYSAYER
NAYSAYING > NAYSAY
NAYSAYS > NAYSAY
NAYTHLES *same as* > NATHELESS
NAYWARD *n* towards denial
NAYWARDS *same as* > NAYWARD
NAYWORD *n* proverb
NAYWORDS > NAYWORD
NAZE *n* flat marshy headland
NAZES > NAZE
NAZI *n* person who thinks or acts in a brutal or dictatorial way
NAZIFIED > NAZIFY
NAZIFIES > NAZIFY
NAZIFY *vb* make nazi in character
NAZIFYING > NAZIFY
NAZIR *n* Muslim official
NAZIRS > NAZIR
NAZIS > NAZI
NE *conj* nor
NEAFE *same as* > NIEVE
NEAFES > NEAFE
NEAFFE *same as* > NIEVE
NEAFFES > NEAFFE
NEAL *same as* > ANNEAL
NEALED > NEAL
NEALING > NEAL
NEALS > NEAL
NEANIC *adj* of or relating to the early stages in the life cycle of an organism
NEAP *adj* of, relating to, or constituting a neap tide ▷ *vb* be grounded by a neap tide
NEAPED > NEAP
NEAPING > NEAP
NEAPS > NEAP
NEAR *adj* indicating a place or time not far away ▷ *vb* draw close (to) ▷ *prep* at or to a place or time not far away from ▷ *adv* at or to a place or time not far away ▷ *n* left side of a horse or vehicle
NEARBY *adj* not far away ▷ *adv* close at hand
NEARED > NEAR
NEARER > NEAR
NEAREST > NEAR
NEARING > NEAR
NEARLIER > NEARLY
NEARLIEST > NEARLY
NEARLY *adv* almost
NEARNESS > NEAR
NEARS > NEAR
NEARSHORE *n* area of coastline water
NEARSIDE *n* side of a vehicle that is nearer the kerb
NEARSIDES > NEARSIDE
NEAT *adj* tidy and clean ▷ *n* domestic bovine animal
NEATEN *vb* make neat
NEATENED > NEATEN
NEATENING > NEATEN
NEATENS > NEATEN
NEATER > NEAT
NEATEST > NEAT
NEATH *short for* > BENEATH
NEATHERD *n* cowherd
NEATHERDS > NEATHERD
NEATLY > NEAT
NEATNESS > NEAT
NEATNIK *n* very neat and tidy person
NEATNIKS > NEATNIK
NEATS > NEAT
NEB *n* beak of a bird or the nose of an animal ▷ *vb* look around nosily
NEBBED > NEB
NEBBICH *same as* > NEBBISH
NEBBICHS > NEBBICH
NEBBING > NEB
NEBBISH *n* unfortunate simpleton
NEBBISHE *same as* > NEBBISH
NEBBISHER *same as* > NEBBISH
NEBBISHES > NEBBISH
NEBBISHY > NEBBISH
NEBBUK *n* type of shrub
NEBBUKS > NEBBUK
NEBECK *same as* > NEBBUK
NEBECKS > NEBECK
NEBEK *same as* > NEBBUK
NEBEKS > NEBEK
NEBEL *n* Hebrew musical instrument
NEBELS > NEBEL
NEBENKERN *n* component of insect sperm
NEBISH *same as* > NEBBISH
NEBISHES > NEBISH
NEBRIS *n* fawn-skin
NEBRISES > NEBRIS
NEBS > NEB
NEBULA *n* hazy cloud of particles and gases
NEBULAE > NEBULA
NEBULAR > NEBULA
NEBULAS > NEBULA
NEBULE *n* cloud
NEBULES > NEBULE
NEBULISE *same as* > NEBULIZE
NEBULISED > NEBULISE
NEBULISER *same as* > NEBULIZER
NEBULISES > NEBULISE
NEBULIUM *n* element
NEBULIUMS > NEBULIUM
NEBULIZE *vb* turn (a liquid) into a fine spray
NEBULIZED > NEBULIZE
NEBULIZER *n* device which turns a drug from a liquid into a fine spray which can be inhaled
NEBULIZES > NEBULIZE
NEBULOSE *same as* > NEBULOUS
NEBULOUS *adj* vague and unclear
NEBULY *adj* wavy
NECESSARY *adj* needed to obtain the desired result
NECESSITY *n* circumstances that inevitably require a certain result
NECK *n* part of the body joining the head to the

shoulders ▷ *vb* kiss and cuddle
NECKATEE *n* piece of ornamental cloth worn around the neck
NECKATEES > NECKATEE
NECKBAND *n* band around the neck of a garment
NECKBANDS > NECKBAND
NECKBEEF *n* cheap cattle flesh
NECKBEEFS > NECKBEEF
NECKCLOTH *n* large ornamental usually white cravat worn formerly by men
NECKED > NECK
NECKER > NECK
NECKERS > NECK
NECKGEAR *n* any neck covering
NECKGEARS > NECKGEAR
NECKING *n* activity of kissing and embracing passionately
NECKINGS > NECKING
NECKLACE *n* decorative piece of jewellery worn around the neck ▷ *vb* kill (someone) by placing a burning tyre round his or her neck
NECKLACED > NECKLACE
NECKLACES > NECKLACE
NECKLESS > NECK
NECKLET *n* ornament worn round the neck
NECKLETS > NECKLET
NECKLIKE > NECK
NECKLINE *n* shape or position of the upper edge of a dress or top
NECKLINES > NECKLINE
NECKPIECE *n* piece of fur, cloth, etc, worn around the neck or neckline
NECKS > NECK
NECKTIE *same as* > TIE
NECKTIES > NECKTIE
NECKVERSE *n* verse read to prove clergy membership
NECKWEAR *n* articles of clothing, such as ties, scarves, etc, worn around the neck
NECKWEARS > NECKWEAR
NECKWEED *n* type of plant
NECKWEEDS > NECKWEED
NECROLOGY *n* list of people recently dead
NECROPHIL *n* person who is sexually attracted to dead bodies
NECROPOLI *pl n* burial sites or cemeteries
NECROPSY *n* postmortem examination ▷ *vb* carry out a necropsy
NECROSE *vb* cause or undergo necrosis
NECROSED > NECROSE
NECROSES > NECROSE
NECROSING > NECROSE
NECROSIS *n* death of cells in the body
NECROTIC > NECROSIS
NECROTISE *same as* > NECROTIZE
NECROTIZE *vb* undergo necrosis
NECROTOMY *n* dissection of a dead body
NECTAR *n* sweet liquid collected from flowers by bees
NECTAREAL > NECTAR
NECTAREAN > NECTAR
NECTARED *adj* filled with nectar
NECTARIAL > NECTARY
NECTARIED *adj* having nectaries
NECTARIES > NECTARY
NECTARINE *n* smooth-skinned peach
NECTAROUS > NECTAR
NECTARS > NECTAR
NECTARY *n* any of various glandular structures secreting nectar in a plant
NED *n* derogatory name for an adolescent hooligan
NEDDIER > NEDDY
NEDDIES > NEDDY
NEDDIEST > NEDDY
NEDDISH > NEDDY
NEDDY *n* donkey ▷ *adj* of or relating to neds
NEDETTE *n* derogatory name for a female adolescent hooligan
NEDETTES > NEDETTE
NEDS > NED
NEE *prep* indicating the maiden name of a married woman ▷ *adj* indicating the maiden name of a married woman
NEED *vb* require or be in want of ▷ *n* condition of lacking something
NEEDED > NEED
NEEDER > NEED
NEEDERS > NEED
NEEDFIRE *n* beacon
NEEDFIRES > NEEDFIRE
NEEDFUL *adj* necessary or required
NEEDFULLY > NEEDFUL
NEEDFULS *n* must-haves
NEEDIER > NEEDY
NEEDIEST > NEEDY
NEEDILY > NEEDY
NEEDINESS *n* state of being needy
NEEDING > NEED
NEEDLE *n* thin pointed piece of metal with an eye through which thread is passed for sewing ▷ *vb* goad or provoke
NEEDLED > NEEDLE
NEEDLEFUL *n* length of thread cut for use in a needle
NEEDLER *n* needle maker
NEEDLERS > NEEDLER
NEEDLES > NEEDLE
NEEDLESS *adj* unnecessary
NEEDLIER > NEEDLE
NEEDLIEST > NEEDLE
NEEDLING > NEEDLE
NEEDLINGS > NEEDLE
NEEDLY > NEEDLE
NEEDMENT > NEED
NEEDMENTS > NEED
NEEDS *adv* necessarily ▷ *pl n* what is required
NEEDY *adj* poor, in need of financial support
NEELD *same as* > NEEDLE
NEELDS > NEELD
NEELE *same as* > NEEDLE
NEELES > NEELE
NEEM *n* type of large Indian tree
NEEMB *same as* > NEEM
NEEMBS > NEEMB
NEEMS > NEEM
NEEP *dialect name for* > TURNIP
NEEPS > NEEP
NEESBERRY *same as* > NASEBERRY
NEESE *same as* > NEEZE
NEESED > NEESE
NEESES > NEESE
NEESING > NEESE
NEEZE *vb* sneeze
NEEZED > NEEZE
NEEZES > NEEZE
NEEZING > NEEZE
NEF *n* church nave
NEFANDOUS *adj* unmentionable
NEFARIOUS *adj* wicked
NEFAST *adj* wicked
NEFS > NEF
NEG *n* photographic negative
NEGATE *vb* invalidate
NEGATED > NEGATE
NEGATER > NEGATE
NEGATERS > NEGATE
NEGATES > NEGATE
NEGATING > NEGATE
NEGATION *n* opposite or absence of something
NEGATIONS > NEGATION
NEGATIVE *adj* expressing a denial or refusal ▷ *n* negative word or statement
NEGATIVED > NEGATIVE
NEGATIVES > NEGATIVE
NEGATON *same as* > NEGATRON
NEGATONS > NEGATON
NEGATOR > NEGATE
NEGATORS > NEGATE
NEGATORY > NEGATION
NEGATRON *obsolete word for* > ELECTRON
NEGATRONS > NEGATRON
NEGLECT *vb* take no care of ▷ *n* neglecting or being neglected
NEGLECTED > NEGLECT
NEGLECTER > NEGLECT
NEGLECTOR > NEGLECT
NEGLECTS > NEGLECT
NEGLIGE *variant of* > NEGLIGEE
NEGLIGEE *n* woman's lightweight usu. lace-trimmed dressing gown
NEGLIGEES > NEGLIGEE
NEGLIGENT *adj* habitually neglecting duties, responsibilities, etc
NEGLIGES > NEGLIGE
NEGOCIANT *n* wine merchant
NEGOTIANT *n* person, nation, organization, etc, involved in a negotiation
NEGOTIATE *vb* discuss in order to reach (an agreement)
NEGRESS *n* old-fashioned offensive name for a Black woman
NEGRESSES > NEGRESS
NEGRITUDE *n* fact of being a Negro
NEGRO *n* old-fashioned offensive name for a Black man
NEGROES > NEGRO
NEGROHEAD *n* type of rubber
NEGROID *n* member of one of the major racial groups of mankind, which is characterized by brown-black skin and tightly-curled hair
NEGROIDAL > NEGROID
NEGROIDS > NEGROID
NEGROISM > NEGRO
NEGROISMS > NEGRO
NEGRONI *n* type of cocktail
NEGRONIS > NEGRONI
NEGROPHIL *n* person who admires Black people and their culture
NEGS > NEG
NEGUS *n* hot drink of port and lemon juice, usually spiced and sweetened
NEGUSES > NEGUS
NEIF *same as* > NIEVE
NEIFS > NEIF
NEIGH *n* loud high-pitched sound made by a horse ▷ *vb* make this sound
NEIGHBOR *same as* > NEIGHBOUR
NEIGHBORS > NEIGHBOR
NEIGHBOUR *n* person who lives or is situated near another ▷ *vb* be or live close (to a person or thing)
NEIGHED > NEIGH
NEIGHING > NEIGH
NEIGHS > NEIGH
NEINEI *n* type of plant
NEINEIS > NEINEI
NEIST *Scots variant of* > NEXT
NEITHER *pron* not one nor the other ▷ *adj* not one nor the other (of two)
NEIVE *same as* > NIEVE
NEIVES > NEIVE
NEK *n* mountain pass

EKS > NEK
EKTON *n* population of free-swimming animals that inhabits the middle depths of a sea or lake
EKTONIC > NEKTON
EKTONS > NEKTON
ELIES *same as* > NELIS
ELIS *n* type of pear
ELLIE *n* effeminate man
ELLIES > NELLIE
ELLY as in *not on your nelly* not under any circumstances
ELSON *n* type of wrestling hold
ELSONS > NELSON
ELUMBIUM *same as* > NELUMBO
ELUMBO *n* type of aquatic plant
ELUMBOS > NELUMBO
EMA *n* filament
EMAS > NEMA
EMATIC *adj* (of a substance) existing in or having a mesomorphic state in which a linear orientation of the molecules causes anisotropic properties
EMATODE *n* slender cylindrical unsegmented worm
EMATODES > NEMATODE
EMATOID > NEMATODE
EMERTEAN *n* type of ribbon-like marine worm ▷ *adj* of this worm
EMERTIAN *same as* > NEMERTEAN
EMERTINE *same as* > NEMERTEAN
EMESES > NEMESIS
EMESIA *n* type of southern African plant
EMESIAS > NEMESIA
EMESIS *n* retribution or vengeance
EMN *vb* name
EMNED > NEMN
EMNING > NEMN
EMNS > NEMN
EMOPHILA *n* any of a genus of low-growing hairy annual plants
EMORAL *adj* of a wood
EMOROUS *adj* woody
EMPT *adj* named
ENE *n* rare black-and-grey short-winged Hawaiian goose
ENES > NENE
ENNIGAI *same as* > NANNYGAI
ENNIGAIS > NENNIGAI
ENUPHAR *n* type of water lily
ENUPHARS > NENUPHAR
EOBLAST *n* worm cell
EOBLASTS > NEOBLAST
EOCON *n* supporter of conservative politics
EOCONS > NEOCON
NEOCORTEX *n* part of the brain
NEODYMIUM *n* silvery-white metallic element of lanthanide series
NEOGENE *adj* of, denoting, or formed during the Miocene and Pliocene epochs
NEOGOTHIC *n* style of architecture popular in Britain in the 18th and 19th centuries
NEOLITH *n* Neolithic stone implement
NEOLITHIC *adj* relating to the Neolithic period
NEOLITHS > NEOLITH
NEOLOGIAN > NEOLOGY
NEOLOGIC > NEOLOGISM
NEOLOGIES > NEOLOGY
NEOLOGISE *same as* > NEOLOGIZE
NEOLOGISM *n* newly-coined word or an established word used in a new sense
NEOLOGIST > NEOLOGISM
NEOLOGIZE *vb* invent or use neologisms
NEOLOGY *same as* > NEOLOGISM
NEOMORPH *n* genetic component
NEOMORPHS > NEOMORPH
NEOMYCIN *n* type of antibiotic obtained from a bacterium
NEOMYCINS > NEOMYCIN
NEON *n* colourless odourless gaseous element used in illuminated signs and lights ▷ *adj* of or illuminated by neon
NEONATAL *adj* relating to the first few weeks of a baby's life
NEONATE *n* newborn child, esp in the first week of life and up to four weeks old
NEONATES > NEONATE
NEONED *adj* lit with neon
NEONOMIAN *n* Christian religious belief
NEONS > NEON
NEOPAGAN *n* advocate of the revival of paganism
NEOPAGANS > NEOPAGAN
NEOPHILE *n* person who welcomes new things
NEOPHILES > NEOPHILE
NEOPHILIA *n* tendency to like anything new
NEOPHOBE > NEOPHOBIA
NEOPHOBES > NEOPHOBIA
NEOPHOBIA *n* tendency to dislike anything new
NEOPHOBIC > NEOPHOBIA
NEOPHYTE *n* beginner or novice
NEOPHYTES > NEOPHYTE
NEOPHYTIC > NEOPHYTE
NEOPILINA *n* type of mollusc
NEOPLASIA *n* abnormal growth of tissue
NEOPLASM *n* any abnormal new growth of tissue
NEOPLASMS > NEOPLASM
NEOPLASTY *n* surgical formation of new tissue structures or repair of damaged structures
NEOPRENE *n* synthetic rubber used in waterproof products
NEOPRENES > NEOPRENE
NEOTEINIA *n* state of prolonged immaturity
NEOTENIC > NEOTENY
NEOTENIES > NEOTENY
NEOTENOUS > NEOTENY
NEOTENY *n* persistence of larval or fetal features in the adult form of an animal
NEOTERIC *adj* belonging to a new fashion or trend ▷ *n* new writer or philosopher
NEOTERICS > NEOTERIC
NEOTERISE *same as* > NEOTERIZE
NEOTERISM > NEOTERIC
NEOTERIST > NEOTERIC
NEOTERIZE *vb* introduce new things
NEOTOXIN *n* harmful agent
NEOTOXINS > NEOTOXIN
NEOTROPIC *adj* of tropical America
NEOTYPE *n* specimen selected to replace a type specimen that has been lost or destroyed
NEOTYPES > NEOTYPE
NEP *n* catmint
NEPENTHE *n* drug that ancient writers referred to as a means of forgetting grief or trouble
NEPENTHES > NEPENTHE
NEPER *n* unit expressing the ratio of two quantities
NEPERS > NEPER
NEPETA *same as* > CATMINT
NEPETAS > NEPETA
NEPHALISM *n* teetotalism
NEPHALIST > NEPHALISM
NEPHELINE *n* whitish mineral
NEPHELITE *same as* > NEPHELINE
NEPHEW *n* son of one's sister or brother
NEPHEWS > NEPHEW
NEPHOGRAM *n* photograph of a cloud
NEPHOLOGY *n* study of clouds
NEPHRALGY *n* pain in a kidney
NEPHRIC *adj* renal
NEPHRIDIA *pl n* simple excretory organs of many invertebrates
NEPHRISM *n* chronic kidney disease
NEPHRISMS > NEPHRISM
NEPHRITE *n* tough fibrous amphibole mineral
NEPHRITES > NEPHRITE
NEPHRITIC *adj* of or relating to the kidneys
NEPHRITIS *n* inflammation of a kidney
NEPHROID *adj* kidney-shaped
NEPHRON *n* minute urine-secreting tubule in the kidney
NEPHRONS > NEPHRON
NEPHROSES > NEPHROSIS
NEPHROSIS *n* any noninflammatory degenerative kidney disease
NEPHROTIC > NEPHROSIS
NEPIONIC *adj* of or relating to the juvenile period in the life cycle of an organism
NEPIT *same as* > NIT
NEPITS > NEPIT
NEPOTIC > NEPOTISM
NEPOTISM *n* favouritism in business shown to relatives and friends
NEPOTISMS > NEPOTISM
NEPOTIST > NEPOTISM
NEPOTISTS > NEPOTISM
NEPS > NEP
NEPTUNIUM *n* synthetic radioactive metallic element
NERAL *n* isomer of citral
NERALS > NERAL
NERD *n* boring person obsessed with a particular subject
NERDIER > NERD
NERDIEST > NERD
NERDINESS > NERD
NERDISH > NERD
NERDS > NERD
NERDY > NERD
NEREID *n* sea nymph in Greek mythology
NEREIDES > NEREID
NEREIDS > NEREID
NEREIS *n* any polychaete worm of the genus *Nereis*
NERINE *n* type of S African plant related to the amaryllis
NERINES > NERINE
NERITE *n* type of sea snail
NERITES > NERITE
NERITIC *adj* of or formed in the region of shallow seas near a coastline
NERK *n* fool
NERKA *n* type of salmon
NERKAS > NERKA
NERKS > NERK
NEROL *n* scented liquid
NEROLI *n* brown oil used in perfumery
NEROLIS > NEROLI
NEROLS > NEROL
NERTS *interj* nuts
NERTZ *same as* > NERTS
NERVAL > NERVE
NERVATE *adj* (of leaves)

with veins
NERVATION *less common word for* > VENATION
NERVATURE *same as* > NERVATION
NERVE *n* cordlike bundle of fibres that conducts impulses between the brain and other parts of the body ▷ *vb* give courage to oneself
NERVED > NERVE
NERVELESS *adj* numb, without feeling
NERVELET *n* small nerve
NERVELETS > NERVELET
NERVER > NERVE
NERVERS > NERVE
NERVES > NERVE
NERVIER > NERVY
NERVIEST > NERVY
NERVILY > NERVY
NERVINE *adj* having a soothing or calming effect upon the nerves ▷ *n* nervine drug or agent
NERVINES > NERVINE
NERVINESS > NERVY
NERVING > NERVE
NERVINGS > NERVE
NERVOSITY *n* nervousness
NERVOUS *adj* apprehensive or worried
NERVOUSLY > NERVOUS
NERVULAR > NERVULE
NERVULE *n* small vein
NERVULES > NERVULE
NERVURE *n* any of the stiff rods that form the supporting framework of an insect's wing
NERVURES > NERVURE
NERVY *adj* excitable or nervous
NESCIENCE *formal or literary word for* > IGNORANCE
NESCIENT > NESCIENCE
NESCIENTS > NESCIENCE
NESH *adj* sensitive to the cold
NESHER > NESH
NESHEST > NESH
NESHNESS > NESH
NESS *n* headland, cape
NESSES > NESS
NEST *n* place or structure in which birds or certain animals lay eggs or give birth to young ▷ *vb* make or inhabit a nest
NESTABLE > NEST
NESTED > NEST
NESTER > NEST
NESTERS > NEST
NESTFUL > NEST
NESTFULS > NEST
NESTING > NEST
NESTINGS > NEST
NESTLE *vb* snuggle
NESTLED > NESTLE
NESTLER > NESTLE
NESTLERS > NESTLE
NESTLES > NESTLE
NESTLIKE > NEST
NESTLING *n* bird too young to leave the nest
NESTLINGS > NESTLING
NESTOR *n* wise old man
NESTORS > NESTOR
NESTS > NEST
NET *n* fabric of meshes of string, thread, or wire with many openings ▷ *vb* catch (a fish or animal) in a net ▷ *adj* left after all deductions
NETBALL *n* team game in which a ball has to be thrown through a net hanging from a ring at the top of a pole
NETBALLER > NETBALL
NETBALLS > NETBALL
NETE *n* lyre string
NETES > NETE
NETFUL > NET
NETFULS > NET
NETHEAD *n* person who is enthusiastic about or an expert on the internet
NETHEADS > NETHEAD
NETHELESS *same as* > NATHELESS
NETHER *adj* lower
NETIZEN *n* person who regularly uses the internet
NETIZENS > NETIZEN
NETLESS > NET
NETLIKE > NET
NETMINDER *n* goalkeeper
NETOP *n* friend
NETOPS > NETOP
NETS > NET
NETSPEAK *n* jargon, abbreviations, and emoticons typically used by frequent internet users
NETSPEAKS > NETSPEAK
NETSUKE *n* (in Japan) a carved toggle worn dangling from the waist
NETSUKES > NETSUKE
NETT *same as* > NET
NETTABLE > NETT
NETTED > NET
NETTER *n* person that makes nets
NETTERS > NETTER
NETTIE *n* habitual and enthusiastic user of the internet
NETTIER > NET
NETTIES > NETTY
NETTIEST > NET
NETTING > NET
NETTINGS > NET
NETTLE *n* plant with stinging hairs on the leaves ▷ *vb* bother or irritate
NETTLED > NETTLE
NETTLER > NETTLE
NETTLERS > NETTLE
NETTLES > NETTLE
NETTLIER > NETTLE
NETTLIEST > NETTLE
NETTLING > NETTLE
NETTLY > NETTLE
NETTS > NETT
NETTY *n* lavatory, originally an earth closet
NETWORK *n* system of intersecting lines, roads, etc ▷ *vb* broadcast (a programme) over a network
NETWORKED > NETWORK
NETWORKER *n* person who forms business contacts through informal social meetings
NETWORKS > NETWORK
NEUK *Scot word for* > NOOK
NEUKS > NEUK
NEUM *same as* > NEUME
NEUMATIC > NEUME
NEUME *n* one of a series of notational symbols used before the 14th century
NEUMES > NEUME
NEUMIC > NEUME
NEUMS > NEUM
NEURAL *adj* of a nerve or the nervous system
NEURALGIA *n* severe pain along a nerve
NEURALGIC > NEURALGIA
NEURALLY > NEURAL
NEURATION *n* arrangement of veins
NEURAXON *n* biological cell component
NEURAXONS > NEURAXON
NEURILITY *n* properties of the nerves
NEURINE *n* poisonous alkaloid
NEURINES > NEURINE
NEURISM *n* nerve force
NEURISMS > NEURISM
NEURITE *n* biological cell component
NEURITES > NEURITE
NEURITIC > NEURITIS
NEURITICS > NEURITIS
NEURITIS *n* inflammation of a nerve or nerves
NEUROCHIP *n* semiconductor chip designed for use in an electronic neural network
NEUROCOEL *n* cavity in brain
NEUROGLIA *another name for* > GLIA
NEUROGRAM *same as* > ENGRAM
NEUROID *adj* nervelike
NEUROLOGY *n* scientific study of the nervous system
NEUROMA *n* any tumour composed of nerve tissue
NEUROMAS > NEUROMA
NEUROMAST *n* sensory cell in fish
NEUROMATA > NEUROMA
NEURON *same as* > NEURONE
NEURONAL > NEURONE
NEURONE *n* cell specialized to conduct nerve impulses
NEURONES > NEURONE
NEURONIC > NEURONE
NEURONS > NEURON
NEUROPATH *n* person suffering from or predisposed to a disorder of the nervous system
NEUROPIL *n* dense network of neurons and glia in the central nervous system
NEUROPILS > NEUROPIL
NEUROSAL > NEUROSIS
NEUROSES > NEUROSIS
NEUROSIS *n* mental disorder producing hysteria, anxiety, depression, or obsessive behaviour
NEUROTIC *adj* emotionally unstable ▷ *n* neurotic person
NEUROTICS > NEUROTIC
NEUROTOMY *n* surgical cutting of a nerve, esp to relieve intractable pain
NEURULA *n* stage of embryonic development
NEURULAE > NEURULA
NEURULAR > NEURULA
NEURULAS > NEURULA
NEUSTIC > NEUSTON
NEUSTON *n* organisms, similar to plankton, that float on the surface film of open water
NEUSTONIC > NEUSTON
NEUSTONS > NEUSTON
NEUTER *adj* belonging to a particular class of grammatical inflections in some languages ▷ *vb* castrate (an animal) ▷ *n* neuter gender
NEUTERED > NEUTER
NEUTERING > NEUTER
NEUTERS > NEUTER
NEUTRAL *adj* taking neither side in a war or dispute ▷ neutral person or nation
NEUTRALLY > NEUTRAL
NEUTRALS > NEUTRAL
NEUTRETTO *n* neutrino associated with the muon
NEUTRINO *n* elementary particle with no mass or electrical charge
NEUTRINOS > NEUTRINO
NEUTRON *n* electrically neutral elementary particle of about the same mass as a proton
NEUTRONIC > NEUTRON
NEUTRONS > NEUTRON
NEVE *n* mass of porous ice formed from snow, that has not yet become frozen into glacier ice
NEVEL *vb* beat with the fists
NEVELLED > NEVEL
NEVELLING > NEVEL
NEVELS > NEVEL
NEVER *adv* at no time ▷ *sentence substitute* at no time ▷ *interj* surely not!

EVERMIND *n* difference
EVERMORE *adv* never again
EVES > NEVE
EVI > NEVUS
EVOID > NAEVUS
EVUS *same as* > NAEVUS
EW *adj* not existing before ▷ *adv* recently ▷ *vb* make new
EWBIE *n* person new to a job, club, etc
EWBIES > NEWBIE
EWBORN *adj* recently or just born ▷ *n* newborn baby
EWBORNS > NEWBORN
EWCOME > NEWCOMER
EWCOMER *n* recent arrival or participant
EWCOMERS > NEWCOMER
EWED > NEW
EWEL *n* post at the top or bottom of a flight of stairs that supports the handrail
EWELL *n* new thing
EWELLED > NEWEL
EWELLS > NEWELL
EWELS > NEWEL
EWER > NEW
EWEST > NEW
EWFANGLE *adj* newly come into existence or fashion
EWFOUND *adj* newly or recently discovered
EWIE *n* fresh idea or thing
EWIES > NEWIE
EWING > NEW
EWISH *adj* fairly new
EWISHLY > NEWISH
EWLY *adv* recently
EWLYWED *n* recently married person
EWLYWEDS > NEWLYWED
EWMARKET *n* double-breasted waisted coat with a full skirt
EWMOWN *adj* freshly cut
EWNESS > NEW
EWNESSES > NEW
EWS *n* important or interesting new happenings ▷ *vb* report
EWSAGENT *n* shopkeeper who sells newspapers and magazines
EWSBEAT *n* particular area of news reporting
EWSBEATS > NEWSBEAT
EWSBOY *n* boy who sells or delivers newspapers
EWSBOYS > NEWSBOY
EWSBREAK *n* newsflash
EWSCAST *n* radio or television broadcast of the news
EWSCASTS > NEWSCAST
EWSDESK *n* news gathering and reporting department
EWSDESKS > NEWSDESK
EWSED > NEWS
EWSES > NEWS
EWSFLASH *n* brief important news item, which interrupts a radio or television programme
NEWSGIRL *n* female newsreader or reporter
NEWSGIRLS > NEWSGIRL
NEWSGROUP *n* forum where subscribers exchange information about a specific subject by e-mail
NEWSHAWK *n* newspaper reporter
NEWSHAWKS > NEWSHAWK
NEWSHOUND *same as* > NEWSHAWK
NEWSIE *same as* > NEWSY
NEWSIER > NEWSY
NEWSIES > NEWSIE
NEWSIEST > NEWSY
NEWSINESS > NEWSY
NEWSING > NEWS
NEWSLESS > NEWS
NEWSMAKER *n* person whose activities are reported in news
NEWSMAN *n* male newsreader or reporter
NEWSMEN > NEWSMAN
NEWSPAPER *n* weekly or daily publication containing news ▷ *vb* do newspaper related work
NEWSPEAK *n* language of politicians and officials regarded as deliberately ambiguous and misleading
NEWSPEAKS > NEWSPEAK
NEWSPRINT *n* inexpensive paper used for newspapers
NEWSREEL *n* short film giving news
NEWSREELS > NEWSREEL
NEWSROOM *n* room where news is received and prepared for publication or broadcasting
NEWSROOMS > NEWSROOM
NEWSSTAND *n* portable stand from which newspapers are sold
NEWSTRADE *n* newspaper retail
NEWSWIRE *n* electronic means of delivering up-to-the-minute news
NEWSWIRES > NEWSWIRE
NEWSWOMAN *n* female newsreader or reporter
NEWSWOMEN > NEWSWOMAN
NEWSY *adj* full of news ▷ *n* newsagent
NEWT *n* small amphibious creature with a long slender body and tail
NEWTON *n* unit of force
NEWTONS > NEWTON
NEWTS > NEWT
NEWWAVER *n* member of new wave
NEWWAVERS > NEWWAVER
NEXT *adv* immediately following ▷ *n* next person or thing
NEXTDOOR *adj* in or at the adjacent house or building
NEXTLY > NEXT
NEXTNESS > NEXT
NEXTS > NEXT
NEXUS *n* connection or link
NEXUSES > NEXUS
NGAIO *n* small New Zealand tree
NGAIOS > NGAIO
NGANA *same as* > NAGANA
NGANAS > NGANA
NGARARA *n* lizard found in New Zealand
NGATI *n* (occurring as part of the tribe name) a tribe or clan
NGATIS > NGATI
NGOMA *n* type of drum
NGOMAS > NGOMA
NGULTRUM *n* standard monetary unit of Bhutan, divided into 100 chetrum
NGULTRUMS > NGULTRUM
NGWEE *n* Zambian monetary unit worth one hundredth of a kwacha
NHANDU *n* type of spider
NHANDUS > NHANDU
NIACIN *n* vitamin of the B complex that occurs in milk, liver, and yeast
NIACINS > NIACIN
NIAISERIE *n* simplicity
NIALAMIDE *n* type of drug
NIB *n* writing point of a pen ▷ *vb* provide with a nib
NIBBED > NIB
NIBBING > NIB
NIBBLE *vb* take little bites (of) ▷ *n* little bite
NIBBLED > NIBBLE
NIBBLER *n* person, animal, or thing that nibbles
NIBBLERS > NIBBLER
NIBBLES > NIBBLE
NIBBLING > NIBBLE
NIBBLINGS > NIBBLE
NIBLICK *n* (formerly) a club, a No. 9 iron, giving a great deal of lift
NIBLICKS > NIBLICK
NIBLIKE > NIB
NIBS > NIB
NICAD *n* rechargeable dry-cell battery
NICADS > NICAD
NICCOLITE *n* copper-coloured mineral
NICE *adj* pleasant
NICEISH > NICE
NICELY > NICE
NICENESS > NICE
NICER > NICE
NICEST > NICE
NICETIES > NICETY
NICETY *n* subtle point
NICHE *n* hollow area in a wall ▷ *adj* of or aimed at a specialist group or market ▷ *vb* place (a statue) in a niche
NICHED > NICHE
NICHER *vb* snigger
NICHERED > NICHER
NICHERING > NICHER
NICHERS > NICHER
NICHES > NICHE
NICHING > NICHE
NICHT *Scot word for* > NIGHT
NICHTS > NICHT
NICISH > NICE
NICK *vb* make a small cut in ▷ *n* small cut
NICKAR *n* hard seed
NICKARS > NICKAR
NICKED > NICK
NICKEL *n* silvery-white metal often used in alloys ▷ *vb* plate with nickel
NICKELED > NICKEL
NICKELIC *adj* of or containing metallic nickel
NICKELINE *another name for* > NICCOLITE
NICKELING > NICKEL
NICKELISE *same as* > NICKELIZE
NICKELIZE *vb* treat with nickel
NICKELLED > NICKEL
NICKELOUS *adj* of or containing nickel, esp in the divalent state
NICKELS > NICKEL
NICKER *n* pound sterling ▷ *vb* (of a horse) to neigh softly
NICKERED > NICKER
NICKERING > NICKER
NICKERS > NICKER
NICKING > NICK
NICKLE *same as* > NICKEL
NICKLED > NICKLE
NICKLES > NICKLE
NICKLING > NICKLE
NICKNACK *n* cheap ornament or trinket
NICKNACKS > NICKNACK
NICKNAME *n* familiar name given to a person or place ▷ *vb* call by a nickname
NICKNAMED > NICKNAME
NICKNAMER > NICKNAME
NICKNAMES > NICKNAME
NICKPOINT *n* break in the slope of a river caused by renewed erosion
NICKS > NICK
NICKSTICK *n* tally
NICKUM *n* mischievous person
NICKUMS > NICKUM
NICOISE *adj* prepared with tomatoes, black olives, garlic and anchovies
NICOL *n* device for producing plane-polarized light
NICOLS > NICOL
NICOMPOOP *n* stupid person
NICOTIAN *n* tobacco user
NICOTIANA *n* any plant of the American and Australian genus *Nicotiana*, such as tobacco
NICOTIANS > NICOTIAN

NICOTIN *same as* > NICOTINE
NICOTINE *n* poisonous substance found in tobacco
NICOTINED > NICOTINE
NICOTINES > NICOTINE
NICOTINIC > NICOTINE
NICOTINS *same as* > NICOTIN
NICTATE *same as* > NICTITATE
NICTATED > NICTATE
NICTATES > NICTATE
NICTATING > NICTATE
NICTATION *n* act of blinking
NICTITANT *adj* blinking
NICTITATE *vb* blink
NID *same as* > NIDE
NIDAL > NIDUS
NIDAMENTA *pl n* egg capsules
NIDATE *vb* undergo nidation
NIDATED > NIDATE
NIDATES > NIDATE
NIDATING > NIDATE
NIDATION *n* implantation
NIDATIONS > NIDATION
NIDDERING *n* coward ▷ *adj* cowardly
NIDDICK *n* nape of the neck
NIDDICKS > NIDDICK
NIDE *vb* nest
NIDED > NIDE
NIDERING *same as* > NIDDERING
NIDERINGS > NIDERING
NIDERLING *same as* > NIDDERING
NIDES > NIDE
NIDGET *n* fool
NIDGETS > NIDGET
NIDI > NIDUS
NIDIFIED > NIDIFY
NIDIFIES > NIDIFY
NIDIFY *vb* (of a bird) to make or build a nest
NIDIFYING > NIDIFY
NIDING *n* coward
NIDINGS > NIDING
NIDOR *n* cooking smell
NIDOROUS > NIDOR
NIDORS > NIDOR
NIDS > NID
NIDUS *n* nest in which insects or spiders deposit their eggs
NIDUSES > NIDUS
NIE *archaic spelling of* > NIGH
NIECE *n* daughter of one's sister or brother
NIECES > NIECE
NIED > NIE
NIEF *same as* > NIEVE
NIEFS > NIEF
NIELLATED > NIELLO
NIELLI > NIELLO
NIELLIST > NIELLO
NIELLISTS > NIELLO
NIELLO *n* black compound of sulphur and silver, lead, or copper ▷ *vb* decorate or treat with niello
NIELLOED > NIELLO
NIELLOING > NIELLO
NIELLOS > NIELLO
NIES > NIE
NIEVE *n* closed hand
NIEVEFUL > NIEVE
NIEVEFULS > NIEVE
NIEVES > NIEVE
NIFE *n* earth's core, thought to be composed of nickel and iron
NIFES > NIFE
NIFF *n* stink ▷ *vb* stink
NIFFED > NIFF
NIFFER *vb* barter
NIFFERED > NIFFER
NIFFERING > NIFFER
NIFFERS > NIFFER
NIFFIER > NIFF
NIFFIEST > NIFF
NIFFING > NIFF
NIFFNAFF *vb* trifle
NIFFNAFFS > NIFFNAFF
NIFFS > NIFF
NIFFY > NIFF
NIFTIER > NIFTY
NIFTIES > NIFTY
NIFTIEST > NIFTY
NIFTILY > NIFTY
NIFTINESS > NIFTY
NIFTY *adj* neat or smart ▷ *n* nifty thing
NIGELLA *n* type of plant the Mediterranean and W Asia
NIGELLAS > NIGELLA
NIGER *n* obsolete offensive term for a Black person
NIGERS > NIGER
NIGGARD *n* stingy person ▷ *adj* miserly ▷ *vb* act in a niggardly way
NIGGARDED > NIGGARD
NIGGARDLY *adj* stingy ▷ *adv* stingily
NIGGARDS > NIGGARD
NIGGER *n* offensive name for a Black person ▷ *vb* burn
NIGGERDOM > NIGGER
NIGGERED > NIGGER
NIGGERING > NIGGER
NIGGERISH > NIGGER
NIGGERISM *n* offensive name for an idiom supposedly characteristic of Black people
NIGGERS > NIGGER
NIGGERY > NIGGER
NIGGLE *vb* worry slightly ▷ *n* small worry or doubt
NIGGLED > NIGGLE
NIGGLER > NIGGLE
NIGGLERS > NIGGLE
NIGGLES > NIGGLE
NIGGLIER > NIGGLE
NIGGLIEST > NIGGLE
NIGGLING *adj* petty ▷ *n* act or instance of niggling
NIGGLINGS > NIGGLING
NIGGLY > NIGGLE
NIGH *prep* near ▷ *adv* nearly ▷ *adj* near ▷ *vb* approach
NIGHED > NIGH
NIGHER > NIGH
NIGHEST > NIGH
NIGHING > NIGH
NIGHLY > NIGH
NIGHNESS > NIGH
NIGHS > NIGH
NIGHT *n* time of darkness between sunset and sunrise ▷ *adj* of, occurring, or working at night
NIGHTBIRD *same as* > NIGHTHAWK
NIGHTCAP *n* drink taken just before bedtime
NIGHTCAPS > NIGHTCAP
NIGHTCLUB *n* establishment for dancing, music, etc, open late at night ▷ *vb* go to nightclubs
NIGHTED *adj* darkened
NIGHTFALL *n* approach of darkness
NIGHTFIRE *n* fire burned at night
NIGHTGEAR *n* nightclothes
NIGHTGLOW *n* faint light from the upper atmosphere in the night sky, esp in low latitudes
NIGHTGOWN *n* loose dress worn in bed by women
NIGHTHAWK *n* type of American nightjar
NIGHTIE *same as* > NIGHTGOWN
NIGHTIES > NIGHTY
NIGHTJAR *n* nocturnal bird with a harsh cry
NIGHTJARS > NIGHTJAR
NIGHTLESS > NIGHT
NIGHTLIFE *n* entertainment and social activities available at night in a town or city
NIGHTLIKE > NIGHT
NIGHTLONG *adv* throughout the night
NIGHTLY *adv* (happening) each night ▷ *adj* happening each night
NIGHTMARE *n* very bad dream
NIGHTMARY > NIGHTMARE
NIGHTS *adv* at night or on most nights
NIGHTSIDE *n* dark side
NIGHTSPOT *n* nightclub
NIGHTTIDE *same as* > NIGHTTIME
NIGHTTIME *n* time from sunset to sunrise
NIGHTWARD > NIGHT
NIGHTWEAR *n* apparel worn in bed or before retiring to bed
NIGHTY *same as* > NIGHTIE
NIGIRI *n* small oval block of cold rice, wasabi and fish, sometimes held together by a seaweed band
NIGIRIS > NIGIRI
NIGRICANT *adj* black
NIGRIFIED > NIGRIFY
NIGRIFIES > NIGRIFY
NIGRIFY *vb* blacken
NIGRITUDE *n* blackness
NIGROSIN *same as* > NIGROSINE
NIGROSINE *n* type of black pigment and dye used in inks and shoe polishes
NIGROSINS > NIGROSIN
NIHIL *n* nil
NIHILISM *n* rejection of a[ll] established authority and institutions
NIHILISMS > NIHILISM
NIHILIST > NIHILISM
NIHILISTS > NIHILISM
NIHILITY *n* state or condition of being nothing
NIHILS > NIHIL
NIHONGA *n* Japanese form of painting
NIHONGAS > NIHONGA
NIKAU *n* palm tree native t[o] New Zealand
NIKAUS > NIKAU
NIL *n* nothing, zero
NILGAI *n* large Indian antelope
NILGAIS > NILGAI
NILGAU *same as* > NILGHAU
NILGAUS > NILGAU
NILGHAI *same as* > NILGAI
NILGHAIS > NILGHAI
NILGHAU *same as* > NILGAI
NILGHAUS > NILGHAU
NILL *vb* be unwilling
NILLED > NILL
NILLING > NILL
NILLS > NILL
NILPOTENT *n* mathematical term
NILS > NIL
NIM *n* game in which two players alternately remov[e] one or more small items from one of several rows [or] piles ▷ *vb* steal
NIMB *n* halo
NIMBED > NIMB
NIMBI > NIMBUS
NIMBLE *adj* agile and quic[k]
NIMBLER > NIMBLE
NIMBLESSE > NIMBLE
NIMBLEST > NIMBLE
NIMBLEWIT *n* alert, bright and clever person
NIMBLY > NIMBLE
NIMBS > NIMB
NIMBUS *n* dark grey rain cloud
NIMBUSED > NIMBUS
NIMBUSES > NIMBUS
NIMBYISM *n* practice of objecting to something that will affect one or tak[e] place in one's locality
NIMBYISMS > NIMBYISM
NIMBYNESS *same as* > NIMBYISM
NIMIETIES > NIMIETY

IMIETY *rare word for* > EXCESS
IMIOUS > NIMIETY
IMMED > NIM
IMMER > NIM
IMMERS > NIM
IMMING > NIM
IMONIC as in *nimonic alloy* type of nickel-based alloy used at high temperature
IMPS *adj* easy
IMROD *n* hunter
IMRODS > NIMROD
IMS > NIM
INCOM *same as* > NICOMPOOP
INCOMS > NINCOM
INCUM *same as* > NICOMPOOP
INCUMS > NINCUM
INE *n* one more than eight
INEBARK *n* North American shrub
INEBARKS > NINEBARK
INEFOLD *adj* having nine times as many or as much ▷ *adv* by nine times as much or as many
INEHOLES *n* type of game
INEPENCE *n* coin worth nine pennies
INEPENNY *same as* > NINEPENCE
INEPIN *n* skittle used in ninepins
INEPINS *n* game of skittles
INES > NINE
INESCORE *n* product of nine times twenty
INETEEN *n* ten and nine
INETEENS > NINETEEN
INETIES > NINETY
NETIETH *adj* being the ordinal number of *ninety* in numbering order ▷ *n* one of 90 approximately equal parts of something
NETY *n* ten times nine ▷ *determiner* amounting to ninety
NHYDRIN *n* chemical reagent used for the detection and analysis of primary amines
NJA *n* person skilled in ninjutsu
NJAS > NINJA
NJITSU *same as* > NINJUTSU
NJITSUS > NINJITSU
NJUTSU *n* Japanese martial art
NJUTSUS > NINJUTSU
NNIES > NINNY
NNY *n* stupid person
NNYISH > NINNY
NON *n* fine strong silky fabric
NONS > NINON
NTH *n* (of) number nine in a series ▷ *adj* coming after the eighth in counting order, position, time, etc ▷ *adv* after the eighth person, position, event, etc
NINTHLY *same as* > NINTH
NINTHS > NINTH
NIOBATE *n* type of salt crystal
NIOBATES > NIOBATE
NIOBIC *adj* of or containing niobium in the pentavalent state
NIOBITE *another name for* > COLUMBITE
NIOBITES > NIOBITE
NIOBIUM *n* white superconductive metallic element
NIOBIUMS > NIOBIUM
NIOBOUS *adj* of or containing niobium in the trivalent state
NIP *vb* hurry ▷ *n* pinch or light bite
NIPA *n* palm tree of S and SE Asia
NIPAS > NIPA
NIPCHEESE *n* ship's purser
NIPPED > NIP
NIPPER *n* small child ▷ *vb* secure with rope
NIPPERED > NIPPER
NIPPERING > NIPPER
NIPPERKIN *n* small quantity of alcohol
NIPPERS *pl n* instrument or tool for snipping, pinching, or squeezing
NIPPIER > NIPPY
NIPPIEST > NIPPY
NIPPILY > NIPPY
NIPPINESS > NIPPY
NIPPING > NIP
NIPPINGLY > NIP
NIPPLE *n* projection in the centre of a breast ▷ *vb* provide with a nipple
NIPPLED > NIPPLE
NIPPLES > NIPPLE
NIPPLING > NIPPLE
NIPPY *adj* frosty or chilly
NIPS > NIP
NIPTER *n* type of religious ceremony
NIPTERS > NIPTER
NIQAB *n* type of veil worn by some Muslim women
NIQABS > NIQAB
NIRAMIAI *n* sumo wrestling procedure
NIRAMIAIS > NIRAMIAI
NIRL *vb* shrivel
NIRLED > NIRL
NIRLIE *variant of* > NIRLY
NIRLIER > NIRLY
NIRLIEST > NIRLY
NIRLING > NIRL
NIRLIT > NIRL
NIRLS > NIRL
NIRLY *adj* shrivelled
NIRVANA *n* absolute spiritual enlightenment and bliss
NIRVANAS > NIRVANA
NIRVANIC > NIRVANA
NIS *n* friendly goblin
NISBERRY *same as* > NASEBERRY
NISEI *n* native-born citizen of the US or Canada whose parents were Japanese immigrants
NISEIS > NISEI
NISGUL *n* smallest and weakest bird in a brood of chickens
NISGULS > NISGUL
NISH *n* nothing
NISHES > NISH
NISI *adj* (of a court order) coming into effect on a specified date
NISSE *same as* > NIS
NISSES > NISSE
NISUS *n* impulse towards or striving after a goal
NIT *n* egg or larva of a louse
NITCHIE *n* offensive term for a Native American person
NITCHIES > NITCHIE
NITE *variant of* > NIGHT
NITER *same as* > NITRE
NITERIE *n* nightclub
NITERIES > NITERIE
NITERS > NITER
NITERY > NITER
NITES > NITE
NITHER *vb* shiver
NITHERED > NITHER
NITHERING > NITHER
NITHERS > NITHER
NITHING *n* coward
NITHINGS > NITHING
NITID *adj* bright
NITINOL *n* metal alloy
NITINOLS > NITINOL
NITON *less common name for* > RADON
NITONS > NITON
NITPICK *vb* criticize unnecessarily
NITPICKED > NITPICK
NITPICKER > NITPICK
NITPICKS > NITPICK
NITPICKY > NITPICK
NITRAMINE *another name for* > TETRYL
NITRATE *n* compound of nitric acid, used as a fertilizer ▷ *vb* treat with nitric acid or a nitrate
NITRATED > NITRATE
NITRATES > NITRATE
NITRATINE *n* type of mineral
NITRATING > NITRATE
NITRATION > NITRATE
NITRATOR > NITRATE
NITRATORS > NITRATE
NITRE *n* potassium nitrate
NITREOUS as in *nitreous silica* quartz glass
NITRES > NITRE
NITRIC *adj* of or containing nitrogen
NITRID *same as* > NITRIDE
NITRIDE *n* compound of nitrogen with a more electropositive element ▷ *vb* make into a nitride
NITRIDED > NITRIDE
NITRIDES > NITRIDE
NITRIDING > NITRIDE
NITRIDS > NITRID
NITRIFIED > NITRIFY
NITRIFIER > NITRIFY
NITRIFIES > NITRIFY
NITRIFY *vb* treat (a substance) or cause (a substance) to react with nitrogen
NITRIL *same as* > NITRILE
NITRILE *n* any one of a particular class of organic compounds
NITRILES > NITRILE
NITRILS > NITRIL
NITRITE *n* salt or ester of nitrous acid
NITRITES > NITRITE
NITRO *n* nitrogylcerine
NITROGEN *n* colourless odourless gas that forms four fifths of the air
NITROGENS > NITROGEN
NITROLIC *adj* pertaining to a group of acids
NITROS > NITRO
NITROSO *adj* of a particular monovalent group
NITROSYL *another word for* > NITROSO
NITROSYLS > NITROSYL
NITROUS *adj* derived from or containing nitrogen in a low valency state
NITROXYL *n* type of chemical
NITROXYLS > NITROXYL
NITRY *adj* nitrous
NITRYL *n* chemical compound
NITRYLS > NITRYL
NITS > NIT
NITTIER > NITTY
NITTIEST > NITTY
NITTY *adj* infested with nits
NITWIT *n* stupid person
NITWITS > NITWIT
NITWITTED > NITWIT
NIVAL *adj* of or growing in or under snow
NIVATION *n* weathering of rock around a patch of snow by alternate freezing and thawing
NIVATIONS > NIVATION
NIVEOUS *adj* resembling snow, esp in colour
NIX *sentence substitute* be careful! watch out! ▷ *n* rejection or refusal ▷ *vb* veto, deny, reject, or forbid (plans, suggestions, etc)
NIXE *n* water sprite
NIXED > NIX
NIXER *n* spare-time job
NIXERS > NIXER
NIXES > NIX
NIXIE *n* female water

sprite, usually unfriendly to humans
NIXIES > NIXIE
NIXING > NIX
NIXY *same as* > NIXIE
NIZAM *n* (formerly) a Turkish regular soldier
NIZAMATE *n* territory of the nizam
NIZAMATES > NIZAMATE
NIZAMS > NIZAM
NKOSI *n* term of address to a superior
NKOSIS > NKOSI
NO *interj* expresses denial, disagreement, or refusal ▷ *adj* not any, not a ▷ *adv* not at all ▷ *n* answer or vote of 'no'
NOAH *n* shark
NOAHS > NOAH
NOB *n* person of wealth or social distinction
NOBBIER > NOB
NOBBIEST > NOB
NOBBILY > NOB
NOBBINESS > NOB
NOBBLE *vb* attract the attention of (someone) in order to talk to him or her
NOBBLED > NOBBLE
NOBBLER > NOBBLE
NOBBLERS > NOBBLE
NOBBLES > NOBBLE
NOBBLING > NOBBLE
NOBBUT *adv* nothing but
NOBBY > NOB
NOBELIUM *n* artificially-produced radioactive element
NOBELIUMS > NOBELIUM
NOBILESSE *same as* > NOBLESSE
NOBILIARY *adj* of or relating to the nobility
NOBILITY *n* quality of being noble
NOBLE *adj* showing or having high moral qualities ▷ *n* member of the nobility
NOBLEMAN *n* person of noble rank
NOBLEMEN > NOBLEMAN
NOBLENESS > NOBLE
NOBLER > NOBLE
NOBLES > NOBLE
NOBLESSE *n* noble birth or condition
NOBLESSES > NOBLESSE
NOBLEST > NOBLE
NOBLY > NOBLE
NOBODIES > NOBODY
NOBODY *pron* no person ▷ *n* person of no importance
NOBS > NOB
NOCAKE *n* Indian meal made from dried corn
NOCAKES > NOCAKE
NOCENT *n* guilty person
NOCENTLY > NOCENT
NOCENTS > NOCENT
NOCHEL *vb* refuse to pay someone else's debt
NOCHELLED > NOCHEL
NOCHELS > NOCHEL
NOCK *n* notch on an arrow or a bow for the bowstring ▷ *vb* fit (an arrow) on a bowstring
NOCKED > NOCK
NOCKET *same as* > NACKET
NOCKETS > NOCKET
NOCKING > NOCK
NOCKS > NOCK
NOCTILIO *n* type of bat
NOCTILIOS > NOCTILIO
NOCTILUCA *n* any bioluminescent marine dinoflagellate of the genus *Noctiluca*
NOCTUA *n* type of moth
NOCTUARY *n* nightly journal
NOCTUAS > NOCTUA
NOCTUID *n* type of nocturnal moth ▷ *adj* of or relating to this type of moth
NOCTUIDS > NOCTUID
NOCTULE *n* any of several large Old World insectivorous bats
NOCTULES > NOCTULE
NOCTUOID > NOCTUA
NOCTURIA *n* excessive urination during the night
NOCTURIAS > NOCTURIA
NOCTURN *n* any of the main sections of the office of matins
NOCTURNAL *adj* of the night ▷ *n* something active at night
NOCTURNE *n* short dreamy piece of music
NOCTURNES > NOCTURNE
NOCTURNS > NOCTURN
NOCUOUS *adj* harmful
NOCUOUSLY > NOCUOUS
NOD *vb* lower and raise (one's head) briefly in agreement or greeting ▷ *n* act of nodding
NODAL *adj* of or like a node
NODALISE *same as* > NODALIZE
NODALISED *same as* > NODALISE
NODALISES *same as* > NODALISE
NODALITY > NODAL
NODALIZE *vb* make something nodal
NODALIZED > NODALIZE
NODALIZES > NODALIZE
NODALLY > NODAL
NODATED *adj* knotted
NODATION *n* knottiness
NODATIONS > NODATION
NODDED > NOD
NODDER > NOD
NODDERS > NOD
NODDIES > NODDY
NODDING > NOD
NODDINGLY > NOD
NODDINGS > NOD
NODDLE *n* head ▷ *vb* nod (the head), as through drowsiness
NODDLED > NODDLE
NODDLES > NODDLE
NODDLING > NODDLE
NODDY *n* tropical tern with a dark plumage ▷ *adj* very easy to use or understand
NODE *n* point on a plant stem from which leaves grow
NODES > NODE
NODI > NODUS
NODICAL *adj* of or relating to the nodes of a celestial body, esp of the moon
NODOSE *adj* having nodes or knotlike swellings
NODOSITY > NODOSE
NODOUS *same as* > NODOSE
NODS > NOD
NODULAR > NODULE
NODULATED > NODULE
NODULE *n* small knot or lump
NODULED > NODULE
NODULES > NODULE
NODULOSE > NODULE
NODULOUS > NODULE
NODUS *n* problematic idea, situation, etc
NOEL *n* Christmas
NOELS > NOEL
NOES > NO
NOESES > NOESIS
NOESIS *n* exercise of reason, esp in the apprehension of universal forms
NOESISES > NOESIS
NOETIC *adj* of or relating to the mind, esp to its rational and intellectual faculties
NOG *same as* > NOGGING
NOGAKU *n* Japanese style of drama
NOGG *same as* > NOG
NOGGED *adj* built with timber and brick
NOGGIN *n* head
NOGGING *n* short horizontal timber member used between the studs of a framed partition
NOGGINGS > NOGGING
NOGGINS > NOGGIN
NOGGS > NOGG
NOGS > NOG
NOH *n* stylized classic drama of Japan
NOHOW *adv* under any conditions
NOHOWISH > NOHOW
NOIL *n* short or knotted fibres that are separated from the long fibres by combing
NOILS > NOIL
NOILY > NOIL
NOINT *vb* anoint
NOINTED > NOINT
NOINTER *n* mischievous child
NOINTERS > NOINTER
NOINTING > NOINT
NOINTS > NOINT
NOIR *adj* (of a film) showi[ng] characteristics of a *film noir*, in plot or style ▷ *n* film noir
NOIRISH > NOIR
NOIRS > NOIR
NOISE *n* sound, usu. a lou[d] or disturbing one
NOISED > NOISE
NOISEFUL > NOISE
NOISELESS *adj* making little or no sound
NOISENIK *n* rock musicia[n] who performs loud harsh music
NOISENIKS > NOISENIK
NOISES > NOISE
NOISETTE *n* hazelnut chocolate ▷ *adj* flavoure[d] or made with hazelnuts
NOISETTES > NOISETTE
NOISIER > NOISY
NOISIEST > NOISY
NOISILY > NOISY
NOISINESS > NOISY
NOISING > NOISE
NOISOME *adj* (of smells) offensive
NOISOMELY > NOISOME
NOISY *adj* making a lot of noise
NOLE *same as* > NOLL
NOLES > NOLE
NOLITION *n* unwillingne[ss]
NOLITIONS > NOLITION
NOLL *n* head
NOLLS > NOLL
NOLO as in *nolo contendere* plea indicating that the defendant does not wish to contest the case
NOLOS > NOLO
NOM *n* name
NOMA *n* gangrenous inflammation of the mouth, esp one affecting malnourished children
NOMAD *n* member of a trib[e] with no fixed dwelling place, wanderer
NOMADE *same as* > NOMAD
NOMADES > NOMADE
NOMADIC *adj* relating to o[r] characteristic of nomad[s] or their way of life
NOMADIES > NOMADY
NOMADISE *same as* > NOMADIZE
NOMADISED > NOMADISE
NOMADISES > NOMADISE
NOMADISM > NOMAD
NOMADISMS > NOMAD
NOMADIZE *vb* live as nomads
NOMADIZED > NOMADIZE
NOMADIZES > NOMADIZE
NOMADS > NOMAD
NOMADY *n* practice of livin[g] like nomads
NOMARCH *n* head of an ancient Egyptian nome
NOMARCHS > NOMARCH

)MARCHY *n* any of the provinces of modern Greece
)MAS > NOMA
)MBLES *variant spelling of* > NUMBLES
)MBRIL *n* point on a shield between the fesse point and the lowest point
)MBRILS > NOMBRIL
)ME *n* any of the former provinces of modern Greece
)MEN *n* ancient Roman's second name, designating his gens or clan
)MES > NOME
)MIC *adj* normal or habitual
)MINA > NOMEN
)MINABLE > NOMINATE
)MINAL *adj* in name only ▷ *n* nominal element
)MINALLY > NOMINAL
)MINALS > NOMINAL
)MINATE *vb* suggest as a candidate ▷ *adj* having a particular name
)MINATED > NOMINATE
)MINATES > NOMINATE
)MINATOR > NOMINATE
)MINEE *n* candidate
)MINEES > NOMINEE
)MISM *n* adherence to a law or laws as a primary exercise of religion
)MISMS > NOMISM
)MISTIC > NOMISM
)MOCRACY *n* government based on the rule of law rather than arbitrary will, terror, etc
)MOGENY *n* law of life originating as a natural process
)MOGRAM *n* arrangement of two linear or logarithmic scales
)MOGRAMS > NOMOGRAM
)MOGRAPH *same* **S** > NOMOGRAM
)MOI > NOMOS
)MOLOGIC > NOMOLOGY
)MOLOGY *n* science of law and law-making
)MOS *n* convention
)MOTHETE *n* legislator
)MS > NOM
)N *adv* not
)NA *n* sleeping sickness
)NACID *adj* not acid ▷ *n* nonacid substance
)NACIDIC *adj* not acidic
)NACIDS > NONACID
)NACTING *adj* not acting
)NACTION *n* not action
)NACTIVE *adj* not active
)NACTOR *n* person who is not an actor
)NACTORS > NONACTOR
)NADDICT *n* person who is not an addict
)NADULT *n* person who is not an adult

NONADULTS > NONADULT
NONAGE *n* state of being under full legal age for various actions
NONAGED > NONAGE
NONAGES > NONAGE
NONAGON *n* geometric figure with nine sides
NONAGONAL > NONAGON
NONAGONS > NONAGON
NONANE *n* type of chemical compound
NONANES > NONANE
NONANIMAL *adj* not animal
NONANOIC as in *nonanoic acid* colourless oily fatty acid with a rancid odour
NONANSWER *n* unsatisfactory reply
NONARABLE *adj* not arable
NONART *n* something that does not constitute art
NONARTIST *n* person who is not an artist
NONARTS > NONART
NONARY *adj* based on the number nine
NONAS > NONES
NONATOMIC *adj* not atomic
NONAUTHOR *n* person who is not the author
NONBANK *n* business or institution that is not a bank but provides similar services
NONBANKS > NONBANK
NONBASIC *adj* not basic
NONBEING *n* philosophical problem relating to the question of existence
NONBEINGS > NONBEING
NONBELIEF *n* state of not believing
NONBINARY *adj* not binary
NONBITING *adj* not biting
NONBLACK *n* person or thing that is not black
NONBLACKS > NONBLACK
NONBODIES > NONBODY
NONBODY *n* nonphysical nature of a person
NONBONDED *adj* not bonded
NONBOOK *n* book with little substance
NONBOOKS > NONBOOK
NONBRAND *adj* not produced by a well-known company
NONBUYING *adj* not buying
NONCAKING *adj* not liable to cake
NONCAMPUS *adj* not on campus
NONCAREER *adj* not career-related
NONCASH *adj* other than cash
NONCASUAL *adj* not casual
NONCAUSAL *adj* not causal
NONCE *n* present time or occasion
NONCEREAL *adj* not cereal
NONCES > NONCE
NONCHURCH *adj* not related to the church

NONCLASS *n* lack of class
NONCLING *adj* not liable to stick
NONCODING *adj* (of DNA) not containing instructions for making protein
NONCOITAL *adj* not involving sexual intercourse
NONCOKING *adj* not liable to coke
NONCOLA *n* soft drink other than cola
NONCOLAS > NONCOLA
NONCOLOR *n* achromatic colour such as black or white
NONCOLORS > NONCOLOR
NONCOM *n* person not involved in combat
NONCOMBAT *adj* not involved in combat
NONCOMS > NONCOM
NONCONCUR *vb* disagree
NONCORE *adj* not central or essential
NONCOUNTY *adj* not controlled or run by a county
NONCREDIT *adj* relating to an educational course not providing a credit towards a degree
NONCRIME *n* incident that is not a crime
NONCRIMES > NONCRIME
NONCRISES > NONCRISIS
NONCRISIS *n* situation that is not a crisis
NONCYCLIC *adj* not cyclic
NONDAIRY *adj* not containing dairy products
NONDANCE *n* series of movements that do not constitute a dance
NONDANCER *n* person who is not a dancer
NONDANCES > NONDANCE
NONDEGREE *adj* not leading to a degree
NONDEMAND *adj* not involving demand
NONDESERT *adj* not belonging to the desert
NONDOCTOR *n* person who is not a doctor
NONDOLLAR *adj* not involving the dollar
NONDRIP *adj* (of paint) specially formulated to minimize dripping during application
NONDRIVER *n* person who does not drive
NONDRUG *adj* not involving the use of drugs
NONDRYING *adj* not drying
NONE *pron* not any
NONEDIBLE *n* not edible
NONEGO *n* everything that is outside one's conscious self, such as one's environment

NONEGOS > NONEGO
NONELECT *n* person not chosen
NONELITE *adj* not elite
NONEMPTY *adj* mathematical term
NONENDING *adj* not ending
NONENERGY *adj* without energy
NONENTITY *n* insignificant person or thing
NONENTRY *n* failure to enter
NONEQUAL *adj* not equal ▷ *n* person who is not the equal of another person
NONEQUALS > NONEQUAL
NONEROTIC *adj* not erotic
NONES *n* (in the Roman calendar) the ninth day before the ides of each month
NONESUCH *n* matchless person or thing
NONET *n* piece of music composed for a group of nine instruments
NONETHNIC *n* not ethnic
NONETS > NONET
NONETTE *same as* > NONET
NONETTES > NONETTE
NONETTI *same as* > NONET
NONETTO *same as* > NONET
NONETTOS > NONETTO
NONEVENT *n* disappointing or insignificant occurrence
NONEVENTS > NONEVENT
NONEXEMPT *adj* not exempt
NONEXOTIC *adj* not exotic
NONEXPERT *n* person who is not an expert
NONEXTANT *adj* no longer in existence
NONFACT *n* event or thing not provable
NONFACTOR *n* something that is not a factor
NONFACTS > NONFACT
NONFADING *adj* colourfast
NONFAMILY *n* household that does not consist of a family
NONFAN *n* person who is not a fan
NONFANS > NONFAN
NONFARM *adj* not connected with a farm
NONFARMER *n* person who is not a farmer
NONFAT *adj* fat free
NONFATAL *adj* not resulting in or capable of causing death
NONFATTY *adj* not fatty
NONFEUDAL *adj* not feudal
NONFILIAL *adj* not involving parent-child relationship
NONFINAL *adj* not final
NONFINITE *adj* not finite
NONFISCAL *adj* not involving government funds
NONFLUID *adj* not fluid ▷ *n*

something that is not a fluid
NONFLUIDS > NONFLUID
NONFLYING *adj* not capable of flying
NONFOCAL *adj* not focal
NONFOOD *n* item that is not food
NONFORMAL *adj* not formal
NONFOSSIL *adj* not consisting of fossils
NONFROZEN *adj* not frozen
NONFUEL *adj* not relating to fuel
NONFUNDED *adj* not receiving funding
NONG *n* stupid or incompetent person
NONGAME *adj* not pursued for competitive sport purposes
NONGAY *n* person who is not gay
NONGAYS > NONGAY
NONGHETTO *adj* not belonging to the ghetto
NONGLARE *adj* not causing glare ▷ *n* any of various nonglare materials
NONGLARES > NONGLARE
NONGLAZED *adj* not glazed
NONGLOSSY *adj* not glossy
NONGOLFER *n* person who is not a golfer
NONGRADED *adj* not graded
NONGREASY *adj* not greasy
NONGREEN *adj* not green
NONGROWTH *n* failure to grow
NONGS > NONG
NONGUEST *n* person who is not a guest
NONGUESTS > NONGUEST
NONGUILT *n* state of being innocent
NONGUILTS > NONGUILT
NONHARDY *adj* fragile
NONHEME *adj* of dietary iron, obtained from vegetable foods
NONHERO *n* person who is not a hero
NONHEROES > NONHERO
NONHEROIC *adj* not heroic
NONHOME *adj* not of the home
NONHUMAN *n* something not human
NONHUMANS > NONHUMAN
NONHUNTER *n* person or thing that does not hunt
NONI *n* type of tree of SE Asia and the Pacific islands whose fruit provides a possibly health-promoting juice
NONIDEAL *adj* not ideal
NONILLION *n* (in Britain, France, and Germany) the number represented as one followed by 54 zeros
NONIMAGE *n* person who is not a celebrity
NONIMAGES > NONIMAGE
NONIMMUNE *adj* not immune
NONIMPACT *adj* not involving impact
NONINERT *adj* not inert
NONINJURY *adj* not involving injury
NONINSECT *n* animal that is not an insect
NONIONIC *adj* not ionic
NONIRON *adj* not requiring ironing
NONIS > NONI
NONISSUE *n* matter of little importance
NONISSUES > NONISSUE
NONJOINER *n* person who does not join (an organisation, etc)
NONJURIES > NONJURY
NONJURING *adj* refusing the oath of allegiance
NONJUROR *n* person who refuses to take an oath, as of allegiance
NONJURORS > NONJUROR
NONJURY *n* trial without a jury
NONKOSHER *adj* not kosher
NONLABOR *adj* not concerned with labour
NONLAWYER *n* person who is not a lawyer
NONLEADED *adj* not leaded
NONLEAFY *adj* not leafy
NONLEAGUE *adj* not belonging to a league
NONLEGAL *adj* not legal
NONLEGUME *n* not a pod of the pea or bean family
NONLETHAL *adj* not resulting in or capable of causing death
NONLEVEL *adj* not level
NONLIABLE *adj* not liable
NONLIFE *n* matter which is not living
NONLINEAL *same as* > NONLINEAR
NONLINEAR *adj* not of, in, along, or relating to a line
NONLIQUID *n* substance which is not liquid
NONLIVES > NONLIFE
NONLIVING *adj* not living
NONLOCAL *adj* not of, affecting, or confined to a limited area or part ▷ *n* person who is not local to an area
NONLOCALS > NONLOCAL
NONLOVING *adj* not loving
NONLOYAL *adj* not loyal
NONLYRIC *adj* without lyrics
NONMAJOR *n* student who is not majoring in a specified subject
NONMAJORS > NONMAJOR
NONMAN *n* being that is not a man
NONMANUAL *adj* not manual
NONMARKET *adj* not relating to markets
NONMATURE *adj* not mature
NONMEAT *n* not containing meat
NONMEMBER *n* person who is not a member of a particular club or organization
NONMEN > NONMAN
NONMENTAL *adj* not mental
NONMETAL *n* chemical element that forms acidic oxides and is a poor conductor of heat and electricity
NONMETALS > NONMETAL
NONMETRIC *adj* not metric
NONMETRO *adj* not metropolitan
NONMOBILE *adj* not mobile
NONMODAL *adj* not modal
NONMODERN *adj* not modern
NONMONEY *adj* not involving money
NONMORAL *adj* not involving morality
NONMORTAL *adj* not fatal
NONMOTILE *adj* not capable of movement
NONMOVING *adj* not moving
NONMUSIC *n* (unpleasant) noise
NONMUSICS > NONMUSIC
NONMUTANT *n* person or thing that is not mutated
NONMUTUAL *adj* not mutual
NONNASAL *adj* not nasal
NONNATIVE *adj* not native ▷ *n* person who is not native to a place
NONNAVAL *adj* not belonging to the navy
NONNEURAL *adj* not neural
NONNEWS *adj* not concerned with news
NONNIES > NONNY
NONNOBLE *adj* not noble
NONNORMAL *adj* not normal
NONNOVEL *n* literary work that is not a novel
NONNOVELS > NONNOVEL
NONNY *n* meaningless word
NONOBESE *adj* not obese
NONOHMIC *adj* not having electrical resistance
NONOILY *adj* not oily
NONORAL *adj* not oral
NONORALLY > NONORAL
NONOWNER *n* person who is not an owner
NONOWNERS > NONOWNER
NONPAGAN *n* person who is not a pagan
NONPAGANS > NONPAGAN
NONPAID *adj* without payment
NONPAPAL *adj* not of the pope
NONPAPIST *adj* not papist
NONPAR *adj* nonparticipating
NONPAREIL *n* person or thing that is unsurpassed ▷ *adj* having no match or equal
NONPARENT *n* person whc is not a parent
NONPARITY *n* state of not being equal
NONPAROUS *adj* never having given birth
NONPARTY *adj* not connected with a politic party
NONPAST *n* grammatical term
NONPASTS > NONPAST
NONPAYING *adj* (of guests customers, etc) not expected or requested to pay
NONPEAK *n* period of low demand
NONPERSON *n* person regarded as nonexistent unimportant
NONPLANAR *adj* not plana
NONPLAY *n* social behaviour that is not classed as play
NONPLAYER *n* person not playing
NONPLAYS > NONPLAY
NONPLIANT *adj* not pliant
NONPLUS *vb* put at a loss ▷ *n* state of utter perplexity prohibiting action or speech
NONPLUSED > NONPLUS
NONPLUSES > NONPLUS
NONPOETIC *adj* not poeti
NONPOINT *adj* without a specific site
NONPOLAR *adj* not polar
NONPOLICE *adj* not relate to the police
NONPOOR *adj* not poor
NONPOROUS *adj* not permeable to water, air, other fluids
NONPOSTAL *adj* not posta
NONPRINT *adj* published i a format other than prin on paper
NONPROFIT *n* organizatic that is not intended to make a profit
NONPROS *vb* enter a judgment of non prosequitur against a plaintiff
NONPROVEN *adj* not tried and tested
NONPUBLIC *adj* not publi
NONQUOTA *adj* not include in a quota
NONRACIAL *adj* not related to racial factors c discrimination
NONRANDOM *adj* not randc
NONRATED *adj* not rated
NONREADER *n* person wh does not or cannot read
NONRETURN *adj* denoting mechanism that permit flow in a pipe in one direction only
NONRHOTIC *adj* denoting or speaking a dialect

f English in which reconsonantal rs are not ronounced
NRIGID *adj* not rigid
NRIOTER *n* person who oes not participate in riot
NRIVAL *n* person or hing not competing for uccess
NRIVALS > NONRIVAL
NROYAL *adj* not royal
NRUBBER *adj* not ontaining rubber
NRULING *adj* not ruling
NRURAL *adj* not rural
NSACRED *adj* not sacred
NSALINE *adj* not ontaining salt
NSCHOOL *adj* not relating o school
NSECRET *adj* not sacred
NSECURE *adj* not secure
NSELF *n* foreign nolecule in the body
NSELVES > NONSELF
NSENSE *n* something hat has or makes no sense *interj* exclamation of isagreement
NSENSES > NONSENSE
NSERIAL *adj* not serial
NSEXIST *adj* not iscriminating on the asis of sex, esp not gainst women
NSEXUAL *adj* not f, relating to, or haracterized by sex or exuality
NSHRINK *adj* not likely o shrink
NSIGNER *n* person who annot use sign language
NSKATER *n* person who oes not skate
NSKED *n* non-scheduled eroplane
NSKEDS > NONSKED
NSKID *adj* designed to educe skidding
NSKIER *n* person who oes not ski
NSKIERS > NONSKIER
NSLIP *adj* designed to revent slipping
NSMOKER *n* person who oes not smoke
NSOCIAL *adj* not social
NSOLAR *adj* not related o the sun
NSOLID *n* substance nat is not a solid
NSOLIDS > NONSOLID
NSPEECH *adj* not nvolving speech
NSTAPLE *adj* not staple
NSTATIC *adj* not static
NSTEADY *adj* not steady
NSTICK *adj* coated with substance that food will ot stick to when cooked
NSTICKY *adj* not sticky
NSTOP *adv* without a stop ▷ *adj* without a stop ▷ *n* nonstop flight
NONSTOPS > NONSTOP
NONSTORY *n* story of little substance or importance
NONSTYLE *n* style that cannot be identified
NONSTYLES > NONSTYLE
NONSUCH *same as* > NONESUCH
NONSUCHES > NONSUCH
NONSUGAR *n* substance that is not a sugar
NONSUGARS > NONSUGAR
NONSUIT *n* order of a judge dismissing a suit when the plaintiff fails to show a good cause of action or to produce any evidence ▷ *vb* order the dismissal of the suit of (a person)
NONSUITED > NONSUIT
NONSUITS > NONSUIT
NONSYSTEM *adj* having no system
NONTALKER *n* person who does not talk
NONTARGET *adj* not being a target
NONTARIFF *adj* without tariff
NONTAX *n* tax that has little real effect
NONTAXES > NONTAX
NONTHEIST *n* person who believes the existence or non-existence of God is irrelevant
NONTIDAL *adj* not having a tide
NONTITLE *adj* without title
NONTONAL *adj* not written in a key
NONTONIC *adj* not tonic
NONTOXIC *adj* not poisonous
NONTRAGIC *adj* not tragic
NONTRIBAL *adj* not tribal
NONTRUMP *adj* not of the trump suit
NONTRUTH *same as* > UNTRUTH
NONTRUTHS > NONTRUTH
NONUNION *adj* (of a company) not employing trade union members ▷ *n* failure of broken bones or bone fragments to heal
NONUNIONS > NONUNION
NONUNIQUE *adj* not unique
NONUPLE *adj* ninefold ▷ *n* ninefold number
NONUPLES > NONUPLE
NONUPLET *n* child born in a multiple birth of nine siblings
NONUPLETS > NONUPLET
NONURBAN *adj* rural
NONURGENT *adj* not urgent
NONUSABLE *adj* not usable
NONUSE *n* failure to use
NONUSER > NONUSE
NONUSERS > NONUSE
NONUSES > NONUSE
NONUSING > NONUSE
NONVACANT *adj* not vacant
NONVALID *adj* not valid
NONVECTOR *n* quantity without size and direction
NONVENOUS *adj* not venous
NONVERBAL *adj* not involving the use of language
NONVESTED *adj* not vested
NONVIABLE *adj* not viable
NONVIEWER *n* person who does not watch (television)
NONVIRAL *adj* not caused by a virus
NONVIRGIN *n* person who is not a virgin
NONVIRILE *adj* not virile
NONVISUAL *adj* not visual
NONVITAL *adj* not vital
NONVOCAL *n* music track without singing
NONVOCALS > NONVOCAL
NONVOTER *n* person who does not vote
NONVOTERS > NONVOTER
NONVOTING *adj* (of shares in a company) not entitling the owner to vote at company meetings
NONWAGE *adj* not part of wages
NONWAR *n* state of nonviolence
NONWARS > NONWAR
NONWHITE *n* person who is not white
NONWHITES > NONWHITE
NONWINGED *adj* without wings
NONWOODY *adj* not woody
NONWOOL *adj* not wool
NONWORD *n* series of letters not recognised as a word
NONWORDS > NONWORD
NONWORK *adj* not involving work
NONWORKER *n* person who does not work
NONWOVEN *n* material made by a method other than weaving
NONWOVENS > NONWOVEN
NONWRITER *n* person who is not a writer
NONYL *n* type of chemical
NONYLS > NONYL
NONZERO *adj* not equal to zero
NOO *n* type of Japanese musical drama
NOODGE *vb* annoy persistently
NOODGED > NOODGE
NOODGES > NOODGE
NOODGING > NOODGE
NOODLE *n* simpleton ▷ *vb* improvise aimlessly on a musical instrument
NOODLED > NOODLE
NOODLEDOM *n* state of being a simpleton
NOODLES > NOODLE
NOODLING *n* aimless musical improvisation
NOODLINGS > NOODLING
NOOGIE *n* act of inflicting pain by rubbing someone's head hard
NOOGIES > NOOGIE
NOOIT *interj* South African exclamation of pleased or shocked surprise
NOOK *n* corner or recess
NOOKIE *same as* > NOOKY
NOOKIER > NOOKY
NOOKIES > NOOKIE
NOOKIEST > NOOKY
NOOKLIKE > NOOK
NOOKS > NOOK
NOOKY *n* sexual intercourse ▷ *adj* resembling a nook
NOOLOGIES > NOOLOGY
NOOLOGY *n* study of intuition
NOOMETRY *n* mind measurement
NOON *n* twelve o'clock midday ▷ *vb* take a rest at noon
NOONDAY *adj* happening at noon ▷ *n* middle of the day
NOONDAYS > NOONDAY
NOONED > NOON
NOONER *n* sexual encounter during a lunch hour
NOONERS > NOONER
NOONING *n* midday break for rest or food
NOONINGS > NOONING
NOONS > NOON
NOONTIDE *same as* > NOONTIME
NOONTIDES > NOONTIDE
NOONTIME *n* middle of the day
NOONTIMES > NOONTIME
NOOP *n* point of the elbow
NOOPS > NOOP
NOOSE *n* loop in the end of a rope, tied with a slipknot
NOOSED > NOOSE
NOOSER *n* person who uses a noose
NOOSERS > NOOSER
NOOSES > NOOSE
NOOSING > NOOSE
NOOSPHERE *n* sphere of human thought
NOOTROPIC *adj* acting on mind
NOPAL *n* type of cactus
NOPALES > NOPAL
NOPALITO *n* small cactus
NOPALITOS > NOPALITO
NOPALS > NOPAL
NOPE *interj* no
NOPLACE *same as* > NOWHERE
NOR *prep* and not
NORDIC *adj* of competitions in cross-country racing and ski-jumping
NORI *n* edible seaweed often used in Japanese cookery, esp for wrapping

sushi or rice balls
NORIA *n* water wheel with buckets attached to its rim for raising water from a stream into irrigation canals
NORIAS > NORIA
NORIMON *n* Japanese passenger vehicle
NORIMONS > NORIMON
NORIS > NORI
NORITE *n* variety of gabbro composed mainly of hypersthene and labradorite feldspar
NORITES > NORITE
NORITIC > NORITE
NORK *n* female breast
NORKS > NORK
NORLAND *n* north part of a country or the earth
NORLANDS > NORLAND
NORM *n* standard that is regarded as normal
NORMA *n* norm or standard
NORMAL *adj* usual, regular, or typical ▷ *n* usual or regular state, degree or form
NORMALCY > NORMAL
NORMALISE *same as* > NORMALIZE
NORMALITY > NORMAL
NORMALIZE *vb* make or become normal
NORMALLY *adv* as a rule
NORMALS > NORMAL
NORMAN *n* post used for winding on a ship
NORMANDE *n* type of cattle
NORMANS > NORMAN
NORMAS > NORMA
NORMATIVE *adj* of or setting a norm or standard
NORMED *n* mathematical term
NORMLESS *adj* without a norm
NORMS > NORM
NORSEL *vb* fit with short lines for fastening hooks
NORSELLED > NORSEL
NORSELLER > NORSEL
NORSELS > NORSEL
NORTENA *same as* > NORTENO
NORTENAS > NORTENA
NORTENO *n* type of Mexican music
NORTENOS > NORTENO
NORTH *n* direction towards the North Pole, opposite south ▷ *adj* or in the north ▷ *adv* in, to, or towards the north ▷ *vb* move north
NORTHEAST *adv* (in or to) direction between north and east ▷ *n* point of the compass or direction midway between north and east ▷ *adj* of or denoting the northeastern part of a specified country, area, etc
NORTHED > NORTH
NORTHER *n* wind or storm from the north ▷ *vb* move north
NORTHERED > NORTHER
NORTHERLY *adj* of or in the north ▷ *adv* towards the north ▷ *n* wind from the north
NORTHERN *adj* situated in or towards the north ▷ *n* person from the north
NORTHERNS > NORTHERN
NORTHERS > NORTHER
NORTHING *n* movement or distance covered in a northerly direction
NORTHINGS > NORTHING
NORTHLAND *n* lands that are far to the north
NORTHMOST *adj* situated furthest north
NORTHS > NORTH
NORTHWARD *adv* towards the north
NORTHWEST *adv* (in or to) direction between north and west ▷ *n* point of the compass or direction midway between north and west ▷ *adj* of or denoting the northwestern part of a specified country, area, etc
NORWARD *same as* > NORTHWARD
NORWARDS *same as* > NORWARD
NOS > NO
NOSE *n* organ of smell, used also in breathing ▷ *vb* move forward slowly and carefully
NOSEAN *n* type of mineral
NOSEANS > NOSEAN
NOSEBAG *n* bag containing feed fastened round a horse's head
NOSEBAGS > NOSEBAG
NOSEBAND *n* part of a horse's bridle that goes around the nose
NOSEBANDS > NOSEBAND
NOSEBLEED *n* bleeding from the nose
NOSED > NOSE
NOSEDIVE *vb* (of an aircraft) plunge suddenly with the nose pointing downwards
NOSEDIVED > NOSEDIVE
NOSEDIVES > NOSEDIVE
NOSEDOVE > NOSEDIVE
NOSEGAY *n* small bunch of flowers
NOSEGAYS > NOSEGAY
NOSEGUARD *n* position in American football
NOSELESS > NOSE
NOSELIKE > NOSE
NOSELITE *same as* > NOSEAN
NOSELITES > NOSELITE
NOSEPIECE *same as* > NOSEBAND
NOSER *n* strong headwind
NOSERS > NOSER
NOSES > NOSE
NOSEWHEEL *n* wheel fitted under the nose of an aircraft
NOSEY *adj* prying or inquisitive ▷ *n* nosey person
NOSEYS > NOSEY
NOSH *n* food ▷ *vb* eat
NOSHED > NOSH
NOSHER > NOSH
NOSHERIE *same as* > NOSHERY
NOSHERIES > NOSHERIE
NOSHERS > NOSH
NOSHERY *n* restaurant or other place where food is served
NOSHES > NOSH
NOSHING > NOSH
NOSIER > NOSY
NOSIES > NOSY
NOSIEST > NOSY
NOSILY > NOSY
NOSINESS > NOSY
NOSING *n* edge of a step or stair tread that projects beyond the riser
NOSINGS > NOSING
NOSODE *n* homeopathic remedy
NOSODES > NOSODE
NOSOLOGIC > NOSOLOGY
NOSOLOGY *n* branch of medicine concerned with the classification of diseases
NOSTALGIA *n* sentimental longing for the past
NOSTALGIC *adj* of or characterized by nostalgia ▷ *n* person who indulges in nostalgia
NOSTOC *n* type of bacterium occurring in moist places
NOSTOCS > NOSTOC
NOSTOI > NOSTOS
NOSTOLOGY *n* scientific study of ageing
NOSTOS *n* story of a return home
NOSTRIL *n* one of the two openings at the end of the nose
NOSTRILS > NOSTRIL
NOSTRO as in *nostro account* bank account conducted by a British bank with a foreign bank
NOSTRUM *n* quack medicine
NOSTRUMS > NOSTRUM
NOSY *adj* prying or inquisitive
NOT *adv* expressing negation, refusal, or denial
NOTA > NOTUM
NOTABILIA *n* things worthy of notice
NOTABLE *adj* worthy of being noted, remarkable ▷ *n* person of distinction
NOTABLES > NOTABLE
NOTABLY *adv* particularly or especially
NOTAEUM *n* back of a bird's body
NOTAEUMS > NOTAEUM
NOTAL > NOTUM
NOTANDA > NOTANDUM
NOTANDUM *n* notable fact
NOTAPHILY *n* study of paper money
NOTARIAL > NOTARY
NOTARIES > NOTARY
NOTARISE *same as* > NOTARIZE
NOTARISED > NOTARISE
NOTARISES > NOTARISE
NOTARIZE *vb* attest to or authenticate (a document, contract, etc), as a notary
NOTARIZED > NOTARIZE
NOTARIZES > NOTARIZE
NOTARY *n* person authorized to witness the signing of legal documents
NOTATE *vb* write (esp music) in notation
NOTATED > NOTATE
NOTATES > NOTATE
NOTATING > NOTATE
NOTATION *n* representation of numbers or quantities in a system by a series of symbols
NOTATIONS > NOTATION
NOTCH *n* V-shaped cut ▷ *vb* make a notch in
NOTCHBACK *n* type of car
NOTCHED > NOTCH
NOTCHEL *vb* refuse to pay another person's debts
NOTCHELS > NOTCHEL
NOTCHER *n* person who cuts notches
NOTCHERS > NOTCHER
NOTCHES > NOTCH
NOTCHIER > NOTCHY
NOTCHIEST > NOTCHY
NOTCHING > NOTCH
NOTCHINGS > NOTCH
NOTCHY *adj* (of a motor vehicle gear mechanism) requiring careful gear-changing
NOTE *n* short letter ▷ *vb* notice, pay attention to
NOTEBOOK *n* book for writing in
NOTEBOOKS > NOTEBOOK
NOTECARD *n* greetings card with space to write note
NOTECARDS > NOTECARD
NOTECASE *same as* > WALL
NOTECASES > NOTECASE
NOTED *adj* well-known
NOTEDLY > NOTED
NOTEDNESS > NOTED
NOTELESS > NOTE
NOTELET *n* small folded card with a design on the front, used for writing informal letters

OTELETS > NOTELET
OTEPAD *n* number of sheets of paper fastened together along one edge
OTEPADS > NOTEPAD
OTEPAPER *n* paper used for writing letters
OTER *n* person who takes notes
OTERS > NOTER
OTES *pl n* short descriptive or summarized jottings taken down for future reference
OTHER *same as* > OTHER
OTHING *pron* not anything ▷ *adv* not at all ▷ *n* person or thing of no importance
OTHINGS > NOTHING
OTICE *n* observation or attention ▷ *vb* observe, become aware of
OTICED > NOTICE
OTICER *n* person who takes notice
OTICERS > NOTICER
OTICES > NOTICE
OTICING > NOTICE
OTIFIED > NOTIFY
OTIFIER > NOTIFY
OTIFIERS > NOTIFY
OTIFIES > NOTIFY
OTIFY *vb* inform
OTIFYING > NOTIFY
OTING > NOTE
OTION *n* idea or opinion
OTIONAL *adj* speculative, imaginary, or unreal
OTIONIST *n* person whose opinions are merely notions
OTIONS *pl n* pins, cotton, ribbon, and similar wares used for sewing
OTITIA *n* register or list, esp of ecclesiastical districts
OTITIAE > NOTITIA
OTITIAS > NOTITIA
OTOCHORD *n* fibrous longitudinal rod in all embryo and some adult chordate animals
OTORIETY > NOTORIOUS
OTORIOUS *adj* well known for something bad
OTORNIS *n* rare flightless rail of New Zealand
OTOUR *adj* notorious
OTT *same as* > NOT
OTTURNI > NOTTURNO
OTTURNO *n* piece of music
OTUM *n* cuticular plate covering the dorsal surface of a thoracic segment of an insect
OUGAT *n* chewy sweet containing nuts and fruit
OUGATS > NOUGAT
OUGHT *n* figure 0
OUGHTIES *pl n* decade from 2000 to 2009
OUGHTS > NOUGHT
OUL *same as* > NOLL
NOULD *vb* would not
NOULDE *same as* > NOULD
NOULE *same as* > NOLL
NOULES > NOULE
NOULS > NOUL
NOUMENA > NOUMENON
NOUMENAL > NOUMENON
NOUMENON *n* (in the philosophy of Kant) a thing as it is in itself, incapable of being known, but only inferred from the nature of experience
NOUN *n* word that refers to a person, place, or thing
NOUNAL > NOUN
NOUNALLY > NOUN
NOUNIER > NOUNY
NOUNIEST > NOUNY
NOUNLESS > NOUN
NOUNS > NOUN
NOUNY *adj* nounlike
NOUP *n* steep headland
NOUPS > NOUP
NOURICE *n* nurse
NOURICES > NOURICE
NOURISH *vb* feed
NOURISHED > NOURISH
NOURISHER > NOURISH
NOURISHES > NOURISH
NOURITURE *n* nourishment
NOURSLE *vb* nurse
NOURSLED > NOURSLE
NOURSLES > NOURSLE
NOURSLING > NOURSLE
NOUS *n* common sense
NOUSELL *vb* foster
NOUSELLED > NOUSELL
NOUSELLS > NOUSELL
NOUSES > NOUS
NOUSLE *vb* nuzzle
NOUSLED > NOUSLE
NOUSLES > NOUSLE
NOUSLING > NOUSLE
NOUT *same as* > NOUGHT
NOUVEAU *adj* having recently become the thing specified
NOUVEAUX *same as* > NOUVEAU
NOUVELLE *n* long short story
NOUVELLES > NOUVELLE
NOVA *n* star that suddenly becomes brighter and then gradually decreases to its original brightness
NOVAE > NOVA
NOVALIA *n* newly reclaimed land
NOVALIKE *adj* resembling a nova
NOVAS > NOVA
NOVATED as in *novated lease* Australian system of employer-aided car purchase
NOVATION *n* substitution of a new obligation for an old one by mutual agreement between the parties
NOVATIONS > NOVATION
NOVEL *n* long fictitious story in book form ▷ *adj* fresh, new, or original
NOVELDOM *n* realm of fiction
NOVELDOMS > NOVELDOM
NOVELESE *n* style of writing characteristic of poor novels
NOVELESES > NOVELESE
NOVELETTE *n* short novel, esp one regarded as trivial or sentimental
NOVELISE *same as* > NOVELIZE
NOVELISED > NOVELISE
NOVELISER *n* person who novelizes
NOVELISES > NOVELISE
NOVELISH *adj* resembling a novel
NOVELISM *n* innovation
NOVELISMS > NOVELISM
NOVELIST *n* writer of novels
NOVELISTS > NOVELIST
NOVELIZE *vb* convert (a true story, film, etc) into a novel
NOVELIZED > NOVELIZE
NOVELIZER *n* person who novelizes
NOVELIZES > NOVELIZE
NOVELLA *n* short novel
NOVELLAE > NOVELLA
NOVELLAS > NOVELLA
NOVELLE > NOVELLA
NOVELLY > NOVEL
NOVELS > NOVEL
NOVELTIES > NOVELTY
NOVELTY *n* newness
NOVENA *n* set of prayers or services on nine consecutive days
NOVENAE > NOVENA
NOVENARY *n* set of nine
NOVENAS > NOVENA
NOVENNIAL *adj* recurring every ninth year
NOVERCAL *adj* stepmotherly
NOVERINT *n* writ
NOVERINTS > NOVERINT
NOVICE *n* beginner
NOVICES > NOVICE
NOVICIATE *same as* > NOVITIATE
NOVITIATE *n* period of being a novice
NOVITIES > NOVITY
NOVITY *n* novelty
NOVOCAINE *n* tradename of a painkilling substance used as a local anaesthetic
NOVODAMUS *n* type of charter
NOVUM *n* game played with dice
NOVUMS > NOVUM
NOW *adv* at or for the present time
NOWADAYS *adv* in these times
NOWAY *adv* in no manner ▷ *sentence substitute* used to make an emphatic refusal, denial etc
NOWAYS *same as* > NOWAY
NOWED *adj* knotted
NOWHENCE *adv* from no place
NOWHERE *adv* not anywhere ▷ *n* nonexistent or insignicant place
NOWHERES > NOWHERE
NOWHITHER *adv* no place
NOWISE *another word for* > NOWAY
NOWL *n* crown of the head
NOWLS > NOWL
NOWN *same as* > OWN
NOWNESS > NOWN
NOWNESSES > NOWN
NOWS > NOW
NOWT *n* nothing
NOWTIER > NOWTY
NOWTIEST > NOWTY
NOWTS > NOWT
NOWTY *adj* bad-tempered
NOWY *adj* having a small projection at the centre (of a cross)
NOX *n* nitrogen oxide
NOXAL *adj* relating to damage done by something belonging to another
NOXES > NOX
NOXIOUS *adj* poisonous or harmful
NOXIOUSLY > NOXIOUS
NOY *vb* harrass
NOYADE *n* execution by drowning
NOYADES > NOYADE
NOYANCE *n* nuisance
NOYANCES > NOYANCE
NOYAU *n* liqueur made from brandy flavoured with nut kernels
NOYAUS > NOYAU
NOYED > NOY
NOYES *archaic form of* > NOISE
NOYESES > NOYES
NOYING > NOY
NOYOUS > NOY
NOYS > NOY
NOYSOME > NOY
NOZZER *n* new recruit (in the Navy)
NOZZERS > NOZZER
NOZZLE *n* projecting spout through which fluid is discharged
NOZZLES > NOZZLE
NTH *adj* of an unspecified number
NU *n* 13th letter in the Greek alphabet
NUANCE *n* subtle difference in colour, meaning, or tone ▷ *vb* give subtle differences to
NUANCED > NUANCE
NUANCES > NUANCE
NUANCING > NUANCE
NUB *n* point or gist (of a story etc) ▷ *vb* hang from

the gallows
NUBBED > NUB
NUBBIER > NUBBY
NUBBIEST > NUBBY
NUBBIN *n* something small or undeveloped, esp a fruit or ear of corn
NUBBINESS > NUBBY
NUBBING > NUB
NUBBINS > NUBBIN
NUBBLE *n* small lump
NUBBLED > NUBBLE
NUBBLES > NUBBLE
NUBBLIER > NUBBLE
NUBBLIEST > NUBBLE
NUBBLING > NUBBLE
NUBBLY > NUBBLE
NUBBY *adj* having small lumps or protuberances
NUBECULA *n* small irregular galaxy near the S celestial pole
NUBECULAE > NUBECULA
NUBIA *n* fleecy scarf for the head, worn by women
NUBIAS > NUBIA
NUBIFORM *adj* cloudlike
NUBILE *adj* sexually attractive
NUBILITY > NUBILE
NUBILOSE *same as* > NUBILOUS
NUBILOUS *adj* cloudy
NUBS > NUB
NUBUCK *n* type of leather with a velvety finish
NUBUCKS > NUBUCK
NUCELLAR > NUCELLUS
NUCELLI > NUCELLUS
NUCELLUS *n* central part of a plant ovule containing the embryo sac
NUCHA *n* back or nape of the neck
NUCHAE > NUCHA
NUCHAL *n* scale on a reptile's neck
NUCHALS > NUCHAL
NUCLEAL > NUCLEUS
NUCLEAR *adj* of nuclear weapons or energy
NUCLEASE *n* any of a group of enzymes that hydrolyse nucleic acids to simple nucleotides
NUCLEASES > NUCLEASE
NUCLEATE *adj* having a nucleus ▷ *vb* form a nucleus
NUCLEATED > NUCLEATE
NUCLEATES > NUCLEATE
NUCLEATOR > NUCLEATE
NUCLEI > NUCLEUS
NUCLEIC as in *nucleic acid* type of complex compound that is a vital constituent of living cells
NUCLEIDE *same as* > NUCLIDE
NUCLEIDES > NUCLEIDE
NUCLEIN *n* any of a group of proteins that occur in the nuclei of living cells
NUCLEINIC > NUCLEIN
NUCLEINS > NUCLEIN
NUCLEOID *n* component of a bacterium
NUCLEOIDS > NUCLEOID
NUCLEOLAR > NUCLEOLUS
NUCLEOLE *variant of* > NUCLEOLUS
NUCLEOLES > NUCLEOLE
NUCLEOLI > NUCLEOLUS
NUCLEOLUS *n* small rounded body within a resting nucleus that contains RNA and proteins
NUCLEON *n* proton or neutron
NUCLEONIC *adj* relating to the branch of physics concerned with the applications of nuclear energy
NUCLEONS > NUCLEON
NUCLEUS *n* centre, esp of an atom or cell
NUCLEUSES > NUCLEUS
NUCLIDE *n* species of atom characterized by its atomic number and its mass number
NUCLIDES > NUCLIDE
NUCLIDIC > NUCLIDE
NUCULE *n* small seed
NUCULES > NUCULE
NUDATION *n* act of stripping
NUDATIONS > NUDATION
NUDDIES > NUDDY
NUDDY as in *in the nuddy* in the nude
NUDE *adj* naked ▷ *n* naked figure in painting, sculpture, or photography
NUDELY > NUDE
NUDENESS > NUDE
NUDER > NUDE
NUDES > NUDE
NUDEST > NUDE
NUDGE *vb* push gently, esp with the elbow ▷ *n* gentle push or touch
NUDGED > NUDGE
NUDGER > NUDGE
NUDGERS > NUDGE
NUDGES > NUDGE
NUDGING > NUDGE
NUDICAUL *adj* (of plants) having stems without leaves
NUDIE *n* film, show, or magazine depicting nudity
NUDIES > NUDIE
NUDISM *n* practice of not wearing clothes
NUDISMS > NUDISM
NUDIST > NUDISM
NUDISTS > NUDISM
NUDITIES > NUDITY
NUDITY *n* state or fact of being nude
NUDNICK *same as* > NUDNIK
NUDNICKS > NUDNICK
NUDNIK *n* boring person
NUDNIKS > NUDNIK
NUDZH *same as* > NUDGE
NUDZHED > NUDZH
NUDZHES > NUDZH
NUDZHING > NUDZH
NUFF *slang form of* > ENOUGH
NUFFIN *slang form of* > NOTHING
NUFFINS > NUFFIN
NUFFS > NUFF
NUGAE *n* jests
NUGATORY *adj* of little value
NUGGAR *n* sailing boat used to carry cargo on the Nile
NUGGARS > NUGGAR
NUGGET *n* small lump of gold in its natural state ▷ *vb* polish footwear
NUGGETED > NUGGET
NUGGETING > NUGGET
NUGGETS > NUGGET
NUGGETTED > NUGGET
NUGGETY *adj* of or resembling a nugget
NUISANCE *n* something or someone that causes annoyance or bother ▷ *adj* causing annoyance or bother
NUISANCER *n* person or thing causing a nuisance
NUISANCES > NUISANCE
NUKE *vb* attack with nuclear weapons ▷ *n* nuclear weapon
NUKED > NUKE
NUKES > NUKE
NUKING > NUKE
NULL *adj* without legal force ▷ *vb* make negative
NULLA *same as* > NULLAH
NULLAH *n* stream or drain
NULLAHS > NULLAH
NULLAS > NULLA
NULLED > NULL
NULLIFIED > NULLIFY
NULLIFIER > NULLIFY
NULLIFIES > NULLIFY
NULLIFY *vb* make ineffective
NULLING *n* knurling
NULLINGS > NULLING
NULLIPARA *n* woman who has never borne a child
NULLIPORE *n* any of several red seaweeds
NULLITIES > NULLITY
NULLITY *n* state of being null
NULLNESS > NULL
NULLS > NULL
NUMB *adj* without feeling, as through cold, shock, or fear ▷ *vb* make numb
NUMBAT *n* small Australian marsupial with a long snout and tongue
NUMBATS > NUMBAT
NUMBED > NUMB
NUMBER *n* sum or quantity ▷ *vb* count
NUMBERED > NUMBER
NUMBERER *n* person who numbers
NUMBERERS > NUMBERER
NUMBERING > NUMBER
NUMBERS > NUMBER
NUMBEST > NUMB
NUMBFISH *n* any of severa[l] electric ray fish
NUMBING > NUMB
NUMBINGLY > NUMB
NUMBLES *pl n* heart, lungs, liver, etc, of a deer or othe[r] animal, cooked for food
NUMBLY > NUMB
NUMBNESS > NUMB
NUMBS > NUMB
NUMBSKULL *n* stupid person
NUMCHUCK *same as* > NUNCHAKU
NUMCHUCKS > NUMCHUCK
NUMDAH *n* coarse felt made esp in India
NUMDAHS > NUMDAH
NUMEN *n* (esp in ancient Roman religion) a deity or spirit presiding over a thing or place
NUMERABLE *adj* able to be numbered or counted
NUMERABLY > NUMERABLE
NUMERACY *n* ability to use numbers, esp in arithmetical operations
NUMERAIRE *n* unit in whic[h] prices are measured
NUMERAL *n* word or symbo[l] used to express a sum or quantity ▷ *adj* of, consisting of, or denoting a number
NUMERALLY > NUMERAL
NUMERALS > NUMERAL
NUMERARY *adj* of or relating to numbers
NUMERATE *adj* able to do basic arithmetic ▷ *vb* rea[d] (a numerical expression)
NUMERATED > NUMERATE
NUMERATES > NUMERATE
NUMERATOR *n* number above the line in a fraction
NUMERIC *n* number or numeral
NUMERICAL *adj* measured or expressed in numbers
NUMERICS > NUMERIC
NUMEROUS *adj* existing or happening in large numbers
NUMINA *plural of* > NUMEN
NUMINOUS *adj* arousing religious or spiritual emotions ▷ *n* something that arouses religious or spiritual emotions
NUMMARY *adj* of or relating to coins
NUMMULAR *adj* shaped like a coin
NUMMULARY > NUMMULAR
NUMMULINE > NUMMULAR
NUMMULITE *n* type of large fossil protozoan
NUMNAH *same as* > NUMDAH
NUMNAHS > NUMNAH
NUMPTIES > NUMPTY

MPTY *n* stupid person
MSKULL *same*
S > NUMBSKULL
MSKULLS > NUMSKULL
N *n* female member of a eligious order
NATAK *n* isolated nountain peak projecting hrough the surface of urrounding glacial ice
NATAKER > NUNATAK
NATAKS > NUNATAK
NCHAKU *n* rice flail used s a weapon
NCHAKUS > NUNCHAKU
NCHEON *n* light snack
NCHEONS > NUNCHEON
NCIO *n* pope's mbassador
NCIOS > NUNCIO
NCLE *archaic or dialect vord for* > UNCLE
NCLES > NUNCLE
NCUPATE *vb* declare ublicly
NDINAL > NUNDINE
NDINE *n* market day
NDINES > NUNDINE
NHOOD *n* condition, ractice, or character of nun
NHOODS > NUNHOOD
NLIKE > NUN
NNATION *n* ronunciation of n at the nd of words
NNERIES > NUNNERY
NNERY *n* convent
NNISH > NUN
NNY as in *nunny bag* mall sealskin haversack ised in Canada
NS > NUN
NSHIP > NUN
NSHIPS > NUN
PTIAL *adj* relating to narriage
PTIALLY > NUPTIAL
PTIALS *pl n* wedding
R *n* wooden ball
RAGHE *n* Sardinian round ower
RAGHI > NURAGHE
RAGHIC > NURAGHE
RD *same as* > NERD
RDIER > NERD
RDIEST > NERD
RDISH > NERD
RDLE *vb* score runs in ricket by deflecting the all rather than striking t hard
RDLED > NURDLE
RDLES > NURDLE
RDLING > NURDLE
RDS > NURD
RDY > NURD
RHAG *n* Sardinian round ower
RHAGS > NURHAG
RL *variant of* > KNURL
RLED > NURL
RLING > NURL
RLS > NURL
NURR *n* wooden ball
NURRS > NURR
NURS > NUR
NURSE *n* person employed to look after sick people, usu. in a hospital ▷ *vb* look after (a sick person)
NURSED > NURSE
NURSELIKE > NURSE
NURSELING *same as* > NURSLING
NURSEMAID *n* woman employed to look after children
NURSER *n* person who treats something carefully
NURSERIES > NURSERY
NURSERS > NURSER
NURSERY *n* room where children sleep or play
NURSES > NURSE
NURSING *n* practice or profession of caring for the sick and injured
NURSINGS > NURSING
NURSLE *vb* nuzzle
NURSLED > NURSLE
NURSLES > NURSLE
NURSLING *n* child or young animal that is being suckled, nursed, or fostered
NURSLINGS > NURSLING
NURTURAL > NURTURE
NURTURANT > NURTURE
NURTURE *n* act or process of promoting the development of a child or young plant ▷ *vb* promote or encourage the development of
NURTURED > NURTURE
NURTURER > NURTURE
NURTURERS > NURTURE
NURTURES > NURTURE
NURTURING > NURTURE
NUS > NU
NUT *n* fruit consisting of a hard shell and a kernel ▷ *vb* to gather nuts
NUTANT *adj* having the apex hanging down
NUTARIAN *n* person whose diet is based around nuts
NUTARIANS > NUTARIAN
NUTATE *vb* nod
NUTATED > NUTATE
NUTATES > NUTATE
NUTATING > NUTATE
NUTATION *n* periodic variation in the precession of the earth's axis
NUTATIONS > NUTATION
NUTBROWN *adj* of a brownish colour, esp a reddish-brown
NUTBUTTER *n* ground nuts blended with butter
NUTCASE *n* insane person
NUTCASES > NUTCASE
NUTGALL *n* nut-shaped gall caused by gall wasps on the oak and other trees
NUTGALLS > NUTGALL
NUTGRASS *n* type of plant
NUTHATCH *n* small songbird
NUTHOUSE *n* mental hospital or asylum
NUTHOUSES > NUTHOUSE
NUTJOBBER *n* nuthatch
NUTLET *n* any of the one-seeded portions of a fruit that fragments when mature
NUTLETS > NUTLET
NUTLIKE > NUT
NUTMEAL *n* type of grain
NUTMEALS > NUTMEAL
NUTMEAT *n* kernel of a nut
NUTMEATS > NUTMEAT
NUTMEG *n* spice made from the seed of a tropical tree ▷ *vb* kick or hit the ball between the legs of (an opposing player)
NUTMEGGED > NUTMEG
NUTMEGGY > NUTMEG
NUTMEGS > NUTMEG
NUTPECKER *n* nuthatch
NUTPICK *n* tool used to dig the meat from nuts
NUTPICKS > NUTPICK
NUTRIA *n* fur of the coypu
NUTRIAS > NUTRIA
NUTRIENT *n* substance that provides nourishment ▷ *adj* providing nourishment
NUTRIENTS > NUTRIENT
NUTRIMENT *n* food or nourishment required by all living things to grow and stay healthy
NUTRITION *n* process of taking in and absorbing nutrients
NUTRITIVE *adj* of nutrition ▷ *n* nutritious food
NUTS > NUT
NUTSEDGE *same as* > NUTGRASS
NUTSEDGES > NUTSEDGE
NUTSHELL *n* shell around the kernel of a nut
NUTSHELLS > NUTSHELL
NUTSIER > NUTSY
NUTSIEST > NUTSY
NUTSO *adj* insane
NUTSY *adj* lunatic
NUTTED > NUT
NUTTER *n* insane person
NUTTERIES > NUTTERY
NUTTERS > NUTTER
NUTTERY *n* place where nut trees grow
NUTTIER > NUTTY
NUTTIEST > NUTTY
NUTTILY > NUTTY
NUTTINESS > NUTTY
NUTTING *n* act of gathering nuts
NUTTINGS > NUTTING
NUTTY *adj* containing or resembling nuts
NUTWOOD *n* any of various nut-bearing trees, such as walnut
NUTWOODS > NUTWOOD
NUZZER *n* present given to a superior in India
NUZZERS > NUZZER
NUZZLE *vb* push or rub gently with the nose or snout
NUZZLED > NUZZLE
NUZZLER *n* person or thing that nuzzles
NUZZLERS > NUZZLER
NUZZLES > NUZZLE
NUZZLING > NUZZLE
NY *same as* > NIGH
NYAFF *n* small or contemptible person ▷ *vb* yelp like a small dog
NYAFFED > NYAFF
NYAFFING > NYAFF
NYAFFS > NYAFF
NYALA *n* spiral-horned southern African antelope
NYALAS > NYALA
NYANZA *n* (in E Africa) a lake
NYANZAS > NYANZA
NYAS *n* young hawk
NYASES > NYAS
NYBBLE *n* small byte
NYBBLES > NYBBLE
NYCTALOPS *n* person or thing with night-vision
NYE *n* flock of pheasants ▷ *vb* near
NYED > NYE
NYES > NYE
NYING > NYE
NYLGHAI *same as* > NILGAI
NYLGHAIS > NYLGHAI
NYLGHAU *same as* > NILGAI
NYLGHAUS > NYLGHAU
NYLON *n* synthetic material used for clothing etc
NYLONS *pl n* stockings made of nylon
NYMPH *n* mythical spirit of nature, represented as a beautiful young woman
NYMPHA *n* either one of the labia minora
NYMPHAE > NYMPHA
NYMPHAEA *n* water lily
NYMPHAEUM *n* shrine of the nymphs
NYMPHAL > NYMPH
NYMPHALID *n* butterfly of the family that includes the fritillaries and red admirals ▷ *adj* of this family of butterflies
NYMPHEAN > NYMPH
NYMPHET *n* sexually precocious young girl
NYMPHETIC > NYMPHET
NYMPHETS > NYMPHET
NYMPHETTE *same as* > NYMPHET
NYMPHIC > NYMPH
NYMPHICAL > NYMPH
NYMPHISH > NYMPH
NYMPHLIKE > NYMPH
NYMPHLY > NYMPH
NYMPHO *n* nymphomaniac
NYMPHOS > NYMPHO
NYMPHS > NYMPH
NYS > NY

NYSSA *n* type of tree
NYSSAS > NYSSA
NYSTAGMIC > NYSTAGMUS
NYSTAGMUS *n* involuntary movement of the eye comprising a smooth drift followed by a flick back
NYSTATIN *n* type of antibiotic obtained from a bacterium
NYSTATINS > NYSTATIN

OAF *n* stupid or clumsy person
OAFISH > OAF
OAFISHLY > OAF
OAFS > OAF
OAK *n* deciduous forest tree
OAKED *adj* relating to wine that is stored for a time in oak barrels prior to bottling
OAKEN *adj* made of the wood of the oak
OAKENSHAW *n* small forest of oaks
OAKER *same as* > OCHRE
OAKERS > OAKER
OAKIER > OAKY
OAKIES > OAKY
OAKIEST > OAKY
OAKLEAF *n* leaf on oak tree
OAKLEAVES > OAKLEAF
OAKLIKE > OAK
OAKLING *n* young oak
OAKLINGS > OAKLING
OAKMOSS *n* type of lichen
OAKMOSSES > OAKMOSS
OAKS > OAK
OAKUM *n* fibre obtained by unravelling old rope
OAKUMS > OAKUM
OAKY *adj* hard like the wood of an oak ▷ *n* ice cream
OANSHAGH *n* foolish girl or woman
OANSHAGHS > OANSHAGH
OAR *n* pole with a broad blade, used for rowing a boat ▷ *vb* propel with oars
OARAGE *n* use or number of oars
OARAGES > OARAGE
OARED *adj* equipped with oars
OARFISH *n* very long ribbonfish with long slender ventral fins
OARFISHES > OARFISH
OARIER > OARY
OARIEST > OARY
OARING > OAR
OARLESS > OAR
OARLIKE > OAR
OARLOCK *n* swivelling device attached to the gunwale of a boat that holds an oar in place
OARLOCKS > OARLOCK
OARS > OAR
OARSMAN *n* person who rows
OARSMEN > OARSMAN
OARSWOMAN *n* female oarsman
OARSWOMEN > OARSWOMAN
OARWEED *n* type of brown seaweed
OARWEEDS > OARWEED
OARY *adj* of or like an oar
OASES > OASIS
OASIS *n* fertile area in a desert
OAST *n* oven for drying hops
OASTHOUSE *n* building with kilns for drying hops
OASTS > OAST
OAT *n* hard cereal grown as food
OATCAKE *n* thin flat biscuit of oatmeal
OATCAKES > OATCAKE
OATEN *adj* made of oats or oat straw
OATER *n* film about the American Wild West
OATERS > OATER
OATH *n* solemn promise, esp to be truthful in court
OATHABLE *adj* able to take an oath
OATHS > OATH
OATLIKE > OAT
OATMEAL *n* coarse flour made from oats ▷ *adj* pale brownish-cream
OATMEALS > OATMEAL
OATS > OAT
OAVES > OAF
OB *n* expression of opposition
OBA *n* (in W Africa) a Yoruba chief or ruler
OBANG *n* former Japanese coin
OBANGS > OBANG
OBAS > OBA
OBBLIGATI > OBBLIGATO
OBBLIGATO *n* essential part or accompaniment ▷ *adj* not to be omitted in performance
OBCONIC *adj* (of a fruit or similar part) shaped like a cone and attached at the pointed end
OBCONICAL *same as* > OBCONIC
OBCORDATE *adj* heart-shaped and attached at the pointed end
OBDURACY > OBDURATE
OBDURATE *adj* hardhearted or stubborn ▷ *vb* make obdurate
OBDURATED > OBDURATE
OBDURATES > OBDURATE
OBDURE *vb* make obdurate
OBDURED > OBDURE
OBDURES > OBDURE
OBDURING > OBDURE
OBE *n* ancient Laconian village
OBEAH *vb* cast spell on
OBEAHED > OBEAH
OBEAHING > OBEAH
OBEAHISM > OBEAH
OBEAHISMS > OBEAH
OBEAHS > OBEAH
OBECHE *n* African tree
OBECHES > OBECHE
OBEDIENCE *n* condition or quality of being obedient
OBEDIENT *adj* obeying or willing to obey
OBEISANCE *n* attitude of respect
OBEISANT > OBEISANCE
OBEISM *n* belief in obeah
OBEISMS > OBEISM
OBELI > OBELUS
OBELIA *n* type of jellyfish
OBELIAS > OBELIA
OBELION *n* area of skull
OBELISCAL > OBELISK
OBELISE *same as* > OBELIZE
OBELISED > OBELISE
OBELISES > OBELISE
OBELISING > OBELISE
OBELISK *n* four-sided stone column tapering to a pyramid at the top
OBELISKS > OBELISK
OBELISM *n* practice of marking passages in text
OBELISMS > OBELISM
OBELIZE *vb* mark (a word or passage) with an obelus
OBELIZED > OBELIZE
OBELIZES > OBELIZE
OBELIZING > OBELIZE
OBELUS *n* mark used in editions of ancient

documents to indicate spurious words or passages
OBENTO *n* Japanese lunch box
OBENTOS > OBENTO
OBES > OBE
OBESE *adj* very fat
OBESELY > OBESE
OBESENESS > OBESE
OBESER > OBESE
OBESEST > OBESE
OBESITIES > OBESE
OBESITY > OBESE
OBEY *vb* carry out instructions or orders
OBEYABLE > OBEY
OBEYED > OBEY
OBEYER > OBEY
OBEYERS > OBEY
OBEYING > OBEY
OBEYS > OBEY
OBFUSCATE *vb* make (something) confusing
OBI *n* broad sash tied in a large flat bow at the back, worn by Japanese women and children ▷ *vb* bewitch
OBIA *same as* > OBEAH
OBIAS > OBIA
OBIED > OBI
OBIING > OBI
OBIISM > OBI
OBIISMS > OBI
OBIIT *vb* died
OBIS > OBI
OBIT *n* memorial service
OBITAL *adj* of obits
OBITER *adv* by the way
OBITS > OBIT
OBITUAL *adj* of obits
OBITUARY *n* announcement of someone's death, esp in a newspaper
OBJECT *n* physical thing ▷ *vb* express disapproval
OBJECTED > OBJECT
OBJECTIFY *vb* represent concretely
OBJECTING > OBJECT
OBJECTION *n* expression or feeling of opposition or disapproval
OBJECTIVE *n* aim or purpose ▷ *adj* not biased
OBJECTOR > OBJECT
OBJECTORS > OBJECT
OBJECTS > OBJECT
OBJET *n* object
OBJETS > OBJET
OBJURE *vb* put on oath
OBJURED > OBJURE
OBJURES > OBJURE
OBJURGATE *vb* scold or reprimand
OBJURING > OBJURE
OBLAST *n* administrative division of the constituent republics of Russia
OBLASTI > OBLAST
OBLASTS > OBLAST
OBLATE *adj* (of a sphere) flattened at the poles ▷ *n* person dedicated to a monastic or religious life
OBLATELY > OBLATE
OBLATES > OBLATE
OBLATION *n* religious offering
OBLATIONS > OBLATION
OBLATORY > OBLATION
OBLIGABLE > OBLIGATE
OBLIGANT *n* person promising to pay a sum
OBLIGANTS > OBLIGANT
OBLIGATE *vb* compel, constrain, or oblige morally or legally ▷ *adj* compelled, bound, or restricted
OBLIGATED > OBLIGATE
OBLIGATES > OBLIGATE
OBLIGATI > OBLIGATO
OBLIGATO *same as* > OBBLIGATO
OBLIGATOR > OBLIGATE
OBLIGATOS > OBLIGATO
OBLIGE *vb* compel (someone) morally or by law to do something
OBLIGED > OBLIGE
OBLIGEE *n* person in whose favour an obligation, contract, or bond is created
OBLIGEES > OBLIGEE
OBLIGER > OBLIGE
OBLIGERS > OBLIGE
OBLIGES > OBLIGE
OBLIGING *adj* ready to help other people
OBLIGOR *n* person who binds himself by contract to perform some obligation
OBLIGORS > OBLIGOR
OBLIQUE *adj* slanting ▷ *n* symbol (/) ▷ *vb* take or have an oblique direction
OBLIQUED > OBLIQUE
OBLIQUELY > OBLIQUE
OBLIQUER > OBLIQUE
OBLIQUES > OBLIQUE
OBLIQUEST > OBLIQUE
OBLIQUID *adj* oblique
OBLIQUING > OBLIQUE
OBLIQUITY *n* state or condition of being oblique
OBLIVION *n* state of being forgotten
OBLIVIONS > OBLIVION
OBLIVIOUS *adj* unaware
OBLONG *adj* having two long sides, two short sides, and four right angles ▷ *n* oblong figure
OBLONGLY > OBLONG
OBLONGS > OBLONG
OBLOQUIAL > OBLOQUY
OBLOQUIES > OBLOQUY
OBLOQUY *n* verbal abuse
OBNOXIOUS *adj* offensive
OBO *n* ship carrying oil and ore
OBOE *n* double-reeded woodwind instrument
OBOES > OBOE
OBOIST > OBOE
OBOISTS > OBOE
OBOL *same as* > OBOLUS
OBOLARY *adj* very poor
OBOLE *n* former weight unit in pharmacy
OBOLES > OBOLE
OBOLI > OBOLUS
OBOLS > OBOL
OBOLUS *n* modern Greek unit of weight equal to one tenth of a gram
OBOS > OBO
OBOVATE *adj* (of a leaf) shaped like the longitudinal section of an egg with the narrower end at the base
OBOVATELY > OBOVATE
OBOVOID *adj* (of a fruit) egg-shaped with the narrower end at the base
OBREPTION *n* obtaining of something by giving false information
OBS > OB
OBSCENE *adj* portraying sex offensively
OBSCENELY > OBSCENE
OBSCENER > OBSCENE
OBSCENEST > OBSCENE
OBSCENITY *n* state or quality of being obscene
OBSCURANT *n* opposer of reform and enlightenment ▷ *adj* of or relating to an obscurant
OBSCURE *adj* not well known ▷ *vb* make (something) obscure
OBSCURED > OBSCURE
OBSCURELY > OBSCURE
OBSCURER > OBSCURE
OBSCURERS > OBSCURE
OBSCURES > OBSCURE
OBSCUREST > OBSCURE
OBSCURING > OBSCURE
OBSCURITY *n* state or quality of being obscure
OBSECRATE *rare word for* > BESEECH
OBSEQUENT *adj* (of a river) flowing into a subsequent stream in the opposite direction to the original slope of the land
OBSEQUIAL > OBSEQUIES
OBSEQUIE *same as* > OBSEQUY
OBSEQUIES *pl n* funeral rites
OBSEQUY *singular of* > OBSEQUIES
OBSERVANT *adj* quick to notice things
OBSERVE *vb* see or notice
OBSERVED > OBSERVE
OBSERVER *n* person who observes, esp one who watches someone or something carefully
OBSERVERS > OBSERVER
OBSERVES > OBSERVE
OBSERVING > OBSERVE
OBSESS *vb* preoccupy (someone) compulsively
OBSESSED > OBSESS
OBSESSES > OBSESS
OBSESSING > OBSESS
OBSESSION *n* something that preoccupies a person to the exclusion of other things
OBSESSIVE *adj* motivated by a persistent overriding idea or impulse ▷ *n* person subject to obsession
OBSESSOR > OBSESS
OBSESSORS > OBSESS
OBSIDIAN *n* dark glassy volcanic rock
OBSIDIANS > OBSIDIAN
OBSIGN *vb* confirm
OBSIGNATE *same as* > OBSIGN
OBSIGNED > OBSIGN
OBSIGNING > OBSIGN
OBSIGNS > OBSIGN
OBSOLESCE *vb* become obsolete
OBSOLETE *adj* no longer in use ▷ *vb* make obsolete
OBSOLETED > OBSOLETE
OBSOLETES > OBSOLETE
OBSTACLE *n* something that makes progress difficult
OBSTACLES > OBSTACLE
OBSTETRIC *adj* of or relating to childbirth
OBSTINACY *n* state or quality of being obstinate
OBSTINATE *adj* stubborn
OBSTRUCT *vb* block with an obstacle
OBSTRUCTS > OBSTRUCT
OBSTRUENT *adj* causing obstruction, esp of the intestinal tract ▷ *n* anything that causes obstruction
OBTAIN *vb* acquire intentionally
OBTAINED > OBTAIN
OBTAINER > OBTAIN
OBTAINERS > OBTAIN
OBTAINING > OBTAIN
OBTAINS > OBTAIN
OBTECT *adj* (of a pupa) encased in a hardened secretion
OBTECTED *same as* > OBTECT
OBTEMPER *vb* comply (with)
OBTEMPERS > OBTEMPER
OBTEND *vb* put forward
OBTENDED > OBTEND
OBTENDING > OBTEND
OBTENDS > OBTEND
OBTENTION *n* act of obtaining
OBTEST *vb* beg (someone) earnestly
OBTESTED > OBTEST
OBTESTING > OBTEST
OBTESTS > OBTEST
OBTRUDE *vb* push oneself or one's ideas on others

TRUDED > OBTRUDE
TRUDER > OBTRUDE
TRUDERS > OBTRUDE
TRUDES > OBTRUDE
TRUDING > OBTRUDE
TRUSION > OBTRUDE
TRUSIVE *adj* npleasantly noticeable
TUND *vb* deaden or dull
TUNDED > OBTUND
TUNDENT > OBTUND
TUNDING > OBTUND
TUNDITY *n* semi-onscious state
TUNDS > OBTUND
TURATE *vb* stop up (an pening, esp the breech of gun)
TURATED > OBTURATE
TURATES > OBTURATE
TURATOR > OBTURATE
TUSE *adj* mentally slow
TUSELY > OBTUSE
TUSER > OBTUSE
TUSEST > OBTUSE
TUSITY > OBTUSE
UMBRATE *vb* overshadow
VENTION *n* incidental xpense
VERSE *n* opposite way of looking at an idea ▷ *adj* acing or turned towards he observer
VERSELY > OBVERSE
VERSES > OBVERSE
VERSION > OBVERT
VERT *vb* deduce the obverse of (a proposition)
VERTED > OBVERT
VERTING > OBVERT
VERTS > OBVERT
VIABLE > OBVIATE
VIATE *vb* make unnecessary
VIATED > OBVIATE
VIATES > OBVIATE
VIATING > OBVIATE
VIATION > OBVIATE
VIATOR > OBVIATE
VIATORS > OBVIATE
VIOUS *adj* easy to see or understand, evident
VIOUSLY *adv* in a way that is easy to see or understand
VOLUTE *adj* (of leaves or petals in the bud) folded so that the margins overlap each other
VOLUTED *same as* > OBVOLUTE
VOLVENT *adj* curving around something
CA *n* any of various South American herbaceous plants
CARINA *n* small oval wind instrument
CARINAS > OCARINA
CAS > OCA
CCAM *n* computer programming language
CCAMIES > OCCAMY
CCAMS > OCCAM
OCCAMY *n* type of alloy
OCCASION *n* time at which a particular thing happens ▷ *vb* cause
OCCASIONS *pl n* needs
OCCIDENT *literary or formal word for* > WEST
OCCIDENTS > OCCIDENT
OCCIES > OCCY
OCCIPITA > OCCIPUT
OCCIPITAL *adj* of or relating to the back of the head or skull
OCCIPUT *n* back of the head
OCCIPUTS > OCCIPUT
OCCLUDE *vb* obstruct
OCCLUDED > OCCLUDE
OCCLUDENT > OCCLUDE
OCCLUDER > OCCLUDE
OCCLUDERS > OCCLUDE
OCCLUDES > OCCLUDE
OCCLUDING > OCCLUDE
OCCLUSAL > OCCLUSION
OCCLUSION *n* act or process of occluding or the state of being occluded
OCCLUSIVE *adj* of or relating to the act of occlusion ▷ *n* occlusive speech sound
OCCLUSOR *n* muscle for closing opening
OCCLUSORS > OCCLUSOR
OCCULT *adj* relating to the supernatural ▷ *vb* (of a celestial body) to hide (another celestial body) from view
OCCULTED > OCCULT
OCCULTER *n* something that obscures
OCCULTERS > OCCULTER
OCCULTING > OCCULT
OCCULTISM *n* belief in and the study and practice of magic, astrology, etc
OCCULTIST > OCCULTISM
OCCULTLY > OCCULT
OCCULTS > OCCULT
OCCUPANCE *same as* > OCCUPANCY
OCCUPANCY *n* (length of) a person's stay in a specified place
OCCUPANT *n* person occupying a specified place
OCCUPANTS > OCCUPANT
OCCUPATE *same as* > OCCUPY
OCCUPATED > OCCUPATE
OCCUPATES > OCCUPATE
OCCUPIED > OCCUPY
OCCUPIER *n* person who lives in a particular house, whether as owner or tenant
OCCUPIERS > OCCUPIER
OCCUPIES > OCCUPY
OCCUPY *vb* live or work in (a building)
OCCUPYING > OCCUPY
OCCUR *vb* happen
OCCURRED > OCCUR
OCCURRENT *adj* (of a property) relating to some observable feature of its bearer
OCCURRING > OCCUR
OCCURS > OCCUR
OCCY as in *all over the occy* dialect expression meaning in every direction
OCEAN *n* vast area of sea between continents
OCEANARIA *pl n* large saltwater aquaria for marine life
OCEANAUT *n* undersea explorer
OCEANAUTS > OCEANAUT
OCEANIC *adj* of or relating to the ocean
OCEANID *n* ocean nymph in Greek mythology
OCEANIDES > OCEANID
OCEANIDS > OCEANID
OCEANS > OCEAN
OCELLAR > OCELLUS
OCELLATE > OCELLUS
OCELLATED > OCELLUS
OCELLI > OCELLUS
OCELLUS *n* simple eye of insects and some other invertebrates
OCELOID *adj* of or like an ocelot
OCELOT *n* American wild cat with a spotted coat
OCELOTS > OCELOT
OCH *interj* expression of surprise, annoyance, or disagreement
OCHE *n* (in darts) mark on the floor behind which a player must stand
OCHER *same as* > OCHRE
OCHERED > OCHER
OCHERING > OCHER
OCHEROUS > OCHER
OCHERS > OCHER
OCHERY > OCHER
OCHES > OCHE
OCHIDORE *n* type of crab
OCHIDORES > OCHIDORE
OCHLOCRAT *n* supporter of rule by the mob
OCHONE *interj* expression of sorrow or regret
OCHRE *n* brownish-yellow earth ▷ *adj* moderate yellow-orange to orange ▷ *vb* colour with ochre
OCHREA *n* cup-shaped structure that sheathes the stems of certain plants
OCHREAE > OCHREA
OCHREATE *same as* > OCREATE
OCHRED > OCHRE
OCHREOUS > OCHRE
OCHRES > OCHRE
OCHREY > OCHRE
OCHRING > OCHRE
OCHROID > OCHRE
OCHROUS > OCHRE
OCHRY > OCHRE
OCICAT *n* breed of large short-haired cat with a spotted coat
OCICATS > OCICAT
OCKER *n* uncultivated or boorish Australian
OCKERISM *n* Australian boorishness
OCKERISMS > OCKERISM
OCKERS > OCKER
OCKODOLS *pl n* one's feet when wearing boots
OCOTILLO *n* cactus-like tree
OCOTILLOS > OCOTILLO
OCREA *same as* > OCHREA
OCREAE > OCREA
OCREATE *adj* possessing an ocrea
OCTA *same as* > OKTA
OCTACHORD *n* eight-stringed musical instrument
OCTAD *n* group or series of eight
OCTADIC > OCTAD
OCTADS > OCTAD
OCTAGON *n* geometric figure with eight sides
OCTAGONAL *adj* having eight sides and eight angles
OCTAGONS > OCTAGON
OCTAHEDRA *pl n* solid eight-sided figures; octahedrons
OCTAL *n* number system with a base 8
OCTALS > OCTAL
OCTAMETER *n* verse line consisting of eight metrical feet
OCTAN *n* illness that occurs weekly
OCTANE *n* hydrocarbon found in petrol
OCTANES > OCTANE
OCTANGLE *same as* > OCTAGON
OCTANGLES > OCTANGLE
OCTANOL *n* alcohol containing eight carbon atoms
OCTANOLS > OCTANOL
OCTANS > OCTAN
OCTANT *n* any of the eight parts into which the three planes containing the Cartesian coordinate axes divide space
OCTANTAL > OCTANT
OCTANTS > OCTANT
OCTAPLA *n* book with eight texts
OCTAPLAS > OCTAPLA
OCTAPLOID *adj* having eight parts
OCTAPODIC > OCTAPODY
OCTAPODY *n* line of verse with eight metrical feet
OCTARCHY *n* government by eight rulers
OCTAROON *same as* > OCTOROON
OCTAROONS > OCTAROON
OCTAS > OCTA
OCTASTICH *n* verse of eight

lines
OCTASTYLE *adj* (of building) having eight columns
OCTAVAL > OCTAVE
OCTAVE *n* (interval between the first and) eighth note of a scale ▷ *adj* consisting of eight parts
OCTAVES > OCTAVE
OCTAVO *n* book size in which the sheets are folded into eight leaves
OCTAVOS > OCTAVO
OCTENNIAL *adj* occurring every eight years
OCTET *n* group of eight performers
OCTETS > OCTET
OCTETT *same as* > OCTET
OCTETTE *same as* > OCTET
OCTETTES > OCTETTE
OCTETTS > OCTETT
OCTILLION *n* (in Britain and Germany) the number represented as one followed by 48 zeros
OCTOFID *adj* divided into eight
OCTOHEDRA *same as* > OCTAHEDRA
OCTONARII *pl n* lines with eight feet
OCTONARY *adj* relating to or based on the number eight ▷ *n* stanza of eight lines
OCTOPI > OCTOPUS
OCTOPLOID *same as* > OCTAPLOID
OCTOPOD *n* type of mollusc ▷ *adj* of these molluscs
OCTOPODAN > OCTOPOD
OCTOPODES > OCTOPOD
OCTOPODS > OCTOPOD
OCTOPUS *n* sea creature with a soft body and eight tentacles
OCTOPUSES > OCTOPUS
OCTOPUSH *n* hockey-like game played underwater
OCTOROON *n* person having one quadroon and one White parent
OCTOROONS > OCTOROON
OCTOSTYLE *same as* > OCTASTYLE
OCTOTHORP *n* type of symbol in printing
OCTROI *n* duty on various goods brought into certain European towns
OCTROIS > OCTROI
OCTUOR *n* octet
OCTUORS > OCTUOR
OCTUPLE *n* quantity or number eight times as great as another ▷ *adj* eight times as much or as many ▷ *vb* multiply by eight
OCTUPLED > OCTUPLE
OCTUPLES > OCTUPLE
OCTUPLET *n* one of eight offspring from one birth
OCTUPLETS > OCTUPLET
OCTUPLEX *n* something made up of eight parts
OCTUPLING > OCTUPLE
OCTUPLY *adv* by eight times
OCTYL *n* group of atoms
OCTYLS > OCTYL
OCULAR *adj* relating to the eyes or sight ▷ *n* lens in an optical instrument
OCULARIST *n* person who makes artificial eyes
OCULARLY > OCULAR
OCULARS > OCULAR
OCULATE *adj* possessing eyes
OCULATED *same as* > OCULATE
OCULI > OCULUS
OCULIST *n* ophthalmologist
OCULISTS > OCULIST
OCULUS *n* round window
OD *n* hypothetical force formerly thought to be responsible for many natural phenomena
ODA *n* room in a harem
ODAH *same as* > ODA
ODAHS > ODAH
ODAL *same as* > UDAL
ODALIQUE *same as* > ODALISQUE
ODALIQUES > ODALIQUE
ODALISK *same as* > ODALISQUE
ODALISKS > ODALISK
ODALISQUE *n* female slave in a harem
ODALLER > ODAL
ODALLERS > ODAL
ODALS > ODAL
ODAS > ODA
ODD *adj* unusual
ODDBALL *n* eccentric person ▷ *adj* strange or peculiar
ODDBALLS > ODDBALL
ODDER > ODD
ODDEST > ODD
ODDISH > ODD
ODDITIES > ODDITY
ODDITY *n* odd person or thing
ODDLY > ODD
ODDMENT *n* odd piece or thing
ODDMENTS > ODDMENT
ODDNESS > ODD
ODDNESSES > ODD
ODDS *pl n* (ratio showing) the probability of something happening
ODDSMAKER *n* person setting odds in betting
ODDSMAN *n* umpire
ODDSMEN > ODDSMAN
ODE *n* lyric poem, usu addressed to a particular subject
ODEA > ODEUM
ODEON *same as* > ODEUM
ODEONS > ODEON
ODES > ODE
ODEUM *n* (esp in ancient Greece and Rome) a building for musical performances
ODEUMS > ODEUM
ODIC > OD
ODIFEROUS *adj* having odour
ODIOUS *adj* offensive
ODIOUSLY > ODIOUS
ODISM > OD
ODISMS > OD
ODIST > OD
ODISTS > OD
ODIUM *n* widespread dislike
ODIUMS > ODIUM
ODOGRAPH *same as* > ODOMETER
ODOGRAPHS > ODOGRAPH
ODOMETER *n* device that records the number of miles that a bicycle or motor vehicle has travelled
ODOMETERS > ODOMETER
ODOMETRY > ODOMETER
ODONATE *n* dragonfly or related insect
ODONATES > ODONATE
ODONATIST *n* dragonfly expert
ODONTALGY *n* toothache
ODONTIC *adj* of teeth
ODONTIST *n* dentist
ODONTISTS > ODONTIST
ODONTOID *adj* toothlike ▷ *n* bone in the spine
ODONTOIDS > ODONTOID
ODONTOMA *n* tumour near teeth
ODONTOMAS > ODONTOMA
ODOR *same as* > ODOUR
ODORANT *n* something with a strong smell
ODORANTS > ODORANT
ODORATE *adj* having a strong smell
ODORED *same as* > ODOURED
ODORFUL *same as* > ODOURFUL
ODORISE *same as* > ODORIZE
ODORISED > ODORISE
ODORISES > ODORISE
ODORISING > ODORISE
ODORIZE *vb* give an odour to
ODORIZED > ODORIZE
ODORIZES > ODORIZE
ODORIZING > ODORIZE
ODORLESS > ODOR
ODOROUS *adj* having or emitting a characteristic smell or odour
ODOROUSLY > ODOROUS
ODORS > ODOR
ODOUR *n* particular smell
ODOURED *adj* having odour
ODOURFUL *adj* full of odour
ODOURLESS > ODOUR
ODOURS > ODOUR
ODS > OD
ODSO *n* cry of suprise
ODSOS > ODSO
ODYL *same as* > OD
ODYLE *same as* > OD
ODYLES > ODYLE
ODYLISM > ODYL
ODYLISMS > ODYL
ODYLS > ODYL
ODYSSEY *n* long eventful journey
ODYSSEYS > ODYSSEY
ODZOOKS *interj* cry of surprise
OE *n* grandchild
OECIST *n* colony founde
OECISTS > OECIST
OECOLOGY *less common spelling of* > ECOLOGY
OECUMENIC *variant of* > ECUMENIC
OEDEMA *n* abnormal swelling
OEDEMAS > OEDEMA
OEDEMATA > OEDEMA
OEDIPAL *adj* relating to an Oedipus complex, whereby a male child wants to replace his fat
OEDIPALLY > OEDIPAL
OEDIPEAN *same as* > OEDIPAL
OEDOMETER *n* instrumen for measuring the consolidation of a soil specimen under pressur
OEILLADE *n* amorous or suggestive glance
OEILLADES > OEILLADE
OENANTHIC *adj* smelling or like wine
OENOLOGY *n* study of wir
OENOMANCY *n* divination by studying the colour o wine
OENOMANIA *n* craving for wine
OENOMEL *n* drink made o wine and honey
OENOMELS > OENOMEL
OENOMETER *n* device for measuring the strength of wine
OENOPHIL *same as* > OENOPHILE
OENOPHILE *n* lover or connoisseur of wines
OENOPHILS > OENOPHIL
OENOPHILY *n* love of wir
OENOTHERA *n* type of American plant with yellow flowers that ope in the evening
OERLIKON *n* type of canr
OERLIKONS > OERLIKON
OERSTED *n* cgs unit of magnetic field strength
OERSTEDS > OERSTED
OES > OE
OESOPHAGI *pl n* gullets
OESTRAL > OESTRUS
OESTRIN *obsolete term for* > OESTROGEN
OESTRINS > OESTRIN
OESTRIOL *n* weak oestrogenic hormone secreted by the mammalian ovary
OESTRIOLS > OESTRIOL

STROGEN *n* female hormone that controls the reproductive cycle
STRONE *n* weak oestrogenic hormone secreted by the mammalian ovary
STRONES > OESTRONE
STROUS > OESTRUS
STRUM *same as* > OESTRUS
STRUMS > OESTRUM
STRUS *n* regularly occurring period of fertility and sexual receptivity in most female mammals
STRUSES > OESTRUS
UVRE *n* work of art, literature, music, etc
UVRES > OEUVRE
prep belonging to
AY *n* derogatory term for a White person
AYS > OFAY
F *prep* away from ▷ *adv* away ▷ *adj* not operating ▷ *n* side of the field to which the batsman's feet point ▷ *vb* kill
FAL *n* edible organs of an animal, such as liver or kidneys
FALS > OFFAL
FBEAT *adj* unusual or eccentric ▷ *n* any of the normally unaccented beats in a bar
FBEATS > OFFBEAT
FCAST *n* cast-off
FCASTS > OFFCAST
FCUT *n* piece remaining after the required parts have been cut out
FCUTS > OFFCUT
FED > OFF
FENCE *n* (cause of) hurt feelings or annoyance
FENCES > OFFENCE
FEND *vb* hurt the feelings of, insult
FENDED > OFFEND
FENDER > OFFEND
FENDERS > OFFEND
FENDING > OFFEND
FENDS > OFFEND
FENSE *same as* > OFFENCE
FENSES > OFFENSE
FENSIVE *adj* disagreeable ▷ *n* position or action of attack
FER *vb* present (something) for acceptance or rejection ▷ *n* something offered
FERABLE > OFFER
FERED > OFFER
FEREE *n* person to whom an offer is made
FEREES > OFFEREE
FERER > OFFER
FERERS > OFFER
FERING *n* thing offered
FERINGS > OFFERING
FEROR > OFFER
OFFERORS > OFFER
OFFERS > OFFER
OFFERTORY *n* offering of the bread and wine for Communion
OFFHAND *adj* casual, curt ▷ *adv* without preparation
OFFHANDED *adj* without care oe consideration
OFFICE *n* room or building where people work at desks
OFFICER *n* person in authority in the armed services ▷ *vb* furnish with officers
OFFICERED > OFFICER
OFFICERS > OFFICER
OFFICES > OFFICE
OFFICIAL *adj* of a position of authority ▷ *n* person who holds a position of authority
OFFICIALS > OFFICIAL
OFFICIANT *n* person who presides and officiates at a religious ceremony
OFFICIARY *n* body of officials ▷ *adj* of, relating to, or derived from office
OFFICIATE *vb* act in an official role
OFFICINAL *adj* (of pharmaceutical products) available without prescription ▷ *n* officinal preparation or plant
OFFICIOUS *adj* interfering unnecessarily
OFFING *n* area of the sea visible from the shore
OFFINGS > OFFING
OFFISH *adj* aloof or distant in manner
OFFISHLY > OFFISH
OFFKEY *adj* out of tune
OFFLINE *adj* disconnected from a computer or the internet
OFFLOAD *vb* pass responsibilty for (something unpleasant) to someone else
OFFLOADED > OFFLOAD
OFFLOADS > OFFLOAD
OFFPEAK *adj* relating to times outside periods of intensive use
OFFPRINT *n* separate reprint of an article that originally appeared in a larger publication ▷ *vb* reprint (an article taken from a larger publication) separately
OFFPRINTS > OFFPRINT
OFFPUT *n* act of putting off
OFFPUTS > OFFPUT
OFFRAMP *n* road allowing traffic to leave a motorway
OFFRAMPS > OFFRAMP
OFFS > OFF
OFFSADDLE *vb* unsaddle
OFFSCREEN *adj* unseen by film viewers
OFFSCUM *n* scum
OFFSCUMS > OFFSCUM
OFFSEASON *n* period of little trade in a business
OFFSET *vb* cancel out, compensate for ▷ *n* printing method in which the impression is made onto a surface which transfers it to the paper
OFFSETS > OFFSET
OFFSHOOT *n* something developed from something else
OFFSHOOTS > OFFSHOOT
OFFSHORE *adv* away from or at some distance from the shore ▷ *adj* sited or conducted at sea ▷ *n* company operating abroad where the tax system is more advantageous than at home
OFFSHORES > OFFSHORE
OFFSIDE *adv* (positioned) illegally ahead of the ball ▷ *n* side of a vehicle nearest the centre of the road
OFFSIDER *n* partner or assistant
OFFSIDERS > OFFSIDER
OFFSIDES > OFFSIDE
OFFSPRING *n* child
OFFSTAGE *adv* out of the view of the audience ▷ *n* something that happens offstage
OFFSTAGES > OFFSTAGE
OFFTAKE *n* act of taking off
OFFTAKES > OFFTAKE
OFFTRACK *adj* not at a racetrack
OFLAG *n* German prisoner-of-war camp for officers in World War II
OFLAGS > OFLAG
OFT *adv* often
OFTEN *adv* frequently, much of the time
OFTENER > OFTEN
OFTENEST > OFTEN
OFTENNESS > OFTEN
OFTER > OFT
OFTEST > OFT
OFTTIMES *same as* > OFTEN
OGAM *same as* > OGHAM
OGAMIC > OGAM
OGAMS > OGAM
OGDOAD *n* group of eight
OGDOADS > OGDOAD
OGEE *n* moulding having a cross section in the form of a letter S
OGEES > OGEE
OGGIN *n* sea
OGGINS > OGGIN
OGHAM *n* ancient alphabetical writing system used by the Celts in Britain and Ireland
OGHAMIC > OGHAM
OGHAMIST > OGHAM
OGHAMISTS > OGHAM
OGHAMS > OGHAM
OGIVAL > OGIVE
OGIVE *n* diagonal rib or groin of a Gothic vault
OGIVES > OGIVE
OGLE *vb* stare at (someone) lustfully ▷ *n* flirtatious or lewd look
OGLED > OGLE
OGLER > OGLE
OGLERS > OGLE
OGLES > OGLE
OGLING > OGLE
OGLINGS > OGLE
OGMIC > OGAM
OGRE *n* giant that eats human flesh
OGREISH > OGRE
OGREISHLY > OGRE
OGREISM > OGRE
OGREISMS > OGRE
OGRES > OGRE
OGRESS > OGRE
OGRESSES > OGRE
OGRISH > OGRE
OGRISHLY > OGRE
OGRISM > OGRE
OGRISMS > OGRE
OH *interj* exclamation of surprise, pain, etc ▷ *vb* say oh
OHED > OH
OHIA *n* Hawaiian plant
OHIAS > OHIA
OHING > OH
OHM *n* unit of electrical resistance
OHMAGE *n* electrical resistance in ohms
OHMAGES > OHMAGE
OHMIC *adj* of or relating to a circuit element
OHMICALLY > OHMIC
OHMMETER *n* instrument for measuring electrical resistance
OHMMETERS > OHMMETER
OHMS > OHM
OHO *n* exclamation expressing surprise, exultation, or derision
OHONE *same as* > OCHONE
OHOS > OHO
OHS > OH
OI *interj* shout to attract attention
OIDIA > OIDIUM
OIDIOID > OIDIUM
OIDIUM *n* type of fungal spore
OIK *n* person regarded as inferior because ignorant or lower-class
OIKIST *same as* > OECIST
OIKISTS > OIKIST
OIKS > OIK
OIL *n* viscous liquid, insoluble in water and usu flammable ▷ *vb* lubricate (a machine) with oil
OILBIRD *n* type of nocturnal gregarious

cave-dwelling bird

OILBIRDS > OILBIRD

OILCAMP *n* camp for oilworkers

OILCAMPS > OILCAMP

OILCAN *n* container with a long nozzle for applying oil to machinery

OILCANS > OILCAN

OILCLOTH *n* waterproof material

OILCLOTHS > OILCLOTH

OILCUP *n* cup-shaped oil reservoir in a machine providing continuous lubrication for a bearing

OILCUPS > OILCUP

OILED > OIL

OILER *n* person, device, etc, that lubricates or supplies oil

OILERIES > OILERY

OILERS > OILER

OILERY *n* oil business

OILFIELD *n* area containing oil reserves

OILFIELDS > OILFIELD

OILFIRED *adj* using oil as fuel

OILGAS *n* gaseous mixture of hydrocarbons used as a fuel

OILGASES > OILGAS

OILHOLE *n* hole for oil

OILHOLES > OILHOLE

OILIER > OILY

OILIEST > OILY

OILILY > OILY

OILINESS > OILY

OILING > OIL

OILLET *same as* > EYELET

OILLETS > OILLET

OILMAN *n* person who owns or operates oil wells

OILMEN > OILMAN

OILNUT *n* nut from which oil is extracted

OILNUTS > OILNUT

OILPAPER *n* oiled paper

OILPAPERS > OILPAPER

OILPROOF *adj* resistant to oil

OILS > OIL

OILSEED *n* seed from which oil is extracted

OILSEEDS > OILSEED

OILSKIN *n* (garment made from) waterproof material

OILSKINS > OILSKIN

OILSTONE *n* stone with a fine grain lubricated with oil and used for sharpening cutting tools

OILSTONES > OILSTONE

OILTIGHT *adj* not allowing oil through

OILWAY *n* channel for oil

OILWAYS > OILWAY

OILY *adj* soaked or covered with oil

OINK *n* grunt of a pig or an imitation of this ▷ *interj* imitation or representation of the grunt of a pig ▷ *vb* make noise of pig

OINKED > OINK

OINKING > OINK

OINKS > OINK

OINOLOGY *same as* > OENOLOGY

OINOMEL *same as* > OENOMEL

OINOMELS > OINOMEL

OINT *vb* anoint

OINTED > OINT

OINTING > OINT

OINTMENT *n* greasy substance used for healing skin or as a cosmetic

OINTMENTS > OINTMENT

OINTS > OINT

OITICICA *n* South American tree

OITICICAS > OITICICA

OJIME *n* Japanese bead used to secure cords

OJIMES > OJIME

OKA *n* unit of weight used in Turkey

OKAPI *n* African animal related to the giraffe but with a shorter neck

OKAPIS > OKAPI

OKAS > OKA

OKAY *adj* satisfactory ▷ *vb* approve or endorse ▷ *n* approval or agreement ▷ *interj* expression of approval

OKAYED > OKAY

OKAYING > OKAY

OKAYS > OKAY

OKE *same as* > OKA

OKEH *variant of* > OKAY

OKEHS > OKEH

OKES > OKE

OKEYDOKE *variant of* > OKAY

OKEYDOKEY *variant of* > OKAY

OKIMONO *n* Japanese ornamental item

OKIMONOS > OKIMONO

OKRA *n* tropical plant with edible green pods

OKRAS > OKRA

OKTA *n* unit used in meteorology to measure cloud cover

OKTAS > OKTA

OLD *adj* having lived or existed for a long time ▷ *n* earlier or past time

OLDEN *adj* old ▷ *vb* grow old

OLDENED > OLDEN

OLDENING > OLDEN

OLDENS > OLDEN

OLDER *adj* having lived or existed longer

OLDEST > OLD

OLDIE *n* old but popular song or film

OLDIES > OLDIE

OLDISH > OLD

OLDNESS > OLD

OLDNESSES > OLD

OLDS > OLD

OLDSQUAW *n* type of long-tailed sea duck

OLDSQUAWS > OLDSQUAW

OLDSTER *n* older person

OLDSTERS > OLDSTER

OLDSTYLE *n* printing type style

OLDSTYLES > OLDSTYLE

OLDWIFE *n* any of various fishes, esp the menhaden or the alewife

OLDWIVES > OLDWIFE

OLDY *same as* > OLDIE

OLE *interj* exclamation of approval or encouragement customary at bullfights ▷ *n* cry of olé

OLEA > OLEUM

OLEACEOUS *adj* relating to a family of trees and shrubs, including the ash, jasmine, and olive

OLEANDER *n* Mediterranean flowering evergreen shrub

OLEANDERS > OLEANDER

OLEARIA *n* daisy bush

OLEARIAS > OLEARIA

OLEASTER *n* type of shrub with silver-white twigs and yellow flowers

OLEASTERS > OLEASTER

OLEATE *n* any salt or ester of oleic acid

OLEATES > OLEATE

OLECRANAL > OLECRANON

OLECRANON *n* bony projection of the ulna behind the elbow joint

OLEFIANT *adj* forming oil

OLEFIN *same as* > OLEFINE

OLEFINE *another name for* > ALKENE

OLEFINES > OLEFINE

OLEFINIC > OLEFINE

OLEFINS > OLEFIN

OLEIC as in *oleic acid* colourless oily liquid used in making soap

OLEIN *another name for* > TRIOLEIN

OLEINE *same as* > OLEIN

OLEINES > OLEINE

OLEINS > OLEIN

OLENT *adj* having smell

OLEO as in *oleo oil* oil extracted from beef fat

OLEOGRAPH *n* chromolithograph printed in oil colours to imitate the appearance of an oil painting

OLEORESIN *n* semisolid mixture of a resin and essential oil

OLEOS > OLEO

OLES > OLE

OLESTRA *n* trademark term for an artificial fat

OLESTRAS > OLESTRA

OLEUM *n* type of sulphuric acid

OLEUMS > OLEUM

OLFACT *vb* smell something

OLFACTED > OLFACT

OLFACTING > OLFACT

OLFACTION *n* sense of smell

OLFACTIVE *adj* of sense of smell

OLFACTORY *adj* relating to the sense of smell ▷ *n* organ or nerve concerned with the sense of smell

OLFACTS > OLFACT

OLIBANUM *n* frankincense

OLIBANUMS > OLIBANUM

OLICOOK *n* doughnut

OLICOOKS > OLICOOK

OLID *adj* foul-smelling

OLIGAEMIA *n* reduction in the volume of the blood, a occurs after haemorrhage

OLIGAEMIC > OLIGAEMIA

OLIGARCH *n* member of an oligarchy

OLIGARCHS > OLIGARCH

OLIGARCHY *n* government by a small group of people

OLIGEMIA *same as* > OLIGAEMIA

OLIGEMIAS > OLIGEMIA

OLIGEMIC > OLIGAEMIA

OLIGIST *n* type of iron ore

OLIGISTS > OLIGIST

OLIGOCENE *adj* belonging to geological time period

OLIGOGENE *n* type of gene

OLIGOMER *n* compound of relatively low molecular weight containing up to five monomer units

OLIGOMERS > OLIGOMER

OLIGOPOLY *n* market situation in which contro over the supply of a commodity is held by a small number of produce

OLIGURIA *n* excretion of a abnormally small volume of urine

OLIGURIAS > OLIGURIA

OLINGO *n* South America mammal

OLINGOS > OLINGO

OLIO *n* dish of many different ingredients

OLIOS > OLIO

OLIPHANT *archaic variant of* > ELEPHANT

OLIPHANTS > OLIPHANT

OLITORIES > OLITORY

OLITORY *n* kitchen garde

OLIVARY *adj* shaped like an olive

OLIVE *n* small green or black fruit used as food or pressed for its oil ▷ *adj* greyish-green

OLIVENITE *n* green to black rare secondary mineral

OLIVER as in *Bath oliver* type of unsweetened biscuit

OLIVERS > OLIVER

LIVES > OLIVE
LIVET *n* button shaped like olive
LIVETS > OLIVET
LIVINE *n* olive-green mineral of the olivine group
LIVINES > OLIVINE
LIVINIC *adj* containing olivine
LLA *n* cooking pot
LLAMH *n* old Irish term for a wise man
LLAMHS > OLLAMH
LLAS > OLLA
LLAV *same as* > OLLAMH
LLAVS > OLLAV
LLER *n* waste ground
LLERS > OLLER
LLIE *n* (in skateboarding and snowboarding) a jump into the air executed by stamping on the tail of the board
LLIES > OLLIE
LM *n* pale blind eel-like salamander
LMS > OLM
LOGIES > OLOGY
LOGIST *n* scientist
LOGISTS > OLOGIST
LOGOAN *vb* complain loudly without reason
LOGOANED > OLOGOAN
LOGOANS > OLOGOAN
LOGY *n* science or other branch of knowledge
LOLIUQUI *n* medicinal plant used by the Aztecs
LOROSO *n* golden-coloured sweet sherry
LOROSOS > OLOROSO
LPAE > OLPE
LPE *n* ancient Greek jug
LPES > OLPE
LYCOOK *same as* > OLYKOEK
LYCOOKS > OLYCOOK
LYKOEK *n* American type of doughnut
LYKOEKS > OLYKOEK
LYMPIAD *n* staging of the modern Olympic Games
LYMPIADS > OLYMPIAD
LYMPICS *pl n* modern revival of the ancient Greek games, featuring sporting contests
M *n* sacred syllable in Hinduism
MADHAUN *n* foolish man or boy
MADHAUNS > OMADHAUN
MASA > OMASUM
MASAL > OMASUM
MASUM *n* compartment in the stomach of a ruminant animal
MBER *same as* > OMBRE
MBERS > OMBER
MBRE *n* 18th-century card game
MBRELLA *old form of* > UMBRELLA
OMBRELLAS > OMBRELLA
OMBRES > OMBRE
OMBROPHIL *n* plant flourishing in rainy conditions
OMBU *n* South American tree
OMBUDSMAN *n* official who investigates complaints against government organizations
OMBUDSMEN > OMBUDSMAN
OMBUS > OMBU
OMEGA *n* last letter in the Greek alphabet
OMEGAS > OMEGA
OMELET *same as* > OMELETTE
OMELETS > OMELET
OMELETTE *n* dish of eggs beaten and fried
OMELETTES > OMELETTE
OMEN *n* happening or object thought to foretell success or misfortune ▷ *vb* portend
OMENED > OMEN
OMENING > OMEN
OMENS > OMEN
OMENTA > OMENTUM
OMENTAL > OMENTUM
OMENTUM *n* double fold of the peritoneum connecting the stomach with other abdominal organs
OMENTUMS > OMENTUM
OMER *n* ancient Hebrew unit of dry measure equal to one tenth of an ephah
OMERS > OMER
OMERTA *n* conspiracy of silence
OMERTAS > OMERTA
OMICRON *n* 15th letter in the Greek alphabet
OMICRONS > OMICRON
OMIGOD *interj* exclamation of surprise, pleasure, dismay, etc
OMIKRON *same as* > OMICRON
OMIKRONS > OMIKRON
OMINOUS *adj* worrying, seeming to foretell misfortune
OMINOUSLY > OMINOUS
OMISSIBLE > OMIT
OMISSION *n* something that has been left out or passed over
OMISSIONS > OMISSION
OMISSIVE > OMISSION
OMIT *vb* leave out
OMITS > OMIT
OMITTANCE *n* omission
OMITTED > OMIT
OMITTER > OMIT
OMITTERS > OMIT
OMITTING > OMIT
OMLAH *n* staff team in India
OMLAHS > OMLAH
OMMATEA > OMMATEUM
OMMATEUM *n* insect eye
OMMATIDIA *pl n* cone-shaped parts of the eyes of some arthropods
OMNEITIES > OMNEITY
OMNEITY *n* state of being all
OMNIANA *n* miscellaneous collection
OMNIARCH *n* ruler of everything
OMNIARCHS > OMNIARCH
OMNIBUS *n* several books or TV or radio programmes made into one ▷ *adj* consisting of or dealing with several different things at once
OMNIBUSES > OMNIBUS
OMNIETIES > OMNIETY
OMNIETY *same as* > OMNEITY
OMNIFIC *adj* creating all things
OMNIFIED > OMNIFY
OMNIFIES > OMNIFY
OMNIFORM *adj* of all forms
OMNIFY *vb* make something universal
OMNIFYING > OMNIFY
OMNIMODE *adj* of all functions
OMNIRANGE *n* very-high-frequency ground radio navigational system
OMNIUM *n* total value
OMNIUMS > OMNIUM
OMNIVORA *n* group of omnivorous mammals
OMNIVORE *n* omnivorous animal
OMNIVORES > OMNIVORE
OMNIVORY *n* state of being omnivorous
OMOHYOID *n* muscle in shoulder
OMOHYOIDS > OMOHYOID
OMOPHAGIA *n* eating of raw food, esp meat
OMOPHAGIC > OMOPHAGIA
OMOPHAGY *same as* > OMOPHAGIA
OMOPHORIA *pl n* stole-like bands worn by some bishops
OMOPLATE *n* shoulder blade
OMOPLATES > OMOPLATE
OMOV *n* one member one vote: a voting system in which each voter has one vote to cast
OMOVS > OMOV
OMPHACITE *n* type of mineral
OMPHALI > OMPHALOS
OMPHALIC > OMPHALOS
OMPHALOID *adj* like navel
OMPHALOS *n* (in the ancient world) a sacred conical object, esp a stone
OMRAH *n* Muslim noble
OMRAHS > OMRAH
OMS > OM
ON *prep* indicating position above, attachment, closeness, etc ▷ *adv* in operation ▷ *adj* operating ▷ *n* side of the field on which the batsman stands ▷ *vb* go on
ONAGER *n* wild ass of Persia
ONAGERS > ONAGER
ONAGRI > ONAGER
ONANISM *n* withdrawal in sexual intercourse before ejaculation
ONANISMS > ONANISM
ONANIST > ONANISM
ONANISTIC > ONANISM
ONANISTS > ONANISM
ONBEAT *n* first and third beats in a bar of four-four time
ONBEATS > ONBEAT
ONBOARD *adj* on a ship or other craft
ONCE *adv* on one occasion ▷ *n* one occasion
ONCER *n* (formerly) a one-pound note
ONCERS > ONCER
ONCES > ONCE
ONCET *dialect form of* > ONCE
ONCIDIUM *n* American orchid
ONCIDIUMS > ONCIDIUM
ONCOGEN *n* substance causing tumours to form
ONCOGENE *n* gene that can cause cancer when abnormally activated
ONCOGENES > ONCOGENE
ONCOGENIC *adj* causing the formation of a tumour
ONCOGENS > ONCOGEN
ONCOLOGIC > ONCOLOGY
ONCOLOGY *n* branch of medicine concerned with the study, classification, and treatment of tumours
ONCOLYSES > ONCOLYSIS
ONCOLYSIS *n* destruction of tumours
ONCOLYTIC *adj* destroying tumours
ONCOME *n* act of coming on
ONCOMES > ONCOME
ONCOMETER *n* instrument for measuring body organs
ONCOMICE > ONCOMOUSE
ONCOMING *adj* approaching from the front ▷ *n* approach or onset
ONCOMINGS > ONCOMING
ONCOMOUSE *n* mouse bred for cancer treatment research
ONCOST *same as* > OVERHEADS
ONCOSTMAN *n* miner paid daily
ONCOSTMEN > ONCOSTMAN
ONCOSTS > ONCOST
ONCOTOMY *n* surgical cutting of a tumour
ONCOVIRUS *n* virus causing cancer
ONCUS *same as* > ONKUS
ONDATRA *same as* > MUSQUASH

ONDATRAS > ONDATRA
ONDINE *same as* > UNDINE
ONDINES > ONDINE
ONDING *Scots word for* > ONSET
ONDINGS > ONDING
ONDOGRAM *n* record made by ondograph
ONDOGRAMS > ONDOGRAM
ONDOGRAPH *n* instrument for producing a graphical recording of an alternating current
ONE *adj* single, lone ▷ *n* number or figure 1 ▷ *pron* any person
ONEFOLD *adj* simple
ONEIRIC *adj* of or relating to dreams
ONELY *same as* > ONLY
ONENESS *n* unity
ONENESSES > ONENESS
ONER *n* single continuous action
ONERIER > ONERY
ONERIEST > ONERY
ONEROUS *adj* (of a task) difficult to carry out
ONEROUSLY > ONEROUS
ONERS > ONER
ONERY *same as* > ORNERY
ONES > ONE
ONESELF *pron* reflexive form of *one*
ONETIME *adj* at some time in the past
ONEYER *old form of* > ONE
ONEYERS > ONEYER
ONEYRE *same as* > ONEYER
ONEYRES > ONEYRE
ONFALL *n* attack or onset
ONFALLS > ONFALL
ONFLOW *n* flowing on
ONFLOWS > ONFLOW
ONGAONGA *n* New Zealand nettle with a severe or fatal sting
ONGAONGAS > ONGAONGA
ONGOING *adj* in progress, continuing
ONGOINGS *pl n* things that are happening
ONIE *variant spelling of* > ONY
ONION *n* strongly flavoured edible bulb ▷ *vb* add onion to
ONIONED > ONION
ONIONIER > ONION
ONIONIEST > ONION
ONIONING > ONION
ONIONS > ONION
ONIONSKIN *n* glazed translucent paper
ONIONY > ONION
ONIRIC *same as* > ONEIRIC
ONISCOID *adj* of or like woodlice
ONIUM as in *onium compound* type of chemical salt
ONIUMS > ONIUM
ONKUS *adj* bad
ONLAY *n* artificial veneer for a tooth
ONLAYS > ONLAY
ONLIEST *same as* > ONLY
ONLINE *adj* connected to a computer or the internet
ONLINER *n* person who uses the internet regularly
ONLINERS > ONLINER
ONLOAD *vb* load files on to a computer
ONLOADED > ONLOAD
ONLOADING > ONLOAD
ONLOADS > ONLOAD
ONLOOKER *n* person who watches without taking part
ONLOOKERS > ONLOOKER
ONLOOKING > ONLOOKER
ONLY *adj* alone of its kind ▷ *adv* exclusively
ONNED > ON
ONNING > ON
ONO *n* Hawaiian fish
ONOMASTIC *adj* of or relating to proper names
ONOS > ONO
ONRUSH *n* forceful forward rush or flow
ONRUSHES > ONRUSH
ONRUSHING *adj* approaching quickly
ONS > ON
ONSCREEN *adj* appearing on screen
ONSET *n* beginning
ONSETS > ONSET
ONSETTER *n* attacker
ONSETTERS > ONSET
ONSETTING *n* attack
ONSHORE *adv* towards the land
ONSHORING *n* practice of employing white-collar workers from abroad
ONSIDE *adv* (of a player in various sports) in a legal position ▷ *adj* taking one's part or side ▷ *n* part of cricket field where a batsman stands
ONSIDES > ONSIDE
ONSLAUGHT *n* violent attack
ONST *same as* > ONCE
ONSTAGE *adj* visible by audience
ONSTEAD *Scots word for* > FARMSTEAD
ONSTEADS > ONSTEAD
ONSTREAM *adj* in operation
ONTIC *adj* having real existence
ONTICALLY > ONTIC
ONTO *prep* a position on
ONTOGENIC > ONTOGENY
ONTOGENY *n* entire sequence of events involved in the development of an individual organism
ONTOLOGIC > ONTOLOGY
ONTOLOGY *n* branch of philosophy concerned with existence
ONUS *n* responsibility or burden
ONUSES > ONUS
ONWARD *same as* > ONWARDS
ONWARDLY > ONWARD
ONWARDS *adv* at or towards a point or position ahead, in advance, etc
ONY *Scots word for* > ANY
ONYCHA *n* part of mollusc
ONYCHAS > ONYCHA
ONYCHIA *n* inflammation of the nails or claws of animals
ONYCHIAS > ONYCHIA
ONYCHITE *n* type of stone
ONYCHITES > ONYCHITE
ONYCHITIS *n* inflammation of nails
ONYCHIUM *n* part of insect foot
ONYCHIUMS > ONYCHIUM
ONYMOUS *adj* (of a book) bearing its author's name
ONYX *n* type of quartz with coloured layers
ONYXES > ONYX
OO *Scots word for* > WOOL
OOBIT *n* hairy caterpillar
OOBITS > OOBIT
OOCYST *n* type of zygote
OOCYSTS > OOCYST
OOCYTE *n* immature female germ cell that gives rise to an ovum
OOCYTES > OOCYTE
OODLES *pl n* great quantities
OODLINS *same as* > OODLES
OOF *n* money
OOFIER > OOF
OOFIEST > OOF
OOFS > OOF
OOFTISH *n* money
OOFTISHES > OOFTISH
OOFY > OOF
OOGAMETE *n* female gamete
OOGAMETES > OOGAMETE
OOGAMIES > OOGAMY
OOGAMOUS > OOGAMY
OOGAMY *n* sexual reproduction involving a small motile male gamete and a large much less motile female gamete
OOGENESES > OOGENESIS
OOGENESIS *n* formation and maturation of ova from undifferentiated cells in the ovary
OOGENETIC > OOGENESIS
OOGENIES > OOGENY
OOGENY *same as* > OOGENESIS
OOGONIA > OOGONIUM
OOGONIAL > OOGONIUM
OOGONIUM *n* immature female germ cell forming oocytes by repeated divisions
OOGONIUMS > OOGONIUM
OOH *interj* exclamation of surprise, pleasure, pain, etc ▷ *vb* say ooh
OOHED > OOH
OOHING > OOH
OOHS > OOH
OOIDAL *adj* shaped like eg
OOLACHAN *same as* > EULACHON
OOLACHANS > OOLACHAN
OOLAKAN *same as* > EULACHON
OOLAKANS > OOLAKAN
OOLITE *n* limestone made up of tiny grains of calciu carbonate
OOLITES > OOLITE
OOLITH *n* any of the tiny spherical grains of sedimentary rock of whic oolite is composed
OOLITHS > OOLITH
OOLITIC > OOLITE
OOLOGIC > OOLOGY
OOLOGICAL > OOLOGY
OOLOGIES > OOLOGY
OOLOGIST > OOLOGY
OOLOGISTS > OOLOGY
OOLOGY *n* branch of ornithology concerned with the study of birds' eggs
OOLONG *n* kind of dark tea that is partly fermented before being dried
OOLONGS > OOLONG
OOM *n* title of respect used to refer to an elderly man
OOMIAC *same as* > UMIAK
OOMIACK *same as* > UMIAK
OOMIACKS > OOMIACK
OOMIACS > OOMIAC
OOMIAK *same as* > UMIAK
OOMIAKS > OOMIAK
OOMPAH *n* representation the sound made by a dee brass instrument ▷ *vb* make the noise of a brass instrument
OOMPAHED > OOMPAH
OOMPAHING > OOMPAH
OOMPAHS > OOMPAH
OOMPH *n* enthusiasm, vigour, or energy
OOMPHS > OOMPH
OOMS > OOM
OOMYCETE *n* organism formerly classified as fun
OOMYCETES > OOMYCETE
OON *Scots word for* > OVEN
OONS > OON
OONT *n* camel
OONTS > OONT
OOP *vb* Scots word meani to bind
OOPED > OOP
OOPHORON *n* ovary
OOPHORONS > OOPHORON
OOPHYTE *n* gametophyte in mosses, liverworts, an ferns
OOPHYTES > OOPHYTE
OOPHYTIC > OOPHYTE
OOPING > OOP
OOPS *interj* exclamation o surprise or apology
OOR *Scots form of* > OUR

ORALI *n* member of Indian people
ORALIS > OORALI
ORIAL *n* Himalayan sheep
ORIALS > OORIAL
ORIE *adj* Scots word meaning shabby
ORIER > OORIE
ORIEST > OORIE
OS > OO
OSE *n* dust
OSES > OOSE
OSIER > OOSE
OSIEST > OOSE
OSPERM *n* fertilized ovum
OSPERMS > OOSPERM
OSPHERE *n* large female gamete produced in the oogonia of algae and fungi
OSPHERES > OOSPHERE
OSPORE *n* thick-walled sexual spore that develops from a fertilized oosphere
OSPORES > OOSPORE
OSPORIC > OOSPORE
OSPOROUS > OOSPORE
OSY > OOSE
OT *Scots word for* > OUT
OTHECA *n* capsule containing eggs that is produced by some insects and molluscs
OTHECAE > OOTHECA
OTHECAL > OOTHECA
OTID *n* immature female gamete that develops into an ovum
OTIDS > OOTID
OTS > OOT
OZE *vb* flow slowly ▷ *n* sluggish flow
OZED > OOZE
OZES > OOZE
OZIER > OOZY
OZIEST > OOZY
OZILY > OOZY
OZINESS > OOZY
OZING > OOZE
OZY *adj* moist or dripping
n operation
PACIFIED > OPACIFY
PACIFIER > OPACIFY
PACIFIES > OPACIFY
PACIFY *vb* become or make opaque
PACITIES > OPACITY
PACITY *n* state or quality of being opaque
PACOUS *same as* > OPAQUE
PAH *n* large soft-finned deep-sea fish
PAHS > OPAH
PAL *n* iridescent precious stone
PALED *adj* made like opal
PALESCE *vb* exhibit a milky iridescence
PALESCED > OPALESCE
PALESCES > OPALESCE
PALINE *adj* opalescent ▷ *n* opaque or semiopaque whitish glass
PALINES > OPALINE
PALISED *same as* > OPALIZED
OPALIZED *adj* made into opal
OPALS > OPAL
OPAQUE *adj* not able to be seen through, not transparent ▷ *n* opaque pigment used to block out particular areas on a negative ▷ *vb* make opaque
OPAQUED > OPAQUE
OPAQUELY > OPAQUE
OPAQUER > OPAQUE
OPAQUES > OPAQUE
OPAQUEST > OPAQUE
OPAQUING > OPAQUE
OPCODE *n* computer code containing operating instructions
OPCODES > OPCODE
OPE *archaic or poetic word for* > OPEN
OPED > OPE
OPEN *adj* not closed ▷ *vb* (cause to) become open ▷ *n* competition which all may enter
OPENABLE > OPEN
OPENCAST as in *opencast mining* mining by excavating from the surface
OPENED > OPEN
OPENER *n* tool for opening cans and bottles
OPENERS > OPENER
OPENEST > OPEN
OPENING *n* beginning ▷ *adj* first
OPENINGS > OPENING
OPENLY > OPEN
OPENNESS > OPEN
OPENS > OPEN
OPENSIDE *n* in rugby, flanker who plays on the open side of the scrum
OPENSIDES > OPENSIDE
OPENWORK *n* ornamental work, as of metal or embroidery, having a pattern of openings or holes
OPENWORKS > OPENWORK
OPEPE *n* African tree
OPEPES > OPEPE
OPERA *n* drama in which the text is sung to an orchestral accompaniment
OPERABLE *adj* capable of being treated by a surgical operation
OPERABLY > OPERABLE
OPERAGOER *n* person who goes to operas
OPERAND *n* quantity, variable, or function upon which an operation is performed
OPERANDS > OPERAND
OPERANT *adj* producing effects ▷ *n* person or thing that operates
OPERANTLY > OPERANT
OPERANTS > OPERANT
OPERAS > OPERA
OPERATE *vb* (cause to) work
OPERATED > OPERATE
OPERATES > OPERATE
OPERATIC *adj* of or relating to opera
OPERATICS *n* performance of operas
OPERATING > OPERATE
OPERATION *n* method or procedure of working
OPERATISE *same as* > OPERATIZE
OPERATIVE *adj* working ▷ *n* worker with a special skill
OPERATIZE *vb* turn (a play, novel, etc) into an opera
OPERATOR *n* person who operates a machine or instrument
OPERATORS > OPERATOR
OPERCELE *same as* > OPERCULE
OPERCELES > OPERCELE
OPERCULA > OPERCULUM
OPERCULAR > OPERCULUM
OPERCULE *n* gill cover
OPERCULES > OPERCULE
OPERCULUM *n* covering flap or lidlike structure in animals or plants
OPERETTA *n* light-hearted comic opera
OPERETTAS > OPERETTA
OPERON *n* group of adjacent genes in bacteria functioning as a unit
OPERONS > OPERON
OPEROSE *adj* laborious
OPEROSELY > OPEROSE
OPEROSITY > OPEROSE
OPES > OPE
OPGEFOK *adj* South African taboo slang for damaged or bungled
OPHIDIAN *adj* snakelike ▷ *n* any reptile of the suborder *Ophidia;* a snake
OPHIDIANS > OPHIDIAN
OPHIOLITE *n* type of mineral
OPHIOLOGY *n* branch of zoology that is concerned with the study of snakes
OPHITE *n* any of several greenish mottled rocks
OPHITES > OPHITE
OPHITIC *adj* having small elongated feldspar crystals enclosed
OPHIURA *n* sea creature like a starfish
OPHIURAN *same as* > OPHIURA
OPHIURANS > OPHIURAN
OPHIURAS > OPHIURA
OPHIURID *same as* > OPHIURA
OPHIURIDS > OPHIURID
OPHIUROID *adj* of or like ophiura
OPIATE *n* narcotic drug containing opium ▷ *adj* containing or consisting of opium ▷ *vb* treat with an opiate
OPIATED > OPIATE
OPIATES > OPIATE
OPIATING > OPIATE
OPIFICER *n* craftsman
OPIFICERS > OPIFICER
OPINABLE *adj* thinkable
OPINE *vb* express an opinion
OPINED > OPINE
OPINES > OPINE
OPING > OPE
OPINICUS *n* mythical monster
OPINING > OPINE
OPINION *n* personal belief or judgment
OPINIONED *adj* having strong opinions
OPINIONS > OPINION
OPIOID *n* substance that resembles morphine in its physiological or pharmacological effect
OPIOIDS > OPIOID
OPIUM *n* addictive narcotic drug made from poppy seeds
OPIUMISM *n* addiction to opium
OPIUMISMS > OPIUMISM
OPIUMS > OPIUM
OPOBALSAM *n* soothing ointment
OPODELDOC *n* medical ointment
OPOPANAX *n* medical resin from plant
OPORICE *n* former medicine made from fruit
OPORICES > OPORICE
OPOSSUM *n* small marsupial of America or Australasia
OPOSSUMS > OPOSSUM
OPPIDAN *adj* of a town ▷ *n* person living in a town
OPPIDANS > OPPIDAN
OPPILANT > OPPILATE
OPPILATE *vb* block (the pores, bowels, etc)
OPPILATED > OPPILATE
OPPILATES > OPPILATE
OPPO *n* counterpart in another organization
OPPONENCY > OPPONENT
OPPONENT *n* person one is working against in a contest, battle, or argument ▷ *adj* opposite, as in position
OPPONENTS > OPPONENT
OPPORTUNE *adj* happening at a suitable time
OPPOS > OPPO
OPPOSABLE *adj* (of the thumb) capable of touching the tip of all the other fingers
OPPOSABLY > OPPOSABLE
OPPOSE *vb* work against

OPPOSED > OPPOSE
OPPOSER > OPPOSE
OPPOSERS > OPPOSE
OPPOSES > OPPOSE
OPPOSING > OPPOSE
OPPOSITE *adj* situated on the other side ▷ *n* person or thing that is opposite ▷ *prep* facing ▷ *adv* on the other side
OPPOSITES > OPPOSITE
OPPRESS *vb* control by cruelty or force
OPPRESSED > OPPRESS
OPPRESSES > OPPRESS
OPPRESSOR > OPPRESS
OPPUGN *vb* call into question
OPPUGNANT *adj* combative, antagonistic, or contrary
OPPUGNED > OPPUGN
OPPUGNER > OPPUGN
OPPUGNERS > OPPUGN
OPPUGNING > OPPUGN
OPPUGNS > OPPUGN
OPS > OP
OPSIMATH *n* person who learns late in life
OPSIMATHS > OPSIMATH
OPSIMATHY > OPSIMATH
OPSIN *n* type of protein
OPSINS > OPSIN
OPSOMANIA *n* extreme enthusiasm for a particular food
OPSONIC > OPSONIN
OPSONIFY *same as* > OPSONIZE
OPSONIN *n* constituent of blood serum
OPSONINS > OPSONIN
OPSONISE *same as* > OPSONIZE
OPSONISED > OPSONISE
OPSONISES > OPSONISE
OPSONIUM *n* relish eaten with bread
OPSONIUMS > OPSONIUM
OPSONIZE *vb* subject (bacteria) to the action of opsonins
OPSONIZED > OPSONIZE
OPSONIZES > OPSONIZE
OPT *vb* show a preference, choose
OPTANT *n* person who opts
OPTANTS > OPTANT
OPTATIVE *adj* indicating or expressing choice, preference, or wish ▷ *n* optative mood
OPTATIVES > OPTATIVE
OPTED > OPT
OPTER > OPT
OPTERS > OPT
OPTIC *adj* relating to the eyes or sight
OPTICAL *adj* of or involving light or optics
OPTICALLY > OPTICAL
OPTICIAN *n* person qualified to prescribe glasses
OPTICIANS > OPTICIAN
OPTICIST *n* optics expert
OPTICISTS > OPTICIST
OPTICS *n* science of sight and light
OPTIMA > OPTIMUM
OPTIMAL *adj* best or most favourable
OPTIMALLY > OPTIMAL
OPTIMATE *n* Roman aristocrat
OPTIMATES > OPTIMATE
OPTIME *n* mathematics student at Cambridge University
OPTIMES > OPTIME
OPTIMISE *same as* > OPTIMIZE
OPTIMISED > OPTIMISE
OPTIMISER > OPTIMISE
OPTIMISES > OPTIMISE
OPTIMISM *n* tendency to take the most hopeful view
OPTIMISMS > OPTIMISM
OPTIMIST > OPTIMISM
OPTIMISTS > OPTIMISM
OPTIMIZE *vb* make the most of
OPTIMIZED > OPTIMIZE
OPTIMIZER > OPTIMIZE
OPTIMIZES > OPTIMIZE
OPTIMUM *n* best possible conditions ▷ *adj* most favourable
OPTIMUMS > OPTIMUM
OPTING > OPT
OPTION *n* choice ▷ *vb* obtain an option on
OPTIONAL *adj* possible but not compulsory ▷ *n* optional thing
OPTIONALS > OPTIONAL
OPTIONED > OPTION
OPTIONEE *n* holder of a financial option
OPTIONEES > OPTIONEE
OPTIONING > OPTION
OPTIONS > OPTION
OPTOLOGY *n* science of sight
OPTOMETER *n* any of various instruments for measuring the refractive power of the eye
OPTOMETRY *n* science or practice of testing visual acuity and prescribing corrective lenses
OPTOPHONE *n* device for blind people that converts printed words into sounds
OPTRONICS *n* science of electronic and light signals
OPTS > OPT
OPULENCE > OPULENT
OPULENCES > OPULENT
OPULENCY > OPULENT
OPULENT *adj* having or indicating wealth
OPULENTLY > OPULENT
OPULUS *n* flowering shrub
OPULUSES > OPULUS
OPUNTIA *n* type of cactus
OPUNTIAS > OPUNTIA
OPUS *n* artistic creation, esp a musical work
OPUSCLE *same as* > OPUSCULE
OPUSCLES > OPUSCLE
OPUSCULA > OPUSCULUM
OPUSCULAR > OPUSCULE
OPUSCULE *n* small or insignificant artistic work
OPUSCULES > OPUSCULE
OPUSCULUM *same as* > OPUSCULE
OPUSES > OPUS
OQUASSA *n* American trout
OQUASSAS > OQUASSA
OR *prep* before ▷ *adj* of the metal gold ▷ *n* gold
ORA > OS
ORACH *same as* > ORACHE
ORACHE *n* type of plant
ORACHES > ORACHE
ORACIES > ORACY
ORACLE *n* shrine of an ancient god ▷ *vb* utter as an oracle
ORACLED > ORACLE
ORACLES > ORACLE
ORACLING > ORACLE
ORACULAR *adj* of or like an oracle
ORACULOUS *adj* of an oracle
ORACY *n* capacity to express oneself in and understand speech
ORAD *adv* towards the mouth
ORAGIOUS *adj* stormy
ORAL *adj* spoken ▷ *n* spoken examination
ORALISM *n* oral method of communicating with deaf people
ORALISMS > ORALISM
ORALIST > ORALISM
ORALISTS > ORALISM
ORALITIES > ORALITY
ORALITY *n* state of being oral
ORALLY > ORAL
ORALS > ORAL
ORANG *n* orangutan
ORANGE *n* reddish-yellow citrus fruit ▷ *adj* reddish-yellow
ORANGEADE *n* orange-flavoured, usu fizzy drink
ORANGER > ORANGE
ORANGERIE *archaic variant of* > ORANGERY
ORANGERY *n* greenhouse for growing orange trees
ORANGES > ORANGE
ORANGEST > ORANGE
ORANGEY > ORANGE
ORANGIER > ORANGE
ORANGIEST > ORANGE
ORANGISH > ORANGE
ORANGS > ORANG
ORANGUTAN *n* large ape with shaggy reddish-brown hair
ORANGY > ORANGE
ORANT *n* artistic representation of worshipper
ORANTS > ORANT
ORARIA > ORARIUM
ORARIAN *n* person who lives on the coast
ORARIANS > ORARIAN
ORARION *n* garment worn by Greek clergyman
ORARIONS > ORARION
ORARIUM *n* handkerchief
ORARIUMS > ORARIUM
ORATE *vb* make or give an oration
ORATED > ORATE
ORATES > ORATE
ORATING > ORATE
ORATION *n* formal speech
ORATIONS > ORATION
ORATOR *n* skilful public speaker
ORATORIAL *adj* of oratory
ORATORIAN *n* clergyman of a particular type of church
ORATORIES > ORATORY
ORATORIO *n* musical composition for choir and orchestra
ORATORIOS > ORATORIO
ORATORS > ORATOR
ORATORY *n* art of making speeches
ORATRESS *n* female orator
ORATRICES > ORATRIX
ORATRIX *n* female orator
ORATRIXES > ORATRIX
ORB *n* ceremonial decorated sphere with a cross on top, carried by a monarch ▷ *vb* make or become circular or spherical
ORBED > ORB
ORBICULAR *adj* circular or spherical
ORBIER > ORBY
ORBIEST > ORBY
ORBING > ORB
ORBIT *n* curved path of a planet, satellite, or spacecraft around another body ▷ *vb* move in an orbit around
ORBITA *same as* > ORBIT
ORBITAL *adj* of or denoting an orbit ▷ *n* region surrounding an atomic nucleus
ORBITALLY > ORBITAL
ORBITALS > ORBITAL
ORBITAS > ORBITA
ORBITED > ORBIT
ORBITER *n* spacecraft or satellite designed to orbit a planet without landing on it
ORBITERS > ORBITER
ORBITIES > ORBITY
ORBITING > ORBIT
ORBITS > ORBIT
ORBITY *n* bereavement
ORBLESS > ORB
ORBS > ORB
ORBY *adj* orb-shaped
ORC *n* any of various

whales, such as the killer and grampus

RCA *n* killer whale

RCAS >ORCA

RCEIN *n* brown crystalline material

RCEINS >ORCEIN

RCHARD *n* area where fruit trees are grown

RCHARDS >ORCHARD

RCHAT *same as* >ORCHARD

RCHATS >ORCHAT

RCHEL *same as* >ORCHIL

RCHELLA *same as* >ORCHIL

RCHELLAS >ORCHELLA

RCHELS >ORCHEL

RCHESES >ORCHESIS

RCHESIS *n* art of dance

RCHESTIC *adj* of dance

RCHESTRA *n* large group of musicians, esp playing a variety of instruments

RCHID *n* plant with flowers that have unusual lip-shaped petals

RCHIDIST *n* orchid grower

RCHIDS >ORCHID

RCHIL *n* any of various lichens

RCHILLA *same as* >ORCHIL

RCHILLAS >ORCHILLA

RCHILS >ORCHIL

RCHIS *n* type of orchid

RCHISES >ORCHIS

RCHITIC >ORCHITIS

RCHITIS *n* inflammation of one or both testicles

RCIN *same as* >ORCINOL

RCINE *same as* >ORCINOL

RCINES >ORCINE

RCINOL *n* colourless crystalline water-soluble solid

RCINOLS >ORCINOL

RCINS >ORCIN

RCS >ORC

RD *n* pointed weapon

RDAIN *vb* make (someone) a member of the clergy

RDAINED >ORDAIN

RDAINER >ORDAIN

RDAINERS >ORDAIN

RDAINING >ORDAIN

RDAINS >ORDAIN

RDALIAN *adj* of an ordeal

RDALIUM *same as* >ORDEAL

RDALIUMS >ORDALIUM

RDEAL *n* painful or difficult experience

RDEALS >ORDEAL

RDER *n* instruction to be carried out ▷ *vb* give an instruction to

RDERABLE >ORDER

RDERED >ORDER

RDERER >ORDER

RDERERS >ORDER

RDERING >ORDER

RDERINGS >ORDER

RDERLESS >ORDER

RDERLIES >ORDERLY

ORDERLY *adj* well-organized ▷ *n* hospital attendant ▷ *adv* according to custom or rule

ORDERS >ORDER

ORDINAIRE *adj* ordinary

ORDINAL *adj* denoting a certain position in a sequence of numbers ▷ *n* book containing the forms of services for the ordination of ministers

ORDINALLY >ORDINAL

ORDINALS >ORDINAL

ORDINANCE *n* official rule or order

ORDINAND *n* candidate for ordination

ORDINANDS >ORDINAND

ORDINANT *n* person who ordains

ORDINANTS >ORDINANT

ORDINAR *Scots word for* >ORDINARY

ORDINARS >ORDINAR

ORDINARY *adj* usual or normal

ORDINATE *n* vertical coordinate of a point in a two-dimensional system of coordinates ▷ *vb* ordain

ORDINATED >ORDINATE

ORDINATES >ORDINATE

ORDINEE *n* person being ordained

ORDINEES >ORDINEE

ORDINES >ORDO

ORDNANCE *n* weapons and military supplies

ORDNANCES >ORDNANCE

ORDO *n* religious order

ORDOS >ORDO

ORDS >ORD

ORDURE *n* excrement

ORDURES >ORDURE

ORDUROUS >ORDURE

ORE *n* (rock containing) a mineral which yields metal

OREAD *n* mountain nymph

OREADES >OREAD

OREADS >OREAD

ORECTIC *adj* of or relating to the desires

ORECTIVE >OREXIS

OREGANO *n* sweet-smelling herb used in cooking

OREGANOS >OREGANO

OREIDE *same as* >OROIDE

OREIDES >OREIDE

OREODONT *n* extinct prehistoric mammal

OREODONTS >OREODONT

OREOLOGY *same as* >OROLOGY

OREPEARCH *same as* >OVERPERCH

ORES >ORE

ORESTUNCK >OVERSTINK

OREWEED *n* seaweed

OREWEEDS >OREWEED

OREXIS *n* appetite

OREXISES >OREXIS

ORF *n* infectious disease of sheep and sometimes goats and cattle

ORFE *n* small slender European fish

ORFES >ORFE

ORFRAY *same as* >ORPHREY

ORFRAYS >ORFRAY

ORFS >ORF

ORGAN *n* part of an animal or plant that has a particular function

ORGANA >ORGANON

ORGANDIE *n* fine cotton fabric

ORGANDIES >ORGANDY

ORGANDY *same as* >ORGANDIE

ORGANELLE *n* structural and functional unit in a cell

ORGANIC *adj* of or produced from animals or plants ▷ *n* substance that is derived from animal or vegetable matter

ORGANICAL *same as* >ORGANIC

ORGANICS >ORGANIC

ORGANISE *same as* >ORGANIZE

ORGANISED *same as* >ORGANIZED

ORGANISER *same as* >ORGANIZER

ORGANISES >ORGANISE

ORGANISM *n* any living animal or plant

ORGANISMS >ORGANISM

ORGANIST *n* organ player

ORGANISTS >ORGANIST

ORGANITY *same as* >ORGANISM

ORGANIZE *vb* make arrangements for

ORGANIZED >ORGANIZE

ORGANIZER *n* person who organizes or is capable of organizing

ORGANIZES >ORGANIZE

ORGANON *n* system of logical or scientific rules, esp that of Aristotle

ORGANONS >ORGANON

ORGANOSOL *n* resin-based coating

ORGANOTIN *adj* of an organic compound used as a pesticide

ORGANS >ORGAN

ORGANUM *same as* >ORGANON

ORGANUMS >ORGANUM

ORGANZA *n* thin stiff fabric of silk, cotton, or synthetic fibre

ORGANZAS >ORGANZA

ORGANZINE *n* strong thread made of twisted strands of raw silk

ORGASM *n* most intense point of sexual pleasure ▷ *vb* experience orgasm

ORGASMED >ORGASM

ORGASMIC >ORGASM

ORGASMING >ORGASM

ORGASMS >ORGASM

ORGASTIC >ORGASM

ORGEAT *n* drink made from barley or almonds, and orange flower water

ORGEATS >ORGEAT

ORGIA *same as* >ORGY

ORGIAC >ORGY

ORGIAS >ORGIA

ORGIAST *n* participant in orgy

ORGIASTIC >ORGY

ORGIASTS >ORGIAST

ORGIC >ORGY

ORGIES >ORGY

ORGILLOUS *same as* >ORGULOUS

ORGONE *n* substance claimed to be needed in people for sexual activity and mental health

ORGONES >ORGONE

ORGUE *n* number of stakes lashed together

ORGUES >ORGUE

ORGULOUS *adj* proud

ORGY *n* party involving promiscuous sexual activity

ORIBATID *n* type of mite

ORIBATIDS >ORIBATID

ORIBI *n* small African antelope

ORIBIS >ORIBI

ORICALCHE *same as* >ORICHALC

ORICHALC *n* type of alloy

ORICHALCS >ORICHALC

ORIEL *n* type of bay window

ORIELLED *adj* having an oriel

ORIELS >ORIEL

ORIENCIES >ORIENCY

ORIENCY *n* state of being orient

ORIENT *vb* position (oneself) according to one's surroundings ▷ *n* eastern sky or the dawn ▷ *adj* eastern

ORIENTAL *adj* eastern ▷ *n* native of the orient

ORIENTALS >ORIENTAL

ORIENTATE *vb* position (oneself) according to one's surroundings

ORIENTED >ORIENT

ORIENTEER *vb* take part in orienteering ▷ *n* person who takes part in orienteering

ORIENTER >ORIENT

ORIENTERS >ORIENT

ORIENTING >ORIENT

ORIENTS >ORIENT

ORIFEX *same as* >ORIFICE

ORIFEXES >ORIFEX

ORIFICE *n* opening or hole

ORIFICES >ORIFICE

ORIFICIAL >ORIFICE

ORIFLAMME *n* scarlet flag

adopted as the national banner of France in the Middle Ages
ORIGAMI *n* Japanese decorative art of paper folding
ORIGAMIS > ORIGAMI
ORIGAN *another name for* > MARJORAM
ORIGANE *same as* > ORIGAN
ORIGANES > ORIGANE
ORIGANS > ORIGAN
ORIGANUM *n* type of aromatic plant
ORIGANUMS > ORIGANUM
ORIGIN *n* point from which something develops
ORIGINAL *adj* first or earliest ▷ *n* first version, from which others are copied
ORIGINALS > ORIGINAL
ORIGINATE *vb* come or bring into existence
ORIGINS > ORIGIN
ORIHOU *n* small New Zealand tree
ORILLION *n* part of bastion
ORILLIONS > ORILLION
ORINASAL *adj* pronounced with simultaneous oral and nasal articulation ▷ *n* orinasal speech sound
ORINASALS > ORINASAL
ORIOLE *n* tropical or American songbird
ORIOLES > ORIOLE
ORISHA *n* any of the minor gods or spirits of traditional Yoruba religion
ORISHAS > ORISHA
ORISON *another word for* > PRAYER
ORISONS > ORISON
ORIXA *same as* > ORISHA
ORIXAS > ORIXA
ORLE *n* border around a shield
ORLEANS *n* type of fabric
ORLEANSES > ORLEANS
ORLES > ORLE
ORLON *n* tradename for a crease-resistant acrylic fibre or fabric used for clothing, furnishings, etc
ORLONS > ORLON
ORLOP *n* (in a vessel with four or more decks) the lowest deck
ORLOPS > ORLOP
ORMER *n* edible marine mollusc
ORMERS > ORMER
ORMOLU *n* gold-coloured alloy used for decoration
ORMOLUS > ORMOLU
ORNAMENT *n* decorative object ▷ *vb* decorate
ORNAMENTS > ORNAMENT
ORNATE *adj* highly decorated, elaborate
ORNATELY > ORNATE
ORNATER > ORNATE
ORNATEST > ORNATE
ORNERIER > ORNERY
ORNERIEST > ORNERY
ORNERY *adj* stubborn or vile-tempered
ORNIS *less common word for* > AVIFAUNA
ORNISES > ORNIS
ORNITHES *n* birds in Greek myth
ORNITHIC *adj* of or relating to birds or a bird fauna
ORNITHINE *n* type of amino acid
ORNITHOID *adj* like bird
OROGEN *n* part of earth subject to orogeny
OROGENIC > OROGENY
OROGENIES > OROGENY
OROGENS > OROGEN
OROGENY *n* formation of mountain ranges by intense upward displacement of the earth's crust
OROGRAPHY *n* study or mapping of relief, esp of mountains
OROIDE *n* alloy containing copper, tin, and other metals, used as imitation gold
OROIDES > OROIDE
OROLOGIES > OROLOGY
OROLOGIST > OROGRAPHY
OROLOGY *same as* > OROGRAPHY
OROMETER *n* aneroid barometer with an altitude scale
OROMETERS > OROMETER
ORONASAL *adj* of or relating to the mouth and nose
OROPESA *n* float used in minesweeping
OROPESAS > OROPESA
OROTUND *adj* (of the voice) resonant and booming
ORPHAN *n* child whose parents are dead ▷ *vb* deprive of parents
ORPHANAGE *n* children's home for orphans
ORPHANED > ORPHAN
ORPHANING > ORPHAN
ORPHANISM *n* state of being an orphan
ORPHANS > ORPHAN
ORPHARION *n* large lute in use during the 16th and 17th centuries
ORPHIC *adj* mystical or occult
ORPHICAL *same as* > ORPHIC
ORPHISM *n* style of abstract art
ORPHISMS > ORPHISM
ORPHREY *n* richly embroidered band or border
ORPHREYED *adj* emroidered with gold
ORPHREYS > ORPHREY
ORPIMENT *n* yellow mineral
ORPIMENTS > ORPIMENT
ORPIN *same as* > ORPINE
ORPINE *n* type of plant
ORPINES > ORPINE
ORPINS > ORPIN
ORRA *adj* odd or unmatched
ORRAMAN *n* man who does odd jobs
ORRAMEN > ORRAMAN
ORRERIES > ORRERY
ORRERY *n* mechanical model of the solar system
ORRICE *same as* > ORRIS
ORRICES > ORRICE
ORRIS *n* kind of iris
ORRISES > ORRIS
ORRISROOT *n* rhizome of a type of iris, used as perfume
ORS > OR
ORSEILLE *same as* > ORCHIL
ORSEILLES > ORSEILLE
ORSELLIC > ORSEILLE
ORT *n* fragment
ORTANIQUE *n* hybrid between an orange and a tangerine
ORTHIAN *adj* having high pitch
ORTHICON *n* type of television camera tube
ORTHICONS > ORTHICON
ORTHO *n* type of photographic plate
ORTHOAXES > ORTHOAXIS
ORTHOAXIS *n* axis in a crystal
ORTHODOX *adj* conforming to established views
ORTHODOXY *n* orthodox belief or practice
ORTHOEPIC > ORTHOEPY
ORTHOEPY *n* study of correct or standard pronunciation
ORTHOPEDY *n* treatment of deformity
ORTHOPOD *n* surgeon
ORTHOPODS > ORTHOPOD
ORTHOPTER *n* type of aircraft propelled by flapping wings
ORTHOPTIC *adj* relating to normal binocular vision
ORTHOS > ORTHO
ORTHOSES > ORTHOSIS
ORTHOSIS *n* artificial or mechanical aid to support a weak part of the body
ORTHOTIC > ORTHOTICS
ORTHOTICS *n* use of artificial or mechanical aids to assist movement of weak joints or muscles
ORTHOTIST *n* person who is qualified to practise orthotics
ORTHOTONE *adj* (of a word) having an independent accent ▷ *n* independently accented word
ORTHROS *n* canonical hour in the Greek Church
ORTHROSES > ORTHROS
ORTOLAN *n* small European songbird eaten as a delicacy
ORTOLANS > ORTOLAN
ORTS *pl n* scraps or leaving
ORVAL *n* plant of sage family
ORVALS > ORVAL
ORYX *n* large African antelope
ORYXES > ORYX
ORZO *n* pasta in small grai shapes
ORZOS > ORZO
OS *n* mouth or mouthlike part or opening
OSAR > OS
OSCAR *n* cash
OSCARS > OSCAR
OSCHEAL *adj* of scrotum
OSCILLATE *vb* swing back and forth
OSCINE *n* songbird ▷ *adj* (songbirds
OSCINES > OSCINE
OSCININE > OSCINE
OSCITANCE *same as* > OSCITANCY
OSCITANCY *n* state of beir drowsy, lazy, or inattentiv
OSCITANT > OSCITANCY
OSCITATE *vb* yawn
OSCITATED > OSCITATE
OSCITATES > OSCITATE
OSCULA > OSCULUM
OSCULANT *adj* possessing some of the characteristi of two different taxonom groups
OSCULAR *adj* of or relating to an osculum
OSCULATE *vb* kiss
OSCULATED > OSCULATE
OSCULATES > OSCULATE
OSCULE *n* small mouth or opening
OSCULES > OSCULE
OSCULUM *n* mouthlike aperture
OSE *same as* > ESKER
OSES > OSE
OSETRA *n* type of caviar
OSETRAS > OSETRA
OSHAC *n* plant smelling of ammonia
OSHACS > OSHAC
OSIER *n* willow tree
OSIERED *adj* covered with osiers
OSIERIES > OSIERY
OSIERS > OSIER
OSIERY *n* work done with osiers
OSMATE *n* salt of osmic ac
OSMATES > OSMATE
OSMATIC *adj* relying on sense of smell
OSMETERIA *pl n* glands in some caterpillars that secrete foul-smelling substances to deter predators
OSMIATE *same as* > OSMAT
OSMIATES > OSMIATE
OSMIC *adj* of or containin

osmium in a high valence state
SMICALLY > OSMIC
SMICS *n* science of smell
SMIOUS *same as* > OSMOUS
SMIUM *n* heaviest known metallic element
SMIUMS > OSMIUM
SMOL *same as* > OSMOLE
SMOLAL > OSMOLE
SMOLAR *adj* containing one osmole per litre
SMOLE *n* unit of osmotic pressure
SMOLES > OSMOLE
SMOLS > OSMOL
SMOMETER *n* instrument for measuring osmotic pressure
SMOMETRY > OSMOMETER
SMOSE *vb* undergo or cause to undergo osmosis
SMOSED > OSMOSE
SMOSES > OSMOSE
SMOSING > OSMOSE
SMOSIS *n* movement of a liquid through a membrane from a lower to a higher concentration
SMOTIC > OSMOSIS
SMOUS *adj* of or containing osmium in a low valence state
SMUND *same as* > OSMUNDA
SMUNDA *n* type of fern
SMUNDAS > OSMUNDA
SMUNDINE *n* type of compost
SMUNDS > OSMUND
SNABURG *n* coarse plain-woven cotton used for sacks, furnishings, etc
SNABURGS > OSNABURG
SPREY *n* large fish-eating bird of prey
SPREYS > OSPREY
SSA > OS
SSARIUM *same as* > OSSUARY
SSARIUMS > OSSARIUM
SSATURE *n* skeleton
SSATURES > OSSATURE
SSEIN *n* protein that forms the organic matrix of bone
SSEINS > OSSEIN
SSELET *n* growth on knee of horse
SSELETS > OSSELET
SSEOUS *adj* consisting of or like bone
SSEOUSLY > OSSEOUS
SSETER *n* sturgeon
SSETERS > OSSETER
SSETRA *same as* > OSETRA
SSETRAS > OSSETRA
SSIA *conj* (in music) or
SSICLE *n* small bone, esp one of those in the middle ear
SSICLES > OSSICLE
SSICULAR > OSSICLE
SSIFIC *adj* making something turn to bone
OSSIFIED *adj* converted into bone
OSSIFIER > OSSIFY
OSSIFIERS > OSSIFY
OSSIFIES > OSSIFY
OSSIFRAGA *n* large sea bird
OSSIFRAGE *n* osprey
OSSIFY *vb* (cause to) become bone, harden
OSSIFYING > OSSIFY
OSSUARIES > OSSUARY
OSSUARY *n* any container for the burial of human bones, such as an urn or vault
OSTEAL *adj* of or relating to bone or to the skeleton
OSTEITIC > OSTEITIS
OSTEITIS *n* inflammation of a bone
OSTENSIVE *adj* directly showing or pointing out
OSTENSORY *n* (in the RC Church) receptacle for displaying the consecrated Host
OSTENT *n* appearance
OSTENTS > OSTENT
OSTEOCYTE *n* bone cell
OSTEODERM *n* bony area in skin
OSTEOGEN *n* material from which bone forms
OSTEOGENS > OSTEOGEN
OSTEOGENY *n* forming of bone
OSTEOID *adj* of or resembling bone ▷ *n* bony deposit
OSTEOIDS > OSTEOID
OSTEOLOGY *n* study of the structure and function of bones
OSTEOMA *n* benign tumour composed of bone or bonelike tissue
OSTEOMAS > OSTEOMA
OSTEOMATA > OSTEOMA
OSTEOPATH *n* person who practises osteopathy
OSTEOSES > OSTEOSIS
OSTEOSIS *n* forming of bony tissue
OSTEOTOME *n* surgical instrument for cutting bone, usually a special chisel
OSTEOTOMY *n* surgical cutting or dividing of bone
OSTIA > OSTIUM
OSTIAL > OSTIUM
OSTIARIES > OSTIARY
OSTIARY *another word for* > PORTER
OSTIATE *adj* having ostium
OSTINATI > OSTINATO
OSTINATO *n* persistently repeated phrase or rhythm
OSTINATOS > OSTINATO
OSTIOLAR > OSTIOLE
OSTIOLATE > OSTIOLE
OSTIOLE *n* pore in the reproductive bodies of certain algae and fungi through which spores pass
OSTIOLES > OSTIOLE
OSTIUM *n* any of the pores in sponges through which water enters the body
OSTLER *n* stableman at an inn
OSTLERESS *n* female ostler
OSTLERS > OSTLER
OSTMARK *n* currency of the former East Germany
OSTMARKS > OSTMARK
OSTOMATE *n* person with an ostomy
OSTOMATES > OSTOMATE
OSTOMIES > OSTOMY
OSTOMY *n* surgically made opening connecting organ to surface of body
OSTOSES > OSTOSIS
OSTOSIS *n* formation of bone
OSTOSISES > OSTOSIS
OSTRACA > OSTRACON
OSTRACEAN *adj* of oysters
OSTRACISE *same as* > OSTRACIZE
OSTRACISM > OSTRACIZE
OSTRACIZE *vb* exclude (a person) from a group
OSTRACOD *n* type of minute crustacean
OSTRACODE *adj* of ostracods
OSTRACODS > OSTRACOD
OSTRACON *n* (in ancient Greece) a potsherd used for ostracizing
OSTRACONS > OSTRACON
OSTRAKA > OSTRAKON
OSTRAKON *same as* > OSTRACON
OSTREGER *n* keeper of hawks
OSTREGERS > OSTREGER
OSTRICH *n* large African bird that runs fast but cannot fly
OSTRICHES > OSTRICH
OTAKU *n* Japanese computer geeks
OTALGIA *technical name for* > EARACHE
OTALGIAS > OTALGIA
OTALGIC > OTALGIA
OTALGIES > OTALGY
OTALGY *same as* > OTALGIA
OTARIES > OTARY
OTARINE > OTARY
OTARY *n* seal with ears
OTHER *adj* remaining in a group of which one or some have been specified ▷ *n* other person or thing
OTHERNESS *n* quality of being different or distinct in appearance, character, etc
OTHERS > OTHER
OTHERWISE *adv* differently, in another way ▷ *adj* of an unexpected nature ▷ *pron* something different in outcome
OTIC *adj* of or relating to the ear
OTIOSE *adj* not useful
OTIOSELY > OTIOSE
OTIOSITY > OTIOSE
OTITIC > OTITIS
OTITIDES > OTITIS
OTITIS *n* inflammation of the ear
OTITISES > OTITIS
OTOCYST *n* embryonic structure in vertebrates that develops into the inner ear in the adult
OTOCYSTIC > OTOCYST
OTOCYSTS > OTOCYST
OTOLITH *n* granule of calcium carbonate in the inner ear of vertebrates
OTOLITHIC > OTOLITH
OTOLITHS > OTOLITH
OTOLOGIES > OTOLOGY
OTOLOGIST > OTOLOGY
OTOLOGY *n* branch of medicine concerned with the ear
OTOPLASTY *n* cosmetic surgery on ears
OTORRHOEA *n* discharge from the ears
OTOSCOPE *another name for* > AURISCOPE
OTOSCOPES > OTOSCOPE
OTOSCOPIC > OTOSCOPY
OTOSCOPY *n* examination of ear using otoscope
OTOTOXIC *adj* toxic to the ear
OTTAR *variant of* > ATTAR
OTTARS > OTTAR
OTTAVA *n* interval of an octave
OTTAVAS > OTTAVA
OTTAVINO *n* piccolo
OTTAVINOS > OTTAVINO
OTTER *n* small brown freshwater mammal that eats fish ▷ *vb* fish using an otter board
OTTERED > OTTER
OTTERING > OTTER
OTTERS > OTTER
OTTO *another name for* > ATTAR
OTTOMAN *n* storage chest with a padded lid for use as a seat
OTTOMANS > OTTOMAN
OTTOS > OTTO
OTTRELITE *n* type of mineral
OU *n* man, bloke, or chap
OUABAIN *n* poisonous white crystalline glycoside
OUABAINS > OUABAIN
OUAKARI *n* South American monkey
OUAKARIS > OUAKARI
OUBAAS *n* man in authority
OUBAASES > OUBAAS
OUBIT *n* hairy caterpillar
OUBITS > OUBIT
OUBLIETTE *n* dungeon entered only by a trapdoor

OUCH *interj* exclamation of sudden pain ▷ *n* brooch or clasp set with gems ▷ *vb* say ouch
OUCHED > OUCH
OUCHES > OUCH
OUCHING > OUCH
OUCHT *Scots word for* > ANYTHING
OUCHTS > OUCHT
OUD *n* Arabic stringed musical instrument resembling a lute or mandolin
OUDS > OUD
OUGHLIED > OUGHLY
OUGHLIES > OUGHLY
OUGHLY *variant of* > UGLY
OUGHLYING > OUGHLIE
OUGHT *vb* have an obligation ▷ *n* zero
OUGHTED > OUGHT
OUGHTING > OUGHT
OUGHTNESS *n* state of being right
OUGHTS > OUGHT
OUGLIE *variant of* > UGLY
OUGLIED > OUGLIE
OUGLIEING > OUGLIE
OUGLIES > OUGLIE
OUGUIYA *n* standard monetary unit of Mauritania
OUGUIYAS > OUGUIYA
OUIJA *n* tradename for a board through which spirits supposedly answer questions
OUIJAS > OUIJA
OUISTITI *n* marmoset
OUISTITIS > OUISTITI
OUK *Scots word for* > WEEK
OUKS > OUK
OULACHON *same as* > EULACHON
OULACHONS > OULACHON
OULAKAN *same as* > EULACHON
OULAKANS > OULAKAN
OULD *Scots or Irish form of* > OLD
OULDER > OULD
OULDEST > OULD
OULK *Scots form of* > WEEK
OULKS > OULK
OULONG *same as* > OOLONG
OULONGS > OULONG
OUMA *n* grandmother, often as a title with a surname
OUMAS > OUMA
OUNCE *n* unit of weight equal to one sixteenth of a pound
OUNCES > OUNCE
OUNDY *adj* wavy
OUP *same as* > OOP
OUPA *n* grandfather, often as a title with a surname
OUPAS > OUPA
OUPED > OUP
OUPH *same as* > OAF
OUPHE *same as* > OAF
OUPHES > OUPHE
OUPHS > OUPH
OUPING > OUP
OUPS > OUP
OUR *adj* belonging to us ▷ *determiner* of, belonging to, or associated in some way with us
OURALI *n* plant from which curare comes
OURALIS > OURALI
OURANG *same as* > ORANG
OURANGS > OURANG
OURARI *same as* > OURALI
OURARIS > OURARI
OUREBI *same as* > ORIBI
OUREBIS > OUREBI
OURIE *same as* > OORIE
OURIER > OURIE
OURIEST > OURIE
OURN *dialect form of* > OUR
OUROBOROS *n* mythical serpent
OUROLOGY *same as* > UROLOGY
OUROSCOPY *same as* > UROSCOPY
OURS *pron* thing(s) belonging to us
OURSELF *pron* formal word for *myself* used by monarchs
OURSELVES *pron* reflexive form of *we* or *us*
OUSEL *same as* > OUZEL
OUSELS > OUSEL
OUST *vb* force (someone) out, expel
OUSTED > OUST
OUSTER *n* act or instance of forcing someone out of a position
OUSTERS > OUSTER
OUSTING > OUST
OUSTITI *n* device for opening locked door
OUSTITIS > OUSTITI
OUSTS > OUST
OUT *adj* denoting movement or distance away from ▷ *vb* name (a public figure) as being homosexual
OUTACT *vb* surpass in acting
OUTACTED > OUTACT
OUTACTING > OUTACT
OUTACTS > OUTACT
OUTADD *vb* beat or surpass at adding
OUTADDED > OUTADD
OUTADDING > OUTADD
OUTADDS > OUTADD
OUTAGE *n* period of power failure
OUTAGES > OUTAGE
OUTARGUE *vb* defeat in argument
OUTARGUED > OUTARGUE
OUTARGUES > OUTARGUE
OUTASIGHT *adj* excellent or wonderful
OUTASK *vb* declare wedding banns
OUTASKED > OUTASK
OUTASKING > OUTASK
OUTASKS > OUTASK
OUTATE > OUTEAT
OUTBACK *n* remote bush country of Australia
OUTBACKER > OUTBACK
OUTBACKS > OUTBACK
OUTBAKE *vb* bake more or better than
OUTBAKED > OUTBAKE
OUTBAKES > OUTBAKE
OUTBAKING > OUTBAKE
OUTBAR *vb* keep out
OUTBARK *vb* bark more or louder than
OUTBARKED > OUTBARK
OUTBARKS > OUTBARK
OUTBARRED > OUTBAR
OUTBARS > OUTBAR
OUTBAWL *vb* bawl more or louder than
OUTBAWLED > OUTBAWL
OUTBAWLS > OUTBAWL
OUTBEAM *vb* beam more or brighter than
OUTBEAMED > OUTBEAM
OUTBEAMS > OUTBEAM
OUTBEG *vb* beg more or better than
OUTBEGGED > OUTBEG
OUTBEGS > OUTBEG
OUTBID *vb* offer a higher price than
OUTBIDDEN > OUTBID
OUTBIDDER > OUTBID
OUTBIDS > OUTBID
OUTBITCH *vb* bitch more or better than
OUTBLAZE *vb* blaze more or hotter than
OUTBLAZED > OUTBLAZE
OUTBLAZES > OUTBLAZE
OUTBLEAT *vb* bleat more or louder than
OUTBLEATS > OUTBLEAT
OUTBLESS *vb* bless more than
OUTBLOOM *vb* bloom more or better than
OUTBLOOMS > OUTBLOOM
OUTBLUFF *vb* surpass in bluffing
OUTBLUFFS > OUTBLUFF
OUTBLUSH *vb* blush more than
OUTBOARD *adj* (of a boat's engine) portable, with its own propeller ▷ *adv* away from the centre line of a vessel or aircraft ▷ *n* outboard motor
OUTBOARDS > OUTBOARD
OUTBOAST *vb* surpass in boasting
OUTBOASTS > OUTBOAST
OUTBOUGHT > OUTBUY
OUTBOUND *adj* going out
OUTBOUNDS *n* boundaries
OUTBOX *vb* surpass in boxing
OUTBOXED > OUTBOX
OUTBOXES > OUTBOX
OUTBOXING > OUTBOX
OUTBRAG *vb* brag more or better than
OUTBRAGS > OUTBRAG
OUTBRAVE *vb* surpass in bravery
OUTBRAVED > OUTBRAVE
OUTBRAVES > OUTBRAVE
OUTBRAWL *vb* defeat in a brawl
OUTBRAWLS > OUTBRAWL
OUTBRAZEN *vb* be more brazen than
OUTBREAK *n* sudden occurrence (of something unpleasant) ▷ *vb* break out
OUTBREAKS > OUTBREAK
OUTBRED > OUTBREED
OUTBREED *vb* produce offspring through sexual relations outside a particular family or tribe
OUTBREEDS > OUTBREED
OUTBRIBE *vb* bribe more than
OUTBRIBED > OUTBRIBE
OUTBRIBES > OUTBRIBE
OUTBROKE > OUTBREAK
OUTBROKEN > OUTBREAK
OUTBUILD *vb* exceed in building
OUTBUILDS > OUTBUILD
OUTBUILT > OUTBUILD
OUTBULGE *vb* bulge outwards
OUTBULGED > OUTBULGE
OUTBULGES > OUTBULGE
OUTBULK *vb* exceed in bulk
OUTBULKED > OUTBULK
OUTBULKS > OUTBULK
OUTBULLY *vb* exceed in bullying
OUTBURN *vb* burn longer or brighter than
OUTBURNED > OUTBURN
OUTBURNS > OUTBURN
OUTBURNT > OUTBURN
OUTBURST *n* sudden expression of emotion ▷ *vb* burst out
OUTBURSTS > OUTBURST
OUTBUY *vb* buy more than
OUTBUYING > OUTBUY
OUTBUYS > OUTBUY
OUTBY *adv* outside
OUTBYE *same as* > OUTBY
OUTCALL *n* visit to customer's home by professional
OUTCALLS > OUTCALL
OUTCAPER *vb* exceed in capering
OUTCAPERS > OUTCAPER
OUTCAST *n* person rejected by a particular group ▷ *adj* rejected, abandoned, or discarded
OUTCASTE *n* person who has been expelled from a caste ▷ *vb* cause (someone) to lose his caste
OUTCASTED > OUTCASTE
OUTCASTES > OUTCASTE
OUTCASTS > OUTCAST
OUTCATCH *vb* catch more than

JTCAUGHT > OUTCATCH
JTCAVIL *vb* exceed in cavilling
JTCAVILS > OUTCAVIL
JTCHARGE *vb* charge more than
JTCHARM *vb* exceed in charming
JTCHARMS > OUTCHARM
JTCHEAT *vb* exceed in cheating
JTCHEATS > OUTCHEAT
JTCHID > OUTCHIDE
JTCHIDE *vb* exceed in chiding
JTCHIDED > OUTCHIDE
JTCHIDES > OUTCHIDE
JTCITIES > OUTCITY
JTCITY *n* anywhere outside a city's confines
JTCLASS *vb* surpass in quality
JTCLIMB *vb* exceed in climbing
JTCLIMBS > OUTCLIMB
JTCLOMB > OUTCLIMB
JTCOACH *vb* exceed in coaching
JTCOME *n* result
JTCOMES > OUTCOME
JTCOOK *vb* cook more or better than
JTCOOKED > OUTCOOK
JTCOOKS > OUTCOOK
JTCOUNT *vb* exceed in counting
JTCOUNTS > OUTCOUNT
JTCRAFTY *vb* be craftier than
JTCRAWL *vb* crawl further or faster than
JTCRAWLS > OUTCRAWL
JTCRIED > OUTCRY
JTCRIES > OUTCRY
JTCROP *n* part of a rock formation that sticks out of the earth ▷ *vb* (of rock strata) to protrude through the surface of the earth
JTCROPS > OUTCROP
JTCROSS *vb* breed (animals or plants of the same breed but different strains) ▷ *n* animal or plant produced as a result of outcrossing
JTCROW *vb* exceed in crowing
JTCROWD *vb* have more crowd than
JTCROWDS > OUTCROWD
JTCROWED > OUTCROW
JTCROWS > OUTCROW
JTCRY *n* vehement or widespread protest ▷ *vb* cry louder or make more noise than (someone or something)
JTCRYING > OUTCRY
JTCURSE *vb* exceed in cursing
JTCURSED > OUTCURSE
JTCURSES > OUTCURSE
OUTCURVE *n* baseball thrown to curve away from batter
OUTCURVES > OUTCURVE
OUTDANCE *vb* surpass in dancing
OUTDANCED > OUTDANCE
OUTDANCES > OUTDANCE
OUTDARE *vb* be more brave than
OUTDARED > OUTDARE
OUTDARES > OUTDARE
OUTDARING > OUTDARE
OUTDATE *vb* make or become old-fashioned or obsolete
OUTDATED *adj* old-fashioned
OUTDATES > OUTDATE
OUTDATING > OUTDATE
OUTDAZZLE *vb* exceed in dazzling
OUTDEBATE *vb* exceed in debate
OUTDESIGN *vb* exceed in designing
OUTDID > OUTDO
OUTDO *vb* surpass in performance
OUTDODGE *vb* surpass in doding
OUTDODGED > OUTDODGE
OUTDODGES > OUTDODGE
OUTDOER > OUTDO
OUTDOERS > OUTDO
OUTDOES > OUTDO
OUTDOING > OUTDO
OUTDONE > OUTDO
OUTDOOR *adj* taking place, existing, or intended for use in the open air
OUTDOORS *adv* in(to) the open air ▷ *n* open air
OUTDOORSY *adj* taking part in activities relating to the outdoors
OUTDRAG *vb* beat in drag race
OUTDRAGS > OUTDRAG
OUTDRANK > OUTDRINK
OUTDRAW *vb* draw (a gun) faster than
OUTDRAWN > OUTDRAW
OUTDRAWS > OUTDRAW
OUTDREAM *vb* exceed in dreaming
OUTDREAMS > OUTDREAM
OUTDREAMT > OUTDREAM
OUTDRESS *vb* dress better than
OUTDREW > OUTDRAW
OUTDRINK *vb* drink more than
OUTDRINKS > OUTDRINK
OUTDRIVE *vb* exceed in driving
OUTDRIVEN > OUTDRIVE
OUTDRIVES > OUTDRIVE
OUTDROP *same as* > OUTCROP
OUTDROPS > OUTDROP
OUTDROVE > OUTDRIVE
OUTDRUNK > OUTDRINK
OUTDUEL *vb* defeat in duel
OUTDUELED > OUTDUEL
OUTDUELS > OUTDUEL
OUTDURE *vb* last longer than
OUTDURED > OUTDURE
OUTDURES > OUTDURE
OUTDURING > OUTDURE
OUTDWELL *vb* live outside something
OUTDWELLS > OUTDWELL
OUTDWELT > OUTDWELL
OUTEARN *vb* earn more than
OUTEARNED > OUTEARN
OUTEARNS > OUTEARN
OUTEAT *vb* eat more than
OUTEATEN > OUTEAT
OUTEATING > OUTEAT
OUTEATS > OUTEAT
OUTECHO *vb* echo more than
OUTECHOED > OUTECHO
OUTECHOES > OUTECHO
OUTED > OUT
OUTEDGE *n* furthest limit
OUTEDGES > OUTEDGE
OUTER *adj* on the outside ▷ *n* white outermost ring on a target
OUTERCOAT *same as* > OVERCOAT
OUTERMOST *adj* furthest out
OUTERS > OUTER
OUTERWEAR *n* clothes worn on top of other clothes
OUTFABLE *vb* exceed in creating fables
OUTFABLED > OUTFABLE
OUTFABLES > OUTFABLE
OUTFACE *vb* subdue or disconcert (someone) by staring
OUTFACED > OUTFACE
OUTFACES > OUTFACE
OUTFACING > OUTFACE
OUTFALL *n* mouth of a river or drain
OUTFALLS > OUTFALL
OUTFAST *vb* fast longer than
OUTFASTED > OUTFAST
OUTFASTS > OUTFAST
OUTFAWN *vb* exceed in fawning
OUTFAWNED > OUTFAWN
OUTFAWNS > OUTFAWN
OUTFEAST *vb* exceed in feasting
OUTFEASTS > OUTFEAST
OUTFEEL *vb* exceed in feeling
OUTFEELS > OUTFEEL
OUTFELT > OUTFEEL
OUTFENCE *vb* surpass at fencing
OUTFENCED > OUTFENCE
OUTFENCES > OUTFENCE
OUTFIELD *n* area far from the pitch
OUTFIELDS > OUTFIELD
OUTFIGHT *vb* surpass in fighting
OUTFIGHTS > OUTFIGHT
OUTFIGURE *same as* > OUTTHINK
OUTFIND *vb* exceed in finding
OUTFINDS > OUTFIND
OUTFIRE *vb* exceed in firing
OUTFIRED > OUTFIRE
OUTFIRES > OUTFIRE
OUTFIRING > OUTFIRE
OUTFISH *vb* catch more fish than
OUTFISHED > OUTFISH
OUTFISHES > OUTFISH
OUTFIT *n* matching set of clothes ▷ *vb* furnish or be furnished with an outfit, equipment, etc
OUTFITS > OUTFIT
OUTFITTED > OUTFIT
OUTFITTER *n* supplier of men's clothes
OUTFLANK *vb* get round the side of (an enemy army)
OUTFLANKS > OUTFLANK
OUTFLASH *vb* be flashier than
OUTFLEW > OUTFLY
OUTFLIES > OUTFLY
OUTFLING *n* cutting remark
OUTFLINGS > OUTFLING
OUTFLOAT *vb* surpass at floating
OUTFLOATS > OUTFLOAT
OUTFLOW *n* anything that flows out, such as liquid or money ▷ *vb* flow faster than
OUTFLOWED > OUTFLOW
OUTFLOWN > OUTFLY
OUTFLOWS > OUTFLOW
OUTFLUSH *n* burst of light
OUTFLY *vb* fly better or faster than
OUTFLYING > OUTFLY
OUTFOOL *vb* be more foolish than
OUTFOOLED > OUTFOOL
OUTFOOLS > OUTFOOL
OUTFOOT *vb* (of a boat) to go faster than (another boat)
OUTFOOTED > OUTFOOT
OUTFOOTS > OUTFOOT
OUTFOUGHT > OUTFIGHT
OUTFOUND > OUTFIND
OUTFOX *vb* defeat or foil (someone) by being more cunning
OUTFOXED > OUTFOX
OUTFOXES > OUTFOX
OUTFOXING > OUTFOX
OUTFROWN *vb* dominate by frowning more than
OUTFROWNS > OUTFROWN
OUTFUMBLE *vb* exceed in fumbling
OUTGAIN *vb* gain more than
OUTGAINED > OUTGAIN
OUTGAINS > OUTGAIN
OUTGALLOP *vb* gallop faster than
OUTGAMBLE *vb* defeat at gambling
OUTGAS *vb* undergo the

removal of adsorbed or absorbed gas from solids
OUTGASES > OUTGAS
OUTGASSED > OUTGAS
OUTGASSES > OUTGAS
OUTGATE *n* way out
OUTGATES > OUTGATE
OUTGAVE > OUTGIVE
OUTGAZE *vb* gaze beyond
OUTGAZED > OUTGAZE
OUTGAZES > OUTGAZE
OUTGAZING > OUTGAZE
OUTGIVE *vb* exceed in giving
OUTGIVEN > OUTGIVE
OUTGIVES > OUTGIVE
OUTGIVING > OUTGIVE
OUTGLARE *vb* exceed in glaring
OUTGLARED > OUTGLARE
OUTGLARES > OUTGLARE
OUTGLEAM *vb* gleam more than
OUTGLEAMS > OUTGLEAM
OUTGLOW *vb* glow more than
OUTGLOWED > OUTGLOW
OUTGLOWS > OUTGLOW
OUTGNAW *vb* exceed in gnawing
OUTGNAWED > OUTGNAW
OUTGNAWN > OUTGNAW
OUTGNAWS > OUTGNAW
OUTGO *vb* exceed or outstrip ▷ *n* cost
OUTGOER > OUTGO
OUTGOERS > OUTGO
OUTGOES > OUTGO
OUTGOING *adj* leaving ▷ *n* act of going out
OUTGOINGS *pl n* expenses
OUTGONE > OUTGO
OUTGREW > OUTGROW
OUTGRIN *vb* exceed in grinning
OUTGRINS > OUTGRIN
OUTGROSS *vb* earn more than
OUTGROUP *n* group of people outside one's own group of people
OUTGROUPS > OUTGROUP
OUTGROW *vb* become too large or too old for
OUTGROWN > OUTGROW
OUTGROWS > OUTGROW
OUTGROWTH *n* natural development
OUTGUARD *n* guard furthest away from main party
OUTGUARDS > OUTGUARD
OUTGUESS *vb* surpass in guessing
OUTGUIDE *n* folder in filing system ▷ *vb* beat or surpass at guiding
OUTGUIDED > OUTGUIDE
OUTGUIDES > OUTGUIDE
OUTGUN *vb* surpass in fire power
OUTGUNNED > OUTGUN
OUTGUNS > OUTGUN
OUTGUSH *vb* gush out
OUTGUSHED > OUTGUSH
OUTGUSHES > OUTGUSH
OUTHANDLE *vb* handle better than
OUTHAUL *n* line or cable for tightening the foot of a sail
OUTHAULER *same as* > OUTHAUL
OUTHAULS > OUTHAUL
OUTHEAR *vb* exceed in hearing
OUTHEARD > OUTHEAR
OUTHEARS > OUTHEAR
OUTHER *same as* > OTHER
OUTHIRE *vb* hire out
OUTHIRED > OUTHIRE
OUTHIRES > OUTHIRE
OUTHIRING > OUTHIRE
OUTHIT *vb* hit something further than (someone else)
OUTHITS > OUTHIT
OUTHOMER *vb* score more home runs than
OUTHOMERS > OUTHOMER
OUTHOUSE *n* building near a main building
OUTHOUSES > OUTHOUSE
OUTHOWL *vb* exceed in howling
OUTHOWLED > OUTHOWL
OUTHOWLS > OUTHOWL
OUTHUMOR *vb* exceed in humouring
OUTHUMORS > OUTHUMOR
OUTHUNT *vb* exceed in hunting
OUTHUNTED > OUTHUNT
OUTHUNTS > OUTHUNT
OUTHUSTLE *vb* be more competitive than
OUTHYRE *same as* > OUTHIRE
OUTHYRED > OUTHYRE
OUTHYRES > OUTHYRE
OUTHYRING > OUTHYRE
OUTING *n* leisure trip
OUTINGS > OUTING
OUTJEST *vb* exceed in jesting
OUTJESTED > OUTJEST
OUTJESTS > OUTJEST
OUTJET *n* projecting part
OUTJETS > OUTJET
OUTJINX *vb* exceed in jinxing
OUTJINXED > OUTJINX
OUTJINXES > OUTJINX
OUTJOCKEY *vb* outwit by deception
OUTJUGGLE *vb* surpass at juggling
OUTJUMP *vb* jump higher or farther than
OUTJUMPED > OUTJUMP
OUTJUMPS > OUTJUMP
OUTJUT *vb* jut out ▷ *n* projecting part
OUTJUTS > OUTJUT
OUTJUTTED > OUTJUT
OUTKEEP *vb* beat or surpass at keeping
OUTKEEPS > OUTKEEP
OUTKEPT > OUTKEEP
OUTKICK *vb* exceed in kicking
OUTKICKED > OUTKICK
OUTKICKS > OUTKICK
OUTKILL *vb* exceed in killing
OUTKILLED > OUTKILL
OUTKILLS > OUTKILL
OUTKISS *vb* exceed in kissing
OUTKISSED > OUTKISS
OUTKISSES > OUTKISS
OUTLAID > OUTLAY
OUTLAIN > OUTLAY
OUTLAND *adj* outlying or distant ▷ *n* outlying areas of a country or region
OUTLANDER *n* foreigner or stranger
OUTLANDS > OUTLAND
OUTLASH *n* sudden attack
OUTLASHES > OUTLASH
OUTLAST *vb* last longer than
OUTLASTED > OUTLAST
OUTLASTS > OUTLAST
OUTLAUGH *vb* laugh longer or louder than
OUTLAUGHS > OUTLAUGH
OUTLAUNCE *same as* > OUTLAUNCH
OUTLAUNCH *vb* send out
OUTLAW *n* criminal deprived of legal protection, bandit ▷ *vb* make illegal
OUTLAWED > OUTLAW
OUTLAWING > OUTLAW
OUTLAWRY *n* act of outlawing or the state of being outlawed
OUTLAWS > OUTLAW
OUTLAY *n* expenditure ▷ *vb* spend (money)
OUTLAYING > OUTLAY
OUTLAYS > OUTLAY
OUTLEAD *vb* be better leader than
OUTLEADS > OUTLEAD
OUTLEAP *vb* leap higher or farther than
OUTLEAPED > OUTLEAP
OUTLEAPS > OUTLEAP
OUTLEAPT > OUTLEAP
OUTLEARN *vb* exceed in learning
OUTLEARNS > OUTLEARN
OUTLEARNT > OUTLEARN
OUTLED > OUTLEAD
OUTLER *n* farm animal kept out of doors
OUTLERS > OUTLER
OUTLET *n* means of expressing emotion
OUTLETS > OUTLET
OUTLIE *vb* lie outside a particular place
OUTLIED > OUTLIE
OUTLIER *n* outcrop of rocks that is entirely surrounded by older rocks
OUTLIERS > OUTLIER
OUTLIES > OUTLIE
OUTLINE *n* short general explanation ▷ *vb* summarize
OUTLINEAR > OUTLINE
OUTLINED > OUTLINE
OUTLINER > OUTLINE
OUTLINERS > OUTLINE
OUTLINES > OUTLINE
OUTLINING > OUTLINE
OUTLIVE *vb* live longer than
OUTLIVED > OUTLIVE
OUTLIVER > OUTLIVE
OUTLIVERS > OUTLIVE
OUTLIVES > OUTLIVE
OUTLIVING > OUTLIVE
OUTLOOK *n* attitude ▷ *vb* look out
OUTLOOKED > OUTLOOK
OUTLOOKS > OUTLOOK
OUTLOVE *vb* exceed in loving
OUTLOVED > OUTLOVE
OUTLOVES > OUTLOVE
OUTLOVING > OUTLOVE
OUTLUSTRE *vb* outshine
OUTLYING *adj* distant from the main area
OUTMAN *vb* surpass in manpower
OUTMANNED > OUTMAN
OUTMANS > OUTMAN
OUTMANTLE *vb* be better dressed than
OUTMARCH *vb* exceed in marching
OUTMASTER *vb* surpass
OUTMATCH *vb* surpass or outdo (someone)
OUTMODE *vb* make unfashionable
OUTMODED *adj* no longer fashionable or accepted
OUTMODES > OUTMODE
OUTMODING > OUTMODE
OUTMOST *another word for* > OUTERMOST
OUTMOVE *vb* move faster o[r] better than
OUTMOVED > OUTMOVE
OUTMOVES > OUTMOVE
OUTMOVING > OUTMOVE
OUTMUSCLE *vb* dominate [by] physical strength
OUTNAME *vb* be more notorious than
OUTNAMED > OUTNAME
OUTNAMES > OUTNAME
OUTNAMING > OUTNAME
OUTNESS *n* state or qualit[y] of being external
OUTNESSES > OUTNESS
OUTNIGHT *vb* refer to nigh[t] more often than
OUTNIGHTS > OUTNIGHT
OUTNUMBER *vb* exceed in number
OUTOFFICE *n* outbuilding
OUTPACE *vb* go faster tha[n] (someone)
OUTPACED > OUTPACE
OUTPACES > OUTPACE
OUTPACING > OUTPACE
OUTPAINT *vb* exceed in painting
OUTPAINTS > OUTPAINT
OUTPART *n* remote region

UTPARTS > OUTPART
UTPASS *vb* exceed in passing
UTPASSED > OUTPASS
UTPASSES > OUTPASS
UTPEEP *vb* peep out
UTPEEPED > OUTPEEP
UTPEEPS > OUTPEEP
UTPEER *vb* surpass
UTPEERED > OUTPEER
UTPEERS > OUTPEER
UTPEOPLE *vb* rid a country of its people
UTPITCH *vb* exceed in pitching
UTPITIED > OUTPITY
UTPITIES > OUTPITY
UTPITY *vb* exceed in pitying
UTPLACE *vb* find job for ex-employee
UTPLACED > OUTPLACE
UTPLACER > OUTPLACE
UTPLACES > OUTPLACE
UTPLAN *vb* exceed in planning
UTPLANS > OUTPLAN
UTPLAY *vb* perform better than one's opponent in a sport or game
UTPLAYED > OUTPLAY
UTPLAYS > OUTPLAY
UTPLOD *vb* exceed in plotting
UTPLODS > OUTPLOD
UTPLOT *vb* exceed in plotting
UTPLOTS > OUTPLOT
UTPOINT *vb* score more points than
UTPOINTS > OUTPOINT
UTPOLL *vb* win more votes than
UTPOLLED > OUTPOLL
UTPOLLS > OUTPOLL
UTPORT *n* isolated fishing village, esp in Newfoundland
UTPORTER *n* inhabitant or native of a Newfoundland outport
UTPORTS > OUTPORT
UTPOST *n* outlying settlement
UTPOSTS > OUTPOST
UTPOUR *n* act of flowing or pouring out ▷ *vb* pour or cause to pour out freely or rapidly
UTPOURED > OUTPOUR
UTPOURER > OUTPOUR
UTPOURS > OUTPOUR
UTPOWER *vb* have more power than
UTPOWERS > OUTPOWER
UTPRAY *vb* exceed in praying
UTPRAYED > OUTPRAY
UTPRAYS > OUTPRAY
UTPREACH *vb* outdo in preaching
UTPREEN *vb* exceed in preening
UTPREENS > OUTPREEN
OUTPRESS *vb* exceed in pressing
OUTPRICE *vb* sell at better price than
OUTPRICED > OUTPRICE
OUTPRICES > OUTPRICE
OUTPRIZE *vb* prize more highly than
OUTPRIZED > OUTPRIZE
OUTPRIZES > OUTPRIZE
OUTPULL *vb* exceed in pulling
OUTPULLED > OUTPULL
OUTPULLS > OUTPULL
OUTPUNCH *vb* punch better than
OUTPUPIL *n* student sent to a different school to the one he or she would normally attend
OUTPUPILS > OUTPUPIL
OUTPURSUE *vb* pursue farther than
OUTPUSH *vb* exceed in pushing
OUTPUSHED > OUTPUSH
OUTPUSHES > OUTPUSH
OUTPUT *n* amount produced ▷ *vb* produce (data) at the end of a process
OUTPUTS > OUTPUT
OUTPUTTED > OUTPUT
OUTQUOTE *vb* exceed in quoting
OUTQUOTED > OUTQUOTE
OUTQUOTES > OUTQUOTE
OUTRACE *vb* surpass in racing
OUTRACED > OUTRACE
OUTRACES > OUTRACE
OUTRACING > OUTRACE
OUTRAGE *n* great moral indignation ▷ *vb* offend morally
OUTRAGED > OUTRAGE
OUTRAGES > OUTRAGE
OUTRAGING > OUTRAGE
OUTRAISE *vb* raise more money than
OUTRAISED > OUTRAISE
OUTRAISES > OUTRAISE
OUTRAN > OUTRUN
OUTRANCE *n* furthest extreme
OUTRANCES > OUTRANCE
OUTRANG > OUTRING
OUTRANGE *vb* have a greater range than
OUTRANGED > OUTRANGE
OUTRANGES > OUTRANGE
OUTRANK *vb* be of higher rank than (someone)
OUTRANKED > OUTRANK
OUTRANKS > OUTRANK
OUTRATE *vb* offer better rate than
OUTRATED > OUTRATE
OUTRATES > OUTRATE
OUTRATING > OUTRATE
OUTRAVE *vb* outdo in raving
OUTRAVED > OUTRAVE
OUTRAVES > OUTRAVE
OUTRAVING > OUTRAVE
OUTRE *adj* shockingly eccentric
OUTREACH *vb* surpass in reach ▷ *n* act or process of reaching out
OUTREAD *vb* outdo in reading
OUTREADS > OUTREAD
OUTREASON *vb* surpass in reasoning
OUTRECKON *vb* surpass in reckoning
OUTRED *vb* be redder than
OUTREDDED > OUTRED
OUTREDDEN *same as* > OUTRED
OUTREDS > OUTRED
OUTREIGN *vb* reign for longer than
OUTREIGNS > OUTREIGN
OUTRELIEF *n* aid given outdoors
OUTREMER *n* land overseas
OUTREMERS > OUTREMER
OUTRIDDEN > OUTRIDE
OUTRIDE *vb* outdo by riding faster, farther, or better than ▷ *n* extra unstressed syllable within a metrical foot
OUTRIDER *n* motorcyclist acting as an escort
OUTRIDERS > OUTRIDER
OUTRIDES > OUTRIDE
OUTRIDING > OUTRIDE
OUTRIG *vb* supply with outfit
OUTRIGGED > OUTRIG
OUTRIGGER *n* stabilizing frame projecting from a boat
OUTRIGHT *adv* absolute(ly) ▷ *adj* complete
OUTRIGS > OUTRIG
OUTRING *vb* exceed in ringing
OUTRINGS > OUTRING
OUTRIVAL *vb* surpass
OUTRIVALS > OUTRIVAL
OUTRO *n* instrumental passage that concludes a piece of music
OUTROAR *vb* roar louder than
OUTROARED > OUTROAR
OUTROARS > OUTROAR
OUTROCK *vb* outdo in rocking
OUTROCKED > OUTROCK
OUTROCKS > OUTROCK
OUTRODE > OUTRIDE
OUTROLL *vb* exceed in rolling
OUTROLLED > OUTROLL
OUTROLLS > OUTROLL
OUTROOP *n* auction
OUTROOPER > OUTROOP
OUTROOPS > OUTROOP
OUTROOT *vb* root out
OUTROOTED > OUTROOT
OUTROOTS > OUTROOT
OUTROPE *same as* > OUTROOP
OUTROPER > OUTROPE
OUTROPERS > OUTROPE
OUTROPES > OUTROPE
OUTROS > OUTRO
OUTROW *vb* outdo in rowing
OUTROWED > OUTROW
OUTROWING > OUTROW
OUTROWS > OUTROW
OUTRUN *vb* run faster than
OUTRUNG > OUTRING
OUTRUNNER *n* attendant who runs in front of a carriage, etc
OUTRUNS > OUTRUN
OUTRUSH *n* flowing or rushing out ▷ *vb* rush out
OUTRUSHED > OUTRUSH
OUTRUSHES > OUTRUSH
OUTS > OUT
OUTSAID > OUTSAY
OUTSAIL *vb* sail better than
OUTSAILED > OUTSAIL
OUTSAILS > OUTSAIL
OUTSANG > OUTSING
OUTSAT > OUTSIT
OUTSAVOR *vb* exceed in savouring
OUTSAVORS > OUTSAVOR
OUTSAW > OUTSEE
OUTSAY *vb* say something out loud
OUTSAYING > OUTSAY
OUTSAYS > OUTSAY
OUTSCHEME *vb* outdo in scheming
OUTSCOLD *vb* outdo in scolding
OUTSCOLDS > OUTSCOLD
OUTSCOOP *vb* outdo in achieving scoops
OUTSCOOPS > OUTSCOOP
OUTSCORE *vb* score more than
OUTSCORED > OUTSCORE
OUTSCORES > OUTSCORE
OUTSCORN *vb* defy with scorn
OUTSCORNS > OUTSCORN
OUTSCREAM *vb* scream louder than
OUTSEE *vb* exceed in seeing
OUTSEEING > OUTSEE
OUTSEEN > OUTSEE
OUTSEES > OUTSEE
OUTSELL *vb* be sold in greater quantities than
OUTSELLS > OUTSELL
OUTSERT *another word for* > WRAPROUND
OUTSERTS > OUTSERT
OUTSERVE *vb* serve better at tennis than
OUTSERVED > OUTSERVE
OUTSERVES > OUTSERVE
OUTSET *n* beginning
OUTSETS > OUTSET
OUTSHAME *vb* greatly shame
OUTSHAMED > OUTSHAME
OUTSHAMES > OUTSHAME
OUTSHINE *vb* surpass (someone) in excellence
OUTSHINED > OUTSHINE
OUTSHINES > OUTSHINE
OUTSHONE > OUTSHINE

OUTSHOOT *vb* surpass or excel in shooting ▷ *n* thing that projects or shoots out
OUTSHOOTS > OUTSHOOT
OUTSHOT > OUTSHOOT *n* projecting part
OUTSHOTS > OUTSHOT
OUTSHOUT *vb* shout louder than
OUTSHOUTS > OUTSHOUT
OUTSIDE *adv* indicating movement to or position on the exterior ▷ *adj* unlikely ▷ *n* external area or surface
OUTSIDER *n* person outside a specific group
OUTSIDERS > OUTSIDER
OUTSIDES > OUTSIDE
OUTSIGHT *n* power of seeing
OUTSIGHTS > OUTSIGHT
OUTSIN *vb* sin more than
OUTSING *vb* sing better or louder than
OUTSINGS > OUTSING
OUTSINNED > OUTSIN
OUTSINS > OUTSIN
OUTSIT *vb* sit longer than
OUTSITS > OUTSIT
OUTSIZE *adj* larger than normal ▷ *n* outsize garment
OUTSIZED *same as* > OUTSIZE
OUTSIZES > OUTSIZE
OUTSKATE *vb* skate better than
OUTSKATED > OUTSKATE
OUTSKATES > OUTSKATE
OUTSKIRT *singular of* > OUTSKIRTS
OUTSKIRTS *pl n* outer areas, esp of a town
OUTSLEEP *vb* sleep longer than
OUTSLEEPS > OUTSLEEP
OUTSLEPT > OUTSLEEP
OUTSLICK *vb* outsmart
OUTSLICKS > OUTSLICK
OUTSMART *vb* outwit
OUTSMARTS > OUTSMART
OUTSMELL *vb* surpass in smelling
OUTSMELLS > OUTSMELL
OUTSMELT > OUTSMELL
OUTSMILE *vb* outdo in smiling
OUTSMILED > OUTSMILE
OUTSMILES > OUTSMILE
OUTSMOKE *vb* smoke more than
OUTSMOKED > OUTSMOKE
OUTSMOKES > OUTSMOKE
OUTSNORE *vb* outdo in snoring
OUTSNORED > OUTSNORE
OUTSNORES > OUTSNORE
OUTSOAR *vb* fly higher than
OUTSOARED > OUTSOAR
OUTSOARS > OUTSOAR
OUTSOLD > OUTSELL
OUTSOLE *n* outermost sole of a shoe
OUTSOLES > OUTSOLE
OUTSOURCE *vb* subcontract (work) to another company
OUTSPAN *vb* relax
OUTSPANS > OUTSPAN
OUTSPEAK *vb* speak better or louder than
OUTSPEAKS > OUTSPEAK
OUTSPED > OUTSPEED
OUTSPEED *vb* go faster than
OUTSPEEDS > OUTSPEED
OUTSPELL *vb* exceed at spelling
OUTSPELLS > OUTSPELL
OUTSPELT > OUTSPELL
OUTSPEND *vb* spend more than
OUTSPENDS > OUTSPEND
OUTSPENT > OUTSPEND
OUTSPOKE > OUTSPEAK
OUTSPOKEN *adj* tending to say what one thinks
OUTSPORT *vb* sport in excess of
OUTSPORTS > OUTSPORT
OUTSPRANG > OUTSPRING
OUTSPREAD *adj* spread or stretched out as far as possible ▷ *vb* spread out or cause to spread out ▷ *n* spreading out
OUTSPRING *vb* spring out
OUTSPRINT *vb* run faster than (someone)
OUTSPRUNG > OUTSPRING
OUTSTAND *vb* be outstanding or excel
OUTSTANDS > OUTSTAND
OUTSTARE *vb* stare longer than
OUTSTARED > OUTSTARE
OUTSTARES > OUTSTARE
OUTSTART *vb* jump out ▷ *n* outset
OUTSTARTS > OUTSTART
OUTSTATE *vb* surpass in stating
OUTSTATED > OUTSTATE
OUTSTATES > OUTSTATE
OUTSTAY *vb* overstay
OUTSTAYED > OUTSTAY
OUTSTAYS > OUTSTAY
OUTSTEER *vb* steer better than
OUTSTEERS > OUTSTEER
OUTSTEP *vb* step farther than
OUTSTEPS > OUTSTEP
OUTSTOOD > OUTSTAND
OUTSTRAIN *vb* strain too much
OUTSTRIDE *vb* surpass in striding
OUTSTRIKE *vb* exceed in striking
OUTSTRIP *vb* surpass
OUTSTRIPS > OUTSTRIP
OUTSTRIVE *vb* strive harder than
OUTSTRODE > OUTSTRIDE
OUTSTROKE *n* outward stroke
OUTSTROVE > OUTSTRIVE
OUTSTRUCK > OUTSTRIKE
OUTSTUDY *vb* outdo in studying
OUTSTUNT *vb* outdo in performing stunts
OUTSTUNTS > OUTSTUNT
OUTSULK *vb* outdo in sulking
OUTSULKED > OUTSULK
OUTSULKS > OUTSULK
OUTSUM *vb* add up to more than
OUTSUMMED > OUTSUM
OUTSUMS > OUTSUM
OUTSUNG > OUTSING
OUTSWAM > OUTSWIM
OUTSWARE > OUTSWEAR
OUTSWEAR *vb* swear more than
OUTSWEARS > OUTSWEAR
OUTSWEEP *n* outward movement of arms in swimming breaststroke
OUTSWEEPS > OUTSWEEP
OUTSWELL *vb* exceed in swelling
OUTSWELLS > OUTSWELL
OUTSWEPT *adj* curving outwards
OUTSWIM *vb* outdo in swimming
OUTSWIMS > OUTSWIM
OUTSWING *n* (in cricket) movement of a ball from leg to off through the air
OUTSWINGS > OUTSWING
OUTSWORE > OUTSWEAR
OUTSWORN > OUTSWEAR
OUTSWUM > OUTSWIM
OUTSWUNG *adj* made to curve outwards
OUTTAKE *n* unreleased take from a recording session, film, or TV programme ▷ *vb* take out
OUTTAKEN > OUTTAKE
OUTTAKES > OUTTAKE
OUTTAKING > OUTTAKE
OUTTALK *vb* talk more, longer, or louder than (someone)
OUTTALKED > OUTTALK
OUTTALKS > OUTTALK
OUTTASK *vb* assign task to staff outside organization
OUTTASKED > OUTTASK
OUTTASKS > OUTTASK
OUTTELL *vb* make known
OUTTELLS > OUTTELL
OUTTHANK *vb* outdo in thanking
OUTTHANKS > OUTTHANK
OUTTHIEVE *vb* surpass in stealing
OUTTHINK *vb* outdo in thinking
OUTTHINKS > OUTTHINK
OUTTHREW > OUTTHROW
OUTTHROB *vb* outdo in throbbing
OUTTHROBS > OUTTHROB
OUTTHROW *vb* throw better than
OUTTHROWN > OUTTHROW
OUTTHROWS > OUTTHROW
OUTTHRUST *vb* extend outwards
OUTTOLD > OUTTELL
OUTTONGUE *vb* speak louder than
OUTTOOK > OUTTAKE
OUTTOP *vb* rise higher than
OUTTOPPED > OUTTOP
OUTTOPS > OUTTOP
OUTTOWER *vb* tower over
OUTTOWERS > OUTTOWER
OUTTRADE *vb* surpass in trading
OUTTRADED > OUTTRADE
OUTTRADES > OUTTRADE
OUTTRAVEL *vb* oudo in travelling
OUTTRICK *vb* outdo in trickery
OUTTRICKS > OUTTRICK
OUTTROT *vb* exceed at trotting
OUTTROTS > OUTTROT
OUTTRUMP *vb* count for more than
OUTTRUMPS > OUTTRUMP
OUTTURN *same as* > OUTPUT
OUTTURNS > OUTTURN
OUTVALUE *vb* surpass in value
OUTVALUED > OUTVALUE
OUTVALUES > OUTVALUE
OUTVAUNT *vb* outdo in boasting
OUTVAUNTS > OUTVAUNT
OUTVENOM *vb* surpass in venomousness
OUTVENOMS > OUTVENOM
OUTVIE *vb* outdo in competition
OUTVIED > OUTVIE
OUTVIES > OUTVIE
OUTVOICE *vb* surpass in noise
OUTVOICED > OUTVOICE
OUTVOICES > OUTVOICE
OUTVOTE *vb* defeat by getting more votes than
OUTVOTED > OUTVOTE
OUTVOTER > OUTVOTE
OUTVOTERS > OUTVOTE
OUTVOTES > OUTVOTE
OUTVOTING > OUTVOTE
OUTVYING > OUTVIE
OUTWAIT *vb* wait longer than
OUTWAITED > OUTWAIT
OUTWAITS > OUTWAIT
OUTWALK *vb* walk farther or longer than
OUTWALKED > OUTWALK
OUTWALKS > OUTWALK
OUTWAR *vb* surpass or exceed in warfare
OUTWARD *same as* > OUTWARDS
OUTWARDLY *adv* in outward appearance
OUTWARDS *adv* towards the outside
OUTWARRED > OUTWAR
OUTWARS > OUTWAR

JTWASH *n* mass of gravel carried and deposited by the water derived from melting glaciers
JTWASHES > OUTWASH
JTWASTE *vb* outdo in wasting
JTWASTED > OUTWASTE
JTWASTES > OUTWASTE
JTWATCH *vb* surpass in watching
JTWEAR *vb* use up or destroy by wearing
JTWEARS > OUTWEAR
JTWEARY *vb* exhaust
JTWEED *vb* root out
JTWEEDED > OUTWEED
JTWEEDS > OUTWEED
JTWEEP *vb* outdo in weeping
JTWEEPS > OUTWEEP
JTWEIGH *vb* be more important, significant, or influential than
JTWEIGHS > OUTWEIGH
JTWELL *vb* pour out
JTWELLED > OUTWELL
JTWELLS > OUTWELL
JTWENT > OUTGO
JTWEPT > OUTWEEP
JTWHIRL *vb* surpass at whirling
JTWHIRLS > OUTWHIRL
JTWICK *vb* move one curling stone by striking with another
JTWICKED > OUTWICK
JTWICKS > OUTWICK
JTWILE *vb* surpass in cunning
JTWILED > OUTWILE
JTWILES > OUTWILE
JTWILING > OUTWILE
JTWILL *vb* demonstrate stronger will than
JTWILLED > OUTWILL
JTWILLS > OUTWILL
JTWIN *vb* get out of
JTWIND *vb* unwind
JTWINDED > OUTWIND
JTWINDS > OUTWIND
JTWING *vb* surpass in flying
JTWINGED > OUTWING
JTWINGS > OUTWING
JTWINS > OUTWIN
JTWISH *vb* surpass in wishing
JTWISHED > OUTWISH
JTWISHES > OUTWISH
JTWIT *vb* get the better of (someone) by cunning
JTWITH *prep* outside
JTWITS > OUTWIT
JTWITTED > OUTWIT
JTWON > OUTWIN
JTWORE > OUTWEAR
JTWORK *n* defences which lie outside main defensive works ▷ *vb* work better, harder, etc, than
JTWORKED > OUTWORK
JTWORKER > OUTWORK
JTWORKS > OUTWORK
OUTWORN *adj* no longer in use
OUTWORTH *vb* be more valuable than
OUTWORTHS > OUTWORTH
OUTWOUND > OUTWIND
OUTWREST *vb* extort
OUTWRESTS > OUTWREST
OUTWRIT > OUTWRITE
OUTWRITE *vb* outdo in writing
OUTWRITES > OUTWRITE
OUTWROTE > OUTWRITE
OUTYELL *vb* outdo in yelling
OUTYELLED > OUTYELL
OUTYELLS > OUTYELL
OUTYELP *vb* outdo in yelping
OUTYELPED > OUTYELP
OUTYELPS > OUTYELP
OUTYIELD *vb* yield more than
OUTYIELDS > OUTYIELD
OUVERT *adj* open
OUVERTE *feminine form of* > OUVERT
OUVRAGE *n* work
OUVRAGES > OUVRAGE
OUVRIER *n* worker
OUVRIERE *feminine form of* > OUVRIER
OUVRIERES > OUVRIERE
OUVRIERS > OUVRIER
OUZEL *n* type of bird
OUZELS > OUZEL
OUZO *n* strong aniseed-flavoured spirit from Greece
OUZOS > OUZO
OVA > OVUM
OVAL *adj* egg-shaped ▷ *n* anything that is oval in shape
OVALBUMIN *n* albumin in egg whites
OVALITIES > OVAL
OVALITY > OVAL
OVALLY > OVAL
OVALNESS > OVAL
OVALS > OVAL
OVARIAL > OVARY
OVARIAN > OVARY
OVARIES > OVARY
OVARIOLE *n* tube in insect ovary
OVARIOLES > OVARIOLE
OVARIOUS *adj* of eggs
OVARITIS *n* inflammation of an ovary
OVARY *n* female egg-producing organ
OVATE *adj* shaped like an egg ▷ *vb* give ovation
OVATED > OVATE
OVATELY > OVATE
OVATES > OVATE
OVATING > OVATE
OVATION *n* enthusiastic round of applause
OVATIONAL > OVATION
OVATIONS > OVATION
OVATOR > OVATE
OVATORS > OVATE
OVEL *n* mourner, esp during the first seven days after a death
OVELS > OVEL
OVEN *n* heated compartment or container for cooking or for drying or firing ceramics ▷ *vb* cook in an oven
OVENABLE *adj* (of food) suitable for cooking in an oven
OVENBIRD *n* type of small brownish South American bird
OVENBIRDS > OVENBIRD
OVENED > OVEN
OVENING > OVEN
OVENLIKE > OVEN
OVENPROOF *adj* able to be used in an oven
OVENS > OVEN
OVENWARE *n* heat-resistant dishes in which food can be both cooked and served
OVENWARES > OVENWARE
OVENWOOD *n* pieces of wood for burning in an oven
OVENWOODS > OVENWOOD
OVER *adv* indicating position on the top of, amount greater than, etc ▷ *adj* finished ▷ *n* (in cricket) series of six balls bowled from one end ▷ *vb* jump over
OVERABLE *adj* too able
OVERACT *vb* act in an exaggerated way
OVERACTED > OVERACT
OVERACTS > OVERACT
OVERACUTE *adj* too acute
OVERAGE *adj* beyond a specified age ▷ *n* amount beyond given limit
OVERAGED *adj* very old
OVERAGES > OVERAGE
OVERALERT *adj* abnormally alert
OVERALL *adv* in total ▷ *n* coat-shaped protective garment ▷ *adj* from one end to the other
OVERALLED *adj* wearing overalls
OVERALLS > OVERALL
OVERAPT *adj* tending excessively
OVERARCH *vb* form an arch over
OVERARM *adv* with the arm above the shoulder ▷ *adj* bowled, thrown, or performed with the arm raised above the shoulder ▷ *vb* throw (a ball) overarm
OVERARMED > OVERARM
OVERARMS > OVERARM
OVERATE > OVEREAT
OVERAWE *vb* affect (someone) with an overpowering sense of awe
OVERAWED > OVERAWE
OVERAWES > OVERAWE
OVERAWING > OVERAWE
OVERBAKE *vb* bake too long
OVERBAKED > OVERBAKE
OVERBAKES > OVERBAKE
OVERBEAR *vb* dominate or overcome
OVERBEARS > OVERBEAR
OVERBEAT *vb* beat too much
OVERBEATS > OVERBEAT
OVERBED *adj* fitting over bed
OVERBET *vb* bet too much
OVERBETS > OVERBET
OVERBID *vb* bid for more tricks than one can expect to win ▷ *n* bid higher than someone else's bid
OVERBIDS > OVERBID
OVERBIG *adj* too big
OVERBILL *vb* charge too much money
OVERBILLS > OVERBILL
OVERBITE *n* extension of the upper front teeth over the lower front teeth when the mouth is closed
OVERBITES > OVERBITE
OVERBLEW > OVERBLOW
OVERBLOW *vb* blow into (a wind instrument) with greater force than normal
OVERBLOWN *adj* excessive
OVERBLOWS > OVERBLOW
OVERBOARD *adv* from a boat into the water
OVERBOIL *vb* boil too much
OVERBOILS > OVERBOIL
OVERBOLD *adj* too bold
OVERBOOK *vb* accept too many bookings
OVERBOOKS > OVERBOOK
OVERBOOT *n* protective boot worn over an ordinary boot or shoe
OVERBOOTS > OVERBOOT
OVERBORE > OVERBEAR
OVERBORN > OVERBEAR
OVERBORNE > OVERBEAR
OVERBOUND *vb* jump over
OVERBRAKE *vb* brake too much
OVERBRED *adj* produced by too much selective breeding
OVERBREED *vb* produce by too much selective breeding
OVERBRIEF *adj* too brief
OVERBRIM *vb* overflow
OVERBRIMS > OVERBRIM
OVERBROAD *adj* not specific enough
OVERBROW *vb* hang over
OVERBROWS > OVERBROW
OVERBUILD *vb* build over or on top of
OVERBUILT > OVERBUILD
OVERBULK *vb* loom large over
OVERBULKS > OVERBULK
OVERBURN *vb* copy

information onto CD
OVERBURNS > OVERBURN
OVERBURNT > OVERBURN
OVERBUSY *adj* too busy ▷ *vb* make too busy
OVERBUY *vb* buy too much or too many
OVERBUYS > OVERBUY
OVERBY *adv* Scots expression meaning over the road or across the way
OVERCALL *n* bid higher than the preceding one ▷ *vb* bid higher than (an opponent)
OVERCALLS > OVERCALL
OVERCAME > OVERCOME
OVERCARRY *vb* carry too far or too many
OVERCAST *adj* (of the sky) covered by clouds ▷ *vb* make or become overclouded or gloomy ▷ *n* covering, as of clouds or mist
OVERCASTS > OVERCAST
OVERCATCH *vb* overtake
OVERCHEAP *adj* too cheap
OVERCHECK *n* thin leather strap attached to a horse's bit to keep its head up
OVERCHILL *vb* make too cold
OVERCIVIL *adj* too civil
OVERCLAD *adj* wearing too many clothes
OVERCLAIM *vb* claim too much
OVERCLASS *n* dominant group in society
OVERCLEAN *adj* too clean
OVERCLEAR *adj* too clear
OVERCLOSE *adj* too close
OVERCLOUD *vb* make or become covered with clouds
OVERCLOY *vb* weary with excess
OVERCLOYS > OVERCLOY
OVERCOACH *vb* coach too much
OVERCOAT *n* heavy coat
OVERCOATS > OVERCOAT
OVERCOLD *adj* too cold
OVERCOLOR *vb* colour too highly
OVERCOME *vb* gain control over after an effort
OVERCOMER > OVERCOME
OVERCOMES > OVERCOME
OVERCOOK *vb* spoil food by cooking it for too long
OVERCOOKS > OVERCOOK
OVERCOOL *vb* cool too much
OVERCOOLS > OVERCOOL
OVERCOUNT *vb* outnumber
OVERCOVER *vb* cover up
OVERCOY *adj* too modest
OVERCRAM *vb* fill too full
OVERCRAMS > OVERCRAM
OVERCRAW *same as* > OVERCROW
OVERCRAWS > OVERCRAW
OVERCROP *vb* exhaust (land) by excessive cultivation
OVERCROPS > OVERCROP
OVERCROW *vb* crow over
OVERCROWD *vb* fill with more people or things than is desirable
OVERCROWS > OVERCROW
OVERCURE *vb* take curing process too far
OVERCURED > OVERCURE
OVERCURES > OVERCURE
OVERCUT *vb* cut too much
OVERCUTS > OVERCUT
OVERDARE *vb* dare too much
OVERDARED > OVERDARE
OVERDARES > OVERDARE
OVERDATED *adj* outdated
OVERDEAR *adj* too dear
OVERDECK *n* upper deck
OVERDECKS > OVERDECK
OVERDID > OVERDO
OVERDIGHT *adj* covered up
OVERDO *vb* do to excess
OVERDOER > OVERDO
OVERDOERS > OVERDO
OVERDOES > OVERDO
OVERDOG *n* person or side in an advantageous position
OVERDOGS > OVERDOG
OVERDOING > OVERDO
OVERDONE > OVERDO
OVERDOSE *n* excessive dose of a drug ▷ *vb* take an overdose
OVERDOSED > OVERDOSE
OVERDOSES > OVERDOSE
OVERDRAFT *n* overdrawing
OVERDRANK > OVERDRINK
OVERDRAW *vb* withdraw more money than is in (one's bank account)
OVERDRAWN > OVERDRAW
OVERDRAWS > OVERDRAW
OVERDRESS *vb* dress (oneself or another) too elaborately or finely ▷ *n* dress that may be worn over a jumper, blouse, etc
OVERDREW > OVERDRAW
OVERDRIED > OVERDRY
OVERDRIES > OVERDRY
OVERDRINK *vb* drink too much alcohol
OVERDRIVE *n* very high gear in a motor vehicle
OVERDROVE > OVERDRIVE
OVERDRUNK > OVERDRINK
OVERDRY *vb* dry too much
OVERDUB *vb* add (new sounds) to a tape so that the old and the new sounds can be heard ▷ *n* sound or series of sounds added by this method
OVERDUBS > OVERDUB
OVERDUE *adj* still due after the time allowed
OVERDUST *vb* dust too much
OVERDUSTS > OVERDUST
OVERDYE *vb* dye (a fabric, yarn, etc) excessively
OVERDYED > OVERDYE
OVERDYER > OVERDYE
OVERDYERS > OVERDYE
OVERDYES > OVERDYE
OVEREAGER *adj* excessively eager or keen
OVEREASY *adj* too easy
OVEREAT *vb* eat more than is necessary or healthy
OVEREATEN > OVEREAT
OVEREATER > OVEREAT
OVEREATS > OVEREAT
OVERED > OVER
OVEREDIT *vb* edit too much
OVEREDITS > OVEREDIT
OVEREGG *vb* exaggerate absurdly
OVEREGGED > OVEREGG
OVEREGGS > OVEREGG
OVEREMOTE *vb* emote too much
OVEREXERT *vb* exhaust or injure (oneself) by doing too much
OVEREYE *vb* survey
OVEREYED > OVEREYE
OVEREYES > OVEREYE
OVEREYING > OVEREYE
OVERFALL *n* turbulent stretch of water caused by marine currents over an underwater ridge
OVERFALLS > OVERFALL
OVERFAR *adv* too far
OVERFAST *adj* too fast
OVERFAT *adj* too fat
OVERFAVOR *vb* favour too much
OVERFEAR *vb* fear too much
OVERFEARS > OVERFEAR
OVERFED > OVERFEED
OVERFEED *vb* give (a person, plant, or animal) more food than is necessary or healthy
OVERFEEDS > OVERFEED
OVERFELL > OVERFALL
OVERFILL *vb* put more into (something) than there is room for
OVERFILLS > OVERFILL
OVERFINE *adj* too fine
OVERFISH *vb* fish too much
OVERFIT *adj* too fit
OVERFLEW > OVERFLY
OVERFLIES > OVERFLY
OVERFLOOD *vb* flood excessively
OVERFLOW *vb* flow over ▷ *n* something that overflows
OVERFLOWN > OVERFLY
OVERFLOWS > OVERFLOW
OVERFLUSH *adj* too flush
OVERFLY *vb* fly over (a territory) or past (a point)
OVERFOCUS *vb* focus too much
OVERFOLD *n* fold in which one or both limbs have been inclined more than 90° from their original orientation
OVERFOLDS > OVERFOLD
OVERFOND *adj* excessively keen (on)
OVERFOUL *adj* too foul
OVERFRANK *adj* too frank
OVERFREE *adj* too forward
OVERFULL *adj* excessively full
OVERFUND *vb* supply with too much money
OVERFUNDS > OVERFUND
OVERFUSSY *adj* too fussy
OVERGALL *vb* make sore all over
OVERGALLS > OVERGALL
OVERGANG *vb* dominate
OVERGANGS > OVERGANG
OVERGAVE > OVERGIVE
OVERGEAR *vb* cause (a company) to have too high a proportion of loan stock
OVERGEARS > OVERGEAR
OVERGET *vb* overtake
OVERGETS > OVERGET
OVERGILD *vb* gild too much
OVERGILDS > OVERGILD
OVERGILT > OVERGILD
OVERGIRD *vb* gird too tightly
OVERGIRDS > OVERGIRD
OVERGIRT > OVERGIRD
OVERGIVE *vb* give up
OVERGIVEN > OVERGIVE
OVERGIVES > OVERGIVE
OVERGLAD *adj* too glad
OVERGLAZE *adj* (of decoration or colours) applied to porcelain above the glaze
OVERGLOOM *vb* make gloomy
OVERGO *vb* go beyond
OVERGOAD *vb* goad too much
OVERGOADS > OVERGOAD
OVERGOES > OVERGO
OVERGOING > OVERGO
OVERGONE > OVERGO
OVERGORGE *vb* overeat
OVERGOT > OVERGET
OVERGRADE *vb* grade too highly
OVERGRAIN *vb* apply grain texture to
OVERGRASS *vb* grow grass on top of
OVERGRAZE *vb* graze (land) too intensively
OVERGREAT *adj* too great
OVERGREEN *vb* cover with vegetation
OVERGREW > OVERGROW
OVERGROW *vb* grow over or across (an area, path, lawn, etc)
OVERGROWN > OVERGROW
OVERGROWS > OVERGROW
OVERHAILE *vb* pull over
OVERHAIR *n* outer coat of animal
OVERHAIRS > OVERHAIR
OVERHALE *same as* > OVERHAILE
OVERHALED > OVERHALE
OVERHALES > OVERHALE

OVERHAND adj thrown or performed with the hand raised above the shoulder ▷ adv with the hand above the shoulder ▷ vb sew with the thread passing over two edges in one direction
OVERHANDS > OVERHAND
OVERHANG vb project beyond something ▷ n overhanging part
OVERHANGS > OVERHANG
OVERHAPPY adj too happy
OVERHARD adj too hard
OVERHASTE n excessive haste
OVERHASTY > OVERHASTE
OVERHATE vb hate too much
OVERHATED > OVERHATE
OVERHATES > OVERHATE
OVERHAUL vb examine and repair ▷ n examination and repair
OVERHAULS > OVERHAUL
OVERHEAD adj above one's head ▷ adv over or above head height ▷ n stroke in racket games played from above head height
OVERHEADS pl n general cost of maintaining a business
OVERHEAP vb supply too much
OVERHEAPS > OVERHEAP
OVERHEAR vb hear (a speaker or remark) unintentionally
OVERHEARD > OVERHEAR
OVERHEARS > OVERHEAR
OVERHEAT vb make or become excessively hot ▷ n condition of being overheated
OVERHEATS > OVERHEAT
OVERHELD > OVERHOLD
OVERHENT vb overtake
OVERHENTS > OVERHENT
OVERHIGH adj too high
OVERHIT vb hit too strongly
OVERHITS > OVERHIT
OVERHOLD vb value too highly
OVERHOLDS > OVERHOLD
OVERHOLY adj too holy
OVERHONOR vb honour too highly
OVERHOPE vb hope too much
OVERHOPED > OVERHOPE
OVERHOPES > OVERHOPE
OVERHOT adj too hot
OVERHUNG > OVERHANG
OVERHUNT vb hunt too much
OVERHUNTS > OVERHUNT
OVERHYPE vb hype too much
OVERHYPED > OVERHYPE
OVERHYPES > OVERHYPE
OVERIDLE adj too idle
OVERING > OVER
OVERINKED adj printed using too much ink
OVERISSUE vb issue (shares, banknotes, etc) in excess of demand or ability to pay ▷ n shares, banknotes, etc, thus issued
OVERJOY vb give great delight to
OVERJOYED adj extremely pleased
OVERJOYS > OVERJOY
OVERJUMP vb jump too far
OVERJUMPS > OVERJUMP
OVERJUST adj too just
OVERKEEN adj too keen
OVERKEEP vb keep too long
OVERKEEPS > OVERKEEP
OVERKEPT > OVERKEEP
OVERKEST same as > OVERCAST
OVERKILL n treatment that is greater than required
OVERKILLS > OVERKILL
OVERKIND adj too kind
OVERKING n supreme king
OVERKINGS > OVERKING
OVERKNEE adj reaching to above knee
OVERLABOR vb spend too much work on
OVERLADE vb overburden
OVERLADED > OVERLADE
OVERLADEN > OVERLADE
OVERLADES > OVERLADE
OVERLAID > OVERLAY
OVERLAIN > OVERLIE
OVERLAND adv by land ▷ vb drive (cattle or sheep) overland
OVERLANDS > OVERLAND
OVERLAP vb share part of the same space or period of time (as) ▷ n area overlapping
OVERLAPS > OVERLAP
OVERLARD vb cover with lard
OVERLARDS > OVERLARD
OVERLARGE adj excessively large
OVERLATE adj too late
OVERLAX adj too lax
OVERLAY vb cover with a thin layer ▷ n something that is laid over something else
OVERLAYS > OVERLAY
OVERLEAF adv on the back of the current page
OVERLEAP vb leap too far
OVERLEAPS > OVERLEAP
OVERLEAPT > OVERLEAP
OVERLEARN vb study too intensely
OVERLEND vb lend too much
OVERLENDS > OVERLEND
OVERLENT > OVERLEND
OVERLET vb let to too many
OVERLETS > OVERLET
OVERLEWD adj too lewd
OVERLIE vb lie on or cover (something or someone)
OVERLIER > OVERLIE
OVERLIERS > OVERLIE
OVERLIES > OVERLIE
OVERLIGHT vb illuminate too brightly
OVERLIT > OVERLIGHT
OVERLIVE vb live longer than (another person)
OVERLIVED > OVERLIVE
OVERLIVES > OVERLIVE
OVERLOAD vb put too large a load on or in ▷ n excessive load
OVERLOADS > OVERLOAD
OVERLOCK vb sew fabric with interlocking stitch
OVERLOCKS > OVERLOCK
OVERLONG adj too or excessively long
OVERLOOK vb fail to notice ▷ n high place affording a view
OVERLOOKS > OVERLOOK
OVERLORD n supreme lord or master
OVERLORDS > OVERLORD
OVERLOUD adj too loud
OVERLOVE vb love too much
OVERLOVED > OVERLOVE
OVERLOVES > OVERLOVE
OVERLUSH adj too lush
OVERLUSTY adj too lusty
OVERLY adv excessively
OVERLYING > OVERLIE
OVERMAN vb provide with too many staff ▷ n man who oversees others
OVERMANS > OVERMAN
OVERMANY adj too many
OVERMAST vb provide mast that is too big
OVERMASTS > OVERMAST
OVERMATCH vb be more than a match for ▷ n person superior in ability
OVERMEEK adj too meek
OVERMELT vb melt too much
OVERMELTS > OVERMELT
OVERMEN > OVERMAN
OVERMERRY adj very merry
OVERMILD adj too mild
OVERMILK vb milk too much
OVERMILKS > OVERMILK
OVERMINE vb mine too much
OVERMINED > OVERMINE
OVERMINES > OVERMINE
OVERMIX vb mix too much
OVERMIXED > OVERMIX
OVERMIXES > OVERMIX
OVERMOUNT vb surmount
OVERMUCH adj too much ▷ n excessive amount
OVERNAME vb repeat (someone's) name
OVERNAMED > OVERNAME
OVERNAMES > OVERNAME
OVERNEAR adj too near
OVERNEAT adj too neat
OVERNET vb cover with net
OVERNETS > OVERNET
OVERNEW adj too new
OVERNICE adj too fastidious, precise, etc
OVERNIGHT adv (taking place) during one night ▷ adj done in, occurring in, or lasting the night ▷ vb stay the night
OVERPACK vb pack too much
OVERPACKS > OVERPACK
OVERPAGE same as > OVERLEAF
OVERPAID > OVERPAY
OVERPAINT vb apply too much paint
OVERPART vb give an actor too difficult a role
OVERPARTS > OVERPART
OVERPASS vb pass over, through, or across
OVERPAST > OVERPASS
OVERPAY vb pay (someone) at too high a rate
OVERPAYS > OVERPAY
OVERPEDAL vb use piano pedal too much
OVERPEER vb look down over
OVERPEERS > OVERPEER
OVERPERCH vb fly up to perch on
OVERPERT adj too insolent
OVERPITCH vb bowl (a cricket ball) so that it pitches too close to the stumps
OVERPLAID n plaid in double layer
OVERPLAN vb plan excessively
OVERPLANS > OVERPLAN
OVERPLANT vb plant more than is necessary
OVERPLAST adj put above
OVERPLAY same as > OVERACT
OVERPLAYS > OVERPLAY
OVERPLIED > OVERPLY
OVERPLIES > OVERPLY
OVERPLOT vb plot onto existing graph or map
OVERPLOTS > OVERPLOT
OVERPLUS n surplus or excess quantity
OVERPLY vb ply too much
OVERPOISE vb weigh more than
OVERPOST vb hurry over
OVERPOSTS > OVERPOST
OVERPOWER vb subdue or overcome (someone)
OVERPRESS vb oppress
OVERPRICE vb put too high a price on
OVERPRINT vb print (additional matter) onto (something already printed) ▷ n additional matter printed onto something already printed

OVERPRIZE *vb* prize too highly
OVERPROOF *adj* containing more alcohol than standard spirit
OVERPROUD *adj* too proud
OVERPUMP *vb* pump too much
OVERPUMPS > OVERPUMP
OVERQUICK *adj* too quick
OVERRACK *vb* strain too much
OVERRACKS > OVERRACK
OVERRAKE *vb* rake over
OVERRAKED > OVERRAKE
OVERRAKES > OVERRAKE
OVERRAN > OVERRUN
OVERRANK *adj* too rank
OVERRASH *adj* too rash
OVERRATE *vb* have too high an opinion of
OVERRATED > OVERRATE
OVERRATES > OVERRATE
OVERREACH *vb* defeat or thwart (oneself) by attempting to do or gain too much
OVERREACT *vb* react more strongly than is necessary
OVERREAD *vb* read over
OVERREADS > OVERREAD
OVERRED *vb* paint over in red
OVERREDS > OVERRED
OVERREN *same as* > OVERRUN
OVERRENS > OVERREN
OVERRICH *adj* (of food) excessively flavoursome or fatty
OVERRIDE *vb* overrule ▷ *n* device or system that can override an automatic control
OVERRIDER > OVERRIDE
OVERRIDES > OVERRIDE
OVERRIFE *adj* too rife
OVERRIGID *adj* too rigid
OVERRIPE *adj* (of a fruit or vegetable) so ripe that it has started to decay
OVERRIPEN *vb* become overripe
OVERROAST *vb* roast too long
OVERRODE > OVERRIDE
OVERRUDE *adj* very rude
OVERRUFF *vb* defeat trump card by playing higher trump
OVERRUFFS > OVERRUFF
OVERRULE *vb* reverse the decision of (a person with less power)
OVERRULED > OVERRULE
OVERRULER > OVERRULE
OVERRULES > OVERRULE
OVERRUN *vb* conquer rapidly ▷ *n* act or an instance of overrunning
OVERRUNS > OVERRUN
OVERS > OVER
OVERSAD *adj* too sad
OVERSAIL *vb* project beyond
OVERSAILS > OVERSAIL
OVERSALE *n* selling of more than is available
OVERSALES > OVERSALE
OVERSALT *vb* put too much salt in
OVERSALTS > OVERSALT
OVERSAUCE *vb* put too much sauce on
OVERSAVE *vb* put too much money in savings
OVERSAVED > OVERSAVE
OVERSAVES > OVERSAVE
OVERSAW > OVERSEE
OVERSCALE *adj* at higher scale than standard
OVERSCORE *vb* cancel by drawing a line or lines over or through
OVERSEA *same as* > OVERSEAS
OVERSEAS *adj* to, of, or from a distant country ▷ *adv* across the sea ▷ *n* foreign country or foreign countries collectively
OVERSEE *vb* watch over from a position of authority
OVERSEED *vb* plant too much seed in
OVERSEEDS > OVERSEED
OVERSEEN > OVERSEE
OVERSEER *n* person who oversees others, esp workmen
OVERSEERS > OVERSEER
OVERSEES > OVERSEE
OVERSELL *vb* exaggerate the merits or abilities of
OVERSELLS > OVERSELL
OVERSET *vb* disturb or upset
OVERSETS > OVERSET
OVERSEW *vb* sew (two edges) with stitches that pass over them both
OVERSEWED > OVERSEW
OVERSEWN > OVERSEW
OVERSEWS > OVERSEW
OVERSEXED *adj* more interested in sex than is thought decent
OVERSHADE *vb* appear more important than
OVERSHARP *adj* too sharp
OVERSHINE *vb* shine down on
OVERSHIRT *n* shirt worn over lighter clothes
OVERSHOE *n* protective shoe worn over an ordinary shoe
OVERSHOES > OVERSHOE
OVERSHONE > OVERSHINE
OVERSHOOT *vb* go beyond (a mark or target) ▷ *n* act or instance of overshooting
OVERSHOT *adj* (of a water wheel) driven by a flow of water that passes over the wheel ▷ *n* type of fishing rod
OVERSHOTS > OVERSHOT
OVERSICK *adj* too sick
OVERSIDE *adv* over the side (of a ship) ▷ *n* top side
OVERSIDES > OVERSIDE
OVERSIGHT *n* mistake caused by not noticing something
OVERSIZE *adj* larger than the usual size ▷ *n* size larger than the usual or proper size
OVERSIZED *same as* > OVERSIZE
OVERSIZES > OVERSIZE
OVERSKIP *vb* skip over
OVERSKIPS > OVERSKIP
OVERSKIRT *n* outer skirt, esp one that reveals a decorative underskirt
OVERSLEEP *vb* sleep beyond the intended time
OVERSLEPT > OVERSLEEP
OVERSLIP *vb* slip past
OVERSLIPS > OVERSLIP
OVERSLIPT > OVERSLIP
OVERSLOW *adj* too slow
OVERSMAN *n* overseer
OVERSMEN > OVERSMAN
OVERSMOKE *vb* smoke something too much
OVERSOAK *vb* soak too much
OVERSOAKS > OVERSOAK
OVERSOFT *adj* too soft
OVERSOLD > OVERSELL
OVERSOON *adv* too soon
OVERSOUL *n* universal divine essence
OVERSOULS > OVERSOUL
OVERSOW *vb* sow again after first sowing
OVERSOWED > OVERSOW
OVERSOWN > OVERSOW
OVERSOWS > OVERSOW
OVERSPEND *vb* spend more than one can afford ▷ *n* amount by which someone or something is overspent
OVERSPENT > OVERSPEND
OVERSPICE *vb* add too much spice to
OVERSPILL *n* rehousing of people from crowded cities in smaller towns ▷ *vb* overflow
OVERSPILT > OVERSPILL
OVERSPIN *n* forward spinning motion
OVERSPINS > OVERSPIN
OVERSTAFF *vb* provide an excessive number of staff for (a factory, hotel, etc)
OVERSTAIN *vb* stain too much
OVERSTAND *vb* remain longer than
OVERSTANK > OVERSTINK
OVERSTARE *vb* outstare
OVERSTATE *vb* state too strongly
OVERSTAY *vb* stay beyond the limit or duration of
OVERSTAYS > OVERSTAY
OVERSTEER *vb* (of a vehicle to turn more sharply than is desirable or anticipated
OVERSTEP *vb* go beyond (a certain limit)
OVERSTEPS > OVERSTEP
OVERSTINK *vb* exceed in stinking
OVERSTIR *vb* stir too much
OVERSTIRS > OVERSTIR
OVERSTOCK *vb* hold or supply (a commodity) in excess of requirements
OVERSTOOD > OVERSTAND
OVERSTORY *n* highest leve of trees in a rainforest
OVERSTREW *vb* scatter ove
OVERSTUDY *vb* study too much
OVERSTUFF *vb* force too much into
OVERSTUNK > OVERSTINK
OVERSUDS *vb* produce too much lather
OVERSUP *vb* sup too much
OVERSUPS > OVERSUP
OVERSURE *adj* too sure
OVERSWAM > OVERSWIM
OVERSWAY *vb* overrule
OVERSWAYS > OVERSWAY
OVERSWEAR *vb* swear agai
OVERSWEET *adj* too sweet
OVERSWELL *vb* overflow
OVERSWIM *vb* swim across
OVERSWIMS > OVERSWIM
OVERSWING *vb* swing too much or too far
OVERSWORE > OVERSWEAR
OVERSWORN > OVERSWEAR
OVERSWUM > OVERSWIM
OVERSWUNG > OVERSWING
OVERT *adj* open, not hidde
OVERTAKE *vb* move past (a vehicle or person) travelling in the same direction
OVERTAKEN > OVERTAKE
OVERTAKES > OVERTAKE
OVERTALK *vb* talk over
OVERTALKS > OVERTALK
OVERTAME *adj* too tame
OVERTART *adj* too bitter
OVERTASK *vb* impose too heavy a task upon
OVERTASKS > OVERTASK
OVERTAX *vb* put too great a strain on
OVERTAXED > OVERTAX
OVERTAXES > OVERTAX
OVERTEACH *vb* teach too much
OVERTEEM *vb* be too full of something
OVERTEEMS > OVERTEEM
OVERTHICK *adj* too thick
OVERTHIN *adj* too thin
OVERTHINK *vb* give too much thought to
OVERTHREW > OVERTHROW
OVERTHROW *vb* defeat and replace ▷ *n* downfall, destruction
OVERTIGHT *adj* too tight

OVERTIME *adv* in addition to one's normal working hours ▷ *n* work at a regular job done in addition to regular working hours ▷ *vb* exceed the required time for (a photographic exposure)
OVERTIMED > OVERTIME
OVERTIMER > OVERTIME
OVERTIMES > OVERTIME
OVERTIMID *adj* too timid
OVERTIP *vb* give too much money as a tip
OVERTIPS > OVERTIP
OVERTIRE *vb* make too tired
OVERTIRED > OVERTIRE
OVERTIRES > OVERTIRE
OVERTLY > OVERT
OVERTNESS > OVERT
OVERTOIL *vb* work too hard
OVERTOILS > OVERTOIL
OVERTONE *n* additional meaning
OVERTONES > OVERTONE
OVERTOOK > OVERTAKE
OVERTOP *vb* exceed in height
OVERTOPS > OVERTOP
OVERTOWER *vb* tower above
OVERTRADE *vb* (of an enterprise) to trade in excess of working capital
OVERTRAIN *vb* train too much
OVERTREAT *vb* give too much medical treatment to
OVERTRICK *n* trick by which a player exceeds his contract
OVERTRIM *vb* trim too much
OVERTRIMS > OVERTRIM
OVERTRIP *vb* tread lightly over
OVERTRIPS > OVERTRIP
OVERTRUMP *vb* (in cards) play a trump higher than (one previously played to the trick)
OVERTRUST *vb* trust too much
OVERTURE *n* orchestral introduction ▷ *vb* make or present an overture to
OVERTURED > OVERTURE
OVERTURES > OVERTURE
OVERTURN *vb* turn upside down ▷ *n* act of overturning or the state of being overturned
OVERTURNS > OVERTURN
OVERTYPE *vb* type over existing text
OVERTYPED > OVERTYPE
OVERTYPES > OVERTYPE
OVERURGE *vb* urge too strongly
OVERURGED > OVERURGE
OVERURGES > OVERURGE
OVERUSE *vb* use excessively ▷ *n* excessive use
OVERUSED > OVERUSE
OVERUSES > OVERUSE
OVERUSING > OVERUSE
OVERVALUE *vb* regard (someone or something) as much more important than is the case
OVERVEIL *vb* cover over
OVERVEILS > OVERVEIL
OVERVIEW *n* general survey
OVERVIEWS > OVERVIEW
OVERVIVID *adj* too vivid
OVERVOTE *vb* vote more times than is allowed
OVERVOTED > OVERVOTE
OVERVOTES > OVERVOTE
OVERWARM *vb* make too warm
OVERWARMS > OVERWARM
OVERWARY *adj* excessively wary
OVERWASH *n* act of washing over something
OVERWATCH *vb* watch over
OVERWATER *vb* give too much water to
OVERWEAK *adj* too weak
OVERWEAR *vb* wear out
OVERWEARS > OVERWEAR
OVERWEARY *vb* make too tired
OVERWEEN *vb* think too highly of
OVERWEENS > OVERWEEN
OVERWEIGH *vb* exceed in weight
OVERWENT > OVERGO
OVERWET *vb* make too wet
OVERWETS > OVERWET
OVERWHELM *vb* overpower, esp emotionally
OVERWIDE *adj* too wide
OVERWILY *adj* too crafty
OVERWIND *vb* wind (a watch) beyond the proper limit
OVERWINDS > OVERWIND
OVERWING *vb* fly above
OVERWINGS > OVERWING
OVERWISE *adj* too wise
OVERWORD *n* repeated word or phrase
OVERWORDS > OVERWORD
OVERWORE > OVERWEAR
OVERWORK *vb* work too much ▷ *n* excessive work
OVERWORKS > OVERWORK
OVERWORN > OVERWEAR
OVERWOUND > OVERWIND
OVERWREST *vb* strain too much
OVERWRITE *vb* write (something) in an excessively ornate or prolix style
OVERWROTE > OVERWRITE
OVERYEAR *vb* keep for later year
OVERYEARS > OVERYEAR
OVERZEAL *n* excess of zeal
OVERZEALS > OVERZEAL
OVIBOS *n* type of ox
OVIBOSES > OVIBOS
OVIBOVINE > OVIBOS
OVICIDAL > OVICIDE
OVICIDE *n* killing of sheep
OVICIDES > OVICIDE
OVIDUCAL > OVIDUCT
OVIDUCT *n* tube through which eggs are conveyed from the ovary
OVIDUCTAL > OVIDUCT
OVIDUCTS > OVIDUCT
OVIFEROUS *adj* carrying or producing eggs or ova
OVIFORM *adj* shaped like an egg
OVIGEROUS *same as* > OVIFEROUS
OVINE *adj* of or like a sheep ▷ *n* member of sheep family
OVINES > OVINE
OVIPARA *n* all oviparous animals
OVIPARITY > OVIPAROUS
OVIPAROUS *adj* producing eggs that hatch outside the body of the mother
OVIPOSIT *vb* (of insects and fishes) to deposit eggs through an ovipositor
OVIPOSITS > OVIPOSIT
OVIRAPTOR *n* egg-eating dinosaur
OVISAC *n* capsule or sac, such as an ootheca, in which egg cells are produced
OVISACS > OVISAC
OVIST *n* person believing ovum contains all subsequent generations
OVISTS > OVIST
OVOID *adj* egg-shaped ▷ *n* something that is ovoid
OVOIDAL *adj* ovoid ▷ *n* something that is ovoid
OVOIDALS > OVOIDAL
OVOIDS > OVOID
OVOLI > OVOLO
OVOLO *n* convex moulding having a cross section in the form of a quarter of a circle or ellipse
OVOLOS > OVOLO
OVONIC *adj* using particular electronic storage batteries
OVONICS *n* science of ovonic equipment
OVOTESTES > OVOTESTIS
OVOTESTIS *n* reproductive organ of snails
OVULAR > OVULE
OVULARY > OVULE
OVULATE *vb* produce or release an egg cell from an ovary
OVULATED > OVULATE
OVULATES > OVULATE
OVULATING > OVULATE
OVULATION > OVULATE
OVULATORY > OVULATE
OVULE *n* plant part that contains the egg cell and becomes the seed after fertilization
OVULES > OVULE
OVUM *n* unfertilized egg cell
OW *interj* exclamation of pain
OWCHE *same as* > OUCH
OWCHES > OWCHE
OWE *vb* be obliged to pay (a sum of money) to (a person)
OWED > OWE
OWELTIES > OWELTY
OWELTY *n* equality, esp in financial transactions
OWER *Scots word for* > OVER
OWERBY *adv* over there
OWERLOUP *n* Scots word meaning encroachment
OWERLOUPS > OWERLOUP
OWES > OWE
OWING > OWE
OWL *n* night bird of prey ▷ *vb* act like an owl
OWLED > OWL
OWLER *vb* smuggler
OWLERIES > OWLERY
OWLERS > OWLER
OWLERY *n* place where owls live
OWLET *n* young or nestling owl
OWLETS > OWLET
OWLIER > OWLY
OWLIEST > OWLY
OWLING > OWL
OWLISH *adj* like an owl
OWLISHLY > OWLISH
OWLLIKE > OWL
OWLS > OWL
OWLY *same as* > OWLISH
OWN *adj* used to emphasize possession ▷ *pron* thing(s) belonging to a particular person ▷ *vb* possess
OWNABLE *adj* able to be owned
OWNED > OWN
OWNER *n* person who owns
OWNERLESS > OWNER
OWNERS > OWNER
OWNERSHIP *n* state or fact of being an owner
OWNING > OWN
OWNS > OWN
OWRE *same as* > OWER
OWRECOME *n* chorus of song
OWRECOMES > OWRECOME
OWRELAY *Scots form of* > OVERLAY
OWRELAYS > OWRELAY
OWRES > OWRE
OWREWORD *variant of* > OVERWORD
OWREWORDS > OWREWORD
OWRIE *same as* > OORIE
OWRIER > OWRIE
OWRIEST > OWRIE
OWSE *Scots form of* > OX
OWSEN *pl n Scots word for* > OXEN
OWT *dialect word for* > ANYTHING
OWTS > OWT

OX *n* castrated bull
OXACILLIN *n* antibiotic drug
OXALATE *n* salt or ester of oxalic acid ▷ *vb* treat with oxalate
OXALATED > OXALATE
OXALATES > OXALATE
OXALATING > OXALATE
OXALIC as in *oxalic acid* poisonous acid found in many plants
OXALIS *n* type of plant
OXALISES > OXALIS
OXAZEPAM *n* drug used to relieve anxiety
OXAZEPAMS > OXAZEPAM
OXAZINE *n* type of chemical compound
OXAZINES > OXAZINE
OXBLOOD *n* dark reddish-brown colour ▷ *adj* of this colour
OXBLOODS > OXBLOOD
OXBOW *n* U-shaped piece of wood fitted around the neck of a harnessed ox and attached to the yoke
OXBOWS > OXBOW
OXCART *n* cart pulled by ox
OXCARTS > OXCART
OXEN > OX
OXER *n* high fence
OXERS > OXER
OXES > OX
OXEYE *n* daisy-like flower
OXEYES > OXEYE
OXFORD *n* type of stout laced shoe with a low heel
OXFORDS > OXFORD
OXGANG *n* old measure of farmland
OXGANGS > OXGANG
OXGATE *same as* > OXGANG
OXGATES > OXGATE
OXHEAD *n* head of an ox
OXHEADS > OXHEAD
OXHEART *n* heart-shaped cherry
OXHEARTS > OXHEART
OXHIDE *n* leather made from the hide of an ox
OXHIDES > OXHIDE
OXID *same as* > OXIDE
OXIDABLE *adj* able to undergo oxidation
OXIDANT *n* substance that acts or is used as an oxidizing agent
OXIDANTS > OXIDANT
OXIDASE *n* any of a group of enzymes that bring about biological oxidation
OXIDASES > OXIDASE
OXIDASIC > OXIDASE
OXIDATE *another word for* > OXIDIZE
OXIDATED > OXIDATE
OXIDATES > OXIDATE
OXIDATING > OXIDATE
OXIDATION *n* oxidizing
OXIDATIVE > OXIDATION
OXIDE *n* compound of oxygen and one other element
OXIDES > OXIDE
OXIDIC > OXIDE
OXIDISE *same as* > OXIDIZE
OXIDISED > OXIDISE
OXIDISER *same as* > OXIDIZER
OXIDISERS > OXIDISER
OXIDISES > OXIDISE
OXIDISING > OXIDISE
OXIDIZE *vb* combine chemically with oxygen, as in burning or rusting
OXIDIZED > OXIDIZE
OXIDIZER *same as* > OXIDANT
OXIDIZERS > OXIDIZER
OXIDIZES > OXIDIZE
OXIDIZING > OXIDIZE
OXIDS > OXID
OXIM *same as* > OXIME
OXIME *n* type of chemical compound
OXIMES > OXIME
OXIMETER *n* instrument for measuring oxygen in blood
OXIMETERS > OXIMETER
OXIMETRY > OXIMETER
OXIMS > OXIM
OXLAND *same as* > OXGANG
OXLANDS > OXLAND
OXLIKE > OX
OXLIP *n* type of woodland plant with small drooping pale yellow flowers
OXLIPS > OXLIP
OXO as in *oxo acid* acid that contains oxygen
OXONIUM as in *oxonium compound* type of salt derived from an organic ether
OXONIUMS > OXONIUM
OXPECKER *n* type of African starling
OXPECKERS > OXPECKER
OXSLIP *same as* > OXLIP
OXSLIPS > OXSLIP
OXTAIL *n* tail of an ox, used in soups and stews
OXTAILS > OXTAIL
OXTER *n* armpit ▷ *vb* grip under arm
OXTERED > OXTER
OXTERING > OXTER
OXTERS > OXTER
OXTONGUE *n* type of plant
OXTONGUES > OXTONGUE
OXY > OX
OXYACID *n* any acid that contains oxygen
OXYACIDS > OXYACID
OXYCODONE as in *oxycodone hydrochloride* opiate drug used as a painkiller
OXYGEN *n* gaseous element essential to life and combustion
OXYGENASE *n* enzyme
OXYGENATE *vb* add oxygen to
OXYGENIC > OXYGEN
OXYGENISE *variant of* > OXYGENIZE
OXYGENIZE *vb* add oxygen to
OXYGENOUS > OXYGEN
OXYGENS > OXYGEN
OXYMEL *n* mixture of vinegar and honey
OXYMELS > OXYMEL
OXYMORA > OXYMORON
OXYMORON *n* figure of speech that combines two apparently contradictory ideas
OXYMORONS > OXYMORON
OXYNTIC *adj* of or denoting stomach cells that secrete acid
OXYPHIL *n* type of cell found in glands
OXYPHILE *same as* > OXYPHIL
OXYPHILES > OXYPHILE
OXYPHILIC > OXYPHIL
OXYPHILS > OXYPHIL
OXYSALT *n* any salt of an oxyacid
OXYSALTS > OXYSALT
OXYSOME *n* group of molecules
OXYSOMES > OXYSOME
OXYTOCIC *adj* accelerating childbirth by stimulating uterine contractions ▷ *n* oxytocic drug or agent
OXYTOCICS > OXYTOCIC
OXYTOCIN *n* hormone that stimulates the ejection of milk in mammals
OXYTOCINS > OXYTOCIN
OXYTONE *adj* having an accent on the final syllable ▷ *n* oxytone word
OXYTONES > OXYTONE
OY *n* grandchild
OYE *same as* > OY
OYER *n* (in the 13th century) an assize
OYERS > OYER
OYES *same as* > OYEZ
OYESES > OYES
OYESSES > OYES
OYEZ *interj* shouted three times by a public crier calling for attention before a proclamation ▷ *n* such a cry
OYEZES > OYEZ
OYS > OY
OYSTER *n* edible shellfish ▷ *vb* dredge for, gather, or raise oysters
OYSTERED > OYSTER
OYSTERER *n* person fishing for oysters
OYSTERERS > OYSTERER
OYSTERING > OYSTER
OYSTERMAN *n* person who gathers, cultivates, or sells oysters
OYSTERMEN > OYSTERMAN
OYSTERS > OYSTER
OYSTRIGE *archaic variant of* > OSTRICH
OYSTRIGES > OYSTRIGE
OZAENA *n* inflammation o nasal mucous membrane
OZAENAS > OZAENA
OZALID *n* method of duplicating writing or illustrations
OZALIDS > OZALID
OZEKI *n* sumo wrestling champion
OZEKIS > OZEKI
OZOCERITE *n* brown or greyish wax
OZOKERITE *same as* > OZOCERITE
OZONATE *vb* add ozone to
OZONATED > OZONATE
OZONATES > OZONATE
OZONATING > OZONATE
OZONATION > OZONATE
OZONE *n* strong-smelling form of oxygen
OZONES > OZONE
OZONIC > OZONE
OZONIDE *n* type of unstabl explosive compound
OZONIDES > OZONIDE
OZONISE *same as* > OZONIZ
OZONISED > OZONISE
OZONISER > OZONISE
OZONISERS > OZONISE
OZONISES > OZONISE
OZONISING > OZONISE
OZONIZE *vb* convert (oxygen) into ozone
OZONIZED > OZONIZE
OZONIZER > OZONIZE
OZONIZERS > OZONIZE
OZONIZES > OZONIZE
OZONIZING > OZONIZE
OZONOUS > OZONE
OZZIE *n* hospital
OZZIES > OZZIE

Pp

A *n* (formerly) fortified Māori settlement
AAL *n* stake driven into the ground
AALS > PAAL
ABLUM *same as* > PABULUM
ABLUMS > PABLUM
ABOUCHE *n* soft shoe
ABOUCHES > PABOUCHE
ABULAR > PABULUM
ABULOUS > PABULUM
ABULUM *n* food
ABULUMS > PABULUM
AC *n* soft shoe
ACA *n* large burrowing hystricomorph rodent of Central and South America
ACABLE *adj* easily appeased
ACAS > PACA
ACATION *n* act of making peace
ACATIONS > PACATION
ACE *n* single step in walking ▷ *vb* walk up and down, esp in anxiety ▷ *prep* with due respect to: used to express polite disagreement
ACED > PACE
ACEMAKER *n* electronic device surgically implanted in a person with heart disease to regulate the heartbeat
ACER *n* horse trained to move at a special gait, esp for racing
ACERS > PACER
ACES > PACE
ACEWAY *n* racecourse for trotting and pacing
ACEWAYS > PACEWAY
PACEY *adj* fast-moving, quick, lively
PACHA *same as* > PASHA
PACHADOM *n* rank of pacha
PACHADOMS > PACHADOM
PACHAK *n* fragrant roots of Asian plant
PACHAKS > PACHAK
PACHALIC *n* jurisdiction of pasha
PACHALICS > PACHALIC
PACHAS > PACHA
PACHINKO *n* Japanese game similar to pinball
PACHINKOS > PACHINKO
PACHISI *n* Indian game somewhat resembling backgammon, played on a cruciform board using six cowries as dice
PACHISIS > PACHISI
PACHOULI *same as* > PATCHOULI
PACHOULIS > PACHOULI
PACHUCO *n* young Mexican living in the US, esp one of low social status who belongs to a street gang
PACHUCOS > PACHUCO
PACHYDERM *n* thick-skinned animal such as an elephant
PACHYTENE *n* third stage of the prophase of meiosis during which the chromosomes become shorter and thicker and divide into chromatids
PACIER > PACY
PACIEST > PACY
PACIFIC *adj* tending to bring peace
PACIFICAL > PACIFIC
PACIFIED > PACIFY
PACIFIER *n* baby's dummy
PACIFIERS > PACIFIER
PACIFIES > PACIFY
PACIFISM *n* belief that violence of any kind is unjustifiable and that one should not participate in war
PACIFISMS > PACIFISM
PACIFIST *n* person who refuses on principle to take part in war ▷ *adj* advocating, relating to, or characterized by pacifism
PACIFISTS > PACIFIST
PACIFY *vb* soothe, calm
PACIFYING > PACIFY
PACING > PACE
PACK *vb* put (clothes etc) together in a suitcase or bag ▷ *n* bag carried on a person's or animal's back
PACKABLE > PACK
PACKAGE *same as* > PACKET
PACKAGED > PACKAGE
PACKAGER *n* independent firm specializing in design and production, as of illustrated books or television programmes which are sold to publishers or television companies as finished products
PACKAGERS > PACKAGER
PACKAGES > PACKAGE
PACKAGING *n* box or wrapping in which a product is offered for sale
PACKBOARD *n* frame for carrying goods
PACKED *adj* completely filled
PACKER *n* person or company whose business is to pack goods, esp food
PACKERS > PACKER
PACKET *n* small container (and contents) ▷ *vb* wrap up in a packet or as a packet
PACKETED > PACKET
PACKETING > PACKET
PACKETS > PACKET
PACKFONG *n* Chinese alloy
PACKFONGS > PACKFONG
PACKFRAME *n* light metal frame with shoulder straps, used for carrying heavy or awkward loads
PACKHORSE *n* horse used for carrying goods
PACKING *n* material, such as paper or plastic, used to protect packed goods
PACKINGS > PACKING
PACKLY > PACK
PACKMAN *n* person carrying pack
PACKMEN > PACKMAN
PACKNESS > PACK
PACKS > PACK
PACKSACK *n* bag carried strapped on the back or shoulder
PACKSACKS > PACKSACK
PACKSHEET *n* cover for pack
PACKSTAFF *n* staff for supporting pack
PACKWAX *n* neck ligament
PACKWAXES > PACKWAX
PACKWAY *n* path for pack animals
PACKWAYS > PACKWAY

PACO *n* S American mammal
PACOS > PACO
PACS > PAC
PACT *n* formal agreement
PACTA > PACTUM
PACTION *vb* concur with
PACTIONAL > PACTION
PACTIONED > PACTION
PACTIONS > PACTION
PACTS > PACT
PACTUM *n* pact
PACY *same as* > PACEY
PAD *n* piece of soft material used for protection, support, absorption of liquid, etc ▷ *vb* protect or fill with soft material
PADANG *n* (in Malaysia) playing field
PADANGS > PADANG
PADAUK *n* tropical African or Asian leguminous tree with reddish wood
PADAUKS > PADAUK
PADDED > PAD
PADDER *n* highwayman who robs on foot
PADDERS > PADDER
PADDIES > PADDY
PADDING > PAD
PADDINGS > PAD
PADDLE *n* short oar with a broad blade at one or each end ▷ *vb* move (a canoe etc) with a paddle
PADDLED > PADDLE
PADDLER > PADDLE
PADDLERS > PADDLE
PADDLES > PADDLE
PADDLING > PADDLE
PADDLINGS > PADDLE
PADDOCK *n* small field or enclosure for horses ▷ *vb* place (a horse) in a paddock
PADDOCKED > PADDOCK
PADDOCKS > PADDOCK
PADDY *n* fit of temper
PADDYWACK *vb* spank or smack
PADELLA *n* type of candle
PADELLAS > PADELLA
PADEMELON *n* small Australian wallaby
PADERERO *same as* > PATERERO
PADEREROS > PADERERO
PADI *same as* > PADDY
PADIS > PADI
PADISHAH *n* Iranian ruler
PADISHAHS > PADISHAH
PADKOS *n* snacks and provisions for a journey
PADLE *another name for* > LUMPFISH
PADLES > PADLE
PADLOCK *n* detachable lock with a hinged hoop fastened over a ring on the object to be secured ▷ *vb* fasten (something) with a padlock
PADLOCKED > PADLOCK
PADLOCKS > PADLOCK
PADMA *n* type of lotus
PADMAS > PADMA
PADNAG *n* ambling horse
PADNAGS > PADNAG
PADOUK *same as* > PADAUK
PADOUKS > PADOUK
PADRE *n* chaplain to the armed forces
PADRES > PADRE
PADRI > PADRE
PADRONE *n* owner or proprietor of an inn, esp in Italy
PADRONES > PADRONE
PADRONI > PADRONE
PADRONISM *n* system of work controlled by a padrone
PADS > PAD
PADSAW *n* small narrow saw used for cutting curves
PADSAWS > PADSAW
PADSHAH *same as* > PADISHAH
PADSHAHS > PADSHAH
PADUASOY *n* rich strong silk fabric used for hangings, vestments, etc
PADUASOYS > PADUASOY
PADYMELON *same as* > PADEMELON
PAEAN *n* song of triumph or thanksgiving
PAEANISM > PAEAN
PAEANISMS > PAEAN
PAEANS > PAEAN
PAEDERAST *same as* > PEDERAST
PAEDEUTIC *adj* of or relating to the study of teaching
PAEDIATRY *n* branch of medical science concerned with children and their diseases
PAEDOLOGY *n* study of the character, growth, and development of children
PAELLA *n* Spanish dish of rice, chicken, shellfish, and vegetables
PAELLAS > PAELLA
PAENULA *n* ancient Roman cloak
PAENULAE > PAENULA
PAENULAS > PAENULA
PAEON *n* metrical foot of four syllables, with one long one and three short ones in any order
PAEONIC > PAEON
PAEONICS > PAEON
PAEONIES > PAEONY
PAEONS > PAEON
PAEONY *same as* > PEONY
PAESAN *n* fellow countryman
PAESANI > PAESANO
PAESANO *n* Italian-American man
PAESANOS > PAESANO
PAESANS > PAESAN
PAGAN *adj* not belonging to one of the world's main religions ▷ *n* pagan person
PAGANDOM > PAGAN
PAGANDOMS > PAGAN
PAGANISE *same as* > PAGANIZE
PAGANISED > PAGANISE
PAGANISER > PAGANISE
PAGANISES > PAGANISE
PAGANISH > PAGAN
PAGANISM > PAGAN
PAGANISMS > PAGAN
PAGANIST > PAGAN
PAGANISTS > PAGAN
PAGANIZE *vb* become pagan, render pagan, or convert to paganism
PAGANIZED > PAGANIZE
PAGANIZER > PAGANIZE
PAGANIZES > PAGANIZE
PAGANS > PAGAN
PAGE *n* (one side of) sheet of paper forming a book etc ▷ *vb* summon (someone) by bleeper or loudspeaker, in order to pass on a message
PAGEANT *n* parade or display of people in costume, usu illustrating a scene from history
PAGEANTRY *n* spectacular display or ceremony
PAGEANTS > PAGEANT
PAGEBOY *n* hairstyle in which the hair is smooth and the same medium length with the ends curled under
PAGEBOYS > PAGEBOY
PAGED > PAGE
PAGEFUL *n* amount (of text, etc) that a page will hold
PAGEFULS > PAGEFUL
PAGEHOOD *n* state of being a page
PAGEHOODS > PAGEHOOD
PAGER *n* small electronic device, capable of receiving short messages
PAGERS > PAGER
PAGES > PAGE
PAGEVIEW *n* electronic page of information displayed at the request of a user
PAGEVIEWS > PAGEVIEW
PAGINAL *adj* page-for-page
PAGINATE *vb* number the pages of (a book, manuscript, etc) in sequence
PAGINATED > PAGINATE
PAGINATES > PAGINATE
PAGING > PAGE
PAGINGS > PAGE
PAGLE *same as* > PAIGLE
PAGLES > PAGLE
PAGOD *n* oriental idol
PAGODA *n* pyramid-shaped Asian temple or tower
PAGODAS > PAGODA
PAGODS > PAGOD
PAGRI *n* type of turban
PAGRIS > PAGRI
PAGURIAN *n* any decapod crustacean of the family *Paguridae*, which includes the hermit crabs ▷ *adj* of relating to, or belonging to the *Paguridae*
PAGURIANS > PAGURIAN
PAGURID *same as* > PAGURIAN
PAGURIDS > PAGURID
PAH *same as* > PA
PAHAUTEA *same as* > KAIKAWAKA
PAHLAVI *n* Iranian coin
PAHLAVIS > PAHLAVI
PAHOEHOE *n* hardened lava
PAHOEHOES > PAHOEHOE
PAHS > PAH
PAID > PAY
PAIDEUTIC *same as* > PAEDEUTIC
PAIDLE *Scots variant of* > PADDLE
PAIDLED > PAIDLE
PAIDLES > PAIDLE
PAIDLING > PAIDLE
PAIGLE *n* cowslip
PAIGLES > PAIGLE
PAIK *vb* thump or whack
PAIKED > PAIK
PAIKING > PAIK
PAIKS > PAIK
PAIL *n* bucket
PAILFUL *same as* > PAIL
PAILFULS > PAILFUL
PAILLARD *n* thin slice of meat
PAILLARDS > PAILLARD
PAILLASSE *same as* > PALLIASSE
PAILLETTE *n* sequin or spangle sewn onto a costume
PAILLON *n* thin leaf of metal
PAILLONS > PAILLON
PAILS > PAIL
PAILSFUL > PAILFUL
PAIN *n* physical or mental suffering ▷ *vb* cause (someone) mental or physical suffering
PAINCH *Scots variant of* > PAUNCH
PAINCHES > PAINCH
PAINED *adj* having or suggesting pain or distress
PAINFUL *adj* causing pain or distress
PAINFULLY > PAINFUL
PAINIM *n* heathen or pagan
PAINIMS > PAINIM
PAINING > PAIN
PAINLESS *adj* not causing pain or distress
PAINS *pl n* care or trouble
PAINT *n* coloured substance, spread on a surface with a brush or roller ▷ *vb* colour or coat with paint
PAINTABLE > PAINT

AINTBALL *n* game in which teams of players simulate a military skirmish, shooting each other with paint pellets
AINTBOX *n* box containing a tray of dry watercolour paints
AINTED > PAINT
AINTER *n* rope at the front of a boat, for tying it up
AINTERLY *adj* having qualities peculiar to painting, esp the depiction of shapes by means of solid masses of colour, rather than by lines
AINTERS > PAINTER
AINTIER > PAINT
AINTIEST > PAINT
AINTING *n* picture produced by using paint
AINTINGS > PAINTING
AINTRESS *n* female painter
AINTS > PAINT
AINTURE *n* art of painting
AINTURES > PAINTURE
AINTWORK *n* covering of paint on parts of a vehicle, building, etc
AINTY > PAINT
AIOCK *obsolete word for* > PEACOCK
AIOCKE *obsolete word for* > PEACOCK
AIOCKES > PAIOCKE
AIOCKS > PAIOCK
IR *n* set of two things matched for use together ▷ *vb* group or be grouped in twos
AIRE *obsolete spelling of* > PAIR
AIRED > PAIR
AIRER > PAIR
IRES > PAIRE
AIREST > PAIR
AIRIAL *variant of* > PRIAL
AIRIALS > PAIRIAL
AIRING > PAIR
AIRINGS > PAIR
IRS > PAIR
AIRWISE *adv* in pairs
AIS *n* country
AISA *n* monetary unit of Bangladesh, Bhutan, India, Nepal, and Pakistan worth one hundredth of a rupee
ISAN *n* fellow countryman
AISANA *n* female peasant
AISANAS > PAISANA
AISANO *n* friend
AISANOS > PAISANO
AISANS > PAISAN
AISAS > PAISA
AISE > PAISA
AISLEY *n* pattern of small curving shapes with intricate detailing, usually printed in bright colours
AISLEYS > PAISLEY
PAITRICK *Scots word for* > PARTRIDGE
PAITRICKS > PAITRICK
PAJAMA *same as* > PYJAMA
PAJAMAED *adj* wearing pajamas
PAJAMAS > PAJAMA
PAJOCK *obsolete word for* > PEACOCK
PAJOCKE *obsolete word for* > PEACOCK
PAJOCKES > PAJOCKE
PAJOCKS > PAJOCK
PAKAHI *n* acid land that is unsuitable for cultivation
PAKAHIS > PAKAHI
PAKAPOO *n* Chinese lottery with betting slips marked with Chinese characters
PAKAPOOS > PAKAPOO
PAKEHA *n* person of European descent, as distinct from a Māori
PAKEHAS > PAKEHA
PAKFONG *same as* > PACKFONG
PAKFONGS > PAKFONG
PAKIHI *n* area of swampy infertile land
PAKIHIS > PAKIHI
PAKKA *variant of* > PUKKA
PAKOKO *n* small freshwater fish
PAKOKOS > PAKOKO
PAKORA *n* Indian dish consisting of pieces of vegetable, chicken, etc, dipped in a spiced batter and deep-fried
PAKORAS > PAKORA
PAKTHONG *n* white alloy containing copper, zinc, and nickel
PAKTHONGS > PAKTHONG
PAKTONG *same as* > PAKTHONG
PAKTONGS > PAKTONG
PAL *n* friend ▷ *vb* associate as friends
PALABRA *n* word
PALABRAS > PALABRA
PALACE *n* residence of a king, bishop, etc
PALACED *adj* having palaces
PALACES > PALACE
PALADIN *n* knight who did battle for a monarch
PALADINS > PALADIN
PALAESTRA *n* (in ancient Greece or Rome) public place devoted to the training of athletes
PALAFITTE *n* prehistoric dwelling
PALAGI *n* (in Samoa) European
PALAGIS > PALAGI
PALAIS *n* dance hall
PALAMA *n* webbing on bird's feet
PALAMAE > PALAMA
PALAMATE > PALAMA
PALAMINO *same as* > PALOMINO
PALAMINOS > PALAMINO
PALAMPORE *same as* > PALEMPORE
PALANKEEN *same as* > PALANQUIN
PALANQUIN *n* (formerly, in the Orient) covered bed in which someone could be carried on the shoulders of four men
PALAPA *n* open-sided tropical building
PALAPAS > PALAPA
PALAS *n* East Indian tree
PALASES > PALAS
PALATABLE *adj* pleasant to taste
PALATABLY > PALATABLE
PALATAL *adj* of or relating to the palate ▷ *n* bony plate that forms the palate
PALATALLY > PALATAL
PALATALS > PALATAL
PALATE *n* roof of the mouth ▷ *vb* perceive by taste
PALATED > PALATE
PALATES > PALATE
PALATIAL *adj* like a palace, magnificent
PALATINE *same as* > PALATAL
PALATINES > PALATINE
PALATING > PALATE
PALAVER *n* time-wasting fuss ▷ *vb* (often used humorously) have a conference
PALAVERED > PALAVER
PALAVERER > PALAVER
PALAVERS > PALAVER
PALAY *n* type of rubber
PALAYS > PALAY
PALAZZI > PALAZZO
PALAZZO *n* Italian palace
PALAZZOS > PALAZZO
PALE *adj* light, whitish ▷ *vb* become pale ▷ *n* wooden or metal post used in fences
PALEA *n* inner of two bracts surrounding each floret in a grass spikelet
PALEAE > PALEA
PALEAL > PALEA
PALEATE *adj* having scales
PALEBUCK *n* small African antelope
PALEBUCKS > PALEBUCK
PALED > PALE
PALEFACE *n* offensive term for a White person, said to have been used by Native Americans of N America
PALEFACES > PALEFACE
PALELY > PALE
PALEMPORE *n* bed covering
PALENESS > PALE
PALEOCENE *adj* belonging to geological time period
PALEOGENE *adj* of early geological time period
PALEOLITH *n* Stone Age artefact
PALEOLOGY *n* study of prehistory
PALEOSOL *n* ancient soil horizon
PALEOSOLS > PALEOSOL
PALEOZOIC *adj* belonging to geological time period
PALER > PALE
PALES > PALE
PALEST > PALE
PALESTRA *same as* > PALAESTRA
PALESTRAE > PALESTRA
PALESTRAL > PALESTRA
PALESTRAS > PALESTRA
PALET *n* perpendicular band on escutcheon
PALETOT *n* loose outer garment
PALETOTS > PALETOT
PALETS > PALET
PALETTE *n* artist's flat board for mixing colours on
PALETTES > PALETTE
PALEWAYS *same as* > PALEWISE
PALEWISE *adv* by perpendicular lines
PALFREY *n* light saddle horse, esp ridden by women ▷ *vb* mount a palfrey
PALFREYED > PALFREY
PALFREYS > PALFREY
PALIER > PALY
PALIEST > PALY
PALIFORM *adj* shaped like a palus
PALIKAR *n* Greek soldier in the war of independence against Turkey
PALIKARS > PALIKAR
PALILALIA *n* speech disorder in which a word or phrase is rapidly repeated
PALILLOGY *n* repetition of word or phrase
PALIMONY *n* alimony awarded to a nonmarried partner after the break-up of a long-term relationship
PALING *n* wooden or metal post used in fences
PALINGS > PALING
PALINKA *n* type of apricot brandy, originating in Central and Eastern Europe
PALINKAS > PALINKA
PALINODE *n* poem in which the poet recants something he has said in a former poem
PALINODES > PALINODE
PALINODY > PALINODE
PALINOPIA *n* visual disorder in which the patient perceives a prolonged afterimage
PALISADE *n* fence made of wooden posts driven into the ground ▷ *vb* enclose

with a palisade
PALISADED > PALISADE
PALISADES > PALISADE
PALISADO *same as* > PALISADE
PALISH *adj* rather pale
PALKEE *n* covered Oriental litter
PALKEES > PALKEE
PALKI *same as* > PALKEE
PALKIS > PALKI
PALL *n* cloth spread over a coffin ▷ *vb* become boring
PALLA *n* ancient Roman cloak
PALLADIA > PALLADIUM
PALLADIC *adj* of or containing palladium in the trivalent or tetravalent state
PALLADIUM *n* silvery-white element of the platinum metal group
PALLADOUS *adj* of or containing palladium in the divalent state
PALLAE > PALLA
PALLAH *n* S African antelope
PALLAHS > PALLAH
PALLED > PALL
PALLET *same as* > PALETTE
PALLETED > PALLET
PALLETING > PALLET
PALLETISE *same as* > PALLETIZE
PALLETIZE *vb* stack or transport on a pallet or pallets
PALLETS > PALLET
PALLETTE *n* armpit plate of a suit of armour
PALLETTES > PALLETTE
PALLIA > PALLIUM
PALLIAL *adj* relating to cerebral cortex
PALLIARD *n* person who begs
PALLIARDS > PALLIARD
PALLIASSE *n* straw-filled mattress
PALLIATE *vb* lessen the severity of (something) without curing it
PALLIATED > PALLIATE
PALLIATES > PALLIATE
PALLIATOR > PALLIATE
PALLID *adj* pale, esp because ill or weak
PALLIDER > PALLID
PALLIDEST > PALLID
PALLIDITY > PALLID
PALLIDLY > PALLID
PALLIER > PALLY
PALLIEST > PALLY
PALLING > PALL
PALLIUM *n* garment worn by men in ancient Greece or Rome, made by draping a large rectangular cloth about the body
PALLIUMS > PALLIUM
PALLONE *n* Italian ball game
PALLONES > PALLONE
PALLOR *n* paleness of complexion, usually because of illness, shock, or fear
PALLORS > PALLOR
PALLS > PALL
PALLY *adj* on friendly terms
PALM *n* inner surface of the hand ▷ *vb* conceal in or about the hand, as in sleight-of-hand tricks
PALMAR *adj* of or relating to the palm of the hand
PALMARIAN *adj* pre-eminent
PALMARY *adj* worthy of praise
PALMATE *adj* shaped like an open hand
PALMATED *same as* > PALMATE
PALMATELY > PALMATE
PALMATION *n* state of being palmate
PALMED > PALM
PALMER *n* (in Medieval Europe) pilgrim bearing a palm branch as a sign of his visit to the Holy Land
PALMERS > PALMER
PALMETTE *n* ornament or design resembling the palm leaf
PALMETTES > PALMETTE
PALMETTO *n* small palm tree with fan-shaped leaves
PALMETTOS > PALMETTO
PALMFUL *n* amount that can be held in the palm of a hand
PALMFULS > PALMFUL
PALMHOUSE *n* greenhouse for palms, etc
PALMIE *n* palmtop computer
PALMIER > PALMY
PALMIES > PALMIE
PALMIEST > PALMY
PALMIET *n* South African rush
PALMIETS > PALMIET
PALMING > PALM
PALMIPED *n* web-footed bird
PALMIPEDE *same as* > PALMIPED
PALMIPEDS > PALMIPED
PALMIST > PALMISTRY
PALMISTER *n* person telling fortunes by reading palms
PALMISTRY *n* fortune-telling from lines on the palm of the hand
PALMISTS > PALMISTRY
PALMITATE *n* any salt or ester of palmitic acid
PALMITIC as in *palmitic acid* white crystalline solid that is a saturated fatty acid
PALMITIN *n* colourless glyceride of palmitic acid
PALMITINS > PALMITIN
PALMLIKE > PALM
PALMS > PALM
PALMTOP *adj* small enough to be held in the hand ▷ *n* computer small enough to be held in the hand
PALMTOPS > PALMTOP
PALMY *adj* successful, prosperous and happy
PALMYRA *n* tall tropical Asian palm
PALMYRAS > PALMYRA
PALOLO *n* polychaete worm of the S Pacific Ocean
PALOLOS > PALOLO
PALOMINO *n* gold-coloured horse with a white mane and tail
PALOMINOS > PALOMINO
PALOOKA *n* stupid or clumsy boxer or other person
PALOOKAS > PALOOKA
PALOVERDE *n* thorny American shrub
PALP *n* either of a pair of sensory appendages that arise from the mouthparts of crustaceans and insects ▷ *vb* feel
PALPABLE *adj* obvious
PALPABLY > PALPABLE
PALPAL > PALP
PALPATE *vb* examine (an area of the body) by touching ▷ *adj* of, relating to, or possessing a palp or palps
PALPATED > PALPATE
PALPATES > PALPATE
PALPATING > PALPATE
PALPATION > PALPATE
PALPATOR *n* type of beetle
PALPATORS > PALPATOR
PALPATORY > PALPATE
PALPEBRA *n* eyelid
PALPEBRAE > PALPEBRA
PALPEBRAL *adj* of or relating to the eyelid
PALPEBRAS > PALPEBRA
PALPED > PALP
PALPI > PALPUS
PALPING > PALP
PALPITANT > PALPITATE
PALPITATE *vb* (of the heart) beat rapidly
PALPS > PALP
PALPUS *same as* > PALP
PALS > PAL
PALSGRAVE *n* German count palatine
PALSHIP *n* state of being pals
PALSHIPS > PALSHIP
PALSIED > PALSY
PALSIER > PALSY
PALSIES > PALSY
PALSIEST > PALSY
PALSTAFF *variant of* > PALSTAVE
PALSTAFFS > PALSTAFF
PALSTAVE *n* kind of celt, usually of bronze, made to fit into a split wooden handle rather than havin[g] a socket for the handle
PALSTAVES > PALSTAVE
PALSY *n* paralysis ▷ *vb* paralyse ▷ *adj* friendly
PALSYING > PALSY
PALSYLIKE > PALSY
PALTER *vb* act or talk insincerely
PALTERED > PALTER
PALTERER > PALTER
PALTERERS > PALTER
PALTERING > PALTER
PALTERS > PALTER
PALTRIER > PALTRY
PALTRIEST > PALTRY
PALTRILY > PALTRY
PALTRY *adj* insignificant
PALUDAL *adj* of, relating to or produced by marshes
PALUDIC *adj* of malaria
PALUDINAL *adj* inhabiting swamps
PALUDINE *adj* relating to marsh
PALUDISM *rare word for* > MALARIA
PALUDISMS > PALUDISM
PALUDOSE *adj* growing or living in marshes
PALUDOUS *adj* marshy
PALUS *n* part of the calicle of certain corals
PALUSTRAL *adj* marshy
PALY *adj* vertically striped
PAM *n* knave of clubs
PAMPA *n* grassland area
PAMPAS *pl n* vast grassy plains in S America
PAMPASES > PAMPAS
PAMPEAN > PAMPAS
PAMPEANS > PAMPAS
PAMPER *vb* treat (someone) with great indulgence, spoil
PAMPERED > PAMPER
PAMPERER > PAMPER
PAMPERERS > PAMPER
PAMPERING > PAMPER
PAMPERO *n* dry cold wind in South America blowing across the pampas from the south or southwest
PAMPEROS > PAMPERO
PAMPERS > PAMPER
PAMPHLET *n* thin paper-covered booklet
PAMPHLETS > PAMPHLET
PAMPHREY *n* cabbage
PAMPHREYS > PAMPHREY
PAMPOEN *n* pumpkin
PAMPOENS > PAMPOEN
PAMPOOTIE *n* rawhide slipper worn by men in the Aran Islands
PAMS > PAM
PAN *n* wide long-handled metal container used in cooking ▷ *vb* sift gravel from (a river) in a pan to search for gold
PANACEA *n* remedy for all

diseases or problems
ANACEAN > PANACEA
ANACEAS > PANACEA
ANACHAEA *variant of* > PANACEA
ANACHE *n* confident elegant style
ANACHES > PANACHE
ANADA *n* mixture of flour, water, etc, or of breadcrumbs soaked in milk, used as a thickening
ANADAS > PANADA
ANAMA *n* hat made of the plaited leaves of the jipijapa plant
ANAMAS > PANAMA
ANARIES > PANARY
ANARY *n* storehouse for bread
ANATELA *same as* > PANATELLA
ANATELAS > PANATELA
ANATELLA *n* long slender cigar
ANAX *n* genus of perennial herbs
ANAXES > PANAX
ANBROIL *vb* broil in a pan
ANBROILS > PANBROIL
ANCAKE *n* thin flat circle of fried batter ▷ *vb* cause (an aircraft) to make a pancake landing or (of an aircraft) to make a pancake landing
ANCAKED > PANCAKE
ANCAKES > PANCAKE
ANCAKING > PANCAKE
ANCE *n* pansy
ANCES > PANCE
ANCETTA *n* lightly spiced cured bacon from Italy
ANCETTAS > PANCETTA
ANCHAX *n* brightly coloured tropical Asian cyprinodont fish
ANCHAXES > PANCHAX
ANCHAYAT *n* village council in India
ANCHEON *n* shallow bowl
ANCHEONS > PANCHEON
ANCHION *same as* > PANCHEON
ANCHIONS > PANCHION
ANCOSMIC *adj* of every cosmos
ANCRATIA *n* wrestling and boxing contests
ANCRATIC > PANCRATIA
ANCREAS *n* large gland behind the stomach that produces insulin and helps digestion
AND *n* valance
ANDA *n* large black-and-white bearlike mammal from China
ANDANI *n* tropical tree
ANDANUS *n* Old World tropical palmlike plant
ANDAR *vb* act as a pimp
ANDARED > PANDAR
ANDARING > PANDAR
PANDARS > PANDAR
PANDAS > PANDA
PANDATION *n* warping
PANDECT *n* treatise covering all aspects of a particular subject
PANDECTS > PANDECT
PANDEMIA *n* epidemic affecting everyone
PANDEMIAN *adj* sensual
PANDEMIAS > PANDEMIA
PANDEMIC *adj* (of a disease) occurring over a wide area ▷ *n* pandemic disease
PANDEMICS > PANDEMIC
PANDER *vb* indulge (a person his or her desires) ▷ *n* person who procures a sexual partner for someone
PANDERED > PANDER
PANDERER *n* person who procures a sexual partner for someone
PANDERERS > PANDERER
PANDERESS *n* female panderer
PANDERING > PANDER
PANDERISM > PANDER
PANDERLY > PANDER
PANDEROUS > PANDER
PANDERS > PANDER
PANDIED > PANDY
PANDIES > PANDY
PANDIT *same as* > PUNDIT
PANDITS > PANDIT
PANDOOR *same as* > PANDOUR
PANDOORS > PANDOOR
PANDORA *n* handsome red sea bream
PANDORAS > PANDORA
PANDORE *another word for* > BANDORE
PANDORES > PANDORE
PANDOUR *n* one of an 18th-century force of Croatian soldiers in the Austrian service, notorious for their brutality
PANDOURS > PANDOUR
PANDOWDY *n* deep-dish pie made from fruit, esp apples, with a cake topping
PANDS > PAND
PANDURA *n* ancient stringed instrument
PANDURAS > PANDURA
PANDURATE *adj* (of plant leaves) shaped like the body of a fiddle
PANDY *n* (in schools) stroke on the hand with a strap as a punishment ▷ *vb* punish with such strokes
PANDYING > PANDY
PANE *n* sheet of glass in a window or door ▷ *adj* (of fish, meat, etc) dipped or rolled in breadcrumbs before cooking
PANED > PANE
PANEER *n* soft white cheese, used in Indian cookery
PANEERS > PANEER
PANEGOISM *n* form of scepticism
PANEGYRIC *n* formal speech or piece of writing in praise of someone or something
PANEGYRY *n* panegyric
PANEITIES > PANEITY
PANEITY *n* state of being bread
PANEL *n* flat distinct section of a larger surface, for example in a door ▷ *vb* cover or decorate with panels ▷ *adj* of a group acting as a panel
PANELED > PANEL
PANELESS > PANE
PANELING *same as* > PANELLING
PANELINGS > PANELING
PANELISED *same as* > PANELIZED
PANELIST *same as* > PANELLIST
PANELISTS > PANELIST
PANELIZED *adj* made in sections for quick assembly
PANELLED > PANEL
PANELLING *n* panels collectively, esp on a wall
PANELLIST *n* member of a panel
PANELS > PANEL
PANES > PANE
PANETELA *same as* > PANATELA
PANETELAS > PANETELA
PANETELLA *n* long thin cigar
PANETTONE *n* kind of Italian spiced brioche containing sultanas
PANETTONI > PANETTONE
PANFISH *n* small food fish
PANFISHES > PANFISH
PANFRIED > PANFRY
PANFRIES > PANFRY
PANFRY *vb* fry in a pan
PANFRYING > PANFRY
PANFUL > PAN
PANFULS > PAN
PANG *n* sudden sharp feeling of pain or sadness ▷ *vb* cause pain
PANGA *n* broad heavy knife of E Africa, used as a tool or weapon
PANGAMIC > PANGAMY
PANGAMIES > PANGAMY
PANGAMY *n* unrestricted mating
PANGAS > PANGA
PANGED > PANG
PANGEN *same as* > PANGENE
PANGENE *n* hypothetical particle of protoplasm
PANGENES > PANGENE
PANGENS > PANGEN
PANGING > PANG
PANGLESS *adj* without pangs
PANGOLIN *n* animal of tropical countries with a scaly body and a long snout for eating ants and termites
PANGOLINS > PANGOLIN
PANGRAM *n* sentence incorporating all the letters of the alphabet
PANGRAMS > PANGRAM
PANGS > PANG
PANHANDLE *n* (in the US) narrow strip of land that projects from one state into another ▷ *vb* accost and beg from (passers-by), esp on the street
PANHUMAN *adj* relating to all humanity
PANIC *n* sudden overwhelming fear, often affecting a whole group of people ▷ *vb* feel or cause to feel panic ▷ *adj* of or resulting from such terror
PANICALLY > PANIC
PANICK *old word for* > PANIC
PANICKED > PANIC
PANICKIER > PANIC
PANICKING > PANIC
PANICKS > PANICK
PANICKY > PANIC
PANICLE *n* loose, irregularly branched cluster of flowers
PANICLED > PANICLE
PANICLES > PANICLE
PANICS > PANIC
PANICUM *n* type of grass
PANICUMS > PANICUM
PANIER *same as* > PANNIER
PANIERS > PANIER
PANIM *n* heathen or pagan
PANIMS > PANIM
PANING > PANE
PANINI > PANINO
PANINO *n* Italian sandwich
PANISC *n* faun; attendant of Pan
PANISCS > PANISC
PANISK *same as* > PANISC
PANISKS > PANISK
PANISLAM *n* all of Islam
PANISLAMS > PANISLAM
PANJANDRA *n* pompous self-important officials of people of rank
PANLOGISM *n* metaphysics of Leibniz
PANMICTIC > PANMIXIA
PANMIXES > PANMIXIA
PANMIXIA *n* (in population genetics) random mating within an interbreeding population
PANMIXIAS > PANMIXIA
PANMIXIS *same as* > PANMIXIA
PANNAGE *n* pasturage for pigs, esp in a forest
PANNAGES > PANNAGE
PANNE *n* lightweight velvet

fabric
PANNED > PAN
PANNELLED *adj* divided into panels
PANNER > PAN
PANNERS > PAN
PANNES > PANNE
PANNICK *old spelling of the noun* > PANIC
PANNICKS > PANNICK
PANNICLE *n* thin layer of body tissue
PANNICLES > PANNICLE
PANNIER *n* bag fixed on the back of a cycle
PANNIERED > PANNIER
PANNIERS > PANNIER
PANNIKEL *n* skull
PANNIKELL *same as* > PANNIKEL
PANNIKELS > PANNIKEL
PANNIKIN *n* small metal cup or pan
PANNIKINS > PANNIKIN
PANNING > PAN
PANNINGS > PAN
PANNOSE *adj* like felt
PANNUS *n* inflammatory fleshy lesion on the surface of the eye
PANNUSES > PANNUS
PANOCHA *n* coarse grade of sugar made in Mexico
PANOCHAS > PANOCHA
PANOCHE *n* type of dark sugar
PANOCHES > PANOCHE
PANOISTIC *adj* producing ova
PANOPLIED > PANOPLY
PANOPLIES > PANOPLY
PANOPLY *n* magnificent array
PANOPTIC *adj* taking in all parts, aspects, etc, in a single view
PANORAMA *n* wide unbroken view of a scene
PANORAMAS > PANORAMA
PANORAMIC > PANORAMA
PANPIPE *n* wind instrument
PANPIPES > PANPIPE
PANS > PAN
PANSEXUAL *n* person open to any sexual activity
PANSIED *adj* covered with pansies
PANSIES > PANSY
PANSOPHIC > PANSOPHY
PANSOPHY *n* universal knowledge
PANSPERMY *n* 19th-century evolutionary theory
PANSY *n* small garden flower with velvety purple, yellow, or white petals
PANT *vb* breathe quickly and noisily during or after exertion ▷ *n* act of panting
PANTABLE *n* soft shoe
PANTABLES > PANTABLE
PANTAGAMY *n* marriage to everyone
PANTALEON *n* percussion instrument
PANTALET *same as* > PANTALETS
PANTALETS *pl n* long drawers, usually trimmed with ruffles, extending below the skirts
PANTALON *n* keyboard instrument
PANTALONE *n* Italian comic character
PANTALONS > PANTALON
PANTALOON *n* (in pantomime) absurd old man, the butt of the clown's tricks
PANTDRESS *n* dress with divided skirt
PANTED > PANT
PANTER *n* person who pants
PANTERS > PANTER
PANTHEISM *n* belief that God is present in everything
PANTHEIST > PANTHEISM
PANTHENOL *n* pantothenyl alcohol
PANTHEON *n* (in ancient Greece and Rome) temple built to honour all the gods
PANTHEONS > PANTHEON
PANTHER *n* leopard, esp a black one
PANTHERS > PANTHER
PANTIE *same as* > PANTY
PANTIES *pl n* women's underpants
PANTIHOSE *same as* > PANTYHOSE
PANTILE *n* roofing tile with an S-shaped cross section ▷ *vb* tile roof with pantiles
PANTILED > PANTILE
PANTILES > PANTILE
PANTILING > PANTILE
PANTINE *n* pasteboard puppet
PANTINES > PANTINE
PANTING > PANT
PANTINGLY > PANT
PANTINGS > PANT
PANTLER *n* pantry servant
PANTLERS > PANTLER
PANTO *same as* > PANTOMIME
PANTOFFLE *same as* > PANTOFLE
PANTOFLE *n* kind of slipper
PANTOFLES > PANTOFLE
PANTOMIME *n* play based on a fairy tale, performed at Christmas time
PANTON *n* type of horseshoe
PANTONS > PANTON
PANTOS > PANTO
PANTOUFLE *same as* > PANTOFLE
PANTOUM *n* verse form
PANTOUMS > PANTOUM
PANTRIES > PANTRY
PANTROPIC *adj* found throughout tropics
PANTRY *n* small room or cupboard for storing food
PANTRYMAN *n* pantry servant
PANTRYMEN > PANTRYMAN
PANTS *pl n* undergarment for the lower part of the body
PANTSUIT *n* woman's suit of a jacket or top and trousers
PANTSUITS > PANTSUIT
PANTUN *n* Malayan poetry
PANTUNS > PANTUN
PANTY *n* woman's undergarment
PANTYHOSE *pl n* women's tights
PANZER *n* German tank
PANZERS > PANZER
PANZOOTIC *n* disease that affects all the animals in a geographical area
PAOLI > PAOLO
PAOLO *n* Italian silver coin
PAP *n* soft food for babies or invalids ▷ *vb* (of the paparazzi) to follow and photograph (a famous person) ▷ *vb* feed with pap
PAPA *n* father
PAPABLE *adj* suitable for papacy
PAPACIES > PAPACY
PAPACY *n* position or term of office of a pope
PAPADAM *variant of* > POPPADOM
PAPADAMS > PAPADAM
PAPADOM *variant of* > POPPADOM
PAPADOMS > PAPADOM
PAPADUM *variant of* > POPPADOM
PAPADUMS > PAPADUM
PAPAIN *n* proteolytic enzyme occurring in the unripe fruit of the papaya tree
PAPAINS > PAPAIN
PAPAL *adj* of the pope
PAPALISE *same as* > PAPALIZE
PAPALISED > PAPALISE
PAPALISES > PAPALISE
PAPALISM *n* papal system
PAPALISMS > PAPALISM
PAPALIST *n* supporter of a pope
PAPALISTS > PAPALIST
PAPALIZE *vb* make papal
PAPALIZED > PAPALIZE
PAPALIZES > PAPALIZE
PAPALLY > PAPAL
PAPARAZZI > PAPARAZZO
PAPARAZZO *n* photographer specializing in candid photographs of famous people
PAPAS > PAPA
PAPAUMA *n* New Zealand word for broadleaf
PAPAW *same as* > PAPAYA
PAPAWS > PAPAW
PAPAYA *n* large sweet Wes Indian fruit
PAPAYAN > PAPAYA
PAPAYAS > PAPAYA
PAPE *n* spiritual father
PAPER *n* material made in sheets from wood pulp or other fibres ▷ *vb* cover (walls) with wallpaper
PAPERBACK *n* book with covers made of flexible card ▷ *adj* of a paperback or publication of paperbacks ▷ *vb* publish in paperback
PAPERBARK *n* Australian tree of swampy regions, with spear-shaped leaves and papery bark
PAPERBOY *n* boy employec to deliver newspapers to people's homes
PAPERBOYS > PAPERBOY
PAPERCLIP *n* bent wire cli for holding sheets of pape together
PAPERED > PAPER
PAPERER > PAPER
PAPERERS > PAPER
PAPERGIRL *n* girl employe to deliver newspapers to people's homes
PAPERIER > PAPERY
PAPERIEST > PAPERY
PAPERING > PAPER
PAPERINGS > PAPER
PAPERLESS *adj* of, relating to, or denoting a means of communication, record keeping, etc, esp electronic, that does not use paper
PAPERS > PAPER
PAPERWARE *n* printed matter
PAPERWORK *n* clerical wor such as writing reports and letters
PAPERY *adj* like paper, esp in thinness, flimsiness, or dryness
PAPES > PAPE
PAPETERIE *n* box or case for papers and other writing materials
PAPHIAN *n* prostitute
PAPHIANS > PAPHIAN
PAPILIO *n* butterfly
PAPILIOS > PAPILIO
PAPILLA *n* small projectic of tissue at the base of a hair, tooth, or feather
PAPILLAE > PAPILLA
PAPILLAR > PAPILLA
PAPILLARY > PAPILLA
PAPILLATE > PAPILLA
PAPILLOMA *n* benign tumour derived from epithelial tissue and forming a rounded or lobulated mass
PAPILLON *n* breed of toy

spaniel with large ears
APILLONS > PAPILLON
APILLOSE > PAPILLA
APILLOTE *n* paper frill around cutlets, etc
APILLOUS > PAPILLA
APILLULE *n* tubercle
APISH *n* Catholic
APISHER *n* derogatory term for a Roman Catholic
APISHERS > PAPISHER
APISHES > PAPISH
APISM *n* derogatory term for Roman Catholicism
APISMS > PAPISM
APIST *n* derogatory term for a Roman Catholic
APISTIC > PAPIST
APISTRY > PAPIST
APISTS > PAPIST
APOOSE *n* Native American child
APOOSES > PAPOOSE
APPADAM *same as* > POPPADOM
APPADAMS > PAPPADAM
APPADOM *same as* > POPPADOM
APPADOMS > PAPPADOM
APPED > PAP
APPI > PAPPUS
APPIER > PAPPY
APPIES > PAPPY
APPIEST > PAPPY
APPING > PAP
APPOOSE *same as* > PAPOOSE
APPOOSES > PAPPOOSE
APPOSE > PAPPUS
APPOUS > PAPPUS
APPUS *n* ring of fine feathery hairs surrounding the fruit in composite plants, such as the thistle
APPUSES > PAPPUS
APPY *adj* resembling pap
APRICA *same as* > PAPRIKA
APRICAS > PAPRICA
APRIKA *n* mild powdered seasoning made from red peppers
APRIKAS > PAPRIKA
APS > PAP
APULA *same as* > PAPULE
APULAE > PAPULA
APULAR > PAPULE
APULE *n* small solid usually round elevation of the skin
APULES > PAPULE
APULOSE > PAPULE
APULOUS > PAPULE
APYRAL > PAPYRUS
APYRI > PAPYRUS
APYRIAN > PAPYRUS
APYRINE > PAPYRUS
APYRUS *n* tall water plant
APYRUSES > PAPYRUS
AR *n* usual or average condition ▷ *vb* play (a golf hole) in par
ARA *n* paratrooper
ARABASES > PARABASIS
ARABASIS *n* (in classical Greek comedy) address from the chorus to the audience
PARABEMA *n* architectural feature
PARABLAST *n* yolk of an egg, such as a hen's egg, that undergoes meroblastic cleavage
PARABLE *n* story that illustrates a religious teaching ▷ *vb* write parable
PARABLED > PARABLE
PARABLES > PARABLE
PARABLING > PARABLE
PARABOLA *n* regular curve resembling the course of an object thrown forward and up
PARABOLAS > PARABOLA
PARABOLE *n* similitude
PARABOLES > PARABOLE
PARABOLIC *adj* of, relating to, or shaped like a parabola
PARABRAKE *n* parachute attached to the rear of a vehicle and opened to assist braking
PARACHOR *n* quantity constant over range of temperatures
PARACHORS > PARACHOR
PARACHUTE *n* large fabric canopy that slows the descent of a person or object from an aircraft ▷ *vb* land or drop by parachute
PARACLETE *n* mediator or advocate
PARACME *n* phase where fever lessens
PARACMES > PARACME
PARACRINE *adj* of signalling between biological cells
PARACUSES > PARACUSIS
PARACUSIS *n* hearing disorder
PARADE *n* procession or march ▷ *vb* display or flaunt
PARADED > PARADE
PARADER > PARADE
PARADERS > PARADE
PARADES > PARADE
PARADIGM *n* example or model
PARADIGMS > PARADIGM
PARADING > PARADE
PARADISAL *adj* of, relating to, or resembling paradise
PARADISE *n* heaven
PARADISES > PARADISE
PARADISIC > PARADISE
PARADOR *n* state-run hotel in Spain
PARADORES > PARADOR
PARADORS > PARADOR
PARADOS *n* bank behind a trench or other fortification, giving protection from being fired on from the rear
PARADOSES > PARADOS
PARADOX *n* person or thing made up of contradictory elements
PARADOXAL *adj* paradoxical
PARADOXER *n* proposer of paradox
PARADOXES > PARADOX
PARADOXY *n* state of being paradoxical
PARADROP *n* delivery of personnel or equipment from an aircraft by parachute
PARADROPS > PARADROP
PARAE *n* type of fish
PARAFFIN *n* liquid mixture distilled from petroleum and used as a fuel or solvent ▷ *vb* treat with paraffin or paraffin wax
PARAFFINE *same as* > PARAFFIN
PARAFFINS > PARAFFIN
PARAFFINY *adj* like paraffin
PARAFFLE *n* extravagant display
PARAFFLES > PARAFFLE
PARAFLE *same as* > PARAFFLE
PARAFLES > PARAFLE
PARAFOIL *n* airfoil used on a paraglider
PARAFOILS > PARAFOIL
PARAFORM *n* paraformaldehyde
PARAFORMS > PARAFORM
PARAGE *n* type of feudal land tenure
PARAGES > PARAGE
PARAGLIDE *vb* glide through the air on a special parachute
PARAGOGE *n* addition of a sound or a syllable to the end of a word, such as *st* in *amongst*
PARAGOGES > PARAGOGE
PARAGOGIC > PARAGOGE
PARAGOGUE *same as* > PARAGOGE
PARAGON *n* model of perfection ▷ *vb* equal or surpass
PARAGONED > PARAGON
PARAGONS > PARAGON
PARAGRAM *n* pun
PARAGRAMS > PARAGRAM
PARAGRAPH *n* section of a piece of writing starting on a new line ▷ *vb* put (a piece of writing) into paragraphs
PARAKEET *n* small long-tailed parrot
PARAKEETS > PARAKEET
PARAKELIA *n* succulent herb of the genus *Calandrinia*, with purple flowers, that thrives in inland Australia
PARAKITE *n* series of linked kites
PARAKITES > PARAKITE
PARALALIA *n* any of various speech disorders, esp the production of a sound different from that intended
PARALEGAL *n* person trained to assist lawyers but not qualified to practise law ▷ *adj* of or designating such a person
PARALEXIA *n* disorder of the ability to read in which words and syllables are meaninglessly transposed
PARALEXIC > PARALEXIA
PARALLAX *n* apparent change in an object's position due to a change in the observer's position
PARALLEL *adj* separated by an equal distance at every point ▷ *n* line separated from another by an equal distance at every point ▷ *vb* correspond to
PARALLELS > PARALLEL
PARALOGIA *n* self-deception
PARALOGY *n* anatomical similarity
PARALYSE *vb* affect with paralysis
PARALYSED > PARALYSE
PARALYSER > PARALYSE
PARALYSES > PARALYSIS
PARALYSIS *n* inability to move or feel, because of damage to the nervous system
PARALYTIC *adj* affected with paralysis ▷ *n* person who is paralysed
PARALYZE *same as* > PARALYSE
PARALYZED > PARALYZE
PARALYZER > PARALYSE
PARALYZES > PARALYZE
PARAMATTA *n* lightweight twill-weave fabric of wool with silk or cotton
PARAMECIA *n* freshwater protozoans
PARAMEDIC *n* person working in support of the medical profession ▷ *adj* of or designating such a person
PARAMENT *n* ecclesiastical vestment or decorative hanging
PARAMENTA > PARAMENT
PARAMENTS > PARAMENT
PARAMESE *n* note in ancient Greek music
PARAMESES > PARAMESE
PARAMETER *n* limiting factor, boundary
PARAMO *n* high plateau in the Andes between the tree line and the permanent snow line
PARAMORPH *n* mineral

that has undergone paramorphism
PARAMOS > PARAMO
PARAMOUNT *adj* of the greatest importance ▷ *n* supreme ruler
PARAMOUR *n* lover, esp of a person married to someone else
PARAMOURS > PARAMOUR
PARAMYLUM *n* starch-like substance
PARANETE *n* note in ancient Greek music
PARANETES > PARANETE
PARANG *n* short stout straight-edged knife used by the Dyaks of Borneo
PARANGS > PARANG
PARANOEA *same as* > PARANOIA
PARANOEAS > PARANOEA
PARANOEIC *same as* > PARANOIAC
PARANOIA *n* mental illness causing delusions of grandeur or persecution
PARANOIAC > PARANOIA
PARANOIAS > PARANOIA
PARANOIC > PARANOIA
PARANOICS > PARANOIA
PARANOID *adj* of, characterized by, or resembling paranoia ▷ *n* person who shows the behaviour patterns associated with paranoia
PARANOIDS > PARANOID
PARANYM *n* euphemism
PARANYMPH *n* bridesmaid or best man
PARANYMS > PARANYM
PARAPARA *n* small carnivorous New Zealand tree
PARAPENTE *n* sport of jumping off high mountains wearing skis and a light parachute
PARAPET *n* low wall or railing along the edge of a balcony or roof ▷ *vb* provide with a parapet
PARAPETED > PARAPET
PARAPETS > PARAPET
PARAPH *n* flourish after a signature, originally to prevent forgery ▷ *vb* embellish signature
PARAPHED > PARAPH
PARAPHING > PARAPH
PARAPHS > PARAPH
PARAPODIA *n* paired unjointed lateral appendages of polychaete worms
PARAQUAT *n* yellow extremely poisonous soluble solid used in solution as a weedkiller
PARAQUATS > PARAQUAT
PARAQUET *n* long-tailed parrot
PARAQUETS > PARAQUET
PARAQUITO *n* parakeet
PARARHYME *n* type of rhyme
PARAS > PARA
PARASAIL *vb* glide through air on parachute towed by boat
PARASAILS > PARASAIL
PARASANG *n* Persian unit of distance equal to about 5.5 km or 3.4 miles
PARASANGS > PARASANG
PARASCEVE *n* preparation
PARASHAH *n* section of the Torah read in the synagogue
PARASHAHS > PARASHAH
PARASHOT > PARASHAH
PARASHOTH > PARASHAH
PARASITE *n* animal or plant living in or on another
PARASITES > PARASITE
PARASITIC > PARASITE
PARASOL *n* umbrella-like sunshade
PARASOLED *adj* having a parasol
PARASOLS > PARASOL
PARATAXES > PARATAXIS
PARATAXIS *n* juxtaposition of clauses in a sentence without the use of a conjunction
PARATHA *n* (in Indian cookery) flat unleavened bread, resembling a small nan bread, that is fried on a griddle
PARATHAS > PARATHA
PARATHION *n* slightly water-soluble toxic oil, odourless and colourless when pure, used as an insecticide
PARATONIC *adj* (of a plant movement) occurring in response to an external stimulus
PARATROOP *n* paratrooper
PARAVAIL *adj* lowest
PARAVANE *n* torpedo-shaped device towed from the bow of a vessel so that the cables will cut the anchors of any moored mines
PARAVANES > PARAVANE
PARAVANT *adv* in front
PARAVAUNT *same as* > PARAVANT
PARAWING *n* paraglider
PARAWINGS > PARAWING
PARAXIAL *adj* (of a light ray) parallel to the axis of an optical system
PARAZOA > PARAZOAN
PARAZOAN *n* sea sponge
PARAZOANS > PARAZOAN
PARAZOON *n* parasitic animal
PARBAKE *vb* partially bake
PARBAKED > PARBAKE
PARBAKES > PARBAKE
PARBAKING > PARBAKE
PARBOIL *vb* boil until partly cooked
PARBOILED > PARBOIL
PARBOILS > PARBOIL
PARBREAK *vb* vomit
PARBREAKS > PARBREAK
PARBUCKLE *n* rope sling for lifting or lowering a heavy cylindrical object, such as a cask or tree trunk ▷ *vb* raise or lower (an object) with such a sling
PARCEL *n* something wrapped up, package ▷ *vb* wrap up
PARCELED > PARCEL
PARCELING > PARCEL
PARCELLED > PARCEL
PARCELS > PARCEL
PARCENARY *n* joint heirship
PARCENER *n* person who takes an equal share with another or others
PARCENERS > PARCENER
PARCH *vb* make very hot and dry
PARCHED > PARCH
PARCHEDLY > PARCH
PARCHEESI *n* modern board game derived from the ancient game of pachisi
PARCHES > PARCH
PARCHESI *same as* > PARCHEESI
PARCHESIS > PARCHESI
PARCHING > PARCH
PARCHISI *same as* > PARCHEESI
PARCHISIS > PARCHISI
PARCHMENT *n* thick smooth writing material made from animal skin
PARCIMONY *obsolete variant of* > PARSIMONY
PARCLOSE *n* screen or railing in a church separating off an altar, chapel, etc
PARCLOSES > PARCLOSE
PARD *n* leopard or panther ▷ *vb* partner
PARDAH *same as* > PURDAH
PARDAHS > PARDAH
PARDAL *variant spelling of* > PARDALE
PARDALE *n* leopard
PARDALES > PARDALE
PARDALIS *n* leopard
PARDALOTE *n* small Australian songbird
PARDALS > PARDAL
PARDED > PARD
PARDEE *adv* certainly
PARDI *same as* > PARDEE
PARDIE *same as* > PARDEE
PARDINE *adj* spotted
PARDING > PARD
PARDNER *n* friend or partner: used as a term of address
PARDNERS > PARDNER
PARDON *vb* forgive, excuse ▷ *n* forgiveness ▷ *interj* sorry ▷ *sentence substitute* sorry
PARDONED > PARDON
PARDONER *n* (before the Reformation) person licensed to sell ecclesiastical indulgence
PARDONERS > PARDONER
PARDONING > PARDON
PARDONS > PARDON
PARDS > PARD
PARDY *same as* > PARDEE
PARE *vb* cut off the skin or top layer of
PARECIOUS *adj* having the male and female reproductive organs at different levels on the same stem
PARECISM *n* state of havin male and female organs close together
PARECISMS > PARECISM
PARED > PARE
PAREGORIC *n* medicine containing opium, benzoic acid, camphor or ammonia, and anise oil
PAREIRA *n* root of a South American menispermaceous climbing plant
PAREIRAS > PAREIRA
PARELLA *n* type of lichen
PARELLAS > PARELLA
PARELLE *same as* > PARELL
PARELLES > PARELLE
PARENESES > PARENESIS
PARENESIS *n* exhortatior
PARENT *n* father or mothe ▷ *vb* raise offspring
PARENTAGE *n* ancestry or family
PARENTAL *adj* of or relatin to a parent or parenthooc
PARENTED > PARENT
PARENTING *n* activity of bringing up children
PARENTS > PARENT
PAREO *same as* > PAREU
PAREOS > PAREU
PARER > PARE
PARERA *n* New Zealand duck with grey-edged brown feathers
PARERGA > PARERGON
PARERGON *n* work that is not one's main employment
PARERS > PARE
PARES > PARE
PARESES > PARESIS
PARESIS *n* incomplete or slight paralysis of motor functions
PARETIC > PARESIS
PARETICS > PARESIS
PAREU *n* rectangle of fabri worn by Polynesians as a skirt or loincloth
PAREUS > PAREU
PAREV *adj* containing neither meat nor milk products and so fit for us

vith either meat or milk dishes
AREVE *same as* > PAREV
ARFAIT *n* dessert consisting of layers of ice cream, fruit, and sauce, topped with whipped cream, and served in a tall glass
ARFAITS > PARFAIT
ARFLECHE *n* sheet of rawhide that has been dried after soaking in lye and water to remove the hair
ARFLESH *same as* > PARFLECHE
ARFOCAL *adj* with focal points in the same plane
ARGANA *n* Indian sub-district
ARGANAS > PARGANA
ARGASITE *n* dark green mineral
ARGE *vb* coat with plaster
ARGED > PARGE
ARGES > PARGE
ARGET *n* plaster, mortar, etc, used to line chimney flues or cover walls ▷ *vb* cover or decorate with parget
ARGETED > PARGET
ARGETER > PARGET
ARGETERS > PARGET
ARGETING *same as* > PARGET
ARGETS > PARGET
ARGETTED > PARGET
ARGING > PARGE
ARGINGS > PARGE
ARGO *n* sea bream
ARGOS > PARGO
ARGYLINE *n* monoamine oxidase inhibitor
ARHELIA > PARHELION
ARHELIC > PARHELION
ARHELION *n* one of several bright spots on the parhelic circle or solar halo
ARHYPATE *n* note in ancient Greek music
ARIAH *n* social outcast
ARIAHS > PARIAH
ARIAL *n* pair royal of playing cards
ARIALS > PARIAL
ARIAN *n* type of marble or porcelain
ARIANS > PARIAN
ARIES *n* wall of an organ or bodily cavity
ARIETAL *adj* of the walls of a body cavity such as the skull ▷ *n* parietal bone
ARIETALS > PARIETAL
ARIETES > PARIES
ARING *n* piece pared off
ARINGS > PARING
ARIS *n* type of herb
ARISCHAN *variant of* > PAROCHIN
ARISES > PARIS
ARISH *n* area that has its own church and a priest or pastor
PARISHAD *n* Indian assembly
PARISHADS > PARISHAD
PARISHEN *n* member of parish
PARISHENS > PARISHEN
PARISHES > PARISH
PARISON *n* unshaped mass of glass before it is moulded into its final form
PARISONS > PARISON
PARITIES > PARITY
PARITOR *n* official who summons witnesses
PARITORS > PARITOR
PARITY *n* equality or equivalence
PARK *n* area of open land for recreational use by the public ▷ *vb* stop and leave (a vehicle) temporarily
PARKA *n* large waterproof jacket with a hood
PARKADE *n* building used as a car park
PARKADES > PARKADE
PARKAS > PARKA
PARKED > PARK
PARKEE *n* Eskimo outer garment
PARKEES > PARKEE
PARKER > PARK
PARKERS > PARK
PARKETTE *n* small public car park
PARKETTES > PARKETTE
PARKI *variant of* > PARKA
PARKIE *n* park keeper
PARKIER > PARKY
PARKIES > PARKIE
PARKIEST > PARKY
PARKIN *n* moist spicy ginger cake usually containing oatmeal
PARKING > PARK
PARKINGS > PARK
PARKINS > PARKIN
PARKIS > PARKI
PARKISH *adj* like a park
PARKLAND *n* grassland with scattered trees
PARKLANDS > PARKLAND
PARKLIKE > PARK
PARKLY *adj* having many parks or resembling a park
PARKOUR *n* sport of running in urban areas performing gymnastics on manmade obstacles
PARKOURS > PARKOUR
PARKS > PARK
PARKWARD *adv* towards a park
PARKWARDS *adv* towards a park
PARKWAY *n* (in the US and Canada) wide road planted with trees, turf, etc
PARKWAYS > PARKWAY
PARKY *adj* (of the weather) chilly
PARLANCE *n* particular way of speaking, idiom
PARLANCES > PARLANCE
PARLANDO *adv* to be performed as though speaking
PARLANTE *same as* > PARLANDO
PARLAY *vb* stake (winnings from one bet) on a subsequent wager ▷ *n* bet in which winnings from one wager are staked on another, or a series of such bets
PARLAYED > PARLAY
PARLAYING > PARLAY
PARLAYS > PARLAY
PARLE *vb* speak
PARLED > PARLE
PARLEMENT *n* parliament
PARLES > PARLE
PARLEY *n* meeting between leaders or representatives of opposing forces to discuss terms ▷ *vb* have a parley
PARLEYED > PARLEY
PARLEYER > PARLEY
PARLEYERS > PARLEY
PARLEYING > PARLEY
PARLEYS > PARLEY
PARLEYVOO *vb* speak French ▷ *n* French language
PARLIES *pl n* small Scottish biscuits
PARLING > PARLE
PARLOR *same as* > PARLOUR
PARLORS > PARLOR
PARLOUR *n* living room for receiving visitors
PARLOURS > PARLOUR
PARLOUS *adj* dire ▷ *adv* extremely
PARLOUSLY > PARLOUS
PARLY *n* short form of parliament
PARMESAN *n* Italian hard cheese
PARMESANS > PARMESAN
PAROCHIAL *adj* narrow in outlook
PAROCHIN *n* old Scottish parish
PAROCHINE *same as* > PAROCHIN
PAROCHINS > PAROCHIN
PARODIC > PARODY
PARODICAL > PARODY
PARODIED > PARODY
PARODIES > PARODY
PARODIST > PARODY
PARODISTS > PARODY
PARODOI *n* path leading to Greek theatre
PARODOS *n* ode sung by Greek chorus
PARODY *n* exaggerated and amusing imitation of someone else's style ▷ *vb* make a parody of
PARODYING > PARODY
PAROEMIA *n* proverb
PAROEMIAC *adj* of proverbs
PAROEMIAL *adj* of proverbs
PAROEMIAS > PAROEMIA
PAROICOUS *same as* > PARECIOUS
PAROL *n* (formerly) pleadings in an action when presented by word of mouth ▷ *adj* (of a contract, lease, etc) made orally or in writing but not under seal
PAROLABLE > PAROLE
PAROLE *n* early freeing of a prisoner on condition that he or she behaves well ▷ *vb* put on parole
PAROLED > PAROLE
PAROLEE > PAROLE
PAROLEES > PAROLE
PAROLES > PAROLE
PAROLING > PAROLE
PAROLS > PAROL
PARONYM *n* cognate word
PARONYMIC > PARONYM
PARONYMS > PARONYM
PARONYMY > PARONYM
PAROQUET *n* small long-tailed parrot
PAROQUETS > PARROQUET
PARORE *n* type of fish found around Australia and New Zealand
PAROSMIA *n* any disorder of the sense of smell
PAROSMIAS > PAROSMIA
PAROTIC *adj* situated near the ear
PAROTID *adj* relating to or situated near the parotid gland ▷ *n* parotid gland
PAROTIDS > PAROTID
PAROTIS *n* parotid gland
PAROTISES > PAROTIS
PAROTITIC > PAROTITIS
PAROTITIS *n* inflammation of the parotid gland
PAROTOID *n* any of various warty poison glands on the head and back of certain toads and salamanders ▷ *adj* resembling a parotid gland
PAROTOIDS > PAROTOID
PAROUS *adj* having given birth
PAROUSIA *n* Second Coming
PAROUSIAS > PAROUSIA
PAROXYSM *n* uncontrollable outburst of rage, delight, etc
PAROXYSMS > PAROXYSM
PARP *vb* make a honking sound
PARPANE *n* parapet on bridge
PARPANES > PARPANE
PARPED > PARP
PARPEN *same as* > PARPEND
PARPEND *same as* > PERPEND
PARPENDS > PARPEND
PARPENS > PARPEN
PARPENT *n* parapet on

bridge
PARPENTS > PARPENT
PARPING > PARP
PARPOINT *n* parapet on bridge
PARPOINTS > PARPOINT
PARPS > PARP
PARQUET *n* floor covering made of wooden blocks arranged in a geometric pattern ▷ *vb* cover with parquet
PARQUETED > PARQUET
PARQUETRY *n* pieces of wood arranged in a geometric pattern, used to cover floors
PARQUETS > PARQUET
PARR *n* salmon up to two years of age
PARRA *n* tourist or non-resident on a beach
PARRAKEET *same as* > PARAKEET
PARRAL *same as* > PARREL
PARRALS > PARRAL
PARRAS > PARRA
PARRED > PAR
PARREL *n* ring that holds the jaws of a boom to the mast but lets it slide up and down
PARRELS > PARREL
PARRHESIA *n* boldness of speech
PARRICIDE *n* crime of killing either of one's parents
PARRIDGE *Scottish variant of* > PORRIDGE
PARRIDGES > PARRIDGE
PARRIED > PARRY
PARRIER > PARRY
PARRIERS > PARRY
PARRIES > PARRY
PARRING > PAR
PARRITCH *Scottish variant of* > PORRIDGE
PARROCK *vb* put (an animal) in a small field
PARROCKED > PARROCK
PARROCKS > PARROCK
PARROKET *n* small long-tailed parrot
PARROKETS > PARROKET
PARROQUET *n* small long-tailed parrot
PARROT *n* tropical bird with a short hooked beak and an ability to imitate human speech ▷ *vb* repeat (someone else's words) without thinking
PARROTED > PARROT
PARROTER *n* person who repeats what is said
PARROTERS > PARROTER
PARROTING > PARROT
PARROTRY > PARROT
PARROTS > PARROT
PARROTY *adj* like a parrot; chattering
PARRS > PARR
PARRY *vb* ward off (an attack) ▷ *n* parrying
PARRYING > PARRY
PARS > PAR
PARSABLE > PARSE
PARSE *vb* analyse (a sentence) in terms of grammar
PARSEC *n* unit of astronomical distance
PARSECS > PARSEC
PARSED > PARSE
PARSER *n* program or part of a program that interprets input to a computer by recognizing key words or analysing sentence structure
PARSERS > PARSER
PARSES > PARSE
PARSIMONY *n* extreme caution in spending money
PARSING > PARSE
PARSINGS > PARSE
PARSLEY *n* herb used for seasoning and decorating food ▷ *vb* garnish with parsley
PARSLEYED > PARSLEY
PARSLEYS > PARSLEY
PARSLIED > PARSLEY
PARSNEP *same as* > PARSNIP
PARSNEPS > PARSNEP
PARSNIP *n* long tapering cream-coloured root vegetable
PARSNIPS > PARSNIP
PARSON *n* Anglican parish priest
PARSONAGE *n* parson's house
PARSONIC > PARSON
PARSONISH *adj* like a parson
PARSONS > PARSON
PART *n* one of the pieces that make up a whole ▷ *vb* divide or separate
PARTAKE *vb* take (food or drink)
PARTAKEN > PARTAKE
PARTAKER > PARTAKE
PARTAKERS > PARTAKE
PARTAKES > PARTAKE
PARTAKING > PARTAKE
PARTAN *Scottish word for* > CRAB
PARTANS > PARTAN
PARTED *adj* divided almost to the base
PARTER *n* thing that parts
PARTERRE *n* formally patterned flower garden
PARTERRES > PARTERRE
PARTERS > PARTER
PARTI *n* concept of architectural design
PARTIAL *adj* not complete ▷ *n* any of the component tones of a single musical sound, including both those that belong to the harmonic series of the sound and those that do not
PARTIALLY > PARTIAL
PARTIALS > PARTIAL
PARTIBLE *adj* (esp of property or an inheritance) divisible
PARTICLE *n* extremely small piece or amount
PARTICLES > PARTICLE
PARTIED > PARTY
PARTIER *n* person who parties
PARTIERS > PARTIER
PARTIES > PARTY
PARTIM *adv* in part
PARTING *same as* > PART
PARTINGS > PARTING
PARTIS > PARTI
PARTISAN *n* strong supporter of a party or group ▷ *adj* prejudiced or one-sided
PARTISANS > PARTISAN
PARTITA *n* type of suite
PARTITAS > PARTITA
PARTITE *adj* composed of or divided into a specified number of parts
PARTITION *n* screen or thin wall that divides a room ▷ *vb* divide with a partition
PARTITIVE *adj* (of a noun) referring to part of something ▷ *n* partitive word, such as *some* or *any*
PARTITURA *n* music score for several parts
PARTIZAN *same as* > PARTISAN
PARTIZANS > PARTIZAN
PARTLET *n* woman's garment covering the neck and shoulders
PARTLETS > PARTLET
PARTLY *adv* not completely
PARTNER *n* either member of a couple in a relationship or activity ▷ *vb* be the partner of
PARTNERED > PARTNER
PARTNERS > PARTNER
PARTON *n* hypothetical elementary particle postulated as a constituent of neutrons and protons
PARTONS > PARTON
PARTOOK > PARTAKE
PARTRIDGE *n* game bird of the grouse family
PARTS *pl n* abilities or talents
PARTURE *n* departure
PARTURES > PARTURE
PARTWAY *adv* some of the way
PARTWORK *n* series of magazines issued at weekly or monthly intervals, which are designed to be bound together to form a complete course or book
PARTWORKS > PARTWORK
PARTY *n* social gathering for pleasure ▷ *vb* celebrate, have fun ▷ *adj* (of a shield) divided vertically into two colours, metals, or furs
PARTYER *n* person who parties
PARTYERS > PARTYER
PARTYGOER *n* person who goes to party
PARTYING > PARTY
PARTYISM *n* devotion to political party
PARTYISMS > PARTYISM
PARULIDES > PARULIS
PARULIS *another name for* > GUMBOIL
PARULISES > PARULIS
PARURA *same as* > PARURE
PARURAS > PARURA
PARURE *n* set of jewels or other ornaments
PARURES > PARURE
PARVE *same as* > PAREV
PARVENU *n* person newly risen to a position of power or wealth ▷ *adj* of or characteristic of a parvenu
PARVENUE *n* woman who, having risen socially or economically, is considered to be an upstart or to lack the appropriate refinement for her new position ▷ *adj* of or characteristic of a parvenue
PARVENUES > PARVENUE
PARVENUS > PARVENU
PARVIS *n* court or portico in front of a building, esp a church
PARVISE *same as* > PARVIS
PARVISES > PARVISE
PARVO *n* disease of cattle and dogs
PARVOLIN *n* substance resulting from the putrefaction of flesh
PARVOLINE *n* liquid derived from coal tar
PARVOLINS > PARVOLIN
PARVOS > PARVO
PAS *n* dance step or movement, esp in ballet
PASCAL *n* unit of pressure
PASCALS > PASCAL
PASCHAL *adj* of the Passover or Easter ▷ *n* Passover or Easter
PASCHALS > PASCHAL
PASCUAL *adj* relating to pasture
PASE *n* movement of the cape or muleta by a matador to attract the bull's attention and guide its attack
PASEAR *vb* go for a rambling walk
PASEARED > PASEAR

SEARING > PASEAR
SEARS > PASEAR
SEO *n* bullfighters' rocession
SEOS > PASEO
SES > PASE
SH *n* infatuation ▷ *vb* hrow or be thrown and reak or be broken to bits
SHA *n* high official of the)ttoman Empire
SHADOM *n* territory of a asha
SHADOMS > PASHADOM
SHALIC *same* s > PASHALIK
SHALICS > PASHALIC
SHALIK *n* province or urisdiction of a pasha
SHALIKS > PASHALIK
SHAS > PASHA
SHED > PASH
SHES > PASH
SHIM *same as* > PASHM
SHIMS > PASHM
SHING > PASH
SHKA *n* rich Russian essert made of cottage heese, cream, almonds, urrants, etc
SHKAS > PASHKA
SHM *n* underfur of arious Tibetan animals, sp goats, used for ashmere shawls
SHMINA *n* type of ashmere scarf or shawl nade from the underfur of ibetan goats
SHMINAS > PASHMINA
SHMS > PASHM
SODOBLE *n* fast modern allroom dance
SPALUM *n* type of grass vith wide leaves
SPALUMS > PASPALUM
SPIES > PASPY
SPY *n* piece of music in riple time
SQUIL *n* abusive ampoon or satire ▷ *vb* idicule with pasquil
SQUILER *n* person who ampoons
SQUILS > PASQUIL
SS *vb* go by, past, or hrough ▷ *n* successful esult in a test or xamination
SSABLE *adj* (just) cceptable
SSABLY *adv* fairly
SSADE *n* act of moving ack and forth in the same lace
SSADES > PASSADE
SSADO *n* forward thrust vith sword
SSADOES > PASSADO
SSADOS > PASSADO
SSAGE *n* channel or pening providing a way hrough ▷ *vb* move or ause to move at a passage

PASSAGED > PASSAGE
PASSAGER as in *passager hawk* young hawk or falcon caught while on migration
PASSAGES > PASSAGE
PASSAGING > PASSAGE
PASSALONG *adj* (of plants) easily propagated and given to others
PASSAMENT *vb* sew border on garment
PASSANT *adj* (of a beast) walking, with the right foreleg raised
PASSATA *n* sauce made from sieved tomatoes, often used in Italian cookery
PASSATAS > PASSATA
PASSBAND *n* band of frequencies that is transmitted with maximum efficiency through a circuit, filter, etc
PASSBANDS > PASSBAND
PASSBOOK *n* book issued by a bank or building society for keeping a record of deposits and withdrawals
PASSBOOKS > PASSBOOK
PASSE *adj* out-of-date
PASSED > PASS
PASSEE *adj* out of fashion
PASSEL *n* group or quantity of no fixed number
PASSELS > PASSEL
PASSEMENT *vb* sew border on garment
PASSENGER *n* person travelling in a vehicle driven by someone else
PASSEPIED *n* lively minuet of Breton origin
PASSER *n* person or thing that passes
PASSERBY *n* person that is passing or going by, esp on foot
PASSERINE *adj* belonging to the order of perching birds ▷ *n* any bird of this order
PASSERS > PASSER
PASSERSBY > PASSERBY
PASSES > PASS
PASSIBLE *adj* susceptible to emotion or suffering
PASSIBLY > PASSIBLE
PASSIM *adv* everywhere, throughout
PASSING *adj* brief or transitory ▷ *n* death
PASSINGLY > PASSING
PASSINGS > PASSING
PASSION *n* intense sexual love ▷ *vb* give passionate character to
PASSIONAL *adj* of, relating to, or due to passion or the passions ▷ *n* book recounting the sufferings of Christian martyrs or saints

PASSIONED > PASSION
PASSIONS > PASSION
PASSIVATE *vb* render (a metal) less susceptible to corrosion by coating the surface with a substance, such as an oxide
PASSIVE *adj* not playing an active part ▷ *n* passive form of a verb
PASSIVELY > PASSIVE
PASSIVES > PASSIVE
PASSIVISM *n* theory, belief, or practice of passive resistance
PASSIVIST > PASSIVISM
PASSIVITY > PASSIVE
PASSKEY *n* private key
PASSKEYS > PASSKEY
PASSLESS *adj* having no pass
PASSMAN *n* student who passes without honours
PASSMEN > PASSMAN
PASSMENT *same as* > PASSEMENT
PASSMENTS > PASSMENT
PASSOUT *n* (in ice hockey) pass by an attacking player from behind the opposition goal line
PASSOUTS > PASSOUT
PASSOVER *n* lamb eaten during Passover
PASSOVERS > PASSOVER
PASSPORT *n* official document of nationality granting permission to travel abroad
PASSPORTS > PASSPORT
PASSUS *n* (esp in medieval literature) division or section of a poem, story, etc
PASSUSES > PASSUS
PASSWORD *n* secret word or phrase that ensures admission
PASSWORDS > PASSWORD
PAST *adj* of the time before the present ▷ *n* period of time before the present ▷ *adv* ago ▷ *prep* beyond
PASTA *n* type of food, such as spaghetti, that is made in different shapes from flour and water
PASTALIKE > PASTA
PASTANCE *n* activity that passes time
PASTANCES > PASTANCE
PASTAS > PASTA
PASTE *n* moist soft mixture, such as toothpaste ▷ *vb* fasten with paste
PASTED > PASTE
PASTEDOWN *n* portion of endpaper pasted to cover of book
PASTEL *n* coloured chalk crayon for drawing ▷ *adj* pale and delicate in colour
PASTELIST > PASTEL

PASTELS > PASTEL
PASTER *n* person or thing that pastes
PASTERN *n* part of a horse's foot between the fetlock and the hoof
PASTERNS > PASTERN
PASTERS > PASTER
PASTES > PASTE
PASTEUP *n* assembly of typeset matter, illustrations, etc, pasted on a sheet of paper or board
PASTEUPS > PASTEUP
PASTICCI > PASTICCIO
PASTICCIO *n* art work borrowing various styles
PASTICHE *n* work of art that mixes styles or copies the style of another artist
PASTICHES > PASTICHE
PASTIE *n* decorative cover for nipple
PASTIER > PASTY
PASTIES > PASTY
PASTIEST > PASTY
PASTIL *same as* > PASTILLE
PASTILLE *n* small fruit-flavoured and sometimes medicated sweet
PASTILLES > PASTILLE
PASTILS > PASTIL
PASTILY > PASTY
PASTIME *n* activity that makes time pass pleasantly
PASTIMES > PASTIME
PASTINA *n* small pieces of pasta
PASTINAS > PASTINA
PASTINESS > PASTY
PASTING *n* heavy defeat
PASTINGS > PASTING
PASTIS *n* anise-flavoured alcoholic drink
PASTISES > PASTIS
PASTITSIO *n* Greek dish consisting of minced meat and macaroni topped with bechamel sauce
PASTITSO *n* Greek dish of baked pasta
PASTITSOS > PASTITSO
PASTLESS *adj* having no past
PASTNESS *n* quality of being past
PASTOR *n* member of the clergy in charge of a congregation ▷ *vb* act as a pastor
PASTORAL *adj* of or depicting country life ▷ *n* poem or picture portraying country life
PASTORALE *n* musical composition that suggests country life
PASTORALI > PASTORALE
PASTORALS > PASTORAL
PASTORATE *n* office or term of office of a pastor
PASTORED > PASTOR

PASTORING > PASTOR
PASTORIUM *n* residence of pastor
PASTORLY > PASTOR
PASTORS > PASTOR
PASTRAMI *n* highly seasoned smoked beef
PASTRAMIS > PASTRAMI
PASTRIES > PASTRY
PASTROMI *same as* > PASTRAMI
PASTROMIS > PASTROMI
PASTRY *n* baking dough made of flour, fat, and water
PASTS > PAST
PASTURAGE *n* business of grazing cattle
PASTURAL *adj* of pasture
PASTURE *n* grassy land for farm animals to graze on ▷ *vb* cause (livestock) to graze or (of livestock) to graze (a pasture)
PASTURED > PASTURE
PASTURER *n* person who tends cattle
PASTURERS > PASTURER
PASTURES > PASTURE
PASTURING > PASTURE
PASTY *adj* (of a complexion) pale and unhealthy ▷ *n* round of pastry folded over a savoury filling
PAT *vb* tap lightly ▷ *n* gentle tap or stroke ▷ *adj* quick, ready, or glib
PATACA *n* monetary unit of Macao
PATACAS > PATACA
PATAGIA > PATAGIUM
PATAGIAL > PATAGIUM
PATAGIUM *n* web of skin between the neck, limbs, and tail in bats and gliding mammals that functions as a wing
PATAKA *n* building on stilts, used for storing provisions
PATAMAR *n* type of boat
PATAMARS > PATAMAR
PATBALL *n* game like squash but using hands instead of rackets
PATBALLS > PATBALL
PATCH *n* piece of material sewn on a garment ▷ *vb* mend with a patch
PATCHABLE > PATCH
PATCHED > PATCH
PATCHER > PATCH
PATCHERS > PATCH
PATCHERY *n* bungling work
PATCHES > PATCH
PATCHIER > PATCHY
PATCHIEST > PATCHY
PATCHILY > PATCHY
PATCHING > PATCH
PATCHINGS > PATCH
PATCHOCKE *Spenserian word for* > CLOWN
PATCHOULI *n* Asiatic tree, the leaves of which yield a heavy fragrant oil
PATCHOULY *same as* > PATCHOULI
PATCHWORK *n* needlework made of pieces of different materials sewn together
PATCHY *adj* of uneven quality or intensity
PATE *n* head
PATED > PATE
PATELA *n* flat-bottomed Indian river boat
PATELAS > PATELA
PATELLA *n* kneecap
PATELLAE > PATELLA
PATELLAR > PATELLA
PATELLAS > PATELLA
PATELLATE *adj* having the shape of a patella
PATEN *n* plate, usually made of silver or gold, used for the bread at Communion
PATENCIES > PATENCY
PATENCY *n* condition of being obvious
PATENS > PATEN
PATENT *n* document giving the exclusive right to make or sell an invention ▷ *adj* open to public inspection ▷ *vb* obtain a patent for
PATENTED > PATENT
PATENTEE *n* person, group, company, etc, that has been granted a patent
PATENTEES > PATENTEE
PATENTING > PATENT
PATENTLY *adv* obviously
PATENTOR *n* person who or official body that grants a patent or patents
PATENTORS > PATENTOR
PATENTS > PATENT
PATER *n* father
PATERA *n* shallow ancient Roman bowl
PATERAE > PATERA
PATERCOVE *n* fraudulent priest
PATERERO *n* type of cannon
PATEREROS > PATERERO
PATERNAL *adj* fatherly
PATERNITY *n* fact or state of being a father
PATERS > PATER
PATES > PATE
PATH *n* surfaced walk or track ▷ *vb* make a path
PATHED > PATH
PATHETIC *adj* causing feelings of pity or sadness ▷ *pl n* pathetic sentiments ▷ *n* pathetic person
PATHETICS > PATHETIC
PATHIC *n* catamite ▷ *adj* of or relating to a catamite
PATHICS > PATHIC
PATHING > PATH
PATHLESS > PATH
PATHNAME *n* name of a file or directory together with its position in relation to other directories traced back in a line to the root
PATHNAMES > PATHNAME
PATHOGEN *n* thing that causes disease
PATHOGENE *same as* > PATHOGEN
PATHOGENS > PATHOGEN
PATHOGENY *n* origin, development, and resultant effects of a disease
PATHOLOGY *n* scientific study of diseases
PATHOS *n* power of arousing pity or sadness
PATHOSES > PATHOS
PATHS > PATH
PATHWAY *n* path
PATHWAYS > PATHWAY
PATIBLE *adj* endurable
PATIENCE *n* quality of being patient
PATIENCES > PATIENCE
PATIENT *adj* enduring difficulties or delays calmly ▷ *n* person receiving medical treatment ▷ *vb* make calm
PATIENTED > PATIENT
PATIENTER > PATIENT
PATIENTLY > PATIENT
PATIENTS > PATIENT
PATIKI *n* New Zealand sand flounder or dab
PATIN *same as* > PATEN
PATINA *n* fine layer on a surface
PATINAE > PATINA
PATINAED *adj* having a patina
PATINAS > PATINA
PATINATE *vb* coat with patina
PATINATED > PATINATE
PATINATES > PATINATE
PATINE *vb* cover with patina
PATINED > PATINE
PATINES > PATINE
PATINING > PATINE
PATINISE *same as* > PATINIZE
PATINISED > PATINISE
PATINISES > PATINISE
PATINIZE *vb* coat with patina
PATINIZED > PATINIZE
PATINIZES > PATINIZE
PATINS > PATIN
PATIO *n* paved area adjoining a house
PATIOS > PATIO
PATISSIER *n* pastry chef
PATLY *adv* fitly
PATNESS *n* appropriateness
PATNESSES > PATNESS
PATOIS *n* regional dialect, esp of French
PATONCE *adj* (of cross) with limbs which broaden from centre
PATOOTIE *n* person's bottom
PATOOTIES > PATOOTIE
PATRIAL *n* (in Britain, formerly) person with a right by statute to live in the United Kingdom, and so not subject to immigration control
PATRIALS > PATRIAL
PATRIARCH *n* male head of a family or tribe
PATRIATE *vb* bring under the authority of an autonomous country
PATRIATED > PATRIATE
PATRIATES > PATRIATE
PATRICIAN *n* member of the nobility ▷ *adj* of noble birth
PATRICIDE *n* crime of killing one's father
PATRICK *n* former Irish coin
PATRICKS > PATRICK
PATRICO *n* fraudulent priest
PATRICOES > PATRICO
PATRILINY *n* tracing of family descent through males
PATRIMONY *n* property inherited from ancestors
PATRIOT *n* person who loves his or her country and supports its interests
PATRIOTIC > PATRIOT
PATRIOTS > PATRIOT
PATRISTIC *adj* of or relating to the Fathers of the Church, their writings or the study of these
PATROL *n* regular circuit by a guard ▷ *vb* go round on guard, or reconnoitring
PATROLLED > PATROL
PATROLLER > PATROL
PATROLMAN *n* man, esp a policeman, who patrols a certain area
PATROLMEN > PATROLMAN
PATROLOGY *n* study of the writings of the Fathers of the Church
PATROLS > PATROL
PATRON *n* person who gives financial support to charities, artists, etc
PATRONAGE *n* support given by a patron
PATRONAL > PATRONESS
PATRONESS *n* woman who sponsors or aids artists, charities, etc
PATRONISE *same as* > PATRONIZE
PATRONIZE *vb* treat in a condescending way
PATRONLY > PATRONESS
PATRONNE *n* woman who owns or manages a hotel, restaurant, or bar
PATRONNES > PATRONNE
PATRONS > PATRON
PATROON *n* Dutch land-holder in New Netherland and New York with

manorial rights in the colonial era
ATROONS > PATROON
ATS > PAT
ATSIES > PATSY
ATSY *n* person who is easily cheated, victimized, etc
ATTAMAR *n* Indian courier
ATTAMARS > PATTAMAR
ATTE *n* band keeping belt in place
ATTED > PAT
ATTEE *adj* (of a cross) having triangular arms widening outwards
ATTEN *n* wooden clog or sandal on a raised wooden platform or metal ring ▷ *vb* wear pattens
ATTENED > PATTEN
ATTENING > PATTEN
ATTENS > PATTEN
ATTER *vb* make repeated soft tapping sounds ▷ *n* quick succession of taps
ATTERED > PATTER
ATTERER > PATTER
ATTERERS > PATTER
ATTERING > PATTER
ATTERN *n* arrangement of repeated parts or decorative designs ▷ *vb* model
ATTERNED > PATTERN
ATTERNS > PATTERN
ATTERS > PATTER
ATTES > PATTE
ATTIE *same as* > PATTY
ATTIES > PATTY
ATTING > PAT
ATTLE *dialect for* > PADDLE
ATTLES > PATTLE
ATTY *n* small flattened cake of minced food
ATTYPAN *n* small round flattish squash
ATTYPANS > PATTYPAN
ATU *n* short Māori club, now used ceremonially
ATULENT *adj* spreading widely
ATULIN *n* toxic antibiotic
ATULINS > PATULIN
ATULOUS *adj* spreading widely or expanded
ATUS > PATU
ATUTUKI *n* blue cod
ATUTUKIS > PATUTUKI
ATY *adj* (of cross) having arms of equal length
ATZER *n* novice chess player
ATZERS > PATZER
AUA *n* edible shellfish of New Zealand, which has a pearly shell used for jewellery
AUAS > PAUA
AUCAL *n* grammatical number occurring in some languages for words in contexts where a few of their referents are described or referred to ▷ *adj* relating to or inflected for this number
PAUCALS > PAUCAL
PAUCITIES > PAUCITY
PAUCITY *n* scarcity
PAUGHTIER > PAUGHTY
PAUGHTY *Scots word for* > HAUGHTY
PAUL *same as* > PAWL
PAULDRON *n* either of two metal plates worn with armour to protect the shoulders
PAULDRONS > PAULDRON
PAULIN *n* tarpaulin
PAULINS > PAULIN
PAULOWNIA *n* Japanese tree with large heart-shaped leaves and clusters of purplish or white flowers
PAULS > PAUL
PAUNCE *n* pansy
PAUNCES > PAUNCE
PAUNCH *n* protruding belly ▷ *vb* stab in the stomach
PAUNCHED > PAUNCH
PAUNCHES > PAUNCH
PAUNCHIER > PAUNCHY
PAUNCHING > PAUNCH
PAUNCHY *adj* having a protruding belly or abdomen
PAUPER *n* very poor person ▷ *vb* reduce to beggary
PAUPERED > PAUPER
PAUPERESS *n* female pauper
PAUPERING > PAUPER
PAUPERISE *same as* > PAUPERIZE
PAUPERISM > PAUPER
PAUPERIZE *vb* make a pauper of
PAUPERS > PAUPER
PAUPIETTE *n* rolled stuffed fish or meat
PAUROPOD *n* minute myriapod
PAUROPODS > PAUROPOD
PAUSAL > PAUSE
PAUSE *vb* stop for a time ▷ *n* stop or rest in speech or action
PAUSED > PAUSE
PAUSEFUL *adj* taking pauses
PAUSELESS *adj* without pauses
PAUSER > PAUSE
PAUSERS > PAUSE
PAUSES > PAUSE
PAUSING > PAUSE
PAUSINGLY *adv* with pauses
PAUSINGS > PAUSE
PAV *short for* > PAVLOVA
PAVAGE *n* tax towards paving streets, or the right to levy such a tax
PAVAGES > PAVAGE
PAVAN *same as* > PAVANE
PAVANE *n* slow and stately dance of the 16th and 17th centuries
PAVANES > PAVANE
PAVANS > PAVAN
PAVE *vb* form (a surface) with stone or brick ▷ *n* paved surface, esp an uneven one
PAVED > PAVE
PAVEED *adj* (of jewels) set close together
PAVEMENT *n* paved path for pedestrians ▷ *vb* provide with pavement
PAVEMENTS > PAVEMENT
PAVEN *same as* > PAVANE
PAVENS > PAVEN
PAVER > PAVE
PAVERS > PAVE
PAVES > PAVE
PAVID *adj* fearful
PAVILION *n* building on a playing field etc ▷ *vb* place or set in or as if in a pavilion
PAVILIONS > PAVILION
PAVILLON *n* bell of wind instrument
PAVILLONS > PAVILLON
PAVIN *same as* > PAVANE
PAVING *n* paved surface ▷ *adj* of or for a paved surface or pavement
PAVINGS > PAVING
PAVINS > PAVIN
PAVIOR *same as* > PAVIOUR
PAVIORS > PAVIOR
PAVIOUR *n* person who lays paving
PAVIOURS > PAVIOUR
PAVIS *n* large square shield, developed in the 15th century, at first portable but later heavy and set up in a permanent position
PAVISE *same as* > PAVIS
PAVISER *n* soldier holding pavise
PAVISERS > PAVISER
PAVISES > PAVISE
PAVISSE *same as* > PAVIS
PAVISSES > PAVISSE
PAVLOVA *n* meringue cake topped with whipped cream and fruit
PAVLOVAS > PAVLOVA
PAVONAZZO *n* white Italian marble
PAVONE *n* peacock
PAVONES > PAVONE
PAVONIAN *same as* > PAVONINE
PAVONINE *adj* of or resembling a peacock or the colours, design, or iridescence of a peacock's tail
PAVS > PAV
PAW *n* animal's foot with claws and pads ▷ *vb* scrape with the paw or hoof
PAWA *old word for* > PEACOCK
PAWAS > PAWA
PAWAW *vb* recite N American incantation
PAWAWED > PAWAW
PAWAWING > PAWAW
PAWAWS > PAWAW
PAWED > PAW
PAWER *n* person or animal that paws
PAWERS > PAWER
PAWING > PAW
PAWK *Scots word for* > TRICK
PAWKIER > PAWKY
PAWKIEST > PAWKY
PAWKILY > PAWKY
PAWKINESS > PAWKY
PAWKS > PAWK
PAWKY *adj* having or characterized by a dry wit
PAWL *n* pivoted lever shaped to engage with a ratchet to prevent motion in a particular direction
PAWLS > PAWL
PAWN *vb* deposit (an article) as security for money borrowed ▷ *n* chessman of the lowest value
PAWNABLE > PAWN
PAWNAGE > PAWN
PAWNAGES > PAWN
PAWNCE *old word for* > PANSY
PAWNCES > PAWNCE
PAWNED > PAWN
PAWNEE *n* one who accepts goods in pawn
PAWNEES > PAWNEE
PAWNER *n* one who pawns his or her possessions
PAWNERS > PAWNER
PAWNING > PAWN
PAWNOR *same as* > PAWNER
PAWNORS > PAWNOR
PAWNS > PAWN
PAWNSHOP *n* premises of a pawnbroker
PAWNSHOPS > PAWNSHOP
PAWPAW *same as* > PAPAW
PAWPAWS > PAWPAW
PAWS > PAW
PAX *n* kiss of peace ▷ *interj* call signalling a desire to end hostilities
PAXES > PAX
PAXIUBA *n* tropical tree
PAXIUBAS > PAXIUBA
PAXWAX *n* strong ligament in the neck of many mammals, which supports the head
PAXWAXES > PAXWAX
PAY *vb* give money etc in return for goods or services ▷ *n* wages or salary
PAYABLE *adj* due to be paid
PAYABLES *n* debts to be paid
PAYABLY > PAYABLE
PAYBACK *n* return on an investment
PAYBACKS > PAYBACK
PAYCHECK *n* payment for work done
PAYCHECKS > PAYCHECK

PAYDAY *n* day on which wages or salaries are paid
PAYDAYS > PAYDAY
PAYED > PAY
PAYEE *n* person to whom money is paid or due
PAYEES > PAYEE
PAYER *n* person who pays
PAYERS > PAYER
PAYFONE *US spelling of* > PAYPHONE
PAYFONES > PAYFONE
PAYGRADE *n* military rank
PAYGRADES > PAYGRADE
PAYING > PAY
PAYINGS > PAY
PAYLOAD *n* passengers or cargo of an aircraft
PAYLOADS > PAYLOAD
PAYMASTER *n* official responsible for the payment of wages and salaries
PAYMENT *n* act of paying
PAYMENTS > PAYMENT
PAYNIM *n* heathen or pagan
PAYNIMRY *n* state of being heathen
PAYNIMS > PAYNIM
PAYOFF *n* final settlement, esp in retribution
PAYOFFS > PAYOFF
PAYOLA *n* bribe to get special treatment, esp to promote a commercial product
PAYOLAS > PAYOLA
PAYOR *same as* > PAYER
PAYORS > PAYOR
PAYOUT *n* sum of money paid out
PAYOUTS > PAYOUT
PAYPHONE *n* coin-operated telephone
PAYPHONES > PAYPHONE
PAYROLL *n* list of employees who receive regular pay ▷ *vb* employ
PAYROLLED > PAYROLL
PAYROLLS > PAYROLL
PAYS > PAY
PAYSAGE *n* landscape
PAYSAGES > PAYSAGE
PAYSAGIST *n* painter of landscapes
PAYSD *Spenserian form of* > POISED
PAYSLIP *n* note of payment given to employee
PAYSLIPS > PAYSLIP
PAZAZZ *same as* > PIZZAZZ
PAZAZZES > PAZAZZ
PAZZAZZ *same as* > PIZZAZZ
PAZZAZZES > PAZZAZZ
PE *n* 17th letter in the Hebrew alphabet
PEA *n* climbing plant with seeds growing in pods
PEABERRY *n* coffee berry containing one seed
PEACE *n* calm, quietness
PEACEABLE *adj* inclined towards peace
PEACEABLY > PEACEABLE
PEACED > PEACE
PEACEFUL *adj* not in a state of war or disagreement
PEACELESS *adj* without peace
PEACENIK *n* activist who opposes war
PEACENIKS > PEACENIK
PEACES > PEACE
PEACETIME *n* period without war
PEACH *n* soft juicy fruit with a stone and a downy skin ▷ *adj* pinkish-orange ▷ *vb* inform against an accomplice
PEACHBLOW *n* type of glaze on porcelain
PEACHED > PEACH
PEACHER > PEACH
PEACHERS > PEACH
PEACHES > PEACH
PEACHIER > PEACHY
PEACHIEST > PEACHY
PEACHILY > PEACHY
PEACHING > PEACH
PEACHY *adj* of or like a peach, esp in colour or texture
PEACING > PEACE
PEACOAT *n* woollen jacket
PEACOATS > PEACOAT
PEACOCK *n* large male bird with a brilliantly coloured fanlike tail ▷ *vb* display (oneself) proudly
PEACOCKED > PEACOCK
PEACOCKS > PEACOCK
PEACOCKY > PEACOCK
PEACOD *same as* > PEACOD
PEACODS > PEACOD
PEAFOWL *n* peacock or peahen
PEAFOWLS > PEAFOWL
PEAG *n* (formerly) money used by North American Indians, made of cylindrical shells strung or woven together
PEAGE *same as* > PEAG
PEAGES > PEAGE
PEAGS > PEAG
PEAHEN > PEACOCK
PEAHENS > PEACOCK
PEAK *n* pointed top, esp of a mountain ▷ *vb* form or reach a peak ▷ *adj* of or at the point of greatest demand
PEAKED *adj* having a peak
PEAKIER > PEAK
PEAKIEST > PEAK
PEAKING > PEAK
PEAKISH *adj* sickly
PEAKLESS > PEAK
PEAKLIKE > PEAK
PEAKS > PEAK
PEAKY > PEAK
PEAL *n* long loud echoing sound, esp of bells or thunder ▷ *vb* sound with a peal or peals
PEALED > PEAL
PEALIKE > PEA
PEALING > PEAL
PEALS > PEAL
PEAN *n* paean ▷ *vb* deliver a pean
PEANED > PEAN
PEANING > PEAN
PEANS > PEAN
PEANUT *n* pea-shaped nut that ripens underground
PEANUTS > PEANUT
PEAPOD *n* pod of the pea plant
PEAPODS > PEAPOD
PEAR *n* sweet juicy fruit with a narrow top and rounded base
PEARCE *old spelling of* > PIERCE
PEARCED > PEARCE
PEARCES > PEARCE
PEARCING > PEARCE
PEARE *obsolete spelling of* > PEAR
PEARES > PEARE
PEARL *same as* > PURL
PEARLASH *n* granular crystalline form of potassium carbonate
PEARLED > PEARL
PEARLER *n* person who dives for or trades in pearls ▷ *adj* excellent
PEARLERS > PEARLER
PEARLIER > PEARLY
PEARLIES > PEARLY
PEARLIEST > PEARLY
PEARLIN *n* type of lace used to trim clothes
PEARLING > PEARL
PEARLINGS > PEARL
PEARLINS *n* type of lace
PEARLISED *same as* > PEARLIZED
PEARLITE *same as* > PERLITE
PEARLITES > PEARLITE
PEARLITIC > PEARLITE
PEARLIZED *adj* having or given a pearly lustre
PEARLS > PEARL
PEARLWORT *n* plant with small white flowers that are spherical in bud
PEARLY *adj* resembling a pearl, esp in lustre ▷ *n* London costermonger who wears on ceremonial occasions a traditional dress of dark clothes covered with pearl buttons
PEARMAIN *n* any of several varieties of apple having a red skin
PEARMAINS > PEARMAIN
PEARS > PEAR
PEARST *archaic variant of* > PIERCED
PEART *adj* lively
PEARTER > PEART
PEARTEST > PEART
PEARTLY > PEART
PEARTNESS > PEART
PEARWOOD *n* wood from pear tree
PEARWOODS > PEARWOOD
PEAS > PEA
PEASANT *n* person workin on the land, esp in poorer countries or in the past
PEASANTRY *n* peasants collectively
PEASANTS > PEASANT
PEASANTY *adj* having qualities ascribed to traditional country life o people
PEASCOD *same as* > COD
PEASCODS > PEASCOD
PEASE *n* archaic or dialect word for pea ▷ *vb* appeas
PEASECOD *n* pod of a pea plant
PEASECODS > PEASECOD
PEASED > PEASE
PEASEN *obsolete plural of* > PEASE
PEASES > PEASE
PEASING > PEASE
PEASON *obsolete plural of* > PEASE
PEASOUPER *n* thick fog
PEAT *n* decayed vegetable material found in bogs, used as fertilizer or fuel
PEATARIES > PEATARY
PEATARY *n* area covered with peat
PEATERIES > PEATERY
PEATERY *same as* > PEATAR
PEATIER > PEAT
PEATIEST > PEAT
PEATLAND *n* area of land consisting of peat bogs, usually containing many species of flora and fauna
PEATLANDS > PEATLAND
PEATMAN *n* person who collects peat
PEATMEN > PEATMAN
PEATS > PEAT
PEATSHIP *n* ship carrying peat
PEATSHIPS > PEATSHIP
PEATY > PEAT
PEAVEY *n* wooden lever with a metal pointed end and a hinged hook, used for handling logs
PEAVEYS > PEAVEY
PEAVIES > PEAVY
PEAVY *same as* > PEAVEY
PEAZE *same as* > PEASE
PEAZED > PEAZE
PEAZES > PEAZE
PEAZING > PEAZE
PEBA *n* type of armadillo
PEBAS > PEBA
PEBBLE *n* small roundish stone ▷ *vb* cover with pebbles
PEBBLED > PEBBLE
PEBBLES > PEBBLE
PEBBLIER > PEBBLE
PEBBLIEST > PEBBLE
PEBBLING *n* act of sprayi the rink with drops of ho water to slow down the stone

:BBLINGS > PEBBLING
:BBLY > PEBBLE
:BRINE *n* disease of silkworms
:BRINES > PEBRINE
:C *n* pectoral muscle
:CAN *n* edible nut of a N American tree
:CANS > PECAN
:CCABLE *adj* liable to sin
:CCANCY > PECCANT
:CCANT *adj* guilty of an offence
:CCANTLY > PECCANT
:CCARIES > PECCARY
:CCARY *n* piglike animal of American forests
:CCAVI *n* confession of guilt
:CCAVIS > PECCAVI
:CH *Scottish word for* > PANT
:CHAN *Scots word for* > STOMACH
:CHANS > PECHAN
:CHED > PECH
:CHING > PECH
:CHS > PECH
:CK *vb* strike or pick up with the beak ▷ *n* pecking movement
:CKE *n* quarter of bushel
:CKED > PECK
:CKER *n* slang word for penis
:CKERS > PECKER
:CKES > PECKE
:CKIER > PECKY
:CKIEST > PECKY
:CKING peck
:CKINGS > PECK
:CKISH *adj* slightly hungry
:CKISHLY > PECKISH
:CKS > PECK
:CKY *adj* discoloured
:CORINI > PECORINO
:CORINO *n* Italian cheese made from ewes' milk
:CORINOS > PECORINO
:CS *pl n* pectoral muscles
:CTASE *n* enzyme occurring in certain ripening fruits
:CTASES > PECTASE
:CTATE *n* salt or ester of pectic acid
:CTATES > PECTATE
:CTEN *n* comblike structure in the eye of birds and reptiles
:CTENS > PECTEN
:CTIC > PECTIN
:CTIN *n* substance in fruit that makes jam set
:CTINAL *adj* resembling a comb
:CTINATE *adj* shaped like a comb
:CTINEAL *adj* relating to pubic bone
:CTINES > PECTEN
:CTINOUS > PECTIN
:CTINS > PECTIN

PECTISE *same as* > PECTIZE
PECTISED > PECTISE
PECTISES > PECTISE
PECTISING > PECTISE
PECTIZE *vb* change into a jelly
PECTIZED > PECTIZE
PECTIZES > PECTIZE
PECTIZING > PECTIZE
PECTOLITE *n* silicate of lime and soda
PECTORAL *adj* of the chest or thorax ▷ *n* pectoral muscle or fin
PECTORALS > PECTORAL
PECTOSE *n* insoluble carbohydrate found in the cell walls of unripe fruit that is converted to pectin by enzymic processes
PECTOSES > PECTOSE
PECULATE *vb* embezzle (public money)
PECULATED > PECULATE
PECULATES > PECULATE
PECULATOR > PECULATE
PECULIA > PECULIUM
PECULIAR *adj* strange ▷ *n* special sort, esp an accented letter
PECULIARS > PECULIAR
PECULIUM *n* property that a father or master allowed his child or slave to hold as his own
PECUNIARY *adj* relating to, or consisting of, money
PECUNIOUS *adj* having lots of money
PED *n* pannier
PEDAGOG *same as* > PEDAGOGUE
PEDAGOGIC > PEDAGOGUE
PEDAGOGS > PEDAGOG
PEDAGOGUE *n* schoolteacher, esp a pedantic one
PEDAGOGY *n* principles, practice, or profession of teaching
PEDAL *n* foot-operated lever used to control a vehicle or machine, or to modify the tone of a musical instrument ▷ *vb* propel (a bicycle) by using its pedals ▷ *adj* of or relating to the foot or the feet
PEDALED > PEDAL
PEDALER > PEDAL
PEDALERS > PEDAL
PEDALFER *n* type of zonal soil deficient in lime but containing deposits of aluminium and iron
PEDALFERS > PEDALFER
PEDALIER *n* pedal piano
PEDALIERS > PEDALIER
PEDALING > PEDAL
PEDALLED > PEDAL
PEDALLER *n* person who pedals
PEDALLERS > PEDALLER

PEDALLING > PEDAL
PEDALO *n* pleasure craft driven by pedal-operated paddle wheels
PEDALOES > PEDALO
PEDALOS > PEDALO
PEDALS > PEDAL
PEDANT *n* person who is excessively concerned with details and rules, esp in academic work
PEDANTIC *adj* of, relating to, or characterized by pedantry
PEDANTISE *same as* > PEDANTIZE
PEDANTISM > PEDANT
PEDANTIZE *vb* make pedantic comments
PEDANTRY *n* practice of being a pedant, esp in the minute observance of petty rules or details
PEDANTS > PEDANT
PEDATE *adj* (of a plant leaf) divided into several lobes arising at a common point, the lobes often being stalked and the lateral lobes sometimes divided into smaller lobes
PEDATELY > PEDATE
PEDATIFID *adj* (of a plant leaf) pedately divided, with the divisions less deep than in a pedate leaf
PEDDER *old form of* > PEDLAR
PEDDERS > PEDDER
PEDDLE *vb* sell (goods) from door to door
PEDDLED > PEDDLE
PEDDLER *same as* > PEDLAR
PEDDLERS > PEDDLER
PEDDLERY *n* business of peddler
PEDDLES > PEDDLE
PEDDLING > PEDDLE
PEDDLINGS > PEDDLE
PEDERAST *n* man who has homosexual relations with boys
PEDERASTS > PEDERAST
PEDERASTY *n* homosexual relations between men and boys
PEDERERO *n* type of cannon
PEDEREROS > PEDERERO
PEDES > PES
PEDESES > PEDESIS
PEDESIS *n* random motion of small particles
PEDESTAL *n* base supporting a column, statue, etc
PEDESTALS > PEDESTAL
PEDETIC *adj* of feet
PEDIATRIC *adj* of or relating to the medical science of children and their diseases
PEDICAB *n* pedal-operated tricycle, available for hire, with an attached seat for one or two passengers

PEDICABS > PEDICAB
PEDICEL *n* stalk bearing a single flower of an inflorescence
PEDICELS > PEDICEL
PEDICLE *n* any small stalk
PEDICLED > PEDICLE
PEDICLES > PEDICLE
PEDICULAR *adj* relating to, infested with, or caused by lice
PEDICULI > PEDICULUS
PEDICULUS *n* wingless parasite
PEDICURE *n* medical or cosmetic treatment of the feet ▷ *vb* give a pedicure
PEDICURED > PEDICURE
PEDICURES > PEDICURE
PEDIFORM *adj* shaped like a foot
PEDIGREE *n* register of ancestors, esp of a purebred animal
PEDIGREED > PEDIGREE
PEDIGREES > PEDIGREE
PEDIMENT *n* triangular part over a door etc
PEDIMENTS > PEDIMENT
PEDIPALP *n* either member of the second pair of head appendages of arachnids
PEDIPALPI > PEDIPALP
PEDIPALPS > PEDIPALP
PEDLAR *n* person who sells goods from door to door
PEDLARIES > PEDLARY
PEDLARS > PEDLAR
PEDLARY *same as* > PEDLERY
PEDLER *same as* > PEDLAR
PEDLERIES > PEDLERY
PEDLERS > PEDLER
PEDLERY *n* business of pedler
PEDOCAL *n* type of zonal soil that is rich in lime and characteristic of relatively dry areas
PEDOCALIC > PEDOCAL
PEDOCALS > PEDOCAL
PEDOGENIC *adj* relating to soil
PEDOLOGIC > PEDOLOGY
PEDOLOGY *same as* > PAEDOLOGY
PEDOMETER *n* instrument which measures the distance walked
PEDOPHILE *n* person who is sexually attracted to children
PEDORTHIC *adj* (of footwear) designed to alleviate foot problems
PEDRAIL *n* device replacing wheel on rough surfaces
PEDRAILS > PEDRAIL
PEDRERO *n* type of cannon
PEDREROES > PEDRERO
PEDREROS > PEDRERO
PEDRO *n* card game
PEDROS > PEDRO
PEDS > PED
PEDUNCLE *same*

as > PEDICEL
PEDUNCLED > PEDUNCLE
PEDUNCLES > PEDUNCLE
PEE *vb* urinate ▷ *n* urine
PEEBEEN *n* type of large evergreen
PEEBEENS > PEEBEEN
PEECE *obsolete variant of* > PIECE
PEECED > PIECE
PEECES > PIECE
PEECING > PIECE
PEED > PEE
PEEING > PEE
PEEK *n* peep or glance ▷ *vb* glance quickly or secretly
PEEKABOO *n* game for young children, in which one person hides his face and suddenly reveals it and cries 'peekaboo' ▷ *adj* (of a garment) made of fabric that is almost transparent or patterned with small holes
PEEKABOOS > PEEKABOO
PEEKAPOO *n* dog which is cross between Pekingese and poodle
PEEKAPOOS > PEEKAPOO
PEEKED > PEEK
PEEKING > PEEK
PEEKS > PEEK
PEEL *vb* remove the skin or rind of (a vegetable or fruit) ▷ *n* rind or skin
PEELABLE > PEEL
PEELED > PEEL
PEELER *n* special knife or mechanical device for peeling vegetables, fruit, etc
PEELERS > PEELER
PEELING *n* strip of skin, rind, bark, etc, that has been peeled off
PEELINGS > PEELING
PEELS > PEEL
PEEN *n* end of a hammer head opposite the striking face, often rounded or wedge-shaped ▷ *vb* strike with the peen of a hammer or with a stream of metal shot in order to bend or shape (a sheet of metal)
PEENED > PEEN
PEENGE *vb* complain
PEENGED > PEENGE
PEENGEING > PEENGE
PEENGES > PEENGE
PEENGING > PEENGE
PEENING > PEEN
PEENS > PEEN
PEEOY *n* homemade firework
PEEOYS > PEEOY
PEEP *vb* look slyly or quickly ▷ *n* peeping look
PEEPE *old spelling of* > PIP
PEEPED > PEEP
PEEPER *n* person who peeps
PEEPERS > PEEPER
PEEPES *archiac spelling of* > PEEPS
PEEPHOLE *n* small aperture, such as one in the door of a flat for observing callers before opening
PEEPHOLES > PEEPHOLE
PEEPING > PEEP
PEEPS > PEEP
PEEPSHOW *n* box containing a series of pictures that can be seen through a small hole
PEEPSHOWS > PEEPSHOW
PEEPUL *n* Indian moraceous tree
PEEPULS > PEEPUL
PEER *n* (in Britain) member of the nobility ▷ *vb* look closely and intently
PEERAGE *n* whole body of peers
PEERAGES > PEERAGE
PEERED > PEER
PEERESS *n* (in Britain) woman holding the rank of a peer
PEERESSES > PEERESS
PEERIE *n* spinning top ▷ *adj* small
PEERIER > PEERIE
PEERIES > PEERIE
PEERIEST > PEERIE
PEERING > PEER
PEERLESS *adj* unequalled, unsurpassed
PEERS > PEER
PEERY *n* child's spinning top
PEES > PEE
PEESWEEP *n* early spring storm
PEESWEEPS > PEESWEEP
PEETWEET *n* spotted sandpiper
PEETWEETS > PEETWEET
PEEVE *vb* irritate or annoy ▷ *n* something that irritates
PEEVED > PEEVE
PEEVER *n* hopscotch
PEEVERS > PEEVER
PEEVES > PEEVE
PEEVING > PEEVE
PEEVISH *adj* fretful or irritable
PEEVISHLY > PEEVISH
PEEWEE *same as* > PEWEE
PEEWEES > PEEWEE
PEEWIT *same as* > LAPWING
PEEWITS > PEEWIT
PEG *n* pin or clip for joining, fastening, marking, etc ▷ *vb* fasten with pegs
PEGASUS *n* winged horse
PEGASUSES > PEGASUS
PEGBOARD *n* board with a pattern of holes into which small pegs can be fitted, used for playing certain games or keeping a score
PEGBOARDS > PEGBOARD
PEGBOX *n* part of stringed instrument that holds tuning pegs
PEGBOXES > PEGBOX
PEGGED > PEG
PEGGIES > PEGGY
PEGGING > PEG
PEGGINGS > PEG
PEGGY *n* ship's steward
PEGH *variant of* > PECH
PEGHED > PEGH
PEGHING > PEGH
PEGHS > PEGH
PEGLEGGED *adj* having wooden leg
PEGLESS > PEG
PEGLIKE > PEG
PEGMATITE *n* exceptionally coarse-grained intrusive igneous rock
PEGS > PEG
PEH *n* letter in the Hebrew alphabet
PEHS > PEH
PEIGNOIR *n* woman's light dressing gown
PEIGNOIRS > PEIGNOIR
PEIN *same as* > PEEN
PEINCT *vb* paint
PEINCTED > PEINCT
PEINCTING > PEINCT
PEINCTS > PEINCT
PEINED > PEIN
PEINING > PEIN
PEINS > PEIN
PEIRASTIC *adj* experimental
PEISE *same as* > PEIZE
PEISED > PEISE
PEISES > PEISE
PEISHWA *n* Indian leader
PEISHWAH *same as* > PEISHWA
PEISHWAHS > PEISHWAH
PEISHWAS > PEISHWA
PEISING > PEISE
PEIZE *vb* weight or poise
PEIZED > PEIZE
PEIZES > PEIZE
PEIZING > PEIZE
PEJORATE *vb* change for the worse
PEJORATED > PEJORATE
PEJORATES > PEJORATE
PEKAN *n* large North American marten
PEKANS > PEKAN
PEKE *n* Pekingese dog
PEKEPOO *same as* > PEEKAPOO
PEKEPOOS > PEKEPOO
PEKES > PEKE
PEKIN *n* silk fabric
PEKINS > PEKIN
PEKOE *n* high-quality tea made from the downy tips of the young buds of the tea plant
PEKOES > PEKOE
PELA *n* insect living on wax
PELAGE *n* coat of a mammal, consisting of hair, wool, fur, etc
PELAGES > PELAGE
PELAGIAL *adj* of the open sea
PELAGIAN *adj* of or inhabiting the open sea ▷ *n* pelagic creature
PELAGIANS > PELAGIAN
PELAGIC *adj* of or relating to the open sea ▷ *n* any pelagic creature
PELAGICS > PELAGIC
PELAS > PELA
PELE *Spenserian variant of* > PEAL
PELECYPOD *another word for* > BIVALVE
PELERINE *n* woman's narrow cape with long pointed ends in front
PELERINES > PELERINE
PELES > PELE
PELF *n* money or wealth
PELFS > PELF
PELHAM *n* horse's bit for a double bridle, less severe than a curb but more severe than a snaffle
PELHAMS > PELHAM
PELICAN *n* large water bi
with a pouch beneath its bill for storing fish
PELICANS > PELICAN
PELISSE *n* cloak or loose coat which is usually fur-trimmed
PELISSES > PELISSE
PELITE *n* any argillaceous
rock such as shale
PELITES > PELITE
PELITIC > PELITE
PELL *vb* knock about
PELLACH *same as* > PELLAC
PELLACHS > PELLACH
PELLACK *n* porpoise
PELLACKS > PELLACK
PELLAGRA *n* disease caus
by lack of vitamin B
PELLAGRAS > PELLAGRA
PELLAGRIN *n* person who suffers from pellagra
PELLED > PELL
PELLET *n* small ball of something ▷ *vb* strike with pellets
PELLETAL > PELLET
PELLETED > PELLET
PELLETIFY *vb* shape into pellets
PELLETING > PELLET
PELLETISE *vb* shape into pellets
PELLETIZE *vb* shape into pellets
PELLETS > PELLET
PELLICLE *n* thin skin or film
PELLICLES > PELLICLE
PELLING > PELL
PELLITORY *n* urticaceous
plant
PELLMELL *n* disorder
PELLMELLS > PELLMELL
PELLOCK *n* porpoise
PELLOCKS > PELLOCK
PELLS > PELL

:LLUCID *adj* very clear
:LLUM *n* dust
:LLUMS > PELLUM
:LMA *n* sole of the foot
:LMANISM *n* memory card game
:LMAS > PELMA
:LMATIC > PELMA
:LMET *n* ornamental drapery or board, concealing a curtain rail
:LMETS > PELMET
:LOID *n* mud used therapeutically
:LOIDS > PELOID
:LOLOGY *n* study of therapeutic uses of mud
:LON *adj* hairless
:LORIA *n* abnormal production of actinomorphic flowers in a plant of a species that usually produces zygomorphic flowers
:LORIAN > PELORIA
:LORIAS > PELORIA
:LORIC > PELORIA
:LORIES > PELORY
:LORISED *adj* affected by peloria
:LORISM *n* floral mutation
:LORISMS > PELORISM
:LORIZED *same as* > PELORISED
:LORUS *n* sighting device used in conjunction with a magnetic compass or a gyrocompass for measuring the relative bearings of observed points
:LORUSES > PELORUS
:LORY *n* floral mutation
:LOTA *n* game played by two players who use a basket strapped to their wrists or a wooden racket to propel a ball against a specially marked wall
:LOTAS > PELOTA
:LOTON *n* main field of riders in a road race
:LOTONS > PELOTON
:LT *vb* throw missiles at ▷ *n* skin of a fur-bearing animal
:LTA *n* small ancient shield
:LTAE > PELTA
:LTAS > PELTA
:LTAST *n* (in ancient Greece) lightly armed foot soldier
:LTASTS > PELTAST
:LTATE *adj* (of leaves) having the stalk attached to the centre of the lower surface
:LTATELY > PELTATE
:LTATION > PELTATE
:LTED > PELT
:LTER > PELT *vb* rain heavily
PELTERED > PELT
PELTERING > PELT
PELTERS > PELT
PELTING > PELT
PELTINGLY > PELT
PELTINGS > PELT
PELTLESS > PELT
PELTRIES > PELTRY
PELTRY *n* pelts of animals collectively
PELTS > PELT
PELVES > PELVIS
PELVIC *adj* of, near, or relating to the pelvis ▷ *n* pelvic bone
PELVICS > PELVIC
PELVIFORM *adj* shaped like pelvis
PELVIS *n* framework of bones at the base of the spine, to which the hips are attached
PELVISES > PELVIS
PEMBINA *n* type of cranberry
PEMBINAS > PEMBINA
PEMBROKE *n* small table
PEMBROKES > PEMBROKE
PEMICAN *same as* > PEMMICAN
PEMICANS > PEMICAN
PEMMICAN *n* small pressed cake of shredded dried meat, pounded into paste with fat and berries or dried fruits
PEMMICANS > PEMMICAN
PEMOLINE *n* mild stimulant
PEMOLINES > PEMOLINE
PEMPHIGUS *n* any of a group of blistering skin diseases
PEMPHIX *n* type of crustacean
PEMPHIXES > PEMPHIX
PEN *n* instrument for writing in ink ▷ *vb* write or compose
PENAL *adj* of or used in punishment
PENALISE *same as* > PENALIZE
PENALISED > PENALISE
PENALISES > PENALISE
PENALITY > PENAL
PENALIZE *vb* impose a penalty on
PENALIZED > PENALIZE
PENALIZES > PENALIZE
PENALLY > PENAL
PENALTIES > PENALTY
PENALTY *n* punishment for a crime or offence
PENANCE *n* voluntary self-punishment to make amends for wrongdoing ▷ *vb* (of ecclesiastical authorities) impose a penance upon (a sinner)
PENANCED > PENANCE
PENANCES > PENANCE
PENANCING > PENANCE
PENANG *variant of* > PINANG
PENANGS > PENANG
PENATES *pl n* household gods
PENCE > PENNY
PENCEL *n* small pennon, originally one carried by a knight's squire
PENCELS > PENCEL
PENCES > PENNY
PENCHANT *n* inclination or liking
PENCHANTS > PENCHANT
PENCIL *n* thin cylindrical instrument containing graphite, for writing or drawing ▷ *vb* draw, write, or mark with a pencil
PENCILED > PENCIL
PENCILER > PENCIL
PENCILERS > PENCIL
PENCILING > PENCIL
PENCILLED > PENCIL
PENCILLER > PENCIL
PENCILS > PENCIL
PENCRAFT *n* skill in writing
PENCRAFTS > PENCRAFT
PEND *vb* await judgment or settlement ▷ *n* archway or vaulted passage
PENDANT *n* ornament worn on a chain round the neck
PENDANTLY > PENDANT
PENDANTS > PENDANT
PENDED > PEND
PENDENCY > PENDENT
PENDENT *adj* hanging ▷ *n* pendant
PENDENTLY > PENDENT
PENDENTS > PENDENT
PENDICLE *n* something dependent on another
PENDICLER *n* person who rents a croft
PENDICLES > PENDICLE
PENDING *prep* while waiting for ▷ *adj* not yet decided or settled
PENDRAGON *n* supreme war chief or leader of the ancient Britons
PENDS > PEND
PENDU *adj* in informal Indian English, culturally backward
PENDULAR *adj* pendulous
PENDULATE *vb* swing as pendulum
PENDULE *n* manoeuvre by which a climber on a rope from above swings in a pendulum-like series of movements to reach another line of ascent
PENDULES > PENDULE
PENDULINE *n* type of titmouse
PENDULOUS *adj* hanging, swinging
PENDULUM *same as* > PENDULE
PENDULUMS > PENDULUM
PENE *variant of* > PEEN
PENED > PENE
PENEPLAIN *n* relatively flat land surface produced by a long period of erosion
PENEPLANE *same as* > PENEPLAIN
PENES > PENIS
PENETRANT *adj* sharp ▷ *n* substance that lowers the surface tension of a liquid and thus causes it to penetrate or be absorbed more easily
PENETRATE *vb* find or force a way into or through
PENFOLD *same as* > PINFOLD
PENFOLDS > PENFOLD
PENFUL *n* contents of pen
PENFULS > PENFUL
PENGO *n* standard monetary unit of Hungary, replaced by the forint in 1946
PENGOS > PENGO
PENGUIN *n* flightless black-and-white sea bird of the southern hemisphere
PENGUINRY *n* breeding place of penguins
PENGUINS > PENGUIN
PENHOLDER *n* container for pens
PENI *old spelling of* > PENNY
PENIAL > PENIS
PENICIL *n* small pad for wounds
PENICILS > PENICIL
PENIE *old spelling of* > PENNY
PENIES > PENIE
PENILE *adj* of or relating to the penis
PENILL > PENILLION
PENILLION *pl n* Welsh art or practice of singing poetry in counterpoint to a traditional melody played on the harp
PENING > PENE
PENINSULA *n* strip of land nearly surrounded by water
PENIS *n* organ of copulation and urination in male mammals
PENISES > PENIS
PENISTONE *n* coarse woollen cloth
PENITENCE > PENITENT
PENITENCY > PENITENT
PENITENT *adj* feeling sorry for having done wrong ▷ *n* someone who is penitent
PENITENTS > PENITENT
PENK *n* small fish
PENKNIFE *n* small knife with blade(s) that fold into the handle
PENKNIVES > PENKNIFE
PENKS > PENK
PENLIGHT *n* small thin flashlight
PENLIGHTS > PENLIGHT
PENLITE *same as* > PENLIGHT
PENLITES > PENLITE
PENMAN *n* person skilled in

handwriting
PENMEN > PENMAN
PENNA *n* any large feather that has a vane and forms part of the main plumage of a bird
PENNAE > PENNA
PENNAL *n* first-year student of Protestant university
PENNALISM *n* menial choring at college
PENNALS > PENNAL
PENNAME *n* author's pseudonym
PENNAMES > PENNAME
PENNANT *same as* > PENDANT
PENNANTS > PENNANT
PENNATE *adj* having feathers, wings, or winglike structures
PENNATED *same as* > PENNATE
PENNATULA *n* sea pen
PENNE *n* pasta in the form of short tubes
PENNED > PEN
PENNEECH *n* card game
PENNEECHS > PENNEECH
PENNEECK *same as* > PENNEECH
PENNEECKS > PENNEECK
PENNER *n* person who writes
PENNERS > PENNER
PENNES > PENNE
PENNI *n* former Finnish monetary unit worth one hundredth of a markka
PENNIA > PENNI
PENNIED *adj* having money
PENNIES > PENNY
PENNIFORM *adj* shaped like a feather
PENNILESS *adj* very poor
PENNILL *n* stanza in a Welsh poem
PENNINE *n* mineral found in the Pennine Alps
PENNINES > PENNINE
PENNING > PEN
PENNINITE *n* bluish-green variety of chlorite occurring in the form of thick crystals
PENNIS > PENNI
PENNON *n* triangular or tapering flag
PENNONCEL *n* small narrow flag
PENNONED *n* equipped with a pennon
PENNONS > PENNON
PENNY *n* British bronze coin worth one hundredth of a pound
PENNYBOY *n* employee whose duties include menial tasks, such as running errands
PENNYBOYS > PENNYBOY
PENNYFEE *n* small payment
PENNYFEES > PENNYFEE
PENNYLAND *n* old Scottish division of land
PENNYWISE *adj* careful with small amounts of money
PENNYWORT *n* Eurasian rock plant with whitish-green tubular flowers and rounded leaves
PENOCHE *n* type of fudge
PENOCHES > PENOCHE
PENOLOGY *n* study of punishment and prison management
PENONCEL *n* small narrow flag
PENONCELS > PENONCEL
PENPOINT *n* tip of pen
PENPOINTS > PENPOINT
PENPUSHER *n* person whose work involves a lot of boring paperwork
PENS > PEN
PENSEE *n* thought put down on paper
PENSEES > PENSEE
PENSEL *same as* > PENCEL
PENSELS > PENSEL
PENSIL *same as* > PENCEL
PENSILE *adj* designating or building a hanging nest
PENSILITY > PENSILE
PENSILS > PENSIL
PENSION *n* regular payment to people above a certain age, retired employees, widows, etc ▷ *vb* grant a pension to
PENSIONE *n* Italian boarding house
PENSIONED > PENSION
PENSIONER *n* person receiving a pension
PENSIONES > PENSIONE
PENSIONS > PENSION
PENSIVE *adj* deeply thoughtful, often with a tinge of sadness
PENSIVELY > PENSIVE
PENSTEMON *n* North American flowering plant with five stamens
PENSTER *n* writer
PENSTERS > PENSTER
PENSTOCK *n* conduit that supplies water to a hydroelectric power plant
PENSTOCKS > PENSTOCK
PENSUM *n* school exercise
PENSUMS > PENSUM
PENT *n* penthouse
PENTACLE *same as* > PENTAGRAM
PENTACLES > PENTACLE
PENTACT *n* sponge spicule with five rays
PENTACTS > PENTACT
PENTAD *n* group or series of five
PENTADIC > PENTAD
PENTADS > PENTAD
PENTAGON *n* geometric figure with five sides
PENTAGONS > PENTAGON
PENTAGRAM *n* five-pointed star
PENTALOGY *n* combination of five closely related symptoms
PENTALPHA *n* five-pointed star
PENTAMERY *n* state of consisting of five parts
PENTANE *n* alkane hydrocarbon with three isomers
PENTANES > PENTANE
PENTANGLE *same as* > PENTAGRAM
PENTANOIC as in *pentanoic acid* colourless liquid carboxylic acid
PENTANOL *n* colourless oily liquid
PENTANOLS > PENTANOL
PENTAPODY *n* series or measure of five feet
PENTARCH *n* member of pentarchy
PENTARCHS > PENTARCH
PENTARCHY *n* government by five rulers
PENTATHLA *n* pentathlons
PENTEL *n* ballpoint pen with free-flowing ink
PENTELS > PENTEL
PENTENE *n* colourless flammable liquid alkene with several straight-chained isomeric forms
PENTENES > PENTENE
PENTHIA *n* child born fifth
PENTHIAS > PENTHIA
PENTHOUSE *n* flat built on the roof or top floor of a building
PENTICE *vb* accommodate in a penthouse
PENTICED > PENTICE
PENTICES > PENTICE
PENTICING > PENTICE
PENTISE *same as* > PENTICE
PENTISED > PENTISE
PENTISES > PENTISE
PENTISING > PENTISE
PENTITI > PENTITO
PENTITO *n* person involved in organized crime who offers information to the police in return for immunity from prosecution
PENTODE *n* electronic valve having five electrodes: a cathode, anode, and three grids
PENTODES > PENTODE
PENTOMIC *adj* denoting or relating to the subdivision of an army division into five battle groups, esp for nuclear warfare
PENTOSAN *n* polysaccharide occuring in plants, humus, etc
PENTOSANE *same as* > PENTOSAN
PENTOSANS > PENTOSAN
PENTOSE *n* monosaccharide containing five atoms of carbon per molecule
PENTOSES > PENTOSE
PENTOSIDE *n* compound containing sugar
PENTOXIDE *n* oxide of an element with five atoms oxygen per molecule
PENTROOF *n* lean-to
PENTROOFS > PENTROOF
PENTS > PENT
PENTYL *n* one of a particular chemical grou
PENTYLENE *n* type of chemical
PENTYLS > PENTYL
PENUCHE *same as* > PANOC
PENUCHES > PENUCHE
PENUCHI *same as* > PANOC
PENUCHIS > PENUCHI
PENUCHLE *same as* > PINOCHLE
PENUCHLES > PENUCHLE
PENUCKLE *same as* > PENUCHLE
PENUCKLES > PENUCKLE
PENULT *n* last syllable but one in a word
PENULTIMA *same as* > PENULT
PENULTS > PENULT
PENUMBRA *n* (in an eclipse partially shadowed regio which surrounds the full shadow
PENUMBRAE > PENUMBRA
PENUMBRAL > PENUMBRA
PENUMBRAS > PENUMBRA
PENURIES > PENURY
PENURIOUS *adj* niggardly with money
PENURY *n* extreme povert
PENWOMAN *n* female write
PENWOMEN > PENWOMAN
PEON *n* Spanish-Americar farm labourer or unskille worker
PEONAGE *n* state of being a peon
PEONAGES > PEONAGE
PEONES > PEON
PEONIES > PEONY
PEONISM *same as* > PEONA
PEONISMS > PEONISM
PEONS > PEON
PEONY *n* garden plant wit showy red, pink, or white flowers
PEOPLE *pl n* persons generally ▷ *vb* provide with inhabitants
PEOPLED > PEOPLE
PEOPLER *n* settler
PEOPLERS > PEOPLER
PEOPLES > PEOPLE
PEOPLING > PEOPLE
PEP *n* high spirits, energy, or enthusiasm ▷ *vb* liver by imbuing with new vigour
PEPERINO *n* type of volcanic rock
PEPERINOS > PEPERINO
PEPEROMIA *n* plant from tropical and subtropical

merica with slightly leshy ornamental leaves
PERONI same s > PEPPERONI
PERONIS > PEPPERONI
PFUL *adj* full of vitality
PINO *n* purple-striped ellow fruit
PINOS > PEPINO
PLA > PEPLUM
PLOS *n* (in ancient reece) top part of a voman's attire, caught at he shoulders and hanging n folds to the waist
PLOSES > PEPLOS
PLUM *same as* > PEPLOS
PLUMED > PEPLUM
PLUMS > PEPLUM
PLUS *same as* > PEPLOS
PLUSES > PEPLUS
PO *n* fruit such as the nelon, squash, cucumber, r pumpkin
PONIDA *variant of* > PEPO
PONIDAS > PEPO
PONIUM *variant of* > PEPO
PONIUMS > PEPONIUM
POS > PEPO
PPED > PEP
PPER *n* sharp hot ondiment made from he fruit of an East Indian limbing plant ▷ *vb* eason with pepper
PPERBOX *n* container for epper
PPERED > PEPPER
PPERER > PEPPER
PPERERS > PEPPER
PPERIER > PEPPERY
PPERING > PEPPER
PPERONI *n* dry sausage f pork and beef spiced vith pepper
PPERS > PEPPER
PPERY *adj* tasting of epper
PPIER > PEPPY
PPIEST > PEPPY
PPILY > PEPPY
PPINESS > PEPPY
PPING > PEP
PPY *adj* full of vitality
PS > PEP
PSIN *n* enzyme roduced in the stomach, vhich, when activated by cid, breaks down proteins
PSINATE *vb* treat (a atient) with pepsin
PSINE *same as* > PEPSIN
PSINES > PEPSINE
PSINS > PEPSIN
PTALK *n* talk meant to nspire ▷ *vb* give a peptalk o
PTALKED > PEPTALK
PTALKS > PEPTALK
PTIC *adj* relating to igestion or the digestive uices ▷ *n* substance that ids digestion
PTICITY > PEPTIC
PEPTICS > PEPTIC
PEPTID *variant of* > PEPTIDE
PEPTIDASE *n* any of a group of proteolytic enzymes that hydrolyse peptides to amino acids
PEPTIDE *n* compound consisting of two or more amino acids linked by chemical bonding between the amino group of one and the carboxyl group of another
PEPTIDES > PEPTIDE
PEPTIDIC *adj* of peptides
PEPTIDS > PEPTID
PEPTISE *same as* > PEPTIZE
PEPTISED > PEPTISE
PEPTISER > PEPTISE
PEPTISERS > PEPTISE
PEPTISES > PEPTISE
PEPTISING > PEPTISE
PEPTIZE *vb* disperse (a substance) into a colloidal state, usually to form a sol
PEPTIZED > PEPTIZE
PEPTIZER > PEPTIZE
PEPTIZERS > PEPTIZE
PEPTIZES > PEPTIZE
PEPTIZING > PEPTIZE
PEPTONE *n* any of a group of compounds that form an intermediary group in the digestion of proteins to amino acids
PEPTONES > PEPTONE
PEPTONIC > PEPTONE
PEPTONISE *same as* > PEPTONIZE
PEPTONIZE *vb* hydrolyse (a protein) to peptones by enzymic action, esp by pepsin or pancreatic extract
PEQUISTE *n* in Canada, member or supporter of the Parti Québécois
PEQUISTES > PEQUISTE
PER *prep* for each
PERACID *n* acid, such as perchloric acid, in which the element forming the acid radical exhibits its highest valency
PERACIDS > PERACID
PERACUTE *adj* very acute
PERAEA > PERAEON
PERAEON *same as* > PEREION
PERAEONS > PERAEON
PERAEOPOD *same as* > PEREIOPOD
PERAI *another name for* > PIRANHA
PERAIS > PERAI
PERBORATE *n* salt derived, or apparently derived, from perboric acid
PERCALE *n* close-textured woven cotton fabric, plain or printed, used esp for sheets
PERCALES > PERCALE
PERCALINE *n* fine light cotton fabric, used esp for linings
PERCASE *adv* perchance
PERCE *obsolete word for* > PIERCE
PERCEABLE *adj* pierceable
PERCEANT *adj* piercing
PERCED > PERCE
PERCEIVE *vb* become aware of (something) through the senses
PERCEIVED > PERCEIVE
PERCEIVER > PERCEIVE
PERCEIVES > PERCEIVE
PERCEN > PERCE
PERCENT *n* percentage or proportion
PERCENTAL > PERCENT
PERCENTS > PERCENT
PERCEPT *n* concept that depends on recognition by the senses, such as sight, of some external object or phenomenon
PERCEPTS > PERCEPT
PERCES > PERCE
PERCH *n* resting place for a bird ▷ *vb* alight, rest, or place on or as if on a perch
PERCHANCE *adv* perhaps
PERCHED > PERCH
PERCHER > PERCH
PERCHERON *n* compact heavy breed of carthorse
PERCHERS > PERCH
PERCHERY *n* barn in which hens are allowed to move without restriction
PERCHES > PERCH
PERCHING > PERCH
PERCHINGS > PERCH
PERCIFORM *adj* of perch-like fishes
PERCINE *adj* of perches
PERCING > PERCE
PERCOCT *adj* well-cooked
PERCOID *adj* of, relating to, or belonging to the *Percoidea*, a suborder of spiny-finned teleost fishes ▷ *n* any fish belonging to the suborder *Percoidea*
PERCOIDS > PERCOID
PERCOLATE *vb* pass or filter through small holes ▷ *n* product of percolation
PERCOLIN *n* pain-relieving drug
PERCOLINS > PERCOLIN
PERCUSS *vb* strike sharply, rapidly, or suddenly
PERCUSSED > PERCUSS
PERCUSSES > PERCUSS
PERCUSSOR > PERCUSS
PERDENDO *adj* (of music) getting gradually quieter and slower
PERDIE *adv* certainly
PERDITION *n* spiritual ruin
PERDU *adj* (of a soldier) placed on hazardous sentry duty ▷ *n* soldier placed on hazardous sentry duty
PERDUE *same as* > PERDU
PERDUES > PERDUE
PERDURE *vb* last for long time
PERDURED > PERDURE
PERDURES > PERDURE
PERDURING > PERDURE
PERDUS > PERDU
PERDY *adv* certainly
PERE *n* addition to a French surname to specify the father rather than the son of the same name
PEREA > PEREON
PEREGAL *adj* equal
PEREGRIN *variant spelling of* > PEREGRIN
PEREGRINE *adj* coming from abroad
PEREGRINS > PEREGRIN
PEREIA > PEREION
PEREION *n* thorax of some crustaceans
PEREIONS > PEREION
PEREIOPOD *n* appendage of the pereion
PEREIRA *n* bark of a South American apocynaceous tree
PEREIRAS > PEREIRA
PERENNATE *vb* (of plants) live from one growing season to another
PERENNIAL *adj* lasting through many years ▷ *n* plant lasting more than two years
PERENNITY *n* state of being perennial
PERENTIE *n* large dark-coloured Australian monitor lizard
PERENTIES > PERENTY
PERENTY *same as* > PERENTIE
PEREON *same as* > PEREION
PEREONS > PEREON
PEREOPOD *same as* > PEREIOPOD
PEREOPODS > PEREOPOD
PERES > PERE
PERFAY *interj* by my faith
PERFECT *adj* having all the essential elements ▷ *n* perfect tense ▷ *vb* improve
PERFECTA *n* bet on the order of the first and second in a race
PERFECTAS > PERFECTA
PERFECTED > PERFECT
PERFECTER *same as* > PERFECTOR
PERFECTI *n* ascetic group of elite Cathars
PERFECTLY *adv* completely, utterly, or absolutely
PERFECTO *n* large cigar that is tapered from both ends
PERFECTOR *n* person who completes or makes something perfect
PERFECTOS > PERFECTO
PERFECTS > PERFECT

PERFERVID *adj* extremely ardent, enthusiastic, or zealous
PERFERVOR *n* zealous person
PERFET *obsolete variant of* > PERFECT
PERFIDIES > PERFIDY
PERFIDY *n* perfidious act
PERFIN *former name for* > SPIF
PERFING *n* practice of taking early retirement, with financial compensation, from the police force
PERFINS > PERFIN
PERFORANS *adj* perforating or penetrating
PERFORANT *adj* perforating
PERFORATE *vb* make holes in ▷ *adj* pierced by small holes
PERFORCE *adv* of necessity
PERFORM *vb* carry out (an action)
PERFORMED > PERFORM
PERFORMER > PERFORM
PERFORMS > PERFORM
PERFUME *n* liquid cosmetic worn for its pleasant smell ▷ *vb* give a pleasant smell to
PERFUMED > PERFUME
PERFUMER *n* person who makes or sells perfume
PERFUMERS > PERFUMER
PERFUMERY *n* perfumes in general
PERFUMES > PERFUME
PERFUMIER *same as* > PERFUMER
PERFUMING > PERFUME
PERFUMY *adj* like perfume
PERFUSATE *n* fluid flowing through tissue or organ
PERFUSE *vb* permeate (a liquid, colour, etc) through or over (something)
PERFUSED > PERFUSE
PERFUSES > PERFUSE
PERFUSING > PERFUSE
PERFUSION > PERFUSE
PERFUSIVE > PERFUSE
PERGOLA *n* arch or framework of trellis supporting climbing plants
PERGOLAS > PERGOLA
PERGUNNAH *same as* > PARGANA
PERHAPS *adv* possibly, maybe ▷ *sentence substitute* it may happen, be so, etc ▷ *n* something that might have happened
PERHAPSES > PERHAPS
PERI *n* (in Persian folklore) one of a race of beautiful supernatural beings
PERIAGUA *n* dugout canoe
PERIAGUAS > PERIAGUA
PERIAKTOI > PERIAKTOS
PERIAKTOS *n* ancient device for changing theatre scenery
PERIANTH *n* outer part of a flower
PERIANTHS > PERIANTH
PERIAPSES > PERIAPSIS
PERIAPSIS *n* closest point to a central body reached by a body in orbit
PERIAPT *n* charm or amulet
PERIAPTS > PERIAPT
PERIBLAST *n* tissue surrounding blastoderm in meroblastic eggs
PERIBLEM *n* layer of meristematic tissue in stems and roots that gives rise to the cortex
PERIBLEMS > PERIBLEM
PERIBOLOI > PERIBOLOS
PERIBOLOS *n* enclosed court surrounding ancient temple
PERIBOLUS *same as* > PERIBOLOS
PERICARP *n* part of a fruit enclosing the seed that develops from the wall of the ovary
PERICARPS > PERICARP
PERICLASE *n* mineral consisting of magnesium oxide in the form of isometric crystals or grains
PERICLINE *n* white translucent variety of albite in the form of elongated crystals
PERICON *n* Argentinian dance
PERICONES > PERICON
PERICOPAE > PERICOPE
PERICOPAL > PERICOPE
PERICOPE *n* selection from a book, esp a passage from the Bible read at religious services
PERICOPES > PERICOPE
PERICOPIC > PERICOPE
PERICYCLE *n* layer of plant tissue beneath the endodermis
PERIDERM *n* outer corky protective layer of woody stems and roots
PERIDERMS > PERIDERM
PERIDIA > PERIDIUM
PERIDIAL > PERIDIUM
PERIDINIA *n* genus of flagellate organisms
PERIDIUM *n* distinct outer layer of the spore-bearing organ in many fungi
PERIDIUMS > PERIDIUM
PERIDOT *n* pale green transparent gemstone
PERIDOTE *same as* > PERIDOT
PERIDOTES > PERIDOTE
PERIDOTIC > PERIDOT
PERIDOTS > PERIDOT
PERIDROME *n* space between the columns and inner room of a classical temple
PERIGEAL > PERIGEE
PERIGEAN > PERIGEE
PERIGEE *n* point in the orbit of the moon or a satellite that is nearest the earth
PERIGEES > PERIGEE
PERIGON *n* angle of 360°
PERIGONE *n* part enclosing the essential organs of a flower
PERIGONES > PERIGONE
PERIGONIA *n* perigones
PERIGONS > PERIGON
PERIGYNY *n* (of a flower) condition of having a concave or flat receptacle with the gynoecium and other floral parts at the same level
PERIHELIA *n* points in the orbits of planets at which they are nearest the sun
PERIKARYA *n* parts of nerve cells that contain the nuclei
PERIL *n* great danger ▷ *vb* expose to danger
PERILED > PERIL
PERILING > PERIL
PERILLA *n* type of mint
PERILLAS > PERILLA
PERILLED > PERIL
PERILLING > PERIL
PERILOUS *adj* very hazardous or dangerous
PERILS > PERIL
PERILUNE *n* point in a lunar orbit when a spacecraft launched from the moon is nearest the moon
PERILUNES > PERILUNE
PERILYMPH *n* fluid filling the space between the membranous and bony labyrinths of the internal ear
PERIMETER *n* outer edge of an area
PERIMETRY > PERIMETER
PERIMORPH *n* mineral that encloses another mineral of a different type
PERIMYSIA *n* sheaths of fibrous connective tissue surrounding the primary bundles of muscle fibres
PERINAEUM *same as* > PERINEUM
PERINATAL *adj* of or in the weeks shortly before or after birth
PERINEA > PERINEUM
PERINEAL > PERINEUM
PERINEUM *n* region of the body between the anus and the genitals
PERINEUMS > PERINEUM
PERIOD *n* particular portion of time ▷ *adj* (of furniture, dress, a play, et dating from or in the styl of an earlier time ▷ *vb* divide into periods
PERIODATE *n* any salt or ester of a periodic acid
PERIODED > PERIOD
PERIODIC *adj* recurring a intervals
PERIODID *n* kind of iodid
PERIODIDE *variant of* > PERIODID
PERIODIDS > PERIODID
PERIODING > PERIOD
PERIODS > PERIOD
PERIOST *n* thick fibrous two-layered membrane covering the surface of bones
PERIOSTEA > PERIOSTS
PERIOSTS > PERIOST
PERIOTIC *adj* of or relatir to the structures situate around the internal ear ▷ *n* periotic bone
PERIOTICS > PERIOTIC
PERIPATUS *n* wormlike arthropod with a segmented body and sho unjointed limbs
PERIPETIA *n* abrupt turn of events or reversal of circumstances
PERIPETY *same as* > PERIPETEIA
PERIPHERY *n* boundary o edge
PERIPLASM *n* region insi wall of biological cell
PERIPLAST *n* nutritive and supporting tissue in animal organ
PERIPLUS *n* circumnavigation
PERIPROCT *n* tough membrane surrounding anus in echinoderms
PERIPTER *n* type of ancie temple
PERIPTERS > PERIPTER
PERIPTERY *n* region surrounding moving bod
PERIQUE *n* strong highly-flavoured tobacco cured its own juices and growr in Louisiana
PERIQUES > PERIQUE
PERIS > PERI
PERISARC *n* outer chitinous layer secreted by colonial hydrozoan coelenterates
PERISARCS > PERISARC
PERISCIAN *adj* person whose shadow moves round every point of compass during day
PERISCOPE *n* instrument used, esp in submarines, to give a view of objects a different level
PERISH *vb* be destroyed or die
PERISHED *adj* (of a perso

part of the body, etc) extremely cold
ERISHER *n* mischievous person
ERISHERS > PERISHER
ERISHES > PERISH
ERISHING *adj* very cold
ERISPERM *n* nutritive tissue surrounding the embryo in certain seeds, and developing from the nucellus of the ovule
ERISTOME *n* fringe of pointed teeth surrounding the opening of a moss capsule
ERISTYLE *n* colonnade that surrounds a court or building
ERITI > PERITUS
ERITONEA *n* thin translucent serous sacs that line the walls of abdominal cavities and cover the viscera
ERITRACK *another name for* > TAXIWAY
ERITRICH *n* ciliate protozoan in which the cilia are restricted to a spiral around the mouth
ERITUS *n* Catholic theology consultant
ERIWIG *same as* > PERUKE
ERIWIGS > PERIWIG
ERJINK *adj* prim or finicky
ERJURE *vb* render (oneself) guilty of perjury
ERJURED *adj* having sworn falsely
ERJURER > PERJURE
ERJURERS > PERJURE
ERJURES > PERJURE
ERJURIES > PERJURY
ERJURING > PERJURE
ERJUROUS > PERJURY
ERJURY *n* act or crime of lying while under oath in a court
ERK *n* incidental benefit gained from a job, such as a company car ▷ *adj* pert ▷ *vb* (of coffee) percolate
ERKED > PERK
ERKIER > PERKY
ERKIEST > PERKY
ERKILY > PERKY
ERKIN *same as* > PARKIN
ERKINESS > PERKY
ERKING > PERK
ERKINS > PERKIN
RKISH *adj* perky
RKS > PERK
RKY *adj* lively or cheerful
RLEMOEN *n* edible sea creature with a shell lined with mother of pearl
RLITE *n* variety of obsidian consisting of masses of small pearly globules
RLITES > PERLITE
RLITIC > PERLITE
RLOUS *same as* > PERILOUS
PERM *n* long-lasting curly hairstyle produced by treating the hair with chemicals ▷ *vb* give (hair) a perm
PERMALLOY *n* any of various alloys containing iron and nickel
PERMANENT *adj* lasting forever
PERMEABLE *adj* able to be permeated, esp by liquid
PERMEABLY > PERMEABLE
PERMEANCE *n* act of permeating
PERMEANT > PERMEANCE
PERMEASE *n* carrier protein
PERMEASES > PERMEASE
PERMEATE *vb* pervade or pass through the whole of (something)
PERMEATED > PERMEATE
PERMEATES > PERMEATE
PERMEATOR > PERMEATE
PERMED > PERM
PERMIAN *adj* of, denoting, or formed in the last period of the Palaeozoic era
PERMIE *n* person, esp an office worker, employed by a firm on a permanent basis
PERMIES > PERMIE
PERMING > PERM
PERMIT *vb* give permission, allow ▷ *n* document giving permission to do something
PERMITS > PERMIT
PERMITTED > PERMIT
PERMITTEE *n* person given a permit
PERMITTER > PERMIT
PERMS > PERM
PERMUTATE *vb* alter the sequence or arrangement (of)
PERMUTE *vb* change the sequence of
PERMUTED > PERMUTE
PERMUTES > PERMUTE
PERMUTING > PERMUTE
PERN *vb* make profitable
PERNANCY *n* receiving of rents
PERNED > PERN
PERNING > PERN
PERNIO *n* chilblain
PERNIONES > PERNIO
PERNOD *n* aniseed-flavoured aperitif from France
PERNODS > PERNOD
PERNS > PERN
PERONE *n* fibula
PERONEAL *adj* of or relating to the fibula or the outer side of the leg
PERONES > PERONE
PERONEUS *n* lateral muscle of the leg
PERORAL *adj* administered through mouth
PERORALLY > PERORAL
PERORATE *vb* speak at length, esp in a formal manner
PERORATED > PERORATE
PERORATES > PERORATE
PERORATOR > PERORATE
PEROVSKIA *n* Russian sage
PEROXID *variant of* > PEROXIDE
PEROXIDE *n* hydrogen peroxide used as a hair bleach ▷ *adj* bleached with or resembling peroxide ▷ *vb* bleach (the hair) with peroxide
PEROXIDED > PEROXIDE
PEROXIDES > PEROXIDE
PEROXIDIC > PEROXIDE
PEROXIDS > PEROXID
PEROXY *adj* containing the peroxide group
PERP *n* informal US and Canadian word for someone who has committed a crime
PERPEND *n* large stone that passes through a wall from one side to the other ▷ *vb* ponder
PERPENDED > PERPEND
PERPENDS > PERPEND
PERPENT *same as* > PERPEND
PERPENTS > PERPENT
PERPETUAL *adj* lasting forever ▷ *n* (of a crop plant) continually producing edible parts
PERPLEX *vb* puzzle, bewilder
PERPLEXED > PERPLEX
PERPLEXER > PERPLEX
PERPLEXES > PERPLEX
PERPS > PERP
PERRADIAL *adj* situated around radii of radiate
PERRADII > PERRADIUS
PERRADIUS *n* primary tentacle of a polyp
PERRIER *n* short mortar
PERRIERS > PERRIER
PERRIES > PERRY
PERRON *n* external flight of steps, esp one at the front entrance of a building
PERRONS > PERRON
PERRUQUE *old spelling of* > PERUKE
PERRUQUES > PERRUQUE
PERRY *n* alcoholic drink made from fermented pears
PERSALT *n* any salt of a peracid
PERSALTS > PERSALT
PERSANT *adj* piercing
PERSAUNT *adj* piercing
PERSE *old variant of* > PIERCE
PERSECUTE *vb* treat cruelly because of race, religion, etc
PERSEITY *n* quality of having substance independently of real objects
PERSELINE *same as* > PURSLANE
PERSES > PERSE
PERSEVERE *vb* keep making an effort despite difficulties
PERSICO *same as* > PERSICOT
PERSICOS > PERSICO
PERSICOT *n* cordial made from apricots
PERSICOTS > PERSICOT
PERSIENNE *n* printed calico
PERSIMMON *n* sweet red tropical fruit
PERSING > PERSE
PERSIST *vb* continue to be or happen, last
PERSISTED > PERSIST
PERSISTER > PERSIST
PERSISTS > PERSIST
PERSON *n* human being
PERSONA *n* someone's personality as presented to others
PERSONAE > PERSONA
PERSONAGE *n* important person
PERSONAL *adj* individual or private ▷ *n* item of movable property
PERSONALS > PERSONAL
PERSONAS > PERSONA
PERSONATE *vb* assume the identity of (another person) with intent to deceive ▷ *adj* (of the corollas of certain flowers) having two lips in the form of a face
PERSONIFY *vb* give human characteristics to
PERSONISE *same as* > PERSONIZE
PERSONIZE *vb* personify
PERSONNED *adj* manned
PERSONNEL *n* people employed in an organization
PERSONS > PERSON
PERSPEX *n* tradename for any of various clear acrylic resins, used chiefly as a substitute for glass
PERSPEXES > PERSPEX
PERSPIRE *vb* sweat
PERSPIRED > PERSPIRE
PERSPIRES > PERSPIRE
PERSPIRY *adj* perspiring
PERST *adj* perished
PERSUADE *vb* make (someone) do something by argument, charm, etc
PERSUADED > PERSUADE
PERSUADER > PERSUADE
PERSUADES > PERSUADE
PERSUE *obsolete form of* > PURSUE
PERSUED > PERSUE
PERSUES > PERSUE
PERSUING > PERSUE
PERSWADE *obsolete form of* > PERSUADE

PERSWADED > PERSWADE
PERSWADES > PERSWADE
PERT *adj* saucy and cheeky ▷ *n* pert person
PERTAIN *vb* belong or be relevant (to)
PERTAINED > PERTAIN
PERTAINS > PERTAIN
PERTAKE *obsolete form of* > PARTAKE
PERTAKEN > PERTAKE
PERTAKES > PERTAKE
PERTAKING > PERTAKE
PERTER > PERT
PERTEST > PERT
PERTHITE *n* type of feldspar
PERTHITES > PERTHITE
PERTHITIC > PERTHITE
PERTINENT *adj* relevant
PERTLY > PERT
PERTNESS > PERT
PERTOOK > PERTAKE
PERTS > PERT
PERTURB *vb* disturb greatly
PERTURBED > PERTURB
PERTURBER > PERTURB
PERTURBS > PERTURB
PERTUSATE *adj* pierced at apex
PERTUSE *adj* having holes
PERTUSED *adj* having holes
PERTUSION *n* punched hole
PERTUSSAL > PERTUSSIS
PERTUSSES > PERTUSSIS
PERTUSSIS *n* whooping cough
PERUKE *n* wig for men worn in the 17th and 18th centuries
PERUKED *adj* wearing wig
PERUKES > PERUKE
PERUSABLE > PERUSE
PERUSAL > PERUSE
PERUSALS > PERUSE
PERUSE *vb* read in a careful or leisurely manner
PERUSED > PERUSE
PERUSER > PERUSE
PERUSERS > PERUSE
PERUSES > PERUSE
PERUSING > PERUSE
PERV *n* pervert ▷ *vb* give a person an erotic look
PERVADE *vb* spread right through (something)
PERVADED > PERVADE
PERVADER > PERVADE
PERVADERS > PERVADE
PERVADES > PERVADE
PERVADING > PERVADE
PERVASION > PERVADE
PERVASIVE *adj* pervading or tending to pervade
PERVE *same as* > PERV
PERVED > PERV
PERVERSE *adj* deliberately doing something different from what is thought normal or proper
PERVERSER > PERVERSE
PERVERT *vb* use or alter for a wrong purpose ▷ *n* person who practises sexual perversion
PERVERTED *adj* deviating greatly from what is regarded as normal or right
PERVERTER > PERVERT
PERVERTS > PERVERT
PERVES > PERV
PERVIATE *vb* perforate or burrow
PERVIATED > PERVIATE
PERVIATES > PERVIATE
PERVICACY *n* obstinacy
PERVING > PERV
PERVIOUS *adj* able to be penetrated, permeable
PERVS > PERV
PES *n* animal part corresponding to the human foot
PESADE *n* position in which the horse stands on the hind legs with the forelegs in the air
PESADES > PESADE
PESANT *obsolete spelling of* > PEASANT
PESANTE *adv* to be performed clumsily
PESANTS > PESANT
PESAUNT *obsolete spelling of* > PEASANT
PESAUNTS > PESAUNT
PESETA *n* former monetary unit of Spain
PESETAS > PESETA
PESEWA *n* Ghanaian monetary unit worth one hundredth of a cedi
PESEWAS > PESEWA
PESHWA *same as* > PEISHWA
PESHWAS > PESHWA
PESKIER > PESKY
PESKIEST > PESKY
PESKILY > PESKY
PESKINESS > PESKY
PESKY *adj* troublesome
PESO *n* monetary unit of Argentina, Mexico, etc
PESOS > PESO
PESSARIES > PESSARY
PESSARY *n* appliance worn in the vagina, either to prevent conception or to support the womb
PESSIMA *n* lowest point
PESSIMAL *adj* (of animal's environment) least favourable for survival
PESSIMISM *n* tendency to expect the worst in all things
PESSIMIST > PESSIMISM
PESSIMUM *same as* > PESSIMAL
PEST *n* annoying person
PESTER *vb* annoy or nag continually
PESTERED > PESTER
PESTERER > PESTER
PESTERERS > PESTER
PESTERING > PESTER
PESTEROUS *adj* inclined to annoy
PESTERS > PESTER
PESTFUL *adj* causing annoyance
PESTHOLE *n* breeding ground for disease
PESTHOLES > PESTHOLE
PESTHOUSE *n* hospital for treating persons with infectious diseases
PESTICIDE *n* chemical for killing insect pests
PESTIER > PESTY
PESTIEST > PESTY
PESTILENT *adj* annoying, troublesome
PESTLE *n* club-shaped implement for grinding things to powder in a mortar ▷ *vb* pound (a substance or object) with or as if with a pestle
PESTLED > PESTLE
PESTLES > PESTLE
PESTLING > PESTLE
PESTO *n* sauce for pasta, consisting of basil leaves, pine nuts, garlic, oil, and Parmesan cheese, all crushed together
PESTOLOGY *n* study of pests
PESTOS > PESTO
PESTS > PEST
PESTY *adj* persistently annoying
PET *n* animal kept for pleasure and companionship ▷ *adj* kept as a pet ▷ *vb* treat as a pet
PETABYTE *n* in computing, 10^{15} or 2^{50} bytes
PETABYTES > PETABYTE
PETAHERTZ *n* very large unit of electrical frequency
PETAL *n* one of the brightly coloured outer parts of a flower
PETALED > PETAL
PETALINE > PETAL
PETALISM *n* ostracism in ancient Syracuse
PETALISMS > PETALISM
PETALLED > PETAL
PETALLIKE > PETAL
PETALODIC > PETALODY
PETALODY *n* condition in certain plants in which stamens or other parts of the flower assume the form and function of petals
PETALOID *adj* resembling a petal, esp in shape
PETALOUS *adj* bearing or having petals
PETALS > PETAL
PETANQUE *n* game, popular in France, in which metal bowls are thrown to land as near as possible to a target ball
PETANQUES > PETANQUE
PETAR *obsolete variant of* > PETARD
PETARA *n* clothes basket
PETARAS > PETARA
PETARD *n* device containing explosives used to breach a wall, doors, etc
PETARDS > PETARD
PETARIES > PETARY
PETARS > PETAR
PETARY *n* weapon for hurling stones
PETASOS *same as* > PETASUS
PETASOSES > PETASOS
PETASUS *n* broad-brimmed hat worn by the ancient Greeks
PETASUSES > PETASUS
PETAURINE *n* animal able to glide
PETAURIST *n* flying phalanger
PETCHARY *n* type of kingbird
PETCOCK *n* small valve for checking the water level in a steam boiler or draining condensed steam from the cylinder of a steam engine
PETCOCKS > PETCOCK
PETECHIA *n* minute discoloured spot on the surface of the skin or mucous membrane, caused by an underlying ruptured blood vessel
PETECHIAE > PETECHIA
PETECHIAL > PETECHIA
PETER *vb* fall (off) in volume, intensity, etc, and finally cease ▷ *n* act of petering
PETERED > PETER
PETERING > PETER
PETERMAN *n* burglar skilled in safe-breaking
PETERMEN > PETERMAN
PETERS > PETER
PETERSHAM *n* thick corded ribbon used to stiffen belts, button bands, etc
PETHER *old variant of* > PEDLAR
PETHERS > PETHER
PETHIDINE *n* white crystalline water-soluble drug used to relieve pain
PETILLANT *adj* (of wine) slightly effervescent
PETIOLAR > PETIOLE
PETIOLATE *adj* (of a plant or leaf) having a leafstalk
PETIOLE *n* stalk which attaches a leaf to a plant
PETIOLED > PETIOLE
PETIOLES > PETIOLE
PETIOLULE *n* stalk of any of the leaflets making up a compound leaf
PETIT *adj* of little or lesser importance
PETITE *adj* (of a woman) small and dainty ▷ *n* clothing size for small women

TITES > PETITE
TITIO as in *petitio principii* form of fallacious reasoning in which the conclusion has been assumed in the premise
TITION *n* formal request, esp one signed by many people and presented to parliament ▷ *vb* present a petition to
TITIONS > PETITION
TITORY *adj* soliciting
TNAP *vb* steal pet
TNAPER > PETNAP
TNAPERS > PETNAP
TNAPING > PETNAP
TNAPPED > PETNAP
TNAPPER > PETNAP
TNAPS > PETNAP
TRALE *n* type of sole
TRALES > PETRALE
TRARIES > PETRARY
TRARY *n* weapon for hurling stones
TRE *same as* > SALTPETRE
TREL *n* sea bird with a hooked bill and tubular nostrils
TRELS > PETREL
TRES > PETRE
TRIFIC *adj* petrifying
TRIFIED > PETRIFY
TRIFIER > PETRIFY
TRIFIES > PETRIFY
TRIFY *vb* frighten severely
TROGENY *n* origin of rocks
TROGRAM *n* prehistoric rock painting
TROL *n* flammable liquid obtained from petroleum, used as fuel in internal-combustion engines ▷ *vb* supply with petrol
TROLAGE *n* addition of petrol (to a body of water) to get rid of mosquitoes
TROLEUM *n* thick dark oil found underground
TROLEUR *n* person using petrol to cause explosions
TROLIC *adj* of, relating to, containing, or obtained from petroleum
TROLLED > PETROL
TROLOGY *n* study of the composition, origin, structure, and formation of rocks
TROLS > PETROL
TRONEL *n* firearm of large calibre used in the 16th and early 17th centuries, esp by cavalry soldiers
TRONELS > PETRONEL
TROSAL *adj* of, relating to, or situated near the dense part of the temporal bone that surrounds the inner ear ▷ *n* petrosal bone
PETROSALS > PETROSAL
PETROUS *adj* denoting the dense part of the temporal bone that surrounds the inner ear
PETS > PET
PETSAI *n* Chinese cabbage
PETSAIS > PETSAI
PETTABLE > PET
PETTED > PET
PETTEDLY > PET
PETTER > PET
PETTERS > PET
PETTI *n* petticoat
PETTICOAT *n* woman's skirt-shaped undergarment
PETTIER > PETTY
PETTIES > PETTI
PETTIEST > PETTY
PETTIFOG *vb* quibble or fuss over details
PETTIFOGS > PETTIFOG
PETTILY > PETTY
PETTINESS > PETTY
PETTING > PET
PETTINGS > PET
PETTISH *adj* peevish or fretful
PETTISHLY > PETTISH
PETTITOES *pl n* pig's trotters, esp when used as food
PETTLE *vb* pat animal
PETTLED > PETTLE
PETTLES > PETTLE
PETTLING > PETTLE
PETTO *n* breast of animal
PETTY *adj* unimportant, trivial
PETULANCE > PETULANT
PETULANCY > PETULANT
PETULANT *adj* childishly irritable or peevish
PETUNIA *n* garden plant with funnel-shaped flowers
PETUNIAS > PETUNIA
PETUNTSE *n* fusible feldspathic mineral used in hard-paste porcelain
PETUNTSES > PETUNTSE
PETUNTZE *same as* > PETUNTSE
PETUNTZES > PETUNTZE
PEW *n* fixed benchlike seat in a church
PEWEE *n* any of several small North American flycatchers of the genus *Contopus*, having a greenish-brown plumage
PEWEES > PEWEE
PEWHOLDER *n* renter of pew
PEWIT *another name for* > LAPWING
PEWITS > PEWIT
PEWS > PEW
PEWTER *n* greyish metal made of tin and lead
PEWTERER > PEWTER
PEWTERERS > PEWTER
PEWTERS > PEWTER
PEYOTE *another name for* > MESCAL
PEYOTES > PEYOTE
PEYOTISM *n* ritual use of peyote
PEYOTISMS > PEYOTISM
PEYOTIST *n* person who uses peyote
PEYOTISTS > PEYOTIST
PEYOTL *same as* > PEYOTE
PEYOTLS > PEYOTL
PEYSE *vb* weight or poise
PEYSED > PEYSE
PEYSES > PEYSE
PEYSING > PEYSE
PEYTRAL *same as* > PEYTREL
PEYTRALS > PEYTRAL
PEYTREL *n* breastplate of horse's armour
PEYTRELS > PEYTREL
PEZANT *obsolete spelling of* > PEASANT
PEZANTS > PEZANT
PEZIZOID *adj* having cup-like form
PFENNIG *n* former German monetary unit worth one hundredth of a mark
PFENNIGE > PFENNIG
PFENNIGS > PFENNIG
PFENNING *old variant of* > PFENNIG
PFENNINGS > PFENNING
PFFT *interj* sound indicating sudden disappearance of something
PFUI *interj* phooey
PHACELIA *n* plant grown for its large, deep blue bell flowers
PHACELIAS > PHACELIA
PHACOID *adj* lentil- or lens-shaped
PHACOIDAL *same as* > PHACOID
PHACOLITE *n* colourless variety of chabazite
PHACOLITH *n* lens-shaped igneous rock structure
PHAEIC *adj* (of animals) having dusky coloration
PHAEISM > PHAEIC
PHAEISMS > PHAEIC
PHAENOGAM *n* seed-bearing plant
PHAETON *n* light four-wheeled horse-drawn carriage with or without a top
PHAETONS > PHAETON
PHAGE *n* virus that is parasitic in a bacterium and multiplies within its host, which is destroyed when the new viruses are released
PHAGEDENA *n* rapidly spreading ulcer that destroys tissues as it increases in size
PHAGES > PHAGE
PHAGOCYTE *n* cell or protozoan that engulfs particles, such as microorganisms
PHAGOSOME *n* part of biological cell
PHALANGAL > PHALANGE
PHALANGE *another name for* > PHALANX
PHALANGER *same as* > POSSUM
PHALANGES > PHALANX
PHALANGID *n* type of arachnid
PHALANX *n* closely grouped mass of people
PHALANXES > PHALANX
PHALAROPE *n* aquatic shore bird of northern oceans and lakes
PHALLI > PHALLUS
PHALLIC *adj* of or resembling a phallus
PHALLIN *n* poisonous substance from mushroom
PHALLINS > PHALLIN
PHALLISM *n* worship or veneration of the phallus
PHALLISMS > PHALLISM
PHALLIST > PHALLICISM
PHALLISTS > PHALLICISM
PHALLOID *adj* resembling penis
PHALLUS *n* penis, esp as a symbol of reproductive power in primitive rites
PHALLUSES > PHALLUS
PHANG *old variant spelling of* > FANG
PHANGED > PHANG
PHANGING > PHANG
PHANGS > PHANG
PHANSIGAR *n* Indian assassin
PHANTASIM *same as* > PHANTASM
PHANTASM *n* unreal vision, illusion
PHANTASMA *same as* > PHANTASM
PHANTASMS > PHANTASM
PHANTAST *same as* > FANTAST
PHANTASTS > PHANTAST
PHANTASY *same as* > FANTASY
PHANTOM *n* ghost ▷ *adj* deceptive or unreal
PHANTOMS > PHANTOM
PHANTOMY *adj* of phantoms
PHANTOSME *old spelling of* > PHANTASM
PHARAOH *n* ancient Egyptian king
PHARAOHS > PHARAOH
PHARAONIC > PHARAOH
PHARE *n* beacon tower
PHARES > PHARE
PHARISAIC *n* righteously hypocritical
PHARISEE *n* self-righteous or hypocritical person
PHARISEES > PHARISEE
PHARMA *n* pharmaceutical companies considered together as an industry

PHARMACY *n* preparation and dispensing of drugs and medicines
PHARMAS > PHARMA
PHARMING *n* practice of rearing or growing genetically-modified animals or plants in order to develop pharmaceutical products
PHARMINGS > PHARMING
PHAROS *n* lighthouse
PHAROSES > PHAROS
PHARYNGAL *adj* of, relating to, or situated in or near the pharynx
PHARYNGES > PHARYNX
PHARYNX *n* cavity forming the back part of the mouth
PHARYNXES > PHARYNX
PHASE *n* any distinct or characteristic stage in a development or chain of events ▷ *vb* arrange or carry out in stages or to coincide with something else
PHASEAL > PHASE
PHASED > PHASE
PHASEDOWN *n* gradual reduction
PHASELESS > PHASE
PHASEOLIN *n* anti-fungal substance from kidney bean
PHASEOUT *n* gradual reduction
PHASEOUTS > PHASEOUT
PHASES > PHASE
PHASIC > PHASE
PHASING *n* tonal sweep achieved by varying the phase relationship of two similar audio signals by mechanical or electronic means
PHASINGS > PHASING
PHASIS *another word for* > PHASE
PHASMID *n* stick insect or leaf insect
PHASMIDS > PHASMID
PHASOR *n* rotating vector representing a quantity, such as an alternating current or voltage, that varies sinusoidally
PHASORS > PHASOR
PHAT *adj* terrific
PHATIC *adj* (of speech, esp of conversational phrases) used to establish social contact and to express sociability rather than specific meaning
PHATTER > PHAT
PHATTEST > PHAT
PHEASANT *n* game bird with bright plumage
PHEASANTS > PHEASANT
PHEAZAR *old variant of* > VIZIER
PHEAZARS > PHEAZAR
PHEER *same as* > FERE
PHEERE *same as* > FERE
PHEERES > PHEERE
PHEERS > PHEER
PHEESE *vb* worry
PHEESED > PHEESE
PHEESES > PHEESE
PHEESING > PHEESE
PHEEZE *same as* > PHEESE
PHEEZED > PHEEZE
PHEEZES > PHEEZE
PHEEZING > PHEEZE
PHELLEM *technical name for* > CORK
PHELLEMS > PHELLEM
PHELLOGEN *n* cork cambium
PHELLOID *adj* like cork
PHELONIA > PHELONION
PHELONION *n* vestment for an Orthodox priest
PHENACITE *n* colourless or white glassy mineral
PHENAKISM *n* deception
PHENAKITE *same as* > PHENACITE
PHENATE *n* ester or salt of phenol
PHENATES > PHENATE
PHENAZIN *same as* > PHENAZINE
PHENAZINE *n* yellow crystalline tricyclic compound
PHENAZINS > PHENAZIN
PHENE *n* genetically determinedcharacteristic of organism
PHENES > PHENE
PHENETIC > PHENETICS
PHENETICS *n* system of classification based on similarities between organisms without regard to their evolutionary relationships
PHENETOL *same as* > PHENETOLE
PHENETOLE *n* colourless oily compound
PHENETOLS > PHENETOL
PHENGITE *n* type of alabaster
PHENGITES > PHENGITE
PHENIC *adj* of phenol
PHENIX *same as* > PHOENIX
PHENIXES > PHENIX
PHENOCOPY *n* noninheritable change in an organism that is caused by environmental influence during development but resembles the effects of a genetic mutation
PHENOGAM *same as* > PHAENOGAM
PHENOGAMS > PHENOGAM
PHENOL *n* chemical used in disinfectants and antiseptics
PHENOLATE *vb* treat or disinfect with phenol
PHENOLIC *adj* of, containing, or derived from phenol ▷ *n* derivative of phenol
PHENOLICS > PHENOLIC
PHENOLOGY *n* study of recurring phenomena, such as animal migration, esp as influenced by climatic conditions
PHENOLS > PHENOL
PHENOM *n* person or thing of outstanding abilities or qualities
PHENOMENA *n* phenomenons
PHENOMS > PHENOM
PHENOTYPE *n* physical form of an organism as determined by the interaction of its genetic make-up and its environment
PHENOXIDE *n* any of a class of salts of phenol
PHENOXY as in *phenoxy resin* any of a class of resins dervied from polyhydroxy ethers
PHENYL *n* chemical substance
PHENYLENE *n* compound derived from benzene
PHENYLIC > PHENYL
PHENYLS > PHENYL
PHENYTOIN *n* anticonvulsant drug
PHEON *n* barbed iron head of dart
PHEONS > PHEON
PHERESES > PHERESIS
PHERESIS *n* specialized form of blood donation
PHEROMONE *n* chemical substance, secreted externally by certain animals, such as insects, affecting the behaviour or physiology of other animals of the same species
PHESE *same as* > PHEESE
PHESED > PHESE
PHESES > PHESE
PHESING > PHESE
PHEW *interj* exclamation of relief, surprise, etc
PHI *n* 21st letter in the Greek alphabet
PHIAL *n* small bottle for medicine etc ▷ *vb* put in phial
PHIALLED > PHIAL
PHIALLING > PHIAL
PHIALS > PHIAL
PHILABEG *same as* > FILIBEG
PHILABEGS > PHILABEG
PHILANDER *vb* (of a man) flirt or have many casual love affairs with women
PHILATELY *n* stamp collecting
PHILHORSE *n* last horse in a team
PHILIBEG *variant spelling of* > FILIBEG
PHILIBEGS > PHILIBEG
PHILIPPIC *n* bitter or impassioned speech of denunciation, invective
PHILISTIA *n* domain of cultural philistine
PHILLABEG *same as* > FILIBEG
PHILLIBEG *same as* > FILIBEG
PHILOGYNY *n* fondness for women
PHILOLOGY *n* science of the structure and development of language
PHILOMATH *n* lover of learning
PHILOMEL *n* nightingale
PHILOMELA *same as* > PHILOMEL
PHILOMELS > PHILOMEL
PHILOMOT *n* colour of dead leaf
PHILOMOTS > PHILOMOT
PHILOPENA *n* gift made as forfeit in game
PHILTER *vb* drink supposed to arouse love, desire, etc ▷ *vb* arouse sexual or romantic feelings by means of a philter
PHILTERED > PHILTER
PHILTERS > PHILTER
PHILTRA > PHILTRUM
PHILTRE *n* magic drink supposed to arouse love in the person who drinks it ▷ *vb* mix with love potion
PHILTRED > PHILTRE
PHILTRES > PHILTRE
PHILTRING > PHILTRE
PHILTRUM *n* indentation above the upper lip
PHIMOSES > PHIMOSIS
PHIMOSIS *n* abnormal tightness of the foreskin, preventing its being retracted over the tip of the penis
PHIMOTIC > PHIMOSIS
PHINNOCK *variant spelling of* > FINNOCK
PHINNOCKS > PHINNOCK
PHIS > PHI
PHISHING *n* use of fraudulent e-mails and lookalike websites to extract personal and financial details for criminal purposes
PHISHINGS > PHISHING
PHISNOMY *n* physiognomy
PHIZ *n* face or a facial expression
PHIZES > PHIZ
PHIZOG *same as* > PHIZ
PHIZOGS > PHIZOG
PHIZZES > PHIZ
PHLEBITIC > PHLEBITIS
PHLEBITIS *n* inflammation of a vein
PHLEGM *n* thick yellowish substance formed in the nose and throat during a

:old
LEGMIER > PHLEGM
LEGMON *n* inflammatory nass that may progress to ıbscess
LEGMONS > PHLEGMON
LEGMS > PHLEGM
LEGMY > PHLEGM
LOEM *n* plant tissue hat acts as a path for he distribution of food ubstances to all parts of he plant
LOEMS > PHLOEM
LOMIS *n* plant of Phlomis genus
LOMISES > PHLOMIS
LORIZIN *n* chemical ound in root bark of fruit rees
LOX *n* flowering garden ılant
LOXES > PHLOX
LYCTENA *n* small blister, esicle, or pustule
O *n* Vietnamese noodle oup
OBIA *n* intense and ınreasoning fear or dislike
OBIAS > PHOBIA
OBIC *adj* of, relating to, r arising from a phobia ▹ *n* person suffering from phobia
OBICS > PHOBIC
OBISM *n* phobia
OBISMS > PHOBISM
OBIST > PHOBISM
OBISTS > PHOBISM
OCA *n* genus of seals
OCAE > PHOCA
OCAS > PHOCA
OCINE *adj* of, relating to, r resembling a seal
OCOMELY *n* congenital eformity resulting from renatal interference with he development of the etal limbs, characterized sp by short stubby hands r feet attached close to he body
OEBE *n* greyish-brown North American flycatcher
OEBES > PHOEBE
OEBUS *n* sun
OEBUSES > PHOEBUS
OENIX *n* legendary bird aid to set fire to itself and ise anew from its ashes
OENIXES > PHOENIX
OH *variant of* > FOH
OHS > PHOH
OLADES > PHOLAS
OLAS *n* type of bivalve nollusc
ON *n* unit of loudness
ONAL *adj* relating to oice
ONATE *vb* articulate peech sounds, esp to ause the vocal cords to ibrate in the execution of voiced speech sound
PHONATED > PHONATE
PHONATES > PHONATE
PHONATHON *n* telephone-based fund-raising campaign
PHONATING > PHONATE
PHONATION > PHONATE
PHONATORY > PHONATE
PHONE *vb* telephone ▹ *n* single uncomplicated speech sound
PHONECAM *n* digital camera incorporated in a mobile phone
PHONECAMS > PHONECAM
PHONECARD *n* card used to operate certain public telephones
PHONED > PHONE
PHONEME *n* one of the set of speech sounds in any given language that serve to distinguish one word from another
PHONEMES > PHONEME
PHONEMIC *adj* of or relating to the phoneme
PHONEMICS *n* classification and analysis of the phonemes of a language
PHONER *n* person making a telephone call
PHONERS > PHONER
PHONES > PHONE
PHONETIC *adj* of speech sounds
PHONETICS *n* science of speech sounds
PHONETISE *same as* > PHONETIZE
PHONETISM *n* phonetic writing
PHONETIST *n* person who advocates or uses a system of phonetic spelling
PHONETIZE *vb* represent by phonetic signs
PHONEY *adj* not genuine ▹ *n* phoney person or thing ▹ *vb* fake
PHONEYED > PHONEY
PHONEYING > PHONEY
PHONEYS > PHONEY
PHONIC > PHONICS
PHONICS *n* method of teaching people to read by training them to associate letters with their phonetic values
PHONIED > PHONY
PHONIER > PHONY
PHONIES > PHONY
PHONIEST > PHONY
PHONILY > PHONY
PHONINESS > PHONY
PHONING > PHONE
PHONMETER *n* instrument measuring sound levels
PHONO *n* phonograph
PHONOGRAM *n* any written symbol standing for a sound, syllable, morpheme, or word
PHONOLITE *n* fine-grained volcanic igneous rock consisting of alkaline feldspars and nepheline
PHONOLOGY *n* study of the speech sounds in a language
PHONON *n* quantum of vibrational energy in the acoustic vibrations of a crystal lattice
PHONONS > PHONON
PHONOPORE *n* device for conveying sound
PHONOS > PHONO
PHONOTYPE *n* letter or symbol representing a sound
PHONOTYPY *n* transcription of speech into phonetic symbols
PHONS > PHON
PHONY *vb* fake
PHONYING > PHONY
PHOOEY *interj* exclamation of scorn or contempt
PHORATE *n* type of insecticide
PHORATES > PHORATE
PHORESIES > PHORESY
PHORESY *n* association in which one animal clings to another to ensure movement from place to place, as some mites use some insects
PHORMINX *n* ancient Greek stringed instrument
PHORMIUM *n* New Zealand plant with leathery evergreen leaves and red or yellow flowers in panicles
PHORMIUMS > PHORMIUM
PHORONID *n* small wormlike marine animal
PHORONIDS > PHORONID
PHOS > PHO
PHOSGENE *n* poisonous gas used in warfare
PHOSGENES > PHOSGENE
PHOSPHATE *n* compound of phosphorus
PHOSPHENE *n* sensation of light caused by pressure on the eyelid of a closed eye or by other mechanical or electrical interference with the visual system
PHOSPHID *same as* > PHOSPHIDE
PHOSPHIDE *n* any compound of phosphorus with another element, esp a more electropositive element
PHOSPHIDS > PHOSPHID
PHOSPHIN *same as* > PHOSPHINE
PHOSPHINE *n* colourless flammable gas that is slightly soluble in water and has a strong fishy odour
PHOSPHINS > PHOSPHIN
PHOSPHITE *n* any salt or ester of phosphorous acid
PHOSPHOR *n* substance capable of emitting light when irradiated with particles of electromagnetic radiation
PHOSPHORE *same as* > PHOSPHOR
PHOSPHORI *n* plural of phosphorus
PHOSPHORS > PHOSPHOR
PHOSSY as in *phossy jaw* gangrenous condition of the lower jawbone caused by prolonged exposure to phosphorus fumes
PHOT *n* unit of illumination equal to one lumen per square centimetre
PHOTIC *adj* of or concerned with light
PHOTICS *n* science of light
PHOTINIA *n* genus of garden plants
PHOTINIAS > PHOTINIA
PHOTISM *n* sensation of light or colour caused by stimulus of another sense
PHOTISMS > PHOTISM
PHOTO *n* photograph ▹ *vb* take a photograph of
PHOTOCELL *n* cell which produces a current or voltage when exposed to light or other electromagnetic radiation
PHOTOCOPY *n* photographic reproduction ▹ *vb* make a photocopy of
PHOTOED > PHOTO
PHOTOFIT *n* method of combining photographs of facial features, hair, etc, into a composite picture of a face
PHOTOFITS > PHOTOFIT
PHOTOG *n* photograph
PHOTOGEN *same as* > PHOTOGENE
PHOTOGENE *n* afterimage
PHOTOGENS > PHOTOGEN
PHOTOGENY *n* photography
PHOTOGRAM *n* picture, usually abstract, produced on a photographic material without the use of a camera, as by placing an object on the material and exposing to light
PHOTOGS > PHOTOG
PHOTOING > PHOTO
PHOTOLYSE *vb* cause to undergo photolysis
PHOTOLYZE *same as* > PHOTOLYZE
PHOTOMAP *n* map constructed by adding grid lines, place names, etc, to one or more aerial photographs ▹ *vb* map (an area) using aerial photography
PHOTOMAPS > PHOTOMAP

PHOTOMASK *n* material on which etching pattern for integrated circuit is drawn
PHOTON *n* quantum of electromagnetic radiation energy, such as light, having both particle and wave behaviour
PHOTONIC > PHOTON
PHOTONICS *n* study and design of devices and systems, such as optical fibres, that depend on the transmission, modulation, or amplification of streams of photons
PHOTONS > PHOTON
PHOTOPHIL *n* light-seeking organism
PHOTOPIA *n* normal adaptation of the eye to light
PHOTOPIAS > PHOTOPIA
PHOTOPIC > PHOTOPIA
PHOTOPLAY *n* play filmed as movie
PHOTOPSIA *n* appearance of flashes due to retinal irritation
PHOTOPSY *same as* > PHOTOPSIA
PHOTOS > PHOTO
PHOTOSCAN *n* photographic scan
PHOTOSET *vb* set (type matter) by photosetting
PHOTOSETS > PHOTOSET
PHOTOSTAT *n* copy made by photocopying machine ▷ *vb* make a photostat copy (of)
PHOTOTAXY *n* movement of an entire organism in response to light
PHOTOTUBE *n* type of photocell in which radiation falling on a photocathode causes electrons to flow to an anode and thus produce an electric current
PHOTOTYPE *n* printing plate produced by photography ▷ *vb* reproduce (an illustration) using a phototype
PHOTOTYPY *n* process of producing phototypes
PHOTS > PHOT
PHPHT *interj* expressing irritation or reluctance
PHRASAL *adj* of, relating to, or composed of phrases
PHRASALLY > PHRASAL
PHRASE *n* group of words forming a unit of meaning, esp within a sentence ▷ *vb* express in words
PHRASED > PHRASE
PHRASEMAN *n* coiner of phrases
PHRASEMEN > PHRASEMAN
PHRASER > PHRASE
PHRASERS > PHRASE
PHRASES > PHRASE
PHRASIER > PHRASY
PHRASIEST > PHRASY
PHRASING *n* exact words used to say or write something
PHRASINGS > PHRASING
PHRASY *adj* containing phrases
PHRATRAL > PHRATRY
PHRATRIC > PHRATRY
PHRATRIES > PHRATRY
PHRATRY *n* group of people within a tribe who have a common ancestor
PHREAK *vb* hack into a telecommunications system
PHREAKED > PHREAK
PHREAKER > PHREAK
PHREAKERS > PHREAK
PHREAKING > PHREAK
PHREAKS > PHREAK
PHREATIC *adj* of or relating to ground water occurring below the water table
PHRENESES > PHRENESIS
PHRENESIS *n* mental confusion
PHRENETIC *obsolete spelling of* > FRENETIC
PHRENIC *adj* of or relating to the diaphragm
PHRENISM *n* belief in non-physical life force
PHRENISMS > PHRENISM
PHRENITIC > PHRENITIS
PHRENITIS *n* state of frenzy
PHRENSIED > PHRENSY
PHRENSIES > PHRENSY
PHRENSY *obsolete spelling of* > FRENZY
PHRENTICK *obsolete spelling of* > PHRENETIC
PHRYGANA *another name for* > GARIGUE
PHRYGANAS > PHRYGANA
PHT *same as* > PHPHT
PHTHALATE *n* salt or ester of phthalic acid
PHTHALEIN *n* any of a class of organic compounds obtained by the reaction of phthalic anhydride with a phenol and used in dyes
PHTHALIC as in *phthalic anhydride* white crystalline substance used mainly in producing dyestuffs
PHTHALIN *n* colourless compound formed by reduction of phthalein
PHTHALINS > PHTHALIN
PHTHISES > PHTHISIS
PHTHISIC *adj* relating to or affected with phthisis ▷ *n* person suffering from phthisis
PHTHISICS > PHTHISIC
PHTHISIS *n* any disease that causes wasting of the body, esp pulmonary tuberculosis
PHUT *vb* make muffled explosive sound
PHUTS > PHUT
PHUTTED > PHUT
PHUTTING > PHUT
PHYCOLOGY *n* study of algae
PHYLA > PHYLUM
PHYLAE > PHYLE
PHYLAR > PHYLUM
PHYLARCH *n* chief of tribe
PHYLARCHS > PHYLARCH
PHYLARCHY > PHYLARCH
PHYLAXIS *n* protection against infection
PHYLE *n* tribe or clan of an ancient Greek people such as the Ionians
PHYLESES > PHYLESIS
PHYLESIS *n* evolutionary events that modify taxon without causing speciation
PHYLETIC *adj* of or relating to the evolution of a species or group of organisms
PHYLETICS *n* study of the evolution of species
PHYLIC > PHYLE
PHYLLARY *n* bract subtending flower head of composite plant
PHYLLID *n* leaf of a liverwort or moss
PHYLLIDS > PHYLLID
PHYLLITE *n* compact lustrous metamorphic rock, rich in mica, derived from a shale or other clay-rich rock
PHYLLITES > PHYLLITE
PHYLLITIC > PHYLLITE
PHYLLO *variant of* > FILO
PHYLLODE *n* flattened leafstalk that resembles and functions as a leaf
PHYLLODES > PHYLLODE
PHYLLODIA > PHYLLODE
PHYLLODY *n* abnormal development of leaves from parts of flower
PHYLLOID *adj* resembling a leaf ▷ *n* leaf-like organ
PHYLLOIDS > PHYLLOID
PHYLLOME *n* leaf or a leaflike organ
PHYLLOMES > PHYLLOME
PHYLLOMIC > PHYLLOME
PHYLLOPOD *n* crustacean with leaf-like appendages
PHYLLOS > PHYLLO
PHYLOGENY *n* sequence of events involved in the evolution of a species, genus, etc
PHYLON *n* tribe
PHYLONS > PHYLON
PHYLUM *n* major taxonomic division of animals and plants that contains one or more classes
PHYSALIA *n* Portuguese man-of-war
PHYSALIAS > PHYSALIA
PHYSALIS *n* strawberry tomato
PHYSED *n* physical education
PHYSEDS > PHYSED
PHYSES > PHYSIS
PHYSETER *n* creature such as the sperm whale
PHYSETERS > PHYSETER
PHYSIATRY *n* treatment of injury by physical means
PHYSIC *n* medicine or drug, esp a cathartic or purge ▷ *vb* treat (a patient) with medicine
PHYSICAL *adj* of the body, as contrasted with the mind or spirit
PHYSICALS *pl n* commodities that can be purchased and used, as opposed to those bought and sold in a futures market
PHYSICIAN *n* doctor of medicine
PHYSICISM *n* belief in the physical as opposed to the spiritual
PHYSICIST *n* person skilled in or studying physics
PHYSICKED > PHYSIC
PHYSICKY > PHYSIC
PHYSICS *n* science of the properties of matter and energy
PHYSIO *n* physiotherapy
PHYSIOS > PHYSIO
PHYSIQUE *n* person's bodily build and muscular development
PHYSIQUED *adj* having particular physique
PHYSIQUES > PHYSIQUE
PHYSIS *n* part of bone responsible for lengthening
PHYTANE *n* hydrocarbon found in some fossilised plant remains
PHYTANES > PHYTANE
PHYTIN *n* substance from plants used as an energy supplement
PHYTINS > PHYTIN
PHYTOGENY *n* branch of botany that is concerned with the detailed description of plants
PHYTOID *adj* resembling plant
PHYTOL *n* alcohol used to synthesize some vitamins
PHYTOLITH *n* microscopic particle in plants
PHYTOLOGY *rare name for* > BOTANY
PHYTOLS > PHYTOL
PHYTON *n* unit of plant structure, usually considered as the smallest part of the plant that is

capable of growth when detached from the parent plant
YTONIC > PHYTON
YTONS > PHYTON
YTOSES > PHYTOSIS
YTOSIS *n* disease caused by vegetable parasite
YTOTOMY *n* dissection of plants
YTOTRON *n* building in which plants can be grown on a large scale, under controlled conditions
n sixteenth letter in the Greek alphabet ▷ *vb* spill and mix (set type) indiscriminately
A *n* innermost of the three membranes that cover the brain and the spinal cord
ACEVOLE *adv* to be performed in playful manner
ACULAR *adj* making expiation for a sacrilege
AFFE *n* passage done on the spot ▷ *vb* strut on the spot
AFFED > PIAFFE
AFFER > PIAFFE
AFFERS > PIAFFE
AFFES > PIAFFE
AFFING > PIAFFE
AL *adj* relating to pia mater
AN *n* contagious tropical skin disease
ANETTE *n* small piano
ANETTES > PIANETTE
ANIC *adj* of piano
ANINO *n* small upright piano
ANINOS > PIANINO
ANISM *n* technique, skill, or artistry in playing the piano
ANISMS > PIANISM
ANIST *n* person who plays the piano
ANISTE *variant* of > PIANIST
ANISTES > PIANISTE
ANISTIC > PIANISM
ANISTS > PIANIST
ANO *n* musical instrument with strings which are struck by hammers worked by a keyboard ▷ *adv* quietly
ANOLIST *n* person who plays the Pianola
ANOS > PIANO
ANS > PIAN
ARIST *n* member of a Roman religious order
ARISTS > PIARIST
AS > PIA
ASABA *same as* > PIASSAVA
ASABAS > PIASABA
ASAVA *same as* > PIASSAVA
ASAVAS > PIASAVA
ASSABA *same* as > PIASSAVA
PIASSABAS > PIASSABA
PIASSAVA *n* South American palm tree
PIASSAVAS > PIASSAVA
PIASTER *same as* > PIASTRE
PIASTERS > PIASTER
PIASTRE *n* standard monetary unit of South Vietnam, divided into 100 cents
PIASTRES > PIASTRE
PIAZZA *n* square or marketplace, esp in Italy
PIAZZAS > PIAZZA
PIAZZE > PIAZZA
PIAZZIAN > PIAZZA
PIBAL *n* method of measuring wind
PIBALS > PIBAL
PIBROCH *n* form of bagpipe music
PIBROCHS > PIBROCH
PIC *n* photograph or illustration
PICA *n* abnormal craving to ingest substances such as clay, dirt, and hair
PICACHO *n* pointed solitary mountain
PICACHOS > PICACHO
PICADILLO *n* Mexican dish
PICADOR *n* mounted bullfighter with a lance
PICADORES > PICADOR
PICADORS > PICADOR
PICAL *adj* relating to pica
PICAMAR *n* hydrocarbon extract of beechwood tar
PICAMARS > PICAMAR
PICANINNY *n* offensive term for a small Black or Aboriginal child
PICANTE *adj* spicy
PICARA *n* female adventurer
PICARAS > PICARA
PICARIAN *n* tree-haunting bird
PICARIANS > PICARIAN
PICARO *n* roguish adventurer
PICAROON *n* adventurer or rogue
PICAROONS > PICAROON
PICAROS > PICARO
PICAS > PICA
PICAYUNE *adj* of small value or importance ▷ *n* any coin of little value, such as a five-cent piece
PICAYUNES > PICAYUNE
PICCADILL *n* high stiff collar
PICCANIN *n* offensive word for a Black African child
PICCANINS > PICCANIN
PICCATA *n* Italian sauce
PICCIES > PICCY
PICCOLO *n* small flute
PICCOLOS > PICCOLO
PICCY *n* picture or photograph
PICE *n* former Indian coin worth one sixty-fourth of a rupee
PICENE *n* type of hydrocarbon
PICENES > PICENE
PICEOUS *adj* of, relating to, or resembling pitch
PICHOLINE *n* variety of olive
PICHURIM *n* S American laurel tree
PICHURIMS > PICHURIM
PICIFORM *adj* relating to certain tree-haunting birds
PICINE *adj* relating to woodpeckers
PICK *vb* choose ▷ *n* choice
PICKABACK *same as* > PIGGYBACK
PICKABLE > PICK
PICKADIL *same as* > PICCADILL
PICKADILL *same as* > PICCADILL
PICKADILS > PICKADIL
PICKAPACK *same as* > PICKABACK
PICKAROON *same as* > PICAROON
PICKAX *same as* > PICKAXE
PICKAXE *n* large pick ▷ *vb* use a pickaxe on (earth, rocks, etc)
PICKAXED > PICKAXE
PICKAXES > PICKAXE
PICKAXING > PICKAXE
PICKBACK *same as* > PICKABACK
PICKBACKS > PICKBACK
PICKED > PICK
PICKEER *vb* make raid for booty
PICKEERED > PICKEER
PICKEERER > PICKEER
PICKEERS > PICKEER
PICKER *n* person or thing that picks, esp that gathers fruit, crops, etc
PICKEREL *n* North American freshwater game fish
PICKERELS > PICKEREL
PICKERIES > PICKERY
PICKERS > PICKER
PICKERY *n* petty theft
PICKET *n* person or group standing outside a workplace to deter would-be workers during a strike ▷ *vb* form a picket outside (a workplace)
PICKETED > PICKET
PICKETER > PICKET
PICKETERS > PICKET
PICKETING > PICKET
PICKETS > PICKET
PICKIER > PICKY
PICKIEST > PICKY
PICKILY > PICKY
PICKIN *n* small child
PICKINESS > PICKY
PICKING > PICK
PICKINGS *pl n* money easily acquired
PICKINS > PICKIN
PICKLE *n* food preserved in vinegar or salt water ▷ *vb* preserve in vinegar or salt water
PICKLED *adj* (of food) preserved
PICKLER > PICKLE
PICKLERS > PICKLE
PICKLES > PICKLE
PICKLING > PICKLE
PICKLOCK *n* person who picks locks, esp one who gains unlawful access to premises by this means
PICKLOCKS > PICKLOCK
PICKMAW *n* type of gull
PICKMAWS > PICKMAW
PICKOFF *n* baseball play
PICKOFFS > PICKOFF
PICKPROOF *adj* (of a lock) unable to be picked
PICKS > PICK
PICKTHANK *n* flatterer
PICKUP *n* small truck with an open body and low sides
PICKUPS > PICKUP
PICKWICK *n* tool for raising the short wick of an oil lamp
PICKWICKS > PICKWICK
PICKY *adj* fussy
PICLORAM *n* type of herbicide
PICLORAMS > PICLORAM
PICNIC *n* informal meal out of doors ▷ *vb* have a picnic
PICNICKED > PICNIC
PICNICKER > PICNIC
PICNICKY > PICNIC
PICNICS > PICNIC
PICOCURIE *n* unit of radioactivity
PICOFARAD *n* unit of capacitance
PICOGRAM *n* trillionth of gram
PICOGRAMS > PICOGRAM
PICOLIN *variant of* > PICOLINE
PICOLINE *n* liquid derivative of pyridine found in bone oil and coal tar
PICOLINES > PICOLINE
PICOLINIC > PICOLINE
PICOLINS > PICOLIN
PICOMETER *same as* > PICOMETRE
PICOMETRE *n* trillionth fraction of metre
PICOMOLE *n* trillionth of a mole
PICOMOLES > PICOMOLE
PICONG *n* any teasing or satirical banter, originally a verbal duel in song
PICONGS > PICONG
PICOT *n* any of pattern of small loops, as on lace ▷ *vb* decorate material with

small loops
PICOTE *adj* (of material) picoted
PICOTED > PICOT
PICOTEE *n* type of carnation having pale petals edged with a darker colour, usually red
PICOTEES > PICOTEE
PICOTING > PICOT
PICOTITE *n* dark-brown mineral
PICOTITES > PICOTITE
PICOTS > PICOT
PICOWAVE *vb* treat food with gamma waves
PICOWAVED > PICOWAVE
PICOWAVES > PICOWAVE
PICQUET *vb* provide early warning of attack
PICQUETED > PICQUET
PICQUETS > PICQUET
PICRA *n* powder of aloes and canella
PICRAS > PICRA
PICRATE *n* any salt or ester of picric acid, such as sodium picrate
PICRATED *adj* containing picrate
PICRATES > PICRATE
PICRIC as in *picric acid* toxic sparingly soluble crystalline yellow acid
PICRITE *n* coarse-grained ultrabasic igneous rock consisting of olivine and augite with small amounts of plagioclase feldspar
PICRITES > PICRITE
PICRITIC > PICRITE
PICS > PIC
PICTARNIE *Scots word for* > TERN
PICTOGRAM *n* picture or symbol standing for a word or group of words, as in written Chinese
PICTORIAL *adj* of or in painting or pictures ▷ *n* newspaper etc with many pictures
PICTURAL *n* picture
PICTURALS > PICTURAL
PICTURE *n* drawing or painting ▷ *vb* visualize, imagine
PICTURED > PICTURE
PICTURES > PICTURE
PICTURING > PICTURE
PICTURISE *same as* > PICTURIZE
PICTURIZE *vb* adorn with pictures
PICUL *n* unit of weight, used in China, Japan, and SE Asia
PICULS > PICUL
PIDDLE *vb* urinate
PIDDLED > PIDDLE
PIDDLER > PIDDLE
PIDDLERS > PIDDLE
PIDDLES > PIDDLE
PIDDLING *adj* small or unimportant
PIDDLY *adj* trivial
PIDDOCK *n* marine bivalve that bores into rock, clay, or wood
PIDDOCKS > PIDDOCK
PIDGEON *variant of* > PIDGIN
PIDGEONS > PIDGEON
PIDGIN *n* language, not a mother tongue, made up of elements of two or more other languages
PIDGINISE *same as* > PIDGINIZE
PIDGINIZE *vb* create pidgin language
PIDGINS > PIDGIN
PIE *n* dish of meat, fruit, etc baked in pastry
PIEBALD *adj* (horse) with irregular black-and-white markings ▷ *n* black-and-white horse
PIEBALDS > PIEBALD
PIECE *n* separate bit or part
PIECED > PIECE
PIECELESS > PIECE
PIECEMEAL *adv* bit by bit ▷ *adj* fragmentary or unsystematic
PIECEN *vb* join broken threads
PIECENED > PIECEN
PIECENER > PIECEN
PIECENERS > PIECEN
PIECENING > PIECEN
PIECENS > PIECEN
PIECER *n* person who mends, repairs, or joins something, esp broken threads on a loom
PIECERS > PIECER
PIECES > PIECE
PIECEWISE *adv* with respect to number of discrete pieces
PIECEWORK *n* work paid for according to the quantity produced
PIECING > PIECE
PIECINGS > PIECE
PIECRUST *n* pastry used for making pies
PIECRUSTS > PIECRUST
PIED > PI
PIEDFORT *n* coin thicker than normal
PIEDFORTS > PIEDFORT
PIEDISH *n* container for baking pies
PIEDISHES > PIEDISH
PIEDMONT *adj* (of glaciers, plains, etc) formed or situated at the foot of a mountain or mountain range ▷ *n* gentle slope leading from mountains to flat land
PIEDMONTS > PIEDMONT
PIEDNESS *n* state of being pied
PIEFORT *same as* > PIEDFORT
PIEFORTS > PIEFORT
PIEHOLE *n* person's mouth
PIEHOLES > PIEHOLE
PIEING > PIE
PIEMAN *n* seller of pies
PIEMEN > PIEMAN
PIEND *same as* > PEEN
PIENDED > PIEND
PIENDING > PIEND
PIENDS > PIEND
PIEPLANT *n* rhubarb
PIEPLANTS > PIEPLANT
PIEPOWDER *n* former court for dealing with certain disputes
PIER *n* platform on stilts sticking out into the sea
PIERAGE *n* accommodation for ships at piers
PIERAGES > PIERAGE
PIERCE *vb* make a hole in or through with a sharp instrument
PIERCED > PIERCE
PIERCER > PIERCE
PIERCERS > PIERCE
PIERCES > PIERCE
PIERCING *adj* (of a sound) shrill and high-pitched ▷ *n* art or practice of piercing body parts for the insertion of jewellery
PIERCINGS > PIERCING
PIERID *n* type of butterfly
PIERIDINE *adj* > PIERID
PIERIDS > PIERID
PIERIS *n* American or Asiatic shrub
PIERISES > PIERIS
PIEROGI *n* Polish dumpling
PIEROGIES > PIEROGI
PIERRETTE *n* female pierrot
PIERROT *n* clown or masquerader with a whitened face, white costume, and pointed hat
PIERROTS > PIERROT
PIERS > PIER
PIERST *archaic spelling of* > PIERCED
PIERT *n* small plant with small greenish flowers
PIERTS > PIERT
PIES > PIE
PIET *n* magpie
PIETA *n* sculpture, painting, or drawing of the dead Christ, supported by the Virgin Mary
PIETAS > PIETA
PIETIES > PIETY
PIETISM *n* exaggerated piety
PIETISMS > PIETISM
PIETIST > PIETISM
PIETISTIC > PIETISM
PIETISTS > PIETISM
PIETS > PIET
PIETY *n* deep devotion to God and religion
PIEZO *adj* piezoelectric
PIFFERARI > PIFFERARO
PIFFERARO *n* player of piffero
PIFFERO *n* small rustic flute
PIFFEROS > PIFFERO
PIFFLE *n* nonsense ▷ *vb* talk or behave feebly
PIFFLED > PIFFLE
PIFFLER *n* talker of nonsense
PIFFLERS > PIFFLER
PIFFLES > PIFFLE
PIFFLING *adj* worthless
PIG *n* animal kept and killed for pork, ham, and bacon ▷ *vb* eat greedily
PIGBOAT *n* submarine
PIGBOATS > PIGBOAT
PIGEON *n* bird with a heavy body and short legs, sometimes trained to carry messages ▷ *vb* pigeonhole
PIGEONED > PIGEON
PIGEONING > PIGEON
PIGEONITE *n* brownish mineral
PIGEONRY *n* loft for keeping pigeons
PIGEONS > PIGEON
PIGFACE *n* creeping succulent plant with bright-coloured flowers and red fruits
PIGFACES > PIGFACE
PIGFEED *n* food for pigs
PIGFEEDS > PIGFEED
PIGFISH *n* grunting fish of the North American Atlantic coast
PIGFISHES > PIGFISH
PIGGED > PIG
PIGGERIES > PIGGERY
PIGGERY *n* place for keeping and breeding pi[gs]
PIGGIE *same as* > PIGGY
PIGGIER > PIGGY
PIGGIES > PIGGY
PIGGIEST > PIGGY
PIGGIN *n* small wooden bucket or tub
PIGGINESS > PIGGY
PIGGING > PIG
PIGGINGS > PIG
PIGGINS > PIGGIN
PIGGISH *adj* like a pig, es[p] in appetite or manners
PIGGISHLY > PIGGISH
PIGGY *n* child's word for a pig, esp a piglet ▷ *adj* lik[e] a pig, esp in appetite
PIGGYBACK *n* ride on someone's shoulders ▷ *a*[dv] carried on someone's shoulders ▷ *adj* on the back and shoulders of another person ▷ *vb* giv[e] (a person) a piggyback o[n] one's back and shoulders
PIGHEADED *adj* stupidly stubborn
PIGHT *vb* pierce

IGHTED > PIGHT
IGHTING > PIGHT
IGHTLE *n* small enclosure
IGHTLES > PIGHTLE
IGHTS > PIGHT
IGLET *n* young pig
IGLETS > PIGLET
IGLIKE > PIG
IGLING *n* young pig
IGLINGS > PIGLING
IGMAEAN *same*
as > PYGMAEAN
IGMEAN *same*
as > PYGMAEAN
IGMEAT *less common name*
for > PORK
IGMEATS > PIGMEAT
IGMENT *n* colouring
matter, paint or dye ▷ *vb*
colour with pigment
IGMENTAL > PIGMENT
IGMENTED > PIGMENT
IGMENTS > PIGMENT
IGMIES > PIGMY
IGMOID *adj* of pygmies
IGMY *same as* > PYGMY
IGNERATE *vb* pledge or
pawn
IGNOLI *same as* > PIGNOLIA
IGNOLIA *n* edible seed of
nut pine
IGNOLIAS > PIGNOLIA
IGNOLIS > PIGNOLI
IGNORA > PIGNUS
IGNORATE *same*
as > PIGNERATE
IGNUS *n* pawn or pledge
IGNUT *n* bitter nut of any
of several North American
hickory trees
IGNUTS > PIGNUT
IGOUT *n* binge
IGOUTS > PIGOUT
IGPEN *same as* > PIGSTY
IGPENS > PIGPEN
IGS > PIG
IGSCONCE *n* foolish
person
IGSKIN *n* skin of the
domestic pig ▷ *adj* made
of pigskin
IGSKINS > PIGSKIN
IGSNEY *same as* > PIGSNY
IGSNEYS > PIGSNEY
IGSNIE *same as* > PIGSNY
IGSNIES > PIGSNIE
IGSNY *n* former pet name
for girl
IGSNYS > PIGSNY
IGSTICK *vb* (esp in India)
hunt and spear wild boar,
esp from horseback
IGSTICKS > PIGSTICK
IGSTIES > PIGSTY
IGSTUCK > PIGSTICK
IGSTY *same as* > PIGPEN
IGSWILL *n* waste food
or other edible matter fed
to pigs
IGSWILLS > PIGSWILL
IGTAIL *n* plait of hair
hanging from the back or
either side of the head ▷ *vb*
twist hair into a pigtail

PIGTAILED > PIGTAIL
PIGTAILS > PIGTAIL
PIGWASH *n* wet feed for pigs
PIGWASHES > PIGWASH
PIGWEED *n* coarse North American amaranthaceous weed
PIGWEEDS > PIGWEED
PIHOIHOI *n* variety of New Zealand pipit
PIING > PI
PIKA *n* burrowing lagomorph mammal of mountainous regions of North America and Asia
PIKAKE *n* type of Asian vine
PIKAKES > PIKAKE
PIKAS > PIKA
PIKAU *n* pack, knapsack, or rucksack
PIKAUS > PIKAU
PIKE *n* large predatory freshwater fish ▷ *vb* stab or pierce using a pike ▷ *adj* (of the body position of a diver) bent at the hips but with the legs straight
PIKED > PIKE
PIKELET *n* small thick pancake
PIKELETS > PIKELET
PIKEMAN *n* (formerly) soldier armed with a pike
PIKEMEN > PIKEMAN
PIKEPERCH *n* pikelike freshwater teleost fish
PIKER *n* shirker
PIKERS > PIKER
PIKES > PIKE
PIKESTAFF *n* wooden handle of a pike
PIKEY *n* in British English, derogatory word for gypsy or vagrant
PIKEYS > PIKEY
PIKI *n* bread made from blue cornmeal
PIKING > PIKE
PIKINGS > PIKE
PIKIS > PIKI
PIKUL *same as* > PICUL
PIKULS > PIKUL
PILA *n* pillar-like anatomical structure
PILAE > PILA
PILAF *same as* > PILAU
PILAFF *same as* > PILAU
PILAFFS > PILAFF
PILAFS > PILAF
PILAO *same as* > PILAU
PILAOS > PILAO
PILAR *adj* relating to hair
PILASTER *n* square column, usu set in a wall
PILASTERS > PILASTER
PILAU *n* Middle Eastern dish of meat, fish, or poultry boiled with rice, spices, etc
PILAUS > PILAU
PILAW *same as* > PILAU
PILAWS > PILAW
PILCH *n* outer garment, originally one made of skin
PILCHARD *n* small edible sea fish of the herring family
PILCHARDS > PILCHARD
PILCHER *n* scabbard for sword
PILCHERS > PILCHER
PILCHES > PILCH
PILCORN *n* type if oat
PILCORNS > PILCORN
PILCROW *n* paragraph mark
PILCROWS > PILCROW
PILE *n* number of things lying on top of each other ▷ *vb* collect into a pile
PILEA *n* artillery or gunpowder plant, which releases a cloud of pollen when shaken
PILEAS > PILEA
PILEATE *adj* (of birds) having a crest
PILEATED *same as* > PILEATE
PILED > PILE
PILEI > PILEUS
PILELESS > PILE
PILEOUS *adj* hairy
PILER *n* placer of things on pile
PILERS > PILER
PILES *pl n* swollen veins in the rectum, haemorrhoids
PILEUM *n* top of a bird's head from the base of the bill to the occiput
PILEUP *n* multiple collision of vehicles
PILEUPS > PILEUP
PILEUS *n* upper cap-shaped part of a mushroom or similar spore-producing body
PILEWORK *n* construction built from heavy stakes or cylinders
PILEWORKS > PILEWORK
PILEWORT *n* any of several plants, such as lesser celandine, thought to be effective in treating piles
PILEWORTS > PILEWORT
PILFER *vb* steal in small quantities
PILFERAGE *n* act or practice of stealing small quantities or articles
PILFERED > PILFER
PILFERER > PILFER
PILFERERS > PILFER
PILFERIES > PILFERY
PILFERING > PILFER
PILFERS > PILFER
PILFERY *n* theft
PILGARLIC *n* bald head or a man with a bald head
PILGRIM *n* person who journeys to a holy place
PILGRIMER *n* one who undertakes a pilgrimage
PILGRIMS > PILGRIM
PILI *n* Philippine tree with edible seeds resembling almonds
PILIFORM *adj* resembling a long hair
PILING *n* act of driving piles
PILINGS > PILING
PILIS > PILI
PILL *n* small ball of medicine swallowed whole ▷ *vb* peel or skin (something)
PILLAGE *vb* steal property by violence in war ▷ *n* violent seizure of goods, esp in war
PILLAGED > PILLAGE
PILLAGER > PILLAGE
PILLAGERS > PILLAGE
PILLAGES > PILLAGE
PILLAGING > PILLAGE
PILLAR *n* upright post, usu supporting a roof ▷ *vb* provide or support with pillars
PILLARED > PILLAR
PILLARING > PILLAR
PILLARIST *n* recluse who sat on high pillar
PILLARS > PILLAR
PILLAU *same as* > PILAU
PILLAUS > PILLAU
PILLBOX *n* small box for pills
PILLBOXES > PILLBOX
PILLED > PILL
PILLHEAD *n* person addicted to pills
PILLHEADS > PILLHEAD
PILLICOCK *n* penis
PILLIE *n* pilchard
PILLIES > PILLIE
PILLING > PILL
PILLINGS > PILL
PILLION *n* seat for a passenger behind the rider of a motorcycle ▷ *adv* on a pillion ▷ *vb* ride pillion
PILLIONED > PILLION
PILLIONS > PILLION
PILLOCK *n* stupid or annoying person
PILLOCKS > PILLOCK
PILLORIED > PILLORY
PILLORIES > PILLORY
PILLORISE *same as* > PILLORIZE
PILLORIZE *vb* put in pillory
PILLORY *n* frame with holes for the head and hands in which an offender was locked and exposed to public abuse ▷ *vb* ridicule publicly
PILLOW *n* stuffed cloth bag for supporting the head in bed ▷ *vb* rest as if on a pillow
PILLOWED > PILLOW
PILLOWING > PILLOW
PILLOWS > PILLOW
PILLOWY > PILLOW
PILLS > PILL
PILLWORM *n* worm that rolls up spirally
PILLWORMS > PILLWORM

PILLWORT *n* small Eurasian water fern
PILLWORTS > PILLWORT
PILOMOTOR *adj* causing movement of hairs
PILONIDAL *adj* of crease above buttocks
PILOSE *adj* covered with fine soft hairs
PILOSITY > PILOSE
PILOT *n* person qualified to fly an aircraft or spacecraft ▷ *adj* experimental and preliminary ▷ *vb* act as the pilot of
PILOTAGE *n* act of piloting an aircraft or ship
PILOTAGES > PILOTAGE
PILOTED > PILOT
PILOTFISH *n* fish that accompanies sharks
PILOTI *n* post that supports a roof
PILOTING *n* navigational handling of a ship near land using buoys, soundings, landmarks, etc, or the finding of a ship's position by such means
PILOTINGS > PILOTING
PILOTIS > PILOTI
PILOTLESS > PILOT
PILOTMAN *n* railway worker who directs trains through hazardous stretches of track
PILOTMEN > PILOTMAN
PILOTS > PILOT
PILOUS *same as* > PILOSE
PILOW *same as* > PILAU
PILOWS > PILOW
PILSENER *same as* > PILSNER
PILSENERS > PILSENER
PILSNER *n* type of pale beer with a strong flavour of hops
PILSNERS > PILSNER
PILULA *n* pill
PILULAE > PILULA
PILULAR > PILULE
PILULAS > PILULA
PILULE *n* small pill
PILULES > PILULE
PILUM *n* ancient Roman javelin
PILUS > PILI
PILY *adj* like wool or pile
PIMA *n* type of cotton
PIMAS > PIMA
PIMENT *n* wine flavoured with spices
PIMENTO *same as* > PIMIENTO
PIMENTON *n* smoked chilli powder
PIMENTONS > PIMENTON
PIMENTOS > PIMENTO
PIMENTS > PIMENT
PIMIENTO *n* Spanish pepper with a red fruit used as a vegetable
PIMIENTOS > PIMIENTO
PIMP *n* man who gets customers for a prostitute in return for a share of his or her earnings ▷ *vb* act as a pimp
PIMPED > PIMP
PIMPERNEL *n* wild plant with small star-shaped flowers
PIMPING > PIMP
PIMPLE *n* small pus-filled spot on the skin
PIMPLED > PIMPLE
PIMPLES > PIMPLE
PIMPLIER > PIMPLE
PIMPLIEST > PIMPLE
PIMPLY > PIMPLE
PIMPS > PIMP
PIN *n* short thin piece of stiff wire with a point and head, for fastening things ▷ *vb* fasten with a pin
PINA *n* cone of silver amalgam
PINACEOUS *adj* of, relating to, or belonging to the *Pinaceae*, a family of conifers with needle-like leaves: includes pine, spruce, fir, larch, and cedar
PINACOID *n* pair of opposite parallel faces of crystal
PINACOIDS > PINACOID
PINAFORE *n* apron ▷ *vb* cover clothes with pinafore
PINAFORED > PINAFORE
PINAFORES > PINAFORE
PINAKOID *same as* > PINACOID
PINAKOIDS > PINAKOID
PINANG *n* areca tree
PINANGS > PINANG
PINAS > PINA
PINASTER *n* Mediterranean pine tree
PINASTERS > PINASTER
PINATA *n* papier-mâché party decoration filled with sweets, hung up during parties, and struck with a stick until it breaks open
PINATAS > PINATA
PINBALL *vb* ricochet
PINBALLED > PINBALL
PINBALLS > PINBALL
PINBONE *n* part of sirloin
PINBONES > PINBONE
PINCASE *n* case for holding pins
PINCASES > PINCASE
PINCER *vb* grip with pincers
PINCERED > PINCER
PINCERING > PINCER
PINCERS *pl n* tool consisting of two hinged arms, for gripping
PINCH *vb* squeeze between finger and thumb ▷ *n* act of pinching
PINCHBECK *n* alloy of zinc and copper, used as imitation gold ▷ *adj* sham or cheap
PINCHBUG *n* type of crab
PINCHBUGS > PINCHBUG
PINCHCOCK *n* clamp used to compress a flexible tube to control the flow of fluid through it
PINCHECK *n* small check woven into fabric
PINCHECKS > PINCHECK
PINCHED > PINCH
PINCHER > PINCH
PINCHERS > PINCH
PINCHES > PINCH
PINCHFIST *n* mean person
PINCHGUT *n* miserly person
PINCHGUTS > PINCHGUT
PINCHING > PINCH
PINCHINGS > PINCH
PINDAN *n* desert region of Western Australia
PINDANS > PINDAN
PINDAREE *same as* > PINDARI
PINDAREES > PINDAREE
PINDARI *n* former irregular Indian horseman
PINDARIS > PINDARI
PINDER *n* person who impounds
PINDERS > PINDER
PINDLING *adj* peevish or fractious
PINDOWN *n* wrestling manoeuvre
PINDOWNS > PINDOWN
PINE *n* evergreen coniferous tree ▷ *vb* feel great longing (for)
PINEAL *adj* resembling a pine cone ▷ *n* pineal gland
PINEALS > PINEAL
PINEAPPLE *n* large tropical fruit with juicy yellow flesh and a hard skin
PINECONE *n* seed-producing structure of a pine tree
PINECONES > PINECONE
PINED > PINE
PINEDROPS *n* parasitic herb of pine trees
PINELAND *n* area covered with pine forest
PINELANDS > PINELAND
PINELIKE > PINE
PINENE *n* isomeric terpene found in many essential oils
PINENES > PINENE
PINERIES > PINERY
PINERY *n* place, esp a hothouse, where pineapples are grown
PINES > PINE
PINESAP *n* red herb of N America
PINESAPS > PINESAP
PINETA > PINETUM
PINETUM *n* area of land where pine trees and other conifers are grown
PINEWOOD *n* wood of pine trees
PINEWOODS > PINEWOOD
PINEY > PINE
PINFALL *another name for* > FALL
PINFALLS > PINFALL
PINFISH *n* small porgy of the SE North American coast of the Atlantic
PINFISHES > PINFISH
PINFOLD *n* pound for stray cattle ▷ *vb* gather or confine in or as if in a pinfold
PINFOLDED > PINFOLD
PINFOLDS > PINFOLD
PING *n* short high-pitched sound ▷ *vb* make such a noise
PINGED > PING
PINGER *n* device, esp a timer, that makes a pinging sound
PINGERS > PINGER
PINGING > PING
PINGLE *vb* enclose small area of ground
PINGLED > PINGLE
PINGLER > PINGLE
PINGLERS > PINGLE
PINGLES > PINGLE
PINGLING > PINGLE
PINGO *n* mound of earth or gravel formed through pressure from a layer of water trapped between newly frozen ice and underlying permafrost in Arctic regions
PINGOES > PINGO
PINGOS > PINGO
PINGPONG *n* table tennis
PINGPONGS > PINGPONG
PINGRASS *n* weed with fernlike leaves
PINGS > PING
PINGUEFY *vb* become greasy or fat
PINGUID *adj* fatty, oily, or greasy
PINGUIN *same as* > PENGUIN
PINGUINS > PINGUIN
PINHEAD *n* head of a pin
PINHEADED *adj* stupid or silly
PINHEADS > PINHEAD
PINHOLE *n* small hole made with or as if with a pin
PINHOLES > PINHOLE
PINHOOKER *n* trader of young thoroughbred horses
PINIER > PINY
PINIES > PINY
PINIEST > PINY
PINING > PINE
PINION *n* bird's wing ▷ *vb* immobilize (someone) by tying or holding his or her arms
PINIONED > PINION
PINIONING > PINION
PINIONS > PINION
PINITE *n* greyish-green or brown mineral containing

amorphous aluminium and potassium sulphates

INITES > PINITE

INITOL *n* compound found in pinewood

INITOLS > PINITOL

INK *n* pale reddish colour ▷ *adj* of the colour pink ▷ *vb* (of an engine) make a metallic noise because not working properly, knock

INKED > PINK

INKEN *vb* turn pink

INKENED > PINKEN

INKENING > PINKEN

INKENS > PINKEN

INKER > PINK

INKERTON *n* private detective

INKEST > PINK

INKEY *variant of* > PINKY

INKEYE *n* acute contagious inflammation of the conjunctiva of the eye

INKEYES > PINKEYE

INKEYS > PINKEY

INKIE *n* little finger

INKIES > PINKIE

INKINESS *n* quality of being pink

INKING > PINK

INKINGS > PINK

INKISH > PINK

INKLY > PINK

INKNESS > PINK

INKO *n* person regarded as mildly left-wing

INKOES > PINKO

INKOS > PINKO

INKROOT *n* plant with red-and-yellow flowers and pink roots

INKROOTS > PINKROOT

INKS > PINK

INKY *same as* > PINKIE

INNA *n* external part of the ear

INNACE *n* ship's boat

INNACES > PINNACE

INNACLE *n* highest point of fame or success ▷ *vb* set on or as if on a pinnacle

INNACLED > PINNACLE

INNACLES > PINNACLE

INNAE > PINNA

INNAL > PINNA

INNAS > PINNA

INNATE *adj* (of compound leaves) having leaflets growing opposite each other in pairs

INNATED *same as* > PINNATE

INNATELY > PINNATE

INNATION > PINNATE

INNED > PIN

INNER *n* person or thing that pins

INNERS > PINNER

INNET *n* pinnacle

INNETS > PINNET

INNIE *same as* > PINNY

INNIES > PINNIE

PINNING > PIN

PINNINGS > PIN

PINNIPED *n* aquatic placental mammal such as the seal, sea lion, walrus, etc

PINNIPEDE *same as* > PINNIPED

PINNIPEDS > PINNIPED

PINNOCK *n* small bird

PINNOCKS > PINNOCK

PINNOED *adj* held or bound by the arms

PINNULA *same as* > PINNULE

PINNULAE > PINNULA

PINNULAR > PINNULE

PINNULAS > PINNULA

PINNULATE > PINNULE

PINNULE *n* any of the lobes of a leaflet of a pinnate compound leaf, which is itself pinnately divided

PINNULES > PINNULE

PINNY *informal or child's name for* > PINAFORE

PINOCHLE *n* card game for two to four players similar to bezique

PINOCHLES > PINOCHLE

PINOCLE *same as* > PINOCHLE

PINOCLES > PINOCLE

PINOCYTIC *adj* of process of pinocytosis

PINOLE *n* (in the southwestern United States) flour made of parched ground corn, mesquite beans, sugar, etc

PINOLES > PINOLE

PINON *n* low-growing pine

PINONES > PINON

PINONS > PINON

PINOT *n* any of several grape varieties

PINOTAGE *n* blended red wine of S Africa

PINOTAGES > PINOTAGE

PINOTS > PINOT

PINPOINT *vb* locate or identify exactly ▷ *adj* exact ▷ *n* insignificant or trifling thing

PINPOINTS > PINPOINT

PINPRICK *n* small irritation or annoyance ▷ *vb* puncture with or as if with a pin

PINPRICKS > PINPRICK

PINS > PIN

PINSCHER *n* breed of dog

PINSCHERS > PINSCHER

PINSETTER *n* device that sets pins in bowling alley

PINSTRIPE *n* very narrow stripe in fabric

PINSWELL *n* small boil

PINSWELLS > PINSWELL

PINT *n* liquid measure, 1/8 gallon (.568 litre)

PINTA *n* pint of milk

PINTABLE *n* pinball machine

PINTABLES > PINTABLE

PINTADA > PINTADO

PINTADERA *n* decorative stamp, usually made of clay, found in the Neolithic of the E Mediterranean and in many American cultures

PINTADO *n* species of seagoing petrel

PINTADOES > PINTADO

PINTADOS > PINTADO

PINTAIL *n* greyish-brown duck with a pointed tail

PINTAILED *adj* having tapered tail

PINTAILS > PINTAIL

PINTANO *n* tropical reef fish

PINTANOS > PINTANO

PINTAS > PINTA

PINTLE *n* pin or bolt forming the pivot of a hinge

PINTLES > PINTLE

PINTO *adj* marked with patches of white ▷ *n* pinto horse

PINTOES > PINTO

PINTOS > PINTO

PINTS > PINT

PINTSIZE *same as* > PINTSIZED

PINTSIZED *adj* very small

PINUP *n* picture of a sexually attractive person, esp when partially or totally undressed

PINUPS > PINUP

PINWALE *n* fabric with narrow ridges

PINWALES > PINWALE

PINWEED *n* herb with tiny flowers

PINWEEDS > PINWEED

PINWHEEL *n* cogwheel whose teeth are formed by small pins projecting either axially or radially from the rim of the wheel

PINWHEELS > PINWHEEL

PINWORK *n* (in needlepoint lace) fine raised stitches

PINWORKS > PINWORK

PINWORM *n* parasitic nematode worm

PINWORMS > PINWORM

PINWRENCH *n* wrench with a projection to fit a hole

PINXIT *vb* (he or she) painted (it): used formerly on paintings next to the artist's name

PINY *variant of* > PEONY

PINYIN *n* system of romanized spelling for the Chinese language

PINYON *n* low-growing pine

PINYONS > PINYON

PIOLET *n* type of ice axe

PIOLETS > PIOLET

PION *n* any of three subatomic particles which are classified as mesons

PIONED *adj* abounding in marsh marigolds

PIONEER *n* explorer or early settler of a new country ▷ *vb* be the pioneer or leader of

PIONEERED > PIONEER

PIONEERS > PIONEER

PIONER *obsolete spelling of* > PIONEER

PIONERS > PIONER

PIONEY *same as* > PEONY

PIONEYS > PIONEY

PIONIC > PION

PIONIES > PIONY

PIONING *n* work of pioneers

PIONINGS > PIONING

PIONS > PION

PIONY *same as* > PEONY

PIOPIO *n* New Zealand thrush, thought to be extinct

PIOSITIES > PIOSITY

PIOSITY *n* grandiose display of piety

PIOTED *adj* pied

PIOUS *adj* deeply religious, devout

PIOUSLY > PIOUS

PIOUSNESS > PIOUS

PIOY *variant of* > PEEOY

PIOYE *variant of* > PEEOY

PIOYES > PIOYE

PIOYS > PIOY

PIP *n* small seed in a fruit ▷ *vb* chirp

PIPA *n* tongueless South American toad, *Pipa pipa*, that carries its young in pits in the skin of its back

PIPAGE *n* pipes collectively

PIPAGES > PIPAGE

PIPAL *same as* > PEEPUL

PIPALS > PIPAL

PIPAS > PIPA

PIPE *n* tube for conveying liquid or gas ▷ *vb* play on a pipe

PIPEAGE *same as* > PIPAGE

PIPEAGES > PIPEAGE

PIPECLAY *n* fine white pure clay, used in tobacco pipes and pottery and to whiten leather and similar materials ▷ *vb* whiten with pipeclay

PIPECLAYS > PIPECLAY

PIPED > PIPE

PIPEFISH *n* teleost fish with a long tubelike snout and an elongated body covered with bony plates

PIPEFUL > PIPE

PIPEFULS > PIPE

PIPELESS > PIPE

PIPELIKE > PIPE

PIPELINE *n* long pipe for transporting oil, water, etc

PIPELINED > PIPELINE

PIPELINES > PIPELINE

PIPER *n* player on a pipe or bagpipes

PIPERIC > PIPERINE

PIPERINE *n* crystalline

insoluble alkaloid that is the active ingredient of pepper
PIPERINES > PIPERINE
PIPERONAL *n* white fragrant aldehyde used in flavourings, perfumery, and suntan lotions
PIPERS > PIPER
PIPES > PIPE
PIPESTEM *n* hollow stem of pipe
PIPESTEMS > PIPESTEM
PIPESTONE *n* variety of consolidated red clay used by American Indians to make tobacco pipes
PIPET *same as* > PIPETTE
PIPETED > PIPET
PIPETING > PIPET
PIPETS > PIPET
PIPETTE *n* slender glass tube used to transfer or measure fluids ▷ *vb* transfer or measure out (a liquid) using a pipette
PIPETTED > PIPETTE
PIPETTES > PIPETTE
PIPETTING > PIPETTE
PIPEWORK *n* stops and flues on pipe organ
PIPEWORKS > PIPEWORK
PIPEWORT *n* perennial plant with a twisted flower stalk and a greenish-grey scaly flower head
PIPEWORTS > PIPEWORT
PIPI *n* edible mollusc often used as bait
PIPIER > PIPE
PIPIEST > PIPE
PIPINESS *n* material's suitability for use as pipe
PIPING *n* system of pipes
PIPINGLY > PIPING
PIPINGS > PIPING
PIPIS > PIPI
PIPISTREL *n* species of bat
PIPIT *n* small brownish songbird
PIPITS > PIPIT
PIPKIN *same as* > PIGGIN
PIPKINS > PIPKIN
PIPLESS > PIP
PIPPED > PIP
PIPPIER > PIPPY
PIPPIEST > PIPPY
PIPPIN *n* type of eating apple
PIPPING > PIP
PIPPINS > PIPPIN
PIPPY *adj* containing many pips
PIPS > PIP
PIPSQUEAK *n* insignificant or contemptible person
PIPUL *n* Indian fig tree
PIPULS > PIPUL
PIPY > PIPE
PIQUANCE *same as* > PIQUANT
PIQUANCES > PIQUANT
PIQUANCY > PIQUANT
PIQUANT *adj* having a pleasant spicy taste
PIQUANTLY > PIQUANT
PIQUE *n* feeling of hurt pride, baffled curiosity, or resentment ▷ *vb* hurt the pride of
PIQUED > PIQUE
PIQUES > PIQUE
PIQUET *n* card game for two ▷ *vb* play game of piquet
PIQUETED > PIQUET
PIQUETING > PIQUET
PIQUETS > PIQUET
PIQUILLO *n* variety of sweet red pepper
PIQUILLOS > PIQUILLO
PIQUING > PIQUE
PIR *n* Sufi master
PIRACETAM *n* drug used to treat muscle spasm
PIRACIES > PIRACY
PIRACY *n* robbery on the seas
PIRAGUA *same as* > PIROGUE
PIRAGUAS > PIRAGUA
PIRAI *n* large S American fish
PIRAIS > PIRAI
PIRANA *same as* > PIRANHA
PIRANAS > PIRANA
PIRANHA *n* small fierce freshwater fish of tropical America
PIRANHAS > PIRANHA
PIRARUCU *n* large S American food fish
PIRARUCUS > PIRARUCU
PIRATE *n* sea robber ▷ *vb* sell or reproduce (artistic work etc) illegally
PIRATED > PIRATE
PIRATES > PIRATE
PIRATIC > PIRATE
PIRATICAL > PIRATE
PIRATING > PIRATE
PIRAYA *same as* > PIRAI
PIRAYAS > PIRAYA
PIRIFORM *adj* shaped like pear
PIRL *vb* spin or twist
PIRLED > PIRL
PIRLICUE *same as* > PURLICUE
PIRLICUED > PIRLICUE
PIRLICUES > PIRLICUE
PIRLING > PIRL
PIRLS > PIRL
PIRN *n* reel or bobbin
PIRNIE > STRIPED
PIRNIT *adj* striped
PIRNS > PIRN
PIROG *n* large pie filled with meat, vegetables, etc
PIROGEN *n* turnovers made from kneaded dough
PIROGHI > PIROG
PIROGI > PIROG
PIROGIES > PIROG
PIROGUE *n* any of various kinds of dugout canoes
PIROGUES > PIROGUE
PIROJKI *same as* > PIROSHKI
PIROPLASM *n* parasite of red blood cells
PIROQUE *same as* > PIROGUE
PIROQUES > PIROQUE
PIROSHKI *same as* > PIROZHKI
PIROUETTE *n* spinning turn balanced on the toes of one foot ▷ *vb* perform a pirouette
PIROZHKI > PIROZHOK
PIROZHOK *n* small triangular pastry filled with meat, vegetables, etc
PIRS > PIR
PIS > PI
PISCARIES > PISCARY
PISCARY *n* place where fishing takes place
PISCATOR *n* fisherman
PISCATORS > PISCATOR
PISCATORY *adj* of or relating to fish, fishing, or fishermen
PISCATRIX *n* female angler
PISCIFORM *adj* having form of fish
PISCINA *n* stone basin, with a drain, in a church or sacristy where water used at Mass is poured away
PISCINAE > PISCINA
PISCINAL > PISCINA
PISCINAS > PISCINA
PISCINE *adj* of or resembling a fish
PISCIVORE *n* eater of fish
PISCO *n* S American brandy
PISCOS > PISCO
PISE *n* rammed earth or clay used to make floors or walls
PISES > PISE
PISH *interj* exclamation of impatience or contempt ▷ *vb* make this exclamation at (someone or something)
PISHED > PISH
PISHER *n* Yiddish term for small boy
PISHERS > PISHER
PISHES > PISH
PISHING > PISH
PISHOGE *same as* > PISHOGUE
PISHOGES > PISHOGE
PISHOGUE *n* sorcery
PISHOGUES > PISHOGUE
PISIFORM *adj* resembling a pea ▷ *n* small pealike bone on the ulnar side of the carpus
PISIFORMS > PISIFORM
PISKIES > PISKY
PISKY *n* Cornish fairy
PISMIRE *archaic or dialect word for* > ANT
PISMIRES > PISMIRE
PISO *n* peso of the Philippines
PISOLITE *n* sedimentary rock
PISOLITES > PISOLITE
PISOLITH *same as* > PISOLITE
PISOLITHS > PISOLITH
PISOLITIC > PISOLITE
PISOS > PISO
PISS *vb* urinate ▷ *n* act o urinating
PISSANT *n* insignificant person
PISSANTS > PISSANT
PISSED *adj* drunk
PISSER *n* someone or something that pisses
PISSERS > PISSER
PISSES > PISS
PISSHEAD *n* drunkard
PISSHEADS > PISSHEAD
PISSING > PISS
PISSOIR *n* public urinal, usu enclosed by a wall or screen
PISSOIRS > PISSOIR
PISTACHE *n* tree yielding pistachio nut
PISTACHES > PISTACHE
PISTACHIO *n* edible nut o a Mediterranean tree ▷ *a* of a yellowish-green colo
PISTAREEN *n* Spanish coi used in the US and the West Indies until the 18th century
PISTE *n* ski slope
PISTES > PISTE
PISTIL *n* seed-bearing part of a flower
PISTILS > PISTIL
PISTOL *n* short-barrelled handgun ▷ *vb* shoot wit a pistol
PISTOLE *n* any of various gold coins of varying valu formerly used in Europe
PISTOLED > PISTOL
PISTOLEER *n* person, esp soldier, who is armed wit or fires a pistol
PISTOLERO *n* shooter of pistols
PISTOLES > PISTOLE
PISTOLET *n* small pistol
PISTOLETS > PISTOLET
PISTOLIER *n* shooter of pistols
PISTOLING > PISTOL
PISTOLLED > PISTOL
PISTOLS > PISTOL
PISTON *n* cylindrical part in an engine that slides t and fro in a cylinder
PISTONS > PISTON
PISTOU *n* French sauce
PISTOUS > PISTOU
PIT *n* deep hole in the ground ▷ *vb* mark with small dents or scars
PITA *n* any of several agav plants yielding a strong fibre
PITAHAYA *n* any giant cactus of Central Americ and the SW United State
PITAHAYAS > PITAHAYA
PITAPAT *adv* with quick

ight taps ▷ *n* such taps ▷ *vb* make quick light taps or beats
TAPATS > PITAPAT
TARA *variant of* > PETARA
TARAH *variant of* > PETARA
TARAHS > PITARAH
TARAS > PITARA
TAS > PITA
TAYA *same as* > PITAHAYA
TAYAS > PITAYA
TCH *vb* throw, hurl ▷ *n* area marked out for playing sport
TCHBEND *n* electronic device that enables a player to bend the pitch of a note being sounded on a synthesizer, usually with a pitch wheel, strip, or lever
TCHED > PITCH
TCHER *n* large jug with a narrow neck
TCHERS > PITCHER
TCHES > PITCH
TCHFORK *n* large long-handled fork for lifting hay ▷ *vb* thrust abruptly or violently
TCHIER > PITCHY
TCHIEST > PITCHY
TCHILY > PITCHY
TCHING > PITCH
TCHINGS > PITCH
TCHMAN *n* itinerant pedlar of small merchandise who operates from a stand at a fair, etc
TCHMEN > PITCHMAN
TCHOUT *n* type of baseball pitch
TCHOUTS > PITCHOUT
TCHPINE *n* large N American pine tree
TCHPIPE *n* small one-note pipe used for tuning instruments
TCHPOLE *vb* turn end over end
TCHY *adj* full of or covered with pitch
TEOUS *adj* arousing pity
TEOUSLY > PITEOUS
TFALL *n* hidden difficulty or danger
TFALLS > PITFALL
TH *n* soft white lining of the rind of oranges etc ▷ *vb* destroy the brain and spinal cord of (a laboratory animal) by piercing or severing
THBALL *n* type of conductor
THBALLS > PITHBALL
THEAD *n* top of a mine shaft and the buildings and hoisting gear around it
THEADS > PITHEAD
THECOID *adj* relating to apes
THED > PITH
PITHFUL > PITH
PITHIER > PITHY
PITHIEST > PITHY
PITHILY > PITHY
PITHINESS > PITHY
PITHING > PITH
PITHLESS > PITH
PITHLIKE > PITH
PITHOI > PITHOS
PITHOS *n* large ceramic container for oil or grain
PITHS > PITH
PITHY *adj* short and full of meaning
PITIABLE *adj* arousing or deserving pity or contempt
PITIABLY > PITIABLE
PITIED > PITY
PITIER > PITY
PITIERS > PITY
PITIES > PITY
PITIFUL *adj* arousing pity
PITIFULLY > PITIFUL
PITILESS *adj* feeling no pity or mercy
PITMAN *n* connecting rod (in a machine)
PITMANS > PITMAN
PITMEN > PITMAN
PITON *n* metal spike used in climbing to secure a rope
PITONS > PITON
PITPROP *n* support beam in mine shaft
PITPROPS > PITPROP
PITS > PIT
PITSAW *n* large saw formerly used for cutting logs into planks, operated by two men, one standing on top of the log and the other in a pit underneath it
PITSAWS > PITSAW
PITTA *n* small brightly coloured ground-dwelling tropical bird
PITTANCE *n* very small amount of money
PITTANCES > PITTANCE
PITTAS > PITTA
PITTED > PIT
PITTEN *adj* having been put
PITTER *vb* make pattering sound
PITTERED > PITTER
PITTERING > PITTER
PITTERS > PITTER
PITTING > PIT
PITTINGS > PIT
PITTITE *n* occupant of a theatre pit
PITTITES > PITTITE
PITUITA *n* thick nasal secretion
PITUITARY *n* gland at the base of the brain, that helps to control growth ▷ *adj* of or relating to the pituitary gland
PITUITAS > PITUITA
PITUITE *n* mucus
PITUITES > PITUITE
PITUITRIN *n* extract from pituitary gland
PITURI *n* Australian solanaceous shrub
PITURIS > PITURI
PITY *n* sympathy or sorrow for others' suffering ▷ *vb* feel pity for
PITYING > PITY
PITYINGLY > PITY
PITYROID *adj* resembling bran
PIU *adv* more (quickly, softly, etc)
PIUM *n* stinging insect
PIUMS > PIUM
PIUPIU *n* skirt made from the leaves of the New Zealand flax, worn by Māoris on ceremonial occasions
PIUPIUS > PIUPIU
PIVOT *n* central shaft on which something turns ▷ *vb* provide with or turn on a pivot
PIVOTABLE > PIVOT
PIVOTAL *adj* of crucial importance
PIVOTALLY > PIVOTAL
PIVOTED > PIVOT
PIVOTER > PIVOT
PIVOTERS > PIVOT
PIVOTING > PIVOT
PIVOTINGS > PIVOT
PIVOTMAN *n* person in rank around whom others wheel
PIVOTMEN > PIVOTMAN
PIVOTS > PIVOT
PIX *less common spelling of* > PYX
PIXEL *n* any of a number of very small picture elements that make up a picture, as on a visual display unit
PIXELS > PIXEL
PIXES > PIX
PIXIE *n* (in folklore) fairy
PIXIEISH > PIXIE
PIXIES > PIXY
PIXILATED *adj* eccentric or whimsical
PIXINESS > PIXIE
PIXY *same as* > PIXIE
PIXYISH > PIXY
PIZAZZ *same as* > PIZZAZZ
PIZAZZES > PIZAZZ
PIZAZZY > PIZAZZ
PIZE *vb* strike (someone a blow)
PIZED > PIZE
PIZES > PIZE
PIZING > PIZE
PIZZA *n* flat disc of dough covered with a wide variety of savoury toppings and baked
PIZZAIOLA *n* type of tomato sauce
PIZZALIKE > PIZZA
PIZZAS > PIZZA
PIZZAZ *same as* > PZAZZ
PIZZAZES > PIZZAZ
PIZZAZZ *n* attractive combination of energy and style
PIZZAZZES > PIZZAZZ
PIZZAZZY > PIZZAZZ
PIZZELLE *n* Italian sweet wafer
PIZZELLES > PIZZELLE
PIZZERIA *n* place where pizzas are made, sold, or eaten
PIZZERIAS > PIZZERIA
PIZZICATI > PIZZICATO
PIZZICATO *adj* played by plucking the string of a violin etc with the finger ▷ *adv* (in music for the violin family) to be plucked with the finger ▷ *n* style or technique of playing a normally bowed stringed instrument in this manner
PIZZLE *n* penis of an animal, esp a bull
PIZZLES > PIZZLE
PLAAS *n* farm
PLAASES > PLAAS
PLACABLE *adj* easily placated or appeased
PLACABLY > PLACABLE
PLACARD *n* notice that is carried or displayed in public ▷ *vb* attach placards to
PLACARDED > PLACARD
PLACARDS > PLACARD
PLACATE *vb* make (someone) stop feeling angry or upset
PLACATED > PLACATE
PLACATER > PLACATE
PLACATERS > PLACATE
PLACATES > PLACATE
PLACATING > PLACATE
PLACATION > PLACATE
PLACATIVE *same as* > PLACATORY
PLACATORY *adj* placating or intended to placate
PLACCAT *variant of* > PLACKET
PLACCATE *variant of* > PLACKET
PLACCATES > PLACCATE
PLACCATS > PLACCAT
PLACE *n* particular part of an area or space ▷ *vb* put in a particular place
PLACEABLE > PLACE
PLACEBO *n* sugar pill etc given to an unsuspecting patient instead of an active drug
PLACEBOES > PLACEBO
PLACEBOS > PLACEBO
PLACED > PLACE
PLACEKICK *n* (in football) kick in which the ball is placed in position before it is kicked ▷ *vb* take a placekick
PLACELESS *adj* not rooted

in a specific place or community
PLACEMAN *n* person who holds a public office, esp for private profit and as a reward for political support
PLACEMEN > PLACEMAN
PLACEMENT *n* arrangement
PLACENTA *n* organ formed in the womb during pregnancy, providing nutrients for the fetus
PLACENTAE > PLACENTA
PLACENTAL *adj* (esp of animals) having a placenta
PLACENTAS > PLACENTA
PLACER *n* surface sediment containing particles of gold or some other valuable mineral
PLACERS > PLACER
PLACES > PLACE
PLACET *n* vote or expression of assent by saying the word *placet*
PLACETS > PLACET
PLACID *adj* not easily excited or upset, calm
PLACIDER > PLACID
PLACIDEST > PLACID
PLACIDITY > PLACID
PLACIDLY > PLACID
PLACING *n* method of issuing securities to the public using an intermediary, such as a stockbroking firm
PLACINGS > PLACING
PLACIT *n* decree or dictum
PLACITA > PLACITUM
PLACITORY > PLACIT
PLACITS > PLACIT
PLACITUM *n* court or assembly in Middle Ages
PLACK *n* small former Scottish coin
PLACKET *n* opening at the waist of a dress or skirt for buttons or zips or for access to a pocket
PLACKETS > PLACKET
PLACKLESS *adj* lacking money
PLACKS > PLACK
PLACODERM *n* extinct bony-plated fishlike vertebrate
PLACOID *adj* platelike or flattened ▷ *n* fish with placoid scales
PLACOIDS > PLACOID
PLAFOND *n* ceiling, esp one having ornamentation
PLAFONDS > PLAFOND
PLAGAL *adj* (of a cadence) progressing from the subdominant to the tonic chord, as in the *Amen* of a hymn
PLAGE *n* bright patch in the sun's chromosphere
PLAGES > PLAGE
PLAGIARY *n* person who plagiarizes or a piece of plagiarism
PLAGIUM *n* crime of kidnapping
PLAGIUMS > PLAGIUM
PLAGUE *n* fast-spreading fatal disease ▷ *vb* trouble or annoy continually
PLAGUED > PLAGUE
PLAGUER > PLAGUE
PLAGUERS > PLAGUE
PLAGUES > PLAGUE
PLAGUEY *same as* > PLAGUY
PLAGUIER > PLAGUEY
PLAGUIEST > PLAGUEY
PLAGUILY > PLAGUY
PLAGUING > PLAGUE
PLAGUY *adj* disagreeable or vexing ▷ *adv* disagreeably or annoyingly
PLAICE *n* edible European flatfish
PLAICES > PLAICE
PLAID *n* long piece of tartan cloth worn as part of Highland dress ▷ *vb* weave cloth into plaid
PLAIDED > PLAID
PLAIDING > PLAID
PLAIDINGS > PLAID
PLAIDMAN *n* wearer of plaid
PLAIDMEN > PLAIDMAN
PLAIDS > PLAID
PLAIN *adj* easy to see or understand ▷ *n* large stretch of level country ▷ *adv* clearly or simply ▷ *vb* complain
PLAINANT *n* plaintiff
PLAINANTS > PLAINANT
PLAINED > PLAIN
PLAINER > PLAIN
PLAINEST > PLAIN
PLAINFUL *adj* apt to complain
PLAINING > PLAIN
PLAININGS > PLAIN
PLAINISH > PLAIN
PLAINLY > PLAIN
PLAINNESS > PLAIN
PLAINS *pl n* extensive tracts of level or almost level treeless countryside
PLAINSMAN *n* person who lives in a plains region, esp in the Great Plains of North America
PLAINSMEN > PLAINSMAN
PLAINSONG *n* unaccompanied singing, esp in a medieval church
PLAINT *n* complaint or lamentation
PLAINTEXT *n* (in telecommunications) message set in a directly readable form rather than in coded groups
PLAINTFUL *adj* complaining
PLAINTIFF *n* person who sues in a court of law
PLAINTIVE *adj* sad, mournful
PLAINTS > PLAINT
PLAINWORK *n* weaving
PLAISTER *n* plaster
PLAISTERS > PLAISTER
PLAIT *n* intertwined length of hair ▷ *vb* intertwine separate strands in a pattern
PLAITED > PLAIT
PLAITER > PLAIT
PLAITERS > PLAIT
PLAITING > PLAIT
PLAITINGS > PLAIT
PLAITS > PLAIT
PLAN *n* way thought out to do or achieve something ▷ *vb* arrange beforehand
PLANAR *adj* of or relating to a plane
PLANARIA *n* free-living flatworms
PLANARIAN *n* free-living flatworm
PLANARITY > PLANAR
PLANATE *adj* having been flattened
PLANATION *n* erosion of a land surface until it is basically flat
PLANCH *vb* cover with planks
PLANCHE *same as* > PLANCH
PLANCHED > PLANCH
PLANCHES > PLANCH
PLANCHET *n* piece of metal ready to be stamped as a coin, medal, etc
PLANCHETS > PLANCHET
PLANCHING > PLANCH
PLANE *n* aeroplane ▷ *adj* perfectly flat or level ▷ *vb* glide or skim
PLANED > PLANE
PLANELOAD *n* amount or number carried by plane
PLANENESS > PLANE
PLANER *n* machine with a cutting tool that makes repeated horizontal strokes across the surface of a workpiece
PLANERS > PLANER
PLANES > PLANE
PLANESIDE *n* area next to aeroplane
PLANET *n* large body in space that revolves round the sun or another star
PLANETARY *adj* of or relating to a planet ▷ *n* train of planetary gears
PLANETIC > PLANET
PLANETOID *See* > ASTEROID
PLANETS > PLANET
PLANFORM *n* outline or silhouette of an object, esp an aircraft, as seen from above
PLANFORMS > PLANFORM
PLANGENCY > PLANGENT
PLANGENT *adj* (of sounds) mournful and resounding
PLANING > PLANE
PLANISH *vb* give a final finish to (metal) by hammering or rolling to produce a smooth surfac
PLANISHED > PLANISH
PLANISHER > PLANISH
PLANISHES > PLANISH
PLANK *n* long flat piece of sawn timber ▷ *vb* cover or provide (an area) with planks
PLANKED > PLANK
PLANKING *n* number of planks
PLANKINGS > PLANKING
PLANKS > PLANK
PLANKTER *n* organism in plankton
PLANKTERS > PLANKTER
PLANKTON *n* minute animals and plants floating in the surface water of a sea or lake
PLANKTONS > PLANKTON
PLANLESS *adj* having no plan
PLANNED > PLAN
PLANNER *n* person who makes plans, esp for the development of a town, building, etc
PLANNERS > PLANNER
PLANNING > PLAN
PLANNINGS > PLAN
PLANOSOL *n* type of intrazonal soil of humid or subhumid uplands having a strongly leache upper layer overlying a cl hardpan
PLANOSOLS > PLANOSOL
PLANS > PLAN
PLANT *n* living organism that grows in the ground and has no power to mov ▷ *vb* put in the ground to grow
PLANTA *n* sole of foot
PLANTABLE > PLANT
PLANTAE > PLANTA
PLANTAGE *n* plants
PLANTAGES > PLANTAGE
PLANTAIN *n* low-growin wild plant with broad leaves
PLANTAINS > PLANTAIN
PLANTAR *adj* of, relating to, or occurring on the sole of the foot or a corresponding part
PLANTAS > PLANTA
PLANTED > PLANT
PLANTER *n* owner of a plantation
PLANTERS > PLANTER
PLANTING > PLANT
PLANTINGS > PLANT
PLANTLESS > PLANT
PLANTLET *n* small plant
PLANTLETS > PLANTLET
PLANTLIKE > PLANT
PLANTLING *n* young plan
PLANTS > PLANT
PLANTSMAN *n* experience gardener who specialize in collecting rare or

nteresting plants
ANTSMEN > PLANTSMAN
ANTULE *n* embryo in act f germination
ANTULES > PLANTULE
ANULA *n* ciliated ree-swimming larva of ydrozoan coelenterates uch as the hydra
ANULAE > PLANULA
ANULAR > PLANULA
ANULATE *adj* flat
ANULOID *adj* of planula
ANURIA *n* expulsion f urine from abnormal pening
ANURIAS > PLANURIA
ANURIES > PLANURY
ANURY *another name or* > PLANURY
ANXTIES > PLANXTY
ANXTY *n* Celtic melody or harp
AP *same as* > PLOP
APPED > PLAP
APPING > PLAP
APS > PLAP
AQUE *n* inscribed ommemorative stone or netal plate
AQUES > PLAQUE
AQUETTE *n* small plaque
ASH *same as* > PLEACH
ASHED > PLASH
ASHER *n* type of farm ool
ASHERS > PLASHER
ASHES > PLASH
ASHET *n* small pond
ASHETS > PLASHET
ASHIER > PLASHY
ASHIEST > PLASHY
ASHING > PLASH
ASHINGS > PLASH
ASHY *adj* wet or marshy
ASM *same as* > PLASMA
ASMA *n* clear liquid part f blood
ASMAGEL *another name or* > ECTOPLASM
ASMAS > PLASMA
ASMASOL *another name or* > ENDOPLASM
ASMATIC > PLASMA
ASMIC > PLASMA
ASMID *n* small circle f bacterial DNA that is ndependent of the main acterial chromosome
ASMIDS > PLASMID
ASMIN *n* proteolytic nzyme that causes ibrinolysis in blood clots
ASMINS > PLASMIN
ASMODIA *n* amoeboid nasses of protoplasm, ach containing many uclei
ASMOID *n* section f a plasma having a haracteristic shape
ASMOIDS > PLASMOID
ASMON *n* sum total of lasmagenes in a cell
PLASMONS > PLASMON
PLASMS > PLASM
PLAST *archaic past participle of* > PLACE
PLASTE *archaic past participle of* > PLACE
PLASTER *n* mixture of lime, sand, etc for coating walls ▷ *vb* cover with plaster
PLASTERED *adj* drunk
PLASTERER > PLASTER
PLASTERS > PLASTER
PLASTERY > PLASTER
PLASTIC *n* synthetic material that can be moulded when soft but sets in a hard long-lasting shape ▷ *adj* made of plastic
PLASTICKY *adj* made of or resembling plastic
PLASTICLY > PLASTIC
PLASTICS > PLASTIC
PLASTID *n* any of various small particles in the cytoplasm of the cells of plants and some animals
PLASTIDS > PLASTID
PLASTIQUE *n* easily-moulded plastic explosive
PLASTISOL *n* suspension of resin particles convertible into solid plastic
PLASTRAL > PLASTRON
PLASTRON *n* bony plate forming the ventral part of the shell of a tortoise or turtle
PLASTRONS > PLASTRON
PLASTRUM *variant of* > PLASTRON
PLASTRUMS > PLASTRUM
PLAT *n* small area of ground
PLATAN *n* plane tree
PLATANE *same as* > PLATAN
PLATANES > PLATANE
PLATANNA *n* S African frog
PLATANNAS > PLATANNA
PLATANS > PLATAN
PLATBAND *n* border of flowers in garden
PLATBANDS > PLATBAND
PLATE *n* shallow dish for holding food ▷ *vb* cover with a thin coating of gold, silver, or other metal
PLATEASM *n* talking with mouth open too wide
PLATEASMS > PLATEASM
PLATEAU *n* area of level high land ▷ *vb* remain stable for a long period
PLATEAUED > PLATEAU
PLATEAUS > PLATEAU
PLATEAUX > PLATEAU
PLATED *adj* coated with a layer of metal
PLATEFUL *same as* > PLATE
PLATEFULS > PLATEFUL
PLATELET *n* minute particle occurring in blood of vertebrates and involved in clotting of blood
PLATELETS > PLATELET
PLATELIKE > PLATE
PLATEMAN *n* one of crew of steam train
PLATEMARK *another name for* > HALLMARK
PLATEMEN > PLATEMAN
PLATEN *n* roller of a typewriter, against which the paper is held
PLATENS > PLATEN
PLATER *n* person or thing that plates
PLATERS > PLATER
PLATES > PLATE
PLATESFUL > PLATEFUL
PLATFORM *n* raised floor
PLATFORMS > PLATFORM
PLATIER > PLATY
PLATIES > PLATY
PLATIEST > PLATY
PLATINA *n* alloy of platinum and several other metals, including palladium, osmium, and iridium
PLATINAS > PLATINA
PLATING *n* coating of metal
PLATINGS > PLATING
PLATINIC *adj* of or containing platinum, esp in the tetravalent state
PLATINISE *same as* > PLATINIZE
PLATINIZE *vb* coat with platinum
PLATINOID *adj* containing or resembling platinum
PLATINOUS *adj* of or containing platinum, esp in the divalent state
PLATINUM *n* valuable silvery-white metal
PLATINUMS > PLATINUM
PLATITUDE *n* remark that is true but not interesting or original
PLATONIC *adj* (of a relationship) friendly or affectionate but not sexual
PLATONISM *n* philosophy of Plato
PLATOON *n* smaller unit within a company of soldiers ▷ *vb* organise into platoons
PLATOONED > PLATOON
PLATOONS > PLATOON
PLATS > PLAT
PLATTED > PLAT
PLATTER *n* large dish
PLATTERS > PLATTER
PLATTING > PLAT
PLATTINGS > PLAT
PLATY *adj* of, relating to, or designating rocks the constituents of which occur in flaky layers ▷ *n* small brightly coloured freshwater cyprinodont fish
PLATYFISH *same as* > PLATY
PLATYPI > PLATYPUS
PLATYPUS *n* Australian egg-laying amphibious mammal, with dense fur, webbed feet, and a ducklike bill
PLATYS > PLATY
PLATYSMA *n* muscle located on side of neck
PLATYSMAS > PLATYSMA
PLAUDIT *n* expression of enthusiastic approval
PLAUDITE *interj* give a round of applause!
PLAUDITS > PLAUDIT
PLAUSIBLE *adj* apparently true or reasonable
PLAUSIBLY > PLAUSIBLE
PLAUSIVE *adj* expressing praise or approval
PLAUSTRAL *adj* relating to wagons
PLAY *vb* occupy oneself in (a game or recreation) ▷ *n* story performed on stage or broadcast
PLAYA *n* (in the US) temporary lake, or its dry often salty bed, in a desert basin
PLAYABLE > PLAY
PLAYACT *vb* pretend or make believe
PLAYACTED > PLAYACT
PLAYACTOR > PLAYACT
PLAYACTS > PLAYACT
PLAYAS > PLAYA
PLAYBACK *n* playing of a recording on magnetic tape ▷ *vb* listen to or watch (something recorded)
PLAYBACKS > PLAYBACK
PLAYBILL *n* poster or bill advertising a play
PLAYBILLS > PLAYBILL
PLAYBOOK *n* book containing a range of possible set plays
PLAYBOOKS > PLAYBOOK
PLAYBOY *n* rich man who lives only for pleasure
PLAYBOYS > PLAYBOY
PLAYBUS *n* mobile playground
PLAYBUSES > PLAYBUS
PLAYDATE *n* gathering of children at house for play
PLAYDATES > PLAYDATE
PLAYDAY *n* day given to play
PLAYDAYS > PLAYDAY
PLAYDOWN *same as* > PLAYOFF
PLAYDOWNS > PLAYDOWN
PLAYED > PLAY
PLAYER *n* person who plays a game or sport
PLAYERS > PLAYER
PLAYFIELD *n* field for sports
PLAYFUL *adj* lively
PLAYFULLY > PLAYFUL
PLAYGIRL *n* rich woman

devoted to pleasure
PLAYGIRLS > PLAYGIRL
PLAYGOER *n* person who goes often to the theatre
PLAYGOERS > PLAYGOER
PLAYGOING > PLAYGOER
PLAYGROUP *same as* > PLAYSCHOOL
PLAYHOUSE *n* theatre
PLAYING
PLAYLAND *US variant of* > PLAYGROUND
PLAYLANDS > PLAYLAND
PLAYLESS > PLAY
PLAYLET *n* short play
PLAYLETS > PLAYLET
PLAYLIKE > PLAY
PLAYLIST *n* list of records chosen for playing, such as on a radio station ▷ *vb* put (a song or record) on a playlist
PLAYLISTS > PLAYLIST
PLAYMAKER *n* player who creates scoring opportunities for his or her team-mates
PLAYMATE *n* companion in play
PLAYMATES > PLAYMATE
PLAYOFF *n* extra contest to decide the winner when two or more competitors are tied
PLAYOFFS > PLAYOFF
PLAYPEN *n* small portable enclosure in which a young child can safely be left to play
PLAYPENS > PLAYPEN
PLAYROOM *n* recreation room, esp for children
PLAYROOMS > PLAYROOM
PLAYS > PLAY
PLAYSOME *adj* playful
PLAYSUIT *n* woman's or child's outfit, usually comprising shorts and a top
PLAYSUITS > PLAYSUIT
PLAYTHING *n* toy
PLAYTIME *n* time for play or recreation, such as a school break
PLAYTIMES > PLAYTIME
PLAYWEAR *n* clothes suitable for playing in
PLAZA *n* open space or square
PLAZAS > PLAZA
PLEA *n* serious or urgent request, entreaty
PLEACH *vb* interlace the stems or boughs of (a tree or hedge)
PLEACHED > PLEACH
PLEACHES > PLEACH
PLEACHING > PLEACH
PLEAD *vb* ask urgently or with deep feeling
PLEADABLE > PLEAD
PLEADED > PLEAD
PLEADER > PLEAD
PLEADERS > PLEAD
PLEADING > PLEAD
PLEADINGS > PLEAD
PLEADS > PLEAD
PLEAED > PLEA
PLEAING > PLEA
PLEAS > PLEA
PLEASABLE > PLEASE
PLEASANCE *n* secluded part of a garden laid out with trees, walks, etc
PLEASANT *adj* pleasing, enjoyable
PLEASE *vb* give pleasure or satisfaction to ▷ *adv* polite word of request
PLEASED > PLEASE
PLEASEDLY > PLEASE
PLEASEMAN *n* person who courts favour
PLEASEMEN > PLEASEMAN
PLEASER > PLEASE
PLEASERS > PLEASE
PLEASES > PLEASE
PLEASETH *obsolete inflection of* > PLEASE
PLEASING *adj* giving pleasure or satisfaction ▷ *n* act of giving pleasure
PLEASINGS > PLEASING
PLEASURE *n* feeling of happiness and satisfaction ▷ *vb* give pleasure to or take pleasure (in)
PLEASURED > PLEASURE
PLEASURER > PLEASURE
PLEASURES > PLEASURE
PLEAT *n* fold made by doubling material back on itself ▷ *vb* arrange (material) in pleats
PLEATED > PLEAT
PLEATER *n* attachment on a sewing machine that makes pleats
PLEATERS > PLEATER
PLEATHER *n* synthetic leather
PLEATHERS > PLEATHER
PLEATING > PLEAT
PLEATLESS > PLEAT
PLEATS > PLEAT
PLEB *n* common vulgar person
PLEBBIER > PLEBBY
PLEBBIEST > PLEBBY
PLEBBY *adj* common or vulgar
PLEBE *n* member of the lowest class at the US Naval Academy or Military Academy
PLEBEAN *old variant of* > PLEBEIAN
PLEBEIAN *adj* of the lower social classes ▷ *n* member of the lower social classes
PLEBEIANS > PLEBEIAN
PLEBES > PLEBE
PLEBIFIED > PLEBIFY
PLEBIFIES > PLEBIFY
PLEBIFY *vb* make plebeian
PLEBS *n* common people
PLECTRA > PLECTRUM
PLECTRE *variant of* > PLECTRUM
PLECTRES > PLECTRE
PLECTRON *same as* > PLECTRUM
PLECTRONS > PLECTRON
PLECTRUM *n* small implement for plucking the strings of a guitar etc
PLECTRUMS > PLECTRUM
PLED > PLEAD
PLEDGABLE > PLEDGE
PLEDGE *n* solemn promise ▷ *vb* promise solemnly
PLEDGED > PLEDGE
PLEDGEE *n* person to whom a pledge is given
PLEDGEES > PLEDGEE
PLEDGEOR *same as* > PLEDGOR
PLEDGEORS > PLEDGEOR
PLEDGER *same as* > PLEDGOR
PLEDGERS > PLEDGER
PLEDGES > PLEDGE
PLEDGET *n* small flattened pad of wool, cotton, etc, esp for use as a pressure bandage to be applied to wounds or sores
PLEDGETS > PLEDGET
PLEDGING > PLEDGE
PLEDGOR *n* person who gives or makes a pledge
PLEDGORS > PLEDGOR
PLEIAD *n* brilliant or talented group, esp one with seven members
PLEIADES > PLEIAD
PLEIADS > PLEIAD
PLEIOCENE *variant spelling of* > PLIOCENE
PLEIOMERY *n* state of having more than normal number
PLEIOTAXY *n* increase in whorls in flower
PLENA > PLENUM
PLENARIES > PLENARY
PLENARILY > PLENARY
PLENARTY *n* state of endowed church office when occupied
PLENARY *adj* (of a meeting) attended by all members ▷ *n* book of the gospels or epistles and homilies read at the Eucharist
PLENCH *n* tool combining wrench and pliers
PLENCHES > PLENCH
PLENILUNE *n* full moon
PLENIPO *n* plenipotentiary diplomat
PLENIPOES > PLENIPO
PLENIPOS > PLENIPO
PLENISH *vb* fill, stock, or resupply
PLENISHED > PLENISH
PLENISHER > PLENISH
PLENISHES > PLENISH
PLENISM *n* philosophical theory
PLENISMS > PLENISM
PLENIST > PLENISM
PLENISTS > PLENISM
PLENITUDE *n* completeness, abundan[ce]
PLENTEOUS *adj* plentiful
PLENTIES > PLENTY
PLENTIFUL *adj* existing i[n] large amounts or numbe[rs]
PLENTY *n* large amount or number ▷ *adj* very many ▷ *adv* more than adequately
PLENUM *n* enclosure containing gas at a higher pressure than the surrounding environme[nt]
PLENUMS > PLENUM
PLEON *n* abdomen of crustacean
PLEONAL *adj* of abdomen [of] crustacean
PLEONASM *n* use of more words than necessary
PLEONASMS > PLEONASM
PLEONAST *n* person using more words than necessary
PLEONASTE *n* type of blac[k] mineral
PLEONASTS > PLEONAST
PLEONEXIA *n* greed
PLEONIC > PLEON
PLEONS > PLEON
PLEOPOD *another name for* > SWIMMERET
PLEOPODS > PLEOPOD
PLERION *n* filled-centre supernova remnant in which radiation is emitt[ed] by the centre as well as t[he] shell
PLERIONS > PLERION
PLEROMA *n* abundance
PLEROMAS > PLEROMA
PLEROME *n* central colum[n] in growing stem or root
PLEROMES > PLEROME
PLESH *n* small pool
PLESHES > PLESH
PLESSOR *same as* > PLEXO[R]
PLESSORS > PLESSOR
PLETHORA *n* excess
PLETHORAS > PLETHORA
PLETHORIC > PLETHORA
PLEUCH *same as* > PLEUGH
PLEUCHED > PLEUCH
PLEUCHING > PLEUCH
PLEUCHS > PLEUCH
PLEUGH *Scottish word for* > PLOUGH
PLEUGHED > PLEUGH
PLEUGHING > PLEUGH
PLEUGHS > PLEUGH
PLEURA > PLEURON
PLEURAE > PLEURON
PLEURAL > PLEURON
PLEURAS > PLEURON
PLEURISY *n* inflammatio[n] of the membrane coveri[ng] the lungs
PLEURITIC > PLEURISY
PLEURITIS *n* pleurisy
PLEURON *n* part of the cuticle of arthropods tha[t] covers the lateral surfac[e] of a body segment

LEUSTON *n* mass of small organisms, esp algae, floating at the surface of shallow pools
LEUSTONS > PLEUSTON
LEW *n* (formerly in Canada) beaver skin used as a standard unit of value in the fur trade
LEWS > PLEW
LEX *n* shortening of multiplex
LEXAL > PLEXUS
LEXES > PLEX
LEXIFORM *adj* like or having the form of a network or plexus
LEXOR *n* small hammer with a rubber head for use in percussion of the chest and testing reflexes
LEXORS > PLEXOR
LEXURE *n* act of weaving together
LEXURES > PLEXURE
LEXUS *n* complex network of nerves or blood vessels
LEXUSES > PLEXUS
LIABLE *adj* easily bent
LIABLY > PLIABLE
LIANCIES > PLIANT
LIANCY > PLIANT
LIANT *adj* pliable
LIANTLY > PLIANT
LICA *n* folding over of parts, such as a fold of skin, muscle, peritoneum, etc
LICAE > PLICA
LICAL > PLICA
LICATE *adj* having or arranged in parallel folds or ridges ▷ *vb* arrange into parallel folds
LICATED > PLICATE
LICATELY > PLICATE
LICATES > PLICATE
LICATING > PLICATE
LICATION *n* act of folding or the condition of being folded or plicate
LICATURE *same as* > PLICATION
LIE *n* classic ballet practice posture with back erect and knees bent
LIED > PLY
LIER *n* person who plies a trade
LIERS *pl n* tool with hinged arms and jaws for gripping
LIES > PLY
LIGHT *n* difficult or dangerous situation
LIGHTED > PLIGHT
LIGHTER > PLIGHT
LIGHTERS > PLIGHT
LIGHTFUL > PLIGHT
LIGHTING > PLIGHT
LIGHTS > PLIGHT
LIM *vb* swell with water
LIMMED > PLIM
LIMMING > PLIM
LIMS > PLIM
PLIMSOL *same as* > PLIMSOLE
PLIMSOLE *same as* > PLIMSOLL
PLIMSOLES > PLIMSOLE
PLIMSOLL *n* light rubber-soled canvas shoe worn for various sports
PLIMSOLLS > PLIMSOLL
PLIMSOLS > PLIMSOL
PLING *n* (in computer jargon) an exclamation mark
PLINGS > PLING
PLINK *n* short sharp often metallic sound as of a string on a musical instrument being plucked or a bullet striking metal ▷ *vb* make such a noise
PLINKED > PLINK
PLINKER > PLINK
PLINKERS > PLINK
PLINKING > PLINK
PLINKS > PLINK
PLINTH *n* slab forming the base of a statue, column, etc
PLINTHS > PLINTH
PLIOCENE *adj* of the Pliocene geological time period
PLIOFILM *n* transparent plastic material
PLIOFILMS > PLIOFILM
PLIOSAUR *n* type of dinosaur
PLIOSAURS > PLIOSAUR
PLIOTRON *n* type of vacuum tube
PLIOTRONS > PLIOTRON
PLISKIE *n* practical joke
PLISKIES > PLISKIE
PLISKY *same as* > PLISKIE
PLISSE *n* fabric with a wrinkled finish, achieved by treatment involving caustic soda
PLISSES > PLISSE
PLOAT *vb* thrash
PLOATED > PLOAT
PLOATING > PLOAT
PLOATS > PLOAT
PLOD *vb* walk with slow heavy steps ▷ *n* act of plodding
PLODDED > PLOD
PLODDER *n* person who plods, esp one who works in a slow and persevering but uninspired manner
PLODDERS > PLODDER
PLODDING > PLOD
PLODDINGS > PLOD
PLODGE *vb* wade in water, esp the sea ▷ *n* act of wading
PLODGED > PLODGE
PLODGES > PLODGE
PLODGING > PLODGE
PLODS > PLOD
PLOIDIES > PLOIDY
PLOIDY *n* number of copies of set of chromosomes in cell
PLONG *obsolete variant of* > PLUNGE
PLONGD > PLONG
PLONGE *vb* clean drains by action of tide
PLONGED > PLONGE
PLONGES > PLONGE
PLONGING > PLONGE
PLONGS > PLONG
PLONK *vb* put (something) down heavily and carelessly ▷ *n* cheap inferior wine ▷ *interj* exclamation imitative of this sound
PLONKED > PLONK
PLONKER *n* stupid person
PLONKERS > PLONKER
PLONKIER > PLONK
PLONKIEST > PLONK
PLONKING > PLONK
PLONKINGS > PLONK
PLONKO *n* alcoholic, esp one who drinks wine
PLONKOS > PLONKO
PLONKS > PLONK
PLONKY > PLONK
PLOOK *same as* > PLOUK
PLOOKIE *same as* > PLOUKY
PLOOKIER > PLOUK
PLOOKIEST > PLOUK
PLOOKS > PLOOK
PLOOKY *same as* > PLOUKY
PLOP *n* sound of an object falling into water without a splash ▷ *vb* make this sound ▷ *interj* exclamation imitative of this sound
PLOPPED > PLOP
PLOPPING > PLOP
PLOPS > PLOP
PLOSION *n* sound of an abrupt break or closure, esp the audible release of a stop
PLOSIONS > PLOSION
PLOSIVE *adj* pronounced with a sudden release of breath ▷ *n* plosive consonant
PLOSIVES > PLOSIVE
PLOT *n* secret plan to do something illegal or wrong ▷ *vb* plan secretly, conspire
PLOTFUL > PLOT
PLOTLESS > PLOT
PLOTLINE *n* literary or dramatic plot
PLOTLINES > PLOTLINE
PLOTS > PLOT
PLOTTAGE *n* land that makes up plot
PLOTTAGES > PLOTTAGE
PLOTTED > PLOT
PLOTTER *same as* > PLOUTER
PLOTTERED > PLOTTER
PLOTTERS > PLOTTER
PLOTTIE *n* hot spiced drink
PLOTTIER > PLOTTY
PLOTTIES > PLOTTIE
PLOTTIEST > PLOTTY
PLOTTING > PLOT
PLOTTINGS > PLOT
PLOTTY *adj* intricately plotted
PLOTZ *vb* faint or collapse
PLOTZED > PLOTZ
PLOTZES > PLOTZ
PLOTZING > PLOTZ
PLOUGH *n* agricultural tool for turning over soil ▷ *vb* turn over (earth) with a plough
PLOUGHBOY *n* boy who guides the animals drawing a plough
PLOUGHED > PLOUGH
PLOUGHER > PLOUGH
PLOUGHERS > PLOUGH
PLOUGHING > PLOUGH
PLOUGHMAN *n* man who ploughs
PLOUGHMEN > PLOUGHMAN
PLOUGHS > PLOUGH
PLOUK *n* pimple
PLOUKIE > PLOUK
PLOUKIER > PLOUK
PLOUKIEST > PLOUK
PLOUKS > PLOUK
PLOUKY > PLOUK
PLOUTER *same as* > PLOWTER
PLOUTERED > PLOUTER
PLOUTERS > PLOUTER
PLOVER *n* shore bird with a straight bill and long pointed wings
PLOVERS > PLOVER
PLOVERY > PLOVER
PLOW *same as* > PLOUGH
PLOWABLE > PLOW
PLOWBACK *n* reinvestment of profits
PLOWBACKS > PLOWBACK
PLOWBOY *same as* > PLOUGHBOY
PLOWBOYS > PLOWBOY
PLOWED > PLOW
PLOWER > PLOW
PLOWERS > PLOW
PLOWHEAD *n* draught iron of plow
PLOWHEADS > PLOWHEAD
PLOWING > PLOW
PLOWLAND *n* land plowed
PLOWLANDS > PLOWLAND
PLOWMAN *same as* > PLOUGHMAN
PLOWMEN > PLOWMAN
PLOWS > PLOW
PLOWSHARE *n* horizontal pointed cutting blade of a mouldboard plow
PLOWSTAFF *n* one of the handles of a plow
PLOWTER *vb* work or play in water or mud ▷ *n* act of plowtering
PLOWTERED > PLOWTER
PLOWTERS > PLOWTER
PLOY *n* manoeuvre designed to gain an advantage ▷ *vb* form a column from a line of troops
PLOYED > PLOY

PLOYING > PLOY
PLOYS > PLOY
PLU *same as* > PLEW
PLUCK *vb* pull or pick off ▷ *n* courage
PLUCKED > PLUCK
PLUCKER > PLUCK
PLUCKERS > PLUCK
PLUCKIER > PLUCKY
PLUCKIEST > PLUCKY
PLUCKILY > PLUCKY
PLUCKING > PLUCK
PLUCKS > PLUCK
PLUCKY *adj* brave
PLUE *same as* > PLEW
PLUES > PLUE
PLUFF *vb* expel in puffs
PLUFFED > PLUFF
PLUFFIER > PLUFF
PLUFFIEST > PLUFF
PLUFFING > PLUFF
PLUFFS > PLUFF
PLUFFY > PLUFF
PLUG *n* thing fitting into and filling a hole ▷ *vb* block or seal (a hole or gap) with a plug
PLUGBOARD *n* device with a large number of sockets in which electrical plugs can be inserted to form many different temporary circuits
PLUGGED > PLUG
PLUGGER > PLUG
PLUGGERS > PLUG
PLUGGING > PLUG
PLUGGINGS > PLUG
PLUGHOLE *n* hole, esp in a bath, basin, or sink, through which waste water drains and which can be closed with a plug
PLUGHOLES > PLUGHOLE
PLUGLESS > PLUG
PLUGOLA *n* plugging of products on television
PLUGOLAS > PLUGOLA
PLUGS > PLUG
PLUGUGLY *n* city tough; ruffian
PLUM *n* oval usu dark red fruit with a stone in the middle ▷ *adj* dark purplish-red
PLUMAGE *n* bird's feathers
PLUMAGED > PLUMAGE
PLUMAGES > PLUMAGE
PLUMATE *adj* of, relating to, or possessing one or more feathers or plumes
PLUMB *vb* understand (something obscure) ▷ *adv* exactly ▷ *n* weight, usually of lead, suspended at the end of a line and used to determine water depth or verticality
PLUMBABLE > PLUMB
PLUMBAGO *n* plant of warm regions with clusters of blue, white, or red flowers
PLUMBAGOS > PLUMBAGO
PLUMBATE *n* compound formed from lead oxide
PLUMBATES > PLUMBATE
PLUMBED > PLUMB
PLUMBEOUS *adj* made of or relating to lead or resembling lead in colour
PLUMBER *n* person who fits and repairs pipes and fixtures for water and drainage systems
PLUMBERS > PLUMBER
PLUMBERY *same as* > PLUMBING
PLUMBIC *adj* of or containing lead in the tetravalent state
PLUMBING *n* pipes and fixtures used in water and drainage systems
PLUMBINGS > PLUMBING
PLUMBISM *n* chronic lead poisoning
PLUMBISMS > PLUMBISM
PLUMBITE *n* substance containing lead oxide
PLUMBITES > PLUMBITE
PLUMBLESS *adj* incapable of being sounded
PLUMBNESS > PLUMB
PLUMBOUS *adj* of or containing lead in the divalent state
PLUMBS > PLUMB
PLUMBUM *n* obsolete name for lead (the metal)
PLUMBUMS > PLUMBUM
PLUMCOT *n* hybrid of apricot and plum
PLUMCOTS > PLUMCOT
PLUMDAMAS *n* prune
PLUME *n* feather, esp one worn as an ornament ▷ *vb* adorn or decorate with feathers or plumes
PLUMED > PLUME
PLUMELESS > PLUME
PLUMELET *n* small plume
PLUMELETS > PLUMELET
PLUMELIKE > PLUME
PLUMERIA *n* tropical tree with candelabra-like branches
PLUMERIAS > PLUMERIA
PLUMERIES > PLUMERY
PLUMERY *n* plumes collectively
PLUMES > PLUME
PLUMIER > PLUMY
PLUMIEST > PLUMY
PLUMING > PLUME
PLUMIPED *n* bird with feathered feet
PLUMIPEDS > PLUMIPED
PLUMIST *n* person who makes plumes
PLUMISTS > PLUMIST
PLUMLIKE > PLUM
PLUMMER > PLUM
PLUMMEST > PLUM
PLUMMET *vb* plunge downward ▷ *n* weight on a plumb line or fishing line
PLUMMETED > PLUMMET
PLUMMETS > PLUMMET
PLUMMIER > PLUMMY
PLUMMIEST > PLUMMY
PLUMMY *adj* of, full of, or like plums
PLUMOSE *same as* > PLUMATE
PLUMOSELY > PLUMOSE
PLUMOSITY > PLUMOSE
PLUMOUS *adj* having plumes or feathers
PLUMP *adj* moderately or attractively fat ▷ *vb* sit or fall heavily and suddenly ▷ *n* heavy abrupt fall or the sound of this ▷ *adv* suddenly or heavily
PLUMPED > PLUMP
PLUMPEN *vb* make or become plump
PLUMPENED > PLUMPEN
PLUMPENS > PLUMPEN
PLUMPER *n* pad carried in the mouth by actors to round out the cheeks
PLUMPERS > PLUMPER
PLUMPEST > PLUMP
PLUMPIER > PLUMPY
PLUMPIEST > PLUMPY
PLUMPING > PLUMP
PLUMPISH *adj* on the plump side
PLUMPLY > PLUMP
PLUMPNESS > PLUMP
PLUMPS > PLUMP
PLUMPY *adj* plump
PLUMS > PLUM
PLUMULA *n* down feather
PLUMULAE > PLUMULA
PLUMULAR > PLUMULE
PLUMULATE *adj* covered with soft fine feathers
PLUMULE *n* embryonic shoot of seed-bearing plants
PLUMULES > PLUMULE
PLUMULOSE *adj* having hairs branching out like feathers
PLUMY *adj* like a feather
PLUNDER *vb* take by force, esp in time of war ▷ *n* things plundered, spoils
PLUNDERED > PLUNDER
PLUNDERER > PLUNDER
PLUNDERS > PLUNDER
PLUNGE *vb* put or throw forcibly or suddenly (into) ▷ *n* plunging dive
PLUNGED > PLUNGE
PLUNGER *n* rubber suction cup used to clear blocked pipes
PLUNGERS > PLUNGER
PLUNGES > PLUNGE
PLUNGING > PLUNGE
PLUNGINGS > PLUNGE
PLUNK *vb* pluck the strings of (a banjo etc) to produce a twanging sound ▷ *n* act or sound of plunking ▷ *interj* exclamation imitative of the sound of something plunking ▷ *adv* exactly
PLUNKED > PLUNK
PLUNKER > PLUNK
PLUNKERS > PLUNK
PLUNKIER > PLUNKY
PLUNKIEST > PLUNKY
PLUNKING > PLUNK
PLUNKS > PLUNK
PLUNKY *adj* sounding like plucked banjo string
PLURAL *adj* of or consisting of more than one ▷ *n* word indicating more than one
PLURALISE *same as* > PLURALIZE
PLURALISM *n* existence and toleration of a variety of peoples, opinions, etc in a society
PLURALIST > PLURALISM
PLURALITY *n* state of being plural
PLURALIZE *vb* make or become plural
PLURALLY > PLURAL
PLURALS > PLURAL
PLURIPARA *n* woman who has borne more than one child
PLURISIE *same as* > PLEURISY
PLURISIES > PLURISIE
PLURRY *euphemism for* > BLOODY
PLUS *vb* make or become greater in value
PLUSAGE *same as* > PLUSSAGE
PLUSAGES > PLUSAGE
PLUSED > PLUS
PLUSES > PLUS
PLUSH *n* fabric with long velvety pile ▷ *adj* luxurious
PLUSHER > PLUSH
PLUSHES > PLUSH
PLUSHEST > PLUSH
PLUSHIER > PLUSHY
PLUSHIEST > PLUSHY
PLUSHILY > PLUSHY
PLUSHLY > PLUSH
PLUSHNESS > PLUSH
PLUSHY *same as* > PLUSH
PLUSING > PLUS
PLUSSAGE *n* amount over and above another amount
PLUSSAGES > PLUSSAGE
PLUSSED > PLUS
PLUSSES > PLUS
PLUSSING > PLUS
PLUTEAL > PLUTEUS
PLUTEI > PLUTEUS
PLUTEUS *n* larva of sea urchin
PLUTEUSES > PLUTEUS
PLUTOCRAT *n* person who is powerful because of being very rich
PLUTOLOGY *n* study of wealth
PLUTON *n* any mass of igneous rock that has solidified below the surface of the earth

LUTONIAN *adj* of or relating to the underworld
LUTONIC *adj* (of igneous rocks) formed from molten rock that has cooled and solidified below the earth's surface
LUTONISM *n* theory that the earth's crust was formed by volcanoes
LUTONIUM *n* radioactive metallic element used esp in nuclear reactors and weapons
LUTONOMY *n* economics
LUTONS > PLUTON
LUVIAL *adj* of or caused by the action of rain ▷ *n* of or relating to rainfall or precipitation
LUVIALS > PLUVIAL
LUVIAN *n* crocodile bird
LUVIOSE *same as* > PLUVIOUS
LUVIOUS *adj* of or relating to rain
LY *vb* work at (a job or trade) ▷ *n* thickness of wool, fabric, etc
LYER *n* person who plies trade
LYERS > PLYER
LYING > PLY
LYINGLY > PLY
LYWOOD *n* board made of thin layers of wood glued together
LYWOODS > PLYWOOD
NEUMA *n* person's vital spirit, soul, or creative energy
NEUMAS > PNEUMA
NEUMATIC *adj* worked by or inflated with wind or air
NEUMONIA *n* inflammation of the lungs
NEUMONIC *adj* of, relating to, or affecting the lungs
O *n* chamber pot
OA *n* type of grass
OACEOUS *adj* of, relating to, or belonging to the plant family *Poaceae* (grasses)
OACH *vb* catch (animals) illegally on someone else's land
OACHABLE > POACH
OACHED > POACH
OACHER *n* person who catches animals illegally on someone else's land
OACHERS > POACHER
OACHES > POACH
OACHIER > POACHY
OACHIEST > POACHY
OACHING > POACH
OACHINGS > POACH
OACHY *adj* (of land) wet and soft
OAKA *n* type of stilt (bird) native to New Zealand
OAKAS > POAKA
OAKE *n* waste matter from tanning of hides
POAKES > POAKE
POAS > POA
POBLANO *n* variety of chilli pepper
POBLANOS > POBLANO
POBOY *n* New Orleans sandwich
POBOYS > POBOY
POCHARD *n* European diving duck
POCHARDS > POCHARD
POCHAY *n* post chaise: a closed horse-drawn four-wheeled coach
POCHAYS > POCHAY
POCHETTE *n* envelope-shaped handbag used by women and men
POCHETTES > POCHETTE
POCHOIR *n* print made from stencils
POCHOIRS > POCHOIR
POCK *n* pus-filled blister resulting from smallpox ▷ *vb* mark with scars
POCKARD *variant of* > POCHARD
POCKARDS > POCKARD
POCKED > POCK
POCKET *n* small bag sewn into clothing for carrying things ▷ *vb* put into one's pocket ▷ *adj* small
POCKETED > POCKET
POCKETER > POCKET
POCKETERS > POCKET
POCKETFUL *n* as much as a pocket will hold
POCKETING > POCKET
POCKETS > POCKET
POCKIER > POCK
POCKIES *pl n* woollen mittens
POCKIEST > POCK
POCKILY > POCK
POCKING > POCK
POCKMANKY *n* portmanteau
POCKMARK *n* pitted scar left on the skin after the healing of a smallpox or similar pustule ▷ *vb* scar or pit (a surface) with pockmarks
POCKMARKS > POCKMARK
POCKPIT *vb* mark with scars
POCKPITS > POCKPIT
POCKS > POCK
POCKY > POCK
POCO *adv* little
POCOSEN *same as* > POCOSIN
POCOSENS > POCOSEN
POCOSIN *n* swamp in US upland coastal region
POCOSINS > POCOSIN
POCOSON *same as* > POCOSIN
POCOSONS > POCOSON
POD *n* long narrow seed case of peas, beans, etc ▷ *vb* remove the pod from
PODAGRA *n* gout of the foot or big toe
PODAGRAL > PODAGRA
PODAGRAS > PODAGRA
PODAGRIC > PODAGRA
PODAGROUS > PODAGRA
PODALIC *adj* relating to feet
PODARGUS *n* bird of SE Asia and Australia
PODCAST *n* audio file similar to a radio broadcast, which can be downloaded and listened to on a computer or MP3 player ▷ *vb* make available in this format
PODCASTED > PODCAST
PODCASTER > PODCAST
PODCASTS > PODCAST
PODDED > POD
PODDIE *n* user of or enthusiast for the iPod, a portable digital music player
PODDIES > PODDY
PODDING > POD
PODDLE *vb* move or travel in a leisurely manner
PODDLED > PODDLE
PODDLES > PODDLE
PODDLING > PODDLE
PODDY *n* handfed calf or lamb
PODESTA *n* (in modern Italy) subordinate magistrate in some towns
PODESTAS > PODESTA
PODEX *n* posterior
PODEXES > PODEX
PODGE *n* short chubby person
PODGES > PODGE
PODGIER > PODGY
PODGIEST > PODGY
PODGILY > PODGY
PODGINESS > PODGY
PODGY *adj* short and fat
PODIA > PODIUM
PODIAL > PODIUM
PODIATRIC > PODIATRY
PODIATRY *another word for* > CHIROPODY
PODITE *n* crustacean leg
PODITES > PODITE
PODITIC *n* segment of limb of arthropod
PODITICS > PODITIC
PODIUM *n* small raised platform for a conductor or speaker
PODIUMS > PODIUM
PODLEY *n* young coalfish
PODLEYS > PODLEY
PODLIKE > POD
PODOCARP *n* stem supporting fruit
PODOCARPS > PODOCARP
PODOLOGY *n* study of feet
PODOMERE *n* segment of limb of arthropod
PODOMERES > PODOMERE
PODS > POD
PODSOL *same as* > PODZOL
PODSOLIC > PODZOL
PODSOLISE *same as* > PODZOLIZE
PODSOLIZE *same as* > PODZOLIZE
PODSOLS > PODSOL
PODZOL *n* type of soil characteristic of coniferous forest regions having a greyish-white colour in its upper leached layers
PODZOLIC > PODZOL
PODZOLISE *same as* > PODZOLIZE
PODZOLIZE *vb* make into or form a podzol
PODZOLS > PODZOL
POECHORE *n* dry region
POECHORES > POECHORE
POEM *n* imaginative piece of writing in rhythmic lines
POEMATIC *adj* of poetry
POEMS > POEM
POENOLOGY *same as* > PENOLOGY
POEP *n* emission of gas from the anus
POEPOL *n* South African slang for anus
POEPOLS > POEPOL
POEPS > POEP
POESIED > POESY
POESIES > POESY
POESY *n* poetry ▷ *vb* write poems
POESYING > POESY
POET *n* writer of poems
POETASTER *n* writer of inferior verse
POETASTRY > POETASTER
POETESS *n* female poet
POETESSES > POETESS
POETIC *adj* of or like poetry
POETICAL *n* poet
POETICALS > POETICAL
POETICISE *same as* > POETICIZE
POETICISM > POETICISE
POETICIZE *vb* put into poetry or make poetic
POETICIZM > POETICIZE
POETICS *n* principles and forms of poetry or the study of these, esp as a form of literary criticism
POETICULE *n* inferior poet
POETISE *same as* > POETICIZE
POETISED > POETISE
POETISER > POETISE
POETISERS > POETISE
POETISES > POETISE
POETISING > POETISE
POETIZE *same as* > POETICIZE
POETIZED > POETIZE
POETIZER > POETIZE
POETIZERS > POETIZE
POETIZES > POETIZE
POETIZING > POETIZE
POETLESS > POET
POETLIKE > POET
POETRESSE *old variant of* > POETESS
POETRIES > POETRY

POETRY *n* poems
POETS > POET
POETSHIP *n* state of being poet
POETSHIPS > POETSHIP
POFFLE *n* small piece of land
POFFLES > POFFLE
POGEY *n* financial or other relief given to the unemployed by the government
POGEYS > POGEY
POGGE *n* European marine scorpaenoid fish
POGGES > POGGE
POGIES > POGY
POGO *vb* jump up and down in one spot, as in a punk dance of the 1970s
POGOED > POGO
POGOER > POGO
POGOERS > POGO
POGOING > POGO
POGONIA *n* orchid with pink or white fragrant flowers
POGONIAS > POGONIA
POGONIP *n* icy winter fog
POGONIPS > POGONIP
POGOS > POGO
POGROM *n* organized persecution and massacre ▷ *vb* carry out a pogrom
POGROMED > POGROM
POGROMING > POGROM
POGROMIST > POGROM
POGROMS > POGROM
POGY *same as* > POGEY
POH *n* exclamation expressing contempt
POHIRI *variant spelling of* > POWHIRI
POHIRIS > POHIRI
POHS > POH
POI *n* ball of woven flax swung rhythmically by Māori women during poi dances
POIGNADO *old variant of* > PONIARD
POIGNANCE > POIGNANT
POIGNANCY > POIGNANT
POIGNANT *adj* sharply painful to the feelings
POILU *n* infantryman in the French Army, esp one in the front lines in World War I
POILUS > POILU
POINADO *old variant of* > PONIARD
POINADOES > POINADO
POINCIANA *n* tropical leguminous tree with large orange or red flowers
POIND *vb* take (property of a debtor) in execution or by way of distress
POINDED > POIND
POINDER > POIND
POINDERS > POIND
POINDING > POIND
POINDINGS > POIND
POINDS > POIND
POINT *n* main idea in a discussion, argument, etc ▷ *vb* show the direction or position of something or draw attention to it by extending a finger or other pointed object towards it
POINTABLE > POINT
POINTE *n* tip of the toe
POINTED *adj* having a sharp end
POINTEDLY > POINTED
POINTEL *n* engraver's tool
POINTELLE *n* fabric design in form of chevrons
POINTELS > POINTEL
POINTER *n* helpful hint
POINTERS > POINTER
POINTES > POINTE
POINTIER > POINTY
POINTIEST > POINTY
POINTILLE *n* dotted lines and curves impressed on cover of book
POINTING *n* insertion of mortar between the joints in brickwork
POINTINGS > POINTING
POINTLESS *adj* meaningless, irrelevant
POINTMAN *n* soldier who walks at the front of an infantry patrol in combat
POINTMEN > POINTMAN
POINTS > POINT
POINTSMAN *n* person who operates railway points
POINTSMEN > POINTSMAN
POINTY *adj* having a sharp point or points
POIS > POI
POISE *n* calm dignified manner ▷ *vb* be balanced or suspended
POISED *adj* absolutely ready
POISER *n* balancing organ of some insects
POISERS > POISER
POISES > POISE
POISHA *n* monetary unit of Bangladesh
POISING > POISE
POISON *n* substance that kills or injures when swallowed or absorbed ▷ *vb* give poison to
POISONED > POISON
POISONER > POISON
POISONERS > POISON
POISONING > POISON
POISONOUS *adj* of or like a poison
POISONS > POISON
POISSON *n* fish
POISSONS > POISSON
POITIN *variant spelling of* > POTEEN
POITINS > POITIN
POITREL *n* breastplate of horse's armour
POITRELS > POITREL
POITRINE *n* woman's bosom
POITRINES > POITRINE
POKABLE > POKE
POKAL *n* tall drinking cup
POKALS > POKAL
POKE *vb* jab or prod with one's finger, a stick, etc ▷ *n* poking
POKEBERRY *same as* > POKEWEED
POKED > POKE
POKEFUL *n* contents of small bag
POKEFULS > POKEFUL
POKELOGAN *another name for* > BOGAN
POKER *n* metal rod for stirring a fire
POKERISH *adj* stiff like poker
POKEROOT *same as* > POKEWEED
POKEROOTS > POKEROOT
POKERS > POKER
POKERWORK *n* art of producing pictures or designs on wood by burning it with a heated metal point
POKES > POKE
POKEWEED *n* tall North American plant that has small white flowers, juicy purple berries, and a poisonous purple root used medicinally
POKEWEEDS > POKEWEED
POKEY *same as* > POKIE
POKEYS > POKEY
POKIE *n* poker machine
POKIER > POKY
POKIES > POKY
POKIEST > POKY
POKILY > POKY
POKINESS > POKY
POKING > POKE
POKY *adj* small and cramped
POL *n* political campaigner
POLACCA *same as* > POLACRE
POLACCAS > POLACCA
POLACRE *n* three-masted sailing vessel used in the Mediterranean
POLACRES > POLACRE
POLAR *adj* of or near either of the earth's poles ▷ *n* type of line in geometry
POLARISE *same as* > POLARIZE
POLARISED > POLARISE
POLARISER *same as* > POLARIZER
POLARISES > POLARISE
POLARITY *n* state of having two directly opposite tendencies or opinions
POLARIZE *vb* form or cause to form into groups with directly opposite views
POLARIZED > POLARIZE
POLARIZER *n* person or a device that causes polarization
POLARIZES > POLARIZE
POLARON *n* kind of electron
POLARONS > POLARON
POLARS > POLAR
POLDER *n* land reclaimed from the sea, esp in the Netherlands ▷ *vb* reclaim land from the sea
POLDERED > POLDER
POLDERING > POLDER
POLDERS > POLDER
POLE *n* long rounded piece of wood etc ▷ *vb* strike or push with a pole
POLEAX *same as* > POLEAXE
POLEAXE *vb* hit or stun with a heavy blow ▷ *n* axe formerly used in battle or used by a butcher
POLEAXED > POLEAXE
POLEAXES > POLEAXE
POLEAXING > POLEAXE
POLECAT *n* small animal of the weasel family
POLECATS > POLECAT
POLED > POLE
POLEIS > POLIS
POLELESS > POLE
POLEMARCH *n* (in ancient Greece) civilian official, originally a supreme general
POLEMIC *n* fierce attack on or defence of a particular opinion, belief, etc ▷ *adj* of or involving dispute or controversy
POLEMICAL > POLEMIC
POLEMICS *n* art of dispute
POLEMISE *same as* > POLEMIZE
POLEMISED > POLEMISE
POLEMISES > POLEMISE
POLEMIST > POLEMIC
POLEMISTS > POLEMIC
POLEMIZE *vb* engage in controversy
POLEMIZED > POLEMIZE
POLEMIZES > POLEMIZE
POLENTA *n* thick porridge made in Italy, usually from maize
POLENTAS > POLENTA
POLER *n* person or thing that poles, esp a punter
POLERS > POLER
POLES > POLE
POLESTAR *n* guiding principle, rule, standard, etc
POLESTARS > POLESTAR
POLEWARD *adv* towards a pole
POLEY *adj* (of cattle) hornless or polled ▷ *n* animal with horns removed
POLEYN *n* piece of armour for protecting the knee
POLEYNS > POLEYN
POLEYS > POLEY
POLIANITE *n* manganese dioxide occurring as hard crystals

LICE *n* organized force n a state which keeps law nd order ▷ *vb* control or vatch over with police or a imilar body
LICED > POLICE
LICEMAN *n* member of a olice force
LICEMEN > POLICEMAN
LICER *n* computer levice controlling use
LICERS > POLICER
LICES > POLICE
LICIES > POLICY
LICING > POLICE
LICINGS > POLICE
LICY *n* plan of action dopted by a person, roup, or state
LIES > POLY
LING > POLE
LINGS > POLE
LIO *n* acute viral disease
LIOS > POLIO
LIS *n* ancient Greek ity-state
LISH *vb* make smooth nd shiny by rubbing › *n* substance used for olishing
LISHED *adj* ccomplished
LISHER > POLISH
LISHERS > POLISH
LISHES > POLISH
LISHING > POLISH
LITBURO *n* supreme olicy-making authority n most communist ountries
LITE *adj* showing onsideration for others in ne's manners, speech, etc
LITELY > POLITE
LITER > POLITE
LITESSE *n* formal or enteel politeness
LITEST > POLITE
LITIC *adj* wise and likely o prove advantageous
LITICAL *adj* of the state, overnment, or public dministration
LITICK *vb* engage in olitics
LITICKS > POLITICK
LITICLY > POLITIC
LITICO *n* politician
LITICOS > POLITICO
LITICS *n* winning and ising of power to govern ociety
LITIES > POLITY
LITIQUE *n* 16th-century rench moderate
LITY *n* politically rganized state, church, or ociety
LJE *n* large elliptical lepression in karst egions, sometimes ontaining a marsh or mall lake
LJES > POLJE
POLK *vb* dance a polka
POLKA *n* lively 19th-century dance ▷ *vb* dance a polka
POLKAED > POLKA
POLKAING > POLKA
POLKAS > POLKA
POLKED > POLK
POLKING > POLK
POLKS > POLK
POLL *n* questioning of a random sample of people to find out general opinion ▷ *vb* receive (votes)
POLLACK *n* food fish related to the cod, found in northern seas
POLLACKS > POLLACK
POLLAN *n* whitefish that occurs in lakes in Northern Ireland
POLLANS > POLLAN
POLLARD *n* animal that has shed its horns or has had them removed ▷ *vb* cut off the top of (a tree) to make it grow bushy
POLLARDED > POLLARD
POLLARDS > POLLARD
POLLED *adj* (of animals, esp cattle) having the horns cut off or being naturally hornless
POLLEE > POLL
POLLEES > POLL
POLLEN *n* fine dust produced by flowers to fertilize other flowers ▷ *vb* collect pollen
POLLENATE *same as* > POLLINATE
POLLENED > POLLEN
POLLENING > POLLEN
POLLENS > POLLEN
POLLENT *adj* strong
POLLER > POLL
POLLERS > POLL
POLLEX *n* first digit of the forelimb of amphibians, reptiles, birds, and mammals, such as the thumb of man and other primates
POLLICAL > POLLEX
POLLICES > POLLEX
POLLICIE *obsolete spelling of* > POLICY
POLLICIES > POLLICIE
POLLICY *obsolete spelling of* > POLICY
POLLIES > POLLY
POLLINATE *vb* fertilize with pollen
POLLING *n* casting or registering of votes at an election
POLLINGS > POLLING
POLLINIA > POLLINIUM
POLLINIC > POLLEN
POLLINISE *same as* > POLLINIZE
POLLINIUM *n* mass of cohering pollen grains, produced by plants such as orchids and transported as a whole during pollination
POLLINIZE *same as* > POLLINATE
POLLIST *n* one advocating the use of polls
POLLISTS > POLLIST
POLLIWIG *same as* > POLLIWOG
POLLIWIGS > POLLIWOG
POLLIWOG *n* sailor who has not crossed the equator
POLLIWOGS > POLLIWOG
POLLMAN *n* one passing a degree without honours
POLLMEN > POLLMAN
POLLOCK *same as* > POLLACK
POLLOCKS > POLLOCK
POLLS > POLL
POLLSTER *n* person who conducts opinion polls
POLLSTERS > POLLSTER
POLLTAKER *n* person conducting poll
POLLUCITE *n* colourless rare mineral consisting of a hydrated caesium aluminium silicate
POLLUSION *n* comic Shakespearian character's version of "allusion"
POLLUTANT *n* something that pollutes
POLLUTE *vb* contaminate with something poisonous or harmful
POLLUTED *adj* made unclean or impure
POLLUTER > POLLUTE
POLLUTERS > POLLUTE
POLLUTES > POLLUTE
POLLUTING > POLLUTE
POLLUTION *n* act of polluting or the state of being polluted
POLLUTIVE *adj* causing pollution
POLLY *n* politician
POLLYANNA *n* person who is constantly or excessively optimistic
POLLYWIG *same as* > POLLIWOG
POLLYWIGS > POLLYWIG
POLLYWOG *same as* > POLLIWOG
POLLYWOGS > POLLYWOG
POLO *n* game like hockey played by teams of players on horseback
POLOIDAL *adj* relating to a type of magnetic field
POLOIST *n* devotee of polo
POLOISTS > POLOIST
POLONAISE *n* old stately dance
POLONIE *same as* > POLONY
POLONIES > POLONY
POLONISE *same as* > POLONIZE
POLONISED > POLONISE
POLONISES > POLONISE
POLONISM > POLONISE
POLONISMS > POLONISE
POLONIUM *n* radioactive element that occurs in trace amounts in uranium ores
POLONIUMS > POLONIUM
POLONIZE *vb* make Polish
POLONIZED > POLONIZE
POLONIZES > POLONIZE
POLONY *n* bologna sausage
POLOS > POLO
POLS > POL
POLT *n* thump or blow ▷ *vb* strike
POLTED > POLT
POLTFOOT *adj* having a club foot
POLTING > POLT
POLTROON *n* utter coward
POLTROONS > POLTROON
POLTS > POLT
POLVERINE *n* glassmakers' potash
POLY *n* polytechnic
POLYACID *n* alcohol or base with two or more hydroxyl groups
POLYACIDS > POLYACID
POLYACT *adj* (of a sea creature) having many tentacles or limb-like protrusions
POLYADIC *adj* (of a relation, operation, etc) having several argument places
POLYAMIDE *n* synthetic polymeric material
POLYAMINE *n* compound containing two or more amine groups
POLYANDRY *n* practice of having more than one husband at the same time
POLYANTHA *n* type of flower
POLYANTHI *n* hybrid garden primroses
POLYARCH *n* member of polyarchy
POLYARCHY *n* political system in which power is dispersed
POLYAXIAL *n* joint in which movement occurs in more than one axis
POLYAXON *n* nerve cell with multiple branches
POLYAXONS > POLYAXON
POLYBASIC *adj* (of an acid) having two or more replaceable hydrogen atoms per molecule
POLYBRID *n* hybrid plant with more than two parental groups
POLYBRIDS > POLYBRID
POLYCARPY *n* condition of being able to produce flowers and fruit several times in successive years or seasons
POLYCHETE *n* variety of worm
POLYCONIC as in *polyconic projection* type of projection used in making maps of large areas

POLYCOT *n* plant that has or appears to have more than two cotyledons
POLYCOTS > POLYCOT
POLYDEMIC *adj* growing in or inhabiting more than two regions
POLYENE *n* chemical compound containing a chain of alternating single and double carbon-carbon bonds
POLYENES > POLYENE
POLYENIC > POLYENE
POLYESTER *n* synthetic material used to make plastics and textile fibres
POLYGALA *n* herbaceous plant or small shrub
POLYGALAS > POLYGALA
POLYGAM *n* plant of the Polygamia class
POLYGAMIC > POLYGAMY
POLYGAMS > POLYGAM
POLYGAMY *n* practice of having more than one husband or wife at the same time
POLYGENE *n* any of a group of genes that each produce a small quantitative effect on a particular characteristic of the phenotype, such as height
POLYGENES > POLYGENE
POLYGENIC *adj* of, relating to, or controlled by polygenes
POLYGENY > POLYGENIC
POLYGLOT *adj* (person) able to speak or write several languages ▷ *n* person who can speak many languages
POLYGLOTS > POLYGLOT
POLYGLOTT *variant of* > POLYGLOT
POLYGON *n* geometrical figure with three or more angles and sides
POLYGONAL > POLYGON
POLYGONS > POLYGON
POLYGONUM *n* plant with stems with knotlike joints and spikes of small white, green, or pink flowers
POLYGONY > POLYGON
POLYGRAPH *n* instrument for recording pulse rate and perspiration, used esp as a lie detector
POLYGYNY *n* practice of having more than one wife at the same time
POLYHEDRA *n* solid figures, each consisting of four or more plane faces
POLYIMIDE *n* type of polymer
POLYLEMMA *n* debate forcing choice between contradictory positions
POLYMASTY *n* condition in which more than two breasts are present
POLYMATH *n* person of great and varied learning
POLYMATHS > POLYMATH
POLYMATHY > POLYMATH
POLYMER *n* chemical compound with large molecules made of simple molecules of the same kind
POLYMERIC *adj* of or being a polymer
POLYMERS > POLYMER
POLYMERY > POLYMER
POLYMORPH *n* species of animal or plant that exhibits polymorphism
POLYMYXIN *n* polypeptide antibiotic
POLYNIA *same as* > POLYNYA
POLYNIAS > POLYNIA
POLYNYA *n* stretch of open water surrounded by ice, esp near the mouths of large rivers, in arctic seas
POLYNYAS > POLYNYA
POLYNYI > POLYNYA
POLYOL *n* type of alcohol
POLYOLS > POLYOL
POLYOMA *n* type of tumour caused by virus
POLYOMAS > POLYOMA
POLYOMINO *n* polygon made from joining identical squares at their edges
POLYONYM *n* object with many names
POLYONYMS > POLYONYM
POLYONYMY > POLYONYM
POLYP *n* small simple sea creature with a hollow cylindrical body
POLYPARIA *n* polyparies
POLYPARY *n* common base and connecting tissue of a colony of coelenterate polyps, esp coral
POLYPE *variant of* > POLYP
POLYPED *same as* > POLYPOD
POLYPEDS > POLYPED
POLYPES > POLYPE
POLYPHAGY *n* insatiable appetite
POLYPHASE *adj* (of an electrical system, circuit, or device) having, generating, or using two or more alternating voltages of the same frequency, the phases of which are cyclically displaced by fractions of a period
POLYPHON *n* musical instrument resembling a lute
POLYPHONE *n* letter or character with more than one phonetic value
POLYPHONS > POLYPHON
POLYPHONY *n* polyphonic style of composition or a piece of music using it
POLYPI > POLYPUS
POLYPIDE *n* polyp forming part of a colonial animal
POLYPIDES > POLYPIDE
POLYPIDOM *same as* > POLYPARY
POLYPILL *n* proposed combined medication intended to reduce the likelihood of heart attacks and strokes
POLYPILLS > POLYPILL
POLYPINE *adj* of or relating to polyps
POLYPITE *same as* > POLYPIDE
POLYPITES > POLYPITE
POLYPLOID *adj* (of cells, organisms, etc) having more than twice the basic (haploid) number of chromosomes ▷ *n* individual or cell of this type
POLYPNEA *n* rapid breathing
POLYPNEAS > POLYPNEA
POLYPNEIC > POLYPNEA
POLYPOD *adj* (esp of insect larvae) having many legs or similar appendages ▷ *n* animal of this type
POLYPODS > POLYPOD
POLYPODY *n* fern with deeply divided leaves and round naked sori
POLYPOID > POLYP
POLYPORE *n* type of fungi
POLYPORES > POLYPORE
POLYPOSES > POLYPOSIS
POLYPOSIS *n* formation of many polyps
POLYPOUS > POLYP
POLYPS > POLYP
POLYPTYCH *n* altarpiece consisting of more than three panels, set with paintings or carvings, and usually hinged for folding
POLYPUS *same as* > POLYP
POLYPUSES > POLYPUS
POLYS > POLY
POLYSEME *n* word with many meanings
POLYSEMES > POLYSEME
POLYSEMIC > POLYSEME
POLYSEMY *n* existence of several meanings in a single word
POLYSOME *n* assemblage of ribosomes associated with a messenger RNA molecule
POLYSOMES > POLYSOME
POLYSOMIC *adj* of, relating to, or designating a basically diploid chromosome complement, in which some but not all the chromosomes are represented more than twice
POLYSOMY > POLYSOME
POLYSTYLE *n* room with many columns
POLYTENE *adj* denoting a type of giant-size chromosome consisting of many replicated genes in parallel, found esp in *Drosophila* larvae
POLYTENY > POLYTENE
POLYTHENE *n* light plasti used for bags etc
POLYTONAL *adj* using mo than two different tones keys simultaneously
POLYTYPE *n* crystal occurring in more than one form
POLYTYPES > POLYTYPE
POLYTYPIC *adj* existing in, consisting of, or incorporating several different types or forms
POLYURIA *n* state or condition of discharging abnormally large quantities of urine, ofte accompanied by a need t urinate frequently
POLYURIAS > POLYURIA
POLYURIC > POLYURIA
POLYVINYL *n* designatin a plastic or resin formed polymerization of a viny derivative
POLYWATER *n* liquid formerly supposed to be polymeric form of water
POLYZOA *n* small mosslik aquatic creatures
POLYZOAN *another word for* > BRYOZOAN
POLYZOANS > POLYZOAN
POLYZOARY *n* colony of bryozoan animals
POLYZOIC *adj* (of certain colonial animals) having many zooids or similar polyps
POLYZONAL *adj* having many zones
POLYZOOID *adj* resembli a polyzoon
POLYZOON *n* individual zooid within polyzoan
POM *same as* > POMMY
POMACE *n* apple pulp left after pressing for juice
POMACEOUS *adj* of, relatin to, or bearing pomes, su as the apple, pear, and quince trees
POMACES > POMACE
POMADE *n* perfumed oil put on the hair to make it smooth and shiny ▷ *vt* put pomade on
POMADED > POMADE
POMADES > POMADE
POMADING > POMADE
POMANDER *n* mixture of sweet-smelling petals, herbs, etc
POMANDERS > POMANDER
POMATO *n* hybrid of toma

nd potato
MATOES > POMATO
MATUM *same as* > POMADE
MATUMS > POMATUM
MBE *n* any alcoholic drink
MBES > POMBE
ME *n* fleshy fruit of the pple and related plants, onsisting of an enlarged eceptacle enclosing the vary and seeds
MELO *n* edible yellow ruit, like a grapefruit, of a ropical tree
MELOS > POMELO
MEROY *n* bullet used to own airships
MEROYS > POMEROY
MES > POME
MFRET *n* small black ounded liquorice sweet
MFRETS > POMFRET
MMEE *adj* (of cross) aving end of each arm nding in disk
MMEL *same as* > PUMMEL
MMELE *adj* having a ommel
MMELED > POMMEL
MMELING > POMMEL
MMELLED > POMMEL
MMELS > POMMEL
MMETTY *adj* having a ommel
MMIE *same as* > POMMY
MMIES > POMMY
MMY *n* word used by ustralians and New ealanders for a British erson
MO *n* postmodernism
MOERIUM *n* space around own within city walls
MOLOGY *n* branch of orticulture that is oncerned with the study nd cultivation of fruit
MOS > POMO
MP *n* stately display or eremony
MPADOUR *n* early 18th-entury hairstyle for vomen, having the front air arranged over a pad o give it greater height nd bulk
MPANO *n* deep-bodied arangid food fish
MPANOS > POMPANO
MPELO *n* large Asian itrus fruit
MPELOS > POMPELO
MPEY *vb* mollycoddle
MPEYED > POMPEY
MPEYING > POMPEY
MPEYS > POMPEY
MPHOLYX *n* type of czema
MPIER *adj* slavishly onventional
MPILID *n* spider-unting wasp
MPILIDS > POMPILID
MPION *n* pumpkin
POMPIONS > POMPION
POMPOM *n* decorative ball of tufted wool, silk, etc
POMPOMS > POMPOM
POMPON *same as* > POMPOM
POMPONS > POMPON
POMPOON *variant of* > POMPOM
POMPOONS > POMPOON
POMPOSITY *n* vain or ostentatious display of dignity or importance
POMPOUS *adj* foolishly serious and grand, self-important
POMPOUSLY > POMPOUS
POMPS > POMP
POMROY *variant of* > POMEROY
POMROYS > POMROY
POMS > POM
POMWATER *n* kind of apple
POMWATERS > POMWATER
PONCE *n* derogatory word for an effeminate man ▷ *vb* act stupidly or waste time
PONCEAU *n* scarlet red
PONCEAUS > PONCEAU
PONCED > PONCE
PONCES > PONCE
PONCEY *adj* ostentatious, pretentious, or effeminate
PONCHO *n* loose circular cloak with a hole for the head
PONCHOED *adj* wearing poncho
PONCHOS > PONCHO
PONCIER > PONCEY
PONCIEST > PONCEY
PONCING > PONCE
PONCY *same as* > PONCEY
POND *n* small area of still water ▷ *vb* hold back (flowing water)
PONDAGE *n* water held in reservoir
PONDAGES > PONDAGE
PONDED > POND
PONDER *vb* think thoroughly or deeply (about)
PONDERAL *adj* relating to weight
PONDERATE *vb* consider
PONDERED > PONDER
PONDERER > PONDER
PONDERERS > PONDER
PONDERING > PONDER
PONDEROSA *n* N American pine tree
PONDEROUS *adj* serious and dull
PONDERS > PONDER
PONDING > POND
PONDOK *n* (in southern Africa) crudely made house or shack
PONDOKKIE *same as* > PONDOK
PONDOKS > PONDOK
PONDS > POND
PONDWEED *n* plant that grows in ponds
PONDWEEDS > PONDWEED
PONE *n* bread made of maize
PONENT *n* west wind
PONES > PONE
PONEY *same as* > PONY
PONEYS > PONEY
PONG *n* strong unpleasant smell ▷ *vb* give off a strong unpleasant smell
PONGA *n* tall New Zealand tree fern with large leathery leaves
PONGAS > PONGA
PONGED > PONG
PONGEE *n* thin plain-weave silk fabric from China or India, left in its natural colour
PONGEES > PONGEE
PONGID *n* any primate of the family *Pongidae*, which includes the gibbons and the great apes ▷ *adj* of, relating to, or belonging to the family *Pongidae*
PONGIDS > PONGID
PONGIER > PONG
PONGIEST > PONG
PONGING > PONG
PONGO *n* anthropoid ape, esp an orang-utan or (formerly) a gorilla
PONGOES > PONGO
PONGOS > PONGO
PONGS > PONG
PONGY > PONG
PONIARD *n* small slender dagger ▷ *vb* stab with a poniard
PONIARDED > PONIARD
PONIARDS > PONIARD
PONIED > PONY
PONIES > PONY
PONK *n* evil spirit
PONKS > PONK
PONS *n* bridge of connecting tissue
PONT *n* (in South Africa) river ferry, esp one that is guided by a cable from one bank to the other
PONTAGE *n* tax paid for repairing bridge
PONTAGES > PONTAGE
PONTAL *adj* of or relating to the pons
PONTES > PONS
PONTIANAC *same as* > PONTIANAK
PONTIANAK *n* (in Malay folklore) female vampire
PONTIC *adj* of or relating to the pons
PONTIES > PONTY
PONTIFEX *n* (in ancient Rome) any of the senior members of the Pontifical College
PONTIFF *n* Pope
PONTIFFS > PONTIFF
PONTIFIC > PONTIFF
PONTIFICE *n* structure of bridge
PONTIFIED > PONTIFY
PONTIFIES > PONTIFY
PONTIFY *vb* speak or behave in a pompous or dogmatic manner
PONTIL *same as* > PUNTY
PONTILE *adj* relating to pons
PONTILS > PONTIL
PONTINE *adj* of or relating to bridges
PONTLEVIS *n* horse rearing repeatedly
PONTON *variant of* > PONTOON
PONTONEER *same as* > PONTONIER
PONTONIER *n* person in charge of or involved in building a pontoon bridge
PONTONS > PONTON
PONTOON *n* floating platform supporting a temporary bridge ▷ *vb* cross a river using pontoons
PONTOONED > PONTOON
PONTOONER > PONTOON
PONTOONS > PONTOON
PONTS > PONT
PONTY *n* rod used for shaping molten glass
PONY *n* small horse ▷ *vb* settle bill or debt
PONYING > PONY
PONYSKIN *n* leather from pony hide
PONYSKINS > PONYSKIN
PONYTAIL *n* long hair tied in one bunch at the back of the head
PONYTAILS > PONYTAIL
PONZU *n* type of Japanese dipping sauce made from orange juice, sake, sugar, soy sauce, and red pepper
PONZUS > PONZU
POO *vb* defecate
POOCH *n* slang word for dog ▷ *vb* bulge or protrude
POOCHED > POOCH
POOCHES > POOCH
POOCHING > POOCH
POOD *n* unit of weight, used in Russia, equal to 36.1 pounds or 16.39 kilograms
POODLE *n* dog with curly hair often clipped fancifully
POODLES > POODLE
POODS > POOD
POOED > POO
POOF *n* derogatory word for a homosexual man
POOFIER > POOF
POOFIEST > POOF
POOFS > POOF
POOFTAH *same as* > POOFTER
POOFTAHS > POOFTAH
POOFTER *n* derogatory word for a man who is considered effeminate or homosexual

POOFTERS > POOFTER
POOFY > POOF
POOGYE *n* Hindu nose-flute
POOGYES > POOGYE
POOH *interj* exclamation of disdain, contempt, or disgust ▷ *vb* make such an exclamation
POOHED > POOH
POOHING > POOH
POOHS > POOH
POOING > POO
POOJA *variant of* > PUJA
POOJAH *variant of* > PUJA
POOJAHS > POOJAH
POOJAS > POOJA
POOK *vb* pluck
POOKA *n* malevolent Irish spirit
POOKAS > POOKA
POOKING > POOK
POOKIT > POOK
POOKS > POOK
POOL *n* small body of still water ▷ *vb* put in a common fund
POOLED > POOL
POOLER *n* person taking part in pool
POOLERS > POOLER
POOLHALL *n* room containing pool tables
POOLHALLS > POOLHALL
POOLING > POOL
POOLROOM *n* hall or establishment where pool, billiards, etc, are played
POOLROOMS > POOLROOM
POOLS *pl n* organized nationwide principally postal gambling pool betting on the result of football matches
POOLSIDE *n* area surrounding swimming pool
POOLSIDES > POOLSIDE
POON *n* SE Asian tree with lightweight hard wood and shiny leathery leaves
POONAC *n* coconut residue
POONACS > POONAC
POONCE *n* derogatory word for a homosexual man ▷ *vb* behave effeminately
POONCED > POONCE
POONCES > POONCE
POONCING > POONCE
POONS > POON
POONTANG *n* taboo word for the female pudenda
POONTANGS > POONTANG
POOP *n* raised part at the back of a sailing ship ▷ *vb* (of a wave or sea) break over the stern of (a vessel)
POOPED > POOP
POOPER as in *party pooper* person whose behaviour or personality spoils other people's enjoyment
POOPERS > POOPER
POOPING > POOP
POOPS > POOP
POOR *adj* having little money and few possessions
POORER > POOR
POOREST > POOR
POORHOUSE *n* (formerly) publicly maintained institution offering accommodation to the poor
POORI *n* unleavened Indian bread
POORIS > POORI
POORISH > POOR
POORLIER > POORLY
POORLIEST > POORLY
POORLY *adv* in a poor manner ▷ *adj* not in good health
POORMOUTH *vb* complain about being poor
POORNESS > POOR
POORT *n* (in South Africa) steep narrow mountain pass, usually following a river or stream
POORTITH *same as* > PUIRTITH
POORTITHS > POORTITH
POORTS > POORT
POORWILL *n* bird of N America
POORWILLS > POORWILL
POOS > POO
POOT *vb* break wind
POOTED > POOT
POOTER > POOT
POOTERS > POOT
POOTING > POOT
POOTLE *vb* travel or go in a relaxed or leisurely manner
POOTLED > POOTLE
POOTLES > POOTLE
POOTLING > POOTLE
POOTS > POOT
POOVE *same as* > POOF
POOVERIES > POOVERY
POOVERY *n* derogatory word for homosexuality
POOVES > POOVE
POOVIER > POOVE
POOVIEST > POOVE
POOVY > POOVE
POP *vb* make or cause to make a small explosive sound ▷ *n* small explosive sound ▷ *adj* popular
POPADUM *same as* > POPPADOM
POPADUMS > POPADUM
POPCORN *n* grains of maize heated until they puff up and burst
POPCORNS > POPCORN
POPE *n* bishop of Rome as head of the Roman Catholic Church
POPEDOM *n* office or dignity of a pope
POPEDOMS > POPEDOM
POPEHOOD > POPE
POPEHOODS > POPE
POPELESS > POPE
POPELIKE > POPE
POPELING *n* deputy or supporter of pope
POPELINGS > POPELING
POPERA *n* music drawing on opera or classical music and aiming for popular appeal
POPERAS > POPERA
POPERIES > POPERY
POPERIN *n* kind of pear
POPERINS > POPERIN
POPERY *n* derogatory word for Roman Catholicism
POPES > POPE
POPESEYE *adj* denoting a cut of steak
POPESHIP > POPE
POPESHIPS > POPE
POPETTE *n* young female fan or performer of pop music
POPETTES > POPETTE
POPEYED *adj* staring in astonishment
POPGUN *n* toy gun that fires a pellet or cork by means of compressed air
POPGUNS > POPGUN
POPINJAY *n* conceited, foppish, or overly talkative person
POPINJAYS > POPINJAY
POPISH *adj* derogatory word for Roman Catholic
POPISHLY > POPISH
POPJOY *vb* amuse oneself
POPJOYED > POPJOY
POPJOYING > POPJOY
POPJOYS > POPJOY
POPLAR *n* tall slender tree
POPLARS > POPLAR
POPLIN *n* ribbed cotton material
POPLINS > POPLIN
POPLITEAL *adj* of, relating to, or near the part of the leg behind the knee
POPLITEI > POPLITEUS
POPLITEUS *n* muscle in leg
POPLITIC *same as* > POPLITEAL
POPOVER *n* individual Yorkshire pudding, often served with roast beef
POPOVERS > POPOVER
POPPA *same as* > PAPA
POPPADOM *n* thin round crisp Indian bread
POPPADOMS > POPPADOM
POPPADUM *same as* > POPPADOM
POPPADUMS > POPPADUM
POPPAS > POPPA
POPPED > POP
POPPER *n* press stud
POPPERING *n* method of fishing
POPPERS > POPPER
POPPET *n* term of affection for a small child or sweetheart
POPPETS > POPPET
POPPIED *adj* covered with poppies
POPPIER > POPPY
POPPIES > POPPY
POPPIEST > POPPY
POPPING > POP
POPPISH *adj* like pop mus
POPPIT *n* bead used to form necklace
POPPITS > POPPIT
POPPLE *vb* (of boiling wat or a choppy sea) to heave or toss
POPPLED > POPPLE
POPPLES > POPPLE
POPPLIER > POPPLY
POPPLIEST > POPPLY
POPPLING > POPPLE
POPPLY *adj* covered in small bumps
POPPY *n* plant with a larg red flower ▷ *adj* reddish orange
POPPYCOCK *n* nonsense
POPPYHEAD *n* hard dry seed-containing capsule of a poppy
POPRIN *same as* > POPERIN
POPRINS > POPRIN
POPS > POP
POPSICLE *n* tradename f a kind of ice lolly
POPSICLES > POPSICLE
POPSIE *same as* > POPSY
POPSIES > POPSY
POPSTER *n* pop star
POPSTERS > POPSTER
POPSY *n* attractive young woman
POPULACE *n* ordinary people
POPULACES > POPULACE
POPULAR *adj* widely liked and admired ▷ *n* cheap newspapers with mass circulation
POPULARLY *adv* by the public as a whole
POPULARS > POPULAR
POPULATE *vb* live in, inhabit
POPULATED > POPULATE
POPULATES > POPULATE
POPULISM *n* political strategy based on a calculated appeal to the interests or prejudices o ordinary people
POPULISMS > POPULISM
POPULIST *adj* (person) appealing to the interes or prejudices of ordinary people ▷ *n* person, esp a politician, who appeals the interests or prejudic of ordinary people
POPULISTS > POPULIST
POPULOUS *adj* densely populated
PORAE *n* large edible sea fish of New Zealand wat
PORAES > PORAE
PORAL *adj* relating to por
PORANGI *adj* crazy
PORBEAGLE *n* kind of sha
PORCELAIN *n* fine china

ORCH *n* covered approach to the entrance of a building
ORCHES > PORCH
ORCINE *adj* of or like a pig
ORCINI > PORCINO
ORCINIS > PORCINO
ORCINO *n* edible woodland fungus
ORCUPINE *n* animal covered with long pointed quills
ORCUPINY > PORCUPINE
ORE *n* tiny opening in the skin or in the surface of a plant ▷ *vb* make a close intent examination or study (of a book, map, etc)
ORED > PORE
ORER *n* person who pores
ORERS > PORE
ORES > PORE
ORGE *vb* cleanse (slaughtered animal) ceremonially
ORGED > PORGE
ORGES > PORGE
ORGIE *same as* > PORGY
ORGIES > PORGY
ORGING > PORGE
ORGY *n* any of various sparid fishes, many of which occur in American Atlantic waters
ORIER > PORY
ORIEST > PORY
ORIFER *n* type of invertebrate
ORIFERAL > PORIFERAN
ORIFERAN *n* sponge ▷ *adj* of, relating to, or belonging to the phylum *Porifera*
ORIFERS > PORIFER
ORINA *n* larva of a moth which causes damage to grassland
ORINAS > PORINA
ORINESS > PORY
ORING > PORE
ORISM *n* type of mathematical proposition, the meaning of which is now obscure
ORISMS > PORISM
ORISTIC > PORISM
ORK *vb* (of eg a raven) make a croaking sound
ORKED > PORK
ORKER *n* pig raised for food
ORKERS > PORKER
ORKIER > PORKY
ORKIES > PORKY
ORKIEST > PORKY
ORKINESS > PORKY
ORKING > PORK
ORKLING *n* pig
ORKLINGS > PORKLING
ORKPIE *n* hat with a round flat crown and a brim that can be turned up or down
ORKPIES > PORKPIE
PORKS > PORK
PORKWOOD *n* wood of small American tree
PORKWOODS > PORKWOOD
PORKY *adj* of or like pork ▷ *n* lie
PORN *n* pornography
PORNIER > PORNY
PORNIEST > PORNY
PORNO *same as* > PORN
PORNOMAG *n* pornographic magazine
PORNOMAGS > PORNOMAG
PORNOS > PORNO
PORNS > PORN
PORNY *adj* pornographic
POROGAMIC > POROGAMY
POROGAMY *n* fertilization of seed plants
POROMERIC *adj* (of a plastic) permeable to water vapour ▷ *n* substance having this characteristic, esp one based on polyurethane and used in place of leather in making shoe uppers
POROSCOPE *n* instrument for assessing porosity
POROSCOPY > POROSCOPE
POROSE *adj* pierced with small pores
POROSES > POROSIS
POROSIS *n* porous condition of bones
POROSITY *n* state or condition of being porous
POROUS *adj* allowing liquid to pass through gradually
POROUSLY > POROUS
PORPESS *n* type of fish
PORPESSE *same as* > PORPOISE
PORPESSES > PORPESS
PORPHYRIA *n* hereditary disease of body metabolism, producing abdominal pain, mental confusion, etc
PORPHYRIC > PORPHYRIA
PORPHYRIN *n* any of a group of pigments occurring widely in animal and plant tissues and having a heterocyclic structure formed from four pyrrole rings linked by four methylene groups
PORPHYRIO *n* aquatic bird
PORPHYRY *n* reddish rock with large crystals in it
PORPOISE *n* fishlike sea mammal ▷ *vb* (of an aeroplane) nose-dive during landing
PORPOISED > PORPOISE
PORPOISES > PORPOISE
PORPORATE *adj* wearing purple
PORRECT *adj* extended forwards ▷ *vb* stretch forward
PORRECTED > PORRECT
PORRECTS > PORRECT
PORRENGER *same as* > PORRINGER
PORRIDGE *n* breakfast food made of oatmeal cooked in water or milk
PORRIDGES > PORRIDGE
PORRIDGY > PORRIDGE
PORRIGO *n* disease of the scalp
PORRIGOS > PORRIGO
PORRINGER *n* small dish, often with a handle, used esp formerly for soup or porridge
PORT *same as* > PORTHOLE
PORTA *n* aperture in an organ, such as the liver, esp one providing an opening for blood vessels
PORTABLE *adj* easily carried ▷ *n* article designed to be easily carried, such as a television or typewriter
PORTABLES > PORTABLE
PORTABLY > PORTABLE
PORTAGE *n* (route for) transporting boats and supplies overland between navigable waterways ▷ *vb* transport (boats and supplies) in this way
PORTAGED > PORTAGE
PORTAGES > PORTAGE
PORTAGING > PORTAGE
PORTAGUE *n* Portuguese gold coin
PORTAGUES > PORTAGUE
PORTAL *n* large imposing doorway or gate ▷ *adj* internet site providing links to other sites ▷ *vb* go from one internet portal to another
PORTALED > PORTAL
PORTALING > PORTAL
PORTALLED > PORTAL
PORTALS > PORTAL
PORTANCE *n* person's bearing
PORTANCES > PORTANCE
PORTAPACK *n* combined videotape recorder and camera
PORTAPAK *same as* > PORTAPACK
PORTAPAKS > PORTAPAK
PORTAS > PORTA
PORTASES *variant of* > PORTESSE
PORTATE *adj* diagonally athwart escutcheon
PORTATILE *adj* portable
PORTATIVE *adj* concerned with the act of carrying
PORTED > PORT
PORTEND *vb* be a sign of
PORTENDED > PORTEND
PORTENDS > PORTEND
PORTENT *n* sign of a future event
PORTENTS > PORTENT
PORTEOUS *variant of* > PORTESSE
PORTER *n* man who carries luggage ▷ *vb* carry luggage
PORTERAGE *n* work of carrying supplies, goods, etc, done by porters
PORTERED > PORTER
PORTERESS *n* female porter
PORTERING > PORTER
PORTERLY > PORTER
PORTERS > PORTER
PORTESS *variant of* > PORTESSE
PORTESSE *n* prayer book
PORTESSES > PORTESSE
PORTFIRE *n* (formerly) slow-burning fuse used for firing rockets and fireworks and, in mining, for igniting explosives
PORTFIRES > PORTFIRE
PORTFOLIO *n* (flat case for carrying) examples of an artist's work
PORTHOLE *n* small round window in a ship or aircraft
PORTHOLES > PORTHOLE
PORTHORS *same as* > PORTESSE
PORTHOSE *same as* > PORTESSE
PORTHOSES > PORTHOSE
PORTHOUSE *n* company producing port
PORTICO *n* porch or covered walkway with columns supporting the roof
PORTICOED > PORTICO
PORTICOES > PORTICO
PORTICOS > PORTICO
PORTIER > PORT
PORTIERE *n* curtain hung in a doorway
PORTIERED > PORTIERE
PORTIERES > PORTIERE
PORTIEST > PORT
PORTIGUE *same as* > PORTAGUE
PORTIGUES > PORTIGUE
PORTING > PORT
PORTION *n* part or share ▷ *vb* divide (something) into shares
PORTIONED > PORTION
PORTIONER > PORTION
PORTIONS > PORTION
PORTLAND *n* type of rose
PORTLANDS > PORTLAND
PORTLAST *n* gunwale of ship
PORTLASTS > PORTLAST
PORTLESS > PORT
PORTLIER > PORTLY
PORTLIEST > PORTLY
PORTLY *adj* rather fat
PORTMAN *n* inhabitant of port
PORTMEN > PORTMAN
PORTOISE *same as* > PORTLAST
PORTOISES > PORTOISE
PORTOLAN *n* book of sailing charts

PORTOLANI > PORTOLANO
PORTOLANO *variant of* > PORTOLAN
PORTOLANS > PORTOLAN
PORTOUS *variant of* > PORTESSE
PORTOUSES > PORTOUS
PORTRAIT *n* picture of a person ▷ *adj* (of a publication or an illustration in a publication) of greater height than width
PORTRAITS > PORTRAIT
PORTRAY *vb* describe or represent by artistic means, as in writing or film
PORTRAYAL > PORTRAY
PORTRAYED > PORTRAY
PORTRAYER > PORTRAY
PORTRAYS > PORTRAY
PORTREEVE *n* Saxon magistrate
PORTRESS *n* female porter, esp a doorkeeper
PORTS > PORT
PORTSIDE *adj* beside port
PORTULACA *n* tropical American plant with yellow, pink, or purple showy flowers
PORTULAN *same as* > PORTOLAN
PORTULANS > PORTULAN
PORTY *adj* like port
PORWIGGLE *n* tadpole
PORY *adj* containing pores
POS > PO
POSABLE > POSE
POSADA *n* inn in a Spanish-speaking country
POSADAS > POSADA
POSAUNE *n* organ chorus reed
POSAUNES > POSAUNE
POSE *vb* place in or take up a particular position to be photographed or drawn ▷ *n* position while posing
POSEABLE *adj* able to be manipulated into poses
POSED > POSE
POSER *n* puzzling question
POSERISH *same as* > POSEY
POSERS > POSER
POSES > POSE
POSEUR *n* person who behaves in an affected way to impress others
POSEURS > POSEUR
POSEUSE *n* female poseur
POSEUSES > POSEUSE
POSEY *adj* (of a place) for, characteristic of, or full of posers
POSH *adj* smart, luxurious ▷ *adv* in a manner associated with the upper class ▷ *vb* make posh
POSHED > POSH
POSHER > POSH
POSHES > POSH
POSHEST > POSH
POSHING > POSH
POSHLY > POSH
POSHNESS > POSH
POSHO *n* corn meal
POSHOS > POSHO
POSHTEEN *same as* > POSTEEN
POSHTEENS > POSHTEEN
POSIER > POSY
POSIES > POSY
POSIEST > POSY
POSIGRADE *n* auxiliary rocket for space craft
POSING > POSE
POSINGLY > POSE
POSINGS > POSE
POSIT *vb* lay down as a basis for argument ▷ *n* fact, idea, etc, that is posited
POSITED > POSIT
POSITIF *n* (on older organs) manual controlling soft stops
POSITIFS > POSITIF
POSITING > POSIT
POSITION *n* place ▷ *vb* place
POSITIONS > POSITION
POSITIVE *same as* > PLUS
POSITIVER > POSITIVE
POSITIVES > POSITIVE
POSITON *n* part of chromosome
POSITONS > POSITON
POSITRON *n* particle with same mass as electron but positive charge
POSITRONS > POSITRON
POSITS > POSIT
POSNET *n* small basin or dish
POSNETS > POSNET
POSOLE *n* hominy
POSOLES > POSOLE
POSOLOGIC > POSOLOGY
POSOLOGY *n* branch of medicine concerned with the determination of appropriate doses of drugs or agents
POSS *vb* wash (clothes) by agitating them with a long rod, pole, etc
POSSE *n* group of men organized to maintain law and order
POSSED > POSS
POSSER *n* short stick used for stirring clothes in a washtub
POSSERS > POSSER
POSSES > POSSE
POSSESS *vb* have as one's property
POSSESSED *adj* owning or having
POSSESSES > POSSESS
POSSESSOR > POSSESS
POSSET *n* drink of hot milk curdled with ale, beer, etc, flavoured with spices, formerly used as a remedy for colds ▷ *vb* treat with a posset
POSSETED > POSSET
POSSETING > POSSET
POSSETS > POSSET
POSSIBLE *adj* able to exist, happen, or be done ▷ *n* person or thing that might be suitable or chosen
POSSIBLER > POSSIBLE
POSSIBLES > POSSIBLE
POSSIBLY *adv* perhaps, not necessarily
POSSIE *n* place
POSSIES > POSSIE
POSSING > POSS
POSSUM *vb* pretend to be dead, asleep, ignorant, etc, to deceive an opponent
POSSUMED > POSSUM
POSSUMING > POSSUM
POSSUMS > POSSUM
POST *n* official system of delivering letters and parcels ▷ *vb* send by post
POSTAGE *n* charge for sending a letter or parcel by post
POSTAGES > POSTAGE
POSTAL *adj* of a Post Office or the mail-delivery service
POSTALLY > POSTAL
POSTANAL *adj* behind the anus
POSTAXIAL *adj* situated or occurring behind the axis of the body
POSTBAG *n* postman's bag
POSTBAGS > POSTBAG
POSTBASE *adv* (in linguistics) coming immediately after a base word
POSTBOX *n* box into which mail is put for collection by the postal service
POSTBOXES > POSTBOX
POSTBOY *n* man or boy who brings the post round to offices
POSTBOYS > POSTBOY
POSTBURN *adj* after injury from burns
POSTBUS *n* (in Britain, esp in rural districts) vehicle carrying the mail that also carries passengers
POSTBUSES > POSTBUS
POSTCARD *n* card for sending a message by post without an envelope
POSTCARDS > POSTCARD
POSTCAVA *n* inferior vena cava
POSTCAVAE > POSTCAVA
POSTCAVAL > POSTCAVA
POSTCAVAS > POSTCAVA
POSTCODE *n* system of letters and numbers used to aid the sorting of mail ▷ *vb* put a postcode on a letter
POSTCODED > POSTCODE
POSTCODES > POSTCODE
POSTCOUP *adj* after coup
POSTCRASH *adj* after a crash
POSTDATE *vb* write a date on (a cheque) that is later than the actual date
POSTDATED > POSTDATE
POSTDATES > POSTDATE
POSTDIVE *adj* following a dive
POSTDOC *n* postdoctoral degree
POSTDOCS > POSTDOC
POSTDRUG *adj* of time afte drug has been taken
POSTED > POST
POSTEEN *n* Afghan leathe jacket
POSTEENS > POSTEEN
POSTER *n* large picture or notice stuck on a wall ▷ v cover with posters
POSTERED > POSTER
POSTERING > POSTER
POSTERIOR *n* buttocks ▷ *adj* behind, at the back
POSTERITY *n* future generations, descendant
POSTERN *n* small back doo or gate ▷ *adj* situated at the rear or the side
POSTERNS > POSTERN
POSTERS > POSTER
POSTFACE *n* note added t the end of a text
POSTFACES > POSTFACE
POSTFAULT *adj* after a fau
POSTFIRE *adj* of the perio after a fire
POSTFIX *vb* add or appen at the end of something
POSTFIXAL > POSTFIX
POSTFIXED > POSTFIX
POSTFIXES > POSTFIX
POSTFORM *vb* mould or shape (plastic) while it h from reheating
POSTFORMS > POSTFORM
POSTGAME *adj* of period after sports match
POSTGRAD *n* graduate taking further degree
POSTGRADS > POSTGRAD
POSTHASTE *adv* with grea speed ▷ *n* great haste
POSTHEAT *n* industrial heating process
POSTHEATS > POSTHEAT
POSTHOLE *n* hole dug in ground to hold fence pos
POSTHOLES > POSTHOLE
POSTHORSE *n* horse kept a an inn or posthouse for u by postriders or for hire t travellers
POSTHOUSE *n* house or in where horses were kept for postriders or for hire t travellers
POSTICAL *adj* (of the position of plant parts) behind another part
POSTICHE *adj* (of architectural ornament)

inappropriately applied > n imitation, counterfeit, or substitute
OSTICHES > POSTICHE
OSTICOUS same as > POSTICAL
OSTIE n postman
OSTIES > POSTIE
OSTIL n commentary or marginal note, as in a Bible ▷ vb annotate (a biblical passage)
OSTILED > POSTIL
OSTILING > POSTIL
OSTILION n person riding one of a pair of horses drawing a carriage
OSTILLED > POSTIL
OSTILLER > POSTIL
OSTILS > POSTIL
OSTIN variant of > POSTEEN
OSTING n job to which someone is assigned by his or her employer which involves moving to a particular town or country
OSTINGS > POSTING
OSTINS > POSTIN
OSTIQUE variant of > POSTICHE
OSTIQUES > POSTIQUE
OSTLUDE n final or concluding piece or movement
OSTLUDES > POSTLUDE
OSTMAN n person who collects and delivers post
OSTMARK n official mark stamped on letters showing place and date of posting ▷ vb put such a mark on (mail)
OSTMARKS > POSTMARK
OSTMEN > POSTMAN
OSTNASAL adj situated at the back of the nose
OSTNATAL adj occurring after childbirth
OSTNATI n those born in Scotland after its union with England
OSTOP n person recovering from surgery
OSTOPS > POSTOP
OSTORAL adj situated at the back of the mouth
OSTPAID adj with the postage prepaid
OSTPONE vb put off to a later time
OSTPONED > POSTPONE
OSTPONER > POSTPONE
OSTPONES > POSTPONE
OSTPOSE vb place (word or phrase) after other constituents in sentence
OSTPOSED > POSTPOSE
OSTPOSES > POSTPOSE
OSTPUNK adj (of pop music) belonging to a style that followed punk rock
OSTRACE adj of the period after a race
POSTRIDER *n* (formerly) person who delivered post on horseback
POSTRIOT *adj* of the period after a riot
POSTS > POST
POSTSHOW *adj* of the period after a show
POSTSYNC *vb* add a sound recording to (and synchronize with) an existing video or film recording
POSTSYNCS > POSTSYNC
POSTTAX *adj* of the period after tax is paid
POSTTEEN *n* young adult
POSTTEENS > POSTTEEN
POSTTEST *n* test taken after a lesson
POSTTESTS > POSTTEST
POSTTRIAL *adj* of the period after a trial
POSTULANT *n* candidate for admission to a religious order
POSTULATA *n* things postulated
POSTULATE *vb* assume to be true as the basis of an argument or theory ▷ *n* something postulated
POSTURAL > POSTURE
POSTURE *n* position or way in which someone stands, walks, etc ▷ *vb* behave in an exaggerated way to get attention
POSTURED > POSTURE
POSTURER > POSTURE
POSTURERS > POSTURE
POSTURES > POSTURE
POSTURING > POSTURE
POSTURISE *same as* > POSTURIZE
POSTURIST > POSTURE
POSTURIZE *less common word for* > POSTURE
POSTVIRAL as in *postviral syndrome* debilitating condition occurring as a sequel to viral illness
POSTWAR *adj* occurring or existing after a war
POSTWOMAN *n* woman who carries and delivers mail as a profession
POSTWOMEN > POSTWOMAN
POSY *n* small bunch of flowers
POT *n* round deep container ▷ *vb* plant in a pot
POTABLE *adj* drinkable ▷ *n* something fit to drink
POTABLES > POTABLE
POTAE *n* hat
POTAES > POTAE
POTAGE *n* thick soup
POTAGER *n* small kitchen garden
POTAGERS > POTAGER
POTAGES > POTAGE
POTAMIC *adj* of or relating to rivers
POTASH *n* white powdery substance obtained from ashes and used as fertilizer ▷ *vb* treat with potash
POTASHED > POTASH
POTASHES > POTASH
POTASHING > POTASH
POTASS *abbreviated form of* > POTASSIUM
POTASSA *n* potassium oxide
POTASSAS > POTASSA
POTASSES > POTASS
POTASSIC > POTASSIUM
POTASSIUM *n* silvery metallic element
POTATION *n* act of drinking
POTATIONS > POTATION
POTATO *n* roundish starchy vegetable that grows underground
POTATOBUG *n* Colorado beetle
POTATOES > POTATO
POTATORY *adj* of, relating to, or given to drinking
POTBELLY *n* bulging belly
POTBOIL *vb* boil in a pot
POTBOILED > POTBOIL
POTBOILER *n* inferior work of art produced quickly to make money
POTBOILS > POTBOIL
POTBOUND *adj* (of plant) unable to grow because pot is too small
POTBOY *n* (esp formerly) youth or man employed at a public house to serve beer, etc
POTBOYS > POTBOY
POTCH *n* inferior quality opal used in jewellery for mounting precious opals
POTCHE *vb* stab
POTCHED > POTCHE
POTCHER > POTCHE
POTCHERS > POTCHE
POTCHES > POTCH
POTCHING > POTCHE
POTE *vb* push
POTED > POTE
POTEEN *n* (in Ireland) illegally made alcoholic drink
POTEENS > POTEEN
POTENCE *same as* > POTENCY
POTENCES > POTENCE
POTENCIES > POTENCY
POTENCY *n* state or quality of being potent
POTENT *adj* having great power or influence ▷ *n* potentate or ruler
POTENTATE *n* ruler or monarch
POTENTIAL *adj* possible but not yet actual ▷ *n* ability or talent not yet fully used
POTENTISE *same as* > POTENTIZE
POTENTIZE *vb* make more potent
POTENTLY > POTENT
POTENTS > POTENT
POTES > POTE
POTFUL *n* amount held by a pot
POTFULS > POTFUL
POTGUN *n* pot-shaped mortar
POTGUNS > POTGUN
POTHEAD *n* habitual user of cannabis
POTHEADS > POTHEAD
POTHECARY *n* pharmacist
POTHEEN *rare variant of* > POTEEN
POTHEENS > POTHEEN
POTHER *n* fuss or commotion ▷ *vb* make or be troubled or upset
POTHERB *n* plant whose leaves, flowers, or stems are used in cooking
POTHERBS > POTHERB
POTHERED > POTHER
POTHERING > POTHER
POTHERS > POTHER
POTHERY *adj* stuffy
POTHOLDER *n* piece of material used to protect hands while lifting pot from oven
POTHOLE *n* hole in the surface of a road
POTHOLED > POTHOLE
POTHOLER > POTHOLING
POTHOLERS > POTHOLING
POTHOLES > POTHOLE
POTHOLING *n* sport of exploring underground caves
POTHOOK *n* S-shaped hook for suspending a pot over a fire
POTHOOKS > POTHOOK
POTHOS *n* climbing plant
POTHOUSE *n* (formerly) small tavern or pub
POTHOUSES > POTHOUSE
POTHUNTER *n* person who hunts for food or for profit without regard to the rules of sport
POTICARY *obsolete spelling of* > POTHECARY
POTICHE *n* tall vase or jar, as of porcelain, with a round or polygonal body that narrows towards the neck and a detached lid or cover
POTICHES > POTICHE
POTIN *n* bronze alloy with high tin content
POTING > POTE
POTINS > POTIN
POTION *n* dose of medicine or poison
POTIONS > POTION
POTLACH *same as* > POTLATCH
POTLACHE *same as* > POTLATCH
POTLACHES > POTLACHE
POTLATCH *n* competitive

ceremonial activity among certain North American Indians
POTLIKE > POT
POTLINE *n* row of electrolytic cells for reducing metals
POTLINES > POTLINE
POTLUCK *n* whatever food happens to be available without special preparation
POTLUCKS > POTLUCK
POTMAN *same as* > POTBOY
POTMEN > POTMAN
POTOMETER *n* apparatus that measures the rate of water uptake by a plant or plant part
POTOO *n* nocturnal tropical bird
POTOOS > POTOO
POTOROO *n* Australian leaping rodent
POTOROOS > POTOROO
POTPIE *n* meat and vegetable stew with a pie crust on top
POTPIES > POTPIE
POTPOURRI *n* fragrant mixture of dried flower petals
POTS > POT
POTSHARD *same as* > POTSHERD
POTSHARDS > POTSHARD
POTSHARE *same as* > POTSHERD
POTSHARES > POTSHARE
POTSHERD *n* broken fragment of pottery
POTSHERDS > POTSHERD
POTSHOP *n* public house
POTSHOPS > POTSHOP
POTSHOT *n* chance shot taken casually, hastily, or without careful aim
POTSHOTS > POTSHOT
POTSIE *same as* > POTSY
POTSIES > POTSY
POTSTONE *n* impure massive variety of soapstone, formerly used for making cooking vessels
POTSTONES > POTSTONE
POTSY *n* hopscotch
POTT *old variant of* > POT
POTTAGE *n* thick soup or stew
POTTAGES > POTTAGE
POTTED > POT
POTTEEN *same as* > POTEEN
POTTEENS > POTTEEN
POTTER *same as* > PUTTER
POTTERED > POTTER
POTTERER > POTTER
POTTERERS > POTTER
POTTERIES > POTTERY
POTTERING > POTTER
POTTERS > POTTER
POTTERY *n* articles made from baked clay
POTTIER > POTTY
POTTIES > POTTY
POTTIEST > POTTY
POTTINESS > POTTY
POTTING > POT
POTTINGAR *same as* > POTTINGER
POTTINGER *n* apothecary
POTTLE *n* liquid measure equal to half a gallon
POTTLES > POTTLE
POTTO *n* short-tailed prosimian primate
POTTOS > POTTO
POTTS > POTT
POTTY *adj* crazy or silly ▷ *n* bowl used by a small child as a toilet
POTWALLER *n* man entitled to the franchise before 1832 by virtue of possession of his own fireplace
POTZER *same as* > PATZER
POTZERS > POTZER
POUCH *n* small bag ▷ *vb* place in or as if in a pouch
POUCHED > POUCH
POUCHES > POUCH
POUCHFUL *n* amount a pouch will hold
POUCHFULS > POUCHFUL
POUCHIER > POUCH
POUCHIEST > POUCH
POUCHING > POUCH
POUCHY > POUCH
POUDER *obsolete spelling of* > POWDER
POUDERS > POUDER
POUDRE *old spelling of* > POWDER
POUDRES > POUDRE
POUF *n* large solid cushion used as a seat ▷ *vb* pile up hair into rolled puffs
POUFED > POUF
POUFFE *same as* > POUF
POUFFED > POUFFE
POUFFES > POUFFE
POUFFING > POUFFE
POUFFS > POUFFE
POUFFY *same as* > POOFY
POUFING > POUF
POUFS > POUF
POUFTAH *same as* > POOFTER
POUFTAHS > POUFTAH
POUFTER *same as* > POOFTER
POUFTERS > POUFTER
POUK *Scots variant of* > POKE
POUKE *n* mischievous spirit
POUKED > POUK
POUKES > POUKE
POUKING > POUK
POUKIT > POUK
POUKS > POUK
POULAINE *n* tapering toe of shoe
POULAINES > POULAINE
POULARD *n* hen that has been spayed for fattening
POULARDE *same as* > POULARD
POULARDES > POULARDE
POULARDS > POULARD
POULDER *obsolete spelling of* > POWDER
POULDERED > POULDER
POULDERS > POULDER
POULDRE *archaic spelling of* > POWDER
POULDRES > POULDRE
POULDRON *same as* > PAULDRON
POULDRONS > POULDRON
POULE *n* fowl suitable for slow stewing
POULES > POULE
POULP *n* octopus
POULPE *variant of* > POULP
POULPES > POULPE
POULPS > POULP
POULT *n* young of a gallinaceous bird, esp of domestic fowl
POULTER *n* poultry dealer
POULTERER *same as* > POULTER
POULTERS > POULTER
POULTICE *n* moist dressing, often heated, applied to inflamed skin ▷ *vb* apply poultice to
POULTICED > POULTICE
POULTICES > POULTICE
POULTRIES > POULTRY
POULTRY *n* domestic fowls
POULTS > POULT
POUNCE *vb* spring upon suddenly to attack or capture ▷ *n* pouncing
POUNCED > POUNCE
POUNCER > POUNCE
POUNCERS > POUNCE
POUNCES > POUNCE
POUNCET *n* box with a perforated top used for perfume
POUNCETS > POUNCET
POUNCHING *old variant of* > PUNCHING
POUNCING > POUNCE
POUND *n* monetary unit of Britain and some other countries ▷ *vb* hit heavily and repeatedly
POUNDAGE *n* charge of so much per pound of weight or sterling
POUNDAGES > POUNDAGE
POUNDAL *n* fps unit of force
POUNDALS > POUNDAL
POUNDCAKE *n* cake containing a pound of each ingredient
POUNDED > POUND
POUNDER > POUND
POUNDERS > POUND
POUNDING > POUND
POUNDS > POUND
POUPE *vb* make sudden blowing sound
POUPED > POUPE
POUPES > POUPE
POUPING > POUPE
POUPT > POUPE
POUR *vb* flow or cause to flow out in a stream
POURABLE > POUR
POURBOIRE *n* tip or gratuity
POURED > POUR
POURER > POUR
POURERS > POUR
POURIE *n* jug
POURIES > POURIE
POURING > POUR
POURINGLY > POUR
POURINGS > POUR
POURPOINT *n* man's stuffe quilted doublet of a kind worn between the Middl Ages and the 17th century
POURS > POUR
POURSEW *obsolete spelling of* > PURSUE
POURSEWED > POURSEW
POURSEWS > POURSEW
POURSUE *obsolete spelling of* > PURSUE
POURSUED > PURSUE
POURSUES > POURSUE
POURSUING > POURSUE
POURSUIT *same as* > PURSUIT
POURSUITS > POURSUIT
POURTRAY *obsolete spelling of* > PORTRAY
POURTRAYD > POURTRAY
POURTRAYS > POURTRAY
POUSOWDIE *n* Scottish ste made from sheep's head
POUSSE *same as* > PEASE
POUSSES > POUSSE
POUSSETTE *n* figure in country dancing in whicl couples hold hands and move up or down the set to change positions ▷ *vb* perform such a figure
POUSSIE *old variant of* > PUSSY
POUSSIES > POUSSIE
POUSSIN *n* young chicken reared for eating
POUSSINS > POUSSIN
POUT *vb* thrust out one's lips, look sulky ▷ *n* pouting look
POUTED > POUT
POUTER *n* pigeon that can puff out its crop
POUTERS > POUTER
POUTFUL *adj* tending to pout
POUTHER *Scots variant of* > POWDER
POUTHERED > POUTHER
POUTHERS > POUTHER
POUTIER > POUT
POUTIEST > POUT
POUTINE *n* dish of chippe potatoes topped with cu cheese and a tomato-based sauce
POUTINES > POUTINE
POUTING > POUT
POUTINGLY > POUT
POUTINGS > POUT
POUTS > POUT
POUTY > POUT
POVERTIES > POVERTY
POVERTY *n* state of being without enough food or money
POW *interj* exclamation to

ndicate that a collision or
explosion has taken place
▷ *n* head or a head of hair
WAN *n* freshwater
whitefish, *Coregonus
lupeoides*, occurring in
some Scottish lakes
WANS > POWAN
WDER *n* substance in the
form of tiny loose particles
▷ *vb* apply powder to
WDERED > POWDER
WDERER > POWDER
WDERERS > POWDER
WDERIER > POWDER
WDERING > POWDER
WDERS > POWDER
WDERY > POWDER
WELLISE > POWELLIZE
WELLITE *n* type of
mineral
WELLIZE *vb* treat wood
with a sugar solution
WER *n* ability to do or
act ▷ *vb* give or provide
power to
WERBOAT *n* fast powerful
motorboat
WERED > POWER
WERFUL *adj* having great
power or influence ▷ *adv*
extremely
WERING > POWER
WERLESS *adj* without
power or authority
WERPLAY *n* behaviour
intended to maximise
person's power
WERS > POWER
WFAGGED *adj* exhausted
WHIRI *n* Māori
ceremony of welcome, esp
to a marae
WHIRIS > POWHIRI
WIN *n* peacock
WINS > POWIN
WN *variant of* > POWIN
WND *obsolete spelling
of* > POUND
WNDED > POWND
WNDING > POWND
WNDS > POWND
WNEY *old Scots spelling
of* > PONY
WNEYS > POWNEY
WNIE *old Scots spelling
of* > PONY
WNIES > POWNIE
WNS > POWN
WNY *old Scots spelling
of* > PONY
WRE *obsolete spelling
of* > POWER
WRED > POWRE
WRES > POWRE
WRING > POWRE
WS > POW
WSOWDY *same
as* > POUSOWDIE
WTER *same as* > POUTER
WTERS > POWTER
WWAW *n* Algonquian
priest
WWAWS > POWWAW

POWWOW *n* talk or conference ▷ *vb* hold a powwow
POWWOWED > POWWOW
POWWOWING > POWWOW
POWWOWS > POWWOW
POX *n* disease in which skin pustules form ▷ *vb* infect with pox
POXED > POX
POXES > POX
POXIER > POXY
POXIEST > POXY
POXING > POX
POXVIRUS *n* virus such as smallpox
POXY *adj* having or having had syphilis
POYNANT *old variant of* > POIGNANT
POYNT *obsolete spelling of* > POINT
POYNTED > POYNT
POYNTING > POYNT
POYNTS > POYNT
POYOU *n* type of armadillo
POYOUS > POYOU
POYSE *obsolete variant of* > POISE
POYSED > POYSE
POYSES > POYSE
POYSING > POYSE
POYSON *obsolete spelling of* > POISON
POYSONED > POYSON
POYSONING > POYSON
POYSONS > POYSON
POZ *adj* positive
POZOLE *same as* > POSOLE
POZOLES > POZOLE
POZZ *adj* positive
POZZIES > POZZY
POZZOLAN *same as* > POZZOLANA
POZZOLANA *n* type of porous volcanic ash
POZZOLANS > POZZOLAN
POZZY *same as* > POSSIE
PRAAM *same as* > PRAM
PRAAMS > PRAAM
PRABBLE *variant of* > BRABBLE
PRABBLES > PRABBLE
PRACHARAK *n* (in India) person appointed to propagate a cause through personal contact, meetings, public lectures, etc
PRACTIC *adj* practical
PRACTICAL *adj* involving experience or actual use rather than theory ▷ *n* examination in which something has to be done or made
PRACTICE *same as* > PRACTISE
PRACTICED > PRACTICE
PRACTICER > PRACTICE
PRACTICES > PRACTICE
PRACTICK *obsolete word for* > PRACTICE
PRACTICKS > PRACTICK

PRACTICUM *n* course in which theory is put into practice
PRACTIQUE *variant of* > PRACTIC
PRACTISE *vb* do repeatedly so as to gain skill
PRACTISED > PRACTISE
PRACTISER > PRACTISE
PRACTISES > PRACTISE
PRACTIVE *obsolete word for* > ACTIVE
PRACTOLOL *n* type of drug
PRAD *n* horse
PRADS > PRAD
PRAEAMBLE *same as* > PREAMBLE
PRAECIPE *n* written request addressed to court
PRAECIPES > PRAECIPE
PRAECOCES *n* division of birds whose young are able to run when first hatched
PRAEDIAL *adj* of or relating to land, farming, etc
PRAEFECT *same as* > PREFECT
PRAEFECTS > PRAEFECT
PRAELECT *same as* > PRAELECT
PRAELECTS > PRAELECT
PRAELUDIA *n* musical preludes
PRAENOMEN *n* ancient Roman's first or given name
PRAESES *n* Roman governor
PRAESIDIA *n* presidiums
PRAETOR *n* (in ancient Rome) senior magistrate ranking just below the consuls
PRAETORS > PRAETOR
PRAGMATIC *adj* concerned with practical consequences rather than theory
PRAHU *same as* > PROA
PRAHUS > PRAHU
PRAIRIE *n* large treeless area of grassland, esp in N America and Canada
PRAIRIES > PRAIRIE
PRAISE *vb* express approval or admiration of (someone or something) ▷ *n* something said or written to show approval or admiration
PRAISEACH *n* type of porridge
PRAISED > PRAISE
PRAISEFUL > PRAISE
PRAISER > PRAISE
PRAISERS > PRAISE
PRAISES > PRAISE
PRAISING > PRAISE
PRAISINGS > PRAISE
PRAJNA *n* wisdom or understanding considered as the goal of Buddhist contemplation

PRAJNAS > PRAJNA
PRALINE *n* sweet made of nuts and caramelized sugar
PRALINES > PRALINE
PRAM *n* four-wheeled carriage for a baby, pushed by hand
PRAMS > PRAM
PRANA *n* (in Oriental medicine, martial arts, etc) cosmic energy believed to come from the sun and connecting the elements of the universe
PRANAS > PRANA
PRANAYAMA *n* breath control in yoga
PRANCE *vb* walk with exaggerated bouncing steps ▷ *n* act of prancing
PRANCED > PRANCE
PRANCER > PRANCE
PRANCERS > PRANCE
PRANCES > PRANCE
PRANCING > PRANCE
PRANCINGS > PRANCE
PRANCK *obsolete variant of* > PRANK
PRANCKE *obsolete variant of* > PRANK
PRANCKED > PRANCK
PRANCKES > PRANCKE
PRANCKING > PRANCK
PRANCKS > PRANCK
PRANDIAL *adj* of or relating to a meal
PRANG *n* crash in a car or aircraft ▷ *vb* crash or damage (an aircraft or car)
PRANGED > PRANG
PRANGING > PRANG
PRANGS > PRANG
PRANK *n* mischievous trick ▷ *vb* dress or decorate showily or gaudily
PRANKED > PRANK
PRANKFUL > PRANK
PRANKIER > PRANK
PRANKIEST > PRANK
PRANKING > PRANK
PRANKINGS > PRANK
PRANKISH > PRANK
PRANKLE *obsolete variant of* > PRANCE
PRANKLED > PRANKLE
PRANKLES > PRANKLE
PRANKLING > PRANKLE
PRANKS > PRANK
PRANKSOME > PRANK
PRANKSTER *n* practical joker
PRANKY > PRANK
PRAO *same as* > PROA
PRAOS > PRAO
PRASE *n* light green translucent variety of chalcedony
PRASES > PRASE
PRAT *n* stupid person
PRATE *vb* talk idly and at length ▷ *n* chatter
PRATED > PRATE
PRATER > PRATE

PRATERS > PRATE
PRATES > PRATE
PRATFALL *n* fall upon one's buttocks
PRATFALLS > PRATFALL
PRATIE *n* potato
PRATIES > PRATIE
PRATING > PRATE
PRATINGLY > PRATE
PRATINGS > PRATE
PRATIQUE *n* formal permission given to a vessel to use a foreign port upon satisfying the requirements of local health authorities
PRATIQUES > PRATIQUE
PRATS > PRAT
PRATT *n* buttocks
PRATTLE *vb* chatter in a childish or foolish way ▷ *n* childish or foolish talk
PRATTLED > PRATTLE
PRATTLER > PRATTLE
PRATTLERS > PRATTLE
PRATTLES > PRATTLE
PRATTLING > PRATTLE
PRATY *obsolete variant of* > PRETTY
PRAU *same as* > PROA
PRAUNCE *obsolete variant of* > PRANCE
PRAUNCED > PRAUNCE
PRAUNCES > PRAUNCE
PRAUNCING > PRAUNCE
PRAUS > PRAU
PRAVITIES > PRAVITY
PRAVITY *n* moral degeneracy
PRAWLE *n* Shakespearian phonetic spelling of "brawl" meant to indicate that the speaker is Welsh
PRAWLES > PRAWLE
PRAWLIN *variant of* > PRALINE
PRAWLINS > PRAWLIN
PRAWN *n* edible shellfish like a large shrimp ▷ *vb* catch prawns
PRAWNED > PRAWN
PRAWNER > PRAWN
PRAWNERS > PRAWN
PRAWNING > PRAWN
PRAWNS > PRAWN
PRAXES > PRAXIS
PRAXIS *n* practice as opposed to theory
PRAXISES > PRAXIS
PRAY *vb* say prayers ▷ *adv* I beg you ▷ *interj* I beg you
PRAYED > PRAY
PRAYER *n* thanks or appeal addressed to one's God
PRAYERFUL *adj* inclined to or characterized by prayer
PRAYERS > PRAYER
PRAYING > PRAY
PRAYINGS > PRAY
PRAYS > PRAY
PRE *prep* before
PREABSORB *vb* absorb beforehand
PREACCUSE *vb* accuse beforehand
PREACE *obsolete variant of* > PRESS
PREACED > PREACE
PREACES > PREACE
PREACH *vb* give a talk on a religious theme as part of a church service
PREACHED > PREACH
PREACHER *n* person who preaches, esp in church
PREACHERS > PREACHER
PREACHES > PREACH
PREACHIER > PREACHY
PREACHIFY *vb* preach or moralize in a tedious manner
PREACHILY > PREACHY
PREACHING > PREACH
PREACHY *adj* inclined to or marked by preaching
PREACING > PREACE
PREACT *vb* act beforehand
PREACTED > PREACT
PREACTING > PREACT
PREACTS > PREACT
PREADAMIC *adj* of or relating to the belief that there were people on earth before Adam
PREADAPT *vb* adapt beforehand
PREADAPTS > PREADAPT
PREADJUST *vb* adjust beforehand
PREADMIT *vb* prepare patient prior to treatment
PREADMITS > PREADMIT
PREADULT *n* animal or person who has not reached adulthood
PREADULTS > PREADULT
PREAGED *adj* treated to appear older
PREALLOT *vb* allot beforehand
PREALLOTS > PREALLOT
PREALTER *vb* alter beforehand
PREALTERS > PREALTER
PREAMBLE *n* introductory part to something said or written ▷ *vb* write a preamble
PREAMBLED > PREAMBLE
PREAMBLES > PREAMBLE
PREAMP *n* electronic amplifier used to improve the signal-to-noise ratio of an electronic device
PREAMPS > PREAMP
PREANAL *adj* situated in front of anus
PREAPPLY *vb* apply beforehand
PREARM *vb* arm beforehand
PREARMED > PREARM
PREARMING > PREARM
PREARMS > PREARM
PREASE *vb* crowd or press
PREASED > PREASE
PREASES > PREASE
PREASING > PREASE
PREASSE *obsolete spelling of* > PRESS
PREASSED > PREASSE
PREASSES > PREASSE
PREASSIGN *vb* assign beforehand
PREASSING > PREASSE
PREASSURE *vb* assure beforehand
PREATOMIC *adj* before the atomic age
PREATTUNE *vb* attune beforehand
PREAUDIT *vb* examine contracts before a transaction
PREAUDITS > PREAUDIT
PREAVER *vb* aver in advance
PREAVERS > PREAVER
PREAXIAL *adj* situated or occurring in front of the axis of the body
PREBADE > PREBID
PREBAKE *vb* bake before further cooking
PREBAKED > PREBAKE
PREBAKES > PREBAKE
PREBAKING > PREBAKE
PREBASAL > PREBASE
PREBASE *n* part of tongue lying anterior to base
PREBATTLE *adj* of the period before a battle
PREBEND *n* allowance paid by a cathedral or collegiate church to a canon or member of the chapter
PREBENDAL > PREBEND
PREBENDS > PREBEND
PREBID *vb* bid beforehand
PREBIDDEN > PREBID
PREBIDS > PREBID
PREBILL *vb* issue an invoice before the service has been provided
PREBILLED > PREBILL
PREBILLS > PREBILL
PREBIND *n* book that has been previously bound
PREBINDS > PREBIND
PREBIOTIC *adj* of the period before the existence of life on earth
PREBIRTH *n* period of life before birth
PREBIRTHS > PREBIRTH
PREBLESS *vb* bless a couple before they marry
PREBOARD *vb* board an aircraft before other passengers
PREBOARDS > PREBOARD
PREBOIL *vb* boil beforehand
PREBOILED > PREBOIL
PREBOILS > PREBOIL
PREBOOK *vb* book well in advance
PREBOOKED > PREBOOK
PREBOOKS > PREBOOK
PREBOOM *adj* of the period before an economic boom
PREBORN *adj* unborn
PREBOUGHT > PREBUY
PREBOUND *adj* previously bound
PREBUDGET *adj* before budget
PREBUILD *vb* build beforehand
PREBUILDS > PREBUILD
PREBUILT > PREBUILD
PREBUTTAL *n* prepared response to an anticipat criticism
PREBUY *vb* buy in advance
PREBUYING > PREBUY
PREBUYS > PREBUY
PRECANCEL *vb* cancel (postage stamps) before placing them on mail ▷ *n* precancelled stamp
PRECANCER *n* condition that may develop into cancer
PRECAST *adj* (esp of concrete when employec as a structural element in building) cast in a particular form before being used ▷ *vb* cast (concrete) in a particular form before use
PRECASTS > PRECAST
PRECATIVE *same as* > PRECATORY
PRECATORY *adj* of, involving, or expressing entreaty
PRECAUDAL *adj* in front of the caudal fin
PRECAVA *n* superior vena cava
PRECAVAE > PRECAVA
PRECAVAL > PRECAVA
PRECEDE *vb* go or be befo
PRECEDED > PRECEDE
PRECEDENT *n* previous ca or occurrence regarded a an example to be followe ▷ *adj* preceding
PRECEDES > PRECEDE
PRECEDING *adj* going or coming before
PRECEESE *Scots variant of* > PRECISE
PRECENSOR *vb* censor (a film, play, book, etc) befo its publication
PRECENT *vb* issue a command or law
PRECENTED > PRECENT
PRECENTOR *n* person whc leads the singing in a church
PRECENTS > PRECENT
PRECEPIT *old word for* > PRECIPICE
PRECEPITS > PRECEPIT
PRECEPT *n* rule of behaviour
PRECEPTOR *n* instructor
PRECEPTS > PRECEPT
PRECESS *vb* undergo or cause to undergo precession
PRECESSED > PRECESS
PRECESSES > PRECESS
PRECHARGE *vb* charge

eforehand
ECHECK *vb* check
eforehand
ECHECKS > PRECHECK
ECHILL *vb* chill
eforehand
ECHILLS > PRECHILL
ECHOOSE *vb* choose in
dvance
ECHOSE > PRECHOOSE
ECHOSEN > PRECHOOSE
ECIEUSE *n* pretentious
emale
ECINCT *n* area in a town
losed to traffic
ECINCTS *pl n*
urrounding region
ECIOUS *adj* of great
alue and importance
adv very
ECIPE *n* type of legal
ocument
ECIPES > PRECIPE
ECIPICE *n* very steep
ace of a cliff
ECIS *n* short written
ummary of a longer piece
vb make a precis of
ECISE *adj* exact,
ccurate in every detail
ECISED > PRECIS
ECISELY *adv* in a precise
nanner
ECISER > PRECISE
ECISES > PRECIS
ECISEST > PRECISE
ECISIAN *n* punctilious
bserver of rules or forms,
sp in the field of religion
ECISING > PRECIS
ECISION *n* quality
f being precise ▷ *adj*
ccurate
ECISIVE *adj* limiting
y cutting off all that is
nnecessary
ECITED *adj* cited
reviously
ECLEAN *vb* clean
eforehand
ECLEANS > PRECLEAN
ECLEAR *vb* approve in
dvance
ECLEARS > PRECLEAR
ECLUDE *vb* make
npossible to happen
ECLUDED > PRECLUDE
ECLUDES > PRECLUDE
ECOCIAL *adj* (of the
oung of some species
f birds after hatching)
overed with down,
aving open eyes, and
apable of leaving the
est within a few days of
atching ▷ *n* precocial
ird
ECOCITY *n* early
naturing or development
ECODE *vb* code
eforehand
ECODED > PRECODE
ECODES > PRECODE
ECODING > PRECODE

PRECOITAL *adj* before sex
PRECONISE *same as* > PRECONIZE
PRECONIZE *vb* announce or commend publicly
PRECOOK *vb* cook (food) beforehand
PRECOOKED > PRECOOK
PRECOOKER *n* device for preparing food before cooking
PRECOOKS > PRECOOK
PRECOOL *vb* cool in advance
PRECOOLED > PRECOOL
PRECOOLS > PRECOOL
PRECOUP *adj* of the period before a coup
PRECRASH *adj* of the period before a crash
PRECREASE *vb* provide with a crease in advance
PRECRISIS *adj* occurring before a crisis
PRECURE *vb* cure in advance
PRECURED > PRECURE
PRECURES > PRECURE
PRECURING > PRECURE
PRECURRER > PRECURE
PRECURSE *n* forerunning
PRECURSES > PRECURSE
PRECURSOR *n* something that precedes and is a signal of something else, forerunner
PRECUT *vb* cut in advance
PRECUTS > PRECUT
PREDACITY *n* predatory nature
PREDATE *vb* occur at an earlier date than
PREDATED > PREDATE
PREDATES > PREDATE
PREDATING > PREDATE
PREDATION *n* relationship between two species of animal in a community, in which one (the predator) hunts, kills, and eats the other (the prey)
PREDATISM *n* state of preying on other animals
PREDATIVE > PREDATE
PREDATOR *n* predatory animal
PREDATORS > PREDATOR
PREDATORY *adj* habitually hunting and killing other animals for food
PREDAWN *n* period before dawn
PREDAWNS > PREDAWN
PREDEATH *n* period immediately before death
PREDEATHS > PREDEATH
PREDEBATE *adj* before a debate
PREDEDUCT *vb* deduct beforehand
PREDEFINE *vb* define in advance
PREDELLA *n* painting or sculpture or a series of small paintings or sculptures in a long narrow strip forming the lower edge of an altarpiece or the face of an altar step or platform
PREDELLAS > PREDELLA
PREDELLE > PREDELLA
PREDESIGN *vb* design beforehand
PREDEVOTE *adj* preordained
PREDIAL *same as* > PRAEDIAL
PREDICANT *same as* > PREDIKANT
PREDICATE *n* part of a sentence in which something is said about the subject ▷ *vb* declare or assert ▷ *adj* of or relating to something that has been predicated
PREDICT *vb* tell about in advance, prophesy
PREDICTED > PREDICT
PREDICTER > PREDICT
PREDICTOR *n* person or thing that predicts
PREDICTS > PREDICT
PREDIGEST *vb* treat (food) artificially to aid subsequent digestion in the body
PREDIKANT *n* minister in the Dutch Reformed Church in South Africa
PREDILECT *vb* choose beforehand
PREDINNER *adj* of the period before dinner
PREDIVE *n* diver's preparation
PREDIVES > PREDIVE
PREDOOM *vb* pronounce (someone or something's) doom beforehand
PREDOOMED > PREDOOM
PREDOOMS > PREDOOM
PREDRAFT *adj* before a draft
PREDRIED > PREDRY
PREDRIES > PREDRY
PREDRILL *vb* drill in advance
PREDRILLS > PREDRILL
PREDRY *vb* dry beforehand
PREDRYING > PREDRY
PREDUSK *n* period before dawn
PREDUSKS > PREDUSK
PREDY *adj* ready; shipshape
PREDYE *vb* dye beforehand
PREDYED > PREDYE
PREDYEING > PREDYE
PREDYES > PREDYE
PREE *vb* try or taste
PREED > PREE
PREEDIT *vb* edit beforehand
PREEDITED > PREEDIT
PREEDITS > PREEDIT
PREEING > PREE
PREELECT *vb* elect beforehand
PREELECTS > PREELECT
PREEMIE *n* premature infant
PREEMIES > PREEMIE
PREEMPT *vb* acquire in advance of or to the exclusion of others
PREEMPTED > PREEMPT
PREEMPTOR > PREEMPT
PREEMPTS > PREEMPT
PREEN *vb* (of a bird) clean or trim (feathers) with the beak ▷ *n* pin, esp a decorative one
PREENACT *vb* enact beforehand
PREENACTS > PREENACT
PREENED > PREEN
PREENER > PREEN
PREENERS > PREEN
PREENING > PREEN
PREENS > PREEN
PREERECT *vb* erect beforehand
PREERECTS > PREERECT
PREES > PREE
PREEVE *old form of* > PROVE
PREEVED > PREEVE
PREEVES > PREEVE
PREEVING > PREEVE
PREEXCITE *vb* stimulate in preparation
PREEXEMPT *vb* exempt beforehand
PREEXILIC *adj* prior to the Babylonian exile of the Jews
PREEXIST *vb* exist beforehand
PREEXISTS > PREEXIST
PREEXPOSE *vb* expose beforehand
PREFAB *n* prefabricated house ▷ *vb* manufacture sections of (building) in factory
PREFABBED > PREFAB
PREFABS > PREFAB
PREFACE *n* introduction to a book ▷ *vb* serve as an introduction to (a book, speech, etc)
PREFACED > PREFACE
PREFACER > PREFACE
PREFACERS > PREFACE
PREFACES > PREFACE
PREFACIAL *adj* anterior to face
PREFACING > PREFACE
PREFADE *vb* fade beforehand
PREFADED > PREFADE
PREFADES > PREFADE
PREFADING > PREFADE
PREFATORY *adj* concerning a preface
PREFECT *n* senior pupil in a school, with limited power over others
PREFECTS > PREFECT
PREFER *vb* like better
PREFERRED > PREFER
PREFERRER > PREFER
PREFERS > PREFER
PREFEUDAL *adj* of the period before the feudal

era
PREFIGHT *adj* of the period before a boxing match
PREFIGURE *vb* represent or suggest in advance
PREFILE *vb* file beforehand
PREFILED > PREFILE
PREFILES > PREFILE
PREFILING > PREFILE
PREFILL *vb* fill beforehand
PREFILLED > PREFILL
PREFILLS > PREFILL
PREFIRE *vb* fire beforehand
PREFIRED > PREFIRE
PREFIRES > PREFIRE
PREFIRING > PREFIRE
PREFIX *n* letter or group of letters put at the beginning of a word to make a new word, such as *un-* in *unhappy* ▷ *vb* put as an introduction or prefix (to)
PREFIXAL > PREFIX
PREFIXED > PREFIX
PREFIXES > PREFIX
PREFIXING > PREFIX
PREFIXION > PREFIX
PREFLAME *adj* of the period before combustion
PREFLIGHT *adj* of or relating to the period just prior to a plane taking off
PREFOCUS *vb* focus in advance
PREFORM *vb* form beforehand
PREFORMAT *vb* format in advance
PREFORMED > PREFORM
PREFORMS > PREFORM
PREFRANK *vb* frank in advance
PREFRANKS > PREFRANK
PREFREEZE *vb* freeze beforehand
PREFROZE > PREFREEZE
PREFROZEN > PREFREEZE
PREFUND *vb* pay for in advance
PREFUNDED > PREFUND
PREFUNDS > PREFUND
PREGAME *adj* of the period before a sports match ▷ *n* such a period
PREGAMES > PREGAME
PREGGERS *informal word for* > PREGNANT
PREGGIER > PREGGY
PREGGIEST > PREGGY
PREGGY *informal word for* > PREGNANT
PREGNABLE *adj* capable of being assailed or captured
PREGNANCE *obsolete word for* > PREGNANCY
PREGNANCY *n* state or condition of being pregnant
PREGNANT *adj* carrying a fetus in the womb
PREGROWTH *n* period before something begins to grow
PREGUIDE *vb* give guidance in advance
PREGUIDED > PREGUIDE
PREGUIDES > PREGUIDE
PREHALLUX *n* extra first toe
PREHANDLE *vb* handle beforehand
PREHARDEN *vb* harden beforehand
PREHEAT *vb* heat (an oven, grill, pan, etc) beforehand
PREHEATED > PREHEAT
PREHEATER > PREHEAT
PREHEATS > PREHEAT
PREHEND *vb* take hold of
PREHENDED > PREHEND
PREHENDS > PREHEND
PREHENSOR *n* part that grasps
PREHNITE *n* green mineral
PREHNITES > PREHNITE
PREHUMAN *n* hominid that predates man
PREHUMANS > PREHUMAN
PREIF *old form of* > PROOF
PREIFE *old form of* > PROOF
PREIFES > PREIFE
PREIFS > PREIF
PREIMPOSE *vb* impose beforehand
PREINFORM *vb* inform beforehand
PREINSERT *vb* insert beforehand
PREINVITE *vb* invite before others
PREJINK *variant of* > PERJINK
PREJUDGE *vb* judge beforehand without sufficient evidence
PREJUDGED > PREJUDGE
PREJUDGER > PREJUDGE
PREJUDGES > PREJUDGE
PREJUDICE *n* unreasonable or unfair dislike or preference ▷ *vb* cause (someone) to have a prejudice
PRELACIES > PRELACY
PRELACY *n* office or status of a prelate
PRELATE *n* bishop or other churchman of high rank
PRELATES > PRELATE
PRELATESS *n* female prelate
PRELATIAL > PRELATE
PRELATIC > PRELATE
PRELATIES > PRELATY
PRELATION *n* setting of one above another
PRELATISE *same as* > PRELATIZE
PRELATISH > PRELATE
PRELATISM *same as* > PRELACY
PRELATIST > PRELATISM
PRELATIZE *vb* exercise prelatical power
PRELATURE *same as* > PRELACY
PRELATY *n* prelacy
PRELAUNCH *adj* of the period before a launch
PRELAW *adj* before taking up study of law
PRELECT *vb* lecture or discourse in public
PRELECTED > PRELECT
PRELECTOR > PRELECT
PRELECTS > PRELECT
PRELEGAL *adj* of the period before the start of a law course
PRELIFE *adj* of the period before life on earth
PRELIM *n* event which precedes another
PRELIMIT *vb* limit beforehand
PRELIMITS > PRELIMIT
PRELIMS *pl n* pages of a book, such as the title page and contents, which come before the main text
PRELOAD *vb* load beforehand
PRELOADED > PRELOAD
PRELOADS > PRELOAD
PRELOCATE *vb* locate beforehand
PRELOVED *adj* previously owned or used
PRELUDE *n* introductory movement in music ▷ *vb* act as a prelude to (something)
PRELUDED > PRELUDE
PRELUDER > PRELUDE
PRELUDERS > PRELUDE
PRELUDES > PRELUDE
PRELUDI > PRELUDIO
PRELUDIAL > PRELUDE
PRELUDING > PRELUDE
PRELUDIO *n* musical prelude
PRELUNCH *adj* of the period before lunch
PRELUSION > PRELUDE
PRELUSIVE > PRELUDE
PRELUSORY > PRELUDE
PREM *n* informal word for a premature infant
PREMADE *adj* made in advance
PREMAN *n* Indonesian gangster
PREMANS > PREMAN
PREMARKET *adj* of the period before a product is available
PREMATURE *adj* happening or done before the normal or expected time
PREMEAL *adj* of the period before a meal
PREMED *n* premedical student
PREMEDIC *same as* > PREMED
PREMEDICS > PREMEDIC
PREMEDS > PREMED
PREMEET *n* meeting prior to another
PREMEETS > PREMEET
PREMERGER *adj* of the period prior to a merger
PREMIA > PREMIUM
PREMIE *same as* > PREEM[illegible]
PREMIER *n* prime minist[illegible] ▷ *adj* chief, leading
PREMIERE *n* first performance of a play, film, etc ▷ *vb* give, or (o[illegible] a film, play, or opera) be[illegible] premiere
PREMIERED > PREMIERE
PREMIERES > PREMIERE
PREMIERS > PREMIER
PREMIES > PREMIE
PREMISE *n* statement assumed to be true and used as the basis of reasoning ▷ *vb* state or assume (a proposition)[illegible] a premise in an argume[illegible] theory, etc
PREMISED > PREMISE
PREMISES > PREMISE
PREMISING > PREMISE
PREMISS *same as* > PREM[illegible]
PREMISSES > PREMISS
PREMIUM *n* additional su[illegible] of money, as on a wage [illegible] charge
PREMIUMS > PREMIUM
PREMIX *vb* mix beforeha[illegible]
PREMIXED > PREMIX
PREMIXES > PREMIX
PREMIXING > PREMIX
PREMODERN *adj* of the period before a modern [illegible]
PREMODIFY *vb* modify in advance
PREMOLAR *n* tooth betwe[illegible] the canine and first mol[illegible] in adult humans ▷ *adj* situated before a molar tooth
PREMOLARS > PREMOLAR
PREMOLD *vb* mold in advance
PREMOLDED > PREMOLD
PREMOLDS > PREMOLD
PREMOLT *n* period before animal molts
PREMOLTS > PREMOLT
PREMONISH *vb* admonis[illegible] beforehand
PREMORAL *adj* not gover[illegible] by sense of right and wrong
PREMORSE *adj* appearing [illegible] though the end had bee[illegible] bitten off
PREMOSAIC *adj* of the period before Moses
PREMOTION *n* previous motion
PREMOVE *vb* prompt to action
PREMOVED > PREMOVE
PREMOVES > PREMOVE
PREMOVING > PREMOVE
PREMS > PREM
PREMUNE *adj* having immunity to a disease a[illegible] result of latent infection
PREMY *variant of* > PREEM[illegible]
PRENAME *n* forename
PRENAMES > PRENAME
PRENASAL *n* bone in the

front of the nose
RENASALS > PRENASAL
RENATAL *adj* before birth, during pregnancy ▷ *n* prenatal examination
RENATALS > PRENATAL
RENOMEN *less common spelling of* > PRAENOMEN
RENOMENS > PRENOMEN
RENOMINA > PRENOMEN
RENOON *adj* of the period before noon
RENOTIFY *vb* notify in advance
RENOTION *n* preconception
RENT *Scots variant of* > PRINT
RENTED > PRENT
RENTICE *vb* bind as an apprentice
RENTICED > PRENTICE
RENTICES > PRENTICE
RENTING > PRENT
RENTS > PRENT
RENUBILE *adj* of the period from birth to puberty
RENUMBER *vb* number in advance
RENUP *n* prenuptial agreement
RENUPS > PRENUP
RENZIE *adj* Shakespearian word, possibly a mistake, supposed by some to mean "princely"
REOBTAIN *vb* obtain in advance
REOCCUPY *vb* fill the thoughts or attention of (someone) to the exclusion of other things
REOCULAR *n* scale in front of eye of reptile or fish
REOP *n* patient being prepared for surgery
REOPS > PREOP
REOPTION *n* right of first choice
REORAL *adj* situated in front of mouth
REORDAIN *vb* ordain, decree, or appoint beforehand
REORDER *vb* order in advance
REORDERS > PREORDER
REOWNED *adj* second-hand
REP *vb* prepare
REPACK *vb* pack in advance of sale
REPACKED *adj* sold already wrapped
REPACKS > PREPACK
REPAID > PREPAY
REPARE *vb* make or get ready
REPARED > PREPARE
REPARER > PREPARE
REPARERS > PREPARE
REPARES > PREPARE
REPARING > PREPARE
PREPASTE *vb* paste in advance
PREPASTED > PREPASTE
PREPASTES > PREPASTE
PREPAVE *vb* pave beforehand
PREPAVED > PREPAVE
PREPAVES > PREPAVE
PREPAVING > PREPAVE
PREPAY *vb* pay for in advance
PREPAYING > PREPAY
PREPAYS > PREPAY
PREPENSE *adj* (usually in legal contexts) arranged in advance ▷ *vb* consider beforehand
PREPENSED > PREPENSE
PREPENSES > PREPENSE
PREPILL *adj* of the period before the contraceptive pill became available
PREPLACE *vb* place in advance
PREPLACED > PREPLACE
PREPLACES > PREPLACE
PREPLAN *vb* plan beforehand
PREPLANS > PREPLAN
PREPLANT *vb* plant in advance
PREPLANTS > PREPLANT
PREPOLLEX *n* additional digit on thumb of some animals
PREPONE *vb* bring forward to an earlier time
PREPONED > PREPONE
PREPONES > PREPONE
PREPONING > PREPONE
PREPOSE *vb* place before
PREPOSED > PREPOSE
PREPOSES > PREPOSE
PREPOSING > PREPOSE
PREPOSTOR *n* prefect in certain public shcools
PREPOTENT *adj* greater in power, force, or influence
PREPPED > PREP
PREPPIE *same as* > PREPPY
PREPPIER > PREPPY
PREPPIES > PREPPY
PREPPIEST > PREPPY
PREPPILY > PREPPY
PREPPING > PREP
PREPPY *adj* characteristic of or denoting a fashion style of neat, understated, and often expensive clothes ▷ *n* person exhibiting such style
PREPREG *n* material already impregnated with synthetic resin
PREPREGS > PREPREG
PREPRESS *adj* before printing
PREPRICE *vb* price in advance
PREPRICED > PREPRICE
PREPRICES > PREPRICE
PREPRINT *vb* print in advance
PREPRINTS > PREPRINT
PREPS > PREP
PREPUBES > PREPUBIS
PREPUBIS *n* animal hip bone
PREPUCE *n* foreskin
PREPUCES > PREPUCE
PREPUEBLO *adj* belonging to the period before the Pueblo Indians
PREPUNCH *vb* pierce with holes in advance
PREPUPA *n* insect in stage of life before pupa
PREPUPAE > PREPUPA
PREPUPAL *adj* of the period between the larval and pupal stages
PREPUPAS > PREPUPA
PREPUTIAL > PREPUCE
PREQUEL *n* film or book about an earlier stage of a story or a character's life, released because the later part of it has already been successful
PREQUELS > PREQUEL
PRERACE *adj* of the period before a race
PRERADIO *adj* before the invention of radio
PRERECORD *vb* record (music or a programme) in advance so that it can be played or broadcast later
PRERECTAL *adj* in front of the rectum
PREREFORM *adj* before reform
PRERENAL *adj* anterior to kidney
PRERETURN *adj* of the period before return
PREREVIEW *adj* of the period before review
PRERINSE *vb* treat before rinsing
PRERINSED > PRERINSE
PRERINSES > PRERINSE
PRERIOT *adj* of the period before a riot
PREROCK *adj* of the era before rock music
PRERUPT *adj* abrupt
PRESA *n* sign or symbol used in a canon, round, etc, to indicate the entry of each part.
PRESAGE *vb* be a sign or warning of ▷ *n* omen
PRESAGED > PRESAGE
PRESAGER > PRESAGE
PRESAGERS > PRESAGE
PRESAGES > PRESAGE
PRESAGING > PRESAGE
PRESALE *n* practice of arranging the sale of a product before it is available
PRESALES > PRESALE
PRESBYOPE *n* person with presbyopy
PRESBYOPY *n* diminishing ability of the eye to focus
PRESBYTE *n* person with presbyopy
PRESBYTER *n* (in some episcopal Churches) official with administrative and priestly duties
PRESBYTES > PRESBYTE
PRESBYTIC > PRESBYTE
PRESCHOOL *adj* of or for children below the age of five
PRESCIENT *adj* having knowledge of events before they take place
PRESCIND *vb* withdraw attention (from something)
PRESCINDS > PRESCIND
PRESCIOUS *adj* prescient
PRESCORE *vb* record (the score of a film) before shooting
PRESCORED > PRESCORE
PRESCORES > PRESCORE
PRESCREEN *vb* screen in advance
PRESCRIBE *vb* recommend the use of (a medicine)
PRESCRIPT *n* something laid down or prescribed ▷ *adj* prescribed as a rule
PRESCUTA > PRESCUTUM
PRESCUTUM *n* part of an insect's thorax
PRESE > PRESA
PRESEASON *n* period before the start of a sport season
PRESELECT *vb* select beforehand
PRESELL *vb* promote (a product, entertainment, etc) with publicity in advance of its appearance
PRESELLS > PRESELL
PRESENCE *n* fact of being in a specified place
PRESENCES > PRESENCE
PRESENILE *adj* occurring before the onset of old age
PRESENT *adj* being in a specified place ▷ *n* present time or tense ▷ *vb* introduce formally or publicly
PRESENTED > PRESENT
PRESENTEE *n* person who is presented, as at court
PRESENTER *n* person introducing a TV or radio show
PRESENTLY *adv* soon
PRESENTS *pl n* used in a deed or document to refer to itself
PRESERVE *vb* keep from being damaged, changed, or ended ▷ *n* area of interest restricted to a particular person or group
PRESERVED > PRESERVE
PRESERVER > PRESERVE
PRESERVES > PRESERVE
PRESES *variant of* > PRAESES
PRESET *vb* set the timer

on a piece of equipment so that it starts to work at a specific time ▷ *adj* (of equipment) with the controls set in advance ▷ *n* control, such as a variable resistor, that is not as accessible as the main controls and is used to set initial conditions

PRESETS > PRESET

PRESETTLE *vb* settle beforehand

PRESHAPE *vb* shape beforehand

PRESHAPED > PRESHAPE

PRESHAPES > PRESHAPE

PRESHIP *vb* ship in advance

PRESHIPS > PRESHIP

PRESHOW *vb* show in advance

PRESHOWED > PRESHOW

PRESHOWN > PRESHOW

PRESHOWS > PRESHOW

PRESHRANK > PRESHRINK

PRESHRINK *vb* subject to a shrinking process so that further shrinkage will not occur

PRESHRUNK > PRESHRINK

PRESIDE *vb* be in charge, esp of a meeting

PRESIDED > PRESIDE

PRESIDENT *n* head of state in many countries

PRESIDER > PRESIDE

PRESIDERS > PRESIDE

PRESIDES > PRESIDE

PRESIDIA > PRESIDIUM

PRESIDIAL *adj* presidential

PRESIDING > PRESIDE

PRESIDIO *n* military post or establishment, esp in countries under Spanish control

PRESIDIOS > PRESIDIO

PRESIDIUM *n* (in Communist countries) permanent administrative committee

PRESIFT *vb* sift beforehand

PRESIFTED > PRESIFT

PRESIFTS > PRESIFT

PRESIGNAL *vb* signal in advance

PRESLEEP *adj* of the period before sleep

PRESLICE *vb* slice in advance

PRESLICED > PRESLICE

PRESLICES > PRESLICE

PRESOAK *vb* soak beforehand

PRESOAKED > PRESOAK

PRESOAKS > PRESOAK

PRESOLD > PRESELL

PRESOLVE *vb* solve beforehand

PRESOLVED > PRESOLVE

PRESOLVES > PRESOLVE

PRESONG *adj* of the period before a song is sung

PRESORT *vb* sort in advance

PRESORTED > PRESORT

PRESORTS > PRESORT

PRESPLIT *adj* of the period prior to a split

PRESS *vb* apply force or weight to ▷ *n* printing machine

PRESSED > PRESS

PRESSER > PRESS

PRESSERS > PRESS

PRESSES > PRESS

PRESSFAT *n* wine vat

PRESSFATS > PRESSFAT

PRESSFUL > PRESS

PRESSGANG *n* squad of sailors forcing others into navy

PRESSIE *informal word for* > PRESENT

PRESSIES > PRESSIE

PRESSING *adj* urgent ▷ *n* large number of gramophone records produced at one time

PRESSINGS > PRESSING

PRESSION *n* act of pressing

PRESSIONS > PRESSION

PRESSMAN *n* person who works for the press

PRESSMARK *n* location mark on a book indicating a specific bookcase

PRESSMEN > PRESSMAN

PRESSOR *adj* relating to or producing an increase in blood pressure

PRESSROOM *n* room in a printing establishment that houses the printing presses

PRESSRUN *n* number of books printed at one time

PRESSRUNS > PRESSRUN

PRESSURE *n* force produced by pressing ▷ *vb* persuade forcefully

PRESSURED > PRESSURE

PRESSURES > PRESSURE

PRESSWORK *n* operation of a printing press

PREST *adj* prepared for action or use ▷ *n* loan of money ▷ *vb* give as a loan

PRESTAMP *vb* stamp in advance

PRESTAMPS > PRESTAMP

PRESTED > PREST

PRESTER > PREST

PRESTERNA *adj* anterior to sternum

PRESTERS > PREST

PRESTIGE *n* high status or respect resulting from success or achievements

PRESTIGES > PRESTIGE

PRESTING > PREST

PRESTO *adv* very quickly ▷ *n* passage to be played very quickly

PRESTORE *vb* store in advance

PRESTORED > PRESTORE

PRESTORES > PRESTORE

PRESTOS > PRESTO

PRESTRESS *vb* apply tensile stress to (the steel cables, wires, etc, of a precast concrete part) before the load is applied

PRESTRIKE *adj* of the period before a strike

PRESTS > PREST

PRESUME *vb* suppose to be the case

PRESUMED > PRESUME

PRESUMER > PRESUME

PRESUMERS > PRESUME

PRESUMES > PRESUME

PRESUMING > PRESUME

PRESUMMIT *n* meeting held prior to a summit

PRESURVEY *vb* survey in advance

PRETAPE *vb* tape in advance

PRETAPED > PRETAPE

PRETAPES > PRETAPE

PRETAPING > PRETAPE

PRETASTE *vb* taste in advance

PRETASTED > PRETASTE

PRETASTES > PRETASTE

PRETAX *adj* before tax

PRETEEN *n* boy or girl approaching his or her teens

PRETEENS > PRETEEN

PRETELL *vb* predict

PRETELLS > PRETELL

PRETENCE *n* behaviour intended to deceive, pretending

PRETENCES > PRETENCE

PRETEND *vb* claim or give the appearance of (something untrue) to deceive or in play ▷ *adj* fanciful

PRETENDED > PRETEND

PRETENDER *n* person who makes a false or disputed claim to a position of power

PRETENDS > PRETEND

PRETENSE *same as* > PRETENCE

PRETENSES > PRETENSE

PRETERIST *n* person interested in past

PRETERIT *same as* > PRETERITE

PRETERITE *n* past tense of verbs, such as *jumped*, *swam* ▷ *adj* expressing such a past tense

PRETERITS > PRETERIT

PRETERM *n* premature baby

PRETERMIT *vb* overlook intentionally

PRETERMS > PRETERM

PRETEST *vb* test (something) before presenting it to its intended public or client ▷ *n* act or instance of pretesting

PRETESTED > PRETEST

PRETESTS > PRETEST

PRETEXT *n* false reason given to hide the real one ▷ *vb* get personal information under false pretences

PRETEXTED > PRETEXT

PRETEXTS > PRETEXT

PRETOLD > PRETELL

PRETONIC *adj* denoting or relating to the syllable before the one bearing th primary stress in a word

PRETOR *same as* > PRAETOR

PRETORIAL > PRETOR

PRETORIAN *n* person wit the rank of praetor

PRETORS > PRETOR

PRETRAIN *vb* train in advance

PRETRAINS > PRETRAIN

PRETRAVEL *adj* of the period before travel

PRETREAT *vb* treat in advance

PRETREATS > PRETREAT

PRETRIAL *n* hearing prio to a trial

PRETRIALS > PRETRIAL

PRETRIM *vb* trim in advance

PRETRIMS > PRETRIM

PRETTIED > PRETTY

PRETTIER > PRETTY

PRETTIES > PRETTY

PRETTIEST > PRETTY

PRETTIFY *vb* make pretty

PRETTILY > PRETTY

PRETTY *adj* pleasing to lo at ▷ *adv* fairly, moderate ▷ *vb* pretty

PRETTYING > PRETTY

PRETTYISH *adj* quite pret

PRETTYISM *n* affectedly pretty style

PRETYPE *vb* type in advance

PRETYPED > PRETYPE

PRETYPES > PRETYPE

PRETYPING > PRETYPE

PRETZEL *n* brittle salted biscuit

PRETZELS > PRETZEL

PREUNION *n* early form of trade union

PREUNIONS > PREUNION

PREUNITE *vb* unite in advance

PREUNITED > PREUNITE

PREUNITES > PREUNITE

PREVAIL *vb* gain mastery

PREVAILED > PREVAIL

PREVAILER > PREVAIL

PREVAILS > PREVAIL

PREVALENT *adj* widespread, common

PREVALUE *vb* value beforehand

PREVALUED > PREVALUE

PREVALUES > PREVALUE

PREVE *vb* prove

PREVED > PREVE

PREVENE *vb* come before

PREVENED > PREVENE

PREVENES > PREVENE
PREVENING > PREVENE
PREVENT *vb* keep from happening or doing
PREVENTED > PREVENT
PREVENTER *n* person or thing that prevents
PREVENTS > PREVENT
PREVERB *n* particle preceding root of verb
PREVERBAL > PREVERB
PREVERBS > PREVERB
PREVES > PREVE
PREVIABLE *adj* not yet viable
PREVIEW *n* advance showing of a film or exhibition before it is shown to the public ▷ *vb* view in advance
PREVIEWED > PREVIEW
PREVIEWER > PREVIEW
PREVIEWS > PREVIEW
PREVING > PREVE
PREVIOUS *adj* coming or happening before
PREVISE *vb* predict or foresee
PREVISED > PREVISE
PREVISES > PREVISE
PREVISING > PREVISE
PREVISION *n* act or power of foreseeing
PREVISIT *vb* visit beforehand
PREVISITS > PREVISIT
PREVISOR > PREVISE
PREVISORS > PREVISE
PREVUE *same as* > PREVIEW
PREVUED > PREVUE
PREVUES > PREVUE
PREVUING > PREVUE
PREWAR *adj* relating to the period before a war, esp before World War I or II
PREWARM *vb* warm beforehand
PREWARMED > PREWARM
PREWARMS > PREWARM
PREWARN *vb* warn in advance
PREWARNED > PREWARN
PREWARNS > PREWARN
PREWASH *vb* give a preliminary wash to (clothes), esp in a washing machine ▷ *n* preliminary wash, esp in a washing machine
PREWASHED > PREWASH
PREWASHES > PREWASH
PREWEIGH *vb* weigh beforehand
PREWEIGHS > PREWEIGH
PREWIRE *vb* wire beforehand
PREWIRED > PREWIRE
PREWIRES > PREWIRE
PREWIRING > PREWIRE
PREWORK *vb* work in advance
PREWORKED > PREWORK
PREWORKS > PREWORK
PREWORN *adj* (of clothes) second-hand
PREWRAP *vb* wrap in advance
PREWRAPS > PREWRAP
PREWYN *obsolete spelling of* > PRUNE
PREWYNS > PREWYN
PREX *same as* > PREXY
PREXES > PREX
PREXIES > PREXY
PREXY *n* US college president
PREY *n* animal hunted and killed for food by another animal ▷ *vb* hunt or seize food by killing other animals
PREYED > PREY
PREYER > PREY
PREYERS > PREY
PREYFUL *adj* rich in prey
PREYING > PREY
PREYS > PREY
PREZ *n* president
PREZZES > PREZ
PREZZIE *same as* > PRESSIE
PREZZIES > PREZZIE
PRIAL *n* pair royal of cards
PRIALS > PRIAL
PRIAPEAN *same as* > PRIAPIC
PRIAPI > PRIAPUS
PRIAPIC *adj* phallic
PRIAPISM *n* prolonged painful erection of the penis, caused by neurological disorders, obstruction of the penile blood vessels, etc
PRIAPISMS > PRIAPISM
PRIAPUS *n* representation of the penis
PRIAPUSES > PRIAPUS
PRIBBLE *variant of* > PRABBLE
PRIBBLES > PRIBBLE
PRICE *n* amount of money for which a thing is bought or sold ▷ *vb* fix or ask the price of
PRICEABLE > PRICE
PRICED > PRICE
PRICELESS *adj* very valuable
PRICER > PRICE
PRICERS > PRICE
PRICES > PRICE
PRICEY *adj* expensive
PRICIER > PRICY
PRICIEST > PRICY
PRICILY > PRICEY
PRICINESS > PRICEY
PRICING > PRICE
PRICINGS > PRICE
PRICK *vb* pierce lightly with a sharp point ▷ *n* sudden sharp pain caused by pricking
PRICKED > PRICK
PRICKER *n* person or thing that pricks
PRICKERS > PRICKER
PRICKET *n* male deer in the second year of life having unbranched antlers
PRICKETS > PRICKET
PRICKIER > PRICKY
PRICKIEST > PRICKY
PRICKING > PRICK
PRICKINGS > PRICK
PRICKLE *n* thorn or spike on a plant ▷ *vb* have a tingling or pricking sensation
PRICKLED > PRICKLE
PRICKLES > PRICKLE
PRICKLIER > PRICKLY
PRICKLING > PRICKLE
PRICKLY *adj* having prickles
PRICKS > PRICK
PRICKWOOD *n* shrub with wood used for skewers
PRICKY *adj* covered with pricks
PRICY *same as* > PRICEY
PRIDE *n* feeling of pleasure and satisfaction when one has done well
PRIDED > PRIDE
PRIDEFUL > PRIDE
PRIDELESS > PRIDE
PRIDES > PRIDE
PRIDIAN *adj* relating to yesterday
PRIDING > PRIDE
PRIED > PRY
PRIEDIEU *n* piece of furniture consisting of a low surface for kneeling upon and a narrow front surmounted by a rest for the elbows or for books, for use when praying
PRIEDIEUS > PRIEDIEU
PRIEDIEUX > PRIEDIEU
PRIEF *obsolete variant of* > PROOF
PRIEFE *obsolete variant of* > PROOF
PRIEFED > PRIEFE
PRIEFES > PRIEFE
PRIEFING > PRIEFE
PRIEFS > PRIEF
PRIER *n* person who pries
PRIERS > PRIER
PRIES > PRY
PRIEST *n* (in the Christian church) person who can administer the sacraments and preach ▷ *vb* make a priest
PRIESTED > PRIEST
PRIESTESS *n* female official who offers sacrifice on behalf of the people and peforms various other religious ceremonies
PRIESTING > PRIEST
PRIESTLY *adj* of, relating to, characteristic of, or befitting a priest
PRIESTS > PRIEST
PRIEVE *obsolete variant of* > PROOF
PRIEVED > PRIEVE
PRIEVES > PRIEVE
PRIEVING > PRIEVE
PRIG *n* self-righteous person who acts as if superior to others
PRIGGED > PRIG
PRIGGER *n* thief
PRIGGERS > PRIGGER
PRIGGERY > PRIG
PRIGGING > PRIG
PRIGGINGS > PRIG
PRIGGISH > PRIG
PRIGGISM > PRIG
PRIGGISMS > PRIG
PRIGS > PRIG
PRILL *vb* convert (a material) into a granular free-flowing form ▷ *n* prilled material
PRILLED > PRILL
PRILLING > PRILL
PRILLS > PRILL
PRIM *adj* formal, proper, and rather prudish ▷ *vb* make prim
PRIMA *same as* > PRIMO
PRIMACIES > PRIMACY
PRIMACY *n* state of being first in rank, grade, etc
PRIMAEVAL *same as* > PRIMEVAL
PRIMAGE *n* tax added to customs duty
PRIMAGES > PRIMAGE
PRIMAL *adj* of basic causes or origins
PRIMALITY *n* state of being prime
PRIMALLY > PRIMAL
PRIMARIES > PRIMARY
PRIMARILY *adv* chiefly or mainly
PRIMARY *adj* chief, most important ▷ *n* person or thing that is first in position, time, or importance
PRIMAS > PRIMA
PRIMATAL > PRIMATE
PRIMATE *n* member of an order of mammals including monkeys and humans ▷ *adj* of, relating to, or belonging to the order *Primates*
PRIMATES > PRIMATE
PRIMATIAL > PRIMATE
PRIMATIC > PRIMATE
PRIMAVERA *n* springtime
PRIME *adj* main, most important ▷ *n* time when someone is at his or her best or most vigorous ▷ *vb* give (someone) information in advance to prepare them for something
PRIMED > PRIME
PRIMELY > PRIME
PRIMENESS > PRIME
PRIMER *n* special paint applied to bare wood etc before the main paint
PRIMERO *n* 16th- and 17th-century card game
PRIMEROS > PRIMERO
PRIMERS > PRIMER

PRIMES > PRIME
PRIMETIME *adj* occurring during or designed for prime time
PRIMEUR *n* anything (esp fruit) produced early
PRIMEURS > PRIMEUR
PRIMEVAL *adj* of the earliest age of the world
PRIMI > PRIMO
PRIMINE *n* integument surrounding an ovule or the outer of two such integuments
PRIMINES > PRIMINE
PRIMING *same as* > PRIMER
PRIMINGS > PRIMING
PRIMIPARA *n* woman who has borne only one child
PRIMITIA *n* first fruit of season
PRIMITIAE > PRIMITIA
PRIMITIAL > PRIMITIA
PRIMITIAS > PRIMITIA
PRIMITIVE *adj* of an early simple stage of development ▷ *n* primitive person or thing
PRIMLY > PRIM
PRIMMED > PRIM
PRIMMER > PRIM
PRIMMERS > PRIM
PRIMMEST > PRIM
PRIMMING > PRIM
PRIMNESS > PRIM
PRIMO *n* upper or right-hand part in a piano duet
PRIMORDIA *n* organs or parts in the earliest stage of development
PRIMOS > PRIMO
PRIMP *vb* tidy (one's hair or clothes) fussily
PRIMPED > PRIMP
PRIMPING > PRIMP
PRIMPS > PRIMP
PRIMROSE *n* pale yellow spring flower ▷ *adj* pale yellow
PRIMROSED > PRIMROSE
PRIMROSES > PRIMROSE
PRIMROSY > PRIMROSE
PRIMS > PRIM
PRIMSIE *Scots variant of* > PRIM
PRIMSIER > PRIMSIE
PRIMSIEST > PRIMSIE
PRIMULA *n* type of primrose with brightly coloured flowers
PRIMULAS > PRIMULA
PRIMULINE *n* type of dye
PRIMUS *n* presiding bishop in the Synod
PRIMUSES > PRIMUS
PRIMY *adj* prime
PRINCE *vb* act the prince
PRINCED > PRINCE
PRINCEDOM *n* dignity, rank, or position of a prince
PRINCEKIN *n* young prince
PRINCELET *n* petty or minor prince
PRINCELY *adj* of or like a prince ▷ *adv* in a princely manner
PRINCES > PRINCE
PRINCESS *n* female member of a royal family, esp the daughter of the king or queen
PRINCING > PRINCE
PRINCIPAL *adj* main, most important ▷ *n* head of a school or college
PRINCIPE *n* prince
PRINCIPI > PRINCIPE
PRINCIPIA *n* principles
PRINCIPLE *n* moral rule guiding behaviour
PRINCOCK *same as* > PRINCOX
PRINCOCKS > PRINCOCK
PRINCOX *n* pert youth
PRINCOXES > PRINCOX
PRINK *vb* dress (oneself) finely
PRINKED > PRINK
PRINKER > PRINK
PRINKERS > PRINK
PRINKING > PRINK
PRINKS > PRINK
PRINT *vb* reproduce (a newspaper, book, etc) in large quantities by mechanical or electronic means ▷ *n* printed words etc
PRINTABLE *adj* capable of being printed or of producing a print
PRINTED > PRINT
PRINTER *n* person or company engaged in printing
PRINTERS > PRINTER
PRINTERY *n* establishment in which printing is carried out
PRINTHEAD *n* component in a printer that forms a printed character
PRINTING *n* process of producing printed matter
PRINTINGS > PRINTING
PRINTLESS > PRINT
PRINTOUT *n* printed information produced by a computer output device
PRINTOUTS > PRINTOUT
PRINTS > PRINT
PRION *n* dovelike petrel with a serrated bill
PRIONS > PRION
PRIOR *adj* earlier ▷ *n* head monk in a priory
PRIORATE *n* office, status, or term of office of a prior
PRIORATES > PRIORATE
PRIORESS *n* deputy head nun in a convent
PRIORIES > PRIORY
PRIORITY *n* most important thing that must be dealt with first
PRIORLY > PRIOR
PRIORS > PRIOR
PRIORSHIP *n* office of prior
PRIORY *n* place where certain orders of monks or nuns live
PRISAGE *n* customs duty levied until 1809 upon wine imported into England
PRISAGES > PRISAGE
PRISE *same as* > PRY
PRISED > PRISE
PRISER > PRISE
PRISERE *n* primary sere or succession from bare ground to the community climax
PRISERES > PRISERE
PRISERS > PRISE
PRISES > PRISE
PRISING > PRISE
PRISM *n* transparent block usu with triangular ends and rectangular sides, used to disperse light into a spectrum or refract it in optical instruments
PRISMATIC *adj* of or shaped like a prism
PRISMOID *n* prismatoid having an equal number of vertices in each of the two parallel planes and whose sides are trapeziums or parallelograms
PRISMOIDS > PRISMOID
PRISMS > PRISM
PRISMY > PRISM
PRISON *n* building where criminals and accused people are held ▷ *vb* imprison
PRISONED > PRISON
PRISONER *n* person held captive
PRISONERS > PRISONER
PRISONING > PRISON
PRISONOUS > PRISON
PRISONS > PRISON
PRISS *n* prissy person ▷ *vb* act prissily
PRISSED > PRISS
PRISSES > PRISS
PRISSIER > PRISSY
PRISSIES > PRISSY
PRISSIEST > PRISSY
PRISSILY > PRISSY
PRISSING > PRISS
PRISSY *adj* prim, correct, and easily shocked ▷ *n* prissy person
PRISTANE *n* colourless combustible liquid
PRISTANES > PRISTANE
PRISTINE *adj* clean, new, and unused
PRITHEE *interj* pray thee
PRIVACIES > PRIVACY
PRIVACY *n* condition of being private
PRIVADO *n* close friend
PRIVADOES > PRIVADO
PRIVADOS > PRIVADO
PRIVATE *adj* for the use of one person or group only ▷ *n* soldier of the lowest rank
PRIVATEER *n* privately owned armed vessel authorized by the government to take part in a war ▷ *vb* competitor esp in motor racing, who is privately financed rather than sponsored by manufacturer
PRIVATELY > PRIVATE
PRIVATER > PRIVATE
PRIVATES > PRIVATE
PRIVATEST > PRIVATE
PRIVATION *n* loss or lack of the necessities of life
PRIVATISE *same as* > PRIVATIZE
PRIVATISM *n* lack of concern for public life
PRIVATIST > PRIVATISM
PRIVATIVE *adj* causing privation
PRIVATIZE *vb* sell (a publicly owned company to individuals or a private company
PRIVET *n* bushy evergreen shrub used for hedges
PRIVETS > PRIVET
PRIVIER > PRIVY
PRIVIES > PRIVY
PRIVIEST > PRIVY
PRIVILEGE *n* advantage or favour that only some people have ▷ *vb* bestow a privilege or privileges upon
PRIVILY *adv* in a secret way
PRIVITIES > PRIVITY
PRIVITY *n* legally recognized relationship existing between two parties, such as that between lessor and lessee and between the parties to a contract
PRIVY *adj* sharing knowledge of something secret ▷ *n* toilet, esp an outside one
PRIZABLE *adj* of worth
PRIZE *n* reward given for success in a competition etc ▷ *adj* winning or likely to win a prize ▷ *vb* value highly
PRIZED > PRIZE
PRIZEMAN *n* winner of prize
PRIZEMEN > PRIZEMAN
PRIZER *n* contender for prize
PRIZERS > PRIZER
PRIZES > PRIZE
PRIZING > PRIZE
PRO *prep* in favour of ▷ *n* professional ▷ *adv* in favour of a motion etc
PROA *n* any of several kinds of canoe-like boats used in the South Pacific, esp one equipped with an

outrigger and sails
ROACTION *n* action that initiates change as opposed to reaction to events
ROACTIVE *adj* tending to initiate change rather than reacting to events
ROAS > PROA
ROB *n* problem
ROBABLE *adj* likely to happen or be true ▷ *n* person who is likely to be chosen for a team, event, etc
ROBABLES > PROBABLE
ROBABLY *adv* in all likelihood ▷ *sentence substitute* I believe such a thing or situation may be the case
ROBALL *adj* believable
ROBAND *n* first patient to be investigated in a family study, to whom all relationships are referred
ROBANDS > PROBAND
ROBANG *n* long flexible rod, often with a small sponge at one end, for inserting into the oesophagus, as to apply medication
ROBANGS > PROBANG
ROBATE *n* process of proving the validity of a will ▷ *vb* establish officially the authenticity and validity of (a will)
ROBATED > PROBATE
ROBATES > PROBATE
ROBATING > PROBATE
ROBATION *n* system of dealing with law-breakers, esp juvenile ones, by placing them under supervision
ROBATIVE *adj* serving to test or designed for testing
ROBATORY *same as* > PROBATIVE
ROBE *vb* search into or examine closely ▷ *n* surgical instrument used to examine a wound, cavity, etc
ROBEABLE > PROBE
ROBED > PROBE
ROBER > PROBE
ROBERS > PROBE
ROBES > PROBE
ROBING > PROBE
ROBINGLY > PROBE
ROBIOTIC *n* bacterium that protects the body from harmful bacteria
ROBIT *n* statistical measurement
ROBITIES > PROBITY
ROBITS > PROBIT
ROBITY *n* honesty, integrity
ROBLEM *n* something difficult to deal with or solve ▷ *adj* of a literary work that deals with difficult moral questions
PROBLEMS > PROBLEM
PROBOSCIS *n* long trunk or snout
PROBS > PROB
PROCACITY *n* insolence
PROCAINE *n* colourless or white crystalline water-soluble substance
PROCAINES > PROCAINE
PROCAMBIA *n* plant part in stem and root
PROCARP *n* female reproductive organ in red algae
PROCARPS > PROCARP
PROCARYON *same as* > PROKARYON
PROCEDURE *n* way of doing something, esp the correct or usual one
PROCEED *vb* start or continue doing
PROCEEDED > PROCEED
PROCEEDER > PROCEED
PROCEEDS *pl n* money obtained from an event or activity
PROCERITY *n* tallness
PROCESS *n* series of actions or changes ▷ *vb* handle or prepare by a special method of manufacture
PROCESSED > PROCESS
PROCESSER *same as* > PROCESSOR
PROCESSES > PROCESS
PROCESSOR *n* person or thing that carries out a process
PROCHAIN *variant of* > PROCHEIN
PROCHEIN *adj* next or nearest
PROCHOICE *adj* in favour of women's right to abortion
PROCHURCH *adj* favourable to church
PROCIDENT *adj* relating to prolapsus
PROCINCT *n* state of preparedness
PROCINCTS > PROCINCT
PROCLAIM *vb* declare publicly
PROCLAIMS > PROCLAIM
PROCLISES > PROCLITIC
PROCLISIS > PROCLITIC
PROCLITIC *adj* relating to or denoting a monosyllabic word or form having no stress or accent and pronounced as a prefix of the following word, as in English *'t* for *it* in *'twas* ▷ *n* proclitic word or form
PROCLIVE *adj* prone
PROCONSUL *n* administrator or governor of a colony, occupied territory, or other dependency
PROCREANT > PROCREATE
PROCREATE *vb* produce offspring
PROCTAL *adj* relating to the rectum
PROCTITIS *n* inflammation of the rectum
PROCTODEA *pl n* parts of the anus
PROCTOR *n* member of the staff of certain universities having duties including the enforcement of discipline ▷ *vb* invigilate (an examination)
PROCTORED > PROCTOR
PROCTORS > PROCTOR
PROCURACY *n* office of a procurator
PROCURAL > PROCURE
PROCURALS > PROCURE
PROCURE *vb* get, provide
PROCURED > PROCURE
PROCURER *n* person who obtains people to act as prostitutes
PROCURERS > PROCURER
PROCURES > PROCURE
PROCURESS *same as* > PROCURER
PROCUREUR *n* law officer in Guernsey
PROCURING > PROCURE
PROD *vb* poke with something pointed ▷ *n* prodding
PRODDED > PROD
PRODDER > PROD
PRODDERS > PROD
PRODDING > PROD
PRODIGAL *adj* recklessly extravagant, wasteful ▷ *n* person who spends lavishly or squanders money
PRODIGALS > PRODIGAL
PRODIGIES > PRODIGY
PRODIGY *n* person with some marvellous talent
PRODITOR *n* traitor
PRODITORS > PRODITOR
PRODITORY > PRODITOR
PRODNOSE *vb* make uninvited inquiries (about someone else's business, for example)
PRODNOSED > PRODNOSE
PRODNOSES > PRODNOSE
PRODROMAL > PRODROME
PRODROME *n* any symptom that signals the impending onset of a disease
PRODROMES > PRODROME
PRODROMI > PRODROME
PRODROMIC > PRODROME
PRODROMUS *same as* > PRODROME
PRODRUG *n* compound that is itself biologically inactive but is metabolized in the body to produce an active therapeutic drug
PRODRUGS > PRODRUG
PRODS > PROD
PRODUCE *vb* bring into existence ▷ *n* food grown for sale
PRODUCED > PRODUCE
PRODUCER *n* person with control over the making of a film, record, etc
PRODUCERS > PRODUCER
PRODUCES > PRODUCE
PRODUCING > PRODUCE
PRODUCT *n* something produced
PRODUCTS > PRODUCT
PROEM *n* introduction or preface
PROEMBRYO *n* stage prior to embryo in plants
PROEMIAL > PROEM
PROEMS > PROEM
PROENZYME *n* inactive form of an enzyme
PROESTRUS *n* period in the estrous cycle that immediately precedes estrus
PROETTE *n* female golfing professional
PROETTES > PROETTE
PROF *short for* > PROFESSOR
PROFACE *interj* much good may it do you
PROFAMILY *adj* in favour of family
PROFANE *adj* showing disrespect for religion or holy things ▷ *vb* treat (something sacred) irreverently, desecrate
PROFANED > PROFANE
PROFANELY > PROFANE
PROFANER > PROFANE
PROFANERS > PROFANE
PROFANES > PROFANE
PROFANING > PROFANE
PROFANITY *n* profane talk or behaviour, blasphemy
PROFESS *vb* state or claim (something as true), sometimes falsely
PROFESSED *adj* supposed
PROFESSES > PROFESS
PROFESSOR *n* teacher of the highest rank in a university
PROFFER *vb* offer ▷ *n* act of proffering
PROFFERED > PROFFER
PROFFERER > PROFFER
PROFFERS > PROFFER
PROFILE *n* outline, esp of the face, as seen from the side ▷ *vb* draw, write, or make a profile of
PROFILED > PROFILE
PROFILER *n* person or device that creates a profile, esp someone with psychological training who assists police investigations by identifying the likely

characteristics of the perpetrator of a particular crime
PROFILERS > PROFILER
PROFILES > PROFILE
PROFILING > PROFILE
PROFILIST > PROFILE
PROFIT *n* money gained ▷ *vb* gain or benefit
PROFITED > PROFIT
PROFITEER *n* person who makes excessive profits at the expense of the public ▷ *vb* make excessive profits
PROFITER > PROFIT
PROFITERS > PROFIT
PROFITING > PROFIT
PROFITS > PROFIT
PROFLUENT *adj* flowing smoothly or abundantly
PROFORMA *n* invoice issued before an order is placed or before the goods are delivered giving all the details and the cost of the goods
PROFORMAS > PROFORMA
PROFOUND *adj* showing or needing great knowledge ▷ *n* great depth
PROFOUNDS > PROFOUND
PROFS > PROF
PROFUSE *adj* plentiful
PROFUSELY > PROFUSE
PROFUSER > PROFUSE
PROFUSERS > PROFUSE
PROFUSION > PROFUSE
PROFUSIVE *same as* > PROFUSE
PROG *vb* prowl about for or as if for food or plunder ▷ *n* food obtained by begging
PROGENIES > PROGENY
PROGENY *n* children
PROGERIA *n* premature old age, a rare condition occurring in children and characterized by small stature, absent or greying hair, wrinkled skin, and other signs of old age
PROGERIAS > PROGERIA
PROGESTIN *n* type of steroid hormone
PROGGED > PROG
PROGGER *n* fan of progressive rock
PROGGERS > PROGGER
PROGGING > PROG
PROGGINS *n* proctor
PROGNOSE *vb* predict course of disease
PROGNOSED > PROGNOSE
PROGNOSES > PROGNOSIS
PROGNOSIS *n* doctor's forecast about the progress of an illness
PROGRADE *vb* (of beach) advance towards sea
PROGRADED > PROGRADE
PROGRADES > PROGRADE
PROGRAM *same as* > PROGRAMME
PROGRAMED > PROGRAM
PROGRAMER *n* US spelling of programmer
PROGRAMME *same as* > PROGRAM
PROGRAMS > PROGRAM
PROGRESS *n* improvement, development ▷ *vb* become more advanced or skilful
PROGS > PROG
PROGUN *adj* in favour of public owning firearms
PROHIBIT *vb* forbid or prevent from happening
PROHIBITS > PROHIBIT
PROIGN *same as* > PROIN
PROIGNED > PROIGN
PROIGNING > PROIGN
PROIGNS > PROIGN
PROIN *vb* trim or prune
PROINE *same as* > PROIN
PROINED > PROIN
PROINES > PROINE
PROINING > PROIN
PROINS > PROIN
PROJECT *n* planned scheme to do or examine something over a period ▷ *vb* make a forecast based on known data
PROJECTED > PROJECT
PROJECTOR *n* apparatus for projecting photographic images, films, or slides on a screen
PROJECTS > PROJECT
PROJET *n* draft of a proposed treaty
PROJETS > PROJET
PROKARYON *n* nucleus of a prokaryote
PROKARYOT *n* any organism having cells in each of which the genetic material is in a single DNA chain, not enclosed in a nucleus
PROKE *vb* thrust or poke
PROKED > PROKE
PROKER > PROKE
PROKERS > PROKE
PROKES > PROKE
PROKING > PROKE
PROLABOR *adj* favouring the Labor party
PROLACTIN *n* gonadotrophic hormone secreted by the anterior lobe of the pituitary gland
PROLAMIN *same as* > PROLAMINE
PROLAMINE *n* any of a group of simple plant proteins, including gliadin, hordein, and zein
PROLAMINS > PROLAMIN
PROLAN *n* constituent of human pregnancy urine
PROLANS > PROLAN
PROLAPSE *n* slipping down of an internal organ of the body from its normal position ▷ *vb* (of an internal organ) slip from its normal position
PROLAPSED > PROLAPSE
PROLAPSES > PROLAPSE
PROLAPSUS *same as* > PROLAPSE
PROLATE *adj* having a polar diameter which is longer than the equatorial diameter ▷ *vb* pronounce or utter
PROLATED > PROLATE
PROLATELY > PROLATE
PROLATES > PROLATE
PROLATING > PROLATE
PROLATION > PROLATE
PROLATIVE > PROLATE
PROLE *old form of* > PROWL
PROLED > PROLE
PROLEG *n* any of the short paired unjointed appendages on each abdominal segment of a caterpillar and any of certain other insect larvae
PROLEGS > PROLEG
PROLEPSES > PROLEPSIS
PROLEPSIS *n* rhetorical device by which objections are anticipated and answered in advance
PROLEPTIC > PROLEPSIS
PROLER *n* prowler
PROLERS > PROLER
PROLES > PROLE
PROLETARY *n* member of the proletariat
PROLICIDE *n* killing of one's child
PROLIFIC *adj* very productive
PROLINE *n* nonessential amino acid that occurs in protein
PROLINES > PROLINE
PROLING > PROLE
PROLIX *adj* (of speech or a piece of writing) overlong and boring
PROLIXITY > PROLIX
PROLIXLY > PROLIX
PROLL *vb* prowl or search
PROLLED > PROLL
PROLLER > PROLL
PROLLERS > PROLL
PROLLING > PROLL
PROLLS > PROLL
PROLOG *same as* > PROLOGUE
PROLOGED > PROLOG
PROLOGING > PROLOG
PROLOGISE *same as* > PROLOGIZE
PROLOGIST *n* prologue writer
PROLOGIZE *vb* write a prologue
PROLOGS > PROLOG
PROLOGUE *n* introduction to a play or book ▷ *vb* introduce or preface with or as if with a prologue
PROLOGUED > PROLOGUE
PROLOGUES > PROLOGUE
PROLONG *vb* make (something) last longer
PROLONGE *n* (formerly) specially fitted rope used as part of the towing equipment of a gun carriage
PROLONGED > PROLONG
PROLONGER > PROLONG
PROLONGES > PROLONGE
PROLONGS > PROLONG
PROLUSION *n* preliminary written exercise
PROLUSORY > PROLUSION
PROM *n* formal dance held at a high school or college
PROMACHOS *n* defender or champion
PROMENADE *n* paved walkway along the seafront at a holiday resort ▷ *vb* take a leisurely walk
PROMETAL *n* type of cast iron
PROMETALS > PROMETAL
PROMETRIC *adj* in favour of the metric system
PROMINE *n* substance promoting cell growth
PROMINENT *adj* very noticeable
PROMINES > PROMINE
PROMISE *vb* say that one will definitely do or not do something ▷ *n* undertaking to do or not to do something
PROMISED > PROMISE
PROMISEE *n* person to whom a promise is made
PROMISEES > PROMISEE
PROMISER > PROMISE
PROMISERS > PROMISE
PROMISES > PROMISE
PROMISING *adj* likely to succeed or turn out well
PROMISOR *n* person who makes a promise
PROMISORS > PROMISOR
PROMISSOR *n* (in law) person who makes a promise
PROMMER *n* spectator at promenade concert
PROMMERS > PROMMER
PROMO *vb* promote (something) using a promo
PROMODERN *adj* in favour of the modern
PROMOED > PROMO
PROMOING > PROMO
PROMOS > PROMO
PROMOTE *vb* help to make (something) happen or increase
PROMOTED > PROMOTE
PROMOTER *n* person who organizes or finances an event etc
PROMOTERS > PROMOTER
PROMOTES > PROMOTE
PROMOTING > PROMOTE
PROMOTION > PROMOTE
PROMOTIVE *adj* tending to

promote
PROMOTOR *variant of* > PROMOTER
PROMOTORS > PROMOTOR
PROMPT *vb* cause (an action) ▷ *adj* done without delay ▷ *adv* exactly ▷ *n* anything that serves to remind
PROMPTED > PROMPT
PROMPTER *n* person offstage who prompts actors
PROMPTERS > PROMPTER
PROMPTEST > PROMPT
PROMPTING > PROMPT
PROMPTLY > PROMPT
PROMPTS > PROMPT
PROMPTURE *n* prompting
PROMS > PROM
PROMULGE *vb* bring to public knowledge
PROMULGED > PROMULGE
PROMULGES > PROMULGE
PROMUSCES > PROMUSCIS
PROMUSCIS *n* proboscis of certain insects
PRONAOI > PRONAOS
PRONAOS *n* inner area of the portico of a classical temple
PRONATE *vb* turn (a limb, hand, or foot) so that the palm or sole is directed downwards
PRONATED > PRONATE
PRONATES > PRONATE
PRONATING > PRONATE
PRONATION > PRONATE
PRONATOR *n* any muscle whose contractions produce or affect pronation
PRONATORS > PRONATOR
PRONE *n* sermon
PRONELY > PRONE
PRONENESS > PRONE
PRONEPHRA *n* parts of the kidneys of lower vertebrates
PRONER > PRONE
PRONES > PRONE
PRONEST > PRONE
PRONEUR *n* flatterer
PRONEURS > PRONEUR
PRONG *n* one spike of a fork or similar instrument ▷ *vb* prick or spear with or as if with a prong
PRONGBUCK *n* horned N American ruminant
PRONGED > PRONG
PRONGHORN *n* ruminant mammal inhabiting rocky deserts of North America and having small branched horns
PRONGING > PRONG
PRONGS > PRONG
PRONK *vb* jump straight up
PRONKED > PRONK
PRONKING > PRONK
PRONKS > PRONK
PRONOTA > PRONOTUM
PRONOTAL > PRONOTUM
PRONOTUM *n* notum of the prothorax of an insect
PRONOUN *n* word, such as *she* or *it*, used to replace a noun
PRONOUNCE *vb* form the sounds of (words or letters), esp clearly or in a particular way
PRONOUNS > PRONOUN
PRONTO *adv* at once
PRONUCLEI *n* nuclei of mature ova or spermatozoa before fertilization
PRONUNCIO *n* papal ambassador
PROO *interj* (to a horse) stop!
PROOEMION *n* preface
PROOEMIUM *n* preface
PROOF *n* evidence that shows that something is true or has happened ▷ *adj* able to withstand ▷ *vb* take a proof from (type matter)
PROOFED > PROOF
PROOFER *n* reader of proofs
PROOFERS > PROOFER
PROOFING > PROOF
PROOFINGS > PROOF
PROOFLESS > PROOF
PROOFREAD *vb* read and correct (printer's proofs)
PROOFROOM *n* room for proofreading
PROOFS > PROOF
PROOTIC *n* bone in front of ear
PROOTICS > PROOTIC
PROP *vb* support (something) so that it stays upright or in place ▷ *n* pole, beam, etc used as a support
PROPAGATE *vb* spread (information and ideas)
PROPAGE *vb* propagate
PROPAGED > PROPAGE
PROPAGES > PROPAGE
PROPAGING > PROPAGE
PROPAGULA > PROPAGULE
PROPAGULE *n* plant part, such as a bud, that becomes detached from the rest of the plant and grows into a new plant
PROPALE *vb* publish (something)
PROPALED > PROPALE
PROPALES > PROPALE
PROPALING > PROPALE
PROPANE *n* flammable gas found in petroleum and used as a fuel
PROPANES > PROPANE
PROPANOIC as in *propanoic acid* colourless liquid carboxylic acid
PROPANOL *n* colourless alcohol
PROPANOLS > PROPANOL
PROPANONE *n* systematic name of acetone
PROPEL *vb* cause to move forward
PROPELLED > PROPEL
PROPELLER *n* revolving shaft with blades for driving a ship or aircraft
PROPELLOR *same as* > PROPELLER
PROPELS > PROPEL
PROPEND *vb* be inclined or disposed
PROPENDED > PROPEND
PROPENDS > PROPEND
PROPENE *n* colourless gaseous alkene obtained by cracking petroleum
PROPENES > PROPENE
PROPENOIC as in *propenoic acid* systematic name of acrylic acid
PROPENOL *n* liquid used to make allylic alcohol
PROPENOLS > PROPENOL
PROPENSE *adj* inclining forward
PROPENYL *n* three-carbon radical
PROPER *adj* real or genuine ▷ *n* service or psalm regarded as appropriate to a specific day, season, etc
PROPERDIN *n* protein present in blood serum that, acting with complement, is involved in the destruction of alien cells, such as bacteria
PROPERER > PROPER
PROPEREST > PROPER
PROPERLY > PROPER
PROPERS > PROPER
PROPERTY *same as* > PROPRIUM
PROPHAGE *n* virus that exists in a bacterial cell and undergoes division with its host without destroying it
PROPHAGES > PROPHAGE
PROPHASE *n* first stage of mitosis, during which the nuclear membrane disappears and the nuclear material resolves itself into chromosomes
PROPHASES > PROPHASE
PROPHASIC > PROPHASE
PROPHECY *n* prediction
PROPHESY *vb* foretell
PROPHET *n* person supposedly chosen by God to spread His word
PROPHETIC *adj* foretelling what will happen
PROPHETS > PROPHET
PROPHYLL *n* leaf-shaped plant structure
PROPHYLLS > PROPHYLL
PROPIONIC as in *propionic acid* former name for propanoic acid
PROPJET *another name for* > TURBOPROP
PROPJETS > PROPJET
PROPMAN *n* member of the stage crew in charge of the stage props
PROPMEN > PROPMAN
PROPODEON *n* part of an insect's thorax
PROPODEUM *variant of* > PROPODEON
PROPOLIS *n* greenish-brown resinous aromatic substance collected by bees from the buds of trees for use in the construction of hives
PROPONE *vb* propose or put forward, esp before a court
PROPONED > PROPONE
PROPONENT *n* person who argues in favour of something
PROPONES > PROPONE
PROPONING > PROPONE
PROPOSAL *n* act of proposing
PROPOSALS > PROPOSAL
PROPOSE *vb* put forward for consideration
PROPOSED > PROPOSE
PROPOSER > PROPOSE
PROPOSERS > PROPOSE
PROPOSES > PROPOSE
PROPOSING > PROPOSE
PROPOSITA *n* woman from whom a line of descent is traced
PROPOSITI *n* people from whom lines of descent are traced
PROPOUND *vb* put forward for consideration
PROPOUNDS > PROPOUND
PROPPANT *n* material used in the oil extraction process
PROPPANTS > PROPPANT
PROPPED > PROP
PROPPING > PROP
PROPRETOR *n* (in ancient Rome) citizen, esp an ex-praetor, granted a praetor's imperium, to be exercised outside Rome
PROPRIA > PROPRIUM
PROPRIETY *n* quality of being appropriate or fitting
PROPRIUM *n* attribute that is not essential to a species but is common and peculiar to it
PROPS > PROP
PROPTOSES > PROPTOSIS
PROPTOSIS *n* forward displacement of an organ or part, such as the eyeball
PROPULSOR *n* propeller
PROPYL *n* of, consisting of, or containing the monovalent group of atoms C_3H_7-
PROPYLA > PROPYLON
PROPYLAEA *n* porticos, esp those that form the

entrances to temples
PROPYLENE *n* gas found in petroleum and used to produce many organic compounds
PROPYLIC > PROPYL
PROPYLITE *n* altered andesite or similar rock containing calcite, chlorite, etc, produced by the action of hot water
PROPYLON *n* portico, esp one that forms the entrance to a temple
PROPYLONS > PROPYLON
PROPYLS > PROPYL
PRORATE *vb* divide, assess, or distribute (something) proportionately
PRORATED > PRORATE
PRORATES > PRORATE
PRORATING > PRORATE
PRORATION > PRORATE
PRORE *n* forward part of ship
PRORECTOR *n* official in German academia
PROREFORM *adj* in favour of or supporting reform, esp within politics
PRORES > PRORE
PROROGATE *vb* discontinue legislative meetings
PROROGUE *vb* suspend (parliament) without dissolving it
PROROGUED > PROROGUE
PROROGUES > PROROGUE
PROS > PRO
PROSAIC *adj* lacking imagination, dull
PROSAICAL *same as* > PROSAIC
PROSAISM *n* prosaic quality or style
PROSAISMS > PROSAISM
PROSAIST > PROSAISM
PROSAISTS > PROSAISM
PROSATEUR *n* writer of prose
PROSCENIA *n* arches or openings separating stages from auditoria together with the areas immediately in front of the arches
PROSCRIBE *vb* prohibit, outlaw
PROSCRIPT *n* proscription or prohibition
PROSE *n* ordinary speech or writing in contrast to poetry ▷ *vb* speak or write in a tedious style
PROSECT *vb* dissect a cadaver for a public demonstration
PROSECTED > PROSECT
PROSECTOR *n* person who prepares or dissects anatomical subjects for demonstration
PROSECTS > PROSECT
PROSECUTE *vb* bring a criminal charge against
PROSED > PROSE
PROSELIKE > PROSE
PROSELYTE *n* recent convert
PROSEMAN *n* writer of prose
PROSEMEN > PROSEMAN
PROSER *n* writer of prose
PROSERS > PROSER
PROSES > PROSE
PROSEUCHA *n* place of prayer
PROSEUCHE *n* prayer
PROSIER > PROSY
PROSIEST > PROSY
PROSIFIED > PROSIFY
PROSIFIES > PROSIFY
PROSIFY *vb* write prose
PROSILY > PROSY
PROSIMIAN *n* any primate of the primitive suborder *Prosimii*, including lemurs, lorises, and tarsiers ▷ *adj* of, relating to, or belonging to the *Prosimii*
PROSINESS > PROSY
PROSING > PROSE
PROSINGS > PROSE
PROSIT *interj* good health! cheers!
PROSO *n* millet
PROSODIAL *adj* of prosody
PROSODIAN *n* writer of prose
PROSODIC > PROSODY
PROSODIES > PROSODY
PROSODIST > PROSODY
PROSODY *n* study of poetic metre and techniques
PROSOMA *n* head and thorax of an arachnid
PROSOMAL > PROSOMA
PROSOMAS > PROSOMA
PROSOMATA > PROSOMA
PROSOPON *n* (in Christianity) manifestation of any of the persons of the Trinity
PROSOPONS > PROSOPON
PROSOS > PROSO
PROSPECT *n* something anticipated ▷ *vb* explore, esp for gold
PROSPECTS > PROSPECT
PROSPER *vb* be successful
PROSPERED > PROSPER
PROSPERS > PROSPER
PROSS *n* prostitute
PROSSES > PROSS
PROSSIE *n* prostitute
PROSSIES > PROSSIE
PROST *same as* > PROSIT
PROSTATE *n* gland in male mammals that surrounds the neck of the bladder ▷ *adj* of or relating to the prostate gland
PROSTATES > PROSTATE
PROSTATIC *same as* > PROSTATE
PROSTERNA *n* sternums or thoraces of insects
PROSTIE *n* prostitute
PROSTIES > PROSTIE
PROSTOMIA *n* lobes at the head ends of earthworms and other annelids
PROSTRATE *adj* lying face downwards ▷ *vb* lie face downwards
PROSTYLE *adj* (of a building) having a row of columns in front, esp as in the portico of a Greek temple ▷ *n* prostyle building, portico, etc
PROSTYLES > PROSTYLE
PROSUMER *n* amateur user of electronic equipment suitable for professionals
PROSUMERS > PROSUMER
PROSY *adj* dull and long-winded
PROTAMIN *same as* > PROTAMINE
PROTAMINE *n* any of a group of basic simple proteins that occur, in association with nucleic acids, in the sperm of some fish
PROTAMINS > PROTAMIN
PROTANDRY *n* condition (in hermaphrodite plants) of maturing the anthers before the stigma
PROTANOPE *n* person with type of colour blindness
PROTASES > PROTASIS
PROTASIS *n* antecedent of a conditional statement
PROTATIC > PROTASIS
PROTEA *n* African shrub with showy flowers
PROTEAN *adj* constantly changing ▷ *n* creature that can change shape
PROTEANS > PROTEAN
PROTEAS > PROTEA
PROTEASE *n* any enzyme involved in proteolysis
PROTEASES > PROTEASE
PROTECT *vb* defend from trouble, harm, or loss
PROTECTED > PROTECT
PROTECTER *same as* > PROTECTOR
PROTECTOR *n* person or thing that protects
PROTECTS > PROTECT
PROTEGE *n* person who is protected and helped by another
PROTEGEE *n* woman or girl who is protected and helped by another
PROTEGEES > PROTEGEE
PROTEGES > PROTEGE
PROTEI > PROTEUS
PROTEID *n* protein
PROTEIDE *variant of* > PROTEID
PROTEIDES > PROTEIDE
PROTEIDS > PROTEID
PROTEIN *n* any of a group of complex organic compounds that are essential for life
PROTEINIC > PROTEIN
PROTEINS > PROTEIN
PROTEND *vb* hold out or stretch
PROTENDED > PROTEND
PROTENDS > PROTEND
PROTENSE *n* extension
PROTENSES > PROTENSE
PROTEOME *n* full complement of proteins that occur within a cell, tissue, or organism
PROTEOMES > PROTEOME
PROTEOMIC > PROTEOME
PROTEOSE *n* compounds formed during proteolysi that is less complex than metaproteins but more s than peptones
PROTEOSES > PROTEOSE
PROTEST *n* declaration or demonstration of objection ▷ *vb* object, disagree
PROTESTED > PROTEST
PROTESTER > PROTEST
PROTESTOR > PROTEST
PROTESTS > PROTEST
PROTEUS *n* aerobic bacterium
PROTEUSES > PROTEUS
PROTHALLI *n* small flat free-living gametophtye in ferns, club mosses etc
PROTHESES > PROTHESIS
PROTHESIS *n* process in the development of a language by which a phoneme or syllable is prefixed to a word to facilitate pronunciation
PROTHETIC > PROTHESIS
PROTHORAX *n* first segme of the thorax of an insect, which bears the first pair of walking legs
PROTHYL *variant of* > PROTYLE
PROTHYLS > PROTHYL
PROTIST *n* (in some classification systems) a organism belonging to t kingdom *Protista*
PROTISTAN > PROTIST
PROTISTIC > PROTIST
PROTISTS > PROTIST
PROTIUM *n* most commor isotope of hydrogen
PROTIUMS > PROTIUM
PROTOAVIS *n* bird-like fossil
PROTOCOL *n* rules of behaviour for formal occasions
PROTOCOLS > PROTOCOL
PROTODERM *n* outer primary meristem of a plant
PROTOGINE *n* type of granite
PROTOGYNY *n* (in hermaphrodite plants and animals) condition c producing female gamet

before male ones
ROTON *n* positively charged particle in the nucleus of an atom
ROTONATE *vb* provide atom with proton
ROTONEMA *n* branched threadlike structure that grows from a moss spore and eventually develops into the moss plant
ROTONIC *adj* (of a solvent, such as water) able to donate hydrogen ions to solute molecules
ROTONS > PROTON
ROTOPOD *n* part of crustacean's leg
ROTOPODS > PROTOPOD
ROTORE *n* primary mineral deposit
ROTORES > PROTORE
ROTOSTAR *n* cloud of interstellar gas and dust that gradually collapses, forming a hot dense core, and evolves into a star once nuclear fusion can occur in the core
ROTOTYPE *n* original or model to be copied or developed
ROTOXID *variant of* > PROTOXIDE
ROTOXIDE *n* oxide of an element that contains the smallest amount of oxygen of any of its oxides
ROTOXIDS > PROTOXID
ROTOZOA > PROTOZOAN
ROTOZOAL > PROTOZOAN
ROTOZOAN *n* microscopic one-celled creature ▷ *adj* of or relating to protozoans
ROTOZOIC > PROTOZOAN
ROTOZOON *same as* > PROTOZOAN
ROTRACT *vb* lengthen or extend (a situation etc)
ROTRACTS > PROTRACT
ROTRADE *adj* in favour of trade
ROTRUDE *vb* stick out, project
ROTRUDED > PROTRUDE
ROTRUDES > PROTRUDE
ROTYL *same as* > PROTYLE
ROTYLE *n* hypothetical primitive substance from which the chemical elements were supposed to have been formed
ROTYLES > PROTYLE
ROTYLS > PROTYL
ROUD *adj* feeling pleasure and satisfaction
ROUDER > PROUD
ROUDEST > PROUD
ROUDFUL *adj* full of pride
ROUDISH *adj* rather proud
ROUDLY > PROUD
ROUDNESS > PROUD
ROUL *variant of* > PROWL
PROULED > PROUL
PROULER *Scots variant of* > PROWLER
PROULERS > PROULER
PROULING > PROUL
PROULS > PROUL
PROUNION *adj* in favour of or supporting the constitutional union between two or more countries
PROUSTITE *n* red mineral consisting of silver arsenic sulphide in hexagonal crystalline form
PROVABLE > PROVE
PROVABLY > PROVE
PROVAND *n* food
PROVANDS > PROVAND
PROVANT *vb* supply with provisions
PROVANTED > PROVANT
PROVANTS > PROVANT
PROVE *vb* establish the validity of
PROVEABLE > PROVE
PROVEABLY > PROVEABLE
PROVED > PROVE
PROVEDOR *variant of* > PROVEDORE
PROVEDORE *n* purveyor
PROVEDORS > PROVEDOR
PROVEN > PROVE
PROVEND *same as* > PROVAND
PROVENDER *n* fodder
PROVENDS > PROVEND
PROVENLY > PROVE
PROVER > PROVE
PROVERB *n* short saying that expresses a truth or gives a warning ▷ *vb* utter or describe (something) in the form of a proverb
PROVERBED > PROVERB
PROVERBS > PROVERB
PROVERS > PROVE
PROVES > PROVE
PROVIANT *variant of* > PROVAND
PROVIANTS > PROVIANT
PROVIDE *vb* make available
PROVIDED > PROVIDE
PROVIDENT *adj* thrifty
PROVIDER > PROVIDE
PROVIDERS > PROVIDE
PROVIDES > PROVIDE
PROVIDING > PROVIDE
PROVIDOR *variant of* > PROVEDORE
PROVIDORS > PROVIDOR
PROVINCE *n* area governed as a unit of a country or empire
PROVINCES > PROVINCE
PROVINE *vb* plant branch of vine in ground for propagation
PROVINED > PROVINE
PROVINES > PROVINE
PROVING > PROVE
PROVINGS > PROVE
PROVINING > PROVINE
PROVIRAL > PROVIRUS
PROVIRUS *n* inactive form of a virus in a host cell
PROVISION *n* act of supplying something ▷ *vb* supply with food
PROVISO *n* condition, stipulation
PROVISOES > PROVISO
PROVISOR *n* person who receives provision
PROVISORS > PROVISOR
PROVISORY *adj* containing a proviso
PROVISOS > PROVISO
PROVOCANT *n* provocateur; one who deliberately behaves controversially to provoke argument or other strong reactions
PROVOKE *vb* deliberately anger
PROVOKED > PROVOKE
PROVOKER > PROVOKE
PROVOKERS > PROVOKE
PROVOKES > PROVOKE
PROVOKING > PROVOKE
PROVOLONE *n* mellow, pale yellow, soft, and sometimes smoked cheese, made of cow's milk: usually moulded in the shape of a pear
PROVOST *n* head of certain university colleges in Britain
PROVOSTRY *n* office of provost
PROVOSTS > PROVOST
PROW *n* bow of a vessel ▷ *adj* gallant
PROWAR *adj* in favour of or supporting war
PROWER > PROW
PROWESS *n* superior skill or ability
PROWESSES > PROWESS
PROWEST > PROW
PROWL *vb* move stealthily around a place as if in search of prey or plunder ▷ *n* prowling
PROWLED > PROWL
PROWLER > PROWL
PROWLERS > PROWL
PROWLING > PROWL
PROWLINGS > PROWL
PROWLS > PROWL
PROWS > PROW
PROXEMIC > PROXEMICS
PROXEMICS *n* study of spatial interrelationships in humans or in populations of animals of the same species
PROXIES > PROXY
PROXIMAL *same as* > PROXIMATE
PROXIMATE *adj* next or nearest in space or time
PROXIMITY *n* nearness in space or time
PROXIMO *adv* in or during the next or coming month
PROXY *n* person authorized to act on behalf of someone else
PROYN *obsolete spelling of* > PRUNE
PROYNE *obsolete spelling of* > PRUNE
PROYNES > PROYNE
PROYNS > PROYNE
PROZYMITE *n* Christian using leavened bread for the Eucharist
PRUDE *n* person who is excessively modest, prim, or proper
PRUDENCE *n* caution in practical affairs
PRUDENCES > PRUDENCE
PRUDENT *adj* cautious, discreet, and sensible
PRUDENTLY > PRUDENT
PRUDERIES > PRUDE
PRUDERY > PRUDE
PRUDES > PRUDE
PRUDISH > PRUDE
PRUDISHLY > PRUDE
PRUH *variant of* > PROO
PRUINA *n* woolly white covering on some lichens
PRUINAS > PRUINA
PRUINE *obsolete spelling of* > PRUNE
PRUINES > PRUINE
PRUINOSE *adj* coated with a powdery or waxy bloom
PRUNABLE > PRUNE
PRUNE *n* dried plum ▷ *vb* cut off dead parts or excessive branches from (a tree or plant)
PRUNED > PRUNE
PRUNELLA *n* strong fabric, esp a twill-weave worsted, used for gowns and the uppers of some shoes
PRUNELLAS > PRUNELLA
PRUNELLE *same as* > PRUNELLA
PRUNELLES > PRUNELLE
PRUNELLO *same as* > PRUNELLA
PRUNELLOS > PRUNELLO
PRUNER > PRUNE
PRUNERS > PRUNE
PRUNES > PRUNE
PRUNING > PRUNE
PRUNINGS > PRUNE
PRUNT *n* glass ornamentation
PRUNTED > PRUNT
PRUNTS > PRUNT
PRUNUS *n* type of ornamental tree or shrub
PRUNUSES > PRUNUS
PRURIENCE > PRURIENT
PRURIENCY *n* sexual desire
PRURIENT *adj* excessively interested in sexual matters
PRURIGO *n* chronic inflammatory disease of the skin characterized by the formation of papules and intense itching
PRURIGOS > PRURIGO
PRURITIC > PRURITUS

PRURITUS *n* any intense sensation of itching
PRUSIK *n* sliding knot that locks under pressure and can be used to form a loop in which a climber can place his or her foot in order to stand or ascend a rope ▷ *vb* climb (up a standing rope) using prusiks
PRUSIKED > PRUSIK
PRUSIKING > PRUSIK
PRUSIKS > PRUSIK
PRUSSIATE *n* any cyanide, ferrocyanide, or ferricyanide
PRUSSIC as in *prussic acid* weakly acidic extremely poisonous aqueous solution of hydrogen cyanide
PRUTA *same as* > PRUTAH
PRUTAH *n* former Israeli coin
PRUTOT > PRUTAH
PRUTOTH > PRUTAH
PRY *vb* make an impertinent or uninvited inquiry into a private matter ▷ *n* act of prying
PRYER *same as* > PRIER
PRYERS > PRYER
PRYING > PRY
PRYINGLY > PRY
PRYINGS > PRY
PRYS *old variant of* > PRICE
PRYSE *old variant of* > PRICE
PRYTANEA > PRYTANEUM
PRYTANEUM *n* public hall of a city in ancient Greece
PRYTHEE *same as* > PRITHEE
PSALM *n* sacred song ▷ *vb* sing a psalm
PSALMBOOK *n* book of psalms
PSALMED > PSALM
PSALMIC > PSALM
PSALMING > PSALM
PSALMIST *n* writer of psalms
PSALMISTS > PSALMIST
PSALMODIC > PSALMODY
PSALMODY *n* singing of sacred music
PSALMS > PSALM
PSALTER *n* devotional or liturgical book containing a version of Psalms
PSALTERIA *n* omasums
PSALTERS > PSALTER
PSALTERY *n* ancient instrument played by plucking strings
PSALTRESS *n* woman who sings psalms
PSALTRIES > PSALTRY
PSALTRY *same as* > PSALTERY
PSAMMITE *rare name for* > SANDSTONE
PSAMMITES > PSAMMITE
PSAMMITIC > PSAMMITE
PSAMMON *n* community of microscopic life forms living between grains of sand on shores
PSAMMONS > PSAMMON
PSCHENT *n* ancient Egyptian crown
PSCHENTS > PSCHENT
PSELLISM *n* stammering
PSELLISMS > PSELLISM
PSEPHISM *n* proposition adopted by a majority vote
PSEPHISMS > PSEPHISM
PSEPHITE *n* any rock, such as a breccia, that consists of large fragments embedded in a finer matrix
PSEPHITES > PSEPHITE
PSEPHITIC > PSEPHITE
PSEUD *n* pretentious person
PSEUDAXES > PSEUDAXIS
PSEUDAXIS *another name for* > SYMPODIUM
PSEUDERY *n* pretentious talk
PSEUDISH > PSEUD
PSEUDO *n* pretentious person
PSEUDONYM *n* fictitious name adopted esp by an author
PSEUDOPOD *n* temporary projection from the body of a single-celled animal
PSEUDOS > PSEUDO
PSEUDS > PSEUD
PSHAW *n* exclamation of disgust, impatience, disbelief, etc
PSHAWS > PSHAW
PSI *n* 23rd letter of the Greek alphabet
PSILOCIN *n* hallucinogenic substance
PSILOCINS > PSILOCIN
PSILOSES > PSILOSIS
PSILOSIS *n* disease of the small intestine
PSILOTIC > PSILOSIS
PSION *n* type of elementary particle
PSIONIC > PSIONICS
PSIONICS *n* study of the practical use of psychic powers
PSIONS > PSION
PSIS > PSI
PSOAE > PSOAS
PSOAI > PSOAS
PSOAS *n* either of two muscles of the loins that aid in flexing and rotating the thigh
PSOATIC > PSOAS
PSOCID *n* tiny wingless insect
PSOCIDS > PSOCID
PSORA *n* itching skin complaint
PSORALEA *n* any plant of the tropical and subtropical leguminous genus *Psoralea*, having curly leaves, white or purple flowers, and short one-seeded pods
PSORALEAS > PSORALEA
PSORALEN *n* treatment for some skin diseases
PSORALENS > PSORALEN
PSORAS > PSORA
PSORIASES > PSORIASIS
PSORIASIS *n* skin disease with reddish spots and patches covered with silvery scales
PSORIATIC > PSORIASIS
PSORIC > PSORA
PSST *n* sound made to attract someone's attention, esp without others noticing
PSSTS > PSST
PST *interj* used to get another person's attention
PSYCH *vb* psychoanalyse
PSYCHE *same as* > PSYCH
PSYCHED > PSYCH
PSYCHES > PSYCH
PSYCHIC *adj* having mental powers which cannot be explained by natural laws ▷ *n* person with psychic powers
PSYCHICAL > PSYCHIC
PSYCHICS > PSYCHIC
PSYCHING > PSYCH
PSYCHISM *n* belief in a universal soul
PSYCHISMS > PSYCHISM
PSYCHIST > PSYCHISM
PSYCHISTS > PSYCHISM
PSYCHO *n* psychopath
PSYCHOGAS *n* gas with a mind-altering effect
PSYCHOID *n* name for an animal's innate impetus to perform actions
PSYCHOIDS > PSYCHOID
PSYCHOS > PSYCHO
PSYCHOSES > PSYCHOSIS
PSYCHOSIS *n* severe mental disorder in which the sufferer's contact with reality becomes distorted
PSYCHOTIC *adj* of, relating to, or characterized by psychosis ▷ *n* person suffering from psychosis
PSYCHS > PSYCH
PSYLLA *same as* > PSYLLID
PSYLLAS > PSYLLA
PSYLLID *n* any homopterous insect of the family *Psyllidae*, which comprises the jumping plant lice
PSYLLIDS > PSYLLID
PSYLLIUM *n* grain, the husks of which are used medicinally as a laxative and to reduce blood cholesterol levels
PSYLLIUMS > PSYLLIUM
PSYOP *n* psychological operation
PSYOPS > PSYOP
PSYWAR *n* psychological warfare
PSYWARS > PSYWAR
PTARMIC *n* material that causes sneezing
PTARMICS > PTARMIC
PTARMIGAN *n* bird of the grouse family which turn[s] white in winter
PTERIA > PTERION
PTERIDINE *n* yellow crystalline base
PTERIN *n* compound such as folic acid
PTERINS > PTERIN
PTERION *n* point on the side of the skull where a number of bones meet
PTEROPOD *n* small marine gastropod mollusc in which the foot is expande[d] into two winglike lobes f[or] swimming and the shell i[s] absent or thin-walled
PTEROPODS > PTEROPOD
PTEROSAUR *n* extinct flyin[g] reptile
PTERYGIA > PTERYGIUM
PTERYGIAL *adj* of or relating to a fin or wing
PTERYGIUM *n* abnormal tissue over corner of eye
PTERYGOID *n* either of two long bony plates extending downwards from each side of the sphenoid bone within th[e] skull
PTERYLA *n* any of the trac[ts] of skin that bear contour feathers, arranged in line[s] along the body of a bird
PTERYLAE > PTERYLA
PTILOSES > PTILOSIS
PTILOSIS *n* falling out of eye lashes
PTISAN *n* grape juice drained off without pressure
PTISANS > PTISAN
PTOMAIN *same as* > PTOMAINE
PTOMAINE *n* any of a grou[p] of poisonous alkaloids found in decaying matte[r]
PTOMAINES > PTOMAINE
PTOMAINIC > PTOMAINE
PTOMAINS > PTOMAIN
PTOOEY *interj* imitation o[f] the sound of spitting
PTOSES > PTOSIS
PTOSIS *n* prolapse or drooping of a part, esp th[e] eyelid
PTOTIC > PTOSIS
PTUI *same as* > PTOOEY
PTYALIN *n* amylase secreted in the saliva of man and other animals
PTYALINS > PTYALIN
PTYALISE *same as* > PTYALIZE
PTYALISED > PTYALISE
PTYALISES > PTYALISE
PTYALISM *n* excessive

secretion of saliva
TYALISMS > PTYALISM
TYALIZE *vb* expel saliva from the mouth
TYALIZED > PTYALIZE
TYALIZES > PTYALIZE
TYXES > PTYXIS
TYXIS *n* folding of a leaf in a bud
JB *n* building with a bar licensed to sell alcoholic drinks ▷ *vb* visit a pub or pubs
JBBED > PUB
JBBING > PUB
JBE *n* pubic hair
JBERAL *adj* relating to puberty
JBERTAL > PUBERTY
JBERTIES > PUBERTY
JBERTY *n* beginning of sexual maturity
JBES > PUBE
JBESCENT *adj* reaching or having reached puberty
JBIC *adj* of the lower abdomen
JBIS *n* one of the three sections of the hipbone that forms part of the pelvis
JBLIC *adj* of or concerning the people as a whole ▷ *n* community, people in general
JBLICAN *n* person who owns or runs a pub
JBLICANS > PUBLICAN
JBLICISE *same as* > PUBLICIZE
JBLICIST *n* person, esp a press agent or journalist, who publicizes something
JBLICITY *n* process or information used to arouse public attention
JBLICIZE *vb* bring to public attention
JBLICLY *adv* in a public manner
JBLICS > PUBLIC
JBLISH *vb* produce and issue (printed matter) for sale
JBLISHED > PUBLISH
JBLISHER *n* company or person that publishes books, periodicals, music, etc
JBLISHES > PUBLISH
JBS > PUB
JCAN *n* traditional Connemara open sailing boat
JCANS > PUCAN
JCCOON *n* any of several North American boraginaceous plants of the genus *Lithospermum*, esp *L. canescens*, that yield a red dye
JCCOONS > PUCCOON
JCE *adj* purplish-brown ▷ *n* colour varying from deep red to dark purplish-brown
PUCELAGE *n* virginity
PUCELAGES > PUCELAGE
PUCELLE *n* maid or virgin
PUCELLES > PUCELLE
PUCER > PUCE
PUCES > PUCE
PUCEST > PUCE
PUCK *n* mischievous or evil spirit ▷ *vb* strike (the ball) in hurling
PUCKA *same as* > PUKKA
PUCKED > PUCK
PUCKER *vb* gather into wrinkles ▷ *n* wrinkle or crease
PUCKERED > PUCKER
PUCKERER > PUCKER
PUCKERERS > PUCKER
PUCKERIER > PUCKERY
PUCKERING > PUCKER
PUCKEROOD *adj* ruined
PUCKERS > PUCKER
PUCKERY *adj* (of wine) high in tannins
PUCKFIST *n* puffball
PUCKFISTS > PUCKFIST
PUCKING > PUCK
PUCKISH > PUCK
PUCKISHLY > PUCK
PUCKLE *n* early type of machine gun
PUCKLES > PUCKLE
PUCKS > PUCK
PUD *short for* > PUDDING
PUDDEN *dialect spelling of* > PUDDING
PUDDENS > PUDDEN
PUDDER *vb* make bother or fuss
PUDDERED > PUDDER
PUDDERING > PUDDER
PUDDERS > PUDDER
PUDDIES > PUDDY
PUDDING *n* dessert, esp a cooked one served hot
PUDDINGS > PUDDING
PUDDINGY > PUDDING
PUDDLE *n* small pool of water, esp of rain ▷ *vb* make (clay etc) into puddle
PUDDLED > PUDDLE
PUDDLER > PUDDLE
PUDDLERS > PUDDLE
PUDDLES > PUDDLE
PUDDLIER > PUDDLE
PUDDLIEST > PUDDLE
PUDDLING *n* process for converting pig iron into wrought iron by heating it with ferric oxide in a furnace to oxidize the carbon
PUDDLINGS > PUDDLING
PUDDLY > PUDDLE
PUDDOCK *same as* > PADDOCK
PUDDOCKS > PUDDOCK
PUDDY *n* paw
PUDENCIES > PUDENCY
PUDENCY *n* modesty, shame, or prudishness
PUDENDA > PUDENDUM
PUDENDAL > PUDENDUM
PUDENDOUS *adj* shameful
PUDENDUM *n* human external genital organs collectively, esp of a female
PUDENT *adj* lacking in ostentation; humble
PUDGE *same as* > PODGE
PUDGES > PUDGE
PUDGIER > PUDGY
PUDGIEST > PUDGY
PUDGILY > PUDGY
PUDGINESS > PUDGY
PUDGY *adj* podgy
PUDIBUND *adj* prudish
PUDIC > PUDENDUM
PUDICITY *n* modesty
PUDOR *n* sense of shame
PUDORS > PUDOR
PUDS > PUD
PUDSEY *variant of* > PUDSY
PUDSIER > PUDSY
PUDSIEST > PUDSY
PUDSY *adj* plump
PUDU *n* diminutive Andean antelope with short straight horns and reddish-brown spotted coat
PUDUS > PUDU
PUEBLO *n* communal village, built by certain Indians of the southwestern US and parts of Latin America, consisting of one or more flat-roofed stone or adobe houses
PUEBLOS > PUEBLO
PUER *vb* steep hides in an alkaline substance from the dung of dogs
PUERED > PUER
PUERILE *adj* silly and childish
PUERILELY > PUERILE
PUERILISM *n* immature or childish behaviour by an adult
PUERILITY > PUERILE
PUERING > PUER
PUERPERA *n* woman who has recently given birth
PUERPERAE > PUERPERA
PUERPERAL *adj* concerning the period following childbirth
PUERPERIA *n* periods of around six weeks following childbirths when uteruses return to their normal size and shape
PUERS > PUER
PUFF *n* (sound of) short blast of breath, wind, etc ▷ *vb* blow or breathe in short quick draughts
PUFFBALL *n* ball-shaped fungus
PUFFBALLS > PUFFBALL
PUFFBIRD *n* brownish tropical American bird with a large head
PUFFBIRDS > PUFFBIRD
PUFFED > PUFF
PUFFER *n* person or thing that puffs
PUFFERIES > PUFFERY
PUFFERS > PUFFER
PUFFERY *n* exaggerated praise, esp in publicity or advertising
PUFFIER > PUFFY
PUFFIEST > PUFFY
PUFFILY > PUFFY
PUFFIN *n* black-and-white sea bird with a brightly-coloured beak
PUFFINESS > PUFFY
PUFFING > PUFF
PUFFINGLY > PUFF
PUFFINGS > PUFF
PUFFINS > PUFFIN
PUFFS > PUFF
PUFFY *adj* short of breath
PUFTALOON *n* Australian fried scone
PUG *n* small snub-nosed dog ▷ *vb* mix or knead (clay) with water to form a malleable mass or paste
PUGAREE *same as* > PUGGREE
PUGAREES > PUGAREE
PUGGAREE *same as* > PUGGREE
PUGGAREES > PUGGAREE
PUGGED > PUG
PUGGERIES > PUGGERY
PUGGERY *same as* > PUGGREE
PUGGIE *n* Scottish word for fruit machine
PUGGIER > PUGGY
PUGGIES > PUGGIE
PUGGIEST > PUGGY
PUGGINESS > PUGGY
PUGGING > PUG
PUGGINGS > PUG
PUGGISH > PUG
PUGGLE *vb* stir up by poking
PUGGLED > PUGGLE
PUGGLES > PUGGLE
PUGGLING > PUGGLE
PUGGREE *n* scarf, usually pleated, around the crown of some hats, esp sun helmets
PUGGREES > PUGGREE
PUGGRIES > PUGGRY
PUGGRY *same as* > PUGGREE
PUGGY *adj* sticky, claylike ▷ *n* term of endearment
PUGH *n* exclamation of disgust
PUGHS > PUGH
PUGIL *n* pinch or small handful
PUGILISM *n* art, practice, or profession of fighting with the fists
PUGILISMS > PUGILISM
PUGILIST > PUGILISM
PUGILISTS > PUGILISM
PUGILS > PUGIL
PUGMARK *n* trail of an animal
PUGMARKS > PUGMARK
PUGNACITY *n* readiness to fight

PUGREE *same as* > PUGGREE
PUGREES > PUGREE
PUGS > PUG
PUH *n* exclamation of contempt
PUHA *n* sow thistle
PUHAS > PUHA
PUHS > PUH
PUIR *Scottish word for* > POOR
PUIRER > PUIR
PUIREST > PUIR
PUIRTITH *n* poverty
PUIRTITHS > PUIRTITH
PUISNE *adj* (esp of a subordinate judge) of lower rank ▷ *n* judge of lower rank
PUISNES > PUISNE
PUISNY *adj* younger or inferior
PUISSANCE *n* showjumping competition that tests a horse's ability to jump large obstacles
PUISSANT *adj* powerful
PUISSAUNT *same as* > PUISSANT
PUJA *n* ritual in honour of the gods, performed either at home or in the mandir (temple)
PUJAH *same as* > PUJA
PUJAHS > PUJAH
PUJAS > PUJA
PUKA *in New Zealand English, same as* > BROADLEAF
PUKATEA *n* aromatic New Zealand tree, valued for its high-quality timber
PUKATEAS > PUKATEA
PUKE *vb* vomit ▷ *n* act of vomiting
PUKED > PUKE
PUKEKO *n* brightly coloured New Zealand wading bird
PUKEKOS > PUKEKO
PUKER *n* person who vomits
PUKERS > PUKER
PUKES > PUKE
PUKING > PUKE
PUKKA *adj* properly done, constructed, etc
PUKU *n* belly or stomach
PUKUS > PUKU
PUL *n* Afghan monetary unit worth one hundredth of an afghani
PULA *n* standard monetary unit of Botswana, divided into 100 thebe
PULAO *same as* > PILAU
PULAOS > PULAO
PULAS > PULA
PULDRON *same as* > PAULDRON
PULDRONS > PULDRON
PULE *vb* whine or whimper
PULED > PULE
PULER > PULE
PULERS > PULE
PULES > PULE
PULI > PUL
PULICENE *adj* flea-ridden
PULICIDE *n* flea-killing substance
PULICIDES > PULICIDE
PULIER > PULY
PULIEST > PULY
PULIK > PUL
PULING > PULE
PULINGLY > PULE
PULINGS > PULE
PULIS > PUL
PULK *same as* > PULKA
PULKA *n* reindeer-drawn sleigh
PULKAS > PULKA
PULKHA *same as* > PULKA
PULKHAS > PULKHA
PULKS > PULK
PULL *vb* exert force on (an object) to move it towards the source of the force ▷ *n* act of pulling
PULLBACK *n* act of pulling back
PULLBACKS > PULLBACK
PULLED > PULL
PULLER > PULL
PULLERS > PULL
PULLET *n* young hen
PULLETS > PULLET
PULLEY *n* wheel with a grooved rim in which a belt, chain, or piece of rope runs in order to lift weights by a downward pull
PULLEYS > PULLEY
PULLI > PULLUS
PULLING > PULL
PULLMAN *n* luxurious railway coach, esp a sleeping car
PULLMANS > PULLMAN
PULLORUM as in *pullorum disease* acute serious bacterial disease of very young birds
PULLOUT *n* removable section of a magazine, etc
PULLOUTS > PULLOUT
PULLOVER *n* sweater that is pulled on over the head
PULLOVERS > PULLOVER
PULLS > PULL
PULLULATE *vb* (of animals, etc) breed rapidly or abundantly
PULLUP *n* exercise in which the body is raised up by the arms pulling on a horizontal bar fixed above the head
PULLUPS > PULLUP
PULLUS *n* technical term for a chick or young bird
PULMO *n* lung
PULMONARY *adj* of the lungs
PULMONATE *adj* having lungs or lung-like organs ▷ *n* any pulmonate mollusc
PULMONES > PULMO
PULMONIC *adj* of or relating to the lungs ▷ *n* person with lung disease
PULMONICS > PULMONIC
PULMOTOR *n* apparatus for pumping oxygen into the lungs during artificial respiration
PULMOTORS > PULMOTOR
PULP *n* soft wet substance made from crushed or beaten matter ▷ *vb* reduce to pulp
PULPAL > PULP
PULPALLY > PULP
PULPBOARD *n* board made from wood pulp
PULPED > PULP
PULPER > PULP
PULPERS > PULP
PULPIER > PULPY
PULPIEST > PULPY
PULPIFIED > PULPIFY
PULPIFIES > PULPIFY
PULPIFY *vb* reduce to pulp
PULPILY > PULPY
PULPINESS > PULPY
PULPING > PULP
PULPIT *n* raised platform for a preacher ▷ *vb* give a sermon
PULPITAL > PULPIT
PULPITED > PULPIT
PULPITEER *n* deliverer of sermon
PULPITER *n* preacher
PULPITERS > PULPITER
PULPITING > PULPIT
PULPITRY *n* art of delivering sermons
PULPITS > PULPIT
PULPITUM *n* stone screen dividing nave and choir
PULPITUMS > PULPITUM
PULPLESS > PULP
PULPMILL *n* mill making raw material for paper
PULPMILLS > PULPMILL
PULPOUS *n* soft and yielding
PULPS > PULP
PULPSTONE *n* calcified mass in a tooth cavity
PULPWOOD *n* pine, spruce, or any other soft wood used to make paper
PULPWOODS > PULPWOOD
PULPY *adj* having a soft or soggy consistency
PULQUE *n* light alcoholic drink from Mexico made from the juice of various agave plants, esp the maguey
PULQUES > PULQUE
PULS > PUL
PULSANT *adj* vibrant
PULSAR *n* small dense star which emits regular bursts of radio waves
PULSARS > PULSAR
PULSATE *vb* throb, quiver
PULSATED > PULSATE
PULSATES > PULSATE
PULSATILE *adj* beating rhythmically
PULSATING > PULSATE
PULSATION *n* act of pulsating
PULSATIVE > PULSATE
PULSATOR *n* device that stimulates rhythmic motion of a body
PULSATORS > PULSATOR
PULSATORY *adj* of or relating to pulsation
PULSE *n* regular beating o blood through the arteri at each heartbeat ▷ *vb* beat, throb, or vibrate
PULSED > PULSE
PULSEJET *n* type of ramje engine
PULSEJETS > PULSEJET
PULSELESS > PULSE
PULSER *n* thing that pulse
PULSERS > PULSER
PULSES > PULSE
PULSIDGE *archaic word for* > PULSE
PULSIDGES > PULSIDGE
PULSIFIC *adj* causing the pulse to increase
PULSING > PULSE
PULSION *n* act of driving forward
PULSIONS > PULSION
PULSOJET *same as* > PULSEJET
PULSOJETS > PULSOJET
PULTAN *n* native Indian regiment
PULTANS > PULTAN
PULTON *same as* > PULTAN
PULTONS > PULTON
PULTOON *same as* > PULTAN
PULTOONS > PULTOON
PULTUN *same as* > PULTAN
PULTUNS > PULTUN
PULTURE *n* food and drink claimed by foresters as their right from anyone within the limits of a give forest
PULTURES > PULTURE
PULU *n* substance from Hawaiian ferns, used for stuffing cushions, etc
PULUS > PULU
PULVER *vb* make into powder
PULVERED > PULVER
PULVERINE *n* ashes of the barilla plant
PULVERING > PULVER
PULVERISE *same as* > PULVERIZE
PULVERIZE *vb* reduce to fine pieces
PULVEROUS *adj* consisting of tiny particles
PULVERS > PULVER
PULVIL *vb* apply perfume powder
PULVILIO *same as* > PULVILLO
PULVILIOS > PULVILIO
PULVILLAR *adj* like cushi
PULVILLE *same as* > PULV

LVILLED > PULVIL
LVILLES > PULVILLE
LVILLI > PULVILLUS
LVILLIO *same* ıs > PULVILLO
LVILLO *n* perfume in the orm of a powder
LVILLOS > PULVILLO
LVILLUS *n* small pad between the claws at the end of an insect's leg
LVILS > PULVIL
LVINAR *n* part of the halamus
LVINARS > PULVINAR
LVINATE *adj* (of a frieze) urved convexly
LVINI > PULVINUS
LVINUS *n* swelling at the base of a leafstalk
LWAR *n* light Indian river boat
LWARS > PULWAR
LY *adj* whiny
MA *n* large American wild cat with a greyish-brown coat
MAS > PUMA
MELO *same as* > POMELO
MELOS > PUMELO
MICATE *vb* pound fruit with pumice to make juice
MICATED > PUMICATE
MICATES > PUMICATE
MICE *n* light porous stone used for scouring ▷ *vb* rub or polish with pumice
MICED > PUMICE
MICEOUS > PUMICE
MICER > PUMICE
MICERS > PUMICE
MICES > PUMICE
MICING > PUMICE
MICITE *n* fine-grained variety of pumice
MICITES > PUMICITE
MIE *n* small stone
MIES > PUMIE
MMEL *vb* strike repeatedly with or as if with the fists
MMELED > PUMMEL
MMELING > PUMMEL
MMELLED > PUMMEL
MMELO *same as* > POMELO
MMELOS > PUMMELO
MMELS > PUMMEL
MP *n* machine used o force a liquid or gas o move in a particular direction ▷ *vb* raise or drive with a pump
MPED > PUMP
MPER > PUMP
MPERS > PUMP
MPHOOD *n* cover for the upper wheel of a chain pump
MPHOODS > PUMPHOOD
MPING > PUMP
MPION *archaic word* or > PUMPKIN
MPIONS > PUMPION
PUMPKIN *n* large round fruit with an orange rind, soft flesh, and many seeds
PUMPKING *n* person involved in a web-based project who has temporary but exclusive authority to make changes to the master source code
PUMPKINGS > PUMPKING
PUMPKINS > PUMPKIN
PUMPLESS > PUMP
PUMPLIKE > PUMP
PUMPS > PUMP
PUMY *adj* large and round
PUN *n* use of words to exploit double meanings for humorous effect ▷ *vb* make puns
PUNA *n* high cold dry plateau, esp in the Andes
PUNALUA *n* marriage between the sisters of one family to the brothers of another
PUNALUAN > PUNALUA
PUNALUAS > PUNALUA
PUNAS > PUNA
PUNCE *n* kick ▷ *vb* kick
PUNCED > PUNCE
PUNCES > PUNCE
PUNCH *vb* strike at with a clenched fist ▷ *n* blow with a clenched fist
PUNCHBAG *n* stuffed or inflated bag suspended by a flexible rod, that is punched for exercise, esp boxing training
PUNCHBAGS > PUNCHBAG
PUNCHBALL *n* stuffed or inflated ball supported by a flexible rod, that is punched for exercise, esp boxing training
PUNCHBOWL *n* large bowl for serving punch
PUNCHED > PUNCH
PUNCHEON *n* large cask of variable capacity, usually between 70 and 120 gallons
PUNCHEONS > PUNCHEON
PUNCHER > PUNCH
PUNCHERS > PUNCH
PUNCHES > PUNCH
PUNCHIER > PUNCHY
PUNCHIEST > PUNCHY
PUNCHILY > PUNCHY
PUNCHING > PUNCH
PUNCHLESS > PUNCH
PUNCHY *adj* forceful
PUNCING > PUNCE
PUNCTA > PUNCTUM
PUNCTATE *adj* having or marked with minute spots, holes, or depressions
PUNCTATED *same as* > PUNCTATE
PUNCTATOR *n* marker of points
PUNCTILIO *n* strict attention to minute points of etiquette
PUNCTO *n* tip of a fencing sword
PUNCTOS > PUNCTO
PUNCTUAL *adj* arriving or taking place at the correct time
PUNCTUATE *vb* put punctuation marks in
PUNCTULE *n* very small opening
PUNCTULES > PUNCTULE
PUNCTUM *n* tip or small point
PUNCTURE *n* small hole made by a sharp object, esp in a tyre ▷ *vb* pierce a hole in
PUNCTURED > PUNCTURE
PUNCTURER > PUNCTURE
PUNCTURES > PUNCTURE
PUNDIT *n* expert who speaks publicly on a subject
PUNDITIC *adj* of pundits
PUNDITRY *n* expressing of expert opinions
PUNDITS > PUNDIT
PUNDONOR *n* point of honour
PUNDONORS > PUNDONOR
PUNG *n* horse-drawn sleigh with a boxlike body on runners
PUNGA *variant spelling of* > PONGA
PUNGAS > PUNGA
PUNGENCE *n* pungency
PUNGENCES > PUNGENCE
PUNGENCY > PUNGENT
PUNGENT *adj* having a strong sharp bitter flavour
PUNGENTLY > PUNGENT
PUNGLE *vb* make payment
PUNGLED > PUNGLE
PUNGLES > PUNGLE
PUNGLING > PUNGLE
PUNGS > PUNG
PUNIER > PUNY
PUNIEST > PUNY
PUNILY > PUNY
PUNINESS > PUNY
PUNISH *vb* cause (someone) to suffer or undergo a penalty for some wrongdoing
PUNISHED > PUNISH
PUNISHER > PUNISH
PUNISHERS > PUNISH
PUNISHES > PUNISH
PUNISHING > PUNISH
PUNITION *n* punishment
PUNITIONS > PUNITION
PUNITIVE *adj* relating to punishment
PUNITORY *same as* > PUNITIVE
PUNJI *n* sharpened bamboo stick
PUNJIS > PUNJI
PUNK *n* anti-Establishment youth movement and style of rock music of the late 1970s ▷ *adj* relating to the punk youth movement of the late 1970s
PUNKA *n* fan made of a palm leaf or leaves
PUNKAH *same as* > PUNKA
PUNKAHS > PUNKAH
PUNKAS > PUNKA
PUNKER > PUNK
PUNKERS > PUNK
PUNKEST > PUNK
PUNKEY *n* small winged insect
PUNKEYS > PUNKEY
PUNKIE *same as* > PUNKEY
PUNKIER > PUNKY
PUNKIES > PUNKIE
PUNKIEST > PUNKY
PUNKIN *same as* > PUMPKIN
PUNKINESS > PUNKY
PUNKINS > PUNKIN
PUNKISH > PUNK
PUNKS > PUNK
PUNKY *adj* of punk music
PUNNED > PUN
PUNNER > PUN
PUNNERS > PUN
PUNNET *n* small basket for fruit
PUNNETS > PUNNET
PUNNIER > PUNNY
PUNNIEST > PUNNY
PUNNING > PUN
PUNNINGLY > PUN
PUNNINGS > PUN
PUNNY *adj* of puns
PUNS > PUN
PUNSTER *n* person who is fond of making puns
PUNSTERS > PUNSTER
PUNT *n* open flat-bottomed boat propelled by a pole ▷ *vb* travel in a punt
PUNTED > PUNT
PUNTEE *same as* > PUNTY
PUNTEES > PUNTEE
PUNTER *n* person who bets
PUNTERS > PUNTER
PUNTIES > PUNTY
PUNTING > PUNT
PUNTO *n* hit in fencing
PUNTOS > PUNTO
PUNTS > PUNT
PUNTSMAN *n* man in charge of a river punt
PUNTSMEN > PUNTSMAN
PUNTY *n* long iron rod used in the finishing process of glass-blowing
PUNY *adj* small and feeble
PUP *n* young of certain animals, such as dogs and seals ▷ *vb* (of dogs, seals, etc) to give birth to pups
PUPA *n* insect at the stage of development between a larva and an adult
PUPAE > PUPA
PUPAL > PUPA
PUPARIA > PUPARIUM
PUPARIAL > PUPARIUM
PUPARIUM *n* hard barrel-shaped case enclosing the pupae of the housefly and other dipterous insects

PUPAS > PUPA
PUPATE *vb* (of an insect larva) to develop into a pupa
PUPATED > PUPATE
PUPATES > PUPATE
PUPATING > PUPATE
PUPATION > PUPATE
PUPATIONS > PUPATE
PUPFISH *n* type of small fish
PUPFISHES > PUPFISH
PUPIL *n* person who is taught by a teacher
PUPILAGE *same as* > PUPILLAGE
PUPILAGES > PUPILAGE
PUPILAR > PUPIL
PUPILARY *same as* > PUPILLARY
PUPILLAGE *n* condition of being a pupil or duration for which one is a pupil
PUPILLAR > PUPIL
PUPILLARY *adj* of or relating to a pupil or a legal ward
PUPILLATE *vb* cry like a peacock
PUPILS > PUPIL
PUPILSHIP *n* state of being a pupil
PUPPED > PUP
PUPPET *n* small doll or figure moved by strings or by the operator's hand
PUPPETEER *n* person who operates puppets
PUPPETRY *n* art of making and manipulating puppets and presenting puppet shows
PUPPETS > PUPPET
PUPPIED > PUPPY
PUPPIES > PUPPY
PUPPING > PUP
PUPPODUM *same as* > POPPADOM
PUPPODUMS > PUPPODUM
PUPPY *n* young dog ▷ *vb* have puppies
PUPPYDOM *n* state of being a puppy
PUPPYDOMS > PUPPYDOM
PUPPYHOOD > PUPPY
PUPPYING > PUPPY
PUPPYISH > PUPPY
PUPPYISM *n* impudence
PUPPYISMS > PUPPYISM
PUPPYLIKE > PUPPY
PUPS > PUP
PUPU *n* Hawaiian dish
PUPUNHA *n* fruit of a type of palm tree
PUPUNHAS > PUPUNHA
PUPUS > PUPU
PUR *same as* > PURR
PURANA *n* any of a class of Sanskrit writings not included in the Vedas, characteristically recounting the birth and deeds of Hindu gods and the creation, destruction, or recreation of the universe
PURANAS > PURANA
PURANIC > PURANA
PURBLIND *adj* partly or nearly blind
PURCHASE *vb* obtain by payment ▷ *n* thing that is bought
PURCHASED > PURCHASE
PURCHASER > PURCHASE
PURCHASES > PURCHASE
PURDA *same as* > PURDAH
PURDAH *n* Muslim and Hindu custom of keeping women in seclusion, with clothing that conceals them completely when they go out
PURDAHED > PURDAH
PURDAHS > PURDAH
PURDAS > PURDA
PURDONIUM *n* type of coal scuttle having a slanted cover that is raised to open it, and an inner removable metal container for the coal
PURE *adj* unmixed, untainted ▷ *vb* make pure
PUREBLOOD *n* purebred animal
PUREBRED *adj* denoting a pure strain obtained through many generations of controlled breeding ▷ *n* purebred animal
PUREBREDS > PUREBRED
PURED > PURE
PUREE *n* smooth thick pulp of cooked and sieved fruit, vegetables, meat, or fish ▷ *vb* make (cooked foods) into a puree
PUREED > PUREE
PUREEING > PUREE
PUREES > PUREE
PURELY *adv* in a pure manner
PURENESS > PURE
PURER > PURE
PURES > PURE
PUREST > PURE
PURFLE *n* ruffled or curved ornamental band, as on clothing, furniture, etc ▷ *vb* decorate with such a band or bands
PURFLED > PURFLE
PURFLER > PURFLE
PURFLERS > PURFLE
PURFLES > PURFLE
PURFLING *same as* > PURFLE
PURFLINGS > PURFLING
PURFLY > PURFLE
PURGATION *n* act of purging or state of being purged
PURGATIVE *adj* (medicine) designed to cause defecation ▷ *n* medicine for emptying the bowels
PURGATORY *n* place or state of temporary suffering
PURGE *vb* rid (a thing or place) of (unwanted things or people) ▷ *n* purging
PURGEABLE > PURGE
PURGED > PURGE
PURGER > PURGE
PURGERS > PURGE
PURGES > PURGE
PURGING > PURGE
PURGINGS > PURGE
PURI *n* unleavened flaky Indian bread, that is deep-fried in ghee and served hot
PURIFIED > PURIFY
PURIFIER *n* device or substance that frees something of extraneous, contaminating, or debasing matter
PURIFIERS > PURIFIER
PURIFIES > PURIFY
PURIFY *vb* make or become pure
PURIFYING > PURIFY
PURIM *n* Jewish holiday
PURIMS > PURIM
PURIN *same as* > PURINE
PURINE *n* colourless crystalline solid that can be prepared from uric acid
PURINES > PURINE
PURING > PURE
PURINS > PURIN
PURIRI *n* forest tree of New Zealand
PURIRIS > PURIRI
PURIS > PURI
PURISM *n* strict insistence on the correct usage or style, such as in grammar or art
PURISMS > PURISM
PURIST > PURISM
PURISTIC > PURISM
PURISTS > PURISM
PURITAN *n* person who follows strict moral or religious principles ▷ *adj* of or like a puritan
PURITANIC > PURITAN
PURITANS > PURITAN
PURITIES > PURITY
PURITY *n* state or quality of being pure
PURL *n* stitch made by knitting a plain stitch backwards ▷ *vb* knit in purl
PURLED > PURL
PURLER *n* headlong or spectacular fall
PURLERS > PURLER
PURLICUE *vb* finish a pen stroke with a flourish
PURLICUED > PURLICUE
PURLICUES > PURLICUE
PURLIEU *n* land on the edge of a royal forest
PURLIEUS > PURLIEU
PURLIN *n* horizontal beam that supports the rafters of a roof
PURLINE *same as* > PURLIN
PURLINES > PURLINE
PURLING > PURL
PURLINGS > PURL
PURLINS > PURLIN
PURLOIN *vb* steal
PURLOINED > PURLOIN
PURLOINER > PURLOIN
PURLOINS > PURLOIN
PURLS > PURL
PUROMYCIN *n* type of antibiotic
PURPIE *old Scots word for* > PURSLANE
PURPIES > PURPIE
PURPLE *n* colour between red and blue ▷ *adj* of a colour between red and blue ▷ *vb* make purple
PURPLED > PURPLE
PURPLER > PURPLE
PURPLES > PURPLE
PURPLEST > PURPLE
PURPLIER > PURPLE
PURPLIEST > PURPLE
PURPLING > PURPLE
PURPLISH > PURPLE
PURPLY > PURPLE
PURPORT *vb* claim (to be or do something) ▷ *n* apparent meaning, significance
PURPORTED *adj* alleged
PURPORTS > PURPORT
PURPOSE *n* reason for which something is done or exists
PURPOSED > PURPOSE
PURPOSELY *adv* intentionally
PURPOSES > PURPOSE
PURPOSING > PURPOSE
PURPOSIVE *adj* having or showing a definite intention
PURPURA *n* any of several blood diseases causing purplish spots or patches on the skin due to subcutaneous bleeding
PURPURAS > PURPURA
PURPURE *n* purple
PURPUREAL *adj* having a purple colour
PURPURES > PURPURE
PURPURIC > PURPURA
PURPURIN *n* red crystalline compound used as a stain for biological specimens
PURPURINS > PURPURIN
PURPY *variant of* > PURPIE
PURR *vb* (of cats) make low vibrant sound, usu when pleased ▷ *n* this sound
PURRED > PURR
PURRING > PURR
PURRINGLY > PURR
PURRINGS > PURR
PURRS > PURR
PURS > PUR
PURSE *n* small bag for money ▷ *vb* draw (one's lips) together into a small round shape
PURSED > PURSE

RSEFUL *n* that which can
e contained in purse
RSEFULS > PURSEFUL
RSELIKE > PURSE
RSER *n* ship's officer who
keeps the accounts
RSERS > PURSER
RSES > PURSE
RSEW *archaic spelling*
f > PURSUE
RSEWED > PURSEW
RSEWING > PURSEW
RSEWS > PURSEW
RSIER > PURSY
RSIEST > PURSY
RSILY > PURSY
RSINESS > PURSY
RSING > PURSE
RSLAIN *same*
s > PURSLANE
RSLAINS > PURSLAIN
RSLANE *n* weedy
ortulacaceous plant,
Portulaca oleracea, with
mall yellow flowers and
eshy leaves, which are
sed in salads and as a
otherb
RSLANES > PURSLANE
RSUABLE > PURSUE
RSUAL *n* act of pursuit
RSUALS > PURSUAL
RSUANCE *n* carrying out
f an action or plan
RSUANT *adj* in
greement or conformity
RSUE *vb* chase
RSUED > PURSUE
RSUER > PURSUE
RSUERS > PURSUE
RSUES > PURSUE
RSUING > PURSUE
RSUINGS > PURSUE
RSUIT *n* pursuing
RSUITS > PURSUIT
RSY *adj* short-winded
RTIER > PURTY
RTIEST > PURTY
RTRAID > PURTRAY
RTRAY *archaic spelling*
f > PORTRAY
RTRAYD > PURTRAY
RTRAYS > PURTRAY
RTY *adj* pretty
RULENCE > PURULENT
RULENCY > PURULENT
RULENT *adj* of or
ontaining pus
RVEY *vb* supply
provisions) ▷ *n* food and
rink laid on at a wedding
eception, etc
RVEYED > PURVEY
RVEYING > PURVEY
RVEYOR *n* person,
rganization, etc,
hat supplies food and
rovisions
RVEYORS > PURVEYOR
RVEYS > PURVEY
RVIEW *n* scope or range
f activity or outlook
RVIEWS > PURVIEW
S *n* yellowish matter
produced by infected
tissue
PUSES > PUS
PUSH *vb* move or try to
move by steady force ▷ *n*
act of pushing
PUSHBALL *n* game in
which two teams try to
push a heavy ball towards
opposite goals
PUSHBALLS > PUSHBALL
PUSHCART *n* handcart,
typically having two
wheels and a canvas roof,
used esp by street vendors
PUSHCARTS > PUSHCART
PUSHCHAIR *n* folding chair
on wheels for a baby
PUSHDOWN *n* list in which
the last item added is at
the top
PUSHDOWNS > PUSHDOWN
PUSHED *adj* short of
PUSHER *n* person who sells
illegal drugs
PUSHERS > PUSHER
PUSHES > PUSH
PUSHFUL > PUSH
PUSHFULLY > PUSH
PUSHIER > PUSHY
PUSHIEST > PUSHY
PUSHILY > PUSHY
PUSHINESS > PUSHY
PUSHING *prep* almost
or nearly (a certain
age, speed, etc) ▷ *adj*
aggressively ambitious
▷ *adv* almost or nearly (a
certain age, speed, etc)
PUSHINGLY > PUSHING
PUSHOVER *n* something
easily achieved
PUSHOVERS > PUSHOVER
PUSHPIN *n* pin with a small
ball-shaped head
PUSHPINS > PUSHPIN
PUSHROD *n* metal rod
transmitting the
reciprocating motion
that operates the valves of
an internal-combustion
engine having the
camshaft in the crankcase
PUSHRODS > PUSHROD
PUSHUP *n* exercise in which
the body is alternately
raised from and lowered
to the floor by the arms
only, the trunk being kept
straight with the toes and
hands resting on the floor
PUSHUPS > PUSHUP
PUSHY *adj* too assertive or
ambitious
PUSLE *old spelling*
of > PUZZLE
PUSLED > PUSLE
PUSLES > PUSLE
PUSLEY *same as* > PURSLANE
PUSLEYS > PUSLEY
PUSLIKE > PUS
PUSLING > PUSLE
PUSS *same as* > PUSSY
PUSSEL *n* slatternly
woman
PUSSELS > PUSSEL
PUSSER *n* naval purser
PUSSERS > PUSSER
PUSSES > PUSS
PUSSIER > PUSSY
PUSSIES > PUSSY
PUSSIEST > PUSSY
PUSSLEY *n* weedy trailing
herb
PUSSLEYS > PUSSLEY
PUSSLIES > PUSSLY
PUSSLIKE > PUSS
PUSSLY *variant of* > PUSSLEY
PUSSY *n* cat ▷ *adj*
containing or full of pus
PUSSYCAT *same as* > PUSSY
PUSSYCATS > PUSSYCAT
PUSSYFOOT *vb* behave too
cautiously ▷ *n* person
who pussyfoots
PUSSYTOES *n* type of low-
growing plant
PUSTULANT *adj* causing
the formation of pustules
▷ *n* agent causing such
formation
PUSTULAR > PUSTULE
PUSTULATE *vb* form into
pustules ▷ *adj* covered
with pustules
PUSTULE *n* pimple
containing pus
PUSTULED > PUSTULE
PUSTULES > PUSTULE
PUSTULOUS > PUSTULE
PUT *vb* cause to be (in a
position, state, or place)
▷ *n* throw in putting the
shot
PUTAMEN *n* hard endocarp
or stone of fruits such
as the peach, plum, and
cherry
PUTAMINA > PUTAMEN
PUTATIVE *adj* reputed,
supposed
PUTCHEON *n* trap for
catching salmon
PUTCHEONS > PUTCHEON
PUTCHER *n* trap for
catching salmon
PUTCHERS > PUTCHER
PUTCHOCK *same as* > PACHAK
PUTCHOCKS > PUTCHOCK
PUTCHUK *same as* > PACHAK
PUTCHUKS > PUTCHUK
PUTDOWN *n* snub or insult
PUTDOWNS > PUTDOWN
PUTEAL *n* enclosure around
a well
PUTEALS > PUTEAL
PUTELI *same as* > PATELA
PUTELIS > PUTELI
PUTID *adj* having an
unpleasant odour
PUTLOCK *same as* > PUTLOG
PUTLOCKS > PUTLOCK
PUTLOG *n* short horizontal
beam that with others
supports the floor planks
of a scaffold
PUTLOGS > PUTLOG
PUTOFF *n* pretext or delay
PUTOFFS > PUTOFF
PUTOIS *n* brush to paint
pottery
PUTOISES > PUTOIS
PUTON *n* hoax or piece of
mockery
PUTONGHUA *n* Chinese
language
PUTONS > PUTON
PUTOUT *n* baseball play in
which the batter or runner
is put out
PUTOUTS > PUTOUT
PUTREFIED > PUTREFY
PUTREFIER > PUTREFY
PUTREFIES > PUTREFY
PUTREFY *vb* rot and
produce an offensive smell
PUTRID *adj* rotten and foul-
smelling
PUTRIDER > PUTRID
PUTRIDEST > PUTRID
PUTRIDITY > PUTRID
PUTRIDLY > PUTRID
PUTS > PUT
PUTSCH *n* sudden violent
attempt to remove a
government from power
PUTSCHES > PUTSCH
PUTSCHIST *n* person
taking part in putsch
PUTT *n* stroke on the
putting green to roll the
ball into or near the hole
▷ *vb* strike (the ball) in
this way
PUTTED > PUTT
PUTTEE *n* (esp as part of a
military uniform) strip of
cloth worn wound around
the leg from the ankle to
the knee
PUTTEES > PUTTEE
PUTTEN *old Scots past*
participle of > PUT
PUTTER *n* golf club for
putting ▷ *vb* busy oneself
in a desultory though
agreeable manner
PUTTERED > PUTTER
PUTTERER > PUTTER
PUTTERERS > PUTTER
PUTTERING > PUTTER
PUTTERS > PUTTER
PUTTI > PUTTO
PUTTIE *same as* > PUTTEE
PUTTIED > PUTTY
PUTTIER *n* glazier
PUTTIERS > PUTTIER
PUTTIES > PUTTY
PUTTING > PUT
PUTTINGS > PUT
PUTTO *n* representation
of a small boy, a cherub
or cupid, esp in baroque
painting or sculpture
PUTTOCK *n* type of bird of
prey
PUTTOCKS > PUTTOCK
PUTTS > PUTT
PUTTY *n* stiff paste of
whiting and linseed oil
▷ *vb* fill, fix, or coat with
putty

PUTTYING > PUTTY
PUTTYLESS > PUTTY
PUTTYLIKE > PUTTY
PUTTYROOT *n* North American orchid
PUTURE *n* claim of foresters for food for men, horses, hawks, and hounds, within the bounds of the forest
PUTURES > PUTURE
PUTZ *n* despicable or stupid person ▷ *vb* waste time
PUTZED > PUTZ
PUTZES > PUTZ
PUTZING > PUTZ
PUY *n* small volcanic cone
PUYS > PUY
PUZZEL *n* prostitute
PUZZELS > PUZZEL
PUZZLE *vb* perplex and confuse or be perplexed or confused ▷ *n* problem that cannot be easily solved
PUZZLED > PUZZLE
PUZZLEDLY > PUZZLE
PUZZLEDOM > PUZZLE
PUZZLER *n* person or thing that puzzles
PUZZLERS > PUZZLER
PUZZLES > PUZZLE
PUZZLING > PUZZLE
PUZZOLANA *same as* > POZZOLANA
PYA *n* monetary unit of Myanmar worth one hundredth of a kyat
PYAEMIA *n* blood poisoning with pus-forming microorganisms in the blood
PYAEMIAS > PYAEMIA
PYAEMIC > PYAEMIA
PYAS > PYA
PYAT *n* magpie ▷ *adj* pied
PYATS > PYAT
PYCNIC *same as* > PYKNIC
PYCNICS > PYCNIC
PYCNIDIA > PYCNIDIUM
PYCNIDIAL > PYCNIDIUM
PYCNIDIUM *n* small flask-shaped structure containing spores that occurs in ascomycetes and certain other fungi
PYCNITE *n* variety of topaz
PYCNITES > PYCNITE
PYCNON *old word for* > SEMITONE
PYCNONS > PYCNON
PYCNOSES > PYCNOSIS
PYCNOSIS *n* process of shrinking in a cell nucleus
PYCNOTIC > PYCNOSIS
PYE *same as* > PIE
PYEBALD *same as* > PIEBALD
PYEBALDS > PYEBALD
PYELITIC > PYELITIS
PYELITIS *n* inflammation of the pelvis of the kidney
PYELOGRAM *n* film produced by pyelography
PYEMIA *same as* > PYAEMIA
PYEMIAS > PYEMIA
PYEMIC > PYAEMIA
PYENGADU *variant of* > PYINKADO
PYENGADUS > PYENGADU
PYES > PYE
PYET *same as* > PYAT
PYETS > PYET
PYGAL *n* relating to the buttocks
PYGARG *n* type of horned mammal
PYGARGS > PYGARG
PYGIDIA > PYGIDIUM
PYGIDIAL > PYGIDIUM
PYGIDIUM *n* terminal segment, division, or other structure in certain annelids, arthropods, and other invertebrates
PYGIDIUMS > PYGIDIUM
PYGMAEAN > PYGMY
PYGMEAN > PYGMY
PYGMIES > PYGMY
PYGMOID *adj* of or like pygmies
PYGMY *n* something that is a very small example of its type ▷ *adj* very small
PYGMYISH > PYGMY
PYGMYISM > PYGMY
PYGMYISMS > PYGMY
PYGOSTYLE *n* vertebral bone in birds
PYIC *adj* relating to pus
PYIN *n* constituent of pus
PYINKADO *n* leguminous tree native to India and Myanmar
PYINKADOS > PYINKADO
PYINS > PYIN
PYJAMA *same as* > PYJAMAS
PYJAMAED > PYJAMAS
PYJAMAS *pl n* loose-fitting trousers and top worn in bed
PYKNIC *adj* (of a physical type) characterized by a broad squat fleshy physique with a large chest and abdomen ▷ *n* person with squat physique
PYKNICS > PYKNIC
PYKNOSES > PYKNOSIS
PYKNOSIS *n* thickening of a cell
PYKNOSOME *n* stocky body type
PYKNOTIC > PYKNOSIS
PYLON *n* steel tower-like structure supporting electrical cables
PYLONS > PYLON
PYLORI > PYLORUS
PYLORIC > PYLORUS
PYLORUS *n* small circular opening at the base of the stomach through which partially digested food (chyme) passes to the duodenum
PYLORUSES > PYLORUS
PYNE *archaic variant of* > PINE
PYNED > PYNE
PYNES > PYNE
PYNING > PYNE
PYODERMA *n* any skin eruption characterized by pustules or the formation of pus
PYODERMAS > PYODERMA
PYODERMIC > PYODERMA
PYOGENIC *adj* of or relating to the formation of pus
PYOID *adj* resembling pus
PYONER *old variant of* > PIONEER
PYORRHEA *same as* > PYORRHOEA
PYORRHEAL > PYORRHOEA
PYORRHEAS > PYORRHEA
PYORRHEIC > PYORRHOEA
PYORRHOEA *n* disease of the gums and tooth sockets which causes bleeding of the gums and the formation of pus
PYOSES > PYOSIS
PYOSIS *n* formation of pus
PYOT *same as* > PYAT
PYOTS > PYOT
PYRACANTH *n* type of thorny shrub
PYRAL > PYRE
PYRALID *n* tropical moth
PYRALIDID *same as* > PYRALID
PYRALIDS > PYRALID
PYRALIS *same as* > PYRALID
PYRALISES > PYRALIS
PYRAMID *n* solid figure with a flat base and triangular sides sloping upwards to a point ▷ *vb* build up or be arranged in the form of a pyramid
PYRAMIDAL > PYRAMID
PYRAMIDED > PYRAMID
PYRAMIDES > PYRAMIS
PYRAMIDIA *n* pyramidal apices of obelisks
PYRAMIDIC > PYRAMID
PYRAMIDON *n* type of pipe for an organ
PYRAMIDS > PYRAMID
PYRAMIS *n* pyramid-shaped structure
PYRAMISES > PYRAMIS
PYRAN *n* unsaturated heterocyclic compound having a ring containing five carbon atoms and one oxygen atom and two double bonds
PYRANOID > PYRAN
PYRANOSE *n* structure in many sugars
PYRANOSES > PYRANOSE
PYRANS > PYRAN
PYRAZOLE *n* crystalline soluble basic heterocyclic compound
PYRAZOLES > PYRAZOLE
PYRE *n* pile of wood for burning a corpse on
PYRENE *n* solid polynuclear aromatic hydrocarbon extracted from coal tar
PYRENEITE *n* dark miner found in the Pyrenees
PYRENES > PYRENE
PYRENOID *n* any of variou small protein granules that occur in certain alg mosses, and protozoans and are involved in the synthesis of starch
PYRENOIDS > PYRENOID
PYRES > PYRE
PYRETHRIN *n* oily water-insoluble compound use as an insecticide
PYRETHRUM *n* Eurasian chrysanthemum with white, pink, red, or purpl flowers
PYRETIC *adj* of, relating t or characterized by fever
PYREX *n* tradename for a of a variety of borosilicat glasses that have low coefficients of expansio making them suitable fo heat-resistant glasswar used in cookery and chemical apparatus
PYREXES > PYREX
PYREXIA *technical name for* > FEVER
PYREXIAL > PYREXIA
PYREXIAS > PYREXIA
PYREXIC > PYREXIA
PYRIC *adj* of or relating tc burning
PYRIDIC > PYRIDINE
PYRIDINE *n* colourless hygroscopic liquid with characteristic odour
PYRIDINES > PYRIDINE
PYRIDOXAL *n* naturally occurring derivative of pyridoxine that is a precursor of a coenzyme involved in several enzymic reactions
PYRIDOXIN *n* derivative pyridine
PYRIFORM *adj* (esp of organs of the body) pear shaped
PYRITE *n* yellow mineral consisting of iron sulphi in cubic crystalline form
PYRITES *same as* > PYRITE
PYRITIC > PYRITE
PYRITICAL > PYRITE
PYRITISE *same as* > PYRITIZE
PYRITISED > PYRITISE
PYRITISES > PYRITISE
PYRITIZE *vb* convert int pyrites
PYRITIZED > PYRITIZE
PYRITIZES > PYRITIZE
PYRITOUS > PYRITE
PYRO *n* pyromaniac
PYROCERAM *n* transparen ceramic material
PYROCLAST *n* piece of lav ejected from a volcano

ROGEN *n* any of a group of substances that cause a rise in temperature in an animal body
ROGENIC *adj* produced by or producing heat
ROGENS > PYROGEN
ROLA *n* evergreen perennial
ROLAS > PYROLA
ROLATER *n* worshipper of fire
ROLATRY > PYROLATER
ROLISE *same as* > PYROLIZE
ROLISED > PYROLISE
ROLISES > PYROLISE
ROLIZE *vb* subject to pyrolysis
ROLIZED > PYROLIZE
ROLIZES > PYROLIZE
ROLOGY *n* study of heat
ROLYSE *vb* subject to pyrolysis
ROLYSED > PYROLYSE
ROLYSER > PYROLYSE
ROLYSES > PYROLYSE
ROLYSIS *n* application of heat to chemical compounds in order to cause decomposition
ROLYTIC > PYROLYSIS
ROLYZE *same as* > PYROLYSE
ROLYZED > PYROLYZE
ROLYZER > PYROLYSE
ROLYZES > PYROLYZE
ROMANCY *n* divination by fire or flames
ROMANIA *n* uncontrollable urge to set things on fire
ROMETER *n* instrument for measuring high temperatures
ROMETRY > PYROMETER
RONE *n* type of heterocyclic compound
RONES > PYRONE
RONINE *n* red dye used as biological stain
RONINES > PYRONINE
ROPE *n* deep yellowish-red garnet that consists of magnesium aluminium silicate and is used as a gemstone
ROPES > PYROPE
ROPHONE *n* musical instrument using hydrogen flames
ROPUS *variant of* > PYROPE
ROPUSES > PYROPUS
ROS > PYRO
ROSCOPE *n* instrument for measuring intensity of heat
ROSES > PYROSIS
ROSIS *technical name for* > HEARTBURN
ROSOME *n* tube-shaped glowing marine creature
ROSOMES > PYROSOME
ROSTAT *n* device that activates an alarm or extinguisher in the event of a fire
PYROSTATS > PYROSTAT
PYROXENE *n* silicate mineral
PYROXENES > PYROXENE
PYROXENIC > PYROXENE
PYROXYLE *same as* > PYROXYLIN
PYROXYLES > PYROXYLE
PYROXYLIC > PYROXYLIN
PYROXYLIN *n* yellow substance obtained by nitrating cellulose with a mixture of nitric and sulphuric acids
PYRRHIC *n* metrical foot of two short or unstressed syllables ▷ *adj* of or relating to such a metrical foot
PYRRHICS > PYRRHIC
PYRRHOUS *adj* ruddy or reddish
PYRROL *same as* > PYRROLE
PYRROLE *n* colourless insoluble toxic liquid with a five-membered ring containing one nitrogen atom
PYRROLES > PYRROLE
PYRROLIC > PYRROLE
PYRROLS > PYRROL
PYRUVATE *n* ester or salt of pyruvic acid
PYRUVATES > PYRUVATE
PYRUVIC as in *pyruvic acid* colourless pleasant-smelling liquid
PYTHIUM *n* type of fungi
PYTHIUMS > PYTHIUM
PYTHON *n* large nonpoisonous snake that crushes its prey
PYTHONESS *n* woman, such as Apollo's priestess at Delphi, believed to be possessed by an oracular spirit
PYTHONIC > PYTHON
PYTHONS > PYTHON
PYURIA *n* any condition characterized by the presence of pus in the urine
PYURIAS > PYURIA
PYX *n* any receptacle for the Eucharistic Host ▷ *vb* put (something) in a pyx
PYXED > PYX
PYXES > PYX
PYXIDES > PYXIS
PYXIDIA > PYXIDIUM
PYXIDIUM *n* dry fruit of such plants as the plantain
PYXIE *n* creeping evergreen shrub of the eastern US with small white or pink star-shaped flowers
PYXIES > PYXIE
PYXING > PYX
PYXIS *same as* > PYXIDIUM
PZAZZ *same as* > PIZZAZZ
PZAZZES > PZAZZ

Qq

QABALA *same as* > KABBALAH
QABALAH *same as* > KABBALAH
QABALAHS > QABALAH
QABALAS > QABALA
QABALISM > QABALAH
QABALISMS > QABALAH
QABALIST > QABALAH
QABALISTS > QABALAH
QADI *variant spelling of* > CADI
QADIS > QADI
QAID *n* chief
QAIDS > QAID
QAIMAQAM *n* Turkish officer or official
QAIMAQAMS > QAIMAQAM
QALAMDAN *n* writing case
QALAMDANS > QALAMDAN
QANAT *n* underground irrigation channel
QANATS > QANAT
QASIDA *n* Arabic verse form
QASIDAS > QASIDA
QAT *variant spelling of* > KHAT
QATS > QAT
QAWWAL *n* qawwali singer
QAWWALI *n* Islamic religious song, esp in Asia
QAWWALIS > QAWWALI
QAWWALS > QAWWAL
QI *variant of* > CHI
QIBLA *variant of* > KIBLAH
QIBLAS > QIBLA
QIGONG *n* system of breathing and exercise designed to benefit both physical and mental health
QIGONGS > QIGONG
QINDAR *n* Albanian monetary unit worth one hundredth of a lek
QINDARKA > QINDAR
QINDARS > QINDAR
QINGHAOSU *n* Chinese herb
QINTAR *same as* > QINDAR
QINTARS > QINTAR
QIS > QI
QIVIUT *n* soft muskox wool
QIVIUTS > QIVIUT
QOPH *variant of* > KOPH
QOPHS > QOPH
QORMA *variant spelling of* > KORMA
QORMAS > QORMA
QUA *prep* in the capacity of
QUAALUDE *n* methaqualone
QUAALUDES > QUAALUDE
QUACK *vb* (of a duck) utter a harsh guttural sound ▷ *n* an unqualified person who claims medical knowledge
QUACKED > QUACK
QUACKER > QUACK
QUACKERS > QUACK
QUACKERY *n* activities or methods of a quack
QUACKIER > QUACK
QUACKIEST > QUACK
QUACKING > QUACK
QUACKISH > QUACK
QUACKISM *same as* > QUACKERY
QUACKISMS > QUACKISM
QUACKLE *same as* > QUACK
QUACKLED > QUACKLE
QUACKLES > QUACKLE
QUACKLING > QUACKLE
QUACKS > QUACK
QUACKY > QUACK
QUAD *n* quadrangle
QUADDED *adj* formed of multiple quads
QUADDING *n* birdwatching in a specified area
QUADPLEX *n* apartment on four floors
QUADRANS *n* Roman coin
QUADRANT *n* quarter of a circle
QUADRANTS > QUADRANT
QUADRAT *n* area of vegetation, often one square metre, marked out for study of the plants in the surrounding area
QUADRATE *n* cube or square, or a square or cubelike object ▷ *vb* make square or rectangular ▷ *adj* of or relating to this bone
QUADRATED > QUADRATE
QUADRATES > QUADRATE
QUADRATIC *n* equation in which the variable is raised to the power of two, but nowhere raised to a higher power ▷ *adj* of the second power
QUADRATS > QUADRAT
QUADRATUS *n* type of muscle
QUADRELLA *n* four nominated horseraces in which the punter bets on selecting the four winners
QUADRIC *adj* having or characterized by an equation of the second degree, usually in two or three variables ▷ *n* quadric curve, surface, or function
QUADRICEP *n* muscle in thigh
QUADRICS > QUADRIC
QUADRIFID *adj* divided into four lobes or other parts
QUADRIGA *n* (in the classical world) a two-wheeled chariot drawn b four horses abreast
QUADRIGAE > QUADRIGA
QUADRIGAS > QUADRIGA
QUADRILLE *n* square danc for four couples
QUADRIVIA *n* higher divisions of the seven liberal arts
QUADROON *n* an offensive term for the offspring of a mulatto and a white person
QUADROONS > QUADROON
QUADRUMAN *n* nonhuman primate
QUADRUPED *n* any animal with four legs ▷ *adj* having four feet
QUADRUPLE *vb* multiply by four ▷ *adj* four times as much or as many ▷ *n* quantity or number four times as great as another
QUADRUPLY > QUADRUPLE
QUADS > QUAD
QUAERE *n* query or questic ▷ *interj* ask or inquire: used esp to introduce a question ▷ *vb* ask
QUAERED > QUAERE
QUAEREING > QUAERE
QUAERES > QUAERE
QUAERITUR *sentence substitute* question is asked
QUAESITUM *n* object sought
QUAESTOR *n* any of severa magistrates of ancient

Rome, usually a financial administrator
'AESTORS > QUAESTOR
'AFF *vb* drink heartily or n one draught
'AFFABLE > QUAFF
'AFFED > QUAFF
'AFFER > QUAFF
'AFFERS > QUAFF
'AFFING > QUAFF
'AFFS > QUAFF
'AG *another word* or > QUAGMIRE
'AGGA *n* recently extinct ebra, striped only on the ead and shoulders
'AGGAS > QUAGGA
'AGGIER > QUAGGY
'AGGIEST > QUAGGY
'AGGY *adj* resembling a narsh or quagmire
'AGMIRE *n* soft wet area of land ▷ *vb* bog down
'AGMIRED > QUAGMIRE
'AGMIRES > QUAGMIRE
'AGMIRY > QUAGMIRE
'AGS > QUAG
'AHAUG *same as* > QUAHOG
'AHAUGS > QUAHAUG
'AHOG *n* edible clam
'AHOGS > QUAHOG
'AI *same as* > QUAY
'AICH *n* small shallow rinking cup, usually with wo handles
'AICHES > QUAICH
'AICHS > QUAICH
'AIGH *same as* > QUAICH
'AIGHS > QUAIGH
'AIL *n* small game bird of he partridge family ▷ *vb* hrink back with fear
'AILED > QUAIL
'AILING > QUAIL
'AILINGS > QUAIL
'AILS > QUAIL
'AINT *adj* attractively nusual, esp in an old-ashioned style
'AINTER > QUAINT
'AINTEST > QUAINT
'AINTLY > QUAINT
'AIR *n* book
'AIRS > QUAIR
'AIS > QUAI
'AKE *vb* shake or tremble vith or as if with fear ▷ *n* earthquake
'AKED > QUAKE
'AKER > QUAKE
'AKERS > QUAKE
'AKES > QUAKE
'AKIER > QUAKY
'AKIEST > QUAKY
'AKILY > QUAKY
'AKINESS > QUAKY
'AKING > QUAKE
'AKINGLY > QUAKE
'AKINGS > QUAKE
'AKY *adj* inclined to quake
'ALE *n* essential property r quality
'ALIA > QUALE
'ALIFIED > QUALIFY

QUALIFIER *n* person or thing that qualifies, esp a contestant in a competition who wins a preliminary heat or contest and so earns the right to take part in the next round
QUALIFIES > QUALIFY
QUALIFY *vb* provide or be provided with the abilities necessary for a task, office, or duty
QUALITIED *adj* possessing qualities
QUALITIES > QUALITY
QUALITY *n* degree or standard of excellence ▷ *adj* excellent or superior
QUALM *n* pang of conscience
QUALMIER > QUALM
QUALMIEST > QUALM
QUALMING *adj* having a qualm
QUALMISH > QUALM
QUALMLESS > QUALM
QUALMS > QUALM
QUALMY > QUALM
QUAMASH *another name for* > CAMASS
QUAMASHES > QUAMASH
QUANDANG *same as* > QUANDONG
QUANDANGS > QUANDANG
QUANDARY *n* difficult situation or dilemma
QUANDONG *n* small Australian tree with edible fruit and nuts used in preserves
QUANDONGS > QUANDONG
QUANGO *n* quasi-autonomous nongovernmental organization: any partly independent official body set up by a government
QUANGOS > QUANGO
QUANNET *n* flat file with handle at one end
QUANNETS > QUANNET
QUANT *n* long pole for propelling a boat, esp a punt, by pushing on the bottom of a river or lake ▷ *vb* propel (a boat) with a quant
QUANTA > QUANTUM
QUANTAL *adj* of or relating to a quantum or an entity that is quantized
QUANTALLY > QUANTAL
QUANTED > QUANT
QUANTIC *n* mathematical function
QUANTICAL > QUANTIC
QUANTICS > QUANTIC
QUANTIFY *vb* discover or express the quantity of
QUANTILE *n* element of a division
QUANTILES > QUANTILE
QUANTING > QUANT

QUANTISE *same as* > QUANTIZE
QUANTISED > QUANTISE
QUANTISER > QUANTISE
QUANTISES > QUANTISE
QUANTITY *n* specified or definite amount or number
QUANTIZE *vb* restrict (a physical quantity) to one of a set of values characterized by quantum numbers
QUANTIZED > QUANTIZE
QUANTIZER > QUANTIZE
QUANTIZES > QUANTIZE
QUANTONG *same as* > QUANDONG
QUANTONGS > QUANTONG
QUANTS > QUANT
QUANTUM *n* desired or required amount, esp a very small one ▷ *adj* of or designating a major breakthrough or sudden advance
QUARE *adj* remarkable or strange
QUARENDEN *n* dark-red apple
QUARENDER *same as* > QUARENDEN
QUARER > QUARE
QUAREST > QUARE
QUARK *n* subatomic particle thought to be the fundamental unit of matter
QUARKS > QUARK
QUARREL *n* angry disagreement ▷ *vb* have a disagreement or dispute
QUARRELED > QUARREL
QUARRELER > QUARREL
QUARRELS > QUARREL
QUARRIAN *n* cockatiel of scrub and woodland regions of inland Australia
QUARRIANS > QUARRIAN
QUARRIED > QUARRY
QUARRIER *another word for* > QUARRYMAN
QUARRIERS > QUARRIER
QUARRIES > QUARRY
QUARRION *same as* > QUARRIAN
QUARRIONS > QUARRION
QUARRY *n* place where stone is dug from the surface of the earth ▷ *vb* extract (stone) from a quarry
QUARRYING > QUARRY
QUARRYMAN *n* man who works in or manages a quarry
QUARRYMEN > QUARRYMAN
QUART *n* unit of liquid measure equal to two pints (1.136 litres)
QUARTAN *adj* (esp of a malarial fever) occurring every third day ▷ *n* quartan malaria

QUARTANS > QUARTAN
QUARTE *n* fourth of eight basic positions from which a parry or attack can be made in fencing
QUARTER *n* one of four equal parts of something ▷ *vb* divide into four equal parts ▷ *adj* being or consisting of one of four equal parts
QUARTERED *adj* (of a shield) divided into four sections, each having contrasting arms or having two sets of arms, each repeated in diagonally opposite corners
QUARTERER > QUARTER
QUARTERLY *adj* occurring, due, or issued at intervals of three months ▷ *n* magazine issued every three months ▷ *adv* once every three months
QUARTERN *n* fourth part of certain weights or measures, such as a peck or a pound
QUARTERNS > QUARTERN
QUARTERS *pl n* accommodation, esp as provided for military personnel
QUARTES > QUARTE
QUARTET *n* group of four performers
QUARTETS > QUARTET
QUARTETT *same as* > QUARTET
QUARTETTE *same as* > QUARTET
QUARTETTI > QUARTETTO
QUARTETTO *same as* > QUARTET
QUARTETTS > QUARTETT
QUARTIC *n* biquadratic equation
QUARTICS > QUARTIC
QUARTIER *n* city district
QUARTIERS > QUARTIER
QUARTILE *n* one of three values of a variable dividing its distribution into four groups with equal frequencies ▷ *adj* of a quartile
QUARTILES > QUARTILE
QUARTO *n* book size in which the sheets are folded into four leaves
QUARTOS > QUARTO
QUARTS > QUART
QUARTZ *n* hard glossy mineral
QUARTZES > QUARTZ
QUARTZIER > QUARTZ
QUARTZITE *n* very hard metamorphic rock consisting of a mosaic of intergrown quartz crystals
QUARTZOSE > QUARTZ
QUARTZOUS > QUARTZ
QUARTZY > QUARTZ

QUASAR *n* extremely distant starlike object that emits powerful radio waves
QUASARS > QUASAR
QUASH *vb* annul or make void
QUASHED > QUASH
QUASHEE *same as* > QUASHIE
QUASHEES > QUASHEE
QUASHER > QUASH
QUASHERS > QUASH
QUASHES > QUASH
QUASHIE *n* in the Carribbean, an unsophisticated or gullible male Black peasant
QUASHIES > QUASHIE
QUASHING > QUASH
QUASI *adv* as if
QUASS *variant of* > KVASS
QUASSES > QUASS
QUASSIA *n* tropical American tree, the wood of which yields a substance used in insecticides
QUASSIAS > QUASSIA
QUASSIN *n* bitter crystalline substance
QUASSINS > QUASSIN
QUAT *n* spot
QUATCH *vb* move
QUATCHED > QUATCH
QUATCHES > QUATCH
QUATCHING > QUATCH
QUATE *n* fortune
QUATORZE *n* cards worth 14 points in piquet
QUATORZES > QUATORZE
QUATRAIN *n* stanza or poem of four lines
QUATRAINS > QUATRAIN
QUATRE *n* playing card with four pips
QUATRES > QUATRE
QUATS > QUAT
QUAVER *vb* (of a voice) quiver or tremble ▷ *n* note half the length of a crotchet
QUAVERED > QUAVER
QUAVERER > QUAVER
QUAVERERS > QUAVER
QUAVERIER > QUAVER
QUAVERING > QUAVER
QUAVERS > QUAVER
QUAVERY > QUAVER
QUAY *n* wharf built parallel to the shore
QUAYAGE *n* system of quays
QUAYAGES > QUAYAGE
QUAYD *archaic past participle of* > QUAIL
QUAYLIKE > QUAY
QUAYS > QUAY
QUAYSIDE *n* edge of a quay along the water
QUAYSIDES > QUAYSIDE
QUAZZIER > QUAZZY
QUAZZIEST > QUAZZY
QUAZZY *adj* unwell
QUBIT *n* quantum bit
QUBITS > QUBIT
QUBYTE *n* unit of eight qubits
QUBYTES > QUBYTE
QUEACH *n* thicket
QUEACHES > QUEACH
QUEACHIER > QUEACHY
QUEACHY *adj* unwell
QUEAN *n* boisterous, impudent, or disreputable woman
QUEANS > QUEAN
QUEASIER > QUEASY
QUEASIEST > QUEASY
QUEASILY > QUEASY
QUEASY *adj* having the feeling that one is about to vomit
QUEAZIER > QUEAZY
QUEAZIEST > QUEAZY
QUEAZY *same as* > QUEASY
QUEBRACHO *n* anacardiaceous South American tree
QUEECHIER > QUEECHY
QUEECHY *same as* > QUEACHY
QUEEN *n* female sovereign who is the official ruler or head of state ▷ *vb* flaunt one's homosexuality
QUEENCAKE *n* small light cake containing currants
QUEENDOM *n* territory, state, people, or community ruled over by a queen
QUEENDOMS > QUEENDOM
QUEENED > QUEEN
QUEENHOOD > QUEEN
QUEENIE *n* scallop
QUEENIER > QUEENY
QUEENIES > QUEENIE
QUEENIEST > QUEENY
QUEENING > QUEEN
QUEENINGS > QUEEN
QUEENITE *n* supporter of a queen
QUEENITES > QUEENITE
QUEENLESS > QUEEN
QUEENLET *n* queen of a small realm
QUEENLETS > QUEENLET
QUEENLIER > QUEENLY
QUEENLY *adj* resembling or appropriate to a queen ▷ *adv* in a manner appropriate to a queen
QUEENS > QUEEN
QUEENSHIP > QUEEN
QUEENSIDE *n* half of a chessboard in which the queen starts
QUEENY *adj* effeminate
QUEER *adj* not normal or usual ▷ *n* derogatory name for a homosexual person ▷ *vb* spoil or thwart
QUEERCORE *n* gay-oriented punk music
QUEERDOM *n* gay culture
QUEERDOMS > QUEERDOM
QUEERED > QUEER
QUEERER > QUEER
QUEEREST > QUEER
QUEERING > QUEER
QUEERISH > QUEER
QUEERITY > QUEER
QUEERLY > QUEER
QUEERNESS > QUEER
QUEERS > QUEER
QUEEST *n* wood pigeon
QUEESTS > QUEEST
QUEINT *same as* > QUAINT
QUELCH *same as* > SQUELCH
QUELCHED > QUELCH
QUELCHES > QUELCH
QUELCHING > QUELCH
QUELEA *n* East African weaver bird
QUELEAS > QUELEA
QUELL *vb* suppress
QUELLABLE > QUELL
QUELLED > QUELL
QUELLER > QUELL
QUELLERS > QUELL
QUELLING > QUELL
QUELLS > QUELL
QUEME *vb* please
QUEMED > QUEME
QUEMES > QUEME
QUEMING > QUEME
QUENA *n* Andean flute
QUENAS > QUENA
QUENCH *vb* satisfy (one's thirst)
QUENCHED > QUENCH
QUENCHER > QUENCH
QUENCHERS > QUENCH
QUENCHES > QUENCH
QUENCHING > QUENCH
QUENELLE *n* finely sieved mixture of cooked meat or fish, shaped into various forms and cooked in stock or fried as croquettes
QUENELLES > QUENELLE
QUEP *interj* expression of derision
QUERCETIC > QUERCETIN
QUERCETIN *n* yellow crystalline pigment found naturally in the rind and bark of many plants
QUERCETUM *n* group of oak trees
QUERCINE *adj* of or relating to oak trees
QUERCITIN *same as* > QUERCETIN
QUERIDA *n* sweetheart
QUERIDAS > QUERIDA
QUERIED > QUERY
QUERIER > QUERY
QUERIERS > QUERY
QUERIES > QUERY
QUERIMONY *n* complaint
QUERIST *n* person who makes inquiries or queries
QUERISTS > QUERIST
QUERN *n* stone hand mill for grinding corn
QUERNS > QUERN
QUERULOUS *adj* complaining or whining
QUERY *n* question, esp one raising doubt ▷ *vb* express uncertainty, doubt, or an objection concerning (something)
QUERYING > QUERY
QUERYINGS > QUERY
QUEST *n* long and difficult search ▷ *vb* go in search
QUESTANT *n* one who quests
QUESTANTS > QUEST
QUESTED > QUEST
QUESTER > QUEST
QUESTERS > QUEST
QUESTING > QUEST
QUESTINGS > QUEST
QUESTION *n* form of words addressed to a person in order to obtain an answer ▷ *vb* put a question or questions to (a person)
QUESTIONS > QUESTION
QUESTOR *same as* > QUAESTOR
QUESTORS > QUESTOR
QUESTRIST *n* one who quests
QUESTS > QUEST
QUETCH *vb* move
QUETCHED > QUETCH
QUETCHES > QUETCH
QUETCHING > QUETCH
QUETHE *vb* say
QUETHES > QUETHE
QUETHING > QUETHE
QUETSCH *n* plum brandy
QUETSCHES > QUETSCH
QUETZAL *n* crested bird of Central and N South America
QUETZALES > QUETZAL
QUETZALS > QUETZAL
QUEUE *n* line of people or vehicles waiting for something ▷ *vb* form or remain in a line while waiting
QUEUED > QUEUE
QUEUEING > QUEUE
QUEUEINGS > QUEUE
QUEUER > QUEUE
QUEUERS > QUEUE
QUEUES > QUEUE
QUEUING > QUEUE
QUEUINGS > QUEUE
QUEY *n* young cow
QUEYN *n* girl
QUEYNIE *same as* > QUEYN
QUEYNIES > QUEYNIE
QUEYNS > QUEYN
QUEYS > QUEY
QUEZAL *same as* > QUETZAL
QUEZALES > QUEZAL
QUEZALS > QUEZAL
QUIBBLE *vb* make trivial objections ▷ *n* trivial objection
QUIBBLED > QUIBBLE
QUIBBLER > QUIBBLE
QUIBBLERS > QUIBBLE
QUIBBLES > QUIBBLE
QUIBBLING > QUIBBLE
QUIBLIN *same as* > QUIBBLE
QUIBLINS > QUIBLIN
QUICH *vb* move
QUICHE *n* savoury flan with an egg custard filling to

vhich vegetables etc are ıdded
ICHED > QUICH
ICHES > QUICHE
ICHING > QUICH
ICK *adj* speedy, fast ▷ *n* rea of sensitive flesh ınder a nail ▷ *adv* in a apid manner
ICKBEAM *n* rowan tree
ICKEN *vb* make or ecome faster ▷ *n* rowan ree
ICKENED > QUICKEN
ICKENER > QUICKEN
ICKENS > QUICKEN
ICKER > QUICK
ICKEST > QUICK
ICKIE *n* anything done r made hurriedly ▷ *adj* nade or done rapidly
ICKIES > QUICKIE
ICKLIME *n* white solid ısed in the manufacture of lass and steel
ICKLY > QUICK
ICKNESS > QUICK
ICKS > QUICK
ICKSAND *n* deep mass of oose wet sand that sucks nything on top of it into it
ICKSET *adj* (of plants or uttings) planted so as to orm a hedge ▷ *n* hedge omposed of such plants
ICKSETS > QUICKSET
ICKSTEP *n* fast modern allroom dance ▷ *vb* erform this dance
ID *n* pound (sterling)
IDAM *n* specified person
IDAMS > QUIDAM
IDDANY *n* quince jelly
IDDIT *same* s > QUIDDITY
IDDITCH *n* imaginary ame in which players fly n broomsticks
IDDITS > QUIDDIT
IDDITY *n* essential ature of something
IDDLE *vb* waste time
IDDLED > QUIDDLE
IDDLER > QUIDDLE
IDDLERS > QUIDDLE
IDDLES > QUIDDLE
IDDLING > QUIDDLE
IDNUNC *n* person eager o learn news and scandal
IDNUNCS > QUIDNUNC
IDS > QUID
IESCE *vb* quieten
IESCED > QUIETEN
IESCENT *adj* quiet, nactive, or dormant
IESCES > QUIESCE
IESCING > QUIESCE
IET *adj* with little noise *n* quietness ▷ *vb* make r become quiet
IETED > QUIET
IETEN *vb* make or ecome quiet
IETENED > QUIETEN
QUIETENER > QUIETEN
QUIETENS > QUIETEN
QUIETER > QUIET
QUIETERS > QUIET
QUIETEST > QUIET
QUIETING > QUIET
QUIETINGS > QUIET
QUIETISM *n* passivity and calmness of mind towards external events
QUIETISMS > QUIETISM
QUIETIST > QUIETISM
QUIETISTS > QUIETISM
QUIETIVE *n* sedative drug
QUIETIVES > QUIETIVE
QUIETLY > QUIET
QUIETNESS > QUIET
QUIETS > QUIET
QUIETSOME > QUIET
QUIETUDE *n* quietness, peace, or tranquillity
QUIETUDES > QUIETUDE
QUIETUS *n* release from life
QUIETUSES > QUIETUS
QUIFF *n* tuft of hair brushed up above the forehead
QUIFFS > QUIFF
QUIGHT *vb* quit
QUIGHTED > QUIGHT
QUIGHTING > QUIGHT
QUIGHTS > QUIGHT
QUILL *n* pen made from the feather of a bird's wing or tail ▷ *vb* wind (thread, yarn, etc) onto a spool or bobbin
QUILLAI *another name for* > SOAPBARK
QUILLAIA *same as* > QUILLAI
QUILLAIAS > QUILLAIA
QUILLAIS > QUILLAI
QUILLAJA *same as* > QUILLAI
QUILLAJAS > QUILLAJA
QUILLBACK *n* freshwater fish
QUILLED > QUILL
QUILLET *n* quibble or subtlety
QUILLETS > QUILLET
QUILLING *n* decorative craftwork in which material such as glass, fabric or paper is formed into small bands or rolls that form the basis of a design
QUILLINGS > QUILLING
QUILLMAN *n* clerk
QUILLMEN > QUILLMAN
QUILLON *n* either half of the extended crosspiece of a sword or dagger
QUILLONS > QUILLON
QUILLS > QUILL
QUILLWORK *n* embroidery using porcupine quills
QUILLWORT *n* aquatic tracheophyte plant with quill-like leaves
QUILT *n* padded covering for a bed ▷ *vb* stitch together two layers of (fabric) with padding between them
QUILTED > QUILT
QUILTER > QUILT
QUILTERS > QUILT
QUILTING *n* material used for making a quilt
QUILTINGS > QUILTING
QUILTS > QUILT
QUIM *n* taboo word for the female genitals
QUIMS > QUIM
QUIN *same as* > QUINT
QUINA *n* quinine
QUINARIES > QUINARY
QUINARY *adj* consisting of fives or by fives ▷ *n* set of five
QUINAS > QUINA
QUINATE *adj* arranged in or composed of five parts
QUINCE *n* acid-tasting pear-shaped fruit
QUINCES > QUINCE
QUINCHE *vb* move
QUINCHED > QUINCHE
QUINCHES > QUINCHE
QUINCHING > QUINCHE
QUINCUNX *n* group of five objects arranged in the shape of a rectangle with one at each corner and the fifth in the centre
QUINE *variant of* > QUEAN
QUINELA *same as* > QUINELLA
QUINELAS > QUINELA
QUINELLA *n* form of betting on a horse race in which the punter bets on selecting the first and second place-winners in any order
QUINELLAS > QUINELLA
QUINES > QUINE
QUINIC as in *quinic acid* white crystalline soluble optically active carboxylic acid
QUINIDINE *n* crystalline alkaloid drug
QUINIE *n* girl
QUINIELA *same as* > QUINELLA
QUINIELAS > QUINIELA
QUINIES > QUINIE
QUININ *same as* > QUININE
QUININA *same as* > QUININE
QUININAS > QUININA
QUININE *n* bitter drug used as a tonic and formerly to treat malaria
QUININES > QUININE
QUININS > QUININ
QUINNAT *n* Pacific salmon
QUINNATS > QUINNAT
QUINO *same as* > KENO
QUINOA *n* type of grain high in nutrients
QUINOAS > QUINOA
QUINOID *same as* > QUINONOID
QUINOIDAL > QUINOID
QUINOIDS > QUINOID
QUINOL *n* white crystalline soluble phenol used as a photographic developer
QUINOLIN *same as* > QUINOLINE
QUINOLINE *n* oily colourless insoluble basic heterocyclic compound
QUINOLINS > QUINOLIN
QUINOLONE *n* any of a group of synthetic antibiotics
QUINOLS > QUINOL
QUINONE *n* yellow crystalline water-soluble unsaturated ketone
QUINONES > QUINONE
QUINONOID *adj* of, resembling, or derived from quinone
QUINOS > QUINO
QUINQUINA *same as* > QUININE
QUINS > QUIN
QUINSIED > QUINSY
QUINSIES > QUINSY
QUINSY *n* inflammation of the throat or tonsils
QUINT *same as* > QUIN
QUINTA *n* Portuguese vineyard where grapes for wine or port are grown
QUINTAIN *n* post or target set up for tilting exercises for mounted knights or foot soldiers
QUINTAINS > QUINTAIN
QUINTAL *n* unit of weight equal to (esp in Britain) 112 pounds (50.85 kg) or (esp in US) 100 pounds (45.36 kg)
QUINTALS > QUINTAL
QUINTAN *adj* (of a fever) occurring every fourth day ▷ *n* quintan fever
QUINTANS > QUINTAN
QUINTAR *n* Albanian unit of currency
QUINTARS > QUINTAR
QUINTAS > QUINTA
QUINTE *n* fifth of eight basic positions from which a parry or attack can be made in fencing
QUINTES > QUINTE
QUINTET *n* group of five performers
QUINTETS > QUINTET
QUINTETT *same as* > QUINTET
QUINTETTE *same as* > QUINTET
QUINTETTI > QUINTETTO
QUINTETTO *same as* > QUINTET
QUINTETTS > QUINTETT
QUINTIC *adj* of or relating to the fifth degree ▷ *n* mathematical function
QUINTICS > QUINTIC
QUINTILE *n* aspect of 72° between two heavenly bodies
QUINTILES > QUINTILE

QUINTIN *same as* > QUINTAIN
QUINTINS > QUINTIN
QUINTROON *n* person with one Black great-great-grandparent
QUINTS > QUINT
QUINTUPLE *vb* multiply by five ▷ *adj* five times as much or as many ▷ *n* quantity or number five times as great as another
QUINTUPLY > QUINTUPLE
QUINZE *n* card game with rules similar to those of vingt-et-un, except that the score aimed at is 15 rather than 21
QUINZES > QUINZE
QUIP *n* witty saying ▷ *vb* make a quip
QUIPO *same as* > QUIPU
QUIPOS > QUIPO
QUIPPED > QUIP
QUIPPER > QUIP
QUIPPERS > QUIP
QUIPPIER > QUIP
QUIPPIEST > QUIP
QUIPPING > QUIP
QUIPPISH > QUIP
QUIPPU *same as* > QUIPU
QUIPPUS > QUIPPU
QUIPPY > QUIP
QUIPS > QUIP
QUIPSTER *n* person inclined to make sarcastic or witty remarks
QUIPSTERS > QUIPSTER
QUIPU *n* device of the Incas of Peru used to record information, consisting of an arrangement of variously coloured and knotted cords attached to a base cord
QUIPUS > QUIPU
QUIRE *n* set of 24 or 25 sheets of paper ▷ *vb* arrange in quires
QUIRED > QUIRE
QUIRES > QUIRE
QUIRING > QUIRE
QUIRISTER *same as* > CHORISTER
QUIRK *n* peculiarity of character ▷ *vb* quip
QUIRKED > QUIRK
QUIRKIER > QUIRK
QUIRKIEST > QUIRK
QUIRKILY > QUIRK
QUIRKING > QUIRK
QUIRKISH > QUIRK
QUIRKS > QUIRK
QUIRKY > QUIRK
QUIRT *n* whip with a leather thong at one end ▷ *vb* strike with a quirt
QUIRTED > QUIRT
QUIRTING > QUIRT
QUIRTS > QUIRT
QUISLING *n* traitor who aids an occupying enemy force
QUISLINGS > QUISLING
QUIST *n* wood pigeon
QUISTS > QUIST
QUIT *vb* stop (doing something) ▷ *adj* free (from)
QUITCH *vb* move
QUITCHED > QUITCH
QUITCHES > QUITCH
QUITCHING > QUITCH
QUITCLAIM *n* formal renunciation of any claim against a person or of a right to land ▷ *vb* renounce (a claim) formally
QUITE *archaic form of* > QUIT
QUITED > QUITE
QUITES > QUITE
QUITING > QUITE
QUITRENT *n* (formerly) a rent payable by a freeholder or copyholder to his lord that released him from liability to perform services
QUITRENTS > QUITRENT
QUITS > QUIT
QUITTAL *n* repayment of an action with a similar action
QUITTALS > QUITTAL
QUITTANCE *n* release from debt or other obligation
QUITTED > QUIT
QUITTER *n* person who lacks perseverance
QUITTERS > QUITTER
QUITTING > QUIT
QUITTOR *n* infection of the cartilages on the side of a horse's foot, characterized by inflammation and the formation of pus
QUITTORS > QUITTOR
QUIVER *vb* shake with a tremulous movement ▷ *n* shaking or trembling
QUIVERED > QUIVER
QUIVERER > QUIVER
QUIVERERS > QUIVER
QUIVERFUL *n* amount that a quiver can hold
QUIVERIER > QUIVER
QUIVERING > QUIVER
QUIVERISH > QUIVER
QUIVERS > QUIVER
QUIVERY > QUIVER
QUIXOTE *n* impractical idealist
QUIXOTES > QUIXOTE
QUIXOTIC *adj* romantic and unrealistic
QUIXOTISM > QUIXOTIC
QUIXOTRY > QUIXOTE
QUIZ *n* entertainment in which the knowledge of the players is tested by a series of questions ▷ *vb* investigate by close questioning
QUIZZED > QUIZ
QUIZZER > QUIZ
QUIZZERS > QUIZ
QUIZZERY > QUIZ
QUIZZES > QUIZ
QUIZZICAL *adj* questioning and mocking
QUIZZIFY > QUIZ
QUIZZING > QUIZ
QUIZZINGS > QUIZ
QUOAD *adv* as far as
QUOD *n* jail ▷ *vb* say
QUODDED > QUOD
QUODDING > QUOD
QUODLIBET *n* light piece of music based on two or more popular tunes
QUODLIN *n* cooking apple
QUODLINS > QUODLIN
QUODS > QUOD
QUOHOG *n* edible clam
QUOHOGS > QUOHOG
QUOIF *vb* arrange (the hair)
QUOIFED > QUOIF
QUOIFING > QUOIF
QUOIFS > QUOIF
QUOIN *n* external corner of a building ▷ *vb* wedge
QUOINED > QUOIN
QUOINING > QUOIN
QUOINS > QUOIN
QUOIST *n* wood pigeon
QUOISTS > QUOIST
QUOIT *n* large ring used in the game of quoits ▷ *vb* throw as a quoit
QUOITED > QUOIT
QUOITER > QUOIT
QUOITERS > QUOIT
QUOITING > QUOIT
QUOITS *n* game in which quoits are tossed at a stake in the ground in attempts to encircle it
QUOKKA *n* small Australian wallaby
QUOKKAS > QUOKKA
QUOLL *n* Australian catlike carnivorous marsupial
QUOLLS > QUOLL
QUOMODO *n* manner
QUOMODOS > QUOMODO
QUONDAM *adj* of an earlier time
QUONK *vb* make an accidental noise while broadcasting
QUONKED > QUONK
QUONKING > QUONK
QUONKS > QUONK
QUOOKE *archaic past participle of* > QUAKE
QUOP *vb* pulsate or throb
QUOPPED > QUOP
QUOPPING > QUOP
QUOPS > QUOP
QUORATE *adj* having or being a quorum
QUORUM *n* minimum number of people required to be present at a meeting before any transactions can take place
QUORUMS > QUORUM
QUOTA *n* share that is due from, due to, or allocated to a group or person
QUOTABLE *adj* apt or suitable for quotation
QUOTABLY > QUOTABLE
QUOTAS > QUOTA
QUOTATION *n* written or spoken passage repeated exactly in a later work, speech, or conversation
QUOTATIVE *n* word indicating quotation
QUOTE *vb* repeat (words) exactly from (an earlier work, speech, or conversation) ▷ *n* quotation ▷ *interj* expression used parenthetically to indicate that the words that follow it form a quotation
QUOTED > QUOTE
QUOTER > QUOTE
QUOTERS > QUOTE
QUOTES > QUOTE
QUOTH *vb* said
QUOTHA *interj* expression of mild sarcasm, used in picking up a word or phrase used by someone else
QUOTIDIAN *adj* daily ▷ *n* malarial fever characterized by attacks that recur daily
QUOTIENT *n* result of the division of one number or quantity by another
QUOTIENTS > QUOTIENT
QUOTING > QUOTE
QUOTITION *n* division by repeated subtraction
QUOTUM *same as* > QUOTA
QUOTUMS > QUOTUM
QURSH *same as* > QURUSH
QURSHES > QURUSH
QURUSH *n* Saudi Arabian currency unit
QURUSHES > QURUSH
QUYTE *same as* > QUIT
QUYTED > QUYTE
QUYTES > QUYTE
QUYTING > QUYTE
QWERTIES > QWERTY
QWERTY *n* standard English language typewriter or computer keyboard
QWERTYS > QWERTY

Rr

BANNA *n* Madagascan
/oven raffia
BANNAS > RABANNA
BAT *vb* rotate so that the
lane rotated coincides
/ith another
BATINE *n* type of collar
BATINES > RABATINE
BATMENT > RABAT
BATO *n* wired or starched
ollar, often of intricate
ice, that stood up at the
ack and sides: worn in
ne 17th century
BATOES > RABATO
BATOS > RABATO
BATS > RABAT
BATTE *same as* > RABAT
BATTED > RABAT
BATTES > RABATTE
BATTING > RABAT
BBET *n* recess, groove, or
tep, usually of rectangular
ection, cut into a surface
r along the edge of a
iece of timber to receive
mating piece ▷ *vb* cut or
orm a rabbet in (timber)
BBETED > RABBET
BBETING > RABBET
BBETS > RABBET
BBI *n* Jewish spiritual
eader
BBIES > RABBI
BBIN *same as* > RABBI
BBINATE *n* position,
unction, or tenure of
ffice of a rabbi
BBINIC *adj* of or
elating to the rabbis,
heir teachings, writings,
iews, language, etc
BBINICS *n* study of
rabbinic literature of the
post-Talmudic period
RABBINISM *n* teachings and traditions of the rabbis of the Talmudic period
RABBINIST > RABBINISM
RABBINITE > RABBINISM
RABBINS > RABBIN
RABBIS > RABBI
RABBIT *n* small burrowing mammal with long ears ▷ *vb* talk too much
RABBITED > RABBIT
RABBITER *n* person who traps and sells rabbits
RABBITERS > RABBITER
RABBITING *n* activity of hunting rabbits
RABBITO *same as* > RABBITOH
RABBITOH *n* (formerly) an itinerant seller of rabbits for eating
RABBITOHS > RABBITOH
RABBITOS > RABBITO
RABBITRY *n* place where tame rabbits are kept and bred
RABBITS > RABBIT
RABBITY *adj* rabbitlike
RABBLE *n* disorderly crowd of noisy people ▷ *vb* stir, mix, or skim (the molten charge) in a roasting furnace
RABBLED > RABBLE
RABBLER *n* iron tool or device for stirring, mixing, or skimming a molten charge in a roasting furnace
RABBLERS > RABBLER
RABBLES > RABBLE
RABBLING > RABBLE
RABBLINGS > RABBLE
RABBONI *n* very respectful Jewish title or form of address meaning my great master
RABBONIS > RABBONI
RABI *n* (in Pakistan, India, etc) a crop that is harvested at the end of winter
RABIC > RABIES
RABID *adj* fanatical
RABIDER > RABID
RABIDEST > RABID
RABIDITY > RABID
RABIDLY > RABID
RABIDNESS > RABID
RABIES *n* usu fatal viral disease transmitted by dogs and certain other animals
RABIETIC > RABIES
RABIS > RABI
RACA *adj* biblical word meaning worthless or empty-headed
RACAHOUT *n* acorn flour or drink made from it
RACAHOUTS > RACAHOUT
RACCAHOUT *same as* > RACAHOUT
RACCOON *n* small N American mammal with a long striped tail
RACCOONS > RACCOON
RACE *n* contest of speed ▷ *vb* compete with in a race
RACECARD *n* card or booklet at a race meeting with the times of the races, names of the runners, etc, printed on it
RACECARDS > RACECARD
RACED > RACE
RACEGOER *n* one who attends a race meeting, esp a habitual frequenter of race meetings
RACEGOERS > RACEGOER
RACEGOING > RACEGOER
RACEHORSE *n* horse specially bred for racing
RACEMATE *n* racemic compound
RACEMATES > RACEMATE
RACEME *n* cluster of flowers along a central stem, as in the foxglove
RACEMED *adj* with or in racemes
RACEMES > RACEME
RACEMIC *adj* of, concerned with, or being a mixture of equal amounts of enantiomers and consequently having no optical activity
RACEMISE *same as* > RACEMIZE
RACEMISED > RACEMISE
RACEMISES > RACEMISE
RACEMISM > RACEMIC
RACEMISMS > RACEMIC
RACEMIZE *vb* change or cause to change into a racemic mixture
RACEMIZED > RACEMIZE
RACEMIZES > RACEMIZE
RACEMOID *adj* resembling a raceme
RACEMOSE *adj* being or resembling a raceme
RACEMOUS *same*

as > RACEMOSE
RACEPATH *same as* > RACETRACK
RACEPATHS > RACEPATH
RACER *n* person, animal, or machine that races
RACERS > RACER
RACES *pl n the.* a series of contests of speed between horses (or sometimes greyhounds) over a set course at prearranged times
RACETRACK *n* track for racing
RACEWALK *vb* race by walking fast rather than running
RACEWALKS > RACEWALK
RACEWAY *n* racetrack, esp one for banger racing
RACEWAYS > RACEWAY
RACH *n* scent hound
RACHE *same as* > RACH
RACHES > RACH
RACHET *same as* > RATCHET
RACHETED > RACHET
RACHETING > RACHET
RACHETS > RACHET
RACHIAL > RACHIS
RACHIDES > RACHIS
RACHIDIAL > RACHIS
RACHIDIAN > RACHIS
RACHILLA *n* (in grasses) the short stem of a spikelet that bears the florets
RACHILLAE > RACHILLA
RACHILLAS > RACHILLA
RACHIS *n* main axis or stem of an inflorescence or compound leaf
RACHISES > RACHIS
RACHITIC > RACHITIS
RACHITIS *another name for* > RICKETS
RACIAL *adj* relating to the division of the human species into races
RACIALISE *same as* > RACIALIZE
RACIALISM *same as* > RACISM
RACIALIST > RACIALISM
RACIALIZE *vb* render racial in tone or content
RACIALLY > RACIAL
RACIATION *n* evolutionary development of races
RACIER > RACY
RACIEST > RACY
RACILY > RACY
RACINESS > RACY
RACING *adj* denoting or associated with horse races ▷ *n* practice of engaging horses (or sometimes greyhounds) in contests of speed
RACINGS > RACING
RACISM *n* hostile attitude or behaviour to members of other races, based on a belief in the innate superiority of one's own race
RACISMS > RACISM
RACIST > RACISM
RACISTS > RACISM
RACK *n* framework for holding particular articles, such as coats or luggage ▷ *vb* cause great suffering to
RACKED > RACK
RACKER > RACK
RACKERS > RACK
RACKET *n* noisy disturbance ▷ *vb* make a commotion
RACKETED > RACKET
RACKETEER *n* person making illegal profits ▷ *vb* operate a racket
RACKETER *n* someone making a racket
RACKETERS > RACKETER
RACKETIER > RACKETY
RACKETING > RACKET
RACKETRY *n* noise and commotion
RACKETS *n* ball game played in a paved walled court
RACKETT *n* early double-reeded wind instrument
RACKETTS > RACKETT
RACKETY *adj* involving noise, commotion and excitement
RACKFUL > RACK
RACKFULS > RACK
RACKING > RACK
RACKINGLY > RACK
RACKINGS > RACK
RACKLE *adj* dialect word meaning rash
RACKS > RACK
RACKWORK *n* mechanism with a rack and pinion
RACKWORKS > RACKWORK
RACLETTE *n* Swiss dish of melted cheese served on boiled potatoes
RACLETTES > RACLETTE
RACLOIR *n* scraper
RACLOIRS > RACLOIR
RACON *n* radar beacon
RACONS > RACON
RACONTEUR *n* skilled storyteller
RACOON *same as* > RACCOON
RACOONS > RACOON
RACQUET *same as* > RACKET
RACQUETED > RACQUET
RACQUETS > RACQUET
RACY *adj* slightly shocking
RAD *n* former unit of absorbed ionizing radiation dose equivalent to an energy absorption per unit mass of 0.01 joule per kilogram of irradiated material. 1 rad is equivalent to 0.01 gray ▷ *vb* fear ▷ *adj* slang term for great
RADAR *n* device for tracking distant objects by bouncing high-frequency radio pulses off them
RADARS > RADAR
RADDED > RAD
RADDER > RAD
RADDEST > RAD
RADDING > RAD
RADDLE *same as* > RUDDLE
RADDLED *adj* (of a person) unkempt or run-down in appearance
RADDLEMAN *same as* > RUDDLEMAN
RADDLEMEN > RADDLEMAN
RADDLES > RADDLE
RADDLING > RADDLE
RADDOCKE *same as* > RUDDOCK
RADDOCKES > RADDOCKE
RADE *(in Scots dialect) past tense of* > RIDE
RADGE *adj* angry or uncontrollable ▷ *n* person acting in such a way
RADGER > RADGE
RADGES > RADGE
RADGEST > RADGE
RADIABLE *adj* able to be x-rayed
RADIAL *adj* spreading out from a common central point ▷ *n* radial-ply tyre
RADIALE *n* bone in the wrist
RADIALIA > RADIALE
RADIALISE *same as* > RADIALIZE
RADIALITY > RADIAL
RADIALIZE *vb* arrange in a pattern of radii
RADIALLY > RADIAL
RADIALS > RADIAL
RADIAN *n* unit for measuring angles, equal to 57.296°
RADIANCE *n* quality or state of being radiant
RADIANCES > RADIANCE
RADIANCY *same as* > RADIANCE
RADIANS > RADIAN
RADIANT *adj* looking happy ▷ *n* point or object that emits radiation, esp the part of a heater that gives out heat
RADIANTLY > RADIANT
RADIANTS > RADIANT
RADIATA as in *radiata pine* type of pine tree
RADIATAS > RADIATA
RADIATE *vb* spread out from a centre ▷ *adj* having rays or a radial structure
RADIATED > RADIATE
RADIATELY > RADIATE
RADIATES > RADIATE
RADIATING > RADIATE
RADIATION *n* transmission of energy from one body to another
RADIATIVE *adj* emitting or causing the emission of radiation
RADIATOR *n* arrangemen[t] of pipes containing hot water or steam to heat a room
RADIATORS > RADIATOR
RADIATORY *same as* > RADIATIVE
RADICAL *adj* fundament[al] ▷ *n* person advocating fundamental (political) change
RADICALLY *adv* thoroug[hly]
RADICALS > RADICAL
RADICAND *n* number or quantity from which a r[oot] is to be extracted, usuall[y] preceded by a radical sig[n]
RADICANDS > RADICAND
RADICANT *adj* forming roots from the stem
RADICATE *vb* root or cau[se] to take root
RADICATED > RADICATE
RADICATES > RADICATE
RADICCHIO *n* Italian variety of chicory, with purple leaves streaked with white that are eate[n] raw in salads
RADICEL *n* very small roo[t]
RADICELS > RADICEL
RADICES > RADIX
RADICLE *n* small or developing root
RADICLES > RADICLE
RADICULAR *adj* root-related
RADICULE *same as* > RADICLE
RADICULES > RADICULE
RADII > RADIUS
RADIO *n* use of electromagnetic waves for broadcasting, communication, etc ▷ *v[b]* transmit (a message) by radio ▷ *adj* of, relating t[o] or using radio
RADIOED > RADIO
RADIOGRAM *n* image produced on a specially sensitized photographi[c] film or plate by radiatio[n] usually by X-rays or gamma rays
RADIOING > RADIO
RADIOLOGY *n* science of using x-rays in medicine
RADIOMAN *n* radio opera[tor]
RADIOMEN > RADIOMAN
RADIONICS *n* dowsing technique using a pendulum to detect the energy fields that are emitted by all forms of matter
RADIOS > RADIO
RADIOTHON *n* lengthy radio programme to rai[se] charity funds, etc
RADISH *n* small hot-flavoured root vegetabl[e] eaten raw in salads
RADISHES > RADISH

ADIUM *n* radioactive metallic element

ADIUMS > RADIUM

ADIUS *n* (length of) a straight line from the centre to the circumference of a circle

ADIUSES > RADIUS

ADIX *n* any number that is the base of a number system or of a system of logarithms

ADIXES > RADIX

ADOME *n* protective housing for a radar antenna made from a material that is transparent to radio waves

ADOMES > RADOME

ADON *n* radioactive gaseous element

ADONS > RADON

ADS > RAD

ADULA *n* horny tooth-bearing strip on the tongue of molluscs that is used for rasping food

ADULAE > RADULA

ADULAR > RADULA

ADULAS > RADULA

ADULATE > RADULA

ADWASTE *n* radioactive wast

ADWASTES > RADWASTE

AFALE *n* burst of artillery fire

AFALES > RAFALE

AFF *n* rubbish

AFFIA *n* prepared palm fibre for weaving mats etc

AFFIAS > RAFFIA

AFFINATE *n* liquid left after a solute has been extracted by solvent extraction

AFFINOSE *n* trisaccharide of fructose, glucose, and galactose that occurs in sugar beet, cotton seed, certain cereals, etc

AFFISH *adj* slightly disreputable

AFFISHLY > RAFFISH

AFFLE *n* lottery with goods as prizes ▷ *vb* offer as a prize in a raffle

AFFLED > RAFFLE

AFFLER > RAFFLE

AFFLERS > RAFFLE

AFFLES > RAFFLE

AFFLESIA *n* any of various tropical Asian parasitic leafless plants whose flowers smell of putrid meat and are pollinated by carrion flies

AFFLING > RAFFLE

AFFS > RAFF

AFT *n* floating platform of logs, planks, etc ▷ *vb* convey on or travel by raft, or make a raft from

AFTED > RAFT

AFTER *n* one of the main beams of a roof ▷ *vb* to fit with rafters

RAFTERED > RAFTER

RAFTERING > RAFTER

RAFTERS > RAFTER

RAFTING > RAFT

RAFTINGS > RAFT

RAFTMAN *same as* > RAFTSMAN

RAFTMEN > RAFTMAN

RAFTS > RAFT

RAFTSMAN *n* someone who does rafting

RAFTSMEN > RAFTSMAN

RAG *n* fragment of cloth ▷ *vb* tease ▷ *adj* (in British universities and colleges) of various events organized to raise money for charity

RAGA *n* any of several conventional patterns of melody and rhythm that form the basis for freely interpreted compositions. Each pattern is associated with different aspects of religious devotion

RAGAS > RAGA

RAGBAG *n* confused assortment, jumble

RAGBAGS > RAGBAG

RAGBOLT *n* bolt that has angled projections on it to prevent it working loose once it has been driven home

RAGBOLTS > RAGBOLT

RAGDE *archaic past form of* > RAGE

RAGE *n* violent anger or passion ▷ *vb* speak or act with fury

RAGED > RAGE

RAGEE *same as* > RAGI

RAGEES > RAGEE

RAGEFUL > RAGE

RAGER > RAGE

RAGERS > RAGE

RAGES > RAGE

RAGG *same as* > RAGSTONE

RAGGA *n* dance-oriented style of reggae

RAGGAS > RAGGA

RAGGED > RAG

RAGGEDER > RAG

RAGGEDEST > RAG

RAGGEDIER > RAGGEDY

RAGGEDLY > RAG

RAGGEDY *adj* somewhat ragged

RAGGEE *same as* > RAGI

RAGGEES > RAGGEE

RAGGERIES > RAGGERY

RAGGERY *n* rags

RAGGIER > RAGGY

RAGGIES > RAGGY

RAGGIEST > RAGGY

RAGGING > RAG

RAGGINGS > RAG

RAGGLE *n* thin groove cut in stone or brickwork, esp to hold the edge of a roof ▷ *vb* cut a raggle in

RAGGLED > RAGGLE

RAGGLES > RAGGLE

RAGGLING > RAGGLE

RAGGS > RAGG

RAGGY *adj* raglike ▷ *n* cereal grass cultivated in Africa and Asia for its edible grain

RAGHEAD *n* offensive term for an Arab person

RAGHEADS > RAGHEAD

RAGI *n* cereal grass cultivated in Africa and Asia for its edible grain

RAGING > RAGE

RAGINGLY > RAGE

RAGINGS > RAGE

RAGINI *n* Indian musical form related to a raga

RAGINIS > RAGINI

RAGIS > RAGI

RAGLAN *adj* (of a sleeve) joined to a garment by diagonal seams from the neck to the underarm ▷ *n* coat with sleeves that continue to the collar instead of having armhole seams

RAGLANS > RAGLAN

RAGMAN *n* rag-and-bone man

RAGMANS > RAGMAN

RAGMEN > RAGMAN

RAGMENT *n* statute, roll, or list

RAGMENTS > RAGMENT

RAGOUT *n* richly seasoned stew of meat and vegetables ▷ *vb* make into a ragout

RAGOUTED > RAGOUT

RAGOUTING > RAGOUT

RAGOUTS > RAGOUT

RAGPICKER *n* rag-and-bone man

RAGS > RAG

RAGSTONE *n* hard sandstone or limestone, esp when used for building

RAGSTONES > RAGSTONE

RAGTAG *n* disparaging term for common people

RAGTAGS > RAGTAG

RAGTIME *n* style of jazz piano music

RAGTIMER > RAGTIME

RAGTIMERS > RAGTIME

RAGTIMES > RAGTIME

RAGTOP *n* informal word for a car with a folding or removable roof

RAGTOPS > RAGTOP

RAGULED *same as* > RAGULY

RAGULY *adj* (in heraldry) having toothlike or stublike projections

RAGWEED *n* any of several plants regarded as weeds, some of which produce a large amount of hay-fever-causing pollen

RAGWEEDS > RAGWEED

RAGWHEEL *n* toothed wheel

RAGWHEELS > RAGWHEEL

RAGWORK *n* weaving or needlework using rags

RAGWORKS > RAGWORK

RAGWORM *n* type of worm that lives chiefly in burrows in sand or mud

RAGWORMS > RAGWORM

RAGWORT *n* plant with ragged leaves and yellow flowers

RAGWORTS > RAGWORT

RAH *informal US word for* > CHEER

RAHED > RAH

RAHING > RAH

RAHS > RAH

RAHUI *n* Māori prohibition

RAHUIS > RAHUI

RAI *n* type of Algerian popular music based on traditional Algerian music influenced by modern Western pop

RAIA *same as* > RAYAH

RAIAS > RAIA

RAID *n* sudden surprise attack or search ▷ *vb* make a raid on

RAIDED > RAID

RAIDER > RAID

RAIDERS > RAID

RAIDING > RAID

RAIDINGS > RAID

RAIDS > RAID

RAIK *n* wander ▷ *vb* wander

RAIKED > RAIK

RAIKING > RAIK

RAIKS > RAIK

RAIL *n* horizontal bar, esp as part of a fence or track ▷ *vb* complain bitterly or loudly

RAILBED *n* ballast layer supporting the sleepers of a railway track

RAILBEDS > RAILBED

RAILBIRD *n* racing aficionado

RAILBIRDS > RAILBIRD

RAILBUS *n* buslike vehicle for use on railway lines

RAILBUSES > RAILBUS

RAILCAR *n* passenger-carrying railway vehicle consisting of a single coach with its own power unit

RAILCARD *n* card which pensioners, young people, etc can buy, entitling them to cheaper rail travel

RAILCARDS > RAILCARD

RAILCARS > RAILCAR

RAILE *archaic spelling of* > RAIL

RAILED > RAIL

RAILER > RAIL

RAILERS > RAIL

RAILES > RAILE

RAILHEAD *n* terminal of a railway

RAILHEADS > RAILHEAD

RAILING *n* fence made of rails supported by posts
RAILINGLY > RAIL
RAILINGS > RAILING
RAILLERY *n* teasing or joking
RAILLESS > RAIL
RAILLIES > RAILLY
RAILLY *old word for* > MOCK
RAILMAN *n* railway employee
RAILMEN > RAILMAN
RAILROAD *same as* > RAILWAY
RAILROADS > RAILROAD
RAILS > RAIL
RAILWAY *n* track of iron rails on which trains run
RAILWAYS > RAILWAY
RAILWOMAN *n* female railway employee
RAILWOMEN > RAILWOMAN
RAIMENT *n* clothing
RAIMENTS > RAIMENT
RAIN *n* water falling in drops from the clouds ▷ *vb* fall or pour down as rain
RAINBAND *n* dark band in the solar spectrum caused by water in the atmosphere
RAINBANDS > RAINBAND
RAINBIRD *n* a bird whose call is believed to be a sign of impending rain
RAINBIRDS > RAINBIRD
RAINBOW *n* arch of colours in the sky
RAINBOWED *adj* resembling or involving a rainbow
RAINBOWS > RAINBOW
RAINBOWY > RAINBOW
RAINCHECK *n* ticket stub allowing readmission to a game on a later date should bad weather prevent play
RAINCOAT *n* water-resistant overcoat
RAINCOATS > RAINCOAT
RAINDATE *n* US term for an alternative date in case of rain
RAINDATES > RAINDATE
RAINDROP *n* water droplet that falls from the sky when it is raining
RAINDROPS > RAINDROP
RAINE *archaic spelling of* > REIGN
RAINED > RAIN
RAINES > RAINE
RAINFALL *n* amount of rain
RAINFALLS > RAINFALL
RAINIER > RAINY
RAINIEST > RAINY
RAINILY > RAINY
RAININESS > RAINY
RAINING > RAIN
RAINLESS > RAIN
RAINMAKER *n* (among American Indians) a professional practitioner of ritual incantations or other actions intended to cause rain to fall
RAINOUT *n* radioactive fallout or atmospheric pollution carried to the earth by rain
RAINOUTS > RAINOUT
RAINPROOF *adj* (of garments, materials, buildings, etc) impermeable to rainwater ▷ *vb* make rainproof
RAINS *pl n the*. the season of heavy rainfall, esp in the tropics
RAINSPOUT *n* waterspout
RAINSTORM *n* storm with heavy rain
RAINTIGHT *same as* > RAINPROOF
RAINWASH *n* action of rain ▷ *vb* erode or wet as a result of rain
RAINWATER *n* water from rain
RAINWEAR *n* protective garments intended for use in wet weather
RAINWEARS > RAINWEAR
RAINY *adj* characterized by a large rainfall
RAIRD *same as* > REIRD
RAIRDS > RAIRD
RAIS > RAI
RAISABLE > RAISE
RAISE *vb* lift up ▷ *n* increase in pay
RAISEABLE > RAISE
RAISED > RAISE
RAISER > RAISE
RAISERS > RAISE
RAISES > RAISE
RAISIN *n* dried grape
RAISING *n* rule that moves a constituent from an embedded clause into the main clause
RAISINGS > RAISING
RAISINS > RAISIN
RAISINY > RAISIN
RAISONNE *adj* carefully thought out
RAIT *same as* > RET
RAITA *n* Indian dish of chopped cucumber, mint, etc, in yogurt, served with curries
RAITAS > RAITA
RAITED > RAIT
RAITING > RAIT
RAITS > RAIT
RAIYAT *same as* > RYOT
RAIYATS > RAIYAT
RAJ *n* (in India) government
RAJA *same as* > RAJAH
RAJAH *n* (in India, formerly) a ruler or landlord: sometimes used as a form of address or as a title preceding a name
RAJAHS > RAJAH
RAJAHSHIP > RAJAH
RAJAS > RAJA
RAJASHIP > RAJA
RAJASHIPS > RAJA
RAJES > RAJ
RAKE *n* tool with a long handle and a crosspiece with teeth, used for smoothing earth or gathering leaves, hay, etc ▷ *vb* gather or smooth with a rake
RAKED > RAKE
RAKEE *same as* > RAKI
RAKEES > RAKEE
RAKEHELL *n* dissolute man ▷ *adj* profligate
RAKEHELLS > RAKEHELL
RAKEHELLY *adj* profligate
RAKEOFF *n* share of profits, esp one that is illegal or given as a bribe
RAKEOFFS > RAKEOFF
RAKER *n* person who rakes
RAKERIES > RAKERY
RAKERS > RAKER
RAKERY *n* rakish behaviour
RAKES > RAKE
RAKESHAME *n* old word for someone shamefully dissolute
RAKI *n* strong spirit distilled in Turkey, the former Yugoslavia, etc, from grain, usually flavoured with aniseed or other aromatics
RAKING *n* offence committed when a player deliberately scrapes an opponent's leg, arm, etc with the studs of his or her boots
RAKINGS > RAKING
RAKIS > RAKI
RAKISH *adj* dashing or jaunty
RAKISHLY > RAKISH
RAKSHAS *same as* > RAKSHASA
RAKSHASA *n* Hindu demon
RAKSHASAS > RAKSHASA
RAKSHASES > RAKSHAS
RAKU *n* type of Japanese pottery
RAKUS > RAKU
RALE *n* abnormal coarse crackling sound heard on auscultation of the chest, usually caused by the accumulation of fluid in the lungs
RALES > RALE
RALLIED > RALLY
RALLIER > RALLY
RALLIERS > RALLY
RALLIES > RALLY
RALLIFORM *adj* of rail family of birds
RALLINE *adj* of, relating to, or belonging to the *Rallidae*, a family of birds that includes the rails, crakes, and coots
RALLY *n* large gathering of people for a meeting ▷ *vb* bring or come together after dispersal or for a common cause
RALLYE *US variant of* > RALLY
RALLYES > RALLYE
RALLYING > RALLY
RALLYINGS > RALLY
RALLYIST > RALLY
RALLYISTS > RALLY
RALPH *vb* slang word meaning vomit
RALPHED > RALPH
RALPHING > RALPH
RALPHS > RALPH
RAM *n* male sheep ▷ *vb* strike against with force
RAMADA *n* outdoor eating area with roof but open sides
RAMADAS > RAMADA
RAMAKIN *same as* > RAMEK
RAMAKINS > RAMAKIN
RAMAL *adj* relating to a branch or branches
RAMATE *adj* with branches
RAMBLA *n* dried-up riverbed
RAMBLAS > RAMBLA
RAMBLE *vb* walk without a definite route ▷ *n* walk, esp in the country
RAMBLED > RAMBLE
RAMBLER *n* person who rambles
RAMBLERS > RAMBLER
RAMBLES > RAMBLE
RAMBLING *adj* large and irregularly shaped ▷ *n* activity of going for long walks in the country
RAMBLINGS > RAMBLING
RAMBUTAN *n* SE Asian tree that has bright red edible fruit
RAMBUTANS > RAMBUTAN
RAMCAT *n* dialect word for male cat
RAMCATS > RAMCAT
RAMEAL *same as* > RAMAL
RAMEE *same as* > RAMIE
RAMEES > RAMEE
RAMEKIN *n* small ovenpro dish for a single serving of food
RAMEKINS > RAMEKIN
RAMEN *n* Japanese dish consisting of a clear brot containing thin white noodles and sometimes vegetables, meat, etc
RAMENS > RAMEN
RAMENTA > RAMENTUM
RAMENTUM *n* any of the th brown scales that cover the stems and leaves of young ferns
RAMEOUS *same as* > RAMAL
RAMEQUIN *same as* > RAMEKIN
RAMEQUINS > RAMEQUIN
RAMET *n* any of the individuals in a group of clones

AMETS > RAMET
AMI *same as* > RAMIE
AMIE *n* woody Asian shrub with broad leaves and a stem that yields a flaxlike fibre
AMIES > RAMIE
AMIFIED > RAMIFY
AMIFIES > RAMIFY
AMIFORM *adj* having a branchlike shape
AMIFY *vb* become complex
AMIFYING > RAMIFY
AMILIE *same as* > RAMILLIE
AMILIES > RAMILIE
AMILLIE *n* wig with a plait at the back fashionable in the 18th century
AMILLIES > RAMILLIE
AMIN *n* swamp-growing tree found in Malaysia and Indonesia
AMINS > RAMIN
AMIS > RAMI
AMJET *n* type of jet engine in which fuel is burned in a duct using air compressed by the forward speed of the aircraft
AMJETS > RAMJET
AMMED > RAM
AMMEL *n* discarded or waste matter
AMMELS > RAMMEL
AMMER > RAM
AMMERS > RAM
AMMIER > RAMMISH
AMMIES > RAMMISH
AMMIEST > RAMMISH
AMMING > RAM
AMMISH *adj* like a ram, esp in being lustful or foul-smelling
AMMISHLY > RAMMISH
AMMLE *n* collection of items saved in case they become useful
AMMLES > RAMMLE
AMMY *n* noisy disturbance or free-for-all ▷ *vb* make a rammy
AMONA *same as* > SAGEBRUSH
AMONAS > RAMONA
AMOSE *adj* having branches
AMOSELY > RAMOSE
AMOSITY > RAMOSE
AMOUS *same as* > RAMOSE
AMOUSLY > RAMOSE
AMP *n* slope joining two level surfaces ▷ *vb* (esp of animals) to rush around in a wild excited manner
AMPAGE *vb* dash about violently
AMPAGED > RAMPAGE
AMPAGER > RAMPAGE
AMPAGERS > RAMPAGE
AMPAGES > RAMPAGE
AMPAGING > RAMPAGE
RAMPANCY > RAMPANT
RAMPANT *adj* growing or spreading uncontrollably
RAMPANTLY > RAMPANT
RAMPART *n* mound or wall for defence ▷ *vb* provide with a rampart
RAMPARTED > RAMPART
RAMPARTS > RAMPART
RAMPAUGE *Scots variant of* > RAMPAGE
RAMPAUGED > RAMPAUGE
RAMPAUGES > RAMPAUGE
RAMPED > RAMP
RAMPER > RAMP
RAMPERS > RAMP
RAMPICK *same as* > RAMPIKE
RAMPICKED > RAMPICK
RAMPICKS > RAMPICK
RAMPIKE *n* US or dialect word for a dead tree
RAMPIKES > RAMPIKE
RAMPING > RAMP
RAMPINGS > RAMP
RAMPION *n* European and Asian plant that has clusters of bluish flowers and an edible white tuberous root used in salads
RAMPIONS > RAMPION
RAMPIRE *archaic variant of* > RAMPART
RAMPIRED > RAMPIRE
RAMPIRES > RAMPIRE
RAMPOLE *same as* > RAMPIKE
RAMPOLES > RAMPOLE
RAMPS > RAMP
RAMPSMAN *n* mugger
RAMPSMEN > RAMPSMAN
RAMROD *n* long thin rod used for cleaning the barrel of a gun or forcing gunpowder into an old-fashioned gun ▷ *adj* (of someone's posture) very straight and upright ▷ *vb* drive
RAMRODDED > RAMROD
RAMRODS > RAMROD
RAMS > RAM
RAMSHORN as in *ramshorn snail* any of various freshwater snails
RAMSHORNS > RAMSHORN
RAMSON *n* type of garlic
RAMSONS > RAMSON
RAMSTAM *adv* headlong ▷ *adj* headlong
RAMTIL *n* African plant grown in India esp for its oil
RAMTILLA *same as* > RAMTIL
RAMTILLAS > RAMTILLA
RAMTILS > RAMTIL
RAMULAR *adj* relating to a branch or branches
RAMULI > RAMULUS
RAMULOSE *adj* (of the parts or organs of animals and plants) having many small branches
RAMULOUS *same as* > RAMULOSE
RAMULUS *n* small branch
RAMUS *n* barb of a bird's feather
RAN > RUN
RANA *n* genus of frogs
RANARIAN *adj* of or relating to frogs
RANARIUM *n* place for keeping frogs
RANARIUMS > RANARIUM
RANAS > RANA
RANCE *Scots word for* > PROP
RANCED > RANCE
RANCEL *vb* (in Shetland and Orkney) carry out a search
RANCELS > RANCEL
RANCES > RANCE
RANCH *n* large cattle farm in the American West ▷ *vb* run a ranch
RANCHED > RANCH
RANCHER *n* person who owns, manages, or works on a ranch
RANCHERIA *n* native American settlement or home of a rancher
RANCHERIE *n* (in British Columbia, Canada) a settlement of North American Indians, esp on a reserve
RANCHERO *another word for* > RANCHER
RANCHEROS > RANCHERO
RANCHERS > RANCHER
RANCHES > RANCH
RANCHING > RANCH
RANCHINGS > RANCH
RANCHLESS > RANCH
RANCHLIKE > RANCH
RANCHMAN *n* man who owns, manages, or works on a ranch
RANCHMEN > RANCHMAN
RANCHO *n* hut or group of huts for housing ranch workers
RANCHOS > RANCHO
RANCID *adj* (of butter, bacon, etc) stale and having an offensive smell
RANCIDER > RANCID
RANCIDEST > RANCID
RANCIDITY > RANCID
RANCIDLY > RANCID
RANCING > RANCE
RANCOR *same as* > RANCOUR
RANCORED > RANCOR
RANCOROUS > RANCOUR
RANCORS > RANCOR
RANCOUR *n* deep bitter hate
RANCOURS > RANCOUR
RAND *n* monetary unit of S Africa; leather strip on the heel of a shoe ▷ *vb* cut into rands
RANDAN *n* boat rowed by three people, in which the person in the middle uses two oars and the people fore and aft use one oar each
RANDANS > RANDAN
RANDED > RAND
RANDEM *adv* with three horses harnessed together as a team ▷ *n* carriage or team of horses so driven
RANDEMS > RANDEM
RANDIE *same as* > RANDY
RANDIER > RANDY
RANDIES > RANDY
RANDIEST > RANDY
RANDILY > RANDY
RANDINESS > RANDY
RANDING > RAND
RANDLORD *n* mining magnate during the 19th-century gold boom in Johannesburg
RANDLORDS > RANDLORD
RANDOM *adj* made or done by chance or without plan ▷ *n* (in mining) the course of a vein of ore
RANDOMISE *same as* > RANDOMIZE
RANDOMIZE *vb* set up (a selection process, sample, etc) in a deliberately random way in order to enhance the statistical validity of any results obtained
RANDOMLY > RANDOM
RANDOMS > RANDOM
RANDON *old variant of* > RANDOM
RANDONS > RANDON
RANDS > RAND
RANDY *adj* sexually aroused ▷ *n* rude or reckless person
RANEE *same as* > RANI
RANEES > RANEE
RANG > RING
RANGATIRA *n* Māori chief of either sex
RANGE *n* limits of effectiveness or variation ▷ *vb* vary between one point and another
RANGED > RANGE
RANGELAND *n* land that naturally produces forage plants suitable for grazing but where rainfall is too low or erratic for growing crops
RANGER *n* official in charge of a nature reserve etc
RANGERS > RANGER
RANGES > RANGE
RANGI *n* sky
RANGIER > RANGY
RANGIEST > RANGY
RANGILY > RANGY
RANGINESS > RANGY
RANGING > RANGE
RANGINGS > RANGE
RANGIORA *n* evergreen New Zealand shrub or small tree with large ovate leaves and small greenish-white flowers
RANGIORAS > RANGIORA
RANGIS > RANGI
RANGOLI *n* traditional

Indian ground decoration using coloured sand or chalks
RANGOLIS > RANGOLI
RANGY *adj* having long slender limbs
RANI *n* wife or widow of a rajah
RANID *n* frog
RANIDS > RANID
RANIFORM *n* froglike
RANINE *adj* relating to frogs
RANIS > RANI
RANK *n* relative place or position ▷ *vb* have a specific rank or position ▷ *adj* complete or absolute
RANKE *archaic variant of* > RANK
RANKED > RANK
RANKER *n* soldier in the ranks
RANKERS > RANKER
RANKES > RANKE
RANKEST > RANK
RANKING *adj* prominent ▷ *n* position on a scale
RANKINGS > RANKING
RANKISH *adj* old word meaning rather rank
RANKISM *n* discrimination against people on the grounds of rank
RANKISMS > RANKISM
RANKLE *vb* continue to cause resentment or bitterness
RANKLED > RANKLE
RANKLES > RANKLE
RANKLESS > RANK
RANKLING > RANKLE
RANKLY > RANK
RANKNESS > RANK
RANKS > RANK
RANKSHIFT *n* phenomenon in which a unit at one rank in the grammar has the function of a unit at a lower rank, as for example in the phrase *the house on the corner*, where the words *on the corner* shift down from the rank of group to the rank of word ▷ *vb* shift or be shifted from one linguistic rank to another
RANPIKE *same as* > RAMPIKE
RANPIKES > RANPIKE
RANSACK *vb* search thoroughly
RANSACKED > RANSACK
RANSACKER > RANSACK
RANSACKS > RANSACK
RANSEL *same as* > RANCEL
RANSELS > RANSEL
RANSHAKLE *Scots word for* > RANSACK
RANSOM *n* money demanded in return for the release of someone who has been kidnapped ▷ *vb* pay money to obtain the release of a captive
RANSOMED > RANSOM
RANSOMER > RANSOM
RANSOMERS > RANSOM
RANSOMING > RANSOM
RANSOMS > RANSOM
RANT *vb* talk in a loud and excited way ▷ *n* loud excited speech
RANTED > RANT
RANTER > RANT
RANTERISM > RANT
RANTERS > RANT
RANTING > RANT
RANTINGLY > RANT
RANTINGS > RANT
RANTIPOLE *n* reckless person ▷ *vb* behave like a rantipole
RANTS > RANT
RANULA *n* saliva-filled cyst that develops under the tongue
RANULAR *n* cyst of lower surface of tongue
RANULAS > RANULA
RANUNCULI *pl n* plants of the genus that includes the buttercup, crowfoot, spearwort, and lesser celandine
RANZEL *same as* > RANCEL
RANZELMAN *n* (in Shetland and Orkney) type of constable
RANZELMEN > RANZELMAN
RANZELS > RANZEL
RAOULIA *n* flowering plant of New Zealand
RAOULIAS > RAOULIA
RAP *vb* hit with a sharp quick blow ▷ *n* quick sharp blow
RAPACIOUS *adj* greedy or grasping
RAPACITY > RAPACIOUS
RAPE *vb* force to submit to sexual intercourse ▷ *n* act of raping
RAPED > RAPE
RAPER > RAPE
RAPERS > RAPE
RAPES > RAPE
RAPESEED *n* seed of the oilseed rape plant
RAPESEEDS > RAPESEED
RAPHAE > RAPHE
RAPHANIA *n* type of ergotism possibly resulting from consumption of radish seeds
RAPHANIAS > RAPHANIA
RAPHE *n* elongated ridge of conducting tissue along the side of certain seeds
RAPHES > RAPHE
RAPHIA *same as* > RAFFIA
RAPHIAS > RAPHIA
RAPHIDE *n* any of numerous needle-shaped crystals, usually of calcium oxalate, that occur in many plant cells as a metabolic product
RAPHIDES > RAPHIDE
RAPHIS *same as* > RAPHIDE
RAPID *adj* quick, swift
RAPIDER > RAPID
RAPIDEST > RAPID
RAPIDITY > RAPID
RAPIDLY > RAPID
RAPIDNESS > RAPID
RAPIDS *pl n* part of a river with a fast turbulent current
RAPIER *n* fine-bladed sword
RAPIERED *adj* carrying a rapier
RAPIERS > RAPIER
RAPINE *n* pillage or plundering
RAPINES > RAPINE
RAPING > RAPE
RAPINI *pl n* type of leafy vegetable
RAPIST *n* person who commits rape
RAPISTS > RAPIST
RAPLOCH *n* Scots word for homespun woollen material ▷ *adj* Scots word meaning coarse or homemade
RAPLOCHS > RAPLOCH
RAPPAREE *n* Irish irregular soldier of the late 17th century
RAPPAREES > RAPPAREE
RAPPE *n* Arcadian dish of grated potatoes and pork or chicken
RAPPED > RAP
RAPPEE *n* moist English snuff of the 18th and 19th centuries
RAPPEES > RAPPEE
RAPPEL *n* (formerly) a drumbeat to call soldiers to arms ▷ *vb* abseil
RAPPELED > RAPPEL
RAPPELING > RAPPEL
RAPPELLED > RAPPEL
RAPPELS > RAPPEL
RAPPEN *n* Swiss coin equal to one hundredth of a franc
RAPPER *n* something used for rapping, such as a knocker on a door
RAPPERS > RAPPER
RAPPES > RAPPE
RAPPING > RAP
RAPPINGS > RAP
RAPPINI *same as* > RAPINI
RAPPORT *n* harmony or agreement
RAPPORTS > RAPPORT
RAPS > RAP
RAPT *adj* engrossed or spellbound
RAPTLY > RAPT
RAPTNESS > RAPT
RAPTOR *n* any bird of prey
RAPTORIAL *adj* (of the feet of birds) adapted for seizing prey
RAPTORS > RAPTOR
RAPTURE *n* ecstasy ▷ *vb* entrance
RAPTURED > RAPTURE
RAPTURES > RAPTURE
RAPTURING > RAPTURE
RAPTURISE *same as* > RAPTURIZE
RAPTURIST > RAPTURE
RAPTURIZE *vb* go into ecstasies
RAPTUROUS *adj* experiencing or manifesting ecstatic joy or delight
RARE *adj* uncommon ▷ *archaic spelling of* > REAR
RAREBIT as in *Welsh rarebit* dish made from melted cheese and sometimes milk and seasonings and served on toast
RAREBITS > RAREBIT
RARED > RARE
RAREE as in *raree show* street show or carnival
RAREFIED *adj* highly specialized, exalted
RAREFIER > RAREFY
RAREFIERS > RAREFY
RAREFIES > RAREFY
RAREFY *vb* make or become rarer or less dense
RAREFYING > RAREFY
RARELY *adv* seldom
RARENESS > RARE
RARER > RARE
RARERIPE *adj* ripening early ▷ *n* fruit or vegetable that ripens early
RARERIPES > RARERIPE
RARES > RARE
RAREST > RARE
RARIFIED *same as* > RAREFIED
RARIFIES > RARIFY
RARIFY *same as* > RAREFY
RARIFYING > RARIFY
RARING *adj* ready
RARITIES > RARITY
RARITY *n* something that is valuable because it is unusual
RARK as in *rark up* informal New Zealand expression meaning reprimand severely
RARKED > RARK
RARKING > RARK
RARKS > RARK
RAS *n* headland
RASBORA *n* often brightly coloured tropical fish
RASBORAS > RASBORA
RASCAILLE *n* rabble
RASCAL *n* rogue ▷ *adj* belonging to the mob or rabble
RASCALDOM > RASCAL
RASCALISM > RASCAL
RASCALITY *n* mischievous disreputable, or dishonest character, behaviour, or action
RASCALLY *adj* dishonest or mean ▷ *adv* in a dishonest

or mean fashion
SCALS > RASCAL
SCASSE *n* any of various fishes with venomous spines on the dorsal and anal fins
SCASSES > RASCASSE
SCHEL *n* type of loosely knitted fabric
SCHELS > RASCHEL
SE *same as* > RAZE
SED > RASE
SER > RASE
SERS > RASE
SES > RASE
SH *adj* hasty, reckless, or ncautious ▷ *n* eruption of spots or patches on the skin ▷ *vb* (in old usage) cut
SHED > RASH
SHER *n* thin slice of bacon
SHERS > RASHER
SHES > RASH
SHEST > RASH
SHIE *n* Australian word for a shirt worn by surfers as protection against sunburn, heat rash, etc
SHIES > RASHIE
SHING > RASH
SHLIKE > RASH
SHLY > RASH
SHNESS > RASH
SING > RASE
SMALAI *n* Indian dessert made from cheese, milk, and almonds
SMALAIS > RASMALAI
SORIAL *adj* (of birds such as domestic poultry) adapted for scratching the ground for food
SP *n* harsh grating noise ▷ *vb* speak in a grating voice
SPATORY *n* surgical instrument for abrading
SPBERRY *n* red juicy edible berry
SPED > RASP
SPER > RASP
SPERS > RASP
SPIER > RASPY
SPIEST > RASPY
SPINESS > RASPY
SPING *adj* (esp of a noise) harsh or grating
SPINGLY > RASPING
SPINGS *pl n* browned breadcrumbs for coating fish and other foods before frying, baking, etc
SPISH > RASP
SPS > RASP
SPY *same as* > RASPING
SSE *n* small S Asian civet
SSES > RASSE
SSLE *dialect variant of* > WRESTLE
SSLED > RASSLE
SSLES > RASSLE
SSLING > RASSLE
RAST *archaic past form of* > RACE
RASTA *n* member of a particular Black religious movement
RASTAFARI *n* Black religious movement
RASTER *n* image consisting of rows of pixel information, such as a JPEG, GIF etc ▷ *vb* use web-based technology to turn a digital image into a large picture composed of a grid of black and white dots
RASTERED > RASTER
RASTERING > RASTER
RASTERISE *same as* > RASTERIZE
RASTERIZE *vb* (in computing) convert into pixels for screen output
RASTERS > RASTER
RASTRUM *n* pen for drawing the five lines of a musical stave simultaneously
RASTRUMS > RASTRUM
RASURE *n* scraping
RASURES > RASURE
RAT *n* small rodent ▷ *vb* inform (on)
RATA *n* New Zealand hardwood forest tree with crimson flowers
RATABLE *adj* able to be rated or evaluated
RATABLES *pl n* property that is liable to rates
RATABLY > RATABLE
RATAFEE *same as* > RATAFIA
RATAFEES > RATAFEE
RATAFIA *n* liqueur made from fruit
RATAFIAS > RATAFIA
RATAL *n* amount on which rates are assessed ▷ *adj* of or relating to rates (local taxation)
RATALS > RATAL
RATAN *same as* > RATTAN
RATANIES > RATANY
RATANS > RATAN
RATANY *n* flowering desert shrub
RATAPLAN *n* drumming sound ▷ *vb* drum
RATAPLANS > RATAPLAN
RATAS > RATA
RATATAT *n* sound of knocking on a door
RATATATS > RATATAT
RATBAG *n* eccentric, stupid, or unreliable person
RATBAGS > RATBAG
RATBITE as in *ratbite fever* acute infectious disease that can be caught from the bite of an infected rat
RATCH *same as* > RATCHET
RATCHED > RATCH
RATCHES > RATCH
RATCHET *n* set of teeth on a bar or wheel allowing motion in one direction only ▷ *vb* move using or as if using a ratchet system
RATCHETED > RATCHET
RATCHETS > RATCHET
RATCHING > RATCH
RATE *n* degree of speed or progress ▷ *vb* consider or value
RATEABLE *same as* > RATABLE
RATEABLY > RATEABLE
RATED > RATE
RATEEN *same as* > RATINE
RATEENS > RATEEN
RATEL *n* large African and S Asian musteline mammal
RATELS > RATEL
RATEMETER *n* device for counting and averaging the number of events in a given time
RATEPAYER *n* person who pays local rates on a building
RATER > RATE
RATERS > RATE
RATES *pl n* (in some countries) a tax on property levied by a local authority
RATFINK *n* contemptible or undesirable person
RATFINKS > RATFINK
RATFISH *n* deep-sea fish with a whiplike tail
RATFISHES > RATFISH
RATH *same as* > RATHE
RATHA *n* (in India) a four-wheeled carriage drawn by horses or bullocks
RATHAS > RATHA
RATHE *adj* blossoming or ripening early in the season
RATHER *adv* some extent ▷ *interj* expression of strong affirmation ▷ *sentence substitute* expression of strong affirmation, often in answer to a question
RATHEREST *adv* archaic word equivalent to soonest
RATHERIPE *same as* > RATHRIPE
RATHERISH *adv* (in informal English) quite or fairly
RATHEST *adv* dialect or archaic word meaning soonest
RATHOLE *n* rat's hiding place or burrow
RATHOLES > RATHOLE
RATHOUSE *n* psychiatric hospital or asylum
RATHOUSES > RATHOUSE
RATHRIPE *adj* dialect word meaning mature or ripe ahead of time ▷ *n* variety of apple or other fruit that is quick to ripen
RATHRIPES > RATHRIPE
RATHS > RATH
RATICIDE *n* rat poison
RATICIDES > RATICIDE
RATIFIED > RATIFY
RATIFIER > RATIFY
RATIFIERS > RATIFY
RATIFIES > RATIFY
RATIFY *vb* give formal approval to
RATIFYING > RATIFY
RATINE *n* coarse loosely woven cloth
RATINES > RATINE
RATING *n* valuation or assessment
RATINGS > RATING
RATIO *n* relationship between two numbers or amounts expressed as a proportion
RATION *n* fixed allowance of food etc ▷ *vb* limit to a certain amount per person
RATIONAL *adj* reasonable, sensible ▷ *n* rational number
RATIONALE *n* reason for an action or decision
RATIONALS > RATIONAL
RATIONED > RATION
RATIONING > RATION
RATIONS *pl n* fixed daily allowance of food, esp to military personnel or when supplies are limited
RATIOS > RATIO
RATITE *adj* (of flightless birds) having a breastbone that lacks a keel for the attachment of flight muscles ▷ *n* bird, such as an ostrich, kiwi, or rhea, that belongs to this group
RATITES > RATITE
RATLIKE > RAT
RATLIN *same as* > RATLINE
RATLINE *n* any of a series of light lines tied across the shrouds of a sailing vessel for climbing aloft
RATLINES > RATLINE
RATLING *n* young rat
RATLINGS > RATLING
RATLINS > RATLIN
RATO *n* rocket-assisted take-off
RATOO *same as* > RATU
RATOON *n* new shoot that grows from near the root or crown of crop plants, esp the sugar cane, after the old growth has been cut back ▷ *vb* propagate or cause to propagate by such a growth
RATOONED > RATOON
RATOONER *n* plant that spreads by ratooning
RATOONERS > RATOONER
RATOONING > RATOON
RATOONS > RATOON
RATOOS > RATOO
RATOS > RATO

RATPACK *n* members of the press who pursue celebrities and give wide coverage of their private lives
RATPACKS > RATPACK
RATPROOF *adj* impenetrable by rats
RATS > RAT
RATSBANE *n* rat poison, esp arsenic oxide
RATSBANES > RATSBANE
RATTAIL *n* type of fish
RATTAILED *adj* having tail like rat
RATTAILS > RATTAIL
RATTAN *n* climbing palm with jointed stems used for canes
RATTANS > RATTAN
RATTED > RAT
RATTEEN *same as* > RATINE
RATTEENS > RATTEEN
RATTEN *vb* sabotage or steal tools in order to disrupt the work of
RATTENED > RATTEN
RATTENER > RATTEN
RATTENERS > RATTEN
RATTENING > RATTEN
RATTENS > RATTEN
RATTER *n* dog or cat that catches and kills rats
RATTERIES > RATTERY
RATTERS > RATTER
RATTERY *n* rats' dwelling area
RATTIER > RATTY
RATTIEST > RATTY
RATTILY > RATTY
RATTINESS > RATTY
RATTING > RAT
RATTINGS > RAT
RATTISH *adj* of, resembling, or infested with rats
RATTLE *vb* give out a succession of short sharp sounds ▷ *n* short sharp sound
RATTLEBAG *n* rattle made out of a bag containing a variety of different things
RATTLEBOX *n* any of various tropical and subtropical leguminous plants that have inflated pods within which the seeds rattle
RATTLED > RATTLE
RATTLER *n* something that rattles
RATTLERS > RATTLER
RATTLES > RATTLE
RATTLIER > RATTLY
RATTLIEST > RATTLY
RATTLIN *same as* > RATLINE
RATTLINE *same as* > RATLINE
RATTLINES > RATTLINE
RATTLING *adv* exceptionally, very ▷ *n* succession of short sharp sounds
RATTLINGS > RATTLING
RATTLINS > RATTLIN
RATTLY *adj* having a rattle
RATTON *n* dialect word for a little rat
RATTONS > RATTON
RATTOON *same as* > RATOON
RATTOONED > RATTOON
RATTOONS > RATTOON
RATTRAP *n* device for catching rats
RATTRAPS > RATTRAP
RATTY *adj* bad-tempered, irritable
RATU *n* title used by Fijian chiefs or nobles
RATUS > RATU
RAUCID *adj* raucous
RAUCITIES > RAUCOUS
RAUCITY > RAUCOUS
RAUCLE *adj* Scots word for rough or tough
RAUCLER > RAUCLE
RAUCLEST > RAUCLE
RAUCOUS *adj* hoarse or harsh
RAUCOUSLY > RAUCOUS
RAUGHT *archaic past form of* > REACH
RAUN *n* fish roe or spawn
RAUNCH *n* lack of polish or refinement ▷ *vb* behave in a raunchy manner
RAUNCHED > RAUNCH
RAUNCHES > RAUNCH
RAUNCHIER > RAUNCHY
RAUNCHILY > RAUNCHY
RAUNCHING > RAUNCH
RAUNCHY *adj* earthy, sexy
RAUNGE *archaic word for* > RANGE
RAUNGED > RAUNGE
RAUNGES > RAUNGE
RAUNGING > RAUNGE
RAUNS > RAUN
RAUPATU *n* confiscation or seizure of land
RAUPATUS > RAUPATU
RAUPO *n* New Zealand bulrush
RAURIKI *n* sow thistle, any of various plants with prickly leaves, milky juice and yellow heads
RAURIKIS > RAURIKI
RAUWOLFIA *n* tropical tree or shrub
RAVAGE *vb* cause extensive damage to ▷ *n* destructive action
RAVAGED > RAVAGE
RAVAGER > RAVAGE
RAVAGERS > RAVAGE
RAVAGES > RAVAGE
RAVAGING > RAVAGE
RAVE *vb* talk wildly or with enthusiasm ▷ *n* enthusiastically good review
RAVED > RAVE
RAVEL *vb* tangle or become entangled ▷ *n* tangle or complication
RAVELED > RAVEL
RAVELER > RAVEL
RAVELERS > RAVEL
RAVELIN *n* outwork having two embankments at a salient angle
RAVELING > RAVEL
RAVELINGS > RAVEL
RAVELINS > RAVELIN
RAVELLED > RAVEL
RAVELLER > RAVEL
RAVELLERS > RAVEL
RAVELLING > RAVEL
RAVELLY > RAVEL
RAVELMENT *n* ravel or tangle
RAVELS > RAVEL
RAVEN *n* black bird like a large crow ▷ *adj* (of hair) shiny black ▷ *vb* seize or seek (plunder, prey, etc)
RAVENED > RAVEN
RAVENER > RAVEN
RAVENERS > RAVEN
RAVENING *adj* (of animals) hungrily searching for prey
RAVENINGS *pl n* rapacious behaviour and activities
RAVENLIKE > RAVEN
RAVENOUS *adj* very hungry
RAVENS > RAVEN
RAVER *n* person who leads a wild or uninhibited social life
RAVERS > RAVER
RAVES > RAVE
RAVIGOTE *n* rich white sauce with herbs and shallots
RAVIGOTES > RAVIGOTE
RAVIGOTTE *n* French salad sauce
RAVIN *archaic spelling of* > RAVEN
RAVINE *n* narrow steep-sided valley worn by a stream
RAVINED > RAVIN
RAVINES > RAVINE
RAVING *adj* delirious ▷ *n* frenzied, irrational, or wildly extravagant talk or utterances
RAVINGLY > RAVING
RAVINGS > RAVING
RAVINING > RAVIN
RAVINS > RAVIN
RAVIOLI *n* small squares of pasta with a savoury filling
RAVIOLIS > RAVIOLI
RAVISH *vb* enrapture
RAVISHED > RAVISH
RAVISHER > RAVISH
RAVISHERS > RAVISH
RAVISHES > RAVISH
RAVISHING *adj* lovely or entrancing
RAW *adj* uncooked ▷ as in *in the raw* without clothes
RAWARU *n* New Zealand name for blue cod
RAWBONE *archaic variant of* > RAWBONED
RAWBONED *adj* having a lean bony physique
RAWER > RAW
RAWEST > RAW
RAWHEAD *n* bogeyman
RAWHEADS > RAWHEAD
RAWHIDE *n* untanned hide ▷ *vb* whip
RAWHIDED > RAWHIDE
RAWHIDES > RAWHIDE
RAWHIDING > RAWHIDE
RAWIN *n* monitoring of winds in the upper atmosphere using radar and a balloon
RAWING *(in dialect) same as* > ROWEN
RAWINGS > RAWING
RAWINS > RAWIN
RAWISH > RAW
RAWLY > RAW
RAWMAISH *n* Irish word for foolish or exaggerated ta[lk]
RAWN *(in dialect) same as* > ROWEN
RAWNESS > RAW
RAWNESSES > RAW
RAWNS > RAWN
RAWS > RAW
RAX *vb* stretch or extend ▷ *n* act of stretching or straining
RAXED > RAX
RAXES > RAX
RAXING > RAX
RAY *n* single line or narrow beam of light ▷ *vb* (of an object) to emit (light) in rays or (of light) to issue in the form of rays
RAYA *same as* > RAYAH
RAYAH *n* (formerly) a non-Muslim subject of the Ottoman Empire
RAYAHS > RAYAH
RAYAS > RAYA
RAYED > RAY
RAYGRASS *same as* > RYEGRASS
RAYING > RAY
RAYLE *archaic spelling of* > RAIL
RAYLED > RAYLE
RAYLES > RAYLE
RAYLESS *adj* dark
RAYLESSLY > RAYLESS
RAYLET *n* small ray
RAYLETS > RAYLET
RAYLIKE *adj* resembling a ray
RAYLING > RAYLE
RAYNE *archaic spelling of* > REIGN
RAYNES > RAYNE
RAYON *n* (fabric made of) synthetic fibre
RAYONS > RAYON
RAYS > RAY
RAZE *vb* destroy (buildings or a town) completely
RAZED > RAZE
RAZEE *n* sailing ship that has had its upper deck or decks removed ▷ *vb* remove the upper deck or decks of (a sailing ship)

ZEED > RAZEE
ZEEING > RAZEE
ZEES > RAZEE
ZER > RAZE
ZERS > RAZE
ZES > RAZE
ZING > RAZE
ZMATAZ *n* noisy or showy uss or activity
ZOO *n* imaginary coin
ZOOS > RAZOO
ZOR *n* sharp instrument or shaving ▷ *vb* cut or have with a razor
ZORABLE *adj* able to be haved
ZORBACK *n* another name for the common orqual
ZORBILL *n* sea bird of he North Atlantic with a tout sideways flattened ill
ZORED > RAZOR
ZORING > RAZOR
ZORS > RAZOR
ZURE *same as* > RASURE
ZURES > RAZURE
ZZ *vb* make fun of
ZZBERRY *US variant f* > RASPBERRY
ZZED > RAZZ
ZZES > RAZZ
ZZIA *n* raid for plunder or slaves, esp one carried out by Moors in North Africa
ZZIAS > RAZZIA
ZZING > RAZZ
ZZLE as in *on the razzle* elebration
ZZLES > RAZZLE
prep concerning
ABSORB *vb* absorb again
ABSORBS > REABSORB
ACCEDE *vb* accede again
ACCEDED > REACCEDE
ACCEDES > REACCEDE
ACCENT *vb* accent again
ACCENTS > REACCENT
ACCEPT *vb* accept again
ACCEPTS > REACCEPT
ACCLAIM *vb* acclaim gain
ACCUSE *vb* accuse again
ACCUSED > REACCUSE
ACCUSES > REACCUSE
ACH *vb* arrive at ▷ *n* istance that one can each
ACHABLE > REACH
ACHED > REACH
ACHER > REACH
ACHERS > REACH
ACHES > REACH
ACHING > REACH
ACHLESS *adj* nreachable or nattainable
ACQUIRE *vb* get or gain something) again which ne has owned
ACT *vb* act in response to)
REACTANCE *n* resistance to the flow of an alternating current caused by the inductance or capacitance of the circuit
REACTANT *n* substance that participates in a chemical reaction
REACTANTS > REACTANT
REACTED > REACT
REACTING > REACT
REACTION *n* physical or emotional response to a stimulus
REACTIONS > REACTION
REACTIVE *adj* chemically active
REACTOR *n* apparatus in which a nuclear reaction is maintained and controlled to produce nuclear energy
REACTORS > REACTOR
REACTS > REACT
REACTUATE *vb* activate again
READ *vb* look at and understand or take in (written or printed matter) ▷ *n* matter suitable for reading
READABLE *adj* enjoyable to read
READABLY > READABLE
READAPT *vb* adapt again
READAPTED > READAPT
READAPTS > READAPT
READD *vb* add again
READDED > READD
READDICT *vb* cause to become addicted again
READDICTS > READDICT
READDING > READD
READDRESS *vb* look at or discuss (an issue, situation, etc) from a new or different point of view
READDS > READD
READER *n* person who reads
READERLY *adj* pertaining to or suitable for a reader
READERS > READER
READIED > READY
READIER > READY
READIES *pl n* ready money
READIEST > READY
READILY *adv* promptly
READINESS *n* state of being ready or prepared
READING > READ
READINGS > READ
READJUST *vb* adapt to a new situation
READJUSTS > READJUST
READMIT *vb* let (a person, country, etc) back in to a place or organization
READMITS > READMIT
READOPT *vb* adopt again
READOPTED > READOPT
READOPTS > READOPT
READORN *vb* adorn again
READORNED > READORN
READORNS > READORN
READOUT *n* act of retrieving information from a computer memory or storage device
READOUTS > READOUT
READS > READ
READVANCE *vb* advance again
READVISE *vb* advise again
READVISED > READVISE
READVISES > READVISE
READY *adj* prepared for use or action ▷ *vb* prepare
READYING > READY
READYMADE *adj* made for purchase and immediate use by any customer
REAEDIFY *vb* rebuild
REAEDIFYE *same as* > REAEDIFY
REAFFIRM *vb* state again, confirm
REAFFIRMS > REAFFIRM
REAFFIX *vb* affix again
REAFFIXED > REAFFIX
REAFFIXES > REAFFIX
REAGENCY > REAGENT
REAGENT *n* chemical substance that reacts with another, used to detect the presence of the other
REAGENTS > REAGENT
REAGIN *n* type of antibody that is formed against an allergen and is attached to the cells of a tissue. The antigen–antibody reaction that occurs on subsequent contact with the allergen causes tissue damage, leading to the release of histamine and other substances responsible for an allergic reaction
REAGINIC > REAGIN
REAGINS > REAGIN
REAK *same as* > RECK
REAKED > REAK
REAKING > REAK
REAKS > REAK
REAL *adj* existing in fact ▷ *n* name of a former small Spanish or Spanish-American silver coin as well as of the standard monetary unit of Brazil
REALER > REAL
REALES > REAL
REALEST > REAL
REALGAR *n* rare orange-red soft mineral consisting of arsenic sulphide in monoclinic crystalline form
REALGARS > REALGAR
REALIA *pl n* real-life facts and material used in teaching
REALIGN *vb* change or put back to a new or former place or position
REALIGNED > REALIGN
REALIGNS > REALIGN
REALISE *same as* > REALIZE
REALISED > REALISE
REALISER > REALISE
REALISERS > REALISE
REALISES > REALISE
REALISING > REALISE
REALISM *n* awareness or acceptance of things as they are
REALISMS > REALISM
REALIST *n* person who is aware of and accepts the physical universe, events, etc, as they are
REALISTIC *adj* seeing and accepting things as they really are, practical
REALISTS > REALIST
REALITIES > REALITY
REALITY *n* state of things as they are
REALIZE *vb* become aware or grasp the significance of
REALIZED > REALIZE
REALIZER > REALIZE
REALIZERS > REALIZE
REALIZES > REALIZE
REALIZING > REALIZE
REALLIE *old or dialect variant of* > REALLY
REALLIED > REALLY
REALLIES > REALLY
REALLOT *vb* allot again
REALLOTS > REALLOT
REALLY *adv* very ▷ *interj* exclamation of dismay, doubt, or surprise ▷ *vb* (in archaic usage) rally
REALLYING > REALLY
REALM *n* kingdom
REALMLESS > REALM
REALMS > REALM
REALNESS > REAL
REALO *n* member of the German Green party with moderate views
REALOS > REALO
REALS > REAL
REALTER *vb* alter again
REALTERED > REALTER
REALTERS > REALTER
REALTIE *n* archaic word meaning sincerity
REALTIES > REALTY
REALTIME *adj* (of a data-processing system) constantly updating to reflect the latest changes in data
REALTOR *n* estate agent
REALTORS > REALTOR
REALTY *n* immovable property
REAM *n* twenty quires of paper, generally 500 sheets ▷ *vb* enlarge (a hole) by use of a reamer
REAME *archaic variant of* > REALM
REAMED > REAM
REAMEND *vb* amend again
REAMENDED > REAMEND
REAMENDS > REAMEND
REAMER *n* steel tool with a cylindrical or tapered

shank around which longitudinal teeth are ground, used for smoothing the bores of holes accurately to size
REAMERS > REAMER
REAMES > REAME
REAMIER > REAMY
REAMIEST > REAMY
REAMING > REAM
REAMS > REAM
REAMY *Scots for* > CREAMY
REAN *same as* > REEN
REANALYSE *vb* analyse again
REANALYZE *US spelling of* > REANALYSE
REANIMATE *vb* refresh or enliven (something) again
REANNEX *vb* annex again
REANNEXED > REANNEX
REANNEXES > REANNEX
REANOINT *vb* anoint again
REANOINTS > REANOINT
REANS > REAN
REANSWER *vb* answer again
REANSWERS > REANSWER
REAP *vb* cut and gather (a harvest)
REAPABLE > REAP
REAPED > REAP
REAPER *n* person who reaps or machine for reaping
REAPERS > REAPER
REAPHOOK *n* sickle
REAPHOOKS > REAPHOOK
REAPING > REAP
REAPPAREL *vb* clothe again
REAPPEAR *vb* appear again
REAPPEARS > REAPPEAR
REAPPLIED > REAPPLY
REAPPLIES > REAPPLY
REAPPLY *vb* put or spread (something) on again
REAPPOINT *vb* assign (a person, committee, etc) to a post or role again
REAPPROVE *vb* approve again
REAPS > REAP
REAR *n* back part ▷ *vb* care for and educate (children)
REARED > REAR
REARER > REAR
REARERS > REAR
REARGUARD *n* troops protecting the rear of an army
REARGUE *vb* argue again
REARGUED > REARGUE
REARGUES > REARGUE
REARGUING > REARGUE
REARHORSE *n* mantis
REARING > REAR
REARISE *vb* arise again
REARISEN > REARISE
REARISES > REARISE
REARISING > REARISE
REARLY *old word for* > EARLY
REARM *vb* arm again
REARMED > REARM
REARMICE > REARMOUSE
REARMING > REARM
REARMOST *adj* nearest the back
REARMOUSE *same as* > REREMOUSE
REARMS > REARM
REAROSE > REARISE
REAROUSAL > REAROUSE
REAROUSE *vb* arouse again
REAROUSED > REAROUSE
REAROUSES > REAROUSE
REARRANGE *vb* organize differently, alter
REARREST *vb* arrest again
REARRESTS > REARREST
REARS > REAR
REARWARD *adj* in the rear ▷ *adv* towards the rear ▷ *n* position in the rear, esp the rear division of a military formation
REARWARDS *same as* > REARWARD
REASCEND *vb* ascend again
REASCENDS > REASCEND
REASCENT *n* new ascent
REASCENTS > REASCENT
REASON *n* cause or motive ▷ *vb* think logically in forming conclusions
REASONED *adj* well thought out or well presented
REASONER > REASON
REASONERS > REASON
REASONING *n* process of drawing conclusions from facts or evidence
REASONS > REASON
REASSAIL *vb* assail again
REASSAILS > REASSAIL
REASSERT *vb* assert (rights, claims, etc) again
REASSERTS > REASSERT
REASSESS *vb* reconsider the value or importance of
REASSIGN *vb* move (personnel, resources, etc) to a new post, department, location, etc
REASSIGNS > REASSIGN
REASSORT *vb* assort again
REASSORTS > REASSORT
REASSUME *vb* assume again
REASSUMED > REASSUME
REASSUMES > REASSUME
REASSURE *vb* restore confidence to
REASSURED > REASSURE
REASSURER > REASSURE
REASSURES > REASSURE
REAST *same as* > REEST
REASTED > REAST
REASTIER > REASTY
REASTIEST > REASTY
REASTING > REAST
REASTS > REAST
REASTY *adj* (in dialect) rancid
REATA *n* lasso
REATAS > REATA
REATE *n* type of crowfoot
REATES > REATE
REATTACH *vb* attach again
REATTACK *vb* attack again
REATTACKS > REATTACK
REATTAIN *vb* attain again
REATTAINS > REATTAIN
REATTEMPT *vb* attempt again
REAVAIL *vb* avail again
REAVAILED > REAVAIL
REAVAILS > REAVAIL
REAVE *vb* carry off (property, prisoners, etc) by force
REAVED > REAVE
REAVER > REAVE
REAVERS > REAVE
REAVES > REAVE
REAVING > REAVE
REAVOW *vb* avow again
REAVOWED > REAVOW
REAVOWING > REAVOW
REAVOWS > REAVOW
REAWAKE *vb* awake again
REAWAKED > REAWAKE
REAWAKEN *vb* emerge or rouse from sleep
REAWAKENS > REAWAKEN
REAWAKES > REAWAKE
REAWAKING > REAWAKE
REAWOKE > REAWAKE
REAWOKEN > REAWAKE
REB *n* Confederate soldier in the American Civil War (1861–65)
REBACK *vb* provide with a new back, backing, or lining
REBACKED > REBACK
REBACKING > REBACK
REBACKS > REBACK
REBADGE *vb* relaunch (a product) under a new name, brand, or logo
REBADGED > REBADGE
REBADGES > REBADGE
REBADGING > REBADGE
REBAIT *vb* bait again
REBAITED > REBAIT
REBAITING > REBAIT
REBAITS > REBAIT
REBALANCE *vb* balance again
REBAPTISE *same as* > REBAPTIZE
REBAPTISM *n* new baptism
REBAPTIZE *vb* baptize again
REBAR *n* rod providing reinforcement in concrete structures
REBARS > REBAR
REBATABLE > REBATE
REBATE *n* discount or refund ▷ *vb* cut a rabbet in
REBATED > REBATE
REBATER > REBATE
REBATERS > REBATE
REBATES > REBATE
REBATING > REBATE
REBATO *same as* > RABATO
REBATOES > REBATO
REBATOS > REBATO
REBBE *n* individual's chosen spiritual mentor
REBBES > REBBE
REBBETZIN *n* wife of a rabbi
REBEC *n* medieval stringed instrument resembling the violin but having a lute-shaped body
REBECK *same as* > REBEC
REBECKS > REBECK
REBECS > REBEC
REBEGAN > REBEGIN
REBEGIN *vb* begin again
REBEGINS > REBEGIN
REBEGUN > REBEGIN
REBEL *vb* revolt against th[e] ruling power ▷ *n* person who rebels ▷ *adj* rebelli[ous]
REBELDOM > REBEL
REBELDOMS > REBEL
REBELLED > REBEL
REBELLER > REBEL
REBELLERS > REBEL
REBELLING > REBEL
REBELLION *n* organized open resistance to authority
REBELLOW *vb* re-echo loudly
REBELLOWS > REBELLOW
REBELS > REBEL
REBID *vb* bid again
REBIDDEN > REBID
REBIDDING > REBID
REBIDS > REBID
REBILL *vb* bill again
REBILLED > REBILL
REBILLING > REBILL
REBILLS > REBILL
REBIND *vb* bind again
REBINDING > REBIND
REBINDS > REBIND
REBIRTH *n* revival or renaissance
REBIRTHS > REBIRTH
REBIT > REBITE
REBITE *vb* (in printing) to give another application of acid in order to cause further cutting of a plate
REBITES > REBITE
REBITING > REBITE
REBITTEN > REBITE
REBLEND *vb* blend again
REBLENDED > REBLEND
REBLENDS > REBLEND
REBLENT *same as* > REBLE[ND]
REBLOOM *vb* bloom again
REBLOOMED > REBLOOM
REBLOOMS > REBLOOM
REBLOSSOM *vb* blossom again
REBOANT *adj* resounding reverberating
REBOARD *vb* board again
REBOARDED > REBOARD
REBOARDS > REBOARD
REBOATION *n* repeated bellow
REBODIED > REBODY
REBODIES > REBODY
REBODY *vb* give a new bo[dy] to
REBODYING > REBODY
REBOIL *vb* boil again
REBOILED > REBOIL
REBOILING > REBOIL
REBOILS > REBOIL
REBOOK *vb* book again

EBOOKED > REBOOK
EBOOKING > REBOOK
EBOOKS > REBOOK
EBOOT *vb* shut down and then restart (a computer system)
EBOOTED > REBOOT
EBOOTING > REBOOT
EBOOTS > REBOOT
EBOP *same as* > BEBOP
EBOPS > REBOP
EBORE *n* boring of a cylinder to restore its true shape ▷ *vb* carry out this process
EBORED > REBORE
EBORES > REBORE
EBORING > REBORE
EBORN *adj* active again after a period of inactivity
EBORROW *vb* borrow again
EBORROWS > REBORROW
EBOTTLE *vb* bottle again
EBOTTLED > REBOTTLE
EBOTTLES > REBOTTLE
EBOUGHT > REBUY
EBOUND *vb* spring back ▷ *n* act of rebounding
EBOUNDED > REBOUND
EBOUNDER > REBOUND
EBOUNDS > REBOUND
EBOZO *n* long wool or linen scarf covering the shoulders and head, worn by Latin American women
EBOZOS > REBOZO
EBRACE *vb* brace again
EBRACED > REBRACE
EBRACES > REBRACE
EBRACING > REBRACE
EBRANCH *vb* branch again
EBRAND *vb* change or update the image of (an organization or product)
EBRANDED > REBRAND
EBRED > REBREED
EBREED *vb* breed again
EBREEDS > REBREED
EBS > REB
EBUFF *vb* reject or snub ▷ *n* blunt refusal, snub
EBUFFED > REBUFF
EBUFFING > REBUFF
EBUFFS > REBUFF
EBUILD *vb* build (a building or town) again, after severe damage
EBUILDED *archaic past form of* > REBUILD
EBUILDS > REBUILD
EBUILT > REBUILD
EBUKABLE > REBUKE
EBUKE *vb* scold sternly ▷ *n* stern scolding
EBUKED > REBUKE
EBUKEFUL > REBUKE
EBUKER > REBUKE
EBUKERS > REBUKE
EBUKES > REBUKE
EBUKING > REBUKE
EBURIAL > REBURY
EBURIALS > REBURY
EBURIED > REBURY
EBURIES > REBURY
REBURY *vb* bury again
REBURYING > REBURY
REBUS *n* puzzle consisting of pictures and symbols representing words or syllables
REBUSES > REBUS
REBUT *vb* prove that (a claim) is untrue
REBUTMENT > REBUT
REBUTS > REBUT
REBUTTAL > REBUT
REBUTTALS > REBUT
REBUTTED > REBUT
REBUTTER *n* defendant's pleading in reply to a claimant's surrejoinder
REBUTTERS > REBUTTER
REBUTTING > REBUT
REBUTTON *vb* button again
REBUTTONS > REBUTTON
REBUY *vb* buy again
REBUYING > REBUY
REBUYS > REBUY
REC *n* short for recreation
RECAL *same as* > RECALL
RECALESCE *vb* glow again
RECALL *vb* recollect or remember ▷ *n* ability to remember
RECALLED > RECALL
RECALLER > RECALL
RECALLERS > RECALL
RECALLING > RECALL
RECALLS > RECALL
RECALMENT > RECAL
RECALS > RECALL
RECAMIER *n* shade of pink
RECAMIERS > RECAMIER
RECANE *vb* cane again
RECANED > RECANE
RECANES > RECANE
RECANING > RECANE
RECANT *vb* withdraw (a statement or belief) publicly
RECANTED > RECANT
RECANTER > RECANT
RECANTERS > RECANT
RECANTING > RECANT
RECANTS > RECANT
RECAP *vb* recapitulate ▷ *n* recapitulation
RECAPPED > RECAP
RECAPPING > RECAP
RECAPS > RECAP
RECAPTION *n* process of taking back one's own wife, child, property, etc, without causing a breach of the peace
RECAPTOR > RECAPTURE
RECAPTORS > RECAPTURE
RECAPTURE *vb* experience again ▷ *n* act of recapturing
RECARPET *vb* replace one carpet with another
RECARPETS > RECARPET
RECARRIED > RECARRY
RECARRIES > RECARRY
RECARRY *vb* carry again
RECAST *vb* organize or set out in a different way
RECASTING > RECAST
RECASTS > RECAST
RECATALOG *vb* catalogue again
RECATCH *vb* catch again
RECATCHES > RECATCH
RECAUGHT > RECATCH
RECAUTION *vb* caution again
RECCE *vb* reconnoitre ▷ *n* reconnaissance
RECCED > RECCE
RECCEED > RECCE
RECCEING > RECCE
RECCES > RECCE
RECCIED > RECCY
RECCIES > RECCY
RECCO *same as* > RECCE
RECCOS > RECCO
RECCY *same as* > RECCE
RECCYING > RECCY
RECEDE *vb* move to a more distant place
RECEDED > RECEDE
RECEDES > RECEDE
RECEDING > RECEDE
RECEIPT *n* written acknowledgment of money or goods received ▷ *vb* acknowledge payment of (a bill), as by marking it
RECEIPTED > RECEIPT
RECEIPTOR *n* person who receipts
RECEIPTS > RECEIPT
RECEIVAL *n* act of receiving or state of being received
RECEIVALS > RECEIVAL
RECEIVE *vb* take, accept, or get
RECEIVED *adj* generally accepted
RECEIVER *n* part of telephone that is held to the ear
RECEIVERS > RECEIVER
RECEIVES > RECEIVE
RECEIVING > RECEIVE
RECEMENT *vb* cement again
RECEMENTS > RECEMENT
RECENCIES > RECENT
RECENCY > RECENT
RECENSE *vb* revise
RECENSED > RECENSE
RECENSES > RECENSE
RECENSING > RECENSE
RECENSION *n* critical revision of a literary work
RECENSOR *vb* censor again
RECENSORS > RECENSOR
RECENT *adj* having happened lately
RECENTER > RECENT
RECENTEST > RECENT
RECENTLY > RECENT
RECENTRE *vb* centre again
RECENTRED > RECENTRE
RECENTRES > RECENTRE
RECEPT *n* idea or image formed in the mind by repeated experience of a particular pattern of sensory stimulation
RECEPTION *n* area for receiving guests, clients, etc
RECEPTIVE *adj* willing to accept new ideas, suggestions, etc
RECEPTOR *n* sensory nerve ending that changes specific stimuli into nerve impulses
RECEPTORS > RECEPTOR
RECEPTS > RECEPT
RECERTIFY *vb* certify again
RECESS *n* niche or alcove ▷ *vb* place or set (something) in a recess
RECESSED > RECESS
RECESSES > RECESS
RECESSING > RECESS
RECESSION *n* period of economic difficulty when little is being bought or sold
RECESSIVE *adj* receding ▷ *n* recessive gene or character
RECHANGE *vb* change again
RECHANGED > RECHANGE
RECHANGES > RECHANGE
RECHANNEL *vb* channel again
RECHARGE *vb* cause (a battery etc) to take in and store electricity again
RECHARGED > RECHARGE
RECHARGER > RECHARGE
RECHARGES > RECHARGE
RECHART *vb* chart again
RECHARTED > RECHART
RECHARTER *vb* charter again
RECHARTS > RECHART
RECHATE *same as* > RECHEAT
RECHATES > RECHATE
RECHAUFFE *n* warmed-up leftover food
RECHEAT *n* (in a hunt) sounding of the horn to call back the hounds ▷ *vb* sound the horn to call back the hounds
RECHEATED > RECHEAT
RECHEATS > RECHEAT
RECHECK *vb* check again
RECHECKED > RECHECK
RECHECKS > RECHECK
RECHERCHE *adj* refined or elegant
RECHEW *vb* chew again
RECHEWED > RECHEW
RECHEWING > RECHEW
RECHEWS > RECHEW
RECHIE *adj* smoky
RECHLESSE *archaic form of* > RECKLESS
RECHOOSE *vb* choose again
RECHOOSES > RECHOOSE
RECHOSE > RECHOOSE
RECHOSEN > RECHOOSE
RECIPE *n* directions for cooking a dish
RECIPES > RECIPE
RECIPIENT *n* person who

receives something
RECIRCLE *vb* circle again
RECIRCLED > RECIRCLE
RECIRCLES > RECIRCLE
RECISION *n* act of cancelling or rescinding
RECISIONS > RECISION
RECIT *n* narrative
RECITABLE > RECITE
RECITAL *n* musical performance by a soloist or soloists
RECITALS > RECITAL
RECITE *vb* repeat (a poem etc) aloud to an audience
RECITED > RECITE
RECITER > RECITE
RECITERS > RECITE
RECITES > RECITE
RECITING > RECITE
RECITS > RECIT
RECK *vb* mind or care about (something)
RECKAN *adj* strained, tormented, or twisted
RECKED > RECK
RECKING > RECK
RECKLESS *adj* heedless of danger
RECKLING *dialect word for* > RUNT
RECKLINGS > RECKLING
RECKON *vb* consider or think
RECKONED > RECKON
RECKONER *n* any of various devices or tables used to facilitate reckoning, esp a ready reckoner
RECKONERS > RECKONER
RECKONING *n* counting or calculating
RECKONS > RECKON
RECKS > RECK
RECLAD > RECLOTHE
RECLAIM *vb* regain possession of ▷ *n* act of reclaiming or state of being reclaimed
RECLAIMED > RECLAIM
RECLAIMER > RECLAIM
RECLAIMS > RECLAIM
RECLAME *n* public acclaim or attention
RECLAMES > RECLAME
RECLASP *vb* clasp again
RECLASPED > RECLASP
RECLASPS > RECLASP
RECLEAN *vb* clean again
RECLEANED > RECLEAN
RECLEANS > RECLEAN
RECLIMB *vb* climb again
RECLIMBED > RECLIMB
RECLIMBS > RECLIMB
RECLINATE *adj* (esp of a leaf or stem) naturally curved or bent backwards so that the upper part rests on the ground
RECLINE *vb* rest in a leaning position
RECLINED > RECLINE
RECLINER *n* type of armchair having a back that can be adjusted to slope at various angles and, usually, a leg rest
RECLINERS > RECLINER
RECLINES > RECLINE
RECLINING > RECLINE
RECLOSE *vb* close again
RECLOSED > RECLOSE
RECLOSES > RECLOSE
RECLOSING > RECLOSE
RECLOTHE *vb* clothe again
RECLOTHED > RECLOTHE
RECLOTHES > RECLOTHE
RECLUSE *n* person who avoids other people ▷ *adj* solitary
RECLUSELY > RECLUSE
RECLUSES > RECLUSE
RECLUSION > RECLUSE
RECLUSIVE > RECLUSE
RECLUSORY *n* recluse's dwelling or cell
RECOAL *vb* supply or be supplied with fresh coal
RECOALED > RECOAL
RECOALING > RECOAL
RECOALS > RECOAL
RECOAT *vb* coat again
RECOATED > RECOAT
RECOATING > RECOAT
RECOATS > RECOAT
RECOCK *vb* cock again
RECOCKED > RECOCK
RECOCKING > RECOCK
RECOCKS > RECOCK
RECODE *vb* put into a new code
RECODED > RECODE
RECODES > RECODE
RECODIFY *vb* codify again
RECODING > RECODE
RECOGNISE *same as* > RECOGNIZE
RECOGNIZE *vb* identify as (a person or thing) already known
RECOIL *vb* jerk or spring back ▷ *n* backward jerk
RECOILED > RECOIL
RECOILER > RECOIL
RECOILERS > RECOIL
RECOILING > RECOIL
RECOILS > RECOIL
RECOIN *vb* coin again
RECOINAGE *n* new coinage
RECOINED > RECOIN
RECOINING > RECOIN
RECOINS > RECOIN
RECOLLECT *vb* call back to mind, remember
RECOLLET *n* member of a particular Franciscan order
RECOLLETS > RECOLLET
RECOLOR *vb* give a new colour to
RECOLORED > RECOLOR
RECOLORS > RECOLOR
RECOLOUR *same as* > RECOLOR
RECOLOURS > RECOLOUR
RECOMB *vb* comb again
RECOMBED > RECOMB
RECOMBINE *vb* join together again
RECOMBING > RECOMB
RECOMBS > RECOMB
RECOMFORT *archaic word for* > COMFORT
RECOMMEND *vb* advise or counsel
RECOMMIT *vb* send (a bill) back to a committee for further consideration
RECOMMITS > RECOMMIT
RECOMPACT *vb* compact again
RECOMPILE *vb* compile again
RECOMPOSE *vb* restore to composure or calmness
RECOMPUTE *vb* compute again
RECON *n* smallest genetic unit capable of recombining
RECONCILE *vb* harmonize (conflicting beliefs etc)
RECONDITE *adj* difficult to understand
RECONDUCT *vb* conduct again
RECONFER *vb* confer again
RECONFERS > RECONFER
RECONFINE *vb* confine again
RECONFIRM *vb* confirm (an arrangement, agreement, etc) again
RECONNECT *vb* link or be linked together again
RECONNED > RECON
RECONNING > RECON
RECONQUER *vb* conquer again
RECONS > RECON
RECONSIGN *vb* consign again
RECONSOLE *vb* console again
RECONSULT *vb* consult again
RECONTACT *vb* contact again
RECONTOUR *vb* contour again
RECONVENE *vb* gather together again after an interval
RECONVERT *vb* change (something) back to a previous state or form
RECONVEY *vb* convey again
RECONVEYS > RECONVEY
RECONVICT *vb* convict again
RECOOK *vb* cook again
RECOOKED > RECOOK
RECOOKING > RECOOK
RECOOKS > RECOOK
RECOPIED > RECOPY
RECOPIES > RECOPY
RECOPY *vb* copy again
RECOPYING > RECOPY
RECORD *n* document or other thing that preserves information ▷ *vb* put in writing
RECORDED > RECORD
RECORDER *n* person or machine that records, esp a video, cassette, or tape recorder
RECORDERS > RECORDER
RECORDING *n* something that has been recorded
RECORDIST *n* person that records
RECORDS > RECORD
RECORK *vb* cork again
RECORKED > RECORK
RECORKING > RECORK
RECORKS > RECORK
RECOUNT *vb* tell in detail
RECOUNTAL > RECOUNT
RECOUNTED > RECOUNT
RECOUNTER *n* narrator
RECOUNTS > RECOUNT
RECOUP *vb* regain or make good (a loss)
RECOUPE *vb* (in law) keep back or withhold
RECOUPED > RECOUP
RECOUPING > RECOUP
RECOUPLE *vb* couple again
RECOUPLED > RECOUPLE
RECOUPLES > RECOUPLE
RECOUPS > RECOUP
RECOURE *archaic variant of* > RECOVER
RECOURED > RECOURE
RECOURES > RECOURE
RECOURING > RECOURE
RECOURSE *archaic word for* > RETURN
RECOURSED > RECOURSE
RECOURSES > RECOURSE
RECOVER *vb* become healthy again
RECOVERED > RECOVER
RECOVEREE *n* (in law) person found against in a recovery case
RECOVERER > RECOVER
RECOVEROR *n* (in law) person successfully demanding a right in a recovery case
RECOVERS > RECOVER
RECOVERY *n* act of recovering from sickness, a shock, or a setback
RECOWER *archaic variant of* > RECOVER
RECOWERED > RECOWER
RECOWERS > RECOWER
RECOYLE *archaic spelling of* > RECOIL
RECOYLED > RECOYLE
RECOYLES > RECOYLE
RECOYLING > RECOYLE
RECRATE *vb* crate again
RECRATED > RECRATE
RECRATES > RECRATE
RECRATING > RECRATE
RECREANCE > RECREANT
RECREANCY > RECREANT
RECREANT *n* disloyal or cowardly person ▷ *adj* cowardly
RECREANTS > RECREANT
RECREATE *vb* amuse

oneself or someone else)
:CREATED > RECREATE
:CREATES > RECREATE
:CREATOR > RECREATE
:CREMENT *n* any substance, such as bile, that is secreted from a part of the body and later reabsorbed instead of being excreted
:CROSS *vb* move or go across (something) again
:CROSSED > RECROSS
:CROSSES > RECROSS
:CROWN *vb* crown again
:CROWNED > RECROWN
:CROWNS > RECROWN
:CRUIT *vb* enlist (new soldiers, members, etc) ▷ *n* newly enlisted soldier
:CRUITAL *n* act of recruiting
:CRUITED > RECRUIT
:CRUITER > RECRUIT
:CRUITS > RECRUIT
:CS > REC
:CTA > RECTUM
:CTAL *adj* of the rectum
:CTALLY > RECTAL
:CTANGLE *n* oblong four-sided figure with four right angles
:CTI > RECTUS
:CTIFIED > RECTIFY
:CTIFIER *n* electronic device, such as a semiconductor diode or valve, that converts an alternating current to a direct current by suppression or inversion of alternate half cycles
CTIFIES > RECTIFY
CTIFY *vb* put right, correct
CTION *n* (in grammar) the determination of the form of one word by another word
CTIONS > RECTION
CTITIC > RECTITIS
CTITIS *n* inflammation of the rectum
:CTITUDE *n* moral correctness
CTO *n* right-hand page of a book
:CTOCELE *n* protrusion or herniation of the rectum into the vagina
CTOR *n* clergyman in charge of a parish
CTORAL *adj* of or relating to God's rule or to a rector
CTORATE > RECTOR
CTORESS *n* female rector or the wife or widow of a rector
CTORIAL *adj* of or relating to a rector ▷ *n* election of a rector
CTORIES > RECTORY
CTORS > RECTOR
CTORY *n* rector's house
RECTOS > RECTO
RECTRESS *same as* > RECTORESS
RECTRICES > RECTRIX
RECTRIX *n* any of the large stiff feathers of a bird's tail, used in controlling the direction of flight
RECTUM *n* final section of the large intestine
RECTUMS > RECTUM
RECTUS *n* straight muscle, esp either of two muscles of the anterior abdominal wall
RECUILE *archaic variant of* > RECOIL
RECUILED > RECUILE
RECUILES > RECUILE
RECUILING > RECUILE
RECULE *archaic variant of* > RECOIL
RECULED > RECULE
RECULES > RECULE
RECULING > RECULE
RECUMBENT *adj* lying down
RECUR *vb* happen again
RECURE *vb* archaic word for cure or recover
RECURED > RECURE
RECURES > RECURE
RECURING > RECURE
RECURRED > RECUR
RECURRENT *adj* happening or tending to happen again or repeatedly
RECURRING > RECUR
RECURS > RECUR
RECURSION *n* act or process of returning or running back
RECURSIVE > RECURSION
RECURVATE *adj* bent back
RECURVE *vb* curve or bend (something) back or down or (of something) to be so curved or bent
RECURVED > RECURVE
RECURVES > RECURVE
RECURVING > RECURVE
RECUSAL *n* withdrawal of a judge from a case
RECUSALS > RECUSAL
RECUSANCE > RECUSANT
RECUSANCY > RECUSANT
RECUSANT *n* Roman Catholic who did not attend the services of the Church of England ▷ *adj* (formerly, of Catholics) refusing to attend services of the Church of England
RECUSANTS > RECUSANT
RECUSE *vb* (in law) object to or withdraw (a judge)
RECUSED > RECUSE
RECUSES > RECUSE
RECUSING > RECUSE
RECUT *vb* cut again
RECUTS > RECUT
RECUTTING > RECUT
RECYCLATE *n* recyclable material
RECYCLE *vb* reprocess (used materials) for further use ▷ *n* repetition of a fixed sequence of events
RECYCLED > RECYCLE
RECYCLER > RECYCLE
RECYCLERS > RECYCLE
RECYCLES > RECYCLE
RECYCLING > RECYCLE
RECYCLIST > RECYCLE
RED *adj* of a colour varying from crimson to orange and seen in blood, fire, etc ▷ *n* red colour
REDACT *vb* compose or draft (an edict, proclamation, etc)
REDACTED > REDACT
REDACTING > REDACT
REDACTION > REDACT
REDACTOR > REDACT
REDACTORS > REDACT
REDACTS > REDACT
REDAMAGE *vb* damage again
REDAMAGED > REDAMAGE
REDAMAGES > REDAMAGE
REDAN *n* fortification of two parapets at a salient angle
REDANS > REDAN
REDARGUE *vb* archaic word for disprove or refute
REDARGUED > REDARGUE
REDARGUES > REDARGUE
REDATE *vb* change date of
REDATED > REDATE
REDATES > REDATE
REDATING > REDATE
REDBACK *n* small venomous Australian spider
REDBACKS > REDBACK
REDBAIT *vb* harass those with leftwing leanings
REDBAITED > REDBAIT
REDBAITER *n* person who deliberately antagonizes communists
REDBAITS > REDBAIT
REDBAY *n* type of tree
REDBAYS > REDBAY
REDBELLY *n* any of various animals having red underparts, especially the char or the redbelly turtle
REDBIRD *n* type of bird, the male of which is distinguished by its bright red plumage and black wings
REDBIRDS > REDBIRD
REDBONE *n* type of American dog
REDBONES > REDBONE
REDBREAST *n* robin
REDBRICK *adj* (of a university in Britain) founded in the late 19th or early 20th century ▷ *n* denoting, relating to, or characteristic of a provincial British university of relatively recent foundation, esp as distinguished from Oxford and Cambridge
REDBRICKS > REDBRICK
REDBUD *n* American leguminous tree with heart-shaped leaves and small budlike pink flowers
REDBUDS > REDBUD
REDBUG *another name for* > CHIGGER
REDBUGS > REDBUG
REDCAP *n* military policeman
REDCAPS > REDCAP
REDCOAT *n* British soldier
REDCOATS > REDCOAT
REDD *vb* bring order to ▷ *n* act or an instance of redding
REDDED > REDD
REDDEN *vb* make or become red
REDDENDA > REDDENDUM
REDDENDO *n* (in Scotland) legal clause specifying what payment or duties are required in exchange for something
REDDENDOS > REDDENDO
REDDENDUM *n* legal clause specifying what shall be given in return for the granting of a lease
REDDENED > REDDEN
REDDENING > REDDEN
REDDENS > REDDEN
REDDER > REDD
REDDERS > REDD
REDDEST > RED
REDDIER > REDDY
REDDIEST > REDDY
REDDING > REDD
REDDINGS > REDD
REDDISH *adj* somewhat red
REDDISHLY > REDDISH
REDDLE *same as* > RUDDLE
REDDLED > REDDLE
REDDLEMAN *same as* > RUDDLEMAN
REDDLEMEN > REDDLEMAN
REDDLES > REDDLE
REDDLING > REDDLE
REDDS > REDD
REDDY *adj* reddish
REDE *n* advice or counsel ▷ *vb* advise
REDEAL *vb* deal again
REDEALING > REDEAL
REDEALS > REDEAL
REDEALT > REDEAL
REDEAR *n* variety of sunfish with a red flash above the gills
REDEARS > REDEAR
REDECIDE *vb* decide again
REDECIDED > REDECIDE
REDECIDES > REDECIDE
REDECRAFT *n* logic
REDED > REDE
REDEEM *vb* make up for
REDEEMED > REDEEM
REDEEMER > REDEEM
REDEEMERS > REDEEM
REDEEMING *adj* making up

for faults or deficiencies
REDEEMS > REDEEM
REDEFEAT *vb* defeat again
REDEFEATS > REDEFEAT
REDEFECT *vb* defect back or again
REDEFECTS > REDEFECT
REDEFIED > REDEFY
REDEFIES > REDEFY
REDEFINE *vb* define (something) again or differently
REDEFINED > REDEFINE
REDEFINES > REDEFINE
REDEFY *vb* defy again
REDEFYING > REDEFY
REDELESS > REDE
REDELIVER *vb* deliver again
REDEMAND *vb* demand again
REDEMANDS > REDEMAND
REDENIED > REDENY
REDENIES > REDENY
REDENY *vb* deny again
REDENYING > REDENY
REDEPLOY *vb* assign to a new position or task
REDEPLOYS > REDEPLOY
REDEPOSIT *vb* deposit again
REDES > REDE
REDESCEND *vb* descend again
REDESIGN *vb* change the design of (something) ▷ *n* something that has been redesigned
REDESIGNS > REDESIGN
REDEVELOP *vb* rebuild or renovate (an area or building)
REDEYE *n* inferior whiskey
REDEYES > REDEYE
REDFIN *n* any of various small fishes with reddish fins that are popular aquarium fishes
REDFINS > REDFIN
REDFISH *n* male salmon that has recently spawned
REDFISHES > REDFISH
REDFOOT *n* fatal disease of newborn lambs of unknown cause in which the horny layers of the feet become separated, exposing the red laminae below
REDFOOTS > REDFOOT
REDHANDED *adj* in the act of doing something criminal, wrong, or shameful
REDHEAD *n* person with reddish hair
REDHEADED > REDHEAD
REDHEADS > REDHEAD
REDHORSE *n* type of fish
REDHORSES > REDHORSE
REDIA *n* parasitic larva of flukes that has simple locomotory organs, pharynx, and intestine and gives rise either to other rediae or to a different larva (the cercaria)
REDIAE > REDIA
REDIAL *vb* dial (a telephone number) again
REDIALED > REDIAL
REDIALING > REDIAL
REDIALLED > REDIAL
REDIALS > REDIAL
REDIAS > REDIA
REDICTATE *vb* dictate again
REDID > REDO
REDIGEST *vb* digest again
REDIGESTS > REDIGEST
REDIGRESS *vb* digress again
REDING > REDE
REDINGOTE *n* woman's coat with a close-fitting top and a full skirt
REDIP *vb* dip again
REDIPPED > REDIP
REDIPPING > REDIP
REDIPS > REDIP
REDIPT *archaic past form of* > REDIP
REDIRECT *vb* send in a new direction or course
REDIRECTS > REDIRECT
REDISCUSS *vb* discuss again
REDISPLAY *vb* display again
REDISPOSE *vb* dispose again
REDISTIL *vb* distil again
REDISTILL *US spelling of* > REDISTIL
REDISTILS > REDISTIL
REDIVIDE *vb* divide again
REDIVIDED > REDIVIDE
REDIVIDES > REDIVIDE
REDIVIVUS *adj* returned to life
REDIVORCE *vb* divorce again
REDLEG *n* derogatory term for poor White
REDLEGS > REDLEG
REDLINE *vb* (esp of a bank or group of banks) to refuse a loan to (a person or country) because of the presumed risks involved
REDLINED > REDLINE
REDLINER > REDLINE
REDLINERS > REDLINE
REDLINES > REDLINE
REDLINING > REDLINE
REDLY > RED
REDNECK *n* (in the southwestern US) derogatory term for a poor uneducated White farm worker ▷ *adj* reactionary and bigoted
REDNECKED *adj* with a red neck
REDNECKS > REDNECK
REDNESS > RED
REDNESSES > RED
REDO *vb* do over again in order to improve ▷ *n* instance of redoing something
REDOCK *vb* dock again
REDOCKED > REDOCK
REDOCKING > REDOCK
REDOCKS > REDOCK
REDOES > REDO
REDOING > REDO
REDOLENCE > REDOLENT
REDOLENCY > REDOLENT
REDOLENT *adj* reminiscent (of)
REDON *vb* don again
REDONE > REDO
REDONNED > REDON
REDONNING > REDON
REDONS > REDON
REDOS > REDO
REDOUBLE *vb* increase, multiply, or intensify ▷ *n* act of redoubling
REDOUBLED > REDOUBLE
REDOUBLER > REDOUBLE
REDOUBLES > REDOUBLE
REDOUBT *n* small fort defending a hilltop or pass ▷ *vb* fear
REDOUBTED > REDOUBT
REDOUBTS > REDOUBT
REDOUND *vb* cause advantage or disadvantage (to)
REDOUNDED > REDOUND
REDOUNDS > REDOUND
REDOUT *n* reddened vision and other symptoms caused by a rush of blood to the head in response to negative gravitational stresses
REDOUTS > REDOUT
REDOWA *n* Bohemian folk dance similar to the waltz
REDOWAS > REDOWA
REDOX *n* chemical reaction in which one substance is reduced and the other is oxidized
REDOXES > REDOX
REDPOLL *n* mostly grey-brown finch with a red crown and pink breast
REDPOLLS > REDPOLL
REDRAFT *vb* write a second copy of (a letter, proposal, essay, etc) ▷ *n* second draft
REDRAFTED > REDRAFT
REDRAFTS > REDRAFT
REDRAW *vb* draw or draw up (something) again or differently
REDRAWER > REDRAW
REDRAWERS > REDRAW
REDRAWING > REDRAW
REDRAWN > REDRAW
REDRAWS > REDRAW
REDREAM *vb* dream again
REDREAMED > REDREAM
REDREAMS > REDREAM
REDREAMT > REDREAM
REDRESS *vb* make amends for ▷ *n* compensation or amends
REDRESSED > REDRESS
REDRESSER > REDRESS
REDRESSES > REDRESS
REDRESSOR > REDRESS
REDREW > REDRAW
REDRIED > REDRY
REDRIES > REDRY
REDRILL *vb* drill again
REDRILLED > REDRILL
REDRILLS > REDRILL
REDRIVE *vb* drive again
REDRIVEN > REDRIVE
REDRIVES > REDRIVE
REDRIVING > REDRIVE
REDROOT *n* yellow-flowere[d] bog plant of E North America whose roots yiel[d] a red dye
REDROOTS > REDROOT
REDROVE > REDRIVE
REDRY *vb* dry again
REDRYING > REDRY
REDS > RED
REDSEAR *same as* > REDSHORT
REDSHANK *n* large Eurasia[n] sandpiper with red legs
REDSHANKS > REDSHANK
REDSHARE *n* red algae
REDSHIFT *n* shift in the lines of the spectrum of a[n] astronomical object
REDSHIFTS > REDSHIFT
REDSHIRE *same as* > REDSHARE
REDSHIRT *vb* take a year out of a sports team
REDSHIRTS > REDSHIRT
REDSHORT *vb* become brittle at red-hot temperatures
REDSKIN *n* offensive term for Native American
REDSKINS > REDSKIN
REDSTART *n* European bird of the thrush family, the male of which has an orange-brown tail and breast
REDSTARTS > REDSTART
REDSTREAK *n* variety of apple
REDTAIL *n* variety of bird with red colouring on its tail
REDTAILS > REDTAIL
REDTOP *n* sensationalist tabloid newspaper
REDTOPS > REDTOP
REDUB *vb* fix or repair
REDUBBED > REDUB
REDUBBING > REDUB
REDUBS > REDUB
REDUCE *vb* bring down, lower
REDUCED > REDUCE
REDUCER *n* chemical solution used to lessen the density of a negative or print by oxidizing som[e] of the blackened silver to soluble silver compound
REDUCERS > REDUCER
REDUCES > REDUCE

EDUCIBLE > REDUCE

EDUCIBLY > REDUCE

EDUCING > REDUCE

EDUCTANT *n* reducing agent

EDUCTASE *n* any enzyme that catalyses a biochemical reduction reaction

EDUCTION *n* act of reducing

EDUCTIVE > REDUCTION

EDUCTOR *n* apparatus in which substances can be reduced

EDUCTORS > REDUCTOR

EDUIT *n* fortified part from which a garrison may fight on once an enemy has taken outworks

EDUITS > REDUIT

EDUNDANT *adj* (of a worker) no longer needed

EDUVIID *n* any hemipterous bug of the family *Reduviidae*, which includes the assassin bugs and the wheel bug ▷ *adj* of, relating to, or belonging to the family *Reduviidae*

EDUVIIDS > REDUVIID

EDUX *adj* brought back or returned

EDWARE *another name for* > KELP

EDWARES > REDWARE

EDWATER *n* tick-borne disease of cattle

EDWATERS > REDWATER

EDWING *n* small European thrush

EDWINGS > REDWING

EDWOOD *n* giant Californian conifer with reddish bark

EDWOODS > REDWOOD

EDYE *vb* dye again

EDYED > REDYE

EDYEING > REDYE

EDYES > REDYE

EE *n* Scots word for walled enclosure

EEARN *vb* earn again

EEARNED > REEARN

EEARNING > REEARN

EEARNS > REEARN

EEBOK *same as* > RHEBOK

EEBOKS > REEBOK

EECH *vb* (in dialect) smoke

EECHED > REECH

EECHES > REECH

EECHIE *same as* > REECHY

EECHIER > REECHY

EECHIEST > REECHY

EECHING > REECH

EECHO *vb* echo again

EECHOED > REECHO

EECHOES > REECHO

EECHOING > REECHO

EECHY *adj* (in dialect) smoky

EED *n* tall grass that grows in swamps and shallow water

REEDBED *n* area of wetland with reeds growing in it

REEDBEDS > REEDBED

REEDBIRD *n* any of several birds that frequent reed beds, esp (in the US and Canada) the bobolink

REEDBIRDS > REEDBIRD

REEDBUCK *n* buff-coloured African antelope with inward-curving horns

REEDBUCKS > REEDBUCK

REEDE *obsolete variant of* > RED

REEDED > REED

REEDEN *adj* of or consisting of reeds

REEDER *n* thatcher

REEDERS > REEDER

REEDES > REEDE

REEDIER > REEDY

REEDIEST > REEDY

REEDIFIED > REEDIFY

REEDIFIES > REEDIFY

REEDIFY *vb* edify again or rebuild

REEDILY > REEDY

REEDINESS > REEDY

REEDING *n* set of small semicircular architectural mouldings

REEDINGS > REEDING

REEDIT *vb* edit again

REEDITED > REEDIT

REEDITING > REEDIT

REEDITION *n* new edition

REEDITS > REEDIT

REEDLIKE *adj* resembling a reed

REEDLING *n* tawny titlike Eurasian songbird common in reed beds

REEDLINGS > REEDLING

REEDMACE *n* tall reedlike marsh plant

REEDMACES > REEDMACE

REEDMAN *n* musician who plays a wind instrument that has a reed

REEDMEN > REEDMAN

REEDS > REED

REEDSTOP *n* organ stop controlling a rank of reed pipes

REEDSTOPS > REEDSTOP

REEDUCATE *vb* educate again

REEDY *adj* harsh and thin in tone

REEF *n* ridge of rock or coral near the surface of the sea ▷ *vb* roll up part of a sail

REEFABLE > REEF

REEFED > REEF

REEFER *n* short thick jacket worn esp by sailors

REEFERS > REEFER

REEFIER > REEFY

REEFIEST > REEFY

REEFING > REEF

REEFINGS > REEF

REEFS > REEF

REEFY *adj* with reefs

REEJECT *vb* eject again

REEJECTED > REEJECT

REEJECTS > REEJECT

REEK *vb* smell strongly ▷ *n* strong unpleasant smell

REEKED > REEK

REEKER > REEK

REEKERS > REEK

REEKIE *same as* > REEKY

REEKIER > REEK

REEKIEST > REEK

REEKING > REEK

REEKINGLY > REEK

REEKS > REEK

REEKY *adj* steamy or smoky

REEL *n* cylindrical object on which film, tape, thread, or wire is wound ▷ *vb* stagger, sway, or whirl

REELABLE > REEL

REELECT *vb* elect again

REELECTED > REELECT

REELECTS > REELECT

REELED > REEL

REELER > REEL

REELERS > REEL

REELEVATE *vb* elevate again

REELING > REEL

REELINGLY > REEL

REELINGS > REEL

REELMAN *n* (formerly) member of a beach life-saving team operating a winch

REELMEN > REELMAN

REELS > REEL

REEMBARK *vb* embark again

REEMBARKS > REEMBARK

REEMBODY *vb* embody again

REEMBRACE *vb* embrace again

REEMERGE *vb* emerge again

REEMERGED > REEMERGE

REEMERGES > REEMERGE

REEMIT *vb* emit again

REEMITS > REEMIT

REEMITTED > REEMIT

REEMPLOY *vb* employ again

REEMPLOYS > REEMPLOY

REEN *n* ditch, esp a drainage channel

REENACT *vb* enact again

REENACTED > REENACT

REENACTOR > REENACT

REENACTS > REENACT

REENDOW *vb* endow again

REENDOWED > REENDOW

REENDOWS > REENDOW

REENFORCE *vb* enforce again

REENGAGE *vb* engage again

REENGAGED > REENGAGE

REENGAGES > REENGAGE

REENGRAVE *vb* engrave again

REENJOY *vb* enjoy again

REENJOYED > REENJOY

REENJOYS > REENJOY

REENLARGE *vb* enlarge again

REENLIST *vb* enlist again

REENLISTS > REENLIST

REENROLL *vb* enrol again

REENROLLS > REENROLL

REENS > REEN

REENSLAVE *vb* enslave again

REENTER *vb* enter again

REENTERED > REENTER

REENTERS > REENTER

REENTRANT *n* reentering angle ▷ *adj* (of an angle) pointing inwards

REENTRIES > REENTRY

REENTRY *n* return of a spacecraft into the earth's atmosphere

REEQUIP *vb* equip again

REEQUIPS > REEQUIP

REERECT *vb* erect again

REERECTED > REERECT

REERECTS > REERECT

REES > REE

REEST *vb* (esp of horses) to be noisily uncooperative

REESTED > REEST

REESTIER > REESTY

REESTIEST > REESTY

REESTING > REEST

REESTS > REEST

REESTY *same as* > REASTY

REEVE *n* local representative of the king in a shire until the early 11th century ▷ *vb* pass (a rope or cable) through an eye or other narrow opening

REEVED > REEVE

REEVES > REEVE

REEVING > REEVE

REEVOKE *vb* evoke again

REEVOKED > REEVOKE

REEVOKES > REEVOKE

REEVOKING > REEVOKE

REEXAMINE *vb* examine again

REEXECUTE *vb* execute again

REEXHIBIT *vb* exhibit again

REEXPEL *vb* expel again

REEXPELS > REEXPEL

REEXPLAIN *vb* explain again

REEXPLORE *vb* explore again

REEXPORT *vb* export again

REEXPORTS > REEXPORT

REEXPOSE *vb* expose again

REEXPOSED > REEXPOSE

REEXPOSES > REEXPOSE

REEXPRESS *vb* express again

REF *n* referee in sport ▷ *vb* referee

REFACE *vb* repair or renew the facing of (a wall)

REFACED > REFACE

REFACES > REFACE

REFACING > REFACE

REFALL *vb* fall again

REFALLEN > REFALL

REFALLING > REFALL

REFALLS > REFALL

REFASHION *vb* give a new

form to (something)
REFASTEN *vb* fasten again
REFASTENS > REFASTEN
REFECT *vb* archaic word for restore or refresh with food and drink
REFECTED > REFECT
REFECTING > REFECT
REFECTION *n* refreshment with food and drink
REFECTIVE > REFECT
REFECTORY *n* room for meals in a college etc
REFECTS > REFECT
REFED > REFEED
REFEED *vb* feed again
REFEEDING > REFEED
REFEEDS > REFEED
REFEEL *vb* feel again
REFEELING > REFEEL
REFEELS > REFEEL
REFEL *vb* refute
REFELL > REFALL
REFELLED > REFEL
REFELLING > REFEL
REFELS > REFEL
REFELT > REFEEL
REFENCE *vb* fence again
REFENCED > REFENCE
REFENCES > REFENCE
REFENCING > REFENCE
REFER *vb* allude (to)
REFERABLE > REFER
REFEREE *n* umpire in sports, esp soccer or boxing ▷ *vb* act as referee of
REFEREED > REFEREE
REFEREES > REFEREE
REFERENCE *n* act of referring
REFERENDA *pl n* polls to determine the view of the electorate on something; referendums
REFERENT *n* object or idea to which a word or phrase refers
REFERENTS > REFERENT
REFERRAL > REFER
REFERRALS > REFER
REFERRED > REFER
REFERRER > REFER
REFERRERS > REFER
REFERRING > REFER
REFERS > REFER
REFFED > REF
REFFING > REF
REFFO *n* offensive name for a European refugee after World War II
REFFOS > REFFO
REFIGHT *vb* fight again ▷ *n* second or new fight
REFIGHTS > REFIGHT
REFIGURE *vb* figure again
REFIGURED > REFIGURE
REFIGURES > REFIGURE
REFILE *vb* file again
REFILED > REFILE
REFILES > REFILE
REFILING > REFILE
REFILL *vb* fill again ▷ *n* second or subsequent filling
REFILLED > REFILL
REFILLING > REFILL
REFILLS > REFILL
REFILM *vb* film again
REFILMED > REFILM
REFILMING > REFILM
REFILMS > REFILM
REFILTER *vb* filter again
REFILTERS > REFILTER
REFINABLE > REFINE
REFINANCE *vb* finance again
REFIND *vb* find again
REFINDING > REFIND
REFINDS > REFIND
REFINE *vb* purify
REFINED *adj* cultured or polite
REFINEDLY > REFINED
REFINER *n* person, device, or substance that removes impurities, sediment, or other unwanted matter from something
REFINERS > REFINER
REFINERY *n* place where sugar, oil, etc is refined
REFINES > REFINE
REFINING > REFINE
REFININGS > REFINE
REFINISH *vb* finish again
REFIRE *vb* fire again
REFIRED > REFIRE
REFIRES > REFIRE
REFIRING > REFIRE
REFIT *vb* make ready for use again by repairing or re-equipping ▷ *n* repair or re-equipping for further use
REFITMENT > REFIT
REFITS > REFIT
REFITTED > REFIT
REFITTING > REFIT
REFIX *vb* fix again
REFIXED > REFIX
REFIXES > REFIX
REFIXING > REFIX
REFLAG *vb* flag again
REFLAGGED > REFLAG
REFLAGS > REFLAG
REFLATE *vb* inflate or be inflated again
REFLATED > REFLATE
REFLATES > REFLATE
REFLATING > REFLATE
REFLATION *n* increase in the supply of money and credit designed to encourage economic activity
REFLECT *vb* throw back, esp rays of light, heat, etc
REFLECTED > REFLECT
REFLECTER *n* archaic word for a critic
REFLECTOR *n* polished surface for reflecting light etc
REFLECTS > REFLECT
REFLET *n* iridescent glow or lustre, as on ceramic ware
REFLETS > REFLET
REFLEW > REFLY
REFLEX *n* involuntary response to a stimulus or situation ▷ *adj* (of a muscular action) involuntary ▷ *vb* bend, turn, or reflect backwards
REFLEXED > REFLEX
REFLEXES > REFLEX
REFLEXING > REFLEX
REFLEXION *n* act of reflecting or the state of being reflected
REFLEXIVE *adj* denoting a pronoun that refers back to the subject of a sentence or clause ▷ *n* reflexive pronoun or verb
REFLEXLY > REFLEX
REFLIES > REFLY
REFLOAT *vb* float again
REFLOATED > REFLOAT
REFLOATS > REFLOAT
REFLOOD *vb* flood again
REFLOODED > REFLOOD
REFLOODS > REFLOOD
REFLOW *vb* flow again
REFLOWED > REFLOW
REFLOWER *vb* flower again
REFLOWERS > REFLOWER
REFLOWING > REFLOW
REFLOWN > REFLY
REFLOWS > REFLOW
REFLUENCE > REFLUENT
REFLUENT *adj* flowing back
REFLUX *vb* boil or be boiled in a vessel attached to a condenser, so that the vapour condenses and flows back into the vessel ▷ *n* act of refluxing
REFLUXED > REFLUX
REFLUXES > REFLUX
REFLUXING > REFLUX
REFLY *vb* fly again
REFLYING > REFLY
REFOCUS *vb* focus again or anew
REFOCUSED > REFOCUS
REFOCUSES > REFOCUS
REFOLD *vb* fold again
REFOLDED > REFOLD
REFOLDING > REFOLD
REFOLDS > REFOLD
REFOOT *vb* foot again
REFOOTED > REFOOT
REFOOTING > REFOOT
REFOOTS > REFOOT
REFOREST *vb* replant (an area that was formerly forested) with trees
REFORESTS > REFOREST
REFORGE *vb* forge again
REFORGED > REFORGE
REFORGES > REFORGE
REFORGING > REFORGE
REFORM *n* improvement ▷ *vb* improve
REFORMADE *archaic variant of* > REFORMADO
REFORMADO *n* formerly, an officer whose men have been disbanded
REFORMAT *vb* format again
REFORMATE *n* gas formed in certain processes
REFORMATS > REFORMAT
REFORMED > REFORM
REFORMER > REFORM
REFORMERS > REFORM
REFORMING > REFORM
REFORMISM *n* doctrine or movement advocating reform, esp political or religious reform, rather than abolition
REFORMIST > REFORMISM
REFORMS > REFORM
REFORTIFY *vb* fortify again or further
REFOUGHT > REFIGHT
REFOUND *vb* found again
REFOUNDED > REFOUND
REFOUNDER > REFOUND
REFOUNDS > REFOUND
REFRACT *vb* change the course of (light etc) passing from one medium to another
REFRACTED > REFRACT
REFRACTOR *n* object or material that refracts
REFRACTS > REFRACT
REFRAIN *n* frequently repeated part of a song ▷ *vb* abstain (from action)
REFRAINED > REFRAIN
REFRAINER > REFRAIN
REFRAINS > REFRAIN
REFRAME *vb* support or enclose (a picture, photograph, etc) in a new or different frame
REFRAMED > REFRAME
REFRAMES > REFRAME
REFRAMING > REFRAME
REFREEZE *vb* freeze or be frozen again after having defrosted
REFREEZES > REFREEZE
REFRESH *vb* revive or reinvigorate, as through food, drink, or rest
REFRESHED > REFRESH
REFRESHEN *vb* freshen again
REFRESHER *n* something that refreshes, such as a cold drink
REFRESHES > REFRESH
REFRIED > REFRY
REFRIES > REFRY
REFRINGE *formerly used to mean* > REFRACT
REFRINGED > REFRINGE
REFRINGES > REFRINGE
REFRONT *vb* put a new front on
REFRONTED > REFRONT
REFRONTS > REFRONT
REFROZE > REFREEZE
REFROZEN > REFREEZE
REFRY *vb* fry again
REFRYING > REFRY
REFS > REF
REFT > REAVE
REFUEL *vb* supply or be

upplied with fresh fuel
FUELED > REFUEL
FUELING > REFUEL
FUELLED > REFUEL
FUELS > REFUEL
FUGE *n* (source of) helter or protection ▷ *vb* ake refuge or give refuge o
FUGED > REFUGE
FUGEE *n* person who eeks refuge, esp in a oreign country
FUGEES > REFUGEE
FUGES > REFUGE
FUGIA > REFUGIUM
FUGING > REFUGE
FUGIUM *n* geographical egion that has remained naltered by a climatic hange affecting urrounding regions and hat therefore forms a aven for relict fauna and lora
FULGENT *adj* shining, adiant
FUND *vb* pay back ▷ *n* eturn of money
FUNDED > REFUND
FUNDER > REFUND
FUNDERS > REFUND
FUNDING > REFUND
FUNDS > REFUND
FURBISH *vb* renovate nd brighten up
FURNISH *vb* furnish gain
FUSABLE > REFUSE
FUSAL *n* denial of nything demanded or ffered
FUSALS > REFUSAL
FUSE *vb* decline, deny, r reject ▷ *n* rubbish or seless matter
FUSED > REFUSE
FUSENIK *n* person who efuses to obey a law r cooperate with the overnment because of trong beliefs
FUSER > REFUSE
FUSERS > REFUSE
FUSES > REFUSE
FUSING > REFUSE
FUSION *n* new or further usion
FUSIONS > REFUSION
FUSNIK *same* s > REFUSENIK
FUSNIKS > REFUSNIK
FUTABLE > REFUTE
FUTABLY > REFUTE
FUTAL *n* act or process of efuting
FUTALS > REFUTAL
FUTE *vb* disprove
FUTED > REFUTE
FUTER > REFUTE
FUTERS > REFUTE
FUTES > REFUTE
FUTING > REFUTE
G *n* large expanse of stony desert terrain
REGAIN *vb* get back or recover ▷ *n* process of getting something back, esp lost weight
REGAINED > REGAIN
REGAINER > REGAIN
REGAINERS > REGAIN
REGAINING > REGAIN
REGAINS > REGAIN
REGAL *adj* of or like a king or queen ▷ *n* portable organ equipped only with small reed pipes, popular from the 15th century and recently revived for modern performance
REGALE *vb* entertain (someone) with stories etc ▷ *n* feast
REGALED > REGALE
REGALER > REGALE
REGALERS > REGALE
REGALES > REGALE
REGALIA *pl n* ceremonial emblems of royalty or high office
REGALIAN *adj* royal
REGALIAS > REGALIA
REGALING > REGALE
REGALISM *n* principle that the sovereign has supremacy in church affairs
REGALISMS > REGALISM
REGALIST > REGALISM
REGALISTS > REGALISM
REGALITY *n* state or condition of being royal
REGALLY > REGAL
REGALNESS > REGAL
REGALS > REGAL
REGAR *same as* > REGUR
REGARD *vb* consider ▷ *n* respect or esteem
REGARDANT *adj* (of a beast) shown looking backwards over its shoulder
REGARDED > REGARD
REGARDER > REGARD
REGARDERS > REGARD
REGARDFUL *adj* showing regard (for)
REGARDING *prep* on the subject of
REGARDS > REGARD
REGARS > REGAR
REGATHER *vb* gather again
REGATHERS > REGATHER
REGATTA *n* meeting for yacht or boat races
REGATTAS > REGATTA
REGAUGE *vb* gauge again
REGAUGED > REGAUGE
REGAUGES > REGAUGE
REGAUGING > REGAUGE
REGAVE > REGIVE
REGEAR *vb* readjust
REGEARED > REGEAR
REGEARING > REGEAR
REGEARS > REGEAR
REGELATE *vb* undergo or cause to undergo regelation
REGELATED > REGELATE
REGELATES > REGELATE
REGENCE *old variant of* > REGENCY
REGENCES > REGENCE
REGENCIES > REGENCY
REGENCY *n* status or period of office of a regent
REGENT *n* ruler of a kingdom during the absence, childhood, or illness of its monarch ▷ *adj* ruling as a regent
REGENTAL > REGENT
REGENTS > REGENT
REGES > REX
REGEST *n* archaic word for register
REGESTS > REGEST
REGGAE *n* style of Jamaican popular music with a strong beat
REGGAES > REGGAE
REGGO *same as* > REGO
REGGOS > REGGO
REGICIDAL > REGICIDE
REGICIDE *n* killing of a king
REGICIDES > REGICIDE
REGIE *n* government-directed management or government monopoly
REGIES > REGIE
REGILD *vb* gild again
REGILDED > REGILD
REGILDING > REGILD
REGILDS > REGILD
REGILT *archaic past form of* > REGILD
REGIME *n* system of government
REGIMEN *n* prescribed system of diet etc
REGIMENS > REGIMEN
REGIMENT *n* organized body of troops as a unit of the army ▷ *vb* force discipline or order on, esp in a domineering manner
REGIMENTS > REGIMENT
REGIMES > REGIME
REGIMINAL *adj* regimen-related
REGINA *n* queen
REGINAE > REGINA
REGINAL *adj* queenly
REGINAS > REGINA
REGION *n* administrative division of a country
REGIONAL *adj* of, characteristic of, or limited to a region ▷ *n* regional heat of a competition
REGIONALS > REGIONAL
REGIONARY *same as* > REGIONAL
REGIONS > REGION
REGISSEUR *n* official in a dance company with varying duties, usually including directing productions
REGISTER *n* (book containing) an official list or record of things ▷ *vb* enter in a register or set down in writing
REGISTERS > REGISTER
REGISTRAR *n* keeper of official records
REGISTRY *n* place where official records are kept
REGIUS as in *regius professor* Crown-appointed holder of a university chair
REGIVE *vb* give again or back
REGIVEN > REGIVE
REGIVES > REGIVE
REGIVING > REGIVE
REGLAZE *vb* glaze again
REGLAZED > REGLAZE
REGLAZES > REGLAZE
REGLAZING > REGLAZE
REGLET *n* flat narrow architectural moulding
REGLETS > REGLET
REGLORIFY *vb* glorify again
REGLOSS *vb* gloss again or give a new gloss to
REGLOSSED > REGLOSS
REGLOSSES > REGLOSS
REGLOW *vb* glow again
REGLOWED > REGLOW
REGLOWING > REGLOW
REGLOWS > REGLOW
REGLUE *vb* glue again
REGLUED > REGLUE
REGLUES > REGLUE
REGLUING > REGLUE
REGMA *n* type of fruit with cells that break open and break away when ripe
REGMAKER *n* drink taken to relieve the symptoms of a hangover
REGMAKERS > REGMAKER
REGMATA > REGMA
REGNA > REGNUM
REGNAL *adj* of a sovereign, reign, or kingdom
REGNANCY > REGNANT
REGNANT *adj* reigning
REGNUM *n* reign or rule
REGO *n* registration of a motor vehicle
REGOLITH *n* layer of loose material covering the bedrock of the earth and moon, etc, comprising soil, sand, rock fragments, volcanic ash, glacial drift, etc
REGOLITHS > REGOLITH
REGORGE *vb* vomit up
REGORGED > REGORGE
REGORGES > REGORGE
REGORGING > REGORGE
REGOS > REGO
REGOSOL *n* type of azonal soil consisting of unconsolidated material derived from freshly deposited alluvium or sands
REGOSOLS > REGOSOL
REGRADE *vb* grade again

REGRADED > REGRADE
REGRADES > REGRADE
REGRADING > REGRADE
REGRAFT *vb* graft again
REGRAFTED > REGRAFT
REGRAFTS > REGRAFT
REGRANT *vb* grant again
REGRANTED > REGRANT
REGRANTS > REGRANT
REGRATE *vb* buy up (commodities) in advance so as to raise their price for profitable resale
REGRATED > REGRATE
REGRATER > REGRATE
REGRATERS > REGRATE
REGRATES > REGRATE
REGRATING > REGRATE
REGRATOR > REGRATE
REGRATORS > REGRATE
REGREDE *vb* go back
REGREDED > REGREDE
REGREDES > REGREDE
REGREDING > REGREDE
REGREEN *vb* green again
REGREENED > REGREEN
REGREENS > REGREEN
REGREET *vb* greet again or return greetings of
REGREETED > REGREET
REGREETS > REGREET
REGRESS *vb* revert to a former worse condition ▷ *n* return to a former and worse condition
REGRESSED > REGRESS
REGRESSES > REGRESS
REGRESSOR > REGRESS
REGRET *vb* feel sorry about ▷ *n* feeling of repentance, guilt, or sorrow
REGRETFUL > REGRET
REGRETS > REGRET
REGRETTED > REGRET
REGRETTER > REGRET
REGREW > REGROW
REGRIND *vb* grind again
REGRINDS > REGRIND
REGROOM *vb* groom again
REGROOMED > REGROOM
REGROOMS > REGROOM
REGROOVE *vb* groove again
REGROOVED > REGROOVE
REGROOVES > REGROOVE
REGROUND > REGRIND
REGROUP *vb* reorganize (military forces) after an attack or a defeat
REGROUPED > REGROUP
REGROUPS > REGROUP
REGROW *vb* grow or be grown again after having been cut or having died or withered
REGROWING > REGROW
REGROWN > REGROW
REGROWS > REGROW
REGROWTH *n* growing back of hair, plants, etc
REGROWTHS > REGROWTH
REGS > REG
REGUERDON *vb* reward
REGULA *n* rule
REGULABLE *adj* able to be regulated
REGULAE > REGULA
REGULAR *adj* normal, customary, or usual ▷ *n* regular soldier
REGULARLY > REGULAR
REGULARS > REGULAR
REGULATE *vb* control, esp by rules
REGULATED > REGULATE
REGULATES > REGULATE
REGULATOR *n* device that automatically controls pressure, temperature, etc
REGULI > REGULUS
REGULINE > REGULUS
REGULISE *variant spelling of* > REGULIZE
REGULISED > REGULISE
REGULISES > REGULISE
REGULIZE *vb* turn into regulus
REGULIZED > REGULIZE
REGULIZES > REGULIZE
REGULO *n* any of a number of temperatures to which a gas oven may be set
REGULOS > REGULO
REGULUS *n* impure metal forming beneath the slag during the smelting of ores
REGULUSES > REGULUS
REGUR *n* black loamy Indian soil
REGURS > REGUR
REH *n* (in India) salty surface crust on the soil
REHAB *vb* help (addict, disabled person, prisoner, etc) to readapt to society or a new job ▷ *n* treatment or help given to an addict, disabled person, or prisoner, etc
REHABBED > REHAB
REHABBER > REHAB
REHABBERS > REHAB
REHABBING > REHAB
REHABS > REHAB
REHAMMER *vb* hammer again
REHAMMERS > REHAMMER
REHANDLE *vb* handle again
REHANDLED > REHANDLE
REHANDLES > REHANDLE
REHANG *vb* hang again
REHANGED > REHANG
REHANGING > REHANG
REHANGS > REHANG
REHARDEN *vb* harden again
REHARDENS > REHARDEN
REHASH *vb* rework or reuse ▷ *n* old ideas presented in a new form
REHASHED > REHASH
REHASHES > REHASH
REHASHING > REHASH
REHEAR *vb* hear again
REHEARD > REHEAR
REHEARING > REHEAR
REHEARS > REHEAR
REHEARSAL *n* preparatory practice session
REHEARSE *vb* practise (a play, concert, etc)
REHEARSED > REHEARSE
REHEARSER > REHEARSE
REHEARSES > REHEARSE
REHEAT *vb* heat or be heated again
REHEATED > REHEAT
REHEATER > REHEAT
REHEATERS > REHEAT
REHEATING > REHEAT
REHEATS > REHEAT
REHEEL *vb* put a new heel or new heels on
REHEELED > REHEEL
REHEELING > REHEEL
REHEELS > REHEEL
REHEM *vb* hem again
REHEMMED > REHEM
REHEMMING > REHEM
REHEMS > REHEM
REHINGE *vb* put a new hinge or new hinges on
REHINGED > REHINGE
REHINGES > REHINGE
REHINGING > REHINGE
REHIRE *vb* hire again
REHIRED > REHIRE
REHIRES > REHIRE
REHIRING > REHIRE
REHOBOAM *n* wine bottle holding the equivalent of six normal bottles (approximately 156 ounces)
REHOBOAMS > REHOBOAM
REHOUSE *vb* provide with a new (and better) home
REHOUSED > REHOUSE
REHOUSES > REHOUSE
REHOUSING > REHOUSE
REHS > REH
REHUNG > REHANG
REHYDRATE *vb* hydrate again
REI *n* name for a former Portuguese coin, more properly called a real
REIF *n* Scots word meaning robbery or plunder
REIFIED > REIFY
REIFIER > REIFY
REIFIERS > REIFY
REIFIES > REIFY
REIFS > REIF
REIFY *vb* consider or make (an abstract idea or concept) real or concrete
REIFYING > REIFY
REIGN *n* period of a sovereign's rule ▷ *vb* rule (a country)
REIGNED > REIGN
REIGNING > REIGN
REIGNITE *vb* catch fire or cause to catch fire again
REIGNITED > REIGNITE
REIGNITES > REIGNITE
REIGNS > REIGN
REIK *Scots word for* > SMOKE
REIKI *n* form of therapy in which the practitioner is believed to channel energy into the patient in order to encourage healing or restore wellbeing
REIKIS > REIKI
REIKS > REIK
REILLUME *vb* relight
REILLUMED > REILLUME
REILLUMES > REILLUME
REIMAGE *vb* image again
REIMAGED > REIMAGE
REIMAGES > REIMAGE
REIMAGINE *vb* imagine again
REIMAGING > REIMAGE
REIMBURSE *vb* refund, pa[y] back
REIMMERSE *vb* immerse again
REIMPLANT *vb* implant again
REIMPORT *vb* import (goods manufactured fro[m] exported raw materials) ▷ *n* act of reimporting
REIMPORTS > REIMPORT
REIMPOSE *vb* establish previously imposed laws[,] controls, etc, again
REIMPOSED > REIMPOSE
REIMPOSES > REIMPOSE
REIN *vb* check or manage with reins
REINCITE *vb* incite again
REINCITED > REINCITE
REINCITES > REINCITE
REINCUR *vb* incur again
REINCURS > REINCUR
REINDEER *n* deer of arctic regions with large branched antlers
REINDEERS > REINDEER
REINDEX *vb* index again
REINDEXED > REINDEX
REINDEXES > REINDEX
REINDICT *vb* indict again
REINDICTS > REINDICT
REINDUCE *vb* induce agai[n]
REINDUCED > REINDUCE
REINDUCES > REINDUCE
REINDUCT *vb* induct agai[n]
REINDUCTS > REINDUCT
REINED > REIN
REINETTE *n* variety of apple
REINETTES > REINETTE
REINFECT *vb* infect or contaminate again
REINFECTS > REINFECT
REINFLAME *vb* inflame again
REINFLATE *vb* inflate aga[in]
REINFORCE *vb* give adde[d] emphasis to
REINFORM *vb* inform agai[n]
REINFORMS > REINFORM
REINFUND *vb* archaic wo[rd] for pour in again
REINFUNDS > REINFUND
REINFUSE *vb* infuse agai[n]
REINFUSED > REINFUSE
REINFUSES > REINFUSE
REINHABIT *vb* inhabit again
REINING > REIN
REINJECT *vb* inject again

INJECTS > REINJECT
INJURE *vb* injure again
INJURED > REINJURE
INJURES > REINJURE
INJURY *n* further injury
INK *vb* ink again
INKED > REINK
INKING > REINK
INKS > REINK
INLESS > REIN
INS *pl n* narrow straps attached to a bit to guide a horse
INSERT *vb* insert again
INSERTS > REINSERT
INSMAN *n* driver in a trotting race
INSMEN > REINSMAN
INSPECT *vb* inspect again
INSPIRE *vb* inspire again
INSTAL *same* as > REINSTALL
INSTALL *vb* put in place and connect (machinery, equipment, etc) again
INSTALS > REINSTAL
INSTATE *vb* restore to a former position
INSURE *vb* insure again
INSURED > REINSURE
INSURER > REINSURE
INSURES > REINSURE
INTER *vb* inter again
INTERS > REINTER
INVADE *vb* invade again
INVADED > REINVADE
INVADES > REINVADE
INVENT *vb* replace (a product, etc) with an entirely new version
INVENTS > REINVENT
INVEST *vb* put back profits from a previous investment into the same enterprise
INVESTS > REINVEST
INVITE *vb* invite again
INVITED > REINVITE
INVITES > REINVITE
INVOKE *vb* invoke again
INVOKED > REINVOKE
INVOKES > REINVOKE
INVOLVE *vb* involve again
IRD *Scots word for* > DIN
IRDS > REIRD
IS > REI
ISES > REI
ISSUE *n* book, record, etc, that is published or released again after being unavailable for a time ▷ *vb* publish or release (a book, record, etc) again after a period of unavailability
ISSUED > REISSUE
ISSUER > REISSUE
ISSUERS > REISSUE
ISSUES > REISSUE
ISSUING > REISSUE
IST *same as* > REEST
ISTAFEL *same* as > RIJSTAFEL
REISTED > REIST
REISTING > REIST
REISTS > REIST
REITBOK *same* as > REEDBUCK
REITBOKS > REITBOK
REITER *n* soldier in the German cavalry
REITERANT > REITERATE
REITERATE *vb* repeat again and again
REITERS > REITER
REIVE *vb* go on a plundering raid
REIVED > REIVE
REIVER > REIVE
REIVERS > REIVE
REIVES > REIVE
REIVING > REIVE
REJACKET *n* put a new jacket on
REJACKETS > REJACKET
REJECT *vb* refuse to accept or believe ▷ *n* person or thing rejected as not up to standard
REJECTED > REJECT
REJECTEE *n* someone who has been rejected
REJECTEES > REJECTEE
REJECTER > REJECT
REJECTERS > REJECT
REJECTING > REJECT
REJECTION > REJECT
REJECTIVE > REJECT
REJECTOR > REJECT
REJECTORS > REJECT
REJECTS > REJECT
REJIG *vb* re-equip (a factory or plant) ▷ *n* act or process of rejigging
REJIGGED > REJIG
REJIGGER > REJIG
REJIGGERS > REJIG
REJIGGING > REJIG
REJIGS > REJIG
REJOICE *vb* feel or express great happiness
REJOICED > REJOICE
REJOICER > REJOICE
REJOICERS > REJOICE
REJOICES > REJOICE
REJOICING > REJOICE
REJOIN *vb* join again
REJOINDER *n* answer, retort
REJOINED > REJOIN
REJOINING > REJOIN
REJOINS > REJOIN
REJON *n* bullfighting lance
REJONEO *n* bullfighting activity in which a mounted bullfighter spears the bull with lances
REJONEOS > REJONEO
REJONES > REJON
REJOURN *vb* archaic word meaning postpone or adjourn
REJOURNED > REJOURN
REJOURNS > REJOURN
REJUDGE *vb* judge again
REJUDGED > REJUDGE
REJUDGES > REJUDGE
REJUDGING > REJUDGE
REJUGGLE *vb* juggle again
REJUGGLED > REJUGGLE
REJUGGLES > REJUGGLE
REJUSTIFY *vb* justify again
REKE *same as* > RECK
REKED > REKE
REKES > REKE
REKEY *vb* key again
REKEYED > REKEY
REKEYING > REKEY
REKEYS > REKEY
REKINDLE *vb* arouse former emotions or interests
REKINDLED > REKINDLE
REKINDLES > REKINDLE
REKING > REKE
REKNIT *vb* knit again
REKNITS > REKNIT
REKNITTED > REKNIT
REKNOT *vb* knot again
REKNOTS > REKNOT
REKNOTTED > REKNOT
RELABEL *vb* label again
RELABELED > RELABEL
RELABELS > RELABEL
RELACE *vb* lace again
RELACED > RELACE
RELACES > RELACE
RELACHE *n* break
RELACHES > RELACHE
RELACING > RELACE
RELACQUER *vb* apply a new coat of lacquer to
RELAID > RELAY
RELAND *vb* land again
RELANDED > RELAND
RELANDING > RELAND
RELANDS > RELAND
RELAPSE *vb* fall back into bad habits, illness, etc ▷ *n* return of bad habits, illness, etc
RELAPSED > RELAPSE
RELAPSER > RELAPSE
RELAPSERS > RELAPSE
RELAPSES > RELAPSE
RELAPSING > RELAPSE
RELATA > RELATUM
RELATABLE > RELATE
RELATE *vb* establish a relation between
RELATED *adj* linked by kinship or marriage
RELATEDLY > RELATED
RELATER > RELATE
RELATERS > RELATE
RELATES > RELATE
RELATING > RELATE
RELATION *n* connection between things
RELATIONS *pl n* social or political dealings between individuals or groups
RELATIVAL *adj* of or relating to a relative
RELATIVE *adj* true to a certain degree or extent ▷ *n* person connected by blood or marriage
RELATIVES > RELATIVE
RELATOR *n* person who relates a story
RELATORS > RELATOR
RELATUM *n* one of the objects between which a relation is said to hold
RELAUNCH *vb* launch again ▷ *n* another launching, or something that is relaunched
RELAUNDER *vb* launder again
RELAX *vb* make or become looser, less tense, or less rigid
RELAXABLE > RELAX
RELAXANT *n* drug or agent that relaxes, esp one that relaxes tense muscles ▷ *adj* of, relating to, or tending to produce relaxation
RELAXANTS > RELAXANT
RELAXED > RELAX
RELAXEDLY > RELAX
RELAXER *n* person or thing that relaxes, esp a substance used to straighten curly hair
RELAXERS > RELAXER
RELAXES > RELAX
RELAXIN *n* mammalian polypeptide hormone secreted by the corpus luteum during pregnancy, which relaxes the pelvic ligaments
RELAXING > RELAX
RELAXINS > RELAXIN
RELAY *n* fresh set of people or animals relieving others ▷ *vb* pass on (a message)
RELAYED > RELAY
RELAYING > RELAY
RELAYS > RELAY
RELEARN *vb* learn (something previously known) again
RELEARNED > RELEARN
RELEARNS > RELEARN
RELEARNT > RELEARN
RELEASE *vb* set free ▷ *n* setting free
RELEASED > RELEASE
RELEASEE *n* someone to whom an estate is released or someone released from captivity
RELEASEES > RELEASEE
RELEASER > RELEASE
RELEASERS > RELEASE
RELEASES > RELEASE
RELEASING > RELEASE
RELEASOR *n* someone releasing an estate to someone else
RELEASORS > RELEASOR
RELEGABLE *adj* able to be relegated
RELEGATE *vb* put in a less important position
RELEGATED > RELEGATE
RELEGATES > RELEGATE
RELEND *vb* lend again
RELENDING > RELEND
RELENDS > RELEND

RELENT *vb* give up a harsh intention, become less severe
RELENTED > RELENT
RELENTING > RELENT
RELENTS > RELENT
RELET *vb* let again
RELETS > RELET
RELETTER *vb* redo lettering of
RELETTERS > RELETTER
RELETTING > RELET
RELEVANCE > RELEVANT
RELEVANCY > RELEVANT
RELEVANT *adj* do with the matter in hand
RELEVE *n* dance move in which heels are off the ground
RELEVES > RELEVE
RELIABLE *adj* able to be trusted, dependable ▷ *n* something or someone believed to be reliable
RELIABLES > RELIABLE
RELIABLY > RELIABLE
RELIANCE *n* dependence, confidence, or trust
RELIANCES > RELIANCE
RELIANT > RELIANCE
RELIANTLY > RELIANCE
RELIC *n* something that has survived from the past
RELICENSE *vb* license again
RELICS > RELIC
RELICT *n* relic
RELICTION *n* process by which sea water or fresh water recedes over time, changing the waterline and leaving land exposed
RELICTS > RELICT
RELIDE *archaic past form of* > RELY
RELIE *archaic spelling of* > RELY
RELIED > RELY
RELIEF *n* gladness at the end or removal of pain, distress, etc
RELIEFS > RELIEF
RELIER > RELY
RELIERS > RELY
RELIES > RELY
RELIEVE *vb* bring relief to
RELIEVED *adj* experiencing relief, esp from worry or anxiety
RELIEVER *n* person or thing that relieves
RELIEVERS > RELIEVER
RELIEVES > RELIEVE
RELIEVING > RELIEVE
RELIEVO *same as* > RELIEF
RELIEVOS > RELIEVO
RELIGHT *vb* ignite or cause to ignite again
RELIGHTED > RELIGHT
RELIGHTS > RELIGHT
RELIGIEUX *n* member of a monastic order or clerical body
RELIGION *n* system of belief in and worship of a supernatural power or god
RELIGIONS > RELIGION
RELIGIOSE *adj* affectedly or extremely pious
RELIGIOSO *adj* religious ▷ *adv* in a religious manner
RELIGIOUS *adj* of religion ▷ *n* monk or nun
RELINE *vb* line again or anew
RELINED > RELINE
RELINES > RELINE
RELINING > RELINE
RELINK *vb* link again
RELINKED > RELINK
RELINKING > RELINK
RELINKS > RELINK
RELIQUARY *n* case or shrine for holy relics
RELIQUE *archaic spelling of* > RELIC
RELIQUEFY *vb* liquefy again
RELIQUES > RELIQUE
RELIQUIAE *pl n* fossil remains of animals or plants
RELISH *vb* enjoy, like very much ▷ *n* liking or enjoyment
RELISHED > RELISH
RELISHES > RELISH
RELISHING > RELISH
RELIST *vb* list again
RELISTED > RELIST
RELISTING > RELIST
RELISTS > RELIST
RELIT > RELIGHT
RELIVABLE > RELIVE
RELIVE *vb* experience (a sensation etc) again, esp in the imagination
RELIVED > RELIVE
RELIVER *vb* deliver up again
RELIVERED > RELIVER
RELIVERS > RELIVER
RELIVES > RELIVE
RELIVING > RELIVE
RELLENO *n* Mexican dish of stuffed vegetable
RELLENOS > RELLENO
RELLIES *pl n* relatives or relations
RELLISH *(in music) variant of* > RELISH
RELLISHED > RELLISH
RELLISHES > RELLISH
RELOAD *vb* put fresh ammunition into (a firearm)
RELOADED > RELOAD
RELOADER > RELOAD
RELOADERS > RELOAD
RELOADING > RELOAD
RELOADS > RELOAD
RELOAN *vb* loan again
RELOANED > RELOAN
RELOANING > RELOAN
RELOANS > RELOAN
RELOCATE *vb* move to a new place to live or work
RELOCATED > RELOCATE
RELOCATEE *n* someone who is relocated
RELOCATES > RELOCATE
RELOCATOR *n* program designed to transfer files from one computer to another
RELOCK *vb* lock again
RELOCKED > RELOCK
RELOCKING > RELOCK
RELOCKS > RELOCK
RELOOK *vb* look again
RELOOKED > RELOOK
RELOOKING > RELOOK
RELOOKS > RELOOK
RELUCENT *adj* bright
RELUCT *vb* struggle or rebel
RELUCTANT *adj* unwilling or disinclined
RELUCTATE *vb* be or appear reluctant
RELUCTED > RELUCT
RELUCTING > RELUCT
RELUCTS > RELUCT
RELUME *vb* light or brighten again
RELUMED > RELUME
RELUMES > RELUME
RELUMINE *same as* > RELUME
RELUMINED > RELUMINE
RELUMINES > RELUMINE
RELUMING > RELUME
RELY *vb* depend (on)
RELYING > RELY
REM *n* dose of ionizing radiation that produces the same effect in man as one roentgen of x- or gamma-radiation
REMADE *n* object that has been reconstructed from original materials
REMADES > REMADE
REMAIL *vb* mail again
REMAILED > REMAIL
REMAILING > REMAIL
REMAILS > REMAIL
REMAIN *vb* continue
REMAINDER *n* part which is left ▷ *vb* offer (copies of a poorly selling book) at reduced prices
REMAINED > REMAIN
REMAINING > REMAIN
REMAINS *pl n* relics, esp of ancient buildings
REMAKE *vb* make again in a different way ▷ *n* new version of an old film
REMAKER > REMAKE
REMAKERS > REMAKE
REMAKES > REMAKE
REMAKING > REMAKE
REMAN *vb* man again or afresh
REMAND *vb* send back into custody or put on bail before trial
REMANDED > REMAND
REMANDING > REMAND
REMANDS > REMAND
REMANENCE *n* ability of a material to retain magnetization, equal to the magnetic flux density of the material after the removal of the magnetizing field
REMANENCY *archaic variant of* > REMANENCE
REMANENT *adj* remaining left over ▷ *n* archaic wo[rd] meaning remainder
REMANENTS > REMANENT
REMANET *n* something lef[t] over
REMANETS > REMANET
REMANIE *n* fragments and fossils of older origin found in a more recent deposit
REMANIES > REMANIE
REMANNED > REMAN
REMANNING > REMAN
REMANS > REMAN
REMAP *vb* map again
REMAPPED > REMAP
REMAPPING > REMAP
REMAPS > REMAP
REMARK *vb* make a casual comment (on) ▷ *n* observation or comment
REMARKED > REMARK
REMARKER > REMARK
REMARKERS > REMARK
REMARKET *vb* market agai[n]
REMARKETS > REMARKET
REMARKING > REMARK
REMARKS > REMARK
REMARQUE *n* printing mar[k] in the margin of a plate
REMARQUED *adj* having ha[d] a remarque put on
REMARQUES > REMARQUE
REMARRIED > REMARRY
REMARRIES > REMARRY
REMARRY *vb* marry again following a divorce or th[e] death of one's previous husband or wife
REMASTER *vb* make a new master audio recording, now usually digital, from (an earlier recording), to produce compact discs or stereo records with improved sound reproduction
REMASTERS > REMASTER
REMATCH *n* second or return game or contest between two players ▷ *v[b]* match (two contestants) again
REMATCHED > REMATCH
REMATCHES > REMATCH
REMATE *vb* mate again ▷ *n* finishing pass in bullfighting
REMATED > REMATE
REMATES > REMATE
REMATING > REMATE
REMBLAI *n* earth used for an embankment or rampart
REMBLAIS > REMBLAI

MBLE *dialect word or* > REMOVE

MBLED > REMBLE

MBLES > REMBLE

MBLING > REMBLE

MEAD *archaic or dialect vord for* > REMEDY

MEADED > REMEAD

MEADING > REMEAD

MEADS > REMEAD

MEASURE *vb* measure again

MEDE *archaic or dialect vord for* > REMEDY

MEDED > REMEDE

MEDES > REMEDE

MEDIAL *adj* intended o correct a specific disability, handicap, etc

MEDIAT *archaic word or* > REMEDIAL

MEDIATE *archaic word or* > REMEDIAL

MEDIED > REMEDY

MEDIES > REMEDY

MEDING > REMEDE

MEDY *n* means of curing pain or disease ▷ *vb* put right

MEDYING > REMEDY

MEET *vb* meet again

MEETING > REMEET

MEETS > REMEET

MEID *archaic or dialect vord for* > REMEDY

MEIDED > REMEID

MEIDING > REMEID

MEIDS > REMEID

MELT *vb* melt again

MELTED > REMELT

MELTING > REMELT

MELTS > REMELT

MEMBER *vb* retain in or recall to one's memory

MEMBERS > REMEMBER

MEN *n* ancient Egyptian measurement unit

MEND *vb* mend again

MENDED > REMEND

MENDING > REMEND

MENDS > REMEND

MENS > REMEN

MERCIED > REMERCY

MERCIES > REMERCY

MERCY *vb* archaic word for thank

MERGE *vb* merge again

MERGED > REMERGE

MERGES > REMERGE

MERGING > REMERGE

MET > REMEET

MEX *n* any of the large flight feathers of a bird's wing

MIGATE *vb* row

MIGATED > REMIGATE

MIGATES > REMIGATE

MIGES > REMEX

MIGIAL > REMEX

MIGRATE *vb* migrate again

MIND *vb* cause to remember

MINDED > REMIND

REMINDER *n* something that recalls the past

REMINDERS > REMINDER

REMINDFUL *adj* serving to remind

REMINDING > REMIND

REMINDS > REMIND

REMINISCE *vb* talk or write of past times, experiences, etc

REMINT *vb* mint again

REMINTED > REMINT

REMINTING > REMINT

REMINTS > REMINT

REMISE *vb* give up or relinquish (a right, claim, etc) ▷ *n* second thrust made on the same lunge after the first has missed

REMISED > REMISE

REMISES > REMISE

REMISING > REMISE

REMISS *adj* negligent or careless

REMISSION *n* reduction in the length of a prison term

REMISSIVE > REMISSION

REMISSLY > REMISS

REMISSORY *adj* liable to or intended to gain remission

REMIT *vb* send (money) for goods, services, etc, esp by post ▷ *n* area of competence or authority

REMITMENT *n* archaic word for remittance or remission

REMITS > REMIT

REMITTAL > REMIT

REMITTALS > REMIT

REMITTED > REMIT

REMITTEE *n* recipient of a remittance

REMITTEES > REMITTEE

REMITTENT *adj* (of a disease) periodically less severe

REMITTER *n* person who remits

REMITTERS > REMITTER

REMITTING > REMIT

REMITTOR *same as* > REMITTER

REMITTORS > REMITTOR

REMIX *vb* change the relative prominence of each performer's part of (a recording) ▷ *n* remixed version of a recording

REMIXED > REMIX

REMIXES > REMIX

REMIXING > REMIX

REMIXT *informal past form of* > REMIX

REMIXTURE > REMIX

REMNANT *n* small piece, esp of fabric, left over ▷ *adj* remaining

REMNANTAL *adj* existing as remnant

REMNANTS > REMNANT

REMODEL *vb* give a different shape or form to ▷ *n* something that has been remodelled

REMODELED > REMODEL

REMODELER > REMODEL

REMODELS > REMODEL

REMODIFY *vb* modify again

REMOISTEN *vb* moisten again

REMOLADE *same as* > REMOULADE

REMOLADES > REMOLADE

REMOLD *US spelling of* > REMOULD

REMOLDED > REMOLD

REMOLDING > REMOLD

REMOLDS > REMOLD

REMONTANT *adj* (esp of cultivated roses) flowering more than once in a single season ▷ *n* rose having such a growth

REMONTOIR *n* any of various devices used in watches, clocks, etc, to compensate for errors arising from the changes in the force driving the escapement

REMORA *n* spiny-finned fish

REMORAS > REMORA

REMORID > REMORA

REMORSE *n* feeling of sorrow and regret for something one did

REMORSES > REMORSE

REMOTE *adj* far away, distant ▷ *n* (in informal usage) remote control

REMOTELY > REMOTE

REMOTER > REMOTE

REMOTES > REMOTE

REMOTEST > REMOTE

REMOTION *n* removal

REMOTIONS > REMOTION

REMOUD *Spenserian variant of* > REMOVED

REMOULADE *n* mayonnaise sauce flavoured with herbs, mustard, and capers, served with salads, cold meat, etc

REMOULD *vb* change completely ▷ *n* renovated tyre

REMOULDED > REMOULD

REMOULDS > REMOULD

REMOUNT *vb* get on (a horse, bicycle, etc) again ▷ *n* fresh horse, esp (formerly) to replace one killed or injured in battle

REMOUNTED > REMOUNT

REMOUNTS > REMOUNT

REMOVABLE > REMOVE

REMOVABLY > REMOVE

REMOVAL *n* removing, esp changing residence

REMOVALS > REMOVAL

REMOVE *vb* take away or off ▷ *n* degree of difference

REMOVED *adj* very different or distant

REMOVEDLY *adv* at a distance

REMOVER > REMOVE

REMOVERS > REMOVE

REMOVES > REMOVE

REMOVING > REMOVE

REMS > REM

REMUAGE *n* (in the making of sparkling wine) process of turning the bottles to let the sediment out

REMUAGES > REMUAGE

REMUDA *n* stock of horses enabling riders to change mounts

REMUDAS > REMUDA

REMUEUR *n* (in the making of sparkling wine) person carrying out remuage, or the turning of bottles

REMUEURS > REMUEUR

REMURMUR *vb* murmur again or murmur in reply

REMURMURS > REMURMUR

REN *archaic variant of* > RUN

RENAGUE *same as* > RENEGE

RENAGUED > RENAGUE

RENAGUES > RENAGUE

RENAGUING > RENAGUE

RENAIL *vb* nail again

RENAILED > RENAIL

RENAILING > RENAIL

RENAILS > RENAIL

RENAL *adj* of the kidneys

RENAME *vb* change the name of (someone or something)

RENAMED > RENAME

RENAMES > RENAME

RENAMING > RENAME

RENASCENT *adj* becoming active or vigorous again

RENATURE *vb* return to natural state

RENATURED > RENATURE

RENATURES > RENATURE

RENAY *vb* archaic word meaning renounce

RENAYED > RENAY

RENAYING > RENAY

RENAYS > RENAY

RENCONTRE *n* unexpected meeting

REND *vb* tear or wrench apart

RENDED > REND

RENDER *vb* cause to become ▷ *n* first thin coat of plaster applied to a surface

RENDERED > RENDER

RENDERER > RENDER

RENDERERS > RENDER

RENDERING *n* act or an instance of performing a play, piece of music, etc

RENDERS > RENDER

RENDIBLE > REND

RENDING > REND

RENDITION *n* performance

RENDS > REND

RENDZINA *n* dark interzonal type of soil found in grassy or formerly grassy areas of moderate rainfall, esp on chalklands

RENDZINAS > RENDZINA
RENEGADE *n* person who deserts a cause ▷ *vb* become a renegade
RENEGADED > RENEGADE
RENEGADES > RENEGADE
RENEGADO *archaic word for* > RENEGADE
RENEGADOS > RENEGADO
RENEGATE *old variant of* > RENEGADE
RENEGATES > RENEGATE
RENEGE *vb* go back (on a promise etc)
RENEGED > RENEGE
RENEGER > RENEGE
RENEGERS > RENEGE
RENEGES > RENEGE
RENEGING > RENEGE
RENEGUE *same as* > RENEGE
RENEGUED > RENEGUE
RENEGUER > RENEGE
RENEGUERS > RENEGE
RENEGUES > RENEGUE
RENEGUING > RENEGUE
RENEST *vb* nest again or form a new nest
RENESTED > RENEST
RENESTING > RENEST
RENESTS > RENEST
RENEW *vb* begin again
RENEWABLE > RENEW
RENEWABLY > RENEW
RENEWAL *n* act of renewing or state of being renewed
RENEWALS > RENEWAL
RENEWED > RENEW
RENEWEDLY > RENEW
RENEWER > RENEW
RENEWERS > RENEW
RENEWING > RENEW
RENEWINGS > RENEW
RENEWS > RENEW
RENEY *same as* > RENAY
RENEYED > RENEY
RENEYING > RENEY
RENEYS > RENEY
RENFIERST *adj* archaic word for turned fierce
RENFORCE *vb* archaic word for reinforce
RENFORCED > RENFORCE
RENFORCES > RENFORCE
RENFORST > RENFORCE
RENGA *n* type of collaborative poetry found in Japan
RENGAS > RENGA
RENIED > RENY
RENIES > RENY
RENIFORM *adj* having the shape or profile of a kidney
RENIG *same as* > RENEGE
RENIGGED > RENIG
RENIGGING > RENIG
RENIGS > RENIG
RENIN *n* proteolytic enzyme secreted by the kidneys, which plays an important part in the maintenance of blood pressure
RENINS > RENIN
RENITENCE > RENITENT
RENITENCY > RENITENT
RENITENT *adj* reluctant
RENK *adj* unpleasant
RENKER > RENK
RENKEST > RENK
RENMINBI *same as* > YUAN
RENMINBIS > RENMINBI
RENNASE *same as* > RENNIN
RENNASES > RENNASE
RENNE *archaic variant of* > RUN
RENNED > REN
RENNES > RENNE
RENNET *n* substance for curdling milk to make cheese
RENNETS > RENNET
RENNIN *n* enzyme that occurs in gastric juice and is a constituent of rennet. It coagulates milk by converting caseinogen to casein
RENNING > REN
RENNINGS > REN
RENNINS > RENNIN
RENOGRAM *n* X-ray kidney image
RENOGRAMS > RENOGRAM
RENOTIFY *vb* notify again
RENOUNCE *vb* give up (a belief, habit, etc) voluntarily ▷ *n* failure to follow suit in a card game
RENOUNCED > RENOUNCE
RENOUNCER > RENOUNCE
RENOUNCES > RENOUNCE
RENOVATE *vb* restore to good condition
RENOVATED > RENOVATE
RENOVATES > RENOVATE
RENOVATOR > RENOVATE
RENOWN *n* widespread good reputation ▷ *vb* make famous
RENOWNED *adj* famous
RENOWNER *n* renown giver
RENOWNERS > RENOWNER
RENOWNING > RENOWN
RENOWNS > RENOWN
RENS > REN
RENT *n* payment made by a tenant to a landlord or owner of a property ▷ *vb* grant the right to use one's property for payment
RENTABLE > REND
RENTAL *n* sum payable as rent ▷ *adj* of or relating to rent
RENTALLER *n* (in Scots law) tenant with very favourable terms
RENTALS > RENTAL
RENTE *n* annual income from capital investment
RENTED > RENT
RENTER *n* person who lets his property in return for rent, esp a landlord
RENTERS > RENTER
RENTES > RENTE
RENTIER *n* person who lives off unearned income such as rents or interest
RENTIERS > RENTIER
RENTING > RENT
RENTINGS > RENT
RENTS > RENT
RENUMBER *vb* number again or afresh
RENUMBERS > RENUMBER
RENVERSE *vb* archaic word meaning overturn
RENVERSED > RENVERSE
RENVERSES > RENVERSE
RENVERST > RENVERSE
RENVOI *n* referring of a dispute or other legal question to a jurisdiction other than that in which it arose
RENVOIS > RENVOI
RENVOY *old variant of* > RENVOI
RENVOYS > RENVOY
RENY *same as* > RENAY
RENYING > RENY
REO *n* language
REOBJECT *vb* object again
REOBJECTS > REOBJECT
REOBSERVE *vb* observe again
REOBTAIN *vb* obtain again
REOBTAINS > REOBTAIN
REOCCUPY *vb* occupy (a building, area, etc) again
REOCCUR *vb* happen, take place, or come about again
REOCCURS > REOCCUR
REOFFEND *vb* commit another offence
REOFFENDS > REOFFEND
REOFFER *vb* offer again
REOFFERED > REOFFER
REOFFERS > REOFFER
REOIL *vb* oil again
REOILED > REOIL
REOILING > REOIL
REOILS > REOIL
REOPEN *vb* open again after a period of being closed or suspended
REOPENED > REOPEN
REOPENER *n* clause in a legal document allowing for an issue to be revisited at a subsequent date
REOPENERS > REOPENER
REOPENING > REOPEN
REOPENS > REOPEN
REOPERATE *vb* operate again
REOPPOSE *vb* oppose again
REOPPOSED > REOPPOSE
REOPPOSES > REOPPOSE
REORDAIN *vb* ordain again
REORDAINS > REORDAIN
REORDER *vb* change the order of
REORDERED > REORDER
REORDERS > REORDER
REORIENT *vb* adjust or align (something) in a new or different way
REORIENTS > REORIENT
REOS > REO
REOUTFIT *vb* outfit again
REOUTFITS > REOUTFIT
REOVIRUS *n* type of virus
REOXIDISE *same as* > REOXIDIZE
REOXIDIZE *vb* oxidize again
REP *n* sales representativ[e] ▷ *vb* work as a representative
REPACIFY *vb* pacify agai[n]
REPACK *vb* place or arran[ge] (articles) in (a container) again or in a different wa[y]
REPACKAGE *vb* wrap or pu[t] (something) in a packag[e] again
REPACKED > REPACK
REPACKING > REPACK
REPACKS > REPACK
REPAID > REPAY
REPAINT *vb* apply a new [or] fresh coat of paint
REPAINTED > REPAINT
REPAINTS > REPAINT
REPAIR *vb* restore to goo[d] condition, mend ▷ *n* act of repairing
REPAIRED > REPAIR
REPAIRER > REPAIR
REPAIRERS > REPAIR
REPAIRING > REPAIR
REPAIRMAN *n* man whose job it is to repair machines, appliances, et[c]
REPAIRMEN > REPAIRMAN
REPAIRS > REPAIR
REPAND *adj* having a wav[y] margin
REPANDLY > REPAND
REPANEL *vb* panel again [or] anew
REPANELED > REPANEL
REPANELS > REPANEL
REPAPER *vb* paper again [or] afresh
REPAPERED > REPAPER
REPAPERS > REPAPER
REPARABLE *adj* able to be repaired or remedied
REPARABLY > REPARABLE
REPARK *vb* park again
REPARKED > REPARK
REPARKING > REPARK
REPARKS > REPARK
REPARTEE *n* interchange [of] witty retorts ▷ *vb* retort
REPARTEED > REPARTEE
REPARTEES > REPARTEE
REPASS *vb* pass again
REPASSAGE *n* passage ba[ck] or return
REPASSED > REPASS
REPASSES > REPASS
REPASSING > REPASS
REPAST *n* meal ▷ *vb* feed (on)
REPASTED > REPAST
REPASTING > REPAST
REPASTS > REPAST
REPASTURE *old word for* > FOOD
REPATCH *vb* patch again
REPATCHED > REPATCH
REPATCHES > REPATCH

PATTERN *vb* pattern gain
PAVE *vb* pave again
PAVED > REPAVE
PAVES > REPAVE
PAVING > REPAVE
PAY *vb* pay back, refund
PAYABLE > REPAY
PAYING > REPAY
PAYMENT > REPAY
PAYS > REPAY
PEAL *vb* cancel (a law) fficially ▷ *n* act of epealing
PEALED > REPEAL
PEALER > REPEAL
PEALERS > REPEAL
PEALING > REPEAL
PEALS > REPEAL
PEAT *vb* say or do again · *n* act or instance of epeating
PEATED *adj* done, made, r said again and again
PEATER *n* firearm that nay be discharged many imes without reloading
PEATERS > REPEATER
PEATING > REPEAT
PEATS > REPEAT
PECHAGE *n* extra heat r test providing second hance to previous losers r failing candidates
PEG *vb* peg again
PEGGED > REPEG
PEGGING > REPEG
PEGS > REPEG
PEL *vb* be disgusting to
PELLANT *same* s > REPELLENT
PELLED > REPEL
PELLENT *adj* distasteful · *n* something that repels, sp a chemical to repel nsects
PELLER > REPEL
PELLERS > REPEL
PELLING > REPEL
PELS > REPEL
PENT *vb* feel regret for a deed or omission) ▷ *adj* ying or creeping along the round
PENTANT *adj* eproaching oneself for ne's past actions or sins
PENTED > REPENT
PENTER > REPENT
PENTERS > REPENT
PENTING > REPENT
PENTS > REPENT
PEOPLE *vb* people again
PEOPLED > REPEOPLE
PEOPLES > REPEOPLE
PERCUSS *vb* have epercussions
PEREPE *n* New Zealand vord for the elephant ish, a large fish of the outhwest Pacific with a runk-like snout
PERK *vb* perk again
PERKED > REPERK
REPERKING > REPERK
REPERKS > REPERK
REPERTORY *n* repertoire
REPERUSAL *n* fresh perusal
REPERUSE *vb* peruse again
REPERUSED > REPERUSE
REPERUSES > REPERUSE
REPETEND *n* digit or series of digits in a recurring decimal that repeats itself
REPETENDS > REPETEND
REPHRASE *vb* express in different words
REPHRASED > REPHRASE
REPHRASES > REPHRASE
REPIGMENT *vb* pigment again
REPIN *vb* pin again
REPINE *vb* fret or complain
REPINED > REPINE
REPINER > REPINE
REPINERS > REPINE
REPINES > REPINE
REPINING > REPINE
REPININGS > REPINE
REPINNED > REPIN
REPINNING > REPIN
REPINS > REPIN
REPIQUE *n* score of 30 points made from the cards held by a player before play begins ▷ *vb* score a repique against (someone)
REPIQUED > REPIQUE
REPIQUES > REPIQUE
REPIQUING > REPIQUE
REPLA > REPLUM
REPLACE *vb* substitute for
REPLACED > REPLACE
REPLACER > REPLACE
REPLACERS > REPLACE
REPLACES > REPLACE
REPLACING > REPLACE
REPLAN *vb* plan again
REPLANNED > REPLAN
REPLANS > REPLAN
REPLANT *vb* plant again
REPLANTED > REPLANT
REPLANTS > REPLANT
REPLASTER *vb* plaster again
REPLATE *vb* plate again
REPLATED > REPLATE
REPLATES > REPLATE
REPLATING > REPLATE
REPLAY *n* immediate reshowing on TV of an incident in sport, esp in slow motion ▷ *vb* play (a match, recording, etc) again
REPLAYED > REPLAY
REPLAYING > REPLAY
REPLAYS > REPLAY
REPLEAD *vb* plead again
REPLEADED > REPLEAD
REPLEADER *n* right to plead again
REPLEADS > REPLEAD
REPLED > REPLEAD
REPLEDGE *vb* pledge again
REPLEDGED > REPLEDGE
REPLEDGES > REPLEDGE
REPLENISH *vb* fill up again, resupply
REPLETE *adj* filled or gorged ▷ *vb* fill again
REPLETED > REPLETE
REPLETELY > REPLETE
REPLETES > REPLETE
REPLETING > REPLETE
REPLETION *n* state or condition of being replete
REPLEVIED > REPLEVY
REPLEVIES > REPLEVY
REPLEVIN *n* recovery of goods unlawfully taken, made subject to establishing the validity of the recovery in a legal action and returning the goods if the decision is adverse
REPLEVINS > REPLEVIN
REPLEVY *vb* recover possession of (goods) by replevin
REPLICA *n* exact copy
REPLICAS > REPLICA
REPLICASE *n* type of enzyme
REPLICATE *vb* make or be a copy of ▷ *adj* folded back on itself
REPLICON *n* region of a DNA molecule that is replicated from a single origin
REPLICONS > REPLICON
REPLIED > REPLY
REPLIER > REPLY
REPLIERS > REPLY
REPLIES > REPLY
REPLOT *vb* plot again
REPLOTS > REPLOT
REPLOTTED > REPLOT
REPLOW *vb* plow again
REPLOWED > REPLOW
REPLOWING > REPLOW
REPLOWS > REPLOW
REPLUM *n* internal separating wall in some fruits
REPLUMB *vb* plumb again
REPLUMBED > REPLUMB
REPLUMBS > REPLUMB
REPLUNGE *vb* plunge again
REPLUNGED > REPLUNGE
REPLUNGES > REPLUNGE
REPLY *vb* answer or respond ▷ *n* answer or response
REPLYING > REPLY
REPO *n* act of repossessing
REPOINT *vb* repair the joints of (brickwork, masonry, etc) with mortar or cement
REPOINTED > REPOINT
REPOINTS > REPOINT
REPOLISH *vb* polish again
REPOLL *vb* poll again
REPOLLED > REPOLL
REPOLLING > REPOLL
REPOLLS > REPOLL
REPOMAN *n* informal word for a man employed to repossess goods in cases of non-payment
REPOMEN > REPOMAN
REPONE *vb* restore (someone) to his former status, office, etc
REPONED > REPONE
REPONES > REPONE
REPONING > REPONE
REPORT *vb* give an account of ▷ *n* account or statement
REPORTAGE *n* act or process of reporting news or other events of general interest
REPORTED > REPORT
REPORTER *n* person who gathers news for a newspaper, TV, etc
REPORTERS > REPORTER
REPORTING > REPORT
REPORTS > REPORT
REPOS > REPO
REPOSAL *n* repose
REPOSALL *archaic spelling of* > REPOSAL
REPOSALLS > REPOSALL
REPOSALS > REPOSE
REPOSE *n* peace ▷ *vb* lie or lay at rest
REPOSED > REPOSE
REPOSEDLY > REPOSE
REPOSEFUL > REPOSE
REPOSER > REPOSE
REPOSERS > REPOSE
REPOSES > REPOSE
REPOSING > REPOSE
REPOSIT *vb* put away, deposit, or store up
REPOSITED > REPOSIT
REPOSITOR *n* any instrument used for correcting the position of displaced organs or bones
REPOSITS > REPOSIT
REPOSSESS *vb* (of a lender) take back property from a customer who is behind with payments
REPOST *vb* post again
REPOSTED > REPOST
REPOSTING > REPOST
REPOSTS > REPOST
REPOSURE *old word for* > REPOSE
REPOSURES > REPOSURE
REPOT *vb* put (a house plant) into a new usually larger pot
REPOTS > REPOT
REPOTTED > REPOT
REPOTTING > REPOT
REPOUR *vb* pour back or again
REPOURED > REPOUR
REPOURING > REPOUR
REPOURS > REPOUR
REPOUSSE *adj* raised in relief, as a design on a thin piece of metal hammered through from the underside ▷ *n* design or surface made in this way
REPOUSSES > REPOUSSE

REPOWER *vb* put new engine in
REPOWERED > REPOWER
REPOWERS > REPOWER
REPP *same as* > REP
REPPED > REP
REPPING > REP
REPPINGS > REP
REPPS > REPP
REPREEVE *archaic spelling of* > REPRIEVE
REPREEVED > REPREEVE
REPREEVES > REPREEVE
REPREHEND *vb* find fault with
REPRESENT *vb* act as a delegate or substitute for
REPRESS *vb* keep (feelings) in check
REPRESSED *adj* (of a person) repressing feelings, instincts, desires, etc
REPRESSER > REPRESS
REPRESSES > REPRESS
REPRESSOR *n* protein synthesized under the control of a repressor gene, which has the capacity to bind to the operator gene and thereby shut off the expression of the structural genes of an operon
REPRICE *vb* price again
REPRICED > REPRICE
REPRICES > REPRICE
REPRICING > REPRICE
REPRIEFE *n* (in archaic usage) reproof
REPRIEFES > REPRIEFE
REPRIEVAL *old word for* > REPRIEVE
REPRIEVE *vb* postpone the execution of (a condemned person) ▷ *n* (document granting) postponement or cancellation of a punishment
REPRIEVED > REPRIEVE
REPRIEVER > REPRIEVE
REPRIEVES > REPRIEVE
REPRIMAND *vb* blame (someone) officially for a fault ▷ *n* official blame
REPRIME *vb* prime again
REPRIMED > REPRIME
REPRIMES > REPRIME
REPRIMING > REPRIME
REPRINT *vb* print further copies of (a book) ▷ *n* reprinted copy
REPRINTED > REPRINT
REPRINTER > REPRINT
REPRINTS > REPRINT
REPRISAL *n* retaliation
REPRISALS > REPRISAL
REPRISE *n* repeating of an earlier theme ▷ *vb* repeat an earlier theme
REPRISED > REPRISE
REPRISES > REPRISE
REPRISING > REPRISE
REPRIVE *archaic spelling of* > REPRIEVE
REPRIVED > REPRIVE
REPRIVES > REPRIVE
REPRIVING > REPRIVE
REPRIZE *archaic spelling of* > REPRISE
REPRIZED > REPRIZE
REPRIZES > REPRIZE
REPRIZING > REPRIZE
REPRO *n* imitation or facsimile of a work of art; reproduction
REPROACH *vb* blame, rebuke
REPROBACY > REPROBATE
REPROBATE *n* depraved or disreputable (person) ▷ *adj* morally unprincipled ▷ *vb* disapprove of
REPROBE *vb* probe again
REPROBED > REPROBE
REPROBES > REPROBE
REPROBING > REPROBE
REPROCESS *vb* treat or prepare (something) by a special method again
REPRODUCE *vb* produce a copy of
REPROGRAM *vb* program again
REPROOF *n* severe blaming of someone for a fault ▷ *vb* treat (a coat, jacket, etc) so as to renew its texture, waterproof qualities, etc
REPROOFED > REPROOF
REPROOFS > REPROOF
REPROS > REPRO
REPROVAL *same as* > REPROOF
REPROVALS > REPROVAL
REPROVE *vb* speak severely to (someone) about a fault
REPROVED > REPROVE
REPROVER > REPROVE
REPROVERS > REPROVE
REPROVES > REPROVE
REPROVING > REPROVE
REPRYVE *archaic spelling of* > REPRIEVE
REPRYVED > REPRYVE
REPRYVES > REPRYVE
REPRYVING > REPRYVE
REPS > REP
REPTANT *adj* creeping, crawling, or lying along the ground
REPTATION *n* creeping action
REPTILE *n* cold-blooded egg-laying vertebrate with horny scales or plates, such as a snake or tortoise ▷ *adj* creeping, crawling, or squirming
REPTILES > REPTILE
REPTILIA > REPTILIUM
REPTILIAN *adj* of, relating to, resembling, or characteristic of reptiles
REPTILIUM *n* place where live reptiles are kept for show
REPTILOID *adj* resembling a reptile
REPUBLIC *n* form of government in which the people or their elected representatives possess the supreme power
REPUBLICS > REPUBLIC
REPUBLISH *vb* publish again
REPUDIATE *vb* reject the authority or validity of
REPUGN *vb* oppose or conflict (with)
REPUGNANT *adj* offensive or distasteful
REPUGNED > REPUGN
REPUGNING > REPUGN
REPUGNS > REPUGN
REPULP *vb* pulp again
REPULPED > REPULP
REPULPING > REPULP
REPULPS > REPULP
REPULSE *vb* be disgusting to ▷ *n* driving back
REPULSED > REPULSE
REPULSER > REPULSE
REPULSERS > REPULSE
REPULSES > REPULSE
REPULSING > REPULSE
REPULSION *n* distaste or aversion
REPULSIVE *adj* loathsome, disgusting
REPUMP *vb* pump again
REPUMPED > REPUMP
REPUMPING > REPUMP
REPUMPS > REPUMP
REPUNIT *n* any number that consists entirely of the same repeated digits, such as 111 or 55,555
REPUNITS > REPUNIT
REPURE *vb* archaic word meaning make pure again
REPURED > REPURE
REPURES > REPURE
REPURIFY *vb* purify again
REPURING > REPURE
REPURPOSE *vb* find new purpose for
REPURSUE *vb* pursue again
REPURSUED > REPURSUE
REPURSUES > REPURSUE
REPUTABLE *adj* of good reputation, respectable
REPUTABLY > REPUTABLE
REPUTE *n* reputation ▷ *vb* consider (a person or thing) to be as specified
REPUTED *adj* supposed
REPUTEDLY *adv* according to general belief or supposition
REPUTES > REPUTE
REPUTING > REPUTE
REPUTINGS > REPUTE
REQUALIFY *vb* qualify again
REQUERE *archaic variant of* > REQUIRE
REQUERED > REQUERE
REQUERES > REQUERE
REQUERING > REQUERE
REQUEST *vb* ask ▷ *n* aski
REQUESTED > REQUEST
REQUESTER > REQUEST
REQUESTOR > REQUEST
REQUESTS > REQUEST
REQUICKEN *vb* quicken again
REQUIEM *n* Mass celebra for the dead
REQUIEMS > REQUIEM
REQUIGHT *archaic spelling of* > REQUITE
REQUIGHTS > REQUIGHT
REQUIN *vb* type of shark
REQUINS > REQUIN
REQUIRE *vb* want or nee
REQUIRED > REQUIRE
REQUIRER > REQUIRE
REQUIRERS > REQUIRE
REQUIRES > REQUIRE
REQUIRING > REQUIRE
REQUISITE *adj* necessar essential ▷ *n* essential thing
REQUIT *vb* quit again
REQUITAL *n* act or an instance of requiting
REQUITALS > REQUITAL
REQUITE *vb* return to someone (the same treatment or feeling as received)
REQUITED > REQUITE
REQUITER > REQUITE
REQUITERS > REQUITE
REQUITES > REQUITE
REQUITING > REQUITE
REQUITS > REQUIT
REQUITTED > REQUIT
REQUOTE *vb* quote again
REQUOTED > REQUOTE
REQUOTES > REQUOTE
REQUOTING > REQUOTE
REQUOYLE *archaic spelling of* > RECOIL
REQUOYLED > REQUOYLE
REQUOYLES > REQUOYLE
RERACK *vb* rack again
RERACKED > RERACK
RERACKING > RERACK
RERACKS > RERACK
RERADIATE *vb* radiate again
RERAIL *vb* put back on a railway line
RERAILED > RERAIL
RERAILING *n* replaceme of existing rails on a railway line
RERAILS > RERAIL
RERAISE *vb* raise again
RERAISED > RERAISE
RERAISES > RERAISE
RERAISING > RERAISE
RERAN > RERUN
REREAD *vb* read (something) again
REREADING > REREAD
REREADS > REREAD
REREBRACE *n* armour wc on the upper arm
RERECORD *vb* record aga
RERECORDS > RERECORD
REREDOS *n* ornamental

creen behind an altar
:**REDOSES** > REREDOS
:**REDOSSE** *same*
'**S** > REREDOS
RELEASE *vb* release again
REMAI *n* New Zealand word for the basking shark
REMICE > REREMOUSE
:**REMIND** *vb* remind again
'**REMINDS** > REREMIND
.**REMOUSE** *n* archaic or dialect word for BAT (the animal)
'**RENT** *vb* rent again
:**RENTED** > RERENT
'**RENTING** > RERENT
:**RENTS** > RERENT
:**REPEAT** *vb* repeat again
REPEATS > REREPEAT
.**REVIEW** *vb* review again
:**REVIEWS** > REREVIEW
'**REVISE** *vb* revise again
REVISED > REREVISE
.**REVISES** > REREVISE
'**REWARD** *archaic spelling of* > REARWARD
REWARDS *archaic spelling of* > REARWARDS
'**RIG** *vb* rig again
RIGGED > RERIG
'**RIGGING** > RERIG
RIGS > RERIG
RISE *vb* rise again
RISEN > RERISE
RISES > RERISE
RISING > RERISE
.**ROLL** *vb* roll again
'**ROLLED** > REROLL
'**ROLLER** > REROLL
ROLLERS > REROLL
ROLLING > REROLL
ROLLS > REROLL
ROOF *vb* put a new roof or roofs on
.**ROOFED** > REROOF
'**ROOFING** > REROOF
'**ROOFS** > REROOF
ROSE > RERISE
ROUTE *vb* send or direct by a different route
ROUTED > REROUTE
ROUTES > REROUTE
'**ROUTING** > REROUTE
.**RUN** *n* film or programme that is broadcast again, repeat ▷ *vb* put on (a film or programme) again
RUNNING > RERUN
RUNS > RERUN
S *informal word for* > RESIDENCE
SADDLE *vb* saddle again
SADDLED > RESADDLE
SADDLES > RESADDLE
SAID > RESAY
SAIL *vb* sail again
SAILED > RESAIL
SAILING > RESAIL
SAILS > RESAIL
SALABLE > RESALE
SALE *n* selling of something purchased earlier
RESALES > RESALE
RESALGAR *archaic variant of* > REALGAR
RESALGARS > RESALGAR
RESALUTE *vb* salute back or again
RESALUTED > RESALUTE
RESALUTES > RESALUTE
RESAMPLE *vb* (in graphics or digital photography) change the size or resolution of
RESAMPLED > RESAMPLE
RESAMPLES > RESAMPLE
RESAT > RESIT
RESAW *vb* saw again
RESAWED > RESAW
RESAWING > RESAW
RESAWN > RESAW
RESAWS > RESAW
RESAY *vb* say again or in response
RESAYING > RESAY
RESAYS > RESAY
RESCALE *vb* resize
RESCALED > RESCALE
RESCALES > RESCALE
RESCALING > RESCALE
RESCHOOL *vb* retrain
RESCHOOLS > RESCHOOL
RESCIND *vb* annul or repeal
RESCINDED > RESCIND
RESCINDER > RESCIND
RESCINDS > RESCIND
RESCORE *vb* score afresh
RESCORED > RESCORE
RESCORES > RESCORE
RESCORING > RESCORE
RESCREEN *vb* screen again
RESCREENS > RESCREEN
RESCRIPT *n* (in ancient Rome) an ordinance taking the form of a reply by the emperor to a question on a point of law
RESCRIPTS > RESCRIPT
RESCUABLE > RESCUE
RESCUE *vb* deliver from danger or trouble, save ▷ *n* rescuing
RESCUED > RESCUE
RESCUER > RESCUE
RESCUERS > RESCUE
RESCUES > RESCUE
RESCUING > RESCUE
RESCULPT *vb* sculpt again
RESCULPTS > RESCULPT
RESEAL *vb* close or secure tightly again
RESEALED > RESEAL
RESEALING > RESEAL
RESEALS > RESEAL
RESEARCH *n* systematic investigation to discover facts or collect information ▷ *vb* carry out investigations
RESEASON *vb* season again
RESEASONS > RESEASON
RESEAT *vb* show (a person) to a new seat
RESEATED > RESEAT
RESEATING > RESEAT
RESEATS > RESEAT
RESEAU *n* mesh background to a lace or other pattern
RESEAUS > RESEAU
RESEAUX > RESEAU
RESECT *vb* cut out part of (a bone, an organ, or other structure or part)
RESECTED > RESECT
RESECTING > RESECT
RESECTION *n* excision of part of a bone, organ, or other part
RESECTS > RESECT
RESECURE *vb* secure again
RESECURED > RESECURE
RESECURES > RESECURE
RESEDA *n* plant that has small spikes of grey-green flowers ▷ *adj* of a greyish-green colour
RESEDAS > RESEDA
RESEE *vb* see again
RESEED *vb* form seed and reproduce naturally, forming a constant plant population
RESEEDED > RESEED
RESEEDING > RESEED
RESEEDS > RESEED
RESEEING > RESEE
RESEEK *vb* seek again
RESEEKING > RESEEK
RESEEKS > RESEEK
RESEEN > RESEE
RESEES > RESEE
RESEIZE *vb* seize again
RESEIZED > RESEIZE
RESEIZES > RESEIZE
RESEIZING > RESEIZE
RESEIZURE > RESEIZE
RESELECT *vb* choose (someone or something) again, esp to choose an existing office-holder as candidate for re-election
RESELECTS > RESELECT
RESELL *vb* sell (something) one has previously bought
RESELLER > RESELL
RESELLERS > RESELL
RESELLING > RESELL
RESELLS > RESELL
RESEMBLE *vb* be or look like
RESEMBLED > RESEMBLE
RESEMBLER > RESEMBLE
RESEMBLES > RESEMBLE
RESEND *vb* send again
RESENDING > RESEND
RESENDS > RESEND
RESENT *vb* feel bitter about
RESENTED > RESENT
RESENTER > RESENT
RESENTERS > RESENT
RESENTFUL *adj* feeling or characterized by resentment
RESENTING > RESENT
RESENTIVE *archaic word for* > RESENTFUL
RESENTS > RESENT
RESERPINE *n* insoluble alkaloid, extracted from the roots of the plant *Rauwolfia serpentina*, used medicinally to lower blood pressure and as a sedative
RESERVE *vb* set aside, keep for future use ▷ *n* something, esp money or troops, kept for emergencies
RESERVED *adj* not showing one's feelings, lacking friendliness
RESERVER > RESERVE
RESERVERS > RESERVE
RESERVES > RESERVE
RESERVICE *vb* service again
RESERVING > RESERVE
RESERVIST *n* member of a military reserve
RESERVOIR *n* natural or artificial lake storing water for community supplies
RESES > RES
RESET *vb* set again (a broken bone, matter in type, a gemstone, etc) ▷ *n* act or an instance of setting again
RESETS > RESET
RESETTED > RESET
RESETTER > RESET
RESETTERS > RESET
RESETTING > RESET
RESETTLE *vb* settle to live in a different place
RESETTLED > RESETTLE
RESETTLES > RESETTLE
RESEW *vb* sew again
RESEWED > RESEW
RESEWING > RESEW
RESEWN > RESEW
RESEWS > RESEW
RESH *n* 20th letter of the Hebrew alphabet
RESHAPE *vb* shape (something) again or differently
RESHAPED > RESHAPE
RESHAPER > RESHAPE
RESHAPERS > RESHAPE
RESHAPES > RESHAPE
RESHAPING > RESHAPE
RESHARPEN *vb* sharpen again
RESHAVE *vb* shave again
RESHAVED > RESHAVE
RESHAVEN > RESHAVE
RESHAVES > RESHAVE
RESHAVING > RESHAVE
RESHES > RESH
RESHINE *vb* shine again
RESHINED > RESHINE
RESHINES > RESHINE
RESHINGLE *vb* put new shingles on
RESHINING > RESHINE
RESHIP *vb* ship again
RESHIPPED > RESHIP
RESHIPPER > RESHIP
RESHIPS > RESHIP
RESHOD > RESHOE
RESHOE *vb* put a new sho or shoes on

RESHOED > RESHOE
RESHOEING > RESHOE
RESHOES > RESHOE
RESHONE > RESHINE
RESHOOT *vb* shoot again
RESHOOTS > RESHOOT
RESHOT > RESHOOT
RESHOW *vb* show again
RESHOWED > RESHOW
RESHOWER *vb* have another shower
RESHOWERS > RESHOWER
RESHOWING > RESHOW
RESHOWN > RESHOW
RESHOWS > RESHOW
RESHUFFLE *n* reorganization ▷ *vb* reorganize
RESIANCE *archaic word for* > RESIDENCE
RESIANCES > RESIANCE
RESIANT *archaic word for* > RESIDENT
RESIANTS > RESIANT
RESID *n* residual oil left over from the petroleum distillation process
RESIDE *vb* dwell permanently
RESIDED > RESIDE
RESIDENCE *n* home or house
RESIDENCY *n* regular series of concerts by a band or singer at one venue
RESIDENT *n* person who lives in a place ▷ *adj* living in a place
RESIDENTS > RESIDENT
RESIDER > RESIDE
RESIDERS > RESIDE
RESIDES > RESIDE
RESIDING > RESIDE
RESIDS > RESID
RESIDUA > RESIDUUM
RESIDUAL *adj* of or being a remainder ▷ *n* something left over as a residue
RESIDUALS > RESIDUAL
RESIDUARY *adj* of, relating to, or constituting a residue
RESIDUE *n* what is left, remainder
RESIDUES > RESIDUE
RESIDUOUS *adj* residual
RESIDUUM *n* residue
RESIDUUMS > RESIDUUM
RESIFT *vb* sift again
RESIFTED > RESIFT
RESIFTING > RESIFT
RESIFTS > RESIFT
RESIGHT *vb* sight again
RESIGHTED > RESIGHT
RESIGHTS > RESIGHT
RESIGN *vb* give up office, a job, etc
RESIGNED *adj* content to endure
RESIGNER > RESIGN
RESIGNERS > RESIGN
RESIGNING > RESIGN
RESIGNS > RESIGN
RESILE *vb* spring or shrink back
RESILED > RESILE
RESILES > RESILE
RESILIENT *adj* (of a person) recovering quickly from a shock etc
RESILIN *n* substance found in insect bodies
RESILING > RESILE
RESILINS > RESILIN
RESILVER *vb* silver again
RESILVERS > RESILVER
RESIN *n* sticky substance from plants, esp pines ▷ *vb* treat or coat with resin
RESINATA *n* type of wine
RESINATAS > RESINATA
RESINATE *vb* impregnate with resin
RESINATED > RESINATE
RESINATES > RESINATE
RESINED > RESIN
RESINER *n* applier or collector of resin
RESINERS > RESINER
RESINIFY *vb* become or cause to be resinous
RESINING > RESIN
RESINISE *variant spelling of* > RESINIZE
RESINISED > RESINISE
RESINISES > RESINISE
RESINIZE *vb* apply resin to
RESINIZED > RESINIZE
RESINIZES > RESINIZE
RESINLIKE > RESIN
RESINOID *adj* resembling, characteristic of, or containing resin ▷ *n* any resinoid substance, esp a synthetic compound
RESINOIDS > RESINOID
RESINOSES > RESINOSIS
RESINOSIS *n* excessive resin loss in diseased or damaged conifers
RESINOUS > RESIN
RESINS > RESIN
RESINY *adj* resembling, containing or covered with resin
RESIST *vb* withstand or oppose ▷ *n* substance used to protect something, esp a coating that prevents corrosion
RESISTANT *adj* characterized by or showing resistance ▷ *n* person or thing that resists
RESISTED > RESIST
RESISTENT *same as* > RESISTANT
RESISTER > RESIST
RESISTERS > RESIST
RESISTING > RESIST
RESISTIVE *adj* exhibiting electrical resistance
RESISTOR *n* component of an electrical circuit producing resistance
RESISTORS > RESISTOR
RESISTS > RESIST
RESIT *vb* take (an exam) again ▷ *n* exam that has to be taken again
RESITE *vb* move to a different site
RESITED > RESITE
RESITES > RESITE
RESITING > RESITE
RESITS > RESIT
RESITTING > RESIT
RESITUATE *vb* situate elsewhere
RESIZE *vb* change size of
RESIZED > RESIZE
RESIZES > RESIZE
RESIZING > RESIZE
RESKETCH *vb* sketch again
RESKEW *archaic spelling of* > RESCUE
RESKEWED > RESKEW
RESKEWING > RESKEW
RESKEWS > RESKEW
RESKILL *vb* train (workers) to acquire new skills
RESKILLED > RESKILL
RESKILLS > RESKILL
RESKUE *archaic spelling of* > RESCUE
RESKUED > RESKUE
RESKUES > RESKUE
RESKUING > RESKUE
RESLATE *vb* slate again
RESLATED > RESLATE
RESLATES > RESLATE
RESLATING > RESLATE
RESMELT *vb* smelt again
RESMELTED > RESMELT
RESMELTS > RESMELT
RESMOOTH *vb* smooth again
RESMOOTHS > RESMOOTH
RESNATRON *n* tetrode used to generate high power at high frequencies
RESOAK *vb* soak again
RESOAKED > RESOAK
RESOAKING > RESOAK
RESOAKS > RESOAK
RESOD *vb* returf
RESODDED > RESOD
RESODDING > RESOD
RESODS > RESOD
RESOFTEN *vb* soften again
RESOFTENS > RESOFTEN
RESOJET *n* type of jet engine
RESOJETS > RESOJET
RESOLD > RESELL
RESOLDER *vb* solder again
RESOLDERS > RESOLDER
RESOLE *vb* put a new sole or new soles on
RESOLED > RESOLE
RESOLES > RESOLE
RESOLING > RESOLE
RESOLUBLE *adj* able to be resolved
RESOLUTE *adj* firm in purpose ▷ *n* someone resolute
RESOLUTER > RESOLUTE
RESOLUTES > RESOLUTE
RESOLVE *vb* decide with an effort of will ▷ *n* absolute determination
RESOLVED *adj* determine[d]
RESOLVENT *adj* serving to dissolve or separate something into its elements ▷ *n* somethin[g] that resolves
RESOLVER > RESOLVE
RESOLVERS > RESOLVE
RESOLVES > RESOLVE
RESOLVING > RESOLVE
RESONANCE *n* echoing, es[p] with a deep sound
RESONANT *adj* resoundin[g] or re-echoing ▷ *n* type of unobstructed speech sound
RESONANTS > RESONANT
RESONATE *vb* resound or cause to resound
RESONATED > RESONATE
RESONATES > RESONATE
RESONATOR *n* any body or system that displays resonance, esp a tuned electrical circuit or a conducting cavity in which microwaves are generated by a resonant current
RESORB *vb* absorb again
RESORBED > RESORB
RESORBENT > RESORB
RESORBING > RESORB
RESORBS > RESORB
RESORCIN *n* substance used principally in dyein[g]
RESORCINS > RESORCIN
RESORT *vb* have recourse (to) for help etc ▷ *n* plac[e] for holidays
RESORTED > RESORT
RESORTER > RESORT
RESORTERS > RESORT
RESORTING > RESORT
RESORTS > RESORT
RESOUGHT > RESEEK
RESOUND *vb* echo or ring with sound
RESOUNDED > RESOUND
RESOUNDS > RESOUND
RESOURCE *n* thing resort[ed] to for support ▷ *vb* provide funding or other resources for
RESOURCED > RESOURCE
RESOURCES > RESOURCE
RESOW *vb* sow again
RESOWED > RESOW
RESOWING > RESOW
RESOWN > RESOW
RESOWS > RESOW
RESPACE *vb* change the spacing of
RESPACED > RESPACE
RESPACES > RESPACE
RESPACING > RESPACE
RESPADE *vb* dig over
RESPADED > RESPADE
RESPADES > RESPADE
RESPADING > RESPADE
RESPEAK *vb* speak furthe[r]
RESPEAKS > RESPEAK
RESPECIFY *vb* specify again

SPECT *n* consideration ·*vb* treat with esteem
SPECTED > RESPECT
SPECTER *n* person who espects someone or omething
SPECTS > RESPECT
SPELL *vb* spell again
SPELLED > RESPELL
SPELLS > RESPELL
SPELT > RESPELL
SPIRE *vb* breathe
SPIRED > RESPIRE
SPIRES > RESPIRE
SPIRING > RESPIRE
SPITE *n* pause, interval f rest ▷ *vb* grant a respite o
SPITED > RESPITE
SPITES > RESPITE
SPITING > RESPITE
SPLEND *vb* be esplendent
SPLENDS > RESPLEND
SPLICE *vb* splice again
SPLICED > RESPLICE
SPLICES > RESPLICE
SPLIT *vb* split again
SPLITS > RESPLIT
SPOKE > RESPEAK
SPOKEN > RESPEAK
SPOND *vb* answer ▷ *n* ilaster or an engaged olumn that supports an rch or a lintel
SPONDED > RESPOND
SPONDER > RESPOND
SPONDS > RESPOND
SPONSA *n* that part f rabbinic literature oncerned with written ulings in answer to uestions
SPONSE *n* answer
SPONSER *n* radio or adar receiver used in onjunction with an nterrogator to receive nd display signals from a ransponder
SPONSES > RESPONSE
SPONSOR *same* S > RESPONSER
SPONSUM *n* written nswer from a rabbinic uthority to a question ubmitted
SPOOL *vb* rewind onto pool
SPOOLED > RESPOOL
SPOOLS > RESPOOL
SPOT *vb* (in billiards) eplace on one of the spots
SPOTS > RESPOT
SPOTTED > RESPOT
SPRANG > RESPRING
SPRAY *n* new coat of aint applied to a car, an, etc ▷ *vb* spray (a car, heels, etc) with a new oat of paint
SPRAYED > RESPRAY
SPRAYS > RESPRAY
SPREAD *vb* spread again
RESPREADS > RESPREAD
RESPRING *vb* put new springs in
RESPRINGS > RESPRING
RESPROUT *vb* sprout again
RESPROUTS > RESPROUT
RESPRUNG > RESPRING
RESSALDAR *n* native cavalry commander in mixed Anglo-Indian army
REST *n* freedom from exertion etc ▷ *vb* take a rest
RESTABLE *vb* put in stable again or elsewhere
RESTABLED > RESTABLE
RESTABLES > RESTABLE
RESTACK *vb* stack again
RESTACKED > RESTACK
RESTACKS > RESTACK
RESTAFF *vb* staff again
RESTAFFED > RESTAFF
RESTAFFS > RESTAFF
RESTAGE *vb* produce or perform a new production of (a play)
RESTAGED > RESTAGE
RESTAGES > RESTAGE
RESTAGING > RESTAGE
RESTAMP *vb* stamp again
RESTAMPED > RESTAMP
RESTAMPS > RESTAMP
RESTART *vb* commence (something) or set (something) in motion again ▷ *n* act or an instance of starting again
RESTARTED > RESTART
RESTARTER > RESTART
RESTARTS > RESTART
RESTATE *vb* state or affirm (something) again or in a different way
RESTATED > RESTATE
RESTATES > RESTATE
RESTATING > RESTATE
RESTATION *vb* station elsewhere
RESTED > REST
RESTEM *vb* stem again
RESTEMMED > RESTEM
RESTEMS > RESTEM
RESTER > REST
RESTERS > REST
RESTFUL *adj* relaxing or soothing
RESTFULLY > RESTFUL
RESTIER > RESTY
RESTIEST > RESTY
RESTIFF *same as* > RESTIVE
RESTIFORM *adj* (esp of bundles of nerve fibres) shaped like a cord or rope
RESTING > REST
RESTINGS > REST
RESTITCH *vb* stitch again
RESTITUTE *vb* restore
RESTIVE *adj* restless or impatient
RESTIVELY > RESTIVE
RESTLESS *adj* bored or dissatisfied
RESTO *n* restored antique, vintage car, etc
RESTOCK *vb* replenish stores or supplies
RESTOCKED > RESTOCK
RESTOCKS > RESTOCK
RESTOKE *vb* stoke again
RESTOKED > RESTOKE
RESTOKES > RESTOKE
RESTOKING > RESTOKE
RESTORAL *n* restoration
RESTORALS > RESTORAL
RESTORE *vb* return (a building, painting, etc) to its original condition
RESTORED > RESTORE
RESTORER > RESTORE
RESTORERS > RESTORE
RESTORES > RESTORE
RESTORING > RESTORE
RESTOS > RESTO
RESTRAIN *vb* hold (someone) back from action
RESTRAINS > RESTRAIN
RESTRAINT *n* something that restrains
RESTRESS *vb* stress again or differently
RESTRETCH *vb* stretch again
RESTRICT *vb* confine to certain limits
RESTRICTS > RESTRICT
RESTRIKE *vb* strike again
RESTRIKES > RESTRIKE
RESTRING *vb* string again or anew
RESTRINGE *vb* restrict
RESTRINGS > RESTRING
RESTRIVE *vb* strive again
RESTRIVEN > RESTRIVE
RESTRIVES > RESTRIVE
RESTROOM *n* room in a public building having lavatories, washing facilities, and sometimes couches
RESTROOMS > RESTROOM
RESTROVE > RESTRIVE
RESTRUCK > RESTRIKE
RESTRUNG > RESTRING
RESTS > REST
RESTUDIED > RESTUDY
RESTUDIES > RESTUDY
RESTUDY *vb* study again
RESTUFF *vb* put new stuffing in
RESTUFFED > RESTUFF
RESTUFFS > RESTUFF
RESTUMP *vb* Australian building term for provide with new stumps
RESTUMPED > RESTUMP
RESTUMPS > RESTUMP
RESTY *adj* restive
RESTYLE *vb* style again
RESTYLED > RESTYLE
RESTYLES > RESTYLE
RESTYLING > RESTYLE
RESUBJECT *vb* subject again
RESUBMIT *vb* submit again
RESUBMITS > RESUBMIT
RESULT *n* outcome or consequence ▷ *vb* be the outcome or consequence (of)
RESULTANT *adj* arising as a result ▷ *n* sum of two or more vectors, such as the force resulting from two or more forces acting on a single point
RESULTED > RESULT
RESULTFUL > RESULT
RESULTING > RESULT
RESULTS > RESULT
RESUMABLE > RESUME
RESUME *vb* begin again ▷ *n* summary
RESUMED > RESUME
RESUMER > RESUME
RESUMERS > RESUME
RESUMES > RESUME
RESUMING > RESUME
RESUMMON *vb* summon again
RESUMMONS > RESUMMON
RESUPINE *adj* lying on the back
RESUPPLY *vb* provide (with something) again
RESURFACE *vb* arise or occur again
RESURGE *vb* rise again from or as if from the dead
RESURGED > RESURGE
RESURGENT *adj* rising again, as to new life, vigour, etc
RESURGES > RESURGE
RESURGING > RESURGE
RESURRECT *vb* restore to life
RESURVEY *vb* survey again
RESURVEYS > RESURVEY
RESUSPEND *vb* put back into suspension
RESWALLOW *vb* swallow again
RET *vb* moisten or soak (flax, hemp, jute, etc) to promote bacterial action in order to facilitate separation of the fibres from the woody tissue by beating
RETABLE *n* ornamental screenlike structure above and behind an altar, esp one used as a setting for a religious picture or carving
RETABLES > RETABLE
RETACK *vb* tack again
RETACKED > RETACK
RETACKING > RETACK
RETACKLE *vb* tackle again
RETACKLED > RETACKLE
RETACKLES > RETACKLE
RETACKS > RETACK
RETAG *vb* tag again
RETAGGED > RETAG
RETAGGING > RETAG
RETAGS > RETAG
RETAIL *n* selling of goods individually or in small amounts to the public ▷ *adj* of or engaged in such

selling ▷ *adv* by retail ▷ *vb* sell or be sold retail
RETAILED > RETAIL
RETAILER > RETAIL
RETAILERS > RETAIL
RETAILING > RETAIL
RETAILOR *vb* tailor afresh
RETAILORS > RETAILOR
RETAILS > RETAIL
RETAIN *vb* keep in one's possession
RETAINED > RETAIN
RETAINER *n* fee to retain someone's services
RETAINERS > RETAINER
RETAINING > RETAIN
RETAINS > RETAIN
RETAKE *vb* recapture ▷ *n* act of rephotographing a scene
RETAKEN > RETAKE
RETAKER > RETAKE
RETAKERS > RETAKE
RETAKES > RETAKE
RETAKING > RETAKE
RETAKINGS > RETAKE
RETALIATE *vb* repay an injury or wrong in kind
RETALLIED > RETALLY
RETALLIES > RETALLY
RETALLY *vb* count up again
RETAMA *n* type of shrub
RETAMAS > RETAMA
RETAPE *vb* tape again
RETAPED > RETAPE
RETAPES > RETAPE
RETAPING > RETAPE
RETARD *vb* delay or slow (progress or development) ▷ *n* offensive term for a retarded person
RETARDANT *n* substance that reduces the rate of a chemical reaction ▷ *adj* having a slowing effect
RETARDATE *n* person who is retarded
RETARDED *adj* underdeveloped, esp mentally
RETARDER *n* person or thing that retards
RETARDERS > RETARDER
RETARDING > RETARD
RETARDS > RETARD
RETARGET *vb* target afresh or differently
RETARGETS > RETARGET
RETASTE *vb* taste again
RETASTED > RETASTE
RETASTES > RETASTE
RETASTING > RETASTE
RETAUGHT > RETEACH
RETAX *vb* tax again
RETAXED > RETAX
RETAXES > RETAX
RETAXING > RETAX
RETCH *vb* try to vomit ▷ *n* involuntary spasm of the stomach
RETCHED > RETCH
RETCHES > RETCH
RETCHING > RETCH
RETCHLESS *archaic variant of* > RECKLESS
RETE *n* any network of nerves or blood vessels
RETEACH *vb* teach again
RETEACHES > RETEACH
RETEAM *vb* team up again
RETEAMED > RETEAM
RETEAMING > RETEAM
RETEAMS > RETEAM
RETEAR *vb* tear again
RETEARING > RETEAR
RETEARS > RETEAR
RETELL *vb* relate (a story, etc) again or differently
RETELLER > RETELL
RETELLERS > RETELL
RETELLING > RETELL
RETELLS > RETELL
RETEM *n* type of shrub
RETEMPER *vb* temper again
RETEMPERS > RETEMPER
RETEMS > RETEM
RETENE *n* yellow crystalline hydrocarbon found in tar oils from pine wood and in certain fossil resins
RETENES > RETENE
RETENTION *n* retaining
RETENTIVE *adj* capable of retaining or remembering
RETES > RETE
RETEST *vb* test (something) again or differently
RETESTED > RETEST
RETESTIFY *vb* testify again
RETESTING > RETEST
RETESTS > RETEST
RETEXTURE *vb* restore natural texture to
RETHINK *vb* consider again, esp with a view to changing one's tactics ▷ *n* act or an instance of thinking again
RETHINKER > RETHINK
RETHINKS > RETHINK
RETHOUGHT > RETHINK
RETHREAD *vb* thread again
RETHREADS > RETHREAD
RETIA > RETE
RETIAL > RETE
RETIARII > RETIARIUS
RETIARIUS *n* (in ancient Rome) a gladiator armed with a net and trident
RETIARY *adj* of, relating to, or resembling a net or web
RETICELLA *n* form of lace
RETICENCE > RETICENT
RETICENCY > RETICENT
RETICENT *adj* uncommunicative, reserved
RETICLE *n* network of fine lines, wires, etc, placed in the focal plane of an optical instrument to assist measurement of the size or position of objects under observation
RETICLES > RETICLE
RETICULA > RETICULUM
RETICULAR *adj* in the form of a network or having a network of parts
RETICULE *same as* > RETICLE
RETICULES > RETICULE
RETICULUM *n* any fine network, esp one in the body composed of cells, fibres, etc
RETIE *vb* tie again
RETIED > RETIE
RETIEING > RETIE
RETIES > RETIE
RETIFORM *adj* netlike
RETIGHTEN *vb* tighten again
RETILE *vb* put new tiles in or on
RETILED > RETILE
RETILES > RETILE
RETILING > RETILE
RETIME *vb* time again or alter time of
RETIMED > RETIME
RETIMES > RETIME
RETIMING > RETIME
RETINA *n* light-sensitive membrane at the back of the eye
RETINAE > RETINA
RETINAL *adj* of or relating to the retina ▷ *n* aldehyde form of the polyene retinol (vitamin A) that associates with the protein opsin to form the visual purple pigment rhodopsin
RETINALS > RETINAL
RETINAS > RETINA
RETINE *n* chemical found in body cells that slows cell growth and division
RETINENE *n* aldehyde form of the polyene retinol (vitamin A) that associates with the protein opsin to form the visual purple pigment rhodopsin
RETINENES > RETINENE
RETINES > RETINE
RETINITE *n* any of various resins of fossil origin, esp one derived from lignite
RETINITES > RETINITE
RETINITIS *n* inflammation of the retina
RETINOID *adj* resinlike ▷ *n* derivative of vitamin A
RETINOIDS > RETINOID
RETINOL *n* another name for vitamin A and rosin oil
RETINOLS > RETINOL
RETINT *vb* tint again or change tint of
RETINTED > RETINT
RETINTING > RETINT
RETINTS > RETINT
RETINUE *n* band of attendants
RETINUED > RETINUE
RETINUES > RETINUE
RETINULA *n* part of the compound eye in certain arthropods
RETINULAE > RETINULA
RETINULAR > RETINULA
RETINULAS > RETINULA
RETIRACY *n* (in US Englis[h]) retirement
RETIRAL *n* act of retiring from office, one's work, e[tc]
RETIRALS > RETIRAL
RETIRANT *n* (in US Englis[h]) retired person
RETIRANTS > RETIRANT
RETIRE *vb* (cause to) give up office or work, esp through age
RETIRED *adj* having retir[ed] from work etc
RETIREDLY > RETIRED
RETIREE *n* person who h[as] retired from work
RETIREES > RETIREE
RETIRER > RETIRE
RETIRERS > RETIRE
RETIRES > RETIRE
RETIRING *adj* shy
RETITLE *vb* give a new title to
RETITLED > RETITLE
RETITLES > RETITLE
RETITLING > RETITLE
RETOLD > RETELL
RETOOK > RETAKE
RETOOL *vb* replace, re-equip, or rearrange the tools in (a factory, etc)
RETOOLED > RETOOL
RETOOLING > RETOOL
RETOOLS > RETOOL
RETORE > RETEAR
RETORN > RETEAR
RETORSION *n* retaliatory action taken by a state whose citizens have bee[n] mistreated by a foreign power by treating the subjects of that power similarly
RETORT *vb* reply quickly, wittily, or angrily ▷ *n* quick, witty, or angry rep[ly]
RETORTED > RETORT
RETORTER > RETORT
RETORTERS > RETORT
RETORTING > RETORT
RETORTION *n* act of retorting
RETORTIVE > RETORT
RETORTS > RETORT
RETOTAL *vb* add up again
RETOTALED > RETOTAL
RETOTALS > RETOTAL
RETOUCH *vb* restore or improve by new touches esp of paint ▷ *n* art or practice of retouching
RETOUCHED > RETOUCH
RETOUCHER > RETOUCH
RETOUCHES > RETOUCH
RETOUR *vb* (in Scottish la[w]) to return as heir
RETOURED > RETOUR
RETOURING > RETOUR
RETOURS > RETOUR
RETRACE *vb* go back over (a route etc) again
RETRACED > RETRACE

TRACER > RETRACE
TRACERS > RETRACE
TRACES > RETRACE
TRACING > RETRACE
TRACK *vb* track again
TRACKED > RETRACK
TRACKS > RETRACK
TRACT *vb* withdraw (a statement etc)
TRACTED > RETRACT
TRACTOR *n* any of various muscles that retract an organ or part
TRACTS > RETRACT
TRAICT *archaic form of* > RETREAT
TRAICTS > RETRAICT
TRAIN *vb* train to do a new or different job
TRAINED > RETRAIN
TRAINEE > RETRAIN
TRAINS > RETRAIN
ETRAIT *archaic form of* > RETREAT
ETRAITE *archaic form of* > RETREAT
ETRAITES > RETRAITE
ETRAITS > RETRAIT
ETRAITT *n* archaic word meaning portrait
ETRAITTS > RETRAITT
ETRAL *adj* at, near, or towards the back
ETRALLY > RETRAL
ETRATE *archaic form of* > RETREAT
ETRATED > RETRATE
ETRATES > RETRATE
ETRATING > RETRATE
ETREAD *n* remould ▷ *vb* remould tread again
ETREADED > RETREAD
ETREADS > RETREAD
ETREAT *vb* move back from a position, withdraw ▷ *n* act of or military signal for retiring or withdrawal
ETREATED > RETREAT
ETREATER > RETREAT
ETREATS > RETREAT
ETREE *n* imperfectly made paper
ETREES > RETREE
ETRENCH *vb* reduce expenditure, cut back
ETRIAL *n* second trial of a case or defendant in a court of law
ETRIALS > RETRIAL
ETRIBUTE *vb* give back
ETRIED > RETRY
ETRIES > RETRY
ETRIEVAL *n* act or process of retrieving
ETRIEVE *vb* fetch back again ▷ *n* chance of being retrieved
ETRIEVED > RETRIEVE
ETRIEVER *n* dog trained to retrieve shot game
ETRIEVES > RETRIEVE
ETRIM *vb* trim again
ETRIMMED > RETRIM
ETRIMS > RETRIM
RETRO *adj* associated with or revived from the past
RETROACT *vb* act in opposition
RETROACTS > RETROACT
RETROCEDE *vb* give back
RETROD > RETREAD
RETRODDEN > RETREAD
RETRODICT *vb* make surmises about the past using information from the present
RETROFIRE *n* act of firing a retrorocket
RETROFIT *vb* equip (a vehicle, piece of equipment, etc) with new parts, safety devices, etc, after manufacture
RETROFITS > RETROFIT
RETROFLEX *adj* bent or curved backwards
RETROJECT *vb* throw backwards (opposed to *project*)
RETRONYM *n* word coined for existing thing to distinguish it from new thing
RETRONYMS > RETRONYM
RETROPACK *n* system of retrorockets on a spacecraft
RETRORSE *adj* (esp of plant parts) pointing backwards or in a direction opposite to normal
RETROS > RETRO
RETROUSSE *adj* (of a nose) turned upwards
RETROVERT *vb* turn back
RETRY *vb* try again (a case already determined)
RETRYING > RETRY
RETS > RET
RETSINA *n* Greek wine flavoured with resin
RETSINAS > RETSINA
RETTED > RET
RETTERIES > RETTERY
RETTERY *n* flax-retting place
RETTING > RET
RETUND *vb* weaken or blunt
RETUNDED > RETUND
RETUNDING > RETUND
RETUNDS > RETUND
RETUNE *vb* tune (a musical instrument) differently or again
RETUNED > RETUNE
RETUNES > RETUNE
RETUNING > RETUNE
RETURF *vb* turf again
RETURFED > RETURF
RETURFING > RETURF
RETURFS > RETURF
RETURN *vb* go or come back ▷ *n* returning ▷ *adj* of or being a return
RETURNED > RETURN
RETURNEE *n* person who returns to his native country, esp after war service
RETURNEES > RETURNEE
RETURNER *n* person or thing that returns
RETURNERS > RETURNER
RETURNIK *n* someone returning or intending to return to their native land, especially when this is in the former Soviet Union
RETURNIKS > RETURNIK
RETURNING > RETURN
RETURNS > RETURN
RETUSE *adj* having a rounded apex and a central depression
RETWIST *vb* twist again
RETWISTED > RETWIST
RETWISTS > RETWIST
RETYING > RETIE
RETYPE *vb* type again
RETYPED > RETYPE
RETYPES > RETYPE
RETYPING > RETYPE
REUNIFIED > REUNIFY
REUNIFIES > REUNIFY
REUNIFY *vb* bring together again something previously divided
REUNION *n* meeting of people who have been apart
REUNIONS > REUNION
REUNITE *vb* bring or come together again after a separation
REUNITED > REUNITE
REUNITER > REUNITE
REUNITERS > REUNITE
REUNITES > REUNITE
REUNITING > REUNITE
REUPTAKE *vb* absorb again
REUPTAKES > REUPTAKE
REURGE *vb* urge again
REURGED > REURGE
REURGES > REURGE
REURGING > REURGE
REUSABLE *adj* able to be used more than once
REUSABLES *pl n* products which can be used more than once
REUSE *vb* use again ▷ *n* act of using something again
REUSED > REUSE
REUSES > REUSE
REUSING > REUSE
REUTILISE *same as* > REUTILIZE
REUTILIZE *vb* utilize again
REUTTER *vb* utter again
REUTTERED > REUTTER
REUTTERS > REUTTER
REV *n* revolution (of an engine) ▷ *vb* increase the speed of revolution of (an engine)
REVALENTA *n* lentil flour
REVALUATE *same as* > REVALUE
REVALUE *vb* adjust the exchange value of (a currency) upwards
REVALUED > REVALUE
REVALUES > REVALUE
REVALUING > REVALUE
REVAMP *vb* renovate or restore ▷ *n* something that has been renovated or revamped
REVAMPED > REVAMP
REVAMPER > REVAMP
REVAMPERS > REVAMP
REVAMPING > REVAMP
REVAMPS > REVAMP
REVANCHE *n* revenge
REVANCHES > REVANCHE
REVARNISH *vb* varnish again
REVEAL *vb* make known ▷ *n* vertical side of an opening in a wall, esp the side of a window or door between the frame and the front of the wall
REVEALED > REVEAL
REVEALER > REVEAL
REVEALERS > REVEAL
REVEALING *adj* disclosing information that one did not know
REVEALS > REVEAL
REVEHENT *adj* (in anatomy) carrying back
REVEILLE *n* morning bugle call to waken soldiers
REVEILLES > REVEILLE
REVEL *vb* take pleasure (in) ▷ *n* occasion of noisy merrymaking
REVELATOR *n* revealer
REVELED > REVEL
REVELER > REVEL
REVELERS > REVEL
REVELING > REVEL
REVELLED > REVEL
REVELLER > REVEL
REVELLERS > REVEL
REVELLING > REVEL
REVELMENT > REVEL
REVELRIES > REVELRY
REVELROUS > REVELRY
REVELRY *n* festivity
REVELS > REVEL
REVENANT *n* something, esp a ghost, that returns
REVENANTS > REVENANT
REVENGE *n* retaliation for wrong done ▷ *vb* make retaliation for
REVENGED > REVENGE
REVENGER > REVENGE
REVENGERS > REVENGE
REVENGES > REVENGE
REVENGING > REVENGE
REVENGIVE > REVENGE
REVENUAL > REVENUE
REVENUE *n* income, esp of a state
REVENUED > REVENUE
REVENUER *n* revenue officer or cutter
REVENUERS > REVENUER
REVENUES > REVENUE
REVERABLE > REVERE
REVERB *n* electronic device that creates artificial acoustics ▷ *vb*

reverberate
REVERBED > REVERB
REVERBING > REVERB
REVERBS > REVERB
REVERE *vb* be in awe of and respect greatly
REVERED > REVERE
REVERENCE *n* awe mingled with respect and esteem
REVEREND *adj* worthy of reverence ▷ *n* clergyman
REVERENDS > REVEREND
REVERENT *adj* showing reverence
REVERER > REVERE
REVERERS > REVERE
REVERES > REVERE
REVERIE *n* absent-minded daydream
REVERIES > REVERIE
REVERIFY *vb* verify again
REVERING > REVERE
REVERIST *n* someone given to reveries
REVERISTS > REVERIST
REVERS *n* turned back part of a garment, such as the lapel
REVERSAL *n* act or an instance of reversing
REVERSALS > REVERSAL
REVERSE *vb* turn upside down or the other way round ▷ *n* opposite ▷ *adj* opposite or contrary
REVERSED > REVERSE
REVERSELY > REVERSE
REVERSER > REVERSE
REVERSERS > REVERSE
REVERSES > REVERSE
REVERSI *n* game played on a draughtboard with 64 pieces, black on one side and white on the other. When pieces are captured they are turned over to join the capturing player's forces
REVERSING > REVERSE
REVERSION *n* return to a former state, practice, or belief
REVERSIS *n* type of card game
REVERSO *another name for* > VERSO
REVERSOS > REVERSO
REVERT *vb* return to a former state
REVERTANT *n* mutant that has reverted to an earlier form ▷ *adj* having mutated to an earlier form
REVERTED > REVERT
REVERTER > REVERT
REVERTERS > REVERT
REVERTING > REVERT
REVERTIVE > REVERT
REVERTS > REVERT
REVERY *same as* > REVERIE
REVEST *vb* restore (former power, authority, status, etc, to a person) or (of power, authority, etc) to be restored
REVESTED > REVEST
REVESTING > REVEST
REVESTRY *same as* > VESTRY
REVESTS > REVEST
REVET *vb* face (a wall or embankment) with stones
REVETMENT *n* facing of stones, sandbags, etc, to protect a wall, embankment, or earthworks
REVETS > REVET
REVETTED > REVET
REVETTING > REVET
REVEUR *n* daydreamer
REVEURS > REVEUR
REVEUSE *n* female daydreamer
REVEUSES > REVEUSE
REVIBRATE *vb* vibrate again
REVICTUAL *vb* victual again
REVIE *vb* archaic cards term meaning challenge by placing a larger stake
REVIED > REVIE
REVIES > REVIE
REVIEW *n* critical assessment of a book, concert, etc ▷ *vb* hold or write a review of
REVIEWAL *same as* > REVIEW
REVIEWALS > REVIEWAL
REVIEWED > REVIEW
REVIEWER > REVIEW
REVIEWERS > REVIEW
REVIEWING > REVIEW
REVIEWS > REVIEW
REVILE *vb* be abusively scornful of
REVILED > REVILE
REVILER > REVILE
REVILERS > REVILE
REVILES > REVILE
REVILING > REVILE
REVILINGS > REVILE
REVIOLATE *vb* violate again
REVISABLE > REVISE
REVISAL > REVISE
REVISALS > REVISE
REVISE *vb* change or alter ▷ *n* act, process, or result of revising
REVISED > REVISE
REVISER > REVISE
REVISERS > REVISE
REVISES > REVISE
REVISING > REVISE
REVISION *n* act of revising
REVISIONS > REVISION
REVISIT *vb* visit again
REVISITED > REVISIT
REVISITS > REVISIT
REVISOR > REVISE
REVISORS > REVISE
REVISORY *adj* of or having the power of revision
REVIVABLE > REVIVE
REVIVABLY > REVIVE
REVIVAL *n* reviving or renewal
REVIVALS > REVIVAL
REVIVE *vb* bring or come back to life, vigour, use, etc
REVIVED > REVIVE
REVIVER > REVIVE
REVIVERS > REVIVE
REVIVES > REVIVE
REVIVIFY *vb* give new life to
REVIVING > REVIVE
REVIVINGS > REVIVE
REVIVOR *n* means of reviving a lawsuit that has been suspended owing to the death or marriage of one of the parties
REVIVORS > REVIVOR
REVOCABLE *adj* capable of being revoked
REVOCABLY > REVOCABLE
REVOICE *vb* utter again
REVOICED > REVOICE
REVOICES > REVOICE
REVOICING > REVOICE
REVOKABLE *same as* > REVOCABLE
REVOKABLY > REVOCABLE
REVOKE *vb* cancel (a will, agreement, etc) ▷ *n* act of revoking
REVOKED > REVOKE
REVOKER > REVOKE
REVOKERS > REVOKE
REVOKES > REVOKE
REVOKING > REVOKE
REVOLT *n* uprising against authority ▷ *vb* rise in rebellion
REVOLTED > REVOLT
REVOLTER > REVOLT
REVOLTERS > REVOLT
REVOLTING *adj* disgusting, horrible
REVOLTS > REVOLT
REVOLUTE *adj* (esp of the margins of a leaf) rolled backwards and downwards
REVOLVE *vb* turn round, rotate ▷ *n* circular section of a stage that can be rotated by electric power to provide a scene change
REVOLVED > REVOLVE
REVOLVER *n* repeating pistol
REVOLVERS > REVOLVER
REVOLVES > REVOLVE
REVOLVING *adj* denoting or relating to an engine, such as a radial aero engine, in which the cylinders revolve about a fixed shaft
REVOTE *vb* decide or grant again by a new vote
REVOTED > REVOTE
REVOTES > REVOTE
REVOTING > REVOTE
REVS > REV
REVUE *n* theatrical entertainment with topical sketches and songs
REVUES > REVUE
REVUIST > REVUE
REVUISTS > REVUE
REVULSED *adj* filled with disgust
REVULSION *n* strong disgust
REVULSIVE *adj* of or causing revulsion ▷ *n* counterirritant
REVVED > REV
REVVING > REV
REVYING > REVIE
REW *archaic spelling of* > RU[E]
REWAKE *vb* awaken again
REWAKED > REWAKE
REWAKEN *vb* awaken agai[n]
REWAKENED > REWAKEN
REWAKENS > REWAKEN
REWAKES > REWAKE
REWAKING > REWAKE
REWAN *archaic past form of* > REWIN
REWARD *n* something give[n] in return for a service ▷ *v[b]* pay or give something to (someone) for a service, information, etc
REWARDED > REWARD
REWARDER > REWARD
REWARDERS > REWARD
REWARDFUL > REWARD
REWARDING *adj* giving personal satisfaction, worthwhile
REWARDS > REWARD
REWAREWA *n* New Zealand tree
REWAREWAS > REWAREWA
REWARM *vb* warm again
REWARMED > REWARM
REWARMING > REWARM
REWARMS > REWARM
REWASH *vb* wash again
REWASHED > REWASH
REWASHES > REWASH
REWASHING > REWASH
REWAX *vb* wax again
REWAXED > REWAX
REWAXES > REWAX
REWAXING > REWAX
REWEAR *vb* wear again
REWEARING > REWEAR
REWEARS > REWEAR
REWEAVE *vb* weave again
REWEAVED > REWEAVE
REWEAVES > REWEAVE
REWEAVING > REWEAVE
REWED *vb* wed again
REWEDDED > REWED
REWEDDING > REWED
REWEDS > REWED
REWEIGH *vb* weigh again
REWEIGHED > REWEIGH
REWEIGHS > REWEIGH
REWELD *vb* weld again
REWELDED > REWELD
REWELDING > REWELD
REWELDS > REWELD
REWET *vb* wet again
REWETS > REWET
REWETTED > REWET
REWETTING > REWET
REWIDEN *vb* widen again
REWIDENED > REWIDEN
REWIDENS > REWIDEN

WIN *vb* win again
WIND *vb* wind again
WINDED > REWIND
WINDER > REWIND
WINDERS > REWIND
WINDING > REWIND
WINDS > REWIND
WINNING > REWIN
WINS > REWIN
WIRABLE > REWIRE
WIRE *vb* provide (a ouse, engine, etc) with ew wiring
WIRED > REWIRE
WIRES > REWIRE
WIRING > REWIRE
WOKE > REWAKE
WOKEN > REWAKE
WON > REWIN
WORD *vb* alter the vording of
WORDED > REWORD
WORDING > REWORD
WORDS > REWORD
WORE > REWEAR
WORK *vb* improve or bring p to date
WORKED > REWORK
WORKING > REWORK
WORKS > REWORK
WORN > REWEAR
WOUND > REWIND
WOVE > REWEAVE
WOVEN > REWEAVE
WRAP *vb* wrap again
WRAPPED > REWRAP
WRAPS > REWRAP
WRAPT > REWRAP
WRITE *vb* write again n a different way ▷ *n* omething rewritten
WRITER > REWRITE
WRITERS > REWRITE
WRITES > REWRITE
WRITING > REWRITE
WRITTEN > REWRITE
WROTE > REWRITE
WROUGHT > REWORK
WS > REW
WTH *archaic variant* f > RUTH
WTHS > REWTH
X *n* king
XES > REX
XINE *n* tradename for a orm of artificial leather
XINES > REXINE
YNARD *n* fox
YNARDS > REYNARD
Z *n* informal word for n instance of reserving; eservation
ZERO *vb* reset to zero
ZEROED > REZERO
ZEROES > REZERO
ZEROING > REZERO
ZEROS > REZERO
ZONE *vb* zone again
ZONED > REZONE
ZONES > REZONE
ZONING > REZONE
ZZES > REZ
ABDOID *adj* rod-shaped ▷ *n* rod-shaped structure found in cells of some plants and animals
RHABDOIDS > RHABDOID
RHABDOM *n* (in insect anatomy) any of many similar rodlike structures found in the eye
RHABDOMAL > RHABDOM
RHABDOME *same as* > RHABDOM
RHABDOMES > RHABDOME
RHABDOMS > RHABDOM
RHABDUS *n* sponge spicule
RHABDUSES > RHABDUS
RHACHIAL > RACHIS
RHACHIDES > RHACHIS
RHACHILLA *same as* > RACHILLA
RHACHIS *same as* > RACHIS
RHACHISES > RHACHIS
RHACHITIS *same as* > RACHITIS
RHAGADES *pl n* cracks found in the skin
RHAMNOSE *n* type of plant sugar
RHAMNOSES > RHAMNOSE
RHAMNUS *n* buckthorn
RHAMNUSES > RHAMNUS
RHAMPHOID *adj* beaklike
RHANJA *n* Indian English word for a male lover
RHANJAS > RHANJA
RHAPHAE > RHAPHE
RHAPHE *same as* > RAPHE
RHAPHES > RHAPHE
RHAPHIDE *same as* > RAPHIDE
RHAPHIDES > RHAPHIDE
RHAPHIS *same as* > RAPHIDE
RHAPONTIC *n* rhubarb
RHAPSODE *n* (in ancient Greece) professional reciter of poetry
RHAPSODES > RHAPSODE
RHAPSODIC *adj* of or like a rhapsody
RHAPSODY *n* freely structured emotional piece of music
RHATANIES > RHATANY
RHATANY *n* South American leguminous shrub
RHEA *n* S American three-toed ostrich
RHEAS > RHEA
RHEBOK *n* woolly brownish-grey southern African antelope
RHEBOKS > RHEBOK
RHEMATIC *adj* of or relating to word formation
RHEME *n* constituent of a sentence that adds most new information, in addition to what has already been said in the discourse. The rheme is usually, but not always, associated with the subject
RHEMES > RHEME
RHENIUM *n* silvery-white metallic element with a high melting point
RHENIUMS > RHENIUM
RHEOBASE *n* minimum nerve impulse required to elicit a response from a tissue
RHEOBASES > RHEOBASE
RHEOBASIC > RHEOBASE
RHEOCHORD *n* wire inserted into an electrical circuit to vary or regulate the current
RHEOCORD *same as* > RHEOCHORD
RHEOCORDS > RHEOCORD
RHEOLOGIC > RHEOLOGY
RHEOLOGY *n* branch of physics concerned with the flow and change of shape of matter
RHEOMETER *n* instrument for measuring the velocity of the blood flow
RHEOMETRY > RHEOMETER
RHEOPHIL *adj* liking flowing water
RHEOSTAT *n* instrument for varying the resistance of an electrical circuit
RHEOSTATS > RHEOSTAT
RHEOTAXES > RHEOTAXIS
RHEOTAXIS *n* movement of an organism towards or away from a current of water
RHEOTOME *n* interrupter
RHEOTOMES > RHEOTOME
RHEOTROPE *n* electric-current-reversing device
RHESUS *n* macaque monkey
RHESUSES > RHESUS
RHETOR *n* teacher of rhetoric
RHETORIC *n* art of effective speaking or writing
RHETORICS > RHETORIC
RHETORISE *same as* > RHETORIZE
RHETORIZE *vb* make use of rhetoric
RHETORS > RHETOR
RHEUM *n* watery discharge from the eyes or nose
RHEUMATIC *adj* (person) affected by rheumatism ▷ *n* person suffering from rheumatism
RHEUMATIZ *n* dialect word meaning rheumatism, any painful disorder of joints, muscles, or connective tissue
RHEUMED *adj* rheumy
RHEUMIC *adj* of or relating to rheum
RHEUMIER > RHEUMY
RHEUMIEST > RHEUMY
RHEUMS > RHEUM
RHEUMY *adj* of the nature of rheum
RHEXES > RHEXIS
RHEXIS *n* rupture
RHEXISES > RHEXIS
RHIES > RHY
RHIGOLENE *n* volatile liquid obtained from petroleum and used as a local anaesthetic
RHIME *old spelling of* > RHYME
RHIMES > RHIME
RHINAL *adj* of or relating to the nose
RHINE *n* dialect word for a ditch
RHINES > RHINE
RHINITIC > RHINITIS
RHINITIS *n* inflammation of the mucous membrane that lines the nose
RHINO *n* rhinoceros
RHINOCERI *n* rhinoceroses
RHINOLITH *n* calculus formed in the nose
RHINOLOGY *n* branch of medical science concerned with the nose and its diseases
RHINOS > RHINO
RHIPIDATE *adj* shaped like a fan
RHIPIDION *n* fan found in Greek Orthodox churches
RHIPIDIUM *n* on a plant, a fan-shaped arrangement of flowers
RHIZIC *adj* of or relating to the root of an equation
RHIZINE *same as* > RHIZOID
RHIZINES > RHIZINE
RHIZOBIA > RHIZOBIUM
RHIZOBIAL > RHIZOBIUM
RHIZOBIUM *n* any rod-shaped bacterium of the genus *Rhizobium*, typically occurring in the root nodules of leguminous plants
RHIZOCARP *n* plant that fruits underground or whose root remains intact while the leaves die off annually
RHIZOCAUL *n* rootlike stem
RHIZOID *n* any of various slender hairlike structures that function as roots in the gametophyte generation of mosses, ferns, and related plants
RHIZOIDAL > RHIZOID
RHIZOIDS > RHIZOID
RHIZOMA *same as* > RHIZOME
RHIZOMATA > RHIZOMA
RHIZOME *n* thick underground stem producing new plants
RHIZOMES > RHIZOME
RHIZOMIC > RHIZOME
RHIZOPI > RHIZOPUS
RHIZOPOD *n* any protozoan of the phylum *Rhizopoda*, characterized by naked protoplasmic processes (pseudopodia). The group includes the amoebas

▷ *adj* of, relating to, or belonging to the *Rhizopoda*
RHIZOPODS > RHIZOPOD
RHIZOPUS *n* any zygomycetous fungus of the genus *Rhizopus*, esp *R. nigricans*, a bread mould
RHIZOTOMY *n* surgical incision into the roots of spinal nerves, esp for the relief of pain
RHO *n* 17th letter in the Greek alphabet, a consonant transliterated as *r* or *rh*
RHODAMIN *same as* > RHODAMINE
RHODAMINE *n* any one of a group of synthetic red or pink basic dyestuffs used for wool and silk. They are made from phthalic anhydride and aminophenols
RHODAMINS > RHODAMIN
RHODANATE *n* sulphocyanate
RHODANIC *adj* of or relating to sulphocyanic acid
RHODANISE *same as* > RHODANIZE
RHODANIZE *vb* plate with rhodium
RHODIC *adj* of or containing rhodium, esp in the tetravalent state
RHODIE *same as* > RHODY
RHODIES > RHODY
RHODINAL *n* substance with a lemon-like smell found esp in citronella and certain eucalyptus oils
RHODINALS > RHODINAL
RHODIUM *n* hard metallic element
RHODIUMS > RHODIUM
RHODOLITE *n* pale violet or red variety of garnet, used as a gemstone
RHODONITE *n* brownish translucent mineral
RHODOPSIN *n* red pigment in the rods of the retina in vertebrates. It is dissociated by light into retinene, the light energy being converted into nerve signals, and is re-formed in the dark
RHODORA *n* type of shrub
RHODORAS > RHODORA
RHODOUS *adj* of or containing rhodium (but proportionally more than a rhodic compound)
RHODY *n* rhododendron
RHOEADINE *n* alkaloid found in the poppy
RHOMB *same as* > RHOMBUS
RHOMBI > RHOMBUS
RHOMBIC *adj* relating to or having the shape of a rhombus
RHOMBICAL *same as* > RHOMBIC
RHOMBOI > RHOMBOS
RHOMBOID *n* parallelogram with adjacent sides of unequal length ▷ *adj* having such a shape
RHOMBOIDS > RHOMBOID
RHOMBOS *n* wooden slat attached to a thong that makes a roaring sound when the thong is whirled
RHOMBS > RHOMB
RHOMBUS *n* parallelogram with sides of equal length but no right angles, diamond-shaped figure
RHOMBUSES > RHOMBUS
RHONCHAL > RHONCHUS
RHONCHI > RHONCHUS
RHONCHIAL > RHONCHUS
RHONCHUS *n* rattling or whistling respiratory sound resembling snoring, caused by secretions in the trachea or bronchi
RHONE *same as* > RONE
RHONES > RHONE
RHOPALIC *adj* describes verse in which each successive word has one more syllable than the word before
RHOPALISM > RHOPALIC
RHOS > RHO
RHOTACISE *same as* > RHOTACIZE
RHOTACISM *n* excessive use or idiosyncratic pronunciation of *r*
RHOTACIST > RHOTACISM
RHOTACIZE *vb* pronounce *r* excessively or idiosyncratically
RHOTIC *adj* denoting or speaking a dialect of English in which postvocalic *r*s are pronounced
RHOTICITY > RHOTIC
RHUBARB *n* garden plant of which the fleshy stalks are cooked as fruit ▷ *interj* noise made by actors to simulate conversation, esp by repeating the word *rhubarb* ▷ *vb* simulate conversation in this way
RHUBARBED > RHUBARB
RHUBARBS > RHUBARB
RHUBARBY > RHUBARB
RHUMB as in *rhumb line* imaginary line on the surface of a sphere, such as the earth, that intersects all meridians at the same angle
RHUMBA *same as* > RUMBA
RHUMBAED > RHUMBA
RHUMBAING > RHUMBA
RHUMBAS > RHUMBA
RHUMBS > RHUMB
RHUS *n* genus of shrubs and small trees, several species of which are cultivated as ornamentals for their colourful autumn foliage
RHUSES > RHUS
RHY *archaic spelling of* > RYE
RHYME *n* sameness of the final sounds at the ends of lines of verse, or in words ▷ *vb* make a rhyme
RHYMED > RHYME
RHYMELESS > RHYME
RHYMER *same as* > RHYMESTER
RHYMERS > RHYMER
RHYMES > RHYME
RHYMESTER *n* mediocre poet
RHYMING > RHYME
RHYMIST > RHYME
RHYMISTS > RHYME
RHYNE *same as* > RHINE
RHYNES > RHYNE
RHYOLITE *n* fine-grained igneous rock consisting of quartz, feldspars, and mica or amphibole. It is the volcanic equivalent of granite
RHYOLITES > RHYOLITE
RHYOLITIC > RHYOLITE
RHYTA > RHYTON
RHYTHM *n* any regular movement or beat
RHYTHMAL *adj* rhythmic
RHYTHMED > RHYTHM
RHYTHMI > RHYTHMUS
RHYTHMIC *adj* of, relating to, or characterized by rhythm, as in movement or sound
RHYTHMICS *n* study of rhythmic movement
RHYTHMISE *same as* > RHYTHMIZE
RHYTHMIST *n* person who has a good sense of rhythm
RHYTHMIZE *vb* make rhythmic
RHYTHMS > RHYTHM
RHYTHMUS *n* rhythm
RHYTIDOME *n* bark
RHYTINA *n* type of sea cow
RHYTINAS > RHYTINA
RHYTON *n* (in ancient Greece) a horn-shaped drinking vessel with a hole in the pointed end through which to drink
RHYTONS > RHYTON
RIA *n* long narrow inlet of the seacoast, being a former valley that was submerged by a rise in the level of the sea. Rias are found esp on the coasts of SW Ireland and NW Spain
RIAL *n* standard monetary unit of Iran
RIALS > RIAL
RIALTO *n* market or exchange
RIALTOS > RIALTO
RIANCIES > RIANT
RIANCY > RIANT
RIANT *adj* laughing
RIANTLY > RIANT
RIAS > RIA
RIATA *same as* > REATA
RIATAS > RIATA
RIB *n* one of the curved bones forming the framework of the upper part of the body ▷ *vb* provide or mark with rib
RIBA *n* (in Islam) interest or usury, as forbidden by the Koran
RIBALD *adj* humorously c mockingly rude or obsce ▷ *n* ribald person
RIBALDLY > RIBALD
RIBALDRY *n* ribald language or behaviour
RIBALDS > RIBALD
RIBAND *n* ribbon awarde for some achievement
RIBANDS > RIBAND
RIBAS > RIBA
RIBATTUTA *n* (in music) type of trill
RIBAUD *archaic variant of* > RIBALD
RIBAUDRED *archaic varian of* > RIBALD
RIBAUDRY *archaic variant of* > RIBALDRY
RIBAUDS > RIBAUD
RIBAVIRIN *n* type of antiviral drug
RIBBAND *same as* > RIBAN
RIBBANDS > RIBBAND
RIBBED > RIB
RIBBER *n* someone who ribs
RIBBERS > RIBBER
RIBBIER > RIBBY
RIBBIEST > RIBBY
RIBBING > RIB
RIBBINGS > RIB
RIBBON *n* narrow band o fabric used for trimming tying, etc ▷ *vb* adorn wi a ribbon or ribbons
RIBBONED > RIBBON
RIBBONING > RIBBON
RIBBONRY *n* ribbons or ribbon work
RIBBONS > RIBBON
RIBBONY > RIBBON
RIBBY *adj* with noticeabl ribs
RIBCAGE *n* bony structur of ribs enclosing the lun
RIBCAGES > RIBCAGE
RIBES *n* genus of shrubs that includes currants
RIBGRASS *same as* > RIBWORT
RIBIBE *n* rebeck
RIBIBES > RIBIBE
RIBIBLE *same as* > RIBIBE
RIBIBLES > RIBIBLE
RIBIER *n* variety of grap
RIBIERS > RIBIER
RIBLESS > RIB
RIBLET *n* small rib
RIBLETS > RIBLET
RIBLIKE > RIB
RIBOSE *n* pentose sugar

ıat is an isomeric form of
rabinose and that occurs
ı RNA and riboflavin
BOSES > RIBOSE
BOSOMAL > RIBOSOME
BOSOME *n* any of
umerous minute
articles in the cytoplasm
f cells, either free
r attached to the
ndoplasmic reticulum,
ıat contain RNA and
rotein and are the site of
rotein synthesis
BOSOMES > RIBOSOME
BOZYMAL > RIBOZYME
BOZYME *n* RNA molecule
apable of catalysing a
hemical reaction, usually
ıe cleavage of another
NA molecule
BOZYMES > RIBOZYME
BS > RIB
BSTON *n* variety of apple
BSTONE *same*
s > RIBSTON
BSTONES > RIBSTONE
BSTONS > RIBSTON
BWORK *n* work or
tructure involving ribs
BWORKS > RIBWORK
BWORT *n* Eurasian plant
rith lancelike ribbed
eaves and a dense spike of
mall white flowers
BWORTS > RIBWORT
CE *n* cereal plant
rown on wet ground
ı warm countries ▷ *vb*
eve (potatoes or other
egetables) to a coarse
ıashed consistency
CEBIRD *n* any of various
irds frequenting rice
elds, esp the Java sparrow
CEBIRDS > RICEBIRD
CED > RICE
CER *n* kitchen utensil
rith small holes through
rhich cooked potatoes
nd similar soft foods are
ressed to form a coarse
ıash
CERCAR *same*
s > RICERCARE
CERCARE *n* elaborate
olyphonic composition
ıaking extensive use of
ontrapuntal imitation
nd usually very slow in
empo
CERCARI > RICERCARE
CERCARS > RICERCAR
CERCATA *same*
s > RICERCARE
CERS > RICER
CES > RICE
CEY *adj* resembling or
ontaining rice
CH *adj* owning a lot
f money or property,
realthy ▷ *vb* (in archaic
sage) enrich
CHED > RICH

RICHEN *vb* enrich
RICHENED > RICHEN
RICHENING > RICHEN
RICHENS > RICHEN
RICHER > RICH
RICHES *pl n* wealth
RICHESSE *n* wealth or richness
RICHESSES > RICHESSE
RICHEST > RICH
RICHING > RICH
RICHLY *adv* elaborately
RICHNESS *n* state or quality of being rich
RICHT *adj, adv, n, vb* right
RICHTED > RICHT
RICHTER > RICHT
RICHTEST > RICHT
RICHTING > RICHT
RICHTS > RICHT
RICHWEED *n* type of plant
RICHWEEDS > RICHWEED
RICIER > RICY
RICIEST > RICY
RICIN *n* highly toxic protein, a lectin, derived from castor-oil seeds: used in experimental cancer therapy
RICING > RICE
RICINS > RICIN
RICINUS *n* genus of plants
RICINUSES > RICINUS
RICK *n* stack of hay etc ▷ *vb* wrench or sprain (a joint)
RICKED > RICK
RICKER *n* young kauri tree of New Zealand
RICKERS > RICKER
RICKETIER > RICKETY
RICKETILY > RICKETY
RICKETS *n* disease of children marked by softening of the bones, bow legs, etc, caused by vitamin D deficiency
RICKETTY *same as* > RICKETY
RICKETY *adj* shaky or unstable
RICKEY *n* cocktail consisting of gin or vodka, lime juice, and soda water, served iced
RICKEYS > RICKEY
RICKING > RICK
RICKLE *n* unsteady or shaky structure, esp a dilapidated building
RICKLES > RICKLE
RICKLY *adj* archaic word for run-down or rickety
RICKRACK *n* zigzag braid used for trimming
RICKRACKS > RICKRACK
RICKS > RICK
RICKSHA *same as* > RICKSHAW
RICKSHAS > RICKSHA
RICKSHAW *n* light two-wheeled man-drawn Asian vehicle
RICKSHAWS > RICKSHAW
RICKSTAND *n* platform on which to put a rick
RICKSTICK *n* tool used when making hayricks
RICKYARD *n* place where hayricks are put
RICKYARDS > RICKYARD
RICOCHET *vb* (of a bullet) rebound from a solid surface ▷ *n* such a rebound
RICOCHETS > RICOCHET
RICOTTA *n* soft white unsalted Italian cheese made from sheep's milk
RICOTTAS > RICOTTA
RICRAC *same as* > RICKRACK
RICRACS > RICRAC
RICTAL > RICTUS
RICTUS *n* gape or cleft of an open mouth or beak
RICTUSES > RICTUS
RICY *same as* > RICEY
RID *vb* clear or relieve (of)
RIDABLE > RIDE
RIDDANCE *n* act of getting rid of something undesirable or unpleasant
RIDDANCES > RIDDANCE
RIDDED > RID
RIDDEN > RIDE
RIDDER > RID
RIDDERS > RID
RIDDING > RID
RIDDLE *n* question made puzzling to test one's ingenuity ▷ *vb* speak in riddles
RIDDLED > RIDDLE
RIDDLER > RIDDLE
RIDDLERS > RIDDLE
RIDDLES > RIDDLE
RIDDLING > RIDDLE
RIDDLINGS > RIDDLE
RIDE *vb* sit on and control or propel (a horse, bicycle, etc) ▷ *n* journey on a horse etc, or in a vehicle
RIDEABLE > RIDE
RIDENT *adj* laughing, smiling, or gay
RIDER *n* person who rides
RIDERED > RIDER
RIDERLESS > RIDER
RIDERS > RIDER
RIDERSHIP > RIDER
RIDES > RIDE
RIDGE *n* long narrow hill ▷ *vb* form into a ridge or ridges
RIDGEBACK as in *Rhodesian ridgeback* large short-haired breed of dog characterized by a ridge of hair growing along the back in the opposite direction to the rest of the coat
RIDGED > RIDGE
RIDGEL *same as* > RIDGELING
RIDGELIKE > RIDGE
RIDGELINE *n* ridge
RIDGELING *n* domestic male animal with one or both testicles undescended, esp a horse
RIDGELS > RIDGEL
RIDGEPOLE *n* timber along the ridge of a roof, to which the rafters are attached
RIDGER *n* plough used to form furrows and ridges
RIDGERS > RIDGER
RIDGES > RIDGE
RIDGETOP *n* summit of ridge
RIDGETOPS > RIDGETOP
RIDGETREE *another name for* > RIDGEPOLE
RIDGEWAY *n* road or track along a ridge, esp one of great antiquity
RIDGEWAYS > RIDGEWAY
RIDGIER > RIDGE
RIDGIEST > RIDGE
RIDGIL *same as* > RIDGELING
RIDGILS > RIDGIL
RIDGING > RIDGE
RIDGINGS > RIDGE
RIDGLING *same as* > RIDGELING
RIDGLINGS > RIDGLING
RIDGY > RIDGE
RIDICULE *n* treatment of a person or thing as ridiculous ▷ *vb* laugh at, make fun of
RIDICULED > RIDICULE
RIDICULER > RIDICULE
RIDICULES > RIDICULE
RIDING > RIDE
RIDINGS > RIDE
RIDLEY *n* marine turtle
RIDLEYS > RIDLEY
RIDOTTO *n* entertainment with music and dancing, often in masquerade: popular in 18th-century England
RIDOTTOS > RIDOTTO
RIDS > RID
RIEL *n* standard monetary unit of Cambodia, divided into 100 sen
RIELS > RIEL
RIEM *n* strip of hide
RIEMPIE *n* leather thong or lace used mainly to make chair seats
RIEMPIES > RIEMPIE
RIEMS > RIEM
RIESLING *n* type of white wine
RIESLINGS > RIESLING
RIEVE *n* archaic word for rob or plunder
RIEVER *n* archaic word for robber or plunderer
RIEVERS > RIEVER
RIEVES > RIEVE
RIEVING > RIEVE
RIF *vb* lay off
RIFAMPIN *n* drug used in the treatment of tuberculosis, meningitis, and leprosy
RIFAMPINS > RIFAMPIN

RIFAMYCIN *n* antibiotic
RIFE *adj* widespread or common
RIFELY > RIFE
RIFENESS > RIFE
RIFER > RIFE
RIFEST > RIFE
RIFF *n* short repeated melodic figure ▷ *vb* play or perform riffs in jazz or rock music
RIFFAGE *n* (in jazz or rock music) act or an instance of playing a short series of chords
RIFFAGES > RIFFAGE
RIFFED > RIFF
RIFFING > RIFF
RIFFLE *vb* flick through (pages etc) quickly ▷ *n* rapid in a stream
RIFFLED > RIFFLE
RIFFLER *n* file with a curved face for filing concave surfaces
RIFFLERS > RIFFLER
RIFFLES > RIFFLE
RIFFLING > RIFFLE
RIFFOLA *n* use of an abundance of dominant riffs
RIFFOLAS > RIFFOLA
RIFFRAFF *n* rabble, disreputable people
RIFFRAFFS > RIFFRAFF
RIFFS > RIFF
RIFLE *n* firearm with a long barrel ▷ *vb* cut spiral grooves inside the barrel of a gun
RIFLEBIRD *n* any of various birds of paradise
RIFLED > RIFLE
RIFLEMAN *n* person skilled in the use of a rifle, esp a soldier
RIFLEMEN > RIFLEMAN
RIFLER > RIFLE
RIFLERIES > RIFLERY
RIFLERS > RIFLE
RIFLERY *n* rifle shots
RIFLES > RIFLE
RIFLING *n* cutting of spiral grooves on the inside of a firearm's barrel
RIFLINGS > RIFLING
RIFLIP *n* genetic difference between two individuals
RIFLIPS > RIFLIP
RIFS > RIF
RIFT *n* break in friendly relations ▷ *vb* burst or cause to burst open
RIFTE *archaic word for* > RIFT
RIFTED > RIFT
RIFTIER > RIFT
RIFTIEST > RIFT
RIFTING > RIFT
RIFTLESS > RIFT
RIFTS > RIFT
RIFTY > RIFT
RIG *vb* arrange in a dishonest way ▷ *n* apparatus for drilling for oil and gas
RIGADOON *n* old Provençal couple dance, light and graceful, in lively duple time
RIGADOONS > RIGADOON
RIGATONI *n* macaroni in the form of short ridged often slightly curved pieces
RIGATONIS > RIGATONI
RIGAUDON *same as* > RIGADOON
RIGAUDONS > RIGAUDON
RIGG *n* type of fish
RIGGALD *same as* > RIDGELING
RIGGALDS > RIGGALD
RIGGED > RIG
RIGGER *n* workman who rigs vessels, etc
RIGGERS > RIGGER
RIGGING > RIG
RIGGINGS > RIG
RIGGISH *adj* dialect word meaning wanton
RIGGS > RIGG
RIGHT *adj* just ▷ *adv* correctly ▷ *n* claim, title, etc allowed or due ▷ *vb* bring or come back to a normal or correct state
RIGHTABLE *adj* capable of being righted
RIGHTABLY > RIGHTABLE
RIGHTED > RIGHT
RIGHTEN *vb* set right
RIGHTENED > RIGHTEN
RIGHTENS > RIGHTEN
RIGHTEOUS *adj* upright, godly, or virtuous
RIGHTER > RIGHT
RIGHTERS > RIGHT
RIGHTEST > RIGHT
RIGHTFUL *adj* in accordance with what is right
RIGHTIES > RIGHTY
RIGHTING > RIGHT
RIGHTINGS > RIGHT
RIGHTISH *adj* somewhat right, esp politically
RIGHTISM > RIGHTIST
RIGHTISMS > RIGHTIST
RIGHTIST *adj* (person) on the political right ▷ *n* supporter of the political right
RIGHTISTS > RIGHTIST
RIGHTLESS > RIGHT
RIGHTLY *adv* in accordance with the true facts or justice
RIGHTMOST > RIGHT
RIGHTNESS *n* state or quality of being right
RIGHTO *n* expression of agreement or compliance
RIGHTOS > RIGHTO
RIGHTS > RIGHT
RIGHTSIZE *vb* restructure (an organization) to cut costs and improve effectiveness without ruthlessly downsizing
RIGHTWARD *adj* situated on or directed towards the right ▷ *adv* towards or on the right
RIGHTY *n* informal word for a right-winger
RIGID *adj* inflexible or strict ▷ *adv* completely or excessively ▷ *n* strict and unbending person
RIGIDER > RIGID
RIGIDEST > RIGID
RIGIDIFY *vb* make or become rigid
RIGIDISE *same as* > RIGIDIZE
RIGIDISED > RIGIDISE
RIGIDISES > RIGIDISE
RIGIDITY > RIGID
RIGIDIZE *vb* make or become rigid
RIGIDIZED > RIGIDIZE
RIGIDIZES > RIGIDIZE
RIGIDLY > RIGID
RIGIDNESS > RIGID
RIGIDS > RIGID
RIGLIN *same as* > RIDGELING
RIGLING *same as* > RIDGELING
RIGLINGS > RIGLING
RIGLINS > RIGLIN
RIGMAROLE *n* long complicated procedure
RIGOL *n* (in dialect) ditch or gutter
RIGOLL *same as* > RIGOL
RIGOLLS > RIGOLL
RIGOLS > RIGOL
RIGOR *same as* > RIGOUR
RIGORISM *n* strictness in judgment or conduct
RIGORISMS > RIGORISM
RIGORIST > RIGORISM
RIGORISTS > RIGORISM
RIGOROUS *adj* harsh, severe, or stern
RIGORS > RIGOR
RIGOUR *n* harshness, severity, or strictness
RIGOURS > RIGOUR
RIGOUT *n* person's clothing
RIGOUTS > RIGOUT
RIGS > RIG
RIGSDALER *n* any of various former Scandinavian or Dutch small silver coins
RIGWIDDIE *n* part of the carthorse's harness to which the shafts of the cart attach
RIGWOODIE *same as* > RIGWIDDIE
RIJSTAFEL *n* assortment of Indonesian rice dishes
RIKISHA *same as* > RICKSHAW
RIKISHAS > RIKISHA
RIKISHI *n* sumo wrestler
RIKSHAW *same as* > RICKSHAW
RIKSHAWS > RIKSHAW
RILE *vb* anger or annoy
RILED > RILE
RILES > RILE
RILEY *adj* cross or irritab
RILIER > RILEY
RILIEST > RILEY
RILIEVI > RILIEVO
RILIEVO *same as* > RELIE
RILING > RILE
RILL *n* small stream ▷ *vb* trickle
RILLE *same as* > RILL
RILLED > RILL
RILLES > RILLE
RILLET *n* little rill
RILLETS > RILLET
RILLETTES *pl n* potted meat
RILLING > RILL
RILLMARK *n* mark left by the trickle of a rill
RILLMARKS > RILLMARK
RILLS > RILL
RIM *n* edge or border ▷ *v* put a rim on (a pot, cup, wheel, etc)
RIMA *n* long narrow opening
RIMAE > RIMA
RIMAYE *n* crevasse at the head of a glacier
RIMAYES > RIMAYE
RIME *same as* > RHYME
RIMED > RIME
RIMELESS > RHYME
RIMER *same as* > RHYMES
RIMERS > RIMER
RIMES > RIME
RIMESTER *same as* > RHYMESTER
RIMESTERS > RIMESTER
RIMFIRE *adj* (of a cartrid having the primer in the rim of the base ▷ *n* cartridge of this type
RIMFIRES > RIMFIRE
RIMIER > RIMY
RIMIEST > RIMY
RIMINESS > RIMY
RIMING > RIME
RIMLAND *n* area situated the outer edges of a regi
RIMLANDS > RIMLAND
RIMLESS > RIM
RIMMED > RIM
RIMMER *n* tool for shapin the edge of something
RIMMERS > RIMMER
RIMMING > RIM
RIMMINGS > RIM
RIMOSE *adj* (esp of plant parts) having the surfac marked by a network of intersecting cracks
RIMOSELY > RIMOSE
RIMOSITY > RIMOSE
RIMOUS *same as* > RIMOSE
RIMPLE *vb* crease or wrinkle
RIMPLED > RIMPLE
RIMPLES > RIMPLE
RIMPLING > RIMPLE

RIMROCK *n* rock forming the boundaries of a sandy or gravelly alluvial deposit
RIMROCKS > RIMROCK
RIMS > RIM
RIMSHOT *n* deliberate simultaneous striking of skin and rim of drum
RIMSHOTS > RIMSHOT
RIMU *n* New Zealand tree whose wood is used for building and furniture
RIMUS > RIMU
RIMY *adj* coated with rime
RIN *Scots variant of* > RUN
RIND *n* tough outer coating of fruits, cheese, or bacon ▷ *vb* take the bark off
RINDED > RIND
RINDIER > RINDY
RINDIEST > RINDY
RINDING > RIND
RINDLESS > RIND
RINDS > RIND
RINDY *adj* with a rind or rindlike skin
RINE *archaic variant of* > RIND
RINES > RINE
RING *vb* give out a clear resonant sound, as a bell ▷ *n* ringing
RINGBARK *same as* > RING
RINGBARKS > RINGBARK
RINGBIT *n* type of bit worn by a horse
RINGBITS > RINGBIT
RINGBOLT *n* bolt with a ring fitted through an eye attached to the bolt head
RINGBOLTS > RINGBOLT
RINGBONE *n* abnormal bony growth affecting the pastern of a horse, often causing lameness
RINGBONES > RINGBONE
RINGDOVE *n* large Eurasian pigeon with white patches on the wings and neck
RINGDOVES > RINGDOVE
RINGED > RING
RINGENT *adj* (of the corolla of plants such as the snapdragon) consisting of two distinct gaping lips
RINGER *n* person or thing apparently identical to another
RINGERS > RINGER
RINGGIT *n* standard monetary unit of Malaysia, divided into 100 sen
RINGGITS > RINGGIT
RINGHALS *n* variety of cobra
RINGING > RING
RINGINGLY > RING
RINGINGS > RING
RINGLESS > RING
RINGLET *n* curly lock of hair
RINGLETED > RINGLET
RINGLETS > RINGLET
RINGLIKE > RING
RINGMAN *n* (in dialect) ring finger
RINGMEN > RINGMAN
RINGNECK *n* any bird that has ringlike markings round its neck
RINGNECKS > RINGNECK
RINGS > RING
RINGSIDE *n* row of seats nearest a boxing or circus ring ▷ *adj* providing a close uninterrupted view
RINGSIDER *n* someone with a ringside seat or position
RINGSIDES > RINGSIDE
RINGSTAND *n* stand for laboratory equipment
RINGSTER *n* member of a ring controlling a market in antiques, art treasures, etc
RINGSTERS > RINGSTER
RINGTAIL *n* possum with a curling tail used to grip branches while climbing
RINGTAILS > RINGTAIL
RINGTAW *n* game of marbles in which the aim is to knock other players' marbles out of a ring
RINGTAWS > RINGTAW
RINGTONE *n* musical tune played by a mobile phone when a call is received
RINGTONES > RINGTONE
RINGTOSS *n* game in which participants try to throw hoops onto an upright stick
RINGWAY *n* bypass
RINGWAYS > RINGWAY
RINGWISE *adj* used to being in the ring and able to respond appropriately
RINGWOMB *n* complication at lambing resulting from failure of the cervix to open
RINGWOMBS > RINGWOMB
RINGWORK *n* circular earthwork
RINGWORKS > RINGWORK
RINGWORM *n* fungal skin disease in circular patches
RINGWORMS > RINGWORM
RINK *n* sheet of ice for skating or curling ▷ *vb* skate on a rink
RINKED > RINK
RINKHALS *n* S African cobra that can spit venom
RINKING > RINK
RINKS > RINK
RINNING > RIN
RINS > RIN
RINSABLE > RINSE
RINSE *vb* remove soap from (washed clothes, hair, etc) by applying clean water ▷ *n* rinsing
RINSEABLE > RINSE
RINSED > RINSE
RINSER > RINSE
RINSERS > RINSE
RINSES > RINSE
RINSIBLE > RINSE
RINSING > RINSE
RINSINGS > RINSE
RIOJA *n* red or white Spanish wine with a vanilla bouquet and flavour
RIOJAS > RIOJA
RIOT *n* disorderly unruly disturbance ▷ *vb* take part in a riot
RIOTED > RIOT
RIOTER > RIOT
RIOTERS > RIOT
RIOTING > RIOT
RIOTINGS > RIOT
RIOTISE *n* archaic word for riotous behaviour and excess
RIOTISES > RIOTISE
RIOTIZE *same as* > RIOTISE
RIOTIZES > RIOTIZE
RIOTOUS *adj* unrestrained
RIOTOUSLY > RIOTOUS
RIOTRIES > RIOTRY
RIOTRY *n* riotous behaviour
RIOTS > RIOT
RIP *vb* tear violently ▷ *n* split or tear
RIPARIAL *adj* riparian
RIPARIAN *adj* of or on the banks of a river ▷ *n* person who owns land on a river bank
RIPARIANS > RIPARIAN
RIPCORD *n* cord pulled to open a parachute
RIPCORDS > RIPCORD
RIPE *adj* ready to be reaped, eaten, etc ▷ *vb* ripen
RIPECK *same as* > RYEPECK
RIPECKS > RIPECK
RIPED > RIPE
RIPELY > RIPE
RIPEN *vb* grow ripe
RIPENED > RIPEN
RIPENER > RIPEN
RIPENERS > RIPEN
RIPENESS > RIPE
RIPENING > RIPEN
RIPENS > RIPEN
RIPER *adj* more ripe ▷ *n* old Scots word meaning plunderer
RIPERS > RIPER
RIPES > RIPE
RIPEST > RIPE
RIPIENI > RIPIENO
RIPIENIST *n* orchestral member who is there to swell the sound rather than play solo
RIPIENO *n* (in baroque concertos and concerti grossi) the full orchestra, as opposed to the instrumental soloists
RIPIENOS > RIPIENO
RIPING > RIPE
RIPOFF *n* grossly overpriced article
RIPOFFS > RIPOFF
RIPOST *same as* > RIPOSTE
RIPOSTE *n* verbal retort ▷ *vb* make a riposte
RIPOSTED > RIPOSTE
RIPOSTES > RIPOSTE
RIPOSTING > RIPOSTE
RIPOSTS > RIPOST
RIPP *n* old Scots word for a handful of grain
RIPPABLE > RIP
RIPPED > RIP
RIPPER *n* person who rips
RIPPERS > RIPPER
RIPPIER *n* archaic word for fish seller
RIPPIERS > RIPPIER
RIPPING > RIP
RIPPINGLY > RIP
RIPPLE *n* slight wave or ruffling of a surface ▷ *vb* flow or form into little waves (on)
RIPPLED > RIPPLE
RIPPLER > RIPPLE
RIPPLERS > RIPPLE
RIPPLES > RIPPLE
RIPPLET *n* tiny ripple
RIPPLETS > RIPPLET
RIPPLIER > RIPPLE
RIPPLIEST > RIPPLE
RIPPLING > RIPPLE
RIPPLINGS > RIPPLE
RIPPLY > RIPPLE
RIPPS > RIPP
RIPRAP *vb* deposit broken stones in or on
RIPRAPPED > RIPRAP
RIPRAPS > RIPRAP
RIPS > RIP
RIPSAW *n* handsaw for cutting along the grain of timber ▷ *vb* saw with a ripsaw
RIPSAWED > RIPSAW
RIPSAWING > RIPSAW
RIPSAWN > RIPSAW
RIPSAWS > RIPSAW
RIPSTOP *n* tear-resistant cloth
RIPSTOPS > RIPSTOP
RIPT *archaic past form of* > RIP
RIPTIDE *n* stretch of turbulent water in the sea, caused by the meeting of currents or abrupt changes in depth
RIPTIDES > RIPTIDE
RIRORIRO *n* small NZ bush bird that hatches the eggs of the shining cuckoo
RIRORIROS > RIRORIRO
RISALDAR *n* Indian cavalry officer
RISALDARS > RISALDAR
RISE *vb* get up from a lying, sitting, or kneeling position ▷ *n* rising
RISEN > RISE
RISER *n* person who rises, esp from bed
RISERS > RISER
RISES > RISE

RISHI *n* Indian seer or sage
RISHIS > RISHI
RISIBLE *adj* causing laughter, ridiculous
RISIBLES *pl n* sense of humour
RISIBLY > RISIBLE
RISING > RISE
RISINGS > RISE
RISK *n* chance of disaster or loss ▷ *vb* act in spite of the possibility of (injury or loss)
RISKED > RISK
RISKER > RISK
RISKERS > RISK
RISKFUL > RISK
RISKIER > RISKY
RISKIEST > RISKY
RISKILY > RISKY
RISKINESS > RISKY
RISKING > RISK
RISKLESS > RISK
RISKS > RISK
RISKY *adj* full of risk, dangerous
RISOLUTO *adj* musical term meaning firm and decisive ▷ *adv* firmly and decisively
RISOTTO *n* dish of rice cooked in stock with vegetables, meat, etc
RISOTTOS > RISOTTO
RISP *vb* Scots word meaning rasp
RISPED > RISP
RISPETTI > RISPETTO
RISPETTO *n* kind of folk song
RISPING > RISP
RISPINGS > RISP
RISPS > RISP
RISQUE *n* risk
RISQUES > RISQUE
RISSOLE *n* cake of minced meat, coated with breadcrumbs and fried
RISSOLES > RISSOLE
RISTRA *n* string of dried chilli peppers
RISTRAS > RISTRA
RISUS *n* involuntary grinning expression
RISUSES > RISUS
RIT *vb* Scots word for cut or slit
RITARD *n* (in music) a slowing down
RITARDS > RITARD
RITE *n* formal practice or custom, esp religious
RITELESS > RITE
RITENUTO *adv* held back momentarily ▷ *n* (in music) a slowing down
RITENUTOS > RITENUTO
RITES > RITE
RITONAVIR *n* drug used to treat HIV
RITORNEL *n* (in music) orchestral passage
RITORNELL *same as* > RITORNEL
RITORNELS > RITORNEL
RITS > RIT
RITT *same as* > RIT
RITTED > RIT
RITTER *n* knight or horseman
RITTERS > RITTER
RITTING > RIT
RITTS > RITT
RITUAL *n* prescribed order of rites ▷ *adj* concerning rites
RITUALISE *same as* > RITUALIZE
RITUALISM *n* exaggerated emphasis on the importance of rites and ceremonies
RITUALIST > RITUALISM
RITUALIZE *vb* engage in ritualism or devise rituals
RITUALLY > RITUAL
RITUALS > RITUAL
RITZ as in *put on the ritz* assume a superior air or make an ostentatious display
RITZES > RITZ
RITZIER > RITZY
RITZIEST > RITZY
RITZILY > RITZY
RITZINESS > RITZY
RITZY *adj* luxurious or elegant
RIVA *n* rock cleft
RIVAGE *n* bank, shore, or coast
RIVAGES > RIVAGE
RIVAL *n* person or thing that competes with or equals another for favour, success, etc ▷ *adj* in the position of a rival ▷ *vb* (try to) equal
RIVALED > RIVAL
RIVALESS *n* female rival
RIVALING > RIVAL
RIVALISE *same as* > RIVALIZE
RIVALISED > RIVALISE
RIVALISES > RIVALISE
RIVALITY > RIVAL
RIVALIZE *vb* become a rival
RIVALIZED > RIVALIZE
RIVALIZES > RIVALIZE
RIVALLED > RIVAL
RIVALLESS > RIVAL
RIVALLING > RIVAL
RIVALRIES > RIVALRY
RIVALROUS > RIVALRY
RIVALRY *n* keen competition
RIVALS > RIVAL
RIVALSHIP > RIVAL
RIVAS > RIVA
RIVE *vb* split asunder
RIVED > RIVE
RIVEL *vb* archaic word meaning wrinkle
RIVELLED > RIVEL
RIVELLING > RIVEL
RIVELS > RIVEL
RIVEN > RIVE
RIVER *n* large natural stream of water
RIVERAIN *same as* > RIPARIAN
RIVERAINS > RIVERAIN
RIVERBANK *n* bank of a river
RIVERBED *n* bed of a river
RIVERBEDS > RIVERBOAT
RIVERBOAT *n* boat, especially a barge, designed for use on rivers
RIVERED *adj* with a river or rivers
RIVERET *n* archaic word for rivulet or stream
RIVERETS > RIVERET
RIVERHEAD *n* source of river
RIVERINE *same as* > RIPARIAN
RIVERLESS > RIVER
RIVERLIKE *adj* resembling a river
RIVERMAN *n* boatman or man earning his living working on a river
RIVERMEN > RIVERMAN
RIVERS > RIVER
RIVERSIDE *n* area beside a river
RIVERWARD *adj* towards the river ▷ *adv* towards the river
RIVERWAY *n* river serving as a waterway
RIVERWAYS > RIVERWAY
RIVERWEED *n* type of plant found growing near rivers
RIVERY *adj* riverlike
RIVES > RIVE
RIVET *n* bolt for fastening metal plates, the end being put through holes and then beaten flat ▷ *vb* fasten with rivets
RIVETED > RIVET
RIVETER > RIVET
RIVETERS > RIVET
RIVETING > RIVET
RIVETINGS > RIVET
RIVETS > RIVET
RIVETTED > RIVET
RIVETTING > RIVET
RIVIERA *n* coastline resembling the Meditteranean Riviera
RIVIERAS > RIVIERA
RIVIERE *n* necklace the diamonds or other precious stones of which gradually increase in size up to a large centre stone
RIVIERES > RIVIERE
RIVING > RIVE
RIVLIN *n* Scots word for rawhide shoe
RIVLINS > RIVLIN
RIVO *interj* (in the past) an informal toast
RIVOS > RIVO
RIVULET *n* small stream
RIVULETS > RIVULET
RIVULOSE *adj* having meandering lines
RIYAL *n* standard monetary unit of Qatar, divided into 100 dirhams
RIYALS > RIYAL
RIZ *(in some dialects) past form of* > RISE
RIZA *n* partial icon cover made from precious met[al]
RIZARD *n* redcurrant
RIZARDS > RIZARD
RIZAS > RIZA
RIZZAR *n* Scots word for red currant ▷ *vb* Scots word for sun-dry
RIZZARED > RIZZAR
RIZZARING > RIZZAR
RIZZARS > RIZZAR
RIZZART *n* Scots word for red currant
RIZZARTS > RIZZART
RIZZER *same as* > RIZZAR
RIZZERED > RIZZER
RIZZERING > RIZZER
RIZZERS > RIZZER
RIZZOR *vb* dry
RIZZORED > RIZZOR
RIZZORING > RIZZOR
RIZZORS > RIZZOR
ROACH *n* Eurasian freshwater fish ▷ *vb* clip (mane) short so that it stands upright
ROACHED *adj* arched convexly, as the back of certain breeds of dog, su[ch] as the whippet
ROACHES > ROACH
ROACHING > ROACH
ROAD *n* way prepared for passengers, vehicles, etc
ROADBED *n* material used to make a road
ROADBEDS > ROADBED
ROADBLOCK *n* barricade across a road to stop traf[fic] for inspection etc
ROADCRAFT *n* skills and knowledge of a road user
ROADEO *n* competition in which drivers or other road users put their skills on the road to the test
ROADEOS > ROADEO
ROADHOUSE *n* pub or restaurant on a country road
ROADIE *n* person who transports and sets up equipment for a band
ROADIES > ROADIE
ROADING *n* road building
ROADINGS > ROADING
ROADKILL *n* remains of a[n] animal or animals killed [on] the road by motor vehicl[es]
ROADKILLS > ROADKILL
ROADLESS > ROAD
ROADMAN *n* someone involved in road repair or construction
ROADMEN > ROADMAN
ROADS > ROAD
ROADSHOW *n* radio show broadcast live from one c[...]

a number of places being visited by a touring disc jockey
[RO]ADSHOWS > ROADSHOW
[RO]ADSIDE *n* side of a road ▷ *adj* situated beside a road
[RO]ADSIDES > ROADSIDE
[RO]ADSMAN *same as* > ROADMAN
[RO]ADSMEN > ROADSMAN
[RO]ADSTEAD *same as* > ROAD
[RO]ADSTER *n* open car with only two seats
[RO]ADSTERS > ROADSTER
[RO]ADWAY *n* part of a road used by vehicles
[RO]ADWAYS > ROADWAY
[RO]ADWORK *n* sports training by running along roads
[RO]ADWORKS *pl n* repairs to a road, esp blocking part of the road
[RO]AM *vb* wander about ▷ *n* act of roaming
[RO]AMED > ROAM
[RO]AMER > ROAM
[RO]AMERS > ROAM
[RO]AMING > ROAM
[RO]AMINGS > ROAM
[RO]AMS > ROAM
[RO]AN *adj* (of a horse) having a brown or black coat sprinkled with white hairs ▷ *n* roan horse
[RO]ANS > ROAN
[RO]AR *vb* make or utter a loud deep hoarse sound like that of a lion ▷ *n* such a sound
[RO]ARED > ROAR
[RO]ARER > ROAR
[RO]ARERS > ROAR
[RO]ARIE *Scots word for* > NOISY
[RO]ARIER > ROARY
[RO]ARIEST > ROARY
[RO]ARING > ROAR
[RO]ARINGLY > ROARING
[RO]ARINGS > ROAR
[RO]ARMING *adj* severe
[RO]ARS > ROAR
[RO]ARY *adj* roarlike or tending to roar
[RO]AST *vb* cook by dry heat, as in an oven ▷ *n* roasted joint of meat ▷ *adj* roasted
[RO]ASTED > ROAST
[RO]ASTER *n* person or thing that roasts
[RO]ASTERS > ROASTER
[RO]ASTING *adj* extremely hot ▷ *n* severe criticism or scolding
[RO]ASTINGS > ROASTING
[RO]ASTS > ROAST
[RO]ATE *archaic form of* > ROTE
[RO]ATED > ROATE
[RO]ATES > ROATE
[RO]ATING > ROATE
[RO]B *vb* steal from
[RO]BALO *n* tropical fish
ROBALOS > ROBALO
ROBAND *n* piece of marline used for fastening a sail to a spar
ROBANDS > ROBAND
ROBBED > ROB
ROBBER > ROB
ROBBERIES > ROBBERY
ROBBERS > ROB
ROBBERY *n* stealing of property from a person by using or threatening to use force
ROBBIN *same as* > ROBAND
ROBBING > ROB
ROBBINS > ROBBIN
ROBE *n* long loose outer garment ▷ *vb* put a robe on
ROBED > ROBE
ROBES > ROBE
ROBIN *n* small brown bird with a red breast
ROBING > ROBE
ROBINGS > ROBE
ROBINIA *n* type of leguminous tree
ROBINIAS > ROBINIA
ROBINS > ROBIN
ROBLE *n* oak tree
ROBLES > ROBLE
ROBORANT *adj* tending to fortify or increase strength ▷ *n* drug or agent that increases strength
ROBORANTS > ROBORANT
ROBOT *n* automated machine, esp one performing functions in a human manner
ROBOTIC > ROBOT
ROBOTICS *n* science of designing and using robots
ROBOTISE *same as* > ROBOTIZE
ROBOTISED > ROBOTISE
ROBOTISES > ROBOTISE
ROBOTISM > ROBOT
ROBOTISMS > ROBOT
ROBOTIZE *vb* automate
ROBOTIZED > ROBOTIZE
ROBOTIZES > ROBOTIZE
ROBOTRIES > ROBOT
ROBOTRY > ROBOT
ROBOTS > ROBOT
ROBS > ROB
ROBURITE *n* flameless explosive
ROBURITES > ROBURITE
ROBUST *adj* very strong and healthy
ROBUSTA *n* species of coffee tree
ROBUSTAS > ROBUSTA
ROBUSTER > ROBUST
ROBUSTEST > ROBUST
ROBUSTLY > ROBUST
ROC *n* monstrous bird of Arabian mythology
ROCAILLE *n* decorative rock or shell work, esp as ornamentation in a rococo fountain, grotto, or interior
ROCAILLES > ROCAILLE
ROCAMBOLE *n* variety of sand leek whose garlic-like bulb is used for seasoning
ROCH *same as* > ROTCH
ROCHES > ROTCH
ROCHET *n* white surplice with tight sleeves, worn by bishops, abbots, and certain other Church dignitaries
ROCHETS > ROCHET
ROCK *n* hard mineral substance that makes up part of the earth's crust, stone ▷ *vb* (cause to) sway to and fro ▷ *adj* of or relating to rock music
ROCKABIES > ROCKABY
ROCKABLE > ROCK
ROCKABY *same as* > ROCKABYE
ROCKABYE *n* lullaby or rocking motion used with a baby during lullabies
ROCKABYES > ROCKABYE
ROCKAWAY *n* four-wheeled horse-drawn carriage, usually with two seats and a hard top
ROCKAWAYS > ROCKAWAY
ROCKBOUND *adj* hemmed in or encircled by rocks
ROCKCRESS *n* low-growing plant with white flowers
ROCKED > ROCK
ROCKER *n* rocking chair
ROCKERIES > ROCKERY
ROCKERS > ROCKER
ROCKERY *n* mound of stones in a garden for rock plants
ROCKET *n* self-propelling device powered by the burning of explosive contents (used as a firework, weapon, etc) ▷ *vb* move fast, esp upwards, like a rocket
ROCKETED > ROCKET
ROCKETEER *n* engineer or scientist concerned with the design, operation, or launching of rockets
ROCKETER *n* bird that launches itself into the air like a rocket when flushed
ROCKETERS > ROCKETER
ROCKETING > ROCKET
ROCKETRY *n* science and technology of the design and operation of rockets
ROCKETS > ROCKET
ROCKFALL *n* instance of rocks breaking away and falling from an outcrop
ROCKFALLS > ROCKFALL
ROCKFISH *n* any of various fishes that live among rocks
ROCKHOUND *n* person interested in rocks and minerals
ROCKIER > ROCKY *n* archaic or dialect word for rock pigeon
ROCKIERS > ROCKY
ROCKIEST > ROCKY
ROCKILY > ROCKY
ROCKINESS > ROCKY
ROCKING > ROCK
ROCKINGLY > ROCKING
ROCKINGS > ROCK
ROCKLAY *same as* > ROKELAY
ROCKLAYS > ROCKLAY
ROCKLESS > ROCK
ROCKLIKE > ROCK
ROCKLING *n* any of various small sea fishes having an elongated body and barbels around the mouth
ROCKLINGS > ROCKLING
ROCKOON *n* rocket carrying scientific equipment for studying the upper atmosphere, fired from a balloon at high altitude
ROCKOONS > ROCKOON
ROCKROSE *n* any of various shrubs or herbaceous plants cultivated for their roselike flowers
ROCKROSES > ROCKROSE
ROCKS > ROCK
ROCKSHAFT *n* shaft that rotates backwards and forwards rather than continuously, esp one used in the valve gear of a steam engine
ROCKSLIDE *n* fall of rocks down hillside
ROCKWATER *n* water that comes out of rock
ROCKWEED *n* any of various seaweeds that grow on rocks exposed at low tide
ROCKWEEDS > ROCKWEED
ROCKWORK *n* structure made of rock
ROCKWORKS > ROCKWORK
ROCKY *adj* having many rocks
ROCOCO *adj* (of furniture, architecture, etc) having much elaborate decoration in an early 18th-century style ▷ *n* style of architecture and decoration that originated in France in the early 18th century, characterized by elaborate but graceful, light, ornamentation, often containing asymmetrical motifs
ROCOCOS > ROCOCO
ROCQUET *n* another name for the salad plant rocket
ROCQUETS > ROCQUET
ROCS > ROC
ROD *n* slender straight bar, stick ▷ *vb* clear with a rod
RODDED > ROD
RODDING > ROD
RODDINGS > ROD
RODE *vb* (of the male

woodcock) to perform a display flight at dusk during the breeding season
RODED > RODE
RODENT *n* animal with teeth specialized for gnawing, such as a rat, mouse, or squirrel
RODENTS > RODENT
RODEO *n* display of skill by cowboys, such as bareback riding ▷ *vb* take part in a rodeo
RODEOED > RODEO
RODEOING > RODEO
RODEOS > RODEO
RODES > RODE
RODEWAY *archaic spelling of* > ROADWAY
RODEWAYS > RODEWAY
RODFISHER *n* angler
RODGERSIA *n* flowering plant
RODING > RODE
RODINGS > RODE
RODLESS > ROD
RODLIKE > ROD
RODMAN *n* someone who uses or fishes with a rod
RODMEN > RODMAN
RODS > ROD
RODSMAN *same as* > RODMAN
RODSMEN > RODSMAN
RODSTER *n* angler
RODSTERS > RODSTER
ROE *n* mass of eggs in a fish, sometimes eaten as food
ROEBUCK *n* male of the roe deer
ROEBUCKS > ROEBUCK
ROED *adj* with roe inside
ROEMER *n* drinking glass, typically having an ovoid bowl on a short stem
ROEMERS > ROEMER
ROENTGEN *n* unit measuring a radiation dose
ROENTGENS > ROENTGEN
ROES > ROE
ROESTONE *same as* > OOLITE
ROESTONES > ROESTONE
ROGALLO *n* flexible fabric delta wing, originally designed as a possible satellite retrieval vehicle but actually developed in the 1960s as the first successful hang-glider
ROGALLOS > ROGALLO
ROGATION *n* solemn supplication, esp in a form of ceremony prescribed by the Church
ROGATIONS > ROGATION
ROGATORY *adj* (esp in legal contexts) seeking or authorized to seek information
ROGER *interj* (used in signalling) message received ▷ *vb* (of a man) to copulate (with)
ROGERED > ROGER
ROGERING > ROGER
ROGERINGS > ROGER
ROGERS > ROGER
ROGNON *n* isolated rock outcrop on a glacier
ROGNONS > ROGNON
ROGUE *n* dishonest or unprincipled person ▷ *adj* (of a wild beast) having a savage temper and living apart from the herd ▷ *vb* rid (a field or crop) of plants that are inferior, diseased, or of an unwanted variety
ROGUED > ROGUE
ROGUEING > ROGUE
ROGUERIES > ROGUERY
ROGUERY *n* dishonest or immoral behaviour
ROGUES > ROGUE
ROGUESHIP *n* being a rogue
ROGUING > ROGUE
ROGUISH *adj* dishonest or unprincipled
ROGUISHLY > ROGUISH
ROGUY *same as* > ROGUISH
ROIL *vb* make (a liquid) cloudy or turbid by stirring up dregs or sediment
ROILED > ROIL
ROILIER > ROILY
ROILIEST > ROILY
ROILING > ROIL
ROILS > ROIL
ROILY *adj* cloudy or muddy
ROIN *same as* > ROYNE
ROINED > ROIN
ROINING > ROIN
ROINISH *same as* > ROYNISH
ROINS > ROIN
ROIST *archaic variant of* > ROISTER
ROISTED > ROIST
ROISTER *vb* make merry noisily or boisterously
ROISTERED > ROISTER
ROISTERER > ROISTER
ROISTERS > ROISTER
ROISTING > ROIST
ROISTS > ROIST
ROJAK *n* (in Malaysia) a salad dish served in chilli sauce
ROJAKS > ROJAK
ROJI *n* Japanese tea garden or its path of stones
ROJIS > ROJI
ROK *same as* > ROC
ROKE *vb* (in dialect) steam or smoke
ROKED > ROKE
ROKELAY *n* type of cloak
ROKELAYS > ROKELAY
ROKER *n* variety of ray
ROKERS > ROKER
ROKES > ROKE
ROKIER > ROKY
ROKIEST > ROKY
ROKING > ROKE
ROKKAKU *n* hexagonal Japanese kite
ROKS > ROK
ROKY *adj* (in dialect) steamy or smoky
ROLAG *n* roll of carded wool ready for spinning
ROLAGS > ROLAG
ROLAMITE *n* type of bearing using two rollers and a moving flexible band
ROLAMITES > ROLAMITE
ROLE *n* task or function
ROLES > ROLE
ROLF *vb* massage following a particular technique
ROLFED > ROLF
ROLFER > ROLF
ROLFERS > ROLF
ROLFING > ROLF
ROLFINGS > ROLF
ROLFS > ROLF
ROLL *vb* move by turning over and over ▷ *n* act of rolling over or from side to side
ROLLABLE > ROLL
ROLLAWAY *n* mounted on rollers so as to be easily moved, esp to be stored away after use
ROLLAWAYS > ROLLAWAY
ROLLBACK *n* reduction to a previous price
ROLLBACKS > ROLLBACK
ROLLBAR *n* bar that reinforces the frame of a car, esp one used for racing, rallying, etc, to protect the driver if the car should turn over
ROLLBARS > ROLLBAR
ROLLED > ROLL
ROLLER *n* rotating cylinder used for smoothing or supporting a thing to be moved, spreading paint, etc
ROLLERS > ROLLER
ROLLICK *vb* behave in a carefree, frolicsome, or boisterous manner ▷ *n* boisterous or carefree escapade or event
ROLLICKED > ROLLICK
ROLLICKS > ROLLICK
ROLLICKY *adj* rollicking
ROLLING > ROLL
ROLLINGS > ROLL
ROLLMOP *n* herring fillet rolled round onion slices and pickled
ROLLMOPS > ROLLMOP
ROLLNECK *adj* (of a garment) having a high neck that is worn rolled over ▷ *n* rollneck sweater or other garment
ROLLNECKS > ROLLNECK
ROLLOCK *same as* > ROWLOCK
ROLLOCKS > ROLLOCK
ROLLOUT *n* presentation to the public of a new aircraft, product, etc; launch
ROLLOUTS > ROLLOUT
ROLLOVER *n* instance of a prize continuing in force for an additional period
ROLLOVERS > ROLLOVER
ROLLS > ROLL
ROLLTOP as in *rolltop desk* desk having a slatted wooden panel that can be pulled down over the writing surface when not in use
ROLLWAY *n* incline down which logs are rolled
ROLLWAYS > ROLLWAY
ROM *n* male gypsy
ROMA *n* gypsy
ROMAGE *archaic variant of* > RUMMAGE
ROMAGES > ROMAGE
ROMAIKA *n* Greek dance
ROMAIKAS > ROMAIKA
ROMAINE *n* usual US and Canadian name for cos (lettuce)
ROMAINES > ROMAINE
ROMAJI *n* Roman alphabet as used to write Japanese
ROMAJIS > ROMAJI
ROMAL *same as* > RUMAL
ROMALS > ROMAL
ROMAN *adj* in or relating to the vertical style of printing type used for most printed matter ▷ *n* roman type
ROMANCE *n* love affair ▷ *vb* exaggerate or fantasize
ROMANCED > ROMANCE
ROMANCER > ROMANCE
ROMANCERS > ROMANCE
ROMANCES > ROMANCE
ROMANCING > ROMANCE
ROMANISE *same as* > ROMANIZE
ROMANISED > ROMANISE
ROMANISES > ROMANISE
ROMANIZE *vb* impart a Roman Catholic character to (a ceremony, practice, etc)
ROMANIZED > ROMANIZE
ROMANIZES > ROMANIZE
ROMANO *n* hard light-coloured sharp-tasting cheese
ROMANOS > ROMANO
ROMANS > ROMAN
ROMANTIC *adj* of or dealing with love ▷ *n* romantic person or artist
ROMANTICS > ROMANTIC
ROMANZA *n* short instrumental piece of song-like character
ROMANZAS > ROMANZA
ROMAS > ROMA
ROMAUNT *n* verse romance
ROMAUNTS > ROMAUNT
ROMCOM *n* film or television comedy based around the romantic relationships of the characters
ROMCOMS > ROMCOM
ROMELDALE *n* type of sheep
ROMEO *n* ardent male lover

OMEOS > ROMEO
OMNEYA *n* bushy type of poppy
OMNEYAS > ROMNEYA
OMP *vb* play wildly and joyfully ▷ *n* boisterous activity
OMPED > ROMP
OMPER *n* playful or boisterous child
OMPERS *pl n* child's overalls
OMPING > ROMP
OMPINGLY > ROMP
OMPISH > ROMP
OMPISHLY > ROMP
OMPS > ROMP
OMS > ROM
ONCADOR *n* any of several types of fish
ONCADORS > RONCADOR
ONDACHE *n* round shield
ONDACHES > RONDACHE
ONDAVEL *n* circular building, often thatched
ONDAVELS > RONDAVEL
ONDE *n* round dance
ONDEAU *n* poem consisting of 13 or 10 lines with the opening words of the first line used as a refrain
ONDEAUX > RONDEAU
ONDEL *n* rondeau consisting of three stanzas of 13 or 14 lines with a two-line refrain appearing twice or three times
ONDELET *n* brief rondeau, having five or seven lines and a refrain taken from the first line
ONDELETS > RONDELET
ONDELLE *n* type of bead
ONDELLES > RONDELLE
ONDELS > RONDEL
ONDES > RONDE
ONDINO *n* short rondo
ONDINOS > RONDINO
ONDO *n* piece of music with a leading theme continually returned to
ONDOS > RONDO
ONDURE *n* circle or curve
ONDURES > RONDURE
ONE *n* drainpipe or gutter for carrying rainwater from a roof
ONEO *vb* duplicate (a document) from a stencil ▷ *n* document reproduced by this process
ONEOED > RONEO
ONEOING > RONEO
ONEOS > RONEO
ONEPIPE *same as* > RONE
ONEPIPES > RONEPIPE
ONES > RONE
ONG *archaic past participle of* > RING
ONGGENG *n* Malay traditional dance
ONGGENGS > RONGGENG
ONIN *n* lordless samurai, esp one whose feudal lord had been deprived of his territory
RONINS > RONIN
RONION *same as* > RUNNION
RONIONS > RONION
RONNE *archaic form of* > RUN
RONNEL *n* type of pesticide
RONNELS > RONNEL
RONNIE *n* Dublin slang word for moustache
RONNIES > RONNIE
RONNING > RONNE
RONT *archaic variant of* > RUNT
RONTE *archaic variant of* > RUNT
RONTES > RONTE
RONTGEN *variant spelling of* > ROENTGEN
RONTGENS > RONTGEN
RONTS > RONT
RONYON *same as* > RUNNION
RONYONS > RUNNION
RONZER *n* New Zealand word for a New Zealander not from Auckland
RONZERS > RONZER
ROO *n* kangaroo
ROOD *n* Cross
ROODS > ROOD
ROOF *n* outside upper covering of a building, car, etc ▷ *vb* put a roof on
ROOFED > ROOF
ROOFER > ROOF
ROOFERS > ROOF
ROOFIE *n* tablet of sedative drug
ROOFIER > ROOFY
ROOFIES > ROOFIE
ROOFIEST > ROOFY
ROOFING *n* material used to build a roof
ROOFINGS > ROOFING
ROOFLESS > ROOF
ROOFLIKE > ROOF
ROOFLINE *n* uppermost edge of a roof
ROOFLINES > ROOFLINE
ROOFS > ROOF
ROOFSCAPE *n* view of the rooftops of a town, city, etc
ROOFTOP *n* outside part of the roof of a building
ROOFTOPS > ROOFTOP
ROOFTREE *same as* > RIDGEPOLE
ROOFTREES > ROOFTREE
ROOFY *adj* with roofs
ROOIBOS *n* tea prepared from the dried leaves of an African plant
ROOIKAT *n* South African lynx
ROOIKATS > ROOIKAT
ROOINEK *n* contemptuous name for an Englishman
ROOINEKS > ROOINEK
ROOK *n* Eurasian bird of the crow family ▷ *vb* swindle
ROOKED > ROOK
ROOKERIES > ROOKERY
ROOKERY *n* colony of rooks, penguins, or seals
ROOKIE *n* new recruit
ROOKIER > ROOKY
ROOKIES > ROOKIE
ROOKIEST > ROOKY
ROOKING > ROOK
ROOKISH > ROOK
ROOKS > ROOK
ROOKY *adj* abounding in rooks
ROOM *n* enclosed area in a building ▷ *vb* occupy or share a room
ROOMED > ROOM
ROOMER > ROOM
ROOMERS > ROOM
ROOMETTE *n* self-contained compartment in a railway sleeping car
ROOMETTES > ROOMETTE
ROOMFUL *n* number or quantity sufficient to fill a room
ROOMFULS > ROOMFUL
ROOMIE *n* roommate
ROOMIER > ROOMY
ROOMIES > ROOMIE
ROOMIEST > ROOMY
ROOMILY > ROOMY
ROOMINESS > ROOMY
ROOMING > ROOM
ROOMMATE *n* person with whom one shares a room or apartment
ROOMMATES > ROOMMATE
ROOMS > ROOM
ROOMSOME *adj* archaic word meaning roomy
ROOMY *adj* spacious
ROON *n* Scots word for shred or strip
ROONS > ROON
ROOP *same as* > ROUP
ROOPED > ROOP
ROOPIER > ROOPY
ROOPIEST > ROOPY
ROOPING > ROOP
ROOPIT *same as* > ROOPY
ROOPS > ROOP
ROOPY *adj* (in dialect) hoarse
ROORBACH *same as* > ROORBACK
ROORBACHS > ROORBACH
ROORBACK *n* false or distorted report or account, used to obtain political advantage
ROORBACKS > ROORBACK
ROOS > ROO
ROOSA *n* type of grass
ROOSAS > ROOSA
ROOSE *vb* flatter
ROOSED > ROOSE
ROOSER > ROOSE
ROOSERS > ROOSE
ROOSES > ROOSE
ROOSING > ROOSE
ROOST *n* perch for fowls ▷ *vb* perch
ROOSTED > ROOST
ROOSTER *n* domestic cock
ROOSTERS > ROOSTER
ROOSTING > ROOST
ROOSTS > ROOST
ROOT *n* part of a plant that grows down into the earth obtaining nourishment ▷ *vb* establish a root and start to grow
ROOTAGE *n* root system
ROOTAGES > ROOTAGE
ROOTCAP *n* layer of cells at root tip
ROOTCAPS > ROOTCAP
ROOTED > ROOT
ROOTEDLY > ROOT
ROOTER > ROOT
ROOTERS > ROOT
ROOTHOLD > ROOT
ROOTHOLDS > ROOT
ROOTIER > ROOT
ROOTIES > ROOTY
ROOTIEST > ROOT
ROOTINESS > ROOT
ROOTING > ROOT
ROOTINGS > ROOT
ROOTLE *same as* > ROOT
ROOTLED > ROOTLE
ROOTLES > ROOTLE
ROOTLESS *adj* having no sense of belonging
ROOTLET *n* small root or branch of a root
ROOTLETS > ROOTLET
ROOTLIKE > ROOT
ROOTLING > ROOTLE
ROOTS *adj* (of popular music) going back to the origins of a style, esp in being unpretentious
ROOTSIER > ROOTS
ROOTSIEST > ROOTS
ROOTSTALK *same as* > RHIZOME
ROOTSTOCK *same as* > RHIZOME
ROOTSY > ROOTS
ROOTWORM *n* beetle larvae feeding on roots
ROOTWORMS > ROOTWORM
ROOTY *adj* rootlike ▷ *n* (in military slang) bread
ROPABLE *adj* capable of being roped
ROPE *n* thick cord
ROPEABLE *same as* > ROPABLE
ROPED > ROPE
ROPELIKE > ROPE
ROPER *n* someone who makes ropes
ROPERIES > ROPERY
ROPERS > ROPER
ROPERY *n* place where ropes are made
ROPES > ROPE
ROPEWALK *n* long narrow usually covered path or shed where ropes are made
ROPEWALKS > ROPEWALK
ROPEWAY *n* type of aerial lift
ROPEWAYS > ROPEWAY
ROPEWORK *n* making, mending, or tying ropes
ROPEWORKS > ROPEWORK
ROPEY *adj* inferior or

inadequate
ROPIER > ROPY
ROPIEST > ROPY
ROPILY > ROPEY
ROPINESS > ROPEY
ROPING > ROPE
ROPINGS > ROPE
ROPY *same as* > ROPEY
ROQUE *n* game developed from croquet, played on a hard surface with a resilient surrounding border from which the ball can rebound
ROQUES > ROQUE
ROQUET *vb* drive one's ball against (another person's ball) in order to be allowed to croquet ▷ *n* act of roqueting
ROQUETED > ROQUET
ROQUETING > ROQUET
ROQUETS > ROQUET
ROQUETTE *n* another name for the salad plant rocket
ROQUETTES > ROQUETTE
RORAL *archaic word for* > DEWY
RORE *archaic spelling of* > ROAR
RORES > RORE
RORIC *same as* > RORAL
RORID *same as* > RORAL
RORIE *same as* > ROARY
RORIER > RORY
RORIEST > RORY
RORQUAL *n* toothless whale with a dorsal fin
RORQUALS > RORQUAL
RORT *n* dishonest scheme ▷ *vb* take unfair advantage of something
RORTED > RORT
RORTER *n* small-scale confidence trickster
RORTERS > RORTER
RORTIER > RORT
RORTIEST > RORT
RORTING > RORT
RORTS > RORT
RORTY > RORT
RORY *adj* dewy
ROSACE *another name for* > ROSETTE
ROSACEA *n* chronic inflammatory disease causing the skin of the face to become abnormally flushed and sometimes pustular
ROSACEAS > ROSACEA
ROSACEOUS *adj* of or belonging to a family of plants typically having five-petalled flowers, which includes the rose, strawberry, and many fruit trees
ROSACES > ROSACE
ROSAKER *archaic word for* > REALGAR
ROSAKERS > ROSAKER
ROSALIA *n* melody which is repeated but at a higher pitch each time
ROSALIAS > ROSALIA
ROSANILIN *n* reddish-brown crystalline insoluble derivative of aniline used as a red dye
ROSARIA > ROSARIUM
ROSARIAN *n* person who cultivates roses, esp professionally
ROSARIANS > ROSARIAN
ROSARIES > ROSARY
ROSARIUM *n* rose garden
ROSARIUMS > ROSARIUM
ROSARY *n* series of prayers
ROSBIF *n* term used in France for an English person
ROSBIFS > ROSBIF
ROSCID *adj* dewy
ROSCOE *slang word for* > GUN
ROSCOES > ROSCOE
ROSE > RISE
ROSEAL *adj* rosy or roselike
ROSEATE *adj* rose-coloured
ROSEATELY > ROSEATE
ROSEBAY as in *rosebay willowherb* perennial plant with spikes of deep pink flowers
ROSEBAYS > ROSEBAY
ROSEBOWL *n* bowl for displaying roses or other flowers
ROSEBOWLS > ROSEBOWL
ROSEBUD *n* rose which has not yet fully opened
ROSEBUDS > ROSEBUD
ROSEBUSH *n* flowering shrub
ROSED > RISE
ROSEFINCH *n* any of various finches with pink patches
ROSEFISH *n* red food fish of North Atlantic coastal waters
ROSEHIP *n* berry-like fruit of a rose plant
ROSEHIPS > ROSEHIP
ROSELESS > RISE
ROSELIKE > RISE
ROSELLA *n* type of Australian parrot
ROSELLAS > ROSELLA
ROSELLE *n* Indian flowering plant
ROSELLES > ROSELLE
ROSEMARY *n* fragrant flowering shrub
ROSEOLA *n* feverish condition of young children that lasts for some five days during the last two of which the patient has a rose-coloured rash. It is caused by the human herpes virus
ROSEOLAR > ROSEOLA
ROSEOLAS > ROSEOLA
ROSERIES > ROSERY
ROSEROOT *n* Eurasian mountain plant
ROSEROOTS > ROSEROOT
ROSERY *n* bed or garden of roses
ROSES > RISE
ROSESLUG *n* one of various types of pest that feed on roses
ROSESLUGS > ROSESLUG
ROSET *n* Scots word meaning rosin ▷ *vb* rub rosin on
ROSETED > ROSET
ROSETING > ROSET
ROSETS > ROSET
ROSETTE *n* rose-shaped ornament, esp a circular bunch of ribbons
ROSETTED > ROSET
ROSETTES > ROSETTE
ROSETTY > ROSET
ROSETY > ROSET
ROSEWATER *n* scented water used as a perfume and in cooking, made by the distillation of rose petals or by impregnation with oil of roses
ROSEWOOD *n* fragrant wood used to make furniture
ROSEWOODS > ROSEWOOD
ROSHI *n* teacher of Zen Buddhism
ROSHIS > ROSHI
ROSIED > ROSY
ROSIER *archaic word for* > ROSEBUSH
ROSIERE *archaic word for* > ROSEBUSH
ROSIERES > ROSIERE
ROSIERS > ROSIER
ROSIES > ROSY
ROSIEST > ROSY
ROSILY > ROSY
ROSIN *n* resin used for treating the bows of violins etc ▷ *vb* apply rosin to
ROSINATE *n* chemical compound
ROSINATES > ROSINATE
ROSINED > ROSIN
ROSINER *n* strong alcoholic drink
ROSINERS > ROSINER
ROSINESS > ROSY
ROSING > RISE
ROSINING > ROSIN
ROSINOL *n* yellowish fluorescent oily liquid obtained from certain resins, used in the manufacture of carbon black, varnishes, and lacquers
ROSINOLS > ROSINOL
ROSINOUS *adj* rosiny
ROSINS > ROSIN
ROSINWEED *n* any of several North American plants of the genus *Silphium* and related genera, having resinous juice, sticky foliage, and a strong smell
ROSINY > ROSIN
ROSIT *same as* > ROSET
ROSITED > ROSIT
ROSITING > ROSIT
ROSITS > ROSIT
ROSMARINE *archaic form of* > ROSEMARY
ROSOGLIO *same as* > ROSOLIO
ROSOGLIOS > ROSOGLIO
ROSOLIO *n* type of cordial
ROSOLIOS > ROSOLIO
ROSSER *n* bark-removing machine
ROSSERS > ROSSER
ROST *archaic spelling of* > ROAST
ROSTED > ROST
ROSTELLA > ROSTELLUM
ROSTELLAR > ROSTELLUM
ROSTELLUM *n* small beaklike process, such as the hooked projection from the top of the head in tapeworms or the outgrowth from the stigma of an orchid
ROSTER *n* list of people an their turns of duty ▷ *vb* place on a roster
ROSTERED > ROSTER
ROSTERING > ROSTER
ROSTERS > ROSTER
ROSTI *n* cheese-topped fried Swiss dish consistir of grated potato and, optionally, onion
ROSTING > ROST
ROSTIS > ROSTI
ROSTRA > ROSTRUM
ROSTRAL *adj* of or like a beak or snout
ROSTRALLY > ROSTRAL
ROSTRATE *adj* having a beak or beaklike process
ROSTRATED *same as* > ROSTRATE
ROSTRUM *n* platform or stage
ROSTRUMS > ROSTRUM
ROSTS > ROST
ROSULA *n* rosette
ROSULAS > ROSULA
ROSULATE *adj* in the form of a rose
ROSY *adj* pink-coloured ▷ *vb* redden or make pinl
ROSYING > ROSY
ROT *vb* decompose or dec ▷ *n* decay
ROTA *n* list of people who take it in turn to do a particular task
ROTACHUTE *n* device serving the same purpos as a parachute, in which the canopy is replaced by freely revolving rotor blades, used for the delivery of stores or recovery of missiles
ROTAL *adj* of or relating to wheels or rotation
ROTAMETER *n* device for measuring the flow of a liquid

OTAN *another name for* > RATTAN
OTANS > ROTAN
OTAPLANE *n* aircraft that derives its lift from freely revolving rotor blades
OTARIES > ROTARY
OTARY *adj* revolving ▷ *n* traffic roundabout
OTAS > ROTA
OTATABLE > ROTATE
OTATE *vb* (cause to) move round a centre or on a pivot ▷ *adj* designating a corolla the united petals of which radiate from a central point like the spokes of a wheel
OTATED > ROTATE
OTATES > ROTATE
OTATING *adj* revolving around a central axis, line, or point
OTATION *n* act of rotating
OTATIONS > ROTATION
OTATIVE *same as* > ROTATORY
OTATOR *n* person, device, or part that rotates or causes rotation
OTATORES > ROTATOR
OTATORS > ROTATOR
OTATORY *adj* of, relating to, possessing, or causing rotation
OTAVATE *same as* > ROTOVATE
OTAVATED > ROTAVATE
OTAVATES > ROTAVATE
OTAVATOR *n* type of machine with rotating blades that will break up soil
OTAVIRUS *n* any member of a genus of viruses that cause worldwide endemic infections. They occur in birds and mammals, cause diarrhoea in children, and are usually transmitted in food prepared with unwashed hands
OTCH *n* little auk
OTCHE *same as* > ROTCH
OTCHES > ROTCH
OTCHIE *same as* > ROTCH
OTCHIES > ROTCHIE
OTE *n* mechanical repetition ▷ *vb* learn by rote
OTED > ROTE
OTENONE *n* white odourless crystalline substance extracted from the roots of derris: a powerful insecticide
OTENONES > ROTENONE
OTES > ROTE
OTGRASS *n* type of grass blamed for sheeprot
OTGUT *n* alcoholic drink of inferior quality
OTGUTS > ROTGUT
OTHER *dialect word for* > OX
ROTHERS > ROTHER
ROTI *n* (in India and the Caribbean) a type of unleavened bread
ROTIFER *n* minute aquatic multicellular invertebrate
ROTIFERAL > ROTIFER
ROTIFERAN > ROTIFER
ROTIFERS > ROTIFER
ROTIFORM *adj* in the shape of a wheel
ROTING > ROTE
ROTIS > ROTI
ROTL *n* unit of weight used in Muslim countries, varying in value between about one and five pounds
ROTLS > ROTL
ROTO *n* printing process using a cylinder etched with many small recesses, from which ink is transferred to a moving web of paper, plastic, etc, in a rotary press
ROTOGRAPH *n* photograph made using a particular method ▷ *vb* photograph using this method
ROTOLO *n* (in Italian cuisine) a roll
ROTOLOS > ROTOLO
ROTON *n* quantum of vortex motion
ROTONS > ROTON
ROTOR *n* revolving portion of a dynamo, motor, or turbine
ROTORS > ROTOR
ROTOS > ROTO
ROTOTILL *vb* break up the soil using a rototiller
ROTOTILLS > ROTOTILL
ROTOVATE *vb* break up (the surface of the earth, or an area of ground) using a rotavator
ROTOVATED > ROTOVATE
ROTOVATES > ROTOVATE
ROTOVATOR *same as* > ROTAVATOR
ROTS > ROT
ROTTAN *n* (in dialect) a rat
ROTTANS > ROTTAN
ROTTE *n* ancient stringed instrument
ROTTED > ROT
ROTTEN *adj* decaying ▷ *adv* extremely ▷ *n* (in dialect) a rat
ROTTENER > ROTTEN
ROTTENEST > ROTTEN
ROTTENLY > ROTTEN
ROTTENS > ROTTEN
ROTTER *n* despicable person
ROTTERS > ROTTER
ROTTES > ROTTE
ROTTING > ROT
ROTULA *n* kneecap
ROTULAE > ROTULA
ROTULAS > ROTULA
ROTUND *adj* round and plump ▷ *vb* make round
ROTUNDA *n* circular building or room, esp with a dome
ROTUNDAS > ROTUNDA
ROTUNDATE *adj* rounded
ROTUNDED > ROTUND
ROTUNDER > ROTUND
ROTUNDEST > ROTUND
ROTUNDING > ROTUND
ROTUNDITY > ROTUND
ROTUNDLY > ROTUND
ROTUNDS > ROTUND
ROTURIER *n* freeholder or ordinary person
ROTURIERS > ROTURIER
ROUBLE *n* monetary unit of Russia, Belarus, and Tajikistan
ROUBLES > ROUBLE
ROUCHE *same as* > RUCHE
ROUCHES > ROUCHE
ROUCOU *another name for* > ANNATTO
ROUCOUS > ROUCOU
ROUE *n* man given to immoral living
ROUEN *n* breed of duck
ROUENS > ROUEN
ROUES > ROUE
ROUGE *n* red cosmetic used to colour the cheeks ▷ *vb* apply rouge to
ROUGED > ROUGE
ROUGES > ROUGE
ROUGH *adj* uneven or irregular ▷ *vb* make rough ▷ *n* rough state or area
ROUGHAGE *n* indigestible constituents of food which aid digestion
ROUGHAGES > ROUGHAGE
ROUGHBACK *n* rough-skinned flatfish
ROUGHCAST *n* mixture of plaster and small stones for outside walls ▷ *vb* coat with this ▷ *adj* covered with or denoting roughcast
ROUGHDRY *vb* dry (clothes or linen) without smoothing
ROUGHED > ROUGH
ROUGHEN *vb* make or become rough
ROUGHENED > ROUGHEN
ROUGHENS > ROUGHEN
ROUGHER *n* person that does the rough preparatory work on something ▷ *adj* more rough
ROUGHERS > ROUGHER
ROUGHEST > ROUGH
ROUGHHEW *vb* cut or hew (timber, stone, etc) roughly without finishing the surfac
ROUGHHEWN > ROUGHHEW
ROUGHHEWS > ROUGHHEW
ROUGHIE *n* small food fish found in southern and western Australian waters
ROUGHIES > ROUGHIE
ROUGHING > ROUGH
ROUGHISH *adj* somewhat rough
ROUGHLEG *n* any of several kinds of large hawk with feathered legs
ROUGHLEGS > ROUGHLEG
ROUGHLY *adv* without being exact or fully authenticated
ROUGHNECK *n* violent person
ROUGHNESS > ROUGH
ROUGHS > ROUGH
ROUGHSHOD *adj* (of a horse) shod with rough-bottomed shoes to prevent slidi
ROUGHT *archaic past form of* > REACH
ROUGHY *spelling variant of* > ROUGHIE
ROUGING > ROUGE
ROUILLE *n* kind of sauce
ROUILLES > ROUILLE
ROUL *archaic form of* > ROLL
ROULADE *n* slice of meat rolled, esp around a stuffing, and cooked
ROULADES > ROULADE
ROULE *archaic form of* > ROLL
ROULEAU *n* roll of paper containing coins
ROULEAUS > ROULEAU
ROULEAUX > ROULEAU
ROULES > ROULE
ROULETTE *n* gambling game played with a revolving wheel and a ball ▷ *vb* use a toothed wheel on (something), as in engraving, making stationery, etc
ROULETTED > ROULETTE
ROULETTES > ROULETTE
ROULS > ROUL
ROUM *archaic spelling of* > ROOM
ROUMING *n* pasture given for an animal
ROUMINGS > ROUMING
ROUMS > ROUM
ROUNCE *n* handle that is turned to move paper and plates on a printing press
ROUNCES > ROUNCE
ROUNCEVAL *n* giant or monster
ROUNCIES > ROUNCY
ROUNCY *archaic word for* > HORSE
ROUND *adj* spherical, cylindrical, circular, or curved ▷ *prep* indicating an encircling movement, presence on all sides, etc ▷ *vb* move round ▷ *n* round shape
ROUNDARCH *adj* with rounded arches
ROUNDBALL *n* form of basketball
ROUNDED *adj* round or curved

ROUNDEDLY > ROUNDED
ROUNDEL *same as* > ROUNDELAY
ROUNDELAY *n* simple song with a refrain
ROUNDELS > ROUNDEL
ROUNDER *n* run round all four bases after one hit in rounders
ROUNDERS *n* bat-and-ball team game
ROUNDEST > ROUND
ROUNDHAND *n* style of handwriting with large rounded curves
ROUNDHEEL *n* immoral woman
ROUNDING *n* process in which a number is approximated as the closest number that can be expressed using the number of bits or digits available
ROUNDINGS > ROUNDING
ROUNDISH *adj* somewhat round
ROUNDLE *same as* > ROUNDEL
ROUNDLES > ROUNDLE
ROUNDLET *n* small circle
ROUNDLETS > ROUNDLET
ROUNDLY *adv* thoroughly
ROUNDNESS > ROUND
ROUNDS > ROUND
ROUNDSMAN *n* person who makes rounds, as for inspection or to deliver goods
ROUNDSMEN > ROUNDSMAN
ROUNDTRIP *n* US term for return trip
ROUNDUP *n* act of gathering together livestock, people, facts, etc
ROUNDUPS > ROUNDUP
ROUNDURE *n* archaic word meaning roundness
ROUNDURES > ROUNDURE
ROUNDWOOD *n* small pieces of timber (about 5–15 cm, or 2–6 in.) in diameter
ROUNDWORM *n* worm that is a common intestinal parasite of man
ROUP *n* any of various chronic respiratory diseases of birds, esp poultry ▷ *vb* sell by auction
ROUPED > ROUP
ROUPET *adj* Scots word meaning hoarse or croaky
ROUPIER > ROUP
ROUPIEST > ROUP
ROUPILY > ROUP
ROUPING > ROUP
ROUPIT *same as* > ROUPET
ROUPS > ROUP
ROUPY > ROUP
ROUSANT *adj* (in heraldry) rising
ROUSE *same as* > REVEILLE
ROUSED > ROUSE
ROUSEMENT *n* stirring up
ROUSER *n* person or thing that rouses people, such as a stirring speech or compelling rock song
ROUSERS > ROUSER
ROUSES > ROUSE
ROUSING *adj* lively, vigorous
ROUSINGLY > ROUSING
ROUSSEAU *n* pemmican fried in its own fat
ROUSSEAUS > ROUSSEAU
ROUSSETTE *n* dogfish
ROUST *vb* rout or stir, as out of bed
ROUSTED > ROUST
ROUSTER *n* unskilled labourer on an oil rig
ROUSTERS > ROUSTER
ROUSTING > ROUST
ROUSTS > ROUST
ROUT *n* overwhelming defeat ▷ *vb* defeat and put to flight
ROUTE *n* roads taken to reach a destination ▷ *vb* send by a particular route
ROUTED > ROUTE
ROUTEING > ROUTE
ROUTEMAN *n* (in US English) delivery man or salesman doing a particular round
ROUTEMEN > ROUTEMAN
ROUTER *n* device that allows data to be moved efficiently between two points on a network
ROUTERS > ROUTER
ROUTES > ROUTE
ROUTEWAY *n* track, road, or waterway, etc, used as a route to somewhere
ROUTEWAYS > ROUTEWAY
ROUTH *n* abundance ▷ *adj* abundant
ROUTHIE *adj* abundant, plentiful, or well filled
ROUTHIER > ROUTHIE
ROUTHIEST > ROUTHIE
ROUTHS > ROUTH
ROUTINE *n* usual or regular method of procedure ▷ *adj* ordinary or regular
ROUTINEER *n* someone who believes in routine
ROUTINELY > ROUTINE
ROUTINES > ROUTINE
ROUTING > ROUT
ROUTINGS > ROUT
ROUTINISE *same as* > ROUTINIZE
ROUTINISM > ROUTINE
ROUTINIST > ROUTINE
ROUTINIZE *vb* make routine
ROUTOUS > ROUT
ROUTOUSLY > ROUT
ROUTS > ROUT
ROUX *n* fat and flour cooked together as a basis for sauces
ROVE > REEVE
ROVED > REEVE
ROVEN > REEVE
ROVER *n* wanderer, traveller
ROVERS > ROVER
ROVES > REEVE
ROVING > ROVE
ROVINGLY > ROVING
ROVINGS > ROVE
ROW *n* straight line of people or things ▷ *vb* propel (a boat) by oars
ROWABLE > ROW
ROWAN *n* tree producing bright red berries, mountain ash
ROWANS > ROWAN
ROWBOAT *n* small boat propelled by one or more pairs of oars
ROWBOATS > ROWBOAT
ROWDEDOW *same as* > ROWDYDOW
ROWDEDOWS > ROWDEDOW
ROWDIER > ROWDY
ROWDIES > ROWDY
ROWDIEST > ROWDY
ROWDILY > ROWDY
ROWDINESS > ROWDY
ROWDY *adj* disorderly, noisy, and rough ▷ *n* person like this
ROWDYDOW *n* hullabaloo
ROWDYDOWS > ROWDYDOW
ROWDYISH > ROWDY
ROWDYISM *n* rowdy behaviour or tendencies or a habitual pattern of rowdy behaviour
ROWDYISMS > ROWDYISM
ROWED > ROW
ROWEL *n* small spiked wheel on a spur ▷ *vb* goad (a horse) using a rowel
ROWELED > ROWEL
ROWELING > ROWEL
ROWELLED > ROWEL
ROWELLING > ROWEL
ROWELS > ROWEL
ROWEN *another word for* > AFTERMATH
ROWENS > ROWEN
ROWER > ROW
ROWERS > ROW
ROWING > ROW
ROWINGS > ROW
ROWLOCK *n* device on a boat that holds an oar in place
ROWLOCKS > ROWLOCK
ROWME *archaic variant of* > ROOM
ROWMES > ROWME
ROWND *archaic variant of* > ROUND
ROWNDED > ROWND
ROWNDELL *archaic variant of* > ROUNDEL
ROWNDELLS > ROWNDELL
ROWNDING > ROWND
ROWNDS > ROWND
ROWOVER *n* act of winning a rowing race unopposed, by rowing the course
ROWOVERS > ROWOVER
ROWS > ROW
ROWT *archaic variant of* > ROUT
ROWTED > ROWT
ROWTH *same as* > ROUTH
ROWTHS > ROWTH
ROWTING > ROWT
ROWTS > ROWT
ROYAL *adj* of, befitting, or supported by a king or queen ▷ *n* member of a royal family
ROYALET *n* minor king
ROYALETS > ROYALET
ROYALISE *same as* > ROYALIZE
ROYALISED > ROYALISE
ROYALISES > ROYALISE
ROYALISM > ROYALIST
ROYALISMS > ROYALIST
ROYALIST *n* supporter of monarchy ▷ *adj* of or relating to royalists
ROYALISTS > ROYALIST
ROYALIZE *vb* make royal
ROYALIZED > ROYALIZE
ROYALIZES > ROYALIZE
ROYALLER > ROYAL
ROYALLEST > ROYAL
ROYALLY > ROYAL
ROYALMAST *n* highest part of mast
ROYALS > ROYAL
ROYALTIES > ROYALTY
ROYALTY *n* royal people
ROYNE *archaic word for* > GNAW
ROYNED > ROYNE
ROYNES > ROYNE
ROYNING > ROYNE
ROYNISH *archaic word for* > MANGY
ROYST *same as* > ROIST
ROYSTED > ROYST
ROYSTER *same as* > ROISTER
ROYSTERED > ROYSTER
ROYSTERER > ROYSTER
ROYSTERS > ROISTER
ROYSTING > ROYST
ROYSTS > ROYST
ROZELLE *same as* > ROSELLE
ROZELLES > ROZELLE
ROZET *same as* > ROSET
ROZETED > ROZET
ROZETING > ROZET
ROZETS > ROZET
ROZIT *same as* > ROSET
ROZITED > ROZIT
ROZITING > ROZIT
ROZITS > ROZIT
ROZZER *n* policeman
ROZZERS > ROZZER
RUANA *n* woollen wrap resembling a poncho
RUANAS > RUANA
RUB *vb* apply pressure and friction to (something) with a circular or backwards-and-forwards movement ▷ *n* act of rubbing
RUBABOO *n* soup or stew made by boiling pemmican with, if available, flour and vegetables

JBABOOS > RUBABOO
JBACE *same as* > RUBASSE
JBACES > RUBACE
JBAI *n* verse form of Persian origin consisting of four-line stanzas
JBAIYAT *n* (in Persian poetry) a verse form consisting of four-line stanzas
JBASSE *n* type of quartz containing red haematite
JBASSES > RUBASSE
JBATI > RUBATO
JBATO *n* (with) expressive flexibility of tempo ▷ *adv* be played with a flexible tempo
JBATOS > RUBATO
JBBABOO *same as* > RUBABOO
JBBABOOS > RUBABOO
JBBED > RUB
JBBER *n* strong waterproof elastic material, orig. made from the dried sap of a tropical tree, now usu synthetic ▷ *adj* made of or producing rubber ▷ *vb* provide with rubber coating
JBBERED > RUBBER
JBBERIER > RUBBERY
JBBERING > RUBBER
JBBERISE *same as* > RUBBERIZE
JBBERIZE *vb* coat or treat with rubber
JBBERS > RUBBER
JBBERY *adj* having the texture of or resembling rubber, esp in flexibility or toughness
JBBET *old Scots past form of* > ROB
JBBIDIES > RUBBIDY
JBBIDY *same as* > RUBBITY
JBBIES > RUBBY
JBBING > RUB
JBBINGS > RUB
JBBISH *n* waste matter ▷ *vb* criticize
JBBISHED > RUBBISH
JBBISHES > RUBBISH
JBBISHLY *variant of* > RUBBISHY
JBBISHY *adj* worthless, of poor quality, or useless
JBBIT *old Scots past form of* > ROB
JBBITIES > RUBBITY
JBBITY *n* pub
JBBLE *n* fragments of broken stone, brick, etc ▷ *vb* turn into rubble
JBBLED > RUBBLE
JBBLES > RUBBLE
JBBLIER > RUBBLE
JBBLIEST > RUBBLE
JBBLING > RUBBLE
JBBLY > RUBBLE
JBBOARD *n* board for scrubbing clothes on
JBBOARDS > RUBBOARD
RUBBY *n* rubbing alcohol, esp when mixed with cheap wine for drinking
RUBDOWN *n* act of drying or cleaning vigorously
RUBDOWNS > RUBDOWN
RUBE *n* unsophisticated countryman
RUBEFIED > RUBEFY
RUBEFIES > RUBEFY
RUBEFY *vb* make red, esp (of a counterirritant) to make the skin go red
RUBEFYING > RUBEFY
RUBEL *n* currency unit of Belarus
RUBELLA *n* mild contagious viral disease characterized by cough, sore throat, and skin rash
RUBELLAN *n* red-coloured mineral
RUBELLANS > RUBELLAN
RUBELLAS > RUBELLA
RUBELLITE *n* red transparent variety of tourmaline, used as a gemstone
RUBELS > RUBEL
RUBEOLA *technical name for* > MEASLES
RUBEOLAR > RUBEOLA
RUBEOLAS > RUBEOLA
RUBES > RUBE
RUBESCENT *adj* reddening
RUBICELLE *n* variety of spinel that is orange or yellow in colour
RUBICON *n* point of no return ▷ *vb* (in bezique) to beat before the loser has managed to gain as many as 1000 points
RUBICONED > RUBICON
RUBICONS > RUBICON
RUBICUND *adj* ruddy
RUBIDIC > RUBIDIUM
RUBIDIUM *n* soft highly reactive radioactive element
RUBIDIUMS > RUBIDIUM
RUBIED > RUBY
RUBIER > RUBY
RUBIES > RUBY
RUBIEST > RUBY
RUBIFIED > RUBIFY
RUBIFIES > RUBIFY
RUBIFY *same as* > RUBEFY
RUBIFYING > RUBIFY
RUBIGO *old Scots word for* > PENIS
RUBIGOS > RUBIGO
RUBIN *archaic word for* > RUBY
RUBINE *archaic word for* > RUBY
RUBINEOUS *same as* > RUBIOUS
RUBINES > RUBINE
RUBINS > RUBIN
RUBIOUS *adj* of the colour ruby
RUBLE *same as* > ROUBLE
RUBLES > RUBLE
RUBOFF *n* resulting effect on something else; consequences
RUBOFFS > RUBOFF
RUBOUT *n* killing or elimination
RUBOUTS > RUBOUT
RUBRIC *n* set of rules for behaviour ▷ *adj* written, printed, or marked in red
RUBRICAL > RUBRIC
RUBRICATE *vb* print (a book or manuscript) with red titles, headings, etc
RUBRICIAN *n* authority on liturgical rubrics
RUBRICS > RUBRIC
RUBS > RUB
RUBSTONE *n* stone used for sharpening or smoothing, esp a whetstone
RUBSTONES > RUBSTONE
RUBUS *n* fruit-bearing genus of shrubs
RUBY *n* red precious gemstone ▷ *adj* deep red ▷ *vb* redden
RUBYING > RUBY
RUBYLIKE > RUBY
RUC *same as* > ROC
RUCHE *n* pleat or frill of lace etc as a decoration ▷ *vb* put a ruche on
RUCHED > RUCHE
RUCHES > RUCHE
RUCHING *n* material used for a ruche
RUCHINGS > RUCHING
RUCK *n* rough crowd of common people ▷ *vb* wrinkle or crease
RUCKED > RUCK
RUCKING > RUCK
RUCKLE *another word for* > RUCK
RUCKLED > RUCKLE
RUCKLES > RUCKLE
RUCKLING > RUCKLE
RUCKMAN *n* person who plays in the ruck
RUCKMEN > RUCKMAN
RUCKS > RUCK
RUCKSACK *n* large pack carried on the back
RUCKSACKS > RUCKSACK
RUCKSEAT *n* seat fixed to or forming part of a rucksack
RUCKSEATS > RUCKSEAT
RUCKUS *n* uproar
RUCKUSES > RUCKUS
RUCOLA *n* another name for the salad plant rocket
RUCOLAS > RUCOLA
RUCS > RUC
RUCTATION *n* archaic word meaning eructation or belch
RUCTION *n* uproar
RUCTIONS > RUCTION
RUCTIOUS *adj* tending or likely to cause ructions
RUD *n* red or redness ▷ *vb* redden
RUDACEOUS *adj* (of conglomerate, breccia, and similar rocks) composed of coarse-grained material
RUDAS *n* Scots word for a coarse, rude old woman
RUDASES > RUDAS
RUDBECKIA *n* any plant of the North American genus *Rudbeckia*, cultivated for their showy flowers
RUDD *n* European freshwater fish
RUDDED > RUD
RUDDER *n* vertical hinged piece at the stern of a boat or at the rear of an aircraft, for steering
RUDDERS > RUDDER
RUDDIED > RUDDY
RUDDIER > RUDDY
RUDDIES > RUDDY
RUDDIEST > RUDDY
RUDDILY > RUDDY
RUDDINESS > RUDDY
RUDDING > RUD
RUDDLE *n* red ochre, used esp to mark sheep ▷ *vb* mark (sheep) with ruddle
RUDDLED > RUDDLE
RUDDLEMAN *n* ruddle dealer
RUDDLEMEN > RUDDLEMAN
RUDDLES > RUDDLE
RUDDLING > RUDDLE
RUDDOCK *dialect name for the* > ROBIN
RUDDOCKS > RUDDOCK
RUDDS > RUDD
RUDDY *adj* of a fresh healthy red colour ▷ *adv* bloody ▷ *vb* redden
RUDDYING > RUDDY
RUDE *archaic spelling of* > ROOD
RUDELY > RUDE
RUDENESS > RUDE
RUDER > RUDE
RUDERAL *n* plant that grows on waste ground ▷ *adj* growing in waste places
RUDERALS > RUDERAL
RUDERIES > RUDE
RUDERY > RUDE
RUDES > RUDE
RUDESBIES > RUDESBY
RUDESBY *n* archaic word for rude person
RUDEST > RUDE
RUDIE *n* member of a youth movement originating in the 1960s
RUDIES > RUDIE
RUDIMENT *n* first principles or elementary stages of a subject
RUDIMENTS > RUDIMENT
RUDISH *adj* somewhat rude
RUDS > RUD
RUE *vb* feel regret for ▷ *n* plant with evergreen bitter leaves
RUED > RUE
RUEFUL *adj* regretful or

sorry
RUEFULLY > RUEFUL
RUEING > RUE
RUEINGS > RUE
RUELLE *n* area between bed and wall, at one time used by French ladies of standing for receiving visitors
RUELLES > RUELLE
RUELLIA *n* genus of plants
RUELLIAS > RUELLIA
RUER > RUE
RUERS > RUE
RUES > RUE
RUFESCENT *adj* tinged with red or becoming red
RUFF *n* circular pleated, gathered, or fluted collar of lawn, muslin, etc, often starched or wired, worn by both men and women in the 16th and 17th centuries ▷ *vb* trump
RUFFE *n* European freshwater fish
RUFFED > RUFF
RUFFES > RUFFE
RUFFIAN *n* violent lawless person ▷ *vb* act like a ruffian
RUFFIANED > RUFFIAN
RUFFIANLY > RUFFIAN
RUFFIANS > RUFFIAN
RUFFIN *archaic name for* > RUFFE
RUFFING > RUFF
RUFFINS > RUFFIN
RUFFLE *vb* disturb the calm of ▷ *n* frill or pleat
RUFFLED > RUFFLE
RUFFLER *n* person or thing that ruffles
RUFFLERS > RUFFLER
RUFFLES > RUFFLE
RUFFLIER > RUFFLY
RUFFLIEST > RUFFLY
RUFFLIKE > RUFF
RUFFLING > RUFFLE
RUFFLINGS > RUFFLE
RUFFLY *adj* ruffled
RUFFS > RUFF
RUFIYAA *n* standard monetary unit of the Maldives, divided into 100 laari
RUFIYAAS > RUFIYAA
RUFOUS *adj* reddish-brown
RUG *n* small carpet ▷ *vb* (in dialect) tug
RUGA *n* fold, wrinkle, or crease
RUGAE > RUGA
RUGAL *adj* (in anatomy) with ridges or folds
RUGALACH *same as* > RUGELACH
RUGATE *same as* > RUGOSE
RUGBIES > RUGBY
RUGBY *n* form of football played with an oval ball which may be handled by the players
RUGELACH *n* fruit and nut pastry shaped like a croissant
RUGGED *adj* rocky or steep
RUGGEDER > RUGGED
RUGGEDEST > RUGGED
RUGGEDISE *same as* > RUGGEDIZE
RUGGEDIZE *vb* make durable, as for military use
RUGGEDLY > RUGGED
RUGGELACH *same as* > RUGELACH
RUGGER *same as* > RUGBY
RUGGERS > RUGGER
RUGGIER > RUGGY
RUGGIEST > RUGGY
RUGGING > RUG
RUGGINGS > RUG
RUGGY *adj* (in dialect) rough or rugged
RUGLIKE > RUG
RUGOLA *n* another name for the salad plant rocket
RUGOLAS > RUGOLA
RUGOSA *n* any of various shrubs descended from a particular type of wild rose
RUGOSAS > RUGOSA
RUGOSE *adj* wrinkled
RUGOSELY > RUGOSE
RUGOSITY > RUGOSE
RUGOUS *same as* > RUGOSE
RUGS > RUG
RUGULOSE *adj* with little wrinkles
RUIN *vb* destroy or spoil completely ▷ *n* destruction or decay
RUINABLE > RUIN
RUINATE *vb* archaic word for bring or come to ruin
RUINATED > RUINATE
RUINATES > RUINATE
RUINATING > RUINATE
RUINATION *n* act of ruining
RUINED > RUIN
RUINER > RUIN
RUINERS > RUIN
RUING > RUE
RUINGS > RUE
RUINING > RUIN
RUININGS > RUIN
RUINOUS *adj* causing ruin
RUINOUSLY > RUINOUS
RUINS > RUIN
RUKH *same as* > ROC
RUKHS > RUKH
RULABLE > RULE
RULE *n* statement of what is allowed, for example in a game or procedure ▷ *vb* govern
RULED > RULE
RULELESS > RULE
RULER *n* person who governs ▷ *vb* punish by hitting with a ruler
RULERED > RULER
RULERING > RULER
RULERS > RULER
RULERSHIP > RULER
RULES > RULE
RULESSE *adj* archaic word meaning ruleless or without rules
RULIER > RULY
RULIEST > RULY
RULING *n* formal decision ▷ *adj* controlling or exercising authority
RULINGS > RULING
RULLION *n* Scots word for rawhide shoe
RULLIONS > RULLION
RULLOCK *same as* > ROWLOCK
RULLOCKS > RULLOCK
RULY *adj* orderly
RUM *n* alcoholic drink distilled from sugar cane ▷ *adj* odd, strange
RUMAKI *n* savoury of chicken liver and sliced water chestnut wrapped in bacon
RUMAKIS > RUMAKI
RUMAL *n* handkerchief or type of cloth
RUMALS > RUMAL
RUMBA *n* lively ballroom dance of Cuban origin ▷ *vb* dance the rumba
RUMBAED > RUMBA
RUMBAING > RUMBA
RUMBAS > RUMBA
RUMBELOW *n* nonsense word used in the refrain of certain sea shanties
RUMBELOWS > RUMBELOW
RUMBLE *vb* make a low continuous noise ▷ *n* deep resonant sound
RUMBLED > RUMBLE
RUMBLER > RUMBLE
RUMBLERS > RUMBLE
RUMBLES > RUMBLE
RUMBLIER > RUMBLY
RUMBLIEST > RUMBLY
RUMBLING > RUMBLE
RUMBLINGS > RUMBLE
RUMBLY *adj* rumbling or liable to rumble
RUMBO *n* rum-based cocktail
RUMBOS > RUMBO
RUME *archaic form of* > RHEUM
RUMEN *n* first compartment of the stomach of ruminants, behind the reticulum, in which food is partly digested before being regurgitated as cud
RUMENS > RUMEN
RUMES > RUME
RUMINA > RUMEN
RUMINAL > RUMEN
RUMINANT *n* cud-chewing (animal, such as a cow, sheep, or deer) ▷ *adj* of ruminants
RUMINANTS > RUMINANT
RUMINATE *vb* chew the cud
RUMINATED > RUMINATE
RUMINATES > RUMINATE
RUMINATOR > RUMINATE
RUMKIN *n* archaic term for a drinking vessel
RUMKINS > RUMKIN
RUMLY > RUM
RUMMAGE *vb* search untidily and at length ▷ *n* untidy search through a collection of things
RUMMAGED > RUMMAGE
RUMMAGER > RUMMAGE
RUMMAGERS > RUMMAGE
RUMMAGES > RUMMAGE
RUMMAGING > RUMMAGE
RUMMER > RUM
RUMMERS > RUM
RUMMEST > RUM
RUMMIER > RUMMY
RUMMIES > RUMMY
RUMMIEST > RUMMY
RUMMILY > RUMMY
RUMMINESS > RUMMY
RUMMISH *adj* rather strange, peculiar or odd
RUMMY *n* card game in which players try to colle sets or sequences ▷ *adj* c or like rum in taste or sm
RUMNESS > RUM
RUMNESSES > RUM
RUMOR *same as* > RUMOUR
RUMORED > RUMOR
RUMORING > RUMOR
RUMOROUS *adj* involving o containing rumours
RUMORS > RUMOR
RUMOUR *n* unproved statement ▷ *vb* pass around or circulate in the form of a rumour
RUMOURED > RUMOUR
RUMOURER *n* someone given to spreading rumours
RUMOURERS > RUMOURER
RUMOURING > RUMOUR
RUMOURS > RUMOUR
RUMP *n* buttocks ▷ *vb* tur back on
RUMPED > RUMP
RUMPIES > RUMPY
RUMPING > RUMP
RUMPLE *vb* make untidy, crumpled, or dishevelled ▷ *n* wrinkle, fold, or creas
RUMPLED > RUMPLE
RUMPLES > RUMPLE
RUMPLESS > RUMP
RUMPLIER > RUMPLE
RUMPLIEST > RUMPLE
RUMPLING > RUMPLE
RUMPLY > RUMPLE
RUMPO *n* slang word for sexual intercourse
RUMPOS > RUMPO
RUMPS > RUMP
RUMPUS *n* noisy commotion
RUMPUSES > RUMPUS
RUMPY *n* tailless Manx cat ▷ *adj* with a large or noticeable rump
RUMRUNNER *n* alcohol smuggler
RUMS > RUM
RUN *vb* move with a more rapid gait than walking

▷ *n* act or spell of running
UNABOUT *n* small car used for short journeys ▷ *vb* move busily from place to place
UNABOUTS > RUNABOUT
UNAGATE *n* vagabond, fugitive, or renegade
JNAGATES > RUNAGATE
UNANGA *n* Māori assembly or council
UNAROUND *n* deceitful or evasive treatment of a person
UNAWAY *n* person or animal that runs away
UNAWAYS > RUNAWAY
UNBACK *n* (in tennis) the areas behind the baselines of the court
UNBACKS > RUNBACK
UNCH *n* another name for white charlock
UNCHES > RUNCH
UNCIBLE as in *runcible spoon* forklike utensil with two prongs and one sharp curved prong
UNCINATE *adj* (of a leaf) having a saw-toothed margin with the teeth or lobes pointing backwards
UND *same as* > ROON
UNDALE *n* (formerly) the name given, esp in Ireland and earlier in Scotland, to the system of land tenure in which each land-holder had several strips of land that were not contiguous
UNDALES > RUNDALE
UNDLE *n* rung of a ladder
UNDLED *adj* rounded
UNDLES > RUNDLE
UNDLET *n* liquid measure, generally about 15 gallons
UNDLETS > RUNDLET
UNDOWN *adj* tired; exhausted ▷ *n* brief review, résumé, or summary
UNDOWNS > RUNDOWN
UNDS > RUND
UNE *n* any character of the earliest Germanic alphabet
JNECRAFT *n* understanding of and skill working with runes
JNED *n* with runes on
JNELIKE *adj* resembling a rune or runes
JNES > RUNE
JNFLAT *adj* having a safety feature that prevents tyres becoming dangerous or liable to damage when flat
JNG > RING
JNGLESS > RING
JNGS > RING
JNIC > RUNE
JNKLE *vb* (in dialect) crease or wrinkle
RUNKLED > RUNKLE
RUNKLES > RUNKLE
RUNKLING > RUNKLE
RUNLESS > RUN
RUNLET *n* cask for wine, beer, etc
RUNLETS > RUNLET
RUNNABLE > RUN
RUNNEL *n* small brook
RUNNELS > RUNNEL
RUNNER *n* competitor in a race
RUNNERS > RUNNER
RUNNET *dialect word for* > RENNET
RUNNETS > RUNNET
RUNNIER > RUNNY
RUNNIEST > RUNNY
RUNNINESS > RUNNY
RUNNING > RUN
RUNNINGLY > RUN
RUNNINGS > RUN
RUNNION *n* archaic pejorative term for a woman
RUNNIONS > RUNNION
RUNNY *adj* tending to flow
RUNOFF *n* extra race to decide the winner after a tie
RUNOFFS > RUNOFF
RUNOUT *n* dismissal of a batsman by running him out
RUNOUTS > RUNOUT
RUNOVER *n* incident in which someone is run over by a vehicle
RUNOVERS > RUNOVER
RUNRIG *same as* > RUNDALE
RUNRIGS > RUNRIG
RUNROUND *same as* > RUNAROUND
RUNROUNDS > RUNROUND
RUNS > RUN
RUNT *n* smallest animal in a litter
RUNTED *adj* stunted
RUNTIER > RUNT
RUNTIEST > RUNT
RUNTINESS > RUNT
RUNTISH > RUNT
RUNTISHLY > RUNT
RUNTS > RUNT
RUNTY > RUNT
RUNWAY *n* hard level roadway where aircraft take off and land
RUNWAYS > RUNWAY
RUPEE *n* monetary unit of India and Pakistan
RUPEES > RUPEE
RUPIA *n* type of skin eruption
RUPIAH *n* standard monetary unit of Indonesia, divided into 100 sen
RUPIAHS > RUPIAH
RUPIAS > RUPIA
RUPTURE *n* breaking, breach ▷ *vb* break, burst, or sever
RUPTURED > RUPTURE
RUPTURES > RUPTURE
RUPTURING > RUPTURE
RURAL *adj* in or of the countryside ▷ *n* country dweller
RURALISE *same as* > RURALIZE
RURALISED > RURALISE
RURALISES > RURALISE
RURALISM > RURAL
RURALISMS > RURAL
RURALIST > RURAL
RURALISTS > RURAL
RURALITE > RURAL
RURALITES > RURAL
RURALITY > RURAL
RURALIZE *vb* make rural in character, appearance, etc
RURALIZED > RURALIZE
RURALIZES > RURALIZE
RURALLY > RURAL
RURALNESS > RURAL
RURALS > RURAL
RURBAN *adj* part country, part urban
RURP *n* very small piton
RURPS > RURP
RURU *another name for* > MOPOKE
RURUS > RURU
RUSA *n* type of deer with a mane
RUSALKA *n* water nymph or spirit
RUSALKAS > RUSALKA
RUSAS > RUSA
RUSCUS *n* type of shrub
RUSCUSES > RUSCUS
RUSE *n* stratagem or trick
RUSES > RUSE
RUSH *vb* move or do very quickly ▷ *n* sudden quick or violent movement ▷ *adj* done with speed, hasty
RUSHED > RUSH
RUSHEE *n* someone interested in gaining fraternity or sorority membership
RUSHEES > RUSHEE
RUSHEN *adj* made of rushes
RUSHER > RUSH
RUSHERS > RUSH
RUSHES *pl n* (in film-making) the initial prints of a scene or scenes before editing, usually prepared daily
RUSHIER > RUSHY
RUSHIEST > RUSHY
RUSHINESS > RUSHY
RUSHING > RUSH
RUSHINGS > RUSH
RUSHLIGHT *n* narrow candle, formerly in use, made of the pith of various types of rush dipped in tallow
RUSHLIKE > RUSH
RUSHY *adj* full of rushes
RUSINE *adj* of or relating to rusa deer
RUSK *n* hard brown crisp biscuit, used esp for feeding babies
RUSKS > RUSK
RUSMA *n* Turkish depilatory
RUSMAS > RUSMA
RUSSE as in *charlotte russe* cold dessert made from whipped cream, custard, etc, surrounded by sponge fingers
RUSSEL *n* type of woollen fabric
RUSSELS > RUSSEL
RUSSET *adj* reddish-brown ▷ *n* apple with rough reddish-brown skin ▷ *vb* become russet-coloured
RUSSETED > RUSSET
RUSSETING > RUSSET
RUSSETS > RUSSET
RUSSETY > RUSSET
RUSSIA *n* Russia leather
RUSSIAS > RUSSIA
RUSSIFIED > RUSSIFY
RUSSIFIES > RUSSIFY
RUSSIFY *vb* cause to become Russian in character
RUSSULA *n* any fungus of the large basidiomycetous genus *Russula*, of typical toadstool shape and often brightly coloured
RUSSULAE > RUSSULA
RUSSULAS > RUSSULA
RUST *n* reddish-brown coating formed on iron etc that has been exposed to moisture ▷ *adj* reddish-brown ▷ *vb* become coated with rust
RUSTABLE *adj* liable to rust
RUSTED > RUST
RUSTIC *adj* of or resembling country people ▷ *n* person from the country
RUSTICAL *n* rustic
RUSTICALS > RUSTICAL
RUSTICANA *pl n* objects, such as agricultural implements, garden furniture, etc, relating to the countryside or made in imitation of rustic styles
RUSTICATE *vb* banish temporarily from university as a punishment
RUSTICIAL *made-up variant of* > RUSTIC
RUSTICISE *same as* > RUSTICIZE
RUSTICISM > RUSTIC
RUSTICITY > RUSTIC
RUSTICIZE *vb* make rustic
RUSTICLY > RUSTIC
RUSTICS > RUSTIC
RUSTIER > RUSTY
RUSTIEST > RUSTY
RUSTILY > RUSTY
RUSTINESS > RUSTY
RUSTING > RUST
RUSTINGS > RUST
RUSTLE *n* (make) a low

whispering sound ▷ *vb* steal (cattle)
RUSTLED > RUSTLE
RUSTLER *n* cattle thief
RUSTLERS > RUSTLER
RUSTLES > RUSTLE
RUSTLESS > RUST
RUSTLING > RUSTLE
RUSTLINGS > RUSTLE
RUSTPROOF *adj* treated against rusting
RUSTRE *n* (in heraldry) lozenge with a round hole in the middle showing the background colour
RUSTRED > RUSTRE
RUSTRES > RUSTRE
RUSTS > RUST
RUSTY *adj* coated with rust
RUT *n* furrow made by wheels ▷ *vb* be in a period of sexual excitability
RUTABAGA *n* Eurasian plant with a bulbous edible root which is used as a vegetable and as cattle fodder
RUTABAGAS > RUTABAGA
RUTACEOUS *adj* of, relating to, or belonging to the *Rutaceae*, a family of tropical and temperate flowering plants many of which have aromatic leaves. The family includes rue and citrus trees
RUTH *n* pity
RUTHENIC *adj* of or containing ruthenium, esp in a high valency state
RUTHENIUM *n* rare hard brittle white element
RUTHFUL *adj* full of or causing sorrow or pity
RUTHFULLY > RUTHFUL
RUTHLESS *adj* pitiless, merciless
RUTHS > RUTH
RUTILANT *adj* of a reddish colour or glow
RUTILATED *adj* (of minerals, esp quartz) containing needles of rutile
RUTILE *n* black, yellowish, or reddish-brown mineral
RUTILES > RUTILE
RUTIN *n* bioflavonoid found in various plants including rue
RUTINS > RUTIN
RUTS > RUT
RUTTED > RUT
RUTTER *n* (in history) type of cavalry soldier
RUTTERS > RUTTER
RUTTIER > RUTTY
RUTTIEST > RUTTY
RUTTILY > RUTTY
RUTTINESS > RUTTY
RUTTING > RUT
RUTTINGS > RUT
RUTTISH *adj* (of an animal) in a condition of rut
RUTTISHLY > RUTTISH
RUTTY *adj* full of ruts or holes
RYA *n* type of rug originating in Scandinavia
RYAL *n* one of several old coins
RYALS > RYAL
RYAS > RYA
RYBAT *n* polished stone piece forming the side of a window or door
RYBATS > RYBAT
RYBAUDRYE *archaic variant of* > RIBALDRY
RYE *n* kind of grain used for fodder and bread
RYEBREAD *n* any of various breads made entirely or partly from rye flour, often with caraway seeds
RYEBREADS > RYEBREAD
RYEFLOUR *n* flour made from rye
RYEFLOURS > RYEFLOUR
RYEGRASS *n* any of various grasses of the genus *Lolium* native to Europe, N Africa, and Asia and widely cultivated as forage crops
RYEPECK *n* punt-mooring pole
RYEPECKS > RYEPECK
RYES > RYE
RYFE *archaic variant of* > RIFE
RYKE *Scots variant of* > REACH
RYKED > RYKE
RYKES > RYKE
RYKING > RYKE
RYMME *same as* > RIM
RYMMED > RYMME
RYMMES > RYMME
RYMMING > RYMME
RYND *n* (in milling) crossbar piece forming part of the support structure of the upper millstone
RYNDS > RYND
RYOKAN *n* traditional Japanese inn
RYOKANS > RYOKAN
RYOT *n* (in India) a peasant or tenant farmer
RYOTS > RYOT
RYOTWARI *n* (in India) system of land tenure in which land taxes are paid to the state
RYOTWARIS > RYOTWARI
RYPE *n* ptarmigan
RYPECK *same as* > RYEPECK
RYPECKS > RYPECK
RYPER > RYPE

Ss

AB *n* person engaged in direct action to prevent a targeted activity taking place ▷ *vb* take part in such action
ABADILLA *n* tropical American liliaceous plant
ABAL *n* variety of palm tree
ABALS > SABAL
ABATON *n* foot covering in suit of armour
ABATONS > SABATON
ABAYON *n* dessert or sweet sauce made with egg yolks, sugar, and wine beaten together over heat till thick
ABAYONS > SABAYON
ABBAT *n* midnight meeting of witches
ABBATH *n* period of rest
ABBATHS > SABBATH
ABBATIC *n* period of leave granted to university staff
ABBATICS > SABBATIC
ABBATINE *adj* of Saturday
ABBATISE *same as* > SABBATIZE
ABBATISM *n* sabbath observance
ABBATIZE *vb* observe as sabbath
ABBATS > SABBAT
ABBED > SAB
ABBING > SAB
ABE *n* very informal word meaning sense or savvy ▷ *vb* very informal word meaning know or savvy
ABED > SABE
ABEING > SABE
ABELLA *n* marine worm
SABELLAS > SABELLA
SABER *same as* > SABRE
SABERED > SABER
SABERING > SABER
SABERLIKE > SABER
SABERS > SABER
SABES > SABE
SABIN *n* unit of acoustic absorption equal to the absorption resulting from one square foot of a perfectly absorbing surface
SABINE *variant of* > SAVIN
SABINES > SABINE
SABINS > SABIN
SABIR *n* member of ancient Turkic people
SABIRS > SABIR
SABKHA *n* flat coastal plain with a salt crust, common in Arabia
SABKHAH *n* sabkha
SABKHAHS > SABKHAH
SABKHAS > SABKHA
SABKHAT *n* sabkha
SABKHATS > SABKHAT
SABLE *n* dark fur from a small weasel-like Arctic animal ▷ *adj* black
SABLED > SABLE
SABLEFISH *n* North American fish
SABLES > SABLE
SABLING > SABLE
SABOT *n* wooden shoe traditionally worn by peasants in France
SABOTAGE *n* intentional damage done to machinery, systems, etc ▷ *vb* damage intentionally
SABOTAGED > SABOTAGE
SABOTAGES > SABOTAGE
SABOTEUR *n* person who commits sabotage
SABOTEURS > SABOTEUR
SABOTIER *n* wearer of wooden clogs
SABOTIERS > SABOTIER
SABOTS > SABOT
SABRA *n* native-born Israeli Jew
SABRAS > SABRA
SABRE *n* curved cavalry sword ▷ *vb* injure or kill with a sabre
SABRED > SABRE
SABRES > SABRE
SABREUR *n* person wielding sabre
SABREURS > SABREUR
SABRING > SABRE
SABS > SAB
SABULINE *same as* > SABULOUS
SABULOSE *same as* > SABULOUS
SABULOUS *adj* like sand in texture
SABURRA *n* granular deposit
SABURRAL > SABURRA
SABURRAS > SABURRA
SAC *n* pouchlike structure in an animal or plant
SACATON *n* coarse grass of the southwestern US and Mexico, grown for hay and pasture
SACATONS > SACATON
SACBUT *n* medieval trombone
SACBUTS > SACBUT
SACCADE *n* movement of the eye when it makes a sudden change of fixation, as in reading
SACCADES > SACCADE
SACCADIC > SACCADE
SACCATE *adj* in the form of a sac
SACCHARIC as in *saccharic acid* white soluble solid acid
SACCHARIN *n* artificial sweetener
SACCHARUM *n* cane sugar
SACCIFORM *adj* like a sac
SACCOI > SACCOS
SACCOS *n* bishop's garment in the Orthodox Church
SACCOSES > SACCOS
SACCULAR *adj* of or resembling a sac
SACCULATE *adj* of, relating to, or possessing a saccule, saccules, or a sacculus
SACCULE *n* small sac
SACCULES > SACCULE
SACCULI > SACCULUS
SACCULUS *same as* > SACCULE
SACELLA > SACELLUM
SACELLUM *n* tomb within a church
SACHEM *same as* > SAGAMORE
SACHEMDOM > SACHEM
SACHEMIC > SACHEM
SACHEMS > SACHEM
SACHET *n* small envelope or bag containing a single portion
SACHETED *adj* contained in a sachet
SACHETS > SACHET
SACK *n* large bag made of coarse material ▷ *vb* dismiss

SACKABLE *adj* of or denoting an offence, infraction of rules, etc, that is sufficiently serious to warrant dismissal from an employment
SACKAGE *n* act of sacking a place
SACKAGES > SACKAGE
SACKBUT *n* medieval form of trombone
SACKBUTS > SACKBUT
SACKCLOTH *n* coarse fabric used for sacks, formerly worn as a penance
SACKED > SACK
SACKER > SACK
SACKERS > SACK
SACKFUL > SACK
SACKFULS > SACKFUL
SACKING *n* rough woven material used for sacks
SACKINGS > SACKING
SACKLESS *adj* old word meaning innocent
SACKLIKE > SACK
SACKS > SACK
SACKSFUL > SACKFUL
SACLESS *adj* old word meaning unchallengeable
SACLIKE > SAC
SACQUE *same as* > SACK
SACQUES > SACQUE
SACRA > SACRUM
SACRAL *adj* of or associated with sacred rites ▷ *n* sacral vertebra
SACRALGIA *n* pain in sacrum
SACRALISE *same as* > SACRALIZE
SACRALIZE *vb* make sacred
SACRALS > SACRAL
SACRAMENT *n* ceremony of the Christian Church, esp Communion
SACRARIA > SACRARIUM
SACRARIAL > SACRARIUM
SACRARIUM *n* sanctuary of a church
SACRED *adj* holy
SACREDLY > SACRED
SACRIFICE *n* giving something up ▷ *vb* offer as a sacrifice
SACRIFIDE *vb* old form of sacrifice
SACRIFIED > SACRIFY
SACRIFIES > SACRIFY
SACRIFY *vb* old form of sacrifice
SACRILEGE *n* misuse or desecration of something sacred
SACRING *n* act or ritual of consecration, esp of the Eucharist or of a bishop
SACRINGS > SACRING
SACRIST *same as* > SACRISTAN
SACRISTAN *n* person in charge of the contents of a church
SACRISTS > SACRIST
SACRISTY *n* room in a church where sacred objects are kept
SACRUM *n* wedge-shaped bone at the base of the spine
SACRUMS > SACRUM
SACS > SAC
SAD *adj* sorrowful, unhappy ▷ *vb* New Zealand word meaning express sadness or displeasure strongly
SADDEN *vb* make (someone) sad
SADDENED > SADDEN
SADDENING > SADDEN
SADDENS > SADDEN
SADDER > SAD
SADDEST > SAD
SADDHU *same as* > SADHU
SADDHUS > SADDHU
SADDISH > SAD
SADDLE *n* rider's seat on a horse or bicycle ▷ *vb* put a saddle on (a horse)
SADDLEBAG *n* pouch or small bag attached to the saddle of a horse, bicycle, or motorcycle
SADDLEBOW *n* pommel of a saddle
SADDLED > SADDLE
SADDLER *n* maker or seller of saddles
SADDLERS > SADDLER
SADDLERY *n* saddles and harness for horses collectively
SADDLES > SADDLE
SADDLING > SADDLE
SADDO *vb* make sad ▷ *n* socially inadequate or pathetic person
SADDOS > SADDO
SADE *same as* > SADHE
SADES > SADE
SADHANA *n* one of a number of spiritual practices or disciplines which lead to perfection, these being contemplation, asceticism, worship of a god, and correct living
SADHANAS > SADHANA
SADHE *n* 18th letter in the Hebrew alphabet
SADHES > SADHE
SADHU *n* Hindu wandering holy man
SADHUS > SADHU
SADI *variant of* > SADHE
SADIRON *n* heavy iron pointed at both ends, for pressing clothes
SADIRONS > SADIRON
SADIS > SADI
SADISM *n* gaining of (sexual) pleasure from inflicting pain
SADISMS > SADISM
SADIST > SADISM
SADISTIC > SADISM
SADISTS > SADISM
SADLY > SAD
SADNESS > SAD
SADNESSES > SAD
SADO *variant of* > CHADO
SADOS > SADO
SADZA *n* southern African porridge
SADZAS > SADZA
SAE *Scot word for* > SO
SAECULUM *n* age in astronomy
SAECULUMS > SAECULUM
SAETER *n* upland pasture in Norway
SAETERS > SAETER
SAFARI *n* expedition to hunt or observe wild animals, esp in Africa ▷ *vb* go on safari
SAFARIED > SAFARI
SAFARIING > SAFARI
SAFARIS > SAFARI
SAFARIST *n* person on safari
SAFARISTS > SAFARIST
SAFE *adj* secure, protected ▷ *n* strong lockable container ▷ *vb* make safe
SAFED > SAFE
SAFEGUARD *vb* protect ▷ *n* protection
SAFELIGHT *n* light that can be used in a room in which photographic material is handled, transmitting only those colours to which a particular type of film, plate, or paper is relatively insensitive
SAFELY > SAFE
SAFENESS > SAFE
SAFER > SAFE
SAFES > SAFE
SAFEST > SAFE
SAFETIED > SAFETY
SAFETIES > SAFETY
SAFETY *n* state of being safe ▷ *vb* make safe
SAFETYING > SAFETY
SAFETYMAN *n* defensive player in American football
SAFETYMEN > SAFETYMAN
SAFFIAN *n* leather tanned with sumach and usually dyed a bright colour
SAFFIANS > SAFFIAN
SAFFLOWER *n* thistle-like plant with flowers used for dye and oil
SAFFRON *n* orange-coloured flavouring obtained from a crocus ▷ *adj* orange
SAFFRONED *adj* containing saffron
SAFFRONS > SAFFRON
SAFFRONY *adj* like saffron
SAFING > SAFE
SAFRANIN *same as* > SAFRANINE
SAFRANINE *n* any of a class of azine dyes, used for textiles and biological stains
SAFRANINS > SAFRANIN
SAFROL *n* oily liquid obtained from sassafras
SAFROLE *n* colourless or yellowish oily water-insoluble liquid
SAFROLES > SAFROLE
SAFROLS > SAFROL
SAFRONAL *n* oily liquid derived from saffron
SAFRONALS > SAFRONAL
SAFT *Scot word for* > SOFT
SAFTER > SAFT
SAFTEST > SAFT
SAG *vb* sink in the middle ▷ *n* droop
SAGA *n* legend of Norse heroes
SAGACIOUS *adj* wise
SAGACITY *n* foresight, discernment, or keen perception
SAGAMAN *n* person reciting Norse sagas
SAGAMEN > SAGAMAN
SAGAMORE *n* (among some Native Americans) a chief or eminent man
SAGAMORES > SAGAMORE
SAGANASH *n* Algonquian term for an Englishman
SAGAPENUM *n* resin formerly used as drug
SAGAS > SAGA
SAGATHIES > SAGATHY
SAGATHY *n* type of light fabric
SAGBUT *n* medieval trombone
SAGBUTS > SAGBUT
SAGE *n* very wise man ▷ *adj* wise
SAGEBRUSH *n* aromatic plant of West N America
SAGELY > SAGE
SAGENE *n* fishing net
SAGENES > SAGENE
SAGENESS > SAGE
SAGENITE *n* mineral found in crystal form
SAGENITES > SAGENITE
SAGENITIC > SAGENITE
SAGER > SAGE
SAGES > SAGE
SAGEST > SAGE
SAGGAR *n* clay box in which fragile ceramic wares are placed for protection during firing ▷ *vb* put in a saggar
SAGGARD *n* saggar
SAGGARDS > SAGGARD
SAGGARED > SAGGAR
SAGGARING > SAGGAR
SAGGARS > SAGGAR
SAGGED > SAG
SAGGER *same as* > SAGGAR
SAGGERED > SAGGER
SAGGERING > SAGGER
SAGGERS > SAGGER
SAGGIER > SAGGY
SAGGIEST > SAGGY
SAGGING > SAG
SAGGINGS > SAG
SAGGY *adj* tending to sag

AGIER > SAGY
AGIEST > SAGY
AGINATE *vb* fatten ivestock
AGINATED > SAGINATE
AGINATES > SAGINATE
AGITTA *n* sine of an arc
AGITTAL *adj* resembling an arrow
AGITTARY *n* centaur
AGITTAS > SAGITTA
AGITTATE *adj* (esp of eaves) shaped like the head of an arrow
AGO *n* starchy cereal from the powdered pith of the sago palm tree
GOIN *n* South American monkey
AGOINS > SAGOIN
AGOS > SAGO
GOUIN *n* South American monkey
AGOUINS > SAGOUIN
AGRADA as in *cascara sagrada* dried bark of the cascara buckthorn, used as a stimulant and laxative
AGS > SAG
AGUARO *n* giant cactus of desert regions of Arizona, S California, and Mexico
AGUAROS > SAGUARO
AGUIN *n* South American monkey
AGUINS > SAGUIN
AGUM *n* Roman soldier's cloak
AGY *adj* like or containing sage
HEB *same as* > SAHIB
HEBS > SAHEB
HIB *n* Indian term of address placed after a man's name as a mark of respect
HIBA *n* respectful Indian term of address for woman
HIBAH *n* sahiba
HIBAHS > SAHIBAH
HIBAS > SAHIBA
HIBS > SAHIB
HIWAL *n* breed of cattle n India
HIWALS > SAHIWAL
HUARO *same as* > SAGUARO
HUAROS > SAHUARO
I *n* South American monkey
IBLING *n* freshwater fish
IBLINGS > SAIBLING
IC *n* boat of eastern Mediterranean
ICE *same as* > SYCE
ICES > SAICE
ICK *n* boat of eastern Mediterranean
ICKS > SAICK
ICS > SAIC
ID *same as* > SAYYID
IDEST > SAY
IDS > SAID
IDST > SAY

SAIGA *n* either of two antelopes of the plains of central Asia
SAIGAS > SAIGA
SAIKEI *n* Japanese ornamental miniature landscape
SAIKEIS > SAIKEI
SAIKLESS *old Scots word for* > INNOCENT
SAIL *n* sheet of fabric stretched to catch the wind for propelling a sailing boat ▷ *vb* travel by water
SAILABLE > SAIL
SAILBOARD *n* board with a mast and single sail, used for windsurfing
SAILBOAT *n* boat propelled chiefly by sail
SAILBOATS > SAILBOAT
SAILCLOTH *n* fabric for making sails
SAILED > SAIL
SAILER *n* vessel, esp one equipped with sails, with specified sailing characteristics
SAILERS > SAILER
SAILFISH *n* large tropical game fish, with a long sail-like fin on its back
SAILING *n* practice, art, or technique of sailing a vessel
SAILINGS > SAILING
SAILLESS > SAIL
SAILMAKER *n* person who makes sails
SAILOR *n* member of a ship's crew
SAILORING *n* activity of working as sailor
SAILORLY > SAILOR
SAILORS > SAILOR
SAILPLANE *n* high-performance glider
SAILROOM *n* space on ship for storing sails
SAILROOMS > SAILROOM
SAILS > SAIL
SAIM *Scots word for* > LARD
SAIMIN *n* Hawaiian dish of noodles
SAIMINS > SAIMIN
SAIMIRI *n* South American monkey
SAIMIRIS > SAIMIRI
SAIMS > SAIM
SAIN *vb* make the sign of the cross over so as to bless or protect from evil or sin
SAINE *vb* old form of say
SAINED > SAIN
SAINFOIN *n* Eurasian plant with pink flowers, widely grown as feed for grazing farm animals
SAINFOINS > SAINFOIN
SAINING > SAIN
SAINS > SAIN
SAINT *n* person venerated after death as specially holy ▷ *vb* canonize
SAINTDOM > SAINT
SAINTDOMS > SAINT
SAINTED *adj* formally recognized by a Christian Church as a saint
SAINTESS *n* female saint
SAINTFOIN *n* sainfoin
SAINTHOOD *n* state or character of being a saint
SAINTING > SAINT
SAINTISH > SAINT
SAINTISM *n* quality of being saint
SAINTISMS > SAINTISM
SAINTLESS > SAINT
SAINTLIER > SAINTLY
SAINTLIKE > SAINT
SAINTLILY > SAINTLY
SAINTLING *n* little saint
SAINTLY *adj* behaving in a very good, patient, or holy way
SAINTS > SAINT
SAINTSHIP > SAINT
SAIQUE *n* boat in eastern Mediterranean
SAIQUES > SAIQUE
SAIR *Scot word for* > SORE
SAIRED > SAIR
SAIRER > SAIR
SAIREST > SAIR
SAIRING > SAIR
SAIRS > SAIR
SAIS > SAI
SAIST > SAY
SAITH *form of the present tense (indicative mood) of* > SAY
SAITHE *n* dark-coloured food fish found in northern seas
SAITHES > SAITHE
SAITHS > SAITH
SAIYID *n* Muslim descended from Mohammed's grandson
SAIYIDS > SAIYID
SAJOU *n* South American monkey
SAJOUS > SAJOU
SAKAI *n* Malaysian aborigine
SAKAIS > SAKAI
SAKE *n* benefit
SAKER *n* large falcon of E Europe and central Asia
SAKERET *n* male saker
SAKERETS > SAKERET
SAKERS > SAKER
SAKES > SAKE
SAKI *same as* > SAKE
SAKIA *n* water wheel in Middle East
SAKIAS > SAKIA
SAKIEH *n* water wheel in Middle East
SAKIEHS > SAKIEH
SAKIS > SAKI
SAKIYEH *n* water wheel in Middle East
SAKIYEHS > SAKIYEH
SAKKOI > SAKKOS
SAKKOS *n* bishop's garment in Orthodox Church
SAKKOSES > SAKKOS
SAKSAUL *n* Asian tree
SAKSAULS > SAKSAUL
SAL *pharmacological term for* > SALT
SALAAM *n* low bow of greeting among Muslims ▷ *vb* make a salaam
SALAAMED > SALAAM
SALAAMING > SALAAM
SALAAMS > SALAAM
SALABLE *same as* > SALEABLE
SALABLY > SALEABLY
SALACIOUS *adj* excessively concerned with sex
SALACITY *n* excessive interest in sex
SALAD *n* dish of raw vegetables, eaten as a meal or part of a meal
SALADANG *n* variety of ox
SALADANGS > SALADANG
SALADE *same as* > SALLET
SALADES > SALADE
SALADING *n* ingredients for salad
SALADINGS > SALADING
SALADS > SALAD
SALAL *n* North American shrub
SALALS > SALAL
SALAMI *n* highly spiced sausage
SALAMIS > SALAMI
SALAMON *n* word used in old oaths
SALAMONS > SALAMON
SALANGANE *n* Asian swift
SALARIAT *n* salary-earning class
SALARIATS > SALARIAT
SALARIED *adj* earning or providing a salary
SALARIES > SALARY
SALARY *n* fixed regular payment, usu monthly, to an employee ▷ *vb* pay a salary to
SALARYING > SALARY
SALARYMAN *n* (in Japan) an office worker
SALARYMEN > SALARYMAN
SALBAND *n* coating of mineral
SALBANDS > SALBAND
SALCHOW *n* type of figure-skating jump
SALCHOWS > SALCHOW
SALE *n* exchange of goods for money
SALEABLE *adj* fit or likely to be sold
SALEABLY > SALEABLE
SALEP *n* dried ground starchy tubers of various orchids, used for food and formerly as drugs
SALEPS > SALEP
SALERATUS *n* sodium bicarbonate when used in baking powder
SALERING *n* enclosed area

for livestock at market
SALERINGS > SALERING
SALEROOM *n* place where goods are sold by auction
SALEROOMS > SALEROOM
SALES > SALE
SALESGIRL *n* person who sells goods
SALESLADY *n* person who sells goods
SALESMAN *n* person who sells goods
SALESMEN > SALESMAN
SALESROOM *n* room in which merchandise on sale is displayed
SALET *same as* > SALLET
SALETS > SALET
SALEWD > SALUE
SALEYARD *n* area with pens for holding animals before auction
SALEYARDS > SALEYARD
SALFERN *n* plant of borage family
SALFERNS > SALFERN
SALIAUNCE *n* old word meaning onslaught
SALIC *adj* (of rocks and minerals) having a high content of silica and alumina
SALICES > SALIX
SALICET *n* soft-toned organ stop
SALICETA > SALICETUM
SALICETS > SALICET
SALICETUM *n* plantation of willows
SALICIN *n* colourless or white crystalline water-soluble glucoside
SALICINE *same as* > SALICIN
SALICINES > SALICINE
SALICINS > SALICIN
SALICYLIC as in *salicylic acid* white crystalline substance with a sweet taste and a bitter aftertaste
SALIENCE > SALIENT
SALIENCES > SALIENT
SALIENCY *n* quality of being prominent
SALIENT *adj* prominent, noticeable ▷ *n* projecting part of a front line
SALIENTLY > SALIENT
SALIENTS > SALIENT
SALIFIED > SALIFY
SALIFIES > SALIFY
SALIFY *vb* treat, mix with, or cause to combine with a salt
SALIFYING > SALIFY
SALIGOT *n* water chestnut
SALIGOTS > SALIGOT
SALIMETER *n* hydrometer for measuring salt in a solution
SALIMETRY > SALIMETER
SALINA *n* salt marsh, lake, or spring
SALINAS > SALINA
SALINE *adj* containing salt ▷ *n* solution of sodium chloride and water
SALINES > SALINE
SALINISE *same as* > SALINIZE
SALINISED > SALINISE
SALINISES > SALINISE
SALINITY > SALINE
SALINIZE *vb* treat with salt
SALINIZED > SALINIZE
SALINIZES > SALINIZE
SALIVA *n* liquid that forms in the mouth, spittle
SALIVAL > SALIVA
SALIVARY > SALIVA
SALIVAS > SALIVA
SALIVATE *vb* produce saliva
SALIVATED > SALIVATE
SALIVATES > SALIVATE
SALIVATOR > SALIVATE
SALIX *n* plant or tree of willow family
SALL *archaic form of* > SHALL
SALLAD *old spelling of* > SALAD
SALLADS > SALLAD
SALLAL *n* North American shrub
SALLALS > SALLAL
SALLE *n* hall
SALLEE *n* SE Australian eucalyptus with a pale grey bark
SALLEES > SALLEE
SALLES > SALLE
SALLET *n* light round helmet extending over the back of the neck
SALLETS > SALLET
SALLIED > SALLY
SALLIER > SALLY
SALLIERS > SALLY
SALLIES > SALLY
SALLOW *adj* of an unhealthy pale or yellowish colour ▷ *vb* make sallow ▷ *n* any of several small willow trees
SALLOWED > SALLOW
SALLOWER > SALLOW
SALLOWEST > SALLOW
SALLOWING > SALLOW
SALLOWISH > SALLOW
SALLOWLY > SALLOW
SALLOWS > SALLOW
SALLOWY > SALLOW
SALLY *n* violent excursion ▷ *vb* set or rush out
SALLYING > SALLY
SALLYPORT *n* opening in a fortified place from which troops may make a sally
SALMI *n* ragout of game stewed in a rich brown sauce
SALMIS *same as* > SALMI
SALMON *n* large fish with orange-pink flesh valued as food ▷ *adj* orange-pink
SALMONET *n* young salmon
SALMONETS > SALMONET
SALMONID *n* any fish of the family *Salmonidae*
SALMONIDS > SALMONID
SALMONOID *adj* belonging to the order of soft-finned teleost fishes that includes the salmon, whitefish, grayling, and char ▷ *n* any of these fish
SALMONS > SALMON
SALOL *n* white sparingly soluble crystalline compound with a slight aromatic odour, used as a preservative and to absorb light in sun-tan lotions, plastics, etc
SALOLS > SALOL
SALOMETER *n* instrument for measuring salt in solution
SALON *n* commercial premises of a hairdresser, beautician, etc
SALONS > SALON
SALOON *n* closed car with four or more seats
SALOONS > SALOON
SALOOP *n* infusion of aromatic herbs or other plant parts formerly used as a tonic or cure
SALOOPS > SALOOP
SALOP *variant of* > SALOOP
SALOPIAN > SALOOP
SALOPS > SALOP
SALP *n* minute animal floating in sea
SALPA *n* any of various minute floating animals of warm oceans
SALPAE > SALPA
SALPAS > SALPA
SALPIAN *n* minute animal floating in sea
SALPIANS > SALPIAN
SALPICON *n* mixture of chopped fish, meat, or vegetables in a sauce
SALPICONS > SALPICON
SALPID *n* minute animal floating in sea
SALPIDS > SALPID
SALPIFORM > SALPA
SALPINGES > SALPINX
SALPINX *n* Fallopian tube or Eustachian tube
SALPINXES > SALPINX
SALPS > SALP
SALS > SAL
SALSA *n* lively Puerto Rican dance ▷ *vb* dance the salsa
SALSAED > SALSA
SALSAING > SALSA
SALSAS > SALSA
SALSE *n* volcano expelling mud
SALSES > SALSE
SALSIFIES > SALSIFY
SALSIFY *n* Mediterranean plant with a long white edible root
SALSILLA *n* tropical American vine
SALSILLAS > SALSILLA
SALT *n* white crystalline substance used to season food ▷ *vb* season or preserve with salt
SALTANDO *n* staccato piec[e] of violin playing
SALTANT *adj* (of an organism) differing from others of its species because of a saltation ▷ *n* saltant organism
SALTANTS > SALTANT
SALTATE *vb* go through saltation
SALTATED > SALTATE
SALTATES > SALTATE
SALTATING > SALTATE
SALTATION *n* abrupt variation in the appearance of an organism, usu caused by genetic mutation
SALTATO *n* saltando
SALTATORY *adj* specialize[d] for jumping
SALTBOX *n* box for salt wit[h] a sloping lid
SALTBOXES > SALTBOX
SALTBUSH *n* shrub that grows in alkaline desert regions
SALTCAT *n* salty medicine for pigeons
SALTCATS > SALTCAT
SALTCHUCK *n* any body of salt water
SALTED *adj* seasoned, preserved, or treated wit[h] salt
SALTER *n* person who dea[ls] in or manufactures salt
SALTERN *n* place where sa[lt] is obtained from pools of evaporated sea water
SALTERNS > SALTERN
SALTERS > SALTER
SALTEST > SALT
SALTFISH *n* salted cod
SALTIE *n* saltwater crocodile
SALTIER *variant of* > SALTIRE
SALTIERS > SALTIER
SALTIES > SALTIE
SALTIEST > SALTY
SALTILY > SALTY
SALTINE *n* salty biscuit
SALTINES > SALTINE
SALTINESS > SALTY
SALTING *n* area of low ground regularly inundated with salt wate[r]
SALTINGS > SALTING
SALTIRE *n* diagonal cross on a shield
SALTIRES > SALTIRE
SALTISH > SALT
SALTISHLY > SALT
SALTLESS > SALT
SALTLIKE > SALT
SALTLY > SALT
SALTNESS > SALT

SALTO *n* daring jump ▷ *vb* perform a daring jump
SALTOED > SALTO
SALTOING > SALTO
SALTOS > SALTO
SALTPAN *n* shallow basin containing salt, gypsum, etc, that was deposited from an evaporated salt lake
SALTPANS > SALTPAN
SALTPETER *same as* > SALTPETRE
SALTPETRE *n* compound used in gunpowder and as a preservative
SALTS > SALT
SALTUS *n* break in the continuity of a sequence, esp the omission of a necessary step in a logical argument
SALTUSES > SALTUS
SALTWATER *adj* living in the sea
SALTWORK *n* place where salt is refined
SALTWORKS *n* place, building, or factory where salt is produced
SALTWORT *n* any of several chenopodiaceous plants with prickly leaves, striped stems, and small green flowers
SALTWORTS > SALTWORT
SALTY *adj* of, tasting of, or containing salt
SALUBRITY *n* quality of being favourable to health or wholesome
SALUE *vb* old word meaning salute
SALUED > SALUE
SALUES > SALUE
SALUING > SALUE
SALUKI *n* type of tall hound with a smooth coat
SALUKIS > SALUKI
SALURETIC *n* drug that increases secretion of salt in urine
SALUTARY *adj* producing a beneficial result
SALUTE *n* motion of the arm as a formal military sign of respect ▷ *vb* greet with a salute
SALUTED > SALUTE
SALUTER > SALUTE
SALUTERS > SALUTE
SALUTES > SALUTE
SALUTING > SALUTE
SALVABLE *adj* capable of or suitable for being saved or salvaged
SALVABLY > SALVABLE
SALVAGE *n* saving of a ship or other property from destruction ▷ *vb* save from destruction or waste
SALVAGED > SALVAGE
SALVAGEE *n* rope on sailing ship
SALVAGEES > SALVAGEE
SALVAGER > SALVAGE
SALVAGERS > SALVAGE
SALVAGES > SALVAGE
SALVAGING > SALVAGE
SALVARSAN *n* old medicine containing arsenic
SALVATION *n* fact or state of being saved from harm or the consequences of sin
SALVATORY *n* place for storing something safely
SALVE *n* healing or soothing ointment ▷ *vb* soothe or appease
SALVED > SALVE
SALVER *same as* > SALVOR
SALVERS > SALVER
SALVES > SALVE
SALVETE *n* Latin greeting
SALVETES > SALVETE
SALVIA *n* plant with blue or red flowers
SALVIAS > SALVIA
SALVIFIC *adj* acting to salve
SALVING > SALVE
SALVINGS > SALVE
SALVO *n* simultaneous discharge of guns etc ▷ *vb* attack with a salvo
SALVOED > SALVO
SALVOES > SALVO
SALVOING > SALVO
SALVOR *n* person instrumental in salvaging a vessel or its cargo
SALVORS > SALVOR
SALVOS > SALVO
SALWAR as in *salwar kameez* long tunic worn over a pair of baggy trousers, usually worn by women, esp in Pakistan
SAM *vb* collect
SAMA *n* Japanese title of respect
SAMAAN *n* South American tree
SAMAANS > SAMAAN
SAMADHI *n* state of deep meditative contemplation which leads to higher consciousness
SAMADHIS > SAMADHI
SAMAN *n* South American tree
SAMANS > SAMAN
SAMARA *n* dry indehiscent one-seeded fruit with a winglike extension to aid dispersal
SAMARAS > SAMARA
SAMARITAN *n* kindly person who helps another in distress
SAMARIUM *n* silvery metallic element
SAMARIUMS > SAMARIUM
SAMAS > SAMA
SAMBA *n* lively Brazilian dance ▷ *vb* perform such a dance
SAMBAED > SAMBA
SAMBAING > SAMBA
SAMBAL *n* Malaysian dish
SAMBALS > SAMBAL
SAMBAR *n* S Asian deer with three-tined antlers
SAMBARS > SAMBAR
SAMBAS > SAMBA
SAMBHAR *n* Indian dish
SAMBHARS > SAMBHAR
SAMBHUR *n* Asian deer
SAMBHURS > SAMBHUR
SAMBO *n* offensive word for a Black person
SAMBOS > SAMBO
SAMBUCA *n* Italian liqueur
SAMBUCAS > SAMBUCA
SAMBUKE *n* ancient Greek stringed instrument
SAMBUKES > SAMBUKE
SAMBUR *same as* > SAMBAR
SAMBURS > SAMBUR
SAME *adj* identical, not different, unchanged ▷ *n* something identical
SAMECH *n* letter in Hebrew alphabet
SAMECHS > SAMECH
SAMEK *variant of* > SAMEKH
SAMEKH *n* 15th letter in the Hebrew alphabet transliterated as *s*
SAMEKHS > SAMEKH
SAMEKS > SAMEK
SAMEL *adj* of brick, not sufficiently fired
SAMELY *adj* the same
SAMEN *old Scots form of* > SAME
SAMENESS *n* state or quality of being the same
SAMES > SAME
SAMEY *adj* monotonous
SAMFOO *n* style of casual dress worn by Chinese women, consisting of a waisted blouse and trousers
SAMFOOS > SAMFOO
SAMFU *n* Chinese female outfit
SAMFUS > SAMFU
SAMIEL *same as* > SIMOOM
SAMIELS > SAMIEL
SAMIER > SAMEY
SAMIEST > SAMEY
SAMISEN *n* Japanese plucked stringed instrument with a long neck, an unfretted fingerboard, and a rectangular soundbox
SAMISENS > SAMISEN
SAMITE *n* heavy fabric of silk, often woven with gold or silver threads, used in the Middle Ages for clothing
SAMITES > SAMITE
SAMITHI *same as* > SAMITI
SAMITHIS > SAMITHI
SAMITI *n* (in India) an association, esp one formed to organize political activity
SAMITIS > SAMITI
SAMIZDAT *n* (in the former Soviet Union) a system of secret printing and distribution of banned literature
SAMIZDATS > SAMIZDAT
SAMLET *n* young salmon
SAMLETS > SAMLET
SAMLOR *n* motor vehicle in Thailand
SAMLORS > SAMLOR
SAMMED > SAM
SAMMIES > SAMMY
SAMMING > SAM
SAMMY *n* (in South Africa) an Indian fruit and vegetable vendor who goes from house to house
SAMNITIS *n* poisonous plant mentioned by Spenser
SAMOSA *n* (in Indian cookery) a small fried triangular spiced meat or vegetable pasty
SAMOSAS > SAMOSA
SAMOVAR *n* Russian tea urn
SAMOVARS > SAMOVAR
SAMOYED *n* Siberian breed of dog of the spitz type, having a dense white or cream coat with a distinct ruff, and a tightly curled tail
SAMOYEDS > SAMOYED
SAMP *n* crushed maize used for porridge
SAMPAN *n* small boat with oars used in China
SAMPANS > SAMPAN
SAMPHIRE *n* plant found on rocks by the seashore
SAMPHIRES > SAMPHIRE
SAMPI *n* old Greek number character
SAMPIRE *n* samphire
SAMPIRES > SAMPIRE
SAMPIS > SAMPI
SAMPLE *n* part taken as representative of a whole ▷ *vb* take and test a sample of
SAMPLED > SAMPLE
SAMPLER *n* piece of embroidery showing the embroiderer's skill
SAMPLERS > SAMPLER
SAMPLERY *n* making of samplers
SAMPLES > SAMPLE
SAMPLING *n* process of selecting a random sample
SAMPLINGS > SAMPLING
SAMPS > SAMP
SAMS > SAM
SAMSARA *n* endless cycle of birth, death, and rebirth
SAMSARAS > SAMSARA
SAMSHOO *n* Chinese alcoholic drink
SAMSHOOS > SAMSHOO
SAMSHU *n* alcoholic drink from China that is made

from fermented rice and resembles sake
SAMSHUS > SAMSHU
SAMURAI *n* member of an ancient Japanese warrior caste
SAMURAIS > SAMURAI
SAN *n* sanatorium
SANATIVE *less common word for* > CURATIVE
SANATORIA *pl n* institutions for the care of chronically ill people
SANATORY *adj* healing
SANBENITO *n* yellow garment bearing a red cross, worn by penitent heretics in the Inquisition
SANCAI *n* glaze in Chinese pottery
SANCAIS > SANCAI
SANCHO *n* African stringed instrument
SANCHOS > SANCHO
SANCTA > SANCTUM
SANCTIFY *vb* make holy
SANCTION *n* permission, authorization ▷ *vb* allow, authorize
SANCTIONS > SANCTION
SANCTITY *n* sacredness, inviolability
SANCTUARY *n* holy place
SANCTUM *n* sacred place
SANCTUMS > SANCTUM
SAND *n* substance consisting of small grains of rock, esp on a beach or in a desert ▷ *vb* smooth with sandpaper
SANDABLE > SAND
SANDAL *n* light shoe consisting of a sole attached by straps ▷ *vb* put sandals on
SANDALED > SANDAL
SANDALING > SANDAL
SANDALLED > SANDAL
SANDALS > SANDAL
SANDARAC *n* either of two coniferous trees having hard fragrant dark wood
SANDARACH *same as* > SANDARAC
SANDARACS > SANDARAC
SANDBAG *n* bag filled with sand, used as protection against gunfire or flood water ▷ *vb* protect with sandbags
SANDBAGS > SANDBAG
SANDBANK *n* bank of sand below the surface of a river or sea
SANDBANKS > SANDBANK
SANDBAR *n* ridge of sand in a river or sea, often exposed at low tide
SANDBARS > SANDBAR
SANDBLAST *n* (clean with) a jet of sand blown from a nozzle under pressure ▷ *vb* clean or decorate (a surface) with a sandblast
SANDBOX *n* container on a railway locomotive from which sand is released onto the rails to assist the traction
SANDBOXES > SANDBOX
SANDBOY as in *happy as a sandboy* very happy or high-spirited
SANDBOYS > SANDBOY
SANDBUR *n* variety of wild grass
SANDBURR *n* variety of wild grass
SANDBURRS > SANDBURR
SANDBURS > SANDBUR
SANDCRACK *n* crack in horse's hoof
SANDDAB *n* type of small Pacific flatfish
SANDDABS > SANDDAB
SANDED > SAND
SANDEK *n* man who holds a baby being circumcised
SANDEKS > SANDEK
SANDER *n* power tool for smoothing surfaces
SANDERS > SANDER
SANDERSES > SANDER
SANDFISH *n* burrowing Pacific fish
SANDFLIES > SANDFLY
SANDFLY *n* any of various small mothlike dipterous flies: the bloodsucking females transmit diseases including leishmaniasis
SANDGLASS *less common word for* > HOURGLASS
SANDHEAP *n* heap of sand
SANDHEAPS > SANDHEAP
SANDHI *n* modification of the form or sound of a word under the influence of an adjacent word
SANDHILL *n* hill of sand
SANDHILLS > SANDHILL
SANDHIS > SANDHI
SANDHOG *n* person who works in underground or underwater construction projects
SANDHOGS > SANDHOG
SANDIER > SANDY
SANDIEST > SANDY
SANDINESS > SANDY
SANDING > SAND
SANDINGS > SAND
SANDIVER *n* scum forming on molten glass
SANDIVERS > SANDIVER
SANDLESS > SAND
SANDLIKE > SAND
SANDLING *n* sand eel
SANDLINGS > SANDLING
SANDLOT *n* area of vacant ground used by children for playing baseball and other games
SANDLOTS > SANDLOT
SANDMAN *n* (in folklore) a magical person supposed to put children to sleep by sprinkling sand in their eyes
SANDMEN > SANDMAN
SANDPAPER *n* paper coated with sand for smoothing a surface ▷ *vb* smooth with sandpaper
SANDPEEP *n* small sandpiper
SANDPEEPS > SANDPEEP
SANDPILE *n* pile of sand
SANDPILES > SANDPILE
SANDPIPER *n* shore bird with a long bill and slender legs
SANDPIT *n* shallow pit or container holding sand for children to play in
SANDPITS > SANDPIT
SANDPUMP *n* pump for wet sand
SANDPUMPS > SANDPUMP
SANDS > SAND
SANDSHOE *n* light canvas shoe with a rubber sole
SANDSHOES > SANDSHOE
SANDSOAP *n* gritty general-purpose soap
SANDSOAPS > SANDSOAP
SANDSPOUT *n* sand sucked into air by whirlwind
SANDSPUR *n* American wild grass
SANDSPURS > SANDSPUR
SANDSTONE *n* rock composed of sand
SANDSTORM *n* desert wind that whips up clouds of sand
SANDWICH *n* two slices of bread with a layer of food between ▷ *vb* insert between two other things
SANDWORM *n* any of various polychaete worms that live in burrows on sandy shores, esp the lugworm
SANDWORMS > SANDWORM
SANDWORT *n* any of numerous caryophyllaceous plants which grow in dense tufts on sandy soil and have white or pink solitary flowers
SANDWORTS > SANDWORT
SANDY *adj* covered with sand
SANE *adj* of sound mind ▷ *vb* heal
SANED > SANE
SANELY > SANE
SANENESS > SANE
SANER > SANE
SANES > SANE
SANEST > SANE
SANG *Scots word for* > SONG
SANGA *n* Ethiopian ox
SANGAR *n* breastwork of stone or sods
SANGAREE *n* spiced drink similar to sangria
SANGAREES > SANGAREE
SANGARS > SANGAR
SANGAS > SANGA
SANGER *n* sandwich
SANGERS > SANGER
SANGFROID *n* composure or self-possession
SANGH *n* Indian union or association
SANGHAT *n* fellowship or assembly, esp a local Sikh community or congregation
SANGHATS > SANGHAT
SANGHS > SANGH
SANGLIER *n* wild boar
SANGLIERS > SANGLIER
SANGO *same as* > SANGER
SANGOMA *n* witch doctor o[r] herbalist
SANGOMAS > SANGOMA
SANGOS > SANGO
SANGRIA *n* Spanish drink [o]f red wine and fruit
SANGRIAS > SANGRIA
SANGS > SANG
SANGUIFY *vb* turn into blood
SANGUINE *adj* cheerful, optimistic ▷ *n* red pencil containing ferric oxide, used in drawing
SANGUINED > SANGUINE
SANGUINES > SANGUINE
SANICLE *n* type of plant with clusters of small white flowers and oval fruits with hooked bristle[s]
SANICLES > SANICLE
SANIDINE *n* alkali feldspa[r] that is found in lavas
SANIDINES > SANIDINE
SANIES *n* thin greenish foul-smelling discharge from a wound, etc, containing pus and blood
SANIFIED > SANIFY
SANIFIES > SANIFY
SANIFY *vb* make healthy
SANIFYING > SANIFY
SANING > SANE
SANIOUS > SANIES
SANITARIA *variant of* > SANATORIA
SANITARY *adj* promoting health by getting rid of di[rt] and germs
SANITATE *vb* make sanitary
SANITATED > SANITATE
SANITATES > SANITATE
SANITIES > SANITY
SANITISE *same as* > SANITIZE
SANITISED > SANITISE
SANITISER > SANITISE
SANITISES > SANITISE
SANITIZE *vb* omit unpleasant details to make (news) more acceptable
SANITIZED > SANITIZE
SANITIZER > SANITIZE
SANITIZES > SANITIZE
SANITORIA *variant of* > SANATORIA
SANITY *n* state of having a

ıormal healthy mind
NJAK *n* (in the Turkish Empire) a subdivision of a vilayet
NJAKS > SANJAK
NK > SINK
NKO *n* African stringed instrument
NKOS > SANKO
NNIE *Scots word for* > SANDSHOE
NNIES > SANNIE
NNOP *n* Native American married man
NNOPS > SANNOP
NNUP *n* Native American married man
NNUPS > SANNUP
NNYASI *n* Brahman who having attained the fourth and last stage of life as a beggar will not be reborn, but will instead be absorbed into the Universal Soul
NNYASIN *same as* > SANNYASI
NNYASIS > SANNYASI
NPAN *n* sampan
NPANS > SANPAN
NPRO *n* sanitary-protection products, collectively
NPROS > SANPRO
NS *archaic word for* > WITHOUT
NSA *n* African musical instrument
NSAR *n* name of a wind that blows in Iran
NSARS > SANSAR
NSAS > SANSA
NSEI *n* American whose parents were Japanese immigrants
NSEIS > SANSEI
NSERIF *n* style of printer's typeface
NSERIFS > SANSERIF
NT *n* devout person in India
NTAL *n* sandalwood
NTALIC *adj* of sandalwood
NTALIN *n* substance giving sandalwood its colour
NTALINS > SANTALIN
NTALOL *n* liquid from sandalwood used in perfume
NTALOLS > SANTALOL
NTALS > SANTAL
NTERA *n* priestess of santeria
NTERAS > SANTERA
NTERIA *n* Caribbean religious cult
NTERIAS > SANTERIA
NTERO *n* priest of santeria
NTEROS > SANTERO
NTIMI > SANTIMS
NTIMS *n* money unit in Latvia
SANTIMU *same as* > SANTIMS
SANTIR *n* Middle Eastern stringed instrument
SANTIRS > SANTIR
SANTO *n* saint or representation of one
SANTOL *n* fruit from Southeast Asia
SANTOLINA *n* any plant of an evergreen Mediterranean genus grown for its silvery-grey felted foliage
SANTOLS > SANTOL
SANTON *n* French figurine
SANTONICA *n* oriental wormwood plant
SANTONIN *n* white crystalline soluble substance extracted from the dried flower heads of santonica
SANTONINS > SANTONIN
SANTONS > SANTON
SANTOOR *same as* > SANTIR
SANTOORS > SANTOOR
SANTOS > SANTO
SANTOUR *n* Middle Eastern stringed instrument
SANTOURS > SANTOUR
SANTS > SANT
SANTUR *n* Middle Eastern stringed instrument
SANTURS > SANTUR
SANYASI *same as* > SANNYASI
SANYASIS > SANNYASI
SAOUARI *n* tropical American tree
SAOUARIS > SAOUARI
SAP *n* moisture that circulates in plants ▷ *vb* undermine
SAPAJOU *n* capuchin monkey
SAPAJOUS > SAPAJOU
SAPAN *n* tropical tree
SAPANS > SAPAN
SAPANWOOD *n* small S Asian tree
SAPEGO *n* skin disease
SAPEGOES > SAPEGO
SAPELE *n* type of W African tree
SAPELES > SAPELE
SAPFUL *adj* full of sap
SAPHEAD *n* simpleton, idiot, or fool
SAPHEADED > SAPHEAD
SAPHEADS > SAPHEAD
SAPHENA *n* either of two large superficial veins of the legs
SAPHENAE > SAPHENA
SAPHENAS > SAPHENA
SAPHENOUS > SAPHENA
SAPID *adj* having a pleasant taste
SAPIDITY > SAPID
SAPIDLESS *adj* lacking flavour
SAPIDNESS > SAPID
SAPIENCE > SAPIENT
SAPIENCES > SAPIENT
SAPIENCY > SAPIENT
SAPIENS *adj* relating to or like modern human beings
SAPIENT *adj* wise, shrewd ▷ *n* wise person
SAPIENTLY > SAPIENT
SAPIENTS > SAPIENT
SAPLESS > SAP
SAPLING *n* young tree
SAPLINGS > SAPLING
SAPODILLA *n* large tropical American evergreen tree
SAPOGENIN *n* substance derived from saponin
SAPONARIA *See* > SOAPWORT
SAPONATED *adj* treated or combined with soap
SAPONIFY *vb* convert (a fat) into a soap by treatment with alkali
SAPONIN *n* any of a group of plant glycosides
SAPONINE *n* saponin
SAPONINES > SAPONINE
SAPONINS > SAPONIN
SAPONITE *n* type of clay mineral
SAPONITES > SAPONITE
SAPOR *n* quality in a substance that is perceived by the sense of taste
SAPORIFIC > SAPOR
SAPOROUS > SAPOR
SAPORS > SAPOR
SAPOTA *same as* > SAPODILLA
SAPOTAS > SAPOTA
SAPOTE *n* Central American tree
SAPOTES > SAPOTE
SAPOUR *variant of* > SAPOR
SAPOURS > SAPOUR
SAPPAN *n* tropical tree
SAPPANS > SAPPAN
SAPPED > SAP
SAPPER *n* soldier in an engineering unit
SAPPERS > SAPPER
SAPPHIC *adj* lesbian ▷ *n* verse written in a particular form
SAPPHICS > SAPPHIC
SAPPHIRE *n* blue precious stone ▷ *adj* deep blue
SAPPHIRED *adj* blue-coloured
SAPPHIRES > SAPPHIRE
SAPPHISM *n* lesbianism
SAPPHISMS > SAPPHISM
SAPPHIST *n* lesbian
SAPPHISTS > SAPPHIST
SAPPIER > SAPPY
SAPPIEST > SAPPY
SAPPILY > SAPPY
SAPPINESS > SAPPY
SAPPING > SAP
SAPPLE *vb* Scots word meaning wash in water
SAPPLED > SAPPLE
SAPPLES > SAPPLE
SAPPLING > SAPPLE
SAPPY *adj* (of plants) full of sap
SAPRAEMIA *n* blood poisoning caused by toxins of putrefactive bacteria
SAPRAEMIC > SAPRAEMIA
SAPREMIA *American spelling of* > SAPRAEMIA
SAPREMIAS > SAPREMIA
SAPREMIC > SAPREMIA
SAPROBE *n* organism that lives on decaying organisms
SAPROBES > SAPROBE
SAPROBIAL > SAPROBE
SAPROBIC > SAPROBE
SAPROLITE *n* deposit of earth, etc, formed by decomposition of rocks that has remained in its original site
SAPROPEL *n* unconsolidated sludge consisting of the decomposed remains of aquatic organisms at the bottoms of lakes and oceans
SAPROPELS > SAPROPEL
SAPROZOIC *adj* (of animals or plants) feeding on dead organic matter
SAPS > SAP
SAPSAGO *n* hard greenish Swiss cheese made with sour skimmed milk and coloured and flavoured with clover
SAPSAGOS > SAPSAGO
SAPSUCKER *n* either of two North American woodpeckers
SAPUCAIA *n* Brazilian tree
SAPUCAIAS > SAPUCAIA
SAPWOOD *n* soft wood, just beneath the bark in tree trunks, that consists of living tissue
SAPWOODS > SAPWOOD
SAR *n* marine fish ▷ *vb* Scots word meaning savour
SARABAND *same as* > SARABANDE
SARABANDE *n* slow stately Spanish dance
SARABANDS > SARABAND
SARAFAN *n* Russian woman's cloak
SARAFANS > SARAFAN
SARAN *n* any one of a class of thermoplastic resins
SARANGI *n* stringed instrument of India played with a bow
SARANGIS > SARANGI
SARANS > SARAN
SARAPE *n* serape
SARAPES > SARAPE
SARBACANE *n* type of blowpipe
SARCASM *n* (use of) bitter or wounding ironic language
SARCASMS > SARCASM
SARCASTIC *adj* full of or

showing sarcasm
SARCENET *n* fine soft silk fabric formerly from Italy and used for clothing, ribbons, etc
SARCENETS > SARCENET
SARCINA *n* type of bacterium
SARCINAE > SARCINA
SARCINAS > SARCINA
SARCOCARP *n* fleshy mesocarp of such fruits as the peach or plum
SARCODE *n* material making up living cell
SARCODES > SARCODE
SARCODIC > SARCODE
SARCOID *adj* of, relating to, or resembling flesh ▷ *n* tumour resembling a sarcoma
SARCOIDS > SARCOID
SARCOLOGY *n* study of flesh
SARCOMA *n* malignant tumour beginning in connective tissue
SARCOMAS > SARCOMA
SARCOMATA > SARCOMA
SARCOMERE *n* any of the units that together comprise skeletal muscle
SARCONET *n* type of silk
SARCONETS > SARCONET
SARCOPTIC *adj* relating to mange
SARCOSOME *n* energy-producing tissue in muscle
SARCOUS *adj* (of tissue) muscular or fleshy
SARD *n* orange, red, or brown variety of chalcedony, used as a gemstone
SARDANA *n* Catalan dance
SARDANAS > SARDANA
SARDAR *n* title used before the name of Sikh men
SARDARS > SARDAR
SARDEL *n* small fish
SARDELLE *n* small fish
SARDELLES > SARDELLE
SARDELS > SARDEL
SARDINE *n* small fish of the herring family, usu preserved tightly packed in tins ▷ *vb* cram together
SARDINED > SARDINE
SARDINES > SARDINE
SARDINING > SARDINE
SARDIUS *same as* > SARD
SARDIUSES > SARDIUS
SARDONIAN *adj* sardonic
SARDONIC *adj* mocking or scornful
SARDONYX *n* brown-and-white gemstone
SARDS > SARD
SARED > SAR
SAREE *same as* > SARI
SAREES > SAREE
SARGASSO *same as* > SARGASSUM
SARGASSOS > SARGASSO
SARGASSUM *n* type of floating seaweed
SARGE *n* sergeant
SARGES > SARGE
SARGO *same as* > SARGUS
SARGOS *variant of* > SARGUS
SARGOSES > SARGOS
SARGUS *n* species of sea fish
SARGUSES > SARGUS
SARI *n* long piece of cloth draped around the body and over one shoulder, worn by Hindu women
SARIN *n* chemical used in warfare as a lethal nerve gas producing asphyxia
SARING > SAR
SARINS > SARIN
SARIS > SARI
SARK *n* shirt or (formerly) chemise
SARKIER > SARKY
SARKIEST > SARKY
SARKING *n* flat planking supporting the roof cladding of a building
SARKINGS > SARKING
SARKS > SARK
SARKY *adj* sarcastic
SARMENT *n* thin twig
SARMENTA > SARMENTUM
SARMENTS > SARMENT
SARMENTUM *n* runner on plant
SARMIE *n* sandwich
SARMIES > SARMIE
SARNEY *n* sandwich
SARNEYS > SARNEY
SARNIE *n* sandwich
SARNIES > SARNIE
SAROD *n* Indian stringed musical instrument that may be played with a bow or plucked
SARODE *n* Indian stringed instrument
SARODES > SARODE
SARODIST *n* sarod player
SARODISTS > SARODIST
SARODS > SAROD
SARONG *n* long piece of cloth tucked around the waist or under the armpits, worn esp in Malaysia
SARONGS > SARONG
SARONIC > SAROS
SAROS *n* cycle of about 18 years 11 days in which eclipses of the sun and moon occur in the same sequence
SAROSES > SAROS
SARPANCH *n* head of a panchayat
SARRASIN *n* buckwheat
SARRASINS > SARRASIN
SARRAZIN *n* buckwheat
SARRAZINS > SARRAZIN
SARS > SAR
SARSAR *same as* > SANSAR
SARSARS > SARSAR
SARSDEN *n* sarsen
SARSDENS > SARSDEN
SARSEN *n* boulder of silicified sandstone found in large numbers in S England
SARSENET *same as* > SARCENET
SARSENETS > SARSENET
SARSENS > SARSEN
SARSNET *n* type of silk
SARSNETS > SARSNET
SARTOR *humorous or literary word for* > TAILOR
SARTORIAL *adj* of men's clothes or tailoring
SARTORIAN *adj* of tailoring
SARTORII > SARTORIUS
SARTORIUS *n* long ribbon-shaped muscle that aids in flexing the knee
SARTORS > SARTOR
SARUS *n* Indian bird of crane family
SARUSES > SARUS
SASARARA *n* scolding
SASARARAS > SASARARA
SASER *n* device for amplifying ultrasound, working on a similar principle to a laser
SASERS > SASER
SASH *n* decorative strip of cloth worn round the waist or over one shoulder ▷ *vb* furnish with a sash, sashes, or sash windows
SASHAY *vb* move or walk in a casual or a showy manner
SASHAYED > SASHAY
SASHAYING > SASHAY
SASHAYS > SASHAY
SASHED > SASH
SASHES > SASH
SASHIMI *n* Japanese dish of thin fillets of raw fish
SASHIMIS > SASHIMI
SASHING > SASH
SASHLESS > SASH
SASIN *another name for* > BLACKBUCK
SASINE *n* granting of legal possession of feudal property
SASINES > SASINE
SASINS > SASIN
SASKATOON *n* species of serviceberry of W Canada
SASQUATCH *n* (in Canadian folklore) hairy beast or manlike monster said to leave huge footprints
SASS *n* insolent or impudent talk or behaviour ▷ *vb* talk or answer back in such a way
SASSABIES > SASSABY
SASSABY *n* African antelope of grasslands and semideserts
SASSAFRAS *n* American tree with aromatic bark used medicinally
SASSARARA *n* scolding
SASSE *n* old word meaning canal lock
SASSED > SASS
SASSES > SASS
SASSIER > SASSY
SASSIES > SASSY
SASSIEST > SASSY
SASSILY > SASSY
SASSINESS > SASSY
SASSING > SASS
SASSOLIN *n* boric acid
SASSOLINS > SASSOLIN
SASSOLITE *n* boric acid
SASSWOOD *same as* > SASSY
SASSWOODS > SASSWOOD
SASSY *adj* insolent, impertinent ▷ *n* W African leguminous tree with poisonous bark
SASSYWOOD *n* trial by orde in Liberia
SASTRA *same as* > SHASTRA
SASTRAS > SASTRA
SASTRUGA *n* one of a serie of ridges on snow-covere plains, caused by the action of wind laden wit ice particles
SASTRUGI > SASTRUGA
SAT > SIT
SATAI *same as* > SATAY
SATAIS > SATAI
SATANG *n* monetary unit of Thailand worth one hundredth of a baht
SATANGS > SATANG
SATANIC *adj* of Satan
SATANICAL *same as* > SATANIC
SATANISM *n* worship of th devil
SATANISMS > SATANISM
SATANIST > SATANISM
SATANISTS > SATANISM
SATANITY *n* quality of being satanic
SATARA *n* type of cloth
SATARAS > SATARA
SATAY *n* Indonesian and Malaysian dish consistin of pieces of chicken, pork etc, grilled on skewers an served with peanut sauc
SATAYS > SATAY
SATCHEL *n* bag, usu with a shoulder strap, for carrying books
SATCHELED *adj* carrying a satchel
SATCHELS > SATCHEL
SATE *vb* satisfy (a desire o appetite) fully
SATED > SATE
SATEDNESS > SATE
SATEEN *n* glossy linen or cotton fabric, woven in such a way that it resembles satin
SATEENS > SATEEN
SATELESS *adj* old word meaning insatiable
SATELLES *n* species of bacteria
SATELLITE *n* man-made device orbiting in space ▷ *adj* of or used in the

.ransmission of television ;ignals from a satellite to .he home ▷ *vb* transmit •y communications ;atellite

.TEM *adj* denoting or)elonging to a particular]roup of Indo-European anguages

.TES > SATE

.TI *n* Indian widow ;uicide

.TIABLE *adj* capable of •eing satiated

.TIABLY > SATIABLE

.TIATE *vb* provide with nore than enough, so as o disgust

.TIATED > SATIATE

.TIATES > SATIATE

.TIATING > SATIATE

.TIATION > SATIATE

.TIETIES > SATIETY

.TIETY *n* feeling of ıaving had too much

.TIN *n* silky fabric with a]lossy surface on one side › *adj* like satin in texture › *vb* cover with satin

.TINED > SATIN

.TINET *n* thin or mitation satin

.TINETS > SATINET

.TINETTA *n* thin satin

.TINETTE *same*

'S > SATINET

.TING > SATE

.TINING > SATIN

.TINPOD *n* honesty (the •lant)

.TINPODS > SATINPOD

.TINS > SATIN

.TINWOOD *n* tropical tree ·ielding hard wood

.TINY > SATIN

.TIRE *n* use of ridicule to ·xpose vice or folly

.TIRES > SATIRE

.TIRIC *same*

'S > SATIRICAL

.TIRICAL *adj* of, relating o, or containing satire

.TIRISE *same*

'S > SATIRIZE

.TIRISED > SATIRISE

.TIRISER > SATIRIZE

.TIRISES > SATIRISE

.TIRIST *n* writer of satire

.TIRISTS > SATIRIST

.TIRIZE *vb* ridicule by neans of satire

.TIRIZED > SATIRIZE

.TIRIZER > SATIRIZE

.TIRIZES > SATIRIZE

.TIS > SATI

.TISFICE *vb* act in such ı way as to satisfy the ninimum requirements or achieving a particular esult

.TISFIED > SATISFY

.TISFIER > SATISFY

.TISFIES > SATISFY

.TISFY *vb* please, content

SATIVE *adj* old word meaning cultivated

SATORI *n* state of sudden indescribable intuitive enlightenment

SATORIS > SATORI

SATRAP *n* (in ancient Persia) a provincial governor or subordinate ruler

SATRAPAL > SATRAP

SATRAPIES > SATRAPY

SATRAPS > SATRAP

SATRAPY *n* province, office, or period of rule of a satrap

SATSUMA *n* kind of small orange

SATSUMAS > SATSUMA

SATURABLE *adj* capable of being saturated

SATURANT *n* substance that causes a solution, etc, to be saturated ▷ *adj* (of a substance) causing saturation

SATURANTS > SATURANT

SATURATE *vb* soak thoroughly

SATURATED *adj* (of a solution or solvent) containing the maximum amount of solute that can normally be dissolved at a given temperature and pressure

SATURATER > SATURATE

SATURATES > SATURATE

SATURATOR > SATURATE

SATURNIC *adj* poisoned by lead

SATURNIID *n* any moth of the mainly tropical family *Saturniidae*, typically having large brightly coloured wings ▷ *adj* of, relating to, or belonging to the *Saturniidae*

SATURNINE *adj* gloomy in temperament or appearance

SATURNISM *n* lead poisoning

SATURNIST *n* old word meaning glum person

SATYR *n* woodland god, part man, part goat

SATYRA *n* female satyr

SATYRAL *n* mythical beast in heraldry

SATYRALS > SATYRAL

SATYRAS > SATYRA

SATYRESS *n* female satyr

SATYRIC > SATYR

SATYRICAL > SATYR

SATYRID *n* butterfly with typically brown or dark wings with paler markings

SATYRIDS > SATYRID

SATYRISK *n* small satyr

SATYRISKS > SATYRISK

SATYRLIKE > SATYR

SATYRS > SATYR

SAU *archaic past tense of* > SEE

SAUBA *n* South American ant

SAUBAS > SAUBA

SAUCE *n* liquid added to food to enhance flavour ▷ *vb* prepare (food) with sauce

SAUCEBOAT *n* gravy boat

SAUCEBOX *n* saucy person

SAUCED > SAUCE

SAUCELESS > SAUCE

SAUCEPAN *n* cooking pot with a long handle

SAUCEPANS > SAUCEPAN

SAUCEPOT *n* cooking pot with lid

SAUCEPOTS > SAUCEPOT

SAUCER *n* small round dish put under a cup

SAUCERFUL > SAUCER

SAUCERS > SAUCER

SAUCES > SAUCE

SAUCH *n* sallow or willow

SAUCHS > SAUCH

SAUCIER *n* chef who makes sauces

SAUCIERS > SAUCIER

SAUCIEST > SAUCY

SAUCILY > SAUCY

SAUCINESS > SAUCY

SAUCING > SAUCE

SAUCISSE *n* type of explosive fuse

SAUCISSES > SAUCISSE

SAUCISSON *n* type of explosive fuse

SAUCY *adj* impudent

SAUFGARD *old form of* > SAFEGUARD

SAUFGARDS > SAUFGARD

SAUGER *n* small North American pikeperch

SAUGERS > SAUGER

SAUGH *same as* > SAUCH

SAUGHS > SAUGH

SAUGHY *adj* Scots word meaning made of willow

SAUL *Scots word for* > SOUL

SAULGE *n* old word for sage plant

SAULGES > SAULGE

SAULIE *n* Scots word meaning professional mourner

SAULIES > SAULIE

SAULS > SAUL

SAULT *n* waterfall in Canada

SAULTS > SAULT

SAUNA *n* Finnish-style steam bath ▷ *vb* have a sauna

SAUNAED > SAUNA

SAUNAING > SAUNA

SAUNAS > SAUNA

SAUNT *Scots form of* > SAINT

SAUNTED > SAUNT

SAUNTER *vb* walk in a leisurely manner, stroll ▷ *n* leisurely walk

SAUNTERED > SAUNTER

SAUNTERER > SAUNTER

SAUNTERS > SAUNTER

SAUNTING > SAUNT

SAUNTS > SAUNT

SAUREL *n* type of mackerel

SAURELS > SAUREL

SAURIAN *adj* of or like a lizard ▷ *n* former name for > LIZARD

SAURIANS > SAURIAN

SAURIES > SAURY

SAUROID *adj* like a lizard

SAUROPOD *n* type of herbivorous dinosaur including the brontosaurus and the diplodocus

SAUROPODS > SAUROPOD

SAURY *n* type of fish of tropical and temperate seas, having an elongated body and long toothed jaws

SAUSAGE *n* minced meat in an edible tube-shaped skin

SAUSAGES > SAUSAGE

SAUT *Scot word for* > SALT

SAUTE *vb* fry quickly in a little fat ▷ *n* dish of sautéed food ▷ *adj* sautéed until lightly brown

SAUTED > SAUT

SAUTEED > SAUTE

SAUTEEING > SAUTE

SAUTEES > SAUTE

SAUTEING > SAUTE

SAUTERNE *n* sauternes

SAUTERNES *n* sweet white French wine

SAUTES > SAUTE

SAUTING > SAUT

SAUTOIR *n* long necklace or pendant

SAUTOIRE *variant of* > SAUTOIR

SAUTOIRES > SAUTOIRE

SAUTOIRS > SAUTOIR

SAUTS > SAUT

SAV *short for* > SAVELOY

SAVABLE > SAVE

SAVAGE *adj* wild, untamed ▷ *n* uncivilized person ▷ *vb* attack ferociously

SAVAGED > SAVAGE

SAVAGEDOM > SAVAGE

SAVAGELY > SAVAGE

SAVAGER > SAVAGE

SAVAGERY *n* viciousness and cruelty

SAVAGES > SAVAGE

SAVAGEST > SAVAGE

SAVAGING > SAVAGE

SAVAGISM > SAVAGE

SAVAGISMS > SAVAGE

SAVANNA *n* open grasslands, usually with scattered bushes or trees, characteristic of much of tropical Africa

SAVANNAH *same as* > SAVANNA

SAVANNAHS > SAVANNAH

SAVANNAS > SAVANNA

SAVANT *n* learned person

SAVANTE > SAVANT

SAVANTES > SAVANT

SAVANTS > SAVANT
SAVARIN *n* type of cake
SAVARINS > SAVARIN
SAVATE *n* form of boxing in which blows may be delivered with the feet as well as the hands
SAVATES > SAVATE
SAVE *vb* rescue or preserve from harm, protect ▷ *n* act of preventing a goal ▷ *prep* except
SAVEABLE > SAVE
SAVED > SAVE
SAVEGARD *vb* old word meaning protect
SAVEGARDS > SAVEGARD
SAVELOY *n* spicy smoked sausage
SAVELOYS > SAVELOY
SAVER > SAVE
SAVERS > SAVE
SAVES > SAVE
SAVEY *vb* understand
SAVEYED > SAVEY
SAVEYING > SAVEY
SAVEYS > SAVEY
SAVIN *n* small spreading juniper bush of Europe, N Asia, and North America
SAVINE *same as* > SAVIN
SAVINES > SAVINE
SAVING *n* economy ▷ *prep* except ▷ *adj* tending to save or preserve
SAVINGLY > SAVING
SAVINGS > SAVING
SAVINS > SAVIN
SAVIOR *same as* > SAVIOUR
SAVIORS > SAVIOR
SAVIOUR *n* person who rescues another
SAVIOURS > SAVIOUR
SAVOR *same as* > SAVOUR
SAVORED > SAVOR
SAVORER > SAVOR
SAVORERS > SAVOR
SAVORIER > SAVORY
SAVORIES > SAVORY
SAVORIEST > SAVORY
SAVORILY > SAVOUR
SAVORING > SAVOR
SAVORLESS > SAVOUR
SAVOROUS > SAVOUR
SAVORS > SAVOR
SAVORY *same as* > SAVOURY
SAVOUR *vb* enjoy, relish ▷ *n* characteristic taste or odour
SAVOURED > SAVOUR
SAVOURER > SAVOUR
SAVOURERS > SAVOUR
SAVOURIER > SAVOURY
SAVOURIES > SAVOURY
SAVOURILY > SAVOURY
SAVOURING > SAVOUR
SAVOURLY *adv* old word meaning refeshingly
SAVOURS > SAVOUR
SAVOURY *adj* salty or spicy ▷ *n* savoury dish served before or after a meal
SAVOY *n* variety of cabbage
SAVOYARD *n* person keenly interested in the operettas of Gilbert and Sullivan
SAVOYARDS > SAVOYARD
SAVOYS > SAVOY
SAVS > SAV
SAVVEY *vb* understand
SAVVEYED > SAVVEY
SAVVEYING > SAVVEY
SAVVEYS > SAVVEY
SAVVIED > SAVVY
SAVVIER > SAVVY
SAVVIES > SAVVY
SAVVIEST > SAVVY
SAVVILY > SAVVY
SAVVINESS > SAVVY
SAVVY *vb* understand ▷ *n* understanding, intelligence ▷ *adj* shrewd
SAVVYING > SAVVY
SAW *n* hand tool for cutting wood and metal ▷ *vb* cut with a saw
SAWAH *n* paddyfield
SAWAHS > SAWAH
SAWBILL *n* any of various hummingbirds of the genus *Ramphodon*
SAWBILLS > SAWBILL
SAWBLADE *n* blade of a saw
SAWBLADES > SAWBLADE
SAWBONES *n* surgeon or doctor
SAWBUCK *n* sawhorse, esp one having an X-shaped supporting structure
SAWBUCKS > SAWBUCK
SAWDER *n* flattery ▷ *vb* flatter
SAWDERED > SAWDER
SAWDERING > SAWDER
SAWDERS > SAWDER
SAWDUST *n* fine wood fragments made in sawing ▷ *vb* cover with sawdust
SAWDUSTED > SAWDUST
SAWDUSTS > SAWDUST
SAWDUSTY > SAWDUST
SAWED > SAW
SAWER > SAW
SAWERS > SAW
SAWFISH *n* fish with a long toothed snout
SAWFISHES > SAWFISH
SAWFLIES > SAWFLY
SAWFLY *n* any of various hymenopterous insects
SAWHORSE *n* structure for supporting wood that is being sawn
SAWHORSES > SAWHORSE
SAWING > SAW
SAWINGS > SAW
SAWLIKE > SAW
SAWLOG *n* log suitable for sawing
SAWLOGS > SAWLOG
SAWMILL *n* mill where timber is sawn into planks
SAWMILLS > SAWMILL
SAWN *past participle of* > SAW
SAWNEY *n* derogatory word for a fool
SAWNEYS > SAWNEY
SAWPIT *n* pit above which a log is sawn into planks
SAWPITS > SAWPIT
SAWS > SAW
SAWSHARK *n* shark with long sawlike snout
SAWSHARKS > SAWSHARK
SAWTEETH > SAWTOOTH
SAWTIMBER *n* wood for sawing
SAWTOOTH *adj* (of a waveform) having an amplitude that varies linearly with time between two values
SAWYER *n* person who saws timber for a living
SAWYERS > SAWYER
SAX *same as* > SAXOPHONE
SAXATILE *adj* living among rocks
SAXAUL *n* Asian tree
SAXAULS > SAXAUL
SAXE as in *saxe blue* light greyish-blue colour
SAXES > SAX
SAXHORN *n* valved brass instrument used chiefly in brass and military bands
SAXHORNS > SAXHORN
SAXICOLE *variant of* > SAXATILE
SAXIFRAGE *n* alpine rock plant with small flowers
SAXITOXIN *n* poison extracted from mollusc
SAXONIES > SAXONY
SAXONITE *n* igneous rock
SAXONITES > SAXONITE
SAXONY *n* fine 3-ply yarn used for knitting and weaving
SAXOPHONE *n* brass wind instrument with keys and a curved body
SAXTUBA *n* bass saxhorn
SAXTUBAS > SAXTUBA
SAY *vb* speak or utter ▷ *n* right or chance to speak
SAYABLE > SAY
SAYED *same as* > SAYYID
SAYEDS > SAYED
SAYER > SAY
SAYERS > SAY
SAYEST > SAY
SAYID *same as* > SAYYID
SAYIDS > SAYID
SAYING > SAY
SAYINGS > SAY
SAYNE > SAY
SAYON *n* type of tunic
SAYONARA *n* Japanese farewell
SAYONARAS > SAYONARA
SAYONS > SAYON
SAYS > SAY
SAYST > SAY
SAYYID *n* Muslim claiming descent from Mohammed's grandson Husain
SAYYIDS > SAYYID
SAZ *n* Middle Eastern stringed instrument
SAZERAC *n* mixed drink of whisky, Pernod, syrup, bitters, and lemon
SAZERACS > SAZERAC
SAZES > SAZ
SAZHEN *n* Russian measu of length
SAZHENS > SAZHEN
SAZZES > SAZ
SBIRRI > SBIRRO
SBIRRO *n* Italian police officer
SCAB *n* crust formed over a wound ▷ *vb* become covered with a scab
SCABBARD *n* sheath for a sword or dagger
SCABBARDS > SCABBARD
SCABBED > SCAB
SCABBIER > SCABBY
SCABBIEST > SCABBY
SCABBILY > SCABBY
SCABBING > SCAB
SCABBLE *vb* shape (stone) roughly
SCABBLED > SCABBLE
SCABBLES > SCABBLE
SCABBLING > SCABBLE
SCABBY *adj* covered with scabs
SCABIES *n* itchy skin disease
SCABIETIC > SCABIES
SCABIOSA *n* flowering plant
SCABIOSAS > SCABIOSA
SCABIOUS *n* plant with showy blue, red, or whiti dome-shaped flower heads ▷ *adj* having or covered with scabs
SCABLAND *n* barren rocky land
SCABLANDS *pl n* type of terrain consisting of bare rock surfaces, with little or no soil cover and scant vegetation
SCABLIKE > SCAB
SCABRID *adj* having a rough or scaly surface
SCABROUS *adj* rough and scaly
SCABS > SCAB
SCAD *n* any of various carangid fishes
SCADS *pl n* large amount c number
SCAFF *n* Scots word meaning food
SCAFFIE *n* Scots word meaning street cleaner
SCAFFIES > SCAFFIE
SCAFFOLD *n* temporary platform for workmen ▷ *vb* provide with a scaffold
SCAFFOLDS > SCAFFOLD
SCAFFS > SCAFF
SCAG *n* tear in a garment c piece of cloth ▷ *vb* make tear in (cloth)
SCAGGED > SCAG
SCAGGING > SCAG
SCAGLIA *n* type of

imestone
AGLIAS > SCAGLIA
AGLIOLA *n* type of mitation marble made of lued gypsum
AGS > SCAG
AIL *vb* Scots word neaning disperse
AILED > SCAIL
AILING > SCAIL
AILS > SCAIL
AITH *vb* old word neaning injure
AITHED > SCAITH
AITHING > SCAITH
AITHS > SCAITH
ALA *n* passage inside the ochlea
ALABLE *adj* capable of eing scaled or climbed
ALABLY > SCALABLE
ALADE *short* or > ESCALADE
ALADES > SCALADE
ALADO *same as* > SCALADE
ALADOS > SCALADO
ALAE > SCALA
ALAGE *n* percentage educted from the price f goods liable to shrink r leak
ALAGES > SCALAGE
ALAR *adj* (variable uantity) having nagnitude but no irection ▷ *n* quantity, uch as time or emperature, that has nagnitude but not irection
ALARE *another name* or > ANGELFISH
ALARES > SCALARE
ALARS > SCALAR
ALATION *n* way scales re arranged
ALAWAG *same* s > SCALLYWAG
ALAWAGS > SCALAWAG
ALD *same as* > SKALD
ALDED > SCALD
ALDER > SCALD
ALDERS > SCALD
ALDFISH *n* small uropean flatfish
ALDHEAD *n* diseased calp
ALDIC > SKALD
ALDING > SCALD
ALDINGS > SCALD
ALDINI > SCALDINO
ALDINO *n* Italian brazier
ALDS > SCALD
ALDSHIP *n* position of eing Scandinavian poet
ALE *n* one of the thin verlapping plates overing fishes and eptiles ▷ *vb* remove cales from
ALED > SCALE
ALELESS > SCALE
ALELIKE > SCALE
ALENE *adj* (of a triangle) with three unequal sides
SCALENI > SCALENUS
SCALENUS *n* any one of the three muscles situated on each side of the neck
SCALEPAN *n* part of scales holding weighed object
SCALEPANS > SCALEPAN
SCALER *n* person or thing that scales
SCALERS > SCALER
SCALES > SCALE
SCALETAIL *n* type of squirrel
SCALEUP *n* increase
SCALEUPS > SCALEUP
SCALEWORK *n* artistic representation of scales
SCALIER > SCALY
SCALIEST > SCALY
SCALINESS > SCALY
SCALING > SCALING
SCALINGS > SCALE
SCALL *n* disease of the scalp characterized by itching and scab formation
SCALLAWAG *same as* > SCALLYWAG
SCALLED > SCALL
SCALLIES > SCALLY
SCALLION *same as* > SHALLOT
SCALLIONS > SCALLION
SCALLOP *n* edible shellfish with two fan-shaped shells ▷ *vb* decorate (an edge) with scallops
SCALLOPED > SCALLOP
SCALLOPER > SCALLOP
SCALLOPS > SCALLOP
SCALLS > SCALL
SCALLY *n* rascal
SCALLYWAG *n* scamp, rascal
SCALOGRAM *n* scale for measuring opinion
SCALP *n* skin and hair on top of the head ▷ *vb* cut off the scalp of
SCALPED > SCALP
SCALPEL *n* small surgical knife
SCALPELS > SCALPEL
SCALPER > SCALP
SCALPERS > SCALP
SCALPING *n* process in which the top portion of a metal ingot is machined away before use
SCALPINGS > SCALPING
SCALPINS *n* small stones
SCALPLESS > SCALP
SCALPRUM *n* large scalpel
SCALPRUMS > SCALPRUM
SCALPS > SCALP
SCALY *adj* resembling or covered in scales
SCAM *n* dishonest scheme ▷ *vb* swindle (someone) by means of a trick
SCAMBLE *vb* scramble
SCAMBLED > SCAMBLE
SCAMBLER > SCAMBLE
SCAMBLERS > SCAMBLE
SCAMBLES > SCAMBLE
SCAMBLING > SCAMBLE
SCAMEL *n* Shakespearian word of uncertain meaning
SCAMELS > SCAMEL
SCAMMED > SCAM
SCAMMER *n* person who perpetrates a scam
SCAMMERS > SCAMMER
SCAMMING > SCAM
SCAMMONY *n* twining Asian convolvulus plant
SCAMP *n* mischievous child ▷ *vb* perform without care
SCAMPED > SCAMP
SCAMPER *vb* run about hurriedly or in play ▷ *n* scampering
SCAMPERED > SCAMP
SCAMPERER > SCAMPER
SCAMPERS > SCAMP
SCAMPI *pl n* large prawns
SCAMPIES > SCAMPI
SCAMPING > SCAMP
SCAMPINGS > SCAMP
SCAMPIS > SCAMPI
SCAMPISH > SCAMP
SCAMPS > SCAMP
SCAMS > SCAM
SCAMSTER *same as* > SCAMMER
SCAMSTERS > SCAMSTER
SCAMTO *n* argot of urban South African Blacks
SCAMTOS > SCAMTO
SCAN *vb* scrutinize carefully ▷ *n* scanning
SCAND > SCAN
SCANDAL *n* disgraceful action or event ▷ *vb* disgrace
SCANDALED > SCANDAL
SCANDALS > SCANDAL
SCANDENT *adj* (of plants) having a climbing habit
SCANDIA *n* scandium oxide
SCANDIAS > SCANDIA
SCANDIC *adj* of or containing scandium
SCANDIUM *n* rare silvery-white metallic element
SCANDIUMS > SCANDIUM
SCANNABLE > SCAN
SCANNED > SCAN
SCANNER *n* electronic device used for scanning
SCANNERS > SCANNER
SCANNING > SCAN
SCANNINGS > SCAN
SCANS > SCAN
SCANSION *n* metrical scanning of verse
SCANSIONS > SCANSION
SCANT *adj* barely sufficient, meagre ▷ *vb* limit in size or quantity ▷ *adv* scarcely
SCANTED > SCANT
SCANTER > SCANT
SCANTEST > SCANT
SCANTIER > SCANTY
SCANTIES *n* women's underwear
SCANTIEST > SCANTY
SCANTILY > SCANTY
SCANTING > SCANT
SCANTITY *n* quality of being scant
SCANTLE *vb* stint
SCANTLED > SCANTLE
SCANTLES > SCANTLE
SCANTLING *n* piece of sawn timber, such as a rafter, that has a small cross section
SCANTLY > SCANT
SCANTNESS > SCANT
SCANTS > SCANT
SCANTY *adj* barely sufficient or not sufficient
SCAPA *variant of* > SCARPER
SCAPAED > SCAPA
SCAPAING > SCAPA
SCAPAS > SCAPA
SCAPE *n* leafless stalk in plants that arises from a rosette of leaves and bears one or more flowers ▷ *vb* archaic word for escape
SCAPED > SCAPE
SCAPEGOAT *n* person made to bear the blame for others ▷ *vb* make a scapegoat of
SCAPELESS *adj* allowing no escape
SCAPEMENT *n* escapement
SCAPES > SCAPE
SCAPHOID *obsolete word for* > NAVICULAR
SCAPHOIDS > SCAPHOID
SCAPHOPOD *n* any marine mollusc of the class *Scaphopoda*
SCAPI > SCAPUS
SCAPING > SCAPE
SCAPOLITE *n* any of a group of colourless, white, grey, or violet fluorescent minerals
SCAPOSE > SCAPE
SCAPPLE *vb* shape roughly
SCAPPLED > SCAPPLE
SCAPPLES > SCAPPLE
SCAPPLING > SCAPPLE
SCAPULA *n* shoulder blade
SCAPULAE > SCAPULA
SCAPULAR *adj* of the scapula ▷ *n* loose sleeveless garment worn by monks over their habits
SCAPULARS > SCAPULAR
SCAPULARY *same as* > SCAPULAR
SCAPULAS > SCAPULA
SCAPUS *n* flower stalk
SCAR *n* mark left by a healed wound ▷ *vb* mark or become marked with a scar
SCARAB *n* sacred beetle of ancient Egypt
SCARABAEI *pl n* scarabs
SCARABEE *n* old word for scarab beetle
SCARABEES > SCARABEE
SCARABOID *adj* resembling a scarab beetle ▷ *n* beetle

that resembles a scarab
SCARABS > SCARAB
SCARCE *adj* insufficient to meet demand
SCARCELY *adv* hardly at all
SCARCER > SCARCE
SCARCEST > SCARCE
SCARCITY *n* inadequate supply
SCARE *vb* frighten or be frightened ▷ *n* fright, sudden panic ▷ *adj* causing (needless) fear or alarm
SCARECROW *n* figure dressed in old clothes, set up to scare birds away from crops
SCARED > SCARE
SCAREDER > SCARE
SCAREDEST > SCARE
SCAREHEAD *n* newspaper headline intended to shock
SCARER > SCARE
SCARERS > SCARE
SCARES > SCARE
SCAREY *adj* frightening
SCARF *n* piece of material worn round the neck, head, or shoulders ▷ *vb* join in this way
SCARFED > SCARF
SCARFER > SCARF
SCARFERS > SCARF
SCARFING > SCARF
SCARFINGS > SCARF
SCARFISH *n* type of fish
SCARFPIN *n* decorative pin securing scarf
SCARFPINS > SCARFPIN
SCARFS > SCARF
SCARFSKIN *n* outermost layer of the skin
SCARFWISE *adv* like scarf
SCARIER > SCARY
SCARIEST > SCARY
SCARIFIED > SCARIFY
SCARIFIER > SCARIFY
SCARIFIES > SCARIFY
SCARIFY *vb* scratch or cut slightly all over
SCARILY > SCARY
SCARINESS > SCARY
SCARING > SCARE
SCARIOSE *same as* > SCARIOUS
SCARIOUS *adj* (of plant parts) membranous, dry, and brownish in colour
SCARLESS > SCAR
SCARLET *n* brilliant red ▷ *adj* bright red ▷ *vb* make scarlet
SCARLETED > SCARLET
SCARLETS > SCARLET
SCARMOGE *n* old form of skirmish
SCARMOGES > SCARMOGE
SCARP *n* steep slope ▷ *vb* wear or cut so as to form a steep slope
SCARPA *vb* run away
SCARPAED > SCARPA
SCARPAING > SCARPA
SCARPAS > SCARPA
SCARPED > SCARP
SCARPER *vb* run away ▷ *n* hasty departure
SCARPERED > SCARPER
SCARPERS > SCARPER
SCARPETTI > SCARPETTO
SCARPETTO *n* type of shoe
SCARPH *vb* join with scarf joint
SCARPHED > SCARPH
SCARPHING > SCARPH
SCARPHS > SCARPH
SCARPINES *n* device for torturing feet
SCARPING > SCARP
SCARPINGS > SCARP
SCARPS > SCARP
SCARRE *n* Shakespearian word of unknown meaning
SCARRED > SCAR
SCARRES > SCARRE
SCARRIER > SCAR
SCARRIEST > SCAR
SCARRING > SCAR
SCARRINGS > SCAR
SCARRY > SCAR
SCARS > SCAR
SCART *vb* scratch or scrape ▷ *n* scratch or scrape
SCARTED > SCART
SCARTH *Scots word for* > CORMORANT
SCARTHS > SCARTH
SCARTING > SCART
SCARTS > SCART
SCARVES > SCARF
SCARY *adj* frightening
SCAT *vb* go away ▷ *n* jazz singing using improvised vocal sounds instead of words
SCATBACK *n* American football player
SCATBACKS > SCATBACK
SCATCH *same as* > STILT
SCATCHES > SCATCH
SCATH *vb* old word meaning injure
SCATHE *vb* attack with severe criticism ▷ *n* harm
SCATHED > SCATHE
SCATHEFUL *adj* old word meaning harmful
SCATHES > SCATHE
SCATHING *adj* harshly critical
SCATHS > SCATH
SCATOLE *n* substance found in coal
SCATOLES > SCATOLE
SCATOLOGY *n* preoccupation with obscenity, esp with references to excrement
SCATS > SCAT
SCATT *n* old word meaning tax ▷ *vb* tax
SCATTED > SCAT
SCATTER *vb* throw about in various directions ▷ *n* scattering
SCATTERED > SCATTER
SCATTERER > SCATTER
SCATTERS > SCATTER
SCATTERY *adj* dispersed
SCATTIER > SCATTY
SCATTIEST > SCATTY
SCATTILY > SCATTY
SCATTING > SCAT
SCATTINGS > SCAT
SCATTS > SCATT
SCATTY *adj* empty-headed
SCAUD *Scot word for* > SCALD
SCAUDED > SCAUD
SCAUDING > SCAUD
SCAUDS > SCAUD
SCAUP *variant of* > SCALP
SCAUPED > SCAUP
SCAUPER *same as* > SCORPER
SCAUPERS > SCAUPER
SCAUPING > SCAUP
SCAUPS > SCAUP
SCAUR *same as* > SCAR
SCAURED > SCAUR
SCAURIES > SCAURY
SCAURING > SCAUR
SCAURS > SCAUR
SCAURY *n* young seagull
SCAVAGE *n* old word meaning toll
SCAVAGER > SCAVAGE
SCAVAGERS > SCAVAGE
SCAVAGES > SCAVAGE
SCAVENGE *vb* search for (anything usable) among discarded material
SCAVENGED > SCAVENGE
SCAVENGER *n* person who scavenges
SCAVENGES > SCAVENGE
SCAW *n* headland
SCAWS > SCAW
SCAWTITE *n* mineral containing calcium
SCAWTITES > SCAWTITE
SCAZON *n* metre in poetry
SCAZONS > SCAZON
SCAZONTES > SCAZON
SCAZONTIC > SCAZON
SCEAT *n* Anglo-Saxon coin
SCEATT *n* Anglo-Saxon coin
SCEATTAS > SCEAT
SCEDULE *old spelling of* > SCHEDULE
SCEDULED > SCEDULE
SCEDULES > SCEDULE
SCEDULING > SCEDULE
SCELERAT *n* villain
SCELERATE *n* villain
SCELERATS > SCELERAT
SCENA *n* scene in an opera, usually longer than a single aria
SCENARIES > SCENARY
SCENARIO *n* summary of the plot of a play or film
SCENARIOS > SCENARIO
SCENARISE *same as* > SCENARIZE
SCENARIST > SCENARIO
SCENARIZE *vb* create scenario
SCENARY *n* scenery
SCENAS > SCENA
SCEND *vb* (of a vessel) to surge upwards in a heavy sea ▷ *n* upward heaving a vessel pitching
SCENDED > SCEND
SCENDING > SCEND
SCENDS > SCEND
SCENE *n* place of action of a real or imaginary event ▷ *vb* set in a scene
SCENED > SCENE
SCENEMAN *n* person shifting stage scenery
SCENEMEN > SCENEMAN
SCENERIES > SCENERY
SCENERY *n* natural featur of a landscape
SCENES > SCENE
SCENIC *adj* picturesque ▷ something scenic
SCENICAL > SCENE
SCENICS > SCENIC
SCENING > SCENE
SCENT *n* pleasant smell ▷ *vb* detect by smell
SCENTED > SCENT
SCENTFUL *adj* old word meaning having scent
SCENTING > SCENT
SCENTINGS > SCENT
SCENTLESS > SCENT
SCENTS > SCENT
SCEPSIS *n* doubt
SCEPSISES > SCEPSIS
SCEPTER *same as* > SCEPTR
SCEPTERED > SCEPTER
SCEPTERS > SCEPTER
SCEPTIC *n* person who habitually doubts generally accepted belief ▷ *adj* of or relating to sceptics
SCEPTICAL *adj* not convinced that somethir is true
SCEPTICS > SCEPTIC
SCEPTRAL *adj* royal
SCEPTRE *n* ornamental rc symbolizing royal power ▷ *vb* invest with authori
SCEPTRED > SCEPTRE
SCEPTRES > SCEPTRE
SCEPTRING > SCEPTRE
SCEPTRY *adj* having scept
SCERNE *vb* old word meaning discern
SCERNED > SCERNE
SCERNES > SCERNE
SCERNING > SCERNE
SCHANSE *n* stones heapec to shelter soldier in battl
SCHANSES > SCHANSE
SCHANTZE *n* stones heape to shelter soldier in battl
SCHANTZES > SCHANTZE
SCHANZE *n* stones heapec to shelter soldier in battl
SCHANZES > SCHANZE
SCHAPPE *n* yarn or fabric made from waste silk
SCHAPPED > SCHAPPE
SCHAPPES > SCHAPPE
SCHAPSKA *n* cap worn by lancer
SCHAPSKAS > SCHAPSKA

CHATCHEN *same as* > SHADCHAN
CHAV *n* Polish soup
CHAVS > SCHAV
CHECHITA *n* slaughter of animals according to Jewish law
CHEDULAR > SCHEDULE
CHEDULE *n* plan of procedure for a project ▷ *vb* plan to occur at a certain time
CHEDULED *adj* arranged or planned according to a programme, timetable, etc
CHEDULER > SCHEDULE
CHEDULES > SCHEDULE
CHEELITE *n* white, brownish, or greenish mineral
CHELLUM *n* Scots word meaning rascal
CHELLUMS > SCHELLUM
CHELM *n* South African word meaning rascal
CHELMS > SCHELM
CHEMA *n* overall plan or diagram
CHEMAS > SCHEMA
CHEMATA > SCHEMA
CHEMATIC *adj* presented as a plan or diagram ▷ *n* schematic diagram, esp of an electrical circuit
CHEME *n* systematic plan ▷ *vb* plan in an underhand manner
CHEMED > SCHEME
CHEMER > SCHEME
CHEMERS > SCHEME
CHEMES > SCHEME
CHEMIE *n* Scots derogatory word for a resident of a housing scheme
CHEMIES > SCHEMIE
CHEMING *adj* given to making plots ▷ *n* intrigues
CHEMINGS > SCHEMING
CHERZI > SCHERZO
CHERZO *n* brisk lively piece of music
CHERZOS > SCHERZO
CHIAVONE *n* type of sword
CHIEDAM *n* type of gin produced in the Netherlands
CHIEDAMS > SCHIEDAM
CHILLER *n* unusual iridescent or metallic lustre in some minerals
CHILLERS > SCHILLER
CHILLING *n* former monetary unit of Austria
CHIMMEL *n* roan horse
CHIMMELS > SCHIMMEL
CHISM *n* (group resulting from) division in an organization
CHISMA *n* musical term
CHISMAS > SCHISMA
CHISMS > SCHISM
SCHIST *n* crystalline rock which splits into layers
SCHISTOSE > SCHIST
SCHISTOUS > SCHIST
SCHISTS > SCHIST
SCHIZIER > SCHIZY
SCHIZIEST > SCHIZY
SCHIZO *n* derogatory term for a schizophrenic (person) ▷ *adj* schizophrenic
SCHIZOID *adj* abnormally introverted ▷ *n* schizoid person
SCHIZOIDS > SCHIZOID
SCHIZONT *n* cell formed from a trophozoite during the asexual stage of the life cycle of sporozoan protozoans
SCHIZONTS > SCHIZONT
SCHIZOPOD *n* any of various shrimplike crustaceans
SCHIZOS > SCHIZO
SCHIZY *adj* slang term meaning schizophrenic
SCHIZZIER > SCHIZZY
SCHIZZY *adj* slang term meaning schizophrenic
SCHLAGER *n* German duelling sword
SCHLAGERS > SCHLAGER
SCHLEMIEL *n* awkward or unlucky person whose endeavours usually fail
SCHLEMIHL *same as* > SCHLEMIEL
SCHLEP *vb* drag or lug (oneself or an object) with difficulty ▷ *n* stupid or clumsy person
SCHLEPP *vb* schlep
SCHLEPPED > SCHLEP
SCHLEPPER *n* incompetent person
SCHLEPPS > SCHLEPP
SCHLEPPY > SCHLEPP
SCHLEPS > SCHLEP
SCHLICH *n* finely crushed ore
SCHLICHS > SCHLICH
SCHLIERE *n* (in physics or geology) streak of different density or composition from surroundings
SCHLIEREN > SCHLIERE
SCHLIERIC > SCHLIERE
SCHLOCK *n* goods or produce of cheap or inferior quality ▷ *adj* cheap, inferior, or trashy
SCHLOCKER *n* thing of poor quality
SCHLOCKS > SCHLOCK
SCHLOCKY *adj* of poor quality
SCHLONG *slang word for* > PENIS
SCHLONGS > SCHLONG
SCHLOSS *n* castle
SCHLOSSES > SCHLOSS
SCHLUB *n* coarse or contemptible person
SCHLUBS > SCHLUB
SCHLUMP *vb* move in lazy way
SCHLUMPED > SCHLUMP
SCHLUMPS > SCHLUMP
SCHLUMPY > SCHLUMP
SCHMALTZ *n* excessive sentimentality
SCHMALTZY *adj* excessively sentimental
SCHMALZ *same as* > SCHMALTZ
SCHMALZES > SCHMALZ
SCHMALZY *adj* schmaltzy
SCHMATTE *same as* > SCHMUTTER
SCHMATTES > SCHMATTE
SCHMEAR *n* situation, matter, or affair ▷ *vb* spread or smear
SCHMEARED > SCHMEAR
SCHMEARS > SCHMEAR
SCHMECK *n* taste
SCHMECKS > SCHMECK
SCHMEER *same as* > SCHMEAR
SCHMEERED > SCHMEER
SCHMEERS > SCHMEER
SCHMELZ *n* ornamental glass
SCHMELZE *variant of* > SCHMELZ
SCHMELZES > SCHMELZ
SCHMICK *n* informal Australian word for excellent, elegant, or stylish
SCHMO *n* dull, stupid, or boring person
SCHMOCK *n* stupid person
SCHMOCKS > SCHMOCK
SCHMOE *n* stupid person
SCHMOES > SCHMO
SCHMOOS *variant of* > SCHMOOSE
SCHMOOSE *vb* chat
SCHMOOSED > SCHMOOSE
SCHMOOSES > SCHMOOSE
SCHMOOZ *n* chat
SCHMOOZE *vb* chat or gossip ▷ *n* trivial conversation
SCHMOOZED > SCHMOOZE
SCHMOOZER > SCHMOOZE
SCHMOOZES > SCHMOOZE
SCHMOOZY > SCHMOOZE
SCHMOS > SCHMO
SCHMUCK *n* stupid or contemptible person
SCHMUCKS > SCHMUCK
SCHMUTTER *n* cloth or clothing
SCHNAPPER *same as* > SNAPPER
SCHNAPPS *n* strong alcoholic spirit
SCHNAPS *same as* > SCHNAPPS
SCHNAPSES > SCHNAPS
SCHNAUZER *n* wire-haired breed of dog of the terrier type, originally from Germany
SCHNECKE > SCHNECKEN
SCHNECKEN *pl n* sweet spiral-shaped bread roll flavoured with cinnamon and nuts
SCHNELL *adj* German word meaning quick
SCHNITZEL *n* thin slice of meat, esp veal
SCHNOOK *n* stupid or gullible person
SCHNOOKS > SCHNOOK
SCHNORKEL *less common variant of* > SNORKEL
SCHNORR *vb* beg
SCHNORRED > SCHNORR
SCHNORRER *n* person who lives off the charity of others
SCHNORRS > SCHNORR
SCHNOZ *n* nose
SCHNOZES > SCHNOZ
SCHNOZZ *n* nose
SCHNOZZES > SCHNOZZ
SCHNOZZLE *slang word for* > NOSE
SCHOLAR *n* learned person
SCHOLARCH *n* head of school
SCHOLARLY > SCHOLAR
SCHOLARS > SCHOLAR
SCHOLIA > SCHOLIUM
SCHOLIAST *n* medieval annotator, esp of classical texts
SCHOLION *n* scholarly annotation
SCHOLIUM *n* commentary or annotation, esp on a classical text
SCHOLIUMS > SCHOLIUM
SCHOOL *n* place where children are taught or instruction is given in a subject ▷ *vb* educate or train
SCHOOLBAG *n* school pupil's bag
SCHOOLBOY *n* child attending school
SCHOOLDAY *n* day for going to school
SCHOOLE *n* old form of shoal
SCHOOLED > SCHOOL
SCHOOLERY *n* old word meaning something taught
SCHOOLES > SCHOOLE
SCHOOLIE *n* schoolteacher or a high-school student
SCHOOLIES > SCHOOLIE
SCHOOLING *n* education
SCHOOLKID *n* child who goes to school
SCHOOLMAN *n* scholar versed in the learning of the Schoolmen
SCHOOLMEN > SCHOOLMAN
SCHOOLS > SCHOOL
SCHOONER *n* sailing ship rigged fore-and-aft
SCHOONERS > SCHOONER
SCHORL *n* type of black tourmaline
SCHORLS > SCHORL

SCHOUT *n* council officer in Netherlands
SCHOUTS > SCHOUT
SCHRIK *variant of* > SKRIK
SCHRIKS > SCHRIK
SCHROD *n* young cod
SCHRODS > SCHROD
SCHTICK *same as* > SHTICK
SCHTICKS > SCHTICK
SCHTIK *n* schtick
SCHTIKS > SCHTIK
SCHTOOK *n* trouble
SCHTOOKS > SCHTOOK
SCHTOOM *adj* silent
SCHTUCK *n* trouble
SCHTUCKS > SCHTUCK
SCHUIT *n* Dutch boat with flat bottom
SCHUITS > SCHUIT
SCHUL *same as* > SHUL
SCHULN > SCHUL
SCHULS > SCHUL
SCHUSS *n* straight high-speed downhill run ▷ *vb* perform a schuss
SCHUSSED > SCHUSS
SCHUSSER > SCHUSS
SCHUSSERS > SCHUSS
SCHUSSES > SCHUSS
SCHUSSING > SCHUSS
SCHUYT *n* Dutch boat with flat bottom
SCHUYTS > SCHUYT
SCHVARTZE *n* Yiddish word for black person
SCHWA *n* central vowel representing the sound that occurs in unstressed syllables in English
SCHWARTZE *same as* > SCHVARTZE
SCHWAS > SCHWA
SCIAENID *adj* of or relating to a family of mainly tropical and subtropical marine percoid fishes ▷ *n* any of these fish
SCIAENIDS > SCIAENID
SCIAENOID *same as* > SCIAENID
SCIAMACHY *n* fight with an imaginary enemy
SCIARID *n* small fly
SCIARIDS > SCIARID
SCIATIC *adj* of the hip ▷ *n* sciatic part of the body
SCIATICA *n* severe pain in the large nerve in the back of the leg
SCIATICAL > SCIATICA
SCIATICAS > SCIATICA
SCIATICS > SCIATIC
SCIENCE *n* systematic study and knowledge of natural or physical phenomena
SCIENCED *adj* old word meaning learned
SCIENCES > SCIENCE
SCIENT *adj* old word meaning scientific
SCIENTER *adv* knowingly
SCIENTIAL *adj* of or relating to science
SCIENTISE *same as* > SCIENTIZE
SCIENTISM *n* application of, or belief in, the scientific method
SCIENTIST *n* person who studies or practises a science
SCIENTIZE *vb* treat scientifically
SCILICET *adv* namely
SCILLA *n* a plant with small bell-shaped flowers
SCILLAS > SCILLA
SCIMETAR *n* scimitar
SCIMETARS > SCIMETAR
SCIMITAR *n* curved oriental sword
SCIMITARS > SCIMITAR
SCIMITER *n* scimitar
SCIMITERS > SCIMITER
SCINCOID *adj* of, relating to, or resembling a skink ▷ *n* any animal, esp a lizard, resembling a skink
SCINCOIDS > SCINCOID
SCINTILLA *n* very small amount
SCIOLISM *n* practice of opinionating on subjects of which one has only superficial knowledge
SCIOLISMS > SCIOLISM
SCIOLIST > SCIOLISM
SCIOLISTS > SCIOLISM
SCIOLOUS > SCIOLISM
SCIOLTO *adv* musical direction meaning freely
SCIOMACHY *same as* > SCIAMACHY
SCIOMANCY *n* divination with the help of ghosts
SCION *n* descendant or heir
SCIONS > SCION
SCIOPHYTE *n* any plant that grows best in the shade
SCIOSOPHY *n* unscientific system of knowledge
SCIROC *n* hot Mediterranean wind
SCIROCCO *n* hot Mediterranean wind
SCIROCCOS > SCIROCCO
SCIROCS > SCIROC
SCIRRHI > SCIRRHUS
SCIRRHOID > SCIRRHUS
SCIRRHOUS *adj* of or resembling a scirrhus
SCIRRHUS *n* hard cancerous growth composed of fibrous tissues
SCISSEL *n* waste metal left over from sheet metal after discs have been punched out of it
SCISSELS > SCISSEL
SCISSIL *n* scissel
SCISSILE *adj* capable of being cut or divided
SCISSILS > SCISSIL
SCISSION *n* act or an instance of cutting, splitting, or dividing
SCISSIONS > SCISSION
SCISSOR *vb* cut (an object) with scissors
SCISSORED > SCISSOR
SCISSORER > SCISSOR
SCISSORS *pl n* cutting instrument with two crossed pivoted blades
SCISSURE *n* longitudinal cleft
SCISSURES > SCISSURE
SCIURID *n* squirrel or related rodent
SCIURIDS > SCIURID
SCIURINE *adj* relating to a family of rodents that includes squirrels, marmots, and chipmunks ▷ *n* any sciurine animal
SCIURINES > SCIURINE
SCIUROID *adj* (of an animal) resembling a squirrel
SCLAFF *vb* cause (the club) to hit (the ground behind the ball) when making a stroke ▷ *n* sclaffing stroke or shot
SCLAFFED > SCLAFF
SCLAFFER > SCLAFF
SCLAFFERS > SCLAFF
SCLAFFING > SCLAFF
SCLAFFS > SCLAFF
SCLATE *vb* Scots word meaning slate
SCLATED > SCLATE
SCLATES > SCLATE
SCLATING > SCLATE
SCLAUNDER *n* old form of slander
SCLAVE *n* old form of slave
SCLAVES > SCLAVE
SCLERA *n* tough white substance that forms the outer covering of the eyeball
SCLERAE > SCLERA
SCLERAL > SCLERA
SCLERAS > SCLERA
SCLERE *n* supporting anatomical structure, esp a sponge spicule
SCLEREID *n* type of biological cell
SCLEREIDE *n* type of biological cell
SCLEREIDS > SCLEREID
SCLEREMA *n* condition in which body tissues harden
SCLEREMAS > SCLEREMA
SCLERES > SCLERE
SCLERITE *n* any of the hard chitinous plates that make up the exoskeleton of an arthropod
SCLERITES > SCLERITE
SCLERITIC > SCLERITE
SCLERITIS *n* inflammation of the sclera
SCLEROID *adj* (of organisms and their parts) hard or hardened
SCLEROMA *n* any small area of abnormally hard tissue, esp in a mucous membrane
SCLEROMAS > SCLEROMA
SCLEROSAL > SCLEROSIS
SCLEROSE *vb* affect with sclerosis
SCLEROSED *adj* hardened
SCLEROSES > SCLEROSIS
SCLEROSIS *n* abnormal hardening of body tissues
SCLEROTAL *n* bony area in sclerotic
SCLEROTIA *pl n* masses of hyphae formed in certain fungi
SCLEROTIC *same as* > SCLERA
SCLEROTIN *n* protein in the cuticle of insects that becomes hard and dark
SCLEROUS *adj* hard
SCLIFF *n* Scots word for small piece
SCLIFFS > SCLIFF
SCLIM *vb* Scots word meaning climb
SCLIMMED > SCLIM
SCLIMMING > SCLIM
SCLIMS > SCLIM
SCODIER > SCODY
SCODIEST > SCODY
SCODY *adj* unkempt
SCOFF *vb* express derision ▷ *n* mocking expression
SCOFFED > SCOFF
SCOFFER > SCOFF
SCOFFERS > SCOFF
SCOFFING > SCOFF
SCOFFINGS > SCOFF
SCOFFLAW *n* person who habitually flouts or violates the law
SCOFFLAWS > SCOFFLAW
SCOFFS > SCOFF
SCOG *vb* shelter
SCOGGED > SCOG
SCOGGING > SCOG
SCOGS > SCOG
SCOINSON *n* part of door or window frame
SCOINSONS > SCOINSON
SCOLD *vb* find fault with, reprimand ▷ *n* person who scolds
SCOLDABLE > SCOLD
SCOLDED > SCOLD
SCOLDER > SCOLD
SCOLDERS > SCOLD
SCOLDING > SCOLD
SCOLDINGS > SCOLD
SCOLDS > SCOLD
SCOLECES > SCOLEX
SCOLECID *n* variety of worm
SCOLECIDS > SCOLECID
SCOLECITE *n* white zeolite mineral
SCOLECOID *adj* like scolex
SCOLEX *n* headlike part of tapeworm
SCOLIA > SCOLION
SCOLICES > SCOLEX
SCOLIOMA *n* condition

with abnormal curvature of spine
OLIOMAS > SCOLIOMA
OLION *n* ancient Greek drinking song
OLIOSES > SCOLIOSIS
OLIOSIS *n* abnormal lateral curvature of the spine
OLIOTIC > SCOLIOSIS
OLLOP *variant* of > SCALLOP
OLLOPED > SCOLLOP
OLLOPS > SCOLLOP
OLYTID *n* type of beetle
OLYTIDS > SCOLYTID
OLYTOID *n* type of beetle
OMBRID *n* fish of mackerel family
OMBRIDS > SCOMBRID
OMBROID *adj* relating to a suborder of marine spiny-finned fishes ▷ *n* any fish belonging to this suborder
OMFISH *vb* Scots word meaning stifle
ONCE *n* bracket on a wall for holding candles or lights ▷ *vb* challenge (a fellow student) on the grounds of a social misdemeanour to drink a large quantity of beer without stopping
ONCED > SCONCE
ONCES > SCONCE
ONCHEON *n* part of door or window frame
ONCING > SCONCE
ONE *n* small plain cake baked in an oven or on a griddle
ONES > SCONE
ONTION *n* part of door or window frame
ONTIONS > SCONTION
OOBIES > SCOOBY
OOBY *n* clue; notion
OOCH *vb* compress one's body into smaller space
OOCHED > SCOOCH
OOCHES > SCOOCH
OOCHING > SCOOCH
OOG *vb* shelter
OOGED > SCOOG
OOGING > SCOOG
OOGS > SCOOG
OOP *n* shovel-like tool for ladling or hollowing out ▷ *vb* take up or hollow out with or as if with a scoop
OOPABLE > SCOOP
OOPED > SCOOP
OOPER > SCOOP
OOPERS > SCOOP
OOPFUL > SCOOP
OOPFULS > SCOOP
OOPING > SCOOP
OOPINGS > SCOOP
OOPS > SCOOP
OOPSFUL > SCOOP
OOSH *vb* squirt ▷ *n* squirt or rush of liquid
SCOOSHED > SCOOSH
SCOOSHES > SCOOSH
SCOOSHING > SCOOSH
SCOOT *vb* leave or move quickly ▷ *n* act of scooting
SCOOTCH *same as* > SCOOCH
SCOOTCHED > SCOOTCH
SCOOTCHES > SCOOTCH
SCOOTED > SCOOT
SCOOTER *n* child's vehicle propelled by pushing on the ground with one foot
SCOOTERS > SCOOTER
SCOOTING > SCOOT
SCOOTS > SCOOT
SCOP *n* (in Anglo-Saxon England) a bard or minstrel
SCOPA *n* tuft of hairs on the abdomen or hind legs of bees, used for collecting pollen
SCOPAE > SCOPA
SCOPAS > SCOPA
SCOPATE *adj* having tuft
SCOPE *n* opportunity for using abilities ▷ *vb* look at or examine carefully
SCOPED > SCOPE
SCOPELID *n* deep-sea fish
SCOPELIDS > SCOPELID
SCOPELOID *n* deep-sea fish
SCOPES > SCOPE
SCOPING > SCOPE
SCOPOLINE *n* soluble crystalline alkaloid
SCOPS > SCOP
SCOPULA *n* small tuft of dense hairs on the legs and chelicerae of some spiders
SCOPULAE > SCOPULA
SCOPULAS > SCOPULA
SCOPULATE > SCOPULA
SCORBUTIC *adj* of or having scurvy
SCORCH *vb* burn on the surface ▷ *n* slight burn
SCORCHED > SCORCH
SCORCHER *n* very hot day
SCORCHERS > SCORCHER
SCORCHES > SCORCH
SCORCHING > SCORCH
SCORDATO *adj* musical term meaning out of tune
SCORE *n* points gained in a game or competition ▷ *vb* gain (points) in a game
SCORECARD *n* card on which scores are recorded in games such as golf
SCORED > SCORE
SCORELESS *adj* without anyone scoring
SCORELINE *n* final score in game
SCOREPAD *n* pad for recording score in game
SCOREPADS > SCOREPAD
SCORER > SCORE
SCORERS > SCORE
SCORES > SCORE
SCORIA *n* mass of solidified lava containing many cavities
SCORIAC > SCORIA
SCORIAE > SCORIA
SCORIFIED > SCORIFY
SCORIFIER > SCORIFY
SCORIFIES > SCORIFY
SCORIFY *vb* remove (impurities) from metals by forming scoria
SCORING *n* act or practice of scoring
SCORINGS > SCORING
SCORIOUS > SCORIA
SCORN *n* open contempt ▷ *vb* despise
SCORNED > SCORN
SCORNER > SCORN
SCORNERS > SCORN
SCORNFUL > SCORN
SCORNING > SCORN
SCORNINGS > SCORN
SCORNS > SCORN
SCORODITE *n* mineral containing iron and aluminium
SCORPER *n* kind of fine chisel with a square or curved tip
SCORPERS > SCORPER
SCORPIOID *adj* of, relating to, or resembling scorpions
SCORPION *n* small lobster-shaped animal with a sting at the end of a jointed tail
SCORPIONS > SCORPION
SCORRENDO *adj* musical term meaning gliding
SCORSE *vb* exchange
SCORSED > SCORSE
SCORSER > SCORSE
SCORSERS > SCORSE
SCORSES > SCORSE
SCORSING > SCORSE
SCOT *n* payment or tax
SCOTCH *vb* put an end to ▷ *n* gash
SCOTCHED > SCOTCH
SCOTCHES > SCOTCH
SCOTCHING > SCOTCH
SCOTER *n* type of sea duck
SCOTERS > SCOTER
SCOTIA *n* deep concave moulding
SCOTIAS > SCOTIA
SCOTOMA *n* blind spot
SCOTOMAS > SCOTOMA
SCOTOMATA > SCOTOMA
SCOTOMIA *n* dizziness
SCOTOMIAS > SCOTOMIA
SCOTOMIES > SCOTOMY
SCOTOMY *n* dizziness
SCOTOPHIL *adj* liking darkness
SCOTOPIA *n* ability of the eye to adjust for night vision
SCOTOPIAS > SCOTOPIA
SCOTOPIC > SCOTOPIA
SCOTS > SCOT
SCOTTIE *n* type of small sturdy terrier
SCOTTIES > SCOTTIE
SCOUG *vb* shelter
SCOUGED > SCOUG
SCOUGING > SCOUG
SCOUGS > SCOUG
SCOUNDREL *n* cheat or deceiver
SCOUP *vb* Scots word meaning jump
SCOUPED > SCOUP
SCOUPING > SCOUP
SCOUPS > SCOUP
SCOUR *vb* clean or polish by rubbing with something rough ▷ *n* scouring
SCOURED > SCOUR
SCOURER > SCOUR
SCOURERS > SCOUR
SCOURGE *n* person or thing causing severe suffering ▷ *vb* cause severe suffering to
SCOURGED > SCOURGE
SCOURGER > SCOURGE
SCOURGERS > SCOURGE
SCOURGES > SCOURGE
SCOURGING > SCOURGE
SCOURIE *n* young seagull
SCOURIES > SCOURIE
SCOURING > SCOUR
SCOURINGS *pl n* residue left after cleaning grain
SCOURS > SCOUR
SCOURSE *vb* exchange
SCOURSED > SCOURSE
SCOURSES > SCOURSE
SCOURSING > SCOURSE
SCOUSE *n* stew made from left-over meat
SCOUSER *n* inhabitant of Liverpool
SCOUSERS > SCOUSER
SCOUSES > SCOUSE
SCOUT *n* person sent out to reconnoitre ▷ *vb* act as a scout
SCOUTED > SCOUT
SCOUTER > SCOUT
SCOUTERS > SCOUT
SCOUTH *n* Scots word meaning plenty of scope
SCOUTHER *vb* Scots word meaning scorch
SCOUTHERS > SCOUTHER
SCOUTHERY > SCOUTHER
SCOUTHS > SCOUTH
SCOUTING > SCOUT
SCOUTINGS > SCOUT
SCOUTS > SCOUT
SCOW *n* unpowered barge used for carrying freight ▷ *vb* transport by scow
SCOWDER *vb* Scots word meaning scorch
SCOWDERED > SCOWDER
SCOWDERS > SCOWDER
SCOWED > SCOW
SCOWING > SCOW
SCOWL *n* (have) an angry or sullen expression ▷ *vb* have an angry or bad-tempered facial expression
SCOWLED > SCOWL
SCOWLER *n* person who scowls
SCOWLERS > SCOWLER
SCOWLING > SCOWL

SCOWLS > SCOWL
SCOWP *vb* Scots word meaning jump
SCOWPED > SCOWP
SCOWPING > SCOWP
SCOWPS > SCOWP
SCOWRER *n* old word meaning hooligan
SCOWRERS > SCOWRER
SCOWRIE *n* young seagull
SCOWRIES > SCOWRIE
SCOWS > SCOW
SCOWTH *n* Scots word meaning plenty of scope
SCOWTHER *vb* Scots word meaning scorch
SCOWTHERS > SCOWTHER
SCOWTHS > SCOWTH
SCOZZA *n* rowdy person, esp one who drinks a lot of alcohol
SCOZZAS > SCOZZA
SCRAB *vb* scratch
SCRABBED > SCRAB
SCRABBING > SCRAB
SCRABBLE *vb* scrape at with the hands, feet, or claws ▷ *n* board game in which words are formed by letter tiles
SCRABBLED > SCRABBLE
SCRABBLER > SCRABBLE
SCRABBLES > SCRABBLE
SCRABBLY *adj* covered with stunted trees
SCRABS > SCRAB
SCRAE *Scots word for* > SCREE
SCRAES > SCRAE
SCRAG *n* thin end of a neck of mutton ▷ *vb* wring the neck of
SCRAGGED > SCRAG
SCRAGGIER > SCRAGGY
SCRAGGILY > SCRAGGY
SCRAGGING > SCRAG
SCRAGGLY *adj* untidy or irregular
SCRAGGY *adj* thin, bony
SCRAGS > SCRAG
SCRAICH *vb* Scots word meaning scream
SCRAICHED > SCRAICH
SCRAICHS > SCRAICH
SCRAIGH *vb* Scots word meaning scream
SCRAIGHED > SCRAIGH
SCRAIGHS > SCRAIGH
SCRAM *vb* go away quickly ▷ *n* emergency shutdown of a nuclear reactor
SCRAMB *vb* scratch with nails or claws
SCRAMBED > SCRAMB
SCRAMBING > SCRAMB
SCRAMBLE *vb* climb or crawl hastily or awkwardly ▷ *n* scrambling
SCRAMBLED > SCRAMBLE
SCRAMBLER *n* electronic device that makes transmitted speech unintelligible
SCRAMBLES > SCRAMBLE
SCRAMBS > SCRAMB
SCRAMJET *n* type of jet engine
SCRAMJETS > SCRAMJET
SCRAMMED > SCRAM
SCRAMMING > SCRAM
SCRAMS > SCRAM
SCRAN *n* food
SCRANCH *vb* crunch
SCRANCHED > SCRANCH
SCRANCHES > SCRANCH
SCRANNEL *adj* thin ▷ *n* thin person or thing
SCRANNELS > SCRANNEL
SCRANNIER > SCRANNY
SCRANNY *adj* scrawny
SCRANS > SCRAN
SCRAP *n* small piece ▷ *vb* discard as useless
SCRAPABLE > SCRAPE
SCRAPBOOK *n* book with blank pages in which newspaper cuttings or pictures are stuck
SCRAPE *vb* rub with something rough or sharp ▷ *n* act or sound of scraping
SCRAPED > SCRAPE
SCRAPEGUT *n* old word for fiddle player
SCRAPER > SCRAPE
SCRAPERS > SCRAPE
SCRAPES > SCRAPE
SCRAPHEAP *n* pile of discarded material
SCRAPIE *n* disease of sheep and goats
SCRAPIES > SCRAPIE
SCRAPING *n* act of scraping
SCRAPINGS > SCRAPING
SCRAPPAGE *n* act of scrapping
SCRAPPED > SCRAP
SCRAPPER *n* person who scraps
SCRAPPERS > SCRAPPER
SCRAPPIER > SCRAPPY
SCRAPPILY > SCRAPPY
SCRAPPING > SCRAP
SCRAPPLE *n* scraps of pork cooked with cornmeal and formed into a loaf
SCRAPPLES > SCRAPPLE
SCRAPPY *adj* fragmentary, disjointed
SCRAPS > SCRAP
SCRAPYARD *n* place for scrap metal
SCRAT *vb* scratch
SCRATCH *vb* mark or cut with claws, nails, or anything rough or sharp ▷ *n* wound, mark, or sound made by scratching ▷ *adj* put together at short notice
SCRATCHED > SCRATCH
SCRATCHER *n* person, animal, or thing that scratches
SCRATCHES *n* disease of horses characterized by dermatitis in the region of the fetlock
SCRATCHIE *n* scratchcard
SCRATCHY > SCRATCH
SCRATS > SCRAT
SCRATTED > SCRAT
SCRATTING > SCRAT
SCRATTLE *vb* dialect word meaning scratch
SCRATTLED > SCRATTLE
SCRATTLES > SCRATTLE
SCRAUCH *vb* squawk
SCRAUCHED > SCRAUCH
SCRAUCHS > SCRAUCH
SCRAUGH *vb* squawk
SCRAUGHED > SCRAUGH
SCRAUGHS > SCRAUGH
SCRAW *n* sod from the surface of a peat bog or from a field
SCRAWL *vb* write carelessly or hastily ▷ *n* scribbled writing
SCRAWLED > SCRAWL
SCRAWLER > SCRAWL
SCRAWLERS > SCRAWL
SCRAWLIER > SCRAWL
SCRAWLING > SCRAWL
SCRAWLS > SCRAWL
SCRAWLY > SCRAWL
SCRAWM *vb* dialect word meaning scratch
SCRAWMED > SCRAWM
SCRAWMING > SCRAWM
SCRAWMS > SCRAWM
SCRAWNIER > SCRAWNY
SCRAWNILY > SCRAWNY
SCRAWNY *adj* thin and bony
SCRAWP *vb* scratch (the skin) to relieve itching
SCRAWPED > SCRAWP
SCRAWPING > SCRAWP
SCRAWPS > SCRAWP
SCRAWS > SCRAW
SCRAY *n* tern
SCRAYE *n* tern
SCRAYES > SCRAYE
SCRAYS > SCRAY
SCREAK *vb* screech or creak ▷ *n* screech or creak
SCREAKED > SCREAK
SCREAKIER > SCREAK
SCREAKING > SCREAK
SCREAKS > SCREAK
SCREAKY > SCREAK
SCREAM *vb* utter a piercing cry, esp of fear or pain ▷ *n* shrill piercing cry
SCREAMED > SCREAM
SCREAMER *n* person or thing that screams
SCREAMERS > SCREAMER
SCREAMING > SCREAM
SCREAMS > SCREAM
SCREE *n* slope of loose shifting stones
SCREECH *n* (utter) a shrill cry ▷ *vb* utter a shrill cry
SCREECHED > SCREECH
SCREECHER > SCREECH
SCREECHES > SCREECH
SCREECHY *adj* loud and shrill
SCREED *n* long tedious piece of writing ▷ *vb* rip
SCREEDED > SCREED
SCREEDER > SCREED
SCREEDERS > SCREED
SCREEDING > SCREED
SCREEDS > SCREED
SCREEN *n* surface of a television set, VDU, etc, on which an image is formed ▷ *vb* shelter or conceal with or as if with a screen
SCREENED > SCREEN
SCREENER > SCREEN
SCREENERS > SCREEN
SCREENFUL > SCREEN
SCREENIE *n* informal Australian word for screensaver
SCREENIES > SCREENIE
SCREENING > SCREEN
SCREENS > SCREEN
SCREES > SCREE
SCREET *vb* shed tears ▷ *n* act or sound of crying
SCREETED > SCREET
SCREETING > SCREET
SCREETS > SCREET
SCREEVE *vb* write
SCREEVED > SCREEVE
SCREEVER > SCREEVE
SCREEVERS > SCREEVE
SCREEVES > SCREEVE
SCREEVING > SCREEVE
SCREICH *same as* > SCREIGH
SCREICHED > SCREICH
SCREICHES > SCREICH
SCREICHS > SCREICH
SCREIGH *Scot word for* > SCREECH
SCREIGHED > SCREIGH
SCREIGHS > SCREIGH
SCREW *n* metal pin with a spiral ridge along its length, twisted into materials to fasten them together ▷ *vb* turn (a screw)
SCREWABLE > SCREW
SCREWBALL *n* odd or eccentric person ▷ *adj* crazy or eccentric
SCREWBEAN *n* variety of mesquite
SCREWED *adj* fastened by a screw or screws
SCREWER > SCREW
SCREWERS > SCREW
SCREWIER > SCREWY
SCREWIEST > SCREWY
SCREWING > SCREW
SCREWINGS > SCREW
SCREWLIKE > SCREW
SCREWS > SCREW
SCREWTOP *n* lid with a threaded rim that is turned to close it securely
SCREWTOPS > SCREWTOP
SCREWUP *n* something done badly
SCREWUPS > SCREWUP
SCREWWORM *n* larva of a fly that develops beneath the skin of living mammals often causing illness or death
SCREWY *adj* crazy or

ccentric
CRIBABLE > SCRIBE
CRIBAL > SCRIBE
CRIBBLE *vb* write hastily or illegibly ▷ *n* something scribbled
CRIBBLED > SCRIBBLE
CRIBBLER *n* often derogatory term for a writer of poetry, novels, journalism, etc
CRIBBLES > SCRIBBLE
CRIBBLY > SCRIBBLE
CRIBE *n* person who copies documents ▷ *vb* to score a line with a pointed instrument
CRIBED > SCRIBE
CRIBER *n* pointed steel tool used to score materials as a guide to cutting, etc
CRIBERS > SCRIBER
CRIBES > SCRIBE
CRIBING > SCRIBE
CRIBINGS > SCRIBE
CRIBISM > SCRIBE
CRIBISMS > SCRIBE
CRIECH *vb* Scots word meaning screech
CRIECHED > SCRIECH
CRIECHS > SCRIECH
CRIED > SCRY
CRIENE *n* old form of screen
CRIENES > SCRIENE
CRIES > SCRY
CRIEVE *vb* Scots word meaning write
CRIEVED > SCRIEVE
CRIEVES > SCRIEVE
CRIEVING > SCRIEVE
CRIGGLE *vb* wriggle
CRIGGLED > SCRIGGLE
CRIGGLES > SCRIGGLE
CRIGGLY > SCRIGGLE
CRIKE *vb* old word meaning shriek
CRIKED > SCRIKE
CRIKES > SCRIKE
CRIKING > SCRIKE
CRIM *n* open-weave muslin or hessian fabric, used in upholstery, lining, building
CRIMMAGE *n* rough or disorderly struggle ▷ *vb* engage in a scrimmage
CRIMP *vb* be very economical
CRIMPED > SCRIMP
CRIMPER > SCRIMP
CRIMPERS > SCRIMP
CRIMPIER > SCRIMP
CRIMPILY > SCRIMP
CRIMPING > SCRIMP
CRIMPIT *adj* Scots word meaning ungenerous
CRIMPLY *adv* sparingly
CRIMPS > SCRIMP
CRIMPY > SCRIMP
CRIMS > SCRIM
CRIMSHAW *n* art of decorating or carving shells, etc, done by sailors as a leisure activity ▷ *vb* produce scrimshaw (from)
SCRIMURE *old word for* > FENCER
SCRIMURES > SCRIMURE
SCRINE *n* old form of shrine
SCRINES > SCRINE
SCRIP *n* certificate representing a claim to stocks or shares
SCRIPPAGE *n* contents of scrip
SCRIPS > SCRIP
SCRIPT *n* text of a film, play, or TV programme ▷ *vb* write a script for
SCRIPTED > SCRIPT
SCRIPTER *n* person who writes scripts for films, play, or television dramas
SCRIPTERS > SCRIPTER
SCRIPTING > SCRIPT
SCRIPTORY *adj* of writing
SCRIPTS > SCRIPT
SCRIPTURE *n* sacred writings of a religion
SCRITCH *vb* screech
SCRITCHED > SCRITCH
SCRITCHES > SCRITCH
SCRIVE *Scots word for* > WRITE
SCRIVED > SCRIVE
SCRIVENER *n* person who writes out deeds, letters, etc
SCRIVES > SCRIVE
SCRIVING > SCRIVE
SCROBE *n* groove
SCROBES > SCROBE
SCROD *n* young cod or haddock, esp one split and prepared for cooking
SCRODDLED *adj* made of scraps of pottery
SCRODS > SCROD
SCROFULA *n* tuberculosis of the lymphatic glands
SCROFULAS > SCROFULA
SCROG *n* Scots word meaning small tree
SCROGGIE *adj* having scrogs upon it
SCROGGIER > SCROGGIE
SCROGGIN *n* mixture of nuts and dried fruits
SCROGGINS > SCROGGIN
SCROGGY *variant of* > SCROGGIE
SCROGS > SCROG
SCROLL *n* roll of parchment or paper ▷ *vb* move (text) up or down on a VDU screen
SCROLLED > SCROLL
SCROLLING > SCROLL
SCROLLS > SCROLL
SCROME *vb* crawl or climb, esp using the hands to aid movement
SCROMED > SCROME
SCROMES > SCROME
SCROMING > SCROME
SCROOCH *vb* scratch (the skin) to relieve itching
SCROOCHED > SCROOCH
SCROOCHES > SCROOCH
SCROOGE *variant of* > SCROUGE
SCROOGED > SCROOGE
SCROOGES > SCROOGE
SCROOGING > SCROOGE
SCROOP *vb* emit a grating or creaking sound ▷ *n* such a sound
SCROOPED > SCROOP
SCROOPING > SCROOP
SCROOPS > SCROOP
SCROOTCH *vb* hunch up
SCRORP *n* deep scratch or weal
SCRORPS > SCRORP
SCROTA > SCROTUM
SCROTAL > SCROTUM
SCROTE *n* slang derogatory word meaning a worthless fellow
SCROTES > SCROTE
SCROTUM *n* pouch of skin containing the testicles
SCROTUMS > SCROTUM
SCROUGE *vb* crowd or press
SCROUGED > SCROUGE
SCROUGER *n* American word meaning whopper
SCROUGERS > SCROUGER
SCROUGES > SCROUGE
SCROUGING > SCROUGE
SCROUNGE *vb* get by cadging or begging
SCROUNGED > SCROUNGE
SCROUNGER > SCROUNGE
SCROUNGES > SCROUNGE
SCROUNGY *adj* shabby
SCROW *n* scroll
SCROWDGE *vb* squeeze
SCROWDGED > SCROWDGE
SCROWDGES > SCROWDGE
SCROWL *vb* old form of scroll
SCROWLE *vb* old form of scroll
SCROWLED > SCROWL
SCROWLES > SCROWLE
SCROWLING > SCROWL
SCROWLS > SCROWL
SCROWS > SCROW
SCROYLE *n* old word meaning wretch
SCROYLES > SCROYLE
SCRUB *vb* clean by rubbing, often with a hard brush and water ▷ *n* scrubbing ▷ *adj* stunted or inferior
SCRUBBED > SCRUB
SCRUBBER *n* woman who has many sexual partners
SCRUBBERS > SCRUBBER
SCRUBBIER > SCRUBBY
SCRUBBILY > SCRUBBY
SCRUBBING > SCRUB
SCRUBBY *adj* covered with scrub
SCRUBLAND *n* area of scrub vegetation
SCRUBS > SCRUB
SCRUFF *same as* > SCUM
SCRUFFIER > SCRUFFY
SCRUFFILY > SCRUFFY
SCRUFFS > SCRUFF
SCRUFFY *adj* unkempt or shabby
SCRUM *n* restarting of play in which opposing packs of forwards push against each other to gain possession of the ball ▷ *vb* form a scrum
SCRUMDOWN *n* forming of scrum in rugby
SCRUMMAGE *same as* > SCRUM
SCRUMMED > SCRUM
SCRUMMIE *n* informal word for a scrum half
SCRUMMIER > SCRUMMY
SCRUMMIES > SCRUMMIE
SCRUMMING > SCRUM
SCRUMMY *adj* delicious
SCRUMP *vb* steal (apples) from an orchard or garden
SCRUMPED > SCRUMP
SCRUMPIES > SCRUMPY
SCRUMPING > SCRUMP
SCRUMPLE *vb* crumple or crush
SCRUMPLED > SCRUMPLE
SCRUMPLES > SCRUMPLE
SCRUMPOX *n* skin infection spread among players in scrum
SCRUMPS > SCRUMP
SCRUMPY *n* rough dry cider
SCRUMS > SCRUM
SCRUNCH *vb* crumple or crunch or be crumpled or crunched ▷ *n* act or sound of scrunching
SCRUNCHED > SCRUNCH
SCRUNCHES > SCRUNCH
SCRUNCHIE *n* loop of elastic covered loosely with fabric, used to hold the hair in a ponytail
SCRUNCHY *adj* crunchy
SCRUNT *n* Scots word meaning stunted thing
SCRUNTIER > SCRUNT
SCRUNTS > SCRUNT
SCRUNTY > SCRUNT
SCRUPLE *n* doubt produced by one's conscience or morals ▷ *vb* have doubts on moral grounds
SCRUPLED > SCRUPLE
SCRUPLER > SCRUPLE
SCRUPLERS > SCRUPLE
SCRUPLES > SCRUPLE
SCRUPLING > SCRUPLE
SCRUTABLE *adj* open to or able to be understood by scrutiny
SCRUTATOR *n* person who examines or scrutinizes
SCRUTINY *n* close examination
SCRUTO *n* trapdoor on stage
SCRUTOIRE *n* writing desk
SCRUTOS > SCRUTO
SCRUZE *vb* old word meaning squeeze
SCRUZED > SCRUZE

SCRUZES > SCRUZE
SCRUZING > SCRUZE
SCRY *vb* divine, esp by crystal gazing
SCRYDE > SCRY
SCRYER > SCRY
SCRYERS > SCRY
SCRYING > SCRY
SCRYINGS > SCRY
SCRYNE *n* old form of shrine
SCRYNES > SCRYNE
SCUBA *n* apparatus used in skin diving, consisting of cylinders containing compressed air attached to a breathing apparatus ▷ *vb* dive using scuba equipment
SCUBAED > SCUBA
SCUBAING > SCUBA
SCUBAS > SCUBA
SCUCHIN *n* old form of scutcheon
SCUCHINS > SCUCHIN
SCUD *vb* move along swiftly ▷ *n* act of scudding
SCUDDALER *n* Scots word meaning leader of festivities
SCUDDED > SCUD
SCUDDER > SCUD
SCUDDERS > SCUD
SCUDDING > SCUD
SCUDDLE *vb* scuttle
SCUDDLED > SCUDDLE
SCUDDLES > SCUDDLE
SCUDDLING > SCUDDLE
SCUDI > SCUDO
SCUDLER *n* Scots word meaning leader of festivities
SCUDLERS > SCUDLER
SCUDO *n* any of several former Italian coins
SCUDS > SCUD
SCUFF *vb* drag (the feet) while walking ▷ *n* mark caused by scuffing
SCUFFED > SCUFF
SCUFFER *n* type of sandal
SCUFFERS > SCUFFER
SCUFFING > SCUFF
SCUFFLE *vb* fight in a disorderly manner ▷ *n* disorderly struggle
SCUFFLED > SCUFFLE
SCUFFLER > SCUFFLE
SCUFFLERS > SCUFFLE
SCUFFLES > SCUFFLE
SCUFFLING > SCUFFLE
SCUFFS > SCUFF
SCUFT *n* dialect word meaning nape of neck
SCUFTS > SCUFT
SCUG *vb* shelter
SCUGGED > SCUG
SCUGGING > SCUG
SCUGS > SCUG
SCUL *n* old form of school
SCULCH *n* rubbish
SCULCHES > SCULCH
SCULK *vb* old form of skulk
SCULKED > SCULK
SCULKER > SCULK
SCULKERS > SCULK
SCULKING > SCULK
SCULKS > SCULK
SCULL *n* small oar ▷ *vb* row (a boat) using sculls
SCULLE *n* old form of school
SCULLED > SCULL
SCULLER > SCULL
SCULLERS > SCULL
SCULLERY *n* small room where washing-up and other kitchen work is done
SCULLES > SCULLE
SCULLING > SCULL
SCULLINGS > SCULL
SCULLION *n* servant employed to do the hard work in a kitchen
SCULLIONS > SCULLION
SCULLS > SCULL
SCULP *variant of* > SCULPTURE
SCULPED > SCULP
SCULPIN *n* any of various fishes of the family *Cottidae*
SCULPING > SCULP
SCULPINS > SCULPIN
SCULPS > SCULP
SCULPSIT (he or she) sculptured it: used formerly on sculptures next to a sculptor's name
SCULPT *same as* > SCULPTURE
SCULPTED > SCULPT
SCULPTING > SCULPT
SCULPTOR *n* person who makes sculptures
SCULPTORS > SCULPTOR
SCULPTS > SCULPT
SCULPTURE *n* art of making figures or designs in wood, stone, etc ▷ *vb* represent in sculpture
SCULS > SCUL
SCULTCH *same as* > SCULCH
SCULTCHES > SCULTCH
SCUM *n* impure or waste matter on the surface of a liquid ▷ *vb* remove scum from
SCUMBAG *n* offensive or despicable person
SCUMBAGS > SCUMBAG
SCUMBER *vb* old word meaning defecate
SCUMBERED > SCUMBER
SCUMBERS > SCUMBER
SCUMBLE *vb* soften or blend (an outline or colour) with a thin upper coat of opaque colour ▷ *n* upper layer of colour applied in this way
SCUMBLED > SCUMBLE
SCUMBLES > SCUMBLE
SCUMBLING > SCUMBLE
SCUMFISH *vb* Scots word meaning disgust
SCUMLESS > SCUM
SCUMLIKE > SCUM
SCUMMED > SCUM
SCUMMER > SCUM
SCUMMERS > SCUM
SCUMMIER > SCUMMY
SCUMMIEST > SCUMMY
SCUMMILY > SCUMMY
SCUMMING > SCUM
SCUMMINGS > SCUM
SCUMMY *adj* of, resembling, consisting of, or covered with scum
SCUMS > SCUM
SCUNCHEON *n* inner part of a door jamb or window frame
SCUNDERED *adj* Irish dialect word for embarrassed
SCUNGE *vb* borrow ▷ *n* dirty or worthless person
SCUNGED > SCUNGE
SCUNGES > SCUNGE
SCUNGIER > SCUNGY
SCUNGIEST > SCUNGY
SCUNGILLI *n* seafood dish of conch
SCUNGING > SCUNGE
SCUNGY *adj* sordid or dirty
SCUNNER *vb* feel aversion ▷ *n* strong aversion
SCUNNERED *adj* annoyed, discontented, or bored
SCUNNERS > SCUNNER
SCUP *n* common sparid fish of American coastal regions of the Atlantic
SCUPPAUG *n* sea fish
SCUPPAUGS > SCUPPAUG
SCUPPER *vb* defeat or ruin ▷ *n* drain in the side of a ship
SCUPPERED > SCUPPER
SCUPPERS > SCUPPER
SCUPS > SCUP
SCUR *n* small unattached growth of horn at the site of a normal horn in cattle
SCURF *n* flaky skin on the scalp
SCURFIER > SCURF
SCURFIEST > SCURF
SCURFS > SCURF
SCURFY > SCURF
SCURRED > SCUR
SCURRIED > SCURRY
SCURRIER *n* old word meaning scout
SCURRIERS > SCURRIER
SCURRIES > SCURRY
SCURRIL *adj* old word meaning vulgar
SCURRILE *adj* old word meaning vulgar
SCURRING > SCUR
SCURRIOUR *n* old word meaning scout
SCURRY *vb* move hastily ▷ *n* act or sound of scurrying
SCURRYING > SCURRY
SCURS > SCUR
SCURVIER > SCURVY
SCURVIES > SCURVY
SCURVIEST > SCURVY
SCURVILY > SCURVY
SCURVY *n* disease caused by lack of vitamin C ▷ *adj* mean and despicable
SCUSE *shortened form of* > EXCUSE
SCUSED > SCUSE
SCUSES > SCUSE
SCUSING > SCUSE
SCUT *n* short tail of the hare, rabbit, or deer
SCUTA > SCUTUM
SCUTAGE *n* payment sometimes exacted by a lord from his vassal in lieu of military service
SCUTAGES > SCUTAGE
SCUTAL > SCUTE
SCUTATE *adj* (of animals) having or covered with large bony or horny plates
SCUTATION > SCUTATE
SCUTCH *vb* separate the fibres from the woody part of (flax) by pounding ▷ *n* tool used for this
SCUTCHED > SCUTCH
SCUTCHEON *same as* > SHIELD
SCUTCHER *same as* > SCUTCH
SCUTCHERS > SCUTCHER
SCUTCHES > SCUTCH
SCUTCHING > SCUTCH
SCUTE *n* horny or chitinous plate that makes up part of the exoskeleton in armadillos, etc
SCUTELLA > SCUTELLUM
SCUTELLAR > SCUTELLUM
SCUTELLUM *n* last of three plates into which the notum of an insect's thorax is divided
SCUTES > SCUTE
SCUTIFORM *adj* (esp of plant parts) shaped like a shield
SCUTIGER *n* species of centipede
SCUTIGERS > SCUTIGER
SCUTS > SCUT
SCUTTER *informal word for* > SCURRY
SCUTTERED > SCUTTER
SCUTTERS > SCUTTER
SCUTTLE *n* fireside container for coal ▷ *vb* run with short quick steps
SCUTTLED > SCUTTLE
SCUTTLER > SCUTTLE
SCUTTLERS > SCUTTLE
SCUTTLES > SCUTTLE
SCUTTLING > SCUTTLE
SCUTUM *n* middle of three plates into which the notum of an insect's thorax is divided
SCUTWORK *n* menial or dull work
SCUTWORKS > SCUTWORK
SCUZZ *n* dirt
SCUZZBALL *n* despicable person
SCUZZES > SCUZZ
SCUZZIER > SCUZZY
SCUZZIEST > SCUZZY
SCUZZY *adj* unkempt, dirty or squalid

YBALA > SCYBALUM
YBALOUS > SCYBALUM
YBALUM *n* hard faeces in tomach
YE *n* Scots word neaning sleeve-hole
YES > SCYE
YPHATE *adj* shaped like up
YPHI > SCYPHUS
YPHUS *n* ancient Greek wo-handled drinking cup without a footed base
YTALE *n* coded message n ancient Sparta
YTALES > SCYTALE
YTHE *n* long-handled ool with a curved blade or cutting grass ▷ *vb* cut with a scythe
YTHED > SCYTHE
YTHEMAN *n* scythe user
YTHEMEN > SCYTHEMAN
YTHER > SCYTHE
YTHERS > SCYTHE
YTHES > SCYTHE
YTHING > SCYTHE
AINE *vb* old form of lisdain
AINED > SDAINE
AINES > SDAINE
AINING > SDAINE
AYN *vb* old form of lisdain
AYNED > SDAYN
AYNING > SDAYN
AYNS > SDAYN
EIGN *vb* old form of lisdain
EIGNE *vb* old form of lisdain
EIGNED > SDEIGN
EIGNES > SDEIGNE
EIGNING > SDEIGN
EIGNS > SDEIGN
EIN *vb* old form of lisdain
EINED > SDEIN
EINING > SDEIN
EINS > SDEIN
A *n* mass of salt water covering three quarters of he earth's surface
ABAG *n* canvas bag or holding a sailor's pelongings
ABAGS > SEABAG
ABANK *n* sea shore
ABANKS > SEABANK
ABEACH *n* beach at seaside
ABED *n* bottom of sea
ABEDS > SEABED
ABIRD *n* bird that lives on the sea
ABIRDS > SEABIRD
ABLITE *n* prostrate annual plant of the goosefoot family
ABLITES > SEABLITE
ABOARD *n* coast
ABOARDS > SEABOARD
ABOOT *n* sailor's waterproof boot
SEABOOTS > SEABOOT
SEABORNE *adj* carried on or by the sea
SEABOTTLE *n* type of seaweed
SEACOAST *n* land bordering on the sea
SEACOASTS > SEACOAST
SEACOCK *n* valve in the hull of a vessel below the water line for admitting sea water or for pumping out bilge water
SEACOCKS > SEACOCK
SEACRAFT *n* skill as sailor
SEACRAFTS > SEACRAFT
SEACUNNY *n* quartermaster on Indian ship
SEADOG *another word for* > FOGBOW
SEADOGS > SEADOG
SEADROME *n* aerodrome floating on sea
SEADROMES > SEADROME
SEAFARER *n* traveller who goes by sea
SEAFARERS > SEAFARER
SEAFARING *adj* working or travelling by sea ▷ *n* act of travelling by sea
SEAFLOOR *n* bottom of the sea
SEAFLOORS > SEAFLOOR
SEAFOLK *n* people who sail sea
SEAFOLKS > SEAFOLK
SEAFOOD *n* edible saltwater fish or shellfish
SEAFOODS > SEAFOOD
SEAFOWL *n* seabird
SEAFOWLS > SEAFOWL
SEAFRONT *n* built-up area facing the sea
SEAFRONTS > SEAFRONT
SEAGIRT *adj* surrounded by the sea
SEAGOING *adj* built for travelling on the sea
SEAGULL *n* gull
SEAGULLS > SEAGULL
SEAHAWK *n* skua
SEAHAWKS > SEAHAWK
SEAHOG *n* porpoise
SEAHOGS > SEAHOG
SEAHORSE *n* marine fish with a horselike head that swims upright
SEAHORSES > SEAHORSE
SEAHOUND *n* dogfish
SEAHOUNDS > SEAHOUND
SEAKALE *n* European coastal plant
SEAKALES > SEAKALE
SEAL *n* piece of wax, lead, etc with a special design impressed upon it, attached to a letter or document as a mark of authentication ▷ *vb* close with or as if with a seal
SEALABLE > SEAL
SEALANT *n* any substance used for sealing
SEALANTS > SEALANT
SEALCH *Scots word for* > SEAL
SEALCHS > SEALCH
SEALED *adj* (of a road) having a hard surface
SEALER *n* person or thing that seals
SEALERIES > SEALERY
SEALERS > SEALER
SEALERY *n* occupation of hunting seals
SEALGH *Scots word for* > SEAL
SEALGHS > SEALGH
SEALIFT *vb* transport by ship
SEALIFTED > SEALIFT
SEALIFTS > SEALIFT
SEALINE *n* company running regular sailings
SEALINES > SEALINE
SEALING > SEAL
SEALINGS > SEAL
SEALLIKE *adj* resembling a seal
SEALPOINT *n* popular variety of Siamese cat
SEALS > SEAL
SEALSKIN *n* skin or prepared fur of a seal, used to make coats
SEALSKINS > SEALSKIN
SEALWAX *n* sealing wax
SEALWAXES > SEALWAX
SEALYHAM *n* type of short-legged terrier
SEALYHAMS > SEALYHAM
SEAM *n* line where two edges are joined, as by stitching ▷ *vb* mark with furrows or wrinkles
SEAMAID *n* mermaid
SEAMAIDS > SEAMAID
SEAMAN *n* sailor
SEAMANLY > SEAMAN
SEAMARK *n* aid to navigation, such as a conspicuous object on a shore used as a guide
SEAMARKS > SEAMARK
SEAME *n* old word meaning grease
SEAMED > SEAM
SEAMEN > SEAMAN
SEAMER *n* fast bowler who makes the ball bounce on its seam so that it will change direction
SEAMERS > SEAMER
SEAMES > SEAME
SEAMIER > SEAMY
SEAMIEST > SEAMY
SEAMINESS > SEAMY
SEAMING > SEAM
SEAMLESS *adj* (of a garment) without seams
SEAMLIKE > SEAM
SEAMOUNT *n* submarine mountain rising more than 1000 metres above the surrounding ocean floor
SEAMOUNTS > SEAMOUNT
SEAMS > SEAM
SEAMSET *n* tool for flattening seams in metal
SEAMSETS > SEAMSET
SEAMSTER *n* person who sews
SEAMSTERS > SEAMSTER
SEAMY *adj* sordid
SEAN *vb* fish with seine net
SEANCE *n* meeting at which spiritualists attempt to communicate with the dead
SEANCES > SEANCE
SEANED > SEAN
SEANING > SEAN
SEANS > SEAN
SEAPIECE *n* artwork depicting sea
SEAPIECES > SEAPIECE
SEAPLANE *n* aircraft designed to take off from and land on water
SEAPLANES > SEAPLANE
SEAPORT *n* town or city with a harbour for boats and ships
SEAPORTS > SEAPORT
SEAQUAKE *n* agitation and disturbance of the sea caused by an earthquake at the sea bed
SEAQUAKES > SEAQUAKE
SEAQUARIA *pl n* areas of salt water where sea animals are kept
SEAR *vb* scorch, burn the surface of ▷ *n* mark caused by searing ▷ *adj* dried up
SEARAT *n* pirate
SEARATS > SEARAT
SEARCE *vb* sift
SEARCED > SEARCE
SEARCES > SEARCE
SEARCH *vb* examine closely in order to find something ▷ *n* searching
SEARCHED > SEARCH
SEARCHER > SEARCH
SEARCHERS > SEARCH
SEARCHES > SEARCH
SEARCHING *adj* keen or thorough
SEARCING > SEARCE
SEARE *adj* old word meaning dry and withered
SEARED > SEAR
SEARER > SEAR
SEAREST > SEAR
SEARING > SEAR
SEARINGLY > SEAR
SEARINGS > SEAR
SEARNESS > SEAR
SEAROBIN *n* type of American gurnard
SEAROBINS > SEAROBIN
SEARS > SEAR
SEAS > SEA
SEASCAPE *n* picture of a scene at sea
SEASCAPES > SEASCAPE
SEASCOUT *n* member of seagoing scouts
SEASCOUTS > SEASCOUT
SEASE *vb* old form of seize
SEASED > SEASE

SEASES > SEASE
SEASHELL *n* empty shell of a mollusc
SEASHELLS > SEASHELL
SEASHORE *n* land bordering on the sea
SEASHORES > SEASHORE
SEASICK *adj* suffering from nausea caused by the motion of a ship
SEASICKER > SEASICK
SEASIDE *n* area, esp a holiday resort, on the coast
SEASIDES > SEASIDE
SEASING > SEASE
SEASON *n* one of four divisions of the year, each of which has characteristic weather conditions ▷ *vb* flavour with salt, herbs, etc
SEASONAL *adj* depending on or varying with the seasons ▷ *n* seasonal thing
SEASONALS > SEASONAL
SEASONED > SEASON
SEASONER > SEASON
SEASONERS > SEASON
SEASONING *n* salt, herbs, etc added to food to enhance flavour
SEASONS > SEASON
SEASPEAK *n* language used by sailors
SEASPEAKS > SEASPEAK
SEASTRAND *n* seashore
SEASURE *n* old form of seizure
SEASURES > SEASURE
SEAT *n* thing designed or used for sitting on ▷ *vb* cause to sit
SEATBACK *n* back of seat
SEATBACKS > SEATBACK
SEATBELT *n* safety belt in vehicle
SEATBELTS > SEATBELT
SEATED > SEAT
SEATER *n* person or thing that seats
SEATERS > SEATER
SEATING *n* supply or arrangement of seats ▷ *adj* of or relating to the provision of places to sit
SEATINGS > SEATING
SEATLESS > SEAT
SEATMATE *n* person sitting in next seat
SEATMATES > SEATMATE
SEATRAIN *n* ship that can carry train
SEATRAINS > SEATRAIN
SEATROUT *n* trout living in the sea
SEATROUTS > SEATROUT
SEATS > SEAT
SEATWORK *n* school work done at pupils' desks
SEATWORKS > SEATWORK
SEAWALL *n* wall built to prevent encroachment or erosion by the sea
SEAWALLS > SEAWALL
SEAWAN *n* shell beads, usually unstrung, used by certain North American Indians as money
SEAWANS > SEAWAN
SEAWANT *n* Native American name for silver coins
SEAWANTS > SEAWANT
SEAWARD *same as* > SEAWARDS
SEAWARDLY > SEAWARD
SEAWARDS *adv* towards the sea
SEAWARE *n* any of numerous large coarse seaweeds
SEAWARES > SEAWARE
SEAWATER *n* water from sea
SEAWATERS > SEAWATER
SEAWAY *n* waterway giving access to an inland port, navigable by ocean-going ships
SEAWAYS > SEAWAY
SEAWEED *n* plant growing in the sea
SEAWEEDS > SEAWEED
SEAWIFE *n* variety of sea fish
SEAWIVES > SEAWIFE
SEAWOMAN *n* mermaid
SEAWOMEN > SEAWOMAN
SEAWORM *n* marine worm
SEAWORMS > SEAWORM
SEAWORTHY *adj* (of a ship) in fit condition for a sea voyage
SEAZE *vb* old form of seize
SEAZED > SEAZE
SEAZES > SEAZE
SEAZING > SEAZE
SEBACEOUS *adj* of, like, or secreting fat or oil
SEBACIC *adj* derived from sebacic acid, a white crystalline acid
SEBASIC *same as* > SEBACIC
SEBATE *n* salt of sebacic acid
SEBATES > SEBATE
SEBESTEN *n* Asian tree
SEBESTENS > SEBESTEN
SEBIFIC *adj* producing fat
SEBORRHEA *n* skin disease in which excessive oil is secreted
SEBUM *n* oily substance secreted by the sebaceous glands
SEBUMS > SEBUM
SEBUNDIES > SEBUNDY
SEBUNDY *n* irregular soldier in India
SEC *same as* > SECANT
SECALOSE *n* type of sugar
SECALOSES > SECALOSE
SECANT *n* (in trigonometry) the ratio of the length of the hypotenuse to the length of the adjacent side in a right-angled triangle
SECANTLY > SECANT
SECANTS > SECANT
SECATEUR *n* secateurs
SECATEURS *pl n* small pruning shears
SECCO *n* wall painting done on dried plaster with tempera or pigments ground in limewater
SECCOS > SECCO
SECEDE *vb* withdraw formally from a political alliance or federation
SECEDED > SECEDE
SECEDER > SECEDE
SECEDERS > SECEDE
SECEDES > SECEDE
SECEDING > SECEDE
SECERN *vb* (of a gland or follicle) to secrete
SECERNED > SECERN
SECERNENT > SECERN
SECERNING > SECERN
SECERNS > SECERN
SECESH *n* secessionist in US Civil War
SECESHER *n* secessionist in US Civil War
SECESHERS > SECESHER
SECESHES > SECESH
SECESSION *n* act of seceding
SECH *n* hyperbolic secant
SECHS > SECH
SECKEL *variant of* > SECKLE
SECKELS > SECKEL
SECKLE *n* type of pear
SECKLES > SECKLE
SECLUDE *vb* keep (a person) from contact with others
SECLUDED *adj* private, sheltered
SECLUDES > SECLUDE
SECLUDING > SECLUDE
SECLUSION *n* state of being secluded
SECLUSIVE *adj* tending to seclude
SECO *adj* (of wine) dry
SECODONT *n* animal with cutting back teeth
SECODONTS > SECODONT
SECONAL *n* tradename for secobarbitol
SECONALS > SECONAL
SECOND *adj* coming directly after the first ▷ *n* person or thing coming second ▷ *vb* express formal support for (a motion proposed in a meeting)
SECONDARY *adj* of less importance ▷ *n* person or thing that is secondary
SECONDE *n* second of eight positions from which a parry or attack can be made in fencing
SECONDED > SECOND
SECONDEE *n* person who is seconded
SECONDEES > SECONDEE
SECONDER > SECOND
SECONDERS > SECOND
SECONDES > SECONDE
SECONDI > SECONDO
SECONDING > SECOND
SECONDLY *same as* > SECO[ND]
SECONDO *n* left-hand part in a piano duet
SECONDS > SECOND
SECPAR *n* distance unit in astronomy
SECPARS > SECPAR
SECRECIES > SECRECY
SECRECY *n* state of being secret
SECRET *adj* kept from the knowledge of others ▷ *n* something kept secret
SECRETA *n* secretions
SECRETAGE *n* use of mercury in treating furs
SECRETARY *n* person who deals with correspondence and general clerical work
SECRETE *vb* (of an organ, gland, etc) produce and release (a substance)
SECRETED > SECRETE
SECRETER > SECRET
SECRETES > SECRETE
SECRETEST > SECRET
SECRETIN *n* peptic hormone secreted by the mucosae of the duodenum and jejunum
SECRETING > SECRETE
SECRETINS > SECRETIN
SECRETION *n* substance that is released from a cell, organ, or gland
SECRETIVE *adj* inclined to keep things secret
SECRETLY > SECRET
SECRETOR > SECRETE
SECRETORS > SECRETE
SECRETORY *adj* of, relating to, or producing a secretion
SECRETS > SECRET
SECS > SEC
SECT *n* often disparaging term for a subdivision of a religious or political group, esp one with extreme beliefs
SECTARIAL > SECT
SECTARIAN *adj* of a sect ▷ member of a sect
SECTARIES > SECTARY
SECTARY *n* member of a sect
SECTATOR *n* member of sect
SECTATORS > SECTATOR
SECTILE *adj* able to be cut smoothly
SECTILITY > SECTILE
SECTION *n* part cut off ▷ cut or divide into sections
SECTIONAL *adj* concerned with a particular area or group within a country or community
SECTIONED > SECTION
SECTIONS > SECTION
SECTOR *n* part or subdivision ▷ *vb* divide

nto sectors
.CTORAL >SECTOR
.CTORED >SECTOR
.CTORIAL *adj* of or elating to a sector
.CTORING >SECTOR
.CTORISE *same* ıs >SECTORIZE
'CTORIZE *vb* split into ectors
.CTORS >SECTOR
.CTS >SECT
'CULAR *adj* worldly, as pposed to sacred ▷*n* nember of the secular lergy
:CULARLY >SECULAR
.CULARS >SECULAR
:CULUM *n* age in stronomy
'CULUMS >SECULUM
:CUND *adj* having or lesignating parts rranged on or turned to ne side of the axis
CUNDINE *n* one of he two integuments urrounding the ovule of plant
'CUNDLY >SECUND
CUNDUM *adj* according to
CURABLE >SECURE
CURANCE >SECURE
'CURE *adj* free from langer ▷*vb* obtain
.CURED >SECURE
'CURELY >SECURE
.CURER >SECURE
'CURERS >SECURE
'CURES >SECURE
CUREST >SECURE
.CURING >SECURE
'CURITAN *n* person elieving they are secure
CURITY *n* precautions gainst theft, espionage, r other danger
D *old spelling of* >SAID
.DAN *same as* >SALOON
DANS >SEDAN
DARIM >SEDER
.DATE *adj* calm and lignified ▷*vb* give a edative drug to
.DATED >SEDATE
.DATELY >SEDATE
'DATER >SEDATE
DATES >SEDATE
.DATEST >SEDATE
DATING >SEDATE
DATION *n* state of calm, sp when brought about y sedatives
DATIONS >SEDATION
DATIVE *adj* having a oothing or calming effect ▷*n* sedative drug
DATIVES >SEDATIVE
DENT *adj* seated
DENTARY *adj* done itting down, involving ttle exercise
DER *n* Jewish ceremonial neal held on the first night or first two nights of Passover
SEDERS >SEDER
SEDERUNT *n* sitting of an ecclesiastical assembly, court, etc
SEDERUNTS >SEDERUNT
SEDES *Latin word for* >SEAT
SEDGE *n* coarse grasslike plant growing on wet ground
SEDGED *adj* having sedge
SEDGELAND *n* land covered with sedge
SEDGES >SEDGE
SEDGIER >SEDGE
SEDGIEST >SEDGE
SEDGY >SEDGE
SEDILE *n* seat for clergy in church
SEDILIA *n* group of three seats where the celebrant and ministers sit at certain points during High Mass
SEDILIUM *n* seat for clergy in church
SEDIMENT *n* matter which settles to the bottom of a liquid
SEDIMENTS >SEDIMENT
SEDITION *n* speech or action encouraging rebellion against the government
SEDITIONS >SEDITION
SEDITIOUS *adj* of, like, or causing sedition
SEDUCE *vb* persuade into sexual intercourse
SEDUCED >SEDUCE
SEDUCER *n* person who entices, allures, or seduces
SEDUCERS >SEDUCER
SEDUCES >SEDUCE
SEDUCIBLE >SEDUCE
SEDUCING >SEDUCE
SEDUCINGS >SEDUCE
SEDUCIVE *adj* seductive
SEDUCTION *n* act of seducing or the state of being seduced
SEDUCTIVE *adj* (of a woman) sexually attractive
SEDUCTOR *n* person who seduces
SEDUCTORS >SEDUCTOR
SEDULITY >SEDULOUS
SEDULOUS *adj* diligent or persevering
SEDUM *n* rock plant
SEDUMS >SEDUM
SEE *vb* perceive with the eyes or mind ▷*n* diocese of a bishop
SEEABLE >SEE
SEECATCH *n* male seal in Aleutians
SEED *n* mature fertilized grain of a plant ▷*vb* sow with seed
SEEDBED *n* area of soil prepared for the growing of seedlings before they are transplanted
SEEDBEDS >SEEDBED
SEEDBOX *n* part of plant that contains seeds
SEEDBOXES >SEEDBED
SEEDCAKE *n* sweet cake flavoured with caraway seeds and lemon rind or essence
SEEDCAKES >SEEDCAKE
SEEDCASE *n* part of a fruit enclosing the seeds
SEEDCASES >SEEDCASE
SEEDEATER *n* bird feeding on seeds
SEEDED >SEED
SEEDER *n* person or thing that seeds
SEEDERS >SEEDER
SEEDIER >SEEDY
SEEDIEST >SEEDY
SEEDILY >SEEDY
SEEDINESS >SEEDY
SEEDING >SEED
SEEDINGS >SEED
SEEDLESS >SEED
SEEDLIKE >SEED
SEEDLING *n* young plant raised from a seed
SEEDLINGS >SEEDLING
SEEDLIP *n* basket holding seeds to be sown
SEEDLIPS >SEEDLIP
SEEDMAN *n* seller of seeds
SEEDMEN >SEEDMAN
SEEDNESS *n* old word meaning sowing of seeds
SEEDPOD *n* carpel enclosing the seeds of a flowering plant
SEEDPODS >SEEDPOD
SEEDS >SEED
SEEDSMAN *n* seller of seeds
SEEDSMEN >SEEDSMAN
SEEDSTOCK *n* livestock used for breeding
SEEDTIME *n* season when seeds are sown
SEEDTIMES >SEEDTIME
SEEDY *adj* shabby
SEEING >SEE
SEEINGS >SEE
SEEK *vb* try to find or obtain
SEEKER >SEEK
SEEKERS >SEEK
SEEKING >SEEK
SEEKS >SEEK
SEEL *vb* sew up the eyelids of (a hawk or falcon) so as to render it quiet and tame
SEELD *adj* old word meaning rare
SEELED >SEEL
SEELIE *pl n* good benevolent fairies
SEELIER >SEELY
SEELIEST >SEELY
SEELING >SEEL
SEELINGS >SEEL
SEELS >SEEL
SEELY *adj* old word meaning happy
SEEM *vb* appear to be
SEEMED >SEEM
SEEMER >SEEM
SEEMERS >SEEM
SEEMING *adj* apparent but not real ▷*n* outward or false appearance
SEEMINGLY *adv* in appearance but not necessarily in actuality
SEEMINGS >SEEMING
SEEMLESS *adj* old word meaning unseemly
SEEMLIER >SEEMLY
SEEMLIEST >SEEMLY
SEEMLIHED *n* old word meaning seemliness
SEEMLY *adj* proper or fitting ▷*adv* properly or decorously
SEEMLYHED *n* old word meaning seemliness
SEEMS >SEEM
SEEN >SEE
SEEP *vb* trickle through slowly, ooze ▷*n* small spring or place where water, oil, etc, has oozed through the ground
SEEPAGE *n* act or process of seeping
SEEPAGES >SEEPAGE
SEEPED >SEEP
SEEPIER >SEEPY
SEEPIEST >SEEPY
SEEPING >SEEP
SEEPS >SEEP
SEEPY *adj* tending to seep
SEER *n* person who sees
SEERESS >SEER
SEERESSES >SEER
SEERS >SEER
SEES >SEE
SEESAW *n* plank balanced in the middle so that two people seated on either end ride up and down alternately ▷*vb* move up and down
SEESAWED >SEESAW
SEESAWING >SEESAW
SEESAWS >SEESAW
SEETHE *vb* be very agitated ▷*n* act or state of seething
SEETHED >SEETHE
SEETHER >SEETHE
SEETHERS >SEETHE
SEETHES >SEETHE
SEETHING *adj* boiling or foaming as if boiling
SEETHINGS >SEETHING
SEEWING *n* suing
SEFER *n* scrolls of the Law
SEG *n* metal stud on shoe sole
SEGAR *n* cigar
SEGARS >SEGAR
SEGETAL *adj* (of weeds) growing amongst crops
SEGGAR *n* box in which pottery is baked
SEGGARS >SEGGAR
SEGHOL *n* pronunciation mark in Hebrew
SEGHOLATE *n* vowel sound

in Hebrew
SEGHOLS > SEGHOL
SEGMENT *n* one of several sections into which something may be divided ▷ *vb* divide into segments
SEGMENTAL *adj* of, like, or having the form of a segment
SEGMENTED > SEGMENT
SEGMENTS > SEGMENT
SEGNI > SEGNO
SEGNO *n* sign at the beginning or end of a section directed to be repeated
SEGNOS > SEGNO
SEGO *n* American variety of lily
SEGOL *variant of* > SEGHOL
SEGOLATE *variant of* > SEGHOLATE
SEGOLATES > SEGOLATE
SEGOLS > SEGOL
SEGOS > SEGO
SEGREANT *adj* having raised wings in heraldry
SEGREGANT *n* organism different because of segregation
SEGREGATE *vb* set apart
SEGS > SEG
SEGUE *vb* proceed from one section or piece of music to another without a break ▷ *n* practice or an instance of playing music in this way
SEGUED > SEGUE
SEGUEING > SEGUE
SEGUES > SEGUE
SEI *n* type of rorqual
SEICENTO *n* 17th century with reference to Italian art and literature
SEICENTOS > SEICENTO
SEICHE *n* periodic oscillation of the surface of an enclosed or semienclosed body of water
SEICHES > SEICHE
SEIDEL *n* vessel for drinking beer
SEIDELS > SEIDEL
SEIF *n* long ridge of blown sand in a desert
SEIFS > SEIF
SEIGNEUR *n* feudal lord
SEIGNEURS > SEIGNEUR
SEIGNEURY *n* estate of a seigneur
SEIGNIOR *n* (in England) the lord of a seigniory
SEIGNIORS > SEIGNIOR
SEIGNIORY *n* (in England) the fee or manor of a seignior
SEIGNORAL *adj* relating to the quality of being a lord
SEIGNORY *n* lordship
SEIK *Scot word for* > SICK
SEIKER > SEIK
SEIKEST > SEIK
SEIL *vb* dialect word meaning strain
SEILED > SEIL
SEILING > SEIL
SEILS > SEIL
SEINE *n* large fishing net that hangs vertically from floats ▷ *vb* catch (fish) using this net
SEINED > SEINE
SEINER > SEINE
SEINERS > SEINE
SEINES > SEINE
SEINING > SEINE
SEININGS > SEINE
SEIR *n* fish of Indian seas
SEIRS > SEIR
SEIS > SEI
SEISABLE > SEISE
SEISE *vb* put into legal possession of (property, etc)
SEISED > SEISE
SEISER > SEISE
SEISERS > SEISE
SEISES > SEISE
SEISIN *n* feudal possession of an estate in land
SEISING > SEISE
SEISINGS > SEISE
SEISINS > SEISIN
SEISM *n* earthquake
SEISMAL *adj* of earthquakes
SEISMIC *adj* relating to earthquakes
SEISMICAL *same as* > SEISMIC
SEISMISM *n* occurrence of earthquakes
SEISMISMS > SEISMISM
SEISMS > SEISM
SEISOR *n* person who takes seisin
SEISORS > SEISOR
SEISURE *n* act of seisin
SEISURES > SEISURE
SEITAN *same as* > SEITEN
SEITANS > SEITAN
SEITEN *n* gluten from wheat
SEITENS > SEITEN
SEITIES > SEITY
SEITY *n* selfhood
SEIZABLE > SEIZE
SEIZE *vb* take hold of forcibly or quickly
SEIZED > SEIZE
SEIZER > SEIZE
SEIZERS > SEIZE
SEIZES > SEIZE
SEIZIN *same as* > SEISIN
SEIZING *n* binding used for holding together two ropes, two spars, etc, esp by lashing with a separate rope
SEIZINGS > SEIZING
SEIZINS > SEIZIN
SEIZOR *n* person who takes seisin
SEIZORS > SEIZOR
SEIZURE *n* sudden violent attack of an illness
SEIZURES > SEIZURE
SEJANT *adj* (of a beast) shown seated
SEJEANT *same as* > SEJANT
SEKOS *n* holy place
SEKOSES > SEKOS
SEKT *n* German sparkling wine
SEKTS > SEKT
SEL *Scot word for* > SELF
SELACHIAN *adj* relating to a large subclass of cartilaginous fishes including the sharks, rays, dogfish, and skates ▷ *n* any fish belonging to this subclass
SELADANG *n* Malaysian tapir
SELADANGS > SELADANG
SELAH *n* Hebrew word of unknown meaning occurring in the Old Testament psalms, and thought to be a musical direction
SELAHS > SELAH
SELAMLIK *n* men's quarters in Turkish house
SELAMLIKS > SELAMLIK
SELCOUTH *adj* old word meaning strange
SELD *adj* old word meaning rare
SELDOM *adv* not often, rarely
SELDOMLY > SELDOM
SELDSEEN *adj* old word meaning seldom seen
SELDSHOWN *adj* old word meaning seldom shown
SELE *n* old word meaning happiness
SELECT *vb* pick out or choose ▷ *adj* chosen in preference to others
SELECTA *n* disc jockey
SELECTAS > SELECTA
SELECTED > SELECT
SELECTEE *n* person who is selected, esp for military service
SELECTEES > SELECTEE
SELECTING > SELECT
SELECTION *n* selecting
SELECTIVE *adj* chosen or choosing carefully
SELECTLY > SELECT
SELECTMAN *n* any of the members of the local boards of most New England towns
SELECTMEN > SELECTMAN
SELECTOR *n* person or thing that selects
SELECTORS > SELECTOR
SELECTS > SELECT
SELENATE *n* any salt or ester formed by replacing one or both of the hydrogens of selenic acid with metal ions or organic groups
SELENATES > SELENATE
SELENIAN *adj* of the moo[n]
SELENIC *adj* of or containing selenium, es[p] in the hexavalent state
SELENIDE *n* compound containing selenium
SELENIDES > SELENIDE
SELENIOUS *adj* of or containing selenium in the divalent or tetravalen[t] state
SELENITE *n* colourless glassy variety of gypsum
SELENITES > SELENITE
SELENITIC > SELENITE
SELENIUM *n* nonmetallic element with photoelectric properties
SELENIUMS > SELENIUM
SELENOSES > SELENOSIS
SELENOSIS *n* poisoned condition caused by selenium
SELENOUS *same as* > SELENIOUS
SELES > SELE
SELF *n* distinct individuality or identity of a person or thing ▷ *pr[on]* myself, yourself, himself, or herself ▷ *vb* reproduc[e] by oneself
SELFDOM *n* selfhood
SELFDOMS > SELFDOM
SELFED > SELF
SELFHEAL *n* low-growin[g] European herbaceous plant
SELFHEALS > SELFHEAL
SELFHOOD *n* state of havi[ng] a distinct identity
SELFHOODS > SELFHOOD
SELFING > SELF
SELFINGS > SELF
SELFISH *adj* caring too much about oneself and not enough about others
SELFISHLY > SELFISH
SELFISM *n* emphasis on self
SELFISMS > SELFISM
SELFIST > SELFISM
SELFISTS > SELFISM
SELFLESS *adj* unselfish
SELFNESS *n* egotism
SELFS > SELF
SELFSAME *adj* very same
SELFWARD *adj* toward self
SELFWARDS *adv* towards self
SELICTAR *n* Turkish swor[d] bearer
SELICTARS > SELICTAR
SELKIE *same as* > SILKIE
SELKIES > SELKIE
SELL *vb* exchange (something) for money ▷ *n* manner of selling
SELLA *n* area of bone in body
SELLABLE > SELL
SELLAE > SELLA
SELLAS > SELLA

ELLE *n* old word meaning seat
ELLER *n* person who sells
ELLERS > SELLER
ELLES > SELLE
ELLING > SELL
ELLOFF *n* act of selling cheaply
ELLOFFS > SELLOFF
ELLOTAPE *n* tradename for a type of transparent adhesive tape
ELLOUT *n* performance of a show etc for which all the tickets are sold
ELLOUTS > SELLOUT
ELLS > SELL
ELS > SEL
ELSYN *same as* > SYNCHRO
ELSYNS > SELSYN
ELTZER *n* natural effervescent water containing minerals
ELTZERS > SELTZER
ELVA *n* dense equatorial forest characterized by tall broad-leaved evergreen trees, lianas, etc
ELVAGE *n* edge of cloth, woven so as to prevent unravelling ▷ *vb* edge or border
ELVAGED > SELVAGE
ELVAGEE *n* rope used as strap
ELVAGEES > SELVAGEE
ELVAGES > SELVAGE
ELVAGING > SELVAGE
ELVAS > SELVA
ELVEDGE *same as* > SELVAGE
ELVEDGED > SELVEDGE
ELVEDGES > SELVEDGE
ELVES > SELF
EMAINIER *n* chest of drawers
EMANTEME *same as* > SEMEME
EMANTIC *adj* relating to the meaning of words
EMANTICS *n* study of linguistic meaning
EMANTIDE *n* type of molecule
EMANTRA > SEMANTRON
EMANTRON *n* bar struck instead of bell in Orthodox church
EMAPHORE *n* system of signalling by holding two flags in different positions to represent letters of the alphabet ▷ *vb* signal (information) by semaphore
EMATIC *adj* (of the conspicuous coloration of certain animals) acting as a warning, esp to potential predators
EMBLABLE *adj* resembling or similar ▷ *n* something that resembles another thing
SEMBLABLY > SEMBLABLE
SEMBLANCE *n* outward or superficial appearance
SEMBLANT *n* semblance
SEMBLANTS > SEMBLANT
SEMBLE *vb* seem
SEMBLED > SEMBLE
SEMBLES > SEMBLE
SEMBLING > SEMBLE
SEME *adj* dotted (with)
SEMEE *variant of* > SEME
SEMEED *adj* seme
SEMEIA > SEMEION
SEMEION *n* unit of metre in ancient poetry
SEMEIOTIC *same as* > SEMIOTIC
SEMEME *n* meaning of a morpheme
SEMEMES > SEMEME
SEMEMIC > SEMEME
SEMEN *n* sperm-carrying fluid produced by male animals
SEMENS > SEMEN
SEMES > SEME
SEMESTER *n* either of two divisions of the academic year
SEMESTERS > SEMESTER
SEMESTRAL > SEMESTER
SEMI *n* semidetached house
SEMIANGLE *n* half angle
SEMIARID *adj* denoting land that lies on the edges of a desert but has a slightly higher rainfall
SEMIBALD *adj* partly bald
SEMIBOLD *adj* denoting a weight of typeface between medium and bold face ▷ *n* semibold type
SEMIBOLDS > SEMIBOLD
SEMIBREVE *n* musical note four beats long
SEMIBULL *n* papal bull issued before coronation
SEMIBULLS > SEMIBULL
SEMICOLON *n* punctuation mark (;)
SEMICOMA *n* condition similar to a coma
SEMICOMAS > SEMICOMA
SEMICURED *adj* partly cured
SEMIDEAF *adj* partly deaf
SEMIDEIFY *vb* treat almost as god
SEMIDOME *n* half-dome, esp one used to cover a semicircular apse
SEMIDOMED *adj* having semidome
SEMIDOMES > SEMIDOME
SEMIDRY *adj* partly dry
SEMIDWARF *adj* smaller than standard variety
SEMIE *n* historical name for a student in second year at a Scottish university
SEMIERECT *adj* partly erect
SEMIES > SEMIE
SEMIFINAL *n* match or round before the final
SEMIFIT *adj* not fully fit
SEMIFLUID *adj* having properties between those of a liquid and those of a solid ▷ *n* substance that has such properties because of high viscosity
SEMIGALA *adj* characterized by quite a lot of celebration and fun
SEMIGLOSS *adj* (of paint) giving finish between matt and gloss
SEMIGROUP *n* type of set in mathematics
SEMIHARD *adj* partly hard
SEMIHIGH *adj* moderately high
SEMIHOBO *n* person looking almost like hobo
SEMIHOBOS > SEMIHOBO
SEMILLON *n* grape used to make wine
SEMILLONS > SEMILLON
SEMILOG *adj* semilogarithmic
SEMILUNAR *adj* shaped like a crescent or half-moon
SEMILUNE *n* half-moon shape
SEMILUNES > SEMILUNE
SEMIMAT *adj* semimatt
SEMIMATT *adj* with surface midway between matt and gloss
SEMIMATTE *adj* semimatt
SEMIMETAL *n* metal not fully malleable
SEMIMICRO *adj* using microwaves
SEMIMILD *adj* somewhat mild
SEMIMOIST *adj* slightly wet
SEMIMUTE *adj* having speech impairment through hearing loss
SEMINA > SEMEN
SEMINAL *adj* original and influential
SEMINALLY > SEMINAL
SEMINAR *n* meeting of a group of students for discussion
SEMINARS > SEMINAR
SEMINARY *n* college for priests
SEMINATE *vb* sow
SEMINATED > SEMINATE
SEMINATES > SEMINATE
SEMINOMA *n* malignant tumour of the testicle
SEMINOMAD *n* person living partly nomadic life
SEMINOMAS > SEMINOMA
SEMINUDE *adj* partly nude
SEMIOLOGY *same as* > SEMIOTICS
SEMIOPEN *adj* half-open
SEMIOSES > SEMIOSIS
SEMIOSIS *n* action involving establishing relationship between signs
SEMIOTIC *adj* relating to signs and symbols, esp spoken or written signs
SEMIOTICS *n* study of human communications, esp signs and symbols
SEMIOVAL *adj* shaped like half of oval
SEMIPED *n* measure in poetic metre
SEMIPEDS > SEMIPED
SEMIPIOUS *adj* quite pious
SEMIPLUME *n* type of bird feather
SEMIPOLAR as in *semipolar bond* type of chemical bond
SEMIPRO *n* semiprofessional
SEMIPROS > SEMIPRO
SEMIRAW *adj* not fully cooked or processed
SEMIRIGID *adj* (of an airship) maintaining shape by means of a main supporting keel and internal gas pressure
SEMIROUND *adj* with one flat side and one round side
SEMIRURAL *adj* partly rural
SEMIS > SEMI
SEMISES > SEMI
SEMISOFT *adj* partly soft
SEMISOLID *adj* having a viscosity and rigidity intermediate between that of a solid and a liquid ▷ *n* substance in this state
SEMISOLUS *n* advertisement that appears on the same page as another advertisement but not adjacent to it
SEMISTIFF *adj* partly stiff
SEMISWEET *adj* partly sweet
SEMITAR *old spelling of* > SCIMITAR
SEMITARS > SEMITAR
SEMITAUR *old spelling of* > SCIMITAR
SEMITAURS > SEMITAR
SEMITIST *n* student of Semitic languages and culture
SEMITISTS > SEMITIST
SEMITONAL > SEMITONE
SEMITONE *n* smallest interval between two notes in Western music
SEMITONES > SEMITONE
SEMITONIC > SEMITONE
SEMITRUCK *n* articulated lorry
SEMIURBAN *adj* suburban
SEMIVOCAL *adj* of or relating to a semivowel
SEMIVOWEL *n* vowel-like sound that acts like a consonant, such as the sound *w* in *well*
SEMIWILD *adj* not fully domesticated
SEMIWORKS *adj* equipped

to manufacture but not in great numbers
SEMMIT *n* vest
SEMMITS > SEMMIT
SEMOLINA *n* hard grains of wheat left after the milling of flour, used to make puddings and pasta
SEMOLINAS > SEMOLINA
SEMPER *adv* Latin word meaning always
SEMPLE *adj* Scots word meaning simple
SEMPLER > SEMPLE
SEMPLEST > SEMPLE
SEMPLICE *adv* be performed in a simple manner
SEMPRE *adv* (preceding a tempo or dynamic marking) always
SEMPSTER *n* person who sews
SEMPSTERS > SEMPSTER
SEMSEM *n* sesame
SEMSEMS > SEMSEM
SEMUNCIA *n* ancient Roman coin
SEMUNCIAE > SEMUNCIA
SEMUNCIAL > SEMUNCIA
SEMUNCIAS > SEMUNCIA
SEN *n* monetary unit of Brunei, Cambodia, Indonesia, Malaysia, and formerly of Japan
SENA *n* (in India) the army: used in the names of certain paramilitary political organizations
SENARIES > SENARY
SENARII > SENARIUS
SENARIUS *n* type of poem
SENARY *adj* of or relating to the number six
SENAS > SENA
SENATE *n* main governing body at some universities
SENATES > SENATE
SENATOR *n* member of a senate
SENATORS > SENATOR
SEND *vb* cause (a person or thing) to go to or be taken or transmitted to a place
SENDABLE > SEND
SENDAL *n* fine silk fabric used, esp in the Middle Ages, for ceremonial clothing, etc
SENDALS > SENDAL
SENDED *vb* old word meaning sent
SENDER > SEND
SENDERS > SEND
SENDING > SEND
SENDINGS > SEND
SENDOFF *n* demonstration of good wishes at a person's departure ▷ *vb* dispatch (something, such as a letter)
SENDOFFS > SENDOFF
SENDS > SEND
SENDUP *n* parody or imitation
SENDUPS > SENDUP
SENE *n* money unit in Samoa
SENECA *variant of* > SENEGA
SENECAS > SENECA
SENECIO *n* any plant of the genus *Senecio*
SENECIOS > SENECIO
SENEGA *n* milkwort plant of the eastern US, with small white flowers
SENEGAS > SENEGA
SENESCENT *adj* growing old
SENESCHAL *n* steward of the household of a medieval prince or nobleman
SENGI *n* African shrew
SENGREEN *n* house leek
SENGREENS > SENGREEN
SENHOR *n* Portuguese term of address for man
SENHORA *n* Portuguese term of address for woman
SENHORAS > SENHORA
SENHORES > SENHOR
SENHORITA *n* Portuguese term of address for girl
SENHORS > SENHOR
SENILE *adj* mentally or physically weak because of old age ▷ *n* senile person
SENILELY > SENILE
SENILES > SENILE
SENILITY > SENILE
SENIOR *adj* superior in rank or standing ▷ *n* senior person
SENIORITY *n* state of being senior
SENIORS > SENIOR
SENITI *n* money unit in Tonga
SENNA *n* tropical plant
SENNACHIE *n* Gaelic storyteller
SENNAS > SENNA
SENNET *n* fanfare: used as a stage direction in Elizabethan drama
SENNETS > SENNET
SENNIGHT *archaic word for* > WEEK
SENNIGHTS > SENNIGHT
SENNIT *n* flat braided cordage used on ships
SENNITS > SENNIT
SENOPIA *n* short-sightedness in old age
SENOPIAS > SENOPIA
SENOR *n* Spanish term of address equivalent to *sir* or *Mr*
SENORA *n* Spanish term of address equivalent to *madam* or *Mrs*
SENORAS > SENORA
SENORES > SENOR
SENORITA *n* Spanish term of address equivalent to *madam* or *Miss*
SENORITAS > SENORITA
SENORS > SENOR
SENRYU *n* Japanese short poem
SENS > SEN
SENSA > SENSUM
SENSATE *adj* perceived by the senses ▷ *vb* make sensate
SENSATED > SENSATE
SENSATELY > SENSATE
SENSATES > SENSATE
SENSATING > SENSATE
SENSATION *n* ability to feel things physically
SENSE *n* any of the faculties of perception or feeling ▷ *vb* perceive
SENSED > SENSE
SENSEFUL *adj* full of sense
SENSEI *n* martial arts teacher
SENSEIS > SENSEI
SENSELESS *adj* foolish
SENSES > SENSE
SENSIBLE *adj* having or showing good sense ▷ *n* sensible thing or person
SENSIBLER > SENSIBLE
SENSIBLES > SENSIBLE
SENSIBLY > SENSIBLE
SENSILE *adj* capable of feeling
SENSILLA > SENSILLUM
SENSILLAE > SENSILLUM
SENSILLUM *n* sense organ in insects
SENSING > SENSE
SENSINGS > SENSE
SENSISM *n* theory that ideas spring from senses
SENSISMS > SENSISM
SENSIST > SENSISM
SENSISTS > SENSISM
SENSITISE *same as* > SENSITIZE
SENSITIVE *adj* easily hurt or offended
SENSITIZE *vb* make sensitive
SENSOR *n* device that detects or measures the presence of something, such as radiation
SENSORIA > SENSORIUM
SENSORIAL *same as* > SENSORY
SENSORILY > SENSORY
SENSORIUM *n* area of the brain considered responsible for receiving and integrating sensations from the outside world
SENSORS > SENSOR
SENSORY *adj* of the senses or sensation
SENSUAL *adj* giving pleasure to the body and senses rather than the mind
SENSUALLY > SENSUAL
SENSUM *n* sensation detached from the information it conveys and also from its source in the external world
SENSUOUS *adj* pleasing to the senses
SENT *n* former monetary unit of Estonia
SENTE *n* money unit in Lesotho
SENTED > SEND
SENTENCE *n* sequence of words capable of standin[g] alone as a statement, question, or command ▷ *vb* pass sentence on (a convicted person)
SENTENCED > SENTENCE
SENTENCER > SENTENCE
SENTENCES > SENTENCE
SENTENTIA *n* opinion
SENTI > SENT
SENTIENCE *n* state or quality of being sentient
SENTIENCY *same as* > SENTIENCE
SENTIENT *adj* capable of feeling ▷ *n* sentient person or thing
SENTIENTS > SENTIENT
SENTIMENT *n* thought, opinion, or attitude
SENTIMO *n* money unit in Philippines
SENTIMOS > SENTIMO
SENTINEL *n* sentry ▷ *vb* guard as a sentinel
SENTINELS > SENTINEL
SENTING > SEND
SENTRIES > SENTRY
SENTRY *n* soldier on watc[h]
SENTS > SENT
SENVIES > SENVY
SENVY *n* mustard
SENZA *prep* without
SEPAD *vb* suppose
SEPADDED > SEPAD
SEPADDING > SEPAD
SEPADS > SEPAD
SEPAL *n* leaflike division [of] the calyx of a flower
SEPALED > SEPAL
SEPALINE *same as* > SEPALOID
SEPALLED > SEPAL
SEPALODY *n* changing of flower part into sepal
SEPALOID *adj* (esp of petals) resembling a sepa[l] in structure and function
SEPALOUS *adj* with sepals
SEPALS > SEPAL
SEPARABLE *adj* able to be separated
SEPARABLY > SEPARABLE
SEPARATA > SEPARATUM
SEPARATE *vb* act as a barrier between ▷ *adj* no[t] the same, different ▷ *n* item of clothing that onl[y] covers half the body
SEPARATED > SEPARATE
SEPARATES > SEPARATE
SEPARATOR *n* person or thing that separates
SEPARATUM *n* separate

printing of article from magazine
EPHEN *n* stingray
EPHENS > SEPHEN
EPIA *n* reddish-brown pigment ▷ *adj* dark reddish-brown, like the colour of very old photographs
EPIAS > SEPIA
EPIC *adj* of sepia
EPIMENT *n* hedge
EPIMENTS > SEPIMENT
EPIOLITE *n* meerschaum
EPIOST *n* cuttlefish bone
EPIOSTS > SEPIOST
EPIUM *n* cuttlefish bone
EPIUMS > SEPIUM
EPMAG *adj* designating a film or television programme for which the sound is recorded on separate magnetic material and run in synchronism with the picture
EPOY *n* (formerly) Indian soldier in the service of the British
EPOYS > SEPOY
EPPUKU *n* Japanese ritual suicide
EPPUKUS > SEPPUKU
EPS *n* species of lizard
EPSES > SEPSIS
EPSIS *n* poisoning caused by pus-forming bacteria
EPT *n* clan, esp in Ireland or Scotland
EPTA > SEPTUM
EPTAGE *n* waste removed from septic tank
EPTAGES > SEPTAGE
EPTAL *adj* of or relating to a septum
EPTARIA > SEPTARIUM
EPTARIAN > SEPTARIUM
EPTARIUM *n* mass of mineral substance having cracks filled with another mineral
EPTATE *adj* divided by septa
EPTATION *n* division by partitions
EPTEMFID *adj* divided into seven
EPTEMVIR *n* member of government of seven men
EPTENARY *adj* of or relating to the number seven ▷ *n* number seven
EPTENNIA *pl n* cycles of seven years
EPTET *n* group of seven performers
EPTETS > SEPTET
EPTETTE *same as* > SEPTET
EPTETTES > SEPTETTE
EPTIC *adj* (of a wound) infected ▷ *n* infected wound
EPTICAL > SEPTIC
SEPTICITY > SEPTIC
SEPTICS > SEPTIC
SEPTIFORM *adj* acting as partition
SEPTIMAL *adj* of number seven
SEPTIME *n* seventh of eight basic positions from which a parry can be made in fencing
SEPTIMES > SEPTIME
SEPTIMOLE *n* group of seven musical notes
SEPTLEVA *n* gambling term from old card game
SEPTLEVAS > SEPTLEVA
SEPTS > SEPT
SEPTUM *n* dividing partition between two cavities in the body
SEPTUMS > SEPTUM
SEPTUOR *n* group of seven musicians
SEPTUORS > SEPTUOR
SEPTUPLE *vb* multiply by seven ▷ *adj* seven times as much or as many ▷ *n* quantity or number seven times as great as another
SEPTUPLED > SEPTUPLE
SEPTUPLES > SEPTUPLE
SEPTUPLET *n* group of seven notes played in a time value of six, eight, etc
SEPULCHER *same as* > SEPULCHRE
SEPULCHRE *n* tomb or burial vault ▷ *vb* bury in a sepulchre
SEPULTURE *n* act of placing in a sepulchre
SEQUACITY quality of being pliant or controllable
SEQUEL *n* novel, play, or film that continues the story of an earlier one
SEQUELA *n* any abnormal bodily condition or disease related to or arising from a pre-existing disease
SEQUELAE > SEQUELA
SEQUELISE *same as* > SEQUELIZE
SEQUELIZE *vb* create sequel to
SEQUELS > SEQUEL
SEQUENCE *n* arrangement of two or more things in successive order ▷ *vb* arrange in a sequence
SEQUENCED > SEQUENCE
SEQUENCER *n* electronic device that determines the order in which a number of operations occur
SEQUENCES > SEQUENCE
SEQUENCY *n* number of changes in mathematical list
SEQUENT *adj* following in order or succession ▷ *n* something that follows
SEQUENTLY > SEQUENT
SEQUENTS > SEQUENT
SEQUESTER *vb* seclude
SEQUESTRA *pl n* detached pieces of necrotic bone that often migrate to wounds
SEQUIN *n* small ornamental metal disc on a garment ▷ *vb* apply sequins
SEQUINED > SEQUIN
SEQUINING > SEQUIN
SEQUINNED > SEQUIN
SEQUINS > SEQUIN
SEQUITUR *n* conclusion that follows from the premises
SEQUITURS > SEQUITUR
SEQUOIA *n* giant Californian coniferous tree
SEQUOIAS > SEQUOIA
SER *n* unit of weight used in India, usually taken as one fortieth of a maund
SERA > SERUM
SERAC *n* pinnacle of ice among crevasses on a glacier, usually on a steep slope
SERACS > SERAC
SERAFILE *n* line of soldiers
SERAFILES > SERAFILE
SERAFIN *n* old silver coin of Goa
SERAFINS > SERAFIN
SERAGLIO *n* harem of a Muslim palace
SERAGLIOS > SERAGLIO
SERAI *n* (in the East) a caravanserai or inn
SERAIL *same as* > SERAGLIO
SERAILS > SERAIL
SERAIS > SERAI
SERAL > SERE
SERANG *n* native captain of a crew of sailors in the East Indies
SERANGS > SERANG
SERAPE *n* blanket-like shawl often of brightly-coloured wool worn by men in Latin America
SERAPES > SERAPE
SERAPH *n* member of the highest order of angels
SERAPHIC *adj* of or resembling a seraph
SERAPHIM > SERAPH
SERAPHIMS > SERAPH
SERAPHIN *n* angel
SERAPHINE *n* old keyboard instrument
SERAPHINS > SERAPHIN
SERAPHS > SERAPH
SERASKIER *n* Turkish military leader
SERDAB *n* secret chamber in an ancient Egyptian tomb
SERDABS > SERDAB
SERE *adj* dried up or withered ▷ *n* series of changes occurring in the ecological succession of a particular community ▷ *vb* sear
SERED > SERE
SEREIN *n* fine rain falling from a clear sky after sunset, esp in the tropics
SEREINS > SEREIN
SERENADE *n* music played or sung to a woman by a lover ▷ *vb* sing or play a serenade to (someone)
SERENADED > SERENADE
SERENADER > SERENADE
SERENADES > SERENADE
SERENATA *n* 18th-century cantata, often dramatic in form
SERENATAS > SERENATA
SERENATE *n* old form of serenade
SERENATES > SERENATE
SERENE *adj* calm, peaceful ▷ *vb* make serene
SERENED > SERENE
SERENELY > SERENE
SERENER > SERENE
SERENES > SERENE
SERENEST > SERENE
SERENING > SERENE
SERENITY *n* state or quality of being serene
SERER > SERE
SERES > SERE
SEREST > SERE
SERF *n* medieval farm labourer who could not leave the land he worked on
SERFAGE > SERF
SERFAGES > SERF
SERFDOM > SERF
SERFDOMS > SERF
SERFHOOD > SERF
SERFHOODS > SERF
SERFISH > SERF
SERFLIKE > SERF
SERFS > SERF
SERFSHIP > SERF
SERFSHIPS > SERF
SERGE *n* strong woollen fabric
SERGEANCY > SERGEANT
SERGEANT *n* noncommissioned officer in the army
SERGEANTS > SERGEANT
SERGEANTY *n* form of feudal tenure
SERGED *adj* with sewn seam
SERGER *n* sewing machine attachment for finishing seams
SERGERS > SERGER
SERGES > SERGE
SERGING *n* type of sewing
SERGINGS > SERGING
SERIAL *n* story or play produced in successive instalments ▷ *adj* of or forming a series
SERIALISE *same as* > SERIALIZE
SERIALISM *n* musical technique using a

sequence of notes in a definite order
SERIALIST *n* writer of serials
SERIALITY > SERIAL
SERIALIZE *vb* publish or present as a serial
SERIALLY > SERIAL
SERIALS > SERIAL
SERIATE *adj* forming a series ▷ *vb* form into a series
SERIATED > SERIATE
SERIATELY > SERIATE
SERIATES > SERIATE
SERIATIM *adv* in a series
SERIATING > SERIATE
SERIATION > SERIATE
SERIC *adj* of silk
SERICEOUS *adj* covered with a layer of small silky hairs
SERICIN *n* gelatinous protein found on the fibres of raw silk
SERICINS > SERICIN
SERICITE *n* type of mica
SERICITES > SERICITE
SERICITIC > SERICITE
SERICON *n* solution used in alchemy
SERICONS > SERICON
SERIEMA *n* either of two cranelike South American birds
SERIEMAS > SERIEMA
SERIES *n* group or succession of related things, usu arranged in order
SERIF *n* small line at the extremities of a main stroke in a type character
SERIFED *adj* having serifs
SERIFFED *adj* having serifs
SERIFS > SERIF
SERIGRAPH *n* colour print made by an adaptation of the silk-screen process
SERIN *n* any of various small yellow-and-brown finches
SERINE *n* sweet-tasting amino acid
SERINES > SERINE
SERINETTE *n* barrel organ
SERING > SERE
SERINGA *n* any of several trees that yield rubber
SERINGAS > SERINGA
SERINS > SERIN
SERIOUS *adj* giving cause for concern
SERIOUSLY *adv* in a serious manner or to a serious degree
SERIPH *same as* > SERIF
SERIPHS > SERIPH
SERJEANCY *n* rank of sergeant
SERJEANT *same as* > SERGEANT
SERJEANTS > SERJEANT
SERJEANTY *n* type of feudal tenure
SERK *Scots word for* > SHIRT
SERKALI *n* government in Africa
SERKALIS > SERKALI
SERKS > SERK
SERMON *n* speech on a religious or moral subject by a clergyman in a church service ▷ *vb* deliver a sermon
SERMONED > SERMON
SERMONEER *n* preacher
SERMONER *variant of* > SERMONEER
SERMONERS > SERMONER
SERMONET *n* short sermon
SERMONETS > SERMONET
SERMONIC > SERMON
SERMONING > SERMON
SERMONISE *same as* > SERMONIZE
SERMONIZE *vb* make a long moralizing speech
SERMONS > SERMON
SEROLOGIC > SEROLOGY
SEROLOGY *n* science concerned with serums
SERON *n* crate
SERONS > SERON
SEROON *n* crate
SEROONS > SEROON
SEROPUS *n* liquid consisting of serum and pus
SEROPUSES > SEROPUS
SEROSA *n* one of the thin membranes surrounding the embryo in an insect's egg
SEROSAE > SEROSA
SEROSAL > SEROSA
SEROSAS > SEROSA
SEROSITY > SEROUS
SEROTINAL *same as* > SEROTINE
SEROTINE *adj* produced, flowering, or developing late in the season ▷ *n* either of two insectivorous bats
SEROTINES > SEROTINE
SEROTINY *n* state of being serotinous
SEROTONIN *n* compound that occurs in the brain, intestines, and blood platelets and acts as a neurotransmitter
SEROTYPE *n* category into which material, usually a bacterium, is placed based on its serological activity ▷ *vb* class according to serotype
SEROTYPED > SEROTYPE
SEROTYPES > SEROTYPE
SEROUS *adj* of, containing, or like serum
SEROVAR *n* subdivision of species
SEROVARS > SEROVAR
SEROW *n* either of two antelopes of mountainous regions of S and SE Asia
SEROWS > SEROW
SERPENT *n* snake
SERPENTRY *n* serpents
SERPENTS > SERPENT
SERPIGO *n* any progressive skin eruption, such as ringworm or herpes
SERPIGOES > SERPIGO
SERPIGOS > SERPIGO
SERPULA *n* marine worm
SERPULAE > SERPULA
SERPULID *n* marine polychaete worm
SERPULIDS > SERPULID
SERPULITE *n* variety of fossil
SERR *vb* press close together
SERRA *n* sawlike part or organ
SERRAE > SERRA
SERRAN *n* species of fish
SERRANID *n* any of numerous marine fishes including the sea basses, and sea perches ▷ *adj* of or belonging to the family *Serranidae*
SERRANIDS > SERRANID
SERRANO *n* type of Spanish ham
SERRANOID *same as* > SERRANID
SERRANOS > SERRANO
SERRANS > SERRAN
SERRAS > SERRA
SERRATE *adj* (of leaves) having a margin of forward pointing teeth ▷ *vb* make serrate
SERRATED *adj* having a notched or sawlike edge
SERRATES > SERRATE
SERRATI > SERRATUS
SERRATING > SERRATE
SERRATION *n* state or condition of being serrated
SERRATURE *same as* > SERRATION
SERRATUS *n* muscle in thorax
SERRE *vb* press close together
SERRED > SERRE
SERREFILE *n* file of soldiers
SERRES > SERRE
SERRICORN *n* with serrate antennae
SERRIED *adj* in close formation
SERRIEDLY > SERRIED
SERRIES > SERRY
SERRIFORM *adj* resembling a notched or sawlike edge
SERRING > SERRE
SERRS > SERR
SERRULATE *adj* (esp of leaves) minutely serrate
SERRY *vb* close together
SERRYING > SERRY
SERS > SER
SERUEWE *vb* old word meaning survey
SERUEWED > SERUEWE
SERUEWES > SERUEWE
SERUEWING > SERUEWE
SERUM *n* watery fluid left after blood has clotted
SERUMAL > SERUM
SERUMS > SERUM
SERVABLE > SERVE
SERVAL *n* feline African mammal
SERVALS > SERVAL
SERVANT *n* person employed to do househol work for another ▷ *vb* work as a servant
SERVANTED > SERVANT
SERVANTRY *n* servants
SERVANTS > SERVANT
SERVE *vb* work for (a person, community, or cause) ▷ *n* act of serving the ball
SERVEABLE > SERVE
SERVED > SERVE
SERVER *n* player who serves in racket games
SERVERIES > SERVERY
SERVERS > SERVER
SERVERY *n* room from which food is served
SERVES > SERVE
SERVEWE *vb* old word meaning survey
SERVEWED > SERVEWE
SERVEWES > SERVEWE
SERVEWING > SERVEWE
SERVICE *n* serving ▷ *adj* serving the public rather than producing goods ▷ *vb* provide a service or services to
SERVICED > SERVICE
SERVICER > SERVICE
SERVICERS > SERVICE
SERVICES > SERVICE
SERVICING > SERVICE
SERVIENT *adj* subordinate
SERVIETTE *n* table napkir
SERVILE *adj* too eager to obey people, fawning ▷ *n* servile person
SERVILELY > SERVILE
SERVILES > SERVILE
SERVILISM *n* condition o being servile
SERVILITY > SERVILE
SERVING *n* portion of fooc
SERVINGS > SERVING
SERVITOR *n* servant or attendant
SERVITORS > SERVITOR
SERVITUDE *n* bondage or slavery
SERVLET *n* small program that runs on a web server often accessing database in response to client inpu
SERVLETS > SERVLET
SERVO *n* servomechanism ▷ *adj* of a servomechanis
SERVOS > SERVO
SERVQUAL *n* provision of

ıigh-quality products by an organization backed by a high level of service for consumers
ERVQUALS > SERVQUAL
SAME *n* plant cultivated for its seeds and oil, which are used in cooking
SAMES > SESAME
SAMOID *adj* of or relating to various small bones formed in tendons ▷ *n* sesamoid bone
SAMOIDS > SESAMOID
SE *interj* exclamation found in Shakespeare
SELI *n* garden plant
SELIS > SESELI
SEY *interj* exclamation found in Shakespeare
SH *short for* > SESSION
SHES > SESH
SS *n* old word meaning tax
SSA *interj* exclamation found in Shakespeare
SSES > SESS
SSILE *adj* (of flowers or leaves) having no stalk
SSILITY > SESSILE
SSION *n* period spent in an activity
SSIONAL > SESSION
SSIONS *pl n* sittings or a sitting of justice in court
SSPOOL *n* cesspool
SSPOOLS > SESSPOOL
STERCE *n* silver or, later, bronze coin of ancient Rome worth a quarter of a denarius
STERCES > SESTERCE
STERTIA *pl n* ancient Roman money accounts
STERTII *pl n* sesterces
STET *n* last six lines of a sonnet
STETS > SESTET
STETT *n* group of six
STETTE *n* group of six
STETTES > SESTETTE
STETTO *n* composition for six musicians
STETTOS > SESTETTO
STETTS > SESTETT
STINA *n* elaborate verse form of Italian origin
STINAS > SESTINA
STINE *n* poem of six lines
STINES > SESTINE
STON *n* type of plankton
STONS > SESTON
T *vb* put in a specified position or state ▷ *n* setting or being set ▷ *adj* fixed or established beforehand
TA *n* (in invertebrates and some plants) any bristle or bristle-like appendage
TACEOUS > SETA
TAE > SETA
SETAL > SETA
SETBACK *n* anything that delays progress
SETBACKS > SETBACK
SETENANT *n* pair of postage stamps of different values joined together
SETENANTS > SETENANT
SETIFORM *adj* shaped like a seta
SETLINE *n* any of various types of fishing line
SETLINES > SETLINE
SETNESS > SET
SETNESSES > SET
SETOFF *n* counterbalance
SETOFFS > SETOFF
SETON *n* surgical thread inserted below the skin
SETONS > SETON
SETOSE *adj* covered with setae
SETOUS > SETA
SETOUT *n* beginning or outset
SETOUTS > SETOUT
SETS > SET
SETSCREW *n* screw that fits into the boss or hub of a wheel, and prevents motion of the part relative to the shaft on which it is mounted
SETSCREWS > SETSCREW
SETT *n* badger's burrow
SETTEE *n* couch
SETTEES > SETTEE
SETTER *n* long-haired gun dog ▷ *vb* treat with a piece of setterwort
SETTERED > SETTER
SETTERING > SETTER
SETTERS > SETTER
SETTING > SET
SETTINGS > SET
SETTLE *vb* arrange or put in order ▷ *n* long wooden bench with high back and arms
SETTLED > SETTLE
SETTLER *n* colonist
SETTLERS > SETTLER
SETTLES > SETTLE
SETTLING > SETTLE
SETTLINGS *pl n* any matter or substance that has settled at the bottom of a liquid
SETTLOR *n* person who settles property on someone
SETTLORS > SETTLOR
SETTS > SETT
SETUALE *n* valerian
SETUALES > SETUALE
SETULE *n* small bristle
SETULES > SETULE
SETULOSE > SETULE
SETULOUS > SETULE
SETUP *n* way in which anything is organized or arranged
SETUPS > SETUP
SETWALL *n* valerian
SETWALLS > SETWALL
SEVEN *n* one more than six ▷ *adj* amounting to seven ▷ *determiner* amounting to seven
SEVENFOLD *adj* having seven times as many or as much ▷ *adv* by seven times as many or as much
SEVENS *n* Rugby Union match or series of matches played with seven players on each side
SEVENTEEN *n* ten and seven ▷ *adj* amounting to seventeen ▷ *determiner* amounting to seventeen
SEVENTH *n* (of) number seven in a series ▷ *adj* coming after the sixth and before the eighth ▷ *adv* after the sixth person, position, event, etc
SEVENTHLY *same as* > SEVENTH
SEVENTHS > SEVENTH
SEVENTIES > SEVENTY
SEVENTY *n* ten times seven ▷ *adj* amounting to seventy ▷ *determiner* amounting to seventy
SEVER *vb* cut through or off
SEVERABLE *adj* able to be severed
SEVERAL *adj* some, a few ▷ *n* individual person
SEVERALLY *adv* separately
SEVERALS > SEVERAL
SEVERALTY *n* state of being several or separate
SEVERANCE *n* act of severing or state of being severed
SEVERE *adj* strict or harsh
SEVERED > SEVER
SEVERELY > SEVERE
SEVERER > SEVERE
SEVEREST > SEVERE
SEVERIES > SEVERY
SEVERING > SEVER
SEVERITY > SEVERE
SEVERS > SEVER
SEVERY *n* part of vaulted ceiling
SEVICHE *n* Mexican fish dish
SEVICHES > SEVICHE
SEVRUGA *n* species of sturgeon
SEVRUGAS > SEVRUGA
SEW *vb* join with thread repeatedly passed through with a needle
SEWABLE > SEW
SEWAGE *n* waste matter or excrement carried away in sewers
SEWAGES > SEWAGE
SEWAN *same as* > SEAWAN
SEWANS > SEWAN
SEWAR *n* Asian dagger
SEWARS > SEWAR
SEWED > SEW
SEWEL *n* scarecrow
SEWELLEL *n* mountain beaver
SEWELLELS > SEWELLEL
SEWELS > SEWEL
SEWEN *same as* > SEWIN
SEWENS > SEWEN
SEWER *n* drain to remove waste water and sewage ▷ *vb* provide with sewers
SEWERAGE *n* system of sewers
SEWERAGES > SEWERAGE
SEWERED > SEWER
SEWERING > SEWER
SEWERINGS > SEWER
SEWERLESS > SEWER
SEWERLIKE > SEWER
SEWERS > SEWER
SEWIN *n* sea trout
SEWING > SEW
SEWINGS > SEW
SEWINS > SEWIN
SEWN > SEW
SEWS > SEW
SEX *n* state of being male or female ▷ *vb* find out the sex of ▷ *adj* of sexual matters
SEXAHOLIC *n* person who is addicted to sex
SEXED *adj* having a specified degree of sexuality
SEXENNIAL *adj* occurring once every six years or over a period of six years ▷ *n* sixth anniversary
SEXER *n* person checking sex of chickens
SEXERCISE *n* sexual activity, regarded as a way of keeping fit
SEXERS > SEXER
SEXES > SEX
SEXFID *adj* split into six
SEXFOIL *n* flower with six petals or leaves
SEXFOILS > SEXFOIL
SEXIER > SEXY
SEXIEST > SEXY
SEXILY > SEXY
SEXINESS > SEXY
SEXING > SEX
SEXISM *n* discrimination on the basis of a person's sex
SEXISMS > SEXISM
SEXIST > SEXISM
SEXISTS > SEXISM
SEXLESS *adj* neither male nor female
SEXLESSLY > SEXLESS
SEXLINKED *adj* (of a gene) found on a sex chromosome
SEXOLOGIC > SEXOLOGY
SEXOLOGY *n* study of sexual behaviour in human beings
SEXPERT *n* person who professes a knowledge of sexual matters
SEXPERTS > SEXPERT
SEXPOT *n* person, esp a

young woman, considered as being sexually very attractive
SEXPOTS > SEXPOT
SEXT *n* fourth of the seven canonical hours of the divine office or the prayers prescribed for it: originally the sixth hour of the day (noon)
SEXTAIN *same as* > SESTINA
SEXTAINS > SEXTAIN
SEXTAN *adj* (of a fever) marked by paroxysms that recur after an interval of five days
SEXTANS *n* Roman coin
SEXTANSES > SEXTANS
SEXTANT *n* navigator's instrument for measuring angles to calculate one's position
SEXTANTAL > SEXTANT
SEXTANTS > SEXTANT
SEXTARII > SEXTARIUS
SEXTARIUS *n* ancient Roman quantity measure
SEXTET *n* group of six performers
SEXTETS > SEXTET
SEXTETT *n* sextet
SEXTETTE *same as* > SEXTET
SEXTETTES > SEXTETTE
SEXTETTS > SEXTETT
SEXTILE *n* one of five values of a variable dividing its distribution into six groups with equal frequencies
SEXTILES > SEXTILE
SEXTO *same as* > SIXMO
SEXTOLET *n* group of six musical notes
SEXTOLETS > SEXTOLET
SEXTON *n* official in charge of a church and churchyard
SEXTONESS *n* female sexton
SEXTONS > SEXTON
SEXTOS > SEXTO
SEXTS > SEXT
SEXTUOR *n* sextet
SEXTUORS > SEXTUOR
SEXTUPLE *vb* multiply by six ▷ *adj* six times as much or as many ▷ *n* quantity or number six times as great as another
SEXTUPLED > SEXTUPLE
SEXTUPLES > SEXTUPLE
SEXTUPLET *n* one of six children born at one birth
SEXTUPLY > SEXTUPLE
SEXUAL *adj* of or characterized by sex
SEXUALISE *same as* > SEXUALIZE
SEXUALISM *n* emphasising of sexuality
SEXUALIST > SEXUALISM
SEXUALITY *n* state or quality of being sexual
SEXUALIZE *vb* make or become sexual or sexually aware
SEXUALLY > SEXUAL
SEXVALENT *adj* with valency of six
SEXY *adj* sexually exciting or attractive
SEY *n* Scots word meaning part of cow carcase
SEYEN *n* old form of scion
SEYENS > SEYEN
SEYS > SEY
SEYSURE *n* old form of seizure
SEYSURES > SEYSURE
SEZ *vb* informal spelling of 'says'
SFERICS *same as* > SPHERICS
SFORZANDI > SFORZANDO
SFORZANDO *adv* be played with strong initial attack ▷ *n* symbol written above a note, indicating this
SFORZATI > SFORZATO
SFORZATO *same as* > SFORZANDO
SFORZATOS > SFORZATO
SFUMATO *n* gradual transition between areas of different colour in painting
SFUMATOS > SFUMATO
SGRAFFITI > SGRAFFITO
SGRAFFITO *n* technique in mural or ceramic decoration in which the top layer of glaze is incised with a design to reveal parts of the ground
SH *same as* > SHILLING
SHA *interj* be quiet
SHABASH *interj* (in Indian English) bravo or well done
SHABBATOT *pl n* Jewish sabbaths
SHABBIER > SHABBY
SHABBIEST > SHABBY
SHABBILY > SHABBY
SHABBLE *n* Scots word meaning old sword
SHABBLES > SHABBLE
SHABBY *adj* worn or dilapidated in appearance
SHABRACK *n* cavalryman's saddle cloth
SHABRACKS > SHABRACK
SHACK *n* rough hut ▷ *vb* evade (work or responsibility)
SHACKED > SHACK
SHACKING > SHACK
SHACKLE *n* metal ring for securing a person's wrists or ankles ▷ *vb* fasten with shackles
SHACKLED > SHACKLE
SHACKLER > SHACKLE
SHACKLERS > SHACKLE
SHACKLES > SHACKLE
SHACKLING > SHACKLE
SHACKO *same as* > SHAKO
SHACKOES > SHACKO
SHACKOS > SHACKO
SHACKS > SHACK
SHAD *n* herring-like fish
SHADBERRY *n* edible purplish berry of the shadbush
SHADBLOW *n* type of shrub
SHADBLOWS > SHADBLOW
SHADBUSH *n* type of N American tree or shrub
SHADCHAN *n* Jewish marriage broker
SHADCHANS > SHADCHAN
SHADDOCK *another name for* > POMELO
SHADDOCKS > SHADDOCK
SHADE *n* relative darkness ▷ *vb* screen from light
SHADED > SHADE
SHADELESS > SHADE
SHADER > SHADE
SHADERS > SHADE
SHADES *pl n* gathering darkness at nightfall
SHADFLIES > SHADFLY
SHADFLY *American name for* > MAYFLY
SHADIER > SHADY
SHADIEST > SHADY
SHADILY > SHADY
SHADINESS > SHADY
SHADING *n* graded areas of tone indicating light and dark in a painting or drawing
SHADINGS > SHADING
SHADKHAN *same as* > SHADCHAN
SHADKHANS > SHADKHAN
SHADOOF *n* mechanism for raising water, esp as used in Egypt and the Near East
SHADOOFS > SHADOOF
SHADOW *n* dark shape cast on a surface when something stands between a light and the surface ▷ *vb* cast a shadow over
SHADOWBOX *vb* practise boxing against an imaginary opponent
SHADOWED > SHADOW
SHADOWER > SHADOW
SHADOWERS > SHADOW
SHADOWIER > SHADOWY
SHADOWILY > SHADOWY
SHADOWING > SHADOW
SHADOWS > SHADOW
SHADOWY *adj* (of a place) full of shadows
SHADRACH *n* lump of iron that has not been melted in the furnace
SHADRACHS > SHADRACH
SHADS > SHAD
SHADUF *same as* > SHADOOF
SHADUFS > SHADUF
SHADY *adj* situated in or giving shade
SHAFT *n* long narrow straight handle of a tool or weapon ▷ *vb* treat badly
SHAFTED > SHAFT
SHAFTER > SHAFT
SHAFTERS > SHAFT
SHAFTING *n* assembly of rotating shafts for transmitting power
SHAFTINGS > SHAFTING
SHAFTLESS > SHAFT
SHAFTS > SHAFT
SHAG *n* coarse shredded tobacco ▷ *adj* (of a carpet) having a long pile ▷ *vb* have sexual intercourse with (a person)
SHAGBARK *n* North American hickory tree
SHAGBARKS > SHAGBARK
SHAGGABLE *adj* sexually attractive
SHAGGED > SHAG
SHAGGIER > SHAGGY
SHAGGIEST > SHAGGY
SHAGGILY > SHAGGY
SHAGGING > SHAG
SHAGGY *adj* covered with rough hair or wool
SHAGPILE *adj* (of carpet) having long fibres
SHAGREEN *n* sharkskin
SHAGREENS > SHAGREEN
SHAGROON *n* nineteenth-century Australian settler in Canterbury
SHAGROONS > SHAGROON
SHAGS > SHAG
SHAH *n* formerly, ruler of Iran
SHAHADA *n* Islamic declaration of faith, repeated daily by Muslims
SHAHADAS > SHAHADA
SHAHDOM > SHAH
SHAHDOMS > SHAH
SHAHS > SHAH
SHAHTOOSH *n* soft wool that comes from the protected Tibetan antelope
SHAIKH *n* sheikh
SHAIKHS > SHAIKH
SHAIRD *n* Scots word meaning shred
SHAIRDS > SHAIRD
SHAIRN *Scots word for* > DUNG
SHAIRNS > SHAIRN
SHAITAN *n* (in Muslim countries) an evil spirit
SHAITANS > SHAITAN
SHAKABLE > SHAKE
SHAKE *vb* move quickly up and down or back and forth ▷ *n* shaking
SHAKEABLE > SHAKE
SHAKED *vb* old form of shook
SHAKEDOWN *n* act of extortion
SHAKEN > SHAKE
SHAKEOUT *n* process of reducing the number of people in a workforce
SHAKEOUTS > SHAKEOUT
SHAKER *n* container in which drinks are mixed or from which powder is shaken
SHAKERS > SHAKER

IAKES > SHAKE
IAKEUP *n* radical reorganization
IAKEUPS > SHAKEUP
IAKIER > SHAKY
IAKIEST > SHAKY
IAKILY > SHAKY
IAKINESS > SHAKY
IAKING > SHAKE
IAKINGS > SHAKE
IAKO *n* tall cylindrical peaked military hat with a plume
IAKOES > SHAKO
IAKOS > SHAKO
IAKT *vb* old form of shook
IAKUDO *n* Japanese alloy of copper and gold
IAKUDOS > SHAKUDO
IAKY *adj* unsteady
IALE *n* flaky sedimentary rock
IALED > SHALE
IALELIKE > SHALE
IALES > SHALE
IALEY > SHALE
IALIER > SHALE
IALIEST > SHALE
IALING > SHALE
IALL *vb* used as an auxiliary to make the future tense
IALLI *n* type of fabric
IALLIS > SHALLI
IALLON *n* American shrub
IALLONS > SHALLON
IALLOON *n* light twill-weave woollen fabric used chiefly for coat linings, etc
IALLOONS > SHALLOON
IALLOP *n* light boat used for rowing in shallow water
IALLOPS > SHALLOP
IALLOT *n* kind of small onion
IALLOTS > SHALLOT
IALLOW *adj* not deep ▷ *n* shallow place in a body of water ▷ *vb* make or become shallow
IALLOWED > SHALLOW
IALLOWER > SHALLOW
IALLOWLY > SHALLOW
IALLOWS > SHALLOW
IALM *n* old woodwind instrument
IALMS > SHALM
IALOM *n* Jewish greeting meaning 'peace be with you'
IALOMS > SHALOM
IALOT *n* shallot
IALOTS > SHALOT
IALT *singular form of the present tense (indicative mood) of* > SHALL
IALWAR *n* pair of loose-fitting trousers tapering to a narrow fit around the ankles, worn in the Indian subcontinent, often with a kameez
IALWARS > SHALWAR
SHALY > SHALE
SHAM *n* thing or person that is not genuine ▷ *adj* not genuine ▷ *vb* fake, feign
SHAMA *n* Indian songbird
SHAMABLE > SHAME
SHAMABLY > SHAME
SHAMAN *n* priest of shamanism
SHAMANIC > SHAMAN
SHAMANISM *n* religion of northern Asia, based on a belief in good and evil spirits
SHAMANIST > SHAMANISM
SHAMANS > SHAMAN
SHAMAS > SHAMA
SHAMATEUR *n* sportsperson who is officially an amateur but accepts payment
SHAMBA *n* (in E Africa) any field used for growing crops
SHAMBAS > SHAMBA
SHAMBLE *vb* walk in a shuffling awkward way ▷ *n* awkward or shuffling walk
SHAMBLED > SHAMBLE
SHAMBLES *n* disorderly event or place
SHAMBLIER > SHAMBLE
SHAMBLING > SHAMBLE
SHAMBLY > SHAMBLE
SHAMBOLIC *adj* completely disorganized
SHAME *n* painful emotion caused by awareness of having done something dishonourable or foolish ▷ *vb* cause to feel shame
SHAMEABLE > SHAME
SHAMEABLY > SHAME
SHAMED > SHAME
SHAMEFAST *adj* old form of shamefaced
SHAMEFUL *adj* causing or deserving shame
SHAMELESS *adj* with no sense of shame
SHAMER *n* cause of shame
SHAMERS > SHAME
SHAMES > SHAME
SHAMIANA *n* tent in India
SHAMIANAH *n* tent in India
SHAMIANAS > SHAMIANA
SHAMINA *n* wool blend of pashm and shahtoosh
SHAMINAS > SHAMINA
SHAMING > SHAME
SHAMISEN *n* Japanese stringed instrument
SHAMISENS > SHAMISEN
SHAMMAS *same as* > SHAMMES
SHAMMASH *same as* > SHAMMES
SHAMMASIM > SHAMMES
SHAMMED > SHAM
SHAMMER > SHAM
SHAMMERS > SHAM
SHAMMES *n* official acting as the beadle, sexton, and caretaker of a synagogue
SHAMMIED > SHAMMY
SHAMMIES > SHAMMY
SHAMMING > SHAM
SHAMMOS *same as* > SHAMMES
SHAMMOSIM > SHAMMES
SHAMMY *n* piece of chamois leather ▷ *vb* rub with a shammy
SHAMMYING > SHAMMY
SHAMOIS *n* chamois
SHAMOS *same as* > SHAMMES
SHAMOSIM > SHAMMES
SHAMOY *n* chamois ▷ *vb* rub with a shamoy
SHAMOYED > SHAMOY
SHAMOYING > SHAMOY
SHAMOYS > SHAMOY
SHAMPOO *n* liquid soap for washing hair, carpets, or upholstery ▷ *vb* wash with shampoo
SHAMPOOED > SHAMPOO
SHAMPOOER > SHAMPOO
SHAMPOOS > SHAMPOO
SHAMROCK *n* clover leaf, esp as the Irish emblem
SHAMROCKS > SHAMROCK
SHAMS > SHAM
SHAMUS *n* police or private detective
SHAMUSES > SHAMUS
SHAN *variant of* > SHAND
SHANACHIE *n* Gaelic storyteller
SHAND *n* old word meaning fake coin
SHANDIES > SHANDY
SHANDRIES > SHANDRY
SHANDRY *n* light horse-drawn cart
SHANDS > SHAND
SHANDY *n* drink made of beer and lemonade
SHANGHAI *vb* force or trick (someone) into doing something ▷ *n* catapult
SHANGHAIS > SHANGHAI
SHANK *n* lower leg ▷ *vb* (of fruits, roots, etc) to show disease symptoms, esp discoloration
SHANKBONE *n* bone in lower leg
SHANKED > SHANK
SHANKING > SHANK
SHANKS > SHANK
SHANNIES > SHANNY
SHANNY *n* European blenny of rocky coastal waters
SHANS > SHAN
SHANTEY *same as* > SHANTY
SHANTEYS > SHANTEY
SHANTI *n* peace
SHANTIES > SHANTY
SHANTIH *same as* > SHANTI
SHANTIHS > SHANTIH
SHANTIS > SHANTI
SHANTUNG *n* soft Chinese silk with a knobbly surface
SHANTUNGS > SHANTUNG
SHANTY *n* shack or crude dwelling
SHANTYMAN *n* man living in shanty
SHANTYMEN > SHANTYMAN
SHAPABLE > SHAPE
SHAPE *n* outward form of an object ▷ *vb* form or mould
SHAPEABLE > SHAPE
SHAPED > SHAPE
SHAPELESS *adj* (of a person or object) lacking a pleasing shape
SHAPELIER > SHAPELY
SHAPELY *adj* having an attractive shape
SHAPEN *vb* old form of shaped
SHAPER > SHAPE
SHAPERS > SHAPE
SHAPES > SHAPE
SHAPEUP *n* system of hiring dockers for a day's work
SHAPEUPS > SHAPEUP
SHAPEWEAR *n* underwear that shapes body
SHAPING > SHAPE
SHAPINGS > SHAPE
SHAPS *n* leather over-trousers worn by cowboys
SHARABLE > SHARE
SHARD *n* broken piece of pottery or glass
SHARDED *adj* old word meaning hidden under dung
SHARDS > SHARD
SHARE *n* part of something that belongs to or is contributed by a person ▷ *vb* give or take a share of (something)
SHAREABLE > SHARE
SHARECROP *vb* cultivate (farmland) as a sharecropper
SHARED > SHARE
SHAREMAN *n* member of fishing-boat crew who shares profits
SHAREMEN > SHAREMAN
SHARER > SHARE
SHARERS > SHARE
SHARES > SHARE
SHARESMAN *n* member of fishing-boat crew who shares profits
SHARESMEN > SHARESMAN
SHAREWARE *n* software available to all users without the need for a licence
SHARIA *n* body of doctrines that regulate the lives of Muslims
SHARIAH *same as* > SHARIA
SHARIAHS > SHARIAH
SHARIAS > SHARIA
SHARIAT *n* Islamic religious law
SHARIATS > SHARIAT
SHARIF *same as* > SHERIF
SHARIFIAN > SHARIF
SHARIFS > SHARIF
SHARING > SHARE

SHARINGS > SHARE
SHARK *n* large usu predatory sea fish ▷ *vb* obtain (something) by cheating or deception
SHARKED > SHARK
SHARKER *n* shark hunter
SHARKERS > SHARKER
SHARKING > SHARK
SHARKINGS > SHARK
SHARKLIKE > SHARK
SHARKS > SHARK
SHARKSKIN *n* stiff glossy fabric
SHARN *Scots word for* > DUNG
SHARNIER > SHARN
SHARNIEST > SHARN
SHARNS > SHARN
SHARNY > SHARN
SHARON as in *sharon fruit* persimmon
SHARP *adj* having a keen cutting edge or fine point ▷ *adv* promptly ▷ *n* symbol raising a note one semitone above natural pitch ▷ *vb* make sharp
SHARPED > SHARP
SHARPEN *vb* make or become sharp or sharper
SHARPENED > SHARPEN
SHARPENER > SHARPEN
SHARPENS > SHARPEN
SHARPER *n* person who cheats
SHARPERS > SHARPER
SHARPEST > SHARP
SHARPIE *n* member of a teenage group having short hair and distinctive clothes
SHARPIES > SHARPIE
SHARPING > SHARP
SHARPINGS > SHARP
SHARPISH *adj* fairly sharp ▷ *adv* promptly
SHARPLY > SHARP
SHARPNESS > SHARP
SHARPS > SHARP
SHARPY *n* swindler
SHASH *vb* old form of sash
SHASHED > SHASH
SHASHES > SHASH
SHASHING > SHASH
SHASHLICK *same as* > SHASHLIK
SHASHLIK *n* type of kebab
SHASHLIKS > SHASHLIK
SHASLIK *n* type of kebab
SHASLIKS > SHASLIK
SHASTER *same as* > SHASTRA
SHASTERS > SHASTER
SHASTRA *n* any of the sacred writings of Hinduism
SHASTRAS > SHASTRA
SHAT *past tense and past participle of* > SHIT
SHATTER *vb* break into pieces ▷ *n* fragment
SHATTERED *adj* completely exhausted
SHATTERER > SHATTER
SHATTERS > SHATTER
SHATTERY *adj* liable to shatter
SHAUCHLE *vb* Scots word meaning shuffle
SHAUCHLED > SHAUCHLE
SHAUCHLES > SHAUCHLE
SHAUCHLY > SHAUCHLE
SHAUGH *n* old word meaning small wood
SHAUGHS > SHAUGH
SHAUL *vb* old form of shawl
SHAULED > SHAUL
SHAULING > SHAUL
SHAULS > SHAUL
SHAVABLE > SHAVE
SHAVE *vb* remove (hair) from (the face, head, or body) with a razor or shaver ▷ *n* shaving
SHAVEABLE > SHAVE
SHAVED > SHAVE
SHAVELING *n* derogatory term for a priest or clergyman with a shaven head
SHAVEN *adj* closely shaved or tonsured
SHAVER *n* electric razor
SHAVERS > SHAVER
SHAVES > SHAUL
SHAVETAIL *n* American slang for second lieutenant
SHAVIE *n* Scots word meaning trick
SHAVIES > SHAVIE
SHAVING > SHAVE
SHAVINGS > SHAVE
SHAW *n* small wood ▷ *vb* show
SHAWED > SHAW
SHAWING > SHAW
SHAWL *n* piece of cloth worn over a woman's shoulders or wrapped around a baby ▷ *vb* cover with a shawl
SHAWLED > SHAWL
SHAWLEY *n* Irish word for woman wearing shawl
SHAWLEYS > SHAWLEY
SHAWLIE *n* disparaging term for a working-class woman who wears a shawl
SHAWLIES > SHAWLIE
SHAWLING > SHAWL
SHAWLINGS > SHAWL
SHAWLLESS > SHAWL
SHAWLS > SHAWL
SHAWM *n* medieval form of the oboe with a conical bore and flaring bell
SHAWMS > SHAWM
SHAWN *variant of* > SHAWM
SHAWS > SHAW
SHAY *dialect word for* > CHAISE
SHAYA *n* Indian plant
SHAYAS > SHAYA
SHAYS > SHAY
SHAZAM *interj* magic slogan
SHCHI *n* Russian cabbage soup
SHCHIS > SHCHI
SHE *pron* female person or animal previously mentioned ▷ *n* female person or animal
SHEA *n* tropical African tree
SHEADING *n* any of the six subdivisions of the Isle of Man
SHEADINGS > SHEADING
SHEAF *n* bundle of papers ▷ *vb* tie into a sheaf
SHEAFED > SHEAF
SHEAFIER > SHEAF
SHEAFIEST > SHEAF
SHEAFING > SHEAF
SHEAFLIKE > SHEAF
SHEAFS > SHEAF
SHEAFY > SHEAF
SHEAL *vb* old word meaning shell
SHEALED > SHEAL
SHEALING > SHEAL
SHEALINGS > SHEAL
SHEALS > SHEAL
SHEAR *vb* clip hair or wool from ▷ *n* breakage caused through strain or twisting
SHEARED > SHEAR
SHEARER > SHEAR
SHEARERS > SHEAR
SHEARING > SHEAR
SHEARINGS > SHEAR
SHEARLEG *n* one spar of shearlegs
SHEARLEGS *same as* > SHEERLEGS
SHEARLING *n* young sheep after its first shearing
SHEARMAN *n* person who trims cloth
SHEARMEN > SHEARMAN
SHEARS > SHEAR
SHEAS > SHEA
SHEATFISH *n* European catfish
SHEATH *n* close-fitting cover, esp for a knife or sword
SHEATHE *vb* put into a sheath
SHEATHED > SHEATHE
SHEATHER > SHEATHE
SHEATHERS > SHEATHE
SHEATHES > SHEATHE
SHEATHIER > SHEATHE
SHEATHING *n* any material used as an outer layer
SHEATHS > SHEATH
SHEATHY > SHEATHE
SHEAVE *vb* gather or bind into sheaves ▷ *n* wheel with a grooved rim, esp one used as a pulley
SHEAVED > SHEAVE
SHEAVES > SHEAF
SHEAVING > SHEAVE
SHEBANG *n* situation, matter, or affair
SHEBANGS > SHEBANG
SHEBEAN *same as* > SHEBEEN
SHEBEANS > SHEBEAN
SHEBEEN *n* place where alcohol is sold illegally ▷ *vb* run a shebeen
SHEBEENED > SHEBEEN
SHEBEENER > SHEBEEN
SHEBEENS > SHEBEEN
SHECHITA *n* Jewish method of killing animal for food
SHECHITAH *same as* > SHECHITA
SHECHITAS > SHECHITA
SHED *n* building used for storage or shelter or as a workshop ▷ *vb* get rid o
SHEDABLE > SHED
SHEDDABLE > SHED
SHEDDED > SHED
SHEDDER *n* person or thin that sheds
SHEDDERS > SHEDDER
SHEDDING > SHED
SHEDDINGS > SHED
SHEDFUL *n* quantity or amount contained in a shed
SHEDFULS > SHEDFUL
SHEDLIKE > SHED
SHEDLOAD *n* very large amount or number
SHEDLOADS > SHEDLOAD
SHEDS > SHED
SHEEL *vb* old word meaning shell
SHEELED > SHEEL
SHEELING > SHEEL
SHEELS > SHEEL
SHEEN *n* glistening brightness on the surfac of something ▷ *adj* shining and beautiful ▷ give a sheen to
SHEENED > SHEEN
SHEENEY *n* offensive wor for Jew
SHEENEYS > SHEENEY
SHEENFUL > SHEEN
SHEENIE *n* offensive wor for Jew
SHEENIER > SHEEN
SHEENIES > SHEENIE
SHEENIEST > SHEEN
SHEENING > SHEEN
SHEENS > SHEEN
SHEENY > SHEEN
SHEEP *n* ruminant anima bred for wool and meat
SHEEPCOT *n* sheepcote
SHEEPCOTE *another word for* > SHEEPFOLD
SHEEPCOTS > SHEEPCOT
SHEEPDOG *n* dog used for herding sheep
SHEEPDOGS > SHEEPDOG
SHEEPFOLD *n* pen or enclosure for sheep
SHEEPHEAD *n* species of fish
SHEEPIER > SHEEP
SHEEPIEST > SHEEP
SHEEPISH *adj* embarrass because of feeling foolish
SHEEPLE *pl n* informal derogatory word for people who follow the majority in matters of opinion, taste, etc

HEEPLIKE >SHEEP
HEEPMAN *n* person who keeps sheep
HEEPMEN >SHEEPMAN
HEEPO *n* person employed to bring sheep to the catching pen in a shearing shed
HEEPOS >SHEEPO
HEEPSKIN *n* skin of a sheep with the fleece still on, used for clothing or rugs
HEEPWALK *n* tract of land for grazing sheep
HEEPY >SHEEP
HEER *adj* absolute, complete ▷ *adv* steeply ▷ *vb* change course suddenly ▷ *n* any transparent fabric used for making garments
HEERED >SHEER
HEERER >SHEER
HEEREST >SHEER
HEERING >SHEER
HEERLEG *n* one spar of sheerlegs
HEERLEGS *n* device for lifting heavy weights
HEERLY >SHEER
HEERNESS >SHEER
HEERS >SHEER
HEESH *interj* exclamation of surprise or annoyance
HEET *n* large piece of cloth used as an inner bed cover ▷ *vb* provide with, cover, or wrap in a sheet
HEETED >SHEET
HEETER >SHEET
HEETERS >SHEET
HEETFED *adj* printing on separate sheets of paper
HEETIER >SHEET
HEETIEST >SHEET
HEETING *n* material from which sheets are made
HEETINGS >SHEETING
HEETLESS >SHEET
HEETLIKE >SHEET
HEETROCK *n* brand name for plasterboard
HEETS >SHEET
HEETY >SHEET
HEEVE *n* part of mine winding gear
HEEVES >SHEEVE
HEGETZ *n* offensive word for non-Jew
HEHITA *n* slaughter of animal according to Jewish religious law
HEHITAH *n* slaughter of animal according to Jewish religious law
HEHITAHS >SHEHITAH
HEHITAS >SHEHITA
HEIK *same as* >SHEIKH
HEIKDOM *same as* >SHEIKHDOM
HEIKDOMS >SHEIKDOM
HEIKH *n* Arab chief
HEIKHA *n* chief wife of sheikh
SHEIKHAS >SHEIKHA
SHEIKHDOM *n* territory ruled by a sheikh
SHEIKHS >SHEIKH
SHEIKS >SHEIK
SHEILA *n* girl or woman
SHEILAS >SHEILA
SHEILING *n* hut used by shepherds
SHEILINGS >SHEILING
SHEITAN *n* Muslim demon
SHEITANS >SHEITAN
SHEKALIM >SHEKEL
SHEKEL *n* monetary unit of Israel
SHEKELIM >SHEKEL
SHEKELS >SHEKEL
SHELDDUCK *n* species of large duck
SHELDRAKE *same as* >SHELDUCK
SHELDUCK *n* large brightly coloured wild duck of Europe and Asia
SHELDUCKS >SHELDUCK
SHELF *n* board fixed horizontally for holding things ▷ *vb* put on a shelf
SHELFED >SHELF
SHELFFUL >SHELF
SHELFFULS >SHELF
SHELFIER >SHELF
SHELFIEST >SHELF
SHELFING >SHELF
SHELFLIKE >SHELF
SHELFROOM *n* space on shelf
SHELFS >SHELF
SHELFY >SHELF
SHELL *n* hard outer covering of an egg, nut, or certain animals ▷ *vb* take the shell from
SHELLAC *n* resin used in varnishes ▷ *vb* coat with shellac
SHELLACK *vb* shellac
SHELLACKS >SHELLAC
SHELLACS >SHELLAC
SHELLBACK *n* sailor who has crossed the equator
SHELLBARK *same as* >SHAGBARK
SHELLDUCK *n* shelduck
SHELLED >SHELL
SHELLER >SHELL
SHELLERS >SHELL
SHELLFIRE *n* firing of artillery shells
SHELLFISH *n* sea-living animal, esp one that can be eaten, with a shell
SHELLFUL >SHELL
SHELLFULS >SHELL
SHELLIER >SHELL
SHELLIEST >SHELL
SHELLING >SHELL
SHELLINGS >SHELL
SHELLS >SHELL
SHELLWORK *n* decoration with shells
SHELLY >SHELL
SHELTA *n* secret language used by some traveling people in Britain and Ireland
SHELTAS >SHELTA
SHELTER *n* structure providing protection from danger or the weather ▷ *vb* give shelter to
SHELTERED *adj* protected from wind and rain
SHELTERER >SHELTER
SHELTERS >SHELTER
SHELTERY >SHELTER
SHELTIE *n* small dog similar to a collie
SHELTIES >SHELTY
SHELTY *same as* >SHELTIE
SHELVE *vb* put aside or postpone
SHELVED >SHELVE
SHELVER >SHELVE
SHELVERS >SHELVE
SHELVES >SHELF
SHELVIER >SHELVY
SHELVIEST >SHELVY
SHELVING *n* (material for) shelves
SHELVINGS >SHELVING
SHELVY *adj* having shelves
SHEMOZZLE *n* noisy confusion or dispute
SHEND *vb* put to shame
SHENDING >SHEND
SHENDS >SHEND
SHENT >SHEND
SHEOL *n* hell
SHEOLS >SHEOL
SHEPHERD *n* person who tends sheep ▷ *vb* guide or watch over (people)
SHEPHERDS >SHEPHERD
SHEQALIM *n* plural of sheqel
SHEQEL *same as* >SHEKEL
SHEQELS >SHEQEL
SHERANG *n* person in charge
SHERANGS >SHERANG
SHERBERT *same as* >SHERBET
SHERBERTS >SHERBET
SHERBET *n* fruit-flavoured fizzy powder
SHERBETS >SHERBET
SHERD *same as* >SHARD
SHERDS >SHERD
SHERE *old spelling of* >SHEER
SHEREEF *same as* >SHERIF
SHEREEFS >SHEREEF
SHERIA *same as* >SHARIA
SHERIAS >SHERIA
SHERIAT *n* Muslim religious law
SHERIATS >SHERIAT
SHERIF *n* descendant of Mohammed through his daughter Fatima
SHERIFF *n* (in the US) chief law enforcement officer of a county
SHERIFFS >SHERIFF
SHERIFIAN >SHERIF
SHERIFS >SHERIF
SHERLOCK *n* detective
SHERLOCKS >SHERLOCK
SHEROOT *n* cheroot
SHEROOTS >SHEROOT
SHERPA *n* official who assists at a summit meeting
SHERPAS >SHERPA
SHERRIES >SHERRY
SHERRIS *n* old form of sherry
SHERRISES >SHERRIS
SHERRY *n* pale or dark brown fortified wine
SHERWANI *n* long coat closed up to the neck, worn by men in India
SHERWANIS >SHERWANI
SHES >SHE
SHET *vb* old form of shut
SHETLAND *n* type of wool spun in the Shetland islands
SHETLANDS >SHETLAND
SHETS >SHET
SHETTING >SHET
SHEUCH *n* ditch or trough ▷ *vb* dig
SHEUCHED >SHEUCH
SHEUCHING >SHEUCH
SHEUCHS >SHEUCH
SHEUGH *same as* >SHEUCH
SHEUGHED >SHEUGH
SHEUGHING >SHEUGH
SHEUGHS >SHEUGH
SHEVA *n* mark in Hebrew writing
SHEVAS >SHEVA
SHEW *archaic spelling of* >SHOW
SHEWBREAD *n* loaves of bread placed every Sabbath on the table beside the altar of incense in the tabernacle of ancient Israel
SHEWED >SHEW
SHEWEL *n* old word meaning scarecrow
SHEWELS >SHEWEL
SHEWER >SHEW
SHEWERS >SHEW
SHEWING >SHEW
SHEWN >SHEW
SHEWS >SHEW
SHH *interj* sound made to ask for silence
SHIAI *n* judo contest
SHIAIS >SHIAI
SHIATSU *n* massage in which pressure is applied to the same points of the body as in acupuncture
SHIATSUS >SHIATSU
SHIATZU *n* shiatzu
SHIATZUS >SHIATZU
SHIBAH *n* Jewish period of mourning
SHIBAHS >SHIBAH
SHIBUICHI *n* Japanese alloy of copper and silver
SHICKER *n* alcoholic drink
SHICKERED *adj* drunk
SHICKERS >SHICKER
SHICKSA *n* non-Jewish girl

SHICKSAS > SHICKSA
SHIDDER *n* old word meaning female animal
SHIDDERS > SHIDDER
SHIDDUCH *n* arranged marriage
SHIED > SHY
SHIEL *vb* sheal
SHIELD *n* piece of armour carried on the arm to protect the body from blows or missiles ▷ *vb* protect
SHIELDED > SHIELD
SHIELDER > SHIELD
SHIELDERS > SHIELD
SHIELDING > SHIELD
SHIELDS > SHIELD
SHIELED > SHIEL
SHIELING *n* rough hut or shelter used by people tending cattle on high or remote ground
SHIELINGS > SHIELING
SHIELS > SHIEL
SHIER *n* horse that shies habitually
SHIERS > SHIER
SHIES > SHY
SHIEST > SHY
SHIFT *vb* move ▷ *n* shifting
SHIFTABLE > SHIFT
SHIFTED > SHIFT
SHIFTER > SHIFT
SHIFTERS > SHIFT
SHIFTIER > SHIFTY
SHIFTIEST > SHIFTY
SHIFTILY > SHIFTY
SHIFTING > SHIFT
SHIFTINGS > SHIFT
SHIFTLESS *adj* lacking in ambition or initiative
SHIFTS > SHIFT
SHIFTWORK *n* system of employment where an individual's normal hours of work are outside the period of normal day working
SHIFTY *adj* evasive or untrustworthy
SHIGELLA *n* any rod-shaped Gram-negative bacterium of the genus *Shigella*
SHIGELLAE > SHIGELLA
SHIGELLAS > SHIGELLA
SHIITAKE *n* kind of mushroom widely used in Oriental cookery
SHIITAKES > SHIITAKE
SHIKAR *n* hunting, esp big-game hunting ▷ *vb* hunt (game, esp big game)
SHIKAREE *same as* > SHIKARI
SHIKAREES > SHIKAREE
SHIKARI *n* (in India) a hunter
SHIKARIS > SHIKARI
SHIKARRED > SHIKAR
SHIKARS > SHIKAR
SHIKKER *n* Yiddish term for drunk person
SHIKKERS > SHIKKER
SHIKSA *n* often derogatory term for a non-Jewish girl
SHIKSAS > SHIKSA
SHIKSE *n* non-Jewish girl
SHIKSEH *same as* > SHIKSE
SHIKSEHS > SHIKSEH
SHIKSES > SHIKSE
SHILINGI *n* money unit in Tanzania
SHILL *n* confidence trickster's assistant ▷ *vb* act as a shill
SHILLABER *n* keen customer
SHILLALA *n* short Irish clud or cudgel
SHILLALAH *same as* > SHILLALA
SHILLALAS > SHILLALA
SHILLED > SHILL
SHILLELAH *same as* > SHILLALA
SHILLING *n* former British coin
SHILLINGS > SHILLING
SHILLS > SHILL
SHILPIT *adj* puny
SHILY > SHY
SHIM *n* thin strip of material placed between two close surfaces to fill a gap ▷ *vb* fit or fill up with a shim
SHIMAAL *n* hot Middle Eastern wind
SHIMAALS > SHIMAAL
SHIMMED > SHIM
SHIMMER *n* (shine with) a faint unsteady light ▷ *vb* shine with a faint unsteady light
SHIMMERED > SHIMMER
SHIMMERS > SHIMMER
SHIMMERY *adj* shining with a glistening or tremulous light
SHIMMEY *n* chemise
SHIMMEYS > SHIMMEY
SHIMMIED > SHIMMY
SHIMMIES > SHIMMY
SHIMMING > SHIM
SHIMMY *n* American ragtime dance with much shaking of the hips and shoulders ▷ *vb* dance the shimmy
SHIMMYING > SHIMMY
SHIMOZZLE *n* predicament
SHIMS > SHIM
SHIN *n* front of the lower leg ▷ *vb* climb by using the hands or arms and legs
SHINBONE *n* tibia
SHINBONES > SHINBONE
SHINDIES > SHINDY
SHINDIG *n* noisy party
SHINDIGS > SHINDIG
SHINDY *n* quarrel or commotion
SHINDYS > SHINDY
SHINE *vb* give out or reflect light; cause to gleam ▷ *n* brightness or lustre
SHINED > SHINE
SHINELESS > SHINE
SHINER *n* black eye
SHINERS > SHINER
SHINES > SHINE
SHINESS > SHY
SHINESSES > SHY
SHINGLE *n* wooden roof tile ▷ *vb* cover (a roof) with shingles
SHINGLED > SHINGLE
SHINGLER > SHINGLE
SHINGLERS > SHINGLE
SHINGLES *n* disease causing a rash of small blisters along a nerve
SHINGLIER > SHINGLE
SHINGLING > SHINGLE
SHINGLY > SHINGLE
SHINGUARD *n* rigid piece of plastic to protect footballer's shin
SHINIER > SHINY
SHINIES > SHINY
SHINIEST > SHINY
SHINILY > SHINY
SHININESS > SHINY
SHINING > SHINE
SHININGLY > SHINE
SHINJU *n* (formerly, in Japan) a ritual double suicide of lovers
SHINJUS > SHINJU
SHINKIN *n* worthless person
SHINKINS > SHINKIN
SHINLEAF *n* wintergreen
SHINLEAFS > SHINLEAF
SHINNE *n* old form of chin
SHINNED > SHIN
SHINNERY *n* American oak tree
SHINNES > SHINNE
SHINNEY *vb* climb with hands and legs
SHINNEYED > SHINNEY
SHINNEYS > SHINNEY
SHINNIED > SHINNY
SHINNIES > SHINNY
SHINNING > SHIN
SHINNY *same as* > SHINTY
SHINNYING > SHINNY
SHINS > SHIN
SHINTIED > SHINTY
SHINTIES > SHINTY
SHINTY *n* game like hockey ▷ *vb* play shinty
SHINTYING > SHINTY
SHINY *adj* bright and polished
SHIP *n* large seagoing vessel ▷ *vb* send or transport by carrier, esp a ship
SHIPBOARD *adj* taking place or used aboard a ship
SHIPBORNE *adj* carried on ship
SHIPFUL *n* amount carried by ship
SHIPFULS > SHIPFUL
SHIPLAP *n* method of constructing ship hull
SHIPLAPS > SHIPLAP
SHIPLESS > SHIP
SHIPLOAD *n* quantity carried by a ship
SHIPLOADS > SHIPLOAD
SHIPMAN *n* master or captain of a ship
SHIPMATE *n* sailor serving on the same ship as another
SHIPMATES > SHIPMATE
SHIPMEN > SHIPMAN
SHIPMENT *n* act of shipping cargo
SHIPMENTS > SHIPMENT
SHIPOWNER *n* person who owns or has shares in a ship or ships
SHIPPABLE > SHIP
SHIPPED > SHIP
SHIPPEN *n* dialect word for cattle shed
SHIPPENS > SHIPPEN
SHIPPER *n* person or company that ships
SHIPPERS > SHIPPER
SHIPPIE *n* prostitute who solicits at a port
SHIPPIES > SHIPPIE
SHIPPING > SHIP
SHIPPINGS > SHIP
SHIPPO *n* Japanese enamel work
SHIPPON *n* dialect word for cattle shed
SHIPPONS > SHIPPON
SHIPPOS > SHIPPO
SHIPPOUND *n* Baltic weight measure
SHIPS > SHIP
SHIPSHAPE *adj* orderly or neat ▷ *adv* in a neat and orderly manner
SHIPSIDE *n* part of wharf next to ship
SHIPSIDES > SHIPSIDE
SHIPWAY *n* structure on which a vessel is built, then launched
SHIPWAYS > SHIPWAY
SHIPWORM *n* any wormlike marine bivalve mollusc of the genus *Teredo*
SHIPWORMS > SHIPWORM
SHIPWRECK *n* destruction of a ship through storm or collision ▷ *vb* cause to undergo shipwreck
SHIPYARD *n* place where ships are built
SHIPYARDS > SHIPYARD
SHIR *n* gathering in material
SHIRALEE *n* swag
SHIRALEES > SHIRALEE
SHIRE *n* county ▷ *vb* refresh or rest
SHIRED > SHIRE
SHIREMAN *n* sheriff
SHIREMEN > SHIREMAN
SHIRES > SHIRE
SHIRING > SHIRE
SHIRK *vb* avoid (duty or work) ▷ *n* person who shirks

HIRKED >SHIRK
HIRKER >SHIRK
HIRKERS >SHIRK
HIRKING >SHIRK
HIRKS >SHIRK
HIRR *vb* gather (fabric) into two or more parallel rows to decorate a dress, etc ▷*n* series of gathered rows decorating a dress, blouse, etc
HIRRA *old Scots word for* >SHERIFF
HIRRALEE *n* swagman's bundle of possessions
HIRRAS >SHIRRA
HIRRED >SHIRR
HIRRING >SHIRR
HIRRINGS >SHIRR
HIRRS >SHIRR
HIRS >SHIR
HIRT *n* garment for the upper part of the body ▷*vb* put a shirt on
HIRTBAND *n* neckband on shirt
HIRTED >SHIRT
HIRTIER >SHIRTY
HIRTIEST >SHIRTY
HIRTILY >SHIRTY
HIRTING *n* fabric used in making men's shirts
HIRTINGS >SHIRTING
HIRTLESS >SHIRT
HIRTS >SHIRT
HIRTTAIL *n* part of a shirt that extends below the waist
HIRTY *adj* bad-tempered or annoyed
HISH as in *shish kebab* dish of meat and vegetables threaded onto skewers and grilled
HISHA *same as* >HOOKAH
HISHAS >SHISHA
HISO *n* Asian plant with aromatic leaves that are used in cooking
HISOS >SHISO
HIST *n* schist
HISTS >SHIST
HIT *taboo vb* defecate ▷*n* excrement ▷*interj* exclamation of anger or disgust
HITAKE *same as* >SHIITAKE
HITAKES >SHITAKE
HITE *same as* >SHIT
HITED >SHITE
HITES >SHITE
HITFACED *adj* drunk
HITHEAD *n taboo slang* fool
HITHEADS >SHITHEAD
HITHOLE *n* dirty place
HITHOLES >SHITHOLE
HITING >SHITE
HITLESS *adj* very frightened
HITLIST *n* list of hated things
HITLISTS >SHITLIST
HITLOAD *n* taboo slang for a lot
SHITLOADS >SHITLOAD
SHITS >SHIT
SHITTAH *n* tree mentioned in the Old Testament
SHITTAHS >SHITTAH
SHITTED >SHIT
SHITTIER >SHIT
SHITTIEST >SHIT
SHITTILY >SHIT
SHITTIM >SHITTAH
SHITTIMS >SHITTAH
SHITTING >SHIT
SHITTY >SHIT
SHIUR *n* lesson in which a passage of the Talmud is studied together by a group of people
SHIURIM >SHIUR
SHIV *variant spelling of* >CHIV
SHIVA *variant of* >SHIVAH
SHIVAH *n* Jewish period of formal mourning
SHIVAHS >SHIVAH
SHIVAREE *n* discordant mock serenade to newlyweds, made with pans, kettles, etc
SHIVAREED >SHIVAREE
SHIVAREES >SHIVAREE
SHIVAS >SHIVA
SHIVE *n* flat cork or bung for wide-mouthed bottles
SHIVER *vb* tremble, as from cold or fear ▷*n* shivering
SHIVERED >SHIVER
SHIVERER >SHIVER
SHIVERERS >SHIVER
SHIVERIER >SHIVERY
SHIVERING >SHIVER
SHIVERS >SHIVER
SHIVERY *adj* inclined to shiver or tremble
SHIVES >SHIVE
SHIVITI *n* Jewish decorative plaque with religious message
SHIVITIS >SHIVITI
SHIVOO *n* Australian word meaning rowdy party
SHIVOOS >SHIVOO
SHIVS >SHIV
SHIVVED >SHIV
SHIVVING >SHIV
SHKOTZIM *n* plural of shegetz
SHLEMIEHL *Yiddish word for* >FOOL
SHLEMIEL *same as* >SCHLEMIEL
SHLEMIELS >SHLEMIEL
SHLEP *vb* schlep
SHLEPP *vb* schlep
SHLEPPED >SHLEP
SHLEPPER >SHLEP
SHLEPPERS >SHLEP
SHLEPPING >SHLEP
SHLEPPS >SHLEPP
SHLEPS >SHLEP
SHLIMAZEL *n* unlucky person
SHLOCK *n* something of poor quality
SHLOCKIER >SHLOCK
SHLOCKS >SHLOCK
SHLOCKY >SHLOCK
SHLOSHIM *n* period of thirty days' deep mourning following a death
SHLOSHIMS >SHLOSHIM
SHLUB *same as* >SCHLUB
SHLUBS >SHLUB
SHLUMP *vb* move in lazy way
SHLUMPED >SHLUMP
SHLUMPING >SHLUMP
SHLUMPS >SHLUMP
SHLUMPY >SHLUMP
SHMALTZ *n* schmaltz
SHMALTZES >SHMALTZ
SHMALTZY >SHMALTZ
SHMATTE *n* rag
SHMATTES >SHMATTE
SHMEAR *n* set of things
SHMEARS >SHMEAR
SHMEK *n* smell
SHMEKS >SHMEK
SHMO *same as* >SCHMO
SHMOCK *n* despicable person
SHMOCKS >SHMOCK
SHMOES >SHMO
SHMOOSE *variant of* >SCHMOOZE
SHMOOSED >SHMOOSE
SHMOOSES >SHMOOSE
SHMOOSING >SHMOOSE
SHMOOZE *variant of* >SCHMOOZE
SHMOOZED >SHMOOZE
SHMOOZES >SHMOOZE
SHMOOZING >SHMOOZE
SHMUCK *n* despicable person
SHMUCKS >SCHMUCK
SHNAPPS *same as* >SCHNAPPS
SHNAPS *n* schnaps
SHNOOK *n* stupid person
SHNOOKS >SHNOOK
SHNORRER *same as* >SCHNORRER
SHNORRERS >SHNORRER
SHOAL *n* large number of fish swimming together ▷*vb* make or become shallow ▷*adj* (of the draught of a vessel) drawing little water
SHOALED >SHOAL
SHOALER >SHOAL
SHOALEST >SHOAL
SHOALIER >SHOALY
SHOALIEST >SHOALY
SHOALING >SHOAL
SHOALINGS >SHOAL
SHOALNESS >SHOAL
SHOALS >SHOAL
SHOALWISE *adv* in a large group or in large groups
SHOALY *adj* shallow
SHOAT *n* piglet that has recently been weaned
SHOATS >SHOAT
SHOCHET *n* (in Judaism) a person who has been specially trained and licensed to slaughter animals and birds in accordance with the laws of shechita
SHOCHETIM >SHOCHET
SHOCHETS >SHOCHET
SHOCK *vb* horrify, disgust, or astonish ▷*n* sudden violent emotional disturbance ▷*adj* bushy
SHOCKABLE >SHOCK
SHOCKED >SHOCK
SHOCKER *n* person or thing that shocks or horrifies
SHOCKERS >SHOCKER
SHOCKING *adj* causing horror, disgust, or astonishment
SHOCKS >SHOCK
SHOD >SHOE
SHODDEN *vb* old form of shod
SHODDIER >SHODDY
SHODDIES >SHODDY
SHODDIEST >SHODDY
SHODDILY >SHODDY
SHODDY *adj* made or done badly ▷*n* yarn or fabric made from wool waste or clippings
SHODER *n* skins used in making gold leaf
SHODERS >SHODER
SHOE *n* outer covering for the foot, ending below the ankle ▷*vb* fit with a shoe or shoes
SHOEBILL *n* large wading bird of tropical E African swamps
SHOEBILLS >SHOEBILL
SHOEBLACK *n* (esp formerly) a person who shines boots and shoes
SHOEBOX *n* cardboard box for shoes
SHOEBOXES >SHOEBOX
SHOED >SHOE
SHOEHORN *n* smooth curved implement inserted at the heel of a shoe to ease the foot into it ▷*vb* cram (people or things) into a very small space
SHOEHORNS >SHOEHORN
SHOEING >SHOE
SHOEINGS >SHOE
SHOELACE *n* cord for fastening shoes
SHOELACES >SHOELACE
SHOELESS >SHOE
SHOEMAKER *n* person who makes or repairs shoes or boots
SHOEPAC *n* waterproof boot
SHOEPACK *n* waterproof boot
SHOEPACKS >SHOEPACK
SHOEPACS >SHOEPAC
SHOER *n* person who shoes horses
SHOERS >SHOER
SHOES >SHOE

SHOESHINE *n* act or an instance of polishing a pair of shoes
SHOETREE *n* piece of metal, wood, or plastic inserted in a shoe to keep its shape
SHOETREES > SHOETREE
SHOFAR *n* ram's horn sounded in the synagogue daily during the month of Elul and repeatedly on Rosh Hashanah
SHOFARS > SHOFAR
SHOFROTH > SHOFAR
SHOG *vb* shake
SHOGGED > SHOG
SHOGGING > SHOG
SHOGGLE *vb* shake
SHOGGLED > SHOGGLE
SHOGGLES > SHOGGLE
SHOGGLIER > SHOGGLE
SHOGGLING > SHOGGLE
SHOGGLY > SHOGGLE
SHOGI *n* Japanese chess
SHOGIS > SHOGI
SHOGS > SHOG
SHOGUN *n* Japanese chief military commander
SHOGUNAL > SHOGUN
SHOGUNATE *n* office or rule of a shogun
SHOGUNS > SHOGUN
SHOJI *n* Japanese rice-paper screen in a sliding wooden frame
SHOJIS > SHOJI
SHOLA *n* Indian plant
SHOLAS > SHOLA
SHOLOM *n* Hebrew greeting
SHOLOMS > SHOLOM
SHONE > SHINE
SHONEEN *n* Irishman who imitates English ways
SHONEENS > SHONEEN
SHONKIER > SHONKY
SHONKIEST > SHONKY
SHONKY *adj* unreliable or unsound
SHOO *interj* go away! ▷ *vb* drive away as by saying 'shoo'
SHOOED > SHOO
SHOOFLIES > SHOOFLY
SHOOFLY as in *shoofly pie* US dessert similar to treacle tart
SHOOGIE *vb* Scots word meaning swing
SHOOGIED > SHOOGIE
SHOOGIES > SHOOGIE
SHOOGLE *vb* shake, sway, or rock back and forth ▷ *n* rocking motion
SHOOGLED > SHOOGLE
SHOOGLES > SHOOGLE
SHOOGLIER > SHOOGLE
SHOOGLING > SHOOGLE
SHOOGLY > SHOOGLE
SHOOING > SHOO
SHOOK *n* set of parts ready for assembly
SHOOKS > SHOOK
SHOOL *dialect word for* > SHOVEL
SHOOLE *dialect word for* > SHOVEL
SHOOLED > SHOOL
SHOOLES > SHOOLE
SHOOLING > SHOOL
SHOOLS > SHOOL
SHOON *plural of* > SHOE
SHOORA *same as* > SHURA
SHOORAS > SHOORA
SHOOS > SHOO
SHOOT *vb* hit, wound, or kill with a missile fired from a weapon ▷ *n* new branch or sprout of a plant
SHOOTABLE > SHOOT
SHOOTDOWN *n* act of shooting down aircraft
SHOOTER *n* person or thing that shoots
SHOOTERS > SHOOTER
SHOOTING > SHOOT
SHOOTINGS > SHOOT
SHOOTIST *n* person who shoots
SHOOTISTS > SHOOTIST
SHOOTOUT *n* conclusive gunfight
SHOOTOUTS > SHOOTOUT
SHOOTS > SHOOT
SHOP *n* place for sale of goods and services ▷ *vb* visit a shop or shops to buy goods
SHOPBOARD *n* shop counter
SHOPBOY *n* boy working in shop
SHOPBOYS > SHOPBOY
SHOPE *n* old form of shape
SHOPFRONT *n* area of shop facing street
SHOPFUL *n* amount stored in shop
SHOPFULS > SHOPFUL
SHOPGIRL *n* girl working in shop
SHOPGIRLS > SHOPGIRL
SHOPHAR *same as* > SHOFAR
SHOPHARS > SHOPHAR
SHOPHROTH > SHOPHAR
SHOPLIFT *vb* steal from shop
SHOPLIFTS > SHOPLIFT
SHOPMAN *n* man working in shop
SHOPMEN > SHOPMAN
SHOPPE *old-fashioned spelling of* > SHOP
SHOPPED > SHOP
SHOPPER *n* person who buys goods in a shop
SHOPPERS > SHOPPER
SHOPPES > SHOPPE
SHOPPIER > SHOPPY
SHOPPIEST > SHOPPY
SHOPPING > SHOP
SHOPPINGS > SHOP
SHOPPY *adj* of a shop
SHOPS > SHOP
SHOPTALK *n* conversation about one's work, carried on outside working hours
SHOPTALKS > SHOPTALK
SHOPWORN *adj* worn or faded from being displayed in a shop
SHORAN *n* short-range radar system
SHORANS > SHORAN
SHORE *n* edge of a sea or lake ▷ *vb* prop or support
SHOREBIRD *n* bird that lives close to the water
SHORED > SHORE
SHORELESS *adj* without a shore suitable for landing
SHORELINE *n* edge of a sea, lake, or wide river
SHOREMAN *n* person who lives on shore
SHOREMEN > SHOREMAN
SHORER > SHORE
SHORERS > SHORE
SHORES > SHORE
SHORESIDE *n* area at shore
SHORESMAN *n* fishing industry worker on shore
SHORESMEN > SHORESMAN
SHOREWARD *adj* near or facing the shore ▷ *adv* towards the shore
SHOREWEED *n* tufty aquatic perennial plant
SHORING > SHORE
SHORINGS > SHORE
SHORL *n* black mineral
SHORLS > SHORL
SHORN *past participle of* > SHEAR
SHORT *adj* not long ▷ *adv* abruptly ▷ *n* drink of spirits ▷ *vb* short-circuit
SHORTAGE *n* deficiency
SHORTAGES > SHORTAGE
SHORTARM *adj* (of a punch) with the arm bent
SHORTCAKE *n* shortbread
SHORTCUT *n* route that is shorter than the usual one
SHORTCUTS > SHORTCUT
SHORTED > SHORT
SHORTEN *vb* make or become shorter
SHORTENED > SHORTEN
SHORTENER > SHORTEN
SHORTENS > SHORTEN
SHORTER > SHORT
SHORTEST > SHORT
SHORTFALL *n* deficit
SHORTGOWN *n* old Scots word meaning woman's jacket
SHORTHAIR *n* cat with short fur
SHORTHAND *n* system of rapid writing using symbols to represent words
SHORTHEAD *n* species of fish
SHORTHOLD *n* as in *shorthold tenancy* letting of a dwelling for between one and five years at a fair rent
SHORTHORN *n* member of a breed of cattle with short horns
SHORTIA *n* American flowering plant
SHORTIAS > SHORTIA
SHORTIE *n* person or thin[g] that is extremely short
SHORTIES > SHORTY
SHORTING > SHORT
SHORTISH > SHORT
SHORTLIST *n* list of suitable applicants for a job, etc
SHORTLY *adv* soon
SHORTNESS > SHORT
SHORTS *pl n* trousers reaching the top of the thigh or partway to the knee
SHORTSTOP *n* fielding position to the left of second base viewed from home plate
SHORTWAVE *n* radio wave with a wavelength in the range 10–100 metres
SHORTY *same as* > SHORTIE
SHOT *vb* load with shot
SHOTE *same as* > SHOAT
SHOTES > SHOTE
SHOTFIRER *n* person detonating blasting charge
SHOTGUN *n* gun for firing a charge of shot at short range ▷ *adj* involving coercion or duress ▷ *vb* shoot or threaten with or as if with a shotgun
SHOTGUNS > SHOTGUN
SHOTHOLE *n* drilled hole i[n]to which explosive is put for blasting
SHOTHOLES > SHOTHOLE
SHOTMAKER *n* sport player making good shots
SHOTPROOF *adj* able to withstand shot
SHOTPUT *n* athletic event which a heavy metal ball thrown
SHOTPUTS > SHOTPUT
SHOTS > SHOT
SHOTT *n* shallow tempora[ry] salt lake or marsh in the North African desert
SHOTTE *n* old form of shoa[t]
SHOTTED > SHOT
SHOTTEN *adj* (of fish, esp herring) having recently spawned
SHOTTES > SHOTTE
SHOTTING > SHOT
SHOTTLE *n* small drawer
SHOTTLES > SHOTTLE
SHOTTS > SHOTT
SHOUGH *n* old word meaning lapdog
SHOUGHS > SHOUGH
SHOULD > SHALL
SHOULDER *n* part of the body to which an arm, foreleg, or wing is attached ▷ *vb* bear (a burden or responsibility)
SHOULDERS > SHOULDER
SHOULDEST *same as* > SHOULDST

OULDST *form of the past* *ense of* > SHALL
OUSE *n* toilet ▷ *adj* unwell or in poor spirits
OUSES > SHOUSE
OUT *n* loud cry ▷ *vb* cry out loudly
OUTED > SHOUT
OUTER > SHOUT
OUTERS > SHOUT
OUTHER *Scots form* *f* > SHOULDER
OUTHERS > SHOUTHER
OUTIER > SHOUTY
OUTIEST > SHOUTY
OUTING > SHOUT
OUTINGS > SHOUT
OUTLINE *n* line in advertisement made prominent to catch attention
OUTS > SHOUT
OUTY *adj* characterized by or involving shouting
OVE *vb* push roughly ▷ *n* rough push
OVED > SHOVE
OVEL *n* tool for lifting or moving loose material ▷ *vb* lift or move as with a shovel
OVELED > SHOVEL
OVELER *n* type of duck
OVELERS > SHOVELER
OVELFUL > SHOVEL
OVELING > SHOVEL
OVELLED > SHOVEL
OVELLER > SHOVEL
OVELS > SHOVEL
OVER > SHOVE
OVERS > SHOVE
OVES > SHOVE
OVING *n* act of pushing hard
OVINGS > SHOVING
OW *vb* make, be, or become noticeable or visible ▷ *n* public exhibition
OWABLE > SHOW
OWBIZ *n* entertainment industry including theatre, films, and TV
OWBIZZY > SHOWBIZ
OWBOAT *n* paddle-wheel river steamer with a theatre and a repertory company ▷ *vb* perform or behave in a showy and flamboyant way
OWBOATS > SHOWBOAT
OWBOX *n* box containing showman's material
OWBOXES > SHOWBOX
OWBREAD *same* *s* > SHEWBREAD
OWCASE *n* situation in which something is displayed to best advantage ▷ *vb* exhibit or display ▷ *adj* displayed or meriting display as in a showcase
OWCASED > SHOWCASE
SHOWCASES > SHOWCASE
SHOWD *vb* rock or sway to and fro ▷ *n* rocking motion
SHOWDED > SHOWD
SHOWDING > SHOWD
SHOWDOWN *n* confrontation that settles a dispute
SHOWDOWNS > SHOWDOWN
SHOWDS > SHOWD
SHOWED > SHOW
SHOWER *n* kind of bath in which a person stands while being sprayed with water ▷ *vb* wash in a shower
SHOWERED > SHOWER
SHOWERER > SHOWER
SHOWERERS > SHOWER
SHOWERFUL > SHOWER
SHOWERIER > SHOWER
SHOWERING > SHOWER
SHOWERS > SHOWER
SHOWERY > SHOWER
SHOWGHE *n* old word meaning lapdog
SHOWGHES > SHOWGHE
SHOWGIRL *n* girl who appears in shows, etc, esp as a singer or dancer
SHOWGIRLS > SHOWGIRL
SHOWIER > SHOWY
SHOWIEST > SHOWY
SHOWILY > SHOWY
SHOWINESS > SHOWY
SHOWING > SHOW
SHOWINGS > SHOW
SHOWMAN *n* man skilled at presenting anything spectacularly
SHOWMANLY > SHOWMAN
SHOWMEN > SHOWMAN
SHOWN > SHOW
SHOWOFF *n* person who makes a vain display of himself or herself
SHOWOFFS > SHOWOFF
SHOWPIECE *n* excellent specimen shown for display or as an example
SHOWPLACE *n* place visited for its beauty or interest
SHOWRING *n* area where animals are displayed for sale or competition
SHOWRINGS > SHOWRING
SHOWROOM *n* room in which goods for sale are on display
SHOWROOMS > SHOWROOM
SHOWS > SHOW
SHOWTIME *n* time when show begins
SHOWTIMES > SHOWTIME
SHOWY *adj* gaudy
SHOWYARD *n* yard where cattle are displayed
SHOWYARDS > SHOWYARD
SHOYU *n* Japanese variety of soy sauce
SHOYUS > SHOYU
SHRADDHA *n* Hindu offering to an ancestor
SHRADDHAS > SHRADDHA
SHRANK > SHRINK
SHRAPNEL *n* artillery shell filled with pellets which scatter on explosion
SHRAPNELS > SHRAPNEL
SHRED *n* long narrow strip torn from something ▷ *vb* tear to shreds
SHREDDED > SHRED
SHREDDER > SHRED
SHREDDERS > SHRED
SHREDDIER > SHRED
SHREDDING > SHRED
SHREDDY > SHRED
SHREDLESS > SHRED
SHREDS > SHRED
SHREEK *old spelling of* > SHRIEK
SHREEKED > SHREEK
SHREEKING > SHREEK
SHREEKS > SHREEK
SHREIK *old spelling of* > SHRIEK
SHREIKED > SHREIK
SHREIKING > SHREIK
SHREIKS > SHREIK
SHREW *n* small mouselike animal ▷ *vb* curse or damn
SHREWD *adj* clever and perceptive
SHREWDER > SHREWD
SHREWDEST > SHREWD
SHREWDIE *n* shrewd person
SHREWDIES > SHREWDIE
SHREWDLY > SHREWD
SHREWED > SHREW
SHREWING > SHREW
SHREWISH *adj* (esp of a woman) bad-tempered and nagging
SHREWLIKE > SHREW
SHREWMICE *pl n* shrews
SHREWS > SHREW
SHRI *n* Indian title of respect
SHRIECH *old spelling of* > SHRIEK
SHRIECHED > SHRIECH
SHRIECHES > SHRIECH
SHRIEK *n* shrill cry ▷ *vb* utter (with) a shriek
SHRIEKED > SHRIEK
SHRIEKER > SHRIEK
SHRIEKERS > SHRIEK
SHRIEKIER > SHRIEK
SHRIEKING > SHRIEK
SHRIEKS > SHRIEK
SHRIEKY > SHRIEK
SHRIEVAL *adj* of or relating to a sheriff
SHRIEVE *archaic word for* > SHERIFF
SHRIEVED > SHRIEVE
SHRIEVES > SHRIEVE
SHRIEVING > SHRIEVE
SHRIFT *n* act or an instance of shriving or being shriven
SHRIFTS > SHRIFT
SHRIGHT *n* old word meaning shriek
SHRIGHTS > SHRIGHT
SHRIKE *n* songbird with a heavy hooked bill ▷ *vb* archaic word for shriek
SHRIKED > SHRIKE
SHRIKES > SHRIKE
SHRIKING > SHRIKE
SHRILL *adj* (of a sound) sharp and high-pitched ▷ *vb* utter shrilly
SHRILLED > SHRILL
SHRILLER > SHRILL
SHRILLEST > SHRILL
SHRILLIER > SHRILL
SHRILLING > SHRILL
SHRILLS > SHRILL
SHRILLY > SHRILL
SHRIMP *n* small edible shellfish ▷ *vb* fish for shrimps
SHRIMPED > SHRIMP
SHRIMPER > SHRIMP
SHRIMPERS > SHRIMP
SHRIMPIER > SHRIMP
SHRIMPING > SHRIMP
SHRIMPS > SHRIMP
SHRIMPY > SHRIMP
SHRINAL > SHRINE
SHRINE *n* place of worship associated with a sacred person or object ▷ *vb* enshrine
SHRINED > SHRINE
SHRINES > SHRINE
SHRINING > SHRINE
SHRINK *vb* become or make smaller ▷ *n* psychiatrist
SHRINKAGE *n* decrease in size, value, or weight
SHRINKER > SHRINK
SHRINKERS > SHRINK
SHRINKING > SHRINK
SHRINKS > SHRINK
SHRIS > SHRI
SHRITCH *vb* old word meaning shriek
SHRITCHED > SHRITCH
SHRITCHES > SHRITCH
SHRIVE *vb* hear the confession of (a penitent)
SHRIVED > SHRIVE
SHRIVEL *vb* shrink and wither
SHRIVELED > SHRIVEL
SHRIVELS > SHRIVEL
SHRIVEN > SHRIVE
SHRIVER > SHRIVE
SHRIVERS > SHRIVE
SHRIVES > SHRIVE
SHRIVING > SHRIVE
SHRIVINGS > SHRIVE
SHROFF *n* (in China and Japan) expert employed to separate counterfeit money from the genuine ▷ *vb* test (money) and separate out the counterfeit and base
SHROFFAGE > SHROFF
SHROFFED > SHROFF
SHROFFING > SHROFF
SHROFFS > SHROFF
SHROOM *n* slang for magic mushroom ▷ *vb* take magic mushrooms
SHROOMED > SHROOM

SHROOMER > SHROOM
SHROOMERS > SHROOM
SHROOMING > SHROOM
SHROOMS > SHROOM
SHROUD *n* piece of cloth used to wrap a dead body ▷ *vb* conceal
SHROUDED > SHROUD
SHROUDIER > SHROUD
SHROUDING > SHROUD
SHROUDS > SHROUD
SHROUDY > SHROUD
SHROVE *vb* dialect word meaning to observe Shrove-tide
SHROVED > SHROVE
SHROVES > SHROVE
SHROVING > SHROVE
SHROW *vb* old form of shrew
SHROWD *adj* old form of shrewd
SHROWED > SHROW
SHROWING > SHROW
SHROWS > SHROW
SHRUB *n* woody plant smaller than a tree ▷ *vb* plant shrubs
SHRUBBED > SHRUB
SHRUBBERY *n* area planted with shrubs
SHRUBBIER > SHRUBBY
SHRUBBING > SHRUB
SHRUBBY *adj* consisting of, planted with, or abounding in shrubs
SHRUBLAND *n* land covered by shrubs
SHRUBLESS > SHRUB
SHRUBLIKE > SHRUB
SHRUBS > SHRUB
SHRUG *vb* raise and then drop (the shoulders) as a sign of indifference or doubt ▷ *n* shrugging
SHRUGGED > SHRUG
SHRUGGING > SHRUG
SHRUGS > SHRUG
SHRUNK > SHRINK
SHRUNKEN *adj* reduced in size
SHTCHI *n* Russian cabbage soup
SHTCHIS > SHTCHI
SHTETEL *n* Jewish community in Eastern Europe
SHTETELS > SHTETEL
SHTETL *n* (formerly) a small Jewish community in Eastern Europe
SHTETLACH > SHTETL
SHTETLS > SHTETL
SHTICK *n* comedian's routine
SHTICKIER > SHTICK
SHTICKS > SHTICK
SHTICKY > SHTICK
SHTIK *n* shtick
SHTIKS > SHTIK
SHTOOK *n* trouble
SHTOOKS > SHTOOK
SHTOOM *adj* silent
SHTUCK *n* trouble
SHTUCKS > SHTUCK
SHTUM *adj* silent
SHTUMM *adj* silent
SHTUP *vb* have sex (with)
SHTUPPED > SHTUP
SHTUPPING > SHTUP
SHTUPS > SHTUP
SHUBUNKIN *n* type of goldfish
SHUCK *n* outer covering of something ▷ *vb* remove the shucks from
SHUCKED > SHUCK
SHUCKER > SHUCK
SHUCKERS > SHUCK
SHUCKING > SHUCK
SHUCKINGS > SHUCK
SHUCKS *pl n* something of little value ▷ *interj* exclamation of disappointment, annoyance, etc
SHUDDER *vb* shake or tremble violently, esp with horror ▷ *n* shaking or trembling
SHUDDERED > SHUDDER
SHUDDERS > SHUDDER
SHUDDERY > SHUDDER
SHUFFLE *vb* walk without lifting the feet ▷ *n* shuffling
SHUFFLED > SHUFFLE
SHUFFLER > SHUFFLE
SHUFFLERS > SHUFFLE
SHUFFLES > SHUFFLE
SHUFFLING > SHUFFLE
SHUFTI *same as* > SHUFTY
SHUFTIES > SHUFTY
SHUFTIS > SHUFTI
SHUFTY *n* look
SHUGGIES > SHUGGY
SHUGGY *n* swing, as at a fairground
SHUL *Yiddish word for* > SYNAGOGUE
SHULE *vb* saunter
SHULED > SHULE
SHULES > SHULE
SHULING > SHULE
SHULN > SHUL
SHULS > SHUL
SHUN *vb* avoid
SHUNLESS *adj* old word meaning not to be shunned
SHUNNABLE > SHUN
SHUNNED > SHUN
SHUNNER > SHUN
SHUNNERS > SHUN
SHUNNING > SHUN
SHUNPIKE *vb* take side road to avoid toll at turnpike
SHUNPIKED > SHUNPIKE
SHUNPIKER > SHUNPIKE
SHUNPIKES > SHUNPIKE
SHUNS > SHUN
SHUNT *vb* move (objects or people) to a different position ▷ *n* shunting
SHUNTED > SHUNT
SHUNTER *n* small railway locomotive used for manoeuvring coaches
SHUNTERS > SHUNTER
SHUNTING > SHUNT
SHUNTINGS > SHUNT
SHUNTS > SHUNT
SHURA *n* consultative council or assembly
SHURAS > SHURA
SHUSH *interj* be quiet! ▷ *vb* quiet by saying 'shush'
SHUSHED > SHUSH
SHUSHER > SHUSH
SHUSHERS > SHUSH
SHUSHES > SHUSH
SHUSHING > SHUSH
SHUT *vb* bring together or fold, close
SHUTDOWN *n* closing of a factory, shop, or other business ▷ *vb* discontinue operations permanently
SHUTDOWNS > SHUTDOWN
SHUTE *variant of* > CHUTE
SHUTED > SHUTE
SHUTES > SHUTE
SHUTEYE *n* sleep
SHUTEYES > SHUTEYE
SHUTING > SHUTE
SHUTOFF *n* device that shuts something off, esp a machine control
SHUTOFFS > SHUTOFF
SHUTOUT *n* game in which the opposing team does not score ▷ *vb* keep out or exclude
SHUTOUTS > SHUTOUT
SHUTS > SHUT
SHUTTER *n* hinged doorlike cover for closing off a window ▷ *vb* close or equip with a shutter
SHUTTERED > SHUTTER
SHUTTERS > SHUTTER
SHUTTING > SHUT
SHUTTLE *n* bobbin-like device used in weaving ▷ *vb* move by or as if by a shuttle
SHUTTLED > SHUTTLE
SHUTTLER > SHUTTLE
SHUTTLERS > SHUTTLE
SHUTTLES > SHUTTLE
SHUTTLING > SHUTTLE
SHVARTZE *same as* > SCHVARTZE
SHVARTZES > SHVARTZE
SHWA *same as* > SCHWA
SHWANPAN *same as* > SWANPAN
SHWANPANS > SHWANPAN
SHWAS > SHWA
SHWESHWE *n* African cotton print fabric
SHWESHWES > SHWESHWE
SHY *adj* not at ease in company ▷ *vb* start back in fear ▷ *n* throw
SHYER > SHY
SHYERS > SHY
SHYEST > SHY
SHYING > SHY
SHYISH > SHY
SHYLOCK *vb* lend money at an exorbitant rate of interest
SHYLOCKED > SHYLOCK
SHYLOCKS > SHYLOCK
SHYLY > SHY
SHYNESS > SHY
SHYNESSES > SHY
SHYPOO *n* liquor of poor quality
SHYPOOS > SHYPOO
SHYSTER *n* person, esp a lawyer or politician, who uses discreditable or unethical methods
SHYSTERS > SHYSTER
SI *same as* > TE
SIAL *n* silicon-rich and aluminium-rich rocks of the earth's continental upper crust
SIALIC > SIAL
SIALID *n* species of fly
SIALIDAN > SIALID
SIALIDANS > SIALID
SIALIDS > SIALID
SIALOGRAM *n* X-ray of salivary gland
SIALOID *adj* resembling saliva
SIALOLITH *n* hard deposit formed in salivary gland
SIALON *n* type of ceramic
SIALONS > SIALON
SIALS > SIAL
SIAMANG *n* large black gibbon
SIAMANGS > SIAMANG
SIAMESE *variant of* > SIAMEZE
SIAMESED > SIAMESE
SIAMESES > SIAMESE
SIAMESING > SIAMESE
SIAMEZE *vb* join together
SIAMEZED > SIAMEZE
SIAMEZES > SIAMEZE
SIAMEZING > SIAMEZE
SIB *n* blood relative
SIBB *n* sib
SIBBS > SIBB
SIBILANCE > SIBILANT
SIBILANCY > SIBILANT
SIBILANT *adj* hissing ▷ *n* consonant pronounced with a hissing sound
SIBILANTS > SIBILANT
SIBILATE *vb* pronounce or utter (words or speech) with a hissing sound
SIBILATED > SIBILATE
SIBILATES > SIBILATE
SIBILATOR > SIBILATE
SIBILOUS > SIBILANT
SIBLING *n* brother or sister
SIBLINGS > SIBLING
SIBS > SIB
SIBSHIP *n* group of children of the same parents
SIBSHIPS > SIBSHIP
SIBYL *n* (in ancient Greece and Rome) prophetess
SIBYLIC > SIBYL
SIBYLLIC > SIBYL
SIBYLLINE > SIBYL
SIBYLS > SIBYL
SIC *adv* thus ▷ *vb* attack

ICCAN *adj* Scots word meaning such
ICCAR *adj* sure
ICCATIVE *n* substance added to a liquid to promote drying
ICCED > sic
ICCING > sic
ICCITIES > siccity
ICCITY *n* dryness
ICE *same as* > syce
ICES > sice
ICH *adj* old form of such
ICHT *Scot word for* > sight
ICHTED > sicht
ICHTING > sicht
ICHTS > sicht
ICILIANA *n* Sicilian dance
ICILIANE > siciliana
ICILIANO *n* old dance in six-beat or twelve-beat time
ICK *adj* vomiting or likely to vomit ▷ *n* vomit ▷ *vb* vomit
ICKBAY *n* room for the treatment of sick people, for example on a ship
ICKBAYS > sickbay
ICKBED *n* bed where sick person lies
ICKBEDS > sickbed
ICKED > sick
ICKEE *n* person off work through illness
ICKEES > sickee
ICKEN *vb* make nauseated or disgusted
ICKENED > sicken
ICKENER *n* something that induces sickness or nausea
ICKENERS > sickener
ICKENING *adj* causing horror or disgust
ICKENS > sicken
ICKER > sick
ICKERLY *adv* Scots word meaning surely
ICKEST > sick
ICKIE *n* day of sick leave from work
ICKIES > sickie
ICKING > sick
ICKISH > sick
ICKISHLY > sick
ICKLE *n* tool with a curved blade for cutting grass or grain ▷ *vb* cut with a sickle
ICKLED > sickle
ICKLEMAN *n* person reaping with sickle
ICKLEMEN > sickleman
ICKLEMIA *n* form of anaemia
ICKLEMIC > sicklemia
ICKLES > sickle
ICKLIED > sickly
ICKLIER > sickly
ICKLIES > sickly
ICKLIEST > sickly
ICKLILY > sickly
SICKLING > sickle
SICKLY *adj* unhealthy, weak ▷ *adv* suggesting sickness ▷ *vb* make sickly
SICKLYING > sickly
SICKNESS *n* particular illness or disease
SICKNURSE *n* person nursing sick person
SICKO *n* person who is mentally disturbed or perverted ▷ *adj* perverted or in bad taste
SICKOS > sicko
SICKOUT *n* form of industrial action in which all workers in a workplace report sick simultaneously
SICKOUTS > sickout
SICKROOM *n* room to which a person who is ill is confined
SICKROOMS > sickroom
SICKS > sick
SICLIKE *adj* Scots word meaning suchlike
SICS > sic
SIDA *n* Australian hemp plant
SIDALCEA *n* type of perennial N American plant
SIDALCEAS > sidalcea
SIDAS > sida
SIDDHA *n* (in Hinduism) person who has achieved perfection
SIDDHAS > siddha
SIDDHI *n* (in Hinduism) power attained with perfection
SIDDHIS > siddhi
SIDDHUISM *n* (in Indian English) any contrived metaphor or simile
SIDDUR *n* Jewish prayer book
SIDDURIM > siddur
SIDDURS > siddur
SIDE *n* line or surface that borders anything ▷ *adj* at or on the side
SIDEARM *n* weapon worn on belt
SIDEARMS > sidearm
SIDEBAND *n* frequency band either above or below the carrier frequency
SIDEBANDS > sideband
SIDEBAR *n* small newspaper article beside larger one
SIDEBARS > sidebar
SIDEBOARD *n* piece of furniture for holding plates, cutlery, etc in a dining room
SIDEBONES *n* part of horse's hoof
SIDEBURNS *pl n* man's side whiskers
SIDECAR *n* small passenger car on the side of a motorcycle
SIDECARS > sidecar
SIDECHECK *n* part of horse's harness
SIDED > side
SIDEDNESS > side
SIDEDRESS *vb* place fertilizer in the soil near the roots of a plant
SIDEHILL *n* side of hill
SIDEHILLS > sidehill
SIDEKICK *n* close friend or associate
SIDEKICKS > sidekick
SIDELIGHT *n* either of two small lights on the front of a vehicle
SIDELINE *n* subsidiary interest or source of income ▷ *vb* prevent (a player) from taking part in a game
SIDELINED > sideline
SIDELINER > sideline
SIDELINES *pl n* area immediately outside the playing area, where substitute players sit
SIDELING *adj* to one side
SIDELOCK *n* long lock of hair on side of head
SIDELOCKS > sidelock
SIDELONG *adj* sideways ▷ *adv* obliquely
SIDEMAN *n* member of a dance band or a jazz group other than the leader
SIDEMEN > sideman
SIDENOTE *n* note written in margin
SIDENOTES > sidenote
SIDEPATH *n* minor path
SIDEPATHS > sidepath
SIDEPIECE *n* part forming side of something
SIDER *n* one who sides with another
SIDERAL *adj* from the stars
SIDERATE *vb* strike violently
SIDERATED > siderate
SIDERATES > siderate
SIDEREAL *adj* of or determined with reference to the stars
SIDERITE *n* pale yellow to brownish-black mineral
SIDERITES > siderite
SIDERITIC > siderite
SIDEROAD *n* (esp in Ontario) a road going at right angles to concession roads
SIDEROADS > sideroad
SIDEROSES > siderosis
SIDEROSIS *n* lung disease caused by breathing in fine particles of iron or other metallic dust
SIDEROTIC > siderosis
SIDERS > sider
SIDES > side
SIDESHOOT *n* minor shoot growing on plant
SIDESHOW *n* entertainment offered along with the main show
SIDESHOWS > sideshow
SIDESLIP *same as* > slip
SIDESLIPS > sideslip
SIDESMAN *n* man elected to help the parish church warden
SIDESMEN > sidesman
SIDESPIN *n* horizontal spin put on ball
SIDESPINS > sidespin
SIDESTEP *vb* dodge (an issue) ▷ *n* movement to one side, such as in dancing or boxing
SIDESTEPS > sidestep
SIDESWIPE *n* unexpected criticism of someone or something while discussing another subject ▷ *vb* make a sideswipe
SIDETRACK *vb* divert from the main topic ▷ *n* railway siding
SIDEWALK *n* paved path for pedestrians, at the side of a road
SIDEWALKS > sidewalk
SIDEWALL *n* either of the sides of a pneumatic tyre between the tread and the rim
SIDEWALLS > sidewall
SIDEWARD *adj* directed or moving towards one side ▷ *adv* towards one side
SIDEWARDS *adv* towards one side
SIDEWAY *variant of* > sideways
SIDEWAYS *adv* or from the side ▷ *adj* moving or directed to or from one side
SIDEWHEEL *n* one of the paddle wheels of a sidewheeler
SIDEWISE *adv* sideways
SIDH *pl n* fairy people
SIDHA *n* (in Hinduism) person who has achieved perfection
SIDHAS > sidha
SIDHE *pl n* inhabitants of fairyland
SIDING *n* short stretch of railway track on which trains are shunted from the main line
SIDINGS > siding
SIDLE *vb* walk in a furtive manner ▷ *n* sideways movement
SIDLED > sidle
SIDLER > sidle
SIDLERS > sidle
SIDLES > sidle
SIDLING > sidle
SIDLINGLY > sidle
SIECLE *n* century, period, or era

SIECLES > SIECLE
SIEGE *n* surrounding and blockading of a place ▷ *vb* lay siege to
SIEGED > SIEGE
SIEGER *n* person who besieges
SIEGERS > SIEGER
SIEGES > SIEGE
SIEGING > SIEGE
SIELD *vb* old word meaning given a ceiling
SIEMENS *n* SI unit of electrical conductance
SIEN *n* old word meaning scion
SIENITE *n* type of igneous rock
SIENITES > SIENITE
SIENNA *n* reddish- or yellowish-brown pigment made from natural earth
SIENNAS > SIENNA
SIENS > SIEN
SIENT *n* old word meaning scion
SIENTS > SIENT
SIEROZEM *n* type of soil
SIEROZEMS > SIEROZEM
SIERRA *n* range of mountains in Spain or America with jagged peaks
SIERRAN > SIERRA
SIERRAS > SIERRA
SIES *same as* > SIS
SIESTA *n* afternoon nap, taken in hot countries
SIESTAS > SIESTA
SIETH *n* old form of scythe
SIETHS > SIETH
SIEUR *n* French word meaning lord
SIEURS > SIEUR
SIEVE *n* utensil with mesh through which a substance is sifted or strained ▷ *vb* sift or strain through a sieve
SIEVED > SIEVE
SIEVELIKE > SIEVE
SIEVERT *n* derived SI unit of dose equivalent, equal to 1 joule per kilogram
SIEVERTS > SIEVERT
SIEVES > SIEVE
SIEVING > SIEVE
SIF *adj* South African slang for disgusting
SIFAKA *n* either of two large rare arboreal lemuroid primates
SIFAKAS > SIFAKA
SIFFLE *vb* whistle
SIFFLED > SIFFLE
SIFFLES > SIFFLE
SIFFLEUR *n* male professional whistler
SIFFLEURS > SIFFLEUR
SIFFLEUSE *n* female professional whistler
SIFFLING > SIFFLE
SIFREI > SEFER
SIFT *vb* remove the coarser particles from a substance with a sieve
SIFTED > SIFT
SIFTER > SIFT
SIFTERS > SIFT
SIFTING > SIFT
SIFTINGLY > SIFT
SIFTINGS *pl n* material or particles separated out by or as if by a sieve
SIFTS > SIFT
SIGANID *n* tropical fish
SIGANIDS > SIGANID
SIGH *n* long audible breath expressing sadness, tiredness, relief, or longing ▷ *vb* utter a sigh
SIGHED > SIGH
SIGHER > SIGH
SIGHERS > SIGH
SIGHFUL > SIGH
SIGHING > SIGH
SIGHINGLY > SIGH
SIGHLESS > SIGH
SIGHLIKE > SIGH
SIGHS > SIGH
SIGHT *n* ability to see ▷ *vb* catch sight of
SIGHTABLE > SIGHT
SIGHTED *adj* not blind
SIGHTER *n* any of six practice shots allowed to each competitor in a tournament
SIGHTERS > SIGHTER
SIGHTING > SIGHT
SIGHTINGS > SIGHT
SIGHTLESS *adj* blind
SIGHTLIER > SIGHTLY
SIGHTLINE *n* uninterrupted line of vision
SIGHTLY *adj* pleasing or attractive to see
SIGHTS > SIGHT
SIGHTSAW > SIGHTSEE
SIGHTSEE *vb* visit the famous or interesting sights of (a place)
SIGHTSEEN > SIGHTSEE
SIGHTSEER > SIGHTSEE
SIGHTSEES > SIGHTSEE
SIGHTSMAN *n* tourist guide
SIGHTSMEN > SIGHTSMAN
SIGIL *n* seal or signet
SIGILLARY > SIGIL
SIGILLATE *adj* closed with seal
SIGILS > SIGIL
SIGISBEI > SIGISBEO
SIGISBEO *n* male escort for a married woman
SIGLA *n* list of symbols used in a book
SIGLAS > SIGLA
SIGLOI > SIGLOS
SIGLOS *n* silver coin of ancient Persia worth one twentieth of a daric
SIGLUM *n* symbol used in book
SIGMA *n* 18th letter in the Greek alphabet
SIGMAS > SIGMA
SIGMATE *adj* shaped like the Greek letter sigma or the Roman S ▷ *n* sigmate thing ▷ *vb* add a sigma
SIGMATED > SIGMATE
SIGMATES > SIGMATE
SIGMATIC > SIGMATE
SIGMATING > SIGMATE
SIGMATION > SIGMATE
SIGMATISM *n* repetition of letter s
SIGMATRON *n* machine for generating X-rays
SIGMOID *adj* shaped like the letter S ▷ *n* S-shaped bend in the final portion of the large intestine
SIGMOIDAL *variant of* > SIGMOID
SIGMOIDS > SIGMOID
SIGN *n* indication of something not immediately or outwardly observable ▷ *vb* write (one's name) on (a document or letter) to show its authenticity or one's agreement
SIGNA *pl n* symbols
SIGNABLE > SIGN
SIGNAGE *n* signs collectively, esp street signs or signs giving directions
SIGNAGES > SIGNAGE
SIGNAL *n* sign or gesture to convey information ▷ *adj* very important ▷ *vb* convey (information) by signal
SIGNALED > SIGNAL
SIGNALER > SIGNAL
SIGNALERS > SIGNAL
SIGNALING > SIGNAL
SIGNALISE *same as* > SIGNALIZE
SIGNALIZE *vb* make noteworthy or conspicuous
SIGNALLED > SIGNAL
SIGNALLER > SIGNAL
SIGNALLY *adv* conspicuously or especially
SIGNALMAN *n* railwayman in charge of signals and points
SIGNALMEN > SIGNALMAN
SIGNALS > SIGNAL
SIGNARIES > SIGNARY
SIGNARY *n* set of symbols
SIGNATORY *n* one of the parties who sign a document ▷ *adj* having signed a document or treaty
SIGNATURE *n* person's name written by himself or herself in signing something
SIGNBOARD *n* board carrying a sign or notice, often to advertise a business or product
SIGNED > SIGN
SIGNEE *n* person signing document
SIGNEES > SIGNEE
SIGNER *n* person who sign something
SIGNERS > SIGNER
SIGNET *n* small seal used to authenticate documents ▷ *vb* stamp o authenticate with a signe
SIGNETED > SIGNET
SIGNETING > SIGNET
SIGNETS > SIGNET
SIGNEUR *old spelling of* > SENIOR
SIGNEURIE *n* old word meaning seniority
SIGNIEUR *n* old word meaning lord
SIGNIEURS > SIGNIEUR
SIGNIFICS *n* study of meaning
SIGNIFIED > SIGNIFY
SIGNIFIER > SIGNIFY
SIGNIFIES > SIGNIFY
SIGNIFY *vb* indicate or suggest
SIGNING *n* system of communication using hand and arm movement such as one used by deaf people
SIGNINGS > SIGNING
SIGNIOR *same as* > SIGNOR
SIGNIORI > SIGNIOR
SIGNIORS > SIGNIOR
SIGNIORY *n* old word meaning lordship
SIGNLESS > SIGN
SIGNOR *n* Italian term of address equivalent to *sir* or *Mr*
SIGNORA *n* Italian term of address equivalent to *madam* or *Mrs*
SIGNORAS > SIGNORA
SIGNORE *n* Italian man: a title of respect equivalent to *sir*
SIGNORES > SIGNORE
SIGNORI > SIGNORE
SIGNORIA *n* government Italian city
SIGNORIAL > SIGNORIA
SIGNORIAS > SIGNORIA
SIGNORIES > SIGNORY
SIGNORINA *n* Italian term of address equivalent to *madam* or *Miss*
SIGNORINE > SIGNORINA
SIGNORINI > SIGNORINO
SIGNORINO *n* young gentleman
SIGNORS > SIGNOR
SIGNORY *same as* > SEIGNIORY
SIGNPOST *n* post bearing a sign that shows the wa ▷ *vb* mark with signpost
SIGNPOSTS > SIGNPOST
SIGNS > SIGN
SIJO *n* Korean poem
SIJOS > SIJO

IK *adj* excellent
IKA *n* Japanese forest-dwelling deer
IKAS > SIKA
IKE *n* small stream
IKER *adj* old spelling of sicker
IKES > SIKE
IKORSKY *n* type of helicopter
ILAGE *n* fodder crop harvested while green and partially fermented in a silo ▷ *vb* make silage
ILAGED > SILAGE
ILAGEING > SILAGE
ILAGES > SILAGE
ILAGING > SILAGE
ILANE *n* gas containing silicon
ILANES > SILANE
ILASTIC *n* tradename for a type of flexible silicone rubber
ILASTICS > SILASTIC
ILD *n* any of various small young herrings, esp when prepared and canned in Norway
ILDS > SILD
ILE *vb* pour with rain
ILED > SILE
ILEN *n* god of woodland
ILENCE *n* absence of noise or speech ▷ *vb* make silent
ILENCED *adj* (of a clergyman) forbidden to preach or perform his clerical functions
ILENCER *n* device to reduce the noise of an engine exhaust or gun
ILENCERS > SILENCER
ILENCES > SILENCE
ILENCING > SILENCE
ILENE *n* any plant of the large perennial genus *Silene*
ILENES > SILENE
ILENI > SILENUS
ILENS > SILEN
ILENT *adj* tending to speak very little ▷ *n* silent film
ILENTER > SILENT
ILENTEST > SILENT
ILENTLY > SILENT
ILENTS > SILENT
ILENUS *n* woodland deity
ILER *n* strainer
ILERS > SILER
ILES > SILE
ILESIA *n* twill-weave fabric of cotton or other fibre
ILESIAS > SILESIA
ILEX *n* type of heat-resistant glass made from fused quartz
ILEXES > SILEX
ILICA *n* hard glossy mineral found as quartz and in sandstone
SILICAS > SILICA
SILICATE *n* compound of silicon, oxygen, and a metal
SILICATED > SILICATE
SILICATES > SILICATE
SILICEOUS *adj* of, relating to, or containing abundant silica
SILICIC *adj* of, concerned with, or containing silicon or an acid obtained from silicon
SILICIDE *n* any one of a class of binary compounds formed between silicon and certain metals
SILICIDES > SILICIDE
SILICIFY *vb* convert or be converted into silica
SILICIOUS *same as* > SILICEOUS
SILICIUM *rare name for* > SILICON
SILICIUMS > SILICIUM
SILICLE *same as* > SILICULA
SILICLES > SILICLE
SILICON *n* brittle nonmetallic element widely used in chemistry and industry ▷ *adj* denoting an area of a country that contains much high-technology industry
SILICONE *n* tough synthetic substance made from silicon and used in lubricants
SILICONES > SILICONE
SILICONS > SILICON
SILICOSES > SILICOSIS
SILICOSIS *n* lung disease caused by inhaling silica dust
SILICOTIC *n* person suffering from silicosis
SILICULA *n* short broad siliqua, occurring in such cruciferous plants as honesty and shepherd's-purse
SILICULAE > SILICULA
SILICULAS > SILICULA
SILICULE *same as* > SILICULA
SILICULES > SILICULE
SILING > SILE
SILIQUA *n* long dry dehiscent fruit of cruciferous plants such as the wallflower
SILIQUAE > SILIQUA
SILIQUAS > SILIQUA
SILIQUE *same as* > SILIQUA
SILIQUES > SILIQUE
SILIQUOSE > SILIQUA
SILIQUOUS > SILIQUA
SILK *n* fibre made by the larva of a certain moth ▷ *vb* (of maize) develop long hairlike styles
SILKALENE *same as* > SILKALINE
SILKALINE *n* fine smooth cotton fabric used for linings, etc
SILKED > SILK
SILKEN *adj* made of silk ▷ *vb* make like silk
SILKENED > SILKEN
SILKENING > SILKEN
SILKENS > SILKEN
SILKIE *n* Scots word for a seal
SILKIER > SILKY
SILKIES > SILKIE
SILKIEST > SILKY
SILKILY > SILKY
SILKINESS > SILKY
SILKING > SILK
SILKLIKE > SILK
SILKOLINE *n* material like silk
SILKS > SILK
SILKTAIL *n* waxwing
SILKTAILS > SILKTAIL
SILKWEED *another name for* > MILKWEED
SILKWEEDS > SILKWEED
SILKWORM *n* caterpillar that spins a cocoon of silk
SILKWORMS > SILKWORM
SILKY *adj* of or like silk
SILL *n* ledge at the bottom of a window or door
SILLABUB *same as* > SYLLABUB
SILLABUBS > SILLABUB
SILLADAR *n* Indian irregular cavalryman
SILLADARS > SILLADAR
SILLER *n* silver ▷ *adj* silver
SILLERS > SILLER
SILLIBUB *n* syllabub
SILLIBUBS > SILLIBUB
SILLIER > SILLY
SILLIES > SILLY
SILLIEST > SILLY
SILLILY > SILLY
SILLINESS > SILLY
SILLOCK *n* young coalfish
SILLOCKS > SILLOCK
SILLS > SILL
SILLY *adj* foolish ▷ *n* foolish person
SILO *n* pit or airtight tower for storing silage or grains ▷ *vb* put in a silo
SILOED > SILO
SILOING > SILO
SILOS > SILO
SILOXANE *n* any of a class of compounds containing alternate silicon and oxygen atoms
SILOXANES > SILOXANE
SILPHIA > SILPHIUM
SILPHIUM *n* American flowering wild plant
SILPHIUMS > SILPHIUM
SILT *n* mud deposited by moving water ▷ *vb* fill or be choked with silt
SILTATION > SILT
SILTED > SILT
SILTIER > SILT
SILTIEST > SILT
SILTING > SILT
SILTS > SILT
SILTSTONE *n* variety of fine sandstone formed from consolidated silt
SILTY > SILT
SILURIAN *n* formed in the third period of the Palaeozoic
SILURID *n* any freshwater fish of the family *Siluridae* including catfish ▷ *adj* of, relating to, or belonging to the family *Siluridae*
SILURIDS > SILURID
SILURIST *n* member of ancient Silurian tribe
SILURISTS > SILURIST
SILUROID *n* freshwater fish
SILUROIDS > SILUROID
SILVA *same as* > SYLVA
SILVAE > SILVA
SILVAN *same as* > SYLVAN
SILVANS > SILVAN
SILVAS > SILVA
SILVATIC *adj* wild, not domestic
SILVER *n* white precious metal ▷ *adj* made of or of the colour of silver ▷ *vb* coat with silver
SILVERED > SILVER
SILVERER > SILVER
SILVERERS > SILVER
SILVEREYE *n* greenish-coloured songbird of Africa, Australia, New Zealand, and Asia
SILVERIER > SILVERY
SILVERING > SILVER
SILVERISE *same as* > SILVERIZE
SILVERIZE *vb* coat with silver
SILVERLY *adv* like silver
SILVERN *adj* silver
SILVERS > SILVER
SILVERY *adj* like silver
SILVEX *n* type of weedkiller
SILVEXES > SILVEX
SILVICAL *adj* of trees
SILVICS *n* study of trees
SIM *n* computer game that simulates an activity such as flying or playing a sport
SIMA *n* silicon-rich and magnesium-rich rocks of the earth's oceanic crust
SIMAR *variant spelling of* > CYMAR
SIMAROUBA *n* any tropical American tree of the genus *Simarouba*
SIMARRE *n* woman's loose gown
SIMARRES > SIMARRE
SIMARS > SIMAR
SIMARUBA *same as* > SIMAROUBA
SIMARUBAS > SIMARUBA
SIMAS > SIMA
SIMATIC > SIMA

SIMAZINE *n* organic weedkiller
SIMAZINES > SIMAZINE
SIMBA *E African word for* > LION
SIMBAS > SIMBA
SIMI *n* East African sword
SIMIAL *adj* of apes
SIMIAN *n* a monkey or ape ▷ *adj* of or resembling a monkey or ape
SIMIANS > SIMIAN
SIMILAR *adj* alike but not identical
SIMILARLY > SIMILAR
SIMILE *n* figure of speech comparing one thing to another, using 'as' or 'like'
SIMILES > SIMILE
SIMILISE *same as* > SIMILIZE
SIMILISED > SIMILISE
SIMILISES > SIMILISE
SIMILIZE *vb* use similes
SIMILIZED > SIMILIZE
SIMILIZES > SIMILIZE
SIMILOR *n* alloy used in cheap jewellery
SIMILORS > SIMILOR
SIMIOID *adj* of apes
SIMIOUS *adj* of apes
SIMIS > SIMI
SIMITAR *same as* > SCIMITAR
SIMITARS > SIMITAR
SIMKIN *word used in India for* > CHAMPAGNE
SIMKINS > SIMKIN
SIMLIN *n* American variety of squash plant
SIMLINS > SIMLIN
SIMMER *vb* cook gently at just below boiling point ▷ *n* state of simmering
SIMMERED > SIMMER
SIMMERING > SIMMER
SIMMERS > SIMMER
SIMNEL as in *simnel cake* fruit cake with marzipan eaten at Easter
SIMNELS > SIMNEL
SIMOLEON *n* American slang for dollar
SIMOLEONS > SIMOLEON
SIMONIAC *n* person who is guilty of practising simony
SIMONIACS > SIMONIAC
SIMONIES > SIMONY
SIMONIOUS > SIMONY
SIMONISE *same as* > SIMONIZE
SIMONISED > SIMONISE
SIMONISES > SIMONISE
SIMONIST > SIMONY
SIMONISTS > SIMONY
SIMONIZE *vb* polish with wax
SIMONIZED > SIMONIZE
SIMONIZES > SIMONIZE
SIMONY *n* practice of buying or selling Church benefits such as pardons
SIMOOM *n* hot suffocating sand-laden desert wind
SIMOOMS > SIMOOM
SIMOON *same as* > SIMOOM
SIMOONS > SIMOON
SIMORG *n* bird in Persian myth
SIMORGS > SIMORG
SIMP *short for* > SIMPLETON
SIMPAI *n* Indonesian monkey
SIMPAIS > SIMPAI
SIMPATICO *adj* pleasant or congenial
SIMPER *vb* smile in a silly or affected way ▷ *n* simpering smile
SIMPERED > SIMPER
SIMPERER > SIMPER
SIMPERERS > SIMPER
SIMPERING > SIMPER
SIMPERS > SIMPER
SIMPKIN *word used in India for* > CHAMPAGNE
SIMPKINS > SIMPKIN
SIMPLE *adj* easy to understand or do ▷ *n* simpleton ▷ *vb* archaic word meaning to look for medicinal herbs
SIMPLED > SIMPLE
SIMPLER > SIMPLE
SIMPLERS > SIMPLE
SIMPLES > SIMPLE
SIMPLESSE *n* old word meaning simplicity
SIMPLEST > SIMPLE
SIMPLETON *n* foolish or half-witted person
SIMPLEX *adj* permitting the transmission of signals in only one direction in a radio circuit ▷ *n* simple not a compound word
SIMPLEXES > SIMPLEX
SIMPLICES > SIMPLEX
SIMPLICIA *n* species of moth
SIMPLIFY *vb* make less complicated
SIMPLING > SIMPLE
SIMPLINGS > SIMPLE
SIMPLISM *n* quality of being extremely naive
SIMPLISMS > SIMPLISM
SIMPLIST *n* old word meaning expert in herbal medicine
SIMPLISTE *adj* simplistic
SIMPLISTS > SIMPLIST
SIMPLY *adv* in a simple manner
SIMPS > SIMP
SIMS > SIM
SIMUL *adj* simultaneous ▷ *n* simultaneous broadcast
SIMULACRA *pl n* representations of things
SIMULACRE *n* resemblance
SIMULANT *adj* simulating ▷ *n* simulant thing
SIMULANTS > SIMULANT
SIMULAR *n* person or thing that simulates or imitates ▷ *adj* fake
SIMULARS > SIMULAR
SIMULATE *vb* make a pretence of ▷ *adj* assumed or simulated
SIMULATED *adj* being an imitation of the genuine article, usually made from cheaper material
SIMULATES > SIMULATE
SIMULATOR *n* device that simulates specific conditions for the purposes of research or training
SIMULCAST *vb* broadcast (a programme) simultaneously on radio and television ▷ *n* programme broadcast in this way
SIMULIUM *n* tropical fly
SIMULIUMS > SIMULIUM
SIMULS > SIMUL
SIMURG *n* bird in Persian myth
SIMURGH *n* bird in Persian myth
SIMURGHS > SIMURGH
SIMURGS > SIMURG
SIN *n* offence or transgression ▷ *vb* commit a sin
SINAPISM *n* mixture of black mustard seeds and an adhesive, applied to the skin
SINAPISMS > SINAPISM
SINCE *prep* during the period of time after ▷ *adv* from that time
SINCERE *adj* without pretence or deceit
SINCERELY > SINCERE
SINCERER > SINCERE
SINCEREST > SINCERE
SINCERITY > SINCERE
SINCIPITA > SINCIPUT
SINCIPUT *n* forward upper part of the skull
SINCIPUTS > SINCIPUT
SIND *variant of* > SYNE
SINDED > SIND
SINDING > SIND
SINDINGS > SIND
SINDON *n* type of cloth
SINDONS > SINDON
SINDS > SIND
SINE *n* ratio of the length of the opposite side to that of the hypotenuse in a right-angled triangle ▷ *vb variant of* > SYNE
SINECURE *n* paid job with minimal duties
SINECURES > SINECURE
SINED > SINE
SINES > SINE
SINEW *n* tough fibrous tissue joining muscle to bone ▷ *vb* make strong
SINEWED *adj* having sinews
SINEWIER > SINEWY
SINEWIEST > SINEWY
SINEWING > SINEW
SINEWLESS > SINEW
SINEWS > SINEW
SINEWY *adj* lean and muscular
SINFONIA *n* symphony orchestra
SINFONIAS > SINFONIA
SINFONIE > SINFONIA
SINFUL *adj* guilty of sin
SINFULLY > SINFUL
SING *vb* make musical sounds with the voice ▷ *n* act or performance of singing
SINGABLE > SING
SINGALONG *n* act of singir along with a performer
SINGE *vb* burn the surface of ▷ *n* superficial burn
SINGED > SINGE
SINGEING > SINGE
SINGER *n* person who sings, esp professionally
SINGERS > SINGER
SINGES > SINGE
SINGING > SING
SINGINGLY > SING
SINGINGS > SING
SINGLE *adj* one only ▷ *n* single thing ▷ *vb* pick ou from others
SINGLED > SINGLE
SINGLEDOM *n* state of beir unmarried or not involve in a long-term relationsh
SINGLES *pl n* match playe with one person on each side
SINGLET *n* sleeveless vest
SINGLETON *n* only card of a particular suit held by a player
SINGLETS > SINGLET
SINGLING > SINGLE
SINGLINGS > SINGLE
SINGLY *adv* one at a time
SINGS > SING
SINGSONG *n* informal singing session ▷ *adj* (of the voice) repeatedly rising and falling in pitch
SINGSONGS > SINGSONG
SINGSONGY > SINGSONG
SINGSPIEL *n* type of German comic opera wit spoken dialogue
SINGULAR *adj* (of a word o form) denoting one pers or thing ▷ *n* singular for of a word
SINGULARS > SINGULAR
SINGULARY *adj* (of an operator) monadic
SINGULT *n* old word meaning sob
SINGULTS > SINGULT
SINGULTUS *technical name for* > HICCUP
SINH *n* hyperbolic sine
SINHS > SINH
SINICAL > SINE
SINICISE *same as* > SINICIZE
SINICISED > SINICISE
SINICISES > SINICISE

NICIZE *vb* make Chinese
NICIZED > SINICIZE
NICIZES > SINICIZE
NING > SINE
NISTER *adj* threatening or suggesting evil or harm
NISTRAL *adj* of, relating o, or located on the left ide, esp the left side of he body
NK *vb* submerge (in iquid) ▷ *n* fixed basin vith a water supply and lrainage pipe
NKABLE > SINK
NKAGE *n* act of sinking or degree to which omething sinks or has unk
NKAGES > SINKAGE
NKER *n* weight for a ishing line
NKERS > SINKER
NKHOLE *n* depression n the ground surface, sp in limestone, where a urface stream disappears nderground
NKHOLES > SINKHOLE
NKIER > SINKY
NKIEST > SINKY
NKING > SINK
NKINGS > SINK
NKS > SINK
NKY *adj* giving underfoot
NLESS *adj* free from sin r guilt
NLESSLY > SINLESS
NNED > SIN
NNER *n* person that sins ▷ *vb* behave like a sinner
NNERED > SINNER
NNERING > SINNER
NNERS > SIN
NNET *n* braided rope
NNETS > SINNET
NNING > SIN
NNINGIA *n* tropical lowering plant
NOLOGUE > SINOLOGY
NOLOGY *n* study of Chinese culture, etc
NOPIA *n* pigment made rom iron ore
NOPIAS > SINOPIA
NOPIE > SINOPIA
NOPIS *n* pigment made rom iron ore
NOPISES > SINOPIS
NOPITE *n* iron ore
NOPITES > SINOPITE
NS > SIN
NSYNE *adv* Scots word neaning since
NTER *n* whitish porous ncrustation that is leposited from hot prings ▷ *vb* form large articles from (metal owders or powdery ores) y heating or pressure
NTERED > SINTER
NTERING > SINTER
NTERS > SINTER
SINTERY > SINTER
SINUATE *vb* wind
SINUATED *same as* > SINUATE
SINUATELY > SINUATE
SINUATES > SINUATE
SINUATING > SINUATE
SINUATION *same as* > SINUOSITY
SINUITIS *variant of* > SINUSITIS
SINUOSE *adj* sinuous
SINUOSITY *n* quality of being sinuous
SINUOUS *adj* full of turns or curves
SINUOUSLY > SINUOUS
SINUS *n* hollow space in a bone, esp an air passage opening into the nose
SINUSES > SINUS
SINUSITIS *n* inflammation of a sinus membrane
SINUSLIKE > SINUS
SINUSOID *n* any of the irregular terminal blood vessels that replace capillaries in certain organs ▷ *adj* resembling a sinus
SINUSOIDS > SINUSOID
SIP *vb* drink in small mouthfuls ▷ *n* amount sipped
SIPE *vb* soak
SIPED > SIPE
SIPES > SIPE
SIPHON *n* bent tube which uses air pressure to draw liquid from a container ▷ *vb* draw off thus
SIPHONAGE > SIPHON
SIPHONAL > SIPHON
SIPHONATE *adj* having a syphon
SIPHONED > SIPHON
SIPHONET *n* sucking tube on an aphid
SIPHONETS > SIPHONET
SIPHONIC > SIPHON
SIPHONING > SIPHON
SIPHONS > SIPHON
SIPHUNCLE *n* tube inside shellfish
SIPING > SIPE
SIPPED > SIP
SIPPER > SIP
SIPPERS > SIP
SIPPET *n* small piece of toast eaten with soup or gravy
SIPPETS > SIPPET
SIPPING > SIP
SIPPLE *vb* sip
SIPPLED > SIPPLE
SIPPLES > SIPPLE
SIPPLING > SIPPLE
SIPPY as in *sippy cup* infant's drinking cup with a tight-fitting lid and perforated spout
SIPS > SIP
SIR *n* polite term of address for a man ▷ *vb* call someone 'sir'
SIRCAR *n* government in India
SIRCARS > SIRCAR
SIRDAR *same as* > SARDAR
SIRDARS > SIRDAR
SIRE *n* male parent of a horse or other domestic animal ▷ *vb* father
SIRED > SIRE
SIREE *emphasized form of* > SIR
SIREES > SIREE
SIREN *n* device making a loud wailing noise as a warning
SIRENIAN *adj* belonging to the *Sirenia*, an order of aquatic herbivorous placental mammals that contains the dugong and manatee ▷ *n* any animal belonging to the order *Sirenia*
SIRENIANS > SIRENIAN
SIRENIC > SIREN
SIRENISE *variant of* > SIRENIZE
SIRENISED > SIRENISE
SIRENISES > SIRENISE
SIRENIZE *vb* bewitch
SIRENIZED > SIRENIZE
SIRENIZES > SIRENIZE
SIRENS > SIREN
SIRES > SIRE
SIRGANG *n* Asian bird
SIRGANGS > SIRGANG
SIRI *n* betel
SIRIASES > SIRIASIS
SIRIASIS *n* sunstroke
SIRIH *n* betel
SIRIHS > SIRIH
SIRING > SIRE
SIRIS > SIRI
SIRKAR *n* government in India
SIRKARS > SIRKAR
SIRLOIN *n* prime cut of loin of beef
SIRLOINS > SIRLOIN
SIRNAME *vb* old form of surname
SIRNAMED > SIRNAME
SIRNAMES > SIRNAME
SIRNAMING > SIRNAME
SIROC *n* sirocco
SIROCCO *n* hot wind blowing from N Africa into S Europe
SIROCCOS > SIROCCO
SIROCS > SIROC
SIRONISE *same as* > SIRONIZE
SIRONISED > SIRONISE
SIRONISES > SIRONISE
SIRONIZE *vb* treat (a woollen fabric) chemically to prevent it wrinkling after being washed
SIRONIZED > SIRONIZE
SIRONIZES > SIRONIZE
SIROSET *adj* of the chemical treatment of woollen fabrics to give a permanent-press effect
SIRRA *disrespectful form of* > SIR
SIRRAH *n* contemptuous term used in addressing a man or boy
SIRRAHS > SIRRAH
SIRRAS > SIRRA
SIRRED > SIR
SIRREE *n* form of 'sir' used for emphasis
SIRREES > SIRREE
SIRRING > SIR
SIRS > SIR
SIRUP *same as* > SYRUP
SIRUPED > SIRUP
SIRUPIER > SIRUP
SIRUPIEST > SIRUP
SIRUPING > SIRUP
SIRUPS > SIRUP
SIRUPY > SIRUP
SIRVENTE *n* verse form employed by the troubadours of Provence to satirize political themes
SIRVENTES > SIRVENTE
SIS *n* sister
SISAL *n* (fibre of) plant used in making ropes
SISALS > SISAL
SISERARY *n* scolding
SISES > SIS
SISKIN *n* yellow-and-black finch
SISKINS > SISKIN
SISS *shortening of* > SISTER
SISSES > SISS
SISSIER > SISSY
SISSIES > SISSY
SISSIEST > SISSY
SISSIFIED > SISSY
SISSINESS > SISSY
SISSOO *n* Indian tree
SISSOOS > SISSOO
SISSY *n* weak or cowardly (person) ▷ *adj* effeminate, weak, or cowardly
SISSYISH > SISSY
SISSYNESS > SISSY
SIST *vb* Scottish law term meaning stop
SISTED > SIST
SISTER *n* girl or woman with the same parents as another person ▷ *adj* closely related, similar ▷ *vb* be or be like a sister
SISTERED > SISTER
SISTERING > SISTER
SISTERLY *adj* of or like a sister
SISTERS > SISTER
SISTING > SIST
SISTRA > SISTRUM
SISTROID *adj* contained between the convex sides of two intersecting curves
SISTRUM *n* musical instrument of ancient Egypt consisting of a metal rattle
SISTRUMS > SISTRUM
SISTS > SIST

SIT *vb* rest one's body upright on the buttocks
SITAR *n* Indian stringed musical instrument
SITARIST > SITAR
SITARISTS > SITAR
SITARS > SITAR
SITATUNGA *another name for* > MARSHBUCK
SITCOM *n* situation comedy
SITCOMS > SITCOM
SITE *n* place where something is, was, or is intended to be located ▷ *vb* provide with a site
SITED > SITE
SITELLA *n* type of small generally black-and-white bird
SITELLAS > SITELLA
SITES > SITE
SITFAST *n* sore on a horse's back caused by rubbing of the saddle
SITFASTS > SITFAST
SITH *archaic word for* > SINCE
SITHE *vb* old form of scythe
SITHED > SITHE
SITHEE *interj* look here! listen!
SITHEN *adv* old word meaning since
SITHENCE *adv* old word meaning since
SITHENS *adv* old word meaning since
SITHES > SITHE
SITHING > SITHE
SITING > SITE
SITIOLOGY *n* study of diet and nutrition
SITKA as in *sitka spruce* tall North American spruce tree
SITKAMER *n* sitting room
SITKAMERS > SITKAMER
SITOLOGY *n* scientific study of food, diet, and nutrition
SITREP *n* military situation report
SITREPS > SITREP
SITS > SIT
SITTAR *n* sitar
SITTARS > SITTAR
SITTELLA *variant spelling of* > SITELLA
SITTELLAS > SITTELLA
SITTEN *adj* dialect word for in the saddle
SITTER *n* baby-sitter
SITTERS > SITTER
SITTINE *adj* of nuthatch bird family
SITTING > SIT
SITTINGS > SIT
SITUATE *vb* place ▷ *adj* (now used esp in legal contexts) situated
SITUATED > SITUATE
SITUATES > SITUATE
SITUATING > SITUATE
SITUATION *n* state of affairs
SITULA *n* bucket-shaped container, usually of metal or pottery and often richly decorated
SITULAE > SITULA
SITUP *n* exercise in which the body is brought into a sitting position from one lying on the back
SITUPS > SITUP
SITUS *n* position or location, esp the usual or right position of an organ or part of the body
SITUSES > SITUS
SITUTUNGA *n* African antelope
SITZ as in *sitz bath* bath in which the buttocks and hips are immersed in hot water
SITZKRIEG *n* period during a war in which both sides change positions very slowly or not at all
SITZMARK *n* depression in the snow where a skier has fallen
SITZMARKS > SITZMARK
SIVER *same as* > SYVER
SIVERS > SIVER
SIWASH *vb* (in the Pacific Northwest) to camp out with only natural shelter
SIWASHED > SIWASH
SIWASHES > SIWASH
SIWASHING > SIWASH
SIX *n* one more than five
SIXAIN *n* stanza or poem of six lines
SIXAINE *n* six-line stanza of poetry
SIXAINES > SIXAINE
SIXAINS > SIXAIN
SIXER *same as* > SIX
SIXERS > SIXER
SIXES > SIX
SIXFOLD *adj* having six times as many or as much ▷ *adv* by six times as many or as much
SIXMO *n* book size resulting from folding a sheet of paper into six leaves or twelve pages, each one sixth the size of the sheet
SIXMOS > SIXMO
SIXPENCE *n* former British and Australian coin worth six pennies
SIXPENCES > SIXPENCE
SIXPENNY *adj* (of a nail) two inches in length
SIXSCORE *n* hundred and twenty
SIXSCORES > SIXSCORE
SIXTE *n* sixth of eight basic positions from which a parry or attack can be made in fencing
SIXTEEN *n* six and ten ▷ *adj* amounting to sixteen ▷ *determiner* amounting to sixteen
SIXTEENER *n* poem verse with sixteen syllables
SIXTEENMO *n* book size resulting from folding a sheet of paper into 16 leaves or 32 pages
SIXTEENS > SIXTEEN
SIXTEENTH *adj* coming after the fifteenth in numbering order ▷ *n* one of 16 equal or nearly equal parts of something
SIXTES > SIXTE
SIXTH *n* (of) number six in a series ▷ *adj* coming after the fifth and before the seventh in numbering order ▷ *adv* after the fifth person, position, etc
SIXTHLY *same as* > SIXTH
SIXTHS > SIXTH
SIXTIES > SIXTY
SIXTIETH *adj* being the ordinal number of *sixty* in numbering order ▷ *n* one of 60 approximately equal parts of something
SIXTIETHS > SIXTIETH
SIXTY *n* six times ten ▷ *adj* amounting to sixty
SIXTYISH > SIXTY
SIZABLE *adj* quite large
SIZABLY > SIZABLE
SIZAR *n* (at certain universities) an undergraduate receiving a maintenance grant from the college
SIZARS > SIZAR
SIZARSHIP > SIZAR
SIZE *n* dimensions, bigness ▷ *vb* arrange according to size
SIZEABLE *same as* > SIZABLE
SIZEABLY > SIZABLE
SIZED *adj* of a specified size
SIZEISM *n* discrimination on the basis of a person's size, esp against people considered to be overweight
SIZEISMS > SIZEISM
SIZEIST > SIZEISM
SIZEISTS > SIZEISM
SIZEL *n* scrap metal clippings
SIZELS > SIZEL
SIZER > SIZE
SIZERS > SIZE
SIZES > SIZE
SIZIER > SIZE
SIZIEST > SIZE
SIZINESS > SIZE
SIZING > SIZE
SIZINGS > SIZE
SIZISM *n* discrimination against people because of weight
SIZISMS > SIZISM
SIZIST > SIZISM
SIZISTS > SIZISM
SIZY > SIZE
SIZZLE *vb* make a hissing sound like frying fat ▷ *n* hissing sound
SIZZLED > SIZZLE
SIZZLER *n* something that sizzles
SIZZLERS > SIZZLER
SIZZLES > SIZZLE
SIZZLING *adj* extremely hot
SIZZLINGS > SIZZLING
SJAMBOK *n* whip or riding crop made of hide ▷ *vb* beat with a sjambok
SJAMBOKED > SJAMBOK
SJAMBOKS > SJAMBOK
SJOE *interj* South African exclamation of surprise, admiration, exhaustion, etc
SKA *n* type of West Indian pop music of the 1960s
SKAG *same as* > SCAG
SKAGS > SKAG
SKAIL *vb* Scots word meaning disperse
SKAILED > SKAIL
SKAILING > SKAIL
SKAILS > SKAIL
SKAITH *vb* Scots word meaning injure
SKAITHED > SKAITH
SKAITHING > SKAITH
SKAITHS > SKAITH
SKALD *n* (in ancient Scandinavia) a bard or minstrel
SKALDIC > SKALD
SKALDS > SKALD
SKALDSHIP > SKALD
SKANGER *n* Irish derogatory slang for a young working class person who wears casual sports clothes
SKANGERS > SKANGER
SKANK *n* fast dance to reggae music ▷ *vb* perform this dance
SKANKED > SKANK
SKANKER > SKANK
SKANKERS > SKANK
SKANKIER > SKANKY
SKANKIEST > SKANKY
SKANKING > SKANK
SKANKINGS > SKANK
SKANKS > SKANK
SKANKY *adj* dirty or unattractive
SKART *Scots word for* > CORMORANT
SKARTH *Scots word for* > CORMORANT
SKARTHS > SKARTH
SKARTS > SKART
SKAS > SKA
SKAT *n* three-handed card game using 32 cards, popular in German-speaking communities
SKATE *n* boot with a steel blade or sets of wheels attached to the sole for gliding over ice or a hard surface ▷ *vb* glide on or

f on skates
KATED > SKATE
KATEPARK *n* place for skateboarding
KATER *n* person who skates
KATERS > SKATER
KATES > SKATE
KATING > SKATE
KATINGS > SKATE
KATOL *n* skatole
KATOLE *n* white or brownish crystalline solid
KATOLES > SKATOLE
KATOLS > SKATOL
KATS > SKAT
KATT *n* dialect word meaning throw
KATTS > SKATT
KAW *variant of* > SCAW
KAWS > SKAW
KEAN *n* kind of double-edged dagger formerly used in Ireland and Scotland
KEANE *same as* > SKEIN
KEANES > SKEANE
KEANS > SKEAN
KEAR *dialect form of* > SCARE
KEARED > SKEAR
KEARIER > SKEARY
KEARIEST > SKEARY
KEARING > SKEAR
KEARS > SKEAR
KEARY *dialect form of* > SCARY
KEDADDLE *vb* run off ▷ *n* hasty retreat
KEE *variant spelling of* > SKI
KEECHAN *n* old Scots type of beer
KEECHANS > SKEECHAN
KEED > SKEE
KEEF *adj, adv* South African slang for at an oblique angle
KEEING > SKEE
KEELIER > SKEELY
KEELIEST > SKEELY
KEELY *adj* Scots word meaning skilful
KEEN *n* type of ibex
KEENS > SKEEN
KEER *dialect form of* > SCARE
KEERED > SKEER
KEERIER > SKEERY
KEERIEST > SKEERY
KEERING > SKEER
KEERS > SKEER
KEERY *dialect form of* > SCARY
KEES > SKEE
KEESICKS *American word meaning* > ROGUE
KEET *n* form of clay-pigeon shooting
KEETER *informal word for* > MOSQUITO
KEETERS > SKEETER
KEETS > SKEET
KEG *n* reinforcing brace between the after end of a keel and the rudderpost
SKEGG *n* skeg
SKEGGER *n* young salmon
SKEGGERS > SKEGGER
SKEGGS > SKEGG
SKEGS > SKEG
SKEIGH *adj* Scots word meaning shy
SKEIGHER > SKEIGH
SKEIGHEST > SKEIGH
SKEIN *n* yarn wound in a loose coil ▷ *vb* wind into a skein
SKEINED > SKEIN
SKEINING > SKEIN
SKEINS > SKEIN
SKELDER *vb* beg
SKELDERED > SKELDER
SKELDERS > SKELDER
SKELETAL > SKELETON
SKELETON *n* framework of bones inside a person's or animal's body ▷ *adj* reduced to a minimum
SKELETONS > SKELETON
SKELF *n* splinter of wood, esp when embedded accidentally in the skin
SKELFS > SKELF
SKELL *n* homeless person
SKELLIE *adj* skelly
SKELLIED > SKELLY
SKELLIER > SKELLY
SKELLIES > SKELLY
SKELLIEST > SKELLY
SKELLOCH *n* Scots word meaning scream
SKELLOCHS > SKELLOCH
SKELLS > SKELL
SKELLUM *n* rogue
SKELLUMS > SKELLUM
SKELLY *n* whitefish of certain lakes in the Lake District ▷ *vb* look sideways or squint ▷ *adj* cross-eyed
SKELLYING > SKELLY
SKELM *n* villain or crook
SKELMS > SKELM
SKELP *vb* slap ▷ *n* slap
SKELPED > SKELP
SKELPING > SKELP
SKELPINGS > SKELP
SKELPIT *vb* Scots word meaning skelped
SKELPS > SKELP
SKELTER *vb* scurry
SKELTERED > SKELTER
SKELTERS > SKELTER
SKELUM *n* Scots word meaning rascal
SKELUMS > SKELUM
SKEN *vb* squint or stare
SKENE *n* Scots word meaning dagger
SKENES > SKENE
SKENNED > SKEN
SKENNING > SKEN
SKENS > SKEN
SKEO *n* Scots dialect word meaning hut
SKEOS > SKEO
SKEP *n* beehive, esp one constructed of straw ▷ *vb* gather into a hive
SKEPFUL *n* amount skep will hold
SKEPFULS > SKEP
SKEPPED > SKEP
SKEPPING > SKEP
SKEPS > SKEP
SKEPSIS *n* doubt
SKEPSISES > SKEPSIS
SKEPTIC *same as* > SCEPTIC
SKEPTICAL > SKEPTIC
SKEPTICS > SKEPTIC
SKER *vb* scour
SKERRED > SKER
SKERRICK *n* small fragment or amount
SKERRICKS > SKERRICK
SKERRIES > SKERRY
SKERRING > SKER
SKERRY *n* rocky island or reef
SKERS > SKER
SKET *vb* splash (water)
SKETCH *n* rough drawing ▷ *vb* make a sketch (of)
SKETCHED > SKETCH
SKETCHER > SKETCH
SKETCHERS > SKETCH
SKETCHES > SKETCH
SKETCHIER > SKETCHY
SKETCHILY > SKETCHY
SKETCHING > SKETCH
SKETCHPAD *n* pad of paper for sketching
SKETCHY *adj* incomplete or inadequate
SKETS > SKET
SKETTED > SKET
SKETTING > SKET
SKEW *vb* make slanting or crooked ▷ *adj* slanting or crooked ▷ *n* slanting position
SKEWBACK *n* sloping surface on both sides of a segmental arch that takes the thrust
SKEWBACKS > SKEWBACK
SKEWBALD *adj* (horse) marked with patches of white and another colour ▷ *n* horse with this marking
SKEWBALDS > SKEWBALD
SKEWED > SKEW
SKEWER *n* pin to hold meat together during cooking ▷ *vb* fasten with a skewer
SKEWERED > SKEWER
SKEWERING > SKEWER
SKEWERS > SKEWER
SKEWEST > SKEW
SKEWING > SKEW
SKEWNESS *n* quality or condition of being skew
SKEWS > SKEW
SKEWWHIFF *adj* crooked or slanting
SKI *n* one of a pair of long runners fastened to boots for gliding over snow or water ▷ *vb* travel on skis
SKIABLE > SKI
SKIAGRAM *n* picture made from shadows
SKIAGRAMS > SKIAGRAM
SKIAGRAPH *n* skiagram
SKIAMACHY *same as* > SCIAMACHY
SKIASCOPE *n* medical instrument for examining the eye to detect errors of refraction
SKIASCOPY *n* retinoscopy
SKIATRON *n* type of cathode ray tube
SKIATRONS > SKIATRON
SKIBOB *n* vehicle made of two short skis for gliding down snow slopes
SKIBOBBED > SKIBOB
SKIBOBBER > SKIBOB
SKIBOBS > SKIBOB
SKID *vb* (of a moving vehicle) slide sideways uncontrollably ▷ *n* skidding
SKIDDED > SKID
SKIDDER > SKID
SKIDDERS > SKID
SKIDDIER > SKID
SKIDDIEST > SKID
SKIDDING > SKID
SKIDDOO *vb* go away quickly
SKIDDOOED > SKIDDOO
SKIDDOOS > SKIDDOO
SKIDDY > SKID
SKIDLID *n* crash helmet
SKIDLIDS > SKIDLID
SKIDOO *n* snowmobile ▷ *vb* travel on a skidoo
SKIDOOED > SKIDOO
SKIDOOING > SKIDOO
SKIDOOS > SKIDOO
SKIDPAN *n* area made slippery so that vehicle drivers can practise controlling skids
SKIDPANS > SKIDPAN
SKIDPROOF *adj* (of a road surface, tyre, etc) preventing or resistant to skidding
SKIDS > SKID
SKIDWAY *n* platform on which logs ready for sawing are piled
SKIDWAYS > SKIDWAY
SKIED > SKY
SKIER > SKI
SKIERS > SKI
SKIES > SKY
SKIEY *adj* of the sky
SKIEYER > SKIEY
SKIEYEST > SKIEY
SKIFF *n* small boat ▷ *vb* travel in a skiff
SKIFFED > SKIFF
SKIFFING > SKIFF
SKIFFLE *n* style of popular music of the 1950s, played chiefly on guitars and improvised percussion instruments ▷ *vb* play this style of music
SKIFFLED > SKIFFLE
SKIFFLES > SKIFFLE

SKIFFLESS > SKIFF
SKIFFLING > SKIFFLE
SKIFFS > SKIFF
SKIING > SKI
SKIINGS > SKI
SKIJORER > SKIJORING
SKIJORERS > SKIJORING
SKIJORING *n* sport in which a skier is pulled over snow or ice, usually by a horse
SKILFUL *adj* having or showing skill
SKILFULLY > SKILFUL
SKILL *n* special ability or expertise
SKILLED *adj* possessing or demonstrating accomplishment, skill, or special training
SKILLESS > SKILL
SKILLET *n* small frying pan or shallow cooking pot
SKILLETS > SKILLET
SKILLFUL *same as* > SKILFUL
SKILLIER > SKILLY
SKILLIES > SKILLY
SKILLIEST > SKILLY
SKILLING *n* former Scandinavian coin of low denomination
SKILLINGS > SKILLING
SKILLION *n* part of a building having a lower, esp sloping, roof
SKILLIONS > SKILLION
SKILLS > SKILL
SKILLY *n* thin soup or gruel ▷ *adj* skilled
SKIM *vb* remove floating matter from the surface of (a liquid) ▷ *n* act or process of skimming
SKIMBOARD *n* type of surfboard, shorter than standard and rounded at both ends ▷ *vb* surf on a skimboard
SKIMMED > SKIM
SKIMMER *n* person or thing that skims
SKIMMERS > SKIMMER
SKIMMIA *n* shrub of S and SE Asia grown for its ornamental red berries and evergreen foliage
SKIMMIAS > SKIMMIA
SKIMMING > SKIM
SKIMMINGS *pl n* material that is skimmed off a liquid
SKIMO *n* informal and offensive word for an Inuit
SKIMOBILE *n* motor vehicle with skis for travelling on snow
SKIMOS > SKIMO
SKIMP *vb* not invest enough time, money, material, etc
SKIMPED > SKIMP
SKIMPIER > SKIMPY
SKIMPIEST > SKIMPY
SKIMPILY > SKIMPY
SKIMPING > SKIMP
SKIMPS > SKIMP
SKIMPY *adj* scanty or insufficient
SKIMS > SKIM
SKIN *n* outer covering of the body ▷ *vb* remove the skin of
SKINCARE *n* use of cosmetics in taking care of skin
SKINCARES > SKINCARE
SKINFLICK *n* film containing much nudity and sex
SKINFLINT *n* miser
SKINFOOD *n* cosmetic cream for the skin
SKINFOODS > SKINFOOD
SKINFUL *n* sufficient alcoholic drink to make one drunk
SKINFULS > SKINFUL
SKINHEAD *n* youth with very short hair
SKINHEADS > SKINHEAD
SKINK *n* any lizard of the family *Scincidae* ▷ *vb* serve a drink
SKINKED > SKINK
SKINKER > SKINK
SKINKERS > SKINK
SKINKING > SKINK
SKINKS > SKINK
SKINLESS > SKIN
SKINLIKE > SKIN
SKINNED > SKIN
SKINNER *n* person who prepares or deals in animal skins
SKINNERS > SKINNER
SKINNIER > SKINNY
SKINNIEST > SKINNY
SKINNING > SKIN
SKINNY *adj* thin
SKINS > SKIN
SKINT *adj* having no money
SKINTER > SKINT
SKINTEST > SKINT
SKINTIGHT *adj* fitting tightly over the body
SKIO *n* Scots dialect word meaning hut
SKIORING *n* sport of being towed on skis by horse
SKIORINGS > SKIORING
SKIOS > SKIO
SKIP *vb* leap lightly from one foot to the other ▷ *n* skipping
SKIPJACK *n* important food fish of tropical seas
SKIPJACKS > SKIPJACK
SKIPLANE *n* aircraft fitted with skis to enable it to land on and take off from snow
SKIPLANES > SKIPLANE
SKIPPABLE > SKIP
SKIPPED > SKIP
SKIPPER *vb* captain ▷ *n* captain of a ship or aircraft
SKIPPERED > SKIPPER
SKIPPERS > SKIPPER
SKIPPET *n* small round box for preserving a document or seal
SKIPPETS > SKIPPET
SKIPPIER > SKIPPY
SKIPPIEST > SKIPPY
SKIPPING > SKIP
SKIPPINGS > SKIP
SKIPPY *adj* in high spirits
SKIPS > SKIP
SKIRL *n* sound of bagpipes ▷ *vb* (of bagpipes) to give out a shrill sound
SKIRLED > SKIRL
SKIRLING > SKIRL
SKIRLINGS > SKIRL
SKIRLS > SKIRL
SKIRMISH *n* brief or minor fight or argument ▷ *vb* take part in a skirmish
SKIRR *vb* move, run, or fly rapidly ▷ *n* whirring or grating sound, as of the wings of birds in flight
SKIRRED > SKIRR
SKIRRET *n* umbelliferous Old World plant
SKIRRETS > SKIRRET
SKIRRING > SKIRR
SKIRRS > SKIRR
SKIRT *n* woman's garment hanging from the waist ▷ *vb* border
SKIRTED > SKIRT
SKIRTER *n* man who skirts fleeces
SKIRTERS > SKIRTER
SKIRTING *n* border fixed round the base of an interior wall to protect it from kicks, dirt, etc
SKIRTINGS *pl n* ragged edges trimmed from the fleece of a sheep
SKIRTLESS > SKIRT
SKIRTLIKE > SKIRT
SKIRTS > SKIRT
SKIS > SKI
SKIT *n* brief satirical sketch
SKITCH *vb* (of a dog) to attack
SKITCHED > SKITCH
SKITCHES > SKITCH
SKITCHING > SKITCH
SKITE *n* boast ▷ *vb* boast
SKITED > SKITE
SKITES > SKITE
SKITING > SKITE
SKITS > SKIT
SKITTER *vb* move or run rapidly or lightly
SKITTERED > SKITTER
SKITTERS > SKITTER
SKITTERY *adj* moving lightly and rapidly
SKITTISH *adj* playful or lively
SKITTLE *n* bottle-shaped object used as a target in some games ▷ *vb* play skittles
SKITTLED > SKITTLE
SKITTLES > SKITTLE
SKITTLING > SKITTLE
SKIVE *vb* evade work or responsibility
SKIVED > SKIVE
SKIVER *n* tanned outer layer split from a skin ▷ *v*[b] cut leather
SKIVERED > SKIVER
SKIVERING > SKIVER
SKIVERS > SKIVER
SKIVES > SKIVE
SKIVIE *adj* old Scots word meaning disarranged
SKIVIER > SKIVIE
SKIVIEST > SKIVIE
SKIVING > SKIVE
SKIVINGS > SKIVE
SKIVVIED > SKIVVY
SKIVVIES > SKIVVY
SKIVVY *n* female servant who does menial work ▷ *vb* work as a skivvy
SKIVVYING > SKIVVY
SKIVY > SKIVE
SKIWEAR *n* clothes for skiing in
SKLATE *Scots word for* > SLATE
SKLATED > SKLATE
SKLATES > SKLATE
SKLATING > SKLATE
SKLENT *Scots word for* > SLANT
SKLENTED > SKLENT
SKLENTING > SKLENT
SKLENTS > SKLENT
SKLIFF *n* Scots word meaning little piece
SKLIFFS > SKLIFF
SKLIM *vb* Scots word meaning climb
SKLIMMED > SKLIM
SKLIMMING > SKLIM
SKLIMS > SKLIM
SKOAL *same as* > SKOL
SKOALED > SKOAL
SKOALING > SKOAL
SKOALS > SKOAL
SKOFF *vb* eat greedily
SKOFFED > SKOFF
SKOFFING > SKOFF
SKOFFS > SKOFF
SKOKIAAN *n* (in South Africa) a potent alcoholic beverage
SKOKIAANS > SKOKIAAN
SKOL *sentence substitute* good health! (a drinking toast) ▷ *vb* down (an alcoholic drink) in one go
SKOLIA > SKOLION
SKOLION *n* ancient Greek drinking song
SKOLLED > SKOL
SKOLLIE *same as* > SKOLLY
SKOLLIES > SKOLLY
SKOLLING > SKOL
SKOLLY *n* hooligan, usually one of a gang
SKOLS > SKOL
SKOOKUM *adj* strong or brave
SKOOL *ironically illiterate or childish spelling of* > SCHOOL

OOLS > SKOOL
OOSH *vb* Scots word meaning squirt
OOSHED > SKOOSH
OOSHES > SKOOSH
OOSHING > SKOOSH
ORT *n* pair of shorts with a front panel which gives he appearance of a skirt
ORTS > SKORT
OSH *n* little bit
OSHES > SKOSH
RAN *n* food
RANS > SKRAN
REEGH *vb* Scots word meaning screech
REEGHED > SKREEGH
REEGHS > SKREEGH
REEN *n* screen
REENS > SKREEN
REIGH *vb* Scots word meaning screech
REIGHED > SKREIGH
REIGHS > SKREIGH
RIECH *vb* Scots word meaning screech
RIECHED > SKRIECH
RIECHS > SKRIECH
RIED > SKRY
RIEGH *vb* Scots word meaning screech
RIEGHED > SKRIEGH
RIEGHS > SKRIEGH
RIES > SKRY
RIK *n* South African word meaning fright
RIKE *vb* cry
RIKED > SKRIKE
RIKES > SKRIKE
RIKING > SKRIKE
RIKS > SKRIK
RIMMAGE *vb* scrimmage
RIMP *vb* steal apples
RIMPED > SKRIMP
RIMPING > SKRIMP
RIMPS > SKRIMP
RUMP *vb* steal apples
RUMPED > SKRUMP
RUMPING > SKRUMP
RUMPS > SKRUMP
RY *vb* try to tell future
RYER > SKRY
RYERS > SKRY
RYING > SKRY
UA *n* large predatory gull
UAS > SKUA
UDLER *n* Scots word meaning leader of estivities
UDLERS > SKUDLER
UG *vb* shelter
UGGED > SKUG
UGGING > SKUG
UGS > SKUG
ULK *vb* move stealthily ▷ *n* person who skulks
ULKED > SKULK
ULKER > SKULK
ULKERS > SKULK
ULKING > SKULK
ULKINGS > SKULK
ULKS > SKULK
ULL *n* bony framework of the head ▷ *vb* strike on the head
SKULLCAP *n* close-fitting brimless cap
SKULLCAPS > SKULLCAP
SKULLED > SKULL
SKULLING > SKULL
SKULLS > SKULL
SKULPIN *n* North American fish
SKULPINS > SKULPIN
SKUMMER *vb* defecate
SKUMMERED > SKUMMER
SKUMMERS > SKUMMER
SKUNK *n* small black-and-white N American mammal which emits a foul-smelling fluid when attacked ▷ *vb* defeat overwhelmingly in a game
SKUNKBIRD *n* North American songbird
SKUNKED > SKUNK
SKUNKIER > SKUNK
SKUNKIEST > SKUNK
SKUNKING > SKUNK
SKUNKS > SKUNK
SKUNKWEED *n* low-growing fetid swamp plant of N America
SKUNKY > SKUNK
SKURRIED > SKURRY
SKURRIES > SKURRY
SKURRY *vb* scurry
SKURRYING > SKURRY
SKUTTLE *vb* scuttle
SKUTTLED > SKUTTLE
SKUTTLES > SKUTTLE
SKUTTLING > SKUTTLE
SKY *n* upper atmosphere as seen from the earth ▷ *vb* hit high in the air
SKYBOARD *n* small board used for skysurfing
SKYBOARDS > SKYBOARD
SKYBORN *adj* born in heaven
SKYBORNE *adj* flying through sky
SKYBOX *n* luxurious suite high up in the stand of a sports stadium
SKYBOXES > SKYBOX
SKYBRIDGE *n* covered, elevated bridge connecting two buildings
SKYCAP *n* luggage porter at American airport
SKYCAPS > SKYCAP
SKYCLAD *adj* naked
SKYDIVE *vb* take part in skydiving
SKYDIVED > SKYDIVE
SKYDIVER > SKYDIVE
SKYDIVERS > SKYDIVE
SKYDIVES > SKYDIVE
SKYDIVING *n* sport of jumping from an aircraft and performing manoeuvres before opening one's parachute
SKYDOVE > SKYDIVE
SKYED > SKY
SKYER *n* cricket ball hit up into air
SKYERS > SKYER
SKYEY *adj* of the sky
SKYF *n* South African slang for a cigarette or substance for smoking ▷ *vb* smoke a cigarette
SKYFED > SKYF
SKYFING > SKYF
SKYFS > SKYF
SKYHOME *n* Australian slang for a sub-penthouse flat in a tall building
SKYHOMES > SKYHOME
SKYHOOK *n* hook hung from helicopter
SKYHOOKS > SKYHOOK
SKYIER > SKYEY
SKYIEST > SKYEY
SKYING > SKY
SKYISH > SKY
SKYJACK *vb* hijack (an aircraft)
SKYJACKED > SKYJACK
SKYJACKER > SKYJACK
SKYJACKS > SKYJACK
SKYLAB *n* orbiting space station
SKYLABS > SKYLAB
SKYLARK *n* lark that sings while soaring at a great height ▷ *vb* play or frolic
SKYLARKED > SKYLARK
SKYLARKER > SKYLARK
SKYLARKS > SKYLARK
SKYLIGHT *n* window in a roof or ceiling
SKYLIGHTS > SKYLIGHT
SKYLIKE > SKY
SKYLINE *n* outline of buildings, trees, etc against the sky
SKYLINES > SKYLINE
SKYLIT *adj* having skylight
SKYMAN *n* paratrooper
SKYMEN > SKYMAN
SKYPHOI > SKYPHOS
SKYPHOS *n* ancient Greek drinking cup
SKYR *n* Scandinavian cheese
SKYRE *vb* Scots word meaning shine
SKYRED > SKYRE
SKYRES > SKYRE
SKYRING > SKYRE
SKYROCKET *vb* rise very quickly
SKYRS > SKYR
SKYSAIL *n* square sail set above the royal on a square-rigger
SKYSAILS > SKYSAIL
SKYSCAPE *n* painting, drawing, photograph, etc, representing or depicting the sky
SKYSCAPES > SKYSCAPE
SKYSURF *vb* perform freefall aerobatics
SKYSURFED > SKYSURF
SKYSURFER *n* someone who performs stunts with a small board attached to his or her feet while in free fall
SKYSURFS > SKYSURF
SKYTE *vb* Scots word meaning slide
SKYTED > SKYTE
SKYTES > SKYTE
SKYTING > SKYTE
SKYWALK *n* tightrope walk at great height
SKYWALKS > SKYWALK
SKYWARD *adj* towards the sky ▷ *adv* towards the sky
SKYWARDS *same as* > SKYWARD
SKYWAY *n* air route
SKYWAYS > SKYWAY
SKYWRITE *vb* write message in sky with smoke from aircraft
SKYWRITER > SKYWRITE
SKYWRITES > SKYWRITE
SKYWROTE > SKYWRITE
SLAB *n* broad flat piece ▷ *vb* cut or make into a slab or slabs
SLABBED > SLAB
SLABBER *vb* dribble from the mouth
SLABBERED > SLABBER
SLABBERER > SLABBER
SLABBERS > SLABBER
SLABBERY > SLABBER
SLABBIER > SLAB
SLABBIEST > SLAB
SLABBING > SLAB
SLABBY > SLAB
SLABLIKE > SLAB
SLABS > SLAB
SLABSTONE *n* flagstone
SLACK *same as* > SLAKE
SLACKED > SLACK
SLACKEN *vb* make or become slack
SLACKENED > SLACKEN
SLACKENER > SLACKEN
SLACKENS > SLACKEN
SLACKER *n* person who evades work or duty
SLACKERS > SLACKER
SLACKEST > SLACK
SLACKING > SLACK
SLACKLY > SLACK
SLACKNESS > SLACK
SLACKS *pl n* casual trousers
SLADANG *n* Malayan tapir
SLADANGS > SLADANG
SLADE *n* little valley
SLADES > SLADE
SLAE *Scots word for* > SLOE
SLAES > SLAE
SLAG *n* waste left after metal is smelted ▷ *vb* criticize
SLAGGED > SLAG
SLAGGIER > SLAG
SLAGGIEST > SLAG
SLAGGING > SLAG
SLAGGINGS > SLAG
SLAGGY > SLAG
SLAGS > SLAG
SLAID *vb* Scots word for 'slid'
SLAIN > SLAY
SLAINTE *interj* cheers!

SLAIRG *Scots word for* > SPREAD
SLAIRGED > SLAIRG
SLAIRGING > SLAIRG
SLAIRGS > SLAIRG
SLAISTER *vb* cover with a sloppy mess ▷ *n* sloppy mess
SLAISTERS > SLAISTER
SLAISTERY > SLAISTER
SLAKABLE > SLAKE
SLAKE *vb* satisfy (thirst or desire)
SLAKEABLE > SLAKE
SLAKED > SLAKE
SLAKELESS *adj* impossible to slake
SLAKER > SLAKE
SLAKERS > SLAKE
SLAKES > SLAKE
SLAKING > SLAKE
SLALOM *n* skiing or canoeing race over a winding course ▷ *vb* take part in a slalom
SLALOMED > SLALOM
SLALOMER > SLALOM
SLALOMERS > SLALOM
SLALOMING > SLALOM
SLALOMIST > SLALOM
SLALOMS > SLALOM
SLAM *vb* shut, put down, or hit violently and noisily ▷ *n* act or sound of slamming
SLAMDANCE *vb* dance aggressively, bumping into others
SLAMMAKIN *n* woman's loose dress
SLAMMED > SLAM
SLAMMER *n* prison
SLAMMERS > SLAMMER
SLAMMING > SLAM
SLAMMINGS > SLAM
SLAMS > SLAM
SLANDER *n* false and malicious statement about a person ▷ *vb* utter slander about
SLANDERED > SLANDER
SLANDERER > SLANDER
SLANDERS > SLANDER
SLANE *n* spade for cutting turf
SLANES > SLANE
SLANG *n* very informal language ▷ *vb* use insulting language to (someone)
SLANGED > SLANG
SLANGER *n* street vendor
SLANGERS > SLANGER
SLANGIER > SLANG
SLANGIEST > SLANG
SLANGILY > SLANG
SLANGING > SLANG
SLANGINGS > SLANG
SLANGISH > SLANG
SLANGS > SLANG
SLANGUAGE *n* language using slang
SLANGULAR *adj* of or using slang
SLANGY > SLANG
SLANK *dialect word for* > LANK
SLANT *vb* lean at an angle, slope ▷ *n* slope
SLANTED > SLANT
SLANTER *same as* > SLINTER
SLANTERS > SLANTER
SLANTING > SLANT
SLANTLY > SLANT
SLANTS > SLANT
SLANTWAYS *same as* > SLANTWISE
SLANTWISE *adj* in a slanting or oblique direction
SLANTY *adj* slanting
SLAP *n* blow with the open hand or a flat object ▷ *vb* strike with the open hand or a flat object
SLAPDASH *adj* careless and hasty ▷ *adv* carelessly or hastily ▷ *n* slapdash activity or work
SLAPHAPPY *adj* cheerfully irresponsible or careless
SLAPHEAD *n* derogatory term for a bald person
SLAPHEADS > SLAPHEAD
SLAPJACK *n* simple card game
SLAPJACKS > SLAPJACK
SLAPPED > SLAP
SLAPPER > SLAP
SLAPPERS > SLAP
SLAPPING > SLAP
SLAPS > SLAP
SLAPSHOT *n* hard, fast, often wild, shot executed with a powerful downward swing
SLAPSHOTS > SLAPSHOT
SLAPSTICK *n* boisterous knockabout comedy
SLART *vb* spill (something)
SLARTED > SLART
SLARTING > SLART
SLARTS > SLART
SLASH *vb* cut with a sweeping stroke ▷ *n* sweeping stroke
SLASHED > SLASH
SLASHER *n* tool or tractor-drawn machine used for cutting scrub or undergrowth in the bush
SLASHERS > SLASHER
SLASHES > SLASH
SLASHFEST *n* film or computer game that features bloody killings involving blades
SLASHING *adj* aggressively critical ▷ *n* act of slashing
SLASHINGS > SLASHING
SLAT *n* narrow strip of wood or metal ▷ *vb* provide with slats
SLATCH *n* slack part of rope
SLATCHES > SLATCH
SLATE *n* rock which splits easily into thin layers ▷ *vb* cover with slates ▷ *adj* dark grey
SLATED > SLATE
SLATELIKE > SLATE
SLATER *n* person trained in laying roof slates
SLATERS > SLATER
SLATES > SLATE
SLATEY *adj* slightly mad
SLATHER *vb* spread quickly or lavishly
SLATHERED > SLATHER
SLATHERS > SLATHER
SLATIER > SLATY
SLATIEST > SLATY
SLATINESS > SLATY
SLATING *n* act or process of laying slates
SLATINGS > SLATING
SLATS > SLAT
SLATTED > SLAT
SLATTER *vb* be slovenly
SLATTERED > SLATTER
SLATTERN *n* slovenly woman
SLATTERNS > SLATTERN
SLATTERS > SLATTER
SLATTERY *adj* slovenly
SLATTING > SLAT
SLATTINGS > SLAT
SLATY *adj* consisting of or resembling slate
SLAUGHTER *vb* kill (animals) for food ▷ *n* slaughtering
SLAVE *n* person owned by another for whom he or she has to work ▷ *vb* work like a slave
SLAVED > SLAVE
SLAVER *n* person or ship engaged in the slave trade ▷ *vb* dribble saliva from the mouth
SLAVERED > SLAVER
SLAVERER > SLAVER
SLAVERERS > SLAVER
SLAVERIES > SLAVERY
SLAVERING > SLAVER
SLAVERS > SLAVER
SLAVERY *n* state or condition of being a slave
SLAVES > SLAVE
SLAVEY *n* female general servant
SLAVEYS > SLAVEY
SLAVING > SLAVE
SLAVISH *adj* of or like a slave
SLAVISHLY > SLAVISH
SLAVOCRAT *n* US slaveholder before the Civil War
SLAVOPHIL *n* person who admires the Slavs or their cultures
SLAW *short for* > COLESLAW
SLAWS > SLAW
SLAY *vb* kill
SLAYABLE > SLAY
SLAYED > SLAY
SLAYER > SLAY
SLAYERS > SLAY
SLAYING > SLAY
SLAYS > SLAY
SLEAVE *n* tangled thread ▷ *vb* disentangle (twiste thread, etc)
SLEAVED > SLEAVE
SLEAVES > SLEAVE
SLEAVING > SLEAVE
SLEAZE *n* behaviour in public life considered immoral, dishonest, or disreputable
SLEAZEBAG *n* disgusting person
SLEAZES > SLEAZE
SLEAZIER > SLEAZY
SLEAZIEST > SLEAZY
SLEAZILY > SLEAZY
SLEAZO *n* sleazy person
SLEAZOID *n* sleazy perso
SLEAZOIDS > SLEAZOID
SLEAZY *adj* run-down or sordid
SLED *same as* > SLEDGE
SLEDDED > SLED
SLEDDER > SLED
SLEDDERS > SLED
SLEDDING > SLED
SLEDDINGS > SLED
SLEDED > SLED
SLEDGE *n* carriage on runners for sliding on snow ▷ *vb* travel by sled
SLEDGED > SLEDGE
SLEDGER > SLEDGE
SLEDGERS > SLEDGE
SLEDGES > SLEDGE
SLEDGING > SLEDGE
SLEDGINGS > SLEDGE
SLEDS > SLED
SLEE *Scots word for* > SLY
SLEECH *n* slippery mud
SLEECHES > SLEECH
SLEECHIER > SLEECH
SLEECHY > SLEECH
SLEEK *adj* glossy, smooth and shiny ▷ *vb* make smooth and glossy, as by grooming, etc
SLEEKED > SLEEK
SLEEKEN *vb* make sleek
SLEEKENED > SLEEKEN
SLEEKENS > SLEEKEN
SLEEKER > SLEEK
SLEEKERS > SLEEK
SLEEKEST > SLEEK
SLEEKIER > SLEEK
SLEEKIEST > SLEEK
SLEEKING > SLEEK
SLEEKINGS > SLEEK
SLEEKIT *adj* smooth
SLEEKLY > SLEEK
SLEEKNESS > SLEEK
SLEEKS > SLEEK
SLEEKY > SLEEK
SLEEP *n* state of rest characterized by unconsciousness ▷ *vb* b in or as if in a state of slee
SLEEPAWAY *n* camp for teenagers
SLEEPER *n* railway car fitted for sleeping in
SLEEPERS > SLEEPER
SLEEPERY *Scots word for* > SLEEPY

.EEPIER > SLEEPY
.EEPIEST > SLEEPY
.EEPILY > SLEEPY
.EEPING > SLEEP
.EEPINGS > SLEEP
.EEPLESS *adj* (of a night) one during which one does not sleep
.EEPLIKE > SLEEP
.EEPOUT *n* small building for sleeping in
.EEPOUTS > SLEEPOUT
.EEPOVER *n* occasion when a person stays overnight at a friend's house
.EEPRY *Scots word for* > SLEEPY
.EEPS > SLEEP
.EEPSUIT *n* baby's sleeping garment
.EEPWALK *vb* walk while asleep
.EEPWEAR *n* clothes for sleeping in
.EEPY *adj* needing sleep
.EER > SLEE
.EEST > SLEE
.EET *n* rain and snow or hail falling together ▷ *vb* fall as sleet
.EETED > SLEET
.EETIER > SLEET
.EETIEST > SLEET
.EETING > SLEET
.EETS > SLEET
.EETY > SLEET
.EEVE *n* part of a garment which covers the arm
.EEVED > SLEEVE
.EEVEEN *n* sly obsequious smooth-tongued person
.EEVEENS > SLEEVEEN
.EEVELET *n* protective covering for forearm
.EEVER *n* old beer measure
.EEVERS > SLEEVER
.EEVES > SLEEVE
.EEVING *n* tubular flexible insulation into which bare wire can be inserted
.EEVINGS > SLEEVING
.EEZIER > SLEEZY
.EEZIEST > SLEEZY
.EEZY *adj* sleazy
.EIDED *adj* old word meaning separated
.EIGH *same as* > SLEDGE
.EIGHED > SLEIGH
.EIGHER > SLEIGH
.EIGHERS > SLEIGH
.EIGHING > SLEIGH
.EIGHS > SLEIGH
.EIGHT *n* skill or cunning
.EIGHTS > SLEIGHT
.ENDER *adj* slim
.ENDERER > SLENDER
.ENDERLY > SLENDER
.ENTER *same as* > SLINTER
.ENTERS > SLENTER
.EPT > SLEEP
.EUTH *n* detective ▷ *vb* track or follow
SLEUTHED > SLEUTH
SLEUTHING > SLEUTH
SLEUTHS > SLEUTH
SLEW *vb* twist sideways, esp awkwardly
SLEWED > SLEW
SLEWING > SLEW
SLEWS > SLEW
SLEY *n* weaver's tool for separating threads
SLEYS > SLEY
SLICE *n* thin flat piece cut from something ▷ *vb* cut into slices
SLICEABLE > SLICE
SLICED > SLICE
SLICER > SLICE
SLICERS > SLICE
SLICES > SLICE
SLICING > SLICE
SLICINGS > SLICE
SLICK *adj* persuasive and glib ▷ *n* patch of oil on water ▷ *vb* make smooth or sleek
SLICKED > SLICK
SLICKEN *vb* make smooth
SLICKENED > SLICKEN
SLICKENER > SLICKEN
SLICKENS > SLICKEN
SLICKER *n* sly or untrustworthy person
SLICKERED *adj* wearing a waterproof jacket
SLICKERS > SLICKER
SLICKEST > SLICK
SLICKING > SLICK
SLICKINGS > SLICK
SLICKLY > SLICK
SLICKNESS > SLICK
SLICKROCK *n* weathered and smooth sandstone or other rock
SLICKS > SLICK
SLICKSTER *n* dishonest person
SLID > SLIDE
SLIDABLE > SLIDE
SLIDDEN > SLIDE
SLIDDER *vb* slip
SLIDDERED > SLIDDER
SLIDDERS > SLIDDER
SLIDDERY *adj* slippery
SLIDE *vb* slip smoothly along (a surface) ▷ *n* sliding
SLIDED > SLIDE
SLIDER > SLIDE
SLIDERS > SLIDE
SLIDES > SLIDE
SLIDEWAY *n* sloping channel down which things are slid
SLIDEWAYS > SLIDEWAY
SLIDING > SLIDE
SLIDINGLY > SLIDE
SLIDINGS > SLIDE
SLIER > SLY
SLIEST > SLY
SLIEVE *n* Irish mountain
SLIEVES > SLIEVE
SLIGHT *adj* small in quantity or extent ▷ *n* snub ▷ *vb* insult (someone) by behaving rudely
SLIGHTED > SLIGHT
SLIGHTER > SLIGHT
SLIGHTERS > SLIGHT
SLIGHTEST > SLIGHT
SLIGHTING *adj* characteristic of a slight
SLIGHTISH > SLIGHT
SLIGHTLY *adv* in small measure or degree
SLIGHTS > SLIGHT
SLILY > SLY
SLIM *adj* not heavy or stout, thin ▷ *vb* make or become slim by diet and exercise
SLIMDOWN *n* instance of an organization cutting staff
SLIMDOWNS > SLIMDOWN
SLIME *n* unpleasant thick slippery substance ▷ *vb* cover with slime
SLIMEBALL *n* odious and contemptible person
SLIMED > SLIME
SLIMES > SLIME
SLIMIER > SLIMY
SLIMIEST > SLIMY
SLIMILY > SLIMY
SLIMINESS > SLIMY
SLIMING > SLIME
SLIMLINE *adj* slim
SLIMLY > SLIM
SLIMMED > SLIM
SLIMMER > SLIM
SLIMMERS > SLIM
SLIMMEST > SLIM
SLIMMING > SLIM
SLIMMINGS > SLIM
SLIMMISH > SLIM
SLIMNESS > SLIM
SLIMPSIER > SLIMPSY
SLIMPSY *adj* thin and flimsy
SLIMS > SLIM
SLIMSIER > SLIMSY
SLIMSIEST > SLIMSY
SLIMSY *adj* frail
SLIMY *adj* of, like, or covered with slime
SLING *n* bandage hung from the neck to support an injured hand or arm ▷ *vb* throw
SLINGBACK *n* shoe with a strap that goes around the back of the heel
SLINGER > SLING
SLINGERS > SLING
SLINGING > SLING
SLINGS > SLING
SLINGSHOT *n* Y-shaped implement with a loop of elastic fastened to the ends of the two prongs, used for shooting small stones, etc
SLINK *vb* move furtively or guiltily ▷ *n* animal, esp a calf, born prematurely
SLINKED > SLINK
SLINKER > SLINK
SLINKERS > SLINK
SLINKIER > SLINKY
SLINKIEST > SLINKY
SLINKILY > SLINKY
SLINKING > SLINK
SLINKS > SLINK
SLINKSKIN *n* skin of premature calf
SLINKWEED *n* plant believed to make cow give birth prematurely
SLINKY *adj* (of clothes) figure-hugging
SLINTER *n* dodge, trick, or stratagem
SLINTERS > SLINTER
SLIOTAR *n* ball used in hurling
SLIOTARS > SLIOTAR
SLIP *vb* lose balance by sliding ▷ *n* slipping
SLIPCASE *n* protective case for a book that is open at one end so that only the spine of the book is visible
SLIPCASED *adj* having a slipcase
SLIPCASES > SLIPCASE
SLIPCOVER *n* fitted but easily removable cloth cover for a chair, sofa, etc
SLIPDRESS *n* silky sleeveless dress
SLIPE *n* wool removed from the pelt of a slaughtered sheep by immersion in a chemical bath ▷ *vb* remove skin
SLIPED > SLIPE
SLIPES > SLIPE
SLIPFORM *n* mould used in building
SLIPFORMS > SLIPFORM
SLIPING > SLIPE
SLIPKNOT *n* knot tied so that it will slip along the rope round which it is made
SLIPKNOTS > SLIPKNOT
SLIPLESS > SLIP
SLIPNOOSE *n* noose made with a slipknot, so that it tightens when pulled
SLIPOUT *n* instance of slipping out
SLIPOUTS > SLIPOUT
SLIPOVER *adj* of or denoting a garment that can be put on easily over the head ▷ *n* such a garment, esp a sleeveless pullover
SLIPOVERS > SLIPOVER
SLIPPAGE *n* act or an instance of slipping
SLIPPAGES > SLIPPAGE
SLIPPED > SLIP
SLIPPER *n* light shoe for indoor wear ▷ *vb* hit or beat with a slipper
SLIPPERED > SLIPPER
SLIPPERS > SLIPPER
SLIPPERY *adj* so smooth or wet as to cause slipping or be difficult to hold

SLIPPIER > SLIPPY
SLIPPIEST > SLIPPY
SLIPPILY > SLIPPY
SLIPPING > SLIP
SLIPPY *adj* slippery
SLIPRAIL *n* rail in a fence that can be slipped out of place to make an opening
SLIPRAILS > SLIPRAIL
SLIPS > SLIP
SLIPSHEET *n* sheet of paper that is interleaved between freshly printed sheets
SLIPSHOD *adj* (of an action) careless
SLIPSLOP *n* weak or unappetizing food or drink
SLIPSLOPS > SLIPSLOP
SLIPSOLE *n* separate sole on shoe
SLIPSOLES > SLIPSOLE
SLIPT *vb* old form of slipped
SLIPUP *n* mistake or mishap
SLIPUPS > SLIPUP
SLIPWARE *n* pottery that has been decorated with slip
SLIPWARES > SLIPWARE
SLIPWAY *n* launching slope on which ships are built or repaired
SLIPWAYS > SLIPWAY
SLISH *n* old word meaning cut
SLISHES > SLISH
SLIT *n* long narrow cut or opening ▷ *vb* make a long straight cut in
SLITHER *vb* slide unsteadily ▷ *n* slithering movement
SLITHERED > SLITHER
SLITHERS > SLITHER
SLITHERY *adj* moving with a slithering motion
SLITLESS > SLIT
SLITLIKE > SLIT
SLITS > SLIT
SLITTED > SLIT
SLITTER > SLIT
SLITTERS > SLIT
SLITTIER > SLIT
SLITTIEST > SLIT
SLITTING > SLIT
SLITTY > SLIT
SLIVE *vb* slip
SLIVED > SLIVE
SLIVEN > SLIVE
SLIVER *n* small thin piece ▷ *vb* cut into slivers
SLIVERED > SLIVER
SLIVERER > SLIVER
SLIVERERS > SLIVER
SLIVERING > SLIVER
SLIVERS > SLIVER
SLIVES > SLIVE
SLIVING > SLIVE
SLIVOVIC *n* plum brandy
SLIVOVICA *n* plum brandy
SLIVOVITZ *n* plum brandy from E Europe
SLIVOWITZ *n* plum brandy
SLOAN *n* severe telling-off
SLOANS > SLOAN
SLOB *n* lazy and untidy person
SLOBBER *vb* dribble or drool ▷ *n* liquid or saliva spilt from the mouth
SLOBBERED > SLOBBER
SLOBBERER > SLOBBER
SLOBBERS > SLOBBER
SLOBBERY > SLOBBER
SLOBBIER > SLOB
SLOBBIEST > SLOB
SLOBBISH > SLOB
SLOBBY > SLOB
SLOBLAND *n* muddy ground
SLOBLANDS > SLOBLAND
SLOBS > SLOB
SLOCKEN *vb* Scots word meaning slake
SLOCKENED > SLOCKEN
SLOCKENS > SLOCKEN
SLOE *n* sour blue-black fruit
SLOEBUSH *n* bush on which sloes grow
SLOES > SLOE
SLOETHORN *n* sloe plant
SLOETREE *n* sloe plant
SLOETREES > SLOETREE
SLOG *vb* work hard and steadily ▷ *n* long and exhausting work or walk
SLOGAN *n* catchword or phrase used in politics or advertising
SLOGANEER *n* person who coins or employs slogans frequently ▷ *vb* coin or employ slogans so as to sway opinion
SLOGANISE *same as* > SLOGANIZE
SLOGANIZE *vb* use slogans
SLOGANS > SLOGAN
SLOGGED > SLOG
SLOGGER > SLOG
SLOGGERS > SLOG
SLOGGING > SLOG
SLOGS > SLOG
SLOID *n* Swedish woodwork
SLOIDS > SLOID
SLOJD *n* Swedish woodwork
SLOJDS > SLOJD
SLOKEN *vb* Scots word meaning slake
SLOKENED > SLOKEN
SLOKENING > SLOKEN
SLOKENS > SLOKEN
SLOMMOCK *vb* walk assertively with a hip-rolling gait
SLOMMOCKS > SLOMMOCK
SLOOM *vb* slumber
SLOOMED > SLOOM
SLOOMIER > SLOOM
SLOOMIEST > SLOOM
SLOOMING > SLOOM
SLOOMS > SLOOM
SLOOMY > SLOOM
SLOOP *n* small single-masted ship
SLOOPS > SLOOP
SLOOSH *vb* wash with water
SLOOSHED > SLOOSH
SLOOSHES > SLOOSH
SLOOSHING > SLOOSH
SLOOT *n* ditch for irrigation or drainage
SLOOTS > SLOOT
SLOP *vb* splash or spill ▷ *n* spilt liquid
SLOPE *vb* slant ▷ *n* sloping surface
SLOPED > SLOPE
SLOPER > SLOPE
SLOPERS > SLOPE
SLOPES > SLOPE
SLOPEWISE > SLOPE
SLOPIER > SLOPE
SLOPIEST > SLOPE
SLOPING > SLOPE
SLOPINGLY > SLOPE
SLOPPED > SLOP
SLOPPIER > SLOPPY
SLOPPIEST > SLOPPY
SLOPPILY > SLOPPY
SLOPPING > SLOP
SLOPPY *adj* careless or untidy
SLOPS > SLOP
SLOPWORK *n* manufacture of cheap shoddy clothing or the clothes so produced
SLOPWORKS > SLOPWORK
SLOPY > SLOPE
SLORM *vb* wipe carelessly
SLORMED > SLORM
SLORMING > SLORM
SLORMS > SLORM
SLOSH *vb* pour carelessly ▷ *n* splashing sound
SLOSHED > SLOSH
SLOSHES > SLOSH
SLOSHIER > SLOSH
SLOSHIEST > SLOSH
SLOSHING > SLOSH
SLOSHINGS > SLOSH
SLOSHY > SLOSH
SLOT *n* narrow opening for inserting something ▷ *vb* make a slot or slots in
SLOTBACK *n* American football player
SLOTBACKS > SLOTBACK
SLOTH *n* slow-moving animal of tropical America ▷ *vb* be lazy
SLOTHED > SLOTH
SLOTHFUL *adj* lazy or idle
SLOTHING > SLOTH
SLOTHS > SLOTH
SLOTS > SLOT
SLOTTED > SLOT
SLOTTER > SLOT
SLOTTERS > SLOT
SLOTTING > SLOT
SLOUCH *vb* sit, stand, or move with a drooping posture ▷ *n* drooping posture
SLOUCHED > SLOUCH
SLOUCHER > SLOUCH
SLOUCHERS > SLOUCH
SLOUCHES > SLOUCH
SLOUCHIER > SLOUCHY
SLOUCHILY > SLOUCHY
SLOUCHING > SLOUCH
SLOUCHY *adj* slouching
SLOUGH *n* bog ▷ *vb* (of a snake) shed (its skin)
SLOUGHED > SLOUGH
SLOUGHIER > SLOUGH
SLOUGHING > SLOUGH
SLOUGHS > SLOUGH
SLOUGHY > SLOUGH
SLOVE > SLIVE
SLOVEN *n* habitually dirty or untidy person
SLOVENLY *adj* dirty or untidy ▷ *adv* in a slovenl manner
SLOVENRY *n* quality of being slovenly
SLOVENS > SLOVEN
SLOW *adj* taking a longer time than is usual or expected ▷ *adv* slowly ▷ *vb* reduce the speed (of
SLOWBACK *n* lazy person
SLOWBACKS > SLOWBACK
SLOWCOACH *n* person wh moves or works slowly
SLOWDOWN *n* any slackeni of pace
SLOWDOWNS > SLOWDOWN
SLOWED > SLOW
SLOWER > SLOW
SLOWEST > SLOW
SLOWING > SLOW
SLOWINGS > SLOW
SLOWISH > SLOW
SLOWLY > SLOW
SLOWNESS > SLOW
SLOWPOKE *same as* > SLOWCOACH
SLOWPOKES > SLOWPOKE
SLOWS > SLOW
SLOWWORM *n* small legless lizard
SLOWWORMS > SLOWWORM
SLOYD *n* Swedish woodwork
SLOYDS > SLOYD
SLUB *n* lump in yarn or fabric, often made intentionally to give a knobbly effect ▷ *vb* drav out and twist (a sliver of fibre) preparatory to spinning ▷ *adj* (of material) having an irregular appearance
SLUBB *same as* > SLUB
SLUBBED > SLUB
SLUBBER *vb* smear
SLUBBERED > SLUBBER
SLUBBERS > SLUBBER
SLUBBIER > SLUB
SLUBBIEST > SLUB
SLUBBING > SLUB
SLUBBINGS > SLUB
SLUBBS > SLUBB
SLUBBY > SLUB
SLUBS > SLUB
SLUDGE *n* thick mud
SLUDGED > SLUDGE
SLUDGES > SLUDGE
SLUDGIER > SLUDGY

UDGIEST > SLUDGY
UDGING > SLUDGE
UDGY *adj* consisting of, containing, or like sludge
UE *same as* > SLEW
UED > SLUE
UEING > SLUE
UES > SLUE
UFF *same as* > SLOUGH
UFFED > SLUFF
UFFING > SLUFF
UFFS > SLUFF
UG *n* land snail with no shell ▷ *vb* hit hard
UGABED *n* person who remains in bed through laziness
UGABEDS > SLUGABED
UGFEST *n* fist fight
UGFESTS > SLUGFEST
UGGABED *same as* > SLUGABED
UGGARD *n* lazy person ▷ *adj* lazy
UGGARDS > SLUGGARD
UGGED > SLUG
UGGER *n* (esp in boxing, baseball, etc) a person who strikes hard
UGGERS > SLUGGER
UGGING > SLUG
UGGISH *adj* slow-moving, lacking energy
UGHORN *same as* > SLOGAN
UGHORNE *same as* > SLOGAN
UGHORNS > SLUGHORN
UGS > SLUG
UICE *n* channel that carries a rapid current of water ▷ *vb* drain water by means of a sluice
UICED > SLUICE
UICES > SLUICE
UICEWAY *same as* > SLUICE
UICIER > SLUICE
UICIEST > SLUICE
UICING > SLUICE
UICY > SLUICE
UING > SLUE
UIT *n* water channel in South Africa
UITS > SLUIT
UM *n* squalid overcrowded house or area ▷ *vb* temporarily and deliberately experience poorer places or conditions than usual
UMBER *n* sleep ▷ *vb* sleep
UMBERED > SLUMBER
UMBERER > SLUMBER
UMBERS > SLUMBER
UMBERY *adj* sleepy
UMBROUS *adj* sleepy
UMBRY *same as* > SLUMBERY
UMGUM *n* material left after wax is extracted from honeycomb
UMGUMS > SLUMGUM
UMISM *n* existence of slums

SLUMISMS > SLUMISM
SLUMLORD *n* absentee landlord of slum property, esp one who profiteers
SLUMLORDS > SLUMLORD
SLUMMED > SLUM
SLUMMER > SLUM
SLUMMERS > SLUM
SLUMMIER > SLUM
SLUMMIEST > SLUM
SLUMMING > SLUM
SLUMMINGS > SLUM
SLUMMOCK *vb* move slowly and heavily
SLUMMOCKS > SLUMMOCK
SLUMMY > SLUM
SLUMP *vb* (of prices or demand) decline suddenly ▷ *n* sudden decline in prices or demand
SLUMPED > SLUMP
SLUMPIER > SLUMPY
SLUMPIEST > SLUMPY
SLUMPING > SLUMP
SLUMPS > SLUMP
SLUMPY *adj* boggy
SLUMS > SLUM
SLUNG > SLING
SLUNGSHOT *n* weight attached to the end of a cord and used as a weapon
SLUNK > SLINK
SLUR *vb* pronounce or utter (words) indistinctly ▷ *n* slurring of words
SLURB *n* suburban slum
SLURBAN > SLURB
SLURBS > SLURB
SLURP *vb* eat or drink noisily ▷ *n* slurping sound
SLURPED > SLURP
SLURPER > SLURP
SLURPERS > SLURP
SLURPING > SLURP
SLURPS > SLURP
SLURRED > SLUR
SLURRIED > SLURRY
SLURRIES > SLURRY
SLURRING > SLUR
SLURRY *n* muddy liquid mixture ▷ *vb* spread slurry
SLURRYING > SLURRY
SLURS > SLUR
SLUSE *same as* > SLUICE
SLUSES > SLUICE
SLUSH *n* watery muddy substance ▷ *vb* make one's way through or as if through slush
SLUSHED > SLUSH
SLUSHES > SLUSH
SLUSHIER > SLUSHY
SLUSHIES > SLUSHY
SLUSHIEST > SLUSHY
SLUSHILY > SLUSHY
SLUSHING > SLUSH
SLUSHY *adj* of, resembling, or consisting of slush ▷ *n* unskilled kitchen assistant
SLUT *n* derogatory term for a dirty or immoral woman
SLUTCH *n* mud
SLUTCHES > SLUTCH
SLUTCHIER > SLUTCH

SLUTCHY > SLUTCH
SLUTS > SLUT
SLUTTERY *n* state of being slut
SLUTTIER > SLUT
SLUTTIEST > SLUT
SLUTTISH > SLUT
SLUTTY > SLUT
SLY *adj* crafty
SLYBOOTS *pl n* person who is sly
SLYER > SLY
SLYEST > SLY
SLYISH > SLY
SLYLY > SLY
SLYNESS > SLY
SLYNESSES > SLY
SLYPE *n* covered passageway in a church that connects the transept to the chapterhouse
SLYPES > SLYPE
SMA *Scots word for* > SMALL
SMAAK *vb* South African slang for like or love
SMAAKED > SMAAK
SMAAKING > SMAAK
SMAAKS > SMAAK
SMACK *vb* slap sharply ▷ *n* sharp slap ▷ *adv* squarely or directly
SMACKED > SMACK
SMACKER *n* loud kiss
SMACKERS > SMACKER
SMACKHEAD *n* person who is addicted to heroin
SMACKING *adj* brisk
SMACKINGS > SMACKING
SMACKS > SMACK
SMAIK *n* Scots word meaning rascal
SMAIKS > SMAIK
SMALL *adj* not large in size, number, or amount ▷ *n* narrow part of the lower back ▷ *adv* into small pieces ▷ *vb* make small
SMALLAGE *n* wild celery
SMALLAGES > SMALLAGE
SMALLBOY *n* steward's assistant or deputy steward in European households in W Africa
SMALLBOYS > SMALLBOY
SMALLED > SMALL
SMALLER > SMALL
SMALLEST > SMALL
SMALLING > SMALL
SMALLISH > SMALL
SMALLNESS > SMALL
SMALLPOX *n* contagious disease with blisters that leave scars
SMALLS > SMALL
SMALLSAT *n* small communications satellite
SMALLSATS > SMALLSAT
SMALLTIME *adj* unimportant
SMALM *same as* > SMARM
SMALMED > SMALM
SMALMILY > SMALMY
SMALMING > SMALM
SMALMS > SMALM

SMALMY *same as* > SMARMY
SMALT *n* type of silica glass coloured deep blue with cobalt oxide
SMALTI > SMALTO
SMALTINE *n* mineral containing cobalt
SMALTINES > SMALTINE
SMALTITE *n* silver-white to greyish mineral
SMALTITES > SMALTITE
SMALTO *n* coloured glass, etc, used in mosaics
SMALTOS > SMALTO
SMALTS > SMALT
SMARAGD *n* any green gemstone, such as the emerald
SMARAGDE *same as* > SMARAGD
SMARAGDES > SMARAGDE
SMARAGDS > SMARAGD
SMARM *vb* bring (oneself) into favour (with) ▷ *n* obsequious flattery
SMARMED > SMARM
SMARMIER > SMARMY
SMARMIEST > SMARMY
SMARMILY > SMARMY
SMARMING > SMARM
SMARMS > SMARM
SMARMY *adj* unpleasantly suave or flattering
SMART *adj* well-kept and neat ▷ *vb* feel or cause stinging pain ▷ *n* stinging pain ▷ *adv* in a smart manner
SMARTARSE *n* derogatory term for a clever person, esp one who parades his knowledge offensively
SMARTASS *same as* > SMARTARSE
SMARTED > SMART
SMARTEN *vb* make or become smart
SMARTENED > SMARTEN
SMARTENS > SMARTEN
SMARTER > SMART
SMARTEST > SMART
SMARTIE *same as* > SMARTY
SMARTIES > SMARTY
SMARTING > SMART
SMARTISH > SMART
SMARTLY > SMART
SMARTNESS > SMART
SMARTS *pl n* know-how, intelligence, or wits
SMARTWEED *n* grass with acrid smell
SMARTY *n* would-be clever person
SMASH *vb* break violently and noisily ▷ *n* act or sound of smashing ▷ *adv* with a smash
SMASHABLE > SMASH
SMASHED *adj* completely intoxicated with alcohol
SMASHER *n* attractive person or thing
SMASHEROO *n* excellent person or thing

SMASHERS > SMASHER
SMASHES > SMASH
SMASHING *adj* excellent
SMASHINGS > SMASHING
SMASHUP *n* bad collision of cars
SMASHUPS > SMASHUP
SMATCH *less common word for* > SMACK
SMATCHED > SMATCH
SMATCHES > SMATCH
SMATCHING > SMATCH
SMATTER *n* smattering ▷ *vb* prattle
SMATTERED > SMATTER
SMATTERER > SMATTER
SMATTERS > SMATTER
SMAZE *n* smoky haze, less damp than fog
SMAZES > SMAZE
SMEAR *vb* spread with a greasy or sticky substance ▷ *n* dirty mark or smudge
SMEARCASE *n* American type of cottage cheese
SMEARED > SMEAR
SMEARER > SMEAR
SMEARERS > SMEAR
SMEARIER > SMEARY
SMEARIEST > SMEARY
SMEARILY > SMEARY
SMEARING > SMEAR
SMEARS > SMEAR
SMEARY *adj* smeared, dirty
SMEATH *n* duck
SMEATHS > SMEATH
SMECTIC *adj* (of a substance) existing in state in which the molecules are oriented in layers
SMECTITE *n* type of clay mineral
SMECTITES > SMECTITE
SMECTITIC > SMECTITE
SMEDDUM *n* any fine powder
SMEDDUMS > SMEDDUM
SMEE *n* duck
SMEECH *Southwest English dialect form of* > SMOKE
SMEECHED > SMEECH
SMEECHES > SMEECH
SMEECHING > SMEECH
SMEEK *vb* smoke
SMEEKED > SMEEK
SMEEKING > SMEECH
SMEEKS > SMEECH
SMEES > SMEE
SMEETH *n* duck
SMEETHS > SMEETH
SMEGMA *n* whitish sebaceous secretion that accumulates beneath the prepuce
SMEGMAS > SMEGMA
SMELL *vb* perceive (a scent or odour) by means of the nose ▷ *n* ability to perceive odours by the nose
SMELLED > SMELL
SMELLER > SMELL
SMELLERS > SMELL
SMELLIER > SMELLY
SMELLIES *pl n* pleasant-smelling products such as perfumes, body lotions, bath salts, etc
SMELLIEST > SMELLY
SMELLING > SMELL
SMELLINGS > SMELL
SMELLS > SMELL
SMELLY *adj* having a nasty smell
SMELT *vb* extract metal from an ore
SMELTED > SMELL
SMELTER *n* industrial plant where smelting is carried out
SMELTERS > SMELTER
SMELTERY *variant of* > SMELTER
SMELTING > SMELL
SMELTINGS > SMELL
SMELTS > SMELL
SMERK *same as* > SMIRK
SMERKED > SMERK
SMERKING > SMERK
SMERKS > SMERK
SMEUSE *n* way through hedge
SMEUSES > SMEUSE
SMEW *n* duck of N Europe and Asia
SMEWS > SMEW
SMICKER *vb* look at someone amorously
SMICKERED > SMICKER
SMICKERS > SMICKER
SMICKET *n* smock
SMICKETS > SMICKET
SMICKLY *adv* amorously
SMIDDIED > SMIDDY
SMIDDIES > SMIDDY
SMIDDY *Scots word for* > SMITHY
SMIDDYING > SMIDDY
SMIDGE *n* very small amount or part
SMIDGEN *n* very small amount or part
SMIDGENS > SMIDGEN
SMIDGEON *same as* > SMIDGEN
SMIDGEONS > SMIDGEON
SMIDGES > SMIDGE
SMIDGIN *same as* > SMIDGEN
SMIDGINS > SMIDGIN
SMIERCASE *same as* > SMEARCASE
SMIGHT *same as* > SMITE
SMIGHTING > SMIGHT
SMIGHTS > SMIGHT
SMILAX *n* type of climbing shrub
SMILAXES > SMILAX
SMILE *n* turning up of the corners of the mouth to show pleasure or friendliness ▷ *vb* give a smile
SMILED > SMILE
SMILEFUL *adj* full of smiles
SMILELESS > SMILE
SMILER > SMILE
SMILERS > SMILE
SMILES > SMILE
SMILET *n* little smile
SMILETS > SMILET
SMILEY *n* symbol depicting a smile or other facial expression, used in e-mail ▷ *adj* cheerful
SMILEYS > SMILEY
SMILING > SMILE
SMILINGLY > SMILE
SMILINGS > SMILE
SMILODON *n* extinct sabre-toothed tiger
SMILODONS > SMILODON
SMIR *n* drizzly rain ▷ *vb* drizzle lightly
SMIRCH *n* stain ▷ *vb* disgrace
SMIRCHED > SMIRCH
SMIRCHER > SMIRCH
SMIRCHERS > SMIRCH
SMIRCHES > SMIRCH
SMIRCHING > SMIRCH
SMIRK *n* smug smile ▷ *vb* give a smirk
SMIRKED > SMIRK
SMIRKER > SMIRK
SMIRKERS > SMIRK
SMIRKIER > SMIRK
SMIRKIEST > SMIRK
SMIRKILY > SMIRK
SMIRKING > SMIRK
SMIRKS > SMIRK
SMIRKY > SMIRK
SMIRR *same as* > SMIR
SMIRRED > SMIRR
SMIRRIER > SMIRR
SMIRRIEST > SMIRR
SMIRRING > SMIRR
SMIRRS > SMIRR
SMIRRY > SMIRR
SMIRS > SMIR
SMIRTING *n* flirting amongst those smoking outside a non-smoking office, pub, etc
SMIRTINGS > SMIRTING
SMIT > SMITE
SMITE *vb* strike hard
SMITER > SMITE
SMITERS > SMITE
SMITES > SMITE
SMITH *n* worker in metal ▷ *vb* work in metal
SMITHED > SMITH
SMITHERS *pl n* little shattered pieces
SMITHERY *n* trade or craft of a blacksmith
SMITHIED > SMITHY
SMITHIES > SMITHY
SMITHING > SMITH
SMITHS > SMITH
SMITHY *n* blacksmith's workshop ▷ *vb* work as a smith
SMITHYING > SMITHY
SMITING > SMITE
SMITS > SMIT
SMITTED > SMIT
SMITTEN > SMITE
SMITTING > SMIT
SMITTLE *adj* infectious
SMOCK *n* loose overall ▷ *vb* gather (material) by sewing in a honeycomb pattern
SMOCKED > SMOCK
SMOCKING *n* ornamental needlework used to gath material
SMOCKINGS > SMOCKING
SMOCKLIKE > SMOCK
SMOCKS > SMOCK
SMOG *n* mixture of smoke and fog
SMOGGIER > SMOG
SMOGGIEST > SMOG
SMOGGY > SMOG
SMOGLESS > SMOG
SMOGS > SMOG
SMOILE *same as* > SMILE
SMOILED > SMOILE
SMOILES > SMOILE
SMOILING > SMOILE
SMOKABLE > SMOKE
SMOKE *n* cloudy mass that rises from something burning ▷ *vb* give off smoke or treat with smo
SMOKEABLE > SMOKE
SMOKEBUSH *n* plant with small light flowers
SMOKED > SMOKE
SMOKEHO *same as* > SMOKO
SMOKEHOOD *n* hood worn keep out smoke
SMOKEHOS > SMOKEHO
SMOKEJACK *n* device formerly used for turning a roasting spit, operated by the movement of ascending gases in a chimney
SMOKELESS *adj* having or producing little or no smoke
SMOKELIKE > SMOKE
SMOKEPOT *n* device for producing smoke
SMOKEPOTS > SMOKEPOT
SMOKER *n* person who habitually smokes tobac
SMOKERS > SMOKER
SMOKES > SMOKE
SMOKETREE *n* shrub with clusters of yellowish flowers
SMOKEY *same as* > SMOKY
SMOKIER > SMOKY
SMOKIES > SMOKY
SMOKIEST > SMOKY
SMOKILY > SMOKY
SMOKINESS > SMOKY
SMOKING > SMOKE
SMOKINGS > SMOKING
SMOKO *n* short break from work for tea or a cigarett
SMOKOS > SMOKO
SMOKY *adj* filled with or giving off smoke, sometimes excessively ▷ *n* haddock that has be smoked
SMOLDER *same as* > SMOULDER
SMOLDERED > SMOLDER
SMOLDERS > SMOLDER
SMOLT *n* young salmon at

he stage when it migrates
o the sea
OLTS > SMOLT
OOCH *vb* kiss and cuddle
› *n* smooching
OOCHED > SMOOCH
OOCHER > SMOOCH
OOCHERS > SMOOCH
OOCHES > SMOOCH
OOCHING > SMOOCH
OOCHY *adj* romantic
OODGE *same as* > SMOOCH
OODGED > SMOODGE
OODGES > SMOODGE
OODGING > SMOODGE
OOGE *same as* > SMOOCH
OOGED > SMOOGE
OOGES > SMOOGE
OOGING > SMOOGE
OOR *vb* Scots word
neaning put out fire
OORED > SMOOR
OORING > SMOOR
OORS > SMOOR
OOSH *vb* paint to give
oftened look
OOSHED > SMOOSH
OOSHES > SMOOSH
OOSHING > SMOOSH
OOT *vb* work as printer
OOTED > SMOOT
OOTH *adj* even in surface,
exture, or consistency
› *vb* make smooth ▷ *adv*
n a smooth manner ▷ *n*
mooth part of something
OOTHED > SMOOTH
OOTHEN *vb* make or
ecome smooth
OOTHENS > SMOOTHEN
OOTHER > SMOOTH
OOTHERS > SMOOTH
OOTHES > SMOOTH
OOTHEST > SMOOTH
OOTHIE *n* slang, usu
erogatory term for a
harming but possibly
nsincere man
OOTHIES > SMOOTHY
OOTHING > SMOOTH
OOTHISH > SMOOTH
OOTHLY > SMOOTH
OOTHS > SMOOTH
OOTHY *same*
S > SMOOTHIE
OOTING > SMOOT
OOTS > SMOOT
ORBROD *n* Danish hors
'oeuvre
ORBRODS > SMORBROD
ORE *same as* > SMOOR
ORED > SMORE
ORES > SMORE
ORING > SMORE
ORZANDO *adv* musical
nstruction meaning
ading away gradually
ORZATO *same*
S > SMORZANDO
OTE > SMITE
OTHER *vb* suffocate or
tifle ▷ *n* anything, such
s a cloud of smoke, that
tifles

SMOTHERED > SMOTHER
SMOTHERER > SMOTHER
SMOTHERS > SMOTHER
SMOTHERY > SMOTHER
SMOUCH *vb* kiss
SMOUCHED > SMOUCH
SMOUCHES > SMOUCH
SMOUCHING > SMOUCH
SMOULDER *vb* burn slowly with smoke but no flame ▷ *n* dense smoke, as from a smouldering fire
SMOULDERS > SMOULDER
SMOULDRY *adj* smouldering
SMOUSE *vb* South African word meaning peddle
SMOUSED > SMOUSE
SMOUSER > SMOUSE
SMOUSERS > SMOUSE
SMOUSES > SMOUSE
SMOUSING > SMOUSE
SMOUT *n* child or undersized person ▷ *vb* creep or sneak
SMOUTED > SMOUT
SMOUTING > SMOUT
SMOUTS > SMOUT
SMOWT *same as* > SMOUT
SMOWTS > SMOWT
SMOYLE *same as* > SMILE
SMOYLED > SMOYLE
SMOYLES > SMOYLE
SMOYLING > SMOYLE
SMRITI *n* class of Hindu sacred literature derived from the Vedas
SMRITIS > SMRITI
SMUDGE *vb* make or become smeared or soiled ▷ *n* dirty mark
SMUDGED > SMUDGE
SMUDGEDLY > SMUDGE
SMUDGER > SMUDGE
SMUDGERS > SMUDGE
SMUDGES > SMUDGE
SMUDGIER > SMUDGY
SMUDGIEST > SMUDGY
SMUDGILY > SMUDGE
SMUDGING > SMUDGE
SMUDGY *adj* smeared, blurred, or soiled, or likely to become so
SMUG *adj* self-satisfied ▷ *vb* make neat
SMUGGED > SMUG
SMUGGER > SMUG
SMUGGERY *n* condition or an instance of being smug
SMUGGEST > SMUG
SMUGGING > SMUG
SMUGGLE *vb* import or export (goods) secretly and illegally
SMUGGLED > SMUGGLE
SMUGGLER > SMUGGLE
SMUGGLERS > SMUGGLE
SMUGGLES > SMUGGLE
SMUGGLING > SMUGGLE
SMUGLY > SMUG
SMUGNESS > SMUG
SMUGS > SMUG
SMUR *same as* > SMIR
SMURFING *n* intentionally flooding and overwhelming a computer network with messages by means of a program
SMURFINGS > SMURFING
SMURRED > SMUR
SMURRIER > SMUR
SMURRIEST > SMUR
SMURRING > SMUR
SMURRY > SMUR
SMURS > SMUR
SMUSH *vb* crush
SMUSHED > SMUSH
SMUSHES > SMUSH
SMUSHING > SMUSH
SMUT *n* obscene jokes, pictures, etc ▷ *vb* mark or become marked or smudged, as with soot
SMUTCH *vb* smudge ▷ *n* mark
SMUTCHED > SMUTCH
SMUTCHES > SMUTCH
SMUTCHIER > SMUTCH
SMUTCHING > SMUTCH
SMUTCHY > SMUTCH
SMUTS > SMUT
SMUTTED > SMUT
SMUTTIER > SMUT
SMUTTIEST > SMUT
SMUTTILY > SMUT
SMUTTING > SMUT
SMUTTY > SMUT
SMYTRIE *n* Scots word meaning collection
SMYTRIES > SMYTRIE
SNAB *same as* > SNOB
SNABBLE *same as* > SNAFFLE
SNABBLED > SNABBLE
SNABBLES > SNABBLE
SNABBLING > SNABBLE
SNABS > SNAB
SNACK *n* light quick meal ▷ *vb* eat a snack
SNACKED > SNACK
SNACKER > SNACK
SNACKERS > SNACK
SNACKETTE *n* snack bar
SNACKING > SNACK
SNACKS > SNACK
SNAFFLE *n* jointed bit for a horse ▷ *vb* steal
SNAFFLED > SNAFFLE
SNAFFLES > SNAFFLE
SNAFFLING > SNAFFLE
SNAFU *n* confusion or chaos regarded as the normal state ▷ *adj* confused or muddled up, as usual ▷ *vb* throw into chaos
SNAFUED > SNAFU
SNAFUING > SNAFU
SNAFUS > SNAFU
SNAG *n* difficulty or disadvantage ▷ *vb* catch or tear on a point
SNAGGED > SNAG
SNAGGIER > SNAGGY
SNAGGIEST > SNAGGY
SNAGGING > SNAG
SNAGGY *adj* having sharp protuberances
SNAGLIKE > SNAG
SNAGS > SNAG
SNAIL *n* slow-moving mollusc with a spiral shell ▷ *vb* move slowly
SNAILED > SNAIL
SNAILERY *n* place where snails are bred
SNAILFISH *n* sea snail
SNAILIER > SNAIL
SNAILIEST > SNAIL
SNAILING > SNAIL
SNAILLIKE *adj* resembling a snail
SNAILS > SNAIL
SNAILY > SNAIL
SNAKE *n* long thin scaly limbless reptile ▷ *vb* move in a winding course like a snake
SNAKEBIRD *n* darter bird
SNAKEBIT *adj* bitten by snake
SNAKEBITE *n* bite of a snake
SNAKED > SNAKE
SNAKEFISH *n* fish resembling snake
SNAKEHEAD *n* Chinese criminal involved in the illegal transport of Chinese citizens to other parts of the world
SNAKELIKE > SNAKE
SNAKEPIT *n* pit filled with snakes
SNAKEPITS > SNAKEPIT
SNAKEROOT *n* any of various North American plants
SNAKES > SNAKE
SNAKESKIN *n* skin of a snake, esp when made into a leather valued for handbags, shoes, etc
SNAKEWEED *same as* > SNAKEROOT
SNAKEWISE *adv* in snakelike way
SNAKEWOOD *n* South American tree
SNAKEY *same as* > SNAKY
SNAKIER > SNAKY
SNAKIEST > SNAKY
SNAKILY > SNAKY
SNAKINESS > SNAKY
SNAKING > SNAKE
SNAKISH > SNAKE
SNAKY *adj* twisted or winding
SNAP *vb* break suddenly ▷ *n* act or sound of snapping ▷ *adj* made on the spur of the moment ▷ *adv* with a snap
SNAPBACK *n* sudden rebound or change in direction
SNAPBACKS > SNAPBACK
SNAPHANCE *n* flintlock gun
SNAPLESS > SNAP
SNAPLINK *n* metal link used in mountaineering
SNAPLINKS > SNAPLINK
SNAPPABLE > SNAP
SNAPPED > SNAP
SNAPPER *n* food fish of

Australia and New Zealand ▷ *vb* stumble
SNAPPERED > SNAPPER
SNAPPERS > SNAPPER
SNAPPIER > SNAPPY
SNAPPIEST > SNAPPY
SNAPPILY > SNAPPY
SNAPPING > SNAP
SNAPPINGS > SNAP
SNAPPISH *same as* > SNAPPY
SNAPPY *adj* irritable
SNAPS > SNAP
SNAPSHOT *n* informal photograph
SNAPSHOTS > SNAPSHOT
SNAPTIN *n* container for food
SNAPTINS > SNAPTIN
SNAPWEED *n* impatiens
SNAPWEEDS > SNAPWEED
SNAR *same as* > SNARL
SNARE *n* trap with a noose ▷ *vb* catch in or as if in a snare
SNARED > SNARE
SNARELESS > SNARE
SNARER > SNARE
SNARERS > SNARE
SNARES > SNARE
SNARF *vb* eat or drink greedily
SNARFED > SNARF
SNARFING > SNARF
SNARFS > SNARF
SNARIER > SNARE
SNARIEST > SNARE
SNARING > SNARE
SNARINGS > SNARE
SNARK *n* imaginary creature in Lewis Carroll's poetry
SNARKIER > SNARKY
SNARKIEST > SNARKY
SNARKILY > SNARKY
SNARKS > SNARK
SNARKY *adj* unpleasant and scornful
SNARL *vb* (of an animal) growl with bared teeth ▷ *n* act or sound of snarling
SNARLED > SNARL
SNARLER > SNARL
SNARLERS > SNARL
SNARLIER > SNARL
SNARLIEST > SNARL
SNARLING > SNARL
SNARLINGS > SNARL
SNARLS > SNARL
SNARLY > SNARL
SNARRED > SNAR
SNARRING > SNAR
SNARS > SNAR
SNARY > SNARE
SNASH *vb* Scots word meaning speak cheekily
SNASHED > SNASH
SNASHES > SNASH
SNASHING > SNASH
SNASTE *n* candle wick
SNASTES > SNASTE
SNATCH *vb* seize or try to seize suddenly ▷ *n* snatching
SNATCHED > SNATCH
SNATCHER > SNATCH
SNATCHERS > SNATCH
SNATCHES > SNATCH
SNATCHIER > SNATCHY
SNATCHILY > SNATCHY
SNATCHING > SNATCH
SNATCHY *adj* disconnected or spasmodic
SNATH *n* handle of a scythe
SNATHE *same as* > SNATH
SNATHES > SNATHE
SNATHS > SNATH
SNAW *Scots variant of* > SNOW
SNAWED > SNAW
SNAWING > SNAW
SNAWS > SNAW
SNAZZIER > SNAZZY
SNAZZIEST > SNAZZY
SNAZZILY > SNAZZY
SNAZZY *adj* stylish and flashy
SNEAD *n* scythe handle
SNEADS > SNEAD
SNEAK *vb* move furtively ▷ *n* cowardly or underhand person ▷ *adj* without warning
SNEAKED > SNEAK
SNEAKER *n* soft shoe
SNEAKERED *adj* wearing sneakers
SNEAKERS *pl n* canvas shoes with rubber soles
SNEAKEUP *n* sneaky person
SNEAKEUPS > SNEAKEUP
SNEAKIER > SNEAK
SNEAKIEST > SNEAK
SNEAKILY > SNEAK
SNEAKING *adj* slight but persistent
SNEAKISH *adj* typical of sneak
SNEAKS > SNEAK
SNEAKSBY *n* sneak
SNEAKY > SNEAK
SNEAP *vb* nip
SNEAPED > SNEAP
SNEAPING > SNEAP
SNEAPS > SNEAP
SNEATH *same as* > SNATH
SNEATHS > SNEATH
SNEB *same as* > SNIB
SNEBBE *same as* > SNUB
SNEBBED > SNEB
SNEBBES > SNEBBE
SNEBBING > SNEB
SNEBS > SNEB
SNECK *n* small squared stone used in a rubble wall to fill spaces between stones ▷ *vb* fasten (a latch)
SNECKED > SNECK
SNECKING > SNECK
SNECKS > SNECK
SNED *vb* prune or trim
SNEDDED > SNED
SNEDDING > SNED
SNEDS > SNED
SNEE *vb* cut
SNEED > SNEE
SNEEING > SNEE
SNEER *n* contemptuous expression or remark ▷ *vb* show contempt by a sneer
SNEERED > SNEER
SNEERER > SNEER
SNEERERS > SNEER
SNEERFUL > SNEER
SNEERIER > SNEERY
SNEERIEST > SNEERY
SNEERING > SNEER
SNEERINGS > SNEER
SNEERS > SNEER
SNEERY *adj* contemptuous or scornful
SNEES > SNEE
SNEESH *n* Scots word meaning pinch of snuff
SNEESHAN *n* Scots word meaning pinch of snuff
SNEESHANS > SNEESHAN
SNEESHES > SNEESH
SNEESHIN *same as* > SNEESHAN
SNEESHING *same as* > SNEESHAN
SNEESHINS > SNEESHIN
SNEEZE *vb* expel air from the nose suddenly, involuntarily, and noisily ▷ *n* act or sound of sneezing
SNEEZED > SNEEZE
SNEEZER > SNEEZE
SNEEZERS > SNEEZE
SNEEZES > SNEEZE
SNEEZIER > SNEEZE
SNEEZIEST > SNEEZE
SNEEZING > SNEEZE
SNEEZINGS > SNEEZE
SNEEZY > SNEEZE
SNELL *adj* biting ▷ *vb* attach hook to fishing line
SNELLED > SNELL
SNELLER > SNELL
SNELLEST > SNELL
SNELLING > SNELL
SNELLS > SNELL
SNELLY > SNELL
SNIB *n* catch of a door or window ▷ *vb* bolt or fasten (a door)
SNIBBED > SNIB
SNIBBING > SNIB
SNIBS > SNIB
SNICK *n* (make) a small cut or notch ▷ *vb* make a small cut or notch in (something)
SNICKED > SNICK
SNICKER *same as* > SNIGGER
SNICKERED > SNICKER
SNICKERER > SNICKER
SNICKERS > SNICKER
SNICKERY > SNICKER
SNICKET *n* passageway between walls or fences
SNICKETS > SNICKET
SNICKING > SNICK
SNICKS > SNICK
SNIDE *adj* critical in an unfair and nasty way ▷ *n* sham jewellery ▷ *vb* fill or load
SNIDELY > SNIDE
SNIDENESS > SNIDE
SNIDER > SNIDE
SNIDES > SNIDE
SNIDEST > SNIDE
SNIDEY *same as* > SNIDE
SNIDIER > SNIDEY
SNIDIEST > SNIDEY
SNIES > SNY
SNIFF *vb* inhale through the nose in short audible breaths ▷ *n* act or sound of sniffing
SNIFFABLE > SNIFF
SNIFFED > SNIFF
SNIFFER *n* device for detecting hidden substances such as drugs or explosives, esp by thei[r] odour
SNIFFERS > SNIFFER
SNIFFIER > SNIFFY
SNIFFIEST > SNIFFY
SNIFFILY > SNIFFY
SNIFFING > SNIFF
SNIFFINGS > SNIFF
SNIFFISH *adj* disdainful
SNIFFLE *vb* sniff repeatedly, as when suffering from a cold ▷ *n* slight cold
SNIFFLED > SNIFFLE
SNIFFLER > SNIFFLE
SNIFFLERS > SNIFFLE
SNIFFLES *pl n* *the*. a cold [in] the head
SNIFFLIER > SNIFFLE
SNIFFLING > SNIFFLE
SNIFFLY > SNIFFLE
SNIFFS > SNIFF
SNIFFY *adj* contemptuou[s] or scornful
SNIFT *same as* > SNIFF
SNIFTED > SNIFT
SNIFTER *n* small quantit[y] of alcoholic drink ▷ *vb* sniff
SNIFTERED > SNIFTER
SNIFTERS > SNIFTER
SNIFTIER > SNIFTY
SNIFTIEST > SNIFTY
SNIFTING > SNIFT
SNIFTS > SNIFT
SNIFTY *adj* slang word meaning excellent
SNIG *vb* drag (a felled log) by a chain or cable
SNIGGED > SNIG
SNIGGER *n* a sly laugh ▷ [vb] laugh slyly
SNIGGERED > SNIGGER
SNIGGERER > SNIGGER
SNIGGERS > SNIGGER
SNIGGING > SNIG
SNIGGLE *vb* fish for eels b[y] dangling or thrusting a baited hook into cavitie[s] ▷ *n* baited hook used for sniggling eels
SNIGGLED > SNIGGLE
SNIGGLER > SNIGGLE
SNIGGLERS > SNIGGLE
SNIGGLES > SNIGGLE
SNIGGLING > SNIGGLE
SNIGLET *n* invented wor[d]
SNIGLETS > SNIGLET
SNIGS > SNIG

IP *vb* cut in small quick trokes with scissors or hears ▷ *n* bargain ▷ *interj* epresentation of the ound of scissors or shears losing
IPE *n* wading bird with a long straight bill ▷ *vb* hoot at (a person) from over
IPED > SNIPE
IPEFISH *n* any eleost fish of the family *Aacrorhamphosidae*
IPELIKE > SNIPE
IPER *n* person who hoots at someone from over
IPERS > SNIPER
IPES > SNIPE
IPIER > SNIPY
IPIEST > SNIPY
IPING > SNIPE
IPINGS > SNIPE
IPPED > SNIP
IPPER > SNIP
IPPERS > SNIP
IPPET *n* small piece
IPPETS > SNIPPET
IPPETY > SNIPPET
IPPIER > SNIPPY
IPPIEST > SNIPPY
IPPILY > SNIPPY
IPPING > SNIP
IPPINGS > SNIP
IPPY *adj* scrappy
IPS > SNIP
IPY *adj* like a snipe
IRT *n* Scots word neaning suppressed laugh
IRTLE *vb* Scots word neaning snicker
IRTLED > SNIRTLE
IRTLES > SNIRTLE
IRTLING > SNIRTLE
IRTS > SNIRT
IT *n* fit of temper
ITCH *vb* act as an nformer ▷ *n* informer
ITCHED > SNITCH
ITCHER > SNITCH
ITCHERS > SNITCH
ITCHES > SNITCH
ITCHIER > SNITCHY
ITCHING > SNITCH
ITCHY *adj* bad-tempered or irritable
ITS > SNIT
IVEL *vb* cry in a whining vay ▷ *n* act of snivelling
IVELED > SNIVEL
IVELER > SNIVEL
IVELERS > SNIVEL
IVELING > SNIVEL
IVELLED > SNIVEL
IVELLER > SNIVEL
IVELLY > SNIVEL
IVELS > SNIVEL
OB *n* person who judges others by social rank
OBBERY > SNOB
OBBIER > SNOB
OBBIEST > SNOB
OBBILY > SNOB
SNOBBISH > SNOB
SNOBBISM > SNOB
SNOBBISMS > SNOB
SNOBBY > SNOB
SNOBLING *n* little snob
SNOBLINGS > SNOBLING
SNOBS > SNOB
SNOD *vb* Scots word meaning make tidy
SNODDED > SNOD
SNODDER > SNOD
SNODDEST > SNOD
SNODDING > SNOD
SNODDIT > SNOD
SNODS > SNOD
SNOEK *n* edible marine fish
SNOEKS > SNOEK
SNOEP *adj* mean or tight-fisted
SNOG *vb* kiss and cuddle ▷ *n* act of kissing and cuddling
SNOGGED > SNOG
SNOGGING > SNOG
SNOGS > SNOG
SNOKE *same as* > SNOOK
SNOKED > SNOKE
SNOKES > SNOKE
SNOKING > SNOKE
SNOOD *n* pouch, often of net, loosely holding a woman's hair at the back ▷ *vb* hold (the hair) in a snood
SNOODED > SNOOD
SNOODING > SNOOD
SNOODS > SNOOD
SNOOK *n* any of several large game fishes ▷ *vb* lurk
SNOOKED > SNOOK
SNOOKER *n* game played on a billiard table ▷ *vb* leave (a snooker opponent) in a position such that another ball blocks the target ball
SNOOKERED > SNOOKER
SNOOKERS > SNOOKER
SNOOKING > SNOOK
SNOOKS > SNOOK
SNOOL *vb* Scots word meaning dominate
SNOOLED > SNOOL
SNOOLING > SNOOL
SNOOLS > SNOOL
SNOOP *vb* pry ▷ *n* snooping
SNOOPED > SNOOP
SNOOPER *n* person who snoops
SNOOPERS > SNOOPER
SNOOPIER > SNOOP
SNOOPIEST > SNOOP
SNOOPILY > SNOOP
SNOOPING > SNOOP
SNOOPS > SNOOP
SNOOPY > SNOOP
SNOOT *n* nose ▷ *vb* look contemptuously at
SNOOTED > SNOOT
SNOOTFUL *n* enough alcohol to make someone drunk
SNOOTFULS > SNOOTFUL
SNOOTIER > SNOOTY
SNOOTIEST > SNOOTY
SNOOTILY > SNOOTY
SNOOTING > SNOOT
SNOOTS > SNOOT
SNOOTY *adj* haughty
SNOOZE *vb* take a brief light sleep ▷ *n* brief light sleep
SNOOZED > SNOOZE
SNOOZER > SNOOZE
SNOOZERS > SNOOZE
SNOOZES > SNOOZE
SNOOZIER > SNOOZE
SNOOZIEST > SNOOZE
SNOOZING > SNOOZE
SNOOZLE *vb* cuddle and sleep
SNOOZLED > SNOOZLE
SNOOZLES > SNOOZLE
SNOOZLING > SNOOZLE
SNOOZY > SNOOZE
SNORE *vb* make snorting sounds while sleeping ▷ *n* sound of snoring
SNORED > SNORE
SNORER > SNORE
SNORERS > SNORE
SNORES > SNORE
SNORING > SNORE
SNORINGS > SNORE
SNORKEL *n* tube allowing a swimmer to breathe while face down on the surface of the water ▷ *vb* swim using a snorkel
SNORKELED > SNORKEL
SNORKELER > SNORKEL
SNORKELS > SNORKEL
SNORT *vb* exhale noisily through the nostrils ▷ *n* act or sound of snorting
SNORTED > SNORT
SNORTER *n* person or animal that snorts
SNORTERS > SNORTER
SNORTIER > SNORT
SNORTIEST > SNORT
SNORTING > SNORT
SNORTINGS > SNORT
SNORTS > SNORT
SNORTY > SNORT
SNOT *n* mucus from the nose ▷ *vb* blow one's nose
SNOTS > SNOT
SNOTTED > SNOT
SNOTTER *vb* breathe through obstructed nostrils
SNOTTERED > SNOTTER
SNOTTERS > SNOTTER
SNOTTERY *n* snot
SNOTTIE *n* midshipman
SNOTTIER > SNOTTY
SNOTTIES > SNOTTY
SNOTTIEST > SNOTTY
SNOTTILY > SNOTTY
SNOTTING > SNOT
SNOTTY *adj* covered with mucus from the nose
SNOUT *n* animal's projecting nose and jaws ▷ *vb* have or give a snout
SNOUTED > SNOUT
SNOUTIER > SNOUT
SNOUTIEST > SNOUT
SNOUTING > SNOUT
SNOUTISH > SNOUT
SNOUTLESS > SNOUT
SNOUTLIKE > SNOUT
SNOUTS > SNOUT
SNOUTY > SNOUT
SNOW *n* frozen vapour falling from the sky in flakes ▷ *vb* fall as or like snow
SNOWBALL *n* snow pressed into a ball for throwing ▷ *vb* increase rapidly
SNOWBALLS > SNOWBALL
SNOWBANK *n* bank of snow
SNOWBANKS > SNOWBANK
SNOWBELL *n* Asian shrub
SNOWBELLS > SNOWBELL
SNOWBELT *n* northern states of USA
SNOWBELTS > SNOWBELT
SNOWBERRY *n* shrub grown for its white berries
SNOWBIRD *n* person addicted to cocaine, or sometimes heroin
SNOWBIRDS > SNOWBIRD
SNOWBLINK *n* whitish glare in the sky reflected from snow
SNOWBOARD *n* board on which a person stands to slide across the snow
SNOWBOOT *n* boot for walking in snow
SNOWBOOTS > SNOWBOOT
SNOWBOUND *adj* shut in by snow
SNOWBRUSH *n* brush for clearing snow
SNOWBUSH *n* North American plant
SNOWCAP *n* cap of snow on top of a mountain
SNOWCAPS > SNOWCAP
SNOWCAT *n* tracked vehicle for travelling over snow
SNOWCATS > SNOWCAT
SNOWDRIFT *n* bank of deep snow
SNOWDROP *n* small white bell-shaped spring flower
SNOWDROPS > SNOWDROP
SNOWED *adj* under the influence of narcotic drugs
SNOWFALL *n* fall of snow
SNOWFALLS > SNOWFALL
SNOWFIELD *n* large area of permanent snow
SNOWFLAKE *n* single crystal of snow
SNOWFLECK *n* snow bunting
SNOWFLICK *same as* > SNOWFLECK
SNOWIER > SNOWY
SNOWIEST > SNOWY
SNOWILY > SNOWY
SNOWINESS > SNOWY
SNOWING > SNOW
SNOWISH *adj* like snow
SNOWK *same as* > SNOOK
SNOWKED > SNOWK
SNOWKING > SNOWK
SNOWKS > SNOWK
SNOWLAND *n* area where

snow lies
SNOWLANDS > SNOWLAND
SNOWLESS > SNOW
SNOWLIKE > SNOW
SNOWLINE *n* limit of permanent snow
SNOWLINES > SNOWLINE
SNOWMAKER *n* machine making artificial snow
SNOWMAN *n* figure shaped out of snow
SNOWMELT *n* melting of snow in spring
SNOWMELTS > SNOWMELT
SNOWMEN > SNOWMAN
SNOWMOLD *n* fungus growing on grass under snow
SNOWMOLDS > SNOWMOLD
SNOWPACK *n* body of hard-packed snow
SNOWPACKS > SNOWPACK
SNOWPLOW *n* implement or vehicle for clearing snow away
SNOWPLOWS > SNOWPLOW
SNOWS > SNOW
SNOWSCAPE *n* snow-covered landscape
SNOWSHED *n* shelter built over an exposed section of railway track to prevent its blockage by snow
SNOWSHEDS > SNOWSHED
SNOWSHOE *n* racket-shaped frame with a network of thongs stretched across it, worn on the feet to make walking on snow less difficult ▷ *vb* walk or go using snowshoes
SNOWSHOED > SNOWSHOE
SNOWSHOER > SNOWSHOE
SNOWSHOES > SNOWSHOE
SNOWSLIDE *n* snow avalanche
SNOWSLIP *n* small snow avalanche
SNOWSLIPS > SNOWSLIP
SNOWSTORM *n* storm with heavy snow
SNOWSUIT *n* one-piece winter outer garment for child
SNOWSUITS > SNOWSUIT
SNOWY *adj* covered with or abounding in snow
SNUB *vb* insult deliberately ▷ *n* deliberate insult ▷ *adj* (of a nose) short and blunt
SNUBBE *n* stub
SNUBBED > SNUB
SNUBBER > SNUB
SNUBBERS > SNUB
SNUBBES > SNUBBE
SNUBBIER > SNUB
SNUBBIEST > SNUB
SNUBBING > SNUB
SNUBBINGS > SNUB
SNUBBISH > SNUB
SNUBBY > SNUB
SNUBNESS > SNUB
SNUBS > SNUB
SNUCK *past tense and past participle of* > SNEAK
SNUDGE *vb* be miserly
SNUDGED > SNUDGE
SNUDGES > SNUDGE
SNUDGING > SNUDGE
SNUFF *n* powdered tobacco for sniffing up the nostrils ▷ *vb* extinguish (a candle)
SNUFFBOX *n* small container for holding snuff
SNUFFED > SNUFF
SNUFFER > SNUFF
SNUFFERS > SNUFF
SNUFFIER > SNUFFY
SNUFFIEST > SNUFFY
SNUFFILY > SNUFFY
SNUFFING > SNUFF
SNUFFINGS > SNUFF
SNUFFLE *vb* breathe noisily or with difficulty ▷ *n* act or the sound of snuffling
SNUFFLED > SNUFFLE
SNUFFLER > SNUFFLE
SNUFFLERS > SNUFFLE
SNUFFLES *same as* > SNIFFLES
SNUFFLIER > SNUFFLE
SNUFFLING > SNUFFLE
SNUFFLY > SNUFFLE
SNUFFS > SNUFF
SNUFFY *adj* of, relating to, or resembling snuff
SNUG *adj* warm and comfortable ▷ *n* (in Britain and Ireland) small room in a pub ▷ *vb* make or become comfortable and warm
SNUGGED > SNUG
SNUGGER > SNUG
SNUGGERIE *n* small bar in pub
SNUGGERY *n* cosy and comfortable place or room
SNUGGEST > SNUG
SNUGGIES *pl n* specially warm underwear
SNUGGING > SNUG
SNUGGLE *vb* nestle into a person or thing for warmth or from affection ▷ *n* act of snuggling
SNUGGLED > SNUGGLE
SNUGGLES > SNUGGLE
SNUGGLING > SNUGGLE
SNUGLY > SNUG
SNUGNESS > SNUG
SNUGS > SNUG
SNUSH *vb* take snuff
SNUSHED > SNUSH
SNUSHES > SNUSH
SNUSHING > SNUSH
SNUZZLE *vb* root in ground
SNUZZLED > SNUZZLE
SNUZZLES > SNUZZLE
SNUZZLING > SNUZZLE
SNY *same as* > SNYE
SNYE *n* side channel of a river
SNYES > SNYE
SO *adv* such an extent ▷ *interj* exclamation of surprise, triumph, or realization
SOAK *vb* make wet ▷ *n* soaking
SOAKAGE *n* process or a period in which a permeable substance is soaked in a liquid
SOAKAGES > SOAKAGE
SOAKAWAY *n* pit filled with rubble, etc, into which rain or waste water drains
SOAKAWAYS > SOAKAWAY
SOAKED > SOAK
SOAKEN > SOAK
SOAKER > SOAK
SOAKERS > SOAK
SOAKING > SOAK
SOAKINGLY > SOAK
SOAKINGS > SOAK
SOAKS > SOAK
SOAP *n* compound of alkali and fat, used with water as a cleaning agent ▷ *vb* apply soap to
SOAPBARK *n* W South American rosaceous tree
SOAPBARKS > SOAPBARK
SOAPBERRY *n* any of various chiefly tropical American sapindaceous trees
SOAPBOX *n* crate used as a platform for speech-making ▷ *vb* deliver a speech from a soapbox
SOAPBOXED > SOAPBOX
SOAPBOXES > SOAPBOX
SOAPED > SOAP
SOAPER *n* soap opera
SOAPERS > SOAPER
SOAPIE *n* soap opera
SOAPIER > SOAPY
SOAPIES > SOAPIE
SOAPIEST > SOAPY
SOAPILY > SOAPY
SOAPINESS > SOAPY
SOAPING > SOAP
SOAPLAND *n* Japanese massage parlour and brothel
SOAPLANDS > SOAPLAND
SOAPLESS > SOAP
SOAPLIKE > SOAP
SOAPROOT *n* plant with roots used as soap substitute
SOAPROOTS > SOAPROOT
SOAPS > SOAP
SOAPSTONE *n* soft mineral used for making table tops and ornaments
SOAPSUDS *pl n* foam or lather produced when soap is mixed with water
SOAPSUDSY > SOAPSUDS
SOAPWORT *n* Eurasian plant with clusters of fragrant pink or white flowers
SOAPWORTS > SOAPWORT
SOAPY *adj* covered with soap
SOAR *vb* rise or fly upwards ▷ *n* act of soaring
SOARAWAY *adj* exceedingly successful
SOARE *n* young hawk
SOARED > SOAR
SOARER > SOAR
SOARERS > SOAR
SOARES > SOARE
SOARING > SOAR
SOARINGLY > SOAR
SOARINGS > SOAR
SOARS > SOAR
SOAVE *n* dry white Italian wine
SOAVES > SOAVE
SOB *vb* weep with convulsive gasps ▷ *n* act or sound of sobbing
SOBA *n* (in Japanese cookery) noodles made from buckwheat flour
SOBAS > SOBA
SOBBED > SOB
SOBBER > SOB
SOBBERS > SOB
SOBBING > SOB
SOBBINGLY > SOB
SOBBINGS > SOB
SOBEIT *conj* provided tha[t]
SOBER *adj* not drunk ▷ *vb* make or become sober
SOBERED > SOBER
SOBERER > SOBER
SOBEREST > SOBER
SOBERING > SOBER
SOBERISE *same as* > SOBERIZE
SOBERISED > SOBERISE
SOBERISES > SOBERISE
SOBERIZE *vb* make sober
SOBERIZED > SOBERIZE
SOBERIZES > SOBERIZE
SOBERLY > SOBER
SOBERNESS > SOBER
SOBERS > SOBER
SOBFUL *adj* tearful
SOBOLE *n* creeping underground stem that produces roots and buds
SOBOLES > SOBOLE
SOBRIETY *n* state of bein[g] sober
SOBRIQUET *n* nickname
SOBS > SOB
SOC *n* feudal right to hold court
SOCA *n* mixture of soul an[d] calypso music popular in the E Caribbean
SOCAGE *n* tenure of land b[y] certain services, esp of a[n] agricultural nature
SOCAGER > SOCAGE
SOCAGERS > SOCAGE
SOCAGES > SOCAGE
SOCAS > SOCA
SOCCAGE *same as* > SOCAG[E]
SOCCAGES > SOCCAGE
SOCCER *n* football played by two teams of eleven kicking a spherical ball
SOCCERS > SOCCER
SOCIABLE *adj* friendly or companionable ▷ *n* typ[e] of open carriage with tw[o] seats facing each other
SOCIABLES > SOCIABLE

CIABLY > SOCIABLE

CIAL *adj* living in a ommunity ▷ *n* informal athering

CIALISE *same s* > SOCIALIZE

CIALISM *n* political ystem which advocates ublic ownership of ndustries, resources, and ransport

CIALIST *n* supporter r advocate of socialism ▷ *adj* of or relating to ocialism

CIALITE *n* member of ashionable society

CIALITY *n* tendency f groups and persons to evelop social links and ive in communities

CIALIZE *vb* meet others ocially

CIALLY > SOCIAL

CIALS > SOCIAL

CIATE *n* associate

CIATES > SOCIATE

CIATION *n* plant ommunity

CIATIVE *adj* of ssociation

CIETAL *adj* of or relating o society, esp human ociety or social relations

CIETIES > SOCIETY

CIETY *n* human beings onsidered as a group

CIOGRAM *n* chart howing social elationships

CIOLECT *n* language poken by particular social lass

CIOLOGY *n* study of uman societies

CIOPATH *n* person vith a personality isorder characterized y a tendency to commit ntisocial acts without ny feelings of guilt

CK *n* knitted covering for he foot ▷ *vb* hit hard

CKED > SOCK

CKET *n* hole or recess nto which something fits ▷ *vb* furnish with or place nto a socket

CKETED > SOCKET

CKETING > SOCKET

CKETS > SOCKET

CKETTE *n* sock not overing ankle

CKETTES > SOCKETTE

CKEYE *n* Pacific salmon vith red flesh

CKEYES > SOCKEYE

CKING > SOCK

CKLESS > SOCK

CKMAN *same as* > SOCMAN

CKMEN > SOCKMAN

CKO *adj* excellent

CKS > SOCK

CLE *another name for* > PLINTH

SOCLES > SOCLE

SOCMAN *n* tenant holding land by socage

SOCMEN > SOCMAN

SOCS > SOC

SOD *n* (piece of) turf ▷ *vb* cover with sods

SODA *n* compound of sodium

SODAIC *adj* containing soda

SODAIN *same as* > SUDDEN

SODAINE *same as* > SUDDEN

SODALESS > SODA

SODALIST *n* member of sodality

SODALISTS > SODALIST

SODALITE *n* blue, grey, yellow, or colourless mineral

SODALITES > SODALITE

SODALITY *n* religious or charitable society

SODAMIDE *n* white crystalline compound used as a dehydrating agent

SODAMIDES > SODAMIDE

SODAS > SODA

SODBUSTER *n* farmer who grows crops

SODDED > SOD

SODDEN *adj* soaked ▷ *vb* make or become sodden

SODDENED > SODDEN

SODDENING > SODDEN

SODDENLY > SODDEN

SODDENS > SODDEN

SODDIER > SODDY

SODDIES > SODDY

SODDIEST > SODDY

SODDING > SOD

SODDY *adj* covered with turf

SODGER *dialect variant of* > SOLDIER

SODGERED > SODGER

SODGERING > SODGER

SODGERS > SODGER

SODIC *adj* containing sodium

SODICITY > SODIC

SODIUM *n* silvery-white metallic element

SODIUMS > SODIUM

SODOM *n* person who performs sodomy

SODOMIES > SODOMY

SODOMISE *same as* > SODOMIZE

SODOMISED > SODOMISE

SODOMISES > SODOMISE

SODOMIST > SODOMY

SODOMISTS > SODOMY

SODOMITE *n* person who practises sodomy

SODOMITES > SODOMITE

SODOMITIC > SODOMY

SODOMIZE *vb* be the active partner in anal intercourse

SODOMIZED > SODOMIZE

SODOMIZES > SODOMIZE

SODOMS > SODOM

SODOMY *n* anal intercourse

SODS > SOD

SOEVER *adv* in any way at all

SOFA *n* couch

SOFABED *n* sofa that converts into a bed

SOFABEDS > SOFABED

SOFAR *n* system for determining a position at sea

SOFARS > SOFAR

SOFAS > SOFA

SOFFIONI *n* holes in volcano that emit steam

SOFFIT *n* underside of a part of a building or a structural component

SOFFITS > SOFFIT

SOFT *adj* easy to shape or cut ▷ *adv* softly ▷ *vb* soften

SOFTA *n* Muslim student of divinity and jurisprudence, esp in Turkey

SOFTAS > SOFTA

SOFTBACK *n* paperback

SOFTBACKS > SOFTBACK

SOFTBALL *n* game similar to baseball, played using a larger softer ball

SOFTBALLS > SOFTBALL

SOFTBOUND *adj* having paperback binding

SOFTCORE *adj* not explicit

SOFTCOVER *n* book with paper covers

SOFTED > SOFT

SOFTEN *vb* make or become soft or softer

SOFTENED > SOFTEN

SOFTENER *n* substance added to another substance to increase its softness

SOFTENERS > SOFTENER

SOFTENING > SOFTEN

SOFTENS > SOFTEN

SOFTER > SOFT

SOFTEST > SOFT

SOFTGOODS *n* clothing and soft furniture

SOFTHEAD *n* half-witted person

SOFTHEADS > SOFTHEAD

SOFTIE *n* person who is easily upset

SOFTIES > SOFTY

SOFTING > SOFT

SOFTISH > SOFT

SOFTLING *n* weakling

SOFTLINGS > SOFTLING

SOFTLY > SOFT

SOFTNESS *n* quality or an instance of being soft

SOFTPASTE artifical porcelain made from clay

SOFTS > SOFT

SOFTSHELL *n* crab or turtle with a soft shell

SOFTWARE *n* computer programs

SOFTWARES > SOFTWARE

SOFTWOOD *n* wood of a coniferous tree

SOFTWOODS > SOFTWOOD

SOFTY *same as* > SOFTIE

SOG *vb* soak

SOGER *same as* > SODGER

SOGERS > SOGER

SOGGED > SOG

SOGGIER > SOGGY

SOGGIEST > SOGGY

SOGGILY > SOGGY

SOGGINESS > SOGGY

SOGGING > SOG

SOGGINGS > SOG

SOGGY *adj* soaked

SOGS > SOG

SOH *n* (in tonic sol-fa) fifth degree of any major scale

SOHO *interj* exclamation announcing the sighting of a hare

SOHS > SOH

SOIGNE *adj* well-groomed, elegant

SOIGNEE *variant of* > SOIGNE

SOIL *n* top layer of earth ▷ *vb* make or become dirty

SOILAGE *n* green fodder, esp when freshly cut and fed to livestock in a confined area

SOILAGES > SOILAGE

SOILBORNE *adj* carried in soil

SOILED > SOIL

SOILIER > SOIL

SOILIEST > SOIL

SOILINESS > SOIL

SOILING > SOIL

SOILINGS > SOIL

SOILLESS > SOIL

SOILS > SOIL

SOILURE *n* act of soiling or the state of being soiled

SOILURES > SOILURE

SOILY > SOIL

SOIREE *n* evening party or gathering

SOIREES > SOIREE

SOJA *same as* > SOYA

SOJAS > SOJA

SOJOURN *n* temporary stay ▷ *vb* stay temporarily

SOJOURNED > SOJOURN

SOJOURNER > SOJOURN

SOJOURNS > SOJOURN

SOKAH *same as* > SOCA

SOKAHS > SOKAH

SOKAIYA *n* Japanese extortionist

SOKE *n* right to hold a local court

SOKEMAN *same as* > SOCMAN

SOKEMANRY *n* feudal tenure by socage

SOKEMEN > SOKEMAN

SOKEN *n* feudal district

SOKENS > SOKEN

SOKES > SOKE

SOKOL *n* Czech gymnastic association

SOKOLS > SOKOL

SOL *n* liquid colloidal solution

SOLA > SOLUM

SOLACE *vb* comfort in distress ▷ *n* comfort in misery or disappointment
SOLACED > SOLACE
SOLACER > SOLACE
SOLACERS > SOLACE
SOLACES > SOLACE
SOLACING > SOLACE
SOLACIOUS *adj* providing solace
SOLAH *n* Indian plant
SOLAHS > SOLAH
SOLAN *archaic name for* > GANNET
SOLAND *n* solan goose
SOLANDER *n* box for botanical specimens, maps, etc, made in the form of a book, the front cover being the lid
SOLANDERS > SOLANDER
SOLANDS > SOLAND
SOLANIN *same as* > SOLANINE
SOLANINE *n* poisonous alkaloid found in various solanaceous plants
SOLANINES > SOLANINE
SOLANINS > SOLANIN
SOLANO *n* hot wind in Spain
SOLANOS > SOLANO
SOLANS > SOLAN
SOLANUM *n* any plant of the mainly tropical genus that includes the potato, aubergine, and certain nightshades
SOLANUMS > SOLANUM
SOLAR *adj* of the sun
SOLARIA > SOLARIUM
SOLARISE *same as* > SOLARIZE
SOLARISED > SOLARISE
SOLARISES > SOLARISE
SOLARISM *n* explanation of myths in terms of the movements and influence of the sun
SOLARISMS > SOLARISM
SOLARIST > SOLARISM
SOLARISTS > SOLARISM
SOLARIUM *n* place with beds and ultraviolet lights used for acquiring an artificial suntan
SOLARIUMS > SOLARIUM
SOLARIZE *vb* treat by exposure to the sun's rays
SOLARIZED > SOLARIZE
SOLARIZES > SOLARIZE
SOLARS > SOLUM
SOLAS > SOLUM
SOLATE *vb* change from gel to liquid
SOLATED > SOLATE
SOLATES > SOLATE
SOLATIA > SOLATIUM
SOLATING > SOLATE
SOLATION *n* liquefaction of a gel
SOLATIONS > SOLATION
SOLATIUM *n* compensation awarded for injury to the feelings
SOLD *n* obsolete word for salary
SOLDADO *n* soldier
SOLDADOS > SOLDADO
SOLDAN *archaic word for* > SULTAN
SOLDANS > SOLDAN
SOLDE *n* wages
SOLDER *n* soft alloy used to join two metal surfaces ▷ *vb* join with solder
SOLDERED > SOLDER
SOLDERER > SOLDER
SOLDERERS > SOLDER
SOLDERING > SOLDER
SOLDERS > SOLDER
SOLDES > SOLDE
SOLDI > SOLDO
SOLDIER *n* member of an army ▷ *vb* serve in an army
SOLDIERED > SOLDIER
SOLDIERLY *adj* of or befitting a good soldier
SOLDIERS > SOLDIER
SOLDIERY *n* soldiers collectively
SOLDO *n* former Italian copper coin worth one twentieth of a lira
SOLDS > SOLD
SOLE *adj* one and only ▷ *n* underside of the foot ▷ *vb* provide (a shoe) with a sole
SOLECISE *variant of* > SOLECIZE
SOLECISED > SOLECISE
SOLECISES > SOLECISE
SOLECISM *n* minor grammatical mistake
SOLECISMS > SOLECISM
SOLECIST > SOLECISM
SOLECISTS > SOLECISM
SOLECIZE *vb* commit a solecism
SOLECIZED *same as* > SOLECIZE
SOLECIZES > SOLECIZE
SOLED > SOLE
SOLEI > SOLEUS
SOLEIN *same as* > SULLEN
SOLELESS > SOLE
SOLELY *adv* only, completely
SOLEMN *adj* serious, deeply sincere
SOLEMNER > SOLEMN
SOLEMNESS > SOLEMN
SOLEMNEST > SOLEMN
SOLEMNIFY *vb* make serious or grave
SOLEMNISE *same as* > SOLEMNIZE
SOLEMNITY *n* state or quality of being solemn
SOLEMNIZE *vb* celebrate or perform (a ceremony)
SOLEMNLY > SOLEMN
SOLENESS > SOLE
SOLENETTE *n* small European sole
SOLENODON *n* either of two rare shrewlike nocturnal mammals of the Caribbean
SOLENOID *n* coil of wire magnetized by passing a current through it
SOLENOIDS > SOLENOID
SOLEPLATE *n* joist forming the lowest member of a timber frame
SOLEPRINT *n* print of sole of foot
SOLER > SOLE
SOLERA *n* system for aging sherry and other fortified wines
SOLERAS > SOLERA
SOLERET *n* armour for foot
SOLERETS > SOLERET
SOLERS > SOLER
SOLES > SOLE
SOLEUS *n* muscle in calf of leg
SOLEUSES > SOLEUS
SOLFATARA *n* volcanic vent emitting only sulphurous gases and water vapour or sometimes hot mud
SOLFEGE *variant of* > SOLFEGGIO
SOLFEGES > SOLFEGE
SOLFEGGI > SOLFEGGIO
SOLFEGGIO *n* voice exercise in which runs, scales, etc, are sung to the same syllable or syllables
SOLFERINO *n* moderate purplish-red colour
SOLGEL *adj* changing between sol and gel
SOLI *adv* (of a piece or passage) to be performed by or with soloists
SOLICIT *vb* request
SOLICITED > SOLICIT
SOLICITOR *n* lawyer who advises clients and prepares documents and cases
SOLICITS > SOLICIT
SOLICITY *n* act of making a request
SOLID *adj* (of a substance) keeping its shape ▷ *n* three-dimensional shape
SOLIDAGO *n* any plant of the chiefly American genus *Solidago*
SOLIDAGOS > SOLIDAGO
SOLIDARE *n* old coin
SOLIDARES > SOLIDARE
SOLIDARY *adj* marked by unity of interests, responsibilities, etc
SOLIDATE *vb* consolidate
SOLIDATED > SOLIDATE
SOLIDATES > SOLIDATE
SOLIDER > SOLID
SOLIDEST > SOLID
SOLIDI > SOLIDUS
SOLIDIFY *vb* make or become solid or firm
SOLIDISH > SOLID
SOLIDISM *n* belief that diseases spring from damage to solid parts of body
SOLIDISMS > SOLIDISM
SOLIDIST > SOLIDISM
SOLIDISTS > SOLIDISM
SOLIDITY > SOLID
SOLIDLY > SOLID
SOLIDNESS > SOLID
SOLIDS > SOLID
SOLIDUM *n* part of pedest
SOLIDUMS > SOLIDUM
SOLIDUS *same as* > SLASH
SOLILOQUY *n* speech mac by a person while alone, esp in a play
SOLING > SOLE
SOLION *n* amplifier used i chemistry
SOLIONS > SOLION
SOLIPED *n* animal whose hooves are not cloven
SOLIPEDS > SOLIPED
SOLIPSISM *n* doctrine th the self is the only thing known to exist
SOLIPSIST > SOLIPSISM
SOLIQUID *n* semi-solid, semi-liquid solution
SOLIQUIDS > SOLIQUID
SOLITAIRE *n* game for or person played with pegs set in a board
SOLITARY *adj* alone, sing ▷ *n* hermit
SOLITO *adv* musical instruction meaning pla in usual manner
SOLITON *n* type of isolate particle-like wave
SOLITONS > SOLITON
SOLITUDE *n* state of bein alone
SOLITUDES > SOLITUDE
SOLIVE *n* type of joist
SOLIVES > SOLIVE
SOLLAR *n* archaic word meaning attic
SOLLARS > SOLLAR
SOLLER *same as* > SOLLAR
SOLLERET *n* protective covering for the foot consisting of riveted plates of armour
SOLLERETS > SOLLERET
SOLLERS > SOLLER
SOLLICKER *n* something very large
SOLO *n* music for one performer ▷ *adj* done alone ▷ *adv* by oneself, alone ▷ *vb* undertake a venture alone, esp to operate an aircraft alone or climb alone
SOLOED > SOLO
SOLOING > SOLO
SOLOIST *n* person who performs a solo
SOLOISTIC > SOLOIST
SOLOISTS > SOLOIST
SOLON *n* US congressmar
SOLONCHAK *n* type of intrazonal soil of arid regions with a greyish

surface crust
)LONETS *same as* > SOLONETZ
)LONETZ *n* type of intrazonal soil with a high saline content characterized by leaching
)LONS > SOLON
)LOS > SOLO
)LPUGID *n* venomous arachnid
)LPUGIDS > SOLPUGID
)LS > SOL
)LSTICE *n* either the shortest (in winter) or longest (in summer) day of the year
)LSTICES > SOLSTICE
)LUBLE *adj* able to be dissolved ▷ *n* soluble substance
)LUBLES > SOLUBLE
)LUBLY > SOLUBLE
)LUM *n* upper layers of the soil profile, affected by climate and vegetation
)LUMS > SOLUM
)LUNAR *adj* relating to sun and moon
)LUS *adj* alone
)LUTE *n* substance in a solution that is dissolved ▷ *adj* loose or unattached
)LUTES > SOLUTE
)LUTION *n* answer to a problem
)LUTIONS > SOLUTION
)LUTIVE *adj* dissolving
)LVABLE *adj* capable of being solved
)LVATE *vb* undergo, cause to undergo, or partake in solvation
)LVATED > SOLVATE
)LVATES > SOLVATE
)LVATING > SOLVATE
)LVATION *n* type of chemical process
)LVE *vb* find the answer to (a problem)
)LVED > SOLVE
)LVENCY *n* ability to pay all debts
)LVENT *adj* having enough money to pay one's debts ▷ *n* liquid capable of dissolving other substances
)LVENTLY > SOLVENT
)LVENTS > SOLVENT
)LVER > SOLVE
)LVERS > SOLVE
)LVES > SOLVE
)LVING > SOLVE
)M *n* currency of Kyrgyzstan and Uzbekistan
)MA *n* body of an organism, esp an animal, as distinct from the germ cells
)MAN *n* organophosphorus compound developed as a nerve gas in Germany during World War II
SOMANS > SOMAN
SOMAS > SOMA
SOMASCOPE *n* instrument for inspecting internal organs
SOMATA > SOMA
SOMATIC *adj* of the body, as distinct from the mind
SOMATISM *n* materialism
SOMATISMS > SOMATISM
SOMATIST > SOMATISM
SOMATISTS > SOMATISM
SOMBER *adj* (in the US) sombre ▷ *vb* (in the US) make sombre
SOMBERED > SOMBER
SOMBERER > SOMBER
SOMBEREST > SOMBER
SOMBERING > SOMBER
SOMBERLY > SOMBER
SOMBERS > SOMBER
SOMBRE *adj* dark, gloomy ▷ *vb* make sombre
SOMBRED > SOMBRE
SOMBRELY > SOMBRE
SOMBRER > SOMBRE
SOMBRERO *n* wide-brimmed Mexican hat
SOMBREROS > SOMBRERO
SOMBRES > SOMBRE
SOMBREST > SOMBRE
SOMBRING > SOMBRE
SOMBROUS > SOMBRE
SOME *adj* unknown or unspecified ▷ *pron* certain unknown or unspecified people or things ▷ *adv* approximately ▷ *determiner* (a) certain unknown or unspecified
SOMEBODY *pron* some person ▷ *n* important person
SOMEDAY *adv* at some unspecified time in the future
SOMEDEAL *adv* to some extent
SOMEDELE *same as* > SOMEDEAL
SOMEGATE *adv* Scots word meaning somehow
SOMEHOW *adv* in some unspecified way
SOMEONE *pron* somebody ▷ *n* significant or important person
SOMEONES > SOMEONE
SOMEPLACE *adv* in, at, or to some unspecified place or region
SOMERSET *variant of* > SOMERSAULT
SOMERSETS > SOMERSET
SOMETHING *pron* unknown or unspecified thing or amount ▷ *n* impressive or important person or thing
SOMETIME *adv* at some unspecified time ▷ *adj* former
SOMETIMES *adv* from time to time, now and then
SOMEWAY *adv* in some unspecified manner
SOMEWAYS *same as* > SOMEWAY
SOMEWHAT *adv* some extent, rather ▷ *n* vague amount
SOMEWHATS > SOMEWHAT
SOMEWHEN *adv* at some time
SOMEWHERE *adv* in, to, or at some unspecified or unknown place
SOMEWHILE *adv* sometimes
SOMEWHY *adv* for some reason
SOMEWISE *adv* in some way or to some degree
SOMITAL > SOMITE
SOMITE *n* any of a series of dorsal paired segments of mesoderm occurring along the notochord in vertebrate embryos
SOMITES > SOMITE
SOMITIC > SOMITE
SOMMELIER *n* wine steward in a restaurant or hotel
SOMNIAL *adj* of dreams
SOMNIATE *vb* dream
SOMNIATED > SOMNIATE
SOMNIATES > SOMNIATE
SOMNIFIC *adj* inducing sleep
SOMNOLENT *adj* drowsy
SOMONI *n* monetary unit of Tajikistan
SOMS > SOM
SOMY > SOM
SON *n* male offspring
SONANCE > SONANT
SONANCES > SONANT
SONANCIES > SONANT
SONANCY > SONANT
SONANT *n* voiced sound able to form a syllable or syllable nucleus ▷ *adj* denoting a voiced sound like this
SONANTAL > SONANT
SONANTIC > SONANT
SONANTS > SONANT
SONAR *n* device for detecting underwater objects by the reflection of sound waves
SONARMAN *n* sonar operator
SONARMEN > SONARMAN
SONARS > SONAR
SONATA *n* piece of music in several movements for one instrument with or without piano
SONATAS > SONATA
SONATINA *n* short sonata
SONATINAS > SONATINA
SONATINE *same as* > SONATINA
SONCE *n* Scots word meaning good luck
SONCES > SONCE
SONDAGE *n* deep trial trench for inspecting stratigraphy
SONDAGES > SONDAGE
SONDE *n* rocket, balloon, or probe used for observing in the upper atmosphere
SONDELI *n* Indian shrew
SONDELIS > SONDELI
SONDER *n* yacht category
SONDERS > SONDER
SONDES > SONDE
SONE *n* subjective unit of loudness
SONERI *n* Indian cloth of gold
SONERIS > SONERI
SONES > SONE
SONG *n* music for the voice
SONGBIRD *n* any bird with a musical call
SONGBIRDS > SONGBIRD
SONGBOOK *n* book of songs
SONGBOOKS > SONGBOOK
SONGCRAFT *n* art of songwriting
SONGFEST *n* event with many songs
SONGFESTS > SONGFEST
SONGFUL *adj* tuneful
SONGFULLY > SONGFUL
SONGKOK *n* (in Malaysia and Indonesia) a kind of oval brimless hat, resembling a skull
SONGKOKS > SONGKOK
SONGLESS > SONG
SONGLIKE > SONG
SONGMAN *n* singer
SONGMEN > SONGMAN
SONGOLOLO *n* kind of millipede
SONGS > SONG
SONGSMITH *n* person who writes songs
SONGSTER *n* singer
SONGSTERS > SONGSTER
SONHOOD > SON
SONHOODS > SON
SONIC *adj* of or producing sound
SONICALLY > SONIC
SONICATE *vb* subject to sound waves
SONICATED > SONICATE
SONICATES > SONICATE
SONICATOR > SONICATE
SONICS *n* study of mechanical vibrations in matter
SONLESS > SON
SONLIKE > SON
SONLY *adj* like a son
SONNE *same as* > SON
SONNES > SONNE
SONNET *n* fourteen-line poem with a fixed rhyme scheme ▷ *vb* compose sonnets
SONNETARY > SONNET
SONNETED > SONNET
SONNETEER *n* writer of sonnets
SONNETING > SONNET
SONNETISE *same as* > SONNETIZE

SONNETIZE *vb* write sonnets
SONNETS > SONNET
SONNETTED > SONNET
SONNIES > SONNY
SONNY *n* term of address to a boy
SONOBUOY *n* buoy equipped to detect underwater noises and transmit them by radio
SONOBUOYS > SONOBUOY
SONOGRAM *n* three-dimensional representation of a sound signal
SONOGRAMS > SONOGRAM
SONOGRAPH *n* device for scanning sound
SONOMETER *same as* > MONOCHORD
SONORANT *n* type of frictionless continuant or nasal
SONORANTS > SONORANT
SONORITY > SONOROUS
SONOROUS *adj* (of sound) deep or resonant
SONOVOX *n* device used to alter sound of human voice in music recordings
SONOVOXES > SONOVOX
SONS > SON
SONSE *same as* > SONCE
SONSES > SONSE
SONSHIP > SON
SONSHIPS > SON
SONSIE *same as* > SONSY
SONSIER > SONSY
SONSIEST > SONSY
SONSY *adj* plump
SONTAG *n* type of knitted women's cape
SONTAGS > SONTAG
SONTIES *n* Shakespearian oath
SOOCHONG *same as* > SOUCHONG
SOOCHONGS > SOOCHONG
SOOEY *interj* call used to summon pigs
SOOGEE *vb* clean ship using a special solution
SOOGEED > SOOGEE
SOOGEEING > SOOGEE
SOOGEES > SOOGEE
SOOGIE *same as* > SOUGEE
SOOGIED > SOOGIE
SOOGIEING > SOOGIE
SOOGIES > SOOGIE
SOOJEY *same as* > SOOGEE
SOOJEYS > SOOJEY
SOOK *n* baby ▷ *vb* suck
SOOKED > SOOK
SOOKING > SOOK
SOOKS > SOOK
SOOL *vb* incite (a dog) to attack
SOOLE *same as* > SOOL
SOOLED > SOOL
SOOLES > SOOLE
SOOLING > SOOL
SOOLS > SOOL
SOOM *Scots word for* > SWIM
SOOMED > SOOM
SOOMING > SOOM
SOOMS > SOOM
SOON *adv* in a short time
SOONER *adv* rather ▷ *n* native of Oklahoma
SOONERS > SOONER
SOONEST *adv* as soon as possible
SOOP *Scots word for* > SWEEP
SOOPED > SOOP
SOOPING > SOOP
SOOPINGS > SOOP
SOOPS > SOOP
SOOPSTAKE *adv* sweeping up all stakes
SOOT *n* black powder formed by the incomplete burning of an organic substance ▷ *vb* cover with soot
SOOTE *n* sweet
SOOTED > SOOT
SOOTERKIN *n* mythical black afterbirth of Dutch women that was believed to result from their warming themselves on stoves
SOOTES > SOOT
SOOTFLAKE *n* speck of soot
SOOTH *n* truth or reality ▷ *adj* true or real
SOOTHE *vb* make calm
SOOTHED > SOOTHE
SOOTHER > SOOTHE *vb* flatter
SOOTHERED > SOOTHE
SOOTHERS > SOOTHE
SOOTHES > SOOTHE
SOOTHEST > SOOTH
SOOTHFAST *adj* truthful
SOOTHFUL *adj* truthful
SOOTHING *adj* having a calming, assuaging, or relieving effect
SOOTHINGS > SOOTHING
SOOTHLICH *adv* truly
SOOTHLY > SOOTH
SOOTHS > SOOTH
SOOTHSAID > SOOTHSAY
SOOTHSAY *vb* predict the future
SOOTHSAYS > SOOTHSAY
SOOTIER > SOOTY
SOOTIEST > SOOTY
SOOTILY > SOOTY
SOOTINESS > SOOTY
SOOTING > SOOT
SOOTLESS > SOOT
SOOTS > SOOT
SOOTY *adj* covered with soot
SOP *n* concession to pacify someone ▷ *vb* mop up or absorb (liquid)
SOPAPILLA *n* Mexican deep-fried pastry
SOPH *shortened form of* > SOPHOMORE
SOPHERIC > SOPHERIM
SOPHERIM *n* Jewish scribes
SOPHIES > SOPHY
SOPHISM *n* argument that seems reasonable but is actually false and misleading
SOPHISMS > SOPHISM
SOPHIST *n* person who uses clever but invalid arguments
SOPHISTER *n* (esp formerly) a second-year undergraduate at certain British universities
SOPHISTIC *adj* of or relating to sophists or sophistry
SOPHISTRY *n* clever but invalid argument
SOPHISTS > SOPHIST
SOPHOMORE *n* student in second year at college
SOPHS > SOPH
SOPHY *n* title of the Persian monarchs
SOPITE *vb* lull to sleep
SOPITED > SOPITE
SOPITES > SOPITE
SOPITING > SOPITE
SOPOR *n* abnormally deep sleep
SOPORIFIC *adj* causing sleep ▷ *n* drug that causes sleep
SOPOROSE *adj* sleepy
SOPOROUS *same as* > SOPOROSE
SOPORS > SOPOR
SOPPED > SOP
SOPPIER > SOPPY
SOPPIEST > SOPPY
SOPPILY > SOPPY
SOPPINESS > SOPPY
SOPPING > SOP
SOPPINGS > SOP
SOPPY *adj* oversentimental
SOPRA *adv* musical instruction meaning above
SOPRANI > SOPRANO
SOPRANINI > SOPRANINO
SOPRANINO *n* instrument with the highest possible pitch in a family of instruments
SOPRANIST *n* soprano
SOPRANO *n* singer with the highest female or boy's voice ▷ *adj* of a musical instrument that is the highest or second highest pitched in its family
SOPRANOS > SOPRANO
SOPS > SOP
SORA *n* North American rail with a yellow bill
SORAGE *n* first year in hawk's life
SORAGES > SORAGE
SORAL > SORUS
SORAS > SORA
SORB *n* any of various related trees, esp the mountain ash ▷ *vb* absorb or adsorb
SORBABLE > SORB
SORBARIA *n* Asian shrub
SORBARIAS > SORBARIA
SORBATE *n* salt of sorbic acid
SORBATES > SORBATE
SORBED > SORB
SORBENT > SORB
SORBENTS > SORB
SORBET *same as* > SHERBET
SORBETS > SORBET
SORBIC > SORB
SORBING > SORB
SORBITE *n* mineral found in steel
SORBITES > SORBITE
SORBITIC > SORBITE
SORBITISE *same as* > SORBITIZE
SORBITIZE *vb* turn metal into form containing sorbite
SORBITOL *n* white water-soluble crystalline alcoh[ol] with a sweet taste
SORBITOLS > SORBITOL
SORBO as in *sorbo rubber* spongy form of rubber
SORBOSE *n* sweet-tasting hexose sugar derived from the berries of the mountain ash
SORBOSES > SORBOSE
SORBS > SORB
SORBUS *n* rowan or relate[d] tree
SORBUSES > SORBUS
SORCERER *n* magician
SORCERERS > SORCERER
SORCERESS *same as* > SORCERER
SORCERIES > SORCERY
SORCEROUS > SORCERY
SORCERY *n* witchcraft or magic
SORD *n* flock of mallard duc[ks]
SORDA *n* deaf woman
SORDES *pl n* dark incrustations on the lips and teeth of patients wit[h] prolonged fever
SORDID *adj* dirty, squalid
SORDIDER > SORDID
SORDIDEST > SORDID
SORDIDLY > SORDID
SORDINE *same as* > SORDI[NO]
SORDINES > SORDINE
SORDINI > SORDINO
SORDINO *n* mute for a stringed or brass musical instrument
SORDO *n* deaf man
SORDOR *n* sordidness
SORDORS > SORDOR
SORDS > SORD
SORE *adj* painful ▷ *n* painful area on the body ▷ *adv* greatly ▷ *vb* make sore
SORED > SORE
SOREDIA > SOREDIUM
SOREDIAL > SOREDIUM
SOREDIATE > SOREDIUM
SOREDIUM *n* organ of vegetative reproduction [in] lichens
SOREE *same as* > SORA

REES > SOREE
REHEAD *n* peevish or disgruntled person
REHEADS > SOREHEAD
REHON *n* old Irish feudal right
REHONS > SOREHON
REL *variant of* > SORREL
RELL *same as* > SORREL
RELLS > SORELL
RELS > SOREL
RELY *adv* greatly
RENESS > SORE
RER > SORE
RES > SORE
REST > SORE
REX *n* shrew or related animal
REXES > SOREX
RGHO *same as* > SORGO
RGHOS > SORGHO
RGHUM *n* kind of grass cultivated for grain
RGHUMS > SORGHUM
RGO *n* any of several varieties of sorghum that have watery sweet juice
RGOS > SORGO
RI > SORUS
RICINE *adj* of or resembling a shrew
RICOID *same* as > SORICINE
RING > SORE
RINGS > SORE
RITES *n* polysyllogism in which the premises are arranged so that intermediate conclusions are omitted, being understood, and only the final conclusion is stated
RITIC > SORITES
RITICAL > SORITES
RN *vb* obtain food, lodging, etc, from another person by presuming on his or her generosity
RNED > SORN
RNER > SORN
RNERS > SORE
RNING > SORN
RNINGS > SORN
RNS > SORN
ROBAN *n* Japanese abacus
ROBANS > SOROBAN
ROCHE *n* altitude sickness
ROCHES > SOROCHE
RORAL *adj* of sister
RORALLY > SORORAL
RORATE *n* custom in some societies of a widower marrying his deceased wife's younger sister
RORATES > SORORATE
RORIAL *same* s > SORORAL
RORISE *same* s > SORORIZE
RORISED > SORORISE
RORISES > SORORISE
SORORITY *n* society for female students
SORORIZE *vb* socialize in sisterly way
SORORIZED > SORORIZE
SORORIZES > SORORIZE
SOROSES > SOROSIS
SOROSIS *n* fleshy multiple fruit
SOROSISES > SOROSIS
SORPTION *n* process in which one substance takes up or holds another
SORPTIONS > SORPTION
SORPTIVE > SORPTION
SORRA *Irish word for* > SORROW
SORRAS > SORRA
SORREL *n* bitter-tasting plant
SORRELS > SORREL
SORRIER > SORRY
SORRIEST > SORRY
SORRILY > SORRY
SORRINESS > SORRY
SORROW *n* grief or sadness ▷ *vb* grieve
SORROWED > SORROW
SORROWER > SORROW
SORROWERS > SORROW
SORROWFUL > SORROW
SORROWING > SORROW
SORROWS > SORROW
SORRY *adj* feeling pity or regret ▷ *interj* exclamation expressing apology or asking someone to repeat what he or she has said
SORRYISH > SORRY
SORT *n* group all sharing certain qualities or characteristics ▷ *vb* arrange according to kind
SORTA *adv* phonetic representation of 'sort of'
SORTABLE > SORT
SORTABLY > SORT
SORTAL *n* type of logical or linguistic concept
SORTALS > SORTAL
SORTANCE *n* suitableness
SORTANCES > SORTANCE
SORTATION *n* act of sorting
SORTED *interj* exclamation of satisfaction, approval, etc ▷ *adj* possessing the desired recreational drugs
SORTER > SORT
SORTERS > SORT
SORTES *n* divination by opening book at random
SORTIE *n* relatively short return trip ▷ *vb* make a sortie
SORTIED > SORTIE
SORTIEING > SORTIE
SORTIES > SORTIE
SORTILEGE *n* act or practice of divination by drawing lots
SORTILEGY *same as* > SORTILEGE
SORTING > SORT
SORTINGS > SORT
SORTITION *n* act of casting lots
SORTMENT *n* assortment
SORTMENTS > SORTMENT
SORTS > SORT
SORUS *n* cluster of sporangia on the undersurface of certain fern leaves
SOS > SO
SOSATIE *n* skewer of curried meat pieces
SOSATIES > SOSATIE
SOSS *vb* make dirty or muddy
SOSSED > SOSS
SOSSES > SOSS
SOSSING > SOSS
SOSSINGS > SOSS
SOSTENUTI > SOSTENUTO
SOSTENUTO *adv* to be performed in a smooth sustained manner
SOT *n* habitual drunkard ▷ *adv* indeed: used to contradict a negative statement ▷ *vb* be a drunkard
SOTERIAL *adj* of salvation
SOTH *archaic variant of* > SOOTH
SOTHS > SOTH
SOTOL *n* American plant related to agave
SOTOLS > SOTOL
SOTS > SOT
SOTTED > SOT
SOTTEDLY > SOT
SOTTING > SOT
SOTTINGS > SOT
SOTTISH > SOT
SOTTISHLY > SOT
SOTTISIER *n* collection of jokes
SOU *n* former French coin
SOUARI *n* tree of tropical America
SOUARIS > SOUARI
SOUBISE *n* purée of onions mixed into a thick white sauce and served over eggs, fish, etc
SOUBISES > SOUBISE
SOUBRETTE *n* minor female role in comedy, often that of a pert maid
SOUCAR *n* Indian banker
SOUCARS > SOUCAR
SOUCE *same as* > SOUSE
SOUCED > SOUCE
SOUCES > SOUCE
SOUCHONG *n* black tea with large leaves
SOUCHONGS > SOUCHONG
SOUCING > SOUCE
SOUCT > SOUCE
SOUDAN *obsolete variaint of* > SULTAN
SOUDANS > SOUDAN
SOUFFLE *n* light fluffy dish made with beaten egg whites and other ingredients ▷ *adj* made light and puffy, as by beating and cooking
SOUFFLED > SOUFFLE
SOUFFLEED > SOUFFLE
SOUFFLES > SOUFFLE
SOUGH *vb* (of the wind) make a sighing sound ▷ *n* soft continuous murmuring sound
SOUGHED > SOUGH
SOUGHING > SOUGH
SOUGHS > SOUGH
SOUGHT > SEEK
SOUK *same as* > SOOK
SOUKED > SOUK
SOUKING > SOUK
SOUKOUS *n* style of African popular music characterized by syncopated rhythms and intricate contrasting guitar melodies
SOUKOUSES > SOUKOUS
SOUKS > SOUK
SOUL *n* spiritual and immortal part of a human being
SOULDAN *same as* > SOLDAN
SOULDANS > SOULDAN
SOULDIER *same as* > SOLDIER
SOULDIERS > SOULDIER
SOULED *adj* having soul
SOULFUL *adj* full of emotion
SOULFULLY > SOULFUL
SOULLESS *adj* lacking human qualities, mechanical
SOULLIKE *adj* resembling a soul
SOULMATE *n* person with whom one has most affinity
SOULMATES > SOULMATE
SOULS > SOUL
SOUM *vb* decide how many animals can graze particular pasture
SOUMED > SOUM
SOUMING > SOUM
SOUMINGS > SOUM
SOUMS > SOUM
SOUND *n* something heard, noise ▷ *vb* make or cause to make a sound ▷ *adj* in good condition ▷ *adv* soundly
SOUNDABLE > SOUND
SOUNDBITE *n* short pithy sentence or phrase extracted from a longer speech
SOUNDBOX *n* resonating chamber of the hollow body of a violin, guitar, etc
SOUNDCARD *n* component giving computer sound effects
SOUNDED > SOUND
SOUNDER *n* electromagnetic device formerly used in telegraphy to convert electric signals into

audible sounds
SOUNDERS > SOUNDER
SOUNDEST > SOUND
SOUNDING *adj* resounding
SOUNDINGS > SOUNDING
SOUNDLESS *adj* extremely still or silent
SOUNDLY > SOUND
SOUNDMAN *n* sound recorder in television crew
SOUNDMEN > SOUNDMAN
SOUNDNESS > SOUND
SOUNDPOST *n* small post on guitars, violins, etc, that joins the front surface to the back and allows the whole body of the instrument to vibrate
SOUNDS > SOUND
SOUP *n* liquid food made from meat, vegetables, etc ▷ *vb* give soup to
SOUPCON *n* small amount
SOUPCONS > SOUPCON
SOUPED > SOUP
SOUPER *n* person dispensing soup
SOUPERS > SOUPER
SOUPFIN *n* Pacific requiem shark valued for its fins
SOUPFINS > SOUPFIN
SOUPIER > SOUPY
SOUPIEST > SOUPY
SOUPING > SOUP
SOUPLE *same as* > SUPPLE
SOUPLED > SOUPLE
SOUPLES > SOUPLE
SOUPLESS > SOUP
SOUPLIKE > SOUP
SOUPLING > SOUPLE
SOUPS > SOUP
SOUPSPOON *n* spoon for eating soup
SOUPY *adj* having the appearance or consistency of soup
SOUR *adj* sharp-tasting ▷ *vb* make or become sour
SOURBALL *n* tart-flavoured boiled sweet
SOURBALLS > SOURBALL
SOURCE *n* origin or starting point ▷ *vb* establish a supplier of (a product, etc)
SOURCED > SOURCE
SOURCEFUL *adj* offering useful things
SOURCES > SOURCE
SOURCING > SOURCE
SOURCINGS > SOURCE
SOURDINE *n* soft stop on an organ or harmonium
SOURDINES > SOURDINE
SOURDOUGH *adj* (of bread) made with fermented dough used as a leaven ▷ *n* (in Western US, Canada, and Alaska) an old-time prospector or pioneer
SOURED > SOUR
SOURER > SOUR
SOUREST > SOUR
SOURING > SOUR
SOURINGS > SOUR
SOURISH > SOUR
SOURISHLY > SOUR
SOURLY > SOUR
SOURNESS > SOUR
SOUROCK *n* Scots word for sorrel plant
SOUROCKS > SOUROCK
SOURPUSS *n* person who is always gloomy, pessimistic, or bitter
SOURS > SOUR
SOURSE *same as* > SOURCE
SOURSES > SOURSE
SOURSOP *n* small West Indian tree
SOURSOPS > SOURSOP
SOURWOOD *n* sorrel tree
SOURWOODS > SOURWOOD
SOUS > SOU
SOUSE *vb* plunge (something) into liquid ▷ *n* liquid used in pickling
SOUSED > SOUSE
SOUSES > SOUSE
SOUSING > SOUSE
SOUSINGS > SOUSE
SOUSLIK *same as* > SUSLIK
SOUSLIKS > SOUSLIK
SOUT *same as* > SOOT
SOUTACHE *n* narrow braid used as a decorative trimming
SOUTACHES > SOUTACHE
SOUTANE *n* Roman Catholic priest's cassock
SOUTANES > SOUTANE
SOUTAR *same as* > SOUTER
SOUTARS > SOUTAR
SOUTENEUR *n* pimp
SOUTER *n* shoemaker or cobbler
SOUTERLY > SOUTER
SOUTERS > SOUTER
SOUTH *n* direction towards the South Pole, opposite north ▷ *adj* or in the south ▷ *adv* in, to, or towards the south ▷ *vb* turn south
SOUTHEAST *adv* (in or to) direction between south and east ▷ *n* point of the compass or the direction midway between south and east ▷ *adj* of or denoting the southeastern part of a specified country, area, etc
SOUTHED > SOUTH
SOUTHER *n* strong wind or storm from the south ▷ *vb* turn south
SOUTHERED > SOUTHER
SOUTHERLY *adj* of or in the south ▷ *adv* towards the south ▷ *n* wind from the south
SOUTHERN *adj* situated in or towards the south ▷ *n* southerner
SOUTHERNS > SOUTHERN
SOUTHERS > SOUTHER
SOUTHING *n* movement, deviation, or distance covered in a southerly direction
SOUTHINGS > SOUTHING
SOUTHLAND *n* southern part of country
SOUTHMOST *adj* situated or occurring farthest south
SOUTHPAW *n* left-handed person, esp a boxer ▷ *adj* left-handed
SOUTHPAWS > SOUTHPAW
SOUTHRON *n* southerner
SOUTHRONS > SOUTHRON
SOUTHS > SOUTH
SOUTHSAID > SOUTHSAY
SOUTHSAY *same as* > SOOTHSAY
SOUTHSAYS > SOUTHSAY
SOUTHWARD *adv* towards the south
SOUTHWEST *adv* (in or to) direction between south and west ▷ *n* point of the compass or the direction midway between west and south ▷ *adj* of or denoting the southwestern part of a specified country, area, etc
SOUTIE *same as* > SOUTPIEL
SOUTIES > SOUTIE
SOUTPIEL *n* South African derogatory slang for an English-speaking South African
SOUTPIELS > SOUTPIEL
SOUTS > SOUT
SOUVENIR *n* keepsake, memento ▷ *vb* steal or keep (something, esp a small article) for one's own use
SOUVENIRS > SOUVENIR
SOUVLAKI *same as* > SOUVLAKIA
SOUVLAKIA *n* Greek dish of kebabs, esp made with lamb
SOUVLAKIS > SOUVLAKI
SOV *shortening of* > SOVEREIGN
SOVENANCE *n* memory
SOVEREIGN *n* king or queen ▷ *adj* (of a state) independent
SOVIET *n* formerly, elected council at various levels of government in the USSR ▷ *adj* of the former USSR
SOVIETIC > SOVIET
SOVIETISE *same as* > SOVIETIZE
SOVIETISM *n* principle or practice of government through soviets
SOVIETIST > SOVIETISM
SOVIETIZE *vb* bring (a country, person, etc) under Soviet control or influence
SOVIETS > SOVIET
SOVKHOZ *n* (in the former Soviet Union) a large mechanized farm owned by the state
SOVKHOZES > SOVKHOZ
SOVKHOZY > SOVKHOZ
SOVRAN *literary word for* > SOVEREIGN
SOVRANLY > SOVRAN
SOVRANS > SOVRAN
SOVRANTY > SOVRAN
SOVS > SOV
SOW *vb* scatter or plant (seed) in or on (the ground) ▷ *n* female adult pig
SOWABLE > SOW
SOWANS *same as* > SOWENS
SOWAR *n* Indian cavalryman
SOWARREE *n* Indian mounted escort
SOWARREES > SOWARREE
SOWARRIES > SOWARRY
SOWARRY *same as* > SOWARREE
SOWARS > SOWAR
SOWBACK *another name for* > HOGBACK
SOWBACKS > SOWBACK
SOWBELLY *n* salt pork from pig's belly
SOWBREAD *n* S European primulaceous plant
SOWBREADS > SOWBREAD
SOWCAR *same as* > SOUCAR
SOWCARS > SOWCAR
SOWCE *same as* > SOUSE
SOWCED > SOWCE
SOWCES > SOWCE
SOWCING > SOWCE
SOWED > SOW
SOWENS *n* pudding made from oatmeal husks steeped and boiled
SOWER > SOW
SOWERS > SOW
SOWF *same as* > SOWTH
SOWFED > SOWF
SOWFF *same as* > SOWTH
SOWFFED > SOWFF
SOWFFING > SOWFF
SOWFFS > SOWFF
SOWFING > SOWF
SOWFS > SOWF
SOWING > SOW
SOWINGS > SOW
SOWL *same as* > SOLE
SOWLE *same as* > SOLE
SOWLED > SOWL
SOWLES > SOWLE
SOWLING > SOWL
SOWLS > SOWL
SOWM *same as* > SOUM
SOWMED > SOWM
SOWMING > SOWM
SOWMS > SOWM
SOWN > SOW
SOWND *vb* wield
SOWNDED > SOWND
SOWNDING > SOWND
SOWNDS > SOWND
SOWNE *same as* > SOUND
SOWNES > SOWNE
SOWP *n* spoonful
SOWPS > SOWP
SOWS > SOW
SOWSE *same as* > SOUSE
SOWSED > SOWSE
SOWSES > SOWSE
SOWSING > SOWSE
SOWSSE *same as* > SOUSE

WSSED > SOWSSE
WSSES > SOWSSE
WSSING > SOWSSE
WTER *same as* > SOUTER
WTERS > SOWTER
WTH *vb* Scots word meaning whistle
WTHED > SOWTH
WTHING > SOWTH
WTHS > SOWTH
X *pl n* informal spelling of 'socks'
Y as in *soy sauce* salty dark brown sauce made from soya beans, used in Chinese and Japanese cookery
YA *n* plant whose edible bean is used for food and as a source of oil
YAS > SOYA
YBEAN *n* soya bean
YBEANS > SOYBEAN
YLE *n* body
YLES > SOYLE
YMILK *n* milk substitute made from soya
YMILKS > SOYMILK
YS > SOY
YUZ *n* Russian spacecraft used to ferry crew to and from space stations
YUZES > SOYUZ
ZIN *n* form of protein
ZINE *same as* > SOZIN
ZINES > SOZINE
ZINS > SOZIN
ZZLE *vb* make wet
ZZLED *adj* drunk
ZZLES > SOZZLE
ZZLIER > SOZZLY
ZZLIEST > SOZZLY
ZZLING > SOZZLE
ZZLY *adj* wet
A *n* resort with a mineral-water spring ▷ *vb* visit a spa
ACE *n* unlimited expanse in which all objects exist and move ▷ *vb* place at intervals
ACEBAND *n* device on a linecaster for evening up the spaces between words
ACED > SPACE
ACELAB *n* laboratory in space where scientific experiments are performed
ACELABS > SPACELAB
ACELESS *adj* having no limits in space
ACEMAN *n* person who travels in space
ACEMEN > SPACEMAN
ACEPORT *n* base equipped to launch, maintain, and test spacecraft
ACER *n* piece of material used to create or maintain a space between two things
ACERS > SPACER
SPACES > SPACE
SPACESHIP *n* (in science fiction) a spacecraft used for travel between planets and galaxies
SPACESUIT *n* sealed pressurized suit worn by an astronaut
SPACEWALK *n* instance of floating and manoeuvring in space, outside but attached by a lifeline to a spacecraft ▷ *vb* float and manoeuvre in space while outside but attached to a spacecraft
SPACEWARD *adv* into space
SPACEY *adj* vague and dreamy, as if under the influence of drugs
SPACIAL *same as* > SPATIAL
SPACIALLY > SPACIAL
SPACIER > SPACEY
SPACIEST > SPACEY
SPACINESS > SPACEY
SPACING *n* arrangement of letters, words, etc, on a page in order to achieve legibility
SPACINGS > SPACING
SPACIOUS *adj* having a large capacity or area
SPACKLE *vb* fill holes in plaster
SPACKLED > SPACKLE
SPACKLES > SPACKLE
SPACKLING > SPACKLE
SPACY *same as* > SPACEY
SPADASSIN *n* swordsman
SPADE *n* tool for digging
SPADED > SPADE
SPADEFISH *n* type of spiny-finned food fish
SPADEFUL *n* amount spade will hold
SPADEFULS > SPADEFUL
SPADELIKE > SPADE
SPADEMAN *n* man who works with spade
SPADEMEN > SPADEMAN
SPADER > SPADE
SPADERS > SPADE
SPADES > SPADE
SPADESMAN *same as* > SPADEMAN
SPADESMEN > SPADEMAN
SPADEWORK *n* hard preparatory work
SPADGER *n* sparrow
SPADGERS > SPADGER
SPADICES > SPADIX
SPADILLE *n* (in ombre and quadrille) the ace of spades
SPADILLES > SPADILLE
SPADILLIO *same as* > SPADILLE
SPADILLO *same as* > SPADILLE
SPADILLOS > SPADILLO
SPADING > SPADE
SPADIX *n* spike of small flowers on a fleshy stem
SPADIXES > SPADIX
SPADO *n* neutered animal
SPADOES > SPADO
SPADONES > SPADO
SPADOS > SPADO
SPADROON *n* type of sword
SPADROONS > SPADROON
SPAE *vb* foretell (the future)
SPAED > SPAE
SPAEING > SPAE
SPAEINGS > SPAE
SPAEMAN *n* man who foretells future
SPAEMEN > SPAEMAN
SPAER > SPAE
SPAERS > SPAE
SPAES > SPAE
SPAETZLE *n* German noodle dish
SPAETZLES > SPAETZLE
SPAEWIFE *n* woman who can supposedly foretell the future
SPAEWIVES > SPAEWIFE
SPAG *vb* (of a cat) to scratch (a person) with the claws ▷ *n* Australian offensive slang for an Italian
SPAGERIC *same as* > SPAGYRIC
SPAGERICS > SPAGERIC
SPAGERIST > SPAGERIC
SPAGGED > SPAG
SPAGGING > SPAG
SPAGHETTI *n* pasta in the form of long strings
SPAGIRIC *same as* > SPAGYRIC
SPAGIRICS > SPAGIRIC
SPAGIRIST > SPAGIRIC
SPAGS > SPAG
SPAGYRIC *adj* of or relating to alchemy ▷ *n* alchemist
SPAGYRICS > SPAGYRIC
SPAGYRIST > SPAGYRIC
SPAHEE *same as* > SPAHI
SPAHEES > SPAHEE
SPAHI *n* (formerly) an irregular cavalryman in the Turkish armed forces
SPAHIS > SPAHI
SPAIL *Scots word for* > SPALL
SPAILS > SPAIL
SPAIN *variant of* > SPANE
SPAINED > SPAIN
SPAING > SPA
SPAINGS > SPA
SPAINING > SPAIN
SPAINS > SPAIN
SPAIRGE *Scots word for* > SPARGE
SPAIRGED > SPAIRGE
SPAIRGES > SPAIRGE
SPAIRGING > SPAIRGE
SPAIT *same as* > SPATE
SPAITS > SPAIT
SPAKE *past tense of* > SPEAK
SPALD *same as* > SPAULD
SPALDEEN *n* ball used in street game
SPALDEENS > SPALDEEN
SPALDS > SPALD
SPALE *Scots word for* > SPALL
SPALES > SPALE
SPALL *n* splinter or chip of ore, rock, or stone ▷ *vb* split or cause to split into such fragments
SPALLABLE > SPALL
SPALLE *same as* > SPAULD
SPALLED > SPALL
SPALLER > SPALL
SPALLERS > SPALL
SPALLES > SPALLE
SPALLING > SPALL
SPALLINGS > SPALL
SPALLS > SPALL
SPALPEEN *n* itinerant seasonal labourer
SPALPEENS > SPALPEEN
SPALT *vb* split
SPALTED > SPALT
SPALTING > SPALT
SPALTS > SPALT
SPAM *vb* send unsolicited e-mail simultaneously to a number of newsgroups on the internet ▷ *n* unsolicited electronic mail or text messages sent in this way
SPAMBOT *n* computer programme that identifies email addresses to send spam to
SPAMBOTS > SPAMBOT
SPAMMED > SPAM
SPAMMER > SPAM
SPAMMERS > SPAM
SPAMMIE *n* love bite
SPAMMIER > SPAMMY
SPAMMIES > SPAMMIE
SPAMMIEST > SPAMMY
SPAMMING > SPAM
SPAMMINGS > SPAM
SPAMMY *adj* bland
SPAMS > SPAM
SPAN *n* space between two points ▷ *vb* stretch or extend across
SPANAEMIA *n* lack of red corpuscles in blood
SPANAEMIC > SPANAEMIA
SPANCEL *n* length of rope for hobbling an animal, esp a horse or cow ▷ *vb* hobble (an animal) with a loose rope
SPANCELED > SPANCEL
SPANCELS > SPANCEL
SPANDEX *n* type of synthetic stretch fabric made from polyurethane fibre
SPANDEXES > SPANDEX
SPANDREL *n* triangular surface bounded by the outer curve of an arch and the adjacent wall
SPANDRELS > SPANDREL
SPANDRIL *same as* > SPANDREL
SPANDRILS > SPANDRIL
SPANE *vb* Scots word meaning wean
SPANED > SPANE
SPANES > SPANE
SPANG *adv* exactly, firmly, or straight ▷ *vb* dash

SPANGED > SPANG
SPANGHEW *vb* throw in air
SPANGHEWS > SPANGHEW
SPANGING > SPANG
SPANGLE *n* small shiny metallic ornament ▷ *vb* decorate with spangles
SPANGLED > SPANGLE
SPANGLER > SPANGLE
SPANGLERS > SPANGLE
SPANGLES > SPANGLE
SPANGLET *n* little spangle
SPANGLETS > SPANGLET
SPANGLIER > SPANGLE
SPANGLING > SPANGLE
SPANGLY > SPANGLE
SPANGS > SPANG
SPANIEL *n* dog with long ears and silky hair
SPANIELS > SPANIEL
SPANING > SPANE
SPANK *vb* slap with the open hand, on the buttocks or legs ▷ *n* such a slap
SPANKED > SPANK
SPANKER *n* fore-and-aft sail or a mast that is aftermost in a sailing vessel
SPANKERS > SPANKER
SPANKING *adj* outstandingly fine or smart ▷ *n* series of spanks, usually as a punishment for children
SPANKINGS > SPANKING
SPANKS > SPANK
SPANLESS *adj* impossible to span
SPANNED > SPAN
SPANNER *n* tool for gripping and turning a nut or bolt
SPANNERS > SPANNER
SPANNING > SPAN
SPANS > SPAN
SPANSPEK *n* cantaloupe melon
SPANSPEKS > SPANSPEK
SPANSULE *n* modified-release capsule of a drug
SPANSULES > SPANSULE
SPANWORM *n* larva of a type of moth
SPANWORMS > SPANWORM
SPAR *n* pole used as a ship's mast, boom, or yard ▷ *vb* box or fight using light blows for practice
SPARABLE *n* small nail with no head, used for fixing the soles and heels of shoes
SPARABLES > SPARABLE
SPARAXIS *n* type of plant with dainty spikes of star-shaped purple, red, or orange flowers
SPARD > SPARE
SPARE *adj* extra ▷ *n* duplicate kept in case of damage or loss ▷ *vb* refrain from punishing or harming
SPAREABLE > SPARE
SPARED > SPARE
SPARELESS *adj* merciless
SPARELY > SPARE
SPARENESS > SPARE
SPARER > SPARE
SPARERIB *n* cut of pork ribs with most of the meat trimmed off
SPARERIBS > SPARERIB
SPARERS > SPARE
SPARES > SPARE
SPAREST > SPARE
SPARGE *vb* sprinkle or scatter (something)
SPARGED > SPARGE
SPARGER > SPARGE
SPARGERS > SPARGE
SPARGES > SPARGE
SPARGING > SPARGE
SPARID *n* type of marine percoid fish ▷ *adj* of or belonging to this family of fish
SPARIDS > SPARID
SPARING *adj* economical
SPARINGLY > SPARING
SPARK *n* fiery particle thrown out from a fire or caused by friction ▷ *vb* give off sparks
SPARKE *n* weapon
SPARKED > SPARK
SPARKER > SPARK
SPARKERS > SPARK
SPARKES > SPARKE
SPARKIE *n* electrician
SPARKIER > SPARKY
SPARKIES > SPARKIE
SPARKIEST > SPARKY
SPARKILY > SPARKY
SPARKING > SPARK
SPARKISH > SPARK
SPARKLE *vb* glitter with many points of light ▷ *n* sparkling points of light
SPARKLED > SPARKLE
SPARKLER *n* hand-held firework that emits sparks
SPARKLERS > SPARKLER
SPARKLES > SPARKLE
SPARKLESS > SPARK
SPARKLET *n* little spark
SPARKLETS > SPARKLET
SPARKLIER > SPARKLY
SPARKLIES > SPARKLY
SPARKLING *adj* (of wine or mineral water) slightly fizzy
SPARKLY *adj* sparkling ▷ *n* sparkling thing
SPARKPLUG *n* device in an engine that ignites the fuel
SPARKS *n* electrician
SPARKY *adj* lively
SPARLIKE > SPAR
SPARLING *n* European smelt
SPARLINGS > SPARLING
SPAROID *same as* > SPARID
SPAROIDS > SPAROID
SPARRE *same as* > SPAR
SPARRED > SPAR
SPARRER > SPAR
SPARRERS > SPAR
SPARRES > SPARRE
SPARRIER > SPARRY
SPARRIEST > SPARRY
SPARRING > SPAR
SPARRINGS > SPAR
SPARROW *n* small brownish bird
SPARROWS > SPARROW
SPARRY *adj* (of minerals) containing, relating to, or resembling spar
SPARS > SPAR
SPARSE *adj* thinly scattered
SPARSEDLY > SPARSE
SPARSELY > SPARSE
SPARSER > SPARSE
SPARSEST > SPARSE
SPARSITY > SPARSE
SPART *n* esparto
SPARTAN *adj* strict and austere ▷ *n* disciplined or brave person
SPARTANS > SPARTAN
SPARTEINE *n* viscous oily alkaloid extracted from the broom plant and lupin seeds
SPARTERIE *n* things made from esparto
SPARTH *n* type of battle-axe
SPARTHE *same as* > SPARTH
SPARTHES > SPARTHE
SPARTHS > SPARTH
SPARTINA *n* grass growing in salt marshes
SPARTINAS > SPARTINA
SPARTS > SPART
SPAS > SPA
SPASM *n* involuntary muscular contraction ▷ *vb* go into spasm
SPASMATIC > SPASM
SPASMED > SPASM
SPASMIC > SPASM
SPASMING > SPASM
SPASMODIC *adj* occurring in spasms
SPASMS > SPASM
SPASTIC *n* offensive slang for a person with cerebral palsy ▷ *adj* suffering from cerebral palsy
SPASTICS > SPASTIC
SPAT *vb* have a quarrel
SPATE *n* large number of things happening within a period of time
SPATES > SPATE
SPATFALL *n* mass of larvae on sea bed
SPATFALLS > SPATFALL
SPATHAL > SPATHE
SPATHE *n* large sheathlike leaf enclosing a flower cluster
SPATHED > SPATHE
SPATHES > SPATHE
SPATHIC *adj* (of minerals) resembling spar, esp in having good cleavage
SPATHOSE *same as* > SPATHIC
SPATIAL *adj* of or in space
SPATIALLY > SPATIAL
SPATLESE *n* type of German wine, usu white
SPATLESEN > SPATLESE
SPATLESES > SPATLESE
SPATS > SPAT
SPATTED > SPAT
SPATTEE *n* type of gaiter
SPATTEES > SPATTEE
SPATTER *vb* scatter or be scattered in drops over (something) ▷ *n* spattering sound
SPATTERED > SPATTER
SPATTERS > SPATTER
SPATTING > SPIT
SPATULA *n* utensil with a broad flat blade for spreading or stirring
SPATULAR > SPATULA
SPATULAS > SPATULA
SPATULATE *adj* shaped lik[e] a spatula
SPATULE *n* spatula
SPATULES > SPATULE
SPATZLE *same as* > SPAETZL[E]
SPATZLES > SPATZLE
SPAUL *same as* > SPAULD
SPAULD *n* shoulder
SPAULDS > SPAULD
SPAULS > SPAUL
SPAVIE *Scots variant of* > SPAVIN
SPAVIES > SPAVIE
SPAVIET *adj* Scots word meaning spavined
SPAVIN *n* enlargement of the hock of a horse by a bony growth
SPAVINED *adj* affected wit[h] spavin
SPAVINS > SPAVIN
SPAW *same as* > SPA
SPAWL *vb* spit
SPAWLED > SPAWL
SPAWLING > SPAWL
SPAWLS > SPAWL
SPAWN *n* jelly-like mass of eggs of fish, frogs, or molluscs ▷ *vb* (of fish, frogs, or molluscs) lay egg[s]
SPAWNED > SPAWN
SPAWNER > SPAWN
SPAWNERS > SPAWN
SPAWNIER > SPAWNY
SPAWNIEST > SPAWNY
SPAWNING > SPAWN
SPAWNINGS > SPAWN
SPAWNS > SPAWN
SPAWNY *adj* like spawn
SPAWS > SPAW
SPAY *vb* remove the ovarie[s] from (a female animal)
SPAYAD *n* male deer
SPAYADS > SPAYAD
SPAYD *same as* > SPAYAD
SPAYDS > SPAYD
SPAYED > SPAY
SPAYING > SPAY
SPAYS > SPAY
SPAZ *vb* offensive slang meaning lose self-contro[l]
SPAZA as in *spaza shop* South African slang for a small shop in a township
SPAZZ *same as* > SPAZ

AZZED > SPAZ
AZZES > SPAZ
AZZING > SPAZ
EAK *vb* say words, talk
EAKABLE > SPEAK
EAKEASY *n* place where alcoholic drink was sold illegally during Prohibition
EAKER *n* person who speaks, esp at a formal occasion
EAKERS > SPEAKER
EAKING > SPEAK
EAKINGS > SPEAK
EAKOUT *n* firm or brave statement of one's beliefs
EAKOUTS > SPEAKOUT
EAKS > SPEAK
EAL *same as* > SPULE
EALS > SPEAL
EAN *same as* > SPANE
EANED > SPEAN
EANING > SPEAN
EANS > SPEAN
EAR *n* weapon consisting of a long shaft with a sharp point ▷ *vb* pierce with or as if with a spear
EARED > SPEAR
EARER > SPEAR
EARERS > SPEAR
EARFISH *n another name for* > MARLIN
EARGUN *n* device for shooting spears underwater
EARGUNS > SPEARGUN
EARHEAD *vb* lead (an attack or campaign) ▷ *n* leading force in an attack or campaign
EARIER > SPEAR
EARIEST > SPEAR
EARING > SPEAR
EARLIKE > SPEAR
EARMAN *n* soldier armed with a spear
EARMEN > SPEARMAN
EARMINT *n* type of mint
EARS > SPEAR
EARWORT *n* any of several Eurasian ranunculaceous plants
EARY > SPEAR
EAT *same as* > SPATE
EATS > SPEAT
EC *vb* set specifications
ECCED > SPEC
ECCIES > SPECCY
ECCING > SPEC
ECCY *n* person wearing spectacles
ECIAL *adj* distinguished from others of its kind ▷ *n* product, programme, etc which is only available at a certain time ▷ *vb.* advertise and sell (an item) at a reduced price
ECIALER > SPECIAL
ECIALLY > SPECIAL
ECIALS > SPECIAL
ECIALTY *n* special interest or skill
SPECIATE *vb* form or develop into a new biological species
SPECIATED > SPECIATE
SPECIATES > SPECIATE
SPECIE *n* coins as distinct from paper money
SPECIES *n* group of plants or animals that are related closely enough to interbreed naturally
SPECIFIC *adj* particular, definite ▷ *n* drug used to treat a particular disease
SPECIFICS > SPECIFIC
SPECIFIED > SPECIFY
SPECIFIER > SPECIFY
SPECIFIES > SPECIFY
SPECIFY *vb* refer to or state specifically
SPECIMEN *n* individual or part typifying a whole
SPECIMENS > SPECIMEN
SPECIOUS *adj* apparently true, but actually false
SPECK *n* small spot or particle ▷ *vb* mark with specks or spots
SPECKED > SPECK
SPECKIER > SPECKY
SPECKIEST > SPECKY
SPECKING > SPECK
SPECKLE *n* small spot ▷ *vb* mark with speckles
SPECKLED > SPECKLE
SPECKLES > SPECKLE
SPECKLESS > SPECK
SPECKLING > SPECKLE
SPECKS > SPECK
SPECKY *same as* > SPECCY
SPECS *pl n* spectacles
SPECTACLE *n* strange, interesting, or ridiculous sight
SPECTATE *vb* watch
SPECTATED > SPECTATE
SPECTATES > SPECTATE
SPECTATOR *n* person viewing anything, onlooker
SPECTER *same as* > SPECTRE
SPECTERS > SPECTER
SPECTRA > SPECTRUM
SPECTRAL *adj* of or like a spectre
SPECTRE *n* ghost
SPECTRES > SPECTRE
SPECTRIN *n* any one of a class of fibrous proteins found in the membranes of red blood cells
SPECTRINS > SPECTRIN
SPECTRUM *n* range of different colours, radio waves, etc in order of their wavelengths
SPECTRUMS > SPECTRUM
SPECULA > SPECULUM
SPECULAR *adj* of, relating to, or having the properties of a mirror
SPECULATE *vb* guess, conjecture
SPECULUM *n* medical instrument for examining body cavities
SPECULUMS > SPECULUM
SPED > SPEED
SPEECH *n* act, power, or manner of speaking ▷ *vb* make a speech
SPEECHED > SPEECH
SPEECHES > SPEECH
SPEECHFUL > SPEECH
SPEECHIFY *vb* make speeches, esp boringly
SPEECHING > SPEECH
SPEED *n* swiftness ▷ *vb* go quickly
SPEEDBALL *n* mixture of heroin with amphetamine or cocaine
SPEEDBOAT *n* light fast motorboat
SPEEDED > SPEED
SPEEDER > SPEED
SPEEDERS > SPEED
SPEEDFUL > SPEED
SPEEDIER > SPEEDY
SPEEDIEST > SPEEDY
SPEEDILY > SPEEDY
SPEEDING > SPEED
SPEEDINGS > SPEED
SPEEDLESS > SPEED
SPEEDO *n* speedometer
SPEEDOS > SPEEDO
SPEEDREAD *vb* read very quickly
SPEEDS > SPEED
SPEEDSTER *n* fast car, esp a sports model
SPEEDUP *n* acceleration
SPEEDUPS > SPEEDUP
SPEEDWAY *n* track for motorcycle racing
SPEEDWAYS > SPEEDWAY
SPEEDWELL *n* plant with small blue flowers
SPEEDY *adj* prompt
SPEEL *n* splinter of wood ▷ *vb* Scots word meaning climb
SPEELED > SPEEL
SPEELER > SPEEL
SPEELERS > SPEEL
SPEELING > SPEEL
SPEELS > SPEEL
SPEER *same as* > SPEIR
SPEERED > SPEER
SPEERING > SPEER
SPEERINGS > SPEER
SPEERS > SPEER
SPEIL *dialect word for* > CLIMB
SPEILED > SPEIL
SPEILING > SPEIL
SPEILS > SPEIL
SPEIR *vb* ask
SPEIRED > SPEIR
SPEIRING > SPEIR
SPEIRINGS > SPEIR
SPEIRS > SPEIR
SPEISE *same as* > SPEISS
SPEISES > SPEISE
SPEISS *n* arsenides and antimonides that form when ores containing arsenic or antimony are smelted
SPEISSES > SPEISS
SPEK *n* bacon, fat, or fatty pork used for larding venison or other game
SPEKBOOM *n* South African shrub
SPEKBOOMS > SPEKBOOM
SPEKS > SPEK
SPELAEAN *adj* of, found in, or inhabiting caves
SPELD *vb* Scots word meaning spread
SPELDED > SPELD
SPELDER *same as* > SPELD
SPELDERED > SPELDER
SPELDERS > SPELDER
SPELDIN *n* fish split and dried
SPELDING *same as* > SPELDIN
SPELDINGS > SPELDING
SPELDINS > SPELDIN
SPELDRIN > VARIANT OF > SPELDIN
SPELDRING *same as* > SPELDIN
SPELDRINS > SPELDRIN
SPELDS > SPELD
SPELEAN *same as* > SPELAEAN
SPELK *n* splinter of wood
SPELKS > SPELK
SPELL *vb* give in correct order the letters that form (a word) ▷ *n* formula of words supposed to have magic power
SPELLABLE > SPELL
SPELLBIND *vb* cause to be spellbound
SPELLDOWN *n* spelling competition
SPELLED > SPELL
SPELLER *n* person who spells words in the manner specified
SPELLERS > SPELLER
SPELLFUL *adj* magical
SPELLICAN *same as* > SPILLIKIN
SPELLING > SPELL
SPELLINGS > SPELL
SPELLS > SPELL
SPELT > SPELL
SPELTER *n* impure zinc, usually containing about 3 per cent of lead and other impurities
SPELTERS > SPELTER
SPELTS > SPELL
SPELTZ *n* wheat variety
SPELTZES > SPELTZ
SPELUNK *vb* explore caves
SPELUNKED > SPELUNK
SPELUNKER *n* person whose hobby is the exploration and study of caves
SPELUNKS > SPELUNK
SPENCE *n* larder or pantry
SPENCER *n* short fitted coat or jacket

SPENCERS > SPENCER
SPENCES > SPENCE
SPEND *vb* pay out (money)
SPENDABLE > SPEND
SPENDALL *n* spendthrift
SPENDALLS > SPENDALL
SPENDER *n* person who spends money in a manner specified
SPENDERS > SPENDER
SPENDIER > SPENDY
SPENDIEST > SPENDY
SPENDING > SPEND
SPENDINGS > SPEND
SPENDS > SPEND
SPENDY *adj* expensive
SPENSE *same as* > SPENCE
SPENSES > SPENSE
SPENT > SPEND
SPEOS *n* (esp in ancient Egypt) a temple or tomb cut into a rock face
SPEOSES > SPEOS
SPERLING *same as* > SPARLING
SPERLINGS > SPERLING
SPERM *n* male reproductive cell released in semen during ejaculation
SPERMARIA *pl n* spermaries
SPERMARY *n* any organ in which spermatozoa are produced, esp a testis
SPERMATIA *pl n* male reproductive cells in red algae and some fungi
SPERMATIC *adj* of or relating to spermatozoa
SPERMATID *n* any of four immature male gametes that are formed from a spermatocyte
SPERMIC *same as* > SPERMATIC
SPERMINE *n* colourless basic water-soluble amine that is found in semen, sputum, and animal tissues
SPERMINES > SPERMINE
SPERMOUS *same as* > SPERMATIC
SPERMS > SPERM
SPERRE *vb* bolt
SPERRED > SPERRE
SPERRES > SPERRE
SPERRING > SPERRE
SPERSE *vb* disperse
SPERSED > SPERSE
SPERSES > SPERSE
SPERSING > SPERSE
SPERST > SPERSE
SPERTHE *same as* > SPARTH
SPERTHES > SPERTHE
SPET *same as* > SPIT
SPETCH *n* piece of animal skin
SPETCHES > SPETCH
SPETS > SPET
SPETSNAZ *n* Soviet intelligence force
SPETTING > SPET
SPETZNAZ *same as* > SPETSNAZ
SPEUG *n* sparrow
SPEUGS > SPEUG
SPEW *vb* vomit ▷ *n* something ejected from the mouth
SPEWED > SPEW
SPEWER > SPEW
SPEWERS > SPEW
SPEWIER > SPEWY
SPEWIEST > SPEWY
SPEWINESS > SPEWY
SPEWING > SPEW
SPEWS > SPEW
SPEWY *adj* marshy
SPHACELUS *n* death of living tissue
SPHAER *same as* > SPHERE
SPHAERE *same as* > SPHERE
SPHAERES > SPHAERE
SPHAERITE *n* aluminium phosphate
SPHAERS > SPHAERE
SPHAGNOUS > SPHAGNUM
SPHAGNUM *n* moss found in bogs
SPHAGNUMS > SPHAGNUM
SPHAIREE *n* game resembling tennis played with wooden bats and a perforated plastic ball
SPHAIREES > SPHAIREE
SPHEAR *same as* > SPHERE
SPHEARE *same as* > SPHERE
SPHEARES > SPHEARE
SPHEARS > SPHEAR
SPHENDONE *n* ancient Greek headband
SPHENE *n* brown, yellow, green, or grey lustrous mineral
SPHENES > SPHENE
SPHENIC *adj* having the shape of a wedge
SPHENODON *technical name for the* > TUATARA
SPHENOID *adj* wedge-shaped ▷ *n* wedge-shaped thing
SPHENOIDS > SPHENOID
SPHERAL *adj* of or shaped like a sphere
SPHERE *n* perfectly round solid object ▷ *vb* surround or encircle
SPHERED > SPHERE
SPHERES > SPHERE
SPHERIC *same as* > SPHERICAL
SPHERICAL *adj* shaped like a sphere
SPHERICS *n* geometry and trigonometry of figures on the surface of a sphere
SPHERIER > SPHERY
SPHERIEST > SPHERY
SPHERING > SPHERE
SPHEROID *n* solid figure that is almost but not exactly a sphere
SPHEROIDS > SPHEROID
SPHERULAR > SPHERULE
SPHERULE *n* very small sphere or globule
SPHERULES > SPHERULE
SPHERY *adj* resembling a sphere
SPHINCTER *n* ring of muscle which controls the opening and closing of a hollow organ
SPHINGES > SPHINX
SPHINGID *n* hawk moth
SPHINGIDS > SPHINGID
SPHINX *n* one of the huge statues built by the ancient Egyptians, with the body of a lion and the head of a man
SPHINXES > SPHINX
SPHYGMIC *adj* of or relating to the pulse
SPHYGMOID *adj* resembling the pulse
SPHYGMUS *n* person's pulse
SPHYNX *n* breed of cat
SPHYNXES > SPHYNX
SPIAL *n* observation
SPIALS > SPIAL
SPIC *n* derogatory word for a Spanish-speaking person
SPICA *n* spiral bandage formed by a series of overlapping figure-of-eight turns
SPICAE > SPICA
SPICAS > SPICA
SPICATE *adj* having, arranged in, or relating to spikes
SPICATED *same as* > SPICATE
SPICCATO *n* style of playing a bowed stringed instrument in which the bow bounces lightly off the strings ▷ *adv* be played in this manner
SPICCATOS > SPICCATO
SPICE *n* aromatic substance used as flavouring ▷ *vb* flavour with spices
SPICEBUSH *n* North American lauraceous shrub
SPICED > SPICE
SPICELESS > SPICE
SPICER > SPICE
SPICERIES > SPICERY
SPICERS > SPICE
SPICERY *n* spices collectively
SPICES > SPICE
SPICEY *same as* > SPICY
SPICIER > SPICY
SPICIEST > SPICY
SPICILEGE *n* anthology
SPICILY > SPICY
SPICINESS > SPICY
SPICING > SPICE
SPICK *adj* neat and clean ▷ *n* spic
SPICKER > SPICK
SPICKEST > SPICK
SPICKNEL *same as* > SPIGNEL
SPICKNELS > SPICKNEL
SPICKS > SPICK
SPICS > SPIC
SPICULA > SPICULUM
SPICULAE > SPICULUM
SPICULAR > SPICULUM
SPICULATE > SPICULE
SPICULE *n* small slender pointed structure or crystal
SPICULES > SPICULE
SPICULUM *same as* > SPICUL
SPICY *adj* flavoured with spices
SPIDE *n* Irish derogatory slang for a young working class man who dresses in casual sports clothes
SPIDER *n* small eight-legged creature which spins a web to catch insects for food
SPIDERIER > SPIDERY
SPIDERISH > SPIDER
SPIDERMAN *n* person who erects the steel structure of a building
SPIDERMEN > SPIDERMAN
SPIDERS > SPIDER
SPIDERWEB *n* spider's wel
SPIDERY *adj* thin and angular like a spider's leg
SPIDES > SPIDE
SPIE *same as* > SPY
SPIED > SPY
SPIEGEL *n* manganese-rich pig iron
SPIEGELS > SPIEGEL
SPIEL *n* speech made to persuade someone to do something ▷ *vb* deliver a prepared spiel
SPIELED > SPIEL
SPIELER > SPIEL
SPIELERS > SPIEL
SPIELING > SPIEL
SPIELS > SPIEL
SPIER *variant of* > SPEIR
SPIERED > SPIER
SPIERING > SPIER
SPIERS > SPIER
SPIES > SPY
SPIF *n* postage stamp perforated with the initials of a firm to avoid theft by employees
SPIFF *vb* make smart
SPIFFED > SPIFF
SPIFFIED > SPIFFY
SPIFFIER > SPIFFY
SPIFFIES > SPIFFY
SPIFFIEST > SPIFFY
SPIFFILY > SPIFFY
SPIFFING *adj* excellent
SPIFFS > SPIFF
SPIFFY *adj* smart ▷ *n* smart thing or person
SPIFFYING > SPIFFY
SPIFS > SPIF
SPIGHT *same as* > SPITE
SPIGHTED > SPIGHT
SPIGHTING > SPIGHT
SPIGHTS > SPIGHT
SPIGNEL *n* European umbelliferous plant
SPIGNELS > SPIGNEL
SPIGOT *n* stopper for, or t

fitted to, a cask
PIGOTS > SPIGOT
PIK *same as* > SPIC
PIKE *n* sharp point ▷ *vb* put spikes on
PIKED > SPIKE
PIKEFISH *n* large sea fish
PIKELET *n* unit of a grass inflorescence
PIKELETS > SPIKELET
PIKELIKE > SPIKE
PIKENARD *n* fragrant Indian plant with rose-purple flowers
PIKER > SPIKE
PIKERIES > SPIKERY
PIKERS > SPIKE
PIKERY *n* High-Church Anglicanism
PIKES > SPIKE
PIKEY *same as* > SPIKY
PIKIER > SPIKY
PIKIEST > SPIKY
PIKILY > SPIKY
PIKINESS > SPIKY
PIKING > SPIKE
PIKS > SPIK
PIKY *adj* resembling a spike
PILE *n* heavy timber stake or pile ▷ *vb* provide or support with a spile
PILED > SPILE
PILES > SPILE
PILIKIN *same as* > SPILLIKIN
PILIKINS > SPILIKIN
PILING > SPILE
PILINGS > SPILE
PILITE *n* type of igneous rock
PILITES > SPILITE
PILITIC > SPILITE
PILL *vb* pour from or as if from a container ▷ *n* fall
PILLABLE > SPILL
PILLAGE *n* instance or the process of spilling
PILLAGES > SPILLAGE
PILLED > SPILL
PILLER > SPILL
PILLERS > SPILL
PILLIKIN *n* thin strip of wood, cardboard, or plastic used in spillikins
PILLING > SPILL
PILLINGS > SPILL
PILLOVER *n* act of splling over
PILLS > SPILL
PILLWAY *n* channel that carries away surplus water, as from a dam
PILLWAYS > SPILLWAY
PILOSITE *n* form of slate
PILT > SPILL
PILTH *n* something spilled
PILTHS > SPILTH
PIM *n* unsolicited commercial communications received on a computer via an instant-messaging system
SPIMS > SPIM
SPIN *vb* revolve or cause to revolve rapidly ▷ *n* revolving motion
SPINA *n* spine
SPINACENE *n* type of vaccine
SPINACH *n* dark green leafy vegetable
SPINACHES > SPINACH
SPINACHY > SPINACH
SPINAE > SPINA
SPINAGE *same as* > SPINACH
SPINAGES > SPINAGE
SPINAL *adj* of the spine ▷ *n* anaesthetic administered in the spine
SPINALLY > SPINAL
SPINALS > SPINAL
SPINAR *n* fast-spinning star
SPINARS > SPINAR
SPINAS > SPINA
SPINATE *adj* having a spine
SPINDLE *n* rotating rod that acts as an axle ▷ *vb* form into a spindle or equip with spindles
SPINDLED > SPINDLE
SPINDLER > SPINDLE
SPINDLERS > SPINDLE
SPINDLES > SPINDLE
SPINDLIER > SPINDLY
SPINDLING *adj* long and slender, esp disproportionately so ▷ *n* spindling person or thing
SPINDLY *adj* long, slender, and frail
SPINDRIFT *n* spray blown up from the sea
SPINE *n* backbone
SPINED > SPINE
SPINEL *n* any of a group of hard glassy minerals of variable colour
SPINELESS *adj* lacking courage
SPINELIKE > SPINE
SPINELLE *same as* > SPINEL
SPINELLES > SPINELLE
SPINELS > SPINEL
SPINES > SPINE
SPINET *n* small harpsichord
SPINETS > SPINET
SPINETTE *same as* > SPINET
SPINETTES > SPINETTE
SPINIER > SPINY
SPINIEST > SPINY
SPINIFEX *n* coarse spiny Australian grass
SPINIFORM *adj* like a thorn
SPININESS > SPINY
SPINK *n* finch
SPINKS > SPINK
SPINLESS > SPIN
SPINNAKER *n* large sail on a racing yacht
SPINNER *n* bowler who specializes in spinning the ball to make it change direction when it bounces or strikes the bat
SPINNERET *n* organ through which silk threads come out of a spider
SPINNERS > SPINNER
SPINNERY *n* spinning mill
SPINNET *same as* > SPINET
SPINNETS > SPINNET
SPINNEY *n* small wood
SPINNEYS > SPINNEY
SPINNIES > SPINNY
SPINNING > SPIN
SPINNINGS > SPIN
SPINNY *same as* > SPINNEY
SPINODE *another name for* > CUSP
SPINODES > SPINODE
SPINOFF *n* development derived incidentally from an existing enterprise
SPINOFFS > SPINOFF
SPINONE as in *Italian spinone* wiry-coated gun dog
SPINONI > SPINONE
SPINOR *n* type of mathematical object
SPINORS > SPINOR
SPINOSE *adj* (esp of plants) bearing many spines
SPINOSELY > SPINOSE
SPINOSITY > SPINOSE
SPINOUS *adj* resembling a spine or thorn
SPINOUT *n* spinning skid that causes a car to run off the road
SPINOUTS > SPINOUT
SPINS > SPIN
SPINSTER *n* unmarried woman
SPINSTERS > SPINSTER
SPINTEXT *n* preacher
SPINTEXTS > SPINTEXT
SPINTO *n* lyrical singing voice
SPINTOS > SPINTO
SPINULA *n* small spine
SPINULAE > SPINULA
SPINULATE *adj* like a spine
SPINULE *n* very small spine, thorn, or prickle
SPINULES > SPINULE
SPINULOSE > SPINULE
SPINULOUS > SPINULE
SPINY *adj* covered with spines
SPIRACLE *n* small blowhole for breathing through, such as that of a whale
SPIRACLES > SPIRACLE
SPIRACULA *pl n* spiracles
SPIRAEA *n* plant with small white or pink flowers
SPIRAEAS > SPIRAEA
SPIRAL *n* continuous curve formed by a point winding about a central axis at an ever-increasing distance from it ▷ *vb* move in a spiral ▷ *adj* having the form of a spiral
SPIRALED > SPIRAL
SPIRALING > SPIRAL
SPIRALISM *n* ascent in spiral structure
SPIRALIST > SPIRALISM
SPIRALITY > SPIRAL
SPIRALLED > SPIRAL
SPIRALLY > SPIRAL
SPIRALS > SPIRAL
SPIRANT *n* fricative consonant
SPIRANTS > SPIRANT
SPIRASTER *n* part of living sponge
SPIRATED *adj* twisted in spiral
SPIRATION *n* breathing
SPIRE *n* pointed part of a steeple ▷ *vb* assume the shape of a spire
SPIREA *same as* > SPIRAEA
SPIREAS > SPIREA
SPIRED > SPIRE
SPIRELESS > SPIRE
SPIRELET *another name for* > FLECHE
SPIRELETS > SPIRELET
SPIREM *same as* > SPIREME
SPIREME *n* tangled mass of chromatin threads into which the nucleus of a cell is resolved at the start of mitosis
SPIREMES > SPIREME
SPIREMS > SPIREM
SPIRES > SPIRE
SPIREWISE > SPIRE
SPIRIC *n* type of curve
SPIRICS > SPIRIC
SPIRIER > SPIRE
SPIRIEST > SPIRE
SPIRILLA > SPIRILLUM
SPIRILLAR > SPIRILLUM
SPIRILLUM *n* any bacterium having a curved or spirally twisted rodlike body
SPIRING > SPIRE
SPIRIT *n* nonphysical aspect of a person concerned with profound thoughts ▷ *vb* carry away mysteriously
SPIRITED *adj* lively
SPIRITFUL > SPIRIT
SPIRITING > SPIRIT
SPIRITISM *n* belief that the spirits of the dead can communicate with the living
SPIRITIST > SPIRITISM
SPIRITOSO *adv* to be played in a spirited or animated manner
SPIRITOUS *adj* high-spirited
SPIRITS > SPIRIT
SPIRITUAL *adj* relating to the spirit ▷ *n* type of religious folk song originating among Black slaves in America
SPIRITUEL *adj* having a refined and lively mind or wit
SPIRITUS *n* spirit

SPIRITY *adj* spirited
SPIRLING *same as* > SPARLING
SPIRLINGS > SPIRLING
SPIROGRAM *n* record made by spirograph
SPIROGYRA *n* green freshwater plant that floats on the surface of ponds and ditches
SPIROID *adj* resembling a spiral or displaying a spiral form
SPIRT *same as* > SPURT
SPIRTED > SPIRT
SPIRTING > SPIRT
SPIRTLE *same as* > SPURTLE
SPIRTLES > SPIRTLE
SPIRTS > SPIRT
SPIRULA *n* tropical cephalopod mollusc
SPIRULAE > SPIRULA
SPIRULAS > SPIRULA
SPIRULINA *n* any filamentous cyanobacterium of the genus *Spirulina*
SPIRY > SPIRE
SPIT *vb* eject (saliva or food) from the mouth ▷ *n* saliva
SPITAL *n* hospital, esp for the needy sick
SPITALS > SPITAL
SPITBALL *n* small missile made from chewed paper
SPITBALLS > SPITBALL
SPITCHER *adj* doomed
SPITE *n* deliberate nastiness ▷ *vb* annoy or hurt from spite
SPITED > SPITE
SPITEFUL *adj* full of or motivated by spite
SPITES > SPITE
SPITFIRE *n* person with a fiery temper
SPITFIRES > SPITFIRE
SPITING > SPITE
SPITS > SPIT
SPITTED > SPIT
SPITTEN > SPIT
SPITTER > SPIT
SPITTERS > SPIT
SPITTING > SPIT
SPITTINGS > SPIT
SPITTLE *n* fluid produced in the mouth, saliva
SPITTLES > SPITTLE
SPITTOON *n* bowl to spit into
SPITTOONS > SPITTOON
SPITZ *n* stockily built dog with a pointed face, erect ears, and a tightly curled tail
SPITZES > SPITZ
SPIV *n* smartly dressed man who makes a living by shady dealings
SPIVS > SPIV
SPIVVERY *n* behaviour of spivs
SPIVVIER > SPIV
SPIVVIEST > SPIV
SPIVVY > SPIV
SPLAKE *n* type of hybrid trout bred by Canadian zoologists
SPLAKES > SPLAKE
SPLASH *vb* scatter liquid on (something) ▷ *n* splashing sound
SPLASHED > SPLASH
SPLASHER *n* anything used for protection against splashes
SPLASHERS > SPLASHER
SPLASHES > SPLASH
SPLASHIER > SPLASHY
SPLASHILY > SPLASHY
SPLASHING > SPLASH
SPLASHY *adj* having irregular marks
SPLAT *n* wet slapping sound ▷ *vb* make wet slapping sound
SPLATCH *vb* splash
SPLATCHED > SPLATCH
SPLATCHES > SPLATCH
SPLATS > SPLAT
SPLATTED > SPLAT
SPLATTER *n* splash ▷ *vb* splash (something or someone) with small blobs
SPLATTERS > SPLATTER
SPLATTING > SPLAT
SPLAY *vb* spread out, with ends spreading in different directions ▷ *adj* spread out ▷ *n* surface of a wall that forms an oblique angle to the main flat surfaces
SPLAYED > SPLAY
SPLAYFEET > SPLAYFOOT
SPLAYFOOT *n* foot of which the toes are spread out
SPLAYING > SPLAY
SPLAYS > SPLAY
SPLEEN *n* abdominal organ which filters bacteria from the blood
SPLEENFUL *adj* bad-tempered or irritable
SPLEENIER > SPLEEN
SPLEENISH > SPLEEN
SPLEENS > SPLEEN
SPLEENY > SPLEEN
SPLENDENT *adj* shining brightly
SPLENDID *adj* excellent
SPLENDOR *same as* > SPLENDOUR
SPLENDORS > SPLENDOR
SPLENDOUR *n* state or quality of being splendid
SPLENETIC *adj* spiteful or irritable ▷ *n* spiteful or irritable person
SPLENIA > SPLENIUM
SPLENIAL > SPLENIUS
SPLENIC *adj* of, relating to, or in the spleen
SPLENII > SPLENIUS
SPLENITIS *n* inflammation of the spleen
SPLENIUM *n* structure in brain
SPLENIUMS > SPLENIUM
SPLENIUS *n* either of two flat muscles situated at the back of the neck
SPLENT *same as* > SPLINT
SPLENTS > SPLENT
SPLEUCHAN *n* pouch for tobacco
SPLICE *vb* join by interweaving or overlapping ends
SPLICED > SPLICE
SPLICER > SPLICE
SPLICERS > SPLICE
SPLICES > SPLICE
SPLICING > SPLICE
SPLIFF *n* cannabis, used as a drug
SPLIFFS > SPLIFF
SPLINE *n* type of narrow key around a shaft that fits into a corresponding groove ▷ *vb* provide (a shaft, part, etc) with splines
SPLINED > SPLINE
SPLINES > SPLINE
SPLINING > SPLINE
SPLINT *n* rigid support for a broken bone ▷ *vb* apply a splint to (a broken arm, etc)
SPLINTED > SPLINT
SPLINTER *n* thin sharp piece broken off, esp from wood ▷ *vb* break into fragments
SPLINTERS > SPLINTER
SPLINTERY *adj* liable to produce or break into splinters
SPLINTING > SPLINT
SPLINTS > SPLINT
SPLIT *vb* break into separate pieces ▷ *n* splitting
SPLITS > SPLIT
SPLITTED > SPLIT
SPLITTER > SPLIT
SPLITTERS > SPLIT
SPLITTING > SPLIT
SPLODGE *n* large uneven spot or stain ▷ *vb* mark (something) with a splodge or splodges
SPLODGED > SPLODGE
SPLODGES > SPLODGE
SPLODGIER > SPLODGE
SPLODGILY > SPLODGE
SPLODGING > SPLODGE
SPLODGY > SPLODGE
SPLOOSH *vb* splash or cause to splash about uncontrollably ▷ *n* instance or sound of splooshing
SPLOOSHED > SPLOOSH
SPLOOSHES > SPLOOSH
SPLORE *n* revel
SPLORES > SPLORE
SPLOSH *vb* scatter (liquid) vigorously about in blobs ▷ *n* instance or sound of sploshing
SPLOSHED > SPLOSH
SPLOSHES > SPLOSH
SPLOSHING > SPLOSH
SPLOTCH *vb* splash, daub
SPLOTCHED > SPLOTCH
SPLOTCHES > SPLOTCH
SPLOTCHY > SPLOTCH
SPLURGE *vb* spend money extravagantly ▷ *n* bout o extravagance
SPLURGED > SPLURGE
SPLURGER > SPLURGE
SPLURGERS > SPLURGE
SPLURGES > SPLURGE
SPLURGIER > SPLURGE
SPLURGING > SPLURGE
SPLURGY > SPLURGE
SPLUTTER *vb* utter with spitting or choking sounc ▷ *n* spluttering
SPLUTTERS > SPLUTTER
SPLUTTERY > SPLUTTER
SPOD *n* boring, unattractive, or overstudious person
SPODDIER > SPOD
SPODDIEST > SPOD
SPODDY > SPOD
SPODE *n* type of English china or porcelain
SPODES > SPODE
SPODIUM *n* black powder
SPODIUMS > SPODIUM
SPODOGRAM *n* ash from plant used in studying it
SPODOSOL *n* ashy soil
SPODOSOLS > SPODOSOL
SPODS > SPOD
SPODUMENE *n* greyish-white, green, or lilac pyroxene mineral
SPOFFISH *adj* officious
SPOFFY *same as* > SPOFFISH
SPOIL *vb* damage
SPOILABLE > SPOIL
SPOILAGE *n* amount of material that has been spoilt
SPOILAGES > SPOILAGE
SPOILED > SPOIL
SPOILER *n* device on an aircraft or car to increase drag
SPOILERS > SPOILER
SPOILFIVE *n* card game f two or more players with five cards each
SPOILFUL *adj* taking spoi
SPOILING > SPOIL
SPOILS > SPOIL
SPOILSMAN *n* person who shares in the spoils of office or advocates the spoils system
SPOILSMEN > SPOILSMAN
SPOILT > SPOIL
SPOKE *n* radial member of a wheel ▷ *vb* equip with spokes
SPOKED > SPOKE
SPOKEN > SPEAK
SPOKES > SPOKE

POKESMAN *n* person chosen to speak on behalf of a group
POKESMEN > SPOKESMAN
POKEWISE > SPEAK
POKING > SPOKE
POLIATE *less common word for* > DESPOIL
POLIATED > SPOLIATE
POLIATES > SPOLIATE
POLIATOR > SPOLIATE
PONDAIC *adj* of, relating to, or consisting of spondees ▷ *n* spondaic line
PONDAICS > SPONDAIC
PONDEE *n* metrical foot of two long syllables
PONDEES > SPONDEE
PONDULIX *n* money
PONDYL *n* vertebra
PONDYLS > SPONDYL
PONGE *n* sea animal with a porous absorbent skeleton ▷ *vb* wipe with a sponge
PONGEBAG *n* small bag for holding toiletries when travelling
PONGED > SPONGE
PONGEOUS *adj* spongy
PONGER *n* person who sponges on others
PONGERS > SPONGER
PONGES > SPONGE
PONGIER > SPONGY
PONGIEST > SPONGY
PONGILY > SPONGY
PONGIN *n* fibrous horny protein that forms the skeletal framework of the bath sponge and related sponges
PONGING > SPONGE
PONGINS > SPONGIN
PONGIOSE > SPONGE
PONGIOUS > SPONGE
PONGOID > SPONGE
PONGY *adj* of or resembling a sponge
PONSAL *n* marriage
PONSALIA *n* marriage ceremony
PONSIBLE *adj* responsible
PONSING *same as* > SPONSON
PONSINGS > SPONSING
PONSION *n* act or process of becoming surety
PONSIONS > SPONSION
PONSON *n* outboard support for a gun enabling it to fire fore and aft
PONSONS > SPONSON
PONSOR *n* person who promotes something ▷ *vb* act as a sponsor for
PONSORED > SPONSOR
PONSORS > SPONSOR
PONTOON *n* form of halberd carried by some junior infantry officers in the 18th and 19th centuries
PONTOONS > SPONTOON
POOF *n* mildly satirical parody ▷ *vb* fool (a person) with a trick or deception
SPOOFED > SPOOF
SPOOFER > SPOOF
SPOOFERS > SPOOF
SPOOFERY > SPOOF
SPOOFING > SPOOF
SPOOFS > SPOOF
SPOOFY > SPOOF
SPOOK *n* ghost ▷ *vb* frighten
SPOOKED > SPOOK
SPOOKERY *n* spooky events
SPOOKIER > SPOOKY
SPOOKIEST > SPOOKY
SPOOKILY > SPOOKY
SPOOKING > SPOOK
SPOOKISH > SPOOK
SPOOKS > SPOOK
SPOOKY *adj* ghostly or eerie
SPOOL *n* cylinder round which something can be wound ▷ *vb* wind or be wound onto a spool or reel
SPOOLED > SPOOL
SPOOLER > SPOOL
SPOOLERS > SPOOL
SPOOLING > SPOOL
SPOOLINGS > SPOOL
SPOOLS > SPOOL
SPOOM *vb* sail fast before wind
SPOOMED > SPOOM
SPOOMING > SPOOM
SPOOMS > SPOOM
SPOON *n* shallow bowl attached to a handle for eating, stirring, or serving food ▷ *vb* lift with a spoon
SPOONBAIT *n* type of lure used in angling
SPOONBILL *n* wading bird of warm regions with a long flat bill
SPOONED > SPOON
SPOONEY *same as* > SPOONY
SPOONEYS > SPOONEY
SPOONFED *adj* having been given someone else's opinions
SPOONFUL *n* amount that a spoon is able to hold
SPOONFULS > SPOONFUL
SPOONIER > SPOONY
SPOONIES > SPOONY
SPOONIEST > SPOONY
SPOONILY > SPOONY
SPOONING > SPOON
SPOONS > SPOON
SPOONSFUL > SPOONFUL
SPOONWAYS *adv* like spoons
SPOONWISE *same as* > SPOONWAYS
SPOONY *adj* foolishly or stupidly amorous ▷ *n* fool or silly person, esp one in love
SPOOR *n* trail of an animal ▷ *vb* track (an animal) by following its trail
SPOORED > SPOOR
SPOORER > SPOOR
SPOORERS > SPOOR
SPOORING > SPOOR
SPOORS > SPOOR
SPOOT *n* razor shell
SPOOTS > SPOOT
SPORADIC *adj* intermittent, scattered
SPORAL > SPORE
SPORANGIA *pl n* organs in fungi in which asexual spores are produced
SPORE *n* minute reproductive body of some plants ▷ *vb* produce, carry, or release spores
SPORED > SPORE
SPORES > SPORE
SPORICIDE *n* substance killing spores
SPORIDESM *n* group of spores
SPORIDIA > SPORIDIUM
SPORIDIAL > SPORIDIUM
SPORIDIUM *n* type of spore
SPORING > SPORE
SPOROCARP *n* specialized leaf branch in certain aquatic ferns that encloses the sori
SPOROCYST *n* thick-walled rounded structure produced by sporozoan protozoans
SPOROCYTE *n* diploid cell that divides by meiosis to produce four haploid spores
SPOROGENY *n* process of spore formation in plants and animals
SPOROGONY *n* process in sporozoans by which sporozoites are formed
SPOROID *adj* of or like a spore
SPOROPHYL *n* leaf in ferns that bears the sporangia
SPOROZOA *n* class of microscopic creature
SPOROZOAL > SPOROZOA
SPOROZOAN *n* any parasitic protozoan of the phylum *Apicomplexa* ▷ *adj* of or relating to sporozoans
SPOROZOIC > SPOROZOA
SPOROZOON *same as* > SPOROZOAN
SPORRAN *n* pouch worn in front of a kilt
SPORRANS > SPORRAN
SPORT *n* activity for pleasure, competition, or exercise ▷ *vb* wear proudly
SPORTABLE *adj* playful
SPORTANCE *n* playing
SPORTED > SPORT
SPORTER > SPORT
SPORTERS > SPORT
SPORTFUL > SPORT
SPORTIER > SPORTY
SPORTIES > SPORTY
SPORTIEST > SPORTY
SPORTIF *adj* sporty
SPORTILY > SPORTY
SPORTING *adj* of sport
SPORTIVE *adj* playful
SPORTLESS > SPORT
SPORTS *adj* of or used in sports ▷ *n* meeting held at a school or college for competitions in athletic events
SPORTSMAN *n* person who plays sports
SPORTSMEN > SPORTSMAN
SPORTY *adj* (of a person) interested in sport ▷ *n* young person who typically wears sportswear, is competitive about sport, and takes an interest in his or her fitness
SPORULAR > SPORULE
SPORULATE *vb* produce spores, esp by multiple fission
SPORULE *n* spore, esp a very small spore
SPORULES > SPORULE
SPOSH *n* slush
SPOSHES > SPOSH
SPOSHIER > SPOSH
SPOSHIEST > SPOSH
SPOSHY > SPOSH
SPOT *n* small mark on a surface ▷ *vb* notice
SPOTLESS *adj* absolutely clean
SPOTLIGHT *n* powerful light illuminating a small area ▷ *vb* draw attention to
SPOTLIT > SPOTLIGHT
SPOTS > SPOT
SPOTTABLE > SPOT
SPOTTED > SPOT
SPOTTER *n* person whose hobby is watching for and noting numbers or types of trains or planes
SPOTTERS > SPOTTER
SPOTTIE *n* young deer of up to three months of age
SPOTTIER > SPOTTY
SPOTTIES > SPOTTIE
SPOTTIEST > SPOTTY
SPOTTILY > SPOTTY
SPOTTING > SPOT
SPOTTINGS > SPOT
SPOTTY *adj* with spots
SPOUSAGE *n* marriage
SPOUSAGES > SPOUSAGE
SPOUSAL *n* marriage ceremony ▷ *adj* of or relating to marriage
SPOUSALLY > SPOUSAL
SPOUSALS > SPOUSAL
SPOUSE *n* husband or wife ▷ *vb* marry
SPOUSED > SPOUSE
SPOUSES > SPOUSE
SPOUSING > SPOUSE
SPOUT *vb* pour out in a stream or jet ▷ *n* projecting tube or lip for pouring liquids
SPOUTED > SPOUT

SPOUTER > SPOUT
SPOUTERS > SPOUT
SPOUTIER > SPOUT
SPOUTIEST > SPOUT
SPOUTING *n* rainwater downpipe on the outside of a building
SPOUTINGS > SPOUTING
SPOUTLESS > SPOUT
SPOUTS > SPOUT
SPOUTY > SPOUT
SPRACK *adj* vigorous
SPRACKLE *vb* clamber
SPRACKLED > SPRACKLE
SPRACKLES > SPRACKLE
SPRAD > SPREAD
SPRADDLE *n* disease of fowl preventing them from standing
SPRADDLED *adj* affected by spraddle
SPRADDLES > SPRADDLE
SPRAG *n* chock or steel bar used to prevent a vehicle from running backwards on an incline ▷ *vb* use sprag to prevent vehicle from moving
SPRAGGED > SPRAG
SPRAGGING > SPRAG
SPRAGS > SPRAG
SPRAID *vb* chapped
SPRAIN *vb* injure (a joint) by a sudden twist ▷ *n* such an injury
SPRAINED > SPRAIN
SPRAINING > SPRAIN
SPRAINS > SPRAIN
SPRAINT *n* piece of otter's dung
SPRAINTS > SPRAINT
SPRANG *n* branch
SPRANGLE *vb* sprawl
SPRANGLED > SPRANGLE
SPRANGLES > SPRANGLE
SPRANGS > SPRANG
SPRAT *n* small sea fish
SPRATS > SPRAT
SPRATTLE *vb* scramble
SPRATTLED > SPRATTLE
SPRATTLES > SPRATTLE
SPRAUCHLE *same as* > SPRACKLE
SPRAUNCY *adj* smart
SPRAWL *vb* lie or sit with the limbs spread out ▷ *n* part of a city that has spread untidily over a large area
SPRAWLED > SPRAWL
SPRAWLER > SPRAWL
SPRAWLERS > SPRAWL
SPRAWLIER > SPRAWL
SPRAWLING > SPRAWL
SPRAWLS > SPRAWL
SPRAWLY > SPRAWL
SPRAY *n* (device for producing) fine drops of liquid ▷ *vb* scatter in fine drops
SPRAYED > SPRAY
SPRAYER > SPRAY
SPRAYERS > SPRAY
SPRAYEY > SPRAY
SPRAYIER > SPRAY
SPRAYIEST > SPRAY
SPRAYING > SPRAY
SPRAYINGS > SPRAY
SPRAYS > SPRAY
SPREAD *vb* open out or be displayed to the fullest extent ▷ *n* spreading ▷ *adj* extended or stretched out, esp to the fullest extent
SPREADER *n* machine or device used for scattering bulk materials over a relatively wide area
SPREADERS > SPREADER
SPREADING > SPREAD
SPREADS > SPREAD
SPREAGH *n* cattle raid
SPREAGHS > SPREAGH
SPREATHE *vb* chap
SPREATHED *adj* sore
SPREATHES > SPREATHE
SPREAZE *same as* > SPREATHE
SPREAZED *same as* > SPREATHED
SPREAZES > SPREAZE
SPREAZING > SPREAZE
SPRECHERY *n* theft of cattle
SPRECKLED *adj* speckled
SPRED *same as* > SPREAD
SPREDD *same as* > SPREAD
SPREDDE *same as* > SPREAD
SPREDDEN > SPREDDE
SPREDDES > SPREDDE
SPREDDING > SPREDDE
SPREDDS > SPREDD
SPREDS > SPRED
SPREE *n* session of overindulgence, usu in drinking or spending money ▷ *vb* go on a spree
SPREED > SPREE
SPREEING > SPREE
SPREES > SPREE
SPREETHE *same as* > SPREATHE
SPREETHED > SPREETHE
SPREETHES > SPREETHE
SPREEZE *same as* > SPREATHE
SPREEZED > SPREEZE
SPREEZES > SPREEZE
SPREEZING > SPREEZE
SPREKELIA *n* bulbous plant grown for its striking crimson or white pendent flowers
SPRENT > SPRINKLE
SPREW *same as* > SPRUE
SPREWS > SPREW
SPRIER > SPRY
SPRIEST > SPRY
SPRIG *n* twig or shoot ▷ *vb* fasten or secure with sprigs
SPRIGGED > SPRIG
SPRIGGER > SPRIG
SPRIGGERS > SPRIG
SPRIGGIER > SPRIG
SPRIGGING > SPRIG
SPRIGGY > SPRIG
SPRIGHT *same as* > SPRITE
SPRIGHTED > SPRIGHT
SPRIGHTLY *adj* lively and brisk ▷ *adv* in a lively manner
SPRIGHTS > SPRIGHT
SPRIGS > SPRIG
SPRIGTAIL *n* species of duck
SPRING *vb* move suddenly upwards or forwards in a single motion, jump ▷ *n* season between winter and summer
SPRINGAL *n* young man
SPRINGALD *same as* > SPRINGAL
SPRINGALS > SPRINGAL
SPRINGBOK *n* S African antelope
SPRINGE *n* type of snare for catching small wild animals or birds ▷ *vb* set such a snare
SPRINGED > SPRINGE
SPRINGER *n* small spaniel
SPRINGERS > SPRINGER
SPRINGES > SPRINGE
SPRINGIER > SPRINGY
SPRINGILY > SPRINGY
SPRINGING > SPRING
SPRINGLE *same as* > SPRINGE
SPRINGLES > SPRINGE
SPRINGLET *n* small spring
SPRINGS > SPRING
SPRINGY *adj* elastic
SPRINKLE *vb* scatter (liquid or powder) in tiny drops or particles over (something) ▷ *n* act or an instance of sprinkling or a quantity that is sprinkled
SPRINKLED > SPRINKLE
SPRINKLER *n* device with small holes that is attached to a garden hose or watering can and used to spray water
SPRINKLES > SPRINKLE
SPRINT *n* short race run at top speed ▷ *vb* run a short distance at top speed
SPRINTED > SPRINT
SPRINTER > SPRINT
SPRINTERS > SPRINT
SPRINTING > SPRINT
SPRINTS > SPRINT
SPRIT *n* small spar set diagonally across a sail to extend it
SPRITE *n* elf
SPRITEFUL > SPRITE
SPRITELY *same as* > SPRIGHTLY
SPRITES > SPRITE
SPRITS > SPRIT
SPRITSAIL *n* sail extended by a sprit
SPRITZ *vb* spray liquid
SPRITZED > SPRITZ
SPRITZER *n* tall drink of wine and soda water
SPRITZERS > SPRITZER
SPRITZES > SPRITZ
SPRITZIG *adj* (of wine) sparkling ▷ *n* sparkling wine
SPRITZIGS > SPRITZIG
SPRITZING > SPRITZ
SPROCKET *n* wheel with teeth on the rim, that drives or is driven by a chain
SPROCKETS > SPROCKET
SPROD *n* young salmon
SPRODS > SPROD
SPROG *n* child
SPROGS > SPROG
SPRONG > SPRING
SPROUT *vb* put forth shoot ▷ *n* shoot
SPROUTED > SPROUT
SPROUTING > SPROUT
SPROUTS > SPROUT
SPRUCE *n* kind of fir ▷ *adj* neat and smart
SPRUCED > SPRUCE
SPRUCELY > SPRUCE
SPRUCER > SPRUCE
SPRUCES > SPRUCE
SPRUCEST > SPRUCE
SPRUCIER > SPRUCE
SPRUCIEST > SPRUCE
SPRUCING > SPRUCE
SPRUCY > SPRUCE
SPRUE *n* vertical channel in a mould through which plastic or molten metal is poured
SPRUES > SPRUE
SPRUG *n* sparrow
SPRUGS > SPRUG
SPRUIK *vb* speak in public (used esp of a showman or salesman)
SPRUIKED > SPRUIK
SPRUIKER > SPRUIK
SPRUIKERS > SPRUIK
SPRUIKING > SPRUIK
SPRUIKS > SPRUIK
SPRUIT *n* small tributary stream or watercourse
SPRUITS > SPRUIT
SPRUNG > SPRING
SPRUSH *Scots form of* > SPRUCE
SPRUSHED > SPRUSH
SPRUSHES > SPRUSH
SPRUSHING > SPRUSH
SPRY *adj* active or nimble
SPRYER > SPRY
SPRYEST > SPRY
SPRYLY > SPRY
SPRYNESS > SPRY
SPUD *n* potato ▷ *vb* remove (bark) or eradicate (weeds) with a spud
SPUDDED > SPUD
SPUDDER *same as* > SPUD
SPUDDERS > SPUDDER
SPUDDIER > SPUDDY
SPUDDIEST > SPUDDY
SPUDDING > SPUD
SPUDDINGS > SPUD
SPUDDLE *n* feeble movement
SPUDDLES > SPUDDLE
SPUDDY *adj* short and fat

SPUDS > SPUD
SPUE same as > SPEW
SPUED > SPUE
SPUEING > SPUE
SPUER > SPUE
SPUERS > SPUE
SPUES > SPUE
SPUG same as > SPUGGY
SPUGGIES > SPUGGY
SPUGGY n house sparrow
SPUGS > SPUG
SPUILZIE vb plunder
SPUILZIED > SPUILZIE
SPUILZIES > SPUILZIE
SPUING > SPUE
SPULE Scots word for > SHOULDER
SPULES > SPULE
SPULYE same as > SPUILZIE
SPULYED > SPULYE
SPULYEING > SPULYE
SPULYES > SPULYE
SPULYIE same as > SPUILZIE
SPULYIED > SPULYIE
SPULYIES > SPULYIE
SPULZIE same as > SPUILZIE
SPULZIED > SPULZIE
SPULZIES > SPULZIE
SPUMANTE n Italian sparkling wine
SPUMANTES > SPUMANTE
SPUME vb froth ▷ n foam or froth on the sea
SPUMED > SPUME
SPUMES > SPUME
SPUMIER > SPUM
SPUMIEST > SPUM
SPUMING > SPUME
SPUMONE n creamy Italian ice cream
SPUMONES > SPUMONE
SPUMONI same as > SPUMONE
SPUMONIS > SPUMONI
SPUMOUS > SPUME
SPUMY > SPUME
SPUN > SPIN
SPUNGE same as > SPONGE
SPUNGES > SPUNGE
SPUNK n courage, spirit ▷ vb catch fire
SPUNKED > SPUNK
SPUNKIE n will-o'-the-wisp
SPUNKIER > SPUNK
SPUNKIES > SPUNKIE
SPUNKIEST > SPUNK
SPUNKILY > SPUNK
SPUNKING > SPUNK
SPUNKS > SPUNK
SPUNKY > SPUNK
SPUNYARN n small stuff made from rope yarns twisted together
SPUNYARNS > SPUNYARN
SPUR n stimulus or incentive ▷ vb urge on, incite (someone)
SPURGALL vb prod with spur
SPURGALLS > SPURGALL
SPURGE n plant with milky sap
SPURGES > SPURGE
SPURIAE n type of bird feathers
SPURIOUS adj not genuine
SPURLESS > SPUR
SPURLING same as > SPARLING
SPURLINGS > SPURLING
SPURN vb reject with scorn ▷ n instance of spurning
SPURNE vb spur
SPURNED > SPURN
SPURNER > SPURN
SPURNERS > SPURN
SPURNES > SPURNE
SPURNING > SPURN
SPURNINGS > SPURN
SPURNS > SPURN
SPURRED > SPUR
SPURRER > SPUR
SPURRERS > SPUR
SPURREY n any of several low-growing European plants
SPURREYS > SPURREY
SPURRIER n maker of spurs
SPURRIERS > SPURRIER
SPURRIES > SPURRY
SPURRIEST > SPURRY
SPURRING > SPUR
SPURRINGS > SPUR
SPURRY n spurrey ▷ adj resembling a spur
SPURS > SPUR
SPURT vb gush or cause to gush out in a jet ▷ n short sudden burst of activity or speed
SPURTED > SPURT
SPURTER > SPURT
SPURTERS > SPURT
SPURTING > SPURT
SPURTLE n wooden spoon for stirring porridge
SPURTLES > SPURTLE
SPURTS > SPURT
SPURWAY n path used by riders
SPURWAYS > SPURWAY
SPUTA > SPUTUM
SPUTNIK n early Soviet artificial satellite
SPUTNIKS > SPUTNIK
SPUTTER n splutter ▷ vb splutter
SPUTTERED > SPUTTER
SPUTTERER > SPUTTER
SPUTTERS > SPUTTER
SPUTTERY > SPUTTER
SPUTUM n spittle, usu mixed with mucus
SPY n person employed to obtain secret information ▷ vb act as a spy
SPYAL n spy
SPYALS > SPYAL
SPYGLASS n small telescope
SPYHOLE n small hole in a door, etc through which one may watch secretly
SPYHOLES > SPYHOLE
SPYING > SPY
SPYINGS > SPY
SPYMASTER n person who controls spy network
SPYPLANE n military aeroplane used to spy on enemy
SPYPLANES > SPYPLANE
SPYRE same as > SPIRE
SPYRES > SPYRE
SPYWARE n software installed via the internet on a computer without the user's knowledge and used to gain information about the user
SPYWARES > SPYWARE
SQUAB n young bird yet to leave the nest ▷ adj (of birds) recently hatched and still unfledged ▷ vb fall
SQUABASH vb crush
SQUABBED > SQUAB
SQUABBER > SQUAB
SQUABBEST > SQUAB
SQUABBIER > SQUAB
SQUABBING > SQUAB
SQUABBISH > SQUAB
SQUABBLE n (engage in) a petty or noisy quarrel ▷ vb quarrel over a small matter
SQUABBLED > SQUABBLE
SQUABBLER > SQUABBLE
SQUABBLES > SQUABBLE
SQUABBY > SQUAB
SQUABS > SQUAB
SQUACCO n S European heron
SQUACCOS > SQUACCO
SQUAD n small group of people working or training together ▷ vb set up squads
SQUADDED > SQUAD
SQUADDIE n private soldier
SQUADDIES > SQUADDY
SQUADDING > SQUAD
SQUADDY same as > SQUADDIE
SQUADRON n division of an air force, fleet, or cavalry regiment ▷ vb assign to squadrons
SQUADRONE n former Scottish political party
SQUADRONS > SQUADRON
SQUADS > SQUAD
SQUAIL vb throw sticks at
SQUAILED > SQUAIL
SQUAILER > SQUAIL
SQUAILERS > SQUAIL
SQUAILING > SQUAIL
SQUAILS > SQUAIL
SQUALENE n terpene first found in the liver of sharks
SQUALENES > SQUALENE
SQUALID adj dirty and unpleasant
SQUALIDER > SQUALID
SQUALIDLY > SQUALID
SQUALL n sudden strong wind ▷ vb cry noisily, yell
SQUALLED > SQUALL
SQUALLER > SQUALL
SQUALLERS > SQUALL
SQUALLIER > SQUALL
SQUALLING > SQUALL
SQUALLISH > SQUALL
SQUALLS > SQUALL
SQUALLY > SQUALL
SQUALOID adj of or like a shark
SQUALOR n disgusting dirt and filth
SQUALORS > SQUALOR
SQUAMA n scale or scalelike structure
SQUAMAE > SQUAMA
SQUAMATE > SQUAMA
SQUAMATES > SQUAMA
SQUAME same as > SQUAMA
SQUAMELLA n small scale
SQUAMES > SQUAME
SQUAMOSAL n thin platelike paired bone in the skull of vertebrates ▷ adj of or relating to this bone
SQUAMOSE same as > SQUAMOUS
SQUAMOUS adj (of epithelium) consisting of one or more layers of flat platelike cells
SQUAMULA same as > SQUAMELLA
SQUAMULAS > SQUAMULA
SQUAMULE same as > SQUAMELLA
SQUAMULES > SQUAMULE
SQUANDER vb waste (money or resources) ▷ n extravagance or dissipation
SQUANDERS > SQUANDER
SQUARE n geometric figure with four equal sides and four right angles ▷ adj square in shape ▷ vb multiply (a number) by itself ▷ adv squarely, directly
SQUARED > SQUARE
SQUARELY adv in a direct way
SQUARER > SQUARE
SQUARERS > SQUARE
SQUARES > SQUARE
SQUAREST > SQUARE
SQUARIAL n type of square dish for receiving satellite television
SQUARIALS > SQUARIAL
SQUARING > SQUARE
SQUARINGS > SQUARE
SQUARISH > SQUARE
SQUARK n hypothetical boson partner of a quark
SQUARKS > SQUARK
SQUARROSE adj having a rough surface
SQUARSON n clergyman who is also landowner
SQUARSONS > SQUARSON
SQUASH vb crush flat ▷ n sweet fruit drink diluted with water
SQUASHED > SQUASH
SQUASHER > SQUASH
SQUASHERS > SQUASH
SQUASHES > SQUASH
SQUASHIER > SQUASHY

SQUASHILY > SQUASHY
SQUASHING > SQUASH
SQUASHY *adj* soft and easily squashed
SQUAT *vb* crouch with the knees bent and the weight on the feet ▷ *n* place where squatters live ▷ *adj* short and broad
SQUATLY > SQUAT
SQUATNESS > SQUAT
SQUATS > SQUAT
SQUATTED > SQUAT
SQUATTER *n* illegal occupier of unused premises
SQUATTERS > SQUATTER
SQUATTEST > SQUAT
SQUATTIER > SQUATTY
SQUATTILY > SQUATTY
SQUATTING > SQUAT
SQUATTLE *vb* squat
SQUATTLED > SQUATTLE
SQUATTLES > SQUATTLE
SQUATTY *adj* short and broad
SQUAW *n* offensive term for a Native American woman
SQUAWBUSH *n* American shrub
SQUAWFISH *n* North American minnow
SQUAWK *n* loud harsh cry ▷ *vb* utter a squawk
SQUAWKED > SQUAWK
SQUAWKER > SQUAWK
SQUAWKERS > SQUAWK
SQUAWKIER > SQUAWK
SQUAWKING > SQUAWK
SQUAWKS > SQUAWK
SQUAWKY > SQUAWK
SQUAWMAN *n* offensive term for a White man married to a Native American woman
SQUAWMEN > SQUAWMAN
SQUAWROOT *n* North American parasitic plant
SQUAWS > SQUAW
SQUEAK *n* short shrill cry or sound ▷ *vb* make or utter a squeak
SQUEAKED > SQUEAK
SQUEAKER > SQUEAK
SQUEAKERS > SQUEAK
SQUEAKERY > SQUEAK
SQUEAKIER > SQUEAK
SQUEAKILY > SQUEAK
SQUEAKING > SQUEAK
SQUEAKS > SQUEAK
SQUEAKY > SQUEAK
SQUEAL *n* long shrill cry or sound ▷ *vb* make or utter a squeal
SQUEALED > SQUEAL
SQUEALER > SQUEAL
SQUEALERS > SQUEAL
SQUEALING > SQUEAL
SQUEALS > SQUEAL
SQUEAMISH *adj* easily sickened or shocked
SQUEEGEE *n* tool with a rubber blade for clearing water from a surface ▷ *vb* remove (water or other liquid) from (something) by use of a squeegee
SQUEEGEED > SQUEEGEE
SQUEEGEES > SQUEEGEE
SQUEEZE *vb* grip or press firmly ▷ *n* squeezing
SQUEEZED > SQUEEZE
SQUEEZER > SQUEEZE
SQUEEZERS > SQUEEZE
SQUEEZES > SQUEEZE
SQUEEZIER > SQUEEZE
SQUEEZING > SQUEEZE
SQUEEZY > SQUEEZE
SQUEG *vb* oscillate
SQUEGGED > SQUEG
SQUEGGER > SQUEG
SQUEGGERS > SQUEG
SQUEGGING > SQUEG
SQUEGS > SQUEG
SQUELCH *vb* make a wet sucking sound, as by walking through mud ▷ *n* squelching sound
SQUELCHED > SQUELCH
SQUELCHER > SQUELCH
SQUELCHES > SQUELCH
SQUELCHY > SQUELCH
SQUIB *n* small firework that hisses before exploding
SQUIBBED > SQUIB
SQUIBBING > SQUIB
SQUIBS > SQUIB
SQUID *n* sea creature with a long soft body and ten tentacles ▷ *vb* (of a parachute) to assume an elongated squidlike shape owing to excess air pressure
SQUIDDED > SQUID
SQUIDDING > SQUID
SQUIDGE *vb* squash
SQUIDGED > SQUIDGE
SQUIDGES > SQUIDGE
SQUIDGIER > SQUIDGY
SQUIDGING > SQUIDGE
SQUIDGY *adj* soft, moist, and squashy
SQUIDS > SQUID
SQUIER *same as* > SQUIRE
SQUIERS > SQUIER
SQUIFF *same as* > SQUIFFY
SQUIFFED *same as* > SQUIFFY
SQUIFFER *n* concertina
SQUIFFERS > SQUIFFER
SQUIFFIER > SQUIFFY
SQUIFFY *adj* slightly drunk
SQUIGGLE *n* wavy line ▷ *vb* wriggle
SQUIGGLED > SQUIGGLE
SQUIGGLER > SQUIGGLE
SQUIGGLES > SQUIGGLE
SQUIGGLY > SQUIGGLE
SQUILGEE *same as* > SQUEEGEE
SQUILGEED > SQUILGEE
SQUILGEES > SQUILGEE
SQUILL *n* Mediterranean plant of the lily family
SQUILLA *n* any mantis shrimp of the genus *Squilla*
SQUILLAE > SQUILLA
SQUILLAS > SQUILLA
SQUILLION *n* extremely large but unspecified number, quantity, or amount
SQUILLS > SQUILL
SQUINANCY *same as* > QUINSY
SQUINCH *n* small arch across an internal corner of a tower, used to support a superstructure such as a spire ▷ *vb* squeeze
SQUINCHED > SQUINCH
SQUINCHES > SQUINCH
SQUINIED > SQUINY
SQUINIES > SQUINY
SQUINNIED > SQUINNY
SQUINNIER > SQUINNY
SQUINNIES > SQUINNY
SQUINNY *vb* squint ▷ *adj* squint
SQUINT *vb* have eyes which face in different directions ▷ *n* squinting condition of the eye ▷ *adj* crooked
SQUINTED > SQUINT
SQUINTER > SQUINT
SQUINTERS > SQUINT
SQUINTEST > SQUINT
SQUINTIER > SQUINT
SQUINTING > SQUINT
SQUINTS > SQUINT
SQUINTY > SQUINT
SQUINY *same as* > SQUINNY
SQUINYING > SQUINY
SQUIRAGE *n* body of squires
SQUIRAGES > SQUIRAGE
SQUIRALTY *same as* > SQUIRAGE
SQUIRARCH *n* person who believes in government by squires
SQUIRE *n* country gentleman, usu the main landowner in a community ▷ *vb* (of a man) escort (a woman)
SQUIREAGE *same as* > SQUIRAGE
SQUIRED > SQUIRE
SQUIREDOM > SQUIRE
SQUIREEN *n* petty squire
SQUIREENS > SQUIREEN
SQUIRELY > SQUIRE
SQUIRES > SQUIRE
SQUIRESS *n* wife of squire
SQUIRING > SQUIRE
SQUIRISH > SQUIRE
SQUIRM *vb* wriggle, writhe ▷ *n* wriggling movement
SQUIRMED > SQUIRM
SQUIRMER > SQUIRM
SQUIRMERS > SQUIRM
SQUIRMIER > SQUIRMY
SQUIRMING > SQUIRM
SQUIRMS > SQUIRM
SQUIRMY *adj* moving with a wriggling motion
SQUIRR *same as* > SKIRR
SQUIRRED > SQUIRR
SQUIRREL *n* small bushy-tailed tree-living animal ▷ *vb* store for future use
SQUIRRELS > SQUIRREL
SQUIRRELY > SQUIRREL
SQUIRRING > SQUIRR
SQUIRRS > SQUIRR
SQUIRT *vb* force (a liquid) or (of a liquid) be forced out of a narrow opening ▷ *n* jet of liquid
SQUIRTED > SQUIRT
SQUIRTER > SQUIRT
SQUIRTERS > SQUIRT
SQUIRTING > SQUIRT
SQUIRTS > SQUIRT
SQUISH *n* (make) a soft squelching sound ▷ *vb* crush (something) with a soft squelching sound
SQUISHED > SQUISH
SQUISHES > SQUISH
SQUISHIER > SQUISHY
SQUISHING > SQUISH
SQUISHY *adj* soft and yielding to the touch
SQUIT *n* insignificant person
SQUITCH *n* couch grass
SQUITCHES > SQUITCH
SQUITS > SQUIT
SQUIZ *n* look or glance, esp an inquisitive one
SQUIZZES > SQUIZ
SQUOOSH *vb* squash
SQUOOSHED > SQUOOSH
SQUOOSHES > SQUOOSH
SQUOOSHY > SQUOOSH
SQUUSH *same as* > SQUOOSH
SQUUSHED > SQUUSH
SQUUSHES > SQUUSH
SQUUSHING > SQUUSH
SRADDHA *n* Hindu offering to ancestor
SRADDHAS > SRADDHA
SRADHA *same as* > SRADHA
SRADHAS > SRADHA
SRI *n* title of respect used when addressing a Hindu
SRIS > SRI
ST *interj* exclamation to attract attention
STAB *vb* pierce with something pointed ▷ *n* stabbing
STABBED > STAB
STABBER > STAB
STABBERS > STAB
STABBING > STAB
STABBINGS > STAB
STABILATE *n* preserved collection of tiny animals
STABILE *n* stationary abstract construction, usually of wire, metal, wood, etc ▷ *adj* fixed
STABILES > STABILE
STABILISE *same as* > STABILIZE
STABILITY *n* quality of being stable
STABILIZE *vb* make or become stable
STABLE *n* building in which horses are kept ▷ *vb* put or keep (a horse) in a stable ▷ *adj* firmly fixed or

established
ABLEBOY *n* boy or man who works in a stable
ABLED > STABLE
ABLEMAN *same as* > STABLEBOY
ABLEMEN > STABLEMAN
ABLER *n* stable owner
ABLERS > STABLER
ABLES > STABLE
ABLEST > STABLE
ABLING *n* stable buildings or accommodation
ABLINGS > STABLING
ABLISH *archaic variant of* > ESTABLISH
ABLY > STABLE
ABS > STAB
ACCATI > STACCATO
ACCATO *adv* with the notes sharply separated ▷ *adj* consisting of short abrupt sounds ▷ *n* staccato note
ACCATOS > STACCATO
ACHYS *n* any plant of the genus *Stachys*
ACHYSES > STACHYS
ACK *n* ordered pile ▷ *vb* pile in a stack
ACKABLE > STACK
ACKED > STACK
ACKER > STACK
ACKERS > STACK
ACKET *n* fence of wooden posts
ACKETS > STACKET
ACKING *n* arrangement of aircraft traffic in busy flight lanes
ACKINGS > STACKING
ACKLESS > STACK
ACKROOM *n* area of library where books are not on open shelves
ACKS > STACK
ACKUP *n* number of aircraft waiting to land
ACKUPS > STACKUP
ACKYARD *n* place where livestock are kept
ACTE *n* one of several sweet-smelling spices used in incense
ACTES > STACTE
ADDA *n* type of saw
ADDAS > STADDA
ADDLE *n* type of support or prop
ADDLES > STADDLE
ADE *same as* > STADIUM
ADES > STADE
ADIA *n* instrument used in surveying
ADIAL *n* stage in development of glacier
ADIALS > STADIAL
ADIAS > STADIA
ADIUM *n* sports arena with tiered seats for spectators
ADIUMS > STADIUM
AFF *n* people employed in an organization ▷ *vb* supply with personnel
STAFFAGE *n* ornamentation in work of art
STAFFAGES > STAFFAGE
STAFFED > STAFF
STAFFER *n* member of staff, esp, in journalism, of editorial staff
STAFFERS > STAFFER
STAFFING > STAFF
STAFFMAN *n* person who holds the levelling staff when a survey is being made
STAFFMEN > STAFFMAN
STAFFROOM *n* common room for teachers
STAFFS > STAFF
STAG *n* adult male deer ▷ *adv* without a female escort ▷ *vb* apply for (shares in a new issue) with the intention of selling them for a quick profit
STAGE *n* step or period of development ▷ *vb* put (a play) on stage
STAGEABLE > STAGE
STAGED > STAGE
STAGEFUL *n* amount that can appear on stage
STAGEFULS > STAGEFUL
STAGEHAND *n* person who moves props and scenery on a stage
STAGELIKE > STAGE
STAGER *n* person of experience
STAGERIES > STAGERY
STAGERS > STAGER
STAGERY *n* theatrical effects or techniques
STAGES > STAGE
STAGEY *same as* > STAGY
STAGGARD *n* male red deer in the fourth year of life
STAGGARDS > STAGGARD
STAGGART *same as* > STAGGARD
STAGGARTS > STAGGART
STAGGED > STAG
STAGGER *vb* walk unsteadily ▷ *n* staggering
STAGGERED > STAGGER
STAGGERER > STAGGER
STAGGERS *n* disease of horses and other domestic animals that causes staggering
STAGGERY > STAGGER
STAGGIE *n* little stag
STAGGIER > STAG
STAGGIES > STAGGIE
STAGGIEST > STAG
STAGGING > STAG
STAGGY > STAG
STAGHORN as in *staghorn fern* type of fern with fronds that resemble antlers
STAGHORNS > STAGHORN
STAGHOUND *n* breed of hound similar in appearance to the foxhound but larger
STAGIER > STAGY
STAGIEST > STAGY
STAGILY > STAGY
STAGINESS > STAGY
STAGING *n* temporary support used in building
STAGINGS > STAGING
STAGNANCE > STAGNANT
STAGNANCY > STAGNANT
STAGNANT *adj* (of water or air) stale from not moving
STAGNATE *vb* be stagnant
STAGNATED > STAGNATE
STAGNATES > STAGNATE
STAGS > STAG
STAGY *adj* too theatrical or dramatic
STAID *adj* sedate, serious, and rather dull
STAIDER > STAID
STAIDEST > STAID
STAIDLY > STAID
STAIDNESS > STAID
STAIG *Scots variant of* > STAG
STAIGS > STAIG
STAIN *vb* discolour, mark ▷ *n* discoloration or mark
STAINABLE > STAIN
STAINED > STAIN
STAINER > STAIN
STAINERS > STAIN
STAINING > STAIN
STAININGS > STAIN
STAINLESS *adj* resistant to discoloration, esp discoloration resulting from corrosion ▷ *n* stainless steel
STAINS > STAIN
STAIR *n* one step in a flight of stairs
STAIRCASE *n* flight of stairs with a handrail or banisters ▷ *vb* buy other houses in same building
STAIRED *adj* having stairs
STAIRFOOT *n* place at foot of stairs
STAIRHEAD *n* top of a flight of stairs
STAIRLESS > STAIR
STAIRLIFT *n* wall-mounted lifting device to carry person up stairs
STAIRLIKE > STAIR
STAIRS *pl n* flight of steps between floors, usu indoors
STAIRSTEP *n* one of the steps in a staircase
STAIRWAY *n* staircase
STAIRWAYS > STAIRWAY
STAIRWELL *n* vertical shaft in a building that contains a staircase
STAIRWISE *adv* by steps
STAIRWORK *n* unseen plotting
STAITH *same as* > STAITHE
STAITHE *n* wharf
STAITHES > STAITHE
STAITHS > STAITH
STAKE *n* pointed stick or post driven into the ground as a support or marker ▷ *vb* support or mark out with stakes
STAKED > STAKE
STAKEOUT *n* police surveillance of an area or house ▷ *vb* keep an area or house under surveillance
STAKEOUTS > STAKEOUT
STAKES > STAKE
STAKING > STAKE
STALACTIC *adj* relating to the masses of calcium carbonate hanging from the roofs of limestone caves
STALAG *n* German prisoner-of-war camp in World War II
STALAGS > STALAG
STALE *adj* not fresh ▷ *vb* make or become stale ▷ *n* urine of horses or cattle
STALED > STALE
STALELY > STALE
STALEMATE *n* (in chess) position in which any of a player's moves would put his king in check, resulting in a draw ▷ *vb* subject to a stalemate
STALENESS > STALE
STALER > STALE
STALES > STALE
STALEST > STALE
STALING > STALE
STALK *n* plant's stem ▷ *vb* follow or approach stealthily
STALKED > STALK
STALKER > STALK
STALKERS > STALK
STALKIER > STALKY
STALKIEST > STALKY
STALKILY > STALKY
STALKING > STALK
STALKINGS > STALK
STALKLESS > STALK
STALKLIKE > STALK
STALKO *n* idle gentleman
STALKOES > STALKO
STALKS > STALK
STALKY *adj* like a stalk
STALL *n* small stand for the display and sale of goods ▷ *vb* stop (a motor vehicle or engine) or (of a motor vehicle or engine) stop accidentally
STALLAGE *n* rent paid for market stall
STALLAGES > STALLAGE
STALLED > STALL
STALLING > STALL
STALLINGS > STALL
STALLION *n* uncastrated male horse
STALLIONS > STALLION
STALLMAN *n* keeper of a stall

STALLMEN > STALLMAN
STALLS > STALL
STALWART *adj* strong and sturdy ▷ *n* stalwart person
STALWARTS > STALWART
STALWORTH *n* stalwart person
STAMEN *n* pollen-producing part of a flower
STAMENED *adj* having stamen
STAMENS > STAMEN
STAMINA *n* enduring energy and strength
STAMINAL > STAMINA
STAMINAS > STAMINA
STAMINATE *adj* (of plants) having stamens, esp having stamens but no carpels
STAMINEAL *adj* having a stamen
STAMINODE *n* stamen that produces no pollen
STAMINODY *n* development of any of various plant organs into stamens
STAMINOID *adj* like a stamen
STAMMEL *n* coarse woollen cloth in former use for undergarments
STAMMELS > STAMMEL
STAMMER *vb* speak or say with involuntary pauses or repetition of syllables ▷ *n* tendency to stammer
STAMMERED > STAMMER
STAMMERER > STAMMER
STAMMERS > STAMMER
STAMNOI > STAMNOS
STAMNOS *n* ancient Greek jar
STAMP *n* piece of gummed paper stuck to an envelope or parcel to show that the postage has been paid ▷ *vb* bring (one's foot) down forcefully
STAMPED > STAMP
STAMPEDE *n* sudden rush of frightened animals or of a crowd ▷ *vb* (cause to) take part in a stampede
STAMPEDED > STAMPEDE
STAMPEDER > STAMPEDE
STAMPEDES > STAMPEDE
STAMPEDO *same as* > STAMPEDE
STAMPEDOS > STAMPEDO
STAMPER > STAMP
STAMPERS > STAMP
STAMPING > STAMP
STAMPINGS > STAMP
STAMPLESS > STAMP
STAMPS > STAMP
STANCE *n* attitude
STANCES > STANCE
STANCH *vb* stem the flow of (a liquid, esp blood) ▷ *adj* loyal and dependable
STANCHED > STANCH
STANCHEL *same as* > STANCHION
STANCHELS > STANCHEL
STANCHER > STANCH
STANCHERS > STANCH
STANCHES > STANCH
STANCHEST > STANCH
STANCHING > STANCH
STANCHION *n* upright bar used as a support ▷ *vb* provide or support with a stanchion or stanchions
STANCHLY > STANCH
STANCK *adj* faint
STAND *vb* be in, rise to, or place in an upright position ▷ *n* stall for the sale of goods
STANDARD *n* level of quality ▷ *adj* usual, regular, or average
STANDARDS > STANDARD
STANDAWAY *adj* erect
STANDBY *n* person or thing that is ready for use
STANDBYS > STANDBY
STANDDOWN *n* return to normal after alert
STANDEE *n* person who stands, esp when there are no vacant seats
STANDEES > STANDEE
STANDEN > STAND
STANDER > STAND
STANDERS > STAND
STANDFAST *n* reliable person or thing
STANDGALE *same as* > STANIEL
STANDING > STAND
STANDINGS > STAND
STANDISH *n* stand, usually of metal, for pens, ink bottles, etc
STANDOFF *n* act or an instance of standing off or apart ▷ *vb* stay at a distance
STANDOFFS > STANDOFF
STANDOUT *n* distinctive or outstanding person or thing
STANDOUTS > STANDOUT
STANDOVER *n* threatening or intimidating act
STANDPAT *n* (in poker) refusal to change one's card
STANDPIPE *n* tap attached to a water main to provide a public water supply
STANDS > STAND
STANDUP *n* comedian who performs solo
STANDUPS > STANDUP
STANE *Scot word for* > STONE
STANED > STANE
STANES > STANE
STANG *vb* sting
STANGED > STANG
STANGING > STANG
STANGS > STANG
STANHOPE *n* light one-seater carriage with two or four wheels
STANHOPES > STANHOPE
STANIEL *n* kestrel
STANIELS > STANIEL
STANINE *n* scale of nine levels
STANINES > STANINE
STANING > STANE
STANK *vb* dam
STANKED > STINK
STANKING > STINK
STANKS > STINK
STANNARY *n* place or region where tin is mined or worked
STANNATE *n* salt of stannic acid
STANNATES > STANNATE
STANNATOR *n* member of old Cornish parliament
STANNEL *same as* > STANIEL
STANNELS > STANNEL
STANNIC *adj* of or containing tin, esp in the tetravalent state
STANNITE *n* grey metallic mineral
STANNITES > STANNITE
STANNOUS *adj* of or containing tin, esp in the divalent state
STANNUM *n* tin (the metal)
STANNUMS > STANNUM
STANOL *n* drug taken to prevent heart disease
STANOLS > STANOL
STANYEL *same as* > STANIEL
STANYELS > STANYEL
STANZA *n* verse of a poem
STANZAED > STANZA
STANZAIC > STANZA
STANZAS > STANZA
STANZE *same as* > STANZA
STANZES > STANZE
STANZO *same as* > STANZA
STANZOES > STANZO
STANZOS > STANZO
STAP *same as* > STOP
STAPEDES > STAPES
STAPEDIAL > STAPES
STAPEDII > STAPEDIUS
STAPEDIUS *n* muscle in stapes
STAPELIA *n* fleshy cactus-like leafless African plant
STAPELIAS > STAPELIA
STAPES *n* stirrup-shaped bone that is the innermost of three small bones in the middle ear of mammals
STAPH *n* staphylococcus
STAPHS > STAPH
STAPLE *n* U-shaped piece of metal used to fasten papers or secure things ▷ *vb* fasten with staples ▷ *adj* of prime importance, principal
STAPLED > STAPLE
STAPLER *n* small device for fastening papers together
STAPLERS > STAPLER
STAPLES > STAPLE
STAPLING > STAPLE
STAPPED > STAP
STAPPING > STAP
STAPPLE *same as* > STOPPL
STAPPLES > STAPPLE
STAPS > STAP
STAR *n* hot gaseous mass space, visible in the night sky as a point of light ▷ *v* feature or be featured as star ▷ *adj* leading, famo
STARAGEN *n* tarragon
STARAGENS > STARAGEN
STARBOARD *n* right-hand side of a ship, when facin forward ▷ *adj* of or on th side ▷ *vb* turn or be turn towards the starboard
STARBURST *n* pattern of rays or lines radiating fro a light source
STARCH *n* carbohydrate forming the main food element in bread, potatoes, etc, and used mixed with water for stiffening fabric ▷ *vb* stiffen (fabric) with starc ▷ *adj* (of a person) forma
STARCHED > STARCH
STARCHER > STARCH
STARCHERS > STARCH
STARCHES > STARCH
STARCHIER > STARCHY
STARCHILY > STARCHY
STARCHING > STARCH
STARCHY *adj* containing starch
STARDOM *n* status of a sta in the entertainment or sports world
STARDOMS > STARDOM
STARDRIFT *n* regular movement of stars
STARDUST *n* dusty materi found between the stars
STARDUSTS > STARDUST
STARE *vb* look or gaze fixedly (at) ▷ *n* fixed gaz
STARED > STARE
STARER > STARE
STARERS > STARE
STARES > STARE
STARETS *n* Russian holy man
STARETSES > STARETS
STARETZ *same as* > STARET
STARETZES > STARETZ
STARFISH *n* star-shaped sea creature
STARFRUIT *n* tree with edible yellow fruit which is star-shaped on cross section
STARGAZE *vb* observe the stars
STARGAZED > STARGAZE
STARGAZER > STARGAZE
STARGAZES > STARGAZE
STARING > STARE
STARINGLY > STARE
STARINGS > STARE
STARK *adj* harsh, unpleasant, and plain ▷ *adv* completely ▷ *vb* stiffen

ARKED > STARK
ARKEN *vb* become or nake stark
ARKENED > STARKEN
ARKENS > STARKEN
ARKER > STARK
ARKERS *adj* completely naked
ARKEST > STARK
ARKING > STARK
ARKLY > STARK
ARKNESS > STARK
ARKS > STARK
ARLESS > STAR
ARLET *n* young actress presented as a future star
ARLETS > STARLET
ARLIGHT *n* light that comes from the stars ▷ *adj* of or like starlight
ARLIKE > STAR
ARLING *n* songbird with glossy black speckled eathers
ARLINGS > STARLING
ARLIT *same* s > STARLIGHT
ARN *same as* > STERN
ARNED > STARN
ARNIE *n* Scots word for ittle star
ARNIES > STARNIE
ARNING > STARN
ARNOSE *n* American nole with starlike nose
ARNOSES > STARNOSE
ARNS > STARN
AROSTA *n* headman of Russian village
AROSTAS > STAROSTA
AROSTY *n* estate of Polish nobleman
ARR *n* (in Judaism) elease from a debt
ARRED > STAR
ARRIER > STARRY
ARRIEST > STARRY
ARRILY > STARRY
ARRING > STAR
ARRINGS > STARE
ARRS > STARR
ARRY *adj* full of or like tars
ARS > STAR
ARSHINE *n* starlight
ARSHIP *n* spacecraft in cience fiction
ARSHIPS > STARSHIP
ARSPOT *n* dark patch on urface of star
ARSPOTS > STARSPOT
ARSTONE *n* precious tone reflecting light in tarlike pattern
ART *vb* take the first tep, begin ▷ *n* first part of something
ARTED > START
ARTER *n* first course of meal
ARTERS > STARTER
ARTFUL *adj* tending to tart
ARTING > START
STARTINGS > START
STARTISH *same as* > STARTFUL
STARTLE *vb* slightly surprise or frighten
STARTLED > STARTLE
STARTLER > STARTLE
STARTLERS > STARTLE
STARTLES > STARTLE
STARTLING *adj* causing surprise or fear
STARTLISH *adj* easily startled
STARTLY *same as* > STARTLISH
STARTS > START
STARTSY > STARETS
STARTUP *n* business enterprise that has been launched recently
STARTUPS > STARTUP
STARVE *vb* die or suffer or cause to die or suffer from hunger
STARVED > STARVE
STARVER > STARVE
STARVERS > STARVE
STARVES > STARVE
STARVING > STARVE
STARVINGS > STARVE
STARWORT *n* plant with star-shaped flowers
STARWORTS > STARWORT
STASES > STASIS
STASH *vb* store in a secret place ▷ *n* secret store
STASHED > STASH
STASHES > STASH
STASHIE *same as* > STUSHIE
STASHIES > STASHIE
STASHING > STASH
STASIDION *n* stall in Greek church
STASIMA > STASIMON
STASIMON *n* ode sung in Greek tragedy
STASIS *n* stagnation in the normal flow of bodily fluids, such as the blood or urine
STAT *n* statistic
STATABLE > STATE
STATAL *adj* of a federal state
STATANT *adj* (of an animal) in profile with all four feet on the ground
STATE *n* condition of a person or thing ▷ *adj* of or concerning the State ▷ *vb* express in words
STATEABLE > STATE
STATED *adj* (esp of a sum) determined by agreement
STATEDLY > STATED
STATEHOOD > STATE
STATELESS *adj* not belonging to any country
STATELET *n* small state
STATELETS > STATELET
STATELIER > STATELY
STATELILY > STATELY
STATELY *adj* dignified or grand ▷ *adv* in a stately manner
STATEMENT *n* something stated ▷ *vb* assess (a pupil) with regard to his or her special educational needs
STATER *n* any of various usually silver coins of ancient Greece
STATEROOM *n* private cabin on a ship
STATERS > STATER
STATES > STATE
STATESIDE *adv* of, in, to, or towards the US
STATESMAN *n* experienced and respected political leader
STATESMEN > STATESMAN
STATEWIDE *adj* throughout a state
STATIC *adj* stationary or inactive ▷ *n* crackling sound or speckled picture caused by interference in radio or television reception
STATICAL > STATIC
STATICE *n* plant name formerly used for both thrift and sea lavender
STATICES > STATICE
STATICKY > STATIC
STATICS *n* branch of mechanics dealing with the forces producing a state of equilibrium
STATIM *adv* right away
STATIN *n* type of drug that lowers the levels of low-density lipoproteins in the blood
STATING > STATE
STATINS > STATIN
STATION *n* place where trains stop for passengers ▷ *vb* assign (someone) to a particular place
STATIONAL > STATION
STATIONED > STATION
STATIONER *n* dealer in stationery
STATIONS > STATION
STATISM *n* theory or practice of concentrating economic and political power in the state
STATISMS > STATISM
STATIST *n* advocate of statism ▷ *adj* of, characteristic of, advocating, or relating to statism
STATISTIC *n* numerical fact collected and classified systematically
STATISTS > STATIST
STATIVE *adj* denoting a verb describing a state rather than an activity, act, or event ▷ *n* stative verb
STATIVES > STATIVE
STATOCYST *n* organ of balance in some invertebrates
STATOLITH *n* any of the granules of calcium carbonate occurring in a statocyst
STATOR *n* stationary part of a rotary machine or device, esp of a motor or generator
STATORS > STATOR
STATS > STAT
STATUA *same as* > STATUE
STATUARY *n* statues collectively ▷ *adj* of, relating to, or suitable for statues
STATUAS > STATUA
STATUE *n* large sculpture of a human or animal figure
STATUED *adj* decorated with or portrayed in a statue or statues
STATUES > STATUE
STATUETTE *n* small statue
STATURE *n* person's height
STATURED *adj* having stature
STATURES > STATURE
STATUS *n* social position
STATUSES > STATUS
STATUSY *adj* conferring or having status
STATUTE *n* written law
STATUTES > STATUTE
STATUTORY *adj* required or authorized by law
STAUMREL *n* stupid person
STAUMRELS > STAUMREL
STAUN *Scot word for* > STAND
STAUNCH *same as* > STANCH
STAUNCHED > STAUNCH
STAUNCHER > STAUNCH
STAUNCHES > STAUNCH
STAUNCHLY > STAUNCH
STAUNING > STAUN
STAUNS > STAUN
STAVE *same as* > STAFF
STAVED > STAVE
STAVES > STAVE
STAVING > STAVE
STAVUDINE *n* drug used to treat HIV
STAW *Scots form of* > STALL
STAWED > STAW
STAWING > STAW
STAWS > STAW
STAY *vb* remain in a place or condition ▷ *n* period of staying in a place
STAYAWAY *n* strike in South Africa
STAYAWAYS > STAYAWAY
STAYED > STAY
STAYER *n* person or thing that stays
STAYERS > STAYER
STAYING > STAY
STAYLESS *adj* with no stays or support
STAYMAKER *n* corset maker
STAYNE *same as* > STAIN
STAYNED > STAYNE
STAYNES > STAYNE
STAYNING > STAYNE

STAYRE *same as* > STAIR
STAYRES > STAYRE
STAYS *pl n* old-fashioned corsets with bones in them
STAYSAIL *n* sail fastened on a stay
STAYSAILS > STAYSAIL
STEAD *n* place or function that should be taken by another ▷ *vb* help or benefit
STEADED > STEAD
STEADFAST *adj* firm, determined
STEADICAM *n* tradename for a mechanism for steadying a hand-held camera
STEADIED > STEADY
STEADIER > STEADY
STEADIERS > STEADY
STEADIES > STEADY
STEADIEST > STEADY
STEADILY > STEADY
STEADING *n* farmstead
STEADINGS > STEADING
STEADS > STEAD
STEADY *adj* not shaky or wavering ▷ *vb* make steady ▷ *adv* in a steady manner
STEADYING > STEADY
STEAK *n* thick slice of meat, esp beef
STEAKS > STEAK
STEAL *vb* take unlawfully or without permission
STEALABLE > STEAL
STEALAGE *n* theft
STEALAGES > STEALAGE
STEALE *n* handle
STEALED > STEAL
STEALER *n* person who steals something
STEALERS > STEALER
STEALES > STEALE
STEALING > STEAL
STEALINGS > STEAL
STEALS > STEAL
STEALT > STEAL
STEALTH *n* moving carefully and quietly ▷ *adj* (of technology) able to render an aircraft almost invisible to radar ▷ *vb* approach undetected
STEALTHED > STEALTH
STEALTHS > STEALTH
STEALTHY *adj* characterized by great caution, secrecy, etc
STEAM *n* vapour into which water changes when boiled ▷ *vb* give off steam
STEAMBOAT *n* boat powered by a steam engine
STEAMED > STEAM
STEAMER *n* steam-propelled ship ▷ *vb* travel by steamer
STEAMERED > STEAMER
STEAMERS > STEAMER
STEAMIE *n* public wash house
STEAMIER > STEAMY
STEAMIES > STEAMIE
STEAMIEST > STEAMY
STEAMILY > STEAMY
STEAMING *adj* very hot ▷ *n* robbery, esp of passengers in a railway carriage or bus, by a large gang of armed youths
STEAMINGS > STEAMING
STEAMROLL *vb* crush (opposition) by overpowering force
STEAMS > STEAM
STEAMSHIP *n* ship powered by steam engines
STEAMY *adj* full of steam
STEAN *n* earthenware vessel
STEANE *same as* > STEEN
STEANED > STEANE
STEANES > STEANE
STEANING > STEANE
STEANINGS > STEANE
STEANS > STEAN
STEAPSIN *n* pancreatic lipase
STEAPSINS > STEAPSIN
STEAR *same as* > STEER
STEARAGE *same as* > STEERAGE
STEARAGES > STEARAGE
STEARATE *n* any salt or ester of stearic acid
STEARATES > STEARATE
STEARD > STEAR
STEARE *same as* > STEER
STEARED > STEARE
STEARES > STEARE
STEARIC *adj* of or relating to suet or fat
STEARIN *n* colourless crystalline ester of glycerol and stearic acid
STEARINE *same as* > STEARIN
STEARINES > STEARINE
STEARING > STEAR
STEARINS > STEARIN
STEARS > STEAR
STEARSMAN *same as* > STEERSMAN
STEARSMEN > STEARSMAN
STEATITE *same as* > SOAPSTONE
STEATITES > STEATITE
STEATITIC > STEATITE
STEATOMA *n* tumour of sebaceous gland
STEATOMAS > STEATOMA
STEATOSES > STEATOSIS
STEATOSIS *n* abnormal accumulation of fat
STED *same as* > STEAD
STEDD *same as* > STEAD
STEDDE *same as* > STEAD
STEDDED > STED
STEDDES > STEDDE
STEDDIED > STEDDY
STEDDIES > STEDDY
STEDDING > STED
STEDDS > STEDD
STEDDY *same as* > STEADY
STEDDYING > STEDDY
STEDE *same as* > STEAD
STEDED > STEDE
STEDES > STEDE
STEDFAST *same as* > STEADFAST
STEDING > STEDE
STEDS > STED
STEED *same as* > STEAD
STEEDED > STEED
STEEDIED > STEEDY
STEEDIES > STEEDY
STEEDING > STEED
STEEDLIKE > STEED
STEEDS > STEED
STEEDY *same as* > STEADY
STEEDYING > STEEDY
STEEK *vb* Scots word meaning shut
STEEKED > STEEK
STEEKING > STEEK
STEEKIT > STEEK
STEEKS > STEEK
STEEL *n* hard malleable alloy of iron and carbon ▷ *vb* prepare (oneself) for something unpleasant
STEELBOW *n* material lent to tenant by landlord
STEELBOWS > STEELBOW
STEELD > STEEL
STEELED > STEEL
STEELHEAD *n* silvery North Pacific variety of the rainbow trout
STEELIE *n* steel ball bearing used as marble
STEELIER > STEEL
STEELIES > STEELIE
STEELIEST > STEELIE
STEELING > STEEL
STEELINGS > STEEL
STEELMAN *n* person working in steel industry
STEELMEN > STEELMAN
STEELS *pl n* shares and bonds of steel companies
STEELWARE *n* things made of steel
STEELWORK *n* frame, foundation, building, or article made of steel
STEELY > STEEL
STEELYARD *n* portable balance consisting of a pivoted bar with two unequal arms
STEEM *variant of* > ESTEEM
STEEMED > STEEM
STEEMING > STEEM
STEEMS > STEEM
STEEN *vb* line with stone
STEENBOK *n* small antelope of central and southern Africa
STEENBOKS > STEENBOK
STEENBRAS *n* variety of sea bream
STEENBUCK *same as* > STEENBOK
STEENED > STEEN
STEENING > STEEN
STEENINGS > STEEN
STEENKIRK *n* type of crav
STEENS > STEEN
STEEP *adj* sloping sharply ▷ *vb* soak or be soaked in liquid ▷ *n* instance or th process of steeping or th condition of being steep
STEEPED > STEEP
STEEPEN *vb* become or cause (something) to become steep or steeper
STEEPENED > STEEPEN
STEEPENS > STEEPEN
STEEPER > STEEP
STEEPERS > STEEP
STEEPEST > STEEP
STEEPEUP *adj* very steep
STEEPIER > STEEPY
STEEPIEST > STEEPY
STEEPING > STEEP
STEEPISH > STEEP
STEEPLE *same as* > SPIRE
STEEPLED > STEEPLE
STEEPLES > STEEPLE
STEEPLY > STEEP
STEEPNESS > STEEP
STEEPS > STEEP
STEEPUP *adj* very steep
STEEPY *same as* > STEEP
STEER *vb* direct the cours of (a vehicle or ship) ▷ *n* castrated male ox
STEERABLE > STEER
STEERAGE *n* cheapest accommodation on a passenger ship
STEERAGES > STEERAGE
STEERED > STEER
STEERER > STEER
STEERERS > STEER
STEERIES > STEERY
STEERING > STEER
STEERINGS > STEER
STEERLING *n* young stee
STEERS > STEER
STEERSMAN *n* person wh steers a vessel
STEERSMEN > STEERSMAN
STEERY *n* commotion
STEEVE *n* spar having a pulley block at one end, used for stowing cargo o a ship ▷ *vb* stow (cargo) securely in the hold of a ship
STEEVED > STEEVE
STEEVELY > STEEVE
STEEVER > STEEVE
STEEVES > STEEVE
STEEVEST > STEEVE
STEEVING > STEEVE
STEEVINGS > STEEVE
STEGNOSES > STEGNOSIS
STEGNOSIS *n* constrictio of bodily pores
STEGNOTIC > STEGNOSIS
STEGODON *n* mammal of Pliocene to Pleistocene times, similar to the mastodon
STEGODONS > STEGODON
STEGODONT *same as* > STEGODON
STEGOMYIA *former name*

or > AEDES
EGOSAUR *n* quadrupedal
ıerbivorous dinosaur
EIL *same as* > STEAL
EILS > STEIL
EIN *same as* > STEEN
EINBOCK *another name*
or > IBEX
EINBOK *same*
s > STEENBOK
EINBOKS > STEINBOK
EINED > STEIN
EINING > STEIN
EININGS > STEIN
EINKIRK *same*
s > STEENKIRK
EINS > STEIN
ELA *same as* > STELE
ELAE > STELE
ELAI > STELE
ELAR > STELE
ELE *n* upright stone slab
r column decorated with
igures or inscriptions
ELENE > STELE
ELES > STELE
ELIC > STELE
ELL *n* shelter for cattle or
heep built on moorland
r hillsides ▷ *vb* position
r place
ELLA *n* star or
omething star-shaped
ELLAR *adj* of stars
ELLAS > STELLA
ELLATE *adj* resembling a
tar in shape
ELLATED *same*
s > STELLATE
ELLED > STELL
ELLERID *n* starfish
ELLIFY *vb* change or be
hanged into a star
ELLING > STELL
ELLION *n*
Mediterranean lizard
ELLIONS > STELLION
ELLITE *n* tradename
or any of various
lloys containing
obalt, chromium,
arbon, tungsten, and
nolybdenum
ELLITES > STELLITE
ELLS > STELL
ELLULAR *adj* displaying
r abounding in small
tars
EM *vb* stop (the flow of
omething) ▷ *n* main axis
f a plant, which bears the
eaves, axillary buds, and
owers
EMBOK *same*
s > STEENBOK
EMBOKS > STEMBOK
EMBUCK *same*
s > STEENBOK
EMBUCKS > STEMBUCK
EME *same as* > STEAM
EMED > STEME
EMES > STEME
EMHEAD *n* head of the
tem of a vessel

STEMHEADS > STEMHEAD
STEMING > STEME
STEMLESS > STEM
STEMLET *n* little stem
STEMLETS > STEMLET
STEMLIKE > STEM
STEMMA *n* family tree
STEMMAS > STEMMA
STEMMATA > STEMMA
STEMMATIC > STEMMA
STEMME *archaic variant of* > STEM
STEMMED > STEM
STEMMER > STEM
STEMMERS > STEM
STEMMERY *n* tobacco factory
STEMMES > STEMME
STEMMIER > STEMMY
STEMMIEST > STEMMY
STEMMING > STEM
STEMMINGS > STEM
STEMMY *adj* (of wine) young and raw
STEMPEL *n* timber support
STEMPELS > STEMPEL
STEMPLE *same as* > STEMPEL
STEMPLES > STEMPLE
STEMS > STEM
STEMSON *n* curved timber scarfed into or bolted to the stem and keelson at the bow of a wooden vessel
STEMSONS > STEMSON
STEMWARE *n* collective term for glasses, goblets, etc, with stems
STEMWARES > STEMWARE
STEN *vb* stride
STENCH *n* foul smell ▷ *vb* cause to smell
STENCHED > STENCH
STENCHES > STENCH
STENCHFUL > STENCH
STENCHIER > STENCH
STENCHING > STENCH
STENCHY > STENCH
STENCIL *n* thin sheet with cut-out pattern through which ink or paint passes to form the pattern on the surface below ▷ *vb* make (a pattern) with a stencil
STENCILED > STENCIL
STENCILER > STENCIL
STENCILS > STENCIL
STEND *vb* Scots word meaning bound
STENDED > STEND
STENDING > STEND
STENDS > STEND
STENGAH *same as* > STINGER
STENGAHS > STENGAH
STENLOCK *n* fish of northern seas
STENLOCKS > STENLOCK
STENNED > STEN
STENNING > STEN
STENO *n* stenographer
STENOBATH *n* stenobathic organism
STENOKIES > STENOKY
STENOKOUS *adj* able to live in narrow range of environments
STENOKY *n* life and survival that is dependent on conditions remaining within a narrow range of variables
STENOPAIC *adj* having narrow opening
STENOS > STENO
STENOSED *adj* abnormally contracted
STENOSES > STENOSIS
STENOSIS *n* abnormal narrowing of a bodily canal or passage
STENOTIC > STENOSIS
STENOTYPE *n* machine with a keyboard for recording speeches in a phonetic shorthand
STENOTYPY *n* form of shorthand in which alphabetic combinations are used to represent groups of sounds or short common words
STENS > STEN
STENT *n* surgical implant used to keep an artery open ▷ *vb* assess
STENTED > STENT
STENTING > STENT
STENTOR *n* person with an unusually loud voice
STENTORS > STENTOR
STENTOUR *n* tax assessor
STENTOURS > STENTOUR
STENTS > STENT
STEP *vb* move and set down the foot, as when walking ▷ *n* stepping
STEPBAIRN *Scots word for* > STEPCHILD
STEPCHILD *n* stepson or stepdaughter
STEPDAME *n* woman married to one's father
STEPDAMES > STEPDAME
STEPHANE *n* ancient Greek headdress
STEPHANES > STEPHANE
STEPLIKE > STEP
STEPNEY *n* spare wheel
STEPNEYS > STEPNEY
STEPPE *n* extensive grassy plain usually without trees
STEPPED > STEP
STEPPER *n* person who or animal that steps, esp a horse or a dancer
STEPPERS > STEPPER
STEPPES > STEPPE
STEPPING > STEP
STEPS > STEP
STEPSON *n* son of one's husband or wife by an earlier relationship
STEPSONS > STEPSON
STEPSTOOL *n* stool able to be used as step
STEPT > STEP
STEPWISE *adj* arranged in the manner of or resembling steps ▷ *adv* with the form or appearance of steps
STERADIAN *n* SI unit of solid angle
STERCORAL *adj* relating to excrement
STERCULIA *n* dietary fibre used as a food stabilizer and denture adhesive
STERE *n* unit used to measure volumes of stacked timber
STEREO *n* stereophonic record player ▷ *adj* (of a sound system) using two or more separate microphones to feed two or more loudspeakers through separate channels ▷ *vb* make stereophonic
STEREOED > STEREO
STEREOING > STEREO
STEREOME *n* tissue of a plant that provides mechanical support
STEREOMES > STEREOME
STEREOS > STEREO
STERES > STERE
STERIC *adj* of or caused by the spatial arrangement of atoms in a molecule
STERICAL *same as* > STERIC
STERIGMA *n* minute stalk bearing a spore or chain of spores in certain fungi
STERIGMAS > STERIGMA
STERILANT *n* any substance or agent used in sterilization
STERILE *adj* free from germs
STERILELY > STERILE
STERILISE *same as* > STERILIZE
STERILITY > STERILE
STERILIZE *vb* make sterile
STERLET *n* small sturgeon of seas and rivers in N Asia and E Europe
STERLETS > STERLET
STERLING *n* British money system ▷ *adj* genuine and reliable
STERLINGS > STERLING
STERN *adj* severe, strict ▷ *n* rear part of a ship ▷ *vb* row boat backward
STERNA > STERNUM
STERNAGE *n* sterns
STERNAGES > STERNAGE
STERNAL > STERNUM
STERNEBRA *n* part of breastbone
STERNED > STERN
STERNER > STERN
STERNEST > STERN
STERNFAST *n* rope for securing boat at stern
STERNING > STERN
STERNITE *n* part of arthropod
STERNITES > STERNITE
STERNITIC > STERNITE

STERNLY > STERN
STERNMOST *adj* farthest to the stern
STERNNESS > STERN
STERNPORT *n* opening in stern of ship
STERNPOST *n* main upright timber or structure at the stern of a vessel
STERNS > STERN
STERNSON *n* timber scarfed into or bolted to the sternpost and keelson at the stern of a wooden vessel
STERNSONS > STERNSON
STERNUM *n* long flat bone in the front of the body, to which the collarbone and most of the ribs are attached
STERNUMS > STERNUM
STERNWARD *adv* towards the stern
STERNWAY *n* movement of a vessel sternforemost
STERNWAYS > STERNWAY
STEROID *n* organic compound containing a carbon ring system, such as many hormones
STEROIDAL > STEROID
STEROIDS > STEROID
STEROL *n* natural insoluble alcohol such as cholesterol and ergosterol
STEROLS > STEROL
STERTOR *n* laborious or noisy breathing caused by obstructed air passages
STERTORS > STERTOR
STERVE *same as* > STARVE
STERVED > STERVE
STERVES > STERVE
STERVING > STERVE
STET *interj* instruction to ignore an alteration previously made by a proofreader ▷ *vb* indicate to a printer that certain deleted matter is to be kept ▷ *n* word or mark indicating that certain deleted written matter is to be retained
STETS > STET
STETTED > STET
STETTING > STET
STEVEDORE *n* person who loads and unloads ships ▷ *vb* load or unload (a ship, ship's cargo, etc)
STEVEN *n* voice
STEVENS > STEVEN
STEW *n* food cooked slowly in a closed pot ▷ *vb* cook slowly in a closed pot
STEWABLE > STEW
STEWARD *n* person who looks after passengers on a ship or aircraft ▷ *vb* act as a steward (of)
STEWARDED > STEWARD
STEWARDRY *n* office of steward
STEWARDS > STEWARD
STEWARTRY *variant of* > STEWARDRY
STEWBUM *n* drunkard
STEWBUMS > STEWBUM
STEWED *adj* (of food) cooked by stewing
STEWER > STEW
STEWERS > STEW
STEWIER > STEW
STEWIEST > STEW
STEWING > STEW
STEWINGS > STEW
STEWPAN *n* pan used for making stew
STEWPANS > STEWPAN
STEWPOND *n* fishpond
STEWPONDS > STEWPOND
STEWPOT *n* pot used for making stew
STEWPOTS > STEWPOT
STEWS > STEW
STEWY > STEW
STEY *adj* Scots word meaning steep
STEYER > STEY
STEYEST > STEY
STHENIA *n* abnormal strength
STHENIAS > STHENIA
STHENIC *adj* abounding in energy or bodily strength
STIBBLE *Scots form of* > STUBBLE
STIBBLER *n* horse allowed to eat stubble
STIBBLERS > STIBBLE
STIBBLES > STIBBLE
STIBIAL > STIBIUM
STIBINE *n* colourless slightly soluble poisonous gas
STIBINES > STIBINE
STIBIUM *obsolete name for* > ANTIMONY
STIBIUMS > STIBIUM
STIBNITE *n* soft greyish mineral
STIBNITES > STIBNITE
STICCADO *n* type of xylophone
STICCADOS > STICCADO
STICCATO *same as* > STICCADO
STICCATOS > STICCATO
STICH *n* line of poetry
STICHARIA *pl n* priest's robes of the Greek Church
STICHERA > STICHERON
STICHERON *n* short hymn in Greek Church
STICHIC > STICH
STICHIDIA *pl n* seaweed branches
STICHOI > STICHOS
STICHOS *n* line of poem
STICHS > STICH
STICK *n* long thin piece of wood ▷ *vb* push (a pointed object) into (something)
STICKABLE > STICK
STICKBALL *n* form of baseball played in street
STICKED > STICK
STICKER *n* adhesive label or sign ▷ *vb* put stickers on
STICKERED > STICKER
STICKERS > STICKER
STICKFUL > STICK
STICKFULS > STICK
STICKIED > STICKY
STICKIER > STICKY
STICKIES > STICKY
STICKIEST > STICKY
STICKILY > STICKY
STICKING > STICK
STICKINGS > STICK
STICKIT *Scots form of* > STUCK
STICKJAW *n* stodgy food
STICKJAWS > STICKJAW
STICKLE *vb* dispute stubbornly, esp about minor points
STICKLED > STICKLE
STICKLER *n* person who insists on something
STICKLERS > STICKLER
STICKLES > STICKLE
STICKLIKE > STICK
STICKLING > STICKLE
STICKMAN *n* human figure drawn in thin strokes
STICKMEN > STICKMAN
STICKOUT *n* conspicuous person or thing
STICKOUTS > STICKOUT
STICKPIN *n* tiepin
STICKPINS > STICKPIN
STICKS > STICK
STICKSEED *n* type of Eurasian and North American plant
STICKUM *n* adhesive
STICKUMS > STICKUM
STICKUP *n* robbery at gun-point
STICKUPS > STICKUP
STICKWEED *n* any of several plants that have clinging fruits or seeds, esp the ragweed
STICKWORK *n* use of stick in hockey
STICKY *adj* covered with an adhesive substance ▷ *vb* make sticky ▷ *n* inquisitive look or stare
STICKYING > STICKY
STICTION *n* frictional force to be overcome to set one object in motion when it is in contact with another
STICTIONS > STICTION
STIDDIE *same as* > STITHY
STIDDIED > STIDDIE
STIDDIES > STIDDIE
STIE *same as* > STY
STIED > STY
STIES > STY
STIEVE *same as* > STEEVE
STIEVELY > STIEVE
STIEVER > STIEVE
STIEVEST > STIEVE
STIFF *adj* not easily bent or moved ▷ *n* corpse ▷ *adv* completely or utterly ▷ *v* fail completely
STIFFED > STIFF
STIFFEN *vb* make or become stiff
STIFFENED > STIFFEN
STIFFENER > STIFFEN
STIFFENS > STIFFEN
STIFFER > STIFF
STIFFEST > STIFF
STIFFIE *n* erection of the penis
STIFFIES > STIFFIE
STIFFING > STIFF
STIFFISH > STIFF
STIFFLY > STIFF
STIFFNESS > STIFF
STIFFS > STIFF
STIFFWARE *n* computer software that is hard to modify
STIFFY *n* erection of the penis
STIFLE *vb* suppress ▷ *n* joint in the hind leg of a horse, dog, etc, between the femur and tibia
STIFLED > STIFLE
STIFLER > STIFLE
STIFLERS > STIFLE
STIFLES > STIFLE
STIFLING *adj* uncomfortably hot and stuffy
STIFLINGS > STIFLING
STIGMA *n* mark of social disgrace
STIGMAL *adj* of part of insect wing
STIGMAS > STIGMA
STIGMATA > STIGMA
STIGMATIC *adj* relating to or having a stigma or stigmata ▷ *n* person marked with the stigmata
STIGME *n* dot in Greek punctuation
STIGMES > STIGME
STILB *n* unit of luminance equal to 1 candela per square centimetre.
STILBENE *n* colourless or slightly yellow crystalline hydrocarbon used in the manufacture of dyes
STILBENES > STILBENE
STILBITE *n* white or yellow zeolite mineral
STILBITES > STILBITE
STILBS > STILB
STILE *same as* > STYLE
STILED > STILE
STILES > STILE
STILET *same as* > STYLET
STILETS > STILET
STILETTO *n* high narrow heel on a woman's shoe ▷ *vb* stab with a stiletto
STILETTOS > STILETTO
STILING > STILE
STILL *adv* now or in the future as before ▷ *adj* motionless ▷ *n* calmness

apparatus for distillation ▷ *vb* make still
TILLAGE *n* frame or stand for keeping things off the ground, such as casks in a brewery
TILLAGES > STILLAGE
TILLBORN *adj* born dead ▷ *n* stillborn fetus or baby
TILLED > STILL
TILLER > STILL
TILLERS > STILL
TILLEST > STILL
TILLIER > STILLY
TILLIEST > STILLY
TILLING > STILL
TILLINGS > STILL
TILLION *n* stand for cask
TILLIONS > STILLION
TILLMAN *n* someone involved in the operation of a still
TILLMEN > STILLMAN
TILLNESS > STILL
TILLROOM *n* room in which distilling is carried out
TILLS > STILL
TILLY *adv* quietly or calmly ▷ *adj* still, quiet, or calm
TILT *n* either of a pair of long poles with footrests for walking raised from the ground ▷ *vb* raise or place on or as if on stilts
TILTBIRD *n* long-legged wading bird
TILTED *adj* stiff and formal in manner
TILTEDLY > STILTED
TILTER > STILT
TILTERS > STILT
TILTIER > STILT
TILTIEST > STILT
TILTING > STILT
TILTINGS > STILT
TILTISH > STILT
TILTS > STILT
TILTY > STILT
TIM *n* very small amount
TIME *same as* > STYME
TIMED > STIME
TIMES > STIME
TIMIE *same as* > STYMIE
TIMIED > STIMIE
TIMIES > STIMIE
TIMING > STIME
TIMS > STIM
TIMULANT *n* something, such as a drug, that acts as a stimulus ▷ *adj* stimulating
TIMULATE *vb* act as a stimulus (on)
TIMULI > STIMULUS
TIMULUS *n* something that rouses a person or thing to activity
TIMY *same as* > STYMIE
TIMYING > STIMY
TING *vb* (of certain animals or plants) wound by injecting with poison ▷ *n* wound or pain caused by or as if by stinging
STINGAREE *popular name for* > STINGRAY
STINGBULL *n* spiny fish
STINGED > STING
STINGER *n* person, plant, animal, etc, that stings or hurts
STINGERS > STINGER
STINGFISH *same as* > STINGBULL
STINGIER > STINGY
STINGIES > STINGY
STINGIEST > STINGY
STINGILY > STINGY
STINGING > STING
STINGINGS > STING
STINGLESS > STING
STINGO *n* strong alcohol
STINGOS > STINGO
STINGRAY *n* flatfish capable of inflicting painful wounds
STINGRAYS > STINGRAY
STINGS > STING
STINGY *adj* mean or miserly ▷ *n* stinging nettle
STINK *n* strong unpleasant smell ▷ *vb* give off a strong unpleasant smell
STINKARD *n* smelly person
STINKARDS > STINKARD
STINKBUG *n* type of insect that releases an unpleasant odour
STINKBUGS > STINKBUG
STINKER *n* difficult or unpleasant person or thing
STINKEROO *n* bad or contemptible person or thing
STINKERS > STINKER
STINKHORN *n* type of fungus with an offensive odour
STINKIER > STINKY
STINKIEST > STINKY
STINKING > STINK
STINKINGS > STINK
STINKO *adj* drunk
STINKPOT *n* person or thing that stinks
STINKPOTS > STINKPOT
STINKS > STINK
STINKWEED *n* plant that has a disagreeable smell when bruised
STINKWOOD *n* any of various trees having offensive-smelling wood
STINKY *adj* having a foul smell
STINT *vb* be miserly with (something) ▷ *n* allotted amount of work
STINTED > STINT
STINTEDLY > STINT
STINTER > STINT
STINTERS > STINT
STINTIER > STINT
STINTIEST > STINT
STINTING > STINT
STINTINGS > STINT
STINTLESS > STINT
STINTS > STINT
STINTY > STINT
STIPA *n* variety of grass
STIPAS > STIPA
STIPE *n* stalk in plants that bears reproductive structures
STIPED *same as* > STIPITATE
STIPEL *n* small paired leaflike structure at the base of certain leaflets
STIPELS > STIPEL
STIPEND *n* regular allowance or salary, esp that paid to a clergyman
STIPENDS > STIPEND
STIPES *n* second maxillary segment in insects and crustaceans
STIPIFORM > STIPES
STIPITATE *adj* possessing or borne on the end of a stipe
STIPITES > STIPES
STIPPLE *vb* paint, draw, or engrave using dots ▷ *n* technique of stippling or a picture produced by or using stippling
STIPPLED > STIPPLE
STIPPLER > STIPPLE
STIPPLERS > STIPPLE
STIPPLES > STIPPLE
STIPPLING > STIPPLE
STIPULAR > STIPULE
STIPULARY > STIPULE
STIPULATE *vb* specify as a condition of an agreement ▷ *adj* (of a plant) having stipules
STIPULE *n* small paired usually leaflike outgrowth occurring at the base of a leaf or its stalk
STIPULED > STIPULE
STIPULES > STIPULE
STIR *vb* mix up (a liquid) by moving a spoon etc around in it ▷ *n* stirring
STIRABOUT *n* kind of porridge orginally made in Ireland
STIRE *same as* > STEER
STIRED > STIRE
STIRES > STIRE
STIRING > STIRE
STIRK *n* heifer of 6 to 12 months old
STIRKS > STIRK
STIRLESS > STIR
STIRP *same as* > STIRPS
STIRPES > STIRPS
STIRPS *n* line of descendants from an ancestor
STIRRA *same as* > SIRRA
STIRRABLE > STIR
STIRRAH *same as* > SIRRAH
STIRRAHS > STIRRAH
STIRRAS > STIRRA
STIRRE *obsolete form of* > STEER
STIRRED > STIR
STIRRER *n* person who deliberately causes trouble
STIRRERS > STIRRER
STIRRES > STIRRE
STIRRING > STIR
STIRRINGS > STIR
STIRRUP *n* metal loop attached to a saddle for supporting a rider's foot
STIRRUPS > STIRRUP
STIRS > STIR
STISHIE *same as* > STUSHIE
STISHIES > STISHIE
STITCH *n* link made by drawing thread through material with a needle ▷ *vb* sew
STITCHED > STITCH
STITCHER > STITCH
STITCHERS > STITCH
STITCHERY *n* needlework, esp modern embroidery
STITCHES > STITCH
STITCHING > STITCH
STITHIED > STITHY
STITHIES > STITHY
STITHY *n* forge or anvil ▷ *vb* forge on an anvil
STITHYING > STITHY
STIVE *vb* stifle
STIVED > STIVE
STIVER *n* former Dutch coin worth one twentieth of a guilder
STIVERS > STIVER
STIVES > STIVE
STIVIER > STIVY
STIVIEST > STIVY
STIVING > STIVE
STIVY *adj* stuffy
STOA *n* covered walk that has a colonnade on one or both sides, esp as used in ancient Greece
STOAE > STOA
STOAI > STOA
STOAS > STOA
STOAT *n* small mammal of the weasel family, with brown fur that turns white in winter
STOATS > STOAT
STOB *same as* > STAB
STOBBED > STOB
STOBBING > STOB
STOBS > STOB
STOCCADO *n* fencing thrust
STOCCADOS > STOCCADO
STOCCATA *same as* > STOCCADO
STOCCATAS > STOCCATA
STOCIOUS *same as* > STOTIOUS
STOCK *n* total amount of goods available for sale in a shop ▷ *adj* kept in stock, standard ▷ *vb* keep for sale or future use
STOCKADE *n* enclosure or barrier made of stakes ▷ *vb* surround with a stockade
STOCKADED > STOCKADE

STOCKADES > STOCKADE
STOCKAGE *n* livestock put to graze on crops
STOCKAGES > STOCKAGE
STOCKCAR *n* car that has been strengthened for a form of racing in which the cars often collide
STOCKCARS > STOCKCAR
STOCKED > STOCK
STOCKER > STOCK
STOCKERS > STOCK
STOCKFISH *n* fish, such as cod or haddock, cured by splitting and drying in the air
STOCKHORN *n* instrument made from animal horn
STOCKIER > STOCKY
STOCKIEST > STOCKY
STOCKILY > STOCKY
STOCKINET *n* machine-knitted elastic fabric
STOCKING *n* close-fitting covering for the foot and leg
STOCKINGS > STOCKING
STOCKISH *adj* stupid or dull
STOCKIST *n* dealer who stocks a particular product
STOCKISTS > STOCKIST
STOCKLESS > STOCK
STOCKLIST *n* list of items in stock
STOCKLOCK *n* lock that is enclosed in a wooden case
STOCKMAN *n* man engaged in the rearing or care of farm livestock, esp cattle
STOCKMEN > STOCKMAN
STOCKPILE *vb* store a large quantity of (something) for future use ▷ *n* accumulated store
STOCKPOT *n* pot in which stock for soup is made
STOCKPOTS > STOCKPOT
STOCKROOM *n* room in which a stock of goods is kept in a shop or factory
STOCKS *pl n* instrument of punishment consisting of a heavy wooden frame with holes in which the feet, hands, or head of an offender were locked
STOCKTAKE *vb* take stock
STOCKTOOK > STOCKTAKE
STOCKWORK *n* group of veins in mine
STOCKY *adj* (of a person) broad and sturdy
STOCKYARD *n* yard where farm animals are sold
STODGE *n* heavy starchy food ▷ *vb* stuff (oneself or another) with food
STODGED > STODGE
STODGER *n* dull person
STODGERS > STODGER
STODGES > STODGE
STODGIER > STODGY
STODGIEST > STODGY
STODGILY > STODGY
STODGING > STODGE
STODGY *adj* (of food) heavy and starchy
STOEP *n* verandah
STOEPS > STOEP
STOGEY *same as* > STOGY
STOGEYS > STOGEY
STOGIE *same as* > STOGY
STOGIES > STOGY
STOGY *n* any long cylindrical inexpensive cigar
STOIC *n* person who suffers hardship without showing his or her feelings ▷ *adj* suffering hardship without showing one's feelings
STOICAL *adj* suffering great difficulties without showing one's feelings
STOICALLY > STOICAL
STOICISM *n* indifference to pleasure and pain
STOICISMS > STOICISM
STOICS > STOIC
STOIT *vb* bounce
STOITED > STOIT
STOITER *vb* stagger
STOITERED > STOITER
STOITERS > STOITER
STOITING > STOIT
STOITS > STOIT
STOKE *vb* feed and tend (a fire or furnace)
STOKED *adj* very pleased
STOKEHOLD *n* hold for a ship's boilers
STOKEHOLE *n* hole in a furnace through which it is stoked
STOKER *n* person employed to tend a furnace on a ship or train powered by steam
STOKERS > STOKER
STOKES *n* cgs unit of kinematic viscosity
STOKESIA *n* American flowering plant
STOKESIAS > STOKESIA
STOKING > STOKE
STOKVEL *n* (in S Africa) informal savings pool or syndicate
STOKVELS > STOKVEL
STOLE *n* long scarf or shawl
STOLED *adj* wearing a stole
STOLEN > STEAL
STOLES > STOLE
STOLID *adj* showing little emotion or interest
STOLIDER > STOLID
STOLIDEST > STOLID
STOLIDITY > STOLID
STOLIDLY > STOLID
STOLLEN *n* rich sweet bread containing nuts, raisins, etc
STOLLENS > STOLLEN
STOLN > STEAL
STOLON *n* long horizontal stem that grows along the surface of the soil and propagates by producing roots and shoots at the nodes or tip
STOLONATE *adj* having a stolon
STOLONIC > STOLON
STOLONS > STOLON
STOLPORT *n* airport for short take-off aircraft
STOLPORTS > STOLPORT
STOMA *n* pore in a plant leaf that controls the passage of gases into and out of the plant
STOMACH *n* organ in the body which digests food ▷ *vb* put up with
STOMACHAL > STOMACH
STOMACHED > STOMACH
STOMACHER *n* decorative V-shaped panel of stiff material worn over the chest and stomach
STOMACHIC *adj* stimulating gastric activity ▷ *n* stomachic medicine
STOMACHS > STOMACH
STOMACHY *adj* having a large belly
STOMACK as in *have a stomack* (in E Africa) be pregnant
STOMACKS > STOMACK
STOMAL > STOMA
STOMAS > STOMA
STOMATA > STOMA
STOMATAL *adj* of, relating to, or possessing stomata or a stoma
STOMATE *n* opening on leaf through which water evaporates
STOMATES > STOMATE
STOMATIC *adj* of or relating to a mouth or mouthlike part
STOMATOUS *same as* > STOMATAL
STOMIA > STOMIUM
STOMIUM *n* part of the sporangium of ferns that ruptures to release the spores
STOMIUMS > STOMIUM
STOMODAEA > STOMODEUM
STOMODEA > STOMODEUM
STOMODEAL > STOMODEUM
STOMODEUM *n* oral cavity of a vertebrate embryo
STOMP *vb* tread heavily ▷ *n* rhythmic stamping jazz dance
STOMPED > STOMP
STOMPER *n* rock or jazz song with a particularly strong and danceable beat
STOMPERS > STOMPER
STOMPIE *n* cigarette butt
STOMPIES > STOMPIE
STOMPING > STOMP
STOMPS > STOMP
STONABLE > STONE
STOND *same as* > STAND
STONDS > STOND
STONE *n* material of which rocks are made ▷ *vb* throw stones at
STONEABLE > STONE
STONEBOAT *n* type of sleig[h] used for moving rocks from fields
STONECAST *n* short distance
STONECHAT *n* songbird tha[t] has black feathers and a reddish-brown breast
STONECROP *n* type of plan[t] with fleshy leaves and red yellow, or white flowers
STONED *adj* under the influence of alcohol or drugs
STONEFISH *n* venomous tropical marine scorpaenid fish
STONEFLY *n* any insect of the order *Plecoptera*, in which the larvae are aquatic
STONEHAND *n* type of compositor
STONELESS > STONE
STONELIKE > STONE
STONEN *adj* of stone
STONER *n* device for removing stones from fru[it]
STONERAG *n* type of lichen
STONERAGS > STONERAG
STONERAW *same as* > STONERAG
STONERAWS > STONERAW
STONERN *same as* > STONE[N]
STONERS > STONER
STONES > STONE
STONESHOT *n* stone's thro[w]
STONEWALL *vb* obstruct or hinder discussion
STONEWARE *n* hard kind of pottery fired at a very hig[h] temperature ▷ *adj* made of stoneware
STONEWASH *vb* wash with stones to give worn appearance
STONEWORK *n* part of a building made of stone
STONEWORT *n* any of various green algae whic[h] grow in brackish or fresh water
STONEY *same as* > STONY
STONG > STING
STONIED > STONY
STONIER > STONY
STONIES > STONY
STONIEST > STONY
STONILY > STONY
STONINESS > STONY
STONING > STONE
STONINGS > STONE
STONISH *same as* > ASTONISH
STONISHED > STONISH
STONISHES > STONISH
STONK *vb* bombard (soldiers, buildings, etc) with artillery ▷ *n* concentrated bombardment by artiller[y]

ONKED > STONK
ONKER *vb* destroy
ONKERED *adj* completely xhausted or beaten
ONKERS > STONKER
ONKING > STONK
ONKS > STONK
ONN *same as* > STUN
ONNE *same as* > STUN
ONNED > STONNE
ONNES > STONNE
ONNING > STONN
ONNS > STONN
ONY *adj* of or like stone vb astonish
ONYING > STONY
OOD > STAND
OODEN > STAND
OOGE *n* actor who feeds ines to a comedian or acts s the butt of his jokes *vb* act as a stooge
OOGED > STOOGE
OOGES > STOOGE
OOGING > STOOGE
OOK *n* number of sheaves et upright in a field to dry vith their heads together *vb* set up (sheaves) in tooks
OOKED > STOOK
OOKER > STOOK
OOKERS > STOOK
OOKIE *n* stucco
OOKIES > STOOKIE
OOKING > STOOK
OOKS > STOOK
OOL *n* chair without rms or back ▷ *vb* (of a lant) send up shoots from he base of the stem
OOLBALL *n* game esembling cricket played y girls
OOLED > STOOL
OOLIE *n* police informer
OOLIES > STOOLIE
OOLING > STOOL
OOLS > STOOL
OOP *vb* bend forward and ownward
OOPBALL *n* American treet game
OOPE *same as* > STOUP
OOPED > STOOP
OOPER > STOOP
OOPERS > STOOP
OOPES > STOOPE
OOPING > STOOP
OOPS > STOOP
OOR *same as* > STOUR
OORS > STOOR
OOSHIE *same* s > STUSHIE
OOSHIES > STOOSHIE
OP *vb* cease or cause o cease from doing something) ▷ *n* stopping r being stopped
OPBANK *n* embankment o prevent flooding
OPBANKS > STOPBANK
OPCOCK *n* valve to ontrol or stop the flow of fluid in a pipe
STOPCOCKS > STOPCOCK
STOPE *n* steplike excavation made in a mine to extract ore ▷ *vb* mine (ore, etc) by cutting stopes
STOPED > STOPE
STOPER *n* drill used in mining
STOPERS > STOPER
STOPES > STOPE
STOPGAP *n* temporary substitute
STOPGAPS > STOPGAP
STOPING *n* process by which country rock is broken up and engulfed by the upward movement of magma
STOPINGS > STOPING
STOPLESS > STOP
STOPLIGHT *n* red light on a traffic signal indicating that vehicles coming towards it should stop
STOPOFF *n* break in a journey
STOPOFFS > STOPOFF
STOPOVER *n* short break in a journey ▷ *vb* make a stopover
STOPOVERS > STOPOVER
STOPPABLE > STOP
STOPPAGE *n* act of stopping something or the state of being stopped
STOPPAGES > STOPPAGE
STOPPED > STOP
STOPPER *n* plug for closing a bottle etc ▷ *vb* close or fit with a stopper
STOPPERED > STOPPER
STOPPERS > STOPPER
STOPPING > STOP
STOPPINGS > STOP
STOPPLE *same as* > STOPPER
STOPPLED > STOPPLE
STOPPLES > STOPPLE
STOPPLING > STOPPLE
STOPS > STOP
STOPT > STOP
STOPWATCH *n* watch which can be stopped instantly for exact timing of a sporting event
STOPWORD *n* common word not used in computer search engines
STOPWORDS > STOPWORD
STORABLE > STORE
STORABLES > STORE
STORAGE *n* storing
STORAGES > STORAGE
STORAX *n* type of tree or shrub with drooping showy white flowers
STORAXES > STORAX
STORE *vb* collect and keep (things) for future use ▷ *n* shop
STORED > STORE
STOREMAN *n* man looking after storeroom
STOREMEN > STOREMAN
STORER > STORE
STOREROOM *n* room in which things are stored
STORERS > STORE
STORES *pl n* supply or stock of food and other essentials for a journey
STORESHIP *n* ship carrying naval stores
STOREWIDE *adj* throughout stores
STOREY *n* floor or level of a building
STOREYED *adj* having a storey or storeys
STOREYS > STOREY
STORGE *n* affection
STORGES > STORGE
STORIATED *adj* decorated with flowers or animals
STORIED > STORY
STORIES > STORY
STORIETTE *n* short story
STORING > STORE
STORK *n* large wading bird
STORKS > STORK
STORM *n* violent weather with wind, rain, or snow ▷ *vb* attack or capture (a place) suddenly
STORMBIRD *n* petrel
STORMED > STORM
STORMER *n* outstanding example of its kind
STORMERS > STORMER
STORMFUL > STORM
STORMIER > STORMY
STORMIEST > STORMY
STORMILY > STORMY
STORMING *adj* characterized by or displaying dynamism, speed, and energy
STORMINGS > STORM
STORMLESS > STORM
STORMLIKE > STORM
STORMS > STORM
STORMY *adj* characterized by storms
STORNELLI > STORNELLO
STORNELLO *n* type of Italian poem
STORY *n* narration of a chain of events ▷ *vb* decorate with scenes from history
STORYBOOK *n* book containing stories for children ▷ *adj* better or happier than in real life
STORYETTE *n* short story
STORYING > STORY
STORYINGS > STORY
STORYLINE *n* plot of a book, film, play, etc
STOSS *adj* (of the side of a hill) facing the onward flow of a glacier ▷ *n* hillside facing glacier flow
STOSSES > STOSS
STOT *n* bullock ▷ *vb* bounce or cause to bounce
STOTIN *n* monetary unit of Slovenia, worth one hundredth of a tolar
STOTINKA *n* monetary unit of Bulgaria, worth one hundredth of a lev
STOTINKI > STOTINKA
STOTINOV > STOTIN
STOTINS > STOTIN
STOTIOUS *adj* drunk
STOTS > STOT
STOTT *same as* > STOT
STOTTED > STOT
STOTTER *same as* > STOT
STOTTERED > STOTTER
STOTTERS > STOTTER
STOTTIE *n* wedge of bread cut from a flat round loaf that has been split and filled with meat, cheese, etc
STOTTIES > STOTTIE
STOTTING > STOT
STOTTS > STOTT
STOUN *same as* > STUN
STOUND *n* short while ▷ *vb* ache
STOUNDED > STOUND
STOUNDING > STOUND
STOUNDS > STOUND
STOUNING > STOUN
STOUNS > STOUN
STOUP *n* small basin for holy water
STOUPS > STOUP
STOUR *n* turmoil or conflict
STOURE *same as* > STOUR
STOURES > STOURE
STOURIE *same as* > STOURY
STOURIER > STOURY
STOURIEST > STOURY
STOURS > STOUR
STOURY *adj* dusty
STOUSH *vb* hit or punch (someone) ▷ *n* fighting or violence
STOUSHED > STOUSH
STOUSHES > STOUSH
STOUSHIE *same as* > STUSHIE
STOUSHIES > STOUSHIE
STOUSHING > STOUSH
STOUT *adj* fat ▷ *n* strong dark beer
STOUTEN *vb* make or become stout
STOUTENED > STOUTEN
STOUTENS > STOUTEN
STOUTER > STOUT
STOUTEST > STOUT
STOUTH *n* Scots word meaning theft
STOUTHS > STOUTH
STOUTISH > STOUT
STOUTLY > STOUT
STOUTNESS > STOUT
STOUTS > STOUT
STOVAINE *n* anaesthetic drug
STOVAINES > STOVAINE
STOVE *n* apparatus for cooking or heating ▷ *vb* process (ceramics, metalwork, etc) by heating in a stove
STOVED > STOVE

STOVEPIPE *n* pipe that takes fumes and smoke away from a stove
STOVER *n* fodder
STOVERS > STOVER
STOVES > STOVE
STOVETOP *US word for* > HOB
STOVETOPS > STOVETOP
STOVIES *pl n* potatoes stewed with onions
STOVING > STOVE
STOVINGS > STOVE
STOW *vb* pack or store
STOWABLE > STOW
STOWAGE *n* space or charge for stowing goods
STOWAGES > STOWAGE
STOWAWAY *n* person who hides on a ship or aircraft in order to travel free ▷ *vb* travel in such a way
STOWAWAYS > STOWAWAY
STOWDOWN *n* packing of ship's hold
STOWDOWNS > STOWDOWN
STOWED > STOW
STOWER > STOW
STOWERS > STOW
STOWING > STOW
STOWINGS > STOW
STOWLINS *adv* stealthily
STOWN > STEAL
STOWND *same as* > STOUND
STOWNDED > STOWND
STOWNDING > STOWND
STOWNDS > STOWND
STOWNLINS *same as* > STOWLINS
STOWP *same as* > STOUP
STOWPS > STOWP
STOWRE *same as* > STOUR
STOWRES > STOWRE
STOWS > STOW
STRABISM *n* abnormal alignment of one or both eyes
STRABISMS > STRABISM
STRAD *n* violin made by Stradivarius
STRADDLE *vb* have one leg or part on each side of (something) ▷ *n* act or position of straddling
STRADDLED > STRADDLE
STRADDLER > STRADDLE
STRADDLES > STRADDLE
STRADIOT *n* Venetian cavalryman
STRADIOTS > STRADIOT
STRADS > STRAD
STRAE *Scots form of* > STRAW
STRAES > STRAE
STRAFE *vb* attack (an enemy) with machine guns from the air ▷ *n* act or instance of strafing
STRAFED > STRAFE
STRAFER > STRAFE
STRAFERS > STRAFE
STRAFES > STRAFE
STRAFF *same as* > STRAFE
STRAFFED > STRAFF
STRAFFING > STRAFF
STRAFFS > STRAFF
STRAFING > STRAFE
STRAG *n* straggler
STRAGGLE *vb* go or spread in a rambling or irregular way
STRAGGLED > STRAGGLE
STRAGGLER > STRAGGLE
STRAGGLES > STRAGGLE
STRAGGLY > STRAGGLE
STRAGS > STRAG
STRAICHT *Scots word for* > STRAIGHT
STRAIGHT *adj* not curved or crooked ▷ *adv* in a straight line ▷ *n* straight part, esp of a racetrack ▷ *vb* tighten
STRAIGHTS > STRAIGHT
STRAIK *Scots word for* > STROKE
STRAIKED > STRAIK
STRAIKING > STRAIK
STRAIKS > STRAIK
STRAIN *vb* subject to mental tension ▷ *n* tension or tiredness
STRAINED *adj* not natural, forced
STRAINER *n* sieve
STRAINERS > STRAINER
STRAINING > STRAIN
STRAINS > STRAIN
STRAINT *n* pressure
STRAINTS > STRAINT
STRAIT *n* narrow channel connecting two areas of sea ▷ *adj* (of spaces, etc) affording little room ▷ *vb* tighten
STRAITED > STRAIT
STRAITEN *vb* embarrass or distress, esp financially
STRAITENS > STRAITEN
STRAITER > STRAIT
STRAITEST > STRAIT
STRAITING > STRAIT
STRAITLY > STRAIT
STRAITS > STRAIT
STRAKE *n* curved metal plate forming part of the metal rim on a wooden wheel
STRAKED *adj* having a strake
STRAKES > STRAKE
STRAMACON *same as* > STRAMAZON
STRAMASH *n* uproar ▷ *vb* destroy
STRAMAZON *n* downward fencing stroke
STRAMMEL *same as* > STRUMMEL
STRAMMELS > STRAMMEL
STRAMONY *n* former asthma medicine made from the dried leaves and flowers of the thorn apple
STRAMP *Scots variant of* > TRAMP
STRAMPED > STRAMP
STRAMPING > STRAMP
STRAMPS > STRAMP
STRAND *vb* run aground ▷ *n* shore
STRANDED > STRAND
STRANDER > STRAND
STRANDERS > STRAND
STRANDING > STRAND
STRANDS > STRAND
STRANG *dialect variant of* > STRONG
STRANGE *adj* odd or unusual ▷ *n* odd or unfamiliar person or thing
STRANGELY > STRANGE
STRANGER *n* person who is not known or is new to a place or experience
STRANGERS > STRANGER
STRANGES > STRANGE
STRANGEST > STRANGE
STRANGLE *vb* kill by squeezing the throat
STRANGLED > STRANGLE
STRANGLER *n* person or thing that strangles
STRANGLES *n* acute bacterial disease of horses
STRANGURY *n* painful excretion of urine caused by muscular spasms of the urinary tract
STRAP *n* strip of flexible material for lifting or holding in place ▷ *vb* fasten with a strap or straps
STRAPHANG *vb* travel standing on public transport
STRAPHUNG > STRAPHANG
STRAPLESS *adj* (of women's clothes) without straps over the shoulders
STRAPLINE *n* subheading in a newspaper or magazine article or in any advertisement
STRAPPADO *n* system of torture in which a victim was hoisted by a rope tied to his wrists and then allowed to drop until his fall was suddenly checked by the rope ▷ *vb* subject to strappado
STRAPPED > STRAP
STRAPPER *n* strapping person
STRAPPERS > STRAPPER
STRAPPIER > STRAPPY
STRAPPING > STRAP
STRAPPY *adj* having straps
STRAPS > STRAP
STRAPWORT *n* plant with leaves like straps
STRASS *another word for* > PASTE
STRASSES > STRASS
STRATA > STRATUM
STRATAGEM *n* clever plan, trick
STRATAL > STRATUM
STRATAS > STRATUM
STRATEGIC *adj* advantageous
STRATEGY *n* overall plan
STRATH *n* flat river valley
STRATHS > STRATH
STRATI > STRATUS
STRATIFY *vb* form or be formed in layers or strata
STRATONIC *adj* of army
STRATOSE *adj* formed in strata
STRATOUS *adj* of stratus
STRATUM *n* layer, esp of ro
STRATUMS > STRATUM
STRATUS *n* grey layer clou
STRAUCHT *Scots word for* > STRETCH
STRAUCHTS > STRAUCHT
STRAUGHT *same as* > STRAUCHT
STRAUGHTS > STRAUGHT
STRAUNGE *same as* > STRANGE
STRAVAGE *same as* > STRAVAIG
STRAVAGED > STRAVAGE
STRAVAGES > STRAVAGE
STRAVAIG *vb* wander aimlessly
STRAVAIGS > STRAVAIG
STRAW *n* dried stalks of grain ▷ *vb* spread aroun
STRAWED > STRAW
STRAWEN *adj* of straw
STRAWHAT *adj* of summer dramatic performance
STRAWIER > STRAWY
STRAWIEST > STRAWY
STRAWING > STRAW
STRAWLESS > STRAW
STRAWLIKE > STRAW
STRAWN > STREW
STRAWS > STRAW
STRAWWORM *n* aquatic larv of a caddis fly
STRAWY *adj* containing straw, or like straw in colour or texture
STRAY *vb* wander ▷ *adj* having strayed ▷ *n* stray animal
STRAYED > STRAY
STRAYER > STRAY
STRAYERS > STRAY
STRAYING > STRAY
STRAYINGS > STRAY
STRAYLING *n* stray
STRAYS > STRAY
STRAYVE *vb* wander aimlessly
STRAYVED > STRAYVE
STRAYVES > STRAYVE
STRAYVING > STRAYVE
STREAK *n* long band of contrasting colour or substance ▷ *vb* mark wi streaks
STREAKED > STREAK
STREAKER > STREAK
STREAKERS > STREAK
STREAKIER > STREAKY
STREAKILY > STREAKY
STREAKING > STREAK
STREAKS > STREAK
STREAKY *adj* marked with streaks
STREAM *n* small river ▷ *vb*

ow steadily
REAMBED *n* bottom of tream
REAMED > STREAM
REAMER *n* strip of oloured paper that nrolls when tossed
REAMERS > STREAMER
REAMIER > STREAMY
REAMING > STREAM
REAMLET > STREAM
REAMS > STREAM
REAMY *adj* (of an area, and, etc) having many treams
REEK *Scots word* or > STRETCH
REEKED > STREEK
REEKER > STREEK
REEKERS > STREEK
REEKING > STREEK
REEKS > STREEK
REEL *n* slovenly woman vb trail
REELED > STREEL
REELING > STREEL
REELS > STREEL
REET *n* public road, usu ined with buildings ▷ *vb* ay out a street or streets
REETAGE *n* toll charged or using a street
REETBOY *n* boy living on he street
REETCAR *n* tram
REETED > STREET
REETFUL *n* amount of eople or things street can old
REETIER > STREETY
REETING > STREET
REETS > STREET
REETY *adj* of streets
REIGHT *same as* > STRAIT
REIGHTS > STREIGHT
REIGNE *same as* > STRAIN
REIGNED > STREIGNE
REIGNES > STREIGNE
RELITZ *n* former ussian soldier
RELITZI > STRELITZ
RENE *same as* > STRAIN
RENES > STRENE
RENGTH *n* quality of eing strong
RENGTHS > STRENGTH
RENUITY > STRENUOUS
RENUOUS *adj* requiring reat energy or effort
REP *n* streptococcus
REPENT *adj* noisy
REPS > STREP
RESS *n* tension or strain vb emphasize
RESSED > STRESS
RESSES > STRESS
RESSFUL > STRESS
RESSING > STRESS
RESSOR *n* event, xperience, etc, that auses stress
RESSORS > STRESSOR
RETCH *vb* extend or be xtended ▷ *n* stretching

STRETCHED > STRETCH
STRETCHER *n* frame covered with canvas, on which an injured person is carried ▷ *vb* transport (a sick or injured person) on a stretcher
STRETCHES > STRETCH
STRETCHY *adj* characterized by elasticity
STRETTA *same as* > STRETTO
STRETTAS > STRETTA
STRETTE > STRETTA
STRETTI > STRETTO
STRETTO *n* (in a fugue) the close overlapping of two parts or voices
STRETTOS > STRETTO
STREUSEL *n* crumbly topping for rich pastries
STREUSELS > STREUSEL
STREW *vb* scatter (things) over a surface
STREWAGE > STREW
STREWAGES > STREW
STREWED > STREW
STREWER > STREW
STREWERS > STREW
STREWING > STREW
STREWINGS > STREW
STREWMENT *n* strewing
STREWN > STREW
STREWS > STREW
STREWTH *interj* expression of surprise or alarm
STRIA *n* scratch or groove on the surface of a rock crystal
STRIAE > STRIA
STRIATA > STRIATUM
STRIATE *adj* marked with striae ▷ *vb* mark with striae
STRIATED *adj* having a pattern of scratches or grooves
STRIATES > STRIATE
STRIATING > STRIATE
STRIATION *same as* > STRIA
STRIATUM *n* part of brain
STRIATUMS > STRIATUM
STRIATURE *n* way something is striated
STRICH *n* screech owl
STRICHES > STRICH
STRICK *n* any bast fibres preparatory to being made into slivers
STRICKEN *adj* seriously affected by disease, grief, pain, etc
STRICKLE *n* board used for sweeping off excess material in a container ▷ *vb* level, form, or sharpen with a strickle
STRICKLED > STRICKLE
STRICKLES > STRICKLE
STRICKS > STRICK
STRICT *adj* stern or severe
STRICTER > STRICT
STRICTEST > STRICT
STRICTION *n* act of restricting

STRICTISH > STRICT
STRICTLY > STRICT
STRICTURE *n* severe criticism
STRIDDEN > STRIDE
STRIDDLE *same as* > STRADDLE
STRIDDLED > STRIDDLE
STRIDDLES > STRIDDLE
STRIDE *vb* walk with long steps ▷ *n* long step
STRIDENCE > STRIDENT
STRIDENCY > STRIDENT
STRIDENT *adj* loud and harsh
STRIDER > STRIDE
STRIDERS > STRIDE
STRIDES > STRIDE
STRIDING > STRIDE
STRIDLING *adv* astride
STRIDOR *n* high-pitched whistling sound made during respiration
STRIDORS > STRIDOR
STRIFE *n* conflict, quarrelling
STRIFEFUL > STRIFE
STRIFES > STRIFE
STRIFT *n* struggle
STRIFTS > STRIFT
STRIG *vb* remove stalk from
STRIGA *same as* > STRIA
STRIGAE > STRIGA
STRIGATE *adj* streaked
STRIGGED > STRIG
STRIGGING > STRIG
STRIGIL *n* curved blade used by the ancient Romans and Greeks to scrape the body after bathing
STRIGILS > STRIGIL
STRIGINE *adj* of or like owl
STRIGOSE *adj* bearing stiff hairs or bristles
STRIGS > STRIG
STRIKE *vb* cease work as a protest ▷ *n* stoppage of work as a protest
STRIKEOUT *n* dismissal in baseball due to three successive failures to hit the ball
STRIKER *n* striking worker
STRIKERS > STRIKER
STRIKES > STRIKE
STRIKING > STRIKE
STRIKINGS > STRIKE
STRING *n* thin cord used for tying ▷ *vb* provide with a string or strings
STRINGED *adj* (of a musical instrument) having strings that are plucked or played with a bow
STRINGENT *adj* strictly controlled or enforced
STRINGER *n* journalist retained by a newspaper to cover a particular town or area
STRINGERS > STRINGER
STRINGIER > STRINGY

STRINGILY > STRINGY
STRINGING > STRING
STRINGS > STRING
STRINGY *adj* like string
STRINKLE *Scots variant of* > SPRINKLE
STRINKLED > STRINKLE
STRINKLES > STRINKLE
STRIP *vb* take (the covering or clothes) off ▷ *n* act of stripping
STRIPE *n* long narrow band of contrasting colour or substance ▷ *vb* mark (something) with stripes
STRIPED *adj* marked or decorated with stripes
STRIPER *n* officer who has a stripe or stripes on his uniform, esp in the navy
STRIPERS > STRIPER
STRIPES > STRIPE
STRIPEY *same as* > STRIPY
STRIPIER > STRIPY
STRIPIEST > STRIPY
STRIPING > STRIPE
STRIPINGS > STRIPE
STRIPLING *n* youth
STRIPPED > STRIP
STRIPPER *n* person who performs a striptease
STRIPPERS > STRIPPER
STRIPPING > STRIP
STRIPS > STRIP
STRIPT > STRIP
STRIPY *adj* marked by or with stripes
STRIVE *vb* make a great effort
STRIVED > STRIVE
STRIVEN > STRIVE
STRIVER > STRIVE
STRIVERS > STRIVE
STRIVES > STRIVE
STRIVING > STRIVE
STRIVINGS > STRIVE
STROAM *vb* wander
STROAMED > STROAM
STROAMING > STROAM
STROAMS > STROAM
STROBE *n* high intensity flashing beam of light ▷ *vb* give the appearance of slow motion by using a strobe
STROBED > STROBE
STROBES > STROBE
STROBIC *adj* spinning or appearing to spin
STROBIL *n* scaly multiple fruit
STROBILA *n* body of a tapeworm, consisting of a string of similar segments
STROBILAE > STROBILA
STROBILAR > STROBILA
STROBILE *same as* > STROBILUS
STROBILES > STROBILE
STROBILI > STROBILUS
STROBILS > STROBIL
STROBILUS *technical name for* > CONE
STROBING > STROBE

STROBINGS > STROBE
STRODDLE *same as* > STRADDLE
STRODDLED > STRODDLE
STRODDLES > STRODDLE
STRODE > STRIDE
STRODLE *same as* > STRADDLE
STRODLED > STRODLE
STRODLES > STRODLE
STRODLING > STRODLE
STROKE *vb* touch or caress lightly with the hand ▷ *n* light touch or caress with the hand
STROKED > STROKE
STROKEN > STRIKE
STROKER > STROKE
STROKERS > STROKE
STROKES > STROKE
STROKING > STROKE
STROKINGS > STROKE
STROLL *vb* walk in a leisurely manner ▷ *n* leisurely walk
STROLLED > STROLL
STROLLER *n* chair-shaped carriage for a baby
STROLLERS > STROLLER
STROLLING > STROLL
STROLLS > STROLL
STROMA *n* gel-like matrix of chloroplasts and certain cells
STROMAL > STROMA
STROMATA > STROMA
STROMATIC > STROMA
STROMB *n* shellfish like a whelk
STROMBS > STROMB
STROMBUS *same as* > STROMB
STROND *same as* > STRAND
STRONDS > STROND
STRONG *adj* having physical power
STRONGARM *adj* involving physical force
STRONGBOX *n* box in which valuables are locked for safety
STRONGER > STRONG
STRONGEST > STRONG
STRONGISH > STRONG
STRONGLY > STRONG
STRONGMAN *n* performer, esp one in a circus, who performs feats of strength
STRONGMEN > STRONGMAN
STRONGYL *same as* > STRONGYLE
STRONGYLE *n* type of parasitic worm chiefly occurring in the intestines of horses
STRONGYLS > STRONGYL
STRONTIA > STRONTIUM
STRONTIAN *n* type of white mineral
STRONTIAS > STRONTIA
STRONTIC > STRONTIUM
STRONTIUM *n* silvery-white metallic element
STROOK > STRIKE
STROOKE *n* stroke
STROOKEN *same as* > STRICKEN
STROOKES > STROOKE
STROP *n* leather strap for sharpening razors ▷ *vb* sharpen (a razor, etc) on a strop
STROPHE *n* first of two movements made by a chorus during the performance of a choral ode
STROPHES > STROPHE
STROPHIC *adj* of, relating to, or employing a strophe or strophes
STROPHOID *n* type of curve on graph
STROPHULI *pl n* skin inflammations seen primarily on small children
STROPPED > STROP
STROPPER > STROP
STROPPERS > STROP
STROPPIER > STROPPY
STROPPILY > STROPPY
STROPPING > STROP
STROPPY *adj* angry or awkward
STROPS > STROP
STROSSERS *same as* > TROUSERS
STROUD *n* coarse woollen fabric
STROUDING *n* woolly material for making strouds
STROUDS > STROUD
STROUP *Scots word for* > SPOUT
STROUPACH *n* cup of tea
STROUPAN *same as* > STROUPACH
STROUPANS > STROUPAN
STROUPS > STROUP
STROUT *vb* bulge
STROUTED > STROUT
STROUTING > STROUT
STROUTS > STROUT
STROVE > STRIVE
STROW *archaic variant of* > STREW
STROWED > STROW
STROWER > STROW
STROWERS > STROW
STROWING > STROW
STROWINGS > STROW
STROWN > STROW
STROWS > STROW
STROY *archaic variant of* > DESTROY
STROYED > STROY
STROYER > STROY
STROYERS > STROY
STROYING > STROY
STROYS > STROY
STRUCK > STRIKE
STRUCKEN *same as* > STRICKEN
STRUCTURE *n* complex construction ▷ *vb* give a structure to
STRUDEL *n* thin sheet of filled dough rolled up and baked, usu with an apple filling
STRUDELS > STRUDEL
STRUGGLE *vb* work, strive, or make one's way with difficulty ▷ *n* striving
STRUGGLED > STRUGGLE
STRUGGLER > STRUGGLE
STRUGGLES > STRUGGLE
STRUM *vb* play (a guitar or banjo) by sweeping the thumb or a plectrum across the strings
STRUMA *n* abnormal enlargement of the thyroid gland
STRUMAE > STRUMA
STRUMAS > STRUMA
STRUMATIC > STRUMA
STRUMITIS *n* inflammation of thyroid gland
STRUMMED > STRUM
STRUMMEL *n* straw
STRUMMELS > STRUMMEL
STRUMMER > STRUM
STRUMMERS > STRUM
STRUMMING > STRUM
STRUMOSE > STRUMA
STRUMOUS > STRUMA
STRUMPET *n* prostitute ▷ *vb* turn into a strumpet
STRUMPETS > STRUMPET
STRUMS > STRUM
STRUNG > STRING
STRUNT *Scots word for* > STRUT
STRUNTED > STRUNT
STRUNTING > STRUNT
STRUNTS > STRUNT
STRUT *vb* walk pompously, swagger ▷ *n* bar supporting a structure
STRUTS > STRUT
STRUTTED > STRUT
STRUTTER > STRUT
STRUTTERS > STRUT
STRUTTING > STRUT
STRYCHNIA *n* strychnine
STRYCHNIC *adj* of, relating to, or derived from strychnine
STUB *n* short piece left after use ▷ *vb* strike (the toe) painfully against an object
STUBBED > STUB
STUBBIE *same as* > STUBBY
STUBBIER > STUBBY
STUBBIES > STUBBY
STUBBIEST > STUBBY
STUBBILY > STUBBY
STUBBING > STUB
STUBBLE *n* short stalks of grain left in a field after reaping
STUBBLED *adj* having the stubs of stalks left after a crop has been cut and harvested
STUBBLES > STUBBLE
STUBBLIER > STUBBLE
STUBBLY > STUBBLE
STUBBORN *adj* refusing to agree or give in ▷ *vb* ma stubborn
STUBBORNS > STUBBORN
STUBBY *adj* short and bro ▷ *n* small bottle of beer
STUBS > STUB
STUCCO *n* plaster used for coating or decorating walls ▷ *vb* apply stucco t (a building)
STUCCOED > STUCCO
STUCCOER > STUCCO
STUCCOERS > STUCCO
STUCCOES > STUCCO
STUCCOING > STUCCO
STUCCOS > STUCCO
STUCK *n* thrust
STUCKS > STUCK
STUD *n* small piece of met attached to a surface for decoration ▷ *vb* set wit studs
STUDBOOK *n* written record of the pedigree of a purebred stock, esp of racehorses
STUDBOOKS > STUDBOOK
STUDDED > STUD
STUDDEN > STAND
STUDDIE *Scots word for* > ANVIL
STUDDIES > STUDDIE
STUDDING > STUD
STUDDINGS > STUD
STUDDLE *n* post
STUDDLES > STUDDLE
STUDENT *n* person who studies a subject, esp at university
STUDENTRY *n* body of students
STUDENTS > STUDENT
STUDENTY *adj* informal, sometimes derogatory term denoting the characteristics believed typical of an undergraduate student
STUDFARM *n* farm where horses are bred
STUDFARMS > STUDFARM
STUDFISH *n* American minnow
STUDHORSE *another word for* > STALLION
STUDIED *adj* carefully practised
STUDIEDLY > STUDIED
STUDIER > STUDY
STUDIERS > STUDY
STUDIES > STUDY
STUDIO *n* workroom of a artist or photographer
STUDIOS > STUDIO
STUDIOUS *adj* fond of stu
STUDLIER > STUDLY
STUDLIEST > STUDLY
STUDLY *adj* strong and virile
STUDS > STUD
STUDWORK *n* work decorated with studs
STUDWORKS > STUDWORK
STUDY *vb* be engaged in

earning (a subject) ▷ *n* ct or process of studying
UDYING > STUDY
UFF *n* substance or naterial ▷ *vb* pack, cram, r fill completely
UFFED > STUFF
UFFER > STUFF
UFFERS > STUFF
UFFIER > STUFFY
UFFIEST > STUFFY
UFFILY > STUFFY
UFFING *n* seasoned nixture with which food s stuffed
UFFINGS > STUFFING
UFFLESS > STUFF
UFFS > STUFF
UFFY *adj* lacking fresh air
UGGIER > STUGGY
UGGIEST > STUGGY
UGGY *adj* stout
UIVER *same as* > STIVER
UIVERS > STUIVER
UKKEND *adj* South frican slang for broken or vrecked
ULL *n* timber prop or latform in a stope
ULLS > STULL
ULM *n* shaft
ULMS > STULM
ULTIFY *vb* dull (the nind) by boring routine
UM *n* partly fermented vine added to fermented vine as a preservative *vb* preserve (wine) by dding stum
UMBLE *vb* trip and nearly all ▷ *n* stumbling
UMBLED > STUMBLE
UMBLER > STUMBLE
UMBLERS > STUMBLE
UMBLES > STUMBLE
UMBLIER > STUMBLY
UMBLING > STUMBLE
UMBLY *adj* tending to tumble
UMER *n* forgery or cheat
UMERS > STUMER
UMM *same as* > SHTOOM
UMMED > STUM
UMMEL *n* bowl of pipe
UMMELS > STUMMEL
UMMING > STUM
UMP *n* base of a tree left vhen the main trunk has een cut away ▷ *vb* baffle
UMPAGE *n* standing imber or its value
UMPAGES > STUMPAGE
UMPED > STUMP
UMPER > STUMP
UMPERS > STUMP
UMPIER > STUMPY
UMPIES > STUMPY
UMPIEST > STUMPY
UMPILY > STUMPY
UMPING > STUMP
UMPS > STUMP
UMPWORK *n* type of mbroidery featuring aised figures, padded with cotton wool or hair
STUMPY *adj* short and thick ▷ *n* stumpy thing
STUMS > STUM
STUN *vb* shock or overwhelm ▷ *n* state or effect of being stunned
STUNG > STING
STUNK > STINK
STUNKARD *adj* sulky
STUNNED > STUN
STUNNER *n* beautiful person or thing
STUNNERS > STUNNER
STUNNING > STUN
STUNNINGS > STUN
STUNS > STUN
STUNSAIL *n* type of light auxiliary sail
STUNSAILS > STUNSAIL
STUNT *vb* prevent or impede the growth of ▷ *n* acrobatic or dangerous action
STUNTED > STUNT
STUNTING > STUNT
STUNTMAN *n* person who performs dangerous acts in a film, etc in place of an actor
STUNTMEN > STUNTMAN
STUNTS > STUNT
STUPA *n* domed edifice housing Buddhist or Jain relics
STUPAS > STUPA
STUPE *n* hot damp cloth applied to the body to relieve pain ▷ *vb* treat with a stupe
STUPED > STUPE
STUPEFIED > STUPEFY
STUPEFIER > STUPEFY
STUPEFIES > STUPEFY
STUPEFY *vb* make insensitive or lethargic
STUPENT *adj* astonished
STUPES > STUPE
STUPID *adj* lacking intelligence ▷ *n* stupid person
STUPIDER > STUPID
STUPIDEST > STUPID
STUPIDITY *n* quality or state of being stupid
STUPIDLY > STUPID
STUPIDS > STUPID
STUPING > STUPE
STUPOR *n* dazed or unconscious state
STUPOROUS > STUPOR
STUPORS > STUPOR
STUPRATE *vb* ravish
STUPRATED > STUPRATE
STUPRATES > STUPRATE
STURDIED > STURDY
STURDIER > STURDY
STURDIES > STURDY
STURDIEST > STURDY
STURDILY > STURDY
STURDY *adj* healthy and robust ▷ *n* disease of sheep
STURE *same as* > STOOR
STURGEON *n* fish from which caviar is obtained
STURGEONS > STURGEON
STURMER *n* type of eating apple with pale green skin
STURMERS > STURMER
STURNINE > STURNUS
STURNOID > STURNUS
STURNUS *n* bird of starling family
STURNUSES > STURNUS
STURT *vb* bother
STURTED > STURT
STURTING > STURT
STURTS > STURT
STUSHIE *n* commotion, rumpus, or row
STUSHIES > STUSHIE
STUTTER *vb* speak with repetition of initial consonants ▷ *n* tendency to stutter
STUTTERED > STUTTER
STUTTERER > STUTTER
STUTTERS > STUTTER
STY *vb* climb
STYE *n* inflammation at the base of an eyelash
STYED > STYE
STYES > STYE
STYGIAN *adj* dark, gloomy, or hellish
STYING > STY
STYLAR > STYLUS
STYLATE *adj* having style
STYLE *n* shape or design ▷ *vb* shape or design
STYLEBOOK *n* book containing rules of punctuation, etc, for the use of writers, editors, and printers
STYLED > STYLE
STYLELESS > STYLE
STYLER > STYLE
STYLERS > STYLE
STYLES > STYLE
STYLET *n* wire for insertion into a flexible cannula or catheter to maintain its rigidity during passage
STYLETS > STYLET
STYLI > STYLUS
STYLIE *adj* fashion-conscious
STYLIER > STYLIE
STYLIEST > STYLIE
STYLIFORM *adj* shaped like a stylus or bristle
STYLING > STYLE
STYLINGS > STYLE
STYLISE *same as* > STYLIZE
STYLISED > STYLISE
STYLISER > STYLISE
STYLISERS > STYLISE
STYLISES > STYLISE
STYLISH *adj* smart, elegant, and fashionable
STYLISHLY > STYLISH
STYLISING > STYLISE
STYLIST *n* hairdresser
STYLISTIC *adj* of literary or artistic style
STYLISTS > STYLIST
STYLITE *n* one of a class of recluses who in ancient times lived on the top of high pillars
STYLITES > STYLITE
STYLITIC > STYLITE
STYLITISM > STYLITE
STYLIZE *vb* cause to conform to an established stylistic form
STYLIZED > STYLIZE
STYLIZER > STYLIZE
STYLIZERS > STYLIZE
STYLIZES > STYLIZE
STYLIZING > STYLIZE
STYLO *n* type of fountain pen
STYLOBATE *n* continuous horizontal course of masonry that supports a colonnade
STYLOID *adj* resembling a stylus ▷ *n* spiny growth
STYLOIDS > STYLOID
STYLOLITE *n* any of the small striated columnar or irregular structures within the strata of some limestones
STYLOPES > STYLOPS
STYLOPISE *same as* > STYLOPIZE
STYLOPIZE *vb* (of a stylops) to parasitize (a host)
STYLOPS *n* type of insect that lives as a parasite in other insects
STYLOS > STYLO
STYLUS *n* needle-like device on a record player that rests in the groove of the record and picks up the sound signals
STYLUSES > STYLUS
STYME *vb* peer
STYMED > STYME
STYMES > STYME
STYMIE *vb* hinder or thwart
STYMIED > STYMY
STYMIEING > STYMIE
STYMIES > STYMY
STYMING > STYME
STYMY *same as* > STYMIE
STYMYING > STYMY
STYPSIS *n* action, application, or use of a styptic
STYPSISES > STYPSIS
STYPTIC *adj* (drug) used to stop bleeding ▷ *n* styptic drug
STYPTICAL > STYPTIC
STYPTICS > STYPTIC
STYRAX *n* type of tropical or subtropical tree
STYRAXES > STYRAX
STYRE *same as* > STIR
STYRED > STYRE
STYRENE *n* colourless oily volatile flammable water-insoluble liquid
STYRENES > STYRENE
STYRES > STYRE
STYRING > STYRE

STYROFOAM *n* tradename for a light expanded polystyrene plastic
STYTE *vb* bounce
STYTED > STYTE
STYTES > STYTE
STYTING > STYTE
SUABILITY > SUABLE
SUABLE *adj* liable to be sued in a court
SUABLY > SUABLE
SUASIBLE > SUASION
SUASION *n* persuasion
SUASIONS > SUASION
SUASIVE > SUASION
SUASIVELY > SUASION
SUASORY > SUASION
SUAVE *adj* smooth and sophisticated in manner
SUAVELY > SUAVE
SUAVENESS > SUAVE
SUAVER > SUAVE
SUAVEST > SUAVE
SUAVITIES > SUAVE
SUAVITY > SUAVE
SUB *n* subeditor ▷ *vb* act as a substitute
SUBA *n* shepherd's cloak
SUBABBOT *n* abbot who is subordinate to another abbot
SUBABBOTS > SUBABBOT
SUBACID *adj* (esp of some fruits) moderately acid or sour
SUBACIDLY > SUBACID
SUBACRID *adj* slightly acrid
SUBACT *vb* subdue
SUBACTED > SUBACT
SUBACTING > SUBACT
SUBACTION > SUBACT
SUBACTS > SUBACT
SUBACUTE *adj* intermediate between acute and chronic
SUBADAR *n* (formerly) the chief native officer of a company of Indian soldiers in the British service
SUBADARS > SUBADAR
SUBADULT *n* animal not quite at adult stage
SUBADULTS > SUBADULT
SUBAERIAL *adj* in open air
SUBAGENCY *n* agency employed by larger agency
SUBAGENT *n* agent who is subordinate to another agent
SUBAGENTS > SUBAGENT
SUBAH *same as* > SUBADAR
SUBAHDAR *same as* > SUBADAR
SUBAHDARS > SUBAHDAR
SUBAHDARY *n* office of subahdar
SUBAHS > SUBAH
SUBAHSHIP > SUBAH
SUBALAR *adj* below a wing
SUBALPINE *adj* situated in or relating to the regions at the foot of mountains
SUBALTERN *n* British army officer below the rank of captain ▷ *adj* of inferior position or rank
SUBAPICAL *adj* below an apex
SUBAQUA *adj* of or relating to underwater sport
SUBARCTIC *adj* of or relating to latitudes immediately south of the Arctic Circle
SUBAREA *n* area within a larger area
SUBAREAS > SUBAREA
SUBARID *adj* receiving slightly more rainfall than arid regions
SUBAS > SUBA
SUBASTRAL *adj* terrestrial
SUBATOM *n* part of an atom
SUBATOMIC *adj* of or being one of the particles which make up an atom
SUBATOMS > SUBATOM
SUBAUDIO *adj* (of sound) low frequency
SUBAURAL *adj* below the ear
SUBAXIAL *adj* below an axis of the body
SUBBASAL > SUBBASE
SUBBASE *same as* > SUBBASS
SUBBASES > SUBBASE
SUBBASIN *n* geographical basin within larger basin
SUBBASINS > SUBBASIN
SUBBASS *another name for* > BOURDON
SUBBASSES > SUBBASS
SUBBED > SUB
SUBBIE *n* subcontractor
SUBBIES > SUBBIE
SUBBING > SUB
SUBBINGS > SUB
SUBBLOCK *n* part of mathematical matrix
SUBBLOCKS > SUBBLOCK
SUBBRANCH *n* branch within another branch
SUBBREED *n* breed within a larger breed
SUBBREEDS > SUBBREED
SUBBUREAU *n* bureau subordinate to the main bureau
SUBBY *same as* > SUBBIE
SUBCANTOR *n* deputy to a cantor
SUBCASTE *n* subdivision of a caste
SUBCASTES > SUBCASTE
SUBCAUDAL *adj* below a tail
SUBCAUSE *n* factor less important than a cause
SUBCAUSES > SUBCAUSE
SUBCAVITY *n* cavity within a larger cavity
SUBCELL *n* cell within a larger cell
SUBCELLAR *n* cellar below another cellar
SUBCELLS > SUBCELL
SUBCENTER *n* secondary center
SUBCHASER *n* anti-submarine warship
SUBCHIEF *n* chief below the main chief
SUBCHIEFS > SUBCHIEF
SUBCHORD *n* part of a curve
SUBCHORDS > SUBCHORD
SUBCLAIM *n* claim that is part of a larger claim
SUBCLAIMS > SUBCLAIM
SUBCLAN *n* clan within a larger clan
SUBCLANS > SUBCLAN
SUBCLASS *n* principal subdivision of a class ▷ *vb* assign to a subclass
SUBCLAUSE *n* subordinate section of a larger clause in a document
SUBCLERK *n* clerk who is subordinate to another clerk
SUBCLERKS > SUBCLERK
SUBCLIMAX *n* community in which development has been arrested before climax has been attained
SUBCODE *n* computer tag identifying data
SUBCODES > SUBCODE
SUBCOLONY *n* colony established by existing colony
SUBCONSUL *n* assistant to a consul
SUBCOOL *vb* make colder
SUBCOOLED > SUBCOOL
SUBCOOLS > SUBCOOL
SUBCORTEX *n* matter of the brain situated beneath the cerebral cortex
SUBCOSTA *n* vein in insect wing
SUBCOSTAE > SUBCOSTA
SUBCOSTAL *adj* below the rib
SUBCOUNTY *n* division of a county
SUBCRUST *n* secondary crust below main crust
SUBCRUSTS > SUBCRUST
SUBCULT *n* cult within larger cult
SUBCULTS > SUBCULT
SUBCUTES > SUBCUTIS
SUBCUTIS *n* layer of tissue beneath outer skin
SUBDEACON *n* cleric who assists at High Mass
SUBDEALER *n* dealer who buys from other dealer
SUBDEAN *n* deputy of dean
SUBDEANS > SUBDEAN
SUBDEB *n* young woman who is not yet a debutante
SUBDEBS > SUBDEB
SUBDEPOT *n* depot within a larger depot
SUBDEPOTS > SUBDEPOT
SUBDEPUTY *n* assistant to a deputy
SUBDERMAL *adj* below the skin
SUBDEW *same as* > SUBDUE
SUBDEWED > SUBDEW
SUBDEWING > SUBDEW
SUBDEWS > SUBDEW
SUBDIVIDE *vb* divide (a part of something) into smaller parts
SUBDOLOUS *adj* clever
SUBDORSAL *adj* situated close to the back
SUBDUABLE > SUBDUE
SUBDUABLY > SUBDUE
SUBDUAL > SUBDUE
SUBDUALS > SUBDUE
SUBDUCE *vb* withdraw
SUBDUCED > SUBDUCE
SUBDUCES > SUBDUCE
SUBDUCING > SUBDUCE
SUBDUCT *vb* draw or turn (the eye, etc) downward
SUBDUCTED > SUBDUCT
SUBDUCTS > SUBDUCT
SUBDUE *vb* overcome
SUBDUED *adj* cowed, passive, or shy
SUBDUEDLY > SUBDUED
SUBDUER > SUBDUE
SUBDUERS > SUBDUE
SUBDUES > SUBDUE
SUBDUING > SUBDUE
SUBDUPLE *adj* in proportion of one to two
SUBDURAL *adj* between the dura mater and the arachnoid
SUBDWARF *n* star smaller than a dwarf star
SUBDWARFS > SUBDWARF
SUBECHO *n* echo resonating more quietly than another echo
SUBECHOES > SUBECHO
SUBEDAR *same as* > SUBADAR
SUBEDARS > SUBEDAR
SUBEDIT *vb* edit and correct (written or printed material)
SUBEDITED > SUBEDIT
SUBEDITOR *n* person who checks and edits text for newspaper or magazine
SUBEDITS > SUBEDIT
SUBENTIRE *adj* slightly indented
SUBENTRY *n* entry within another entry
SUBEPOCH *n* epoch within another epoch
SUBEPOCHS > SUBEPOCH
SUBEQUAL *adj* not quite equal
SUBER *n* cork
SUBERATE *n* salt of suberic acid
SUBERATES > SUBERATE
SUBERECT *adj* not quite erect
SUBEREOUS *same as* > SUBEROSE
SUBERIC *same as* > SUBEROSE
SUBERIN *n* fatty or waxy substance that is present in the walls of cork cells
SUBERINS > SUBERIN
SUBERISE *same*

as >SUBERIZE
JBERISED >SUBERISE
JBERISES >SUBERISE
JBERIZE *vb* impregnate (cell walls) with suberin during the formation of corky tissue
JBERIZED >SUBERIZE
JBERIZES >SUBERIZE
JBEROSE *adj* relating to, resembling, or consisting of cork
JBEROUS *same as* >SUBEROSE
JBERS >SUBER
JBFAMILY *n* taxonomic group that is a subdivision of a family
JBFEU *vb* grant feu to vassal
JBFEUED >SUBFEU
JBFEUING >SUBFEU
JBFEUS >SUBFEU
JBFIELD *n* subdivision of a field
JBFIELDS >SUBFIELD
JBFILE *n* file within another file
JBFILES >SUBFILE
JBFIX *n* suffix
JBFIXES >SUBFIX
JBFLOOR *n* rough floor that forms a base for a finished floor
JBFLOORS >SUBFLOOR
JBFLUID *adj* viscous
JBFOSSIL *n* something partly fossilized
JBFRAME *n* frame on which car body is built
JBFRAMES >SUBFRAME
JBFUSC *adj* devoid of brightness or appeal ▷*n* (at Oxford University) formal academic dress
JBFUSCS >SUBFUSC
JBFUSK *same as* >SUBFUSC
JBFUSKS >SUBFUSK
JBGENERA >SUBGENUS
JBGENRE *n* genre within a larger genre
JBGENRES >SUBGENRE
JBGENUS *n* taxonomic group that is a subdivision of a genus but of higher rank than a species
JBGOAL *n* secondary goal
JBGOALS >SUBGOAL
JBGRADE *n* ground beneath a roadway or pavement
JBGRADES >SUBGRADE
JBGRAPH *n* graph sharing vertices of other graph
JBGRAPHS >SUBGRAPH
JBGROUP *n* small group that is part of a larger group
JBGROUPS >SUBGROUP
JBGUM *n* Chinese dish
JBGUMS >SUBGUM
JBHA *n* string of beads used in praying and meditating
SUBHAS >SUBHA
SUBHEAD *n* heading of a subsection in a printed work
SUBHEADS >SUBHEAD
SUBHEDRAL *adj* with some characteristics of crystal
SUBHUMAN *adj* less than human
SUBHUMANS >SUBHUMAN
SUBHUMID *adj* not wet enough for trees to grow
SUBIDEA *n* secondary idea
SUBIDEAS >SUBIDEA
SUBIMAGO *n* first winged stage of the mayfly
SUBIMAGOS >SUBIMAGO
SUBINCISE *vb* perform subincision
SUBINDEX *same as* >SUBSCRIPT
SUBINFEUD *vb* grant by feudal tenant to further tenant
SUBITEM *n* item that is less important than another item
SUBITEMS >SUBITEM
SUBITISE *same as* >SUBITIZE
SUBITISED >SUBITISE
SUBITISES >SUBITISE
SUBITIZE *vb* perceive the number of (a group of items) at a glance and without counting
SUBITIZED >SUBITIZE
SUBITIZES >SUBITIZE
SUBITO *adv* (preceding or following a dynamic marking, etc) suddenly
SUBJACENT *adj* forming a foundation
SUBJECT *n* person or thing being dealt with or studied ▷*adj* being under the rule of a monarch or government ▷*vb* cause to undergo
SUBJECTED >SUBJECT
SUBJECTS >SUBJECT
SUBJOIN *vb* add or attach at the end of something spoken, written, etc
SUBJOINED >SUBJOIN
SUBJOINS >SUBJOIN
SUBJUGATE *vb* bring (a group of people) under one's control
SUBLATE *vb* deny
SUBLATED >SUBLATE
SUBLATES >SUBLATE
SUBLATING >SUBLATE
SUBLATION >SUBLATE
SUBLEASE *n* lease of property made by a person who is himself or herself a lessee or tenant of that property ▷*vb* grant a sublease of (property)
SUBLEASED >SUBLEASE
SUBLEASES >SUBLEASE
SUBLESSEE >SUBLEASE
SUBLESSOR >SUBLEASE
SUBLET *vb* rent out (property rented from someone else) ▷*n* sublease
SUBLETHAL *adj* not strong enough to kill
SUBLETS >SUBLET
SUBLETTER >SUBLET
SUBLEVEL *n* subdivision of a level
SUBLEVELS >SUBLEVEL
SUBLIMATE *vb* direct the energy of (a strong desire, esp a sexual one) into socially acceptable activities ▷*n* material obtained when a substance is sublimed ▷*adj* exalted or purified
SUBLIME *adj* of high moral, intellectual, or spiritual value ▷*vb* change from a solid to a vapour without first melting
SUBLIMED >SUBLIME
SUBLIMELY >SUBLIME
SUBLIMER >SUBLIME
SUBLIMERS >SUBLIME
SUBLIMES >SUBLIME
SUBLIMEST >SUBLIME
SUBLIMING >SUBLIME
SUBLIMISE *same as* >SUBLIMIZE
SUBLIMIT *n* limit on a subcategory
SUBLIMITS >SUBLIMIT
SUBLIMITY >SUBLIME
SUBLIMIZE *vb* make sublime
SUBLINE *n* secondary headline
SUBLINEAR *adj* beneath a line
SUBLINES >SUBLINE
SUBLOT *n* subdivision of a lot
SUBLOTS >SUBLOT
SUBLUNAR *same as* >SUBLUNARY
SUBLUNARY *adj* situated between the moon and the earth
SUBLUNATE *adj* almost crescent-shaped
SUBLUXATE *vb* partially dislocate
SUBMAN *n* primitive form of human
SUBMARINE *n* vessel which can operate below the surface of the sea ▷*adj* below the surface of the sea ▷*vb* slide beneath seatbelt in car crash
SUBMARKET *n* specialized market within larger market
SUBMATRIX *n* part of matrix
SUBMEN >SUBMAN
SUBMENTA >SUBMENTUM
SUBMENTAL *adj* situated beneath the chin
SUBMENTUM *n* base of insect lip
SUBMENU *n* further list of options within computer menu
SUBMENUS >SUBMENU
SUBMERGE *vb* put or go below the surface of water or other liquid
SUBMERGED *adj* (of plants or plant parts) growing beneath the surface of the water
SUBMERGES >SUBMERGE
SUBMERSE *same as* >SUBMERGE
SUBMERSED *same as* >SUBMERGED
SUBMERSES >SUBMERSE
SUBMICRON *n* object only visible through powerful microscope
SUBMISS *adj* docile
SUBMISSLY *adv* submissively
SUBMIT *vb* surrender
SUBMITS >SUBMIT
SUBMITTAL >SUBMIT
SUBMITTED >SUBMIT
SUBMITTER >SUBMIT
SUBMUCOSA *n* connective tissue beneath a mucous membrane
SUBMUCOUS >SUBMUCOSA
SUBNASAL *adj* beneath nose
SUBNET *n* part of network
SUBNETS >SUBNET
SUBNEURAL *adj* beneath a nerve centre
SUBNICHE *n* subdivision of a niche
SUBNICHES >SUBNICHE
SUBNIVEAL *adj* beneath the snow
SUBNIVEAN *same as* >SUBNIVEAL
SUBNODAL *adj* below the level of a node
SUBNORMAL *adj* less than normal, esp in intelligence ▷*n* subnormal person
SUBNUCLEI *pl n* plural of subnucleus, secondary nucleus
SUBOCEAN *adj* beneath the ocean
SUBOCTAVE *n* octave below another
SUBOCULAR *adj* below the eye
SUBOFFICE *n* office that is subordinate to another office
SUBOPTIC *adj* below the eye
SUBORAL *adj* not quite oral
SUBORDER *n* taxonomic group that is a subdivision of an order
SUBORDERS >SUBORDER
SUBORN *vb* bribe or incite (a person) to commit a wrongful act
SUBORNED >SUBORN

SUBORNER > SUBORN
SUBORNERS > SUBORN
SUBORNING > SUBORN
SUBORNS > SUBORN
SUBOSCINE *adj* belonging to a subfamily of birds
SUBOVAL *adj* not quite oval
SUBOVATE *adj* almost egg-shaped
SUBOXIDE *n* oxide of an element containing less oxygen than the common oxide formed by the element
SUBOXIDES > SUBOXIDE
SUBPANEL *n* panel that is part of larger panel
SUBPANELS > SUBPANEL
SUBPAR *adj* not up to standard
SUBPART *n* part within another part
SUBPARTS > SUBPART
SUBPENA *same as* > SUBPOENA
SUBPENAED > SUBPENA
SUBPENAS > SUBPENA
SUBPERIOD *n* subdivision of time period
SUBPHASE *n* subdivision of phase
SUBPHASES > SUBPHASE
SUBPHYLA > SUBPHYLUM
SUBPHYLAR > SUBPHYLUM
SUBPHYLUM *n* taxonomic group that is a subdivision of a phylum
SUBPLOT *n* secondary plot in a novel, play, or film
SUBPLOTS > SUBPLOT
SUBPOENA *n* writ requiring a person to appear before a lawcourt ▷ *vb* summon (someone) with a subpoena
SUBPOENAS > SUBPOENA
SUBPOLAR *adj* not quite polar
SUBPOTENT *adj* not at full strength
SUBPRIOR *n* monk junior to a prior
SUBPRIORS > SUBPRIOR
SUBPUBIC *adj* beneath the pubic bone
SUBRACE *n* race of people considered to be inferior
SUBRACES > SUBRACE
SUBREGION *n* subdivision of a region, esp a zoogeographical or ecological region
SUBRENT *n* rent paid to renter who rents to another
SUBRENTS > SUBRENT
SUBRING *n* mathematical ring that is a subset of another ring
SUBRINGS > SUBRING
SUBROGATE *vb* put (one person or thing) in the place of another in respect of a right or claim
SUBRULE *n* rule within another rule
SUBRULES > SUBRULE
SUBS > SUB
SUBSACRAL *adj* below the sacrum
SUBSALE *n* sale carried out within the process of a larger sale
SUBSALES > SUBSALE
SUBSAMPLE *vb* take further sample from existing sample
SUBSCALE *n* scale within a scale
SUBSCALES > SUBSCALE
SUBSCHEMA *n* part of computer database used by an individual
SUBSCRIBE *vb* pay (a subscription)
SUBSCRIPT *adj* (character) printed below the line ▷ *n* subscript character
SUBSEA *adj* undersea
SUBSECIVE *adj* left over
SUBSECT *n* sect within a larger sect
SUBSECTOR *n* subdivision of sector
SUBSECTS > SUBSECT
SUBSELLIA *pl n* ledges underneath the hinged seats in a church
SUBSENSE *n* definition that is division of wider definition
SUBSENSES > SUBSENSE
SUBSERE *n* secondary sere arising when the progress of a sere towards its climax has been interrupted
SUBSERES > SUBSERE
SUBSERIES *n* series within a larger series
SUBSERVE *vb* be helpful or useful to
SUBSERVED > SUBSERVE
SUBSERVES > SUBSERVE
SUBSET *n* mathematical set contained within a larger set
SUBSETS > SUBSET
SUBSHAFT *n* secondary shaft in mine
SUBSHAFTS > SUBSHAFT
SUBSHELL *n* part of a shell of an atom
SUBSHELLS > SUBSHELL
SUBSHRUB *n* small bushy plant that is woody except for the tips of the branches
SUBSHRUBS > SUBSHRUB
SUBSIDE *vb* become less intense
SUBSIDED > SUBSIDE
SUBSIDER > SUBSIDE
SUBSIDERS > SUBSIDE
SUBSIDES > SUBSIDE
SUBSIDIES > SUBSIDY
SUBSIDING > SUBSIDE
SUBSIDISE *same as* > SUBSIDIZE
SUBSIDIZE *vb* help financially
SUBSIDY *n* financial aid
SUBSIST *vb* manage to live
SUBSISTED > SUBSIST
SUBSISTER > SUBSIST
SUBSISTS > SUBSIST
SUBSITE *n* location within a website
SUBSITES > SUBSITE
SUBSIZAR *n* type of undergraduate at Cambridge
SUBSIZARS > SUBSIZAR
SUBSKILL *n* element of a wider skill
SUBSKILLS > SUBSKILL
SUBSOCIAL *adj* lacking a complex or definite social structure
SUBSOIL *n* earth just below the surface soil ▷ *vb* plough (land) to a depth below the normal ploughing level
SUBSOILED > SUBSOIL
SUBSOILER > SUBSOIL
SUBSOILS > SUBSOIL
SUBSOLAR *adj* (of a point on the earth) directly below the sun
SUBSONG *n* subdued form of birdsong modified from the full territorial song
SUBSONGS > SUBSONG
SUBSONIC *adj* moving at a speed less than that of sound
SUBSPACE *n* part of a mathematical matrix
SUBSPACES > SUBSPACE
SUBSTAGE *n* part of a microscope below the stage
SUBSTAGES > SUBSTAGE
SUBSTANCE *n* physical composition of something
SUBSTATE *n* subdivision of state
SUBSTATES > SUBSTATE
SUBSTRACT *same as* > SUBTRACT
SUBSTRATA *pl n* layers lying underneath other layers
SUBSTRATE *n* substance upon which an enzyme acts
SUBSTRUCT *vb* build as a foundation
SUBSTYLAR > SUBSTYLE
SUBSTYLE *n* line on a dial
SUBSTYLES > SUBSTYLE
SUBSULTUS *n* abnormal twitching
SUBSUME *vb* include (an idea, case, etc) under a larger classification or group
SUBSUMED > SUBSUME
SUBSUMES > SUBSUME
SUBSUMING > SUBSUME
SUBSYSTEM *n* system operating within a larger system
SUBTACK *Scots word for* > SUBLEASE
SUBTACKS > SUBTACK
SUBTASK *n* task that is par of a larger task
SUBTASKS > SUBTASK
SUBTAXA > SUBTAXON
SUBTAXON *n* supplementary piece of identifying information i plant or animal scientific name
SUBTAXONS > SUBTAXON
SUBTEEN *n* young person who has not yet become a teenager
SUBTEENS > SUBTEEN
SUBTENANT *n* person who rents property from a tenant
SUBTEND *vb* be opposite (an angle or side)
SUBTENDED > SUBTEND
SUBTENDS > SUBTEND
SUBTENSE *n* line that subtends
SUBTENSES > SUBTENSE
SUBTENURE *n* tenancy given by other tenant
SUBTEST *n* test that is par of larger test
SUBTESTS > SUBTEST
SUBTEXT *n* underlying theme in a piece of writin
SUBTEXTS > SUBTEXT
SUBTHEME *n* secondary theme
SUBTHEMES > SUBTHEME
SUBTIDAL *adj* below the level of low tide
SUBTIL *same as* > SUBTLE
SUBTILE *rare spelling of* > SUBTLE
SUBTILELY > SUBTILE
SUBTILER > SUBTILE
SUBTILEST > SUBTILE
SUBTILIN *n* antibiotic drug
SUBTILINS > SUBTILIN
SUBTILISE *same as* > SUBTILIZE
SUBTILITY > SUBTILE
SUBTILIZE *vb* bring to a purer state
SUBTILTY > SUBTILE
SUBTITLE *n* secondary tit of a book ▷ *vb* provide with a subtitle or subtitle
SUBTITLED > SUBTITLE
SUBTITLES > SUBTITLE
SUBTLE *adj* not immediately obvious
SUBTLER > SUBTLE
SUBTLEST > SUBTLE
SUBTLETY *n* fine distinction
SUBTLY > SUBTLE
SUBTONE *n* subdivision of a tone
SUBTONES > SUBTONE
SUBTONIC *n* seventh degree of a major or minc scale
SUBTONICS > SUBTONIC
SUBTOPIA *n* suburban

development that encroaches on rural areas yet appears to offer the attractions of country life to suburban dwellers
JBTOPIAN > SUBTOPIA
UBTOPIAS > SUBTOPIA
JBTOPIC *n* topic within a larger topic
UBTOPICS > SUBTOPIC
UBTORRID *same as* > SUBTROPIC
UBTOTAL *n* total made up by a column of figures, forming part of the total made up by a larger column or group ▷ *vb* establish or work out a subtotal for (a column, group, etc)
JBTOTALS > SUBTOTAL
JBTRACT *vb* take (one number or quantity) from another
JBTRACTS > SUBTRACT
JBTREND *n* minor trend
JBTRENDS > SUBTREND
JBTRIBE *n* tribe within a larger tribe
JBTRIBES > SUBTRIBE
JBTRIST *adj* slightly sad
JBTROPIC *adj* relating to the region lying between the tropics and the temperate lands
JBTRUDE *vb* intrude stealthily
JBTRUDED > SUBTRUDE
JBTRUDES > SUBTRUDE
JBTUNIC *adj* below membrane ▷ *n* garment worn under a tunic
JBTUNICS > SUBTUNIC
JBTYPE *n* secondary or subordinate type or genre
JBTYPES > SUBTYPE
JBUCULA *n* ancient Roman man's undergarment
JBUCULAS > SUBUCULA
JBULATE *adj* (esp of plant parts) tapering to a point
JBUNIT *n* distinct part or component of something larger
JBUNITS > SUBUNIT
JBURB *n* residential area on the outskirts of a city
JBURBAN *adj* mildly derogatory term for inhabiting a suburb ▷ *n* mildly derogatory term for a person who lives in a suburb
JBURBANS > SUBURBAN
JBURBED > SUBURB
JBURBIA *n* suburbs and their inhabitants
JBURBIAS > SUBURBIA
JBURBS > SUBURB
JBURSINE *adj* of a bear subspecies
JBVASSAL *n* vassal of a vassal
SUBVENE *vb* happen in such a way as to be of assistance, esp in preventing something
SUBVENED > SUBVENE
SUBVENES > SUBVENE
SUBVENING > SUBVENE
SUBVERSAL > SUBVERT
SUBVERSE *same as* > SUBVERT
SUBVERSED > SUBVERSE
SUBVERSES > SUBVERSE
SUBVERST > SUBVERSE
SUBVERT *vb* overthrow the authority of
SUBVERTED > SUBVERT
SUBVERTER > SUBVERT
SUBVERTS > SUBVERT
SUBVICAR *n* assistant to a vicar
SUBVICARS > SUBVICAR
SUBVIRAL *adj* of, caused by, or denoting a part of the structure of a virus
SUBVIRUS *n* organism smaller than a virus
SUBVISUAL *adj* not visible to the naked eye
SUBVOCAL *adj* formed in mind without being spoken aloud
SUBWARDEN *n* assistant to a warden
SUBWAY *n* passage under a road or railway ▷ *vb* travel by subway
SUBWAYED > SUBWAY
SUBWAYING > SUBWAY
SUBWAYS > SUBWAY
SUBWOOFER *n* loudspeaker for very low tones
SUBWORLD *n* underworld
SUBWORLDS > SUBWORLD
SUBWRITER *n* person carrying out writing tasks for other writer
SUBZERO *adj* lower than zero
SUBZONAL > SUBZONE
SUBZONE *n* subdivision of a zone
SUBZONES > SUBZONE
SUCCADE *n* piece of candied fruit
SUCCADES > SUCCADE
SUCCAH *same as* > SUKKAH
SUCCAHS > SUCCAH
SUCCEDENT *adj* following
SUCCEED *vb* accomplish an aim
SUCCEEDED > SUCCEED
SUCCEEDER > SUCCEED
SUCCEEDS > SUCCEED
SUCCENTOR *n* deputy of the precentor of a cathedral that has retained its statutes from pre-Reformation days
SUCCES *French word for* > SUCCESS
SUCCESS *n* achievement of something attempted
SUCCESSES > SUCCESS
SUCCESSOR *n* person who succeeds someone in a position
SUCCI > SUCCUS
SUCCINATE *n* any salt or ester of succinic acid
SUCCINCT *adj* brief and clear
SUCCINIC *adj* of, relating to, or obtained from amber
SUCCINITE *n* type of amber
SUCCINYL *n* constituent of succinic acid
SUCCINYLS > SUCCINYL
SUCCISE *adj* ending abruptly, as if cut off
SUCCOR *same as* > SUCCOUR
SUCCORED > SUCCOR
SUCCORER > SUCCOR
SUCCORERS > SUCCOR
SUCCORIES > SUCCORY
SUCCORING > SUCCOR
SUCCORS > SUCCOR
SUCCORY *another name for* > CHICORY
SUCCOS *same as* > SUCCOTH
SUCCOSE > SUCCUS
SUCCOT *same as* > SUKKOTH
SUCCOTASH *n* mixture of cooked sweet corn kernels and lima beans, served as a vegetable
SUCCOTH *variant of* > SUKKOTH
SUCCOUR *n* help in distress ▷ *vb* give aid to (someone in time of difficulty)
SUCCOURED > SUCCOUR
SUCCOURER > SUCCOUR
SUCCOURS > SUCCOUR
SUCCOUS > SUCCUS
SUCCUBA *same as* > SUCCUBUS
SUCCUBAE > SUCCUBA
SUCCUBAS > SUCCUBA
SUCCUBI > SUCCUBUS
SUCCUBINE > SUCCUBUS
SUCCUBOUS *adj* having the leaves arranged so that the upper margin of each leaf is covered by the lower margin of the next leaf along
SUCCUBUS *n* female demon believed to have sex with sleeping men
SUCCULENT *adj* juicy and delicious ▷ *n* succulent plant
SUCCUMB *vb* give way (to something overpowering)
SUCCUMBED > SUCCUMB
SUCCUMBER > SUCCUMB
SUCCUMBS > SUCCUMB
SUCCURSAL *adj* (esp of a religious establishment) subsidiary ▷ *n* subsidiary establishment
SUCCUS *n* fluid
SUCCUSS *vb* shake (a patient) to detect the sound of fluid in the thoracic or another bodily cavity
SUCCUSSED > SUCCUSS
SUCCUSSES > SUCCUSS
SUCH *adj* of the kind specified ▷ *pron* such things
SUCHLIKE *pron* such or similar things ▷ *n* such or similar things ▷ *adj* of such a kind
SUCHNESS > SUCH
SUCHWISE > SUCH
SUCK *vb* draw (liquid or air) into the mouth ▷ *n* sucking
SUCKED > SUCK
SUCKEN *Scots word for* > DISTRICT
SUCKENER *n* tenant
SUCKENERS > SUCKENER
SUCKENS > SUCKEN
SUCKER *n* person who is easily deceived or swindled ▷ *vb* strip off the suckers from (a plant)
SUCKERED > SUCKER
SUCKERING > SUCKER
SUCKERS > SUCKER
SUCKET *same as* > SUCCADE
SUCKETS > SUCKET
SUCKFISH *n* type of spiny-finned marine fish
SUCKIER > SUCKY
SUCKIEST > SUCKY
SUCKING *adj* not yet weaned
SUCKINGS > SUCKING
SUCKLE *vb* feed at the breast
SUCKLED > SUCKLE
SUCKLER > SUCKLE
SUCKLERS > SUCKLE
SUCKLES > SUCKLE
SUCKLESS > SUCK
SUCKLING *n* unweaned baby or young animal
SUCKLINGS > SUCKLING
SUCKS *interj* expression of disappointment
SUCKY *adj* despicable
SUCRALOSE *n* artificial sweetener
SUCRASE *another name for* > INVERTASE
SUCRASES > SUCRASE
SUCRE *n* former standard monetary unit of Ecuador
SUCRES > SUCRE
SUCRIER *n* small container for sugar at table
SUCRIERS > SUCRIER
SUCROSE *same as* > SUGAR
SUCROSES > SUCROSE
SUCTION *n* sucking ▷ *vb* subject to suction
SUCTIONAL > SUCTION
SUCTIONED > SUCTION
SUCTIONS > SUCTION
SUCTORIAL *adj* specialized for sucking or adhering
SUCTORIAN *n* microscopic creature
SUCURUJU *n* anaconda
SUCURUJUS > SUCURUJU
SUD *singular of* > SUDS
SUDAMEN *n* small cavity in

the skin
SUDAMINA > SUDAMEN
SUDAMINAL > SUDAMEN
SUDARIA > SUDARIUM
SUDARIES > SUDARY
SUDARIUM *n* room in a Roman bathhouse where sweating is induced by heat
SUDARY *same as* > SUDARIUM
SUDATE *vb* sweat
SUDATED > SUDATE
SUDATES > SUDATE
SUDATING > SUDATE
SUDATION > SUDATE
SUDATIONS > SUDATE
SUDATORIA *same as* > SUDARIA
SUDATORY > SUDORIUM
SUDD *n* floating masses of reeds and weeds that occur on the White Nile
SUDDEN *adj* done or occurring quickly and unexpectedly
SUDDENLY *adv* quickly and without warning
SUDDENS > SUDDEN
SUDDENTY *n* suddenness
SUDDER *n* supreme court in India
SUDDERS > SUDDER
SUDDS > SUDD
SUDOR *technical name for* > SWEAT
SUDORAL > SUDOR
SUDORIFIC *adj* (drug) causing sweating ▷ *n* drug that causes sweating
SUDOROUS > SUDOR
SUDORS > SUDOR
SUDS *pl n* froth of soap and water, lather ▷ *vb* wash in suds
SUDSED > SUDS
SUDSER *n* soap opera
SUDSERS > SUDSER
SUDSES > SUDS
SUDSIER > SUDS
SUDSIEST > SUDS
SUDSING > SUDS
SUDSLESS > SUDS
SUDSY > SUDS
SUE *vb* start legal proceedings against
SUEABLE > SUE
SUED > SUE
SUEDE *n* leather with a velvety finish on one side ▷ *vb* give a suede finish to
SUEDED > SUEDE
SUEDES > SUEDE
SUEDETTE *n* imitation suede fabric
SUEDETTES > SUEDETTE
SUEDING > SUEDE
SUENT *adj* smooth
SUER > SUE
SUERS > SUE
SUES > SUE
SUET *n* hard fat obtained from sheep and cattle, used in cooking
SUETIER > SUET
SUETIEST > SUET
SUETS > SUET
SUETTIER > SUET
SUETTIEST > SUET
SUETTY > SUET
SUETY > SUET
SUFFARI *same as* > SAFARI
SUFFARIS > SUFFARI
SUFFECT *adj* additional
SUFFER *vb* undergo or be subjected to
SUFFERED > SUFFER
SUFFERER > SUFFER
SUFFERERS > SUFFER
SUFFERING *n* pain, misery, or loss experienced by a person who suffers
SUFFERS > SUFFER
SUFFETE *n* official in ancient Carthage
SUFFETES > SUFFETE
SUFFICE *vb* be enough for a purpose
SUFFICED > SUFFICE
SUFFICER > SUFFICE
SUFFICERS > SUFFICE
SUFFICES > SUFFICE
SUFFICING > SUFFICE
SUFFIX *n* letter or letters added to the end of a word to form another word ▷ *vb* add (a letter or letters) to the end of a word to form another word
SUFFIXAL > SUFFIX
SUFFIXED > SUFFIX
SUFFIXES > SUFFIX
SUFFIXING > SUFFIX
SUFFIXION > SUFFIX
SUFFLATE *archaic word for* > INFLATE
SUFFLATED > SUFFLATE
SUFFLATES > SUFFLATE
SUFFOCATE *vb* kill or be killed by deprivation of oxygen
SUFFRAGAN *n* bishop appointed to assist an archbishop ▷ *adj* (of any bishop of a diocese) subordinate to and assisting his superior archbishop
SUFFRAGE *n* right to vote in public elections
SUFFRAGES > SUFFRAGE
SUFFUSE *vb* spread through or over (something)
SUFFUSED > SUFFUSE
SUFFUSES > SUFFUSE
SUFFUSING > SUFFUSE
SUFFUSION > SUFFUSE
SUFFUSIVE > SUFFUSE
SUGAN *n* straw rope
SUGANS > SUGAN
SUGAR *n* sweet crystalline carbohydrate used to sweeten food and drinks ▷ *vb* sweeten or cover with sugar
SUGARALLY *n* liquorice
SUGARBUSH *n* area covered in sugar maple trees
SUGARCANE *n* coarse grass that yields sugar
SUGARCOAT *vb* cover with sugar
SUGARED *adj* made sweeter or more appealing with or as with sugar
SUGARER > SUGAR
SUGARERS > SUGAR
SUGARIER > SUGARY
SUGARIEST > SUGARY
SUGARING *n* method of removing unwanted body hair
SUGARINGS > SUGARING
SUGARLESS > SUGAR
SUGARLIKE > SUGAR
SUGARLOAF *n* large conical mass of unrefined sugar
SUGARPLUM *n* crystallized plum
SUGARS > SUGAR
SUGARY *adj* of, like, or containing sugar
SUGGEST *vb* put forward (an idea) for consideration
SUGGESTED > SUGGEST
SUGGESTER > SUGGEST
SUGGESTS > SUGGEST
SUGGING *n* practice of selling products under the pretence of conducting market research
SUGGINGS > SUGGING
SUGH *same as* > SOUGH
SUGHED > SUGH
SUGHING > SUGH
SUGHS > SUGH
SUI *adj* of itself
SUICIDAL *adj* liable to commit suicide
SUICIDE *n* killing oneself intentionally ▷ *vb* commit suicide
SUICIDED > SUICIDE
SUICIDES > SUICIDE
SUICIDING > SUICIDE
SUID *n* pig or related animal
SUIDIAN > SUID
SUIDIANS > SUID
SUIDS > SUID
SUILLINE *adj* of or like a pig
SUING > SUE
SUINGS > SUE
SUINT *n* water-soluble substance found in the fleece of sheep
SUINTS > SUINT
SUIPLAP *n* South African slang for a drunkard
SUIPLAPS > SUIPLAP
SUIT *n* set of clothes designed to be worn together ▷ *vb* be appropriate for
SUITABLE *adj* appropriate or proper
SUITABLY > SUITABLE
SUITCASE *n* portable travelling case for clothing
SUITCASES > SUITCASE
SUITE *n* set of connected rooms in a hotel
SUITED > SUIT
SUITER *n* piece of luggage for carrying suits and dresses
SUITERS > SUITER
SUITES > SUITE
SUITING *n* fabric used for suits
SUITINGS > SUITING
SUITLIKE > SUIT
SUITOR *n* man who is courting a woman ▷ *vb* act as a suitor
SUITORED > SUITOR
SUITORING > SUITOR
SUITORS > SUITOR
SUITRESS *n* female suitor
SUITS > SUIT
SUIVANTE *n* lady's maid
SUIVANTES > SUIVANTE
SUIVEZ *vb* musical direction meaning follow
SUJEE *same as* > SOOGEE
SUJEES > SUJEE
SUK *same as* > SOUK
SUKH *same as* > SOUK
SUKHS > SUKH
SUKIYAKI *n* Japanese dish consisting of very thinly sliced beef, vegetables, and seasonings cooked together quickly
SUKIYAKIS > SUKIYAKI
SUKKAH *n* temporary structure with a roof of branches in which orthodox Jews eat and, if possible, sleep during the festival of Sukkoth
SUKKAHS > SUKKAH
SUKKOS *same as* > SUKKOTH
SUKKOT *same as* > SUKKOTH
SUKKOTH *n* eight-day Jewish harvest festival
SUKS > SUK
SULCAL > SULCUS
SULCALISE *same as* > SULCALIZE
SULCALIZE *vb* furrow
SULCATE *adj* marked with longitudinal parallel grooves
SULCATED *same as* > SULCATE
SULCATION > SULCATE
SULCI > SULCUS
SULCUS *n* linear groove, furrow, or slight depression
SULDAN *same as* > SULTAN
SULDANS > SULDAN
SULFA *same as* > SULPHA
SULFAS > SULFA
SULFATASE *n* type of enzyme
SULFATE *same as* > SULPHATE
SULFATED > SULFATE
SULFATES > SULFATE
SULFATIC *adj* relating to sulphate
SULFATING > SULFATE
SULFATION > SULFATE
SULFID *same as* > SULPHIDE

JLFIDE *same as* >SULPHIDE
JLFIDES >SULFIDE
ILFIDS >SULFID
JLFINYL *same as* >SULPHINYL
JLFINYLS >SULFINYL
ILFITE *same as* >SULPHITE
ILFITES >SULFITE
JLFITIC >SULFITE
ILFO *same as* >SULPHONIC
JLFONATE *n* salt or ester of sulphonic acid
JLFONE *same as* >SULPHONE
JLFONES >SULFONE
JLFONIC >SULFONE
JLFONIUM *n* one of a type of salts
JLFONYL *same as* >SULPHURYL
JLFONYLS >SULFONYL
ILFOXIDE *n* compound containing sulphur
ILFUR *variant of* >SULPHUR
ILFURATE *vb* treat with sulphur
ILFURED >SULFUR
JLFURET *same as* >SULPHURET
JLFURETS >SULFURET
ILFURIC >SULFUR
JLFURING >SULFUR
ILFURISE *variant of* >SULFURIZE
JLFURIZE *vb* combine or treat with sulphur
JLFUROUS *adj* resembling sulphur
JLFURS >SULFUR
JLFURY >SULFUR
JLFURYL *same as* >SULPHURYL
JLFURYLS >SULFURYL
JLK *vb* be silent and sullen because of resentment or bad temper ▷ *n* resentful or sullen mood
JLKED >SULK
ILKER *same as* >SULK
JLKERS >SULKER
ILKIER >SULKY
JLKIES >SULKY
ILKIEST >SULKY
JLKILY >SULKY
ILKINESS >SULKY
JLKING >SULK
ILKS >SULK
JLKY *adj* moody or silent because of anger or resentment ▷ *n* light two-wheeled vehicle for one person, usually drawn by one horse
ILLAGE *n* filth or waste, esp sewage
ILLAGES >SULLAGE
ILLEN *adj* unwilling to talk or be sociable ▷ *n* sullen mood
ILLENER >SULLEN
ILLENEST >SULLEN
SULLENLY >SULLEN
SULLENS >SULLEN
SULLIABLE >SULLY
SULLIED >SULLY
SULLIES >SULLY
SULLY *vb* ruin (someone's reputation) ▷ *n* stain
SULLYING >SULLY
SULPHA *n* any of a group of sulphonamides that prevent the growth of bacteria
SULPHAS >SULPHA
SULPHATE *n* salt or ester of sulphuric acid ▷ *vb* treat with a sulphate or convert into a sulphate
SULPHATED >SULPHATE
SULPHATES >SULPHATE
SULPHATIC >SULPHATE
SULPHID *same as* >SULPHIDE
SULPHIDE *n* compound of sulphur with another element
SULPHIDES >SULPHIDE
SULPHIDS >SULPHID
SULPHINYL *another term for* >THIONYL
SULPHITE *n* salt or ester of sulphurous acid
SULPHITES >SULPHITE
SULPHITIC >SULPHITE
SULPHONE *n* type of organic compound
SULPHONES >SULPHONE
SULPHONIC as in *sulphonic acid* type of strong organic acid
SULPHONYL *same as* >SULPHURYL
SULPHUR *n* pale yellow nonmetallic element ▷ *vb* treat with sulphur
SULPHURED >SULPHUR
SULPHURET *vb* treat or combine with sulphur
SULPHURIC >SULPHUR
SULPHURS >SULPHUR
SULPHURY >SULPHUR
SULPHURYL *n* particular chemical divalent group
SULTAN *n* sovereign of a Muslim country
SULTANA *n* kind of raisin
SULTANAS >SULTANA
SULTANATE *n* territory of a sultan
SULTANESS *same as* >SULTANA
SULTANIC >SULTAN
SULTANS >SULTAN
SULTRIER >SULTRY
SULTRIEST >SULTRY
SULTRILY >SULTRY
SULTRY *adj* (of weather or climate) hot and humid
SULU *n* type of sarong worn in Fiji
SULUS >SULU
SUM *n* result of addition, total ▷ *vb* add or form a total of (something)
SUMAC *same as* >SUMACH
SUMACH *n* type of temperate or subtropical shrub or small tree
SUMACHS >SUMACH
SUMACS >SUMAC
SUMATRA *n* violent storm blowing from the direction of Sumatra
SUMATRAS >SUMATRA
SUMLESS *adj* uncountable
SUMMA *n* compendium of theology, philosophy, or canon law, or sometimes of all three together
SUMMABLE >SUM
SUMMAE >SUMMA
SUMMAND *n* number or quantity forming part of a sum
SUMMANDS >SUMMAND
SUMMAR *Scots variant of* >SUMMER
SUMMARIES >SUMMARY
SUMMARILY >SUMMARY
SUMMARISE *same as* >SUMMARIZE
SUMMARIST >SUMMARIZE
SUMMARIZE *vb* make or be a summary of (something)
SUMMARY *n* brief account giving the main points of something ▷ *adj* done quickly, without formalities
SUMMAS >SUMMA
SUMMAT *pron* something ▷ *n* impressive or important person or thing
SUMMATE *vb* add up
SUMMATED >SUMMATE
SUMMATES >SUMMATE
SUMMATING >SUMMATE
SUMMATION *n* summary
SUMMATIVE >SUMMATION
SUMMATS >SUMMAT
SUMMED >SUM
SUMMER *n* warmest season of the year, between spring and autumn ▷ *vb* spend the summer (at a place)
SUMMERED >SUMMER
SUMMERIER >SUMMER
SUMMERING >SUMMER
SUMMERLY >SUMMER
SUMMERS >SUMMER
SUMMERSET *n* somersault
SUMMERY >SUMMER
SUMMING >SUM
SUMMINGS >SUM
SUMMIST *n* writer of summae
SUMMISTS >SUMMIST
SUMMIT *n* top of a mountain or hill ▷ *vb* reach summit
SUMMITAL >SUMMIT
SUMMITED >SUMMIT
SUMMITEER *n* person who participates in a summit conference
SUMMITING >SUMMIT
SUMMITRY *n* practice of conducting international negotiations by summit conferences
SUMMITS >SUMMIT
SUMMON *vb* order (someone) to come
SUMMONED >SUMMON
SUMMONER >SUMMON
SUMMONERS >SUMMON
SUMMONING >SUMMON
SUMMONS *n* command summoning someone ▷ *vb* order (someone) to appear in court
SUMMONSED >SUMMONS
SUMMONSES >SUMMONS
SUMO *n* Japanese style of wrestling
SUMOIST >SUMO
SUMOISTS >SUMO
SUMOS >SUMO
SUMOTORI *n* sumo wrestler
SUMOTORIS >SUMOTORI
SUMP *n* container in an internal-combustion engine into which oil can drain
SUMPH *n* stupid person
SUMPHISH >SUMPH
SUMPHS >SUMPH
SUMPIT *n* Malay blowpipe
SUMPITAN *same as* >SUMPIT
SUMPITANS >SUMPITAN
SUMPITS >SUMPIT
SUMPS >SUMP
SUMPSIMUS *n* correct form of expression
SUMPTER *n* packhorse, mule, or other beast of burden
SUMPTERS >SUMPTER
SUMPTUARY *adj* controlling expenditure or extravagant use of resources
SUMPTUOUS *adj* lavish, magnificent
SUMPWEED *n* American weed
SUMPWEEDS >SUMPWEED
SUMS >SUM
SUN *n* star around which the earth and other planets revolve ▷ *vb* expose (oneself) to the sun's rays
SUNBACK *adj* (of dress) cut low at back
SUNBAKE *vb* sunbathe, esp in order to become tanned ▷ *n* period of sunbaking
SUNBAKED *adj* (esp of roads, etc) dried or cracked by the sun's heat
SUNBAKES >SUNBAKE
SUNBAKING >SUNBAKE
SUNBATH *n* exposure of the body to the sun to get a suntan
SUNBATHE *vb* lie in the sunshine in order to get a suntan
SUNBATHED >SUNBATHE
SUNBATHER >SUNBATHE
SUNBATHES >SUNBATHE
SUNBATHS >SUNBATH

SUNBEAM *n* ray of sun
SUNBEAMED > SUNBEAM
SUNBEAMS > SUNBEAM
SUNBEAMY > SUNBEAM
SUNBEAT *adj* exposed to sun
SUNBEATEN *same as* > SUNBEAT
SUNBED *n* machine for giving an artificial tan
SUNBEDS > SUNBED
SUNBELT *n* southern states of the US
SUNBELTS > SUNBELT
SUNBERRY *n* red fruit like the blackberry
SUNBIRD *n* any small songbird of the family *Nectariniidae*
SUNBIRDS > SUNBIRD
SUNBLIND *n* blind that shades a room from the sun's glare
SUNBLINDS > SUNBLIND
SUNBLOCK *n* cream applied to the skin to protect it from the sun's rays
SUNBLOCKS > SUNBLOCK
SUNBONNET *n* hat that shades the face and neck from the sun
SUNBOW *n* bow of prismatic colours similar to a rainbow, produced when sunlight shines through spray
SUNBOWS > SUNBOW
SUNBRIGHT *adj* bright as the sun
SUNBURN *n* painful reddening of the skin caused by overexposure to the sun ▷ *vb* become sunburnt
SUNBURNED > SUNBURN
SUNBURNS > SUNBURN
SUNBURNT > SUNBURN
SUNBURST *n* burst of sunshine, as through a break in the clouds
SUNBURSTS > SUNBURST
SUNCHOKE *n* Jerusalem artichoke
SUNCHOKES > SUNCHOKE
SUNDAE *n* ice cream topped with fruit etc
SUNDAES > SUNDAE
SUNDARI *n* Indian tree
SUNDARIS > SUNDARI
SUNDECK *n* upper open deck on a passenger ship
SUNDECKS > SUNDECK
SUNDER *vb* break apart
SUNDERED > SUNDER
SUNDERER > SUNDER
SUNDERERS > SUNDER
SUNDERING > SUNDER
SUNDERS > SUNDER
SUNDEW *n* any of several bog plants of the genus *Drosera*
SUNDEWS > SUNDEW
SUNDIAL *n* device showing the time by means of a pointer that casts a shadow on a marked dial
SUNDIALS > SUNDIAL
SUNDOG *n* small rainbow or halo near the horizon
SUNDOGS > SUNDOG
SUNDOWN *same as* > SUNSET
SUNDOWNED > SUNDOWN
SUNDOWNER *n* tramp, esp one who seeks food and lodging at sundown when it is too late to work
SUNDOWNS > SUNDOWN
SUNDRA *same as* > SUNDARI
SUNDRAS > SUNDRA
SUNDRESS *n* dress for hot weather that exposes the shoulders, arms, and back, esp one with straps over the shoulders
SUNDRI *same as* > SUNDARI
SUNDRIES > SUNDRY
SUNDRILY > SUNDRY
SUNDRIS > SUNDRI
SUNDROPS *n* American primrose
SUNDRY *adj* several, various
SUNFAST *adj* not fading in sunlight
SUNFISH *n* large sea fish with a rounded body
SUNFISHES > SUNFISH
SUNFLOWER *n* tall plant with large golden flowers
SUNG > SING
SUNGAR *same as* > SANGAR
SUNGARS > SUNGAR
SUNGLASS *n* convex lens used to focus the sun's rays and thus produce heat or ignition
SUNGLOW *n* pinkish glow often seen in the sky before sunrise or after sunset
SUNGLOWS > SUNGLOW
SUNGREBE *another name for* > FINFOOT
SUNGREBES > SUNGREBE
SUNHAT *n* hat that shades the face and neck from the sun
SUNHATS > SUNHAT
SUNK *n* bank or pad
SUNKEN *adj* unhealthily hollow
SUNKET *n* something good to eat
SUNKETS > SUNKET
SUNKIE *n* little stool
SUNKIES > SUNKIE
SUNKS > SUNK
SUNLAMP *n* lamp that generates ultraviolet rays
SUNLAMPS > SUNLAMP
SUNLAND *n* sunny area
SUNLANDS > SUNLAND
SUNLESS *adj* without sun or sunshine
SUNLESSLY > SUNLESS
SUNLIGHT *n* light that comes from the sun
SUNLIGHTS > SUNLIGHT
SUNLIKE > SUN
SUNLIT > SUNLIGHT
SUNN *n* leguminous plant of the East Indies, having yellow flowers
SUNNA *n* body of traditional Islamic law
SUNNAH *same as* > SUNNA
SUNNAHS > SUNNAH
SUNNAS > SUNNA
SUNNED > SUN
SUNNIER > SUNNY
SUNNIES *pl n* pair of sunglasses
SUNNIEST > SUNNY
SUNNILY > SUNNY
SUNNINESS > SUNNY
SUNNING > SUN
SUNNS > SUNN
SUNNY *adj* full of or exposed to sunlight
SUNPORCH *n* porch for sunbathing on
SUNPROOF > SUN
SUNRAY *n* ray of light from the sun
SUNRAYS > SUNRAY
SUNRISE *n* daily appearance of the sun above the horizon
SUNRISES > SUNRISE
SUNRISING *same as* > SUNRISE
SUNROOF *n* panel in the roof of a car that opens to let in air
SUNROOFS > SUNROOF
SUNROOM *n* room or glass-enclosed porch designed to display beautiful views
SUNROOMS > SUNROOM
SUNS > SUN
SUNSCALD *n* sun damage on tomato plants
SUNSCALDS > SUNSCALD
SUNSCREEN *n* cream or lotion applied to exposed skin to protect it from the ultraviolet rays of the sun
SUNSEEKER *n* person looking for sunny weather
SUNSET *n* daily disappearance of the sun below the horizon
SUNSETS > SUNSET
SUNSHADE *n* anything used to shade people from the sun, such as a parasol or awning
SUNSHADES > SUNSHADE
SUNSHINE *n* light and warmth from the sun
SUNSHINES > SUNSHINE
SUNSHINY > SUNSHINE
SUNSPOT *n* dark patch appearing temporarily on the sun's surface
SUNSPOTS > SUNSPOT
SUNSTAR *n* any starfish of the genus *Solaster*, having up to 13 arms radiating from a central disc
SUNSTARS > SUNSTAR
SUNSTONE *n* type of translucent feldspar with reddish-gold speckles
SUNSTONES > SUNSTONE
SUNSTROKE *n* illness caused by prolonged exposure to intensely hot sunlight
SUNSTRUCK *adj* suffering from sunstroke
SUNSUIT *n* child's outfit consisting of a brief top and shorts or a short skirt
SUNSUITS > SUNSUIT
SUNTAN *n* browning of the skin caused by exposure t[o] the sun
SUNTANNED > SUNTAN
SUNTANS > SUNTAN
SUNTRAP *n* very sunny sheltered place
SUNTRAPS > SUNTRAP
SUNUP *same as* > SUNRISE
SUNUPS > SUNUP
SUNWARD *same as* > SUNWARDS
SUNWARDS *adv* towards the sun
SUNWISE *adv* moving in th[e] same direction as the sur[n]
SUP *same as* > SUPINE
SUPAWN *same as* > SUPPAW[N]
SUPAWNS > SUPAWN
SUPE *n* superintendent
SUPER *adj* excellent ▷ *n* superannuation ▷ *interj* enthusiastic expression of approval or assent ▷ *v[b]* work as superintendent
SUPERABLE *adj* able to be surmounted or overcome
SUPERABLY > SUPERABLE
SUPERADD *vb* add (something) to somethin[g] that has already been added
SUPERADDS > SUPERADD
SUPERATE *vb* overcome
SUPERATED > SUPERATE
SUPERATES > SUPERATE
SUPERATOM *n* cluster of atoms behaving like a single atom
SUPERB *adj* excellent, impressive, or splendid
SUPERBAD *adj* exceptionally bad
SUPERBANK *n* bank that owns other banks
SUPERBER > SUPERB
SUPERBEST > SUPERB
SUPERBIKE *n* high-performance motorcycle
SUPERBITY > SUPERB
SUPERBLY > SUPERB
SUPERBOLD *adj* exceptionally bold
SUPERBOMB *n* large bomb
SUPERBRAT *n* exceptiona[lly] unpleasant child
SUPERBUG *n* bacterium resistant to antibiotics
SUPERBUGS > SUPERBUG
SUPERCAR *n* very expensi[ve] fast or powerful car with centrally located engine
SUPERCARS > SUPERCAR

UPERCEDE *former variant of* > SUPERSEDE
UPERCHIC *adj* highly chic
UPERCITY *n* very large ity
UPERCLUB *n* large and mportant club
UPERCOIL *vb* form a omplex coil
UPERCOLD *adj* very cold
UPERCOOL *vb* cool or be ooled to a temperature below that at which freezing or crystallization should occur
UPERCOP *n* high-ranking police officer
UPERCOPS > SUPERCOP
UPERCOW *n* dairy cow that produces a very high milk yield
UPERCOWS > SUPERCOW
UPERCUTE *adj* very cute
UPERED > SUPER
UPEREGO *n* that part of the unconscious mind that governs ideas about what is right and wrong
UPEREGOS > SUPEREGO
UPERETTE *n* small store or dairy laid out along the ines of a supermarket
UPERFAN *n* very devoted an
UPERFANS > SUPERFAN
UPERFARM *n* very large arm
UPERFAST *adj* very fast
UPERFINE *adj* of exceptional fineness or quality
UPERFIRM *adj* very firm
UPERFIT *adj* highly fit
UPERFIX *n* lingustic eature distinguishing the meaning of one word that of another
UPERFLUX *n* superfluity
UPERFUND *n* large fund
UPERFUSE *vb* pour or be poured so as to cover something
UPERGENE *n* cluster of genes
UPERGLUE *n* extremely strong and quick-drying glue ▷ *vb* fix with superglue
UPERGOOD *adj* very good
UPERGUN *n* large powerful gun
UPERGUNS > SUPERGUN
UPERHEAT *vb* heat (a vapour, esp steam) to a emperature above its saturation point for a given pressure
UPERHERO *n* any of various comic-strip characters with superhuman abilities or magical powers
UPERHET *n* type of radio eceiver
SUPERHETS > SUPERHET
SUPERHIGH *adj* extremely high
SUPERHIT *n* very popular hit
SUPERHITS > SUPERHIT
SUPERHIVE *n* upper part of beehive
SUPERHOT *adj* very hot
SUPERHYPE *n* exaggerated hype
SUPERING > SUPER
SUPERIOR *adj* greater in quality, quantity, or merit ▷ *n* person of greater rank or status
SUPERIORS > SUPERIOR
SUPERJET *n* supersonic aircraft
SUPERJETS > SUPERJET
SUPERJOCK *n* very athletic person
SUPERLAIN > SUPERLIE
SUPERLAY > SUPERLIE
SUPERLIE *vb* lie above
SUPERLIES > SUPERLIE
SUPERLOAD *n* variable weight on a structure
SUPERLONG *adj* very long
SUPERLOO *n* automated public toilet
SUPERLOOS > SUPERLOO
SUPERMALE *former name for* > METAMALE
SUPERMAN *n* man with great physical or mental powers
SUPERMART *n* large self-service store selling food and household supplies
SUPERMAX *n* having or relating to the very highest levels of security
SUPERMEN > SUPERMAN
SUPERMIND *n* very powerful brain
SUPERMINI *n* small car, usually a hatchback, that is economical to run but has a high level of performance
SUPERMOM *n* very capable and busy mother
SUPERMOMS > SUPERMOM
SUPERMOTO *n* form of motorcycle racing over part-tarmac and part-dirt circuits
SUPERNAL *adj* of or from the world of the divine
SUPERNATE *n* liquid lying above a sediment
SUPERNOVA *n* star that explodes and briefly becomes exceptionally bright
SUPERPIMP *n* pimp controlling many prostitutes
SUPERPLUS *n* surplus
SUPERPORT *n* large port
SUPERPOSE *vb* transpose (the coordinates of one geometric figure) to coincide with those of another
SUPERPRO *n* person regarded as a real professional
SUPERPROS > SUPERPRO
SUPERRACE *n* important race
SUPERREAL *adj* surreal
SUPERRICH *adj* exceptionally wealthy
SUPERROAD *n* very large road
SUPERS > SUPER
SUPERSAFE *adj* very safe
SUPERSALE *n* large sale
SUPERSALT *n* acid salt
SUPERSAUR *n* very large dinosaur
SUPERSEDE *vb* replace, supplant
SUPERSELL *vb* sell in very large numbers
SUPERSEX *n* sterile organism in which the ratio between the sex chromosomes is disturbed
SUPERSHOW *n* very impressive show
SUPERSIZE *vb* make larger
SUPERSOFT *adj* very soft
SUPERSOLD > SUPERSELL
SUPERSPY *n* highly accomplished spy
SUPERSTAR *n* very famous entertainer or sportsperson
SUPERSTUD *n* highly virile man
SUPERTAX *n* extra tax on incomes above a certain level
SUPERTHIN *adj* very thin
SUPERVENE *vb* occur as an unexpected development
SUPERVISE *vb* watch over to direct or check
SUPERWAIF *n* very young and very thin supermodel
SUPERWAVE *n* large wave
SUPERWEED *n* hybrid plant that contains genes for herbicide resistance
SUPERWIDE *n* very wide lens
SUPERWIFE *n* highly accomplished wife
SUPES > SUPE
SUPINATE *vb* turn (the hand and forearm) so that the palm faces up or forwards
SUPINATED > SUPINATE
SUPINATES > SUPINATE
SUPINATOR *n* muscle of the forearm that can produce the motion of supination
SUPINE *adj* lying flat on one's back ▷ *n* noun form derived from a verb in Latin
SUPINELY > SUPINE
SUPINES > SUPINE
SUPLEX *n* wrestling hold in which a wrestler grasps his opponent round the waist from behind and carries him backwards
SUPLEXES > SUPLEX
SUPPAWN *n* kind of porridge
SUPPAWNS > SUPPAWN
SUPPEAGO *same as* > SERPIGO
SUPPED > SUP
SUPPER *n* light evening meal ▷ *vb* eat supper
SUPPERED > SUPPER
SUPPERING > SUPPER
SUPPERS > SUPPER
SUPPING > SUP
SUPPLANT *vb* take the place of, oust
SUPPLANTS > SUPPLANT
SUPPLE *adj* (of a person) moving and bending easily and gracefully ▷ *vb* make or become supple
SUPPLED > SUPPLE
SUPPLELY *same as* > SUPPLY
SUPPLER > SUPPLE
SUPPLES > SUPPLE
SUPPLEST > SUPPLE
SUPPLIAL *n* instance of supplying
SUPPLIALS > SUPPLIAL
SUPPLIANT *n* person who requests humbly
SUPPLICAT *n* university petition
SUPPLIED > SUPPLY
SUPPLIER > SUPPLY
SUPPLIERS > SUPPLY
SUPPLIES > SUPPLY
SUPPLING > SUPPLE
SUPPLY *vb* provide with something required ▷ *n* supplying ▷ *adj* acting as a temporary substitute ▷ *adv* in a supple manner
SUPPLYING > SUPPLY
SUPPORT *vb* bear the weight of ▷ *n* supporting
SUPPORTED > SUPPORT
SUPPORTER *n* person who supports a team, principle, etc
SUPPORTS > SUPPORT
SUPPOSAL *n* supposition
SUPPOSALS > SUPPOSAL
SUPPOSE *vb* presume to be true
SUPPOSED *adj* presumed to be true without proof, doubtful
SUPPOSER > SUPPOSE
SUPPOSERS > SUPPOSE
SUPPOSES > SUPPOSE
SUPPOSING > SUPPOSE
SUPPRESS *vb* put an end to
SUPPURATE *vb* (of a wound etc) produce pus
SUPRA *adv* above, esp referring to earlier parts of a book etc
SUPREMACY *n* supreme power
SUPREME *adj* highest in authority, rank, or degree

▷ *n* rich velouté sauce made with a base of veal or chicken stock, with cream or egg yolks added
SUPREMELY > SUPREME
SUPREMER > SUPREME
SUPREMES > SUPREME
SUPREMEST > SUPREME
SUPREMITY *n* supremeness
SUPREMO *n* person in overall authority
SUPREMOS > SUPREMO
SUPS > SUP
SUQ *same as* > SOUK
SUQS > SUQ
SUR *prep* above
SURA *n* any of the 114 chapters of the Koran
SURAH *n* twill-weave fabric of silk or rayon, used for dresses, blouses, etc
SURAHS > SURAH
SURAL *adj* of or relating to the calf of the leg
SURAMIN *n* drug used in treating sleeping sickness
SURAMINS > SURAMIN
SURANCE *same as* > ASSURANCE
SURANCES > SURANCE
SURAS > SURA
SURAT *n* (formerly) a cotton fabric from the Surat area of India
SURATS > SURAT
SURBAHAR *n* Indian string instrument
SURBAHARS > SURBAHAR
SURBASE *n* uppermost part, such as a moulding, of a pedestal, base, or skirting
SURBASED *adj* having a surbase
SURBASES > SURBASE
SURBATE *vb* make feet sore through walking
SURBATED > SURBATE
SURBATES > SURBATE
SURBATING > SURBATE
SURBED *vb* put something on its edge
SURBEDDED > SURBED
SURBEDS > SURBED
SURBET > SURBATE
SURCEASE *n* cessation or intermission ▷ *vb* desist from (some action)
SURCEASED > SURCEASE
SURCEASES > SURCEASE
SURCHARGE *n* additional charge ▷ *vb* charge (someone) an additional sum or tax
SURCINGLE *n* girth for a horse which goes around the body, used esp with a racing saddle ▷ *vb* put a surcingle on or over (a horse)
SURCOAT *n* tunic worn by a knight over his armour during the Middle Ages
SURCOATS > SURCOAT
SURCULI > SURCULUS
SURCULOSE *adj* (of a plant) bearing suckers
SURCULUS *n* sucker on plant
SURD *n* number that cannot be expressed in whole numbers ▷ *adj* of or relating to a surd
SURDITIES > SURDITY
SURDITY *n* deafness
SURDS > SURD
SURE *adj* free from uncertainty or doubt ▷ *interj* certainly ▷ *vb* archaic form of sewer
SURED > SURE
SUREFIRE *adj* certain to succeed
SURELY *adv* it must be true that
SURENESS > SURE
SURER > SURE
SURES > SURE
SUREST > SURE
SURETIED > SURETY
SURETIES > SURETY
SURETY *n* person who takes responsibility for the fulfilment of another's obligation ▷ *vb* be surety for
SURETYING > SURETY
SURF *n* foam caused by waves breaking on the shore ▷ *vb* take part in surfing
SURFABLE > SURF
SURFACE *n* outside or top of an object ▷ *vb* become apparent
SURFACED > SURFACE
SURFACER > SURFACE
SURFACERS > SURFACE
SURFACES > SURFACE
SURFACING > SURFACE
SURFBIRD *n* American shore bird
SURFBIRDS > SURFBIRD
SURFBOARD *n* long smooth board used in surfing
SURFBOAT *n* boat with a high bow and stern and flotation chambers
SURFBOATS > SURFBOAT
SURFED > SURF
SURFEIT *n* excessive amount ▷ *vb* supply or feed excessively
SURFEITED > SURFEIT
SURFEITER > SURFEIT
SURFEITS > SURFEIT
SURFER > SURFING
SURFERS > SURFING
SURFFISH *n* fish of American coastal seas
SURFICIAL *adj* superficial
SURFIE *n* young person whose main interest is in surfing
SURFIER > SURF
SURFIES > SURFIE
SURFIEST > SURF
SURFING *n* sport of riding towards the shore on a surfboard on the crest of a wave
SURFINGS > SURFING
SURFLIKE > SURF
SURFMAN *n* sailor skilled in sailing through surf
SURFMEN > SURFMAN
SURFPERCH *n* type of marine fish of North American Pacific coastal waters
SURFRIDER > SURFING
SURFS > SURF
SURFSIDE *adj* next to the sea
SURFY > SURF
SURGE *n* sudden powerful increase ▷ *vb* increase suddenly
SURGED > SURGE
SURGEFUL > SURGE
SURGELESS > SURGE
SURGENT > SURGE
SURGEON *n* doctor who specializes in surgery
SURGEONCY *n* office, duties, or position of a surgeon, esp in the army or navy
SURGEONS > SURGEON
SURGER > SURGE
SURGERIES > SURGERY
SURGERS > SURGE
SURGERY *n* treatment in which the patient's body is cut open in order to treat the affected part
SURGES > SURGE
SURGICAL *adj* involving or used in surgery
SURGIER > SURGE
SURGIEST > SURGE
SURGING > SURGE
SURGINGS > SURGE
SURGY > SURGE
SURICATE *n* type of meerkat
SURICATES > SURICATE
SURIMI *n* blended seafood product made from precooked fish, restructured into stick shapes
SURIMIS > SURIMI
SURING > SURE
SURLIER > SURLY
SURLIEST > SURLY
SURLILY > SURLY
SURLINESS > SURLY
SURLOIN *same as* > SIRLOIN
SURLOINS > SURLOIN
SURLY *adj* ill-tempered and rude
SURMASTER *n* deputy headmaster
SURMISAL > SURMISE
SURMISALS > SURMISE
SURMISE *n* guess, conjecture ▷ *vb* guess (something) from incomplete or uncertain evidence
SURMISED > SURMISE
SURMISER > SURMISE
SURMISERS > SURMISE
SURMISES > SURMISE
SURMISING > SURMISE
SURMOUNT *vb* overcome (a problem)
SURMOUNTS > SURMOUNT
SURMULLET *n* red mullet
SURNAME *n* family name ▷ *vb* furnish with or call b[y] a surname
SURNAMED > SURNAME
SURNAMER > SURNAME
SURNAMERS > SURNAME
SURNAMES > SURNAME
SURNAMING > SURNAME
SURPASS *vb* be greater tha[n] or superior to
SURPASSED > SURPASS
SURPASSER > SURPASS
SURPASSES > SURPASS
SURPLICE *n* loose white robe worn by clergymen and choristers
SURPLICED > SURPLICE
SURPLICES > SURPLICE
SURPLUS *n* amount left over in excess of what is required ▷ *adj* extra ▷ *vb* be left over in excess of what is required
SURPLUSED > SURPLUS
SURPLUSES > SURPLUS
SURPRINT *vb* print (additional matter) over something already printe[d] ▷ *n* marks, printed matte[r] etc, that have been surprinted
SURPRINTS > SURPRINT
SURPRISAL > SURPRISE
SURPRISE *n* unexpected event ▷ *vb* cause to feel amazement or wonder
SURPRISED > SURPRISE
SURPRISER > SURPRISE
SURPRISES > SURPRISE
SURPRIZE *same as* > SURPRISE
SURPRIZED > SURPRIZE
SURPRIZES > SURPRIZE
SURQUEDRY *n* arrogance
SURQUEDY *same as* > SURQUEDRY
SURRA *n* tropical febrile disease of animals
SURRAS > SURRA
SURREAL *adj* bizarre ▷ *n* atmosphere or qualities evoked by surrealism
SURREALLY > SURREAL
SURREBUT *vb* give eviden[ce] to support the surrebutt[er]
SURREBUTS > SURREBUT
SURREINED *adj* (of horse) ridden too much
SURREJOIN *vb* reply to le[gal] rejoinder
SURRENDER *vb* give onese[lf] up ▷ *n* surrendering
SURRENDRY *same as* > SURRENDER
SURREY *n* light four-wheeled horse-drawn carriage having two or

four seats
URREYS > SURREY
URROGACY > SURROGATE
URROGATE *n* substitute ▷ *adj* acting as a substitute ▷ *vb* put in another's position as a deputy, substitute, etc
URROUND *vb* be, come, or place all around (a person or thing) ▷ *n* border or edging
URROUNDS > SURROUND
URROYAL *n* high point on stag's horns
URROYALS > SURROYAL
URTAX *n* extra tax on incomes above a certain level ▷ *vb* assess for liability to surtax
URTAXED > SURTAX
URTAXES > SURTAX
URTAXING > SURTAX
URTITLE *singular of* > SURTITLE
URTITLES *pl n* brief translations of the text of an opera or play projected above the stage
URTOUT *n* man's overcoat resembling a frock coat, popular in the late 19th century
URTOUTS > SURTOUT
URUCUCU *n* South American snake
URUCUCUS > SURUCUCU
URVEIL *same as* > SURVEILLE
JRVEILED > SURVEIL
JRVEILLE *vb* observe closely
JRVEILS > SURVEIL
JRVEY *vb* view or consider in a general way ▷ *n* surveying
JRVEYAL > SURVEY
JRVEYALS > SURVEY
JRVEYED > SURVEY
JRVEYING *n* practice of measuring altitudes, angles, and distances on the land surface so that they can be accurately plotted on a map
JRVEYOR *n* person whose occupation is to survey land or buildings
JRVEYORS > SURVEYOR
JRVEYS > SURVEY
JRVIEW *vb* survey
JRVIEWED > SURVIEW
JRVIEWS > SURVIEW
JRVIVAL *n* condition of having survived ▷ *adj* of, relating to, or assisting the act of surviving
JRVIVALS > SURVIVAL
JRVIVE *vb* continue to live or exist after (a difficult experience)
JRVIVED > SURVIVE
JRVIVER *same as* > SURVIVOR
SURVIVERS > SURVIVER
SURVIVES > SURVIVE
SURVIVING > SURVIVE
SURVIVOR *n* person or thing that survives
SURVIVORS > SURVIVOR
SUS *same as* > SUSS
SUSCEPTOR *n* sponsor
SUSCITATE *vb* excite
SUSES > SUS
SUSHI *n* Japanese dish of small cakes of cold rice with a topping of raw fish
SUSHIS > SUSHI
SUSLIK *n* central Eurasian ground squirrel
SUSLIKS > SUSLIK
SUSPECT *vb* believe (someone) to be guilty without having any proof ▷ *adj* not to be trusted ▷ *n* person who is suspected
SUSPECTED > SUSPECT
SUSPECTER > SUSPECT
SUSPECTS > SUSPECT
SUSPENCE *same as* > SUSPENSE
SUSPEND *vb* hang from a high place
SUSPENDED > SUSPEND
SUSPENDER *n* elastic strap for holding up women's stockings
SUSPENDS > SUSPEND
SUSPENS *same as* > SUSPENSE
SUSPENSE *n* state of uncertainty while awaiting news, an event, etc
SUSPENSER *n* film that creates a feeling of suspense
SUSPENSES > SUSPENSE
SUSPENSOR *n* ligament or muscle that holds a part in position
SUSPICION *n* feeling of not trusting a person or thing
SUSPIRE *vb* sigh or utter with a sigh
SUSPIRED > SUSPIRE
SUSPIRES > SUSPIRE
SUSPIRING > SUSPIRE
SUSS *vb* attempt to work out (a situation, etc), using one's intuition ▷ *n* sharpness of mind
SUSSED > SUSS
SUSSES > SUSS
SUSSING > SUSS
SUSTAIN *vb* maintain or prolong ▷ *n* prolongation of a note, by playing technique or electronics
SUSTAINED > SUSTAIN
SUSTAINER *n* rocket engine that maintains the velocity of a space vehicle after the booster has been jettisoned
SUSTAINS > SUSTAIN
SUSTINENT *adj* sustaining
SUSU *n* (in the Caribbean) savings fund shared by friends
SUSURRANT > SUSURRATE
SUSURRATE *vb* make a soft rustling sound
SUSURROUS *adj* full of murmuring sounds
SUSURRUS > SUSURRATE
SUSUS > SUSU
SUTILE *adj* involving sewing
SUTLER *n* (formerly) a merchant who accompanied an army in order to sell provisions to the soldiers
SUTLERIES > SUTLER
SUTLERS > SUTLER
SUTLERY > SUTLER
SUTOR *n* cobbler
SUTORIAL > SUTOR
SUTORIAN > SUTOR
SUTORS > SUTOR
SUTRA *n* Sanskrit sayings or collections of sayings
SUTRAS > SUTRA
SUTTA *n* Buddhist scripture
SUTTAS > SUTTA
SUTTEE *n* former Hindu custom whereby a widow burnt herself to death on her husband's funeral pyre
SUTTEEISM > SUTTEE
SUTTEES > SUTTEE
SUTTLE *vb* work as sutler
SUTTLED > SUTTLE
SUTTLES > SUTTLE
SUTTLETIE *same as* > SUBTLETY
SUTTLING > SUTTLE
SUTTLY > SUBTLE
SUTURAL > SUTURE
SUTURALLY > SUTURE
SUTURE *n* stitch joining the edges of a wound ▷ *vb* join (the edges of a wound, etc) by means of sutures
SUTURED > SUTURE
SUTURES > SUTURE
SUTURING > SUTURE
SUZERAIN *n* state or sovereign with limited authority over another self-governing state
SUZERAINS > SUZERAIN
SVARAJ *same as* > SWARAJ
SVARAJES > SVARAJ
SVASTIKA *same as* > SWASTIKA
SVASTIKAS > SVASTIKA
SVEDBERG *n* unit used in physics
SVEDBERGS > SVEDBERG
SVELTE *adj* attractively or gracefully slim
SVELTELY > SVELTE
SVELTER > SVELTE
SVELTEST > SVELTE
SWAB *n* small piece of cotton wool used to apply medication, clean a wound, etc ▷ *vb* clean (a wound) with a swab
SWABBED > SWAB
SWABBER *n* person who uses a swab
SWABBERS > SWABBER
SWABBIE *same as* > SWABBY
SWABBIES > SWABBY
SWABBING > SWAB
SWABBY *n* seaman
SWABS > SWAB
SWACK *adj* flexible
SWACKED *adj* in a state of intoxication, stupor, or euphoria induced by drugs or alcohol
SWAD *n* loutish person
SWADDIE *same as* > SWADDY
SWADDIES > SWADDY
SWADDLE *vb* wrap (a baby) in swaddling clothes ▷ *n* swaddling clothes
SWADDLED > SWADDLE
SWADDLER > SWADDLE
SWADDLERS > SWADDLE
SWADDLES > SWADDLE
SWADDLING > SWADDLE
SWADDY *n* private soldier
SWADS > SWADDLE
SWAG *n* stolen property ▷ *vb* sway from side to side
SWAGE *n* shaped tool or die used in forming cold metal by hammering ▷ *vb* form (metal) with a swage
SWAGED > SWAGE
SWAGER > SWAGE
SWAGERS > SWAGE
SWAGES > SWAGE
SWAGGED > SWAG
SWAGGER *vb* walk or behave arrogantly ▷ *n* arrogant walk or manner ▷ *adj* elegantly fashionable
SWAGGERED > SWAGGER
SWAGGERER > SWAGGER
SWAGGERS > SWAGGER
SWAGGIE *same as* > SWAGGER
SWAGGIES > SWAGGIE
SWAGGING > SWAG
SWAGING > SWAGE
SWAGMAN *n* tramp who carries his belongings in a bundle on his back
SWAGMEN > SWAGMAN
SWAGS > SWAG
SWAGSHOP *n* shop selling cheap goods
SWAGSHOPS > SWAGSHOP
SWAGSMAN *same as* > SWAGMAN
SWAGSMEN > SWAGSMAN
SWAIL *same as* > SWALE
SWAILS > SWAIL
SWAIN *n* suitor
SWAINING *n* acting as suitor
SWAININGS > SWAINING
SWAINISH > SWAIN
SWAINS > SWAIN
SWALE *n* moist depression in a tract of land, usually with rank vegetation ▷ *vb* sway
SWALED > SWALE
SWALES > SWALE
SWALIER > SWALE

SWALIEST > SWALE
SWALING > SWALE
SWALINGS > SWALE
SWALLET *n* hole where water goes underground
SWALLETS > SWALLET
SWALLOW *vb* cause to pass down one's throat ▷ *n* swallowing
SWALLOWED > SWALLOW
SWALLOWER > SWALLOW
SWALLOWS > SWALLOW
SWALY > SWALE
SWAM > SWIM
SWAMI *n* Hindu religious teacher
SWAMIES > SWAMI
SWAMIS > SWAMI
SWAMP *n* watery area of land, bog ▷ *vb* cause (a boat) to fill with water and sink
SWAMPED > SWAMP
SWAMPER *n* person who lives or works in a swampy region, esp in the southern US
SWAMPERS > SWAMPER
SWAMPIER > SWAMP
SWAMPIEST > SWAMP
SWAMPING > SWAMP
SWAMPISH > SWAMP
SWAMPLAND *n* permanently waterlogged area
SWAMPLESS > SWAMP
SWAMPS > SWAMP
SWAMPY > SWAMP
SWAMY *same as* > SWAMI
SWAN *n* large usu white water bird with a long graceful neck ▷ *vb* wander about idly
SWANG > SWING
SWANHERD *n* person who herds swans
SWANHERDS > SWANHERD
SWANK *vb* show off or boast ▷ *n* showing off or boasting
SWANKED > SWANK
SWANKER > SWANK
SWANKERS > SWANK
SWANKEST > SWANK
SWANKEY *same as* > SWANKY
SWANKEYS > SWANKY
SWANKIE *same as* > SWANKY
SWANKIER > SWANKY
SWANKIES > SWANKY
SWANKIEST > SWANKY
SWANKILY > SWANKY
SWANKING > SWANK
SWANKPOT *same as* > SWANK
SWANKPOTS > SWANKPOT
SWANKS > SWANK
SWANKY *adj* expensive and showy, stylish ▷ *n* lively person
SWANLIKE > SWAN
SWANNED > SWAN
SWANNERY *n* place where swans are kept and bred
SWANNIE *n* (in NZ) type of all-weather heavy woollen shirt
SWANNIER > SWANNY
SWANNIES > SWANNIE
SWANNIEST > SWANNY
SWANNING > SWAN
SWANNINGS > SWAN
SWANNY *adj* swanlike
SWANPAN *n* Chinese abacus
SWANPANS > SWANPAN
SWANS > SWAN
SWANSDOWN *n* fine soft feathers of a swan
SWANSKIN *n* skin of a swan with the feathers attached
SWANSKINS > SWANSKIN
SWAP *vb* exchange (something) for something else ▷ *n* exchange
SWAPPED > SWAP
SWAPPER > SWAP
SWAPPERS > SWAP
SWAPPING > SWAP
SWAPPINGS > SWAP
SWAPS > SWAP
SWAPT > SWAP
SWAPTION *another name for* > SWAP
SWAPTIONS > SWAPTION
SWARAJ *n* (in British India) self-government
SWARAJES > SWARAJ
SWARAJISM > SWARAJ
SWARAJIST > SWARAJ
SWARD *n* stretch of short grass ▷ *vb* cover or become covered with grass
SWARDED > SWARD
SWARDIER > SWARDY
SWARDIEST > SWARDY
SWARDING > SWARD
SWARDS > SWARD
SWARDY *adj* covered with sward
SWARE > SWEAR
SWARF *n* material removed by cutting tools in the machining of metals, stone, etc ▷ *vb* faint
SWARFED > SWARF
SWARFING > SWARF
SWARFS > SWARF
SWARM *n* large group of bees or other insects ▷ *vb* move in a swarm
SWARMED > SWARM
SWARMER > SWARM
SWARMERS > SWARM
SWARMING > SWARM
SWARMINGS > SWARM
SWARMS > SWARM
SWART *adj* swarthy
SWARTH *same as* > SWART
SWARTHIER > SWARTHY
SWARTHILY > SWARTHY
SWARTHS > SWARTH
SWARTHY *adj* dark-complexioned
SWARTNESS > SWART
SWARTY > SWART
SWARVE *same as* > SWARF
SWARVED > SWARF
SWARVES > SWARF
SWARVING > SWARF
SWASH *n* rush of water up a beach following each break of the waves ▷ *vb* (esp of water or things in water) to wash or move with noisy splashing
SWASHED > SWASH
SWASHER *n* braggart
SWASHERS > SWASHER
SWASHES > SWASH
SWASHIER > SWASHY
SWASHIEST > SWASHY
SWASHING > SWASH
SWASHINGS > SWASH
SWASHWORK *n* type of work done on lathe
SWASHY *adj* slushy
SWASTICA *same as* > SWASTIKA
SWASTICAS > SWASTICA
SWASTIKA *n* symbol in the shape of a cross with the arms bent at right angles, used as the emblem of Nazi Germany
SWASTIKAS > SWASTIKA
SWAT *vb* strike or hit sharply ▷ *n* swatter
SWATCH *n* sample of cloth
SWATCHES > SWATCH
SWATH *n* width of one sweep of a scythe or of the blade of a mowing machine
SWATHABLE > SWATHE
SWATHE *vb* bandage or wrap completely ▷ *n* bandage or wrapping
SWATHED > SWATHE
SWATHER > SWATHE
SWATHERS > SWATHE
SWATHES > SWATHE
SWATHIER > SWATH
SWATHIEST > SWATH
SWATHING > SWATHE
SWATHS > SWATH
SWATHY > SWATH
SWATS > SWAT
SWATTED > SWAT
SWATTER *n* device for killing insects, esp a meshed flat attached to a handle ▷ *vb* splash
SWATTERED > SWATTER
SWATTERS > SWATTER
SWATTING > SWAT
SWATTINGS > SWAT
SWAY *vb* swing to and fro or from side to side ▷ *n* power or influence
SWAYABLE > SWAY
SWAYBACK *n* abnormal sagging in the spine of older horses
SWAYBACKS > SWAYBACK
SWAYED > SWAY
SWAYER > SWAY
SWAYERS > SWAY
SWAYFUL > SWAY
SWAYING > SWAY
SWAYINGS > SWAY
SWAYL *same as* > SWEAL
SWAYLED > SWAYL
SWAYLING > SWAYL
SWAYLINGS > SWAYL
SWAYLS > SWAYL
SWAYS > SWAY
SWAZZLE *n* small metal instrument used to produce a shrill voice
SWAZZLES > SWAZZLE
SWEAL *vb* scorch
SWEALED > SWEAL
SWEALING > SWEAL
SWEALINGS > SWEAL
SWEALS > SWEAL
SWEAR *vb* use obscene or blasphemous language
SWEARD *same as* > SWORD
SWEARDS > SWEARD
SWEARER > SWEAR
SWEARERS > SWEAR
SWEARING > SWEAR
SWEARINGS > SWEAR
SWEARS > SWEAR
SWEARWORD *n* word considered obscene or blasphemous
SWEAT *n* salty liquid given off through the pores of the skin ▷ *vb* have sweat coming through the pores
SWEATBAND *n* strip of cloth tied around the forehead or wrist to absorb sweat
SWEATBOX *n* device for causing tobacco leaves, fruit, or hides to sweat
SWEATED *adj* made by exploited labour
SWEATER *n* (woollen) garment for the upper part of the body
SWEATERS > SWEATER
SWEATIER > SWEATY
SWEATIEST > SWEATY
SWEATILY > SWEATY
SWEATING > SWEAT
SWEATINGS > SWEAT
SWEATLESS > SWEAT
SWEATS > SWEAT
SWEATSHOP *n* place where employees work long hours in poor conditions for low pay
SWEATSUIT *n* knitted suit worn by athletes for training
SWEATY *adj* covered with sweat
SWEDE *n* kind of turnip
SWEDES > SWEDE
SWEDGER *n* Scots dialect word for sweet
SWEDGERS > SWEDGER
SWEE *vb* sway
SWEED > SWEE
SWEEING > SWEE
SWEEL *same as* > SWEAL
SWEELED > SWEEL
SWEELING > SWEEL
SWEELS > SWEEL
SWEENEY *n* police flying squad
SWEENEYS > SWEENEY
SWEENIES > SWEENY
SWEENY *n* wasting of the shoulder muscles of a

horse
WEEP *vb* remove dirt from (a floor) with a broom ▷ *n* sweeping
WEEPBACK *n* rearward inclination of a component or surface
WEEPER *n* device used to sweep carpets, consisting of a long handle attached to a revolving brush
WEEPERS > SWEEPER
WEEPIER > SWEEP
WEEPIEST > SWEEP
WEEPING > SWEEP
WEEPINGS *pl n* debris, litter, or refuse
WEEPS > SWEEP
WEEPY > SWEEP
WEER *variant of* > SWEIR
WEERED > SWEER
WEERER > SWEER
WEEREST > SWEER
WEERING > SWEER
WEERS > SWEER
WEERT > SWEER
WEES > SWEE
EET *adj* tasting of or like sugar ▷ *n* shaped piece of food consisting mainly of sugar ▷ *vb* sweeten
EETCORN *n* variety of maize, the kernels of which are eaten when young
EETED > SWEET
EETEN *vb* make (food or drink) sweet or sweeter
EETENED > SWEETEN
EETENER *n* sweetening agent that does not contain sugar
EETENS > SWEETEN
EETER > SWEET
EETEST > SWEET
EETFISH *n* small Japanese fish
EETIE *n* lovable person
EETIES > SWEETIE
EETING *n* variety of sweet apple
EETINGS > SWEETING
EETISH > SWEET
EETLY > SWEET
EETMAN *n* (in the Caribbean) a man kept by a woman
EETMEAL *adj* (of biscuits) sweet and wholemeal
EETMEAT *n* sweet delicacy such as a small cake
EETMEN > SWEETMAN
EETNESS > SWEET
EETPEA *n* climbing plant with fragrant flowers of delicate pastel colours
EETPEAS > SWEETPEA
EETS > SWEET
EETSHOP *n* shop selling confectionery
EETSOP *n* small West Indian tree
EETSOPS > SWEETSOP
SWEETWOOD *n* tropical tree
SWEETY *same as* > SWEETIE
SWEIR *vb* swear ▷ *adj* lazy
SWEIRED > SWEIR
SWEIRER > SWEIR
SWEIREST > SWEIR
SWEIRING > SWEIR
SWEIRNESS > SWEIR
SWEIRS > SWEIR
SWEIRT > SWEIR
SWELCHIE *n* whirlpool in Orkney
SWELCHIES > SWELCHIE
SWELL *vb* expand or increase ▷ *n* swelling or being swollen ▷ *adj* excellent or fine
SWELLDOM *n* fashionable society
SWELLDOMS > SWELLDOM
SWELLED > SWELL
SWELLER > SWELL
SWELLERS > SWELL
SWELLEST > SWELL
SWELLFISH *popular name for* > PUFFER
SWELLHEAD *n* conceited person
SWELLING > SWELL
SWELLINGS > SWELL
SWELLISH > SWELL
SWELLS > SWELL
SWELT *vb* die
SWELTED > SWELT
SWELTER *vb* feel uncomfortably hot ▷ *n* hot and uncomfortable condition
SWELTERED > SWELTER
SWELTERS > SWELTER
SWELTING > SWELT
SWELTRIER > SWELTRY
SWELTRY *adj* sultry
SWELTS > SWELT
SWEPT > SWEEP
SWEPTBACK *adj* (of an aircraft wing) having the leading edge inclined backwards towards the rear
SWEPTWING *adj* (of an aircraft) having wings swept backwards
SWERF *same as* > SWARF
SWERFED > SWERF
SWERFING > SWERF
SWERFS > SWERF
SWERVABLE > SWERVE
SWERVE *vb* turn aside from a course sharply or suddenly ▷ *n* swerving
SWERVED > SWERVE
SWERVER > SWERVE
SWERVERS > SWERVE
SWERVES > SWERVE
SWERVING > SWERVE
SWERVINGS > SWERVE
SWEVEN *n* vision or dream
SWEVENS > SWEVEN
SWEY *same as* > SWEE
SWEYED > SWEY
SWEYING > SWEY
SWEYS > SWEY
SWIDDEN *n* area of land where slash-and-burn techniques have been used to prepare it for cultivation
SWIDDENS > SWIDDEN
SWIES > SWY
SWIFT *adj* moving or able to move quickly ▷ *n* fast-flying bird with pointed wings ▷ *adv* swiftly or quickly ▷ *vb* make tight
SWIFTED > SWIFT
SWIFTER *n* line run around the ends of capstan bars to prevent their falling out of their sockets
SWIFTERS > SWIFTER
SWIFTEST > SWIFT
SWIFTIE *n* trick, ruse, or deception
SWIFTIES > SWIFTY
SWIFTING > SWIFT
SWIFTLET *n* type of small Asian swift
SWIFTLETS > SWIFTLET
SWIFTLY > SWIFT
SWIFTNESS > SWIFT
SWIFTS > SWIFT
SWIFTY *same as* > SWIFTIE
SWIG *n* large mouthful of drink ▷ *vb* drink in large mouthfuls
SWIGGED > SWIG
SWIGGER > SWIG
SWIGGERS > SWIG
SWIGGING > SWIG
SWIGS > SWIG
SWILER *n* (in Newfoundland) a seal hunter
SWILERS > SWILER
SWILL *vb* drink greedily ▷ *n* sloppy mixture containing waste food, fed to pigs
SWILLED > SWILL
SWILLER > SWILL
SWILLERS > SWILL
SWILLING > SWILL
SWILLINGS > SWILL
SWILLS > SWILL
SWIM *vb* move along in water by movements of the limbs ▷ *n* act or period of swimming
SWIMMABLE > SWIM
SWIMMER > SWIM
SWIMMERET *n* any of the small paired appendages on the abdomen of crustaceans
SWIMMERS *pl n* swimming costume
SWIMMIER > SWIMMY
SWIMMIEST > SWIMMY
SWIMMILY > SWIMMY
SWIMMING > SWIM
SWIMMINGS > SWIM
SWIMMY *adj* dizzy
SWIMS > SWIM
SWIMSUIT *n* woman's swimming garment that leaves the arms and legs bare
SWIMSUITS > SWIMSUIT
SWIMWEAR *n* swimming costumes
SWIMWEARS > SWIMWEAR
SWINDGE *same as* > SWINGE
SWINDGED > SWINDGE
SWINDGES > SWINDGE
SWINDGING > SWINDGE
SWINDLE *vb* cheat (someone) out of money ▷ *n* instance of swindling
SWINDLED > SWINDLE
SWINDLER > SWINDLE
SWINDLERS > SWINDLE
SWINDLES > SWINDLE
SWINDLING > SWINDLE
SWINE *n* contemptible person
SWINEHERD *n* person who looks after pigs
SWINEHOOD > SWINE
SWINELIKE > SWINE
SWINEPOX *n* acute infectious viral disease of pigs
SWINERIES > SWINERY
SWINERY *n* pig farm
SWINES > SWINE
SWING *vb* move to and fro, sway ▷ *n* swinging
SWINGBEAT *n* type of modern dance music that combines soul, rhythm and blues, and hip-hop
SWINGBOAT *n* piece of fairground equipment consisting of a boat-shaped carriage for swinging in
SWINGBY *n* act of spacecraft passing close to planet
SWINGBYS > SWINGBY
SWINGE *vb* beat, flog, or punish
SWINGED > SWINGE
SWINGEING > SWINGE
SWINGER *n* person regarded as being modern and lively
SWINGERS > SWINGER
SWINGES > SWINGE
SWINGIER > SWINGY
SWINGIEST > SWINGY
SWINGING > SWING
SWINGINGS > SWING
SWINGISM *n* former resistance to use of agricultural machines
SWINGISMS > SWINGISM
SWINGLE *n* flat-bladed wooden instrument used for beating and scraping flax ▷ *vb* use a swingle on
SWINGLED > SWINGLE
SWINGLES > SWINGLE
SWINGLING > SWINGLE
SWINGMAN *n* musician specializing in swing music
SWINGMEN > SWINGMAN
SWINGS > SWING
SWINGTREE *n* crossbar in a horse's harness
SWINGY *adj* lively and modern
SWINISH > SWINE
SWINISHLY > SWINE

SWINK *vb* toil or drudge ▷ *n* toil or drudgery
SWINKED > SWINK
SWINKER > SWINK
SWINKERS > SWINK
SWINKING > SWINK
SWINKS > SWINK
SWINNEY *variant of* > SWEENY
SWINNEYS > SWINNEY
SWIPE *vb* strike (at) with a sweeping blow ▷ *n* hard blow
SWIPED > SWIPE
SWIPER > SWIPE
SWIPERS > SWIPE
SWIPES *pl n* beer, esp when poor or weak
SWIPEY *adj* drunk
SWIPIER > SWIPEY
SWIPIEST > SWIPEY
SWIPING > SWIPE
SWIPLE *same as* > SWIPPLE
SWIPLES > SWIPLE
SWIPPLE *n* part of a flail that strikes the grain
SWIPPLES > SWIPPLE
SWIRE *n* neck
SWIRES > SWIRE
SWIRL *vb* turn with a whirling motion ▷ *n* whirling motion
SWIRLED > SWIRL
SWIRLIER > SWIRL
SWIRLIEST > SWIRL
SWIRLING > SWIRL
SWIRLS > SWIRL
SWIRLY > SWIRL
SWISH *vb* move with a whistling or hissing sound ▷ *n* whistling or hissing sound ▷ *adj* fashionable, smart
SWISHED > SWISH
SWISHER > SWISH
SWISHERS > SWISH
SWISHES > SWISH
SWISHEST > SWISH
SWISHIER > SWISHY
SWISHIEST > SWISHY
SWISHING > SWISH
SWISHINGS > SWISH
SWISHY *adj* moving with a swishing sound
SWISS *n* type of muslin
SWISSES > SWISS
SWISSING *n* method of treating cloth
SWISSINGS > SWISSING
SWITCH *n* device for opening and closing an electric circuit ▷ *vb* change abruptly
SWITCHED > SWITCH
SWITCHEL *n* type of beer
SWITCHELS > SWITCHEL
SWITCHER > SWITCH
SWITCHERS > SWITCH
SWITCHES > SWITCH
SWITCHIER > SWITCH
SWITCHING > SWITCH
SWITCHMAN *n* person who operates railway points
SWITCHMEN > SWITCHMAN
SWITCHY > SWITCH
SWITH *adv* swiftly
SWITHE *same as* > SWITH
SWITHER *vb* hesitate or be indecisive ▷ *n* state of hesitation or uncertainty
SWITHERED > SWITHER
SWITHERS > SWITHER
SWITHLY > SWITH
SWITS *same as* > SWITCH
SWITSES > SWITS
SWIVE *vb* have sexual intercourse with (a person)
SWIVED > SWIVE
SWIVEL *vb* turn on a central point ▷ *n* coupling device that allows an attached object to turn freely
SWIVELED > SWIVEL
SWIVELING > SWIVEL
SWIVELLED > SWIVEL
SWIVELS > SWIVEL
SWIVES > SWIVE
SWIVET *n* nervous state
SWIVETS > SWIVET
SWIVING > SWIVE
SWIZ *n* swindle or disappointment
SWIZZ *same as* > SWIZ
SWIZZED > SWIZZ
SWIZZES > SWIZZ
SWIZZING > SWIZZ
SWIZZLE *n* unshaken cocktail ▷ *vb* stir a swizzle stick in (a drink)
SWIZZLED > SWIZZLE
SWIZZLER > SWIZZLE
SWIZZLERS > SWIZZLE
SWIZZLES > SWIZZLE
SWIZZLING > SWIZZLE
SWOB *less common word for* > SWAB
SWOBBED > SWOB
SWOBBER > SWOB
SWOBBERS > SWOB
SWOBBING > SWOB
SWOBS > SWOB
SWOFFER > SWOFFING
SWOFFERS > SWOFFING
SWOFFING *n* sport of saltwater fly-fishing
SWOFFINGS > SWOFFING
SWOLLEN > SWELL
SWOLLENLY > SWELL
SWOLN > SWELL
SWONE *archaic variant of* > SWOON
SWONES > SWONE
SWOON *n* faint ▷ *vb* faint because of shock or strong emotion
SWOONED > SWOON
SWOONER > SWOON
SWOONERS > SWOON
SWOONIER > SWOONY
SWOONIEST > SWOONY
SWOONING > SWOON
SWOONINGS > SWOON
SWOONS > SWOON
SWOONY *adj* romantic or sexy
SWOOP *vb* sweep down or pounce on suddenly ▷ *n* swooping
SWOOPED > SWOOP
SWOOPER > SWOOP
SWOOPERS > SWOOP
SWOOPIER > SWOOP
SWOOPIEST > SWOOP
SWOOPING > SWOOP
SWOOPS > SWOOP
SWOOPY > SWOOP
SWOOSH *vb* make a swirling or rustling sound when moving or pouring out ▷ *n* swirling or rustling sound or movement
SWOOSHED > SWOOSH
SWOOSHES > SWOOSH
SWOOSHING > SWOOSH
SWOP *same as* > SWAP
SWOPPED > SWOP
SWOPPER > SWOP
SWOPPERS > SWOP
SWOPPING > SWOP
SWOPPINGS > SWOP
SWOPS > SWOP
SWOPT > SWOP
SWORD *n* weapon with a long sharp blade ▷ *vb* bear a sword
SWORDBILL *n* South American hummingbird
SWORDED > SWORD
SWORDER *n* fighter with sword
SWORDERS > SWORDER
SWORDFISH *n* large fish with a very long upper jaw
SWORDING > SWORD
SWORDLESS > SWORD
SWORDLIKE > SWORD
SWORDMAN *same as* > SWORDSMAN
SWORDMEN > SWORDMAN
SWORDPLAY *n* action or art of fighting with a sword
SWORDS > SWORD
SWORDSMAN *n* person skilled in the use of a sword
SWORDSMEN > SWORDSMAN
SWORDTAIL *n* type of small freshwater fish of Central America
SWORE > SWEAR
SWORN > SWEAR
SWOT *vb* study (a subject) intensively ▷ *n* person who studies hard
SWOTS > SWOT
SWOTTED > SWOT
SWOTTER > SWOT
SWOTTERS > SWOT
SWOTTIER > SWOTTY
SWOTTIEST > SWOTTY
SWOTTING > SWOT
SWOTTINGS > SWOT
SWOTTY *adj* given to studying hard, esp to the exclusion of other activities
SWOUN *same as* > SWOON
SWOUND *same as* > SWOON
SWOUNDED > SWOUND
SWOUNDING > SWOUND
SWOUNDS *less common spellings of* > ZOUNDS
SWOUNE *same as* > SWOON
SWOUNED > SWOUNE
SWOUNES > SWOUNE
SWOUNING > SWOUNE
SWOUNS > SWOUN
SWOWND *same as* > SWOON
SWOWNDS > SWOWND
SWOWNE *same as* > SWOON
SWOWNES > SWOWNE
SWOZZLE *same as* > SWAZZLE
SWOZZLES > SWOZZLE
SWUM > SWIM
SWUNG > SWING
SWY *n* Australian gambling game involving two coins
SYBARITE *n* lover of luxury ▷ *adj* luxurious or sensuous
SYBARITES > SYBARITE
SYBARITIC > SYBARITE
SYBBE *same as* > SIB
SYBBES > SYBBE
SYBIL *same as* > SIBYL
SYBILS > SYBIL
SYBO *n* spring onion
SYBOE *same as* > SYBO
SYBOES > SYBOE
SYBOTIC *adj* of a swineherd
SYBOTISM > SYBOTIC
SYBOTISMS > SYBOTIC
SYBOW *same as* > SYBO
SYBOWS > SYBOW
SYCAMINE *n* mulberry tree mentioned in the Bible, thought to be the black mulberry
SYCAMINES > SYCAMINE
SYCAMORE *n* tree with five-pointed leaves and two-winged fruits
SYCAMORES > SYCAMORE
SYCE *n* (formerly, in India) servant employed to look after horses, etc
SYCEE *n* silver ingots formerly used as a medium of exchange in China
SYCEES > SYCEE
SYCES > SYCE
SYCOMORE *same as* > SYCAMORE
SYCOMORES > SYCOMORE
SYCONIA > SYCONIUM
SYCONIUM *n* fleshy fruit of the fig
SYCOPHANT *n* person who uses flattery to win favour from people with power or influence
SYCOSES > SYCOSIS
SYCOSIS *n* chronic inflammation of the hair follicles
SYE *vb* strain
SYED > SYE
SYEING > SYE
SYEN *same as* > SCION
SYENITE *n* light-coloured coarse-grained plutonic igneous rock
SYENITES > SYENITE
SYENITIC > SYENITE
SYENS > SYEN

YES > SYE
YKE *same as* > SIKE
YKER *adv* surely
YKES > SYKE
YLI *n* Finnish unit of volume
YLIS > SYLI
YLLABARY *n* table or list of syllables
YLLABI > SYLLABUS
YLLABIC *adj* of or relating to syllables ▷ *n* syllabic consonant
YLLABICS > SYLLABIC
YLLABIFY *vb* divide (a word) into syllables
YLLABISE *same as* > SYLLABIZE
YLLABISM *n* use of a writing system consisting of characters for syllables
YLLABIZE *vb* divide into syllables
YLLABLE *n* part of a word pronounced as a unit
YLLABLED > SYLLABLE
YLLABLES > SYLLABLE
YLLABUB *n* dessert of beaten cream, sugar, and wine
YLLABUBS > SYLLABUB
YLLABUS *n* list of subjects for a course of study
YLLEPSES > SYLLEPSIS
YLLEPSIS *n* (in grammar or rhetoric) the use of a single sentence construction in which a verb, adjective, etc is made to cover two syntactical functions
YLLEPTIC > SYLLEPSIS
YLLOGISE *same as* > SYLLOGIZE
YLLOGISM *n* form of logical reasoning consisting of two premises and a conclusion
YLLOGIST > SYLLOGISM
YLLOGIZE *vb* reason or infer by using syllogisms
YLPH *n* slender graceful girl or woman
YLPHIC *sylph*
YLPHID *n* little sylph
YLPHIDE *same as* > SYLPHID
YLPHIDES > SYLPHIDE
YLPHIDS > SYLPHID
YLPHIER > SYLPH
YLPHIEST > SYLPH
YLPHINE > SYLPH
YLPHISH > SYLPH
YLPHLIKE > SYLPH
YLPHS > SYLPH
YLPHY > SYLPH
YLVA *n* trees growing in a particular region
YLVAE > SYLVA
YLVAN *adj* relating to woods and trees ▷ *n* inhabitant of the woods, esp a spirit
YLVANER *n* German variety of grape
SYLVANERS > SYLVANER
SYLVANITE *n* silver-white mineral
SYLVANS > SYLVAN
SYLVAS > SYLVA
SYLVATIC *adj* growing, living, or occurring in a wood or beneath a tree
SYLVIA *n* songbird
SYLVIAS > SYLVIA
SYLVIINE > SYLVIA
SYLVIN *same as* > SYLVITE
SYLVINE *same as* > SYLVITE
SYLVINES > SYLVINE
SYLVINITE *n* rock containing sylvine
SYLVINS > SYLVIN
SYLVITE *n* soluble colourless, white, or coloured mineral
SYLVITES > SYLVITE
SYMAR *same as* > CYMAR
SYMARS > SYMAR
SYMBION *same as* > SYMBIONT
SYMBIONS > SYMBION
SYMBIONT *n* organism living in a state of symbiosis
SYMBIONTS > SYMBIONT
SYMBIOSES > SYMBIOSIS
SYMBIOSIS *n* close association of two species living together to their mutual benefit
SYMBIOT *same as* > SYMBIONT
SYMBIOTE *same as* > SYMBIONT
SYMBIOTES > SYMBIOTE
SYMBIOTIC > SYMBIOSIS
SYMBIOTS > SYMBIOT
SYMBOL *n* sign or thing that stands for something else ▷ *vb* be a symbol
SYMBOLE *same as* > CYMBAL
SYMBOLED > SYMBOL
SYMBOLES > SYMBOLE
SYMBOLIC *adj* of or relating to a symbol or symbols
SYMBOLICS *n* study of beliefs
SYMBOLING > SYMBOL
SYMBOLISE *same as* > SYMBOLIZE
SYMBOLISM *n* representation of something by symbols
SYMBOLIST *n* person who uses or can interpret symbols ▷ *adj* of, relating to, or characterizing symbolism or symbolists
SYMBOLIZE *vb* be a symbol of
SYMBOLLED > SYMBOL
SYMBOLOGY *n* use, study, or interpretation of symbols
SYMBOLS > SYMBOL
SYMITAR *same as* > SCIMITAR
SYMITARE *same as* > SCIMITAR
SYMITARES > SYMITARE
SYMITARS > SYMITAR
SYMMETRAL > SYMMETRY
SYMMETRIC *adj* (of a disease) affecting both sides of the body
SYMMETRY *n* state of having two halves that are mirror images of each other
SYMPATHIN *n* substance released at certain sympathetic nerve endings
SYMPATHY *n* compassion for someone's pain or distress
SYMPATICO *adj* nice
SYMPATRIC *adj* (of biological speciation or species) existing in the same geographical areas
SYMPATRY *n* existing of organisms together without interbreeding
SYMPETALY *n* quality of having petals that are united
SYMPHILE *n* insect that lives in the nests of social insects and is fed and reared by the inmates
SYMPHILES > SYMPHILE
SYMPHILY *n* presence of different kinds of animal in ants' nests
SYMPHONIC > SYMPHONY
SYMPHONY *n* composition for orchestra, with several movements
SYMPHYSES > SYMPHYSIS
SYMPHYSIS *n* growing together of parts or structures
SYMPHYTIC > SYMPHYSIS
SYMPLAST *n* continuous system of protoplasts, linked by plasmodesmata and bounded by the cell wall
SYMPLASTS > SYMPLAST
SYMPLOCE *n* word repetition in successive clauses
SYMPLOCES > SYMPLOCE
SYMPODIA > SYMPODIUM
SYMPODIAL > SYMPODIUM
SYMPODIUM *n* main axis of growth in the grapevine and similar plants
SYMPOSIA > SYMPOSIUM
SYMPOSIAC *adj* of, suitable for, or occurring at a symposium
SYMPOSIAL > SYMPOSIUM
SYMPOSIUM *n* conference for discussion of a particular topic
SYMPTOM *n* sign indicating the presence of an illness
SYMPTOMS > SYMPTOM
SYMPTOSES > SYMPTOSIS
SYMPTOSIS *n* wasting condition
SYMPTOTIC > SYMPTOSIS
SYN *adv Scots word for* > SINCE
SYNAGOG *same as* > SYNAGOGUE
SYNAGOGAL > SYNAGOGUE
SYNAGOGS > SYNAGOG
SYNAGOGUE *n* Jewish place of worship and religious instruction
SYNALEPHA *n* elision of vowels in speech
SYNANDRIA *pl n* peculiar bunchings of stamens
SYNANGIA > SYNANGIUM
SYNANGIUM *n* junction between arteries
SYNANON *n* type of therapy given to drug addicts
SYNANONS > SYNANON
SYNANTHIC > SYNANTHY
SYNANTHY *n* abnormal joining between flowers
SYNAPHEA *n* continuity in metre of verses of poem
SYNAPHEAS > SYNAPHEA
SYNAPHEIA *same as* > SYNAPHEA
SYNAPSE *n* gap where nerve impulses pass between two nerve cells ▷ *vb* create a synapse
SYNAPSED > SYNAPSE
SYNAPSES > SYNAPSIS
SYNAPSID *n* prehistoric mammal-like reptile
SYNAPSIDS > SYNAPSID
SYNAPSING > SYNAPSE
SYNAPSIS *n* association in pairs of homologous chromosomes at the start of meiosis
SYNAPTASE *n* type of enzyme
SYNAPTE *n* litany in Greek Orthodox Church
SYNAPTES > SYNAPTE
SYNAPTIC *adj* of or relating to a synapse
SYNARCHY *n* joint rule
SYNASTRY *n* coincidence of astrological influences
SYNAXARIA *pl n* readings in the Greek Orthodox Church
SYNAXES > SYNAXIS
SYNAXIS *n* early Christian meeting
SYNC *n* synchronization ▷ *vb* synchronize
SYNCARP *n* fleshy multiple fruit
SYNCARPS > SYNCARP
SYNCARPY *n* quality of consisting of united carpels
SYNCED > SYNC
SYNCH *same as* > SYNC
SYNCHED > SYNCH
SYNCHING > SYNCH
SYNCHRO *n* type of electrical device
SYNCHRONY *n* state of being synchronous
SYNCHROS > SYNCHRO
SYNCHS > SYNCH

SYNCHYSES > SYNCHYSIS
SYNCHYSIS *n* muddled meaning
SYNCING > SYNC
SYNCLINAL > SYNCLINE
SYNCLINE *n* downward slope of stratified rock in which the layers dip towards each other from either side
SYNCLINES > SYNCLINE
SYNCOM *n* communications satellite in stationary orbit
SYNCOMS > SYNCOM
SYNCOPAL > SYNCOPE
SYNCOPATE *vb* stress the weak beats in (a rhythm) instead of the strong ones
SYNCOPE *n* omission of one or more sounds or letters from the middle of a word
SYNCOPES > SYNCOPE
SYNCOPIC > SYNCOPE
SYNCOPTIC > SYNCOPE
SYNCRETIC *adj* of the tendency of languages to reduce their use of inflection
SYNCS > SYNC
SYNCYTIA > SYNCYTIUM
SYNCYTIAL > SYNCYTIUM
SYNCYTIUM *n* mass of cytoplasm containing many nuclei and enclosed in a cell membrane
SYND *same as* > SYNE
SYNDACTYL *adj* (of certain animals) having two or more digits growing fused together ▷ *n* animal with this arrangement of digits
SYNDED > SYND
SYNDESES > SYNDESIS
SYNDESIS *n* use of syndetic constructions
SYNDET *n* synthetic detergent
SYNDETIC *adj* denoting a grammatical construction in which two clauses are connected by a conjunction
SYNDETON *n* syndetic construction
SYNDETONS > SYNDETON
SYNDETS > SYNDET
SYNDIC *n* business or legal agent of some universities or other institutions
SYNDICAL *adj* relating to the theory that syndicates of workers should seize the means of production
SYNDICATE *n* group of people or firms undertaking a joint business project ▷ *vb* publish (material) in several newspapers
SYNDICS > SYNDIC
SYNDING > SYND
SYNDINGS > SYND
SYNDROME *n* combination of symptoms indicating a particular disease
SYNDROMES > SYNDROME
SYNDROMIC > SYNDROME
SYNDS > SYND
SYNE *vb* rinse ▷ *n* rinse ▷ *adv* since
SYNECHIA *n* abnormality of the eye
SYNECHIAS > SYNECHIA
SYNECIOUS *adj* having male and female organs together on a branch
SYNECTIC > SYNECTICS
SYNECTICS *n* method of identifying and solving problems that depends on creative thinking
SYNED > SYNE
SYNEDRIA > SYNEDRION
SYNEDRIAL > SYNEDRION
SYNEDRION *n* assembly of judges
SYNEDRIUM *same as* > SYNEDRION
SYNERESES > SYNERESIS
SYNERESIS *n* process in which a gel contracts on standing and exudes liquid
SYNERGIA *same as* > SYNERGY
SYNERGIAS > SYNERGIA
SYNERGIC > SYNERGY
SYNERGID *n* type of cell in embryo
SYNERGIDS > SYNERGID
SYNERGIES > SYNERGY
SYNERGISE *same as* > SYNERGIZE
SYNERGISM *same as* > SYNERGY
SYNERGIST *n* drug, muscle, etc, that increases the action of another ▷ *adj* of or relating to synergism
SYNERGIZE *vb* act in synergy
SYNERGY *n* working together of two or more people, substances, or things to produce an effect greater than the sum of their individual effects
SYNES > SYNE
SYNESES > SYNESIS
SYNESIS *n* grammatical construction in which the inflection or form of a word is conditioned by the meaning rather than the syntax
SYNESISES > SYNESIS
SYNFUEL *n* synthetic fuel
SYNFUELS > SYNFUEL
SYNGAMIC > SYNGAMY
SYNGAMIES > SYNGAMY
SYNGAMOUS > SYNGAMY
SYNGAMY *n* sexual reproduction
SYNGAS *n* mixture of carbon monoxide and hydrogen
SYNGASES > SYNGAS
SYNGASSES > SYNGAS
SYNGENEIC *adj* with identical genes
SYNGENIC *adj* with the same genetic makeup
SYNGRAPH *n* document signed by several parties
SYNGRAPHS > SYNGRAPH
SYNING > SYNE
SYNIZESES > SYNIZESIS
SYNIZESIS *n* contraction of two vowels originally belonging to separate syllables into a single syllable
SYNKARYA > SYNKARYON
SYNKARYON *n* nucleus of a fertilized egg
SYNOD *n* church council
SYNODAL *adj* of or relating to a synod ▷ *n* money paid to a bishop by less senior members of the clergy at a synod
SYNODALS > SYNOD
SYNODIC *adj* relating to or involving a conjunction or two successive conjunctions of the same star, planet, or satellite
SYNODICAL > SYNOD
SYNODS > SYNOD
SYNODSMAN *n* layman at synod
SYNODSMEN > SYNODSMAN
SYNOECETE *same as* > SYNOEKETE
SYNOECISE *same as* > SYNOECIZE
SYNOECISM *n* union
SYNOECIZE *vb* unite
SYNOEKETE *n* insect that lives in the nests of social insects without receiving any attentions from the inmates
SYNOICOUS *variant of* > SYNECIOUS
SYNONYM *n* word with the same meaning as another
SYNONYME *same as* > SYNONYM
SYNONYMES > SYNONYME
SYNONYMIC > SYNONYM
SYNONYMS > SYNONYM
SYNONYMY *n* study of synonyms
SYNOPSES > SYNOPSIS
SYNOPSIS *n* summary or outline
SYNOPSISE *same as* > SYNOPSIZE
SYNOPSIZE *vb* make a synopsis of
SYNOPTIC *adj* of or relating to a synopsis ▷ *n* any of the three synoptic Gospels
SYNOPTICS > SYNOPTIC
SYNOPTIST > SYNOPTIC
SYNOVIA *n* clear thick fluid that lubricates the body joints
SYNOVIAL *adj* of or relating to the synovia
SYNOVIAS > SYNOVIA
SYNOVITIC > SYNOVITIS
SYNOVITIS *n* inflammation of the membrane surrounding a joint
SYNROC *n* titanium-ceramic substance that can incorporate nuclear waste in its crystals
SYNROCS > SYNROC
SYNTACTIC *adj* relating to or determined by syntax
SYNTAGM *same as* > SYNTAGMA
SYNTAGMA *n* syntactic unit or a word or phrase forming a syntactic unit
SYNTAGMAS > SYNTAGMA
SYNTAGMIC > SYNTAGMA
SYNTAGMS > SYNTAGM
SYNTAN *n* synthetic tanning substance
SYNTANS > SYNTAN
SYNTAX *n* way in which words are arranged to form phrases and sentences
SYNTAXES > SYNTAX
SYNTECTIC > SYNTEXIS
SYNTENIC > SYNTENY
SYNTENIES > SYNTENY
SYNTENY *n* presence of tw[o] or more genes on the sam[e] chromosome
SYNTEXIS *n* liquefaction
SYNTH *n* type of electrophonic musical instrument operated by a keyboard and pedals
SYNTHESES > SYNTHESIS
SYNTHESIS *n* combinatio[n] of objects or ideas into a whole
SYNTHETIC *adj* (of a substance) made artificially ▷ *n* synthetic substance or material
SYNTHON *n* molecule used in synthesis
SYNTHONS > SYNTHON
SYNTHPOP *n* pop music using synthesizers
SYNTHPOPS > SYNTHPOP
SYNTHRONI *pl n* combine[d] thrones for bishops and their subordinates
SYNTHS > SYNTH
SYNTONIC *adj* emotionall[y] in harmony with one's environment
SYNTONIES > SYNTONY
SYNTONIN *n* substance in muscle
SYNTONINS > SYNTONIN
SYNTONISE *same as* > SYNTONIZE
SYNTONIZE *vb* make frequencies match
SYNTONOUS *same as* > SYNTONIC
SYNTONY *n* matching of frequencies
SYNURA *n* variety of microbe
SYNURAE > SYNURA

SYPE *same as* > SIPE
SYPED > SYPE
SYPES > SYPE
SYPH *shortening of* > SYPHILIS
SYPHER *vb* lap (a chamfered edge of one plank over that of another) in order to form a flush surface
SYPHERED > SYPHER
SYPHERING > SYPHER
SYPHERS > SYPHER
SYPHILIS *n* serious sexually transmitted disease
SYPHILISE *same as* > SYPHILIZE
SYPHILIZE *vb* infect with syphilis
SYPHILOID > SYPHILIS
SYPHILOMA *n* tumour or gumma caused by infection with syphilis
SYPHON *same as* > SIPHON
SYPHONED > SYPHON
SYPHONING > SYPHON
SYPHONS > SYPHON
SYPHS > SYPH
SYPING > SYPE
SYRAH *n* type of French red wine
SYRAHS > SYRAH
SYREN *same as* > SIREN
SYRENS > SYREN
SYRETTE *n* small disposable syringe
SYRETTES > SYRETTE
SYRINGA *n* mock orange or lilac
SYRINGAS > SYRINGA
SYRINGE *n* device for withdrawing or injecting fluids, consisting of a hollow cylinder, a piston, and a hollow needle ▷ *vb* wash out or inject with a syringe
SYRINGEAL > SYRINX
SYRINGED > SYRINGE
SYRINGES > SYRINX
SYRINGING > SYRINGE
SYRINX *n* vocal organ of a bird, which is situated in the lower part of the trachea
SYRINXES > SYRINX
SYRPHIAN *same as* > SYRPHID
SYRPHIANS > SYRPHIAN
SYRPHID *n* type of fly
SYRPHIDS > SYRPHID
SYRTES > SYRTIS
SYRTIS *n* area of quicksand
SYRUP *n* solution of sugar in water ▷ *vb* bring to the consistency of syrup
SYRUPED > SYRUP
SYRUPIER > SYRUPY
SYRUPIEST > SYRUPY
SYRUPING > SYRUP
SYRUPLIKE > SYRUP
SYRUPS > SYRUP
SYRUPY *adj* thick and sweet
SYSADMIN *n* computer system administrator
SYSADMINS > SYSADMIN
SYSOP *n* person who runs a system or network
SYSOPS > SYSOP
SYSSITIA *n* ancient Spartan communal meal
SYSSITIAS > SYSSITIA
SYSTALTIC *adj* (esp of the action of the heart) characterized by alternate contractions and dilations
SYSTEM *n* method or set of methods
SYSTEMED *adj* having system
SYSTEMIC *adj* affecting the entire animal or body ▷ *n* systemic pesticide, fungicide, etc
SYSTEMICS > SYSTEMIC
SYSTEMISE *same as* > SYSTEMIZE
SYSTEMIZE *vb* give a system to
SYSTEMS > SYSTEM
SYSTOLE *n* regular contraction of the heart as it pumps blood
SYSTOLES > SYSTOLE
SYSTOLIC > SYSTOLE
SYSTYLE *n* building with different types of columns
SYSTYLES > SYSTYLE
SYTHE *same as* > SITH
SYTHES > SYTHE
SYVER *n* street drain or the grating over it
SYVERS > SYVER
SYZYGAL > SYZYGY
SYZYGETIC > SYZYGY
SYZYGIAL > SYZYGY
SYZYGIES > SYZYGY
SYZYGY *n* either of the two positions of a celestial body when sun, earth, and the body lie in a straight line

Tt

TA *interj* thank you
TAAL *n* language: usually, by implication, Afrikaans
TAALS > TAAL
TAATA *child's word for* > FATHER
TAATAS > TAATA
TAB *n* small flap or projecting label ▷ *vb* supply with a tab
TABANID *n* stout-bodied fly, the females of which have mouthparts specialized for sucking blood
TABANIDS > TABANID
TABARD *n* short sleeveless tunic decorated with a coat of arms, worn in medieval times
TABARDED *adj* wearing a tabard
TABARDS > TABARD
TABARET *n* hard-wearing fabric of silk or similar cloth with stripes of satin or moire, used esp for upholstery
TABARETS > TABARET
TABASHEER *n* dried bamboo sap, used medicinally
TABASHIR *same as* > TABASHEER
TABASHIRS > TABASHIR
TABBED > TAB
TABBIED > TABBY
TABBIES > TABBY
TABBINET *same as* > TABINET
TABBINETS > TABBINET
TABBING > TAB
TABBIS *n* silken cloth
TABBISES > TABBIS
TABBOULEH *n* kind of Middle Eastern salad made with cracked wheat, mint, parsley, and usually cucumber
TABBOULI *same as* > TABBOULEH
TABBOULIS > TABBOULI
TABBY *vb* make (eg a material) appear wavy ▷ *n* female domestic cat
TABBYHOOD *n* spinsterhood
TABBYING > TABBY
TABEFIED > TABEFY
TABEFIES > TABEFY
TABEFY *vb* emaciate or become emaciated
TABEFYING > TABEFY
TABELLION *n* scribe or notary authorized by the Roman Empire
TABER *old variant of* > TABOR
TABERD *same as* > TABARD
TABERDAR *n* holder of a scholarship at Queen's College, Oxford
TABERDARS > TABERDAR
TABERDS > TABERD
TABERED > TABER
TABERING > TABER
TABERS > TABER
TABES *n* wasting of a bodily organ or part
TABESCENT *adj* progressively emaciating
TABETIC > TABES
TABETICS > TABES
TABI *n* thick-soled Japanese sock, worn with sandals
TABID *adj* emaciated
TABINET *n* type of tabbied fabric
TABINETS > TABINET
TABIS > TABI
TABLA *n* one of a pair of Indian drums played with the hands
TABLAS > TABLA
TABLATURE *n* any of a number of forms of musical notation, esp for playing the lute, consisting of letters and signs indicating rhythm and fingering
TABLE *n* piece of furniture with a flat top supported by legs ▷ *vb* submit (a motion) for discussion by a meeting
TABLEAU *n* silent motionless group arranged to represent some scene
TABLEAUS > TABLEAU
TABLEAUX > TABLEAU
TABLED > TABLE
TABLEFUL > TABLE
TABLEFULS > TABLE
TABLELAND *n* high plateau
TABLELESS > TABLE
TABLEMATE *n* someone with whom one shares a table
TABLES > TABLE
TABLESFUL > TABLE
TABLET *n* medicinal pill ▷ *vb* make (something) into a tablet
TABLETED > TABLET
TABLETING > TABLET
TABLETOP *n* upper surface of a table
TABLETOPS > TABLETOP
TABLETS > TABLET
TABLETTED > TABLET
TABLEWARE *n* articles such as dishes, plates, knives, forks, etc, used at meals
TABLEWISE *adv* in the form of a table
TABLIER *n* (formerly) part of a dress resembling an apron
TABLIERS > TABLIER
TABLING > TABLE
TABLINGS > TABLE
TABLOID *n* small-sized newspaper with many photographs and a concise, usu sensational style
TABLOIDS > TABLOID
TABLOIDY *adj* characteristic of a tabloid newspaper; trashy
TABOGGAN *same as* > TOBOGGAN
TABOGGANS > TABOGGAN
TABOO *n* prohibition resulting from religious or social conventions ▷ *adj* forbidden by a taboo ▷ *vb* place under a taboo
TABOOED > TABOO
TABOOING > TABOO
TABOOLEY *variant of* > TABBOULEH
TABOOLEYS > TABOOLEY
TABOOS > TABOO
TABOR *vb* play the tabor
TABORED > TABOR
TABORER > TABOR
TABORERS > TABOR
TABORET *n* low stool, originally in the shape of a drum

ABORETS > TABORET
ABORIN *same as* > TABORET
ABORINE *same as* > TABOURIN
ABORINES > TABORINE
ABORING > TABOR
ABORINS > TABORIN
ABORS > TABOR
ABOULEH *variant of* > TABBOULEH
ABOULEHS > TABOULEH
ABOULI *same as* > TABBOULEH
ABOULIS > TABOULI
ABOUR *same as* > TABOR
ABOURED > TABOUR
ABOURER > TABOUR
ABOURERS > TABOUR
ABOURET *same as* > TABORET
ABOURETS > TABOURET
ABOURIN *same as* > TABORET
ABOURING > TABOUR
ABOURINS > TABOURIN
ABOURS > TABOUR
BRERE *same as* > TABOR
BRERES > TABRERE
BRET *n* smaller version of a tabor
BRETS > TABRET
BS > TAB
BU *same as* > TABOO
BUED > TABU
BUING > TABU
BULA *n* tablet for writing on
BULABLE > TABULATE
BULAE > TABULA
BULAR *adj* arranged in a table
BULARLY > TABULAR
BULATE *vb* arrange (information) in a table ▷ *adj* having a flat surface
BULATED > TABULATE
BULATES > TABULATE
BULATOR *n* key on a typewriter or word processor that sets stops so that data can be arranged and presented in columns
BULI *variant of* > TABBOULEH
BULIS > TABULI
BUN *n* organic compound used in chemical warfare as a lethal nerve gas
BUNS > TABUN
BUS > TABU
CAHOUT *n* abnormal outgrowth on the tamarisk plant
CAHOUTS > TACAHOUT
CAMAHAC *n* any of several strong-smelling resinous gums obtained from certain trees, used in making ointments, incense, etc
CAN *n* electronic ultrahigh-frequency navigation system for aircraft which gives a continuous indication of bearing and distance from a transmitting station
TACANS > TACAN
TACE *same as* > TASSET
TACES > TACE
TACET *vb* (on a musical score) a direction indicating that a particular instrument or singer does not take part in a movement or part of a movement
TACETED > TACET
TACETING > TACET
TACETS > TACET
TACH *n* device for measuring speed
TACHE *n* buckle, clasp, or hook
TACHES > TACHE
TACHINA as in *tachina fly* bristly fly
TACHINID *n* type of fly
TACHINIDS > TACHINID
TACHISM *same as* > TACHISME
TACHISME *n* type of action painting evolved in France in which haphazard dabs and blots of colour are treated as a means of instinctive or unconscious expression
TACHISMES > TACHISME
TACHISMS > TACHISM
TACHIST > TACHISM
TACHISTE > TACHISME
TACHISTES > TACHISME
TACHISTS > TACHIST
TACHO *same as* > TACHOGRAM
TACHOGRAM *n* graphical record of readings
TACHOS > TACHO
TACHS > TACH
TACHYLITE *same as* > TACHYLYTE
TACHYLYTE *n* black basaltic glass often found on the edges of intrusions of basalt
TACHYON *n* hypothetical elementary particle capable of travelling faster than the velocity of light
TACHYONIC > TACHYON
TACHYONS > TACHYON
TACHYPNEA *n* abnormally rapid breathing
TACIT *adj* implied but not spoken
TACITLY > TACIT
TACITNESS > TACIT
TACITURN *adj* habitually uncommunicative
TACK *n* short nail with a large head ▷ *vb* fasten with tacks
TACKBOARD *n* noticeboard
TACKED > TACK
TACKER > TACK
TACKERS > TACK
TACKET *n* nail, esp a hobnail
TACKETS > TACKET
TACKETY > TACKET
TACKEY *same as* > TACKY
TACKIER > TACKY
TACKIES *pl n* tennis shoes or plimsolls
TACKIEST > TACKY
TACKIFIED > TACKIFY
TACKIFIER > TACKIFY
TACKIFIES > TACKIFY
TACKIFY *vb* give (eg rubber) a sticky feel
TACKILY > TACKY
TACKINESS > TACKY
TACKING > TACK
TACKINGS > TACK
TACKLE *vb* deal with (a task) ▷ *n* act of tackling an opposing player
TACKLED > TACKLE
TACKLER > TACKLE
TACKLERS > TACKLE
TACKLES > TACKLE
TACKLESS > TACK
TACKLING > TACKLE
TACKLINGS > TACKLE
TACKS > TACK
TACKSMAN *n* leaseholder, esp a tenant in the Highlands who sublets
TACKSMEN > TACKSMAN
TACKY *adj* slightly sticky
TACMAHACK *same as* > TACAMAHAC
TACNODE *n* in maths, point at which two branches of a curve have a common tangent, each branch extending in both directions of the tangent
TACNODES > TACNODE
TACO *n* tortilla fried until crisp, served with a filling
TACONITE *n* fine-grained sedimentary rock containing magnetite, haematite, and silica, which occurs in the Lake Superior region: a low-grade iron ore
TACONITES > TACONITE
TACOS > TACO
TACRINE *n* drug used to treat Alzheimer's disease
TACRINES > TACRINE
TACT *n* skill in avoiding giving offence
TACTFUL > TACT
TACTFULLY > TACT
TACTIC *n* method or plan to achieve an end
TACTICAL *adj* of or employing tactics
TACTICIAN > TACTICS
TACTICITY *n* quality of regularity in the arrangement of repeated units within a polymer chain
TACTICS *n* art of directing military forces in battle
TACTILE *adj* of or having the sense of touch
TACTILELY > TACTILE
TACTILIST *n* artist whose work strives to appeal to the sense of touch
TACTILITY > TACTILE
TACTION *n* act of touching
TACTIONS > TACTION
TACTISM *another word for* > TAXIS
TACTISMS > TACTISM
TACTLESS > TACT
TACTS > TACT
TACTUAL *adj* caused by touch
TACTUALLY > TACTUAL
TAD *n* small bit or piece
TADDIE *short for* > TADPOLE
TADDIES > TADDIE
TADPOLE *n* limbless tailed larva of a frog or toad
TADPOLES > TADPOLE
TADS > TAD
TADVANCE *vb* Spenserian form of advance
TAE *Scots form of the verb* > TOE
TAED > TAE
TAEDIUM *archaic spelling of* > TEDIUM
TAEDIUMS > TAEDIUM
TAEING > TAE
TAEKWONDO *n* Korean martial art
TAEL *n* unit of weight, used in the Far East, having various values between one to two and a half ounces
TAELS > TAEL
TAENIA *n* (in ancient Greece) a narrow fillet or headband for the hair
TAENIAE > TAENIA
TAENIAS > TAENIA
TAENIASES > TAENIASIS
TAENIASIS *n* infestation with tapeworms
TAENIATE *adj* ribbon-like
TAENIOID *adj* ribbon-like
TAES > TAE
TAFFAREL *same as* > TAFFRAIL
TAFFARELS > TAFFAREL
TAFFEREL *same as* > TAFFRAIL
TAFFERELS > TAFFEREL
TAFFETA *n* shiny silk or rayon fabric
TAFFETAS *same as* > TAFFETA
TAFFETIES > TAFFETY
TAFFETY *same as* > TAFFETA
TAFFIA *same as* > TAFIA
TAFFIAS > TAFFIA
TAFFIES > TAFFY
TAFFRAIL *n* rail at the back of a ship or boat
TAFFRAILS > TAFFRAIL
TAFFY *same as* > TOFFEE
TAFIA *n* type of rum, esp from Guyana or the Caribbean
TAFIAS > TAFIA

TAG *n* label bearing information ▷ *vb* attach a tag to
TAGALONG *n* one who trails behind, esp uninvited; a hanger-on
TAGALONGS > TAGALONG
TAGAREEN *n* junk shop
TAGAREENS > TAGAREEN
TAGBOARD *n* sturdy form of cardboard
TAGBOARDS > TAGBOARD
TAGETES *n* any of a genus of plants with yellow or orange flowers, including the French and African marigolds
TAGGANT *n* microscopic material added to substance to identify it
TAGGANTS > TAGGANT
TAGGED > TAG
TAGGEE *n* one who has been made to wear a tag
TAGGEES > TAGGEE
TAGGER *n* one who marks with a tag
TAGGERS > TAGGER
TAGGIER > TAGGY
TAGGIEST > TAGGY
TAGGING > TAG
TAGGINGS > TAG
TAGGY *adj* (of wool, hair, etc) matted
TAGHAIRM *n* form of divination once practised in the Highlands of Scotland
TAGHAIRMS > TAGHAIRM
TAGINE *n* large, heavy N African cooking pot with a conical lid
TAGINES > TAGINE
TAGLIKE *adj* resembling a tag
TAGLINE *n* funny line of joke
TAGLINES > TAGLINE
TAGLIONI *n* type of coat
TAGLIONIS > TAGLIONI
TAGMA *n* distinct region of the body of an arthropod, such as the head, thorax, or abdomen of an insect
TAGMATA > TAGMA
TAGMEME *n* class of speech elements all of which may fulfil the same grammatical role in a sentence
TAGMEMES > TAGMEME
TAGMEMIC > TAGMEME
TAGMEMICS > TAGMEME
TAGRAG *same as* > RAGTAG
TAGRAGS > TAGRAG
TAGS > TAG
TAGUAN *n* large nocturnal flying squirrel of high forests in the East Indies that uses its long tail as a rudder
TAGUANS > TAGUAN
TAHA *n* type of South African bird
TAHAS > TAHA
TAHINA *same as* > TAHINI
TAHINAS > TAHINA
TAHINI *n* paste made from ground sesame seeds, used esp in Middle Eastern cookery
TAHINIS > TAHINI
TAHOU *same as* > SILVEREYE
TAHOUS > TAHOU
TAHR *n* goatlike bovid mammal of mountainous regions of S and SW Asia, having a shaggy coat and curved horns
TAHRS > TAHR
TAHSIL *n* administrative division of a zila in certain states in India
TAHSILDAR *n* officer in charge of the collection of revenues, etc, in a tahsil
TAHSILS > TAHSIL
TAI as in *tai chi chuan* Chinese system of callisthenics characterized by coordinated and rhythmic movements
TAIAHA *n* carved weapon in the form of a staff, now used in Māori ceremonial oratory
TAIAHAS > TAIAHA
TAIG *n* often derogatory term for Roman Catholic
TAIGA *n* belt of coniferous forest extending across much of subarctic North America, Europe, and Asia
TAIGAS > TAIGA
TAIGLACH *same as* > TEIGLACH
TAIGLE *vb* entangle or impede
TAIGLED > TAIGLE
TAIGLES > TAIGLE
TAIGLING > TAIGLE
TAIGS > TAIG
TAIHOA *interj* hold on! no hurry!
TAIKONAUT *n* astronaut from the People's Republic of China
TAIL *n* rear part of an animal's body, usu forming a flexible appendage ▷ *adj* at the rear ▷ *vb* follow (someone) secretly
TAILARD *n* one having a tail
TAILARDS > TAILARD
TAILBACK *n* queue of traffic stretching back from an obstruction
TAILBACKS > TAILBACK
TAILBOARD *n* removable or hinged rear board on a truck etc
TAILBONE *nontechnical name for* > COCCYX
TAILBONES > TAILBONE
TAILCOAT *n* man's black coat having a horizontal cut over the hips and a tapering tail with a vertical slit up to the waist
TAILCOATS > TAILCOAT
TAILED > TAIL
TAILENDER *n* (in cricket) the batter last in the batting order
TAILER *n* one that tails
TAILERON *n* aileron located on the tailplane of an aircraft
TAILERONS > TAILERON
TAILERS > TAILER
TAILFAN *n* fanned structure at the hind end of a lobster or related crustacean, formed from the telson and uropods
TAILFANS > TAILFAN
TAILFIN *n* decorative projection at back of car
TAILFINS > TAILFIN
TAILFLIES > TAILFLY
TAILFLY *n* in angling, the lowest fly on a wet-fly cast
TAILGATE *n* door at the rear of a hatchback vehicle ▷ *vb* drive very close behind (a vehicle)
TAILGATED > TAILGATE
TAILGATER > TAILGATE
TAILGATES > TAILGATE
TAILING *n* part of a beam, rafter, projecting brick or stone, etc, embedded in a wall
TAILINGS *pl n* waste left over after certain processes, such as from an ore-crushing plant or in milling grain
TAILLAMP *n* rear light
TAILLAMPS > TAILLAMP
TAILLE *n* (in France before 1789) a tax levied by a king or overlord on his subjects
TAILLES > TAILLE
TAILLESS > TAIL
TAILLEUR *n* woman's suit
TAILLEURS > TAILLEUR
TAILLIE *n* (in law) the limitation of an estate or interest to a person and the heirs of his body
TAILLIES > TAILLIE
TAILLIGHT *same as* > TAILLAMP
TAILLIKE *adj* resembling a tail
TAILOR *n* person who makes men's clothes ▷ *vb* cut or style (a garment) to specific requirements
TAILORED > TAILOR
TAILORESS *n* female tailor
TAILORING > TAILOR
TAILORS > TAILOR
TAILPIECE *n* piece added at the end of something, for example a report
TAILPIPE *vb* attach an object, esp a tin can, to the tail of an animal
TAILPIPED > TAILPIPE
TAILPIPES > TAILPIPE
TAILPLANE *n* small stabilizing wing at the re of an aircraft
TAILRACE *n* channel that carries water away from a water wheel, turbine, etc
TAILRACES > TAILRACE
TAILS *adv* with the side of a coin that does not have a portrait of a head on it uppermost
TAILSKID *n* runner under the tail of an aircraft
TAILSKIDS > TAILSKID
TAILSLIDE *n* backwards descent of an aeroplane after stalling while in an upward trajectory
TAILSPIN *n* uncontrolled spinning dive of an aircra
TAILSPINS > TAILSPIN
TAILSTOCK *n* casting tha slides on the bed of a lath in alignment with the headstock and is locked in position to support the free end of a workpiece
TAILWATER *n* water flowing in a tailrace
TAILWHEEL *n* wheel fittec to the rear of a vehicle, es the landing wheel under the tail of an aircraft
TAILWIND *n* wind coming from the rear
TAILWINDS > TAILWIND
TAILYE *same as* > TAILLIE
TAILYES > TAILYE
TAILZIE *same as* > TAILLIE
TAILZIES > TAILZIE
TAIN *n* tinfoil used in backing mirrors
TAINS > TAIN
TAINT *vb* spoil with a small amount of decay, contamination, or other bad quality ▷ *n* something that taints
TAINTED > TAINT
TAINTING > TAINT
TAINTLESS > TAINT
TAINTS > TAINT
TAINTURE *n* contamination; staining
TAINTURES > TAINTURE
TAIPAN *n* large poisonous Australian snake
TAIPANS > TAIPAN
TAIRA *same as* > TAYRA
TAIRAS > TAIRA
TAIS > TAI
TAISCH *n* (in Scotland) apparition of a person whose death is imminen
TAISCHES > TAISCH
TAISH *same as* > TAISCH
TAISHES > TAISH
TAIT *same as* > TATE
TAITS > TAIT
TAIVER *same as* > TAVER
TAIVERED > TAIVER
TAIVERING > TAIVER
TAIVERS > TAIVER

AIVERT *adj* Scots word meaning confused or bewildered
AJ *n* tall conical cap worn as a mark of distinction by Muslims
AJES >TAJ
AJINE *same as* >TAGINE
AJINES >TAJINE
AK *Scots variant spelling of* >TAKE
AKA *n* standard monetary unit of Bangladesh, divided into 100 paise
AKABLE >TAKE
AKAHE *n* very rare flightless New Zealand bird
AKAHES >TAKAHE
AKAMAKA *same as* >TACAMAHAC
AKAMAKAS >TAKAMAKA
AKAS >TAKA
AKE *vb* remove from a place ▷ *n* one of a series of recordings from which the best will be used
AKEABLE >TAKE
AKEAWAY *adj* (of food) sold for consumption away from the premises ▷ *n* shop or restaurant selling meals for eating elsewhere
KEAWAYS >TAKEAWAY
AKEDOWN *n* disassembly
AKEDOWNS >TAKEDOWN
AKEN >TAKE
AKEOFF *n* act or process of making an aircraft airborne
AKEOFFS >TAKEOFF
AKEOUT *n* shop or restaurant that sells such food
AKEOUTS >TAKEOUT
AKEOVER *n* act of taking control of a company by buying a large number of its shares
AKEOVERS >TAKEOVER
AKER *n* person who agrees to take something that is offered
AKERS >TAKER
AKES >TAKE
AKEUP *n* the claiming or acceptance of something, esp a state benefit, that is due or available
AKEUPS >TAKEUP
AKHI *n* type of wild Mongolian horse
AKHIS >TAKHI
AKI *same as* >TAKHIW
AKIER >TAKY
AKIEST >TAKY
AKIN *n* massive bovid mammal of mountainous regions of S Asia, having a shaggy coat, short legs, and horns that point backwards and upwards
AKING >TAKE
AKINGLY >TAKE
AKINGS >TAKE
TAKINS >TAKIN
TAKIS >TAKI
TAKKIES *same as* >TACKIES
TAKS >TAK
TAKY *adj* appealing
TALA *n* standard monetary unit of Samoa, divided into 100 sene
TALAK *same as* >TALAQ
TALAKS >TALAK
TALANT *old variant of* >TALON
TALANTS >TALANT
TALAPOIN *n* smallest of the guenon monkeys of swampy central W African forests, having olive-green fur and slightly webbed digits
TALAPOINS >TALAPOIN
TALAQ *n* Muslim form of divorce
TALAQS >TALAQ
TALAR *n* ankle-length robe
TALARIA *pl n* winged sandals, such as those worn by Hermes
TALARS >TALAR
TALAS >TALA
TALAUNT *old variant of* >TALON
TALAUNTS >TALAUNT
TALAYOT *n* ancient Balearic stone tower
TALAYOTS >TALAYOT
TALBOT *n* (formerly) an ancient breed of large hound, usually white or light-coloured, having pendulous ears and strong powers of scent
TALBOTS >TALBOT
TALBOTYPE *n* early type of photographic process (invented by W H Fox Talbot) or a photograph produced using it
TALC *n* talcum powder ▷ *vb* apply talc to ▷ *adj* of, or relating to, talc
TALCED >TALC
TALCIER >TALCY
TALCIEST >TALCY
TALCING >TALC
TALCKED >TALCKY
TALCKIER >TALCKY
TALCKIEST >TALCKY
TALCKING >TALCKY
TALCKY *same as* >TALCY
TALCOSE >TALC
TALCOUS >TALC
TALCS >TALC
TALCUM *n* white, grey, brown, or pale green mineral, found in metamorphic rocks. It is used in the manufacture of talcum powder and electrical insulatorsr
TALCUMS >TALCUM
TALCY *adj* like, containing, or covered in talc
TALE *n* story
TALEA *n* rhythmic pattern in certain mediaeval choral compositions
TALEAE >TALEA
TALEFUL *adj* having many tales
TALEGALLA *n* brush turkey, of New Guinea and Australia
TALEGGIO *n* Italian cheese
TALEGGIOS >TALEGGIO
TALENT *n* natural ability
TALENTED >TALENT
TALENTS >TALENT
TALER *same as* >THALER
TALERS >TALER
TALES *n* group of persons summoned from among those present in court or from bystanders to fill vacancies on a jury panel
TALESMAN >TALES
TALESMEN >TALES
TALEYSIM >TALLITH
TALI >TALUS
TALIGRADE *adj* (of mammals) walking on the outer side of the foot
TALION *n* system or legal principle of making the punishment correspond to the crime
TALIONIC *adj* of or relating to talion
TALIONS >TALION
TALIPAT *same as* >TALIPOT
TALIPATS >TALIPAT
TALIPED *adj* having a club foot ▷ *n* club-footed person
TALIPEDS >TALIPED
TALIPES *n* congenital deformity of the foot by which it is twisted in any of various positions
TALIPOT *n* palm tree of the East Indies, having large leaves that are used for fans, thatching houses, etc
TALIPOTS >TALIPOT
TALISMAN *n* object believed to have magic power
TALISMANS >TALISMAN
TALK *vb* express ideas or feelings by means of speech ▷ *n* speech or lecture
TALKABLE >TALK
TALKATHON *n* epic bout of discussion or speechifying
TALKATIVE *adj* fond of talking
TALKBACK *n* broadcast in which telephone comments or questions from the public are transmitted live
TALKBACKS >TALKBACK
TALKBOX *n* voice box
TALKBOXES >TALKBOX
TALKED >TALK
TALKER >TALK
TALKERS >TALK
TALKFEST *n* lengthy discussion
TALKFESTS >TALKFEST
TALKIE *n* early film with a soundtrack
TALKIER >TALKY
TALKIES >TALKIE
TALKIEST >TALKY
TALKINESS *n* quality or condition of being talky
TALKING *n* speech; the act of speaking
TALKINGS >TALKING
TALKS >TALK
TALKY *adj* containing too much dialogue or inconsequential talk
TALL *adj* higher than average
TALLAGE *n* tax levied by the Norman and early Angevin kings on their Crown lands and royal towns ▷ *vb* levy a tax (upon)
TALLAGED >TALLAGE
TALLAGES >TALLAGE
TALLAGING >TALLAGE
TALLAISIM >TALLITH
TALLAT *same as* >TALLET
TALLATS >TALLAT
TALLBOY *n* high chest of drawers
TALLBOYS >TALLBOY
TALLENT *n* plenty
TALLENTS >TALLENT
TALLER >TALL
TALLEST >TALL
TALLET *n* loft
TALLETS >TALLET
TALLGRASS *n* long grass in North American prairie
TALLIABLE *adj* taxable
TALLIATE *vb* levy a tax
TALLIATED >TALLIATE
TALLIATES >TALLIATE
TALLIED >TALLY
TALLIER >TALLY
TALLIERS >TALLY
TALLIES >TALLY
TALLIS *variant of* >TALLITH
TALLISES >TALLIS
TALLISH *adj* quite tall
TALLISIM >TALLITH
TALLIT *variant of* >TALLITH
TALLITES >TALLIT
TALLITH *n* white shawl with fringed corners worn over the head and shoulders by Jewish males during religious services
TALLITHES >TALLITH
TALLITHIM >TALLITH
TALLITHS >TALLITH
TALLITIM >TALLIT
TALLITOT >TALLIT
TALLITOTH >TALLITH
TALLITS >TALLIT
TALLNESS >TALL
TALLOL *n* oily liquid used for making soaps, lubricants, etc
TALLOLS >TALLOL
TALLOT *same as* >TALLET
TALLOTS >TALLOT
TALLOW *n* hard animal fat

used to make candles ▷ *vb* cover or smear with tallow
TALLOWED > TALLOW
TALLOWING > TALLOW
TALLOWISH > TALLOW
TALLOWS > TALLOW
TALLOWY > TALLOW
TALLS > TALL
TALLY *vb* (of two things) correspond ▷ *n* record of a debt or score
TALLYHO *n* cry of a participant at a hunt to encourage the hounds when the quarry is sighted ▷ *vb* to make the cry of tallyho
TALLYHOED > TALLYHO
TALLYHOS > TALLYHO
TALLYING > TALLY
TALLYMAN *n* scorekeeper or recorder
TALLYMEN > TALLYMAN
TALLYSHOP *n* shop that allows customers to pay in instalments
TALMA *n* short cloak
TALMAS > TALMA
TALMUD *n* primary source of Jewish religious law, consisting of the Mishnah and the Gemara
TALMUDIC > TALMUD
TALMUDISM > TALMUD
TALMUDS > TALMUD
TALON *n* bird's hooked claw
TALONED > TALON
TALONS > TALON
TALOOKA *same as* > TALUK
TALOOKAS > TALOOKA
TALPA *n* sebaceous cyst
TALPAE > TALPA
TALPAS > TALPA
TALUK *n* subdivision of a district
TALUKA *same as* > TALUK
TALUKAS > TALUKA
TALUKDAR *n* person in charge of a taluk
TALUKDARS > TALUKDAR
TALUKS > TALUK
TALUS *n* bone of the ankle that articulates with the leg bones to form the ankle joint
TALUSES > TALUS
TALWEG *same as* > THALWEG
TALWEGS > TALWEG
TAM *n* tam-o'-shanter
TAMABLE > TAME
TAMAL *same as* > TAMALE
TAMALE *n* Mexican dish made of minced meat mixed with crushed maize and seasonings, wrapped in maize husks and steamed
TAMALES > TAMALE
TAMALS > TAMAL
TAMANDU *same as* > TAMANDUA
TAMANDUA *n* small arboreal edentate mammal
TAMANDUAS > TAMANDUA
TAMANDUS > TAMANDU
TAMANOIR *n* anteater
TAMANOIRS > TAMANOIR
TAMANU *n* poon tree
TAMANUS > TAMANU
TAMARA *n* powder consisting of cloves, cinnamon, fennel, coriander, etc, used in certain cuisines
TAMARACK *n* North American larch, with reddish-brown bark, bluish-green needle-like leaves, and shiny oval cones
TAMARACKS > TAMARACK
TAMARAO *same as* > TAMARAU
TAMARAOS > TAMARAO
TAMARAS > TAMARA
TAMARAU *n* small rare member of the cattle tribe of lowland areas of Mindoro in the Philippines
TAMARAUS > TAMARAU
TAMARI *n* Japanese variety of soy sauce
TAMARILLO *n* shrub with a red oval edible fruit
TAMARIN *n* small monkey of South and Central American forests
TAMARIND *n* tropical tree
TAMARINDS > TAMARIND
TAMARINS > TAMARIN
TAMARIS > TAMARI
TAMARISK *n* evergreen shrub with slender branches and feathery flower clusters
TAMARISKS > TAMARISK
TAMASHA *n* (in India) a show
TAMASHAS > TAMASHA
TAMBAC *same as* > TOMBAC
TAMBACS > TAMBAC
TAMBAK *same as* > TOMBAC
TAMBAKS > TAMBAK
TAMBALA *n* unit of Malawian currency
TAMBALAS > TAMBALA
TAMBER *same as* > TIMBRE
TAMBERS > TAMBER
TAMBOUR *n* embroidery frame, consisting of two hoops over which the fabric is stretched while being worked ▷ *vb* embroider (fabric or a design) on a tambour
TAMBOURA *n* instrument with a long neck, four strings, and no frets, used in Indian music to provide a drone
TAMBOURAS > TAMBOURA
TAMBOURED > TAMBOUR
TAMBOURER *n* one who embroiders on a tambour
TAMBOURIN *n* 18th-century Provençal folk dance
TAMBOURS > TAMBOUR
TAMBUR *n* old Turkish stringed instrument
TAMBURA *n* Middle-Eastern stringed instrument with a long neck, related to the tambur
TAMBURAS > TAMBURA
TAMBURIN *same as* > TAMBURIN
TAMBURINS > TAMBURIN
TAMBURS > TAMBUR
TAME *adj* (of animals) brought under human control ▷ *vb* make tame
TAMEABLE > TAME
TAMED > TAME
TAMEIN *n* Burmese skirt
TAMEINS > TAMEIN
TAMELESS > TAME
TAMELY > TAME
TAMENESS > TAME
TAMER > TAME
TAMERS > TAME
TAMES > TAME
TAMEST > TAME
TAMIN *n* thin woollen fabric
TAMINE *same as* > TAMIN
TAMINES > TAMINE
TAMING *n* act of making (something) tame
TAMINGS > TAMING
TAMINS > TAMIN
TAMIS *same as* > TAMMY
TAMISE *n* type of thin cloth
TAMISES > TAMIS
TAMMAR *n* small scrub wallaby of Australia, with a thick dark-coloured coat
TAMMARS > TAMMAR
TAMMIE *n* short for tam-o'shanter, a traditional Scottish hat
TAMMIED > TAMMY
TAMMIES > TAMMY
TAMMY *n* glazed woollen or mixed fabric, used for linings, undergarments, etc ▷ *vb* (esp formerly) to strain (sauce, soup, etc) through a tammy
TAMMYING > TAMMY
TAMOXIFEN *n* drug that antagonizes the action of oestrogen and is used to treat breast cancer and some types of infertility in women
TAMP *vb* pack down by repeated taps
TAMPALA *n* Asian plant (Amaranthus tricolor), eaten as food
TAMPALAS > TAMPALA
TAMPAN *n* biting mite
TAMPANS > TAMPAN
TAMPED > TAMP
TAMPER *vb* interfere ▷ *n* person or thing that tamps, esp an instrument for packing down tobacco in a pipe
TAMPERED > TAMPER
TAMPERER > TAMPER
TAMPERERS > TAMPER
TAMPERING > TAMPER
TAMPERS > TAMPER
TAMPING *adj* very angry ▷ act or instance of tampin
TAMPINGS > TAMPING
TAMPION *n* plug placed in a gun's muzzle when the gun is not in use to keep out moisture and dust
TAMPIONS > TAMPION
TAMPON *n* absorbent plug of cotton wool inserted into the vagina during menstruation ▷ *vb* use a tampon
TAMPONADE > TAMPON
TAMPONAGE > TAMPON
TAMPONED > TAMPON
TAMPONING > TAMPON
TAMPONS > TAMPON
TAMPS > TAMP
TAMS > TAM
TAMWORTH *n* any of a hard rare breed of long-bodied reddish pigs
TAMWORTHS > TAMWORTH
TAN *n* brown coloration o the skin from exposure tc sunlight ▷ *vb* (of skin) gc brown from exposure to sunlight ▷ *adj* yellowish brown
TANA *n* small Madagascar lemur
TANADAR *n* commanding officer of an Indian police station
TANADARS > TANADAR
TANAGER *n* any American songbird of the family *Thraupidae*, having a shor thick bill and a brilliantly coloured male plumage
TANAGERS > TANAGER
TANAGRA *n* type of tanage
TANAGRAS > TANAGRA
TANAGRINE *adj* of or relating to the tanager
TANAISTE *n* prime minister of the Republic Ireland
TANAISTES > TANAISTE
TANALISED *adj* having been treated with the trademarked timber preservative Tanalith
TANALIZED *same as* > TANALISED
TANAS > TANA
TANBARK *n* bark of certai trees, esp the oak and hemlock, used as a sourc of tannin
TANBARKS > TANBARK
TANDEM *n* bicycle for two riders, one behind the other
TANDEMS > TANDEM
TANDOOR *n* type of Indian clay oven
TANDOORI *adj* (of food) cooked in an Indian clay oven ▷ *n* Indian method of cooking meat or vegetables on a spit in a clay oven

NDOORIS >TANDOORI
NDOORS >TANDOOR
NE *old Scottish variant* f >TAKEN
NG *n* strong taste or mell ▷ *vb* cause to ring
NGA *n* triangular oincloth worn by ndigenous peoples in ropical America
NGAS >TANGA
NGED >TANG
NGELO *n* hybrid roduced by crossing tangerine tree with a rapefruit tree
NGELOS >TANGELO
NGENCE *n* touching
NGENCES >TANGENCE
NGENCY >TANGENT
NGENT *n* line that ouches a curve without ntersecting it
NGENTAL >TANGENT
NGENTS >TANGENT
NGERINE *n* small range-like fruit of an sian citrus tree ▷ *adj* eddish-orange
NGHIN *n* strong oison formerly used in adagascar to determine he guilt or otherwise of rime suspects
NGHININ *n* active ngredient in tanghin
NGHINS >TANGHIN
NGI *n* Māori funeral eremony
NGIBLE *adj* able to be ouched ▷ *n* tangible hing or asset
NGIBLES >TANGIBLE
NGIBLY >TANGIBLE
NGIE *n* water spirit of rkney, appearing as a igure draped in seaweed, r as a seahorse
NGIER >TANGY
NGIES >TANGIE
NGIEST >TANGY
NGINESS >TANGY
NGING >TANG
NGIS >TANGI
NGLE *n* confused mass r situation ▷ *vb* twist ogether in a tangle
NGLED >TANGLE
NGLER >TANGLE
NGLERS >TANGLE
NGLES >TANGLE
NGLIER >TANGLE
NGLIEST >TANGLE
NGLING *n* act or ondition of tangling
NGLINGS >TANGLING
NGLY >TANGLE
NGO *n* S American dance ▷ *vb* dance a tango
NGOED >TANGO
NGOES >TANGO
NGOING >TANGO
NGOIST >TANGO
NGOISTS >TANGO
TANGOLIKE >TANGO
TANGOS >TANGO
TANGRAM *n* Chinese puzzle in which a square, cut into a parallelogram, a square, and five triangles, is formed into figures
TANGRAMS >TANGRAM
TANGS >TANG
TANGUN *n* small and sturdy Tibetan pony
TANGUNS >TANGUN
TANGY *adj* having a pungent, fresh, or briny flavour or aroma
TANH *n* hyperbolic tangent
TANHS >TANH
TANIST *n* heir apparent of a Celtic chieftain chosen by election during the chief's lifetime: usually the worthiest of his kin
TANISTRY >TANIST
TANISTS >TANIST
TANIWHA *n* mythical Māori monster that lives in water
TANIWHAS >TANIWHA
TANK *n* container for liquids or gases ▷ *vb* put or keep in a tank
TANKA *n* Japanese verse form consisting of five lines, the first and third having five syllables, the others seven
TANKAGE *n* capacity or contents of a tank or tanks
TANKAGES >TANKAGE
TANKARD *n* large beer-mug, often with a hinged lid
TANKARDS >TANKARD
TANKAS >TANKA
TANKED >TANK
TANKER *n* ship or truck for carrying liquid in bulk
TANKERS >TANKER
TANKFUL *n* quantity contained in a tank
TANKFULS >TANKFUL
TANKIA *n* type of boat used in Canton
TANKIAS >TANKIA
TANKIES >TANKY
TANKING *n* heavy defeat
TANKINGS >TANKING
TANKINI *n* woman's two-piece swimming costume consisting of a vest or camisole top and bikini briefs
TANKINIS >TANKINI
TANKLESS >TANK
TANKLIKE >TANK
TANKS >TANK
TANKSHIP *same as* >TANKER
TANKSHIPS >TANKSHIP
TANKY *n* die-hard communist
TANLING *n* suntanned person
TANLINGS >TANLING
TANNA *n* Indian police station or army base
TANNABLE >TAN
TANNAGE *n* act or process of tanning
TANNAGES >TANNAGE
TANNAH *same as* >TANNA
TANNAHS >TANNAH
TANNAS >TANNA
TANNATE *n* any salt or ester of tannic acid
TANNATES >TANNATE
TANNED >TAN
TANNER >TAN
TANNERIES >TANNERY
TANNERS >TAN
TANNERY *n* place where hides are tanned
TANNEST >TAN
TANNIC *adj* of, containing, or produced from tannin or tannic acid
TANNIE *n* in S Africa, title of respect used to refer to an elderly woman
TANNIES >TANNIE
TANNIN *n* vegetable substance used in tanning
TANNING >TAN
TANNINGS >TAN
TANNINS >TANNIN
TANNISH >TAN
TANNOY *n* sound-amplifying apparatus used as a public-address system esp in a large building, such as a university ▷ *vb* announce (something) using a Tannoy system
TANNOYED >TANNOY
TANNOYING >TANNOY
TANNOYS >TANNOY
TANREC *same as* >TENREC
TANRECS >TANREC
TANS >TAN
TANSIES >TANSY
TANSY *n* yellow-flowered plant
TANTALATE *n* any of various salts of tantalic acid formed when the pentoxide of tantalum dissolves in an alkali
TANTALIC *adj* of or containing tantalum, esp in the pentavalent state
TANTALISE *same as* >TANTALIZE
TANTALISM >TANTALISE
TANTALITE *n* heavy brownish mineral consisting of a tantalum oxide of iron and manganese in orthorhombic crystalline form
TANTALIZE *vb* torment by showing but withholding something desired
TANTALOUS *adj* of or containing tantalum in the trivalent state
TANTALUM *n* hard greyish-white metallic element
TANTALUMS >TANTALUM
TANTALUS *n* case in which bottles of wine and spirits may be locked with their contents tantalizingly visible
TANTARA *n* blast, as on a trumpet or horn
TANTARARA *same as* >TANTARA
TANTARAS >TANTARA
TANTI *adj* old word for worthwhile
TANTIVIES >TANTIVY
TANTIVY *adv* at full speed ▷ *interj* hunting cry, esp at full gallop
TANTO *adv* too much
TANTONIES >TANTONY
TANTONY *n* runt
TANTRA *n* sacred books of Tantrism, written between the 7th and 17th centuries AD, mainly in the form of a dialogue between Siva and his wife
TANTRAS >TANTRA
TANTRIC >TANTRA
TANTRISM *n* teaching of tantra
TANTRISMS >TANTRISM
TANTRUM *n* childish outburst of temper
TANTRUMS >TANTRUM
TANUKI *n* animal similar to a raccoon, found in Japan
TANUKIS >TANUKI
TANYARD *n* part of a tannery
TANYARDS >TANYARD
TANZANITE *n* blue gemstone
TAO *n* (in Confucian philosophy) the correct course of action
TAOISEACH *n* prime minister of the Republic of Ireland
TAONGA *n* treasure
TAONGAS >TAONGA
TAOS >TAO
TAP *vb* knock lightly and usu repeatedly ▷ *n* light knock
TAPA *n* inner bark of the paper mulberry
TAPACOLO *n* small bird of Chile and Argentina
TAPACOLOS >TAPACOLO
TAPACULO *same as* >TAPACOLO
TAPACULOS >TAPACULO
TAPADERA *n* leather covering for the stirrup on an American saddle
TAPADERAS >TAPADERA
TAPADERO *same as* >TAPADERA
TAPADEROS >TAPADERO
TAPALO *n* Latin American scarf, often patterned and brightly coloured
TAPALOS >TAPALO
TAPAS *pl n* (in Spanish cookery) light snacks or appetizers, usually eaten with drinks

TAPE *n* narrow long strip of material ▷ *vb* record on magnetic tape
TAPEABLE >TAPE
TAPED >TAPE
TAPELESS >TAPE
TAPELIKE >TAPE
TAPELINE *n* tape or length of metal marked off in inches, centimetres, etc, used principally for measuring and fitting garments
TAPELINES >TAPELINE
TAPEN *adj* made of tape
TAPENADE *n* savoury paste made from capers, olives, and anchovies, with olive oil and lemon juice
TAPENADES >TAPENADE
TAPER >TAPE
TAPERED >TAPE
TAPERER >TAPE
TAPERERS >TAPE
TAPERING >TAPE
TAPERINGS >TAPE
TAPERNESS *n* state or quality of being tapered
TAPERS >TAPE
TAPERWISE *adv* in the manner of a taper
TAPES >TAPE
TAPESTRY *n* fabric decorated with coloured woven designs ▷ *vb* portray in tapestry
TAPET *n* example of tapestry
TAPETA >TAPETUM
TAPETAL >TAPETUM
TAPETI *n* forest rabbit of Brazil
TAPETIS >TAPETI
TAPETS >TAPET
TAPETUM *n* layer of nutritive cells in the sporangia of ferns and anthers of flowering plants that surrounds developing spore cells
TAPEWORM *n* long flat parasitic worm living in the intestines of vertebrates
TAPEWORMS >TAPEWORM
TAPHOLE *n* hole in a furnace for running off molten metal or slag
TAPHOLES >TAPHOLE
TAPHONOMY *n* study of the processes affecting an organism after death that result in its fossilization
TAPHOUSE *n* inn or bar
TAPHOUSES >TAPHOUSE
TAPING >TAPE
TAPIOCA *n* beadlike starch made from cassava root, used in puddings
TAPIOCAS >TAPIOCA
TAPIR *n* piglike mammal of tropical America and SE Asia, with a long snout
TAPIROID >TAPIR
TAPIRS >TAPIR
TAPIS *n* tapestry or carpeting, esp as formerly used to cover a table in a council chamber
TAPISES >TAPIS
TAPIST *n* person who records (read out) printed matter in an audio format for the benefit of visually impaired people
TAPISTS >TAPIST
TAPLASH *n* dregs of beer
TAPLASHES >TAPLASH
TAPPA *same as* >TAPA
TAPPABLE >TAP
TAPPAS >TAPPA
TAPPED >TAP
TAPPER *n* person who taps
TAPPERS >TAPPER
TAPPET *n* short steel rod in an engine, transferring motion from one part to another
TAPPETS >TAPPET
TAPPICE *vb* hide
TAPPICED >TAPPICE
TAPPICES >TAPPICE
TAPPICING >TAPPICE
TAPPING >TAP
TAPPINGS >TAP
TAPPIT *adj* crested; topped
TAPROOM *n* public bar in a hotel or pub
TAPROOMS >TAPROOM
TAPROOT *n* main root of a plant, growing straight down
TAPROOTED >TAPROOT
TAPROOTS >TAPROOT
TAPS >TAP
TAPSMAN *n* old word for a barman
TAPSMEN >TAPSMAN
TAPSTER *n* barman
TAPSTERS >TAPSTER
TAPSTRESS >TAPSTER
TAPSTRY *adj* relating to tapestry
TAPU *adj* sacred ▷ *n* Māori religious or superstitious restriction on something
TAPUS >TAPU
TAQUERIA *n* restaurant specializing in tacos
TAQUERIAS >TAQUERIA
TAR *n* thick black liquid distilled from coal etc ▷ *vb* coat with tar
TARA *same as* >TARO
TARAIRE *n* type of New Zealand tree
TARAKIHI *n* common edible sea fish of New Zealand waters
TARAKIHIS >TARAKIHI
TARAMA *n* cod roe
TARAMAS >TARAMA
TARAMEA *n* variety of New Zealand speargrass
TARAMEAS >TARAMEA
TARAND *n* northern animal of legend, now supposed to have been the reindeer
TARANDS >TARAND
TARANTARA *same as* >TANTARA
TARANTAS *same as* >TARANTASS
TARANTASS *n* large horse-drawn four-wheeled Russian carriage without springs
TARANTISM *n* nervous disorder marked by uncontrollable bodily movement, widespread in S Italy during the 15th to 17th centuries: popularly thought to be caused by the bite of a tarantula
TARANTIST >TARANTISM
TARANTULA *n* large hairy spider with a poisonous bite
TARAS >TARA
TARAXACUM *n* perennial plant with dense heads of small yellow flowers and seeds with a feathery attachment
TARBOGGIN *same as* >TOBOGGAN
TARBOOSH *n* felt or cloth brimless cap, usually red and often with a silk tassel, formerly worn by Muslim men
TARBOUCHE *same as* >TARBOOSH
TARBOUSH *same as* >TARBOOSH
TARBOY *n* boy who applies tar to the skin of sheep cut during shearing
TARBOYS >TARBOY
TARBUSH *same as* >TARBOOSH
TARBUSHES >TARBUSH
TARCEL *same as* >TARCEL
TARCELS >TARCEL
TARDIED >TARDY
TARDIER >TARDY
TARDIES >TARDY
TARDIEST >TARDY
TARDILY >TARDY
TARDINESS >TARDY
TARDIVE *adj* tending to develop late
TARDO *adj* (of music) slow; to be played slowly
TARDY *adj* slow or late ▷ *vb* delay or impede (something or someone)
TARDYING >TARDY
TARDYON *n* particle travelling slower than the speed of light
TARDYONS >TARDYON
TARE *n* weight of the wrapping or container of goods ▷ *vb* weigh (a package, etc) in order to calculate the amount of tare
TARED >TARE
TARES >TARE
TARGE *vb* interrogate
TARGED >TARGE
TARGES >TARGE
TARGET *n* object or perso[n] a missile is aimed at ▷ *vb* aim or direct
TARGETED >TARGET
TARGETEER *n* soldier armed with a small roun[d] shield
TARGETING >TARGET
TARGETS >TARGET
TARGING >TARGE
TARIFF *n* tax levied on imports ▷ *vb* impose punishment for a crimina[l] offence
TARIFFED >TARIFF
TARIFFING >TARIFF
TARIFFS >TARIFF
TARING >TARE
TARINGS >TARE
TARLATAN *n* open-weave cotton fabric, used for stiffening garments
TARLATANS >TARLATAN
TARLETAN *same as* >TARLATAN
TARLETANS >TARLETAN
TARMAC *See also* >MACADA[M]
TARMACKED >TARMAC
TARMACS >TARMAC
TARN *n* small mountain lake
TARNAL *adj* damned ▷ *adv* extremely
TARNALLY >TARNAL
TARNATION *euphemism for* >DAMNATION
TARNISH *vb* make or become stained or less bright ▷ *n* discoloration or blemish
TARNISHED >TARNISH
TARNISHER >TARNISH
TARNISHES >TARNISH
TARNS >TARN
TARO *n* plant with a large edible rootstock
TAROC *old variant of* >TAR[OT]
TAROCS >TAROC
TAROK *old variant of* >TAR[OT]
TAROKS >TAROK
TAROS >TARO
TAROT *n* special pack of cards used mainly in fortune-telling ▷ *adj* relating to tarot cards
TAROTS >TAROT
TARP *informal word for* >TARPAULIN
TARPAN *n* European wild horse common in prehistoric times but no[w] extinct
TARPANS >TARPAN
TARPAPER *n* paper coate[d] or impregnated with tar
TARPAPERS >TARPAPER
TARPAULIN *n* (sheet of) heavy waterproof fabric
TARPON *n* large silvery clupeoid game fish foun[d] in warm Atlantic waters
TARPONS >TARPON

RPS > TARP
RRAGON *n* aromatic herb
RRAGONS > TARRAGON
RRAS *same as* > TRASS
RRASES > TARRAS
RRE *vb* old word
neaning to provoke or
oad
RRED > TAR
RRES > TARRE
RRIANCE *archaic word*
or > DELAY
RRIED > TARRY
RRIER > TARRY
RRIERS > TARRY
RRIES > TARRY
RRIEST > TARRY
RRINESS > TAR
RRING > TAR
RRINGS > TAR
RROCK *n* seabird
RROCKS > TARROCK
RROW *vb* exhibit
eluctance
RROWED > TARROW
RROWING > TARROW
RROWS > TARROW
RRY *vb* linger or delay
▷ *n* stay ▷ *adj* covered in
r resembling tar
RRYING > TAR
RS > TAR
RSAL *adj* of the tarsus or
arsi ▷ *n* tarsal bone
RSALGIA *n* pain in the
arsus
RSALS > TARSAL
RSEAL *n* bitumen
urface of a road
RSEALS > TARSEAL
RSEL *same as* > TERCEL
RSELS > TARSEL
RSI > TARSUS
RSIA *another term*
or > INTARSIA
RSIAS > TARSIA
RSIER *n* small nocturnal
rimate of the E Indies,
vhich has very large eyes
RSIERS > TARSIER
RSIOID *adj* resembling
tarsier
RSIPED *n* generic term
or a number of marsupials
RSIPEDS > TARSIPED
RSUS *n* bones of the heel
nd ankle collectively
RT *n* pie or flan with a
weet filling ▷ *adj* sharp
r bitter ▷ *adj* (of a flavour,
ood, etc) sour, acid, or
stringent ▷ *vb* (of food,
rink, etc) become tart
sour)
RTAN *n* design of straight
nes crossing at right
ngles, esp one associated
vith a Scottish clan
RTANA *n* small
Mediterranean sailing
oat
RTANAS > TARTANA
RTANE *same as* > TARTANA
RTANED > TARTAN

TARTANES > TARTANE
TARTANRY *n* derogatory term for excessive use of tartan and other Scottish imagery to produce a distorted sentimental view of Scotland and its history
TARTANS > TARTAN
TARTAR *n* hard deposit on the teeth
TARTARE *n* mayonnaise sauce mixed with hard-boiled egg yolks, chopped herbs, capers, and gherkins
TARTARES > TARTARE
TARTARIC *adj* of or derived from tartar or tartaric acid
TARTARISE *same as* > TARTARIZE
TARTARIZE *vb* impregnate or treat with tartar or tartar emetic
TARTARLY *adj* resembling a tartar
TARTAROUS *adj* consisting of, containing, or resembling tartar
TARTARS > TARTAR
TARTED > TART
TARTER > TART
TARTEST > TART
TARTIER > TARTY
TARTIEST > TARTY
TARTILY > TARTY
TARTINE *n* slice of bread with butter or jam spread on it
TARTINES > TARTINE
TARTINESS > TARTY
TARTING > TART
TARTISH > TART
TARTISHLY > TART
TARTLET *n* individual pastry case with a filling of fruit or other sweet or savoury mixture
TARTLETS > TARTLET
TARTLY > TART
TARTNESS > TART
TARTRATE *n* any salt or ester of tartaric acid
TARTRATED *adj* being in the form of a tartrate
TARTRATES > TARTRATE
TARTS > TART
TARTUFE *same as* > TARTUFFE
TARTUFES > TARTUFE
TARTUFFE *n* person who hypocritically pretends to be deeply pious
TARTUFFES > TARTUFFE
TARTY *adj* resembling a promiscuous woman; provocative in a cheap and bawdy way
TARWEED *n* resinous Californian plant with a pungent scent
TARWEEDS > TARWEED
TARWHINE *n* bream of E Australia, silver in colour with gold streaks
TARWHINES > TARWHINE
TARZAN *n* man with great physical strength, agility, and virility
TARZANS > TARZAN
TAS *old form of* > TASS
TASAR *same as* > TUSSORE
TASARS > TASAR
TASER *vb* use a Taser (trademark) stun gun on (someone)
TASERED > TASER
TASERING > TASER
TASERS > TASER
TASH *vb* stain or besmirch
TASHED > TASH
TASHES > TASH
TASHING > TASH
TASIMETER *n* device for measuring small temperature changes. It depends on the changes of pressure resulting from expanding or contracting solids
TASIMETRY > TASIMETER
TASK *n* piece of work to be done ▷ *vb* give someone a task to do
TASKBAR *n* area of computer screen showing what programs are running
TASKBARS > TASKBAR
TASKED > TASK
TASKER > TASK
TASKERS > TASK
TASKING > TASK
TASKINGS > TASK
TASKLESS > TASK
TASKS > TASK
TASKWORK *n* hard or unpleasant work
TASKWORKS > TASKWORK
TASLET *same as* > TASSET
TASLETS > TASLET
TASS *n* cup, goblet, or glass
TASSE *same as* > TASSET
TASSEL *n* decorative fringed knot of threads ▷ *vb* adorn with a tassel or tassels
TASSELED > TASSEL
TASSELING > TASSEL
TASSELL *same as* > TASSEL
TASSELLED > TASSEL
TASSELLS > TASSELL
TASSELLY > TASSEL
TASSELS > TASSEL
TASSES > TASSE
TASSET *n* piece of armour consisting of one or more plates fastened on to the bottom of a cuirass to protect the thigh
TASSETS > TASSET
TASSIE *same as* > TASS
TASSIES > TASSIE
TASSWAGE *vb* old poetic contraction of "to assuage"
TASTABLE > TASTE
TASTE *n* sense by which the flavour of a substance is distinguished in the mouth ▷ *vb* distinguish the taste of (a substance)
TASTEABLE > TASTE
TASTED > TASTE
TASTEFUL *adj* having or showing good taste
TASTELESS *adj* bland or insipid
TASTER *n* person employed to test the quality of food or drink by tasting it
TASTERS > TASTER
TASTES > TASTE
TASTEVIN *n* small shallow cup for wine tasting
TASTEVINS > TASTEVIN
TASTIER > TASTY
TASTIEST > TASTY
TASTILY > TASTY
TASTINESS > TASTY
TASTING > TASTE
TASTINGS > TASTE
TASTY *adj* pleasantly flavoured
TAT *n* tatty or tasteless article(s) ▷ *vb* make (something) by tatting
TATAHASH *n* stew containing potatoes and cheap cuts of meat
TATAMI *n* thick rectangular mat of woven straw, used as a standard to measure a Japanese room
TATAMIS > TATAMI
TATAR *n* brutal person
TATARS > TATAR
TATE *n* small tuft of fibre
TATER *n* potato
TATERS > TATER
TATES > TATE
TATH *vb* (of cattle) to defecate
TATHED > TATH
TATHING > TATH
TATHS > TATH
TATIE *same as* > TATTIE
TATIES > TATIE
TATLER *old variant of* > TATTLER
TATLERS > TATLER
TATOU *n* armadillo
TATOUAY *n* large armadillo of South America
TATOUAYS > TATOUAY
TATOUS > TATOU
TATS > TAT
TATSOI *n* variety of Chinese cabbage
TATSOIS > TATSOI
TATT *same as* > TAT
TATTED > TAT
TATTER *vb* make or become torn
TATTERED > TATTER
TATTERING > TATTER
TATTERS > TATTER
TATTERY *same as* > TATTERED
TATTIE *Scot or dialect word for* > POTATO
TATTIER > TATTY
TATTIES > TATTIE

TATTIEST > TATTY
TATTILY > TATTY
TATTINESS > TATTY
TATTING > TAT
TATTINGS > TAT
TATTLE *n* gossip or chatter ▷ *vb* gossip or chatter
TATTLED > TATTLE
TATTLER *n* person who tattles
TATTLERS > TATTLER
TATTLES > TATTLE
TATTLING > TATTLE
TATTLINGS > TATTLE
TATTOO *n* pattern made on the body by pricking the skin and staining it with indelible inks ▷ *vb* make such a pattern on the skin
TATTOOED > TATTOO
TATTOOER > TATTOO
TATTOOERS > TATTOO
TATTOOING > TATTOO
TATTOOIST > TATTOO
TATTOOS > TATTOO
TATTOW *old variant of* > TATTOO
TATTOWED > TATTOW
TATTOWING > TATTOW
TATTOWS > TATTOW
TATTS > TATT
TATTY *adj* worn out, shabby, tawdry, or unkempt
TATU *old variant of* > TATTOO
TATUED > TATU
TATUING > TATU
TATUS > TATU
TAU *n* 19th letter in the Greek alphabet
TAUBE *n* type of German aeroplane
TAUBES > TAUBE
TAUGHT > TEACH
TAUHINU *New Zealand name for* > POPLAR
TAUHINUS > TAUHINU
TAUHOU *same as* > SILVEREYE
TAUIWI *n* Māori term for the non-Māori people of New Zealand
TAUIWIS > TAUIWI
TAULD *vb* old Scots variant of told
TAUNT *vb* tease with jeers ▷ *n* jeering remark ▷ *adj* (of the mast or masts of a sailing vessel) unusually tall
TAUNTED > TAUNT
TAUNTER > TAUNT
TAUNTERS > TAUNT
TAUNTING > TAUNT
TAUNTINGS > TAUNT
TAUNTS > TAUNT
TAUON *n* negatively charged elementary particle
TAUONS > TAUON
TAUPATA *n* New Zealand shrub or tree, with shiny dark green leaves
TAUPE *adj* brownish-grey ▷ *n* brownish-grey colour
TAUPES > TAUPE
TAUPIE *same as* > TAWPIE
TAUPIES > TAUPIE
TAUREAN *adj* born under or characteristic of Taurus
TAURIC *same as* > TAUREAN
TAURIFORM *adj* in the form of a bull
TAURINE *adj* of, relating to, or resembling a bull ▷ *n* derivative of the amino acid, cysteine, obtained from the bile of animals
TAURINES > TAURINE
TAUS > TAU
TAUT *adj* drawn tight ▷ *vb* Scots word meaning to tangle
TAUTAUG *same as* > TAUTOG
TAUTAUGS > TAUTAUG
TAUTED > TAUT
TAUTEN *vb* make or become taut
TAUTENED > TAUTEN
TAUTENING > TAUTEN
TAUTENS > TAUTEN
TAUTER > TAUT
TAUTEST > TAUT
TAUTING > TAUT
TAUTIT *adj* Scots word meaning tangled
TAUTLY > TAUT
TAUTNESS > TAUT
TAUTOG *n* large dark-coloured wrasse, used as a food fish
TAUTOGS > TAUTOG
TAUTOLOGY *n* use of words which merely repeat something already stated
TAUTOMER *n* either of the two forms of a chemical compound that exhibits tautomerism
TAUTOMERS > TAUTOMER
TAUTONYM *n* taxonomic name in which the generic and specific components are the same
TAUTONYMS > TAUTONYM
TAUTONYMY > TAUTONYM
TAUTS > TAUT
TAV *n* 23rd and last letter in the Hebrew alphabet
TAVA *n* thick Indian frying pan
TAVAH *variant of* > TAVA
TAVAHS > TAVAH
TAVAS > TAVA
TAVER *vb* wander about
TAVERED > TAVER
TAVERING > TAVER
TAVERN *n* pub
TAVERNA *n* (in Greece) a guesthouse that has its own bar
TAVERNAS > TAVERNA
TAVERNER *n* keeper of a tavern
TAVERNERS > TAVERNER
TAVERNS > TAVERN
TAVERS > TAVER
TAVERT *adj* bewildered or confused
TAVS > TAV
TAW *vb* convert skins into leather
TAWA *n* tall timber tree from New Zealand, with edible purple berries
TAWAI *n* any of various species of beech of the genus *Nothofagus* of New Zealand, originally called "birches" by the settlers
TAWAIS > TAWAI
TAWAS > TAWA
TAWDRIER > TAWDRY
TAWDRIES > TAWDRY
TAWDRIEST > TAWDRY
TAWDRILY > TAWDRY
TAWDRY *adj* cheap, showy, and of poor quality ▷ *n* gaudy finery of poor quality
TAWED > TAW
TAWER > TAW
TAWERIES > TAWERY
TAWERS > TAW
TAWERY *n* place where tawing is carried out
TAWHAI *same as* > TAWAI
TAWHAIS > TAWHAI
TAWHIRI *n* small New Zealand tree with wavy green glossy leaves
TAWIE *adj* easily persuaded or managed
TAWIER > TAWIE
TAWIEST > TAWIE
TAWING > TAW
TAWINGS > TAW
TAWNEY *same as* > TAWNY
TAWNEYS > TAWNEY
TAWNIER > TAWNY
TAWNIES > TAWNY
TAWNIEST > TAWNY
TAWNILY > TAWNY
TAWNINESS > TAWNY
TAWNY *adj* yellowish-brown ▷ *n* light brown to brownish-orange colour
TAWPIE *n* foolish or maladroit girl
TAWPIES > TAWPIE
TAWS *same as* > TAWSE
TAWSE *n* leather strap with one end cut into thongs, formerly used by schoolteachers to hit children who had misbehaved ▷ *vb* punish (someone) with or as if with a tawse
TAWSED > TAWSE
TAWSES > TAWSE
TAWSING > TAWSE
TAWT *same as* > TAUT
TAWTED > TAWT
TAWTIE > TAWT
TAWTIER > TAWT
TAWTIEST > TAWT
TAWTING > TAWT
TAWTS > TAWT
TAX *n* compulsory payment levied by a government on income, property, etc to raise revenue ▷ *vb* levy a tax on
TAXA > TAXON
TAXABLE *adj* capable of being taxed ▷ *n* person, income, property, etc, th[at] is subject to tax
TAXABLES > TAXABLE
TAXABLY > TAXABLE
TAXACEOUS *adj* of, relatin[g] to, or belonging to the *Taxaceae*, a family of coniferous trees that includes the yews
TAXAMETER *old variant of* > TAXIMETER
TAXATION *n* levying of taxes
TAXATIONS > TAXATION
TAXATIVE > TAXATION
TAXED > TAX
TAXEME *n* any element of speech that may differentiate one utterance from another with a different meanin[g]
TAXEMES > TAXEME
TAXEMIC > TAXEME
TAXER > TAX
TAXERS > TAX
TAXES > TAX
TAXI *n* car with a driver that may be hired to tak[e] people to any specified destination ▷ *vb* (of an aircraft) run along the ground before taking off after landing
TAXIARCH *n* soldier in charge of a Greek taxis
TAXIARCHS > TAXIARCH
TAXICAB *same as* > TAXI
TAXICABS > TAXICAB
TAXIDERMY *n* art of stuffing and mounting animal skins to give the[m] a lifelike appearance
TAXIED > TAXI
TAXIES > TAXIS
TAXIING > TAXI
TAXIMAN *n* taxi driver
TAXIMEN > TAXIMAN
TAXIMETER *n* meter fitte[d] to a taxi to register the fare, based on the length [of] the journey
TAXING *adj* demanding, onerous
TAXINGLY > TAXING
TAXINGS > TAX
TAXIPLANE *n* aircraft tha[t] is available for hire
TAXIS *n* movement of a c[ell] or organism in a particu[lar] direction in response to [an] external stimulus ancie[nt] Greek army unit
TAXITE *n* type of volcani[c] rock
TAXITES > TAXITE
TAXITIC > TAXITE
TAXIWAY *n* marked path along which aircraft taxi to or from a runway, parking area, etc

XIWAYS > TAXIWAY
XLESS > TAX
XMAN *n* collector of taxes
XMEN > TAXMAN
XOL *n* trademarked anti-cancer drug
XOLS > TAXOL
XON *n* any taxonomic group or rank
XONOMER > TAXONOMY
XONOMIC > TAXONOMY
XONOMY *n* classification of plants and animals into groups
XONS > TAXON
XOR > TAX
XORS > TAX
XPAID *adj* (of taxable products, esp wine) having had the applicable tax paid already
XPAYER *n* person or organization that pays taxes
XPAYERS > TAXPAYER
XPAYING > TAXPAYER
XUS *n* genus of conifers
XWISE *adv* regarding tax
XYING > TAXI
Y *Irish dialect word for* > TEA
YASSUID *n* peccary
YBERRY *n* hybrid shrub produced by crossing a blackberry, raspberry, and loganberry
YRA *n* large arboreal musteline mammal, of Central and South America, with a dark brown body and paler head
YRAS > TAYRA
YS > TAY
ZZA *n* wine cup with a shallow bowl and a circular foot
ZZAS > TAZZA
ZZE > TAZZA
HICK *vb* make a click by creating a vacuum in the mouth with the tongue pressed againt the palate then suddenly breaking the seal by withdrawing part of the tongue from the palate
HICKED > TCHICK
HICKING > TCHICK
HICKS > TCHICK
HOTCHKE *n* trinket
n (in tonic sol-fa) seventh degree of any major scale
A *n* drink made from infusing the dried leaves of an Asian bush in boiling water ▷ *vb* take tea
ABERRY *n* berry of the wintergreen
ABOARD *n* tea tray
ABOARDS > TEABOARD
ABOWL *n* small bowl used (instead of a teacup) for serving tea
TEABOWLS > TEABOWL
TEABOX *n* box for storing tea
TEABOXES > TEABOX
TEABREAD *n* loaf-shaped cake that contains dried fruit which has been steeped in cold tea before baking: served sliced and buttered
TEABREADS > TEABREAD
TEACAKE *n* flat bun, usually eaten toasted and buttered
TEACAKES > TEACAKE
TEACART *n* trolley from which tea is served
TEACARTS > TEACART
TEACH *vb* tell or show (someone) how to do something
TEACHABLE > TEACH
TEACHABLY > TEACH
TEACHER *n* person who teaches, esp in a school
TEACHERLY > TEACHER
TEACHERS > TEACHER
TEACHES > TEACH
TEACHIE *old form of* > TETCHY
TEACHING > TEACH
TEACHINGS > TEACH
TEACHLESS *adj* unable to be taught
TEACUP *n* cup out of which tea may be drunk
TEACUPFUL *n* amount a teacup will hold, about four fluid ounces
TEACUPS > TEACUP
TEAD *old word for* > TORCH
TEADE *same as* > TEAD
TEADES > TEADE
TEADS > TEAD
TEAED > TEA
TEAGLE *vb* raise or hoist using a tackle
TEAGLED > TEAGLE
TEAGLES > TEAGLE
TEAGLING > TEAGLE
TEAHOUSE *n* restaurant, esp in Japan or China, where tea and light refreshments are served
TEAHOUSES > TEAHOUSE
TEAING > TEA
TEAK *n* very hard wood of an E Indian tree
TEAKETTLE *n* kettle for boiling water to make tea
TEAKS > TEAK
TEAKWOOD *another word for* > TEAK
TEAKWOODS > TEAKWOOD
TEAL *n* kind of small duck
TEALIKE *adj* resembling tea
TEALS > TEAL
TEAM *n* group of people forming one side in a game ▷ *vb* make or cause to make a team
TEAMAKER *n* person or thing that makes tea
TEAMAKERS > TEAMAKER
TEAMED > TEAM
TEAMER > TEAM
TEAMERS > TEAM
TEAMING > TEAM
TEAMINGS > TEAM
TEAMMATE *n* fellow member of a team
TEAMMATES > TEAMMATE
TEAMS > TEAM
TEAMSTER *n* commercial vehicle driver
TEAMSTERS > TEAMSTER
TEAMWISE *adv* in respect of a team; in the manner of a team
TEAMWORK *n* cooperative work by a team
TEAMWORKS > TEAMWORK
TEAPOT *n* container with a lid, spout, and handle for making and serving tea
TEAPOTS > TEAPOT
TEAPOY *n* small table or stand with a tripod base
TEAPOYS > TEAPOY
TEAR *n* drop of fluid appearing in and falling from the eye ▷ *vb* rip a hole in ▷ *vb* shed tears
TEARABLE > TEAR
TEARAWAY *n* wild or unruly person
TEARAWAYS > TEARAWAY
TEARDOWN *n* demolition; disassembly
TEARDOWNS > TEARDOWN
TEARDROP *same as* > TEAR
TEARDROPS > TEARDROP
TEARED > TEAR
TEARER > TEAR
TEARERS > TEAR
TEARFUL *adj* weeping or about to weep
TEARFULLY > TEARFUL
TEARGAS *n* gas or vaopr that makes the eyes smart and water ▷ *vb* deploy teargas against
TEARGASES > TEARGAS
TEARIER > TEARY
TEARIEST > TEARY
TEARILY > TEARY
TEARINESS > TEARY
TEARING > TEAR
TEARLESS > TEAR
TEAROOM *same as* > TEASHOP
TEAROOMS > TEAROOM
TEARS > TEAR
TEARSHEET *n* page in a newspaper or periodical that is cut or perforated so that it can be easily torn out
TEARSTAIN *n* stain or streak left by tears
TEARSTRIP *n* part of packaging torn to open it
TEARY *adj* characterized by, covered with, or secreting tears
TEAS > TEA
TEASABLE > TEASE
TEASE *vb* make fun of (someone) in a provoking or playful way ▷ *n* person who teases
TEASED > TEASE
TEASEL *n* plant with prickly leaves and flowers ▷ *vb* tease (a fabric)
TEASELED > TEASEL
TEASELER > TEASEL
TEASELERS > TEASEL
TEASELING > TEASEL
TEASELLED > TEASEL
TEASELLER > TEASEL
TEASELS > TEASEL
TEASER *n* annoying or difficult problem
TEASERS > TEASER
TEASES > TEASE
TEASHOP *n* restaurant where tea and light refreshments are served
TEASHOPS > TEASHOP
TEASING > TEASE
TEASINGLY > TEASE
TEASINGS > TEASE
TEASPOON *n* small spoon for stirring tea
TEASPOONS > TEASPOON
TEAT *n* nipple of a breast or udder
TEATASTER *n* person assessing teas by tasting them
TEATED > TEAT
TEATIME *n* late afternoon
TEATIMES > TEATIME
TEATS > TEAT
TEAWARE *n* implements and vessels for brewing and serving tea
TEAWARES > TEAWARE
TEAZE *old variant of* > TEASE
TEAZED > TEAZE
TEAZEL *same as* > TEASEL
TEAZELED > TEAZEL
TEAZELING > TEAZEL
TEAZELLED > TEAZEL
TEAZELS > TEAZEL
TEAZES > TEAZE
TEAZING > TEAZE
TEAZLE *same as* > TEASEL
TEAZLED > TEAZLE
TEAZLES > TEAZLE
TEAZLING > TEAZLE
TEBBAD *n* sandstorm
TEBBADS > TEBBAD
TEC *short for* > DETECTIVE
TECH *n* technical college
TECHED *adj* showing slight insanity
TECHIE *n* person who is skilled in the use of technology ▷ *adj* relating to or skilled in the use of technology
TECHIER > TECHY
TECHIES > TECHIE
TECHIEST > TECHY
TECHILY > TECHY
TECHINESS > TECHY
TECHNIC *another word for* > TECHNIQUE
TECHNICAL *adj* of or specializing in industrial,

practical, or mechanical arts and applied sciences ▷ *n* small armed military truck
TECHNICS *n* study or theory of industry and industrial arts
TECHNIKON *n* technical college
TECHNIQUE *n* method or skill used for a particular task
TECHNO *n* type of electronic dance music with a very fast beat
TECHNOPOP *n* pop music sharing certain features with techno
TECHNOS >TECHNO
TECHS >TECH
TECHY *same as* >TECHIE
TECKEL *n* dachshund
TECKELS >TECKEL
TECS >TEC
TECTA >TECTUM
TECTAL >TECTUM
TECTIFORM *adj* in the form of a roof
TECTITE *same as* >TEKTITE
TECTITES >TECTITE
TECTONIC *adj* denoting or relating to construction or building
TECTONICS *n* study of the earth's crust and the forces affecting it
TECTONISM >TECTONIC
TECTORIAL as in *tectorial membrane* membrane in the inner ear that covers the organ of Corti
TECTRICES >TECTRIX
TECTRIX *another name for* >COVERT
TECTUM *n* any roof-like structure in the body, esp the dorsal area of the midbrain
TECTUMS >TECTUM
TED *vb* shake out (hay), so as to dry it
TEDDED >TED
TEDDER *n* machine equipped with a series of small rotating forks for tedding hay
TEDDERED >TEDDER
TEDDERING >TEDDER
TEDDERS >TEDDER
TEDDIE *same as* >TEDDY
TEDDIES >TEDDY
TEDDING >TED
TEDDY *n* teddy bear
TEDESCA *adj* (of a piece of music) in German style
TEDESCHE >TEDESCA
TEDESCHI >TEDESCO
TEDESCO *adj* German
TEDIER >TEDY
TEDIEST >TEDY
TEDIOSITY >TEDIOUS
TEDIOUS *adj* causing fatigue or boredom
TEDIOUSLY >TEDIOUS
TEDISOME *old Scottish variant of* >TEDIOUS
TEDIUM *n* monotony
TEDIUMS >TEDIUM
TEDS >TED
TEDY *same as* >TEDIOUS
TEE *n* small peg from which a golf ball can be played at the start of each hole ▷ *vb* position (the ball) ready for striking, on or as if on a tee
TEED >TEE
TEEING >TEE
TEEK *adj* in Indian English, well
TEEL *same as* >SESAME
TEELS >TEEL
TEEM *vb* be full of
TEEMED >TEEM
TEEMER >TEEM
TEEMERS >TEEM
TEEMFUL >TEEM
TEEMING >TEEM
TEEMINGLY >TEEM
TEEMLESS >TEEM
TEEMS >TEEM
TEEN *n* affliction or woe ▷ *n* teenager ▷ *vb* set alight
TEENAGE *adj* (of a person) aged between 13 and 19 ▷ *n* this period of time
TEENAGED *adj* (of a person) aged between 13 and 19
TEENAGER *n* person aged between 13 and 19
TEENAGERS >TEENAGER
TEEND *same as* >TIND
TEENDED >TEEND
TEENDING >TEEND
TEENDS >TEEND
TEENE *same as* >TEEN
TEENED >TEEN
TEENER >TEEN
TEENERS >TEEN
TEENES >TEENE
TEENFUL >TEEN
TEENIER >TEENY
TEENIEST >TEENY
TEENING >TEEN
TEENS >TEEN
TEENSIER >TEENSY
TEENSIEST >TEENSY
TEENSY *same as* >TEENY
TEENTIER >TEENTY
TEENTIEST >TEENTY
TEENTSIER >TEENTSY
TEENTSY *same as* >TEENY
TEENTY *same as* >TEENY
TEENY *adj* extremely small
TEENYBOP *adj* of, or relating to, a young teenager who avidly follows fashions in music and clothes
TEEPEE *same as* >TEPEE
TEEPEES >TEEPEE
TEER *vb* smear; daub
TEERED >TEER
TEERING >TEER
TEERS >TEER
TEES >TEE
TEETER *vb* wobble or move unsteadily
TEETERED >TEETER
TEETERING >TEETER
TEETERS >TEETER
TEETH >TOOTH
TEETHE *vb* (of a baby) grow his or her first teeth
TEETHED >TEETHE
TEETHER *n* object for an infant to bite on during teething
TEETHERS >TEETHER
TEETHES >TEETHE
TEETHING >TEETHE
TEETHINGS >TEETHING
TEETHLESS >TEETH
TEETOTAL *adj* drinking no alcohol ▷ *vb* advocate total abstinence from alcohol
TEETOTALS >TEETOTAL
TEETOTUM *n* spinning top bearing letters of the alphabet on its four sides
TEETOTUMS >TEETOTUM
TEF *n* annual grass, of NE Africa, grown for its grain
TEFF *same as* >TEF
TEFFS >TEFF
TEFILLAH *n* either of the pair of blackened square cases containing parchments inscribed with biblical passages, bound by leather thongs to the head and left arm, and worn by Jewish men during weekday morning prayers
TEFILLIN >TEFILLAH
TEFLON *n* a trademark for polytetrafluoroethylene when used in nonstick cooking vessels
TEFLONS >TEFLON
TEFS >TEF
TEG *n* two-year-old sheep
TEGG *same as* >TEG
TEGGS >TEGG
TEGMEN *n* either of the leathery forewings of the cockroach and related insects
TEGMENTA >TEGMENTUM
TEGMENTAL >TEGMENTUM
TEGMENTUM *n* one of the hard protective sometimes hairy or resinous specialized leaves surrounding the buds of certain plants
TEGMINA >TEGMEN
TEGMINAL >TEGMEN
TEGS >TEG
TEGU *n* large South American lizard
TEGUA *n* type of moccasin
TEGUAS >TEGUA
TEGUEXIN *same as* >TEGU
TEGUEXINS >TEGUEXIN
TEGULA *n* one of a pair of coverings of the forewings of certain insects
TEGULAE >TEGULA
TEGULAR *adj* of, relating to, or resembling a tile or tiles
TEGULARLY >TEGULAR
TEGULATED *adj* overlappi in the manner of roof tiles
TEGUMEN *same as* >TEGME
TEGUMENT *n* protective layer around an ovule
TEGUMENTS >TEGUMENT
TEGUMINA >TEGUMEN
TEGUS >TEGU
TEHR *same as* >TAHR
TEHRS >TEHR
TEIGLACH *n* dish consisting of morsels of dough boiled in honey
TEIID *n* member of the Teiidae family of lizards
TEIIDS >TEIID
TEIL *n* lime tree
TEILS >TEIL
TEIND *Scot and northern English word for* >TITHE
TEINDED >TEIND
TEINDING >TEIND
TEINDS >TEIND
TEKKIE *variant of* >TECHIE
TEKKIES >TEKKIE
TEKNONYMY *n* practice of naming a child after his o her parent
TEKTITE *n* small dark glassy object found in several areas around the world, thought to be a product of meteorite impact
TEKTITES >TEKTITE
TEKTITIC >TEKTITE
TEL *same as* >TELL
TELA *n* any delicate tissue or weblike structure
TELAE >TELA
TELAMON *n* column in the form of a male figure, use to support an entablatur
TELAMONES >TELAMON
TELAMONS >TELAMON
TELARY *adj* capable of spinning a web
TELCO *n* telecommunications company
TELCOS >TELCO
TELD *same as* >TAULD
TELE *same as* >TELLY
TELECAST *vb* broadcast b television ▷ *n* television broadcast
TELECASTS >TELECAST
TELECHIR *n* robot arm controlled by a human operator
TELECHIRS >TELECHIR
TELECINE *n* apparatus for producing a television signal from cinematograph film
TELECINES >TELECINE
TELECOM *n* telecommunications
TELECOMS *same as* >TELECOM
TELEDU *n* badger of SE As and Indonesia, having dark brown hair with a

white stripe along the back and producing a fetid secretion from the anal glands when attacked

LEDUS > TELEDU

LEFAX *another word for* > FAX

LEFAXED > TELEFAX

LEFAXES > TELEFAX

LEFILM *n* TV movie

LEFILMS > TELEFILM

LEGA *n* rough four-wheeled cart used in Russia

LEGAS > TELEGA

LEGENIC *adj* having or showing a pleasant television image

LEGONIC > TELEGONY

LEGONY *n* supposed influence of a previous sire on offspring borne by a female to other sires

LEGRAM *n* formerly, a message sent by telegraph ▷ *vb* send a telegram

LEGRAMS > TELEGRAM

LEGRAPH *n* formerly, a system for sending messages over a distance along a cable ▷ *vb* communicate by telegraph

LEMAN *n* noncommissioned officer in the US navy, usually charged with communications duties

LEMARK *n* turn in which one ski is placed far forward of the other and turned gradually inwards ▷ *vb* perform a telemark turn

LEMARKS > TELEMARK

LEMATIC *adj* of, or relating to, the branch of science concerned with the use of technological devices to transmit information over long distances

LEMEN > TELEMAN

LEMETER *n* any device for recording or measuring a distant event and transmitting the data to a receiver or observer ▷ *vb* obtain and transmit (data) from a distant source, esp from a spacecraft

LEMETRY *n* use of electronic devices to record or measure a distant event and transmit the data to a receiver

LEOLOGY *n* belief that all things have a predetermined purpose

LEONOMY *n* condition of having a fundamental purpose

LEOSAUR *n* type of crocodile from the Jurassic period

TELEOST *n* bony fish with rayed fins and a swim bladder ▷ *adj* of, relating to, or belonging to this type of fish

TELEOSTS > TELEOST

TELEPATH *n* person who is telepathic ▷ *vb* practise telepathy

TELEPATHS > TELEPATH

TELEPATHY *n* direct communication between minds

TELEPHEME *n* any message sent by telephone

TELEPHONE *n* device for transmitting sound over a distance along wires ▷ *vb* call or talk to (a person) by telephone ▷ *adj* of or using a telephone

TELEPHONY *n* system of telecommunications for the transmission of speech or other sounds

TELEPHOTO *n* short for telephoto lens: a compound camera lens that produces a magnified image of distant objects

TELEPLAY *n* play written for television

TELEPLAYS > TELEPLAY

TELEPOINT *n* system providing a place where a cordless telephone can be connected to a telephone network

TELEPORT *vb* (in science fiction) to transport (a person or object) across a distance instantaneously

TELEPORTS > TELEPORT

TELERAN *n* electronic navigational aid in which the image of a ground-based radar system is televised to aircraft in flight so that a pilot can see the position of his aircraft in relation to others

TELERANS > TELERAN

TELERGIC > TELERGY

TELERGIES > TELERGY

TELERGY *n* name for the form of energy supposedly transferred during telepathy

TELES > TELE

TELESALE > TELESALES

TELESALES *n* selling of a product or service by telephone

TELESCOPE *n* optical instrument for magnifying distant objects ▷ *vb* shorten

TELESCOPY *n* branch of astronomy concerned with the use and design of telescopes

TELESEME *n* old-fashioned electric signalling system

TELESEMES > TELESEME

TELESES > TELESIS

TELESHOP *vb* buy goods by telephone or Internet

TELESHOPS > TELESHOP

TELESIS *n* purposeful use of natural and social processes to obtain specific social goals

TELESM *n* talisman

TELESMS > TELESM

TELESTIC *adj* relating to a hierophant

TELESTICH *n* short poem in which the last letters of each successive line form a word

TELESTICS *n* ancient pseudoscientific art of animating statues, idols, etc, or causing them to be inhabited by a diety

TELETEX *n* international means of communicating text between a variety of terminals

TELETEXES > TELETEX

TELETEXT *n* system which shows information and news on television screens

TELETEXTS > TELETEXT

TELETHON *n* lengthy television programme to raise charity funds, etc

TELETHONS > TELETHON

TELETRON *n* system for showing enlarged televisual images in eg sports stadiums

TELETRONS > TELETRON

TELETYPE *vb* send typed message by telegraph

TELETYPED > TELETYPE

TELETYPES > TELETYPE > TELETYPESETTING

TELEVIEW *vb* watch television

TELEVIEWS > TELEVIEW

TELEVISE *vb* broadcast on television

TELEVISED > TELEVISE

TELEVISER > TELEVISE

TELEVISES > TELEVISE

TELEVISOR *n* apparatus through which one transmits or receives televisual images

TELEX *n* international communication service using teleprinters ▷ *vb* transmit by telex

TELEXED > TELEX

TELEXES > TELEX

TELEXING > TELEX

TELFER *same as* > TELPHERAGE

TELFERAGE *n* overhead transport system in which an electrically driven truck runs along a single rail or cable, the load being suspended in a separate car beneath

TELFERED > TELFER

TELFERIC > TELFER

TELFERING > TELFER

TELFERS > TELFER

TELFORD *n* road built using a method favoured by Thomas Telford (1757-1834)

TELFORDS > TELFORD

TELIA > TELIUM

TELIAL > TELIUM

TELIC *adj* directed or moving towards some goal

TELICALLY > TELIC

TELIUM *n* spore-producing body of some rust fungi in which the teliospores are formed

TELL *vb* make known in words ▷ *n* large mound resulting from the accumulation of rubbish on a long-settled site, esp one with mudbrick buildings, particularly in the Middle East

TELLABLE > TELL

TELLAR *same as* > TILLER

TELLARED > TELLAR

TELLARING > TELLAR

TELLARS > TELLAR

TELLEN *same as* > TELLIN

TELLENS > TELLEN

TELLER *n* narrator ▷ *vb* (of a plant) to produce tillers

TELLERED > TELLER

TELLERING > TELLER

TELLERS > TELLER

TELLIES > TELLY

TELLIN *n* slim marine bivalve molluscs that live in intertidal sand

TELLING > TELL

TELLINGLY > TELL

TELLINGS > TELL

TELLINOID > TELLIN

TELLINS > TELLIN

TELLS > TELL

TELLTALE *n* person who reveals secrets ▷ *adj* revealing

TELLTALES > TELLTALE

TELLURAL *adj* tellurial; of or relating to the earth

TELLURATE *n* any salt or ester of telluric acid

TELLURIAN *same as* > TELLURION

TELLURIC *adj* of, relating to, or originating on or in the earth or soil

TELLURIDE *n* any compound of tellurium, esp one formed between tellurium and a more electropositive element or group

TELLURION *n* instrument that shows how day and night and the seasons result from the tilt of the earth, its rotation on its axis, and its revolution around the sun

TELLURISE *same as* >TELLURIZE
TELLURITE *n* any salt or ester of tellurous acid
TELLURIUM *n* brittle silvery-white nonmetallic element
TELLURIZE *vb* mix or combine with tellurium
TELLUROUS *adj* of or containing tellurium, esp in a low valence state
TELLUS *n* earth
TELLUSES >TELLUS
TELLY *n* television
TELLYS >TELLY
TELNET *n* computer system allowing one user to access remotely other computers on the same network ▷ *vb* use a telnet system
TELNETED >TELNET
TELNETING >TELNET
TELNETS >TELNET
TELNETTED >TELNET
TELOI >TELOS
TELOME *n* fundamental unit of a plant's structure
TELOMERE *n* either of the ends of a chromosome
TELOMERES >TELOMERE
TELOMES >TELOME
TELOMIC >TELOME
TELOPHASE *n* final stage of mitosis, during which a set of chromosomes is present at each end of the cell and a nuclear membrane forms around each, producing two new nuclei
TELOS *n* objective; ultimate purpose
TELOSES >TELOS
TELOTAXES >TELOTAXIS
TELOTAXIS *n* movement of an organism in response to one particular stimulus, overriding any response to other stimuli present
TELPHER *same as* >TELFERAGE
TELPHERED >TELPHER
TELPHERIC >TELPHER
TELPHERS >TELPHER
TELS >TEL
TELSON *n* last segment or an appendage on the last segment of the body of crustaceans and arachnids
TELSONIC >TELSON
TELSONS >TELSON
TELT *same as* >TAULD
TEMAZEPAM *n* sedative in the form of a gel-like capsule, which is taken orally or melted and injected by drug users
TEMBLOR *n* earthquake or earth tremor
TEMBLORES >TEMBLOR
TEMBLORS >TEMBLOR
TEME *old variant of* >TEAM
TEMED >TEME
TEMENE >TEMENOS
TEMENOS *n* sacred area, esp one surrounding a temple
TEMERITY *n* boldness or audacity
TEMEROUS >TEMERITY
TEMES >TEME
TEMP *same as* >TEMPORARY
TEMPED >TEMP
TEMPEH *n* fermented soya beans
TEMPEHS >TEMPEH
TEMPER *n* outburst of anger ▷ *vb* make less extreme
TEMPERA *n* painting medium for powdered pigments
TEMPERAS >TEMPERA
TEMPERATE *adj* (of climate) not extreme ▷ *vb* temper
TEMPERED *adj* (of a scale) having the frequency differences between notes adjusted in accordance with the system of equal temperament
TEMPERER >TEMPER
TEMPERERS >TEMPER
TEMPERING >TEMPER
TEMPERS >TEMPER
TEMPEST *n* violent storm ▷ *vb* agitate or disturb violently
TEMPESTED >TEMPEST
TEMPESTS >TEMPEST
TEMPI >TEMPO
TEMPING >TEMP
TEMPLAR *n* lawyer, esp a barrister, who lives or has chambers in the Inner or Middle Temple in London
TEMPLARS >TEMPLAR
TEMPLATE *n* pattern used to cut out shapes accurately
TEMPLATES >TEMPLATE
TEMPLE *n* building for worship
TEMPLED >TEMPLE
TEMPLES >TEMPLE
TEMPLET *same as* >TEMPLATE
TEMPLETS >TEMPLET
TEMPO *n* rate or pace
TEMPORAL *adj* of time ▷ *n* any body part relating to or near the temple or temples
TEMPORALS >TEMPORAL
TEMPORARY *adj* lasting only for a short time ▷ *n* person, esp a secretary or other office worker, employed on a temporary basis
TEMPORE *adv* in the time of
TEMPORISE *same as* >TEMPORIZE
TEMPORIZE *vb* gain time by negotiation or evasiveness
TEMPOS >TEMPO
TEMPS >TEMP
TEMPT *vb* entice (a person) to do something wrong
TEMPTABLE >TEMPT
TEMPTED >TEMPT
TEMPTER >TEMPT
TEMPTERS >TEMPT
TEMPTING *adj* attractive or inviting
TEMPTINGS >TEMPTING
TEMPTRESS *n* woman who sets out to allure or seduce a man or men
TEMPTS >TEMPT
TEMPURA *n* Japanese dish of seafood or vegetables dipped in batter and deep-fried, often at the table
TEMPURAS >TEMPURA
TEMS *same as* >TEMSE
TEMSE *vb* sieve
TEMSED >TEMSE
TEMSES >TEMSE
TEMSING >TEMSE
TEMULENCE *n* drunkenness
TEMULENCY *same as* >TEMULENCE
TEMULENT >TEMULENCE
TEN *n* one more than nine ▷ *adj* amounting to ten
TENABLE *adj* able to be upheld or maintained
TENABLY >TENABLE
TENACE *n* holding of two nonconsecutive high cards of a suit, such as the ace and queen
TENACES >TENACE
TENACIOUS *adj* holding fast
TENACITY >TENACIOUS
TENACULA >TENACULUM
TENACULUM *n* surgical or dissecting instrument for grasping and holding parts, consisting of a slender hook mounted in a handle
TENAIL *same as* >TENAILLE
TENAILLE *n* low outwork in the main ditch between two bastions
TENAILLES >TENAILLE
TENAILLON *n* outwork shoring up a ravelin
TENAILS >TENAIL
TENANCIES >TENANCY
TENANCY *n* temporary possession or use of lands or property owned by somebody else, in return for payment
TENANT *n* person who rents land or a building ▷ *vb* hold (land or property) as a tenant
TENANTED >TENANT
TENANTING >TENANT
TENANTRY *n* tenants collectively
TENANTS >TENANT
TENCH *n* freshwater game fish of the carp family
TENCHES >TENCH
TEND *vb* be inclined
TENDANCE *n* care and attention
TENDANCES >TENDANCE
TENDED >TEND
TENDENCE *same as* >TENDENCY
TENDENCES >TENDENCE >TENDENCIOUSNESS
TENDENCY *n* inclination to act in a certain way
TENDENZ *same as* >TENDENCY
TENDENZEN >TENDENZ
TENDER *adj* not tough ▷ *vb* offer ▷ *n* such an offer
TENDERED >TENDER
TENDERER >TENDER
TENDERERS >TENDER
TENDEREST >TENDER
TENDERING >TENDER
TENDERISE *same as* >TENDERIZE
TENDERIZE *vb* soften (meat) by pounding or treatment with a special substance
TENDERLY >TENDER
TENDERS >TENDER
TENDING >TEND
TENDINOUS *adj* of, relating to, possessing, or resembling tendons
TENDON *n* strong tissue attaching a muscle to a bone
TENDONS >TENDON
TENDRE *n* care
TENDRES >TENDRE
TENDRESSE *n* feeling of love; tenderness
TENDRIL *n* slender stem by which a climbing plant clings
TENDRILED >TENDRIL
TENDRILS >TENDRIL
TENDRON *n* shoot
TENDRONS >TENDRON
TENDS >TEND
TENDU *n* position in ballet
TENDUS >TENDU
TENE *same as* >TEEN
TENEBRAE *n* darkness
TENEBRIO *n* type of small mealworm
TENEBRIOS >TENEBRIO >TENEBRIOUSNESS
TENEBRISM *n* school, style, or method of painting, adopted chiefly by 17th-century Spanish and Neapolitan painters, esp Caravaggio, characterized by large areas of dark colours, usually relieved with a shaft of light
TENEBRIST >TENEBRISM
TENEBRITY *n* darkness; gloominess
TENEBROSE *same as* >TENEBROUS
TENEBROUS *adj* gloomy, shadowy, or dark
TENEMENT *n* (esp in Scotland or the US) building divided into several flats

NEMENTS >TENEMENT
NENDUM *n* part of a deed hat specifies the terms of enure
NENDUMS >TENENDUM
NES >TENE
NESMIC >TENESMUS
NESMUS *n* bowel disorder
NET *n* doctrine or belief
NETS >TENET
NFOLD *n* one tenth
NFOLDS >TENFOLD
NGE *n* standard nonetary unit of Kazakhstan, divided into oo tiyn
NGES >TENGE
NIA *same as* >TAENIA
NIACIDE *n* substance, sp a drug, that kills apeworms
NIAE >TENIA
NIAFUGE *same* S >TENIACIDE
NIAS >TENIA
NIASES >TENIASIS
NIASIS *same* S >TAENIASIS
NIOID >TENIA
NNE *n* tawny colour
NNER *n* ten-pound note
NNERS >TENNER
NNES >TENNE
NNIES >TENNY
NNIS *n* game in which layers use rackets to hit ball back and forth over net
NNISES >TENNIS
NNIST *n* tennis player
NNISTS >TENNIST
NNO *n* formal title of the apanese emperor, esp when regarded as a divine eligious leader
NNOS >TENNO
NNY *same as* >TENNE
NON *n* projecting end n a piece of wood fitting nto a slot in another ▷ *vb* orm a tenon on (a piece of wood)
NONED >TENON
NONER >TENON
NONERS >TENON
NONING >TENON
NONS >TENON
NOR *n* (singer with) he second highest male oice ▷ *adj* (of a voice or nstrument) between alto nd baritone
NORIST *n* musician laying any tenor nstrument
NORISTS >TENORIST
NORITE *n* black mineral ound in copper deposits nd consisting of copper xide in the form of either netallic scales or earthy nasses. Formula: CuO
NORITES >TENORITE
NORLESS >TENOR
TENOROON *n* tenor bassoon
TENOROONS >TENOROON
TENORS >TENOR
TENOTOMY *n* surgical division of a tendon
TENOUR *old variant of* >TENOR
TENOURS >TENOUR
TENPENCE *n* sum of money equivalent to ten pennies
TENPENCES >TENPENCE
TENPENNY *adj* (of a nail) three inches in length
TENPIN *n* one of the pins used in tenpin bowling
TENPINS >TENPIN
TENREC *n* small mammal resembling hedgehogs or shrews
TENRECS >TENREC
TENS >TEN
TENSE *adj* emotionally strained ▷ *vb* make or become tense ▷ *n* form of a verb showing the time of action
TENSED >TENSE
TENSELESS >TENSE
TENSELY >TENSE
TENSENESS >TENSE
TENSER >TENSE
TENSES >TENSE
TENSEST >TENSE
TENSIBLE *adj* capable of being stretched
TENSIBLY >TENSIBLE
TENSILE *adj* of tension
TENSILELY >TENSILE
TENSILITY >TENSILE
TENSING >TENSE
TENSION *n* hostility or suspense ▷ *vb* tighten
TENSIONAL >TENSION
TENSIONED >TENSION
TENSIONER >TENSION
TENSIONS >TENSION
TENSITIES >TENSITY
TENSITY *rare word for* >TENSION
TENSIVE *adj* of or causing tension or strain
TENSON *n* type of French lyric poem
TENSONS >TENSON
TENSOR *n* any muscle that can cause a part to become firm or tense
TENSORIAL >TENSOR
TENSORS >TENSOR
TENT *n* portable canvas shelter ▷ *vb* camp in a tent
TENTACLE *n* flexible organ of many invertebrates, used for grasping, feeding, etc
TENTACLED >TENTACLE
TENTACLES >TENTACLE
TENTACULA >TENTACLE
TENTAGE *n* tents collectively
TENTAGES >TENTAGE
TENTATION *n* method of achieving the correct adjustment of a mechanical device by a series of trials
TENTATIVE *adj* provisional or experimental ▷ *n* investigative attempt
TENTED >TENT
TENTER >TENT
TENTERED >TENT
TENTERING >TENT
TENTERS >TENT
TENTFUL *n* number of people or objects that can fit in a tent
TENTFULS >TENTFUL
TENTH *n* (of) number ten in a series ▷ *adj* coming after the ninth in numbering or counting order, position, time, etc ▷ *adv* after the ninth person, position, event, etc
TENTHLY *same as* >TENTH
TENTHS >TENTH
TENTIE *adj* wary
TENTIER >TENTIE
TENTIEST >TENTIE
TENTIGO *n* morbid preoccupation with sex
TENTIGOS >TENTIGO
TENTING >TENT
TENTINGS >TENT
TENTLESS >TENT
TENTLIKE >TENT
TENTMAKER *n* maker of tents
TENTORIA >TENTORIUM
TENTORIAL >TENTORIUM
TENTORIUM *n* tough membrane covering the upper part of the cerebellum
TENTS >TENT
TENTWISE *adv* in the manner of a tent
TENTY *same as* >TENTIE
TENUE *n* deportment
TENUES >TENUIS
TENUIOUS *same as* >TENUOUS
TENUIS *n* (in the grammar of classical Greek) any of the voiceless stops as represented by kappa, pi, or tau (k, p, t)
TENUITIES >TENUOUS
TENUITY >TENUOUS
TENUOUS *adj* slight or flimsy
TENUOUSLY >TENUOUS
TENURABLE >TENURE
TENURE *n* (period of) the holding of an office or position
TENURED *adj* having tenure of office
TENURES >TENURE
TENURIAL >TENURE
TENURING *n* process of making tenured
TENUTI >TENUTO
TENUTO *adv* (of a note) to be held for or beyond its full time value ▷ *vb* note sustained thus
TENUTOS >TENUTO
TENZON *same as* >TENSON
TENZONS >TENZON
TEOCALLI *n* any of various truncated pyramids built by the Aztecs as bases for their temples
TEOCALLIS >TEOCALLI
TEOPAN *n* enclosure surrounding a teocalli
TEOPANS >TEOPAN
TEOSINTE *n* tall Central American annual grass, related to maize and grown for forage in the southern US
TEOSINTES >TEOSINTE
TEPA *n* type of tree native to South America
TEPAL *n* any of the subdivisions of a perianth that is not clearly differentiated into calyx and corolla
TEPALS >TEPAL
TEPAS >TEPA
TEPEE *n* cone-shaped tent, formerly used by Native Americans
TEPEES >TEPEE
TEPEFIED >TEPEFY
TEPEFIES >TEPEFY
TEPEFY *vb* make or become tepid
TEPEFYING >TEPEFY
TEPHIGRAM *n* chart depicting variations in atmospheric conditions relative to altitude
TEPHILLAH *same as* >TEFILLAH
TEPHILLIN >TEPHILLAH
TEPHRA *n* solid matter ejected during a volcanic eruption
TEPHRAS >TEPHRA
TEPHRITE *n* variety of basalt
TEPHRITES >TEPHRITE
TEPHRITIC >TEPHRITE
TEPHROITE *n* manganese silicate
TEPID *adj* slightly warm
TEPIDARIA *pl n* in Ancient Rome, the warm rooms of the baths
TEPIDER >TEPID
TEPIDEST >TEPID
TEPIDITY >TEPID
TEPIDLY >TEPID
TEPIDNESS >TEPID
TEPOY *same as* >TEAPOY
TEPOYS >TEPOY
TEQUILA *n* Mexican alcoholic drink
TEQUILAS >TEQUILA
TEQUILLA *same as* >TEQUILA
TEQUILLAS >TEQUILLA
TERABYTE *n* large unit of computer memory
TERABYTES >TERABYTE
TERAFLOP *n* measure

of processing speed, consisting of a thousand billion floating-point operations a second
TERAFLOPS >TERAFLOP
TERAGLIN *n* edible marine fish of Australia which has fine scales and is blue in colour
TERAGLINS >TERAGLIN
TERAHERTZ *n* large unit of electrical frequency
TERAI *n* felt hat with a wide brim worn in subtropical regions
TERAIS >TERAI
TERAKIHI *same as* >TARAKIHI
TERAKIHIS >TERAKIHI
TERAOHM *n* unit of resistance equal to 10^{12} ohms
TERAOHMS >TERAOHM
TERAPH *n* any of various small household gods or images venerated by ancient Semitic peoples
TERAPHIM >TERAPH
TERAPHIMS >TERAPH
TERAS *n* monstrosity; teratism
TERATA >TERAS
TERATISM *n* malformed animal or human, esp in the fetal stage
TERATISMS >TERATISM
TERATOGEN *n* any substance, organism, or process that causes malformations in a fetus
TERATOID *adj* resembling a monster
TERATOMA *n* tumour or group of tumours composed of tissue foreign to the site of growth
TERATOMAS >TERATOMA
TERAWATT *n* unit of power equal to one million megawatts
TERAWATTS >TERAWATT
TERBIA *n* amorphous white insoluble powder
TERBIAS >TERBIA
TERBIC >TERBIUM
TERBIUM *n* rare metallic element
TERBIUMS >TERBIUM
TERCE *n* third of the seven canonical hours of the divine office, originally fixed at the third hour of the day, about 9 am
TERCEL *n* male falcon or hawk, esp as used in falconry
TERCELET *same as* >TERCEL
TERCELETS >TERCELET
TERCELS >TERCEL
TERCES >TERCE
TERCET *n* group of three lines of verse that rhyme together or are connected by rhyme with adjacent groups of three lines
TERCETS >TERCET
TERCIO *n* regiment of Spanish or Italian infantry
TERCIOS >TERCIO
TEREBENE *n* mixture of hydrocarbons prepared from oil of turpentine and sulphuric acid, used to make paints and varnishes and medicinally as an expectorant and antiseptic
TEREBENES >TEREBENE
TEREBIC as in *terebic acid* white crystalline carboxylic acid produced by the action of nitric acid on turpentin
TEREBINTH *n* small anacardiaceous tree with winged leafstalks and clusters of small flowers, and yielding a turpentine
TEREBRA *n* ancient Roman device used for boring holes in defensive walls
TEREBRAE >TEREBRA
TEREBRANT *n* type of hymenopterous insect
TEREBRAS >TEREBRA
TEREBRATE *adj* (of animals, esp insects) having a boring or penetrating organ, such as a sting ▷ *vb* bore
TEREDINES >TEREDO
TEREDO *n* marine mollusc that bores into and destroys submerged timber
TEREDOS >TEREDO
TEREFA *same as* >TREF
TEREFAH *same as* >TREF
TEREK *n* type of sandpiper
TEREKS >TEREK
TERES *n* shoulder muscle
TERETE *adj* (esp of plant parts) smooth and usually cylindrical and tapering
TERETES >TERETE
TERF *old variant of* >TURF
TERFE *old variant of* >TURF
TERFES >TERFE
TERFS >TERF
TERGA >TERGUM
TERGAL >TERGUM
TERGITE *n* constituent part of a tergum
TERGITES >TERGITE
TERGUM *n* cuticular plate covering the dorsal surface of a body segment of an arthropod
TERIYAKI *adj* basted with soy sauce and rice wine and broiled over an open fire ▷ *n* dish prepared in this way
TERIYAKIS >TERIYAKI
TERM *n* word or expression ▷ *vb* name or designate
TERMAGANT *n* unpleasant and bad-tempered woman
TERMED >TERM
TERMER *same as* >TERMOR
TERMERS >TERMER
TERMINAL *adj* (of an illness) ending in death ▷ *n* place where people or vehicles begin or end a journey
TERMINALS >TERMINAL
TERMINATE *vb* bring or come to an end
TERMINER *n* person or thing that limits or determines
TERMINERS >TERMINER
TERMING >TERM
TERMINI >TERMINUS
TERMINISM *n* philosophical theory
TERMINIST >TERMINISM
TERMINUS *n* railway or bus station at the end of a line
TERMITARY *n* termite nest
TERMITE *n* white antlike insect that destroys timber
TERMITES >TERMITE
TERMITIC >TERMITE
TERMLESS *adj* without limit or boundary
TERMLIES >TERMLY
TERMLY *n* publication issued once a term
TERMOR *n* person who holds an estate for a term of years or until he dies
TERMORS >TERMOR
TERMS >TERM
TERMTIME *n* time during a term, esp a school or university term
TERMTIMES >TERMTIME
TERN *n* gull-like sea bird with a forked tail and pointed wings
TERNAL >TERN
TERNARIES >TERNARY
TERNARY *adj* consisting of three parts ▷ *n* group of three
TERNATE *adj* (esp of a leaf) consisting of three leaflets or other parts
TERNATELY >TERNATE
TERNE *n* alloy of lead containing tin (10–20 per cent) and antimony (1.5–2 per cent) ▷ *vb* coat with this alloy
TERNED >TERNE
TERNES >TERNE
TERNING >TERNE
TERNION *n* group of three
TERNIONS >TERNION
TERNS >TERN
TERPENE *n* any one of a class of unsaturated hydrocarbons, such as the carotenes, that are found in the essential oils of many plants
TERPENES >TERPENE
TERPENIC >TERPENE
TERPENOID >TERPENE
TERPINEOL *n* terpene alcohol with an odour of lilac, present in several essential oils
TERPINOL *same as* >TERPINEOL
TERPINOLS >TERPINOL
TERRA *n* (in legal contexts earth or land
TERRACE *n* row of houses built as one block ▷ *vb* form into or provide with a terrace
TERRACED >TERRACE
TERRACES >TERRACE
TERRACING *n* series of terraces, esp one dividin a slope into a steplike system of flat narrow fie
TERRAE >TERRA
TERRAFORM *vb* engage in planetary engineering to enhance the capacity of extraterrestrial planetar environment to sustain life
TERRAIN *same as* >TERRA
TERRAINS >TERRAIN
TERRAMARA *n* neolithic Italian pile-dwelling
TERRAMARE >TERRAMARA
TERRANE *n* series of rock formations, esp one having a prevalent type of rock
TERRANES >TERRANE
TERRAPIN *n* small turtle-like reptile
TERRAPINS >TERRAPIN
TERRARIA >TERRARIUM
TERRARIUM *n* enclosed container for small plant or animals
TERRAS *same as* >TRASS
TERRASES >TERRAS
TERRAZZO *n* floor of mar chips set in mortar and polished
TERRAZZOS >TERRAZZO
TERREEN *old variant of* >TUREEN
TERREENS >TERREEN
TERRELLA *n* magnetic globe designed to simulate and demonstra the earth's magnetic fie
TERRELLAS >TERRELLA
TERRENE *adj* of or relatin to the earth ▷ *n* land
TERRENELY >TERRENE
TERRENES >TERRENE
>TERRESTRIAL
TERRET *n* either of the tw metal rings on a harness saddle through which th reins are passed
TERRETS >TERRET
TERRIBLE *adj* very seriou ▷ *n* something terrible
TERRIBLES >TERRIBLE
TERRIBLY *adv* in a terrib manner
TERRICOLE *n* plant or animal living on land
TERRIER *n* any of variou

reeds of small active dog
RRIERS >TERRIER
RRIES >TERRY
RRIFIC *adj* great or ntense
RRIFIED >TERRIFY
RRIFIER >TERRIFY
RRIFIES >TERRIFY
RRIFY *vb* fill with fear
RRINE *n* earthenware ish with a lid
RRINES >TERRINE
RRIT *same as* >TERRET
RRITORY *n* district
RRITS >TERRIT
RROIR *n* combination f factors, including soil, limate, and environment, hat gives a wine its istinctive character
RROIRS >TERROIR
RROR *n* great fear
RRORFUL >TERROR
RRORISE *same* s >TERRORIZE
RRORISM *n* use of iolence and intimidation o achieve political ends
RRORIST *n* person vho employs terror or errorism, esp as a political veapon
RRORIZE *vb* force or ppress by fear or violence
RRORS >TERROR
RRY *n* fabric with small oops covering both sides, sed esp for making owels
RSE *adj* neat and concise
RSELY >TERSE
RSENESS >TERSE
RSER >TERSE
RSEST >TERSE
RSION *n* action of ubbing off or wiping
RSIONS >TERSION
RTIA *same as* >TERCIO
RTIAL *same as* >TERTIARY
RTIALS >TERTIAL
RTIAN *adj* (of a fever or he symptoms of a disease, sp malaria) occurring very other day ▷*n* ertian fever or symptoms
RTIANS >TERTIAN
RTIARY *adj* third in egree, order, etc ▷*n* any f the tertiary feathers
RTIAS >TERTIA
RTIUM as in *tertium quid* nknown or indefinite ning related in some way o two known or definite nings, but distinct from oth
RTIUS *n* third (in a roup)
RTIUSES >TERTIUS
RTS *n* card game using 2 cards
RVALENT *same* s >TRIVALENT
RYLENE *n* tradename for a synthetic polyester fibre or fabric based on terephthalic acid, characterized by lightness and crease resistance and used for clothing, sheets, ropes, sails, etc
TERYLENES >TERYLENE
TERZETTA *n* tercet
TERZETTAS >TERZETTA
TERZETTI >TERZETTO
TERZETTO *n* trio, esp a vocal one
TERZETTOS >TERZETTO
TES >TE
TESLA *n* derived SI unit of magnetic flux density equal to a flux of 1 weber in an area of 1 square metre.
TESLAS >TESLA
TESSELATE *vb* cover with small tiles
TESSELLA *n* little tessera
TESSELLAE >TESSELLA
TESSELLAR *adj* of or relating to tessellae
TESSERA *n* small square tile used in mosaics
TESSERACT *n* cube inside another cube
TESSERAE >TESSERA
TESSERAL >TESSERA
TESSITURA *n* general pitch level of a piece of vocal music
TESSITURE >TESSITURA
TEST *vb* try out to ascertain the worth, capability, or endurance of ▷*n* critical examination
TESTA *n* hard outer layer of a seed
TESTABLE >TEST
TESTACEAN *n* microscopic animal with hard shell
TESTACIES >TESTATE
TESTACY >TESTATE
TESTAE >TESTA
TESTAMENT *n* proof or tribute
TESTAMUR *n* certificate proving an examination has been passed
TESTAMURS >TESTAMUR
TESTATE *adj* having left a valid will ▷*n* person who dies and leaves a legally valid will
TESTATES >TESTATE
TESTATION >TESTATOR
TESTATOR *n* maker of a will
TESTATORS >TESTATOR
TESTATRIX *same as* >TESTATOR
TESTATUM *n* part of a purchase deed
TESTATUMS >TESTATUM
TESTCROSS *vb* subject to a testcross, a genetic test for ascertaining whether an individual is homozygous or heterozygous
TESTE *n* witness
TESTED >TEST
TESTEE *n* person subjected to a test
TESTEES >TESTEE
TESTER *n* person or thing that tests or is used for testing
TESTERN *vb* give (someone) a teston
TESTERNED >TESTERN
TESTERNS >TESTERN
TESTERS >TESTER
TESTES >TESTIS
TESTICLE *n* either of the two male reproductive glands
TESTICLES >TESTICLE
TESTIER >TESTY
TESTIEST >TESTY
TESTIFIED >TESTIFY
TESTIFIER >TESTIFY
TESTIFIES >TESTIFY
TESTIFY *vb* give evidence under oath
TESTILY >TESTY
TESTIMONY *n* declaration of truth or fact ▷*vb* testify
TESTINESS >TESTY
TESTING >TEST
TESTINGS >TEST
TESTIS *same as* >TESTICLE
TESTON *n* French silver coin of the 16th century
TESTONS >TESTON
TESTOON *same as* >TESTON
TESTOONS >TESTOON
TESTRIL *same as* >TESTRILL
TESTRILL *n* sixpence
TESTRILLS >TESTRILL
TESTRILS >TESTRIL
TESTS >TEST
TESTUDO *n* form of shelter used by the ancient Roman Army for protection against attack from above, consisting either of a mobile arched structure or of overlapping shields held by the soldiers over their heads
TESTUDOS >TESTUDO
TESTY *adj* irritable or touchy
TET *same as* >TETH
TETANAL >TETANUS
TETANIC *adj* of, relating to, or producing tetanus or the spasms of tetanus ▷*n* tetanic drug or agent
TETANICAL >TETANUS
TETANICS >TETANIC
TETANIES >TETANY
TETANISE *same as* >TETANIZE
TETANISED >TETANISE
TETANISES >TETANISE
TETANIZE *vb* induce tetanus in (a muscle)
TETANIZED >TETANIZE
TETANIZES >TETANIZE
TETANOID >TETANUS
TETANUS *n* acute infectious disease producing muscular spasms and convulsions
TETANUSES >TETANUS
TETANY *n* abnormal increase in the excitability of nerves and muscles resulting in spasms of the arms and legs, caused by a deficiency of parathyroid secretion
TETCHED *same as* >TECHED
TETCHIER >TETCHY
TETCHIEST >TETCHY
TETCHILY >TETCHY
TETCHY *adj* cross and irritable
TETE *n* elaborate hairstyle
TETES >TETE
TETH *n* ninth letter of the Hebrew alphabet transliterated as *t* and pronounced more or less like English *t* with pharyngeal articulation
TETHER *n* rope or chain for tying an animal to a spot ▷*vb* tie up with rope
TETHERED >TETHER
TETHERING >TETHER
TETHERS >TETHER
TETHS >TETH
TETOTUM *same as* >TEETOTUM
TETOTUMS >TETOTUM
TETRA *n* brightly coloured tropical freshwater fish
TETRACID *adj* (of a base) capable of reacting with four molecules of a monobasic acid
TETRACIDS >TETRACID
TETRACT *n* sponge spicule with four rays
TETRACTS >TETRACT
TETRAD *n* group or series of four
TETRADIC >TETRAD
TETRADITE *n* person who believes that the number four has supernatural significance
TETRADS >TETRAD
TETRAGON *n* figure with four angles and four sides >TETRAGONAL
TETRAGONS >TETRAGON
TETRAGRAM *n* any word of four letters
TETRALOGY *n* series of four related works
TETRAMER *n* four-molecule polymer
TETRAMERS >TETRAMER
TETRAPLA *n* book containing versions of the same text in four languages
TETRAPLAS >TETRAPLA
TETRAPOD *n* any vertebrate that has four limbs
TETRAPODS >TETRAPOD
TETRAPODY *n* metrical unit consisting of four feet
TETRARCH *n* ruler of one fourth of a country
TETRARCHS >TETRARCH

TETRARCHY >TETRARCH
TETRAS >TETRA
TETRAXON *n* four-pointed spicule
TETRAXONS >TETRAXON
TETRI *n* currency unit of Georgia
TETRIS >TETRI
TETRODE *n* electronic valve having four electrodes, namely a cathode, control grid, screen grid, and anode
TETRODES >TETRODE
TETRONAL *n* sedative drug
TETRONALS >TETRONAL
TETROXID *same as* >TETROXIDE
TETROXIDE *n* any oxide that contains four oxygen atoms per molecule
TETROXIDS >TETROXID
TETRYL *n* yellow crystalline explosive solid used in detonators
TETRYLS >TETRYL
TETS >TET
TETTER *n* blister or pimple ▷ *vb* cause a tetter to erupt (on)
TETTERED >TETTER
TETTERING >TETTER
TETTEROUS >TETTER
TETTERS >TETTER
TETTIX *n* cicada
TETTIXES >TETTIX
TEUCH *Scots variant of* >TOUGH
TEUCHAT *Scots variant of* >TEWIT
TEUCHATS >TEUCHAT
TEUCHER >TEUCH
TEUCHEST >TEUCH
TEUCHTER *n* in Scotland, derogatory word used by Lowlanders for a Highlander
TEUCHTERS >TEUCHTER
TEUGH *same as* >TEUCH
TEUGHER >TEUGH
TEUGHEST >TEUGH
TEUGHLY >TEUGH
TEUTONISE *same as* >TEUTONIZE
TEUTONIZE *vb* make or become German or Germanic
TEVATRON *n* machine used in nuclear research
TEVATRONS >TEVATRON
TEW *vb* work hard
TEWART *same as* >TUART
TEWARTS >TEWART
TEWED >TEW
TEWEL *n* horse's rectum
TEWELS >TEWEL
TEWHIT *same as* >TEWIT
TEWHITS >TEWHIT
TEWING >TEW
TEWIT *n* lapwing
TEWITS >TEWIT
TEWS >TEW
TEX *n* unit of weight used to measure yarn density
TEXAS *n* structure on the upper deck of a paddle-steamer containing the officers' quarters and the wheelhouse
TEXASES >TEXAS
TEXES >TEX
TEXT *n* main body of a book as distinct from illustrations etc ▷ *vb* send a text message to (someone)
TEXTBOOK *n* standard book on a particular subject ▷ *adj* perfect
TEXTBOOKS >TEXTBOOK
TEXTER *n* person who communicates by text messaging
TEXTERS >TEXTER
TEXTILE *n* fabric or cloth, esp woven ▷ *adj* of (the making of) fabrics
TEXTILES >TEXTILE
TEXTLESS >TEXT
TEXTORIAL *adj* of or relating to weaving or weavers
TEXTPHONE *n* phone designed to translate speech into text and vice versa
TEXTS >TEXT
TEXTUAL *adj* of, based on, or relating to, a text or texts
TEXTUALLY >TEXTUAL
TEXTUARY *adj* of, relating to, or contained in a text ▷ *n* textual critic
TEXTURAL >TEXTURE
TEXTURE *n* structure, feel, or consistency ▷ *vb* give a distinctive texture to (something)
TEXTURED >TEXTURE
TEXTURES >TEXTURE
TEXTURING >TEXTURE
TEXTURISE *same as* >TEXTURIZE
TEXTURIZE *vb* texture
THACK *Scots word for* >THATCH
THACKED >THACK
THACKING >THACK
THACKS >THACK
THAE *Scots word for* >THOSE
THAGI *same as* >THUGGEE
THAGIS >THAGI
THAIM *Scots variant of* >THEM
THAIRM *n* catgut
THAIRMS >THAIRM
THALAMI >THALAMUS
THALAMIC >THALAMUS
THALAMUS *n* either of the two contiguous egg-shaped masses of grey matter at the base of the brain
THALASSIC *adj* of or relating to the sea
THALER *n* former German, Austrian, or Swiss silver coin
THALERS >THALER
THALI *n* meal consisting of several small meat or vegetable dishes accompanied by rice, bread, etc, and sometimes by a starter or a sweet
THALIAN *adj* of or relating to comedy
THALIS >THALI
THALLI >THALLUS
THALLIC *adj* of or containing thallium, esp in the trivalent state
THALLINE >THALLUS
THALLIOUS >THALLIUM
THALLIUM *n* highly toxic metallic element
THALLIUMS >THALLIUM
THALLOID >THALLUS
THALLOUS *adj* of or containing thallium, esp in the monovalent state
THALLUS *n* undifferentiated vegetative body of algae, fungi, and lichens
THALLUSES >THALLUS
THALWEG *n* longitudinal outline of a riverbed from source to mouth
THALWEGS >THALWEG
THAN *prep* used to introduce the second element of a comparison ▷ *n* old variant of "then" (that time)
THANA *same as* >TANA
THANADAR *same as* >TANADAR
THANADARS >THANADAR
THANAGE *n* state of being a thane
THANAGES >THANAGE
THANAH *same as* >TANA
THANAHS >THANAH
THANAS >THANA
THANATISM *n* belief that the soul ceases to exist when the body dies
THANATIST >THANATISM
THANATOID *adj* like death
THANATOS *n* Greek personification of death
THANE *n* Anglo-Saxon or medieval Scottish nobleman
THANEDOM >THANE
THANEDOMS >THANE
THANEHOOD >THANE
THANES >THANE
THANESHIP >THANE
THANGKA *n* (in Tibetan Buddhism) a religious painting on a scroll
THANGKAS >THANGKA
THANK *vb* express gratitude to
THANKED >THANK
THANKEE *interj* thank you
THANKER >THANK
THANKERS >THANK
THANKFUL *adj* grateful
THANKING >THANK
THANKINGS >THANK
THANKLESS *adj* unrewarding or unappreciated
THANKS *pl n* words of gratitude ▷ *interj* polite expression of gratitude
THANKYOU *n* conventiona expression of gratitude
THANKYOUS >THANKYOU
THANNA *same as* >TANA
THANNAH *same as* >TANA
THANNAHS >THANNAH
THANNAS >THANNA
THANS >THAN
THAR *same as* >TAHR
THARM *n* stomach
THARMS >THARM
THARS >THAR
THAT *pron* used to refer to something already mentioned or familiar, o further away
THATAWAY *adv* that way
THATCH *n* roofing materi of reeds or straw ▷ *vb* ro (a house) with reeds or straw
THATCHED >THATCH
THATCHER >THATCH
THATCHERS >THATCH
THATCHES >THATCH
THATCHIER >THATCH
THATCHING >THATCH
THATCHT *old variant of* >THATCHED
THATCHY >THATCH
THATNESS *n* state or quality of being 'that'
THAUMATIN *n* type of natural sweetener
THAW *vb* make or become unfrozen ▷ *n* thawing
THAWED >THAW
THAWER >THAW
THAWERS >THAW
THAWIER >THAWY
THAWIEST >THAWY
THAWING >THAW
THAWINGS >THAW
THAWLESS >THAW
THAWS >THAW
THAWY *adj* tending to tha
THE *determiner* definite article, used before a no
THEACEOUS *adj* of, relatin to, or belonging to the *Theaceae*, a family of evergreen trees and shru of tropical and warm regions: includes the tea plant
THEANDRIC *adj* both divi and human
THEARCHIC >THEARCHY
THEARCHY *n* rule or government by God or gods
THEATER *same as* >THEAT
THEATERS >THEATER
THEATRAL *adj* of or relati to the theatre
THEATRE *n* place where

plays etc are performed
HEATRES >THEATRE
HEATRIC *adj* of or relating to the theatre
HEATRICS *n* art of staging plays
HEAVE *n* young ewe
HEAVES >THEAVE
HEBAINE *n* poisonous white crystalline alkaloid, found in opium but without opioid actions
HEBAINES >THEBAINE
HEBE *n* inner satellite of Jupiter discovered in 1979
HEBES >THEBE
HECA *n* enclosing organ, cell, or spore case, esp the capsule of a moss
HECAE >THECA
HECAL >THECA
HECATE >THECA
HECODONT *adj* (of mammals and certain reptiles) having teeth that grow in sockets ▷ *n* extinct reptile
HEE *pron* refers to the person addressed: used mainly by members of the Society of Friends ▷ *vb* use the word "thee"
HEED >THEE
HEEING >THEE
HEEK *Scots variant of* >THATCH
HEEKED >THEEK
HEEKING >THEEK
HEEKS >THEEK
HEELIN *trade name for* >ESTRONE
HEELINS >THEELIN
HEELOL *n* estriol
HEELOLS >THEELOL
HEES >THEE
HEFT *n* act or an instance of stealing
HEFTLESS >THEFT
HEFTS >THEFT
HEFTUOUS *adj* tending to commit theft
HEGITHER *Scots variant of* >TOGETHER
HEGN *same as* >THANE
HEGNLY >THEGN
HEGNS >THEGN
HEIC *n* person who drinks excessive amounts of tea
HEICS >THEIC
HEIN *old variant of* >THANE
HEINE *another name for* >CAFFEINE
HEINES >THEINE
HEINS >THEIN
HEIR *determiner* of, belonging to, or associated in some way with them
HEIRS *pron* (thing or person) belonging to them
HEIRSELF *pron* dialect form of themselves: reflexive form of they or them
THEISM *n* belief in a God or gods
THEISMS >THEISM
THEIST >THEISM
THEISTIC >THEISM
THEISTS >THEISM
THELEMENT *n* old contraction of "the element"
THELF *n* old contraction of "the element"
THELITIS *n* inflammation of the nipple
THELVES >THELF
THELYTOKY *n* type of reproduction resulting in female offspring only
THEM *pron* refers to people or things other than the speaker or those addressed
THEMA *n* theme
THEMATA >THEMA
THEMATIC *adj* of, relating to, or consisting of a theme or themes ▷ *n* thematic vowel
THEMATICS >THEMATIC
THEME *n* main idea or subject being discussed ▷ *vb* design, decorate, arrange, etc, in accordance with a theme
THEMED >THEME
THEMELESS >THEME
THEMES >THEME
THEMING >THEME
THEMSELF *pron* reflexive form of one, whoever, anybody
THEN *adv* at that time ▷ *pron* that time ▷ *adj* existing or functioning at that time ▷ *n* that time
THENABOUT *adv* around then
THENAGE *old variant of* >THANAGE
THENAGES >THENAGE
THENAL *adj* of or relating to the thenar
THENAR *n* palm of the hand ▷ *adj* of or relating to the palm or the region at the base of the thumb
THENARS >THENAR
THENCE *adv* from that place or time
THENS >THEN
THEOCRACY *n* government by a god or priests
THEOCRASY *n* mingling into one of deities or divine attributes previously regarded as distinct
THEOCRAT >THEOCRACY
THEOCRATS >THEOCRACY
THEODICY *n* branch of theology concerned with defending the attributes of God against objections resulting from physical and moral evil
THEOGONIC >THEOGONY
THEOGONY *n* origin and descent of the gods
THEOLOG *same as* >THEOLOGUE
THEOLOGER *n* theologian
THEOLOGIC >THEOLOGY
THEOLOGS >THEOLOG
THEOLOGUE *n* theologian
THEOLOGY *n* study of religions and religious beliefs
THEOMACHY *n* battle among the gods or against them
THEOMANCY *n* divination or prophecy by an oracle or by people directly inspired by a god
THEOMANIA *n* religious madness, esp when it takes the form of believing oneself to be a god
THEONOMY *n* state of being governed by God
THEOPATHY *n* religious emotion engendered by the contemplation of or meditation upon God
THEOPHAGY *n* sacramental eating of a god
THEOPHANY *n* manifestation of a deity to man in a form that, though visible, is not necessarily material
THEORBIST >THEORBO
THEORBO *n* obsolete form of the lute, having two necks, one above the other, the second neck carrying a set of unstopped sympathetic bass strings
THEORBOS >THEORBO
THEOREM *n* proposition that can be proved by reasoning
THEOREMIC >THEOREM
THEOREMS >THEOREM
THEORETIC *adj* of, or based on, a theory
THEORIC *n* theory; conjecture
THEORICS >THEORIC
THEORIES >THEORY
THEORIQUE *same as* >THEORIC
THEORISE *same as* >THEORIZE
THEORISED >THEORISE
THEORISER >THEORISE
THEORISES >THEORISE
THEORIST *n* originator of a theory
THEORISTS >THEORIST
THEORIZE *vb* form theories, speculate
THEORIZED >THEORIZE
THEORIZER >THEORIZE
THEORIZES >THEORIZE
THEORY *n* set of ideas to explain something
THEOSOPH *n* proponent of theosophy
THEOSOPHS >THEOSOPH
THEOSOPHY *n* religious or philosophical system claiming to be based on intuitive insight into the divine nature
THEOTOKOI >THEOTOKOS
THEOTOKOS *n* mother of God
THEOW *n* slave in Anglo-Saxon Britain
THEOWS >THEOW
THERALITE *n* type of igneous rock
THERAPIES >THERAPY
THERAPIST *n* person skilled in a particular type of therapy
THERAPSID *n* extinct reptile: considered to be the ancestors of mammals
THERAPY *n* curing treatment
THERBLIG *n* basic unit of work in an industrial process
THERBLIGS >THERBLIG
THERE *adv* in or to that place ▷ *n* that place
THEREAT *adv* at that point or time
THEREAWAY *adv* in that direction
THEREBY *adv* by that means
THEREFOR *adv* for this, that, or it
THEREFORE *adv* consequently, that being so
THEREFROM *adv* from that or there
THEREIN *adv* in or into that place or thing
THEREINTO *adv* into that place, circumstance, etc
THEREMIN *n* electronic musical instrument, played by moving the hands through electromagnetic fields created by two metal rods
THEREMINS >THEREMIN
THERENESS *n* quality of having existence
THEREOF *adv* of or concerning that or it
THEREON *archaic word for* >THEREUPON
THEREOUT *another word for* >THEREFROM
THERES >THERE
THERETO *adv* that or it
THEREUNTO *adv* to that
THEREUPON *adv* immediately after that
THEREWITH *adv* with or in addition to that
THERIAC *n* ointment or potion of varying composition, used as an antidote to a poison
THERIACA *same as* >THERIAC
THERIACAL >THERIAC
THERIACAS >THERIACA

THERIACS > THERIAC
THERIAN *n* animal of the class Theria, a subclass of mammals
THERIANS > THERIAN
THERM *n* unit of measurement of heat public bath
THERMAE *pl n* public baths or hot springs, esp in ancient Greece or Rome
THERMAL *adj* of heat ▷ *n* rising current of warm air
THERMALLY > THERMAL
THERMALS > THERMAL
THERME *old variant of* > THERM
THERMEL *n* type of thermometer measuring temperature by means of thermoelectic current
THERMELS > THERMEL
THERMES > THERME
THERMETTE *n* device, used outdoors, for boiling water rapidly
THERMIC *same as* > THERMAL
THERMICAL *same as* > THERMAL
THERMIDOR as in *lobster thermidor* dish of cooked lobster
THERMION *n* electron or ion emitted by a body at high temperature
THERMIONS > THERMION
THERMIT *variant of* > THERMITE
THERMITE as in *thermite process* process for reducing metallic oxides
THERMITES > THERMITE
THERMITS > THERMIT
THERMOS *n* trademark term for a type of stoppered vacuum flask used to preserve the temperature of its contents
THERMOSES > THERMOS
THERMOSET *n* material (esp a synthetic plastic or resin) that hardens permanently after one application of heat and pressure
THERMOTIC *adj* of or because of heat
THERMS > THERM
THEROID *adj* of, relating to, or resembling a beast
THEROLOGY *n* study of mammals
THEROPOD *n* bipedal carnivorous saurischian dinosaur with strong hind legs and grasping hands
THEROPODS > THEROPOD
THESAURAL > THESAURUS
THESAURI > THESAURUS
THESAURUS *n* book containing lists of synonyms and related words
THESE *determiner* form of this used before a plural noun
THESES > THESIS
THESIS *n* written work submitted for a degree
THESP *short for* > THESPIAN
THESPIAN *adj* of or relating to drama and the theatre ▷ *n* actor or actress
THESPIANS > THESPIAN
THESPS > THESP
THETA *n* eighth letter of the Greek alphabet
THETAS > THETA
THETCH *old variant spelling of* > THATCH
THETCHED > THETCH
THETCHES > THETCH
THETCHING > THETCH
THETE *n* member of the lowest order of freeman in ancient Athens
THETES > THETE
THETHER *old variant of* > THITHER
THETIC *adj* (in classical prosody) of, bearing, or relating to a metrical stress
THETICAL *another word for* > THETIC
THEURGIC > THEURGY
THEURGIES > THEURGY
THEURGIST > THEURGY
THEURGY *n* intervention of a divine or supernatural agency in the affairs of man
THEW *n* muscle, esp if strong or well-developed
THEWED *adj* strong; muscular
THEWES > THEW
THEWIER > THEW
THEWIEST > THEW
THEWLESS > THEW
THEWS > THEW
THEWY > THEW
THEY *pron* people or things other than the speaker or people addressed
THIAMIN *same as* > THIAMINE
THIAMINE *n* vitamin found in the outer coat of rice and other grains
THIAMINES > THIAMINE
THIAMINS > THIAMIN
THIASUS *n* congregation of people who have gathered to sing and dance in honour of a god
THIASUSES > THIASUS
THIAZIDE *n* diuretic drug
THIAZIDES > THIAZIDE
THIAZIN *same as* > THIAZINE
THIAZINE *n* any of a group of organic compounds containing a ring system composed of four carbon atoms, a sulphur atom, and a nitrogen atom
THIAZINES > THIAZINE
THIAZINS > THIAZIN
THIAZOL *same as* > THIAZOLE
THIAZOLE *n* colourless liquid with a pungent smell that contains a ring system composed of three carbon atoms, a sulphur atom, and a nitrogen atom
THIAZOLES > THIAZOLE
THIAZOLS > THIAZOL
THIBET *n* coloured woollen cloth
THIBETS > THIBET
THIBLE *n* stick for stirring porridge
THIBLES > THIBLE
THICK *adj* of great or specified extent from one side to the other ▷ *vb* thicken
THICKED > THICK
THICKEN *vb* make or become thick or thicker
THICKENED > THICKEN
THICKENER > THICKEN
THICKENS > THICKEN
THICKER > THICK
THICKEST > THICK
THICKET *n* dense growth of small trees
THICKETED *adj* covered in thicket
THICKETS > THICKET
THICKETY > THICKET
THICKHEAD *n* stupid or ignorant person
THICKIE *same as* > THICKO
THICKIES > THICKY
THICKING > THICK
THICKISH > THICK
THICKLEAF *n* succulent plant with sessile or short-stalked fleshy leaves
THICKLY > THICK
THICKNESS *n* state of being thick
THICKO *n* slow-witted unintelligent person
THICKOES > THICKO
THICKOS > THICKO
THICKS > THICK
THICKSET *adj* stocky in build
THICKSETS > THICKSET
THICKSKIN *n* insensitive person
THICKY *same as* > THICKO
THIEF *n* person who steals
THIEVE *vb* steal
THIEVED > THIEVE
THIEVERY > THIEVE
THIEVES > THIEVE
THIEVING *adj* given to stealing other people's possessions
THIEVINGS > THIEVING
THIEVISH > THIEF
THIG *vb* beg
THIGGER > THIG
THIGGERS > THIG
THIGGING > THIG
THIGGINGS > THIG
THIGGIT *Scots inflection of* > THIG
THIGH *n* upper part of the human leg
THIGHBONE *same as* > FEMUR
THIGHED *adj* having thigh
THIGHS > THIGH
THIGS > THIG
THILK *pron* that same
THILL *another word for* > SHAFT
THILLER *n* horse that goes between the thills of a cart
THILLERS > THILLER
THILLS > THILL
THIMBLE *n* cap protecting the end of the finger when sewing ▷ *vb* use a thimble
THIMBLED > THIMBLE
THIMBLES > THIMBLE
THIMBLING > THIMBLE
THIN *adj* not thick ▷ *vb* make or become thin ▷ *adv* in order to produce something thin
THINCLAD *n* track-and-field athlete
THINCLADS > THINCLAD
THINDOWN *n* reduction in the amount of particles, esp protons, of very high energy reaching and penetrating the earth's atmosphere from outer space
THINDOWNS > THINDOWN
THINE *adj* (something) of or associated with you (thou) ▷ *pron* something belonging to you (thou) ▷ *determiner* of, belonging to, or associated in some way with you (thou)
THING *n* material object
THINGAMY *n* person or thing the name of which unknown
THINGHOOD *n* existence; state or condition of being a thing
THINGIER > THINGY
THINGIES > THINGY
THINGIEST > THINGY
THINGNESS *n* state of being a thing
THINGS > THING
THINGUMMY *n* person or thing the name of which is unknown, temporarily forgotten, or deliberately overlooked
THINGY *adj* existing in reality; actual
THINK *vb* consider, judge, or believe
THINKABLE *adj* able to be conceived or considered
THINKABLY > THINKABLE
THINKER > THINK
THINKERS > THINK
THINKING > THINK
THINKINGS > THINK
THINKS > THINK

HINLY >THIN
HINNED >THIN
HINNER >THIN
HINNERS >THIN
HINNESS >THIN
HINNEST >THIN
HINNING >THIN
HINNINGS >THIN
HINNISH >THIN
HINS >THIN
HIO *adj* of, or relating to, sulphur
HIOFURAN *another name for* >THIOPHEN
HIOL *n* any of a class of sulphur-containing organic compounds with the formula RSH, where R is an organic group
HIOLIC >THIOL
HIOLS >THIOL
HIONATE *n* any salt or ester of thionic acid
HIONATES >THIONATE
HIONIC *adj* of, relating to, or containing sulphur
HIONIN *same as* >THIONINE
HIONINE *n* crystalline derivative of thiazine used as a violet dye to stain microscope specimens
HIONINES >THIONINE
HIONINS >THIONIN
HIONYL *n* of, consisting of, or containing the divalent group SO
IONYLS >THIONYL
IOPHEN *n* colourless liquid heterocyclic compound found in the benzene fraction of coal tar and manufactured from butane and sulphur
IOPHENE *same as* >THIOPHEN
IOPHENS >THIOPHEN
IOPHIL *adj* having an attraction to sulphur
IOTEPA *n* drug used in chemotherapy
IOTEPAS >THIOTEPA
IOUREA *n* white water-soluble crystalline substance with a bitter taste
IOUREAS >THIOUREA
IR *Scots word for* >THESE
IRAM *n* antifungal agent
IRAMS >THIRAM
IRD *adj* of number three in a series ▷ *n* one of three equal parts ▷ *adv* in the third place ▷ *vb* divide (something) by three
IRDED >THIRD
IRDHAND *adv* from the second of two intermediaries
IRDING >THIRD
IRDINGS >THIRD
IRDLY >THIRD
IRDS >THIRD
IRDSMAN *n* intermediary
THIRDSMEN >THIRDSMAN
THIRL *vb* bore or drill
THIRLAGE *n* obligation imposed upon tenants of certain lands requiring them to have their grain ground at a specified mill
THIRLAGES >THIRLAGE
THIRLED >THIRL
THIRLING >THIRL
THIRLS >THIRL
THIRST *n* desire to drink ▷ *vb* feel thirst
THIRSTED >THIRST
THIRSTER >THIRST
THIRSTERS >THIRSTER
THIRSTFUL >THIRST
THIRSTIER >THIRSTY
THIRSTILY >THIRSTY
THIRSTING >THIRST
THIRSTS >THIRST
THIRSTY *adj* feeling a desire to drink
THIRTEEN *n* three plus ten ▷ *adj* amounting to thirteen ▷ *determiner* amounting to thirteen
THIRTEENS >THIRTEEN
THIRTIES >THIRTY
THIRTIETH *adj* being the ordinal number of *thirty* in counting order, position, time, etc: often written 30th ▷ *n* one of 30 approximately equal parts of something
THIRTY *n* three times ten ▷ *adj* amounting to thirty ▷ *determiner* amounting to thirty
THIRTYISH *adj* around thirty years of age
THIS *pron* used to refer to a thing or person nearby, just mentioned, or about to be mentioned ▷ *adj* used to refer to the present time
THISAWAY *adv* this way
THISNESS *n* state or quality of being *this*
THISTLE *n* prickly plant with dense flower heads
THISTLES >THISTLE
THISTLIER >THISTLE
THISTLY >THISTLE
THITHER *adv* or towards that place
THITHERTO *adv* until that time
THIVEL *same as* >THIBLE
THIVELS >THIVEL
THLIPSES >THLIPSIS
THLIPSIS *n* compression, esp of part of the body
THO *short for* >THOUGH
THOFT *n* bench (in a boat) upon which a rower sits
THOFTS >THOFT
THOLE *n* wooden pin set in the side of a rowing boat to serve as a fulcrum for rowing ▷ *vb* bear or put up with
THOLED >THOLE
THOLEIITE *n* type of volcanic rock
THOLEPIN *same as* >THOLE
THOLEPINS >THOLEPIN
THOLES >THOLE
THOLI >THOLUS
THOLING >THOLE
THOLOBATE *n* structure supporting a dome
THOLOI >THOLOS
THOLOS *n* dry-stone beehive-shaped tomb associated with the Mycenaean culture of Greece in the 16th to the 12th century BC
THOLUS *n* domed tomb
THON *Scot word for* >YON
THONDER *Scot word for* >YONDER
THONG *n* thin strip of leather etc
THONGED *adj* fastened with a thong
THONGS >THONG
THORACAL *another word for* >THORACIC
THORACES >THORAX
THORACIC *adj* of, near, or relating to the thorax
THORAX *n* part of the body between the neck and the abdomen
THORAXES >THORAX
THORIA >THORIUM
THORIAS >THORIUM
THORIC >THORIUM
THORITE *n* yellow, brownish, or black radioactive mineral consisting of tetragonal thorium silicate. It occurs in coarse granite and is a source of thorium
THORITES >THORITE
THORIUM *n* radioactive metallic element
THORIUMS >THORIUM
THORN *n* prickle on a plant ▷ *vb* jag or prick (something) as if with a thorn
THORNBACK *n* European ray with a row of spines along the back and tail
THORNBILL *n* South American hummingbirds
THORNBUSH *n* tree, shrub, or bush with thorns
THORNED >THORN
THORNIER >THORNY
THORNIEST >THORNY
THORNILY >THORNY
THORNING >THORN
THORNLESS >THORN
THORNLIKE >THORN
THORNS >THORN
THORNSET *adj* set with thorns
THORNTREE *n* tree with thorns
THORNY *adj* covered with thorns
THORO *(nonstandard) variant spelling of* >THOROUGH
THORON *n* radioisotope of radon that is a decay product of thorium
THORONS >THORON
THOROUGH *adj* complete ▷ *n* passage
THOROUGHS >THOROUGH
THORP *n* small village
THORPE *same as* >THORP
THORPES >THORPE
THORPS >THORP
THOSE *determiner* form of that used before a plural noun
THOTHER *pron* old contraction of *the other*
THOU *pron* used when talking to one person ▷ *n* one thousandth of an inch ▷ *vb* use the word *thou*
THOUED >THOU
THOUGH *adv* nevertheless
THOUGHT >THINK
THOUGHTED *adj* with thoughts
THOUGHTEN *adj* convinced
THOUGHTS >THINK
THOUING >THOU
THOUS >THOU
THOUSAND *n* ten hundred ▷ *adj* amounting to a thousand ▷ *determiner* amounting to a thousand
THOUSANDS >THOUSAND
THOWEL *old variant of* >THOLE
THOWELS >THOWEL
THOWL *old variant of* >THOLE
THOWLESS *adj* lacking in vigour
THOWLS >THOWEL
THRAE *same as* >FRAE
THRAIPING *n* thrashing
THRALDOM *same as* >THRALL
THRALDOMS >THRALDOM
THRALL *n* state of being in the power of another person ▷ *vb* enslave or dominate
THRALLDOM *same as* >THRALL
THRALLED >THRALL
THRALLING >THRALL
THRALLS >THRALL
THRANG *n* throng ▷ *vb* throng ▷ *adj* crowded
THRANGED >THRANG
THRANGING >THRANG
THRANGS >THRANG
THRAPPLE *n* throat or windpipe ▷ *vb* throttle
THRAPPLED >THRAPPLE
THRAPPLES >THRAPPLE
THRASH *vb* beat, esp with a stick or whip ▷ *n* party
THRASHED >THRASH
THRASHER *same as* >THRESHER
THRASHERS >THRASHER
THRASHES >THRASH
THRASHING *n* severe beating

THRASONIC *adj* bragging or boastful
THRAVE *n* twenty-four sheaves of corn
THRAVES > THRAVE
THRAW *vb* twist (something); make something thrawn
THRAWARD *adj* contrary or stubborn
THRAWART *same as* > THRAWARD
THRAWED > THRAW
THRAWING > THRAW
THRAWN *adj* crooked or twisted
THRAWNLY > THRAWN
THRAWS > THRAW
THREAD *n* fine strand or yarn ▷ *vb* pass thread through
THREADED > THREAD
THREADEN *adj* made of thread
THREADER > THREAD
THREADERS > THREAD
THREADFIN *n* spiny-finned tropical marine fish
THREADIER > THREADY
THREADING > THREAD
THREADS *slang word for* > CLOTHES
THREADY *adj* of, relating to, or resembling a thread or threads
THREAP *vb* scold
THREAPED > THREAP
THREAPER > THREAP
THREAPERS > THREAP
THREAPING > THREAP
THREAPIT *variant past participle of* > THREAP
THREAPS > THREAP
THREAT *n* declaration of intent to harm
THREATED > THREAT
THREATEN *vb* make or be a threat to
THREATENS > THREATEN
THREATFUL > THREAT
THREATING > THREAT
THREATS > THREAT
THREAVE *same as* > THRAVE
THREAVES > THREAVE
THREE *n* one more than two ▷ *adj* amounting to three ▷ *determiner* amounting to three
THREEFOLD *adv* (having) three times as many or as much ▷ *adj* having three times as many or as much
THREENESS *n* state or quality of being three
THREEP *same as* > THREAP
THREEPED > THREEP
THREEPER > THREAP
THREEPERS > THREAP
THREEPING > THREEP
THREEPIT *variant past participle of* > THREEP
THREEPS > THREEP
THREES > THREE
THREESOME *n* group of three
THRENE *n* dirge; threnody
THRENES > THRENE
THRENETIC > THRENE
THRENODE *same as* > THRENODY
THRENODES > THRENODE
THRENODIC > THRENODY
THRENODY *n* lament for the dead
THRENOS *n* threnody; lamentation
THRENOSES > THRENOS
THREONINE *n* essential amino acid that occurs in certain proteins
THRESH *vb* beat (wheat etc) to separate the grain from the husks and straw ▷ *n* act of threshing
THRESHED > THRESH
THRESHEL *n* flail
THRESHELS > THRESHEL
THRESHER *n* any of a genus of large sharks occurring in tropical and temperate seas. They have a very long whiplike tail
THRESHERS > THRESHER
THRESHES > THRESH
THRESHING > THRESH
THRESHOLD *n* bar forming the bottom of a doorway
THRETTIES > THRETTY
THRETTY *nonstandard variant of* > THIRTY
THREW > THROW
THRICE *adv* three times
THRID *old variant of* > THREAD
THRIDACE *n* sedative made from lettuce juice
THRIDACES > THRIDACE
THRIDDED > THRID
THRIDDING > THRID
THRIDS > THRID
THRIFT *n* wisdom and caution with money
THRIFTIER > THRIFTY
THRIFTILY > THRIFTY
THRIFTS > THRIFT
THRIFTY *adj* not wasteful with money
THRILL *n* sudden feeling of excitement ▷ *vb* (cause to) feel a thrill
THRILLANT *another word for* > THRILLING
THRILLED > THRILL
THRILLER *n* book, film, etc with an atmosphere of mystery or suspense
THRILLERS > THRILLER
THRILLIER > THRILLY
THRILLING *adj* very exciting or stimulating
THRILLS > THRILL
THRILLY *adj* causing thrills
THRIMSA *same as* > THRYMSA
THRIMSAS > THRIMSA
THRIP *same as* > THRIPS
THRIPS *n* small slender-bodied insect with piercing mouthparts that feeds on plant sap
THRIPSES > THRIPS
THRISSEL *Scots variant of* > THISTLE
THRISSELS > THRISSEL
THRIST *old variant of* > THIRST
THRISTED > THRIST
THRISTING > THRIST
THRISTLE *Scots variant of* > THISTLE
THRISTLES > THRISTLE
THRISTS > THRIST
THRISTY > THRIST
THRIVE *vb* flourish or prosper
THRIVED > THRIVE
THRIVEN > THRIVE
THRIVER > THRIVE
THRIVERS > THRIVE
THRIVES > THRIVE
THRIVING > THRIVE
THRIVINGS > THRIVE
THRO *same as* > THROUGH
THROAT *n* passage from the mouth and nose to the stomach and lungs ▷ *vb* vocalize in the throat
THROATED > THROAT
THROATIER > THROATY
THROATILY > THROATY
THROATING > THROAT
THROATS > THROAT
THROATY *adj* (of the voice) hoarse
THROB *vb* pulsate repeatedly ▷ *n* throbbing
THROBBED > THROB
THROBBER > THROB
THROBBERS > THROB
THROBBING > THROB
THROBLESS > THROB
THROBS > THROB
THROE *n* pang or pain ▷ *n* endure throes
THROED > THROE
THROEING > THROE
THROES *pl n* violent pangs or pains
THROMBI > THROMBUS
THROMBIN *n* enzyme that acts on fibrinogen in blood causing it to clot
THROMBINS > THROMBIN
THROMBOSE *vb* become or affect with a thrombus
THROMBUS *n* clot of coagulated blood that forms within a blood vessel or inside the heart and remains at the site of its formation, often impeding the flow of blood
THRONE *n* ceremonial seat of a monarch or bishop ▷ *vb* place or be placed on a throne
THRONED > THRONE
THRONES > THRONE
THRONG *vb* crowd ▷ *n* great number of people or things crowded together ▷ *adj* busy
THRONGED > THRONG
THRONGFUL > THRONG
THRONGING > THRONG
THRONGS > THRONG
THRONING > THRONE
THRONNER *n* person who i[s] good at doing odd jobs
THRONNERS > THRONNER
THROPPLE *vb* strangle or choke
THROPPLED > THROPPLE
THROPPLES > THROPPLE
THROSTLE *n* song thrush
THROSTLES > THROSTLE
THROTTLE *n* device controlling the amount of fuel entering an engine ▷ *vb* strangle
THROTTLED > THROTTLE
THROTTLER > THROTTLE
THROTTLES > THROTTLE
THROUGH *prep* from end to end or side to side of ▷ *ad[j]* finished
THROUGHLY *adv* thorough[ly]
THROVE > THRIVE
THROW *vb* hurl through the air ▷ *n* throwing
THROWAWAY *adj* done or sa[id] casually ▷ *vb* get rid of or discard ▷ *n* handbill or advertisement distribute[d] in a public place
THROWBACK *n* person or thing that reverts to an earlier type ▷ *vb* remind someone of (something he or she said or did previously) in order to upset him or her
THROWE *old variant of* > THROE
THROWER > THROW
THROWERS > THROW
THROWES > THROWE
THROWING > THROW
THROWINGS > THROW
THROWN > THROW
THROWS > THROW
THROWSTER *n* person who twists silk or other fibres into yarn
THRU *same as* > THROUGH
THRUM *vb* strum rhythmically but without expression on (a musical instrument) ▷ *n* in textiles, unwoven ends o[f] wap thread
THRUMMED > THRUM
THRUMMER > THRUM
THRUMMERS > THRUM
THRUMMIER > THRUMMY
THRUMMING > THRUM
THRUMMY *adj* made of thrums
THRUMS > THRUM
THRUPENNY as in *thrupenn[y] bit* twelve-sided British coin of nickel-brass, valued at three old pence obsolete since 1971
THRUPUT *n* quantity of ra[w] material or information processed in a given peri[od]

HRUPUTS >THRUPUT
HRUSH *n* brown songbird
HRUSHES >THRUSH
HRUST *vb* push forcefully ▷ *n* forceful stab
HRUSTED >THRUST
HRUSTER *n* person or thing that thrusts
HRUSTERS >THRUSTER
HRUSTFUL >THRUST
HRUSTING >THRUST
HRUSTOR *variant of* >THRUSTER
HRUSTORS >THRUSTOR
HRUSTS >THRUST
HRUTCH *n* narrow, fast-moving stream ▷ *vb* thrust
HRUTCHED >THRUTCH
HRUTCHES >THRUTCH
HRUWAY *n* thoroughfare
HRUWAYS >THRUWAY
HRYMSA *n* gold coin used in Anglo-Saxon England
HRYMSAS >THRYMSA
UD *n* dull heavy sound ▷ *vb* make such a sound
UDDED >THUD
UDDING >THUD
UDS >THUD
UG *n* violent man, esp a criminal
UGGEE *n* methods and practices of the thugs of India
UGGEES >THUGGEE
UGGERY >THUG
UGGISH >THUG
UGGISM >THUG
UGGISMS >THUG
UGGO *n* tough and violent person
UGGOS >THUGGO
UGS >THUG
UJA *n* coniferous tree of North America and East Asia, with scalelike leaves, small cones, and an aromatic wood
UJAS >THUJA
ULIA *n* oxide of thulium
ULIAS >THULIA
ULITE *n* rose-coloured zoisite sometimes incorporated into jewellery
ULITES >THULITE
ULIUM *n* malleable ductile silvery-grey element
ULIUMS >THULIUM
UMB *n* short thick finger set apart from the others ▷ *vb* touch or handle with the thumb
UMBED >THUMB
UMBHOLE *n* hole for putting the thumb into
UMBIER >THUMBY
UMBIEST >THUMBY
UMBING >THUMB
UMBKIN *same as* >THUMBKIN
UMBKINS *n* thumbscrew
THUMBLESS >THUMB
THUMBLIKE >THUMB
THUMBLING *n* extremely small person
THUMBNAIL *n* nail of the thumb ▷ *adj* concise and brief
THUMBNUT *n* nut with projections enabling it to be turned by the thumb and forefinger
THUMBNUTS >THUMBNUT
THUMBPOT *n* tiny flowerpot
THUMBPOTS >THUMBPOT
THUMBS >THUMB
THUMBTACK *n* short tack with a broad smooth head for fastening papers to a drawing board, etc
THUMBY *adj* clumsy; uncoordinated
THUMP *n* (sound of) a dull heavy blow ▷ *vb* strike heavily
THUMPED >THUMP
THUMPER >THUMP
THUMPERS >THUMP
THUMPING *adj* huge or excessive
THUMPS >THUMP
THUNDER *n* loud noise accompanying lightning ▷ *vb* rumble with thunder
THUNDERED >THUNDER
THUNDERER >THUNDER
THUNDERS >THUNDER
THUNDERY >THUNDER
THUNDROUS >THUNDER
THUNK *another word for* >THUD
THUNKED >THUNK
THUNKING >THUNK
THUNKS >THUNK
THURIBLE *same as* >CENSER
THURIBLES >THURIBLE
THURIFER *n* person appointed to carry the censer at religious ceremonies
THURIFERS >THURIFER
THURIFIED >THURIFY
THURIFIES >THURIFY
THURIFY *vb* burn incense near or before an altar, shrine, etc
THURL *same as* >THIRL
THURLS >THURL
THUS *adv* in this manner ▷ *n* aromatic gum resin
THUSES >THUS
THUSLY *adv* in such a way; thus
THUSNESS *n* state or quality of being *thus*
THUSWISE *adj* in this way; thus
THUYA *same as* >THUJA
THUYAS >THUYA
THWACK *n* whack ▷ *vb* beat with something flat ▷ *interj* exclamation imitative of this sound
THWACKED >THWACK
THWACKER >THWACK
THWACKERS >THWACK
THWACKING >THWACK
THWACKS >THWACK
THWAITE *n* piece of land cleared from forest or reclaimed from wasteland
THWAITES >THWAITE
THWART *vb* foil or frustrate ▷ *n* seat across a boat ▷ *adj* passing or being situated across ▷ *adv* across
THWARTED >THWART
THWARTER >THWART
THWARTERS >THWART
THWARTING >THWART
THWARTLY >THWART
THWARTS >THWART
THY *adj* of or associated with you (thou) ▷ *determiner* belonging to or associated in some way with you (thou)
THYINE *adj* of relating to the sandarac tree
THYLACINE *n* extinct doglike Tasmanian marsupial
THYLAKOID *n* small membranous sac within a chloroplast
THYLOSE *old variant of* >TYLOSIS
THYLOSES >THYLOSIS
THYLOSIS *same as* >TYLOSIS
THYME *n* aromatic herb
THYMES >THYME
THYMEY >THYME
THYMI >THYMUS
THYMIC *adj* of or relating to the thymus
THYMIDINE *n* crystalline nucleoside of thymine, found in DNA
THYMIER >THYME
THYMIEST >THYME
THYMINE *n* white crystalline pyrimidine base found in DNA
THYMINES >THYMINE
THYMOCYTE *n* lymphocyte found in the thymus
THYMOL *n* substance obtained from thyme, used as an antiseptic
THYMOLS >THYMOL
THYMOSIN *n* hormone secreted by the thymus
THYMOSINS >THYMOSIN
THYMUS *n* small gland at the base of the neck
THYMUSES >THYMUS
THYMY >THYME
THYRATRON *n* gas-filled tube that has three electrodes and can be switched between an 'off' state and an 'on' state. It has been superseded, except for application involving high-power switching, by the thyristor
THYREOID *same as* >THYROID
THYREOIDS >THYREOID
THYRISTOR *n* any of a group of semiconductor devices, such as the silicon-controlled rectifier, that can be switched between two states
THYROID *n* (of) a gland in the neck controlling body growth ▷ *adj* of or relating to the thyroid gland
THYROIDAL >THYROID
THYROIDS >THYROID
THYROXIN *same as* >THYROXINE
THYROXINE *n* principal hormone produced by the thyroid gland
THYROXINS >THYROXIN
THYRSE *n* type of inflorescence, occurring in the lilac and grape, in which the main branch is racemose and the lateral branches cymose
THYRSES >THYRSE
THYRSI >THYRSUS
THYRSOID >THYRSE
THYRSUS *same as* >THYRSE
THYSELF *pron* reflexive form of thou
TI *same as* >TE
TIAR *same as* >TIARA
TIARA *n* semicircular jewelled headdress
TIARAED >TIARA
TIARAS >TIARA
TIARS >TIAR
TIBIA *n* inner bone of the lower leg
TIBIAE >TIBIA
TIBIAL >TIBIA
TIBIAS >TIBIA
TIC *n* spasmodic muscular twitch
TICAL *n* former standard monetary unit of Thailand, replaced by the baht in 1928
TICALS >TICAL
TICCA *adj* (of a thing or the services of a person) having been acquired for temporary use in exchange for payment
TICCED >TIC
TICCING >TIC
TICE *vb* tempt or allure; entice
TICED >TICE
TICES >TICE
TICH *same as* >TITCH
TICHES >TICH
TICHIER >TICHY
TICHIEST >TICHY
TICHY *same as* >TITCHY
TICING >TICE
TICK *n* mark (✓) used to check off or indicate the correctness of something ▷ *vb* mark with a tick
TICKED >TICK
TICKEN *same as* >TICKING
TICKENS >TICKEN

TICKER *n* heart
TICKERS > TICKER
TICKET *n* card or paper entitling the holder to admission, travel, etc ▷ *vb* attach or issue a ticket to
TICKETED > TICKET
TICKETING > TICKET
TICKETS *pl n* death or ruin
TICKEY *n* South African threepenny piece, which was replaced by the five-cent coin in 1961
TICKEYS > TICKEY
TICKIES > TICKY
TICKING *n* strong material for mattress covers
TICKINGS > TICKING
TICKLACE *n* (in Newfoundland) a kittiwake
TICKLACES > TICKLACE
TICKLE *vb* touch or stroke (a person) to produce laughter ▷ *n* tickling
TICKLED > TICKLE
TICKLER *n* difficult or delicate problem
TICKLERS > TICKLER
TICKLES > TICKLE
TICKLIER > TICKLE
TICKLIEST > TICKLE
TICKLING > TICKLE
TICKLINGS > TICKLE
TICKLISH *adj* sensitive to tickling
TICKLY > TICKLE
TICKS > TICK
TICKSEED *another name for* > COREOPSIS
TICKSEEDS > TICKSEED
TICKTACK *n* bookmakers' sign language ▷ *vb* make a ticking sound
TICKTACKS > TICKTACK
TICKTOCK *n* ticking sound made by a clock ▷ *vb* make a ticking sound
TICKTOCKS > TICKTOCK
TICKY *same as* > TICKEY
TICS > TIC
TICTAC *same as* > TICKTACK
TICTACKED > TICTAC
TICTACS > TICTAC
TICTOC *same as* > TICKTOCK
TICTOCKED > TICTOC
TICTOCS > TICTOC
TID *n* girl
TIDAL *adj* (of a river, lake, or sea) having tides
TIDALLY > TIDAL
TIDBIT *same as* > TITBIT
TIDBITS > TIDBIT
TIDDIER > TIDDY
TIDDIES > TIDDY
TIDDIEST > TIDDY
TIDDLE *vb* busy oneself with inconsequential tasks
TIDDLED > TIDDLE
TIDDLER *n* very small fish
TIDDLERS > TIDDLER
TIDDLES > TIDDLE
TIDDLEY *same as* > TIDDLY
TIDDLEYS > TIDDLEY
TIDDLIER > TIDDLY
TIDDLIES > TIDDLY
TIDDLIEST > TIDDLY
TIDDLING > TIDDLE
TIDDLY *adj* tiny ▷ *n* alcoholic beverage
TIDDY *n* four of trumps in the card game gleek
TIDE *n* rise and fall of the sea caused by the gravitational pull of the sun and moon ▷ *vb* carry or be carried with or as if with the tide
TIDED > TIDE
TIDELAND *n* land between high-water and low-water marks
TIDELANDS > TIDELAND
TIDELESS > TIDE
TIDELIKE > TIDE
TIDEMARK *n* mark left by the highest or lowest point of a tide
TIDEMARKS > TIDEMARK
TIDEMILL *n* watermill powered by the force of the tide
TIDEMILLS > TIDEMILL
TIDERIP *same as* > RIPTIDE
TIDERIPS > TIDERIP
TIDES > TIDE
TIDESMAN *n* customs official at a port
TIDESMEN > TIDESMAN
TIDEWATER *n* water that advances and recedes with the tide
TIDEWAVE *n* undulation of the earth's water levels as the tide moves around it
TIDEWAVES > TIDEWAVE
TIDEWAY *n* strong tidal current or its channel, esp the tidal part of a river
TIDEWAYS > TIDEWAY
TIDIED > TIDY
TIDIER > TIDY
TIDIERS > TIDY
TIDIES > TIDY
TIDIEST > TIDY
TIDILY > TIDY
TIDINESS > TIDY
TIDING > TIDE
TIDINGS *pl n* news
TIDIVATE *same as* > TITIVATE
TIDIVATED > TITIVATE
TIDIVATES > TITIVATE
TIDS > TID
TIDY *adj* neat and orderly ▷ *vb* put in order ▷ *n* small container for odds and ends
TIDYING > TIDY
TIDYTIPS *n* herb with flowers resembling those of the daisy
TIE *vb* fasten or be fastened with string, rope, etc ▷ *n* long narrow piece of material worn knotted round the neck
TIEBACK *n* length of cord, ribbon, or other fabric used for tying a curtain to one side
TIEBACKS > TIEBACK
TIEBREAK *n* deciding game in drawn match
TIEBREAKS > TIEBREAK
TIECLASP *n* clip, often ornamental, which holds a tie in place against a shirt
TIECLASPS > TIECLASP
TIED > TIE
TIEING > TIE
TIELESS > TIE
TIEPIN *n* ornamental pin used to pin the two ends of a tie to a shirt
TIEPINS > TIEPIN
TIER *n* one of a set of rows placed one above and behind the other ▷ *vb* be or arrange in tiers
TIERCE *same as* > TERCE
TIERCED *adj* (of a shield) divided into three sections of similar size but different colour
TIERCEL *same as* > TERCEL
TIERCELET *another name for* > TERCEL
TIERCELS > TIERCEL
TIERCERON *n* (in Gothic architecture) a type of rib on a vault
TIERCES > TIERCE
TIERCET *same as* > TERCET
TIERCETS > TIERCET
TIERED > TIER
TIERING > TIER
TIEROD *n* any rod- or bar-shaped structural member designed to prevent the separation of two parts, as in a vehicle
TIERODS > TIEROD
TIERS > TIER
TIES > TIE
TIETAC *n* fastener for holding a tie in place
TIETACK *same as* > TIETAC
TIETACKS > TIETACK
TIETACS > TIETAC
TIFF *n* petty quarrel ▷ *vb* have or be in a tiff
TIFFANIES > TIFFANY
TIFFANY *n* sheer fine gauzy fabric
TIFFED > TIFF
TIFFIN *n* (in India) a light meal, esp at midday ▷ *vb* take tiffin
TIFFINED > TIFFIN
TIFFING > TIFF
TIFFINGS > TIFF
TIFFINING > TIFFIN
TIFFINS > TIFFIN
TIFFS > TIFF
TIFOSI > TIFOSO
TIFOSO *n* fanatical fan (esp an Italian F1 fan)
TIFT *(Scots) variant of* > TIFF
TIFTED > TIFT
TIFTING > TIFT
TIFTS > TIFT
TIG *n* child's game
TIGE *n* trunk of an architectural column
TIGER *n* large yellow-and-black striped Asian cat
TIGEREYE *n* golden brown silicified variety of crocidolite, used as an ornamental stone
TIGEREYES > TIGEREYE
TIGERISH > TIGER
TIGERISM *n* arrogant and showy manner
TIGERISMS > TIGERISM
TIGERLIKE *adj* resembling a tiger
TIGERLY *adj* of or like a tiger
TIGERS > TIGER
TIGERY > TIGER
TIGES > TIGE
TIGGED > TIG
TIGGING > TIG
TIGHT *adj* stretched or drawn taut ▷ *adv* in a close, firm, or secure way
TIGHTASS *n* inhibited or excessively self-controlled person
TIGHTEN *vb* make or become tight or tighter
TIGHTENED > TIGHTEN
TIGHTENER > TIGHTEN
TIGHTENS > TIGHTEN
TIGHTER > TIGHT
TIGHTEST > TIGHT
TIGHTISH > TIGHT
TIGHTKNIT *adj* closely integrated
TIGHTLY > TIGHT
TIGHTNESS > TIGHT
TIGHTROPE *n* rope stretched taut on which acrobats perform
TIGHTS *pl n* one-piece clinging garment covering the body from the waist to the feet
TIGHTWAD *n* stingy person
TIGHTWADS > TIGHTWAD
TIGHTWIRE *n* wire tightrope
TIGLIC as in *tiglic acid* syrupy liquid or crystalline colourless unsaturated carboxylic acid
TIGLON *same as* > TIGON
TIGLONS > TIGLON
TIGON *n* hybrid offspring of a male tiger and a female lion
TIGONS > TIGON
TIGRESS *n* female tiger
TIGRESSES > TIGRESS
TIGRIDIA *n* type of tropical American plant
TIGRIDIAS > TIGRIDIA
TIGRINE *adj* of, characteristic of, or resembling a tiger
TIGRISH > TIGER
TIGRISHLY > TIGER
TIGROID *adj* resembling

a tiger
GS >TIG
KA *same as* >TIKKA
KANGA *n* Māori ways or customs
KANGAS >TIKANGA
KAS >TIKA
KE *same as* >TYKE
KES >TIKE
KI *n* small carving of a grotesque person worn as a pendant ▷ *vb* take a scenic tour around an area
KIED >TIKI
KIING >TIKI
KIS >TIKI
KKA *adj* marinated in spices and dry-roasted ▷ *n* act of marking a tikka on the forehead
KKAS >TIKKA
KOLOSHE *same* as >TOKOLOSHE
L *another name* for >SESAME
LAK *n* coloured spot or mark worn by Hindus, esp on the forehead, often indicating membership of a religious sect, caste, etc, or (in the case of a woman) marital status
LAKS >TILAK
LAPIA *n* type of fish
LAPIAS >TILAPIA
LBURIES >TILBURY
LBURY *n* light two-wheeled horse-drawn open carriage, seating two people
LDE *n* mark (~) used in Spanish to indicate that the letter 'n' is to be pronounced in a particular way
LDES >TILDE
LE *n* flat piece of ceramic, plastic, etc used to cover a roof, floor, or wall ▷ *vb* cover with tiles
LED >TILE
LEFISH *n* large brightly coloured deep-sea percoid food fish
LELIKE *adj* like a tile
LER >TILE
LERIES >TILERY
LERS >TILE
LERY *n* place where tiles are produced
LES >TILE
LING *n* tiles collectively
LINGS >TILING
LL *prep* until ▷ *vb* cultivate (land) ▷ *n* drawer for money, usu in a cash register ▷ *n* unstratified glacial deposit consisting of rock fragments of various sizes
LLABLE >TILL
LLAGE *n* act, process, or art of tilling
LLAGES >TILLAGE
TILLED >TILL
TILLER *n* on boats, a handle fixed to the top of a rudderpost to serve as a lever in steering ▷ *vb* use a tiller
TILLERED >TILLER
TILLERING >TILLER
TILLERMAN *n* one working a tiller
TILLERMEN >TILLERMAN
TILLERS >TILL
TILLICUM *n* (in the Pacific Northwest) a friend
TILLICUMS >TILLICUM
TILLIER >TILL
TILLIEST >TILL
TILLING >TILL
TILLINGS >TILL
TILLITE *n* rock formed from hardened till
TILLITES >TILLITE
TILLS >TILL
TILLY >TILL
TILS >TIL
TILT *vb* slant at an angle ▷ *n* slope
TILTABLE >TILT
TILTED >TILT
TILTER >TILT
TILTERS >TILT
TILTH *n* (condition of) land that has been tilled
TILTHS >TILTH
TILTING >TILT
TILTINGS >TILT
TILTMETER *n* instrument for measuring the tilt of the earth's surface
TILTROTOR *n* aircraft with rotors that can be tilted
TILTS >TILT
TILTYARD *n* (formerly) an enclosed area for tilting
TILTYARDS >TILTYARD
TIMARAU *same as* >TAMARAU
TIMARAUS >TIMARAU
TIMARIOT *n* one holding a fief in feudal Turkey
TIMARIOTS >TIMARIOT
TIMBAL *n* type of kettledrum
TIMBALE *n* mixture of meat, fish, etc, in a rich sauce, cooked in a mould lined with potato or pastry
TIMBALES >TIMBALE
TIMBALS >TIMBAL
TIMBER *n* wood as a building material ▷ *adj* made out of timber ▷ *vb* provide with timbers ▷ *interj* lumberjack's shouted warning when a tree is about to fall
TIMBERED *adj* made of or containing timber or timbers
TIMBERING *n* timbers collectively
TIMBERMAN *n* any of various longicorn beetles that have destructive wood-eating larvae
TIMBERMEN >TIMBERMAN
TIMBERS >TIMBER
TIMBERY >TIMBER
TIMBO *n* Amazonian vine from which a useful insecticide can be derived
TIMBOS >TIMBO
TIMBRAL *adj* relating to timbre
TIMBRE *n* distinctive quality of sound of a voice or instrument
TIMBREL *n* tambourine
TIMBRELS >TIMBREL
TIMBRES >TIMBRE
TIME *n* past, present, and future as a continuous whole ▷ *vb* note the time taken by
TIMEBOMB *n* bomb containing a timing mechanism that determines the time it will detonate
TIMEBOMBS >TIMEBOMB
TIMECARD *n* card used with a time clock
TIMECARDS >TIMECARD
TIMED >TIME
TIMEFRAME *n* period of time within which certain events are scheduled to occur
TIMELESS *adj* unaffected by time
TIMELIER >TIMELY
TIMELIEST >TIMELY
TIMELINE *n* graphic representation showing the passage of time as a line
TIMELINES >TIMELINE
TIMELY *adj* at the appropriate time ▷ *adv* at the right or an appropriate time
TIMENOGUY *n* taut rope on a ship
TIMEOUS *adj* in good time
TIMEOUSLY >TIMEOUS
TIMEOUT *n* in sport, interruption in play during which players rest, discuss tactics, or make substitutions
TIMEOUTS >TIMEOUT
TIMEPASS *n* way of passing the time ▷ *vb* pass the time
TIMEPIECE *n* watch or clock
TIMER *n* device for measuring time, esp a switch or regulator that causes a mechanism to operate at a specific time
TIMERS >TIMER
TIMES >TIME
TIMESAVER *n* something that saves time
TIMESCALE *n* period of time within which events occur or are due to occur
TIMETABLE *n* plan showing the times when something takes place, the departure and arrival times of trains or buses, etc ▷ *vb* set a time when a particular thing should be done
TIMEWORK *n* work paid for by the length of time taken, esp by the hour or the day
TIMEWORKS >TIMEWORK
TIMEWORN *adj* showing the adverse effects of overlong use or of old age
TIMID *adj* easily frightened
TIMIDER >TIMID
TIMIDEST >TIMID
TIMIDITY >TIMID
TIMIDLY >TIMID
TIMIDNESS >TIMID
TIMING *n* ability to judge when to do or say something so as to make the best effect
TIMINGS >TIMING
TIMIST *n* one concerned with time
TIMISTS >TIMIST
TIMOCRACY *n* political unit or system in which possession of property serves as the first requirement for participation in government
TIMOLOL *n* relaxant medicine used (for example) to reduce blood pressure
TIMOLOLS >TIMOLOL
TIMON *n* apparatus by which a vessel is steered
TIMONEER *n* helmsman; tillerman
TIMONEERS >TIMONEER
TIMONS >TIMON
TIMOROUS *adj* timid
TIMORSOME *adj* timorous; timid
TIMOTHIES >TIMOTHY
TIMOTHY as in *timothy grass* perennial grass of temperate regions, having erect stiff stems and cylindrical flower spikes: grown for hay and pasture
TIMOUS *same as* >TIMEOUS
TIMOUSLY >TIMOUS
TIMPANA *n* traditional Maltese baked pasta and pastry dish
TIMPANI *pl n* set of kettledrums
TIMPANIST >TIMPANI
TIMPANO *n* kettledrum
TIMPANUM *same as* >TYMPANUM
TIMPANUMS >TIMPANUM
TIMPS *same as* >TIMPANI
TIN *n* soft metallic element ▷ *vb* put (food) into tins
TINAJA *n* large jar for cooling water

TINAJAS >TINAJA
TINAMOU n any bird of the order *Tinamiformes* of Central and South America, having small wings, a heavy body, and an inconspicuous plumage
TINAMOUS >TINAMOU
TINCAL another name for >BORAX
TINCALS >TINCAL
TINCHEL n in Scotland, a circle of deer hunters who gradually close in on their quarry
TINCHELS >TINCHEL
TINCT vb tint ▷ adj tinted or coloured
TINCTED >TINCT
TINCTING >TINCT
TINCTS >TINCT
TINCTURE n medicinal extract in a solution of alcohol ▷ vb give a tint or colour to
TINCTURED >TINCTURE
TINCTURES >TINCTURE
TIND vb set alight
TINDAL n petty officer
TINDALS >TINDAL
TINDED >TIND
TINDER n dry easily-burning material used to start a fire
TINDERBOX n formerly, small box for tinder, esp one fitted with a flint and steel
TINDERS >TINDER
TINDERY >TINDER
TINDING >TIND
TINDS >TIND
TINE n prong of a fork or antler ▷ vb lose
TINEA n any fungal skin disease, esp ringworm
TINEAL >TINEA
TINEAS >TINEA
TINED >TINE
TINEID n any moth of the family *Tineidae*, which includes the clothes moths ▷ adj of, relating to, or belonging to the family *Tineidae*
TINEIDS >TINEID
TINES >TINE
TINFOIL n paper-thin sheet of metal, used for wrapping foodstuffs
TINFOILS >TINFOIL
TINFUL n contents of a tin or the amount a tin will hold
TINFULS >TINFUL
TING same as >THING
TINGE n slight tint ▷ vb give a slight tint or trace to
TINGED >TINGE
TINGEING >TINGE
TINGES >TINGE
TINGING >TINGE
TINGLE n (feel) a prickling or stinging sensation ▷ vb feel a mild prickling or stinging sensation, as from cold or excitement
TINGLED >TINGLE
TINGLER >TINGLE
TINGLERS >TINGLE
TINGLES >TINGLE
TINGLIER >TINGLE
TINGLIEST >TINGLE
TINGLING >TINGLE
TINGLINGS >TINGLE
TINGLISH adj exciting
TINGLY >TINGLE
TINGS >TING
TINGUAITE n type of igneous rock
TINHORN n cheap pretentious person, esp a gambler with extravagant claims ▷ adj cheap and showy
TINHORNS >TINHORN
TINIER >TINY
TINIES pl n small children
TINIEST >TINY
TINILY >TINY
TININESS >TINY
TINING >TINE
TINK shortened form of >TINKER
TINKED >TINK
TINKER n derogatory term for travelling mender of pots and pans ▷ vb fiddle with (an engine etc) in an attempt to repair it
TINKERED >TINKER
TINKERER >TINKER
TINKERERS >TINKER
TINKERING >TINKER
TINKERS >TINKER
TINKERTOY n children's construction set
TINKING >TINK
TINKLE vb ring with a high tinny sound like a small bell ▷ n this sound or action
TINKLED >TINKLE
TINKLER same as >TINKER
TINKLERS >TINKLER
TINKLES >TINKLE
TINKLIER >TINKLE
TINKLIEST >TINKLE
TINKLING >TINKLE
TINKLINGS >TINKLE
TINKLY >TINKLE
TINKS >TINK
TINLIKE >TIN
TINMAN n one who works with tin or tin plate
TINMEN >TINMAN
TINNED >TIN
TINNER n tin miner
TINNERS >TINNER
TINNIE same as >TINNY
TINNIER >TINNY
TINNIES >TINNY
TINNIEST >TINNY
TINNILY >TINNY
TINNINESS >TINNY
TINNING >TIN
TINNINGS >TIN
TINNITUS n ringing, hissing, or booming sensation in one or both ears, caused by infection of the middle or inner ear, a side effect of certain drugs, etc
TINNY adj (of sound) thin and metallic ▷ n can of beer
TINPLATE n thin steel sheet coated with a layer of tin that protects the steel from corrosion ▷ vb coat (a metal or object) with a layer of tin, usually either by electroplating or by dipping in a bath of molten tin
TINPLATED >TINPLATE
TINPLATES >TINPLATE
TINPOT adj worthless or unimportant ▷ n pot made of tin
TINPOTS >TINPOT
TINS >TIN
TINSEL n decorative metallic strips or threads ▷ adj made of or decorated with tinsel ▷ vb decorate with or as if with tinsel
TINSELED >TINSEL
TINSELING >TINSEL
TINSELLED >TINSEL
TINSELLY >TINSEL
TINSELRY n tinsel-like material
TINSELS >TINSEL
TINSEY old variant of >TINSEL
TINSEYS >TINSEY
TINSMITH n person who works with tin or tin plate
TINSMITHS >TINSMITH
TINSNIPS n metal cutters
TINSTONE n black or brown stone
TINSTONES >TINSTONE
TINT n (pale) shade of a colour ▷ vb give a tint to
TINTACK n tin-plated tack
TINTACKS >TINTACK
TINTED >TINT
TINTER >TINT
TINTERS >TINT
TINTIER >TINTY
TINTIEST >TINTY
TINTINESS >TINTY
TINTING >TINT
TINTINGS >TINT
TINTLESS >TINT
TINTOOKIE n in informal Australian English, fawning or servile person
TINTS >TINT
TINTY adj having many tints
TINTYPE another name for >FERROTYPE
TINTYPES >TINTYPE
TINWARE n objects made of tin plate
TINWARES >TINWARE
TINWORK n objects made of tin
TINWORKS n place where tin is mined, smelted, or rolled
TINY adj very small
TIP n narrow or pointed end of anything ▷ vb put a tip on
TIPCART n cart that can be tipped to empty out its contents
TIPCARTS >TIPCART
TIPCAT n game in which a short sharp-ended piece of wood (the cat) is tipped in the air with a stick
TIPCATS >TIPCAT
TIPI variant spelling of >TEPEE
TIPIS >TIPI
TIPLESS >TIP
TIPOFF n warning or hint esp given confidentially and based on inside information
TIPOFFS >TIPOFF
TIPPABLE >TIP
TIPPED >TIP
TIPPEE n person who receives a tip, esp regarding share prices
TIPPEES >TIPPEE
TIPPER n person who gives or leaves a tip
TIPPERS >TIPPER
TIPPET n scarflike piece of fur, often made from a whole animal skin, worn, esp formerly, round a woman's shoulders
TIPPETS >TIPPET
TIPPIER >TIPPY
TIPPIEST >TIPPY
TIPPING >TIP
TIPPINGS >TIP
TIPPLE vb drink alcohol habitually, esp in small quantities ▷ n alcoholic drink
TIPPLED >TIPPLE
TIPPLER >TIPPLE
TIPPLERS >TIPPLE
TIPPLES >TIPPLE
TIPPLING >TIPPLE
TIPPY adj extremely fashionable or stylish
TIPPYTOE same as >TIPTOE
TIPPYTOED >TIPPYTOE
TIPPYTOES >TIPPYTOE
TIPS >TIP
TIPSHEET n list of advice instructions
TIPSHEETS >TIPSHEET
TIPSIER >TIPSY
TIPSIEST >TIPSY
TIPSIFIED >TIPSIFY
TIPSIFIES >TIPSIFY
TIPSIFY vb make tipsy
TIPSILY >TIPSY
TIPSINESS >TIPSY
TIPSTAFF n court official
TIPSTAFFS >TIPSTAFF
TIPSTAVES >TIPSTAFF
TIPSTER n person who

sells tips about races
IPSTERS > TIPSTER
IPSTOCK *n* detachable section of a gunstock, usually gripped by the left hand of the user
IPSTOCKS > TIPSTOCK
IPSY *adj* slightly drunk
IPT > TIP
IPTOE *vb* walk quietly with the heels off the ground
IPTOED > TIPTOE
IPTOEING > TIPTOE
IPTOES > TIPTOE
IPTOP *adj* of the highest quality or condition ▷ *adv* of the highest quality or condition ▷ *n* best in quality ▷ *n* very top; pinnacle
IPTOPS > TIPTOP
IPTRONIC *n* type of gearbox that has both automatic and manual options
IPULA *n* crane fly
IPULAS > TIPULA
IPUNA *n* ancestor
IPUNAS > TIPUNA
IRADE *n* long angry speech
IRADES > TIRADE
IRAGE *n* drawing of wine from a barrel prior to bottling
IRAGES > TIRAGE
IRAMISU *n* Italian dessert made with sponge soaked in coffee and Marsala, topped with soft cheese and powdered chocolate
IRAMISUS > TIRAMISU
IRASSE *n* mechanism in an organ connecting two pedals, so that both may be depressed at once
IRASSES > TIRASSE
IRE *vb* reduce the energy of, as by exertion
IRED *adj* exhausted
IREDER > TIRED
IREDEST > TIRED
IREDLY > TIRED
IREDNESS > TIRED
IRELESS *adj* energetic and determined
IRELING *n* fatigued person or animal
IRELINGS > TIRELING
IRES > TIRE
IRESOME *adj* boring and irritating
IREWOMAN *n* an obsolete term for lady's maid
IREWOMEN > TIREWOMAN
IRING > TIRE
IRINGS > TIRE
IRITI *n* another name for the Treaty of Waitangi
IRITIS > TIRITI
IRL *vb* turn
IRLED > TIRL
IRLING > TIRL
TIRLS > TIRL
TIRO *same as* > TYRO
TIROES > TIRO
TIRONIC *variant of* > TYRONIC
TIROS > TIRO
TIRR *vb* strip or denude
TIRRED > TIRR
TIRRING > TIRR
TIRRIT *n* panic; scare
TIRRITS > TIRRIT
TIRRIVEE *n* outburst of bad temper; rumpus
TIRRIVEES > TIRRIVEE
TIRRIVIE *same as* > TIRRIVEE
TIRRIVIES > TIRRIVIE
TIRRS > TIRR
TIS > TI
TISANE *n* infusion of dried or fresh leaves or flowers, as camomile
TISANES > TISANE
TISICK *n* splutter; cough
TISICKS > TISICK
TISSUAL *adj* relating to tissue
TISSUE *n* substance of an animal body or plant ▷ *vb* weave into tissue
TISSUED > TISSUE
TISSUES > TISSUE
TISSUEY > TISSUE
TISSUING > TISSUE
TISSULAR *adj* relating to tissue
TISWAS *n* state of anxiety or excitement
TISWASES > TISWAS
TIT *n* any of various small songbirds; informal term for a female breast ▷ *vb* jerk or tug
TITAN *n* person who is huge, strong, or very important
TITANATE *n* any salt or ester of titanic acid
TITANATES > TITANATE
TITANESS *n* person who is huge, strong, or very important
TITANIA > TITANIUM
TITANIAS > TITANIA
TITANIC *adj* huge or very important
TITANIS *n* large predatory flightless prehistoric bird
TITANISES > TITANIS
TITANISM *n* titanic power
TITANISMS > TITANISM
TITANITE *another name for* > SPHENE
TITANITES > TITANITE
TITANIUM *n* strong light metallic element used to make alloys
TITANIUMS > TITANIUM
TITANOUS *adj* of or containing titanium, esp in the trivalent state
TITANS > TITAN
TITBIT *n* tasty piece of food
TITBITS > TITBIT
TITCH *n* small person
TITCHES > TITCH
TITCHIER > TITCHY
TITCHIEST > TITCHY
TITCHY *adj* very small
TITE *adj* immediately
TITELY *adv* immediately
TITER *same as* > TITRE
TITERS > TITER
TITFER *n* hat
TITFERS > TITFER
TITHABLE *adj* (until 1936) liable to pay tithes
TITHE *n* esp formerly, one tenth of one's income or produce paid to the church as a tax ▷ *vb* charge or pay a tithe
TITHED > TITHE
TITHER > TITHE
TITHERS > TITHE
TITHES > TITHE
TITHING > TITHE
TITHINGS > TITHING
TITHONIA *n* Central American herb with flowers resembling sunflowers
TITHONIAS > TITHONIA
TITI *n* small omnivorous New World monkey of South America, with long beautifully coloured fur and a long nonprehensile tail
TITIAN *n* reddish gold colour
TITIANS > TITIAN
TITILLATE *vb* excite or stimulate pleasurably
TITIS > TITI
TITIVATE *vb* smarten up
TITIVATED > TITIVATE
TITIVATES > TITIVATE
TITIVATOR > TITIVATE
TITLARK *another name for* > PIPIT
TITLARKS > TITLARK
TITLE *n* name of a book, film, etc ▷ *vb* give a title to
TITLED *adj* aristocratic
TITLELESS > TITLE
TITLER *n* one who writes titles
TITLERS > TITLE
TITLES > TITLE
TITLING > TITLE
TITLINGS > TITLE
TITLIST *n* titleholder
TITLISTS > TITLIST
TITMAN *n* (of pigs) the runt of a litter
TITMEN > TITMAN
TITMICE > TITMOUSE
TITMOSE *old spelling of* > TITMOUSE
TITMOUSE *n* any small active songbird
TITOKI *n* New Zealand evergreen tree with a spreading crown and glossy green leaves
TITOKIS > TITOKI
TITRABLE > TITRATE
TITRANT *n* solution in a titration that is added from a burette to a measured quantity of another solution
TITRANTS > TITRANT
TITRATE *vb* measure the volume or concentration of (a solution) by titration
TITRATED > TITRATE
TITRATES > TITRATE
TITRATING > TITRATE
TITRATION *n* operation in which a measured amount of one solution is added to a known quantity of another solution until the reaction between the two is complete
TITRATOR *n* device used to perform titration
TITRATORS > TITRATOR
TITRE *n* concentration of a solution as determined by titration
TITRES > TITRE
TITS > TIT
TITTED > TIT
TITTER *vb* laugh in a suppressed way ▷ *n* suppressed laugh
TITTERED > TITTER
TITTERER > TITTER
TITTERERS > TITTER
TITTERING > TITTER
TITTERS > TITTER
TITTIE *n* sister; young woman
TITTIES > TITTIE
TITTING > TIT
TITTISH *adj* testy
TITTIVATE *same as* > TITIVATE
TITTLE *n* very small amount ▷ *vb* chatter; tattle
TITTLEBAT *n* child's name for the stickleback fish
TITTLED > TITTLE
TITTLES > TITTLE
TITTLING > TITTLE
TITTUP *vb* prance or frolic ▷ *n* caper
TITTUPED > TITTUP
TITTUPING > TITTUP
TITTUPPED > TITTUP
TITTUPPY *same as* > TITTUPY
TITTUPS > TITTUP
TITTUPY *adj* spritely; lively
TITTY *same as* > TITTIE
TITUBANCY *n* staggering or stumbling
TITUBANT *adj* staggering
TITUBATE *vb* stagger
TITUBATED > TITUBATE
TITUBATES > TITUBATE
TITULAR *adj* in name only ▷ *n* bearer of a title
TITULARLY > TITULAR
TITULARS > TITULAR
TITULARY *same as* > TITULAR
TITULE *same as* > TITLE

TITULED > TITULE
TITULES > TITULE
TITULI > TITULUS
TITULING > TITULE
TITULUS *n* (in crucifixion) a sign attached to the top of the cross on which were written the condemned man's name and crime
TITUP *same as* > TITTUP
TITUPED > TITUP
TITUPING > TITUP
TITUPPED > TITUP
TITUPPING > TITUP
TITUPS > TITUP
TITUPY *same as* > TITTUPY
TIVY *same as* > TANTIVY
TIX *pl n* tickets
TIZWAS *same as* > TISWAS
TIZWASES > TIZWAS
TIZZ *same as* > TIZZY
TIZZES > TIZZ
TIZZIES > TIZZY
TIZZY *n* confused or agitated state
TJANTING *n* pen-like tool used in batik for applying molten wax to fabric
TJANTINGS > TJANTING
TMESES > TMESIS
TMESIS *n* interpolation of a word or group of words between the parts of a compound word
TO *prep* indicating movement towards, equality or comparison, etc ▷ *adv* a closed position
TOAD *n* animal like a large frog
TOADEATER *rare word for* > TOADY
TOADFISH *n* spiny-finned bottom-dwelling marine fish of tropical and temperate seas, with a flattened tapering body and a wide mouth
TOADFLAX *n* plant with narrow leaves and yellow-orange flowers
TOADGRASS *another name for* > TOADRUSH
TOADIED > TOADY
TOADIES > TOADY
TOADISH > TOAD
TOADLESS *adj* having no toads
TOADLIKE > TOAD
TOADRUSH *n* annual rush growing in damp lowlands
TOADS > TOAD
TOADSTONE *n* amygdaloidal basalt occurring in the limestone regions of Derbyshire
TOADSTOOL *n* poisonous fungus like a mushroom
TOADY *n* ingratiating person ▷ *vb* be ingratiating
TOADYING > TOADY
TOADYISH > TOADY
TOADYISM > TOADY
TOADYISMS > TOADY
TOAST *n* sliced bread browned by heat ▷ *vb* brown (bread) by heat
TOASTED > TOAST
TOASTER > TOAST
TOASTERS > TOAST
TOASTIE *same as* > TOASTY
TOASTIER > TOASTY
TOASTIES > TOASTY
TOASTIEST > TOASTY
TOASTING > TOAST
TOASTINGS > TOAST
TOASTS > TOAST
TOASTY *n* toasted sandwich ▷ *adj* tasting or smelling like toast
TOAZE *variant spelling of* > TOZE
TOAZED > TOAZE
TOAZES > TOAZE
TOAZING > TOAZE
TOBACCO *n* plant with large leaves dried for smoking
TOBACCOES > TOBACCO
TOBACCOS > TOBACCO
TOBIES > TOBY
TOBOGGAN *n* narrow sledge for sliding over snow ▷ *vb* ride a toboggan
TOBOGGANS > TOBOGGAN
TOBOGGIN *variant spelling of* > TOBOGGAN
TOBOGGINS > TOBOGGIN
TOBY *n* water stopcock at the boundary of a street and house section
TOC *n* in communications code, signal for letter t
TOCCATA *n* rapid piece of music for a keyboard instrument
TOCCATAS > TOCCATA
TOCCATE > TOCCATA
TOCCATINA *n* short toccata
TOCHER *n* dowry ▷ *vb* give a dowry to
TOCHERED > TOCHER
TOCHERING > TOCHER
TOCHERS > TOCHER
TOCK *n* sound made by a clock ▷ *vb* (of a clock) make such a sound
TOCKED > TOCK
TOCKIER > TOCKY
TOCKIEST > TOCKY
TOCKING > TOCK
TOCKLEY *slang word for* > PENIS
TOCKLEYS > TOCKLEY
TOCKS > TOCK
TOCKY *adj* muddy
TOCO *n* punishment
TOCOLOGY *n* branch of medicine concerned with childbirth
TOCOS > TOCO
TOCS > TOC
TOCSIN *n* warning signal
TOCSINS > TOCSIN
TOD *n* unit of weight, used for wool, etc, usually equal to 28 pounds ▷ *vb* produce a tod
TODAY *n* this day ▷ *adv* on this day
TODAYS > TODAY
TODDE *same as* > TOD
TODDED > TOD
TODDES > TODDE
TODDIES > TODDY
TODDING > TOD
TODDLE *vb* walk with short unsteady steps ▷ *n* act or an instance of toddling
TODDLED > TODDLE
TODDLER *n* child beginning to walk
TODDLERS > TODDLER
TODDLES > TODDLE
TODDLING > TODDLE
TODDY *n* sweetened drink of spirits and hot water
TODIES > TODY
TODS > TOD
TODY *n* small bird of the Caribbean, with a red-and-green plumage and long straight bill
TOE *n* digit of the foot ▷ *vb* touch or kick with the toe
TOEA *n* monetary unit of Papua New Guinea, worth one-hundredth of a kina
TOEAS > TOEA
TOEBIE *n* South African slang for sandwich
TOEBIES > TOEBIE
TOECAP *n* strengthened covering for the toe of a shoe
TOECAPS > TOECAP
TOECLIP *n* clip on a bicycle pedal into which the toes are inserted to prevent the foot from slipping
TOECLIPS > TOECLIP
TOED > TOE
TOEHOLD *n* small space on a mountain for supporting the toe of the foot in climbing
TOEHOLDS > TOEHOLD
TOEIER > TOEY
TOEIEST > TOEY
TOEING > TOE
TOELESS *adj* not having toes
TOELIKE > TOE
TOENAIL *n* thin hard clear plate covering part of the upper surface of the end of each toe ▷ *vb* join (beams) by driving nails obliquely
TOENAILED > TOENAIL
TOENAILS > TOENAIL
TOEPIECE *n* part of a shoe that covers the toes
TOEPIECES > TOEPIECE
TOEPLATE *n* metal reinforcement of the part of the sole of a shoe or boot underneath the toes
TOEPLATES > TOEPLATE
TOERAG *n* contemptible person
TOERAGGER *same as* > TOERAG
TOERAGS > TOERAG
TOES > TOE
TOESHOE *n* ballet pump with padded toes
TOESHOES > TOESHOE
TOETOE *same as* > TOITOI
TOETOES > TOETOE
TOEY *adj* (of a person) nervous or anxious
TOFF *n* well-dressed or upper-class person
TOFFEE *n* chewy sweet made of boiled sugar
TOFFEES > TOFFEE
TOFFIER > TOFFY
TOFFIES > TOFFY
TOFFIEST > TOFFY
TOFFISH *adj* belonging to or characteristic of the upper class
TOFFS *adj* like a toff
TOFFY *same as* > TOFFEE
TOFORE *prep* before
TOFT *n* homestead
TOFTS > TOFT
TOFU *n* soft food made fro[m] soya-bean curd
TOFUS > TOFU
TOFUTTI *n* tradename for any of a variety of nondairy, soya-based food products, esp frozen desserts
TOFUTTIS > TOFUTTI
TOG *n* unit for measuring the insulating power of duvets ▷ *vb* dress onesel[f] esp in smart clothes
TOGA *n* garment worn by citizens of ancient Rome ▷ *vb* wear a toga
TOGAE > TOGA
TOGAED > TOGA
TOGAS > TOGA
TOGATE *adj* clad in a toga
TOGATED *same as* > TOGATE
TOGAVIRUS *n* one of famil[y] of viruses
TOGE *old variant of* > TOGA
TOGED > TOGE
TOGES > TOGE
TOGETHER *adv* in compan[y] ▷ *adj* organized
TOGGED > TOG
TOGGER *vb* play football ▷ football player
TOGGERIES > TOGGERY
TOGGERS > TOGGER
TOGGERY *n* clothes
TOGGING > TOG
TOGGLE *n* small bar-shape[d] button inserted through a loop for fastening ▷ *vb* supply or fasten with a toggle or toggles
TOGGLED > TOGGLE
TOGGLER > TOGGLE
TOGGLERS > TOGGLE
TOGGLES > TOGGLE
TOGGLING > TOGGLE
TOGS > TOG
TOGUE *n* large North American freshwater game fish

TOGUES >TOGUE
TOHEROA *n* large edible mollusc of New Zealand with a distinctive flavour
TOHEROAS >TOHEROA
TOHO *n* (to a hunting dog) an instruction to stop
TOHOS >TOHO
TOHUNGA *n* Māori priest
TOHUNGAS >TOHUNGA
TOIL *n* hard work ▷ *vb* work hard
TOILE *n* transparent linen or cotton fabric
TOILED >TOIL
TOILER >TOIL
TOILERS >TOIL
TOILES >TOILE
TOILET *n* a bowl connected to a drain for receiving and disposing of urine and faeces ▷ *vb* go to the toilet
TOILETED >TOILET
TOILETING >TOILET
TOILETRY *n* object or cosmetic used to clean or groom oneself
TOILETS >TOILET
TOILETTE *same as* >TOILET
TOILETTES >TOILETTE
TOILFUL *same as* >TOILSOME
TOILFULLY >TOILFUL
TOILINET *n* type of fabric with a woollen weft and a cotton or silk warp
TOILINETS >TOILINET
TOILING >TOIL
TOILINGS >TOIL
TOILLESS >TOIL
TOILS >TOIL
TOILSOME *adj* requiring hard work
TOILWORN *adj* fatigued, wearied by work
TOING as in *toing and froing* state of going back and forth
TOINGS >TOING
TOISE *n* obsolete French unit of length roughly equal to 2m
TOISEACH *n* ancient Celtic nobleman
TOISEACHS >TOISEACH
TOISECH *same as* >TOISEACH
TOISECHS >TOISECH
TOISES >TOISE
TOISON *n* fleece
TOISONS >TOISON
TOIT *vb* walk or move in an unsteady manner, as from old age
TOITED >TOIT
TOITING >TOIT
TOITOI *n* tall grasses with feathery fronds
TOITOIS >TOITOI
TOITS >TOIT
TOKAMAK *n* reactor used in thermonuclear experiments
TOKAMAKS >TOKAMAK
TOKAY *n* small gecko of S and SE Asia, having a retractile claw at the tip of each digit
TOKAYS >TOKAY
TOKE *n* draw on a cannabis cigarette ▷ *vb* take a draw on a cannabis cigarette
TOKED >TOKE
TOKEN *n* sign or symbol ▷ *adj* nominal or slight
TOKENED >TOKEN
TOKENING >TOKEN
TOKENISM *n* policy of making only a token effort, esp to comply with a law
TOKENISMS >TOKENISM
TOKENS >TOKEN
TOKER >TOKE
TOKERS >TOKE
TOKES >TOKE
TOKING >TOKE
TOKO *same as* >TOCO
TOKOLOGY *same as* >TOCOLOGY
TOKOLOSHE *n* (in Bantu folklore) a malevolent mythical manlike animal of short stature
TOKOLOSHI *variant of* >TOKOLOSHE
TOKOMAK *variant spelling of* >TOKAMAK
TOKOMAKS >TOKOMAK
TOKONOMA *n* recess off a living room
TOKONOMAS >TOKONOMA
TOKOS >TOKO
TOKOTOKO *n* ceremonial carved Māori walking stick
TOKOTOKOS >TOKOTOKO
TOKTOKKIE *n* large South African beetle
TOLA *n* unit of weight, used in India, equal to 180 ser or 180 grains
TOLAN *n* white crystalline derivative of acetylene
TOLANE *same as* >TOLAN
TOLANES >TOLANE
TOLANS >TOLAN
TOLAR *n* standard monetary unit of Slovenia, divided into 100 stotin
TOLARJEV >TOLAR
TOLARJI >TOLAR
TOLARS >TOLAR
TOLAS >TOLA
TOLBOOTH *same as* >TOLLBOOTH
TOLBOOTHS >TOLBOOTH
TOLD >TELL
TOLE *same as* >TOLL
TOLED >TOLE
TOLEDO *n* type of sword originally made in Toledo
TOLEDOS >TOLEDO
TOLERABLE *adj* bearable
TOLERABLY >TOLERABLE
TOLERANCE *n* acceptance of other people's rights to their own opinions or actions
TOLERANT *adj* able to tolerate the beliefs, actions, opinions, etc, of others
TOLERATE *vb* allow to exist or happen
TOLERATED >TOLERATE
TOLERATES >TOLERATE
TOLERATOR >TOLERATE
TOLES >TOLE
TOLEWARE *n* enamelled or lacquered metal ware, usually gilded
TOLEWARES >TOLEWARE
TOLIDIN *same as* >TOLIDINE
TOLIDINE *n* compound used in dying and in chemical analysis, esp as an indicator of the presence of free chlorine in water
TOLIDINES >TOLIDINE
TOLIDINS >TOLIDIN
TOLING >TOLE
TOLINGS >TOLE
TOLL *vb* ring (a bell) slowly and regularly, esp to announce a death ▷ *n* tolling
TOLLABLE >TOLL
TOLLAGE *same as* >TOLL
TOLLAGES >TOLLAGE
TOLLBAR *n* bar blocking passage of a thoroughfare, raised on payment of a toll
TOLLBARS >TOLLBAR
TOLLBOOTH *n* booth or kiosk at which a toll is collected
TOLLDISH *n* dish used to measure out the portion of grain given to a miller as payment for his or her work
TOLLED >TOLL
TOLLER >TOLL
TOLLERS >TOLLER
TOLLGATE *n* gate across a toll road or bridge at which travellers must pay
TOLLGATES >TOLLGATE
TOLLHOUSE *n* small house at a tollgate occupied by a toll collector
TOLLIE *same as* >TOLLY
TOLLIES >TOLLY
TOLLING >TOLL
TOLLINGS >TOLL
TOLLMAN *n* man who collects tolls
TOLLMEN >TOLLMAN
TOLLS >TOLL
TOLLWAY *n* road on which users must pay tolls to travel
TOLLWAYS >TOLLWAY
TOLLY *n* castrated calf
TOLSEL *n* tolbooth
TOLSELS >TOLSEL
TOLSEY *n* tolbooth
TOLSEYS >TOLBOOTH
TOLT *n* type of obsolete English writ
TOLTER *vb* struggle or move with difficulty, as in mud
TOLTERED >TOLTER
TOLTERING >TOLTER
TOLTERS >TOLTER
TOLTS >TOLT
TOLU *n* sweet-smelling balsam obtained from a South American tree, used in medicine and perfume
TOLUATE *n* any salt or ester of any of the three isomeric forms of toluic acid
TOLUATES >TOLUATE
TOLUENE *n* colourless volatile flammable liquid obtained from petroleum and coal tar
TOLUENES >TOLUENE
TOLUIC as in *toluic acid* white crystalline derivative of toluene existing in three isomeric forms
TOLUID *n* white crystalline derivative of glycocoll
TOLUIDE *variant of* >TOLUID
TOLUIDES >TOLUIDE
TOLUIDIDE *n* chemical deriving from toluene
TOLUIDIN *n* type of dye
TOLUIDINE *n* compound used in dye production
TOLUIDINS >TOLUIDIN
TOLUIDS >TOLUID
TOLUOL *another name for* >TOLUENE
TOLUOLE *another name for* >TOLUENE
TOLUOLES >TOLUOLE
TOLUOLS >TOLUOL
TOLUS >TOLU
TOLUYL *n* of, consisting of, or containing any of three isomeric groups $CH_3C_6H_4CO$–, derived from a toluic acid by removal of the hydroxyl group
TOLUYLS >TOLUYL
TOLYL *n* of, consisting of, or containing any of three isomeric groups, $CH_3C_6H_4$–, derived from toluene
TOLYLS >TOLYL
TOLZEY *n* tolbooth
TOLZEYS >TOLZEY
TOM *n* male cat ▷ *adj* (of an animal) male ▷ *vb* prostitute oneself
TOMAHAWK *n* fighting axe of the Native Americans
TOMAHAWKS >TOMAHAWK
TOMALLEY *n* fat from a lobster, called "liver", and eaten as a delicacy
TOMALLEYS >TOMALLEY
TOMAN *n* gold coin formerly issued in Persia
TOMANS >TOMAN
TOMATILLO *n* Mexican plant bearing edible berries of the same name
TOMATO *n* red fruit used in

salads and as a vegetable
TOMATOES > TOMATO
TOMATOEY > TOMATO
TOMB *n* grave
TOMBAC *n* any of various brittle alloys containing copper and zinc and sometimes tin and arsenic: used for making cheap jewellery, etc
TOMBACK *variant spelling of* > TOMBAC
TOMBACKS > TOMBAC
TOMBACS > TOMBAC
TOMBAK *same as* > TOMBAC
TOMBAKS > TOMBAK
TOMBAL *adj* like or relating to a tomb
TOMBED > TOMB
TOMBIC *adj* of or relating to tombs
TOMBING > TOMB
TOMBLESS > TOMB
TOMBLIKE > TOMB
TOMBOC *n* weapon
TOMBOCS > TOMBOC
TOMBOLA *n* lottery with tickets drawn from a revolving drum
TOMBOLAS > TOMBOLA
TOMBOLO *n* narrow sand or shingle bar linking a small island with another island or the mainland
TOMBOLOS > TOMBOLO
TOMBOY *n* girl who acts or dresses like a boy
TOMBOYISH > TOMBOY
TOMBOYS > TOMBOY
TOMBS > TOMB
TOMBSTONE *n* gravestone
TOMCAT *vb* (of a man) to be promiscuous
TOMCATS > TOMCAT
TOMCATTED > TOMCAT
TOMCOD *n* small fish resembling the cod
TOMCODS > TOMCOD
TOME *n* large heavy book
TOMENTA > TOMENTUM
TOMENTOSE > TOMENTUM
TOMENTOUS > TOMENTUM
TOMENTUM *n* feltlike covering of downy hairs on leaves and other plant parts
TOMES > TOME
TOMFOOL *n* fool ▷ *vb* act the fool
TOMFOOLED > TOMFOOL
TOMFOOLS > TOMFOOL
TOMIA > TOMIUM
TOMIAL > TOMIUM
TOMIUM *n* sharp edge of a bird's beak
TOMMED > TOM
TOMMIED > TOMMY
TOMMIES > TOMMY
TOMMING > TOM
TOMMY *n* private in the British Army ▷ *vb* (formerly) to exploit workers by paying them in goods rather than in money
TOMMYING > TOMMY
TOMMYROT *n* utter nonsense
TOMMYROTS > TOMMYROT
TOMO *n* shaft formed by the action of water on limestone or volcanic rock
TOMOGRAM *n* x-ray photograph of a selected plane section of the human body or some other solid object
TOMOGRAMS > TOMOGRAM
TOMOGRAPH *n* device for making tomograms
TOMORROW *n* (on) the day after today ▷ *adv* on the day after today
TOMORROWS > TOMORROW
TOMOS > TOMO
TOMPION *same as* > TAMPION
TOMPIONS > TOMPION
TOMPON *same as* > TAMPON
TOMPONED > TOMPON
TOMPONING > TOMPON
TOMPONS > TOMPON
TOMS > TOM
TOMTIT *n* small European bird that eats insects and seeds
TOMTITS > TOMTIT
TON *n* unit of weight equal to 2240 pounds or 1016 kilograms (long ton) or, in the US, 2000 pounds or 907 kilograms (short ton); style, distinction
TONAL *adj* written in a key
TONALITE *n* igneous rock found in the Italian Alps
TONALITES > TONALITE
TONALITY *n* presence of a musical key in a composition
TONALLY > TONAL
TONANT *adj* very loud
TONDI > TONDO
TONDINI > TONDINO
TONDINO *n* small tondo
TONDINOS > TONDINO
TONDO *n* circular easel painting or relief carving
TONDOS > TONDO
TONE *n* sound with reference to its pitch, volume, etc ▷ *vb* harmonize (with)
TONEARM *same as* > PICKUP
TONEARMS > TONEARM
TONED > TONE
TONELESS *adj* having no tone
TONEME *n* phoneme that is distinguished from another phoneme only by its tone
TONEMES > TONEME
TONEMIC > TONEME
TONEPAD *n* keypad used to transmit information by generating tones that can be recognised by a central system as corresponding to particular digits
TONEPADS > TONEPAD
TONER *n* cosmetic applied to the skin to reduce oiliness
TONERS > TONER
TONES > TONE
TONETIC *adj* (of a language) distinguishing words semantically by distinction of tone as well as by other sounds
TONETICS *pl n* area of linguistics concentrating on the use of tone to distinguish words semantically
TONETTE *n* small musical instrument resembling a recorder
TONETTES > TONETTE
TONEY *variant spelling of* > TONY
TONG *n* (formerly) a secret society of Chinese Americans ▷ *vb* gather or seize with tongs ▷ *n* (formerly) a Chinese secret society
TONGA *n* light two-wheeled vehicle used in rural areas of India
TONGAS > TONGA
TONGED > TONG
TONGER *n* one who uses tongs to gather oysters
TONGERS > TONGER
TONGING > TONG
TONGMAN *another word for* > TONGER
TONGMEN > TONGMAN
TONGS *pl n* large pincers for grasping and lifting
TONGSTER *n* tong member
TONGSTERS > TONGSTER
TONGUE *n* muscular organ in the mouth, used in speaking and tasting ▷ *vb* use the tongue
TONGUED > TONGUE
TONGUELET *n* small tongue
TONGUES > TONGUE
TONGUING > TONGUE
TONGUINGS > TONGUE
TONIC *n* medicine to improve body tone ▷ *adj* invigorating
TONICALLY > TONIC
TONICITY *n* state, condition, or quality of being tonic
TONICS > TONIC
TONIER > TONY
TONIES > TONY
TONIEST > TONY
TONIGHT *n* (in or during) the night or evening of this day ▷ *adv* in or during the night or evening of this day
TONIGHTS > TONIGHT
TONING > TONE
TONINGS > TONE
TONISH > TON
TONISHLY > TON
TONITE *n* explosive used i[n] quarrying
TONITES > TONITE
TONK *vb* strike with a heavy blow ▷ *n* effete or effeminate man
TONKA as in *tonka bean* tall leguminous tree of tropical America, having fragrant black almond-shaped seeds
TONKED > TONK
TONKER > TONK
TONKERS > TONK
TONKING > TONK
TONKS > TONK
TONLET *n* skirt of a suit of armour, consisting of overlapping metal bands
TONLETS > TONLET
TONNAG *n* type of (usually tartan) shawl
TONNAGE *n* weight capaci[ty] of a ship
TONNAGES > TONNAGE
TONNAGS > TONNAG
TONNE *same as* > TON
TONNEAU *n* detachable cover to protect the rear part of an open car when is not carrying passenger[s]
TONNEAUS > TONNEAU
TONNEAUX > TONNEAU
TONNELL *old spelling of* > TUNNEL
TONNELLS > TONNELL
TONNER *n* something, for example a vehicle, that weighs one ton
TONNERS > TONNE
TONNES > TONNE
TONNISH > TON
TONNISHLY > TON
TONOMETER *n* instrument for measuring the pitch of a sound, esp one consisting of a set of tuning forks
TONOMETRY > TONOMETER
TONOPLAST *n* membrane enclosing a vacuole in a plant cell
TONS > TON
TONSIL *n* small gland in th[e] throat
TONSILAR > TONSIL
TONSILLAR > TONSIL
TONSILS > TONSIL
TONSOR *n* barber
TONSORIAL *adj* of a barbe[r] or his trade
TONSORS > TONSOR
TONSURE *n* shaving of all or the top of the head as a religious or monastic practice ▷ *vb* shave the head of
TONSURED > TONSURE
TONSURES > TONSURE
TONSURING > TONSURE
TONTINE *n* annuity scheme by which several subscribers accumulate and invest a common fu[nd]

out of which they receive an annuity that increases as subscribers die until the last survivor takes the whole
ONTINER *n* subscriber to a tontine
ONTINERS > TONTINER
ONTINES > TONTINE
ONUS *n* normal tension of a muscle at rest
ONUSES > TONUS
ONY *adj* stylish or distinctive ▷ *n* stylish or distinctive person
OO *adv* also, as well
OOART *variant spelling of* > TUART
OOARTS > TOOART
OOK > TAKE
OOL *n* implement used by hand ▷ *vb* work on with a tool
OOLBAG *n* bag for storing or carrying tools
OOLBAGS > TOOLBAG
OOLBAR *n* horizontal row or vertical column of selectable buttons displayed on a computer screen, allowing the user to select a variety of functions
OOLBARS > TOOLBAR
OOLBOX *n* box for storing or carrying tools
OOLBOXES > TOOLBOX
OOLED > TOOL
OOLER > TOOL
OOLERS > TOOL
OOLHEAD *n* adjustable attachment for a machine tool that holds the tool in position
OOLHEADS > TOOLHEAD
OOLHOUSE *another word for* > TOOLSHED
OOLING *n* any decorative work done with a tool, esp a design stamped onto a book cover, piece of leatherwork, etc
OOLINGS > TOOLING
OOLKIT *n* set of tools designed to be used together or for a particular purpose
OOLKITS > TOOLKIT
OOLLESS *adj* having no tools
OOLMAKER *n* person who makes tools
OOLMAN *n* person who works with tools
OOLMEN > TOOLMAN
OOLROOM *n* room, as in a machine shop, where tools are made or stored
OOLROOMS > TOOLROOM
OOLS > TOOL
OOLSET *n* set of predefined tools associated with a particular computer application
TOOLSETS > TOOLSET
TOOLSHED *n* small shed in the garden or yard of a house used for storing tools, esp those for gardening
TOOLSHEDS > TOOLSHED
TOOM *vb* empty (something) ▷ *adj* empty
TOOMED > TOOM
TOOMER > TOOM
TOOMEST > TOOM
TOOMING > TOOM
TOOMS > TOOM
TOON *n* large meliaceous tree of the East Indies and Australia, having clusters of flowers from which a dye is obtained
TOONIE *n* Canadian two-dollar coin
TOONIES > TOONIE
TOONS > TOON
TOORIE *n* tassel or bobble on a bonnet
TOORIES > TOORIE
TOOSHIE *adj* angry
TOOT *n* short hooting sound ▷ *vb* (cause to) make such a sound
TOOTED > TOOT
TOOTER > TOOT
TOOTERS > TOOT
TOOTH *n* bonelike projection in the jaws of most vertebrates for biting and chewing
TOOTHACHE *n* pain in or near a tooth
TOOTHCOMB *n* comb with fine teeth set closely together
TOOTHED *adj* having a tooth or teeth
TOOTHFISH as in *Patagonian toothfish* Chilean sea bass
TOOTHFUL *n* little (esp alcoholic) drink
TOOTHFULS > TOOTHFUL
TOOTHIER > TOOTHY
TOOTHIEST > TOOTHY
TOOTHILY > TOOTHY
TOOTHING > TOOTH
TOOTHINGS > TOOTH
TOOTHLESS > TOOTH
TOOTHLIKE > TOOTH
TOOTHPICK *n* small stick for removing scraps of food from between the teeth
TOOTHS > TOOTH
TOOTHSOME *adj* delicious or appetizing in appearance, flavour, or smell
TOOTHWASH *n* tooth-cleaning liquid
TOOTHWORT *n* parasitic plant
TOOTHY *adj* having or showing numerous, large, or prominent teeth
TOOTING > TOOT
TOOTLE *vb* hoot softly or repeatedly ▷ *n* soft hoot or series of hoots
TOOTLED > TOOTLE
TOOTLER > TOOTLE
TOOTLERS > TOOTLE
TOOTLES > TOOTLE
TOOTLING > TOOTLE
TOOTS *Scots version of* > TUT
TOOTSED > TOOTS
TOOTSES > TOOTS
TOOTSIE *same as* > TOOTSY
TOOTSIES > TOOTSY
TOOTSING > TOOTS
TOOTSY *same as* > TOOTS
TOP *n* highest point or part ▷ *adj* at or of the top ▷ *vb* form a top on
TOPALGIA *n* pain restricted to a particular spot: a neurotic or hysterical symptom
TOPALGIAS > TOPALGIA
TOPARCH *n* ruler of a small state or realm
TOPARCHS > TOPARCH
TOPARCHY > TOPARCH
TOPAZ *n* semiprecious stone in various colours
TOPAZES > TOPAZ
TOPAZINE *adj* like topaz
TOPCOAT *n* overcoat
TOPCOATS > TOPCOAT
TOPCROSS *n* class of hybrid
TOPE *vb* drink alcohol regularly ▷ *n* small European shark
TOPECTOMY *n* (formerly) the surgical removal of part of the cerebral cortex to relieve certain psychiatric disorders
TOPED > TOPE
TOPEE *n* lightweight hat worn in tropical countries
TOPEES > TOPEE
TOPEK *same as* > TUPIK
TOPEKS > TOPEK
TOPER > TOPE
TOPERS > TOPE
TOPES > TOPE
TOPFLIGHT *adj* superior or excellent quality; outstanding
TOPFUL *variant spelling of* > TOPFULL
TOPFULL *adj* full to the top
TOPH *n* variety of sandstone
TOPHE *variant spelling of* > TOPH
TOPHES > TOPHE
TOPHI > TOPHUS
TOPHS > TOPH
TOPHUS *n* deposit of sodium urate in the helix of the ear or surrounding a joint
TOPI *same as* > TOPEE
TOPIARIAN > TOPIARY
TOPIARIES > TOPIARY
TOPIARIST > TOPIARY
TOPIARY *n* art of trimming trees and bushes into decorative shapes ▷ *adj* of or relating to topiary
TOPIC *n* subject of a conversation, book, etc
TOPICAL *adj* relating to current events
TOPICALLY > TOPICAL
TOPICS > TOPIC
TOPING > TOPE
TOPIS > TOPI
TOPKICK *n* (formerly) sergeant
TOPKICKS > TOPKICK
TOPKNOT *n* crest, tuft, decorative bow, etc, on the top of the head
TOPKNOTS > TOPKNOT
TOPLESS *adj* (of a costume or woman) with no covering for the breasts
TOPLINE *vb* headline; be the main focus of a newspaper story
TOPLINED > TOPLINE
TOPLINER > TOPLINE
TOPLINERS > TOPLINE
TOPLINES > TOPLINE
TOPLINING > TOPLINE
TOPLOFTY *adj* haughty or pretentious
TOPMAKER *n* wool dealer
TOPMAKERS > TOPMAKER
TOPMAKING > TOPMAKER
TOPMAN *n* sailor positioned in the rigging of the topsail
TOPMAST *n* mast next above a lower mast on a sailing vessel
TOPMASTS > TOPMAST
TOPMEN > TOPMAN
TOPMINNOW *n* small American freshwater cyprinodont fish
TOPMOST *adj* highest or best
TOPNOTCH *adj* excellent
TOPO *n* picture of a mountain with details of climbing routes superimposed on it
TOPOGRAPH *n* type of x-ray photograph
TOPOI > TOPO
TOPOLOGIC > TOPOLOGY
TOPOLOGY *n* geometry of the properties of a shape which are unaffected by continuous distortion
TOPONYM *n* name of a place
TOPONYMAL > TOPONYMY
TOPONYMIC > TOPONYMY
TOPONYMS > TOPONYM
TOPONYMY *n* study of place names
TOPOS > TOPO
TOPOTYPE *n* specimen plant or animal taken from an area regarded as the typical habitat
TOPOTYPES > TOPOTYPE
TOPPED > TOP
TOPPER *n* top hat
TOPPERS > TOPPER
TOPPING > TOP

TOPPINGLY >TOP
TOPPINGS >TOP
TOPPLE *vb* (cause to) fall over
TOPPLED >TOPPLE
TOPPLES >TOPPLE
TOPPLING >TOPPLE
TOPS >TOP
TOPSAIL *n* square sail carried on a yard set on a topmast
TOPSAILS >TOPSAIL
TOPSIDE *n* lean cut of beef from the thigh containing no bone
TOPSIDER *n* person in charge
TOPSIDERS >TOPSIDER
TOPSIDES >TOPSIDE
TOPSMAN *n* chief drover
TOPSMEN >TOPSMAN
TOPSOIL *n* surface layer of soil ▷ *vb* spread topsoil on (land)
TOPSOILED >TOPSOIL
TOPSOILS >TOPSOIL
TOPSPIN *n* spin imparted to make a ball bounce or travel exceptionally far, high, or quickly, as by hitting it with a sharp forward and upward stroke
TOPSPINS >TOPSPIN
TOPSTITCH *vb* stitch a line the outside of a garment, running close to a seam
TOPSTONE *n* stone forming the top of something
TOPSTONES >TOPSTONE
TOPWORK *vb* graft shoots or twigs onto the main branches of (for example, a fruit tree) to modify its yield
TOPWORKED >TOPWORK
TOPWORKS >TOPWORK
TOQUE *same as* >TUQUE
TOQUES >TOQUE
TOQUET *same as* >TOQUE
TOQUETS >TOQUET
TOQUILLA *another name for* >JIPIJAPA
TOQUILLAS >TOQUILLA
TOR *n* high rocky hill
TORA *variant spelling of* >TORAH
TORAH *n* whole body of traditional Jewish teaching, including the Oral Law
TORAHS >TORAH
TORAN *n* (in Indian architecture) an archway, usually wooden and often ornately carved
TORANA *same as* >TORAN
TORANAS >TORANA
TORANS >TORAN
TORAS >TORA
TORBANITE *n* type of oil shale
TORC *same as* >TORQUE
TORCH *n* small portable battery-powered lamp ▷ *vb* deliberately set (a building) on fire
TORCHABLE >TORCH
TORCHED >TORCH
TORCHER >TORCH
TORCHERE *n* tall narrow stand for holding a candelabrum
TORCHERES >TORCHERE
TORCHERS >TORCH
TORCHES >TORCH
TORCHIER *n* standing lamp with a bowl for casting light upwards and so giving all-round indirect illumination
TORCHIERE *same as* >TORCHIER
TORCHIERS >TORCHIER
TORCHIEST >TORCHY
TORCHING >TORCH
TORCHINGS >TORCH
TORCHLIKE >TORCH
TORCHON as in *torchon lace* coarse linen or cotton lace with a simple openwork pattern
TORCHONS >TORCHON
TORCHWOOD *n* rutaceous tree or shrub of Florida and the Caribbean, with hard resinous wood used for torches
TORCHY *adj* sentimental; maudlin; characteristic of a torch song
TORCS >TORC
TORCULAR *n* tourniquet
TORCULARS >TORCULAR
TORDION *n* old triple-time dance for two people
TORDIONS >TORDION
TORE *same as* >TORUS
TOREADOR *n* bullfighter
TOREADORS >TOREADOR
TORERO *n* bullfighter, esp one on foot
TOREROS >TORERO
TORES >TORE
TOREUTIC >TOREUTICS
TOREUTICS *n* art of making detailed ornamental reliefs, esp in metal, by embossing and chasing
TORGOCH *n* type of char
TORGOCHS >TORGOCH
TORI >TORUS
TORIC *adj* of, relating to, or having the form of a torus
TORICS >TORIC
TORIES >TORY
TORII *n* gateway, esp one at the entrance to a Japanese Shinto temple
TORMENT *vb* cause (someone) great suffering ▷ *n* great suffering
TORMENTA >TORMENTUM
TORMENTED >TORMENT
TORMENTER *same as* >TORMENTOR
TORMENTIL *n* creeping plant with yellow four-petalled flowers
TORMENTOR *n* person or thing that torments
TORMENTS >TORMENT
TORMENTUM *n* type of Roman catapult
TORMINA *n* complaints
TORMINAL >TORMINA
TORMINOUS >TORMINA
TORN >TEAR
TORNADE *same as* >TORNADO
TORNADES >TORNADE
TORNADIC >TORNADO
TORNADO *n* violent whirlwind
TORNADOES >TORNADO
TORNADOS >TORNADO
TORNILLO *n* shrub found in Mexico and some southwestern states of the US
TORNILLOS >TORNILLO
TORO *n* bull
TOROID *n* surface generated by rotating a closed plane curve about a coplanar line that does not intersect the curve
TOROIDAL >TOROID
TOROIDS >TOROID
TOROS >TORO
TOROSE *adj* (of a cylindrical part) having irregular swellings
TOROSITY >TOROSE
TOROT >TORAH
TOROTH >TORAH
TOROUS *same as* >TOROSE
TORPEDO *n* self-propelled underwater missile ▷ *vb* attack or destroy with or as if with torpedoes
TORPEDOED >TORPEDO
TORPEDOER >TORPEDO
TORPEDOES >TORPEDO
TORPEDOS >TORPEDO
TORPEFIED >TORPEFY
TORPEFIES >TORPEFY
TORPEFY *n* make torpid
TORPID *adj* sluggish and inactive
TORPIDITY >TORPID
TORPIDLY >TORPID
TORPIDS *n* series of boat races held at Oxford University during Lent
TORPITUDE *another word for* >TORPOR
TORPOR *n* torpid state
TORPORS >TORPOR
TORQUATE >TORQUES
TORQUATED >TORQUES
TORQUE *n* force causing rotation ▷ *vb* apply torque to (something)
TORQUED >TORQUE
TORQUER >TORQUE
TORQUERS >TORQUE
TORQUES *n* distinctive band of hair, feathers, skin, or colour around the neck of an animal
TORQUESES >TORQUES
TORQUING >TORQUE
TORR *n* unit of pressure equal to one millimetre of mercury (133.3 newtons p[er] square metre)
TORREFIED >TORREFY
TORREFIES >TORREFY
TORREFY *vb* dry (drugs, ores, etc) by subjection to intense heat
TORRENT *n* rushing stream ▷ *adj* like or relating to a torrent
TORRENTS >TORRENT
TORRET *same as* >TERRET
TORRETS >TORRET
TORRID *adj* very hot and dr[y]
TORRIDER >TORRID
TORRIDEST >TORRID
TORRIDITY >TORRID
TORRIDLY >TORRID
TORRIFIED >TORRIEFY
TORRIFIES >TORRIFY
TORRIFY *same as* >TORREF[Y]
TORRS >TORR
TORS >TOR
TORSADE *n* ornamental twist or twisted cord, as on hats
TORSADES >TORSADE
TORSE *same as* >TORSO
TORSEL *n* wooden beam along the top of a wall for distributing the weight o[f] something laid upon it
TORSELS >TORSEL
TORSES >TORSE
TORSI >TORSO
TORSION *n* twisting of a part by equal forces being applied at both ends but i[n] opposite directions
TORSIONAL >TORSION
TORSIONS >TORSION
TORSIVE *adj* twisted
TORSK *n* fish with a single long dorsal fin
TORSKS >TORSK
TORSO *n* trunk of the human body
TORSOS >TORSO
TORT *n* civil wrong or inju[ry] for which damages may b[e] claimed
TORTA *n* (in mining) a flat circular pile of silver ore
TORTAS >TORTA
TORTE *n* rich cake, originating in Austria, usually decorated or fille[d] with cream, fruit, nuts, and jam
TORTEN >TORTE
TORTES >TORTE
TORTILE *adj* twisted or coiled
TORTILITY >TORTILE
TORTILLA *n* thin Mexican pancake
TORTILLAS >TORTILLA
TORTILLON *another word for* >STUMP
TORTIOUS *adj* having the nature of or involving a

tort
ORTIVE *adj* twisted
ORTOISE *n* slow-moving land reptile with a dome-shaped shell
ORTOISES > TORTOISE
ORTONI *n* rich ice cream often flavoured with sherry
ORTONIS > TORTONI
ORTRICES > TORTRIX
ORTRICID *n* small moth of the chiefly temperate family *Tortricidae*, ▷ *adj* of, relating to, or belonging to the family *Tortricidae*
ORTRIX *n* type of moth
ORTRIXES > TORTRIX
ORTS > TORT
ORTUOUS *adj* winding or twisting
ORTURE *vb* cause (someone) severe pain or mental anguish ▷ *n* severe physical or mental pain
ORTURED > TORTURE
ORTURER > TORTURE
ORTURERS > TORTURE
ORTURES > TORTURE
ORTURING > TORTURE
ORTUROUS > TORTURE
ORULA *n* species of fungal microorganisms
ORULAE > TORULA
ORULAS > TORULA
ORULI > TORULUS
ORULIN *n* vitamin found in yeast
ORULINS > TORULIN
ORULOSE *adj* (of something cylindrical) alternately swollen and pinched along its length
ORULOSES > TORULOSIS
ORULOSIS *n* infection by one of the torula
ORULUS *n* socket in an insect's head in which its antenna is attached
RUS *n* large convex moulding approximately semicircular in cross section, esp one used on the base of a classical column
RY *n* ultraconservative or reactionary person ▷ *adj* ultraconservative or reactionary
SA *n* large reddish dog, originally bred for fighting
SAS > TOSA
SE *same as* > TOZE
SED > TOSE
SES > TOSE
SH *n* nonsense ▷ *vb* tidy or trim
SHACH *n* military leader of a clan
SHACHS > TOSHACH
SHED > TOSH
SHER > TOSH
SHERS > TOSH
TOSHES > TOSH
TOSHIER > TOSHY
TOSHIEST > TOSHY
TOSHING > TOSH
TOSHY *adj* neat; trim
TOSING > TOSE
TOSS *vb* throw lightly ▷ *n* tossing
TOSSED > TOSS
TOSSEN *old past participle of* > TOSS
TOSSER *n* stupid or despicable person
TOSSERS > TOSSER
TOSSES > TOSS
TOSSIER > TOSSY
TOSSIEST > TOSSY
TOSSILY > TOSSY
TOSSING > TOSS
TOSSINGS > TOSS
TOSSPOT *n* habitual drinker
TOSSPOTS > TOSSPOT
TOSSUP *n* an instance of tossing up a coin
TOSSUPS > TOSSUP
TOSSY *adj* impudent
TOST *old past participle of* > TOSS
TOSTADA *n* crispy deep-fried tortilla topped with meat, cheese, and refried beans
TOSTADAS > TOSTADA
TOSTADO *same as* > TOSTADA
TOSTADOS > TOSTADO
TOT *n* small child ▷ *vb* total
TOTABLE > TOTE
TOTAL *n* whole, esp a sum of parts ▷ *adj* complete ▷ *vb* amount to
TOTALED > TOTAL
TOTALING > TOTAL
TOTALISE *same as* > TOTALIZE
TOTALISED > TOTALISE
TOTALISER > TOTALISE
TOTALISES > TOTALISE
TOTALISM *n* practice of a dictatorial one party state that regulates every form of life
TOTALISMS > TOTALISM
TOTALIST > TOTALISM
TOTALISTS > TOTALISM
TOTALITY *n* whole amount
TOTALIZE *vb* combine or make into a total
TOTALIZED > TOTALIZE
TOTALIZER > TOTALIZE
TOTALIZES > TOTALIZE
TOTALLED > TOTAL
TOTALLING > TOTAL
TOTALLY > TOTAL
TOTALS > TOTAL
TOTANUS *another name for* > REDSHANK
TOTANUSES > TOTANUS
TOTAQUINE *n* mixture of quinine and other alkaloids derived from cinchona bark, used as a substitute for quinine in treating malaria
TOTARA *n* tall coniferous forest tree of New Zealand, with a hard durable wood
TOTARAS > TOTARA
TOTE *vb* carry (a gun etc) ▷ *n* act of or an instance of toting
TOTEABLE > TOTE
TOTED > TOTE
TOTEM *n* tribal badge or emblem
TOTEMIC > TOTEM
TOTEMISM *n* belief in kinship of groups or individuals having a common totem
TOTEMISMS > TOTEMISM
TOTEMIST > TOTEMISM
TOTEMISTS > TOTEMISM
TOTEMITE > TOTEMISM
TOTEMITES > TOTEMITE
TOTEMS > TOTEM
TOTER > TOTE
TOTERS > TOTE
TOTES > TOTE
TOTHER *n* other
TOTIENT *n* quantity of numbers less than, and sharing no common factors with, a given number
TOTIENTS > TOTIENT
TOTING > TOTE
TOTITIVE *n* number less than, and having no common factors with, a given number
TOTITIVES > TOTITIVE
TOTS > TOT
TOTTED > TOT
TOTTER *vb* move unsteadily ▷ *n* act or an instance of tottering
TOTTERED > TOTTER
TOTTERER > TOTTER
TOTTERERS > TOTTER
TOTTERING > TOTTER
TOTTERS > TOTTER
TOTTERY > TOTTER
TOTTIE *adj* very small
TOTTIER > TOTTY
TOTTIES > TOTTY
TOTTIEST > TOTTY
TOTTING > TOT
TOTTINGS > TOT
TOTTY *n* people, esp women, collectively considered as sexual objects ▷ *adj* very small
TOUCAN *n* tropical American bird with a large bill
TOUCANET *n* type of small toucan
TOUCANETS > TOUCAN
TOUCANS > TOUCAN
TOUCH *vb* come into contact with ▷ *n* sense by which an object's qualities are perceived when they come into contact with part of the body ▷ *adj* of a non-contact version of particular sport
TOUCHABLE > TOUCH
TOUCHBACK *n* play in which the ball is put down by a player behind his own goal line when the ball has been put across the goal line by an opponent
TOUCHDOWN *n* moment at which a landing aircraft or spacecraft comes into contact with the landing surface ▷ *vb* (of an aircraft or spacecraft) to land
TOUCHE *interj* acknowledgment of the striking home of a remark or witty reply
TOUCHED *adj* emotionally moved
TOUCHER > TOUCH
TOUCHERS > TOUCH
TOUCHES > TOUCH
TOUCHHOLE *n* hole in the breech of early cannon and firearms through which the charge was ignited
TOUCHIER > TOUCHY
TOUCHIEST > TOUCHY
TOUCHILY > TOUCHY
TOUCHING *adj* emotionally moving ▷ *prep* relating to or concerning
TOUCHINGS > TOUCH
TOUCHLESS > TOUCH
TOUCHLINE *n* side line of the pitch in some games
TOUCHMARK *n* maker's mark stamped on pewter objects
TOUCHPAD *n* part of laptop computer functioning like mouse
TOUCHPADS > TOUCHPAD
TOUCHTONE *adj* of or relating to a telephone dialling system in which each of the buttons pressed generates a tone of a different pitch, which is transmitted to the exchange
TOUCHUP *n* renovation or retouching, as of a painting
TOUCHUPS > TOUCHUP
TOUCHWOOD *n* something, esp dry wood, used as tinder
TOUCHY *adj* easily offended
TOUGH *adj* strong or resilient ▷ *n* rough violent person
TOUGHED > TOUGH
TOUGHEN *vb* make or become tough or tougher
TOUGHENED > TOUGHEN
TOUGHENER > TOUGHEN
TOUGHENS > TOUGHEN
TOUGHER > TOUGH
TOUGHEST > TOUGH
TOUGHIE *n* person who is tough
TOUGHIES > TOUGHIE
TOUGHING > TOUGH
TOUGHISH > TOUGH

TOUGHLY > TOUGH
TOUGHNESS *n* quality or an instance of being tough
TOUGHS > TOUGH
TOUGHY *same as* > TOUGHIE
TOUK *same as* > TUCK
TOUKED > TOUK
TOUKING > TOUK
TOUKS > TOUK
TOUN *n* town
TOUNS > TOUN
TOUPEE *n* small wig
TOUPEES > TOUPEE
TOUPET *same as* > TOUPEE
TOUPETS > TOUPET
TOUR *n* journey visiting places of interest along the way ▷ *vb* make a tour (of)
TOURACO *n* any brightly coloured crested arboreal African bird of the family *Musophagidae*: order *Cuculiformes* (cuckoos, etc)
TOURACOS > TOURACO
TOURED > TOUR
TOURER *n* large open car with a folding top, usually seating a driver and four passengers
TOURERS > TOURER
TOURIE *same as* > TOORIE
TOURIES > TOURIE
TOURING > TOUR
TOURINGS > TOUR
TOURISM *n* tourist travel as an industry
TOURISMS > TOURISM
TOURIST *n* person travelling for pleasure ▷ *adj* of or relating to tourists or tourism
TOURISTA *variant of* > TOURIST
TOURISTAS > TOURISTA
TOURISTED *adj* busy with tourists
TOURISTIC > TOURIST
TOURISTS > TOURIST
TOURISTY *adj* informal term for full of tourists or tourist attractions
TOURNEDOS *n* thick round steak of beef
TOURNEY *n* knightly tournament ▷ *vb* engage in a tourney
TOURNEYED > TOURNEY
TOURNEYER > TOURNEY
TOURNEYS > TOURNEY
TOURNURE *n* outline or contour
TOURNURES > TOURNURE
TOURS > TOUR
TOURTIERE *n* type of meat pie
TOUSE *vb* tangle, ruffle, or disarrange; treat roughly
TOUSED > TOUSE
TOUSER > TOUSE
TOUSERS > TOUSE
TOUSES > TOUSE
TOUSIER > TOUSY
TOUSIEST > TOUSY
TOUSING > TOUSE
TOUSINGS > TOUSE
TOUSLE *vb* make (hair or clothes) ruffled and untidy ▷ *n* disorderly, tangled, or rumpled state
TOUSLED > TOUSLE
TOUSLES > TOUSLE
TOUSLING > TOUSLE
TOUSTIE *adj* irritable; testy
TOUSTIER > TOUSTIE
TOUSTIEST > TOUSTIE
TOUSY *adj* tousled
TOUT *vb* seek business in a persistent manner ▷ *n* person who sells tickets for a popular event at inflated prices
TOUTED > TOUT
TOUTER > TOUT
TOUTERS > TOUT
TOUTIE childishly irritable or sullen
TOUTIER > TOUTIE
TOUTIEST > TOUTIE
TOUTING > TOUT
TOUTS > TOUT
TOUZE *variant spelling of* > TOUSE
TOUZED > TOUZE
TOUZES > TOUZE
TOUZIER > TOUZY
TOUZIEST > TOUZY
TOUZING > TOUZE
TOUZLE *rare spelling of* > TOUSLE
TOUZLED > TOUZLE
TOUZLES > TOUZLE
TOUZLING > TOUZLE
TOUZY *variant spelling of* > TOUSY
TOVARICH *same as* > TOVARISCH
TOVARISCH *n* comrade: a term of address
TOVARISH *same as* > TOVARISCH
TOW *vb* drag, esp by means of a rope ▷ *n* towing
TOWABLE > TOW
TOWAGE *n* charge made for towing
TOWAGES > TOWAGE
TOWARD *same as* > TOWARDS
TOWARDLY *adj* compliant
TOWARDS *prep* in the direction of
TOWAWAY *n* vehicle which has been towed away (because, for example, it was illegally parked)
TOWAWAYS > TOWAWAY
TOWBAR *n* metal bar on a car for towing vehicles
TOWBARS > TOWBAR
TOWBOAT *n* another word for tug (the boat)
TOWBOATS > TOWBOAT
TOWED > TOW
TOWEL *n* cloth for drying things ▷ *vb* dry or wipe with a towel
TOWELED > TOWEL
TOWELETTE *n* paper towel
TOWELHEAD *n* offensive term for someone who wears a turban
TOWELING > TOWEL
TOWELINGS > TOWEL
TOWELLED > TOWEL
TOWELLING *n* material used for making towels
TOWELS > TOWEL
TOWER *n* tall structure, often forming part of a larger building
TOWERED *adj* having a tower or towers
TOWERIER > TOWERY
TOWERIEST > TOWERY
TOWERING *adj* very tall or impressive
TOWERLESS *adj* not having a tower
TOWERLIKE *adj* like a tower
TOWERS > TOWER
TOWERY *adj* with towers
TOWHEAD *n* often disparaging term for a person with blond or yellowish hair
TOWHEADED *adj* having blonde or yellowish hair
TOWHEADS > TOWHEAD
TOWHEE *n* any of various North American brownish-coloured sparrows of the genera *Pipilo* and *Chlorura*
TOWHEES > TOWHEE
TOWIE *n* truck used for towing
TOWIER > TOW
TOWIES > TOWIE
TOWIEST > TOW
TOWING > TOW
TOWINGS > TOW
TOWKAY *n* sir
TOWKAYS > TOWKAY
TOWLINE *same as* > TOWROPE
TOWLINES > TOWLINE
TOWMON *same as* > TOWMOND
TOWMOND *n* old word for year
TOWMONDS > TOWMOND
TOWMONS > TOWMON
TOWMONT *same as* > TOWMOND
TOWMONTS > TOWMONT
TOWN *n* group of buildings larger than a village
TOWNEE *same as* > TOWNIE
TOWNEES > TOWNEE
TOWNFOLK *same as* > TOWNSFOLK
TOWNHALL *n* chief building in which municipal business is transacted, often with a hall for public meetings
TOWNHOME *another word for* > TOWNHOUSE
TOWNHOMES > TOWNHOME
TOWNHOUSE *n* terraced house in an urban area, esp a fashionable one, often having the main living room on the first floor with an integral garage on the ground floor
TOWNIE *n* often disparaging term for a resident in a town, esp as distinct from country dwellers
TOWNIER > TOWNY
TOWNIES > TOWNY
TOWNIEST > TOWNY
TOWNISH > TOWN
TOWNLAND *n* division of land of various sizes
TOWNLANDS > TOWNLAND
TOWNLESS > TOWN
TOWNLET *n* small town
TOWNLETS > TOWNLET
TOWNLIER > TOWNLY
TOWNLIEST > TOWNLY
TOWNLING *n* person who lives in a town
TOWNLINGS > TOWNLING
TOWNLY *adj* characteristic of a town
TOWNS > TOWN
TOWNSCAPE *n* view of an urban scene
TOWNSFOLK *n* people of a town
TOWNSHIP *n* small town
TOWNSHIPS > TOWNSHIP
TOWNSKIP *n* old term for a mischievous and roguish child who frequents city streets
TOWNSKIPS > TOWNSKIP
TOWNSMAN *n* inhabitant of a town
TOWNSMEN > TOWNSMAN
TOWNWEAR *n* clothes suitable for wearing whil persuing activities usuall associated with towns
TOWNY *adj* characteristic o a town
TOWPATH *n* path beside a canal or river, originally fo horses towing boats
TOWPATHS > TOWPATH
TOWPLANE *n* aeroplane tha tows gliders
TOWPLANES > TOWPLANE
TOWROPE *n* rope or cable used for towing a vehicle or vessel
TOWROPES > TOWROPE
TOWS > TOW
TOWSACK *n* sack made fron tow
TOWSACKS > TOWSACK
TOWSE *same as* > TOUSE
TOWSED > TOWSE
TOWSER > TOWSE
TOWSERS > TOWSE
TOWSES > TOWSE
TOWSIER > TOWSY
TOWSIEST > TOWSY
TOWSING > TOWSE
TOWSY *same as* > TOUSY
TOWT *vb* sulk
TOWTED > TOWT
TOWTING > TOWT
TOWTS > TOWT
TOWY > TOW
TOWZE *same as* > TOUSE

OWZED > TOWZE
OWZES > TOWZE
OWZIER > TOWZY
OWZIEST > TOWZY
OWZING > TOWZE
OWZY *same as* > TOUSY
OXAEMIA *n* blood poisoning
OXAEMIAS > TOXAEMIA
OXAEMIC > TOXAEMIA
OXAPHENE *n* amber waxy solid with a pleasant pine odour, consisting of chlorinated terpenes, esp chlorinated camphene: used as an insecticide
OXEMIA *same as* > TOXAEMIA
OXEMIAS > TOXEMIA
OXEMIC > TOXAEMIA
OXIC *adj* poisonous ▷ *n* toxic substance
OXICAL *adj* toxic
OXICALLY > TOXIC
OXICANT *n* toxic substance ▷ *adj* poisonous
OXICANTS > TOXICANT
OXICITY *n* degree of strength of a poison
OXICOSES > TOXICOSIS
OXICOSIS *n* any disease or condition caused by poisoning
OXICS > TOXIC
OXIGENIC *adj* producing poison
OXIN *n* poison of bacterial origin
OXINE *nonstandard variant spelling of* > TOXIN
OXINES > TOXINE
OXINS > TOXIN
OXOCARA *n* parasitic worm infesting the intestines of cats and dogs
OXOCARAS > TOXOCARA
OXOID *n* toxin that has been treated to reduce its toxicity and is used in immunization to stimulate production of antitoxins
OXOIDS > TOXOID
OXOPHILY *n* archer
OY *n* something designed to be played with ▷ *adj* designed to be played with ▷ *vb* play, fiddle, or flirt
OYED > TOY
OYER > TOY
OYERS > TOY
OYING > TOY
OYINGS > TOY
OYISH *adj* resembling a toy
OYISHLY > TOYISH
OYLESOME *old spelling of* > TOILSOME
OYLESS > TOY
OYLIKE > TOY
OYLSOM *old spelling of* > TOILSOME
OYMAN *n* man who sells toys
TOYMEN > TOYMAN
TOYO *n* Japanese straw-like material made out of rice paper and used to make hats
TOYON *n* shrub related to the rose
TOYONS > TOYON
TOYOS > TOYO
TOYS > TOY
TOYSHOP *n* shop selling toys
TOYSHOPS > TOYSHOP
TOYSOME *adj* playful
TOYTOWN *adj* having an unreal and picturesque appearance
TOYWOMAN *n* woman who sells toys
TOYWOMEN > TOYWOMAN
TOZE *vb* tease out; (of wool, etc) card
TOZED > TOZE
TOZES > TOZE
TOZIE *n* type of shawl
TOZIES > TOZIE
TOZING > TOZE
TRABEATE *same as* > TRABEATED
TRABEATED *adj* constructed with horizontal beams as opposed to arches
TRABECULA *n* any of various rod-shaped structures that divide organs into separate chambers
TRABS *pl n* training shoes
TRACE *vb* locate or work out (the cause of something) ▷ *n* track left by something
TRACEABLE > TRACE
TRACEABLY > TRACE
TRACED > TRACE
TRACELESS > TRACE
TRACER *n* projectile which leaves a visible trail
TRACERIED > TRACERY
TRACERIES > TRACERY
TRACERS > TRACER
TRACERY *n* pattern of interlacing lines
TRACES > TRACE
TRACEUR *n* parkour participant
TRACEURS > TRACEUR
TRACHEA *n* windpipe
TRACHEAE > TRACHEA
TRACHEAL > TRACHEA
TRACHEARY *adj* using tracheae to breathe
TRACHEAS > TRACHEA
TRACHEATE > TRACHEA
TRACHEID *n* element of xylem tissue consisting of an elongated lignified cell with tapering ends and large pits
TRACHEIDE *same as* > TRACHEID
TRACHEIDS > TRACHEID
TRACHEOLE *n* small trachea found in some insects
TRACHINUS *n* weever fish
TRACHITIS *n* another spelling of tracheitis (inflammation of the trachea)
TRACHLE *vb* (of hair, clothing, etc) make untidy; dishevel; rumple
TRACHLED > TRACHLE
TRACHLES > TRACHLE
TRACHLING > TRACHLE
TRACHOMA *n* chronic contagious disease of the eye characterized by inflammation of the inner surface of the lids and the formation of scar tissue
TRACHOMAS > TRACHOMA
TRACHYTE *n* light-coloured fine-grained volcanic rock
TRACHYTES > TRACHYTE
TRACHYTIC *adj* (of the texture of certain igneous rocks) characterized by a parallel arrangement of crystals, which mark the flow of the lava when still molten
TRACING *n* traced copy
TRACINGS > TRACING
TRACK *n* rough road or path ▷ *vb* follow the trail or path of
TRACKABLE > TRACK
TRACKAGE *n* collective term for the railway tracks in general, or those in a given area or belonging to a particular company, etc
TRACKAGES > TRACKAGE
TRACKBALL *n* device consisting of a small ball, mounted in a cup, which can be rotated to move the cursor around the screen
TRACKED > TRACK
TRACKER > TRACK
TRACKERS > TRACK
TRACKING *n* act or process of following something or someone
TRACKINGS > TRACKING
TRACKLESS *adj* having or leaving no trace or trail
TRACKMAN *n* workman who lays and maintains railway track
TRACKMEN > TRACKMAN
TRACKPAD *same as* > TOUCHPAD
TRACKPADS > TRACKPAD
TRACKROAD *another word for* > TOWPATH
TRACKS > TRACK
TRACKSIDE *n* area alongside a track
TRACKSUIT *n* warm loose-fitting suit worn by athletes etc, esp during training
TRACKWAY *n* path or track
TRACKWAYS > TRACKWAY
TRACT *n* wide area ▷ *vb* track
TRACTABLE *adj* easy to manage or control
TRACTABLY > TRACTABLE
TRACTATE *n* short tract
TRACTATES > TRACTATE
TRACTATOR *n* person who writes tracts
TRACTED > TRACT
TRACTILE *adj* capable of being drawn out
TRACTING > TRACT
TRACTION *n* pulling, esp by engine power
TRACTIONS > TRACTION
TRACTIVE > TRACTION
TRACTOR *n* motor vehicle with large rear wheels for pulling farm machinery
TRACTORS > TRACTOR
TRACTRIX *n* (in geometry) type of curve
TRACTS > TRACT
TRACTUS *n* anthem sung in some RC masses
TRACTUSES > TRACTUS
TRAD *n* traditional jazz, as revived in the 1950s
TRADABLE > TRADE
TRADE *n* buying, selling, or exchange of goods ▷ *vb* buy and sell ▷ *adj* intended for or available only to people in industry or business
TRADEABLE > TRADE
TRADED > TRADE
TRADEFUL *adj* (of shops, for example) full of trade
TRADELESS > TRADE
TRADEMARK *n* (legally registered) name or symbol used by a firm to distinguish its goods ▷ *vb* label with a trademark
TRADENAME *n* name used by a trade to refer to a commodity, service, etc
TRADEOFF *n* exchange, esp as a compromise
TRADEOFFS > TRADEOFF
TRADER *n* person who engages in trade
TRADERS > TRADER
TRADES > TRADE
TRADESMAN *n* skilled worker
TRADESMEN > TRADESMAN
TRADING > TRADE
TRADINGS > TRADE
TRADITION *n* handing down from generation to generation of customs and beliefs
TRADITIVE *adj* traditional
TRADITOR *n* Christian who betrayed his fellow Christians at the time of the Roman persecutions
TRADITORS > TRADITOR
TRADS > TRAD
TRADUCE *vb* slander
TRADUCED > TRADUCE

TRADUCER > TRADUCE
TRADUCERS > TRADUCE
TRADUCES > TRADUCE
TRADUCIAN > TRADUCE
TRADUCING > TRADUCE
TRAFFIC *n* vehicles coming and going on a road ▷ *vb* trade, usu illicitly
TRAFFICKY *adj* (of a street, area, town, etc) busy with motor vehicles
TRAFFICS > TRAFFIC
TRAGAL > TRAGUS
TRAGEDIAN *n* person who acts in or writes tragedies
TRAGEDIES > TRAGEDY
TRAGEDY *n* shocking or sad event
TRAGELAPH *n* mythical animal: a cross between a goat and a stag
TRAGI > TRAGUS
TRAGIC *adj* of or like a tragedy ▷ *n* tragedian
TRAGICAL *same as* > TRAGIC
TRAGICS > TRAGIC
TRAGOPAN *n* pheasant of S and SE Asia, with a brilliant plumage and brightly coloured fleshy processes on the head
TRAGOPANS > TRAGOPAN
TRAGULE *n* mouse deer
TRAGULES > TRAGULE
TRAGULINE *adj* like or characteristic of a tragule
TRAGUS *n* cartilaginous fleshy projection that partially covers the entrance to the external ear
TRAHISON *n* treason
TRAHISONS > TRAHISON
TRAIK *vb* trudge; trek with difficulty
TRAIKED > TRAIK
TRAIKING > TRAIK
TRAIKIT > TRAIK
TRAIKS > TRAIK
TRAIL *n* path, track, or road ▷ *vb* drag along the ground
TRAILABLE *adj* capable of being trailed
TRAILED > TRAIL
TRAILER *n* vehicle designed to be towed by another vehicle ▷ *vb* use a trailer to advertise (something)
TRAILERED > TRAILER
TRAILERS > TRAILER
TRAILHEAD *n* place where a trail begins
TRAILING *adj* (of a plant) having a long stem which spreads over the ground or hangs loosely
TRAILLESS *adj* without trail
TRAILS > TRAIL
TRAILSIDE *adj* beside a trail
TRAIN *vb* instruct in a skill ▷ *n* line of railway coaches or wagons drawn by an engine
TRAINABLE > TRAIN
TRAINBAND *n* company of English militia from the 16th to the 18th century
TRAINED > TRAIN
TRAINEE *n* person being trained ▷ *adj* (of a person) undergoing training
TRAINEES > TRAINEE
TRAINER *n* person who trains an athlete or sportsman
TRAINERS *pl n* shoes in the style of those used for sports training
TRAINFUL *n* quantity of people or cargo that would be capable of filling a train
TRAINFULS > TRAINFUL
TRAINING *n* process of bringing a person to an agreed standard of proficiency by practice and instruction
TRAININGS > TRAINING
TRAINLESS > TRAIN
TRAINLOAD *n* quantity of people or cargo sufficient to fill a train
TRAINMAN *n* man who works on a train
TRAINMEN > TRAINMAN
TRAINS > TRAIN
TRAINWAY *n* railway track; channel in a built-up area through which a train passes
TRAINWAYS > TRAINWAY
TRAIPSE *vb* walk wearily ▷ *n* long or tiring walk
TRAIPSED > TRAIPSE
TRAIPSES > TRAIPSE
TRAIPSING > TRAIPSE
TRAIT *n* characteristic feature
TRAITOR *n* person guilty of treason or treachery
TRAITORLY *adj* of or characteristic of a traitor
TRAITORS > TRAITOR
TRAITRESS > TRAITOR
TRAITS > TRAIT
TRAJECT *vb* transport or transmit
TRAJECTED > TRAJECT
TRAJECTS > TRAJECT
TRAM *same as* > TRAMMEL
TRAMCAR *same as* > TRAM
TRAMCARS > TRAMCAR
TRAMEL *variant spelling of* > TRAMMEL
TRAMELED > TRAMEL
TRAMELING > TRAMEL
TRAMELL *variant spelling of* > TRAMMEL
TRAMELLED > TRAMELL
TRAMELLS > TRAMELL
TRAMELS > TRAMEL
TRAMLESS > TRAM
TRAMLINE *n* tracks on which a tram runs
TRAMLINED *adj* having tramlines
TRAMLINES > TRAMLINE
TRAMMED > TRAM
TRAMMEL *n* hindrance to free action or movement ▷ *vb* hinder or restrain
TRAMMELED > TRAMMEL
TRAMMELER > TRAMMEL
TRAMMELS > TRAMMEL
TRAMMIE *n* conductor or driver of a tram
TRAMMIES > TRAMMIE
TRAMMING > TRAM
TRAMP *vb* travel on foot, hike ▷ *n* homeless person who travels on foot
TRAMPED > TRAMP
TRAMPER *n* person who tramps
TRAMPERS > TRAMPER
TRAMPET *variant spelling of* > TRAMPETTE
TRAMPETS > TRAMPET
TRAMPETTE *n* small trampoline
TRAMPIER > TRAMPY
TRAMPIEST > TRAMPY
TRAMPING > TRAMP
TRAMPINGS > TRAMP
TRAMPISH > TRAMP
TRAMPLE *vb* tread on and crush ▷ *n* action or sound of trampling
TRAMPLED > TRAMPLE
TRAMPLER > TRAMPLE
TRAMPLERS > TRAMPLE
TRAMPLES > TRAMPLE
TRAMPLING > TRAMPLE
TRAMPOLIN *n* variant of trampoline: a tough canvass sheet suspended by springs from a frame, used by acrobats, gymnasts, etc
TRAMPS > TRAMP
TRAMPY *adj* (of woman) disreputable
TRAMROAD *same as* > TRAMWAY
TRAMROADS > TRAMROAD
TRAMS > TRAM
TRAMWAY *same as* > TRAMLINE
TRAMWAYS > TRAMWAY
TRANCE *n* unconscious or dazed state ▷ *vb* put into or as into a trance
TRANCED > TRANCE
TRANCEDLY > TRANCE
TRANCES > TRANCE
TRANCHE *n* portion of something large, esp a sum of money
TRANCHES > TRANCHE
TRANCHET *n* stoneage cutting tool
TRANCHETS > TRANCHET
TRANCING > TRANCE
TRANECT *n* ferry
TRANECTS > TRANECT
TRANGAM *n* bauble or trinket
TRANGAMS > TRANGAM
TRANGLE *n* (in heraldry) a small fesse
TRANGLES > TRANGLE
TRANK *n* short form of tranquillizer: drug that calms a person
TRANKS > TRANK
TRANKUM *same as* > TRANGAM
TRANKUMS > TRANKUM
TRANNIE *n* transistor radio
TRANNIES > TRANNY
TRANNY *same as* > TRANNIE
TRANQ *same as* > TRANK
TRANQS > TRANQ
TRANQUIL *adj* calm and quiet
TRANS *n* short from of translation
TRANSACT *vb* conduct or negotiate (a business deal)
TRANSACTS > TRANSACT
TRANSAXLE *n* combined axle and gearbox
TRANSCEND *vb* rise above
TRANSDUCE *vb* change one form of energy to another
TRANSE *n* way through; passage
TRANSECT *n* sample strip of land used to monitor plant distribution and animal populations within a given area ▷ *vb* cut or divide crossways
TRANSECTS > TRANSECT
TRANSENNA *n* screen around a shrine
TRANSEPT *n* either of the two shorter wings of a cross-shaped church
TRANSEPTS > TRANSEPT
TRANSES > TRANSE
TRANSEUNT *adj* (of a mental act) causing effects outside the mind
TRANSFARD *old past participle of* > TRANSFER
TRANSFECT *vb* transfer genetic material isolated from a cell or virus into another cell
TRANSFER *vb* move or send from one person or place to another ▷ *n* transferring
TRANSFERS > TRANSFER
TRANSFIX *vb* astound or stun
TRANSFIXT > TRANSFIX
TRANSFORM *vb* change the shape or character of ▷ *n* result of a mathematical transformation
TRANSFUSE *vb* give a transfusion to
TRANSGENE *n* gene that is transferred from an organism of one species to an organism of another species by genetic engineering
TRANSHIP *same as* > TRANSSHIP

RANSHIPS > TRANSHIP
RANSHUME *vb* (of livestock) move to suitable grazing grounds according to the season
RANSIENT *same as* > TRANSEUNT
RANSIRE *n* document allowing goods to pass through customs
RANSIRES > TRANSIRE
RANSIT *n* passage or conveyance of goods or people ▷ *vb* make transit
RANSITED > TRANSIT
RANSITS > TRANSIT
RANSLATE *vb* turn from one language into another
RANSMEW *old variant of* > TRANSMUTE
RANSMEWS > TRANSMEW
RANSMIT *vb* pass (something) from one person or place to another
RANSMITS > TRANSMIT
> TRANSMITTIVITY
RANSMOVE *vb* change the form, character, or substance of
RANSMUTE *vb* change the form or nature of
RANSOM *n* horizontal bar across a window
RANSOMED > TRANSOM
RANSOMS > TRANSOM
RANSONIC *adj* of or relating to conditions when travelling at or near the speed of sound
RANSPIRE *vb* become known
RANSPORT *vb* convey from one place to another ▷ *n* business or system of transporting
RANSPOSE *vb* interchange two things ▷ *n* matrix resulting from interchanging the rows and columns of a given matrix
RANSSHIP *vb* transfer or be transferred from one ship or vehicle to another
RANSUDE *vb* (of a fluid) ooze or pass through interstices, pores, or small holes
RANSUDED > TRANSUDE
RANSUDES > TRANSUDE
RANSUME *vb* make an official transcription of
RANSUMED > TRANSUME
RANSUMES > TRANSUME
RANSUMPT *n* official transcription
RANSVEST *vb* wear clothes traditionally associated with the opposite sex
RANT *vb* travel from place to place selling goods
RANTED > TRANT
RANTER > TRANT
RANTERS > TRANT
TRANTING > TRANT
TRANTS > TRANT
TRAP *n* device for catching animals ▷ *vb* catch
TRAPAN *same as* > TREPAN
TRAPANNED > TRAPAN
TRAPANNER > TRAPAN
TRAPANS > TRAPAN
TRAPBALL *n* old ball game in which a ball is placed in a see-saw device called a trap, flicked up by a batsman hitting one end of the trap, and then hit with a bat
TRAPBALLS > TRAPBALL
TRAPDOOR *n* door in floor or roof
TRAPDOORS > TRAPDOOR
TRAPE *same as* > TRAIPSE
TRAPED > TRAPE
TRAPES *same as* > TRAIPSE
TRAPESED > TRAPES
TRAPESES > TRAPES
TRAPESING > TRAPES
TRAPEZE *n* horizontal bar suspended from two ropes, used by circus acrobats ▷ *vb* swing on a trapeze
TRAPEZED > TRAPEZE
TRAPEZES > TRAPEZE
TRAPEZIA > TRAPEZIUM
TRAPEZIAL > TRAPEZIUM
TRAPEZII > TRAPEZIUS
TRAPEZING > TRAPEZE
TRAPEZIST *n* trapeze artist
TRAPEZIUM *same as* > TRAPEZOID
TRAPEZIUS *n* either of two flat triangular muscles, one covering each side of the back and shoulders, that rotate the shoulder blades
TRAPEZOID *same as* > TRAPEZIUM
TRAPING > TRAPE
TRAPLIKE > TRAP
TRAPLINE *n* line of traps
TRAPLINES > TRAPLINE
TRAPNEST *n* nest that holds a hen in place so that the number of eggs it alone produces can be counted
TRAPNESTS > TRAPNEST
TRAPPEAN *adj* of, relating to, or consisting of igneous rock, esp a basalt
TRAPPED > TRAP
TRAPPER *n* person who traps animals for their fur
TRAPPERS > TRAPPER
TRAPPIER > TRAPPY
TRAPPIEST > TRAPPY
TRAPPING > TRAP
TRAPPINGS *pl n* accessories that symbolize an office or position
TRAPPOSE *adj* of or relating to traprock
TRAPPOUS *same as* > TRAPPOSE
TRAPPY *adj* having many traps
TRAPROCK *another name for* > TRAP
TRAPROCKS > TRAPROCK
TRAPS > TRAP
TRAPT *old past participle of* > TRAP
TRAPUNTO *n* type of quilting that is only partly padded in a design
TRAPUNTOS > TRAPUNTO
TRASH *n* anything worthless ▷ *vb* attack or destroy maliciously
TRASHCAN *n* dustbin
TRASHCANS > TRASHCAN
TRASHED *adj* drunk
TRASHER > TRASH
TRASHERS > TRASH
TRASHERY > TRASH
TRASHES > TRASH
TRASHIER > TRASHY
TRASHIEST > TRASHY
TRASHILY > TRASHY
TRASHING > TRASH
TRASHMAN *another name for* > BINMAN
TRASHMEN > TRASHMAN
TRASHTRIE *n* trash
TRASHY *adj* cheap, worthless, or badly made
TRASS *n* variety of the volcanic rock tuff, used to make a hydraulic cement
TRASSES > TRASS
TRAT *n* type of fishing line holding a series of baited hooks
TRATS > TRAT
TRATT *short for* > TRATTORIA
TRATTORIA *n* Italian restaurant
TRATTORIE > TRATTORIA
TRATTS > TRATT
TRAUCHLE *n* work or a task that is tiring, monotonous, and lengthy ▷ *vb* walk or work slowly and wearily
TRAUCHLED *adj* exhausted by long hard work or concern
TRAUCHLES > TRAUCHLE
TRAUMA *n* emotional shock
TRAUMAS > TRAUMA
TRAUMATA > TRAUMA
TRAUMATIC > TRAUMA
TRAVAIL *n* labour or toil ▷ *vb* suffer or labour painfully, esp in childbirth
TRAVAILED > TRAVAIL
TRAVAILS > TRAVAIL
TRAVE *n* stout wooden cage in which difficult horses are shod
TRAVEL *vb* go from one place to another, through an area, or for a specified distance ▷ *n* travelling, esp as a tourist
TRAVELED *same as* > TRAVELLED
TRAVELER *same as* > TRAVELLER
TRAVELERS > TRAVELER
TRAVELING > TRAVEL
TRAVELLED *adj* having experienced or undergone much travelling
TRAVELLER *n* person who makes a journey or travels a lot
TRAVELOG *n* film, lecture, or brochure on travel
TRAVELOGS > TRAVELOG
TRAVELS > TRAVEL
TRAVERSAL > TRAVERSE
TRAVERSE *vb* pass or go over
TRAVERSED > TRAVERSE
TRAVERSER > TRAVERSE
TRAVERSES > TRAVERSE
TRAVERTIN *n* porous rock
TRAVES > TRAVE
TRAVESTY *n* grotesque imitation or mockery ▷ *vb* make or be a travesty of
TRAVIS *same as* > TREVISS
TRAVISES > TRAVIS
TRAVOIS *n* sled used for dragging logs
TRAVOISE *same as* > TRAVOIS
TRAVOISES > TRAVOISE
TRAWL *n* net dragged at deep levels behind a fishing boat ▷ *vb* fish with such a net
TRAWLED > TRAWL
TRAWLER *n* trawling boat
TRAWLERS > TRAWLER
TRAWLEY *same as* > TROLLEY
TRAWLEYS > TRAWLEY
TRAWLING > TRAWL
TRAWLINGS > TRAWL
TRAWLNET *n* large net, usually in the shape of a sock or bag, drawn at deep levels behind special boats (trawlers)
TRAWLNETS > TRAWLNET
TRAWLS > TRAWL
TRAY *n* flat board, usu with a rim, for carrying things
TRAYBIT *n* threepenny bit
TRAYBITS > TRAYBIT
TRAYFUL *n* as many or as much as will fit on a tray
TRAYFULS > TRAYFUL
TRAYNE *old spelling of* > TRAIN
TRAYNED > TRAIN
TRAYNES > TRAYNE
TRAYNING > TRAYNE
TRAYS > TRAY
TRAZODONE *n* drug used to treat depression
TREACHER *n* traitor; treacherous person
TREACHERS > TREACHER
TREACHERY *n* wilful betrayal
TREACHOUR *same as* > TREACHER
TREACLE *n* thick dark syrup produced when sugar is refined ▷ *vb* add treacle to
TREACLED > TREACLE

TREACLES >TREACLE
TREACLIER >TREACLE
TREACLING >TREACLE
TREACLY >TREACLE
TREAD *vb* set one's foot on ▷ *n* way of walking or dancing
TREADED >TREAD
TREADER >TREAD
TREADERS >TREAD
TREADING >TREAD
TREADINGS >TREAD
TREADLE *n* lever worked by the foot to turn a wheel ▷ *vb* work (a machine) with a treadle
TREADLED >TREADLE
TREADLER >TREADLE
TREADLERS >TREADLE
TREADLES >TREADLE
TREADLESS *adj* (of a tyre, for example) having no tread
TREADLING >TREADLE
TREADMILL *n* cylinder turned by treading on steps projecting from it
TREADS >TREAD
TREAGUE *n* agreement to stop fighting
TREAGUES >TREAGUE
TREASON *n* betrayal of one's sovereign or country
TREASONS >TREASON
TREASURE *n* collection of wealth, esp gold or jewels ▷ *vb* prize or cherish
TREASURED >TREASURE
TREASURER *n* official in charge of funds
TREASURES >TREASURE
TREASURY *n* storage place for treasure
TREAT *vb* deal with or regard in a certain manner ▷ *n* pleasure, entertainment, etc given or paid for by someone else
TREATABLE >TREAT
TREATED >TREAT
TREATER >TREAT
TREATERS >TREAT
TREATIES >TREATY
TREATING >TREAT
TREATINGS >TREAT
TREATISE *n* formal piece of writing on a particular subject
TREATISES >TREATISE
TREATMENT *n* medical care
TREATS >TREAT
TREATY *n* signed contract between states
TREBBIANO *n* grape used to make wine
TREBLE *adj* triple ▷ *n* (singer with or part for) a soprano voice ▷ *vb* increase three times
TREBLED >TREBLE
TREBLES >TREBLE
TREBLING >TREBLE
TREBLY >TREBLE
TREBUCHET *n* large medieval siege engine for hurling missiles consisting of a sling on a pivoted wooden arm set in motion by the fall of a weight
TREBUCKET *same as* >TREBUCHET
TRECENTO *n* 14th century, esp with reference to Italian art and literature
TRECENTOS >TRECENTO
TRECK *same as* >TREK
TRECKED >TRECK
TRECKING >TRECK
TRECKS >TRECK
TREDDLE *variant spelling of* >TREADLE
TREDDLED >TREDDLE
TREDDLES >TREDDLE
TREDDLING >TREDDLE
TREDILLE *same as* >TREDRILLE
TREDILLES >TREDILLE
TREDRILLE *n* card game for three players
TREE *n* large perennial plant with a woody trunk
TREED >TREE
TREEHOUSE *n* house built in tree
TREEING >TREE
TREELAWN *n* narrow band of grass between a road and a pavement, usually planted with trees
TREELAWNS >TREELAWN
TREELESS >TREE
TREELIKE >TREE
TREEN *adj* made of wood ▷ *n* art of making treenware
TREENAIL *n* dowel used for pinning planks or timbers together
TREENAILS >TREENAIL
TREENS >TREEN
TREENWARE *n* dishes and other household utensils made of wood, as by pioneers in North America
TREES >TREE
TREESHIP *n* state of being a tree
TREESHIPS >TREESHIP
TREETOP *n* top of a tree
TREETOPS >TREETOP
TREEWARE *n* books, magazines, or other reading materials that are printed on paper made from wood pulp as opposed to texts in the form of computer software, CD-ROM, audio books, etc
TREEWARES >TREEWARE
TREEWAX *n* yellowish wax secreted by an oriental scale insect
TREEWAXES >TREEWAX
TREF *adj* in Judaism, ritually unfit to be eaten
TREFA *same as* >TREF
TREFAH *same as* >TREF
TREFOIL *n* plant, such as clover, with a three-lobed leaf
TREFOILED >TREFOIL
TREFOILS >TREFOIL
TREGETOUR *n* juggler
TREHALA *n* edible sugary substance obtained from the pupal cocoon of an Asian weevil
TREHALAS >TREHALA
TREHALOSE *n* white crystalline disaccharide that occurs in yeast and certain fungi
TREIF *same as* >TREF
TREIFA *same as* >TREF
TREILLAGE *n* latticework
TREILLE *another word for* >TRELLIS
TREILLES >TREILLE
TREK *n* long difficult journey, esp on foot ▷ *vb* make such a journey
TREKKED >TREK
TREKKER >TREK
TREKKERS >TREK
TREKKING >TREK
TREKS >TREK
TRELLIS *n* framework of horizontal and vertical strips of wood ▷ *vb* interweave (strips of wood, etc) to make a trellis
TRELLISED >TRELLIS
TRELLISES >TRELLIS
TREMA *n* mark consisting of two dots placed over the second of two adjacent vowels to indicate it is to be pronounced separately rather than forming a diphthong with the first
TREMAS >TREMA
TREMATIC *adj* relating to the gills
TREMATODE *n* parasitic flatworm
TREMATOID >TREMATODE
TREMBLANT *adj* (of jewels) set in such a way that they shake when the wearer moves
TREMBLE *vb* shake or quiver ▷ *n* trembling
TREMBLED >TREMBLE
TREMBLER *n* device that vibrates to make or break an electrical circuit
TREMBLERS >TREMBLER
TREMBLES *n* disease of cattle and sheep characterized by muscular incoordination and tremor, caused by ingestion of white snakeroot or rayless goldenrod
TREMBLIER >TREMBLE
TREMBLING >TREMBLE
TREMBLY >TREMBLE
TREMIE *n* large metal hopper and pipe used to distribute freshly mixed concrete over an underwater site.
TREMIES >TREMIE
TREMOLANT *another word for* >TREMOLO
TREMOLITE *n* white or pale green mineral of the amphibole group consisting of calcium magnesium silicate
TREMOLO *n* quivering effec in singing or playing
TREMOLOS >TREMOLO
TREMOR *n* involuntary shaking ▷ *vb* tremble
TREMORED >TREMOR
TREMORING >TREMOR
TREMOROUS >TREMOR
TREMORS >TREMOR
TREMULANT *n* device on an organ by which the wind stream is made to fluctuate in intensity producing a tremolo effec
TREMULATE *vb* produce a tremulous sound
TREMULOUS *adj* trembling, as from fear or excitemen
TRENAIL *same as* >TREENAIL
TRENAILS >TRENAIL
TRENCH *n* long narrow ditch, esp one used as a shelter in war ▷ *adj* of or involving military trenches ▷ *vb* make a trench in (a place)
TRENCHAND *old variant of* >TRENCHANT
TRENCHANT *adj* incisive
TRENCHARD *same as* >TRENCHER
TRENCHED >TRENCH
TRENCHER *n* wooden plate for serving food
TRENCHERS >TRENCHER
TRENCHES >TRENCH
TRENCHING >TRENCH
TREND *n* general tendency or direction ▷ *vb* take a certain trend
TRENDED >TREND
TRENDIER >TRENDY
TRENDIES >TRENDY
TRENDIEST >TRENDY
TRENDIFY *vb* render fashionable
TRENDILY >TRENDY
TRENDING >TREND
TRENDOID *n* follower of trends
TRENDOIDS >TRENDOID
TRENDS >TREND
TRENDY *n* consciously fashionable (person) ▷ *ac* consciously fashionable
TRENDYISM >TRENDY
TRENISE *n* one of the figures in a quadrille
TRENISES >TRENISE
TRENTAL *n* mass said in remembrance of a person 30 days after his or her

leath
ENTALS >TRENTAL
EPAN *same as* >TREPHINE
EPANG *n* any of various arge sea cucumbers of ropical Oriental seas, he body walls of which re used as food by the apanese and Chinese
EPANGS >TREPANG
EPANNED >TREPAN
EPANNER >TREPAN
EPANS >TREPAN
EPHINE *n* surgical awlike instrument for emoving circular sections of bone, esp from the skull ▷ *vb* remove a circular ection of bone from (esp he skull)
EPHINED >TREPHINE
EPHINER >TREPHINE
EPHINES >TREPHINE
EPID *adj* trembling
EPIDANT *adj* trembling
EPONEMA *n* anaerobic pirochaete bacterium hat causes syphilis
EPONEME *same s* >TREPONEMA
ES *adj* very
ESPASS *vb* go onto nother's property vithout permission ▷ *n* respassing
ESS *n* lock of hair, esp a ong lock of woman's hair ▷ *vb* arrange in tresses
ESSED *adj* having a tress r tresses as specified
ESSEL *variant spelling f* >TRESTLE
ESSELS >TRESSEL
ESSES >TRESS
ESSIER >TRESS
ESSIEST >TRESS
ESSING >TRESS
ESSOUR *same s* >TRESSURE
ESSOURS >TRESSOUR
ESSURE *n* narrow inner order on a shield, usually ecorated with fleurs-le-lys
ESSURED >TRESSURE
ESSURES >TRESSURE
ESSY >TRESS
EST *old variant f* >TRESTLE
ESTLE *n* board fixed on airs of spreading legs, sed as a support
ESTLES >TRESTLE
ESTS >TREST
ET *n* (formerly) an llowance according o weight granted to urchasers for waste due o transportation
ETINOIN *n* retinoid drug sed to treat certain skin onditions
ETS >TRET
EVALLY *n* any of various food and game fishes
TREVALLYS >TREVALLY
TREVET *same as* >TRIVET
TREVETS >TREVET
TREVIS *variant spelling of* >TREVISS
TREVISES >TREVIS
TREVISS *n* partition in a stable for keeping animals apart
TREVISSES >TREVISS
TREW *old variant spelling of* >TRUE
TREWS *pl n* close-fitting tartan trousers
TREWSMAN *n* Highlander
TREWSMEN >TREWSMAN
TREY *n* any card or dice throw with three spots
TREYBIT *same as* >TRAYBIT
TREYBITS >TREYBIT
TREYS >TREY
TREZ *same as* >TREY
TREZES >TREZ
TRIABLE *adj* liable to be tried judicially
TRIAC *n* device for regulating the amount of electric current allowed to reach a circuit
TRIACID *adj* (of a base) capable of reacting with three molecules of a monobasic acid
TRIACIDS >TRIACID
TRIACS >TRIAC
TRIACT *adj* having three rays
TRIACTINE *same as* >TRIACT
TRIAD *n* group of three
TRIADIC *n* something that has the characteristics of a triad
TRIADICS >TRIADIC
TRIADISM >TRIAD
TRIADISMS >TRIAD
TRIADIST >TRIAD
TRIADISTS >TRIAD
TRIADS >TRIAD
TRIAGE *n* (in a hospital) the principle or practice of sorting emergency patients into categories of priority for treatment ▷ *vb* sort (patients) into categories of priority for treatment
TRIAGED >TRIAGE
TRIAGES >TRIAGE
TRIAGING >TRIAGE
TRIAL *n* investigation of a case before a judge
TRIALISM *n* belief that man consists of body, soul, and spirit
TRIALISMS >TRIALISM
TRIALIST *same as* >TRIALLIST
TRIALISTS >TRIALIST
TRIALITY >TRIALISM
TRIALLED >TRIAL
TRIALLING >TRIAL
TRIALLIST *n* person who takes part in a competition
TRIALOGUE *n* dialogue between three people
TRIALS >TRIAL
TRIALWARE *n* computer software that can be used without charge for a limited evaluation period
TRIANGLE *n* geometric figure with three sides
TRIANGLED >TRIANGLE
TRIANGLES >TRIANGLE
TRIAPSAL *adj* (of a church) having three apses
TRIARCH *n* one of three rulers of a triarchy
TRIARCHS >TRIARCH
TRIARCHY *n* government by three people
TRIASSIC *adj* of, denoting, or formed in the first period of the Mesozoic era
TRIATHLON *n* athletic contest in which each athlete competes in three different events: swimming, cycling, and running
TRIATIC *n* rope between a ship's mastheads
TRIATICS >TRIATIC
TRIATOMIC *adj* a molecule having three atoms
TRIAXIAL *adj* having three axes ▷ *n* sponge spicule with three axes
TRIAXIALS >TRIAXIAL
TRIAXON *another name for* >TRIAXIAL
TRIAXONS >TRIAXON
TRIAZIN *same as* >TRIAZINE
TRIAZINE *n* any of three azines that contain three nitrogen atoms in their molecules
TRIAZINES >TRIAZINE
TRIAZINS >TRIAZIN
TRIAZOLE *n* heterocyclic compound
TRIAZOLES >TRIAZOLE
TRIAZOLIC >TRIAZOLE
TRIBADE *n* lesbian, esp one who practises tribadism
TRIBADES >TRIBADE
TRIBADIC >TRIBADE
TRIBADIES >TRIBADY
TRIBADISM *n* lesbian practice in which one partner lies on top of the other and simulates the male role in heterosexual intercourse
TRIBADY *another word for* >TRIBADISM
TRIBAL *adj* of or denoting a tribe or tribes
TRIBALISM *n* loyalty to a tribe
TRIBALIST >TRIBALISM
TRIBALLY >TRIBAL
TRIBALS >TRIBAL
TRIBASIC *adj* (of an acid) containing three replaceable hydrogen atoms in the molecule
TRIBBLE *n* frame for drying paper
TRIBBLES >TRIBBLE
TRIBE *n* group of clans or families believed to have a common ancestor
TRIBELESS >TRIBE
TRIBES >TRIBE
TRIBESMAN *n* member of a tribe
TRIBESMEN >TRIBESMAN
TRIBLET *n* spindle or mandrel used in making rings, tubes, etc
TRIBLETS >TRIBLET
TRIBOLOGY *n* study of friction, lubrication, and wear between moving surfaces
TRIBRACH *n* metrical foot of three short syllables
TRIBRACHS >TRIBRACH
TRIBULATE *vb* trouble
TRIBUNAL *n* board appointed to inquire into a specific matter
TRIBUNALS >TRIBUNAL
TRIBUNARY >TRIBUNE
TRIBUNATE *n* office or rank of a tribune
TRIBUNE *n* people's representative, esp in ancient Rome
TRIBUNES >TRIBUNE
TRIBUTARY *n* stream or river flowing into a larger one ▷ *adj* (of a stream or river) flowing into a larger one
TRIBUTE *n* sign of respect or admiration
TRIBUTER *n* miner
TRIBUTERS >TRIBUTER
TRIBUTES >TRIBUTE
TRICAR *n* car with three wheels
TRICARS >TRICAR
TRICE *n* moment ▷ *vb* haul up or secure
TRICED >TRICE
TRICEP *same as* >TRICEPS
TRICEPS *n* muscle at the back of the upper arm
TRICEPSES >TRICEPS
TRICERION *n* candlestick with three arms
TRICES >TRICE
TRICHINA *n* parasitic nematode worm, occurring in the intestines of pigs, rats, and man and producing larvae that form cysts in skeletal muscle
TRICHINAE >TRICHINA
TRICHINAL >TRICHINA
TRICHINAS >TRICHINA
TRICHITE *n* any of various needle-shaped crystals that occur in some glassy volcanic rocks
TRICHITES >TRICHITE
TRICHITIC >TRICHITE

TRICHOID *adj* resembling a hair
TRICHOME *n* any hairlike outgrowth from the surface of a plant
TRICHOMES > TRICHOME
TRICHOMIC > TRICHOME
TRICHORD *n* musical instrument with three strings
TRICHORDS > TRICHORD
TRICHOSES > TRICHOSIS
TRICHOSIS *n* any abnormal condition or disease of the hair
TRICHROIC *n* state of having three colours
TRICHROME *adj* three-coloured
TRICING > TRICE
TRICK *n* deceitful or cunning action or plan ▷ *vb* cheat or deceive
TRICKED > TRICK
TRICKER > TRICK
TRICKERS > TRICK
TRICKERY *n* practice or an instance of using tricks
TRICKIE *Scots form of* > TRICKY
TRICKIER > TRICKY
TRICKIEST > TRICKY
TRICKILY > TRICKY
TRICKING > TRICK
TRICKINGS > TRICK
TRICKISH *same as* > TRICKY
TRICKLE *vb* (cause to) flow in a thin stream or drops ▷ *n* gradual flow
TRICKLED > TRICKLE
TRICKLES > TRICKLE
TRICKLESS > TRICK
TRICKLET *n* tiny trickle
TRICKLETS > TRICKLET
TRICKLIER > TRICKLE
TRICKLING > TRICKLE
TRICKLY > TRICKLE
TRICKS > TRICK
TRICKSIER > TRICKSY
TRICKSOME *adj* full of tricks
TRICKSTER *n* person who deceives or plays tricks
TRICKSY *adj* playing tricks habitually
TRICKY *adj* difficult, needing careful handling
TRICLAD *n* type of worm having a tripartite intestine
TRICLADS > TRICLAD
TRICLINIA *n* plural of triclinium: in Ancient Rome, reclining couch
TRICLINIC *adj* relating to or belonging to the crystal system characterized by three unequal axes, no pair of which are perpendicular
TRICLOSAN *n* drug used to treat skin infections
TRICOLOR *same as* > TRICOLOUR
TRICOLORS > TRICOLOR
TRICOLOUR *n* three-coloured striped flag ▷ *adj* having or involving three colours
TRICORN *n* cocked hat with opposing brims turned back and caught in three places ▷ *adj* having three horns or corners
TRICORNE *same as* > TRICORN
TRICORNES > TRICORNE
TRICORNS > TRICORN
TRICOT *n* thin rayon or nylon fabric knitted or resembling knitting, used for dresses, etc
TRICOTINE *n* twill-weave woollen fabric resembling gabardine
TRICOTS > TRICOT
TRICROTIC *adj* (of the pulse) having a tracing characterized by three elevations with each beat
TRICTRAC *n* game similar to backgammon
TRICTRACS > TRICTRAC
TRICUSPID *adj* having three points, cusps, or segments ▷ *n* tooth having three cusps
TRICYCLE *n* three-wheeled cycle ▷ *vb* ride a tricycle
TRICYCLED > TRICYCLE
TRICYCLER > TRICYCLE
TRICYCLES > TRICYCLE
TRICYCLIC *adj* (of a chemical compound) containing three rings in the molecular structure ▷ *n* antidepressant drug having a tricyclic molecular structure
TRIDACNA *n* giant clam
TRIDACNAS > TRIDACNA
TRIDACTYL *adj* having three digits on one hand or foot
TRIDARN *n* sideboard with three levels
TRIDARNS > TRIDARN
TRIDE *old spelling of the past tense of* > TRY
TRIDENT *n* three-pronged spear ▷ *adj* having three prongs
TRIDENTAL *adj* having three prongs, teeth, etc
TRIDENTED *adj* having three prongs
TRIDENTS > TRIDENT
TRIDUAN *adj* three days long
TRIDUUM *n* period of three days for prayer before a feast
TRIDUUMS > TRIDUUM
TRIDYMITE *n* form of silica
TRIE *old spelling of* > TRY
TRIECIOUS *adj* (of a plant) having male, female, and hermaphroditic flowers
TRIED > TRY
TRIELLA *n* three nominated horse races in which the punter bets on selecting the three winners
TRIELLAS > TRIELLA
TRIENE *n* chemical compound containing three double bonds
TRIENES > TRIENE
TRIENNIA > TRIENNIUM
TRIENNIAL *adj* happening every three years ▷ *n* relating to, lasting for, or occurring every three years
TRIENNIUM *n* period or cycle of three years
TRIENS *n* Byzantine gold goin worth one third of a solidus
TRIENTES > TRIENS
TRIER *n* person or thing that tries
TRIERARCH *n* citizen responsible for fitting out a state trireme, esp in Athens
TRIERS > TRIER
TRIES > TRY
TRIETERIC *adj* occurring once every two years
TRIETHYL *adj* consisting of three groups of ethyls
TRIFACIAL *adj* relating to the trigeminal nerve
TRIFECTA *n* form of betting in which the punter selects the first three place-winners in a horse race in the correct order
TRIFECTAS > TRIFECTA
TRIFF *adj* terrific; very good indeed
TRIFFER > TRIFF
TRIFFEST > TRIFF
TRIFFIC *adj* terrific; very good indeed
TRIFFID *n* any of a species of fictional plants that supposedly grew to a gigantic size, were capable of moving about, and could kill humans
TRIFFIDS > TRIFFID
TRIFFIDY *adj* resembling a triffid
TRIFID *adj* divided or split into three parts or lobes
TRIFLE *n* insignificant thing or amount ▷ *vb* deal (with) as if worthless
TRIFLED > TRIFLE
TRIFLER > TRIFLE
TRIFLERS > TRIFLE
TRIFLES > TRIFLE
TRIFLING *adj* insignificant
TRIFLINGS > TRIFLE
TRIFOCAL *adj* having three focuses ▷ *n* glasses that have trifocal lenses
TRIFOCALS > TRIFOCAL
TRIFOLD *less common word for* > TRIPLE
TRIFOLIES > TRIFOLY
TRIFOLIUM *n* leguminous plant with leaves divided into three leaflets and dense heads of small white, yellow, red, or purple flowers
TRIFOLY *same as* > TREFO[IL]
TRIFORIA > TRIFORIUM
TRIFORIAL > TRIFORIUM
TRIFORIUM *n* arcade abov[e] the arches of the nave, choir, or transept of a church
TRIFORM *adj* having three parts
TRIFORMED *same as* > TRIFORM
TRIG *adj* neat or spruce ▷ *vb* make or become spruce
TRIGAMIES > TRIGAMY
TRIGAMIST > TRIGAMY
TRIGAMOUS > TRIGAMY
TRIGAMY *n* condition of having three spouses
TRIGGED > TRIG
TRIGGER *n* small lever releasing a catch on a gun or machine ▷ *vb* set (an action or process) in motion
TRIGGERED > TRIGGER
TRIGGERS > TRIGGER
TRIGGEST > TRIG
TRIGGING > TRIG
TRIGLOT *n* person who ca[n] speak three languages
TRIGLOTS > TRIGLOT
TRIGLY > TRIG
TRIGLYPH *n* stone block i[n] a Doric frieze, having thr[ee] vertical channels
TRIGLYPHS > TRIGLYPH
TRIGNESS > TRIG
TRIGO *n* wheat field
TRIGON *n* (in classical Greece or Rome) a triangular harp or lyre
TRIGONAL *adj* triangular
TRIGONIC > TRIGON
TRIGONOUS *adj* (of stems, seeds, and similar parts) having a triangular cross section
TRIGONS > TRIGON
TRIGOS > TRIGO
TRIGRAM *n* three-letter inscription
TRIGRAMS > TRIGRAM
TRIGRAPH *n* combinatio[n] of three letters used to represent a single speech sound or phoneme, such as *eau* in French *beau*
TRIGRAPHS > TRIGRAPH
TRIGS > TRIG
TRIGYNIAN *adj* relating t[o] the Trigynia order of plan[ts]
TRIGYNOUS *adj* (of a plant) having three pistils
TRIHEDRA > TRIHEDRON
TRIHEDRAL *adj* having or formed by three plane

aces meeting at a point
▸ *n* figure formed by the
ntersection of three lines
n different planes
:IHEDRON *n* figure
letermined by the
ntersection of three
planes
.IHYBRID *n* hybrid that
liffers from its parents in
hree genetic traits
:IHYDRIC *adj* (of
n alcohol or similar
ompound) containing
hree hydroxyl groups
:IJET *n* jet with three
engines
:IJETS >TRIJET
.IJUGATE *adj* in three
pairs
:IJUGOUS *same*
'S >TRIJUGATE
.IKE *n* tricycle
IKES >TRIKE
.ILBIES >TRILBY
ILBY *n* man's soft felt hat
.ILBYS >TRILBY
ILD *old past tense*
f >TRILL
ILEMMA *n* quandary
posed by three alternative
ourses of action
ILEMMAS >TRILEMMA
ILINEAR *adj* consisting
f, bounded by, or relating
o three lines
ILITH *same*
S >TRILITHON
ILITHIC >TRILITHON
ILITHON *n* structure
onsisting of two upright
tones with a third placed
cross the top, such as
hose of Stonehenge
ILITHS >TRILITH
ILL *n* rapid alternation
etween two notes ▷ *vb*
lay or sing a trill
ILLED >TRILL
ILLER >TRILL
ILLERS >TRILL
ILLING >TRILL
ILLINGS >TRILL
ILLION *n* one million
nillion ▷ *adj* amounting
o a trillion
ILLIONS >TRILLION
ILLIUM *n* plant of Asia
nd North America that
as three leaves at the top
f the stem with a single
white, pink, or purple
hree-petalled flower
ILLIUMS >TRILLIUM
ILLO *n* (in music) a trill
ILLOES >TRILL
ILLS >TRILL
ILOBAL >TRILOBE
ILOBATE *adj* (esp of
leaf) consisting of or
aving three lobes or parts
ILOBE *n* three-lobed
hing
ILOBED *adj* having three
lobes

TRILOBES >TRILOBE
TRILOBITE *n* small prehistoric sea animal
TRILOGIES >TRILOGY
TRILOGY *n* series of three related books, plays, etc
TRIM *adj* neat and smart ▷ *vb* cut or prune into good shape ▷ *n* decoration
TRIMARAN *n* three-hulled boat
TRIMARANS >TRIMARAN
TRIMER *n* polymer or a molecule of a polymer consisting of three identical monomers
TRIMERIC >TRIMER
TRIMERISM >TRIMER
TRIMEROUS *adj* (of plants) having parts arranged in groups of three
TRIMERS >TRIMER
TRIMESTER *n* period of three months
TRIMETER *n* verse line consisting of three metrical feet ▷ *adj* designating such a line
TRIMETERS >TRIMETER
TRIMETHYL *adj* having three methyl groups
TRIMETRIC *adj* of, relating to, or consisting of a trimeter or trimeters
TRIMLY >TRIM
TRIMMED >TRIM
TRIMMER >TRIM
TRIMMERS >TRIM
TRIMMEST >TRIM
TRIMMING >TRIM
TRIMMINGS >TRIM
TRIMNESS >TRIM
TRIMORPH *n* substance, esp a mineral, that exists in three distinct forms
TRIMORPHS >TRIMORPH
TRIMOTOR *n* vehicle with three motors
TRIMOTORS >TRIMOTOR
TRIMS >TRIM
TRIMTAB *n* small control surface attached to the trailing edge of a main control surface to enable the pilot to balance an aircraft
TRIMTABS >TRIMTAB
TRIN *n* triplet
TRINAL >TRINE
TRINARY *adj* made up of three parts
TRINDLE *vb* move heavily on (or as if on) wheels
TRINDLED >TRINDLE
TRINDLES >TRINDLE
TRINDLING >TRINDLE
TRINE *n* aspect of 120° between two planets, an orb of 8° being allowed ▷ *adj* of or relating to a trine ▷ *vb* put in a trine aspect

TRINED >TRINE
TRINES >TRINE
TRINGLE *n* slim rod
TRINGLES >TRINGLE
TRINING >TRINE
TRINITIES >TRINITY
TRINITRIN *n* pale yellow viscous explosive liquid substance made from glycerol and nitric and sulphuric acids
TRINITY *n* group of three
TRINKET *n* small or worthless ornament or piece of jewellery ▷ *vb* ornament with trinkets
TRINKETED >TRINKET
TRINKETER >TRINKET
TRINKETRY >TRINKET
TRINKETS >TRINKET
TRINKUM *n* trinket or bauble
TRINKUMS >TRINKUM
TRINODAL *adj* having three nodes
TRINOMIAL *adj* consisting of or relating to three terms ▷ *n* polynomial consisting of three terms, such as $ax^2 + bx + c$
TRINS >TRIN
TRIO *n* group of three
TRIODE *n* electronic valve having three electrodes, a cathode, an anode, and a grid
TRIODES >TRIODE
TRIOL *n* any of a class of alcohols that have three hydroxyl groups per molecule
TRIOLEIN *n* naturally occurring glyceride of oleic acid, found in fats and oils
TRIOLEINS >TRIOLEIN
TRIOLET *n* verse form of eight lines
TRIOLETS >TRIOLET
TRIOLS >TRIOL
TRIONES *n* seven stars of the constellation Ursa Major
TRIONYM *another name for* >TRINOMIAL
TRIONYMAL >TRIONYM
TRIONYMS >TRIONYM
TRIOR *old form of* >TRIER
TRIORS >TRIOR
TRIOS >TRIO
TRIOSE *n* simple monosaccharide produced by the oxidation of glycerol
TRIOSES >TRIOSE
TRIOXID *same as* >TRIOXIDE
TRIOXIDE *n* any oxide that contains three oxygen atoms per molecule
TRIOXIDES >TRIOXIDE
TRIOXIDS >TRIOXIDE
TRIOXYGEN *technical name for* >OXYGEN
TRIP *n* journey to a place and back, esp for pleasure ▷ *vb* (cause to) stumble

TRIPACK *n* pack of three
TRIPACKS >TRIPACK
TRIPART *adj* composed of three parts
TRIPE *n* stomach of a cow used as food
TRIPEDAL *adj* having three feet
TRIPERIES >TRIPERY
TRIPERY *n* place where tripe is prepared
TRIPES >TRIPE
TRIPEY >TRIPE
TRIPHASE *adj* having three phases
TRIPHONE *n* group of three phonemes
TRIPHONES >TRIPHONE
TRIPIER >TRIPE
TRIPIEST >TRIPE
TRIPITAKA *n* three collections of books making up the Buddhist canon of scriptures
TRIPLANE *n* aeroplane having three wings arranged one above the other
TRIPLANES >TRIPLANE
TRIPLE *adj* having three parts ▷ *vb* increase three times ▷ *n* something that is, or contains, three times as much as normal
TRIPLED >TRIPLE
TRIPLES >TRIPLE
TRIPLET *n* one of three babies born at one birth
TRIPLETS >TRIPLET
TRIPLEX *n* building divided into three separate dwellings
TRIPLEXES >TRIPLEX
TRIPLIED >TRIPLY
TRIPLIES >TRIPLY
TRIPLING >TRIPLE
TRIPLINGS >TRIPLE
TRIPLITE *n* brownish-red phosphate
TRIPLITES >TRIPLITE
TRIPLOID *adj* having or relating to three times the haploid number of chromosomes ▷ *n* triploid organism
TRIPLOIDS >TRIPLOID
TRIPLOIDY *n* triploid state
TRIPLY *vb* give a reply to a duply
TRIPLYING >TRIPLY
TRIPOD *n* three-legged stand, stool, etc
TRIPODAL >TRIPOD
TRIPODIC >TRIPOD
TRIPODIES >TRIPODY
TRIPODS >TRIPOD
TRIPODY *n* metrical unit consisting of three feet
TRIPOLI *n* lightweight porous siliceous rock derived by weathering and used in a powdered form as a polish, filter, etc
TRIPOLIS >TRIPOLI

TRIPOS *n* final examinations for an honours degree at Cambridge University
TRIPOSES > TRIPOS
TRIPPANT *adj* (in heraldry) in the process of tripping
TRIPPED > TRIP
TRIPPER *n* tourist
TRIPPERS > TRIPPER
TRIPPERY *adj* like a tripper
TRIPPET *n* any mechanism that strikes or is struck at regular intervals, as by a cam
TRIPPETS > TRIPPET
TRIPPIER > TRIPPY
TRIPPIEST > TRIPPY
TRIPPING > TRIP
TRIPPINGS > TRIP
TRIPPLE *vb* canter
TRIPPLED > TRIPPLE
TRIPPLER > TRIPPLE
TRIPPLERS > TRIPPLE
TRIPPLES > TRIPPLE
TRIPPLING > TRIPPLE
TRIPPY *adj* suggestive of or resembling the effect produced by a hallucinogenic drug
TRIPS > TRIP
TRIPSES > TRIPSIS
TRIPSIS *n* act of kneading the body to promote circulation, suppleness, etc
TRIPTAN *n* drug used to treat migraine
TRIPTANE *n* colourless highly flammable liquid
TRIPTANES > TRIPTANE
TRIPTANS > TRIPTAN
TRIPTOTE *n* word that has only three cases
TRIPTOTES > TRIPTOTE
TRIPTYCA *variant of* > TRIPTYCH
TRIPTYCAS > TRIPTYCA
TRIPTYCH *n* painting or carving on three hinged panels, often forming an altarpiece
TRIPTYCHS > TRIPTYCH
TRIPTYQUE *n* customs permit for the temporary importation of a motor vehicle
TRIPUDIA > TRIPUDIUM
TRIPUDIUM *n* ancient religious dance
TRIPWIRE *n* wire that activates a trap, mine, etc, when tripped over
TRIPWIRES > TRIPWIRE
TRIPY > TRIPE
TRIQUETRA *n* ornament in the shape of three intersecting ellipses roughly forming a triangle
TRIRADIAL *adj* having or consisting of three rays or radiating branches
TRIREME *n* ancient Greek warship with three rows of oars on each side
TRIREMES > TRIREME
TRISAGION *n* old hymn
TRISCELE *variant spelling of* > TRISKELE
TRISCELES > TRISCELE
TRISECT *vb* divide into three parts, esp three equal parts
TRISECTED > TRISECT
TRISECTOR > TRISECT
TRISECTS > TRISECT
TRISEME *n* metrical foot of a length equal to three short syllables
TRISEMES > TRISEME
TRISEMIC > TRISEME
TRISERIAL *adj* arranged in three rows or series
TRISHAW *another name for* > RICKSHAW
TRISHAWS > TRISHAW
TRISKELE *n* three-limbed symbol
TRISKELES > TRISKELE
TRISKELIA *n* plural of singular triskelion: three-limbed symbol
TRISMIC > TRISMUS
TRISMUS *n* state of being unable to open the mouth because of sustained contractions of the jaw muscles, caused by tetanus
TRISMUSES > TRISMUS
TRISODIUM *adj* containing three sodium atoms
TRISOME *n* chromosome occurring three times (rather than twice) in a cell
TRISOMES > TRISOME
TRISOMIC > TRISOMY
TRISOMICS *n* study of trisomy
TRISOMIES > TRISOMY
TRISOMY *n* condition of having one chromosome of the set represented three times in an otherwise diploid organism, cell, etc
TRIST *variant spelling of* > TRISTE
TRISTATE *adj* (of a digital computer chip) having high, low, and floating output states
TRISTE *adj* sad
TRISTESSE *n* sadness
TRISTEZA *n* disease affecting citrus trees
TRISTEZAS > TRISTEZA
TRISTFUL *same as* > TRISTE
TRISTICH *n* poem, stanza, or strophe that consists of three lines
TRISTICHS > TRISTICH
TRISUL *n* trident symbol of Siva
TRISULA *same as* > TRISUL
TRISULAS > TRISULA
TRISULS > TRISUL
TRITE *adj* (of a remark or idea) commonplace and unoriginal ▷ *n* (on a lyre) the third string from the highest in pitch
TRITELY > TRITE
TRITENESS > TRITE
TRITER > TRITE
TRITES > TRITE
TRITEST > TRITE
TRITHEISM *n* belief in three gods, esp in the Trinity as consisting of three distinct gods
TRITHEIST > TRITHEISM
TRITHING *n* tripartition
TRITHINGS > TRITHING
TRITIATE *vb* replace normal hydrogen atoms in (a compound) by those of tritium
TRITIATED > TRITIATE
TRITIATES > TRITIATE
TRITICAL *n* trite; hackneyed
TRITICALE *n* fertile hybrid cereal
TRITICISM *n* something trite
TRITICUM *n* any annual cereal grass of the genus *Triticum*, which includes the wheats
TRITICUMS > TRITICUM
TRITIDE *n* tritium compound
TRITIDES > TRITIDE
TRITIUM *n* radioactive isotope of hydrogen
TRITIUMS > TRITIUM
TRITOMA *another name for* > KNIPHOFIA
TRITOMAS > TRITOMA
TRITON *n* any of various chiefly tropical marine gastropod molluscs, having large beautifully-coloured spiral shells
TRITONE *n* musical interval consisting of three whole tones
TRITONES > TRITONE
TRITONIA *n* any plant of the perennial cormous S. African genus *Tritonia*, with typically scarlet or orange flowers
TRITONIAS > TRITONIA
TRITONS > TRITON
TRITURATE *vb* grind or rub into a fine powder or pulp ▷ *n* powder or pulp resulting from this grinding
TRIUMPH *n* (happiness caused by) victory or success ▷ *vb* be victorious or successful
TRIUMPHAL *adj* celebrating a triumph
TRIUMPHED > TRIUMPH
TRIUMPHER > TRIUMPH
TRIUMPHS > TRIUMPH
TRIUMVIR *n* (esp in ancient Rome) a member of a triumvirate
TRIUMVIRI > TRIUMVIR
TRIUMVIRS > TRIUMVIR
TRIUMVIRY *n* triumvirate
TRIUNE *adj* constituting three in one, esp the thre persons in one God of the Trinity ▷ *n* group of thre
TRIUNES > TRIUNE
TRIUNITY > TRIUNE
TRIVALENT *adj* having a valency of three
TRIVALVE *n* animal havin three valves
TRIVALVED *adj* having three valves
TRIVALVES > TRIVALVE
TRIVET *n* metal stand for pot or kettle
TRIVETS > TRIVET
TRIVIA *pl n* trivial things or details
TRIVIAL *adj* of little importance
TRIVIALLY > TRIVIAL
TRIVIUM *n* (in medieval learning) the lower division of the seven liberal arts, consisting of grammar, rhetoric, and logic
TRIVIUMS > TRIVIUM
TRIWEEKLY *adv* every thre weeks ▷ *n* triweekly publication
TRIZONAL > TRIZONE
TRIZONE *n* area comprisi three zones
TRIZONES > TRIZONE
TROAD *same as* > TROD
TROADE *same as* > TROD
TROADES > TROADE
TROADS > TROAD
TROAK *old form of* > TRUCK
TROAKED > TROAK
TROAKING > TROAK
TROAKS > TROAK
TROAT *vb* (of a rutting buc to call or bellow
TROATED > TROAT
TROATING > TROAT
TROATS > TROAT
TROCAR *n* surgical instrument for removing fluid from bodily cavities consisting of a puncturi device situated inside a tube
TROCARS > TROCAR
TROCHAIC *adj* of, relating to, or consisting of trochees ▷ *n* verse composed of trochees
TROCHAICS > TROCHAIC
TROCHAL *adj* shaped like a wheel
TROCHAR *old variant spellin of* > TROCAR
TROCHARS > TROCHAR
TROCHE *another name for* > LOZENGE
TROCHEE *n* metrical foot of one long and one shor syllable

ROCHEES >TROCHEE
ROCHES >TROCHE
ROCHI >TROCHUS
ROCHIL *same as* >TROCHILUS
ROCHILI >TROCHILUS
ROCHILIC *adj* relating to the movement of a hummingbird's wings
ROCHILS >TROCHIL
ROCHILUS *n* any of several Old World warblers
ROCHISK *another word for* >TROCHE
ROCHISKS >TROCHISK
ROCHITE *n* joint of a crinoid
ROCHITES >TROCHITE
ROCHLEA *n* any bony or cartilaginous part with a grooved surface over which a bone, tendon, etc, may slide or articulate
ROCHLEAE >TROCHLEA
ROCHLEAR as in *trochlear nerve* either one of the fourth pair of cranial nerves, which supply the superior oblique muscle of the eye
ROCHLEAS >TROCHLEA
ROCHOID *n* curve described by a fixed point on the radius or extended radius of a circle as the circle rolls along a straight line ▷ *adj* rotating or capable of rotating about a central axis
ROCHOIDS >TROCHOID
ROCHUS *n* hoop (used in exercise)
ROCHUSES >TROCHUS
ROCK *same as* >TRUCK
ROCKED >TROCK
ROCKEN *adj* dry (used of wine, esp German wine)
ROCKING >TROCK
ROCKS >TROCK
ROD *vb* past participle of tread ▷ *n* path
RODDEN >TREAD
RODE *same as* >TROD
RODES >TRODE
RODS >TROD
ROELIE *same as* >TROOLIE
ROELIES >TROELIE
ROELY *same as* >TROOLIE
ROFFER *n* trough-like fixture for holding in place and reflecting light from a fluorescent tube
ROFFERS >TROFFER
ROG *vb* walk, esp aimlessly or heavily
ROGGED >TROG
ROGGING >TROG
ROGGS *n* loyalty; fidelity
ROGON *n* bird of tropical and subtropical regions of America, Africa, and Asia. They have a brilliant plumage, short hooked bill, and long tail
TROGONS >TROGON
TROGS >TROG
TROIKA *n* Russian vehicle drawn by three horses abreast
TROIKAS >TROIKA
TROILISM *n* sexual activity involving three people
TROILISMS >TROILISM
TROILIST >TROILISM
TROILISTS >TROILISM
TROILITE *n* iron sulphide present in most meteorites
TROILITES >TROILITE
TROILUS *n* type of large butterfly
TROILUSES >TROILUS
TROIS *Scots form of* >TROY
TROKE *same as* >TRUCK
TROKED >TROKE
TROKES >TROKE
TROKING >TROKE
TROLAND *n* unit of light intensity in the eye
TROLANDS >TROLAND
TROLL *n* giant or dwarf in Scandinavian folklore ▷ *vb* fish by dragging a lure through the water
TROLLED >TROLL
TROLLER >TROLL
TROLLERS >TROLL
TROLLEY *n* small wheeled table for food and drink
TROLLEYED >TROLLEY
TROLLEYS *pl n* men's underpants
TROLLIED >TROLLY
TROLLIES >TROLLY
TROLLING >TROLL
TROLLINGS >TROLL
TROLLIUS *n* plant with globe-shaped flowers
TROLLOP *n* promiscuous or slovenly woman ▷ *vb* behave like a trollop
TROLLOPED >TROLLOP
TROLLOPEE *n* loose dress or gown
TROLLOPS >TROLLOP
TROLLOPY >TROLLOP
TROLLS >TROLL
TROLLY *same as* >TROLLEY
TROLLYING >TROLLY
TROMBONE *n* brass musical instrument with a sliding tube
TROMBONES >TROMBONE
TROMINO *n* shape made from three squares, each joined to the next along one full side
TROMINOES >TROMINO
TROMINOS >TROMINO
TROMMEL *n* revolving cylindrical sieve used to screen crushed ore
TROMMELS >TROMMEL
TROMP *vb* trample
TROMPE *n* apparatus for supplying the blast of air in a forge, consisting of a thin column down which water falls, drawing in air through side openings
TROMPED >TROMP
TROMPES >TROMPE
TROMPING >TROMP
TROMPS >TROMP
TRON *n* public weighing machine
TRONA *n* greyish mineral that consists of hydrated sodium carbonate and occurs in salt deposits
TRONAS >TRONA
TRONC *n* pool into which waiters, waitresses, hotel workers, etc, pay their tips
TRONCS >TRONC
TRONE *same as* >TRON
TRONES >TRONE
TRONK *n* jail
TRONKS >TRONK
TRONS >TRON
TROOLIE *n* large palm leaf
TROOLIES >TROOLIE
TROOP *n* large group ▷ *vb* move in a crowd
TROOPED >TROOP
TROOPER *n* cavalry soldier
TROOPERS >TROOPER
TROOPIAL *same as* >TROUPIAL
TROOPIALS >TROOPIAL
TROOPING >TROOP
TROOPS >TROOP
TROOPSHIP *n* ship used to transport military personnel
TROOSTITE *n* reddish or greyish mineral that is a variety of willemite in which some of the zinc is replaced by manganese
TROOZ *same as* >TREWS
TROP *adv* too, too much
TROPAEOLA *n* plural of singular tropaeolum (a garden plant)
TROPARIA >TROPARION
TROPARION *n* short hymn
TROPE *n* figure of speech ▷ *vb* use tropes (in speech or writing)
TROPED >TROPE
TROPEOLIN *n* type of dye
TROPES >TROPE
TROPHESY *n* disorder of the nerves relating to nutrition
TROPHI *n* collective term for the mandibles other parts of an insect's mouth
TROPHIC *adj* of or relating to nutrition
TROPHIED >TROPHY
TROPHIES >TROPHY
TROPHY *n* cup, shield, etc given as a prize ▷ *adj* regraded as a highly desirable symbol of wealth or success ▷ *vb* award a trophy to (someone)
TROPHYING >TROPHY
TROPIC *n* either of two lines of latitude at 23½°N (tropic of Cancer) or 23½°S (tropic of Capricorn)
TROPICAL *adj* of or in the tropics ▷ *n* tropical thing or place
TROPICALS >TROPICAL
TROPICS >TROPIC
TROPIN *n* andrenal androgen
TROPINE *n* white crystalline poisonous hygroscopic alkaloid obtained by heating atropine or hyoscyamine with barium hydroxide
TROPINES >TROPINE
TROPING >TROPE
TROPINS >TROPIN
TROPISM *n* tendency of a plant or animal to turn or curve in response to an external stimulus
TROPISMS >TROPISM
TROPIST >TROPISM
TROPISTIC >TROPISM
TROPISTS >TROPISM
TROPOLOGY *n* use of figurative language in speech or writing
TROPONIN *n* muscle-tissue protein involved in the controlling of muscle contraction
TROPONINS >TROPONIN
TROPPO *adv* too much ▷ *adj* mentally affected by a tropical climate
TROSSERS *old form of* >TROUSERS
TROT *vb* (of a horse) move at a medium pace, lifting the feet in diagonal pairs ▷ *n* trotting
TROTH *n* pledge of devotion, esp a betrothal ▷ *vb* promise to marry (someone)
TROTHED >TROTH
TROTHFUL >TROTH
TROTHING >TROTH
TROTHLESS >TROTH
TROTHS >TROTH
TROTLINE *n* long line suspended across a stream, river, etc, to which shorter hooked and baited lines are attached
TROTLINES >TROTLINE
TROTS >TROT
TROTTED >TROT
TROTTER *n* pig's foot
TROTTERS >TROTTER
TROTTING >TROT
TROTTINGS >TROT
TROTTOIR *n* pavement
TROTTOIRS >TROTTOIR
TROTYL *n* trinitrotoluene; a yellow solid: used chiefly as a high explosive and is also an intermediate in the manufacture of dyestuffs
TROTYLS >TROTYL
TROUBLE *n* (cause of) distress or anxiety ▷ *vb*

(cause to) worry
TROUBLED > TROUBLE
TROUBLER > TROUBLE
TROUBLERS > TROUBLE
TROUBLES > TROUBLE
TROUBLING > TROUBLE
TROUBLOUS *adj* unsettled or agitated
TROUCH *n* rubbish
TROUCHES > TROUCH
TROUGH *n* long open container, esp for animals' food or water ▷ *vb* eat, consume, or take greedily
TROUGHS > TROUGH
TROULE *old variant of* > TROLL
TROULED > TROULE
TROULES > TROULE
TROULING > TROULE
TROUNCE *vb* defeat utterly
TROUNCED > TROUNCE
TROUNCER > TROUNCE
TROUNCERS > TROUNCE
TROUNCES > TROUNCE
TROUNCING > TROUNCE
TROUPE *n* company of performers ▷ *vb* (esp of actors) to move or travel in a group
TROUPED > TROUPE
TROUPER *n* member of a troupe
TROUPERS > TROUPER
TROUPES > TROUPE
TROUPIAL *n* any of various American orioles
TROUPIALS > TROUPIAL
TROUPING > TROUPE
TROUSE *pl n* close-fitting breeches worn in Ireland
TROUSER *adj* of trousers ▷ *vb* take (something, esp money), often surreptitiously or unlawfully ▷ *n* of or relating to trousers
TROUSERED > TROUSERS
TROUSERS *pl n* two-legged outer garment with legs reaching usu to the ankles
TROUSES > TROUSE
TROUSSEAU *n* bride's collection of clothing etc for her marriage
TROUT *n* game fish related to the salmon ▷ *vb* fish for trout
TROUTER > TROUT
TROUTERS > TROUT
TROUTFUL *adj* (of a body of water) full of trout
TROUTIER > TROUT
TROUTIEST > TROUT
TROUTING > TROUT
TROUTINGS > TROUT
TROUTLESS > TROUT
TROUTLET *n* small trout
TROUTLETS > TROUTLET
TROUTLING *n* small trout
TROUTS > TROUT
TROUTY > TROUT
TROUVERE *n* any of a group of poets of N France during the 12th and 13th centuries who composed chiefly narrative works
TROUVERES > TROUVERE
TROUVEUR *same as* > TROUVERE
TROUVEURS > TROUVEUR
TROVE as in *treasure-trove* valuable articles, such as coins, bullion, etc, found hidden in the earth or elsewhere and of unknown ownership
TROVER *n* (formerly) the act of wrongfully assuming proprietary rights over personal goods or property belonging to another
TROVERS > TROVER
TROVES > TROVE
TROW *vb* think, believe, or trust
TROWED > TROW
TROWEL *n* hand tool with a wide blade for spreading mortar, lifting plants, etc ▷ *vb* use a trowel on (plaster, soil, etc)
TROWELED > TROWEL
TROWELER > TROWEL
TROWELERS > TROWEL
TROWELING > TROWEL
TROWELLED > TROWEL
TROWELLER > TROWEL
TROWELS > TROWEL
TROWING > TROW
TROWS > TROW
TROWSERS *old spelling of* > TROUSERS
TROWTH *variant spelling of* > TROTH
TROWTHS > TROWTH
TROY as in *troy weight* system of weights used for precious metals and gemstones, based on the grain, which is identical to the avoirdupois grain
TROYS > TROY
TRUANCIES > TRUANT
TRUANCY > TRUANT
TRUANT *n* pupil who stays away from school without permission ▷ *adj* being or relating to a truant ▷ *vb* play truant
TRUANTED > TRUANT
TRUANTING > TRUANT
TRUANTLY > TRUANT
TRUANTRY > TRUANT
TRUANTS > TRUANT
TRUCAGE *n* art forgery
TRUCAGES > TRUCAGE
TRUCE *n* temporary agreement to stop fighting ▷ *vb* make a truce
TRUCED > TRUCE
TRUCELESS > TRUCE
TRUCES > TRUCE
TRUCHMAN *n* interpreter; translator
TRUCHMANS > TRUCHMAN
TRUCHMEN > TRUCHMAN
TRUCIAL > TRUCE
TRUCING > TRUCE
TRUCK *n* railway goods wagon ▷ *vb* exchange (goods); barter
TRUCKABLE > TRUCK
TRUCKAGE *n* conveyance of cargo by truck
TRUCKAGES > TRUCKAGE
TRUCKED > TRUCK
TRUCKER *n* truck driver
TRUCKERS > TRUCKER
TRUCKFUL *n* amount of something that can be conveyed in a truck
TRUCKFULS > TRUCKFUL
TRUCKIE *n* truck driver
TRUCKIES > TRUCKIE
TRUCKING *n* transportation of goods by lorry
TRUCKINGS > TRUCKING
TRUCKLE *vb* yield weakly or give in ▷ *n* small wheel
TRUCKLED > TRUCKLE
TRUCKLER > TRUCKLE
TRUCKLERS > TRUCKLE
TRUCKLES > TRUCKLE
TRUCKLINE *n* organisation that conveys freight by truck
TRUCKLING > TRUCKLE
TRUCKLOAD *n* amount carried by a truck
TRUCKMAN *n* truck driver
TRUCKMEN > TRUCKMAN
TRUCKS > TRUCK
TRUCKSTOP *n* place providing fuel, oil, and often service facilities for truck drivers
TRUCULENT *adj* aggressively defiant
TRUDGE *vb* walk heavily or wearily ▷ *n* long tiring walk
TRUDGED > TRUDGE
TRUDGEN *n* type of swimming stroke that uses overarm action, as in the crawl, and a scissors kick
TRUDGENS > TRUDGEN
TRUDGEON *nonstandard variant of* > TRUDGEN
TRUDGEONS > TRUDGEON
TRUDGER > TRUDGE
TRUDGERS > TRUDGE
TRUDGES > TRUDGE
TRUDGING > TRUDGE
TRUDGINGS > TRUDGE
TRUE *adj* in accordance with facts
TRUEBLUE *n* staunch royalist or Conservative
TRUEBLUES > TRUEBLUE
TRUEBORN *adj* being such by birth
TRUEBRED *adj* thoroughbred
TRUED > TRUE
TRUEING > TRUE
TRUELOVE *n* person that one loves
TRUELOVES > TRUELOVE
TRUEMAN *n* honest person
TRUEMEN > TRUEMAN
TRUENESS > TRUE
TRUEPENNY *n* truthful person
TRUER > TRUE
TRUES > TRUE
TRUEST > TRUE
TRUFFE *rare word for* > TRUFFLE
TRUFFES > TRUFFE
TRUFFLE *n* edible underground fungus ▷ *vb* hunt for truffles
TRUFFLED > TRUFFLE
TRUFFLES > TRUFFLE
TRUFFLING > TRUFFLE
TRUG *n* long shallow baske used by gardeners
TRUGO *n* game similar to croquet, originally improvised in Victoria from the rubber discs used as buffers on railway carriages
TRUGOS > TRUGO
TRUGS > TRUG
TRUING > TRUE
TRUISM *n* self-evident trut
TRUISMS > TRUISM
TRUISTIC > TRUISM
TRULL *n* prostitute
TRULLS > TRULL
TRULY *adv* in a true manne
TRUMEAU *n* section of a wall or pillar between tw openings
TRUMEAUX > TRUMEAU
TRUMP *adj* (card) of the sui outranking the others ▷ *vb* play a trump card on (another card) ▷ *pl n* suit outranking the others
TRUMPED > TRUMP
TRUMPERY *n* something useless or worthless ▷ *ad* useless or worthless
TRUMPET *n* valved brass instrument with a flared tube ▷ *vb* proclaim loudl
TRUMPETED > TRUMPET
TRUMPETER *n* person who plays the trumpet, esp on whose duty it is to play fanfares, signals, etc
TRUMPETS > TRUMPET
TRUMPING > TRUMP
TRUMPINGS > TRUMP
TRUMPLESS > TRUMP
TRUMPS > TRUMP
TRUNCAL *adj* of or relating to the trunk
TRUNCATE *vb* cut short ▷ *adj* cut short
TRUNCATED *adj* (of a cone, pyramid, prism, etc) having an apex or end removed by a plane intersection that is usual nonparallel to the base
TRUNCATES > TRUNCATE
TRUNCHEON *n* club formerly carried by a policeman ▷ *vb* beat wit

a truncheon
RUNDLE *vb* move heavily on wheels ▷ *n* act or an instance of trundling
RUNDLED > TRUNDLE
RUNDLER *n* golf or shopping trolley
RUNDLERS > TRUNDLER
RUNDLES > TRUNDLE
RUNDLING > TRUNDLE
RUNK *n* main stem of a tree ▷ *vb* lop or truncate
RUNKED > TRUNK
RUNKFISH *n* tropical fish, having the body encased in bony plates with openings for the fins, eyes, mouth, etc
RUNKFUL > TRUNK
RUNKFULS > TRUNK
RUNKING *n* cables that take a common route through an exchange building linking ranks of selectors
RUNKINGS > TRUNKING
RUNKLESS > TRUNK
RUNKS *pl n* shorts worn by a man for swimming
RUNNEL *same as* > TREENAIL
RUNNELS > TRUNNEL
RUNNION *n* one of a pair of coaxial projections attached to opposite sides of a container, cannon, etc, to provide a support about which it can turn in a vertical
RUNNIONS > TRUNNION
RUQUAGE *variant of* > TRUCAGE
RUQUAGES > TRUQUAGE
RUQUEUR *n* art forger
RUQUEURS > TRUQUEUR
RUSS *vb* tie or bind up ▷ *n* device for holding a hernia, etc in place
RUSSED > TRUSS
RUSSER > TRUSS
RUSSERS > TRUSS
RUSSES > TRUSS
RUSSING *n* system of trusses, esp for strengthening or reinforcing a structure
RUSSINGS > TRUSSING
RUST *vb* believe in and rely on ▷ *n* confidence in the truth, reliability, etc of a person or thing ▷ *adj* of or relating to a trust or trusts
RUSTABLE > TRUST
RUSTED > TRUST
RUSTEE *n* person holding property on another's behalf ▷ *vb* act as a trustee
RUSTEED > TRUSTEE
RUSTEES > TRUSTEE
RUSTER > TRUST
RUSTERS > TRUST
RUSTFUL *adj* inclined to trust others
TRUSTIER > TRUSTY
TRUSTIES > TRUSTY
TRUSTIEST > TRUSTY
TRUSTILY > TRUSTY
TRUSTING *same as* > TRUSTFUL
TRUSTLESS *adj* untrustworthy
TRUSTOR *n* person who sets up a trust
TRUSTORS > TRUSTOR
TRUSTS > TRUST
TRUSTY *adj* faithful or reliable ▷ *n* trustworthy convict to whom special privileges are granted
TRUTH *n* state of being true
TRUTHFUL *adj* honest
TRUTHIER > TRUTHY
TRUTHIEST > TRUTHY
TRUTHLESS > TRUTH
TRUTHLIKE *n* truthful
TRUTHS > TRUTH
TRUTHY *adj* truthful
TRY *vb* make an effort or attempt ▷ *n* attempt or effort
TRYE *adj* very good; select
TRYER *variant of* > TRIER
TRYERS > TRYER
TRYING > TRY
TRYINGLY > TRY
TRYINGS > TRY
TRYKE *variant spelling of* > TRIKE
TRYKES > TRYKE
TRYMA *n* drupe produced by the walnut and similar plants, in which the endocarp is a hard shell and the epicarp is dehiscent
TRYMATA > TRYMA
TRYOUT *n* a trial or test, as of an athlete or actor
TRYOUTS > TRYOUT
TRYP *n* parastitic protozoan
TRYPAN as in *trypan blue* dye obtained from tolidine that is absorbed by the macrophages of the reticuloendothelial system and is therefore used for staining cells in biological research
TRYPS > TRYP
TRYPSIN *n* enzyme occurring in pancreatic juice
TRYPSINS > TRYPSIN
TRYPTIC > TRYPSIN
TRYSAIL *n* small fore-and-aft sail set on a sailing vessel to help keep her head to the wind in a storm
TRYSAILS > TRYSAIL
TRYST *n* arrangement to meet ▷ *vb* meet at or arrange a tryst
TRYSTE *variant spelling of* > TRYST
TRYSTED > TRYST
TRYSTER > TRYST
TRYSTERS > TRYST
TRYSTES > TRYSTE
TRYSTING > TRYST
TRYSTS > TRYST
TRYWORKS *n* furnace for rendering blubber
TSADDIK *variant of* > ZADDIK
TSADDIKIM > TSADDIK
TSADDIKS > TSADDIK
TSADDIQ *variant of* > ZADDIK
TSADDIQIM > TSADDIQ
TSADDIQS > TSADDIQ
TSADE *variant spelling of* > SADHE
TSADES > TSADE
TSADI *variant of* > SADHE
TSADIS > TSADI
TSAMBA *n* Tibetan dish made from roasted barley and tea
TSAMBAS > TSAMBA
TSANTSA *n* (among the Shuar subgroup of the Jivaro people of Ecuador) shrunken head of an enemy kept as a trophy
TSANTSAS > TSANTSA
TSAR *n* Russian emperor
TSARDOM > TSAR
TSARDOMS > TSAR
TSAREVICH *n* tsar's son
TSAREVNA *n* daughter of a Russian tsar
TSAREVNAS > TSAREVNA
TSARINA *n* wife of a Russian tsar
TSARINAS > TSARINA
TSARISM *n* system of government by a tsar, esp in Russia until 1917
TSARISMS > TSARISM
TSARIST > TSARISM
TSARISTS > TSARISM
TSARITSA *same as* > TSARINA
TSARITSAS > TSARITSA
TSARITZA *variant spelling of* > TSARITSA
TSARITZAS > TSARITZA
TSARS > TSAR
TSATSKE *variant of* > TCHOTCHKE
TSATSKES > TSATSKE
TSESSEBE *South African variant of* > SASSABY
TSESSEBES > TSESSEBE
TSETSE *n* any of various bloodsucking African dipterous flies which transmit the pathogens of various diseases
TSETSES > TSETSE
TSIGANE *variant of* > TZIGANE
TSIGANES > TSIGANE
TSIMMES *variant spelling of* > TZIMMES
TSITSITH *n* tassels or fringes of thread attached to the four corners of the tallith
TSK *vb* utter the sound "tsk", usu in disapproval
TSKED > TSK
TSKING > TSK
TSKS > TSK
TSKTSK *same as* > TSK
TSKTSKED > TSKTSK
TSKTSKING > TSKTSK
TSKTSKS > TSKTSK
TSOORIS *variant of* > TSURIS
TSORES *variant of* > TSURIS
TSORIS *variant of* > TSURIS
TSORRISS *variant of* > TSURIS
TSOTSI *n* Black street thug or gang member
TSOTSIS > TSOTSI
TSOURIS *variant of* > TSURIS
TSOURISES > TSOURIS
TSUBA *n* sword guard of a Japanese sword
TSUBAS > TSUBA
TSUNAMI *n* tidal wave, usu caused by an earthquake under the sea
TSUNAMIC > TSUNAMI
TSUNAMIS > TSUNAMI
TSURIS *n* grief or strife
TSURISES > TSURIS
TSUTSUMU *n* Japanese art of wrapping gifts
TSUTSUMUS > TSUTSUMU
TUAN *n* lord
TUANS > TUAN
TUART *n* eucalyptus tree of Australia, yielding a very durable light-coloured timber
TUARTS > TUART
TUATARA *n* large lizard-like New Zealand reptile
TUATARAS > TUATARA
TUATERA *variant spelling of* > TUATARA
TUATERAS > TUATERA
TUATH *n* territory of an ancient Irish tribe
TUATHS > TUATH
TUATUA *n* edible marine bivalve of New Zealand waters
TUB *n* open, usu round container ▷ *vb* wash (oneself or another) in a tub
TUBA *n* valved low-pitched brass instrument
TUBAE > TUBA
TUBAGE *n* insertion of a tube
TUBAGES > TUBAGE
TUBAIST > TUBA
TUBAISTS > TUBA
TUBAL *adj* of or relating to a tube
TUBAR *another word for* > TUBULAR
TUBAS > TUBA
TUBATE *less common word for* > TUBULAR
TUBBABLE > TUB
TUBBED > TUB
TUBBER > TUB
TUBBERS > TUB
TUBBIER > TUBBY
TUBBIEST > TUBBY

TUBBINESS > TUBBY
TUBBING > TUB
TUBBINGS > TUB
TUBBISH *adj* fat
TUBBY *adj* (of a person) short and fat
TUBE *n* hollow cylinder
TUBECTOMY *n* excision of the Fallopian tubes
TUBED > TUBE
TUBEFUL *n* quantity (of something) that a tube can hold
TUBEFULS > TUBEFUL
TUBELESS *adj* without a tube
TUBELIKE *adj* resembling a tube
TUBENOSE *n* seabird with tubular nostrils on its beak
TUBENOSES > TUBENOSE
TUBER *n* fleshy underground root of a plant such as a potato
TUBERCLE *n* small rounded swelling
TUBERCLED *adj* having tubercles
TUBERCLES > TUBERCLE
TUBERCULA *n* plural of tuberculum (another name for "turbercle")
TUBERCULE *variant of* > TUBERCLE
TUBEROID *adj* resembling a tuber
TUBEROSE *same as* > TUBEROUS
TUBEROSES > TUBEROSE
TUBEROUS *adj* (of plants) forming, bearing, or resembling a tuber or tubers
TUBERS > TUBER
TUBES > TUBE
TUBEWORK *n* collective term for tubes or tubing
TUBEWORKS > TUBEWORK
TUBEWORM *n* undersea worm
TUBEWORMS > TUBEWORM
TUBFAST *n* period of fasting and sweating in a tub, intended as a cure for disease
TUBFASTS > TUBFAST
TUBFISH *another name for* > GURNARD
TUBFISHES > TUBFISH
TUBFUL *n* amount a tub will hold
TUBFULS > TUBFUL
TUBICOLAR *adj* tube-dwelling
TUBICOLE *n* tube-dwelling creature
TUBICOLES > TUBICOLE
TUBIFEX *n* any small reddish freshwater oligochaete worm of the genus *Tubifex*
TUBIFEXES > TUBIFEX
TUBIFICID *n* type of threadlike annelid worm
TUBIFORM *same as* > TUBULAR
TUBING *n* length of tube
TUBINGS > TUBING
TUBIST > TUBA
TUBISTS > TUBA
TUBLIKE > TUB
TUBS > TUB
TUBULAR *adj* of or shaped like a tube
TUBULARLY > TUBULAR
TUBULATE *vb* form or shape into a tube
TUBULATED > TUBULATE
TUBULATES > TUBULATE
TUBULATOR > TUBULATE
TUBULE *n* any small tubular structure, esp in an animal or plant
TUBULES > TUBULE
TUBULIN *n* protein forming the basis of microtubules
TUBULINS > TUBULIN
TUBULOSE *adj* tube-shaped; consisting of tubes
TUBULOUS *adj* tube-shaped
TUBULURE *n* tube leading into a retort or other receptacle
TUBULURES > TUBULURE
TUCHUN *n* (formerly) a Chinese military governor or warlord
TUCHUNS > TUCHUN
TUCK *vb* push or fold into a small space ▷ *n* stitched fold ▷ *vb* touch or strike
TUCKAHOE *n* type of edible root
TUCKAHOES > TUCKAHOE
TUCKED > TUCK
TUCKER *n* food ▷ *vb* weary or tire completely
TUCKERBAG *n* in Australia, bag or box used for carrying food
TUCKERBOX *same as* > TUCKERBAG
TUCKERED > TUCKER
TUCKERING > TUCKER
TUCKERS > TUCKER
TUCKET *n* flourish on a trumpet
TUCKETS > TUCKET
TUCKING > TUCK
TUCKS > TUCK
TUCKSHOP *n* shop, esp one in or near a school, where food such as cakes and sweets are sold
TUCKSHOPS > TUCKSHOP
TUCOTUCO *n* colonial burrowing South American rodent
TUCOTUCOS > TUCOTUCO
TUCUTUCO *variant spelling of* > TUCOTUCO
TUCUTUCOS > TUCUTUCO
TUCUTUCU *same as* > TUCOTUCO
TUCUTUCUS > TUCUTUCU
TUFA *n* porous rock formed as a deposit from springs
TUFACEOUS > TUFA
TUFAS > TUFA
TUFF *n* porous rock formed from volcanic dust or ash
TUFFE *old form of* > TUFT
TUFFES > TUFFE
TUFFET *n* small mound or seat
TUFFETS > TUFFET
TUFFS > TUFF
TUFOLI *n* type of tubular pasta
TUFT *n* bunch of feathers, grass, hair, etc held or growing together at the base ▷ *vb* provide or decorate with a tuft or tufts
TUFTED *adj* having a tuft or tufts
TUFTER > TUFT
TUFTERS > TUFT
TUFTIER > TUFT
TUFTIEST > TUFT
TUFTILY > TUFT
TUFTING > TUFT
TUFTINGS > TUFT
TUFTS > TUFT
TUFTY > TUFT
TUG *vb* pull hard ▷ *n* hard pull
TUGBOAT *same as* > TUG
TUGBOATS > TUGBOAT
TUGGED > TUG
TUGGER > TUG
TUGGERS > TUG
TUGGING > TUG
TUGGINGLY > TUG
TUGGINGS > TUG
TUGHRA *n* Turkish Sultan's official emblem
TUGHRAS > TUGHRA
TUGHRIK *same as* > TUGRIK
TUGHRIKS > TUGHRIK
TUGLESS > TUG
TUGRA *variant of* > TUGHRA
TUGRAS > TUGRA
TUGRIK *n* standard monetary unit of Mongolia, divided into 100 möngös
TUGRIKS > TUGRIK
TUGS > TUG
TUI *n* New Zealand honeyeater that mimics human speech and the songs of other birds
TUILLE *n* (in a suit of armour) hanging plate protecting the thighs
TUILLES > TUILLE
TUILLETTE *n* little tuille
TUILYIE *vb* fight
TUILYIED > TUILYIE
TUILYIES > TUILYIE
TUILZIE *variant form of* > TUILYIE
TUILZIED > TUILZIE
TUILZIES > TUILZIE
TUINA *n* form of massage originating in China
TUINAS > TUINA
TUIS > TUI
TUISM *n* practice of putting the interests of another before one's own
TUISMS > TUISM
TUITION *n* instruction, es[p] received individually or i[n] a small group
TUITIONAL > TUITION
TUITIONS > TUITION
TUKTOO *same as* > TUKTU
TUKTOOS > TUKTOO
TUKTU *(in Canada) another name for* > CARIBOU
TUKTUS > TUKTU
TULADI *n* large trout foun[d] in Canada and northern areas of the US
TULADIS > TULADI
TULAREMIA *n* infectious disease of rodents
TULAREMIC > TULAREMIA
TULBAN *old form of* > TURBAN
TULBANS > TULBAN
TULCHAN *n* skin of a calf placed next to a cow to induce it to give milk
TULCHANS > TULCHAN
TULE *n* type of bulrush found in California
TULES > TULE
TULIP *n* plant with bright cup-shaped flowers
TULIPANT *n* turban
TULIPANTS > TULIPANT
TULIPLIKE > TULIP
TULIPS > TULIP
TULIPWOOD *n* light soft wood of the tulip tree, used in making furniture and veneer
TULLE *n* fine net fabric of silk etc
TULLES > TULLE
TULLIBEE *n* cisco of the Great Lakes of Canada
TULLIBEES > TULLIBEE
TULPA *n* being or object created through willpow[er] and visualization techniques
TULPAS > TULPA
TULWAR *n* Indian sabre
TULWARS > TULWAR
TUM *informal or childish word for* > STOMACH
TUMBLE *vb* (cause to) fall, esp awkwardly or violent[ly] ▷ *n* fall
TUMBLEBUG *n* type of dung beetle
TUMBLED > TUMBLE
TUMBLER *n* stemless drinking glass
TUMBLERS > TUMBLER
TUMBLES > TUMBLE
TUMBLESET *n* somersault
TUMBLING > TUMBLE
TUMBLINGS > TUMBLING
TUMBREL *n* farm cart for carrying dung, esp one that tilts backwards to deposit its load
TUMBRELS > TUMBREL
TUMBRIL *same as* > TUMBREL

MBRILS > TUMBRIL
MEFIED > TUMEFY
MEFIES > TUMEFY
MEFY vb make or become umid
MEFYING > TUMEFY
MESCE vb swell
MESCED > TUMESCE
MESCENT adj swollen or ecoming swollen
MESCES > TUMESCE
MESCING > TUMESCE
MID adj (of an organ or art of the body) enlarged r swollen
MIDITY > TUMID
MIDLY > TUMID
MIDNESS > TUMID
MMIES > TUMMY
MMLER n comedian r other entertainer mployed to encourage udience participation r to encourage guests t a resort to take part in ommunal activities
MMLERS > TUMMLER
MMY n stomach
MOR same as > TUMOUR
MORAL > TUMOUR
MORLIKE > TUMOUR
MOROUS > TUMOUR
MORS > TUMOR
MOUR n abnormal rowth in or on the body
MOURS > TUMOUR
MP n small mound or lump ▷ vb make a tump round
MPED > TUMP
MPHIES > TUMPHY
MPHY n dolt; fool
MPIER > TUMP
MPIEST > TUMP
MPING > TUMP
MPLINE n (in the US and Canada, esp formerly) eather or cloth band trung across the forehead r chest and attached to pack or load in order to upport it
MPLINES > TUMPLINE
MPS > TUMP
MPY > TUMP
MS > TUM
MSHIE n turnip
MSHIES > TUMSHIE
MULAR adj of, relating to, r like a mound
MULARY same s > TUMULAR
MULI > TUMULUS
MULOSE adj abounding n small hills or mounds
MULOUS same s > TUMULOSE
MULT n uproar or ommotion ▷ vb stir up a ommotion
MULTED > TUMULT
MULTING > TUMULT
MULTS > TUMULT
MULUS n burial mound

TUMULUSES > TUMULUS
TUN n large beer cask ▷ vb put into or keep in tuns
TUNA n large marine food fish
TUNABLE adj able to be tuned
TUNABLY > TUNABLE
TUNAS > TUNA
TUNBELLY n large round belly
TUND vb beat; strike
TUNDED > TUND
TUNDING > TUND
TUNDISH n type of funnel
TUNDISHES > TUNDISH
TUNDRA n vast treeless Arctic region with permanently frozen subsoil
TUNDRAS > TUNDRA
TUNDS > TUND
TUNDUN n wooden instrument used by Native Australians in religious rites
TUNDUNS > TUNDUN
TUNE n (pleasing) sequence of musical notes ▷ vb adjust (a musical instrument) so that it is in tune
TUNEABLE same as > TUNABLE
TUNEABLY > TUNEABLE
TUNED > TUNE
TUNEFUL adj having a pleasant tune
TUNEFULLY > TUNEFUL
TUNELESS adj having no melody or tune
TUNER n part of a radio or television receiver for selecting channels
TUNERS > TUNER
TUNES > TUNE
TUNESMITH n composer of light or popular music and songs
TUNEUP n adjustments made to an engine to improve its performance
TUNEUPS > TUNEUP
TUNG as in tung oil fast-drying oil obtained from the seeds of a central Asian euphorbiaceous tree, used in paints, varnishes, etc, as a drying agent and to give a water-resistant finish
TUNGS > TUNG
TUNGSTATE n salt of tungstic acid
TUNGSTEN n greyish-white metal
TUNGSTENS > TUNGSTEN
TUNGSTIC adj of or containing tungsten, esp in a high valence state
TUNGSTITE n yellow earthy rare secondary mineral that consists of tungsten oxide and occurs with tungsten ores

TUNGSTOUS adj of or containing tungsten in a low valence state
TUNIC n close-fitting jacket forming part of some uniforms
TUNICA n tissue forming a layer or covering of an organ or part, such as any of the tissue layers of a blood vessel wall
TUNICAE > TUNICA
TUNICATE n minute primitive marine chordate animal ▷ adj of, relating to this animal ▷ vb wear a tunic
TUNICATED > TUNICATE
TUNICATES > TUNICATE
TUNICIN n cellulose-like substance found in tunicates
TUNICINS > TUNICIN
TUNICKED adj wearing a tunic
TUNICLE n liturgical vestment worn by the subdeacon and bishops at High Mass and other religious ceremonies
TUNICLES > TUNICLE
TUNICS > TUNIC
TUNIER > TUNY
TUNIEST > TUNY
TUNING n set of pitches to which the open strings of a guitar, violin, etc, are tuned
TUNINGS > TUNING
TUNNAGE same as > TONNAGE
TUNNAGES > TUNNAGE
TUNNED > TUN
TUNNEL n underground passage ▷ vb make a tunnel (through)
TUNNELED > TUNNEL
TUNNELER > TUNNEL
TUNNELERS > TUNNEL
TUNNELING > TUNNEL
TUNNELLED > TUNNEL
TUNNELLER > TUNNEL
TUNNELS > TUNNEL
TUNNIES > TUNNY
TUNNING > TUN
TUNNINGS > TUN
TUNNY same as > TUNA
TUNS > TUN
TUNY adj having an easily discernable melody
TUP n male sheep ▷ vb cause (a ram) to mate with a ewe, or (of a ram) to mate with (a ewe)
TUPEK same as > TUPIK
TUPEKS > TUPEK
TUPELO n large tree of deep swamps and rivers of the southern US
TUPELOS > TUPELO
TUPIK n tent of seal or caribou skin used for shelter by the Inuit in summer

TUPIKS > TUPIK
TUPLE n row of values in a relational database
TUPLES > TUPLE
TUPPED > TUP
TUPPENCE same as > TWOPENCE
TUPPENCES > TUPPENCE
TUPPENNY same as > TWOPENNY
TUPPING > TUP
TUPS > TUP
TUPTOWING n study of Greek grammar
TUPUNA same as > TIPUNA
TUPUNAS > TUPUNA
TUQUE n knitted cap with a long tapering end
TUQUES > TUQUE
TURACIN n red pigment found in touraco feathers
TURACINS > TURACIN
TURACO same as > TOURACO
TURACOS > TURACO
TURACOU variant of > TOURACO
TURACOUS > TURACOU
TURBAN n Muslim, Hindu, or Sikh man's head covering, made by winding cloth round the head
TURBAND old variant of > TURBAN
TURBANDS > TURBAND
TURBANED > TURBAN
TURBANNED > TURBAN
TURBANS > TURBAN
TURBANT old variant of > TURBAN
TURBANTS > TURBANT
TURBARIES > TURBARY
TURBARY n land where peat or turf is cut or has been cut
TURBETH variant of > TURPETH
TURBETHS > TURBETH
TURBID adj muddy, not clear
TURBIDITE n sediment deposited by a turbidity current
TURBIDITY > TURBID
TURBIDLY > TURBID
TURBINAL same as > TURBINATE
TURBINALS > TURBINAL
TURBINATE adj of or relating to any of the thin scroll-shaped bones situated on the walls of the nasal passages ▷ n turbinate bone
TURBINE n machine or generator driven by gas, water, etc turning blades
TURBINED adj having a turbine
TURBINES > TURBINE
TURBIT n crested breed of domestic pigeon
TURBITH variant of > TURPETH

TURBITHS > TURBITH
TURBITS > TURBIT
TURBO *n* compressor in an engine
TURBOCAR *n* car driven by a gas turbine
TURBOCARS > TURBOCAR
TURBOFAN *n* engine in which a large fan driven by a turbine forces air rearwards to increase the thrust
TURBOFANS > TURBOFAN
TURBOJET *n* gas turbine in which the exhaust gases provide the propulsive thrust to drive an aircraft
TURBOJETS > TURBOJET
TURBOND *old variant of* > TURBAN
TURBONDS > TURBOND
TURBOPROP *n* gas turbine for driving an aircraft propeller
TURBOS > TURBO
TURBOT *n* large European edible flatfish
TURBOTS > TURBOT
TURBULENT *adj* involving a lot of sudden changes and conflicting elements
TURCOPOLE *n* lightly armed and highly mobile class of Crusader
TURD *n* piece of excrement
TURDINE *adj* of, relating to, or characteristic of thrushes
TURDION *variant of* > TORDION
TURDIONS > TURDION
TURDOID *same as* > TURDINE
TURDS > TURD
TUREEN *n* serving dish for soup
TUREENS > TUREEN
TURF *n* short thick even grass ▷ *vb* cover with turf
TURFED > TURF
TURFEN *adj* made of turf
TURFGRASS *n* grass grown for lawns
TURFIER > TURFY
TURFIEST > TURFY
TURFINESS > TURFY
TURFING > TURF
TURFINGS > TURF
TURFITE *same as* > TURFMAN
TURFITES > TURFITE
TURFLESS > TURF
TURFLIKE > TURF
TURFMAN *n* person devoted to horse racing
TURFMEN > TURFMAN
TURFS > TURF
TURFSKI *n* ski down a grassy hill on skis modified with integral wheels
TURFSKIS > TURFSKI
TURFY *adj* of, covered with, or resembling turf
TURGENCY > TURGENT
TURGENT *obsolete word for* > TURGID
TURGENTLY > TURGENT
TURGID *adj* (of language) pompous
TURGIDER > TURGID
TURGIDEST > TURGID
TURGIDITY > TURGID
TURGIDLY > TURGID
TURGITE *n* red or black mineral consisting of hydrated ferric oxide
TURGITES > TURGITE
TURGOR *n* normal rigid state of a cell, caused by pressure of the cell contents against the cell wall or membrane
TURGORS > TURGOR
TURION *n* perennating bud produced by many aquatic plants
TURIONS > TURION
TURISTA *n* traveller's diarrhoea
TURISTAS > TURISTA
TURK *n* obsolete derogatory term for a violent, brutal, or domineering person
TURKEY *n* large bird bred for food
TURKEYS > TURKEY
TURKIES *old form of* > TURQUOISE
TURKIESES > TURKIES
TURKIS *old form of* > TURQUOISE
TURKISES > TURKIS
TURKOIS *old form of* > TURQUOISE
TURKOISES > TURKOIS
TURKS > TURK
TURLOUGH *n* seasonal lake or pond
TURLOUGHS > TURLOUGH
TURM *n* troop of horsemen
TURME *variant of* > TURM
TURMERIC *n* yellow spice obtained from the root of an Asian plant
TURMERICS > TURMERIC
TURMES > TURME
TURMOIL *n* agitation or confusion ▷ *vb* make or become turbulent
TURMOILED > TURMOIL
TURMOILS > TURMOIL
TURMS > TURM
TURN *vb* change the position or direction (of) ▷ *n* turning
TURNABLE > TURN
TURNABOUT *n* act of turning so as to face a different direction
TURNAGAIN *n* revolution
TURNBACK *n* one who turns back (from a challenge, for example)
TURNBACKS > TURNBACK
TURNCOAT *n* person who deserts one party or cause to join another
TURNCOATS > TURNCOAT
TURNCOCK *n* (formerly) official employed to turn on the water for the mains supply
TURNCOCKS > TURNCOCK
TURNDOWN *vb, adj*
TURNDOWN capable of being or designed to be folded or doubled down *n* instance of turning down
TURNDOWNS > TURNDOWN
TURNDUN *another name for* > TUNDUN
TURNDUNS > TURNDUN
TURNED > TURN
TURNER *n* person or thing that turns, esp a person who operates a lathe
TURNERIES > TURNERY
TURNERS > TURNER
TURNERY *n* objects made on a lathe
TURNHALL *n* building in which gymnastics is taught and practised
TURNHALLS > TURNHALL
TURNING *n* road or path leading off a main route
TURNINGS > TURNING
TURNIP *n* root vegetable with orange or white flesh ▷ *vb* sow (a field) with turnips
TURNIPED > TURNIP
TURNIPING > TURNIP
TURNIPS > TURNIP
TURNKEY *n* jailer ▷ *adj* denoting a project, as in civil engineering, in which a single contractor has responsibility for the complete job from the start to the time of installation or occupancy
TURNKEYS > TURNKEY
TURNOFF
TURN OFF *n* a road or other way branching off from the main
TURNOFFS > TURNOFF
TURNON *n* something sexually exciting
TURNONS > TURNON
TURNOUT *n* number of people appearing at a gathering
TURNOUTS > TURNOUT
TURNOVER *n* total sales made by a business over a certain period
TURNOVERS > TURNOVER
TURNPIKE *n* road where a toll is collected at barriers
TURNPIKES > TURNPIKE
TURNROUND *n* act or process in which a ship, aircraft, etc, unloads passengers and freight at end of a trip and reloads for next trip
TURNS > TURN
TURNSKIN *n* old name for a werewolf
TURNSKINS > TURNSKIN
TURNSOLE *n* any of various plants having flowers that are said to turn towards the sun
TURNSOLES > TURNSOLE
TURNSPIT *n* (formerly) a servant or small dog whose job was to turn the spit on which meat, poultry, etc, was roasting
TURNSPITS > TURNSPIT
TURNSTILE *n* revolving gate for admitting one person at a time
TURNSTONE *n* shore bird
TURNTABLE *n* revolving platform
TURNUP *n* the turned-up fold at the bottom of som[e] trouser legs
TURNUPS > TURNUP
TUROPHILE *n* person wh[o] loves cheese
TURPETH *n* convolvulaceous plant o[f] the East Indies, having roots with purgative properties
TURPETHS > TURPETH
TURPITUDE *n* wickednes[s]
TURPS *n* colourless, flammable liquid
TURQUOIS *variant of* > TURQUOISE
TURQUOISE *adj* blue-gree[n] ▷ *n* blue-green precious stone
TURRET *n* small tower
TURRETED *adj* having or resembling a turret or turrets
TURRETS > TURRET
TURRIBANT *old variant of* > TURBAN
TURRICAL *adj* of, relating to, or resembling a turre[t]
TURTLE *n* sea tortoise
TURTLED > TURTLE
TURTLER > TURTLE
TURTLERS > TURTLE
TURTLES > TURTLE
TURTLING > TURTLE
TURTLINGS > TURTLE
TURVES > TURF
TUSCHE *n* substance use[d] in lithography for drawi[ng] the design and as a resis[t] in silk-screen printing a[nd] lithography
TUSCHES > TUSCHE
TUSH *interj* exclamation o[f] disapproval or contempt ▷ *n* small tusk ▷ *vb* utte[r] the interjection "tush"
TUSHED > TUSH
TUSHERIES > TUSHERY
TUSHERY *n* use of affecte[d] archaic language in novels, etc
TUSHES > TUSH
TUSHIE *n* pair of buttock[s]
TUSHIES > TUSHIE
TUSHING > TUSH
TUSHKAR *variant of* > TUSK[ER]
TUSHKARS > TUSHKAR
TUSHKER *variant of* > TUSK[ER]

SHKERS > TUSHKER
SHY *variant of* > TUSHIE
SK *n* long pointed tooth
f an elephant, walrus,
tc ▷ *vb* stab, tear, or gore
vith the tusks
SKAR *n* peat-cutting
pade
SKARS > TUSKAR
SKED > TUSK
SKER *n* any animal with
rominent tusks, esp a
vild boar or elephant
SKERS > TUSKER
SKIER > TUSK
SKIEST > TUSK
SKING > TUSK
SKINGS > TUSK
SKLESS > TUSK
SKLIKE > TUSK
SKS > TUSK
SKY > TUSK
SSAH *same as* > TUSSORE
SSAHS > TUSSAH
SSAL > TUSSIS
SSAR *variant of* > TUSSORE
SSARS > TUSSAR
SSEH *variant of* > TUSSORE
SSEHS > TUSSEH
SSER *same as* > TUSSORE
SSERS > TUSSER
SSES > TUSSIS
SSIS *technical name for* > COUGH
SSISES > TUSSIS
SSIVE > TUSSIS
SSLE *vb* fight or scuffle
▸ *n* energetic fight,
truggle, or argument
SSLED > TUSSLE
SSLES > TUSSLE
SSLING > TUSSLE
SSOCK *n* tuft of grass
SSOCKED *adj* having
ussocks
SSOCKS > TUSSOCK
SSOCKY > TUSSOCK
SSOR *variant of* > TUSSORE
SSORE *n* strong coarse
rownish Indian silk
btained from the cocoons
f an Oriental saturniid
ilkworm
SSORES > TUSSORE
SSORS > TUSSOR
SSUCK *variant*
f > TUSSOCK
SSUCKS > TUSSUCK
SSUR *variant of* > TUSSORE
SSURS > TUSSUR
T *interj* an exclamation
f mild reprimand,
isapproval, or surprise
▸ *vb* express disapproval
y the exclamation of "tut-
ut." ▷ *n* payment system
ased on measurable work
one rather that time
pent doing it
TANIA *n* alloy of low
nelting point containing
in, antimony, copper and
sed mostly for decorative
urposes

TUTANIAS > TUTANIA
TUTEE *n* one who is tutored, esp in a university
TUTEES > TUTEE
TUTELAGE *n* instruction or guidance, esp by a tutor
TUTELAGES > TUTELAGE
TUTELAR *same as* > TUTELARY
TUTELARS > TUTELAR
TUTELARY *adj* having the role of guardian or protector ▷ *n* tutelary person, deity, or saint
TUTENAG *n* zinc alloy
TUTENAGS > TUTENAG
TUTIORISM *n* (in Roman Catholic moral theology) the doctrine that in cases of moral doubt it is best to follow the safer course or that in agreement with the law
TUTIORIST > TUTIORISM
TUTMAN *n* one who does tutwork
TUTMEN > TUTMAN
TUTOR *n* person teaching individuals or small groups ▷ *vb* act as a tutor to
TUTORAGE > TUTOR
TUTORAGES > TUTOR
TUTORED > TUTOR
TUTORESS *n* female tutor
TUTORIAL *n* period of instruction with a tutor ▷ *adj* of or relating to a tutor
TUTORIALS > TUTORIAL
TUTORING > TUTOR
TUTORINGS > TUTOR
TUTORISE *variant spelling of* > TUTORIZE
TUTORISED > TUTORISE
TUTORISES > TUTORISE
TUTORISM > TUTOR
TUTORISMS > TUTOR
TUTORIZE *vb* tutor
TUTORIZED > TUTOR
TUTORIZES > TUTORIZE
TUTORS > TUTOR
TUTORSHIP > TUTOR
TUTOYED > TUTOY
TUTOYER *vb* speak to someone on familiar terms
TUTOYERED > TUTOYER
TUTOYERS > TUTOYER
TUTRESS *same as* > TUTORESS
TUTRESSES > TUTRESS
TUTRICES > TUTRIX
TUTRIX *n* female tutor; tutoress
TUTRIXES > TUTRIX
TUTS *Scots version of* > TUT
TUTSAN *n* woodland shrub of Europe and W Asia
TUTSANS > TUTSAN
TUTSED > TUTS
TUTSES > TUTS
TUTSING > TUTS
TUTTED > TUT
TUTTI *adv* be performed by the whole orchestra or choir ▷ *n* piece of tutti music
TUTTIES > TUTTY
TUTTING > TUT
TUTTINGS > TUT
TUTTIS > TUTTI
TUTTY *n* finely powdered impure zinc oxide obtained from the flues of zinc-smelting furnaces and used as a polishing powder
TUTU *n* short stiff skirt worn by ballerinas
TUTUED *adj* wearing tutu
TUTUS > TUTU
TUTWORK *n* work paid using a tut system
TUTWORKER > TUTWORK
TUTWORKS > TUTWORK
TUX *short for* > TUXEDO
TUXEDO *n* dinner jacket
TUXEDOED *adj* wearing a tuxedo
TUXEDOES > TUXEDO
TUXEDOS > TUXEDO
TUXES > TUX
TUYER *variant of* > TUYERE
TUYERE *n* water-cooled nozzle through which air is blown into a cupola, blast furnace, or forge
TUYERES > TUYERE
TUYERS > TUYER
TUZZ *n* tuft or clump of hair
TUZZES > TUZZ
TWA *Scots word for* > TWO
TWADDLE *n* silly or pretentious talk or writing ▷ *vb* talk or write in a silly or pretentious way
TWADDLED > TWADDLE
TWADDLER > TWADDLE
TWADDLERS > TWADDLE
TWADDLES > TWADDLE
TWADDLIER > TWADDLE
TWADDLING > TWADDLE
TWADDLY > TWADDLE
TWAE *same as* > TWA
TWAES > TWAE
TWAFALD *Scots variant of* > TWOFOLD
TWAIN *n* two
TWAINS > TWAIN
TWAITE *n* herring-like food fish
TWAITES > TWAITE
TWAL *n* twelve
TWALPENNY *n* shilling
TWALS > TWAL
TWANG *n* sharp ringing sound ▷ *vb* (cause to) make a twang
TWANGED > TWANG
TWANGER > TWANG
TWANGERS > TWANG
TWANGIER > TWANG
TWANGIEST > TWANG
TWANGING > TWANG
TWANGINGS > TWANG
TWANGLE *vb* make a continuous loose twanging sound (on a musical instrument, for example)
TWANGLED > TWANGLE
TWANGLER > TWANGLE
TWANGLERS > TWANGLE
TWANGLES > TWANGLE
TWANGLING > TWANGLE
TWANGS > TWANG
TWANGY > TWANG
TWANK *vb* make an sharply curtailed twang
TWANKAY *n* variety of Chinese green tea
TWANKAYS > TWANKAY
TWANKIES > TWANKY
TWANKS > TWANK
TWANKY *same as* > TWANKAY
TWAS > TWA
TWASOME *same as* > TWOSOME
TWASOMES > TWASOME
TWAT *n* taboo term for female genitals
TWATS > TWAT
TWATTLE *rare word for* > TWADDLE
TWATTLED > TWATTLE
TWATTLER > TWATTLE
TWATTLERS > TWATTLE
TWATTLES > TWATTLE
TWATTLING > TWATTLE
TWAY *old variant of* > TWAIN
TWAYBLADE *n* type of orchid
TWAYS > TWAY
TWEAK *vb* pinch or twist sharply ▷ *n* tweaking
TWEAKED > TWEAK
TWEAKER *n* engineer's small screwdriver, used for fine adjustments
TWEAKERS > TWEAKER
TWEAKIER > TWEAK
TWEAKIEST > TWEAK
TWEAKING > TWEAK
TWEAKINGS > TWEAK
TWEAKS > TWEAK
TWEAKY > TWEAK
TWEE *adj* too sentimental, sweet, or pretty
TWEED *n* thick woollen cloth
TWEEDIER > TWEEDY
TWEEDIEST > TWEEDY
TWEEDLE *vb* improvise aimlessly on a musical instrument
TWEEDLED > TWEEDLE
TWEEDLER > TWEEDLE
TWEEDLERS > TWEEDLE
TWEEDLES > TWEEDLE
TWEEDLING > TWEEDLE
TWEEDS > TWEED
TWEEDY *adj* of or made of tweed
TWEEL *variant of* > TWILL
TWEELED > TWEEL
TWEELING > TWEEL
TWEELS > TWEEL
TWEELY > TWEE
TWEEN *same as* > BETWEEN
TWEENAGER *n* child of approximately eight to fourteen years of age
TWEENER *same*

as >TWEENAGER
TWEENERS >TWEENER
TWEENESS >TWEE
TWEENIE *same as* >TWEENY
TWEENIES >TWEENY
TWEENS >TWEEN
TWEENY *n* maid who assists both cook and housemaid
TWEER *variant of* >TWIRE
TWEERED >TWEER
TWEERING >TWEER
TWEERS >TWEER
TWEEST >TWEE
TWEET *vb* chirp ▷ *interj* imitation of the thin chirping sound made by small birds
TWEETED >TWEET
TWEETER *n* loudspeaker reproducing high-frequency sounds
TWEETERS >TWEETER
TWEETING >TWEET
TWEETS >TWEET
TWEEZE *vb* take hold of or pluck (hair, small objects, etc) with or as if with tweezers
TWEEZED >TWEEZE
TWEEZER *same as* >TWEEZERS
TWEEZERS *pl n* small pincer-like tool
TWEEZES >TWEEZE
TWEEZING >TWEEZE
TWELFTH *n* (of) number twelve in a series ▷ *adj* of or being number twelve in a series
TWELFTHLY *adv* after the eleventh person, position, event, etc
TWELFTHS >TWELFTH
TWELVE *n* two more than ten ▷ *adj* amounting to twelve ▷ *determiner* amounting to twelve
TWELVEMO *another word for* >DUODECIMO
TWELVEMOS >TWELVEMO
TWELVES >TWELVE
TWENTIES >TWENTY
TWENTIETH *adj* coming after the nineteenth in numbering or counting order, position, time, etc ▷ *n* one of 20 approximately equal parts of something
TWENTY *n* two times ten ▷ *adj* amounting to twenty ▷ *determiner* amounting to twenty
TWENTYISH *adj* around 20
TWERP *n* silly person
TWERPIER >TWERP
TWERPIEST >TWERP
TWERPS >TWERP
TWERPY >TWERP
TWIBIL *same as* >TWIBILL
TWIBILL *n* mattock with a blade shaped like an adze at one end and like an axe at the other
TWIBILLS >TWIBILL
TWIBILS >TWIBIL
TWICE *adv* two times
TWICER *n* someone who does something twice
TWICERS >TWICER
TWICHILD *n* person in his or her dotage
TWIDDLE *vb* fiddle or twirl in an idle way ▷ *n* act or instance of twiddling
TWIDDLED >TWIDDLE
TWIDDLER >TWIDDLE
TWIDDLERS >TWIDDLE
TWIDDLES >TWIDDLE
TWIDDLIER >TWIDDLE
TWIDDLING >TWIDDLE
TWIDDLY >TWIDDLE
TWIER *variant of* >TUYERE
TWIERS >TWIER
TWIFOLD *variant of* >TWOFOLD
TWIFORKED *adj* having two forks; bifurcate
TWIFORMED *adj* having two forms
TWIG *n* small branch or shoot ▷ *vb* realize or understand
TWIGGED >TWIG
TWIGGEN *adj* made of twigs
TWIGGER >TWIG
TWIGGERS >TWIG
TWIGGIER >TWIGGY
TWIGGIEST >TWIGGY
TWIGGING >TWIG
TWIGGY *adj* of or relating to a twig or twigs
TWIGHT *old variant of* >TWIT
TWIGHTED >TWIGHT
TWIGHTING >TWIGHT
TWIGHTS >TWIGHT
TWIGLESS >TWIG
TWIGLIKE >TWIG
TWIGLOO *n* temporary shelter made from twigs, branches, leaves, etc
TWIGLOOS >TWIGLOO
TWIGS >TWIG
TWIGSOME *adj* covered with twigs; twiggy
TWILIGHT *n* soft dim light just after sunset ▷ *adj* of or relating to the period towards the end of the day
TWILIGHTS >TWILIGHT
TWILIT >TWILIGHT
TWILL *n* fabric woven to produce parallel ridges ▷ *adj* (in textiles) of or designating a weave in which the weft yarns are worked around two or more warp yarns to produce an effect of parallel diagonal lines or ribs ▷ *vb* weave in this fashion
TWILLED >TWILL
TWILLIES >TWILLY
TWILLING >TWILL
TWILLINGS >TWILL
TWILLS >TWILL
TWILLY *n* machine having a system of revolving spikes for opening and cleaning raw textile fibres
TWILT *variant of* >QUILT
TWILTED >TWILT
TWILTING >TWILT
TWILTS >TWILT
TWIN *n* one of a pair, esp of two children born at one birth ▷ *vb* pair or be paired
TWINBERRY *n* creeping wooden plant
TWINBORN *adj* born as a twin
TWINE *n* string or cord ▷ *vb* twist or coil round
TWINED >TWINE
TWINER >TWINE
TWINERS >TWINE
TWINES >TWINE
TWINGE *n* sudden sharp pain or emotional pang ▷ *vb* have or cause to have a twinge
TWINGED >TWINGE
TWINGEING >TWINGE
TWINGES >TWINGE
TWINGING >TWINGE
TWINIER >TWINE
TWINIEST >TWINE
TWINIGHT *adj* (of a baseball double-header) held in the late afternoon and evening
TWINING >TWINE
TWININGLY >TWINE
TWININGS >TWINE
TWINJET *n* jet aircraft with two engines
TWINJETS >TWINJET
TWINK *n* white correction fluid for deleting written text ▷ *vb* twinkle
TWINKED >TWINK
TWINKIE *n* stupid person
TWINKIES >TWINKIE
TWINKING >TWINK
TWINKLE *vb* shine brightly but intermittently ▷ *n* flickering brightness
TWINKLED >TWINKLE
TWINKLER >TWINKLE
TWINKLERS >TWINKLE
TWINKLES >TWINKLE
TWINKLING *n* very short time
TWINKLY >TWINKLE
TWINKS >TWINK
TWINLING *old name for* >TWIN
TWINLINGS >TWINLING
TWINNED >TWIN
TWINNING >TWIN
TWINNINGS >TWIN
TWINS >TWIN
TWINSET *n* matching jumper and cardigan
TWINSETS >TWINSET
TWINSHIP *n* condition of being a twin or twins
TWINSHIPS >TWIN
TWINTER *n* animal that is 2 years old
TWINTERS >TWINTER
TWINY >TWINE
TWIRE *vb* look intently at with (or as if with) difficulty
TWIRED >TWIRE
TWIRES >TWIRE
TWIRING >TWIRE
TWIRL *vb* turn or spin around quickly ▷ *n* whirl or twist
TWIRLED >TWIRL
TWIRLER >TWIRL
TWIRLERS >TWIRL
TWIRLIER >TWIRL
TWIRLIEST >TWIRL
TWIRLING >TWIRL
TWIRLS >TWIRL
TWIRLY >TWIRL
TWIRP *same as* >TWERP
TWIRPIER >TWIRP
TWIRPIEST >TWIRP
TWIRPS >TWIRP
TWIRPY >TWIRP
TWISCAR *variant of* >TUSK
TWISCARS >TWISCAR
TWIST *vb* turn out of the natural position ▷ *n* twisting
TWISTABLE >TWIST
TWISTED >TWIST
TWISTER *n* swindler
TWISTERS >TWISTER
TWISTIER >TWIST
TWISTIEST >TWIST
TWISTING >TWIST
TWISTINGS >TWIST
TWISTOR *n* variable corresponding to the coordinates of a point in space and time
TWISTORS >TWISTOR
TWISTS >TWIST
TWISTY >TWIST
TWIT *vb* poke fun at (someone) ▷ *n* foolish person
TWITCH *vb* move spasmodically ▷ *n* nervous muscular spasm
TWITCHED >TWITCH
TWITCHER *n* bird-watcher who tries to spot as many rare varieties as possible
TWITCHERS >TWITCHER
TWITCHES >TWITCH
TWITCHIER >TWITCHY
TWITCHILY >TWITCHY
TWITCHING >TWITCH
TWITCHY *adj* nervous, worried, and ill-at-ease
TWITE *n* N European finch with a brown streaked plumage
TWITES >TWITE
TWITS >TWIT
TWITTED >TWIT
TWITTEN *n* narrow alleyway
TWITTENS >TWITTEN
TWITTER *vb* (of birds) utter chirping sounds ▷ *n* act or sound of twittering
TWITTERED >TWITTER
TWITTERER >TWITTER

ITTERS >TWITTER
ITTERY >TWITTER
ITTING >TWIT
ITTINGS >TWIT
IXT *same as* >BETWIXT
IZZLE *vb* spin around
IZZLED >TWIZZLE
IZZLES >TWIZZLE
IZZLING >TWIZZLE
O *n* one more than one
OCCER >TWOCCING
OCCERS >TWOCCING
OCCING *n* act of breaking nto a motor vehicle and driving it away
OCCINGS >TWOCCING
OCKER >TWOCCING
OCKERS >TWOCCING
OCKING *same* as >TWOCCING
OCKINGS >TWOCKING
OER *n* (in a game) something that scores two
OERS >TWOER
OFER *n* single ticket allowing the buyer entrance to two events, attractions, etc, for substantially less than the cost were he or she to pay for each individually
OFERS >TWOFER
OFOLD *adj* having twice as many or as much ▷ *adv* by twice as many or as much ▷ *n* folding piece of theatrical scenery
OFOLDS >TWOFOLD
ONESS *n* state or condition of being two
ONESSES >TWONESS
ONIE *same as* >TOONIE
ONIES >TWONIE
OONIE *variant* of >TOONIE
OONIES >TWOONIE
OPENCE *n* sum of two pennies
OPENCES >TWOPENCE
OPENNY *adj* cheap or tawdry
OS >TWO
OSEATER *n* vehicle providing seats for two people
OSOME *n* group of two people
OSOMES >TWOSOME
OSTROKE *adj* relating to or designating an internal-combustion engine whose piston makes two strokes for every explosion
P *adj* stupid
YER *same as* >TUYERE
YERE *variant of* >TUYERE
YERES >TWYERE
YERS >TWYER
YFOLD *adj* twofold
CHISM *n* theory that chance is an objective reality at work in the universe, esp in evolutionary adaptations

TYCHISMS >TYCHISM
TYCOON *n* powerful wealthy businessman; shogun
TYCOONATE *n* office or rule of a tycoon
TYCOONERY >TYCOON
TYCOONS >TYCOON
TYDE *old variant of the past participle of* >TIE
TYE *n* trough used in mining to separate valuable material from dross ▷ *vb* (in mining) isolate valuable material from dross using a tye
TYED >TYE
TYEE *n* large northern Pacific salmon
TYEES >TYEE
TYEING >TYE
TYER >TYE
TYERS >TYE
TYES >TYE
TYG *n* mug with two handles
TYGS >TYG
TYIN *variant of* >TYIYN
TYING >TIE
TYIYN *n* money unit of Kyrgyzstan
TYKE *n* often offensive term for small cheeky child
TYKES >TYKE
TYKISH >TYKE
TYLECTOMY *n* excision of a breast tumour
TYLER *variant of* >TILER
TYLERS >TYLER
TYLOPOD *n* mammal with padded feet, such as a camel or llama
TYLOPODS >TYLOPOD
TYLOSES >TYLOSIS
TYLOSIN *n* broad spectrum antibiotic
TYLOSINS >TYLOSIN
TYLOSIS *n* bladder-like outgrowth from certain cells in woody tissue that extends into and blocks adjacent conducting xylem cells
TYLOTE *n* knobbed sponge spicule
TYLOTES >TYLOTE
TYMBAL *same as* >TIMBAL
TYMBALS >TYMBAL
TYMP *n* blast furnace outlet through which molten metal flows
TYMPAN *same as* >TYMPANUM
TYMPANA >TYMPANUM
TYMPANAL *adj* relating to the tympanum
TYMPANI *same as* >TIMPANI
TYMPANIC *adj* of, relating to, or having a tympanum ▷ *n* part of the temporal bone in the mammalian skull that surrounds the auditory canal
TYMPANICS >TYMPANIC
TYMPANIES >TYMPANY

TYMPANIST >TIMPANI
TYMPANO >TYMPANI
TYMPANS >TYMPAN
TYMPANUM *n* cavity of the middle ear
TYMPANUMS >TYMPANUM
TYMPANY *n* distention of the abdomen
TYMPS >TYMP
TYND *variant of* >TIND
TYNDE *variant of* >TIND
TYNE *variant of* >TINE
TYNED *variant of* >TYNE
TYNES >TYNE
TYNING >TYNE
TYPABLE >TYPE
TYPAL *rare word for* >TYPICAL
TYPE *n* class or category ▷ *vb* print with a typewriter or word processor
TYPEABLE >TYPE
TYPEBAR *n* one of the bars in a typewriter that carry the type and are operated by keys
TYPEBARS >TYPEBAR
TYPECASE *n* compartmental tray for storing printer's type
TYPECASES >TYPECASE
TYPECAST *vb* continually cast (an actor or actress) in similar roles
TYPECASTS >TYPECAST
TYPED >TYPE
TYPEFACE *n* style of the type
TYPEFACES >TYPEFACE
TYPES >TYPE
TYPESET *vb* set (text for printing) in type
TYPESETS >TYPESET
TYPESTYLE *another word for* >TYPEFACE
TYPEWRITE *vb* write by means of a typewriter
TYPEWROTE >TYPEWRITE
TYPEY *variant of* >TYPY
TYPHLITIC >TYPHLITIS
TYPHLITIS *n* inflammation of the caecum
TYPHOID *adj* of or relating to typhoid fever
TYPHOIDAL >TYPHOID
TYPHOIDIN *n* culture of dead typhoid bacillus for injection into the skin to test for typhoid fever
TYPHOIDS >TYPHOID
TYPHON *n* whirlwind
TYPHONIAN >TYPHON
TYPHONIC >TYPHOON
TYPHONS >TYPHON
TYPHOON *n* violent tropical storm
TYPHOONS >TYPHOON
TYPHOSE *adj* relating to typhoid
TYPHOUS >TYPHUS
TYPHUS *n* infectious feverish disease

TYPHUSES >TYPHUS
TYPIC *same as* >TYPICAL
TYPICAL *adj* true to type, characteristic
TYPICALLY >TYPICAL
TYPIER >TYPY
TYPIEST >TYPY
TYPIFIED >TYPIFY
TYPIFIER >TYPIFY
TYPIFIERS >TYPIFY
TYPIFIES >TYPIFY
TYPIFY *vb* be typical of
TYPIFYING >TYPIFY
TYPING *n* work or activity of using a typewriter or word processor
TYPINGS >TYPING
TYPIST *n* person who types with a typewriter or word processor
TYPISTS >TYPIST
TYPO *n* typographical error
TYPOGRAPH *n* person skilled in the art of composing type and printing from it
TYPOLOGIC >TYPOLOGY
TYPOLOGY *n* doctrine or study of types or of the correspondence between them and the realities which they typify
TYPOMANIA *n* obsession with typology
TYPOS >TYPO
TYPP *n* unit of thickness of yarn
TYPPS >TYPP
TYPTO *vb* learn Greek conjugations
TYPTOED >TYPTO
TYPTOING >TYPTO
TYPTOS >TYPTO
TYPY *adj* (of an animal) typifying the breed
TYRAMINE *n* colourless crystalline amine derived from phenol
TYRAMINES >TYRAMINE
TYRAN *vb* act as a tyrant
TYRANED >TYRAN
TYRANING >TYRAN
TYRANNE *variant of* >TYRAN
TYRANNED >TYRANNE
TYRANNES >TYRANNE
TYRANNESS *n* female tyrant
TYRANNIC >TYRANNY
TYRANNIES >TYRANNY
TYRANNING >TYRANNE
TYRANNIS *n* tyrannical government
TYRANNISE *same as* >TYRANNIZE
TYRANNIZE *vb* exert power (over) oppressively or cruelly
TYRANNOUS >TYRANNY
TYRANNY *n* tyrannical rule
TYRANS >TYRAN
TYRANT *n* oppressive or cruel ruler ▷ *vb* act the tyrant
TYRANTED >TYRANT
TYRANTING >TYRANT

TYRANTS > TYRANT
TYRE *n* rubber ring, usu inflated, over the rim of a vehicle's wheel to grip the road ▷ *vb* fit a tyre or tyres to (a wheel, vehicle, etc)
TYRED > TYRE
TYRELESS > TYRE
TYRES > TYRE
TYRING > TYRE
TYRO *n* novice or beginner
TYROCIDIN *n* antibiotic
TYROES > TYRO
TYRONES > TYRO
TYRONIC > TYRO
TYROPITTA *n* Greek cheese pie
TYROS > TYRO
TYROSINE *n* aromatic nonessential amino acid
TYROSINES > TYROSINE
TYSTIE *n* black guillemot
TYSTIES > TYSTIE
TYTE *variant spelling of* > TITE
TYTHE *variant of* > TITHE
TYTHED > TYTHE
TYTHES > TYTHE
TYTHING > TYTHE
TZADDIK *variant of* > ZADDIK
TZADDIKIM > TZADDIK
TZADDIKS > TZADDIK
TZADDIQ *variant of* > ZADDIK
TZADDIQIM > TZADDIQ
TZADDIQS > TZADDIQ
TZAR *same as* > TSAR
TZARDOM > TZAR
TZARDOMS > TZAR
TZAREVNA *variant of* > TSAREVNA
TZAREVNAS > TZAREVNA
TZARINA *variant of* > TSARINA
TZARINAS > TZARINA
TZARISM *variant of* > TSARISM
TZARISMS > TZARISM
TZARIST > TZARISM
TZARISTS > TZARISM
TZARITZA *variant of* > TSARITSA
TZARITZAS > TZARITZA
TZARS > TZAR
TZATZIKI *n* Greek dip made from yogurt, chopped cucumber, and mint
TZATZIKIS > TZATZIKI
TZETSE *variant of* > TSETSE
TZETSES > TZETSE
TZETZE *variant of* > TSETSE
TZETZES > TZETZE
TZIGANE *n* type of Gypsy music
TZIGANES > TZIGANE
TZIGANIES > TZIGANY
TZIGANY *variant of* > TZIGANE
TZIMMES *n* traditional Jewish stew
TZITZIS *variant of* > TSITSITH
TZITZIT *variant of* > TZITZIT
TZITZITH *variant of* > TSITSITH
TZURIS *variant of* > TSURIS

Uu

AKARI *n* type of monkey
AKARIS > UAKARI
BEROUS *adj* abundant
BERTIES > UBERTY
BERTY *n* abundance
BIETIES > UBIETY
BIETY *n* condition of being in a particular place
BIQUE *adv* everywhere
BIQUITIN *n* type of polypeptide
BIQUITY *n* state of apparently being everywhere at once; omnipresence
CKERS *n* type of naval game
DAL *n* form of freehold possession of land existing in northern Europe before the introduction of the feudal system and still used in Orkney and Shetland
DALLER *n* person possessing a udal
DALLERS > UDALLER
DALS > UDAL
DDER *n* large baglike milk-producing gland of cows, sheep, or goats
DDERED > UDDER
DDERFUL > UDDER
DDERLESS > UDDER
DDERS > UDDER
DO *n* stout perennial plant of Japan and China with berry-like black fruits and young shoots that are edible when blanched
DOMETER *n* archaic term for an instrument for measuring rainfall or snowfall
UDOMETERS > UDOMETER
UDOMETRIC > UDOMETER
UDOMETRY > UDOMETER
UDON *n* (in Japanese cookery) large noodles made of wheat flour
UDONS > UDON
UDOS > UDO
UDS *interj* God's or God save
UEY *n* u-turn
UEYS > UEY
UFO *n* flying saucer
UFOLOGIES > UFOLOGY
UFOLOGIST > UFOLOGY
UFOLOGY *n* study of UFOs
UFOS > UFO
UG *vb* hate
UGALI *n* type of stiff porridge made by mixing corn meal with boiling water: the basic starch constituent of a meal
UGALIS > UGALI
UGGED > UG
UGGING > UG
UGH *interj* exclamation of disgust ▷ *n* sound made to indicate disgust
UGHS > UGH
UGLIED > UGLY
UGLIER > UGLY
UGLIES > UGLY
UGLIEST > UGLY
UGLIFIED > UGLIFY
UGLIFIER > UGLIFY
UGLIFIERS > UGLIFY
UGLIFIES > UGLIFY
UGLIFY *vb* make or become ugly or more ugly
UGLIFYING > UGLIFY
UGLILY > UGLY
UGLINESS > UGLY
UGLY *adj* of unpleasant appearance ▷ *vb* make ugly
UGLYING > UGLY
UGS > UG
UGSOME *adj* loathsome
UH *interj* used to express hesitation
UHLAN *n* member of a body of lancers first employed in the Polish army and later in W European armies
UHLANS > UHLAN
UHURU *n* national independence
UHURUS > UHURU
UILLEAN as in *uillean pipes* bagpipes developed in Ireland and operated by squeezing bellows under the arm
UINTAHITE *same as* > UINTAITE
UINTAITE *n* variety of asphalt
UINTAITES > UINTAITE
UITLANDER *n* foreigner
UJAMAA as in *ujamaa village* communally organized village in Tanzania
UJAMAAS > UJAMAA
UKASE *n* (in imperial Russia) a decree from the tsar
UKASES > UKASE
UKE *short form of* > UKULELE
UKELELE *same as* > UKULELE
UKELELES > UKELELE
UKES > UKE
UKULELE *n* small guitar with four strings
UKULELES > UKULELE
ULAMA *n* body of Muslim scholars or religious leaders
ULAMAS > ULAMA
ULAN *same as* > UHLAN
ULANS > ULAN
ULCER *n* open sore on the surface of the skin or mucous membrane. ▷ *vb* make or become ulcerous
ULCERATE *vb* make or become ulcerous
ULCERATED > ULCERATE
ULCERATES > ULCERATE
ULCERED > ULCER
ULCERING > ULCER
ULCEROUS *adj* of, like, or characterized by ulcers
ULCERS > ULCER
ULE *n* rubber tree
ULEMA *same as* > ULAMA
ULEMAS > ULEMA
ULES > ULE
ULEX *n* variety of shrub
ULEXES > ULEX
ULEXITE *n* type of mineral
ULEXITES > ULEXITE
ULICON *same as* > EULACHON
ULICONS > ULICON
ULIGINOSE *same as* > ULIGINOUS
ULIGINOUS *adj* marshy
ULIKON *same as* > EULACHON
ULIKONS > ULIKON
ULITIS *n* gingivitis
ULITISES > ULITIS
ULLAGE *n* volume by which a liquid container falls short of being full ▷ *vb* create ullage in
ULLAGED > ULLAGE
ULLAGES > ULLAGE

ULLAGING > ULLAGE
ULLING *n* process of filling
ULLINGS > ULLING
ULMACEOUS *adj* of, relating to, or belonging to the *Ulmaceae*, a temperate and tropical family of deciduous trees and shrubs having scaly buds, simple serrated leaves, and typically winged fruits: includes the elms
ULMIN *n* substance found in decaying vegetation
ULMINS > ULMIN
ULNA *n* inner and longer of the two bones of the human forearm
ULNAD *adv* towards the ulna
ULNAE > ULNA
ULNAR > ULNA
ULNARE *n* bone in the wrist
ULNARIA > ULNARE
ULNAS > ULNA
ULOSES > ULOSIS
ULOSIS *n* formation of a scar
ULOTRICHY *n* state of having woolly or curly hair
ULPAN *n* Israeli study centre
ULPANIM > ULPAN
ULSTER *n* man's heavy double-breasted overcoat
ULSTERED *adj* wearing an ulster
ULSTERS > ULSTER
ULTERIOR *adj* (of an aim, reason, etc) concealed or hidden
ULTIMA *n* final syllable of a word
ULTIMACY > ULTIMATE
ULTIMAS > ULTIMA
ULTIMATA > ULTIMATUM
ULTIMATE *adj* final in a series or process ▷ *n* most significant, highest, furthest, or greatest thing ▷ *vb* end
ULTIMATED > ULTIMATE
ULTIMATES > ULTIMATE
ULTIMATUM *n* final warning stating that action will be taken unless certain conditions are met
ULTIMO *adv* in or during the previous month
ULTION *n* vengeance
ULTIONS > ULTION
ULTRA *n* person who has extreme or immoderate beliefs or opinions ▷ *adj* extreme or immoderate, esp in beliefs or opinions
ULTRACHIC *adj* extremely chic
ULTRACOLD *adj* extremely cold
ULTRACOOL *adj* extremely cool
ULTRADRY *adj* extremely dry
ULTRAFAST *adj* extremely fast
ULTRAFINE *adj* extremely fine
ULTRAHEAT *vb* sterilize through extreme heat treatment
ULTRAHIGH as in *ultrahigh frequency* radio-frequency band or radio frequency lying between 3000 and 300 megahertz
ULTRAHIP *adj* extremely trendy
ULTRAHOT *adj* extremely hot
ULTRAISM *n* extreme philosophy, belief, or action
ULTRAISMS > ULTRAISM
ULTRAIST > ULTRAISM
ULTRAISTS > ULTRAISM
ULTRALEFT *adj* of the extreme political Left or extremely radical
ULTRALOW *adj* extremely low
ULTRAPOSH *adj* extremely posh
ULTRAPURE *adj* extremely pure
ULTRARARE *adj* extremely rare
ULTRARED *obsolete word for* > INFRARED
ULTRAREDS > ULTRARED
ULTRARICH *adj* extremely rich
ULTRAS > ULTRA
ULTRASAFE *adj* extremely safe
ULTRASLOW *adj* extremely slow
ULTRASOFT *adj* extremely soft
ULTRATHIN *adj* extremely thin
ULTRATINY *adj* extremely small
ULTRAWIDE *adj* extremely wide
ULU *n* type of knife
ULULANT > ULULATE
ULULATE *vb* howl or wail
ULULATED > ULULATE
ULULATES > ULULATE
ULULATING > ULULATE
ULULATION > ULULATE
ULUS > ULU
ULVA *n* genus of seaweed
ULVAS > ULVA
ULYIE *Scots variant of* > OIL
ULYIES > ULYIE
ULZIE *Scots variant of* > OIL
ULZIES > ULZIE
UM *interj* representation of a common sound made when hesitating in speech
UMAMI *n* savoury flavour
UMAMIS > UMAMI
UMANGITE *n* type of mineral
UMANGITES > UMANGITE
UMBEL *n* umbrella-like flower cluster with the stalks springing from the central point
UMBELED *same as* > UMBELLED
UMBELLAR > UMBEL
UMBELLATE > UMBEL
UMBELLED *adj* having umbels
UMBELLET *same as* > UMBELLULE
UMBELLETS > UMBELLET
UMBELLULE *n* any of the small secondary umbels that make up a compound umbel
UMBELS > UMBEL
UMBER *adj* dark brown to reddish-brown ▷ *n* type of dark brown earth containing ferric oxide (rust) ▷ *vb* stain with umber
UMBERED > UMBER
UMBERING > UMBER
UMBERS > UMBER
UMBERY > UMBER
UMBILICAL *adj* of the navel
UMBILICI > UMBILICUS
UMBILICUS *n* navel
UMBLE as in *umble pie* (formerly) a pie made from the heart, entrails, etc, of a deer
UMBLES *another term for* > NUMBLES
UMBO *n* small hump projecting from the centre of the cap in certain mushrooms
UMBONAL > UMBO
UMBONATE > UMBO
UMBONES > UMBO
UMBONIC > UMBO
UMBOS > UMBO
UMBRA *n* shadow, esp the shadow cast by the moon onto the earth during a solar eclipse
UMBRACULA *pl n* umbrella-like structures
UMBRAE > UMBRA
UMBRAGE *n* displeasure or resentment ▷ *vb* shade
UMBRAGED > UMBRAGE
UMBRAGES > UMBRAGE
UMBRAGING > UMBRAGE
UMBRAL > UMBRA
UMBRAS > UMBRA
UMBRATED *adj* shown in a faint manner
UMBRATIC > UMBRA
UMBRATILE *adj* shadowy
UMBRE *same as* > UMBRETTE
UMBREL *n* umbrella
UMBRELLA *n* portable device used for protection against rain, consisting of a folding frame covered in material attached to a central rod ▷ *adj* containing or covering many different organizations, ideas, etc
UMBRELLAS > UMBRELLA
UMBRELLO *same as* > UMBRELLA
UMBRELLOS > UMBRELLO
UMBRELS > UMBREL
UMBRERE *n* helmet visor
UMBRERES > UMBRERE
UMBRES > UMBRE
UMBRETTE *n* African wading bird
UMBRETTES > UMBRETTE
UMBRIERE *same as* > UMBRERE
UMBRIERES > UMBRIERE
UMBRIL *same as* > UMBRER[E]
UMBRILS > UMBRIL
UMBROSE *same as* > UMBROUS
UMBROUS *adj* shady
UMFAZI *n* African married woman
UMFAZIS > UMFAZI
UMIAC *variant of* > UMIAK
UMIACK *variant of* > UMIAK
UMIACKS > UMIACK
UMIACS > UMIAC
UMIAK *n* Inuit boat made of skins
UMIAKS > UMIAK
UMIAQ *same as* > UMIAK
UMIAQS > UMIAQ
UMLAUT *n* mark (¨) placed over a vowel, esp in German, to indicate a change in its sound ▷ *vb* modify by umlaut
UMLAUTED > UMLAUT
UMLAUTING > UMLAUT
UMLAUTS > UMLAUT
UMLUNGU *n* White man: used esp as a term of address
UMLUNGUS > UMLUNGU
UMM *same as* > UM
UMP *short for* > UMPIRE
UMPED > UMP
UMPH *same as* > HUMPH
UMPIE *informal word for* > UMPIRE
UMPIES > UMPY
UMPING > UMP
UMPIRAGE > UMPIRE
UMPIRAGES > UMPIRE
UMPIRE *n* official who rul[es] on the playing of a game ▷ *vb* act as umpire in (a game)
UMPIRED > UMPIRE
UMPIRES > UMPIRE
UMPIRING > UMPIRE
UMPS > UMP
UMPTEEN *adj* very many ▷ *determiner* very many
UMPTEENTH *adj* latest in a tediously long series
UMPTIETH *same as* > UMPTEENTH
UMPTY *same as* > UMPTEEN
UMPY *same as* > UMPIE
UMQUHILE *adv* formerly
UMTEENTH *same as* > UMPTEENTH
UMU *n* type of oven
UMWELT *n* environmental factors, collectively, that are capable of affecting t[he]

ehaviour of an animal or ndividual
WELTS > UMWELT
WHILE *same*
S > UMQUHILE
pron spelling of ONE ntended to reflect a ialectal or informal ronunciation
ABASHED *adj* not shamed or embarrassed
ABATED *adv* without ny reduction in force *adj* without losing any riginal force or violence
ABATING *adj* not rowing less in strength
ABETTED *adj* without ssistance
ABIDING *adj* not lasting
ABJURED *adj* not denied
ABLE *adj* lacking the ecessary power, ability, r authority (to do omething)
ABORTED *adj* not aborted
ABRADED *adj* not eroded
ABUSED *adj* not abused
ABUSIVE *adj* not abusive
ACCRUED *adj* not accrued
ACCUSED *adj* not charged ith wrongdoing
ACERBIC *adj* not acerbic
ACHING *adj* not aching
ACIDIC *adj* not acidic
ACTABLE *adj* unable to e acted
ACTED *adj* not acted or erformed
ACTIVE *adj* inactive
ADAPTED *adj* not dapted
ADDED *adj* not added
ADEPT *adj* not adept
ADEPTLY > UNADEPT
ADMIRED *adj* not dmired
ADOPTED *adj* (of a road) ot maintained by a local uthority
ADORED *adj* not adored
ADORNED *adj* not ecorated
ADULT *adj* not mature
ADVISED *adj* rash or nwise
AFRAID *adj* not ightened or nervous
AGED *adj* not old
AGEING *adj* not ageing
AGILE *adj* not agile
AGING *same*
S > UNAGEING
AGREED *adj* not agreed
AI *same as* > UNAU
AIDABLE *adj* unable to e helped
AIDED *adv* without any elp or assistance ▷ *adj* ithout having received ny help
AIDEDLY > UNAIDED
AIMED *adj* not aimed or ecifically targeted

UNAIRED *adj* not aired
UNAIS > UNAI
UNAKIN *adj* not related
UNAKING *Shakespearean form of* > UNACHING
UNAKITE *n* type of mineral
UNAKITES > UNAKITE
UNALARMED *adj* not alarmed
UNALERTED *adj* not alerted
UNALIGNED *adj* not aligned
UNALIKE *adj* not similar
UNALIST *n* priest holding only one benefice
UNALISTS > UNALIST
UNALIVE *adj* unaware
UNALLAYED *adj* not allayed
UNALLEGED *adj* not alleged
UNALLIED *adj* not allied
UNALLOWED *adj* not allowed
UNALLOYED *adj* not spoiled by being mixed with anything else
UNALTERED *adj* not altered
UNAMASSED *adj* not amassed
UNAMAZED *adj* not greatly surprised
UNAMENDED *adj* not amended
UNAMERCED *adj* not amerced
UNAMIABLE *adj* not amiable
UNAMUSED *adj* not entertained, diverted, or laughing
UNAMUSING *adj* not entertaining
UNANCHOR *vb* remove anchor
UNANCHORS > UNANCHOR
UNANELED *adj* not having received extreme unction
UNANIMITY > UNANIMOUS
UNANIMOUS *adj* in complete agreement
UNANNEXED *adj* not annexed
UNANNOYED *adj* not annoyed
UNANXIOUS *adj* not anxious
UNAPPAREL *vb* undress
UNAPPLIED *adj* not applied
UNAPT *adj* not suitable or qualified
UNAPTLY > UNAPT
UNAPTNESS > UNAPT
UNARCHED *adj* not arched
UNARGUED *adj* not debated
UNARISEN *adj* not having risen
UNARM *less common word for* > DISARM
UNARMED *adj* without weapons
UNARMING > UNARM
UNARMORED *adj* without armour
UNARMS > UNARM
UNAROUSED *adj* not aroused
UNARRAYED *adj* not arrayed
UNARTFUL *adj* not artful
UNARY *adj* consisting of, or affecting, a single element or component
UNASHAMED *adj* not embarrassed, esp when doing something some people might find offensive
UNASKED *adv* without being asked to do something ▷ *adj* (of a question) not asked, although sometimes implied
UNASSAYED *adj* untried
UNASSUMED *adj* not assumed
UNASSURED *adj* insecure
UNATONED *adj* not atoned for
UNATTIRED *adj* unclothed
UNATTUNED *adj* unaccustomed
UNAU *n* two-toed sloth
UNAUDITED *adj* not having been audited
UNAUS > UNAU
UNAVENGED *adj* not avenged
UNAVERAGE *adj* not average
UNAVERTED *adj* not averted
UNAVOIDED *adj* not avoided
UNAVOWED *adj* not openly admitted
UNAWAKE *adj* not awake
UNAWAKED *adj* not aroused
UNAWARDED *adj* not awarded
UNAWARE *adj* not aware or conscious ▷ *adv* by surprise
UNAWARELY > UNAWARE
UNAWARES *adv* by surprise
UNAWED *adj* not awed
UNAWESOME *adj* not awesome
UNAXED *adj* not axed
UNBACKED *adj* (of a book, chair, etc) not having a back
UNBAFFLED *adj* not baffled
UNBAG *vb* take out of a bag
UNBAGGED > UNBAG
UNBAGGING > UNBAG
UNBAGS > UNBAG
UNBAITED *adj* not baited
UNBAKED *adj* not having been baked
UNBALANCE *vb* upset the equilibrium or balance of ▷ *n* imbalance or instability
UNBALE *vb* remove from bale
UNBALED > UNBALE
UNBALES > UNBALE
UNBALING > UNBALE
UNBAN *vb* stop banning or permit again
UNBANDAGE *vb* remove bandage from
UNBANDED *adj* not fastened with a band
UNBANKED *adj* not having been banked
UNBANNED > UNBAN
UNBANNING > UNBAN
UNBANS > UNBAN
UNBAPTISE *same as* > UNBAPTIZE
UNBAPTIZE *vb* remove the effect of baptism
UNBAR *vb* take away a bar or bars from
UNBARBED *adj* without barbs
UNBARE *vb* expose
UNBARED > UNBARE
UNBARES > UNBARE
UNBARING > UNBARE
UNBARK *vb* strip bark from
UNBARKED > UNBARK
UNBARKING > UNBARK
UNBARKS > UNBARK
UNBARRED > UNBAR
UNBARRING > UNBAR
UNBARS > UNBAR
UNBASED *adj* not having a base
UNBASHFUL *adj* not shy
UNBASTED *adj* not basted
UNBATED *adj* (of a sword, lance, etc) not covered with a protective button
UNBATHED *adj* unwashed
UNBE *vb* make non-existent
UNBEAR *vb* release (horse) from the bearing rein
UNBEARDED *adj* not having a beard
UNBEARED > UNBEAR
UNBEARING > UNBEAR
UNBEARS > UNBEAR
UNBEATEN *adj* having suffered no defeat
UNBED *vb* remove from bed
UNBEDDED > UNBED
UNBEDDING > UNBED
UNBEDS > UNBED
UNBEEN > UNBE
UNBEGET *vb* deprive of existence
UNBEGETS > UNBEGET
UNBEGGED *adj* not obtained by begging
UNBEGOT *adj* unbegotten
UNBEGUILE *vb* undeceive
UNBEGUN *adj* not commenced
UNBEING *n* non-existence
UNBEINGS > UNBEING
UNBEKNOWN *adv* without the knowledge (of a person) ▷ *adj* not known (to)
UNBELIEF *n* disbelief or rejection of belief
UNBELIEFS > UNBELIEF
UNBELIEVE *vb* disbelieve
UNBELOVED *adj* unhappy in love
UNBELT *vb* unbuckle the belt of (a garment)
UNBELTED > UNBELT
UNBELTING > UNBELT
UNBELTS > UNBELT
UNBEMUSED *adj* not bemused
UNBEND *vb* become less strict or more informal

in one's attitudes or behaviour
UNBENDED > UNBEND
UNBENDING *adj* rigid or inflexible
UNBENDS > UNBEND
UNBENIGN *adj* not benign
UNBENT *adj* not bent or bowed
UNBEREFT *adj* not bereft
UNBERUFEN *adj* not called for
UNBESEEM *vb* be unbefitting to
UNBESEEMS > UNBESEEM
UNBESPEAK *vb* annul
UNBESPOKE *adj* not bespoken
UNBIAS *vb* free from prejudice
UNBIASED *adj* not having or showing prejudice or favouritism
UNBIASES > UNBIAS
UNBIASING > UNBIAS
UNBIASSED *same as* > UNBIASED
UNBIASSES > UNBIAS
UNBID *same as* > UNBIDDEN
UNBIDDEN *adj* not ordered or asked
UNBIGOTED *adj* not bigoted
UNBILLED *adj* not having been billed
UNBIND *vb* set free from bonds or chains
UNBINDING > UNBIND
UNBINDS > UNBIND
UNBISHOP *vb* remove from the position of bishop
UNBISHOPS > UNBISHOP
UNBITT *vb* remove (cable) from the bitts
UNBITTED > UNBITT
UNBITTEN *adj* not having been bitten
UNBITTER *adj* not bitter
UNBITTING > UNBITT
UNBITTS > UNBITT
UNBLAMED *vb* not blamed
UNBLENDED *adj* not blended
UNBLENT *same as* > UNBLENDED
UNBLESS *vb* deprive of a blessing
UNBLESSED *adj* deprived of blessing
UNBLESSES > UNBLESS
UNBLEST *same as* > UNBLESSED
UNBLIND *vb* rid of blindness
UNBLINDED > UNBLIND
UNBLINDS > UNBLIND
UNBLOCK *vb* remove a blockage from
UNBLOCKED > UNBLOCK
UNBLOCKS > UNBLOCK
UNBLOODED *adj* not bloodied
UNBLOODY *adj* not covered with blood
UNBLOTTED *adj* not blotted
UNBLOWED *same as* > UNBLOWN
UNBLOWN *adj* (of a flower) still in the bud
UNBLUNTED *adj* not blunted
UNBLURRED *adj* not blurred
UNBOARDED *adj* not boarded
UNBOBBED *adj* not bobbed
UNBODIED *adj* having no body
UNBODING *adj* having no presentiment
UNBOILED *adj* not boiled
UNBOLT *vb* unfasten a bolt of (a door)
UNBOLTED *adj* (of grain, meal, or flour) not sifted
UNBOLTING > UNBOLT
UNBOLTS > UNBOLT
UNBONDED *adj* not bonded
UNBONE *vb* remove bone from
UNBONED *adj* (of meat, fish, etc) not having had the bones removed
UNBONES > UNBONE
UNBONING > UNBONE
UNBONNET *vb* remove the bonnet from
UNBONNETS > UNBONNET
UNBOOKED *adj* not reserved
UNBOOKISH *adj* not studious
UNBOOT *vb* remove boots from
UNBOOTED > UNBOOT
UNBOOTING > UNBOOT
UNBOOTS > UNBOOT
UNBORE *adj* unborn
UNBORN *adj* not yet born
UNBORNE *adj* not borne
UNBOSOM *vb* relieve (oneself) of (secrets or feelings) by telling someone
UNBOSOMED > UNBOSOM
UNBOSOMER > UNBOSOM
UNBOSOMS > UNBOSOM
UNBOTTLE *vb* allow out of bottle
UNBOTTLED > UNBOTTLE
UNBOTTLES > UNBOTTLE
UNBOUGHT *adj* not purchased
UNBOUNCY *adj* not bouncy
UNBOUND *adj* (of a book) not bound within a cover
UNBOUNDED *adj* having no boundaries or limits
UNBOWED *adj* not giving in or submitting
UNBOWING *adj* not bowing
UNBOX *vb* empty a box
UNBOXED > UNBOX
UNBOXES > UNBOX
UNBOXING > UNBOX
UNBRACE *vb* remove tension or strain from
UNBRACED > UNBRACE
UNBRACES > UNBRACE
UNBRACING > UNBRACE
UNBRAID *vb* remove braids from
UNBRAIDED > UNBRAID
UNBRAIDS > UNBRAID
UNBRAKE *vb* stop reducing speed by releasing brake
UNBRAKED > UNBRAKE
UNBRAKES > UNBRAKE
UNBRAKING > UNBRAKE
UNBRANDED *adj* not having a brand name
UNBRASTE *archaic past form of* > UNBRACE
UNBRED *adj* not taught or instructed
UNBREECH *vb* remove breech from
UNBRIDGED *adj* not spanned by a bridge
UNBRIDLE *vb* remove the bridle from (a horse)
UNBRIDLED *adj* (of feelings or behaviour) not controlled in any way
UNBRIDLES > UNBRIDLE
UNBRIEFED *adj* not instructed
UNBRIGHT *adj* not bright
UNBRIZZED *same as* > UNBRUISED
UNBROILED *adj* not broiled
UNBROKE *same as* > UNBROKEN
UNBROKEN *adj* complete or whole
UNBROWNED *adj* not browned
UNBRUISED *adj* not bruised
UNBRUSED *same as* > UNBRUISED
UNBRUSHED *adj* not brushed
UNBUCKLE *vb* undo the buckle or buckles of
UNBUCKLED > UNBUCKLE
UNBUCKLES > UNBUCKLE
UNBUDDED *adj* not having buds
UNBUDGING *adj* not moving
UNBUILD *vb* destroy
UNBUILDS > UNBUILD
UNBUILT > UNBUILD
UNBULKY *adj* not bulky
UNBUNDLE *vb* separate (hardware from software) for sales purposes
UNBUNDLED > UNBUNDLE
UNBUNDLER > UNBUNDLE
UNBUNDLES > UNBUNDLE
UNBURDEN *vb* relieve (one's mind or oneself) of a worry by confiding in someone
UNBURDENS > UNBURDEN
UNBURIED > UNBURY
UNBURIES > UNBURY
UNBURNED *same as* > UNBURNT
UNBURNT *adj* not burnt
UNBURROW *vb* remove from a burrow
UNBURROWS > UNBURROW
UNBURTHEN *same as* > UNBURDEN
UNBURY *vb* unearth
UNBURYING > UNBURY
UNBUSTED *adj* unbroken
UNBUSY *adj* not busy
UNBUTTON *vb* undo by unfastening the buttons (a garment)
UNBUTTONS > UNBUTTON
UNCAGE *vb* release from a cage
UNCAGED *adj* at liberty
UNCAGES > UNCAGE
UNCAGING > UNCAGE
UNCAKE *vb* remove compacted matter from
UNCAKED > UNCAKE
UNCAKES > UNCAKE
UNCAKING > UNCAKE
UNCALLED *adj* not called
UNCANDID *adj* not frank
UNCANDLED *adj* not illuminated by candle
UNCANDOUR *n* lack of candour
UNCANNED *adj* not canne
UNCANNIER > UNCANNY
UNCANNILY > UNCANNY
UNCANNY *adj* weird or mysterious
UNCANONIC *adj* unclerica
UNCAP *vb* remove a cap or top from (a container)
UNCAPABLE *same as* > INCAPABLE
UNCAPE *vb* remove the ca from
UNCAPED > UNCAPE
UNCAPES > UNCAPE
UNCAPING > UNCAPE
UNCAPPED > UNCAP
UNCAPPING > UNCAP
UNCAPS > UNCAP
UNCARDED *adj* not carded
UNCAREFUL *adj* careless
UNCARING *adj* thoughtle
UNCART *vb* remove from a cart
UNCARTED > UNCART
UNCARTING > UNCART
UNCARTS > UNCART
UNCARVED *adj* not carved
UNCASE *vb* display
UNCASED > UNCASE
UNCASES > UNCASE
UNCASHED *adj* not cashec
UNCASING > UNCASE
UNCASKED *adj* removed from a cask
UNCAST *adj* not cast
UNCATCHY *adj* not catchy
UNCATE *same as* > UNCINA
UNCATERED *adj* not cater
UNCAUGHT *adj* not caugh
UNCAUSED *adj* not broug into existence by any cause
UNCE *same as* > OUNCE
UNCEASING *adj* continui without a break
UNCEDED *adj* not ceded
UNCERTAIN *adj* not able t be accurately known or predicted
UNCES > UNCE
UNCESSANT *same as* > INCESSANT
UNCHAIN *vb* remove a ch or chains from
UNCHAINED > UNCHAIN

CHAINS > UNCHAIN
CHAIR *vb* unseat from hair
CHAIRED > UNCHAIR
CHAIRS > UNCHAIR
CHANCY *adj* unlucky, ill-mened, or dangerous
CHANGED *adj* remaining he same
CHARGE *vb* unload
CHARGED *adj* (of land r other property) not ubject to a charge
CHARGES > UNCHARGE
CHARITY *n* lack of harity
CHARM *vb* disenchant
CHARMED > UNCHARM
CHARMS > UNCHARM
CHARNEL *vb* exhume
CHARRED *adj* not charred
CHARTED *adj* (of an area f sea or land) not having ad a map made of it, esp ecause it is unexplored
CHARY *adj* not cautious
CHASTE *adj* not chaste
CHASTER > UNCHASTE
CHECK *vb* remove check nark from
CHECKED *adj* not revented from ontinuing or growing ▷ *adv* without being topped or hindered
CHECKS > UNCHECK
CHEERED *adj* miserable
CHEWED *adj* not chewed
CHIC *adj* not chic
CHICLY > UNCHIC
CHILD *vb* deprive of hildren
CHILDED > UNCHILD
CHILDS > UNCHILD
CHILLED *adj* not chilled
CHOKE *vb* unblock
CHOKED > UNCHOKE
CHOKES > UNCHOKE
CHOKING > UNCHOKE
CHOSEN *adj* not chosen
CHRISOM *adj* nchristened
CHURCH *vb* xcommunicate
CI > UNCUS
CIA *n* twelfth part
CIAE > UNCIA
CIAL *adj* of or written n letters that resemble odern capitals, as sed in Greek and Latin anuscripts of the third to inth centuries ▷ *n* uncial etter or manuscript
CIALLY > UNCIAL
CIALS > UNCIAL
CIFORM *adj* having the hape of a hook ▷ *n* any ook-shaped structure or art, esp a small bone of he wrist
CIFORMS > UNCIFORM
CINAL *same* s > UNCINATE
UNCINARIA *same as* > HOOKWORM
UNCINATE *adj* shaped like a hook
UNCINATED > UNCINATE
UNCINI > UNCINUS
UNCINUS *n* small hooked structure, such as any of the hooked chaetae of certain polychaete worms
UNCIPHER *vb* decode
UNCIPHERS > UNCIPHER
UNCITED *adj* not quoted
UNCIVIL *adj* impolite, rude or bad-mannered
UNCIVILLY > UNCIVIL
UNCLAD *adj* having no clothes on
UNCLAIMED *adj* not having been claimed
UNCLAMP *vb* remove clamp from
UNCLAMPED > UNCLAMP
UNCLAMPS > UNCLAMP
UNCLARITY *adj* lack of clarity
UNCLASP *vb* unfasten the clasp of (something)
UNCLASPED > UNCLASP
UNCLASPS > UNCLASP
UNCLASSED *adj* not divided into classes
UNCLASSY *adj* not classy
UNCLAWED *adj* not clawed
UNCLE *n* brother of one's father or mother ▷ *vb* refer to as uncle
UNCLEAN *adj* lacking moral, spiritual, or physical cleanliness
UNCLEANED *adj* not cleaned
UNCLEANER > UNCLEAN
UNCLEANLY *adv* in an unclean manner ▷ *adj* characterized by an absence of cleanliness
UNCLEAR *adj* confusing or hard to understand
UNCLEARED *adj* not cleared
UNCLEARER > UNCLEAR
UNCLEARLY > UNCLEAR
UNCLED > UNCLE
UNCLEFT *adj* not cleft
UNCLENCH *vb* relax from a clenched position
UNCLES > UNCLE
UNCLESHIP *n* position of an uncle
UNCLEW *vb* undo
UNCLEWED > UNCLEW
UNCLEWING > UNCLEW
UNCLEWS > UNCLEW
UNCLICHED *adj* not cliched
UNCLINCH *same as* > UNCLENCH
UNCLING > UNCLE
UNCLIP *vb* remove clip from
UNCLIPPED > UNCLIP
UNCLIPS > UNCLIP
UNCLIPT *archaic past form of* > UNCLIP
UNCLOAK *vb* remove cloak from
UNCLOAKED > UNCLOAK
UNCLOAKS > UNCLOAK
UNCLOG *vb* remove an obstruction from (a drain, etc)
UNCLOGGED > UNCLOG
UNCLOGS > UNCLOG
UNCLOSE *vb* open or cause to open
UNCLOSED > UNCLOSE
UNCLOSES > UNCLOSE
UNCLOSING > UNCLOSE
UNCLOTHE *vb* take off garments from
UNCLOTHED > UNCLOTHE
UNCLOTHES > UNCLOTHE
UNCLOUD *vb* clear clouds from
UNCLOUDED > UNCLOUD
UNCLOUDS > UNCLOUD
UNCLOUDY *adj* not cloudy
UNCLOVEN *adj* not cleaved
UNCLOYED *adj* not cloyed
UNCLOYING *adj* not cloying
UNCLUTCH *vb* open from tight grip
UNCLUTTER *vb* tidy and straighten up
UNCO *adj* awkward ▷ *n* awkward or clumsy person
UNCOATED *adj* not covered with a layer
UNCOATING *n* process whereby a virus exposes its genome in order to replicate
UNCOBBLED *adj* not cobbled
UNCOCK *vb* remove from a cocked position
UNCOCKED > UNCOCK
UNCOCKING > UNCOCK
UNCOCKS > UNCOCK
UNCODED *adj* not coded
UNCOER > UNCO
UNCOERCED *adj* unforced
UNCOEST > UNCO
UNCOFFIN *vb* take out of a coffin
UNCOFFINS > UNCOFFIN
UNCOIL *vb* unwind or untwist
UNCOILED > UNCOIL
UNCOILING > UNCOIL
UNCOILS > UNCOIL
UNCOINED *adj* (of a metal) not made into coin
UNCOLORED *adj* not coloured
UNCOLT *vb* divest of a horse
UNCOLTED > UNCOLT
UNCOLTING > UNCOLT
UNCOLTS > UNCOLT
UNCOMBED *adj* not combed
UNCOMBINE *vb* break apart
UNCOMELY *adj* not attractive
UNCOMIC *adj* not comical
UNCOMMON *adj* not happening or encountered often
UNCONCERN *n* apathy or indifference
UNCONFINE *vb* remove restrictions from
UNCONFORM *adj* dissimilar
UNCONFUSE *vb* remove confusion from
UNCONGEAL *vb* become liquid again
UNCOOKED *adj* raw
UNCOOL *adj* unsophisticated
UNCOOLED *adj* not cooled
UNCOPE *vb* unmuzzle
UNCOPED > UNCOPE
UNCOPES > UNCOPE
UNCOPING > UNCOPE
UNCORD *vb* release from cords
UNCORDED > UNCORD
UNCORDIAL *adj* unfriendly
UNCORDING > UNCORD
UNCORDS > UNCORD
UNCORK *vb* remove the cork from (a bottle)
UNCORKED > UNCORK
UNCORKING > UNCORK
UNCORKS > UNCORK
UNCORRUPT *adj* not corrupt
UNCOS > UNCO
UNCOSTLY *adj* inexpensive
UNCOUNTED *adj* unable to be counted
UNCOUPLE *vb* disconnect or become disconnected
UNCOUPLED > UNCOUPLE
UNCOUPLER > UNCOUPLE
UNCOUPLES > UNCOUPLE
UNCOURTLY *adj* not courtly
UNCOUTH *adj* lacking in good manners, refinement, or grace
UNCOUTHER > UNCOUTH
UNCOUTHLY > UNCOUTH
UNCOVER *vb* reveal or disclose
UNCOVERED *adj* not covered
UNCOVERS > UNCOVER
UNCOWL *vb* remove hood from
UNCOWLED > UNCOWL
UNCOWLING > UNCOWL
UNCOWLS > UNCOWL
UNCOY *adj* not modest
UNCOYNED *same as* > UNCOINED
UNCRACKED *adj* not cracked
UNCRATE *vb* remove from a crate
UNCRATED > UNCRATE
UNCRATES > UNCRATE
UNCRATING > UNCRATE
UNCRAZY *adj* not crazy
UNCREATE *vb* unmake
UNCREATED > UNCREATE
UNCREATES > UNCREATE
UNCREWED *adj* not crewed
UNCROPPED *adj* not cropped
UNCROSS *vb* cease to cross
UNCROSSED > UNCROSS
UNCROSSES > UNCROSS
UNCROWDED *adj* (of a confined space, area, etc) not containing too many people or things
UNCROWN *vb* take the crown from
UNCROWNED *adj* having the

powers, but not the title, of royalty
UNCROWNS > UNCROWN
UNCRUDDED *adj* uncurdled
UNCRUMPLE *vb* remove creases from
UNCRUSHED *adj* not crushed
UNCTION *n* act of anointing with oil in sacramental ceremonies
UNCTIONS > UNCTION
UNCTUOUS *adj* pretending to be kind and concerned
UNCUFF *vb* remove handcuffs from
UNCUFFED > UNCUFF
UNCUFFING > UNCUFF
UNCUFFS > UNCUFF
UNCULLED *adj* not culled
UNCURABLE *same as* > INCURABLE
UNCURABLY > UNCURABLE
UNCURB *vb* remove curbs from (a horse)
UNCURBED > UNCURB
UNCURBING > UNCURB
UNCURBS > UNCURB
UNCURDLED *adj* not curdled
UNCURED *adj* not cured
UNCURIOUS *adj* not curious
UNCURL *vb* move or cause to move out of a curled or rolled up position
UNCURLED > UNCURL
UNCURLING > UNCURL
UNCURLS > UNCURL
UNCURRENT *adj* not current
UNCURSE *vb* remove curse from
UNCURSED > UNCURSE
UNCURSES > UNCURSE
UNCURSING > UNCURSE
UNCURTAIN *vb* reveal
UNCURVED *adj* not curved
UNCUS *n* hooked part or process, as in the human cerebrum
UNCUT *adj* not shortened or censored
UNCUTE *adj* not cute
UNCYNICAL *adj* not cynical
UNDAM *vb* free from a dam
UNDAMAGED *adj* not spoilt or damaged
UNDAMMED > UNDAM
UNDAMMING > UNDAM
UNDAMNED *adj* not damned
UNDAMPED *adj* (of an oscillating system) having unrestricted motion
UNDAMS > UNDAM
UNDARING *adj* not daring
UNDASHED *adj* not dashed
UNDATABLE *adj* not able to be dated
UNDATE *vb* remove date from
UNDATED *adj* (of a manuscript, letter, etc) not having an identifying date
UNDAUNTED *adj* not put off, discouraged, or beaten
UNDAWNING *adj* not dawning
UNDAZZLE *vb* recover from a daze
UNDAZZLED > UNDAZZLE
UNDAZZLES > UNDAZZLE
UNDE *same as* > UNDEE
UNDEAD *adj* alive
UNDEAF *vb* restore hearing to
UNDEAFED > UNDEAF
UNDEAFING > UNDEAF
UNDEAFS > UNDEAF
UNDEALT *adj* not dealt (with)
UNDEAR *adj* not dear
UNDEBASED *adj* not debased
UNDEBATED *adj* not debated
UNDECAGON *n* polygon having eleven sides
UNDECAYED *adj* not rotten
UNDECEIVE *vb* reveal the truth to (someone previously misled or deceived)
UNDECENT *same as* > INDECENT
UNDECIDED *adj* not having made up one's mind
UNDECIMAL *adj* based on the number 11
UNDECK *vb* remove decorations from
UNDECKED > UNDECK
UNDECKING > UNDECK
UNDECKS > UNDECK
UNDEE *adj* wavy
UNDEEDED *adj* not transferred by deed
UNDEFACED *adj* not spoilt
UNDEFIDE *same as* > UNDEFIED
UNDEFIED *adj* not challenged
UNDEFILED *adj* not defiled
UNDEFINED *adj* not defined or made clear
UNDEIFIED > UNDEIFY
UNDEIFIES > UNDEIFY
UNDEIFY *vb* strip of the status of a deity
UNDELAYED *adj* not delayed
UNDELETED *adj* not deleted, or restored after being deleted
UNDELIGHT *n* absence of delight
UNDELUDED *adj* not deluded
UNDENIED *adj* not denied
UNDENTED *adj* not dented
UNDER *adv* indicating movement to or position beneath the underside or base ▷ *prep* less than
UNDERACT *vb* play (a role) without adequate emphasis
UNDERACTS > UNDERACT
UNDERAGE *adj* below the required or standard age ▷ *n* shortfall
UNDERAGED *adj* not old enough
UNDERAGES > UNDERAGE
UNDERARM *adj* denoting a style of throwing, bowling, or serving in which the hand is swung below shoulder level ▷ *adv* in an underarm style ▷ *n* armpit
UNDERARMS > UNDERARM
UNDERATE > UNDEREAT
UNDERBAKE *vb* bake insufficiently
UNDERBEAR *vb* endure
UNDERBID *vb* submit a bid lower than that of (others)
UNDERBIDS > UNDERBID
UNDERBIT > UNDERBITE
UNDERBITE *vb* use insufficient acid in etching
UNDERBODY *n* underpart of a body, as of an animal or motor vehicle
UNDERBORE > UNDERBEAR
UNDERBOSS *n* person who is second in command
UNDERBRED *adj* of impure stock
UNDERBRIM *n* part of a hat
UNDERBUD *vb* produce fewer buds than expected
UNDERBUDS > UNDERBUD
UNDERBUSH *n* undergrowth or underbrush
UNDERBUY *vb* buy (stock in trade) in amounts lower than required
UNDERBUYS > UNDERBUY
UNDERCARD *n* event supporting a main event
UNDERCART *n* aircraft undercarriage
UNDERCAST *vb* cast beneath
UNDERCLAD *adj* not wearing enough clothes
UNDERCLAY *n* grey or whitish clay rock containing fossilized plant roots and occurring beneath coal seams. When used as a refractory, it is known as fireclay
UNDERCLUB *vb* use a golf club that will not hit the ball as far as required
UNDERCOAT *n* coat of paint applied before the final coat ▷ *vb* apply an undercoat to a surface
UNDERCOOK *vb* cook for too short a time or at too low a temperature
UNDERCOOL *vb* cool insufficiently
UNDERCUT *vb* charge less than (a competitor) to obtain trade ▷ *n* act or an instance of cutting underneath
UNDERCUTS > UNDERCUT
UNDERDAKS *pl n* underpants
UNDERDECK *n* lower deck of a vessel
UNDERDID > UNDERDO
UNDERDO *vb* do (something) inadequate
UNDERDOER > UNDERDO
UNDERDOES > UNDERDO
UNDERDOG *n* person or team in a weak or underprivileged positior
UNDERDOGS > UNDERDOG
UNDERDONE *adj* not cooke enough
UNDERDOSE *vb* give insufficient dose
UNDERDRAW *vb* sketch the subject before painting i on the same surface
UNDERDREW > UNDERDRAW
UNDEREAT *vb* not eat enough
UNDEREATS > UNDEREAT
UNDERFED > UNDERFEED
UNDERFEED *vb* give too little food to ▷ *n* apparatus by which fuel, etc, is supplied from belo
UNDERFELT *n* thick felt la under a carpet to increas insulation
UNDERFIRE *vb* bake insufficiently
UNDERFISH *vb* catch fewe fish than the permitted maximum amount
UNDERFLOW *n* undercurre
UNDERFONG *vb* receive
UNDERFOOT *adv* under the feet
UNDERFUND *vb* provide insufficient funding
UNDERFUR *n* layer of dens soft fur occurring beneat the outer coarser fur in certain mammals, such the otter and seal
UNDERFURS > UNDERFUR
UNDERGIRD *vb* strengthe or reinforce by passing a rope, cable, or chain around the underside of (an object, load, etc)
UNDERGIRT > UNDERGIRD
UNDERGO *vb* experience, endure, or sustain
UNDERGOD *n* subordinate god
UNDERGODS > UNDERGOD
UNDERGOER > UNDERGO
UNDERGOES > UNDERGO
UNDERGONE > UNDERGO
UNDERGOWN *n* gown worr under another article of clothing
UNDERGRAD *n* person studying for a first degre undergraduate
UNDERHAIR *n* lower layer animal's hair
UNDERHAND *adj* sly, deceitful, and secretive ▷ *adv* in an underhand manner or style
UNDERHEAT *vb* heat insufficiently
UNDERHUNG *adj* (of the lower jaw) projecting

beyond the upper jaw
NDERIVED *adj* not derived
NDERJAW *n* lower jaw
NDERJAWS > UNDERJAW
NDERKEEP *vb* suppress
NDERKEPT > UNDERKEEP
NDERKILL *n* less force than is needed to defeat enemy
NDERKING *n* ruler subordinate to a king
NDERLAID *adj* laid underneath
NDERLAIN > UNDERLIE
NDERLAP *vb* project under the edge of
NDERLAPS > UNDERLAP
NDERLAY *n* felt or rubber laid beneath a carpet to increase insulation and resilience ▷ *vb* place (something) under or beneath
NDERLAYS > UNDERLAY
NDERLEAF *n* (in liverworts) any of the leaves forming a row on the underside of the stem: usually smaller than the two rows of lateral leaves and sometimes absent
NDERLET *vb* let for a price lower than expected or justified
NDERLETS > UNDERLET
NDERLIE *vb* lie or be placed under
NDERLIER > UNDERLIE
NDERLIES > UNDERLIE
NDERLINE *vb* draw a line under ▷ *n* line underneath, esp under written matter
NDERLING *n* subordinate
NDERLIP *n* lower lip
NDERLIPS > UNDERLIP
NDERLIT *adj* lit from beneath
NDERLOAD *vb* load incompletely
NDERMAN *vb* supply with insufficient staff ▷ *n* subordinate man
NDERMANS > UNDERMAN
NDERMEN > UNDERMAN
NDERMINE *vb* weaken gradually
NDERMOST *adj* being the furthest under ▷ *adv* in the lowest place
NDERN *n* time between sunrise and noon
NDERNOTE *n* undertone
NDERNS > UNDERN
NDERPAID *adj* not paid as much as the job deserves
NDERPART *n* lower part or underside of something such as an animal
NDERPASS *n* section of a road that passes under another road or a railway line
NDERPAY *vb* pay someone insufficiently
UNDERPAYS > UNDERPAY
UNDERPEEP *vb* peep under
UNDERPIN *vb* give strength or support to
UNDERPINS > UNDERPIN
UNDERPLAY *vb* achieve (an effect) by deliberate lack of emphasis
UNDERPLOT *n* subsidiary plot in a literary or dramatic work
UNDERPROP *vb* prop up from beneath
UNDERRAN > UNDERRUN
UNDERRATE *vb* underestimate
UNDERRIPE *adj* not quite ripe
UNDERRUN *vb* run beneath
UNDERRUNS > UNDERRUN
UNDERSAID > UNDERSAY
UNDERSAY *vb* say by way of response
UNDERSAYS > UNDERSAY
UNDERSEA *adv* below the surface of the sea
UNDERSEAL *n* coating of tar etc applied to the underside of a motor vehicle to prevent corrosion ▷ *vb* apply such a coating to a motor vehicle
UNDERSEAS *same as* > UNDERSEA
UNDERSELF *n* subconscious or person within
UNDERSELL *vb* sell at a price lower than that of another seller
UNDERSET *n* ocean undercurrent ▷ *vb* support from underneath
UNDERSETS > UNDERSET
UNDERSHOT *adj* (of the lower jaw) projecting beyond the upper jaw
UNDERSIDE *n* bottom or lower surface
UNDERSIGN *vb* sign the bottom (of a document)
UNDERSIZE *adj* smaller than normal
UNDERSKY *n* lower sky
UNDERSOIL *another word for* > SUBSOIL
UNDERSOLD > UNDERSELL
UNDERSONG *n* accompanying secondary melody
UNDERSPIN *n* backspin
UNDERTAKE *vb* agree or commit oneself to (something) or to do (something)
UNDERTANE *Shakespearean past participle of* > UNDERTAKE
UNDERTAX *vb* tax insufficiently
UNDERTIME *n* time spent by an employee at work in non-work-related activities like socializing, surfing the internet, making personal telephone calls, etc
UNDERTINT *n* slight, subdued, or delicate tint
UNDERTONE *n* quiet tone of voice
UNDERTOOK *past tense of* > UNDERTAKE
UNDERTOW *n* strong undercurrent flowing in a different direction from the surface current
UNDERTOWS > UNDERTOW
UNDERUSE *vb* use less than normal
UNDERUSED > UNDERUSE
UNDERUSES > UNDERUSE
UNDERVEST *another name for* > VEST
UNDERVOTE *n* vote cast but invalid
UNDERWAY *adj* in progress ▷ *adv* in progress
UNDERWEAR *n* clothing worn under the outer garments and next to the skin
UNDERWENT *past tense of* > UNDERGO
UNDERWING *n* hind wing of an insect, esp when covered by the forewing
UNDERWIRE *vb* support with wire underneath
UNDERWIT *n* half-wit
UNDERWITS > UNDERWIT
UNDERWOOD *n* small trees, bushes, ferns, etc growing beneath taller trees in a wood or forest
UNDERWOOL *n* lower layer of an animal's coat
UNDERWORK *vb* do less work than expected
UNDESERT *n* lack of worth
UNDESERTS > UNDESERT
UNDESERVE *vb* fail to deserve
UNDESIRED *adj* not desired
UNDEVOUT *adj* not devout
UNDID > UNDO
UNDIES *pl n* underwear, esp women's
UNDIGHT *vb* remove
UNDIGHTS > UNDIGHT
UNDIGNIFY *vb* divest of dignity
UNDILUTED *adj* (of a liquid) not having any water added to it
UNDIMMED *adj* (of eyes, light, etc) still bright or shining
UNDINE *n* female water spirit
UNDINES > UNDINE
UNDINISM *n* obsession with water
UNDINISMS > UNDINISM
UNDINTED *adj* not dinted
UNDIPPED *adj* not dipped
UNDIVIDED *adj* total and whole-hearted
UNDIVINE *adj* not divine
UNDO *vb* open, unwrap
UNDOABLE *adj* impossible
UNDOCILE *adj* not docile
UNDOCK *vb* take out of a dock
UNDOCKED > UNDOCK
UNDOCKING > UNDOCK
UNDOCKS > UNDOCK
UNDOER > UNDO
UNDOERS > UNDO
UNDOES > UNDO
UNDOING *n* cause of someone's downfall
UNDOINGS > UNDOING
UNDONE *adj* not done or completed
UNDOOMED *adj* not doomed
UNDOTTED *adj* not dotted
UNDOUBLE *vb* stretch out
UNDOUBLED > UNDOUBLE
UNDOUBLES > UNDOUBLE
UNDOUBTED *adj* certain or indisputable
UNDRAINED *adj* not drained
UNDRAPE *vb* remove drapery from
UNDRAPED > UNDRAPE
UNDRAPES > UNDRAPE
UNDRAPING > UNDRAPE
UNDRAW *vb* open (curtains)
UNDRAWING > UNDRAW
UNDRAWN > UNDRAW
UNDRAWS > UNDRAW
UNDREADED *adj* not feared
UNDREAMED *adj* not thought of or imagined
UNDREAMT *same as* > UNDREAMED
UNDRESS *vb* take off clothes from (oneself or another) ▷ *n* partial or complete nakedness ▷ *adj* characterized by or requiring informal or normal working dress or uniform
UNDRESSED *adj* partially or completely naked
UNDRESSES > UNDRESS
UNDREST *same as* > UNDRESSED
UNDREW > UNDRAW
UNDRIED *adj* not dried
UNDRILLED *adj* not drilled
UNDRIVEN *adj* not driven
UNDROSSY *adj* pure
UNDROWNED *adj* not drowned
UNDRUNK *adj* not drunk
UNDUBBED *adj* (of a film, etc) not dubbed
UNDUE *adj* greater than is reasonable; excessive
UNDUG *adj* not having been dug
UNDULANCE > UNDULANT
UNDULANCY > UNDULANT
UNDULANT *adj* resembling waves
UNDULAR > UNDULATE
UNDULATE *vb* move in waves ▷ *adj* having a wavy

or rippled appearance, margin, or form
UNDULATED > UNDULATE
UNDULATES > UNDULATE
UNDULATOR > UNDULATE
UNDULLED *adj* not dulled
UNDULOSE *same as* > UNDULOUS
UNDULOUS *adj* undulate
UNDULY *adv* excessively
UNDUTEOUS *same as* > UNDUTIFUL
UNDUTIFUL *adj* not dutiful
UNDY *same as* > UNDEE
UNDYED *adj* not dyed
UNDYING *adj* never ending, eternal
UNDYINGLY > UNDYING
UNDYNAMIC *adj* not dynamic
UNEAGER *adj* nonchalant
UNEAGERLY > UNEAGER
UNEARED *adj* not ploughed
UNEARNED *adj* not deserved
UNEARTH *vb* reveal or discover by searching
UNEARTHED > UNEARTH
UNEARTHLY *adj* ghostly or eerie
UNEARTHS > UNEARTH
UNEASE > UNEASY
UNEASES > UNEASY
UNEASIER > UNEASY
UNEASIEST > UNEASY
UNEASILY > UNEASY
UNEASY *adj* (of a person) anxious or apprehensive
UNEATABLE *adj* (of food) so rotten or unattractive as to be unfit to eat
UNEATEN *adj* (of food) not having been consumed
UNEATH *adv* not easily
UNEATHES *same as* > UNEATH
UNEDGE *vb* take the edge off
UNEDGED > UNEDGE
UNEDGES > UNEDGE
UNEDGING > UNEDGE
UNEDIBLE *variant of* > INEDIBLE
UNEDITED *adj* not edited
UNEFFACED *adj* not destroyed
UNELATED *adj* not elated
UNELECTED *adj* not elected
UNEMPTIED *adj* not emptied
UNENDED *adj* without end
UNENDING *adj* not showing any signs of ever stopping
UNENDOWED *adj* not endowed
UNENGAGED *adj* not engaged
UNENJOYED *adj* not enjoyed
UNENSURED *adj* not ensured
UNENTERED *adj* not having been entered previously
UNENVIED *adj* not envied
UNENVIOUS *adj* not envious
UNENVYING *adj* not envying
UNEQUABLE *adj* unstable
UNEQUAL *adj* not equal in quantity, size, rank, value, etc ▷ *n* person who is not equal
UNEQUALED *adj* (in US English) not equalled
UNEQUALLY > UNEQUAL
UNEQUALS > UNEQUAL
UNERASED *adj* not rubbed out
UNEROTIC *adj* not erotic
UNERRING *adj* never mistaken, consistently accurate
UNESPIED *adj* unnoticed
UNESSAYED *adj* untried
UNESSENCE *vb* deprive of being
UNETH *same as* > UNEATH
UNETHICAL *adj* morally wrong
UNEVADED *adj* not evaded
UNEVEN *adj* not level or flat
UNEVENER > UNEVEN
UNEVENEST > UNEVEN
UNEVENLY > UNEVEN
UNEVOLVED *adj* not evolved
UNEXALTED *adj* not exalted
UNEXCITED *adj* not aroused to pleasure, interest, agitation, etc
UNEXCUSED *adj* not excused
UNEXOTIC *adj* not exotic
UNEXPERT *same as* > INEXPERT
UNEXPIRED *adj* not having expired
UNEXPOSED *adj* not having been exhibited or brought to public notice
UNEXTINCT *adj* not extinct
UNEXTREME *adj* not extreme
UNEYED *adj* unseen
UNFABLED *adj* not fictitious
UNFACT *n* event or thing not provable
UNFACTS > UNFACT
UNFADABLE *adj* incapable of fading
UNFADED *adj* not faded
UNFADING *adj* not fading
UNFAILING *adj* continuous or reliable
UNFAIR *adj* not right, fair, or just ▷ *vb* disfigure
UNFAIRED > UNFAIR
UNFAIRER > UNFAIR
UNFAIREST > UNFAIR
UNFAIRING > UNFAIR
UNFAIRLY > UNFAIR
UNFAIRS > UNFAIR
UNFAITH *n* lack of faith
UNFAITHS > UNFAITH
UNFAKED *adj* not faked
UNFALLEN *adj* not fallen
UNFAMED *adj* not famous
UNFAMOUS *adj* not famous
UNFANCY *adj* not fancy
UNFANNED *adj* not fanned
UNFASTEN *vb* undo, untie, or open or become undone, untied, or opened
UNFASTENS > UNFASTEN
UNFAULTY *adj* not faulty
UNFAVORED *adj* (in US English) not favoured
UNFAZED *adj* not disconcerted
UNFEARED *adj* unafraid
UNFEARFUL *adj* not scared
UNFEARING *adj* having no fear
UNFED *adj* not fed
UNFEED *adj* unpaid
UNFEELING *adj* without sympathy
UNFEIGNED *adj* not feigned
UNFELLED *adj* not cut down
UNFELT *adj* not felt
UNFELTED *adj* not felted
UNFENCE *vb* remove a fence from
UNFENCED *adj* not enclosed by a fence
UNFENCES > UNFENCE
UNFENCING > UNFENCE
UNFERTILE *same as* > INFERTILE
UNFETTER *vb* release from fetters, bonds, etc
UNFETTERS > UNFETTER
UNFEUDAL *adj* not feudal
UNFEUED *adj* not feued
UNFIGURED *adj* not numbered
UNFILDE *archaic form of* > UNFILED
UNFILED *adj* not filed
UNFILIAL *adj* not filial
UNFILLED *adj* (of a container, receptacle, etc) not having become or been made full
UNFILMED *adj* not filmed
UNFINE *adj* not fine
UNFIRED *adj* not fired
UNFIRM *adj* soft or unsteady
UNFISHED *adj* not used for fishing
UNFIT *adj* unqualified or unsuitable ▷ *vb* make unfit
UNFITLY *adv* in an unfit way
UNFITNESS > UNFIT
UNFITS > UNFIT
UNFITTED *adj* unsuitable
UNFITTER > UNFIT
UNFITTEST > UNFIT
UNFITTING *adj* not fitting
UNFIX *vb* unfasten, detach, or loosen
UNFIXED *adj* not fixed
UNFIXES > UNFIX
UNFIXING > UNFIX
UNFIXITY *n* instability
UNFIXT *variant of* > UNFIXED
UNFLAPPED *adj* not agitated or excited
UNFLASHY *adj* not flashy
UNFLAWED *adj* perfect
UNFLEDGED *adj* (of a young bird) not having developed adult feathers
UNFLESH *vb* remove flesh from
UNFLESHED > UNFLESH
UNFLESHES > UNFLESH
UNFLESHLY *adj* immateri
UNFLEXED *adj* unbent
UNFLOORED *adj* without flooring
UNFLUSH *vb* lose the colou caused by flushing
UNFLUSHED > UNFLUSH
UNFLUSHES > UNFLUSH
UNFLUTED *adj* not fluted
UNFLYABLE *adj* unable to be flown
UNFOCUSED *adj* blurry
UNFOILED *adj* not thwarted
UNFOLD *vb* open or spread out from a folded state
UNFOLDED > UNFOLD
UNFOLDER > UNFOLD
UNFOLDERS > UNFOLD
UNFOLDING > UNFOLD
UNFOLDS > UNFOLD
UNFOND *adj* not fond
UNFOOL *vb* undeceive
UNFOOLED > UNFOOL
UNFOOLING > UNFOOL
UNFOOLS > UNFOOL
UNFOOTED *adj* untrodden
UNFORBID *adj* archaic wo meaning unforbidden
UNFORCED *adj* not forced o having been forced
UNFORGED *adj* genuine
UNFORGOT *adj* archaic wo meaning unforgotten
UNFORKED *adj* not forked
UNFORM *vb* make formless
UNFORMAL *same as* > INFORMAL
UNFORMED *adj* in an early stage of development
UNFORMING > UNFORM
UNFORMS > UNFORM
UNFORTUNE *n* misfortune
UNFOUGHT *adj* not fought
UNFOUND *adj* not found
UNFOUNDED *adj* not based on facts or evidence
UNFRAMED *adj* not framed
UNFRANKED *adj* not frank
UNFRAUGHT *adj* not fraugh
UNFREE *vb* remove freedo from
UNFREED > UNFREE
UNFREEDOM *n* lack of freedom
UNFREEING > UNFREE
UNFREEMAN *n* person whc is not a freeman
UNFREEMEN > UNFREEMAN
UNFREES > UNFREE
UNFREEZE *vb* thaw or cau to thaw
UNFREEZES > UNFREEZE
UNFRETTED *adj* not worri
UNFRIEND *n* enemy
UNFRIENDS > UNFRIEND
UNFROCK *vb* deprive (a priest in holy orders) of h or her priesthood
UNFROCKED > UNFROCK
UNFROCKS > UNFROCK
UNFROZE > UNFREEZE
UNFROZEN > UNFREEZE

NFUELLED *adj* not fuelled
NFUMED *adj* not fumigated
NFUNDED *adj* not funded
NFUNNY *adj* not funny
NFURL *vb* unroll or unfold
NFURLED >UNFURL
NFURLING >UNFURL
NFURLS >UNFURL
NFURNISH *vb* clear
NFURRED *adj* not adorned with fur
NFUSED *adj* not fused
NFUSSIER >UNFUSSY
NFUSSILY >UNFUSSY
NFUSSY *adj* not characterized by overelaborate detail
NGAG *vb* restore freedom of speech to
NGAGGED >UNGAG
NGAGGING >UNGAG
NGAGS >UNGAG
NGAIN *adj* inconvenient
NGAINFUL >UNGAIN
NGAINLY *adj* lacking grace when moving ▷ *adv* clumsily
NGALLANT *adj* not gallant
NGALLED *adj* not annoyed
NGARBED *adj* undressed
NGARBLED *adj* clear
NGATED *adj* without gate
NGAUGED *adj* not measured
NGAZING *adj* not gazing
NGEAR *vb* disengage
NGEARED >UNGEAR
NGEARING >UNGEAR
NGEARS >UNGEAR
NGELDED *adj* not gelded
NGENIAL *adj* unfriendly
NGENTEEL *adj* impolite
NGENTLE *adj* not gentle
NGENTLY >UNGENTLE
NGENUINE *adj* false
NGERMANE *adj* inappropriate
NGET *vb* get rid of
NGETS >UNGET
NGETTING >UNGET
NGHOSTLY *adj* not ghostly
NGIFTED *adj* not talented
NGILD *vb* remove gilding from
NGILDED >UNGILD
NGILDING >UNGILD
NGILDS >UNGILD
NGILT >UNGILD
NGIRD *vb* remove belt from
NGIRDED >UNGIRD
NGIRDING >UNGIRD
NGIRDS >UNGIRD
NGIRT *adj* not belted
NGIRTH *vb* release from a girth
NGIRTHED >UNGIRTH
NGIRTHS >UNGIRTH
NGIVING *adj* inflexible
NGLAD *adj* not glad
NGLAZED *adj* not glazed
NGLOSSED *adj* not glossed
NGLOVE *vb* remove glove(s)
UNGLOVED >UNGLOVE
UNGLOVES >UNGLOVE
UNGLOVING >UNGLOVE
UNGLUE *vb* remove adhesive from
UNGLUED >UNGLUE
UNGLUES >UNGLUE
UNGLUING >UNGLUE
UNGOD *vb* remove status of being a god from
UNGODDED >UNGOD
UNGODDING >UNGOD
UNGODLIER >UNGODLY
UNGODLIKE *adj* not godlike
UNGODLILY >UNGODLY
UNGODLY *adj* unreasonable or outrageous
UNGODS >UNGOD
UNGORD *same as* >UNGORED
UNGORED *adj* not gored
UNGORGED *same as* >UNGORED
UNGOT *same as* >UNGOTTEN
UNGOTTEN *adj* not obtained or won
UNGOWN *vb* remove gown (from)
UNGOWNED >UNGOWN
UNGOWNING >UNGOWN
UNGOWNS >UNGOWN
UNGRACED *adj* not graced
UNGRADED *adj* not graded
UNGRASSED *adj* not covered with grass
UNGRAVELY *adj* in a light-hearted manner
UNGRAZED *adj* not grazed
UNGREASED *adj* not greased
UNGREEDY *adj* not greedy
UNGROOMED *adj* not groomed
UNGROUND *adj* not crushed
UNGROUPED *adj* not placed in a group
UNGROWN *adj* not fully developed
UNGRUDGED *adj* not grudged
UNGUAL *adj* of, relating to, or affecting the fingernails or toenails
UNGUARD *vb* expose (to attack)
UNGUARDED *adj* not protected
UNGUARDS >UNGUARD
UNGUENT *n* ointment
UNGUENTA >UNGUENTUM
UNGUENTS >UNGUENT
UNGUENTUM *same as* >UNGUENT
UNGUES >UNGUIS
UNGUESSED *adj* unexpected
UNGUIDED *adj* (of a missile, bomb, etc) not having a flight path controlled either by radio signals or internal preset or self-actuating homing devices
UNGUIFORM *adj* shaped like a nail or claw
UNGUILTY *adj* innocent
UNGUINOUS *adj* fatty
UNGUIS *n* nail, claw, or hoof, or the part of the digit giving rise to it
UNGULA *n* truncated cone, cylinder, etc
UNGULAE >UNGULA
UNGULAR >UNGULA
UNGULATE *n* hoofed mammal
UNGULATES >UNGULATE
UNGULED *adj* hoofed
UNGUM *vb* remove adhesive from
UNGUMMED >UNGUM
UNGUMMING >UNGUM
UNGUMS >UNGUM
UNGYVE *vb* release from shackles
UNGYVED >UNGYVE
UNGYVES >UNGYVE
UNGYVING >UNGYVE
UNHABLE *same as* >UNABLE
UNHACKED *adj* not hacked
UNHAILED *adj* not hailed
UNHAIR *vb* remove the hair from (a hide)
UNHAIRED >UNHAIR
UNHAIRER >UNHAIR
UNHAIRERS >UNHAIR
UNHAIRING >UNHAIR
UNHAIRS >UNHAIR
UNHALLOW *vb* desecrate
UNHALLOWS >UNHALLOW
UNHALSED *adj* not hailed
UNHALVED *adj* not divided in half
UNHAND *vb* release from one's grasp
UNHANDED >UNHAND
UNHANDIER >UNHANDY
UNHANDILY >UNHANDY
UNHANDING >UNHAND
UNHANDLED *adj* not handled
UNHANDS >UNHAND
UNHANDY *adj* not skilful with one's hands
UNHANG *vb* take down from hanging position
UNHANGED *adj* not executed by hanging
UNHANGING >UNHANG
UNHANGS >UNHANG
UNHAPPIED >UNHAPPY
UNHAPPIER >UNHAPPY
UNHAPPIES >UNHAPPY
UNHAPPILY >UNHAPPY
UNHAPPY *adj* sad or depressed ▷ *vb* make unhappy
UNHARBOUR *vb* force out of shelter
UNHARDY *adj* fragile
UNHARMED *adj* not hurt or damaged in any way
UNHARMFUL *adj* not harmful
UNHARMING *adj* not capable of harming
UNHARNESS *vb* remove the harness from (a horse, etc)
UNHARRIED *adj* not harried
UNHASP *vb* unfasten
UNHASPED >UNHASP
UNHASPING >UNHASP
UNHASPS >UNHASP
UNHASTING *adj* not rushing
UNHASTY *adj* not speedy
UNHAT *vb* doff one's hat
UNHATCHED *adj* (of an egg) not having broken to release the fully developed young
UNHATS >UNHAT
UNHATTED >UNHAT
UNHATTING >UNHAT
UNHAUNTED *adj* not haunted
UNHEAD *vb* remove the head from
UNHEADED *adj* not having a heading
UNHEADING >UNHEAD
UNHEADS >UNHEAD
UNHEAL *vb* expose
UNHEALED *adj* not having healed physically, mentally, or emotionally
UNHEALING *adj* not healing
UNHEALS >UNHEAL
UNHEALTH *n* illness
UNHEALTHS >UNHEALTH
UNHEALTHY *adj* likely to cause poor health
UNHEARD *adj* not listened to
UNHEARSE *vb* remove from a hearse
UNHEARSED >UNHEARSE
UNHEARSES >UNHEARSE
UNHEART *vb* discourage
UNHEARTED >UNHEART
UNHEARTS >UNHEART
UNHEATED *adj* not having been warmed up
UNHEDGED *adj* unprotected
UNHEEDED *adj* noticed but ignored
UNHEEDFUL *adj* not heedful
UNHEEDILY *adv* carelessly
UNHEEDING *adj* not heeding
UNHEEDY *adj* not heedful
UNHELE *same as* >UNHEAL
UNHELED >UNHELE
UNHELES >UNHELE
UNHELING >UNHELE
UNHELM *vb* remove the helmet of (oneself or another)
UNHELMED >UNHELM
UNHELMING >UNHELM
UNHELMS >UNHELM
UNHELPED *adj* without help
UNHELPFUL *adj* doing nothing to improve a situation
UNHEPPEN *adj* awkward
UNHEROIC *adj* not heroic
UNHERST *archaic past form of* >UNHEARSE
UNHEWN *adj* not hewn
UNHIDDEN *adj* not hidden
UNHINGE *vb* derange or unbalance (a person or his or her mind)
UNHINGED >UNHINGE
UNHINGES >UNHINGE
UNHINGING >UNHINGE
UNHIP *adj* not at all fashionable or up to date
UNHIPPER >UNHIP

UNHIPPEST > UNHIP
UNHIRABLE *adj* not fit to be hired
UNHIRED *adj* not hired
UNHITCH *vb* unfasten or detach
UNHITCHED > UNHITCH
UNHITCHES > UNHITCH
UNHIVE *vb* remove from a hive
UNHIVED > UNHIVE
UNHIVES > UNHIVE
UNHIVING > UNHIVE
UNHOARD *vb* remove from a hoard
UNHOARDED > UNHOARD
UNHOARDS > UNHOARD
UNHOLIER > UNHOLY
UNHOLIEST > UNHOLY
UNHOLILY > UNHOLY
UNHOLPEN *same as* > UNHELPED
UNHOLY *adj* immoral or wicked
UNHOMELY *adj* not homely
UNHONEST *same as* > DISHONEST
UNHONORED *adj* not honoured
UNHOOD *vb* remove hood from
UNHOODED > UNHOOD
UNHOODING > UNHOOD
UNHOODS > UNHOOD
UNHOOK *vb* unfasten the hooks of (a garment)
UNHOOKED > UNHOOK
UNHOOKING > UNHOOK
UNHOOKS > UNHOOK
UNHOOP *vb* remove hoop(s) from
UNHOOPED > UNHOOP
UNHOOPING > UNHOOP
UNHOOPS > UNHOOP
UNHOPED *adj* unhoped-for
UNHOPEFUL *adj* not hopeful
UNHORSE *vb* knock or throw from a horse
UNHORSED > UNHORSE
UNHORSES > UNHORSE
UNHORSING > UNHORSE
UNHOSTILE *adj* not hostile
UNHOUSE *vb* remove from a house
UNHOUSED > UNHOUSE
UNHOUSES > UNHOUSE
UNHOUSING > UNHOUSE
UNHUMAN *adj* inhuman or not human
UNHUMANLY > UNHUMAN
UNHUMBLED *adj* not humbled
UNHUNG > UNHANG
UNHUNTED *adj* not hunted
UNHURRIED *adj* done at a leisurely pace, without any rush or anxiety
UNHURT *adj* not injured in an accident, attack, etc
UNHURTFUL *adj* not hurtful
UNHUSK *vb* remove the husk from
UNHUSKED > UNHUSK
UNHUSKING > UNHUSK
UNHUSKS > UNHUSK
UNI *n* (in informal English) university
UNIALGAL *adj* microbiological term
UNIAXIAL *adj* (esp of plants) having an unbranched main axis
UNIBODY *n* vehicle in which frame and body are one unit
UNIBROW *n* informal word for eyebrows that meet above the nose
UNIBROWS > UNIBROW
UNICITIES > UNICITY
UNICITY *n* oneness
UNICOLOR *same as* > UNICOLOUR
UNICOLOUR *adj* of one colour
UNICORN *n* imaginary horselike creature with one horn growing from its forehead
UNICORNS > UNICORN
UNICYCLE *n* one-wheeled vehicle driven by pedals, used in a circus ▷ *vb* ride a unicycle
UNICYCLED > UNICYCLE
UNICYCLES > UNICYCLE
UNIDEAED *adj* not having ideas
UNIDEAL *adj* not ideal
UNIFACE *n* type of tool
UNIFACES > UNIFACE
UNIFIABLE > UNIFY
UNIFIC *adj* unifying
UNIFIED > UNIFY
UNIFIER > UNIFY
UNIFIERS > UNIFY
UNIFIES > UNIFY
UNIFILAR *adj* composed of, having, or using only one wire, thread, filament, etc
UNIFORM *n* special identifying set of clothes for the members of an organization, such as soldiers ▷ *adj* regular and even throughout, unvarying ▷ *vb* fit out (a body of soldiers, etc) with uniforms
UNIFORMED > UNIFORM
UNIFORMER > UNIFORM
UNIFORMLY > UNIFORM
UNIFORMS > UNIFORM
UNIFY *vb* make or become one
UNIFYING > UNIFY
UNIFYINGS > UNIFY
UNIJUGATE *adj* (of a compound leaf) having only one pair of leaflets
UNILINEAL *same as* > UNILINEAR
UNILINEAR *adj* developing in a progressive sequence
UNILLUMED *adj* not illuminated
UNILOBAR *adj* having one lobe
UNILOBED *same as* > UNILOBAR
UNIMBUED *adj* not imbued
UNIMPEDED *adj* not stopped or disrupted by anything
UNIMPOSED *adj* not imposed
UNINCITED *adj* unprovoked
UNINDEXED *adj* not indexed
UNINJURED *adj* not having sustained any injury
UNINSTALL *vb* remove from a computer system
UNINSURED *adj* not covered by insurance
UNINURED *adj* unaccustomed
UNINVITED *adj* not having been asked ▷ *adv* without having been asked
UNINVOKED *adj* not invoked
UNION *n* uniting or being united ▷ *adj* of a trade union
UNIONISE *same as* > UNIONIZE
UNIONISED > UNIONISE
UNIONISER > UNIONISE
UNIONISES > UNIONISE
UNIONISM *n* principles of trade unions
UNIONISMS > UNIONISM
UNIONIST *n* member or supporter of a trade union ▷ *adj* of or relating to union or unionism, esp trade unionism
UNIONISTS > UNIONIST
UNIONIZE *vb* organize (workers) into a trade union
UNIONIZED > UNIONIZE
UNIONIZER > UNIONIZE
UNIONIZES > UNIONIZE
UNIONS > UNION
UNIPAROUS *adj* (of certain animals) producing a single offspring at each birth
UNIPED *n* person or thing with one foot
UNIPEDS > UNIPED
UNIPLANAR *adj* situated in one plane
UNIPOD *n* one-legged support, as for a camera
UNIPODS > UNIPOD
UNIPOLAR *adj* of, concerned with, or having a single magnetic or electric pole
UNIPOTENT *adj* able to form only one type of cell
UNIQUE *n* person or thing that is unique
UNIQUELY > UNIQUE
UNIQUER > UNIQUE
UNIQUES > UNIQUE
UNIQUEST > UNIQUE
UNIRAMOSE *same as* > UNIRAMOUS
UNIRAMOUS *adj* (esp of the appendages of crustaceans) consisting of a single branch
UNIRONED *adj* not ironed
UNIRONIC *adj* not ironic
UNIS > UNI
UNISERIAL *adj* in or relating to a single series
UNISEX *adj* designed for use by both sexes ▷ *n* condition of seeming not to belong obviously either to one sex or the other from the way one behaves or dresses
UNISEXES > UNISEX
UNISEXUAL *adj* of one sex only
UNISIZE *adj* in one size only
UNISON *n* complete agreement
UNISONAL > UNISON
UNISONANT > UNISON
UNISONOUS > UNISON
UNISONS > UNISON
UNISSUED *adj* not issued
UNIT *n* single undivided entity or whole
UNITAGE > UNIT
UNITAGES > UNIT
UNITAL > UNIT
UNITARD *n* all-in-one skintight suit
UNITARDS > UNITARD
UNITARIAN *n* supporter of unity or centralization ▷ *adj* of or relating to unity or centralization
UNITARILY > UNITARY
UNITARY *adj* consisting of single undivided whole
UNITE *vb* make or become an integrated whole ▷ *n* English gold coin minted in the Stuart period, originally worth 20 shillings
UNITED *adj* produced by two or more people or things in combination
UNITEDLY > UNITED
UNITER > UNITE
UNITERS > UNITE
UNITES > UNITE
UNITIES > UNITY
UNITING > UNITE
UNITINGS > UNITE
UNITION *n* joining
UNITIONS > UNITION
UNITISE *same as* > UNITIZE
UNITISED > UNITISE
UNITISER *same as* > UNITIZER
UNITISERS > UNITISER
UNITISES > UNITISE
UNITISING > UNITISE
UNITIVE *adj* tending to unite or capable of uniting
UNITIVELY > UNITIVE
UNITIZE *vb* convert (an investment trust) into a unit trust
UNITIZED > UNITIZE
UNITIZER *n* person or thing that arranges units into batches

ITIZERS > UNITIZER
ITIZES > UNITIZE
ITIZING > UNITIZE
ITRUST *n* type of ncome-producing trust und
ITRUSTS > UNITRUST
ITS > UNIT
ITY *n* state of being one
IVALENT *adj* (of a hromosome during neiosis) not paired with ts homologue
IVALVE *adj* relating to, esignating, or possessing mollusc shell that onsists of a single piece valve) ▷ *n* gastropod nollusc or its shell
IVALVED > UNIVALVE
IVALVES > UNIVALVE
IVERSAL *adj* of or typical f the whole of mankind or f nature ▷ *n* something which exists or is true in all laces and all situations
IVERSE *n* whole of all xisting matter, energy, nd space
IVERSES > UNIVERSE
IVOCAL *adj* nambiguous or nmistakable ▷ *n* word r term that has only one neaning
IVOCALS > UNIVOCAL
JADED *adj* not jaded
JAM *vb* remove blockage om
JAMMED > UNJAM
JAMMING > UNJAM
JAMS > UNJAM
JEALOUS *adj* not jealous
JOINED *adj* not joined
JOINT *vb* disjoint
JOINTED > UNJOINT
JOINTS > UNJOINT
JOYFUL *adj* not joyful
JOYOUS *adj* not joyous
JUDGED *adj* not judged
JUST *adj* not fair or just
JUSTER > UNJUST
JUSTEST > UNJUST
JUSTLY > UNJUST
KED *adj* alien
KEELED *adj* without a eel
KEMPT *adj* (of the hair) ot combed
KEMPTLY > UNKEMPT
KEND *same* s > UNKENNED
KENNED *adj* unknown
KENNEL *vb* release from kennel
KENNELS > UNKENNEL
KENT *same* s > UNKENNED
KEPT *adj* not kept
KET *same as* > UNKED
KID *same as* > UNKED
KIND *adj* unsympathetic r cruel
KINDER > UNKIND
UNKINDEST > UNKIND
UNKINDLED *adj* not kindled
UNKINDLY > UNKIND
UNKING *vb* strip of sovereignty
UNKINGED > UNKING
UNKINGING > UNKING
UNKINGLY *adj* not kingly
UNKINGS > UNKING
UNKINK *vb* straighten out
UNKINKED > UNKINK
UNKINKING > UNKINK
UNKINKS > UNKINK
UNKISS *vb* cancel (a previous action) with a kiss
UNKISSED *adj* not kissed
UNKISSES > UNKISS
UNKISSING > UNKISS
UNKNELLED *adj* not tolled
UNKNIGHT *vb* strip of knighthood
UNKNIGHTS > UNKNIGHT
UNKNIT *vb* make or become undone, untied, or unravelled
UNKNITS > UNKNIT
UNKNITTED > UNKNIT
UNKNOT *vb* disentangle or undo a knot or knots in
UNKNOTS > UNKNOT
UNKNOTTED > UNKNOT
UNKNOWING *adj* unaware or ignorant
UNKNOWN *adj* not known ▷ *n* unknown person, quantity, or thing
UNKNOWNS > UNKNOWN
UNKOSHER *adj* not conforming to Jewish religious law
UNLABELED *adj* not labelled
UNLABORED *adj* not laboured
UNLACE *vb* loosen or undo the lacing of (shoes, garments, etc)
UNLACED *adj* not laced
UNLACES > UNLACE
UNLACING > UNLACE
UNLADE *less common word for* > UNLOAD
UNLADED > UNLADE
UNLADEN *adj* not laden
UNLADES > UNLADE
UNLADING > UNLADE
UNLADINGS > UNLADE
UNLAID > UNLAY
UNLASH *vb* untie or unfasten
UNLASHED > UNLASH
UNLASHES > UNLASH
UNLASHING > UNLASH
UNLAST *archaic variant of* > UNLACED
UNLASTE *archaic variant of* > UNLACED
UNLATCH *vb* open or unfasten or come open or unfastened by the lifting or release of a latch
UNLATCHED > UNLATCH
UNLATCHES > UNLATCH
UNLAW *vb* penalize
UNLAWED > UNLAW
UNLAWFUL *adj* not permitted by law
UNLAWING > UNLAW
UNLAWS > UNLAW
UNLAY *vb* untwist (a rope or cable) to separate its strands
UNLAYING > UNLAY
UNLAYS > UNLAY
UNLEAD *vb* strip off lead
UNLEADED *adj* (of petrol) containing less tetraethyl lead, in order to reduce environmental pollution ▷ *n* petrol containing a reduced amount of tetraethyl lead
UNLEADEDS > UNLEADED
UNLEADING > UNLEAD
UNLEADS > UNLEAD
UNLEAL *adj* treacherous
UNLEARN *vb* try to forget something learnt or to discard accumulated knowledge
UNLEARNED *same as* > UNLEARNT
UNLEARNS > UNLEARN
UNLEARNT *adj* denoting knowledge or skills innately present rather than learnt
UNLEASED *adj* not leased
UNLEASH *vb* set loose or cause (something bad)
UNLEASHED > UNLEASH
UNLEASHES > UNLEASH
UNLED *adj* not led
UNLESS *conj* except under the circumstances that ▷ *prep* except
UNLET *adj* not rented
UNLETHAL *adj* not deadly
UNLETTED *adj* unimpeded
UNLEVEL *adj* not level ▷ *vb* make unbalanced
UNLEVELED > UNLEVEL
UNLEVELS > UNLEVEL
UNLEVIED *adj* not levied
UNLICH *Spenserian form of* > UNLIKE
UNLICKED *adj* not licked
UNLID *vb* remove lid from
UNLIDDED > UNLID
UNLIDDING > UNLID
UNLIDS > UNLID
UNLIGHTED *adj* not lit
UNLIKABLE *adj* not likable
UNLIKE *adj* dissimilar or different ▷ *prep* not like or typical of ▷ *n* person or thing that is unlike another
UNLIKED *adj* not liked
UNLIKELY *adj* improbable
UNLIKES > UNLIKE
UNLIMBER *vb* disengage (a gun) from its limber
UNLIMBERS > UNLIMBER
UNLIME *vb* detach
UNLIMED > UNLIME
UNLIMES > UNLIME
UNLIMING > UNLIME
UNLIMITED *adj* apparently endless
UNLINE *vb* remove the lining from
UNLINEAL *adj* not lineal
UNLINED *adj* not having any lining
UNLINES > UNLINE
UNLINING > UNLINE
UNLINK *vb* undo the link or links between
UNLINKED > UNLINK
UNLINKING > UNLINK
UNLINKS > UNLINK
UNLISTED *adj* not entered on a list
UNLIT *adj* (of a fire, cigarette, etc) not lit and therefore not burning
UNLIVABLE *adj* not fit for living in
UNLIVE *vb* live so as to nullify, undo, or live down (past events or times)
UNLIVED > UNLIVE
UNLIVELY *adj* lifeless
UNLIVES > UNLIVE
UNLIVING > UNLIVE
UNLOAD *vb* remove (cargo) from (a ship, truck, or plane)
UNLOADED > UNLOAD
UNLOADER > UNLOAD
UNLOADERS > UNLOAD
UNLOADING > UNLOAD
UNLOADS > UNLOAD
UNLOBED *adj* without lobes
UNLOCATED *adj* not located
UNLOCK *vb* unfasten (a lock or door)
UNLOCKED *adj* not locked
UNLOCKING > UNLOCK
UNLOCKS > UNLOCK
UNLOGICAL *same as* > ILLOGICAL
UNLOOKED *adj* not looked (at)
UNLOOSE *vb* set free or release
UNLOOSED > UNLOOSE
UNLOOSEN *same as* > UNLOOSE
UNLOOSENS > UNLOOSEN
UNLOOSES > UNLOOSE
UNLOOSING > UNLOOSE
UNLOPPED *adj* not chopped off
UNLORD *vb* remove from position of being lord
UNLORDED > UNLORD
UNLORDING > UNLORD
UNLORDLY *adv* not in a lordlike manner
UNLORDS > UNLORD
UNLOSABLE *adj* unable to be lost
UNLOST *adj* not lost
UNLOVABLE *adj* too unpleasant or unattractive to be loved
UNLOVE *vb* stop loving
UNLOVED *adj* not loved by anyone
UNLOVELY *adj* unpleasant

in appearance or character
UNLOVES > UNLOVE
UNLOVING *adj* not feeling or showing love and affection
UNLUCKIER > UNLUCKY
UNLUCKILY > UNLUCKY
UNLUCKY *adj* having bad luck, unfortunate
UNLYRICAL *adj* not lyrical
UNMACHO *adj* not macho
UNMADE *adj* (of a bed) with the bedclothes not smoothed and tidied
UNMAILED *adj* not sent by post
UNMAIMED *adj* not injured
UNMAKABLE *adj* unable to be made
UNMAKE *vb* undo or destroy
UNMAKER > UNMAKE
UNMAKERS > UNMAKE
UNMAKES > UNMAKE
UNMAKING > UNMAKE
UNMAKINGS > UNMAKE
UNMAN *vb* cause to lose courage or nerve
UNMANACLE *vb* release from manacles
UNMANAGED *adj* not managed
UNMANFUL *adj* unmanly
UNMANLIER > UNMANLY
UNMANLIKE *adj* not worthy of a man
UNMANLY *adj* not masculine or virile
UNMANNED *adj* having no personnel or crew
UNMANNING > UNMAN
UNMANNISH *adj* not mannish
UNMANS > UNMAN
UNMANTLE *vb* remove mantle from
UNMANTLED > UNMANTLE
UNMANTLES > UNMANTLE
UNMANURED *adj* not treated with manure
UNMAPPED *adj* not charted
UNMARD *same as* > UNMARRED
UNMARKED *adj* having no signs of damage or injury
UNMARRED *adj* not marred
UNMARRIED *adj* not married
UNMARRIES > UNMARRY
UNMARRY *vb* divorce
UNMASK *vb* remove the mask or disguise from
UNMASKED > UNMASK
UNMASKER > UNMASK
UNMASKERS > UNMASK
UNMASKING > UNMASK
UNMASKS > UNMASK
UNMATCHED *adj* not equalled or surpassed
UNMATED *adj* not mated
UNMATTED *adj* not matted
UNMATURED *adj* not matured
UNMEANING *adj* having no meaning
UNMEANT *adj* unintentional
UNMEEK *adj* not submissive
UNMEET *adj* not meet
UNMEETLY > UNMEET
UNMELLOW *adj* not mellow
UNMELTED *adj* not melted
UNMENDED *adj* not mended
UNMERITED *adj* not merited or deserved
UNMERRY *adj* not merry
UNMESH *vb* release from mesh
UNMESHED > UNMESH
UNMESHES > UNMESH
UNMESHING > UNMESH
UNMET *adj* unfulfilled
UNMETED *adj* unmeasured
UNMEW *vb* release from confinement
UNMEWED > UNMEW
UNMEWING > UNMEW
UNMEWS > UNMEW
UNMILKED *adj* not milked
UNMILLED *adj* not milled
UNMINDED *adj* disregarded
UNMINDFUL *adj* careless, heedless, or forgetful
UNMINED *adj* not mined
UNMINGLE *vb* separate
UNMINGLED > UNMINGLE
UNMINGLES > UNMINGLE
UNMIRY *adj* not swampy
UNMISSED *adj* unnoticed
UNMITER *same as* > UNMITRE
UNMITERED > UNMITER
UNMITERS > UNMITER
UNMITRE *vb* divest of a mitre
UNMITRED > UNMITRE
UNMITRES > UNMITRE
UNMITRING > UNMITRE
UNMIX *vb* separate
UNMIXABLE *adj* incapable of being mixed
UNMIXED > UNMIX
UNMIXEDLY > UNMIXED
UNMIXES > UNMIX
UNMIXING > UNMIX
UNMIXT *archaic past form of* > UNMIX
UNMOANED *adj* unmourned
UNMODISH *adj* passé
UNMOLD *same as* > UNMOULD
UNMOLDED > UNMOLD
UNMOLDING > UNMOLD
UNMOLDS > UNMOLD
UNMOLTEN *adj* not molten
UNMONEYED *adj* poor
UNMONIED *same as* > UNMONEYED
UNMOOR *vb* weigh the anchor or drop the mooring of (a vessel)
UNMOORED > UNMOOR
UNMOORING > UNMOOR
UNMOORS > UNMOOR
UNMORAL *adj* outside morality
UNMORALLY > UNMORAL
UNMORTISE *vb* release from mortise
UNMOTIVED *adj* without motive
UNMOULD *vb* change shape of
UNMOULDED > UNMOULD
UNMOULDS > UNMOULD
UNMOUNT *vb* dismount
UNMOUNTED > UNMOUNT
UNMOUNTS > UNMOUNT
UNMOURNED *adj* not mourned
UNMOVABLE *adj* not movable
UNMOVABLY > UNMOVABLE
UNMOVED *adj* not affected by emotion, indifferent
UNMOVEDLY > UNMOVED
UNMOVING *adj* still and motionless
UNMOWN *adj* not mown
UNMUFFLE *vb* remove a muffle or muffles from
UNMUFFLED > UNMUFFLE
UNMUFFLES > UNMUFFLE
UNMUSICAL *adj* (of a person) unable to appreciate or play music
UNMUZZLE *vb* take the muzzle off (a dog, etc)
UNMUZZLED > UNMUZZLE
UNMUZZLES > UNMUZZLE
UNNAIL *vb* unfasten by removing nails
UNNAILED > UNNAIL
UNNAILING > UNNAIL
UNNAILS > UNNAIL
UNNAMABLE *adj* that cannot or must not be named
UNNAMED *adj* not mentioned by name
UNNANELD *same as* > UNANELED
UNNATIVE *adj* not native
UNNATURAL *adj* strange and frightening because not usual
UNNEATH *adj* archaic word for underneath
UNNEEDED *adj* not needed
UNNEEDFUL *adj* not needful
UNNERVE *vb* cause to lose courage, confidence, or self-control
UNNERVED > UNNERVE
UNNERVES > UNNERVE
UNNERVING > UNNERVE
UNNEST *vb* remove from a nest
UNNESTED > UNNEST
UNNESTING > UNNEST
UNNESTS > UNNEST
UNNETHES *same as* > UNNEATH
UNNETTED *adj* not having or not enclosed in a net
UNNOBLE *vb* strip of nobility
UNNOBLED > UNNOBLE
UNNOBLES > UNNOBLE
UNNOBLING > UNNOBLE
UNNOISY *adj* quiet
UNNOTED *adj* not noted
UNNOTICED *adj* without being seen or noticed
UNNUANCED *adj* without nuances
UNOBEYED *adj* not obeyed
UNOBVIOUS *adj* unapparent
UNOFFERED *adj* not offered
UNOFTEN *adv* infrequentl
UNOILED *adj* not lubricat with oil
UNOPEN *adj* not open
UNOPENED *adj* closed, barred, or sealed
UNOPPOSED *adj* not opposed
UNORDER *vb* cancel an ord
UNORDERED *adj* not order
UNORDERLY *adj* not order or disorderly
UNORDERS > UNORDER
UNORNATE *same as* > INORNATE
UNOWED *same as* > UNOWN
UNOWNED *adj* not owned
UNPACED *adj* without the aid of a pacemaker
UNPACK *vb* remove the contents of (a suitcase, trunk, etc)
UNPACKED > UNPACK
UNPACKER > UNPACK
UNPACKERS > UNPACK
UNPACKING > UNPACK
UNPACKS > UNPACK
UNPADDED *adj* not padde
UNPAGED *adj* (of a book) having no page numbers
UNPAID *adj* without a salary or wage
UNPAINED *adj* not sufferi pain
UNPAINFUL *adj* painless
UNPAINT *vb* remove pain from
UNPAINTED > UNPAINT
UNPAINTS > UNPAINT
UNPAIRED *adj* not paired
UNPALSIED *adj* not affect with palsy
UNPANEL *vb* unsaddle
UNPANELS > UNPANEL
UNPANGED *adj* without pa or sadness
UNPANNEL *same as* > UNPANEL
UNPANNELS > UNPANNEL
UNPAPER *vb* remove pape from
UNPAPERED > UNPAPER
UNPAPERS > UNPAPER
UNPARED *adj* not pared
UNPARTED *adj* not parted
UNPARTIAL *same as* > IMPARTIAL
UNPATCHED *adj* not patched
UNPATHED *adj* not having a path
UNPAVED *adj* not covered paving
UNPAY *vb* undo
UNPAYABLE *adj* incapabl of being paid
UNPAYING > UNPAY
UNPAYS > UNPAY
UNPEELED *adj* not peeled
UNPEERED *adj* unparallel
UNPEG *vb* remove the peg pegs from, esp to unfast
UNPEGGED > UNPEG
UNPEGGING > UNPEG

PEGS > UNPEG
PEN *vb* release from a pen
PENNED > UNPEN
PENNIED *adj* not having pennies
PENNING > UNPEN
PENS > UNPEN
PENT *archaic past form* of > UNPEN
PEOPLE *vb* empty of people
PEOPLED > UNPEOPLE
PEOPLES > UNPEOPLE
PERCH *vb* remove from a perch
PERCHED > UNPERCH
PERCHES > UNPERCH
PERFECT *same* as > IMPERFECT
PERPLEX *vb* remove confusion from
PERSON *n* person whose existence is officially denied or ignored
PERSONS > UNPERSON
PERVERT *vb* free (someone) from perversion
PICK *vb* undo (the stitches) of (a piece of sewing)
PICKED *adj* (of knitting, sewing, etc) having been unravelled or picked out
PICKING > UNPICK
PICKS > UNPICK
PIERCED *adj* not pierced
PILE *vb* remove from a pile
PILED > UNPILE
PILES > UNPILE
PILING > UNPILE
PILOTED *adj* unguided
PIN *vb* remove a pin or pins from
PINKED *adj* not decorated with a perforated pattern
PINKT *same* as > UNPINKED
PINNED > UNPIN
PINNING > UNPIN
PINS > UNPIN
PITIED *adj* not pitied
PITIFUL *adj* pitiless
PITTED *adj* not having had pits removed
PITYING *adj* not pitying
PLACE *same as* > DISPLACE
PLACED *adj* not given or put in a particular place
PLACES > UNPLACE
PLACING > UNPLACE
PLAGUED *adj* not plagued
PLAINED *adj* unmourned
PLAIT *vb* remove plaits from
PLAITED > UNPLAIT
PLAITS > UNPLAIT
PLANKED *adj* not planked
PLANNED *adj* not intentional or deliberate
PLANTED *adj* not planted
PLAYED *adj* not played
UNPLEASED *adj* not pleased or displeased
UNPLEATED *adj* not pleated
UNPLEDGED *adj* not pledged
UNPLIABLE *adj* not easily bent
UNPLIABLY > UNPLIABLE
UNPLIANT *adj* not pliant
UNPLOWED *adj* not ploughed
UNPLUCKED *adj* not plucked
UNPLUG *vb* disconnect (a piece of electrical equipment) by taking the plug out of the socket
UNPLUGGED *adj* using acoustic rather than electric instruments
UNPLUGS > UNPLUG
UNPLUMB *vb* remove lead from
UNPLUMBED *adj* not measured
UNPLUMBS > UNPLUMB
UNPLUME *vb* remove feathers from
UNPLUMED > UNPLUME
UNPLUMES > UNPLUME
UNPLUMING > UNPLUME
UNPOETIC *adj* not poetic
UNPOINTED *adj* not pointed
UNPOISED *adj* not poised
UNPOISON *vb* extract poison from
UNPOISONS > UNPOISON
UNPOLICED *adj* without police control
UNPOLISH *vb* remove polish from
UNPOLITE *same* as > IMPOLITE
UNPOLITIC *another word* for > IMPOLITIC
UNPOLLED *adj* not included in an opinion poll
UNPOPE *vb* strip of popedom
UNPOPED > UNPOPE
UNPOPES > UNPOPE
UNPOPING > UNPOPE
UNPOPULAR *adj* generally disliked or disapproved of
UNPOSED *adj* not posed
UNPOSTED *adj* not sent by post
UNPOTABLE *adj* undrinkable
UNPOTTED *adj* not planted in a pot
UNPRAISE *vb* withhold praise from
UNPRAISED > UNPRAISE
UNPRAISES > UNPRAISE
UNPRAY *vb* withdraw (a prayer)
UNPRAYED > UNPRAY
UNPRAYING > UNPRAY
UNPRAYS > UNPRAY
UNPREACH *vb* retract (a sermon)
UNPRECISE *same* as > IMPRECISE
UNPREDICT *vb* retract (a previous prediction)
UNPREPARE *vb* make unprepared
UNPRESSED *adj* not pressed
UNPRETTY *adj* unattractive
UNPRICED *adj* having no fixed or marked price
UNPRIEST *vb* strip of priesthood
UNPRIESTS > UNPRIEST
UNPRIMED *adj* not primed
UNPRINTED *adj* not printed
UNPRISON *vb* release from prison
UNPRISONS > UNPRISON
UNPRIZED *adj* not treasured
UNPROBED *adj* not examined
UNPROP *vb* remove support from
UNPROPER *same* as > IMPROPER
UNPROPPED > UNPROP
UNPROPS > UNPROP
UNPROVED *adj* not having been established as true, valid, or possible
UNPROVEN *adj* not established as true by evidence or demonstration
UNPROVIDE *vb* fail to supply requirements for
UNPROVOKE *vb* remove provocation from
UNPRUNED *adj* not pruned
UNPUCKER *vb* remove wrinkles from
UNPUCKERS > UNPUCKER
UNPULLED *adj* not pulled
UNPURE *same as* > IMPURE
UNPURELY > UNPURE
UNPURGED *adj* not purged
UNPURSE *vb* relax (lips) from pursed position
UNPURSED > UNPURSE
UNPURSES > UNPURSE
UNPURSING > UNPURSE
UNPURSUED *adj* not followed
UNPUZZLE *vb* figure out
UNPUZZLED > UNPUZZLE
UNPUZZLES > UNPUZZLE
UNQUAKING *adj* not quaking
UNQUALIFY *vb* disqualify
UNQUEEN *vb* depose from the position of queen
UNQUEENED > UNQUEEN
UNQUEENLY *adv* not in a queenlike manner
UNQUEENS > UNQUEEN
UNQUELLED *adj* not quelled
UNQUIET *adj* anxious or uneasy ▷ *n* state of unrest ▷ *vb* disquiet
UNQUIETED > UNQUIET
UNQUIETER > UNQUIET
UNQUIETLY > UNQUIET
UNQUIETS > UNQUIET
UNQUOTE *interj* expression used to indicate the end of a quotation that was introduced with the word 'quote' ▷ *vb* close (a quotation), esp in printing
UNQUOTED > UNQUOTE
UNQUOTES > UNQUOTE
UNQUOTING > UNQUOTE
UNRACED *adj* not raced
UNRACKED *adj* not stretched
UNRAISED *adj* not raised
UNRAKE *vb* unearth through raking
UNRAKED *adj* not raked
UNRAKES > UNRAKE
UNRAKING > UNRAKE
UNRANKED *adj* not ranked
UNRATED *adj* not rated
UNRAVAGED *adj* not ravaged
UNRAVEL *vb* reduce (something knitted or woven) to separate strands
UNRAVELED > UNRAVEL
UNRAVELS > UNRAVEL
UNRAZED *adj* not razed
UNRAZORED *adj* unshaven
UNREACHED *adj* not reached
UNREAD *adj* (of a book or article) not yet read
UNREADIER > UNREADY
UNREADILY > UNREADY
UNREADY *adj* not ready or prepared
UNREAL *adj* (as if) existing only in the imagination
UNREALISE *same* as > UNREALIZE
UNREALISM *n* abstractionism
UNREALITY *n* quality or state of being unreal, fanciful, or impractical
UNREALIZE *vb* make unreal
UNREALLY > UNREAL
UNREAPED *adj* not reaped
UNREASON *n* irrationality or madness ▷ *vb* deprive of reason
UNREASONS > UNREASON
UNREAVE *vb* unwind
UNREAVED > UNREAVE
UNREAVES > UNREAVE
UNREAVING > UNREAVE
UNREBATED *adj* not refunded
UNREBUKED *adj* not rebuked
UNRECKED *adj* disregarded
UNRED *same as* > UNREAD
UNREDREST *adj* not redressed
UNREDUCED *adj* not reduced
UNREDY *same as* > UNREADY
UNREEL *vb* unwind from a reel
UNREELED > UNREEL
UNREELER *n* machine that unwinds something from a reel
UNREELERS > UNREELER
UNREELING > UNREEL
UNREELS > UNREEL
UNREEVE *vb* withdraw (a rope) from a block, thimble, etc

UNREEVED >UNREEVE
UNREEVES >UNREEVE
UNREEVING >UNREEVE
UNREFINED *adj* (of substances such as petroleum, ores, and sugar) not processed into a pure or usable form
UNREFUTED *adj* not refuted
UNREIN *vb* free from reins
UNREINED >UNREIN
UNREINING >UNREIN
UNREINS >UNREIN
UNRELATED *adj* not connected with each other
UNRELAXED *adj* not relaxed
UNREMOVED *adj* not removed
UNRENEWED *adj* not renewed
UNRENT *adj* not torn
UNRENTED *adj* not rented
UNREPAID *adj* not repaid
UNREPAIR *less common word for* >DISREPAIR
UNREPAIRS >UNREPAIR
UNRESERVE *n* candour
UNREST *n* rebellious state of discontent
UNRESTED *adj* not rested
UNRESTFUL *adj* restless
UNRESTING *adj* not resting
UNRESTS >UNREST
UNRETIRE *vb* resume work after retiring
UNRETIRED >UNRETIRE
UNRETIRES >UNRETIRE
UNREVISED *adj* not revised
UNREVOKED *adj* not revoked
UNRHYMED *adj* not rhymed
UNRIBBED *adj* not ribbed
UNRID *adj* unridden
UNRIDABLE *adj* not capable of being ridden
UNRIDDEN *adj* not or never ridden
UNRIDDLE *vb* solve or puzzle out
UNRIDDLED >UNRIDDLE
UNRIDDLER >UNRIDDLE
UNRIDDLES >UNRIDDLE
UNRIFLED *adj* (of a firearm or its bore) not rifled
UNRIG *vb* strip (a vessel) of standing and running rigging
UNRIGGED >UNRIG
UNRIGGING >UNRIG
UNRIGHT *n* wrong
UNRIGHTS >UNRIGHT
UNRIGS >UNRIG
UNRIMED *same as* >UNRHYMED
UNRINGED *adj* not having or wearing a ring
UNRINSED *adj* not rinsed
UNRIP *vb* rip open
UNRIPE *adj* not fully matured
UNRIPELY >UNRIPE
UNRIPENED *same as* >UNRIPE
UNRIPER >UNRIPE
UNRIPEST >UNRIPE
UNRIPPED >UNRIP
UNRIPPING >UNRIP
UNRIPS >UNRIP
UNRISEN *adj* not risen
UNRIVALED *adj* (in US English) matchless or unrivalled
UNRIVEN *adj* not torn apart
UNRIVET *vb* remove rivets from
UNRIVETED >UNRIVET
UNRIVETS >UNRIVET
UNROASTED *adj* not roasted
UNROBE *same as* >DISROBE
UNROBED >UNROBE
UNROBES >UNROBE
UNROBING >UNROBE
UNROLL *vb* open out or unwind (something rolled or coiled) or (of something rolled or coiled) become opened out or unwound
UNROLLED >UNROLL
UNROLLING >UNROLL
UNROLLS >UNROLL
UNROOF *vb* remove the roof from
UNROOFED >UNROOF
UNROOFING >UNROOF
UNROOFS >UNROOF
UNROOST *vb* remove from a perch
UNROOSTED >UNROOST
UNROOSTS >UNROOST
UNROOT *less common word for* >UPROOT
UNROOTED >UNROOT
UNROOTING >UNROOT
UNROOTS >UNROOT
UNROPE *vb* release from a rope
UNROPED >UNROPE
UNROPES >UNROPE
UNROPING >UNROPE
UNROSINED *adj* not coated with rosin
UNROTTED *adj* not rotted
UNROTTEN *adj* not rotten
UNROUGED *adj* not coloured with rouge
UNROUGH *adj* not rough
UNROUND *vb* release (lips) from a rounded position
UNROUNDED *adj* articulated with the lips spread
UNROUNDS >UNROUND
UNROUSED *adj* not roused
UNROVE >UNREEVE
UNROVEN >UNREEVE
UNROYAL *adj* not royal
UNROYALLY >UNROYAL
UNRUBBED *adj* not rubbed
UNRUDE *adj* not rude
UNRUFFE *same as* >UNROUGH
UNRUFFLE *vb* calm
UNRUFFLED *adj* calm and unperturbed
UNRUFFLES >UNRUFFLE
UNRULE *n* lack of authority
UNRULED *adj* not ruled
UNRULES >UNRULE
UNRULIER >UNRULY
UNRULIEST >UNRULY
UNRULY *adj* difficult to control or organize
UNRUMPLED *adj* neat
UNRUSHED *adj* unhurried
UNRUSTED *adj* not rusted
UNS >UN
UNSADDLE *vb* remove the saddle from (a horse)
UNSADDLED >UNSADDLE
UNSADDLES >UNSADDLE
UNSAFE *adj* dangerous
UNSAFELY >UNSAFE
UNSAFER >UNSAFE
UNSAFEST >UNSAFE
UNSAFETY *n* lack of safety
UNSAID *adj* not said or expressed
UNSAILED *adj* not sailed
UNSAINED *adj* not blessed
UNSAINT *vb* remove status of being a saint from
UNSAINTED >UNSAINT
UNSAINTLY *adj* not saintly
UNSAINTS >UNSAINT
UNSALABLE *adj* not capable of being sold
UNSALABLY >UNSALABLE
UNSALTED *adj* not seasoned, preserved, or treated with salt
UNSALUTED *adj* not saluted
UNSAMPLED *adj* not sampled
UNSAPPED *adj* not undermined
UNSASHED *adj* not furnished with a sash
UNSATABLE *adj* not able to be sated; insatiable
UNSATED *adj* not sated
UNSATIATE *same as* >INSATIABLE
UNSATING *adj* not satisfying
UNSAVED *adj* not saved
UNSAVORY *same as* >UNSAVOURY
UNSAVOURY *adj* distasteful or objectionable
UNSAWED *same as* >UNSAWN
UNSAWN *adj* not cut with a saw
UNSAY *vb* retract or withdraw (something said or written)
UNSAYABLE *adj* that cannot be said
UNSAYING >UNSAY
UNSAYS >UNSAY
UNSCALE *same as* >DESCALE
UNSCALED >UNSCALE
UNSCALES >UNSCALE
UNSCALING >UNSCALE
UNSCANNED *adj* not scanned
UNSCARRED *adj* not scarred
UNSCARY *adj* not scary
UNSCATHED *adj* not harmed or injured
UNSCENTED *adj* not filled or impregnated with odour or fragrance
UNSCOURED *adj* not scoured
UNSCREW *vb* loosen (a screw or lid) by turning it
UNSCREWED >UNSCREW
UNSCREWS >UNSCREW
UNSCYTHED *adj* not cut with a scythe
UNSEAL *vb* remove or brea[k] the seal of
UNSEALED >UNSEAL
UNSEALING >UNSEAL
UNSEALS >UNSEAL
UNSEAM *vb* open or undo the seam of
UNSEAMED >UNSEAM
UNSEAMING >UNSEAM
UNSEAMS >UNSEAM
UNSEARED *adj* not seared
UNSEASON *vb* affect unfavourably
UNSEASONS >UNSEASON
UNSEAT *vb* throw or displace from a seat or saddle
UNSEATED >UNSEAT
UNSEATING >UNSEAT
UNSEATS >UNSEAT
UNSECRET *adj* not secret
UNSECULAR *adj* not secula[r]
UNSECURED *adj* (of a loan, etc) secured only against general assets and not against a specific asset
UNSEDUCED *adj* not seduced
UNSEEABLE *adj* not able t[o] be seen
UNSEEDED *adj* (of a player in a sport) not given a top player's position in the opening rounds of a tournament
UNSEEING *adj* not noticin[g] or looking at anything
UNSEEL *vb* undo seeling
UNSEELED >UNSEEL
UNSEELIE *pl n* evil malevolent fairies ▷ *adj* of or belonging to the unseelie
UNSEELING >UNSEEL
UNSEELS >UNSEEL
UNSEEMING *adj* unseemly
UNSEEMLY *adj* not according to expected standards of behaviour ▷ *adv* in an unseemly manner
UNSEEN *adj* hidden or invisible ▷ *adv* without being seen ▷ *n* passage which is given to studen[ts] for translation without them having seen it in advance
UNSEENS >UNSEEN
UNSEIZED *adj* not seized
UNSELDOM *adv* frequently
UNSELF *vb* remove self-centredness from ▷ *n* la[ck] of self
UNSELFED >UNSELF
UNSELFING >UNSELF
UNSELFISH *adj* concerne[d] about other people's wishes and needs rather

han one's own
ISELFS > UNSELF
ISELL *vb* speak nfavourably and off-uttingly of (something or omeone)
ISELLING > UNSELL
ISELLS > UNSELL
ISELVES > UNSELF
ISENSE *vb* remove sense rom
ISENSED > UNSENSE
ISENSES > UNSENSE
ISENSING > UNSENSE
ISENT *adj* not sent
ISERIOUS *adj* not serious
ISERVED *adj* not served
ISET *adj* not yet solidified r firm ▷ *vb* displace
ISETS > UNSET
ISETTING > UNSET
ISETTLE *vb* change or ecome changed from a ixed or settled condition
ISETTLED *adj* lacking rder or stability
ISETTLES > UNSETTLE
ISEVERED *adj* not severed
ISEW *vb* undo stitching of
ISEWED *same as* > UNSEW
ISEWING > UNSEW
ISEWN > UNSEW
ISEWS > UNSEW
ISEX *vb* deprive (a person) f the attributes of his r her sex, esp to make a voman more callous
ISEXED > UNSEX
ISEXES > UNSEX
ISEXING > UNSEX
ISEXIST *adj* not sexist
ISEXUAL *adj* not sexual
ISEXY *adj* not sexually ttractive
ISHACKLE *vb* release from hackles
ISHADED *adj* not shaded
ISHADOW *vb* remove hadow from
ISHADOWS > UNSHADOW
ISHAKED *same* s > UNSHAKEN
ISHAKEN *adj* (of faith or eelings) not having been veakened
ISHALE *vb* expose
ISHALED > UNSHALE
ISHALES > UNSHALE
ISHALING > UNSHALE
ISHAMED *same* s > UNASHAMED
ISHAPE *vb* make hapeless
ISHAPED > UNSHAPE
ISHAPELY *adj* not shapely
ISHAPEN *adj* having no lefinite shape
ISHAPES > UNSHAPE
ISHAPING > UNSHAPE
ISHARED *adj* not shared
ISHARP *adj* not sharp
ISHAVED *adj* not shaved
ISHAVEN *adj* (of a man vho does not have a beard) having stubble on his chin because he has not shaved recently
UNSHEATHE *vb* pull (a weapon) from a sheath
UNSHED *adj* not shed
UNSHELL *vb* remove from a shell
UNSHELLED > UNSHELL
UNSHELLS > UNSHELL
UNSHENT *adj* undamaged
UNSHEWN *adj* unshown
UNSHIFT *vb* release the shift key on a keyboard
UNSHIFTED > UNSHIFT
UNSHIFTS > UNSHIFT
UNSHIP *vb* be or cause to be unloaded, discharged, or disembarked from a ship
UNSHIPPED > UNSHIP
UNSHIPS > UNSHIP
UNSHIRTED *adj* not wearing a shirt
UNSHOCKED *adj* not shocked
UNSHOD *adj* not wearing shoes
UNSHOE *vb* remove shoes from
UNSHOED *same as* > UNSHOD
UNSHOEING > UNSHOE
UNSHOES > UNSHOE
UNSHOOT *Shakespearean variant of* > UNSHOUT
UNSHOOTED > UNSHOOT
UNSHOOTS > UNSHOOT
UNSHORN *adj* not cut
UNSHOT *adj* not shot
UNSHOUT *vb* revoke (an earlier statement) by shouting a contrary one
UNSHOUTED > UNSHOUT
UNSHOUTS > UNSHOUT
UNSHOWN *adj* not shown
UNSHOWY *adj* not showy
UNSHRIVED *same as* > UNSHRIVEN
UNSHRIVEN *adj* not shriven
UNSHROUD *vb* uncover
UNSHROUDS > UNSHROUD
UNSHRUBD *adj* not having shrubs
UNSHRUNK *adj* not shrunk
UNSHUNNED *adj* not shunned
UNSHUT *vb* open
UNSHUTS > UNSHUT
UNSHUTTER *vb* remove shutters from
UNSICKER *adj* unsettled
UNSICKLED *adj* not cut with a sickle
UNSIFTED *adj* not strained
UNSIGHING *adj* not lamented
UNSIGHT *vb* obstruct vision of
UNSIGHTED *adj* not sighted
UNSIGHTLY *adj* unpleasant to look at
UNSIGHTS > UNSIGHT
UNSIGNED *adj* (of a letter etc) anonymous
UNSILENT *adj* not silent
UNSIMILAR *adj* not similar
UNSINEW *vb* weaken
UNSINEWED > UNSINEW
UNSINEWS > UNSINEW
UNSINFUL *adj* without sin
UNSISTING *adj* Shakespearean term, possibly meaning insisting
UNSIZABLE *adj* of inadequate size
UNSIZED *adj* not made or sorted according to size
UNSKILFUL *adj* lacking dexterity or proficiency
UNSKILLED *adj* not having or requiring any special skill or training
UNSKIMMED *adj* not skimmed
UNSKINNED *adj* not skinned
UNSLAIN *adj* not killed
UNSLAKED *adj* not slaked
UNSLICED *adj* not sliced
UNSLICK *adj* not slick
UNSLING *vb* remove or release from a slung position
UNSLINGS > UNSLING
UNSLUICE *vb* let flow
UNSLUICED > UNSLUICE
UNSLUICES > UNSLUICE
UNSLUNG > UNSLING
UNSMART *adj* not smart
UNSMILING *adj* not wearing or assuming a smile
UNSMITTEN *adj* not smitten
UNSMOKED *adj* not smoked
UNSMOOTH *vb* roughen
UNSMOOTHS > UNSMOOTH
UNSMOTE *same as* > UNSMITTEN
UNSNAG *vb* remove snags from
UNSNAGGED > UNSNAG
UNSNAGS > UNSNAG
UNSNAP *vb* unfasten (the snap or catch) of (something)
UNSNAPPED > UNSNAP
UNSNAPS > UNSNAP
UNSNARL *vb* free from a snarl or tangle
UNSNARLED > UNSNARL
UNSNARLS > UNSNARL
UNSNECK *vb* unlatch
UNSNECKED > UNSNECK
UNSNECKS > UNSNECK
UNSNUFFED *adj* not snuffed
UNSOAKED *adj* not soaked
UNSOAPED *adj* not rubbed with soap
UNSOBER *adj* not sober
UNSOBERLY > UNSOBER
UNSOCIAL *adj* avoiding the company of other people
UNSOCKET *vb* remove from a socket
UNSOCKETS > UNSOCKET
UNSOD *same as* > UNSODDEN
UNSODDEN *adj* not soaked
UNSOFT *adj* hard
UNSOILED *adj* not soiled
UNSOLACED *adj* not comforted
UNSOLD *adj* not sold
UNSOLDER *vb* remove soldering from
UNSOLDERS > UNSOLDER
UNSOLEMN *adj* unceremonious
UNSOLID *adj* not solid
UNSOLIDLY > UNSOLID
UNSOLVED *adj* not having been solved or explained
UNSONCY *same as* > UNSONSY
UNSONSIE *same as* > UNSONSY
UNSONSY *adj* unfortunate
UNSOOTE *adj* not sweet
UNSOOTHED *adj* not soothed
UNSORTED *adj* not sorted
UNSOUGHT *adj* not sought after
UNSOUL *vb* cause to be soulless
UNSOULED > UNSOUL
UNSOULING > UNSOUL
UNSOULS > UNSOUL
UNSOUND *adj* unhealthy or unstable
UNSOUNDED *adj* not sounded
UNSOUNDER > UNSOUND
UNSOUNDLY > UNSOUND
UNSOURCED *adj* without a source
UNSOURED *adj* not soured
UNSOWED *same as* > UNSOWN
UNSOWN *adj* not sown
UNSPAR *vb* open
UNSPARED *adj* not spared
UNSPARING *adj* very generous
UNSPARRED > UNSPAR
UNSPARS > UNSPAR
UNSPEAK *obsolete word for* > UNSAY
UNSPEAKS > UNSPEAK
UNSPED *adj* not achieved
UNSPELL *vb* release from a spell
UNSPELLED > UNSPELL
UNSPELLS > UNSPELL
UNSPENT *adj* not spent
UNSPHERE *vb* remove from its, one's, etc, sphere or place
UNSPHERED > UNSPHERE
UNSPHERES > UNSPHERE
UNSPIDE *same as* > UNSPIED
UNSPIED *adj* unnoticed
UNSPILLED *same as* > UNSPILT
UNSPILT *adj* not spilt
UNSPLIT *adj* not split
UNSPOILED *adj* not damaged or harmed
UNSPOILT *same as* > UNSPOILED
UNSPOKE > UNSPEAK
UNSPOKEN *adj* not openly expressed
UNSPOOL *vb* unwind from spool
UNSPOOLED > UNSPOOL

UNSPOOLS > UNSPOOL
UNSPOTTED *adj* without spots or stains
UNSPRAYED *adj* not sprayed
UNSPRUNG *adj* without springs
UNSPUN *adj* not spun
UNSQUARED *adj* not made into a square shape
UNSTABLE *adj* lacking stability or firmness
UNSTABLER > UNSTABLE
UNSTABLY > UNSTABLE
UNSTACK *vb* remove from a stack
UNSTACKED > UNSTACK
UNSTACKS > UNSTACK
UNSTAID *adj* not staid
UNSTAINED *adj* not stained
UNSTALKED *adj* without a stalk
UNSTAMPED *adj* not stamped
UNSTARCH *vb* remove starch from
UNSTARRED *adj* not marked with a star
UNSTARRY *adj* not resembling or characteristic of a star from the entertainment world
UNSTATE *vb* deprive of state
UNSTATED *adj* not having been articulated or uttered
UNSTATES > UNSTATE
UNSTATING > UNSTATE
UNSTAYED *adj* unhindered
UNSTAYING *adj* nonstop
UNSTEADY *adj* not securely fixed ▷ *vb* make unsteady
UNSTEEL *vb* make (the heart, feelings, etc) more gentle or compassionate
UNSTEELED > UNSTEEL
UNSTEELS > UNSTEEL
UNSTEMMED *adj* without a stem
UNSTEP *vb* remove (a mast) from its step
UNSTEPPED > UNSTEP
UNSTEPS > UNSTEP
UNSTERILE *adj* not free from living, esp pathogenic, microorganisms
UNSTICK *vb* free or loosen (something stuck)
UNSTICKS > UNSTICK
UNSTIFLED *adj* not suppressed
UNSTILLED *adj* not reduced
UNSTINTED *adj* not stinted
UNSTIRRED *adj* not stirred
UNSTITCH *vb* remove stitching from
UNSTOCK *vb* remove stock from
UNSTOCKED *adj* without stock
UNSTOCKS > UNSTOCK
UNSTONED *adj* not stoned
UNSTOP *vb* remove the stop or stopper from
UNSTOPPED *adj* not obstructed or stopped up
UNSTOPPER *vb* unplug
UNSTOPS > UNSTOP
UNSTOW *vb* remove from storage
UNSTOWED > UNSTOW
UNSTOWING > UNSTOW
UNSTOWS > UNSTOW
UNSTRAP *vb* undo the straps fastening (something) in position
UNSTRAPS > UNSTRAP
UNSTRESS *n* weak syllable
UNSTRING *vb* remove the strings of
UNSTRINGS > UNSTRING
UNSTRIP *vb* strip
UNSTRIPED *adj* (esp of smooth muscle) not having stripes
UNSTRIPS > UNSTRIP
UNSTRUCK *adj* not struck
UNSTRUNG *adj* emotionally distressed
UNSTUCK *adj* freed from being stuck, glued, fastened, etc
UNSTUDIED *adj* natural or spontaneous
UNSTUFFED *adj* not stuffed
UNSTUFFY *adj* well-ventilated
UNSTUFT *same as* > UNSTUFFED
UNSTUNG *adj* not stung
UNSTYLISH *adj* unfashionable
UNSUBDUED *adj* not subdued
UNSUBJECT *adj* not subject
UNSUBTLE *adj* not subtle
UNSUBTLY > UNSUBTLE
UNSUCCESS *n* failure
UNSUCKED *adj* not sucked
UNSUIT *vb* make unsuitable
UNSUITED *adj* not appropriate for a particular task or situation
UNSUITING > UNSUIT
UNSUITS > UNSUIT
UNSULLIED *adj* (of a reputation, etc) not stained or tarnished
UNSUMMED *adj* not calculated
UNSUNG *adj* not acclaimed or honoured
UNSUNK *adj* not sunken
UNSUNNED *adj* not subjected to sunlight
UNSUNNY *adj* not sunny
UNSUPPLE *adj* rigid
UNSURE *adj* lacking assurance or self-confidence
UNSURED *adj* not assured
UNSURELY > UNSURE
UNSURER > UNSURE
UNSUREST > UNSURE
UNSUSPECT *adj* not open to suspicion
UNSWADDLE *same as* > UNSWATHE
UNSWATHE *vb* unwrap
UNSWATHED > UNSWATHE
UNSWATHES > UNSWATHE
UNSWAYED *adj* not swayed
UNSWEAR *vb* retract or revoke (a sworn oath)
UNSWEARS > UNSWEAR
UNSWEET *adj* not sweet
UNSWEPT *adj* not swept
UNSWOLLEN *adj* not swollen
UNSWORE > UNSWEAR
UNSWORN > UNSWEAR
UNTACK *vb* remove saddle and harness, etc, from
UNTACKED > UNTACK
UNTACKING > UNTACK
UNTACKLE *vb* remove tackle from
UNTACKLED > UNTACKLE
UNTACKLES > UNTACKLE
UNTACKS > UNTACK
UNTACTFUL *adj* not tactful
UNTAGGED *adj* without a label
UNTAILED *adj* tailless
UNTAINTED *adj* not tarnished, contaminated, or polluted
UNTAKEN *adj* not taken
UNTAMABLE *adj* (of an animal or person) not capable of being tamed, subdued, or made obedient
UNTAMABLY > UNTAMABLE
UNTAME *vb* undo the taming of
UNTAMED *adj* not brought under human control
UNTAMES > UNTAME
UNTAMING > UNTAME
UNTANGLE *vb* free from tangles or confusion
UNTANGLED > UNTANGLE
UNTANGLES > UNTANGLE
UNTANNED *adj* not tanned
UNTAPPED *adj* not yet used
UNTARRED *adj* not coated with tar
UNTASTED *adj* not tasted
UNTAUGHT *adj* without training or education
UNTAX *vb* stop taxing
UNTAXED *adj* not subject to taxation
UNTAXES > UNTAX
UNTAXING > UNTAX
UNTEACH *vb* cause to disbelieve (teaching)
UNTEACHES > UNTEACH
UNTEAM *vb* disband a team
UNTEAMED > UNTEAM
UNTEAMING > UNTEAM
UNTEAMS > UNTEAM
UNTEMPER *vb* soften
UNTEMPERS > UNTEMPER
UNTEMPTED *adj* not tempted
UNTENABLE *adj* (of a theory, idea, etc) incapable of being defended
UNTENABLY > UNTENABLE
UNTENANT *vb* remove (a tenant)
UNTENANTS > UNTENANT
UNTENDED *adj* not cared fo[r] or attended to
UNTENDER *adj* not tender
UNTENT *vb* remove from a tent
UNTENTED > UNTENT
UNTENTING > UNTENT
UNTENTS > UNTENT
UNTENTY *adj* inattentive
UNTENURED *adj* not havin[g] tenure
UNTESTED *adj* not having been tested or examined
UNTETHER *vb* untie
UNTETHERS > UNTETHER
UNTHANKED *adj* not thanked
UNTHATCH *vb* remove the thatch from
UNTHAW *same as* > THAW
UNTHAWED *adj* not thawed
UNTHAWING > UNTHAW
UNTHAWS > UNTHAW
UNTHINK *vb* reverse one's opinion about
UNTHINKS > UNTHINK
UNTHOUGHT > UNTHINK
UNTHREAD *vb* draw out th[e] thread or threads from (a needle, etc)
UNTHREADS > UNTHREAD
UNTHRIFT *n* unthrifty person
UNTHRIFTS > UNTHRIFT
UNTHRIFTY *adj* careless with money
UNTHRONE *less common wo[rd] for* > DETHRONE
UNTHRONED > UNTHRONE
UNTHRONES > UNTHRONE
UNTIDIED > UNTIDY
UNTIDIER > UNTIDY
UNTIDIES > UNTIDY
UNTIDIEST > UNTIDY
UNTIDILY > UNTIDY
UNTIDY *adj* messy and disordered ▷ *vb* make untidy
UNTIDYING > UNTIDY
UNTIE *vb* open or free (something that is tied)
UNTIED > UNTIE
UNTIEING > UNTIE
UNTIES > UNTIE
UNTIL *prep* in or throughout the period before
UNTILE *vb* strip tiles from
UNTILED > UNTILE
UNTILES > UNTILE
UNTILING > UNTILE
UNTILLED *adj* not tilled
UNTILTED *adj* not tilted
UNTIMED *adj* not timed
UNTIMELY *adj* occurring before the expected or normal time ▷ *adv* prematurely or inopportunely
UNTIMEOUS *same*

S > UNTIMELY
TIN *vb* remove tin from
TINGED *adj* not tinged
TINNED > UNTIN
TINNING > UNTIN
TINS > UNTIN
TIPPED *adj* not tipped
TIRABLE *adj* not able to e fatigued
TIRED *adj* not tired
TIRING *adj* (of a erson or their actions) ontinuing or persisting vithout declining in trength or vigour
TITLED *adj* without a itle
TO *prep* to
TOILING *adj* not abouring
TOLD *adj* incapable of escription
TOMB *vb* exhume
TOMBED > UNTOMB
TOMBING > UNTOMB
TOMBS > UNTOMB
TONED *adj* not toned
TORN *adj* not torn
TOUCHED *adj* not hanged, moved, or ffected
TOWARD *adj* causing nisfortune or annoyance
TRACE *vb* remove traces rom
TRACED *adj* not traced
TRACES > UNTRACE
TRACING > UNTRACE
TRACK *vb* remove from rack
TRACKED *adj* not tracked
TRACKS > UNTRACK
TRADED *adj* not traded
TRAINED *adj* without ormal or adequate raining or education
TRAPPED *adj* not trapped
TREAD *vb* retrace (a ourse, path, etc)
TREADED > UNTREAD
TREADS > UNTREAD
TREATED *adj* (of an llness, etc) not having een dealt with
TRENDY *adj* not trendy
TRESSED *adj* not having tress
TRIDE *same as* > UNTRIED
TRIED *adj* not yet used, one, or tested
TRIM *vb* deprive of legance or adornment
TRIMMED > UNTRIM
TRIMS > UNTRIM
TROD > UNTREAD
TRODDEN > UNTREAD
TRUE *adj* incorrect or alse
TRUER > UNTRUE
TRUEST > UNTRUE
TRUISM *n* something hat is false
TRUISMS > UNTRUISM
TRULY > UNTRUE

UNTRUSS *vb* release from or as if from a truss
UNTRUSSED > UNTRUSS
UNTRUSSER *n* person who untrusses
UNTRUSSES > UNTRUSS
UNTRUST *n* mistrust
UNTRUSTS > UNTRUST
UNTRUSTY *adj* not trusty
UNTRUTH *n* statement that is not true, lie
UNTRUTHS > UNTRUTH
UNTUCK *vb* become or cause to become loose or not tucked in
UNTUCKED > UNTUCK
UNTUCKING > UNTUCK
UNTUCKS > UNTUCK
UNTUFTED *adj* not having tufts
UNTUMBLED *adj* not tumbled
UNTUNABLE *adj* not tuneful
UNTUNABLY > UNTUNABLE
UNTUNE *vb* make out of tune
UNTUNED > UNTUNE
UNTUNEFUL *adj* not tuneful
UNTUNES > UNTUNE
UNTUNING > UNTUNE
UNTURBID *adj* clear
UNTURF *vb* remove turf from
UNTURFED > UNTURF
UNTURFING > UNTURF
UNTURFS > UNTURF
UNTURN *vb* turn in a reverse direction
UNTURNED *adj* not turned
UNTURNING > UNTURN
UNTURNS > UNTURN
UNTUTORED *adj* without formal education
UNTWILLED *adj* not twilled
UNTWINE *vb* untwist, unravel, and separate
UNTWINED > UNTWINE
UNTWINES > UNTWINE
UNTWINING > UNTWINE
UNTWIST *vb* twist apart and loosen
UNTWISTED > UNTWIST
UNTWISTS > UNTWIST
UNTYING > UNTIE
UNTYINGS > UNTIE
UNTYPABLE *adj* incapable of being typed
UNTYPICAL *adj* not representative or characteristic of a particular type, person, etc
UNUNBIUM *n* chemical element
UNUNBIUMS > UNUNBIUM
UNUNITED *adj* separated
UNUNUNIUM *n* chemical element
UNURGED *adj* not urged
UNUSABLE *adj* not in good enough condition to be used
UNUSABLY > UNUSABLE
UNUSED *adj* not being or never having been used

UNUSEFUL *adj* useless
UNUSHERED *adj* not escorted
UNUSUAL *adj* uncommon or extraordinary
UNUSUALLY > UNUSUAL
UNUTTERED *adj* not uttered
UNVAIL *same as* > UNVEIL
UNVAILE *same as* > UNVEIL
UNVAILED > UNVAIL
UNVAILES > UNVAIL
UNVAILING > UNVAIL
UNVAILS > UNVAIL
UNVALUED *adj* not appreciated or valued
UNVARIED *adj* not varied
UNVARYING *adj* always staying the same
UNVEIL *vb* ceremonially remove the cover from (a new picture, plaque, etc)
UNVEILED > UNVEIL
UNVEILER *n* person who removes a veil
UNVEILERS > UNVEILER
UNVEILING *n* ceremony involving the removal of a veil covering a statue
UNVEILS > UNVEIL
UNVEINED *adj* without veins
UNVENTED *adj* not vented
UNVERSED *adj* not versed
UNVESTED *adj* not vested
UNVETTED *adj* not thoroughly examined
UNVEXED *adj* not annoyed
UNVEXT *same as* > UNVEXED
UNVIABLE *adj* not capable of succeeding, esp financially
UNVIEWED *adj* not viewed
UNVIRTUE *n* state of having no virtue
UNVIRTUES > UNVIRTUE
UNVISITED *adj* not visited
UNVISOR *vb* remove visor from
UNVISORED > UNVISOR
UNVISORS > UNVISOR
UNVITAL *adj* not vital
UNVIZARD *same as* > UNVISOR
UNVIZARDS > UNVIZARD
UNVOCAL *adj* not vocal
UNVOICE *vb* pronounce without vibration of the vocal cords
UNVOICED *adj* not expressed or spoken
UNVOICES > UNVOICE
UNVOICING > UNVOICE
UNVULGAR *adj* not vulgar
UNWAGED *adj* (of a person) not having a paid job
UNWAKED *same as* > UNWAKENED
UNWAKENED *adj* not roused from sleep
UNWALLED *adj* not surrounded by walls
UNWANING *adj* not waning
UNWANTED *adj* not wanted or welcome

UNWARDED *adj* not warded
UNWARE *same as* > UNAWARE
UNWARELY > UNWARE
UNWARES *same as* > UNAWARES
UNWARIE *same as* > UNWARY
UNWARIER > UNWARY
UNWARIEST > UNWARY
UNWARILY > UNWARY
UNWARLIKE *adj* not warlike
UNWARMED *adj* not warmed
UNWARNED *adj* not warned
UNWARPED *adj* not warped
UNWARY *adj* not careful or cautious and therefore likely to be harmed
UNWASHED *adj* not washed ▷ *pl n* the masses
UNWASHEDS > UNWASHED
UNWASHEN *same as* > UNWASHED
UNWASTED *adj* not wasted
UNWASTING *adj* not wasting
UNWATCHED *adj* (of an automatic device, such as a beacon) not manned
UNWATER *vb* dry out
UNWATERED > UNWATER
UNWATERS > UNWATER
UNWATERY *adj* not watery
UNWAXED *adj* not treated with wax, esp of oranges or lemons, not sprayed with a protective coating of wax
UNWAYED *adj* having no routes
UNWEAL *n* ill or sorrow
UNWEALS > UNWEAL
UNWEANED *adj* not weaned
UNWEAPON *vb* disarm
UNWEAPONS > UNWEAPON
UNWEARIED *adj* not abating or tiring
UNWEARY *adj* not weary
UNWEAVE *vb* undo (weaving)
UNWEAVES > UNWEAVE
UNWEAVING > UNWEAVE
UNWEBBED *adj* not webbed
UNWED *adj* not wed
UNWEDDED *adj* not wedded
UNWEEDED *adj* not weeded
UNWEENED *adj* unknown
UNWEETING *same as* > UNWITTING
UNWEIGHED *adj* (of quantities purchased, etc) not measured for weight
UNWEIGHT *vb* remove weight from
UNWEIGHTS > UNWEIGHT
UNWELCOME *adj* unpleasant and unwanted
UNWELDED *adj* not welded
UNWELDY *same as* > UNWIELDY
UNWELL *adj* not healthy, ill
UNWEPT *adj* not wept for or lamented
UNWET *adj* not wet
UNWETTED *same as* > UNWET
UNWHIPPED *adj* not

whipped
UNWHIPT *same as* > UNWHIPPED
UNWHITE *adj* not white
UNWIELDLY *same as* > UNWIELDY
UNWIELDY *adj* too heavy, large, or awkward to be easily handled
UNWIFELY *adj* not like a wife
UNWIGGED *adj* without a wig
UNWILFUL *adj* complaisant
UNWILL *vb* will the reversal of (something that has already occurred)
UNWILLED *adj* not intentional
UNWILLING *adj* reluctant
UNWILLS > UNWILL
UNWIND *vb* relax after a busy or tense time
UNWINDER > UNWIND
UNWINDERS > UNWIND
UNWINDING > UNWIND
UNWINDS > UNWIND
UNWINGED *adj* without wings
UNWINKING *adj* vigilant
UNWIPED *adj* not wiped
UNWIRE *vb* remove wiring from
UNWIRED > UNWIRE
UNWIRES > UNWIRE
UNWIRING > UNWIRE
UNWISDOM *n* imprudence
UNWISDOMS > UNWISDOM
UNWISE *adj* foolish
UNWISELY > UNWISE
UNWISER > UNWISE
UNWISEST > UNWISE
UNWISH *vb* retract or revoke (a wish)
UNWISHED *adj* not desired
UNWISHES > UNWISH
UNWISHFUL *adj* not wishful
UNWISHING > UNWISH
UNWIST *adj* unknown
UNWIT *vb* divest of wit
UNWITCH *vb* release from witchcraft
UNWITCHED > UNWITCH
UNWITCHES > UNWITCH
UNWITS > UNWIT
UNWITTED > UNWIT
UNWITTILY > UNWITTY
UNWITTING *adj* not intentional
UNWITTY *adj* not clever and amusing
UNWIVE *vb* remove a wife from
UNWIVED > UNWIVE
UNWIVES > UNWIVE
UNWIVING > UNWIVE
UNWOMAN *vb* remove womanly qualities from
UNWOMANED > UNWOMAN
UNWOMANLY *adj* not womanly
UNWOMANS > UNWOMAN
UNWON *adj* not won
UNWONT *adj* unaccustomed
UNWONTED *adj* out of the ordinary
UNWOODED *adj* not wooded
UNWOOED *adj* not wooed
UNWORDED *adj* not expressed in words
UNWORK *vb* destroy (work previously done)
UNWORKED *adj* not worked
UNWORKING > UNWORK
UNWORKS > UNWORK
UNWORLDLY *adj* not concerned with material values or pursuits
UNWORMED *adj* not rid of worms
UNWORN *adj* not having deteriorated through use or age
UNWORRIED *adj* not bothered or perturbed
UNWORTH *n* lack of value
UNWORTHS > UNWORTH
UNWORTHY *adj* not deserving or worthy
UNWOUND *past tense and past participle of* > UNWIND
UNWOUNDED *adj* not wounded
UNWOVE > UNWEAVE
UNWOVEN > UNWEAVE
UNWRAP *vb* remove the wrapping from (something)
UNWRAPPED > UNWRAP
UNWRAPS > UNWRAP
UNWREAKED *adj* unavenged
UNWREATHE *vb* untwist from a wreathed shape
UNWRINKLE *vb* remove wrinkles from
UNWRITE *vb* cancel (what has been written)
UNWRITES > UNWRITE
UNWRITING > UNWRITE
UNWRITTEN *adj* not printed or in writing
UNWROTE > UNWRITE
UNWROUGHT *adj* not worked
UNWRUNG *adj* not twisted
UNYEANED *adj* not having given birth
UNYOKE *vb* release (an animal, etc) from a yoke
UNYOKED > UNYOKE
UNYOKES > UNYOKE
UNYOKING > UNYOKE
UNYOUNG *adj* not young
UNZEALOUS *adj* unenthusiastic
UNZIP *vb* unfasten the zip of (a garment) or (of a zip or a garment with a zip) to become unfastened
UNZIPPED > UNZIP
UNZIPPING > UNZIP
UNZIPS > UNZIP
UNZONED *adj* not divided into zones
UP *adv* indicating movement to or position at a higher place ▷ *adj* of a high or higher position ▷ *vb* increase or raise
UPADAISY *same as* > UPSADAISY
UPAITHRIC *adj* without a roof
UPAS *n* large Javan tree with whitish bark and poisonous milky sap
UPASES > UPAS
UPBEAR *vb* sustain
UPBEARER > UPBEAR
UPBEARERS > UPBEAR
UPBEARING > UPBEAR
UPBEARS > UPBEAR
UPBEAT *adj* cheerful and optimistic ▷ *n* unaccented beat
UPBEATS > UPBEAT
UPBIND *vb* bind up
UPBINDING > UPBIND
UPBINDS > UPBIND
UPBLEW > UPBLOW
UPBLOW *vb* inflate
UPBLOWING > UPBLOW
UPBLOWN > UPBLOW
UPBLOWS > UPBLOW
UPBOIL *vb* boil up
UPBOILED > UPBOIL
UPBOILING > UPBOIL
UPBOILS > UPBOIL
UPBORE > UPBEAR
UPBORNE *adj* held up
UPBOUND *adj* travelling upwards
UPBOUNDEN *same as* > UPBOUND
UPBOW *n* stroke of the bow from its tip to its nut on a stringed instrument
UPBOWS > UPBOW
UPBRAID *vb* scold or reproach
UPBRAIDED > UPBRAID
UPBRAIDER > UPBRAID
UPBRAIDS > UPBRAID
UPBRAST *same as* > UPBURST
UPBRAY *vb* shame
UPBRAYED > UPBRAY
UPBRAYING > UPBRAY
UPBRAYS > UPBRAY
UPBREAK *vb* escape upwards
UPBREAKS > UPBREAK
UPBRING *vb* rear
UPBRINGS > UPBRING
UPBROKE > UPBREAK
UPBROKEN > UPBREAK
UPBROUGHT > UPBRING
UPBUILD *vb* build up
UPBUILDER > UPBUILD
UPBUILDS > UPBUILD
UPBUILT > UPBUILD
UPBURNING *adj* burning upwards
UPBURST *vb* burst upwards
UPBURSTS > UPBURST
UPBY *same as* > UPBYE
UPBYE *adv* yonder
UPCAST *n* material cast or thrown up ▷ *adj* directed or thrown upwards ▷ *vb* throw or cast up
UPCASTING > UPCAST
UPCASTS > UPCAST
UPCATCH *vb* catch up
UPCATCHES > UPCATCH
UPCAUGHT > UPCATCH
UPCHEER *vb* cheer up
UPCHEERED > UPCHEER
UPCHEERS > UPCHEER
UPCHUCK *vb* vomit
UPCHUCKED > UPCHUCK
UPCHUCKS > UPCHUCK
UPCLIMB *vb* ascend
UPCLIMBED > UPCLIMB
UPCLIMBS > UPCLIMB
UPCLOSE *vb* close up
UPCLOSED > UPCLOSE
UPCLOSES > UPCLOSE
UPCLOSING > UPCLOSE
UPCOAST *adv* up the coast
UPCOIL *vb* make into a co
UPCOILED > UPCOIL
UPCOILING > UPCOIL
UPCOILS > UPCOIL
UPCOME *vb* come up
UPCOMES > UPCOME
UPCOMING *adj* coming soo
UPCOUNTRY *adj* of or from the interior of a country ▷ *adv* towards or in the interior of a country ▷ *n* interior part of a region c country
UPCOURT *adv* up basketba court
UPCURL *vb* curl up
UPCURLED > UPCURL
UPCURLING > UPCURL
UPCURLS > UPCURL
UPCURVE *vb* curve upwar
UPCURVED > UPCURVE
UPCURVES > UPCURVE
UPCURVING > UPCURVE
UPDART *vb* dart upwards
UPDARTED > UPDART
UPDARTING > UPDART
UPDARTS > UPDART
UPDATE *vb* bring up to da ▷ *n* act of updating or something that is updat
UPDATED > UPDATE
UPDATER > UPDATE
UPDATERS > UPDATE
UPDATES > UPDATE
UPDATING > UPDATE
UPDIVE *vb* leap upwards
UPDIVED > UPDIVE
UPDIVES > UPDIVE
UPDIVING > UPDIVE
UPDO *n* type of hairstyle
UPDOS > UPDO
UPDOVE > UPDIVE
UPDRAFT *n* upwards air current
UPDRAFTS > UPDRAFT
UPDRAG *vb* drag up
UPDRAGGED > UPDRAG
UPDRAGS > UPDRAG
UPDRAUGHT *n* upward movement of air or othe gas
UPDRAW *vb* draw up
UPDRAWING > UPDRAW
UPDRAWN > UPDRAW
UPDRAWS > UPDRAW
UPDREW > UPDRAW
UPDRIED > UPDRY
UPDRIES > UPDRY

DRY *vb* dry up
DRYING > UPDRY
END *vb* turn or set something) on its end
ENDED > UPEND
ENDING > UPEND
ENDS > UPEND
FIELD *adj* in sport, away rom the defending team's joal
FILL *vb* fill up
FILLED > UPFILL
FILLING > UPFILL
FILLS > UPFILL
FLING *vb* throw upwards
FLINGS > UPFLING
FLOW *vb* flow upwards
FLOWED > UPFLOW
FLOWING > UPFLOW
FLOWS > UPFLOW
FLUNG > UPFLING
FOLD *vb* fold up
FOLDED > UPFOLD
FOLDING > UPFOLD
FOLDS > UPFOLD
FOLLOW *vb* follow
FOLLOWS > UPFOLLOW
FRONT *adj* open and rank ▷ *adv* (of money) paid out at the beginning of a business arrangement
FURL *vb* roll up
FURLED > UPFURL
FURLING > UPFURL
FURLS > UPFURL
GANG *n* climb
GANGS > UPGANG
GATHER *vb* draw together
GATHERS > UPGATHER
GAZE *vb* gaze upwards
GAZED > UPGAZE
GAZES > UPGAZE
GAZING > UPGAZE
GIRD *vb* belt up
GIRDED > UPGIRD
GIRDING > UPGIRD
GIRDS > UPGIRD
GIRT > UPGIRD
GO *vb* ascend
GOES > UPGO
GOING > UPGO
GOINGS > UPGO
GONE > UPGO
GRADE *vb* promote (a person or job) to a higher rank
GRADED > UPGRADE
GRADER > UPGRADE
GRADERS > UPGRADE
GRADES > UPGRADE
GRADING > UPGRADE
GREW > UPGROW
GROW *vb* grow up
GROWING > UPGROW
GROWN > UPGROW
GROWS > UPGROW
GROWTH *n* process of developing or growing upwards
GROWTHS > UPGROWTH
GUSH *vb* flow upwards
GUSHED > UPGUSH
GUSHES > UPGUSH
UPGUSHING > UPGUSH
UPHAND *adj* lifted by hand
UPHANG *vb* hang up
UPHANGING > UPHANG
UPHANGS > UPHANG
UPHAUD *Scots variant of* > UPHOLD
UPHAUDING > UPHAUD
UPHAUDS > UPHAUD
UPHEAP *vb* computing term
UPHEAPED > UPHEAP
UPHEAPING > UPHEAP
UPHEAPS > UPHEAP
UPHEAVAL *n* strong, sudden, or violent disturbance
UPHEAVALS > UPHEAVAL
UPHEAVE *vb* heave or rise upwards
UPHEAVED > UPHEAVE
UPHEAVER > UPHEAVE
UPHEAVERS > UPHEAVE
UPHEAVES > UPHEAVE
UPHEAVING > UPHEAVE
UPHELD > UPHOLD
UPHILD *archaic past form of* > UPHOLD
UPHILL *adj* sloping or leading upwards ▷ *adv* up a slope ▷ *n* difficulty
UPHILLS > UPHILL
UPHOARD *vb* hoard up
UPHOARDED > UPHOARD
UPHOARDS > UPHOARD
UPHOIST *vb* raise
UPHOISTED > UPHOIST
UPHOISTS > UPHOIST
UPHOLD *vb* maintain or defend against opposition
UPHOLDER > UPHOLD
UPHOLDERS > UPHOLD
UPHOLDING > UPHOLD
UPHOLDS > UPHOLD
UPHOLSTER *vb* fit (a chair or sofa) with padding, springs, and covering
UPHOORD *vb* heap up
UPHOORDED > UPHOORD
UPHOORDS > UPHOORD
UPHOVE > UPHEAVE
UPHROE *variant spelling of* > EUPHROE
UPHROES > UPHROE
UPHUDDEN > UPHAUD
UPHUNG > UPHANG
UPHURL *vb* throw upwards
UPHURLED > UPHURL
UPHURLING > UPHURL
UPHURLS > UPHURL
UPJET *vb* stream upwards
UPJETS > UPJET
UPJETTED > UPJET
UPJETTING > UPJET
UPKEEP *n* act, process, or cost of keeping something in good repair
UPKEEPS > UPKEEP
UPKNIT *vb* bind
UPKNITS > UPKNIT
UPKNITTED > UPKNIT
UPLAID > UPLAY
UPLAND *adj* of or in an area of high or relatively high ground ▷ *n* area of high or relatively high ground
UPLANDER *n* person hailing from the uplands
UPLANDERS > UPLANDER
UPLANDISH > UPLAND
UPLANDS > UPLAND
UPLAY *vb* stash
UPLAYING > UPLAY
UPLAYS > UPLAY
UPLEAD *vb* lead upwards
UPLEADING > UPLEAD
UPLEADS > UPLEAD
UPLEAN *vb* lean on something
UPLEANED > UPLEAN
UPLEANING > UPLEAN
UPLEANS > UPLEAN
UPLEANT > UPLEAN
UPLEAP *vb* jump upwards
UPLEAPED > UPLEAP
UPLEAPING > UPLEAP
UPLEAPS > UPLEAP
UPLEAPT > UPLEAP
UPLED > UPLEAD
UPLIFT *vb* raise or lift up ▷ *n* act or process of improving moral, social, or cultural conditions ▷ *adj* (of a bra) designed to lift and support the breasts
UPLIFTED > UPLIFT
UPLIFTER > UPLIFT
UPLIFTERS > UPLIFT
UPLIFTING *adj* acting to raise moral, spiritual, cultural, etc, levels
UPLIFTS > UPLIFT
UPLIGHT *n* lamp or wall light designed or positioned to cast its light upwards ▷ *vb* light in an upward direction
UPLIGHTED > UPLIGHT
UPLIGHTER *n* lamp or wall light designed or positioned to cast its light upwards
UPLIGHTS > UPLIGHT
UPLINK *n* transmitter on the ground that sends signals up to a communications satellite ▷ *vb* send (data) to a communications satellite
UPLINKED > UPLINK
UPLINKING > UPLINK
UPLINKS > UPLINK
UPLIT > UPLIGHT
UPLOAD *vb* transfer (data or a program) from one's own computer into the memory of another computer
UPLOADED > UPLOAD
UPLOADING > UPLOAD
UPLOADS > UPLOAD
UPLOCK *vb* lock up
UPLOCKED > UPLOCK
UPLOCKING > UPLOCK
UPLOCKS > UPLOCK
UPLOOK *vb* look up
UPLOOKED > UPLOOK
UPLOOKING > UPLOOK
UPLOOKS > UPLOOK
UPLYING *adj* raised
UPMAKE *vb* make up
UPMAKER > UPMAKE
UPMAKERS > UPMAKE
UPMAKES > UPMAKE
UPMAKING > UPMAKE
UPMAKINGS > UPMAKE
UPMANSHIP *n* one-upmanship
UPMARKET *adj* expensive and of superior quality
UPMOST *another word for* > UPPERMOST
UPO *prep* upon
UPON *prep* on
UPPED > UP
UPPER *adj* higher or highest in physical position, wealth, rank, or status ▷ *n* part of a shoe above the sole
UPPERCASE *adj* capitalized ▷ *vb* capitalize or print in capitals
UPPERCUT *n* short swinging upward punch delivered to the chin ▷ *vb* hit (an opponent) with an uppercut
UPPERCUTS > UPPERCUT
UPPERMOST *adj* highest in position, power, or importance ▷ *adv* in or into the highest place or position
UPPERPART *n* highest part
UPPERS > UPPER
UPPILE *vb* pile up
UPPILED > UPPILE
UPPILES > UPPILE
UPPILING > UPPILE
UPPING > UP
UPPINGS > UP
UPPISH *adj* snobbish, arrogant, or presumptuous
UPPISHLY > UPPISH
UPPITY *adj* snobbish, arrogant, or presumptuous
UPPROP *vb* support
UPPROPPED > UPPROP
UPPROPS > UPPROP
UPRAISE *vb* lift up
UPRAISED > UPRAISE
UPRAISER > UPRAISE
UPRAISERS > UPRAISE
UPRAISES > UPRAISE
UPRAISING > UPRAISE
UPRAN > UPRUN
UPRATE *vb* raise the value, rate, or size of, upgrade
UPRATED > UPRATE
UPRATES > UPRATE
UPRATING > UPRATE
UPREACH *vb* reach up
UPREACHED > UPREACH
UPREACHES > UPREACH
UPREAR *vb* lift up
UPREARED > UPREAR
UPREARING > UPREAR
UPREARS > UPREAR
UPREST *n* uprising
UPRESTS > UPREST

UPRIGHT *adj* vertical or erect ▷ *adv* vertically or in an erect position ▷ *n* vertical support, such as a post ▷ *vb* make upright
UPRIGHTED >UPRIGHT
UPRIGHTLY >UPRIGHT
UPRIGHTS >UPRIGHT
UPRISAL >UPRISE
UPRISALS >UPRISE
UPRISE *vb* rise up
UPRISEN >UPRISE
UPRISER >UPRISE
UPRISERS >UPRISE
UPRISES >UPRISE
UPRISING *n* rebellion or revolt
UPRISINGS >UPRISING
UPRIST *same as* >UPREST
UPRISTS >UPRIST
UPRIVER *adv* towards or near the source of a river ▷ *n* area located upstream
UPRIVERS >UPRIVER
UPROAR *n* disturbance characterized by loud noise and confusion ▷ *vb* cause an uproar
UPROARED >UPROAR
UPROARING >UPROAR
UPROARS >UPROAR
UPROLL *vb* roll up
UPROLLED >UPROLL
UPROLLING >UPROLL
UPROLLS >UPROLL
UPROOT *vb* pull up by or as if by the roots
UPROOTAL >UPROOT
UPROOTALS >UPROOT
UPROOTED >UPROOT
UPROOTER >UPROOT
UPROOTERS >UPROOT
UPROOTING >UPROOT
UPROOTS >UPROOT
UPROSE >UPRISE
UPROUSE *vb* rouse or stir up
UPROUSED >UPROUSE
UPROUSES >UPROUSE
UPROUSING >UPROUSE
UPRUN *vb* run up
UPRUNNING >UPRUN
UPRUNS >UPRUN
UPRUSH *n* upward rush, as of consciousness ▷ *vb* rush upwards
UPRUSHED >UPRUSH
UPRUSHES >UPRUSH
UPRUSHING >UPRUSH
UPRYST *same as* >UPREST
UPS >UP
UPSADAISY *interj* expression of reassurance often uttered when someone stumbles or is lifted up
UPSCALE *adj* of or for the upper end of an economic or social scale ▷ *vb* upgrade
UPSCALED >UPSCALE
UPSCALES >UPSCALE
UPSCALING >UPSCALE
UPSEE *n* drunken revel
UPSEES >UPSEE
UPSEND *vb* send up
UPSENDING >UPSEND
UPSENDS >UPSEND
UPSENT >UPSEND
UPSET *adj* emotionally or physically disturbed or distressed ▷ *vb* tip over ▷ *n* unexpected defeat or reversal
UPSETS >UPSET
UPSETTER >UPSET
UPSETTERS >UPSET
UPSETTING >UPSET
UPSEY *same as* >UPSEE
UPSEYS >UPSEY
UPSHIFT *vb* move up (a gear)
UPSHIFTED >UPSHIFT
UPSHIFTS >UPSHIFT
UPSHOOT *vb* shoot upwards
UPSHOOTS >UPSHOOT
UPSHOT *n* final result or conclusion
UPSHOTS >UPSHOT
UPSIDE *n* upper surface or part
UPSIDES >UPSIDE
UPSIES >UPSY
UPSILON *n* 20th letter in the Greek alphabet
UPSILONS >UPSILON
UPSITTING *n* sitting up of a woman after childbirth
UPSIZE *vb* increase in size
UPSIZED >UPSIZE
UPSIZES >UPSIZE
UPSIZING >UPSIZE
UPSKILL *vb* improve the aptitude for work of (a person) by additional training
UPSKILLED >UPSKILL
UPSKILLS >UPSKILL
UPSLOPE *adv* up a or the slope
UPSOAR *vb* soar up
UPSOARED >UPSOAR
UPSOARING >UPSOAR
UPSOARS >UPSOAR
UPSPAKE >UPSPEAK
UPSPEAK *vb* speak with rising intonation
UPSPEAKS >UPSPEAK
UPSPEAR *vb* grow upwards in a spear-like manner
UPSPEARED >UPSPEAR
UPSPEARS >UPSPEAR
UPSPOKE >UPSPEAK
UPSPOKEN >UPSPEAK
UPSPRANG >UPSPRING
UPSPRING *vb* spring up or come into existence ▷ *n* leap forwards or upwards
UPSPRINGS >UPSPRING
UPSPRUNG >UPSPRING
UPSTAGE *adj* at the back half of the stage ▷ *vb* draw attention to oneself from (someone else) ▷ *adv* on, at, or to the rear of the stage ▷ *n* back half of the stage
UPSTAGED >UPSTAGE
UPSTAGER >UPSTAGE
UPSTAGERS >UPSTAGE
UPSTAGES >UPSTAGE
UPSTAGING >UPSTAGE
UPSTAIR *same as* >UPSTAIRS
UPSTAIRS *adv* or on an upper floor of a building ▷ *n* upper floor ▷ *adj* situated on an upper floor
UPSTAND *vb* rise
UPSTANDS >UPSTAND
UPSTARE *vb* stare upwards
UPSTARED >UPSTARE
UPSTARES >UPSTARE
UPSTARING >UPSTARE
UPSTART *n* person who has risen suddenly to a position of power and behaves arrogantly ▷ *vb* start up, as in surprise, etc
UPSTARTED >UPSTART
UPSTARTS >UPSTART
UPSTATE *adv* towards, in, from, or relating to the outlying or northern sections of a state, esp of New York State ▷ *n* outlying, esp northern, sections of a state
UPSTATER >UPSTATE
UPSTATERS >UPSTATE
UPSTATES >UPSTATE
UPSTAY *vb* support
UPSTAYED >UPSTAY
UPSTAYING >UPSTAY
UPSTAYS >UPSTAY
UPSTEP *n* type of vocal intonation
UPSTEPPED >UPSTEP
UPSTEPS >UPSTEP
UPSTIR *vb* stir up ▷ *n* commotion
UPSTIRRED >UPSTIR
UPSTIRS >UPSTIR
UPSTOOD >UPSTAND
UPSTREAM *adj* in or towards the higher part of a stream ▷ *vb* stream upwards
UPSTREAMS >UPSTREAM
UPSTROKE *n* upward stroke or movement, as of a pen or brush
UPSTROKES >UPSTROKE
UPSURGE *n* rapid rise or swell ▷ *vb* surge up
UPSURGED >UPSURGE
UPSURGES >UPSURGE
UPSURGING >UPSURGE
UPSWARM *vb* rise in a swarm
UPSWARMED >UPSWARM
UPSWARMS >UPSWARM
UPSWAY *vb* swing in the air
UPSWAYED >UPSWAY
UPSWAYING >UPSWAY
UPSWAYS >UPSWAY
UPSWEEP *n* curve or sweep upwards ▷ *vb* sweep, curve, or brush or be swept, curved, or brushed upwards
UPSWEEPS >UPSWEEP
UPSWELL *vb* swell up or cause to swell up
UPSWELLED >UPSWELL
UPSWELLS >UPSWELL
UPSWEPT >UPSWEEP
UPSWING *n* recovery perio in the trade cycle ▷ *vb* swing or move up
UPSWINGS >UPSWING
UPSWOLLEN >UPSWELL
UPSWUNG >UPSWING
UPSY *same as* >UPSEE
UPTA *same as* >UPTER
UPTAK *same as* >UPTAKE
UPTAKE *n* numbers taking up something such as an offer or the act of taking i up ▷ *vb* take up
UPTAKEN >UPTAKE
UPTAKES >UPTAKE
UPTAKING >UPTAKE
UPTAKS >UPTAK
UPTALK *n* style of speech i which every sentence en with a rising tone, as if th speaker is always asking question ▷ *vb* talk in thi manner
UPTALKED >UPTALK
UPTALKING >UPTALK
UPTALKS >UPTALK
UPTEAR *vb* tear up
UPTEARING >UPTEAR
UPTEARS >UPTEAR
UPTEMPO *adj* fast ▷ *n* uptempo piece
UPTEMPOS >UPTEMPO
UPTER *adj* of poor quality
UPTHREW >UPTHROW
UPTHROW *n* upward movement of rocks on one side of a fault plane relative to rocks on the other side ▷ *vb* throw upwards
UPTHROWN >UPTHROW
UPTHROWS >UPTHROW
UPTHRUST *n* upward push
UPTHRUSTS >UPTHRUST
UPTHUNDER *vb* make a noise like thunder
UPTICK *n* rise or increase
UPTICKS >UPTICK
UPTIE *vb* tie up
UPTIED >UPTIE
UPTIES >UPTIE
UPTIGHT *adj* nervously tense, irritable, or angry
UPTIGHTER >UPTIGHT
UPTILT *vb* tilt up
UPTILTED >UPTILT
UPTILTING >UPTILT
UPTILTS >UPTILT
UPTIME *n* time during which a machine, such as a computer, actually operates
UPTIMES >UPTIME
UPTITLING *n* practice of conferring grandiose job titles to employees performing relatively menial jobs
UPTOOK >UPTAKE
UPTORE >UPTEAR
UPTORN >UPTEAR
UPTOSS *vb* throw upward
UPTOSSED >UPTOSS

TOSSES > UPTOSS
TOSSING > UPTOSS
TOWN *adv* towards, in, or elating to some part of a town that is away from he centre ▷ *n* such a part of town, esp a residential part
TOWNER > UPTOWN
TOWNERS > UPTOWN
TOWNS > UPTOWN
TRAIN *vb* train up
TRAINED > UPTRAIN
TRAINS > UPTRAIN
TREND *n* upward trend
TRENDS > UPTREND
TRILLED *adj* trilled high
TURN *n* upward trend or mprovement ▷ *vb* turn or cause to turn over or upside down
TURNED > UPTURN
TURNING > UPTURN
TURNS > UPTURN
TYING > UPTIE
VALUE *vb* raise the value of
VALUED > UPVALUE
VALUES > UPVALUE
VALUING > UPVALUE
WAFT *vb* waft upwards
WAFTED > UPWAFT
WAFTING > UPWAFT
WAFTS > UPWAFT
WARD *same as* > UPWARDS
WARDLY > UPWARD
WARDS *adv* from a lower o a higher place, level, condition, etc
WELL *vb* well up
WELLED > UPWELL
WELLING > UPWELL
WELLS > UPWELL
WENT > UPGO
WHIRL *vb* spin upwards
WHIRLED > UPWHIRL
WHIRLS > UPWHIRL
WIND *adv* into or against he wind ▷ *adj* going against the wind ▷ *vb* wind up
WINDING > UPWIND
WINDS > UPWIND
WOUND > UPWIND
WRAP *vb* wrap up
WRAPS > UPWRAP
WROUGHT *adj* wrought up
interj hesitant utterance used to fill gaps in talking
ACHI > URACHUS
ACHUS *n* cord of tissue connected to the bladder
ACHUSES > URACHUS
ACIL *n* pyrimidine present in all living cells, usually in a combined orm, as in RNA
ACILS > URACIL
AEI > URAEUS
AEMIA *n* accumulation of waste products, normally excreted in he urine, in the blood: causes severe headaches, vomiting, etc
URAEMIAS > URAEMIA
URAEMIC > URAEMIA
URAEUS *n* sacred serpent represented on the headdresses of ancient Egyptian kings and gods
URAEUSES > URAEUS
URALI *n* type of plant
URALIS > URALI
URALITE *n* amphibole mineral, similar to hornblende, that replaces pyroxene in some igneous and metamorphic rocks
URALITES > URALITE
URALITIC > URALITE
URALITISE *same as* > URALITIZE
URALITIZE *vb* turn into uralite
URANIA *n* uranium dioxide
URANIAN *adj* heavenly
URANIAS > URANIA
URANIC *adj* of or containing uranium, esp in a high valence state
URANIDE *n* any element having an atomic number greater than that of protactinium
URANIDES > URANIDE
URANIN *n* type of alkaline substance
URANINITE *n* blackish heavy radioactive mineral consisting of uranium oxide in cubic crystalline form together with radium, lead, helium, etc: occurs in coarse granite
URANINS > URANIN
URANISCI > URANISCUS
URANISCUS *n* palate
URANISM *n* homosexuality
URANISMS > URANISM
URANITE *n* any of various minerals containing uranium, esp torbernite or autunite
URANITES > URANITE
URANITIC > URANITE
URANIUM *n* radioactive silvery-white metallic element, used chiefly as a source of nuclear energy
URANIUMS > URANIUM
URANOLOGY *n* study of the universe and planets
URANOUS *adj* of or containing uranium, esp in a low valence state
URANYL *n* of, consisting of, or containing the divalent ion UO_2^{2+} or the group $-UO_2$
URANYLIC > URANYL
URANYLS > URANYL
URAO *n* type of mineral
URAOS > URAO
URARE *same as* > URALI
URARES > URARE
URARI *same as* > URALI
URARIS > URARI
URASE *same as* > UREASE
URASES > URASE
URATE *n* any salt or ester of uric acid
URATES > URATE
URATIC > URATE
URB *n* urban area
URBAN *adj* of or living in a city or town
URBANE *adj* characterized by courtesy, elegance, and sophistication
URBANELY > URBANE
URBANER > URBANE
URBANEST > URBANE
URBANISE *same as* > URBANIZE
URBANISED > URBANISE
URBANISES > URBANISE
URBANISM *n* character of city life
URBANISMS > URBANISM
URBANIST *n* person who studies towns and cities
URBANISTS > URBANIST
URBANITE *n* resident of an urban community
URBANITES > URBANITE
URBANITY *n* quality of being urbane
URBANIZE *vb* make (a rural area) more industrialized and urban
URBANIZED > URBANIZE
URBANIZES > URBANIZE
URBIA *n* urban area
URBIAS > URBIA
URBS > URB
URCEOLATE *adj* shaped like an urn or pitcher
URCEOLI > URCEOLUS
URCEOLUS *n* organ of a plant
URCHIN *n* mischievous child
URCHINS > URCHIN
URD *n* type of plant with edible seeds
URDE *adj* (in heraldry) having points
URDEE *same as* > URDE
URDS > URD
URDY *n* heraldic line pattern
URE *same as* > AUROCHS
UREA *n* white soluble crystalline compound found in urine
UREAL > UREA
UREAS > UREA
UREASE *n* enzyme occurring in many plants, esp fungi, that converts urea to ammonium carbonate
UREASES > UREASE
UREDIA > UREDIUM
UREDIAL > UREDIUM
UREDINE > UREDO
UREDINES > UREDO
UREDINIA > UREDINIUM
UREDINIAL > UREDINIUM
UREDINIUM *same as* > UREDIUM
UREDINOUS > UREDO
UREDIUM *n* spore-producing body of some rust fungi in which uredospores are formed
UREDO *less common name for* > URTICARIA
UREDOS > UREDO
UREDOSORI *pl n* spore-producing bodies of some rust fungi in which uredospores are formed; uredia
UREIC > UREA
UREIDE *n* any of a class of organic compounds derived from urea by replacing one or more of its hydrogen atoms by organic groups
UREIDES > UREIDE
UREMIA *same as* > URAEMIA
UREMIAS > UREMIA
UREMIC > UREMIA
URENA *n* plant genus
URENAS > URENA
URENT *adj* burning
UREOTELIC *adj* excreting urea
URES > URE
URESES > URESIS
URESIS *n* urination
URETER *n* tube that conveys urine from the kidney to the bladder
URETERAL > URETER
URETERIC > URETER
URETERS > URETER
URETHAN *same as* > URETHANE
URETHANE *n* short for the synthetic material polyurethane
URETHANES > URETHANE
URETHANS > URETHAN
URETHRA *n* canal that carries urine from the bladder out of the body
URETHRAE > URETHRA
URETHRAL > URETHRA
URETHRAS > URETHRA
URETIC *adj* of or relating to the urine
URGE *n* strong impulse, inner drive, or yearning ▷ *vb* plead with or press (a person to do something)
URGED > URGE
URGENCE > URGENT
URGENCES > URGENT
URGENCIES > URGENT
URGENCY > URGENT
URGENT *adj* requiring speedy action or attention
URGENTLY > URGENT
URGER > URGE
URGERS > URGE
URGES > URGE
URGING > URGE
URGINGLY > URGE
URGINGS > URGE
URIAL *n* type of sheep
URIALS > URIAL
URIC *adj* of or derived from

urine
URICASE *n* type of enzyme
URICASES > URICASE
URIDINE *n* nucleoside present in all living cells in a combined form, esp in RNA
URIDINES > URIDINE
URIDYLIC as in *uridylic acid* nucleotide consisting of uracil, ribose, and a phosphate group. It is a constituent of RNA
URINAL *n* sanitary fitting used by men for urination
URINALS > URINAL
URINANT *adj* having the head downwards
URINARIES > URINARY
URINARY *adj* of urine or the organs that secrete and pass urine ▷ *n* reservoir for urine
URINATE *vb* discharge urine
URINATED > URINATE
URINATES > URINATE
URINATING > URINATE
URINATION > URINATE
URINATIVE > URINATE
URINATOR > URINATE
URINATORS > URINATE
URINE *n* pale yellow fluid excreted by the kidneys to the bladder and passed as waste from the body ▷ *vb* urinate
URINED > URINE
URINEMIA *same as* > UREMIA
URINEMIAS > URINEMIA
URINEMIC > URINEMIA
URINES > URINE
URINING > URINE
URINOLOGY *same as* > UROLOGY
URINOSE *same as* > URINOUS
URINOUS *adj* of, resembling, or containing urine
URITE *n* part of the abdomen
URITES > URITE
URMAN *n* forest
URMANS > URMAN
URN *n* vase used as a container for the ashes of the dead ▷ *vb* put in an urn
URNAL > URN
URNED > URN
URNFIELD *n* cemetery full of individual cremation urns ▷ *adj* (of a number of Bronze Age cultures) characterized by cremation in urns, which began in E Europe about the second millennium BC and by the seventh century BC had covered almost all of mainland Europe
URNFIELDS > URNFIELD
URNFUL *n* capacity of an urn
URNFULS > URNFUL
URNING *n* homosexual man
URNINGS > URNING
URNLIKE > URN
URNS > URN
UROBILIN *n* brownish pigment found in faeces and sometimes in urine
UROBILINS > UROBILIN
UROCHORD *n* notochord of a larval tunicate, typically confined to the tail region
UROCHORDS > UROCHORD
UROCHROME *n* yellowish pigment that colours urine
URODELAN > URODELE
URODELANS > URODELAN
URODELE *n* any amphibian of the order *Urodela*, having a long body and tail and four short limbs: includes the salamanders and newts ▷ *adj* of, relating to, or belonging to the *Urodela*
URODELES > URODELE
URODELOUS > URODELE
UROGENOUS *adj* producing or derived from urine
UROGRAPHY *n* branch of radiology concerned with X-ray examination of the kidney and associated structures
UROKINASE *n* biochemical catalyst
UROLAGNIA *n* sexual arousal involving urination
UROLITH *n* calculus in the urinary tract
UROLITHIC > UROLITH
UROLITHS > UROLITH
UROLOGIC > UROLOGY
UROLOGIES > UROLOGY
UROLOGIST > UROLOGY
UROLOGY *n* branch of medicine concerned with the urinary system and its diseases
UROMERE *n* part of the abdomen
UROMERES > UROMERE
UROPOD *n* paired appendage that arises from the last segment of the body in lobsters and related crustaceans and forms part of the tail fan
UROPODAL > UROPOD
UROPODOUS > UROPOD
UROPODS > UROPOD
UROPYGIA > UROPYGIUM
UROPYGIAL > UROPYGIUM
UROPYGIUM *n* hindmost part of a bird's body, from which the tail feathers grow
UROSCOPIC > UROSCOPY
UROSCOPY *n* examination of the urine
UROSES > UROSIS
UROSIS *n* urinary disease
UROSOME *n* abdomen of arthropods
UROSOMES > UROSOME
UROSTEGE *n* part of a serpent's tail
UROSTEGES > UROSTEGE
UROSTOMY *n* type of urinary surgery
UROSTYLE *n* bony rod forming the last segment of the vertebral column of frogs, toads, and related amphibians
UROSTYLES > UROSTYLE
URP *dialect word for* > VOMIT
URPED > URP
URPING > URP
URPS > URP
URSA *n* she-bear
URSAE > URSA
URSID *n* meteor
URSIDS > URSID
URSIFORM *adj* bear-shaped or bearlike in form
URSINE *adj* of or like a bear
URSON *n* type of porcupine
URSONS > URSON
URTEXT *n* earliest form of a text as established by linguistic scholars as a basis for variants in later texts still in existence
URTEXTS > URTEXT
URTICA *n* type of nettle
URTICANT *n* something that causes itchiness and irritation
URTICANTS > URTICANT
URTICARIA *n* skin condition characterized by the formation of itchy red or whitish raised patches, usually caused by an allergy
URTICAS > URTICA
URTICATE *adj* characterized by the presence of weals ▷ *vb* sting
URTICATED > URTICATE
URTICATES > URTICATE
URUBU *n* type of bird
URUBUS > URUBU
URUS *another name for the* > AUROCHS
URUSES > URUS
URUSHIOL *n* poisonous pale yellow liquid occurring in poison ivy and the lacquer tree
URUSHIOLS > URUSHIOL
URVA *n* Indian mongoose
URVAS > URVA
US *pron* refers to the speaker or writer and another person or other people
USABILITY > USABLE
USABLE *adj* able to be used
USABLY > USABLE
USAGE *n* regular or constant use
USAGER *n* person who has the use of something in trust
USAGERS > USAGER
USAGES > USAGE
USANCE *n* period of time permitted by commercia usage for the redemptior of foreign bills of exchang
USANCES > USANCE
USAUNCE *same as* > USANCE
USAUNCES > USAUNCE
USE *vb* put into service or action ▷ *n* using or bein used
USEABLE *same as* > USABLE
USEABLY > USABLE
USED *adj* second-hand
USEFUL *adj* able to be use advantageously or for several different purpose ▷ *n* odd-jobman or gener factotum
USEFULLY > USEFUL
USEFULS > USEFUL
USELESS *adj* having no practical use
USELESSLY > USELESS
USER *n* continued exercis use, or enjoyment of a right, esp in property
USERNAME *n* name given by computer user to gain access
USERNAMES > USERNAME
USERS > USER
USES > USE
USHER *n* official who show people to their seats, as i a church ▷ *vb* conduct o escort
USHERED > USHER
USHERESS *n* female usher
USHERETTE *n* female assistant in a cinema wh shows people to their seats
USHERING > USHER
USHERINGS > USHER
USHERS > USHER
USHERSHIP > USHER
USING > USE
USNEA *n* type of lichen
USNEAS > USNEA
USQUABAE *n* whisky
USQUABAES > USQUABAE
USQUE *n* whisky
USQUEBAE *same as* > USQUABAE
USQUEBAES > USQUEBAE
USQUES > USQUE
USTION *n* burning
USTIONS > USTION
USTULATE *adj* charred
USUAL *adj* of the most normal, frequent, or regular type ▷ *n* ordinar or commonplace events
USUALLY *adv* most often, most cases
USUALNESS > USUAL
USUALS > USUAL
USUCAPION *n* method of acquiring property
USUCAPT > USUCAPION
USUCAPTED > USUCAPION
USUCAPTS > USUCAPION

UFRUCT *n* right
o use and derive
rofit from a piece of
roperty belonging to
nother, provided the
roperty itself remains
ndiminished and
ninjured in any way
UFRUCTS > USUFRUCT
URE *vb* be involved in
sury
URED > USURE
URER *n* person who lends
unds at an exorbitant rate
f interest
URERS > USURER
URES > USURE
URESS *n* female usurer
URESSES > USURESS
URIES > USURY
URING > USURE
URIOUS > USURY
UROUS > USURY
URP *vb* seize (a position
r power) without
uthority
URPED > USURP
URPEDLY > USURP
URPER > USURP
URPERS > USURP
URPING > USURP
URPINGS > USURP
URPS > USURP
URY *n* practice of lending
noney at an extremely
igh rate of interest
WARD *adv* towards us
WARDS *same as* > USWARD
n syllable used in
ne fixed system of
olmization for the note C
A *n* side-blotched lizard
AS *n* eighth day of a
estival
ASES > UTAS
E *same as* > UTILITY
ENSIL *n* tool or
ontainer for practical use
ENSILS > UTENSIL
ERI > UTERUS
ERINE *adj* of or affecting
ne womb
ERITIS *n* inflammation
f the womb
EROTOMY *n* surgery on
ne uterus
ERUS *n* womb
ERUSES > UTERUS
ES > UTE
ILE *obsolete word*
r > USEFUL
ILIDOR *n* above-ground
nsulated casing for
ipes carrying water,
ewerage and electricity in
ermafrost regions
ILIDORS > UTILIDOR
ILISE *same as* > UTILIZE
ILISED > UTILISE
ILISER > UTILISE
ILISERS > UTILISE
ILISES > UTILISE
ILISING > UTILISE
ILITIES > UTILITY

UTILITY *n* usefulness ▷ *adj* designed for use rather than beauty
UTILIZE *vb* make practical use of
UTILIZED > UTILIZE
UTILIZER > UTILIZE
UTILIZERS > UTILIZE
UTILIZES > UTILIZE
UTILIZING > UTILIZE
UTIS *n* uproar
UTISES > UTIS
UTMOST *n* the greatest possible degree or amount ▷ *adj* of the greatest possible degree or amount
UTMOSTS > UTMOST
UTOPIA *n* real or imaginary society, place, state, etc, considered to be perfect or ideal
UTOPIAN *adj* of or relating to a perfect or ideal existence ▷ *n* idealistic social reformer
UTOPIANS > UTOPIAN
UTOPIAS > UTOPIA
UTOPIAST > UTOPIA
UTOPIASTS > UTOPIA
UTOPISM > UTOPIA
UTOPISMS > UTOPIA
UTOPIST > UTOPIA
UTOPISTIC > UTOPIA
UTOPISTS > UTOPIA
UTRICLE *n* larger of the two parts of the membranous labyrinth of the internal ear
UTRICLES > UTRICLE
UTRICULAR > UTRICLE
UTRICULI > UTRICULUS
UTRICULUS *same as* > UTRICLE
UTS > UT
UTTER *vb* express (something) in sounds or words ▷ *adj* total or absolute
UTTERABLE > UTTER
UTTERANCE *n* something uttered
UTTERED > UTTER
UTTERER > UTTER
UTTERERS > UTTER
UTTEREST > UTTER
UTTERING > UTTER
UTTERINGS > UTTER
UTTERLESS > UTTER
UTTERLY *adv* extrremely
UTTERMOST *same as* > UTMOST
UTTERNESS > UTTER
UTTERS > UTTER
UTU *n* reward
UTUS > UTU
UVA *n* grape or fruit resembling this
UVAE > UVA
UVAROVITE *n* emerald-green garnet found in chromium deposits: consists of calcium chromium silicate
UVAS > UVA

UVEA *n* part of the eyeball consisting of the iris, ciliary body, and choroid
UVEAL > UVEA
UVEAS > UVEA
UVEITIC > UVEITIS
UVEITIS *n* inflammation of the uvea
UVEITISES > UVEITIS
UVEOUS > UVEA
UVULA *n* small fleshy part of the soft palate that hangs in the back of the throat
UVULAE > UVULA
UVULAR *adj* of or relating to the uvula ▷ *n* uvular consonant
UVULARLY > UVULAR
UVULARS > UVULAR
UVULAS > UVULA
UVULITIS *n* inflammation of the uvula
UXORIAL *adj* of or relating to a wife
UXORIALLY > UXORIAL
UXORICIDE *n* act of killing one's wife
UXORIOUS *adj* excessively fond of or dependent on one's wife

Vv

VAC *vb* clean with a vacuum cleaner
VACANCE *n* vacant period
VACANCES > VACANCE
VACANCIES > VACANCY
VACANCY *n* unfilled job
VACANT *adj* (of a toilet, room, etc) unoccupied
VACANTLY > VACANT
VACATABLE > VACATE
VACATE *vb* cause (something) to be empty by leaving
VACATED > VACATE
VACATES > VACATE
VACATING > VACATE
VACATION *n* time when universities and law courts are closed ▷ *vb* take a vacation
VACATIONS > VACATION
VACATUR *n* annulment
VACATURS > VACATUR
VACCINA *same as* > VACCINIA
VACCINAL *adj* of or relating to vaccine or vaccination
VACCINAS > VACCINA
VACCINATE *vb* inject with a vaccine
VACCINE *n* substance designed to cause a mild form of a disease to make a person immune to the disease itself
VACCINEE *n* person who has been vaccinated
VACCINEES > VACCINEE
VACCINES > VACCINE
VACCINIA *technical name for* > COWPOX
VACCINIAL > VACCINIA
VACCINIAS > VACCINIA
VACCINIUM *n* shrub genus
VACHERIN *n* soft cheese made from cows' milk
VACHERINS > VACHERIN
VACILLANT *adj* indecisive
VACILLATE *vb* keep changing one's mind or opinions
VACKED > VAC
VACKING > VAC
VACS > VAC
VACUA > VACUUM
VACUATE *vb* empty
VACUATED > VACUATE
VACUATES > VACUATE
VACUATING > VACUATE
VACUATION > VACUATE
VACUIST *n* person believing in the existence of vacuums in nature
VACUISTS > VACUIST
VACUITIES > VACUITY
VACUITY *n* absence of intelligent thought or ideas
VACUOLAR > VACUOLE
VACUOLATE > VACUOLE
VACUOLE *n* fluid-filled cavity in the cytoplasm of a cell
VACUOLES > VACUOLE
VACUOUS *adj* not expressing intelligent thought
VACUOUSLY > VACUOUS
VACUUM *n* empty space from which all or most air or gas has been removed ▷ *vb* clean with a vacuum cleaner
VACUUMED > VACUUM
VACUUMING > VACUUM
VACUUMS > VACUUM
VADE *vb* fade
VADED > VADE
VADES > VADE
VADING > VADE
VADOSE *adj* of or derived from water occurring above the water table
VAE *same as* > VOE
VAES > VAE
VAG *n* vagrant
VAGABOND *n* person with no fixed home, esp a beggar
VAGABONDS > VAGABOND
VAGAL *adj* of, relating to, or affecting the vagus nerve
VAGALLY > VAGAL
VAGARIES > VAGARY
VAGARIOUS *adj* characterized or caused by vagaries
VAGARISH > VAGARY
VAGARY *n* unpredictable change
VAGGED > VAG
VAGGING > VAG
VAGI > VAGUS
VAGILE *adj* able to move freely
VAGILITY > VAGILE
VAGINA *n* (in female mammals) passage from the womb to the external genitals
VAGINAE > VAGINA
VAGINAL > VAGINA
VAGINALLY > VAGINA
VAGINANT *adj* sheathing
VAGINAS > VAGINA
VAGINATE *adj* (esp of plant parts) having a sheath
VAGINATED > VAGINATE
VAGINITIS *n* inflammation of the vagina
VAGINOSES > VAGINOSIS
VAGINOSIS *n* bacterial vaginal infection
VAGINULA *n* little sheath
VAGINULAE > VAGINULA
VAGINULE *same as* > VAGINULA
VAGINULES > VAGINULE
VAGITUS *n* new-born baby's cry
VAGITUSES > VAGITUS
VAGOTOMY *n* surgical division of the vagus ner[ve]
VAGOTONIA *n* pathologic[al] overactivity of the vagus nerve
VAGOTONIC > VAGOTONIA
VAGRANCY *n* state or condition of being a vagrant
VAGRANT *n* person with no settled home ▷ *adj* wandering
VAGRANTLY > VAGRANT
VAGRANTS > VAGRANT
VAGROM *same as* > VAGRAN[T]
VAGROMS > VAGROM
VAGS > VAG
VAGUE *adj* not clearly explained ▷ *vb* wander
VAGUED > VAGUE
VAGUELY > VAGUE
VAGUENESS > VAGUE
VAGUER > VAGUE
VAGUES > VAGUE
VAGUEST > VAGUE
VAGUING > VAGUE
VAGUS *n* tenth cranial nerve, which supplies th[e] heart, lungs, and viscera
VAHANA *n* vehicle
VAHANAS > VAHANA
VAHINE *n* Polynesian

voman
HINES > VAHINE
IL *vb* lower (something,
uch as a weapon), esp
s a sign of deference or
ubmission
ILED > VAIL
ILING > VAIL
ILS > VAIL
IN *adj* excessively proud,
sp of one's appearance
INER > VAIN
INESSE *n* vainness
INESSES > VAINESSE
INEST > VAIN
INGLORY *n* boastfulness
r vanity
INLY > VAIN
INNESS > VAIN
IR *n* fur, probably
ussian squirrel, used to
rim robes in the Middle
ges
IRE *same as* > VAIR
IRIER > VAIR
IRIEST > VAIR
IRS > VAIR
IRY > VAIR
IVODE *n* European ruler
IVODES > VAIVODE
KASS *n* type of cloak
KASSES > VAKASS
KEEL *n* ambassador
KEELS > VAKEEL
KIL *same as* > VAKEEL
KILS > VAKIL
LANCE *n* piece of drapery
ound the edge of a
ed ▷ *vb* provide with a
alance
LANCED > VALANCE
LANCES > VALANCE
LANCING > VALANCE
LE *n* valley ▷ *sentence*
ubstitute farewell
LENCE *same as* > VALENCY
LENCES > VALENCE
LENCIA *n* type of fabric
LENCIAS > VALENCIA
LENCIES > VALENCY
LENCY *n* power of an
tom to make molecular
onds
LENTINE *n* (person
o whom one sends) a
omantic card on Saint
alentine's Day, 14th
ebruary
LERATE *n* salt of valeric
cid
LERATES > VALERATE
LERIAN *n* herb used as a
edative
LERIANS > VALERIAN
LERIC *adj* of, relating to,
r derived from valerian
LES > VALE
LET *n* man's personal
nale servant ▷ *vb* act as a
alet (for)
LETA *n* old-time dance in
riple time
LETAS > VALETA
LETE *n* farewell

VALETED > VALET
VALETES > VALETE
VALETING > VALET
VALETINGS > VALET
VALETS > VALET
VALGOID > VALGUS
VALGOUS *same as* > VALGUS
VALGUS *adj* denoting a deformity of a limb ▷ *n* abnormal position of a limb
VALGUSES > VALGUS
VALI *n* Turkish civil governor
VALIANCE > VALIANT
VALIANCES > VALIANT
VALIANCY > VALIANT
VALIANT *adj* brave or courageous ▷ *n* brave person
VALIANTLY > VALIANT
VALIANTS > VALIANT
VALID *adj* soundly reasoned
VALIDATE *vb* make valid
VALIDATED > VALIDATE
VALIDATES > VALIDATE
VALIDER > VALID
VALIDEST > VALID
VALIDITY > VALID
VALIDLY > VALID
VALIDNESS > VALID
VALINE *n* essential amino acid
VALINES > VALINE
VALIS > VALI
VALISE *n* small suitcase
VALISES > VALISE
VALKYR *variant of* > VALKYRIE
VALKYRIE *n* (in Norse mythology) beatiful maiden who collects dead heroes on the battlefield to take to Valhalla
VALKYRIES > VALKYRIES
VALKYRS > VALKYR
VALLAR *adj* pertaining to a rampart
VALLARY > VALLAR
VALLATE *adj* surrounded with a wall
VALLATION *n* act or process of building fortifications
VALLECULA *n* any of various natural depressions or crevices
VALLEY *n* low area between hills, often with a river running through it
VALLEYED *adj* having a valley
VALLEYS > VALLEY
VALLHUND as in *Swedish vallhund* breed of dog
VALLHUNDS > VALLHUND
VALLONIA *same as* > VALONIA
VALLONIAS > VALLONIA
VALLUM *n* Roman rampart or earthwork
VALLUMS > VALLUM
VALONEA *same as* > VALONIA
VALONEAS > VALONEA

VALONIA *n* acorn cups and unripe acorns of a particular oak
VALONIAS > VALONIA
VALOR *same as* > VALOUR
VALORISE *same as* > VALORIZE
VALORISED > VALORISE
VALORISES > VALORISE
VALORIZE *vb* fix and maintain an artificial price for (a commodity) by governmental action
VALORIZED > VALORIZE
VALORIZES > VALORIZE
VALOROUS > VALOUR
VALORS > VALOR
VALOUR *n* bravery ▷ *n* courageous person
VALOURS > VALOUR
VALPROATE *n* medicament derived from valproic acid
VALPROIC as in *valproic acid* synthetic crystalline compound, used as an anticonvulsive
VALSE *another word for* > WALTZ
VALSED > VALSE
VALSES > VALSE
VALSING > VALSE
VALUABLE *adj* having great worth ▷ *n* valuable article of personal property, esp jewellery
VALUABLES > VALUABLE
VALUABLY > VALUABLE
VALUATE *vb* value or evaluate
VALUATED > VALUATE
VALUATES > VALUATE
VALUATING > VALUATE
VALUATION *n* assessment of worth
VALUATOR *n* person who estimates the value of objects, paintings, etc
VALUATORS > VALUATOR
VALUE *n* importance, usefulness ▷ *vb* assess the worth or desirability of
VALUED > VALUE
VALUELESS *adj* having or possessing no value
VALUER > VALUE
VALUERS > VALUE
VALUES > VALUE
VALUING > VALUE
VALUTA *n* value of one currency in terms of its exchange rate with another
VALUTAS > VALUTA
VALVAL *same as* > VALVULAR
VALVAR *same as* > VALVULAR
VALVASSOR *same as* > VAVASOR
VALVATE *adj* furnished with a valve or valves
VALVE *n* device to control the movement of fluid through a pipe ▷ *vb* provide with a valve
VALVED > VALVE

VALVELESS > VALVE
VALVELET *same as* > VALVULE
VALVELETS > VALVELET
VALVELIKE > VALVE
VALVES > VALVE
VALVING > VALVE
VALVULA *same as* > VALVULE
VALVULAE > VALVULA
VALVULAR *adj* of or having valves
VALVULE *n* small valve or a part resembling one
VALVULES > VALVULE
VAMBRACE *n* piece of armour used to protect the arm
VAMBRACED > VAMBRACE
VAMBRACES > VAMBRACE
VAMOOSE *vb* leave a place hurriedly
VAMOOSED > VAMOSE
VAMOOSES > VAMOSE
VAMOOSING > VAMOSE
VAMOSE *same as* > VAMOOSE
VAMOSED > VAMOSE
VAMOSES > VAMOSE
VAMOSING > VAMOSE
VAMP *n* sexually attractive woman who seduces men ▷ *vb* (of a woman) to seduce (a man)
VAMPED > VAMP
VAMPER > VAMP
VAMPERS > VAMP
VAMPIER > VAMP
VAMPIEST > VAMP
VAMPING > VAMP
VAMPINGS > VAMP
VAMPIRE *n* (in folklore) corpse that rises at night to drink the blood of the living ▷ *vb* assail
VAMPIRED > VAMPIRE
VAMPIRES > VAMPIRE
VAMPIRIC > VAMPIRE
VAMPIRING > VAMPIRE
VAMPIRISE *same as* > VAMPIRIZE
VAMPIRISH > VAMPIRE
VAMPIRISM *n* belief in the existence of vampires
VAMPIRIZE *vb* suck blood from
VAMPISH > VAMP
VAMPISHLY > VAMP
VAMPLATE *n* piece of metal mounted on a lance to protect the hand
VAMPLATES > VAMPLATE
VAMPS > VAMP
VAMPY > VAMP
VAN *n* motor vehicle for transporting goods ▷ *vb* send in a van
VANADATE *n* any salt or ester of a vanadic acid
VANADATES > VANADATE
VANADIATE *same as* > VANADATE
VANADIC *adj* of or containing vanadium, esp in a trivalent or pentavalent state

VANADIUM *n* metallic element, used in steel
VANADIUMS > VANADIUM
VANADOUS *adj* of or containing vanadium
VANASPATI *n* hydrogenated vegetable fat commonly used in India as a substitute for butter
VANDA *n* type of orchid
VANDAL *n* person who deliberately damages property
VANDALIC > VANDAL
VANDALISE *same as* > VANDALIZE
VANDALISH > VANDAL
VANDALISM *n* wanton or deliberate destruction caused by a vandal or an instance of such destruction
VANDALIZE *vb* cause damage to (personal or public property) deliberately
VANDALS > VANDAL
VANDAS > VANDA
VANDYKE *n* short pointed beard ▷ *vb* cut with deep zigzag indentations
VANDYKED > VANDYKE
VANDYKES > VANDYKE
VANDYKING > VANDYKE
VANE *n* flat blade on a rotary device such as a weathercock or propeller
VANED > VANE
VANELESS > VANE
VANES > VANE
VANESSA *n* type of butterfly
VANESSAS > VANESSA
VANESSID *n* type of butterfly ▷ *adj* relating to this butterfly
VANESSIDS > VANESSID
VANG *n* type of rope or tackle on a sailing ship
VANGS > VANG
VANGUARD *n* unit of soldiers leading an army
VANGUARDS > VANGUARD
VANILLA *n* seed pod of a tropical climbing orchid, used for flavouring ▷ *adj* flavoured with vanilla
VANILLAS > VANILLA
VANILLIC *adj* of, resembling, containing, or derived from vanilla or vanillin
VANILLIN *n* white crystalline aldehyde found in vanilla
VANILLINS > VANILLIN
VANISH *vb* disappear suddenly or mysteriously ▷ *n* second and weaker of the two vowels in a falling diphthong
VANISHED > VANISH
VANISHER > VANISH
VANISHERS > VANISH
VANISHES > VANISH
VANISHING > VANISH
VANITAS *n* type of Dutch painting
VANITASES > VANITAS
VANITIED *adj* with vanity units or mirrors
VANITIES > VANITY
VANITORY *n* vanity unit
VANITY *n* (display of) excessive pride
VANLOAD *n* amount van will carry
VANLOADS > VANLOAD
VANMAN *n* man in control of a van
VANMEN > VANMAN
VANNED > VAN
VANNER *n* horse used to pull delivery vehicles
VANNERS > VANNER
VANNING > VAN
VANNINGS > VAN
VANPOOL *n* van-sharing group
VANPOOLS > VANPOOL
VANQUISH *vb* defeat (someone) utterly
VANS > VAN
VANT *archaic word for* > VANGUARD
VANTAGE *n* state, position, or opportunity offering advantage ▷ *vb* benefit
VANTAGED > VANTAGE
VANTAGES > VANTAGE
VANTAGING > VANTAGE
VANTBRACE *n* armour for the arm
VANTS > VANT
VANWARD *adv* in or towards the front
VAPID *adj* lacking character, dull
VAPIDER > VAPID
VAPIDEST > VAPID
VAPIDITY > VAPID
VAPIDLY > VAPID
VAPIDNESS > VAPID
VAPOR *same as* > VAPOUR
VAPORABLE > VAPOR
VAPORED > VAPOR
VAPORER > VAPOR
VAPORERS > VAPOR
VAPORETTI > VAPORETTO
VAPORETTO *n* steam-powered passenger boat, as used on the canals in Venice
VAPORIFIC *adj* producing, causing, or tending to produce vapour
VAPORING > VAPOR
VAPORINGS > VAPOR
VAPORISE *same as* > VAPORIZE
VAPORISED > VAPORISE
VAPORISER *same as* > VAPORIZER
VAPORISES > VAPORISE
VAPORISH > VAPOR
VAPORIZE *vb* change into a vapour
VAPORIZED > VAPORIZE
VAPORIZER *n* substance that vaporizes or a device that causes vaporization
VAPORIZES > VAPORIZE
VAPORLESS > VAPOR
VAPORLIKE > VAPOR
VAPOROUS *same as* > VAPORIFIC
VAPORS > VAPOR
VAPORWARE *n* new software that has not yet been produced
VAPORY > VAPOUR
VAPOUR *n* moisture suspended in air as steam or mist ▷ *vb* evaporate
VAPOURED > VAPOUR
VAPOURER > VAPOUR
VAPOURERS > VAPOUR
VAPOURING > VAPOUR
VAPOURISH > VAPOUR
VAPOURS > VAPOUR
VAPOURY > VAPOUR
VAPULATE *vb* strike
VAPULATED > VAPULATE
VAPULATES > VAPULATE
VAQUERO *n* cattlehand
VAQUEROS > VAQUERO
VAR *n* unit of reactive power of an alternating current
VARA *n* unit of length used in Spain, Portugal, and South America
VARACTOR *n* semiconductor diode that acts as a voltage-dependent capacitor
VARACTORS > VARACTOR
VARAN *n* type of lizard
VARANS > VARAN
VARAS > VARA
VARDIES > VARDY
VARDY *n* verdict
VARE *n* rod
VAREC *n* ash obtained from kelp
VARECH *same as* > VAREC
VARECHS > VARECH
VARECS > VAREC
VARES > VARE
VAREUSE *n* type of coat
VAREUSES > VAREUSE
VARGUENO *n* type of Spanish cabinet
VARGUENOS > VARGUENO
VARIA *n* collection or miscellany, esp of literary works
VARIABLE *adj* not always the same, changeable ▷ *n* something that is subject to variation
VARIABLES > VARIABLE
VARIABLY > VARIABLE
VARIANCE *n* act of varying
VARIANCES > VARIANCE
VARIANT *adj* differing from a standard or type ▷ *n* something that differs from a standard or type
VARIANTS > VARIANT
VARIAS > VARIA
VARIATE *n* random variable or a numerical value taken by it ▷ *vb* va[ry]
VARIATED > VARIATE
VARIATES > VARIATE
VARIATING > VARIATE
VARIATION *n* something presented in a slightly different form
VARIATIVE > VARIATE
VARICELLA n chickenpox
VARICES > VARIX
VARICOID *same as* > CIRSOID
VARICOSE *adj* of or resulting from varicose veins
VARICOSED *same as* > VARICOSE
VARICOSES > VARICOSIS
VARICOSIS *n* any condition characterized [by] distension of the veins
VARIED > VARY
VARIEDLY > VARY
VARIEGATE *vb* alter the appearance of, esp by adding different colours
VARIER *n* person who varies
VARIERS > VARIER
VARIES > VARY
VARIETAL *adj* of or formi[ng] a variety, esp a biologica[l] variety ▷ *n* wine labelle[d] with the name of the gra[pe] from which it is pressed
VARIETALS > VARIETAL
VARIETIES > VARIETY
VARIETY *n* state of being diverse or various
VARIFOCAL *adj* gradated [to] permit any length of visi[on] between near and distan[t] ▷ *n* lens of this type
VARIFORM *adj* varying in form or shape
VARIOLA *n* smallpox
VARIOLAR > VARIOLA
VARIOLAS > VARIOLA
VARIOLATE *vb* inoculate with the smallpox virus ▷ *adj* marked or pitted with or as if with the sca[rs] of smallpox
VARIOLE *n* any of the rounded masses that make up the rock variolit[e]
VARIOLES > VARIOLE
VARIOLITE *n* type of basi[c] igneous rock
VARIOLOID *adj* resembli[ng] smallpox ▷ *n* mild form of smallpox occurring in persons with partial immunity
VARIOLOUS *adj* relating t[o] or resembling smallpox
VARIORUM *adj* containing notes by various scholar[s] or critics or various versions of the text ▷ *n* edition or text of this kin[d]
VARIORUMS > VARIORUM
VARIOUS *adj* of several

inds
RIOUSLY > VARIOUS
RISCITE *n* green econdary mineral
RISIZED *adj* of different izes
RISTOR *n* type of emiconductor device
RISTORS > VARISTOR
RITYPE *vb* produce :opy) on a Varityper *n* copy produced on a arityper
RITYPED > VARITYPE
RITYPES > VARITYPE
RIX *n* tortuous dilated ein
RLET *n* menial servant
RLETESS *n* female varlet
RLETRY *n* the rabble
RLETS > VARLET
RLETTO *same as* > VARLET
RLETTOS > VARLETTO
RMENT *same as* > VARMINT
RMENTS > VARMENT
RMINT *n* irritating or bnoxious person or nimal
RMINTS > VARMINT
RNA *n* any of the four indu castes
RNAS > VARNA
RNISH *n* solution of oil nd resin, put on a surface) make it hard and glossy *vb* apply varnish to
RNISHED > VARNISH
RNISHER > VARNISH
RNISHES > VARNISH
RNISHY > VARNISH
ROOM *same as* > VROOM
ROOMED > VAROOM
ROOMING > VAROOM
ROOMS > VAROOM
RROA *n* small parasite
RROAS > VARROA
RS > VAR
RSAL *adj* universal
RSITIES > VARSITY
RSITY *n* university
RTABED *n* position in the rmenian church
RTABEDS > VARTABED
RUS *adj* denoting a eformity of a limb ▷ *n* ɔnormal position of a mb
RUSES > VARUS
RVE *n* typically thin band f sediment deposited nnually in glacial lakes
RVED *adj* having layers of edimentary deposit
RVEL *n* piece of falconry quipment
RVELLED *adj* having arvels
RVELS > VARVEL
RVES > VARVE
RY *vb* change
RYING > VARY
RYINGLY > VARY
RYINGS > VARY
; *n* vessel or tube that carries a fluid
VASA > VAS
VASAL > VAS
VASCULA > VASCULUM
VASCULAR *adj* relating to vessels
VASCULUM *n* metal box used by botanists in the field for carrying botanical specimens
VASCULUMS > VASCULUM
VASE *n* ornamental jar, esp for flowers
VASECTOMY *n* surgical removal of part of the vas deferens, as a contraceptive method
VASELIKE > VASE
VASELINE *n* translucent gelatinous substance obtained from petroleum
VASELINES > VASELINE
VASES > VASE
VASIFORM > VAS
VASOMOTOR *adj* (of a drug, agent, nerve, etc) affecting the diameter of blood vessels
VASOSPASM *n* sudden contraction of a blood vessel
VASOTOCIN *n* chemical found in birds, reptiles, and some amphibians
VASOTOMY *n* surgery on the vas deferens
VASOVAGAL *adj* relating to blood vessels and the vagus nerve
VASSAIL *archaic variant of* > VASSAL
VASSAILS > VASSAIL
VASSAL *n* man given land by a lord in return for military service ▷ *adj* of or relating to a vassal ▷ *vb* vassalize
VASSALAGE *n* condition of being a vassal or the obligations to which a vassal was liable
VASSALESS > VASSAL
VASSALISE *same as* > VASSALIZE
VASSALIZE *vb* make a vassal of
VASSALLED > VASSAL
VASSALRY *n* vassalage
VASSALS > VASSAL
VAST *adj* extremely large ▷ *n* immense or boundless space
VASTER > VAST
VASTEST > VAST
VASTIDITY *n* vastness
VASTIER > VASTY
VASTIEST > VASTY
VASTITIES > VAST
VASTITUDE *n* condition or quality of being vast
VASTITY > VAST
VASTLY > VAST
VASTNESS > VAST
VASTS > VAST
VASTY *archaic or poetic word for* > VAST
VAT *n* large container for liquids ▷ *vb* place, store, or treat in a vat
VATABLE *adj* subject to VAT
VATFUL *n* amount enough to fill a vat
VATFULS > VATFUL
VATIC *adj* of, relating to, or characteristic of a prophet
VATICAL *same as* > VATIC
VATICIDE *n* murder of a prophet
VATICIDES > VATICIDE
VATICINAL *adj* foretelling or prophesying
VATMAN *n* Customs and Excise employee
VATMEN > VATMAN
VATS > VAT
VATTED > VAT
VATTER *n* person who works with vats; blender
VATTERS > VATTER
VATTING > VAT
VATU *n* standard monetary unit of Vanuatu
VATUS > VATU
VAU *same as* > VAV
VAUCH *vb* move fast
VAUCHED > VAUCH
VAUCHES > VAUCH
VAUCHING > VAUCH
VAUDOO *same as* > VOODOO
VAUDOOS > VAUDOO
VAUDOUX *same as* > VOODOO
VAULT *n* secure room for storing valuables ▷ *vb* jump over (something) by resting one's hand(s) on it.
VAULTAGE *n* group of vaults
VAULTAGES > VAULTAGE
VAULTED > VAULT
VAULTER > VAULT
VAULTERS > VAULT
VAULTIER > VAULTY
VAULTIEST > VAULTY
VAULTING *n* arrangement of ceiling vaults in a building ▷ *adj* excessively confident
VAULTINGS > VAULTING
VAULTLIKE > VAULT
VAULTS > VAULT
VAULTY *adj* arched
VAUNCE > ADVANCE
VAUNCED > VAUNCE
VAUNCES > VAUNCE
VAUNCING > VAUNCE
VAUNT *vb* describe or display (success or possessions) boastfully ▷ *n* boast
VAUNTAGE *archaic variant of* > VANTAGE
VAUNTAGES > VAUNTAGE
VAUNTED > VAUNT
VAUNTER > VAUNT
VAUNTERS > VAUNT
VAUNTERY *n* bravado
VAUNTFUL > VAUNT
VAUNTIE *same as* > VAUNTY
VAUNTIER > VAUNT
VAUNTIEST > VAUNT
VAUNTING > VAUNT
VAUNTINGS > VAUNT
VAUNTS > VAUNT
VAUNTY *adj* proud
VAURIEN *n* rascal
VAURIENS > VAURIEN
VAUS > VAU
VAUT *same as* > VAULT
VAUTE *same as* > VAULT
VAUTED > VAUTE
VAUTES > VAUTE
VAUTING > VAUT
VAUTS > VAUT
VAV *n* sixth letter of the Hebrew alphabet
VAVASOR *n* (in feudal society) vassal who also has vassals himself
VAVASORS > VAVASOR
VAVASORY *n* lands held by a vavasor
VAVASOUR *same as* > VAVASOR
VAVASOURS > VAVASOUR
VAVASSOR *same as* > VAVASOR
VAVASSORS > VAVASSOR
VAVS > VAV
VAW *n* Hebrew letter
VAWARD *n* vanguard
VAWARDS > VAWARD
VAWNTIE *same as* > VAUNT
VAWS > VAW
VAWTE *same as* > VAULT
VAWTED > VAWTE
VAWTES > VAWTE
VAWTING > VAWTE
VEAL *n* calf meat ▷ *vb* cover with a veil
VEALE *same as* > VEIL
VEALED > VEAL
VEALER *n* young bovine animal of up to 14 months old grown for veal
VEALERS > VEALER
VEALES > VEALE
VEALIER > VEAL
VEALIEST > VEAL
VEALING > VEAL
VEALS > VEAL
VEALY > VEAL
VECTOR *n* quantity that has size and direction, such as force ▷ *vb* direct or guide (a pilot) by directions transmitted by radio
VECTORED > VECTOR
VECTORIAL > VECTOR
VECTORING > VECTOR
VECTORISE *same as* > VECTORIZE
VECTORIZE *vb* computing term
VECTORS > VECTOR
VEDALIA *n* Australian ladybird which is a pest of citrus fruits
VEDALIAS > VEDALIA
VEDETTE *n* small patrol vessel
VEDETTES > VEDETTE
VEDUTA *n* painting of a town or city

VEDUTE >VEDUTA
VEDUTISTA *n* artist who creates vedutas
VEDUTISTI >VEDUTISTA
VEE *n* letter 'v'
VEEJAY *n* video jockey
VEEJAYS >VEEJAY
VEENA *same as* >VINA
VEENAS >VEENA
VEEP *n* vice president
VEEPEE *n* vice president
VEEPEES >VEEPEE
VEEPS >VEEP
VEER *vb* change direction suddenly ▷ *n* change of course or direction
VEERED >VEER
VEERIES >VEERY
VEERING >VEER
VEERINGLY >VEER
VEERINGS >VEER
VEERS >VEER
VEERY *n* tawny brown North American thrush
VEES >VEE
VEG *n* vegetable or vegetables ▷ *vb* relax
VEGA *n* tobacco plantation
VEGAN *n* person who eats no meat, fish, eggs, or dairy products ▷ *adj* suitable for a vegan
VEGANIC *adj* farmed without the use of animal products or byproducts
VEGANISM >VEGAN
VEGANISMS >VEGAN
VEGANS >VEGAN
VEGAS >VEGA
VEGELATE *n* type of chocolate
VEGELATES >VEGELATE
VEGEMITE *n* informal word for a child
VEGEMITES >VEGEMITE
VEGES >VEG
VEGETABLE *n* edible plant ▷ *adj* of or like plants or vegetables
VEGETABLY >VEGETABLE
VEGETAL *adj* of or relating to plant life ▷ *n* vegetable
VEGETALLY >VEGETAL
VEGETALS >VEGETAL
VEGETANT *adj* causing growth or vegetation-like
VEGETATE *vb* live a dull boring life with no mental stimulation
VEGETATED >VEGETATE
VEGETATES >VEGETATE
VEGETE *adj* lively
VEGETIST *n* vegetable cultivator or enthusiast
VEGETISTS >VEGETIST
VEGETIVE *adj* dull or passive ▷ *n* vegetable
VEGETIVES >VEGETIVE
VEGGED >VEG
VEGGES >VEG
VEGGIE *n* vegetable ▷ *adj* vegetarian
VEGGIES >VEGGIE
VEGGING >VEG
VEGIE *variant of* >VEGGIE
VEGIES >VEGIE
VEGO *adj* vegetarian ▷ *n* vegetarian
VEGOS >VEGO
VEHEMENCE >VEHEMENT
VEHEMENCY >VEHEMENT
VEHEMENT *adj* expressing strong feelings
VEHICLE *n* machine for carrying people or objects
VEHICLES >VEHICLE
VEHICULAR >VEHICLE
VEHM *n* type of medieval German court
VEHME >VEHM
VEHMIC >VEHM
VEHMIQUE >VEHM
VEIL *n* piece of thin cloth covering the head or face ▷ *vb* cover with or as if with a veil
VEILED *adj* disguised
VEILEDLY >VEILED
VEILER >VEIL
VEILERS >VEIL
VEILIER >VEIL
VEILIEST >VEIL
VEILING *n* veil or the fabric used for veils
VEILINGS >VEILING
VEILLESS >VEIL
VEILLEUSE *n* small night-light
VEILLIKE >VEIL
VEILS >VEIL
VEILY >VEIL
VEIN *n* tube that takes blood to the heart ▷ *vb* diffuse over or cause to diffuse over in streaked patterns
VEINAL >VEIN
VEINED >VEIN
VEINER *n* wood-carving tool
VEINERS >VEINER
VEINIER >VEIN
VEINIEST >VEIN
VEINING *n* pattern or network of veins or streaks
VEININGS >VEINING
VEINLESS >VEIN
VEINLET *n* any small vein or venule
VEINLETS >VEINLET
VEINLIKE >VEIN
VEINOUS >VEIN
VEINS >VEIN
VEINSTONE *another word for* >GANGUE
VEINSTUFF *another word for* >GANGUE
VEINULE *less common spelling of* >VENULE
VEINULES >VEINULE
VEINULET *same as* >VEINLET
VEINULETS >VEINULET
VEINY >VEIN
VELA >VELUM
VELAMEN *n* thick layer of dead cells that covers the aerial roots of certain orchids
VELAMINA >VELAMEN
VELAR *adj* of, relating to, or attached to a velum ▷ *n* velar sound
VELARIA >VELARIUM
VELARIC >VELAR
VELARISE *same as* >VELARIZE
VELARISED >VELARISE
VELARISES >VELARISE
VELARIUM *n* awning used to protect the audience in ancient Roman theatres and amphitheatres
VELARIZE *vb* pronounce or supplement the pronunciation of (a speech sound) with articulation at the soft palate
VELARIZED >VELARIZE
VELARIZES >VELARIZE
VELARS >VELAR
VELATE *adj* having or covered with velum
VELATED *same as* >VELATE
VELATURA *n* overglaze
VELATURAS >VELATURA
VELCRO *n* tradename for a fastening consisting of two strips of nylon fabric that form a strong bond when pressed together
VELCROS >VELCRO
VELD *n* high grassland in southern Africa
VELDS >VELD
VELDSKOEN *n* leather ankle boot
VELDT *same as* >VELD
VELDTS >VELDT
VELE *same as* >VEIL
VELES >VELE
VELETA *same as* >VALETA
VELETAS >VELETA
VELIGER *n* free-swimming larva of many molluscs
VELIGERS >VELIGER
VELITES *pl n* light-armed troops in ancient Rome, drawn from the poorer classes
VELL *vb* cut turf
VELLEITY *n* weakest level of desire or volition
VELLENAGE *n* (in Medieval Europe) status of being a villein
VELLET *n* velvet
VELLETS >VELLET
VELLICATE *vb* twitch, pluck, or pinch
VELLON *n* silver and copper alloy used in old Spanish coins
VELLONS >VELLON
VELLS >VELL
VELLUM *n* fine calfskin parchment ▷ *adj* made of or resembling vellum
VELLUMS >VELLUM
VELOCE *adv* be played rapidly
VELOCITY *n* speed of movement in a given direction
VELODROME *n* arena with a banked track for cycle racing
VELOUR *n* fabric similar t[o] velvet
VELOURS *same as* >VELOU[R]
VELOUTE *n* rich white sauce or soup made fro[m] stock, egg yolks, and cream
VELOUTES >VELOUTE
VELOUTINE *n* type of velvety fabric
VELSKOEN *n* type of shoe
VELSKOENS >VELSKOEN
VELUM *n* any of various membranous structures
VELURE *n* velvet or a simi[lar] fabric ▷ *vb* cover with velure
VELURED >VELURE
VELURES >VELURE
VELURING >VELURE
VELVERET *n* type of velve[t]-like fabric
VELVERETS >VELVERET
VELVET *n* fabric with a thick soft pile ▷ *vb* cove[r] with velvet
VELVETED >VELVET
VELVETEEN *n* cotton velv[et]
VELVETIER >VELVET
VELVETING >VELVET
VELVETS >VELVET
VELVETY >VELVET
VENA *n* vein in the body
VENAE >VENA
VENAL *adj* easily bribed
VENALITY >VENAL
VENALLY >VENAL
VENATIC *adj* of, relating t[o] or used in hunting
VENATICAL *same as* >VENATIC
VENATION *n* arrangemen[t] of the veins in a leaf or in the wing of an insect
VENATIONS >VENATION
VENATOR *n* hunter
VENATORS >VENATOR
VEND *vb* sell
VENDABLE >VEND
VENDABLES >VEND
VENDACE *n* either of two small whitefish occurri[ng] in lakes in Scotland and NW England
VENDACES >VENDACE
VENDAGE *n* vintage
VENDAGES >VENDAGE
VENDANGE *same as* >VENDAGE
VENDANGES >VENDANGE
VENDED >VEND
VENDEE *n* person to who[m] something, esp real property, is sold
VENDEES >VENDEE
VENDER *same as* >VENDO[R]
VENDERS >VENDER
VENDETTA *n* long-lasting quarrel between people

n which they attempt to arm each other
NDETTAS >VENDETTA
NDEUSE *n* female alesperson
NDEUSES >VENDEUSE
NDIBLE *adj* saleable or narketable ▷ *n* saleable bject
NDIBLES >VENDIBLE
NDIBLY >VENDIBLE
NDING >VEND
NDINGS >VEND
NDIS *same as* >VENDACE
NDISES >VENDIS
NDISS *same as* >VENDACE
NDISSES >VENDIS
NDITION >VEND
NDOR *n* person who sells oods such as newspapers r hamburgers from a stall r cart
NDORS >VENDOR
NDS >VEND
NDUE *n* public sale
NDUES >VENDUE
NEER *n* thin layer of vood etc covering a heaper material ▷ *vb* over (a surface) with a eneer
NEERED >VENEER
NEERER >VENEER
NEERERS >VENEER
NEERING *n* material sed as veneer or a eneered surface
NEERS >VENEER
NEFIC *adj* having oisonous effects
NEFICAL *same* s >VENEFIC
NENATE *vb* poison
NENATED >VENENATE
NENATES >VENENATE
NENE *n* medicine from nake venom
NENES >VENENE
NENOSE *adj* poisonous
NERABLE *adj* worthy of eep respect
NERABLY >VENERABLE
NERATE *vb* hold (a erson) in deep respect
NERATED >VENERATE
NERATES >VENERATE
NERATOR >VENERATE
NEREAL *adj* transmitted y sexual intercourse
NEREAN *n* sex addict
NEREANS >VENEREAN
NEREOUS *adj* libidinous
NERER *n* hunter
NERERS >VENERER
NERIES >VENERY
NERY *n* pursuit of sexual ratification
NETIAN *n* Venetian blind
NETIANS >VENETIAN
NEWE *same as* >VENUE
NEWES >VENEWE
NEY *n* thrust
NEYS >VENEY
NGE *vb* avenge

VENGEABLE >VENGE
VENGEABLY >VENGE
VENGEANCE *n* revenge
VENGED >VENGE
VENGEFUL *adj* wanting revenge
VENGEMENT >VENGE
VENGER >VENGE
VENGERS >VENGE
VENGES >VENGE
VENGING >VENGE
VENIAL *adj* (of a sin or fault) easily forgiven
VENIALITY >VENIAL
VENIALLY >VENIAL
VENIDIUM *n* genus of flowering plants
VENIDIUMS >VENIDIUM
VENIN *n* any of the poisonous constituents of animal venoms
VENINE *same as* >VENIN
VENINES >VENINE
VENINS >VENIN
VENIRE *n* list from which jurors are selected
VENIREMAN *n* person summoned for jury service
VENIREMEN >VENIREMAN
VENIRES >VENIRE
VENISON *n* deer meat
VENISONS >VENISON
VENITE *n* musical setting for the 95th psalm
VENITES >VENITE
VENNEL *n* lane
VENNELS >VENNEL
VENOGRAM *n* X-ray of a vein
VENOGRAMS >VENOGRAM
VENOLOGY *n* study of veins
VENOM *n* malice or spite ▷ *vb* poison
VENOMED >VENOM
VENOMER >VENOM
VENOMERS >VENOM
VENOMING >VENOM
VENOMLESS >VENOM
VENOMOUS >VENOM
VENOMS >VENOM
VENOSE *adj* having veins
VENOSITY *n* excessive quantity of blood in the venous system or in an organ or part
VENOUS *adj* of veins
VENOUSLY >VENOUS
VENT *n* outlet releasing fumes or fluid ▷ *vb* express (an emotion) freely
VENTAGE *n* small opening
VENTAGES >VENTAGE
VENTAIL *n* (in medieval armour) a covering for the lower part of the face
VENTAILE *same as* >VENTAIL
VENTAILES >VENTAILE
VENTAILS >VENTAIL
VENTANA *n* window
VENTANAS >VENTANA
VENTAYLE *same as* >VENTAIL
VENTAYLES >VENTAYLE
VENTED >VENT

VENTER >VENT
VENTERS >VENT
VENTIDUCT *n* air pipe
VENTIFACT *n* pebble that has been shaped by wind-blown sand
VENTIGE *same as* >VENTAGE
VENTIGES >VENTIGE
VENTIL *n* valve on a musical instrument
VENTILATE *vb* let fresh air into
VENTILS >VENTIL
VENTING >VENT
VENTINGS >VENT
VENTLESS >VENT
VENTOSE *adj* full of wind
VENTOSITY *n* flatulence
VENTOUSE *n* apparatus sometimes used to assist the delivery of a baby
VENTOUSES >VENTOUSE
VENTRAL *adj* relating to the front of the body ▷ *n* ventral fin
VENTRALLY >VENTRAL
VENTRALS >VENTRAL
VENTRE *same as* >VENTURE
VENTRED >VENTRE
VENTRES >VENTRE
VENTRICLE *n* cavity in an organ such as the heart
VENTRING >VENTRE
VENTRINGS >VENTRE
VENTROUS >VENTRE
VENTS >VENT
VENTURE *n* risky undertaking, esp in business ▷ *vb* do something risky
VENTURED >VENTURE
VENTURER >VENTURE
VENTURERS >VENTURE
VENTURES >VENTURE
VENTURI *n* tube used to control the flow of fluid
VENTURING >VENTURE
VENTURIS >VENTURI
VENTUROUS *adj* adventurous
VENUE *n* place where an organized gathering is held
VENUES >VENUE
VENULAR >VENULE
VENULE *n* any of the small branches of a vein
VENULES >VENULE
VENULOSE >VENULE
VENULOUS >VENULE
VENUS *n* type of marine bivalve mollusc
VENUSES >VENUS
VENVILLE *n* type of parish tenure
VENVILLES >VENVILLE
VERA as in *aloe vera* plant substance used in skin and hair preparations
VERACIOUS *adj* habitually truthful
VERACITY *n* truthfulness
VERANDA *n* porch or portico along the outside of a building
VERANDAED >VERANDA
VERANDAH *same as* >VERANDA
VERANDAHS >VERANDAH
VERANDAS >VERANDA
VERAPAMIL *n* calcium-channel blocker used in the treatment of some types of irregular heart rhythm
VERATRIA *same as* >VERATRINE
VERATRIAS >VERATRIA
VERATRIN *same as* >VERATRINE
VERATRINE *n* white poisonous mixture obtained from the seeds of sabadilla
VERATRINS >VERATRIN
VERATRUM *n* genus of herbs
VERATRUMS >VERATRUM
VERB *n* word that expresses the idea of action, happening, or being
VERBAL *adj* spoken ▷ *n* abuse or invective ▷ *vb* implicate (someone) in a crime by quoting alleged admission of guilt in court
VERBALISE *same as* >VERBALIZE
VERBALISM *n* exaggerated emphasis on the importance of words
VERBALIST *n* person who deals with words alone, rather than facts, ideas, feeling, etc
VERBALITY >VERBAL
VERBALIZE *vb* express (something) in words
VERBALLED >VERBAL
VERBALLY >VERBAL
VERBALS >VERBAL
VERBARIAN *n* inventor of words
VERBASCUM *See* >MULLEIN
VERBATIM *adj* word for word ▷ *adv* using exactly the same words
VERBENA *n* plant with sweet-smelling flowers
VERBENAS >VERBENA
VERBERATE *vb* lash
VERBIAGE *n* excessive use of words
VERBIAGES >VERBIAGE
VERBICIDE *n* person who destroys a word
VERBID *n* any nonfinite form of a verb or any nonverbal word derived from a verb
VERBIDS >VERBID
VERBIFIED >VERBIFY
VERBIFIES >VERBIFY
VERBIFY *another word for* >VERBALIZE
VERBILE *n* person who is best stimulated by words
VERBILES >VERBILE
VERBING *n* use of nouns as

verbs
VERBINGS >VERBING
VERBLESS >VERB
VERBOSE *adj* speaking at tedious length
VERBOSELY >VERBOSE
VERBOSER >VERBOSE
VERBOSEST >VERBOSE
VERBOSITY >VERBOSE
VERBOTEN *adj* forbidden
VERBS >VERB
VERD as in *verd antique* dark green mottled impure variety of serpentine marble
VERDANCY >VERDANT
VERDANT *adj* covered in green vegetation
VERDANTLY >VERDANT
VERDELHO *n* type of grape
VERDELHOS >VERDELHO
VERDERER *n* judicial officer responsible for the maintenance of law and order in the royal forests
VERDERERS >VERDERER
VERDEROR *same as* >VERDERER
VERDERORS >VERDEROR
VERDET *n* type of verdigris
VERDETS >VERDET
VERDICT *n* decision of a jury
VERDICTS >VERDICT
VERDIGRIS *n* green film on copper, brass, or bronze
VERDIN *n* small W North American tit having grey plumage with a yellow head
VERDINS >VERDIN
VERDIT *same as* >VERDICT
VERDITE *n* type of rock used in jewellery
VERDITER *n* blue-green pigment made from copper
VERDITERS >VERDITER
VERDITES >VERDITE
VERDITS >VERDIT
VERDOY *n* floral or leafy shield decoration
VERDURE *n* flourishing green vegetation
VERDURED >VERDURE
VERDURES >VERDURE
VERDUROUS >VERDURE
VERECUND *adj* shy or modest
VERGE *n* grass border along a road ▷ *vb* move in a specified direction
VERGED >VERGE
VERGENCE *n* inward or outward turning movement of the eyes in convergence or divergence
VERGENCES >VERGENCE
VERGENCY *adj* inclination
VERGER *n* church caretaker
VERGERS >VERGER
VERGES >VERGE
VERGING >VERGE
VERGLAS *n* thin film of ice on rock
VERGLASES >VERGLAS
VERIDIC *same as* >VERIDICAL
VERIDICAL *adj* truthful
VERIER >VERY
VERIEST >VERY
VERIFIED >VERIFY
VERIFIER >VERIFY
VERIFIERS >VERIFY
VERIFIES >VERIFY
VERIFY *vb* check the truth or accuracy of
VERIFYING >VERIFY
VERILY *adv* in truth
VERISM *n* extreme naturalism in art or literature
VERISMO *n* school of composition that originated in Italian opera
VERISMOS >VERISMO
VERISMS >VERISM
VERIST >VERISM
VERISTIC >VERISM
VERISTS >VERISM
VERITABLE *adj* rightly called, without exaggeration
VERITABLY >VERITABLE
VERITAS *n* truth
VERITATES >VERITAS
VERITE *adj* involving a high degree of realism or naturalism ▷ *n* this kind of realism in film
VERITES >VERITE
VERITIES >VERITY
VERITY *n* true statement or principle
VERJUICE *n* acid juice of unripe grapes, apples, or crab apples ▷ *vb* make sour
VERJUICED >VERJUICE
VERJUICES >VERJUICE
VERKRAMP *adj* bigoted or illiberal
VERLAN *n* variety of French slang in which the syllables are inverted
VERLANS >VERLAN
VERLIG *adj* enlightened
VERLIGTE *n* (during apartheid) a White political liberal
VERLIGTES >VERLIGTE
VERMAL >VERMIS
VERMEIL *n* gilded silver, bronze, or other metal, used esp in the 19th century ▷ *vb* decorate with vermeil ▷ *adj* vermilion
VERMEILED >VERMEIL
VERMEILLE *variant of* >VERMEIL
VERMEILS >VERMEIL
VERMELL *same as* >VERMEIL
VERMELLS >VERMELL
VERMES >VERMIS
VERMIAN >VERMIS
VERMICIDE *n* any substance used to kill worms
VERMICULE *n* small worm
VERMIFORM *adj* shaped like a worm
VERMIFUGE *n* any drug or agent able to destroy or expel intestinal worms
VERMIL *same as* >VERMEIL
VERMILIES >VERMILY
VERMILION *adj* orange-red ▷ *n* mercuric sulphide, used as an orange-red pigment
VERMILLED >VERMIL
VERMILS >VERMIL
VERMILY *variant of* >VERMEIL
VERMIN *pl n* animals, esp insects and rodents, that spread disease or cause damage
VERMINATE *vb* breed vermin
VERMINED *adj* plagued with vermin
VERMINOUS *adj* relating to, infested with, or suggestive of vermin
VERMINS >VERMIN
VERMINY >VERMIN
VERMIS *n* middle lobe connecting the two halves of the cerebellum
VERMOULU *adj* worm-eaten
VERMOUTH *n* wine flavoured with herbs
VERMOUTHS >VERMOUTH
VERMUTH *same as* >VERMOUTH
VERMUTHS >VERMUTH
VERNACLE *same as* >VERNICLE
VERNACLES >VERNACLE
VERNAL *adj* occurring in spring
VERNALISE *same as* >VERNALIZE
VERNALITY >VERNAL
VERNALIZE *vb* subject (ungerminated or germinating seeds) to low temperatures
VERNALLY >VERNAL
VERNANT >VERNAL
VERNATION *n* way in which leaves are arranged in the bud
VERNICLE *n* veronica
VERNICLES >VERNICLE
VERNIER *n* movable scale on a graduated measuring instrument for taking readings in fractions
VERNIERS >VERNIER
VERNIX *n* white substance covering the skin of a foetus
VERNIXES >VERNIX
VERONAL *n* a long-acting barbiturate used medicinally
VERONALS >VERONAL
VERONICA *n* plant with small blue, pink, or white flowers
VERONICAS >VERONICA
VERONIQUE *adj* (of a dish) garnished with seedless white grapes
VERQUERE *n* type of backgammon game
VERQUERES >VERQUERE
VERQUIRE *variant of* >VERQUERE
VERQUIRES >VERQUIRE
VERRA *Scot word for* >VERY
VERREL *n* ferrule
VERRELS >VERREL
VERREY *same as* >VAIR
VERRUCA *n* wart, usu on the foot
VERRUCAE >VERRUCA
VERRUCAS >VERRUCA
VERRUCOSE *adj* covered with warts
VERRUCOUS *same as* >VERRUCOSE
VERRUGA *same as* >VERRU
VERRUGAS >VERRUGA
VERRY *same as* >VAIR
VERS *n* verse
VERSAL *n* embellished letter
VERSALS >VERSAL
VERSANT *n* side or slope of a mountain or mountain range
VERSANTS >VERSANT
VERSATILE *adj* having many skills or uses
VERSE *n* group of lines forming part of a song or poem ▷ *vb* write verse
VERSED *adj* thoroughly knowledgeable (about)
VERSELET *n* small verse
VERSELETS >VERSELET
VERSEMAN *n* man who writes verse
VERSEMEN >VERSEMAN
VERSER *n* versifier
VERSERS >VERSER
VERSES >VERSE
VERSET *n* short, often sacred, verse
VERSETS >VERSET
VERSICLE *n* short verse
VERSICLES >VERSICLE
VERSIFIED >VERSIFY
VERSIFIER >VERSIFY
VERSIFIES >VERSIFY
VERSIFORM *adj* changing in form
VERSIFY *vb* write in verse
VERSIN *same as* >VERSINE
VERSINE *n* mathematical term
VERSINES >VERSINE
VERSING >VERSE
VERSINGS >VERSE
VERSINS >VERSIN
VERSION *n* form of something, such as a piece of writing, with some differences from other forms
VERSIONAL >VERSION
VERSIONER *n* translator

:RSIONS >VERSION
:RSO *n* left-hand page of
ı book
:RSOS >VERSO
:RST *n* unit of length used
n Russia
:RSTE *same as* >VERST
:RSTES >VERSTE
:RSTS >VERST
.RSUS *prep* in opposition
:o or in contrast with
.RSUTE *adj* cunning
:RT *n* right to cut green
vood in a forest ▷ *vb* turn
:RTEBRA *n* one of the
ɔones that form the spine
.RTEBRAE >VERTEBRA
.RTEBRAL >VERTEBRA
:RTEBRAS >VERTEBRA
:RTED >VERT
:RTEX *n* point on a
jeometric figure where
'he sides form an angle
.RTEXES >VERTEX
:RTICAL *adj* straight up
ınd down ▷ *n* vertical
lirection
RTICALS >VERTICAL
RTICES >VERTEX
.RTICIL *n* circular
ırrangement of parts
ıbout an axis, esp leaves
ıround a stem
.RTICILS >VERTICIL
:RTICITY *n* ability to
urn
'RTIGO *n* dizziness, usu
vhen looking down from a
ıigh place
RTIGOES >VERTIGO
RTIGOS >VERTIGO
:RTING >VERT
:RTIPORT *n* type of
ıirport
RTS >VERT
RTU *same as* >VIRTU
RTUE *same as* >VIRTU
RTUES >VERTUE
RTUOUS >VERTU
RTUS >VERTU
RVAIN *n* plant with
pikes of blue, purple, or
vhite flowers
RVAINS >VERVAIN
RVE *n* enthusiasm or
iveliness
RVEL *same as* >VARVEL
RVELLED >VERVEL
RVELS >VERVEL
RVEN *same as* >VERVAIN
RVENS >VERVEN
RVES >VERVE
RVET *n* variety of a South
ıfrican guenon monkey
RVETS >VERVET
RY *adv* more than
ısually, extremely ▷ *adj*
ıbsolute, exact
SICA *n* bladder
SICAE >VESICA
SICAL *adj* of or relating
o a vesica, esp the urinary
ıladder
SICANT *n* any substance
that causes blisters ▷ *adj*
acting as a vesicant
VESICANTS >VESICANT
VESICATE *vb* blister
VESICATED >VESICATE
VESICATES >VESICATE
VESICLE *n* sac or small
cavity, esp one containing
fluid
VESICLES >VESICLE
VESICULA *n* vesicle
VESICULAE >VESICULA
VESICULAR >VESICLE
VESPA *n* type of wasp
VESPAS >VESPA
VESPER *n* evening prayer,
service, or hymn
VESPERAL *n* liturgical book
containing the prayers,
psalms, and hymns used at
vespers
VESPERALS >VESPERAL
VESPERS *pl n* service of
evening prayer
VESPIARY *n* nest or colony
of social wasps or hornets
VESPID *n* insect of the
family that includes the
common wasp and hornet
▷ *adj* of or belonging to
this family
VESPIDS >VESPID
VESPINE *adj* of, relating to,
or resembling a wasp or
wasps
VESPOID *adj* like a wasp
VESSAIL *archaic variant
of* >VESSEL
VESSAILS >VESSAIL
VESSEL *n* container or ship
▷ *adj* contained in a vessel
VESSELED >VESSEL
VESSELS >VESSEL
VEST *n* undergarment
worn on the top half of the
body ▷ *vb* give (authority)
to (someone)
VESTA *n* short friction
match, usually of wood
VESTAL *adj* pure, chaste
▷ *n* chaste woman
VESTALLY >VESTAL
VESTALS >VESTAL
VESTAS >VESTA
VESTED *adj* having an
existing right to the
immediate or future
possession of property
VESTEE *n* person having a
vested interest something
VESTEES >VESTEE
VESTIARY *n* room for
storing clothes or dressing
in, such as a vestry ▷ *adj* of
or relating to clothes
VESTIBULA >VESTIBULE
VESTIBULE *n* small
entrance hall
VESTIGE *n* small amount
or trace
VESTIGES >VESTIGE
VESTIGIA >VESTIGIUM
VESTIGIAL *adj* remaining
after a larger or more
important thing has gone
VESTIGIUM *n* trace
VESTIMENT *same
as* >VESTMENT
VESTING >VEST
VESTINGS >VEST
VESTITURE *n* investiture
VESTLESS >VEST
VESTLIKE >VEST
VESTMENT *n* garment or
robe, esp one denoting
office, authority, or rank
VESTMENTS >VESTMENT
VESTRAL >VESTRY
VESTRIES >VESTRY
VESTRY *n* room in a church
used as an office by the
priest or minister
VESTRYMAN *n* member of a
church vestry
VESTRYMEN >VESTRYMAN
VESTS >VEST
VESTURAL >VESTURE
VESTURE *n* garment or
something that seems like
a garment ▷ *vb* clothe
VESTURED >VESTURE
VESTURER *n* person
in charge of church
vestments
VESTURERS >VESTURER
VESTURES >VESTURE
VESTURING >VESTURE
VESUVIAN *n* match for
lighting cigars
VESUVIANS >VESUVIAN
VET *vb* check the suitability
of ▷ *n* military veteran
VETCH *n* climbing plant
with a beanlike fruit used
as fodder
VETCHES >VETCH
VETCHIER >VETCHY
VETCHIEST >VETCHY
VETCHLING *n* type of
climbing plant
VETCHY *adj* consisting of
vetches
VETERAN *n* person with
long experience in a
particular activity, esp
military service ▷ *adj*
long-serving
VETERANS >VETERAN
VETIVER *n* tall hairless
grass of tropical and
subtropical Asia
VETIVERS >VETIVER
VETIVERT *n* oil from the
vetiver
VETIVERTS >VETIVERT
VETKOEK *n* South African
cake
VETKOEKS >VETKOEK
VETO *n* official power to
cancel a proposal ▷ *vb*
enforce a veto against
VETOED >VETO
VETOER >VETO
VETOERS >VETO
VETOES >VETO
VETOING >VETO
VETOLESS >VETO
VETS >VET
VETTED >VET
VETTER >VET
VETTERS >VET
VETTING >VET
VETTURA *n* Italian mode of
transport
VETTURAS >VETTURA
VETTURINI >VETTURINO
VETTURINO *n* person who
drives a vettura
VEX *vb* frustrate, annoy
VEXATION *n* something
annoying
VEXATIONS >VEXATION
VEXATIOUS *adj* vexing
VEXATORY >VEX
VEXED *adj* annoyed and
puzzled
VEXEDLY >VEXED
VEXEDNESS >VEXED
VEXER >VEX
VEXERS >VEX
VEXES >VEX
VEXIL *same as* >VEXILLUM
VEXILLA >VEXILLUM
VEXILLAR >VEXILLUM
VEXILLARY >VEXILLUM
VEXILLATE >VEXILLUM
VEXILLUM *n* vane of a
feather
VEXILS >VEXIL
VEXING >VEX
VEXINGLY >VEX
VEXINGS >VEX
VEXT *same as* >VEXED
VEZIR *same as* >VIZIER
VEZIRS >VEZIR
VIA *prep* by way of ▷ *n* road
VIABILITY >VIABLE
VIABLE *adj* able to be put
into practice
VIABLY >VIABLE
VIADUCT *n* bridge over a
valley
VIADUCTS >VIADUCT
VIAE >VIA
VIAL *n* small bottle for
liquids ▷ *vb* put into a vial
VIALED >VIAL
VIALFUL >VIAL
VIALFULS >VIAL
VIALING >VIAL
VIALLED >VIAL
VIALLING >VIAL
VIALS >VIAL
VIAMETER *n* device to
measure distance travelled
VIAMETERS >VIAMETER
VIAND *n* type of food, esp a
delicacy
VIANDS >VIAND
VIAS >VIA
VIATIC *same as* >VIATICAL
VIATICA >VIATICUM
VIATICAL *adj* of or
denoting a road or a
journey ▷ *n* purchase of
a terminal patient's life
assurance policy so that he
or she may make use of the
proceeds
VIATICALS >VIATICAL
VIATICUM *n* Holy
Communion given to a

person who is dying or in danger of death
VIATICUMS > VIATICUM
VIATOR *n* traveller
VIATORES > VIATOR
VIATORIAL *adj* pertaining to travelling
VIATORS > VIATOR
VIBE *n* feeling or flavour of the kind specified
VIBES *pl n* vibrations
VIBEX *n* mark under the skin
VIBEY *adj* lively and vibrant
VIBICES > VIBEX
VIBIER > VIBEY
VIBIEST > VIBEY
VIBIST *n* person who plays a vibraphone in a jazz band or group
VIBISTS > VIBIST
VIBRACULA *pl n* bristle-like polyps in certain bryozoans
VIBRAHARP *n* type of percussion instrument
VIBRANCE *n* vibrancy
VIBRANCES > VIBRANCE
VIBRANCY > VIBRANT
VIBRANT *adj* vigorous in appearance, energetic ▷ *n* trilled or rolled speech sound
VIBRANTLY > VIBRANT
VIBRANTS > VIBRANT
VIBRATE *vb* move back and forth rapidly
VIBRATED > VIBRATE
VIBRATES > VIBRATE
VIBRATILE > VIBRATE
VIBRATING > VIBRATE
VIBRATION *n* vibrating
VIBRATIVE > VIBRATE
VIBRATO *n* rapid fluctuation in the pitch of a note
VIBRATOR *n* device that produces vibratory motion
VIBRATORS > VIBRATOR
VIBRATORY > VIBRATE
VIBRATOS > VIBRATO
VIBRIO *n* curved or spiral rodlike bacterium
VIBRIOID > VIBRIO
VIBRION *same as* > VIBRIO
VIBRIONIC > VIBRIO
VIBRIONS > VIBRION
VIBRIOS > VIBRIO
VIBRIOSES > VIBRIOSIS
VIBRIOSIS *n* bacterial disease
VIBRISSA *n* any of the bristle-like sensitive hairs on the face of many mammals
VIBRISSAE > VIBRISSA
VIBRISSAL > VIBRISSA
VIBRONIC *adj* of, concerned with, or involving both electronic and vibrational energy levels of a molecule
VIBS *pl n* type of climbing shoes
VIBURNUM *n* subtropical shrub with white flowers and berry-like fruits
VIBURNUMS > VIBURNUM
VICAR *n* member of the clergy in charge of a parish
VICARAGE *n* vicar's house
VICARAGES > VICARAGE
VICARATE *same as* > VICARIATE
VICARATES > VICARATE
VICARESS *n* rank of nun
VICARIAL *adj* of or relating to a vicar, vicars, or a vicariate
VICARIANT *n* any of several closely related species, etc, each of which exists in a separate geographical area
VICARIATE *n* office, rank, or authority of a vicar
VICARIES > VICARY
VICARIOUS *adj* felt indirectly by imagining what another person experiences
VICARLY > VICAR
VICARS > VICAR
VICARSHIP *same as* > VICARIATE
VICARY *n* office of a vicar
VICE *n* immoral or evil habit or action ▷ *adj* serving in place of ▷ *vb* grip (something) with or as if with a vice ▷ *prep* instead of
VICED > VICE
VICEGERAL *adj* of or relating to a person who deputizes for another
VICELESS > VICE
VICELIKE > VICE
VICENARY *adj* relating to or consisting of 20
VICENNIAL *adj* occurring every 20 years
VICEREGAL *adj* of a viceroy
VICEREINE *n* wife of a viceroy
VICEROY *n* governor of a colony who represents the monarch
VICEROYS > VICEROY
VICES > VICE
VICESIMAL *same as* > VIGESIMAL
VICHIES > VICHY
VICHY *n* French mineral water
VICIATE *same as* > VITIATE
VICIATED > VICIATE
VICIATES > VICIATE
VICIATING > VICIATE
VICINAGE *n* residents of a particular neighbourhood
VICINAGES > VICINAGE
VICINAL *adj* neighbouring
VICING > VICE
VICINITY *n* surrounding area
VICIOSITY *same as* > VITIOSITY
VICIOUS *adj* cruel and violent
VICIOUSLY > VICIOUS
VICOMTE *n* French nobleman
VICOMTES > VICOMTE
VICTIM *n* person or thing harmed or killed
VICTIMISE *same as* > VICTIMIZE
VICTIMIZE *vb* punish unfairly
VICTIMS > VICTIM
VICTOR *n* person who has defeated an opponent, esp in war or in sport
VICTORESS *same as* > VICTRESS
VICTORIA *n* large sweet plum, red and yellow in colour
VICTORIAS > VICTORIA
VICTORIES > VICTORY
VICTORINE *n* woman's article of clothing
VICTORS > VICTOR
VICTORY *n* winning of a battle or contest
VICTRESS *n* female victor
VICTRIX *same as* > VICTRESS
VICTRIXES > VICTRIX
VICTROLLA *n* type of gramophone
VICTUAL *vb* supply with or obtain victuals
VICTUALED > VICTUAL
VICTUALER > VICTUAL
VICTUALS *pl n* food and drink
VICUGNA *same as* > VICUNA
VICUGNAS > VICUGNA
VICUNA *n* S American animal like the llama
VICUNAS > VICUNA
VID *informal word for* > VIDEO
VIDAME *n* French nobleman
VIDAMES > VIDAME
VIDE *interj* look
VIDELICET *adv* namely: used to specify items
VIDENDA > VIDENDUM
VIDENDUM *n* that which is to be seen
VIDEO *vb* record (a TV programme or event) on video ▷ *adj* relating to or used in producing television images ▷ *n* recording and showing of films and events using a television set, video tapes, and a video recorder
VIDEODISC *variant of* > VIDEODISK
VIDEODISK *n* disk on which information is stored in digital form
VIDEOED > VIDEO
VIDEOFIT *n* computer-generated picture of a person sought by the police
VIDEOFITS > VIDEOFIT
VIDEOGRAM *n* audiovisual recording
VIDEOING > VIDEO
VIDEOLAND *n* world of television and televised images
VIDEOS > VIDEO
VIDEOTAPE *vb* record (a TV programme) on video tap
VIDEOTEX *n* information system that displays data from a distant computer on a screen
VIDEOTEXT *n* means of representing on a TV screen information that i held in a computer
VIDETTE *same as* > VEDETT
VIDETTES > VIDETTE
VIDICON *n* small televisio camera tube used in closed-circuit television
VIDICONS > VIDICON
VIDIMUS *n* inspection
VIDIMUSES > VIDIMUS
VIDS > VID
VIDUAGE *n* widows collectively
VIDUAGES > VIDUAGE
VIDUAL *adj* widowed
VIDUITIES > VIDUITY
VIDUITY *n* widowhood
VIDUOUS *adj* empty
VIE *vb* compete (with someone)
VIED > VIE
VIELLE *n* stringed musica instrument
VIELLES > VIELLE
VIER > VIE
VIERS > VIE
VIES > VIE
VIEW *n* opinion or belief ▷ *vb* think of (something in a particular way
VIEWABLE > VIEW
VIEWDATA *n* interactive form of videotext
VIEWDATAS > VIEWDATA
VIEWED > VIEW
VIEWER *n* person who watches television
VIEWERS > VIEWER
VIEWIER > VIEWY
VIEWIEST > VIEWY
VIEWINESS > VIEWY
VIEWING *n* act of watchir television
VIEWINGS > VIEWING
VIEWLESS *adj* (of window etc) not affording a view
VIEWLY *adj* pleasant on the eye
VIEWPHONE *n* videophone
VIEWPOINT *n* person's attitude towards somethi
VIEWS > VIEW
VIEWY *adj* having fanciful opinions or ideas
VIFDA *same as* > VIVDA
VIFDAS > VIFDA
VIG *n* interest on a loan that is paid to a moneylender
VIGA *n* rafter
VIGAS > VIGA

IGESIMAL *adj* relating to or based on the number 20
IGIA *n* navigational hazard marked on a chart although its existence has not been confirmed
IGIAS >VIGIA
IGIL *n* night-time period of staying awake to look after a sick person, pray, etc
IGILANCE *n* careful attention
IGILANT *adj* watchful in case of danger
IGILANTE *n* person who takes it upon himself or herself to enforce the law
IGILS >VIGIL
IGNERON *n* person who grows grapes for winemaking
IGNERONS >VIGNERON
IGNETTE *n* small illustration placed at the beginning or end of a chapter or book ▷ *vb* portray in a vignette
IGNETTED >VIGNETTE
IGNETTER *n* device used in printing vignettes
IGNETTES >VIGNETTE
IGOR *same as* >VIGOUR
IGORISH *n* type of commission
IGORO *n* women's game similar to cricket
IGOROS >VIGORO
IGOROSO *adv* in music, emphatically
IGOROUS *adj* having physical or mental energy
IGORS >VIGOR
IGOUR *n* physical or mental energy
IGOURS >VIGOUR
IGS >VIG
VIHARA *n* type of Buddhist temple
VIHARAS >VIHARA
VIHUELA *n* obsolete plucked stringed instrument of Spain, related to the guitar
VIHUELAS >VIHUELA
VIKING *n* Dane, Norwegian, or Swede who raided by sea most of N and W Europe between the 8th and 11th centuries
VIKINGISM >VIKING
VIKINGS >VIKING
VILAYET *n* major administrative division of Turkey
VILAYETS >VILAYET
VILD *same as* >VILE
VILDE *same as* >VILE
VILDLY >VILD
VILDNESS >VILD
VILE *adj* very wicked
VILELY >VILE
VILENESS >VILE
VILER >VILE
VILEST >VILE
VILIACO *n* scoundrel
VILIACOES >VILIACO
VILIACOS >VILIACO
VILIAGO *same as* >VILIACO
VILIAGOES >VILIAGO
VILIAGOS >VILIAGO
VILIFIED >VILIFY
VILIFIER >VILIFY
VILIFIERS >VILIFY
VILIFIES >VILIFY
VILIFY *vb* attack the character of
VILIFYING >VILIFY
VILIPEND *vb* treat or regard with contempt
VILIPENDS >VILIPEND
VILL *n* township
VILLA *n* large house with gardens
VILLADOM >VILLA
VILLADOMS >VILLA
VILLAE >VILLA
VILLAGE *n* small group of houses in a country area
VILLAGER *n* inhabitant of a village ▷ *adj* backward, unsophisticated, or illiterate
VILLAGERS >VILLAGER
VILLAGERY *n* villages
VILLAGES >VILLAGE
VILLAGIO *same as* >VILIACO
VILLAGIOS >VILLAGIO
VILLAGREE *variant of* >VILLAGERY
VILLAIN *n* wicked person
VILLAINS >VILLAIN
VILLAINY *n* evil or vicious behaviour
VILLAN *same as* >VILLEIN
VILLANAGE >VILLAN
VILLANIES >VILLANY
VILLANOUS >VILLAIN
VILLANS >VILLAN
VILLANY *same as* >VILLAINY
VILLAR >VILL
VILLAS >VILLA
VILLATIC *adj* of or relating to a villa, village, or farm
VILLEIN *n* peasant bound in service to his lord
VILLEINS >VILLEIN
VILLENAGE *n* villein's status
VILLI >VILLUS
VILLIAGO *same as* >VILIACO
VILLIAGOS >VILLIAGO
VILLIFORM *adj* having the form of a villus or a series of villi
VILLOSE *same as* >VILLOUS
VILLOSITY *n* state of being villous
VILLOUS *adj* (of plant parts) covered with long hairs
VILLOUSLY >VILLOUS
VILLS >VILL
VILLUS *n* one of the finger-like projections in the small intestine of many vertebrates
VIM *n* force, energy
VIMANA *n* Indian mythological chariot of the gods
VIMANAS >VIMANA
VIMEN *n* long flexible shoot that occurs in certain plants
VIMINA >VIMEN
VIMINAL >VIMEN
VIMINEOUS *adj* having, producing, or resembling long flexible shoots
VIMS >VIM
VIN *n* French wine
VINA *n* stringed musical instrument related to the sitar
VINACEOUS *adj* of, relating to, or containing wine
VINAL *n* type of manmade fibre
VINALS >VINAL
VINAS >VINA
VINASSE *n* residue left in a still after distilling spirits, esp brandy
VINASSES >VINASSE
VINCA *n* type of trailing plant with blue flowers
VINCAS >VINCA
VINCIBLE *adj* capable of being defeated or overcome
VINCIBLY >VINCIBLE
VINCULA >VINCULUM
VINCULUM *n* horizontal line drawn above a group of mathematical terms
VINCULUMS >VINCULUM
VINDALOO *n* type of very hot Indian curry
VINDALOOS >VINDALOO
VINDEMIAL *adj* relating to a grape harvest
VINDICATE *vb* clear (someone) of guilt
VINE *n* climbing plant, esp one producing grapes ▷ *vb* form like a vine
VINEAL *adj* relating to wines
VINED >VINE
VINEGAR *n* acid liquid made from wine, beer, or cider ▷ *vb* apply vinegar to
VINEGARED >VINEGAR
VINEGARS >VINEGAR
VINEGARY *adj* containing vinegar
VINELESS >VINE
VINELIKE >VINE
VINER *n* vinedresser
VINERIES >VINERY
VINERS >VINER
VINERY *n* hothouse for growing grapes
VINES >VINE
VINEW *vb* become mouldy
VINEWED >VINEW
VINEWING >VINEW
VINEWS >VINEW
VINEYARD *n* plantation of grape vines, esp for making wine
VINEYARDS >VINEYARD
VINIC *adj* of, relating to, or contained in wine
VINIER >VINE
VINIEST >VINE
VINIFERA *n* species of vine
VINIFERAS >VINIFERA
VINIFIED >VINIFY
VINIFIES >VINIFY
VINIFY *vb* convert into wine
VINIFYING >VINIFY
VINING >VINE
VINO *n* wine
VINOLENT *adj* drunken
VINOLOGY *n* scientific study of vines
VINOS >VINO
VINOSITY *n* distinctive and essential quality and flavour of wine
VINOUS *adj* of or characteristic of wine
VINOUSLY >VINOUS
VINS >VIN
VINT *vb* sell (wine)
VINTAGE *n* wine from a particular harvest of grapes ▷ *adj* best and most typical ▷ *vb* gather (grapes) or make (wine)
VINTAGED >VINTAGE
VINTAGER *n* grape harvester
VINTAGERS >VINTAGER
VINTAGES >VINTAGE
VINTAGING >VINTAGE
VINTED >VINT
VINTING >VINT
VINTNER *n* dealer in wine
VINTNERS >VINTNER
VINTRIES >VINTRY
VINTRY *n* place where wine is sold
VINTS >VINT
VINY >VINE
VINYL *n* type of plastic, used in mock leather and records ▷ *adj* of or containing a particular group of atoms
VINYLIC >VINYL
VINYLS >VINYL
VIOL *n* early stringed instrument preceding the violin
VIOLA *n* stringed instrument lower in pitch than a violin
VIOLABLE >VIOLATE
VIOLABLY >VIOLATE
VIOLAS >VIOLA
VIOLATE *vb* break (a law or agreement) ▷ *adj* violated or dishonoured
VIOLATED >VIOLATE
VIOLATER >VIOLATE
VIOLATERS >VIOLATE
VIOLATES >VIOLATE
VIOLATING >VIOLATE
VIOLATION >VIOLATE
VIOLATIVE >VIOLATE
VIOLATOR >VIOLATE
VIOLATORS >VIOLATE

VIOLD *archaic or poetic past form of* > VIAL
VIOLENCE *n* use of physical force, usu intended to cause injury or destruction
VIOLENCES > VIOLENCE
VIOLENT *adj* using or involving physical force with the intention of causing injury or destruction ▷ *vb* coerce
VIOLENTED > VIOLENT
VIOLENTLY > VIOLENT
VIOLENTS > VIOLENT
VIOLER *n* person who plays the viol
VIOLERS > VIOLER
VIOLET *n* plant with bluish-purple flowers ▷ *adj* bluish-purple
VIOLETS > VIOLET
VIOLIN *n* small four-stringed musical instrument played with a bow.
VIOLINIST *n* person who plays the violin
VIOLINS > VIOLIN
VIOLIST *n* person who plays the viola
VIOLISTS > VIOLIST
VIOLONE *n* double-bass member of the viol family
VIOLONES > VIOLONE
VIOLS > VIOL
VIOMYCIN *n* type of antibiotic
VIOMYCINS > VIOMYCIN
VIOSTEROL *n* type of vitamin
VIPER *n* poisonous snake
VIPERFISH *n* predatory deep-sea fish
VIPERINE *same as* > VIPEROUS
VIPERISH *same as* > VIPEROUS
VIPEROUS *adj* of, relating to, or resembling a viper
VIPERS > VIPER
VIRAEMIA *n* condition in which virus particles circulate and reproduce in the bloodstream
VIRAEMIAS > VIRAEMIA
VIRAEMIC > VIRAEMIA
VIRAGO *n* aggressive woman
VIRAGOES > VIRAGO
VIRAGOISH > VIRAGO
VIRAGOS > VIRAGO
VIRAL *adj* of or caused by a virus
VIRALLY > VIRAL
VIRANDA *same as* > VERANDA
VIRANDAS > VIRANDA
VIRANDO *same as* > VERANDA
VIRANDOS > VIRANDO
VIRE *vb* turn
VIRED > VIRE
VIRELAI *same as* > VIRELAY
VIRELAIS > VIRELAI
VIRELAY *n* old French verse form
VIRELAYS > VIRELAY
VIREMENT *n* administrative transfer of funds from one part of a budget to another
VIREMENTS > VIREMENT
VIREMIA *same as* > VIRAEMIA
VIREMIAS > VIREMIA
VIREMIC > VIREMIA
VIRENT *adj* green
VIREO *n* American songbird
VIREONINE > VIREO
VIREOS > VIREO
VIRES > VIRE
VIRESCENT *adj* greenish or becoming green
VIRETOT as in *on the viretot* in a rush
VIRETOTS > VIRETOT
VIRGA *n* wisps of rain or snow that evaporate before reaching the earth
VIRGAS > VIRGA
VIRGATE *adj* long, straight, and thin ▷ *n* obsolete measure of land area, usually taken as equivalent to 30 acres
VIRGATES > VIRGATE
VIRGE *n* rod
VIRGER *n* rod-bearer
VIRGERS > VIRGER
VIRGES > VIRGE
VIRGIN *n* person, esp a woman, who has not had sexual intercourse ▷ *adj* not having had sexual intercourse ▷ *vb* behave like a virgin
VIRGINAL *adj* like a virgin ▷ *n* early keyboard instrument like a small harpsichord
VIRGINALS > VIRGINAL
VIRGINED > VIRGIN
VIRGINIA *n* type of flue-cured tobacco grown originally in Virginia
VIRGINIAS > VIRGINIA
VIRGINING > VIRGIN
VIRGINITY *n* condition or fact of being a virgin
VIRGINIUM *former name for* > FRANCIUM
VIRGINLY > VIRGIN
VIRGINS > VIRGIN
VIRGULATE *adj* rod-shaped or rodlike
VIRGULE *another name for* > SLASH
VIRGULES > VIRGULE
VIRICIDAL > VIRICIDE
VIRICIDE *n* substance that destroys viruses
VIRICIDES > VIRICIDE
VIRID *adj* verdant
VIRIDIAN *n* green pigment consisting of a hydrated form of chromic oxide
VIRIDIANS > VIRIDIAN
VIRIDITE *n* greenish mineral
VIRIDITES > VIRIDITE
VIRIDITY *n* quality or state of being green
VIRILE *adj* having the traditional male characteristics of physical strength and a high sex drive
VIRILELY > VIRILE
VIRILISE *same as* > VIRILIZE
VIRILISED > VIRILISE
VIRILISES > VIRILISE
VIRILISM *n* abnormal development in a woman of male secondary sex characteristics
VIRILISMS > VIRILISM
VIRILITY > VIRILE
VIRILIZE *vb* cause male characteristics to appear in female
VIRILIZED > VIRILIZE
VIRILIZES > VIRILIZE
VIRILOCAL *adj* living with husband's family
VIRING > VIRE
VIRINO *n* entity postulated to be the causative agent of BSE
VIRINOS > VIRINO
VIRION *n* virus in infective form, consisting of an RNA particle within a protein covering
VIRIONS > VIRION
VIRL *same as* > FERRULE
VIRLS > VIRL
VIROGENE *n* type of viral gene
VIROGENES > VIROGENE
VIROID *n* any of various infective RNA particles
VIROIDS > VIROID
VIROLOGIC > VIROLOGY
VIROLOGY *n* study of viruses
VIROSE *adj* poisonous
VIROSES > VIROSIS
VIROSIS *n* viral disease
VIROUS *same as* > VIROSE
VIRTU *n* taste or love for curios or works of fine art
VIRTUAL *adj* having the effect but not the form of
VIRTUALLY *adv* practically, almost
VIRTUE *n* moral goodness
VIRTUES > VIRTUE
VIRTUOSA *n* female virtuoso
VIRTUOSAS > VIRTUOSA
VIRTUOSE > VIRTUOSA
VIRTUOSI > VIRTUOSO
VIRTUOSIC > VIRTUOSO
VIRTUOSO *n* person with impressive esp musical skill ▷ *adj* showing exceptional skill or brilliance
VIRTUOSOS > VIRTUOSO
VIRTUOUS *adj* morally good
VIRTUS > VIRTU
VIRUCIDAL > VIRUCIDE
VIRUCIDE *same as* > VIRICIDE
VIRUCIDES > VIRUCIDE
VIRULENCE *n* quality of being virulent
VIRULENCY *same as* > VIRULENCE
VIRULENT *adj* extremely bitter or hostile
VIRUS *n* microorganism that causes disease in humans, animals, and plants
VIRUSES > VIRUS
VIRUSLIKE > VIRUS
VIRUSOID *n* small plant virus
VIRUSOIDS > VIRUSOID
VIS *n* power, force, or strength
VISA *n* permission to enter a country, shown by a stamp on the passport ▷ *vb* enter a visa into (a passport)
VISAED > VISA
VISAGE *n* face
VISAGED > VISAGE
VISAGES > VISAGE
VISAGIST *same as* > VISAGISTE
VISAGISTE *n* person who designs and applies face make-up
VISAGISTS > VISAGIST
VISAING > VISA
VISARD *same as* > VIZARD
VISARDS > VISARD
VISAS > VISA
VISCACHA *n* South American rodent
VISCACHAS > VISCACHA
VISCARIA *n* type of perennial plant
VISCARIAS > VISCARIA
VISCERA *pl n* large abdominal organs
VISCERAL *adj* instinctive
VISCERATE *vb* disembow[el]
VISCID *adj* sticky
VISCIDITY > VISCID
VISCIDLY > VISCID
VISCIN *n* sticky substanc[e] found on plants
VISCINS > VISCIN
VISCOID *adj* (of a fluid) somewhat viscous
VISCOIDAL *same as* > VISCOID
VISCOSE *same as* > VISCOU[S]
VISCOSES > VISCOSE
VISCOSITY *n* state of bei[ng] viscous
VISCOUNT *n* British nobleman ranking between an earl and a baron
VISCOUNTS > VISCOUNT
VISCOUNTY > VISCOUNT
VISCOUS *adj* thick and sticky
VISCOUSLY > VISCOUS
VISCUM *n* shrub genus
VISCUMS > VISCUM
VISCUS *n* internal organ

ISE *vb* advise or award a visa to ▷ *n* (in US English) vice
ISED >VISE
ISEED >VISE
ISEING >VISE
ISELIKE >VICE
ISES >VISE
ISIBLE *adj* able to be seen ▷ *n* visible item of trade
ISIBLES >VISIBLE
ISIBLY >VISIBLE
ISIE *same as* >VIZY
ISIED >VISIE
ISIEING >VISIE
ISIER >VISIE
ISIERS >VISIE
ISIES >VISIE
ISILE *n* person best stimulated by vision
ISILES >VISILE
ISING >VISE
ISION *n* ability to see ▷ *vb* see or show in or as if in a vision
ISIONAL *adj* of, relating to, or seen in a vision, apparition, etc
ISIONARY *adj* showing foresight ▷ *n* visionary person
ISIONED >VISION
ISIONER *n* visionary
ISIONERS >VISIONER
ISIONING >VISION
ISIONIST *n* type of visionary
ISIONS >VISION
ISIT *vb* go or come to see ▷ *n* instance of visiting
ISITABLE >VISIT
ISITANT *n* ghost or apparition ▷ *adj* paying a visit
ISITANTS >VISITANT
ISITATOR *n* official visitor
ISITE *n* type of cape
ISITED >VISIT
ISITEE *n* person who is visited
ISITEES >VISITEE
ISITER *variant of* >VISITOR
ISITERS >VISITER
ISITES >VISITE
ISITING >VISIT
ISITINGS >VISIT
ISITOR *n* person who visits a person or place
ISITORS >VISITOR
ISITRESS *n* female visitor
ISITS >VISIT
ISIVE *adj* visual
ISNE *n* neighbourhood
ISNES >VISNE
ISNOMIE *same as* >VISNOMY
ISNOMIES >VISNOMY
ISNOMY *n* method of judging character from facial features
ISON *n* type of mink
VISONS >VISON
VISOR *n* transparent part of a helmet that pulls down over the face ▷ *vb* cover, provide, or protect with a visor
VISORED >VISOR
VISORING >VISOR
VISORLESS >VISOR
VISORS >VISOR
VISTA *n* (beautiful) extensive view ▷ *vb* make into vistas
VISTAED >VISTA
VISTAING >VISTA
VISTAL >VISTA
VISTALESS >VISTA
VISTAS >VISTA
VISTO *same as* >VISTA
VISTOS >VISTO
VISUAL *adj* done by or used in seeing ▷ *n* sketch to show the proposed layout of an advertisement, as in a newspaper
VISUALISE *same as* >VISUALIZE
VISUALIST *n* visualiser
VISUALITY >VISUAL
VISUALIZE *vb* form a mental image of
VISUALLY >VISUAL
VISUALS >VISUAL
VITA *n* curriculum vitae
VITACEOUS *adj* of a family of flowering plants that includes the grapevine
VITAE >VITA
VITAL *adj* essential or highly important ▷ *n* bodily organs that are necessary to maintain life
VITALISE *same as* >VITALIZE
VITALISED >VITALISE
VITALISER >VITALISE
VITALISES >VITALISE
VITALISM *n* philosophical doctrine that the phenomena of life cannot be explained in purely mechanical terms
VITALISMS >VITALISM
VITALIST >VITALISM
VITALISTS >VITALISM
VITALITY *n* physical or mental energy
VITALIZE *vb* fill with life or vitality
VITALIZED >VITALIZE
VITALIZER >VITALIZE
VITALIZES >VITALIZE
VITALLY >VITAL
VITALNESS >VITAL
VITALS >VITAL
VITAMER *n* type of chemical
VITAMERS >VITAMER
VITAMIN *n* one of a group of substances that are essential in the diet for specific body processes
VITAMINE *same as* >VITAMIN
VITAMINES >VITAMINE
VITAMINIC >VITAMIN
VITAMINS >VITAMIN
VITAS >VITA
VITASCOPE *n* early type of film projector
VITATIVE *adj* fond of life
VITE *adv* musical direction
VITELLARY >VITELLUS
VITELLI >VITELLUS
VITELLIN *n* phosphoprotein that is the major protein in egg yolk
VITELLINE *adj* of or relating to the yolk of an egg
VITELLINS >VITELLIN
VITELLUS *n* yolk of an egg
VITESSE *n* speed
VITESSES >VITESSE
VITEX *n* type of herb
VITEXES >VITEX
VITIABLE >VITIATE
VITIATE *vb* spoil the effectiveness of
VITIATED >VITIATE
VITIATES >VITIATE
VITIATING >VITIATE
VITIATION >VITIATE
VITIATOR >VITIATE
VITIATORS >VITIATE
VITICETA >VITICETUM
VITICETUM *n* place where vines are cultivated
VITICIDE *n* vine killer
VITICIDES >VITICIDE
VITILIGO *n* area of skin that is white from albinism or loss of melanin pigmentation
VITILIGOS >VITILIGO
VITIOSITY *n* viciousness
VITRAGE *n* light fabric
VITRAGES >VITRAGE
VITRAIL *n* stained glass
VITRAIN *n* type of coal occurring as horizontal glassy bands of a nonsoiling friable material
VITRAINS >VITRAIN
VITRAUX >VITRAIL
VITREOUS *adj* like or made from glass
VITREUM *n* vitreous body
VITREUMS >VITREUM
VITRIC *adj* of, relating to, resembling, or having the nature of glass
VITRICS *n* glassware
VITRIFIED >VITRIFY
VITRIFIES >VITRIFY
VITRIFORM *adj* having the form or appearance of glass
VITRIFY *vb* change or be changed into glass or a glassy substance
VITRINE *n* glass display case or cabinet for works of art, curios, etc
VITRINES >VITRINE
VITRIOL *n* language expressing bitterness and hatred ▷ *vb* attack or injure with or as if with vitriol
VITRIOLED >VITRIOL
VITRIOLIC *adj* (of language) severely bitter or harsh
VITRIOLS >VITRIOL
VITTA *n* tubelike cavity containing oil that occurs in the fruits of certain plants
VITTAE >VITTA
VITTATE >VITTA
VITTLE *obsolete or dialect spelling of* >VICTUAL
VITTLED >VITTLE
VITTLES *obsolete or dialect spelling of* >VICTUALS
VITTLING >VITTLE
VITULAR *same as* >VITULINE
VITULINE *adj* of or resembling a calf or veal
VIVA *interj* long live (a person or thing) ▷ *n* examination in the form of an interview ▷ *vb* examine (a candidate) in a spoken interview
VIVACE *adv* in a lively manner ▷ *adj* be performed in a lively manner ▷ *n* piece of music to be performed in this way
VIVACES >VIVACE
VIVACIOUS *adj* full of energy and enthusiasm
VIVACITY *n* quality of being vivacious
VIVAED >VIVA
VIVAING >VIVA
VIVAMENTE *adv* in a lively manner
VIVANDIER *n* sutler
VIVARIA >VIVARIUM
VIVARIES >VIVARY
VIVARIUM *n* place where animals are kept in natural conditions
VIVARIUMS >VIVARIUM
VIVARY *same as* >VIVARIUM
VIVAS >VIVA
VIVAT *interj* long live ▷ *n* expression of acclamation
VIVATS >VIVAT
VIVDA *n* method of drying meat
VIVDAS >VIVDA
VIVE *interj* long live
VIVELY *adv* in a lively manner
VIVENCIES >VIVENCY
VIVENCY *n* physical or mental energy
VIVER *n* fish pond
VIVERRA *n* civet genus
VIVERRAS >VIVERRA
VIVERRID >VIVERRINE
VIVERRIDS >VIVERRINE
VIVERRINE *n* type of mammal of Eurasia and Africa ▷ *adj* of this family of mammals
VIVERS >VIVER
VIVES *n* disease found in

horses
VIVIANITE *n* type of mineral
VIVID *adj* very bright
VIVIDER >VIVID
VIVIDEST >VIVID
VIVIDITY >VIVID
VIVIDLY >VIVID
VIVIDNESS >VIVID
VIVIFIC *adj* giving life
VIVIFIED >VIVIFY
VIVIFIER >VIVIFY
VIVIFIERS >VIVIFY
VIVIFIES >VIVIFY
VIVIFY *vb* animate, inspire
VIVIFYING >VIVIFY
VIVIPARA *n* animal that produces offspring that develop as embryos within the female parent
VIVIPARY *n* act of giving birth producing offspring that have developed as embryos
VIVISECT *vb* subject (an animal) to vivisection
VIVISECTS >VIVISECT
VIVO *adv* with life and vigour
VIVRES *n* provisions
VIXEN *n* female fox
VIXENISH >VIXEN
VIXENLY >VIXEN
VIXENS >VIXEN
VIZAMENT *n* consultation
VIZAMENTS >VIZAMENT
VIZARD *n* means of disguise ▷ *vb* conceal by means of a disguise
VIZARDED >VIZARD
VIZARDING >VIZARD
VIZARDS >VIZARD
VIZCACHA *same as* >VISCACHA
VIZCACHAS >VIZCACHA
VIZIED >VIZY
VIZIER *n* high official in certain Muslim countries
VIZIERATE *n* position, rank, or authority of a vizier
VIZIERIAL >VIZIER
VIZIERS >VIZIER
VIZIES >VIZY
VIZIR *same as* >VIZIER
VIZIRATE >VIZIR
VIZIRATES >VIZIR
VIZIRIAL >VIZIR
VIZIRS >VIZIR
VIZIRSHIP >VIZIR
VIZOR *same as* >VISOR
VIZORED >VIZOR
VIZORING >VIZOR
VIZORLESS >VIZOR
VIZORS >VIZOR
VIZSLA *n* breed of Hungarian hunting dog with a smooth rusty-gold coat
VIZSLAS >VIZSLA
VIZY *vb* look
VIZYING >VIZY
VIZZIE *same as* >VIZY
VIZZIED >VIZZIE
VIZZIEING >VIZZIE
VIZZIES >VIZZIE
VLEI *n* area of low marshy ground, esp one that feeds a stream
VLEIS >VLEI
VLIES >VLY
VLY *same as* >VLEI
VOAR *n* spring
VOARS >VOAR
VOCAB *n* vocabulary
VOCABLE *n* word regarded simply as a sequence of letters or spoken sounds ▷ *adj* capable of being uttered
VOCABLES >VOCABLE
VOCABLY >VOCABLE
VOCABS >VOCAB
VOCABULAR >VOCABLE
VOCAL *adj* relating to the voice ▷ *n* piece of jazz or pop music that is sung
VOCALESE *n* style of jazz singing
VOCALESES >VOCALESE
VOCALIC *adj* of, relating to, or containing a vowel or vowels
VOCALICS *n* non-verbal aspects of voice
VOCALION *n* type of musical instrument
VOCALIONS >VOCALION
VOCALISE *same as* >VOCALIZE
VOCALISED >VOCALISE
VOCALISER >VOCALISE
VOCALISES >VOCALISE
VOCALISM *n* exercise of the voice, as in singing or speaking
VOCALISMS >VOCALISM
VOCALIST *n* singer
VOCALISTS >VOCALIST
VOCALITY >VOCAL
VOCALIZE *vb* express with the voice
VOCALIZED >VOCALIZE
VOCALIZER >VOCALIZE
VOCALIZES >VOCALIZE
VOCALLY >VOCAL
VOCALNESS >VOCAL
VOCALS >VOCAL
VOCATION *n* profession or trade
VOCATIONS >VOCATION
VOCATIVE *n* (in some languages) case of nouns used when addressing a person ▷ *adj* relating to, used in, or characterized by calling
VOCATIVES >VOCATIVE
VOCES >VOX
VOCODER *n* type of synthesizer that uses the human voice as an oscillator
VOCODERS >VOCODER
VOCULAR >VOCULE
VOCULE *n* faint noise made when articulating certain sounds
VOCULES >VOCULE
VODKA *n* (Russian) spirit distilled from potatoes or grain
VODKAS >VODKA
VODOU *variant of* >VOODOO
VODOUN *same as* >VODUN
VODOUNS >VODOUN
VODOUS >VODOU
VODUN *n* voodoo
VODUNS >VODUN
VOE *n* (in Orkney and Shetland) a small bay or narrow creek
VOEMA *n* vigour or energy
VOEMAS >VOEMA
VOERTSAK *variant of* >VOETSEK
VOERTSEK *variant of* >VOETSEK
VOES >VOE
VOETSAK *same as* >VOETSEK
VOETSEK *interj* S African offensive expression of rejection
VOGIE *adj* conceited
VOGIER >VOGIE
VOGIEST >VOGIE
VOGUE *n* popular style ▷ *adj* popular or fashionable ▷ *vb* bring into vogue
VOGUED >VOGUE
VOGUEING *n* dance style of the late 1980s
VOGUEINGS >VOGUEING
VOGUER >VOGUE
VOGUERS >VOGUE
VOGUES >VOGUE
VOGUEY >VOGUE
VOGUIER >VOGUE
VOGUIEST >VOGUE
VOGUING *same as* >VOGUEING
VOGUINGS >VOGUING
VOGUISH >VOGUE
VOGUISHLY >VOGUE
VOICE *n* (quality of) sound made when speaking or singing ▷ *vb* express verbally
VOICED *adj* articulated with accompanying vibration of the vocal cords
VOICEFUL >VOICE
VOICELESS *adj* without a voice
VOICEMAIL *n* facility of leaving recorded message by telephone
VOICEOVER *n* spoken commentary by unseen narrator on film
VOICER >VOICE
VOICERS >VOICE
VOICES >VOICE
VOICING >VOICE
VOICINGS >VOICE
VOID *adj* not legally binding ▷ *n* feeling of deprivation ▷ *vb* make invalid
VOIDABLE *adj* capable of being voided
VOIDANCE *n* annulment, as of a contract
VOIDANCES >VOIDANCE
VOIDED *adj* (of a design) with a hole in the centre of the same shape as the design
VOIDEE *n* light meal eaten before bed
VOIDEES >VOIDEE
VOIDER >VOID
VOIDERS >VOID
VOIDING >VOID
VOIDINGS >VOID
VOIDNESS >VOID
VOIDS >VOID
VOILA *interj* word used to express satisfaction
VOILE *n* light semitransparent fabric
VOILES >VOILE
VOISINAGE *n* district or neighbourhood
VOITURE *n* type of vehicle
VOITURES >VOITURE
VOITURIER *n* driver of a voiture
VOIVODE *n* type of military leader
VOIVODES >VOIVODE
VOL *n* volume
VOLA *n* palm of hand or sole of foot
VOLABLE *adj* quick-witted
VOLAE >VOLA
VOLAGE *adj* changeable
VOLANT *adj* in a flying position
VOLANTE *n* Spanish horse carriage
VOLANTES >VOLANTE
VOLAR *adj* of or relating to the palm of the hand or the sole of the foot
VOLARIES >VOLARY
VOLARY *n* large bird enclosure
VOLATIC *adj* flying
VOLATILE *adj* liable to sudden change, esp in behaviour ▷ *n* volatile substance
VOLATILES >VOLATILE
VOLCANIAN *same as* >VOLCANIC
VOLCANIC *adj* of or relating to volcanoes
VOLCANICS *n* types of rock
VOLCANISE *same as* >VOLCANIZE
VOLCANISM *n* processes that result in the formation of volcanoes
VOLCANIST *n* person who studies volcanoes
VOLCANIZE *vb* subject to the effects of or change by volcanic heat
VOLCANO *n* mountain with a vent through which lava is ejected
VOLCANOES >VOLCANO
VOLCANOS >VOLCANO
VOLE *n* small rodent ▷ *vb* to win by taking all the tricks in a deal

LED >VOLE
LENS as in *nolens volens* whether willing or unwilling
LERIES >VOLERY
LERY *same as* >VOLARY
LES >VOLE
LET *n* type of veil
LETS >VOLET
LING >VOLE
LITANT *adj* flying or moving about rapidly
LITATE *vb* flutter
LITATED >VOLITATE
LITATES >VOLITATE
LITIENT >VOLITION
LITION *n* ability to decide things for oneself
LITIONS >VOLITION
LITIVE *adj* of, relating to, or emanating from the will ▷ *n* (in some languages) a verb form or mood used to express a wish or desire
LITIVES >VOLITIVE
LK *n* people or nation, esp the nation of Afrikaners
LKS >VOLK
LKSLIED *n* German folk song
LKSRAAD *n* Boer assembly in South Africa in the 19th century
LLEY *n* simultaneous discharge of ammunition ▷ *vb* discharge (ammunition) in a volley
LLEYED >VOLLEY
LLEYER >VOLLEY
LLEYERS >VOLLEY
LLEYING >VOLLEY
LLEYS >VOLLEY
LOST *n* (in the former Soviet Union) a rural soviet
LOSTS >VOLOST
LPINO *n* Italian breed of dog
LPINOS >VOLPINO
LPLANE *vb* glide in an aeroplane
LPLANED >VOLPLANE
LPLANES >VOLPLANE
LS >VOL
LT *n* unit of electric potential
LTA *n* quick-moving Italian dance popular during the 16th and 17th centuries
LTAGE *n* electric potential difference expressed in volts
LTAGES >VOLTAGE
LTAIC *adj* producing an electric current
LTAISM *another name for* >GALVANISM
LTAISMS >VOLTAISM
LTE *same as* >VOLT
LTES >VOLTE
LTI *adv* musical direction
VOLTIGEUR *n* French infantry member
VOLTINISM *n* number of annual broods of an animal
VOLTMETER *n* instrument for measuring voltage
VOLTS >VOLT
VOLUBIL *same as* >VOLUBLE
VOLUBLE *adj* talking easily and at length
VOLUBLY >VOLUBLE
VOLUCRINE *adj* relating to birds
VOLUME *n* size of the space occupied by something ▷ *vb* billow or surge in volume
VOLUMED >VOLUME
VOLUMES >VOLUME
VOLUMETER *n* any instrument for measuring the volume of a solid, liquid, or gas
VOLUMETRY *n* act of measuring by volume
VOLUMINAL >VOLUME
VOLUMING >VOLUME
VOLUMISE *same as* >VOLUMIZE
VOLUMISED >VOLUMISE
VOLUMISES >VOLUMISE
VOLUMIST *n* author
VOLUMISTS >VOLUMIST
VOLUMIZE *vb* create volume in something
VOLUMIZED >VOLUMIZE
VOLUMIZES >VOLUMIZE
VOLUNTARY *adj* done by choice ▷ *n* organ solo in a church service
VOLUNTEER *n* person who offers voluntarily to do something ▷ *vb* offer one's services
VOLUSPA *n* Icelandic mythological poem
VOLUSPAS >VOLUSPA
VOLUTE *n* spiral or twisting turn, form, or object ▷ *adj* having the form of a volute
VOLUTED >VOLUTE
VOLUTES >VOLUTE
VOLUTIN *n* granular substance found in cells
VOLUTINS >VOLUTIN
VOLUTION *n* rolling, revolving, or spiral form or motion
VOLUTIONS >VOLUTION
VOLUTOID >VOLUTE
VOLVA *n* cup-shaped structure that sheathes the base of the stalk of certain mushrooms
VOLVAE >VOLVA
VOLVAS >VOLVA
VOLVATE >VOLVA
VOLVE *vb* turn over
VOLVED >VOLVE
VOLVES >VOLVE
VOLVING >VOLVE
VOLVOX *n* freshwater protozoan
VOLVOXES >VOLVOX
VOLVULI >VOLVULUS
VOLVULUS *n* abnormal twisting of the intestines causing obstruction
VOMER *n* thin flat bone forming part of the separation between the nasal passages in mammals
VOMERINE >VOMER
VOMERS >VOMER
VOMICA *n* pus-containing cavity
VOMICAE >VOMICA
VOMICAS >VOMICA
VOMIT *vb* eject (the contents of the stomach) through the mouth ▷ *n* matter vomited
VOMITED >VOMIT
VOMITER >VOMIT
VOMITERS >VOMIT
VOMITING >VOMIT
VOMITINGS >VOMIT
VOMITIVE *same as* >VOMITORY
VOMITIVES >VOMITIVE
VOMITO *n* form of yellow fever
VOMITORIA *n* entrances in an amphitheatre
VOMITORY *adj* causing vomiting ▷ *n* vomitory agent
VOMITOS >VOMITO
VOMITOUS *adj* arousing feelings of disgust
VOMITS >VOMIT
VOMITUS *n* matter that has been vomited
VOMITUSES >VOMITUS
VOODOO *n* religion involving ancestor worship and witchcraft ▷ *adj* of or relating to voodoo ▷ *vb* affect by or as if by the power of voodoo
VOODOOED >VOODOO
VOODOOING >VOODOO
VOODOOISM *same as* >VOODOO
VOODOOIST >VOODOO
VOODOOS >VOODOO
VOORKAMER *n* front room of a house
VOORSKOT *n* advance payment made to a farmer for crops
VOORSKOTS >VOORSKOT
VOR *vb* (in dialect) warn
VORACIOUS *adj* craving great quantities of food
VORACITY >VORACIOUS
VORAGO *n* chasm
VORAGOES >VORAGO
VORANT *adj* devouring
VORLAGE *n* skiing position
VORLAGES >VORLAGE
VORPAL *adj* sharp
VORRED >VOR
VORRING >VOR
VORS >VOR
VORTEX *n* whirlpool
VORTEXES >VORTEX
VORTICAL >VORTEX
VORTICES >VORTEX
VORTICISM *n* art movement in 20th-century England
VORTICIST >VORTICISM
VORTICITY *n* rotational spin in a fluid
VORTICOSE *adj* rotating quickly
VOSTRO as in *vostro account* bank account held by a foreign bank with a British bank
VOTABLE >VOTE
VOTARESS *n* female votary
VOTARIES >VOTARY
VOTARIST *variant of* >VOTARY
VOTARISTS >VOTARIST
VOTARY *n* person dedicated to religion or to a cause ▷ *adj* ardently devoted to the services or worship of God
VOTE *n* choice made by a participant in a shared decision ▷ *vb* make a choice by a vote
VOTEABLE >VOTE
VOTED >VOTE
VOTEEN *n* devotee
VOTEENS >VOTEEN
VOTELESS >VOTE
VOTER *n* person who can or does vote
VOTERS >VOTER
VOTES >VOTE
VOTING >VOTE
VOTINGS >VOTE
VOTIVE *adj* done or given to fulfil a vow ▷ *n* votive offering
VOTIVELY >VOTIVE
VOTIVES >VOTIVE
VOTRESS >VOTARESS
VOTRESSES >VOTRESS
VOUCH *vb* give personal assurance ▷ *n* act of vouching
VOUCHED >VOUCH
VOUCHEE *n* person summoned to court to defend a title
VOUCHEES >VOUCHEE
VOUCHER *n* ticket used instead of money to buy specified goods ▷ *vb* summon someone to court as a vouchee
VOUCHERED >VOUCHER
VOUCHERS >VOUCHER
VOUCHES >VOUCH
VOUCHING >VOUCH
VOUCHSAFE *vb* give, entrust
VOUDON *variant of* >VOODOO
VOUDONS >VOUDON
VOUDOU *same as* >VOODOO
VOUDOUED >VOUDOU
VOUDOUING >VOUDOU
VOUDOUN *variant of* >VOODOO

VOUDOUNS > VOUDOUN
VOUDOUS > VOUDOU
VOUGE *n* form of pike used by foot soldiers in the 14th century and later
VOUGES > VOUGE
VOULGE *n* type of medieval weapon
VOULGES > VOULGE
VOULU *adj* deliberate
VOUSSOIR *n* wedge-shaped stone or brick that is used with others to construct an arch
VOUSSOIRS > VOUSSOIR
VOUTSAFE *same as* > VOUCHSAFE
VOUTSAFED > VOUTSAFE
VOUTSAFES > VOUTSAFE
VOUVRAY *n* dry white French wine
VOUVRAYS > VOUVRAY
VOW *n* solemn and binding promise ▷ *vb* promise solemnly
VOWED > VOW
VOWEL *n* speech sound made without obstructing the flow of breath ▷ *vb* say as a vowel
VOWELISE *same as* > VOWELIZE
VOWELISED > VOWELISE
VOWELISES > VOWELISE
VOWELIZE *vb* mark the vowel points in (a Hebrew word or text)
VOWELIZED > VOWELIZE
VOWELIZES > VOWELIZE
VOWELLED > VOWEL
VOWELLESS > VOWEL
VOWELLING > VOWEL
VOWELLY > VOWEL
VOWELS > VOWEL
VOWER > VOW
VOWERS > VOW
VOWESS *n* nun
VOWESSES > VOWESS
VOWING > VOW
VOWLESS > VOW
VOWS > VOW
VOX *n* voice or sound
VOXEL *n* term used in computing imaging
VOXELS > VOXEL
VOYAGE *n* long journey by sea or in space ▷ *vb* make a voyage
VOYAGED > VOYAGE
VOYAGER > VOYAGE
VOYAGERS > VOYAGE
VOYAGES > VOYAGE
VOYAGEUR *n* French canoeman who transported furs from trading posts in the North American interior
VOYAGEURS > VOYAGEUR
VOYAGING > VOYAGE
VOYEUR *n* person who obtains pleasure from watching people undressing or having sex
VOYEURISM > VOYEUR
VOYEURS > VOYEUR
VOZHD *n* Russian leader
VOZHDS > VOZHD
VRAIC *n* type of seaweed
VRAICKER *n* person who gathers vraic
VRAICKERS > VRAICKER
VRAICKING *n* act of gathering vraic
VRAICS > VRAIC
VRIL *n* life force
VRILS > VRIL
VROOM *interj* exclamation imitative of a car engine revving up ▷ *vb* move noisily and at high speed
VROOMED > VROOM
VROOMING > VROOM
VROOMS > VROOM
VROT *adj* South African slang for rotten
VROU *n* Afrikaner woman, esp a married woman
VROUS > VROU
VROUW *n* woman
VROUWS > VROUW
VROW *same as* > VROUW
VROWS > VROW
VUG *n* small cavity in a rock or vein, usually lined with crystals
VUGG *same as* > VUG
VUGGIER > VUG
VUGGIEST > VUG
VUGGS > VUGG
VUGGY > VUG
VUGH *same as* > VUG
VUGHIER > VUGH
VUGHIEST > VUGH
VUGHS > VUGH
VUGHY > VUG
VUGS > VUG
VULCAN *n* blacksmith
VULCANIAN *adj* of or relating to a volcanic eruption
VULCANIC *same as* > VOLCANIC
VULCANISE *same as* > VULCANIZE
VULCANISM *same as* > VOLCANISM
VULCANIST *same as* > VOLCANIST
VULCANITE *n* vulcanized rubber
VULCANIZE *vb* strengthen (rubber) by treating it with sulphur
VULCANS > VULCAN
VULGAR *adj* showing lack of good taste, decency, or refinement ▷ *n* common and ignorant person
VULGARER > VULGAR
VULGAREST > VULGAR
VULGARIAN *n* vulgar (rich) person
VULGARISE *same as* > VULGARIZE
VULGARISM *n* coarse word or phrase
VULGARITY *n* condition of being vulgar
VULGARIZE *vb* make vulgar or too common
VULGARLY > VULGAR
VULGARS > VULGAR
VULGATE *n* commonly recognized text or version ▷ *adj* generally accepted
VULGATES > VULGATE
VULGO *adv* generally
VULGUS *n* the common people
VULGUSES > VULGUS
VULN *vb* wound
VULNED > VULN
VULNERARY *adj* of, relating to, or used to heal a wound ▷ *n* vulnerary drug or agent
VULNERATE *vb* wound
VULNING > VULN
VULNS > VULN
VULPICIDE *n* person who kills foxes
VULPINE *adj* of or like a fox
VULPINISM > VULPINE
VULPINITE *n* type of granular anhydrite
VULSELLA *n* forceps
VULSELLAE > VULSELLA
VULSELLUM *variant of* > VULSELLA
VULTURE *n* large bird that feeds on the flesh of dead animals
VULTURES > VULTURE
VULTURINE *adj* of, relating to, or resembling a vulture
VULTURISH > VULTURE
VULTURISM *n* greed
VULTURN *n* type of turkey
VULTURNS > VULTURN
VULTUROUS *same as* > VULTURINE
VULVA *n* woman's external genitals
VULVAE > VULVA
VULVAL > VULVA
VULVAR > VULVA
VULVAS > VULVA
VULVATE > VULVA
VULVIFORM > VULVA
VULVITIS *n* inflammation of the vulva
VUM *vb* swear
VUMMED > VUM
VUMMING > VUM
VUMS > VUM
VUTTIER > VUTTY
VUTTIEST > VUTTY
VUTTY *adj* dirty
VUVUZELA *n* South African instrument blown by football fans
VUVUZELAS > VUVUZELA
VYING > VIE
VYINGLY > VIE

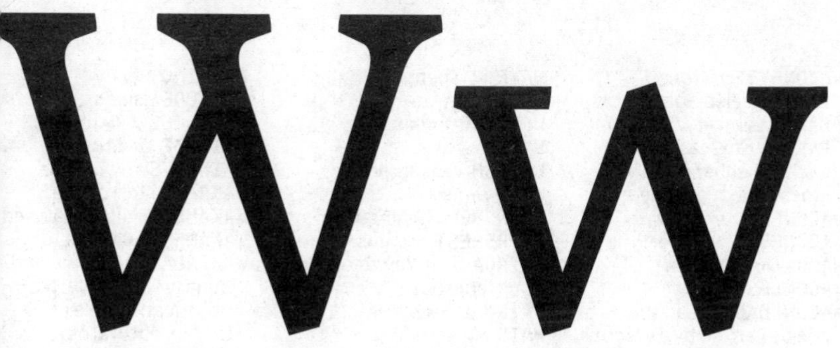

AC *n* (formerly) member of the Women's Auxiliary Army Corp
ACS >WAAC
B *n* offensive term for Mexican living in US
BAIN *same as* >OUABAIN
BAINS >WABAIN
BBIT *adj* weary
BBLE *same as* >WOBBLE
BBLED >WABBLE
BBLER >WABBLE
BBLERS >WABBLE
BBLES >WABBLE
BBLIER >WABBLE
BBLIEST >WABBLE
BBLING >WABBLE
BBLY >WABBLE
BOOM *another word for* >WAGENBOOM
BOOMS >WABOOM
BS >WAB
BSTER *Scots form of* >WEBSTER
BSTERS >WABSTER
CK *n* friend
CKE *n* any of various soft earthy rocks that resemble or are derived from basaltic rocks
CKER *same as* >WACK
CKERS >WACKER
CKES >WACKE
CKEST >WACK
CKIER >WACKY
CKIEST >WACKY
CKILY >WACKY
CKINESS >WACKY
CKO *adj* mad or eccentric ▷ *n* mad or eccentric person
CKOS >WACKO
CKS >WACK
WACKY *adj* eccentric or funny
WAD *n* black earthy ore of manganese ▷ *n* small mass of soft material ▷ *vb* form (something) into a wad
WADABLE >WADE
WADD *same as* >WAD
WADDED >WAD
WADDER >WAD
WADDERS >WAD
WADDIE *same as* >WADDY
WADDIED >WADDY
WADDIES >WADDY
WADDING >WAD
WADDINGS >WAD
WADDLE *vb* walk with short swaying steps ▷ *n* swaying walk
WADDLED >WADDLE
WADDLER >WADDLE
WADDLERS >WADDLE
WADDLES >WADDLE
WADDLING >WADDLE
WADDLY >WADDLE
WADDS >WADD
WADDY *n* heavy wooden club used by Australian Aborigines ▷ *vb* hit with a waddy
WADDYING >WADDY
WADE *vb* walk with difficulty through water or mud ▷ *n* act or an instance of wading
WADEABLE >WADE
WADED >WADE
WADER *n* long-legged water bird
WADERS *pl n* long waterproof boots which completely cover the legs, worn by anglers for standing in water
WADES >WADE
WADI *n* (in N Africa and Arabia) river which is dry except in the wet season
WADIES >WADY
WADING >WADE
WADINGS >WADE
WADIS >WADI
WADMAAL *same as* >WADMAL
WADMAALS >WADMAAL
WADMAL *n* coarse thick woollen fabric, formerly woven esp in Orkney and Shetland, for outer garments
WADMALS >WADMAL
WADMEL *same as* >WADMAL
WADMELS >WADMEL
WADMOL *same as* >WADMAL
WADMOLL *same as* >WADMAL
WADMOLLS >WADMOLL
WADMOLS >WADMOL
WADS >WAD
WADSET *vb* pledge or mortgage
WADSETS >WADSET
WADSETT *same as* >WADSET
WADSETTED >WADSET
WADSETTER >WADSET
WADSETTS >WADSETT
WADT *same as* >WAD
WADTS >WADT
WADY *same as* >WADI
WAE *old form of* >WOE
WAEFUL *old form of* >WOEFUL
WAENESS *n* sorrow
WAENESSES >WAENESS
WAES >WAE
WAESOME *adj* sorrowful
WAESUCK *interj* alas
WAESUCKS *interj* alas
WAFER *n* thin crisp biscuit ▷ *vb* seal, fasten, or attach with a wafer
WAFERED >WAFER
WAFERING >WAFER
WAFERS >WAFER
WAFERY >WAFER
WAFF *n* gust or puff of air ▷ *vb* flutter or cause to flutter
WAFFED >WAFF
WAFFIE *n* person regarded as having little worth to society
WAFFIES >WAFFIE
WAFFING >WAFF
WAFFLE *vb* speak or write in a vague wordy way ▷ *n* vague wordy talk or writing
WAFFLED >WAFFLE
WAFFLER >WAFFLE
WAFFLERS >WAFFLE
WAFFLES >WAFFLE
WAFFLIER >WAFFLE
WAFFLIEST >WAFFLE
WAFFLING >WAFFLE
WAFFLINGS >WAFFLE
WAFFLY >WAFFLE
WAFFS >WAFF
WAFT *vb* drift or carry gently through the air ▷ *n* something wafted
WAFTAGE >WAFT
WAFTAGES >WAFT
WAFTED >WAFT
WAFTER *n* device that causes a draught
WAFTERS >WAFTER
WAFTING >WAFT
WAFTINGS >WAFT
WAFTS >WAFT

WAFTURE *n* act of wafting or waving
WAFTURES >WAFTURE
WAG *vb* move rapidly from side to side ▷ *n* wagging movement
WAGE *n* payment for work done, esp when paid weekly ▷ *vb* engage in (an activity)
WAGED >WAGE
WAGELESS >WAGE
WAGENBOOM *n* S African tree
WAGER *vb* bet on the outcome of something ▷ *n* bet on the outcome of an event or activity
WAGERED >WAGER
WAGERER >WAGER
WAGERERS >WAGER
WAGERING >WAGER
WAGERS >WAGER
WAGES >WAGE
WAGGA *n* blanket or bed covering made out of sacks stitched together
WAGGAS >WAGGA
WAGGED >WAG
WAGGER >WAG
WAGGERIES >WAGGERY
WAGGERS >WAG
WAGGERY *n* quality of being humorous
WAGGING >WAG
WAGGISH *adj* jocular or humorous
WAGGISHLY >WAGGISH
WAGGLE *vb* move with a rapid shaking or wobbling motion ▷ *n* rapid shaking or wobbling motion
WAGGLED >WAGGLE
WAGGLER *n* float only the bottom of which is attached to the fishing line
WAGGLERS >WAGGLER
WAGGLES >WAGGLE
WAGGLIER >WAGGLE
WAGGLIEST >WAGGLE
WAGGLING >WAGGLE
WAGGLY >WAGGLE
WAGGON *same as* >WAGON
WAGGONED >WAGGON
WAGGONER *same as* >WAGONER
WAGGONERS >WAGGONER
WAGGONING >WAGGON
WAGGONS >WAGGON
WAGHALTER *n* person likely to be hanged
WAGING >WAGE
WAGMOIRE *obsolete word for* >QUAGMIRE
WAGMOIRES >WAGMOIRE
WAGON *n* four-wheeled vehicle for heavy loads ▷ *vb* transport by wagon
WAGONAGE *n* money paid for transport by wagon
WAGONAGES >WAGONAGE
WAGONED >WAGON
WAGONER *n* person who drives a wagon
WAGONERS >WAGONER
WAGONETTE *n* light four-wheeled horse-drawn vehicle with two lengthwise seats facing each other behind a crosswise driver's seat
WAGONFUL >WAGON
WAGONFULS >WAGON
WAGONING >WAGON
WAGONLESS >WAGON
WAGONLOAD *n* load that is or can be carried by a wagon
WAGONS >WAGON
WAGS >WAG
WAGSOME *another word for* >WAGGISH
WAGTAIL *n* small long-tailed bird
WAGTAILS >WAGTAIL
WAHCONDA *n* supreme being
WAHCONDAS >WAHCONDA
WAHINE *n* Māori woman, esp a wife
WAHINES >WAHINE
WAHOO *n* food and game fish of tropical seas
WAHOOS >WAHOO
WAI *n* in New Zealand, water
WAIATA *n* Māori song
WAIATAS >WAIATA
WAID >WEIGH
WAIDE >WEIGH
WAIF *n* young person who is, or seems, homeless or neglected ▷ *vb* treat as a waif
WAIFED >WAIF
WAIFING >WAIF
WAIFISH >WAIF
WAIFLIKE >WAIF
WAIFS >WAIF
WAIFT *n* piece of lost property found by someone other than the owner
WAIFTS >WAIFT
WAIL *vb* cry out in pain or misery ▷ *n* mournful cry
WAILED >WAIL
WAILER >WAIL
WAILERS >WAIL
WAILFUL >WAIL
WAILFULLY >WAIL
WAILING >WAIL
WAILINGLY >WAIL
WAILINGS >WAIL
WAILS >WAIL
WAILSOME >WAIL
WAIN *vb* transport ▷ *n* farm wagon
WAINAGE *n* carriages, etc, for transportation of goods
WAINAGES >WAINAGE
WAINED >WAIN
WAINING >WAIN
WAINS >WAIN
WAINSCOT *n* wooden lining of the lower part of the walls of a room ▷ *vb* line (a wall of a room) with a wainscot
WAINSCOTS >WAINSCOT
WAIR *vb* spend
WAIRED >WAIR
WAIRING >WAIR
WAIRS >WAIR
WAIRSH *variant spelling of* >WERSH
WAIRSHER >WAIRSH
WAIRSHEST >WAIRSH
WAIRUA *n* in New Zealand, spirit or soul
WAIRUAS >WAIRUA
WAIS >WAI
WAIST *n* part of the trunk between the ribs and the hips
WAISTBAND *n* band of material sewn on to the waist of a garment to strengthen it
WAISTBELT *n* belt
WAISTCOAT *n* sleeveless garment which buttons up the front, usu worn over a shirt and under a jacket
WAISTED *adj* having a waist or waistlike part
WAISTER *n* sailor performing menial duties
WAISTERS >WAISTER
WAISTING *n* act of wasting
WAISTINGS >WAISTING
WAISTLESS >WAIST
WAISTLINE *n* (size of) the waist of a person or garment
WAISTS >WAIST
WAIT *vb* remain inactive in expectation (of something) ▷ *n* act or period of waiting
WAITE *old form of* >WAIT
WAITED >WAIT
WAITER *n* man who serves in a restaurant etc ▷ *vb* serve at table
WAITERAGE *n* service
WAITERED >WAITER
WAITERING *n* act of serving at table
WAITERS >WAITER
WAITES >WAITE
WAITING >WAIT
WAITINGLY >WAIT
WAITINGS >WAIT
WAITLIST *n* waiting list
WAITLISTS >WAITLIST
WAITRESS *n* woman who serves people with food and drink in a restaurant ▷ *vb* work as a waitress
WAITRON *n* waiter or waitress
WAITRONS >WAITRON
WAITS >WAIT
WAITSTAFF *n* waiters and waitresses collectively
WAIVE *vb* refrain from enforcing (a law, right, etc)
WAIVED >WAIVE
WAIVER *n* act or instance of voluntarily giving up a claim, right, etc
WAIVERS >WAIVER
WAIVES >WAIVE
WAIVING >WAIVE
WAIVODE *same as* >VOIVOD
WAIVODES >WAIVODE
WAIWODE *same as* >VOIVOD
WAIWODES >WAIWODE
WAKA *n* Māori canoe
WAKAME *n* edible seaweed
WAKAMES >WAKAME
WAKANDA *n* supernatural quality said by Native American people to be held by natural objects
WAKANDAS >WAKANDA
WAKANE *n* type of seaweed
WAKANES >WAKANE
WAKAS >WAKA
WAKE *vb* rouse from sleep c inactivity ▷ *n* vigil besid a corpse the night before the funeral
WAKEBOARD *n* short surfboard for a rider towe behind a motorboat
WAKED >WAKE
WAKEFUL *adj* unable to sleep
WAKEFULLY >WAKEFUL
WAKELESS *adj* (of sleep) deep or unbroken
WAKEMAN *n* watchman
WAKEMEN >WAKEMAN
WAKEN *vb* wake
WAKENED >WAKEN
WAKENER >WAKEN
WAKENERS >WAKEN
WAKENING >WAKEN
WAKENINGS >WAKEN
WAKENS >WAKEN
WAKER >WAKE
WAKERIFE *adj* watchful
WAKERS >WAKE
WAKES >WAKE
WAKF *same as* >WAQF
WAKFS >WAKF
WAKIKI *n* Melanesian she currency
WAKIKIS >WAKIKI
WAKING >WAKE
WAKINGS >WAKE
WALD *Scots form of* >WELD
WALDFLUTE *n* organ flute stop
WALDGRAVE *n* (in medieva Germany) an officer with jurisdiction over a royal forest
WALDHORN *n* organ reed stop
WALDHORNS >WALDHORN
WALDO *n* gadget for manipulating objects by remote control
WALDOES >WALDO
WALDOS >WALDO
WALDRAPP *n* type of ibis
WALDRAPPS >WALDRAPP
WALDS >WALD
WALE *same as* >WEAL
WALED >WALE
WALER >WALE
WALERS >WALE
WALES >WALE
WALI *same as* >VALI
WALIER >WALY

ALIES >WALY
ALIEST >WALY
ALING >WALE
ALIS >WALI
ALISE *same as* >VALISE
ALISES >WALISE
ALK *vb* move on foot with at least one foot always on the ground ▷*n* short journey on foot, usu for pleasure
ALKABLE >WALK
ALKABOUT *n* informal walk among the public by royalty etc
ALKATHON *n* long walk done, esp for charity
ALKAWAY *n* easily achieved victory
ALKAWAYS >WALKAWAY
ALKED >WALK
ALKER *n* person who walks
ALKERS >WALKER
ALKING *adj* (of a person) considered to possess the qualities of something inanimate as specified ▷*n* act of walking
ALKINGS >WALKING
ALKMILL *same as* >WAULKMILL
ALKMILLS >WALKMILL
ALKOUT *n* strike
ALKOUTS >WALKOUT
ALKOVER *n* easy victory
ALKOVERS >WALKOVER
ALKS >WALK
ALKUP *n* building with stairs to upper floors
ALKUPS >WALKUP
ALKWAY *n* path designed for use by pedestrians
ALKWAYS >WALKWAY
ALKYRIE *variant of* >VALKYRIE
ALKYRIES >WALKYRIE
ALL *n* structure of brick, stone, etc used to enclose, divide, or support ▷*vb* enclose or seal with a wall or walls
ALLA *same as* >WALLAH
ALLABA *n* type of S American tree
ALLABAS >WALLABA
ALLABIES >WALLABY
ALLABY *n* marsupial like a small kangaroo
ALLAH *n* person involved with or in charge of a specified thing
ALLAHS >WALLAH
ALLAROO *n* large stocky Australian kangaroo of rocky regions
ALLAROOS >WALLAROO
ALLAS >WALLA
ALLBOARD *n* thin board made of materials, such as compressed wood fibres or gypsum plaster, between stiff paper, and used to cover walls, partitions, etc
WALLCHART *n* chart on wall
WALLED >WALL
WALLER >WALL
WALLERS >WALL
WALLET *n* small folding case for paper money, documents, etc
WALLETS >WALLET
WALLEYE *n* fish with large staring eyes
WALLEYED >WALLEYE
WALLEYES >WALLEYE
WALLFISH *n* snail
WALLIE *same as* >WALLY
WALLIER >WALLY
WALLIES >WALLY
WALLIEST >WALLY
WALLING >WALL
WALLINGS >WALL
WALLOP *vb* hit hard ▷*n* hard blow
WALLOPED >WALLOP
WALLOPER *n* person or thing that wallops
WALLOPERS >WALLOPER
WALLOPING *n* thrashing ▷*adj* large or great
WALLOPS >WALLOP
WALLOW *vb* revel in an emotion ▷*n* act or instance of wallowing
WALLOWED >WALLOW
WALLOWER >WALLOW
WALLOWERS >WALLOW
WALLOWING >WALLOW
WALLOWS >WALLOW
WALLPAPER *n* decorative paper to cover interior walls ▷*vb* cover (walls) with wallpaper
WALLS >WALL
WALLSEND *n* type of coal
WALLSENDS >WALLSEND
WALLWORT *n* type of plant
WALLWORTS >WALLWORT
WALLY *n* stupid person ▷*adj* fine, pleasing, or splendid
WALLYBALL *n* ball game played on court
WALLYDRAG *n* worthless person or animal
WALNUT *n* edible nut with a wrinkled shell ▷*adj* made from the wood of a walnut tree
WALNUTS >WALNUT
WALRUS *n* large sea mammal with long tusks
WALRUSES >WALRUS
WALTIER >WALTY
WALTIEST >WALTY
WALTY *adj* (of a ship) likely to roll over
WALTZ *n* ballroom dance ▷*vb* dance a waltz
WALTZED >WALTZ
WALTZER *n* person who waltzes
WALTZERS >WALTZER
WALTZES >WALTZ
WALTZING >WALTZ
WALTZINGS >WALTZ
WALTZLIKE >WALTZ
WALY *same as* >WALLY
WAMBENGER *another name for* >TUAN
WAMBLE *vb* move unsteadily ▷*n* unsteady movement
WAMBLED >WAMBLE
WAMBLES >WAMBLE
WAMBLIER >WAMBLE
WAMBLIEST >WAMBLE
WAMBLING >WAMBLE
WAMBLINGS >WAMBLE
WAMBLY >WAMBLE
WAME *n* belly, abdomen, or womb
WAMED >WAME
WAMEFOU *Scots variant of* >WAMEFUL
WAMEFOUS
WAMEFUL *n* bellyful
WAMEFULS >WAMEFUL
WAMES >WAME
WAMMUL *n* dog
WAMMULS >WAMMUL
WAMMUS *same as* >WAMUS
WAMMUSES >WAMMUS
WAMPEE *n* type of Asian fruit tree
WAMPEES >WAMPEE
WAMPISH *vb* wave
WAMPISHED >WAMPISH
WAMPISHES >WAMPISH
WAMPUM *n* shells woven together, formerly used by Native Americans for money and ornament
WAMPUMS >WAMPUM
WAMPUS *same as* >WAMUS
WAMPUSES >WAMPUS
WAMUS *n* type of cardigan or jacket
WAMUSES >WAMUS
WAN *adj* pale and sickly looking ▷*vb* make or become wan
WANCHANCY *adj* infelicitous
WAND *n* thin rod, esp one used in performing magic tricks
WANDER *vb* move about without a definite destination or aim ▷*n* act or instance of wandering
WANDERED >WANDER
WANDERER >WANDER
WANDERERS >WANDER
WANDERING >WANDER
WANDEROO *n* macaque monkey of India and Sri Lanka, having black fur with a ruff of long greyish fur on each side of the face
WANDEROOS >WANDEROO
WANDERS >WANDER
WANDLE *adj* supple
WANDLIKE >WAND
WANDOO *n* eucalyptus tree of W Australia, having white bark and durable wood
WANDOOS >WANDOO
WANDS >WAND
WANE *vb* decrease gradually in size or strength
WANED >WANE
WANES >WANE
WANEY >WANE
WANG *n* cheekbone
WANGAN *same as* >WANIGAN
WANGANS >WANGAN
WANGLE *vb* get by devious methods ▷*n* act or an instance of wangling
WANGLED >WANGLE
WANGLER >WANGLE
WANGLERS >WANGLE
WANGLES >WANGLE
WANGLING >WANGLE
WANGLINGS >WANGLE
WANGS >WANG
WANGUN *same as* >WANIGAN
WANGUNS >WANGUN
WANHOPE *n* delusion
WANHOPES >WANHOPE
WANIER >WANY
WANIEST >WANY
WANIGAN *n* provisions for camp
WANIGANS >WANIGAN
WANING >WANE
WANINGS >WANE
WANION *n* vehemence
WANIONS >WANION
WANK *vb* slang word for masturbate ▷*n* instance of masturbating ▷*adj* bad, useless, or worthless
WANKED >WANK
WANKER *n* slang word for worthless or stupid person
WANKERS >WANKER
WANKIER >WANKY
WANKIEST >WANKY
WANKING >WANK
WANKLE *adj* unstable
WANKS >WANK
WANKSTA *n* derogatory slang word for a person who acts or dresses like a gangster but who is not involved in crime
WANKSTAS >WANKSTA
WANKY *adj* slang word for pretentious
WANLE *same as* >WANDLE
WANLY >WAN
WANNA *vb* spelling of **want to** intended to reflect a dialectal or informal pronunciation
WANNABE *adj* wanting to be, or be like, a particular person or thing ▷*n* person who wants to be, or be like, a particular person or thing
WANNABEE *same as* >WANNABE
WANNABEES >WANNABEE
WANNABES >WANNABE
WANNED >WAN
WANNEL *same as* >WANDLE
WANNER >WAN
WANNESS >WAN
WANNESSES >WAN
WANNEST >WAN
WANNIGAN *same as* >WANIGAN
WANNIGANS >WANNIGAN

WANNING > WAN
WANNISH *adj* rather wan
WANS > WAN
WANT *vb* need or long for ▷ *n* act or instance of wanting
WANTAGE *n* shortage
WANTAGES > WANTAGE
WANTED > WANT
WANTER > WANT
WANTERS > WANT
WANTHILL *n* molehill
WANTHILLS > WANTHILL
WANTIES > WANTY
WANTING *adj* lacking ▷ *prep* without
WANTINGS > WANT
WANTON *adj* without motive, provocation, or justification ▷ *n* sexually unrestrained or immodest woman ▷ *vb* behave in a wanton manner
WANTONED > WANTON
WANTONER > WANTON
WANTONERS > WANTON
WANTONEST > WANTON
WANTONING > WANTON
WANTONISE *same as* > WANTONIZE
WANTONIZE *vb* behave wantonly
WANTONLY > WANTON
WANTONS > WANTON
WANTS > WANT
WANTY *adj* belt
WANWORDY *adj* without merit
WANWORTH *n* inexpensive purchase
WANWORTHS > WANWORTH
WANY > WANE
WANZE *vb* wane
WANZED > WANZE
WANZES > WANZE
WANZING > WANZE
WAP *vb* strike
WAPENSHAW *n* showing of weapons
WAPENTAKE *n* subdivision of certain shires or counties, esp in the Midlands and North of England
WAPINSHAW *same as* > WAPENSHAW
WAPITI *n* large N American deer, now also common in New Zealand
WAPITIS > WAPITI
WAPPED > WAP
WAPPEND *adj* tired
WAPPER *vb* blink
WAPPERED > WAPPER
WAPPERING > WAPPER
WAPPERS > WAPPER
WAPPING > WAP
WAPS > WAP
WAQF *n* endowment in Muslim law
WAQFS > WAQF
WAR *n* fighting between nations ▷ *adj* of, like, or caused by war ▷ *vb* conduct a war
WARAGI *n* Ugandan alcoholic drink made from bananas
WARAGIS > WARAGI
WARATAH *n* Australian shrub with crimson flowers
WARATAHS > WARATAH
WARB *n* dirty or insignificant person
WARBIER > WARB
WARBIEST > WARB
WARBLE *vb* sing in a trilling voice ▷ *n* act or an instance of warbling
WARBLED > WARBLE
WARBLER *n* any of various small songbirds
WARBLERS > WARBLER
WARBLES > WARBLE
WARBLING > WARBLE
WARBLINGS > WARBLE
WARBONNET *n* headband with trailing feathers worn by certain North American Indian warriors
WARBS > WARB
WARBY > WARB
WARCRAFT *n* skill in warfare
WARCRAFTS > WARCRAFT
WARD *n* room in a hospital for patients needing a similar kind of care ▷ *vb* guard or protect
WARDCORN *n* payment of corn
WARDCORNS > WARDCORN
WARDED > WARD
WARDEN *n* person in charge of a building and its occupants ▷ *vb* act as a warden
WARDENED > WARDEN
WARDENING > WARDEN
WARDENRY > WARDEN
WARDENS > WARDEN
WARDER *vb* guard ▷ *n* prison officer
WARDERED > WARDER
WARDERING > WARDER
WARDERS > WARDER
WARDIAN as in *wardian case* type of glass container for housing delicate plants
WARDING > WARD
WARDINGS > WARD
WARDLESS > WARD
WARDMOTE *n* assembly of the citizens or liverymen of an area
WARDMOTES > WARDMOTE
WARDOG *n* veteran warrior
WARDOGS > WARDOG
WARDRESS *n* female officer in charge of prisoners in a jail
WARDROBE *n* cupboard for hanging clothes in
WARDROBED > WARDROBE
WARDROBER *n* person in charge of someone's wardrobe
WARDROBES > WARDROBE
WARDROOM *n* officers' quarters on a warship
WARDROOMS > WARDROOM
WARDROP *obsolete form of* > WARDROBE
WARDROPS > WARDROP
WARDS > WARD
WARDSHIP *n* state of being a ward
WARDSHIPS > WARDSHIP
WARE *n* articles of a specified type or material ▷ *vb* spend or squander
WARED > WARE
WAREHOU *n* any of several edible saltwater New Zealand fish
WAREHOUSE *n* building for storing goods prior to sale or distribution ▷ *vb* store or place in a warehouse, esp a bonded warehouse
WARELESS *adj* careless
WAREROOM *n* store-room
WAREROOMS > WAREROOM
WARES *pl n* goods for sale
WAREZ *pl n* illegally copied computer software which has had its protection codes de-activated
WARFARE *vb* engage in war ▷ *n* fighting or hostilities
WARFARED > WARFARE
WARFARER > WARFARE
WARFARERS > WARFARE
WARFARES > WARFARE
WARFARIN *n* crystalline compound, used as a medical anticoagulant
WARFARING > WARFARE
WARFARINS > WARFARIN
WARHABLE *adj* able to fight in war
WARHEAD *n* explosive front part of a missile
WARHEADS > WARHEAD
WARHORSE *n* (formerly) a horse used in battle
WARHORSES > WARHORSE
WARIBASHI *n* disposable chopsticks
WARIER > WARY
WARIEST > WARY
WARILY > WARY
WARIMENT *n* caution
WARIMENTS > WARIMENT
WARINESS > WARY
WARING > WARE
WARISON *n* (esp formerly) a bugle note used as an order to a military force to attack
WARISONS > WARISON
WARK *Scots form of* > WORK
WARKED > WARK
WARKING > WARK
WARKS > WARK
WARLESS > WAR
WARLIKE *adj* of or relating to war
WARLING *n* one who is not liked
WARLINGS > WARLING
WARLOCK *n* man who practises black magic
WARLOCKRY *n* witchcraft
WARLOCKS > WARLOCK
WARLORD *n* military leader of a nation or part of a nation
WARLORDS > WARLORD
WARM *adj* moderately hot ▷ *vb* make or become warm ▷ *n* warm place or area
WARMAKER *n* one who wages war
WARMAKERS > WARMAKER
WARMAN *n* one experienced in warfare
WARMBLOOD *n* type of horse
WARMED > WARM
WARMEN > WARMAN
WARMER > WARM
WARMERS > WARM
WARMEST > WARM
WARMING > WARM
WARMINGS > WARM
WARMISH > WARM
WARMLY > WARM
WARMNESS > WARM
WARMONGER *n* person who encourages war
WARMOUTH *n* type of fish
WARMOUTHS > WARMOUTH
WARMS > WARM
WARMTH *n* mild heat
WARMTHS > WARMTH
WARMUP *n* preparatory exercise routine
WARMUPS > WARMUP
WARN *vb* make aware of possible danger or harm
WARNED > WARN
WARNER > WARN
WARNERS > WARN
WARNING *n* something that warns ▷ *adj* giving or serving as a warning
WARNINGLY > WARNING
WARNINGS > WARNING
WARNS > WARN
WARP *vb* twist out of shape ▷ *n* state of being warped
WARPAGE > WARP
WARPAGES > WARP
WARPATH *n* route taken by Native Americans on a warlike expedition
WARPATHS > WARPATH
WARPED > WARP
WARPER > WARP
WARPERS > WARP
WARPING > WARP
WARPINGS > WARP
WARPLANE *n* any aircraft designed for and used in warfare
WARPLANES > WARPLANE
WARPOWER *n* ability to wage war
WARPOWERS > WARPOWER
WARPS > WARP
WARPWISE *adv* (weaving) in the direction of the warp
WARRAGAL *same as* > WARRIGAL
WARRAGALS > WARRAGAL

WARRAGLE *same as* >WARRIGAL
WARRAGLES >WARRAGLE
WARRAGUL *same as* >WARRIGAL
WARRAGULS >WARRAGUL
WARRAN *same as* >WARRANT
WARRAND *same as* >WARRANT
WARRANDED >WARRAND
WARRANDS >WARRAND
WARRANED >WARRAN
WARRANING >WARRAN
WARRANS >WARRAN
WARRANT *n* (document giving) official authorization ▷ *vb* make necessary
WARRANTED >WARRANT
WARRANTEE *n* person to whom a warranty is given
WARRANTER >WARRANT
WARRANTOR *n* person or company that provides a warranty
WARRANTS >WARRANT
WARRANTY *n* (document giving) a guarantee
WARRAY *vb* wage war on
WARRAYED >WARRAY
WARRAYING >WARRAY
WARRAYS >WARRAY
WARRE *same as* >WAR
WARRED >WAR
WARREN *n* series of burrows in which rabbits live
WARRENER *n* gamekeeper or keeper of a warren
WARRENERS >WARRENER
WARRENS >WARREN
WARREY *same as* >WARRAY
WARREYED >WARREY
WARREYING >WARREY
WARREYS >WARREY
WARRIGAL *n* dingo ▷ *adj* wild
WARRIGALS >WARRIGAL
WARRING >WAR
WARRIOR *n* person who fights in a war
WARRIORS >WARRIOR
WARRISON *same as* >WARISON
WARRISONS >WARRISON
WARS >WAR
WARSAW *n* type of grouper fish
WARSAWS >WARSAW
WARSHIP *n* ship designed and equipped for naval combat
WARSHIPS >WARSHIP
WARSLE *dialect word for* >WRESTLE
WARSLED >WARSLE
WARSLER >WARSLE
WARSLERS >WARSLE
WARSLES >WARSLE
WARSLING >WARSLE
WARST *obsolete form of* >WORST
WARSTLE *dialect form of* >WRESTLE
WARSTLED >WARSTLE
WARSTLER >WARSTLE
WARSTLERS >WARSTLE
WARSTLES >WARSTLE
WARSTLING >WARSTLE
WART *n* small hard growth on the skin
WARTED >WART
WARTHOG *n* wild African pig with heavy tusks, wartlike lumps on the face, and a mane of coarse hair
WARTHOGS >WARTHOG
WARTIER >WART
WARTIEST >WART
WARTIME *n* time of war ▷ *adj* of or in a time of war
WARTIMES >WARTIME
WARTLESS >WART
WARTLIKE >WART
WARTS >WART
WARTWEED *n* type of plant
WARTWEEDS >WARTWEED
WARTWORT *another word for* >WARTWEED
WARTWORTS >WARTWORT
WARTY >WART
WARWOLF *n* Roman engine of war
WARWOLVES >WARWOLF
WARWORK *n* work contributing to war effort
WARWORKS >WARWORK
WARWORN *adj* worn down by war
WARY *adj* watchful or cautious
WARZONE *n* area where a war is taking place or there is some other violent conflict
WARZONES >WARZONE
WAS *vb* form of the subjunctive mood used in place of *were*, esp in conditional sentences
WASABI *n* Japanese cruciferous plant cultivated for its thick green pungent root
WASABIS >WASABI
WASE *n* pad to relieve pressure of load carried on head
WASES >WASE
WASH *vb* clean (oneself, clothes, etc) with water and usu soap ▷ *n* act or process of washing
WASHABLE *n* thing that can be washed ▷ *adj* (esp of fabrics or clothes) capable of being washed without deteriorating
WASHABLES >WASHABLE
WASHAWAY *another word for* >WASHOUT
WASHAWAYS >WASHAWAY
WASHBALL *n* ball of soap
WASHBALLS >WASHBALL
WASHBASIN *n* basin for washing the face and hands
WASHBOARD *n* board having a surface, usually of corrugated metal, on which esp formerly, clothes were scrubbed
WASHBOWL *same as* >WASHBASIN
WASHBOWLS >WASHBOWL
WASHCLOTH *n* small piece of cloth used to wash the face and hands
WASHDAY *n* day on which clothes and linen are washed, often the same day each week
WASHDAYS >WASHDAY
WASHED >WASH
WASHEN >WASH
WASHER *n* ring put under a nut or bolt or in a tap as a seal ▷ *vb* fit with a washer
WASHERED >WASHER
WASHERIES >WASHERY
WASHERING >WASHER
WASHERMAN *n* man who washes clothes for a living
WASHERMEN >WASHERMAN
WASHERS >WASHER
WASHERY *n* plant at a mine where water or other liquid is used to remove dirt from a mineral, esp coal
WASHES >WASH
WASHHOUSE *n* (formerly) building in which laundry was done
WASHIER >WASHY
WASHIEST >WASHY
WASHILY >WASHY
WASHIN *n* increase in the angle of attack of an aircraft wing towards the wing tip
WASHINESS >WASHY
WASHING *n* clothes to be washed
WASHINGS >WASHING
WASHINS >WASHIN
WASHLAND *n* frequently-flooded plain
WASHLANDS >WASHLAND
WASHOUT *n* complete failure
WASHOUTS >WASHOUT
WASHPOT *n* pot for washing things in
WASHPOTS >WASHPOT
WASHRAG *same as* >WASHCLOTH
WASHRAGS >WASHRAG
WASHROOM *n* toilet
WASHROOMS >WASHROOM
WASHSTAND *n* piece of furniture designed to hold a basin for washing the face and hands in
WASHTUB *n* tub or large container used for washing anything, esp clothes
WASHTUBS >WASHTUB
WASHUP *n* outcome of a process
WASHUPS >WASHUP
WASHWIPE *n* windscreen spray-cleaning mechanism
WASHWIPES >WASHWIPE
WASHWOMAN *n* woman who washes clothes for a living
WASHWOMEN >WASHWOMAN
WASHY *adj* overdiluted or weak
WASM *n* obsolete belief
WASMS >WASM
WASP *n* stinging insect with a slender black-and-yellow striped body
WASPIE *n* tight-waited corset
WASPIER >WASP
WASPIES >WASPIE
WASPIEST >WASP
WASPILY >WASP
WASPINESS >WASP
WASPISH *adj* bad-tempered
WASPISHLY >WASPISH
WASPLIKE >WASP
WASPNEST *n* nest of wasp
WASPNESTS >WASPNEST
WASPS >WASP
WASPY >WASP
WASSAIL *n* formerly, festivity when much drinking took place ▷ *vb* drink health of (a person) at a wassail
WASSAILED >WASSAIL
WASSAILER >WASSAIL
WASSAILRY >WASSAIL
WASSAILS >WASSAIL
WASSERMAN *n* man-shaped sea monster
WASSERMEN >WASSERMAN
WASSUP *sentence substitute* what is happening?
WAST *singular form of the past tense of* >BE
WASTABLE >WASTE
WASTAGE *n* loss by wear or waste
WASTAGES >WASTAGE
WASTE *vb* use pointlessly or thoughtlessly ▷ *n* act of wasting or state of being wasted ▷ *adj* rejected as worthless or surplus to requirements
WASTED >WASTE
WASTEFUL *adj* extravagant
WASTEL *n* fine bread or cake
WASTELAND *n* barren or desolate area of land
WASTELOT *n* piece of waste ground in a city
WASTELOTS >WASTELOT
WASTELS >WASTEL
WASTENESS >WASTE
WASTER *vb* waste ▷ *n* layabout
WASTERED >WASTER
WASTERFUL *Scots variant of* >WASTEFUL
WASTERIE *same as* >WASTERY
WASTERIES >WASTERIE
WASTERING >WASTER
WASTERS >WASTER
WASTERY *n* extravagance

WASTES >WASTE
WASTEWAY *n* open ditch
WASTEWAYS >WASTEWAY
WASTEWEIR *another name for* >SPILLWAY
WASTFULL *obsolete form of* >WASTEFUL
WASTING *adj* reducing the vitality and strength of the body
WASTINGLY >WASTING
WASTINGS >WASTE
WASTNESS *n* obsolete form of wasteness
WASTREL *n* lazy or worthless person
WASTRELS >WASTREL
WASTRIE *same as* >WASTERY
WASTRIES >WASTRIE
WASTRIFE *n* wastefulness
WASTRIFES >WASTRIFE
WASTRY *n* wastefulness
WASTS >WAST
WAT *n* Thai Buddhist monastery or temple
WATAP *n* stringy thread made by Native Americans from the roots of conifers
WATAPE *same as* >WATAP
WATAPES >WATAPE
WATAPS >WATAP
WATCH *vb* look at closely ▷ *n* portable timepiece for the wrist or pocket
WATCHABLE *adj* interesting, enjoyable, or entertaining
WATCHBAND *n* watch strap
WATCHBOX *n* sentry's box
WATCHCASE *n* protective case for a watch, generally of metal such as gold, silver, brass, or gunmetal
WATCHCRY *n* slogan used to rally support
WATCHDOG *n* dog kept to guard property
WATCHDOGS >WATCHDOG
WATCHED >WATCH
WATCHER *n* person who watches
WATCHERS >WATCHER
WATCHES >WATCH
WATCHET *n* shade of blue
WATCHETS >WATCHET
WATCHEYE *n* eye with a light-coloured iris
WATCHEYES >WATCHEYE
WATCHFUL *adj* vigilant or alert
WATCHING >WATCH
WATCHLIST *n* list of things to be monitored
WATCHMAN *n* man employed to guard a building or property
WATCHMEN >WATCHMAN
WATCHOUT *n* lookout
WATCHOUTS >WATCHOUT
WATCHWORD *n* word or phrase that sums up the attitude of a particular group
WATE >WIT
WATER *n* clear colourless tasteless liquid that falls as rain and forms rivers etc ▷ *vb* put water on or into
WATERAGE *n* transportation of cargo by means of ships, or the charges for such transportation
WATERAGES >WATERAGE
WATERBED *n* watertight mattress filled with water
WATERBEDS >WATERBED
WATERBIRD *n* any aquatic bird
WATERBUCK *n* any of various antelopes of the swampy areas of Africa, having long curved ridged horns
WATERBUS *n* boat offering regular transport service
WATERDOG *n* dog trained to hunt in water
WATERDOGS >WATERDOG
WATERED >WATER
WATERER >WATER
WATERERS >WATER
WATERFALL *n* place where the waters of a river drop vertically
WATERFOWL *n* bird that swims on water, such as a duck or swan
WATERHEAD *n* source of river
WATERHEN *another name for* >GALLINULE
WATERHENS >WATERHEN
WATERIER >WATERY
WATERIEST >WATERY
WATERILY >WATERY
WATERING >WATER
WATERINGS >WATER
WATERISH >WATER
WATERJET *n* jet of water
WATERJETS >WATERJET
WATERLEAF *n* carved column design
WATERLESS >WATER
WATERLILY *n* any of various aquatic plants having large leaves and showy flowers that float on the surface of the water
WATERLINE *n* level to which a ship's hull will be immersed when afloat
WATERLOG *vb* flood with water
WATERLOGS >WATERLOG
WATERLOO *n* total defeat
WATERLOOS >WATERLOO
WATERMAN *n* skilled boatman
WATERMARK *n* faint translucent design in a sheet of paper ▷ *vb* mark (paper) with a watermark
WATERMEN >WATERMAN
WATERPOX *n* chickenpox
WATERS >WATER
WATERSHED *n* important period or factor serving as a dividing line
WATERSIDE *n* area of land beside a river or lake
WATERSKI *vb* ski on water towed behind motorboat
WATERSKIS >WATERSKI
WATERWAY *n* river, canal, or other navigable channel used as a means of travel or transport
WATERWAYS >WATERWAY
WATERWEED *n* any of various weedy aquatic plants
WATERWORK *n* machinery, etc for storing, purifying, and distributing water
WATERWORN *adj* worn smooth by the action or passage of water
WATERY *adj* of, like, or containing water
WATERZOOI *n* type of Flemish stew
WATS >WAT
WATT *n* unit of power
WATTAGE *n* electrical power expressed in watts
WATTAGES >WATTAGE
WATTAPE *same as* >WATAP
WATTAPES >WATTAPE
WATTER >WAT
WATTEST >WAT
WATTHOUR *n* unit of energy equal to the power of one watt operating for an hour
WATTHOURS >WATTHOUR
WATTLE *n* branches woven over sticks to make a fence ▷ *adj* made of, formed by, or covered with wattle ▷ *vb* construct from wattle
WATTLED >WATTLE
WATTLES >WATTLE
WATTLESS >WATT
WATTLING >WATTLE
WATTLINGS >WATTLE
WATTMETER *n* meter for measuring electric power in watts
WATTS >WATT
WAUCHT *same as* >WAUGHT
WAUCHTED >WAUCHT
WAUCHTING >WAUCHT
WAUCHTS >WAUCHT
WAUFF *same as* >WAFF
WAUFFED >WAUFF
WAUFFING >WAUFF
WAUFFS >WAUFF
WAUGH *vb* bark
WAUGHED >WAUGH
WAUGHING >WAUGH
WAUGHS >WAUGH
WAUGHT *vb* drink in large amounts
WAUGHTED >WAUGHT
WAUGHTING >WAUGHT
WAUGHTS >WAUGHT
WAUK *vb* full (cloth)
WAUKED >WAUK
WAUKER >WAUK
WAUKERS >WAUK
WAUKING >WAUK
WAUKMILL *same as* >WAULKMILL
WAUKMILLS >WAUKMILL
WAUKRIFE *variant of* >WAKERIFE
WAUKS >WAUK
WAUL *vb* cry or wail plaintively like a cat
WAULED >WAUL
WAULING >WAUL
WAULINGS >WAUL
WAULK *same as* >WAUK
WAULKED >WAULK
WAULKER >WAULK
WAULKERS >WAULK
WAULKING >WAULK
WAULKMILL *n* cloth-fulling mill
WAULKS >WAULK
WAULS >WAUL
WAUR *obsolete form of* >WAR
WAURED >WAUR
WAURING >WAUR
WAURS >WAUR
WAURST >WAUR
WAVE *vb* move the hand to and fro as a greeting or signal ▷ *n* moving ridge on water
WAVEBAND *n* range of wavelengths or frequencies used for a particular type of radio transmission
WAVEBANDS >WAVEBAND
WAVED >WAVE
WAVEFORM *n* shape of the graph of a wave or oscillation obtained by plotting the value of some changing quantity against time
WAVEFORMS >WAVEFORM
WAVEFRONT *n* surface associated with a propagating wave and passing through all points in the wave that have the same phase
WAVEGUIDE *n* solid rod of dielectric or a hollow metal tube, usually of rectangular cross section, used as a path to guide microwaves
WAVELESS >WAVE
WAVELET *n* small wave
WAVELETS >WAVELET
WAVELIKE >WAVE
WAVELLITE *n* greyish-white, yellow, or brown mineral
WAVEMETER *n* instrument for measuring the frequency or wavelength of radio waves
WAVEOFF *n* signal or instruction to an aircraft not to land
WAVEOFFS >WAVEOFF
WAVER *vb* hesitate or be irresolute ▷ *n* act or an instance of wavering
WAVERED >WAVER
WAVERER >WAVER
WAVERERS >WAVER

AVERIER >WAVERY
AVERIEST >WAVERY
AVERING >WAVER
AVERINGS >WAVER
AVEROUS *same as* >WAVERY
AVERS >WAVER
AVERY *adj* lacking firmness
AVES >WAVE
AVESHAPE *another word for* >WAVEFORM
AVESON *n* goods floating on waves after shipwreck
AVESONS >WAVESON
AVEY *n* snow goose or other wild goose
AVEYS >WAVEY
AVICLE *n* origin of wave
AVICLES >WAVICLE
AVIER >WAVY
AVIES >WAVY
AVIEST >WAVY
AVILY >WAVY
AVINESS >WAVY
AVING >WAVE
AVINGS >WAVE
AVY *adj* having curves ▷ *n* snow goose or other wild goose
AW *another name for* >VAV
AWA *n* speech ▷ *vb* speak
AWAED >WAWA
AWAING >WAWA
AWAS >WAWA
AWE *same as* >WAW
AWES >WAWE
AWL *same as* >WAUL
AWLED >WAWL
AWLING >WAWL
AWLINGS >WAWL
AWLS >WAWL
AWS >WAW
AX *n* solid shiny fatty or oily substance used for sealing, making candles, etc ▷ *vb* coat or polish with wax
AXABLE >WAX
AXBERRY *n* waxy fruit of the wax myrtle or the snowberry
AXBILL *n* any of various chiefly African finchlike weaverbirds
AXBILLS >WAXBILL
AXCLOTH *another name for* >OILCLOTH
AXCLOTHS >WAXCLOTH
AXED >WAX
AXEN *adj* made of or like wax
AXER >WAX
AXERS >WAX
AXES >WAX
AXEYE *n* small New Zealand bird with a white circle round its eye
AXEYES >WAXEYE
AXFLOWER *n* any of various plants with waxy flowers
AXIER >WAXY
AXIEST >WAXY
AXILY >WAXY
WAXINESS >WAXY
WAXING >WAX
WAXINGS >WAX
WAXLIKE >WAX
WAXPLANT *n* climbing shrub of E Asia and Australia
WAXPLANTS >WAXPLANT
WAXWEED *n* type of wild flower
WAXWEEDS >WAXWEED
WAXWING *n* type of songbird
WAXWINGS >WAXWING
WAXWORK *n* lifelike wax model of a (famous) person
WAXWORKER >WAXWORK
WAXWORKS >WAXWORK
WAXWORM *n* waxmoth larva
WAXWORMS >WAXWORM
WAXY *adj* resembling wax in colour, appearance, or texture
WAY *n* manner or method ▷ *vb* travel
WAYBILL *n* document stating the nature, origin, and destination of goods being transported
WAYBILLS >WAYBILL
WAYBOARD *n* thin geological seam separating larger strata
WAYBOARDS >WAYBOARD
WAYBREAD *n* plantain
WAYBREADS >WAYBREAD
WAYED >WAY
WAYFARE *vb* travel
WAYFARED >WAYFARE
WAYFARER *n* traveller
WAYFARERS >WAYFARER
WAYFARES >WAYFARE
WAYFARING >WAYFARE
WAYGOING *n* leaving
WAYGOINGS >WAYGOING
WAYGONE *adj* travel-weary
WAYGOOSE *same as* >WAYZGOOSE
WAYGOOSES >WAYGOOSE
WAYING >WAY
WAYLAID >WAYLAY
WAYLAY *vb* lie in wait for and accost or attack
WAYLAYER >WAYLAY
WAYLAYERS >WAYLAY
WAYLAYING >WAYLAY
WAYLAYS >WAYLAY
WAYLEAVE *n* access to property granted by a landowner for payment
WAYLEAVES >WAYLEAVE
WAYLEGGO *interj* away here! let go!
WAYLESS >WAY
WAYMARK *n* symbol or signpost marking the route of a footpath ▷ *vb* mark out with waymarks
WAYMARKED >WAYMARK
WAYMARKS >WAYMARK
WAYMENT *vb* express grief
WAYMENTED >WAYMENT
WAYMENTS >WAYMENT
WAYPOINT *n* stopping point on route
WAYPOINTS >WAYPOINT
WAYPOST *n* signpost
WAYPOSTS >WAYPOST
WAYS >WAY
WAYSIDE *n* side of a road
WAYSIDES >WAYSIDE
WAYWARD *adj* erratic, selfish, or stubborn
WAYWARDLY >WAYWARD
WAYWISER *n* device for measuring distance
WAYWISERS >WAYWISER
WAYWODE *n* Slavonic governor
WAYWODES >WAYWODE
WAYWORN *adj* worn or tired by travel
WAYZGOOSE *n* works outing made annually by a printing house
WAZIR *another word for* >VIZIER
WAZIRS >WAZIR
WAZOO *n* slang word for person's bottom
WAZOOS >WAZOO
WAZZOCK *n* foolish or annoying person
WAZZOCKS >WAZZOCK
WE *pron* speaker or writer and one or more others
WEAK *adj* lacking strength
WEAKEN *vb* make or become weak
WEAKENED >WEAKEN
WEAKENER >WEAKEN
WEAKENERS >WEAKEN
WEAKENING >WEAKEN
WEAKENS >WEAKEN
WEAKER >WEAK
WEAKEST >WEAK
WEAKFISH *n* any of several sea trouts
WEAKISH >WEAK
WEAKISHLY >WEAK
WEAKLIER >WEAKLY
WEAKLIEST >WEAKLY
WEAKLING *n* feeble person or animal
WEAKLINGS >WEAKLING
WEAKLY *adv* feebly ▷ *adj* weak or sickly
WEAKNESS *n* being weak
WEAKON *n* subatomic particle
WEAKONS >WEAKON
WEAKSIDE *n* (in basketball) side of court away from ball
WEAKSIDES >WEAKSIDE
WEAL *n* raised mark left on the skin by a blow
WEALD *n* open or forested country
WEALDS >WEALD
WEALS >WEAL
WEALSMAN *n* statesman
WEALSMEN >WEALSMAN
WEALTH *n* state of being rich
WEALTHIER >WEALTHY
WEALTHILY >WEALTHY
WEALTHS >WEALTH
WEALTHY *adj* possessing wealth
WEAMB *same as* >WAME
WEAMBS >WEAMB
WEAN *vb* accustom (a baby or young mammal) to food other than mother's milk
WEANED >WEAN
WEANEL *n* recently-weaned child or animal
WEANELS >WEANEL
WEANER *n* person or thing that weans
WEANERS >WEANER
WEANING >WEAN
WEANLING *n* child or young animal recently weaned
WEANLINGS >WEANLING
WEANS >WEAN
WEAPON *vb* arm ▷ *n* object used in fighting
WEAPONED >WEAPON
WEAPONEER *n* person associated with the use or maintenance of weapons, esp nuclear weapons
WEAPONING >WEAPON
WEAPONISE *same as* >WEAPONIZE
WEAPONIZE *vb* adapt (a chemical, bacillus, etc) in such a way that it can be used as a weapon
WEAPONRY *n* weapons collectively
WEAPONS >WEAPON
WEAR *vb* have on the body as clothing or ornament ▷ *n* clothes suitable for a particular time or purpose
WEARABLE *adj* suitable for wear or able to be worn ▷ *n* any garment that can be worn
WEARABLES >WEARABLE
WEARED >WEAR
WEARER >WEAR
WEARERS >WEAR
WEARIED >WEARY
WEARIER >WEARY
WEARIES >WEARY
WEARIEST >WEARY
WEARIFUL *same as* >WEARISOME
WEARILESS *adj* not wearied or able to be wearied
WEARILY >WEARY
WEARINESS >WEARY
WEARING *adj* tiring ▷ *n* act of wearing
WEARINGLY >WEARING
WEARINGS >WEAR
WEARISH *adj* withered
WEARISOME *adj* tedious
WEARPROOF *adj* resistant to damage from normal wear or usage
WEARS >WEAR
WEARY *adj* tired or exhausted ▷ *vb* make or become weary
WEARYING >WEARY
WEASAND *former name for the* >TRACHEA

WEASANDS > WEASAND
WEASEL *n* small carnivorous mammal with a long body and short legs ▷ *vb* use ambiguous language to avoid speaking directly or honestly
WEASELED > WEASEL
WEASELER > WEASEL
WEASELERS > WEASEL
WEASELING > WEASEL
WEASELLED > WEASEL
WEASELLER > WEASEL
WEASELLY > WEASEL
WEASELS > WEASEL
WEASELY > WEASEL
WEASON *Scots form of* > WEASAND
WEASONS > WEASON
WEATHER *n* day-to-day atmospheric conditions of a place ▷ *vb* (cause to) be affected by the weather
WEATHERED *adj* affected by exposure to the action of the weather
WEATHERER > WEATHER
WEATHERLY *adj* (of a sailing vessel) making very little leeway when close-hauled, even in a stiff breeze
WEATHERS > WEATHER
WEAVE *vb* make (fabric) by interlacing (yarn) on a loom
WEAVED > WEAVE
WEAVER *n* person who weaves, esp as a means of livelihood
WEAVERS > WEAVER
WEAVES > WEAVE
WEAVING > WEAVE
WEAVINGS > WEAVE
WEAZAND *same as* > WEASAND
WEAZANDS > WEAZAND
WEAZEN *same as* > WIZEN
WEAZENED > WEAZEN
WEAZENING > WEAZEN
WEAZENS > WEAZEN
WEB *n* net spun by a spider ▷ *vb* cover with or as if with a web
WEBBED > WEB
WEBBIE *n* person who is well versed in the use the World Wide Web
WEBBIER > WEBBY
WEBBIES > WEBBIE
WEBBIEST > WEBBY
WEBBING *n* anything that forms a web
WEBBINGS > WEBBING
WEBBY *adj* of, relating to, resembling, or consisting of a web
WEBCAM *n* camera that transmits images over the internet
WEBCAMS > WEBCAM
WEBCAST *n* broadcast of an event over the internet ▷ *vb* make such a broadcast
WEBCASTED > WEBCAST
WEBCASTER > WEBCAST
WEBCASTS > WEBCAST
WEBER *n* SI unit of magnetic flux
WEBERS > WEBER
WEBFED *adj* (of printing press) printing from rolls of paper
WEBFEET > WEBFOOT
WEBFOOT *n* foot having the toes connected by folds of skin
WEBFOOTED > WEBFOOT
WEBINAR *n* interactive seminar conducted over the World Wide Web
WEBINARS > WEBINAR
WEBLESS > WEB
WEBLIKE > WEB
WEBLISH *n* shorthand form of English that is used in text messaging, chat rooms, etc
WEBLISHES > WEBLISH
WEBLOG *n* person's online journal
WEBLOGGER > WEBLOG
WEBLOGS > WEBLOG
WEBMAIL *n* system of electronic mail that allows account holders to access their mail via an internet site rather than downloading it
WEBMAILS > WEBMAIL
WEBMASTER *n* person responsible for the administration of a website on the World Wide Web
WEBPAGE *n* page on website
WEBPAGES > WEBPAGE
WEBS > WEB
WEBSITE *n* group of connected pages on the World Wide Web
WEBSITES > WEBSITE
WEBSTER *archaic word for* > WEAVER
WEBSTERS > WEBSTER
WEBWHEEL *n* wheel containing a plate or web instead of spokes
WEBWHEELS > WEBWHEEL
WEBWORK *n* work done using the World Wide Web
WEBWORKS > WEBWORK
WEBWORM *n* type of caterpillar
WEBWORMS > WEBWORM
WECHT *n* agricultural tool
WECHTS > WECHT
WED *vb* marry
WEDDED > WED
WEDDER *dialect form of* > WEATHER
WEDDERED > WEDDER
WEDDERING > WEDDER
WEDDERS > WEDDER
WEDDING > WED
WEDDINGS > WEDDING
WEDEL *variant of* > WEDELN
WEDELED > WEDEL
WEDELING > WEDEL
WEDELN *n* succession of high-speed turns performed in skiing ▷ *vb* perform a wedeln
WEDELNED > WEDELN
WEDELNING > WEDELN
WEDELNS > WEDELN
WEDELS > WEDEL
WEDGE *n* piece of material thick at one end and thin at the other ▷ *vb* fasten or split with a wedge
WEDGED > WEDGE
WEDGELIKE > WEDGE
WEDGES > WEDGE
WEDGEWISE *adv* in manner of a wedge
WEDGIE *n* wedge-heeled shoe
WEDGIER > WEDGE
WEDGIES > WEDGIE
WEDGIEST > WEDGE
WEDGING > WEDGE
WEDGINGS > WEDGE
WEDGY > WEDGE
WEDLOCK *n* marriage
WEDLOCKS > WEDLOCK
WEDS > WED
WEE *adj* small or short ▷ *n* instance of urinating ▷ *vb* urinate
WEED *n* plant growing where undesired ▷ *vb* clear of weeds
WEEDED > WEED
WEEDER > WEED
WEEDERIES > WEEDERY
WEEDERS > WEED
WEEDERY *n* weed-ridden area
WEEDICIDE *n* weed-killer
WEEDIER > WEEDY
WEEDIEST > WEEDY
WEEDILY > WEEDY
WEEDINESS > WEEDY
WEEDING > WEED
WEEDINGS > WEED
WEEDLESS > WEED
WEEDLIKE > WEED
WEEDS *pl n* widow's mourning clothes
WEEDY *adj* (of a person) thin and weak
WEEING > WEE
WEEK *n* period of seven days, esp one beginning on a Sunday ▷ *adv* seven days before or after a specified day
WEEKDAY *n* any day of the week except Saturday or Sunday
WEEKDAYS > WEEKDAY
WEEKE *same as* > WICK
WEEKEND *n* Saturday and Sunday ▷ *vb* spend or pass a weekend
WEEKENDED > WEEKEND
WEEKENDER *n* person spending a weekend holiday in a place, esp habitually
WEEKENDS *adv* at the weekend, esp regularly or during every weekend
WEEKES > WEEKE
WEEKLIES > WEEKLY
WEEKLONG *adj* lasting a week
WEEKLY *adv* happening, done, etc once a week ▷ *n* newspaper or magazine published once a week ▷ *adj* happening once a week or every week
WEEKNIGHT *n* evening or night of a weekday
WEEKS > WEEK
WEEL *Scot word for* > WELL
WEELS > WEEL
WEEM *n* underground home
WEEMS > WEEM
WEEN *vb* think or imagine (something)
WEENED > WEEN
WEENIE *adj* very small ▷ *n* wiener
WEENIER > WEENY
WEENIES > WEENIE
WEENIEST > WEENY
WEENING > WEEN
WEENS > WEEN
WEENSIER > WEENSY
WEENSIEST > WEENSY
WEENSY *same as* > WEENY
WEENY *adj* very small
WEEP *vb* shed tears ▷ *n* spell of weeping
WEEPER *n* person who weeps, esp a hired mourner
WEEPERS > WEEPER
WEEPHOLE *n* small drain hole in wall
WEEPHOLES > WEEPHOLE
WEEPIE *same as* > WEEPY
WEEPIER > WEEPY
WEEPIES > WEEPY
WEEPIEST > WEEPY
WEEPILY > WEEPY
WEEPINESS > WEEPY
WEEPING *adj* (of plants) having slender hanging branches
WEEPINGLY > WEEPING
WEEPINGS > WEEPING
WEEPS > WEEP
WEEPY *adj* liable to cry ▷ *n* sentimental film or book
WEER > WEE
WEES > WEE
WEEST > WEE
WEET *dialect form of* > WET
WEETE *same as* > WIT
WEETED > WEETE
WEETEN *same as* > WIT
WEETER > WEET
WEETEST > WEET
WEETING > WEET
WEETINGLY > WEET
WEETLESS *obsolete variant of* > WITLESS
WEETS > WEET
WEEVER *n* type of small fish
WEEVERS > WEEVER

EEVIL *n* small beetle that eats grain etc
EEVILED *same as* >WEEVILLED
EEVILLED *adj* weevil-ridden
EEVILLY *another word for* >WEEVILLED
EEVILS >WEEVIL
EEVILY *another word for* >WEEVILLED
EEWEE *vb* urinate
EEWEED >WEEWEE
EEWEEING >WEEWEE
EEWEES >WEEWEE
EFT *n* cross threads in weaving ▷ *vb* form weft
EFTAGE *n* texture
EFTAGES >WEFTAGE
EFTE *n* forsaken child
EFTED >WEFT
EFTES >WEFTE
EFTING >WEFT
EFTS >WEFT
EFTWISE *adv* in the direction of the weft
EID *n* sudden illness
EIDS >WEID
EIGELA *n* type of shrub
EIGELAS >WEIGELA
EIGELIA *same as* >WEIGELA
EIGELIAS >WEIGELIA
EIGH *vb* have a specified weight
EIGHABLE >WEIGH
EIGHAGE *n* duty paid for weighing goods
EIGHAGES >WEIGHAGE
EIGHED >WEIGH
EIGHER >WEIGH
EIGHERS >WEIGH
EIGHING >WEIGH
EIGHINGS >WEIGH
EIGHMAN *n* person responsible for weighing goods
EIGHMEN >WEIGHMAN
EIGHS >WEIGH
EIGHT *n* heaviness of an object ▷ *vb* add weight to
EIGHTED >WEIGHT
EIGHTER >WEIGHT
EIGHTERS >WEIGHT
EIGHTIER >WEIGHTY
EIGHTILY >WEIGHTY
EIGHTING *n* extra allowance paid in special circumstances
EIGHTS >WEIGHT
EIGHTY *adj* important or serious
EIL *n* whirlpool
EILS >WEIL
EINER *same as* >WIENER
EINERS >WEINER
EIR *vb* ward off ▷ *n* river dam
EIRD *adj* strange or bizarre ▷ *vb* warn beforehand
EIRDED >WEIRD
EIRDER >WEIRD
EIRDEST >WEIRD
WEIRDIE *same as* >WEIRDO
WEIRDIES >WEIRDIE
WEIRDING >WEIRD
WEIRDLY >WEIRD
WEIRDNESS >WEIRD
WEIRDO *n* peculiar person
WEIRDOES >WEIRDO
WEIRDOS >WEIRDO
WEIRDS >WEIRD
WEIRDY *n* weird person
WEIRED >WEIR
WEIRING >WEIR
WEIRS >WEIR
WEISE *same as* >WISE
WEISED >WEISE
WEISES >WEISE
WEISING >WEISE
WEIZE *same as* >WISE
WEIZED >WEIZE
WEIZES >WEIZE
WEIZING >WEIZE
WEKA *n* flightless New Zealand rail
WEKAS >WEKA
WELAWAY *same as* >WELLAWAY
WELCH *same as* >WELSH
WELCHED >WELCH
WELCHER >WELCH
WELCHERS >WELCH
WELCHES >WELCH
WELCHING >WELCH
WELCOME *vb* greet with pleasure ▷ *n* kindly greeting ▷ *adj* received gladly
WELCOMED >WELCOME
WELCOMELY >WELCOME
WELCOMER >WELCOME
WELCOMERS >WELCOME
WELCOMES >WELCOME
WELCOMING >WELCOME
WELD *vb* join (pieces of metal or plastic) by softening with heat ▷ *n* welded joint
WELDABLE >WELD
WELDED >WELD
WELDER >WELD
WELDERS >WELD
WELDING >WELD
WELDINGS >WELD
WELDLESS >WELD
WELDMENT *n* unit composed of welded pieces
WELDMENTS >WELDMENT
WELDMESH *n* type of metal fencing
WELDOR >WELD
WELDORS >WELDOR
WELDS >WELD
WELFARE *n* wellbeing
WELFARES >WELFARE
WELFARISM *n* policies or attitudes associated with a welfare state
WELFARIST >WELFARISM
WELK *vb* wither; dry up
WELKE *obsolete form of* >WELK
WELKED >WELK
WELKES >WELKE
WELKIN *n* sky, heavens, or upper air
WELKING >WELK
WELKINS >WELKIN
WELKS >WELK
WELKT *adj* twisted
WELL *adv* satisfactorily ▷ *adj* in good health ▷ *interj* exclamation of surprise, interrogation, etc ▷ *n* hole sunk into the earth to reach water, oil, or gas ▷ *vb* flow upwards or outwards
WELLADAY *interj* alas
WELLADAYS *interj* alas
WELLANEAR *interj* alas
WELLAWAY *interj* alas!
WELLAWAYS *interj* alas
WELLBEING *n* state of being well, happy, or prosperous
WELLBORN *adj* having been born into a wealthy family
WELLCURB *n* stone surround at top of well
WELLCURBS >WELLCURB
WELLDOER *n* moral person
WELLDOERS >WELLDOER
WELLED >WELL
WELLHEAD *n* source of a well or stream
WELLHEADS >WELLHEAD
WELLHOLE *n* well shaft
WELLHOLES >WELLHOLE
WELLHOUSE *n* housing for well
WELLIE *n* wellington boot
WELLIES >WELLY
WELLING >WELL
WELLINGS >WELL
WELLNESS *n* state of being in good physical and mental health
WELLS >WELL
WELLSITE *n* site of well
WELLSITES >WELLSITE
WELLY *n* energy or commitment
WELSH *vb* fail to pay a debt or fulfil an obligation
WELSHED >WELSH
WELSHER >WELSH
WELSHERS >WELSH
WELSHES >WELSH
WELSHING >WELSH
WELT *same as* >WEAL
WELTED >WELT
WELTER *n* jumbled mass ▷ *vb* roll about, writhe, or wallow
WELTERED >WELTER
WELTERING >WELTER
WELTERS >WELTER
WELTING >WELT
WELTINGS >WELT
WELTS >WELT
WEM *same as* >WAME
WEMB *same as* >WAME
WEMBS >WEMB
WEMS >WEM
WEN *n* cyst on the scalp
WENA *n* South African word for you
WENCH *n* young woman ▷ *vb* frequent the company of prostitutes
WENCHED >WENCH
WENCHER >WENCH
WENCHERS >WENCH
WENCHES >WENCH
WENCHING >WENCH
WEND *vb* go or travel
WENDED >WEND
WENDIGO *n* evil spirit or cannibal
WENDIGOS >WENDIGO
WENDING >WEND
WENDS >WEND
WENGE *n* type of tree found in central and West Africa
WENGES >WENGE
WENNIER >WEN
WENNIEST >WEN
WENNISH >WEN
WENNY >WEN
WENS >WEN
WENT *n* path
WENTS >WENT
WEPT >WEEP
WERE *vb* form of the past tense of **be** used after *we*, *you*, *they*, or a plural noun
WEREGILD *same as* >WERGILD
WEREGILDS >WEREGILD
WEREWOLF *n* (in folklore) person who can turn into a wolf
WERGELD *same as* >WERGILD
WERGELDS >WERGELD
WERGELT *same as* >WERGELD
WERGELTS >WERGELT
WERGILD *n* price set on a man's life in successive Anglo-Saxon and Germanic law codes, to be paid as compensation by his slayer
WERGILDS >WERGILD
WERNERITE *another name for* >SCAPOLITE
WERO *n* challenge made by an armed Māori warrior to a visitor to a marae
WEROS >WERO
WERRIS *slang word for* >URINATION
WERRISES >WERRIS
WERSH *adj* tasteless
WERSHER >WERSH
WERSHEST >WERSH
WERT *singular form of the past tense of* >BE
WERWOLF *same as* >WEREWOLF
WERWOLVES >WERWOLF
WESAND *same as* >WEASAND
WESANDS >WESAND
WESKIT *informal word for* >WAISTCOAT
WESKITS >WESKIT
WESSAND *same as* >WEASAND
WESSANDS >WESSAND
WEST *n* part of the horizon where the sun sets ▷ *adj* or in the west ▷ *adv* in, to, or towards the west ▷ *vb* move in westerly direction

WESTBOUND *adj* going towards the west
WESTED > WEST
WESTER *vb* move or appear to move towards the west ▷ *n* strong wind or storm from the west
WESTERED > WESTER
WESTERING > WESTER
WESTERLY *adj* of or in the west ▷ *adv* towards the west ▷ *n* wind blowing from the west
WESTERN *adj* of or in the west ▷ *n* film or story about cowboys in the western US
WESTERNER *n* person from the west of a country or area
WESTERNS > WESTERN
WESTERS > WESTER
WESTIE *n* informal word for a young working-class person from the western suburbs of Sydney
WESTIES > WESTIE
WESTING *n* movement, deviation, or distance covered in a westerly direction
WESTINGS > WESTING
WESTLIN *Scots word for* > WESTERN
WESTLINS *adv* to or in west
WESTMOST *adj* most western
WESTS > WEST
WESTWARD *adv* towards the west ▷ *n* westward part or direction ▷ *adj* moving, facing, or situated in the west
WESTWARDS *same as* > WESTWARD
WET *adj* covered or soaked with water or another liquid ▷ *n* moisture or rain ▷ *vb* make wet
WETA *n* type of wingless insect
WETAS > WETA
WETBACK *n* Mexican labourer who enters the US illegally
WETBACKS > WETBACK
WETHER *n* male sheep, esp a castrated one
WETHERS > WETHER
WETLAND *n* area of marshy land
WETLANDS > WETLAND
WETLY > WET
WETNESS > WET
WETNESSES > WET
WETPROOF *adj* waterproof
WETS > WET
WETSUIT *n* body suit for diving
WETSUITS > WETSUIT
WETTABLE > WET
WETTED > WET
WETTER > WET
WETTERS > WET
WETTEST > WET
WETTIE *n* wetsuit
WETTIES > WETTIE
WETTING > WET
WETTINGS > WET
WETTISH > WET
WETWARE *n* humorous term for the brain
WETWARES > WETWARE
WEX *obsolete form of* > WAX
WEXE *obsolete form of* > WAX
WEXED > WEX
WEXES > WEX
WEXING > WEX
WEY *n* measurement of weight
WEYARD *obsolete form of* > WEIRD
WEYS > WEY
WEYWARD *obsolete form of* > WEIRD
WEZAND *obsolete form of* > WEASAND
WEZANDS > WEZAND
WHA *Scot word for* > WHO
WHACK *vb* strike with a resounding blow ▷ *n* such a blow
WHACKED > WHACK
WHACKER > WHACK
WHACKERS > WHACK
WHACKIER > WHACKY
WHACKIEST > WHACKY
WHACKING *adj* huge ▷ *n* severe beating ▷ *adv* extremely
WHACKINGS > WHACKING
WHACKO *n* mad person
WHACKOES > WHACKO
WHACKOS > WHACKO
WHACKS > WHACK
WHACKY *variant spelling of* > WACKY
WHAE *same as* > WHA
WHAISLE *Scots form of* > WHEEZE
WHAISLED > WHAISLE
WHAISLES > WHAISLE
WHAISLING > WHAISLE
WHAIZLE *same as* > WHAISLE
WHAIZLED > WHAIZLE
WHAIZLES > WHAIZLE
WHAIZLING > WHAIZLE
WHAKAIRO *n* art of carving
WHAKAIROS > WHAKAIRO
WHAKAPAPA *n* genealogy
WHALE *n* large fish-shaped sea mammal ▷ *vb* hunt for whales
WHALEBACK *n* something shaped like the back of a whale
WHALEBOAT *n* narrow boat from 20 to 30 feet long having a sharp prow and stern, formerly used in whaling
WHALEBONE *n* horny substance hanging from the upper jaw of toothless whales
WHALED > WHALE
WHALELIKE > WHALE
WHALEMAN *n* person employed in whaling
WHALEMEN > WHALEMAN
WHALER *n* ship or person involved in whaling
WHALERIES > WHALERY
WHALERS > WHALER
WHALERY *n* whaling
WHALES > WHALE
WHALING *n* hunting of whales for food and oil ▷ *adv* extremely
WHALINGS > WHALING
WHALLY *adj* (of eyes) with light-coloured irises
WHAM *interj* expression indicating suddenness or forcefulness ▷ *n* forceful blow or impact or the sound produced by such a blow or impact ▷ *vb* strike or cause to strike with great force
WHAMMED > WHAM
WHAMMIES > WHAMMY
WHAMMING > WHAM
WHAMMO *n* sound of a sudden collision
WHAMMOS > WHAMMO
WHAMMY *n* devastating setback
WHAMO *same as* > WHAMMO
WHAMPLE *n* strike
WHAMPLES > WHAMPLE
WHAMS > WHAM
WHANAU *n* (in Māori societies) a family, esp an extended family
WHANAUS > WHANAU
WHANG *vb* strike or be struck so as to cause a resounding noise ▷ *n* resounding noise produced by a heavy blow
WHANGAM *n* imaginary creature
WHANGAMS > WHANGAM
WHANGED > WHANG
WHANGEE *n* tall woody grass grown for its stems, which are used for bamboo canes
WHANGEES > WHANGEE
WHANGING > WHANG
WHANGS > WHANG
WHAP *same as* > WHOP
WHAPPED > WHAP
WHAPPER *same as* > WHOPPER
WHAPPERS > WHAPPER
WHAPPING > WHAP
WHAPS > WHAP
WHARE *n* Māori hut or dwelling place
WHARENUI *n* (in New Zealand) meeting house
WHARENUIS > WHARENUI
WHAREPUNI *n* (in a Māori community) a tall carved building used as a guesthouse
WHARES > WHARE
WHARF *n* platform at a harbour for loading and unloading ships ▷ *vb* put (goods, etc) on a wharf
WHARFAGE *n* accommodation for ships at wharves
WHARFAGES > WHARFAGE
WHARFED > WHARF
WHARFIE *n* person employed to load and unload ships
WHARFIES > WHARFIE
WHARFING > WHARF
WHARFINGS > WHARF
WHARFS > WHARF
WHARVE *n* wooden disc or wheel on a shaft serving as a flywheel or pulley
WHARVES > WHARVE
WHAT *pron* which thing ▷ *interj* exclamation of anger, surprise, etc ▷ *adv* in which way, how much ▷ *n* part; portion
WHATA *n* building on stilts or a raised platform for storing provisions
WHATAS > WHATA
WHATEN *adj* what; what kind of
WHATEVER *pron* everything or anything that ▷ *adj* intensive form of *what* ▷ *determiner* intensive form of *what* ▷ *interj* expression used to show indifference or dismissal
WHATNA *another word for* > WHATEN
WHATNESS *n* what something is
WHATNOT *n* similar unspecified thing
WHATNOTS > WHATNOT
WHATS > WHAT
WHATSIS *US form of* > WHATSIT
WHATSISES > WHATSIS
WHATSIT *n* person or thing the name of which is unknown, temporarily forgotten, or deliberately overlooked
WHATSITS > WHATSIT
WHATSO *n* of whatever kind
WHATTEN *same as* > WHATEN
WHAUP *n* curlew
WHAUPS > WHAUP
WHAUR *Scot word for* > WHERE
WHAURS > WHAUR
WHEAL *same as* > WEAL
WHEALS > WHEAL
WHEAR *obsolete variant of* > WHERE
WHEARE *obsolete variant of* > WHERE
WHEAT *n* grain used in making flour, bread, and pasta
WHEATEAR *n* small songbird
WHEATEARS > WHEATEAR
WHEATEN *n* type of dog ▷ *adj* made of the grain or flour of wheat
WHEATENS > WHEATEN
WHEATIER > WHEATY

IEATIEST >WHEATY
IEATLAND *n* region where wheat is grown
IEATLESS >WHEAT
IEATMEAL *n* brown, but not wholemeal, flour
IEATS >WHEAT
IEATWORM *n* parasitic nematode worm that forms galls in the seeds of wheat
IEATY *adj* having a wheat-like taste
IEE *interj* exclamation of joy, thrill, etc
IEECH *vb* move quickly
IEECHED >WHEECH
IEECHING >WHEECH
IEECHS >WHEECH
IEEDLE *vb* coax or cajole
IEEDLED >WHEEDLE
IEEDLER >WHEEDLE
IEEDLERS >WHEEDLE
IEEDLES >WHEEDLE
IEEDLING >WHEEDLE
IEEL *n* disc that revolves on an axle ▷ *vb* push or pull (something with wheels)
IEELBASE *n* distance between a vehicle's front and back axles
IEELED *adj* having or equipped with a wheel or wheels
IEELER *n* horse or other draught animal nearest the wheel
IEELERS >WHEELER
IEELIE *n* manoeuvre on a bike in which the front wheel is raised off the ground
IEELIER >WHEELY
IEELIES >WHEELIE
IEELIEST >WHEELY
IEELING >WHEEL
IEELINGS >WHEEL
IEELLESS *adj* having no wheels
IEELMAN *n* helmsman
IEELMEN >WHEELMAN
IEELS >WHEEL
IEELSMAN *same as* >WHEELMAN
IEELSMEN >WHEELSMAN
IEELWORK *n* arrangement of wheels in a machine, esp a train of gears
IEELY *adj* resembling a wheel
IEEN *n* few
IEENGE *Scots form of* >WHINGE
IEENGED >WHEENGE
IEENGES >WHEENGE
IEENGING >WHEENGE
IEENS >WHEEN
IEEP *vb* fly quickly and lightly
IEEPED >WHEEP
IEEPING >WHEEP
IEEPLE *vb* whistle weakly
IEEPLED >WHEEPLE
WHEEPLES >WHEEPLE
WHEEPLING >WHEEPLE
WHEEPS >WHEEP
WHEESH *vb* silence (a person, noise, etc) or be silenced
WHEESHED >WHEESH
WHEESHES >WHEESH
WHEESHING >WHEESH
WHEESHT *same as* >WHEESH
WHEESHTED >WHEESHT
WHEESHTS >WHEESHT
WHEEZE *vb* breathe with a hoarse whistling noise ▷ *n* wheezing sound
WHEEZED >WHEEZE
WHEEZER >WHEEZE
WHEEZERS >WHEEZE
WHEEZES >WHEEZE
WHEEZIER >WHEEZE
WHEEZIEST >WHEEZE
WHEEZILY >WHEEZE
WHEEZING >WHEEZE
WHEEZINGS >WHEEZE
WHEEZLE *vb* make hoarse breathing sound
WHEEZLED >WHEEZLE
WHEEZLES >WHEEZLE
WHEEZLING >WHEEZLE
WHEEZY >WHEEZE
WHEFT *same as* >WAFT
WHEFTS >WHEFT
WHELK *n* edible snail-like shellfish
WHELKED *adj* having or covered with whelks
WHELKIER >WHELK
WHELKIEST >WHELK
WHELKS >WHELK
WHELKY >WHELK
WHELM *vb* engulf entirely with or as if with water
WHELMED >WHELM
WHELMING >WHELM
WHELMS >WHELM
WHELP *n* pup or cub ▷ *vb* (of an animal) give birth
WHELPED >WHELP
WHELPING >WHELP
WHELPLESS >WHELP
WHELPS >WHELP
WHEMMLE *vb* overturn
WHEMMLED >WHEMMLE
WHEMMLES >WHEMMLE
WHEMMLING >WHEMMLE
WHEN *adv* at what time? ▷ *pron* at which time ▷ *n* question of when
WHENAS *conj* while; inasamuch as
WHENCE *n* point of origin ▷ *adv* from what place or source ▷ *pron* from what place, cause, or origin
WHENCES >WHENCE
WHENCEVER *adv* out of whatsoever place, cause or origin
WHENEVER *adv* at whatever time
WHENS >WHEN
WHENUA *n* land
WHENUAS >WHENUA
WHENWE *n* White immigrant from Zimbabwe, caricatured as being tiresomely over-reminiscent of happier times
WHENWES >WHENWE
WHERE *adv* in, at, or to what place? ▷ *pron* in, at, or to which place ▷ *n* question as to the position, direction, or destination of something
WHEREAS *n* testimonial introduced by whereas
WHEREASES >WHEREAS
WHEREAT *adv* at or to which place
WHEREBY *pron* by which ▷ *adv* how? by what means?
WHEREFOR *adv* for which
WHEREFORE *adv* why ▷ *n* explanation or reason
WHEREFROM *adv* from what or where? whence? ▷ *pron* from which place
WHEREIN *adv* in what place or respect? ▷ *pron* in which place or thing
WHEREINTO *adv* into what place? ▷ *pron* into which place
WHERENESS *n* state of having a place
WHEREOF *adv* of what or which person or thing? ▷ *pron* of which person or thing
WHEREON *adv* on what thing or place? ▷ *pron* on which thing, place, etc
WHEREOUT *adv* out of which
WHERES >WHERE
WHERESO *adv* in or to unspecified place
WHERETO *adv* towards what (place, end, etc)? ▷ *pron* which
WHEREUNTO *same as* >WHERETO
WHEREUPON *adv* upon what?
WHEREVER *adv* at whatever place ▷ *pron* at, in, or to every place or point which
WHEREWITH *pron* with or by which ▷ *adv* with what?
WHERRET *vb* strike (someone) a blow ▷ *n* blow, esp a slap on the face
WHERRETED >WHERRET
WHERRETS >WHERRET
WHERRIED >WHERRY
WHERRIES >WHERRY
WHERRIT *vb* worry or cause to worry
WHERRITED >WHERRIT
WHERRITS >WHERRIT
WHERRY *n* any of certain kinds of half-decked commercial boats, such as barges, used in Britain ▷ *vb* travel in a wherry
WHERRYING >WHERRY
WHERRYMAN >WHERRY
WHERRYMEN >WHERRY
WHERVE *same as* >WHARVE
WHERVES >WHERVE
WHET *vb* sharpen (a tool) ▷ *n* act of whetting
WHETHER *conj* used to introduce any indirect question
WHETS >WHET
WHETSTONE *n* stone for sharpening tools
WHETTED >WHET
WHETTER >WHET
WHETTERS >WHET
WHETTING >WHET
WHEUGH *same as* >WHEW
WHEUGHED >WHEUGH
WHEUGHING >WHEUGH
WHEUGHS >WHEUGH
WHEW *interj* exclamation expressing relief, delight, etc ▷ *vb* express relief
WHEWED >WHEW
WHEWING >WHEW
WHEWS >WHEW
WHEY *n* watery liquid that separates from the curd when milk is clotted
WHEYEY >WHEY
WHEYFACE *n* pale bloodless face
WHEYFACED >WHEYFACE
WHEYFACES >WHEYFACE
WHEYIER >WHEY
WHEYIEST >WHEY
WHEYISH >WHEY
WHEYLIKE >WHEY
WHEYS >WHEY
WHICH *pron* used to request or refer to a choice from different possibilities ▷ *adj* used with a noun in requesting that the particular thing being referred to is further identified or distinguished
WHICHEVER *pron* any out of several ▷ *adj* any out of several ▷ *determiner* any (one, two, etc, out of several)
WHICKER *vb* (of a horse) to whinny or neigh
WHICKERED >WHICKER
WHICKERS >WHICKER
WHID *vb* move quickly
WHIDAH *same as* >WHYDAH
WHIDAHS >WHIDAH
WHIDDED >WHID
WHIDDER *vb* move with force
WHIDDERED >WHIDDER
WHIDDERS >WHIDDER
WHIDDING >WHID
WHIDS >WHID
WHIFF *n* puff of air or odour ▷ *vb* come, convey, or go in whiffs
WHIFFED >WHIFF
WHIFFER >WHIFF
WHIFFERS >WHIFF
WHIFFET *n* insignificant person

WHIFFETS > WHIFFET
WHIFFIER > WHIFFY
WHIFFIEST > WHIFFY
WHIFFING > WHIFF
WHIFFINGS > WHIFF
WHIFFLE *vb* think or behave in an erratic or unpredictable way
WHIFFLED > WHIFFLE
WHIFFLER *n* person who whiffles
WHIFFLERS > WHIFFLER
WHIFFLERY *n* frivolity
WHIFFLES > WHIFFLE
WHIFFLING > WHIFFLE
WHIFFS > WHIFF
WHIFFY *adj* smelly
WHIFT *n* brief emission of air
WHIFTS > WHIFT
WHIG *vb* go quickly
WHIGGED > WHIG
WHIGGING > WHIG
WHIGS > WHIG
WHILE *n* period of time
WHILED > WHILE
WHILERE *adv* a while ago
WHILES *adv* at times
WHILING > WHILE
WHILK *archaic and dialect word for* > WHICH
WHILLIED > WHILLY
WHILLIES > WHILLY
WHILLY *vb* influence by flattery
WHILLYING > WHILLY
WHILLYWHA *variant of* > WHILLY
WHILOM *adv* formerly ▷ *adj* one-time
WHILST *same as* > WHILE
WHIM *n* sudden fancy ▷ *vb* have a whim
WHIMBERRY *n* whortleberry
WHIMBREL *n* small European curlew with a striped head
WHIMBRELS > WHIMBREL
WHIMMED > WHIM
WHIMMIER > WHIMMY
WHIMMIEST > WHIMMY
WHIMMING > WHIM
WHIMMY *adj* having whims
WHIMPER *vb* cry in a soft whining way ▷ *n* soft plaintive whine
WHIMPERED > WHIMPER
WHIMPERER > WHIMPER
WHIMPERS > WHIMPER
WHIMPLE *same as* > WIMPLE
WHIMPLED > WHIMPLE
WHIMPLES > WHIMPLE
WHIMPLING > WHIMPLE
WHIMS > WHIM
WHIMSEY *same as* > WHIMSY
WHIMSEYS > WHIMSEY
WHIMSICAL *adj* unusual, playful, and fanciful
WHIMSIED > WHIMSY
WHIMSIER > WHIMSY
WHIMSIES > WHIMSY
WHIMSIEST > WHIMSY
WHIMSILY > WHIMSY
WHIMSY *n* capricious idea ▷ *adj* quaint, comical, or unusual, often in a tasteless way
WHIN *n* gorse
WHINBERRY *same as* > WHIMBERRY
WHINCHAT *n* type of songbird
WHINCHATS > WHINCHAT
WHINE *n* high-pitched plaintive cry ▷ *vb* make such a sound
WHINED > WHINE
WHINER > WHINE
WHINERS > WHINE
WHINES > WHINE
WHINEY *same as* > WHINY
WHINGDING *same as* > WINGDING
WHINGE *vb* complain ▷ *n* complaint
WHINGED > WHINGE
WHINGEING > WHINGE
WHINGER > WHINGE
WHINGERS > WHINGE
WHINGES > WHINGE
WHINGING > WHINGE
WHINIARD *same as* > WHINYARD
WHINIARDS > WHINIARD
WHINIER > WHINY
WHINIEST > WHINY
WHININESS > WHINY
WHINING > WHINE
WHININGLY > WHINE
WHININGS > WHINE
WHINNIED > WHINNY
WHINNIER > WHINNY
WHINNIES > WHINNY
WHINNIEST > WHINNY
WHINNY *vb* neigh softly ▷ *n* soft neigh ▷ *adj* covered in whin
WHINNYING > WHINNY
WHINS > WHIN
WHINSTONE *n* any dark hard fine-grained rock, such as basalt
WHINY *adj* high-pitched and plaintive
WHINYARD *n* sword
WHINYARDS > WHINYARD
WHIO *n* New Zealand mountain duck with blue plumage
WHIP *n* cord attached to a handle, used for beating animals or people ▷ *vb* strike with a whip, strap, or cane
WHIPBIRD *n* any of several birds having a whistle ending in a whipcrack note
WHIPBIRDS > WHIPBIRD
WHIPCAT *n* tailor
WHIPCATS > WHIPCAT
WHIPCORD *n* strong worsted or cotton fabric with a diagonally ribbed surface
WHIPCORDS > WHIPCORD
WHIPCORDY *adj* whipcord-like
WHIPJACK *n* beggar imitating a sailor
WHIPJACKS > WHIPJACK
WHIPLASH *n* quick lash of a whip
WHIPLIKE > WHIP
WHIPPED > WHIP
WHIPPER > WHIP
WHIPPERS > WHIP
WHIPPET *n* racing dog like a small greyhound
WHIPPETS > WHIPPET
WHIPPIER > WHIPPY
WHIPPIEST > WHIPPY
WHIPPING > WHIP
WHIPPINGS > WHIP
WHIPPY *adj* springy
WHIPRAY *n* stingray
WHIPRAYS > WHIPRAY
WHIPS > WHIP
WHIPSAW *n* any saw with a flexible blade, such as a bandsaw ▷ *vb* saw with a whipsaw
WHIPSAWED > WHIPSAW
WHIPSAWN > WHIPSAW
WHIPSAWS > WHIPSAW
WHIPSNAKE *n* thin snake like leather whip
WHIPSTAFF *n* ship's steering bar
WHIPSTALL *n* stall in which an aircraft goes into a nearly vertical climb, pauses, slips backwards momentarily, and drops suddenly with its nose down
WHIPSTER *n* insignificant but pretentious or cheeky person, esp a young one
WHIPSTERS > WHIPSTER
WHIPSTOCK *n* handle of a whip
WHIPT *old past tense of* > WHIP
WHIPTAIL *n* type of lizard
WHIPTAILS > WHIPTAIL
WHIPWORM *n* parasitic worm living in the intestines of mammals
WHIPWORMS > WHIPWORM
WHIR *n* prolonged soft swish or buzz, as of a motor working or wings flapping ▷ *vb* make or cause to make a whir
WHIRL *vb* spin or revolve ▷ *n* whirling movement
WHIRLBAT *n* thing moved with a whirl
WHIRLBATS > WHIRLBAT
WHIRLED > WHIRL
WHIRLER > WHIRL
WHIRLERS > WHIRL
WHIRLIER > WHIRLY
WHIRLIES *n* illness induced by excessive use of alcohol or drugs
WHIRLIEST > WHIRLY
WHIRLIGIG *same as* > WINDMILL
WHIRLING > WHIRL
WHIRLINGS > WHIRL
WHIRLPOOL *n* strong circular current of water
WHIRLS > WHIRL
WHIRLWIND *n* column of air whirling violently upwards in a spiral ▷ *adj* much quicker than norma
WHIRLY *adj* characterized by whirling
WHIRR *same as* > WHIR
WHIRRED > WHIR
WHIRRET *vb* strike with sharp blow
WHIRRETED > WHIRRET
WHIRRETS > WHIRRET
WHIRRIED > WHIRRY
WHIRRIES > WHIRRY
WHIRRING > WHIR
WHIRRINGS > WHIR
WHIRRS > WHIRR
WHIRRY *vb* move quickly
WHIRRYING > WHIRRY
WHIRS > WHIR
WHIRTLE *same as* > WORTLE
WHIRTLES > WHIRTLE
WHISH *less common word for* > SWISH
WHISHED > WHISH
WHISHES > WHISH
WHISHING > WHISH
WHISHT *interj* hush! be quiet! ▷ *adj* silent or still ▷ *vb* make or become silent
WHISHTED > WHISHT
WHISHTING > WHISHT
WHISHTS > WHISHT
WHISK *vb* move or remove quickly ▷ *n* quick movement
WHISKED > WHISK
WHISKER *n* any of the long stiff hairs on the face of a cat or other mammal
WHISKERED *adj* having whiskers
WHISKERS > WHISKER
WHISKERY *adj* having whiskers
WHISKET *same as* > WISKET
WHISKETS > WHISKET
WHISKEY *n* Irish or American whisky
WHISKEYS > WHISKEY
WHISKIES > WHISKY
WHISKING > WHISK
WHISKS > WHISK
WHISKY *n* spirit distilled from fermented cereals
WHISPER *vb* speak softly, without vibration of the vocal cords ▷ *n* soft voice
WHISPERED > WHISPER
WHISPERER *n* person or thing that whispers
WHISPERS > WHISPER
WHISPERY > WHISPER
WHISS *vb* hiss
WHISSED > WHISS
WHISSES > WHISS
WHISSING > WHISS
WHIST *same as* > WHISHT
WHISTED > WHIST
WHISTING > WHIST

ISTLE *vb* produce a shrill sound, esp by forcing the breath through pursed lips ▷ *n* whistling sound
ISTLED > WHISTLE
ISTLER *n* person or thing that whistles
ISTLERS > WHISTLER
ISTLES > WHISTLE
ISTLING > WHISTLE
ISTS > WHIST
IT *n* smallest particle
ITE *adj* of the colour of snow ▷ *n* colour of snow
ITEBAIT *n* small edible fish
ITEBASS *n* type of fish
ITEBEAM *n* type of tree
ITECAP *n* wave with a white broken crest
ITECAPS > WHITECAP
ITECOAT *n* person who wears a white coat
ITECOMB *n* fungal disease infecting the combs of certain fowls
ITED as in *whited sepulchre* hypocrite
ITEDAMP *n* mixture of poisonous gases, mainly carbon monoxide, occurring in coal mines
ITEFACE *n* white stage make-up
ITEFISH *n* type of fish
ITEFLY *n* tiny whitish insect that is harmful to greenhouse plants
ITEHEAD *n* type of pimple with a white head
ITELY > WHITE
ITEN *vb* make or become white or whiter
ITENED > WHITEN
ITENER *n* substance that makes something white or whiter
ITENERS > WHITENER
ITENESS > WHITE
ITENING > WHITEN
ITENS > WHITEN
ITEOUT *n* atmospheric condition in which blizzards or low clouds make it very difficult to see
ITEOUTS > WHITEOUT
ITEPOT *n* custard or milk pudding
ITEPOTS > WHITEPOT
ITER > WHITE
ITES *pl n* white clothes, as worn for playing cricket
ITEST > WHITE
ITETAIL *n* type of deer
ITEWALL *n* pneumatic tyre having white sidewalls
ITEWARE *n* white ceramics
ITEWASH *n* substance for whitening walls ▷ *vb* cover with whitewash
ITEWING *n* type of bird
ITEWOOD *n* light-coloured wood often prepared for staining
WHITEY *same as* > WHITY
WHITEYS > WHITEY
WHITHER *same as* > WUTHER
WHITHERED > WHITHER
WHITHERS > WHITHER
WHITIER > WHITY
WHITIES > WHITY
WHITIEST > WHITY
WHITING *n* edible sea fish
WHITINGS > WHITING
WHITISH > WHITE
WHITLING *n* type of trout
WHITLINGS > WHITLING
WHITLOW *n* inflamed sore on a finger or toe, esp round a nail
WHITLOWS > WHITLOW
WHITRACK *n* weasel or stoat
WHITRACKS > WHITRACK
WHITRET *n* variant of whittret
WHITRETS > WHITRET
WHITRICK *n* dialect word for a male weasel
WHITRICKS > WHITRICK
WHITS > WHIT
WHITSTER *n* person who whitens clothes
WHITSTERS > WHITSTER
WHITTAW *same as* > WHITTAWER
WHITTAWER *n* person who treats leather
WHITTAWS > WHITTAW
WHITTER *variant spelling of* > WITTER
WHITTERED > WHITTER
WHITTERS > WHITTER
WHITTLE *vb* cut or carve (wood) with a knife ▷ *n* knife, esp a large one
WHITTLED > WHITTLE
WHITTLER > WHITTLE
WHITTLERS > WHITTLE
WHITTLES > WHITTLE
WHITTLING > WHITTLE
WHITTRET *n* male weasel
WHITTRETS > WHITTRET
WHITY *adj* of a white colour ▷ *n* derogatory term for a White person
WHIZ *same as* > WHIZZ
WHIZBANG *n* small-calibre shell
WHIZBANGS > WHIZBANG
WHIZZ *vb* make a loud buzzing sound ▷ *n* loud buzzing sound
WHIZZBANG *same as* > WHIZBANG
WHIZZED > WHIZZ
WHIZZER > WHIZZ
WHIZZERS > WHIZZ
WHIZZES > WHIZZ
WHIZZIER > WHIZZY
WHIZZIEST > WHIZZY
WHIZZING > WHIZZ
WHIZZINGS > WHIZZ
WHIZZY *adj* using sophisticated technology to produce vivid effects
WHO *pron* which person
WHOA *interj* command used, esp to horses, to stop or slow down
WHODUNIT *same as* > WHODUNNIT
WHODUNITS > WHODUNIT
WHODUNNIT *n* detective story, play, or film
WHOEVER *pron* any person who
WHOLE *adj* containing all the elements or parts ▷ *n* complete thing or system
WHOLEFOOD *n* food that has been processed as little as possible ▷ *adj* of or relating to wholefood
WHOLEMEAL *adj* (of flour) made from the whole wheat grain
WHOLENESS > WHOLE
WHOLES > WHOLE
WHOLESALE *adv* dealing by selling goods in large quantities to retailers ▷ *n* business of selling goods in large quantities and at lower prices to retailers for resale
WHOLESOME *adj* physically or morally beneficial
WHOLISM *same as* > HOLISM
WHOLISMS > WHOLISM
WHOLIST *same as* > HOLIST
WHOLISTIC *same as* > HOLISTIC
WHOLISTS > WHOLIST
WHOLLY *adv* completely or totally
WHOM *pron* objective form of *who*
WHOMBLE *same as* > WHEMMLE
WHOMBLED > WHOMBLE
WHOMBLES > WHOMBLE
WHOMBLING > WHOMBLE
WHOMEVER *pron* objective form of *whoever*
WHOMMLE *same as* > WHEMMLE
WHOMMLED > WHOMMLE
WHOMMLES > WHOMMLE
WHOMMLING > WHOMMLE
WHOMP *vb* strike; thump
WHOMPED > WHOMP
WHOMPING > WHOMP
WHOMPS > WHOMP
WHOMSO *pron* whom; whomever
WHOOBUB *same as* > HUBBUB
WHOOBUBS > WHOOBUB
WHOOF *same as* > WOOF
WHOOFED > WHOOF
WHOOFING > WHOOF
WHOOFS > WHOOF
WHOOP *n* shout or cry to express excitement ▷ *vb* emit a whoop
WHOOPED > WHOOP
WHOOPEE *n* cry of joy
WHOOPEES > WHOOPEE
WHOOPER *n* type of swan
WHOOPERS > WHOOPER
WHOOPIE *same as* > WHOOPEE
WHOOPIES > WHOOPIE
WHOOPING > WHOOP
WHOOPINGS > WHOOPING
WHOOPLA *n* commotion; fuss
WHOOPLAS > WHOOPLA
WHOOPS *interj* exclamation of surprise or of apology
WHOOPSIE *n* animal excrement
WHOOPSIES > WHOOPSIE
WHOOSH *n* hissing or rushing sound ▷ *vb* make or move with a hissing or rushing sound
WHOOSHED > WHOOSH
WHOOSHES > WHOOSH
WHOOSHING > WHOOSH
WHOOSIS *n* thingamajig
WHOOSISES > WHOOSIS
WHOOT *obsolete variant of* > HOOT
WHOOTED > WHOOT
WHOOTING > WHOOT
WHOOTS > WHOOT
WHOP *vb* strike, beat, or thrash ▷ *n* heavy blow or the sound made by such a blow
WHOPPED > WHOP
WHOPPER *n* anything unusually large
WHOPPERS > WHOPPER
WHOPPING *n* beating as punishment ▷ *adj* unusually large ▷ *adv* extremely
WHOPPINGS > WHOPPING
WHOPS > WHOP
WHORE *n* prostitute ▷ *vb* be or act as a prostitute
WHORED > WHORE
WHOREDOM *n* activity of whoring or state of being a whore
WHOREDOMS > WHOREDOM
WHORES > WHORE
WHORESON *n* bastard ▷ *adj* vile or hateful
WHORESONS > WHORESON
WHORING > WHORE
WHORISH > WHORE
WHORISHLY > WHORE
WHORL *n* ring of leaves or petals
WHORLBAT *same as* > WHIRLBAT
WHORLBATS > WHORLBAT
WHORLED > WHORL
WHORLS > WHORL
WHORT *n* small shrub bearing blackish edible sweet berries
WHORTLE *n* whortleberry
WHORTLES > WHORTLE
WHORTS > WHORT
WHOSE *pron* of whom or of which ▷ *determiner* of whom? belonging to whom?
WHOSEVER *pron* belonging to whoever

WHOSIS *n* thingamajig
WHOSISES >WHOSIS
WHOSO *archaic word for* >WHOEVER
WHOSOEVER *same as* >WHOEVER
WHOT *obsolete variant of* >HOT
WHOW *interj* wow
WHUMMLE *vb* variant of whemmle
WHUMMLED >WHUMMLE
WHUMMLES >WHUMMLE
WHUMMLING >WHUMMLE
WHUMP *vb* make a dull thud ▷ *n* dull thud
WHUMPED >WHUMP
WHUMPING >WHUMP
WHUMPS >WHUMP
WHUNSTANE *Scots variant of* >WHINSTONE
WHUP *vb* defeat totally
WHUPPED >WHUP
WHUPPING >WHUP
WHUPS >WHUP
WHY *adv* for what reason ▷ *pron* because of which ▷ *n* reason, purpose, or cause of something
WHYDAH *n* type of black African bird
WHYDAHS >WHYDAH
WHYDUNIT *same as* >WHYDUNNIT
WHYDUNITS >WHYDUNIT
WHYDUNNIT *n* novel, film, etc, concerned with the motives of the criminal rather than his or her identity
WHYEVER *adv* for whatever reason
WHYS >WHY
WIBBLE *vb* wobble
WIBBLED >WIBBLE
WIBBLES >WIBBLE
WIBBLING >WIBBLE
WICCA *n* cult or practice of witchcraft
WICCAN *n* member of wicca
WICCANS >WICCAN
WICCAS >WICCA
WICE *Scots form of* >WISE
WICH *n* variant of wych
WICHES >WICH
WICK *n* cord through a lamp or candle which carries fuel to the flame ▷ *adj* lively or active ▷ *vb* (of a material) draw in (water, fuel, etc)
WICKAPE *same as* >WICOPY
WICKAPES >WICKAPE
WICKED *adj* morally bad ▷ *n* wicked person
WICKEDER >WICKED
WICKEDEST >WICKED
WICKEDLY >WICKED
WICKEDS >WICKED
WICKEN *variant of* >QUICKEN
WICKENS >WICKEN
WICKER *adj* made of woven cane ▷ *n* slender flexible twig or shoot, esp of willow
WICKERED >WICKER
WICKERS >WICKER
WICKET *n* set of three cricket stumps and two bails
WICKETS >WICKET
WICKIES >WICKY
WICKING >WICK
WICKINGS >WICK
WICKIUP *n* crude shelter made of brushwood, mats, or grass and having an oval frame
WICKIUPS >WICKIUP
WICKLESS >WICK
WICKS >WICK
WICKTHING *n* creeping animal, such as a woodlouse
WICKY *same as* >QUICKEN
WICKYUP *same as* >WICKIUP
WICKYUPS >WICKYUP
WICOPIES >WICOPY
WICOPY *n* any of various N American trees, shrubs, or herbaceous plants
WIDDER *same as* >WIDOW
WIDDERS >WIDDER
WIDDIE *same as* >WIDDY
WIDDIES >WIDDY
WIDDLE *vb* urinate ▷ *n* urine
WIDDLED >WIDDLE
WIDDLES >WIDDLE
WIDDLING >WIDDLE
WIDDY *vb* rope made of twigs
WIDE *adj* large from side to side ▷ *adv* the full extent ▷ *n* (in cricket) a bowled ball ruled to be outside a batsman's reach
WIDEAWAKE *n* hat with a low crown and a very wide brim
WIDEBAND *n* wide bandwidth transmission medium
WIDEBODY *n* aircraft with a wide fuselage
WIDELY >WIDE
WIDEN *vb* make or become wider
WIDENED >WIDEN
WIDENER >WIDEN
WIDENERS >WIDEN
WIDENESS >WIDE
WIDENING >WIDEN
WIDENS >WIDEN
WIDEOUT *n* footballer who catches passes from the quarterback
WIDEOUTS >WIDEOUT
WIDER >WIDE
WIDES >WIDE
WIDEST >WIDE
WIDGEON *same as* >WIGEON
WIDGEONS >WIDGEON
WIDGET *n* any small device, the name of which is unknown or forgotten
WIDGETS >WIDGET
WIDGIE *n* female larrikin or bodgie
WIDGIES >WIDGIE
WIDISH >WIDE
WIDOW *n* woman whose husband is dead and who has not remarried ▷ *vb* cause to become a widow
WIDOWBIRD *n* whydah
WIDOWED >WIDOW
WIDOWER *n* man whose wife is dead and who has not remarried
WIDOWERED >WIDOWER
WIDOWERS >WIDOWER
WIDOWHOOD >WIDOW
WIDOWING >WIDOW
WIDOWMAN *n* widower
WIDOWMEN >WIDOWMAN
WIDOWS >WIDOW
WIDTH *n* distance from side to side
WIDTHS >WIDTH
WIDTHWAY *adj* across the width
WIDTHWAYS *same as* >WIDTHWISE
WIDTHWISE *adv* in the direction of the width
WIEL *same as* >WEEL
WIELD *vb* hold and use (a weapon)
WIELDABLE >WIELD
WIELDED >WIELD
WIELDER >WIELD
WIELDERS >WIELD
WIELDIER >WIELDY
WIELDIEST >WIELDY
WIELDING >WIELD
WIELDLESS *adj* unwieldy
WIELDS >WIELD
WIELDY *adj* easily handled, used, or managed
WIELS >WIEL
WIENER *n* kind of smoked beef or pork sausage, similar to a frankfurter
WIENERS >WIENER
WIENIE *same as* >WIENER
WIENIES >WIENIE
WIFE *n* woman to whom a man is married ▷ *vb* marry
WIFED >WIFE
WIFEDOM *n* state of being a wife
WIFEDOMS >WIFEDOM
WIFEHOOD >WIFE
WIFEHOODS >WIFE
WIFELESS >WIFE
WIFELIER >WIFE
WIFELIEST >WIFE
WIFELIKE >WIFE
WIFELY >WIFE
WIFES >WIFE
WIFEY *n* wife
WIFEYS >WIFEY
WIFIE *n* woman
WIFIES >WIFIE
WIFING >WIFE
WIFTIER >WIFTY
WIFTIEST >WIFTY
WIFTY *adj* scatterbrained
WIG *n* artificial head of hair ▷ *vb* furnish with a wig
WIGAN *n* stiff fabric
WIGANS >WIGAN
WIGEON *n* duck found in marshland
WIGEONS >WIGEON
WIGGA *same as* >WIGGER
WIGGAS >WIGGA
WIGGED >WIG
WIGGER *n* white youth wh[o] adopts Black youth cultu[re]
WIGGERIES >WIGGERY
WIGGERS >WIGGER
WIGGERY *n* wigs
WIGGIER >WIGGY
WIGGIEST >WIGGY
WIGGING >WIG
WIGGINGS >WIG
WIGGLE *vb* move jerkily from side to side ▷ *n* wiggling movement
WIGGLED >WIGGLE
WIGGLER >WIGGLE
WIGGLERS >WIGGLE
WIGGLES >WIGGLE
WIGGLIER >WIGGLE
WIGGLIEST >WIGGLE
WIGGLING >WIGGLE
WIGGLY >WIGGLE
WIGGY *adj* eccentric
WIGHT *vb* blame ▷ *n* human being ▷ *adj* stron[g] and brave
WIGHTED >WIGHT
WIGHTING >WIGHT
WIGHTLY *adv* swiftly
WIGHTS >WIGHT
WIGLESS >WIG
WIGLET *n* small wig
WIGLETS >WIGLET
WIGLIKE >WIG
WIGMAKER *n* person who makes wigs
WIGMAKERS >WIGMAKER
WIGS >WIG
WIGWAG *vb* move (something) back and forth ▷ *n* system of communication by flag semaphore
WIGWAGGED >WIGWAG
WIGWAGGER >WIGWAG
WIGWAGS >WIGWAG
WIGWAM *n* Native American's tent
WIGWAMS >WIGWAM
WIKIUP *same as* >WICKIUP
WIKIUPS >WIKIUP
WILCO *interj* expression in telecommunications etc, indicating that the message just received wi[ll] be complied with
WILD *same as* >WIELD
WILDCARD *n* person given entry to competition without qualifying
WILDCARDS >WILDCARD
WILDCAT *n* European wild animal like a large domestic cat ▷ *adj* risky and financially unsound ▷ *vb* drill for petroleum or natural gas in an area having no known reserve[s]

LDCATS >WILDCAT
LDED >WILD
LDER *vb* lead or be led astray
LDERED >WILDER
LDERING >WILDER
LDERS >WILDER
LDEST >WILD
LDFIRE *n* highly flammable material, such as Greek fire, formerly used in warfare
LDFIRES >WILDFIRE
LDFOWL *n* wild bird that is hunted for sport or food
LDFOWLS >WILDFOWL
LDGRAVE *same as* >WALDGRAVE
LDING *n* uncultivated plant, esp the crab apple, or a cultivated plant that has become wild
LDINGS >WILDING
LDISH >WILD
LDLAND *n* land which has not been cultivated
LDLANDS >WILDLAND
LDLIFE *n* wild animals and plants collectively
LDLIFES >WILDLIFE
LDLING *same as* >WILDING
LDLINGS >WILDLING
LDLY >WILD
LDNESS >WILD
LDS >WILD
LDWOOD *n* wood or forest growing in a natural uncultivated state
LDWOODS >WILDWOOD
LE *n* trickery, cunning, or craftiness ▷ *vb* lure, beguile, or entice
LED >WILE
LEFUL *adj* deceitful
LES >WILE
LFUL *adj* headstrong or obstinate
LFULLY >WILFUL
LGA *n* small drought-resistant tree of Australia
LGAS >WILGA
LI *n* spirit
LIER >WILY
LIEST >WILY
LILY >WILY
LINESS >WILY
LING >WILE
LIS >WILI
LJA *n* variety of potato
LJAS >WILJA
ILL *vb* used as an auxiliary to form the future tense or to indicate intention, ability, or expectation ▷ *n* strong determination
ILLABLE *adj* able to be wished or determined by the will
ILLED *adj* having a will as specified
ILLEMITE *n* secondary mineral consisting of zinc silicate
WILLER >WILL
WILLERS >WILL
WILLEST >WILL
WILLET *n* large American shore bird
WILLETS >WILLET
WILLEY *same as* >WILLY
WILLEYED >WILLEY
WILLEYING >WILLEY
WILLEYS >WILLEY
WILLFUL *same as* >WILFUL
WILLFULLY >WILLFUL
WILLIAM as in *sweet william* flowering plant
WILLIAMS >WILLIAM
WILLIE *n* informal word for a penis
WILLIED >WILLY
WILLIES >WILLY
WILLING *adj* ready or inclined (to do something)
WILLINGER >WILLING
WILLINGLY >WILLING
WILLIWAU *same as* >WILLIWAW
WILLIWAUS >WILLIWAU
WILLIWAW *n* sudden strong gust of cold wind blowing offshore from a mountainous coast
WILLIWAWS >WILLIWAW
WILLOW *n* tree with thin flexible branches ▷ *vb* (of raw textile fibres) to open and clean in a machine having a system of rotating spikes
WILLOWED >WILLOW
WILLOWER *n* willow
WILLOWERS >WILLOWER
WILLOWIER >WILLOWY
WILLOWING >WILLOW
WILLOWISH >WILLOW
WILLOWS >WILLOW
WILLOWY *adj* slender and graceful
WILLPOWER *n* ability to control oneself and one's actions
WILLS >WILL
WILLY *vb* clean in willowing-machine
WILLYARD *adj* timid
WILLYART *same as* >WILLYARD
WILLYING >WILLY
WILLYWAW *same as* >WILLIWAW
WILLYWAWS >WILLYWAW
WILT *vb* (cause to) become limp or lose strength ▷ *n* act of wilting or state of becoming wilted
WILTED >WILT
WILTING >WILT
WILTJA *n* Aboriginal shelter
WILTJAS >WILTJA
WILTS >WILT
WILY *adj* crafty or sly
WIMBLE *n* any of a number of hand tools, such as a brace and bit or a gimlet, used for boring holes ▷ *vb* bore (a hole) with or as if with a wimble
WIMBLED >WIMBLE
WIMBLES >WIMBLE
WIMBLING >WIMBLE
WIMBREL *same as* >WHIMBREL
WIMBRELS >WIMBREL
WIMMIN *n* common intentional literary misspelling spelling of 'women'
WIMP *n* feeble ineffectual person ▷ *vb* fail to complete something through fear
WIMPED >WIMP
WIMPIER >WIMP
WIMPIEST >WIMP
WIMPINESS >WIMP
WIMPING >WIMP
WIMPISH >WIMP
WIMPISHLY >WIMP
WIMPLE *n* garment framing the face, worn by medieval women and now by nuns ▷ *vb* ripple or cause to ripple or undulate
WIMPLED >WIMPLE
WIMPLES >WIMPLE
WIMPLING >WIMPLE
WIMPS >WIMP
WIMPY >WIMP
WIN *vb* come first in (a competition, fight, etc) ▷ *n* victory, esp in a game
WINCE *vb* draw back, as if in pain ▷ *n* wincing
WINCED >WINCE
WINCER >WINCE
WINCERS >WINCE
WINCES >WINCE
WINCEY *n* plain- or twill-weave cloth, usually having a cotton or linen warp and a wool filling
WINCEYS >WINCEY
WINCH *n* machine for lifting or hauling using a cable or chain wound round a drum ▷ *vb* lift or haul using a winch
WINCHED >WINCH
WINCHER >WINCH
WINCHERS >WINCH
WINCHES >WINCH
WINCHING >WINCH
WINCHMAN *n* man who operates winch
WINCHMEN >WINCHMAN
WINCING >WINCE
WINCINGS >WINCE
WINCOPIPE *n* type of plant
WIND *n* current of air ▷ *vb* render short of breath
WINDABLE *n* able to be wound
WINDAC *same as* >WINDAS
WINDACS >WINDAC
WINDAGE *n* deflection of a projectile as a result of the effect of the wind
WINDAGES >WINDAGE
WINDAS *n* windlass
WINDASES >WINDAS
WINDBAG *n* person who talks much but uninterestingly
WINDBAGS >WINDBAG
WINDBELL *n* light bell made to be sounded by wind
WINDBELLS >WINDBELL
WINDBILL *n* bill of exchange cosigned by a guarantor
WINDBILLS >WINDBILL
WINDBLAST *n* strong gust of wind
WINDBLOW *n* trees uprooted by wind
WINDBLOWN *adj* blown about by the wind
WINDBLOWS >WINDBLOW
WINDBORNE *adj* (of plant seeds, etc) borne on the wind
WINDBOUND *adj* (of a sailing vessel) prevented from sailing by an unfavourable wind
WINDBREAK *n* fence or line of trees providing shelter from the wind
WINDBURN *n* irritation and redness of the skin caused by prolonged exposure to winds of high velocity
WINDBURNS >WINDBURN
WINDBURNT >WINDBURN
WINDCHILL *n* chilling effect of wind and low temperature
WINDED >WIND
WINDER *n* person or device that winds, as an engine for hoisting the cages in a mine shaft
WINDERS >WINDER
WINDFALL *n* unexpected good luck
WINDFALLS >WINDFALL
WINDFLAW *n* squall
WINDFLAWS >WINDFLAW
WINDGALL *n* soft swelling in the area of the fetlock joint of a horse
WINDGALLS >WINDGALL
WINDGUN *n* air gun
WINDGUNS >WINDGUN
WINDHOVER *dialect name for* >KESTREL
WINDIER >WINDY
WINDIEST >WINDY
WINDIGO *same as* >WENDIGO
WINDIGOS >WINDIGO
WINDILY >WINDY
WINDINESS >WINDY
WINDING >WIND
WINDINGLY >WINDING
WINDINGS >WIND
WINDLASS *n* winch worked by a crank ▷ *vb* raise or haul (a weight, etc) by means of a windlass
WINDLE *vb* wind something round continuously

WINDLED >WINDLE
WINDLES >WINDLE
WINDLESS >WIND
WINDLING >WINDLE
WINDLINGS >WINDLE
WINDMILL *n* machine for grinding or pumping driven by sails turned by the wind ▷ *vb* move or cause to move like the arms of a windmill
WINDMILLS >WINDMILL
WINDOCK *same as* >WINNOCK
WINDOCKS >WINDOCK
WINDORE *n* window
WINDORES >WINDORE
WINDOW *n* opening in a wall to let in light or air ▷ *vb* furnish with windows
WINDOWED >WINDOW
WINDOWING >WINDOW
WINDOWS >WINDOW
WINDOWY >WINDOW
WINDPIPE *n* tube linking the throat and the lungs
WINDPIPES >WINDPIPE
WINDPROOF *n* wind-resistant
WINDRING *adj* winding
WINDROSE *n* diagram with radiating lines showing the strength and frequency of winds from each direction affecting a specific place
WINDROSES >WINDROSE
WINDROW *n* long low ridge or line of hay or a similar crop, designed to achieve the best conditions for drying or curing ▷ *vb* put (hay or a similar crop) into windrows
WINDROWED >WINDROW
WINDROWER >WINDROW
WINDROWS >WINDROW
WINDS >WIND
WINDSAIL *n* sail rigged as an air scoop over a hatch or companionway to catch breezes and divert them below
WINDSAILS >WINDSAIL
WINDSES *pl n* ventilation shafts within mines
WINDSHAKE *n* crack between the annual rings in wood
WINDSHIP *n* ship propelled by wind
WINDSHIPS >WINDSHIP
WINDSOCK *n* cloth cone on a mast at an airfield to indicate wind direction
WINDSOCKS >WINDSOCK
WINDSTORM *n* storm consisting of violent winds
WINDSURF *vb* sail standing on a board equipped with a mast, sail, and boom
WINDSURFS >WINDSURF
WINDSWEPT *adj* exposed to the wind
WINDTHROW *n* uprooting of trees by wind
WINDTIGHT *adj* impenetrable by wind
WINDUP *n* prank or hoax
WINDUPS >WINDUP
WINDWARD *n* direction from which the wind is blowing ▷ *adj* of or in the direction from which the wind blows ▷ *adv* towards the wind
WINDWARDS *adv* in the direction of the wind
WINDWAY *n* part of wind instrument
WINDWAYS >WINDWAY
WINDY *adj* denoting a time or conditions in which there is a strong wind
WINE *n* alcoholic drink made from fermented grapes ▷ *adj* of a dark purplish-red colour ▷ *vb* give wine to
WINEBERRY *another name for* >MAKO
WINED >WINE
WINEGLASS *n* glass for wine, usually with a small bowl on a stem with a flared base
WINELESS >WINE
WINEMAKER *n* maker of wine
WINEPRESS *n* any equipment used for squeezing the juice from grapes in order to make wine
WINERIES >WINERY
WINERY *n* place where wine is made
WINES >WINE
WINESAP *n* variety of apple
WINESAPS >WINESAP
WINESHOP *n* shop where wine is sold
WINESHOPS >WINESHOP
WINESKIN *n* skin of a sheep or goat sewn up and used as a holder for wine
WINESKINS >WINESKIN
WINESOP *n* old word for an alcoholic
WINESOPS >WINESOP
WINEY *adj* having the taste or qualities of wine
WING *n* one of the limbs or organs of a bird, insect, or bat that are used for flying ▷ *vb* fly
WINGBACK *n* football position
WINGBACKS >WINGBACK
WINGBEAT *n* complete cycle of moving the wing by a bird in flight
WINGBEATS >WINGBEAT
WINGBOW *n* distinctive band of colour marking the wing of a bird
WINGBOWS >WINGBOW
WINGCHAIR *n* chair with forward projections from back
WINGDING *n* noisy lively party or festivity
WINGDINGS >WINGDING
WINGE *same as* >WHINGE
WINGED *adj* furnished with wings
WINGEDLY >WINGED
WINGEING >WINGE
WINGER *n* player positioned on a wing
WINGERS >WINGER
WINGES >WINGE
WINGIER >WINGY
WINGIEST >WINGY
WINGING >WING
WINGLESS *adj* having no wings or vestigial wings
WINGLET *n* small wing
WINGLETS >WINGLET
WINGLIKE >WING
WINGMAN *n* player in the wing position in Australian Rules
WINGMEN >WINGMAN
WINGOVER *n* manoeuvre in which the direction of flight of an aircraft is reversed by putting it into a climbing turn until nearly stalled, the nose then being allowed to fall while continuing the turn
WINGOVERS >WINGOVER
WINGS >WING
WINGSPAN *n* distance between the wing tips of an aircraft, bird, or insect
WINGSPANS >WINGSPAN
WINGSUIT *n* type of skydiving suit
WINGSUITS >WINGSUIT
WINGTIP *n* outermost edge of a wing
WINGTIPS >WINGTIP
WINGY *adj* having wings
WINIER >WINY
WINIEST >WINY
WINING >WINE
WINISH >WINE
WINK *vb* close and open (an eye) quickly as a signal ▷ *n* winking
WINKED >WINK
WINKER *n* person or thing that winks
WINKERS >WINKER
WINKING >WINK
WINKINGLY >WINK
WINKINGS >WINK
WINKLE *n* shellfish with a spiral shell ▷ *vb* extract or prise out
WINKLED >WINKLE
WINKLER *n* one who forces person or thing out
WINKLERS >WINKLER
WINKLES >WINKLE
WINKLING >WINKLE
WINKS >WINK
WINLESS *adj* not having won anything
WINN *n* penny
WINNA *vb* will not
WINNABLE >WIN
WINNARD *n* heron
WINNARDS >WINNARD
WINNED >WIN
WINNER *n* person or thing that wins
WINNERS >WINNER
WINNING *adj* (of a person) charming, attractive, etc
WINNINGLY >WINNING
WINNINGS >WIN
WINNLE *same as* >WINNLE
WINNLES >WINNLE
WINNOCK *n* window
WINNOCKS >WINNOCK
WINNOW *vb* separate (chaff from (grain) ▷ *n* device f winnowing
WINNOWED >WINNOW
WINNOWER >WINNOW
WINNOWERS >WINNOW
WINNOWING >WINNOW
WINNOWS >WINNOW
WINNS >WINN
WINO *n* destitute person who habitually drinks cheap wine
WINOES >WINO
WINOS >WINO
WINS >WIN
WINSEY *same as* >WINCEY
WINSEYS >WINSEY
WINSOME *adj* charming or winning
WINSOMELY >WINSOME
WINSOMER >WINSOME
WINSOMEST >WINSOME
WINTER *n* coldest season ▷ *vb* spend the winter
WINTERED >WINTER
WINTERER >WINTER
WINTERERS >WINTER
WINTERFED *vb* past tense of 'winterfeed' (to feed (livestock) in winter whe the grazing is not rich enough)
WINTERIER >WINTERY
WINTERING >WINTER
WINTERISE *same as* >WINTERIZE
WINTERISH >WINTER
WINTERIZE *vb* prepare (a house, car, etc) to withstand winter conditions
WINTERLY *same as* >WINT
WINTERS >WINTER
WINTERY *same as* >WINTR
WINTLE *vb* reel; stagger
WINTLED >WINTLE
WINTLES >WINTLE
WINTLING >WINTLE
WINTRIER >WINTRY
WINTRIEST >WINTRY
WINTRILY >WINTRY
WINTRY *adj* of or like wint
WINY *same as* >WINEY
WINZE *n* steeply inclined shaft, as for ventilation between levels
WINZES >WINZE

IPE *vb* clean or dry by rubbing ▷ *n* wiping
IPED >WIPE
IPEOUT *n* instance of wiping out
IPEOUTS >WIPEOUT
IPER *n* any piece of cloth, such as a handkerchief, towel, etc, used for wiping
IPERS >WIPER
IPES >WIPE
IPING >WIPE
IPINGS >WIPE
IPPEN *n* part of hammer action in piano
IPPENS >WIPPEN
IRABLE *adj* that can be wired
IRE *n* thin flexible strand of metal ▷ *vb* fasten with wire
IRED *adj* excited or nervous
IREDRAW *vb* convert (metal) into wire by drawing through successively smaller dies
IREDRAWN >WIREDRAW
IREDRAWS >WIREDRAW
IREDREW >WIREDRAW
IREGRASS *n* fine variety of grass
IREHAIR *n* type of terrier
IREHAIRS >WIREHAIR
IRELESS *adj* (of a computer network) connected by radio rather than by cables or fibre optics
IRELIKE >WIRE
IREMAN *n* person who installs and maintains electric wiring, cables, etc
IREMEN >WIREMAN
IREPHOTO *n* facsimile of a photograph transmitted electronically via a telephone system
IRER *n* person who sets or uses wires to snare rabbits and similar animals
IRERS >WIRER
IRES >WIRE
IRETAP *vb* make a connection to a telegraph or telephone wire in order to obtain information secretly
IRETAPS >WIRETAP
IREWAY *n* tube for electric wires
IREWAYS >WIREWAY
IREWORK *n* functional or decorative work made of wire
IREWORKS *n* factory where wire or articles of wire are made
IREWORM *n* destructive wormlike beetle larva
IREWORMS >WIREWORM
IREWOVE *adj* woven out of wire
IRIER >WIRY
WIRIEST >WIRY
WIRILDA *n* acacia tree, *Acacia retinoides*, of SE Australia with edible seeds
WIRILDAS >WIRILDA
WIRILY >WIRY
WIRINESS >WIRY
WIRING *n* system of wires ▷ *adj* used in wiring
WIRINGS >WIRING
WIRRA *interj* exclamation of sorrow or deep concern
WIRRAH *n* saltwater fish, *Acanthistius serratus*, of Australia, with bright blue spots
WIRRAHS >WIRRAH
WIRRICOW *same as* >WORRICOW
WIRRICOWS >WIRRICOW
WIRY *adj* lean and tough
WIS *vb* know or suppose (something)
WISARD *obsolete spelling of* >WIZARD
WISARDS >WISARD
WISDOM *n* good sense and judgment
WISDOMS >WISDOM
WISE *vb* guide ▷ *adj* having wisdom ▷ *n* manner
WISEACRE *n* person who wishes to seem wise
WISEACRES >WISEACRE
WISEASS *n* person who thinks he or she is being witty or clever
WISEASSES >WISEASS
WISECRACK *n* clever, sometimes unkind, remark ▷ *vb* make a wisecrack
WISED >WISE
WISEGUY *n* person who wants to seem clever
WISEGUYS >WISEGUY
WISELIER >WISE
WISELIEST >WISE
WISELING *n* one who claims to be wise
WISELINGS >WISELING
WISELY >WISE
WISENESS >WISE
WISENT *n* European bison
WISENTS >WISENT
WISER >WISE
WISES >WISE
WISEST >WISE
WISEWOMAN *n* witch
WISEWOMEN >WISEWOMAN
WISH *vb* want or desire ▷ *n* expression of a desire
WISHA *interj* expression of surprise
WISHBONE *n* V-shaped bone above the breastbone of a fowl
WISHBONES >WISHBONE
WISHED >WISH
WISHER >WISH
WISHERS >WISH
WISHES >WISH
WISHFUL *adj* too optimistic
WISHFULLY >WISHFUL
WISHING >WISH
WISHINGS >WISH
WISHLESS >WISH
WISHT *variant of* >WHISHT
WISING >WISE
WISKET *n* basket
WISKETS >WISKET
WISP *n* light delicate streak ▷ *vb* move or act like a wisp
WISPED >WISP
WISPIER >WISPY
WISPIEST >WISPY
WISPILY >WISPY
WISPINESS >WISPY
WISPING >WISP
WISPISH >WISP
WISPLIKE >WISP
WISPS >WISP
WISPY *adj* thin, fine, or delicate
WISS *vb* urinate
WISSED >WIS
WISSES >WIS
WISSING >WIS
WIST *vb* know
WISTARIA *same as* >WISTERIA
WISTARIAS >WISTARIA
WISTED >WIST
WISTERIA *n* climbing shrub with blue or purple flowers
WISTERIAS >WISTERIA
WISTFUL *adj* sadly longing
WISTFULLY >WISTFUL
WISTING >WIST
WISTITI *n* marmoset
WISTITIS >WISTITI
WISTLY *adv* intently
WISTS >WIST
WIT *vb* detect ▷ *n* ability to use words or ideas in a clever and amusing way
WITAN *n* assembly of higher ecclesiastics and important laymen, including king's thegns, that met to counsel the king on matters such as judicial problems
WITANS >WITAN
WITBLITS *n* illegally distilled strong alcoholic drink
WITCH *n* person, usu female, who practises (black) magic ▷ *vb* cause or change by or as if by witchcraft
WITCHED >WITCH
WITCHEN *n* rowan tree
WITCHENS >WITCHEN
WITCHERY *n* practice of witchcraft
WITCHES >WITCH
WITCHETTY *n* edible larva of certain Australian moths and beetles
WITCHHOOD >WITCH
WITCHIER >WITCHY
WITCHIEST >WITCHY
WITCHING *adj* relating to or appropriate for witchcraft ▷ *n* witchcraft
WITCHINGS >WITCHING
WITCHKNOT *n* knot in hair
WITCHLIKE >WITCH
WITCHWEED *n* any of several scrophulariaceous plants of the genus *Striga*, esp *S. hermonthica*, that are serious pests of grain crops in parts of Africa and Asia
WITCHY *adj* like a witch
WITE *vb* blame
WITED >WITE
WITELESS *adj* witless
WITES >WITE
WITGAT *n* type of S African tree
WITGATS >WITGAT
WITH *prep* indicating presence alongside, possession, means of performance, characteristic manner, etc ▷ *n* division between flues in chimney
WITHAL *adv* as well
WITHDRAW *vb* take or move out or away
WITHDRAWN *adj* unsociable
WITHDRAWS >WITHDRAW
WITHDREW *past tense of* >WITHDRAW
WITHE *n* strong flexible twig, esp of willow, suitable for binding things together ▷ *vb* bind with withes
WITHED >WITHE
WITHER *vb* wilt or dry up
WITHERED >WITHER
WITHERER >WITHER
WITHERERS >WITHER
WITHERING >WITHER
WITHERITE *n* white, grey, or yellowish mineral
WITHEROD *n* American shrub
WITHERODS >WITHEROD
WITHERS *pl n* ridge between a horse's shoulder blades
WITHES >WITHE
WITHHAULT >WITHHOLD
WITHHELD >WITHHOLD
WITHHOLD *vb* refrain from giving
WITHHOLDS >WITHHOLD
WITHIER >WITHY
WITHIES >WITHY
WITHIEST >WITHY
WITHIN *adv* in or inside ▷ *prep* in or inside ▷ *n* something that is within
WITHING >WITHE
WITHINS >WITHIN
WITHOUT *prep* not accompanied by, using, or having ▷ *adv* outside ▷ *n* person who is without
WITHOUTEN *obsolete form of* >WITHOUT
WITHOUTS >WITHOUT
WITHS >WITH

WITHSTAND *vb* oppose or resist successfully
WITHSTOOD > WITHSTAND
WITHWIND *n* bindweed
WITHWINDS > WITHWIND
WITHY *n* willow tree, esp an osier ▷ *adj* (of people) tough and agile
WITHYWIND *same as* > WITHWIND
WITING > WITE
WITLESS *adj* foolish
WITLESSLY > WITLESS
WITLING *n* person who thinks himself witty
WITLINGS > WITLING
WITLOOF *n* chicory
WITLOOFS > WITLOOF
WITNESS *n* person who has seen something happen ▷ *vb* see at first hand
WITNESSED > WITNESS
WITNESSER > WITNESS
WITNESSES > WITNESS
WITNEY *n* type of blanket; heavy cloth
WITNEYS > WITNEY
WITS > WIT
WITTED *adj* having wit
WITTER *vb* chatter pointlessly or at unnecessary length ▷ *n* pointless chat
WITTERED > WITTER
WITTERING > WITTER
WITTERS > WITTER
WITTICISM *n* witty remark
WITTIER > WITTY
WITTIEST > WITTY
WITTILY > WITTY
WITTINESS > WITTY
WITTING *adj* deliberate
WITTINGLY > WITTING
WITTINGS > WIT
WITTOL *n* man who tolerates his wife's unfaithfulness
WITTOLLY > WITTOL
WITTOLS > WITTOL
WITTY *adj* clever and amusing
WITWALL *n* golden oriole
WITWALLS > WITWALL
WITWANTON *n* be disrespectfully witty
WIVE *vb* marry (a woman)
WIVED > WIVE
WIVEHOOD *obsolete variant of* > WIFEHOOD
WIVEHOODS > WIVEHOOD
WIVER *another word for* > WIVERN
WIVERN *same as* > WYVERN
WIVERNS > WIVERN
WIVERS > WIVER
WIVES > WIFE
WIVING > WIVE
WIZ *shortened form of* > WIZARD
WIZARD *n* magician ▷ *adj* superb
WIZARDLY > WIZARD
WIZARDRY *n* magic or sorcery
WIZARDS > WIZARD
WIZEN *vb* make or become shrivelled ▷ *n* archaic word for WEASAND (the gullet)
WIZENED *adj* shrivelled or wrinkled
WIZENING > WIZEN
WIZENS > WIZEN
WIZES > WIZ
WIZIER *same as* > VIZIER
WIZIERS > WIZIER
WIZZEN *same as* > WIZEN
WIZZENS > WIZEN
WIZZES > WIZ
WO *archaic spelling of* > WOE
WOAD *n* blue dye obtained from a plant, used by the ancient Britons as a body dye
WOADED *adj* coloured blue with woad
WOADS > WOAD
WOADWAX *n* small Eurasian leguminous shrub
WOADWAXEN *n* small leguminous shrub with yellow flowers producing a yellow dye
WOADWAXES > WOADWAX
WOALD *same as* > WELD
WOALDS > WOALD
WOBBEGONG *n* Australian shark with brown-and-white skin
WOBBLE *vb* move unsteadily ▷ *n* wobbling movement or sound
WOBBLED > WOBBLE
WOBBLER > WOBBLE
WOBBLERS > WOBBLE
WOBBLES > WOBBLE
WOBBLIER > WOBBLY
WOBBLIES > WOBBLY
WOBBLIEST > WOBBLY
WOBBLING > WOBBLE
WOBBLINGS > WOBBLE
WOBBLY *adj* unsteady ▷ *n* temper tantrum
WOBEGONE *same as* > WOEBEGONE
WOCK *same as* > WOK
WOCKS > WOCK
WODGE *n* thick lump or chunk
WODGES > WODGE
WOE *n* grief
WOEBEGONE *adj* looking miserable
WOEFUL *adj* extremely sad
WOEFULLER > WOEFUL
WOEFULLY > WOEFUL
WOENESS > WOE
WOENESSES > WOE
WOES > WOE
WOESOME *adj* woeful
WOF *n* fool
WOFS > WOF
WOFUL *same as* > WOEFUL
WOFULLER > WOFUL
WOFULLEST > WOFUL
WOFULLY > WOFUL
WOFULNESS > WOFUL
WOG *n* derogatory word for a foreigner, esp one who is not White
WOGGISH > WOG
WOGGLE *n* ring of leather through which a Scout neckerchief is threaded
WOGGLES > WOGGLE
WOGS > WOG
WOIWODE *same as* > VOIVODE
WOIWODES > WOIWODE
WOK *n* bowl-shaped Chinese cooking pan, used for stir-frying
WOKE > WAKE
WOKEN > WAKE
WOKKA as in *wokka board* wobble board: a piece of fibreboard used as a musical instrument
WOKS > WOK
WOLD *same as* > WELD
WOLDS > WOLD
WOLF *n* wild predatory canine mammal ▷ *vb* eat ravenously
WOLFBERRY *n* type of shrub
WOLFED > WOLF
WOLFER *same as* > WOLVER
WOLFERS > WOLFER
WOLFFISH *n* any large northern deep-sea blennioid fish of the family *Anarhichadidae* with large sharp teeth and no pelvic fins
WOLFHOUND *n* very large breed of dog
WOLFING > WOLF
WOLFINGS > WOLF
WOLFISH > WOLF
WOLFISHLY > WOLF
WOLFKIN *n* young wolf
WOLFKINS > WOLFKIN
WOLFLIKE > WOLF
WOLFLING *n* young wolf
WOLFLINGS > WOLFLING
WOLFRAM *another name for* > TUNGSTEN
WOLFRAMS > WOLFRAM
WOLFS > WOLF
WOLFSBANE *n* any of several poisonous N temperate plants of the ranunculaceous genus *Aconitum*, esp *A. lycoctonum*, which has yellow hoodlike flowers
WOLFSKIN *n* skin of wolf used for clothing, etc
WOLFSKINS > WOLFSKIN
WOLLIES > WOLLY
WOLLY *n* pickled cucumber or olive
WOLVE *vb* hunt for wolves
WOLVED > WOLVE
WOLVER *n* person who hunts wolves
WOLVERENE *same as* > WOLVERINE
WOLVERINE *n* carnivorous mammal of Arctic regions
WOLVERS > WOLVER
WOLVES > WOLF
WOLVING > WOLVE
WOLVINGS > WOLVE
WOLVISH *same as* > WOLFIS[H]
WOLVISHLY > WOLVISH
WOMAN *n* adult human female ▷ *adj* female ▷ *vb* provide with a woman or women
WOMANED > WOMAN
WOMANHOOD *n* state of bein[g] a woman
WOMANING > WOMAN
WOMANISE *same as* > WOMANIZE
WOMANISED > WOMANISE
WOMANISER > WOMANISE
WOMANISES > WOMANISE
WOMANISH *adj* effeminate
WOMANISM *n* feminism among black women
WOMANISMS > WOMANISM
WOMANIST > WOMANISM
WOMANISTS > WOMANISM
WOMANIZE *vb* (of a man) to indulge in many casual affairs with women
WOMANIZED > WOMANIZE
WOMANIZER > WOMANIZE
WOMANIZES > WOMANIZE
WOMANKIND *n* all women considered as a group
WOMANLESS > WOMAN
WOMANLIER > WOMANLY
WOMANLIKE *adj* like a woman
WOMANLY *adj* having qualities traditionally associated with a woman
WOMANNESS > WOMAN
WOMANS > WOMAN
WOMB *vb* enclose ▷ *n* hollow organ in female mammals where babies are conceived and develo[p]
WOMBAT *n* small heavily-built burrowing Australia[n] marsupial
WOMBATS > WOMBAT
WOMBED > WOMB
WOMBIER > WOMBY
WOMBIEST > WOMBY
WOMBING > WOMB
WOMBLIKE > WOMB
WOMBS > WOMB
WOMBY *adj* hollow; spaciou[s]
WOMEN > WOMAN
WOMENFOLK *pl n* women collectively
WOMENKIND *same as* > WOMANKIND
WOMERA *same as* > WOOMER[A]
WOMERAS > WOMERA
WOMMERA *same as* > WOOMERA
WOMMERAS > WOMMERA
WOMMIT *n* foolish person
WOMMITS > WOMMIT
WOMYN *same as* > WOMAN
WON *n* standard monetary unit of North Korea, divided into 100 chon ▷ *v[b]* live or dwell
WONDER *vb* be curious about ▷ *n* wonderful thing ▷ *adj* spectacularl[y]

uccessful
NDERED > WONDER
NDERER > WONDER
NDERERS > WONDER
NDERFUL *adj* very fine
NDERING > WONDER
NDERKID *n* informal vord for an exceptionally uccessful young person
NDEROUS *obsolete variant* of > WONDROUS
NDERS > WONDER
NDRED *adj* splendid
NDROUS *adj* wonderful ▷ *adv* (intensifier)
NGA *n* money
NGAS > WONGA
NGI *vb* talk informally
NGIED > WONGI
NGIING > WONGI
NGIS > WONGI
NING > WON
NINGS > WON
NK *n* person who is obsessively interested in a pecified subject
NKIER > WONKY
NKIEST > WONKY
NKS > WONK
NKY *adj* shaky or unsteady
NNED > WON
NNER > WON
NNERS > WON
NNING > WON
NNINGS > WON
NS > WON
NT *adj* accustomed ▷ *n* custom ▷ *vb* become or cause to become accustomed
NTED *adj* accustomed or habituated (to doing something)
NTEDLY > WONTED
NTING > WONT
NTLESS > WONT
NTON *n* dumpling filled with spiced minced pork
NTONS > WONTON
NTS > WONT
O *vb* seek the love or affection of (a woman)
OBUT *same as* > WOUBIT
OBUTS > WOOBUT
OD *n* substance trees are made of, used in carpentry and as fuel ▷ *adj* made of or using wood ▷ *vb* (of and) plant with trees
ODBIN *n* box for firewood
ODBIND *same* as > WOODBINE
ODBINDS > WOODBIND
ODBINE *n* honeysuckle
ODBINES > WOODBINE
ODBINS > WOODBIN
ODBLOCK *n* hollow block of wood used as a percussion instrument
ODBORER *n* any of various beetles of the amilies *Anobiidae*, *Buprestidae*, etc, the larvae of which bore into and damage wood
WOODBOX *n* box for firewood
WOODBOXES > WOODBOX
WOODCHAT *n* songbird, *Lanius senator*, of Europe and N Africa, having a black-and-white plumage with a reddish-brown crown and a hooked bill
WOODCHATS > WOODCHAT
WOODCHIP *n* textured wallpaper
WOODCHIPS > WOODCHIP
WOODCHOP *n* wood-chopping competition, esp at a show
WOODCHOPS > WOODCHOP
WOODCHUCK *n* North American marmot, *Marmota monax*, having coarse reddish-brown fur
WOODCOCK *n* game bird
WOODCOCKS > WOODCOCK
WOODCRAFT *n* ability and experience in matters concerned with living in a wood or forest
WOODCUT *n* (print made from) an engraved block of wood
WOODCUTS > WOODCUT
WOODED *adj* covered with trees
WOODEN *adj* made of wood ▷ *vb* fell or kill (a person or animal)
WOODENED > WOODEN
WOODENER > WOODEN
WOODENEST > WOODEN
WOODENING > WOODEN
WOODENLY > WOODEN
WOODENS > WOODEN
WOODENTOP *n* dull, foolish, or unintelligent person
WOODFREE *adj* (of high-quality paper) made from pulp that has been treated chemically, removing impurities
WOODGRAIN *n* grain in wood
WOODHEN *another name for* > WEKA
WOODHENS > WOODHEN
WOODHOLE *n* store area for wood
WOODHOLES > WOODHOLE
WOODHORSE *n* frame for holding wood being sawn
WOODHOUSE *n* shed for firewood
WOODIE *n* gallows rope
WOODIER > WOODY
WOODIES > WOODIE
WOODIEST > WOODY
WOODINESS > WOODY
WOODING > WOOD
WOODLAND *n* forest ▷ *adj* living in woods
WOODLANDS > WOODLAND
WOODLARK *n* Old World lark, *Lullula arborea*, similar to but slightly smaller than the skylark
WOODLARKS > WOODLARK
WOODLESS > WOOD
WOODLICE > WOODLOUSE
WOODLORE *n* woodcraft skills
WOODLORES > WOODLORE
WOODLOT *n* area restricted to the growing of trees
WOODLOTS > WOODLOT
WOODLOUSE *n* small insect-like creature with many legs
WOODMAN *same as* > WOODSMAN
WOODMEAL *n* sawdust powder
WOODMEALS > WOODMEAL
WOODMEN > WOODMAN
WOODMICE > WOODMOUSE
WOODMOUSE *n* field mouse
WOODNESS > WOOD
WOODNOTE *n* natural musical note or song, like that of a wild bird
WOODNOTES > WOODNOTE
WOODPILE *n* heap of firewood
WOODPILES > WOODPILE
WOODPRINT *another name for* > WOODCUT
WOODREEVE *n* steward responsible for wood
WOODROOF *same as* > WOODRUFF
WOODROOFS > WOODROOF
WOODRUFF *n* plant with small sweet-smelling white flowers and sweet-smelling leaves
WOODRUFFS > WOODRUFF
WOODRUSH *n* any of various juncaceous plants of the genus *Luzula*, chiefly of cold and temperate regions of the N hemisphere, having grasslike leaves and small brown flowers
WOODS *pl n* closely packed trees forming a forest or wood
WOODSCREW *n* metal screw that tapers to a point so that it can be driven into wood by a screwdriver
WOODSHED *n* small outbuilding where firewood, garden tools, etc, are stored
WOODSHEDS > WOODSHED
WOODSHOCK *n* type of bird
WOODSIA *n* any small fern of the genus *Woodsia*, of temperate and cold regions, having tufted rhizomes and numerous wiry fronds
WOODSIAS > WOODSIA
WOODSIER > WOODSY
WOODSIEST > WOODSY
WOODSKIN *n* canoe made of bark
WOODSKINS > WOODSKIN
WOODSMAN *n* person who lives in a wood or who is skilled at woodwork or carving
WOODSMEN > WOODSMAN
WOODSPITE *n* green woodpecker
WOODSTONE *n* type of stone resembling wood
WOODSTOVE *n* wood-burning stove
WOODSY *adj* of, reminiscent of, or connected with woods
WOODTONE *n* colour matching that of wood
WOODTONES > WOODTONE
WOODWALE *n* green woodpecker
WOODWALES > WOODWALE
WOODWARD *n* person in charge of a forest or wood
WOODWARDS > WOODWARD
WOODWAX *same as* > WOODWAXEN
WOODWAXEN *same as* > WOADWAXEN
WOODWAXES > WOODWAX
WOODWIND *n* (of) a type of wind instrument made of wood ▷ *adj* of or denoting a type of wind instrument, such as the oboe
WOODWINDS > WOODWIND
WOODWORK *n* parts of a room or building made of wood
WOODWORKS > WOODWORK
WOODWORM *n* insect larva that bores into wood
WOODWORMS > WOODWORM
WOODWOSE *n* hairy wildman of the woods
WOODWOSES > WOODWOSE
WOODY *adj* (of a plant) having a very hard stem
WOODYARD *n* place where timber is cut and stored
WOODYARDS > WOODYARD
WOOED > WOO
WOOER > WOO
WOOERS > WOO
WOOF *vb* (of dogs) bark or growl
WOOFED > WOOF
WOOFER *n* loudspeaker reproducing low-frequency sounds
WOOFERS > WOOFER
WOOFIER > WOOFY
WOOFIEST > WOOFY
WOOFING > WOOF
WOOFS > WOOF
WOOFTER *n* derogatory term for a male homosexual
WOOFTERS > WOOFTER
WOOFY *adj* with close, dense texture
WOOING > WOO
WOOINGLY > WOO
WOOINGS > WOO
WOOL *n* soft hair of sheep, goats, etc
WOOLD *vb* wind (rope)

WOOLDED > WOOLD
WOOLDER *n* stick for winding rope
WOOLDERS > WOOLDER
WOOLDING > WOOLD
WOOLDINGS > WOOLD
WOOLDS > WOOLD
WOOLED *same as* > WOOLLED
WOOLEN *same as* > WOOLLEN
WOOLENS > WOOLEN
WOOLER *same as* > WOOLDER
WOOLERS > WOOLER
WOOLFAT *same as* > LANOLIN
WOOLFATS > WOOLFAT
WOOLFELL *n* skin of a sheep or similar animal with the fleece still attached
WOOLFELLS > WOOLFELL
WOOLHAT *n* poor white person in S States
WOOLHATS > WOOLHAT
WOOLIE *n* wool garment
WOOLIER > WOOLY
WOOLIES > WOOLY
WOOLIEST > WOOLY
WOOLINESS > WOOLY
WOOLLED *adj* (of animals) having wool
WOOLLEN *adj* relating to or consisting partly or wholly of wool ▷ *n* garment or piece of cloth made wholly or partly of wool, esp a knitted one
WOOLLENS > WOOLLEN
WOOLLIER > WOOLLY
WOOLLIES > WOOLLY
WOOLLIEST > WOOLLY
WOOLLIKE > WOOL
WOOLLILY > WOOLLY
WOOLLY *adj* of or like wool ▷ *n* knitted woollen garment
WOOLMAN *n* wool trader
WOOLMEN > WOOLMAN
WOOLPACK *n* cloth or canvas wrapping used to pack a bale of wool
WOOLPACKS > WOOLPACK
WOOLS > WOOL
WOOLSACK *n* sack containing or intended to contain wool
WOOLSACKS > WOOLSACK
WOOLSEY *n* cotton and wool blend
WOOLSEYS > WOOLSEY
WOOLSHED *n* large building in which sheep shearing takes place
WOOLSHEDS > WOOLSHED
WOOLSKIN *n* sheepskin with wool still on
WOOLSKINS > WOOLSKIN
WOOLWARD *adv* with woollen side touching the skin
WOOLWORK *n* embroidery with wool
WOOLWORKS > WOOLWORK
WOOLY *same as* > WOOLLY
WOOMERA *n* notched stick used by Australian Aborigines to aid the propulsion of a spear
WOOMERANG *same as* > WOOMERA
WOOMERAS > WOOMERA
WOON *same as* > WON
WOONED > WOON
WOONING > WOON
WOONS > WOON
WOOPIE *n* well-off older person
WOOPIES > WOOPIE
WOOPS *vb* (esp of small child) vomit
WOOPSED > WOOPS
WOOPSES > WOOPS
WOOPSING > WOOPS
WOORALI *less common name for* > CURARE
WOORALIS > WOORALI
WOORARA *same as* > WOURALI
WOORARAS > WOORARA
WOORARI *same as* > WOURALI
WOORARIS > WOORARI
WOOS > WOO
WOOSE *same as* > WUSS
WOOSEL *same as* > OUZEL
WOOSELL *same as* > OUZEL
WOOSELLS > WOOSELL
WOOSELS > WOOSEL
WOOSES > WOOSE
WOOSH *same as* > WHOOSH
WOOSHED > WOOSH
WOOSHES > WOOSH
WOOSHING > WOOSH
WOOT *vb* wilt thou?
WOOTZ *n* Middle-Eastern steel
WOOTZES > WOOTZ
WOOZIER > WOOZY
WOOZIEST > WOOZY
WOOZILY > WOOZY
WOOZINESS > WOOZY
WOOZY *adj* weak, dizzy, and confused
WOP *same as* > WHOP
WOPPED > WOP
WOPPING > WOP
WOPS > WOP
WORCESTER *n* type of woollen fabric
WORD *n* smallest single meaningful unit of speech or writing ▷ *vb* express in words
WORDAGE *n* words considered collectively, esp a quantity of words
WORDAGES > WORDAGE
WORDBOOK *n* book containing words, usually with their meanings
WORDBOOKS > WORDBOOK
WORDBOUND *adj* unable to find words to express sth
WORDBREAK *n* point at which a word is divided when it runs over from one line of print to the next
WORDED > WORD
WORDGAME *n* any game involving the formation, discovery, or alteration of a word or words
WORDGAMES > WORDGAME
WORDIER > WORDY
WORDIEST > WORDY
WORDILY > WORDY
WORDINESS > WORDY
WORDING *n* choice and arrangement of words
WORDINGS > WORDING
WORDISH *adj* talkative
WORDLESS *adj* inarticulate or silent
WORDLORE *n* knowledge about words
WORDLORES > WORDLORE
WORDPLAY *n* verbal wit based on the meanings and ambiguities of words
WORDPLAYS > WORDPLAY
WORDS > WORD
WORDSMITH *n* person skilled in using words
WORDY *adj* using too many words
WORE > WEAR
WORK *n* physical or mental effort directed to making or doing something ▷ *adj* of or for work ▷ *vb* (cause to) do work
WORKABLE *adj* able to operate efficiently
WORKABLY > WORKABLE
WORKADAY *n* working day ▷ *adj* ordinary
WORKADAYS > WORKADAY
WORKBAG *n* container for implements, tools, or materials, esp sewing equipment
WORKBAGS > WORKBAG
WORKBENCH *n* heavy table at which a craftsman or mechanic works
WORKBOAT *n* boat used for tasks
WORKBOATS > WORKBOAT
WORKBOOK *n* exercise book or textbook used for study, esp a textbook with spaces for answers
WORKBOOKS > WORKBOOK
WORKBOX *same as* > WORKBAG
WORKBOXES > WORKBOX
WORKDAY *another word for* > WORKADAY
WORKDAYS > WORKDAY
WORKED *adj* made or decorated with evidence of workmanship
WORKER *n* person who works in a specified way
WORKERIST *n* supporter of working-class politics
WORKERS > WORKER
WORKFARE *n* scheme under which the government of a country requires unemployed people to do community work or undergo job training in return for social-security payments
WORKFARES > WORKFARE
WORKFLOW *n* rate of progress of work
WORKFLOWS > WORKFLOW
WORKFOLK *pl n* working people, esp labourers on a farm
WORKFOLKS *same as* > WORKFOLK
WORKFORCE *n* total numb
of workers
WORKFUL *adj* hardworking
WORKGIRL *n* young femal
manual worker
WORKGIRLS > WORKGIRL
WORKGROUP *n* collection o
networked computers
WORKHORSE *n* person or thing that does a lot of du
or routine work
WORKHOUR *n* time set asid
for work
WORKHOURS > WORKHOUR
WORKHOUSE *n* (in England formerly) institution where the poor were given food and lodgings i
return for work
WORKING *n* operation or mode of operation of something ▷ *adj* relatin
to or concerned with a person or thing that wor
WORKINGS > WORKING
WORKLESS > WORK
WORKLOAD *n* amount of work to be done, esp in a specified period
WORKLOADS > WORKLOAD
WORKMAN *n* manual worke
WORKMANLY *adj* appropria
to or befitting a good workman
WORKMATE *n* person who works with another person
WORKMATES > WORKMATE
WORKMEN > WORKMAN
WORKOUT *n* session of physical exercise for training or fitness
WORKOUTS > WORKOUT
WORKPIECE *n* piece of metal or other material that is in the process of being worked on or mad
or has actually been cut c
shaped by a hand tool or machine
WORKPLACE *n* place, such
a factory or office, where
people work
WORKPRINT *n* unfinished print of cinema film
WORKROOM *n* room in whic
work, usually manual labour, is done
WORKROOMS > WORKROOM
WORKS > WORK
WORKSHEET *n* sheet of paper containing exercis
to be completed by a student
WORKSHOP *n* room or building for a manufacturing process

> *vb* perform (a play) with no costumes, set, or musical accompaniment
RKSHOPS > WORKSHOP
RKSHY *adj* not inclined to work
RKSOME *adj* hardworking
RKSPACE *n* area set aside for work
RKTABLE *n* table at which writing, sewing, or other work may be done
RKTOP *n* surface in a kitchen, used for food preparation
RKTOPS > WORKTOP
RKUP *n* medical examination
RKUPS > WORKUP
RKWEAR *n* clothes, such as overalls, as worn for work in a factory, shop, etc
RKWEARS > WORKWEAR
RKWEEK *n* number of hours or days in a week actually or officially allocated to work
RKWEEKS > WORKWEEK
RKWOMAN *n* female manual worker
RKWOMEN > WORKWOMAN
RLD *n* planet earth ▷ *adj* of the whole world
RLDBEAT *n* popular music from outside western mainstream
RLDED *adj* incorporating worlds
RLDLIER > WORLDLY
RLDLING *n* person who is primarily concerned with worldly matters or material things
RLDLY *adj* not spiritual ▷ *adv* in a worldly manner
RLDS > WORLD
RLDVIEW *n* comprehensive view of human life and the universe
RLDWIDE *adj* applying or extending throughout the world
RM *n* small limbless invertebrate animal ▷ *vb* rid of worms
RMCAST *n* coil of earth excreted by a burrowing worm
RMCASTS > WORMCAST
RMED > WORM
RMER > WORM
RMERIES > WORMERY
RMERS > WORM
RMERY *n* piece of apparatus, having a glass side or sides, in which worms are kept for study
RMFLIES > WORMFLY
RMFLY *n* type of lure dressed on a double hook, the barbs of which sit one above the other and back-to-back

WORMGEAR *n* gear with screw thread
WORMGEARS > WORMGEAR
WORMHOLE *n* hole made by a worm in timber, plants, or fruit
WORMHOLED > WORMHOLE
WORMHOLES > WORMHOLE
WORMIER > WORMY
WORMIEST > WORMY
WORMIL *n* burrowing larva of type of fly
WORMILS > WORMIL
WORMINESS > WORMY
WORMING > WORM
WORMISH > WORM
WORMLIKE > WORM
WORMROOT *n* plant used to cure worms
WORMROOTS > WORMROOT
WORMS *n* disease caused by parasitic worms living in the intestines
WORMSEED *n* any of various plants having seeds or other parts used in medicine to treat worm infestation
WORMSEEDS > WORMSEED
WORMWOOD *n* bitter plant
WORMWOODS > WORMWOOD
WORMY *adj* infested with or eaten by worms
WORN > WEAR
WORNNESS *n* quality or condition of being worn
WORRAL *n* type of lizard
WORRALS > WORRAL
WORREL *same as* > WORRAL
WORRELS > WORREL
WORRICOW *n* frightening creature
WORRICOWS > WORRICOW
WORRIED > WORRY
WORRIEDLY > WORRY
WORRIER > WORRY
WORRIERS > WORRY
WORRIES > WORRY
WORRIMENT *n* anxiety or the trouble that causes it
WORRISOME *adj* causing worry
WORRIT *vb* tease or worry
WORRITED > WORRIT
WORRITING > WORRIT
WORRITS > WORRIT
WORRY *vb* (cause to) be anxious or uneasy ▷ *n* (cause of) anxiety or concern
WORRYCOW *same as* > WORRICOW
WORRYCOWS > WORRYCOW
WORRYGUTS *n* person who tends to worry, esp about insignificant matters
WORRYING > WORRY
WORRYINGS > WORRY
WORRYWART *same as* > WORRYGUTS
WORSE *vb* defeat
WORSED > WORSE
WORSEN *vb* make or grow worse

WORSENED > WORSEN
WORSENESS *n* state or condition of being worse
WORSENING > WORSEN
WORSENS > WORSEN
WORSER *archaic or nonstandard word for* > WORSE
WORSES > WORSE
WORSET *n* worsted fabric
WORSETS > WORSET
WORSHIP *vb* show religious devotion to ▷ *n* act or instance of worshipping
WORSHIPED > WORSHIP
WORSHIPER *same as* > WORSHIPPER
WORSHIPS > WORSHIP
WORSING > WORSE
WORST *n* worst thing ▷ *vb* defeat
WORSTED *n* type of woollen yarn or fabric
WORSTEDS > WORSTED
WORSTING > WORST
WORSTS > WORST
WORT *n* any of various unrelated plants, esp ones formerly used to cure diseases
WORTH *prep* having a value of ▷ *n* value or price ▷ *vb* happen or betide
WORTHED > WORTH
WORTHFUL *adj* worthy
WORTHIED > WORTHY
WORTHIER > WORTHY
WORTHIES > WORTHY
WORTHIEST > WORTHY
WORTHILY > WORTHY
WORTHING > WORTH
WORTHLESS *adj* without value or usefulness
WORTHS > WORTH
WORTHY *adj* deserving admiration or respect ▷ *n* notable person ▷ *vb* make worthy
WORTHYING > WORTHY
WORTLE *n* plate with holes for drawing wire through
WORTLES > WORTLE
WORTS > WORT
WOS > WO
WOSBIRD *n* illegitimate child
WOSBIRDS > WOSBIRD
WOST *obsolete 2nd pers sing of* wit, to know
WOT *form of the present tense (indicative mood) of* wit, to know
WOTCHER *sentence substitute* slang term of greeting
WOTS > WOT
WOTTED > WOT
WOTTEST > WOT
WOTTETH > WOT
WOTTING > WOT
WOUBIT *n* type of caterpillar
WOUBITS > WOUBIT
WOULD > WILL
WOULDEST *same as* > WOULDST

WOULDS *same as* > WOULDST
WOULDST *singular form of the past tense of* > WILL
WOUND *vb* injure ▷ *n* injury
WOUNDABLE > WOUND
WOUNDED *adj* suffering from wounds
WOUNDEDLY > WOUNDED
WOUNDER > WOUND
WOUNDERS > WOUND
WOUNDILY > WOUNDY
WOUNDING > WOUND
WOUNDINGS > WOUND
WOUNDLESS > WOUND
WOUNDS > WOUND
WOUNDWORT *n* type of plant formerly used for dressing wounds
WOUNDY *adj* extreme
WOURALI *n* plant from which curare is obtained
WOURALIS > WOURALI
WOVE > WEAVE
WOVEN *n* article made from woven cloth
WOVENS > WOVEN
WOW *interj* exclamation of astonishment ▷ *n* astonishing person or thing ▷ *vb* be a great success with
WOWED > WOW
WOWEE *stronger form of* > WOW
WOWF *adj* mad
WOWFER > WOWF
WOWFEST > WOWF
WOWING > WOW
WOWS > WOW
WOWSER *n* puritanical person
WOWSERS > WOWSER
WOX > WAX
WOXEN > WAX
WRACK *n* seaweed ▷ *vb* strain or shake (something) violently
WRACKED > WRACK
WRACKFUL *n* ruinous
WRACKING > WRACK
WRACKS > WRACK
WRAITH *n* ghost
WRAITHS > WRAITH
WRANG *Scot word for* > WRONG
WRANGED > WRANG
WRANGING > WRANG
WRANGLE *vb* argue noisily ▷ *n* noisy argument
WRANGLED > WRANGLE
WRANGLER *n* one who wrangles
WRANGLERS > WRANGLER
WRANGLES > WRANGLE
WRANGLING > WRANGLE
WRANGS > WRANG
WRAP *vb* fold (something) round (a person or thing) so as to cover ▷ *n* garment wrapped round the shoulders
WRAPOVER *adj* (of a garment, esp a skirt) not sewn up at one side, but

worn wrapped round the body and fastened so that the open edges overlap ▷ *n* such a garment
WRAPOVERS > WRAPOVER
WRAPPAGE *n* material for wrapping
WRAPPAGES > WRAPPAGE
WRAPPED > WRAP
WRAPPER *vb* cover with wrapping ▷ *n* cover for a product
WRAPPERED > WRAPPER
WRAPPERS > WRAPPER
WRAPPING > WRAP
WRAPPINGS > WRAP
WRAPROUND *same as* > WRAPOVER
WRAPS > WRAP
WRAPT *same as* > RAPT
WRASSE *n* colourful sea fish
WRASSES > WRASSE
WRASSLE *same as* > WRESTLE
WRASSLED > WRASSLE
WRASSLES > WRASSLE
WRASSLING > WRASSLE
WRAST *same as* > WREST
WRASTED > WRAST
WRASTING > WRAST
WRASTLE *same as* > WRESTLE
WRASTLED > WRASTLE
WRASTLES > WRASTLE
WRASTLING > WRASTLE
WRASTS > WRAST
WRATE > WRITE
WRATH *n* intense anger ▷ *adj* incensed ▷ *vb* make angry
WRATHED > WRATH
WRATHFUL *adj* full of wrath
WRATHIER > WRATHY
WRATHIEST > WRATHY
WRATHILY > WRATHY
WRATHING > WRATH
WRATHLESS > WRATH
WRATHS > WRATH
WRATHY *same as* > WRATHFUL
WRAWL *vb* howl
WRAWLED > WRAWL
WRAWLING > WRAWL
WRAWLS > WRAWL
WRAXLE *vb* wrestle
WRAXLED > WRAXLE
WRAXLES > WRAXLE
WRAXLING > WRAXLE
WRAXLINGS > WRAXLE
WREAK *vb* inflict (vengeance, etc) or to cause (chaos, etc)
WREAKED > WREAK
WREAKER > WREAK
WREAKERS > WREAK
WREAKFUL *adj* seeking revenge
WREAKING > WREAK
WREAKLESS *adj* unrevengeful
WREAKS > WREAK
WREATH *n* twisted ring or band of flowers or leaves used as a memorial or tribute
WREATHE *vb* form into or take the form of a wreath by intertwining or twisting together
WREATHED > WREATHE
WREATHEN *adj* twisted into wreath
WREATHER > WREATHE
WREATHERS > WREATHE
WREATHES > WREATHE
WREATHIER > WREATHY
WREATHING > WREATHE
WREATHS > WREATH
WREATHY *adj* twisted into wreath
WRECK *vb* destroy ▷ *n* remains of something that has been destroyed or badly damaged, esp a ship
WRECKAGE *n* wrecked remains
WRECKAGES > WRECKAGE
WRECKED *adj* in a state of intoxication, stupor, or euphoria, induced by drugs or alcohol
WRECKER *n* formerly, person who lured ships onto the rocks in order to plunder them
WRECKERS > WRECKER
WRECKFISH *n* large sea perch
WRECKFUL *adj* causing wreckage
WRECKING > WRECK
WRECKINGS > WRECK
WRECKS > WRECK
WREN *n* small brown songbird
WRENCH *vb* twist or pull violently ▷ *n* violent twist or pull
WRENCHED > WRENCH
WRENCHER > WRENCH
WRENCHERS > WRENCH
WRENCHES > WRENCH
WRENCHING > WRENCH
WRENS > WREN
WREST *vb* twist violently ▷ *n* act or an instance of wresting
WRESTED > WREST
WRESTER > WREST
WRESTERS > WREST
WRESTING > WREST
WRESTLE *vb* fight, esp as a sport, by grappling with and trying to throw down an opponent ▷ *n* act of wrestling
WRESTLED > WRESTLE
WRESTLER > WRESTLE
WRESTLERS > WRESTLE
WRESTLES > WRESTLE
WRESTLING *n* sport in which each contestant tries to overcome the other either by throwing or pinning him or her to the ground or by forcing a submission
WRESTS > WREST
WRETCH *n* despicable person
WRETCHED *adj* miserable or unhappy
WRETCHES > WRETCH
WRETHE *same as* > WREATHE
WRETHED > WRETHE
WRETHES > WRETHE
WRETHING > WRETHE
WRICK *variant spelling (chiefly Brit) of* > RICK
WRICKED > WRICK
WRICKING > WRICK
WRICKS > WRICK
WRIED > WRY
WRIER > WRY
WRIES > WRY
WRIEST > WRY
WRIGGLE *vb* move with a twisting action ▷ *n* wriggling movement
WRIGGLED > WRIGGLE
WRIGGLER > WRIGGLE
WRIGGLERS > WRIGGLE
WRIGGLES > WRIGGLE
WRIGGLIER > WRIGGLE
WRIGGLING > WRIGGLE
WRIGGLY > WRIGGLE
WRIGHT *n* maker
WRIGHTS > WRIGHT
WRING *vb* twist, esp to squeeze liquid out of
WRINGED > WRING
WRINGER *same as* > MANGLE
WRINGERS > WRINGER
WRINGING > WRING
WRINGINGS > WRING
WRINGS > WRING
WRINKLE *n* slight crease, esp one in the skin due to age ▷ *vb* make or become slightly creased
WRINKLED > WRINKLE
WRINKLES > WRINKLE
WRINKLIER > WRINKLE
WRINKLIES *pl n* derogatory word for old people
WRINKLING > WRINKLE
WRINKLY > WRINKLE
WRIST *n* joint between the hand and the arm
WRISTBAND *n* band around the wrist, esp one attached to a watch or forming part of a long sleeve
WRISTIER > WRISTY
WRISTIEST > WRISTY
WRISTLET *n* band or bracelet worn around the wrist
WRISTLETS > WRISTLET
WRISTLOCK *n* wrestling hold in which a wrestler seizes his opponent's wrist and exerts pressure against the joints of his hand, arm, or shoulder
WRISTS > WRIST
WRISTY *adj* (of a player's style of hitting the ball in cricket, tennis, etc) characterized by considerable movement of the wrist
WRIT *n* written legal command
WRITABLE > WRITE
WRITATIVE *adj* inclined to write a lot
WRITE *vb* mark paper etc with symbols or words
WRITEABLE > WRITE
WRITER *n* author
WRITERESS *n* female writ
WRITERLY *adj* of or characteristic of a writer
WRITERS > WRITER
WRITES > WRITE
WRITHE *vb* twist or squirm in or as if in pain ▷ *n* act or an instance of writhing
WRITHED > WRITHE
WRITHEN *adj* twisted
WRITHER > WRITHE
WRITHERS > WRITHE
WRITHES > WRITHE
WRITHING > WRITHE
WRITHINGS > WRITHE
WRITHLED *adj* wrinkled
WRITING > WRITE
WRITINGS > WRITE
WRITS > WRIT
WRITTEN > WRITE
WRIZLED *adj* wrinkled
WROATH *n* unforeseen trouble
WROATHS > WROATH
WROKE > WREAK
WROKEN > WREAK
WRONG *adj* incorrect or mistaken ▷ *adv* in a wrong manner ▷ *n* something immoral or unjust ▷ *vb* treat unjust
WRONGDOER *n* person who acts immorally or illegall
WRONGED > WRONG
WRONGER > WRONG
WRONGERS > WRONG
WRONGEST > WRONG
WRONGFUL *adj* unjust or illegal
WRONGING > WRONG
WRONGLY > WRONG
WRONGNESS > WRONG
WRONGOUS *adj* unfair
WRONGS > WRONG
WROOT *obsolete form of* > ROOT
WROOTED > WROOT
WROOTING > WROOT
WROOTS > WROOT
WROTE > WRITE
WROTH *adj* angry
WROTHFUL *same as* > WRATHFUL
WROUGHT *adj* (of metals) shaped by hammering or beating
WRUNG > WRING
WRY *adj* drily humorous ▷ *vb* twist or contort
WRYBILL *n* New Zealand plover whose bill is bent to one side enabling it to search for food beneath stones
WRYBILLS > WRYBILL
WRYER > WRY
WRYEST > WRY

RYING >WRY
RYLY >WRY
RYNECK *n* woodpecker that has a habit of twisting its neck round
RYNECKS >WRYNECK
RYNESS >WRY
RYNESSES >WRY
RYTHEN *adj* twisted
D *Scots form of* >WOOD
JDDED >WUD
DDING >WUD
JDJULA *n* Australian word for a non-Aboriginal person
DJULAS >WUDJULA
JDS >WUD
DU *n* practice of ritual washing before daily prayer
JDUS >WUDU
KKAS *pl n* Australian taboo slang expression for no problems
JLFENITE *n* yellow, orange, red, or grey lustrous secondary mineral
JLL *obsolete form of* >WILL
LLED >WILL
JLLING >WILL
LLS >WILL
JNNER *same as* >ONER
NNERS >WUNNER
JRLEY *n* Aboriginal hut
RLEYS >WURLEY
JRLIE *same as* >WURLEY
RLIES >WURLIE
JRST *n* large sausage, esp of a type made in Germany, Austria, etc
RSTS >WURST
JRTZITE *n* zinc sulphide
RTZITES >WURTZITE
JRZEL *n* root
RZELS >WURZEL
JS *n* casual term of address
JSES >WUS
SHU *n* Chinese martial arts
SHUS >WUSHU
JSS *n* feeble or effeminate person
JSSES >WUSS
SSIER >WUSSY
JSSIES >WUSSY
SSIEST >WUSSY
JSSY *adj* feeble or effeminate ▷ *n* feeble person
THER *vb* (of wind) blow and roar
THERED >WUTHER
JTHERING *adj* (of a wind) blowing strongly with a roaring sound
THERS >WUTHER
JXIA *n* genre of Chinese fiction and film, concerning the adventures of sword-wielding chivalrous heroes
XIAS >WUXIA
WUZZLE *vb* mix up
WUZZLED >WUZZLE
WUZZLES >WUZZLE
WUZZLING >WUZZLE
WYANDOTTE *n* heavy American breed of domestic fowl
WYCH *n* type of tree having flexible branches
WYCHES >WYCH
WYE *n* y-shaped pipe
WYES >WYE
WYLE *vb* entice
WYLED >WYLE
WYLES >WYLE
WYLIECOAT *n* petticoat
WYLING >WYLE
WYN *n* rune equivalent to English 'w'
WYND *n* narrow lane or alley
WYNDS >WYND
WYNN *same as* >WYN
WYNNS >WYNN
WYNS >WYN
WYSIWYG *adj* (of text and images displayed on a computer screen) being the same as what will be printed out
WYTE *vb* blame
WYTED >WYTE
WYTES >WYTE
WYTING >WYTE
WYVERN *n* heraldic beast having a serpent's tail and a dragon's head and a body with wings and two legs
WYVERNS >WYVERN

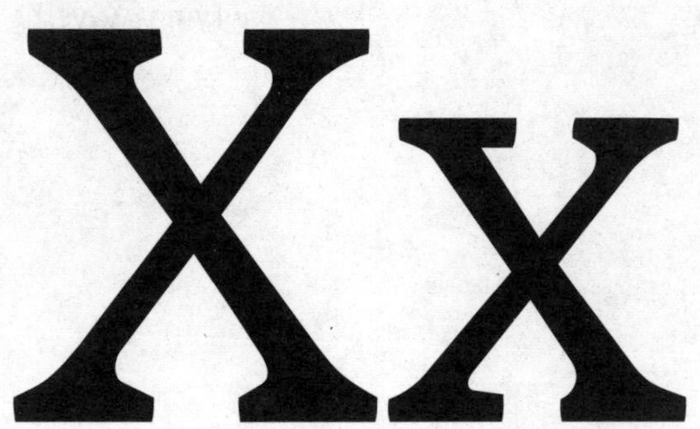

XANTHAM *n* acacia gum
XANTHAMS > XANTHAM
XANTHAN *same as* > XANTHAM
XANTHANS > XANTHAN
XANTHATE *n* any salt or ester of xanthic acid
XANTHATES > XANTHATE
XANTHEIN *n* soluble part of the yellow pigment that is found in the cell sap of some flowers
XANTHEINS > XANTHEIN
XANTHENE *n* yellowish crystalline heterocyclic compound used as a fungicide
XANTHENES > XANTHENE
XANTHIC *adj* of, containing, or derived from xanthic acid
XANTHIN *n* any of a group of yellow or orange carotene derivatives that occur in the fruit and flowers of certain plants
XANTHINE *n* crystalline compound related in structure to uric acid and found in urine, blood, certain plants, and certain animal tissues
XANTHINES > XANTHINE
XANTHINS > XANTHIN
XANTHISM *n* condition of skin, fur, or feathers in which yellow coloration predominates
XANTHISMS > XANTHISM
XANTHOMA *n* presence in the skin of fatty yellow or brownish plaques or nodules, esp on the eyelids, caused by a disorder of lipid metabolism
XANTHOMAS > XANTHOMA
XANTHONE *n* crystalline compound
XANTHONES > XANTHONE
XANTHOUS *adj* of, relating to, or designating races with yellowish hair and a light complexion
XANTHOXYL *n* South American plant
XEBEC *n* small three-masted Mediterranean vessel with both square and lateen sails, formerly used by Algerian pirates and later used for commerce
XEBECS > XEBEC
XENIA *n* influence of pollen upon the form of the fruit developing after pollination
XENIAL > XENIA
XENIAS > XENIA
XENIC *adj* denoting the presence of bacteria
XENIUM *n* diplomatic gift
XENOBLAST *n* type of mineral deposit
XENOCRYST *n* crystal included within an igneous rock as the magma cooled but not formed from it
XENOGAMY *n* fertilization by the fusion of male and female gametes from different individuals of the same species
XENOGENIC *adj* relating to the supposed production of offspring completely unlike either parent
XENOGENY *n* offspring unlike either parent
XENOGRAFT *n* tissue graft obtained from a donor of a different species from the recipient
XENOLITH *n* fragment of rock differing in origin, composition, structure, etc, from the igneous rock enclosing it
XENOLITHS > XENOLITH
XENOMANIA *n* passion for foreign things
XENOMENIA *n* menstruation from unusual orifices
XENON *n* colourless odourless gas found in very small quantities in the air
XENONS > XENON
XENOPHILE *n* person who likes foreigners or things foreign
XENOPHOBE *n* person who hates or fears foreigners or strangers
XENOPHOBY *n* hatred or fear of foreigners or strangers
XENOPHYA *n* parts of shell or skeleton formed by foreign bodies
XENOPUS *n* African frog
XENOPUSES > XENOPUS
XENOTIME *n* yellow-brown mineral
XENOTIMES > XENOTIME
XENURINE *n* type of armadillo
XENURINES > XENURINE
XERAFIN *n* Indian coin
XERAFINS > XERAFIN
XERANSES > XERANSIS
XERANSIS *n* gradual loss c tissue moisture
XERANTIC > XERANSIS
XERAPHIM *same as* > XERAFIN
XERAPHIMS > XERAPHIM
XERARCH *adj* (of a sere) having its origin in a dry habitat
XERASIA *n* dryness of the hair
XERASIAS > XERASIA
XERIC *adj* of, relating to, c growing in dry condition
XERICALLY > XERIC
XERISCAPE *n* landscape designed to conserve water
XEROCHASY *n* release of seeds or pollen on drying
XERODERMA *n* any abnormal dryness of the skin as the result of diminished secretions from the sweat or sebaceous glands
XEROMA *n* excessive dryne of the cornea
XEROMAS > XEROMA
XEROMATA > XEROMA
XEROMORPH *n* xerophilous plant
XEROPHAGY *n* fasting by eating only dry food
XEROPHILE *n* plant or animal who likes living ir dry surroundings
XEROPHILY > XEROPHILE
XEROPHYTE *n* xerophilous

plant, such as a cactus
ROSERE *n* sere that
originates in dry
surroundings
ROSERES > XEROSERE
ROSES > XEROSIS
ROSIS *n* abnormal
dryness of bodily tissues,
esp the skin, eyes, or
mucous membranes
ROSTOMA *n* abnormal
lack of saliva; dryness of
the mouth
ROTES *same as* > XEROSIS
ROTIC > XEROSIS
ROX *n* tradename for
a machine employing
a xerographic copying
process ▷ *vb* produce a
copy (of a document, etc)
using such a machine
ROXED > XEROX
ROXES > XEROX
ROXING > XEROX
RUS *n* ground squirrel
RUSES > XERUS
n 14th letter in the Greek
alphabet
PHOID *adj* shaped like
a sword ▷ *n* part of the
sternum
PHOIDAL > XIPHOID
PHOIDS > XIPHOID
PHOPAGI *n* Siamese
twins joined at the lower
sternum
S > XI
ANA > XOANON
ANON *n* primitive image
of a god, carved, esp
originally, in wood, and
supposed to have fallen
from heaven
n Vietnamese currency
unit
LAN *n* yellow
polysaccharide consisting
of xylose units: occurs in
straw husks and other
woody tissue
LANS > XYLAN
LEM *n* plant tissue that
conducts water and
minerals from the roots to
all other parts
LEMS > XYLEM
LENE *n* type of
hydrocarbon
LENES > XYLENE
LENOL *n* synthetic resin
made from xylene
LENOLS > XYLENOL
LIC > XYLEM
LIDIN *same as* > XYLIDINE
LIDINE *n* mixture of six
isomeric amines derived
from xylene and used in
dyes
LIDINES > XYLIDINE
LIDINS > XYLIDIN
LITOL *n* crystalline
alcohol used as sweetener
LITOLS > XYLITOL
LOCARP *n* fruit, such as
a coconut, having a hard
woody pericarp
XYLOCARPS > XYLOCARP
XYLOGEN *same as* > XYLEM
XYLOGENS > XYLOGEN
XYLOGRAPH *n* engraving in
wood ▷ *vb* print (a design,
illustration, etc) from a
wood engraving
XYLOID *adj* of, relating to,
or resembling wood
XYLOIDIN *n* type of
explosive
XYLOIDINE *same*
as > XYLOIDIN
XYLOIDINS > XYLOIDIN
XYLOL *another name*
(not in technical usage)
for > XYLENE
XYLOLOGY *n* study of the
composition of wood
XYLOLS > XYLOL
XYLOMA *n* hard growth in
fungi
XYLOMAS > XYLOMA
XYLOMATA > XYLOMA
XYLOMETER *n* device for
measuring the specific
gravity of wood
XYLONIC *adj* denoting an
acid formed from xylose
XYLONITE *n* type of plastic
XYLONITES > XYLONITE
XYLOPHAGE *n* creature that
eats wood
XYLOPHONE *n* musical
instrument made of a row
of wooden bars played
with hammers
XYLORIMBA *n* large
xylophone with an
extended range of five
octaves
XYLOSE *n* white crystalline
dextrorotatory sugar
found in the form of xylan
in wood and straw
XYLOSES > XYLOSE
XYLOTOMY *n* preparation
of sections of wood
for examination by
microscope
XYLYL *n* group of atoms
XYLYLS > XYLYL
XYST *n* long portico, esp
one used in ancient Greece
for athletics
XYSTER *n* surgical
instrument for scraping
bone
XYSTERS > XYSTER
XYSTI > XYSTUS
XYSTOI > XYSTOS
XYSTOS *same as* > XYST
XYSTS > XYST
XYSTUS *same as* > XYST

Yy

YA *pron* you
YAAR *n* in informal Indian English, a friend
YAARS > YAAR
YABA *n* informal word for 'yet another bloody acronym'
YABBA *n* form of methamphetamine
YABBAS > YABBA
YABBER *vb* talk or jabber ▷ *n* talk or jabber
YABBERED > YABBER
YABBERING > YABBER
YABBERS > YABBER
YABBIE *same as* > YABBY
YABBIED > YABBY
YABBIES > YABBY
YABBY *n* small freshwater crayfish ▷ *vb* go out to catch yabbies
YABBYING > YABBY
YACCA *n* Australian plant with a woody stem, stiff grasslike leaves, and a spike of small white flowers
YACCAS > YACCA
YACHT *n* large boat with sails or an engine, used for racing or pleasure cruising ▷ *vb* sail in a yacht
YACHTED > YACHT
YACHTER > YACHT
YACHTERS > YACHT
YACHTIE *n* yachtsman
YACHTIES > YACHTIE
YACHTING *n* sport or practice of navigating a yacht
YACHTINGS > YACHTING
YACHTMAN *same as* > YACHTSMAN
YACHTMEN > YACHTMAN
YACHTS > YACHT
YACHTSMAN *n* person who sails a yacht
YACHTSMEN > YACHTSMAN
YACK *same as* > YAK
YACKA *same as* > YACCA
YACKAS > YACKA
YACKED > YACK
YACKER *same as* > YAKKA
YACKERS > YACKER
YACKING > YACK
YACKS > YACK
YAD *n* hand-held pointer used for reading the sefer torah
YADS > YAD
YAE *same as* > AE
YAFF *vb* bark
YAFFED > YAFF
YAFFING > YAFF
YAFFLE *n* woodpecker with a green back and wings, and a red crown
YAFFLES > YAFFLE
YAFFS > YAFF
YAG *n* artificial crystal
YAGER *same as* > JAEGER
YAGERS > YAGER
YAGGER *n* pedlar
YAGGERS > YAGGER
YAGI *n* type of highly directional aerial
YAGIS > YAGI
YAGS > YAG
YAH *interj* exclamation of derision or disgust ▷ *n* affected upper-class person
YAHOO *n* crude coarse person
YAHOOISM > YAHOO
YAHOOISMS > YAHOO
YAHOOS > YAHOO
YAHRZEIT *n* (in Judaism) the anniversary of the death of a close relative, on which it is customary to kindle a light and recite the Kaddish
YAHRZEITS > YAHRZEIT
YAHS > YAH
YAIRD *Scots form of* > YARD
YAIRDS > YAIRD
YAK *n* Tibetan ox with long shaggy hair ▷ *vb* talk continuously about unimportant matters
YAKHDAN *n* box for carrying ice on a pack animal
YAKHDANS > YAKHDAN
YAKIMONO *n* grilled food
YAKIMONOS > YAKIMONO
YAKITORI *n* Japanese dish consisting of small pieces of chicken skewered and grilled
YAKITORIS > YAKITORI
YAKKA *n* work
YAKKAS > YAKKA
YAKKED > YAK
YAKKER *same as* > YAKKA
YAKKERS > YAKKER
YAKKING > YAK
YAKOW *n* animal bred from a male yak and a domestic cow
YAKOWS > YAKOW
YAKS > YAK
YAKUZA *n* Japanese criminal organization involved in illegal gambling, extortion, gun-running, etc
YALD *adj* vigorous
YALE *n* mythical beast with the body of an antelope (or similar animal) and swivelling horns
YALES > YALE
YAM *n* tropical root vegetable
YAMALKA *same as* > YARMULKE
YAMALKAS > YAMALKA
YAMEN *n* (in imperial Chin the office or residence of public official
YAMENS > YAMEN
YAMMER *vb* whine in a complaining manner ▷ yammering sound
YAMMERED > YAMMER
YAMMERER > YAMMER
YAMMERERS > YAMMER
YAMMERING > YAMMER
YAMMERS > YAMMER
YAMPIES > YAMPY
YAMPY *n* foolish person
YAMS > YAM
YAMULKA *same as* > YARMULKE
YAMULKAS > YAMULKA
YAMUN *same as* > YAMEN
YAMUNS > YAMUN
YANG *n* (in Chinese philosophy) one of two complementary principl maintaining harmony in the universe
YANGS > YANG
YANK *vb* pull or jerk suddenly ▷ *n* sudden pu or jerk
YANKED > YANK
YANKER > YANK
YANKERS > YANK
YANKIE *n* shrewish wom
YANKIES > YANKIE

ANKING > YANK
ANKS > YANK
ANQUI *n* slang word for American
ANQUIS > YANQUI
ANTRA *n* diagram used in meditation
ANTRAS > YANTRA
OURT *n* yoghurt
OURTS > YAOURT
AP *vb* bark with a high-pitched sound ▷ *n* high-pitched bark ▷ *interj* imitation or representation of the sound of a dog yapping or people jabbering
APOCK *same as* > YAPOK
APOCKS > YAPOCK
APOK *n* type of opossum
APOKS > YAPOK
APON *same as* > YAUPON
APONS > YAPON
APP *n* type of book binding
APPED > YAP
APPER > YAP
APPERS > YAP
APPIE *n* young aspiring professional
APPIER > YAP
APPIES > YAPPIE
APPIEST > YAP
APPING > YAP
PINGLY > YAP
APPS > YAPP
APPY > YAP
APS > YAP
APSTER > YAP
APSTERS > YAP
AQONA *n* Polynesian shrub
AQONAS > YAQONA
AR *adj* nimble
ARCO *n* derogatory dialect word for a young working-class person who wears casual sports clothes
ARCOS > YARCO
ARD *n* unit of length equal to 36 inches or about 91.4 centimetres ▷ *vb* draft (animals), esp to a saleyard
ARDAGE *n* length measured in yards
ARDAGES > YARDAGE
ARDANG *n* ridge formed by wind erosion
ARDANGS > YARDANG
ARDARM *n* outer end of a ship's yard
ARDARMS > YARDARM
ARDBIRD *n* inexperienced, untrained, or clumsy soldier, esp one employed on menial duties
ARDBIRDS > YARDBIRD
ARDED > YARD
ARDER > YARD
ARDERS > YARD
ARDING *n* group of animals displayed for sale
ARDINGS > YARDING
ARDLAND *n* archaic unit of land
YARDLANDS > YARDLAND
YARDMAN *n* farm overseer
YARDMEN > YARDMAN
YARDS > YARD
YARDSTICK *n* standard against which to judge other people or things
YARDWAND *same as* > YARDSTICK
YARDWANDS > YARDWAND
YARDWORK *n* garden work
YARDWORKS > YARDWORK
YARE *adj* ready, brisk, or eager ▷ *adv* readily or eagerly
YARELY > YARE
YARER > YARE
YAREST > YARE
YARFA *n* peat
YARFAS > YARFA
YARK *vb* make ready
YARKED > YARK
YARKING > YARK
YARKS > YARK
YARMELKE *same as* > YARMULKE
YARMELKES > YARMELKE
YARMULKA *same as* > YARMULKE
YARMULKAS > YARMULKA
YARMULKE *n* skullcap worn by Jewish men
YARMULKES > YARMULKE
YARN *n* thread used for knitting or making cloth ▷ *vb* thread with yarn
YARNED > YARN
YARNER > YARN
YARNERS > YARN
YARNING > YARN
YARNS > YARN
YARPHA *n* peat
YARPHAS > YARPHA
YARR *n* wild white flower
YARRAMAN *n* horse
YARRAMANS > YARRAMAN
YARRAMEN > YARRAMAN
YARRAN *n* small hardy tree, *Acacia homalophylla*, of inland Australia
YARRANS > YARRAN
YARROW *n* wild plant with flat clusters of white flowers
YARROWS > YARROW
YARRS > YARR
YARTA *Shetland word for* > HEART
YARTAS > YARTA
YARTO *same as* > YARTA
YARTOS > YARTO
YASHMAC *same as* > YASHMAK
YASHMACS > YASHMAC
YASHMAK *n* veil worn by a Muslim woman to cover her face in public
YASHMAKS > YASHMAK
YASMAK *same as* > YASHMAK
YASMAKS > YASHMAK
YATAGAN *same as* > YATAGHAN
YATAGANS > YATAGAN
YATAGHAN *n* Turkish sword with a curved single-edged blade
YATAGHANS > YATAGHAN
YATE *n* any of several small eucalyptus trees, esp *Eucalyptus cornuta*, yielding a very hard timber
YATES > YATE
YATTER *vb* talk at length ▷ *n* continuous chatter
YATTERED > YATTER
YATTERING > YATTER
YATTERS > YATTER
YAUD *Scots word for* > MARE
YAUDS > YAUD
YAULD *adj* alert, spritely, or nimble
YAUP *variant spelling of* > YAWP
YAUPED > YAUP
YAUPER > YAUP
YAUPERS > YAUP
YAUPING > YAUP
YAUPON *n* southern US evergreen holly shrub, *Ilex vomitoria*, with spreading branches, scarlet fruits, and oval leaves
YAUPONS > YAUPON
YAUPS > YAUP
YAUTIA *n* any of several Caribbean aroid plants of the genus *Xanthosoma*, cultivated for their edible leaves and underground stems
YAUTIAS > YAUTIA
YAW *vb* (of an aircraft or ship) turn to one side or from side to side while moving ▷ *n* act or movement of yawing
YAWED > YAW
YAWEY > YAWS
YAWING > YAW
YAWL *n* two-masted sailing boat ▷ *vb* howl, weep, or scream harshly
YAWLED > YAWL
YAWLING > YAWL
YAWLS > YAWL
YAWMETER *n* instrument for measuring an aircraft's yaw
YAWMETERS > YAWMETER
YAWN *vb* open the mouth wide and take in air deeply, often when sleepy or bored ▷ *n* act of yawning
YAWNED > YAWN
YAWNER > YAWN
YAWNERS > YAWN
YAWNIER > YAWN
YAWNIEST > YAWN
YAWNING > YAWN
YAWNINGLY > YAWN
YAWNINGS > YAWN
YAWNS > YAWN
YAWNY > YAWN
YAWP *vb* gape or yawn, esp audibly ▷ *n* shout, bark, yelp, or cry
YAWPED > YAWP
YAWPER > YAWP
YAWPERS > YAWP
YAWPING > YAWP
YAWPINGS > YAWP
YAWPS > YAWP
YAWS *n* infectious tropical skin disease
YAWY > YAWS
YAY *interj* exclamation indicating approval, congratulation, or triumph ▷ *n* cry of approval
YAYS > YAY
YBET *archaic past participle of* > BEAT
YBLENT *archaic past participle of* > BLEND
YBORE *archaic past participle of* > BEAR
YBOUND *archaic past participle of* > BIND
YBOUNDEN *archaic past participle of* > BIND
YBRENT *archaic past participle of* > BURN
YCLAD *archaic past participle of* > CLOTHE
YCLED *archaic past participle of* > CLOTHE
YCLEEPE *archaic form of* > CLEPE
YCLEEPED > YCLEEPE
YCLEEPES > YCLEEPE
YCLEEPING > YCLEEPE
YCLEPED *same as* > YCLEPT
YCLEPT *adj* having the name of
YCOND *archaic past participle of* > CON
YDRAD *archaic past participle of* > DREAD
YDRED *archaic past participle of* > DREAD
YE *pron* you ▷ *adj* the
YEA *interj* yes ▷ *adv* indeed or truly ▷ *sentence substitute* > AYE ▷ *n* cry of agreement
YEAD *vb* proceed
YEADING > YEAD
YEADS > YEAD
YEAH *n* positive affirmation
YEAHS > YEAH
YEALDON *n* fuel
YEALDONS > YEALDON
YEALING *n* person of the same age as oneself
YEALINGS > YEALING
YEALM *vb* prepare for thatching
YEALMED > YEALM
YEALMING > YEALM
YEALMS > YEALM
YEAN *vb* (of a sheep or goat) to give birth to (offspring)
YEANED > YEAN
YEANING > YEAN
YEANLING *n* young of a goat or sheep
YEANLINGS > YEANLING
YEANS > YEAN
YEAR *n* time taken for the earth to make one revolution around the sun, about 365 days

YEARBOOK *n* reference book published annually containing details of the previous year's events
YEARBOOKS > YEARBOOK
YEARD *vb* bury
YEARDED > YEARD
YEARDING > YEARD
YEARDS > YEARD
YEAREND *n* end of the year
YEARENDS > YEAREND
YEARLIES > YEARLY
YEARLING *n* animal between one and two years old ▷ *adj* being a year old
YEARLINGS > YEARLING
YEARLONG *adj* throughout a whole year
YEARLY *adv* (happening) every year or once a year ▷ *adj* occurring, done, or appearing once a year or every year ▷ *n* publication, event, etc, that occurs once a year
YEARN *vb* want (something) very much
YEARNED > YEARN
YEARNER > YEARN
YEARNERS > YEARN
YEARNING *n* intense or overpowering longing, desire, or need
YEARNINGS > YEARNING
YEARNS > YEARN
YEARS > YEAR
YEAS > YEA
YEASAYER *n* person who usually agrees with proposals
YEASAYERS > YEASAYER
YEAST *n* fungus used to make bread rise and to ferment alcoholic drinks ▷ *vb* froth or foam
YEASTED > YEAST
YEASTIER > YEASTY
YEASTIEST > YEASTY
YEASTILY > YEASTY
YEASTING > YEAST
YEASTLESS > YEAST
YEASTLIKE > YEAST
YEASTS > YEAST
YEASTY *adj* of, resembling, or containing yeast
YEBO *interj* yes ▷ *sentence substitute* expression of affirmation
YECCH *same as* > YECH
YECCHS > YECCH
YECH *n* expression of disgust
YECHS > YECH
YECHY > YECH
YEDE *same as* > YEAD
YEDES > YEDE
YEDING > YEDE
YEED *same as* > YEAD
YEEDING > YEED
YEEDS > YEED
YEELIN *n* person of the same age as oneself
YEELINS > YEELIN
YEGG *n* burglar or safe-breaker
YEGGMAN *same as* > YEGG
YEGGMEN > YEGGMAN
YEGGS > YEGG
YEH *same as* > YEAH
YELD *adj* (of an animal) barren or too young to bear young
YELDRING *n* yellowhammer (bird)
YELDRINGS > YELDRING
YELDROCK *same as* > YELDRING
YELDROCKS > YELDROCK
YELK *n* yolk of an egg
YELKS > YELK
YELL *vb* shout or scream in a loud or piercing way ▷ *n* loud cry of pain, anger, or fear
YELLED > YELL
YELLER > YELL
YELLERS > YELL
YELLING > YELL
YELLINGS > YELL
YELLOCH *vb* yell
YELLOCHED > YELLOCH
YELLOCHS > YELLOCH
YELLOW *n* colour of gold, a lemon, etc ▷ *adj* of this colour ▷ *vb* make or become yellow
YELLOWED > YELLOW
YELLOWER > YELLOW
YELLOWEST > YELLOW
YELLOWFIN *n* type of tuna
YELLOWIER > YELLOW
YELLOWING > YELLOW
YELLOWISH > YELLOW
YELLOWLY > YELLOW
YELLOWS *n* any of various fungal or viral diseases of plants, characterized by yellowish discoloration and stunting
YELLOWY > YELLOW
YELLS > YELL
YELM *same as* > YEALM
YELMED > YELM
YELMING > YELM
YELMS > YELM
YELP *n* a short sudden cry ▷ *vb* utter a sharp or high-pitched cry of pain
YELPED > YELP
YELPER > YELP
YELPERS > YELP
YELPING > YELP
YELPINGS > YELP
YELPS > YELP
YELT *n* young sow
YELTS > YELT
YEMMER *southwest English form of* > EMBER
YEMMERS > YEMMER
YEN *n* monetary unit of Japan ▷ *vb* have a longing
YENNED > YEN
YENNING > YEN
YENS > YEN
YENTA *n* meddlesome woman
YENTAS > YENTA
YENTE *same as* > YENTA
YENTES > YENTE
YEOMAN *n* farmer owning and farming his own land
YEOMANLY *adj* of, relating to, or like a yeoman ▷ *adv* in a yeomanly manner, as in being brave, staunch, or loyal
YEOMANRY *n* yeomen
YEOMEN > YEOMAN
YEP *n* affirmative statement
YEPS > YEP
YERBA *n* stimulating South American drink made from dried leaves
YERBAS > YERBA
YERD *vb* bury
YERDED > YERD
YERDING > YERD
YERDS > YERD
YERK *vb* tighten stitches
YERKED > YERK
YERKING > YERK
YERKS > YERK
YERSINIA *n* plague bacterium
YERSINIAE > YERSINIA
YERSINIAS > YERSINIA
YES *interj* expresses consent, agreement, or approval ▷ *n* answer or vote of yes ▷ *sentence substitute* used to express acknowledgment, affirmation, consent, agreement, or approval or to answer when one is addressed ▷ *vb* reply in the affirmative
YESES > YES
YESHIVA *n* traditional Jewish school devoted chiefly to the study of rabbinic literature and the Talmud
YESHIVAH *same as* > YESHIVA
YESHIVAHS > YESHIVAH
YESHIVAS > YESHIVA
YESHIVOT > YESHIVA
YESHIVOTH > YESHIVA
YESK *vb* hiccup
YESKED > YESK
YESKING > YESK
YESKS > YESK
YESSED > YES
YESSES > YES
YESSING > YES
YEST *archaic form of* > YEAST
YESTER *adj* of or relating to yesterday
YESTERDAY *n* the day before today ▷ *adv* on or during the day before today
YESTEREVE *n* yesterday evening
YESTERN *same as* > YESTER
YESTREEN *n* yesterday evening
YESTREENS > YESTREEN
YESTS > YEST
YESTY *archaic form of* > YEASTY
YET *adv* up until then or now
YETI *n* large legendary manlike creature alleged to inhabit the Himalayan Mountains
YETIS > YETI
YETT *n* gate or door
YETTIE *n* young, entrepreneurial, and technology-based (perso
YETTIES > YETTIE
YETTS > YETT
YEUK *vb* itch
YEUKED > YEUK
YEUKING > YEUK
YEUKS > YEUK
YEUKY > YEUK
YEVE *vb* give
YEVEN > YEVE
YEVES > YEVE
YEVING > YEVE
YEW *n* evergreen tree with needle-like leaves and re berries
YEWEN *adj* made of yew
YEWS > YEW
YEX *vb* hiccup
YEXED > YEX
YEXES > YEX
YEXING > YEX
YFERE *adv* together
YGLAUNST *archaic past participle of* > GLANCE
YGO *archaic past participle of* > GO
YGOE *archaic past participle of* > GO
YIBBLES *adv* perhaps
YICKER *vb* squeal or sque
YICKERED > YICKER
YICKERING > YICKER
YICKERS > YICKER
YID *n* offensive word for a Jew
YIDAKI *n* long wooden wind instrument played the Aboriginal peoples of Arnhem Land
YIDAKIS > YIDAKI
YIDS > YID
YIELD *vb* produce or bear ▷ *n* amount produced
YIELDABLE > YIELD
YIELDED > YIELD
YIELDER > YIELD
YIELDERS > YIELD
YIELDING *adj* submissive
YIELDINGS > YIELD
YIELDS > YIELD
YIKE *n* argument, squabble, or fight ▷ *vb* argue, squabble, or fight
YIKED > YIKE
YIKES *interj* expression of surprise, fear, or alarm
YIKING > YIKE
YIKKER *vb* squeal or sque
YIKKERED > YIKKER
YIKKERING > YIKKER
YIKKERS > YIKKER
YILL *n* ale

ILLS >YILL
IN *Scots word for* >ONE
INCE *Scots form of* >ONCE
INS >YIN
IP *n* emit a high-pitched bark
IPE *same as* >YIPES
IPES *interj* expression of surprise, fear, or alarm
IPPED >YIP
IPPEE *interj* exclamation of joy or pleasure
IPPER *n* golfer who suffers from a failure of nerve
IPPERS >YIPPER
IPPIE *n* young person sharing hippy ideals
IPPIES >YIPPIE
IPPING >YIP
IPPY *same as* >YIPPIE
IPS >YIP
IRD *vb* bury
IRDED >YIRD
IRDING >YIRD
IRDS >YIRD
IRK *same as* >YERK
IRKED >YIRK
IRKING >YIRK
IRKS >YIRK
IRR *vb* snarl, growl, or yell
IRRED >YIRR
IRRING >YIRR
IRRS >YIRR
IRTH *n* earth
IRTHS >YIRTH
ITE *n* European bunting with a yellowish head and body and brown streaked wings and tail
ITES >YITE
ITIE *same as* >YITE
ITIES >YITIE
ITTEN *adj* frightened
LEM *n* original matter from which the basic elements are said to have been formed following the explosion postulated in the big bang theory of cosmology
LEMS >YLEM
LIKE *Spenserian form of* >ALIKE
LKE *archaic spelling of* >ILK
LKES >YLKE
MOLT *Spenserian past participle of* >MELT
MOLTEN *Spenserian past participle of* >MELT
MPE *Spenserian form of* >IMP
MPES >YMPE
MPING >YMPE
MPT >YMPE
NAMBU *n* South American bird
NAMBUS >YNAMBU
O *interj* expression used as a greeting or to attract someone's attention ▷ *sentence substitute* expression used as a greeting, to attract someone's attention, etc ▷ *n* cry of greeting
YOB *n* bad-mannered aggressive youth
YOBBERIES >YOBBERY
YOBBERY *n* behaviour typical of aggressive surly youths
YOBBISH *adj* typical of aggressive surly youths
YOBBISHLY >YOBBISH
YOBBISM >YOB
YOBBISMS >YOB
YOBBO *same as* >YOB
YOBBOES >YOBBO
YOBBOS >YOBBO
YOBS >YOB
YOCK *vb* chuckle
YOCKED >YOCK
YOCKING >YOCK
YOCKS >YOCK
YOD *n* tenth letter in the Hebrew alphabet
YODE >YEAD
YODEL *vb* sing with abrupt changes between a normal and a falsetto voice ▷ *n* act or sound of yodelling
YODELED >YODEL
YODELER >YODEL
YODELERS >YODEL
YODELING >YODEL
YODELLED >YODEL
YODELLER >YODEL
YODELLERS >YODEL
YODELLING >YODEL
YODELS >YODEL
YODH *same as* >YOD
YODHS >YODH
YODLE *variant spelling of* >YODEL
YODLED >YODLE
YODLER >YODLE
YODLERS >YODLE
YODLES >YODLE
YODLING >YODLE
YODS >YOD
YOGA *n* Hindu method of exercise and discipline aiming at spiritual, mental, and physical wellbeing
YOGAS >YOGA
YOGEE *same as* >YOGI
YOGEES >YOGEE
YOGH *n* character used in Old and Middle English to represent a palatal fricative
YOGHOURT *variant form of* >YOGURT
YOGHOURTS >YOGHOURT
YOGHS >YOGH
YOGHURT *same as* >YOGURT
YOGHURTS >YOGHURT
YOGI *n* person who practises yoga
YOGIC >YOGA
YOGIN *same as* >YOGI
YOGINI >YOGI
YOGINIS >YOGI
YOGINS >YOGIN
YOGIS >YOGI
YOGISM >YOGI
YOGISMS >YOGI
YOGURT *n* slightly sour custard-like food made from milk that has had bacteria added to it, often sweetened and flavoured with fruit
YOGURTS >YOGURT
YOHIMBE *n* bark used in herbal medicine
YOHIMBES >YOHIMBE
YOHIMBINE *n* alkaloid found in the bark of the tree *Corynanthe yohimbe*
YOICK *vb* urge on foxhounds
YOICKED >YOICK
YOICKING >YOICK
YOICKS *interj* cry used by huntsmen to urge on the hounds to the fox ▷ *vb* urge on foxhounds
YOICKSED >YOICKS
YOICKSES >YOICKS
YOICKSING >YOICKS
YOJAN *n* Indian unit of distance
YOJANA *same as* >YOJAN
YOJANAS >YOJANA
YOJANS >YOJAN
YOK *vb* chuckle
YOKE *n* wooden bar put across the necks of two animals to hold them together ▷ *vb* put a yoke on
YOKED >YOKE
YOKEL *n* derogatory term for a person who lives in the country and is usu simple and old-fashioned
YOKELESS >YOKE
YOKELISH >YOKEL
YOKELS >YOKEL
YOKEMATE *n* colleague
YOKEMATES >YOKEMATE
YOKER >YOKE
YOKERS >YOKE
YOKES >YOKE
YOKING >YOKE
YOKINGS >YOKE
YOKKED >YOK
YOKKING >YOK
YOKOZUNA *n* grand champion sumo wrestler
YOKOZUNAS >YOKOZUNA
YOKS >YOK
YOKUL *Shetland word for* >YES
YOLD *archaic past participle of* >YIELD
YOLDRING *n* yellowhammer (bird)
YOLDRINGS >YOLDRING
YOLK *n* yellow part of an egg that provides food for the developing embryo
YOLKED >YOLK
YOLKIER >YOLK
YOLKIEST >YOLK
YOLKLESS >YOLK
YOLKS >YOLK
YOLKY >YOLK
YOM *n* day
YOMIM >YOM
YOMP *vb* walk or trek laboriously, esp heavily laden and over difficult terrain
YOMPED >YOMP
YOMPING >YOMP
YOMPS >YOMP
YON *adj* that or those over there ▷ *adv* yonder ▷ *pron* that person or thing
YOND *same as* >YON
YONDER *adv* over there ▷ *adj* situated over there ▷ *determiner* being at a distance, either within view or as if within view ▷ *n* person
YONDERLY >YONDER
YONDERS >YONDER
YONI *n* female genitalia, regarded as a divine symbol of sexual pleasure
YONIC *adj* resembling a vulva
YONIS >YONI
YONKER *same as* >YOUNKER
YONKERS >YONKER
YONKS *pl n* very long time
YONNIE *n* stone
YONNIES >YONNIE
YONT *same as* >YON
YOOF *n* non-standard spelling of youth, used humorously or facetiously
YOOFS >YOOF
YOOP *n* sob
YOOPS >YOOP
YOPPER *n* (formerly in Britain) a youth employed under the Youth Opportunities Programme)
YOPPERS >YOPPER
YORE *n* time long past ▷ *adv* in the past
YORES >YORE
YORK *vb* bowl or try to bowl (a batsman) by pitching the ball under or just beyond the bat
YORKED >YORK
YORKER *n* ball that pitches just under the bat
YORKERS >YORKER
YORKIE *n* Yorkshire terrier
YORKIES >YORKIE
YORKING >YORK
YORKS >YORK
YORP *vb* shout
YORPED >YORP
YORPING >YORP
YORPS >YORP
YOS >YO
YOTTABYTE *n* very large unit of computer memory
YOU *pron* person or people addressed ▷ *n* personality of the person being addressed
YOUK *vb* itch
YOUKED >YOUK
YOUKING >YOUK
YOUKS >YOUK

YOUNG *adj* in an early stage of life or growth ▷ *n* young people in general; offspring
YOUNGER > YOUNG
YOUNGERS *n* young people
YOUNGEST > YOUNG
YOUNGISH > YOUNG
YOUNGLING *n* young person, animal, or plant
YOUNGLY *adv* youthfully
YOUNGNESS > YOUNG
YOUNGS > YOUNG
YOUNGSTER *n* young person
YOUNGTH *n* youth
YOUNGTHLY *adj* youthful
YOUNGTHS > YOUNGTH
YOUNKER *n* young man
YOUNKERS > YOUNKER
YOUPON *same as* > YAUPON
YOUPONS > YOUPON
YOUR *adj* of, belonging to, or associated with you
YOURN *dialect form of* > YOURS
YOURS *pron* something belonging to you
YOURSELF *pron* reflexive form of *you*
YOURT *same as* > YURT
YOURTS > YOURT
YOUS *pron* refers to more than one person including the person or persons addressed but not including the speaker
YOUSE *same as* > YOUS
YOUTH *n* time of being young
YOUTHEN *vb* render more youthful-seeming
YOUTHENED > YOUTHEN
YOUTHENS > YOUTHEN
YOUTHFUL *adj* vigorous or active
YOUTHHEAD *same as* > YOUTHHOOD
YOUTHHOOD *n* youth
YOUTHIER > YOUTHY
YOUTHIEST > YOUTHY
YOUTHLESS > YOUTH
YOUTHLY *adv* young
YOUTHS > YOUTH
YOUTHSOME *archaic variant of* > YOUTHFUL
YOUTHY *Scots word for* > YOUNG
YOW *vb* howl
YOWE *Scot word for* > EWE
YOWED > YOW
YOWES > YOWE
YOWIE *n* legendary Australian apelike creature
YOWIES > YOWIE
YOWING > YOW
YOWL *n* loud mournful cry ▷ *vb* produce a loud mournful wail or cry
YOWLED > YOWL
YOWLER > YOWL
YOWLERS > YOWL
YOWLEY *n* yellowhammer (bird)
YOWLEYS > YOWLEY
YOWLING > YOWL
YOWLINGS > YOWL
YOWLS > YOWL
YOWS > YOW
YPERITE *n* mustard gas
YPERITES > YPERITE
YPIGHT *archaic past participle of* > PITCH
YPLAST *archaic past participle of* > PLACE
YPLIGHT *archaic past participle of* > PLIGHT
YPSILOID > YPSILON
YPSILON *same as* > UPSILON
YPSILONS > YPSILON
YRAPT *Spenserian form of* > RAPT
YRAVISHED *archaic past participle of* > RAVISH
YRENT *archaic past participle of* > REND
YRIVD *archaic past participle of* > RIVE
YRNEH *n* unit of reciprocal inductance
YRNEHS > YRNEH
YSAME *Spenserian word for* > TOGETHER
YSHEND *Spenserian form of* > SHEND
YSHENDING > YSHEND
YSHENDS > YSHEND
YSHENT > YSHEND
YSLAKED *archaic past participle of* > SLAKE
YTOST *archaic past participle of* > TOSS
YTTERBIA *n* colourless hygroscopic substance used in certain alloys and ceramics
YTTERBIAS > YTTERBIA
YTTERBIC > YTTERBIUM
YTTERBITE *n* rare mineral
YTTERBIUM *n* soft silvery element
YTTERBOUS > YTTERBIUM
YTTRIA *n* insoluble solid used mainly in incandescent mantles
YTTRIAS > YTTRIA
YTTRIC > YTTRIUM
YTTRIOUS > YTTRIUM
YTTRIUM *n* silvery metallic element used in various alloys
YTTRIUMS > YTTRIUM
YU *n* jade
YUAN *n* standard monetary unit of the People's Republic of China
YUANS > YUAN
YUCA *same as* > YUCCA
YUCAS > YUCA
YUCCA *n* tropical plant with spikes of white leaves
YUCCAS > YUCCA
YUCCH *interj* expression of disgust
YUCH *interj* expression of disgust
YUCK *interj* exclamation indicating contempt, dislike, or disgust ▷ *vb* chuckle
YUCKED > YUCK
YUCKER > YUCK
YUCKERS > YUCK
YUCKIER > YUCKY
YUCKIEST > YUCKY
YUCKINESS > YUCKY
YUCKING > YUCK
YUCKO *adj* disgusting ▷ *interj* exclamation of disgust
YUCKS > YUCK
YUCKY *adj* disgusting, nasty
YUFT *n* Russia leather
YUFTS > YUFT
YUG *same as* > YUGA
YUGA *n* (in Hindu cosmology) one of the four ages of mankind
YUGARIE *variant spelling of* > EUGARIE
YUGARIES > YUGARIE
YUGAS > YUGA
YUGS > YUG
YUK *same as* > YUCK
YUKATA *n* light kimono
YUKATAS > YUKATA
YUKE *vb* itch
YUKED > YUKE
YUKES > YUKE
YUKIER > YUKY
YUKIEST > YUKY
YUKING > YUKE
YUKKED > YUK
YUKKIER > YUKKY
YUKKIEST > YUKKY
YUKKING > YUK
YUKKY *same as* > YUCKY
YUKO *n* score of five points in judo
YUKOS > YUKO
YUKS > YUK
YUKY *adj* itchy
YULAN *n* Chinese magnolia, *Magnolia denudata*, that is often cultivated for its showy white flowers
YULANS > YULAN
YULE *n* Christmas, the Christmas season, or Christmas festivities
YULES > YULE
YULETIDE *n* Christmas season
YULETIDES > YULETIDE
YUM *interj* expression of delight
YUMMIER > YUMMY
YUMMIES > YUMMY
YUMMIEST > YUMMY
YUMMINESS > YUMMY
YUMMO *adj* tasty ▷ *interj* exclamation of delight or approval
YUMMY *adj* delicious ▷ *interj* exclamation indicating pleasure or delight, as in anticipation of delicious food ▷ *n* delicious food item
YUMP *vb* leave the ground when driving over a ridge
YUMPED > YUMP
YUMPIE *n* young upwardly mobile person
YUMPIES > YUMPIE
YUMPING > YUMP
YUMPS > YUMP
YUNX *n* wryneck
YUNXES > YUNX
YUP *n* informal affirmative statement
YUPON *same as* > YAUPON
YUPONS > YUPON
YUPPIE *n* young highly-paid professional person, esp one who has a materialistic way of life ▷ *adj* typical of or reflecting the values of yuppies
YUPPIEDOM > YUPPIE
YUPPIEISH > YUPPIE
YUPPIES > YUPPY
YUPPIFIED > YUPPIFY
YUPPIFIES > YUPPIFY
YUPPIFY *vb* make yuppie in nature
YUPPY *same as* > YUPPIE
YUPS > YUP
YURT *n* circular tent consisting of a framework of poles covered with felt or skins, used by Mongolian and Turkic nomads of E and central Asia
YURTA *same as* > YURT
YURTAS > YURT
YURTS > YURT
YUS > YU
YUTZ *n* Yiddish word meaning fool
YUTZES > YUTZ
YUZU *n* type of citrus fruit
YUZUS > YUZU
YWIS *adv* certainly
YWROKE *archaic past participle of* > WREAK

Zz

A *n* pizza
ABAIONE *n* light foamy dessert
ABAIONES > ZABAIONE
ABAJONE *same as* > ZABAIONE
ABAJONES > ZABAJONE
ABETA *n* tariff
ABETAS > ZABETA
ABRA *n* small sailing vessel
ABRAS > ZABRA
ABTIEH *n* Turkish police officer
ABTIEHS > ZABTIEH
ACATON *n* coarse grass
ACATONS > ZACATON
ACK *n* Australian five-cent piece
ACKS > ZACK
ADDICK *adj* righteous
ADDIK *n* Hasidic Jewish leader
ADDIKIM > ZADDIK
ADDIKS > ZADDIK
AFFAR *same as* > ZAFFER
AFFARS > ZAFFAR
AFFER *n* impure cobalt oxide, used to impart a blue colour to enamels
ZAFFERS > ZAFFER
ZAFFIR *same as* > ZAFFER
ZAFFIRS > ZAFFIR
ZAFFRE *same as* > ZAFFER
ZAFFRES > ZAFFRE
ZAFTIG *adj* ripe or curvaceous
ZAG *vb* change direction sharply
ZAGGED > ZAG
ZAGGING > ZAG
ZAGS > ZAG
ZAIBATSU *n* group or combine comprising a few wealthy families that controls industry, business, and finance in Japan
ZAIKAI *n* Japanese business community
ZAIKAIS > ZAIKAI
ZAIRE *n* currency used in the former Zaïre
ZAIRES > ZAIRE
ZAITECH *n* investment in financial markets by a company to supplement its main income
ZAITECHS > ZAITECH
ZAKAT *n* annual tax on Muslims to aid the poor in the Muslim community
ZAKATS > ZAKAT
ZAKOUSKA > ZAKOUSKI
ZAKOUSKI *same as* > ZAKUSKI
ZAKUSKA > ZAKUSKI
ZAKUSKI *pl n* hors d'œuvres, consisting of tiny open sandwiches spread with caviar, smoked sausage, etc
ZAMAN *n* tropical tree
ZAMANG *same as* > ZAMAN
ZAMANGS > ZAMANG
ZAMANS > ZAMAN
ZAMARRA *n* sheepskin coat
ZAMARRAS > ZAMARRA
ZAMARRO *same as* > ZAMARRA
ZAMARROS > ZAMARRO
ZAMBO *n* offensive word for a Black person
ZAMBOMBA *n* drum-like musical instrument
ZAMBOMBAS > ZAMBOMBA
ZAMBOORAK *n* small swivel-mounted cannon
ZAMBOS > ZAMBO
ZAMBUCK *n* St John ambulance attendant, esp at a sports meeting
ZAMBUCKS > ZAMBUCK
ZAMBUK *same as* > ZAMBUCK
ZAMBUKS > ZAMBUK
ZAMIA *n* any cycadaceous plant of the genus *Zamia*, of tropical and subtropical America, having a short thick trunk, palmlike leaves, and short stout cones
ZAMIAS > ZAMIA
ZAMINDAR *n* (in India) the owner of an agricultural estate
ZAMINDARI *n* (in India) a large agricultural estate
ZAMINDARS > ZAMINDAR
ZAMINDARY *same as* > ZAMINDARI
ZAMOUSE *n* West African buffalo
ZAMOUSES > ZAMOUSE
ZAMPOGNA *n* Italian bagpipes
ZAMPOGNAS > ZAMPOGNA
ZAMPONE *n* sausage made from pig's trotters
ZAMPONI > ZAMPONE
ZAMZAWED *adj* (of tea) having been left in the pot to stew
ZANANA *same as* > ZENANA
ZANANAS > ZANANA
ZANDER *n* freshwater teleost pikeperch of Europe, *Stizostedion lucioperca*, valued as a food fish
ZANDERS > ZANDER
ZANELLA *n* twill fabric
ZANELLAS > ZANELLA
ZANIED > ZANY
ZANIER > ZANY
ZANIES > ZANY
ZANIEST > ZANY
ZANILY > ZANY
ZANINESS > ZANY
ZANJA *n* irrigation canal
ZANJAS > ZANJA
ZANJERO *n* irrigation supervisor
ZANJEROS > ZANJERO
ZANTE *n* type of wood
ZANTES > ZANTE
ZANTHOXYL *variant spelling of* > XANTHOXYL
ZANY *adj* comical in an endearing way ▷ *n* clown or buffoon, esp one in old comedies who imitated other performers with ludicrous effect ▷ *vb* clown
ZANYING > ZANY
ZANYISH > ZANY
ZANYISM > ZANY
ZANYISMS > ZANY
ZANZA *same as* > ZANZE
ZANZAS > ZANZA
ZANZE *n* African musical instrument
ZANZES > ZANZE
ZAP *vb* kill (by shooting) ▷ *n* energy, vigour, or pep ▷ *interj* exclamation used to express sudden or swift action
ZAPATA *adj* (of a moustache) drooping
ZAPATEADO *n* Spanish dance with stamping and

very fast footwork
ZAPATEO *n* Cuban folk dance
ZAPATEOS > ZAPATEO
ZAPOTILLA *n* shoe
ZAPPED > ZAP
ZAPPER *n* remote control for a television etc
ZAPPERS > ZAPPER
ZAPPIER > ZAPPY
ZAPPIEST > ZAPPY
ZAPPING > ZAP
ZAPPY *adj* energetic
ZAPS > ZAP
ZAPTIAH *same as* > ZAPTIEH
ZAPTIAHS > ZAPTIAH
ZAPTIEH *n* Turkish police officer
ZAPTIEHS > ZAPTIEH
ZARAPE *n* blanket-like shawl
ZARAPES > ZARAPE
ZARATITE *n* green amorphous mineral
ZARATITES > ZARATITE
ZAREBA *n* stockade or enclosure of thorn bushes around a village or campsite
ZAREBAS > ZAREBA
ZAREEBA *same as* > ZAREBA
ZAREEBAS > ZAREEBA
ZARF *n* (esp in the Middle East) a holder, usually ornamental, for a hot coffee cup
ZARFS > ZARF
ZARIBA *same as* > ZAREBA
ZARIBAS > ZARIBA
ZARNEC *n* sulphide of arsenic
ZARNECS > ZARNEC
ZARNICH *same as* > ZARNEC
ZARNICHS > ZARNICH
ZARZUELA *n* type of Spanish vaudeville or operetta, usually satirical in nature
ZARZUELAS > ZARZUELA
ZAS > ZA
ZASTRUGA *variant spelling of* > SASTRUGA
ZASTRUGI > ZASTRUGA
ZATI *n* type of macaque
ZATIS > ZATI
ZAX *variant of* > SAX
ZAXES > ZAX
ZAYIN *n* seventh letter of the Hebrew alphabet
ZAYINS > ZAYIN
ZAZEN *n* (in Zen Buddhism) deep meditation undertaken whilst sitting upright with legs crossed
ZAZENS > ZAZEN
ZEA *n* corn silk
ZEAL *n* great enthusiasm or eagerness
ZEALANT *archaic variant of* > ZEALOT
ZEALANTS > ZEALANT
ZEALFUL > ZEAL
ZEALLESS > ZEAL
ZEALOT *n* fanatic or extreme enthusiast
ZEALOTISM > ZEALOT
ZEALOTRY *n* extreme or excessive zeal or devotion
ZEALOTS > ZEALOT
ZEALOUS *adj* extremely eager or enthusiastic
ZEALOUSLY > ZEALOUS
ZEALS > ZEAL
ZEAS > ZEAL
ZEATIN *n* cytokinin derived from corn
ZEATINS > ZEATIN
ZEBEC *variant spelling of* > XEBEC
ZEBECK *same as* > ZEBEC
ZEBECKS > ZEBECK
ZEBECS > ZEBEC
ZEBRA *n* black-and-white striped African animal of the horse family
ZEBRAFISH *n* striped tropical fish
ZEBRAIC *adj* like a zebra
ZEBRANO *n* type of striped wood
ZEBRANOS > ZEBRANO
ZEBRAS > ZEBRA
ZEBRASS *n* offspring of a male zebra and a female ass
ZEBRASSES > ZEBRASS
ZEBRAWOOD *n* tree yielding striped hardwood used in cabinetwork
ZEBRINA *n* trailing herbaceous plant
ZEBRINAS > ZEBRINA
ZEBRINE > ZEBRA
ZEBRINES > ZEBRA
ZEBRINNY *n* offspring of a male horse and a female zebra
ZEBROID > ZEBRA
ZEBRULA *n* offspring of a male zebra and a female horse
ZEBRULAS > ZEBRULA
ZEBRULE *same as* > ZEBRULA
ZEBRULES > ZEBRULE
ZEBU *n* Asian ox with a humped back and long horns
ZEBUB *n* large African fly
ZEBUBS > ZEBUB
ZEBUS > ZEBU
ZECCHIN *same as* > ZECCHINO
ZECCHINE *same as* > ZECCHINO
ZECCHINES > ZECCHINE
ZECCHINI > ZECCHINO
ZECCHINO *n* former gold coin
ZECCHINOS > ZECCHINO
ZECCHINS > ZECCHIN
ZECHIN *same as* > ZECCHINO
ZECHINS > ZECHIN
ZED *n* British and New Zealand spoken form of the letter *z*
ZEDOARIES > ZEDOARY
ZEDOARY *n* dried rhizome of the tropical Asian plant *Curcuma zedoaria*, used as a stimulant and a condiment
ZEDS > ZED
ZEE *same as* > ZED
ZEES > ZEE
ZEIN *n* protein occurring in maize and used in the manufacture of plastics
ZEINS > ZEIN
ZEITGEBER *n* agent or event that sets or resets the biological clock
ZEITGEIST *n* spirit or attitude of a specific time or period
ZEK *n* Soviet prisoner
ZEKS > ZEK
ZEL *n* Turkish cymbal
ZELANT *alternative form of* > ZEALANT
ZELANTS > ZELANT
ZELATOR *same as* > ZELATRIX
ZELATORS > ZELATOR
ZELATRICE *same as* > ZELATRIX
ZELATRIX *n* nun who monitors the behaviour of younger nuns
ZELKOVA *n* type of elm tree
ZELKOVAS > ZELKOVA
ZELOSO *adv* with zeal
ZELOTYPIA *n* morbid zeal
ZELS > ZEL
ZEMINDAR *same as* > ZAMINDAR
ZEMINDARI > ZEMINDAR
ZEMINDARS > ZEMINDAR
ZEMINDARY *n* jurisdiction of a zemindar
ZEMSTVA > ZEMSTVO
ZEMSTVO *n* (in tsarist Russia) an elective provincial or district council established in most provinces of Russia by Alexander II in 1864 as part of his reform policy
ZEMSTVOS > ZEMSTVO
ZENAIDA *n* dove
ZENAIDAS > ZENAIDA
ZENANA *n* (in the East, esp in Muslim and Hindu homes) part of a house reserved for the women and girls of a household
ZENANAS > ZENANA
ZENDIK *n* unbeliever or heretic
ZENDIKS > ZENDIK
ZENITH *n* highest point of success or power
ZENITHAL > ZENITH
ZENITHS > ZENITH
ZEOLITE *n* any of a large group of glassy secondary minerals
ZEOLITES > ZEOLITE
ZEOLITIC > ZEOLITE
ZEP *n* type of long sandwich
ZEPHYR *n* soft gentle breeze
ZEPHYRS > ZEPHYR
ZEPPELIN *n* large cylindrical airship
ZEPPELINS > ZEPPELIN
ZEPPOLE *n* Italian fritter
ZEPPOLES > ZEPPOLE
ZEPPOLI > ZEPPOLE
ZEPS > ZEP
ZERDA *n* fennec
ZERDAS > ZERDA
ZEREBA *same as* > ZAREBA
ZEREBAS > ZEREBA
ZERIBA *same as* > ZAREBA
ZERIBAS > ZERIBA
ZERK *n* grease fitting
ZERKS > ZERK
ZERO *n* (symbol representing) the number 0 ▷ *adj* having no measurable quantity or size ▷ *vb* adjust (an instrument or scale) so a to read zero ▷ *determiner* no (thing) at all
ZEROED > ZERO
ZEROES > ZERO
ZEROING > ZERO
ZEROS > ZERO
ZEROTH *adj* denoting a term in a series that precedes the term otherwise regarded as th first term
ZERUMBET *n* plant stem used as stimulant and condiment
ZERUMBETS > ZERUMBET
ZEST *n* enjoyment or excitement ▷ *vb* give flavour, interest, or piquancy to
ZESTED > ZEST
ZESTER *n* kitchen utensil used to scrape fine shred of peel from citrus fruits
ZESTERS > ZESTER
ZESTFUL > ZEST
ZESTFULLY > ZEST
ZESTIER > ZEST
ZESTIEST > ZEST
ZESTILY > ZEST
ZESTING > ZEST
ZESTLESS > ZEST
ZESTS > ZEST
ZESTY > ZEST
ZETA *n* sixth letter in the Greek alphabet, a consonant, transliterate as *z*
ZETAS > ZETA
ZETETIC *adj* proceeding inquiry ▷ *n* investigatio
ZETETICS > ZETETIC
ZETTABYTE *n* 10^{21} or 2^{70} bytes
ZEUGMA *n* figure of speec in which a word is used to modify or govern two or more words although appropriate to only one them or making a differe sense with each, as in th sentence *Mr Pickwick too his hat and his leave* (Char Dickens)

:UGMAS >ZEUGMA
:UGMATIC >ZEUGMA
:UXITE *n* ferriferous mineral
:UXITES >ZEUXITE
:X *n* tool for cutting oofing slate
XES >ZEX
ZE *n* stringed musical nstrument
ZES >ZEZE
IO *same as* >ZO
IOMO *n* female zho
IOMOS >ZHOMO
IOS >ZHO
BELINE *n* sable or the ur of this animal ▷ *adj* of, elating to, or resembling sable
BELINES >ZIBELINE
BELLINE *same* S >ZIBELINE
BET *n* large civet of S and SE Asia, having tawny fur narked with black spots nd stripes
BETH *same as* >ZIBET
BETHS >ZIBETH
BETS >ZIBET
FF *n* beard
FFIUS *n* sea monster
FFIUSES >ZIFFIUS
FFS >ZIFF
G *same as* >ZAG
GAN *n* gypsy
GANKA *n* Russian dance
GANKAS >ZIGANKA
GANS >ZIGAN
GGED >ZIG
GGING >ZIG
GGURAT *n* (in ancient Mesopotamia) a temple in he shape of a pyramid
GGURATS >ZIGGURAT
GS >ZIG
GZAG *n* line or course aving sharp turns in lternating directions ▷ *vb* move in a zigzag ▷ *adj* ormed in or proceeding in zigzag ▷ *adv* in a zigzag nanner
GZAGGED >ZIGZAG
GZAGGER >ZIGZAG
GZAGGY >ZIGZAG
GZAGS >ZIGZAG
KKURAT *same* S >ZIGGURAT
KKURATS >ZIKKURAT
KURAT *same* S >ZIGGURAT
KURATS >ZIKURAT
LA *n* administrative istrict in India
LAS >ZILA
LCH *n* nothing
LCHES >ZILCH
LL *n* finger cymbal
LLA *same as* >ZILA
LLAH *same as* >ZILA
LLAHS >ZILLAH
LLAS >ZILLA
LLION *n* extremely large ut unspecified number

ZILLIONS >ZILLION
ZILLIONTH >ZILLION
ZILLS >ZILL
ZIMB *same as* >ZEBUB
ZIMBI *n* cowrie shell used as money
ZIMBIS >ZIMBI
ZIMBS >ZIMB
ZIMMER *n* tradename for a kind of walking frame
ZIMMERS >ZIMMER
ZIMOCCA *n* bath sponge
ZIMOCCAS >ZIMOCCA
ZIN *short form of* >ZINFANDEL
ZINC *n* bluish-white metallic element used in alloys and to coat metal ▷ *vb* coat with zinc
ZINCATE *n* any of a class of salts derived from the amphoteric hydroxide of zinc
ZINCATES >ZINCATE
ZINCED >ZINC
ZINCIC >ZINC
ZINCIER >ZINC
ZINCIEST >ZINC
ZINCIFIED >ZINCIFY
ZINCIFIES >ZINCIFY
ZINCIFY *vb* coat with zinc
ZINCING >ZINC
ZINCITE *n* red or yellow mineral consisting of zinc oxide in hexagonal crystalline form
ZINCITES >ZINCITE
ZINCKED >ZINC
ZINCKIER >ZINC
ZINCKIEST >ZINC
ZINCKIFY *same as* >ZINCIFY
ZINCKING >ZINC
ZINCKY >ZINC
ZINCO *n* printing plate made from zincography
ZINCODE *n* positive electrode
ZINCODES >ZINCODE
ZINCOID >ZINC
ZINCOS >ZINCO
ZINCOUS >ZINC
ZINCS >ZINC
ZINCY >ZINC
ZINDABAD *vb* long live: used as part of a slogan in India, Pakistan, etc
ZINE *n* magazine or fanzine
ZINEB *n* organic insecticide
ZINEBS >ZINEB
ZINES >ZINE
ZINFANDEL *n* type of Californian wine
ZING *n* quality in something that makes it lively or interesting ▷ *vb* make or move with or as if with a high-pitched buzzing sound
ZINGANI >ZINGANO
ZINGANO *n* gypsy
ZINGARA *same as* >ZINGARO
ZINGARE >ZINGARA

ZINGARI >ZINGARO
ZINGARO *n* Italian Gypsy
ZINGED >ZING
ZINGEL *n* small freshwater perch
ZINGELS >ZINGEL
ZINGER >ZING
ZINGERS >ZING
ZINGIBER *n* ginger plant
ZINGIBERS >ZINGIBER
ZINGIER >ZINGY
ZINGIEST >ZINGY
ZINGING >ZING
ZINGS >ZING
ZINGY *adj* vibrant
ZINKE *n* cornett
ZINKED >ZINC
ZINKENITE *n* steel-grey metallic mineral consisting of a sulphide of lead and antimony
ZINKES >ZINKE
ZINKIER >ZINC
ZINKIEST >ZINC
ZINKIFIED >ZINCIFY
ZINKIFIES >ZINKIFY
ZINKIFY *vb* coat with zinc
ZINKING >ZINC
ZINKY >ZINC
ZINNIA *n* plant of tropical and subtropical America, with solitary heads of brightly coloured flowers
ZINNIAS >ZINNIA
ZINS >ZIN
ZIP *same as* >ZIPPER
ZIPLESS >ZIP
ZIPLOCK *adj* fastened with interlocking plastic strips
ZIPPED >ZIP
ZIPPER *n* fastening device operating by means of two parallel rows of metal or plastic teeth on either side of a closure that are interlocked by a sliding tab ▷ *vb* fasten with a zipper
ZIPPERED *adj* provided or fastened with a zip
ZIPPERING >ZIPPER
ZIPPERS >ZIPPER
ZIPPIER >ZIPPY
ZIPPIEST >ZIPPY
ZIPPING >ZIP
ZIPPO *n* nothing
ZIPPOS >ZIPPO
ZIPPY *adj* full of energy
ZIPS >ZIP
ZIPTOP *adj* (of a bag) closed with a zip
ZIRAM *n* industrial fungicide
ZIRAMS >ZIRAM
ZIRCALLOY *n* alloy of zirconium containing small amounts of tin, chromium, and nickel. It is used in pressurized-water reactors
ZIRCALOY *same as* >ZIRCALLOY
ZIRCALOYS >ZIRCALOY
ZIRCON *n* mineral used as a gemstone and in industry

ZIRCONIA *n* white oxide of zirconium, used as a pigment for paints, a catalyst, and an abrasive
ZIRCONIAS >ZIRCONIA
ZIRCONIC >ZIRCONIUM
ZIRCONIUM *n* greyish-white metallic element that is resistant to corrosion
ZIRCONS >ZIRCON
ZIT *n* spot or pimple
ZITE *same as* >ZITI
ZITHER *n* musical instrument consisting of strings stretched over a flat box and plucked to produce musical notes
ZITHERIST >ZITHER
ZITHERN *same as* >ZITHER
ZITHERNS >ZITHERN
ZITHERS >ZITHER
ZITI *n* type of pasta
ZITIS >ZITI
ZITS >ZIT
ZIZ *same as* >ZIZZ
ZIZANIA *n* aquatic grass
ZIZANIAS >ZIZANIA
ZIZEL *n* chipmunk
ZIZELS >ZIZEL
ZIZIT *same as* >ZIZITH
ZIZITH *variant spelling of* >TSITSITH
ZIZYPHUS *n* jubejube tree
ZIZZ *n* short sleep ▷ *vb* take a short sleep, snooze
ZIZZED >ZIZZ
ZIZZES >ZIZZ
ZIZZING >ZIZZ
ZIZZLE *vb* sizzle
ZIZZLED >ZIZZLE
ZIZZLES >ZIZZLE
ZIZZLING >ZIZZLE
ZLOTE >ZLOTY
ZLOTIES >ZLOTY
ZLOTY *n* monetary unit of Poland
ZLOTYCH *same as* >ZLOTY
ZLOTYS >ZLOTY
ZO *n* Tibetan breed of cattle, developed by crossing the yak with common cattle
ZOA >ZOON
ZOAEA *same as* >ZOEA
ZOAEAE >ZOAEA
ZOAEAS >ZOAEA
ZOARIA >ZOARIUM
ZOARIAL >ZOARIUM
ZOARIUM *n* colony of zooids
ZOBO *same as* >ZO
ZOBOS >ZOBO
ZOBU *same as* >ZO
ZOBUS >ZOBU
ZOCALO *n* plaza in Mexico
ZOCALOS >ZOCALO
ZOCCO *n* plinth
ZOCCOLO *same as* >ZOCCO
ZOCCOLOS >ZOCCOLO
ZOCCOS >ZOCCO
ZODIAC *n* imaginary belt in the sky within which the sun, moon, and planets appear to move,

divided into twelve equal areas, called signs of the zodiac, each named after a constellation
ZODIACAL > ZODIAC
ZODIACS > ZODIAC
ZOEA *n* free-swimming larva of a crab or related crustacean, which has well-developed abdominal appendages and may bear one or more spines
ZOEAE > ZOEA
ZOEAL > ZOEA
ZOEAS > ZOAEA
ZOECHROME *same as* > ZOETROPE
ZOECIA > ZOECIUM
ZOECIUM *same as* > ZOOECIUM
ZOEFORM > ZOEA
ZOETIC *adj* pertaining to life
ZOETROPE *n* cylinder-shaped toy with a sequence of pictures on its inner surface which, when viewed through the vertical slits spaced regularly around it while the toy is rotated, produce an illusion of animation
ZOETROPES > ZOETROPE
ZOETROPIC > ZOETROPE
ZOFTIG *adj* ripe or curvaceous
ZOIATRIA *n* veterinary surgery
ZOIATRIAS > ZOIATRIA
ZOIATRICS *n* veterinary surgery
ZOIC *adj* relating to or having animal life
ZOISITE *n* grey, brown, or pink mineral
ZOISITES > ZOISITE
ZOISM *n* belief in magical animal powers
ZOISMS > ZOISM
ZOIST > ZOISM
ZOISTS > ZOISM
ZOL *n* South African slang for a cannabis cigarette
ZOLS > ZOL
ZOMBI *same as* > ZOMBIE
ZOMBIE *n* person who appears to be lifeless, apathetic, or totally lacking in independent judgment
ZOMBIES > ZOMBIE
ZOMBIFIED > ZOMBIFY
ZOMBIFIES > ZOMBIFY
ZOMBIFY *vb* turn into a zombie
ZOMBIISM > ZOMBIE
ZOMBIISMS > ZOMBIE
ZOMBIS > ZOMBI
ZOMBORUK *n* small swivel-mounted cannon
ZOMBORUKS > ZOMBORUK
ZONA *n* zone or belt
ZONAE > ZONA
ZONAL *adj* of, relating to, or of the nature of a zone
ZONALLY > ZONAL
ZONARY *same as* > ZONAL
ZONATE *adj* marked with, divided into, or arranged in zones
ZONATED *same as* > ZONATE
ZONATION *n* arrangement in zones
ZONATIONS > ZONATION
ZONDA *n* South American wind
ZONDAS > ZONDA
ZONE *n* area with particular features or properties ▷ *vb* divide into zones
ZONED > ZONE
ZONELESS > ZONE
ZONER *n* something which divides other things into zones
ZONERS > ZONER
ZONES > ZONE
ZONETIME *n* standard time of the time zone in which a ship is located at sea, each zone extending 7½° to each side of a meridian
ZONETIMES > ZONETIME
ZONING > ZONE
ZONINGS > ZONE
ZONK *vb* strike resoundingly
ZONKED *adj* highly intoxicated with drugs or alcohol
ZONKING > ZONK
ZONKS > ZONK
ZONOID *adj* resembling a zone
ZONULA *n* small zone or belt
ZONULAE > ZONULA
ZONULAR > ZONULE
ZONULAS > ZONULA
ZONULE *n* small zone, band, or area
ZONULES > ZONULE
ZONULET *n* small belt
ZONULETS > ZONULET
ZONURE *n* lizard with ringed tail
ZONURES > ZONURE
ZOO *n* place where live animals are kept for show
ZOOBIOTIC *adj* parasitic on or living in association with an animal
ZOOBLAST *n* animal cell
ZOOBLASTS > ZOOBLAST
ZOOCHORE *n* plant with the spores or seeds dispersed by animals
ZOOCHORES > ZOOCHORE
ZOOCHORY > ZOOCHORE
ZOOCYTIA > ZOOCYTIUM
ZOOCYTIUM *n* outer sheath of some social infusorians
ZOOEA *same as* > ZOEA
ZOOEAE > ZOOEA
ZOOEAL > ZOOEA
ZOOEAS > ZOOEA
ZOOECIA > ZOOECIUM
ZOOECIUM *n* part of a polyzoan colony that houses the feeding zooids
ZOOEY > ZOO
ZOOGAMETE *n* gamete that can move independently
ZOOGAMIES > ZOOGAMY
ZOOGAMOUS > ZOOGAMY
ZOOGAMY *n* sexual reproduction in animals
ZOOGENIC *adj* produced from animals
ZOOGENIES > ZOOGENY
ZOOGENOUS *same as* > ZOOGENIC
ZOOGENY *n* doctrine of formation of animals
ZOOGLEA *same as* > ZOOGLOEA
ZOOGLEAE > ZOOGLEA
ZOOGLEAL > ZOOGLEA
ZOOGLEAS > ZOOGLEA
ZOOGLOEA *n* mass of bacteria adhering together by a jelly-like substance derived from their cell walls
ZOOGLOEAE > ZOOGLOEA
ZOOGLOEAL > ZOOGLOEA
ZOOGLOEAS > ZOOGLOEA
ZOOGLOEIC > ZOOGLOEA
ZOOGONIES > ZOOGONY
ZOOGONOUS > ZOOGONY
ZOOGONY *same as* > ZOOGENY
ZOOGRAFT *n* animal tissue grafted onto a human body
ZOOGRAFTS > ZOOGRAFT
ZOOGRAPHY *n* branch of zoology concerned with the description of animals
ZOOID *n* any independent animal body, such as an individual of a coral colony
ZOOIDAL > ZOOID
ZOOIDS > ZOOID
ZOOIER > ZOO
ZOOIEST > ZOO
ZOOKEEPER *n* person who cares for animals in a zoo
ZOOKS *short form of* > GADZOOKS
ZOOLATER > ZOOLATRY
ZOOLATERS > ZOOLATRY
ZOOLATRIA *same as* > ZOOLATRY
ZOOLATRY *n* (esp in ancient or primitive religions) the worship of animals as the incarnations of certain deities, symbols of particular qualities or natural forces, etc
ZOOLITE *n* fossilized animal
ZOOLITES > ZOOLITE
ZOOLITH *n* fossilized animal
ZOOLITHIC > ZOOLITH
ZOOLITHS > ZOOLITH
ZOOLITIC > ZOOLITE
ZOOLOGIC > ZOOLOGY
ZOOLOGIES > ZOOLOGY
ZOOLOGIST > ZOOLOGY
ZOOLOGY *n* study of animals
ZOOM *vb* move or rise very rapidly ▷ *n* sound or act of zooming
ZOOMANCY *n* divination through observing the actions of animals
ZOOMANIA *n* extreme or excessive devotion to animals
ZOOMANIAS > ZOOMANIA
ZOOMANTIC > ZOOMANCY
ZOOMED > ZOOM
ZOOMETRIC > ZOOMETRY
ZOOMETRY *n* branch of zoology concerned with the relative length or size of the different parts of an animal or animals
ZOOMING > ZOOM
ZOOMORPH *n* representation of an animal form
ZOOMORPHS > ZOOMORPH
ZOOMORPHY > ZOOMORPH
ZOOMS > ZOOM
ZOON *less common term for* > ZOOID ▷ *vb* zoom
ZOONAL > ZOON
ZOONED > ZOON
ZOONIC *adj* concerning animals
ZOONING > ZOON
ZOONITE *n* segment of an articulated animal
ZOONITES > ZOONITE
ZOONITIC > ZOONITE
ZOONOMIA *same as* > ZOONOMY
ZOONOMIAS > ZOONOMIA
ZOONOMIC > ZOONOMY
ZOONOMIES > ZOONOMY
ZOONOMIST > ZOONOMY
ZOONOMY *n* science of animal life
ZOONOSES > ZOONOSIS
ZOONOSIS *n* any infection or disease that is transmitted to man from lower vertebrates
ZOONOTIC > ZOONOSIS
ZOONS > ZOON
ZOOPATHY *n* science of animal diseases
ZOOPERAL > ZOOPERY
ZOOPERIES > ZOOPERY
ZOOPERIST > ZOOPERY
ZOOPERY *n* experimentation on animals
ZOOPHAGAN *n* carnivore
ZOOPHAGY *n* eating other animals
ZOOPHILE *n* person who is devoted to animals and their protection from practices such as vivisection
ZOOPHILES > ZOOPHILE
ZOOPHILIA *n* morbid condition in which a person has a sexual attraction to animals
ZOOPHILIC > ZOOPHILE
ZOOPHILY *same*

as >ZOOPHILIA
OPHOBE >ZOOPHOBIA
OPHOBES >ZOOPHOBIA
OPHOBIA *n* unusual or morbid dread of animals
OPHORI >ZOOPHORUS
OPHORIC >ZOOPHORUS
OPHORUS *n* frieze with animal figures
OPHYTE *n* any animal resembling a plant, such as a sea anemone
OPHYTES >ZOOPHYTE
OPHYTIC >ZOOPHYTE
OPLASTY *n* surgical transplantation to man of animal tissues
OS >ZOO
OSCOPIC >ZOOSCOPY
OSCOPY *n* condition causing hallucinations of animals
OSPERM *n* any of the male reproductive cells released in the semen during ejaculation
OSPERMS >ZOOSPERM
OSPORE *n* asexual spore of some algae and fungi that moves by means of flagella
OSPORES >ZOOSPORE
OSPORIC >ZOOSPORE
OSTEROL *n* any of a group of animal sterols, such as cholesterol
OT as in *zoot suit* man's suit consisting of baggy trousers with tapered bottoms and a long jacket with wide padded shoulders
OTAXIES >ZOOTAXY
OTAXY *n* science of the classification of animals
OTECHNY *n* science of breeding animals
OTHECIA *n* outer layers of certain protozoans
OTHEISM *n* treatment of an animal as a god
OTHOME *n* group of zooids
OTHOMES >ZOOTHOME
OTIER >ZOOTY
OTIEST >ZOOTY
OTOMIC >ZOOTOMY
OTOMIES >ZOOTOMY
OTOMIST >ZOOTOMY
OTOMY *n* branch of zoology concerned with the dissection and anatomy of animals
OTOXIC >ZOOTOXIN
OTOXIN *n* toxin, such as snake venom, that is produced by an animal
OTOXINS >ZOOTOXIN
OTROPE *same as* >ZOETROPE
OTROPES >ZOOTROPE
OTROPHY *n* nourishment of animals
OTY *adj* showy
ZOOTYPE *n* animal figure used as a symbol
ZOOTYPES >ZOOTYPE
ZOOTYPIC >ZOOTYPE
ZOOZOO *n* wood pigeon
ZOOZOOS >ZOOZOO
ZOPILOTE *n* small American vulture
ZOPILOTES >ZOPILOTE
ZOPPA *adj* syncopated
ZOPPO *same as* >ZOPPA
ZORBING *n* activity of travelling downhill inside a large air-cushioned hollow ball
ZORBINGS >ZORBING
ZORBONAUT *n* person who engages in the activity of zorbing
ZORGITE *n* copper-lead selenide
ZORGITES >ZORGITE
ZORI *n* Japanese sandal
ZORIL *same as* >ZORILLA
ZORILLA *n* skunk-like African musteline mammal having a long black-and-white coat
ZORILLAS >ZORILLA
ZORILLE *same as* >ZORILLA
ZORILLES >ZORILLE
ZORILLO *same as* >ZORILLE
ZORILLOS >ZORILLO
ZORILS >ZORIL
ZORINO *n* skunk fur
ZORINOS >ZORINO
ZORIS >ZORI
ZORRO *n* hoary fox
ZORROS >ZORRO
ZOS >ZO
ZOSTER *n* shingles; herpes zoster
ZOSTERS >ZOSTER
ZOUAVE *n* (formerly) member of a body of French infantry composed of Alge rian recruits
ZOUAVES >ZOUAVE
ZOUK *n* style of dance music that combines African and Latin American rhythms and uses electronic instruments and modern studio technology
ZOUKS >ZOUK
ZOUNDS *interj* mild oath indicating surprise or indignation
ZOWIE *interj* expression of pleasurable surprise
ZOYSIA *n* any creeping perennial grass of the genus *Zoysia*, of warm dry regions, having short stiffly pointed leaves: often used for lawns
ZOYSIAS >ZOYSIA
ZUCCHETTI >ZUCCHETTO
ZUCCHETTO *n* small round skullcap worn by clergymen and varying in colour according to the rank of the wearer
ZUCCHINI *n* courgette
ZUCCHINIS >ZUCCHINI
ZUCHETTA *same as* >ZUCCHETTO
ZUCHETTAS >ZUCHETTA
ZUCHETTO *same as* >ZUCCHETTO
ZUCHETTOS >ZUCHETTO
ZUFFOLI >ZUFFOLO
ZUFFOLO *same as* >ZUFOLO
ZUFOLI >ZUFOLO
ZUFOLO *n* small flute
ZUGZWANG *n* (in chess) position in which one player can move only with loss or severe disadvantage ▷ *vb* manoeuvre (one's opponent) into a zugzwang
ZUGZWANGS >ZUGZWANG
ZULU *n* (in the NATO phonetic alphabet) used to represent z
ZULUS >ZULU
ZUMBOORUK *n* small swivel-mounted cannon
ZUPA *n* confederation of Serbian villages
ZUPAN *n* head of a zupa
ZUPANS >ZUPAN
ZUPAS >ZUPA
ZURF *same as* >ZARF
ZURFS >ZURF
ZUZ *n* ancient Hebrew silver coin
ZUZIM >ZUZ
ZWIEBACK *n* small type of rusk, which has been baked first as a loaf, then sliced and toasted, usually bought ready-made
ZWIEBACKS >ZWIEBACK
ZYDECO *n* type of Black Cajun music
ZYDECOS >ZYDECO
ZYGA >ZYGON
ZYGAENID *adj* of the burnet moth genus
ZYGAENOID *same as* >ZYGAENID
ZYGAL >ZYGON
ZYGANTRA >ZYGANTRUM
ZYGANTRUM *n* vertebral articulation in snakes and some lizards
ZYGOCACTI *n* branching cactuses
ZYGODONT *adj* possessing paired molar cusps
ZYGOID *same as* >DIPLOID
ZYGOMA *n* slender arch of bone that forms a bridge between the cheekbone and the temporal bone on each side of the skull of mammals
ZYGOMAS >ZYGOMA
ZYGOMATA >ZYGOMA
ZYGOMATIC *adj* of or relating to the zygoma
ZYGON *n* brain fissure
ZYGOPHYTE *n* plant that reproduces by means of zygospores
ZYGOSE >ZYGOSIS
ZYGOSES >ZYGOSIS
ZYGOSIS *n* (in bacteria) the direct transfer of DNA between two cells that are temporarily joined
ZYGOSITY >ZYGOSIS
ZYGOSPERM *same as* >ZYGOSPORE
ZYGOSPORE *n* thick-walled sexual spore formed from the zygote of some fungi and algae
ZYGOTE *n* fertilized egg cell
ZYGOTENE *n* second stage of the prophase of meiosis, during which homologous chromosomes become associated in pairs (bivalents)
ZYGOTENES >ZYGOTENE
ZYGOTES >ZYGOTE
ZYGOTIC >ZYGOTE
ZYLONITE *variant spelling of* >XYLONITE
ZYLONITES >ZYLONITE
ZYMASE *n* mixture of enzymes that is obtained as an extract from yeast and ferments sugars
ZYMASES >ZYMASE
ZYME *n* ferment
ZYMES >ZYME
ZYMIC >ZYME
ZYMITE *n* priest who uses leavened bread during communion
ZYMITES >ZYMITE
ZYMOGEN *n* any of a group of compounds that are inactive precursors of enzymes and are activated by a kinase
ZYMOGENE *same as* >ZYMOGEN
ZYMOGENES >ZYMOGENE
ZYMOGENIC *adj* of, or relating to a zymogen
ZYMOGENS >ZYMOGEN
ZYMOGRAM *n* band of electrophoretic medium showing a pattern of enzymes following electrophoresis
ZYMOGRAMS >ZYMOGRAM
ZYMOID *adj* relating to a ferment
ZYMOLOGIC >ZYMOLOGY
ZYMOLOGY *n* chemistry of fermentation
ZYMOLYSES >ZYMOLYSIS
ZYMOLYSIS *n* process of fermentation
ZYMOLYTIC >ZYMOLYSIS
ZYMOME *n* glutinous substance that is insoluble in alcohol
ZYMOMES >ZYMOME
ZYMOMETER *n* instrument for estimating the degree of fermentation
ZYMOSAN *n* insoluble carbohydrate found in yeast

ZYMOSANS > ZYMOSAN
ZYMOSES > ZYMOSIS
ZYMOSIS *same as* > ZYMOLYSIS
ZYMOTIC *adj* of, relating to, or causing fermentation ▷ *n* disease
ZYMOTICS > ZYMOTIC
ZYMURGIES > ZYMURGY
ZYMURGY *n* branch of chemistry concerned with fermentation processes in brewing, etc
ZYTHUM *n* Ancient Egyptian beer
ZYTHUMS > ZYTHUM
ZYZZYVA *n* American weevil
ZYZZYVAS > ZYZZYVA

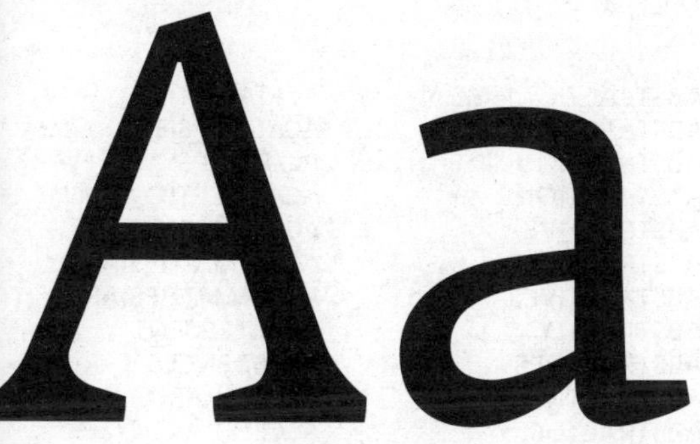

ARDWOLVES
BACTERIAL
BACTINALLY
BANDONEDLY
BANDONEES
BANDONERS
BANDONING
BANDONMENT
BANDONMENTS
BANDONWARE
BANDONWARES
BASEMENTS
BASHMENTS
BATEMENTS
BBOTSHIPS
BBREVIATE
BBREVIATED
BBREVIATES
BBREVIATING
BBREVIATION
BBREVIATIONS
BBREVIATOR
BBREVIATORS
BBREVIATORY
BBREVIATURE
BBREVIATURES
BCOULOMBS
BDICATING
BDICATION
BDICATIONS
BDICATIVE
BDICATORS
BDOMINALLY
BDOMINALS
BDOMINOPLASTY
BDOMINOUS
BDUCENTES
BDUCTIONS

ABDUCTORES
ABECEDARIAN
ABECEDARIANS
ABERDEVINE
ABERDEVINES
ABERNETHIES
ABERRANCES
ABERRANCIES
ABERRANTLY
ABERRATING
ABERRATION
ABERRATIONAL
ABERRATIONS
ABEYANCIES
ABHOMINABLE
ABHORRENCE
ABHORRENCES
ABHORRENCIES
ABHORRENCY
ABHORRENTLY
ABHORRINGS
ABIOGENESES
ABIOGENESIS
ABIOGENETIC
ABIOGENETICALLY
ABIOGENICALLY
ABIOGENIST
ABIOGENISTS
ABIOLOGICAL
ABIOTICALLY
ABIOTROPHIC
ABIOTROPHIES
ABIOTROPHY
ABIRRITANT
ABIRRITANTS
ABIRRITATE
ABIRRITATED
ABIRRITATES

ABIRRITATING
ABITURIENT
ABITURIENTS
ABJECTIONS
ABJECTNESS
ABJECTNESSES
ABJOINTING
ABJUNCTION
ABJUNCTIONS
ABJURATION
ABJURATIONS
ABLACTATION
ABLACTATIONS
ABLATITIOUS
ABLATIVELY
ABLUTIONARY
ABLUTOMANE
ABLUTOMANES
ABNEGATING
ABNEGATION
ABNEGATIONS
ABNEGATORS
ABNORMALISM
ABNORMALISMS
ABNORMALITIES
ABNORMALITY
ABNORMALLY
ABNORMITIES
ABODEMENTS
ABOLISHABLE
ABOLISHERS
ABOLISHING
ABOLISHMENT
ABOLISHMENTS
ABOLITIONAL
ABOLITIONARY
ABOLITIONISM
ABOLITIONISMS

ABOLITIONIST
ABOLITIONISTS
ABOLITIONS
ABOMASUSES
ABOMINABLE
ABOMINABLENESS
ABOMINABLY
ABOMINATED
ABOMINATES
ABOMINATING
ABOMINATION
ABOMINATIONS
ABOMINATOR
ABOMINATORS
ABONDANCES
ABONNEMENT
ABONNEMENTS
ABORIGINAL
ABORIGINALISM
ABORIGINALISMS
ABORIGINALITIES
ABORIGINALITY
ABORIGINALLY
ABORIGINALS
ABORIGINES
ABORTICIDE
ABORTICIDES
ABORTIFACIENT
ABORTIFACIENTS
ABORTIONAL
ABORTIONIST
ABORTIONISTS
ABORTIVELY
ABORTIVENESS
ABORTIVENESSES
ABORTUARIES
ABOVEBOARD
ABOVEGROUND

ABRACADABRA
ABRACADABRAS
ABRANCHIAL
ABRANCHIATE
ABRASIVELY
ABRASIVENESS
ABRASIVENESSES
ABREACTING
ABREACTION
ABREACTIONS
ABREACTIVE
ABRIDGABLE
ABRIDGEABLE
ABRIDGEMENT
ABRIDGEMENTS
ABRIDGMENT
ABRIDGMENTS
ABROGATING
ABROGATION
ABROGATIONS
ABROGATIVE
ABROGATORS
ABRUPTIONS
ABRUPTNESS
ABRUPTNESSES
ABSCESSING
ABSCINDING
ABSCISSINS
ABSCISSION
ABSCISSIONS
ABSCONDENCE
ABSCONDENCES
ABSCONDERS
ABSCONDING
ABSEILINGS
ABSENTEEISM
ABSENTEEISMS
ABSENTMINDED
ABSENTMINDEDLY
ABSINTHIATED
ABSINTHISM
ABSINTHISMS
ABSOLUTELY
ABSOLUTENESS
ABSOLUTENESSES
ABSOLUTEST
ABSOLUTION
ABSOLUTIONS
ABSOLUTISE
ABSOLUTISED
ABSOLUTISES
ABSOLUTISING
ABSOLUTISM
ABSOLUTISMS
ABSOLUTIST
ABSOLUTISTIC
ABSOLUTISTS
ABSOLUTIVE
ABSOLUTIZE
ABSOLUTIZED
ABSOLUTIZES
ABSOLUTIZING
ABSOLUTORY
ABSOLVABLE
ABSOLVENTS
ABSOLVITOR
ABSOLVITORS
ABSORBABILITIES
ABSORBABILITY
ABSORBABLE
ABSORBANCE
ABSORBANCES
ABSORBANCIES
ABSORBANCY
ABSORBANTS
ABSORBATES
ABSORBEDLY
ABSORBEFACIENT
ABSORBEFACIENTS
ABSORBENCIES
ABSORBENCY
ABSORBENTS
ABSORBINGLY
ABSORPTANCE
ABSORPTANCES
ABSORPTIOMETER
ABSORPTIOMETERS
ABSORPTION
ABSORPTIONS
ABSORPTIVE
ABSORPTIVENESS
ABSORPTIVITIES
ABSORPTIVITY
ABSQUATULATE
ABSQUATULATED
ABSQUATULATES
ABSQUATULATING
ABSTAINERS
ABSTAINING
ABSTEMIOUS
ABSTEMIOUSLY
ABSTEMIOUSNESS
ABSTENTION
ABSTENTIONISM
ABSTENTIONISMS
ABSTENTIONIST
ABSTENTIONISTS
ABSTENTIONS
ABSTENTIOUS
ABSTERGENT
ABSTERGENTS
ABSTERGING
ABSTERSION
ABSTERSIONS
ABSTERSIVE
ABSTERSIVES
ABSTINENCE
ABSTINENCES
ABSTINENCIES
ABSTINENCY
ABSTINENTLY
ABSTRACTABLE
ABSTRACTED
ABSTRACTEDLY
ABSTRACTEDNESS
ABSTRACTER
ABSTRACTERS
ABSTRACTEST
ABSTRACTING
ABSTRACTION
ABSTRACTIONAL
ABSTRACTIONISM
ABSTRACTIONISMS
ABSTRACTIONIST
ABSTRACTIONISTS
ABSTRACTIONS
ABSTRACTIVE
ABSTRACTIVELY
ABSTRACTIVES
ABSTRACTLY
ABSTRACTNESS
ABSTRACTNESSES
ABSTRACTOR
ABSTRACTORS
ABSTRICTED
ABSTRICTING
ABSTRICTION
ABSTRICTIONS
ABSTRUSELY
ABSTRUSENESS
ABSTRUSENESSES
ABSTRUSEST
ABSTRUSITIES
ABSTRUSITY
ABSURDISMS
ABSURDISTS
ABSURDITIES
ABSURDNESS
ABSURDNESSES
ABUNDANCES
ABUNDANCIES
ABUNDANTLY
ABUSIVENESS
ABUSIVENESSES
ABYSSOPELAGIC
ACADEMICAL
ACADEMICALISM
ACADEMICALISMS
ACADEMICALLY
ACADEMICALS
ACADEMICIAN
ACADEMICIANS
ACADEMICISM
ACADEMICISMS
ACADEMISMS
ACADEMISTS
ACALCULIAS
ACALEPHANS
ACANACEOUS
ACANTHACEOUS
ACANTHOCEPHALAN
ACANTHUSES
ACARICIDAL
ACARICIDES
ACARIDEANS
ACARIDIANS
ACARIDOMATIA
ACARIDOMATIUM
ACARODOMATIA
ACARODOMATIUM
ACAROLOGIES
ACAROLOGIST
ACAROLOGISTS
ACAROPHILIES
ACAROPHILY
ACARPELLOUS
ACARPELOUS
ACATALECTIC
ACATALECTICS
ACATALEPSIES
ACATALEPSY
ACATALEPTIC
ACATALEPTICS
ACATAMATHESIA
ACATAMATHESIAS
ACAULESCENT
ACCEDENCES
ACCELERABLE
ACCELERANDO
ACCELERANDOS
ACCELERANT
ACCELERANTS
ACCELERATE
ACCELERATED
ACCELERATES
ACCELERATING
ACCELERATINGLY
ACCELERATION
ACCELERATIONS
ACCELERATIVE
ACCELERATOR
ACCELERATORS
ACCELERATORY
ACCELEROMETER
ACCELEROMETERS
ACCENSIONS
ACCENTLESS
ACCENTUALITIES
ACCENTUALITY
ACCENTUALLY
ACCENTUATE
ACCENTUATED
ACCENTUATES
ACCENTUATING
ACCENTUATION
ACCENTUATIONS
ACCEPTABILITIES
ACCEPTABILITY
ACCEPTABLE
ACCEPTABLENESS
ACCEPTABLY
ACCEPTANCE
ACCEPTANCES
ACCEPTANCIES
ACCEPTANCY
ACCEPTANTS
ACCEPTATION
ACCEPTATIONS
ACCEPTEDLY
ACCEPTILATION
ACCEPTILATIONS
ACCEPTINGLY
ACCEPTINGNESS
ACCEPTINGNESSES
ACCEPTIVITIES
ACCEPTIVITY
ACCESSARIES
ACCESSARILY
ACCESSARINESS
ACCESSIBILITIES
ACCESSIBILITY
ACCESSIBLE
ACCESSIBLENESS
ACCESSIBLY

CESSIONAL
CESSIONED
CESSIONING
CESSIONS
CESSORIAL
CESSORIES
CESSORII
CESSORILY
CESSORINESS
CESSORISE
CESSORISED
CESSORISES
CESSORISING
CESSORIUS
CESSORIZE
CESSORIZED
CESSORIZES
CESSORIZING
CIACCATURA
CIACCATURAS
CIACCATURE
CIDENCES
CIDENTAL
CIDENTALISM
CIDENTALISMS
CIDENTALITIES
CIDENTALITY
CIDENTALLY
CIDENTALNESS
CIDENTALS
CIDENTED
CIDENTLY
CIDENTOLOGIST
CIDENTOLOGY
CIPITERS
CIPITRAL
CIPITRINE
CIPITRINES
CLAIMERS
CLAIMING
CLAMATION
CLAMATIONS
CLAMATORY
CLIMATABILITY
CLIMATABLE
CLIMATATION
CLIMATATIONS
CLIMATED
CLIMATES
CLIMATING
CLIMATION
CLIMATIONS
CLIMATISABLE
CLIMATISATION
CLIMATISE
CLIMATISED
CLIMATISER
CLIMATISERS
CLIMATISES
CLIMATISING
CLIMATIZABLE
CLIMATIZATION
CLIMATIZE
CLIMATIZED
CLIMATIZER
CLIMATIZERS

ACCLIMATIZES
ACCLIMATIZING
ACCLIVITIES
ACCLIVITOUS
ACCOASTING
ACCOLADING
ACCOMMODABLE
ACCOMMODATE
ACCOMMODATED
ACCOMMODATES
ACCOMMODATING
ACCOMMODATINGLY
ACCOMMODATION
ACCOMMODATIONAL
ACCOMMODATIONS
ACCOMMODATIVE
ACCOMMODATOR
ACCOMMODATORS
ACCOMPANIED
ACCOMPANIER
ACCOMPANIERS
ACCOMPANIES
ACCOMPANIMENT
ACCOMPANIMENTS
ACCOMPANIST
ACCOMPANISTS
ACCOMPANYING
ACCOMPANYIST
ACCOMPANYISTS
ACCOMPLICE
ACCOMPLICES
ACCOMPLISH
ACCOMPLISHABLE
ACCOMPLISHED
ACCOMPLISHER
ACCOMPLISHERS
ACCOMPLISHES
ACCOMPLISHING
ACCOMPLISHMENT
ACCOMPLISHMENTS
ACCOMPTABLE
ACCOMPTANT
ACCOMPTANTS
ACCOMPTING
ACCORAGING
ACCORDABLE
ACCORDANCE
ACCORDANCES
ACCORDANCIES
ACCORDANCY
ACCORDANTLY
ACCORDINGLY
ACCORDIONIST
ACCORDIONISTS
ACCORDIONS
ACCOSTABLE
ACCOUCHEMENT
ACCOUCHEMENTS
ACCOUCHEUR
ACCOUCHEURS
ACCOUCHEUSE
ACCOUCHEUSES
ACCOUNTABILITY
ACCOUNTABLE
ACCOUNTABLENESS
ACCOUNTABLY

ACCOUNTANCIES
ACCOUNTANCY
ACCOUNTANT
ACCOUNTANTS
ACCOUNTANTSHIP
ACCOUNTANTSHIPS
ACCOUNTING
ACCOUNTINGS
ACCOUPLEMENT
ACCOUPLEMENTS
ACCOURAGED
ACCOURAGES
ACCOURAGING
ACCOURTING
ACCOUSTREMENT
ACCOUSTREMENTS
ACCOUTERED
ACCOUTERING
ACCOUTERMENT
ACCOUTERMENTS
ACCOUTREMENT
ACCOUTREMENTS
ACCOUTRING
ACCREDITABLE
ACCREDITATION
ACCREDITATIONS
ACCREDITED
ACCREDITING
ACCRESCENCE
ACCRESCENCES
ACCRESCENT
ACCRETIONARY
ACCRETIONS
ACCRUEMENT
ACCRUEMENTS
ACCUBATION
ACCUBATIONS
ACCULTURAL
ACCULTURATE
ACCULTURATED
ACCULTURATES
ACCULTURATING
ACCULTURATION
ACCULTURATIONAL
ACCULTURATIONS
ACCULTURATIVE
ACCUMBENCIES
ACCUMBENCY
ACCUMULABLE
ACCUMULATE
ACCUMULATED
ACCUMULATES
ACCUMULATING
ACCUMULATION
ACCUMULATIONS
ACCUMULATIVE
ACCUMULATIVELY
ACCUMULATOR
ACCUMULATORS
ACCURACIES
ACCURATELY
ACCURATENESS
ACCURATENESSES
ACCURSEDLY
ACCURSEDNESS
ACCURSEDNESSES

ACCUSATION
ACCUSATIONS
ACCUSATIVAL
ACCUSATIVE
ACCUSATIVELY
ACCUSATIVES
ACCUSATORIAL
ACCUSATORY
ACCUSEMENT
ACCUSEMENTS
ACCUSINGLY
ACCUSTOMARY
ACCUSTOMATION
ACCUSTOMATIONS
ACCUSTOMED
ACCUSTOMEDNESS
ACCUSTOMING
ACCUSTREMENT
ACCUSTREMENTS
ACEPHALOUS
ACERACEOUS
ACERBATING
ACERBICALLY
ACERBITIES
ACERVATELY
ACERVATION
ACERVATIONS
ACESCENCES
ACESCENCIES
ACETABULAR
ACETABULUM
ACETABULUMS
ACETALDEHYDE
ACETALDEHYDES
ACETAMIDES
ACETAMINOPHEN
ACETAMINOPHENS
ACETANILID
ACETANILIDE
ACETANILIDES
ACETANILIDS
ACETAZOLAMIDE
ACETAZOLAMIDES
ACETIFICATION
ACETIFICATIONS
ACETIFIERS
ACETIFYING
ACETOMETER
ACETOMETERS
ACETONAEMIA
ACETONAEMIAS
ACETONEMIA
ACETONEMIAS
ACETONITRILE
ACETONITRILES
ACETONURIA
ACETONURIAS
ACETOPHENETIDIN
ACETYLATED
ACETYLATES
ACETYLATING
ACETYLATION
ACETYLATIONS
ACETYLATIVE
ACETYLCHOLINE
ACETYLCHOLINES

ACETYLENES
ACETYLENIC
ACETYLIDES
ACETYLSALICYLIC
ACHAENIUMS
ACHAENOCARP
ACHAENOCARPS
ACHALASIAS
ACHIEVABLE
ACHIEVEMENT
ACHIEVEMENTS
ACHINESSES
ACHLAMYDEOUS
ACHLORHYDRIA
ACHLORHYDRIAS
ACHLORHYDRIC
ACHONDRITE
ACHONDRITES
ACHONDRITIC
ACHONDROPLASIA
ACHONDROPLASIAS
ACHONDROPLASTIC
ACHROMATIC
ACHROMATICALLY
ACHROMATICITIES
ACHROMATICITY
ACHROMATIN
ACHROMATINS
ACHROMATISATION
ACHROMATISE
ACHROMATISED
ACHROMATISES
ACHROMATISING
ACHROMATISM
ACHROMATISMS
ACHROMATIZATION
ACHROMATIZE
ACHROMATIZED
ACHROMATIZES
ACHROMATIZING
ACHROMATOPSIA
ACHROMATOPSIAS
ACHROMATOUS
ACICULATED
ACIDANTHERA
ACIDANTHERAS
ACIDFREAKS
ACIDIFIABLE
ACIDIFICATION
ACIDIFICATIONS
ACIDIFIERS
ACIDIFYING
ACIDIMETER
ACIDIMETERS
ACIDIMETRIC
ACIDIMETRICAL
ACIDIMETRICALLY
ACIDIMETRIES
ACIDIMETRY
ACIDNESSES
ACIDOMETER
ACIDOMETERS
ACIDOPHILE
ACIDOPHILES
ACIDOPHILIC
ACIDOPHILOUS
ACIDOPHILS
ACIDOPHILUS
ACIDOPHILUSES
ACIDULATED
ACIDULATES
ACIDULATING
ACIDULATION
ACIDULATIONS
ACIERATING
ACIERATION
ACIERATIONS
ACINACEOUS
ACINACIFORM
ACKNOWLEDGE
ACKNOWLEDGEABLE
ACKNOWLEDGEABLY
ACKNOWLEDGED
ACKNOWLEDGEDLY
ACKNOWLEDGEMENT
ACKNOWLEDGER
ACKNOWLEDGERS
ACKNOWLEDGES
ACKNOWLEDGING
ACKNOWLEDGMENT
ACKNOWLEDGMENTS
ACOELOMATE
ACOELOMATES
ACOLOUTHIC
ACOLOUTHITE
ACOLOUTHITES
ACOLOUTHOS
ACOLOUTHOSES
ACONITINES
ACOTYLEDON
ACOTYLEDONOUS
ACOTYLEDONS
ACOUSTICAL
ACOUSTICALLY
ACOUSTICIAN
ACOUSTICIANS
ACQUAINTANCE
ACQUAINTANCES
ACQUAINTED
ACQUAINTING
ACQUIESCED
ACQUIESCENCE
ACQUIESCENCES
ACQUIESCENT
ACQUIESCENTLY
ACQUIESCENTS
ACQUIESCES
ACQUIESCING
ACQUIESCINGLY
ACQUIGHTING
ACQUIRABILITIES
ACQUIRABILITY
ACQUIRABLE
ACQUIREMENT
ACQUIREMENTS
ACQUISITION
ACQUISITIONAL
ACQUISITIONS
ACQUISITIVE
ACQUISITIVELY
ACQUISITIVENESS
ACQUISITOR
ACQUISITORS
ACQUITMENT
ACQUITMENTS
ACQUITTALS
ACQUITTANCE
ACQUITTANCED
ACQUITTANCES
ACQUITTANCING
ACQUITTERS
ACQUITTING
ACRIDITIES
ACRIDNESSES
ACRIFLAVIN
ACRIFLAVINE
ACRIFLAVINES
ACRIFLAVINS
ACRIMONIES
ACRIMONIOUS
ACRIMONIOUSLY
ACRIMONIOUSNESS
ACRITARCHS
ACROAMATIC
ACROAMATICAL
ACROBATICALLY
ACROBATICS
ACROBATISM
ACROBATISMS
ACROCARPOUS
ACROCENTRIC
ACROCENTRICS
ACROCYANOSES
ACROCYANOSIS
ACRODROMOUS
ACROGENOUS
ACROGENOUSLY
ACROLITHIC
ACROMEGALIC
ACROMEGALICS
ACROMEGALIES
ACROMEGALY
ACRONICALLY
ACRONYCALLY
ACRONYCHAL
ACRONYCHALLY
ACRONYMANIA
ACRONYMANIAS
ACRONYMICALLY
ACRONYMOUS
ACROPARESTHESIA
ACROPETALLY
ACROPHOBES
ACROPHOBIA
ACROPHOBIAS
ACROPHOBIC
ACROPHONETIC
ACROPHONIC
ACROPHONIES
ACROPOLISES
ACROSPIRES
ACROSTICAL
ACROSTICALLY
ACROTERIAL
ACROTERION
ACROTERIUM
ACROTERIUMS
ACRYLAMIDE
ACRYLAMIDES
ACRYLONITRILE
ACRYLONITRILES
ACTABILITIES
ACTABILITY
ACTINICALLY
ACTINIFORM
ACTINOBACILLI
ACTINOBACILLUS
ACTINOBIOLOGIES
ACTINOBIOLOGY
ACTINOCHEMISTRY
ACTINOLITE
ACTINOLITES
ACTINOMERE
ACTINOMERES
ACTINOMETER
ACTINOMETERS
ACTINOMETRIC
ACTINOMETRICAL
ACTINOMETRIES
ACTINOMETRY
ACTINOMORPHIC
ACTINOMORPHIES
ACTINOMORPHOUS
ACTINOMORPHY
ACTINOMYCES
ACTINOMYCETE
ACTINOMYCETES
ACTINOMYCETOUS
ACTINOMYCIN
ACTINOMYCINS
ACTINOMYCOSES
ACTINOMYCOSIS
ACTINOMYCOTIC
ACTINOPODS
ACTINOTHERAPIES
ACTINOTHERAPY
ACTINOURANIUM
ACTINOURANIUMS
ACTINOZOAN
ACTIONABLE
ACTIONABLY
ACTIONISTS
ACTIONLESS
ACTIVATING
ACTIVATION
ACTIVATIONS
ACTIVATORS
ACTIVENESS
ACTIVENESSES
ACTIVISING
ACTIVISTIC
ACTIVITIES
ACTIVIZING
ACTOMYOSIN
ACTOMYOSINS
ACTUALISATION
ACTUALISATIONS
ACTUALISED
ACTUALISES
ACTUALISING
ACTUALISTS
ACTUALITES
ACTUALITIES
ACTUALIZATION

CTUALIZATIONS
CTUALIZED
CTUALIZES
CTUALIZING
CTUARIALLY
CTUATIONS
CUMINATED
CUMINATES
CUMINATING
CUMINATION
CUMINATIONS
CUPRESSURE
CUPRESSURES
CUPUNCTURAL
CUPUNCTURE
CUPUNCTURES
CUPUNCTURIST
CUPUNCTURISTS
CUTENESSES
CYCLOVIRS
CYLATIONS
DACTYLOUS
DAMANCIES
DAMANTEAN
DAMANTINE
DAPTABILITIES
DAPTABILITY
DAPTABLENESS
DAPTABLENESSES
DAPTATION
DAPTATIONAL
DAPTATIONALLY
DAPTATIONS
DAPTATIVE
DAPTEDNESS
DAPTEDNESSES
DAPTIVELY
DAPTIVENESS
DAPTIVENESSES
DAPTIVITIES
DAPTIVITY
DAPTOGENIC
DAPTOGENS
DDERSTONE
DDERSTONES
DDERWORTS
DDICTEDNESS
DDICTEDNESSES
DDICTIONS
DDITAMENT
DDITAMENTS
DDITIONAL
DDITIONALITY
DDITIONALLY
DDITITIOUS
DDITIVELY
DDITIVITIES
DDITIVITY
DDLEMENTS
DDLEPATED
DDRESSABILITY
DDRESSABLE
DDRESSEES
DDRESSERS
DDRESSING
DDRESSORS

ADDUCEABLE
ADDUCTIONS
ADELANTADO
ADELANTADOS
ADEMPTIONS
ADENECTOMIES
ADENECTOMY
ADENITISES
ADENOCARCINOMA
ADENOCARCINOMAS
ADENOHYPOPHYSES
ADENOHYPOPHYSIS
ADENOIDECTOMIES
ADENOIDECTOMY
ADENOMATOUS
ADENOPATHIES
ADENOPATHY
ADENOSINES
ADENOVIRAL
ADENOVIRUS
ADENOVIRUSES
ADEPTNESSES
ADEQUACIES
ADEQUATELY
ADEQUATENESS
ADEQUATENESSES
ADEQUATIVE
ADHERENCES
ADHERENTLY
ADHESIONAL
ADHESIVELY
ADHESIVENESS
ADHESIVENESSES
ADHIBITING
ADHIBITION
ADHIBITIONS
ADHOCRACIES
ADIABATICALLY
ADIABATICS
ADIACTINIC
ADIAPHORISM
ADIAPHORISMS
ADIAPHORIST
ADIAPHORISTIC
ADIAPHORISTS
ADIAPHORON
ADIAPHOROUS
ADIATHERMANCIES
ADIATHERMANCY
ADIATHERMANOUS
ADIATHERMIC
ADIPOCERES
ADIPOCEROUS
ADIPOCYTES
ADIPOSITIES
ADJACENCES
ADJACENCIES
ADJACENTLY
ADJECTIVAL
ADJECTIVALLY
ADJECTIVELY
ADJECTIVES
ADJOURNING
ADJOURNMENT
ADJOURNMENTS
ADJUDGEMENT

ADJUDGEMENTS
ADJUDGMENT
ADJUDGMENTS
ADJUDICATE
ADJUDICATED
ADJUDICATES
ADJUDICATING
ADJUDICATION
ADJUDICATIONS
ADJUDICATIVE
ADJUDICATOR
ADJUDICATORS
ADJUDICATORY
ADJUNCTION
ADJUNCTIONS
ADJUNCTIVE
ADJUNCTIVELY
ADJURATION
ADJURATIONS
ADJURATORY
ADJUSTABILITIES
ADJUSTABILITY
ADJUSTABLE
ADJUSTABLY
ADJUSTMENT
ADJUSTMENTAL
ADJUSTMENTS
ADJUTANCIES
ADJUVANCIES
ADMEASURED
ADMEASUREMENT
ADMEASUREMENTS
ADMEASURES
ADMEASURING
ADMINICLES
ADMINICULAR
ADMINICULATE
ADMINICULATED
ADMINICULATES
ADMINICULATING
ADMINISTER
ADMINISTERED
ADMINISTERING
ADMINISTERS
ADMINISTRABLE
ADMINISTRANT
ADMINISTRANTS
ADMINISTRATE
ADMINISTRATED
ADMINISTRATES
ADMINISTRATING
ADMINISTRATION
ADMINISTRATIONS
ADMINISTRATIVE
ADMINISTRATOR
ADMINISTRATORS
ADMINISTRATRIX
ADMIRABILITIES
ADMIRABILITY
ADMIRABLENESS
ADMIRABLENESSES
ADMIRALSHIP
ADMIRALSHIPS
ADMIRALTIES
ADMIRANCES
ADMIRATION

ADMIRATIONS
ADMIRATIVE
ADMIRAUNCE
ADMIRAUNCES
ADMIRINGLY
ADMISSIBILITIES
ADMISSIBILITY
ADMISSIBLE
ADMISSIBLENESS
ADMISSIONS
ADMITTABLE
ADMITTANCE
ADMITTANCES
ADMITTEDLY
ADMIXTURES
ADMONISHED
ADMONISHER
ADMONISHERS
ADMONISHES
ADMONISHING
ADMONISHINGLY
ADMONISHMENT
ADMONISHMENTS
ADMONITION
ADMONITIONS
ADMONITIVE
ADMONITORILY
ADMONITORS
ADMONITORY
ADNOMINALS
ADOLESCENCE
ADOLESCENCES
ADOLESCENT
ADOLESCENTLY
ADOLESCENTS
ADOPTABILITIES
ADOPTABILITY
ADOPTIANISM
ADOPTIANISMS
ADOPTIANIST
ADOPTIANISTS
ADOPTIONISM
ADOPTIONISMS
ADOPTIONIST
ADOPTIONISTS
ADOPTIVELY
ADORABILITIES
ADORABILITY
ADORABLENESS
ADORABLENESSES
ADORATIONS
ADORNMENTS
ADPRESSING
ADRENALECTOMIES
ADRENALECTOMY
ADRENALINE
ADRENALINES
ADRENALINS
ADRENALISED
ADRENALIZED
ADRENERGIC
ADRENERGICALLY
ADRENOCHROME
ADRENOCHROMES
ADRENOCORTICAL
ADRIAMYCIN

ADRIAMYCINS
ADROITNESS
ADROITNESSES
ADSCITITIOUS
ADSCITITIOUSLY
ADSCRIPTION
ADSCRIPTIONS
ADSORBABILITIES
ADSORBABILITY
ADSORBABLE
ADSORBATES
ADSORBENTS
ADSORPTION
ADSORPTIONS
ADSORPTIVE
ADULARESCENCE
ADULARESCENCES
ADULARESCENT
ADULATIONS
ADULTERANT
ADULTERANTS
ADULTERATE
ADULTERATED
ADULTERATES
ADULTERATING
ADULTERATION
ADULTERATIONS
ADULTERATOR
ADULTERATORS
ADULTERERS
ADULTERESS
ADULTERESSES
ADULTERIES
ADULTERINE
ADULTERINES
ADULTERISE
ADULTERISED
ADULTERISES
ADULTERISING
ADULTERIZE
ADULTERIZED
ADULTERIZES
ADULTERIZING
ADULTEROUS
ADULTEROUSLY
ADULTESCENT
ADULTESCENTS
ADULTHOODS
ADULTNESSES
ADULTRESSES
ADUMBRATED
ADUMBRATES
ADUMBRATING
ADUMBRATION
ADUMBRATIONS
ADUMBRATIVE
ADUMBRATIVELY
ADUNCITIES
ADVANCEMENT
ADVANCEMENTS
ADVANCINGLY
ADVANTAGEABLE
ADVANTAGED
ADVANTAGEOUS
ADVANTAGEOUSLY
ADVANTAGES
ADVANTAGING
ADVECTIONS
ADVENTITIA
ADVENTITIAL
ADVENTITIAS
ADVENTITIOUS
ADVENTITIOUSLY
ADVENTIVES
ADVENTURED
ADVENTUREFUL
ADVENTURER
ADVENTURERS
ADVENTURES
ADVENTURESOME
ADVENTURESS
ADVENTURESSES
ADVENTURING
ADVENTURISM
ADVENTURISMS
ADVENTURIST
ADVENTURISTIC
ADVENTURISTS
ADVENTUROUS
ADVENTUROUSLY
ADVENTUROUSNESS
ADVERBIALISE
ADVERBIALISED
ADVERBIALISES
ADVERBIALISING
ADVERBIALIZE
ADVERBIALIZED
ADVERBIALIZES
ADVERBIALIZING
ADVERBIALLY
ADVERBIALS
ADVERSARIA
ADVERSARIAL
ADVERSARIES
ADVERSARINESS
ADVERSARINESSES
ADVERSATIVE
ADVERSATIVELY
ADVERSATIVES
ADVERSENESS
ADVERSENESSES
ADVERSITIES
ADVERTENCE
ADVERTENCES
ADVERTENCIES
ADVERTENCY
ADVERTENTLY
ADVERTISED
ADVERTISEMENT
ADVERTISEMENTS
ADVERTISER
ADVERTISERS
ADVERTISES
ADVERTISING
ADVERTISINGS
ADVERTIZED
ADVERTIZEMENT
ADVERTIZEMENTS
ADVERTIZER
ADVERTIZERS
ADVERTIZES
ADVERTIZING
ADVERTORIAL
ADVERTORIALS
ADVISABILITIES
ADVISABILITY
ADVISABLENESS
ADVISABLENESSES
ADVISATORY
ADVISEDNESS
ADVISEDNESSES
ADVISEMENT
ADVISEMENTS
ADVISERSHIP
ADVISERSHIPS
ADVISORATE
ADVISORATES
ADVISORIES
ADVOCACIES
ADVOCATING
ADVOCATION
ADVOCATIONS
ADVOCATIVE
ADVOCATORS
ADVOCATORY
ADVOUTRERS
ADVOUTRIES
AECIDIOSPORE
AECIDIOSPORES
AECIDOSPORE
AECIDOSPORES
AECIOSPORE
AECIOSPORES
AEDILESHIP
AEDILESHIPS
AEOLIPILES
AEOLIPYLES
AEOLOTROPIC
AEOLOTROPIES
AEOLOTROPY
AEPYORNISES
AERENCHYMA
AERENCHYMAS
AERENCHYMATOUS
AERIALISTS
AERIALITIES
AERIFICATION
AERIFICATIONS
AEROACOUSTICS
AEROBALLISTICS
AEROBATICS
AEROBICALLY
AEROBICISE
AEROBICISED
AEROBICISES
AEROBICISING
AEROBICIST
AEROBICISTS
AEROBICIZE
AEROBICIZED
AEROBICIZES
AEROBICIZING
AEROBIOLOGICAL
AEROBIOLOGIES
AEROBIOLOGIST
AEROBIOLOGISTS
AEROBIOLOGY
AEROBIONTS
AEROBIOSES
AEROBIOSIS
AEROBIOTIC
AEROBIOTICALLY
AEROBRAKED
AEROBRAKES
AEROBRAKING
AEROBRAKINGS
AEROBUSSES
AERODONETICALLY
AERODONETICS
AERODROMES
AERODYNAMIC
AERODYNAMICAL
AERODYNAMICALLY
AERODYNAMICIST
AERODYNAMICISTS
AERODYNAMICS
AEROELASTIC
AEROELASTICIAN
AEROELASTICIANS
AEROELASTICITY
AEROEMBOLISM
AEROEMBOLISMS
AEROGENERATOR
AEROGENERATORS
AEROGRAMME
AEROGRAMMES
AEROGRAPHIES
AEROGRAPHS
AEROGRAPHY
AEROHYDROPLANE
AEROHYDROPLANES
AEROLITHOLOGIES
AEROLITHOLOGY
AEROLOGICAL
AEROLOGIES
AEROLOGIST
AEROLOGISTS
AEROMAGNETIC
AEROMANCIES
AEROMECHANIC
AEROMECHANICAL
AEROMECHANICS
AEROMEDICAL
AEROMEDICINE
AEROMEDICINES
AEROMETERS
AEROMETRIC
AEROMETRIES
AEROMOTORS
AERONAUTIC
AERONAUTICAL
AERONAUTICALLY
AERONAUTICS
AERONEUROSES
AERONEUROSIS
AERONOMERS
AERONOMICAL
AERONOMIES
AERONOMIST
AERONOMISTS
AEROPAUSES
AEROPHAGIA
AEROPHAGIAS
AEROPHAGIES

EROPHOBES
EROPHOBIA
EROPHOBIAS
EROPHOBIC
EROPHONES
EROPHORES
EROPHYTES
EROPLANES
EROPLANKTON
EROPLANKTONS
EROPULSES
EROSCOPES
EROSHELLS
EROSIDERITE
EROSIDERITES
EROSOLISATION
EROSOLISATIONS
EROSOLISE
EROSOLISED
EROSOLISES
EROSOLISING
EROSOLIZATION
EROSOLIZATIONS
EROSOLIZE
EROSOLIZED
EROSOLIZES
EROSOLIZING
EROSPACES
EROSPHERE
EROSPHERES
EROSTATIC
EROSTATICAL
EROSTATICS
EROSTATION
EROSTATIONS
EROSTRUCTURE
EROSTRUCTURES
EROTACTIC
EROTRAINS
EROTROPIC
EROTROPISM
EROTROPISMS
ERUGINOUS
ESTHESIAS
ESTHESIOGEN
ESTHESIOGENIC
ESTHESIOGENS
ESTHETICAL
ESTHETICALLY
ESTHETICIAN
ESTHETICIANS
ESTHETICISE
ESTHETICISED
ESTHETICISES
ESTHETICISING
ESTHETICISM
ESTHETICISMS
ESTHETICIST
ESTHETICISTS
ESTHETICIZE
ESTHETICIZED
ESTHETICIZES
ESTHETICIZING
ESTHETICS
ESTIVATED
ESTIVATES

AESTIVATING
AESTIVATION
AESTIVATIONS
AESTIVATOR
AESTIVATORS
AETHEREALITIES
AETHEREALITY
AETHEREALLY
AETHRIOSCOPE
AETHRIOSCOPES
AETIOLOGICAL
AETIOLOGICALLY
AETIOLOGIES
AETIOLOGIST
AETIOLOGISTS
AFFABILITIES
AFFABILITY
AFFECTABILITIES
AFFECTABILITY
AFFECTABLE
AFFECTATION
AFFECTATIONS
AFFECTEDLY
AFFECTEDNESS
AFFECTEDNESSES
AFFECTINGLY
AFFECTIONAL
AFFECTIONALLY
AFFECTIONATE
AFFECTIONATELY
AFFECTIONED
AFFECTIONING
AFFECTIONLESS
AFFECTIONS
AFFECTIVELY
AFFECTIVENESS
AFFECTIVITIES
AFFECTIVITY
AFFECTLESS
AFFECTLESSNESS
AFFEERMENT
AFFEERMENTS
AFFENPINSCHER
AFFENPINSCHERS
AFFERENTLY
AFFETTUOSO
AFFETTUOSOS
AFFIANCING
AFFICIONADO
AFFICIONADOS
AFFIDAVITS
AFFILIABLE
AFFILIATED
AFFILIATES
AFFILIATING
AFFILIATION
AFFILIATIONS
AFFINITIES
AFFINITIVE
AFFIRMABLE
AFFIRMANCE
AFFIRMANCES
AFFIRMANTS
AFFIRMATION
AFFIRMATIONS
AFFIRMATIVE

AFFIRMATIVELY
AFFIRMATIVES
AFFIRMATORY
AFFIRMINGLY
AFFIXATION
AFFIXATIONS
AFFIXMENTS
AFFIXTURES
AFFLATIONS
AFFLATUSES
AFFLICTERS
AFFLICTING
AFFLICTINGS
AFFLICTION
AFFLICTIONS
AFFLICTIVE
AFFLICTIVELY
AFFLUENCES
AFFLUENCIES
AFFLUENTIAL
AFFLUENTIALS
AFFLUENTLY
AFFLUENTNESS
AFFLUENTNESSES
AFFLUENZAS
AFFLUXIONS
AFFOORDING
AFFORCEMENT
AFFORCEMENTS
AFFORDABILITIES
AFFORDABILITY
AFFORDABLE
AFFORDABLY
AFFORESTABLE
AFFORESTATION
AFFORESTATIONS
AFFORESTED
AFFORESTING
AFFRANCHISE
AFFRANCHISED
AFFRANCHISEMENT
AFFRANCHISES
AFFRANCHISING
AFFRAPPING
AFFREIGHTMENT
AFFREIGHTMENTS
AFFRICATED
AFFRICATES
AFFRICATING
AFFRICATION
AFFRICATIONS
AFFRICATIVE
AFFRICATIVES
AFFRIGHTED
AFFRIGHTEDLY
AFFRIGHTEN
AFFRIGHTENED
AFFRIGHTENING
AFFRIGHTENS
AFFRIGHTFUL
AFFRIGHTING
AFFRIGHTMENT
AFFRIGHTMENTS
AFFRONTING
AFFRONTINGLY
AFFRONTINGS

AFFRONTIVE
AFICIONADA
AFICIONADAS
AFICIONADO
AFICIONADOS
AFLATOXINS
AFOREMENTIONED
AFORETHOUGHT
AFORETHOUGHTS
AFRORMOSIA
AFRORMOSIAS
AFTERBIRTH
AFTERBIRTHS
AFTERBODIES
AFTERBRAIN
AFTERBRAINS
AFTERBURNER
AFTERBURNERS
AFTERBURNING
AFTERBURNINGS
AFTERCARES
AFTERCLAPS
AFTERDAMPS
AFTERDECKS
AFTEREFFECT
AFTEREFFECTS
AFTEREYEING
AFTEREYING
AFTERGAMES
AFTERGLOWS
AFTERGRASS
AFTERGRASSES
AFTERGROWTH
AFTERGROWTHS
AFTERHEATS
AFTERIMAGE
AFTERIMAGES
AFTERLIFES
AFTERLIVES
AFTERMARKET
AFTERMARKETS
AFTERMATHS
AFTERNOONS
AFTERPAINS
AFTERPEAKS
AFTERPIECE
AFTERPIECES
AFTERSALES
AFTERSENSATION
AFTERSENSATIONS
AFTERSHAFT
AFTERSHAFTS
AFTERSHAVE
AFTERSHAVES
AFTERSHOCK
AFTERSHOCKS
AFTERSHOWS
AFTERSUPPER
AFTERSUPPERS
AFTERSWARM
AFTERSWARMS
AFTERTASTE
AFTERTASTES
AFTERTHOUGHT
AFTERTHOUGHTS
AFTERTIMES

AFTERWARDS
AFTERWORDS
AFTERWORLD
AFTERWORLDS
AGALACTIAS
AGALMATOLITE
AGALMATOLITES
AGAMICALLY
AGAMOGENESES
AGAMOGENESIS
AGAMOGENETIC
AGAMOGONIES
AGAMOSPERMIES
AGAMOSPERMY
AGAPANTHUS
AGAPANTHUSES
AGARICACEOUS
AGATEWARES
AGATHODAIMON
AGATHODAIMONS
AGEDNESSES
AGELESSNESS
AGELESSNESSES
AGENDALESS
AGENTIVITIES
AGENTIVITY
AGGIORNAMENTI
AGGIORNAMENTO
AGGIORNAMENTOS
AGGLOMERATE
AGGLOMERATED
AGGLOMERATES
AGGLOMERATING
AGGLOMERATION
AGGLOMERATIONS
AGGLOMERATIVE
AGGLUTINABILITY
AGGLUTINABLE
AGGLUTINANT
AGGLUTINANTS
AGGLUTINATE
AGGLUTINATED
AGGLUTINATES
AGGLUTINATING
AGGLUTINATION
AGGLUTINATIONS
AGGLUTINATIVE
AGGLUTININ
AGGLUTININS
AGGLUTINOGEN
AGGLUTINOGENIC
AGGLUTINOGENS
AGGRADATION
AGGRADATIONS
AGGRANDISE
AGGRANDISED
AGGRANDISEMENT
AGGRANDISEMENTS
AGGRANDISER
AGGRANDISERS
AGGRANDISES
AGGRANDISING
AGGRANDIZE
AGGRANDIZED
AGGRANDIZEMENT
AGGRANDIZEMENTS
AGGRANDIZER
AGGRANDIZERS
AGGRANDIZES
AGGRANDIZING
AGGRAVATED
AGGRAVATES
AGGRAVATING
AGGRAVATINGLY
AGGRAVATION
AGGRAVATIONS
AGGREGATED
AGGREGATELY
AGGREGATENESS
AGGREGATENESSES
AGGREGATES
AGGREGATING
AGGREGATION
AGGREGATIONAL
AGGREGATIONS
AGGREGATIVE
AGGREGATIVELY
AGGREGATOR
AGGREGATORS
AGGRESSING
AGGRESSION
AGGRESSIONS
AGGRESSIVE
AGGRESSIVELY
AGGRESSIVENESS
AGGRESSIVITIES
AGGRESSIVITY
AGGRESSORS
AGGRIEVEDLY
AGGRIEVEMENT
AGGRIEVEMENTS
AGGRIEVING
AGILENESSES
AGISTMENTS
AGITATEDLY
AGITATIONAL
AGITATIONS
AGNATICALLY
AGNOIOLOGICALLY
AGNOIOLOGIES
AGNOIOLOGY
AGNOSTICISM
AGNOSTICISMS
AGONISEDLY
AGONISINGLY
AGONISTICAL
AGONISTICALLY
AGONISTICS
AGONIZEDLY
AGONIZINGLY
AGONOTHETES
AGORAPHOBE
AGORAPHOBES
AGORAPHOBIA
AGORAPHOBIAS
AGORAPHOBIC
AGORAPHOBICS
AGRANULOCYTE
AGRANULOCYTES
AGRANULOCYTOSES
AGRANULOCYTOSIS
AGRANULOSES
AGRANULOSIS
AGRARIANISM
AGRARIANISMS
AGREEABILITIES
AGREEABILITY
AGREEABLENESS
AGREEABLENESSES
AGREEMENTS
AGREGATION
AGREGATIONS
AGRIBUSINESS
AGRIBUSINESSES
AGRIBUSINESSMAN
AGRIBUSINESSMEN
AGRICHEMICAL
AGRICHEMICALS
AGRICULTURAL
AGRICULTURALIST
AGRICULTURALLY
AGRICULTURE
AGRICULTURES
AGRICULTURIST
AGRICULTURISTS
AGRIMONIES
AGRIOLOGIES
AGRIPRODUCT
AGRIPRODUCTS
AGRITOURISM
AGRITOURISMS
AGRITOURIST
AGRITOURISTS
AGROBIOLOGICAL
AGROBIOLOGIES
AGROBIOLOGIST
AGROBIOLOGISTS
AGROBIOLOGY
AGROBUSINESS
AGROBUSINESSES
AGROCHEMICAL
AGROCHEMICALS
AGRODOLCES
AGROFORESTER
AGROFORESTERS
AGROFORESTRIES
AGROFORESTRY
AGROINDUSTRIAL
AGROINDUSTRIES
AGROINDUSTRY
AGROLOGICAL
AGROLOGIES
AGROLOGIST
AGROLOGISTS
AGRONOMIAL
AGRONOMICAL
AGRONOMICALLY
AGRONOMICS
AGRONOMIES
AGRONOMIST
AGRONOMISTS
AGROSTEMMA
AGROSTEMMAS
AGROSTEMMATA
AGROSTOLOGICAL
AGROSTOLOGIES
AGROSTOLOGIST
AGROSTOLOGISTS
AGROSTOLOGY
AGROTERRORISM
AGROTERRORISMS
AGROTOURISM
AGROTOURISMS
AGROTOURIST
AGROTOURISTS
AGRYPNOPTICALLY
AGRYPNOTIC
AGRYPNOTICS
AGTERSKOTS
AGUARDIENTE
AGUARDIENTES
AHISTORICAL
AHORSEBACK
AICHMOPHOBIA
AICHMOPHOBIAS
AIGUILLETTE
AIGUILLETTES
AILANTHUSES
AILOUROPHILE
AILOUROPHILES
AILOUROPHILIA
AILOUROPHILIAS
AILOUROPHILIC
AILOUROPHOBE
AILOUROPHOBES
AILOUROPHOBIA
AILOUROPHOBIAS
AILOUROPHOBIC
AILUROPHILE
AILUROPHILES
AILUROPHILIA
AILUROPHILIAS
AILUROPHILIC
AILUROPHOBE
AILUROPHOBES
AILUROPHOBIA
AILUROPHOBIAS
AILUROPHOBIC
AIMLESSNESS
AIMLESSNESSES
AIRBRUSHED
AIRBRUSHES
AIRBRUSHING
AIRCOACHES
AIRCRAFTMAN
AIRCRAFTMEN
AIRCRAFTSMAN
AIRCRAFTSMEN
AIRCRAFTSWOMAN
AIRCRAFTSWOMEN
AIRCRAFTWOMAN
AIRCRAFTWOMEN
AIRDROPPED
AIRDROPPING
AIRFREIGHT
AIRFREIGHTED
AIRFREIGHTING
AIRFREIGHTS
AIRINESSES
AIRLESSNESS
AIRLESSNESSES
AIRLIFTING
AIRMAILING
AIRMANSHIP

IRMANSHIPS
IRPROOFED
IRPROOFING
IRSICKNESS
IRSICKNESSES
IRSTREAMS
IRSTRIKES
IRTIGHTNESS
IRTIGHTNESSES
IRWORTHIER
IRWORTHIEST
IRWORTHINESS
IRWORTHINESSES
ITCHBONES
KATHISIAS
KOLOUTHOS
KOLOUTHOSES
KOLUTHOSES
LABAMINES
LABANDINE
LABANDINES
LABANDITE
LABANDITES
LABASTERS
LABASTRINE
LABLASTER
LABLASTERS
LACRITIES
LACRITOUS
LARMINGLY
LBARELLOS
LBATROSSES
LBERTITES
LBESCENCE
LBESCENCES
LBESPINES
LBESPYNES
LBINESSES
LBINISTIC
LBINOISMS
LBITISING
LBITIZING
LBUGINEOUS
LBUMBLATT
LBUMBLATTER
LBUMBLATTS
LBUMENISE
LBUMENISED
LBUMENISES
LBUMENISING
LBUMENIZE
LBUMENIZED
LBUMENIZES
LBUMENIZING
LBUMINATE
LBUMINATES
LBUMINISE
LBUMINISED
LBUMINISES
LBUMINISING
LBUMINIZE
LBUMINIZED
LBUMINIZES
LBUMINIZING
LBUMINOID
LBUMINOIDS

ALBUMINOUS
ALBUMINURIA
ALBUMINURIAS
ALBUMINURIC
ALBUTEROLS
ALCAICERIA
ALCAICERIAS
ALCARRAZAS
ALCATRASES
ALCHEMICAL
ALCHEMICALLY
ALCHEMISED
ALCHEMISES
ALCHEMISING
ALCHEMISTIC
ALCHEMISTICAL
ALCHEMISTS
ALCHEMIZED
ALCHEMIZES
ALCHEMIZING
ALCHERINGA
ALCHERINGAS
ALCOHOLICALLY
ALCOHOLICITIES
ALCOHOLICITY
ALCOHOLICS
ALCOHOLISATION
ALCOHOLISATIONS
ALCOHOLISE
ALCOHOLISED
ALCOHOLISES
ALCOHOLISING
ALCOHOLISM
ALCOHOLISMS
ALCOHOLIZATION
ALCOHOLIZATIONS
ALCOHOLIZE
ALCOHOLIZED
ALCOHOLIZES
ALCOHOLIZING
ALCOHOLOMETER
ALCOHOLOMETERS
ALCOHOLOMETRIES
ALCOHOLOMETRY
ALCYONARIAN
ALCYONARIANS
ALDERFLIES
ALDERMANIC
ALDERMANITIES
ALDERMANITY
ALDERMANLIKE
ALDERMANLY
ALDERMANRIES
ALDERMANRY
ALDERMANSHIP
ALDERMANSHIPS
ALDERWOMAN
ALDERWOMEN
ALDOHEXOSE
ALDOHEXOSES
ALDOLISATION
ALDOLISATIONS
ALDOLIZATION
ALDOLIZATIONS
ALDOPENTOSE
ALDOPENTOSES

ALDOSTERONE
ALDOSTERONES
ALDOSTERONISM
ALDOSTERONISMS
ALEATORIES
ALEBENCHES
ALECTRYONS
ALEGGEAUNCE
ALEGGEAUNCES
ALEMBICATED
ALEMBICATION
ALEMBICATIONS
ALEMBROTHS
ALERTNESSES
ALEXANDERS
ALEXANDERSES
ALEXANDRINE
ALEXANDRINES
ALEXANDRITE
ALEXANDRITES
ALEXIPHARMAKON
ALEXIPHARMAKONS
ALEXIPHARMIC
ALEXIPHARMICS
ALFILARIAS
ALFILERIAS
ALGAECIDES
ALGARROBAS
ALGARROBOS
ALGEBRAICAL
ALGEBRAICALLY
ALGEBRAIST
ALGEBRAISTS
ALGIDITIES
ALGIDNESSES
ALGOLAGNIA
ALGOLAGNIAC
ALGOLAGNIACS
ALGOLAGNIAS
ALGOLAGNIC
ALGOLAGNIST
ALGOLAGNISTS
ALGOLOGICAL
ALGOLOGICALLY
ALGOLOGIES
ALGOLOGIST
ALGOLOGISTS
ALGOMETERS
ALGOMETRICALLY
ALGOMETRIES
ALGOPHOBIA
ALGOPHOBIAS
ALGORISMIC
ALGORITHMIC
ALGORITHMICALLY
ALGORITHMS
ALIENABILITIES
ALIENABILITY
ALIENATING
ALIENATION
ALIENATIONS
ALIENATORS
ALIENNESSES
ALIGHTMENT
ALIGHTMENTS
ALIGNMENTS

ALIKENESSES
ALIMENTARY
ALIMENTATION
ALIMENTATIONS
ALIMENTATIVE
ALIMENTING
ALIMENTIVENESS
ALINEATION
ALINEATIONS
ALINEMENTS
ALISMACEOUS
ALITERACIES
ALITERATES
ALIVENESSES
ALIZARINES
ALKAHESTIC
ALKALESCENCE
ALKALESCENCES
ALKALESCENCIES
ALKALESCENCY
ALKALESCENT
ALKALIFIED
ALKALIFIES
ALKALIFYING
ALKALIMETER
ALKALIMETERS
ALKALIMETRIC
ALKALIMETRIES
ALKALIMETRY
ALKALINISATION
ALKALINISATIONS
ALKALINISE
ALKALINISED
ALKALINISES
ALKALINISING
ALKALINITIES
ALKALINITY
ALKALINIZATION
ALKALINIZATIONS
ALKALINIZE
ALKALINIZED
ALKALINIZES
ALKALINIZING
ALKALISABLE
ALKALISERS
ALKALISING
ALKALIZABLE
ALKALIZERS
ALKALIZING
ALKALOIDAL
ALKYLATING
ALKYLATION
ALKYLATIONS
ALLANTOIDAL
ALLANTOIDES
ALLANTOIDS
ALLANTOINS
ALLANTOISES
ALLARGANDO
ALLAYMENTS
ALLEGATION
ALLEGATIONS
ALLEGEANCE
ALLEGEANCES
ALLEGIANCE
ALLEGIANCES

ALLEGIANTS
ALLEGORICAL
ALLEGORICALLY
ALLEGORICALNESS
ALLEGORIES
ALLEGORISATION
ALLEGORISATIONS
ALLEGORISE
ALLEGORISED
ALLEGORISER
ALLEGORISERS
ALLEGORISES
ALLEGORISING
ALLEGORIST
ALLEGORISTS
ALLEGORIZATION
ALLEGORIZATIONS
ALLEGORIZE
ALLEGORIZED
ALLEGORIZER
ALLEGORIZERS
ALLEGORIZES
ALLEGORIZING
ALLEGRETTO
ALLEGRETTOS
ALLELOMORPH
ALLELOMORPHIC
ALLELOMORPHISM
ALLELOMORPHISMS
ALLELOMORPHS
ALLELOPATHIC
ALLELOPATHIES
ALLELOPATHY
ALLELUIAHS
ALLEMANDES
ALLERGENIC
ALLERGENICITIES
ALLERGENICITY
ALLERGISTS
ALLETHRINS
ALLEVIANTS
ALLEVIATED
ALLEVIATES
ALLEVIATING
ALLEVIATION
ALLEVIATIONS
ALLEVIATIVE
ALLEVIATOR
ALLEVIATORS
ALLEVIATORY
ALLHALLOND
ALLHALLOWEN
ALLHALLOWN
ALLHOLLOWN
ALLIACEOUS
ALLICHOLIES
ALLIGARTAS
ALLIGATING
ALLIGATION
ALLIGATIONS
ALLIGATORS
ALLINEATION
ALLINEATIONS
ALLITERATE
ALLITERATED
ALLITERATES
ALLITERATING
ALLITERATION
ALLITERATIONS
ALLITERATIVE
ALLITERATIVELY
ALLNIGHTER
ALLNIGHTERS
ALLOANTIBODIES
ALLOANTIBODY
ALLOANTIGEN
ALLOANTIGENS
ALLOCARPIES
ALLOCATABLE
ALLOCATING
ALLOCATION
ALLOCATIONS
ALLOCATORS
ALLOCHEIRIA
ALLOCHEIRIAS
ALLOCHIRIA
ALLOCHIRIAS
ALLOCHTHONOUS
ALLOCUTION
ALLOCUTIONS
ALLOGAMIES
ALLOGAMOUS
ALLOGENEIC
ALLOGRAFTED
ALLOGRAFTING
ALLOGRAFTS
ALLOGRAPHIC
ALLOGRAPHS
ALLOIOSTROPHOS
ALLOMERISM
ALLOMERISMS
ALLOMEROUS
ALLOMETRIC
ALLOMETRIES
ALLOMORPHIC
ALLOMORPHISM
ALLOMORPHISMS
ALLOMORPHS
ALLONYMOUS
ALLOPATHIC
ALLOPATHICALLY
ALLOPATHIES
ALLOPATHIST
ALLOPATHISTS
ALLOPATRIC
ALLOPATRICALLY
ALLOPATRIES
ALLOPHANES
ALLOPHONES
ALLOPHONIC
ALLOPLASMIC
ALLOPLASMS
ALLOPLASTIC
ALLOPOLYPLOID
ALLOPOLYPLOIDS
ALLOPOLYPLOIDY
ALLOPURINOL
ALLOPURINOLS
ALLOSAURUS
ALLOSAURUSES
ALLOSTERIC
ALLOSTERICALLY
ALLOSTERIES
ALLOTETRAPLOID
ALLOTETRAPLOIDS
ALLOTETRAPLOIDY
ALLOTHEISM
ALLOTHEISMS
ALLOTMENTS
ALLOTRIOMORPHIC
ALLOTROPES
ALLOTROPIC
ALLOTROPICALLY
ALLOTROPIES
ALLOTROPISM
ALLOTROPISMS
ALLOTROPOUS
ALLOTTERIES
ALLOTYPICALLY
ALLOTYPIES
ALLOWABILITIES
ALLOWABILITY
ALLOWABLENESS
ALLOWABLENESSES
ALLOWABLES
ALLOWANCED
ALLOWANCES
ALLOWANCING
ALLUREMENT
ALLUREMENTS
ALLURINGLY
ALLUSIVELY
ALLUSIVENESS
ALLUSIVENESSES
ALLYCHOLLIES
ALLYCHOLLY
ALMACANTAR
ALMACANTARS
ALMANDINES
ALMANDITES
ALMIGHTILY
ALMIGHTINESS
ALMIGHTINESSES
ALMSGIVERS
ALMSGIVING
ALMSGIVINGS
ALMSHOUSES
ALMUCANTAR
ALMUCANTARS
ALOGICALLY
ALONENESSES
ALONGSHORE
ALONGSHOREMAN
ALONGSHOREMEN
ALOOFNESSES
ALPARGATAS
ALPENGLOWS
ALPENHORNS
ALPENSTOCK
ALPENSTOCKS
ALPESTRINE
ALPHABETARIAN
ALPHABETARIANS
ALPHABETED
ALPHABETIC
ALPHABETICAL
ALPHABETICALLY
ALPHABETIFORM
ALPHABETING
ALPHABETISATION
ALPHABETISE
ALPHABETISED
ALPHABETISER
ALPHABETISERS
ALPHABETISES
ALPHABETISING
ALPHABETIZATION
ALPHABETIZE
ALPHABETIZED
ALPHABETIZER
ALPHABETIZERS
ALPHABETIZES
ALPHABETIZING
ALPHAMERIC
ALPHAMERICAL
ALPHAMERICALLY
ALPHAMETIC
ALPHAMETICS
ALPHANUMERIC
ALPHANUMERICAL
ALPHANUMERICS
ALPHASORTED
ALPHASORTING
ALPHASORTS
ALPHOSISES
ALSTROEMERIA
ALSTROEMERIAS
ALTALTISSIMO
ALTALTISSIMOS
ALTARPIECE
ALTARPIECES
ALTAZIMUTH
ALTAZIMUTHS
ALTERABILITIES
ALTERABILITY
ALTERATION
ALTERATIONS
ALTERATIVE
ALTERATIVES
ALTERCATED
ALTERCATES
ALTERCATING
ALTERCATION
ALTERCATIONS
ALTERCATIVE
ALTERITIES
ALTERNANCE
ALTERNANCES
ALTERNANTS
ALTERNATED
ALTERNATELY
ALTERNATES
ALTERNATIM
ALTERNATING
ALTERNATION
ALTERNATIONS
ALTERNATIVE
ALTERNATIVELY
ALTERNATIVENESS
ALTERNATIVES
ALTERNATOR
ALTERNATORS
ALTIGRAPHS
ALTIMETERS

TIMETRICAL
TIMETRICALLY
TIMETRIES
TIPLANOS
TISONANT
TITONANT
TITUDINAL
TITUDINARIAN
TITUDINARIANS
TITUDINOUS
TOCUMULI
TOCUMULUS
TOGETHER
TOGETHERS
TORUFFLED
TOSTRATI
TOSTRATUS
TRICIALS
TRUISTIC
TRUISTICALLY
UMINATES
UMINIFEROUS
UMINISED
UMINISES
UMINISING
UMINIUMS
UMINIZED
UMINIZES
UMINIZING
UMINOSILICATE
UMINOSITIES
UMINOSITY
UMINOTHERMY
UMSTONES
VEOLARLY
VEOLATION
VEOLATIONS
VEOLITIS
VEOLITISES
YCOMPAINE
YCOMPAINES
AKWEREKWERE
ALGAMATE
ALGAMATED
ALGAMATES
ALGAMATING
ALGAMATION
ALGAMATIONS
ALGAMATIVE
ALGAMATOR
ALGAMATORS
ANTADINE
ANTADINES
ANUENSES
ANUENSIS
ARACUSES
ARANTACEOUS
ARANTHACEOUS
ARANTHINE
ARANTINE
ARYLLIDACEOUS
ARYLLIDS
ARYLLISES
ASSMENTS
ATEURISH
ATEURISHLY

AMATEURISHNESS
AMATEURISM
AMATEURISMS
AMATEURSHIP
AMATEURSHIPS
AMATIVENESS
AMATIVENESSES
AMATORIALLY
AMATORIOUS
AMAZEDNESS
AMAZEDNESSES
AMAZEMENTS
AMAZONIANS
AMAZONITES
AMAZONSTONE
AMAZONSTONES
AMBAGITORY
AMBASSADOR
AMBASSADORIAL
AMBASSADORS
AMBASSADORSHIP
AMBASSADORSHIPS
AMBASSADRESS
AMBASSADRESSES
AMBASSAGES
AMBERGRISES
AMBERJACKS
AMBIDENTATE
AMBIDEXTER
AMBIDEXTERITIES
AMBIDEXTERITY
AMBIDEXTEROUS
AMBIDEXTERS
AMBIDEXTROUS
AMBIDEXTROUSLY
AMBIGUITIES
AMBIGUOUSLY
AMBIGUOUSNESS
AMBIGUOUSNESSES
AMBILATERAL
AMBIOPHONICALLY
AMBIOPHONIES
AMBIOPHONY
AMBISEXUAL
AMBISEXUALITIES
AMBISEXUALITY
AMBISEXUALS
AMBISONICS
AMBITIONED
AMBITIONING
AMBITIONLESS
AMBITIOUSLY
AMBITIOUSNESS
AMBITIOUSNESSES
AMBIVALENCE
AMBIVALENCES
AMBIVALENCIES
AMBIVALENCY
AMBIVALENT
AMBIVALENTLY
AMBIVERSION
AMBIVERSIONS
AMBLYGONITE
AMBLYGONITES
AMBLYOPIAS
AMBOCEPTOR

AMBOCEPTORS
AMBOSEXUAL
AMBROSIALLY
AMBROTYPES
AMBULACRAL
AMBULACRUM
AMBULANCEMAN
AMBULANCEMEN
AMBULANCES
AMBULANCEWOMAN
AMBULANCEWOMEN
AMBULATING
AMBULATION
AMBULATIONS
AMBULATORIES
AMBULATORILY
AMBULATORS
AMBULATORY
AMBULETTES
AMBUSCADED
AMBUSCADER
AMBUSCADERS
AMBUSCADES
AMBUSCADING
AMBUSCADOES
AMBUSCADOS
AMBUSHMENT
AMBUSHMENTS
AMEBOCYTES
AMELIORABLE
AMELIORANT
AMELIORANTS
AMELIORATE
AMELIORATED
AMELIORATES
AMELIORATING
AMELIORATION
AMELIORATIONS
AMELIORATIVE
AMELIORATOR
AMELIORATORS
AMELIORATORY
AMELOBLAST
AMELOBLASTS
AMELOGENESES
AMELOGENESIS
AMENABILITIES
AMENABILITY
AMENABLENESS
AMENABLENESSES
AMENAUNCES
AMENDATORY
AMENDMENTS
AMENORRHEA
AMENORRHEAS
AMENORRHEIC
AMENORRHOEA
AMENORRHOEAS
AMENTACEOUS
AMENTIFEROUS
AMERCEABLE
AMERCEMENT
AMERCEMENTS
AMERCIABLE
AMERCIAMENT
AMERCIAMENTS

AMERICIUMS
AMETABOLIC
AMETABOLISM
AMETABOLISMS
AMETABOLOUS
AMETHYSTINE
AMETROPIAS
AMIABILITIES
AMIABILITY
AMIABLENESS
AMIABLENESSES
AMIANTHINE
AMIANTHOID
AMIANTHOIDAL
AMIANTHUSES
AMIANTUSES
AMICABILITIES
AMICABILITY
AMICABLENESS
AMICABLENESSES
AMINOACIDURIA
AMINOACIDURIAS
AMINOBENZOIC
AMINOBUTENE
AMINOBUTENES
AMINOPEPTIDASE
AMINOPEPTIDASES
AMINOPHENAZONE
AMINOPHENAZONES
AMINOPHENOL
AMINOPHENOLS
AMINOPHYLLINE
AMINOPHYLLINES
AMINOPTERIN
AMINOPTERINS
AMINOPYRINE
AMINOPYRINES
AMISSIBILITIES
AMISSIBILITY
AMITOTICALLY
AMITRIPTYLINE
AMITRIPTYLINES
AMITRYPTYLINE
AMITRYPTYLINES
AMMOCOETES
AMMONIACAL
AMMONIACUM
AMMONIACUMS
AMMONIATED
AMMONIATES
AMMONIATING
AMMONIATION
AMMONIATIONS
AMMONIFICATION
AMMONIFICATIONS
AMMONIFIED
AMMONIFIES
AMMONIFYING
AMMONOLYSES
AMMONOLYSIS
AMMOPHILOUS
AMMUNITION
AMMUNITIONED
AMMUNITIONING
AMMUNITIONS
AMNESTYING

AMNIOCENTESES
AMNIOCENTESIS
AMNIOTOMIES
AMOBARBITAL
AMOBARBITALS
AMOEBIASES
AMOEBIASIS
AMOEBIFORM
AMOEBOCYTE
AMOEBOCYTES
AMONTILLADO
AMONTILLADOS
AMORALISMS
AMORALISTS
AMORALITIES
AMOROSITIES
AMOROUSNESS
AMOROUSNESSES
AMORPHISMS
AMORPHOUSLY
AMORPHOUSNESS
AMORPHOUSNESSES
AMORTISABLE
AMORTISATION
AMORTISATIONS
AMORTISEMENT
AMORTISEMENTS
AMORTISING
AMORTIZABLE
AMORTIZATION
AMORTIZATIONS
AMORTIZEMENT
AMORTIZEMENTS
AMORTIZING
AMOURETTES
AMOXICILLIN
AMOXICILLINS
AMOXYCILLIN
AMOXYCILLINS
AMPELOGRAPHIES
AMPELOGRAPHY
AMPELOPSES
AMPELOPSIS
AMPEROMETRIC
AMPERSANDS
AMPERZANDS
AMPHETAMINE
AMPHETAMINES
AMPHIARTHROSES
AMPHIARTHROSIS
AMPHIASTER
AMPHIASTERS
AMPHIBIANS
AMPHIBIOTIC
AMPHIBIOTICALLY
AMPHIBIOUS
AMPHIBIOUSLY
AMPHIBIOUSNESS
AMPHIBLASTIC
AMPHIBLASTULA
AMPHIBLASTULAE
AMPHIBOLES
AMPHIBOLIC
AMPHIBOLIES
AMPHIBOLITE
AMPHIBOLITES
AMPHIBOLOGICAL
AMPHIBOLOGIES
AMPHIBOLOGY
AMPHIBOLOUS
AMPHIBRACH
AMPHIBRACHIC
AMPHIBRACHS
AMPHICHROIC
AMPHICHROICALLY
AMPHICHROMATIC
AMPHICHROMATISM
AMPHICOELOUS
AMPHICTYON
AMPHICTYONIC
AMPHICTYONIES
AMPHICTYONS
AMPHICTYONY
AMPHIDENTATE
AMPHIDIPLOID
AMPHIDIPLOIDIES
AMPHIDIPLOIDS
AMPHIDIPLOIDY
AMPHIGASTRIA
AMPHIGASTRIUM
AMPHIGORIC
AMPHIGORIES
AMPHIGOURI
AMPHIGOURIS
AMPHIMACER
AMPHIMACERS
AMPHIMICTIC
AMPHIMIXES
AMPHIMIXIS
AMPHIOXUSES
AMPHIPATHIC
AMPHIPHILE
AMPHIPHILES
AMPHIPHILIC
AMPHIPLOID
AMPHIPLOIDIES
AMPHIPLOIDS
AMPHIPLOIDY
AMPHIPODOUS
AMPHIPROSTYLAR
AMPHIPROSTYLE
AMPHIPROSTYLES
AMPHIPROTIC
AMPHISBAENA
AMPHISBAENAE
AMPHISBAENAS
AMPHISBAENIC
AMPHISCIAN
AMPHISCIANS
AMPHISTOMATAL
AMPHISTOMATALLY
AMPHISTOMATIC
AMPHISTOMOUS
AMPHISTYLAR
AMPHISTYLARS
AMPHITHEATER
AMPHITHEATERS
AMPHITHEATRAL
AMPHITHEATRE
AMPHITHEATRES
AMPHITHEATRIC
AMPHITHEATRICAL
AMPHITHECIA
AMPHITHECIUM
AMPHITRICHA
AMPHITRICHOUS
AMPHITROPOUS
AMPHOLYTES
AMPHOTERIC
AMPICILLIN
AMPICILLINS
AMPLENESSES
AMPLEXICAUL
AMPLEXUSES
AMPLIATION
AMPLIATIONS
AMPLIATIVE
AMPLIDYNES
AMPLIFIABLE
AMPLIFICATION
AMPLIFICATIONS
AMPLIFIERS
AMPLIFYING
AMPLITUDES
AMPLOSOMES
AMPULLACEAL
AMPULLACEOUS
AMPULLOSITIES
AMPULLOSITY
AMPUTATING
AMPUTATION
AMPUTATIONS
AMPUTATORS
AMRITATTVA
AMRITATTVAS
AMSINCKIAS
AMUSEMENTS
AMUSINGNESS
AMUSINGNESSES
AMUSIVENESS
AMUSIVENESSES
AMYGDALACEOUS
AMYGDALATE
AMYGDALINE
AMYGDALINS
AMYGDALOID
AMYGDALOIDAL
AMYGDALOIDS
AMYLACEOUS
AMYLOIDOSES
AMYLOIDOSIS
AMYLOLYSES
AMYLOLYSIS
AMYLOLYTIC
AMYLOPECTIN
AMYLOPECTINS
AMYLOPLAST
AMYLOPLASTS
AMYLOPSINS
AMYOTONIAS
AMYOTROPHIC
AMYOTROPHIES
AMYOTROPHY
ANABANTIDS
ANABAPTISE
ANABAPTISED
ANABAPTISES
ANABAPTISING
ANABAPTISM
ANABAPTISMS
ANABAPTIST
ANABAPTISTIC
ANABAPTISTS
ANABAPTIZE
ANABAPTIZED
ANABAPTIZES
ANABAPTIZING
ANABLEPSES
ANABOLISMS
ANABOLITES
ANABOLITIC
ANABRANCHES
ANACARDIACEOUS
ANACARDIUM
ANACARDIUMS
ANACATHARSES
ANACATHARSIS
ANACATHARTIC
ANACATHARTICS
ANACHARISES
ANACHORISM
ANACHORISMS
ANACHRONIC
ANACHRONICAL
ANACHRONICALLY
ANACHRONISM
ANACHRONISMS
ANACHRONISTIC
ANACHRONOUS
ANACHRONOUSLY
ANACLASTIC
ANACOLUTHA
ANACOLUTHIA
ANACOLUTHIAS
ANACOLUTHIC
ANACOLUTHICALLY
ANACOLUTHON
ANACOLUTHONS
ANACOUSTIC
ANACREONTIC
ANACREONTICALLY
ANACREONTICS
ANACRUSTIC
ANADIPLOSES
ANADIPLOSIS
ANADROMOUS
ANADYOMENE
ANAEROBICALLY
ANAEROBIONT
ANAEROBIONTS
ANAEROBIOSES
ANAEROBIOSIS
ANAEROBIOTIC
ANAEROBIUM
ANAESTHESES
ANAESTHESIA
ANAESTHESIAS
ANAESTHESIOLOGY
ANAESTHESIS
ANAESTHETIC
ANAESTHETICALLY
ANAESTHETICS
ANAESTHETISE
ANAESTHETISED

NAESTHETISES
NAESTHETISING
NAESTHETIST
NAESTHETISTS
NAESTHETIZE
NAESTHETIZED
NAESTHETIZES
NAESTHETIZING
NAGENESES
NAGENESIS
NAGLYPHIC
NAGLYPHICAL
NAGLYPHICALLY
NAGLYPHIES
NAGLYPTIC
NAGLYPTICAL
NAGNORISES
NAGNORISIS
NAGOGICAL
NAGOGICALLY
NAGRAMMATIC
NAGRAMMATICAL
NAGRAMMATISE
NAGRAMMATISED
NAGRAMMATISES
NAGRAMMATISING
NAGRAMMATISM
NAGRAMMATISMS
NAGRAMMATIST
NAGRAMMATISTS
NAGRAMMATIZE
NAGRAMMATIZED
NAGRAMMATIZES
NAGRAMMATIZING
NAGRAMMED
NAGRAMMER
NAGRAMMERS
NAGRAMMING
NALEMMATA
NALEMMATIC
NALEPTICS
NALGESIAS
NALGESICS
NALGETICS
NALOGICAL
NALOGICALLY
NALOGISED
NALOGISES
NALOGISING
NALOGISMS
NALOGISTS
NALOGIZED
NALOGIZES
NALOGIZING
NALOGOUSLY
NALOGOUSNESS
NALOGOUSNESSES
NALPHABET
NALPHABETE
NALPHABETES
NALPHABETIC
NALPHABETICS
NALPHABETISM
NALPHABETISMS
NALPHABETS
NALYSABLE
ANALYSANDS
ANALYSATION
ANALYSATIONS
ANALYTICAL
ANALYTICALLY
ANALYTICITIES
ANALYTICITY
ANALYZABILITIES
ANALYZABILITY
ANALYZABLE
ANALYZATION
ANALYZATIONS
ANAMNESTIC
ANAMNESTICALLY
ANAMNIOTES
ANAMNIOTIC
ANAMORPHIC
ANAMORPHISM
ANAMORPHISMS
ANAMORPHOSCOPE
ANAMORPHOSCOPES
ANAMORPHOSES
ANAMORPHOSIS
ANAMORPHOUS
ANANDAMIDE
ANANDAMIDES
ANAPAESTIC
ANAPAESTICAL
ANAPESTICS
ANAPHORESES
ANAPHORESIS
ANAPHORICAL
ANAPHORICALLY
ANAPHRODISIA
ANAPHRODISIAC
ANAPHRODISIACS
ANAPHRODISIAS
ANAPHYLACTIC
ANAPHYLACTOID
ANAPHYLAXES
ANAPHYLAXIES
ANAPHYLAXIS
ANAPHYLAXY
ANAPLASIAS
ANAPLASMOSES
ANAPLASMOSIS
ANAPLASTIC
ANAPLASTIES
ANAPLEROSES
ANAPLEROSIS
ANAPLEROTIC
ANAPTYCTIC
ANAPTYCTICAL
ANARCHICAL
ANARCHICALLY
ANARCHISED
ANARCHISES
ANARCHISING
ANARCHISMS
ANARCHISTIC
ANARCHISTS
ANARCHIZED
ANARCHIZES
ANARCHIZING
ANARTHRIAS
ANARTHROUS
ANARTHROUSLY
ANARTHROUSNESS
ANASARCOUS
ANASTIGMAT
ANASTIGMATIC
ANASTIGMATISM
ANASTIGMATISMS
ANASTIGMATS
ANASTOMOSE
ANASTOMOSED
ANASTOMOSES
ANASTOMOSING
ANASTOMOSIS
ANASTOMOTIC
ANASTROPHE
ANASTROPHES
ANASTROZOLE
ANASTROZOLES
ANATHEMATA
ANATHEMATICAL
ANATHEMATISE
ANATHEMATISED
ANATHEMATISES
ANATHEMATISING
ANATHEMATIZE
ANATHEMATIZED
ANATHEMATIZES
ANATHEMATIZING
ANATOMICAL
ANATOMICALLY
ANATOMISATION
ANATOMISATIONS
ANATOMISED
ANATOMISER
ANATOMISERS
ANATOMISES
ANATOMISING
ANATOMISTS
ANATOMIZATION
ANATOMIZATIONS
ANATOMIZED
ANATOMIZER
ANATOMIZERS
ANATOMIZES
ANATOMIZING
ANATROPIES
ANATROPOUS
ANCESTORED
ANCESTORIAL
ANCESTORING
ANCESTRALLY
ANCESTRESS
ANCESTRESSES
ANCESTRIES
ANCHORAGES
ANCHORESSES
ANCHORETIC
ANCHORETICAL
ANCHORETTE
ANCHORETTES
ANCHORITES
ANCHORITIC
ANCHORITICAL
ANCHORITICALLY
ANCHORLESS
ANCHORPEOPLE
ANCHORPERSON
ANCHORPERSONS
ANCHORWOMAN
ANCHORWOMEN
ANCHOVETAS
ANCHOVETTA
ANCHOVETTAS
ANCHYLOSED
ANCHYLOSES
ANCHYLOSING
ANCHYLOSIS
ANCHYLOTIC
ANCIENTEST
ANCIENTNESS
ANCIENTNESSES
ANCIENTRIES
ANCILLARIES
ANCIPITOUS
ANCYLOSTOMIASES
ANCYLOSTOMIASIS
ANDALUSITE
ANDALUSITES
ANDANTINOS
ANDOUILLES
ANDOUILLETTE
ANDOUILLETTES
ANDRADITES
ANDROCENTRIC
ANDROCENTRISM
ANDROCENTRISMS
ANDROCEPHALOUS
ANDROCLINIA
ANDROCLINIUM
ANDRODIOECIOUS
ANDRODIOECISM
ANDRODIOECISMS
ANDROECIAL
ANDROECIUM
ANDROECIUMS
ANDROGENESES
ANDROGENESIS
ANDROGENETIC
ANDROGENIC
ANDROGENOUS
ANDROGYNES
ANDROGYNIES
ANDROGYNOPHORE
ANDROGYNOPHORES
ANDROGYNOUS
ANDROLOGIES
ANDROLOGIST
ANDROLOGISTS
ANDROMEDAS
ANDROMEDOTOXIN
ANDROMEDOTOXINS
ANDROMONOECIOUS
ANDROMONOECISM
ANDROMONOECISMS
ANDROPAUSE
ANDROPAUSES
ANDROPHORE
ANDROPHORES
ANDROSPHINGES
ANDROSPHINX
ANDROSPHINXES
ANDROSTERONE

ANDROSTERONES
ANECDOTAGE
ANECDOTAGES
ANECDOTALISM
ANECDOTALISMS
ANECDOTALIST
ANECDOTALISTS
ANECDOTALLY
ANECDOTICAL
ANECDOTICALLY
ANECDOTIST
ANECDOTISTS
ANELASTICITIES
ANELASTICITY
ANEMICALLY
ANEMOCHORE
ANEMOCHORES
ANEMOCHOROUS
ANEMOGRAMS
ANEMOGRAPH
ANEMOGRAPHIC
ANEMOGRAPHIES
ANEMOGRAPHS
ANEMOGRAPHY
ANEMOLOGIES
ANEMOMETER
ANEMOMETERS
ANEMOMETRIC
ANEMOMETRICAL
ANEMOMETRIES
ANEMOMETRY
ANEMOPHILIES
ANEMOPHILOUS
ANEMOPHILY
ANEMOPHOBIA
ANEMOPHOBIAS
ANEMOSCOPE
ANEMOSCOPES
ANEMOSCOPICALLY
ANENCEPHALIA
ANENCEPHALIAS
ANENCEPHALIC
ANENCEPHALIES
ANENCEPHALY
ANESTHESIA
ANESTHESIAS
ANESTHESIOLOGY
ANESTHETIC
ANESTHETICALLY
ANESTHETICS
ANESTHETISE
ANESTHETISED
ANESTHETISES
ANESTHETISING
ANESTHETIST
ANESTHETISTS
ANESTHETIZATION
ANESTHETIZE
ANESTHETIZED
ANESTHETIZES
ANESTHETIZING
ANEUPLOIDIES
ANEUPLOIDS
ANEUPLOIDY
ANEURISMAL
ANEURISMALLY
ANEURISMATIC
ANEURYSMAL
ANEURYSMALLY
ANEURYSMATIC
ANFRACTUOSITIES
ANFRACTUOSITY
ANFRACTUOUS
ANGASHORES
ANGELFISHES
ANGELHOODS
ANGELICALLY
ANGELOLATRIES
ANGELOLATRY
ANGELOLOGIES
ANGELOLOGIST
ANGELOLOGISTS
ANGELOLOGY
ANGELOPHANIES
ANGELOPHANY
ANGIOCARPOUS
ANGIOGENESES
ANGIOGENESIS
ANGIOGENIC
ANGIOGRAMS
ANGIOGRAPHIC
ANGIOGRAPHIES
ANGIOGRAPHY
ANGIOLOGIES
ANGIOMATOUS
ANGIOPLASTIES
ANGIOPLASTY
ANGIOSARCOMA
ANGIOSARCOMAS
ANGIOSARCOMATA
ANGIOSPERM
ANGIOSPERMAL
ANGIOSPERMOUS
ANGIOSPERMS
ANGIOSTOMATOUS
ANGIOSTOMOUS
ANGIOTENSIN
ANGIOTENSINS
ANGLEBERRIES
ANGLEBERRY
ANGLEDOZER
ANGLEDOZERS
ANGLERFISH
ANGLERFISHES
ANGLESITES
ANGLETWITCH
ANGLETWITCHES
ANGLEWORMS
ANGLICISATION
ANGLICISATIONS
ANGLICISED
ANGLICISES
ANGLICISING
ANGLICISMS
ANGLICISTS
ANGLICIZATION
ANGLICIZATIONS
ANGLICIZED
ANGLICIZES
ANGLICIZING
ANGLIFYING
ANGLISTICS
ANGLOMANIA
ANGLOMANIAC
ANGLOMANIACS
ANGLOMANIAS
ANGLOPHILE
ANGLOPHILES
ANGLOPHILIA
ANGLOPHILIAS
ANGLOPHILIC
ANGLOPHILS
ANGLOPHOBE
ANGLOPHOBES
ANGLOPHOBIA
ANGLOPHOBIAC
ANGLOPHOBIAS
ANGLOPHOBIC
ANGLOPHONE
ANGLOPHONES
ANGLOPHONIC
ANGOPHORAS
ANGOSTURAS
ANGRINESSES
ANGUIFAUNA
ANGUIFAUNAE
ANGUIFAUNAS
ANGUILLIFORM
ANGUISHING
ANGULARITIES
ANGULARITY
ANGULARNESS
ANGULARNESSES
ANGULATING
ANGULATION
ANGULATIONS
ANGUSTIFOLIATE
ANGUSTIROSTRATE
ANGWANTIBO
ANGWANTIBOS
ANHARMONIC
ANHEDONIAS
ANHELATION
ANHELATIONS
ANHIDROSES
ANHIDROSIS
ANHIDROTIC
ANHIDROTICS
ANHUNGERED
ANHYDRASES
ANHYDRIDES
ANHYDRITES
ANICONISMS
ANICONISTS
ANILINCTUS
ANILINCTUSES
ANILINGUSES
ANIMADVERSION
ANIMADVERSIONS
ANIMADVERT
ANIMADVERTED
ANIMADVERTER
ANIMADVERTERS
ANIMADVERTING
ANIMADVERTS
ANIMALCULA
ANIMALCULAR
ANIMALCULE
ANIMALCULES
ANIMALCULISM
ANIMALCULISMS
ANIMALCULIST
ANIMALCULISTS
ANIMALCULUM
ANIMALIERS
ANIMALISATION
ANIMALISATIONS
ANIMALISED
ANIMALISES
ANIMALISING
ANIMALISMS
ANIMALISTIC
ANIMALISTS
ANIMALITIES
ANIMALIZATION
ANIMALIZATIONS
ANIMALIZED
ANIMALIZES
ANIMALIZING
ANIMALLIKE
ANIMATEDLY
ANIMATENESS
ANIMATENESSES
ANIMATINGLY
ANIMATIONS
ANIMATISMS
ANIMATISTS
ANIMATRONIC
ANIMATRONICALLY
ANIMATRONICS
ANIMOSITIES
ANISEIKONIA
ANISEIKONIAS
ANISEIKONIC
ANISOCERCAL
ANISODACTYL
ANISODACTYLOUS
ANISODACTYLS
ANISOGAMIES
ANISOGAMOUS
ANISOMERIC
ANISOMEROUS
ANISOMETRIC
ANISOMETRICALLY
ANISOMETROPIA
ANISOMETROPIAS
ANISOMETROPIC
ANISOMORPHIC
ANISOPHYLLIES
ANISOPHYLLOUS
ANISOPHYLLY
ANISOTROPIC
ANISOTROPICALLY
ANISOTROPIES
ANISOTROPISM
ANISOTROPISMS
ANISOTROPY
ANKLEBONES
ANKYLOSAUR
ANKYLOSAURS
ANKYLOSAURUS
ANKYLOSAURUSES
ANKYLOSING
ANKYLOSTOMIASES

NKYLOSTOMIASIS
NNABERGITE
NNABERGITES
NNALISING
NNALISTIC
NNALIZING
NNEALINGS
NNELIDANS
NNEXATION
NNEXATIONAL
NNEXATIONISM
NNEXATIONISMS
NNEXATIONIST
NNEXATIONISTS
NNEXATIONS
NNEXMENTS
NNIHILABLE
NNIHILATE
NNIHILATED
NNIHILATES
NNIHILATING
NNIHILATION
NNIHILATIONISM
NNIHILATIONS
NNIHILATIVE
NNIHILATOR
NNIHILATORS
NNIHILATORY
NNIVERSARIES
NNIVERSARY
NNOTATABLE
NNOTATING
NNOTATION
NNOTATIONS
NNOTATIVE
NNOTATORS
NNOUNCEMENT
NNOUNCEMENTS
NNOUNCERS
NNOUNCING
NNOYANCES
NNOYINGLY
NNUALISED
NNUALISES
NNUALISING
NNUALIZED
NNUALIZES
NNUALIZING
NNUITANTS
NNULARITIES
NNULARITY
NNULATION
NNULATIONS
NNULLABLE
NNULMENTS
NNUNCIATE
NNUNCIATED
NNUNCIATES
NNUNCIATING
NNUNCIATION
NNUNCIATIONS
NNUNCIATIVE
NNUNCIATOR
NNUNCIATORS
NNUNCIATORY
NNUNTIATE

ANNUNTIATED
ANNUNTIATES
ANNUNTIATING
ANODICALLY
ANODISATION
ANODISATIONS
ANODIZATION
ANODIZATIONS
ANODONTIAS
ANOESTROUS
ANOINTMENT
ANOINTMENTS
ANOMALISTIC
ANOMALISTICAL
ANOMALISTICALLY
ANOMALOUSLY
ANOMALOUSNESS
ANOMALOUSNESSES
ANONACEOUS
ANONYMISED
ANONYMISES
ANONYMISING
ANONYMITIES
ANONYMIZED
ANONYMIZES
ANONYMIZING
ANONYMOUSLY
ANONYMOUSNESS
ANONYMOUSNESSES
ANOPHELESES
ANOPHELINE
ANOPHELINES
ANORECTICS
ANOREXIGENIC
ANORTHITES
ANORTHITIC
ANORTHOSITE
ANORTHOSITES
ANORTHOSITIC
ANOTHERGUESS
ANOVULANTS
ANOVULATORY
ANOXAEMIAS
ANSWERABILITIES
ANSWERABILITY
ANSWERABLE
ANSWERABLENESS
ANSWERABLY
ANSWERLESS
ANSWERPHONE
ANSWERPHONES
ANTAGONISABLE
ANTAGONISATION
ANTAGONISATIONS
ANTAGONISE
ANTAGONISED
ANTAGONISES
ANTAGONISING
ANTAGONISM
ANTAGONISMS
ANTAGONIST
ANTAGONISTIC
ANTAGONISTS
ANTAGONIZABLE
ANTAGONIZATION
ANTAGONIZATIONS

ANTAGONIZE
ANTAGONIZED
ANTAGONIZES
ANTAGONIZING
ANTALKALIES
ANTALKALINE
ANTALKALINES
ANTALKALIS
ANTAPHRODISIAC
ANTAPHRODISIACS
ANTARTHRITIC
ANTARTHRITICS
ANTASTHMATIC
ANTASTHMATICS
ANTEBELLUM
ANTECEDENCE
ANTECEDENCES
ANTECEDENT
ANTECEDENTLY
ANTECEDENTS
ANTECEDING
ANTECESSOR
ANTECESSORS
ANTECHAMBER
ANTECHAMBERS
ANTECHAPEL
ANTECHAPELS
ANTECHOIRS
ANTEDATING
ANTEDILUVIAL
ANTEDILUVIALLY
ANTEDILUVIAN
ANTEDILUVIANS
ANTEMERIDIAN
ANTEMORTEM
ANTEMUNDANE
ANTENATALLY
ANTENATALS
ANTENNIFEROUS
ANTENNIFORM
ANTENNULAR
ANTENNULES
ANTENUPTIAL
ANTEORBITAL
ANTEPENDIA
ANTEPENDIUM
ANTEPENDIUMS
ANTEPENULT
ANTEPENULTIMA
ANTEPENULTIMAS
ANTEPENULTIMATE
ANTEPENULTS
ANTEPOSITION
ANTEPOSITIONS
ANTEPRANDIAL
ANTERIORITIES
ANTERIORITY
ANTERIORLY
ANTEROGRADE
ANTEVERSION
ANTEVERSIONS
ANTEVERTED
ANTEVERTING
ANTHELICES
ANTHELIONS
ANTHELIXES

ANTHELMINTHIC
ANTHELMINTHICS
ANTHELMINTIC
ANTHELMINTICS
ANTHEMWISE
ANTHERIDIA
ANTHERIDIAL
ANTHERIDIUM
ANTHEROZOID
ANTHEROZOIDS
ANTHEROZOOID
ANTHEROZOOIDS
ANTHERSMUT
ANTHERSMUTS
ANTHOCARPOUS
ANTHOCARPS
ANTHOCHLORE
ANTHOCHLORES
ANTHOCYANIN
ANTHOCYANINS
ANTHOCYANS
ANTHOLOGICAL
ANTHOLOGIES
ANTHOLOGISE
ANTHOLOGISED
ANTHOLOGISER
ANTHOLOGISERS
ANTHOLOGISES
ANTHOLOGISING
ANTHOLOGIST
ANTHOLOGISTS
ANTHOLOGIZE
ANTHOLOGIZED
ANTHOLOGIZER
ANTHOLOGIZERS
ANTHOLOGIZES
ANTHOLOGIZING
ANTHOMANIA
ANTHOMANIAC
ANTHOMANIACS
ANTHOMANIAS
ANTHOPHILOUS
ANTHOPHORE
ANTHOPHORES
ANTHOPHYLLITE
ANTHOPHYLLITES
ANTHOTAXIES
ANTHOXANTHIN
ANTHOXANTHINS
ANTHOZOANS
ANTHRACENE
ANTHRACENES
ANTHRACITE
ANTHRACITES
ANTHRACITIC
ANTHRACNOSE
ANTHRACNOSES
ANTHRACOID
ANTHRACOSES
ANTHRACOSIS
ANTHRANILATE
ANTHRANILATES
ANTHRAQUINONE
ANTHRAQUINONES
ANTHROPICAL
ANTHROPOBIOLOGY

ANTHROPOCENTRIC
ANTHROPOGENESES
ANTHROPOGENESIS
ANTHROPOGENETIC
ANTHROPOGENIC
ANTHROPOGENIES
ANTHROPOGENY
ANTHROPOGONIES
ANTHROPOGONY
ANTHROPOGRAPHY
ANTHROPOID
ANTHROPOIDAL
ANTHROPOIDS
ANTHROPOLATRIES
ANTHROPOLATRY
ANTHROPOLOGICAL
ANTHROPOLOGIES
ANTHROPOLOGIST
ANTHROPOLOGISTS
ANTHROPOLOGY
ANTHROPOMETRIC
ANTHROPOMETRIES
ANTHROPOMETRIST
ANTHROPOMETRY
ANTHROPOMORPH
ANTHROPOMORPHIC
ANTHROPOMORPHS
ANTHROPOPATHIC
ANTHROPOPATHIES
ANTHROPOPATHISM
ANTHROPOPATHY
ANTHROPOPHAGI
ANTHROPOPHAGIC
ANTHROPOPHAGIES
ANTHROPOPHAGITE
ANTHROPOPHAGOUS
ANTHROPOPHAGUS
ANTHROPOPHAGY
ANTHROPOPHOBIA
ANTHROPOPHOBIAS
ANTHROPOPHOBIC
ANTHROPOPHOBICS
ANTHROPOPHUISM
ANTHROPOPHUISMS
ANTHROPOPHYTE
ANTHROPOPHYTES
ANTHROPOPSYCHIC
ANTHROPOSOPHIC
ANTHROPOSOPHIES
ANTHROPOSOPHIST
ANTHROPOSOPHY
ANTHROPOTOMIES
ANTHROPOTOMY
ANTHURIUMS
ANTIABORTION
ANTIABORTIONIST
ANTIACADEMIC
ANTIADITIS
ANTIADITISES
ANTIAGGRESSION
ANTIAIRCRAFT
ANTIAIRCRAFTS
ANTIALCOHOL
ANTIALCOHOLISM
ANTIALLERGENIC
ANTIANEMIA
ANTIANXIETY
ANTIAPARTHEID
ANTIAPHRODISIAC
ANTIARRHYTHMIC
ANTIARRHYTHMICS
ANTIARTHRITIC
ANTIARTHRITICS
ANTIARTHRITIS
ANTIASTHMA
ANTIASTHMATIC
ANTIASTHMATICS
ANTIAUTHORITY
ANTIAUXINS
ANTIBACCHII
ANTIBACCHIUS
ANTIBACKLASH
ANTIBACTERIAL
ANTIBACTERIALS
ANTIBALLISTIC
ANTIBARBARUS
ANTIBARBARUSES
ANTIBARYON
ANTIBARYONS
ANTIBILIOUS
ANTIBILLBOARD
ANTIBIOSES
ANTIBIOSIS
ANTIBIOTIC
ANTIBIOTICALLY
ANTIBIOTICS
ANTIBLACKISM
ANTIBLACKISMS
ANTIBODIES
ANTIBOURGEOIS
ANTIBOYCOTT
ANTIBURGLAR
ANTIBURGLARY
ANTIBUSERS
ANTIBUSINESS
ANTIBUSING
ANTICAKING
ANTICANCER
ANTICAPITALISM
ANTICAPITALISMS
ANTICAPITALIST
ANTICAPITALISTS
ANTICARCINOGEN
ANTICARCINOGENS
ANTICARIES
ANTICATALYST
ANTICATALYSTS
ANTICATHODE
ANTICATHODES
ANTICATHOLIC
ANTICELLULITE
ANTICENSORSHIP
ANTICENSORSHIPS
ANTICHLORISTIC
ANTICHLORS
ANTICHOICE
ANTICHOICER
ANTICHOICERS
ANTICHOLESTEROL
ANTICHOLINERGIC
ANTICHRIST
ANTICHRISTIAN
ANTICHRISTIANLY
ANTICHRISTS
ANTICHTHONES
ANTICHURCH
ANTICIGARETTE
ANTICIPANT
ANTICIPANTS
ANTICIPATABLE
ANTICIPATE
ANTICIPATED
ANTICIPATES
ANTICIPATING
ANTICIPATION
ANTICIPATIONS
ANTICIPATIVE
ANTICIPATIVELY
ANTICIPATOR
ANTICIPATORILY
ANTICIPATORS
ANTICIPATORY
ANTICISING
ANTICIVISM
ANTICIVISMS
ANTICIZING
ANTICLASSICAL
ANTICLASTIC
ANTICLASTICALLY
ANTICLERICAL
ANTICLERICALISM
ANTICLERICALS
ANTICLIMACTIC
ANTICLIMACTICAL
ANTICLIMAX
ANTICLIMAXES
ANTICLINAL
ANTICLINALS
ANTICLINES
ANTICLINORIA
ANTICLINORIUM
ANTICLINORIUMS
ANTICLOCKWISE
ANTICLOTTING
ANTICOAGULANT
ANTICOAGULANTS
ANTICOAGULATING
ANTICODONS
ANTICOINCIDENCE
ANTICOLLISION
ANTICOLONIAL
ANTICOLONIALISM
ANTICOLONIALIST
ANTICOMMERCIAL
ANTICOMMUNISM
ANTICOMMUNISMS
ANTICOMMUNIST
ANTICOMMUNISTS
ANTICOMPETITIVE
ANTICONSUMER
ANTICONVULSANT
ANTICONVULSANTS
ANTICONVULSIVE
ANTICONVULSIVES
ANTICORPORATE
ANTICORROSION
ANTICORROSIVE
ANTICORROSIVES
ANTICORRUPTION
ANTICREATIVE
ANTICRUELTY
ANTICULTURAL
ANTICYCLONE
ANTICYCLONES
ANTICYCLONIC
ANTIDANDRUFF
ANTIDAZZLE
ANTIDEFAMATION
ANTIDEMOCRATIC
ANTIDEPRESSANT
ANTIDEPRESSANTS
ANTIDEPRESSION
ANTIDERIVATIVE
ANTIDERIVATIVES
ANTIDESICCANT
ANTIDESICCANTS
ANTIDEVELOPMENT
ANTIDIABETIC
ANTIDIARRHEAL
ANTIDIARRHEALS
ANTIDILUTION
ANTIDIURETIC
ANTIDIURETICS
ANTIDOGMATIC
ANTIDOTALLY
ANTIDOTING
ANTIDROMIC
ANTIDROMICALLY
ANTIDUMPING
ANTIECONOMIC
ANTIEDUCATIONAL
ANTIEGALITARIAN
ANTIELECTRON
ANTIELECTRONS
ANTIELITES
ANTIELITISM
ANTIELITISMS
ANTIELITIST
ANTIEMETIC
ANTIEMETICS
ANTIENTROPIC
ANTIEPILEPSY
ANTIEPILEPTIC
ANTIEPILEPTICS
ANTIEROTIC
ANTIESTROGEN
ANTIESTROGENS
ANTIEVOLUTION
ANTIFAMILY
ANTIFASCISM
ANTIFASCISMS
ANTIFASCIST
ANTIFASCISTS
ANTIFASHION
ANTIFASHIONABLE
ANTIFASHIONS
ANTIFATIGUE
ANTIFEBRILE
ANTIFEBRILES
ANTIFEDERALIST
ANTIFEDERALISTS
ANTIFEMALE
ANTIFEMININE
ANTIFEMINISM

NTIFEMINISMS
NTIFEMINIST
NTIFEMINISTS
NTIFERROMAGNET
NTIFERTILITY
NTIFILIBUSTER
NTIFOAMING
NTIFOGGING
NTIFORECLOSURE
NTIFOREIGN
NTIFOREIGNER
NTIFORMALIST
NTIFOULING
NTIFOULINGS
NTIFREEZE
NTIFREEZES
NTIFRICTION
NTIFUNGAL
NTIFUNGALS
NTIGAMBLING
NTIGENICALLY
NTIGENICITIES
NTIGENICITY
NTIGLOBULIN
NTIGLOBULINS
NTIGOVERNMENT
NTIGRAVITIES
NTIGRAVITY
NTIGROPELOES
NTIGROPELOS
NTIGROWTH
NTIGUERRILLA
NTIHALATION
NTIHALATIONS
NTIHELICES
NTIHELIXES
NTIHELMINTHIC
NTIHEROES
NTIHEROIC
NTIHEROINE
NTIHEROINES
NTIHERPES
NTIHIJACK
NTIHISTAMINE
NTIHISTAMINES
NTIHISTAMINIC
NTIHISTAMINICS
NTIHISTORICAL
NTIHOMOSEXUAL
NTIHUMANISM
NTIHUMANISMS
NTIHUMANISTIC
NTIHUNTER
NTIHUNTING
NTIHYDROGEN
NTIHYDROGENS
NTIHYSTERIC
NTIHYSTERICS
NTIJACOBIN
NTIJACOBINS
NTIJAMMING
NTIJAMMINGS
NTIKICKBACK
NTIKNOCKS
NTILEGOMENA
NTILEPROSY

ANTILEPTON
ANTILEPTONS
ANTILEUKEMIC
ANTILIBERAL
ANTILIBERALISM
ANTILIBERALISMS
ANTILIBERALS
ANTILIBERTARIAN
ANTILIFERS
ANTILITERATE
ANTILITTER
ANTILITTERING
ANTILOGARITHM
ANTILOGARITHMIC
ANTILOGARITHMS
ANTILOGICAL
ANTILOGIES
ANTILOGOUS
ANTILOPINE
ANTILYNCHING
ANTIMACASSAR
ANTIMACASSARS
ANTIMAGNETIC
ANTIMALARIA
ANTIMALARIAL
ANTIMALARIALS
ANTIMANAGEMENT
ANTIMARIJUANA
ANTIMARKET
ANTIMASQUE
ANTIMASQUES
ANTIMATERIALISM
ANTIMATERIALIST
ANTIMATTER
ANTIMATTERS
ANTIMECHANIST
ANTIMECHANISTS
ANTIMERGER
ANTIMERISM
ANTIMERISMS
ANTIMETABOLE
ANTIMETABOLES
ANTIMETABOLIC
ANTIMETABOLITE
ANTIMETABOLITES
ANTIMETATHESES
ANTIMETATHESIS
ANTIMICROBIAL
ANTIMICROBIALS
ANTIMILITARISM
ANTIMILITARISMS
ANTIMILITARIST
ANTIMILITARISTS
ANTIMILITARY
ANTIMISSILE
ANTIMISSILES
ANTIMITOTIC
ANTIMITOTICS
ANTIMNEMONIC
ANTIMNEMONICS
ANTIMODERN
ANTIMODERNIST
ANTIMODERNISTS
ANTIMONARCHICAL
ANTIMONARCHIST
ANTIMONARCHISTS

ANTIMONATE
ANTIMONATES
ANTIMONIAL
ANTIMONIALS
ANTIMONIATE
ANTIMONIATES
ANTIMONIDE
ANTIMONIDES
ANTIMONIES
ANTIMONIOUS
ANTIMONITE
ANTIMONITES
ANTIMONOPOLIST
ANTIMONOPOLISTS
ANTIMONOPOLY
ANTIMONOUS
ANTIMONYLS
ANTIMOSQUITO
ANTIMUSICAL
ANTIMUSICS
ANTIMUTAGEN
ANTIMUTAGENS
ANTIMYCINS
ANTIMYCOTIC
ANTINARRATIVE
ANTINARRATIVES
ANTINATIONAL
ANTINATIONALIST
ANTINATURAL
ANTINATURE
ANTINAUSEA
ANTINEOPLASTIC
ANTINEPHRITIC
ANTINEPHRITICS
ANTINEPOTISM
ANTINEUTRINO
ANTINEUTRINOS
ANTINEUTRON
ANTINEUTRONS
ANTINOMIAN
ANTINOMIANISM
ANTINOMIANISMS
ANTINOMIANS
ANTINOMICAL
ANTINOMICALLY
ANTINOMIES
ANTINOVELIST
ANTINOVELISTS
ANTINOVELS
ANTINUCLEAR
ANTINUCLEARIST
ANTINUCLEARISTS
ANTINUCLEON
ANTINUCLEONS
ANTINUKERS
ANTIOBESITY
ANTIOBSCENITY
ANTIODONTALGIC
ANTIODONTALGICS
ANTIOXIDANT
ANTIOXIDANTS
ANTIOZONANT
ANTIOZONANTS
ANTIPARALLEL
ANTIPARALLELS
ANTIPARASITIC

ANTIPARTICLE
ANTIPARTICLES
ANTIPARTIES
ANTIPASTOS
ANTIPATHETIC
ANTIPATHETICAL
ANTIPATHIC
ANTIPATHIES
ANTIPATHIST
ANTIPATHISTS
ANTIPERIODIC
ANTIPERIODICS
ANTIPERISTALSES
ANTIPERISTALSIS
ANTIPERISTALTIC
ANTIPERISTASES
ANTIPERISTASIS
ANTIPERSONNEL
ANTIPERSPIRANT
ANTIPERSPIRANTS
ANTIPESTICIDE
ANTIPETALOUS
ANTIPHLOGISTIC
ANTIPHLOGISTICS
ANTIPHONAL
ANTIPHONALLY
ANTIPHONALS
ANTIPHONARIES
ANTIPHONARY
ANTIPHONER
ANTIPHONERS
ANTIPHONIC
ANTIPHONICAL
ANTIPHONICALLY
ANTIPHONIES
ANTIPHRASES
ANTIPHRASIS
ANTIPHRASTIC
ANTIPHRASTICAL
ANTIPIRACY
ANTIPLAGUE
ANTIPLAQUE
ANTIPLEASURE
ANTIPOACHING
ANTIPODALS
ANTIPODEAN
ANTIPODEANS
ANTIPOETIC
ANTIPOLICE
ANTIPOLITICAL
ANTIPOLITICS
ANTIPOLLUTION
ANTIPOLLUTIONS
ANTIPOPULAR
ANTIPORNOGRAPHY
ANTIPOVERTY
ANTIPREDATOR
ANTIPROGRESSIVE
ANTIPROHIBITION
ANTIPROTON
ANTIPROTONS
ANTIPRURITIC
ANTIPRURITICS
ANTIPSYCHIATRIC
ANTIPSYCHIATRY
ANTIPSYCHOTIC

ANTIPSYCHOTICS
ANTIPYRESES
ANTIPYRESIS
ANTIPYRETIC
ANTIPYRETICS
ANTIPYRINE
ANTIPYRINES
ANTIQUARIAN
ANTIQUARIANISM
ANTIQUARIANISMS
ANTIQUARIANS
ANTIQUARIES
ANTIQUARKS
ANTIQUATED
ANTIQUATEDNESS
ANTIQUATES
ANTIQUATING
ANTIQUATION
ANTIQUATIONS
ANTIQUENESS
ANTIQUENESSES
ANTIQUITARIAN
ANTIQUITARIANS
ANTIQUITIES
ANTIRABIES
ANTIRACHITIC
ANTIRACHITICS
ANTIRACISM
ANTIRACISMS
ANTIRACIST
ANTIRACISTS
ANTIRADARS
ANTIRADICAL
ANTIRADICALISM
ANTIRADICALISMS
ANTIRATIONAL
ANTIRATIONALISM
ANTIRATIONALIST
ANTIRATIONALITY
ANTIREALISM
ANTIREALISMS
ANTIREALIST
ANTIREALISTS
ANTIRECESSION
ANTIREFLECTION
ANTIREFLECTIVE
ANTIREFORM
ANTIREGULATORY
ANTIREJECTION
ANTIRELIGION
ANTIRELIGIOUS
ANTIREPUBLICAN
ANTIREPUBLICANS
ANTIRHEUMATIC
ANTIRHEUMATICS
ANTIRITUALISM
ANTIRITUALISMS
ANTIROMANTIC
ANTIROMANTICISM
ANTIROMANTICS
ANTIROYALIST
ANTIROYALISTS
ANTIRRHINUM
ANTIRRHINUMS
ANTISATELLITE
ANTISCIANS
ANTISCIENCE
ANTISCIENCES
ANTISCIENTIFIC
ANTISCORBUTIC
ANTISCORBUTICS
ANTISCRIPTURAL
ANTISECRECY
ANTISEGREGATION
ANTISEIZURE
ANTISENTIMENTAL
ANTISEPALOUS
ANTISEPARATIST
ANTISEPARATISTS
ANTISEPSES
ANTISEPSIS
ANTISEPTIC
ANTISEPTICALLY
ANTISEPTICISE
ANTISEPTICISED
ANTISEPTICISES
ANTISEPTICISING
ANTISEPTICISM
ANTISEPTICISMS
ANTISEPTICIZE
ANTISEPTICIZED
ANTISEPTICIZES
ANTISEPTICIZING
ANTISEPTICS
ANTISERUMS
ANTISEXIST
ANTISEXISTS
ANTISEXUAL
ANTISEXUALITIES
ANTISEXUALITY
ANTISHOCKS
ANTISHOPLIFTING
ANTISLAVERY
ANTISMOKER
ANTISMOKERS
ANTISMOKING
ANTISMUGGLING
ANTISOCIAL
ANTISOCIALISM
ANTISOCIALISMS
ANTISOCIALIST
ANTISOCIALISTS
ANTISOCIALITIES
ANTISOCIALITY
ANTISOCIALLY
ANTISPASMODIC
ANTISPASMODICS
ANTISPASTIC
ANTISPASTS
ANTISPECULATION
ANTISPECULATIVE
ANTISPENDING
ANTISPIRITUAL
ANTISTATIC
ANTISTATICS
ANTISTORIES
ANTISTRESS
ANTISTRIKE
ANTISTROPHE
ANTISTROPHES
ANTISTROPHIC
ANTISTROPHON
ANTISTROPHONS
ANTISTUDENT
ANTISTYLES
ANTISUBMARINE
ANTISUBSIDY
ANTISUBVERSION
ANTISUBVERSIVE
ANTISUICIDE
ANTISYMMETRIC
ANTISYPHILITIC
ANTISYPHILITICS
ANTISYZYGIES
ANTISYZYGY
ANTITAKEOVER
ANTITARNISH
ANTITECHNOLOGY
ANTITERRORISM
ANTITERRORISMS
ANTITERRORIST
ANTITERRORISTS
ANTITHALIAN
ANTITHEISM
ANTITHEISMS
ANTITHEIST
ANTITHEISTIC
ANTITHEISTS
ANTITHEORETICAL
ANTITHESES
ANTITHESIS
ANTITHETIC
ANTITHETICAL
ANTITHETICALLY
ANTITHROMBIN
ANTITHROMBINS
ANTITHROMBOTIC
ANTITHROMBOTICS
ANTITHYROID
ANTITOBACCO
ANTITOXINS
ANTITRADES
ANTITRADITIONAL
ANTITRAGUS
ANTITRANSPIRANT
ANTITRINITARIAN
ANTITRUSTER
ANTITRUSTERS
ANTITUBERCULAR
ANTITUBERCULOUS
ANTITUMORAL
ANTITUMORS
ANTITUSSIVE
ANTITUSSIVES
ANTITYPHOID
ANTITYPICAL
ANTITYPICALLY
ANTIUNIVERSITY
ANTIVENENE
ANTIVENENES
ANTIVENINS
ANTIVENOMS
ANTIVIOLENCE
ANTIVIRUSES
ANTIVITAMIN
ANTIVITAMINS
ANTIVIVISECTION
ANTIWELFARE
ANTIWHALING
ANTIWORLDS
ANTIWRINKLE
ANTONINIANUS
ANTONINIANUSES
ANTONOMASIA
ANTONOMASIAS
ANTONOMASTIC
ANTONYMIES
ANTONYMOUS
ANTRORSELY
ANTSINESSES
ANUCLEATED
ANXIOLYTIC
ANXIOLYTICS
ANXIOUSNESS
ANXIOUSNESSES
ANYTHINGARIAN
ANYTHINGARIANS
ANYWHITHER
AORISTICALLY
AORTITISES
AORTOGRAPHIC
AORTOGRAPHIES
AORTOGRAPHY
APAGOGICAL
APAGOGICALLY
APARTHEIDS
APARTHOTEL
APARTHOTELS
APARTMENTAL
APARTMENTS
APARTNESSES
APATHATONS
APATHETICAL
APATHETICALLY
APATOSAURS
APATOSAURUS
APATOSAURUSES
APERIODICALLY
APERIODICITIES
APERIODICITY
APERITIVES
APERTNESSES
APFELSTRUDEL
APFELSTRUDELS
APHAERESES
APHAERESIS
APHAERETIC
APHANIPTEROUS
APHELANDRA
APHELANDRAS
APHELIOTROPIC
APHELIOTROPISM
APHELIOTROPISMS
APHETICALLY
APHETISING
APHETIZING
APHIDICIDE
APHIDICIDES
APHORISERS
APHORISING
APHORISTIC
APHORISTICALLY
APHORIZERS
APHORIZING

PHRODISIA
PHRODISIAC
PHRODISIACAL
PHRODISIACS
PHRODISIAS
PHRODITES
PICULTURAL
PICULTURE
PICULTURES
PICULTURIST
PICULTURISTS
PIOLOGIES
PISHNESSES
PITHERAPIES
PITHERAPY
PLACENTAL
PLANATICALLY
PLANATISM
PLANATISMS
PLANOGAMETE
PLANOGAMETES
PLANOSPORE
PLANOSPORES
POAPSIDES
POCALYPSE
POCALYPSES
POCALYPTIC
POCALYPTICAL
POCALYPTICALLY
POCALYPTICISM
POCALYPTICISMS
POCALYPTISM
POCALYPTISMS
POCALYPTIST
POCALYPTISTS
POCARPIES
POCARPOUS
POCATASTASES
POCATASTASIS
POCHROMAT
POCHROMATIC
POCHROMATISM
POCHROMATISMS
POCHROMATS
POCOPATED
POCOPATES
POCOPATING
POCOPATION
POCOPATIONS
POCRYPHAL
POCRYPHALLY
POCRYPHALNESS
POCRYPHON
POCYNACEOUS
POCYNTHION
POCYNTHIONS
PODEICTIC
PODEICTICAL
PODEICTICALLY
PODICTICAL
PODICTICALLY
PODYTERIUM
PODYTERIUMS
POENZYMES
POGAMOUSLY
POGEOTROPIC

APOGEOTROPISM
APOGEOTROPISMS
APOLAUSTIC
APOLAUSTICS
APOLIPOPROTEIN
APOLIPOPROTEINS
APOLITICAL
APOLITICALITIES
APOLITICALITY
APOLITICALLY
APOLITICISM
APOLITICISMS
APOLLONIAN
APOLLONICON
APOLLONICONS
APOLOGETIC
APOLOGETICAL
APOLOGETICALLY
APOLOGETICS
APOLOGISED
APOLOGISER
APOLOGISERS
APOLOGISES
APOLOGISING
APOLOGISTS
APOLOGIZED
APOLOGIZER
APOLOGIZERS
APOLOGIZES
APOLOGIZING
APOMICTICAL
APOMICTICALLY
APOMORPHIA
APOMORPHIAS
APOMORPHINE
APOMORPHINES
APONEUROSES
APONEUROSIS
APONEUROTIC
APOPEMPTIC
APOPHLEGMATIC
APOPHLEGMATICS
APOPHONIES
APOPHTHEGM
APOPHTHEGMATIC
APOPHTHEGMATISE
APOPHTHEGMATIST
APOPHTHEGMATIZE
APOPHTHEGMS
APOPHYLLITE
APOPHYLLITES
APOPHYSATE
APOPHYSEAL
APOPHYSIAL
APOPLECTIC
APOPLECTICAL
APOPLECTICALLY
APOPLECTICS
APOPLEXIES
APOPLEXING
APOPROTEIN
APOPROTEINS
APOSEMATIC
APOSEMATICALLY
APOSIOPESES
APOSIOPESIS

APOSIOPETIC
APOSPORIES
APOSPOROUS
APOSTACIES
APOSTASIES
APOSTATICAL
APOSTATISE
APOSTATISED
APOSTATISES
APOSTATISING
APOSTATIZE
APOSTATIZED
APOSTATIZES
APOSTATIZING
APOSTILLES
APOSTLESHIP
APOSTLESHIPS
APOSTOLATE
APOSTOLATES
APOSTOLICAL
APOSTOLICALLY
APOSTOLICISM
APOSTOLICISMS
APOSTOLICITIES
APOSTOLICITY
APOSTOLISE
APOSTOLISED
APOSTOLISES
APOSTOLISING
APOSTOLIZE
APOSTOLIZED
APOSTOLIZES
APOSTOLIZING
APOSTROPHE
APOSTROPHES
APOSTROPHIC
APOSTROPHISE
APOSTROPHISED
APOSTROPHISES
APOSTROPHISING
APOSTROPHIZE
APOSTROPHIZED
APOSTROPHIZES
APOSTROPHIZING
APOSTROPHUS
APOSTROPHUSES
APOTHECARIES
APOTHECARY
APOTHECIAL
APOTHECIUM
APOTHEGMATIC
APOTHEGMATICAL
APOTHEGMATISE
APOTHEGMATISED
APOTHEGMATISES
APOTHEGMATISING
APOTHEGMATIST
APOTHEGMATISTS
APOTHEGMATIZE
APOTHEGMATIZED
APOTHEGMATIZES
APOTHEGMATIZING
APOTHEOSES
APOTHEOSIS
APOTHEOSISE
APOTHEOSISED

APOTHEOSISES
APOTHEOSISING
APOTHEOSIZE
APOTHEOSIZED
APOTHEOSIZES
APOTHEOSIZING
APOTROPAIC
APOTROPAICALLY
APOTROPAISM
APOTROPAISMS
APOTROPOUS
APPALLINGLY
APPALOOSAS
APPARATCHIK
APPARATCHIKI
APPARATCHIKS
APPARATUSES
APPARELING
APPARELLED
APPARELLING
APPARELMENT
APPARELMENTS
APPARENCIES
APPARENTLY
APPARENTNESS
APPARENTNESSES
APPARITION
APPARITIONAL
APPARITIONS
APPARITORS
APPARTEMENT
APPARTEMENTS
APPASSIONATO
APPEACHING
APPEACHMENT
APPEACHMENTS
APPEALABILITIES
APPEALABILITY
APPEALABLE
APPEALINGLY
APPEALINGNESS
APPEALINGNESSES
APPEARANCE
APPEARANCES
APPEASABLE
APPEASEMENT
APPEASEMENTS
APPEASINGLY
APPELLANTS
APPELLATION
APPELLATIONAL
APPELLATIONS
APPELLATIVE
APPELLATIVELY
APPELLATIVES
APPENDAGES
APPENDANTS
APPENDECTOMIES
APPENDECTOMY
APPENDENTS
APPENDICECTOMY
APPENDICES
APPENDICITIS
APPENDICITISES
APPENDICLE
APPENDICLES

APPENDICULAR
APPENDICULARIAN
APPENDICULATE
APPENDIXES
APPERCEIVE
APPERCEIVED
APPERCEIVES
APPERCEIVING
APPERCEPTION
APPERCEPTIONS
APPERCEPTIVE
APPERCIPIENT
APPERTAINANCE
APPERTAINANCES
APPERTAINED
APPERTAINING
APPERTAINMENT
APPERTAINMENTS
APPERTAINS
APPERTINENT
APPERTINENTS
APPETEEZEMENT
APPETEEZEMENTS
APPETENCES
APPETENCIES
APPETISEMENT
APPETISEMENTS
APPETISERS
APPETISING
APPETISINGLY
APPETITION
APPETITIONS
APPETITIVE
APPETIZERS
APPETIZING
APPETIZINGLY
APPLAUDABLE
APPLAUDABLY
APPLAUDERS
APPLAUDING
APPLAUDINGLY
APPLAUSIVE
APPLAUSIVELY
APPLECARTS
APPLEDRAIN
APPLEDRAINS
APPLEJACKS
APPLERINGIE
APPLERINGIES
APPLESAUCE
APPLESAUCES
APPLIANCES
APPLICABILITIES
APPLICABILITY
APPLICABLE
APPLICABLENESS
APPLICABLY
APPLICANTS
APPLICATION
APPLICATIONS
APPLICATIVE
APPLICATIVELY
APPLICATOR
APPLICATORS
APPLICATORY
APPLIQUEING
APPOGGIATURA
APPOGGIATURAS
APPOGGIATURE
APPOINTEES
APPOINTERS
APPOINTING
APPOINTIVE
APPOINTMENT
APPOINTMENTS
APPOINTORS
APPORTIONABLE
APPORTIONED
APPORTIONER
APPORTIONERS
APPORTIONING
APPORTIONMENT
APPORTIONMENTS
APPORTIONS
APPOSITELY
APPOSITENESS
APPOSITENESSES
APPOSITION
APPOSITIONAL
APPOSITIONS
APPOSITIVE
APPOSITIVELY
APPOSITIVES
APPRAISABLE
APPRAISALS
APPRAISEES
APPRAISEMENT
APPRAISEMENTS
APPRAISERS
APPRAISING
APPRAISINGLY
APPRAISIVE
APPRAISIVELY
APPRECIABLE
APPRECIABLY
APPRECIATE
APPRECIATED
APPRECIATES
APPRECIATING
APPRECIATION
APPRECIATIONS
APPRECIATIVE
APPRECIATIVELY
APPRECIATOR
APPRECIATORILY
APPRECIATORS
APPRECIATORY
APPREHENDED
APPREHENDING
APPREHENDS
APPREHENSIBLE
APPREHENSIBLY
APPREHENSION
APPREHENSIONS
APPREHENSIVE
APPREHENSIVELY
APPRENTICE
APPRENTICED
APPRENTICEHOOD
APPRENTICEHOODS
APPRENTICEMENT
APPRENTICEMENTS
APPRENTICES
APPRENTICESHIP
APPRENTICESHIPS
APPRENTICING
APPRESSING
APPRESSORIA
APPRESSORIUM
APPRISINGS
APPRIZINGS
APPROACHABILITY
APPROACHABLE
APPROACHED
APPROACHES
APPROACHING
APPROBATED
APPROBATES
APPROBATING
APPROBATION
APPROBATIONS
APPROBATIVE
APPROBATORY
APPROPINQUATE
APPROPINQUATED
APPROPINQUATES
APPROPINQUATING
APPROPINQUATION
APPROPINQUE
APPROPINQUED
APPROPINQUES
APPROPINQUING
APPROPINQUITIES
APPROPINQUITY
APPROPRIABLE
APPROPRIACIES
APPROPRIACY
APPROPRIATE
APPROPRIATED
APPROPRIATELY
APPROPRIATENESS
APPROPRIATES
APPROPRIATING
APPROPRIATION
APPROPRIATIONS
APPROPRIATIVE
APPROPRIATOR
APPROPRIATORS
APPROVABLE
APPROVABLY
APPROVANCE
APPROVANCES
APPROVINGLY
APPROXIMAL
APPROXIMATE
APPROXIMATED
APPROXIMATELY
APPROXIMATES
APPROXIMATING
APPROXIMATION
APPROXIMATIONS
APPROXIMATIVE
APPULSIVELY
APPURTENANCE
APPURTENANCES
APPURTENANT
APPURTENANTS
APRICATING
APRICATION
APRICATIONS
APRIORISMS
APRIORISTS
APRIORITIES
APSIDIOLES
APTERYGIAL
APTITUDINAL
APTITUDINALLY
AQUABATICS
AQUABOARDS
AQUACEUTICAL
AQUACEUTICALS
AQUACULTURAL
AQUACULTURE
AQUACULTURES
AQUACULTURIST
AQUACULTURISTS
AQUADROMES
AQUAEROBICS
AQUAFARMED
AQUAFARMING
AQUAFITNESS
AQUAFITNESSES
AQUAFORTIS
AQUAFORTISES
AQUAFORTIST
AQUAFORTISTS
AQUALEATHER
AQUALEATHERS
AQUAMANALE
AQUAMANALES
AQUAMANILE
AQUAMANILES
AQUAMARINE
AQUAMARINES
AQUANAUTICS
AQUAPHOBES
AQUAPHOBIA
AQUAPHOBIAS
AQUAPHOBIC
AQUAPHOBICS
AQUAPLANED
AQUAPLANER
AQUAPLANERS
AQUAPLANES
AQUAPLANING
AQUAPLANINGS
AQUAPORINS
AQUARELLES
AQUARELLIST
AQUARELLISTS
AQUARIISTS
AQUAROBICS
AQUATICALLY
AQUATINTAS
AQUATINTED
AQUATINTER
AQUATINTERS
AQUATINTING
AQUATINTIST
AQUATINTISTS
AQUICULTURAL
AQUICULTURE
AQUICULTURES
AQUICULTURIST

QUICULTURISTS
QUIFEROUS
QUIFOLIACEOUS
QUILEGIAS
QUILINITIES
QUILINITY
RABESQUED
RABESQUES
RABICISATION
RABICISATIONS
RABICISED
RABICISES
RABICISING
RABICIZATION
RABICIZATIONS
RABICIZED
RABICIZES
RABICIZING
RABILITIES
RABINOSES
RABINOSIDE
RABINOSIDES
RABISATION
RABISATIONS
RABIZATION
RABIZATIONS
RACHIDONIC
RACHNIDAN
RACHNIDANS
RACHNOIDAL
RACHNOIDITIS
RACHNOIDITISES
RACHNOIDS
RACHNOLOGICAL
RACHNOLOGIES
RACHNOLOGIST
RACHNOLOGISTS
RACHNOLOGY
RACHNOPHOBE
RACHNOPHOBES
RACHNOPHOBIA
RACHNOPHOBIAS
RAEOMETER
RAEOMETERS
RAEOMETRIC
RAEOMETRICAL
RAEOMETRIES
RAEOMETRY
RAEOSTYLE
RAEOSTYLES
RAEOSYSTYLE
RAEOSYSTYLES
RAGONITES
RAGONITIC
RALIACEOUS
RAUCARIAN
RAUCARIAS
RBALESTER
RBALESTERS
RBALISTER
RBALISTERS
RBITRABLE
RBITRAGED
RBITRAGER
RBITRAGERS
RBITRAGES
ARBITRAGEUR
ARBITRAGEURS
ARBITRAGING
ARBITRAMENT
ARBITRAMENTS
ARBITRARILY
ARBITRARINESS
ARBITRARINESSES
ARBITRATED
ARBITRATES
ARBITRATING
ARBITRATION
ARBITRATIONAL
ARBITRATIONS
ARBITRATIVE
ARBITRATOR
ARBITRATORS
ARBITRATRICES
ARBITRATRIX
ARBITRATRIXES
ARBITREMENT
ARBITREMENTS
ARBITRESSES
ARBITRIUMS
ARBLASTERS
ARBORACEOUS
ARBOREALLY
ARBORESCENCE
ARBORESCENCES
ARBORESCENT
ARBORETUMS
ARBORICULTURAL
ARBORICULTURE
ARBORICULTURES
ARBORICULTURIST
ARBORISATION
ARBORISATIONS
ARBORISING
ARBORIZATION
ARBORIZATIONS
ARBORIZING
ARBORVITAE
ARBORVITAES
ARBOVIRUSES
ARBUSCULAR
ARCANENESS
ARCANENESSES
ARCCOSINES
ARCHAEBACTERIA
ARCHAEBACTERIUM
ARCHAEOBOTANIST
ARCHAEOBOTANY
ARCHAEOLOGICAL
ARCHAEOLOGIES
ARCHAEOLOGIST
ARCHAEOLOGISTS
ARCHAEOLOGY
ARCHAEOMETRIC
ARCHAEOMETRIES
ARCHAEOMETRIST
ARCHAEOMETRISTS
ARCHAEOMETRY
ARCHAEOPTERYX
ARCHAEOPTERYXES
ARCHAEORNIS
ARCHAEORNISES
ARCHAEOZOOLOGY
ARCHAEZOOLOGIES
ARCHAEZOOLOGY
ARCHAICALLY
ARCHAICISM
ARCHAICISMS
ARCHAISERS
ARCHAISING
ARCHAISTIC
ARCHAIZERS
ARCHAIZING
ARCHANGELIC
ARCHANGELS
ARCHBISHOP
ARCHBISHOPRIC
ARCHBISHOPRICS
ARCHBISHOPS
ARCHDEACON
ARCHDEACONRIES
ARCHDEACONRY
ARCHDEACONS
ARCHDIOCESAN
ARCHDIOCESE
ARCHDIOCESES
ARCHDUCHESS
ARCHDUCHESSES
ARCHDUCHIES
ARCHDUKEDOM
ARCHDUKEDOMS
ARCHEGONIA
ARCHEGONIAL
ARCHEGONIATE
ARCHEGONIATES
ARCHEGONIUM
ARCHENEMIES
ARCHENTERA
ARCHENTERIC
ARCHENTERON
ARCHENTERONS
ARCHEOASTRONOMY
ARCHEOBOTANICAL
ARCHEOBOTANIES
ARCHEOBOTANIST
ARCHEOBOTANISTS
ARCHEOBOTANY
ARCHEOLOGICAL
ARCHEOLOGICALLY
ARCHEOLOGIES
ARCHEOLOGIST
ARCHEOLOGISTS
ARCHEOLOGY
ARCHEOMAGNETISM
ARCHEOMETRIES
ARCHEOMETRY
ARCHEOZOOLOGIST
ARCHEOZOOLOGY
ARCHERESSES
ARCHERFISH
ARCHERFISHES
ARCHESPORE
ARCHESPORES
ARCHESPORIA
ARCHESPORIAL
ARCHESPORIUM
ARCHETYPAL
ARCHETYPALLY
ARCHETYPES
ARCHETYPICAL
ARCHETYPICALLY
ARCHFIENDS
ARCHGENETHLIAC
ARCHGENETHLIACS
ARCHICARPS
ARCHIDIACONAL
ARCHIDIACONATE
ARCHIDIACONATES
ARCHIEPISCOPACY
ARCHIEPISCOPAL
ARCHIEPISCOPATE
ARCHILOWES
ARCHIMAGES
ARCHIMANDRITE
ARCHIMANDRITES
ARCHIPELAGIAN
ARCHIPELAGIC
ARCHIPELAGO
ARCHIPELAGOES
ARCHIPELAGOS
ARCHIPHONEME
ARCHIPHONEMES
ARCHIPLASM
ARCHIPLASMIC
ARCHIPLASMS
ARCHITECTED
ARCHITECTING
ARCHITECTONIC
ARCHITECTONICS
ARCHITECTS
ARCHITECTURAL
ARCHITECTURALLY
ARCHITECTURE
ARCHITECTURES
ARCHITRAVE
ARCHITRAVED
ARCHITRAVES
ARCHITYPES
ARCHIVISTS
ARCHIVOLTS
ARCHNESSES
ARCHOLOGIES
ARCHONSHIP
ARCHONSHIPS
ARCHONTATE
ARCHONTATES
ARCHOPLASM
ARCHOPLASMIC
ARCHOPLASMS
ARCHOSAURIAN
ARCHOSAURS
ARCHPRIEST
ARCHPRIESTHOOD
ARCHPRIESTHOODS
ARCHPRIESTS
ARCHPRIESTSHIP
ARCHPRIESTSHIPS
ARCHRIVALS
ARCOGRAPHS
ARCOLOGIES
ARCSECONDS
ARCTANGENT
ARCTANGENTS
ARCTICALLY

ARCTOPHILE
ARCTOPHILES
ARCTOPHILIA
ARCTOPHILIAS
ARCTOPHILIES
ARCTOPHILIST
ARCTOPHILISTS
ARCTOPHILS
ARCTOPHILY
ARCUATIONS
ARCUBALIST
ARCUBALISTS
ARDUOUSNESS
ARDUOUSNESSES
ARECOLINES
AREFACTION
AREFACTIONS
ARENACEOUS
ARENATIONS
ARENICOLOUS
AREOCENTRIC
AREOGRAPHIC
AREOGRAPHIES
AREOGRAPHY
AREOLATION
AREOLATIONS
AREOLOGIES
AREOMETERS
AREOSTYLES
AREOSYSTILE
AREOSYSTILES
ARFVEDSONITE
ARFVEDSONITES
ARGENTIFEROUS
ARGENTINES
ARGENTITES
ARGILLACEOUS
ARGILLIFEROUS
ARGILLITES
ARGILLITIC
ARGONAUTIC
ARGUMENTATION
ARGUMENTATIONS
ARGUMENTATIVE
ARGUMENTATIVELY
ARGUMENTIVE
ARGUMENTUM
ARGUMENTUMS
ARGUTENESS
ARGUTENESSES
ARGYRODITE
ARGYRODITES
ARHATSHIPS
ARHYTHMIAS
ARIBOFLAVINOSES
ARIBOFLAVINOSIS
ARIDNESSES
ARISTOCRACIES
ARISTOCRACY
ARISTOCRAT
ARISTOCRATIC
ARISTOCRATICAL
ARISTOCRATISM
ARISTOCRATISMS
ARISTOCRATS
ARISTOLOCHIA
ARISTOLOCHIAS
ARISTOLOGIES
ARISTOLOGY
ARISTOTLES
ARITHMETIC
ARITHMETICAL
ARITHMETICALLY
ARITHMETICIAN
ARITHMETICIANS
ARITHMETICS
ARITHMOMANIA
ARITHMOMANIAS
ARITHMOMETER
ARITHMOMETERS
ARITHMOPHOBIA
ARITHMOPHOBIAS
ARMADILLOS
ARMAMENTARIA
ARMAMENTARIUM
ARMAMENTARIUMS
ARMATURING
ARMIGEROUS
ARMILLARIA
ARMILLARIAS
ARMIPOTENCE
ARMIPOTENCES
ARMIPOTENT
ARMISTICES
ARMLOCKING
ARMORIALLY
ARMOURLESS
AROMATASES
AROMATHERAPIES
AROMATHERAPIST
AROMATHERAPISTS
AROMATHERAPY
AROMATICALLY
AROMATICITIES
AROMATICITY
AROMATISATION
AROMATISATIONS
AROMATISED
AROMATISES
AROMATISING
AROMATIZATION
AROMATIZATIONS
AROMATIZED
AROMATIZES
AROMATIZING
ARPEGGIATE
ARPEGGIATED
ARPEGGIATES
ARPEGGIATING
ARPEGGIATION
ARPEGGIATIONS
ARPEGGIONE
ARPEGGIONES
ARPILLERAS
ARQUEBUSADE
ARQUEBUSADES
ARQUEBUSES
ARQUEBUSIER
ARQUEBUSIERS
ARRACACHAS
ARRAGONITE
ARRAGONITES
ARRAIGNERS
ARRAIGNING
ARRAIGNINGS
ARRAIGNMENT
ARRAIGNMENTS
ARRANGEABLE
ARRANGEMENT
ARRANGEMENTS
ARRAYMENTS
ARREARAGES
ARRESTABLE
ARRESTANTS
ARRESTATION
ARRESTATIONS
ARRESTINGLY
ARRESTMENT
ARRESTMENTS
ARRHENOTOKIES
ARRHENOTOKY
ARRHYTHMIA
ARRHYTHMIAS
ARRHYTHMIC
ARRIVANCES
ARRIVANCIES
ARRIVEDERCI
ARRIVISMES
ARRIVISTES
ARROGANCES
ARROGANCIES
ARROGANTLY
ARROGATING
ARROGATION
ARROGATIONS
ARROGATIVE
ARROGATORS
ARRONDISSEMENT
ARRONDISSEMENTS
ARROWGRASS
ARROWGRASSES
ARROWHEADS
ARROWROOTS
ARROWWOODS
ARROWWORMS
ARSENIATES
ARSENICALS
ARSENOPYRITE
ARSENOPYRITES
ARSMETRICK
ARSMETRICKS
ARSPHENAMINE
ARSPHENAMINES
ARTEFACTUAL
ARTEMISIAS
ARTEMISININ
ARTEMISININS
ARTERIALISATION
ARTERIALISE
ARTERIALISED
ARTERIALISES
ARTERIALISING
ARTERIALIZATION
ARTERIALIZE
ARTERIALIZED
ARTERIALIZES
ARTERIALIZING
ARTERIALLY
ARTERIOGRAM
ARTERIOGRAMS
ARTERIOGRAPHIC
ARTERIOGRAPHIES
ARTERIOGRAPHY
ARTERIOLAR
ARTERIOLES
ARTERIOTOMIES
ARTERIOTOMY
ARTERIOVENOUS
ARTERITIDES
ARTERITISES
ARTFULNESS
ARTFULNESSES
ARTHRALGIA
ARTHRALGIAS
ARTHRALGIC
ARTHRECTOMIES
ARTHRECTOMY
ARTHRITICALLY
ARTHRITICS
ARTHRITIDES
ARTHRITISES
ARTHRODESES
ARTHRODESIS
ARTHRODIAE
ARTHRODIAL
ARTHROGRAPHIES
ARTHROGRAPHY
ARTHROMERE
ARTHROMERES
ARTHROMERIC
ARTHROPATHIES
ARTHROPATHY
ARTHROPLASTIES
ARTHROPLASTY
ARTHROPODAL
ARTHROPODAN
ARTHROPODOUS
ARTHROPODS
ARTHROSCOPE
ARTHROSCOPES
ARTHROSCOPIC
ARTHROSCOPIES
ARTHROSCOPY
ARTHROSPORE
ARTHROSPORES
ARTHROSPORIC
ARTHROSPOROUS
ARTICHOKES
ARTICULABLE
ARTICULACIES
ARTICULACY
ARTICULATE
ARTICULATED
ARTICULATELY
ARTICULATENESS
ARTICULATES
ARTICULATING
ARTICULATION
ARTICULATIONS
ARTICULATIVE
ARTICULATOR
ARTICULATORS
ARTICULATORY
ARTIFACTUAL

RTIFICERS
RTIFICIAL
RTIFICIALISE
RTIFICIALISED
RTIFICIALISES
RTIFICIALISING
RTIFICIALITIES
RTIFICIALITY
RTIFICIALIZE
RTIFICIALIZED
RTIFICIALIZES
RTIFICIALIZING
RTIFICIALLY
RTIFICIALNESS
RTILLERIES
RTILLERIST
RTILLERISTS
RTILLERYMAN
RTILLERYMEN
RTINESSES
RTIODACTYL
RTIODACTYLOUS
RTIODACTYLS
RTISANSHIP
RTISANSHIPS
RTISTICAL
RTISTICALLY
RTISTRIES
RTLESSNESS
RTLESSNESSES
RTOCARPUS
RTOCARPUSES
RTSINESSES
RUNDINACEOUS
RVICOLINE
RYBALLOID
RYBALLOSES
RYTAENOID
RYTAENOIDS
RYTENOIDAL
RYTENOIDS
SAFETIDAS
SAFOETIDA
SAFOETIDAS
SARABACCA
SARABACCAS
SBESTIFORM
SBESTOSES
SBESTOSIS
SBESTUSES
SCARIASES
SCARIASIS
SCENDABLE
SCENDANCE
SCENDANCES
SCENDANCIES
SCENDANCY
SCENDANTLY
SCENDANTS
SCENDENCE
SCENDENCES
SCENDENCIES
SCENDENCY
SCENDENTS
SCENDEURS
SCENDIBLE
ASCENSIONAL
ASCENSIONIST
ASCENSIONISTS
ASCENSIONS
ASCERTAINABLE
ASCERTAINABLY
ASCERTAINED
ASCERTAINING
ASCERTAINMENT
ASCERTAINMENTS
ASCERTAINS
ASCETICALLY
ASCETICISM
ASCETICISMS
ASCITITIOUS
ASCLEPIADACEOUS
ASCLEPIADS
ASCLEPIASES
ASCOCARPIC
ASCOGONIUM
ASCOMYCETE
ASCOMYCETES
ASCOMYCETOUS
ASCORBATES
ASCOSPORES
ASCOSPORIC
ASCRIBABLE
ASCRIPTION
ASCRIPTIONS
ASCRIPTIVE
ASEPTICALLY
ASEPTICISE
ASEPTICISED
ASEPTICISES
ASEPTICISING
ASEPTICISM
ASEPTICISMS
ASEPTICIZE
ASEPTICIZED
ASEPTICIZES
ASEPTICIZING
ASEXUALITIES
ASEXUALITY
ASHAMEDNESS
ASHAMEDNESSES
ASHINESSES
ASHLARINGS
ASHLERINGS
ASHRAMITES
ASININITIES
ASKEWNESSES
ASPARAGINASE
ASPARAGINASES
ASPARAGINE
ASPARAGINES
ASPARAGUSES
ASPARTAMES
ASPARTATES
ASPECTABLE
ASPENDICITIS
ASPENDICITISES
ASPERATING
ASPERGATION
ASPERGATIONS
ASPERGILLA
ASPERGILLI
ASPERGILLOSES
ASPERGILLOSIS
ASPERGILLS
ASPERGILLUM
ASPERGILLUMS
ASPERGILLUS
ASPERITIES
ASPERSIONS
ASPERSIVELY
ASPERSOIRS
ASPERSORIA
ASPERSORIES
ASPERSORIUM
ASPERSORIUMS
ASPHALTERS
ASPHALTING
ASPHALTITE
ASPHALTITES
ASPHALTUMS
ASPHERICAL
ASPHETERISE
ASPHETERISED
ASPHETERISES
ASPHETERISING
ASPHETERISM
ASPHETERISMS
ASPHETERIZE
ASPHETERIZED
ASPHETERIZES
ASPHETERIZING
ASPHYXIANT
ASPHYXIANTS
ASPHYXIATE
ASPHYXIATED
ASPHYXIATES
ASPHYXIATING
ASPHYXIATION
ASPHYXIATIONS
ASPHYXIATOR
ASPHYXIATORS
ASPIDISTRA
ASPIDISTRAS
ASPIRATING
ASPIRATION
ASPIRATIONAL
ASPIRATIONS
ASPIRATORS
ASPIRATORY
ASPIRINGLY
ASPIRINGNESS
ASPIRINGNESSES
ASPLANCHNIC
ASPLENIUMS
ASPORTATION
ASPORTATIONS
ASSAFETIDA
ASSAFETIDAS
ASSAFOETIDA
ASSAFOETIDAS
ASSAGAIING
ASSAILABLE
ASSAILANTS
ASSAILMENT
ASSAILMENTS
ASSASSINATE
ASSASSINATED
ASSASSINATES
ASSASSINATING
ASSASSINATION
ASSASSINATIONS
ASSASSINATOR
ASSASSINATORS
ASSAULTERS
ASSAULTING
ASSAULTIVE
ASSAULTIVELY
ASSAULTIVENESS
ASSEGAAIED
ASSEGAAIING
ASSEGAIING
ASSEMBLAGE
ASSEMBLAGES
ASSEMBLAGIST
ASSEMBLAGISTS
ASSEMBLANCE
ASSEMBLANCES
ASSEMBLAUNCE
ASSEMBLAUNCES
ASSEMBLERS
ASSEMBLIES
ASSEMBLING
ASSEMBLYMAN
ASSEMBLYMEN
ASSEMBLYWOMAN
ASSEMBLYWOMEN
ASSENTANEOUS
ASSENTATION
ASSENTATIONS
ASSENTATOR
ASSENTATORS
ASSENTIENT
ASSENTIENTS
ASSENTINGLY
ASSENTIVENESS
ASSENTIVENESSES
ASSERTABLE
ASSERTEDLY
ASSERTIBLE
ASSERTIONS
ASSERTIVELY
ASSERTIVENESS
ASSERTIVENESSES
ASSERTORIC
ASSESSABLE
ASSESSMENT
ASSESSMENTS
ASSESSORIAL
ASSESSORSHIP
ASSESSORSHIPS
ASSEVERATE
ASSEVERATED
ASSEVERATES
ASSEVERATING
ASSEVERATINGLY
ASSEVERATION
ASSEVERATIONS
ASSEVERATIVE
ASSEVERING
ASSIBILATE
ASSIBILATED
ASSIBILATES
ASSIBILATING

ASSIBILATION
ASSIBILATIONS
ASSIDUITIES
ASSIDUOUSLY
ASSIDUOUSNESS
ASSIDUOUSNESSES
ASSIGNABILITIES
ASSIGNABILITY
ASSIGNABLE
ASSIGNABLY
ASSIGNATION
ASSIGNATIONS
ASSIGNMENT
ASSIGNMENTS
ASSIMILABILITY
ASSIMILABLE
ASSIMILABLY
ASSIMILATE
ASSIMILATED
ASSIMILATES
ASSIMILATING
ASSIMILATION
ASSIMILATIONISM
ASSIMILATIONIST
ASSIMILATIONS
ASSIMILATIVE
ASSIMILATIVELY
ASSIMILATOR
ASSIMILATORS
ASSIMILATORY
ASSISTANCE
ASSISTANCES
ASSISTANTS
ASSISTANTSHIP
ASSISTANTSHIPS
ASSOCIABILITIES
ASSOCIABILITY
ASSOCIABLE
ASSOCIATED
ASSOCIATES
ASSOCIATESHIP
ASSOCIATESHIPS
ASSOCIATING
ASSOCIATION
ASSOCIATIONAL
ASSOCIATIONISM
ASSOCIATIONISMS
ASSOCIATIONIST
ASSOCIATIONISTS
ASSOCIATIONS
ASSOCIATIVE
ASSOCIATIVELY
ASSOCIATIVITIES
ASSOCIATIVITY
ASSOCIATOR
ASSOCIATORS
ASSOCIATORY
ASSOILMENT
ASSOILMENTS
ASSOILZIED
ASSOILZIEING
ASSOILZIES
ASSONANCES
ASSONANTAL
ASSONATING
ASSORTATIVE
ASSORTATIVELY
ASSORTEDNESS
ASSORTEDNESSES
ASSORTMENT
ASSORTMENTS
ASSUAGEMENT
ASSUAGEMENTS
ASSUAGINGS
ASSUBJUGATE
ASSUBJUGATED
ASSUBJUGATES
ASSUBJUGATING
ASSUEFACTION
ASSUEFACTIONS
ASSUETUDES
ASSUMABILITIES
ASSUMABILITY
ASSUMINGLY
ASSUMPSITS
ASSUMPTION
ASSUMPTIONS
ASSUMPTIVE
ASSUMPTIVELY
ASSURANCES
ASSUREDNESS
ASSUREDNESSES
ASSURGENCIES
ASSURGENCY
ASSYTHMENT
ASSYTHMENTS
ASTACOLOGICAL
ASTACOLOGIES
ASTACOLOGIST
ASTACOLOGISTS
ASTACOLOGY
ASTARBOARD
ASTATICALLY
ASTATICISM
ASTEREOGNOSES
ASTEREOGNOSIS
ASTERIATED
ASTERIDIAN
ASTERIDIANS
ASTERISKED
ASTERISKING
ASTERISKLESS
ASTEROIDAL
ASTEROIDEAN
ASTEROIDEANS
ASTHENOPIA
ASTHENOPIAS
ASTHENOPIC
ASTHENOSPHERE
ASTHENOSPHERES
ASTHENOSPHERIC
ASTHMATICAL
ASTHMATICALLY
ASTHMATICS
ASTIGMATIC
ASTIGMATICALLY
ASTIGMATICS
ASTIGMATISM
ASTIGMATISMS
ASTOMATOUS
ASTONISHED
ASTONISHES
ASTONISHING
ASTONISHINGLY
ASTONISHMENT
ASTONISHMENTS
ASTOUNDING
ASTOUNDINGLY
ASTOUNDMENT
ASTOUNDMENTS
ASTRACHANS
ASTRAGALUS
ASTRAGALUSES
ASTRAKHANS
ASTRANTIAS
ASTRAPHOBIA
ASTRAPHOBIAS
ASTRAPHOBIC
ASTRAPOPHOBIA
ASTRAPOPHOBIAS
ASTRICTING
ASTRICTION
ASTRICTIONS
ASTRICTIVE
ASTRICTIVELY
ASTRINGENCE
ASTRINGENCES
ASTRINGENCIES
ASTRINGENCY
ASTRINGENT
ASTRINGENTLY
ASTRINGENTS
ASTRINGERS
ASTRINGING
ASTROBIOLOGIES
ASTROBIOLOGIST
ASTROBIOLOGISTS
ASTROBIOLOGY
ASTROBLEME
ASTROBLEMES
ASTROBOTANIES
ASTROBOTANY
ASTROCHEMISTRY
ASTROCOMPASS
ASTROCOMPASSES
ASTROCYTES
ASTROCYTIC
ASTROCYTOMA
ASTROCYTOMAS
ASTROCYTOMATA
ASTRODOMES
ASTRODYNAMICIST
ASTRODYNAMICS
ASTROFELLS
ASTROGEOLOGIES
ASTROGEOLOGIST
ASTROGEOLOGISTS
ASTROGEOLOGY
ASTROHATCH
ASTROHATCHES
ASTROLABES
ASTROLATRIES
ASTROLATRY
ASTROLOGER
ASTROLOGERS
ASTROLOGIC
ASTROLOGICAL
ASTROLOGICALLY
ASTROLOGIES
ASTROLOGIST
ASTROLOGISTS
ASTROMETRIC
ASTROMETRICAL
ASTROMETRICALLY
ASTROMETRIES
ASTROMETRY
ASTRONAUTIC
ASTRONAUTICAL
ASTRONAUTICALLY
ASTRONAUTICS
ASTRONAUTS
ASTRONAVIGATION
ASTRONAVIGATOR
ASTRONAVIGATORS
ASTRONOMER
ASTRONOMERS
ASTRONOMIC
ASTRONOMICAL
ASTRONOMICALLY
ASTRONOMIES
ASTRONOMISE
ASTRONOMISED
ASTRONOMISES
ASTRONOMISING
ASTRONOMIZE
ASTRONOMIZED
ASTRONOMIZES
ASTRONOMIZING
ASTROPHELS
ASTROPHOBIA
ASTROPHOBIAS
ASTROPHOBIC
ASTROPHOTOGRAPH
ASTROPHYSICAL
ASTROPHYSICALLY
ASTROPHYSICIST
ASTROPHYSICISTS
ASTROPHYSICS
ASTROSPHERE
ASTROSPHERES
ASTROTOURISM
ASTROTOURISMS
ASTROTOURIST
ASTROTOURISTS
ASTUCIOUSLY
ASTUCITIES
ASTUTENESS
ASTUTENESSES
ASYMMETRIC
ASYMMETRICAL
ASYMMETRICALLY
ASYMMETRIES
ASYMPTOMATIC
ASYMPTOTES
ASYMPTOTIC
ASYMPTOTICAL
ASYMPTOTICALLY
ASYNARTETE
ASYNARTETES
ASYNARTETIC
ASYNCHRONIES
ASYNCHRONISM
ASYNCHRONISMS
ASYNCHRONOUS

SYNCHRONOUSLY
SYNCHRONY
SYNDETICALLY
SYNDETONS
SYNERGIAS
SYNERGIES
SYNTACTIC
SYSTOLISM
SYSTOLISMS
TACAMITES
TARACTICS
TAVISTICALLY
TCHIEVING
TELECTASES
TELECTASIS
TELECTATIC
TELEIOSES
TELEIOSIS
THANASIES
THEISTICAL
THEISTICALLY
THEMATICALLY
THENAEUMS
THEOLOGICAL
THEOLOGIES
THEORETICAL
THERMANCIES
THERMANCY
THERMANOUS
THEROGENESES
THEROGENESIS
THEROGENIC
THEROMATA
THEROMATOUS
THEROSCLEROSES
THEROSCLEROSIS
THEROSCLEROTIC
THETISING
THETIZING
THLETICALLY
THLETICISM
THLETICISMS
THROCYTES
THROCYTOSES
THROCYTOSIS
THWARTSHIP
THWARTSHIPS
TMOLOGIES
TMOLOGIST
TMOLOGISTS
TMOLYSING
TMOLYZING
TMOMETERS
TMOMETRIES
TMOSPHERE
TMOSPHERED
TMOSPHERES
TMOSPHERIC
TMOSPHERICAL
TMOSPHERICALLY
TMOSPHERICS
TOMICALLY
TOMICITIES
TOMISATION
TOMISATIONS
TOMISTICAL

ATOMISTICALLY
ATOMIZATION
ATOMIZATIONS
ATONALISMS
ATONALISTS
ATONALITIES
ATONEMENTS
ATONICITIES
ATRABILIAR
ATRABILIOUS
ATRABILIOUSNESS
ATRACURIUM
ATRACURIUMS
ATRAMENTAL
ATRAMENTOUS
ATROCIOUSLY
ATROCIOUSNESS
ATROCIOUSNESSES
ATROCITIES
ATROPHYING
ATTACHABLE
ATTACHMENT
ATTACHMENTS
ATTACKABLE
ATTAINABILITIES
ATTAINABILITY
ATTAINABLE
ATTAINABLENESS
ATTAINDERS
ATTAINMENT
ATTAINMENTS
ATTAINTING
ATTAINTMENT
ATTAINTMENTS
ATTAINTURE
ATTAINTURES
ATTEMPERED
ATTEMPERING
ATTEMPERMENT
ATTEMPERMENTS
ATTEMPTABILITY
ATTEMPTABLE
ATTEMPTERS
ATTEMPTING
ATTENDANCE
ATTENDANCES
ATTENDANCIES
ATTENDANCY
ATTENDANTS
ATTENDEMENT
ATTENDEMENTS
ATTENDINGS
ATTENDMENT
ATTENDMENTS
ATTENTIONAL
ATTENTIONS
ATTENTIVELY
ATTENTIVENESS
ATTENTIVENESSES
ATTENUANTS
ATTENUATED
ATTENUATES
ATTENUATING
ATTENUATION
ATTENUATIONS
ATTENUATOR

ATTENUATORS
ATTESTABLE
ATTESTANTS
ATTESTATION
ATTESTATIONS
ATTESTATIVE
ATTESTATOR
ATTESTATORS
ATTICISING
ATTICIZING
ATTIREMENT
ATTIREMENTS
ATTITUDINAL
ATTITUDINALLY
ATTITUDINARIAN
ATTITUDINARIANS
ATTITUDINISE
ATTITUDINISED
ATTITUDINISER
ATTITUDINISERS
ATTITUDINISES
ATTITUDINISING
ATTITUDINISINGS
ATTITUDINIZE
ATTITUDINIZED
ATTITUDINIZER
ATTITUDINIZERS
ATTITUDINIZES
ATTITUDINIZING
ATTITUDINIZINGS
ATTOLASERS
ATTOLLENTS
ATTOPHYSICS
ATTORNEYDOM
ATTORNEYDOMS
ATTORNEYED
ATTORNEYING
ATTORNEYISM
ATTORNEYISMS
ATTORNEYSHIP
ATTORNEYSHIPS
ATTORNMENT
ATTORNMENTS
ATTRACTABLE
ATTRACTANCE
ATTRACTANCES
ATTRACTANCIES
ATTRACTANCY
ATTRACTANT
ATTRACTANTS
ATTRACTERS
ATTRACTING
ATTRACTINGLY
ATTRACTION
ATTRACTIONS
ATTRACTIVE
ATTRACTIVELY
ATTRACTIVENESS
ATTRACTORS
ATTRAHENTS
ATTRAPPING
ATTRIBUTABLE
ATTRIBUTED
ATTRIBUTER
ATTRIBUTERS
ATTRIBUTES

ATTRIBUTING
ATTRIBUTION
ATTRIBUTIONAL
ATTRIBUTIONS
ATTRIBUTIVE
ATTRIBUTIVELY
ATTRIBUTIVENESS
ATTRIBUTIVES
ATTRIBUTOR
ATTRIBUTORS
ATTRISTING
ATTRITIONAL
ATTRITIONS
ATTRITTING
ATTUITIONAL
ATTUITIONS
ATTUITIVELY
ATTUNEMENT
ATTUNEMENTS
ATYPICALITIES
ATYPICALITY
ATYPICALLY
AUBERGINES
AUBERGISTE
AUBERGISTES
AUBRIETIAS
AUCTIONARY
AUCTIONEER
AUCTIONEERED
AUCTIONEERING
AUCTIONEERS
AUCTIONING
AUDACIOUSLY
AUDACIOUSNESS
AUDACIOUSNESSES
AUDACITIES
AUDIBILITIES
AUDIBILITY
AUDIBLENESS
AUDIBLENESSES
AUDIENCIAS
AUDIOBOOKS
AUDIOCASSETTE
AUDIOCASSETTES
AUDIOGENIC
AUDIOGRAMS
AUDIOGRAPH
AUDIOGRAPHS
AUDIOLOGIC
AUDIOLOGICAL
AUDIOLOGICALLY
AUDIOLOGIES
AUDIOLOGIST
AUDIOLOGISTS
AUDIOMETER
AUDIOMETERS
AUDIOMETRIC
AUDIOMETRICALLY
AUDIOMETRICIAN
AUDIOMETRICIANS
AUDIOMETRIES
AUDIOMETRIST
AUDIOMETRISTS
AUDIOMETRY
AUDIOPHILE
AUDIOPHILES

AUDIOPHILS
AUDIOTAPED
AUDIOTAPES
AUDIOTAPING
AUDIOTYPING
AUDIOTYPINGS
AUDIOTYPIST
AUDIOTYPISTS
AUDIOVISUAL
AUDIOVISUALLY
AUDIOVISUALS
AUDIPHONES
AUDITIONED
AUDITIONER
AUDITIONERS
AUDITIONING
AUDITORIAL
AUDITORIES
AUDITORILY
AUDITORIUM
AUDITORIUMS
AUDITORSHIP
AUDITORSHIPS
AUDITRESSES
AUGMENTABLE
AUGMENTATION
AUGMENTATIONS
AUGMENTATIVE
AUGMENTATIVELY
AUGMENTATIVES
AUGMENTERS
AUGMENTING
AUGMENTORS
AUGURSHIPS
AUGUSTNESS
AUGUSTNESSES
AURALITIES
AUREATENESS
AUREATENESSES
AURICULARLY
AURICULARS
AURICULATE
AURICULATED
AURICULATELY
AURIFEROUS
AURISCOPES
AURISCOPIC
AUSCULTATE
AUSCULTATED
AUSCULTATES
AUSCULTATING
AUSCULTATION
AUSCULTATIONS
AUSCULTATIVE
AUSCULTATOR
AUSCULTATORS
AUSCULTATORY
AUSFORMING
AUSLANDERS
AUSPICATED
AUSPICATES
AUSPICATING
AUSPICIOUS
AUSPICIOUSLY
AUSPICIOUSNESS
AUSTENITES
AUSTENITIC
AUSTERENESS
AUSTERENESSES
AUSTERITIES
AUSTRALITE
AUSTRALITES
AUSTRINGER
AUSTRINGERS
AUTARCHICAL
AUTARCHIES
AUTARCHIST
AUTARCHISTS
AUTARKICAL
AUTARKISTS
AUTECOLOGIC
AUTECOLOGICAL
AUTECOLOGIES
AUTECOLOGY
AUTEURISMS
AUTEURISTS
AUTHENTICAL
AUTHENTICALLY
AUTHENTICATE
AUTHENTICATED
AUTHENTICATES
AUTHENTICATING
AUTHENTICATION
AUTHENTICATIONS
AUTHENTICATOR
AUTHENTICATORS
AUTHENTICITIES
AUTHENTICITY
AUTHIGENIC
AUTHORCRAFT
AUTHORCRAFTS
AUTHORESSES
AUTHORINGS
AUTHORISABLE
AUTHORISATION
AUTHORISATIONS
AUTHORISED
AUTHORISER
AUTHORISERS
AUTHORISES
AUTHORISING
AUTHORISMS
AUTHORITARIAN
AUTHORITARIANS
AUTHORITATIVE
AUTHORITATIVELY
AUTHORITIES
AUTHORIZABLE
AUTHORIZATION
AUTHORIZATIONS
AUTHORIZED
AUTHORIZER
AUTHORIZERS
AUTHORIZES
AUTHORIZING
AUTHORLESS
AUTHORSHIP
AUTHORSHIPS
AUTISTICALLY
AUTOALLOGAMIES
AUTOALLOGAMY
AUTOANTIBODIES
AUTOANTIBODY
AUTOBAHNEN
AUTOBIOGRAPHER
AUTOBIOGRAPHERS
AUTOBIOGRAPHIC
AUTOBIOGRAPHIES
AUTOBIOGRAPHY
AUTOBUSSES
AUTOCATALYSE
AUTOCATALYSED
AUTOCATALYSES
AUTOCATALYSING
AUTOCATALYSIS
AUTOCATALYTIC
AUTOCATALYZE
AUTOCATALYZED
AUTOCATALYZES
AUTOCATALYZING
AUTOCEPHALIC
AUTOCEPHALIES
AUTOCEPHALOUS
AUTOCEPHALY
AUTOCHANGER
AUTOCHANGERS
AUTOCHTHON
AUTOCHTHONAL
AUTOCHTHONES
AUTOCHTHONIC
AUTOCHTHONIES
AUTOCHTHONISM
AUTOCHTHONISMS
AUTOCHTHONOUS
AUTOCHTHONOUSLY
AUTOCHTHONS
AUTOCHTHONY
AUTOCLAVED
AUTOCLAVES
AUTOCLAVING
AUTOCOPROPHAGY
AUTOCORRELATION
AUTOCRACIES
AUTOCRATIC
AUTOCRATICAL
AUTOCRATICALLY
AUTOCRIMES
AUTOCRITIQUE
AUTOCRITIQUES
AUTOCROSSES
AUTOCUTIES
AUTOCYCLES
AUTODESTRUCT
AUTODESTRUCTED
AUTODESTRUCTING
AUTODESTRUCTIVE
AUTODESTRUCTS
AUTODIDACT
AUTODIDACTIC
AUTODIDACTICISM
AUTODIDACTS
AUTOECIOUS
AUTOECIOUSLY
AUTOECISMS
AUTOEROTIC
AUTOEROTICISM
AUTOEROTICISMS
AUTOEROTISM
AUTOEROTISMS
AUTOEXPOSURE
AUTOEXPOSURES
AUTOFLARES
AUTOFOCUSES
AUTOGAMIES
AUTOGAMOUS
AUTOGENESES
AUTOGENESIS
AUTOGENETIC
AUTOGENETICALLY
AUTOGENICS
AUTOGENIES
AUTOGENOUS
AUTOGENOUSLY
AUTOGRAFTED
AUTOGRAFTING
AUTOGRAFTS
AUTOGRAPHED
AUTOGRAPHIC
AUTOGRAPHICAL
AUTOGRAPHICALLY
AUTOGRAPHIES
AUTOGRAPHING
AUTOGRAPHS
AUTOGRAPHY
AUTOGRAVURE
AUTOGRAVURES
AUTOGUIDES
AUTOHYPNOSES
AUTOHYPNOSIS
AUTOHYPNOTIC
AUTOIMMUNE
AUTOIMMUNITIES
AUTOIMMUNITY
AUTOINFECTION
AUTOINFECTIONS
AUTOINOCULATION
AUTOINOCULATORY
AUTOIONISATION
AUTOIONISATIONS
AUTOIONIZATION
AUTOIONIZATIONS
AUTOJUMBLE
AUTOJUMBLES
AUTOKINESES
AUTOKINESIS
AUTOKINETIC
AUTOLATRIES
AUTOLOADING
AUTOLOGIES
AUTOLOGOUS
AUTOLYSATE
AUTOLYSATES
AUTOLYSING
AUTOLYSINS
AUTOLYZATE
AUTOLYZATES
AUTOLYZING
AUTOMAKERS
AUTOMATABLE
AUTOMATICAL
AUTOMATICALLY
AUTOMATICITIES
AUTOMATICITY
AUTOMATICS

UTOMATING
UTOMATION
UTOMATIONS
UTOMATISATION
UTOMATISATIONS
UTOMATISE
UTOMATISED
UTOMATISES
UTOMATISING
UTOMATISM
UTOMATISMS
UTOMATIST
UTOMATISTS
UTOMATIZATION
UTOMATIZATIONS
UTOMATIZE
UTOMATIZED
UTOMATIZES
UTOMATIZING
UTOMATONS
UTOMATOUS
UTOMETERS
UTOMOBILE
UTOMOBILED
UTOMOBILES
UTOMOBILIA
UTOMOBILING
UTOMOBILISM
UTOMOBILISMS
UTOMOBILIST
UTOMOBILISTS
UTOMOBILITIES
UTOMOBILITY
UTOMORPHIC
UTOMORPHICALLY
UTOMORPHISM
UTOMORPHISMS
UTOMOTIVE
UTONOMICAL
UTONOMICALLY
UTONOMICS
UTONOMIES
UTONOMIST
UTONOMISTS
UTONOMOUS
UTONOMOUSLY
UTOPHAGIA
UTOPHAGIAS
UTOPHAGIES
UTOPHAGOUS
UTOPHANOUS
UTOPHOBIA
UTOPHOBIAS
UTOPHOBIES
UTOPHONIES
UTOPHYTES
UTOPHYTIC
UTOPHYTICALLY
UTOPILOTS
UTOPISTAS
UTOPLASTIC
UTOPLASTIES
UTOPLASTY
UTOPOINTS
UTOPOLYPLOID
UTOPOLYPLOIDS

AUTOPOLYPLOIDY
AUTOPSISTS
AUTOPSYING
AUTOPTICAL
AUTOPTICALLY
AUTORADIOGRAM
AUTORADIOGRAMS
AUTORADIOGRAPH
AUTORADIOGRAPHS
AUTORADIOGRAPHY
AUTORICKSHAW
AUTORICKSHAWS
AUTOROTATE
AUTOROTATED
AUTOROTATES
AUTOROTATING
AUTOROTATION
AUTOROTATIONS
AUTOROUTES
AUTOSCHEDIASM
AUTOSCHEDIASMS
AUTOSCHEDIASTIC
AUTOSCHEDIAZE
AUTOSCHEDIAZED
AUTOSCHEDIAZES
AUTOSCHEDIAZING
AUTOSCOPIC
AUTOSCOPIES
AUTOSEXING
AUTOSOMALLY
AUTOSPORES
AUTOSTABILITY
AUTOSTRADA
AUTOSTRADAS
AUTOSTRADE
AUTOSUGGEST
AUTOSUGGESTED
AUTOSUGGESTING
AUTOSUGGESTION
AUTOSUGGESTIONS
AUTOSUGGESTIVE
AUTOSUGGESTS
AUTOTELLER
AUTOTELLERS
AUTOTETRAPLOID
AUTOTETRAPLOIDS
AUTOTETRAPLOIDY
AUTOTHEISM
AUTOTHEISMS
AUTOTHEIST
AUTOTHEISTS
AUTOTIMERS
AUTOTOMIES
AUTOTOMISE
AUTOTOMISED
AUTOTOMISES
AUTOTOMISING
AUTOTOMIZE
AUTOTOMIZED
AUTOTOMIZES
AUTOTOMIZING
AUTOTOMOUS
AUTOTOXAEMIA
AUTOTOXAEMIAS
AUTOTOXEMIA
AUTOTOXEMIAS

AUTOTOXINS
AUTOTRANSFORMER
AUTOTRANSFUSION
AUTOTROPHIC
AUTOTROPHICALLY
AUTOTROPHIES
AUTOTROPHS
AUTOTROPHY
AUTOTYPIES
AUTOTYPING
AUTOTYPOGRAPHY
AUTOWINDER
AUTOWINDERS
AUTOWORKER
AUTOWORKERS
AUTOXIDATION
AUTOXIDATIONS
AUTUMNALLY
AUXANOMETER
AUXANOMETERS
AUXILIARIES
AUXOCHROME
AUXOCHROMES
AUXOMETERS
AUXOSPORES
AUXOTROPHIC
AUXOTROPHIES
AUXOTROPHS
AUXOTROPHY
AVAILABILITIES
AVAILABILITY
AVAILABLENESS
AVAILABLENESSES
AVAILINGLY
AVALANCHED
AVALANCHES
AVALANCHING
AVANTURINE
AVANTURINES
AVARICIOUS
AVARICIOUSLY
AVARICIOUSNESS
AVASCULARITIES
AVASCULARITY
AVENACEOUS
AVENGEMENT
AVENGEMENTS
AVENGERESS
AVENGERESSES
AVENTAILES
AVENTURINE
AVENTURINES
AVENTURINS
AVERAGENESS
AVERAGENESSES
AVERAGINGS
AVERRUNCATE
AVERRUNCATED
AVERRUNCATES
AVERRUNCATING
AVERRUNCATION
AVERRUNCATIONS
AVERRUNCATOR
AVERRUNCATORS
AVERSENESS
AVERSENESSES

AVERSIVELY
AVERSIVENESS
AVERSIVENESSES
AVERTIMENT
AVERTIMENTS
AVGOLEMONO
AVGOLEMONOS
AVIANISING
AVIANIZING
AVIATRESSES
AVIATRICES
AVIATRIXES
AVICULTURE
AVICULTURES
AVICULTURIST
AVICULTURISTS
AVIDNESSES
AVISANDUMS
AVISEMENTS
AVITAMINOSES
AVITAMINOSIS
AVITAMINOTIC
AVIZANDUMS
AVOCATIONAL
AVOCATIONALLY
AVOCATIONS
AVOIDANCES
AVOIRDUPOIS
AVOIRDUPOISES
AVOUCHABLE
AVOUCHMENT
AVOUCHMENTS
AVOUTERERS
AVOWABLENESS
AVOWABLENESSES
AVUNCULARITIES
AVUNCULARITY
AVUNCULARLY
AVUNCULATE
AVUNCULATES
AVVOGADORE
AVVOGADORES
AWAKENINGS
AWARENESSES
AWAYNESSES
AWELESSNESS
AWELESSNESSES
AWESOMENESS
AWESOMENESSES
AWESTRICKEN
AWESTRIKES
AWESTRIKING
AWFULNESSES
AWKWARDEST
AWKWARDISH
AWKWARDNESS
AWKWARDNESSES
AXENICALLY
AXEROPHTHOL
AXEROPHTHOLS
AXIALITIES
AXILLARIES
AXINOMANCIES
AXINOMANCY
AXIOLOGICAL
AXIOLOGICALLY

AXIOLOGIES
AXIOLOGIST
AXIOLOGISTS
AXIOMATICAL
AXIOMATICALLY
AXIOMATICS
AXIOMATISATION
AXIOMATISATIONS
AXIOMATISE
AXIOMATISED
AXIOMATISES
AXIOMATISING
AXIOMATIZATION
AXIOMATIZATIONS
AXIOMATIZE
AXIOMATIZED
AXIOMATIZES
AXIOMATIZING
AXISYMMETRIC
AXISYMMETRICAL
AXISYMMETRIES
AXISYMMETRY
AXOLEMMATA
AXONOMETRIC
AXONOMETRICALLY
AXONOMETRIES
AXONOMETRY
AXOPLASMIC
AYAHUASCAS
AYAHUASCOS
AYATOLLAHS
AYUNTAMIENTO
AYUNTAMIENTOS
AYURVEDICS
AZATHIOPRINE
AZATHIOPRINES
AZEDARACHS
AZEOTROPES
AZEOTROPIC
AZEOTROPIES
AZIDOTHYMIDINE
AZIDOTHYMIDINES
AZIMUTHALLY
AZOBENZENE
AZOBENZENES
AZOOSPERMIA
AZOOSPERMIAS
AZOOSPERMIC
AZOTAEMIAS
AZOTOBACTER
AZOTOBACTERS
AZYGOSPORE
AZYGOSPORES

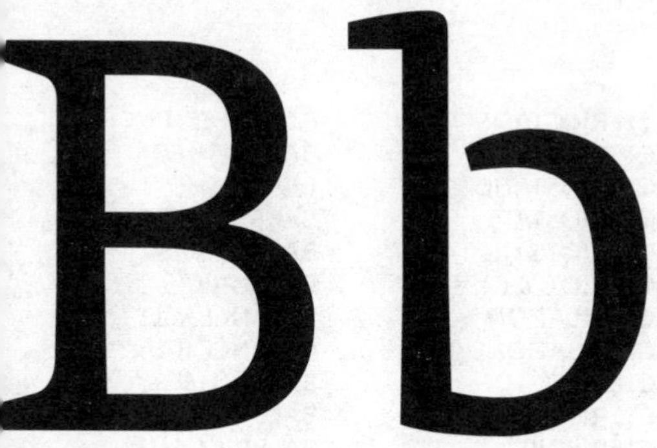

AALEBATIM
ABACOOTES
ABBITRIES
ABBITTING
ABBITTRIES
ABBLATIVE
ABBLEMENT
ABBLEMENTS
ABELESQUE
ABESIASES
ABESIASIS
ABESIOSES
ABESIOSIS
ABINGTONITE
ABINGTONITES
ABIROUSSA
ABIROUSSAS
ABIRUSSAS
ABOONERIES
ABYPROOFED
ABYPROOFING
ABYPROOFS
ABYSITTING
ACCALAUREAN
ACCALAUREATE
ACCALAUREATES
ACCHANALIA
ACCHANALIAN
ACCHANALIANISM
ACCHANALIANS
ACCHANALS
ACCHANTES
ACCIFEROUS
ACCIVOROUS
ACHARACHS
ACHELORDOM
ACHELORDOMS
ACHELORETTE
BACHELORETTES
BACHELORHOOD
BACHELORHOODS
BACHELORISM
BACHELORISMS
BACHELORSHIP
BACHELORSHIPS
BACILLAEMIA
BACILLAEMIAS
BACILLEMIA
BACILLEMIAS
BACILLICIDE
BACILLICIDES
BACILLIFORM
BACILLURIA
BACILLURIAS
BACITRACIN
BACITRACINS
BACKBENCHER
BACKBENCHERS
BACKBENCHES
BACKBITERS
BACKBITING
BACKBITINGS
BACKBITTEN
BACKBLOCKER
BACKBLOCKERS
BACKBLOCKS
BACKBOARDS
BACKBONELESS
BACKBREAKER
BACKBREAKERS
BACKBREAKING
BACKBURNED
BACKBURNING
BACKCHATTED
BACKCHATTING
BACKCHECKED
BACKCHECKING
BACKCHECKS
BACKCLOTHS
BACKCOMBED
BACKCOMBING
BACKCOUNTRIES
BACKCOUNTRY
BACKCOURTMAN
BACKCOURTMEN
BACKCOURTS
BACKCROSSED
BACKCROSSES
BACKCROSSING
BACKDATING
BACKDRAFTS
BACKDRAUGHT
BACKDRAUGHTS
BACKDROPPED
BACKDROPPING
BACKFIELDS
BACKFILLED
BACKFILLING
BACKFIRING
BACKFISCHES
BACKFITTED
BACKFITTING
BACKFITTINGS
BACKFLIPPED
BACKFLIPPING
BACKGAMMON
BACKGAMMONED
BACKGAMMONING
BACKGAMMONS
BACKGROUND
BACKGROUNDED
BACKGROUNDER
BACKGROUNDERS
BACKGROUNDING
BACKGROUNDS
BACKHANDED
BACKHANDEDLY
BACKHANDEDNESS
BACKHANDER
BACKHANDERS
BACKHANDING
BACKHAULED
BACKHAULING
BACKHOEING
BACKHOUSES
BACKLASHED
BACKLASHER
BACKLASHERS
BACKLASHES
BACKLASHING
BACKLIGHTED
BACKLIGHTING
BACKLIGHTS
BACKLISTED
BACKLISTING
BACKLOADED
BACKLOADING
BACKLOGGED
BACKLOGGING
BACKMARKER
BACKMARKERS
BACKPACKED
BACKPACKER
BACKPACKERS
BACKPACKING
BACKPACKINGS
BACKPEDALED
BACKPEDALING
BACKPEDALLED
BACKPEDALLING
BACKPEDALS
BACKPIECES

BACKRUSHES
BACKSCATTER
BACKSCATTERED
BACKSCATTERING
BACKSCATTERINGS
BACKSCATTERS
BACKSCRATCH
BACKSCRATCHED
BACKSCRATCHER
BACKSCRATCHERS
BACKSCRATCHES
BACKSCRATCHING
BACKSCRATCHINGS
BACKSHEESH
BACKSHEESHED
BACKSHEESHES
BACKSHEESHING
BACKSHISHED
BACKSHISHES
BACKSHISHING
BACKSHORES
BACKSIGHTS
BACKSLAPPED
BACKSLAPPER
BACKSLAPPERS
BACKSLAPPING
BACKSLASHES
BACKSLIDDEN
BACKSLIDER
BACKSLIDERS
BACKSLIDES
BACKSLIDING
BACKSLIDINGS
BACKSPACED
BACKSPACER
BACKSPACERS
BACKSPACES
BACKSPACING
BACKSPEERED
BACKSPEERING
BACKSPEERS
BACKSPEIRED
BACKSPEIRING
BACKSPEIRS
BACKSPLASH
BACKSPLASHES
BACKSTABBED
BACKSTABBER
BACKSTABBERS
BACKSTABBING
BACKSTABBINGS
BACKSTAGES
BACKSTAIRS
BACKSTALLS
BACKSTAMPED
BACKSTAMPING
BACKSTAMPS
BACKSTARTING
BACKSTITCH
BACKSTITCHED
BACKSTITCHES
BACKSTITCHING
BACKSTOPPED
BACKSTOPPING
BACKSTORIES
BACKSTREET
BACKSTREETS
BACKSTRETCH
BACKSTRETCHES
BACKSTROKE
BACKSTROKES
BACKSWINGS
BACKSWORDMAN
BACKSWORDMEN
BACKSWORDS
BACKSWORDSMAN
BACKSWORDSMEN
BACKTRACKED
BACKTRACKING
BACKTRACKINGS
BACKTRACKS
BACKVELDER
BACKVELDERS
BACKWARDATION
BACKWARDATIONS
BACKWARDLY
BACKWARDNESS
BACKWARDNESSES
BACKWASHED
BACKWASHES
BACKWASHING
BACKWATERS
BACKWOODSMAN
BACKWOODSMEN
BACKWOODSY
BACKWORKER
BACKWORKERS
BACTERAEMIA
BACTERAEMIAS
BACTEREMIA
BACTEREMIAS
BACTEREMIC
BACTERIALLY
BACTERIALS
BACTERICIDAL
BACTERICIDALLY
BACTERICIDE
BACTERICIDES
BACTERIOCIN
BACTERIOCINS
BACTERIOID
BACTERIOIDS
BACTERIOLOGIC
BACTERIOLOGICAL
BACTERIOLOGIES
BACTERIOLOGIST
BACTERIOLOGISTS
BACTERIOLOGY
BACTERIOLYSES
BACTERIOLYSIN
BACTERIOLYSINS
BACTERIOLYSIS
BACTERIOLYTIC
BACTERIOPHAGE
BACTERIOPHAGES
BACTERIOPHAGIC
BACTERIOPHAGIES
BACTERIOPHAGOUS
BACTERIOPHAGY
BACTERIOSES
BACTERIOSIS
BACTERIOSTASES
BACTERIOSTASIS
BACTERIOSTAT
BACTERIOSTATIC
BACTERIOSTATS
BACTERIOTOXIN
BACTERIOTOXINS
BACTERISATION
BACTERISATIONS
BACTERISED
BACTERISES
BACTERISING
BACTERIURIA
BACTERIURIAS
BACTERIZATION
BACTERIZATIONS
BACTERIZED
BACTERIZES
BACTERIZING
BACTEROIDS
BACTERURIA
BACTERURIAS
BACULIFORM
BACULOVIRUS
BACULOVIRUSES
BADDELEYITE
BADDELEYITES
BADDERLOCK
BADDERLOCKS
BADINAGING
BADINERIES
BADMINTONS
BADMOUTHED
BADMOUTHING
BAFFLEGABS
BAFFLEMENT
BAFFLEMENTS
BAFFLINGLY
BAGASSOSES
BAGASSOSIS
BAGATELLES
BAGGINESSES
BAGPIPINGS
BAGSWINGER
BAGSWINGERS
BAHUVRIHIS
BAIGNOIRES
BAILIESHIP
BAILIESHIPS
BAILIFFSHIP
BAILIFFSHIPS
BAILIWICKS
BAILLIAGES
BAILLIESHIP
BAILLIESHIPS
BAIRNLIEST
BAISEMAINS
BAITFISHES
BAKEAPPLES
BAKEBOARDS
BAKEHOUSES
BAKESTONES
BAKHSHISHED
BAKHSHISHES
BAKHSHISHING
BAKSHEESHED
BAKSHEESHES
BAKSHEESHING
BAKSHISHED
BAKSHISHES
BAKSHISHING
BALACLAVAS
BALALAIKAS
BALANCEABLE
BALANCINGS
BALANITISES
BALBRIGGAN
BALBRIGGANS
BALBUTIENT
BALCONETTE
BALCONETTES
BALDACHINO
BALDACHINOS
BALDACHINS
BALDAQUINS
BALDERDASH
BALDERDASHES
BALDERLOCKS
BALDERLOCKSES
BALDHEADED
BALDICOOTS
BALDMONEYS
BALDNESSES
BALECTIONS
BALEFULNESS
BALEFULNESSES
BALIBUNTAL
BALIBUNTALS
BALKANISATION
BALKANISATIONS
BALKANISED
BALKANISES
BALKANISING
BALKANIZATION
BALKANIZATIONS
BALKANIZED
BALKANIZES
BALKANIZING
BALKINESSES
BALLABILES
BALLADEERED
BALLADEERING
BALLADEERS
BALLADINES
BALLADISTS
BALLADMONGER
BALLADMONGERS
BALLADRIES
BALLANTING
BALLANWRASSE
BALLANWRASSES
BALLASTERS
BALLASTING
BALLBREAKER
BALLBREAKERS
BALLCARRIER
BALLCARRIERS
BALLERINAS
BALLETICALLY
BALLETOMANE
BALLETOMANES
BALLETOMANIA
BALLETOMANIAS

ALLFLOWER
ALLFLOWERS
ALLHANDLING
ALLHANDLINGS
ALLICATTER
ALLICATTERS
ALLISTICALLY
ALLISTICS
ALLISTITE
ALLISTITES
ALLISTOSPORE
ALLISTOSPORES
ALLOCKSED
ALLOCKSES
ALLOCKSING
ALLOONING
ALLOONINGS
ALLOONIST
ALLOONISTS
ALLOTTEMENT
ALLOTTEMENTS
ALLPLAYER
ALLPLAYERS
ALLPOINTS
ALLSINESS
ALLSINESSES
ALLYHOOED
ALLYHOOING
ALLYRAGGED
ALLYRAGGING
ALMACAANS
ALMINESSES
ALMORALITIES
ALMORALITY
ALNEARIES
ALNEATION
ALNEATIONS
ALNEOLOGICAL
ALNEOLOGIES
ALNEOLOGIST
ALNEOLOGISTS
ALNEOLOGY
ALNEOTHERAPIES
ALNEOTHERAPY
ALSAMIFEROUS
ALSAMINACEOUS
ALSAWOODS
ALTHASARS
ALTHAZARS
ALUSTERED
ALUSTRADE
ALUSTRADED
ALUSTRADES
ALZARINES
AMBOOZLED
AMBOOZLEMENT
AMBOOZLEMENTS
AMBOOZLER
AMBOOZLERS
AMBOOZLES
AMBOOZLING
ANALISATION
ANALISATIONS
ANALISING
ANALITIES
ANALIZATION
BANALIZATIONS
BANALIZING
BANCASSURANCE
BANCASSURANCES
BANCASSURER
BANCASSURERS
BANDALORES
BANDBRAKES
BANDEIRANTE
BANDEIRANTES
BANDELIERS
BANDERILLA
BANDERILLAS
BANDERILLERO
BANDERILLEROS
BANDEROLES
BANDERSNATCH
BANDERSNATCHES
BANDICOOTED
BANDICOOTING
BANDICOOTS
BANDINESSES
BANDITRIES
BANDLEADER
BANDLEADERS
BANDMASTER
BANDMASTERS
BANDOBASTS
BANDOBUSTS
BANDOLEERED
BANDOLEERS
BANDOLEONS
BANDOLEROS
BANDOLIERED
BANDOLIERS
BANDOLINED
BANDOLINES
BANDOLINING
BANDONEONS
BANDONIONS
BANDSHELLS
BANDSPREADING
BANDSPREADINGS
BANDSTANDS
BANDWAGONS
BANDWIDTHS
BANEBERRIES
BANEFULNESS
BANEFULNESSES
BANGSRINGS
BANISHMENT
BANISHMENTS
BANISTERED
BANJULELES
BANKABILITIES
BANKABILITY
BANKROLLED
BANKROLLER
BANKROLLERS
BANKROLLING
BANKRUPTCIES
BANKRUPTCY
BANKRUPTED
BANKRUPTING
BANNERALLS
BANNERETTE
BANNERETTES
BANNISTERS
BANQUETEER
BANQUETEERS
BANQUETERS
BANQUETING
BANQUETINGS
BANQUETTES
BANTAMWEIGHT
BANTAMWEIGHTS
BANTERINGLY
BANTERINGS
BANTINGISM
BANTINGISMS
BAPHOMETIC
BAPTISMALLY
BAPTISTERIES
BAPTISTERY
BAPTISTRIES
BARACHOISES
BARAESTHESIA
BARAESTHESIAS
BARAGOUINS
BARASINGAS
BARASINGHA
BARASINGHAS
BARATHRUMS
BARBARESQUE
BARBARIANISM
BARBARIANISMS
BARBARIANS
BARBARICALLY
BARBARISATION
BARBARISATIONS
BARBARISED
BARBARISES
BARBARISING
BARBARISMS
BARBARITIES
BARBARIZATION
BARBARIZATIONS
BARBARIZED
BARBARIZES
BARBARIZING
BARBAROUSLY
BARBAROUSNESS
BARBAROUSNESSES
BARBASCOES
BARBASTELLE
BARBASTELLES
BARBASTELS
BARBECUERS
BARBECUING
BARBELLATE
BARBEQUING
BARBERRIES
BARBERSHOP
BARBERSHOPS
BARBITONES
BARBITURATE
BARBITURATES
BARBITURIC
BARBOTINES
BARCAROLES
BARCAROLLE
BARCAROLLES
BARDOLATER
BARDOLATERS
BARDOLATRIES
BARDOLATROUS
BARDOLATRY
BAREBACKED
BAREFACEDLY
BAREFACEDNESS
BAREFACEDNESSES
BAREFOOTED
BAREHANDED
BAREHANDING
BAREHEADED
BARELEGGED
BARENESSES
BARESTHESIA
BARESTHESIAS
BARGAINERS
BARGAINING
BARGAININGS
BARGANDERS
BARGEBOARD
BARGEBOARDS
BARGEMASTER
BARGEMASTERS
BARGEPOLES
BARHOPPING
BARKANTINE
BARKANTINES
BARKEEPERS
BARKENTINE
BARKENTINES
BARLEYCORN
BARLEYCORNS
BARMBRACKS
BARMINESSES
BARMITSVAH
BARMITSVAHS
BARMITZVAH
BARMITZVAHS
BARNBRACKS
BARNSBREAKING
BARNSBREAKINGS
BARNSTORMED
BARNSTORMER
BARNSTORMERS
BARNSTORMING
BARNSTORMINGS
BARNSTORMS
BAROCEPTOR
BAROCEPTORS
BARODYNAMICS
BAROGNOSES
BAROGNOSIS
BAROGRAPHIC
BAROGRAPHS
BAROMETERS
BAROMETRIC
BAROMETRICAL
BAROMETRICALLY
BAROMETRIES
BAROMETZES
BARONESSES
BARONETAGE
BARONETAGES
BARONETCIES

BARONETESS
BARONETESSES
BARONETICAL
BAROPHILES
BAROPHILIC
BAROPHORESES
BAROPHORESIS
BARORECEPTOR
BARORECEPTORS
BAROSCOPES
BAROSCOPIC
BAROTRAUMA
BAROTRAUMAS
BAROTRAUMATA
BARPERSONS
BARQUANTINE
BARQUANTINES
BARQUENTINE
BARQUENTINES
BARQUETTES
BARRACKERS
BARRACKING
BARRACKINGS
BARRACOONS
BARRACOOTA
BARRACOOTAS
BARRACOUTA
BARRACOUTAS
BARRACUDAS
BARRAMUNDA
BARRAMUNDAS
BARRAMUNDI
BARRAMUNDIES
BARRAMUNDIS
BARRATRIES
BARRATROUS
BARRATROUSLY
BARRELAGES
BARRELFULS
BARRELHEAD
BARRELHEADS
BARRELHOUSE
BARRELHOUSES
BARRELLING
BARRELSFUL
BARRENNESS
BARRENNESSES
BARRENWORT
BARRENWORTS
BARRETRIES
BARRETROUS
BARRETROUSLY
BARRETTERS
BARRICADED
BARRICADER
BARRICADERS
BARRICADES
BARRICADING
BARRICADOED
BARRICADOES
BARRICADOING
BARRICADOS
BARRIERING
BARRISTERIAL
BARRISTERS
BARRISTERSHIP
BARRISTERSHIPS
BARROWFULS
BARTENDERS
BARTENDING
BARTIZANED
BARYCENTRE
BARYCENTRES
BARYCENTRIC
BARYSPHERE
BARYSPHERES
BASALTWARE
BASALTWARES
BASEBALLER
BASEBALLERS
BASEBOARDS
BASEBURNER
BASEBURNERS
BASELESSLY
BASELESSNESS
BASELESSNESSES
BASELINERS
BASEMENTLESS
BASENESSES
BASEPLATES
BASERUNNER
BASERUNNERS
BASERUNNING
BASERUNNINGS
BASHAWISMS
BASHAWSHIP
BASHAWSHIPS
BASHFULNESS
BASHFULNESSES
BASHIBAZOUK
BASHIBAZOUKS
BASICITIES
BASICRANIAL
BASIDIOCARP
BASIDIOCARPS
BASIDIOMYCETE
BASIDIOMYCETES
BASIDIOMYCETOUS
BASIDIOSPORE
BASIDIOSPORES
BASIDIOSPOROUS
BASIFICATION
BASIFICATIONS
BASILICONS
BASIPETALLY
BASKETBALL
BASKETBALLS
BASKETFULS
BASKETLIKE
BASKETRIES
BASKETSFUL
BASKETWEAVE
BASKETWEAVER
BASKETWEAVERS
BASKETWEAVES
BASKETWORK
BASKETWORKS
BASMITZVAH
BASMITZVAHS
BASOPHILES
BASOPHILIA
BASOPHILIAS
BASOPHILIC
BASSETTING
BASSNESSES
BASSOONIST
BASSOONISTS
BASTARDIES
BASTARDISATION
BASTARDISATIONS
BASTARDISE
BASTARDISED
BASTARDISES
BASTARDISING
BASTARDISM
BASTARDISMS
BASTARDIZATION
BASTARDIZATIONS
BASTARDIZE
BASTARDIZED
BASTARDIZES
BASTARDIZING
BASTARDRIES
BASTINADED
BASTINADES
BASTINADING
BASTINADOED
BASTINADOES
BASTINADOING
BASTNAESITE
BASTNAESITES
BASTNASITE
BASTNASITES
BATFOWLERS
BATFOWLING
BATFOWLINGS
BATHETICALLY
BATHHOUSES
BATHMITSVAH
BATHMITSVAHS
BATHMITZVAH
BATHMITZVAHS
BATHMIZVAH
BATHMIZVAHS
BATHOCHROME
BATHOCHROMES
BATHOCHROMIC
BATHOLITES
BATHOLITHIC
BATHOLITHS
BATHOLITIC
BATHOMETER
BATHOMETERS
BATHOMETRIC
BATHOMETRICALLY
BATHOMETRIES
BATHOMETRY
BATHOPHILOUS
BATHOPHOBIA
BATHOPHOBIAS
BATHWATERS
BATHYBIUSES
BATHYGRAPHICAL
BATHYLIMNETIC
BATHYLITES
BATHYLITHIC
BATHYLITHS
BATHYLITIC
BATHYMETER
BATHYMETERS
BATHYMETRIC
BATHYMETRICAL
BATHYMETRICALLY
BATHYMETRIES
BATHYMETRY
BATHYPELAGIC
BATHYSCAPE
BATHYSCAPES
BATHYSCAPH
BATHYSCAPHE
BATHYSCAPHES
BATHYSCAPHS
BATHYSPHERE
BATHYSPHERES
BATMITZVAH
BATMITZVAHS
BATOLOGICAL
BATOLOGIES
BATOLOGIST
BATOLOGISTS
BATRACHIAN
BATRACHIANS
BATRACHOPHOBIA
BATRACHOPHOBIAS
BATRACHOPHOBIC
BATSMANSHIP
BATSMANSHIPS
BATTAILOUS
BATTALIONS
BATTEILANT
BATTELLING
BATTEMENTS
BATTENINGS
BATTERINGS
BATTILLING
BATTINESSES
BATTLEBUSES
BATTLEBUSSES
BATTLEDOOR
BATTLEDOORS
BATTLEDORE
BATTLEDORES
BATTLEDRESS
BATTLEDRESSES
BATTLEFIELD
BATTLEFIELDS
BATTLEFRONT
BATTLEFRONTS
BATTLEGROUND
BATTLEGROUNDS
BATTLEMENT
BATTLEMENTED
BATTLEMENTS
BATTLEPIECE
BATTLEPIECES
BATTLEPLANE
BATTLEPLANES
BATTLESHIP
BATTLESHIPS
BATTLEWAGON
BATTLEWAGONS
BATTOLOGICAL
BATTOLOGIES
BAUDRICKES

AUDRONSES
AULKINESS
AULKINESSES
AVARDAGES
AVAROISES
AWDINESSES
AWDYHOUSE
AWDYHOUSES
AYBERRIES
AYONETING
AYONETTED
AYONETTING
AZILLIONS
EACHBALLS
EACHCOMBED
EACHCOMBER
EACHCOMBERS
EACHCOMBING
EACHCOMBINGS
EACHCOMBS
EACHFRONT
EACHFRONTS
EACHGOERS
EACHHEADS
EADBLASTED
EADBLASTER
EADBLASTERS
EADBLASTING
EADBLASTS
EADHOUSES
EADINESSES
EADLEDOMS
EADLEHOOD
EADLEHOODS
EADLESHIP
EADLESHIPS
EADSWOMAN
EADSWOMEN
EAMINESSES
EANFEASTS
EANSTALKS
EARABILITIES
EARABILITY
EARABLENESS
EARABLENESSES
EARBAITING
EARBAITINGS
EARBERRIES
EARDEDNESS
EARDEDNESSES
EARDLESSNESS
EARDLESSNESSES
EARDTONGUE
EARDTONGUES
EARGRASSES
EARISHNESS
EARISHNESSES
EARNAISES
EASTHOODS
EASTLIEST
EASTLINESS
EASTLINESSES
EATIFICAL
EATIFICALLY
EATIFICATION
EATIFICATIONS

BEATIFYING
BEATITUDES
BEAUJOLAIS
BEAUJOLAISES
BEAUMONTAGE
BEAUMONTAGES
BEAUMONTAGUE
BEAUMONTAGUES
BEAUTEOUSLY
BEAUTEOUSNESS
BEAUTEOUSNESSES
BEAUTICIAN
BEAUTICIANS
BEAUTIFICATION
BEAUTIFICATIONS
BEAUTIFIED
BEAUTIFIER
BEAUTIFIERS
BEAUTIFIES
BEAUTIFULLER
BEAUTIFULLEST
BEAUTIFULLY
BEAUTIFULNESS
BEAUTIFULNESSES
BEAUTIFYING
BEAVERBOARD
BEAVERBOARDS
BEBEERINES
BEBLOODING
BEBLUBBERED
BECARPETED
BECARPETING
BECCACCIAS
BECCAFICOS
BECHALKING
BECHANCING
BECHARMING
BECLAMORED
BECLAMORING
BECLASPING
BECLOAKING
BECLOGGING
BECLOTHING
BECLOUDING
BECLOWNING
BECOMINGLY
BECOMINGNESS
BECOMINGNESSES
BECOWARDED
BECOWARDING
BECQUERELS
BECRAWLING
BECROWDING
BECRUSTING
BECUDGELED
BECUDGELING
BECUDGELLED
BECUDGELLING
BEDABBLING
BEDAGGLING
BEDARKENED
BEDARKENING
BEDAZZLEMENT
BEDAZZLEMENTS
BEDAZZLING
BEDCHAMBER

BEDCHAMBERS
BEDCLOTHES
BEDCOVERING
BEDCOVERINGS
BEDEAFENED
BEDEAFENING
BEDEHOUSES
BEDELLSHIP
BEDELLSHIPS
BEDELSHIPS
BEDEVILING
BEDEVILLED
BEDEVILLING
BEDEVILMENT
BEDEVILMENTS
BEDFELLOWS
BEDIAPERED
BEDIAPERING
BEDIGHTING
BEDIMMINGS
BEDIMPLING
BEDIRTYING
BEDIZENING
BEDIZENMENT
BEDIZENMENTS
BEDLAMISMS
BEDLAMITES
BEDPRESSER
BEDPRESSERS
BEDRAGGLED
BEDRAGGLES
BEDRAGGLING
BEDRENCHED
BEDRENCHES
BEDRENCHING
BEDRIVELED
BEDRIVELING
BEDRIVELLED
BEDRIVELLING
BEDROPPING
BEDRUGGING
BEDSITTERS
BEDSITTING
BEDSPREADS
BEDSPRINGS
BEDWARFING
BEDWARMERS
BEDWETTERS
BEECHDROPS
BEECHMASTS
BEECHWOODS
BEEFBURGER
BEEFBURGERS
BEEFEATERS
BEEFINESSES
BEEFSTEAKS
BEEKEEPERS
BEEKEEPING
BEEKEEPINGS
BEERINESSES
BEESWAXING
BEESWINGED
BEETLEBRAIN
BEETLEBRAINED
BEETLEBRAINS
BEETLEHEAD

BEETLEHEADED
BEETLEHEADS
BEETMASTER
BEETMASTERS
BEETMISTER
BEETMISTERS
BEFINGERED
BEFINGERING
BEFITTINGLY
BEFLAGGING
BEFLECKING
BEFLOWERED
BEFLOWERING
BEFLUMMING
BEFOREHAND
BEFORETIME
BEFORTUNED
BEFORTUNES
BEFORTUNING
BEFOULMENT
BEFOULMENTS
BEFRETTING
BEFRIENDED
BEFRIENDER
BEFRIENDERS
BEFRIENDING
BEFRINGING
BEFUDDLEMENT
BEFUDDLEMENTS
BEFUDDLING
BEGGARDOMS
BEGGARHOOD
BEGGARHOODS
BEGGARLINESS
BEGGARLINESSES
BEGGARWEED
BEGGARWEEDS
BEGINNINGLESS
BEGINNINGS
BEGIRDLING
BEGLADDING
BEGLAMORED
BEGLAMORING
BEGLAMOURED
BEGLAMOURING
BEGLAMOURS
BEGLERBEGS
BEGLOOMING
BEGRIMMING
BEGROANING
BEGRUDGERIES
BEGRUDGERS
BEGRUDGERY
BEGRUDGING
BEGRUDGINGLY
BEGUILEMENT
BEGUILEMENTS
BEGUILINGLY
BEGUINAGES
BEHAPPENED
BEHAPPENING
BEHAVIORAL
BEHAVIORALLY
BEHAVIORISM
BEHAVIORISMS
BEHAVIORIST

BEHAVIORISTIC
BEHAVIORISTS
BEHAVIOURAL
BEHAVIOURALLY
BEHAVIOURISM
BEHAVIOURISMS
BEHAVIOURIST
BEHAVIOURISTIC
BEHAVIOURISTS
BEHAVIOURS
BEHEADINGS
BEHIGHTING
BEHINDHAND
BEHOLDINGS
BEINGNESSES
BEINNESSES
BEJESUITED
BEJESUITING
BEJEWELING
BEJEWELLED
BEJEWELLING
BEJUMBLING
BEKNIGHTED
BEKNIGHTING
BEKNOTTING
BELABORING
BELABOURED
BELABOURING
BELAMOURES
BELATEDNESS
BELATEDNESSES
BELEAGUERED
BELEAGUERING
BELEAGUERMENT
BELEAGUERMENTS
BELEAGUERS
BELEMNITES
BELIEFLESS
BELIEVABILITIES
BELIEVABILITY
BELIEVABLE
BELIEVABLY
BELIEVINGLY
BELIQUORED
BELIQUORING
BELITTLEMENT
BELITTLEMENTS
BELITTLERS
BELITTLING
BELITTLINGLY
BELLADONNA
BELLADONNAS
BELLAMOURE
BELLAMOURES
BELLARMINE
BELLARMINES
BELLETRISM
BELLETRISMS
BELLETRIST
BELLETRISTIC
BELLETRISTICAL
BELLETRISTS
BELLETTRIST
BELLETTRISTS
BELLFLOWER
BELLFLOWERS
BELLFOUNDER
BELLFOUNDERS
BELLFOUNDRIES
BELLFOUNDRY
BELLHANGER
BELLHANGERS
BELLIBONES
BELLICOSELY
BELLICOSITIES
BELLICOSITY
BELLIGERATI
BELLIGERENCE
BELLIGERENCES
BELLIGERENCIES
BELLIGERENCY
BELLIGERENT
BELLIGERENTLY
BELLIGERENTS
BELLOCKING
BELLPUSHES
BELLWETHER
BELLWETHERS
BELLYACHED
BELLYACHER
BELLYACHERS
BELLYACHES
BELLYACHING
BELLYBANDS
BELLYBUTTON
BELLYBUTTONS
BELOMANCIES
BELONGINGNESS
BELONGINGNESSES
BELONGINGS
BELOWDECKS
BELOWGROUND
BELOWSTAIRS
BELSHAZZAR
BELSHAZZARS
BELTCOURSE
BELTCOURSES
BELVEDERES
BEMADAMING
BEMADDENED
BEMADDENING
BEMEDALLED
BEMEDALLING
BEMINGLING
BEMOANINGS
BEMONSTERED
BEMONSTERING
BEMONSTERS
BEMOUTHING
BEMUDDLING
BEMUFFLING
BEMURMURED
BEMURMURING
BEMUSEMENT
BEMUSEMENTS
BEMUZZLING
BENCHERSHIP
BENCHERSHIPS
BENCHLANDS
BENCHMARKED
BENCHMARKING
BENCHMARKINGS
BENCHMARKS
BENCHWARMER
BENCHWARMERS
BENEDICITE
BENEDICITES
BENEDICTION
BENEDICTIONAL
BENEDICTIONS
BENEDICTIVE
BENEDICTORY
BENEDICTUS
BENEDICTUSES
BENEFACTED
BENEFACTING
BENEFACTION
BENEFACTIONS
BENEFACTOR
BENEFACTORS
BENEFACTORY
BENEFACTRESS
BENEFACTRESSES
BENEFICENCE
BENEFICENCES
BENEFICENT
BENEFICENTIAL
BENEFICENTLY
BENEFICIAL
BENEFICIALLY
BENEFICIALNESS
BENEFICIALS
BENEFICIARIES
BENEFICIARY
BENEFICIATE
BENEFICIATED
BENEFICIATES
BENEFICIATING
BENEFICIATION
BENEFICIATIONS
BENEFICING
BENEFITERS
BENEFITING
BENEFITTED
BENEFITTING
BENEPLACITO
BENEVOLENCE
BENEVOLENCES
BENEVOLENT
BENEVOLENTLY
BENEVOLENTNESS
BENGALINES
BENIGHTEDLY
BENIGHTEDNESS
BENIGHTEDNESSES
BENIGHTENED
BENIGHTENING
BENIGHTENINGS
BENIGHTENS
BENIGHTERS
BENIGHTING
BENIGHTINGS
BENIGHTMENT
BENIGHTMENTS
BENIGNANCIES
BENIGNANCY
BENIGNANTLY
BENIGNITIES
BENTGRASSES
BENTHOPELAGIC
BENTHOSCOPE
BENTHOSCOPES
BENTONITES
BENTONITIC
BENUMBEDNESS
BENUMBEDNESSES
BENUMBINGLY
BENUMBMENT
BENUMBMENTS
BENZALDEHYDE
BENZALDEHYDES
BENZANTHRACENE
BENZANTHRACENES
BENZENECARBONYL
BENZENOIDS
BENZIDINES
BENZIMIDAZOLE
BENZIMIDAZOLES
BENZOAPYRENE
BENZOAPYRENES
BENZOCAINE
BENZOCAINES
BENZODIAZEPINE
BENZODIAZEPINES
BENZOFURAN
BENZOFURANS
BENZOLINES
BENZOPHENONE
BENZOPHENONES
BENZOQUINONE
BENZOQUINONES
BENZPYRENE
BENZPYRENES
BENZYLIDINE
BENZYLIDINES
BEPAINTING
BEPEARLING
BEPEPPERED
BEPEPPERING
BEPESTERED
BEPESTERING
BEPIMPLING
BEPLASTERED
BEPLASTERING
BEPLASTERS
BEPOMMELLED
BEPOMMELLING
BEPOWDERED
BEPOWDERING
BEPRAISING
BEQUEATHABLE
BEQUEATHAL
BEQUEATHALS
BEQUEATHED
BEQUEATHER
BEQUEATHERS
BEQUEATHING
BEQUEATHMENT
BEQUEATHMENTS
BERASCALED
BERASCALING
BERBERIDACEOUS
BERBERINES
BERBERISES

EREAVEMENT
EREAVEMENTS
ERGAMASKS
ERGANDERS
ERGOMASKS
ERGSCHRUND
ERGSCHRUNDS
ERIBBONED
ERKELIUMS
ERRYFRUIT
ERRYFRUITS
ERSAGLIERE
ERSAGLIERI
ERSERKERS
ERTILLONAGE
ERTILLONAGES
ERYLLIOSES
ERYLLIOSIS
ERYLLIUMS
ESAINTING
ESCATTERED
ESCATTERING
ESCATTERS
ESCORCHED
ESCORCHES
ESCORCHING
ESCOURING
ESCRAWLED
ESCRAWLING
ESCREENED
ESCREENING
ESCRIBBLE
ESCRIBBLED
ESCRIBBLES
ESCRIBBLING
ESEECHERS
ESEECHING
ESEECHINGLY
ESEECHINGNESS
ESEECHINGS
ESEEMINGLY
ESEEMINGNESS
ESEEMINGNESSES
ESEEMINGS
ESETMENTS
ESHADOWED
ESHADOWING
ESHIVERED
ESHIVERING
ESHOUTING
ESHREWING
ESHROUDED
ESHROUDING
ESIEGEMENT
ESIEGEMENTS
ESIEGINGLY
ESIEGINGS
ESLAVERED
ESLAVERING
ESLOBBERED
ESLOBBERING
ESLOBBERS
ESLUBBERED
ESLUBBERING
ESLUBBERS
ESMEARERS

BESMEARING
BESMIRCHED
BESMIRCHES
BESMIRCHING
BESMOOTHED
BESMOOTHING
BESMUDGING
BESMUTCHED
BESMUTCHES
BESMUTCHING
BESMUTTING
BESOOTHING
BESOTTEDLY
BESOTTEDNESS
BESOTTEDNESSES
BESPANGLED
BESPANGLES
BESPANGLING
BESPATTERED
BESPATTERING
BESPATTERS
BESPEAKING
BESPECKLED
BESPECKLES
BESPECKLING
BESPECTACLED
BESPEEDING
BESPITTING
BESPORTING
BESPOTTEDNESS
BESPOTTEDNESSES
BESPOTTING
BESPOUSING
BESPOUTING
BESPREADING
BESPRINKLE
BESPRINKLED
BESPRINKLES
BESPRINKLING
BESTAINING
BESTARRING
BESTEADING
BESTIALISE
BESTIALISED
BESTIALISES
BESTIALISING
BESTIALISM
BESTIALISMS
BESTIALITIES
BESTIALITY
BESTIALIZE
BESTIALIZED
BESTIALIZES
BESTIALIZING
BESTIARIES
BESTICKING
BESTILLING
BESTIRRING
BESTORMING
BESTOWMENT
BESTOWMENTS
BESTRADDLE
BESTRADDLED
BESTRADDLES
BESTRADDLING
BESTRAUGHT

BESTREAKED
BESTREAKING
BESTREWING
BESTRIDABLE
BESTRIDDEN
BESTRIDING
BESTROWING
BESTSELLER
BESTSELLERDOM
BESTSELLERDOMS
BESTSELLERS
BESTSELLING
BESTUDDING
BESWARMING
BETACAROTENE
BETACAROTENES
BETACYANIN
BETACYANINS
BETATTERED
BETATTERING
BETHANKING
BETHANKITS
BETHINKING
BETHORNING
BETHRALLED
BETHRALLING
BETHUMBING
BETHUMPING
BETHWACKED
BETHWACKING
BETOKENING
BETREADING
BETRIMMING
BETROTHALS
BETROTHEDS
BETROTHING
BETROTHMENT
BETROTHMENTS
BETTERINGS
BETTERMENT
BETTERMENTS
BETTERMOST
BETTERNESS
BETTERNESSES
BETULACEOUS
BETWEENBRAIN
BETWEENBRAINS
BETWEENITIES
BETWEENITY
BETWEENNESS
BETWEENNESSES
BETWEENTIME
BETWEENTIMES
BETWEENWHILES
BEVELLINGS
BEVELMENTS
BEVOMITING
BEWAILINGLY
BEWAILINGS
BEWEARYING
BEWELTERED
BEWHISKERED
BEWILDERED
BEWILDEREDLY
BEWILDEREDNESS
BEWILDERING

BEWILDERINGLY
BEWILDERMENT
BEWILDERMENTS
BEWITCHERIES
BEWITCHERS
BEWITCHERY
BEWITCHING
BEWITCHINGLY
BEWITCHMENT
BEWITCHMENTS
BEWORRYING
BEWRAPPING
BHIKKHUNIS
BIANNUALLY
BIANNULATE
BIASNESSES
BIATHLETES
BIAURICULAR
BIAURICULATE
BIBLICALLY
BIBLICISMS
BIBLICISTS
BIBLIOGRAPHER
BIBLIOGRAPHERS
BIBLIOGRAPHIC
BIBLIOGRAPHICAL
BIBLIOGRAPHIES
BIBLIOGRAPHY
BIBLIOLATER
BIBLIOLATERS
BIBLIOLATRIES
BIBLIOLATRIST
BIBLIOLATRISTS
BIBLIOLATROUS
BIBLIOLATRY
BIBLIOLOGICAL
BIBLIOLOGIES
BIBLIOLOGIST
BIBLIOLOGISTS
BIBLIOLOGY
BIBLIOMANCIES
BIBLIOMANCY
BIBLIOMANE
BIBLIOMANES
BIBLIOMANIA
BIBLIOMANIAC
BIBLIOMANIACAL
BIBLIOMANIACS
BIBLIOMANIAS
BIBLIOPEGIC
BIBLIOPEGIES
BIBLIOPEGIST
BIBLIOPEGISTS
BIBLIOPEGY
BIBLIOPHAGIST
BIBLIOPHAGISTS
BIBLIOPHIL
BIBLIOPHILE
BIBLIOPHILES
BIBLIOPHILIC
BIBLIOPHILIES
BIBLIOPHILISM
BIBLIOPHILISMS
BIBLIOPHILIST
BIBLIOPHILISTIC
BIBLIOPHILISTS

BIBLIOPHILS
BIBLIOPHILY
BIBLIOPHOBIA
BIBLIOPHOBIAS
BIBLIOPOLE
BIBLIOPOLES
BIBLIOPOLIC
BIBLIOPOLICAL
BIBLIOPOLIES
BIBLIOPOLIST
BIBLIOPOLISTS
BIBLIOPOLY
BIBLIOTHECA
BIBLIOTHECAE
BIBLIOTHECAL
BIBLIOTHECARIES
BIBLIOTHECARY
BIBLIOTHECAS
BIBLIOTHERAPIES
BIBLIOTHERAPY
BIBLIOTICS
BIBLIOTIST
BIBLIOTISTS
BIBULOUSLY
BIBULOUSNESS
BIBULOUSNESSES
BICAMERALISM
BICAMERALISMS
BICAMERALIST
BICAMERALISTS
BICAPSULAR
BICARBONATE
BICARBONATES
BICARPELLARY
BICENTENARIES
BICENTENARY
BICENTENNIAL
BICENTENNIALS
BICEPHALOUS
BICHLORIDE
BICHLORIDES
BICHROMATE
BICHROMATED
BICHROMATES
BICKERINGS
BICOLLATERAL
BICOLOURED
BICOMPONENT
BICONCAVITIES
BICONCAVITY
BICONDITIONAL
BICONDITIONALS
BICONVEXITIES
BICONVEXITY
BICORNUATE
BICORPORATE
BICULTURAL
BICULTURALISM
BICULTURALISMS
BICUSPIDATE
BICUSPIDATES
BICYCLICAL
BICYCLISTS
BIDDABILITIES
BIDDABILITY
BIDDABLENESS
BIDDABLENESSES
BIDENTATED
BIDIALECTAL
BIDIALECTALISM
BIDIALECTALISMS
BIDIRECTIONAL
BIDIRECTIONALLY
BIDONVILLE
BIDONVILLES
BIENNIALLY
BIENSEANCE
BIENSEANCES
BIERKELLER
BIERKELLERS
BIFACIALLY
BIFARIOUSLY
BIFIDITIES
BIFLAGELLATE
BIFOLIOLATE
BIFUNCTIONAL
BIFURCATED
BIFURCATES
BIFURCATING
BIFURCATION
BIFURCATIONS
BIGAMOUSLY
BIGARREAUS
BIGEMINIES
BIGFOOTING
BIGHEADEDLY
BIGHEADEDNESS
BIGHEADEDNESSES
BIGHEARTED
BIGHEARTEDLY
BIGHEARTEDNESS
BIGMOUTHED
BIGNONIACEOUS
BIGUANIDES
BIJECTIONS
BIJOUTERIE
BIJOUTERIES
BILATERALISM
BILATERALISMS
BILATERALLY
BILBERRIES
BILDUNGSROMAN
BILDUNGSROMANS
BILECTIONS
BILESTONES
BILGEWATER
BILGEWATERS
BILHARZIAL
BILHARZIAS
BILHARZIASES
BILHARZIASIS
BILHARZIOSES
BILHARZIOSIS
BILIMBINGS
BILINGUALISM
BILINGUALISMS
BILINGUALLY
BILINGUALS
BILINGUIST
BILINGUISTS
BILIOUSNESS
BILIOUSNESSES
BILIRUBINS
BILIVERDIN
BILIVERDINS
BILLABONGS
BILLBOARDED
BILLBOARDING
BILLBOARDS
BILLFISHES
BILLINGSGATE
BILLINGSGATES
BILLIONAIRE
BILLIONAIRES
BILLIONTHS
BILLOWIEST
BILLOWINESS
BILLOWINESSES
BILLPOSTER
BILLPOSTERS
BILLPOSTING
BILLPOSTINGS
BILLSTICKER
BILLSTICKERS
BILLSTICKING
BILLSTICKINGS
BILLYCOCKS
BILOCATION
BILOCATIONS
BILOCULATE
BIMANUALLY
BIMESTRIAL
BIMESTRIALLY
BIMETALLIC
BIMETALLICS
BIMETALLISM
BIMETALLISMS
BIMETALLIST
BIMETALLISTIC
BIMETALLISTS
BIMILLENARIES
BIMILLENARY
BIMILLENNIA
BIMILLENNIAL
BIMILLENNIALS
BIMILLENNIUM
BIMILLENNIUMS
BIMODALITIES
BIMODALITY
BIMOLECULAR
BIMOLECULARLY
BIMONTHLIES
BIMORPHEMIC
BINATIONAL
BINAURALLY
BINDINGNESS
BINDINGNESSES
BINOCULARITIES
BINOCULARITY
BINOCULARLY
BINOCULARS
BINOMIALLY
BINOMINALS
BINTURONGS
BINUCLEATE
BINUCLEATED
BIOACCUMULATE
BIOACCUMULATED
BIOACCUMULATES
BIOACCUMULATING
BIOACCUMULATION
BIOACOUSTICS
BIOACTIVITIES
BIOACTIVITY
BIOAERATION
BIOAERATIONS
BIOAERONAUTICS
BIOASSAYED
BIOASSAYING
BIOASTRONAUTICS
BIOAVAILABILITY
BIOAVAILABLE
BIOCATALYST
BIOCATALYSTS
BIOCATALYTIC
BIOCELLATE
BIOCENOLOGIES
BIOCENOLOGY
BIOCENOSES
BIOCENOSIS
BIOCENOTIC
BIOCHEMICAL
BIOCHEMICALLY
BIOCHEMICALS
BIOCHEMIST
BIOCHEMISTRIES
BIOCHEMISTRY
BIOCHEMISTS
BIOCLASTIC
BIOCLIMATIC
BIOCLIMATOLOGY
BIOCOENOLOGIES
BIOCOENOLOGY
BIOCOENOSES
BIOCOENOSIS
BIOCOENOTIC
BIOCOMPATIBLE
BIOCOMPUTING
BIOCOMPUTINGS
BIOCONTROL
BIOCONTROLS
BIOCONVERSION
BIOCONVERSIONS
BIODEGRADABLE
BIODEGRADATION
BIODEGRADATIONS
BIODEGRADE
BIODEGRADED
BIODEGRADES
BIODEGRADING
BIODESTRUCTIBLE
BIODIESELS
BIODIVERSITIES
BIODIVERSITY
BIODYNAMIC
BIODYNAMICAL
BIODYNAMICS
BIOECOLOGICAL
BIOECOLOGICALLY
BIOECOLOGIES
BIOECOLOGIST
BIOECOLOGISTS
BIOECOLOGY
BIOELECTRIC

IOELECTRICAL
IOELECTRICITY
IOENERGETIC
IOENERGETICS
IOENGINEER
IOENGINEERED
IOENGINEERING
IOENGINEERINGS
IOENGINEERS
IOETHICAL
IOETHICIST
IOETHICISTS
IOFEEDBACK
IOFEEDBACKS
IOFLAVONOID
IOFLAVONOIDS
IOFOULERS
IOFOULING
IOFOULINGS
IOGENESES
IOGENESIS
IOGENETIC
IOGENETICAL
IOGENETICALLY
IOGENETICS
IOGEOCHEMICAL
IOGEOCHEMICALS
IOGEOCHEMISTRY
IOGEOGRAPHER
IOGEOGRAPHERS
IOGEOGRAPHIC
IOGEOGRAPHICAL
IOGEOGRAPHIES
IOGEOGRAPHY
IOGRAPHED
IOGRAPHEE
IOGRAPHEES
IOGRAPHER
IOGRAPHERS
IOGRAPHIC
IOGRAPHICAL
IOGRAPHICALLY
IOGRAPHIES
IOGRAPHING
IOGRAPHISE
IOGRAPHISED
IOGRAPHISES
IOGRAPHISING
IOGRAPHIZE
IOGRAPHIZED
IOGRAPHIZES
IOGRAPHIZING
IOHAZARDOUS
IOHAZARDS
IOINDUSTRIES
IOINDUSTRY
IOINFORMATICS
IOLOGICAL
IOLOGICALLY
IOLOGICALS
IOLOGISMS
IOLOGISTIC
IOLOGISTS
IOLUMINESCENCE
IOLUMINESCENT
IOMAGNETICS

BIOMARKERS
BIOMATERIAL
BIOMATERIALS
BIOMATHEMATICAL
BIOMATHEMATICS
BIOMECHANICAL
BIOMECHANICALLY
BIOMECHANICS
BIOMEDICAL
BIOMEDICINE
BIOMEDICINES
BIOMETEOROLOGY
BIOMETRICAL
BIOMETRICALLY
BIOMETRICIAN
BIOMETRICIANS
BIOMETRICS
BIOMETRIES
BIOMIMETIC
BIOMIMETICS
BIOMIMICRIES
BIOMIMICRY
BIOMININGS
BIOMOLECULAR
BIOMOLECULE
BIOMOLECULES
BIOMORPHIC
BIONOMICALLY
BIONOMISTS
BIOPARENTS
BIOPESTICIDAL
BIOPESTICIDE
BIOPESTICIDES
BIOPHILIAS
BIOPHYSICAL
BIOPHYSICALLY
BIOPHYSICIST
BIOPHYSICISTS
BIOPHYSICS
BIOPIRACIES
BIOPIRATES
BIOPLASMIC
BIOPOIESES
BIOPOIESIS
BIOPOLYMER
BIOPOLYMERS
BIOPROSPECTING
BIOPROSPECTINGS
BIOPSYCHOLOGIES
BIOPSYCHOLOGY
BIOREACTOR
BIOREACTORS
BIOREAGENT
BIOREAGENTS
BIOREGIONAL
BIOREGIONALISM
BIOREGIONALISMS
BIOREGIONALIST
BIOREGIONALISTS
BIOREGIONS
BIOREMEDIATION
BIOREMEDIATIONS
BIORHYTHMIC
BIORHYTHMICALLY
BIORHYTHMICS
BIORHYTHMS

BIOSAFETIES
BIOSATELLITE
BIOSATELLITES
BIOSCIENCE
BIOSCIENCES
BIOSCIENTIFIC
BIOSCIENTIST
BIOSCIENTISTS
BIOSCOPIES
BIOSENSORS
BIOSOCIALLY
BIOSPHERES
BIOSPHERIC
BIOSTATICALLY
BIOSTATICS
BIOSTATISTICAL
BIOSTATISTICIAN
BIOSTATISTICS
BIOSTRATIGRAPHY
BIOSTROMES
BIOSURGERIES
BIOSURGERY
BIOSYNTHESES
BIOSYNTHESIS
BIOSYNTHETIC
BIOSYSTEMATIC
BIOSYSTEMATICS
BIOSYSTEMATIST
BIOSYSTEMATISTS
BIOTECHNICAL
BIOTECHNOLOGIES
BIOTECHNOLOGIST
BIOTECHNOLOGY
BIOTELEMETRIC
BIOTELEMETRIES
BIOTELEMETRY
BIOTERRORS
BIOTICALLY
BIOTURBATION
BIOTURBATIONS
BIOWEAPONS
BIPARENTAL
BIPARENTALLY
BIPARIETAL
BIPARTISAN
BIPARTISANISM
BIPARTISANISMS
BIPARTISANSHIP
BIPARTISANSHIPS
BIPARTITELY
BIPARTITION
BIPARTITIONS
BIPEDALISM
BIPEDALISMS
BIPEDALITIES
BIPEDALITY
BIPETALOUS
BIPINNARIA
BIPINNARIAS
BIPINNATELY
BIPOLARISATION
BIPOLARISATIONS
BIPOLARISE
BIPOLARISED
BIPOLARISES
BIPOLARISING

BIPOLARITIES
BIPOLARITY
BIPOLARIZATION
BIPOLARIZATIONS
BIPOLARIZE
BIPOLARIZED
BIPOLARIZES
BIPOLARIZING
BIPROPELLANT
BIPROPELLANTS
BIPYRAMIDAL
BIPYRAMIDS
BIQUADRATE
BIQUADRATES
BIQUADRATIC
BIQUADRATICS
BIQUARTERLY
BIQUINTILE
BIQUINTILES
BIRACIALISM
BIRACIALISMS
BIRACIALLY
BIRADICALS
BIRDBRAINED
BIRDBRAINS
BIRDDOGGED
BIRDDOGGING
BIRDHOUSES
BIRDLIMING
BIRDWATCHED
BIRDWATCHER
BIRDWATCHERS
BIRDWATCHES
BIRDWATCHING
BIREFRINGENCE
BIREFRINGENCES
BIREFRINGENT
BIROSTRATE
BIRTHMARKS
BIRTHNAMES
BIRTHNIGHT
BIRTHNIGHTS
BIRTHPLACE
BIRTHPLACES
BIRTHRATES
BIRTHRIGHT
BIRTHRIGHTS
BIRTHROOTS
BIRTHSTONE
BIRTHSTONES
BIRTHWORTS
BISECTIONAL
BISECTIONALLY
BISECTIONS
BISECTRICES
BISEXUALISM
BISEXUALISMS
BISEXUALITIES
BISEXUALITY
BISEXUALLY
BISHOPBIRD
BISHOPBIRDS
BISHOPDOMS
BISHOPESSES
BISHOPRICS
BISHOPWEED

BISHOPWEEDS
BISMUTHINITE
BISMUTHINITES
BISMUTHOUS
BISOCIATION
BISOCIATIONS
BISOCIATIVE
BISPHOSPHONATE
BISPHOSPHONATES
BISSEXTILE
BISSEXTILES
BISTOURIES
BISULFATES
BISULFIDES
BISULFITES
BISULPHATE
BISULPHATES
BISULPHIDE
BISULPHIDES
BISULPHITE
BISULPHITES
BISYMMETRIC
BISYMMETRICAL
BISYMMETRICALLY
BISYMMETRIES
BISYMMETRY
BITARTRATE
BITARTRATES
BITCHERIES
BITCHFESTS
BITCHINESS
BITCHINESSES
BITEPLATES
BITMAPPING
BITONALITIES
BITONALITY
BITSTREAMS
BITTERBARK
BITTERBARKS
BITTERBRUSH
BITTERBRUSHES
BITTERCRESS
BITTERCRESSES
BITTERLING
BITTERLINGS
BITTERNESS
BITTERNESSES
BITTERNUTS
BITTERROOT
BITTERROOTS
BITTERSWEET
BITTERSWEETLY
BITTERSWEETNESS
BITTERSWEETS
BITTERWEED
BITTERWEEDS
BITTERWOOD
BITTERWOODS
BITTINESSES
BITUMINATE
BITUMINATED
BITUMINATES
BITUMINATING
BITUMINISATION
BITUMINISATIONS
BITUMINISE
BITUMINISED
BITUMINISES
BITUMINISING
BITUMINIZATION
BITUMINIZATIONS
BITUMINIZE
BITUMINIZED
BITUMINIZES
BITUMINIZING
BITUMINOUS
BIUNIQUENESS
BIUNIQUENESSES
BIVALENCES
BIVALENCIES
BIVALVULAR
BIVARIANTS
BIVARIATES
BIVOUACKED
BIVOUACKING
BIWEEKLIES
BIZARRENESS
BIZARRENESSES
BIZARRERIE
BIZARRERIES
BLABBERING
BLABBERMOUTH
BLABBERMOUTHS
BLACKAMOOR
BLACKAMOORS
BLACKBALLED
BLACKBALLING
BLACKBALLINGS
BLACKBALLS
BLACKBANDS
BLACKBERRIED
BLACKBERRIES
BLACKBERRY
BLACKBERRYING
BLACKBERRYINGS
BLACKBIRDED
BLACKBIRDER
BLACKBIRDERS
BLACKBIRDING
BLACKBIRDINGS
BLACKBIRDS
BLACKBOARD
BLACKBOARDS
BLACKBODIES
BLACKBUCKS
BLACKBUTTS
BLACKCOCKS
BLACKCURRANT
BLACKCURRANTS
BLACKDAMPS
BLACKENERS
BLACKENING
BLACKENINGS
BLACKFACED
BLACKFACES
BLACKFISHES
BLACKFLIES
BLACKGAMES
BLACKGUARD
BLACKGUARDED
BLACKGUARDING
BLACKGUARDISM
BLACKGUARDISMS
BLACKGUARDLY
BLACKGUARDS
BLACKHANDER
BLACKHANDERS
BLACKHEADED
BLACKHEADS
BLACKHEART
BLACKHEARTS
BLACKISHLY
BLACKJACKED
BLACKJACKING
BLACKJACKS
BLACKLANDS
BLACKLEADS
BLACKLEGGED
BLACKLEGGING
BLACKLISTED
BLACKLISTER
BLACKLISTERS
BLACKLISTING
BLACKLISTINGS
BLACKLISTS
BLACKMAILED
BLACKMAILER
BLACKMAILERS
BLACKMAILING
BLACKMAILS
BLACKNESSES
BLACKPOLLS
BLACKSMITH
BLACKSMITHING
BLACKSMITHINGS
BLACKSMITHS
BLACKSNAKE
BLACKSNAKES
BLACKSTRAP
BLACKTAILS
BLACKTHORN
BLACKTHORNS
BLACKTOPPED
BLACKTOPPING
BLACKWASHED
BLACKWASHES
BLACKWASHING
BLACKWATER
BLACKWATERS
BLACKWOODS
BLADDERLIKE
BLADDERNOSE
BLADDERNOSES
BLADDERNUT
BLADDERNUTS
BLADDERWORT
BLADDERWORTS
BLADDERWRACK
BLADDERWRACKS
BLADEWORKS
BLAEBERRIES
BLAMABLENESS
BLAMABLENESSES
BLAMEABLENESS
BLAMEABLENESSES
BLAMEFULLY
BLAMEFULNESS
BLAMEFULNESSES
BLAMELESSLY
BLAMELESSNESS
BLAMELESSNESSES
BLAMEWORTHINESS
BLAMEWORTHY
BLANCHISSEUSE
BLANCHISSEUSES
BLANCMANGE
BLANCMANGES
BLANDISHED
BLANDISHER
BLANDISHERS
BLANDISHES
BLANDISHING
BLANDISHMENT
BLANDISHMENTS
BLANDNESSES
BLANKETFLOWER
BLANKETFLOWERS
BLANKETIES
BLANKETING
BLANKETINGS
BLANKETLIKE
BLANKETWEED
BLANKETWEEDS
BLANKNESSES
BLANQUETTE
BLANQUETTES
BLARNEYING
BLASPHEMED
BLASPHEMER
BLASPHEMERS
BLASPHEMES
BLASPHEMIES
BLASPHEMING
BLASPHEMOUS
BLASPHEMOUSLY
BLASPHEMOUSNESS
BLASTEMATA
BLASTEMATIC
BLASTMENTS
BLASTOCHYLE
BLASTOCHYLES
BLASTOCOEL
BLASTOCOELE
BLASTOCOELES
BLASTOCOELIC
BLASTOCOELS
BLASTOCYST
BLASTOCYSTS
BLASTODERM
BLASTODERMIC
BLASTODERMS
BLASTODISC
BLASTODISCS
BLASTOGENESES
BLASTOGENESIS
BLASTOGENETIC
BLASTOGENIC
BLASTOMATA
BLASTOMERE
BLASTOMERES
BLASTOMERIC
BLASTOMYCOSES
BLASTOMYCOSIS
BLASTOPORAL

LASTOPORE
LASTOPORES
LASTOPORIC
LASTOPORS
LASTOSPHERE
LASTOSPHERES
LASTOSPORE
LASTOSPORES
LASTULATION
LASTULATIONS
LATANCIES
LATHERERS
LATHERING
LATHERSKITE
LATHERSKITES
LATTERING
LAXPLOITATION
LAXPLOITATIONS
LAZONINGS
LAZONRIES
LEACHABLE
LEACHERIES
LEACHERITE
LEACHERITES
LEACHINGS
LEAKNESSES
LEARINESS
LEARINESSES
LEMISHERS
LEMISHING
LEMISHMENT
LEMISHMENTS
LENNIOIDS
LENNORRHEA
LENNORRHEAS
LENNORRHOEA
LENNORRHOEAS
LEPHARISM
LEPHARISMS
LEPHARITIC
LEPHARITIS
LEPHARITISES
LEPHAROPLAST
LEPHAROPLASTS
LEPHAROPLASTY
LEPHAROSPASM
LEPHAROSPASMS
LESSEDEST
LESSEDNESS
LESSEDNESSES
LETHERANSKATE
LETHERANSKATES
LETHERATION
LETHERATIONS
LETHERERS
LETHERING
LETHERINGS
LETHERSKATE
LETHERSKATES
LIGHTINGLY
LIGHTINGS
LIMPISHLY
LIMPISHNESS
LIMPISHNESSES
LINDFISHES
LINDFOLDED
BLINDFOLDING
BLINDFOLDS
BLINDINGLY
BLINDNESSES
BLINDSIDED
BLINDSIDES
BLINDSIDING
BLINDSIGHT
BLINDSIGHTS
BLINDSTOREY
BLINDSTOREYS
BLINDSTORIES
BLINDSTORY
BLINDWORMS
BLINGLISHES
BLINKERING
BLISSFULLY
BLISSFULNESS
BLISSFULNESSES
BLISTERIER
BLISTERIEST
BLISTERING
BLISTERINGLY
BLITHENESS
BLITHENESSES
BLITHERING
BLITHESOME
BLITHESOMELY
BLITHESOMENESS
BLITZKRIEG
BLITZKRIEGS
BLIZZARDLY
BLOATEDNESS
BLOATEDNESSES
BLOATWARES
BLOCKADERS
BLOCKADING
BLOCKBOARD
BLOCKBOARDS
BLOCKBUSTED
BLOCKBUSTER
BLOCKBUSTERS
BLOCKBUSTING
BLOCKBUSTINGS
BLOCKBUSTS
BLOCKHEADED
BLOCKHEADEDLY
BLOCKHEADEDNESS
BLOCKHEADS
BLOCKHOLES
BLOCKHOUSE
BLOCKHOUSES
BLOCKINESS
BLOCKINESSES
BLOCKISHLY
BLOCKISHNESS
BLOCKISHNESSES
BLOCKWORKS
BLOKEISHNESS
BLOKEISHNESSES
BLOKISHNESS
BLOKISHNESSES
BLONDENESS
BLONDENESSES
BLONDINING
BLONDNESSES
BLOODBATHS
BLOODCURDLING
BLOODCURDLINGLY
BLOODGUILT
BLOODGUILTINESS
BLOODGUILTS
BLOODGUILTY
BLOODHEATS
BLOODHOUND
BLOODHOUNDS
BLOODINESS
BLOODINESSES
BLOODLESSLY
BLOODLESSNESS
BLOODLESSNESSES
BLOODLETTER
BLOODLETTERS
BLOODLETTING
BLOODLETTINGS
BLOODLINES
BLOODLUSTS
BLOODMOBILE
BLOODMOBILES
BLOODROOTS
BLOODSHEDS
BLOODSPRENT
BLOODSTAIN
BLOODSTAINED
BLOODSTAINS
BLOODSTOCK
BLOODSTOCKS
BLOODSTONE
BLOODSTONES
BLOODSTREAM
BLOODSTREAMS
BLOODSUCKER
BLOODSUCKERS
BLOODSUCKING
BLOODTHIRSTIER
BLOODTHIRSTIEST
BLOODTHIRSTILY
BLOODTHIRSTY
BLOODWOODS
BLOODWORMS
BLOODWORTS
BLOOMERIES
BLOQUISTES
BLOSSOMING
BLOSSOMINGS
BLOSSOMLESS
BLOTCHIEST
BLOTCHINESS
BLOTCHINESSES
BLOTCHINGS
BLOTTESQUE
BLOTTESQUES
BLOVIATING
BLOVIATION
BLOVIATIONS
BLOWFISHES
BLOWINESSES
BLOWKARTING
BLOWKARTINGS
BLOWSINESS
BLOWSINESSES
BLOWTORCHED
BLOWTORCHES
BLOWTORCHING
BLOWZINESS
BLOWZINESSES
BLUBBERERS
BLUBBERING
BLUDGEONED
BLUDGEONER
BLUDGEONERS
BLUDGEONING
BLUEBEARDS
BLUEBERRIES
BLUEBLOODS
BLUEBONNET
BLUEBONNETS
BLUEBOTTLE
BLUEBOTTLES
BLUEBREAST
BLUEBREASTS
BLUEBUSHES
BLUEFISHES
BLUEGRASSES
BLUEISHNESS
BLUEISHNESSES
BLUEJACKET
BLUEJACKETS
BLUEJACKING
BLUEJACKINGS
BLUELINERS
BLUENESSES
BLUEPOINTS
BLUEPRINTED
BLUEPRINTING
BLUEPRINTS
BLUESHIFTED
BLUESHIFTS
BLUESNARFING
BLUESNARFINGS
BLUESTOCKING
BLUESTOCKINGS
BLUESTONES
BLUETHROAT
BLUETHROATS
BLUETONGUE
BLUETONGUES
BLUFFNESSES
BLUISHNESS
BLUISHNESSES
BLUNDERBUSS
BLUNDERBUSSES
BLUNDERERS
BLUNDERING
BLUNDERINGLY
BLUNDERINGS
BLUNTHEADS
BLUNTNESSES
BLURREDNESS
BLURREDNESSES
BLURRINESS
BLURRINESSES
BLURRINGLY
BLUSHINGLY
BLUSHLESSLY
BLUSTERERS
BLUSTERIER
BLUSTERIEST

BLUSTERING
BLUSTERINGLY
BLUSTERINGS
BLUSTEROUS
BLUSTEROUSLY
BLUTWURSTS
BOARDINGHOUSE
BOARDINGHOUSES
BOARDROOMS
BOARDSAILING
BOARDSAILINGS
BOARDSAILOR
BOARDSAILORS
BOARDWALKS
BOARFISHES
BOARHOUNDS
BOARISHNESS
BOARISHNESSES
BOASTFULLY
BOASTFULNESS
BOASTFULNESSES
BOASTINGLY
BOATBUILDER
BOATBUILDERS
BOATBUILDING
BOATBUILDINGS
BOATHOUSES
BOATLIFTED
BOATLIFTING
BOATSWAINS
BOBBEJAANS
BOBBITTING
BOBBYSOCKS
BOBBYSOXER
BOBBYSOXERS
BOBSLEDDED
BOBSLEDDER
BOBSLEDDERS
BOBSLEDDING
BOBSLEDDINGS
BOBSLEIGHED
BOBSLEIGHING
BOBSLEIGHS
BOBTAILING
BOBWEIGHTS
BOCCONCINI
BODACIOUSLY
BODDHISATTVA
BODDHISATTVAS
BODEGUEROS
BODHISATTVA
BODHISATTVAS
BODYBOARDED
BODYBOARDING
BODYBOARDINGS
BODYBOARDS
BODYBUILDER
BODYBUILDERS
BODYBUILDING
BODYBUILDINGS
BODYCHECKED
BODYCHECKING
BODYCHECKS
BODYGUARDED
BODYGUARDING
BODYGUARDS
BODYSHELLS
BODYSURFED
BODYSURFER
BODYSURFERS
BODYSURFING
BODYWORKER
BODYWORKERS
BOEREMUSIEK
BOEREMUSIEKS
BOEREWORSES
BOGGINESSES
BOGTROTTER
BOGTROTTERS
BOGTROTTING
BOGTROTTINGS
BOGUSNESSES
BOHEMIANISM
BOHEMIANISMS
BOILERMAKER
BOILERMAKERS
BOILERPLATE
BOILERPLATED
BOILERPLATES
BOILERPLATING
BOILERSUIT
BOILERSUITS
BOISTEROUS
BOISTEROUSLY
BOISTEROUSNESS
BOKMAKIERIE
BOKMAKIERIES
BOLDFACING
BOLDNESSES
BOLECTIONS
BOLIVIANOS
BOLLETRIES
BOLLOCKING
BOLLOCKINGS
BOLLOCKSED
BOLLOCKSES
BOLLOCKSING
BOLOGRAPHS
BOLOMETERS
BOLOMETRIC
BOLOMETRICALLY
BOLOMETRIES
BOLSHEVIKI
BOLSHEVIKS
BOLSHEVISE
BOLSHEVISED
BOLSHEVISES
BOLSHEVISING
BOLSHEVISM
BOLSHEVISMS
BOLSHEVIST
BOLSHEVISTS
BOLSHEVIZE
BOLSHEVIZED
BOLSHEVIZES
BOLSHEVIZING
BOLSTERERS
BOLSTERING
BOLSTERINGS
BOMBACACEOUS
BOMBARDERS
BOMBARDIER
BOMBARDIERS
BOMBARDING
BOMBARDMENT
BOMBARDMENTS
BOMBARDONS
BOMBASINES
BOMBASTERS
BOMBASTICALLY
BOMBASTING
BOMBAZINES
BOMBILATED
BOMBILATES
BOMBILATING
BOMBILATION
BOMBILATIONS
BOMBINATED
BOMBINATES
BOMBINATING
BOMBINATION
BOMBINATIONS
BOMBPROOFED
BOMBPROOFING
BOMBPROOFS
BOMBSHELLS
BOMBSIGHTS
BONAMIASES
BONAMIASIS
BONASSUSES
BONBONNIERE
BONBONNIERES
BONDHOLDER
BONDHOLDERS
BONDMANSHIP
BONDMANSHIPS
BONDSERVANT
BONDSERVANTS
BONDSTONES
BONDSWOMAN
BONDSWOMEN
BONEBLACKS
BONEFISHES
BONEFISHING
BONEFISHINGS
BONEHEADED
BONEHEADEDNESS
BONESETTER
BONESETTERS
BONESHAKER
BONESHAKERS
BONHOMMIES
BONILASSES
BONINESSES
BONKBUSTER
BONKBUSTERS
BONNIBELLS
BONNILASSE
BONNILASSES
BONNINESSES
BONNYCLABBER
BONNYCLABBERS
BOOBIALLAS
BOOBOISIES
BOOKBINDER
BOOKBINDERIES
BOOKBINDERS
BOOKBINDERY
BOOKBINDING
BOOKBINDINGS
BOOKCROSSING
BOOKCROSSINGS
BOOKISHNESS
BOOKISHNESSES
BOOKKEEPER
BOOKKEEPERS
BOOKKEEPING
BOOKKEEPINGS
BOOKLIGHTS
BOOKMAKERS
BOOKMAKING
BOOKMAKINGS
BOOKMARKED
BOOKMARKER
BOOKMARKERS
BOOKMARKING
BOOKMOBILE
BOOKMOBILES
BOOKPLATES
BOOKSELLER
BOOKSELLERS
BOOKSELLING
BOOKSELLINGS
BOOKSHELVES
BOOKSTALLS
BOOKSTANDS
BOOKSTORES
BOOMERANGED
BOOMERANGING
BOOMERANGS
BOOMSLANGS
BOONDOGGLE
BOONDOGGLED
BOONDOGGLER
BOONDOGGLERS
BOONDOGGLES
BOONDOGGLING
BOONGARIES
BOORISHNESS
BOORISHNESSES
BOOSTERISH
BOOSTERISM
BOOSTERISMS
BOOTBLACKS
BOOTLEGGED
BOOTLEGGER
BOOTLEGGERS
BOOTLEGGING
BOOTLEGGINGS
BOOTLESSLY
BOOTLESSNESS
BOOTLESSNESSES
BOOTLICKED
BOOTLICKER
BOOTLICKERS
BOOTLICKING
BOOTLICKINGS
BOOTLOADER
BOOTLOADERS
BOOTMAKERS
BOOTMAKING
BOOTMAKINGS
BOOTSTRAPPED
BOOTSTRAPPING

OOTSTRAPS
OOTYLICIOUS
OOZINESSES
ORAGINACEOUS
ORBORYGMAL
ORBORYGMI
ORBORYGMIC
ORBORYGMUS
ORBORYGMUSES
ORDEREAUX
ORDERLAND
ORDERLANDS
ORDERLESS
ORDERLINE
ORDERLINES
ORDRAGING
ORDRAGINGS
ORESCOPES
ORGHETTOS
ORINGNESS
ORINGNESSES
OROHYDRIDE
OROHYDRIDES
OROSILICATE
OROSILICATES
ORROWINGS
OSBERAADS
OSCHVARKS
OSCHVELDS
OSKINESSES
OSSINESSES
OSSYBOOTS
OTANICALLY
OTANICALS
OTANISERS
OTANISING
OTANIZERS
OTANIZING
OTANOMANCIES
OTANOMANCY
OTCHERIES
OTCHINESS
OTCHINESSES
OTHERATION
OTHERATIONS
OTHERSOME
OTRYOIDAL
OTRYTISES
OTTLEBRUSH
OTTLEBRUSHES
OTTLEFULS
OTTLENECK
OTTLENECKED
OTTLENECKING
OTTLENECKS
OTTLENOSE
OTTOMLAND
OTTOMLANDS
OTTOMLESS
OTTOMLESSLY
OTTOMLESSNESS
OTTOMMOST
OTTOMNESS
OTTOMNESSES
OTTOMRIES
OTULINUMS

BOTULINUSES
BOUGAINVILIA
BOUGAINVILIAS
BOUGAINVILLAEA
BOUGAINVILLAEAS
BOUGAINVILLEA
BOUGAINVILLEAS
BOUILLABAISSE
BOUILLABAISSES
BOUILLOTTE
BOUILLOTTES
BOULDERERS
BOULDERING
BOULDERINGS
BOULEVARDIER
BOULEVARDIERS
BOULEVARDS
BOULEVERSEMENT
BOULEVERSEMENTS
BOULLEWORK
BOULLEWORKS
BOUNCINESS
BOUNCINESSES
BOUNCINGLY
BOUNDARIES
BOUNDEDNESS
BOUNDEDNESSES
BOUNDERISH
BOUNDLESSLY
BOUNDLESSNESS
BOUNDLESSNESSES
BOUNDNESSES
BOUNTEOUSLY
BOUNTEOUSNESS
BOUNTEOUSNESSES
BOUNTIFULLY
BOUNTIFULNESS
BOUNTIFULNESSES
BOUNTYHEDS
BOUQUETIERE
BOUQUETIERES
BOURASQUES
BOURBONISM
BOURBONISMS
BOURGEOISE
BOURGEOISES
BOURGEOISIE
BOURGEOISIES
BOURGEOISIFIED
BOURGEOISIFIES
BOURGEOISIFY
BOURGEOISIFYING
BOURGEONED
BOURGEONING
BOURGUIGNON
BOURGUIGNONNE
BOUSINGKEN
BOUSINGKENS
BOUSTROPHEDON
BOUSTROPHEDONIC
BOUSTROPHEDONS
BOUTONNIERE
BOUTONNIERES
BOUVARDIAS
BOVINITIES
BOWDLERISATION

BOWDLERISATIONS
BOWDLERISE
BOWDLERISED
BOWDLERISER
BOWDLERISERS
BOWDLERISES
BOWDLERISING
BOWDLERISM
BOWDLERISMS
BOWDLERIZATION
BOWDLERIZATIONS
BOWDLERIZE
BOWDLERIZED
BOWDLERIZER
BOWDLERIZERS
BOWDLERIZES
BOWDLERIZING
BOWERBIRDS
BOWERWOMAN
BOWERWOMEN
BOWHUNTERS
BOWSTRINGED
BOWSTRINGING
BOWSTRINGS
BOXBERRIES
BOXERCISES
BOXHAULING
BOXINESSES
BOXKEEPERS
BOXWALLAHS
BOYCOTTERS
BOYCOTTING
BOYFRIENDS
BOYISHNESS
BOYISHNESSES
BOYSENBERRIES
BOYSENBERRY
BRAAIVLEIS
BRAAIVLEISES
BRABBLEMENT
BRABBLEMENTS
BRACHIATED
BRACHIATES
BRACHIATING
BRACHIATION
BRACHIATIONS
BRACHIATOR
BRACHIATORS
BRACHIOCEPHALIC
BRACHIOPOD
BRACHIOPODS
BRACHIOSAURUS
BRACHIOSAURUSES
BRACHISTOCHRONE
BRACHYAXES
BRACHYAXIS
BRACHYCEPHAL
BRACHYCEPHALIC
BRACHYCEPHALICS
BRACHYCEPHALIES
BRACHYCEPHALISM
BRACHYCEPHALOUS
BRACHYCEPHALS
BRACHYCEPHALY
BRACHYCEROUS
BRACHYDACTYL

BRACHYDACTYLIC
BRACHYDACTYLIES
BRACHYDACTYLISM
BRACHYDACTYLOUS
BRACHYDACTYLY
BRACHYDIAGONAL
BRACHYDIAGONALS
BRACHYDOME
BRACHYDOMES
BRACHYGRAPHIES
BRACHYGRAPHY
BRACHYLOGIES
BRACHYLOGOUS
BRACHYLOGY
BRACHYODONT
BRACHYPINAKOID
BRACHYPINAKOIDS
BRACHYPRISM
BRACHYPRISMS
BRACHYPTERISM
BRACHYPTERISMS
BRACHYPTEROUS
BRACHYTHERAPIES
BRACHYTHERAPY
BRACHYURAL
BRACHYURAN
BRACHYURANS
BRACHYUROUS
BRACKETING
BRACKETINGS
BRACKISHNESS
BRACKISHNESSES
BRACTEATES
BRACTEOLATE
BRACTEOLES
BRADYCARDIA
BRADYCARDIAC
BRADYCARDIAS
BRADYKINESIA
BRADYKINESIAS
BRADYKININ
BRADYKININS
BRADYPEPTIC
BRADYPEPTICS
BRADYSEISM
BRADYSEISMS
BRAGADISME
BRAGADISMES
BRAGGADOCIO
BRAGGADOCIOS
BRAGGADOCIOUS
BRAGGARTISM
BRAGGARTISMS
BRAGGARTLY
BRAGGINGLY
BRAHMANISM
BRAHMANISMS
BRAHMANIST
BRAHMANISTS
BRAHMINISM
BRAHMINISMS
BRAHMINIST
BRAHMINISTS
BRAILLEWRITER
BRAILLEWRITERS
BRAILLISTS

BRAINBOXES
BRAINCASES
BRAINCHILD
BRAINCHILDREN
BRAINFARTS
BRAININESS
BRAININESSES
BRAINLESSLY
BRAINLESSNESS
BRAINLESSNESSES
BRAINPOWER
BRAINPOWERS
BRAINSICKLY
BRAINSICKNESS
BRAINSICKNESSES
BRAINSTEMS
BRAINSTORM
BRAINSTORMED
BRAINSTORMER
BRAINSTORMERS
BRAINSTORMING
BRAINSTORMINGS
BRAINSTORMS
BRAINTEASER
BRAINTEASERS
BRAINWASHED
BRAINWASHER
BRAINWASHERS
BRAINWASHES
BRAINWASHING
BRAINWASHINGS
BRAINWAVES
BRAMBLIEST
BRAMBLINGS
BRANCHERIES
BRANCHIATE
BRANCHIEST
BRANCHINGS
BRANCHIOPOD
BRANCHIOPODS
BRANCHIOSTEGAL
BRANCHLESS
BRANCHLETS
BRANCHLIKE
BRANCHLINE
BRANCHLINES
BRANDERING
BRANDISHED
BRANDISHER
BRANDISHERS
BRANDISHES
BRANDISHING
BRANDLINGS
BRANDRETHS
BRANFULNESS
BRANFULNESSES
BRANGLINGS
BRANKURSINE
BRANKURSINES
BRANNIGANS
BRASHINESS
BRASHINESSES
BRASHNESSES
BRASILEINS
BRASSBOUND
BRASSERIES
BRASSFOUNDER
BRASSFOUNDERS
BRASSFOUNDING
BRASSFOUNDINGS
BRASSICACEOUS
BRASSIERES
BRASSINESS
BRASSINESSES
BRASSWARES
BRATPACKER
BRATPACKERS
BRATTICING
BRATTICINGS
BRATTINESS
BRATTINESSES
BRATTISHED
BRATTISHES
BRATTISHING
BRATTISHINGS
BRATTLINGS
BRATWURSTS
BRAUNCHING
BRAUNSCHWEIGER
BRAUNSCHWEIGERS
BRAVADOING
BRAVENESSES
BRAVISSIMO
BRAWNINESS
BRAWNINESSES
BRAZENNESS
BRAZENNESSES
BRAZENRIES
BRAZIERIES
BRAZILEINS
BRAZILWOOD
BRAZILWOODS
BREADBASKET
BREADBASKETS
BREADBERRIES
BREADBERRY
BREADBOARD
BREADBOARDED
BREADBOARDING
BREADBOARDS
BREADBOXES
BREADCRUMB
BREADCRUMBED
BREADCRUMBING
BREADCRUMBS
BREADFRUIT
BREADFRUITS
BREADHEADS
BREADLINES
BREADROOMS
BREADROOTS
BREADSTICKS
BREADSTUFF
BREADSTUFFS
BREADTHWAYS
BREADTHWISE
BREADWINNER
BREADWINNERS
BREADWINNING
BREADWINNINGS
BREAKABLENESS
BREAKABLENESSES
BREAKABLES
BREAKAWAYS
BREAKBEATS
BREAKDANCE
BREAKDANCED
BREAKDANCER
BREAKDANCERS
BREAKDANCES
BREAKDANCING
BREAKDANCINGS
BREAKDOWNS
BREAKEVENS
BREAKFASTED
BREAKFASTER
BREAKFASTERS
BREAKFASTING
BREAKFASTS
BREAKFRONT
BREAKFRONTS
BREAKPOINT
BREAKPOINTS
BREAKTHROUGH
BREAKTHROUGHS
BREAKTIMES
BREAKWALLS
BREAKWATER
BREAKWATERS
BREASTBONE
BREASTBONES
BREASTFEED
BREASTFEEDING
BREASTFEEDS
BREASTPINS
BREASTPLATE
BREASTPLATES
BREASTPLOUGH
BREASTPLOUGHS
BREASTRAIL
BREASTRAILS
BREASTSTROKE
BREASTSTROKER
BREASTSTROKERS
BREASTSTROKES
BREASTSUMMER
BREASTSUMMERS
BREASTWORK
BREASTWORKS
BREATHABILITIES
BREATHABILITY
BREATHABLE
BREATHALYSE
BREATHALYSED
BREATHALYSER
BREATHALYSERS
BREATHALYSES
BREATHALYSING
BREATHALYZE
BREATHALYZED
BREATHALYZER
BREATHALYZERS
BREATHALYZES
BREATHALYZING
BREATHARIAN
BREATHARIANISM
BREATHARIANISMS
BREATHARIANS
BREATHIEST
BREATHINESS
BREATHINESSES
BREATHINGS
BREATHLESS
BREATHLESSLY
BREATHLESSNESS
BREATHTAKING
BREATHTAKINGLY
BRECCIATED
BRECCIATES
BRECCIATING
BRECCIATION
BRECCIATIONS
BREECHBLOCK
BREECHBLOCKS
BREECHCLOTH
BREECHCLOTHS
BREECHCLOUT
BREECHCLOUTS
BREECHINGS
BREECHLESS
BREECHLOADER
BREECHLOADERS
BREEZELESS
BREEZEWAYS
BREEZINESS
BREEZINESSES
BREMSSTRAHLUNG
BREMSSTRAHLUNGS
BRESSUMMER
BRESSUMMERS
BRETASCHES
BRETTICING
BREUNNERITE
BREUNNERITES
BREVETCIES
BREVETTING
BREVIARIES
BREVIPENNATE
BREWMASTER
BREWMASTERS
BRIARROOTS
BRIARWOODS
BRICABRACS
BRICKCLAYS
BRICKEARTH
BRICKEARTHS
BRICKFIELD
BRICKFIELDER
BRICKFIELDERS
BRICKFIELDS
BRICKKILNS
BRICKLAYER
BRICKLAYERS
BRICKLAYING
BRICKLAYINGS
BRICKMAKER
BRICKMAKERS
BRICKMAKING
BRICKMAKINGS
BRICKSHAPED
BRICKWALLS
BRICKWORKS
BRICKYARDS
BRICOLAGES

RIDECAKES
RIDEGROOM
RIDEGROOMS
RIDEMAIDEN
RIDEMAIDENS
RIDEMAIDS
RIDESMAID
RIDESMAIDS
RIDEWEALTH
RIDEWEALTHS
RIDEWELLS
RIDGEABLE
RIDGEBOARD
RIDGEBOARDS
RIDGEHEAD
RIDGEHEADS
RIDGELESS
RIDGEWORK
RIDGEWORKS
RIDLEWAYS
RIDLEWISE
RIEFCASES
RIEFNESSES
RIERROOTS
RIERWOODS
RIGADIERS
RIGANDAGE
RIGANDAGES
RIGANDINE
RIGANDINES
RIGANDRIES
RIGANTINE
RIGANTINES
RIGHTENED
RIGHTENER
RIGHTENERS
RIGHTENING
RIGHTNESS
RIGHTNESSES
RIGHTSOME
RIGHTWORK
RIGHTWORKS
RILLIANCE
RILLIANCES
RILLIANCIES
RILLIANCY
RILLIANTE
RILLIANTED
RILLIANTINE
RILLIANTINES
RILLIANTING
RILLIANTLY
RILLIANTNESS
RILLIANTNESSES
RILLIANTS
RIMFULLNESS
RIMFULLNESSES
RIMFULNESS
RIMFULNESSES
RIMSTONES
RINELLING
RINELLINGS
RINGDOWNS
RININESSES
RINJARRIES
RINKMANSHIP

BRINKMANSHIPS
BRINKSMANSHIP
BRINKSMANSHIPS
BRIOLETTES
BRIQUETING
BRIQUETTED
BRIQUETTES
BRIQUETTING
BRISKENING
BRISKNESSES
BRISTLECONE
BRISTLECONES
BRISTLELIKE
BRISTLETAIL
BRISTLETAILS
BRISTLIEST
BRISTLINESS
BRISTLINESSES
BRITANNIAS
BRITSCHKAS
BRITTANIAS
BRITTLENESS
BRITTLENESSES
BROADBANDS
BROADBEANS
BROADBILLS
BROADBRIMS
BROADBRUSH
BROADCASTED
BROADCASTER
BROADCASTERS
BROADCASTING
BROADCASTINGS
BROADCASTS
BROADCLOTH
BROADCLOTHS
BROADENERS
BROADENING
BROADLEAVES
BROADLINES
BROADLOOMS
BROADMINDED
BROADMINDEDLY
BROADMINDEDNESS
BROADNESSES
BROADPIECE
BROADPIECES
BROADSCALE
BROADSHEET
BROADSHEETS
BROADSIDED
BROADSIDES
BROADSIDING
BROADSWORD
BROADSWORDS
BROADTAILS
BROBDINGNAGIAN
BROCATELLE
BROCATELLES
BROCHETTES
BROGUERIES
BROIDERERS
BROIDERIES
BROIDERING
BROIDERINGS
BROKENHEARTED

BROKENHEARTEDLY
BROKENNESS
BROKENNESSES
BROKERAGES
BROKERINGS
BROMEGRASS
BROMEGRASSES
BROMELAINS
BROMELIACEOUS
BROMELIADS
BROMEOSINS
BROMHIDROSES
BROMHIDROSIS
BROMIDROSES
BROMIDROSIS
BROMINATED
BROMINATES
BROMINATING
BROMINATION
BROMINATIONS
BROMINISMS
BROMOCRIPTINE
BROMOCRIPTINES
BROMOFORMS
BROMOURACIL
BROMOURACILS
BRONCHIALLY
BRONCHIECTASES
BRONCHIECTASIS
BRONCHIOLAR
BRONCHIOLE
BRONCHIOLES
BRONCHIOLITIS
BRONCHIOLITISES
BRONCHITIC
BRONCHITICS
BRONCHITIS
BRONCHITISES
BRONCHODILATOR
BRONCHODILATORS
BRONCHOGENIC
BRONCHOGRAPHIES
BRONCHOGRAPHY
BRONCHOSCOPE
BRONCHOSCOPES
BRONCHOSCOPIC
BRONCHOSCOPICAL
BRONCHOSCOPIES
BRONCHOSCOPIST
BRONCHOSCOPISTS
BRONCHOSCOPY
BRONCHOSPASM
BRONCHOSPASMS
BRONCHOSPASTIC
BRONCOBUSTER
BRONCOBUSTERS
BRONDYRONS
BRONTOBYTE
BRONTOBYTES
BRONTOSAUR
BRONTOSAURS
BRONTOSAURUS
BRONTOSAURUSES
BRONZIFIED
BRONZIFIES
BRONZIFYING

BROODINESS
BROODINESSES
BROODINGLY
BROODMARES
BROOKLIMES
BROOKWEEDS
BROOMBALLER
BROOMBALLERS
BROOMBALLS
BROOMCORNS
BROOMRAPES
BROOMSTAFF
BROOMSTAFFS
BROOMSTICK
BROOMSTICKS
BROTHERHOOD
BROTHERHOODS
BROTHERING
BROTHERLIKE
BROTHERLINESS
BROTHERLINESSES
BROUGHTASES
BROWALLIAS
BROWBEATEN
BROWBEATER
BROWBEATERS
BROWBEATING
BROWBEATINGS
BROWNFIELD
BROWNFIELDS
BROWNNESSES
BROWNNOSED
BROWNNOSER
BROWNNOSERS
BROWNNOSES
BROWNNOSING
BROWNSHIRT
BROWNSHIRTS
BROWNSTONE
BROWNSTONES
BROWRIDGES
BROWSABLES
BRUCELLOSES
BRUCELLOSIS
BRUGMANSIA
BRUGMANSIAS
BRUMMAGEMS
BRUSCHETTA
BRUSCHETTAS
BRUSCHETTE
BRUSHABILITIES
BRUSHABILITY
BRUSHBACKS
BRUSHFIRES
BRUSHLANDS
BRUSHMARKS
BRUSHWHEEL
BRUSHWHEELS
BRUSHWOODS
BRUSHWORKS
BRUSQUENESS
BRUSQUENESSES
BRUSQUERIE
BRUSQUERIES
BRUTALISATION
BRUTALISATIONS

BRUTALISED
BRUTALISES
BRUTALISING
BRUTALISMS
BRUTALISTS
BRUTALITIES
BRUTALIZATION
BRUTALIZATIONS
BRUTALIZED
BRUTALIZES
BRUTALIZING
BRUTENESSES
BRUTIFYING
BRUTISHNESS
BRUTISHNESSES
BRYOLOGICAL
BRYOLOGIES
BRYOLOGIST
BRYOLOGISTS
BRYOPHYLLUM
BRYOPHYLLUMS
BRYOPHYTES
BRYOPHYTIC
BUBBLEGUMS
BUBBLEHEAD
BUBBLEHEADED
BUBBLEHEADS
BUBONOCELE
BUBONOCELES
BUCCANEERED
BUCCANEERING
BUCCANEERINGS
BUCCANEERISH
BUCCANEERS
BUCCANIERED
BUCCANIERING
BUCCANIERS
BUCCINATOR
BUCCINATORS
BUCCINATORY
BUCELLASES
BUCENTAURS
BUCKBOARDS
BUCKBRUSHES
BUCKETFULS
BUCKETINGS
BUCKETSFUL
BUCKHOUNDS
BUCKJUMPER
BUCKJUMPERS
BUCKJUMPING
BUCKJUMPINGS
BUCKLERING
BUCKRAMING
BUCKSHISHED
BUCKSHISHES
BUCKSHISHING
BUCKSKINNED
BUCKTHORNS
BUCKTOOTHED
BUCKWHEATS
BUCKYBALLS
BUCKYTUBES
BUCOLICALLY
BUDGERIGAR
BUDGERIGARS
BUDGETEERS
BUFFALOBERRIES
BUFFALOBERRY
BUFFALOFISH
BUFFALOFISHES
BUFFALOING
BUFFETINGS
BUFFLEHEAD
BUFFLEHEADS
BUFFOONERIES
BUFFOONERY
BUFFOONISH
BUFOTALINS
BUFOTENINE
BUFOTENINES
BUGGINESSES
BUGLEWEEDS
BUHRSTONES
BUILDDOWNS
BUIRDLIEST
BULBIFEROUS
BULBOSITIES
BULBOUSNESS
BULBOUSNESSES
BULGINESSES
BULKINESSES
BULLBAITING
BULLBAITINGS
BULLBRIERS
BULLDOGGED
BULLDOGGER
BULLDOGGERS
BULLDOGGING
BULLDOGGINGS
BULLDOZERS
BULLDOZING
BULLETINED
BULLETINING
BULLETPROOF
BULLETPROOFED
BULLETPROOFING
BULLETPROOFS
BULLETRIES
BULLETWOOD
BULLETWOODS
BULLFIGHTER
BULLFIGHTERS
BULLFIGHTING
BULLFIGHTINGS
BULLFIGHTS
BULLFINCHES
BULLHEADED
BULLHEADEDLY
BULLHEADEDNESS
BULLIONIST
BULLIONISTS
BULLISHNESS
BULLISHNESSES
BULLMASTIFF
BULLMASTIFFS
BULLNECKED
BULLOCKIES
BULLOCKING
BULLROARER
BULLROARERS
BULLRUSHES
BULLSHITTED
BULLSHITTER
BULLSHITTERS
BULLSHITTING
BULLSHITTINGS
BULLSNAKES
BULLTERRIER
BULLTERRIERS
BULLWADDIE
BULLWADDIES
BULLWHACKED
BULLWHACKING
BULLWHACKS
BULLWHIPPED
BULLWHIPPING
BULLYRAGGED
BULLYRAGGING
BULWADDEES
BULWADDIES
BULWARKING
BUMBAILIFF
BUMBAILIFFS
BUMBERSHOOT
BUMBERSHOOTS
BUMBLEBEES
BUMBLEDOMS
BUMBLINGLY
BUMFREEZER
BUMFREEZERS
BUMFUZZLED
BUMFUZZLES
BUMFUZZLING
BUMMALOTIS
BUMPINESSES
BUMPKINISH
BUMPOLOGIES
BUMPSADAISY
BUMPTIOUSLY
BUMPTIOUSNESS
BUMPTIOUSNESSES
BUMSUCKERS
BUMSUCKING
BUMSUCKINGS
BUNCHBERRIES
BUNCHBERRY
BUNCHGRASS
BUNCHGRASSES
BUNCHINESS
BUNCHINESSES
BUNDOBUSTS
BUNGALOIDS
BUNGLESOME
BUNGLINGLY
BUNKHOUSES
BUOYANCIES
BUOYANTNESS
BUOYANTNESSES
BUPIVACAINE
BUPIVACAINES
BUPRENORPHINE
BUPRENORPHINES
BUPRESTIDS
BURDENSOME
BUREAUCRACIES
BUREAUCRACY
BUREAUCRAT
BUREAUCRATESE
BUREAUCRATESES
BUREAUCRATIC
BUREAUCRATISE
BUREAUCRATISED
BUREAUCRATISES
BUREAUCRATISING
BUREAUCRATISM
BUREAUCRATISMS
BUREAUCRATIST
BUREAUCRATISTS
BUREAUCRATIZE
BUREAUCRATIZED
BUREAUCRATIZES
BUREAUCRATIZING
BUREAUCRATS
BURGEONING
BURGLARIES
BURGLARING
BURGLARIOUS
BURGLARIOUSLY
BURGLARISE
BURGLARISED
BURGLARISES
BURGLARISING
BURGLARIZE
BURGLARIZED
BURGLARIZES
BURGLARIZING
BURGLARPROOF
BURGOMASTER
BURGOMASTERS
BURGUNDIES
BURLADEROS
BURLESQUED
BURLESQUELY
BURLESQUER
BURLESQUERS
BURLESQUES
BURLESQUING
BURLEYCUES
BURLINESSES
BURNETTISE
BURNETTISED
BURNETTISES
BURNETTISING
BURNETTIZE
BURNETTIZED
BURNETTIZES
BURNETTIZING
BURNISHABLE
BURNISHERS
BURNISHING
BURNISHINGS
BURNISHMENT
BURNISHMENTS
BURRAMUNDI
BURRAMUNDIS
BURRAMYSES
BURRAWANGS
BURROWSTOWN
BURROWSTOWNS
BURRSTONES
BURSARSHIP
BURSARSHIPS
BURSERACEOUS

URSICULATE
URSITISES
URTHENING
URTHENSOME
USHBABIES
USHBASHING
USHBASHINGS
USHCRAFTS
USHELLERS
USHELLING
USHELLINGS
USHELWOMAN
USHELWOMEN
USHHAMMER
USHHAMMERS
USHINESSES
USHMANSHIP
USHMANSHIPS
USHMASTER
USHMASTERS
USHRANGER
USHRANGERS
USHRANGING
USHRANGINGS
USHWALKED
USHWALKER
USHWALKERS
USHWALKING
USHWALKINGS
USHWHACKED
USHWHACKER
USHWHACKERS
USHWHACKING
USHWHACKINGS
USHWHACKS
USINESSES
USINESSLIKE
USINESSMAN
USINESSMEN
USINESSPEOPLE
USINESSPERSON
USINESSPERSONS
USINESSWOMAN
USINESSWOMEN
USTICATED
USTICATES
USTICATING
USTINESSES
USTLINGLY
USYBODIED
USYBODIES
USYBODYING
USYNESSES
UTADIENES
UTCHERBIRD
UTCHERBIRDS
UTCHERERS
UTCHERIES
UTCHERING
UTCHERINGS
UTCHNESSES
UTENEDIOIC
UTEONINES
UTLERAGES
UTLERSHIP
UTLERSHIPS
BUTTERBALL
BUTTERBALLS
BUTTERBURS
BUTTERCUPS
BUTTERDOCK
BUTTERDOCKS
BUTTERFATS
BUTTERFINGERED
BUTTERFINGERS
BUTTERFISH
BUTTERFISHES
BUTTERFLIED
BUTTERFLIES
BUTTERFLYER
BUTTERFLYERS
BUTTERFLYING
BUTTERIEST
BUTTERINES
BUTTERINESS
BUTTERINESSES
BUTTERLESS
BUTTERMILK
BUTTERMILKS
BUTTERNUTS
BUTTERSCOTCH
BUTTERSCOTCHES
BUTTERWEED
BUTTERWEEDS
BUTTERWORT
BUTTERWORTS
BUTTINSKIES
BUTTINSKIS
BUTTOCKING
BUTTONBALL
BUTTONBALLS
BUTTONBUSH
BUTTONBUSHES
BUTTONHELD
BUTTONHOLD
BUTTONHOLDING
BUTTONHOLDS
BUTTONHOLE
BUTTONHOLED
BUTTONHOLER
BUTTONHOLERS
BUTTONHOLES
BUTTONHOLING
BUTTONHOOK
BUTTONHOOKED
BUTTONHOOKING
BUTTONHOOKS
BUTTONLESS
BUTTONMOULD
BUTTONMOULDS
BUTTONWOOD
BUTTONWOODS
BUTTRESSED
BUTTRESSES
BUTTRESSING
BUTTSTOCKS
BUTYLATING
BUTYLATION
BUTYLATIONS
BUTYRACEOUS
BUTYRALDEHYDE
BUTYRALDEHYDES
BUTYROPHENONE
BUTYROPHENONES
BUXOMNESSES
BYPRODUCTS
BYSSACEOUS
BYSSINOSES
BYSSINOSIS
BYSTANDERS
BYTOWNITES

Cc

CABALETTAS
CABALISTIC
CABALISTICAL
CABALLEROS
CABBAGETOWN
CABBAGETOWNS
CABBAGEWORM
CABBAGEWORMS
CABBALISMS
CABBALISTIC
CABBALISTICAL
CABBALISTS
CABDRIVERS
CABINETMAKER
CABINETMAKERS
CABINETMAKING
CABINETMAKINGS
CABINETRIES
CABINETWORK
CABINETWORKS
CABINMATES
CABLECASTED
CABLECASTING
CABLECASTS
CABLEGRAMS
CABLEVISION
CABLEVISIONS
CABRIOLETS
CACAFUEGOS
CACCIATORA
CACCIATORE
CACHAEMIAS
CACHECTICAL
CACHINNATE
CACHINNATED
CACHINNATES
CACHINNATING
CACHINNATION
CACHINNATIONS
CACHINNATORY
CACHOLONGS
CACIQUISMS
CACKERMANDER
CACKERMANDERS
CACKLEBERRIES
CACKLEBERRY
CACODAEMON
CACODAEMONS
CACODEMONIC
CACODEMONS
CACODOXIES
CACOEPISTIC
CACOGASTRIC
CACOGENICS
CACOGRAPHER
CACOGRAPHERS
CACOGRAPHIC
CACOGRAPHICAL
CACOGRAPHIES
CACOGRAPHY
CACOLOGIES
CACOMISTLE
CACOMISTLES
CACOMIXLES
CACONYMIES
CACOPHONIC
CACOPHONICAL
CACOPHONICALLY
CACOPHONIES
CACOPHONIOUS
CACOPHONOUS
CACOPHONOUSLY
CACOTOPIAN
CACOTOPIAS
CACOTROPHIES
CACOTROPHY
CACTACEOUS
CACTOBLASTES
CACTOBLASTIS
CACUMINALS
CACUMINOUS
CADASTRALLY
CADAVERINE
CADAVERINES
CADAVEROUS
CADAVEROUSLY
CADAVEROUSNESS
CADDISFLIES
CADDISHNESS
CADDISHNESSES
CADDISWORM
CADDISWORMS
CADETSHIPS
CADUCITIES
CAECILIANS
CAECITISES
CAENOGENESES
CAENOGENESIS
CAENOGENETIC
CAESALPINOID
CAESAREANS
CAESARIANS
CAESARISMS
CAESAROPAPISM
CAESAROPAPISMS
CAESPITOSE
CAESPITOSELY
CAFETERIAS
CAFETIERES
CAFETORIUM
CAFETORIUMS
CAFFEINATED
CAFFEINISM
CAFFEINISMS
CAGEYNESSES
CAGINESSES
CAGMAGGING
CAGYNESSES
CAILLEACHS
CAILLIACHS
CAINOGENESES
CAINOGENESIS
CAINOGENETIC
CAIRNGORMS
CAJOLEMENT
CAJOLEMENTS
CAJOLERIES
CAJOLINGLY
CAKEWALKED
CAKEWALKER
CAKEWALKERS
CAKEWALKING
CAKINESSES
CALABASHES
CALABOGUSES
CALABOOSES
CALABRESES
CALAMANCOES
CALAMANCOS
CALAMANDER
CALAMANDERS
CALAMARIES
CALAMINING
CALAMITIES
CALAMITOUS
CALAMITOUSLY
CALAMITOUSNESS
CALAMONDIN
CALAMONDINS
CALANDRIAS
CALAVANCES
CALAVERITE

CALAVERITES
CALCAREOUS
CALCAREOUSLY
CALCARIFEROUS
CALCARIFORM
CALCEAMENTA
CALCEAMENTUM
CALCEATING
CALCEDONIES
CALCEDONIO
CALCEDONIOS
CALCEIFORM
CALCEOLARIA
CALCEOLARIAS
CALCEOLATE
CALCICOLES
CALCICOLOUS
CALCIFEROL
CALCIFEROLS
CALCIFEROUS
CALCIFICATION
CALCIFICATIONS
CALCIFUGAL
CALCIFUGES
CALCIFUGOUS
CALCIFYING
CALCIGEROUS
CALCIMINED
CALCIMINES
CALCIMINING
CALCINABLE
CALCINATION
CALCINATIONS
CALCINOSES
CALCINOSIS
CALCITONIN
CALCITONINS
CALCSINTER
CALCSINTERS
CALCULABILITIES
CALCULABILITY
CALCULABLE
CALCULABLY
CALCULATED
CALCULATEDLY
CALCULATEDNESS
CALCULATES
CALCULATING
CALCULATINGLY
CALCULATION
CALCULATIONAL
CALCULATIONS
CALCULATIVE
CALCULATOR
CALCULATORS
CALCULUSES
CALEFACIENT
CALEFACIENTS
CALEFACTION
CALEFACTIONS
CALEFACTIVE
CALEFACTOR
CALEFACTORIES
CALEFACTORS
CALEFACTORY
CALEMBOURS
CALENDARED
CALENDARER
CALENDARERS
CALENDARING
CALENDARISATION
CALENDARISE
CALENDARISED
CALENDARISES
CALENDARISING
CALENDARIST
CALENDARISTS
CALENDARIZATION
CALENDARIZE
CALENDARIZED
CALENDARIZES
CALENDARIZING
CALENDERED
CALENDERER
CALENDERERS
CALENDERING
CALENDERINGS
CALENDRERS
CALENDRICAL
CALENDRIES
CALENDULAS
CALENTURES
CALESCENCE
CALESCENCES
CALFDOZERS
CALIATOURS
CALIBRATED
CALIBRATER
CALIBRATERS
CALIBRATES
CALIBRATING
CALIBRATION
CALIBRATIONS
CALIBRATOR
CALIBRATORS
CALIDITIES
CALIFORNIUM
CALIFORNIUMS
CALIGINOSITIES
CALIGINOSITY
CALIGINOUS
CALIOLOGIES
CALIPASHES
CALIPERING
CALIPHATES
CALISTHENIC
CALISTHENICS
CALLBOARDS
CALLIATURE
CALLIATURES
CALLIDITIES
CALLIGRAMME
CALLIGRAMMES
CALLIGRAMS
CALLIGRAPHER
CALLIGRAPHERS
CALLIGRAPHIC
CALLIGRAPHICAL
CALLIGRAPHIES
CALLIGRAPHIST
CALLIGRAPHISTS
CALLIGRAPHY
CALLIOPSIS
CALLIPASHES
CALLIPERED
CALLIPERING
CALLIPYGEAN
CALLIPYGIAN
CALLIPYGOUS
CALLISTEMON
CALLISTEMONS
CALLISTHENIC
CALLISTHENICS
CALLITHUMP
CALLITHUMPIAN
CALLITHUMPS
CALLOSITIES
CALLOUSING
CALLOUSNESS
CALLOUSNESSES
CALLOWNESS
CALLOWNESSES
CALMATIVES
CALMNESSES
CALMODULIN
CALMODULINS
CALMSTONES
CALORESCENCE
CALORESCENCES
CALORESCENT
CALORICALLY
CALORICITIES
CALORICITY
CALORIFICALLY
CALORIFICATION
CALORIFICATIONS
CALORIFIER
CALORIFIERS
CALORIMETER
CALORIMETERS
CALORIMETRIC
CALORIMETRICAL
CALORIMETRIES
CALORIMETRY
CALORISING
CALORIZING
CALOTYPIST
CALOTYPISTS
CALUMNIABLE
CALUMNIATE
CALUMNIATED
CALUMNIATES
CALUMNIATING
CALUMNIATION
CALUMNIATIONS
CALUMNIATOR
CALUMNIATORS
CALUMNIATORY
CALUMNIOUS
CALUMNIOUSLY
CALVADOSES
CALVARIUMS
CALYCANTHEMIES
CALYCANTHEMY
CALYCANTHUS
CALYCANTHUSES
CALYCIFORM
CALYCOIDEOUS
CALYCULATE
CALYPSONIAN
CALYPSONIANS
CALYPTERAS
CALYPTRATE
CALYPTROGEN
CALYPTROGENS
CAMANACHDS
CAMARADERIE
CAMARADERIES
CAMARILLAS
CAMBERINGS
CAMBISTRIES
CAMCORDERS
CAMELBACKS
CAMELEOPARD
CAMELEOPARDS
CAMELHAIRS
CAMELOPARD
CAMELOPARDS
CAMERAPERSON
CAMERAPERSONS
CAMERATION
CAMERATIONS
CAMERAWOMAN
CAMERAWOMEN
CAMERAWORK
CAMERAWORKS
CAMERLENGO
CAMERLENGOS
CAMERLINGO
CAMERLINGOS
CAMIKNICKERS
CAMIKNICKS
CAMISADOES
CAMORRISTA
CAMORRISTI
CAMORRISTS
CAMOUFLAGE
CAMOUFLAGEABLE
CAMOUFLAGED
CAMOUFLAGES
CAMOUFLAGIC
CAMOUFLAGING
CAMOUFLETS
CAMOUFLEUR
CAMOUFLEURS
CAMPAIGNED
CAMPAIGNER
CAMPAIGNERS
CAMPAIGNING
CAMPANEROS
CAMPANIFORM
CAMPANILES
CAMPANISTS
CAMPANOLOGER
CAMPANOLOGERS
CAMPANOLOGICAL
CAMPANOLOGIES
CAMPANOLOGIST
CAMPANOLOGISTS
CAMPANOLOGY
CAMPANULACEOUS
CAMPANULAR
CAMPANULAS
CAMPANULATE

CAMPCRAFTS
CAMPEADORS
CAMPESINOS
CAMPESTRAL
CAMPESTRIAN
CAMPGROUND
CAMPGROUNDS
CAMPHORACEOUS
CAMPHORATE
CAMPHORATED
CAMPHORATES
CAMPHORATING
CAMPIMETRIES
CAMPIMETRY
CAMPINESSES
CAMPNESSES
CAMPODEIDS
CAMPODEIFORM
CAMPSHIRTS
CAMPSTOOLS
CAMPYLOBACTER
CAMPYLOBACTERS
CAMPYLOTROPOUS
CAMSTEERIE
CANALBOATS
CANALICULAR
CANALICULATE
CANALICULATED
CANALICULI
CANALICULUS
CANALISATION
CANALISATIONS
CANALISING
CANALIZATION
CANALIZATIONS
CANALIZING
CANCELABLE
CANCELATION
CANCELATIONS
CANCELEERED
CANCELEERING
CANCELEERS
CANCELIERED
CANCELIERING
CANCELIERS
CANCELLABLE
CANCELLARIAL
CANCELLARIAN
CANCELLARIATE
CANCELLARIATES
CANCELLATE
CANCELLATED
CANCELLATION
CANCELLATIONS
CANCELLERS
CANCELLING
CANCELLOUS
CANCERATED
CANCERATES
CANCERATING
CANCERATION
CANCERATIONS
CANCEROPHOBIA
CANCEROPHOBIAS
CANCEROUSLY
CANCERPHOBIA
CANCERPHOBIAS
CANCIONERO
CANCIONEROS
CANCRIFORM
CANCRIZANS
CANDELABRA
CANDELABRAS
CANDELABRUM
CANDELABRUMS
CANDELILLA
CANDELILLAS
CANDESCENCE
CANDESCENCES
CANDESCENT
CANDESCENTLY
CANDIDACIES
CANDIDATES
CANDIDATESHIP
CANDIDATESHIPS
CANDIDATURE
CANDIDATURES
CANDIDIASES
CANDIDIASIS
CANDIDNESS
CANDIDNESSES
CANDLEBERRIES
CANDLEBERRY
CANDLEFISH
CANDLEFISHES
CANDLEHOLDER
CANDLEHOLDERS
CANDLELIGHT
CANDLELIGHTED
CANDLELIGHTER
CANDLELIGHTERS
CANDLELIGHTS
CANDLENUTS
CANDLEPINS
CANDLEPOWER
CANDLEPOWERS
CANDLESNUFFER
CANDLESNUFFERS
CANDLESTICK
CANDLESTICKS
CANDLEWICK
CANDLEWICKS
CANDLEWOOD
CANDLEWOODS
CANDYFLOSS
CANDYFLOSSES
CANDYGRAMS
CANDYTUFTS
CANEBRAKES
CANEFRUITS
CANEPHORAS
CANEPHORES
CANEPHORUS
CANEPHORUSES
CANESCENCE
CANESCENCES
CANINITIES
CANISTERED
CANISTERING
CANISTERISATION
CANISTERISE
CANISTERISED
CANISTERISES
CANISTERISING
CANISTERIZATION
CANISTERIZE
CANISTERIZED
CANISTERIZES
CANISTERIZING
CANKEREDLY
CANKEREDNESS
CANKEREDNESSES
CANKERWORM
CANKERWORMS
CANNABINOID
CANNABINOIDS
CANNABINOL
CANNABINOLS
CANNABISES
CANNELLINI
CANNELLONI
CANNELURES
CANNIBALISATION
CANNIBALISE
CANNIBALISED
CANNIBALISES
CANNIBALISING
CANNIBALISM
CANNIBALISMS
CANNIBALISTIC
CANNIBALIZATION
CANNIBALIZE
CANNIBALIZED
CANNIBALIZES
CANNIBALIZING
CANNIBALLY
CANNINESSES
CANNISTERS
CANNONADED
CANNONADES
CANNONADING
CANNONBALL
CANNONBALLED
CANNONBALLING
CANNONBALLS
CANNONEERS
CANNONIERS
CANNONRIES
CANNULATED
CANNULATES
CANNULATING
CANNULATION
CANNULATIONS
CANOEWOODS
CANONESSES
CANONICALLY
CANONICALS
CANONICATE
CANONICATES
CANONICITIES
CANONICITY
CANONISATION
CANONISATIONS
CANONISERS
CANONISING
CANONISTIC
CANONIZATION
CANONIZATIONS
CANONIZERS
CANONIZING
CANOODLERS
CANOODLING
CANOPHILIA
CANOPHILIAS
CANOPHILIST
CANOPHILISTS
CANOPHOBIA
CANOPHOBIAS
CANOROUSLY
CANOROUSNESS
CANOROUSNESSES
CANTABANKS
CANTABILES
CANTALOUPE
CANTALOUPES
CANTALOUPS
CANTANKEROUS
CANTANKEROUSLY
CANTATRICE
CANTATRICES
CANTATRICI
CANTERBURIES
CANTERBURY
CANTERBURYS
CANTHARIDAL
CANTHARIDES
CANTHARIDIAN
CANTHARIDIC
CANTHARIDIN
CANTHARIDINE
CANTHARIDINES
CANTHARIDINS
CANTHARIDS
CANTHAXANTHIN
CANTHAXANTHINE
CANTHAXANTHINES
CANTHAXANTHINS
CANTHITISES
CANTICOING
CANTICOYED
CANTICOYING
CANTILENAS
CANTILEVER
CANTILEVERED
CANTILEVERING
CANTILEVERS
CANTILLATE
CANTILLATED
CANTILLATES
CANTILLATING
CANTILLATION
CANTILLATIONS
CANTILLATORY
CANTINESSES
CANTONISATION
CANTONISATIONS
CANTONISED
CANTONISES
CANTONISING
CANTONIZATION
CANTONIZATIONS
CANTONIZED
CANTONIZES
CANTONIZING

ANTONMENT
ANTONMENTS
ANULATING
ANULATION
ANULATIONS
ANVASBACK
ANVASBACKS
ANVASLIKE
ANVASSERS
ANVASSING
ANYONEERS
ANYONINGS
ANZONETTA
ANZONETTAS
ANZONETTE
AOUTCHOUC
AOUTCHOUCS
APABILITIES
APABILITY
APABLENESS
APABLENESSES
APACIOUSLY
APACIOUSNESS
APACIOUSNESSES
APACITANCE
APACITANCES
APACITATE
APACITATED
APACITATES
APACITATING
APACITATION
APACITATIONS
APACITIES
APACITIVE
APACITIVELY
APACITORS
APARISONED
APARISONING
APARISONS
APELLINES
APELLMEISTER
APELLMEISTERS
APERCAILLIE
APERCAILLIES
APERCAILZIE
APERCAILZIES
APERINGLY
APERNOITED
APERNOITIE
APERNOITIES
APERNOITY
APILLACEOUS
APILLAIRE
APILLAIRES
APILLARIES
APILLARITIES
APILLARITY
APILLITIA
APILLITIUM
APILLITIUMS
APITALISATION
APITALISATIONS
APITALISE
APITALISED
APITALISES
APITALISING

CAPITALISM
CAPITALISMS
CAPITALIST
CAPITALISTIC
CAPITALISTS
CAPITALIZATION
CAPITALIZATIONS
CAPITALIZE
CAPITALIZED
CAPITALIZES
CAPITALIZING
CAPITATION
CAPITATIONS
CAPITATIVE
CAPITELLUM
CAPITOLIAN
CAPITOLINE
CAPITULANT
CAPITULANTS
CAPITULARIES
CAPITULARLY
CAPITULARS
CAPITULARY
CAPITULATE
CAPITULATED
CAPITULATES
CAPITULATING
CAPITULATION
CAPITULATIONS
CAPITULATOR
CAPITULATORS
CAPITULATORY
CAPNOMANCIES
CAPNOMANCY
CAPOCCHIAS
CAPODASTRO
CAPODASTROS
CAPONIERES
CAPONISING
CAPONIZING
CAPOTASTOS
CAPPARIDACEOUS
CAPPELLETTI
CAPPERNOITIES
CAPPERNOITY
CAPPUCCINO
CAPPUCCINOS
CAPREOLATE
CAPRICCIOS
CAPRICCIOSO
CAPRICIOUS
CAPRICIOUSLY
CAPRICIOUSNESS
CAPRIFICATION
CAPRIFICATIONS
CAPRIFOILS
CAPRIFOLES
CAPRIFOLIACEOUS
CAPRIFYING
CAPRIOLING
CAPROLACTAM
CAPROLACTAMS
CAPRYLATES
CAPSAICINS
CAPSIZABLE
CAPSOMERES

CAPSULATED
CAPSULATION
CAPSULATIONS
CAPSULISED
CAPSULISES
CAPSULISING
CAPSULIZED
CAPSULIZES
CAPSULIZING
CAPTAINCIES
CAPTAINING
CAPTAINRIES
CAPTAINSHIP
CAPTAINSHIPS
CAPTIONING
CAPTIONLESS
CAPTIOUSLY
CAPTIOUSNESS
CAPTIOUSNESSES
CAPTIVANCE
CAPTIVANCES
CAPTIVATED
CAPTIVATES
CAPTIVATING
CAPTIVATINGLY
CAPTIVATION
CAPTIVATIONS
CAPTIVATOR
CAPTIVATORS
CAPTIVAUNCE
CAPTIVAUNCES
CAPTIVITIES
CAPTOPRILS
CARABINEER
CARABINEERS
CARABINERO
CARABINEROS
CARABINERS
CARABINIER
CARABINIERE
CARABINIERI
CARABINIERS
CARACOLERS
CARACOLING
CARACOLLED
CARACOLLING
CARAGEENAN
CARAGEENANS
CARAMBOLAS
CARAMBOLED
CARAMBOLES
CARAMBOLING
CARAMELISATION
CARAMELISATIONS
CARAMELISE
CARAMELISED
CARAMELISES
CARAMELISING
CARAMELIZATION
CARAMELIZATIONS
CARAMELIZE
CARAMELIZED
CARAMELIZES
CARAMELIZING
CARAMELLED
CARAMELLING

CARANGOIDS
CARAPACIAL
CARAVANCES
CARAVANEER
CARAVANEERS
CARAVANERS
CARAVANETTE
CARAVANETTES
CARAVANING
CARAVANINGS
CARAVANNED
CARAVANNER
CARAVANNERS
CARAVANNING
CARAVANNINGS
CARAVANSARAI
CARAVANSARAIS
CARAVANSARIES
CARAVANSARY
CARAVANSERAI
CARAVANSERAIS
CARAVELLES
CARBACHOLS
CARBAMATES
CARBAMAZEPINE
CARBAMAZEPINES
CARBAMIDES
CARBAMIDINE
CARBAMIDINES
CARBAMOYLS
CARBANIONS
CARBAZOLES
CARBIMAZOLE
CARBIMAZOLES
CARBINEERS
CARBINIERS
CARBOCYCLIC
CARBOHYDRASE
CARBOHYDRASES
CARBOHYDRATE
CARBOHYDRATES
CARBOLATED
CARBOLISED
CARBOLISES
CARBOLISING
CARBOLIZED
CARBOLIZES
CARBOLIZING
CARBONACEOUS
CARBONADES
CARBONADOED
CARBONADOES
CARBONADOING
CARBONADOS
CARBONARAS
CARBONATED
CARBONATES
CARBONATING
CARBONATION
CARBONATIONS
CARBONATITE
CARBONATITES
CARBONETTE
CARBONETTES
CARBONIFEROUS
CARBONISATION

CARBONISATIONS
CARBONISED
CARBONISER
CARBONISERS
CARBONISES
CARBONISING
CARBONIUMS
CARBONIZATION
CARBONIZATIONS
CARBONIZED
CARBONIZER
CARBONIZERS
CARBONIZES
CARBONIZING
CARBONLESS
CARBONNADE
CARBONNADES
CARBONYLATE
CARBONYLATED
CARBONYLATES
CARBONYLATING
CARBONYLATION
CARBONYLATIONS
CARBONYLIC
CARBOXYLASE
CARBOXYLASES
CARBOXYLATE
CARBOXYLATED
CARBOXYLATES
CARBOXYLATING
CARBOXYLATION
CARBOXYLATIONS
CARBOXYLIC
CARBUNCLED
CARBUNCLES
CARBUNCULAR
CARBURATED
CARBURATES
CARBURATING
CARBURATION
CARBURATIONS
CARBURETED
CARBURETER
CARBURETERS
CARBURETING
CARBURETION
CARBURETIONS
CARBURETOR
CARBURETORS
CARBURETTED
CARBURETTER
CARBURETTERS
CARBURETTING
CARBURETTOR
CARBURETTORS
CARBURISATION
CARBURISATIONS
CARBURISED
CARBURISES
CARBURISING
CARBURIZATION
CARBURIZATIONS
CARBURIZED
CARBURIZES
CARBURIZING
CARBYLAMINE
CARBYLAMINES
CARCASSING
CARCINOGEN
CARCINOGENESES
CARCINOGENESIS
CARCINOGENIC
CARCINOGENICITY
CARCINOGENS
CARCINOIDS
CARCINOLOGICAL
CARCINOLOGIES
CARCINOLOGIST
CARCINOLOGISTS
CARCINOLOGY
CARCINOMAS
CARCINOMATA
CARCINOMATOID
CARCINOMATOSES
CARCINOMATOSIS
CARCINOMATOUS
CARCINOSARCOMA
CARCINOSARCOMAS
CARCINOSES
CARCINOSIS
CARDAMINES
CARDBOARDS
CARDBOARDY
CARDCASTLE
CARDCASTLES
CARDHOLDER
CARDHOLDERS
CARDIALGIA
CARDIALGIAS
CARDIALGIC
CARDIALGIES
CARDIGANED
CARDINALATE
CARDINALATES
CARDINALATIAL
CARDINALITIAL
CARDINALITIES
CARDINALITY
CARDINALLY
CARDINALSHIP
CARDINALSHIPS
CARDIOCENTESES
CARDIOCENTESIS
CARDIOGENIC
CARDIOGRAM
CARDIOGRAMS
CARDIOGRAPH
CARDIOGRAPHER
CARDIOGRAPHERS
CARDIOGRAPHIC
CARDIOGRAPHICAL
CARDIOGRAPHIES
CARDIOGRAPHS
CARDIOGRAPHY
CARDIOLOGICAL
CARDIOLOGIES
CARDIOLOGIST
CARDIOLOGISTS
CARDIOLOGY
CARDIOMEGALIES
CARDIOMEGALY
CARDIOMOTOR
CARDIOMYOPATHY
CARDIOPATHIES
CARDIOPATHY
CARDIOPLEGIA
CARDIOPLEGIAS
CARDIOPULMONARY
CARDIOTHORACIC
CARDIOTONIC
CARDIOTONICS
CARDIOVASCULAR
CARDITISES
CARDOPHAGI
CARDOPHAGUS
CARDPHONES
CARDPLAYER
CARDPLAYERS
CARDPUNCHES
CARDSHARPER
CARDSHARPERS
CARDSHARPING
CARDSHARPINGS
CARDSHARPS
CARDUACEOUS
CAREENAGES
CAREERISMS
CAREERISTS
CAREFREENESS
CAREFREENESSES
CAREFULLER
CAREFULLEST
CAREFULNESS
CAREFULNESSES
CAREGIVERS
CAREGIVING
CAREGIVINGS
CARELESSLY
CARELESSNESS
CARELESSNESSES
CARESSINGLY
CARESSINGS
CARESSIVELY
CARETAKERS
CARETAKING
CARETAKINGS
CAREWORKER
CAREWORKERS
CARFUFFLED
CARFUFFLES
CARFUFFLING
CARHOPPING
CARICATURA
CARICATURAL
CARICATURAS
CARICATURE
CARICATURED
CARICATURES
CARICATURING
CARICATURIST
CARICATURISTS
CARILLONED
CARILLONING
CARILLONIST
CARILLONISTS
CARILLONNED
CARILLONNEUR
CARILLONNEURS
CARILLONNING
CARIOGENIC
CARIOSITIES
CARIOUSNESS
CARIOUSNESSES
CARJACKERS
CARJACKING
CARJACKINGS
CARMAGNOLE
CARMAGNOLES
CARMELITES
CARMINATIVE
CARMINATIVES
CARNAHUBAS
CARNALISED
CARNALISES
CARNALISING
CARNALISMS
CARNALISTS
CARNALITIES
CARNALIZED
CARNALIZES
CARNALIZING
CARNALLING
CARNALLITE
CARNALLITES
CARNAPTIOUS
CARNAROLIS
CARNASSIAL
CARNASSIALS
CARNATIONED
CARNATIONS
CARNELIANS
CARNIFEXES
CARNIFICATION
CARNIFICATIONS
CARNIFICIAL
CARNIFYING
CARNITINES
CARNIVALESQUE
CARNIVORES
CARNIVORIES
CARNIVOROUS
CARNIVOROUSLY
CARNIVOROUSNESS
CARNOSAURS
CARNOSITIES
CARNOTITES
CAROLLINGS
CAROMELLED
CAROMELLING
CAROTENOID
CAROTENOIDS
CAROTINOID
CAROTINOIDS
CAROUSINGLY
CARPACCIOS
CARPELLARY
CARPELLATE
CARPELLATES
CARPENTARIA
CARPENTARIAS
CARPENTERED
CARPENTERING
CARPENTERS
CARPENTRIES

ARPETBAGGED
ARPETBAGGER
ARPETBAGGERIES
ARPETBAGGERS
ARPETBAGGERY
ARPETBAGGING
ARPETBAGS
ARPETINGS
ARPETMONGER
ARPETMONGERS
ARPETWEED
ARPETWEEDS
ARPHOLOGIES
ARPHOLOGY
ARPOGONIA
ARPOGONIAL
ARPOGONIUM
ARPOLOGICAL
ARPOLOGIES
ARPOLOGIST
ARPOLOGISTS
ARPOMETACARPI
ARPOMETACARPUS
ARPOOLERS
ARPOOLING
ARPOPHAGOUS
ARPOPHORE
ARPOPHORES
ARPOSPORE
ARPOSPORES
ARRAGEENAN
ARRAGEENANS
ARRAGEENIN
ARRAGEENINS
ARRAGEENS
ARRAGHEEN
ARRAGHEENAN
ARRAGHEENANS
ARRAGHEENIN
ARRAGHEENINS
ARRAGHEENS
ARREFOURS
ARRIAGEABLE
ARRIAGEWAY
ARRIAGEWAYS
ARRITCHES
ARRIWITCHET
ARRIWITCHETS
ARRONADES
ARROTIEST
ARROTTOPPED
ARROTTOPS
ARROUSELS
ARRYBACKS
ARRYFORWARD
ARRYFORWARDS
ARRYOVERS
ARRYTALES
ARSICKNESS
ARSICKNESSES
ARTELISATION
ARTELISATIONS
ARTELISED
ARTELISES
ARTELISING
ARTELISMS
CARTELISTS
CARTELIZATION
CARTELIZATIONS
CARTELIZED
CARTELIZES
CARTELIZING
CARTHAMINE
CARTHAMINES
CARTHORSES
CARTILAGES
CARTILAGINOUS
CARTOGRAMS
CARTOGRAPHER
CARTOGRAPHERS
CARTOGRAPHIC
CARTOGRAPHICAL
CARTOGRAPHIES
CARTOGRAPHY
CARTOLOGICAL
CARTOLOGIES
CARTOMANCIES
CARTOMANCY
CARTONAGES
CARTONNAGE
CARTONNAGES
CARTOONING
CARTOONINGS
CARTOONISH
CARTOONISHLY
CARTOONIST
CARTOONISTS
CARTOONLIKE
CARTOPHILE
CARTOPHILES
CARTOPHILIC
CARTOPHILIES
CARTOPHILIST
CARTOPHILISTS
CARTOPHILY
CARTOPPERS
CARTOUCHES
CARTRIDGES
CARTULARIES
CARTWHEELED
CARTWHEELER
CARTWHEELERS
CARTWHEELING
CARTWHEELS
CARTWRIGHT
CARTWRIGHTS
CARUNCULAR
CARUNCULATE
CARUNCULATED
CARUNCULOUS
CARVACROLS
CARYATIDAL
CARYATIDEAN
CARYATIDES
CARYATIDIC
CARYOPSIDES
CARYOPTERIS
CARYOPTERISES
CASCADURAS
CASCARILLA
CASCARILLAS
CASEATIONS
CASEBEARER
CASEBEARERS
CASEINATES
CASEINOGEN
CASEINOGENS
CASEMAKERS
CASEMENTED
CASEWORKER
CASEWORKERS
CASHIERERS
CASHIERING
CASHIERINGS
CASHIERMENT
CASHIERMENTS
CASHPOINTS
CASINGHEAD
CASINGHEADS
CASKSTANDS
CASSAREEPS
CASSATIONS
CASSEROLED
CASSEROLES
CASSEROLING
CASSIMERES
CASSINGLES
CASSIOPEIUM
CASSIOPEIUMS
CASSITERITE
CASSITERITES
CASSOLETTE
CASSOLETTES
CASSONADES
CASSOULETS
CASSOWARIES
CASSUMUNAR
CASSUMUNARS
CASTABILITIES
CASTABILITY
CASTANOSPERMINE
CASTELLANS
CASTELLATED
CASTELLATION
CASTELLATIONS
CASTELLUMS
CASTIGATED
CASTIGATES
CASTIGATING
CASTIGATION
CASTIGATIONS
CASTIGATOR
CASTIGATORS
CASTIGATORY
CASTOREUMS
CASTRAMETATION
CASTRAMETATIONS
CASTRATERS
CASTRATING
CASTRATION
CASTRATIONS
CASTRATORS
CASTRATORY
CASUALISATION
CASUALISATIONS
CASUALISED
CASUALISES
CASUALISING
CASUALISMS
CASUALIZATION
CASUALIZATIONS
CASUALIZED
CASUALIZES
CASUALIZING
CASUALNESS
CASUALNESSES
CASUALTIES
CASUARINAS
CASUISTICAL
CASUISTICALLY
CASUISTRIES
CATABOLICALLY
CATABOLISE
CATABOLISED
CATABOLISES
CATABOLISING
CATABOLISM
CATABOLISMS
CATABOLITE
CATABOLITES
CATABOLIZE
CATABOLIZED
CATABOLIZES
CATABOLIZING
CATACAUSTIC
CATACAUSTICS
CATACHRESES
CATACHRESIS
CATACHRESTIC
CATACHRESTICAL
CATACLASES
CATACLASIS
CATACLASMIC
CATACLASMS
CATACLASTIC
CATACLINAL
CATACLYSMAL
CATACLYSMIC
CATACLYSMICALLY
CATACLYSMS
CATACOUSTICS
CATACUMBAL
CATADIOPTRIC
CATADIOPTRICAL
CATADROMOUS
CATAFALCOES
CATAFALQUE
CATAFALQUES
CATALECTIC
CATALECTICS
CATALEPSIES
CATALEPTIC
CATALEPTICALLY
CATALEPTICS
CATALLACTIC
CATALLACTICALLY
CATALLACTICS
CATALOGERS
CATALOGING
CATALOGISE
CATALOGISED
CATALOGISES
CATALOGISING
CATALOGIZE

CATALOGIZED
CATALOGIZES
CATALOGIZING
CATALOGUED
CATALOGUER
CATALOGUERS
CATALOGUES
CATALOGUING
CATALOGUISE
CATALOGUISED
CATALOGUISES
CATALOGUISING
CATALOGUIST
CATALOGUISTS
CATALOGUIZE
CATALOGUIZED
CATALOGUIZES
CATALOGUIZING
CATALYSERS
CATALYSING
CATALYTICAL
CATALYTICALLY
CATALYZERS
CATALYZING
CATAMARANS
CATAMENIAL
CATAMOUNTAIN
CATAMOUNTAINS
CATAMOUNTS
CATANANCHE
CATANANCHES
CATAPHONIC
CATAPHONICS
CATAPHORAS
CATAPHORESES
CATAPHORESIS
CATAPHORETIC
CATAPHORIC
CATAPHRACT
CATAPHRACTIC
CATAPHRACTS
CATAPHYLLARY
CATAPHYLLS
CATAPHYSICAL
CATAPLASIA
CATAPLASIAS
CATAPLASMS
CATAPLASTIC
CATAPLECTIC
CATAPLEXIES
CATAPULTED
CATAPULTIC
CATAPULTIER
CATAPULTIERS
CATAPULTING
CATARACTOUS
CATARRHALLY
CATARRHINE
CATARRHINES
CATARRHOUS
CATASTASES
CATASTASIS
CATASTROPHE
CATASTROPHES
CATASTROPHIC
CATASTROPHISM
CATASTROPHISMS
CATASTROPHIST
CATASTROPHISTS
CATATONIAS
CATATONICALLY
CATATONICS
CATATONIES
CATCALLERS
CATCALLING
CATCHCRIES
CATCHFLIES
CATCHINESS
CATCHINESSES
CATCHMENTS
CATCHPENNIES
CATCHPENNY
CATCHPHRASE
CATCHPHRASES
CATCHPOLES
CATCHPOLLS
CATCHWATER
CATCHWEEDS
CATCHWEIGHT
CATCHWORDS
CATECHESES
CATECHESIS
CATECHETIC
CATECHETICAL
CATECHETICALLY
CATECHETICS
CATECHISATION
CATECHISATIONS
CATECHISED
CATECHISER
CATECHISERS
CATECHISES
CATECHISING
CATECHISINGS
CATECHISMAL
CATECHISMS
CATECHISTIC
CATECHISTICAL
CATECHISTICALLY
CATECHISTS
CATECHIZATION
CATECHIZATIONS
CATECHIZED
CATECHIZER
CATECHIZERS
CATECHIZES
CATECHIZING
CATECHIZINGS
CATECHOLAMINE
CATECHOLAMINES
CATECHUMEN
CATECHUMENAL
CATECHUMENATE
CATECHUMENATES
CATECHUMENICAL
CATECHUMENISM
CATECHUMENISMS
CATECHUMENS
CATECHUMENSHIP
CATECHUMENSHIPS
CATEGOREMATIC
CATEGORIAL
CATEGORIALLY
CATEGORICAL
CATEGORICALLY
CATEGORICALNESS
CATEGORIES
CATEGORISATION
CATEGORISATIONS
CATEGORISE
CATEGORISED
CATEGORISES
CATEGORISING
CATEGORIST
CATEGORISTS
CATEGORIZATION
CATEGORIZATIONS
CATEGORIZE
CATEGORIZED
CATEGORIZES
CATEGORIZING
CATENACCIO
CATENACCIOS
CATENARIAN
CATENARIES
CATENATING
CATENATION
CATENATIONS
CATENULATE
CATERCORNER
CATERCORNERED
CATERESSES
CATERPILLAR
CATERPILLARS
CATERWAULED
CATERWAULER
CATERWAULERS
CATERWAULING
CATERWAULINGS
CATERWAULS
CATFACINGS
CATHARISED
CATHARISES
CATHARISING
CATHARIZED
CATHARIZES
CATHARIZING
CATHARTICAL
CATHARTICALLY
CATHARTICS
CATHECTING
CATHEDRALS
CATHEDRATIC
CATHEPSINS
CATHETERISATION
CATHETERISE
CATHETERISED
CATHETERISES
CATHETERISING
CATHETERISM
CATHETERISMS
CATHETERIZATION
CATHETERIZE
CATHETERIZED
CATHETERIZES
CATHETERIZING
CATHETOMETER
CATHETOMETERS
CATHETUSES
CATHODALLY
CATHODICAL
CATHODICALLY
CATHODOGRAPH
CATHODOGRAPHER
CATHODOGRAPHERS
CATHODOGRAPHIES
CATHODOGRAPHS
CATHODOGRAPHY
CATHOLICALLY
CATHOLICATE
CATHOLICATES
CATHOLICISATION
CATHOLICISE
CATHOLICISED
CATHOLICISES
CATHOLICISING
CATHOLICISM
CATHOLICISMS
CATHOLICITIES
CATHOLICITY
CATHOLICIZATION
CATHOLICIZE
CATHOLICIZED
CATHOLICIZES
CATHOLICIZING
CATHOLICLY
CATHOLICOI
CATHOLICON
CATHOLICONS
CATHOLICOS
CATHOLICOSES
CATHOLYTES
CATILINARIAN
CATIONICALLY
CATNAPPERS
CATNAPPING
CATOPTRICAL
CATOPTRICS
CATTINESSES
CATTISHNESS
CATTISHNESSES
CAUCHEMARS
CAUCUSSING
CAUDATIONS
CAUDILLISMO
CAUDILLISMOS
CAULESCENT
CAULICOLOUS
CAULICULATE
CAULICULUS
CAULICULUSES
CAULIFLORIES
CAULIFLOROUS
CAULIFLORY
CAULIFLOWER
CAULIFLOWERET
CAULIFLOWERETS
CAULIFLOWERS
CAULIGENOUS
CAUMSTONES
CAUSABILITIES
CAUSABILITY
CAUSALGIAS
CAUSALITIES

AUSATIONAL
AUSATIONISM
AUSATIONISMS
AUSATIONIST
AUSATIONISTS
AUSATIONS
AUSATIVELY
AUSATIVENESS
AUSATIVENESSES
AUSATIVES
AUSELESSLY
AUSELESSNESS
AUSELESSNESSES
AUSEWAYED
AUSEWAYING
AUSTICALLY
AUSTICITIES
AUSTICITY
AUSTICNESS
AUSTICNESSES
AUTERANTS
AUTERISATION
AUTERISATIONS
AUTERISED
AUTERISES
AUTERISING
AUTERISMS
AUTERIZATION
AUTERIZATIONS
AUTERIZED
AUTERIZES
AUTERIZING
AUTIONARY
AUTIONERS
AUTIONING
AUTIONRIES
AUTIOUSLY
AUTIOUSNESS
AUTIOUSNESSES
AVALCADED
AVALCADES
AVALCADING
AVALIERED
AVALIERING
AVALIERISH
AVALIERISM
AVALIERISMS
AVALIERLY
AVALLETTI
AVALRYMAN
AVALRYMEN
AVEFISHES
AVENDISHES
AVERNICOLOUS
AVERNOUSLY
AVERNULOUS
AVILLATION
AVILLATIONS
AVILLINGS
AVITATING
AVITATION
AVITATIONS
EANOTHUSES
EASEFIRES
EASELESSLY
EASELESSNESS
CEASELESSNESSES
CEBADILLAS
CECUTIENCIES
CECUTIENCY
CEDARBIRDS
CEDARWOODS
CEDRELACEOUS
CEILOMETER
CEILOMETERS
CELANDINES
CELEBRANTS
CELEBRATED
CELEBRATEDNESS
CELEBRATES
CELEBRATING
CELEBRATION
CELEBRATIONS
CELEBRATIVE
CELEBRATOR
CELEBRATORS
CELEBRATORY
CELEBRITIES
CELERITIES
CELESTIALLY
CELESTIALS
CELESTINES
CELESTITES
CELIBACIES
CELIBATARIAN
CELLARAGES
CELLARETTE
CELLARETTES
CELLARISTS
CELLARWAYS
CELLBLOCKS
CELLENTANI
CELLENTANIS
CELLIFEROUS
CELLOBIOSE
CELLOBIOSES
CELLOIDINS
CELLOPHANE
CELLOPHANES
CELLPHONES
CELLULARITIES
CELLULARITY
CELLULASES
CELLULATED
CELLULIFEROUS
CELLULITES
CELLULITIS
CELLULITISES
CELLULOIDS
CELLULOLYTIC
CELLULOSES
CELLULOSIC
CELLULOSICS
CELSITUDES
CEMBALISTS
CEMENTATION
CEMENTATIONS
CEMENTATORY
CEMENTITES
CEMENTITIOUS
CEMETERIES
CENESTHESES
CENESTHESIA
CENESTHESIAS
CENESTHESIS
CENESTHETIC
CENOBITICAL
CENOGENESES
CENOGENESIS
CENOGENETIC
CENOGENETICALLY
CENOSPECIES
CENOTAPHIC
CENSORABLE
CENSORIOUS
CENSORIOUSLY
CENSORIOUSNESS
CENSORSHIP
CENSORSHIPS
CENSURABILITIES
CENSURABILITY
CENSURABLE
CENSURABLENESS
CENSURABLY
CENTAUREAS
CENTAURIAN
CENTAURIES
CENTENARIAN
CENTENARIANISM
CENTENARIANISMS
CENTENARIANS
CENTENARIES
CENTENIERS
CENTENNIAL
CENTENNIALLY
CENTENNIALS
CENTERBOARD
CENTERBOARDS
CENTEREDNESS
CENTEREDNESSES
CENTERFOLD
CENTERFOLDS
CENTERINGS
CENTERLESS
CENTERLINE
CENTERLINES
CENTERPIECE
CENTERPIECES
CENTESIMAL
CENTESIMALLY
CENTESIMALS
CENTESIMOS
CENTIGRADE
CENTIGRAMME
CENTIGRAMMES
CENTIGRAMS
CENTILITER
CENTILITERS
CENTILITRE
CENTILITRES
CENTILLION
CENTILLIONS
CENTILLIONTH
CENTILLIONTHS
CENTIMETER
CENTIMETERS
CENTIMETRE
CENTIMETRES
CENTIMETRIC
CENTIMORGAN
CENTIMORGANS
CENTINELLS
CENTIPEDES
CENTIPOISE
CENTIPOISES
CENTONELLS
CENTONISTS
CENTRALEST
CENTRALISATION
CENTRALISATIONS
CENTRALISE
CENTRALISED
CENTRALISER
CENTRALISERS
CENTRALISES
CENTRALISING
CENTRALISM
CENTRALISMS
CENTRALIST
CENTRALISTIC
CENTRALISTS
CENTRALITIES
CENTRALITY
CENTRALIZATION
CENTRALIZATIONS
CENTRALIZE
CENTRALIZED
CENTRALIZER
CENTRALIZERS
CENTRALIZES
CENTRALIZING
CENTREBOARD
CENTREBOARDS
CENTREFOLD
CENTREFOLDS
CENTREINGS
CENTRELINE
CENTRELINES
CENTREPIECE
CENTREPIECES
CENTRICALLY
CENTRICALNESS
CENTRICALNESSES
CENTRICITIES
CENTRICITY
CENTRIFUGAL
CENTRIFUGALISE
CENTRIFUGALISED
CENTRIFUGALISES
CENTRIFUGALIZE
CENTRIFUGALIZED
CENTRIFUGALIZES
CENTRIFUGALLY
CENTRIFUGALS
CENTRIFUGATION
CENTRIFUGATIONS
CENTRIFUGE
CENTRIFUGED
CENTRIFUGENCE
CENTRIFUGENCES
CENTRIFUGES
CENTRIFUGING
CENTRIOLES
CENTRIPETAL

CENTRIPETALISM
CENTRIPETALISMS
CENTRIPETALLY
CENTROBARIC
CENTROCLINAL
CENTROIDAL
CENTROLECITHAL
CENTROMERE
CENTROMERES
CENTROMERIC
CENTROSOME
CENTROSOMES
CENTROSOMIC
CENTROSPHERE
CENTROSPHERES
CENTROSYMMETRIC
CENTUMVIRATE
CENTUMVIRATES
CENTUMVIRI
CENTUPLICATE
CENTUPLICATED
CENTUPLICATES
CENTUPLICATING
CENTUPLICATION
CENTUPLICATIONS
CENTUPLING
CENTURIATION
CENTURIATIONS
CENTURIATOR
CENTURIATORS
CENTURIONS
CEPHALAGRA
CEPHALAGRAS
CEPHALALGIA
CEPHALALGIAS
CEPHALALGIC
CEPHALEXIN
CEPHALEXINS
CEPHALICALLY
CEPHALISATION
CEPHALISATIONS
CEPHALITIS
CEPHALITISES
CEPHALIZATION
CEPHALIZATIONS
CEPHALOCELE
CEPHALOCELES
CEPHALOCHORDATE
CEPHALOMETER
CEPHALOMETERS
CEPHALOMETRIC
CEPHALOMETRIES
CEPHALOMETRY
CEPHALOPOD
CEPHALOPODAN
CEPHALOPODANS
CEPHALOPODIC
CEPHALOPODOUS
CEPHALOPODS
CEPHALORIDINE
CEPHALORIDINES
CEPHALOSPORIN
CEPHALOSPORINS
CEPHALOTHIN
CEPHALOTHINS
CEPHALOTHORACES
CEPHALOTHORACIC
CEPHALOTHORAX
CEPHALOTHORAXES
CEPHALOTOMIES
CEPHALOTOMY
CERAMICIST
CERAMICISTS
CERAMOGRAPHIES
CERAMOGRAPHY
CERARGYRITE
CERARGYRITES
CERASTIUMS
CERATITISES
CERATODUSES
CERATOPSIAN
CERATOPSIANS
CERATOPSID
CERATOPSIDS
CERCARIANS
CERCOPITHECID
CERCOPITHECIDS
CERCOPITHECOID
CERCOPITHECOIDS
CEREALISTS
CEREBELLAR
CEREBELLIC
CEREBELLOUS
CEREBELLUM
CEREBELLUMS
CEREBRALISM
CEREBRALISMS
CEREBRALIST
CEREBRALISTS
CEREBRALLY
CEREBRATED
CEREBRATES
CEREBRATING
CEREBRATION
CEREBRATIONS
CEREBRIFORM
CEREBRITIS
CEREBRITISES
CEREBROSIDE
CEREBROSIDES
CEREBROSPINAL
CEREBROTONIA
CEREBROTONIAS
CEREBROTONIC
CEREBROVASCULAR
CERECLOTHS
CEREMONIAL
CEREMONIALISM
CEREMONIALISMS
CEREMONIALIST
CEREMONIALISTS
CEREMONIALLY
CEREMONIALS
CEREMONIES
CEREMONIOUS
CEREMONIOUSLY
CEREMONIOUSNESS
CERIFEROUS
CEROGRAPHIC
CEROGRAPHICAL
CEROGRAPHIES
CEROGRAPHIST
CEROGRAPHISTS
CEROGRAPHS
CEROGRAPHY
CEROMANCIES
CEROPLASTIC
CEROPLASTICS
CERTAINEST
CERTAINTIES
CERTIFIABLE
CERTIFIABLY
CERTIFICATE
CERTIFICATED
CERTIFICATES
CERTIFICATING
CERTIFICATION
CERTIFICATIONS
CERTIFICATORIES
CERTIFICATORY
CERTIFIERS
CERTIFYING
CERTIORARI
CERTIORARIS
CERTITUDES
CERULOPLASMIN
CERULOPLASMINS
CERUMINOUS
CERUSSITES
CERVELASES
CERVICITIS
CERVICITISES
CERVICOGRAPHIES
CERVICOGRAPHY
CESAREVICH
CESAREVICHES
CESAREVITCH
CESAREVITCHES
CESAREVNAS
CESAREWICH
CESAREWICHES
CESAREWITCH
CESAREWITCHES
CESPITOSELY
CESSATIONS
CESSIONARIES
CESSIONARY
CESTOIDEAN
CESTOIDEANS
CETEOSAURUS
CETEOSAURUSES
CETOLOGICAL
CETOLOGIES
CETOLOGIST
CETOLOGISTS
CETRIMIDES
CEVADILLAS
CEYLANITES
CEYLONITES
CHABAZITES
CHAENOMELES
CHAENOMELESES
CHAETIFEROUS
CHAETODONS
CHAETOGNATH
CHAETOGNATHS
CHAETOPODS
CHAFFERERS
CHAFFERIES
CHAFFERING
CHAFFINCHES
CHAFFINGLY
CHAGRINING
CHAGRINNED
CHAGRINNING
CHAINBRAKE
CHAINBRAKES
CHAINFALLS
CHAINPLATE
CHAINPLATES
CHAINSAWED
CHAINSAWING
CHAINSHOTS
CHAINSTITCH
CHAINSTITCHES
CHAINWHEEL
CHAINWHEELS
CHAINWORKS
CHAIRBORNE
CHAIRBOUND
CHAIRLIFTS
CHAIRMANED
CHAIRMANING
CHAIRMANNED
CHAIRMANNING
CHAIRMANSHIP
CHAIRMANSHIPS
CHAIRPERSON
CHAIRPERSONS
CHAIRWOMAN
CHAIRWOMEN
CHAISELESS
CHAKALAKAS
CHALAZIONS
CHALAZOGAMIC
CHALAZOGAMIES
CHALAZOGAMY
CHALCANTHITE
CHALCANTHITES
CHALCEDONIC
CHALCEDONIES
CHALCEDONY
CHALCEDONYX
CHALCEDONYXES
CHALCOCITE
CHALCOCITES
CHALCOGENIDE
CHALCOGENIDES
CHALCOGENS
CHALCOGRAPHER
CHALCOGRAPHERS
CHALCOGRAPHIC
CHALCOGRAPHICAL
CHALCOGRAPHIES
CHALCOGRAPHIST
CHALCOGRAPHISTS
CHALCOGRAPHY
CHALCOLITHIC
CHALCOPYRITE
CHALCOPYRITES
CHALICOTHERE
CHALICOTHERES
CHALKBOARD
CHALKBOARDS

HALKFACES
HALKINESS
HALKINESSES
HALKSTONE
HALKSTONES
HALLANING
HALLENGEABLE
HALLENGED
HALLENGER
HALLENGERS
HALLENGES
HALLENGING
HALLENGINGLY
HALUMEAUS
HALUMEAUX
HALYBEATE
HALYBEATES
HALYBITES
HAMAELEON
HAMAELEONS
HAMAEPHYTE
HAMAEPHYTES
HAMBERERS
HAMBERHAND
HAMBERHANDS
HAMBERING
HAMBERINGS
HAMBERLAIN
HAMBERLAINS
HAMBERLAINSHIP
HAMBERMAID
HAMBERMAIDS
HAMBERPOT
HAMBERPOTS
HAMBRANLE
HAMBRANLES
HAMELEONIC
HAMELEONLIKE
HAMELEONS
HAMFERERS
HAMFERING
HAMFRAINS
HAMOISING
HAMOMILES
HAMPAGNES
HAMPAIGNS
HAMPERTIES
HAMPERTOUS
HAMPIGNON
HAMPIGNONS
HAMPIONED
HAMPIONESS
HAMPIONESSES
HAMPIONING
HAMPIONSHIP
HAMPIONSHIPS
HAMPLEVES
HANCELESS
HANCELLERIES
HANCELLERY
HANCELLOR
HANCELLORIES
HANCELLORS
HANCELLORSHIP
HANCELLORSHIPS
HANCELLORY

CHANCERIES
CHANCINESS
CHANCINESSES
CHANCROIDAL
CHANCROIDS
CHANDELIER
CHANDELIERED
CHANDELIERS
CHANDELLED
CHANDELLES
CHANDELLING
CHANDLERIES
CHANDLERING
CHANDLERINGS
CHANDLERLY
CHANGEABILITIES
CHANGEABILITY
CHANGEABLE
CHANGEABLENESS
CHANGEABLY
CHANGEFULLY
CHANGEFULNESS
CHANGEFULNESSES
CHANGELESS
CHANGELESSLY
CHANGELESSNESS
CHANGELING
CHANGELINGS
CHANGEOVER
CHANGEOVERS
CHANGEROUND
CHANGEROUNDS
CHANNELERS
CHANNELING
CHANNELISATION
CHANNELISATIONS
CHANNELISE
CHANNELISED
CHANNELISES
CHANNELISING
CHANNELIZATION
CHANNELIZATIONS
CHANNELIZE
CHANNELIZED
CHANNELIZES
CHANNELIZING
CHANNELLED
CHANNELLER
CHANNELLERS
CHANNELLING
CHANSONETTE
CHANSONETTES
CHANSONNIER
CHANSONNIERS
CHANTARELLE
CHANTARELLES
CHANTECLER
CHANTECLERS
CHANTERELLE
CHANTERELLES
CHANTEUSES
CHANTICLEER
CHANTICLEERS
CHANTINGLY
CHANTRESSES
CHANUKIAHS

CHAOLOGIES
CHAOLOGIST
CHAOLOGISTS
CHAOTICALLY
CHAPARAJOS
CHAPAREJOS
CHAPARRALS
CHAPATTIES
CHAPELRIES
CHAPERONAGE
CHAPERONAGES
CHAPERONED
CHAPERONES
CHAPERONING
CHAPFALLEN
CHAPLAINCIES
CHAPLAINCY
CHAPLAINRIES
CHAPLAINRY
CHAPLAINSHIP
CHAPLAINSHIPS
CHAPMANSHIP
CHAPMANSHIPS
CHAPPESSES
CHAPRASSIES
CHAPRASSIS
CHAPSTICKS
CHAPTALISATION
CHAPTALISATIONS
CHAPTALISE
CHAPTALISED
CHAPTALISES
CHAPTALISING
CHAPTALIZATION
CHAPTALIZATIONS
CHAPTALIZE
CHAPTALIZED
CHAPTALIZES
CHAPTALIZING
CHAPTERHOUSE
CHAPTERHOUSES
CHAPTERING
CHARABANCS
CHARACINOID
CHARACTERED
CHARACTERFUL
CHARACTERIES
CHARACTERING
CHARACTERISABLE
CHARACTERISE
CHARACTERISED
CHARACTERISER
CHARACTERISERS
CHARACTERISES
CHARACTERISING
CHARACTERISM
CHARACTERISMS
CHARACTERISTIC
CHARACTERISTICS
CHARACTERIZABLE
CHARACTERIZE
CHARACTERIZED
CHARACTERIZER
CHARACTERIZERS
CHARACTERIZES
CHARACTERIZING

CHARACTERLESS
CHARACTEROLOGY
CHARACTERS
CHARACTERY
CHARBROILED
CHARBROILER
CHARBROILERS
CHARBROILING
CHARBROILS
CHARCOALED
CHARCOALING
CHARCUTERIE
CHARCUTERIES
CHARDONNAY
CHARDONNAYS
CHARGEABILITIES
CHARGEABILITY
CHARGEABLE
CHARGEABLENESS
CHARGEABLY
CHARGEHAND
CHARGEHANDS
CHARGELESS
CHARGENURSE
CHARGENURSES
CHARGESHEET
CHARGESHEETS
CHARGRILLED
CHARGRILLING
CHARGRILLS
CHARINESSES
CHARIOTEER
CHARIOTEERED
CHARIOTEERING
CHARIOTEERS
CHARIOTING
CHARISMATA
CHARISMATIC
CHARISMATICS
CHARITABLE
CHARITABLENESS
CHARITABLY
CHARIVARIED
CHARIVARIING
CHARIVARIS
CHARLADIES
CHARLATANIC
CHARLATANICAL
CHARLATANISM
CHARLATANISMS
CHARLATANISTIC
CHARLATANRIES
CHARLATANRY
CHARLATANS
CHARLESTON
CHARLESTONED
CHARLESTONING
CHARLESTONS
CHARLOTTES
CHARMEUSES
CHARMINGER
CHARMINGEST
CHARMINGLY
CHARMLESSLY
CHARMONIUM
CHAROSETHS

CHARTACEOUS
CHARTERERS
CHARTERING
CHARTERPARTIES
CHARTERPARTY
CHARTHOUSE
CHARTHOUSES
CHARTOGRAPHER
CHARTOGRAPHERS
CHARTOGRAPHIC
CHARTOGRAPHICAL
CHARTOGRAPHIES
CHARTOGRAPHY
CHARTREUSE
CHARTREUSES
CHARTULARIES
CHARTULARY
CHASEPORTS
CHASMOGAMIC
CHASMOGAMIES
CHASMOGAMOUS
CHASMOGAMY
CHASSEPOTS
CHASTENERS
CHASTENESS
CHASTENESSES
CHASTENING
CHASTENINGLY
CHASTENMENT
CHASTENMENTS
CHASTISABLE
CHASTISEMENT
CHASTISEMENTS
CHASTISERS
CHASTISING
CHASTITIES
CHATEAUBRIAND
CHATEAUBRIANDS
CHATELAINE
CHATELAINES
CHATELAINS
CHATOYANCE
CHATOYANCES
CHATOYANCIES
CHATOYANCY
CHATOYANTS
CHATTERATI
CHATTERBOX
CHATTERBOXES
CHATTERERS
CHATTERING
CHATTERINGS
CHATTINESS
CHATTINESSES
CHAUDFROID
CHAUDFROIDS
CHAUFFEURED
CHAUFFEURING
CHAUFFEURS
CHAUFFEUSE
CHAUFFEUSED
CHAUFFEUSES
CHAUFFEUSING
CHAULMOOGRA
CHAULMOOGRAS
CHAULMUGRA
CHAULMUGRAS
CHAUNTRESS
CHAUNTRESSES
CHAUNTRIES
CHAUSSURES
CHAUTAUQUA
CHAUTAUQUAS
CHAUVINISM
CHAUVINISMS
CHAUVINIST
CHAUVINISTIC
CHAUVINISTS
CHAVENDERS
CHAVTASTIC
CHAWBACONS
CHEAPENERS
CHEAPENING
CHEAPISHLY
CHEAPJACKS
CHEAPNESSES
CHEAPSKATE
CHEAPSKATES
CHEATERIES
CHEATINGLY
CHECHAKOES
CHECHAQUOS
CHECKBOOKS
CHECKCLERK
CHECKCLERKS
CHECKERBERRIES
CHECKERBERRY
CHECKERBLOOM
CHECKERBLOOMS
CHECKERBOARD
CHECKERBOARDS
CHECKERING
CHECKLATON
CHECKLATONS
CHECKLISTED
CHECKLISTING
CHECKLISTS
CHECKMARKED
CHECKMARKING
CHECKMARKS
CHECKMATED
CHECKMATES
CHECKMATING
CHECKPOINT
CHECKPOINTS
CHECKRAILS
CHECKREINS
CHECKROOMS
CHECKROWED
CHECKROWING
CHECKWEIGHER
CHECKWEIGHERS
CHEECHAKOES
CHEECHAKOS
CHEECHALKO
CHEECHALKOES
CHEECHALKOS
CHEEKBONES
CHEEKINESS
CHEEKINESSES
CHEEKPIECE
CHEEKPIECES
CHEEKPOUCH
CHEEKPOUCHES
CHEEKTEETH
CHEEKTOOTH
CHEERFULLER
CHEERFULLEST
CHEERFULLY
CHEERFULNESS
CHEERFULNESSES
CHEERINESS
CHEERINESSES
CHEERINGLY
CHEERISHNESS
CHEERISHNESSES
CHEERLEADER
CHEERLEADERS
CHEERLEADING
CHEERLEADS
CHEERLESSLY
CHEERLESSNESS
CHEERLESSNESSES
CHEESEBOARD
CHEESEBOARDS
CHEESEBURGER
CHEESEBURGERS
CHEESECAKE
CHEESECAKES
CHEESECLOTH
CHEESECLOTHS
CHEESECUTTER
CHEESECUTTERS
CHEESEHOPPER
CHEESEHOPPERS
CHEESEMITE
CHEESEMITES
CHEESEMONGER
CHEESEMONGERS
CHEESEPARER
CHEESEPARERS
CHEESEPARING
CHEESEPARINGS
CHEESEPRESS
CHEESEPRESSES
CHEESETASTER
CHEESETASTERS
CHEESEVATS
CHEESEWIRE
CHEESEWIRES
CHEESEWOOD
CHEESEWOODS
CHEESEWRING
CHEESEWRINGS
CHEESINESS
CHEESINESSES
CHEILITISES
CHELASHIPS
CHELATABLE
CHELATIONS
CHELICERAE
CHELICERAL
CHELICERATE
CHELICERATES
CHELIFEROUS
CHELONIANS
CHELUVIATION
CHELUVIATIONS
CHEMAUTOTROPH
CHEMAUTOTROPHIC
CHEMAUTOTROPHS
CHEMIATRIC
CHEMICALLY
CHEMICKING
CHEMIOSMOSES
CHEMIOSMOSIS
CHEMIOSMOTIC
CHEMISETTE
CHEMISETTES
CHEMISORBED
CHEMISORBING
CHEMISORBS
CHEMISORPTION
CHEMISORPTIONS
CHEMISTRIES
CHEMITYPES
CHEMITYPIES
CHEMOATTRACTANT
CHEMOAUTOTROPH
CHEMOAUTOTROPHS
CHEMOAUTOTROPHY
CHEMOAUTROPH
CHEMOAUTROPHS
CHEMOCEPTOR
CHEMOCEPTORS
CHEMOKINES
CHEMOKINESES
CHEMOKINESIS
CHEMOLITHOTROPH
CHEMONASTIES
CHEMONASTY
CHEMOPSYCHIATRY
CHEMORECEPTION
CHEMORECEPTIONS
CHEMORECEPTIVE
CHEMORECEPTOR
CHEMORECEPTORS
CHEMOSMOSES
CHEMOSMOSIS
CHEMOSMOTIC
CHEMOSORBED
CHEMOSORBING
CHEMOSORBS
CHEMOSPHERE
CHEMOSPHERES
CHEMOSPHERIC
CHEMOSTATS
CHEMOSURGERIES
CHEMOSURGERY
CHEMOSURGICAL
CHEMOSYNTHESES
CHEMOSYNTHESIS
CHEMOSYNTHETIC
CHEMOTACTIC
CHEMOTACTICALLY
CHEMOTAXES
CHEMOTAXIS
CHEMOTAXONOMIC
CHEMOTAXONOMIES
CHEMOTAXONOMIST
CHEMOTAXONOMY
CHEMOTHERAPIES
CHEMOTHERAPIST
CHEMOTHERAPISTS

HEMOTHERAPY
HEMOTROPIC
HEMOTROPICALLY
HEMOTROPISM
HEMOTROPISMS
HEMPADUKS
HEMURGICAL
HEMURGIES
HENOPODIACEOUS
HEONGSAMS
HEQUEBOOK
HEQUEBOOKS
HEQUERBOARD
HEQUERBOARDS
HEQUERING
HEQUERWISE
HEQUERWORK
HEQUERWORKS
HERALITES
HERIMOYAS
HERIMOYER
HERIMOYERS
HERISHABLE
HERISHERS
HERISHING
HERISHINGLY
HERISHMENT
HERISHMENTS
HERNOZEMIC
HERNOZEMS
HERRYLIKE
HERRYSTONE
HERRYSTONES
HERSONESE
HERSONESES
HERUBICAL
HERUBICALLY
HERUBIMIC
HERUBLIKE
HERVONETS
HESSBOARD
HESSBOARDS
HESSPIECE
HESSPIECES
HESSYLITE
HESSYLITES
HESTERFIELD
HESTERFIELDS
HESTINESS
HESTINESSES
HEVALIERS
HEVELURES
HEVESAILE
HEVESAILES
HEVISANCE
HEVISANCES
HEVRETTES
HEVROTAIN
HEVROTAINS
HEWINESSES
HIACKINGS
HIAROSCURISM
HIAROSCURISMS
HIAROSCURIST
HIAROSCURISTS
HIAROSCURO
CHIAROSCUROS
CHIASMATIC
CHIASTOLITE
CHIASTOLITES
CHIBOUQUES
CHICALOTES
CHICANERIES
CHICANINGS
CHICCORIES
CHICKABIDDIES
CHICKABIDDY
CHICKADEES
CHICKAREES
CHICKENHEARTED
CHICKENING
CHICKENPOX
CHICKENPOXES
CHICKENSHIT
CHICKENSHITS
CHICKLINGS
CHICKORIES
CHICKWEEDS
CHICNESSES
CHIEFERIES
CHIEFESSES
CHIEFLINGS
CHIEFSHIPS
CHIEFTAINCIES
CHIEFTAINCY
CHIEFTAINESS
CHIEFTAINESSES
CHIEFTAINRIES
CHIEFTAINRY
CHIEFTAINS
CHIEFTAINSHIP
CHIEFTAINSHIPS
CHIFFCHAFF
CHIFFCHAFFS
CHIFFONADE
CHIFFONADES
CHIFFONIER
CHIFFONIERS
CHIFFONNIER
CHIFFONNIERS
CHIFFOROBE
CHIFFOROBES
CHIHUAHUAS
CHILBLAINED
CHILBLAINS
CHILDBEARING
CHILDBEARINGS
CHILDBIRTH
CHILDBIRTHS
CHILDCARES
CHILDCROWING
CHILDCROWINGS
CHILDERMAS
CHILDERMASES
CHILDHOODS
CHILDISHLY
CHILDISHNESS
CHILDISHNESSES
CHILDLESSNESS
CHILDLESSNESSES
CHILDLIEST
CHILDLIKENESS
CHILDLIKENESSES
CHILDMINDER
CHILDMINDERS
CHILDNESSES
CHILDPROOF
CHILIAGONS
CHILIAHEDRA
CHILIAHEDRON
CHILIAHEDRONS
CHILIARCHIES
CHILIARCHS
CHILIARCHY
CHILIASTIC
CHILLINESS
CHILLINESSES
CHILLINGLY
CHILLNESSES
CHILOPODAN
CHILOPODANS
CHILOPODOUS
CHILTEPINS
CHIMAERISM
CHIMAERISMS
CHIMERICAL
CHIMERICALLY
CHIMERICALNESS
CHIMERISMS
CHIMICHANGA
CHIMICHANGAS
CHIMNEYBOARD
CHIMNEYBOARDS
CHIMNEYBREAST
CHIMNEYBREASTS
CHIMNEYING
CHIMNEYLIKE
CHIMNEYPIECE
CHIMNEYPIECES
CHIMNEYPOT
CHIMNEYPOTS
CHIMPANZEE
CHIMPANZEES
CHINABERRIES
CHINABERRY
CHINACHINA
CHINACHINAS
CHINAROOTS
CHINAWARES
CHINCAPINS
CHINCHERINCHEE
CHINCHERINCHEES
CHINCHIEST
CHINCHILLA
CHINCHILLAS
CHINCOUGHS
CHINKAPINS
CHINKERINCHEE
CHINKERINCHEES
CHINOISERIE
CHINOISERIES
CHINOVNIKS
CHINQUAPIN
CHINQUAPINS
CHINSTRAPS
CHINTZIEST
CHINWAGGED
CHINWAGGING
CHIONODOXA
CHIONODOXAS
CHIPBOARDS
CHIPOCHIAS
CHIPOLATAS
CHIPPERING
CHIPPINESS
CHIPPINESSES
CHIQUICHIQUI
CHIQUICHIQUIS
CHIRAGRICAL
CHIRALITIES
CHIRIMOYAS
CHIROGNOMIES
CHIROGNOMY
CHIROGRAPH
CHIROGRAPHER
CHIROGRAPHERS
CHIROGRAPHIC
CHIROGRAPHICAL
CHIROGRAPHIES
CHIROGRAPHIST
CHIROGRAPHISTS
CHIROGRAPHS
CHIROGRAPHY
CHIROLOGIES
CHIROLOGIST
CHIROLOGISTS
CHIROMANCER
CHIROMANCERS
CHIROMANCIES
CHIROMANCY
CHIROMANTIC
CHIROMANTICAL
CHIRONOMER
CHIRONOMERS
CHIRONOMIC
CHIRONOMID
CHIRONOMIDS
CHIRONOMIES
CHIROPODIAL
CHIROPODIES
CHIROPODIST
CHIROPODISTS
CHIROPRACTIC
CHIROPRACTICS
CHIROPRACTOR
CHIROPRACTORS
CHIROPTERAN
CHIROPTERANS
CHIROPTEROUS
CHIROPTERS
CHIRPINESS
CHIRPINESSES
CHIRRUPERS
CHIRRUPING
CHIRRUPPED
CHIRRUPPING
CHIRURGEON
CHIRURGEONLY
CHIRURGEONS
CHIRURGERIES
CHIRURGERY
CHIRURGICAL
CHISELLERS
CHISELLING

CHISELLINGS
CHITARRONE
CHITARRONI
CHITCHATTED
CHITCHATTING
CHITTAGONG
CHITTAGONGS
CHITTERING
CHITTERINGS
CHITTERLING
CHITTERLINGS
CHIVALRIES
CHIVALROUS
CHIVALROUSLY
CHIVALROUSNESS
CHIVAREEING
CHIVARIING
CHIYOGAMIS
CHLAMYDATE
CHLAMYDEOUS
CHLAMYDIAE
CHLAMYDIAL
CHLAMYDIAS
CHLAMYDOMONADES
CHLAMYDOMONAS
CHLAMYDOSPORE
CHLAMYDOSPORES
CHLOANTHITE
CHLOANTHITES
CHLOASMATA
CHLORACETIC
CHLORACNES
CHLORALISM
CHLORALISMS
CHLORALOSE
CHLORALOSED
CHLORALOSES
CHLORAMBUCIL
CHLORAMBUCILS
CHLORAMINE
CHLORAMINES
CHLORAMPHENICOL
CHLORARGYRITE
CHLORARGYRITES
CHLORDANES
CHLORELLAS
CHLORENCHYMA
CHLORENCHYMAS
CHLORHEXIDINE
CHLORHEXIDINES
CHLORIDATE
CHLORIDATED
CHLORIDATES
CHLORIDATING
CHLORIDISE
CHLORIDISED
CHLORIDISES
CHLORIDISING
CHLORIDIZE
CHLORIDIZED
CHLORIDIZES
CHLORIDIZING
CHLORIMETER
CHLORIMETERS
CHLORIMETRIC
CHLORIMETRIES
CHLORIMETRY
CHLORINATE
CHLORINATED
CHLORINATES
CHLORINATING
CHLORINATION
CHLORINATIONS
CHLORINATOR
CHLORINATORS
CHLORINISE
CHLORINISED
CHLORINISES
CHLORINISING
CHLORINITIES
CHLORINITY
CHLORINIZE
CHLORINIZED
CHLORINIZES
CHLORINIZING
CHLORITISATION
CHLORITISATIONS
CHLORITIZATION
CHLORITIZATIONS
CHLOROACETIC
CHLOROARGYRITE
CHLOROBENZENE
CHLOROBENZENES
CHLOROBROMIDE
CHLOROBROMIDES
CHLOROCRUORIN
CHLOROCRUORINS
CHLORODYNE
CHLORODYNES
CHLOROFORM
CHLOROFORMED
CHLOROFORMER
CHLOROFORMERS
CHLOROFORMING
CHLOROFORMIST
CHLOROFORMISTS
CHLOROFORMS
CHLOROHYDRIN
CHLOROHYDRINS
CHLOROMETER
CHLOROMETERS
CHLOROMETHANE
CHLOROMETHANES
CHLOROMETRIC
CHLOROMETRIES
CHLOROMETRY
CHLOROPHYL
CHLOROPHYLL
CHLOROPHYLLOID
CHLOROPHYLLOUS
CHLOROPHYLLS
CHLOROPHYLS
CHLOROPHYTUM
CHLOROPHYTUMS
CHLOROPICRIN
CHLOROPICRINS
CHLOROPLAST
CHLOROPLASTAL
CHLOROPLASTIC
CHLOROPLASTS
CHLOROPRENE
CHLOROPRENES
CHLOROQUIN
CHLOROQUINE
CHLOROQUINES
CHLOROQUINS
CHLOROTHIAZIDE
CHLOROTHIAZIDES
CHLORPICRIN
CHLORPICRINS
CHLORPROMAZINE
CHLORPROMAZINES
CHLORPROPAMIDE
CHLORPROPAMIDES
CHLORTHALIDONE
CHLORTHALIDONES
CHOANOCYTE
CHOANOCYTES
CHOCAHOLIC
CHOCAHOLICS
CHOCKABLOCK
CHOCKSTONE
CHOCKSTONES
CHOCOHOLIC
CHOCOHOLICS
CHOCOLATES
CHOCOLATEY
CHOCOLATIER
CHOCOLATIERS
CHOCOLATIEST
CHOICENESS
CHOICENESSES
CHOIRGIRLS
CHOIRMASTER
CHOIRMASTERS
CHOIRSCREEN
CHOIRSCREENS
CHOIRSTALLS
CHOKEBERRIES
CHOKEBERRY
CHOKEBORES
CHOKECHERRIES
CHOKECHERRY
CHOKECOILS
CHOKEDAMPS
CHOKEHOLDS
CHOLAEMIAS
CHOLAGOGIC
CHOLAGOGUE
CHOLAGOGUES
CHOLANGIOGRAM
CHOLANGIOGRAMS
CHOLANGIOGRAPHY
CHOLECALCIFEROL
CHOLECYSTECTOMY
CHOLECYSTITIS
CHOLECYSTITISES
CHOLECYSTOKININ
CHOLECYSTOSTOMY
CHOLECYSTOTOMY
CHOLECYSTS
CHOLELITHIASES
CHOLELITHIASIS
CHOLELITHS
CHOLERICALLY
CHOLERICLY
CHOLESTASES
CHOLESTASIS
CHOLESTATIC
CHOLESTERIC
CHOLESTERIN
CHOLESTERINS
CHOLESTEROL
CHOLESTEROLEMIA
CHOLESTEROLS
CHOLESTYRAMINE
CHOLESTYRAMINES
CHOLIAMBIC
CHOLIAMBICS
CHOLINERGIC
CHOLINERGICALLY
CHOLINESTERASE
CHOLINESTERASES
CHOMOPHYTE
CHOMOPHYTES
CHONDRICHTHYAN
CHONDRICHTHYANS
CHONDRIFICATION
CHONDRIFIED
CHONDRIFIES
CHONDRIFYING
CHONDRIOSOMAL
CHONDRIOSOME
CHONDRIOSOMES
CHONDRITES
CHONDRITIC
CHONDRITIS
CHONDRITISES
CHONDROBLAST
CHONDROBLASTS
CHONDROCRANIA
CHONDROCRANIUM
CHONDROCRANIUMS
CHONDROGENESES
CHONDROGENESIS
CHONDROITIN
CHONDROITINS
CHONDROMAS
CHONDROMATA
CHONDROMATOSES
CHONDROMATOSIS
CHONDROMATOUS
CHONDROPHORINE
CHONDROPHORINES
CHONDROSKELETON
CHONDROSTIAN
CHONDROSTIANS
CHONDRULES
CHOPFALLEN
CHOPHOUSES
CHOPLOGICS
CHOPPERING
CHOPPINESS
CHOPPINESSES
CHOPSOCKIES
CHOPSTICKS
CHORAGUSES
CHORALISTS
CHORDAMESODERM
CHORDAMESODERMS
CHORDOPHONE
CHORDOPHONES
CHORDOPHONIC
CHORDOTOMIES

HORDOTOMY
HOREGRAPH
HOREGRAPHED
HOREGRAPHER
HOREGRAPHERS
HOREGRAPHIC
HOREGRAPHIES
HOREGRAPHING
HOREGRAPHS
HOREGRAPHY
HOREGUSES
HOREIFORM
HOREODRAMA
HOREODRAMAS
HOREOGRAPH
HOREOGRAPHED
HOREOGRAPHER
HOREOGRAPHERS
HOREOGRAPHIC
HOREOGRAPHIES
HOREOGRAPHING
HOREOGRAPHS
HOREOGRAPHY
HOREOLOGIES
HOREOLOGIST
HOREOLOGISTS
HOREOLOGY
HOREPISCOPAL
HORIAMBIC
HORIAMBICS
HORIAMBUS
HORIAMBUSES
HORIOALLANTOIC
HORIOALLANTOIS
HORIOCARCINOMA
HORISATION
HORISATIONS
HORISTERS
HORIZATION
HORIZATIONS
HORIZONTIST
HORIZONTISTS
HORIZONTS
HOROGRAPHER
HOROGRAPHERS
HOROGRAPHIC
HOROGRAPHICAL
HOROGRAPHIES
HOROGRAPHY
HOROIDITIS
HOROIDITISES
HOROLOGICAL
HOROLOGIES
HOROLOGIST
HOROLOGISTS
HOROPLETH
HOROPLETHS
HORUSMASTER
HORUSMASTERS
HORUSSING
HOUCROUTE
HOUCROUTES
HOULTRIES
HOUNTERED
HOUNTERING
HOWDERHEAD
CHOWDERHEADED
CHOWDERHEADS
CHOWDERING
CHOWHOUNDS
CHOWKIDARS
CHREMATIST
CHREMATISTIC
CHREMATISTICS
CHREMATISTS
CHRESTOMATHIC
CHRESTOMATHICAL
CHRESTOMATHIES
CHRESTOMATHY
CHRISMATION
CHRISMATIONS
CHRISMATORIES
CHRISMATORY
CHRISTCROSS
CHRISTCROSSES
CHRISTENED
CHRISTENER
CHRISTENERS
CHRISTENING
CHRISTENINGS
CHRISTIANIA
CHRISTIANIAS
CHRISTIANISE
CHRISTIANISED
CHRISTIANISER
CHRISTIANISERS
CHRISTIANISES
CHRISTIANISING
CHRISTIANIZE
CHRISTIANIZED
CHRISTIANIZER
CHRISTIANIZERS
CHRISTIANIZES
CHRISTIANIZING
CHRISTIANLY
CHRISTIANS
CHRISTINGLE
CHRISTINGLES
CHRISTOPHANIES
CHRISTOPHANY
CHROMAFFIN
CHROMAKEYS
CHROMATICALLY
CHROMATICISM
CHROMATICISMS
CHROMATICITIES
CHROMATICITY
CHROMATICNESS
CHROMATICNESSES
CHROMATICS
CHROMATIDS
CHROMATINIC
CHROMATINS
CHROMATIST
CHROMATISTS
CHROMATOGRAM
CHROMATOGRAMS
CHROMATOGRAPH
CHROMATOGRAPHED
CHROMATOGRAPHER
CHROMATOGRAPHIC
CHROMATOGRAPHS
CHROMATOGRAPHY
CHROMATOID
CHROMATOLOGIES
CHROMATOLOGIST
CHROMATOLOGISTS
CHROMATOLOGY
CHROMATOLYSES
CHROMATOLYSIS
CHROMATOLYTIC
CHROMATOPHORE
CHROMATOPHORES
CHROMATOPHORIC
CHROMATOPHOROUS
CHROMATOPSIA
CHROMATOPSIAS
CHROMATOSPHERE
CHROMATOSPHERES
CHROMATYPE
CHROMATYPES
CHROMIDIUM
CHROMINANCE
CHROMINANCES
CHROMISING
CHROMIZING
CHROMOCENTER
CHROMOCENTERS
CHROMODYNAMICS
CHROMOGENIC
CHROMOGENS
CHROMOGRAM
CHROMOGRAMS
CHROMOMERE
CHROMOMERES
CHROMOMERIC
CHROMONEMA
CHROMONEMAL
CHROMONEMATA
CHROMONEMATIC
CHROMONEMIC
CHROMOPHIL
CHROMOPHILIC
CHROMOPHOBE
CHROMOPHONIC
CHROMOPHORE
CHROMOPHORES
CHROMOPHORIC
CHROMOPHOROUS
CHROMOPLAST
CHROMOPLASTS
CHROMOPROTEIN
CHROMOPROTEINS
CHROMOSCOPE
CHROMOSCOPES
CHROMOSOMAL
CHROMOSOMALLY
CHROMOSOME
CHROMOSOMES
CHROMOSPHERE
CHROMOSPHERES
CHROMOSPHERIC
CHROMOTHERAPIES
CHROMOTHERAPY
CHROMOTYPE
CHROMOTYPES
CHROMOXYLOGRAPH
CHRONAXIES
CHRONICALLY
CHRONICITIES
CHRONICITY
CHRONICLED
CHRONICLER
CHRONICLERS
CHRONICLES
CHRONICLING
CHRONOBIOLOGIC
CHRONOBIOLOGIES
CHRONOBIOLOGIST
CHRONOBIOLOGY
CHRONOGRAM
CHRONOGRAMMATIC
CHRONOGRAMS
CHRONOGRAPH
CHRONOGRAPHER
CHRONOGRAPHERS
CHRONOGRAPHIC
CHRONOGRAPHIES
CHRONOGRAPHS
CHRONOGRAPHY
CHRONOLOGER
CHRONOLOGERS
CHRONOLOGIC
CHRONOLOGICAL
CHRONOLOGICALLY
CHRONOLOGIES
CHRONOLOGISE
CHRONOLOGISED
CHRONOLOGISES
CHRONOLOGISING
CHRONOLOGIST
CHRONOLOGISTS
CHRONOLOGIZE
CHRONOLOGIZED
CHRONOLOGIZES
CHRONOLOGIZING
CHRONOLOGY
CHRONOMETER
CHRONOMETERS
CHRONOMETRIC
CHRONOMETRICAL
CHRONOMETRIES
CHRONOMETRY
CHRONOSCOPE
CHRONOSCOPES
CHRONOSCOPIC
CHRONOTHERAPIES
CHRONOTHERAPY
CHRONOTRON
CHRONOTRONS
CHRYSALIDAL
CHRYSALIDES
CHRYSALIDS
CHRYSALISES
CHRYSANTHEMUM
CHRYSANTHEMUMS
CHRYSANTHS
CHRYSAROBIN
CHRYSAROBINS
CHRYSOBERYL
CHRYSOBERYLS
CHRYSOCOLLA
CHRYSOCOLLAS
CHRYSOCRACIES

CHRYSOCRACY
CHRYSOLITE
CHRYSOLITES
CHRYSOLITIC
CHRYSOMELID
CHRYSOMELIDS
CHRYSOPHAN
CHRYSOPHANS
CHRYSOPHILITE
CHRYSOPHILITES
CHRYSOPHYTE
CHRYSOPHYTES
CHRYSOPRASE
CHRYSOPRASES
CHRYSOTILE
CHRYSOTILES
CHUBBINESS
CHUBBINESSES
CHUCKAWALLA
CHUCKAWALLAS
CHUCKHOLES
CHUCKLEHEAD
CHUCKLEHEADED
CHUCKLEHEADS
CHUCKLESOME
CHUCKLINGLY
CHUCKLINGS
CHUCKWALLA
CHUCKWALLAS
CHUFFINESS
CHUFFINESSES
CHUGALUGGED
CHUGALUGGING
CHUMMINESS
CHUMMINESSES
CHUNDERING
CHUNDEROUS
CHUNKINESS
CHUNKINESSES
CHUNNERING
CHUNTERING
CHUPATTIES
CHUPRASSIES
CHURCHGOER
CHURCHGOERS
CHURCHGOING
CHURCHGOINGS
CHURCHIANITIES
CHURCHIANITY
CHURCHIEST
CHURCHINGS
CHURCHISMS
CHURCHLESS
CHURCHLIER
CHURCHLIEST
CHURCHLINESS
CHURCHLINESSES
CHURCHMANLY
CHURCHMANSHIP
CHURCHMANSHIPS
CHURCHPEOPLE
CHURCHWARD
CHURCHWARDEN
CHURCHWARDENS
CHURCHWARDS
CHURCHWAYS
CHURCHWOMAN
CHURCHWOMEN
CHURCHYARD
CHURCHYARDS
CHURLISHLY
CHURLISHNESS
CHURLISHNESSES
CHURNMILKS
CHURRIGUERESCO
CHURRIGUERESQUE
CHYLACEOUS
CHYLIFEROUS
CHYLIFICATION
CHYLIFICATIONS
CHYLIFYING
CHYLOMICRON
CHYLOMICRONS
CHYMIFEROUS
CHYMIFICATION
CHYMIFICATIONS
CHYMIFYING
CHYMISTRIES
CHYMOTRYPSIN
CHYMOTRYPSINS
CHYMOTRYPTIC
CIBACHROME
CIBACHROMES
CICADELLID
CICADELLIDS
CICATRICES
CICATRICHULE
CICATRICHULES
CICATRICIAL
CICATRICLE
CICATRICLES
CICATRICOSE
CICATRICULA
CICATRICULAS
CICATRISANT
CICATRISATION
CICATRISATIONS
CICATRISED
CICATRISER
CICATRISERS
CICATRISES
CICATRISING
CICATRIXES
CICATRIZANT
CICATRIZATION
CICATRIZATIONS
CICATRIZED
CICATRIZER
CICATRIZERS
CICATRIZES
CICATRIZING
CICERONEING
CICHORACEOUS
CICINNUSES
CICISBEISM
CICISBEISMS
CICLATOUNS
CICLOSPORIN
CICLOSPORINS
CIGARETTES
CIGARILLOS
CIGUATERAS
CILIATIONS
CIMETIDINE
CIMETIDINES
CINCHONACEOUS
CINCHONIDINE
CINCHONIDINES
CINCHONINE
CINCHONINES
CINCHONINIC
CINCHONISATION
CINCHONISATIONS
CINCHONISE
CINCHONISED
CINCHONISES
CINCHONISING
CINCHONISM
CINCHONISMS
CINCHONIZATION
CINCHONIZATIONS
CINCHONIZE
CINCHONIZED
CINCHONIZES
CINCHONIZING
CINCINNATE
CINCINNUSES
CINCTURING
CINEANGIOGRAPHY
CINEMAGOER
CINEMAGOERS
CINEMATHEQUE
CINEMATHEQUES
CINEMATICALLY
CINEMATISE
CINEMATISED
CINEMATISES
CINEMATISING
CINEMATIZE
CINEMATIZED
CINEMATIZES
CINEMATIZING
CINEMATOGRAPH
CINEMATOGRAPHED
CINEMATOGRAPHER
CINEMATOGRAPHIC
CINEMATOGRAPHS
CINEMATOGRAPHY
CINEMICROGRAPHY
CINEPHILES
CINEPLEXES
CINERARIAS
CINERARIUM
CINERATION
CINERATIONS
CINERATORS
CINERITIOUS
CINGULATED
CINNABARIC
CINNABARINE
CINNAMONIC
CINNARIZINE
CINNARIZINES
CINQUECENTIST
CINQUECENTISTS
CINQUECENTO
CINQUECENTOS
CINQUEFOIL
CINQUEFOILS
CIPHERINGS
CIPHERTEXT
CIPHERTEXTS
CIPOLLINOS
CIPROFLOXACIN
CIPROFLOXACINS
CIRCASSIAN
CIRCASSIANS
CIRCASSIENNE
CIRCASSIENNES
CIRCENSIAL
CIRCENSIAN
CIRCINATELY
CIRCUITEER
CIRCUITEERS
CIRCUITIES
CIRCUITING
CIRCUITOUS
CIRCUITOUSLY
CIRCUITOUSNESS
CIRCUITRIES
CIRCULABLE
CIRCULARISATION
CIRCULARISE
CIRCULARISED
CIRCULARISER
CIRCULARISERS
CIRCULARISES
CIRCULARISING
CIRCULARITIES
CIRCULARITY
CIRCULARIZATION
CIRCULARIZE
CIRCULARIZED
CIRCULARIZER
CIRCULARIZERS
CIRCULARIZES
CIRCULARIZING
CIRCULARLY
CIRCULARNESS
CIRCULARNESSES
CIRCULATABLE
CIRCULATED
CIRCULATES
CIRCULATING
CIRCULATINGS
CIRCULATION
CIRCULATIONS
CIRCULATIVE
CIRCULATOR
CIRCULATORS
CIRCULATORY
CIRCUMAMBAGES
CIRCUMAMBAGIOUS
CIRCUMAMBIENCE
CIRCUMAMBIENCES
CIRCUMAMBIENCY
CIRCUMAMBIENT
CIRCUMAMBIENTLY
CIRCUMAMBULATE
CIRCUMAMBULATED
CIRCUMAMBULATES
CIRCUMAMBULATOR
CIRCUMBENDIBUS
CIRCUMCENTER

IRCUMCENTERS
IRCUMCENTRE
IRCUMCENTRES
IRCUMCIRCLE
IRCUMCIRCLES
IRCUMCISE
IRCUMCISED
IRCUMCISER
IRCUMCISERS
IRCUMCISES
IRCUMCISING
IRCUMCISION
IRCUMCISIONS
IRCUMDUCE
IRCUMDUCED
IRCUMDUCES
IRCUMDUCING
IRCUMDUCT
IRCUMDUCTED
IRCUMDUCTING
IRCUMDUCTION
IRCUMDUCTIONS
IRCUMDUCTORY
IRCUMDUCTS
IRCUMFERENCE
IRCUMFERENCES
IRCUMFERENTIAL
IRCUMFERENTOR
IRCUMFERENTORS
IRCUMFLECT
IRCUMFLECTED
IRCUMFLECTING
IRCUMFLECTS
IRCUMFLEX
IRCUMFLEXES
IRCUMFLEXION
IRCUMFLEXIONS
IRCUMFLUENCE
IRCUMFLUENCES
IRCUMFLUENT
IRCUMFLUOUS
IRCUMFORANEAN
IRCUMFORANEOUS
IRCUMFUSE
IRCUMFUSED
IRCUMFUSES
IRCUMFUSILE
IRCUMFUSING
IRCUMFUSION
IRCUMFUSIONS
IRCUMGYRATE
IRCUMGYRATED
IRCUMGYRATES
IRCUMGYRATING
IRCUMGYRATION
IRCUMGYRATIONS
IRCUMGYRATORY
IRCUMINCESSION
IRCUMINSESSION
IRCUMJACENCIES
IRCUMJACENCY
IRCUMJACENT
IRCUMLITTORAL
IRCUMLOCUTE
IRCUMLOCUTED
IRCUMLOCUTES
CIRCUMLOCUTING
CIRCUMLOCUTION
CIRCUMLOCUTIONS
CIRCUMLOCUTORY
CIRCUMLUNAR
CIRCUMMURE
CIRCUMMURED
CIRCUMMURES
CIRCUMMURING
CIRCUMNAVIGABLE
CIRCUMNAVIGATE
CIRCUMNAVIGATED
CIRCUMNAVIGATES
CIRCUMNAVIGATOR
CIRCUMNUTATE
CIRCUMNUTATED
CIRCUMNUTATES
CIRCUMNUTATING
CIRCUMNUTATION
CIRCUMNUTATIONS
CIRCUMNUTATORY
CIRCUMPOLAR
CIRCUMPOSE
CIRCUMPOSED
CIRCUMPOSES
CIRCUMPOSING
CIRCUMPOSITION
CIRCUMPOSITIONS
CIRCUMSCISSILE
CIRCUMSCRIBABLE
CIRCUMSCRIBE
CIRCUMSCRIBED
CIRCUMSCRIBER
CIRCUMSCRIBERS
CIRCUMSCRIBES
CIRCUMSCRIBING
CIRCUMSCRIPTION
CIRCUMSCRIPTIVE
CIRCUMSOLAR
CIRCUMSPECT
CIRCUMSPECTION
CIRCUMSPECTIONS
CIRCUMSPECTIVE
CIRCUMSPECTLY
CIRCUMSPECTNESS
CIRCUMSTANCE
CIRCUMSTANCED
CIRCUMSTANCES
CIRCUMSTANCING
CIRCUMSTANTIAL
CIRCUMSTANTIALS
CIRCUMSTANTIATE
CIRCUMSTELLAR
CIRCUMVALLATE
CIRCUMVALLATED
CIRCUMVALLATES
CIRCUMVALLATING
CIRCUMVALLATION
CIRCUMVENT
CIRCUMVENTED
CIRCUMVENTER
CIRCUMVENTERS
CIRCUMVENTING
CIRCUMVENTION
CIRCUMVENTIONS
CIRCUMVENTIVE
CIRCUMVENTOR
CIRCUMVENTORS
CIRCUMVENTS
CIRCUMVOLUTION
CIRCUMVOLUTIONS
CIRCUMVOLUTORY
CIRCUMVOLVE
CIRCUMVOLVED
CIRCUMVOLVES
CIRCUMVOLVING
CIRRHIPEDE
CIRRHIPEDES
CIRRHOTICS
CIRRIGRADE
CIRRIPEDES
CIRROCUMULI
CIRROCUMULUS
CIRROSTRATI
CIRROSTRATIVE
CIRROSTRATUS
CISMONTANE
CISPLATINS
CISPONTINE
CISTACEOUS
CITATIONAL
CITHARISTIC
CITHARISTS
CITIFICATION
CITIFICATIONS
CITIZENESS
CITIZENESSES
CITIZENISE
CITIZENISED
CITIZENISES
CITIZENISING
CITIZENIZE
CITIZENIZED
CITIZENIZES
CITIZENIZING
CITIZENRIES
CITIZENSHIP
CITIZENSHIPS
CITRICULTURE
CITRICULTURES
CITRICULTURIST
CITRICULTURISTS
CITRONELLA
CITRONELLAL
CITRONELLALS
CITRONELLAS
CITRONELLOL
CITRONELLOLS
CITRULLINE
CITRULLINES
CITYFICATION
CITYFICATIONS
CITYSCAPES
CIVILIANISATION
CIVILIANISE
CIVILIANISED
CIVILIANISES
CIVILIANISING
CIVILIANIZATION
CIVILIANIZE
CIVILIANIZED
CIVILIANIZES
CIVILIANIZING
CIVILISABLE
CIVILISATION
CIVILISATIONAL
CIVILISATIONS
CIVILISERS
CIVILISING
CIVILITIES
CIVILIZABLE
CIVILIZATION
CIVILIZATIONAL
CIVILIZATIONS
CIVILIZERS
CIVILIZING
CIVILNESSES
CLABBERING
CLACKBOXES
CLACKDISHES
CLADISTICALLY
CLADISTICS
CLADOCERAN
CLADOCERANS
CLADOGENESES
CLADOGENESIS
CLADOGENETIC
CLADOGRAMS
CLADOPHYLL
CLADOPHYLLS
CLADOSPORIA
CLADOSPORIUM
CLADOSPORIUMS
CLAIRAUDIENCE
CLAIRAUDIENCES
CLAIRAUDIENT
CLAIRAUDIENTLY
CLAIRAUDIENTS
CLAIRCOLLE
CLAIRCOLLES
CLAIRSCHACH
CLAIRSCHACHS
CLAIRVOYANCE
CLAIRVOYANCES
CLAIRVOYANCIES
CLAIRVOYANCY
CLAIRVOYANT
CLAIRVOYANTLY
CLAIRVOYANTS
CLAMANCIES
CLAMATORIAL
CLAMBERERS
CLAMBERING
CLAMJAMFRIES
CLAMJAMFRY
CLAMJAMPHRIE
CLAMJAMPHRIES
CLAMMINESS
CLAMMINESSES
CLAMOROUSLY
CLAMOROUSNESS
CLAMOROUSNESSES
CLAMOURERS
CLAMOURING
CLAMPDOWNS
CLAMPERING
CLAMSHELLS
CLANDESTINE

CLANDESTINELY
CLANDESTINENESS
CLANDESTINITIES
CLANDESTINITY
CLANGBOXES
CLANGORING
CLANGOROUS
CLANGOROUSLY
CLANGOURED
CLANGOURING
CLANJAMFRAY
CLANJAMFRAYS
CLANKINGLY
CLANNISHLY
CLANNISHNESS
CLANNISHNESSES
CLANSWOMAN
CLANSWOMEN
CLAPBOARDED
CLAPBOARDING
CLAPBOARDS
CLAPBREADS
CLAPDISHES
CLAPOMETER
CLAPOMETERS
CLAPPERBOARD
CLAPPERBOARDS
CLAPPERBOY
CLAPPERBOYS
CLAPPERCLAW
CLAPPERCLAWED
CLAPPERCLAWER
CLAPPERCLAWERS
CLAPPERCLAWING
CLAPPERCLAWS
CLAPPERING
CLAPPERINGS
CLAPTRAPPERIES
CLAPTRAPPERY
CLARABELLA
CLARABELLAS
CLARENDONS
CLARIBELLA
CLARIBELLAS
CLARICHORD
CLARICHORDS
CLARIFICATION
CLARIFICATIONS
CLARIFIERS
CLARIFYING
CLARINETIST
CLARINETISTS
CLARINETTIST
CLARINETTISTS
CLARIONETS
CLARIONING
CLARTHEADS
CLASHINGLY
CLASSICALISM
CLASSICALISMS
CLASSICALIST
CLASSICALISTS
CLASSICALITIES
CLASSICALITY
CLASSICALLY
CLASSICALNESS
CLASSICALNESSES
CLASSICALS
CLASSICISE
CLASSICISED
CLASSICISES
CLASSICISING
CLASSICISM
CLASSICISMS
CLASSICIST
CLASSICISTIC
CLASSICISTS
CLASSICIZE
CLASSICIZED
CLASSICIZES
CLASSICIZING
CLASSIFIABLE
CLASSIFICATION
CLASSIFICATIONS
CLASSIFICATORY
CLASSIFIED
CLASSIFIER
CLASSIFIERS
CLASSIFIES
CLASSIFYING
CLASSINESS
CLASSINESSES
CLASSLESSNESS
CLASSLESSNESSES
CLASSMATES
CLASSROOMS
CLASSWORKS
CLATHRATES
CLATTERERS
CLATTERING
CLATTERINGLY
CLAUCHTING
CLAUDICATION
CLAUDICATIONS
CLAUGHTING
CLAUSTRATION
CLAUSTRATIONS
CLAUSTROPHOBE
CLAUSTROPHOBES
CLAUSTROPHOBIA
CLAUSTROPHOBIAS
CLAUSTROPHOBIC
CLAVATIONS
CLAVECINIST
CLAVECINISTS
CLAVICEMBALO
CLAVICEMBALOS
CLAVICHORD
CLAVICHORDIST
CLAVICHORDISTS
CLAVICHORDS
CLAVICORNS
CLAVICULAE
CLAVICULAR
CLAVICULATE
CLAVICYTHERIA
CLAVICYTHERIUM
CLAVIERIST
CLAVIERISTIC
CLAVIERISTS
CLAVIGEROUS
CLAWHAMMER
CLAYMATION
CLAYMATIONS
CLAYSTONES
CLAYTONIAS
CLEANABILITIES
CLEANABILITY
CLEANHANDED
CLEANLIEST
CLEANLINESS
CLEANLINESSES
CLEANNESSES
CLEANSABLE
CLEANSINGS
CLEANSKINS
CLEARANCES
CLEARCOLED
CLEARCOLES
CLEARCOLING
CLEARCUTTING
CLEARHEADED
CLEARHEADEDLY
CLEARHEADEDNESS
CLEARINGHOUSE
CLEARINGHOUSES
CLEARNESSES
CLEARSKINS
CLEARSTORIED
CLEARSTORIES
CLEARSTORY
CLEARWEEDS
CLEARWINGS
CLEAVABILITIES
CLEAVABILITY
CLEAVABLENESS
CLEAVABLENESSES
CLEISTOGAMIC
CLEISTOGAMIES
CLEISTOGAMOUS
CLEISTOGAMOUSLY
CLEISTOGAMY
CLEMATISES
CLEMENCIES
CLEMENTINE
CLEMENTINES
CLENBUTEROL
CLENBUTEROLS
CLEOPATRAS
CLEPSYDRAE
CLEPSYDRAS
CLEPTOCRACIES
CLEPTOCRACY
CLEPTOMANIA
CLEPTOMANIAC
CLEPTOMANIACS
CLEPTOMANIAS
CLERESTORIED
CLERESTORIES
CLERESTORY
CLERGIABLE
CLERGYABLE
CLERGYWOMAN
CLERGYWOMEN
CLERICALISM
CLERICALISMS
CLERICALIST
CLERICALISTS
CLERICALLY
CLERICATES
CLERICITIES
CLERKESSES
CLERKLIEST
CLERKLINESS
CLERKLINESSES
CLERKLINGS
CLERKSHIPS
CLEROMANCIES
CLEROMANCY
CLERUCHIAL
CLERUCHIAS
CLERUCHIES
CLEVERALITIES
CLEVERALITY
CLEVERDICK
CLEVERDICKS
CLEVERNESS
CLEVERNESSES
CLIANTHUSES
CLICKETING
CLICKSTREAM
CLICKSTREAMS
CLIENTAGES
CLIENTELES
CLIENTLESS
CLIENTSHIP
CLIENTSHIPS
CLIFFHANGER
CLIFFHANGERS
CLIFFHANGING
CLIFFHANGINGS
CLIFFHANGS
CLIMACTERIC
CLIMACTERICAL
CLIMACTERICALLY
CLIMACTERICS
CLIMACTICAL
CLIMACTICALLY
CLIMATICAL
CLIMATICALLY
CLIMATISED
CLIMATISES
CLIMATISING
CLIMATIZED
CLIMATIZES
CLIMATIZING
CLIMATOGRAPHIES
CLIMATOGRAPHY
CLIMATOLOGIC
CLIMATOLOGICAL
CLIMATOLOGIES
CLIMATOLOGIST
CLIMATOLOGISTS
CLIMATOLOGY
CLIMATURES
CLIMAXLESS
CLIMBDOWNS
CLINANDRIA
CLINANDRIUM
CLINCHINGLY
CLINDAMYCIN
CLINDAMYCINS
CLINGFILMS
CLINGFISHES

LINGINESS
LINGINESSES
LINGINGLY
LINGINGNESS
LINGINGNESSES
LINGSTONE
LINGSTONES
LINICALLY
LINICALNESS
LINICALNESSES
LINICIANS
LINKERING
CLINKSTONE
CLINKSTONES
CLINOCHLORE
CLINOCHLORES
CLINODIAGONAL
CLINODIAGONALS
CLINOMETER
CLINOMETERS
CLINOMETRIC
CLINOMETRICAL
CLINOMETRIES
CLINOMETRY
CLINOPINACOID
CLINOPINACOIDS
CLINOPINAKOID
CLINOPINAKOIDS
CLINOPYROXENE
CLINOPYROXENES
CLINOSTATS
CLINQUANTS
CLINTONIAS
CLIOMETRIC
CLIOMETRICAL
CLIOMETRICIAN
CLIOMETRICIANS
CLIOMETRICS
CLIPBOARDS
CLIPSHEARS
CLIPSHEETS
CLIQUINESS
CLIQUINESSES
CLIQUISHLY
CLIQUISHNESS
CLIQUISHNESSES
CLISHMACLAVER
CLISHMACLAVERS
CLISTOGAMIES
CLISTOGAMY
CLITICISED
CLITICISES
CLITICISING
CLITICIZED
CLITICIZES
CLITICIZING
CLITORECTOMIES
CLITORECTOMY
CLITORIDECTOMY
CLITORIDES
CLITORISES
CLITTERING
CLOACALINE
CLOACITISES
CLOAKROOMS
CLOBBERING
CLOCKMAKER
CLOCKMAKERS
CLOCKWORKS
CLODDISHLY
CLODDISHNESS
CLODDISHNESSES
CLODHOPPER
CLODHOPPERS
CLODHOPPING
CLOFIBRATE
CLOFIBRATES
CLOGDANCES
CLOGGINESS
CLOGGINESSES
CLOISONNAGE
CLOISONNAGES
CLOISONNES
CLOISTERED
CLOISTERER
CLOISTERERS
CLOISTERING
CLOISTRESS
CLOISTRESSES
CLOMIPHENE
CLOMIPHENES
CLONAZEPAM
CLONAZEPAMS
CLONICITIES
CLONIDINES
CLOSEDOWNS
CLOSEFISTED
CLOSEHEADS
CLOSEMOUTHED
CLOSENESSES
CLOSESTOOL
CLOSESTOOLS
CLOSETFULS
CLOSTRIDIA
CLOSTRIDIAL
CLOSTRIDIAN
CLOSTRIDIUM
CLOSTRIDIUMS
CLOTHBOUND
CLOTHESHORSE
CLOTHESHORSES
CLOTHESLINE
CLOTHESLINED
CLOTHESLINES
CLOTHESLINING
CLOTHESPIN
CLOTHESPINS
CLOTHESPRESS
CLOTHESPRESSES
CLOTTERING
CLOTTINESS
CLOTTINESSES
CLOUDBERRIES
CLOUDBERRY
CLOUDBURST
CLOUDBURSTS
CLOUDINESS
CLOUDINESSES
CLOUDLANDS
CLOUDLESSLY
CLOUDLESSNESS
CLOUDLESSNESSES
CLOUDSCAPE
CLOUDSCAPES
CLOUDTOWNS
CLOVEPINKS
CLOVERGRASS
CLOVERGRASSES
CLOVERLEAF
CLOVERLEAFS
CLOVERLEAVES
CLOWNERIES
CLOWNISHLY
CLOWNISHNESS
CLOWNISHNESSES
CLOXACILLIN
CLOXACILLINS
CLOZAPINES
CLUBABILITIES
CLUBABILITY
CLUBBABILITIES
CLUBBABILITY
CLUBBINESS
CLUBBINESSES
CLUBFOOTED
CLUBHAULED
CLUBHAULING
CLUBHOUSES
CLUBMANSHIP
CLUBMANSHIPS
CLUBMASTER
CLUBMASTERS
CLUBRUSHES
CLUMPINESS
CLUMPINESSES
CLUMSINESS
CLUMSINESSES
CLUSTERING
CLUSTERINGLY
CLUTTERING
CLYPEIFORM
CNIDARIANS
CNIDOBLAST
CNIDOBLASTS
COACERVATE
COACERVATED
COACERVATES
COACERVATING
COACERVATION
COACERVATIONS
COACHBUILDER
COACHBUILDERS
COACHBUILDING
COACHBUILDINGS
COACHBUILT
COACHLINES
COACHLOADS
COACHWHIPS
COACHWOODS
COACHWORKS
COACTIVELY
COACTIVITIES
COACTIVITY
COADAPTATION
COADAPTATIONS
COADJACENCIES
COADJACENCY
COADJACENT
COADJUTANT
COADJUTANTS
COADJUTORS
COADJUTORSHIP
COADJUTORSHIPS
COADJUTRESS
COADJUTRESSES
COADJUTRICES
COADJUTRIX
COADJUTRIXES
COADMIRING
COADMITTED
COADMITTING
COADUNATED
COADUNATES
COADUNATING
COADUNATION
COADUNATIONS
COADUNATIVE
COAGENCIES
COAGULABILITIES
COAGULABILITY
COAGULABLE
COAGULANTS
COAGULASES
COAGULATED
COAGULATES
COAGULATING
COAGULATION
COAGULATIONS
COAGULATIVE
COAGULATOR
COAGULATORS
COAGULATORY
COALESCENCE
COALESCENCES
COALESCENT
COALESCING
COALFIELDS
COALFISHES
COALHOUSES
COALIFICATION
COALIFICATIONS
COALIFYING
COALITIONAL
COALITIONER
COALITIONERS
COALITIONISM
COALITIONISMS
COALITIONIST
COALITIONISTS
COALITIONS
COALMASTER
COALMASTERS
COALMINERS
COANCHORED
COANCHORING
COANNEXING
COAPPEARED
COAPPEARING
COAPTATION
COAPTATIONS
COARCTATED
COARCTATES
COARCTATING
COARCTATION

COARCTATIONS
COARSENESS
COARSENESSES
COARSENING
COASSISTED
COASSISTING
COASSUMING
COASTEERING
COASTEERINGS
COASTGUARD
COASTGUARDMAN
COASTGUARDMEN
COASTGUARDS
COASTGUARDSMAN
COASTGUARDSMEN
COASTLANDS
COASTLINES
COASTWARDS
COATDRESSES
COATIMUNDI
COATIMUNDIS
COATSTANDS
COATTENDED
COATTENDING
COATTESTED
COATTESTING
COAUTHORED
COAUTHORING
COAUTHORSHIP
COAUTHORSHIPS
COBALAMINS
COBALTIFEROUS
COBALTINES
COBALTITES
COBBLERIES
COBBLESTONE
COBBLESTONED
COBBLESTONES
COBBLESTONING
COBELLIGERENT
COBELLIGERENTS
COBWEBBERIES
COBWEBBERY
COBWEBBIER
COBWEBBIEST
COBWEBBING
COCAINISATION
COCAINISATIONS
COCAINISED
COCAINISES
COCAINISING
COCAINISMS
COCAINISTS
COCAINIZATION
COCAINIZATIONS
COCAINIZED
COCAINIZES
COCAINIZING
COCAPTAINED
COCAPTAINING
COCAPTAINS
COCARBOXYLASE
COCARBOXYLASES
COCARCINOGEN
COCARCINOGENIC
COCARCINOGENS
COCATALYST
COCATALYSTS
COCCIDIOSES
COCCIDIOSIS
COCCIDIOSTAT
COCCIDIOSTATS
COCCIFEROUS
COCCINEOUS
COCCOLITES
COCCOLITHS
COCHAIRING
COCHAIRMAN
COCHAIRMEN
COCHAIRPERSON
COCHAIRPERSONS
COCHAIRWOMAN
COCHAIRWOMEN
COCHAMPION
COCHAMPIONS
COCHINEALS
COCHLEARES
COCHLEARIFORM
COCHLEATED
COCKABULLIES
COCKABULLY
COCKALEEKIE
COCKALEEKIES
COCKALORUM
COCKALORUMS
COCKAMAMIE
COCKATEELS
COCKATIELS
COCKATRICE
COCKATRICES
COCKBILLED
COCKBILLING
COCKCHAFER
COCKCHAFERS
COCKCROWING
COCKCROWINGS
COCKERNONIES
COCKERNONY
COCKEYEDLY
COCKEYEDNESS
COCKEYEDNESSES
COCKFIGHTING
COCKFIGHTINGS
COCKFIGHTS
COCKHORSES
COCKIELEEKIE
COCKIELEEKIES
COCKINESSES
COCKLEBOAT
COCKLEBOATS
COCKLEBURS
COCKLEERTS
COCKLESHELL
COCKLESHELLS
COCKMATCHES
COCKNEYDOM
COCKNEYDOMS
COCKNEYFICATION
COCKNEYFIED
COCKNEYFIES
COCKNEYFYING
COCKNEYISH
COCKNEYISM
COCKNEYISMS
COCKNIFICATION
COCKNIFICATIONS
COCKNIFIED
COCKNIFIES
COCKNIFYING
COCKROACHES
COCKSCOMBS
COCKSFOOTS
COCKSINESS
COCKSINESSES
COCKSUCKER
COCKSUCKERS
COCKSURELY
COCKSURENESS
COCKSURENESSES
COCKSWAINED
COCKSWAINING
COCKSWAINS
COCKTAILED
COCKTAILING
COCKTEASER
COCKTEASERS
COCKTHROWING
COCKTHROWINGS
COCKYLEEKIES
COCKYLEEKY
COCOMPOSER
COCOMPOSERS
COCONSCIOUS
COCONSCIOUSES
COCONSCIOUSNESS
COCONSPIRATOR
COCONSPIRATORS
COCOONERIES
COCOONINGS
COCOUNSELED
COCOUNSELING
COCOUNSELLED
COCOUNSELLING
COCOUNSELS
COCOZELLES
COCREATING
COCREATORS
COCULTIVATE
COCULTIVATED
COCULTIVATES
COCULTIVATING
COCULTIVATION
COCULTIVATIONS
COCULTURED
COCULTURES
COCULTURING
COCURATORS
COCURRICULAR
COCUSWOODS
CODECLINATION
CODECLINATIONS
CODEFENDANT
CODEFENDANTS
CODEPENDENCE
CODEPENDENCES
CODEPENDENCIES
CODEPENDENCY
CODEPENDENT
CODEPENDENTS
CODERIVING
CODESIGNED
CODESIGNING
CODETERMINATION
CODEVELOPED
CODEVELOPER
CODEVELOPERS
CODEVELOPING
CODEVELOPS
CODICILLARY
CODICOLOGICAL
CODICOLOGIES
CODICOLOGY
CODIFIABILITIES
CODIFIABILITY
CODIFICATION
CODIFICATIONS
CODIRECTED
CODIRECTING
CODIRECTION
CODIRECTIONS
CODIRECTOR
CODIRECTORS
CODISCOVER
CODISCOVERED
CODISCOVERER
CODISCOVERERS
CODISCOVERING
CODISCOVERS
CODOLOGIES
CODOMINANCE
CODOMINANCES
CODOMINANT
CODOMINANTS
CODSWALLOP
CODSWALLOPS
COEDUCATION
COEDUCATIONAL
COEDUCATIONALLY
COEDUCATIONS
COEFFICIENT
COEFFICIENTS
COELACANTH
COELACANTHIC
COELACANTHS
COELANAGLYPHIC
COELENTERA
COELENTERATE
COELENTERATES
COELENTERIC
COELENTERON
COELOMATES
COELOMATIC
COELOSTATS
COELUROSAUR
COELUROSAURS
COEMBODIED
COEMBODIES
COEMBODYING
COEMPLOYED
COEMPLOYING
COEMPTIONS
COENACTING
COENAESTHESES
COENAESTHESIA

COENAESTHESIAS
COENAESTHESIS
COENAMORED
COENAMORING
COENDURING
COENENCHYMA
COENENCHYMAS
COENENCHYMATA
COENESTHESES
COENESTHESIA
COENESTHESIAS
COENESTHESIS
COENESTHETIC
COENOBITES
COENOBITIC
COENOBITICAL
COENOBITISM
COENOBITISMS
COENOCYTES
COENOCYTIC
COENOSARCS
COENOSPECIES
COENOSTEUM
COENOSTEUMS
COENZYMATIC
COENZYMATICALLY
COEQUALITIES
COEQUALITY
COEQUALNESS
COEQUALNESSES
COEQUATING
COERCIMETER
COERCIMETERS
COERCIONIST
COERCIONISTS
COERCIVELY
COERCIVENESS
COERCIVENESSES
COERCIVITIES
COERCIVITY
COERECTING
COESSENTIAL
COESSENTIALITY
COESSENTIALLY
COESSENTIALNESS
COETANEOUS
COETANEOUSLY
COETANEOUSNESS
COETERNALLY
COETERNITIES
COETERNITY
COEVALITIES
COEVOLUTION
COEVOLUTIONARY
COEVOLUTIONS
COEVOLVING
COEXECUTOR
COEXECUTORS
COEXECUTRICES
COEXECUTRIX
COEXECUTRIXES
COEXERTING
COEXISTENCE
COEXISTENCES
COEXISTENT
COEXISTING
COEXTENDED
COEXTENDING
COEXTENSION
COEXTENSIONS
COEXTENSIVE
COEXTENSIVELY
COFAVORITE
COFAVORITES
COFEATURED
COFEATURES
COFEATURING
COFFEEHOUSE
COFFEEHOUSES
COFFEEMAKER
COFFEEMAKERS
COFFEEPOTS
COFFERDAMS
COFFINITES
COFINANCED
COFINANCES
COFINANCING
COFOUNDERS
COFOUNDING
COFUNCTION
COFUNCTIONS
COGENERATION
COGENERATIONS
COGENERATOR
COGENERATORS
COGITATING
COGITATINGLY
COGITATION
COGITATIONS
COGITATIVE
COGITATIVELY
COGITATIVENESS
COGITATORS
COGNATENESS
COGNATENESSES
COGNATIONS
COGNISABLE
COGNISABLY
COGNISANCE
COGNISANCES
COGNITIONAL
COGNITIONS
COGNITIVELY
COGNITIVISM
COGNITIVISMS
COGNITIVITIES
COGNITIVITY
COGNIZABLE
COGNIZABLY
COGNIZANCE
COGNIZANCES
COGNOMINAL
COGNOMINALLY
COGNOMINATE
COGNOMINATED
COGNOMINATES
COGNOMINATING
COGNOMINATION
COGNOMINATIONS
COGNOSCENTE
COGNOSCENTI
COGNOSCIBLE
COGNOSCING
COHABITANT
COHABITANTS
COHABITATION
COHABITATIONS
COHABITEES
COHABITERS
COHABITING
COHABITORS
COHEIRESSES
COHERENCES
COHERENCIES
COHERENTLY
COHERITORS
COHESIBILITIES
COHESIBILITY
COHESIONLESS
COHESIVELY
COHESIVENESS
COHESIVENESSES
COHIBITING
COHIBITION
COHIBITIONS
COHIBITIVE
COHOBATING
COHOMOLOGICAL
COHOMOLOGIES
COHOMOLOGY
COHORTATIVE
COHORTATIVES
COHOSTESSED
COHOSTESSES
COHOSTESSING
COHOUSINGS
COHYPONYMS
COIFFEUSES
COIFFURING
COILABILITIES
COILABILITY
COINCIDENCE
COINCIDENCES
COINCIDENCIES
COINCIDENCY
COINCIDENT
COINCIDENTAL
COINCIDENTALLY
COINCIDENTLY
COINCIDING
COINFECTED
COINFECTING
COINFERRED
COINFERRING
COINHERENCE
COINHERENCES
COINHERING
COINHERITANCE
COINHERITANCES
COINHERITOR
COINHERITORS
COINSTANTANEITY
COINSTANTANEOUS
COINSURANCE
COINSURANCES
COINSURERS
COINSURING
COINTERRED
COINTERRING
COINTREAUS
COINVENTED
COINVENTING
COINVENTOR
COINVENTORS
COINVESTIGATOR
COINVESTIGATORS
COINVESTOR
COINVESTORS
COKULORISES
COLATITUDE
COLATITUDES
COLCANNONS
COLCHICINE
COLCHICINES
COLCHICUMS
COLCOTHARS
COLDBLOODS
COLDCOCKED
COLDCOCKING
COLDHEARTED
COLDHEARTEDLY
COLDHEARTEDNESS
COLDHOUSES
COLDNESSES
COLECTOMIES
COLEMANITE
COLEMANITES
COLEOPTERA
COLEOPTERAL
COLEOPTERAN
COLEOPTERANS
COLEOPTERIST
COLEOPTERISTS
COLEOPTERON
COLEOPTERONS
COLEOPTEROUS
COLEOPTERS
COLEOPTILE
COLEOPTILES
COLEORHIZA
COLEORHIZAE
COLEORHIZAS
COLEORRHIZA
COLEORRHIZAS
COLESTIPOL
COLESTIPOLS
COLICKIEST
COLICROOTS
COLICWEEDS
COLINEARITIES
COLINEARITY
COLIPHAGES
COLLABORATE
COLLABORATED
COLLABORATES
COLLABORATING
COLLABORATION
COLLABORATIONS
COLLABORATIVE
COLLABORATIVELY
COLLABORATIVES
COLLABORATOR
COLLABORATORS
COLLAGENASE

COLLAGENASES
COLLAGENIC
COLLAGENOUS
COLLAGISTS
COLLAPSABILITY
COLLAPSABLE
COLLAPSARS
COLLAPSIBILITY
COLLAPSIBLE
COLLAPSING
COLLARBONE
COLLARBONES
COLLARETTE
COLLARETTES
COLLARLESS
COLLATABLE
COLLATERAL
COLLATERALISE
COLLATERALISED
COLLATERALISES
COLLATERALISING
COLLATERALITIES
COLLATERALITY
COLLATERALIZE
COLLATERALIZED
COLLATERALIZES
COLLATERALIZING
COLLATERALLY
COLLATERALS
COLLATIONS
COLLEAGUED
COLLEAGUES
COLLEAGUESHIP
COLLEAGUESHIPS
COLLEAGUING
COLLECTABLE
COLLECTABLES
COLLECTANEA
COLLECTEDLY
COLLECTEDNESS
COLLECTEDNESSES
COLLECTIBLE
COLLECTIBLES
COLLECTING
COLLECTINGS
COLLECTION
COLLECTIONS
COLLECTIVE
COLLECTIVELY
COLLECTIVENESS
COLLECTIVES
COLLECTIVISE
COLLECTIVISED
COLLECTIVISES
COLLECTIVISING
COLLECTIVISM
COLLECTIVISMS
COLLECTIVIST
COLLECTIVISTIC
COLLECTIVISTS
COLLECTIVITIES
COLLECTIVITY
COLLECTIVIZE
COLLECTIVIZED
COLLECTIVIZES
COLLECTIVIZING
COLLECTORATE
COLLECTORATES
COLLECTORS
COLLECTORSHIP
COLLECTORSHIPS
COLLEGIALISM
COLLEGIALISMS
COLLEGIALITIES
COLLEGIALITY
COLLEGIALLY
COLLEGIANER
COLLEGIANERS
COLLEGIANS
COLLEGIATE
COLLEGIATELY
COLLEGIATES
COLLEGIUMS
COLLEMBOLAN
COLLEMBOLANS
COLLEMBOLOUS
COLLENCHYMA
COLLENCHYMAS
COLLENCHYMATA
COLLENCHYMATOUS
COLLETERIAL
COLLICULUS
COLLICULUSES
COLLIERIES
COLLIESHANGIE
COLLIESHANGIES
COLLIGATED
COLLIGATES
COLLIGATING
COLLIGATION
COLLIGATIONS
COLLIGATIVE
COLLIMATED
COLLIMATES
COLLIMATING
COLLIMATION
COLLIMATIONS
COLLIMATOR
COLLIMATORS
COLLINEARITIES
COLLINEARITY
COLLINEARLY
COLLINSIAS
COLLIQUABLE
COLLIQUANT
COLLIQUATE
COLLIQUATED
COLLIQUATES
COLLIQUATING
COLLIQUATION
COLLIQUATIONS
COLLIQUATIVE
COLLIQUESCENCE
COLLIQUESCENCES
COLLISIONAL
COLLISIONALLY
COLLISIONS
COLLOCATED
COLLOCATES
COLLOCATING
COLLOCATION
COLLOCATIONAL
COLLOCATIONS
COLLOCUTOR
COLLOCUTORS
COLLOCUTORY
COLLODIONS
COLLODIUMS
COLLOGUING
COLLOIDALITIES
COLLOIDALITY
COLLOIDALLY
COLLOQUIAL
COLLOQUIALISM
COLLOQUIALISMS
COLLOQUIALIST
COLLOQUIALISTS
COLLOQUIALITIES
COLLOQUIALITY
COLLOQUIALLY
COLLOQUIALNESS
COLLOQUIALS
COLLOQUIED
COLLOQUIES
COLLOQUING
COLLOQUISE
COLLOQUISED
COLLOQUISES
COLLOQUISING
COLLOQUIST
COLLOQUISTS
COLLOQUIUM
COLLOQUIUMS
COLLOQUIZE
COLLOQUIZED
COLLOQUIZES
COLLOQUIZING
COLLOQUYING
COLLOTYPES
COLLOTYPIC
COLLOTYPIES
COLLUCTATION
COLLUCTATIONS
COLLUSIONS
COLLUSIVELY
COLLUVIUMS
COLLYRIUMS
COLLYWOBBLES
COLOBOMATA
COLOCATING
COLOCYNTHS
COLOGARITHM
COLOGARITHMS
COLOMBARDS
COLONELCIES
COLONELLING
COLONELLINGS
COLONELSHIP
COLONELSHIPS
COLONIALISE
COLONIALISED
COLONIALISES
COLONIALISING
COLONIALISM
COLONIALISMS
COLONIALIST
COLONIALISTIC
COLONIALISTS
COLONIALIZE
COLONIALIZED
COLONIALIZES
COLONIALIZING
COLONIALLY
COLONIALNESS
COLONIALNESSES
COLONISABLE
COLONISATION
COLONISATIONS
COLONISATIONIST
COLONISERS
COLONISING
COLONITISES
COLONIZABLE
COLONIZATION
COLONIZATIONIST
COLONIZATIONS
COLONIZERS
COLONIZING
COLONNADED
COLONNADES
COLONOSCOPE
COLONOSCOPES
COLONOSCOPIES
COLONOSCOPY
COLOPHONIES
COLOQUINTIDA
COLOQUINTIDAS
COLORATION
COLORATIONS
COLORATURA
COLORATURAS
COLORATURE
COLORATURES
COLORBREED
COLORBREEDING
COLORBREEDS
COLORCASTED
COLORCASTING
COLORCASTS
COLORECTAL
COLORFASTNESS
COLORFASTNESSES
COLORFULLY
COLORFULNESS
COLORFULNESSES
COLORIMETER
COLORIMETERS
COLORIMETRIC
COLORIMETRICAL
COLORIMETRIES
COLORIMETRY
COLORISATION
COLORISATIONS
COLORISERS
COLORISING
COLORISTIC
COLORISTICALLY
COLORIZATION
COLORIZATIONS
COLORIZERS
COLORIZING
COLORLESSLY
COLORLESSNESS
COLORLESSNESSES

OLORPOINT
OLORPOINTS
OLOSSALLY
OLOSSEUMS
OLOSSUSES
OLOSTOMIES
OLOSTROUS
OLOSTRUMS
OLOTOMIES
OLOURABILITIES
OLOURABILITY
OLOURABLE
OLOURABLENESS
OLOURABLY
OLOURANTS
OLOURATION
OLOURATIONS
OLOURFAST
OLOURFASTNESS
OLOURFULLY
OLOURFULNESS
OLOURFULNESSES
OLOURINGS
OLOURISATION
OLOURISATIONS
OLOURISED
OLOURISES
OLOURISING
OLOURISTIC
OLOURISTS
OLOURIZATION
OLOURIZATIONS
OLOURIZED
OLOURIZES
OLOURIZING
OLOURLESS
OLOURLESSLY
OLOURLESSNESS
OLOURPOINT
OLOURPOINTS
OLOURWASH
OLOURWASHED
OLOURWASHES
OLOURWASHING
OLOURWAYS
OLPITISES
OLPORTAGE
OLPORTAGES
OLPORTEUR
OLPORTEURS
OLPOSCOPE
OLPOSCOPES
OLPOSCOPICAL
OLPOSCOPICALLY
OLPOSCOPIES
OLPOSCOPY
OLPOTOMIES
OLTISHNESS
OLTISHNESSES
OLTSFOOTS
OLUBRIADS
OLUBRIFORM
OLUMBARIA
OLUMBARIES
OLUMBARIUM
OLUMBATES

COLUMBINES
COLUMBITES
COLUMBIUMS
COLUMELLAE
COLUMELLAR
COLUMNARITIES
COLUMNARITY
COLUMNATED
COLUMNIATED
COLUMNIATION
COLUMNIATIONS
COLUMNISTIC
COLUMNISTS
COMANAGEMENT
COMANAGEMENTS
COMANAGERS
COMANAGING
COMANCHERO
COMANCHEROS
COMATOSELY
COMATULIDS
COMBATABLE
COMBATANTS
COMBATIVELY
COMBATIVENESS
COMBATIVENESSES
COMBATTING
COMBINABILITIES
COMBINABILITY
COMBINABLE
COMBINATION
COMBINATIONAL
COMBINATIONS
COMBINATIVE
COMBINATORIAL
COMBINATORIALLY
COMBINATORICS
COMBINATORY
COMBININGS
COMBRETUMS
COMBURGESS
COMBURGESSES
COMBUSTIBILITY
COMBUSTIBLE
COMBUSTIBLENESS
COMBUSTIBLES
COMBUSTIBLY
COMBUSTING
COMBUSTION
COMBUSTIONS
COMBUSTIOUS
COMBUSTIVE
COMBUSTIVES
COMBUSTORS
COMEDDLING
COMEDICALLY
COMEDIENNE
COMEDIENNES
COMEDIETTA
COMEDIETTAS
COMEDOGENIC
COMELINESS
COMELINESSES
COMESTIBLE
COMESTIBLES
COMETOGRAPHIES

COMETOGRAPHY
COMETOLOGIES
COMETOLOGY
COMEUPPANCE
COMEUPPANCES
COMFINESSES
COMFITURES
COMFORTABLE
COMFORTABLENESS
COMFORTABLY
COMFORTERS
COMFORTING
COMFORTINGLY
COMFORTLESS
COMFORTLESSLY
COMFORTLESSNESS
COMICALITIES
COMICALITY
COMICALNESS
COMICALNESSES
COMINGLING
COMITADJIS
COMITATIVE
COMITATIVES
COMITATUSES
COMMANDABLE
COMMANDANT
COMMANDANTS
COMMANDANTSHIP
COMMANDANTSHIPS
COMMANDEER
COMMANDEERED
COMMANDEERING
COMMANDEERS
COMMANDERIES
COMMANDERS
COMMANDERSHIP
COMMANDERSHIPS
COMMANDERY
COMMANDING
COMMANDINGLY
COMMANDMENT
COMMANDMENTS
COMMANDOES
COMMEASURABLE
COMMEASURE
COMMEASURED
COMMEASURES
COMMEASURING
COMMEMORABLE
COMMEMORATE
COMMEMORATED
COMMEMORATES
COMMEMORATING
COMMEMORATION
COMMEMORATIONAL
COMMEMORATIONS
COMMEMORATIVE
COMMEMORATIVELY
COMMEMORATIVES
COMMEMORATOR
COMMEMORATORS
COMMEMORATORY
COMMENCEMENT
COMMENCEMENTS
COMMENCERS

COMMENCING
COMMENDABLE
COMMENDABLENESS
COMMENDABLY
COMMENDAMS
COMMENDATION
COMMENDATIONS
COMMENDATOR
COMMENDATORS
COMMENDATORY
COMMENDERS
COMMENDING
COMMENSALISM
COMMENSALISMS
COMMENSALITIES
COMMENSALITY
COMMENSALLY
COMMENSALS
COMMENSURABLE
COMMENSURABLY
COMMENSURATE
COMMENSURATELY
COMMENSURATION
COMMENSURATIONS
COMMENTARIAL
COMMENTARIAT
COMMENTARIATS
COMMENTARIES
COMMENTARY
COMMENTATE
COMMENTATED
COMMENTATES
COMMENTATING
COMMENTATION
COMMENTATIONS
COMMENTATOR
COMMENTATORIAL
COMMENTATORS
COMMENTERS
COMMENTING
COMMENTORS
COMMERCIAL
COMMERCIALESE
COMMERCIALESES
COMMERCIALISE
COMMERCIALISED
COMMERCIALISES
COMMERCIALISING
COMMERCIALISM
COMMERCIALISMS
COMMERCIALIST
COMMERCIALISTIC
COMMERCIALISTS
COMMERCIALITIES
COMMERCIALITY
COMMERCIALIZE
COMMERCIALIZED
COMMERCIALIZES
COMMERCIALIZING
COMMERCIALLY
COMMERCIALS
COMMERCING
COMMERGING
COMMINATED
COMMINATES
COMMINATING

COMMINATION
COMMINATIONS
COMMINATIVE
COMMINATORY
COMMINGLED
COMMINGLES
COMMINGLING
COMMINUTED
COMMINUTES
COMMINUTING
COMMINUTION
COMMINUTIONS
COMMISERABLE
COMMISERATE
COMMISERATED
COMMISERATES
COMMISERATING
COMMISERATINGLY
COMMISERATION
COMMISERATIONS
COMMISERATIVE
COMMISERATIVELY
COMMISERATOR
COMMISERATORS
COMMISSAIRE
COMMISSAIRES
COMMISSARIAL
COMMISSARIAT
COMMISSARIATS
COMMISSARIES
COMMISSARS
COMMISSARY
COMMISSARYSHIP
COMMISSARYSHIPS
COMMISSION
COMMISSIONAIRE
COMMISSIONAIRES
COMMISSIONAL
COMMISSIONARY
COMMISSIONED
COMMISSIONER
COMMISSIONERS
COMMISSIONING
COMMISSIONS
COMMISSURAL
COMMISSURE
COMMISSURES
COMMITMENT
COMMITMENTS
COMMITTABLE
COMMITTALS
COMMITTEEMAN
COMMITTEEMEN
COMMITTEES
COMMITTEESHIP
COMMITTEESHIPS
COMMITTEEWOMAN
COMMITTEEWOMEN
COMMITTERS
COMMITTING
COMMIXTION
COMMIXTIONS
COMMIXTURE
COMMIXTURES
COMMODIFICATION
COMMODIFIED
COMMODIFIES
COMMODIFYING
COMMODIOUS
COMMODIOUSLY
COMMODIOUSNESS
COMMODITIES
COMMODITISE
COMMODITISED
COMMODITISES
COMMODITISING
COMMODITIZE
COMMODITIZED
COMMODITIZES
COMMODITIZING
COMMODORES
COMMONABLE
COMMONAGES
COMMONALITIES
COMMONALITY
COMMONALTIES
COMMONALTY
COMMONHOLD
COMMONHOLDS
COMMONINGS
COMMONNESS
COMMONNESSES
COMMONPLACE
COMMONPLACED
COMMONPLACENESS
COMMONPLACES
COMMONPLACING
COMMONSENSE
COMMONSENSIBLE
COMMONSENSICAL
COMMONWEAL
COMMONWEALS
COMMONWEALTH
COMMONWEALTHS
COMMORANTS
COMMORIENTES
COMMOTIONAL
COMMOTIONS
COMMUNALISATION
COMMUNALISE
COMMUNALISED
COMMUNALISER
COMMUNALISERS
COMMUNALISES
COMMUNALISING
COMMUNALISM
COMMUNALISMS
COMMUNALIST
COMMUNALISTIC
COMMUNALISTS
COMMUNALITIES
COMMUNALITY
COMMUNALIZATION
COMMUNALIZE
COMMUNALIZED
COMMUNALIZER
COMMUNALIZERS
COMMUNALIZES
COMMUNALIZING
COMMUNALLY
COMMUNARDS
COMMUNAUTAIRE
COMMUNAUTAIRES
COMMUNICABILITY
COMMUNICABLE
COMMUNICABLY
COMMUNICANT
COMMUNICANTS
COMMUNICATE
COMMUNICATED
COMMUNICATEE
COMMUNICATEES
COMMUNICATES
COMMUNICATING
COMMUNICATION
COMMUNICATIONAL
COMMUNICATIONS
COMMUNICATIVE
COMMUNICATIVELY
COMMUNICATOR
COMMUNICATORS
COMMUNICATORY
COMMUNINGS
COMMUNIONAL
COMMUNIONALLY
COMMUNIONS
COMMUNIQUE
COMMUNIQUES
COMMUNISATION
COMMUNISATIONS
COMMUNISED
COMMUNISES
COMMUNISING
COMMUNISMS
COMMUNISTIC
COMMUNISTICALLY
COMMUNISTS
COMMUNITAIRE
COMMUNITAIRES
COMMUNITARIAN
COMMUNITARIANS
COMMUNITIES
COMMUNIZATION
COMMUNIZATIONS
COMMUNIZED
COMMUNIZES
COMMUNIZING
COMMUTABILITIES
COMMUTABILITY
COMMUTABLE
COMMUTABLENESS
COMMUTATED
COMMUTATES
COMMUTATING
COMMUTATION
COMMUTATIONS
COMMUTATIVE
COMMUTATIVELY
COMMUTATIVITIES
COMMUTATIVITY
COMMUTATOR
COMMUTATORS
COMONOMERS
COMPACTEDLY
COMPACTEDNESS
COMPACTEDNESSES
COMPACTERS
COMPACTEST
COMPACTIBLE
COMPACTIFIED
COMPACTIFIES
COMPACTIFY
COMPACTIFYING
COMPACTING
COMPACTION
COMPACTIONS
COMPACTNESS
COMPACTNESSES
COMPACTORS
COMPACTURE
COMPACTURES
COMPAGINATE
COMPAGINATED
COMPAGINATES
COMPAGINATING
COMPAGINATION
COMPAGINATIONS
COMPANDERS
COMPANDING
COMPANDORS
COMPANIABLE
COMPANIONABLE
COMPANIONABLY
COMPANIONATE
COMPANIONED
COMPANIONHOOD
COMPANIONHOODS
COMPANIONING
COMPANIONLESS
COMPANIONS
COMPANIONSHIP
COMPANIONSHIPS
COMPANIONWAY
COMPANIONWAYS
COMPANYING
COMPARABILITIES
COMPARABILITY
COMPARABLE
COMPARABLENESS
COMPARABLY
COMPARATIST
COMPARATISTS
COMPARATIVE
COMPARATIVELY
COMPARATIVENESS
COMPARATIVES
COMPARATIVIST
COMPARATIVISTS
COMPARATOR
COMPARATORS
COMPARISON
COMPARISONS
COMPARTING
COMPARTMENT
COMPARTMENTAL
COMPARTMENTALLY
COMPARTMENTED
COMPARTMENTING
COMPARTMENTS
COMPASSABLE
COMPASSING
COMPASSINGS
COMPASSION
COMPASSIONABLE

OMPASSIONATE
OMPASSIONATED
OMPASSIONATELY
OMPASSIONATES
OMPASSIONATING
OMPASSIONED
OMPASSIONING
OMPASSIONLESS
OMPASSIONS
OMPATIBILITIES
OMPATIBILITY
OMPATIBLE
OMPATIBLENESS
OMPATIBLES
OMPATIBLY
OMPATRIOT
OMPATRIOTIC
OMPATRIOTISM
OMPATRIOTISMS
OMPATRIOTS
OMPEARANCE
OMPEARANCES
OMPEARANT
OMPEARANTS
OMPEARING
OMPEERING
OMPELLABLE
OMPELLABLY
OMPELLATION
OMPELLATIONS
OMPELLATIVE
OMPELLATIVES
OMPELLERS
OMPELLING
OMPELLINGLY
OMPENDIOUS
OMPENDIOUSLY
OMPENDIOUSNESS
OMPENDIUM
OMPENDIUMS
OMPENSABILITY
OMPENSABLE
OMPENSATE
OMPENSATED
OMPENSATES
OMPENSATING
OMPENSATION
OMPENSATIONAL
OMPENSATIONS
OMPENSATIVE
OMPENSATOR
OMPENSATORS
OMPENSATORY
OMPESCING
OMPETENCE
OMPETENCES
OMPETENCIES
OMPETENCY
OMPETENTLY
OMPETENTNESS
OMPETENTNESSES
OMPETITION
OMPETITIONS
OMPETITIVE
OMPETITIVELY
OMPETITIVENESS
COMPETITOR
COMPETITORS
COMPILATION
COMPILATIONS
COMPILATOR
COMPILATORS
COMPILATORY
COMPILEMENT
COMPILEMENTS
COMPLACENCE
COMPLACENCES
COMPLACENCIES
COMPLACENCY
COMPLACENT
COMPLACENTLY
COMPLAINANT
COMPLAINANTS
COMPLAINED
COMPLAINER
COMPLAINERS
COMPLAINING
COMPLAININGLY
COMPLAININGS
COMPLAINTS
COMPLAISANCE
COMPLAISANCES
COMPLAISANT
COMPLAISANTLY
COMPLANATE
COMPLANATION
COMPLANATIONS
COMPLECTED
COMPLECTING
COMPLEMENT
COMPLEMENTAL
COMPLEMENTALLY
COMPLEMENTARIES
COMPLEMENTARILY
COMPLEMENTARITY
COMPLEMENTARY
COMPLEMENTATION
COMPLEMENTED
COMPLEMENTING
COMPLEMENTISER
COMPLEMENTISERS
COMPLEMENTIZER
COMPLEMENTIZERS
COMPLEMENTS
COMPLETABLE
COMPLETELY
COMPLETENESS
COMPLETENESSES
COMPLETERS
COMPLETEST
COMPLETING
COMPLETION
COMPLETIONS
COMPLETIST
COMPLETISTS
COMPLETIVE
COMPLETORY
COMPLEXATION
COMPLEXATIONS
COMPLEXEDNESS
COMPLEXEDNESSES
COMPLEXEST
COMPLEXIFIED
COMPLEXIFIES
COMPLEXIFY
COMPLEXIFYING
COMPLEXING
COMPLEXION
COMPLEXIONAL
COMPLEXIONED
COMPLEXIONLESS
COMPLEXIONS
COMPLEXITIES
COMPLEXITY
COMPLEXNESS
COMPLEXNESSES
COMPLEXOMETRIC
COMPLEXONE
COMPLEXONES
COMPLEXUSES
COMPLIABLE
COMPLIABLENESS
COMPLIABLY
COMPLIANCE
COMPLIANCES
COMPLIANCIES
COMPLIANCY
COMPLIANTLY
COMPLIANTNESS
COMPLIANTNESSES
COMPLICACIES
COMPLICACY
COMPLICANT
COMPLICATE
COMPLICATED
COMPLICATEDLY
COMPLICATEDNESS
COMPLICATES
COMPLICATING
COMPLICATION
COMPLICATIONS
COMPLICATIVE
COMPLICITIES
COMPLICITOUS
COMPLICITY
COMPLIMENT
COMPLIMENTAL
COMPLIMENTARILY
COMPLIMENTARY
COMPLIMENTED
COMPLIMENTER
COMPLIMENTERS
COMPLIMENTING
COMPLIMENTS
COMPLISHED
COMPLISHES
COMPLISHING
COMPLOTTED
COMPLOTTER
COMPLOTTERS
COMPLOTTING
COMPLUVIUM
COMPLUVIUMS
COMPONENCIES
COMPONENCY
COMPONENTAL
COMPONENTIAL
COMPONENTS
COMPORTANCE
COMPORTANCES
COMPORTING
COMPORTMENT
COMPORTMENTS
COMPOSEDLY
COMPOSEDNESS
COMPOSEDNESSES
COMPOSITED
COMPOSITELY
COMPOSITENESS
COMPOSITENESSES
COMPOSITES
COMPOSITING
COMPOSITION
COMPOSITIONAL
COMPOSITIONALLY
COMPOSITIONS
COMPOSITIVE
COMPOSITOR
COMPOSITORIAL
COMPOSITORS
COMPOSITOUS
COMPOSSIBILITY
COMPOSSIBLE
COMPOSTABLE
COMPOSTERS
COMPOSTING
COMPOSTURE
COMPOSTURED
COMPOSTURES
COMPOSTURING
COMPOSURES
COMPOTATION
COMPOTATIONS
COMPOTATIONSHIP
COMPOTATOR
COMPOTATORS
COMPOTATORY
COMPOTIERS
COMPOUNDABLE
COMPOUNDED
COMPOUNDER
COMPOUNDERS
COMPOUNDING
COMPRADORE
COMPRADORES
COMPRADORS
COMPREHEND
COMPREHENDED
COMPREHENDIBLE
COMPREHENDING
COMPREHENDS
COMPREHENSIBLE
COMPREHENSIBLY
COMPREHENSION
COMPREHENSIONS
COMPREHENSIVE
COMPREHENSIVELY
COMPREHENSIVES
COMPREHENSIVISE
COMPREHENSIVIZE
COMPRESSED
COMPRESSEDLY
COMPRESSES
COMPRESSIBILITY

COMPRESSIBLE
COMPRESSIBLY
COMPRESSING
COMPRESSION
COMPRESSIONAL
COMPRESSIONS
COMPRESSIVE
COMPRESSIVELY
COMPRESSOR
COMPRESSORS
COMPRESSURE
COMPRESSURES
COMPRIMARIO
COMPRIMARIOS
COMPRINTED
COMPRINTING
COMPRISABLE
COMPRISALS
COMPRISING
COMPRIZING
COMPROMISE
COMPROMISED
COMPROMISER
COMPROMISERS
COMPROMISES
COMPROMISING
COMPROMISINGLY
COMPROVINCIAL
COMPTROLLED
COMPTROLLER
COMPTROLLERS
COMPTROLLERSHIP
COMPTROLLING
COMPTROLLS
COMPULSATIVE
COMPULSATORY
COMPULSING
COMPULSION
COMPULSIONIST
COMPULSIONISTS
COMPULSIONS
COMPULSITOR
COMPULSITORS
COMPULSIVE
COMPULSIVELY
COMPULSIVENESS
COMPULSIVES
COMPULSIVITIES
COMPULSIVITY
COMPULSORIES
COMPULSORILY
COMPULSORINESS
COMPULSORY
COMPUNCTION
COMPUNCTIONS
COMPUNCTIOUS
COMPUNCTIOUSLY
COMPURGATION
COMPURGATIONS
COMPURGATOR
COMPURGATORIAL
COMPURGATORS
COMPURGATORY
COMPURSION
COMPURSIONS
COMPUTABILITIES
COMPUTABILITY
COMPUTABLE
COMPUTANTS
COMPUTATION
COMPUTATIONAL
COMPUTATIONALLY
COMPUTATIONS
COMPUTATIVE
COMPUTATOR
COMPUTATORS
COMPUTERATE
COMPUTERDOM
COMPUTERDOMS
COMPUTERESE
COMPUTERESES
COMPUTERISABLE
COMPUTERISATION
COMPUTERISE
COMPUTERISED
COMPUTERISES
COMPUTERISING
COMPUTERIST
COMPUTERISTS
COMPUTERIZABLE
COMPUTERIZATION
COMPUTERIZE
COMPUTERIZED
COMPUTERIZES
COMPUTERIZING
COMPUTERLESS
COMPUTERLIKE
COMPUTERNIK
COMPUTERNIKS
COMPUTERPHOBE
COMPUTERPHOBES
COMPUTERPHOBIA
COMPUTERPHOBIAS
COMPUTERPHOBIC
COMPUTISTS
COMRADELINESS
COMRADELINESSES
COMRADERIES
COMRADESHIP
COMRADESHIPS
COMSTOCKER
COMSTOCKERIES
COMSTOCKERS
COMSTOCKERY
COMSTOCKISM
COMSTOCKISMS
CONACREISM
CONACREISMS
CONATIONAL
CONCANAVALIN
CONCANAVALINS
CONCATENATE
CONCATENATED
CONCATENATES
CONCATENATING
CONCATENATION
CONCATENATIONS
CONCAVENESS
CONCAVENESSES
CONCAVITIES
CONCEALABLE
CONCEALERS
CONCEALING
CONCEALINGLY
CONCEALMENT
CONCEALMENTS
CONCEDEDLY
CONCEITEDLY
CONCEITEDNESS
CONCEITEDNESSES
CONCEITFUL
CONCEITING
CONCEITLESS
CONCEIVABILITY
CONCEIVABLE
CONCEIVABLENESS
CONCEIVABLY
CONCEIVERS
CONCEIVING
CONCELEBRANT
CONCELEBRANTS
CONCELEBRATE
CONCELEBRATED
CONCELEBRATES
CONCELEBRATING
CONCELEBRATION
CONCELEBRATIONS
CONCENTERED
CONCENTERING
CONCENTERS
CONCENTRATE
CONCENTRATED
CONCENTRATEDLY
CONCENTRATES
CONCENTRATING
CONCENTRATION
CONCENTRATIONS
CONCENTRATIVE
CONCENTRATIVELY
CONCENTRATOR
CONCENTRATORS
CONCENTRED
CONCENTRES
CONCENTRIC
CONCENTRICAL
CONCENTRICALLY
CONCENTRICITIES
CONCENTRICITY
CONCENTRING
CONCEPTACLE
CONCEPTACLES
CONCEPTION
CONCEPTIONAL
CONCEPTIONS
CONCEPTIOUS
CONCEPTIVE
CONCEPTUAL
CONCEPTUALISE
CONCEPTUALISED
CONCEPTUALISER
CONCEPTUALISERS
CONCEPTUALISES
CONCEPTUALISING
CONCEPTUALISM
CONCEPTUALISMS
CONCEPTUALIST
CONCEPTUALISTIC
CONCEPTUALISTS
CONCEPTUALITIES
CONCEPTUALITY
CONCEPTUALIZE
CONCEPTUALIZED
CONCEPTUALIZER
CONCEPTUALIZERS
CONCEPTUALIZES
CONCEPTUALIZING
CONCEPTUALLY
CONCEPTUSES
CONCERNANCIES
CONCERNANCY
CONCERNEDLY
CONCERNEDNESS
CONCERNEDNESSES
CONCERNING
CONCERNMENT
CONCERNMENTS
CONCERTANTE
CONCERTANTES
CONCERTANTI
CONCERTEDLY
CONCERTEDNESS
CONCERTEDNESSES
CONCERTGOER
CONCERTGOERS
CONCERTGOING
CONCERTGOINGS
CONCERTINA
CONCERTINAED
CONCERTINAING
CONCERTINAS
CONCERTING
CONCERTINI
CONCERTINIST
CONCERTINISTS
CONCERTINO
CONCERTINOS
CONCERTISE
CONCERTISED
CONCERTISES
CONCERTISING
CONCERTIZE
CONCERTIZED
CONCERTIZES
CONCERTIZING
CONCERTMASTER
CONCERTMASTERS
CONCERTMEISTER
CONCERTMEISTERS
CONCERTSTUCK
CONCERTSTUCKS
CONCESSIBLE
CONCESSION
CONCESSIONAIRE
CONCESSIONAIRES
CONCESSIONAL
CONCESSIONARIES
CONCESSIONARY
CONCESSIONER
CONCESSIONERS
CONCESSIONIST
CONCESSIONISTS
CONCESSIONNAIRE
CONCESSIONS
CONCESSIVE

ONCESSIVELY
ONCETTISM
ONCETTISMS
ONCETTIST
ONCETTISTS
ONCHIFEROUS
ONCHIFORM
ONCHIGLIE
ONCHIOLIN
ONCHIOLINS
ONCHITISES
ONCHOIDAL
ONCHOIDALLY
ONCHOLOGICAL
ONCHOLOGIES
ONCHOLOGIST
ONCHOLOGISTS
ONCHOLOGY
ONCIERGES
ONCILIABLE
ONCILIARLY
ONCILIARY
ONCILIATE
ONCILIATED
ONCILIATES
ONCILIATING
ONCILIATION
ONCILIATIONS
ONCILIATIVE
ONCILIATOR
ONCILIATORILY
ONCILIATORS
ONCILIATORY
ONCINNITIES
ONCINNITY
ONCINNOUS
ONCIPIENCIES
ONCIPIENCY
ONCIPIENT
ONCISENESS
ONCISENESSES
ONCISIONS
ONCLAMATION
ONCLAMATIONS
ONCLAVIST
ONCLAVISTS
ONCLUDERS
ONCLUDING
ONCLUSION
ONCLUSIONARY
ONCLUSIONS
ONCLUSIVE
ONCLUSIVELY
ONCLUSIVENESS
ONCLUSORY
ONCOCTERS
ONCOCTING
ONCOCTION
ONCOCTIONS
ONCOCTIVE
ONCOCTORS
ONCOLORATE
ONCOLOROUS
ONCOMITANCE
ONCOMITANCES
ONCOMITANCIES
CONCOMITANCY
CONCOMITANT
CONCOMITANTLY
CONCOMITANTS
CONCORDANCE
CONCORDANCES
CONCORDANT
CONCORDANTLY
CONCORDATS
CONCORDIAL
CONCORDING
CONCORPORATE
CONCORPORATED
CONCORPORATES
CONCORPORATING
CONCOURSES
CONCREATED
CONCREATES
CONCREATING
CONCREMATION
CONCREMATIONS
CONCRESCENCE
CONCRESCENCES
CONCRESCENT
CONCRETELY
CONCRETENESS
CONCRETENESSES
CONCRETING
CONCRETION
CONCRETIONARY
CONCRETIONS
CONCRETISATION
CONCRETISATIONS
CONCRETISE
CONCRETISED
CONCRETISES
CONCRETISING
CONCRETISM
CONCRETISMS
CONCRETIST
CONCRETISTS
CONCRETIVE
CONCRETIVELY
CONCRETIZATION
CONCRETIZATIONS
CONCRETIZE
CONCRETIZED
CONCRETIZES
CONCRETIZING
CONCREWING
CONCUBINAGE
CONCUBINAGES
CONCUBINARY
CONCUBINES
CONCUBITANCIES
CONCUBITANCY
CONCUBITANT
CONCUBITANTS
CONCUPISCENCE
CONCUPISCENCES
CONCUPISCENT
CONCUPISCIBLE
CONCURRENCE
CONCURRENCES
CONCURRENCIES
CONCURRENCY
CONCURRENT
CONCURRENTLY
CONCURRENTS
CONCURRING
CONCURRINGLY
CONCUSSING
CONCUSSION
CONCUSSIONS
CONCUSSIVE
CONCYCLICALLY
CONDEMNABLE
CONDEMNABLY
CONDEMNATION
CONDEMNATIONS
CONDEMNATORY
CONDEMNERS
CONDEMNING
CONDEMNINGLY
CONDEMNORS
CONDENSABILITY
CONDENSABLE
CONDENSATE
CONDENSATED
CONDENSATES
CONDENSATING
CONDENSATION
CONDENSATIONAL
CONDENSATIONS
CONDENSERIES
CONDENSERS
CONDENSERY
CONDENSIBILITY
CONDENSIBLE
CONDENSING
CONDESCEND
CONDESCENDED
CONDESCENDENCE
CONDESCENDENCES
CONDESCENDING
CONDESCENDINGLY
CONDESCENDS
CONDESCENSION
CONDESCENSIONS
CONDIDDLED
CONDIDDLES
CONDIDDLING
CONDIGNNESS
CONDIGNNESSES
CONDIMENTAL
CONDIMENTED
CONDIMENTING
CONDIMENTS
CONDISCIPLE
CONDISCIPLES
CONDITIONABLE
CONDITIONAL
CONDITIONALITY
CONDITIONALLY
CONDITIONALS
CONDITIONATE
CONDITIONATED
CONDITIONATES
CONDITIONATING
CONDITIONED
CONDITIONER
CONDITIONERS
CONDITIONING
CONDITIONINGS
CONDITIONS
CONDOLATORY
CONDOLEMENT
CONDOLEMENTS
CONDOLENCE
CONDOLENCES
CONDOLINGLY
CONDOMINIUM
CONDOMINIUMS
CONDONABLE
CONDONATION
CONDONATIONS
CONDOTTIERE
CONDOTTIERI
CONDUCEMENT
CONDUCEMENTS
CONDUCIBLE
CONDUCINGLY
CONDUCIVENESS
CONDUCIVENESSES
CONDUCTANCE
CONDUCTANCES
CONDUCTIBILITY
CONDUCTIBLE
CONDUCTIMETRIC
CONDUCTING
CONDUCTIOMETRIC
CONDUCTION
CONDUCTIONAL
CONDUCTIONS
CONDUCTIVE
CONDUCTIVELY
CONDUCTIVITIES
CONDUCTIVITY
CONDUCTOMETRIC
CONDUCTORIAL
CONDUCTORS
CONDUCTORSHIP
CONDUCTORSHIPS
CONDUCTRESS
CONDUCTRESSES
CONDUPLICATE
CONDUPLICATION
CONDUPLICATIONS
CONDYLOMAS
CONDYLOMATA
CONDYLOMATOUS
CONEFLOWER
CONEFLOWERS
CONFABBING
CONFABULAR
CONFABULATE
CONFABULATED
CONFABULATES
CONFABULATING
CONFABULATION
CONFABULATIONS
CONFABULATOR
CONFABULATORS
CONFABULATORY
CONFARREATE
CONFARREATION
CONFARREATIONS
CONFECTING

CONFECTION
CONFECTIONARIES
CONFECTIONARY
CONFECTIONER
CONFECTIONERIES
CONFECTIONERS
CONFECTIONERY
CONFECTIONS
CONFEDERACIES
CONFEDERACY
CONFEDERAL
CONFEDERATE
CONFEDERATED
CONFEDERATES
CONFEDERATING
CONFEDERATION
CONFEDERATIONS
CONFEDERATIVE
CONFERENCE
CONFERENCES
CONFERENCIER
CONFERENCIERS
CONFERENCING
CONFERENCINGS
CONFERENTIAL
CONFERMENT
CONFERMENTS
CONFERRABLE
CONFERRALS
CONFERREES
CONFERRENCE
CONFERRENCES
CONFERRERS
CONFERRING
CONFERVOID
CONFERVOIDS
CONFESSABLE
CONFESSANT
CONFESSANTS
CONFESSEDLY
CONFESSING
CONFESSION
CONFESSIONAL
CONFESSIONALISM
CONFESSIONALIST
CONFESSIONALLY
CONFESSIONALS
CONFESSIONARIES
CONFESSIONARY
CONFESSIONS
CONFESSORESS
CONFESSORESSES
CONFESSORS
CONFESSORSHIP
CONFESSORSHIPS
CONFIDANTE
CONFIDANTES
CONFIDANTS
CONFIDENCE
CONFIDENCES
CONFIDENCIES
CONFIDENCY
CONFIDENTIAL
CONFIDENTIALITY
CONFIDENTIALLY
CONFIDENTLY
CONFIDENTS
CONFIDINGLY
CONFIDINGNESS
CONFIDINGNESSES
CONFIGURATE
CONFIGURATED
CONFIGURATES
CONFIGURATING
CONFIGURATION
CONFIGURATIONAL
CONFIGURATIONS
CONFIGURATIVE
CONFIGURED
CONFIGURES
CONFIGURING
CONFINABLE
CONFINEABLE
CONFINEDLY
CONFINEDNESS
CONFINEDNESSES
CONFINELESS
CONFINEMENT
CONFINEMENTS
CONFIRMABILITY
CONFIRMABLE
CONFIRMAND
CONFIRMANDS
CONFIRMATION
CONFIRMATIONAL
CONFIRMATIONS
CONFIRMATIVE
CONFIRMATOR
CONFIRMATORS
CONFIRMATORY
CONFIRMEDLY
CONFIRMEDNESS
CONFIRMEDNESSES
CONFIRMEES
CONFIRMERS
CONFIRMING
CONFIRMINGS
CONFIRMORS
CONFISCABLE
CONFISCATABLE
CONFISCATE
CONFISCATED
CONFISCATES
CONFISCATING
CONFISCATION
CONFISCATIONS
CONFISCATOR
CONFISCATORS
CONFISCATORY
CONFISERIE
CONFISERIES
CONFISEURS
CONFITEORS
CONFITURES
CONFLAGRANT
CONFLAGRATE
CONFLAGRATED
CONFLAGRATES
CONFLAGRATING
CONFLAGRATION
CONFLAGRATIONS
CONFLAGRATIVE
CONFLATING
CONFLATION
CONFLATIONS
CONFLICTED
CONFLICTFUL
CONFLICTING
CONFLICTINGLY
CONFLICTION
CONFLICTIONS
CONFLICTIVE
CONFLICTORY
CONFLICTUAL
CONFLUENCE
CONFLUENCES
CONFLUENTLY
CONFLUENTS
CONFOCALLY
CONFORMABILITY
CONFORMABLE
CONFORMABLENESS
CONFORMABLY
CONFORMANCE
CONFORMANCES
CONFORMATION
CONFORMATIONAL
CONFORMATIONS
CONFORMERS
CONFORMING
CONFORMINGLY
CONFORMISM
CONFORMISMS
CONFORMIST
CONFORMISTS
CONFORMITIES
CONFORMITY
CONFOUNDABLE
CONFOUNDED
CONFOUNDEDLY
CONFOUNDEDNESS
CONFOUNDER
CONFOUNDERS
CONFOUNDING
CONFOUNDINGLY
CONFRATERNAL
CONFRATERNITIES
CONFRATERNITY
CONFRERIES
CONFRONTAL
CONFRONTALS
CONFRONTATION
CONFRONTATIONAL
CONFRONTATIONS
CONFRONTED
CONFRONTER
CONFRONTERS
CONFRONTING
CONFRONTMENT
CONFRONTMENTS
CONFUSABILITIES
CONFUSABILITY
CONFUSABLE
CONFUSABLES
CONFUSEDLY
CONFUSEDNESS
CONFUSEDNESSES
CONFUSIBLE
CONFUSIBLES
CONFUSINGLY
CONFUSIONAL
CONFUSIONS
CONFUTABLE
CONFUTATION
CONFUTATIONS
CONFUTATIVE
CONFUTEMENT
CONFUTEMENTS
CONGEALABLE
CONGEALABLENESS
CONGEALERS
CONGEALING
CONGEALMENT
CONGEALMENTS
CONGELATION
CONGELATIONS
CONGENERIC
CONGENERICAL
CONGENERICS
CONGENEROUS
CONGENETIC
CONGENIALITIES
CONGENIALITY
CONGENIALLY
CONGENIALNESS
CONGENIALNESSES
CONGENITAL
CONGENITALLY
CONGENITALNESS
CONGESTIBLE
CONGESTING
CONGESTION
CONGESTIONS
CONGESTIVE
CONGIARIES
CONGLOBATE
CONGLOBATED
CONGLOBATES
CONGLOBATING
CONGLOBATION
CONGLOBATIONS
CONGLOBING
CONGLOBULATE
CONGLOBULATED
CONGLOBULATES
CONGLOBULATING
CONGLOBULATION
CONGLOBULATIONS
CONGLOMERATE
CONGLOMERATED
CONGLOMERATES
CONGLOMERATEUR
CONGLOMERATEURS
CONGLOMERATIC
CONGLOMERATING
CONGLOMERATION
CONGLOMERATIONS
CONGLOMERATIVE
CONGLOMERATOR
CONGLOMERATORS
CONGLUTINANT
CONGLUTINATE
CONGLUTINATED
CONGLUTINATES

ONGLUTINATING
ONGLUTINATION
ONGLUTINATIONS
ONGLUTINATIVE
ONGLUTINATOR
ONGLUTINATORS
ONGRATTERS
ONGRATULABLE
ONGRATULANT
ONGRATULANTS
ONGRATULATE
ONGRATULATED
ONGRATULATES
ONGRATULATING
ONGRATULATION
ONGRATULATIONS
ONGRATULATIVE
ONGRATULATOR
ONGRATULATORS
ONGRATULATORY
ONGREEING
ONGREETED
ONGREETING
ONGREGANT
ONGREGANTS
ONGREGATE
ONGREGATED
ONGREGATES
ONGREGATING
ONGREGATION
ONGREGATIONAL
ONGREGATIONS
ONGREGATIVE
ONGREGATOR
ONGREGATORS
ONGRESSED
ONGRESSES
ONGRESSING
ONGRESSIONAL
ONGRESSIONALLY
ONGRESSMAN
ONGRESSMEN
ONGRESSPEOPLE
ONGRESSPERSON
ONGRESSPERSONS
ONGRESSWOMAN
ONGRESSWOMEN
ONGRUENCE
ONGRUENCES
ONGRUENCIES
ONGRUENCY
ONGRUENTLY
ONGRUITIES
ONGRUOUSLY
ONGRUOUSNESS
ONGRUOUSNESSES
ONICITIES
ONIDIOPHORE
ONIDIOPHORES
ONIDIOPHOROUS
ONIDIOSPORE
ONIDIOSPORES
ONIFEROUS
ONIOLOGIES
ONIROSTRAL
ONJECTING
CONJECTURABLE
CONJECTURABLY
CONJECTURAL
CONJECTURALLY
CONJECTURE
CONJECTURED
CONJECTURER
CONJECTURERS
CONJECTURES
CONJECTURING
CONJOINERS
CONJOINING
CONJOINTLY
CONJUGABLE
CONJUGALITIES
CONJUGALITY
CONJUGALLY
CONJUGANTS
CONJUGATED
CONJUGATELY
CONJUGATENESS
CONJUGATENESSES
CONJUGATES
CONJUGATING
CONJUGATINGS
CONJUGATION
CONJUGATIONAL
CONJUGATIONALLY
CONJUGATIONS
CONJUGATIVE
CONJUGATOR
CONJUGATORS
CONJUNCTION
CONJUNCTIONAL
CONJUNCTIONALLY
CONJUNCTIONS
CONJUNCTIVA
CONJUNCTIVAE
CONJUNCTIVAL
CONJUNCTIVAS
CONJUNCTIVE
CONJUNCTIVELY
CONJUNCTIVENESS
CONJUNCTIVES
CONJUNCTIVITIS
CONJUNCTLY
CONJUNCTURAL
CONJUNCTURE
CONJUNCTURES
CONJURATION
CONJURATIONS
CONJURATOR
CONJURATORS
CONJUREMENT
CONJUREMENTS
CONJURINGS
CONNASCENCE
CONNASCENCES
CONNASCENCIES
CONNASCENCY
CONNASCENT
CONNATENESS
CONNATENESSES
CONNATIONS
CONNATURAL
CONNATURALISE
CONNATURALISED
CONNATURALISES
CONNATURALISING
CONNATURALITIES
CONNATURALITY
CONNATURALIZE
CONNATURALIZED
CONNATURALIZES
CONNATURALIZING
CONNATURALLY
CONNATURALNESS
CONNATURES
CONNECTABLE
CONNECTEDLY
CONNECTEDNESS
CONNECTEDNESSES
CONNECTERS
CONNECTIBLE
CONNECTING
CONNECTION
CONNECTIONAL
CONNECTIONISM
CONNECTIONISMS
CONNECTIONS
CONNECTIVE
CONNECTIVELY
CONNECTIVES
CONNECTIVITIES
CONNECTIVITY
CONNECTORS
CONNEXIONAL
CONNEXIONS
CONNIPTION
CONNIPTIONS
CONNIVANCE
CONNIVANCES
CONNIVANCIES
CONNIVANCY
CONNIVENCE
CONNIVENCES
CONNIVENCIES
CONNIVENCY
CONNIVENTLY
CONNIVERIES
CONNIVINGLY
CONNOISSEUR
CONNOISSEURS
CONNOISSEURSHIP
CONNOTATED
CONNOTATES
CONNOTATING
CONNOTATION
CONNOTATIONAL
CONNOTATIONS
CONNOTATIVE
CONNOTATIVELY
CONNOTIVELY
CONNUBIALISM
CONNUBIALISMS
CONNUBIALITIES
CONNUBIALITY
CONNUBIALLY
CONNUMERATE
CONNUMERATED
CONNUMERATES
CONNUMERATING
CONNUMERATION
CONNUMERATIONS
CONOIDALLY
CONOIDICAL
CONOMINEES
CONOSCENTE
CONOSCENTI
CONQUERABLE
CONQUERABLENESS
CONQUERERS
CONQUERESS
CONQUERESSES
CONQUERING
CONQUERINGLY
CONQUERORS
CONQUISTADOR
CONQUISTADORES
CONQUISTADORS
CONSANGUINE
CONSANGUINEOUS
CONSANGUINITIES
CONSANGUINITY
CONSCIENCE
CONSCIENCELESS
CONSCIENCES
CONSCIENTIOUS
CONSCIENTIOUSLY
CONSCIENTISE
CONSCIENTISED
CONSCIENTISES
CONSCIENTISING
CONSCIENTIZE
CONSCIENTIZED
CONSCIENTIZES
CONSCIENTIZING
CONSCIONABLE
CONSCIONABLY
CONSCIOUSES
CONSCIOUSLY
CONSCIOUSNESS
CONSCIOUSNESSES
CONSCRIBED
CONSCRIBES
CONSCRIBING
CONSCRIPTED
CONSCRIPTING
CONSCRIPTION
CONSCRIPTIONAL
CONSCRIPTIONIST
CONSCRIPTIONS
CONSCRIPTS
CONSECRATE
CONSECRATED
CONSECRATEDNESS
CONSECRATES
CONSECRATING
CONSECRATION
CONSECRATIONS
CONSECRATIVE
CONSECRATOR
CONSECRATORS
CONSECRATORY
CONSECTANEOUS
CONSECTARIES
CONSECTARY
CONSECUTION

CONSECUTIONS
CONSECUTIVE
CONSECUTIVELY
CONSECUTIVENESS
CONSENESCENCE
CONSENESCENCES
CONSENESCENCIES
CONSENESCENCY
CONSENSION
CONSENSIONS
CONSENSUAL
CONSENSUALLY
CONSENSUSES
CONSENTANEITIES
CONSENTANEITY
CONSENTANEOUS
CONSENTANEOUSLY
CONSENTERS
CONSENTIENCE
CONSENTIENCES
CONSENTIENT
CONSENTING
CONSENTINGLY
CONSEQUENCE
CONSEQUENCED
CONSEQUENCES
CONSEQUENCING
CONSEQUENT
CONSEQUENTIAL
CONSEQUENTIALLY
CONSEQUENTLY
CONSEQUENTS
CONSERVABLE
CONSERVANCIES
CONSERVANCY
CONSERVANT
CONSERVATION
CONSERVATIONAL
CONSERVATIONIST
CONSERVATIONS
CONSERVATISE
CONSERVATISED
CONSERVATISES
CONSERVATISING
CONSERVATISM
CONSERVATISMS
CONSERVATIVE
CONSERVATIVELY
CONSERVATIVES
CONSERVATIZE
CONSERVATIZED
CONSERVATIZES
CONSERVATIZING
CONSERVATOIRE
CONSERVATOIRES
CONSERVATOR
CONSERVATORIA
CONSERVATORIAL
CONSERVATORIES
CONSERVATORIUM
CONSERVATORIUMS
CONSERVATORS
CONSERVATORSHIP
CONSERVATORY
CONSERVATRICES
CONSERVATRIX
CONSERVATRIXES
CONSERVERS
CONSERVING
CONSIDERABLE
CONSIDERABLES
CONSIDERABLY
CONSIDERANCE
CONSIDERANCES
CONSIDERATE
CONSIDERATELY
CONSIDERATENESS
CONSIDERATION
CONSIDERATIONS
CONSIDERATIVE
CONSIDERATIVELY
CONSIDERED
CONSIDERER
CONSIDERERS
CONSIDERING
CONSIDERINGLY
CONSIGLIERE
CONSIGLIERI
CONSIGNABLE
CONSIGNATION
CONSIGNATIONS
CONSIGNATORIES
CONSIGNATORY
CONSIGNEES
CONSIGNERS
CONSIGNIFIED
CONSIGNIFIES
CONSIGNIFY
CONSIGNIFYING
CONSIGNING
CONSIGNMENT
CONSIGNMENTS
CONSIGNORS
CONSILIENCE
CONSILIENCES
CONSILIENT
CONSIMILAR
CONSIMILARITIES
CONSIMILARITY
CONSIMILITIES
CONSIMILITUDE
CONSIMILITUDES
CONSIMILITY
CONSISTENCE
CONSISTENCES
CONSISTENCIES
CONSISTENCY
CONSISTENT
CONSISTENTLY
CONSISTING
CONSISTORIAL
CONSISTORIAN
CONSISTORIES
CONSISTORY
CONSOCIATE
CONSOCIATED
CONSOCIATES
CONSOCIATING
CONSOCIATION
CONSOCIATIONAL
CONSOCIATIONS
CONSOLABLE
CONSOLATED
CONSOLATES
CONSOLATING
CONSOLATION
CONSOLATIONS
CONSOLATORIES
CONSOLATORY
CONSOLATRICES
CONSOLATRIX
CONSOLATRIXES
CONSOLEMENT
CONSOLEMENTS
CONSOLIDATE
CONSOLIDATED
CONSOLIDATES
CONSOLIDATING
CONSOLIDATION
CONSOLIDATIONS
CONSOLIDATIVE
CONSOLIDATOR
CONSOLIDATORS
CONSOLINGLY
CONSONANCE
CONSONANCES
CONSONANCIES
CONSONANCY
CONSONANTAL
CONSONANTALLY
CONSONANTLY
CONSONANTS
CONSORTABLE
CONSORTERS
CONSORTIAL
CONSORTING
CONSORTISM
CONSORTISMS
CONSORTIUM
CONSORTIUMS
CONSPECIFIC
CONSPECIFICS
CONSPECTUITIES
CONSPECTUITY
CONSPECTUS
CONSPECTUSES
CONSPICUITIES
CONSPICUITY
CONSPICUOUS
CONSPICUOUSLY
CONSPICUOUSNESS
CONSPIRACIES
CONSPIRACY
CONSPIRANT
CONSPIRATION
CONSPIRATIONAL
CONSPIRATIONS
CONSPIRATOR
CONSPIRATORIAL
CONSPIRATORS
CONSPIRATORY
CONSPIRATRESS
CONSPIRATRESSES
CONSPIRERS
CONSPIRING
CONSPIRINGLY
CONSPURCATION
CONSPURCATIONS
CONSTABLES
CONSTABLESHIP
CONSTABLESHIPS
CONSTABLEWICK
CONSTABLEWICKS
CONSTABULARIES
CONSTABULARY
CONSTANCIES
CONSTANTAN
CONSTANTANS
CONSTANTLY
CONSTATATION
CONSTATATIONS
CONSTATING
CONSTATIVE
CONSTATIVES
CONSTELLATE
CONSTELLATED
CONSTELLATES
CONSTELLATING
CONSTELLATION
CONSTELLATIONAL
CONSTELLATIONS
CONSTELLATORY
CONSTERING
CONSTERNATE
CONSTERNATED
CONSTERNATES
CONSTERNATING
CONSTERNATION
CONSTERNATIONS
CONSTIPATE
CONSTIPATED
CONSTIPATES
CONSTIPATING
CONSTIPATION
CONSTIPATIONS
CONSTITUENCIES
CONSTITUENCY
CONSTITUENT
CONSTITUENTLY
CONSTITUENTS
CONSTITUTE
CONSTITUTED
CONSTITUTER
CONSTITUTERS
CONSTITUTES
CONSTITUTING
CONSTITUTION
CONSTITUTIONAL
CONSTITUTIONALS
CONSTITUTIONIST
CONSTITUTIONS
CONSTITUTIVE
CONSTITUTIVELY
CONSTITUTOR
CONSTITUTORS
CONSTRAINABLE
CONSTRAINED
CONSTRAINEDLY
CONSTRAINER
CONSTRAINERS
CONSTRAINING
CONSTRAINS
CONSTRAINT
CONSTRAINTS

CONSTRICTED
CONSTRICTING
CONSTRICTION
CONSTRICTIONS
CONSTRICTIVE
CONSTRICTIVELY
CONSTRICTOR
CONSTRICTORS
CONSTRICTS
CONSTRINGE
CONSTRINGED
CONSTRINGENCE
CONSTRINGENCES
CONSTRINGENCIES
CONSTRINGENCY
CONSTRINGENT
CONSTRINGES
CONSTRINGING
CONSTRUABILITY
CONSTRUABLE
CONSTRUALS
CONSTRUCTABLE
CONSTRUCTED
CONSTRUCTER
CONSTRUCTERS
CONSTRUCTIBLE
CONSTRUCTING
CONSTRUCTION
CONSTRUCTIONAL
CONSTRUCTIONISM
CONSTRUCTIONIST
CONSTRUCTIONS
CONSTRUCTIVE
CONSTRUCTIVELY
CONSTRUCTIVISM
CONSTRUCTIVISMS
CONSTRUCTIVIST
CONSTRUCTIVISTS
CONSTRUCTOR
CONSTRUCTORS
CONSTRUCTS
CONSTRUCTURE
CONSTRUCTURES
CONSTRUERS
CONSTRUING
CONSTUPRATE
CONSTUPRATED
CONSTUPRATES
CONSTUPRATING
CONSTUPRATION
CONSTUPRATIONS
CONSUBSIST
CONSUBSISTED
CONSUBSISTING
CONSUBSISTS
CONSUBSTANTIAL
CONSUBSTANTIATE
CONSUETUDE
CONSUETUDES
CONSUETUDINARY
CONSULAGES
CONSULATES
CONSULSHIP
CONSULSHIPS
CONSULTABLE
CONSULTANCIES
CONSULTANCY
CONSULTANT
CONSULTANTS
CONSULTANTSHIP
CONSULTANTSHIPS
CONSULTATION
CONSULTATIONS
CONSULTATIVE
CONSULTATIVELY
CONSULTATORY
CONSULTEES
CONSULTERS
CONSULTING
CONSULTIVE
CONSULTORS
CONSULTORY
CONSUMABLE
CONSUMABLES
CONSUMEDLY
CONSUMERISM
CONSUMERISMS
CONSUMERIST
CONSUMERISTIC
CONSUMERISTS
CONSUMERSHIP
CONSUMERSHIPS
CONSUMINGLY
CONSUMINGS
CONSUMMATE
CONSUMMATED
CONSUMMATELY
CONSUMMATES
CONSUMMATING
CONSUMMATION
CONSUMMATIONS
CONSUMMATIVE
CONSUMMATOR
CONSUMMATORS
CONSUMMATORY
CONSUMPTION
CONSUMPTIONS
CONSUMPTIVE
CONSUMPTIVELY
CONSUMPTIVENESS
CONSUMPTIVES
CONSUMPTIVITIES
CONSUMPTIVITY
CONTABESCENCE
CONTABESCENCES
CONTABESCENT
CONTACTABLE
CONTACTEES
CONTACTING
CONTACTORS
CONTACTUAL
CONTACTUALLY
CONTADINAS
CONTAGIONIST
CONTAGIONISTS
CONTAGIONS
CONTAGIOUS
CONTAGIOUSLY
CONTAGIOUSNESS
CONTAINABLE
CONTAINERBOARD
CONTAINERBOARDS
CONTAINERISE
CONTAINERISED
CONTAINERISES
CONTAINERISING
CONTAINERIZE
CONTAINERIZED
CONTAINERIZES
CONTAINERIZING
CONTAINERLESS
CONTAINERPORT
CONTAINERPORTS
CONTAINERS
CONTAINERSHIP
CONTAINERSHIPS
CONTAINING
CONTAINMENT
CONTAINMENTS
CONTAMINABLE
CONTAMINANT
CONTAMINANTS
CONTAMINATE
CONTAMINATED
CONTAMINATES
CONTAMINATING
CONTAMINATION
CONTAMINATIONS
CONTAMINATIVE
CONTAMINATOR
CONTAMINATORS
CONTANGOED
CONTANGOES
CONTANGOING
CONTEMNERS
CONTEMNIBLE
CONTEMNIBLY
CONTEMNING
CONTEMNORS
CONTEMPERATION
CONTEMPERATIONS
CONTEMPERATURE
CONTEMPERATURES
CONTEMPERED
CONTEMPERING
CONTEMPERS
CONTEMPLABLE
CONTEMPLANT
CONTEMPLANTS
CONTEMPLATE
CONTEMPLATED
CONTEMPLATES
CONTEMPLATING
CONTEMPLATION
CONTEMPLATIONS
CONTEMPLATIST
CONTEMPLATISTS
CONTEMPLATIVE
CONTEMPLATIVELY
CONTEMPLATIVES
CONTEMPLATOR
CONTEMPLATORS
CONTEMPORANEAN
CONTEMPORANEANS
CONTEMPORANEITY
CONTEMPORANEOUS
CONTEMPORARIES
CONTEMPORARILY
CONTEMPORARY
CONTEMPORISE
CONTEMPORISED
CONTEMPORISES
CONTEMPORISING
CONTEMPORIZE
CONTEMPORIZED
CONTEMPORIZES
CONTEMPORIZING
CONTEMPTIBILITY
CONTEMPTIBLE
CONTEMPTIBLY
CONTEMPTUOUS
CONTEMPTUOUSLY
CONTENDENT
CONTENDENTS
CONTENDERS
CONTENDING
CONTENDINGLY
CONTENDINGS
CONTENEMENT
CONTENEMENTS
CONTENTATION
CONTENTATIONS
CONTENTEDLY
CONTENTEDNESS
CONTENTEDNESSES
CONTENTING
CONTENTION
CONTENTIONS
CONTENTIOUS
CONTENTIOUSLY
CONTENTIOUSNESS
CONTENTLESS
CONTENTMENT
CONTENTMENTS
CONTERMINAL
CONTERMINALLY
CONTERMINANT
CONTERMINATE
CONTERMINOUS
CONTERMINOUSLY
CONTESSERATION
CONTESSERATIONS
CONTESTABILITY
CONTESTABLE
CONTESTABLENESS
CONTESTABLY
CONTESTANT
CONTESTANTS
CONTESTATION
CONTESTATIONS
CONTESTERS
CONTESTING
CONTESTINGLY
CONTEXTLESS
CONTEXTUAL
CONTEXTUALISE
CONTEXTUALISED
CONTEXTUALISES
CONTEXTUALISING
CONTEXTUALIZE
CONTEXTUALIZED
CONTEXTUALIZES
CONTEXTUALIZING
CONTEXTUALLY

CONTEXTURAL
CONTEXTURE
CONTEXTURES
CONTIGNATION
CONTIGNATIONS
CONTIGUITIES
CONTIGUITY
CONTIGUOUS
CONTIGUOUSLY
CONTIGUOUSNESS
CONTINENCE
CONTINENCES
CONTINENCIES
CONTINENCY
CONTINENTAL
CONTINENTALISM
CONTINENTALISMS
CONTINENTALIST
CONTINENTALISTS
CONTINENTALLY
CONTINENTALS
CONTINENTLY
CONTINENTS
CONTINGENCE
CONTINGENCES
CONTINGENCIES
CONTINGENCY
CONTINGENT
CONTINGENTLY
CONTINGENTS
CONTINUABLE
CONTINUALITIES
CONTINUALITY
CONTINUALLY
CONTINUALNESS
CONTINUALNESSES
CONTINUANCE
CONTINUANCES
CONTINUANT
CONTINUANTS
CONTINUATE
CONTINUATION
CONTINUATIONS
CONTINUATIVE
CONTINUATIVELY
CONTINUATIVES
CONTINUATOR
CONTINUATORS
CONTINUEDLY
CONTINUEDNESS
CONTINUEDNESSES
CONTINUERS
CONTINUING
CONTINUINGLY
CONTINUITIES
CONTINUITY
CONTINUOUS
CONTINUOUSLY
CONTINUOUSNESS
CONTINUUMS
CONTORNIATE
CONTORNIATES
CONTORTEDLY
CONTORTEDNESS
CONTORTEDNESSES
CONTORTING
CONTORTION
CONTORTIONAL
CONTORTIONATE
CONTORTIONED
CONTORTIONISM
CONTORTIONISMS
CONTORTIONIST
CONTORTIONISTIC
CONTORTIONISTS
CONTORTIONS
CONTORTIVE
CONTOURING
CONTRABAND
CONTRABANDISM
CONTRABANDISMS
CONTRABANDIST
CONTRABANDISTS
CONTRABANDS
CONTRABASS
CONTRABASSES
CONTRABASSI
CONTRABASSIST
CONTRABASSISTS
CONTRABASSO
CONTRABASSOON
CONTRABASSOONS
CONTRABASSOS
CONTRABBASSI
CONTRABBASSO
CONTRABBASSOS
CONTRACEPTION
CONTRACEPTIONS
CONTRACEPTIVE
CONTRACEPTIVES
CONTRACLOCKWISE
CONTRACTABILITY
CONTRACTABLE
CONTRACTED
CONTRACTEDLY
CONTRACTEDNESS
CONTRACTIBILITY
CONTRACTIBLE
CONTRACTIBLY
CONTRACTILE
CONTRACTILITIES
CONTRACTILITY
CONTRACTING
CONTRACTION
CONTRACTIONAL
CONTRACTIONARY
CONTRACTIONS
CONTRACTIVE
CONTRACTIVELY
CONTRACTIVENESS
CONTRACTOR
CONTRACTORS
CONTRACTUAL
CONTRACTUALLY
CONTRACTURAL
CONTRACTURE
CONTRACTURES
CONTRACYCLICAL
CONTRADANCE
CONTRADANCES
CONTRADICT
CONTRADICTABLE
CONTRADICTED
CONTRADICTER
CONTRADICTERS
CONTRADICTING
CONTRADICTION
CONTRADICTIONS
CONTRADICTIOUS
CONTRADICTIVE
CONTRADICTIVELY
CONTRADICTOR
CONTRADICTORIES
CONTRADICTORILY
CONTRADICTORS
CONTRADICTORY
CONTRADICTS
CONTRAFAGOTTO
CONTRAFAGOTTOS
CONTRAFLOW
CONTRAFLOWS
CONTRAGESTION
CONTRAGESTIONS
CONTRAGESTIVE
CONTRAGESTIVES
CONTRAHENT
CONTRAHENTS
CONTRAINDICANT
CONTRAINDICANTS
CONTRAINDICATE
CONTRAINDICATED
CONTRAINDICATES
CONTRALATERAL
CONTRALTOS
CONTRANATANT
CONTRAOCTAVE
CONTRAOCTAVES
CONTRAPLEX
CONTRAPOSITION
CONTRAPOSITIONS
CONTRAPOSITIVE
CONTRAPOSITIVES
CONTRAPPOSTO
CONTRAPPOSTOS
CONTRAPROP
CONTRAPROPELLER
CONTRAPROPS
CONTRAPTION
CONTRAPTIONS
CONTRAPUNTAL
CONTRAPUNTALIST
CONTRAPUNTALLY
CONTRAPUNTIST
CONTRAPUNTISTS
CONTRARIAN
CONTRARIANS
CONTRARIED
CONTRARIES
CONTRARIETIES
CONTRARIETY
CONTRARILY
CONTRARINESS
CONTRARINESSES
CONTRARIOUS
CONTRARIOUSLY
CONTRARIOUSNESS
CONTRARIWISE
CONTRARYING
CONTRASEXUAL
CONTRASEXUALS
CONTRASTABLE
CONTRASTABLY
CONTRASTED
CONTRASTING
CONTRASTIVE
CONTRASTIVELY
CONTRATERRENE
CONTRAVALLATION
CONTRAVENE
CONTRAVENED
CONTRAVENER
CONTRAVENERS
CONTRAVENES
CONTRAVENING
CONTRAVENTION
CONTRAVENTIONS
CONTRAYERVA
CONTRAYERVAS
CONTRECOUP
CONTRECOUPS
CONTREDANCE
CONTREDANCES
CONTREDANSE
CONTREDANSES
CONTRETEMPS
CONTRIBUTABLE
CONTRIBUTARIES
CONTRIBUTARY
CONTRIBUTE
CONTRIBUTED
CONTRIBUTES
CONTRIBUTING
CONTRIBUTION
CONTRIBUTIONS
CONTRIBUTIVE
CONTRIBUTIVELY
CONTRIBUTOR
CONTRIBUTORIES
CONTRIBUTORS
CONTRIBUTORY
CONTRISTATION
CONTRISTATIONS
CONTRISTED
CONTRISTING
CONTRITELY
CONTRITENESS
CONTRITENESSES
CONTRITION
CONTRITIONS
CONTRITURATE
CONTRITURATED
CONTRITURATES
CONTRITURATING
CONTRIVABLE
CONTRIVANCE
CONTRIVANCES
CONTRIVEMENT
CONTRIVEMENTS
CONTRIVERS
CONTRIVING
CONTROLLABILITY
CONTROLLABLE
CONTROLLABLY
CONTROLLED

ONTROLLER
ONTROLLERS
ONTROLLERSHIP
ONTROLLERSHIPS
ONTROLLING
ONTROLMENT
ONTROLMENTS
ONTROULED
ONTROULING
ONTROVERSE
ONTROVERSES
ONTROVERSIAL
ONTROVERSIALLY
ONTROVERSIES
ONTROVERSY
ONTROVERT
ONTROVERTED
ONTROVERTER
ONTROVERTERS
ONTROVERTIBLE
ONTROVERTIBLY
ONTROVERTING
ONTROVERTIST
ONTROVERTISTS
ONTROVERTS
ONTUBERNAL
ONTUBERNYAL
ONTUMACIES
ONTUMACIOUS
ONTUMACIOUSLY
ONTUMACITIES
ONTUMACITY
ONTUMELIES
ONTUMELIOUS
ONTUMELIOUSLY
ONTUNDING
ONTUSIONED
ONTUSIONS
ONUNDRUMS
ONURBATION
ONURBATIONS
ONVALESCE
ONVALESCED
ONVALESCENCE
ONVALESCENCES
ONVALESCENCIES
ONVALESCENCY
ONVALESCENT
ONVALESCENTLY
ONVALESCENTS
ONVALESCES
ONVALESCING
ONVECTING
ONVECTION
ONVECTIONAL
ONVECTIONS
ONVECTIVE
ONVECTORS
ONVENABLE
ONVENANCE
ONVENANCES
ONVENERSHIP
ONVENERSHIPS
ONVENIENCE
ONVENIENCES
ONVENIENCIES

CONVENIENCY
CONVENIENT
CONVENIENTLY
CONVENORSHIP
CONVENORSHIPS
CONVENTICLE
CONVENTICLED
CONVENTICLER
CONVENTICLERS
CONVENTICLES
CONVENTICLING
CONVENTING
CONVENTION
CONVENTIONAL
CONVENTIONALISE
CONVENTIONALISM
CONVENTIONALIST
CONVENTIONALITY
CONVENTIONALIZE
CONVENTIONALLY
CONVENTIONALS
CONVENTIONARY
CONVENTIONEER
CONVENTIONEERS
CONVENTIONER
CONVENTIONERS
CONVENTIONIST
CONVENTIONISTS
CONVENTIONS
CONVENTUAL
CONVENTUALLY
CONVENTUALS
CONVERGENCE
CONVERGENCES
CONVERGENCIES
CONVERGENCY
CONVERGENT
CONVERGING
CONVERSABLE
CONVERSABLENESS
CONVERSABLY
CONVERSANCE
CONVERSANCES
CONVERSANCIES
CONVERSANCY
CONVERSANT
CONVERSANTLY
CONVERSATION
CONVERSATIONAL
CONVERSATIONISM
CONVERSATIONIST
CONVERSATIONS
CONVERSATIVE
CONVERSAZIONE
CONVERSAZIONES
CONVERSAZIONI
CONVERSELY
CONVERSERS
CONVERSING
CONVERSION
CONVERSIONAL
CONVERSIONARY
CONVERSIONS
CONVERTAPLANE
CONVERTAPLANES
CONVERTEND

CONVERTENDS
CONVERTERS
CONVERTIBILITY
CONVERTIBLE
CONVERTIBLENESS
CONVERTIBLES
CONVERTIBLY
CONVERTING
CONVERTIPLANE
CONVERTIPLANES
CONVERTITE
CONVERTITES
CONVERTIVE
CONVERTOPLANE
CONVERTOPLANES
CONVERTORS
CONVEXEDLY
CONVEXITIES
CONVEXNESS
CONVEXNESSES
CONVEYABLE
CONVEYANCE
CONVEYANCER
CONVEYANCERS
CONVEYANCES
CONVEYANCING
CONVEYANCINGS
CONVEYORISATION
CONVEYORISE
CONVEYORISED
CONVEYORISES
CONVEYORISING
CONVEYORIZATION
CONVEYORIZE
CONVEYORIZED
CONVEYORIZES
CONVEYORIZING
CONVICINITIES
CONVICINITY
CONVICTABLE
CONVICTIBLE
CONVICTING
CONVICTION
CONVICTIONAL
CONVICTIONS
CONVICTISM
CONVICTISMS
CONVICTIVE
CONVICTIVELY
CONVINCEMENT
CONVINCEMENTS
CONVINCERS
CONVINCIBLE
CONVINCING
CONVINCINGLY
CONVINCINGNESS
CONVIVIALIST
CONVIVIALISTS
CONVIVIALITIES
CONVIVIALITY
CONVIVIALLY
CONVOCATED
CONVOCATES
CONVOCATING
CONVOCATION
CONVOCATIONAL

CONVOCATIONIST
CONVOCATIONISTS
CONVOCATIONS
CONVOCATIVE
CONVOCATOR
CONVOCATORS
CONVOLUTED
CONVOLUTEDLY
CONVOLUTEDNESS
CONVOLUTELY
CONVOLUTES
CONVOLUTING
CONVOLUTION
CONVOLUTIONAL
CONVOLUTIONARY
CONVOLUTIONS
CONVOLVING
CONVOLVULACEOUS
CONVOLVULI
CONVOLVULUS
CONVOLVULUSES
CONVULSANT
CONVULSANTS
CONVULSIBLE
CONVULSING
CONVULSION
CONVULSIONAL
CONVULSIONARIES
CONVULSIONARY
CONVULSIONIST
CONVULSIONISTS
CONVULSIONS
CONVULSIVE
CONVULSIVELY
CONVULSIVENESS
COOKHOUSES
COOKSHACKS
COOKSTOVES
COOLHEADED
COOLHOUSES
COOLINGNESS
COOLINGNESSES
COOLNESSES
COOMCEILED
COONHOUNDS
COOPERAGES
COOPERATED
COOPERATES
COOPERATING
COOPERATION
COOPERATIONIST
COOPERATIONISTS
COOPERATIONS
COOPERATIVE
COOPERATIVELY
COOPERATIVENESS
COOPERATIVES
COOPERATIVITY
COOPERATOR
COOPERATORS
COOPERINGS
COOPTATION
COOPTATIONS
COOPTATIVE
COORDINANCE
COORDINANCES

COORDINATE
COORDINATED
COORDINATELY
COORDINATENESS
COORDINATES
COORDINATING
COORDINATION
COORDINATIONS
COORDINATIVE
COORDINATOR
COORDINATORS
COPARCENARIES
COPARCENARY
COPARCENER
COPARCENERIES
COPARCENERS
COPARCENERY
COPARCENIES
COPARENTED
COPARENTING
COPARTNERED
COPARTNERIES
COPARTNERING
COPARTNERS
COPARTNERSHIP
COPARTNERSHIPS
COPARTNERY
COPATRIOTS
COPAYMENTS
COPESETTIC
COPESTONES
COPINGSTONE
COPINGSTONES
COPIOUSNESS
COPIOUSNESSES
COPLANARITIES
COPLANARITY
COPLOTTING
COPOLYMERIC
COPOLYMERISE
COPOLYMERISED
COPOLYMERISES
COPOLYMERISING
COPOLYMERIZE
COPOLYMERIZED
COPOLYMERIZES
COPOLYMERIZING
COPOLYMERS
COPPERASES
COPPERHEAD
COPPERHEADS
COPPERINGS
COPPERPLATE
COPPERPLATES
COPPERSKIN
COPPERSKINS
COPPERSMITH
COPPERSMITHS
COPPERWORK
COPPERWORKS
COPPERWORM
COPPERWORMS
COPPICINGS
COPRESENCE
COPRESENCES
COPRESENTED
COPRESENTING
COPRESENTS
COPRESIDENT
COPRESIDENTS
COPRINCIPAL
COPRINCIPALS
COPRISONER
COPRISONERS
COPROCESSING
COPROCESSOR
COPROCESSORS
COPRODUCED
COPRODUCER
COPRODUCERS
COPRODUCES
COPRODUCING
COPRODUCTION
COPRODUCTIONS
COPRODUCTS
COPROLALIA
COPROLALIAC
COPROLALIAS
COPROLITES
COPROLITHS
COPROLITIC
COPROLOGIES
COPROMOTER
COPROMOTERS
COPROPHAGAN
COPROPHAGANS
COPROPHAGIC
COPROPHAGIES
COPROPHAGIST
COPROPHAGISTS
COPROPHAGOUS
COPROPHAGY
COPROPHILIA
COPROPHILIAC
COPROPHILIACS
COPROPHILIAS
COPROPHILIC
COPROPHILOUS
COPROPRIETOR
COPROPRIETORS
COPROSPERITIES
COPROSPERITY
COPROSTEROL
COPROSTEROLS
COPSEWOODS
COPUBLISHED
COPUBLISHER
COPUBLISHERS
COPUBLISHES
COPUBLISHING
COPULATING
COPULATION
COPULATIONS
COPULATIVE
COPULATIVELY
COPULATIVES
COPULATORY
COPURIFIED
COPURIFIES
COPURIFYING
COPYCATTED
COPYCATTING
COPYEDITED
COPYEDITING
COPYGRAPHS
COPYHOLDER
COPYHOLDERS
COPYREADER
COPYREADERS
COPYREADING
COPYREADINGS
COPYRIGHTABLE
COPYRIGHTED
COPYRIGHTER
COPYRIGHTERS
COPYRIGHTING
COPYRIGHTS
COPYTAKERS
COPYWRITER
COPYWRITERS
COPYWRITING
COPYWRITINGS
COQUELICOT
COQUELICOTS
COQUETRIES
COQUETTING
COQUETTISH
COQUETTISHLY
COQUETTISHNESS
COQUIMBITE
COQUIMBITES
CORACIIFORM
CORADICATE
CORALBELLS
CORALBERRIES
CORALBERRY
CORALLACEOUS
CORALLIFEROUS
CORALLIFORM
CORALLIGENOUS
CORALLINES
CORALLITES
CORALLOIDAL
CORALROOTS
CORALWORTS
CORBEILLES
CORBELINGS
CORBELLING
CORBELLINGS
CORBICULAE
CORBICULATE
CORDECTOMIES
CORDECTOMY
CORDELLING
CORDGRASSES
CORDIALISE
CORDIALISED
CORDIALISES
CORDIALISING
CORDIALITIES
CORDIALITY
CORDIALIZE
CORDIALIZED
CORDIALIZES
CORDIALIZING
CORDIALNESS
CORDIALNESSES
CORDIERITE
CORDIERITES
CORDILLERA
CORDILLERAN
CORDILLERAS
CORDLESSES
CORDOCENTESES
CORDOCENTESIS
CORDONNETS
CORDOTOMIES
CORDUROYED
CORDUROYING
CORDWAINER
CORDWAINERIES
CORDWAINERS
CORDWAINERY
CORDYLINES
CORECIPIENT
CORECIPIENTS
COREDEEMED
COREDEEMING
COREFERENTIAL
COREGONINE
CORELATING
CORELATION
CORELATIONS
CORELATIVE
CORELATIVES
CORELIGIONIST
CORELIGIONISTS
COREOPSISES
COREPRESSOR
COREPRESSORS
COREQUISITE
COREQUISITES
CORESEARCHER
CORESEARCHERS
CORESIDENT
CORESIDENTIAL
CORESIDENTS
CORESPONDENT
CORESPONDENTS
CORFHOUSES
CORIACEOUS
CORIANDERS
CORINTHIANISE
CORINTHIANISED
CORINTHIANISES
CORINTHIANISING
CORINTHIANIZE
CORINTHIANIZED
CORINTHIANIZES
CORINTHIANIZING
CORIVALLED
CORIVALLING
CORIVALRIES
CORIVALSHIP
CORIVALSHIPS
CORKBOARDS
CORKBORERS
CORKINESSES
CORKSCREWED
CORKSCREWING
CORKSCREWS
CORMOPHYTE
CORMOPHYTES
CORMOPHYTIC

CORMORANTS
CORNACEOUS
CORNBORERS
CORNBRAIDED
CORNBRAIDING
CORNBRAIDS
CORNBRANDIES
CORNBRANDY
CORNBRASHES
CORNBREADS
CORNCOCKLE
CORNCOCKLES
CORNCRAKES
CORNEITISES
CORNELIANS
CORNEMUSES
CORNERBACK
CORNERBACKS
CORNERSTONE
CORNERSTONES
CORNERWAYS
CORNERWISE
CORNETCIES
CORNETISTS
CORNETTINO
CORNETTINOS
CORNETTIST
CORNETTISTS
CORNFIELDS
CORNFLAKES
CORNFLOURS
CORNFLOWER
CORNFLOWERS
CORNHUSKER
CORNHUSKERS
CORNHUSKING
CORNHUSKINGS
CORNICHONS
CORNICULATE
CORNICULUM
CORNICULUMS
CORNIFEROUS
CORNIFICATION
CORNIFICATIONS
CORNIFYING
CORNIGEROUS
CORNINESSES
CORNOPEANS
CORNROWING
CORNSTALKS
CORNSTARCH
CORNSTARCHES
CORNSTONES
CORNUCOPIA
CORNUCOPIAN
CORNUCOPIAS
COROLLACEOUS
COROLLARIES
COROLLIFLORAL
COROLLIFLOROUS
COROLLIFORM
COROMANDEL
COROMANDELS
CORONAGRAPH
CORONAGRAPHS
CORONARIES
CORONATING
CORONATION
CORONATIONS
CORONAVIRUS
CORONAVIRUSES
CORONERSHIP
CORONERSHIPS
CORONOGRAPH
CORONOGRAPHS
COROTATING
COROTATION
COROTATIONS
CORPORALES
CORPORALITIES
CORPORALITY
CORPORALLY
CORPORALSHIP
CORPORALSHIPS
CORPORASES
CORPORATELY
CORPORATENESS
CORPORATENESSES
CORPORATES
CORPORATION
CORPORATIONS
CORPORATISE
CORPORATISED
CORPORATISES
CORPORATISING
CORPORATISM
CORPORATISMS
CORPORATIST
CORPORATISTS
CORPORATIVE
CORPORATIVISM
CORPORATIVISMS
CORPORATIZE
CORPORATIZED
CORPORATIZES
CORPORATIZING
CORPORATOR
CORPORATORS
CORPOREALISE
CORPOREALISED
CORPOREALISES
CORPOREALISING
CORPOREALISM
CORPOREALISMS
CORPOREALIST
CORPOREALISTS
CORPOREALITIES
CORPOREALITY
CORPOREALIZE
CORPOREALIZED
CORPOREALIZES
CORPOREALIZING
CORPOREALLY
CORPOREALNESS
CORPOREALNESSES
CORPOREITIES
CORPOREITY
CORPORIFICATION
CORPORIFIED
CORPORIFIES
CORPORIFYING
CORPOSANTS
CORPULENCE
CORPULENCES
CORPULENCIES
CORPULENCY
CORPULENTLY
CORPUSCLES
CORPUSCULAR
CORPUSCULARIAN
CORPUSCULARIANS
CORPUSCULARITY
CORPUSCULE
CORPUSCULES
CORRALLING
CORRASIONS
CORRECTABLE
CORRECTEST
CORRECTIBLE
CORRECTING
CORRECTION
CORRECTIONAL
CORRECTIONER
CORRECTIONERS
CORRECTIONS
CORRECTITUDE
CORRECTITUDES
CORRECTIVE
CORRECTIVELY
CORRECTIVES
CORRECTNESS
CORRECTNESSES
CORRECTORS
CORRECTORY
CORREGIDOR
CORREGIDORS
CORRELATABLE
CORRELATED
CORRELATES
CORRELATING
CORRELATION
CORRELATIONAL
CORRELATIONS
CORRELATIVE
CORRELATIVELY
CORRELATIVENESS
CORRELATIVES
CORRELATIVITIES
CORRELATIVITY
CORRELATOR
CORRELATORS
CORRELIGIONIST
CORRELIGIONISTS
CORREPTION
CORREPTIONS
CORRESPOND
CORRESPONDED
CORRESPONDENCE
CORRESPONDENCES
CORRESPONDENCY
CORRESPONDENT
CORRESPONDENTLY
CORRESPONDENTS
CORRESPONDING
CORRESPONDINGLY
CORRESPONDS
CORRESPONSIVE
CORRIGENDA
CORRIGENDUM
CORRIGENTS
CORRIGIBILITIES
CORRIGIBILITY
CORRIGIBLE
CORRIGIBLY
CORRIVALLED
CORRIVALLING
CORRIVALRIES
CORRIVALRY
CORRIVALSHIP
CORRIVALSHIPS
CORROBORABLE
CORROBORANT
CORROBORATE
CORROBORATED
CORROBORATES
CORROBORATING
CORROBORATION
CORROBORATIONS
CORROBORATIVE
CORROBORATIVELY
CORROBORATIVES
CORROBORATOR
CORROBORATORS
CORROBORATORY
CORROBOREE
CORROBOREED
CORROBOREEING
CORROBOREES
CORRODANTS
CORRODENTS
CORRODIBILITIES
CORRODIBILITY
CORRODIBLE
CORROSIBILITIES
CORROSIBILITY
CORROSIBLE
CORROSIONS
CORROSIVELY
CORROSIVENESS
CORROSIVENESSES
CORROSIVES
CORRUGATED
CORRUGATES
CORRUGATING
CORRUGATION
CORRUGATIONS
CORRUGATOR
CORRUGATORS
CORRUPTERS
CORRUPTEST
CORRUPTIBILITY
CORRUPTIBLE
CORRUPTIBLENESS
CORRUPTIBLY
CORRUPTING
CORRUPTION
CORRUPTIONIST
CORRUPTIONISTS
CORRUPTIONS
CORRUPTIVE
CORRUPTIVELY
CORRUPTNESS
CORRUPTNESSES
CORRUPTORS

CORSELETTE
CORSELETTES
CORSETIERE
CORSETIERES
CORSETIERS
CORSETRIES
CORTICALLY
CORTICATED
CORTICATION
CORTICATIONS
CORTICOIDS
CORTICOLOUS
CORTICOSTEROID
CORTICOSTEROIDS
CORTICOSTERONE
CORTICOSTERONES
CORTICOTROPHIC
CORTICOTROPHIN
CORTICOTROPHINS
CORTICOTROPIC
CORTICOTROPIN
CORTICOTROPINS
CORTISONES
CORUSCATED
CORUSCATES
CORUSCATING
CORUSCATION
CORUSCATIONS
CORVETTING
CORYBANTES
CORYBANTIC
CORYBANTISM
CORYBANTISMS
CORYDALINE
CORYDALINES
CORYDALISES
CORYLOPSES
CORYLOPSIS
CORYMBOSELY
CORYNEBACTERIA
CORYNEBACTERIAL
CORYNEBACTERIUM
CORYNEFORM
CORYPHAEUS
CORYPHENES
COSCINOMANCIES
COSCINOMANCY
COSCRIPTED
COSCRIPTING
COSEISMALS
COSEISMICS
COSENTIENT
COSHERINGS
COSIGNATORIES
COSIGNATORY
COSIGNIFICATIVE
COSINESSES
COSMECEUTICAL
COSMECEUTICALS
COSMETICAL
COSMETICALLY
COSMETICIAN
COSMETICIANS
COSMETICISE
COSMETICISED
COSMETICISES
COSMETICISING
COSMETICISM
COSMETICISMS
COSMETICIZE
COSMETICIZED
COSMETICIZES
COSMETICIZING
COSMETICOLOGIES
COSMETICOLOGY
COSMETOLOGIES
COSMETOLOGIST
COSMETOLOGISTS
COSMETOLOGY
COSMICALLY
COSMOCHEMICAL
COSMOCHEMIST
COSMOCHEMISTRY
COSMOCHEMISTS
COSMOCRATIC
COSMOCRATS
COSMODROME
COSMODROMES
COSMOGENIC
COSMOGENIES
COSMOGONAL
COSMOGONIC
COSMOGONICAL
COSMOGONIES
COSMOGONIST
COSMOGONISTS
COSMOGRAPHER
COSMOGRAPHERS
COSMOGRAPHIC
COSMOGRAPHICAL
COSMOGRAPHIES
COSMOGRAPHIST
COSMOGRAPHISTS
COSMOGRAPHY
COSMOLATRIES
COSMOLATRY
COSMOLINED
COSMOLINES
COSMOLINING
COSMOLOGIC
COSMOLOGICAL
COSMOLOGICALLY
COSMOLOGIES
COSMOLOGIST
COSMOLOGISTS
COSMONAUTICS
COSMONAUTS
COSMOPLASTIC
COSMOPOLIS
COSMOPOLISES
COSMOPOLITAN
COSMOPOLITANISM
COSMOPOLITANS
COSMOPOLITE
COSMOPOLITES
COSMOPOLITIC
COSMOPOLITICAL
COSMOPOLITICS
COSMOPOLITISM
COSMOPOLITISMS
COSMORAMAS
COSMORAMIC
COSMOSPHERE
COSMOSPHERES
COSMOTHEISM
COSMOTHEISMS
COSMOTHETIC
COSMOTHETICAL
COSMOTRONS
COSPONSORED
COSPONSORING
COSPONSORS
COSPONSORSHIP
COSPONSORSHIPS
COSTALGIAS
COSTARDMONGER
COSTARDMONGERS
COSTARRING
COSTEANING
COSTEANINGS
COSTERMONGER
COSTERMONGERS
COSTIVENESS
COSTIVENESSES
COSTLESSLY
COSTLINESS
COSTLINESSES
COSTMARIES
COSTOTOMIES
COSTUMERIES
COSTUMIERS
COSURFACTANT
COSURFACTANTS
COTANGENTIAL
COTANGENTS
COTELETTES
COTEMPORANEOUS
COTEMPORARY
COTENANCIES
COTERMINOUS
COTERMINOUSLY
COTILLIONS
COTONEASTER
COTONEASTERS
COTRANSDUCE
COTRANSDUCED
COTRANSDUCES
COTRANSDUCING
COTRANSDUCTION
COTRANSDUCTIONS
COTRANSFER
COTRANSFERS
COTRANSPORT
COTRANSPORTED
COTRANSPORTING
COTRANSPORTS
COTRUSTEES
COTTABUSES
COTTAGINGS
COTTERLESS
COTTIERISM
COTTIERISMS
COTTONADES
COTTONMOUTH
COTTONMOUTHS
COTTONOCRACIES
COTTONOCRACY
COTTONSEED
COTTONSEEDS
COTTONTAIL
COTTONTAILS
COTTONWEED
COTTONWEEDS
COTTONWOOD
COTTONWOODS
COTURNIXES
COTYLEDONAL
COTYLEDONARY
COTYLEDONOID
COTYLEDONOUS
COTYLEDONS
COTYLIFORM
COTYLOIDAL
COTYLOIDALS
COTYLOSAUR
COTYLOSAURS
COUCHETTES
COULIBIACA
COULIBIACAS
COULIBIACS
COULOMBMETER
COULOMBMETERS
COULOMETER
COULOMETERS
COULOMETRIC
COULOMETRICALLY
COULOMETRIES
COULOMETRY
COUMARILIC
COUMARONES
COUNCILLOR
COUNCILLORS
COUNCILLORSHIP
COUNCILLORSHIPS
COUNCILMAN
COUNCILMANIC
COUNCILMEN
COUNCILORS
COUNCILORSHIP
COUNCILORSHIPS
COUNCILWOMAN
COUNCILWOMEN
COUNSELABLE
COUNSELEES
COUNSELING
COUNSELINGS
COUNSELLABLE
COUNSELLED
COUNSELLING
COUNSELLINGS
COUNSELLOR
COUNSELLORS
COUNSELLORSHIP
COUNSELLORSHIPS
COUNSELORS
COUNSELORSHIP
COUNSELORSHIPS
COUNTABILITIES
COUNTABILITY
COUNTBACKS
COUNTDOWNS
COUNTENANCE
COUNTENANCED
COUNTENANCER

OUNTENANCERS
OUNTENANCES
OUNTENANCING
OUNTERACT
OUNTERACTED
OUNTERACTING
OUNTERACTION
OUNTERACTIONS
OUNTERACTIVE
OUNTERACTIVELY
OUNTERACTS
OUNTERAGENT
OUNTERAGENTS
OUNTERARGUE
OUNTERARGUED
OUNTERARGUES
OUNTERARGUING
OUNTERARGUMENT
OUNTERASSAULT
OUNTERASSAULTS
OUNTERATTACK
OUNTERATTACKED
OUNTERATTACKER
OUNTERATTACKS
OUNTERBALANCE
OUNTERBALANCED
OUNTERBALANCES
OUNTERBASE
OUNTERBASES
OUNTERBID
OUNTERBIDDER
OUNTERBIDDERS
OUNTERBIDS
OUNTERBLAST
OUNTERBLASTS
OUNTERBLOCKADE
OUNTERBLOW
OUNTERBLOWS
OUNTERBLUFF
OUNTERBLUFFS
OUNTERBOND
OUNTERBONDS
OUNTERBORE
OUNTERBORED
OUNTERBORES
OUNTERBORING
OUNTERBRACE
OUNTERBRACED
OUNTERBRACES
OUNTERBRACING
OUNTERBUFF
OUNTERBUFFED
OUNTERBUFFING
OUNTERBUFFS
OUNTERCAMPAIGN
OUNTERCHANGE
OUNTERCHANGED
OUNTERCHANGES
OUNTERCHANGING
OUNTERCHARGE
OUNTERCHARGED
OUNTERCHARGES
OUNTERCHARGING
OUNTERCHARM
OUNTERCHARMED
OUNTERCHARMING
COUNTERCHARMS
COUNTERCHECK
COUNTERCHECKED
COUNTERCHECKING
COUNTERCHECKS
COUNTERCLAIM
COUNTERCLAIMANT
COUNTERCLAIMED
COUNTERCLAIMING
COUNTERCLAIMS
COUNTERCOUP
COUNTERCOUPS
COUNTERCRIES
COUNTERCRY
COUNTERCULTURAL
COUNTERCULTURE
COUNTERCULTURES
COUNTERCURRENT
COUNTERCURRENTS
COUNTERCYCLICAL
COUNTERDEMAND
COUNTERDEMANDS
COUNTERDRAW
COUNTERDRAWING
COUNTERDRAWN
COUNTERDRAWS
COUNTERDREW
COUNTEREFFORT
COUNTEREFFORTS
COUNTEREVIDENCE
COUNTEREXAMPLE
COUNTEREXAMPLES
COUNTERFACTUAL
COUNTERFACTUALS
COUNTERFECT
COUNTERFEISANCE
COUNTERFEIT
COUNTERFEITED
COUNTERFEITER
COUNTERFEITERS
COUNTERFEITING
COUNTERFEITLY
COUNTERFEITS
COUNTERFESAUNCE
COUNTERFIRE
COUNTERFIRES
COUNTERFLOW
COUNTERFLOWS
COUNTERFOIL
COUNTERFOILS
COUNTERFORCE
COUNTERFORCES
COUNTERFORT
COUNTERFORTS
COUNTERGLOW
COUNTERGLOWS
COUNTERGUERILLA
COUNTERIMAGE
COUNTERIMAGES
COUNTERING
COUNTERINSTANCE
COUNTERION
COUNTERIONS
COUNTERIRRITANT
COUNTERLIGHT
COUNTERLIGHTS
COUNTERMAN
COUNTERMAND
COUNTERMANDABLE
COUNTERMANDED
COUNTERMANDING
COUNTERMANDS
COUNTERMARCH
COUNTERMARCHED
COUNTERMARCHES
COUNTERMARCHING
COUNTERMARK
COUNTERMARKS
COUNTERMEASURE
COUNTERMEASURES
COUNTERMELODIES
COUNTERMELODY
COUNTERMEMO
COUNTERMEMOS
COUNTERMEN
COUNTERMINE
COUNTERMINED
COUNTERMINES
COUNTERMINING
COUNTERMOTION
COUNTERMOTIONS
COUNTERMOVE
COUNTERMOVED
COUNTERMOVEMENT
COUNTERMOVES
COUNTERMOVING
COUNTERMURE
COUNTERMURED
COUNTERMURES
COUNTERMURING
COUNTERMYTH
COUNTERMYTHS
COUNTEROFFER
COUNTEROFFERS
COUNTERORDER
COUNTERORDERED
COUNTERORDERING
COUNTERORDERS
COUNTERPACE
COUNTERPACES
COUNTERPANE
COUNTERPANES
COUNTERPART
COUNTERPARTIES
COUNTERPARTS
COUNTERPARTY
COUNTERPEISE
COUNTERPEISED
COUNTERPEISES
COUNTERPEISING
COUNTERPETITION
COUNTERPICKET
COUNTERPICKETED
COUNTERPICKETS
COUNTERPLAN
COUNTERPLANS
COUNTERPLAY
COUNTERPLAYER
COUNTERPLAYERS
COUNTERPLAYS
COUNTERPLEA
COUNTERPLEAD
COUNTERPLEADED
COUNTERPLEADING
COUNTERPLEADS
COUNTERPLEAS
COUNTERPLED
COUNTERPLOT
COUNTERPLOTS
COUNTERPLOTTED
COUNTERPLOTTING
COUNTERPLOY
COUNTERPLOYS
COUNTERPOINT
COUNTERPOINTED
COUNTERPOINTING
COUNTERPOINTS
COUNTERPOISE
COUNTERPOISED
COUNTERPOISES
COUNTERPOISING
COUNTERPOSE
COUNTERPOSED
COUNTERPOSES
COUNTERPOSING
COUNTERPOWER
COUNTERPOWERS
COUNTERPRESSURE
COUNTERPROJECT
COUNTERPROJECTS
COUNTERPROOF
COUNTERPROOFS
COUNTERPROPOSAL
COUNTERPROTEST
COUNTERPROTESTS
COUNTERPUNCH
COUNTERPUNCHED
COUNTERPUNCHER
COUNTERPUNCHERS
COUNTERPUNCHES
COUNTERPUNCHING
COUNTERQUESTION
COUNTERRAID
COUNTERRAIDS
COUNTERRALLIED
COUNTERRALLIES
COUNTERRALLY
COUNTERRALLYING
COUNTERREACTION
COUNTERREFORM
COUNTERREFORMER
COUNTERREFORMS
COUNTERRESPONSE
COUNTERSANK
COUNTERSCARP
COUNTERSCARPS
COUNTERSEAL
COUNTERSEALED
COUNTERSEALING
COUNTERSEALS
COUNTERSHADING
COUNTERSHADINGS
COUNTERSHAFT
COUNTERSHAFTS
COUNTERSHOT
COUNTERSHOTS
COUNTERSIGN
COUNTERSIGNED

COUNTERSIGNING
COUNTERSIGNS
COUNTERSINK
COUNTERSINKING
COUNTERSINKS
COUNTERSNIPER
COUNTERSNIPERS
COUNTERSPELL
COUNTERSPELLS
COUNTERSPIES
COUNTERSPY
COUNTERSPYING
COUNTERSPYINGS
COUNTERSTAIN
COUNTERSTAINED
COUNTERSTAINING
COUNTERSTAINS
COUNTERSTATE
COUNTERSTATED
COUNTERSTATES
COUNTERSTATING
COUNTERSTEP
COUNTERSTEPS
COUNTERSTRATEGY
COUNTERSTREAM
COUNTERSTREAMS
COUNTERSTRICKEN
COUNTERSTRIKE
COUNTERSTRIKES
COUNTERSTRIKING
COUNTERSTROKE
COUNTERSTROKES
COUNTERSTRUCK
COUNTERSTYLE
COUNTERSTYLES
COUNTERSUBJECT
COUNTERSUBJECTS
COUNTERSUE
COUNTERSUED
COUNTERSUES
COUNTERSUING
COUNTERSUIT
COUNTERSUITS
COUNTERSUNK
COUNTERTACTIC
COUNTERTACTICS
COUNTERTENDENCY
COUNTERTENOR
COUNTERTENORS
COUNTERTERROR
COUNTERTERRORS
COUNTERTHREAT
COUNTERTHREATS
COUNTERTHRUST
COUNTERTHRUSTS
COUNTERTOP
COUNTERTOPS
COUNTERTRADE
COUNTERTRADED
COUNTERTRADES
COUNTERTRADING
COUNTERTREND
COUNTERTRENDS
COUNTERTYPE
COUNTERTYPES
COUNTERVAIL
COUNTERVAILABLE
COUNTERVAILED
COUNTERVAILING
COUNTERVAILS
COUNTERVIEW
COUNTERVIEWS
COUNTERVIOLENCE
COUNTERWEIGH
COUNTERWEIGHED
COUNTERWEIGHING
COUNTERWEIGHS
COUNTERWEIGHT
COUNTERWEIGHTED
COUNTERWEIGHTS
COUNTERWORD
COUNTERWORDS
COUNTERWORK
COUNTERWORKED
COUNTERWORKER
COUNTERWORKERS
COUNTERWORKING
COUNTERWORKS
COUNTERWORLD
COUNTERWORLDS
COUNTESSES
COUNTINGHOUSE
COUNTINGHOUSES
COUNTLESSLY
COUNTLINES
COUNTRIFIED
COUNTROLLED
COUNTROLLING
COUNTRYFIED
COUNTRYISH
COUNTRYMAN
COUNTRYMEN
COUNTRYSEAT
COUNTRYSEATS
COUNTRYSIDE
COUNTRYSIDES
COUNTRYWIDE
COUNTRYWOMAN
COUNTRYWOMEN
COUNTSHIPS
COUPLEDOMS
COUPLEMENT
COUPLEMENTS
COUPONINGS
COURAGEFUL
COURAGEOUS
COURAGEOUSLY
COURAGEOUSNESS
COURANTOES
COURBARILS
COURBETTES
COURGETTES
COURSEBOOK
COURSEBOOKS
COURSEWARE
COURSEWARES
COURSEWORK
COURSEWORKS
COURTCRAFT
COURTCRAFTS
COURTEOUSLY
COURTEOUSNESS
COURTEOUSNESSES
COURTESANS
COURTESIED
COURTESIES
COURTESYING
COURTEZANS
COURTHOUSE
COURTHOUSES
COURTIERISM
COURTIERISMS
COURTIERLIKE
COURTIERLY
COURTLIEST
COURTLINESS
COURTLINESSES
COURTLINGS
COURTMARTIALLED
COURTROOMS
COURTSHIPS
COURTSIDES
COURTYARDS
COUSCOUSES
COUSCOUSOU
COUSCOUSOUS
COUSINAGES
COUSINHOOD
COUSINHOODS
COUSINRIES
COUSINSHIP
COUSINSHIPS
COUTURIERE
COUTURIERES
COUTURIERS
COVALENCES
COVALENCIES
COVALENTLY
COVARIANCE
COVARIANCES
COVARIANTS
COVARIATES
COVARIATION
COVARIATIONS
COVELLINES
COVELLITES
COVENANTAL
COVENANTALLY
COVENANTED
COVENANTEE
COVENANTEES
COVENANTER
COVENANTERS
COVENANTING
COVENANTOR
COVENANTORS
COVERALLED
COVERMOUNT
COVERMOUNTED
COVERMOUNTING
COVERMOUNTS
COVERSINES
COVERSLIPS
COVERTNESS
COVERTNESSES
COVERTURES
COVETINGLY
COVETIVENESS
COVETIVENESSES
COVETOUSLY
COVETOUSNESS
COVETOUSNESSES
COWARDICES
COWARDLINESS
COWARDLINESSES
COWARDRIES
COWARDSHIP
COWARDSHIPS
COWBERRIES
COWCATCHER
COWCATCHERS
COWERINGLY
COWFEEDERS
COWFETERIA
COWFETERIAS
COWGRASSES
COWLSTAFFS
COWLSTAVES
COWPUNCHER
COWPUNCHERS
COXCOMBICAL
COXCOMBICALITY
COXCOMBICALLY
COXCOMBRIES
COXCOMICAL
COXINESSES
COXSWAINED
COXSWAINING
COYISHNESS
COYISHNESSES
COYOTILLOS
COZINESSES
CRABABBLES
CRABBEDNESS
CRABBEDNESSES
CRABBINESS
CRABBINESSES
CRABEATERS
CRABGRASSES
CRABSTICKS
CRACKAJACK
CRACKAJACKS
CRACKBACKS
CRACKBERRIES
CRACKBERRY
CRACKBRAIN
CRACKBRAINED
CRACKBRAINS
CRACKDOWNS
CRACKERJACK
CRACKERJACKS
CRACKHEADS
CRACKLEWARE
CRACKLEWARES
CRACKLIEST
CRACKLINGS
CRACOVIENNE
CRACOVIENNES
CRADLESONG
CRADLESONGS
CRADLEWALK
CRADLEWALKS
CRAFTINESS
CRAFTINESSES

RAFTMANSHIP
RAFTMANSHIPS
RAFTSMANLIKE
RAFTSMANLY
RAFTSMANSHIP
RAFTSMANSHIPS
RAFTSPEOPLE
RAFTSPERSON
RAFTSPERSONS
RAFTSWOMAN
RAFTSWOMEN
RAFTWORKS
RAGGEDNESS
RAGGEDNESSES
RAGGINESS
RAGGINESSES
RAIGFLUKE
RAIGFLUKES
RAKEBERRIES
RAKEBERRY
RAMBOCLINK
RAMBOCLINKS
RAMOISIES
RAMPBARKS
RAMPFISHES
RAMPONING
RANBERRIES
RANEFLIES
RANESBILL
RANESBILLS
RANIECTOMIES
RANIECTOMY
RANIOCEREBRAL
RANIOFACIAL
RANIOGNOMIES
RANIOGNOMY
RANIOLOGICAL
RANIOLOGICALLY
RANIOLOGIES
RANIOLOGIST
RANIOLOGISTS
RANIOLOGY
RANIOMETER
RANIOMETERS
RANIOMETRIC
RANIOMETRICAL
RANIOMETRIES
RANIOMETRIST
RANIOMETRISTS
RANIOMETRY
RANIOPAGI
RANIOPAGUS
RANIOSACRAL
RANIOSCOPIES
RANIOSCOPIST
RANIOSCOPISTS
RANIOSCOPY
RANIOTOMIES
RANIOTOMY
RANKCASES
RANKHANDLE
RANKHANDLES
RANKINESS
RANKINESSES
RANKNESSES
RANKSHAFT
CRANKSHAFTS
CRANREUCHS
CRAPEHANGER
CRAPEHANGERS
CRAPEHANGING
CRAPEHANGINGS
CRAPSHOOTER
CRAPSHOOTERS
CRAPSHOOTS
CRAPULENCE
CRAPULENCES
CRAPULENTLY
CRAPULOSITIES
CRAPULOSITY
CRAPULOUSLY
CRAPULOUSNESS
CRAPULOUSNESSES
CRAQUELURE
CRAQUELURES
CRASHINGLY
CRASHLANDED
CRASHLANDING
CRASHLANDS
CRASHWORTHINESS
CRASHWORTHY
CRASSAMENTA
CRASSAMENTUM
CRASSITUDE
CRASSITUDES
CRASSNESSES
CRASSULACEAN
CRASSULACEOUS
CRATERIFORM
CRATERINGS
CRATERLESS
CRATERLETS
CRATERLIKE
CRAUNCHABLE
CRAUNCHIER
CRAUNCHIEST
CRAUNCHINESS
CRAUNCHINESSES
CRAUNCHING
CRAVATTING
CRAVENNESS
CRAVENNESSES
CRAWDADDIES
CRAWFISHED
CRAWFISHES
CRAWFISHING
CRAWLINGLY
CRAYFISHES
CRAYONISTS
CRAZINESSES
CRAZYWEEDS
CREAKINESS
CREAKINESSES
CREAKINGLY
CREAMERIES
CREAMINESS
CREAMINESSES
CREAMPUFFS
CREAMWARES
CREASELESS
CREASOTING
CREATIANISM
CREATIANISMS
CREATININE
CREATININES
CREATIONAL
CREATIONISM
CREATIONISMS
CREATIONIST
CREATIONISTIC
CREATIONISTS
CREATIVELY
CREATIVENESS
CREATIVENESSES
CREATIVITIES
CREATIVITY
CREATORSHIP
CREATORSHIPS
CREATRESSES
CREATRIXES
CREATUREHOOD
CREATUREHOODS
CREATURELINESS
CREATURELY
CREATURESHIP
CREATURESHIPS
CREDENTIAL
CREDENTIALED
CREDENTIALING
CREDENTIALISM
CREDENTIALISMS
CREDENTIALLED
CREDENTIALLING
CREDENTIALS
CREDIBILITIES
CREDIBILITY
CREDIBLENESS
CREDIBLENESSES
CREDITABILITIES
CREDITABILITY
CREDITABLE
CREDITABLENESS
CREDITABLY
CREDITLESS
CREDITWORTHY
CREDULITIES
CREDULOUSLY
CREDULOUSNESS
CREDULOUSNESSES
CREEPINESS
CREEPINESSES
CREEPINGLY
CREEPMOUSE
CREESHIEST
CREMAILLERE
CREMAILLERES
CREMASTERS
CREMATIONISM
CREMATIONISMS
CREMATIONIST
CREMATIONISTS
CREMATIONS
CREMATORIA
CREMATORIAL
CREMATORIES
CREMATORIUM
CREMATORIUMS
CREMOCARPS
CRENATIONS
CRENATURES
CRENELATED
CRENELATES
CRENELATING
CRENELATION
CRENELATIONS
CRENELLATE
CRENELLATED
CRENELLATES
CRENELLATING
CRENELLATION
CRENELLATIONS
CRENELLING
CRENULATED
CRENULATION
CRENULATIONS
CREOLISATION
CREOLISATIONS
CREOLISING
CREOLIZATION
CREOLIZATIONS
CREOLIZING
CREOPHAGIES
CREOPHAGOUS
CREOSOTING
CREPEHANGER
CREPEHANGERS
CREPEHANGING
CREPEHANGINGS
CREPINESSES
CREPITATED
CREPITATES
CREPITATING
CREPITATION
CREPITATIONS
CREPITATIVE
CREPITUSES
CREPOLINES
CREPUSCLES
CREPUSCULAR
CREPUSCULE
CREPUSCULES
CREPUSCULOUS
CRESCENDOED
CRESCENDOES
CRESCENDOING
CRESCENDOS
CRESCENTADE
CRESCENTADES
CRESCENTED
CRESCENTIC
CRESCIVELY
CRESCOGRAPH
CRESCOGRAPHS
CRESTFALLEN
CRESTFALLENLY
CRESTFALLENNESS
CRETACEOUS
CRETACEOUSES
CRETACEOUSLY
CRETINISED
CRETINISES
CRETINISING
CRETINISMS
CRETINIZED

CRETINIZES
CRETINIZING
CRETINOIDS
CREVASSING
CREWELISTS
CREWELLERIES
CREWELLERY
CREWELLING
CREWELWORK
CREWELWORKS
CRIBRATION
CRIBRATIONS
CRIBRIFORM
CRICKETERS
CRICKETING
CRICKETINGS
CRIMEWAVES
CRIMINALESE
CRIMINALESES
CRIMINALISATION
CRIMINALISE
CRIMINALISED
CRIMINALISES
CRIMINALISING
CRIMINALIST
CRIMINALISTICS
CRIMINALISTS
CRIMINALITIES
CRIMINALITY
CRIMINALIZATION
CRIMINALIZE
CRIMINALIZED
CRIMINALIZES
CRIMINALIZING
CRIMINALLY
CRIMINATED
CRIMINATES
CRIMINATING
CRIMINATION
CRIMINATIONS
CRIMINATIVE
CRIMINATOR
CRIMINATORS
CRIMINATORY
CRIMINOGENIC
CRIMINOLOGIC
CRIMINOLOGICAL
CRIMINOLOGIES
CRIMINOLOGIST
CRIMINOLOGISTS
CRIMINOLOGY
CRIMINOUSNESS
CRIMINOUSNESSES
CRIMSONING
CRIMSONNESS
CRIMSONNESSES
CRINGELING
CRINGELINGS
CRINGEWORTHY
CRINGINGLY
CRINICULTURAL
CRINIGEROUS
CRINKLEROOT
CRINKLEROOTS
CRINKLIEST
CRINOIDEAN
CRINOIDEANS
CRINOLETTE
CRINOLETTES
CRINOLINED
CRINOLINES
CRIPPLEDOM
CRIPPLEDOMS
CRIPPLEWARE
CRIPPLEWARES
CRIPPLINGLY
CRIPPLINGS
CRISPATION
CRISPATIONS
CRISPATURE
CRISPATURES
CRISPBREAD
CRISPBREADS
CRISPENING
CRISPHEADS
CRISPINESS
CRISPINESSES
CRISPNESSES
CRISSCROSS
CRISSCROSSED
CRISSCROSSES
CRISSCROSSING
CRISTIFORM
CRISTOBALITE
CRISTOBALITES
CRITERIONS
CRITERIUMS
CRITHIDIAL
CRITHOMANCIES
CRITHOMANCY
CRITICALITIES
CRITICALITY
CRITICALLY
CRITICALNESS
CRITICALNESSES
CRITICASTER
CRITICASTERS
CRITICISABLE
CRITICISED
CRITICISER
CRITICISERS
CRITICISES
CRITICISING
CRITICISINGLY
CRITICISMS
CRITICIZABLE
CRITICIZED
CRITICIZER
CRITICIZERS
CRITICIZES
CRITICIZING
CRITICIZINGLY
CRITIQUING
CROAKINESS
CROAKINESSES
CROCHETERS
CROCHETING
CROCHETINGS
CROCIDOLITE
CROCIDOLITES
CROCKERIES
CROCODILES
CROCODILIAN
CROCODILIANS
CROCOISITE
CROCOISITES
CROCOSMIAS
CROISSANTS
CROKINOLES
CROOKBACKED
CROOKBACKS
CROOKEDEST
CROOKEDNESS
CROOKEDNESSES
CROOKERIES
CROOKNECKS
CROPDUSTER
CROPDUSTERS
CROQUANTES
CROQUETING
CROQUETTES
CROQUIGNOLE
CROQUIGNOLES
CROSSABILITIES
CROSSABILITY
CROSSANDRA
CROSSANDRAS
CROSSBANDED
CROSSBANDING
CROSSBANDINGS
CROSSBANDS
CROSSBARRED
CROSSBARRING
CROSSBEAMS
CROSSBEARER
CROSSBEARERS
CROSSBENCH
CROSSBENCHER
CROSSBENCHERS
CROSSBENCHES
CROSSBILLS
CROSSBIRTH
CROSSBIRTHS
CROSSBITES
CROSSBITING
CROSSBITTEN
CROSSBONES
CROSSBOWER
CROSSBOWERS
CROSSBOWMAN
CROSSBOWMEN
CROSSBREDS
CROSSBREED
CROSSBREEDING
CROSSBREEDINGS
CROSSBREEDS
CROSSBUCKS
CROSSCHECK
CROSSCHECKED
CROSSCHECKING
CROSSCHECKS
CROSSCLAIM
CROSSCLAIMS
CROSSCOURT
CROSSCURRENT
CROSSCURRENTS
CROSSCUTTING
CROSSCUTTINGS
CROSSETTES
CROSSFALLS
CROSSFIELD
CROSSFIRES
CROSSFISHES
CROSSHAIRS
CROSSHATCH
CROSSHATCHED
CROSSHATCHES
CROSSHATCHING
CROSSHEADS
CROSSJACKS
CROSSLIGHT
CROSSLIGHTS
CROSSLINGUISTIC
CROSSNESSES
CROSSOPTERYGIAN
CROSSOVERS
CROSSPATCH
CROSSPATCHES
CROSSPIECE
CROSSPIECES
CROSSROADS
CROSSRUFFED
CROSSRUFFING
CROSSRUFFS
CROSSTALKS
CROSSTREES
CROSSWALKS
CROSSWINDS
CROSSWORDS
CROSSWORTS
CROTALARIA
CROTALARIAS
CROTALISMS
CROTCHETED
CROTCHETEER
CROTCHETEERS
CROTCHETIER
CROTCHETIEST
CROTCHETINESS
CROTCHETINESSES
CROTONBUGS
CROUPINESS
CROUPINESSES
CROUSTADES
CROWBARRED
CROWBARRING
CROWBERRIES
CROWDEDNESS
CROWDEDNESSES
CROWKEEPER
CROWKEEPERS
CROWNLANDS
CROWNPIECE
CROWNPIECES
CROWNWORKS
CROWSTEPPED
CRUCIATELY
CRUCIFEROUS
CRUCIFIERS
CRUCIFIXES
CRUCIFIXION
CRUCIFIXIONS
CRUCIFORMLY
CRUCIFORMS

RUCIFYING
RUCIVERBAL
RUCIVERBALISM
RUCIVERBALISMS
RUCIVERBALIST
RUCIVERBALISTS
RUDENESSES
RUELNESSES
RUISERWEIGHT
RUISERWEIGHTS
RUISEWAYS
RUISEWEAR
RUISEWEARS
RUMBCLOTH
RUMBCLOTHS
RUMBLIEST
RUMBLINESS
RUMBLINESSES
RUMBLINGS
RUMMINESS
RUMMINESSES
RUMPLIEST
RUMPLINGS
RUNCHABLE
RUNCHIEST
RUNCHINESS
RUNCHINESSES
RUNCHINGS
RUSHABILITIES
RUSHABILITY
RUSHINGLY
RUSHPROOF
RUSTACEAN
RUSTACEANS
RUSTACEOUS
RUSTATION
RUSTATIONS
RUSTINESS
RUSTINESSES
RUTCHINGS
RYMOTHERAPIES
RYMOTHERAPY
RYOBIOLOGICAL
RYOBIOLOGIES
RYOBIOLOGIST
RYOBIOLOGISTS
RYOBIOLOGY
RYOCABLES
RYOCONITE
RYOCONITES
RYOGENICALLY
RYOGENICS
RYOGENIES
RYOGLOBULIN
RYOGLOBULINS
RYOHYDRATE
RYOHYDRATES
RYOMETERS
RYOMETRIC
RYOMETRIES
RYOPHILIC
RYOPHORUS
RYOPHORUSES
RYOPHYSICS
RYOPHYTES
RYOPLANKTON

CRYOPLANKTONS
CRYOPRECIPITATE
CRYOPRESERVE
CRYOPRESERVED
CRYOPRESERVES
CRYOPRESERVING
CRYOPROBES
CRYOPROTECTANT
CRYOPROTECTANTS
CRYOPROTECTIVE
CRYOSCOPES
CRYOSCOPIC
CRYOSCOPIES
CRYOSTATIC
CRYOSURGEON
CRYOSURGEONS
CRYOSURGERIES
CRYOSURGERY
CRYOSURGICAL
CRYOTHERAPIES
CRYOTHERAPY
CRYPTAESTHESIA
CRYPTAESTHESIAS
CRYPTAESTHETIC
CRYPTANALYSES
CRYPTANALYSIS
CRYPTANALYST
CRYPTANALYSTS
CRYPTANALYTIC
CRYPTANALYTICAL
CRYPTARITHM
CRYPTARITHMS
CRYPTESTHESIA
CRYPTESTHESIAS
CRYPTICALLY
CRYPTOBIONT
CRYPTOBIONTS
CRYPTOBIOSES
CRYPTOBIOSIS
CRYPTOCLASTIC
CRYPTOCOCCAL
CRYPTOCOCCI
CRYPTOCOCCOSES
CRYPTOCOCCOSIS
CRYPTOCOCCUS
CRYPTOGAMIAN
CRYPTOGAMIC
CRYPTOGAMIES
CRYPTOGAMIST
CRYPTOGAMISTS
CRYPTOGAMOUS
CRYPTOGAMS
CRYPTOGAMY
CRYPTOGENIC
CRYPTOGRAM
CRYPTOGRAMS
CRYPTOGRAPH
CRYPTOGRAPHER
CRYPTOGRAPHERS
CRYPTOGRAPHIC
CRYPTOGRAPHICAL
CRYPTOGRAPHIES
CRYPTOGRAPHIST
CRYPTOGRAPHISTS
CRYPTOGRAPHS
CRYPTOGRAPHY

CRYPTOLOGIC
CRYPTOLOGICAL
CRYPTOLOGIES
CRYPTOLOGIST
CRYPTOLOGISTS
CRYPTOLOGY
CRYPTOMERIA
CRYPTOMERIAS
CRYPTOMETER
CRYPTOMETERS
CRYPTOMNESIA
CRYPTOMNESIAS
CRYPTOMNESIC
CRYPTONYMOUS
CRYPTONYMS
CRYPTOPHYTE
CRYPTOPHYTES
CRYPTOPHYTIC
CRYPTORCHID
CRYPTORCHIDISM
CRYPTORCHIDISMS
CRYPTORCHIDS
CRYPTORCHISM
CRYPTORCHISMS
CRYPTOSPORIDIA
CRYPTOSPORIDIUM
CRYPTOZOIC
CRYPTOZOITE
CRYPTOZOITES
CRYPTOZOOLOGIES
CRYPTOZOOLOGIST
CRYPTOZOOLOGY
CRYSTALISABLE
CRYSTALISATION
CRYSTALISATIONS
CRYSTALISE
CRYSTALISED
CRYSTALISER
CRYSTALISERS
CRYSTALISES
CRYSTALISING
CRYSTALIZABLE
CRYSTALIZATION
CRYSTALIZATIONS
CRYSTALIZE
CRYSTALIZED
CRYSTALIZER
CRYSTALIZERS
CRYSTALIZES
CRYSTALIZING
CRYSTALLINE
CRYSTALLINES
CRYSTALLINITIES
CRYSTALLINITY
CRYSTALLISABLE
CRYSTALLISATION
CRYSTALLISE
CRYSTALLISED
CRYSTALLISER
CRYSTALLISERS
CRYSTALLISES
CRYSTALLISING
CRYSTALLITE
CRYSTALLITES
CRYSTALLITIC
CRYSTALLITIS

CRYSTALLITISES
CRYSTALLIZABLE
CRYSTALLIZATION
CRYSTALLIZE
CRYSTALLIZED
CRYSTALLIZER
CRYSTALLIZERS
CRYSTALLIZES
CRYSTALLIZING
CRYSTALLOGRAPHY
CRYSTALLOID
CRYSTALLOIDAL
CRYSTALLOIDS
CRYSTALLOMANCY
CTENOPHORAN
CTENOPHORANS
CTENOPHORE
CTENOPHORES
CUADRILLAS
CUBANELLES
CUBBYHOLES
CUBICALNESS
CUBICALNESSES
CUBICITIES
CUBISTICALLY
CUCKOLDING
CUCKOLDISE
CUCKOLDISED
CUCKOLDISES
CUCKOLDISING
CUCKOLDIZE
CUCKOLDIZED
CUCKOLDIZES
CUCKOLDIZING
CUCKOLDOMS
CUCKOLDRIES
CUCKOOFLOWER
CUCKOOFLOWERS
CUCKOOPINT
CUCKOOPINTS
CUCULIFORM
CUCULLATED
CUCULLATELY
CUCUMIFORM
CUCURBITACEOUS
CUCURBITAL
CUDDLESOME
CUDGELLERS
CUDGELLING
CUDGELLINGS
CUFFUFFLES
CUIRASSIER
CUIRASSIERS
CUIRASSING
CUISINARTS
CUISINIERS
CULICIFORM
CULINARIAN
CULINARIANS
CULINARILY
CULLENDERS
CULMIFEROUS
CULMINATED
CULMINATES
CULMINATING
CULMINATION

CULMINATIONS
CULPABILITIES
CULPABILITY
CULPABLENESS
CULPABLENESSES
CULTISHNESS
CULTISHNESSES
CULTIVABILITIES
CULTIVABILITY
CULTIVABLE
CULTIVATABLE
CULTIVATED
CULTIVATES
CULTIVATING
CULTIVATION
CULTIVATIONS
CULTIVATOR
CULTIVATORS
CULTRIFORM
CULTURABLE
CULTURALLY
CULTURELESS
CULTURISTS
CULVERINEER
CULVERINEERS
CULVERTAGE
CULVERTAGES
CULVERTAILED
CUMBERBUND
CUMBERBUNDS
CUMBERLESS
CUMBERMENT
CUMBERMENTS
CUMBERSOME
CUMBERSOMELY
CUMBERSOMENESS
CUMBRANCES
CUMBROUSLY
CUMBROUSNESS
CUMBROUSNESSES
CUMMERBUND
CUMMERBUNDS
CUMMINGTONITE
CUMMINGTONITES
CUMULATELY
CUMULATING
CUMULATION
CUMULATIONS
CUMULATIVE
CUMULATIVELY
CUMULATIVENESS
CUMULIFORM
CUMULOCIRRI
CUMULOCIRRUS
CUMULONIMBI
CUMULONIMBUS
CUMULONIMBUSES
CUMULOSTRATI
CUMULOSTRATUS
CUNCTATION
CUNCTATIONS
CUNCTATIOUS
CUNCTATIVE
CUNCTATORS
CUNCTATORY
CUNEIFORMS
CUNNILINCTUS
CUNNILINCTUSES
CUNNILINGUS
CUNNILINGUSES
CUNNINGEST
CUNNINGNESS
CUNNINGNESSES
CUPBEARERS
CUPBOARDED
CUPBOARDING
CUPELLATION
CUPELLATIONS
CUPFERRONS
CUPIDINOUS
CUPIDITIES
CUPRAMMONIUM
CUPRAMMONIUMS
CUPRESSUSES
CUPRIFEROUS
CUPRONICKEL
CUPRONICKELS
CUPULIFEROUS
CURABILITIES
CURABILITY
CURABLENESS
CURABLENESSES
CURANDERAS
CURANDEROS
CURARISATION
CURARISATIONS
CURARISING
CURARIZATION
CURARIZATIONS
CURARIZING
CURATESHIP
CURATESHIPS
CURATIVELY
CURATIVENESS
CURATIVENESSES
CURATORIAL
CURATORSHIP
CURATORSHIPS
CURATRIXES
CURBSTONES
CURCUMINES
CURDINESSES
CURETTAGES
CURETTEMENT
CURETTEMENTS
CURFUFFLED
CURFUFFLES
CURFUFFLING
CURIALISMS
CURIALISTIC
CURIALISTS
CURIETHERAPIES
CURIETHERAPY
CURIOSITIES
CURIOUSEST
CURIOUSNESS
CURIOUSNESSES
CURLICUING
CURLIEWURLIE
CURLIEWURLIES
CURLINESSES
CURLPAPERS
CURMUDGEON
CURMUDGEONLY
CURMUDGEONS
CURMURRING
CURMURRINGS
CURNAPTIOUS
CURRAJONGS
CURRANTIER
CURRANTIEST
CURRAWONGS
CURREJONGS
CURRENCIES
CURRENTNESS
CURRENTNESSES
CURRICULAR
CURRICULUM
CURRICULUMS
CURRIERIES
CURRIJONGS
CURRISHNESS
CURRISHNESSES
CURRYCOMBED
CURRYCOMBING
CURRYCOMBS
CURSEDNESS
CURSEDNESSES
CURSELARIE
CURSIVENESS
CURSIVENESSES
CURSORINESS
CURSORINESSES
CURSTNESSES
CURTAILERS
CURTAILING
CURTAILMENT
CURTAILMENTS
CURTAINING
CURTAINLESS
CURTALAXES
CURTATIONS
CURTILAGES
CURTNESSES
CURTSEYING
CURVACEOUS
CURVACEOUSLY
CURVACIOUS
CURVATIONS
CURVATURES
CURVEBALLED
CURVEBALLING
CURVEBALLS
CURVEDNESS
CURVEDNESSES
CURVETTING
CURVICAUDATE
CURVICOSTATE
CURVIFOLIATE
CURVILINEAL
CURVILINEAR
CURVILINEARITY
CURVILINEARLY
CURVIROSTRAL
CUSHINESSES
CUSHIONETS
CUSHIONING
CUSHIONLESS
CUSPIDATED
CUSPIDATION
CUSPIDATIONS
CUSPIDORES
CUSSEDNESS
CUSSEDNESSES
CUSTODIANS
CUSTODIANSHIP
CUSTODIANSHIPS
CUSTODIERS
CUSTOMABLE
CUSTOMARIES
CUSTOMARILY
CUSTOMARINESS
CUSTOMARINESSES
CUSTOMHOUSE
CUSTOMHOUSES
CUSTOMISATION
CUSTOMISATIONS
CUSTOMISED
CUSTOMISER
CUSTOMISERS
CUSTOMISES
CUSTOMISING
CUSTOMIZATION
CUSTOMIZATIONS
CUSTOMIZED
CUSTOMIZER
CUSTOMIZERS
CUSTOMIZES
CUSTOMIZING
CUSTOMSHOUSE
CUSTOMSHOUSES
CUSTUMARIES
CUTABILITIES
CUTABILITY
CUTANEOUSLY
CUTCHERIES
CUTCHERRIES
CUTENESSES
CUTGRASSES
CUTINISATION
CUTINISATIONS
CUTINISING
CUTINIZATION
CUTINIZATIONS
CUTINIZING
CUTTHROATS
CUTTLEBONE
CUTTLEBONES
CUTTLEFISH
CUTTLEFISHES
CYANAMIDES
CYANIDATION
CYANIDATIONS
CYANIDINGS
CYANOACETYLENE
CYANOACETYLENES
CYANOACRYLATE
CYANOACRYLATES
CYANOBACTERIA
CYANOBACTERIUM
CYANOCOBALAMIN
CYANOCOBALAMINE
CYANOCOBALAMINS
CYANOETHYLATE

YANOETHYLATED
YANOETHYLATES
YANOETHYLATING
YANOETHYLATION
YANOGENAMIDE
YANOGENAMIDES
YANOGENESES
YANOGENESIS
YANOGENETIC
YANOGENIC
YANOHYDRIN
YANOHYDRINS
YANOMETER
YANOMETERS
YANOPHYTE
YANOPHYTES
YANOTYPES
YANURATES
YATHIFORM
BERATHLETE
BERATHLETES
BERATHLETICS
BERCAFES
BERCASTS
BERCRIME
BERCRIMES
BERCRIMINAL
BERCRIMINALS
BERNATED
BERNATES
BERNATING
BERNATION
BERNATIONS
BERNAUTS
BERNETIC
BERNETICAL
BERNETICALLY
BERNETICIAN
BERNETICIANS
BERNETICIST
BERNETICISTS
BERNETICS
BERPHOBIA
BERPHOBIAS
BERPHOBIC
BERPORNS
BERPUNKS
BERSECURITIES
BERSECURITY
BERSEXES
BERSPACE
BERSPACES
BERSQUATTER
BERSQUATTERS
BERSQUATTING
BERSQUATTINGS
BERTERRORISM
BERTERRORISMS
BERTERRORIST
BERTERRORISTS
BRARIANS
CADACEOUS
CADEOIDS
CADOPHYTE
CADOPHYTES
CLAMATES
CYCLANDELATE
CYCLANDELATES
CYCLANTHACEOUS
CYCLAZOCINE
CYCLAZOCINES
CYCLICALITIES
CYCLICALITY
CYCLICALLY
CYCLICISMS
CYCLICITIES
CYCLISATION
CYCLISATIONS
CYCLIZATION
CYCLIZATIONS
CYCLIZINES
CYCLOADDITION
CYCLOADDITIONS
CYCLOALIPHATIC
CYCLOALKANE
CYCLOALKANES
CYCLOBARBITONE
CYCLOBARBITONES
CYCLODEXTRIN
CYCLODEXTRINS
CYCLODIALYSES
CYCLODIALYSIS
CYCLODIENE
CYCLODIENES
CYCLOGENESES
CYCLOGENESIS
CYCLOGIROS
CYCLOGRAPH
CYCLOGRAPHIC
CYCLOGRAPHS
CYCLOHEXANE
CYCLOHEXANES
CYCLOHEXANONE
CYCLOHEXANONES
CYCLOHEXIMIDE
CYCLOHEXIMIDES
CYCLOHEXYLAMINE
CYCLOIDALLY
CYCLOIDIAN
CYCLOIDIANS
CYCLOLITHS
CYCLOMETER
CYCLOMETERS
CYCLOMETRIES
CYCLOMETRY
CYCLONICAL
CYCLONICALLY
CYCLONITES
CYCLOOLEFIN
CYCLOOLEFINIC
CYCLOOLEFINS
CYCLOPAEDIA
CYCLOPAEDIAS
CYCLOPAEDIC
CYCLOPAEDIST
CYCLOPAEDISTS
CYCLOPARAFFIN
CYCLOPARAFFINS
CYCLOPEDIA
CYCLOPEDIAS
CYCLOPEDIC
CYCLOPEDIST
CYCLOPEDISTS
CYCLOPENTADIENE
CYCLOPENTANE
CYCLOPENTANES
CYCLOPENTOLATE
CYCLOPENTOLATES
CYCLOPLEGIA
CYCLOPLEGIAS
CYCLOPLEGIC
CYCLOPROPANE
CYCLOPROPANES
CYCLORAMAS
CYCLORAMIC
CYCLOSERINE
CYCLOSERINES
CYCLOSPERMOUS
CYCLOSPORIN
CYCLOSPORINE
CYCLOSPORINES
CYCLOSPORINS
CYCLOSTOMATE
CYCLOSTOMATOUS
CYCLOSTOME
CYCLOSTOMES
CYCLOSTOMOUS
CYCLOSTYLE
CYCLOSTYLED
CYCLOSTYLES
CYCLOSTYLING
CYCLOTHYME
CYCLOTHYMES
CYCLOTHYMIA
CYCLOTHYMIAC
CYCLOTHYMIACS
CYCLOTHYMIAS
CYCLOTHYMIC
CYCLOTHYMICS
CYCLOTOMIC
CYCLOTRONS
CYLINDERED
CYLINDERING
CYLINDRACEOUS
CYLINDRICAL
CYLINDRICALITY
CYLINDRICALLY
CYLINDRICALNESS
CYLINDRICITIES
CYLINDRICITY
CYLINDRIFORM
CYLINDRITE
CYLINDRITES
CYLINDROID
CYLINDROIDS
CYMAGRAPHS
CYMBALEERS
CYMBALISTS
CYMBIDIUMS
CYMIFEROUS
CYMOGRAPHIC
CYMOGRAPHS
CYMOPHANES
CYMOPHANOUS
CYMOTRICHIES
CYMOTRICHOUS
CYMOTRICHY
CYNGHANEDD
CYNGHANEDDS
CYNICALNESS
CYNICALNESSES
CYNOMOLGUS
CYNOPHILIA
CYNOPHILIAS
CYNOPHILIST
CYNOPHILISTS
CYNOPHOBIA
CYNOPHOBIAS
CYNOPODOUS
CYPERACEOUS
CYPRINODONT
CYPRINODONTS
CYPRINOIDS
CYPRIPEDIA
CYPRIPEDIUM
CYPRIPEDIUMS
CYPROHEPTADINE
CYPROHEPTADINES
CYPROTERONE
CYPROTERONES
CYSTEAMINE
CYSTEAMINES
CYSTECTOMIES
CYSTECTOMY
CYSTICERCI
CYSTICERCOID
CYSTICERCOIDS
CYSTICERCOSES
CYSTICERCOSIS
CYSTICERCUS
CYSTIDEANS
CYSTINOSES
CYSTINOSIS
CYSTINURIA
CYSTINURIAS
CYSTITIDES
CYSTITISES
CYSTOCARPIC
CYSTOCARPS
CYSTOCELES
CYSTOGENOUS
CYSTOGRAPHIES
CYSTOGRAPHY
CYSTOLITHIASES
CYSTOLITHIASIS
CYSTOLITHS
CYSTOSCOPE
CYSTOSCOPES
CYSTOSCOPIC
CYSTOSCOPIES
CYSTOSCOPY
CYSTOSTOMIES
CYSTOSTOMY
CYSTOTOMIES
CYTOCHALASIN
CYTOCHALASINS
CYTOCHEMICAL
CYTOCHEMISTRIES
CYTOCHEMISTRY
CYTOCHROME
CYTOCHROMES
CYTODIAGNOSES
CYTODIAGNOSIS
CYTOGENESES

CYTOGENESIS
CYTOGENETIC
CYTOGENETICAL
CYTOGENETICALLY
CYTOGENETICIST
CYTOGENETICISTS
CYTOGENETICS
CYTOGENIES
CYTOKINESES
CYTOKINESIS
CYTOKINETIC
CYTOKININS
CYTOLOGICAL
CYTOLOGICALLY
CYTOLOGIES
CYTOLOGIST
CYTOLOGISTS
CYTOLYSINS
CYTOMEGALIC
CYTOMEGALOVIRUS
CYTOMEMBRANE
CYTOMEMBRANES
CYTOMETERS
CYTOMETRIC
CYTOMETRIES
CYTOPATHIC
CYTOPATHOGENIC
CYTOPATHOLOGIES
CYTOPATHOLOGY
CYTOPENIAS
CYTOPHILIC
CYTOPHOTOMETRIC
CYTOPHOTOMETRY
CYTOPLASMIC
CYTOPLASMICALLY
CYTOPLASMS
CYTOPLASTIC
CYTOPLASTS
CYTOSKELETAL
CYTOSKELETON
CYTOSKELETONS
CYTOSTATIC
CYTOSTATICALLY
CYTOSTATICS
CYTOTAXONOMIC
CYTOTAXONOMIES
CYTOTAXONOMIST
CYTOTAXONOMISTS
CYTOTAXONOMY
CYTOTECHNOLOGY
CYTOTOXICITIES
CYTOTOXICITY
CYTOTOXINS
CZAREVICHES
CZAREVITCH
CZAREVITCHES

Dd

ABBLINGLY
ACHSHUNDS
ACOITAGES
ACQUOISES
ACTYLICALLY
ACTYLIOGRAPHY
ACTYLIOLOGIES
ACTYLIOLOGY
ACTYLIOMANCIES
ACTYLIOMANCY
ACTYLISTS
ACTYLOGRAM
ACTYLOGRAMS
ACTYLOGRAPHER
ACTYLOGRAPHERS
ACTYLOGRAPHIC
ACTYLOGRAPHIES
ACTYLOGRAPHY
ACTYLOLOGIES
ACTYLOLOGY
ACTYLOSCOPIES
ACTYLOSCOPY
AFFADOWNDILLY
AFFINESSES
AFFODILLIES
AFFODILLY
AFTNESSES
AGGERBOARD
AGGERBOARDS
AGGERLIKE
AGUERREAN
AGUERREOTYPE
AGUERREOTYPED
AGUERREOTYPER
AGUERREOTYPERS
AGUERREOTYPES
AGUERREOTYPIES
AGUERREOTYPING
DAGUERREOTYPIST
DAGUERREOTYPY
DAHABEEAHS
DAHABEEYAH
DAHABEEYAHS
DAHABIYAHS
DAHABIYEHS
DAILINESSES
DAILYNESSES
DAINTINESS
DAINTINESSES
DAIRYMAIDS
DAISYWHEEL
DAISYWHEELS
DALLIANCES
DALMATIANS
DALTONISMS
DAMAGEABILITIES
DAMAGEABILITY
DAMAGEABLE
DAMAGINGLY
DAMASCEENE
DAMASCEENED
DAMASCEENES
DAMASCEENING
DAMASCENED
DAMASCENES
DAMASCENING
DAMASCENINGS
DAMASKEENED
DAMASKEENING
DAMASKEENS
DAMASKINED
DAMASKINING
DAMASQUINED
DAMASQUINING
DAMASQUINS
DAMINOZIDE
DAMINOZIDES
DAMNABILITIES
DAMNABILITY
DAMNABLENESS
DAMNABLENESSES
DAMNATIONS
DAMNEDESTS
DAMNIFICATION
DAMNIFICATIONS
DAMNIFYING
DAMOISELLE
DAMOISELLES
DAMPCOURSE
DAMPCOURSES
DAMPISHNESS
DAMPISHNESSES
DAMPNESSES
DAMSELFISH
DAMSELFISHES
DAMSELFLIES
DANCEHALLS
DANDELIONS
DANDIFICATION
DANDIFICATIONS
DANDIFYING
DANDIPRATS
DANDYFUNKS
DANDYISHLY
DANDYPRATS
DANGERLESS
DANGEROUSLY
DANGEROUSNESS
DANGEROUSNESSES
DANGLINGLY
DANKNESSES
DANNEBROGS
DANTHONIAS
DAPPERLING
DAPPERLINGS
DAPPERNESS
DAPPERNESSES
DAREDEVILRIES
DAREDEVILRY
DAREDEVILS
DAREDEVILTRIES
DAREDEVILTRY
DARINGNESS
DARINGNESSES
DARKNESSES
DARLINGNESS
DARLINGNESSES
DARNATIONS
DARNEDESTS
DARRAIGNED
DARRAIGNES
DARRAIGNING
DARRAIGNMENT
DARRAIGNMENTS
DARRAINING
DARRAYNING
DARTBOARDS
DASHBOARDS
DASTARDIES
DASTARDLINESS
DASTARDLINESSES
DASTARDNESS
DASTARDNESSES
DASYMETERS
DASYPAEDAL
DASYPHYLLOUS
DATABASING
DATABUSSES
DATAGLOVES
DATAMATION
DATAMATIONS
DATEDNESSES

DATELINING
DAUGHTERHOOD
DAUGHTERHOODS
DAUGHTERLESS
DAUGHTERLINESS
DAUGHTERLING
DAUGHTERLINGS
DAUGHTERLY
DAUNDERING
DAUNOMYCIN
DAUNOMYCINS
DAUNORUBICIN
DAUNORUBICINS
DAUNTINGLY
DAUNTLESSLY
DAUNTLESSNESS
DAUNTLESSNESSES
DAUNTONING
DAUPHINESS
DAUPHINESSES
DAVENPORTS
DAWDLINGLY
DAWSONITES
DAYCENTRES
DAYDREAMED
DAYDREAMER
DAYDREAMERS
DAYDREAMING
DAYDREAMLIKE
DAYFLOWERS
DAYLIGHTED
DAYLIGHTING
DAYLIGHTINGS
DAYSPRINGS
DAYWORKERS
DAZEDNESSES
DAZZLEMENT
DAZZLEMENTS
DAZZLINGLY
DEACIDIFICATION
DEACIDIFIED
DEACIDIFIES
DEACIDIFYING
DEACONESSES
DEACONHOOD
DEACONHOODS
DEACONRIES
DEACONSHIP
DEACONSHIPS
DEACTIVATE
DEACTIVATED
DEACTIVATES
DEACTIVATING
DEACTIVATION
DEACTIVATIONS
DEACTIVATOR
DEACTIVATORS
DEADENINGLY
DEADENINGS
DEADHEADED
DEADHEADING
DEADHOUSES
DEADLIFTED
DEADLIFTING
DEADLIGHTS
DEADLINESS
DEADLINESSES
DEADLINING
DEADLOCKED
DEADLOCKING
DEADNESSES
DEADPANNED
DEADPANNER
DEADPANNERS
DEADPANNING
DEADSTOCKS
DEADSTROKE
DEADWEIGHT
DEADWEIGHTS
DEAERATING
DEAERATION
DEAERATIONS
DEAERATORS
DEAFENINGLY
DEAFENINGS
DEAFNESSES
DEALATIONS
DEALBATION
DEALBATIONS
DEALERSHIP
DEALERSHIPS
DEALFISHES
DEAMBULATORIES
DEAMBULATORY
DEAMINASES
DEAMINATED
DEAMINATES
DEAMINATING
DEAMINATION
DEAMINATIONS
DEAMINISATION
DEAMINISATIONS
DEAMINISED
DEAMINISES
DEAMINISING
DEAMINIZATION
DEAMINIZATIONS
DEAMINIZED
DEAMINIZES
DEAMINIZING
DEARBOUGHT
DEARNESSES
DEARTICULATE
DEARTICULATED
DEARTICULATES
DEARTICULATING
DEASPIRATE
DEASPIRATED
DEASPIRATES
DEASPIRATING
DEASPIRATION
DEASPIRATIONS
DEATHBLOWS
DEATHLESSLY
DEATHLESSNESS
DEATHLESSNESSES
DEATHLIEST
DEATHLINESS
DEATHLINESSES
DEATHTRAPS
DEATHWARDS
DEATHWATCH
DEATHWATCHES
DEATTRIBUTE
DEATTRIBUTED
DEATTRIBUTES
DEATTRIBUTING
DEBAGGINGS
DEBARCATION
DEBARCATIONS
DEBARKATION
DEBARKATIONS
DEBARMENTS
DEBARRASSED
DEBARRASSES
DEBARRASSING
DEBASEDNESS
DEBASEDNESSES
DEBASEMENT
DEBASEMENTS
DEBASINGLY
DEBATEABLE
DEBATEMENT
DEBATEMENTS
DEBATINGLY
DEBAUCHEDLY
DEBAUCHEDNESS
DEBAUCHEDNESSES
DEBAUCHEES
DEBAUCHERIES
DEBAUCHERS
DEBAUCHERY
DEBAUCHING
DEBAUCHMENT
DEBAUCHMENTS
DEBEARDING
DEBENTURED
DEBENTURES
DEBILITATE
DEBILITATED
DEBILITATES
DEBILITATING
DEBILITATION
DEBILITATIONS
DEBILITATIVE
DEBILITIES
DEBONAIRLY
DEBONAIRNESS
DEBONAIRNESSES
DEBONNAIRE
DEBOUCHING
DEBOUCHMENT
DEBOUCHMENTS
DEBOUCHURE
DEBOUCHURES
DEBRIDEMENT
DEBRIDEMENTS
DEBRIEFERS
DEBRIEFING
DEBRIEFINGS
DEBRUISING
DEBUTANTES
DECACHORDS
DECADENCES
DECADENCIES
DECADENTLY
DECAFFEINATE
DECAFFEINATED
DECAFFEINATES
DECAFFEINATING
DECAGONALLY
DECAGRAMME
DECAGRAMMES
DECAGYNIAN
DECAGYNOUS
DECAHEDRAL
DECAHEDRON
DECAHEDRONS
DECALCIFICATION
DECALCIFIED
DECALCIFIER
DECALCIFIERS
DECALCIFIES
DECALCIFYING
DECALCOMANIA
DECALCOMANIAS
DECALESCENCE
DECALESCENCES
DECALESCENT
DECALITERS
DECALITRES
DECALOGIST
DECALOGISTS
DECALOGUES
DECAMERONIC
DECAMEROUS
DECAMETERS
DECAMETHONIUM
DECAMETHONIUMS
DECAMETRES
DECAMETRIC
DECAMPMENT
DECAMPMENTS
DECANDRIAN
DECANDROUS
DECANEDIOIC
DECANICALLY
DECANTATED
DECANTATES
DECANTATING
DECANTATION
DECANTATIONS
DECAPITALISE
DECAPITALISED
DECAPITALISES
DECAPITALISING
DECAPITALIZE
DECAPITALIZED
DECAPITALIZES
DECAPITALIZING
DECAPITATE
DECAPITATED
DECAPITATES
DECAPITATING
DECAPITATION
DECAPITATIONS
DECAPITATOR
DECAPITATORS
DECAPODANS
DECAPODOUS
DECAPSULATE
DECAPSULATED
DECAPSULATES
DECAPSULATING

ECAPSULATION
ECAPSULATIONS
ECARBONATE
ECARBONATED
ECARBONATES
ECARBONATING
ECARBONATION
ECARBONATIONS
ECARBONATOR
ECARBONATORS
ECARBONISATION
ECARBONISE
ECARBONISED
ECARBONISER
ECARBONISERS
ECARBONISES
ECARBONISING
ECARBONIZATION
ECARBONIZE
ECARBONIZED
ECARBONIZER
ECARBONIZERS
ECARBONIZES
ECARBONIZING
ECARBOXYLASE
ECARBOXYLASES
ECARBOXYLATE
ECARBOXYLATED
ECARBOXYLATES
ECARBOXYLATING
ECARBOXYLATION
ECARBURATION
ECARBURATIONS
ECARBURISATION
ECARBURISE
ECARBURISED
ECARBURISES
ECARBURISING
ECARBURIZATION
ECARBURIZE
ECARBURIZED
ECARBURIZES
ECARBURIZING
ECASTERES
ECASTICHS
ECASTYLES
ECASUALISATION
ECASUALIZATION
ECASYLLABIC
ECASYLLABICS
ECASYLLABLE
ECASYLLABLES
ECATHLETE
ECATHLETES
ECATHLONS
ECAUDATED
ECAUDATES
ECAUDATING
ECEITFULLY
ECEITFULNESS
ECEITFULNESSES
ECEIVABILITIES
ECEIVABILITY
ECEIVABLE
ECEIVABLENESS
ECEIVABLY
DECEIVINGLY
DECELERATE
DECELERATED
DECELERATES
DECELERATING
DECELERATION
DECELERATIONS
DECELERATOR
DECELERATORS
DECELEROMETER
DECELEROMETERS
DECELERONS
DECEMVIRAL
DECEMVIRATE
DECEMVIRATES
DECENARIES
DECENNARIES
DECENNIALLY
DECENNIALS
DECENNIUMS
DECENNOVAL
DECENTERED
DECENTERING
DECENTNESS
DECENTNESSES
DECENTRALISE
DECENTRALISED
DECENTRALISES
DECENTRALISING
DECENTRALIST
DECENTRALISTS
DECENTRALIZE
DECENTRALIZED
DECENTRALIZES
DECENTRALIZING
DECENTRING
DECEPTIBILITIES
DECEPTIBILITY
DECEPTIBLE
DECEPTIONAL
DECEPTIONS
DECEPTIOUS
DECEPTIVELY
DECEPTIVENESS
DECEPTIVENESSES
DECEREBRATE
DECEREBRATED
DECEREBRATES
DECEREBRATING
DECEREBRATION
DECEREBRATIONS
DECEREBRISE
DECEREBRISED
DECEREBRISES
DECEREBRISING
DECEREBRIZE
DECEREBRIZED
DECEREBRIZES
DECEREBRIZING
DECERTIFICATION
DECERTIFIED
DECERTIFIES
DECERTIFYING
DECESSIONS
DECHEANCES
DECHLORINATE
DECHLORINATED
DECHLORINATES
DECHLORINATING
DECHLORINATION
DECHLORINATIONS
DECHRISTIANISE
DECHRISTIANISED
DECHRISTIANISES
DECHRISTIANIZE
DECHRISTIANIZED
DECHRISTIANIZES
DECIDABILITIES
DECIDABILITY
DECIDEDNESS
DECIDEDNESSES
DECIDUOUSLY
DECIDUOUSNESS
DECIDUOUSNESSES
DECIGRAMME
DECIGRAMMES
DECILITERS
DECILITRES
DECILLIONS
DECILLIONTH
DECILLIONTHS
DECIMALISATION
DECIMALISATIONS
DECIMALISE
DECIMALISED
DECIMALISES
DECIMALISING
DECIMALISM
DECIMALISMS
DECIMALIST
DECIMALISTS
DECIMALIZATION
DECIMALIZATIONS
DECIMALIZE
DECIMALIZED
DECIMALIZES
DECIMALIZING
DECIMATING
DECIMATION
DECIMATIONS
DECIMATORS
DECIMETERS
DECIMETRES
DECIMETRIC
DECINORMAL
DECIPHERABILITY
DECIPHERABLE
DECIPHERED
DECIPHERER
DECIPHERERS
DECIPHERING
DECIPHERMENT
DECIPHERMENTS
DECISIONAL
DECISIONED
DECISIONING
DECISIVELY
DECISIVENESS
DECISIVENESSES
DECISTERES
DECITIZENISE
DECITIZENISED
DECITIZENISES
DECITIZENISING
DECITIZENIZE
DECITIZENIZED
DECITIZENIZES
DECITIZENIZING
DECIVILISE
DECIVILISED
DECIVILISES
DECIVILISING
DECIVILIZE
DECIVILIZED
DECIVILIZES
DECIVILIZING
DECKCHAIRS
DECKHOUSES
DECLAIMANT
DECLAIMANTS
DECLAIMERS
DECLAIMING
DECLAIMINGS
DECLAMATION
DECLAMATIONS
DECLAMATORILY
DECLAMATORY
DECLARABLE
DECLARANTS
DECLARATION
DECLARATIONS
DECLARATIVE
DECLARATIVELY
DECLARATOR
DECLARATORILY
DECLARATORS
DECLARATORY
DECLAREDLY
DECLASSIFIABLE
DECLASSIFIED
DECLASSIFIES
DECLASSIFY
DECLASSIFYING
DECLASSING
DECLENSION
DECLENSIONAL
DECLENSIONALLY
DECLENSIONS
DECLINABLE
DECLINATION
DECLINATIONAL
DECLINATIONS
DECLINATOR
DECLINATORS
DECLINATORY
DECLINATURE
DECLINATURES
DECLINISTS
DECLINOMETER
DECLINOMETERS
DECLIVITIES
DECLIVITOUS
DECLUTCHED
DECLUTCHES
DECLUTCHING
DECLUTTERED
DECLUTTERING
DECLUTTERS

DECOCTIBLE
DECOCTIONS
DECOCTURES
DECOHERENCE
DECOHERENCES
DECOHERERS
DECOLLATED
DECOLLATES
DECOLLATING
DECOLLATION
DECOLLATIONS
DECOLLATOR
DECOLLATORS
DECOLLETAGE
DECOLLETAGES
DECOLLETES
DECOLONISATION
DECOLONISATIONS
DECOLONISE
DECOLONISED
DECOLONISES
DECOLONISING
DECOLONIZATION
DECOLONIZATIONS
DECOLONIZE
DECOLONIZED
DECOLONIZES
DECOLONIZING
DECOLORANT
DECOLORANTS
DECOLORATE
DECOLORATED
DECOLORATES
DECOLORATING
DECOLORATION
DECOLORATIONS
DECOLORING
DECOLORISATION
DECOLORISATIONS
DECOLORISE
DECOLORISED
DECOLORISER
DECOLORISERS
DECOLORISES
DECOLORISING
DECOLORIZATION
DECOLORIZATIONS
DECOLORIZE
DECOLORIZED
DECOLORIZER
DECOLORIZERS
DECOLORIZES
DECOLORIZING
DECOLOURED
DECOLOURING
DECOLOURISATION
DECOLOURISE
DECOLOURISED
DECOLOURISES
DECOLOURISING
DECOLOURIZATION
DECOLOURIZE
DECOLOURIZED
DECOLOURIZES
DECOLOURIZING
DECOMMISSION
DECOMMISSIONED
DECOMMISSIONER
DECOMMISSIONERS
DECOMMISSIONING
DECOMMISSIONS
DECOMMITTED
DECOMMITTING
DECOMPENSATE
DECOMPENSATED
DECOMPENSATES
DECOMPENSATING
DECOMPENSATION
DECOMPENSATIONS
DECOMPOSABILITY
DECOMPOSABLE
DECOMPOSED
DECOMPOSER
DECOMPOSERS
DECOMPOSES
DECOMPOSING
DECOMPOSITE
DECOMPOSITION
DECOMPOSITIONS
DECOMPOUND
DECOMPOUNDABLE
DECOMPOUNDED
DECOMPOUNDING
DECOMPOUNDS
DECOMPRESS
DECOMPRESSED
DECOMPRESSES
DECOMPRESSING
DECOMPRESSION
DECOMPRESSIONS
DECOMPRESSIVE
DECOMPRESSOR
DECOMPRESSORS
DECONCENTRATE
DECONCENTRATED
DECONCENTRATES
DECONCENTRATING
DECONCENTRATION
DECONDITION
DECONDITIONED
DECONDITIONING
DECONDITIONS
DECONGESTANT
DECONGESTANTS
DECONGESTED
DECONGESTING
DECONGESTION
DECONGESTIONS
DECONGESTIVE
DECONGESTS
DECONSECRATE
DECONSECRATED
DECONSECRATES
DECONSECRATING
DECONSECRATION
DECONSECRATIONS
DECONSTRUCT
DECONSTRUCTED
DECONSTRUCTING
DECONSTRUCTION
DECONSTRUCTIONS
DECONSTRUCTIVE
DECONSTRUCTOR
DECONSTRUCTORS
DECONSTRUCTS
DECONTAMINANT
DECONTAMINANTS
DECONTAMINATE
DECONTAMINATED
DECONTAMINATES
DECONTAMINATING
DECONTAMINATION
DECONTAMINATIVE
DECONTAMINATOR
DECONTAMINATORS
DECONTROLLED
DECONTROLLING
DECONTROLS
DECORATING
DECORATION
DECORATIONS
DECORATIVE
DECORATIVELY
DECORATIVENESS
DECORATORS
DECOROUSLY
DECOROUSNESS
DECOROUSNESSES
DECORTICATE
DECORTICATED
DECORTICATES
DECORTICATING
DECORTICATION
DECORTICATIONS
DECORTICATOR
DECORTICATORS
DECOUPAGED
DECOUPAGES
DECOUPAGING
DECOUPLERS
DECOUPLING
DECOUPLINGS
DECRASSIFIED
DECRASSIFIES
DECRASSIFY
DECRASSIFYING
DECREASING
DECREASINGLY
DECREEABLE
DECREMENTAL
DECREMENTED
DECREMENTING
DECREMENTS
DECREPITATE
DECREPITATED
DECREPITATES
DECREPITATING
DECREPITATION
DECREPITATIONS
DECREPITLY
DECREPITNESS
DECREPITNESSES
DECREPITUDE
DECREPITUDES
DECRESCENCE
DECRESCENCES
DECRESCENDO
DECRESCENDOS
DECRESCENT
DECRETALIST
DECRETALISTS
DECRETISTS
DECRIMINALISE
DECRIMINALISED
DECRIMINALISES
DECRIMINALISING
DECRIMINALIZE
DECRIMINALIZED
DECRIMINALIZES
DECRIMINALIZING
DECROWNING
DECRUSTATION
DECRUSTATIONS
DECRYPTING
DECRYPTION
DECRYPTIONS
DECUMBENCE
DECUMBENCES
DECUMBENCIES
DECUMBENCY
DECUMBENTLY
DECUMBITURE
DECUMBITURES
DECURIONATE
DECURIONATES
DECURRENCIES
DECURRENCY
DECURRENTLY
DECURSIONS
DECURSIVELY
DECURVATION
DECURVATIONS
DECUSSATED
DECUSSATELY
DECUSSATES
DECUSSATING
DECUSSATION
DECUSSATIONS
DEDICATEDLY
DEDICATEES
DEDICATING
DEDICATION
DEDICATIONAL
DEDICATIONS
DEDICATIVE
DEDICATORIAL
DEDICATORS
DEDICATORY
DEDIFFERENTIATE
DEDRAMATISE
DEDRAMATISED
DEDRAMATISES
DEDRAMATISING
DEDRAMATIZE
DEDRAMATIZED
DEDRAMATIZES
DEDRAMATIZING
DEDUCEMENT
DEDUCEMENTS
DEDUCIBILITIES
DEDUCIBILITY
DEDUCIBLENESS
DEDUCIBLENESSES
DEDUCTIBILITIES

EDUCTIBILITY
EDUCTIBLE
EDUCTIBLES
EDUCTIONS
EDUCTIVELY
EEMSTERSHIP
EEMSTERSHIPS
EEPFREEZE
EEPFREEZES
EEPFREEZING
EEPFROZEN
EEPNESSES
EEPWATERMAN
EEPWATERMEN
EERBERRIES
EERGRASSES
EERHOUNDS
EERSTALKER
EERSTALKERS
EERSTALKING
EERSTALKINGS
EFACEABLE
EFACEMENT
EFACEMENTS
EFACINGLY
EFAECATED
EFAECATES
EFAECATING
EFAECATION
EFAECATIONS
EFAECATOR
EFAECATORS
EFALCATED
EFALCATES
EFALCATING
EFALCATION
EFALCATIONS
EFALCATOR
EFALCATORS
EFAMATION
EFAMATIONS
EFAMATORILY
EFAMATORY
EFAULTERS
EFAULTING
EFEASANCE
EFEASANCED
EFEASANCES
EFEASIBILITIES
EFEASIBILITY
EFEASIBLE
EFEASIBLENESS
EFEATISMS
EFEATISTS
EFEATURED
EFEATURES
EFEATURING
EFECATING
EFECATION
EFECATIONS
EFECATORS
EFECTIBILITIES
EFECTIBILITY
EFECTIBLE
EFECTIONIST
EFECTIONISTS

DEFECTIONS
DEFECTIVELY
DEFECTIVENESS
DEFECTIVENESSES
DEFECTIVES
DEFEMINISATION
DEFEMINISATIONS
DEFEMINISE
DEFEMINISED
DEFEMINISES
DEFEMINISING
DEFEMINIZATION
DEFEMINIZATIONS
DEFEMINIZE
DEFEMINIZED
DEFEMINIZES
DEFEMINIZING
DEFENCELESS
DEFENCELESSLY
DEFENCELESSNESS
DEFENCEMAN
DEFENCEMEN
DEFENDABLE
DEFENDANTS
DEFENESTRATE
DEFENESTRATED
DEFENESTRATES
DEFENESTRATING
DEFENESTRATION
DEFENESTRATIONS
DEFENSATIVE
DEFENSATIVES
DEFENSELESS
DEFENSELESSLY
DEFENSELESSNESS
DEFENSEMAN
DEFENSEMEN
DEFENSIBILITIES
DEFENSIBILITY
DEFENSIBLE
DEFENSIBLENESS
DEFENSIBLY
DEFENSIVELY
DEFENSIVENESS
DEFENSIVENESSES
DEFENSIVES
DEFERENCES
DEFERENTIAL
DEFERENTIALLY
DEFERMENTS
DEFERRABLE
DEFERRABLES
DEFERVESCENCE
DEFERVESCENCES
DEFERVESCENCIES
DEFERVESCENCY
DEFEUDALISE
DEFEUDALISED
DEFEUDALISES
DEFEUDALISING
DEFEUDALIZE
DEFEUDALIZED
DEFEUDALIZES
DEFEUDALIZING
DEFIANTNESS
DEFIANTNESSES

DEFIBRILLATE
DEFIBRILLATED
DEFIBRILLATES
DEFIBRILLATING
DEFIBRILLATION
DEFIBRILLATIONS
DEFIBRILLATOR
DEFIBRILLATORS
DEFIBRINATE
DEFIBRINATED
DEFIBRINATES
DEFIBRINATING
DEFIBRINATION
DEFIBRINATIONS
DEFIBRINISE
DEFIBRINISED
DEFIBRINISES
DEFIBRINISING
DEFIBRINIZE
DEFIBRINIZED
DEFIBRINIZES
DEFIBRINIZING
DEFICIENCE
DEFICIENCES
DEFICIENCIES
DEFICIENCY
DEFICIENTLY
DEFICIENTNESS
DEFICIENTNESSES
DEFICIENTS
DEFILADING
DEFILEMENT
DEFILEMENTS
DEFILIATION
DEFILIATIONS
DEFINABILITIES
DEFINABILITY
DEFINEMENT
DEFINEMENTS
DEFINIENDA
DEFINIENDUM
DEFINIENTIA
DEFINITELY
DEFINITENESS
DEFINITENESSES
DEFINITION
DEFINITIONAL
DEFINITIONS
DEFINITISE
DEFINITISED
DEFINITISES
DEFINITISING
DEFINITIVE
DEFINITIVELY
DEFINITIVENESS
DEFINITIVES
DEFINITIZE
DEFINITIZED
DEFINITIZES
DEFINITIZING
DEFINITUDE
DEFINITUDES
DEFLAGRABILITY
DEFLAGRABLE
DEFLAGRATE
DEFLAGRATED

DEFLAGRATES
DEFLAGRATING
DEFLAGRATION
DEFLAGRATIONS
DEFLAGRATOR
DEFLAGRATORS
DEFLATIONARY
DEFLATIONIST
DEFLATIONISTS
DEFLATIONS
DEFLECTABLE
DEFLECTING
DEFLECTION
DEFLECTIONAL
DEFLECTIONS
DEFLECTIVE
DEFLECTORS
DEFLEXIONAL
DEFLEXIONS
DEFLEXURES
DEFLOCCULANT
DEFLOCCULANTS
DEFLOCCULATE
DEFLOCCULATED
DEFLOCCULATES
DEFLOCCULATING
DEFLOCCULATION
DEFLOCCULATIONS
DEFLORATED
DEFLORATES
DEFLORATING
DEFLORATION
DEFLORATIONS
DEFLOWERED
DEFLOWERER
DEFLOWERERS
DEFLOWERING
DEFLUXIONS
DEFOCUSING
DEFOCUSSED
DEFOCUSSES
DEFOCUSSING
DEFOLIANTS
DEFOLIATED
DEFOLIATES
DEFOLIATING
DEFOLIATION
DEFOLIATIONS
DEFOLIATOR
DEFOLIATORS
DEFORCEMENT
DEFORCEMENTS
DEFORCIANT
DEFORCIANTS
DEFORCIATION
DEFORCIATIONS
DEFORESTATION
DEFORESTATIONS
DEFORESTED
DEFORESTER
DEFORESTERS
DEFORESTING
DEFORMABILITIES
DEFORMABILITY
DEFORMABLE
DEFORMALISE

DEFORMALISED
DEFORMALISES
DEFORMALISING
DEFORMALIZE
DEFORMALIZED
DEFORMALIZES
DEFORMALIZING
DEFORMATION
DEFORMATIONAL
DEFORMATIONS
DEFORMATIVE
DEFORMEDLY
DEFORMEDNESS
DEFORMEDNESSES
DEFORMITIES
DEFRAGGERS
DEFRAGGING
DEFRAGMENT
DEFRAGMENTED
DEFRAGMENTING
DEFRAGMENTS
DEFRAUDATION
DEFRAUDATIONS
DEFRAUDERS
DEFRAUDING
DEFRAUDMENT
DEFRAUDMENTS
DEFRAYABLE
DEFRAYMENT
DEFRAYMENTS
DEFREEZING
DEFROCKING
DEFROSTERS
DEFROSTING
DEFTNESSES
DEFUELLING
DEFUNCTION
DEFUNCTIONS
DEFUNCTIVE
DEFUNCTNESS
DEFUNCTNESSES
DEGARNISHED
DEGARNISHES
DEGARNISHING
DEGAUSSERS
DEGAUSSING
DEGEARINGS
DEGENDERED
DEGENDERING
DEGENERACIES
DEGENERACY
DEGENERATE
DEGENERATED
DEGENERATELY
DEGENERATENESS
DEGENERATES
DEGENERATING
DEGENERATION
DEGENERATIONIST
DEGENERATIONS
DEGENERATIVE
DEGENEROUS
DEGLACIATED
DEGLACIATION
DEGLACIATIONS
DEGLAMORISATION
DEGLAMORISE
DEGLAMORISED
DEGLAMORISES
DEGLAMORISING
DEGLAMORIZATION
DEGLAMORIZE
DEGLAMORIZED
DEGLAMORIZES
DEGLAMORIZING
DEGLUTINATE
DEGLUTINATED
DEGLUTINATES
DEGLUTINATING
DEGLUTINATION
DEGLUTINATIONS
DEGLUTITION
DEGLUTITIONS
DEGLUTITIVE
DEGLUTITORY
DEGRADABILITIES
DEGRADABILITY
DEGRADABLE
DEGRADATION
DEGRADATIONS
DEGRADATIVE
DEGRADEDLY
DEGRADINGLY
DEGRADINGNESS
DEGRADINGNESSES
DEGRANULATION
DEGRANULATIONS
DEGREASANT
DEGREASANTS
DEGREASERS
DEGREASING
DEGREELESS
DEGRESSION
DEGRESSIONS
DEGRESSIVE
DEGRESSIVELY
DEGRINGOLADE
DEGRINGOLADED
DEGRINGOLADES
DEGRINGOLADING
DEGRINGOLER
DEGRINGOLERED
DEGRINGOLERING
DEGRINGOLERS
DEGUSTATED
DEGUSTATES
DEGUSTATING
DEGUSTATION
DEGUSTATIONS
DEGUSTATORY
DEHISCENCE
DEHISCENCES
DEHORTATION
DEHORTATIONS
DEHORTATIVE
DEHORTATORY
DEHUMANISATION
DEHUMANISATIONS
DEHUMANISE
DEHUMANISED
DEHUMANISES
DEHUMANISING
DEHUMANIZATION
DEHUMANIZATIONS
DEHUMANIZE
DEHUMANIZED
DEHUMANIZES
DEHUMANIZING
DEHUMIDIFIED
DEHUMIDIFIER
DEHUMIDIFIERS
DEHUMIDIFIES
DEHUMIDIFY
DEHUMIDIFYING
DEHYDRATED
DEHYDRATER
DEHYDRATERS
DEHYDRATES
DEHYDRATING
DEHYDRATION
DEHYDRATIONS
DEHYDRATOR
DEHYDRATORS
DEHYDROGENASE
DEHYDROGENASES
DEHYDROGENATE
DEHYDROGENATED
DEHYDROGENATES
DEHYDROGENATING
DEHYDROGENATION
DEHYDROGENISE
DEHYDROGENISED
DEHYDROGENISES
DEHYDROGENISING
DEHYDROGENIZE
DEHYDROGENIZED
DEHYDROGENIZES
DEHYDROGENIZING
DEHYDRORETINOL
DEHYDRORETINOLS
DEHYPNOTISATION
DEHYPNOTISE
DEHYPNOTISED
DEHYPNOTISES
DEHYPNOTISING
DEHYPNOTIZATION
DEHYPNOTIZE
DEHYPNOTIZED
DEHYPNOTIZES
DEHYPNOTIZING
DEICTICALLY
DEIFICATION
DEIFICATIONS
DEINDEXING
DEINDIVIDUATION
DEINDUSTRIALISE
DEINDUSTRIALIZE
DEINONYCHUS
DEINONYCHUSES
DEINOSAURS
DEINOTHERE
DEINOTHERES
DEINOTHERIUM
DEINOTHERIUMS
DEIONISATION
DEIONISATIONS
DEIONISERS
DEIONISING
DEIONIZATION
DEIONIZATIONS
DEIONIZERS
DEIONIZING
DEIPNOSOPHIST
DEIPNOSOPHISTS
DEISTICALLY
DEJECTEDLY
DEJECTEDNESS
DEJECTEDNESSES
DEJECTIONS
DEKALITERS
DEKALITRES
DEKALOGIES
DEKAMETERS
DEKAMETRES
DEKAMETRIC
DELAMINATE
DELAMINATED
DELAMINATES
DELAMINATING
DELAMINATION
DELAMINATIONS
DELAPSIONS
DELASSEMENT
DELASSEMENTS
DELAYERING
DELAYERINGS
DELAYINGLY
DELECTABILITIES
DELECTABILITY
DELECTABLE
DELECTABLENESS
DELECTABLES
DELECTABLY
DELECTATED
DELECTATES
DELECTATING
DELECTATION
DELECTATIONS
DELEGACIES
DELEGATEES
DELEGATING
DELEGATION
DELEGATIONS
DELEGATORS
DELEGITIMATION
DELEGITIMATIONS
DELEGITIMISE
DELEGITIMISED
DELEGITIMISES
DELEGITIMISING
DELEGITIMIZE
DELEGITIMIZED
DELEGITIMIZES
DELEGITIMIZING
DELETERIOUS
DELETERIOUSLY
DELETERIOUSNESS
DELFTWARES
DELIBATING
DELIBATION
DELIBATIONS
DELIBERATE
DELIBERATED
DELIBERATELY

ELIBERATENESS
ELIBERATES
ELIBERATING
ELIBERATION
ELIBERATIONS
ELIBERATIVE
ELIBERATIVELY
ELIBERATOR
ELIBERATORS
ELICACIES
ELICATELY
ELICATENESS
ELICATENESSES
ELICATESSEN
ELICATESSENS
ELICIOUSLY
ELICIOUSNESS
ELICIOUSNESSES
ELIGATION
ELIGATIONS
ELIGHTEDLY
ELIGHTEDNESS
ELIGHTEDNESSES
ELIGHTERS
ELIGHTFUL
ELIGHTFULLY
ELIGHTFULNESS
ELIGHTING
ELIGHTLESS
ELIGHTSOME
ELIMITATE
ELIMITATED
ELIMITATES
ELIMITATING
ELIMITATION
ELIMITATIONS
ELIMITATIVE
ELIMITERS
ELIMITING
ELINEABLE
ELINEATED
ELINEATES
ELINEATING
ELINEATION
ELINEATIONS
ELINEATIVE
ELINEATOR
ELINEATORS
ELINEAVIT
ELINQUENCIES
ELINQUENCY
ELINQUENT
ELINQUENTLY
ELINQUENTS
ELIQUESCE
ELIQUESCED
ELIQUESCENCE
ELIQUESCENCES
ELIQUESCENT
ELIQUESCES
ELIQUESCING
ELIQUIUMS
ELIRATION
ELIRATIONS
ELIRIFACIENT
ELIRIFACIENTS
DELIRIOUSLY
DELIRIOUSNESS
DELIRIOUSNESSES
DELITESCENCE
DELITESCENCES
DELITESCENT
DELIVERABILITY
DELIVERABLE
DELIVERANCE
DELIVERANCES
DELIVERERS
DELIVERIES
DELIVERING
DELIVERYMAN
DELIVERYMEN
DELOCALISATION
DELOCALISATIONS
DELOCALISE
DELOCALISED
DELOCALISES
DELOCALISING
DELOCALIZATION
DELOCALIZATIONS
DELOCALIZE
DELOCALIZED
DELOCALIZES
DELOCALIZING
DELPHICALLY
DELPHINIUM
DELPHINIUMS
DELPHINOID
DELTIOLOGIES
DELTIOLOGIST
DELTIOLOGISTS
DELTIOLOGY
DELTOIDEUS
DELUDINGLY
DELUNDUNGS
DELUSIONAL
DELUSIONARY
DELUSIONIST
DELUSIONISTS
DELUSIVELY
DELUSIVENESS
DELUSIVENESSES
DELUSTERED
DELUSTERING
DELUSTRANT
DELUSTRANTS
DEMAGNETISATION
DEMAGNETISE
DEMAGNETISED
DEMAGNETISER
DEMAGNETISERS
DEMAGNETISES
DEMAGNETISING
DEMAGNETIZATION
DEMAGNETIZE
DEMAGNETIZED
DEMAGNETIZER
DEMAGNETIZERS
DEMAGNETIZES
DEMAGNETIZING
DEMAGOGICAL
DEMAGOGICALLY
DEMAGOGIES
DEMAGOGING
DEMAGOGISM
DEMAGOGISMS
DEMAGOGUED
DEMAGOGUERIES
DEMAGOGUERY
DEMAGOGUES
DEMAGOGUING
DEMAGOGUISM
DEMAGOGUISMS
DEMANDABLE
DEMANDANTS
DEMANDINGLY
DEMANDINGNESS
DEMANDINGNESSES
DEMANNINGS
DEMANTOIDS
DEMARCATED
DEMARCATES
DEMARCATING
DEMARCATION
DEMARCATIONS
DEMARCATOR
DEMARCATORS
DEMARKATION
DEMARKATIONS
DEMARKETED
DEMARKETING
DEMATERIALISE
DEMATERIALISED
DEMATERIALISES
DEMATERIALISING
DEMATERIALIZE
DEMATERIALIZED
DEMATERIALIZES
DEMATERIALIZING
DEMEANOURS
DEMEASNURE
DEMEASNURES
DEMENTATED
DEMENTATES
DEMENTATING
DEMENTEDLY
DEMENTEDNESS
DEMENTEDNESSES
DEMERGERED
DEMERGERING
DEMERITING
DEMERITORIOUS
DEMERITORIOUSLY
DEMERSIONS
DEMIBASTION
DEMIBASTIONS
DEMICANTON
DEMICANTONS
DEMIGODDESS
DEMIGODDESSES
DEMIGRATION
DEMIGRATIONS
DEMILITARISE
DEMILITARISED
DEMILITARISES
DEMILITARISING
DEMILITARIZE
DEMILITARIZED
DEMILITARIZES
DEMILITARIZING
DEMIMONDAINE
DEMIMONDAINES
DEMIMONDES
DEMINERALISE
DEMINERALISED
DEMINERALISER
DEMINERALISERS
DEMINERALISES
DEMINERALISING
DEMINERALIZE
DEMINERALIZED
DEMINERALIZER
DEMINERALIZERS
DEMINERALIZES
DEMINERALIZING
DEMIPIQUES
DEMIRELIEF
DEMIRELIEFS
DEMIREPDOM
DEMIREPDOMS
DEMISEMIQUAVER
DEMISEMIQUAVERS
DEMISSIONS
DEMITASSES
DEMIURGEOUS
DEMIURGICAL
DEMIURGICALLY
DEMIURGUSES
DEMIVEGGES
DEMIVIERGE
DEMIVIERGES
DEMIVOLTES
DEMIWORLDS
DEMOBILISATION
DEMOBILISATIONS
DEMOBILISE
DEMOBILISED
DEMOBILISES
DEMOBILISING
DEMOBILIZATION
DEMOBILIZATIONS
DEMOBILIZE
DEMOBILIZED
DEMOBILIZES
DEMOBILIZING
DEMOCRACIES
DEMOCRATIC
DEMOCRATICAL
DEMOCRATICALLY
DEMOCRATIES
DEMOCRATIFIABLE
DEMOCRATISATION
DEMOCRATISE
DEMOCRATISED
DEMOCRATISER
DEMOCRATISERS
DEMOCRATISES
DEMOCRATISING
DEMOCRATIST
DEMOCRATISTS
DEMOCRATIZATION
DEMOCRATIZE
DEMOCRATIZED
DEMOCRATIZER
DEMOCRATIZERS

DEMOCRATIZES
DEMOCRATIZING
DEMODULATE
DEMODULATED
DEMODULATES
DEMODULATING
DEMODULATION
DEMODULATIONS
DEMODULATOR
DEMODULATORS
DEMOGRAPHER
DEMOGRAPHERS
DEMOGRAPHIC
DEMOGRAPHICAL
DEMOGRAPHICALLY
DEMOGRAPHICS
DEMOGRAPHIES
DEMOGRAPHIST
DEMOGRAPHISTS
DEMOGRAPHY
DEMOISELLE
DEMOISELLES
DEMOLISHED
DEMOLISHER
DEMOLISHERS
DEMOLISHES
DEMOLISHING
DEMOLISHMENT
DEMOLISHMENTS
DEMOLITION
DEMOLITIONIST
DEMOLITIONISTS
DEMOLITIONS
DEMOLOGIES
DEMONESSES
DEMONETARISE
DEMONETARISED
DEMONETARISES
DEMONETARISING
DEMONETARIZE
DEMONETARIZED
DEMONETARIZES
DEMONETARIZING
DEMONETISATION
DEMONETISATIONS
DEMONETISE
DEMONETISED
DEMONETISES
DEMONETISING
DEMONETIZATION
DEMONETIZATIONS
DEMONETIZE
DEMONETIZED
DEMONETIZES
DEMONETIZING
DEMONIACAL
DEMONIACALLY
DEMONIACISM
DEMONIACISMS
DEMONIANISM
DEMONIANISMS
DEMONICALLY
DEMONISATION
DEMONISATIONS
DEMONISING
DEMONIZATION
DEMONIZATIONS
DEMONIZING
DEMONOCRACIES
DEMONOCRACY
DEMONOLATER
DEMONOLATERS
DEMONOLATRIES
DEMONOLATRY
DEMONOLOGIC
DEMONOLOGICAL
DEMONOLOGIES
DEMONOLOGIST
DEMONOLOGISTS
DEMONOLOGY
DEMONOMANIA
DEMONOMANIAS
DEMONSTRABILITY
DEMONSTRABLE
DEMONSTRABLY
DEMONSTRATE
DEMONSTRATED
DEMONSTRATES
DEMONSTRATING
DEMONSTRATION
DEMONSTRATIONAL
DEMONSTRATIONS
DEMONSTRATIVE
DEMONSTRATIVELY
DEMONSTRATIVES
DEMONSTRATOR
DEMONSTRATORS
DEMONSTRATORY
DEMORALISATION
DEMORALISATIONS
DEMORALISE
DEMORALISED
DEMORALISER
DEMORALISERS
DEMORALISES
DEMORALISING
DEMORALISINGLY
DEMORALIZATION
DEMORALIZATIONS
DEMORALIZE
DEMORALIZED
DEMORALIZER
DEMORALIZERS
DEMORALIZES
DEMORALIZING
DEMORALIZINGLY
DEMOTICIST
DEMOTICISTS
DEMOTIVATE
DEMOTIVATED
DEMOTIVATES
DEMOTIVATING
DEMOUNTABLE
DEMOUNTING
DEMULCENTS
DEMULSIFICATION
DEMULSIFIED
DEMULSIFIER
DEMULSIFIERS
DEMULSIFIES
DEMULSIFYING
DEMULTIPLEXER
DEMULTIPLEXERS
DEMURENESS
DEMURENESSES
DEMURRABLE
DEMURRAGES
DEMUTUALISATION
DEMUTUALISE
DEMUTUALISED
DEMUTUALISES
DEMUTUALISING
DEMUTUALIZATION
DEMUTUALIZE
DEMUTUALIZED
DEMUTUALIZES
DEMUTUALIZING
DEMYELINATE
DEMYELINATED
DEMYELINATES
DEMYELINATING
DEMYELINATION
DEMYELINATIONS
DEMYSTIFICATION
DEMYSTIFIED
DEMYSTIFIES
DEMYSTIFYING
DEMYTHOLOGISE
DEMYTHOLOGISED
DEMYTHOLOGISER
DEMYTHOLOGISERS
DEMYTHOLOGISES
DEMYTHOLOGISING
DEMYTHOLOGIZE
DEMYTHOLOGIZED
DEMYTHOLOGIZER
DEMYTHOLOGIZERS
DEMYTHOLOGIZES
DEMYTHOLOGIZING
DENATIONALISE
DENATIONALISED
DENATIONALISES
DENATIONALISING
DENATIONALIZE
DENATIONALIZED
DENATIONALIZES
DENATIONALIZING
DENATURALISE
DENATURALISED
DENATURALISES
DENATURALISING
DENATURALIZE
DENATURALIZED
DENATURALIZES
DENATURALIZING
DENATURANT
DENATURANTS
DENATURATION
DENATURATIONS
DENATURING
DENATURISE
DENATURISED
DENATURISES
DENATURISING
DENATURIZE
DENATURIZED
DENATURIZES
DENATURIZING
DENAZIFICATION
DENAZIFICATIONS
DENAZIFIED
DENAZIFIES
DENAZIFYING
DENDRACHATE
DENDRACHATES
DENDRIFORM
DENDRIMERS
DENDRITICAL
DENDRITICALLY
DENDROBIUM
DENDROBIUMS
DENDROGLYPH
DENDROGLYPHS
DENDROGRAM
DENDROGRAMS
DENDROIDAL
DENDROLATRIES
DENDROLATRY
DENDROLOGIC
DENDROLOGICAL
DENDROLOGIES
DENDROLOGIST
DENDROLOGISTS
DENDROLOGOUS
DENDROLOGY
DENDROMETER
DENDROMETERS
DENDROPHIS
DENDROPHISES
DENEGATION
DENEGATIONS
DENERVATED
DENERVATES
DENERVATING
DENERVATION
DENERVATIONS
DENIABILITIES
DENIABILITY
DENIGRATED
DENIGRATES
DENIGRATING
DENIGRATION
DENIGRATIONS
DENIGRATIVE
DENIGRATOR
DENIGRATORS
DENIGRATORY
DENISATION
DENISATIONS
DENITRATED
DENITRATES
DENITRATING
DENITRATION
DENITRATIONS
DENITRIFICATION
DENITRIFICATOR
DENITRIFICATORS
DENITRIFIED
DENITRIFIER
DENITRIFIERS
DENITRIFIES
DENITRIFYING
DENIZATION
DENIZATIONS

ENIZENING
ENIZENSHIP
ENIZENSHIPS
ENOMINABLE
ENOMINATE
ENOMINATED
ENOMINATES
ENOMINATING
ENOMINATION
ENOMINATIONAL
ENOMINATIONS
ENOMINATIVE
ENOMINATIVELY
ENOMINATIVES
ENOMINATOR
ENOMINATORS
ENOTATING
ENOTATION
ENOTATIONS
ENOTATIVE
ENOTATIVELY
ENOTEMENT
ENOTEMENTS
ENOUEMENT
ENOUEMENTS
ENOUNCEMENT
ENOUNCEMENTS
ENOUNCERS
ENOUNCING
ENSENESSES
ENSIFICATION
ENSIFICATIONS
ENSIFIERS
ENSIFYING
ENSIMETER
ENSIMETERS
ENSIMETRIC
ENSIMETRIES
ENSIMETRY
ENSITOMETER
ENSITOMETERS
ENSITOMETRIC
ENSITOMETRIES
ENSITOMETRY
ENTALITIES
ENTALIUMS
ENTATIONS
ENTICULATE
ENTICULATED
ENTICULATELY
ENTICULATION
ENTICULATIONS
ENTIFRICE
ENTIFRICES
ENTIGEROUS
ENTILABIAL
ENTILINGUAL
ENTILINGUALS
ENTIROSTRAL
ENTISTRIES
ENTITIONS
ENTURISTS
ENUCLEARISE
ENUCLEARISED
ENUCLEARISES
ENUCLEARISING
DENUCLEARIZE
DENUCLEARIZED
DENUCLEARIZES
DENUCLEARIZING
DENUDATING
DENUDATION
DENUDATIONS
DENUDEMENT
DENUDEMENTS
DENUMERABILITY
DENUMERABLE
DENUMERABLY
DENUNCIATE
DENUNCIATED
DENUNCIATES
DENUNCIATING
DENUNCIATION
DENUNCIATIONS
DENUNCIATIVE
DENUNCIATOR
DENUNCIATORS
DENUNCIATORY
DEOBSTRUENT
DEOBSTRUENTS
DEODORANTS
DEODORISATION
DEODORISATIONS
DEODORISED
DEODORISER
DEODORISERS
DEODORISES
DEODORISING
DEODORIZATION
DEODORIZATIONS
DEODORIZED
DEODORIZER
DEODORIZERS
DEODORIZES
DEODORIZING
DEONTOLOGICAL
DEONTOLOGIES
DEONTOLOGIST
DEONTOLOGISTS
DEONTOLOGY
DEOPPILATE
DEOPPILATED
DEOPPILATES
DEOPPILATING
DEOPPILATION
DEOPPILATIONS
DEOPPILATIVE
DEORBITING
DEOXIDATED
DEOXIDATES
DEOXIDATING
DEOXIDATION
DEOXIDATIONS
DEOXIDISATION
DEOXIDISATIONS
DEOXIDISED
DEOXIDISER
DEOXIDISERS
DEOXIDISES
DEOXIDISING
DEOXIDIZATION
DEOXIDIZATIONS
DEOXIDIZED
DEOXIDIZER
DEOXIDIZERS
DEOXIDIZES
DEOXIDIZING
DEOXYCORTONE
DEOXYCORTONES
DEOXYGENATE
DEOXYGENATED
DEOXYGENATES
DEOXYGENATING
DEOXYGENATION
DEOXYGENATIONS
DEOXYGENISE
DEOXYGENISED
DEOXYGENISES
DEOXYGENISING
DEOXYGENIZE
DEOXYGENIZED
DEOXYGENIZES
DEOXYGENIZING
DEOXYRIBOSE
DEOXYRIBOSES
DEPAINTING
DEPANNEURS
DEPARTEMENT
DEPARTEMENTS
DEPARTINGS
DEPARTMENT
DEPARTMENTAL
DEPARTMENTALISE
DEPARTMENTALISM
DEPARTMENTALIZE
DEPARTMENTALLY
DEPARTMENTS
DEPARTURES
DEPASTURED
DEPASTURES
DEPASTURING
DEPAUPERATE
DEPAUPERATED
DEPAUPERATES
DEPAUPERATING
DEPAUPERISE
DEPAUPERISED
DEPAUPERISES
DEPAUPERISING
DEPAUPERIZE
DEPAUPERIZED
DEPAUPERIZES
DEPAUPERIZING
DEPEINCTED
DEPEINCTING
DEPENDABILITIES
DEPENDABILITY
DEPENDABLE
DEPENDABLENESS
DEPENDABLY
DEPENDACIE
DEPENDACIES
DEPENDANCE
DEPENDANCES
DEPENDANCIES
DEPENDANCY
DEPENDANTS
DEPENDENCE
DEPENDENCES
DEPENDENCIES
DEPENDENCY
DEPENDENTLY
DEPENDENTS
DEPENDINGLY
DEPEOPLING
DEPERSONALISE
DEPERSONALISED
DEPERSONALISES
DEPERSONALISING
DEPERSONALIZE
DEPERSONALIZED
DEPERSONALIZES
DEPERSONALIZING
DEPHLEGMATE
DEPHLEGMATED
DEPHLEGMATES
DEPHLEGMATING
DEPHLEGMATION
DEPHLEGMATIONS
DEPHLEGMATOR
DEPHLEGMATORS
DEPHLOGISTICATE
DEPHOSPHORYLATE
DEPICTIONS
DEPICTURED
DEPICTURES
DEPICTURING
DEPIGMENTATION
DEPIGMENTATIONS
DEPILATING
DEPILATION
DEPILATIONS
DEPILATORIES
DEPILATORS
DEPILATORY
DEPLETABLE
DEPLETIONS
DEPLORABILITIES
DEPLORABILITY
DEPLORABLE
DEPLORABLENESS
DEPLORABLY
DEPLORATION
DEPLORATIONS
DEPLORINGLY
DEPLOYABLE
DEPLOYMENT
DEPLOYMENTS
DEPLUMATION
DEPLUMATIONS
DEPOLARISATION
DEPOLARISATIONS
DEPOLARISE
DEPOLARISED
DEPOLARISER
DEPOLARISERS
DEPOLARISES
DEPOLARISING
DEPOLARIZATION
DEPOLARIZATIONS
DEPOLARIZE
DEPOLARIZED
DEPOLARIZER
DEPOLARIZERS

DEPOLARIZES
DEPOLARIZING
DEPOLISHED
DEPOLISHES
DEPOLISHING
DEPOLITICISE
DEPOLITICISED
DEPOLITICISES
DEPOLITICISING
DEPOLITICIZE
DEPOLITICIZED
DEPOLITICIZES
DEPOLITICIZING
DEPOLYMERISE
DEPOLYMERISED
DEPOLYMERISES
DEPOLYMERISING
DEPOLYMERIZE
DEPOLYMERIZED
DEPOLYMERIZES
DEPOLYMERIZING
DEPOPULATE
DEPOPULATED
DEPOPULATES
DEPOPULATING
DEPOPULATION
DEPOPULATIONS
DEPOPULATOR
DEPOPULATORS
DEPORTABLE
DEPORTATION
DEPORTATIONS
DEPORTMENT
DEPORTMENTS
DEPOSITARIES
DEPOSITARY
DEPOSITATION
DEPOSITATIONS
DEPOSITING
DEPOSITION
DEPOSITIONAL
DEPOSITIONS
DEPOSITIVE
DEPOSITORIES
DEPOSITORS
DEPOSITORY
DEPRAVATION
DEPRAVATIONS
DEPRAVEDLY
DEPRAVEDNESS
DEPRAVEDNESSES
DEPRAVEMENT
DEPRAVEMENTS
DEPRAVINGLY
DEPRAVITIES
DEPRECABLE
DEPRECATED
DEPRECATES
DEPRECATING
DEPRECATINGLY
DEPRECATION
DEPRECATIONS
DEPRECATIVE
DEPRECATIVELY
DEPRECATOR
DEPRECATORILY
DEPRECATORS
DEPRECATORY
DEPRECIABLE
DEPRECIATE
DEPRECIATED
DEPRECIATES
DEPRECIATING
DEPRECIATINGLY
DEPRECIATION
DEPRECIATIONS
DEPRECIATIVE
DEPRECIATOR
DEPRECIATORS
DEPRECIATORY
DEPREDATED
DEPREDATES
DEPREDATING
DEPREDATION
DEPREDATIONS
DEPREDATOR
DEPREDATORS
DEPREDATORY
DEPREHENDED
DEPREHENDING
DEPREHENDS
DEPRESSANT
DEPRESSANTS
DEPRESSIBLE
DEPRESSING
DEPRESSINGLY
DEPRESSION
DEPRESSIONS
DEPRESSIVE
DEPRESSIVELY
DEPRESSIVENESS
DEPRESSIVES
DEPRESSOMOTOR
DEPRESSOMOTORS
DEPRESSORS
DEPRESSURISE
DEPRESSURISED
DEPRESSURISES
DEPRESSURISING
DEPRESSURIZE
DEPRESSURIZED
DEPRESSURIZES
DEPRESSURIZING
DEPRIVABLE
DEPRIVATION
DEPRIVATIONS
DEPRIVATIVE
DEPRIVEMENT
DEPRIVEMENTS
DEPROGRAMED
DEPROGRAMING
DEPROGRAMME
DEPROGRAMMED
DEPROGRAMMER
DEPROGRAMMERS
DEPROGRAMMES
DEPROGRAMMING
DEPROGRAMS
DEPURATING
DEPURATION
DEPURATIONS
DEPURATIVE
DEPURATIVES
DEPURATORS
DEPURATORY
DEPUTATION
DEPUTATIONS
DEPUTISATION
DEPUTISATIONS
DEPUTISING
DEPUTIZATION
DEPUTIZATIONS
DEPUTIZING
DERACIALISE
DERACIALISED
DERACIALISES
DERACIALISING
DERACIALIZE
DERACIALIZED
DERACIALIZES
DERACIALIZING
DERACINATE
DERACINATED
DERACINATES
DERACINATING
DERACINATION
DERACINATIONS
DERAIGNING
DERAIGNMENT
DERAIGNMENTS
DERAILLEUR
DERAILLEURS
DERAILMENT
DERAILMENTS
DERANGEMENT
DERANGEMENTS
DERATIONED
DERATIONING
DEREALISATION
DEREALISATIONS
DEREALIZATION
DEREALIZATIONS
DERECOGNISE
DERECOGNISED
DERECOGNISES
DERECOGNISING
DERECOGNITION
DERECOGNITIONS
DERECOGNIZE
DERECOGNIZED
DERECOGNIZES
DERECOGNIZING
DEREGISTER
DEREGISTERED
DEREGISTERING
DEREGISTERS
DEREGISTRATION
DEREGISTRATIONS
DEREGULATE
DEREGULATED
DEREGULATES
DEREGULATING
DEREGULATION
DEREGULATIONS
DEREGULATOR
DEREGULATORS
DEREGULATORY
DERELICTION
DERELICTIONS
DERELIGIONISE
DERELIGIONISED
DERELIGIONISES
DERELIGIONISING
DERELIGIONIZE
DERELIGIONIZED
DERELIGIONIZES
DERELIGIONIZING
DEREPRESSED
DEREPRESSES
DEREPRESSING
DEREPRESSION
DEREPRESSIONS
DEREQUISITION
DEREQUISITIONED
DEREQUISITIONS
DERESTRICT
DERESTRICTED
DERESTRICTING
DERESTRICTION
DERESTRICTIONS
DERESTRICTS
DERIDINGLY
DERISIVELY
DERISIVENESS
DERISIVENESSES
DERIVATION
DERIVATIONAL
DERIVATIONIST
DERIVATIONISTS
DERIVATIONS
DERIVATISATION
DERIVATISATIONS
DERIVATISE
DERIVATISED
DERIVATISES
DERIVATISING
DERIVATIVE
DERIVATIVELY
DERIVATIVENESS
DERIVATIVES
DERIVATIZATION
DERIVATIZATIONS
DERIVATIZE
DERIVATIZED
DERIVATIZES
DERIVATIZING
DERMABRASION
DERMABRASIONS
DERMAPTERAN
DERMAPTERANS
DERMATITIS
DERMATITISES
DERMATOGEN
DERMATOGENS
DERMATOGLYPHIC
DERMATOGLYPHICS
DERMATOGRAPHIA
DERMATOGRAPHIAS
DERMATOGRAPHIC
DERMATOGRAPHIES
DERMATOGRAPHY
DERMATOLOGIC
DERMATOLOGICAL
DERMATOLOGIES

ERMATOLOGIST
ERMATOLOGISTS
ERMATOLOGY
ERMATOMAL
ERMATOMES
ERMATOMIC
ERMATOMICALLY
ERMATOMYOSITIS
ERMATOPHYTE
ERMATOPHYTES
ERMATOPHYTIC
ERMATOPHYTOSES
ERMATOPHYTOSIS
ERMATOPLASTIC
ERMATOPLASTIES
ERMATOPLASTY
ERMATOSES
ERMATOSIS
ERMESTIDS
ERMOGRAPHIES
ERMOGRAPHY
EROGATELY
EROGATING
EROGATION
EROGATIONS
EROGATIVE
EROGATIVELY
EROGATORILY
EROGATORINESS
EROGATORY
ERRICKING
ERRINGERS
ESACRALISATION
ESACRALISE
ESACRALISED
ESACRALISES
ESACRALISING
ESACRALIZATION
ESACRALIZE
ESACRALIZED
ESACRALIZES
ESACRALIZING
ESAGREMENT
ESAGREMENTS
ESALINATE
ESALINATED
ESALINATES
ESALINATING
ESALINATION
ESALINATIONS
ESALINATOR
ESALINATORS
ESALINISATION
ESALINISATIONS
ESALINISE
ESALINISED
ESALINISES
ESALINISING
ESALINIZATION
ESALINIZATIONS
ESALINIZE
ESALINIZED
ESALINIZES
ESALINIZING
ESALTINGS
ESATURATION
DESATURATIONS
DESCANTERS
DESCANTING
DESCENDABLE
DESCENDANT
DESCENDANTS
DESCENDENT
DESCENDENTS
DESCENDERS
DESCENDEUR
DESCENDEURS
DESCENDIBLE
DESCENDING
DESCENDINGS
DESCENSION
DESCENSIONAL
DESCENSIONS
DESCHOOLED
DESCHOOLER
DESCHOOLERS
DESCHOOLING
DESCHOOLINGS
DESCRAMBLE
DESCRAMBLED
DESCRAMBLER
DESCRAMBLERS
DESCRAMBLES
DESCRAMBLING
DESCRIBABLE
DESCRIBERS
DESCRIBING
DESCRIPTION
DESCRIPTIONS
DESCRIPTIVE
DESCRIPTIVELY
DESCRIPTIVENESS
DESCRIPTIVISM
DESCRIPTIVISMS
DESCRIPTIVIST
DESCRIPTOR
DESCRIPTORS
DESCRIVING
DESECRATED
DESECRATER
DESECRATERS
DESECRATES
DESECRATING
DESECRATION
DESECRATIONS
DESECRATOR
DESECRATORS
DESEGREGATE
DESEGREGATED
DESEGREGATES
DESEGREGATING
DESEGREGATION
DESEGREGATIONS
DESELECTED
DESELECTING
DESELECTION
DESELECTIONS
DESENSITISATION
DESENSITISE
DESENSITISED
DESENSITISER
DESENSITISERS
DESENSITISES
DESENSITISING
DESENSITIZATION
DESENSITIZE
DESENSITIZED
DESENSITIZER
DESENSITIZERS
DESENSITIZES
DESENSITIZING
DESERPIDINE
DESERPIDINES
DESERTIFICATION
DESERTIFIED
DESERTIFIES
DESERTIFYING
DESERTIONS
DESERTISATION
DESERTISATIONS
DESERTIZATION
DESERTIZATIONS
DESERTLESS
DESERVEDLY
DESERVEDNESS
DESERVEDNESSES
DESERVINGLY
DESERVINGNESS
DESERVINGNESSES
DESERVINGS
DESEXUALISATION
DESEXUALISE
DESEXUALISED
DESEXUALISES
DESEXUALISING
DESEXUALIZATION
DESEXUALIZE
DESEXUALIZED
DESEXUALIZES
DESEXUALIZING
DESHABILLE
DESHABILLES
DESICCANTS
DESICCATED
DESICCATES
DESICCATING
DESICCATION
DESICCATIONS
DESICCATIVE
DESICCATIVES
DESICCATOR
DESICCATORS
DESIDERATA
DESIDERATE
DESIDERATED
DESIDERATES
DESIDERATING
DESIDERATION
DESIDERATIONS
DESIDERATIVE
DESIDERATIVES
DESIDERATUM
DESIDERIUM
DESIDERIUMS
DESIGNABLE
DESIGNATED
DESIGNATES
DESIGNATING
DESIGNATION
DESIGNATIONS
DESIGNATIVE
DESIGNATOR
DESIGNATORS
DESIGNATORY
DESIGNEDLY
DESIGNINGLY
DESIGNINGS
DESIGNLESS
DESIGNMENT
DESIGNMENTS
DESILVERED
DESILVERING
DESILVERISATION
DESILVERISE
DESILVERISED
DESILVERISES
DESILVERISING
DESILVERIZATION
DESILVERIZE
DESILVERIZED
DESILVERIZES
DESILVERIZING
DESINENCES
DESINENTIAL
DESIPIENCE
DESIPIENCES
DESIPRAMINE
DESIPRAMINES
DESIRABILITIES
DESIRABILITY
DESIRABLENESS
DESIRABLENESSES
DESIRABLES
DESIRELESS
DESIROUSLY
DESIROUSNESS
DESIROUSNESSES
DESISTANCE
DESISTANCES
DESISTENCE
DESISTENCES
DESKILLING
DESMODIUMS
DESMODROMIC
DESMOSOMAL
DESMOSOMES
DESNOODING
DESOBLIGEANTE
DESOBLIGEANTES
DESOLATELY
DESOLATENESS
DESOLATENESSES
DESOLATERS
DESOLATING
DESOLATINGLY
DESOLATION
DESOLATIONS
DESOLATORS
DESOLATORY
DESORIENTE
DESORPTION
DESORPTIONS
DESOXYRIBOSE
DESOXYRIBOSES

DESPAIRERS
DESPAIRFUL
DESPAIRING
DESPAIRINGLY
DESPATCHED
DESPATCHER
DESPATCHERS
DESPATCHES
DESPATCHING
DESPERADOES
DESPERADOS
DESPERATELY
DESPERATENESS
DESPERATENESSES
DESPERATION
DESPERATIONS
DESPICABILITIES
DESPICABILITY
DESPICABLE
DESPICABLENESS
DESPICABLY
DESPIRITUALISE
DESPIRITUALISED
DESPIRITUALISES
DESPIRITUALIZE
DESPIRITUALIZED
DESPIRITUALIZES
DESPISABLE
DESPISEDNESS
DESPISEDNESSES
DESPISEMENT
DESPISEMENTS
DESPITEFUL
DESPITEFULLY
DESPITEFULNESS
DESPITEOUS
DESPITEOUSLY
DESPOILERS
DESPOILING
DESPOILMENT
DESPOILMENTS
DESPOLIATION
DESPOLIATIONS
DESPONDENCE
DESPONDENCES
DESPONDENCIES
DESPONDENCY
DESPONDENT
DESPONDENTLY
DESPONDING
DESPONDINGLY
DESPONDINGS
DESPOTATES
DESPOTICAL
DESPOTICALLY
DESPOTICALNESS
DESPOTISMS
DESPOTOCRACIES
DESPOTOCRACY
DESPUMATED
DESPUMATES
DESPUMATING
DESPUMATION
DESPUMATIONS
DESQUAMATE
DESQUAMATED
DESQUAMATES
DESQUAMATING
DESQUAMATION
DESQUAMATIONS
DESQUAMATIVE
DESQUAMATORY
DESSERTSPOON
DESSERTSPOONFUL
DESSERTSPOONS
DESSIATINE
DESSIATINES
DESSIGNMENT
DESSIGNMENTS
DESSYATINE
DESSYATINES
DESTABILISATION
DESTABILISE
DESTABILISED
DESTABILISER
DESTABILISERS
DESTABILISES
DESTABILISING
DESTABILIZATION
DESTABILIZE
DESTABILIZED
DESTABILIZER
DESTABILIZERS
DESTABILIZES
DESTABILIZING
DESTAINING
DESTEMPERED
DESTEMPERING
DESTEMPERS
DESTINATED
DESTINATES
DESTINATING
DESTINATION
DESTINATIONS
DESTITUTED
DESTITUTENESS
DESTITUTENESSES
DESTITUTES
DESTITUTING
DESTITUTION
DESTITUTIONS
DESTOCKING
DESTROYABLE
DESTROYERS
DESTROYING
DESTRUCTED
DESTRUCTIBILITY
DESTRUCTIBLE
DESTRUCTING
DESTRUCTION
DESTRUCTIONAL
DESTRUCTIONIST
DESTRUCTIONISTS
DESTRUCTIONS
DESTRUCTIVE
DESTRUCTIVELY
DESTRUCTIVENESS
DESTRUCTIVES
DESTRUCTIVIST
DESTRUCTIVISTS
DESTRUCTIVITIES
DESTRUCTIVITY
DESTRUCTOR
DESTRUCTORS
DESTRUCTOS
DESUETUDES
DESUGARING
DESULFURED
DESULFURING
DESULFURISATION
DESULFURISE
DESULFURISED
DESULFURISES
DESULFURISING
DESULFURIZATION
DESULFURIZE
DESULFURIZED
DESULFURIZES
DESULFURIZING
DESULPHURATE
DESULPHURATED
DESULPHURATES
DESULPHURATING
DESULPHURATION
DESULPHURATIONS
DESULPHURED
DESULPHURING
DESULPHURISE
DESULPHURISED
DESULPHURISER
DESULPHURISERS
DESULPHURISES
DESULPHURISING
DESULPHURIZE
DESULPHURIZED
DESULPHURIZER
DESULPHURIZERS
DESULPHURIZES
DESULPHURIZING
DESULPHURS
DESULTORILY
DESULTORINESS
DESULTORINESSES
DETACHABILITIES
DETACHABILITY
DETACHABLE
DETACHABLY
DETACHEDLY
DETACHEDNESS
DETACHEDNESSES
DETACHMENT
DETACHMENTS
DETAILEDLY
DETAILEDNESS
DETAILEDNESSES
DETAILINGS
DETAINABLE
DETAINMENT
DETAINMENTS
DETASSELED
DETASSELING
DETASSELLED
DETASSELLING
DETECTABILITIES
DETECTABILITY
DETECTABLE
DETECTIBLE
DETECTIONS
DETECTIVELIKE
DETECTIVES
DETECTIVIST
DETECTIVISTS
DETECTOPHONE
DETECTOPHONES
DETECTORIST
DETECTORISTS
DETENTIONS
DETENTISTS
DETERGENCE
DETERGENCES
DETERGENCIES
DETERGENCY
DETERGENTS
DETERIORATE
DETERIORATED
DETERIORATES
DETERIORATING
DETERIORATION
DETERIORATIONS
DETERIORATIVE
DETERIORISM
DETERIORISMS
DETERIORITIES
DETERIORITY
DETERMENTS
DETERMINABILITY
DETERMINABLE
DETERMINABLY
DETERMINACIES
DETERMINACY
DETERMINANT
DETERMINANTAL
DETERMINANTS
DETERMINATE
DETERMINATED
DETERMINATELY
DETERMINATENESS
DETERMINATES
DETERMINATING
DETERMINATION
DETERMINATIONS
DETERMINATIVE
DETERMINATIVELY
DETERMINATIVES
DETERMINATOR
DETERMINATORS
DETERMINED
DETERMINEDLY
DETERMINEDNESS
DETERMINER
DETERMINERS
DETERMINES
DETERMINING
DETERMINISM
DETERMINISMS
DETERMINIST
DETERMINISTIC
DETERMINISTS
DETERRABILITIES
DETERRABILITY
DETERRABLE
DETERRENCE
DETERRENCES
DETERRENTLY

ETERRENTS
ETERSIONS
ETERSIVES
ETESTABILITIES
ETESTABILITY
ETESTABLE
ETESTABLENESS
ETESTABLY
ETESTATION
ETESTATIONS
ETHATCHED
ETHATCHES
ETHATCHING
ETHRONEMENT
ETHRONEMENTS
ETHRONERS
ETHRONING
ETHRONINGS
ETONABILITIES
ETONABILITY
ETONATABLE
ETONATING
ETONATION
ETONATIONS
ETONATIVE
ETONATORS
ETORSIONS
ETORTIONS
ETOXICANT
ETOXICANTS
ETOXICATE
ETOXICATED
ETOXICATES
ETOXICATING
ETOXICATION
ETOXICATIONS
ETOXIFICATION
ETOXIFICATIONS
ETOXIFIED
ETOXIFIES
ETOXIFYING
ETRACTING
ETRACTINGLY
ETRACTINGS
ETRACTION
ETRACTIONS
ETRACTIVE
ETRACTIVELY
ETRACTORS
ETRACTORY
ETRACTRESS
ETRACTRESSES
ETRAINING
ETRAINMENT
ETRAINMENTS
ETRAQUEES
ETRIBALISATION
ETRIBALISE
ETRIBALISED
ETRIBALISES
ETRIBALISING
ETRIBALIZATION
ETRIBALIZE
ETRIBALIZED
ETRIBALIZES
ETRIBALIZING

DETRIMENTAL
DETRIMENTALLY
DETRIMENTALS
DETRIMENTS
DETRITIONS
DETRITOVORE
DETRITOVORES
DETRUNCATE
DETRUNCATED
DETRUNCATES
DETRUNCATING
DETRUNCATION
DETRUNCATIONS
DETRUSIONS
DETUMESCENCE
DETUMESCENCES
DETUMESCENT
DEUTERAGONIST
DEUTERAGONISTS
DEUTERANOMALIES
DEUTERANOMALOUS
DEUTERANOMALY
DEUTERANOPE
DEUTERANOPES
DEUTERANOPIA
DEUTERANOPIAS
DEUTERANOPIC
DEUTERATED
DEUTERATES
DEUTERATING
DEUTERATION
DEUTERATIONS
DEUTERIDES
DEUTERIUMS
DEUTEROGAMIES
DEUTEROGAMIST
DEUTEROGAMISTS
DEUTEROGAMY
DEUTEROPLASM
DEUTEROPLASMS
DEUTEROSCOPIC
DEUTEROSCOPIES
DEUTEROSCOPY
DEUTEROSTOME
DEUTEROSTOMES
DEUTEROTOKIES
DEUTEROTOKY
DEUTOPLASM
DEUTOPLASMIC
DEUTOPLASMS
DEUTOPLASTIC
DEVALORISATION
DEVALORISATIONS
DEVALORISE
DEVALORISED
DEVALORISES
DEVALORISING
DEVALORIZATION
DEVALORIZATIONS
DEVALORIZE
DEVALORIZED
DEVALORIZES
DEVALORIZING
DEVALUATED
DEVALUATES
DEVALUATING

DEVALUATION
DEVALUATIONS
DEVANAGARI
DEVANAGARIS
DEVASTATED
DEVASTATES
DEVASTATING
DEVASTATINGLY
DEVASTATION
DEVASTATIONS
DEVASTATIVE
DEVASTATOR
DEVASTATORS
DEVASTAVIT
DEVASTAVITS
DEVELOPABLE
DEVELOPERS
DEVELOPING
DEVELOPMENT
DEVELOPMENTAL
DEVELOPMENTALLY
DEVELOPMENTS
DEVERBATIVE
DEVERBATIVES
DEVIANCIES
DEVIATIONISM
DEVIATIONISMS
DEVIATIONIST
DEVIATIONISTS
DEVIATIONS
DEVILESSES
DEVILFISHES
DEVILISHLY
DEVILISHNESS
DEVILISHNESSES
DEVILMENTS
DEVILSHIPS
DEVILTRIES
DEVILWOODS
DEVIOUSNESS
DEVIOUSNESSES
DEVITALISATION
DEVITALISATIONS
DEVITALISE
DEVITALISED
DEVITALISES
DEVITALISING
DEVITALIZATION
DEVITALIZATIONS
DEVITALIZE
DEVITALIZED
DEVITALIZES
DEVITALIZING
DEVITRIFICATION
DEVITRIFIED
DEVITRIFIES
DEVITRIFYING
DEVOCALISE
DEVOCALISED
DEVOCALISES
DEVOCALISING
DEVOCALIZE
DEVOCALIZED
DEVOCALIZES
DEVOCALIZING
DEVOLUTION

DEVOLUTIONARY
DEVOLUTIONIST
DEVOLUTIONISTS
DEVOLUTIONS
DEVOLVEMENT
DEVOLVEMENTS
DEVONPORTS
DEVOTEDNESS
DEVOTEDNESSES
DEVOTEMENT
DEVOTEMENTS
DEVOTIONAL
DEVOTIONALIST
DEVOTIONALISTS
DEVOTIONALITIES
DEVOTIONALITY
DEVOTIONALLY
DEVOTIONALNESS
DEVOTIONALS
DEVOTIONIST
DEVOTIONISTS
DEVOURINGLY
DEVOURMENT
DEVOURMENTS
DEVOUTNESS
DEVOUTNESSES
DEVVELLING
DEWATERERS
DEWATERING
DEWATERINGS
DEWBERRIES
DEWINESSES
DEXAMETHASONE
DEXAMETHASONES
DEXAMPHETAMINE
DEXAMPHETAMINES
DEXIOTROPIC
DEXTERITIES
DEXTEROUSLY
DEXTEROUSNESS
DEXTEROUSNESSES
DEXTERWISE
DEXTRALITIES
DEXTRALITY
DEXTRANASE
DEXTRANASES
DEXTROCARDIA
DEXTROCARDIAC
DEXTROCARDIACS
DEXTROCARDIAS
DEXTROGLUCOSE
DEXTROGLUCOSES
DEXTROGYRATE
DEXTROGYRE
DEXTROPHOSPHATE
DEXTROROTARY
DEXTROROTATION
DEXTROROTATIONS
DEXTROROTATORY
DEXTRORSAL
DEXTRORSELY
DEXTROUSLY
DEXTROUSNESS
DEXTROUSNESSES
DEZINCKING
DHARMSALAS

DHARMSHALA
DHARMSHALAS
DIABETICAL
DIABETOGENIC
DIABETOLOGIST
DIABETOLOGISTS
DIABLERIES
DIABOLICAL
DIABOLICALLY
DIABOLICALNESS
DIABOLISED
DIABOLISES
DIABOLISING
DIABOLISMS
DIABOLISTS
DIABOLIZED
DIABOLIZES
DIABOLIZING
DIABOLOGIES
DIABOLOLOGIES
DIABOLOLOGY
DIACATHOLICON
DIACATHOLICONS
DIACAUSTIC
DIACAUSTICS
DIACHRONIC
DIACHRONICALLY
DIACHRONIES
DIACHRONISM
DIACHRONISMS
DIACHRONISTIC
DIACHRONOUS
DIACHYLONS
DIACHYLUMS
DIACODIONS
DIACODIUMS
DIACONATES
DIACONICON
DIACONICONS
DIACOUSTIC
DIACOUSTICS
DIACRITICAL
DIACRITICALLY
DIACRITICS
DIACTINISM
DIACTINISMS
DIADELPHOUS
DIADOCHIES
DIADROMOUS
DIAGENESES
DIAGENESIS
DIAGENETIC
DIAGENETICALLY
DIAGEOTROPIC
DIAGEOTROPISM
DIAGEOTROPISMS
DIAGNOSABILITY
DIAGNOSABLE
DIAGNOSEABLE
DIAGNOSING
DIAGNOSTIC
DIAGNOSTICAL
DIAGNOSTICALLY
DIAGNOSTICIAN
DIAGNOSTICIANS
DIAGNOSTICS
DIAGOMETER
DIAGOMETERS
DIAGONALISABLE
DIAGONALISATION
DIAGONALISE
DIAGONALISED
DIAGONALISES
DIAGONALISING
DIAGONALIZABLE
DIAGONALIZATION
DIAGONALIZE
DIAGONALIZED
DIAGONALIZES
DIAGONALIZING
DIAGONALLY
DIAGRAMING
DIAGRAMMABLE
DIAGRAMMATIC
DIAGRAMMATICAL
DIAGRAMMED
DIAGRAMMING
DIAGRAPHIC
DIAHELIOTROPIC
DIAHELIOTROPISM
DIAKINESES
DIAKINESIS
DIALECTALLY
DIALECTICAL
DIALECTICALLY
DIALECTICIAN
DIALECTICIANS
DIALECTICISM
DIALECTICISMS
DIALECTICS
DIALECTOLOGICAL
DIALECTOLOGIES
DIALECTOLOGIST
DIALECTOLOGISTS
DIALECTOLOGY
DIALLAGOID
DIALOGICAL
DIALOGICALLY
DIALOGISED
DIALOGISES
DIALOGISING
DIALOGISMS
DIALOGISTIC
DIALOGISTICAL
DIALOGISTS
DIALOGITES
DIALOGIZED
DIALOGIZES
DIALOGIZING
DIALOGUERS
DIALOGUING
DIALYPETALOUS
DIALYSABILITIES
DIALYSABILITY
DIALYSABLE
DIALYSATES
DIALYSATION
DIALYSATIONS
DIALYTICALLY
DIALYZABILITIES
DIALYZABILITY
DIALYZABLE
DIALYZATES
DIALYZATION
DIALYZATIONS
DIAMAGNETIC
DIAMAGNETICALLY
DIAMAGNETISM
DIAMAGNETISMS
DIAMAGNETS
DIAMANTIFEROUS
DIAMANTINE
DIAMETRALLY
DIAMETRICAL
DIAMETRICALLY
DIAMONDBACK
DIAMONDBACKS
DIAMONDIFEROUS
DIAMONDING
DIAMORPHINE
DIAMORPHINES
DIANTHUSES
DIAPASONAL
DIAPASONIC
DIAPAUSING
DIAPEDESES
DIAPEDESIS
DIAPEDETIC
DIAPERINGS
DIAPHANEITIES
DIAPHANEITY
DIAPHANOMETER
DIAPHANOMETERS
DIAPHANOUS
DIAPHANOUSLY
DIAPHANOUSNESS
DIAPHONIES
DIAPHORASE
DIAPHORASES
DIAPHORESES
DIAPHORESIS
DIAPHORETIC
DIAPHORETICS
DIAPHOTOTROPIC
DIAPHOTOTROPIES
DIAPHOTOTROPISM
DIAPHOTOTROPY
DIAPHRAGMAL
DIAPHRAGMATIC
DIAPHRAGMATITIS
DIAPHRAGMED
DIAPHRAGMING
DIAPHRAGMS
DIAPHYSEAL
DIAPHYSIAL
DIAPIRISMS
DIAPOPHYSES
DIAPOPHYSIAL
DIAPOPHYSIS
DIAPOSITIVE
DIAPOSITIVES
DIAPYETICS
DIARCHICAL
DIARRHETIC
DIARRHOEAL
DIARRHOEAS
DIARRHOEIC
DIARTHRODIAL
DIARTHROSES
DIARTHROSIS
DIASCORDIUM
DIASCORDIUMS
DIASKEUAST
DIASKEUASTS
DIASTALSES
DIASTALSIS
DIASTALTIC
DIASTEMATA
DIASTEMATIC
DIASTEREOISOMER
DIASTEREOMER
DIASTEREOMERIC
DIASTEREOMERS
DIASTROPHIC
DIASTROPHICALLY
DIASTROPHISM
DIASTROPHISMS
DIATESSARON
DIATESSARONS
DIATHERMACIES
DIATHERMACY
DIATHERMAL
DIATHERMANCIES
DIATHERMANCY
DIATHERMANEITY
DIATHERMANOUS
DIATHERMIA
DIATHERMIAS
DIATHERMIC
DIATHERMIES
DIATHERMOUS
DIATOMACEOUS
DIATOMICITIES
DIATOMICITY
DIATOMISTS
DIATOMITES
DIATONICALLY
DIATONICISM
DIATONICISMS
DIATRETUMS
DIATRIBIST
DIATRIBISTS
DIATROPISM
DIATROPISMS
DIAZEUCTIC
DIAZOMETHANE
DIAZOMETHANES
DIAZONIUMS
DIAZOTISATION
DIAZOTISATIONS
DIAZOTISED
DIAZOTISES
DIAZOTISING
DIAZOTIZATION
DIAZOTIZATIONS
DIAZOTIZED
DIAZOTIZES
DIAZOTIZING
DIBASICITIES
DIBASICITY
DIBENZOFURAN
DIBENZOFURANS
DIBRANCHIATE
DIBRANCHIATES

DIBROMIDES
DICACITIES
DICACODYLS
DICARBOXYLIC
DICARPELLARY
DICASTERIES
DICENTRICS
DICEPHALISM
DICEPHALISMS
DICEPHALOUS
DICHASIALLY
DICHLAMYDEOUS
DICHLORIDE
DICHLORIDES
DICHLOROBENZENE
DICHLOROETHANE
DICHLOROETHANES
DICHLOROMETHANE
DICHLORVOS
DICHLORVOSES
DICHOGAMIC
DICHOGAMIES
DICHOGAMOUS
DICHONDRAS
DICHOTICALLY
DICHOTOMIC
DICHOTOMIES
DICHOTOMISATION
DICHOTOMISE
DICHOTOMISED
DICHOTOMISES
DICHOTOMISING
DICHOTOMIST
DICHOTOMISTS
DICHOTOMIZATION
DICHOTOMIZE
DICHOTOMIZED
DICHOTOMIZES
DICHOTOMIZING
DICHOTOMOUS
DICHOTOMOUSLY
DICHOTOMOUSNESS
DICHROISCOPE
DICHROISCOPES
DICHROISCOPIC
DICHROISMS
DICHROITES
DICHROITIC
DICHROMATE
DICHROMATES
DICHROMATIC
DICHROMATICISM
DICHROMATICISMS
DICHROMATICS
DICHROMATISM
DICHROMATISMS
DICHROMATS
DICHROMISM
DICHROMISMS
DICHROOSCOPE
DICHROOSCOPES
DICHROOSCOPIC
DICHROSCOPE
DICHROSCOPES
DICHROSCOPIC
DICKCISSEL
DICKCISSELS
DICKEYBIRD
DICKEYBIRDS
DICKYBIRDS
DICLINISMS
DICOTYLEDON
DICOTYLEDONOUS
DICOTYLEDONS
DICOUMARIN
DICOUMARINS
DICOUMAROL
DICOUMAROLS
DICROTISMS
DICTATIONAL
DICTATIONS
DICTATORIAL
DICTATORIALLY
DICTATORIALNESS
DICTATORSHIP
DICTATORSHIPS
DICTATRESS
DICTATRESSES
DICTATRICES
DICTATRIXES
DICTATURES
DICTIONALLY
DICTIONARIES
DICTIONARY
DICTYOGENS
DICTYOPTERAN
DICTYOPTERANS
DICTYOSOME
DICTYOSOMES
DICTYOSTELE
DICTYOSTELES
DICUMAROLS
DICYNODONT
DICYNODONTS
DIDACTICAL
DIDACTICALLY
DIDACTICISM
DIDACTICISMS
DIDACTYLISM
DIDACTYLISMS
DIDACTYLOUS
DIDASCALIC
DIDELPHIAN
DIDELPHIDS
DIDELPHINE
DIDELPHOUS
DIDGERIDOO
DIDGERIDOOS
DIDJERIDOO
DIDJERIDOOS
DIDJERIDUS
DIDRACHMAS
DIDYNAMIAN
DIDYNAMIES
DIDYNAMOUS
DIECIOUSLY
DIECIOUSNESS
DIECIOUSNESSES
DIEFFENBACHIA
DIEFFENBACHIAS
DIELECTRIC
DIELECTRICALLY
DIELECTRICS
DIENCEPHALA
DIENCEPHALIC
DIENCEPHALON
DIENCEPHALONS
DIESELINGS
DIESELISATION
DIESELISATIONS
DIESELISED
DIESELISES
DIESELISING
DIESELIZATION
DIESELIZATIONS
DIESELIZED
DIESELIZES
DIESELIZING
DIESINKERS
DIESTRUSES
DIETARIANS
DIETETICAL
DIETETICALLY
DIETHYLAMIDE
DIETHYLAMIDES
DIETHYLAMINE
DIETHYLAMINES
DIETHYLENE
DIETHYLENES
DIETICIANS
DIETITIANS
DIFFARREATION
DIFFARREATIONS
DIFFERENCE
DIFFERENCED
DIFFERENCES
DIFFERENCIED
DIFFERENCIES
DIFFERENCING
DIFFERENCY
DIFFERENCYING
DIFFERENTIA
DIFFERENTIABLE
DIFFERENTIAE
DIFFERENTIAL
DIFFERENTIALLY
DIFFERENTIALS
DIFFERENTIATE
DIFFERENTIATED
DIFFERENTIATES
DIFFERENTIATING
DIFFERENTIATION
DIFFERENTIATOR
DIFFERENTIATORS
DIFFERENTLY
DIFFERENTNESS
DIFFERENTNESSES
DIFFICULTIES
DIFFICULTLY
DIFFICULTY
DIFFIDENCE
DIFFIDENCES
DIFFIDENTLY
DIFFORMITIES
DIFFORMITY
DIFFRACTED
DIFFRACTING
DIFFRACTION
DIFFRACTIONS
DIFFRACTIVE
DIFFRACTIVELY
DIFFRACTIVENESS
DIFFRACTOMETER
DIFFRACTOMETERS
DIFFRACTOMETRIC
DIFFRACTOMETRY
DIFFRANGIBILITY
DIFFRANGIBLE
DIFFUSEDLY
DIFFUSEDNESS
DIFFUSEDNESSES
DIFFUSENESS
DIFFUSENESSES
DIFFUSIBILITIES
DIFFUSIBILITY
DIFFUSIBLE
DIFFUSIBLENESS
DIFFUSIONAL
DIFFUSIONISM
DIFFUSIONISMS
DIFFUSIONIST
DIFFUSIONISTS
DIFFUSIONS
DIFFUSIVELY
DIFFUSIVENESS
DIFFUSIVENESSES
DIFFUSIVITIES
DIFFUSIVITY
DIFUNCTIONAL
DIFUNCTIONALS
DIGASTRICS
DIGESTANTS
DIGESTEDLY
DIGESTIBILITIES
DIGESTIBILITY
DIGESTIBLE
DIGESTIBLENESS
DIGESTIBLY
DIGESTIONAL
DIGESTIONS
DIGESTIVELY
DIGESTIVES
DIGITALINS
DIGITALISATION
DIGITALISATIONS
DIGITALISE
DIGITALISED
DIGITALISES
DIGITALISING
DIGITALISM
DIGITALISMS
DIGITALIZATION
DIGITALIZATIONS
DIGITALIZE
DIGITALIZED
DIGITALIZES
DIGITALIZING
DIGITATELY
DIGITATION
DIGITATIONS
DIGITIFORM
DIGITIGRADE
DIGITIGRADES
DIGITISATION

DIGITISATIONS
DIGITISERS
DIGITISING
DIGITIZATION
DIGITIZATIONS
DIGITIZERS
DIGITIZING
DIGITONINS
DIGITORIUM
DIGITORIUMS
DIGITOXIGENIN
DIGITOXIGENINS
DIGITOXINS
DIGLADIATE
DIGLADIATED
DIGLADIATES
DIGLADIATING
DIGLADIATION
DIGLADIATIONS
DIGLADIATOR
DIGLADIATORS
DIGLOSSIAS
DIGLYCERIDE
DIGLYCERIDES
DIGNIFICATION
DIGNIFICATIONS
DIGNIFIEDLY
DIGNIFIEDNESS
DIGNIFIEDNESSES
DIGNIFYING
DIGNITARIES
DIGONEUTIC
DIGONEUTISM
DIGONEUTISMS
DIGRAPHICALLY
DIGRESSERS
DIGRESSING
DIGRESSION
DIGRESSIONAL
DIGRESSIONARY
DIGRESSIONS
DIGRESSIVE
DIGRESSIVELY
DIGRESSIVENESS
DIHYBRIDISM
DIHYBRIDISMS
DIJUDICATE
DIJUDICATED
DIJUDICATES
DIJUDICATING
DIJUDICATION
DIJUDICATIONS
DILACERATE
DILACERATED
DILACERATES
DILACERATING
DILACERATION
DILACERATIONS
DILAPIDATE
DILAPIDATED
DILAPIDATES
DILAPIDATING
DILAPIDATION
DILAPIDATIONS
DILAPIDATOR
DILAPIDATORS
DILATABILITIES
DILATABILITY
DILATABLENESS
DILATABLENESSES
DILATANCIES
DILATATION
DILATATIONAL
DILATATIONS
DILATATORS
DILATOMETER
DILATOMETERS
DILATOMETRIC
DILATOMETRIES
DILATOMETRY
DILATORILY
DILATORINESS
DILATORINESSES
DILEMMATIC
DILETTANTE
DILETTANTEISH
DILETTANTEISM
DILETTANTEISMS
DILETTANTES
DILETTANTI
DILETTANTISH
DILETTANTISM
DILETTANTISMS
DILIGENCES
DILIGENTLY
DILLYDALLIED
DILLYDALLIES
DILLYDALLY
DILLYDALLYING
DILTIAZEMS
DILUCIDATE
DILUCIDATED
DILUCIDATES
DILUCIDATING
DILUCIDATION
DILUCIDATIONS
DILUTABLES
DILUTENESS
DILUTENESSES
DILUTIONARY
DILUVIALISM
DILUVIALISMS
DILUVIALIST
DILUVIALISTS
DIMENHYDRINATE
DIMENHYDRINATES
DIMENSIONAL
DIMENSIONALITY
DIMENSIONALLY
DIMENSIONED
DIMENSIONING
DIMENSIONLESS
DIMENSIONS
DIMERCAPROL
DIMERCAPROLS
DIMERISATION
DIMERISATIONS
DIMERISING
DIMERIZATION
DIMERIZATIONS
DIMERIZING
DIMETHOATE
DIMETHOATES
DIMETHYLAMINE
DIMETHYLAMINES
DIMETHYLANILINE
DIMIDIATED
DIMIDIATES
DIMIDIATING
DIMIDIATION
DIMIDIATIONS
DIMINISHABLE
DIMINISHED
DIMINISHES
DIMINISHING
DIMINISHINGLY
DIMINISHINGS
DIMINISHMENT
DIMINISHMENTS
DIMINUENDO
DIMINUENDOES
DIMINUENDOS
DIMINUTION
DIMINUTIONS
DIMINUTIVAL
DIMINUTIVE
DIMINUTIVELY
DIMINUTIVENESS
DIMINUTIVES
DIMORPHISM
DIMORPHISMS
DIMORPHOUS
DIMPLEMENT
DIMPLEMENTS
DINANDERIE
DINANDERIES
DINARCHIES
DINGDONGED
DINGDONGING
DINGINESSES
DINGLEBERRIES
DINGLEBERRY
DINITROBENZENE
DINITROBENZENES
DINITROGEN
DINITROPHENOL
DINITROPHENOLS
DINNERLESS
DINNERTIME
DINNERTIMES
DINNERWARE
DINNERWARES
DINOCERASES
DINOFLAGELLATE
DINOFLAGELLATES
DINOMANIAS
DINOSAURIAN
DINOSAURIC
DINOTHERES
DINOTHERIUM
DINOTHERIUMS
DINOTURBATION
DINOTURBATIONS
DINUCLEOTIDE
DINUCLEOTIDES
DIOECIOUSLY
DIOECIOUSNESS
DIOECIOUSNESSES
DIOESTRUSES
DIOICOUSLY
DIOICOUSNESS
DIOICOUSNESSES
DIOPHYSITE
DIOPHYSITES
DIOPTOMETER
DIOPTOMETERS
DIOPTOMETRIES
DIOPTOMETRY
DIOPTRICAL
DIOPTRICALLY
DIORISTICAL
DIORISTICALLY
DIORTHOSES
DIORTHOSIS
DIORTHOTIC
DIOSCOREACEOUS
DIOSGENINS
DIOTHELETE
DIOTHELETES
DIOTHELETIC
DIOTHELETICAL
DIOTHELISM
DIOTHELISMS
DIOTHELITE
DIOTHELITES
DIPEPTIDASE
DIPEPTIDASES
DIPEPTIDES
DIPETALOUS
DIPHENHYDRAMINE
DIPHENYLAMINE
DIPHENYLAMINES
DIPHENYLENIMINE
DIPHENYLKETONE
DIPHENYLKETONES
DIPHOSGENE
DIPHOSGENES
DIPHOSPHATE
DIPHOSPHATES
DIPHTHERIA
DIPHTHERIAL
DIPHTHERIAS
DIPHTHERIC
DIPHTHERITIC
DIPHTHERITIS
DIPHTHERITISES
DIPHTHEROID
DIPHTHEROIDS
DIPHTHONGAL
DIPHTHONGALLY
DIPHTHONGED
DIPHTHONGIC
DIPHTHONGING
DIPHTHONGISE
DIPHTHONGISED
DIPHTHONGISES
DIPHTHONGISING
DIPHTHONGIZE
DIPHTHONGIZED
DIPHTHONGIZES
DIPHTHONGIZING
DIPHTHONGS
DIPHYCERCAL
DIPHYLETIC

PHYLLOUS
PHYODONT
PHYODONTS
PHYSITES
PHYSITISM
PHYSITISMS
PLEIDOSCOPE
PLEIDOSCOPES
PLOBIONT
PLOBIONTIC
PLOBIONTS
PLOBLASTIC
PLOCARDIAC
PLOCOCCAL
PLOCOCCI
PLOCOCCIC
PLOCOCCUS
PLODOCUS
PLODOCUSES
PLOGENESES
PLOGENESIS
PLOIDIES
PLOMACIES
PLOMAING
PLOMATED
PLOMATES
PLOMATESE
PLOMATESES
PLOMATIC
PLOMATICAL
PLOMATICALLY
PLOMATICS
PLOMATING
PLOMATISE
PLOMATISED
PLOMATISES
PLOMATISING
PLOMATIST
PLOMATISTS
PLOMATIZE
PLOMATIZED
PLOMATIZES
PLOMATIZING
PLOMATOLOGIES
PLOMATOLOGY
PLONEMAS
PLOPHASE
PLOPHASES
PLOSTEMONOUS
PLOTENES
PNETTING
PPERFULS
PPINESSES
PRIONIDIAN
PROPELLANT
PROPELLANTS
PROTODON
PROTODONS
PROTODONT
PROTODONTID
PROTODONTIDS
PROTODONTS
PSOMANIA
PSOMANIAC
PSOMANIACAL
PSOMANIACS
DIPSOMANIAS
DIPTERISTS
DIPTEROCARP
DIPTEROCARPOUS
DIPTEROCARPS
DIPTEROSES
DIRECTEDNESS
DIRECTEDNESSES
DIRECTIONAL
DIRECTIONALITY
DIRECTIONLESS
DIRECTIONS
DIRECTIVES
DIRECTIVITIES
DIRECTIVITY
DIRECTNESS
DIRECTNESSES
DIRECTORATE
DIRECTORATES
DIRECTORIAL
DIRECTORIALLY
DIRECTORIES
DIRECTORSHIP
DIRECTORSHIPS
DIRECTRESS
DIRECTRESSES
DIRECTRICE
DIRECTRICES
DIRECTRIXES
DIREFULNESS
DIREFULNESSES
DIREMPTING
DIREMPTION
DIREMPTIONS
DIRENESSES
DIRIGIBILITIES
DIRIGIBILITY
DIRIGIBLES
DIRIGISMES
DIRTINESSES
DISABILITIES
DISABILITY
DISABLEMENT
DISABLEMENTS
DISABUSALS
DISABUSING
DISACCHARID
DISACCHARIDASE
DISACCHARIDASES
DISACCHARIDE
DISACCHARIDES
DISACCHARIDS
DISACCOMMODATE
DISACCOMMODATED
DISACCOMMODATES
DISACCORDANT
DISACCORDED
DISACCORDING
DISACCORDS
DISACCREDIT
DISACCREDITED
DISACCREDITING
DISACCREDITS
DISACCUSTOM
DISACCUSTOMED
DISACCUSTOMING
DISACCUSTOMS
DISACKNOWLEDGE
DISACKNOWLEDGED
DISACKNOWLEDGES
DISADORNED
DISADORNING
DISADVANCE
DISADVANCED
DISADVANCES
DISADVANCING
DISADVANTAGE
DISADVANTAGED
DISADVANTAGEOUS
DISADVANTAGES
DISADVANTAGING
DISADVENTURE
DISADVENTURES
DISADVENTUROUS
DISAFFECTED
DISAFFECTEDLY
DISAFFECTEDNESS
DISAFFECTING
DISAFFECTION
DISAFFECTIONATE
DISAFFECTIONS
DISAFFECTS
DISAFFILIATE
DISAFFILIATED
DISAFFILIATES
DISAFFILIATING
DISAFFILIATION
DISAFFILIATIONS
DISAFFIRMANCE
DISAFFIRMANCES
DISAFFIRMATION
DISAFFIRMATIONS
DISAFFIRMED
DISAFFIRMING
DISAFFIRMS
DISAFFOREST
DISAFFORESTED
DISAFFORESTING
DISAFFORESTMENT
DISAFFORESTS
DISAGGREGATE
DISAGGREGATED
DISAGGREGATES
DISAGGREGATING
DISAGGREGATION
DISAGGREGATIONS
DISAGGREGATIVE
DISAGREEABILITY
DISAGREEABLE
DISAGREEABLES
DISAGREEABLY
DISAGREEING
DISAGREEMENT
DISAGREEMENTS
DISALLOWABLE
DISALLOWANCE
DISALLOWANCES
DISALLOWED
DISALLOWING
DISALLYING
DISAMBIGUATE
DISAMBIGUATED
DISAMBIGUATES
DISAMBIGUATING
DISAMBIGUATION
DISAMBIGUATIONS
DISAMENITIES
DISAMENITY
DISANALOGIES
DISANALOGOUS
DISANALOGY
DISANCHORED
DISANCHORING
DISANCHORS
DISANIMATE
DISANIMATED
DISANIMATES
DISANIMATING
DISANNEXED
DISANNEXES
DISANNEXING
DISANNULLED
DISANNULLER
DISANNULLERS
DISANNULLING
DISANNULLINGS
DISANNULMENT
DISANNULMENTS
DISANOINTED
DISANOINTING
DISANOINTS
DISAPPAREL
DISAPPARELLED
DISAPPARELLING
DISAPPARELS
DISAPPEARANCE
DISAPPEARANCES
DISAPPEARED
DISAPPEARING
DISAPPEARS
DISAPPLICATION
DISAPPLICATIONS
DISAPPLIED
DISAPPLIES
DISAPPLYING
DISAPPOINT
DISAPPOINTED
DISAPPOINTEDLY
DISAPPOINTING
DISAPPOINTINGLY
DISAPPOINTMENT
DISAPPOINTMENTS
DISAPPOINTS
DISAPPROBATION
DISAPPROBATIONS
DISAPPROBATIVE
DISAPPROBATORY
DISAPPROPRIATE
DISAPPROPRIATED
DISAPPROPRIATES
DISAPPROVAL
DISAPPROVALS
DISAPPROVE
DISAPPROVED
DISAPPROVER
DISAPPROVERS
DISAPPROVES
DISAPPROVING

DISAPPROVINGLY
DISARMAMENT
DISARMAMENTS
DISARMINGLY
DISARRANGE
DISARRANGED
DISARRANGEMENT
DISARRANGEMENTS
DISARRANGES
DISARRANGING
DISARRAYED
DISARRAYING
DISARTICULATE
DISARTICULATED
DISARTICULATES
DISARTICULATING
DISARTICULATION
DISARTICULATOR
DISARTICULATORS
DISASSEMBLE
DISASSEMBLED
DISASSEMBLER
DISASSEMBLERS
DISASSEMBLES
DISASSEMBLIES
DISASSEMBLING
DISASSEMBLY
DISASSIMILATE
DISASSIMILATED
DISASSIMILATES
DISASSIMILATING
DISASSIMILATION
DISASSIMILATIVE
DISASSOCIATE
DISASSOCIATED
DISASSOCIATES
DISASSOCIATING
DISASSOCIATION
DISASSOCIATIONS
DISASTROUS
DISASTROUSLY
DISATTIRED
DISATTIRES
DISATTIRING
DISATTRIBUTION
DISATTRIBUTIONS
DISATTUNED
DISATTUNES
DISATTUNING
DISAUTHORISE
DISAUTHORISED
DISAUTHORISES
DISAUTHORISING
DISAUTHORIZE
DISAUTHORIZED
DISAUTHORIZES
DISAUTHORIZING
DISAVAUNCE
DISAVAUNCED
DISAVAUNCES
DISAVAUNCING
DISAVENTROUS
DISAVENTURE
DISAVENTURES
DISAVOUCHED
DISAVOUCHES
DISAVOUCHING
DISAVOWABLE
DISAVOWALS
DISAVOWEDLY
DISAVOWERS
DISAVOWING
DISBANDING
DISBANDMENT
DISBANDMENTS
DISBARKING
DISBARMENT
DISBARMENTS
DISBARRING
DISBELIEFS
DISBELIEVE
DISBELIEVED
DISBELIEVER
DISBELIEVERS
DISBELIEVES
DISBELIEVING
DISBELIEVINGLY
DISBENCHED
DISBENCHES
DISBENCHING
DISBENEFIT
DISBENEFITS
DISBOSOMED
DISBOSOMING
DISBOWELED
DISBOWELING
DISBOWELLED
DISBOWELLING
DISBRANCHED
DISBRANCHES
DISBRANCHING
DISBUDDING
DISBURDENED
DISBURDENING
DISBURDENMENT
DISBURDENMENTS
DISBURDENS
DISBURSABLE
DISBURSALS
DISBURSEMENT
DISBURSEMENTS
DISBURSERS
DISBURSING
DISBURTHEN
DISBURTHENED
DISBURTHENING
DISBURTHENS
DISCALCEATE
DISCALCEATES
DISCANDERING
DISCANDERINGS
DISCANDIED
DISCANDIES
DISCANDYING
DISCANDYINGS
DISCANTERS
DISCANTING
DISCAPACITATE
DISCAPACITATED
DISCAPACITATES
DISCAPACITATING
DISCARDABLE
DISCARDERS
DISCARDING
DISCARDMENT
DISCARDMENTS
DISCARNATE
DISCEPTATION
DISCEPTATIONS
DISCEPTATIOUS
DISCEPTATOR
DISCEPTATORIAL
DISCEPTATORS
DISCEPTING
DISCERNABLE
DISCERNABLY
DISCERNERS
DISCERNIBLE
DISCERNIBLY
DISCERNING
DISCERNINGLY
DISCERNMENT
DISCERNMENTS
DISCERPIBILITY
DISCERPIBLE
DISCERPING
DISCERPTIBLE
DISCERPTION
DISCERPTIONS
DISCERPTIVE
DISCHARGEABLE
DISCHARGED
DISCHARGEE
DISCHARGEES
DISCHARGER
DISCHARGERS
DISCHARGES
DISCHARGING
DISCHUFFED
DISCHURCHED
DISCHURCHES
DISCHURCHING
DISCIPLESHIP
DISCIPLESHIPS
DISCIPLINABLE
DISCIPLINAL
DISCIPLINANT
DISCIPLINANTS
DISCIPLINARIAN
DISCIPLINARIANS
DISCIPLINARILY
DISCIPLINARITY
DISCIPLINARIUM
DISCIPLINARIUMS
DISCIPLINARY
DISCIPLINE
DISCIPLINED
DISCIPLINER
DISCIPLINERS
DISCIPLINES
DISCIPLING
DISCIPLINING
DISCIPULAR
DISCISSION
DISCISSIONS
DISCLAIMED
DISCLAIMER
DISCLAIMERS
DISCLAIMING
DISCLAMATION
DISCLAMATIONS
DISCLIMAXES
DISCLOSERS
DISCLOSING
DISCLOSURE
DISCLOSURES
DISCOBOLOS
DISCOBOLUS
DISCOBOLUSES
DISCOGRAPHER
DISCOGRAPHERS
DISCOGRAPHIC
DISCOGRAPHICAL
DISCOGRAPHIES
DISCOGRAPHY
DISCOLOGIES
DISCOLOGIST
DISCOLOGISTS
DISCOLORATION
DISCOLORATIONS
DISCOLORED
DISCOLORING
DISCOLORMENT
DISCOLORMENTS
DISCOLOURATION
DISCOLOURATIONS
DISCOLOURED
DISCOLOURING
DISCOLOURMENT
DISCOLOURMENTS
DISCOLOURS
DISCOMBOBERATE
DISCOMBOBERATED
DISCOMBOBERATES
DISCOMBOBULATE
DISCOMBOBULATED
DISCOMBOBULATES
DISCOMEDUSAN
DISCOMEDUSANS
DISCOMFITED
DISCOMFITER
DISCOMFITERS
DISCOMFITING
DISCOMFITS
DISCOMFITURE
DISCOMFITURES
DISCOMFORT
DISCOMFORTABLE
DISCOMFORTED
DISCOMFORTING
DISCOMFORTS
DISCOMMEND
DISCOMMENDABLE
DISCOMMENDATION
DISCOMMENDED
DISCOMMENDING
DISCOMMENDS
DISCOMMISSION
DISCOMMISSIONED
DISCOMMISSIONS
DISCOMMODE
DISCOMMODED
DISCOMMODES
DISCOMMODING

DISCOMMODIOUS
DISCOMMODIOUSLY
DISCOMMODITIES
DISCOMMODITY
DISCOMMONED
DISCOMMONING
DISCOMMONS
DISCOMMUNITIES
DISCOMMUNITY
DISCOMPOSE
DISCOMPOSED
DISCOMPOSEDLY
DISCOMPOSES
DISCOMPOSING
DISCOMPOSINGLY
DISCOMPOSURE
DISCOMPOSURES
DISCOMYCETE
DISCOMYCETES
DISCOMYCETOUS
DISCONCERT
DISCONCERTED
DISCONCERTEDLY
DISCONCERTING
DISCONCERTINGLY
DISCONCERTION
DISCONCERTIONS
DISCONCERTMENT
DISCONCERTMENTS
DISCONCERTS
DISCONFIRM
DISCONFIRMATION
DISCONFIRMED
DISCONFIRMING
DISCONFIRMS
DISCONFORMABLE
DISCONFORMITIES
DISCONFORMITY
DISCONNECT
DISCONNECTED
DISCONNECTEDLY
DISCONNECTER
DISCONNECTERS
DISCONNECTING
DISCONNECTION
DISCONNECTIONS
DISCONNECTIVE
DISCONNECTS
DISCONNEXION
DISCONNEXIONS
DISCONSENT
DISCONSENTED
DISCONSENTING
DISCONSENTS
DISCONSOLATE
DISCONSOLATELY
DISCONSOLATION
DISCONSOLATIONS
DISCONTENT
DISCONTENTED
DISCONTENTEDLY
DISCONTENTFUL
DISCONTENTING
DISCONTENTMENT
DISCONTENTMENTS
DISCONTENTS
DISCONTIGUITIES
DISCONTIGUITY
DISCONTIGUOUS
DISCONTINUANCE
DISCONTINUANCES
DISCONTINUATION
DISCONTINUE
DISCONTINUED
DISCONTINUER
DISCONTINUERS
DISCONTINUES
DISCONTINUING
DISCONTINUITIES
DISCONTINUITY
DISCONTINUOUS
DISCONTINUOUSLY
DISCOPHILE
DISCOPHILES
DISCOPHORAN
DISCOPHORANS
DISCOPHOROUS
DISCORDANCE
DISCORDANCES
DISCORDANCIES
DISCORDANCY
DISCORDANT
DISCORDANTLY
DISCORDFUL
DISCORDING
DISCORPORATE
DISCOTHEQUE
DISCOTHEQUES
DISCOUNSEL
DISCOUNSELLED
DISCOUNSELLING
DISCOUNSELS
DISCOUNTABLE
DISCOUNTED
DISCOUNTENANCE
DISCOUNTENANCED
DISCOUNTENANCES
DISCOUNTER
DISCOUNTERS
DISCOUNTING
DISCOURAGE
DISCOURAGEABLE
DISCOURAGED
DISCOURAGEMENT
DISCOURAGEMENTS
DISCOURAGER
DISCOURAGERS
DISCOURAGES
DISCOURAGING
DISCOURAGINGLY
DISCOURAGINGS
DISCOURING
DISCOURSAL
DISCOURSED
DISCOURSER
DISCOURSERS
DISCOURSES
DISCOURSING
DISCOURSIVE
DISCOURTEISE
DISCOURTEOUS
DISCOURTEOUSLY
DISCOURTESIES
DISCOURTESY
DISCOVERABLE
DISCOVERED
DISCOVERER
DISCOVERERS
DISCOVERIES
DISCOVERING
DISCOVERTURE
DISCOVERTURES
DISCREDITABLE
DISCREDITABLY
DISCREDITED
DISCREDITING
DISCREDITS
DISCREETER
DISCREETEST
DISCREETLY
DISCREETNESS
DISCREETNESSES
DISCREPANCE
DISCREPANCES
DISCREPANCIES
DISCREPANCY
DISCREPANT
DISCREPANTLY
DISCRETELY
DISCRETENESS
DISCRETENESSES
DISCRETEST
DISCRETION
DISCRETIONAL
DISCRETIONALLY
DISCRETIONARILY
DISCRETIONARY
DISCRETIONS
DISCRETIVE
DISCRETIVELY
DISCRIMINABLE
DISCRIMINABLY
DISCRIMINANT
DISCRIMINANTS
DISCRIMINATE
DISCRIMINATED
DISCRIMINATELY
DISCRIMINATES
DISCRIMINATING
DISCRIMINATION
DISCRIMINATIONS
DISCRIMINATIVE
DISCRIMINATOR
DISCRIMINATORS
DISCRIMINATORY
DISCROWNED
DISCROWNING
DISCULPATE
DISCULPATED
DISCULPATES
DISCULPATING
DISCUMBERED
DISCUMBERING
DISCUMBERS
DISCURSION
DISCURSIONS
DISCURSIST
DISCURSISTS
DISCURSIVE
DISCURSIVELY
DISCURSIVENESS
DISCURSORY
DISCURSUSES
DISCUSSABLE
DISCUSSANT
DISCUSSANTS
DISCUSSERS
DISCUSSIBLE
DISCUSSING
DISCUSSION
DISCUSSIONAL
DISCUSSIONS
DISCUSSIVE
DISCUTIENT
DISCUTIENTS
DISDAINFUL
DISDAINFULLY
DISDAINFULNESS
DISDAINING
DISEASEDNESS
DISEASEDNESSES
DISEASEFUL
DISECONOMIES
DISECONOMY
DISEMBARKATION
DISEMBARKATIONS
DISEMBARKED
DISEMBARKING
DISEMBARKMENT
DISEMBARKMENTS
DISEMBARKS
DISEMBARRASS
DISEMBARRASSED
DISEMBARRASSES
DISEMBARRASSING
DISEMBELLISH
DISEMBELLISHED
DISEMBELLISHES
DISEMBELLISHING
DISEMBITTER
DISEMBITTERED
DISEMBITTERING
DISEMBITTERS
DISEMBODIED
DISEMBODIES
DISEMBODIMENT
DISEMBODIMENTS
DISEMBODYING
DISEMBOGUE
DISEMBOGUED
DISEMBOGUEMENT
DISEMBOGUEMENTS
DISEMBOGUES
DISEMBOGUING
DISEMBOSOM
DISEMBOSOMED
DISEMBOSOMING
DISEMBOSOMS
DISEMBOWEL
DISEMBOWELED
DISEMBOWELING
DISEMBOWELLED
DISEMBOWELLING
DISEMBOWELMENT

DISEMBOWELMENTS
DISEMBOWELS
DISEMBRANGLE
DISEMBRANGLED
DISEMBRANGLES
DISEMBRANGLING
DISEMBROIL
DISEMBROILED
DISEMBROILING
DISEMBROILS
DISEMBURDEN
DISEMBURDENED
DISEMBURDENING
DISEMBURDENS
DISEMPLOYED
DISEMPLOYING
DISEMPLOYMENT
DISEMPLOYMENTS
DISEMPLOYS
DISEMPOWER
DISEMPOWERED
DISEMPOWERING
DISEMPOWERMENT
DISEMPOWERMENTS
DISEMPOWERS
DISENABLED
DISENABLEMENT
DISENABLEMENTS
DISENABLES
DISENABLING
DISENCHAIN
DISENCHAINED
DISENCHAINING
DISENCHAINS
DISENCHANT
DISENCHANTED
DISENCHANTER
DISENCHANTERS
DISENCHANTING
DISENCHANTINGLY
DISENCHANTMENT
DISENCHANTMENTS
DISENCHANTRESS
DISENCHANTS
DISENCLOSE
DISENCLOSED
DISENCLOSES
DISENCLOSING
DISENCUMBER
DISENCUMBERED
DISENCUMBERING
DISENCUMBERMENT
DISENCUMBERS
DISENCUMBRANCE
DISENCUMBRANCES
DISENDOWED
DISENDOWER
DISENDOWERS
DISENDOWING
DISENDOWMENT
DISENDOWMENTS
DISENFRANCHISE
DISENFRANCHISED
DISENFRANCHISES
DISENGAGED
DISENGAGEDNESS
DISENGAGEMENT
DISENGAGEMENTS
DISENGAGES
DISENGAGING
DISENNOBLE
DISENNOBLED
DISENNOBLES
DISENNOBLING
DISENROLLED
DISENROLLING
DISENSHROUD
DISENSHROUDED
DISENSHROUDING
DISENSHROUDS
DISENSLAVE
DISENSLAVED
DISENSLAVES
DISENSLAVING
DISENTAILED
DISENTAILING
DISENTAILMENT
DISENTAILMENTS
DISENTAILS
DISENTANGLE
DISENTANGLED
DISENTANGLEMENT
DISENTANGLES
DISENTANGLING
DISENTHRAL
DISENTHRALL
DISENTHRALLED
DISENTHRALLING
DISENTHRALLMENT
DISENTHRALLS
DISENTHRALMENT
DISENTHRALMENTS
DISENTHRALS
DISENTHRONE
DISENTHRONED
DISENTHRONES
DISENTHRONING
DISENTITLE
DISENTITLED
DISENTITLES
DISENTITLING
DISENTOMBED
DISENTOMBING
DISENTOMBS
DISENTRAIL
DISENTRAILED
DISENTRAILING
DISENTRAILS
DISENTRAIN
DISENTRAINED
DISENTRAINING
DISENTRAINMENT
DISENTRAINMENTS
DISENTRAINS
DISENTRANCE
DISENTRANCED
DISENTRANCEMENT
DISENTRANCES
DISENTRANCING
DISENTRAYLE
DISENTRAYLED
DISENTRAYLES
DISENTRAYLING
DISENTWINE
DISENTWINED
DISENTWINES
DISENTWINING
DISENVELOP
DISENVELOPED
DISENVELOPING
DISENVELOPS
DISENVIRON
DISENVIRONED
DISENVIRONING
DISENVIRONS
DISEPALOUS
DISEQUILIBRATE
DISEQUILIBRATED
DISEQUILIBRATES
DISEQUILIBRIA
DISEQUILIBRIUM
DISEQUILIBRIUMS
DISESPOUSE
DISESPOUSED
DISESPOUSES
DISESPOUSING
DISESTABLISH
DISESTABLISHED
DISESTABLISHES
DISESTABLISHING
DISESTEEMED
DISESTEEMING
DISESTEEMS
DISESTIMATION
DISESTIMATIONS
DISFAVORED
DISFAVORING
DISFAVOURED
DISFAVOURER
DISFAVOURERS
DISFAVOURING
DISFAVOURS
DISFEATURE
DISFEATURED
DISFEATUREMENT
DISFEATUREMENTS
DISFEATURES
DISFEATURING
DISFELLOWSHIP
DISFELLOWSHIPS
DISFIGURATION
DISFIGURATIONS
DISFIGURED
DISFIGUREMENT
DISFIGUREMENTS
DISFIGURER
DISFIGURERS
DISFIGURES
DISFIGURING
DISFLESHED
DISFLESHES
DISFLESHING
DISFLUENCIES
DISFLUENCY
DISFORESTATION
DISFORESTATIONS
DISFORESTED
DISFORESTING
DISFORESTS
DISFORMING
DISFRANCHISE
DISFRANCHISED
DISFRANCHISES
DISFRANCHISING
DISFROCKED
DISFROCKING
DISFUNCTION
DISFUNCTIONS
DISFURNISH
DISFURNISHED
DISFURNISHES
DISFURNISHING
DISFURNISHMENT
DISFURNISHMENTS
DISGARNISH
DISGARNISHED
DISGARNISHES
DISGARNISHING
DISGARRISON
DISGARRISONED
DISGARRISONING
DISGARRISONS
DISGAVELLED
DISGAVELLING
DISGESTING
DISGESTION
DISGESTIONS
DISGLORIFIED
DISGLORIFIES
DISGLORIFY
DISGLORIFYING
DISGORGEMENT
DISGORGEMENTS
DISGORGERS
DISGORGING
DISGOSPELLING
DISGOWNING
DISGRACEFUL
DISGRACEFULLY
DISGRACEFULNESS
DISGRACERS
DISGRACING
DISGRACIOUS
DISGRADATION
DISGRADATIONS
DISGRADING
DISGREGATION
DISGREGATIONS
DISGRUNTLE
DISGRUNTLED
DISGRUNTLEMENT
DISGRUNTLEMENTS
DISGRUNTLES
DISGRUNTLING
DISGUISABLE
DISGUISEDLY
DISGUISEDNESS
DISGUISEDNESSES
DISGUISELESS
DISGUISEMENT
DISGUISEMENTS
DISGUISERS
DISGUISING
DISGUISINGS

ISGUSTEDLY
ISGUSTEDNESS
ISGUSTEDNESSES
ISGUSTFUL
ISGUSTFULLY
ISGUSTFULNESS
ISGUSTING
ISGUSTINGLY
ISGUSTINGNESS
ISHABILITATE
ISHABILITATED
ISHABILITATES
ISHABILITATING
ISHABILITATION
ISHABILLE
ISHABILLES
ISHABITED
ISHABITING
ISHABLING
ISHALLOWED
ISHALLOWING
ISHALLOWS
ISHARMONIC
ISHARMONIES
ISHARMONIOUS
ISHARMONIOUSLY
ISHARMONISE
ISHARMONISED
ISHARMONISES
ISHARMONISING
ISHARMONIZE
ISHARMONIZED
ISHARMONIZES
ISHARMONIZING
ISHARMONY
ISHCLOTHS
ISHCLOUTS
ISHDASHAS
ISHEARTEN
ISHEARTENED
ISHEARTENING
ISHEARTENINGLY
ISHEARTENMENT
ISHEARTENMENTS
ISHEARTENS
ISHELMING
ISHERISON
ISHERISONS
ISHERITED
ISHERITING
ISHERITOR
ISHERITORS
ISHEVELED
ISHEVELING
ISHEVELLED
ISHEVELLING
ISHEVELMENT
ISHEVELMENTS
ISHONESTIES
ISHONESTLY
ISHONESTY
ISHONORABLE
ISHONORABLY
ISHONORARY
ISHONORED
ISHONORER
DISHONORERS
DISHONORING
DISHONOURABLE
DISHONOURABLY
DISHONOURED
DISHONOURER
DISHONOURERS
DISHONOURING
DISHONOURS
DISHORNING
DISHORSING
DISHOUSING
DISHTOWELS
DISHUMOURED
DISHUMOURING
DISHUMOURS
DISHWASHER
DISHWASHERS
DISHWATERS
DISILLUDED
DISILLUDES
DISILLUDING
DISILLUMINATE
DISILLUMINATED
DISILLUMINATES
DISILLUMINATING
DISILLUSION
DISILLUSIONARY
DISILLUSIONED
DISILLUSIONING
DISILLUSIONISE
DISILLUSIONISED
DISILLUSIONISES
DISILLUSIONIZE
DISILLUSIONIZED
DISILLUSIONIZES
DISILLUSIONMENT
DISILLUSIONS
DISILLUSIVE
DISIMAGINE
DISIMAGINED
DISIMAGINES
DISIMAGINING
DISIMMURED
DISIMMURES
DISIMMURING
DISIMPASSIONED
DISIMPRISON
DISIMPRISONED
DISIMPRISONING
DISIMPRISONMENT
DISIMPRISONS
DISIMPROVE
DISIMPROVED
DISIMPROVES
DISIMPROVING
DISINCARCERATE
DISINCARCERATED
DISINCARCERATES
DISINCENTIVE
DISINCENTIVES
DISINCLINATION
DISINCLINATIONS
DISINCLINE
DISINCLINED
DISINCLINES
DISINCLINING
DISINCLOSE
DISINCLOSED
DISINCLOSES
DISINCLOSING
DISINCORPORATE
DISINCORPORATED
DISINCORPORATES
DISINFECTANT
DISINFECTANTS
DISINFECTED
DISINFECTING
DISINFECTION
DISINFECTIONS
DISINFECTOR
DISINFECTORS
DISINFECTS
DISINFESTANT
DISINFESTANTS
DISINFESTATION
DISINFESTATIONS
DISINFESTED
DISINFESTING
DISINFESTS
DISINFLATION
DISINFLATIONARY
DISINFLATIONS
DISINFORMATION
DISINFORMATIONS
DISINFORMED
DISINFORMING
DISINFORMS
DISINGENUITIES
DISINGENUITY
DISINGENUOUS
DISINGENUOUSLY
DISINHERISON
DISINHERISONS
DISINHERIT
DISINHERITANCE
DISINHERITANCES
DISINHERITED
DISINHERITING
DISINHERITS
DISINHIBIT
DISINHIBITED
DISINHIBITING
DISINHIBITION
DISINHIBITIONS
DISINHIBITORY
DISINHIBITS
DISINHUMED
DISINHUMES
DISINHUMING
DISINTEGRABLE
DISINTEGRATE
DISINTEGRATED
DISINTEGRATES
DISINTEGRATING
DISINTEGRATION
DISINTEGRATIONS
DISINTEGRATIVE
DISINTEGRATOR
DISINTEGRATORS
DISINTEREST
DISINTERESTED
DISINTERESTEDLY
DISINTERESTING
DISINTERESTS
DISINTERMENT
DISINTERMENTS
DISINTERRED
DISINTERRING
DISINTHRAL
DISINTHRALLED
DISINTHRALLING
DISINTHRALS
DISINTOXICATE
DISINTOXICATED
DISINTOXICATES
DISINTOXICATING
DISINTOXICATION
DISINTRICATE
DISINTRICATED
DISINTRICATES
DISINTRICATING
DISINURING
DISINVESTED
DISINVESTING
DISINVESTITURE
DISINVESTITURES
DISINVESTMENT
DISINVESTMENTS
DISINVESTS
DISINVIGORATE
DISINVIGORATED
DISINVIGORATES
DISINVIGORATING
DISINVITED
DISINVITES
DISINVITING
DISINVOLVE
DISINVOLVED
DISINVOLVES
DISINVOLVING
DISJECTING
DISJECTION
DISJECTIONS
DISJOINABLE
DISJOINING
DISJOINTED
DISJOINTEDLY
DISJOINTEDNESS
DISJOINTING
DISJUNCTION
DISJUNCTIONS
DISJUNCTIVE
DISJUNCTIVELY
DISJUNCTIVES
DISJUNCTOR
DISJUNCTORS
DISJUNCTURE
DISJUNCTURES
DISLEAFING
DISLEAVING
DISLIKABLE
DISLIKEABLE
DISLIKEFUL
DISLIKENED
DISLIKENESS
DISLIKENESSES
DISLIKENING

DISLIMBING
DISLIMNING
DISLINKING
DISLOADING
DISLOCATED
DISLOCATEDLY
DISLOCATES
DISLOCATING
DISLOCATION
DISLOCATIONS
DISLODGEMENT
DISLODGEMENTS
DISLODGING
DISLODGMENT
DISLODGMENTS
DISLOIGNED
DISLOIGNING
DISLOYALLY
DISLOYALTIES
DISLOYALTY
DISLUSTRED
DISLUSTRES
DISLUSTRING
DISMALITIES
DISMALLEST
DISMALNESS
DISMALNESSES
DISMANNING
DISMANTLED
DISMANTLEMENT
DISMANTLEMENTS
DISMANTLER
DISMANTLERS
DISMANTLES
DISMANTLING
DISMASKING
DISMASTING
DISMASTMENT
DISMASTMENTS
DISMAYEDNESS
DISMAYEDNESSES
DISMAYFULLY
DISMAYINGLY
DISMAYLING
DISMEMBERED
DISMEMBERER
DISMEMBERERS
DISMEMBERING
DISMEMBERMENT
DISMEMBERMENTS
DISMEMBERS
DISMISSALS
DISMISSIBLE
DISMISSING
DISMISSION
DISMISSIONS
DISMISSIVE
DISMISSIVELY
DISMISSORY
DISMOUNTABLE
DISMOUNTED
DISMOUNTING
DISMUTATION
DISMUTATIONS
DISNATURALISE
DISNATURALISED
DISNATURALISES
DISNATURALISING
DISNATURALIZE
DISNATURALIZED
DISNATURALIZES
DISNATURALIZING
DISNATURED
DISNESTING
DISOBEDIENCE
DISOBEDIENCES
DISOBEDIENT
DISOBEDIENTLY
DISOBEYERS
DISOBEYING
DISOBLIGATION
DISOBLIGATIONS
DISOBLIGATORY
DISOBLIGED
DISOBLIGEMENT
DISOBLIGEMENTS
DISOBLIGES
DISOBLIGING
DISOBLIGINGLY
DISOBLIGINGNESS
DISOPERATION
DISOPERATIONS
DISORDERED
DISORDEREDLY
DISORDEREDNESS
DISORDERING
DISORDERLIES
DISORDERLINESS
DISORDERLY
DISORDINATE
DISORDINATELY
DISORGANIC
DISORGANISATION
DISORGANISE
DISORGANISED
DISORGANISER
DISORGANISERS
DISORGANISES
DISORGANISING
DISORGANIZATION
DISORGANIZE
DISORGANIZED
DISORGANIZER
DISORGANIZERS
DISORGANIZES
DISORGANIZING
DISORIENTATE
DISORIENTATED
DISORIENTATES
DISORIENTATING
DISORIENTATION
DISORIENTATIONS
DISORIENTED
DISORIENTING
DISORIENTS
DISOWNMENT
DISOWNMENTS
DISPARAGED
DISPARAGEMENT
DISPARAGEMENTS
DISPARAGER
DISPARAGERS
DISPARAGES
DISPARAGING
DISPARAGINGLY
DISPARATELY
DISPARATENESS
DISPARATENESSES
DISPARATES
DISPARITIES
DISPARKING
DISPARTING
DISPASSION
DISPASSIONATE
DISPASSIONATELY
DISPASSIONS
DISPATCHED
DISPATCHER
DISPATCHERS
DISPATCHES
DISPATCHFUL
DISPATCHING
DISPATHIES
DISPAUPERED
DISPAUPERING
DISPAUPERISE
DISPAUPERISED
DISPAUPERISES
DISPAUPERISING
DISPAUPERIZE
DISPAUPERIZED
DISPAUPERIZES
DISPAUPERIZING
DISPAUPERS
DISPELLERS
DISPELLING
DISPENCING
DISPENDING
DISPENSABILITY
DISPENSABLE
DISPENSABLENESS
DISPENSABLY
DISPENSARIES
DISPENSARY
DISPENSATION
DISPENSATIONAL
DISPENSATIONS
DISPENSATIVE
DISPENSATIVELY
DISPENSATOR
DISPENSATORIES
DISPENSATORILY
DISPENSATORS
DISPENSATORY
DISPENSERS
DISPENSING
DISPEOPLED
DISPEOPLES
DISPEOPLING
DISPERMOUS
DISPERSALS
DISPERSANT
DISPERSANTS
DISPERSEDLY
DISPERSEDNESS
DISPERSEDNESSES
DISPERSERS
DISPERSIBLE
DISPERSING
DISPERSION
DISPERSIONS
DISPERSIVE
DISPERSIVELY
DISPERSIVENESS
DISPERSOID
DISPERSOIDS
DISPIRITED
DISPIRITEDLY
DISPIRITEDNESS
DISPIRITING
DISPIRITINGLY
DISPIRITMENT
DISPIRITMENTS
DISPITEOUS
DISPITEOUSLY
DISPITEOUSNESS
DISPLACEABLE
DISPLACEMENT
DISPLACEMENTS
DISPLACERS
DISPLACING
DISPLANTATION
DISPLANTATIONS
DISPLANTED
DISPLANTING
DISPLAYABLE
DISPLAYERS
DISPLAYING
DISPLEASANCE
DISPLEASANCES
DISPLEASANT
DISPLEASED
DISPLEASEDLY
DISPLEASEDNESS
DISPLEASES
DISPLEASING
DISPLEASINGLY
DISPLEASINGNESS
DISPLEASURE
DISPLEASURED
DISPLEASURES
DISPLEASURING
DISPLENISH
DISPLENISHED
DISPLENISHES
DISPLENISHING
DISPLENISHMENT
DISPLENISHMENTS
DISPLODING
DISPLOSION
DISPLOSIONS
DISPLUMING
DISPONDAIC
DISPONDEES
DISPONGING
DISPORTING
DISPORTMENT
DISPORTMENTS
DISPOSABILITIES
DISPOSABILITY
DISPOSABLE
DISPOSABLENESS
DISPOSABLES
DISPOSEDLY

ISPOSINGLY
ISPOSINGS
ISPOSITION
ISPOSITIONAL
ISPOSITIONED
ISPOSITIONS
ISPOSITIVE
ISPOSITIVELY
ISPOSITOR
ISPOSITORS
ISPOSSESS
ISPOSSESSED
ISPOSSESSES
ISPOSSESSING
ISPOSSESSION
ISPOSSESSIONS
ISPOSSESSOR
ISPOSSESSORS
ISPOSSESSORY
ISPOSTING
ISPOSURES
ISPRAISED
ISPRAISER
ISPRAISERS
ISPRAISES
ISPRAISING
ISPRAISINGLY
ISPREADING
ISPREDDEN
ISPREDDING
ISPRINCED
ISPRISONED
ISPRISONING
ISPRISONS
ISPRIVACIED
ISPRIVILEGE
ISPRIVILEGED
ISPRIVILEGES
ISPRIVILEGING
ISPRIZING
ISPROFESS
ISPROFESSED
ISPROFESSES
ISPROFESSING
ISPROFITS
ISPROOVED
ISPROOVES
ISPROOVING
ISPROPERTIED
ISPROPERTIES
ISPROPERTY
ISPROPERTYING
ISPROPORTION
ISPROPORTIONAL
ISPROPORTIONED
ISPROPORTIONS
ISPROPRIATE
ISPROPRIATED
ISPROPRIATES
ISPROPRIATING
ISPROVABLE
ISPROVALS
ISPROVERS
ISPROVIDE
ISPROVIDED
ISPROVIDES
DISPROVIDING
DISPROVING
DISPUNGING
DISPURSING
DISPURVEYANCE
DISPURVEYANCES
DISPURVEYED
DISPURVEYING
DISPURVEYS
DISPUTABILITIES
DISPUTABILITY
DISPUTABLE
DISPUTABLENESS
DISPUTABLY
DISPUTANTS
DISPUTATION
DISPUTATIONS
DISPUTATIOUS
DISPUTATIOUSLY
DISPUTATIVE
DISPUTATIVELY
DISPUTATIVENESS
DISQUALIFIABLE
DISQUALIFIED
DISQUALIFIER
DISQUALIFIERS
DISQUALIFIES
DISQUALIFY
DISQUALIFYING
DISQUANTITIED
DISQUANTITIES
DISQUANTITY
DISQUANTITYING
DISQUIETED
DISQUIETEDLY
DISQUIETEDNESS
DISQUIETEN
DISQUIETENED
DISQUIETENING
DISQUIETENS
DISQUIETFUL
DISQUIETING
DISQUIETINGLY
DISQUIETIVE
DISQUIETLY
DISQUIETNESS
DISQUIETNESSES
DISQUIETOUS
DISQUIETUDE
DISQUIETUDES
DISQUISITION
DISQUISITIONAL
DISQUISITIONARY
DISQUISITIONS
DISQUISITIVE
DISQUISITORY
DISRANKING
DISREGARDED
DISREGARDER
DISREGARDERS
DISREGARDFUL
DISREGARDFULLY
DISREGARDING
DISREGARDS
DISRELATED
DISRELATION
DISRELATIONS
DISRELISHED
DISRELISHES
DISRELISHING
DISREMEMBER
DISREMEMBERED
DISREMEMBERING
DISREMEMBERS
DISREPAIRS
DISREPUTABILITY
DISREPUTABLE
DISREPUTABLY
DISREPUTATION
DISREPUTATIONS
DISREPUTES
DISRESPECT
DISRESPECTABLE
DISRESPECTED
DISRESPECTFUL
DISRESPECTFULLY
DISRESPECTING
DISRESPECTS
DISROBEMENT
DISROBEMENTS
DISROOTING
DISRUPTERS
DISRUPTING
DISRUPTION
DISRUPTIONS
DISRUPTIVE
DISRUPTIVELY
DISRUPTIVENESS
DISRUPTORS
DISSATISFACTION
DISSATISFACTORY
DISSATISFIED
DISSATISFIEDLY
DISSATISFIES
DISSATISFY
DISSATISFYING
DISSAVINGS
DISSEATING
DISSECTIBLE
DISSECTING
DISSECTINGS
DISSECTION
DISSECTIONS
DISSECTIVE
DISSECTORS
DISSEISEES
DISSEISING
DISSEISINS
DISSEISORS
DISSEIZEES
DISSEIZING
DISSEIZINS
DISSEIZORS
DISSELBOOM
DISSELBOOMS
DISSEMBLANCE
DISSEMBLANCES
DISSEMBLED
DISSEMBLER
DISSEMBLERS
DISSEMBLES
DISSEMBLIES
DISSEMBLING
DISSEMBLINGLY
DISSEMBLINGS
DISSEMINATE
DISSEMINATED
DISSEMINATES
DISSEMINATING
DISSEMINATION
DISSEMINATIONS
DISSEMINATIVE
DISSEMINATOR
DISSEMINATORS
DISSEMINULE
DISSEMINULES
DISSENSION
DISSENSIONS
DISSENSUSES
DISSENTERISH
DISSENTERISM
DISSENTERISMS
DISSENTERS
DISSENTIENCE
DISSENTIENCES
DISSENTIENCIES
DISSENTIENCY
DISSENTIENT
DISSENTIENTLY
DISSENTIENTS
DISSENTING
DISSENTINGLY
DISSENTION
DISSENTIONS
DISSENTIOUS
DISSEPIMENT
DISSEPIMENTAL
DISSEPIMENTS
DISSERTATE
DISSERTATED
DISSERTATES
DISSERTATING
DISSERTATION
DISSERTATIONAL
DISSERTATIONIST
DISSERTATIONS
DISSERTATIVE
DISSERTATOR
DISSERTATORS
DISSERTING
DISSERVICE
DISSERVICEABLE
DISSERVICES
DISSERVING
DISSEVERANCE
DISSEVERANCES
DISSEVERATION
DISSEVERATIONS
DISSEVERED
DISSEVERING
DISSEVERMENT
DISSEVERMENTS
DISSHEATHE
DISSHEATHED
DISSHEATHES
DISSHEATHING
DISSHIVERED
DISSHIVERING

DISSHIVERS
DISSIDENCE
DISSIDENCES
DISSIDENTLY
DISSIDENTS
DISSILIENCE
DISSILIENCES
DISSILIENT
DISSIMILAR
DISSIMILARITIES
DISSIMILARITY
DISSIMILARLY
DISSIMILARS
DISSIMILATE
DISSIMILATED
DISSIMILATES
DISSIMILATING
DISSIMILATION
DISSIMILATIONS
DISSIMILATIVE
DISSIMILATORY
DISSIMILES
DISSIMILITUDE
DISSIMILITUDES
DISSIMULATE
DISSIMULATED
DISSIMULATES
DISSIMULATING
DISSIMULATION
DISSIMULATIONS
DISSIMULATIVE
DISSIMULATOR
DISSIMULATORS
DISSIPABLE
DISSIPATED
DISSIPATEDLY
DISSIPATEDNESS
DISSIPATER
DISSIPATERS
DISSIPATES
DISSIPATING
DISSIPATION
DISSIPATIONS
DISSIPATIVE
DISSIPATOR
DISSIPATORS
DISSOCIABILITY
DISSOCIABLE
DISSOCIABLENESS
DISSOCIABLY
DISSOCIALISE
DISSOCIALISED
DISSOCIALISES
DISSOCIALISING
DISSOCIALITIES
DISSOCIALITY
DISSOCIALIZE
DISSOCIALIZED
DISSOCIALIZES
DISSOCIALIZING
DISSOCIATE
DISSOCIATED
DISSOCIATES
DISSOCIATING
DISSOCIATION
DISSOCIATIONS
DISSOCIATIVE
DISSOLUBILITIES
DISSOLUBILITY
DISSOLUBLE
DISSOLUBLENESS
DISSOLUTELY
DISSOLUTENESS
DISSOLUTENESSES
DISSOLUTES
DISSOLUTION
DISSOLUTIONISM
DISSOLUTIONISMS
DISSOLUTIONIST
DISSOLUTIONISTS
DISSOLUTIONS
DISSOLUTIVE
DISSOLVABILITY
DISSOLVABLE
DISSOLVABLENESS
DISSOLVENT
DISSOLVENTS
DISSOLVERS
DISSOLVING
DISSOLVINGS
DISSONANCE
DISSONANCES
DISSONANCIES
DISSONANCY
DISSONANTLY
DISSUADABLE
DISSUADERS
DISSUADING
DISSUASION
DISSUASIONS
DISSUASIVE
DISSUASIVELY
DISSUASIVENESS
DISSUASIVES
DISSUASORIES
DISSUASORY
DISSUNDERED
DISSUNDERING
DISSUNDERS
DISSYLLABIC
DISSYLLABLE
DISSYLLABLES
DISSYMMETRIC
DISSYMMETRICAL
DISSYMMETRIES
DISSYMMETRY
DISTAINING
DISTANCELESS
DISTANCING
DISTANTNESS
DISTANTNESSES
DISTASTEFUL
DISTASTEFULLY
DISTASTEFULNESS
DISTASTING
DISTELFINK
DISTELFINKS
DISTEMPERATE
DISTEMPERATURE
DISTEMPERATURES
DISTEMPERED
DISTEMPERING
DISTEMPERS
DISTENDERS
DISTENDING
DISTENSIBILITY
DISTENSIBLE
DISTENSILE
DISTENSION
DISTENSIONS
DISTENSIVE
DISTENTION
DISTENTIONS
DISTHRONED
DISTHRONES
DISTHRONING
DISTHRONISE
DISTHRONISED
DISTHRONISES
DISTHRONISING
DISTHRONIZE
DISTHRONIZED
DISTHRONIZES
DISTHRONIZING
DISTICHOUS
DISTICHOUSLY
DISTILLABLE
DISTILLAND
DISTILLANDS
DISTILLATE
DISTILLATES
DISTILLATION
DISTILLATIONS
DISTILLATORY
DISTILLERIES
DISTILLERS
DISTILLERY
DISTILLING
DISTILLINGS
DISTILMENT
DISTILMENTS
DISTINCTER
DISTINCTEST
DISTINCTION
DISTINCTIONS
DISTINCTIVE
DISTINCTIVELY
DISTINCTIVENESS
DISTINCTIVES
DISTINCTLY
DISTINCTNESS
DISTINCTNESSES
DISTINCTURE
DISTINCTURES
DISTINGUEE
DISTINGUISH
DISTINGUISHABLE
DISTINGUISHABLY
DISTINGUISHED
DISTINGUISHER
DISTINGUISHERS
DISTINGUISHES
DISTINGUISHING
DISTINGUISHMENT
DISTORTEDLY
DISTORTEDNESS
DISTORTEDNESSES
DISTORTERS
DISTORTING
DISTORTION
DISTORTIONAL
DISTORTIONS
DISTORTIVE
DISTRACTABLE
DISTRACTED
DISTRACTEDLY
DISTRACTEDNESS
DISTRACTER
DISTRACTERS
DISTRACTIBILITY
DISTRACTIBLE
DISTRACTING
DISTRACTINGLY
DISTRACTION
DISTRACTIONS
DISTRACTIVE
DISTRACTIVELY
DISTRAINABLE
DISTRAINED
DISTRAINEE
DISTRAINEES
DISTRAINER
DISTRAINERS
DISTRAINING
DISTRAINMENT
DISTRAINMENTS
DISTRAINOR
DISTRAINORS
DISTRAINTS
DISTRAUGHT
DISTRAUGHTLY
DISTRESSED
DISTRESSER
DISTRESSERS
DISTRESSES
DISTRESSFUL
DISTRESSFULLY
DISTRESSFULNESS
DISTRESSING
DISTRESSINGLY
DISTRIBUEND
DISTRIBUENDS
DISTRIBUTABLE
DISTRIBUTARIES
DISTRIBUTARY
DISTRIBUTE
DISTRIBUTED
DISTRIBUTEE
DISTRIBUTEES
DISTRIBUTER
DISTRIBUTERS
DISTRIBUTES
DISTRIBUTING
DISTRIBUTION
DISTRIBUTIONAL
DISTRIBUTIONS
DISTRIBUTIVE
DISTRIBUTIVELY
DISTRIBUTIVES
DISTRIBUTIVITY
DISTRIBUTOR
DISTRIBUTORS
DISTRICTED
DISTRICTING

DISTRINGAS
DISTRINGASES
DISTROUBLE
DISTROUBLED
DISTROUBLES
DISTROUBLING
DISTRUSTED
DISTRUSTER
DISTRUSTERS
DISTRUSTFUL
DISTRUSTFULLY
DISTRUSTFULNESS
DISTRUSTING
DISTRUSTLESS
DISTURBANCE
DISTURBANCES
DISTURBANT
DISTURBANTS
DISTURBATIVE
DISTURBERS
DISTURBING
DISTURBINGLY
DISUBSTITUTED
DISULFATES
DISULFIDES
DISULFIRAM
DISULFIRAMS
DISULFOTON
DISULFOTONS
DISULPHATE
DISULPHATES
DISULPHIDE
DISULPHIDES
DISULPHURET
DISULPHURETS
DISULPHURIC
DISUNIONIST
DISUNIONISTS
DISUNITERS
DISUNITIES
DISUNITING
DISUTILITIES
DISUTILITY
DISVALUING
DISVOUCHED
DISVOUCHES
DISVOUCHING
DISWORSHIP
DISWORSHIPS
DISYLLABIC
DISYLLABIFIED
DISYLLABIFIES
DISYLLABIFY
DISYLLABIFYING
DISYLLABISM
DISYLLABISMS
DISYLLABLE
DISYLLABLES
DITCHDIGGER
DITCHDIGGERS
DITCHWATER
DITCHWATERS
DITHEISTIC
DITHEISTICAL
DITHELETES
DITHELETIC
DITHELETICAL
DITHELETISM
DITHELETISMS
DITHELISMS
DITHELITISM
DITHELITISMS
DITHERIEST
DITHIOCARBAMATE
DITHIONATE
DITHIONATES
DITHIONITE
DITHIONITES
DITHIONOUS
DITHYRAMBIC
DITHYRAMBICALLY
DITHYRAMBIST
DITHYRAMBISTS
DITHYRAMBS
DITRANSITIVE
DITRANSITIVES
DITRIGLYPH
DITRIGLYPHIC
DITRIGLYPHS
DITROCHEAN
DITROCHEES
DITSINESSES
DITTANDERS
DITTOGRAPHIC
DITTOGRAPHIES
DITTOGRAPHY
DITTOLOGIES
DITZINESSES
DIURETICALLY
DIURETICALNESS
DIURNALIST
DIURNALISTS
DIUTURNITIES
DIUTURNITY
DIVAGATING
DIVAGATION
DIVAGATIONS
DIVALENCES
DIVALENCIES
DIVARICATE
DIVARICATED
DIVARICATELY
DIVARICATES
DIVARICATING
DIVARICATINGLY
DIVARICATION
DIVARICATIONS
DIVARICATOR
DIVARICATORS
DIVEBOMBED
DIVEBOMBING
DIVELLICATE
DIVELLICATED
DIVELLICATES
DIVELLICATING
DIVERGEMENT
DIVERGEMENTS
DIVERGENCE
DIVERGENCES
DIVERGENCIES
DIVERGENCY
DIVERGENTLY
DIVERGINGLY
DIVERSENESS
DIVERSENESSES
DIVERSIFIABLE
DIVERSIFICATION
DIVERSIFIED
DIVERSIFIER
DIVERSIFIERS
DIVERSIFIES
DIVERSIFORM
DIVERSIFYING
DIVERSIONAL
DIVERSIONARY
DIVERSIONIST
DIVERSIONISTS
DIVERSIONS
DIVERSITIES
DIVERTIBILITIES
DIVERTIBILITY
DIVERTIBLE
DIVERTICULA
DIVERTICULAR
DIVERTICULATE
DIVERTICULATED
DIVERTICULITIS
DIVERTICULOSES
DIVERTICULOSIS
DIVERTICULUM
DIVERTIMENTI
DIVERTIMENTO
DIVERTIMENTOS
DIVERTINGLY
DIVERTISEMENT
DIVERTISEMENTS
DIVERTISSEMENT
DIVERTISSEMENTS
DIVESTIBLE
DIVESTITURE
DIVESTITURES
DIVESTMENT
DIVESTMENTS
DIVESTURES
DIVIDEDNESS
DIVIDEDNESSES
DIVIDENDLESS
DIVINATION
DIVINATIONS
DIVINATORIAL
DIVINATORS
DIVINATORY
DIVINENESS
DIVINENESSES
DIVINERESS
DIVINERESSES
DIVINIFIED
DIVINIFIES
DIVINIFYING
DIVINISATION
DIVINISATIONS
DIVINISING
DIVINITIES
DIVINIZATION
DIVINIZATIONS
DIVINIZING
DIVISIBILITIES
DIVISIBILITY
DIVISIBLENESS
DIVISIBLENESSES
DIVISIONAL
DIVISIONALLY
DIVISIONARY
DIVISIONISM
DIVISIONISMS
DIVISIONIST
DIVISIONISTS
DIVISIVELY
DIVISIVENESS
DIVISIVENESSES
DIVORCEABLE
DIVORCEMENT
DIVORCEMENTS
DIVULGATED
DIVULGATER
DIVULGATERS
DIVULGATES
DIVULGATING
DIVULGATION
DIVULGATIONS
DIVULGATOR
DIVULGATORS
DIVULGEMENT
DIVULGEMENTS
DIVULGENCE
DIVULGENCES
DIVULSIONS
DIZENMENTS
DIZZINESSES
DIZZYINGLY
DJELLABAHS
DOBSONFLIES
DOCENTSHIP
DOCENTSHIPS
DOCHMIACAL
DOCHMIUSES
DOCIBILITIES
DOCIBILITY
DOCIBLENESS
DOCIBLENESSES
DOCILITIES
DOCIMASIES
DOCIMASTIC
DOCIMOLOGIES
DOCIMOLOGY
DOCKISATION
DOCKISATIONS
DOCKIZATION
DOCKIZATIONS
DOCKMASTER
DOCKMASTERS
DOCKWORKER
DOCKWORKERS
DOCQUETING
DOCTORANDS
DOCTORATED
DOCTORATES
DOCTORATING
DOCTORESSES
DOCTORLESS
DOCTORSHIP
DOCTORSHIPS
DOCTRESSES
DOCTRINAIRE

DOCTRINAIRES
DOCTRINAIRISM
DOCTRINAIRISMS
DOCTRINALITIES
DOCTRINALITY
DOCTRINALLY
DOCTRINARIAN
DOCTRINARIANISM
DOCTRINARIANS
DOCTRINARISM
DOCTRINARISMS
DOCTRINISM
DOCTRINISMS
DOCTRINIST
DOCTRINISTS
DOCUDRAMAS
DOCUMENTABLE
DOCUMENTAL
DOCUMENTALIST
DOCUMENTALISTS
DOCUMENTARIAN
DOCUMENTARIANS
DOCUMENTARIES
DOCUMENTARILY
DOCUMENTARISE
DOCUMENTARISED
DOCUMENTARISES
DOCUMENTARISING
DOCUMENTARIST
DOCUMENTARISTS
DOCUMENTARIZE
DOCUMENTARIZED
DOCUMENTARIZES
DOCUMENTARIZING
DOCUMENTARY
DOCUMENTATION
DOCUMENTATIONAL
DOCUMENTATIONS
DOCUMENTED
DOCUMENTER
DOCUMENTERS
DOCUMENTING
DODDERIEST
DODDIPOLLS
DODDYPOLLS
DODECAGONAL
DODECAGONS
DODECAGYNIAN
DODECAGYNOUS
DODECAHEDRA
DODECAHEDRAL
DODECAHEDRON
DODECAHEDRONS
DODECANDROUS
DODECANOIC
DODECAPHONIC
DODECAPHONIES
DODECAPHONISM
DODECAPHONISMS
DODECAPHONIST
DODECAPHONISTS
DODECAPHONY
DODECASTYLE
DODECASTYLES
DODECASYLLABIC
DODECASYLLABLE
DODECASYLLABLES
DODGEBALLS
DODGINESSES
DOGARESSAS
DOGBERRIES
DOGBERRYISM
DOGBERRYISMS
DOGCATCHER
DOGCATCHERS
DOGFIGHTING
DOGGEDNESS
DOGGEDNESSES
DOGGINESSES
DOGGISHNESS
DOGGISHNESSES
DOGGONEDER
DOGGONEDEST
DOGLEGGING
DOGMATICAL
DOGMATICALLY
DOGMATICALNESS
DOGMATISATION
DOGMATISATIONS
DOGMATISED
DOGMATISER
DOGMATISERS
DOGMATISES
DOGMATISING
DOGMATISMS
DOGMATISTS
DOGMATIZATION
DOGMATIZATIONS
DOGMATIZED
DOGMATIZER
DOGMATIZERS
DOGMATIZES
DOGMATIZING
DOGMATOLOGIES
DOGMATOLOGY
DOGNAPPERS
DOGNAPPING
DOGROBBERS
DOGSBODIED
DOGSBODIES
DOGSBODYING
DOGSLEDDED
DOGSLEDDER
DOGSLEDDERS
DOGSLEDDING
DOGTROTTED
DOGTROTTING
DOGWATCHES
DOLABRIFORM
DOLCELATTE
DOLCELATTES
DOLCEMENTE
DOLEFULLER
DOLEFULLEST
DOLEFULNESS
DOLEFULNESSES
DOLESOMELY
DOLICHOCEPHAL
DOLICHOCEPHALIC
DOLICHOCEPHALS
DOLICHOCEPHALY
DOLICHOSAURUS
DOLICHOSAURUSES
DOLICHOSES
DOLICHURUS
DOLICHURUSES
DOLLARBIRD
DOLLARBIRDS
DOLLARFISH
DOLLARFISHES
DOLLARISATION
DOLLARISATIONS
DOLLARISED
DOLLARISES
DOLLARISING
DOLLARIZATION
DOLLARIZATIONS
DOLLARIZED
DOLLARIZES
DOLLARIZING
DOLLARLESS
DOLLAROCRACIES
DOLLAROCRACY
DOLLARSHIP
DOLLARSHIPS
DOLLHOUSES
DOLLINESSES
DOLLISHNESS
DOLLISHNESSES
DOLLYBIRDS
DOLOMITISATION
DOLOMITISATIONS
DOLOMITISE
DOLOMITISED
DOLOMITISES
DOLOMITISING
DOLOMITIZATION
DOLOMITIZATIONS
DOLOMITIZE
DOLOMITIZED
DOLOMITIZES
DOLOMITIZING
DOLORIFEROUS
DOLORIMETRIES
DOLORIMETRY
DOLOROUSLY
DOLOROUSNESS
DOLOROUSNESSES
DOLOSTONES
DOLPHINARIA
DOLPHINARIUM
DOLPHINARIUMS
DOLPHINETS
DOLPHINFISH
DOLPHINFISHES
DOLTISHNESS
DOLTISHNESSES
DOMESTICABLE
DOMESTICAL
DOMESTICALLY
DOMESTICATE
DOMESTICATED
DOMESTICATES
DOMESTICATING
DOMESTICATION
DOMESTICATIONS
DOMESTICATIVE
DOMESTICATOR
DOMESTICATORS
DOMESTICISE
DOMESTICISED
DOMESTICISES
DOMESTICISING
DOMESTICITIES
DOMESTICITY
DOMESTICIZE
DOMESTICIZED
DOMESTICIZES
DOMESTICIZING
DOMICILIARY
DOMICILIATE
DOMICILIATED
DOMICILIATES
DOMICILIATING
DOMICILIATION
DOMICILIATIONS
DOMICILING
DOMINANCES
DOMINANCIES
DOMINANTLY
DOMINATING
DOMINATINGLY
DOMINATION
DOMINATIONS
DOMINATIVE
DOMINATORS
DOMINATRICES
DOMINATRIX
DOMINATRIXES
DOMINEERED
DOMINEERING
DOMINEERINGLY
DOMINEERINGNESS
DOMINICKER
DOMINICKERS
DOMINIQUES
DONATARIES
DONATISTIC
DONATISTICAL
DONATORIES
DONENESSES
DONKEYWORK
DONKEYWORKS
DONNICKERS
DONNISHNESS
DONNISHNESSES
DONNYBROOK
DONNYBROOKS
DONORSHIPS
DOODLEBUGS
DOOHICKEYS
DOOHICKIES
DOOMSAYERS
DOOMSAYING
DOOMSAYINGS
DOOMSDAYER
DOOMSDAYERS
DOOMWATCHED
DOOMWATCHER
DOOMWATCHERS
DOOMWATCHES
DOOMWATCHING
DOOMWATCHINGS
DOORFRAMES

OORKEEPER
OORKEEPERS
OORKNOCKED
OORKNOCKER
OORKNOCKERS
OORKNOCKING
OORKNOCKS
OORPLATES
OORSTEPPED
OORSTEPPER
OORSTEPPERS
OORSTEPPING
OORSTEPPINGS
OORSTONES
OPAMINERGIC
OPESHEETS
OPEYNESSES
OPINESSES
OPPELGANGER
OPPELGANGERS
OPPLERITE
OPPLERITES
ORBEETLES
ORKINESSES
ORMANCIES
ORMITIONS
ORMITIVES
ORMITORIES
ORONICUMS
ORSIBRANCHIATE
ORSIFEROUS
ORSIFIXED
ORSIFLEXION
ORSIFLEXIONS
ORSIGRADE
ORSIVENTRAL
ORSIVENTRALITY
ORSIVENTRALLY
ORSOLATERAL
ORSOLUMBAR
ORSOVENTRAL
ORSOVENTRALITY
ORSOVENTRALLY
ORTINESSES
OSEMETERS
OSIMETERS
OSIMETRIC
OSIMETRICIAN
OSIMETRICIANS
OSIMETRIES
OSIMETRIST
OSIMETRISTS
OSIOLOGIES
OSOLOGIES
OSSHOUSES
OTCOMMERS
OTTINESSES
OUBLEHEADER
OUBLEHEADERS
OUBLENESS
OUBLENESSES
OUBLESPEAK
OUBLESPEAKER
OUBLESPEAKERS
OUBLESPEAKS
OUBLETHINK
DOUBLETHINKS
DOUBLETONS
DOUBLETREE
DOUBLETREES
DOUBTFULLY
DOUBTFULNESS
DOUBTFULNESSES
DOUBTINGLY
DOUBTLESSLY
DOUBTLESSNESS
DOUBTLESSNESSES
DOUCENESSES
DOUCEPERES
DOUCHEBAGS
DOUGHFACED
DOUGHFACES
DOUGHINESS
DOUGHINESSES
DOUGHNUTLIKE
DOUGHNUTTED
DOUGHNUTTING
DOUGHNUTTINGS
DOUGHTIEST
DOUGHTINESS
DOUGHTINESSES
DOULOCRACIES
DOULOCRACY
DOUPPIONIS
DOURNESSES
DOUROUCOULI
DOUROUCOULIS
DOVEISHNESS
DOVEISHNESSES
DOVETAILED
DOVETAILING
DOVETAILINGS
DOVISHNESS
DOVISHNESSES
DOWDINESSES
DOWELLINGS
DOWFNESSES
DOWITCHERS
DOWNBURSTS
DOWNCOMERS
DOWNDRAFTS
DOWNDRAUGHT
DOWNDRAUGHTS
DOWNFALLEN
DOWNFORCES
DOWNGRADED
DOWNGRADES
DOWNGRADING
DOWNHEARTED
DOWNHEARTEDLY
DOWNHEARTEDNESS
DOWNHILLER
DOWNHILLERS
DOWNINESSES
DOWNLIFTING
DOWNLIGHTER
DOWNLIGHTERS
DOWNLIGHTS
DOWNLINKED
DOWNLINKING
DOWNLOADABLE
DOWNLOADED
DOWNLOADING
DOWNLOOKED
DOWNPLAYED
DOWNPLAYING
DOWNREGULATION
DOWNREGULATIONS
DOWNRIGHTLY
DOWNRIGHTNESS
DOWNRIGHTNESSES
DOWNRUSHES
DOWNSCALED
DOWNSCALES
DOWNSCALING
DOWNSHIFTED
DOWNSHIFTER
DOWNSHIFTERS
DOWNSHIFTING
DOWNSHIFTINGS
DOWNSHIFTS
DOWNSIZING
DOWNSLIDES
DOWNSPOUTS
DOWNSTAGES
DOWNSTAIRS
DOWNSTAIRSES
DOWNSTATER
DOWNSTATERS
DOWNSTATES
DOWNSTREAM
DOWNSTROKE
DOWNSTROKES
DOWNSWINGS
DOWNTHROWS
DOWNTOWNER
DOWNTOWNERS
DOWNTRENDED
DOWNTRENDING
DOWNTRENDS
DOWNTRODDEN
DOWNTURNED
DOWNWARDLY
DOWNWARDNESS
DOWNWARDNESSES
DOWNWASHES
DOWNZONING
DOXOGRAPHER
DOXOGRAPHERS
DOXOGRAPHIC
DOXOGRAPHIES
DOXOGRAPHY
DOXOLOGICAL
DOXOLOGICALLY
DOXOLOGIES
DOXORUBICIN
DOXORUBICINS
DOXYCYCLINE
DOXYCYCLINES
DOZINESSES
DRABBINESS
DRABBINESSES
DRABBLINGS
DRABNESSES
DRACONIANISM
DRACONIANISMS
DRACONICALLY
DRACONISMS
DRACONITES
DRACONTIASES
DRACONTIASIS
DRACUNCULUS
DRACUNCULUSES
DRAFTINESS
DRAFTINESSES
DRAFTSMANSHIP
DRAFTSMANSHIPS
DRAFTSPERSON
DRAFTSPERSONS
DRAFTSWOMAN
DRAFTSWOMEN
DRAGGINGLY
DRAGGLETAILED
DRAGHOUNDS
DRAGONESSES
DRAGONFLIES
DRAGONHEAD
DRAGONHEADS
DRAGONISED
DRAGONISES
DRAGONISING
DRAGONISMS
DRAGONIZED
DRAGONIZES
DRAGONIZING
DRAGONLIKE
DRAGONNADE
DRAGONNADED
DRAGONNADES
DRAGONNADING
DRAGONROOT
DRAGONROOTS
DRAGOONAGE
DRAGOONAGES
DRAGOONING
DRAGSTRIPS
DRAINLAYER
DRAINLAYERS
DRAINPIPES
DRAKESTONE
DRAKESTONES
DRAMATICAL
DRAMATICALLY
DRAMATICISM
DRAMATICISMS
DRAMATISABLE
DRAMATISATION
DRAMATISATIONS
DRAMATISED
DRAMATISER
DRAMATISERS
DRAMATISES
DRAMATISING
DRAMATISTS
DRAMATIZABLE
DRAMATIZATION
DRAMATIZATIONS
DRAMATIZED
DRAMATIZER
DRAMATIZERS
DRAMATIZES
DRAMATIZING
DRAMATURGE
DRAMATURGES

DRAMATURGIC
DRAMATURGICAL
DRAMATURGICALLY
DRAMATURGIES
DRAMATURGIST
DRAMATURGISTS
DRAMATURGS
DRAMATURGY
DRAPABILITIES
DRAPABILITY
DRAPEABILITIES
DRAPEABILITY
DRAPERYING
DRASTICALLY
DRATCHELLS
DRAUGHTBOARD
DRAUGHTBOARDS
DRAUGHTERS
DRAUGHTIER
DRAUGHTIEST
DRAUGHTILY
DRAUGHTINESS
DRAUGHTINESSES
DRAUGHTING
DRAUGHTMAN
DRAUGHTMEN
DRAUGHTSMAN
DRAUGHTSMANSHIP
DRAUGHTSMEN
DRAUGHTSWOMAN
DRAUGHTSWOMEN
DRAWBRIDGE
DRAWBRIDGES
DRAWERFULS
DRAWKNIVES
DRAWLINGLY
DRAWLINGNESS
DRAWLINGNESSES
DRAWNWORKS
DRAWPLATES
DRAWSHAVES
DRAWSTRING
DRAWSTRINGS
DRAYHORSES
DREADFULLY
DREADFULNESS
DREADFULNESSES
DREADLESSLY
DREADLESSNESS
DREADLESSNESSES
DREADLOCKS
DREADNAUGHT
DREADNAUGHTS
DREADNOUGHT
DREADNOUGHTS
DREAMBOATS
DREAMERIES
DREAMFULLY
DREAMFULNESS
DREAMFULNESSES
DREAMHOLES
DREAMINESS
DREAMINESSES
DREAMINGLY
DREAMLANDS
DREAMLESSLY
DREAMLESSNESS
DREAMLESSNESSES
DREAMTIMES
DREAMWHILE
DREAMWHILES
DREAMWORLD
DREAMWORLDS
DREARIHEAD
DREARIHEADS
DREARIHOOD
DREARIHOODS
DREARIMENT
DREARIMENTS
DREARINESS
DREARINESSES
DREARISOME
DRECKSILLS
DREGGINESS
DREGGINESSES
DREIKANTER
DREIKANTERS
DRENCHINGS
DREPANIUMS
DRERIHEADS
DRESSGUARD
DRESSGUARDS
DRESSINESS
DRESSINESSES
DRESSMAKER
DRESSMAKERS
DRESSMAKES
DRESSMAKING
DRESSMAKINGS
DRIBBLIEST
DRICKSIEST
DRIFTINGLY
DRIFTWOODS
DRILLABILITIES
DRILLABILITY
DRILLMASTER
DRILLMASTERS
DRILLSHIPS
DRILLSTOCK
DRILLSTOCKS
DRINKABILITIES
DRINKABILITY
DRINKABLENESS
DRINKABLENESSES
DRINKABLES
DRIPSTONES
DRIVABILITIES
DRIVABILITY
DRIVEABILITIES
DRIVEABILITY
DRIVELINES
DRIVELLERS
DRIVELLING
DRIVENNESS
DRIVENNESSES
DRIVERLESS
DRIVESHAFT
DRIVESHAFTS
DRIVETHROUGH
DRIVETHROUGHS
DRIVETRAIN
DRIVETRAINS
DRIZZLIEST
DRIZZLINGLY
DROICHIEST
DROLLERIES
DROLLNESSES
DROMEDARES
DROMEDARIES
DROMOPHOBIA
DROMOPHOBIAS
DRONISHNESS
DRONISHNESSES
DRONKVERDRIET
DROOPINESS
DROOPINESSES
DROOPINGLY
DROPCLOTHS
DROPFORGED
DROPFORGES
DROPFORGING
DROPKICKER
DROPKICKERS
DROPLIGHTS
DROPPERFUL
DROPPERFULS
DROPPERSFUL
DROPSICALLY
DROPSONDES
DROPSTONES
DROSERACEOUS
DROSOMETER
DROSOMETERS
DROSOPHILA
DROSOPHILAE
DROSOPHILAS
DROSSINESS
DROSSINESSES
DROUGHTIER
DROUGHTIEST
DROUGHTINESS
DROUGHTINESSES
DROUTHIEST
DROUTHINESS
DROUTHINESSES
DROWSIHEAD
DROWSIHEADS
DROWSIHEDS
DROWSINESS
DROWSINESSES
DRUCKENNESS
DRUCKENNESSES
DRUDGERIES
DRUDGINGLY
DRUGMAKERS
DRUGSTORES
DRUIDESSES
DRUMBEATER
DRUMBEATERS
DRUMBEATING
DRUMBEATINGS
DRUMBLEDOR
DRUMBLEDORS
DRUMBLEDRANE
DRUMBLEDRANES
DRUMFISHES
DRUMSTICKS
DRUNKATHON
DRUNKATHONS
DRUNKENNESS
DRUNKENNESSES
DRUPACEOUS
DRYASDUSTS
DRYBEATING
DRYOPITHECINE
DRYOPITHECINES
DRYSALTERIES
DRYSALTERS
DRYSALTERY
DRYWALLING
DUALISTICALLY
DUBIOSITIES
DUBIOUSNESS
DUBIOUSNESSES
DUBITANCIES
DUBITATING
DUBITATION
DUBITATIONS
DUBITATIVE
DUBITATIVELY
DUCHESSING
DUCKBOARDS
DUCKSHOVED
DUCKSHOVER
DUCKSHOVERS
DUCKSHOVES
DUCKSHOVING
DUCKWALKED
DUCKWALKING
DUCTILENESS
DUCTILENESSES
DUCTILITIES
DUENNASHIP
DUENNASHIPS
DUFFERDOMS
DUFFERISMS
DUIKERBOKS
DUKKERIPEN
DUKKERIPENS
DULCAMARAS
DULCETNESS
DULCETNESSES
DULCIFICATION
DULCIFICATIONS
DULCIFLUOUS
DULCIFYING
DULCILOQUIES
DULCILOQUY
DULCIMORES
DULCITUDES
DULLNESSES
DULLSVILLE
DULLSVILLES
DULOCRACIES
DUMBFOUNDED
DUMBFOUNDER
DUMBFOUNDERED
DUMBFOUNDERING
DUMBFOUNDERS
DUMBFOUNDING
DUMBFOUNDS
DUMBLEDORE
DUMBLEDORES
DUMBNESSES

UMBSTRICKEN
UMBSTRUCK
UMBWAITER
UMBWAITERS
UMFOUNDED
UMFOUNDER
UMFOUNDERED
UMFOUNDERING
UMFOUNDERS
UMFOUNDING
UMMELHEAD
UMMELHEADS
UMMINESSES
UMORTIERITE
UMORTIERITES
UMOSITIES
UMPINESSES
UMPISHNESS
UMPISHNESSES
UMPTRUCKS
UNDERFUNK
UNDERFUNKS
UNDERHEAD
UNDERHEADED
UNDERHEADISM
UNDERHEADISMS
UNDERHEADS
UNDERPATE
UNDERPATES
UNDREARIES
UNGEONERS
UNGEONING
UNIEWASSAL
UNIEWASSALS
UNIWASSAL
UNIWASSALS
UNNIEWASSAL
UNNIEWASSALS
UODECENNIAL
UODECILLION
UODECILLIONS
UODECIMAL
UODECIMALLY
UODECIMALS
UODECIMOS
UODENECTOMIES
UODENECTOMY
UODENITIS
UODENITISES
UOPOLISTIC
UOPSONIES
UPABILITIES
UPABILITY
UPLEXITIES
UPLICABILITIES
UPLICABILITY
UPLICABLE
UPLICANDS
UPLICATED
UPLICATELY
UPLICATES
UPLICATING
UPLICATION
UPLICATIONS
UPLICATIVE
UPLICATOR
DUPLICATORS
DUPLICATURE
DUPLICATURES
DUPLICIDENT
DUPLICITIES
DUPLICITOUS
DUPLICITOUSLY
DURABILITIES
DURABILITY
DURABLENESS
DURABLENESSES
DURALUMINIUM
DURALUMINIUMS
DURALUMINS
DURATIONAL
DURCHKOMPONIERT
DURCHKOMPONIRT
DURICRUSTS
DUROMETERS
DUSKINESSES
DUSKISHNESS
DUSKISHNESSES
DUSKNESSES
DUSTCOVERS
DUSTINESSES
DUSTSHEETS
DUSTSTORMS
DUTEOUSNESS
DUTEOUSNESSES
DUTIABILITIES
DUTIABILITY
DUTIFULNESS
DUTIFULNESSES
DUUMVIRATE
DUUMVIRATES
DWARFISHLY
DWARFISHNESS
DWARFISHNESSES
DWARFNESSES
DWINDLEMENT
DWINDLEMENTS
DYADICALLY
DYARCHICAL
DYEABILITIES
DYEABILITY
DYINGNESSES
DYNAMETERS
DYNAMICALLY
DYNAMICIST
DYNAMICISTS
DYNAMISING
DYNAMISTIC
DYNAMITARD
DYNAMITARDS
DYNAMITERS
DYNAMITING
DYNAMIZING
DYNAMOELECTRIC
DYNAMOGENESES
DYNAMOGENESIS
DYNAMOGENIES
DYNAMOGENY
DYNAMOGRAPH
DYNAMOGRAPHS
DYNAMOMETER
DYNAMOMETERS
DYNAMOMETRIC
DYNAMOMETRICAL
DYNAMOMETRIES
DYNAMOMETRY
DYNAMOTORS
DYNASTICAL
DYNASTICALLY
DYNORPHINS
DYOPHYSITE
DYOPHYSITES
DYOTHELETE
DYOTHELETES
DYOTHELETIC
DYOTHELETICAL
DYOTHELETISM
DYOTHELETISMS
DYOTHELISM
DYOTHELISMS
DYOTHELITE
DYOTHELITES
DYOTHELITIC
DYOTHELITICAL
DYSAESTHESIA
DYSAESTHESIAS
DYSAESTHETIC
DYSARTHRIA
DYSARTHRIAS
DYSBINDINS
DYSCALCULIA
DYSCALCULIAS
DYSCHROIAS
DYSCRASIAS
DYSCRASITE
DYSCRASITES
DYSENTERIC
DYSENTERIES
DYSFUNCTION
DYSFUNCTIONAL
DYSFUNCTIONS
DYSGENESES
DYSGENESIS
DYSGRAPHIA
DYSGRAPHIAS
DYSGRAPHIC
DYSHARMONIC
DYSKINESIA
DYSKINESIAS
DYSKINETIC
DYSLECTICS
DYSLOGISTIC
DYSLOGISTICALLY
DYSMENORRHEA
DYSMENORRHEAL
DYSMENORRHEAS
DYSMENORRHEIC
DYSMENORRHOEA
DYSMENORRHOEAL
DYSMENORRHOEAS
DYSMENORRHOEIC
DYSMORPHIC
DYSMORPHOPHOBIA
DYSPAREUNIA
DYSPAREUNIAS
DYSPATHETIC
DYSPATHIES
DYSPEPSIAS
DYSPEPSIES
DYSPEPTICAL
DYSPEPTICALLY
DYSPEPTICS
DYSPHAGIAS
DYSPHAGIES
DYSPHASIAS
DYSPHASICS
DYSPHEMISM
DYSPHEMISMS
DYSPHEMISTIC
DYSPHONIAS
DYSPHORIAS
DYSPLASIAS
DYSPLASTIC
DYSPRAXIAS
DYSPROSIUM
DYSPROSIUMS
DYSRHYTHMIA
DYSRHYTHMIAS
DYSRHYTHMIC
DYSSYNERGIA
DYSSYNERGIAS
DYSTELEOLOGICAL
DYSTELEOLOGIES
DYSTELEOLOGIST
DYSTELEOLOGISTS
DYSTELEOLOGY
DYSTHESIAS
DYSTHYMIAC
DYSTHYMIACS
DYSTHYMIAS
DYSTHYMICS
DYSTOPIANS
DYSTROPHIA
DYSTROPHIAS
DYSTROPHIC
DYSTROPHIES
DYSTROPHIN
DYSTROPHINS
DZIGGETAIS

Ee

EAGERNESSES
EAGLESTONE
EAGLESTONES
EAGLEWOODS
EARBASHERS
EARBASHING
EARBASHINGS
EARLIERISE
EARLIERISED
EARLIERISES
EARLIERISING
EARLIERIZE
EARLIERIZED
EARLIERIZES
EARLIERIZING
EARLINESSES
EARLYWOODS
EARMARKING
EARNESTNESS
EARNESTNESSES
EARSPLITTING
EARTHBOUND
EARTHENWARE
EARTHENWARES
EARTHFALLS
EARTHFLAXES
EARTHINESS
EARTHINESSES
EARTHLIEST
EARTHLIGHT
EARTHLIGHTS
EARTHLINESS
EARTHLINESSES
EARTHLINGS
EARTHMOVER
EARTHMOVERS
EARTHMOVING
EARTHMOVINGS
EARTHQUAKE
EARTHQUAKED
EARTHQUAKES
EARTHQUAKING
EARTHRISES
EARTHSHAKER
EARTHSHAKERS
EARTHSHAKING
EARTHSHAKINGLY
EARTHSHATTERING
EARTHSHINE
EARTHSHINES
EARTHSTARS
EARTHWARDS
EARTHWAXES
EARTHWOLVES
EARTHWOMAN
EARTHWOMEN
EARTHWORKS
EARTHWORMS
EARWIGGING
EARWIGGINGS
EARWITNESS
EARWITNESSES
EASEFULNESS
EASEFULNESSES
EASINESSES
EASSELGATE
EASSELWARD
EASTERLIES
EASTERLING
EASTERLINGS
EASTERMOST
EASTERNERS
EASTERNMOST
EASTWARDLY
EASYGOINGNESS
EASYGOINGNESSES
EAVESDRIPS
EAVESDROPPED
EAVESDROPPER
EAVESDROPPERS
EAVESDROPPING
EAVESDROPPINGS
EAVESDROPS
EAVESTROUGH
EAVESTROUGHS
EBIONISING
EBIONITISM
EBIONITISMS
EBIONIZING
EBOULEMENT
EBOULEMENTS
EBRACTEATE
EBRACTEOLATE
EBRILLADES
EBRIOSITIES
EBULLIENCE
EBULLIENCES
EBULLIENCIES
EBULLIENCY
EBULLIENTLY
EBULLIOMETER
EBULLIOMETERS
EBULLIOMETRIES
EBULLIOMETRY
EBULLIOSCOPE
EBULLIOSCOPES
EBULLIOSCOPIC
EBULLIOSCOPICAL
EBULLIOSCOPIES
EBULLIOSCOPY
EBULLITION
EBULLITIONS
EBURNATION
EBURNATIONS
EBURNIFICATION
EBURNIFICATIONS
ECARDINATE
ECBLASTESES
ECBLASTESIS
ECCALEOBION
ECCALEOBIONS
ECCENTRICAL
ECCENTRICALLY
ECCENTRICITIES
ECCENTRICITY
ECCENTRICS
ECCHYMOSED
ECCHYMOSES
ECCHYMOSIS
ECCHYMOTIC
ECCLESIARCH
ECCLESIARCHS
ECCLESIAST
ECCLESIASTIC
ECCLESIASTICAL
ECCLESIASTICISM
ECCLESIASTICS
ECCLESIASTS
ECCLESIOLATER
ECCLESIOLATERS
ECCLESIOLATRIES
ECCLESIOLATRY
ECCLESIOLOGICAL
ECCLESIOLOGIES
ECCLESIOLOGIST
ECCLESIOLOGISTS
ECCLESIOLOGY
ECCOPROTIC
ECCOPROTICS
ECCREMOCARPUS
ECCREMOCARPUSES
ECCRINOLOGIES

CCRINOLOGY
CDYSIASTS
CHELONING
CHEVERIAS
CHIDNINES
CHINACEAS
CHINOCOCCI
CHINOCOCCOSES
CHINOCOCCOSIS
CHINOCOCCUS
CHINODERM
CHINODERMAL
CHINODERMATOUS
CHINODERMS
CHIUROIDS
CHOCARDIOGRAM
CHOCARDIOGRAMS
CHOGRAPHIES
CHOGRAPHY
CHOLALIAS
CHOLOCATION
CHOLOCATIONS
CHOPRAXES
CHOPRAXIA
CHOPRAXIAS
CHOPRAXIS
CHOVIRUSES
CLAIRCISSEMENT
CLAMPSIAS
CLAMPSIES
CLECTICALLY
CLECTICISM
CLECTICISMS
CLIPSISES
CLIPTICALLY
COCATASTROPHE
COCATASTROPHES
COCENTRIC
COCLIMATE
COCLIMATES
COFEMINISM
COFEMINISMS
COFEMINIST
COFEMINISTS
COFRIENDLY
COLOGICAL
COLOGICALLY
COLOGISTS
COMMERCES
CONOBOXES
CONOMETRIC
CONOMETRICAL
CONOMETRICALLY
CONOMETRICIAN
CONOMETRICIANS
CONOMETRICS
CONOMETRIST
CONOMETRISTS
CONOMICAL
CONOMICALLY
CONOMISATION
CONOMISATIONS
CONOMISED
CONOMISER
CONOMISERS
CONOMISES
ECONOMISING
ECONOMISMS
ECONOMISTIC
ECONOMISTS
ECONOMIZATION
ECONOMIZATIONS
ECONOMIZED
ECONOMIZER
ECONOMIZERS
ECONOMIZES
ECONOMIZING
ECOPHOBIAS
ECOPHYSIOLOGIES
ECOPHYSIOLOGY
ECOREGIONS
ECOSPECIES
ECOSPECIFIC
ECOSPHERES
ECOSSAISES
ECOSYSTEMS
ECOTERRORISM
ECOTERRORISMS
ECOTERRORIST
ECOTERRORISTS
ECOTOURISM
ECOTOURISMS
ECOTOURIST
ECOTOURISTS
ECOTOXICOLOGIES
ECOTOXICOLOGIST
ECOTOXICOLOGY
ECOTYPICALLY
ECPHONESES
ECPHONESIS
ECPHRACTIC
ECPHRACTICS
ECRITOIRES
ECSTASISED
ECSTASISES
ECSTASISING
ECSTASIZED
ECSTASIZES
ECSTASIZING
ECSTASYING
ECSTATICALLY
ECTHLIPSES
ECTHLIPSIS
ECTOBLASTIC
ECTOBLASTS
ECTOCRINES
ECTODERMAL
ECTODERMIC
ECTOENZYME
ECTOENZYMES
ECTOGENESES
ECTOGENESIS
ECTOGENETIC
ECTOGENICALLY
ECTOGENIES
ECTOGENOUS
ECTOMORPHIC
ECTOMORPHIES
ECTOMORPHS
ECTOMORPHY
ECTOMYCORRHIZA
ECTOMYCORRHIZAE
ECTOMYCORRHIZAS
ECTOPARASITE
ECTOPARASITES
ECTOPARASITIC
ECTOPHYTES
ECTOPHYTIC
ECTOPICALLY
ECTOPLASMIC
ECTOPLASMS
ECTOPLASTIC
ECTOPROCTS
ECTOSARCOUS
ECTOTHERMIC
ECTOTHERMS
ECTOTROPHIC
ECTROPIONS
ECTROPIUMS
ECTYPOGRAPHIES
ECTYPOGRAPHY
ECUMENICAL
ECUMENICALISM
ECUMENICALISMS
ECUMENICALLY
ECUMENICISM
ECUMENICISMS
ECUMENICIST
ECUMENICISTS
ECUMENICITIES
ECUMENICITY
ECUMENISMS
ECUMENISTS
ECZEMATOUS
EDACIOUSLY
EDACIOUSNESS
EDACIOUSNESSES
EDAPHICALLY
EDAPHOLOGIES
EDAPHOLOGY
EDELWEISSES
EDENTULATE
EDENTULOUS
EDGINESSES
EDIBILITIES
EDIBLENESS
EDIBLENESSES
EDIFICATION
EDIFICATIONS
EDIFICATORY
EDIFYINGLY
EDITORIALISE
EDITORIALISED
EDITORIALISER
EDITORIALISERS
EDITORIALISES
EDITORIALISING
EDITORIALIST
EDITORIALISTS
EDITORIALIZE
EDITORIALIZED
EDITORIALIZER
EDITORIALIZERS
EDITORIALIZES
EDITORIALIZING
EDITORIALLY
EDITORIALS
EDITORSHIP
EDITORSHIPS
EDITRESSES
EDRIOPHTHALMIAN
EDRIOPHTHALMIC
EDRIOPHTHALMOUS
EDUCABILITIES
EDUCABILITY
EDUCATABILITIES
EDUCATABILITY
EDUCATABLE
EDUCATEDNESS
EDUCATEDNESSES
EDUCATIONAL
EDUCATIONALIST
EDUCATIONALISTS
EDUCATIONALLY
EDUCATIONESE
EDUCATIONESES
EDUCATIONIST
EDUCATIONISTS
EDUCATIONS
EDUCEMENTS
EDULCORANT
EDULCORATE
EDULCORATED
EDULCORATES
EDULCORATING
EDULCORATION
EDULCORATIONS
EDULCORATIVE
EDULCORATOR
EDULCORATORS
EDUSKUNTAS
EDUTAINMENT
EDUTAINMENTS
EELGRASSES
EERINESSES
EFFACEABLE
EFFACEMENT
EFFACEMENTS
EFFECTIBLE
EFFECTIVELY
EFFECTIVENESS
EFFECTIVENESSES
EFFECTIVES
EFFECTIVITIES
EFFECTIVITY
EFFECTLESS
EFFECTUALITIES
EFFECTUALITY
EFFECTUALLY
EFFECTUALNESS
EFFECTUALNESSES
EFFECTUATE
EFFECTUATED
EFFECTUATES
EFFECTUATING
EFFECTUATION
EFFECTUATIONS
EFFEMINACIES
EFFEMINACY
EFFEMINATE
EFFEMINATED
EFFEMINATELY
EFFEMINATENESS
EFFEMINATES

EFFEMINATING
EFFEMINISE
EFFEMINISED
EFFEMINISES
EFFEMINISING
EFFEMINIZE
EFFEMINIZED
EFFEMINIZES
EFFEMINIZING
EFFERENCES
EFFERENTLY
EFFERVESCE
EFFERVESCED
EFFERVESCENCE
EFFERVESCENCES
EFFERVESCENCIES
EFFERVESCENCY
EFFERVESCENT
EFFERVESCENTLY
EFFERVESCES
EFFERVESCIBLE
EFFERVESCING
EFFERVESCINGLY
EFFETENESS
EFFETENESSES
EFFICACIES
EFFICACIOUS
EFFICACIOUSLY
EFFICACIOUSNESS
EFFICACITIES
EFFICACITY
EFFICIENCE
EFFICIENCES
EFFICIENCIES
EFFICIENCY
EFFICIENTLY
EFFICIENTS
EFFIERCING
EFFIGURATE
EFFIGURATION
EFFIGURATIONS
EFFLEURAGE
EFFLEURAGED
EFFLEURAGES
EFFLEURAGING
EFFLORESCE
EFFLORESCED
EFFLORESCENCE
EFFLORESCENCES
EFFLORESCENT
EFFLORESCES
EFFLORESCING
EFFLUENCES
EFFLUVIUMS
EFFLUXIONS
EFFORTFULLY
EFFORTFULNESS
EFFORTFULNESSES
EFFORTLESS
EFFORTLESSLY
EFFORTLESSNESS
EFFRONTERIES
EFFRONTERY
EFFULGENCE
EFFULGENCES
EFFULGENTLY
EFFUSIOMETER
EFFUSIOMETERS
EFFUSIVELY
EFFUSIVENESS
EFFUSIVENESSES
EGALITARIAN
EGALITARIANISM
EGALITARIANISMS
EGALITARIANS
EGAREMENTS
EGGBEATERS
EGGHEADEDNESS
EGGHEADEDNESSES
EGLANDULAR
EGLANDULOSE
EGLANTINES
EGOCENTRIC
EGOCENTRICALLY
EGOCENTRICITIES
EGOCENTRICITY
EGOCENTRICS
EGOCENTRISM
EGOCENTRISMS
EGOISTICAL
EGOISTICALLY
EGOMANIACAL
EGOMANIACALLY
EGOMANIACS
EGOTHEISMS
EGOTISTICAL
EGOTISTICALLY
EGREGIOUSLY
EGREGIOUSNESS
EGREGIOUSNESSES
EGRESSIONS
EGURGITATE
EGURGITATED
EGURGITATES
EGURGITATING
EICOSANOID
EICOSANOIDS
EIDERDOWNS
EIDETICALLY
EIDOGRAPHS
EIGENFREQUENCY
EIGENFUNCTION
EIGENFUNCTIONS
EIGENMODES
EIGENTONES
EIGENVALUE
EIGENVALUES
EIGENVECTOR
EIGENVECTORS
EIGHTBALLS
EIGHTEENMO
EIGHTEENMOS
EIGHTEENTH
EIGHTEENTHLY
EIGHTEENTHS
EIGHTFOILS
EIGHTIETHS
EIGHTPENCE
EIGHTPENCES
EIGHTPENNY
EIGHTSCORE
EIGHTSCORES
EIGHTSOMES
EINSTEINIUM
EINSTEINIUMS
EIRENICALLY
EIRENICONS
EISTEDDFOD
EISTEDDFODAU
EISTEDDFODIC
EISTEDDFODS
EJACULATED
EJACULATES
EJACULATING
EJACULATION
EJACULATIONS
EJACULATIVE
EJACULATOR
EJACULATORS
EJACULATORY
EJECTAMENTA
EJECTIVELY
EJECTMENTS
EKISTICIAN
EKISTICIANS
ELABORATED
ELABORATELY
ELABORATENESS
ELABORATENESSES
ELABORATES
ELABORATING
ELABORATION
ELABORATIONS
ELABORATIVE
ELABORATOR
ELABORATORIES
ELABORATORS
ELABORATORY
ELAEOLITES
ELAEOPTENE
ELAEOPTENES
ELAIOSOMES
ELASMOBRANCH
ELASMOBRANCHS
ELASMOSAUR
ELASMOSAURS
ELASTANCES
ELASTICALLY
ELASTICATE
ELASTICATED
ELASTICATES
ELASTICATING
ELASTICATION
ELASTICATIONS
ELASTICISE
ELASTICISED
ELASTICISES
ELASTICISING
ELASTICITIES
ELASTICITY
ELASTICIZE
ELASTICIZED
ELASTICIZES
ELASTICIZING
ELASTICNESS
ELASTICNESSES
ELASTOMERIC
ELASTOMERS
ELATEDNESS
ELATEDNESSES
ELATERITES
ELATERIUMS
ELBOWROOMS
ELDERBERRIES
ELDERBERRY
ELDERCARES
ELDERLINESS
ELDERLINESSES
ELDERSHIPS
ELECAMPANE
ELECAMPANES
ELECTABILITIES
ELECTABILITY
ELECTIONEER
ELECTIONEERED
ELECTIONEERER
ELECTIONEERERS
ELECTIONEERING
ELECTIONEERINGS
ELECTIONEERS
ELECTIVELY
ELECTIVENESS
ELECTIVENESSES
ELECTIVITIES
ELECTIVITY
ELECTORALLY
ELECTORATE
ELECTORATES
ELECTORESS
ELECTORESSES
ELECTORIAL
ELECTORSHIP
ELECTORSHIPS
ELECTRESSES
ELECTRICAL
ELECTRICALLY
ELECTRICIAN
ELECTRICIANS
ELECTRICITIES
ELECTRICITY
ELECTRIFIABLE
ELECTRIFICATION
ELECTRIFIED
ELECTRIFIER
ELECTRIFIERS
ELECTRIFIES
ELECTRIFYING
ELECTRISATION
ELECTRISATIONS
ELECTRISED
ELECTRISES
ELECTRISING
ELECTRIZATION
ELECTRIZATIONS
ELECTRIZED
ELECTRIZES
ELECTRIZING
ELECTROACOUSTIC
ELECTROACTIVE
ELECTROACTIVITY
ELECTROANALYSES
ELECTROANALYSIS
ELECTROANALYTIC
ELECTROBIOLOGY

LECTROCAUTERY
LECTROCEMENT
LECTROCEMENTS
LECTROCHEMIC
LECTROCHEMICAL
LECTROCHEMIST
LECTROCHEMISTS
LECTROCLASH
LECTROCLASHES
LECTROCULTURE
LECTROCULTURES
LECTROCUTE
LECTROCUTED
LECTROCUTES
LECTROCUTING
LECTROCUTION
LECTROCUTIONS
LECTROCYTE
LECTROCYTES
LECTRODEPOSIT
LECTRODEPOSITS
LECTRODERMAL
LECTRODES
LECTRODIALYSES
LECTRODIALYSIS
LECTRODIALYTIC
LECTRODYNAMIC
LECTRODYNAMICS
LECTROFISHING
LECTROFISHINGS
LECTROFLUOR
LECTROFLUORS
LECTROFORM
LECTROFORMED
LECTROFORMING
LECTROFORMINGS
LECTROFORMS
LECTROGEN
LECTROGENESES
LECTROGENESIS
LECTROGENIC
LECTROGENS
LECTROGILDING
LECTROGILDINGS
LECTROGRAM
LECTROGRAMS
LECTROGRAPH
LECTROGRAPHIC
LECTROGRAPHIES
LECTROGRAPHS
LECTROGRAPHY
LECTROING
LECTROJET
LECTROJETS
LECTROKINETIC
LECTROKINETICS
LECTROLESS
LECTROLIER
LECTROLIERS
LECTROLOGIES
LECTROLOGIST
LECTROLOGISTS
LECTROLOGY
LECTROLYSATION
LECTROLYSE
LECTROLYSED
ELECTROLYSER
ELECTROLYSERS
ELECTROLYSES
ELECTROLYSING
ELECTROLYSIS
ELECTROLYTE
ELECTROLYTES
ELECTROLYTIC
ELECTROLYTICS
ELECTROLYZATION
ELECTROLYZE
ELECTROLYZED
ELECTROLYZER
ELECTROLYZERS
ELECTROLYZES
ELECTROLYZING
ELECTROMAGNET
ELECTROMAGNETIC
ELECTROMAGNETS
ELECTROMER
ELECTROMERIC
ELECTROMERISM
ELECTROMERISMS
ELECTROMERS
ELECTROMETER
ELECTROMETERS
ELECTROMETRIC
ELECTROMETRICAL
ELECTROMETRIES
ELECTROMETRY
ELECTROMOTANCE
ELECTROMOTANCES
ELECTROMOTIVE
ELECTROMOTOR
ELECTROMOTORS
ELECTROMYOGRAM
ELECTROMYOGRAMS
ELECTROMYOGRAPH
ELECTRONEGATIVE
ELECTRONIC
ELECTRONICA
ELECTRONICALLY
ELECTRONICAS
ELECTRONICS
ELECTRONVOLT
ELECTRONVOLTS
ELECTROOSMOSES
ELECTROOSMOSIS
ELECTROOSMOTIC
ELECTROPHILE
ELECTROPHILES
ELECTROPHILIC
ELECTROPHONE
ELECTROPHONES
ELECTROPHONIC
ELECTROPHORESE
ELECTROPHORESED
ELECTROPHORESES
ELECTROPHORESIS
ELECTROPHORETIC
ELECTROPHORI
ELECTROPHORUS
ELECTROPHORUSES
ELECTROPLATE
ELECTROPLATED
ELECTROPLATER
ELECTROPLATERS
ELECTROPLATES
ELECTROPLATING
ELECTROPLATINGS
ELECTROPOLAR
ELECTROPOSITIVE
ELECTRORECEPTOR
ELECTRORHEOLOGY
ELECTROSCOPE
ELECTROSCOPES
ELECTROSCOPIC
ELECTROSHOCK
ELECTROSHOCKS
ELECTROSONDE
ELECTROSONDES
ELECTROSTATIC
ELECTROSTATICS
ELECTROSURGERY
ELECTROSURGICAL
ELECTROTECHNICS
ELECTROTHERAPY
ELECTROTHERMAL
ELECTROTHERMIC
ELECTROTHERMICS
ELECTROTHERMIES
ELECTROTHERMY
ELECTROTINT
ELECTROTINTS
ELECTROTONIC
ELECTROTONUS
ELECTROTONUSES
ELECTROTYPE
ELECTROTYPED
ELECTROTYPER
ELECTROTYPERS
ELECTROTYPES
ELECTROTYPIC
ELECTROTYPIES
ELECTROTYPING
ELECTROTYPIST
ELECTROTYPISTS
ELECTROTYPY
ELECTROVALENCE
ELECTROVALENCES
ELECTROVALENCY
ELECTROVALENT
ELECTROVALENTLY
ELECTROWEAK
ELECTROWINNING
ELECTROWINNINGS
ELECTUARIES
ELEDOISINS
ELEEMOSYNARY
ELEGANCIES
ELEGIACALLY
ELEMENTALISM
ELEMENTALISMS
ELEMENTALLY
ELEMENTALS
ELEMENTARILY
ELEMENTARINESS
ELEMENTARY
ELEOPTENES
ELEPHANTIASES
ELEPHANTIASIC
ELEPHANTIASIS
ELEPHANTINE
ELEPHANTOID
ELEUTHERARCH
ELEUTHERARCHS
ELEUTHERIAN
ELEUTHEROCOCCI
ELEUTHEROCOCCUS
ELEUTHERODACTYL
ELEUTHEROMANIA
ELEUTHEROMANIAS
ELEUTHEROPHOBIA
ELEUTHEROPHOBIC
ELEVATIONAL
ELEVATIONS
ELEVENTHLY
ELFISHNESS
ELFISHNESSES
ELICITABLE
ELICITATION
ELICITATIONS
ELIGIBILITIES
ELIGIBILITY
ELIMINABILITIES
ELIMINABILITY
ELIMINABLE
ELIMINANTS
ELIMINATED
ELIMINATES
ELIMINATING
ELIMINATION
ELIMINATIONS
ELIMINATIVE
ELIMINATOR
ELIMINATORS
ELIMINATORY
ELLIPSOGRAPH
ELLIPSOGRAPHS
ELLIPSOIDAL
ELLIPSOIDS
ELLIPTICAL
ELLIPTICALLY
ELLIPTICALNESS
ELLIPTICALS
ELLIPTICITIES
ELLIPTICITY
ELOCUTIONARY
ELOCUTIONIST
ELOCUTIONISTS
ELOCUTIONS
ELOIGNMENT
ELOIGNMENTS
ELOINMENTS
ELONGATING
ELONGATION
ELONGATIONS
ELOPEMENTS
ELOQUENCES
ELOQUENTLY
ELSEWHITHER
ELUCIDATED
ELUCIDATES
ELUCIDATING
ELUCIDATION
ELUCIDATIONS
ELUCIDATIVE
ELUCIDATOR

ELUCIDATORS
ELUCIDATORY
ELUCUBRATE
ELUCUBRATED
ELUCUBRATES
ELUCUBRATING
ELUCUBRATION
ELUCUBRATIONS
ELUSIVENESS
ELUSIVENESSES
ELUSORINESS
ELUSORINESSES
ELUTRIATED
ELUTRIATES
ELUTRIATING
ELUTRIATION
ELUTRIATIONS
ELUTRIATOR
ELUTRIATORS
ELUVIATING
ELUVIATION
ELUVIATIONS
ELVISHNESS
ELVISHNESSES
ELYTRIFORM
ELYTRIGEROUS
EMACIATING
EMACIATION
EMACIATIONS
EMALANGENI
EMANATIONAL
EMANATIONS
EMANATISTS
EMANCIPATE
EMANCIPATED
EMANCIPATES
EMANCIPATING
EMANCIPATION
EMANCIPATIONIST
EMANCIPATIONS
EMANCIPATIVE
EMANCIPATOR
EMANCIPATORS
EMANCIPATORY
EMANCIPIST
EMANCIPISTS
EMARGINATE
EMARGINATED
EMARGINATELY
EMARGINATES
EMARGINATING
EMARGINATION
EMARGINATIONS
EMASCULATE
EMASCULATED
EMASCULATES
EMASCULATING
EMASCULATION
EMASCULATIONS
EMASCULATIVE
EMASCULATOR
EMASCULATORS
EMASCULATORY
EMBALLINGS
EMBALMINGS
EMBALMMENT
EMBALMMENTS
EMBANKMENT
EMBANKMENTS
EMBARCADERO
EMBARCADEROS
EMBARCATION
EMBARCATIONS
EMBARGOING
EMBARKATION
EMBARKATIONS
EMBARKMENT
EMBARKMENTS
EMBARQUEMENT
EMBARQUEMENTS
EMBARRASSABLE
EMBARRASSED
EMBARRASSEDLY
EMBARRASSES
EMBARRASSING
EMBARRASSINGLY
EMBARRASSMENT
EMBARRASSMENTS
EMBARRINGS
EMBASEMENT
EMBASEMENTS
EMBASSADES
EMBASSADOR
EMBASSADORS
EMBASSAGES
EMBATTLEMENT
EMBATTLEMENTS
EMBATTLING
EMBAYMENTS
EMBEDDINGS
EMBEDMENTS
EMBELLISHED
EMBELLISHER
EMBELLISHERS
EMBELLISHES
EMBELLISHING
EMBELLISHINGLY
EMBELLISHMENT
EMBELLISHMENTS
EMBEZZLEMENT
EMBEZZLEMENTS
EMBEZZLERS
EMBEZZLING
EMBITTERED
EMBITTERER
EMBITTERERS
EMBITTERING
EMBITTERINGS
EMBITTERMENT
EMBITTERMENTS
EMBLAZONED
EMBLAZONER
EMBLAZONERS
EMBLAZONING
EMBLAZONMENT
EMBLAZONMENTS
EMBLAZONRIES
EMBLAZONRY
EMBLEMATIC
EMBLEMATICAL
EMBLEMATICALLY
EMBLEMATISE
EMBLEMATISED
EMBLEMATISES
EMBLEMATISING
EMBLEMATIST
EMBLEMATISTS
EMBLEMATIZE
EMBLEMATIZED
EMBLEMATIZES
EMBLEMATIZING
EMBLEMENTS
EMBLEMISED
EMBLEMISES
EMBLEMISING
EMBLEMIZED
EMBLEMIZES
EMBLEMIZING
EMBLOOMING
EMBLOSSOMED
EMBLOSSOMING
EMBLOSSOMS
EMBODIMENT
EMBODIMENTS
EMBOITEMENT
EMBOITEMENTS
EMBOLDENED
EMBOLDENER
EMBOLDENERS
EMBOLDENING
EMBOLECTOMIES
EMBOLECTOMY
EMBOLISATION
EMBOLISATIONS
EMBOLISING
EMBOLISMAL
EMBOLISMIC
EMBOLIZATION
EMBOLIZATIONS
EMBOLIZING
EMBONPOINT
EMBONPOINTS
EMBORDERED
EMBORDERING
EMBOSCATAS
EMBOSOMING
EMBOSSABLE
EMBOSSMENT
EMBOSSMENTS
EMBOTHRIUM
EMBOTHRIUMS
EMBOUCHURE
EMBOUCHURES
EMBOUNDING
EMBOURGEOISE
EMBOURGEOISED
EMBOURGEOISES
EMBOURGEOISING
EMBOWELING
EMBOWELLED
EMBOWELLING
EMBOWELMENT
EMBOWELMENTS
EMBOWERING
EMBOWERMENT
EMBOWERMENTS
EMBOWMENTS
EMBRACEABLE
EMBRACEMENT
EMBRACEMENTS
EMBRACEORS
EMBRACERIES
EMBRACINGLY
EMBRACINGNESS
EMBRACINGNESSES
EMBRAIDING
EMBRANCHMENT
EMBRANCHMENTS
EMBRANGLED
EMBRANGLEMENT
EMBRANGLEMENTS
EMBRANGLES
EMBRANGLING
EMBRASURED
EMBRASURES
EMBRAZURES
EMBREADING
EMBREATHED
EMBREATHES
EMBREATHING
EMBRITTLED
EMBRITTLEMENT
EMBRITTLEMENTS
EMBRITTLES
EMBRITTLING
EMBROCATED
EMBROCATES
EMBROCATING
EMBROCATION
EMBROCATIONS
EMBROGLIOS
EMBROIDERED
EMBROIDERER
EMBROIDERERS
EMBROIDERIES
EMBROIDERING
EMBROIDERS
EMBROIDERY
EMBROILERS
EMBROILING
EMBROILMENT
EMBROILMENTS
EMBROWNING
EMBRUEMENT
EMBRUEMENTS
EMBRYECTOMIES
EMBRYECTOMY
EMBRYOGENESES
EMBRYOGENESIS
EMBRYOGENETIC
EMBRYOGENIC
EMBRYOGENIES
EMBRYOGENY
EMBRYOLOGIC
EMBRYOLOGICAL
EMBRYOLOGICALLY
EMBRYOLOGIES
EMBRYOLOGIST
EMBRYOLOGISTS
EMBRYOLOGY
EMBRYONATE
EMBRYONATED
EMBRYONICALLY
EMBRYOPHYTE

MBRYOPHYTES
MBRYOTOMIES
MBRYOTOMY
MBRYULCIA
MBRYULCIAS
MENDATING
MENDATION
MENDATIONS
MENDATORS
MENDATORY
MERGENCES
MERGENCIES
MERGENTLY
METICALLY
METOPHOBIA
METOPHOBIAS
MICATIONS
MIGRATING
MIGRATION
MIGRATIONAL
MIGRATIONIST
MIGRATIONISTS
MIGRATIONS
MIGRATORY
MINENCIES
MINENTIAL
MISSARIES
MISSIVITIES
MISSIVITY
MITTANCES
MMARBLING
MMENAGOGIC
MMENAGOGUE
MMENAGOGUES
MMENOLOGIES
MMENOLOGY
MMETROPES
MMETROPIA
MMETROPIAS
MMETROPIC
MOLLESCENCE
MOLLESCENCES
MOLLIATED
MOLLIATES
MOLLIATING
MOLLIENCE
MOLLIENCES
MOLLIENTS
MOLLITION
MOLLITIONS
MOLUMENTAL
MOLUMENTARY
MOLUMENTS
MOTIONABLE
MOTIONALISE
MOTIONALISED
MOTIONALISES
MOTIONALISING
MOTIONALISM
MOTIONALISMS
MOTIONALIST
MOTIONALISTIC
MOTIONALISTS
MOTIONALITIES
MOTIONALITY
MOTIONALIZE
EMOTIONALIZED
EMOTIONALIZES
EMOTIONALIZING
EMOTIONALLY
EMOTIONLESS
EMOTIONLESSLY
EMOTIONLESSNESS
EMOTIVENESS
EMOTIVENESSES
EMOTIVISMS
EMOTIVITIES
EMPACKETED
EMPACKETING
EMPALEMENT
EMPALEMENTS
EMPANELING
EMPANELLED
EMPANELLING
EMPANELMENT
EMPANELMENTS
EMPANOPLIED
EMPANOPLIES
EMPANOPLYING
EMPARADISE
EMPARADISED
EMPARADISES
EMPARADISING
EMPARLAUNCE
EMPARLAUNCES
EMPASSIONATE
EMPASSIONED
EMPATHETIC
EMPATHETICALLY
EMPATHICALLY
EMPATHISED
EMPATHISES
EMPATHISING
EMPATHISTS
EMPATHIZED
EMPATHIZES
EMPATHIZING
EMPATRONED
EMPATRONING
EMPEACHING
EMPENNAGES
EMPEOPLING
EMPERISHED
EMPERISHES
EMPERISHING
EMPERISING
EMPERIZING
EMPERORSHIP
EMPERORSHIPS
EMPHASISED
EMPHASISES
EMPHASISING
EMPHASIZED
EMPHASIZES
EMPHASIZING
EMPHATICAL
EMPHATICALLY
EMPHATICALNESS
EMPHRACTIC
EMPHRACTICS
EMPHYSEMAS
EMPHYSEMATOUS
EMPHYSEMIC
EMPHYSEMICS
EMPHYTEUSES
EMPHYTEUSIS
EMPHYTEUTIC
EMPIECEMENT
EMPIECEMENTS
EMPIERCING
EMPIRICALLY
EMPIRICALNESS
EMPIRICALNESSES
EMPIRICISM
EMPIRICISMS
EMPIRICIST
EMPIRICISTS
EMPIRICUTIC
EMPLACEMENT
EMPLACEMENTS
EMPLASTERED
EMPLASTERING
EMPLASTERS
EMPLASTICS
EMPLASTRON
EMPLASTRONS
EMPLASTRUM
EMPLASTRUMS
EMPLEACHED
EMPLEACHES
EMPLEACHING
EMPLECTONS
EMPLECTUMS
EMPLONGING
EMPLOYABILITIES
EMPLOYABILITY
EMPLOYABLE
EMPLOYABLES
EMPLOYMENT
EMPLOYMENTS
EMPOISONED
EMPOISONING
EMPOISONMENT
EMPOISONMENTS
EMPOLDERED
EMPOLDERING
EMPOVERISH
EMPOVERISHED
EMPOVERISHER
EMPOVERISHERS
EMPOVERISHES
EMPOVERISHING
EMPOVERISHMENT
EMPOVERISHMENTS
EMPOWERING
EMPOWERMENT
EMPOWERMENTS
EMPRESSEMENT
EMPRESSEMENTS
EMPTINESSES
EMPURPLING
EMPYREUMATA
EMPYREUMATIC
EMPYREUMATICAL
EMPYREUMATISE
EMPYREUMATISED
EMPYREUMATISES
EMPYREUMATISING
EMPYREUMATIZE
EMPYREUMATIZED
EMPYREUMATIZES
EMPYREUMATIZING
EMULATIONS
EMULATIVELY
EMULATRESS
EMULATRESSES
EMULGENCES
EMULOUSNESS
EMULOUSNESSES
EMULSIFIABLE
EMULSIFICATION
EMULSIFICATIONS
EMULSIFIED
EMULSIFIER
EMULSIFIERS
EMULSIFIES
EMULSIFYING
EMULSIONISE
EMULSIONISED
EMULSIONISES
EMULSIONISING
EMULSIONIZE
EMULSIONIZED
EMULSIONIZES
EMULSIONIZING
EMULSOIDAL
EMUNCTIONS
EMUNCTORIES
ENABLEMENT
ENABLEMENTS
ENACTMENTS
ENALAPRILS
ENAMELISTS
ENAMELLERS
ENAMELLING
ENAMELLINGS
ENAMELLIST
ENAMELLISTS
ENAMELWARE
ENAMELWARES
ENAMELWORK
ENAMELWORKS
ENAMORADOS
ENAMOURING
ENANTIODROMIA
ENANTIODROMIAS
ENANTIODROMIC
ENANTIOMER
ENANTIOMERIC
ENANTIOMERS
ENANTIOMORPH
ENANTIOMORPHIC
ENANTIOMORPHIES
ENANTIOMORPHISM
ENANTIOMORPHOUS
ENANTIOMORPHS
ENANTIOMORPHY
ENANTIOPATHIES
ENANTIOPATHY
ENANTIOSES
ENANTIOSIS
ENANTIOSTYLIES
ENANTIOSTYLOUS
ENANTIOSTYLY

ENANTIOTROPIC
ENANTIOTROPIES
ENANTIOTROPY
ENARRATION
ENARRATIONS
ENARTHRODIAL
ENARTHROSES
ENARTHROSIS
ENCAMPMENT
ENCAMPMENTS
ENCANTHISES
ENCAPSULATE
ENCAPSULATED
ENCAPSULATES
ENCAPSULATING
ENCAPSULATION
ENCAPSULATIONS
ENCAPSULED
ENCAPSULES
ENCAPSULING
ENCARNALISE
ENCARNALISED
ENCARNALISES
ENCARNALISING
ENCARNALIZE
ENCARNALIZED
ENCARNALIZES
ENCARNALIZING
ENCARPUSES
ENCASEMENT
ENCASEMENTS
ENCASHABLE
ENCASHMENT
ENCASHMENTS
ENCAUSTICALLY
ENCAUSTICS
ENCEPHALALGIA
ENCEPHALALGIAS
ENCEPHALIC
ENCEPHALIN
ENCEPHALINE
ENCEPHALINES
ENCEPHALINS
ENCEPHALITIC
ENCEPHALITIDES
ENCEPHALITIS
ENCEPHALITISES
ENCEPHALITOGEN
ENCEPHALITOGENS
ENCEPHALOCELE
ENCEPHALOCELES
ENCEPHALOGRAM
ENCEPHALOGRAMS
ENCEPHALOGRAPH
ENCEPHALOGRAPHS
ENCEPHALOGRAPHY
ENCEPHALOID
ENCEPHALOMA
ENCEPHALOMAS
ENCEPHALOMATA
ENCEPHALON
ENCEPHALONS
ENCEPHALOPATHIC
ENCEPHALOPATHY
ENCEPHALOTOMIES
ENCEPHALOTOMY
ENCEPHALOUS
ENCHAINING
ENCHAINMENT
ENCHAINMENTS
ENCHANTERS
ENCHANTING
ENCHANTINGLY
ENCHANTMENT
ENCHANTMENTS
ENCHANTRESS
ENCHANTRESSES
ENCHARGING
ENCHARMING
ENCHEASONS
ENCHEERING
ENCHEIRIDION
ENCHEIRIDIONS
ENCHILADAS
ENCHIRIDIA
ENCHIRIDION
ENCHIRIDIONS
ENCHONDROMA
ENCHONDROMAS
ENCHONDROMATA
ENCHONDROMATOUS
ENCINCTURE
ENCINCTURED
ENCINCTURES
ENCINCTURING
ENCIPHERED
ENCIPHERER
ENCIPHERERS
ENCIPHERING
ENCIPHERMENT
ENCIPHERMENTS
ENCIRCLEMENT
ENCIRCLEMENTS
ENCIRCLING
ENCIRCLINGS
ENCLASPING
ENCLITICALLY
ENCLOISTER
ENCLOISTERED
ENCLOISTERING
ENCLOISTERS
ENCLOSABLE
ENCLOSURES
ENCLOTHING
ENCLOUDING
ENCODEMENT
ENCODEMENTS
ENCOIGNURE
ENCOIGNURES
ENCOLOURED
ENCOLOURING
ENCOLPIONS
ENCOLPIUMS
ENCOMENDERO
ENCOMENDEROS
ENCOMIASTIC
ENCOMIASTICAL
ENCOMIASTICALLY
ENCOMIASTS
ENCOMIENDA
ENCOMIENDAS
ENCOMPASSED
ENCOMPASSES
ENCOMPASSING
ENCOMPASSMENT
ENCOMPASSMENTS
ENCOPRESES
ENCOPRESIS
ENCOPRETIC
ENCOUNTERED
ENCOUNTERER
ENCOUNTERERS
ENCOUNTERING
ENCOUNTERS
ENCOURAGED
ENCOURAGEMENT
ENCOURAGEMENTS
ENCOURAGER
ENCOURAGERS
ENCOURAGES
ENCOURAGING
ENCOURAGINGLY
ENCOURAGINGS
ENCRADLING
ENCREASING
ENCRIMSONED
ENCRIMSONING
ENCRIMSONS
ENCRINITAL
ENCRINITES
ENCRINITIC
ENCROACHED
ENCROACHER
ENCROACHERS
ENCROACHES
ENCROACHING
ENCROACHINGLY
ENCROACHMENT
ENCROACHMENTS
ENCRUSTATION
ENCRUSTATIONS
ENCRUSTING
ENCRUSTMENT
ENCRUSTMENTS
ENCRYPTING
ENCRYPTION
ENCRYPTIONS
ENCULTURATE
ENCULTURATED
ENCULTURATES
ENCULTURATING
ENCULTURATION
ENCULTURATIONS
ENCULTURATIVE
ENCUMBERED
ENCUMBERING
ENCUMBERINGLY
ENCUMBERMENT
ENCUMBERMENTS
ENCUMBRANCE
ENCUMBRANCER
ENCUMBRANCERS
ENCUMBRANCES
ENCURTAINED
ENCURTAINING
ENCURTAINS
ENCYCLICAL
ENCYCLICALS
ENCYCLOPAEDIA
ENCYCLOPAEDIAS
ENCYCLOPAEDIC
ENCYCLOPAEDISM
ENCYCLOPAEDISMS
ENCYCLOPAEDIST
ENCYCLOPAEDISTS
ENCYCLOPEDIA
ENCYCLOPEDIAN
ENCYCLOPEDIAS
ENCYCLOPEDIC
ENCYCLOPEDICAL
ENCYCLOPEDISM
ENCYCLOPEDISMS
ENCYCLOPEDIST
ENCYCLOPEDISTS
ENCYSTATION
ENCYSTATIONS
ENCYSTMENT
ENCYSTMENTS
ENDAMAGEMENT
ENDAMAGEMENTS
ENDAMAGING
ENDAMOEBAE
ENDAMOEBAS
ENDANGERED
ENDANGERER
ENDANGERERS
ENDANGERING
ENDANGERMENT
ENDANGERMENTS
ENDARCHIES
ENDARTERECTOMY
ENDEARINGLY
ENDEARINGNESS
ENDEARINGNESSES
ENDEARMENT
ENDEARMENTS
ENDEAVORED
ENDEAVORER
ENDEAVORERS
ENDEAVORING
ENDEAVOURED
ENDEAVOURER
ENDEAVOURERS
ENDEAVOURING
ENDEAVOURMENT
ENDEAVOURMENTS
ENDEAVOURS
ENDECAGONS
ENDEIXISES
ENDEMICALLY
ENDEMICITIES
ENDEMICITY
ENDEMIOLOGIES
ENDEMIOLOGY
ENDENIZENED
ENDENIZENING
ENDENIZENS
ENDERGONIC
ENDERMATIC
ENDERMICAL
ENDLESSNESS
ENDLESSNESSES
ENDOBIOTIC
ENDOBLASTIC

NDOBLASTS
NDOCARDIA
NDOCARDIAC
NDOCARDIAL
NDOCARDITIC
NDOCARDITIS
NDOCARDITISES
NDOCARDIUM
NDOCARPAL
NDOCARPIC
NDOCENTRIC
NDOCHONDRAL
NDOCHYLOUS
NDOCRANIA
NDOCRANIAL
NDOCRANIUM
NDOCRINAL
NDOCRINES
NDOCRINIC
NDOCRINOLOGIC
NDOCRINOLOGIES
NDOCRINOLOGIST
NDOCRINOLOGY
NDOCRINOPATHIC
NDOCRINOPATHY
NDOCRINOUS
NDOCRITIC
NDOCUTICLE
NDOCUTICLES
NDOCYTOSES
NDOCYTOSIS
NDOCYTOTIC
NDODERMAL
NDODERMIC
NDODERMIS
NDODERMISES
NDODONTAL
NDODONTIC
NDODONTICALLY
NDODONTICS
NDODONTIST
NDODONTISTS
NDOENZYME
NDOENZYMES
NDOGAMIES
NDOGAMOUS
NDOGENIES
NDOGENOUS
NDOGENOUSLY
NDOLITHIC
NDOLYMPHATIC
NDOLYMPHS
NDOMETRIA
NDOMETRIAL
NDOMETRIOSES
NDOMETRIOSIS
NDOMETRITIS
NDOMETRITISES
NDOMETRIUM
NDOMITOSES
NDOMITOSIS
NDOMITOTIC
NDOMIXISES
NDOMORPHIC
NDOMORPHIES
NDOMORPHISM
ENDOMORPHISMS
ENDOMORPHS
ENDOMORPHY
ENDOMYCORRHIZA
ENDONEURIA
ENDONEURIUM
ENDONUCLEASE
ENDONUCLEASES
ENDONUCLEOLYTIC
ENDOPARASITE
ENDOPARASITES
ENDOPARASITIC
ENDOPARASITISM
ENDOPARASITISMS
ENDOPEPTIDASE
ENDOPEPTIDASES
ENDOPEROXIDE
ENDOPEROXIDES
ENDOPHAGIES
ENDOPHAGOUS
ENDOPHYLLOUS
ENDOPHYTES
ENDOPHYTIC
ENDOPHYTICALLY
ENDOPLASMIC
ENDOPLASMS
ENDOPLASTIC
ENDOPLEURA
ENDOPLEURAS
ENDOPODITE
ENDOPODITES
ENDOPOLYPLOID
ENDOPOLYPLOIDY
ENDOPROCTS
ENDORADIOSONDE
ENDORADIOSONDES
ENDORHIZAL
ENDORPHINS
ENDORSABLE
ENDORSEMENT
ENDORSEMENTS
ENDOSCOPES
ENDOSCOPIC
ENDOSCOPICALLY
ENDOSCOPIES
ENDOSCOPIST
ENDOSCOPISTS
ENDOSKELETAL
ENDOSKELETON
ENDOSKELETONS
ENDOSMOMETER
ENDOSMOMETERS
ENDOSMOMETRIC
ENDOSMOSES
ENDOSMOSIS
ENDOSMOTIC
ENDOSMOTICALLY
ENDOSPERMIC
ENDOSPERMS
ENDOSPORES
ENDOSPOROUS
ENDOSTEALLY
ENDOSTOSES
ENDOSTOSIS
ENDOSTYLES
ENDOSULFAN
ENDOSULFANS
ENDOSYMBIONT
ENDOSYMBIONTS
ENDOSYMBIOSES
ENDOSYMBIOSIS
ENDOSYMBIOTIC
ENDOTHECIA
ENDOTHECIAL
ENDOTHECIUM
ENDOTHELIA
ENDOTHELIAL
ENDOTHELIOID
ENDOTHELIOMA
ENDOTHELIOMAS
ENDOTHELIOMATA
ENDOTHELIUM
ENDOTHERMAL
ENDOTHERMIC
ENDOTHERMICALLY
ENDOTHERMIES
ENDOTHERMISM
ENDOTHERMISMS
ENDOTHERMS
ENDOTHERMY
ENDOTOXINS
ENDOTRACHEAL
ENDOTROPHIC
ENDOWMENTS
ENDPLAYING
ENDUNGEONED
ENDUNGEONING
ENDUNGEONS
ENDURABILITIES
ENDURABILITY
ENDURABLENESS
ENDURABLENESSES
ENDURANCES
ENDURINGLY
ENDURINGNESS
ENDURINGNESSES
ENERGETICAL
ENERGETICALLY
ENERGETICS
ENERGISATION
ENERGISATIONS
ENERGISERS
ENERGISING
ENERGIZATION
ENERGIZATIONS
ENERGIZERS
ENERGIZING
ENERGUMENS
ENERVATING
ENERVATION
ENERVATIONS
ENERVATIVE
ENERVATORS
ENFACEMENT
ENFACEMENTS
ENFEEBLEMENT
ENFEEBLEMENTS
ENFEEBLERS
ENFEEBLING
ENFELONING
ENFEOFFING
ENFEOFFMENT
ENFEOFFMENTS
ENFESTERED
ENFETTERED
ENFETTERING
ENFEVERING
ENFIERCING
ENFILADING
ENFLESHING
ENFLEURAGE
ENFLEURAGES
ENFLOWERED
ENFLOWERING
ENFOLDMENT
ENFOLDMENTS
ENFORCEABILITY
ENFORCEABLE
ENFORCEDLY
ENFORCEMENT
ENFORCEMENTS
ENFORESTED
ENFORESTING
ENFOULDERED
ENFRAMEMENT
ENFRAMEMENTS
ENFRANCHISE
ENFRANCHISED
ENFRANCHISEMENT
ENFRANCHISER
ENFRANCHISERS
ENFRANCHISES
ENFRANCHISING
ENFREEDOMED
ENFREEDOMING
ENFREEDOMS
ENFREEZING
ENGAGEMENT
ENGAGEMENTS
ENGAGINGLY
ENGAGINGNESS
ENGAGINGNESSES
ENGARLANDED
ENGARLANDING
ENGARLANDS
ENGARRISON
ENGARRISONED
ENGARRISONING
ENGARRISONS
ENGENDERED
ENGENDERER
ENGENDERERS
ENGENDERING
ENGENDERMENT
ENGENDERMENTS
ENGENDRURE
ENGENDRURES
ENGENDURES
ENGINEERED
ENGINEERING
ENGINEERINGS
ENGINERIES
ENGIRDLING
ENGISCOPES
ENGLACIALLY
ENGLISHING
ENGLOOMING
ENGLUTTING

ENGORGEMENT
ENGORGEMENTS
ENGOUEMENT
ENGOUEMENTS
ENGOUMENTS
ENGRAFFING
ENGRAFTATION
ENGRAFTATIONS
ENGRAFTING
ENGRAFTMENT
ENGRAFTMENTS
ENGRAILING
ENGRAILMENT
ENGRAILMENTS
ENGRAINEDLY
ENGRAINEDNESS
ENGRAINEDNESSES
ENGRAINERS
ENGRAINING
ENGRAMMATIC
ENGRASPING
ENGRAVERIES
ENGRAVINGS
ENGRENAGES
ENGRIEVING
ENGROOVING
ENGROSSEDLY
ENGROSSERS
ENGROSSING
ENGROSSINGLY
ENGROSSMENT
ENGROSSMENTS
ENGUARDING
ENGULFMENT
ENGULFMENTS
ENGULPHING
ENGYSCOPES
ENHANCEMENT
ENHANCEMENTS
ENHARMONIC
ENHARMONICAL
ENHARMONICALLY
ENHEARSING
ENHEARTENED
ENHEARTENING
ENHEARTENS
ENHUNGERED
ENHUNGERING
ENHYDRITES
ENHYDRITIC
ENHYDROSES
ENHYPOSTASIA
ENHYPOSTASIAS
ENHYPOSTATIC
ENHYPOSTATISE
ENHYPOSTATISED
ENHYPOSTATISES
ENHYPOSTATISING
ENHYPOSTATIZE
ENHYPOSTATIZED
ENHYPOSTATIZES
ENHYPOSTATIZING
ENIGMATICAL
ENIGMATICALLY
ENIGMATISE
ENIGMATISED
ENIGMATISES
ENIGMATISING
ENIGMATIST
ENIGMATISTS
ENIGMATIZE
ENIGMATIZED
ENIGMATIZES
ENIGMATIZING
ENIGMATOGRAPHY
ENJAMBEMENT
ENJAMBEMENTS
ENJAMBMENT
ENJAMBMENTS
ENJOINDERS
ENJOINMENT
ENJOINMENTS
ENJOYABLENESS
ENJOYABLENESSES
ENJOYMENTS
ENKEPHALIN
ENKEPHALINE
ENKEPHALINES
ENKEPHALINS
ENKERNELLED
ENKERNELLING
ENKINDLERS
ENKINDLING
ENLACEMENT
ENLACEMENTS
ENLARGEABLE
ENLARGEDLY
ENLARGEDNESS
ENLARGEDNESSES
ENLARGEMENT
ENLARGEMENTS
ENLARGENED
ENLARGENING
ENLEVEMENT
ENLEVEMENTS
ENLIGHTENED
ENLIGHTENER
ENLIGHTENERS
ENLIGHTENING
ENLIGHTENMENT
ENLIGHTENMENTS
ENLIGHTENS
ENLIGHTING
ENLISTMENT
ENLISTMENTS
ENLIVENERS
ENLIVENING
ENLIVENMENT
ENLIVENMENTS
ENLUMINING
ENMESHMENT
ENMESHMENTS
ENNEAGONAL
ENNEAHEDRA
ENNEAHEDRAL
ENNEAHEDRON
ENNEAHEDRONS
ENNEANDRIAN
ENNEANDROUS
ENNEASTYLE
ENNOBLEMENT
ENNOBLEMENTS
ENOKIDAKES
ENOKITAKES
ENOLOGICAL
ENOLOGISTS
ENORMITIES
ENORMOUSLY
ENORMOUSNESS
ENORMOUSNESSES
ENOUNCEMENT
ENOUNCEMENTS
ENPHYTOTIC
ENQUIRATION
ENQUIRATIONS
ENRAGEMENT
ENRAGEMENTS
ENRANCKLED
ENRANCKLES
ENRANCKLING
ENRAPTURED
ENRAPTURES
ENRAPTURING
ENRAUNGING
ENRAVISHED
ENRAVISHES
ENRAVISHING
ENREGIMENT
ENREGIMENTED
ENREGIMENTING
ENREGIMENTS
ENREGISTER
ENREGISTERED
ENREGISTERING
ENREGISTERS
ENRHEUMING
ENRICHMENT
ENRICHMENTS
ENROLLMENT
ENROLLMENTS
ENROLMENTS
ENROUGHING
ENROUNDING
ENSAMPLING
ENSANGUINATED
ENSANGUINE
ENSANGUINED
ENSANGUINES
ENSANGUINING
ENSCHEDULE
ENSCHEDULED
ENSCHEDULES
ENSCHEDULING
ENSCONCING
ENSCROLLED
ENSCROLLING
ENSEPULCHRE
ENSEPULCHRED
ENSEPULCHRES
ENSEPULCHRING
ENSERFMENT
ENSERFMENTS
ENSHEATHED
ENSHEATHES
ENSHEATHING
ENSHELLING
ENSHELTERED
ENSHELTERING
ENSHELTERS
ENSHIELDED
ENSHIELDING
ENSHRINEES
ENSHRINEMENT
ENSHRINEMENTS
ENSHRINING
ENSHROUDED
ENSHROUDING
ENSIGNCIES
ENSIGNSHIP
ENSIGNSHIPS
ENSILABILITIES
ENSILABILITY
ENSILAGEING
ENSILAGING
ENSLAVEMENT
ENSLAVEMENTS
ENSNAREMENT
ENSNAREMENTS
ENSNARLING
ENSORCELED
ENSORCELING
ENSORCELLED
ENSORCELLING
ENSORCELLMENT
ENSORCELLMENTS
ENSORCELLS
ENSOULMENT
ENSOULMENTS
ENSPHERING
ENSTAMPING
ENSTATITES
ENSTEEPING
ENSTRUCTURED
ENSWATHEMENT
ENSWATHEMENTS
ENSWATHING
ENSWEEPING
ENTABLATURE
ENTABLATURES
ENTABLEMENT
ENTABLEMENTS
ENTAILMENT
ENTAILMENTS
ENTAMOEBAE
ENTAMOEBAS
ENTANGLEMENT
ENTANGLEMENTS
ENTANGLERS
ENTANGLING
ENTELECHIES
ENTELLUSES
ENTENDERED
ENTENDERING
ENTERCHAUNGE
ENTERCHAUNGED
ENTERCHAUNGES
ENTERCHAUNGING
ENTERDEALE
ENTERDEALED
ENTERDEALES
ENTERDEALING
ENTERECTOMIES
ENTERECTOMY
ENTERITIDES

ENTERITISES
ENTEROBACTERIA
ENTEROBACTERIAL
ENTEROBACTERIUM
ENTEROBIASES
ENTEROBIASIS
ENTEROCELE
ENTEROCELES
ENTEROCENTESES
ENTEROCENTESIS
ENTEROCOCCAL
ENTEROCOCCI
ENTEROCOCCUS
ENTEROCOEL
ENTEROCOELE
ENTEROCOELES
ENTEROCOELIC
ENTEROCOELOUS
ENTEROCOELS
ENTEROCOLITIS
ENTEROCOLITISES
ENTEROGASTRONE
ENTEROGASTRONES
ENTEROHEPATITIS
ENTEROKINASE
ENTEROKINASES
ENTEROLITH
ENTEROLITHS
ENTEROPATHIES
ENTEROPATHY
ENTEROPNEUST
ENTEROPNEUSTAL
ENTEROPNEUSTS
ENTEROPTOSES
ENTEROPTOSIS
ENTEROSTOMAL
ENTEROSTOMIES
ENTEROSTOMY
ENTEROTOMIES
ENTEROTOMY
ENTEROTOXIN
ENTEROTOXINS
ENTEROVIRAL
ENTEROVIRUS
ENTEROVIRUSES
ENTERPRISE
ENTERPRISED
ENTERPRISER
ENTERPRISERS
ENTERPRISES
ENTERPRISING
ENTERPRISINGLY
ENTERTAINED
ENTERTAINER
ENTERTAINERS
ENTERTAINING
ENTERTAININGLY
ENTERTAININGS
ENTERTAINMENT
ENTERTAINMENTS
ENTERTAINS
ENTERTAKEN
ENTERTAKES
ENTERTAKING
ENTERTISSUED
ENTHALPIES
ENTHRALDOM
ENTHRALDOMS
ENTHRALLED
ENTHRALLER
ENTHRALLERS
ENTHRALLING
ENTHRALLMENT
ENTHRALLMENTS
ENTHRALMENT
ENTHRALMENTS
ENTHRONEMENT
ENTHRONEMENTS
ENTHRONING
ENTHRONISATION
ENTHRONISATIONS
ENTHRONISE
ENTHRONISED
ENTHRONISES
ENTHRONISING
ENTHRONIZATION
ENTHRONIZATIONS
ENTHRONIZE
ENTHRONIZED
ENTHRONIZES
ENTHRONIZING
ENTHUSIASM
ENTHUSIASMS
ENTHUSIAST
ENTHUSIASTIC
ENTHUSIASTICAL
ENTHUSIASTS
ENTHYMEMATIC
ENTHYMEMATICAL
ENTHYMEMES
ENTICEABLE
ENTICEMENT
ENTICEMENTS
ENTICINGLY
ENTICINGNESS
ENTICINGNESSES
ENTIRENESS
ENTIRENESSES
ENTIRETIES
ENTITATIVE
ENTITLEMENT
ENTITLEMENTS
ENTOBLASTIC
ENTOBLASTS
ENTODERMAL
ENTODERMIC
ENTOILMENT
ENTOILMENTS
ENTOMBMENT
ENTOMBMENTS
ENTOMOFAUNA
ENTOMOFAUNAE
ENTOMOFAUNAS
ENTOMOLOGIC
ENTOMOLOGICAL
ENTOMOLOGICALLY
ENTOMOLOGIES
ENTOMOLOGISE
ENTOMOLOGISED
ENTOMOLOGISES
ENTOMOLOGISING
ENTOMOLOGIST
ENTOMOLOGISTS
ENTOMOLOGIZE
ENTOMOLOGIZED
ENTOMOLOGIZES
ENTOMOLOGIZING
ENTOMOLOGY
ENTOMOPHAGIES
ENTOMOPHAGOUS
ENTOMOPHAGY
ENTOMOPHILIES
ENTOMOPHILOUS
ENTOMOPHILY
ENTOMOSTRACAN
ENTOMOSTRACANS
ENTOMOSTRACOUS
ENTOPHYTAL
ENTOPHYTES
ENTOPHYTIC
ENTOPHYTOUS
ENTOPLASTRA
ENTOPLASTRAL
ENTOPLASTRON
ENTOPROCTS
ENTOURAGES
ENTRAILING
ENTRAINEMENT
ENTRAINEMENTS
ENTRAINERS
ENTRAINING
ENTRAINMENT
ENTRAINMENTS
ENTRAMMELLED
ENTRAMMELLING
ENTRAMMELS
ENTRANCEMENT
ENTRANCEMENTS
ENTRANCEWAY
ENTRANCEWAYS
ENTRANCING
ENTRAPMENT
ENTRAPMENTS
ENTRAPPERS
ENTRAPPING
ENTREASURE
ENTREASURED
ENTREASURES
ENTREASURING
ENTREATABLE
ENTREATIES
ENTREATING
ENTREATINGLY
ENTREATIVE
ENTREATMENT
ENTREATMENTS
ENTRECHATS
ENTRECOTES
ENTREMESSE
ENTREMESSES
ENTRENCHED
ENTRENCHER
ENTRENCHERS
ENTRENCHES
ENTRENCHING
ENTRENCHMENT
ENTRENCHMENTS
ENTREPRENEUR
ENTREPRENEURIAL
ENTREPRENEURS
ENTREPRENEUSE
ENTREPRENEUSES
ENTROPICALLY
ENTROPIONS
ENTROPIUMS
ENTRUSTING
ENTRUSTMENT
ENTRUSTMENTS
ENTWINEMENT
ENTWINEMENTS
ENTWISTING
ENUCLEATED
ENUCLEATES
ENUCLEATING
ENUCLEATION
ENUCLEATIONS
ENUMERABILITIES
ENUMERABILITY
ENUMERABLE
ENUMERATED
ENUMERATES
ENUMERATING
ENUMERATION
ENUMERATIONS
ENUMERATIVE
ENUMERATOR
ENUMERATORS
ENUNCIABLE
ENUNCIATED
ENUNCIATES
ENUNCIATING
ENUNCIATION
ENUNCIATIONS
ENUNCIATIVE
ENUNCIATIVELY
ENUNCIATOR
ENUNCIATORS
ENUNCIATORY
ENUREDNESS
ENUREDNESSES
ENUREMENTS
ENURESISES
ENVASSALLED
ENVASSALLING
ENVAULTING
ENVEIGLING
ENVELOPERS
ENVELOPING
ENVELOPMENT
ENVELOPMENTS
ENVENOMING
ENVENOMISATION
ENVENOMISATIONS
ENVENOMIZATION
ENVENOMIZATIONS
ENVERMEILED
ENVERMEILING
ENVERMEILS
ENVIABLENESS
ENVIABLENESSES
ENVIOUSNESS
ENVIOUSNESSES
ENVIRONICS
ENVIRONING

ENVIRONMENT
ENVIRONMENTAL
ENVIRONMENTALLY
ENVIRONMENTS
ENVISAGEMENT
ENVISAGEMENTS
ENVISAGING
ENVISIONED
ENVISIONING
ENVOYSHIPS
ENWALLOWED
ENWALLOWING
ENWHEELING
ENWRAPMENT
ENWRAPMENTS
ENWRAPPING
ENWRAPPINGS
ENWREATHED
ENWREATHES
ENWREATHING
ENZOOTICALLY
ENZYMATICALLY
ENZYMICALLY
ENZYMOLOGICAL
ENZYMOLOGIES
ENZYMOLOGIST
ENZYMOLOGISTS
ENZYMOLOGY
ENZYMOLYSES
ENZYMOLYSIS
ENZYMOLYTIC
EOHIPPUSES
EOSINOPHIL
EOSINOPHILE
EOSINOPHILES
EOSINOPHILIA
EOSINOPHILIAS
EOSINOPHILIC
EOSINOPHILOUS
EOSINOPHILS
EPAGOMENAL
EPANADIPLOSES
EPANADIPLOSIS
EPANALEPSES
EPANALEPSIS
EPANALEPTIC
EPANAPHORA
EPANAPHORAL
EPANAPHORAS
EPANODOSES
EPANORTHOSES
EPANORTHOSIS
EPANORTHOTIC
EPARCHATES
EPAULEMENT
EPAULEMENTS
EPAULETTED
EPAULETTES
EPEIROGENESES
EPEIROGENESIS
EPEIROGENETIC
EPEIROGENIC
EPEIROGENICALLY
EPEIROGENIES
EPEIROGENY
EPENCEPHALA
EPENCEPHALIC
EPENCEPHALON
EPENCEPHALONS
EPENTHESES
EPENTHESIS
EPENTHETIC
EPEOLATRIES
EPEXEGESES
EPEXEGESIS
EPEXEGETIC
EPEXEGETICAL
EPEXEGETICALLY
EPHEBOPHILIA
EPHEBOPHILIAS
EPHEDRINES
EPHEMERALITIES
EPHEMERALITY
EPHEMERALLY
EPHEMERALNESS
EPHEMERALNESSES
EPHEMERALS
EPHEMERIDES
EPHEMERIDIAN
EPHEMERIDS
EPHEMERIST
EPHEMERISTS
EPHEMERONS
EPHEMEROPTERAN
EPHEMEROPTERANS
EPHEMEROUS
EPHORALTIES
EPIBLASTIC
EPICALYCES
EPICALYXES
EPICANTHIC
EPICANTHUS
EPICARDIAC
EPICARDIAL
EPICARDIUM
EPICENISMS
EPICENTERS
EPICENTRAL
EPICENTRES
EPICENTRUM
EPICHEIREMA
EPICHEIREMAS
EPICHLOROHYDRIN
EPICONDYLE
EPICONDYLES
EPICONDYLITIS
EPICONDYLITISES
EPICONTINENTAL
EPICRANIUM
EPICUREANISM
EPICUREANISMS
EPICUREANS
EPICURISED
EPICURISES
EPICURISING
EPICURISMS
EPICURIZED
EPICURIZES
EPICURIZING
EPICUTICLE
EPICUTICLES
EPICUTICULAR
EPICYCLICAL
EPICYCLOID
EPICYCLOIDAL
EPICYCLOIDS
EPIDEICTIC
EPIDEICTICAL
EPIDEMICAL
EPIDEMICALLY
EPIDEMICITIES
EPIDEMICITY
EPIDEMIOLOGIC
EPIDEMIOLOGICAL
EPIDEMIOLOGIES
EPIDEMIOLOGIST
EPIDEMIOLOGISTS
EPIDEMIOLOGY
EPIDENDRONE
EPIDENDRONES
EPIDENDRUM
EPIDENDRUMS
EPIDERMISES
EPIDERMOID
EPIDERMOLYSES
EPIDERMOLYSIS
EPIDIASCOPE
EPIDIASCOPES
EPIDIDYMAL
EPIDIDYMIDES
EPIDIDYMIS
EPIDIDYMITIS
EPIDIDYMITISES
EPIDIORITE
EPIDIORITES
EPIDOSITES
EPIDOTISATION
EPIDOTISATIONS
EPIDOTISED
EPIDOTIZATION
EPIDOTIZATIONS
EPIDOTIZED
EPIGASTRIA
EPIGASTRIAL
EPIGASTRIC
EPIGASTRIUM
EPIGENESES
EPIGENESIS
EPIGENESIST
EPIGENESISTS
EPIGENETIC
EPIGENETICALLY
EPIGENETICIST
EPIGENETICISTS
EPIGENETICS
EPIGENISTS
EPIGLOTTAL
EPIGLOTTIC
EPIGLOTTIDES
EPIGLOTTIS
EPIGLOTTISES
EPIGNATHOUS
EPIGONISMS
EPIGRAMMATIC
EPIGRAMMATICAL
EPIGRAMMATISE
EPIGRAMMATISED
EPIGRAMMATISER
EPIGRAMMATISERS
EPIGRAMMATISES
EPIGRAMMATISING
EPIGRAMMATISM
EPIGRAMMATISMS
EPIGRAMMATIST
EPIGRAMMATISTS
EPIGRAMMATIZE
EPIGRAMMATIZED
EPIGRAMMATIZER
EPIGRAMMATIZERS
EPIGRAMMATIZES
EPIGRAMMATIZING
EPIGRAPHED
EPIGRAPHER
EPIGRAPHERS
EPIGRAPHIC
EPIGRAPHICAL
EPIGRAPHICALLY
EPIGRAPHIES
EPIGRAPHING
EPIGRAPHIST
EPIGRAPHISTS
EPILATIONS
EPILEPSIES
EPILEPTICAL
EPILEPTICALLY
EPILEPTICS
EPILEPTIFORM
EPILEPTOGENIC
EPILEPTOID
EPILIMNION
EPILIMNIONS
EPILOBIUMS
EPILOGISED
EPILOGISES
EPILOGISING
EPILOGISTIC
EPILOGISTS
EPILOGIZED
EPILOGIZES
EPILOGIZING
EPILOGUING
EPILOGUISE
EPILOGUISED
EPILOGUISES
EPILOGUISING
EPILOGUIZE
EPILOGUIZED
EPILOGUIZES
EPILOGUIZING
EPIMELETIC
EPIMERASES
EPIMERISMS
EPIMORPHIC
EPIMORPHOSES
EPIMORPHOSIS
EPINASTICALLY
EPINASTIES
EPINEPHRIN
EPINEPHRINE
EPINEPHRINES
EPINEPHRINS
EPINEURIAL
EPINEURIUM
EPINEURIUMS

EPINICIONS
EPINIKIONS
EPIPELAGIC
EPIPETALOUS
EPIPHANIES
EPIPHANOUS
EPIPHENOMENA
EPIPHENOMENAL
EPIPHENOMENALLY
EPIPHENOMENON
EPIPHONEMA
EPIPHONEMAS
EPIPHRAGMS
EPIPHYLLOUS
EPIPHYSEAL
EPIPHYSIAL
EPIPHYTICAL
EPIPHYTICALLY
EPIPHYTISM
EPIPHYTISMS
EPIPHYTOLOGIES
EPIPHYTOLOGY
EPIPHYTOTIC
EPIPHYTOTICS
EPIPLASTRA
EPIPLASTRAL
EPIPLASTRON
EPIPOLISMS
EPIROGENETIC
EPIROGENIC
EPIROGENIES
EPIRRHEMAS
EPIRRHEMATIC
EPISCOPACIES
EPISCOPACY
EPISCOPALIAN
EPISCOPALIANISM
EPISCOPALIANS
EPISCOPALISM
EPISCOPALISMS
EPISCOPALLY
EPISCOPANT
EPISCOPANTS
EPISCOPATE
EPISCOPATED
EPISCOPATES
EPISCOPATING
EPISCOPIES
EPISCOPISE
EPISCOPISED
EPISCOPISES
EPISCOPISING
EPISCOPIZE
EPISCOPIZED
EPISCOPIZES
EPISCOPIZING
EPISEMATIC
EPISEPALOUS
EPISIOTOMIES
EPISIOTOMY
EPISODICAL
EPISODICALLY
EPISOMALLY
EPISPASTIC
EPISPASTICS
EPISTASIES
EPISTAXISES
EPISTEMICALLY
EPISTEMICS
EPISTEMOLOGICAL
EPISTEMOLOGIES
EPISTEMOLOGIST
EPISTEMOLOGISTS
EPISTEMOLOGY
EPISTERNAL
EPISTERNUM
EPISTERNUMS
EPISTILBITE
EPISTILBITES
EPISTOLARIAN
EPISTOLARIANS
EPISTOLARIES
EPISTOLARY
EPISTOLATORY
EPISTOLERS
EPISTOLETS
EPISTOLICAL
EPISTOLISE
EPISTOLISED
EPISTOLISES
EPISTOLISING
EPISTOLIST
EPISTOLISTS
EPISTOLIZE
EPISTOLIZED
EPISTOLIZES
EPISTOLIZING
EPISTOLOGRAPHY
EPISTROPHE
EPISTROPHES
EPITAPHERS
EPITAPHIAL
EPITAPHIAN
EPITAPHING
EPITAPHIST
EPITAPHISTS
EPITAXIALLY
EPITHALAMIA
EPITHALAMIC
EPITHALAMION
EPITHALAMIUM
EPITHALAMIUMS
EPITHELIAL
EPITHELIALISE
EPITHELIALISED
EPITHELIALISES
EPITHELIALISING
EPITHELIALIZE
EPITHELIALIZED
EPITHELIALIZES
EPITHELIALIZING
EPITHELIOID
EPITHELIOMA
EPITHELIOMAS
EPITHELIOMATA
EPITHELIOMATOUS
EPITHELISATION
EPITHELISATIONS
EPITHELISE
EPITHELISED
EPITHELISES
EPITHELISING
EPITHELIUM
EPITHELIUMS
EPITHELIZATION
EPITHELIZATIONS
EPITHELIZE
EPITHELIZED
EPITHELIZES
EPITHELIZING
EPITHEMATA
EPITHERMAL
EPITHETICAL
EPITHETING
EPITHETONS
EPITHYMETIC
EPITOMICAL
EPITOMISATION
EPITOMISATIONS
EPITOMISED
EPITOMISER
EPITOMISERS
EPITOMISES
EPITOMISING
EPITOMISTS
EPITOMIZATION
EPITOMIZATIONS
EPITOMIZED
EPITOMIZER
EPITOMIZERS
EPITOMIZES
EPITOMIZING
EPITRACHELION
EPITRACHELIONS
EPITROCHOID
EPITROCHOIDS
EPIZEUXISES
EPIZOOTICALLY
EPIZOOTICS
EPIZOOTIES
EPIZOOTIOLOGIC
EPIZOOTIOLOGIES
EPIZOOTIOLOGY
EPONYCHIUM
EPONYCHIUMS
EPONYMOUSLY
EPOXIDATION
EPOXIDATIONS
EPOXIDISED
EPOXIDISES
EPOXIDISING
EPOXIDIZED
EPOXIDIZES
EPOXIDIZING
EPROUVETTE
EPROUVETTES
EPULATIONS
EPURATIONS
EQUABILITIES
EQUABILITY
EQUABLENESS
EQUABLENESSES
EQUALISATION
EQUALISATIONS
EQUALISERS
EQUALISING
EQUALITARIAN
EQUALITARIANISM
EQUALITARIANS
EQUALITIES
EQUALIZATION
EQUALIZATIONS
EQUALIZERS
EQUALIZING
EQUALNESSES
EQUANIMITIES
EQUANIMITY
EQUANIMOUS
EQUANIMOUSLY
EQUATABILITIES
EQUATABILITY
EQUATIONAL
EQUATIONALLY
EQUATORIAL
EQUATORIALLY
EQUATORIALS
EQUATORWARD
EQUESTRIAN
EQUESTRIANISM
EQUESTRIANISMS
EQUESTRIANS
EQUESTRIENNE
EQUESTRIENNES
EQUIANGULAR
EQUIANGULARITY
EQUIBALANCE
EQUIBALANCED
EQUIBALANCES
EQUIBALANCING
EQUICALORIC
EQUIDIFFERENT
EQUIDISTANCE
EQUIDISTANCES
EQUIDISTANT
EQUIDISTANTLY
EQUILATERAL
EQUILATERALLY
EQUILATERALS
EQUILIBRANT
EQUILIBRANTS
EQUILIBRATE
EQUILIBRATED
EQUILIBRATES
EQUILIBRATING
EQUILIBRATION
EQUILIBRATIONS
EQUILIBRATOR
EQUILIBRATORS
EQUILIBRATORY
EQUILIBRIA
EQUILIBRIST
EQUILIBRISTIC
EQUILIBRISTS
EQUILIBRITIES
EQUILIBRITY
EQUILIBRIUM
EQUILIBRIUMS
EQUIMOLECULAR
EQUIMULTIPLE
EQUIMULTIPLES
EQUINITIES
EQUINOCTIAL
EQUINOCTIALLY
EQUINOCTIALS

EQUINUMEROUS
EQUIPAGING
EQUIPARATE
EQUIPARATED
EQUIPARATES
EQUIPARATING
EQUIPARATION
EQUIPARATIONS
EQUIPARTITION
EQUIPARTITIONS
EQUIPMENTS
EQUIPOISED
EQUIPOISES
EQUIPOISING
EQUIPOLLENCE
EQUIPOLLENCES
EQUIPOLLENCIES
EQUIPOLLENCY
EQUIPOLLENT
EQUIPOLLENTLY
EQUIPOLLENTS
EQUIPONDERANCE
EQUIPONDERANCES
EQUIPONDERANCY
EQUIPONDERANT
EQUIPONDERATE
EQUIPONDERATED
EQUIPONDERATES
EQUIPONDERATING
EQUIPOTENT
EQUIPOTENTIAL
EQUIPROBABILITY
EQUIPROBABLE
EQUISETACEOUS
EQUISETIFORM
EQUISETUMS
EQUITABILITIES
EQUITABILITY
EQUITABLENESS
EQUITABLENESSES
EQUITATION
EQUITATIONS
EQUIVALENCE
EQUIVALENCES
EQUIVALENCIES
EQUIVALENCY
EQUIVALENT
EQUIVALENTLY
EQUIVALENTS
EQUIVOCALITIES
EQUIVOCALITY
EQUIVOCALLY
EQUIVOCALNESS
EQUIVOCALNESSES
EQUIVOCATE
EQUIVOCATED
EQUIVOCATES
EQUIVOCATING
EQUIVOCATINGLY
EQUIVOCATION
EQUIVOCATIONS
EQUIVOCATOR
EQUIVOCATORS
EQUIVOCATORY
EQUIVOQUES
ERADIATING
ERADIATION
ERADIATIONS
ERADICABLE
ERADICABLY
ERADICANTS
ERADICATED
ERADICATES
ERADICATING
ERADICATION
ERADICATIONS
ERADICATIVE
ERADICATOR
ERADICATORS
ERASABILITIES
ERASABILITY
ERASEMENTS
ERECTILITIES
ERECTILITY
ERECTNESSES
EREMACAUSES
EREMACAUSIS
EREMITICAL
EREMITISMS
EREMURUSES
ERETHISMIC
ERETHISTIC
ERGASTOPLASM
ERGASTOPLASMIC
ERGASTOPLASMS
ERGATANDROMORPH
ERGATANERS
ERGATIVITIES
ERGATIVITY
ERGATOCRACIES
ERGATOCRACY
ERGATOGYNE
ERGATOGYNES
ERGATOMORPH
ERGATOMORPHIC
ERGATOMORPHS
ERGODICITIES
ERGODICITY
ERGOGRAPHS
ERGOMANIAC
ERGOMANIACS
ERGOMANIAS
ERGOMETERS
ERGOMETRIC
ERGOMETRIES
ERGONOMICALLY
ERGONOMICS
ERGONOMIST
ERGONOMISTS
ERGONOVINE
ERGONOVINES
ERGOPHOBIA
ERGOPHOBIAS
ERGOSTEROL
ERGOSTEROLS
ERGOTAMINE
ERGOTAMINES
ERGOTISING
ERGOTIZING
ERICACEOUS
ERINACEOUS
ERIOMETERS
ERIOPHOROUS
ERIOPHORUM
ERIOPHORUMS
ERIOPHYIDS
ERIOSTEMON
ERIOSTEMONS
ERISTICALLY
ERODIBILITIES
ERODIBILITY
EROGENEITIES
EROGENEITY
EROSIONALLY
EROSIVENESS
EROSIVENESSES
EROSIVITIES
EROTICALLY
EROTICISATION
EROTICISATIONS
EROTICISED
EROTICISES
EROTICISING
EROTICISMS
EROTICISTS
EROTICIZATION
EROTICIZATIONS
EROTICIZED
EROTICIZES
EROTICIZING
EROTISATION
EROTISATIONS
EROTIZATION
EROTIZATIONS
EROTOGENIC
EROTOGENOUS
EROTOLOGICAL
EROTOLOGIES
EROTOLOGIST
EROTOLOGISTS
EROTOMANIA
EROTOMANIAC
EROTOMANIACS
EROTOMANIAS
EROTOPHOBIA
EROTOPHOBIAS
ERRANTRIES
ERRATICALLY
ERRATICISM
ERRATICISMS
ERRONEOUSLY
ERRONEOUSNESS
ERRONEOUSNESSES
ERUBESCENCE
ERUBESCENCES
ERUBESCENCIES
ERUBESCENCY
ERUBESCENT
ERUBESCITE
ERUBESCITES
ERUCTATING
ERUCTATION
ERUCTATIONS
ERUCTATIVE
ERUDITENESS
ERUDITENESSES
ERUDITIONS
ERUPTIONAL
ERUPTIVELY
ERUPTIVENESS
ERUPTIVENESSES
ERUPTIVITIES
ERUPTIVITY
ERVALENTAS
ERYSIPELAS
ERYSIPELASES
ERYSIPELATOUS
ERYSIPELOID
ERYSIPELOIDS
ERYTHEMATIC
ERYTHEMATOUS
ERYTHORBATE
ERYTHORBATES
ERYTHRAEMIA
ERYTHRAEMIAS
ERYTHREMIA
ERYTHREMIAS
ERYTHRINAS
ERYTHRISMAL
ERYTHRISMS
ERYTHRISTIC
ERYTHRITES
ERYTHRITIC
ERYTHRITOL
ERYTHRITOLS
ERYTHROBLAST
ERYTHROBLASTIC
ERYTHROBLASTS
ERYTHROCYTE
ERYTHROCYTES
ERYTHROCYTIC
ERYTHROMELALGIA
ERYTHROMYCIN
ERYTHROMYCINS
ERYTHRONIUM
ERYTHRONIUMS
ERYTHROPENIA
ERYTHROPENIAS
ERYTHROPHOBIA
ERYTHROPHOBIAS
ERYTHROPOIESES
ERYTHROPOIESIS
ERYTHROPOIETIC
ERYTHROPOIETIN
ERYTHROPOIETINS
ERYTHROPSIA
ERYTHROPSIAS
ERYTHROSIN
ERYTHROSINE
ERYTHROSINES
ERYTHROSINS
ESCADRILLE
ESCADRILLES
ESCALADERS
ESCALADING
ESCALADOES
ESCALATING
ESCALATION
ESCALATIONS
ESCALATORS
ESCALATORY
ESCALLONIA
ESCALLONIAS
ESCALLOPED

ESCALLOPING
ESCALOPING
ESCAMOTAGE
ESCAMOTAGES
ESCAPADOES
ESCAPELESS
ESCAPEMENT
ESCAPEMENTS
ESCAPOLOGIES
ESCAPOLOGIST
ESCAPOLOGISTS
ESCAPOLOGY
ESCARMOUCHE
ESCARMOUCHES
ESCARPMENT
ESCARPMENTS
ESCHAROTIC
ESCHAROTICS
ESCHATOLOGIC
ESCHATOLOGICAL
ESCHATOLOGIES
ESCHATOLOGIST
ESCHATOLOGISTS
ESCHATOLOGY
ESCHEATABLE
ESCHEATAGE
ESCHEATAGES
ESCHEATING
ESCHEATMENT
ESCHEATMENTS
ESCHEATORS
ESCHSCHOLTZIA
ESCHSCHOLTZIAS
ESCHSCHOLZIA
ESCHSCHOLZIAS
ESCLANDRES
ESCOPETTES
ESCORTAGES
ESCRIBANOS
ESCRITOIRE
ESCRITOIRES
ESCRITORIAL
ESCUTCHEON
ESCUTCHEONED
ESCUTCHEONS
ESEMPLASIES
ESEMPLASTIC
ESOPHAGEAL
ESOPHAGOSCOPE
ESOPHAGOSCOPES
ESOPHAGUSES
ESOTERICALLY
ESOTERICISM
ESOTERICISMS
ESOTERICIST
ESOTERICISTS
ESOTERISMS
ESOTROPIAS
ESPADRILLE
ESPADRILLES
ESPAGNOLES
ESPAGNOLETTE
ESPAGNOLETTES
ESPALIERED
ESPALIERING
ESPECIALLY
ESPERANCES
ESPIEGLERIE
ESPIEGLERIES
ESPIONAGES
ESPLANADES
ESPRESSIVO
ESQUIRESSES
ESSAYETTES
ESSAYISTIC
ESSENTIALISE
ESSENTIALISED
ESSENTIALISES
ESSENTIALISING
ESSENTIALISM
ESSENTIALISMS
ESSENTIALIST
ESSENTIALISTS
ESSENTIALITIES
ESSENTIALITY
ESSENTIALIZE
ESSENTIALIZED
ESSENTIALIZES
ESSENTIALIZING
ESSENTIALLY
ESSENTIALNESS
ESSENTIALNESSES
ESSENTIALS
ESTABLISHABLE
ESTABLISHED
ESTABLISHER
ESTABLISHERS
ESTABLISHES
ESTABLISHING
ESTABLISHMENT
ESTABLISHMENTS
ESTAFETTES
ESTAMINETS
ESTANCIERO
ESTANCIEROS
ESTATESMAN
ESTATESMEN
ESTERIFICATION
ESTERIFICATIONS
ESTERIFIED
ESTERIFIES
ESTERIFYING
ESTHESIOGEN
ESTHESIOGENS
ESTHESISES
ESTHETICAL
ESTHETICALLY
ESTHETICIAN
ESTHETICIANS
ESTHETICISM
ESTHETICISMS
ESTIMABLENESS
ESTIMABLENESSES
ESTIMATING
ESTIMATION
ESTIMATIONS
ESTIMATIVE
ESTIMATORS
ESTIPULATE
ESTIVATING
ESTIVATION
ESTIVATIONS
ESTIVATORS
ESTOPPAGES
ESTRADIOLS
ESTRAMAZONE
ESTRAMAZONES
ESTRANGEDNESS
ESTRANGEDNESSES
ESTRANGELO
ESTRANGELOS
ESTRANGEMENT
ESTRANGEMENTS
ESTRANGERS
ESTRANGHELO
ESTRANGHELOS
ESTRANGING
ESTRAPADES
ESTREATING
ESTREPEMENT
ESTREPEMENTS
ESTRILDIDS
ESTROGENIC
ESTROGENICALLY
ESURIENCES
ESURIENCIES
ESURIENTLY
ETEPIMELETIC
ETERNALISATION
ETERNALISATIONS
ETERNALISE
ETERNALISED
ETERNALISES
ETERNALISING
ETERNALIST
ETERNALISTS
ETERNALITIES
ETERNALITY
ETERNALIZATION
ETERNALIZATIONS
ETERNALIZE
ETERNALIZED
ETERNALIZES
ETERNALIZING
ETERNALNESS
ETERNALNESSES
ETERNISATION
ETERNISATIONS
ETERNISING
ETERNITIES
ETERNIZATION
ETERNIZATIONS
ETERNIZING
ETHAMBUTOL
ETHAMBUTOLS
ETHANEDIOIC
ETHANEDIOL
ETHANEDIOLS
ETHANOATES
ETHANOLAMINE
ETHANOLAMINES
ETHEOSTOMINE
ETHEREALISATION
ETHEREALISE
ETHEREALISED
ETHEREALISES
ETHEREALISING
ETHEREALITIES
ETHEREALITY
ETHEREALIZATION
ETHEREALIZE
ETHEREALIZED
ETHEREALIZES
ETHEREALIZING
ETHEREALLY
ETHEREALNESS
ETHEREALNESSES
ETHERIFICATION
ETHERIFICATIONS
ETHERIFIED
ETHERIFIES
ETHERIFYING
ETHERISATION
ETHERISATIONS
ETHERISERS
ETHERISING
ETHERIZATION
ETHERIZATIONS
ETHERIZERS
ETHERIZING
ETHEROMANIA
ETHEROMANIAC
ETHEROMANIACS
ETHEROMANIAS
ETHICALITIES
ETHICALITY
ETHICALNESS
ETHICALNESSES
ETHICISING
ETHICIZING
ETHIONAMIDE
ETHIONAMIDES
ETHIONINES
ETHNARCHIES
ETHNICALLY
ETHNICISMS
ETHNICITIES
ETHNOBIOLOGY
ETHNOBOTANICAL
ETHNOBOTANIES
ETHNOBOTANIST
ETHNOBOTANISTS
ETHNOBOTANY
ETHNOCENTRIC
ETHNOCENTRICITY
ETHNOCENTRISM
ETHNOCENTRISMS
ETHNOCIDES
ETHNOGENIC
ETHNOGENIES
ETHNOGENIST
ETHNOGENISTS
ETHNOGRAPHER
ETHNOGRAPHERS
ETHNOGRAPHIC
ETHNOGRAPHICA
ETHNOGRAPHICAL
ETHNOGRAPHIES
ETHNOGRAPHY
ETHNOHISTORIAN
ETHNOHISTORIANS
ETHNOHISTORIC
ETHNOHISTORICAL
ETHNOHISTORIES

ETHNOHISTORY
ETHNOLINGUIST
ETHNOLINGUISTIC
ETHNOLINGUISTS
ETHNOLOGIC
ETHNOLOGICAL
ETHNOLOGICALLY
ETHNOLOGIES
ETHNOLOGIST
ETHNOLOGISTS
ETHNOMUSICOLOGY
ETHNOSCIENCE
ETHNOSCIENCES
ETHOLOGICAL
ETHOLOGICALLY
ETHOLOGIES
ETHOLOGIST
ETHOLOGISTS
ETHOXYETHANE
ETHOXYETHANES
ETHYLAMINE
ETHYLAMINES
ETHYLATING
ETHYLATION
ETHYLATIONS
ETHYLBENZENE
ETHYLBENZENES
ETIOLATING
ETIOLATION
ETIOLATIONS
ETIOLOGICAL
ETIOLOGICALLY
ETIOLOGIES
ETIOLOGIST
ETIOLOGISTS
ETIQUETTES
ETONOGESTREL
ETONOGESTRELS
ETOURDERIE
ETOURDERIES
ETRANGERES
ETYMOLOGICA
ETYMOLOGICAL
ETYMOLOGICALLY
ETYMOLOGICON
ETYMOLOGICUM
ETYMOLOGIES
ETYMOLOGISE
ETYMOLOGISED
ETYMOLOGISES
ETYMOLOGISING
ETYMOLOGIST
ETYMOLOGISTS
ETYMOLOGIZE
ETYMOLOGIZED
ETYMOLOGIZES
ETYMOLOGIZING
EUBACTERIA
EUBACTERIUM
EUCALYPTOL
EUCALYPTOLE
EUCALYPTOLES
EUCALYPTOLS
EUCALYPTUS
EUCALYPTUSES
EUCARYOTES
EUCARYOTIC
EUCHARISES
EUCHARISTIC
EUCHARISTICAL
EUCHLORINE
EUCHLORINES
EUCHLORINS
EUCHOLOGIA
EUCHOLOGIES
EUCHOLOGION
EUCHROMATIC
EUCHROMATIN
EUCHROMATINS
EUCRYPHIAS
EUDAEMONIA
EUDAEMONIAS
EUDAEMONIC
EUDAEMONICS
EUDAEMONIES
EUDAEMONISM
EUDAEMONISMS
EUDAEMONIST
EUDAEMONISTIC
EUDAEMONISTICAL
EUDAEMONISTS
EUDAIMONISM
EUDAIMONISMS
EUDEMONIAS
EUDEMONICS
EUDEMONISM
EUDEMONISMS
EUDEMONIST
EUDEMONISTIC
EUDEMONISTICAL
EUDEMONISTS
EUDIALYTES
EUDICOTYLEDON
EUDICOTYLEDONS
EUDIOMETER
EUDIOMETERS
EUDIOMETRIC
EUDIOMETRICAL
EUDIOMETRICALLY
EUDIOMETRIES
EUDIOMETRY
EUGENECIST
EUGENECISTS
EUGENICALLY
EUGENICIST
EUGENICISTS
EUGEOSYNCLINAL
EUGEOSYNCLINE
EUGEOSYNCLINES
EUGLENOIDS
EUGLOBULIN
EUGLOBULINS
EUHARMONIC
EUHEMERISE
EUHEMERISED
EUHEMERISES
EUHEMERISING
EUHEMERISM
EUHEMERISMS
EUHEMERIST
EUHEMERISTIC
EUHEMERISTS
EUHEMERIZE
EUHEMERIZED
EUHEMERIZES
EUHEMERIZING
EUKARYOTES
EUKARYOTIC
EULOGISERS
EULOGISING
EULOGISTIC
EULOGISTICAL
EULOGISTICALLY
EULOGIZERS
EULOGIZING
EUMELANINS
EUNUCHISED
EUNUCHISES
EUNUCHISING
EUNUCHISMS
EUNUCHIZED
EUNUCHIZES
EUNUCHIZING
EUNUCHOIDISM
EUNUCHOIDISMS
EUNUCHOIDS
EUONYMUSES
EUPATORIUM
EUPATORIUMS
EUPATRIDAE
EUPEPTICITIES
EUPEPTICITY
EUPHAUSIACEAN
EUPHAUSIACEANS
EUPHAUSIDS
EUPHAUSIID
EUPHAUSIIDS
EUPHEMISED
EUPHEMISER
EUPHEMISERS
EUPHEMISES
EUPHEMISING
EUPHEMISMS
EUPHEMISTIC
EUPHEMISTICALLY
EUPHEMISTS
EUPHEMIZED
EUPHEMIZER
EUPHEMIZERS
EUPHEMIZES
EUPHEMIZING
EUPHONICAL
EUPHONICALLY
EUPHONIOUS
EUPHONIOUSLY
EUPHONIOUSNESS
EUPHONISED
EUPHONISES
EUPHONISING
EUPHONISMS
EUPHONIUMS
EUPHONIZED
EUPHONIZES
EUPHONIZING
EUPHORBIACEOUS
EUPHORBIAS
EUPHORBIUM
EUPHORBIUMS
EUPHORIANT
EUPHORIANTS
EUPHORICALLY
EUPHRASIES
EUPHUISING
EUPHUISTIC
EUPHUISTICAL
EUPHUISTICALLY
EUPHUIZING
EUPLASTICS
EUPLOIDIES
EURHYTHMIC
EURHYTHMICAL
EURHYTHMICS
EURHYTHMIES
EURHYTHMIST
EURHYTHMISTS
EUROCHEQUE
EUROCHEQUES
EUROCREEPS
EUROCURRENCIES
EUROCURRENCY
EURODEPOSIT
EURODEPOSITS
EURODOLLAR
EURODOLLARS
EUROMARKET
EUROMARKETS
EUROPEANISE
EUROPEANISED
EUROPEANISES
EUROPEANISING
EUROPEANIZE
EUROPEANIZED
EUROPEANIZES
EUROPEANIZING
EUROPHILES
EUROPHILIA
EUROPHILIAS
EUROPHOBIA
EUROPHOBIAS
EUROPHOBIC
EUROTERMINAL
EUROTERMINALS
EURYBATHIC
EURYHALINE
EURYPTERID
EURYPTERIDS
EURYPTEROID
EURYPTEROIDS
EURYTHERMAL
EURYTHERMIC
EURYTHERMOUS
EURYTHERMS
EURYTHMICAL
EURYTHMICS
EURYTHMIES
EUSPORANGIATE
EUSTATICALLY
EUTECTOIDS
EUTHANASIA
EUTHANASIAS
EUTHANASIAST
EUTHANASIASTS
EUTHANASIC
EUTHANASIES

EUTHANATISE
EUTHANATISED
EUTHANATISES
EUTHANATISING
EUTHANATIZE
EUTHANATIZED
EUTHANATIZES
EUTHANATIZING
EUTHANISED
EUTHANISES
EUTHANISING
EUTHANIZED
EUTHANIZES
EUTHANIZING
EUTHENISTS
EUTHERIANS
EUTHYROIDS
EUTRAPELIA
EUTRAPELIAS
EUTRAPELIES
EUTROPHICATION
EUTROPHICATIONS
EUTROPHIES
EVACUATING
EVACUATION
EVACUATIONS
EVACUATIVE
EVACUATORS
EVAGATIONS
EVAGINATED
EVAGINATES
EVAGINATING
EVAGINATION
EVAGINATIONS
EVALUATING
EVALUATION
EVALUATIONS
EVALUATIVE
EVALUATORS
EVANESCENCE
EVANESCENCES
EVANESCENT
EVANESCENTLY
EVANESCING
EVANGELIAR
EVANGELIARIES
EVANGELIARION
EVANGELIARIONS
EVANGELIARIUM
EVANGELIARIUMS
EVANGELIARS
EVANGELIARY
EVANGELICAL
EVANGELICALISM
EVANGELICALISMS
EVANGELICALLY
EVANGELICALNESS
EVANGELICALS
EVANGELICISM
EVANGELICISMS
EVANGELIES
EVANGELISATION
EVANGELISATIONS
EVANGELISE
EVANGELISED
EVANGELISER
EVANGELISERS
EVANGELISES
EVANGELISING
EVANGELISM
EVANGELISMS
EVANGELIST
EVANGELISTARIES
EVANGELISTARION
EVANGELISTARY
EVANGELISTIC
EVANGELISTS
EVANGELIZATION
EVANGELIZATIONS
EVANGELIZE
EVANGELIZED
EVANGELIZER
EVANGELIZERS
EVANGELIZES
EVANGELIZING
EVANISHING
EVANISHMENT
EVANISHMENTS
EVANITIONS
EVAPORABILITIES
EVAPORABILITY
EVAPORABLE
EVAPORATED
EVAPORATES
EVAPORATING
EVAPORATION
EVAPORATIONS
EVAPORATIVE
EVAPORATOR
EVAPORATORS
EVAPORIMETER
EVAPORIMETERS
EVAPORITES
EVAPORITIC
EVAPOROGRAPH
EVAPOROGRAPHS
EVAPOROMETER
EVAPOROMETERS
EVASIVENESS
EVASIVENESSES
EVECTIONAL
EVENEMENTS
EVENHANDED
EVENHANDEDLY
EVENHANDEDNESS
EVENNESSES
EVENTFULLY
EVENTFULNESS
EVENTFULNESSES
EVENTISING
EVENTIZING
EVENTRATED
EVENTRATES
EVENTRATING
EVENTRATION
EVENTRATIONS
EVENTUALISE
EVENTUALISED
EVENTUALISES
EVENTUALISING
EVENTUALITIES
EVENTUALITY
EVENTUALIZE
EVENTUALIZED
EVENTUALIZES
EVENTUALIZING
EVENTUALLY
EVENTUATED
EVENTUATES
EVENTUATING
EVENTUATION
EVENTUATIONS
EVERBLOOMING
EVERDURING
EVERGLADES
EVERGREENS
EVERLASTING
EVERLASTINGLY
EVERLASTINGNESS
EVERLASTINGS
EVERYDAYNESS
EVERYDAYNESSES
EVERYPLACE
EVERYTHING
EVERYWHENCE
EVERYWHERE
EVERYWHITHER
EVERYWOMAN
EVERYWOMEN
EVIDENCING
EVIDENTIAL
EVIDENTIALLY
EVIDENTIARY
EVILDOINGS
EVILNESSES
EVINCEMENT
EVINCEMENTS
EVISCERATE
EVISCERATED
EVISCERATES
EVISCERATING
EVISCERATION
EVISCERATIONS
EVISCERATOR
EVISCERATORS
EVITATIONS
EVITERNALLY
EVITERNITIES
EVITERNITY
EVOCATIONS
EVOCATIVELY
EVOCATIVENESS
EVOCATIVENESSES
EVOLUTIONAL
EVOLUTIONARILY
EVOLUTIONARY
EVOLUTIONISM
EVOLUTIONISMS
EVOLUTIONIST
EVOLUTIONISTIC
EVOLUTIONISTS
EVOLUTIONS
EVOLVEMENT
EVOLVEMENTS
EVONYMUSES
EVULGATING
EXACERBATE
EXACERBATED
EXACERBATES
EXACERBATING
EXACERBATION
EXACERBATIONS
EXACERBESCENCE
EXACERBESCENCES
EXACTINGLY
EXACTINGNESS
EXACTINGNESSES
EXACTITUDE
EXACTITUDES
EXACTMENTS
EXACTNESSES
EXACTRESSES
EXAGGERATE
EXAGGERATED
EXAGGERATEDLY
EXAGGERATEDNESS
EXAGGERATES
EXAGGERATING
EXAGGERATINGLY
EXAGGERATION
EXAGGERATIONS
EXAGGERATIVE
EXAGGERATOR
EXAGGERATORS
EXAGGERATORY
EXAHERTZES
EXALBUMINOUS
EXALTATION
EXALTATIONS
EXALTEDNESS
EXALTEDNESSES
EXAMINABILITIES
EXAMINABILITY
EXAMINABLE
EXAMINANTS
EXAMINATES
EXAMINATION
EXAMINATIONAL
EXAMINATIONS
EXAMINATOR
EXAMINATORS
EXAMINERSHIP
EXAMINERSHIPS
EXANIMATION
EXANIMATIONS
EXANTHEMAS
EXANTHEMATA
EXANTHEMATIC
EXANTHEMATOUS
EXARATIONS
EXARCHATES
EXARCHISTS
EXASPERATE
EXASPERATED
EXASPERATEDLY
EXASPERATER
EXASPERATERS
EXASPERATES
EXASPERATING
EXASPERATINGLY
EXASPERATION
EXASPERATIONS
EXASPERATIVE
EXASPERATOR

EXASPERATORS
EXCAMBIONS
EXCAMBIUMS
EXCARNATED
EXCARNATES
EXCARNATING
EXCARNATION
EXCARNATIONS
EXCAVATING
EXCAVATION
EXCAVATIONAL
EXCAVATIONS
EXCAVATORS
EXCEEDABLE
EXCEEDINGLY
EXCELLENCE
EXCELLENCES
EXCELLENCIES
EXCELLENCY
EXCELLENTLY
EXCELSIORS
EXCENTRICS
EXCEPTANTS
EXCEPTIONABLE
EXCEPTIONABLY
EXCEPTIONAL
EXCEPTIONALISM
EXCEPTIONALISMS
EXCEPTIONALITY
EXCEPTIONALLY
EXCEPTIONALNESS
EXCEPTIONALS
EXCEPTIONS
EXCEPTIOUS
EXCEPTLESS
EXCERPTERS
EXCERPTIBLE
EXCERPTING
EXCERPTINGS
EXCERPTION
EXCERPTIONS
EXCERPTORS
EXCESSIVELY
EXCESSIVENESS
EXCESSIVENESSES
EXCHANGEABILITY
EXCHANGEABLE
EXCHANGEABLY
EXCHANGERS
EXCHANGING
EXCHEQUERED
EXCHEQUERING
EXCHEQUERS
EXCIPIENTS
EXCISIONAL
EXCITABILITIES
EXCITABILITY
EXCITABLENESS
EXCITABLENESSES
EXCITANCIES
EXCITATION
EXCITATIONS
EXCITATIVE
EXCITATORY
EXCITEDNESS
EXCITEDNESSES
EXCITEMENT
EXCITEMENTS
EXCITINGLY
EXCLAIMERS
EXCLAIMING
EXCLAMATION
EXCLAMATIONAL
EXCLAMATIONS
EXCLAMATIVE
EXCLAMATORILY
EXCLAMATORY
EXCLAUSTRATION
EXCLAUSTRATIONS
EXCLOSURES
EXCLUDABILITIES
EXCLUDABILITY
EXCLUDABLE
EXCLUDIBLE
EXCLUSIONARY
EXCLUSIONISM
EXCLUSIONISMS
EXCLUSIONIST
EXCLUSIONISTS
EXCLUSIONS
EXCLUSIVELY
EXCLUSIVENESS
EXCLUSIVENESSES
EXCLUSIVES
EXCLUSIVISM
EXCLUSIVISMS
EXCLUSIVIST
EXCLUSIVISTS
EXCLUSIVITIES
EXCLUSIVITY
EXCOGITABLE
EXCOGITATE
EXCOGITATED
EXCOGITATES
EXCOGITATING
EXCOGITATION
EXCOGITATIONS
EXCOGITATIVE
EXCOGITATOR
EXCOGITATORS
EXCOMMUNICABLE
EXCOMMUNICATE
EXCOMMUNICATED
EXCOMMUNICATES
EXCOMMUNICATING
EXCOMMUNICATION
EXCOMMUNICATIVE
EXCOMMUNICATOR
EXCOMMUNICATORS
EXCOMMUNICATORY
EXCOMMUNION
EXCOMMUNIONS
EXCORIATED
EXCORIATES
EXCORIATING
EXCORIATION
EXCORIATIONS
EXCORTICATE
EXCORTICATED
EXCORTICATES
EXCORTICATING
EXCORTICATION
EXCORTICATIONS
EXCREMENTA
EXCREMENTAL
EXCREMENTITIAL
EXCREMENTITIOUS
EXCREMENTS
EXCREMENTUM
EXCRESCENCE
EXCRESCENCES
EXCRESCENCIES
EXCRESCENCY
EXCRESCENT
EXCRESCENTIAL
EXCRESCENTLY
EXCRETIONS
EXCRETORIES
EXCRUCIATE
EXCRUCIATED
EXCRUCIATES
EXCRUCIATING
EXCRUCIATINGLY
EXCRUCIATION
EXCRUCIATIONS
EXCULPABLE
EXCULPATED
EXCULPATES
EXCULPATING
EXCULPATION
EXCULPATIONS
EXCULPATORY
EXCURSIONED
EXCURSIONING
EXCURSIONISE
EXCURSIONISED
EXCURSIONISES
EXCURSIONISING
EXCURSIONIST
EXCURSIONISTS
EXCURSIONIZE
EXCURSIONIZED
EXCURSIONIZES
EXCURSIONIZING
EXCURSIONS
EXCURSIVELY
EXCURSIVENESS
EXCURSIVENESSES
EXCURSUSES
EXCUSABLENESS
EXCUSABLENESSES
EXCUSATORY
EXECRABLENESS
EXECRABLENESSES
EXECRATING
EXECRATION
EXECRATIONS
EXECRATIVE
EXECRATIVELY
EXECRATORS
EXECRATORY
EXECUTABLE
EXECUTABLES
EXECUTANCIES
EXECUTANCY
EXECUTANTS
EXECUTARIES
EXECUTIONER
EXECUTIONERS
EXECUTIONS
EXECUTIVELY
EXECUTIVES
EXECUTORIAL
EXECUTORSHIP
EXECUTORSHIPS
EXECUTRESS
EXECUTRESSES
EXECUTRICES
EXECUTRIES
EXECUTRIXES
EXEGETICAL
EXEGETICALLY
EXEGETISTS
EXEMPLARILY
EXEMPLARINESS
EXEMPLARINESSES
EXEMPLARITIES
EXEMPLARITY
EXEMPLIFIABLE
EXEMPLIFICATION
EXEMPLIFICATIVE
EXEMPLIFIED
EXEMPLIFIER
EXEMPLIFIERS
EXEMPLIFIES
EXEMPLIFYING
EXEMPTIONS
EXENTERATE
EXENTERATED
EXENTERATES
EXENTERATING
EXENTERATION
EXENTERATIONS
EXEQUATURS
EXERCISABLE
EXERCISERS
EXERCISING
EXERCITATION
EXERCITATIONS
EXERCYCLES
EXFOLIANTS
EXFOLIATED
EXFOLIATES
EXFOLIATING
EXFOLIATION
EXFOLIATIONS
EXFOLIATIVE
EXFOLIATOR
EXFOLIATORS
EXHALATION
EXHALATIONS
EXHAUSTERS
EXHAUSTIBILITY
EXHAUSTIBLE
EXHAUSTING
EXHAUSTION
EXHAUSTIONS
EXHAUSTIVE
EXHAUSTIVELY
EXHAUSTIVENESS
EXHAUSTIVITIES
EXHAUSTIVITY
EXHAUSTLESS
EXHAUSTLESSLY

XHAUSTLESSNESS
XHEREDATE
XHEREDATED
XHEREDATES
XHEREDATING
XHEREDATION
XHEREDATIONS
XHIBITERS
XHIBITING
XHIBITION
XHIBITIONER
XHIBITIONERS
XHIBITIONISM
XHIBITIONISMS
XHIBITIONIST
XHIBITIONISTIC
XHIBITIONISTS
XHIBITIONS
XHIBITIVE
XHIBITIVELY
XHIBITORS
XHIBITORY
XHILARANT
XHILARANTS
XHILARATE
XHILARATED
XHILARATES
XHILARATING
XHILARATINGLY
XHILARATION
XHILARATIONS
XHILARATIVE
XHILARATOR
XHILARATORS
XHILARATORY
XHORTATION
XHORTATIONS
XHORTATIVE
XHORTATORY
XHUMATING
XHUMATION
XHUMATIONS
XIGENCIES
XIGUITIES
XIGUOUSLY
XIGUOUSNESS
XIGUOUSNESSES
XILEMENTS
XIMIOUSLY
XISTENCES
XISTENTIAL
XISTENTIALISM
XISTENTIALISMS
XISTENTIALIST
XISTENTIALISTS
XISTENTIALLY
XOBIOLOGICAL
XOBIOLOGIES
XOBIOLOGIST
XOBIOLOGISTS
XOBIOLOGY
XOCENTRIC
XOCUTICLE
XOCUTICLES
XOCYTOSED
XOCYTOSES
EXOCYTOSING
EXOCYTOSIS
EXOCYTOTIC
EXODERMISES
EXODONTIAS
EXODONTICS
EXODONTIST
EXODONTISTS
EXOENZYMES
EXOERYTHROCYTIC
EXOGENETIC
EXOGENISMS
EXOGENOUSLY
EXONERATED
EXONERATES
EXONERATING
EXONERATION
EXONERATIONS
EXONERATIVE
EXONERATOR
EXONERATORS
EXONUCLEASE
EXONUCLEASES
EXONUMISTS
EXOPARASITE
EXOPARASITES
EXOPARASITIC
EXOPEPTIDASE
EXOPEPTIDASES
EXOPHAGIES
EXOPHAGOUS
EXOPHTHALMIA
EXOPHTHALMIAS
EXOPHTHALMIC
EXOPHTHALMOS
EXOPHTHALMOSES
EXOPHTHALMUS
EXOPHTHALMUSES
EXOPLANETS
EXOPODITES
EXOPODITIC
EXORABILITIES
EXORABILITY
EXORATIONS
EXORBITANCE
EXORBITANCES
EXORBITANCIES
EXORBITANCY
EXORBITANT
EXORBITANTLY
EXORBITATE
EXORBITATED
EXORBITATES
EXORBITATING
EXORCISERS
EXORCISING
EXORCISTIC
EXORCISTICAL
EXORCIZERS
EXORCIZING
EXOSKELETAL
EXOSKELETON
EXOSKELETONS
EXOSPHERES
EXOSPHERIC
EXOSPHERICAL
EXOSPORIUM
EXOSPOROUS
EXOTERICAL
EXOTERICALLY
EXOTERICISM
EXOTERICISMS
EXOTHERMAL
EXOTHERMALLY
EXOTHERMIC
EXOTHERMICALLY
EXOTHERMICITIES
EXOTHERMICITY
EXOTICALLY
EXOTICISMS
EXOTICISTS
EXOTICNESS
EXOTICNESSES
EXOTROPIAS
EXPANDABILITIES
EXPANDABILITY
EXPANDABLE
EXPANSIBILITIES
EXPANSIBILITY
EXPANSIBLE
EXPANSIBLY
EXPANSIONAL
EXPANSIONARY
EXPANSIONISM
EXPANSIONISMS
EXPANSIONIST
EXPANSIONISTIC
EXPANSIONISTS
EXPANSIONS
EXPANSIVELY
EXPANSIVENESS
EXPANSIVENESSES
EXPANSIVITIES
EXPANSIVITY
EXPATIATED
EXPATIATES
EXPATIATING
EXPATIATION
EXPATIATIONS
EXPATIATIVE
EXPATIATOR
EXPATIATORS
EXPATIATORY
EXPATRIATE
EXPATRIATED
EXPATRIATES
EXPATRIATING
EXPATRIATION
EXPATRIATIONS
EXPATRIATISM
EXPATRIATISMS
EXPECTABLE
EXPECTABLY
EXPECTANCE
EXPECTANCES
EXPECTANCIES
EXPECTANCY
EXPECTANTLY
EXPECTANTS
EXPECTATION
EXPECTATIONAL
EXPECTATIONS
EXPECTATIVE
EXPECTATIVES
EXPECTEDLY
EXPECTEDNESS
EXPECTEDNESSES
EXPECTINGLY
EXPECTINGS
EXPECTORANT
EXPECTORANTS
EXPECTORATE
EXPECTORATED
EXPECTORATES
EXPECTORATING
EXPECTORATION
EXPECTORATIONS
EXPECTORATIVE
EXPECTORATOR
EXPECTORATORS
EXPEDIENCE
EXPEDIENCES
EXPEDIENCIES
EXPEDIENCY
EXPEDIENTIAL
EXPEDIENTIALLY
EXPEDIENTLY
EXPEDIENTS
EXPEDITATE
EXPEDITATED
EXPEDITATES
EXPEDITATING
EXPEDITATION
EXPEDITATIONS
EXPEDITELY
EXPEDITERS
EXPEDITING
EXPEDITION
EXPEDITIONARY
EXPEDITIONS
EXPEDITIOUS
EXPEDITIOUSLY
EXPEDITIOUSNESS
EXPEDITIVE
EXPEDITORS
EXPELLABLE
EXPELLANTS
EXPELLENTS
EXPENDABILITIES
EXPENDABILITY
EXPENDABLE
EXPENDABLES
EXPENDITURE
EXPENDITURES
EXPENSIVELY
EXPENSIVENESS
EXPENSIVENESSES
EXPERIENCE
EXPERIENCEABLE
EXPERIENCED
EXPERIENCELESS
EXPERIENCER
EXPERIENCERS
EXPERIENCES
EXPERIENCING
EXPERIENTIAL
EXPERIENTIALISM
EXPERIENTIALIST

EXPERIENTIALLY
EXPERIMENT
EXPERIMENTAL
EXPERIMENTALISE
EXPERIMENTALISM
EXPERIMENTALIST
EXPERIMENTALIZE
EXPERIMENTALLY
EXPERIMENTATION
EXPERIMENTATIVE
EXPERIMENTED
EXPERIMENTER
EXPERIMENTERS
EXPERIMENTING
EXPERIMENTIST
EXPERIMENTISTS
EXPERIMENTS
EXPERTISED
EXPERTISES
EXPERTISING
EXPERTISMS
EXPERTIZED
EXPERTIZES
EXPERTIZING
EXPERTNESS
EXPERTNESSES
EXPIATIONS
EXPIRATION
EXPIRATIONS
EXPIRATORY
EXPISCATED
EXPISCATES
EXPISCATING
EXPISCATION
EXPISCATIONS
EXPISCATORY
EXPLAINABLE
EXPLAINERS
EXPLAINING
EXPLANATION
EXPLANATIONS
EXPLANATIVE
EXPLANATIVELY
EXPLANATORILY
EXPLANATORY
EXPLANTATION
EXPLANTATIONS
EXPLANTING
EXPLETIVELY
EXPLETIVES
EXPLICABLE
EXPLICABLY
EXPLICATED
EXPLICATES
EXPLICATING
EXPLICATION
EXPLICATIONS
EXPLICATIVE
EXPLICATIVELY
EXPLICATOR
EXPLICATORS
EXPLICATORY
EXPLICITLY
EXPLICITNESS
EXPLICITNESSES
EXPLOITABLE
EXPLOITAGE
EXPLOITAGES
EXPLOITATION
EXPLOITATIONS
EXPLOITATIVE
EXPLOITATIVELY
EXPLOITERS
EXPLOITING
EXPLOITIVE
EXPLORATION
EXPLORATIONAL
EXPLORATIONIST
EXPLORATIONISTS
EXPLORATIONS
EXPLORATIVE
EXPLORATIVELY
EXPLORATORY
EXPLOSIBLE
EXPLOSIONS
EXPLOSIVELY
EXPLOSIVENESS
EXPLOSIVENESSES
EXPLOSIVES
EXPONENTIAL
EXPONENTIALLY
EXPONENTIALS
EXPONENTIATION
EXPONENTIATIONS
EXPORTABILITIES
EXPORTABILITY
EXPORTABLE
EXPORTATION
EXPORTATIONS
EXPOSEDNESS
EXPOSEDNESSES
EXPOSITING
EXPOSITION
EXPOSITIONAL
EXPOSITIONS
EXPOSITIVE
EXPOSITIVELY
EXPOSITORILY
EXPOSITORS
EXPOSITORY
EXPOSITRESS
EXPOSITRESSES
EXPOSTULATE
EXPOSTULATED
EXPOSTULATES
EXPOSTULATING
EXPOSTULATINGLY
EXPOSTULATION
EXPOSTULATIONS
EXPOSTULATIVE
EXPOSTULATOR
EXPOSTULATORS
EXPOSTULATORY
EXPOSTURES
EXPOUNDERS
EXPOUNDING
EXPRESSAGE
EXPRESSAGES
EXPRESSERS
EXPRESSIBLE
EXPRESSING
EXPRESSION
EXPRESSIONAL
EXPRESSIONISM
EXPRESSIONISMS
EXPRESSIONIST
EXPRESSIONISTIC
EXPRESSIONISTS
EXPRESSIONLESS
EXPRESSIONS
EXPRESSIVE
EXPRESSIVELY
EXPRESSIVENESS
EXPRESSIVITIES
EXPRESSIVITY
EXPRESSMAN
EXPRESSMEN
EXPRESSNESS
EXPRESSNESSES
EXPRESSURE
EXPRESSURES
EXPRESSWAY
EXPRESSWAYS
EXPROBRATE
EXPROBRATED
EXPROBRATES
EXPROBRATING
EXPROBRATION
EXPROBRATIONS
EXPROBRATIVE
EXPROBRATORY
EXPROMISSION
EXPROMISSIONS
EXPROMISSOR
EXPROMISSORS
EXPROPRIABLE
EXPROPRIATE
EXPROPRIATED
EXPROPRIATES
EXPROPRIATING
EXPROPRIATION
EXPROPRIATIONS
EXPROPRIATOR
EXPROPRIATORS
EXPUGNABLE
EXPUGNATION
EXPUGNATIONS
EXPULSIONS
EXPUNCTING
EXPUNCTION
EXPUNCTIONS
EXPURGATED
EXPURGATES
EXPURGATING
EXPURGATION
EXPURGATIONS
EXPURGATOR
EXPURGATORIAL
EXPURGATORS
EXPURGATORY
EXQUISITELY
EXQUISITENESS
EXQUISITENESSES
EXQUISITES
EXSANGUINATE
EXSANGUINATED
EXSANGUINATES
EXSANGUINATING
EXSANGUINATION
EXSANGUINATIONS
EXSANGUINE
EXSANGUINED
EXSANGUINEOUS
EXSANGUINITIES
EXSANGUINITY
EXSANGUINOUS
EXSCINDING
EXSECTIONS
EXSERTIONS
EXSICCATED
EXSICCATES
EXSICCATING
EXSICCATION
EXSICCATIONS
EXSICCATIVE
EXSICCATOR
EXSICCATORS
EXSOLUTION
EXSOLUTIONS
EXSTIPULATE
EXSTROPHIES
EXSUFFLATE
EXSUFFLATED
EXSUFFLATES
EXSUFFLATING
EXSUFFLATION
EXSUFFLATIONS
EXSUFFLICATE
EXTEMPORAL
EXTEMPORALLY
EXTEMPORANEITY
EXTEMPORANEOUS
EXTEMPORARILY
EXTEMPORARINESS
EXTEMPORARY
EXTEMPORES
EXTEMPORISATION
EXTEMPORISE
EXTEMPORISED
EXTEMPORISER
EXTEMPORISERS
EXTEMPORISES
EXTEMPORISING
EXTEMPORIZATION
EXTEMPORIZE
EXTEMPORIZED
EXTEMPORIZER
EXTEMPORIZERS
EXTEMPORIZES
EXTEMPORIZING
EXTENDABILITIES
EXTENDABILITY
EXTENDABLE
EXTENDEDLY
EXTENDEDNESS
EXTENDEDNESSES
EXTENDIBILITIES
EXTENDIBILITY
EXTENDIBLE
EXTENSIBILITIES
EXTENSIBILITY
EXTENSIBLE
EXTENSIBLENESS
EXTENSIFICATION

EXTENSIMETER
EXTENSIMETERS
EXTENSIONAL
EXTENSIONALISM
EXTENSIONALISMS
EXTENSIONALITY
EXTENSIONALLY
EXTENSIONIST
EXTENSIONISTS
EXTENSIONS
EXTENSITIES
EXTENSIVELY
EXTENSIVENESS
EXTENSIVENESSES
EXTENSIVISATION
EXTENSIVIZATION
EXTENSOMETER
EXTENSOMETERS
EXTENUATED
EXTENUATES
EXTENUATING
EXTENUATINGLY
EXTENUATINGS
EXTENUATION
EXTENUATIONS
EXTENUATIVE
EXTENUATOR
EXTENUATORS
EXTENUATORY
EXTERIORISATION
EXTERIORISE
EXTERIORISED
EXTERIORISES
EXTERIORISING
EXTERIORITIES
EXTERIORITY
EXTERIORIZATION
EXTERIORIZE
EXTERIORIZED
EXTERIORIZES
EXTERIORIZING
EXTERIORLY
EXTERMINABLE
EXTERMINATE
EXTERMINATED
EXTERMINATES
EXTERMINATING
EXTERMINATION
EXTERMINATIONS
EXTERMINATIVE
EXTERMINATOR
EXTERMINATORS
EXTERMINATORY
EXTERMINED
EXTERMINES
EXTERMINING
EXTERNALISATION
EXTERNALISE
EXTERNALISED
EXTERNALISES
EXTERNALISING
EXTERNALISM
EXTERNALISMS
EXTERNALIST
EXTERNALISTS
EXTERNALITIES
EXTERNALITY
EXTERNALIZATION
EXTERNALIZE
EXTERNALIZED
EXTERNALIZES
EXTERNALIZING
EXTERNALLY
EXTERNSHIP
EXTERNSHIPS
EXTEROCEPTIVE
EXTEROCEPTOR
EXTEROCEPTORS
EXTERRITORIAL
EXTERRITORIALLY
EXTINCTING
EXTINCTION
EXTINCTIONS
EXTINCTIVE
EXTINCTURE
EXTINCTURES
EXTINGUISH
EXTINGUISHABLE
EXTINGUISHANT
EXTINGUISHANTS
EXTINGUISHED
EXTINGUISHER
EXTINGUISHERS
EXTINGUISHES
EXTINGUISHING
EXTINGUISHMENT
EXTINGUISHMENTS
EXTIRPABLE
EXTIRPATED
EXTIRPATES
EXTIRPATING
EXTIRPATION
EXTIRPATIONS
EXTIRPATIVE
EXTIRPATOR
EXTIRPATORS
EXTIRPATORY
EXTOLLINGLY
EXTOLMENTS
EXTORSIVELY
EXTORTIONARY
EXTORTIONATE
EXTORTIONATELY
EXTORTIONER
EXTORTIONERS
EXTORTIONIST
EXTORTIONISTS
EXTORTIONS
EXTRABOLDS
EXTRACANONICAL
EXTRACELLULAR
EXTRACELLULARLY
EXTRACORPOREAL
EXTRACRANIAL
EXTRACTABILITY
EXTRACTABLE
EXTRACTANT
EXTRACTANTS
EXTRACTIBLE
EXTRACTING
EXTRACTION
EXTRACTIONS
EXTRACTIVE
EXTRACTIVELY
EXTRACTIVES
EXTRACTORS
EXTRACURRICULAR
EXTRADITABLE
EXTRADITED
EXTRADITES
EXTRADITING
EXTRADITION
EXTRADITIONS
EXTRADOSES
EXTRADOTAL
EXTRADURAL
EXTRAEMBRYONIC
EXTRAFLORAL
EXTRAFORANEOUS
EXTRAGALACTIC
EXTRAHEPATIC
EXTRAJUDICIAL
EXTRAJUDICIALLY
EXTRALEGAL
EXTRALEGALLY
EXTRALIMITAL
EXTRALIMITARY
EXTRALINGUISTIC
EXTRALITERARY
EXTRALITIES
EXTRALOGICAL
EXTRAMARITAL
EXTRAMETRICAL
EXTRAMUNDANE
EXTRAMURAL
EXTRAMURALLY
EXTRAMUSICAL
EXTRANEITIES
EXTRANEITY
EXTRANEOUS
EXTRANEOUSLY
EXTRANEOUSNESS
EXTRANUCLEAR
EXTRAORDINAIRE
EXTRAORDINARIES
EXTRAORDINARILY
EXTRAORDINARY
EXTRAPOLATE
EXTRAPOLATED
EXTRAPOLATES
EXTRAPOLATING
EXTRAPOLATION
EXTRAPOLATIONS
EXTRAPOLATIVE
EXTRAPOLATOR
EXTRAPOLATORS
EXTRAPOLATORY
EXTRAPOSED
EXTRAPOSES
EXTRAPOSING
EXTRAPOSITION
EXTRAPOSITIONS
EXTRAPYRAMIDAL
EXTRASENSORY
EXTRASOLAR
EXTRASYSTOLE
EXTRASYSTOLES
EXTRATEXTUAL
EXTRATROPICAL
EXTRAUTERINE
EXTRAVAGANCE
EXTRAVAGANCES
EXTRAVAGANCIES
EXTRAVAGANCY
EXTRAVAGANT
EXTRAVAGANTLY
EXTRAVAGANZA
EXTRAVAGANZAS
EXTRAVAGATE
EXTRAVAGATED
EXTRAVAGATES
EXTRAVAGATING
EXTRAVAGATION
EXTRAVAGATIONS
EXTRAVASATE
EXTRAVASATED
EXTRAVASATES
EXTRAVASATING
EXTRAVASATION
EXTRAVASATIONS
EXTRAVASCULAR
EXTRAVEHICULAR
EXTRAVERSION
EXTRAVERSIONS
EXTRAVERSIVE
EXTRAVERTED
EXTRAVERTING
EXTRAVERTS
EXTREMENESS
EXTREMENESSES
EXTREMISMS
EXTREMISTS
EXTREMITIES
EXTREMOPHILE
EXTREMOPHILES
EXTRICABLE
EXTRICATED
EXTRICATES
EXTRICATING
EXTRICATION
EXTRICATIONS
EXTRINSICAL
EXTRINSICALITY
EXTRINSICALLY
EXTROVERSION
EXTROVERSIONS
EXTROVERSIVE
EXTROVERSIVELY
EXTROVERTED
EXTROVERTING
EXTROVERTS
EXTRUDABILITIES
EXTRUDABILITY
EXTRUDABLE
EXTRUSIBLE
EXTRUSIONS
EXTUBATING
EXUBERANCE
EXUBERANCES
EXUBERANCIES
EXUBERANCY
EXUBERANTLY
EXUBERATED
EXUBERATES

EXUBERATING
EXUDATIONS
EXULCERATE
EXULCERATED
EXULCERATES
EXULCERATING
EXULCERATION
EXULCERATIONS
EXULTANCES
EXULTANCIES
EXULTANTLY
EXULTATION
EXULTATIONS
EXULTINGLY
EXURBANITE
EXURBANITES
EXUVIATING
EXUVIATION
EXUVIATIONS
EYEBALLING
EYEBRIGHTS
EYEBROWING
EYEBROWLESS
EYEDNESSES
EYEDROPPER
EYEDROPPERS
EYEGLASSES
EYELETEERS
EYELETTING
EYEOPENERS
EYEPOPPERS
EYESHADOWS
EYESTRAINS
EYESTRINGS
EYEWITNESS
EYEWITNESSES

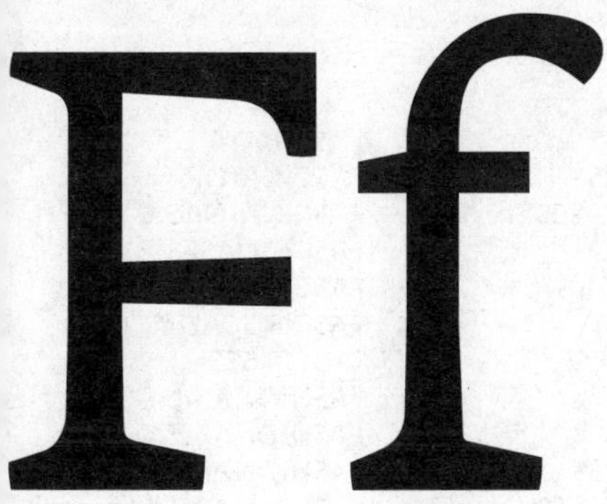

ABRICANTS
ABRICATED
ABRICATES
ABRICATING
ABRICATION
ABRICATIONS
ABRICATIVE
ABRICATOR
ABRICATORS
ABRICKING
ABULATING
ABULATORS
ABULISING
ABULISTIC
ABULIZING
ABULOSITIES
ABULOSITY
ABULOUSLY
ABULOUSNESS
ABULOUSNESSES
ACECLOTHS
ACELESSNESS
ACELESSNESSES
ACELIFTED
ACELIFTING
ACEPLATES
ACEPRINTS
ACETIOUSLY
ACETIOUSNESS
ACETIOUSNESSES
ACEWORKER
ACEWORKERS
ACILENESS
ACILENESSES
ACILITATE
ACILITATED
ACILITATES
ACILITATING

FACILITATION
FACILITATIONS
FACILITATIVE
FACILITATOR
FACILITATORS
FACILITATORY
FACILITIES
FACINERIOUS
FACINOROUS
FACINOROUSNESS
FACSIMILED
FACSIMILEING
FACSIMILES
FACSIMILIST
FACSIMILISTS
FACTICITIES
FACTIONALISM
FACTIONALISMS
FACTIONALIST
FACTIONALISTS
FACTIONALLY
FACTIONARIES
FACTIONARY
FACTIONIST
FACTIONISTS
FACTIOUSLY
FACTIOUSNESS
FACTIOUSNESSES
FACTITIOUS
FACTITIOUSLY
FACTITIOUSNESS
FACTITIVELY
FACTORABILITIES
FACTORABILITY
FACTORABLE
FACTORAGES
FACTORIALLY
FACTORIALS

FACTORINGS
FACTORISATION
FACTORISATIONS
FACTORISED
FACTORISES
FACTORISING
FACTORIZATION
FACTORIZATIONS
FACTORIZED
FACTORIZES
FACTORIZING
FACTORSHIP
FACTORSHIPS
FACTORYLIKE
FACTSHEETS
FACTUALISM
FACTUALISMS
FACTUALIST
FACTUALISTIC
FACTUALISTS
FACTUALITIES
FACTUALITY
FACTUALNESS
FACTUALNESSES
FACULTATIVE
FACULTATIVELY
FACUNDITIES
FADDINESSES
FADDISHNESS
FADDISHNESSES
FADEDNESSES
FADELESSLY
FADOMETERS
FAGGOTINGS
FAGGOTRIES
FAGOTTISTS
FAINEANCES
FAINEANCIES

FAINEANTISE
FAINEANTISES
FAINNESSES
FAINTHEARTED
FAINTHEARTEDLY
FAINTINGLY
FAINTISHNESS
FAINTISHNESSES
FAINTNESSES
FAIRGROUND
FAIRGROUNDS
FAIRLEADER
FAIRLEADERS
FAIRNESSES
FAIRNITICKLE
FAIRNITICKLES
FAIRNITICLE
FAIRNITICLES
FAIRNYTICKLE
FAIRNYTICKLES
FAIRNYTICLE
FAIRNYTICLES
FAIRYFLOSS
FAIRYFLOSSES
FAIRYHOODS
FAIRYLANDS
FAIRYTALES
FAITHCURES
FAITHFULLY
FAITHFULNESS
FAITHFULNESSES
FAITHLESSLY
FAITHLESSNESS
FAITHLESSNESSES
FAITHWORTHINESS
FAITHWORTHY
FALANGISMS
FALANGISTS

FALCATIONS
FALCONIFORM
FALCONRIES
FALDISTORIES
FALDISTORY
FALDSTOOLS
FALLACIOUS
FALLACIOUSLY
FALLACIOUSNESS
FALLALERIES
FALLALISHLY
FALLBOARDS
FALLFISHES
FALLIBILISM
FALLIBILISMS
FALLIBILIST
FALLIBILISTS
FALLIBILITIES
FALLIBILITY
FALLIBLENESS
FALLIBLENESSES
FALLOWNESS
FALLOWNESSES
FALSEFACES
FALSEHOODS
FALSENESSES
FALSEWORKS
FALSIDICAL
FALSIFIABILITY
FALSIFIABLE
FALSIFICATION
FALSIFICATIONS
FALSIFIERS
FALSIFYING
FALTERINGLY
FALTERINGS
FAMILIARISATION
FAMILIARISE
FAMILIARISED
FAMILIARISER
FAMILIARISERS
FAMILIARISES
FAMILIARISING
FAMILIARITIES
FAMILIARITY
FAMILIARIZATION
FAMILIARIZE
FAMILIARIZED
FAMILIARIZER
FAMILIARIZERS
FAMILIARIZES
FAMILIARIZING
FAMILIARLY
FAMILIARNESS
FAMILIARNESSES
FAMILISTIC
FAMISHMENT
FAMISHMENTS
FAMOUSNESS
FAMOUSNESSES
FANATICALLY
FANATICALNESS
FANATICALNESSES
FANATICISE
FANATICISED
FANATICISES
FANATICISING
FANATICISM
FANATICISMS
FANATICIZE
FANATICIZED
FANATICIZES
FANATICIZING
FANCIFULLY
FANCIFULNESS
FANCIFULNESSES
FANCIFYING
FANCINESSES
FANCYWORKS
FANDANGLES
FANDANGOES
FANFARADES
FANFARONADE
FANFARONADED
FANFARONADES
FANFARONADING
FANFARONAS
FANFOLDING
FANTABULOUS
FANTASISED
FANTASISER
FANTASISERS
FANTASISES
FANTASISING
FANTASISTS
FANTASIZED
FANTASIZER
FANTASIZERS
FANTASIZES
FANTASIZING
FANTASMALLY
FANTASMICALLY
FANTASQUES
FANTASTICAL
FANTASTICALITY
FANTASTICALLY
FANTASTICALNESS
FANTASTICATE
FANTASTICATED
FANTASTICATES
FANTASTICATING
FANTASTICATION
FANTASTICATIONS
FANTASTICISM
FANTASTICISMS
FANTASTICO
FANTASTICOES
FANTASTICS
FANTASTRIES
FANTASYING
FANTASYLAND
FANTASYLANDS
FANTOCCINI
FARADISATION
FARADISATIONS
FARADISERS
FARADISING
FARADIZATION
FARADIZATIONS
FARADIZERS
FARADIZING
FARANDINES
FARANDOLES
FARAWAYNESS
FARAWAYNESSES
FARBOROUGH
FARBOROUGHS
FARCEMEATS
FARCICALITIES
FARCICALITY
FARCICALLY
FARCICALNESS
FARCICALNESSES
FARCIFYING
FAREWELLED
FAREWELLING
FARFETCHEDNESS
FARINACEOUS
FARINOSELY
FARKLEBERRIES
FARKLEBERRY
FARMERESSES
FARMERETTE
FARMERETTES
FARMHOUSES
FARMSTEADS
FARMWORKER
FARMWORKERS
FARNARKELED
FARNARKELING
FARNARKELINGS
FARNARKELS
FARRAGINOUS
FARRANDINE
FARRANDINES
FARRIERIES
FARSIGHTED
FARSIGHTEDLY
FARSIGHTEDNESS
FARTHERMORE
FARTHERMOST
FARTHINGALE
FARTHINGALES
FARTHINGLAND
FARTHINGLANDS
FARTHINGLESS
FARTHINGSWORTH
FARTHINGSWORTHS
FASCIATELY
FASCIATION
FASCIATIONS
FASCICULAR
FASCICULARLY
FASCICULATE
FASCICULATED
FASCICULATELY
FASCICULATION
FASCICULATIONS
FASCICULES
FASCICULUS
FASCIITISES
FASCINATED
FASCINATEDLY
FASCINATES
FASCINATING
FASCINATINGLY
FASCINATION
FASCINATIONS
FASCINATIVE
FASCINATOR
FASCINATORS
FASCIOLIASES
FASCIOLIASIS
FASCISTICALLY
FASCITISES
FASHIONABILITY
FASHIONABLE
FASHIONABLENESS
FASHIONABLES
FASHIONABLY
FASHIONERS
FASHIONING
FASHIONIST
FASHIONISTA
FASHIONISTAS
FASHIONISTS
FASHIONMONGER
FASHIONMONGERS
FASHIONMONGING
FASHIOUSNESS
FASHIOUSNESSES
FASTBALLER
FASTBALLERS
FASTENINGS
FASTIDIOUS
FASTIDIOUSLY
FASTIDIOUSNESS
FASTIGIATE
FASTIGIATED
FASTIGIUMS
FASTNESSES
FATALISTIC
FATALISTICALLY
FATALITIES
FATALNESSES
FATBRAINED
FATEFULNESS
FATEFULNESSES
FATHEADEDLY
FATHEADEDNESS
FATHEADEDNESSES
FATHERHOOD
FATHERHOODS
FATHERLAND
FATHERLANDS
FATHERLESS
FATHERLESSNESS
FATHERLIKE
FATHERLINESS
FATHERLINESSES
FATHERSHIP
FATHERSHIPS
FATHOMABLE
FATHOMETER
FATHOMETERS
FATHOMLESS
FATHOMLESSLY
FATHOMLESSNESS
FATIDICALLY
FATIGABILITIES
FATIGABILITY
FATIGABLENESS
FATIGABLENESSES
FATIGATING

ATIGUABLE
ATIGUABLENESS
ATIGUELESS
ATIGUINGLY
ATISCENCE
ATISCENCES
ATSHEDERA
ATSHEDERAS
ATTENABLE
ATTENINGS
ATTINESSES
ATUOUSNESS
ATUOUSNESSES
AULCHIONS
AULTFINDER
AULTFINDERS
AULTFINDING
AULTFINDINGS
AULTINESS
AULTINESSES
AULTLESSLY
AULTLESSNESS
AULTLESSNESSES
AUNISTICALLY
AUXBOURDON
AUXBOURDONS
AVORABLENESS
AVORABLENESSES
AVOREDNESS
AVOREDNESSES
AVORINGLY
AVORITISM
AVORITISMS
AVOURABLE
AVOURABLENESS
AVOURABLY
AVOUREDNESS
AVOUREDNESSES
AVOURINGLY
AVOURITES
AVOURITISM
AVOURITISMS
AVOURLESS
AWNINGNESS
AWNINGNESSES
AZENDEIRO
AZENDEIROS
EARFULLER
EARFULLEST
EARFULNESS
EARFULNESSES
EARLESSLY
EARLESSNESS
EARLESSNESSES
EARNAUGHT
EARNAUGHTS
EARNOUGHT
EARNOUGHTS
EARSOMELY
EARSOMENESS
EARSOMENESSES
EASIBILITIES
EASIBILITY
EASIBLENESS
EASIBLENESSES
EATEOUSLY

FEATHERBED
FEATHERBEDDED
FEATHERBEDDING
FEATHERBEDDINGS
FEATHERBEDS
FEATHERBRAIN
FEATHERBRAINED
FEATHERBRAINS
FEATHEREDGE
FEATHEREDGED
FEATHEREDGES
FEATHEREDGING
FEATHERHEAD
FEATHERHEADED
FEATHERHEADS
FEATHERIER
FEATHERIEST
FEATHERINESS
FEATHERINESSES
FEATHERING
FEATHERINGS
FEATHERLESS
FEATHERLIGHT
FEATHERSTITCH
FEATHERSTITCHED
FEATHERSTITCHES
FEATHERWEIGHT
FEATHERWEIGHTS
FEATLINESS
FEATLINESSES
FEATURELESS
FEATURELESSNESS
FEATURETTE
FEATURETTES
FEBRICITIES
FEBRICULAS
FEBRICULES
FEBRIFACIENT
FEBRIFACIENTS
FEBRIFEROUS
FEBRIFUGAL
FEBRIFUGES
FEBRILITIES
FECKLESSLY
FECKLESSNESS
FECKLESSNESSES
FECULENCES
FECULENCIES
FECUNDATED
FECUNDATES
FECUNDATING
FECUNDATION
FECUNDATIONS
FECUNDATOR
FECUNDATORS
FECUNDATORY
FECUNDITIES
FEDERACIES
FEDERALESE
FEDERALESES
FEDERALISATION
FEDERALISATIONS
FEDERALISE
FEDERALISED
FEDERALISES
FEDERALISING

FEDERALISM
FEDERALISMS
FEDERALIST
FEDERALISTIC
FEDERALISTS
FEDERALIZATION
FEDERALIZATIONS
FEDERALIZE
FEDERALIZED
FEDERALIZES
FEDERALIZING
FEDERARIES
FEDERATING
FEDERATION
FEDERATIONS
FEDERATIVE
FEDERATIVELY
FEDERATORS
FEEBLEMINDED
FEEBLEMINDEDLY
FEEBLENESS
FEEBLENESSES
FEEDGRAINS
FEEDINGSTUFF
FEEDINGSTUFFS
FEEDSTOCKS
FEEDSTUFFS
FEEDTHROUGH
FEEDTHROUGHS
FEEDWATERS
FEELINGLESS
FEELINGNESS
FEELINGNESSES
FEIGNEDNESS
FEIGNEDNESSES
FEIGNINGLY
FEISTINESS
FEISTINESSES
FELDSCHARS
FELDSCHERS
FELDSPATHIC
FELDSPATHOID
FELDSPATHOIDS
FELDSPATHOSE
FELDSPATHS
FELICITATE
FELICITATED
FELICITATES
FELICITATING
FELICITATION
FELICITATIONS
FELICITATOR
FELICITATORS
FELICITIES
FELICITOUS
FELICITOUSLY
FELICITOUSNESS
FELINENESS
FELINENESSES
FELINITIES
FELLATIONS
FELLATRICES
FELLATRIXES
FELLMONGER
FELLMONGERED
FELLMONGERIES

FELLMONGERING
FELLMONGERINGS
FELLMONGERS
FELLMONGERY
FELLNESSES
FELLOWSHIP
FELLOWSHIPED
FELLOWSHIPING
FELLOWSHIPPED
FELLOWSHIPPING
FELLOWSHIPS
FELLWALKER
FELLWALKERS
FELONIOUSLY
FELONIOUSNESS
FELONIOUSNESSES
FELSPATHIC
FELSPATHOID
FELSPATHOIDS
FELSPATHOSE
FEMALENESS
FEMALENESSES
FEMALITIES
FEMETARIES
FEMINACIES
FEMINALITIES
FEMINALITY
FEMINEITIES
FEMINILITIES
FEMINILITY
FEMININELY
FEMININENESS
FEMININENESSES
FEMININISM
FEMININISMS
FEMININITIES
FEMININITY
FEMINISATION
FEMINISATIONS
FEMINISING
FEMINISTIC
FEMINITIES
FEMINIZATION
FEMINIZATIONS
FEMINIZING
FEMTOSECOND
FEMTOSECONDS
FENCELESSNESS
FENCELESSNESSES
FENDERLESS
FENESTELLA
FENESTELLAE
FENESTELLAS
FENESTRALS
FENESTRATE
FENESTRATED
FENESTRATION
FENESTRATIONS
FENNELFLOWER
FENNELFLOWERS
FENUGREEKS
FEOFFMENTS
FERACITIES
FERETORIES
FERMENTABILITY
FERMENTABLE

FERMENTATION
FERMENTATIONS
FERMENTATIVE
FERMENTATIVELY
FERMENTERS
FERMENTESCIBLE
FERMENTING
FERMENTITIOUS
FERMENTIVE
FERMENTORS
FERNITICKLE
FERNITICKLES
FERNITICLE
FERNITICLES
FERNTICKLE
FERNTICKLED
FERNTICKLES
FERNTICLED
FERNTICLES
FERNYTICKLE
FERNYTICKLES
FERNYTICLE
FERNYTICLES
FEROCIOUSLY
FEROCIOUSNESS
FEROCIOUSNESSES
FEROCITIES
FERRANDINE
FERRANDINES
FERREDOXIN
FERREDOXINS
FERRELLING
FERRETINGS
FERRICYANIC
FERRICYANIDE
FERRICYANIDES
FERRICYANOGEN
FERRICYANOGENS
FERRIFEROUS
FERRIMAGNET
FERRIMAGNETIC
FERRIMAGNETISM
FERRIMAGNETISMS
FERRIMAGNETS
FERROCENES
FERROCHROME
FERROCHROMES
FERROCHROMIUM
FERROCHROMIUMS
FERROCONCRETE
FERROCONCRETES
FERROCYANIC
FERROCYANIDE
FERROCYANIDES
FERROCYANOGEN
FERROCYANOGENS
FERROELECTRIC
FERROELECTRICS
FERROGRAMS
FERROGRAPHIES
FERROGRAPHY
FERROMAGNESIAN
FERROMAGNET
FERROMAGNETIC
FERROMAGNETISM
FERROMAGNETISMS
FERROMAGNETS
FERROMANGANESE
FERROMANGANESES
FERROMOLYBDENUM
FERRONICKEL
FERRONICKELS
FERRONIERE
FERRONIERES
FERRONNIERE
FERRONNIERES
FERROPRUSSIATE
FERROPRUSSIATES
FERROSILICON
FERROSILICONS
FERROSOFERRIC
FERROTYPED
FERROTYPES
FERROTYPING
FERRUGINEOUS
FERRUGINOUS
FERRYBOATS
FERTIGATED
FERTIGATES
FERTIGATING
FERTIGATION
FERTIGATIONS
FERTILENESS
FERTILENESSES
FERTILISABLE
FERTILISATION
FERTILISATIONS
FERTILISED
FERTILISER
FERTILISERS
FERTILISES
FERTILISING
FERTILITIES
FERTILIZABLE
FERTILIZATION
FERTILIZATIONS
FERTILIZED
FERTILIZER
FERTILIZERS
FERTILIZES
FERTILIZING
FERULACEOUS
FERVENCIES
FERVENTEST
FERVENTNESS
FERVENTNESSES
FERVESCENT
FERVIDITIES
FERVIDNESS
FERVIDNESSES
FESCENNINE
FESTILOGIES
FESTINATED
FESTINATELY
FESTINATES
FESTINATING
FESTINATION
FESTINATIONS
FESTIVALGOER
FESTIVALGOERS
FESTIVENESS
FESTIVENESSES
FESTIVITIES
FESTOLOGIES
FESTOONERIES
FESTOONERY
FESTOONING
FESTSCHRIFT
FESTSCHRIFTEN
FESTSCHRIFTS
FETCHINGLY
FETICHISED
FETICHISES
FETICHISING
FETICHISMS
FETICHISTIC
FETICHISTS
FETICHIZED
FETICHIZES
FETICHIZING
FETIDITIES
FETIDNESSES
FETIPAROUS
FETISHISATION
FETISHISATIONS
FETISHISED
FETISHISES
FETISHISING
FETISHISMS
FETISHISTIC
FETISHISTICALLY
FETISHISTS
FETISHIZATION
FETISHIZATIONS
FETISHIZED
FETISHIZES
FETISHIZING
FETOLOGIES
FETOLOGIST
FETOLOGISTS
FETOPROTEIN
FETOPROTEINS
FETOSCOPES
FETOSCOPIES
FETTERLESS
FETTERLOCK
FETTERLOCKS
FETTUCCINE
FETTUCCINES
FETTUCCINI
FETTUCINES
FETTUCINIS
FEUDALISATION
FEUDALISATIONS
FEUDALISED
FEUDALISES
FEUDALISING
FEUDALISMS
FEUDALISTIC
FEUDALISTS
FEUDALITIES
FEUDALIZATION
FEUDALIZATIONS
FEUDALIZED
FEUDALIZES
FEUDALIZING
FEUDATORIES
FEUILLETES
FEUILLETON
FEUILLETONISM
FEUILLETONISMS
FEUILLETONIST
FEUILLETONISTIC
FEUILLETONISTS
FEUILLETONS
FEVERISHLY
FEVERISHNESS
FEVERISHNESSES
FEVEROUSLY
FEVERROOTS
FEVERWEEDS
FEVERWORTS
FIANCAILLES
FIANCHETTI
FIANCHETTO
FIANCHETTOED
FIANCHETTOES
FIANCHETTOING
FIANCHETTOS
FIBERBOARD
FIBERBOARDS
FIBERFILLS
FIBERGLASS
FIBERGLASSED
FIBERGLASSES
FIBERGLASSING
FIBERISATION
FIBERISATIONS
FIBERISING
FIBERIZATION
FIBERIZATIONS
FIBERIZING
FIBERSCOPE
FIBERSCOPES
FIBREBOARD
FIBREBOARDS
FIBREFILLS
FIBREGLASS
FIBREGLASSES
FIBREOPTIC
FIBRESCOPE
FIBRESCOPES
FIBRILLARY
FIBRILLATE
FIBRILLATED
FIBRILLATES
FIBRILLATING
FIBRILLATION
FIBRILLATIONS
FIBRILLIFORM
FIBRILLINS
FIBRILLOSE
FIBRILLOUS
FIBRINOGEN
FIBRINOGENIC
FIBRINOGENOUS
FIBRINOGENS
FIBRINOIDS
FIBRINOLYSES
FIBRINOLYSIN
FIBRINOLYSINS
FIBRINOLYSIS
FIBRINOLYTIC
FIBRINOPEPTIDE

IBRINOPEPTIDES
IBROBLAST
IBROBLASTIC
IBROBLASTS
IBROCARTILAGE
IBROCARTILAGES
IBROCEMENT
IBROCEMENTS
IBROCYSTIC
IBROCYTES
IBROLINES
IBROLITES
IBROMATOUS
IBROMYALGIA
IBROMYALGIAS
IBRONECTIN
IBRONECTINS
IBROSARCOMA
IBROSARCOMAS
IBROSARCOMATA
IBROSITIS
IBROSITISES
IBROUSNESS
IBROUSNESSES
IBROVASCULAR
ICKLENESS
ICKLENESSES
ICTIONALISE
ICTIONALISED
ICTIONALISES
ICTIONALISING
ICTIONALITIES
ICTIONALITY
ICTIONALIZE
ICTIONALIZED
ICTIONALIZES
ICTIONALIZING
ICTIONALLY
ICTIONEER
ICTIONEERING
ICTIONEERINGS
ICTIONEERS
ICTIONISATION
ICTIONISATIONS
ICTIONISE
ICTIONISED
ICTIONISES
ICTIONISING
ICTIONIST
ICTIONISTS
ICTIONIZATION
ICTIONIZATIONS
ICTIONIZE
ICTIONIZED
ICTIONIZES
ICTIONIZING
ICTITIOUS
ICTITIOUSLY
ICTITIOUSNESS
ICTIVENESS
ICTIVENESSES
IDDIOUSED
IDDIOUSES
IDDIOUSING
IDDLEBACK
IDDLEBACKS
FIDDLEDEDEE
FIDDLEDEEDEE
FIDDLEHEAD
FIDDLEHEADS
FIDDLENECK
FIDDLENECKS
FIDDLESTICK
FIDDLESTICKS
FIDDLEWOOD
FIDDLEWOODS
FIDEICOMMISSA
FIDEICOMMISSARY
FIDEICOMMISSUM
FIDELISMOS
FIDELISTAS
FIDELITIES
FIDGETIEST
FIDGETINESS
FIDGETINESSES
FIDGETINGLY
FIDUCIALLY
FIDUCIARIES
FIDUCIARILY
FIELDBOOTS
FIELDCRAFT
FIELDCRAFTS
FIELDFARES
FIELDMOUSE
FIELDPIECE
FIELDPIECES
FIELDSTONE
FIELDSTONES
FIELDSTRIP
FIELDSTRIPPED
FIELDSTRIPPING
FIELDSTRIPS
FIELDVOLES
FIELDWARDS
FIELDWORKER
FIELDWORKERS
FIELDWORKS
FIENDISHLY
FIENDISHNESS
FIENDISHNESSES
FIERCENESS
FIERCENESSES
FIERINESSES
FIFTEENERS
FIFTEENTHLY
FIFTEENTHS
FIGHTBACKS
FIGURABILITIES
FIGURABILITY
FIGURANTES
FIGURATELY
FIGURATION
FIGURATIONS
FIGURATIVE
FIGURATIVELY
FIGURATIVENESS
FIGUREHEAD
FIGUREHEADS
FIGURELESS
FIGUREWORK
FIGUREWORKS
FILAGREEING
FILAMENTARY
FILAMENTOUS
FILARIASES
FILARIASIS
FILATORIES
FILCHINGLY
FILEFISHES
FILIALNESS
FILIALNESSES
FILIATIONS
FILIBUSTER
FILIBUSTERED
FILIBUSTERER
FILIBUSTERERS
FILIBUSTERING
FILIBUSTERINGS
FILIBUSTERISM
FILIBUSTERISMS
FILIBUSTEROUS
FILIBUSTERS
FILICINEAN
FILIGRAINS
FILIGRANES
FILIGREEING
FILIOPIETISTIC
FILIPENDULOUS
FILLAGREED
FILLAGREEING
FILLAGREES
FILLESTERS
FILLIPEENS
FILLISTERS
FILMICALLY
FILMINESSES
FILMMAKERS
FILMMAKING
FILMMAKINGS
FILMOGRAPHIES
FILMOGRAPHY
FILMSETTER
FILMSETTERS
FILMSETTING
FILMSETTINGS
FILMSTRIPS
FILOPLUMES
FILOPODIUM
FILOSELLES
FILOVIRUSES
FILTERABILITIES
FILTERABILITY
FILTERABLE
FILTERABLENESS
FILTHINESS
FILTHINESSES
FILTRABILITIES
FILTRABILITY
FILTRATABLE
FILTRATING
FILTRATION
FILTRATIONS
FIMBRIATED
FIMBRIATES
FIMBRIATING
FIMBRIATION
FIMBRIATIONS
FIMBRILLATE
FIMICOLOUS
FINABLENESS
FINABLENESSES
FINALISATION
FINALISATIONS
FINALISERS
FINALISING
FINALISTIC
FINALITIES
FINALIZATION
FINALIZATIONS
FINALIZERS
FINALIZING
FINANCIALIST
FINANCIALISTS
FINANCIALLY
FINANCIERED
FINANCIERING
FINANCIERS
FINANCINGS
FINEABLENESS
FINEABLENESSES
FINENESSES
FINESSINGS
FINGERBOARD
FINGERBOARDS
FINGERBOWL
FINGERBOWLS
FINGERBREADTH
FINGERBREADTHS
FINGERGLASS
FINGERGLASSES
FINGERGUARD
FINGERGUARDS
FINGERHOLD
FINGERHOLDS
FINGERHOLE
FINGERHOLES
FINGERINGS
FINGERLESS
FINGERLIKE
FINGERLING
FINGERLINGS
FINGERMARK
FINGERMARKS
FINGERNAIL
FINGERNAILS
FINGERPICK
FINGERPICKED
FINGERPICKING
FINGERPICKINGS
FINGERPICKS
FINGERPLATE
FINGERPLATES
FINGERPOST
FINGERPOSTS
FINGERPRINT
FINGERPRINTED
FINGERPRINTING
FINGERPRINTINGS
FINGERPRINTS
FINGERSTALL
FINGERSTALLS
FINGERTIPS
FINICALITIES
FINICALITY

FINICALNESS
FINICALNESSES
FINICKETIER
FINICKETIEST
FINICKIEST
FINICKINESS
FINICKINESSES
FINICKINGS
FINISHINGS
FINITENESS
FINITENESSES
FINNICKIER
FINNICKIEST
FINNOCHIOS
FINOCCHIOS
FIORATURAE
FIREBALLER
FIREBALLERS
FIREBALLING
FIREBOARDS
FIREBOMBED
FIREBOMBING
FIREBRANDS
FIREBREAKS
FIREBRICKS
FIREBUSHES
FIRECRACKER
FIRECRACKERS
FIRECRESTS
FIREDRAGON
FIREDRAGONS
FIREDRAKES
FIREFANGED
FIREFANGING
FIREFIGHTER
FIREFIGHTERS
FIREFIGHTING
FIREFIGHTINGS
FIREFIGHTS
FIREFLOATS
FIREFLOODS
FIREGUARDS
FIREHOUSES
FIRELIGHTER
FIRELIGHTERS
FIRELIGHTS
FIREPLACED
FIREPLACES
FIREPOWERS
FIREPROOFED
FIREPROOFING
FIREPROOFINGS
FIREPROOFS
FIRESCREEN
FIRESCREENS
FIRESTONES
FIRESTORMS
FIRETHORNS
FIRETRUCKS
FIREWARDEN
FIREWARDENS
FIREWATERS
FIRMAMENTAL
FIRMAMENTS
FIRMNESSES
FIRSTBORNS
FIRSTFRUITS
FIRSTLINGS
FIRSTNESSES
FISCALISTS
FISHABILITIES
FISHABILITY
FISHBURGER
FISHBURGERS
FISHERFOLK
FISHERWOMAN
FISHERWOMEN
FISHFINGER
FISHFINGERS
FISHIFYING
FISHINESSES
FISHMONGER
FISHMONGERS
FISHPLATES
FISHTAILED
FISHTAILING
FISHWIFELY
FISHYBACKS
FISSICOSTATE
FISSILINGUAL
FISSILITIES
FISSIONABILITY
FISSIONABLE
FISSIONABLES
FISSIONING
FISSIPALMATE
FISSIPARISM
FISSIPARISMS
FISSIPARITIES
FISSIPARITY
FISSIPAROUS
FISSIPAROUSLY
FISSIPAROUSNESS
FISSIPEDAL
FISSIPEDES
FISSIROSTRAL
FISTFIGHTS
FISTICUFFS
FITFULNESS
FITFULNESSES
FITTINGNESS
FITTINGNESSES
FIVEFINGER
FIVEFINGERS
FIVEPENCES
FIXEDNESSES
FIXTURELESS
FIZZENLESS
FIZZINESSES
FLABBERGAST
FLABBERGASTED
FLABBERGASTING
FLABBERGASTS
FLABBINESS
FLABBINESSES
FLABELLATE
FLABELLATION
FLABELLATIONS
FLABELLIFORM
FLABELLUMS
FLACCIDEST
FLACCIDITIES
FLACCIDITY
FLACCIDNESS
FLACCIDNESSES
FLACKERIES
FLACKERING
FLAFFERING
FLAGELLANT
FLAGELLANTISM
FLAGELLANTISMS
FLAGELLANTS
FLAGELLATE
FLAGELLATED
FLAGELLATES
FLAGELLATING
FLAGELLATION
FLAGELLATIONS
FLAGELLATOR
FLAGELLATORS
FLAGELLATORY
FLAGELLIFEROUS
FLAGELLIFORM
FLAGELLINS
FLAGELLOMANIA
FLAGELLOMANIAC
FLAGELLOMANIACS
FLAGELLOMANIAS
FLAGELLUMS
FLAGEOLETS
FLAGGINESS
FLAGGINESSES
FLAGGINGLY
FLAGITATED
FLAGITATES
FLAGITATING
FLAGITATION
FLAGITATIONS
FLAGITIOUS
FLAGITIOUSLY
FLAGITIOUSNESS
FLAGRANCES
FLAGRANCIES
FLAGRANTLY
FLAGRANTNESS
FLAGRANTNESSES
FLAGSTAFFS
FLAGSTAVES
FLAGSTICKS
FLAGSTONES
FLAKINESSES
FLAMBEEING
FLAMBOYANCE
FLAMBOYANCES
FLAMBOYANCIES
FLAMBOYANCY
FLAMBOYANT
FLAMBOYANTE
FLAMBOYANTES
FLAMBOYANTLY
FLAMBOYANTS
FLAMEPROOF
FLAMEPROOFED
FLAMEPROOFER
FLAMEPROOFERS
FLAMEPROOFING
FLAMEPROOFS
FLAMETHROWER
FLAMETHROWERS
FLAMINGOES
FLAMINICAL
FLAMMABILITIES
FLAMMABILITY
FLAMMABLES
FLAMMIFEROUS
FLAMMULATED
FLAMMULATION
FLAMMULATIONS
FLANCHINGS
FLANCONADE
FLANCONADES
FLANGELESS
FLANKERING
FLANNELBOARD
FLANNELBOARDS
FLANNELETS
FLANNELETTE
FLANNELETTES
FLANNELGRAPH
FLANNELGRAPHS
FLANNELING
FLANNELINGS
FLANNELLED
FLANNELLING
FLANNELLINGS
FLANNELMOUTHED
FLAPDOODLE
FLAPDOODLES
FLAPPERHOOD
FLAPPERHOODS
FLAPPERISH
FLAPTRACKS
FLAREBACKS
FLASHBACKED
FLASHBACKING
FLASHBACKS
FLASHBOARD
FLASHBOARDS
FLASHBULBS
FLASHCARDS
FLASHCUBES
FLASHFORWARD
FLASHFORWARDED
FLASHFORWARDING
FLASHFORWARDS
FLASHINESS
FLASHINESSES
FLASHLAMPS
FLASHLIGHT
FLASHLIGHTS
FLASHMOBBING
FLASHMOBBINGS
FLASHOVERS
FLASHTUBES
FLATBREADS
FLATFISHES
FLATFOOTED
FLATFOOTING
FLATLANDER
FLATLANDERS
FLATLINERS
FLATLINING
FLATNESSES
FLATSCREEN

LATSCREENS
LATSHARES
LATTENERS
LATTENING
LATTERABLE
LATTERERS
LATTERIES
LATTERING
LATTERINGLY
LATTEROUS
LATTEROUSLY
LATULENCE
LATULENCES
LATULENCIES
LATULENCY
LATULENTLY
LATWASHES
LAUGHTERED
LAUGHTERING
LAUGHTERS
LAUGHTING
LAUNCHING
LAUNCHINGS
LAUNTIEST
LAUNTINESS
LAUNTINESSES
LAUNTINGLY
LAVANONES
LAVESCENT
LAVIVIRUS
LAVIVIRUSES
LAVONOIDS
LAVOPROTEIN
LAVOPROTEINS
LAVOPURPURIN
LAVOPURPURINS
LAVORFULLY
LAVORINGS
LAVORISTS
LAVORLESS
LAVORSOME
LAVOURDYNAMICS
LAVOURERS
LAVOURFUL
LAVOURFULLY
LAVOURING
LAVOURINGS
LAVOURLESS
LAVOURSOME
LAWLESSLY
LAWLESSNESS
LAWLESSNESSES
LEAHOPPER
LEAHOPPERS
LEAMARKET
LEAMARKETS
LECHETTES
LECKERING
LECTIONAL
LECTIONLESS
LEDGELING
LEDGELINGS
LEDGLINGS
LEECELESS
LEECHINGS
LEECHMENT

FLEECHMENTS
FLEECINESS
FLEECINESSES
FLEERINGLY
FLEETINGLY
FLEETINGNESS
FLEETINGNESSES
FLEETNESSES
FLEHMENING
FLEMISHING
FLESHHOODS
FLESHINESS
FLESHINESSES
FLESHLIEST
FLESHLINESS
FLESHLINESSES
FLESHLINGS
FLESHMENTS
FLESHMONGER
FLESHMONGERS
FLESHWORMS
FLETCHINGS
FLEURETTES
FLEXECUTIVE
FLEXECUTIVES
FLEXIBILITIES
FLEXIBILITY
FLEXIBLENESS
FLEXIBLENESSES
FLEXIHOURS
FLEXIONLESS
FLEXITARIAN
FLEXITARIANISM
FLEXITARIANISMS
FLEXITARIANS
FLEXITIMES
FLEXOGRAPHIC
FLEXOGRAPHIES
FLEXOGRAPHY
FLEXTIMERS
FLEXUOUSLY
FLIBBERTIGIBBET
FLICHTERED
FLICHTERING
FLICKERING
FLICKERINGLY
FLICKERTAIL
FLICKERTAILS
FLIGHTIEST
FLIGHTINESS
FLIGHTINESSES
FLIGHTLESS
FLIMFLAMMED
FLIMFLAMMER
FLIMFLAMMERIES
FLIMFLAMMERS
FLIMFLAMMERY
FLIMFLAMMING
FLIMSINESS
FLIMSINESSES
FLINCHINGLY
FLINCHINGS
FLINDERSIA
FLINDERSIAS
FLINTHEADS
FLINTIFIED

FLINTIFIES
FLINTIFYING
FLINTINESS
FLINTINESSES
FLINTLOCKS
FLIPFLOPPED
FLIPFLOPPING
FLIPPANCIES
FLIPPANTLY
FLIPPANTNESS
FLIPPANTNESSES
FLIRTATION
FLIRTATIONS
FLIRTATIOUS
FLIRTATIOUSLY
FLIRTATIOUSNESS
FLIRTINGLY
FLITTERING
FLITTERMICE
FLITTERMOUSE
FLOATABILITIES
FLOATABILITY
FLOATATION
FLOATATIONS
FLOATINGLY
FLOATPLANE
FLOATPLANES
FLOCCILLATION
FLOCCILLATIONS
FLOCCULANT
FLOCCULANTS
FLOCCULATE
FLOCCULATED
FLOCCULATES
FLOCCULATING
FLOCCULATION
FLOCCULATIONS
FLOCCULATOR
FLOCCULATORS
FLOCCULENCE
FLOCCULENCES
FLOCCULENCIES
FLOCCULENCY
FLOCCULENT
FLOCCULENTLY
FLOODGATES
FLOODLIGHT
FLOODLIGHTED
FLOODLIGHTING
FLOODLIGHTINGS
FLOODLIGHTS
FLOODMARKS
FLOODPLAIN
FLOODPLAINS
FLOODTIDES
FLOODWALLS
FLOODWATER
FLOODWATERS
FLOORBOARD
FLOORBOARDS
FLOORCLOTH
FLOORCLOTHS
FLOORHEADS
FLOORSHOWS
FLOORWALKER
FLOORWALKERS

FLOPHOUSES
FLOPPINESS
FLOPPINESSES
FLORENTINE
FLORENTINES
FLORESCENCE
FLORESCENCES
FLORESCENT
FLORIATION
FLORIATIONS
FLORIBUNDA
FLORIBUNDAS
FLORICANES
FLORICULTURAL
FLORICULTURE
FLORICULTURES
FLORICULTURIST
FLORICULTURISTS
FLORIDEANS
FLORIDEOUS
FLORIDITIES
FLORIDNESS
FLORIDNESSES
FLORIFEROUS
FLORIFEROUSNESS
FLORIGENIC
FLORILEGIA
FLORILEGIUM
FLORISTICALLY
FLORISTICS
FLORISTRIES
FLOSCULOUS
FLOTATIONS
FLOUNCIEST
FLOUNCINGS
FLOUNDERED
FLOUNDERING
FLOURISHED
FLOURISHER
FLOURISHERS
FLOURISHES
FLOURISHING
FLOURISHINGLY
FLOUTINGLY
FLOUTINGSTOCK
FLOUTINGSTOCKS
FLOWCHARTING
FLOWCHARTINGS
FLOWCHARTS
FLOWERAGES
FLOWERBEDS
FLOWERETTE
FLOWERETTES
FLOWERIEST
FLOWERINESS
FLOWERINESSES
FLOWERINGS
FLOWERLESS
FLOWERLIKE
FLOWERPOTS
FLOWINGNESS
FLOWINGNESSES
FLOWMETERS
FLOWSTONES
FLUCTUATED
FLUCTUATES

FLUCTUATING
FLUCTUATION
FLUCTUATIONAL
FLUCTUATIONS
FLUEGELHORN
FLUEGELHORNS
FLUENTNESS
FLUENTNESSES
FLUFFINESS
FLUFFINESSES
FLUGELHORN
FLUGELHORNIST
FLUGELHORNISTS
FLUGELHORNS
FLUIDEXTRACT
FLUIDEXTRACTS
FLUIDIFIED
FLUIDIFIES
FLUIDIFYING
FLUIDISATION
FLUIDISATIONS
FLUIDISERS
FLUIDISING
FLUIDITIES
FLUIDIZATION
FLUIDIZATIONS
FLUIDIZERS
FLUIDIZING
FLUIDNESSES
FLUKINESSES
FLUMMERIES
FLUMMOXING
FLUNITRAZEPAM
FLUNITRAZEPAMS
FLUNKEYDOM
FLUNKEYDOMS
FLUNKEYISH
FLUNKEYISM
FLUNKEYISMS
FLUNKYISMS
FLUORAPATITE
FLUORAPATITES
FLUORESCED
FLUORESCEIN
FLUORESCEINE
FLUORESCEINES
FLUORESCEINS
FLUORESCENCE
FLUORESCENCES
FLUORESCENT
FLUORESCENTS
FLUORESCER
FLUORESCERS
FLUORESCES
FLUORESCING
FLUORIDATE
FLUORIDATED
FLUORIDATES
FLUORIDATING
FLUORIDATION
FLUORIDATIONS
FLUORIDISE
FLUORIDISED
FLUORIDISES
FLUORIDISING
FLUORIDIZE
FLUORIDIZED
FLUORIDIZES
FLUORIDIZING
FLUORIMETER
FLUORIMETERS
FLUORIMETRIC
FLUORIMETRIES
FLUORIMETRY
FLUORINATE
FLUORINATED
FLUORINATES
FLUORINATING
FLUORINATION
FLUORINATIONS
FLUOROACETATE
FLUOROACETATES
FLUOROCARBON
FLUOROCARBONS
FLUOROCHROME
FLUOROCHROMES
FLUOROGRAPHIC
FLUOROGRAPHIES
FLUOROGRAPHY
FLUOROMETER
FLUOROMETERS
FLUOROMETRIC
FLUOROMETRIES
FLUOROMETRY
FLUOROPHORE
FLUOROPHORES
FLUOROSCOPE
FLUOROSCOPED
FLUOROSCOPES
FLUOROSCOPIC
FLUOROSCOPIES
FLUOROSCOPING
FLUOROSCOPIST
FLUOROSCOPISTS
FLUOROSCOPY
FLUOROTYPE
FLUOROTYPES
FLUOROURACIL
FLUOROURACILS
FLUORSPARS
FLUOXETINE
FLUOXETINES
FLUPHENAZINE
FLUPHENAZINES
FLUSHNESSES
FLUSHWORKS
FLUSTEREDLY
FLUSTERING
FLUSTERMENT
FLUSTERMENTS
FLUSTRATED
FLUSTRATES
FLUSTRATING
FLUSTRATION
FLUSTRATIONS
FLUTEMOUTH
FLUTEMOUTHS
FLUTTERBOARD
FLUTTERBOARDS
FLUTTERERS
FLUTTERING
FLUTTERINGLY
FLUVIALIST
FLUVIALISTS
FLUVIATILE
FLUVIOMARINE
FLUVOXAMINE
FLUVOXAMINES
FLUXIONALLY
FLUXIONARY
FLUXIONIST
FLUXIONISTS
FLUXMETERS
FLYBLOWING
FLYBRIDGES
FLYCATCHER
FLYCATCHERS
FLYPITCHER
FLYPITCHERS
FLYPITCHES
FLYPOSTING
FLYPOSTINGS
FLYRODDERS
FLYSCREENS
FLYSPECKED
FLYSPECKING
FLYSTRIKES
FLYSWATTER
FLYSWATTERS
FLYWEIGHTS
FOAMFLOWER
FOAMFLOWERS
FOAMINESSES
FOCALISATION
FOCALISATIONS
FOCALISING
FOCALIZATION
FOCALIZATIONS
FOCALIZING
FOCIMETERS
FOCOMETERS
FODDERINGS
FOEDERATUS
FOETATIONS
FOETICIDAL
FOETICIDES
FOETIDNESS
FOETIDNESSES
FOETIPAROUS
FOETOSCOPIES
FOETOSCOPY
FOGGINESSES
FOGRAMITES
FOGRAMITIES
FOISONLESS
FOLIACEOUS
FOLIATIONS
FOLIATURES
FOLKISHNESS
FOLKISHNESSES
FOLKLORISH
FOLKLORIST
FOLKLORISTIC
FOLKLORISTS
FOLKSINESS
FOLKSINESSES
FOLKSINGER
FOLKSINGERS
FOLKSINGING
FOLKSINGINGS
FOLLICULAR
FOLLICULATE
FOLLICULATED
FOLLICULIN
FOLLICULINS
FOLLICULITIS
FOLLICULITISES
FOLLICULOSE
FOLLICULOUS
FOLLOWABLE
FOLLOWERSHIP
FOLLOWERSHIPS
FOLLOWINGS
FOLLOWSHIP
FOLLOWSHIPS
FOMENTATION
FOMENTATIONS
FONCTIONNAIRE
FONCTIONNAIRES
FONDLINGLY
FONDNESSES
FONTANELLE
FONTANELLES
FONTICULUS
FONTICULUSES
FONTINALIS
FONTINALISES
FOODLESSNESS
FOODLESSNESSES
FOODSTUFFS
FOOLBEGGED
FOOLFISHES
FOOLHARDIER
FOOLHARDIEST
FOOLHARDILY
FOOLHARDINESS
FOOLHARDINESSES
FOOLHARDISE
FOOLHARDISES
FOOLHARDIZE
FOOLHARDIZES
FOOLISHEST
FOOLISHNESS
FOOLISHNESSES
FOOTBALLENE
FOOTBALLENES
FOOTBALLER
FOOTBALLERS
FOOTBALLING
FOOTBALLIST
FOOTBALLISTS
FOOTBOARDS
FOOTBREADTH
FOOTBREADTHS
FOOTBRIDGE
FOOTBRIDGES
FOOTCLOTHS
FOOTDRAGGER
FOOTDRAGGERS
FOOTFAULTED
FOOTFAULTING
FOOTFAULTS
FOOTGUARDS
FOOTLAMBERT

OOTLAMBERTS
OOTLESSLY
OOTLESSNESS
OOTLESSNESSES
OOTLIGHTS
OOTLOCKER
OOTLOCKERS
OOTNOTING
OOTPLATEMAN
OOTPLATEMEN
OOTPLATES
OOTPLATEWOMAN
OOTPLATEWOMEN
OOTPRINTS
OOTSLOGGED
OOTSLOGGER
OOTSLOGGERS
OOTSLOGGING
OOTSLOGGINGS
OOTSORENESS
OOTSORENESSES
OOTSTALKS
OOTSTALLS
OOTSTOCKS
OOTSTONES
OOTSTOOLED
OOTSTOOLS
OPPISHNESS
OPPISHNESSES
ORAMINATED
ORAMINIFER
ORAMINIFERA
ORAMINIFERAL
ORAMINIFERAN
ORAMINIFERANS
ORAMINIFEROUS
ORAMINIFERS
ORAMINOUS
ORBEARANCE
ORBEARANCES
ORBEARANT
ORBEARERS
ORBEARING
ORBEARINGLY
ORBIDDALS
ORBIDDANCE
ORBIDDANCES
ORBIDDENLY
ORBIDDERS
ORBIDDING
ORBIDDINGLY
ORBIDDINGNESS
ORBIDDINGS
ORCEDNESS
ORCEDNESSES
ORCEFULLY
ORCEFULNESS
ORCEFULNESSES
ORCEMEATS
ORCEPSLIKE
ORCIBILITIES
ORCIBILITY
ORCIBLENESS
ORCIBLENESSES
ORCIPATED
ORCIPATION
FORCIPATIONS
FOREARMING
FOREBITTER
FOREBITTERS
FOREBODEMENT
FOREBODEMENTS
FOREBODERS
FOREBODIES
FOREBODING
FOREBODINGLY
FOREBODINGNESS
FOREBODINGS
FOREBRAINS
FORECABINS
FORECADDIE
FORECADDIES
FORECARRIAGE
FORECARRIAGES
FORECASTABLE
FORECASTED
FORECASTER
FORECASTERS
FORECASTING
FORECASTLE
FORECASTLES
FORECHECKED
FORECHECKER
FORECHECKERS
FORECHECKING
FORECHECKS
FORECHOSEN
FORECLOSABLE
FORECLOSED
FORECLOSES
FORECLOSING
FORECLOSURE
FORECLOSURES
FORECLOTHS
FORECOURSE
FORECOURSES
FORECOURTS
FOREDAMNED
FOREDATING
FOREDOOMED
FOREDOOMING
FOREFATHER
FOREFATHERLY
FOREFATHERS
FOREFEELING
FOREFEELINGLY
FOREFENDED
FOREFENDING
FOREFINGER
FOREFINGERS
FOREFRONTS
FOREGATHER
FOREGATHERED
FOREGATHERING
FOREGATHERS
FOREGLEAMS
FOREGOINGS
FOREGONENESS
FOREGONENESSES
FOREGROUND
FOREGROUNDED
FOREGROUNDING
FOREGROUNDS
FOREHANDED
FOREHANDEDLY
FOREHANDEDNESS
FOREHANDING
FOREHENTING
FOREHOOVES
FOREIGNERS
FOREIGNISM
FOREIGNISMS
FOREIGNNESS
FOREIGNNESSES
FOREJUDGED
FOREJUDGEMENT
FOREJUDGEMENTS
FOREJUDGES
FOREJUDGING
FOREJUDGMENT
FOREJUDGMENTS
FOREKNOWABLE
FOREKNOWING
FOREKNOWINGLY
FOREKNOWLEDGE
FOREKNOWLEDGES
FORELADIES
FORELAYING
FORELENDING
FORELIFTED
FORELIFTING
FORELOCKED
FORELOCKING
FOREMANSHIP
FOREMANSHIPS
FOREMASTMAN
FOREMASTMEN
FOREMEANING
FOREMENTIONED
FOREMOTHER
FOREMOTHERS
FORENIGHTS
FORENSICALITIES
FORENSICALITY
FORENSICALLY
FOREORDAIN
FOREORDAINED
FOREORDAINING
FOREORDAINMENT
FOREORDAINMENTS
FOREORDAINS
FOREORDINATION
FOREORDINATIONS
FOREPASSED
FOREPAYMENT
FOREPAYMENTS
FOREPLANNED
FOREPLANNING
FOREPOINTED
FOREPOINTING
FOREPOINTS
FOREQUARTER
FOREQUARTERS
FOREREACHED
FOREREACHES
FOREREACHING
FOREREADING
FOREREADINGS
FORERUNNER
FORERUNNERS
FORERUNNING
FORESAYING
FORESEEABILITY
FORESEEABLE
FORESEEING
FORESEEINGLY
FORESHADOW
FORESHADOWED
FORESHADOWER
FORESHADOWERS
FORESHADOWING
FORESHADOWINGS
FORESHADOWS
FORESHANKS
FORESHEETS
FORESHEWED
FORESHEWING
FORESHOCKS
FORESHORES
FORESHORTEN
FORESHORTENED
FORESHORTENING
FORESHORTENINGS
FORESHORTENS
FORESHOWED
FORESHOWING
FORESIGHTED
FORESIGHTEDLY
FORESIGHTEDNESS
FORESIGHTFUL
FORESIGHTLESS
FORESIGHTS
FORESIGNIFIED
FORESIGNIFIES
FORESIGNIFY
FORESIGNIFYING
FORESKIRTS
FORESLACKED
FORESLACKING
FORESLACKS
FORESLOWED
FORESLOWING
FORESPEAKING
FORESPEAKS
FORESPENDING
FORESPENDS
FORESPOKEN
FORESTAGES
FORESTAIRS
FORESTALLED
FORESTALLER
FORESTALLERS
FORESTALLING
FORESTALLINGS
FORESTALLMENT
FORESTALLMENTS
FORESTALLS
FORESTALMENT
FORESTALMENTS
FORESTATION
FORESTATIONS
FORESTAYSAIL
FORESTAYSAILS
FORESTLAND

FORESTLANDS
FORESTLESS
FORESTRIES
FORESWEARING
FORESWEARS
FORETASTED
FORETASTES
FORETASTING
FORETAUGHT
FORETEACHES
FORETEACHING
FORETELLER
FORETELLERS
FORETELLING
FORETHINKER
FORETHINKERS
FORETHINKING
FORETHINKS
FORETHOUGHT
FORETHOUGHTFUL
FORETHOUGHTS
FORETOKENED
FORETOKENING
FORETOKENINGS
FORETOKENS
FORETOPMAN
FORETOPMAST
FORETOPMASTS
FORETOPMEN
FORETRIANGLE
FORETRIANGLES
FOREVERMORE
FOREVERNESS
FOREVERNESSES
FOREVOUCHED
FOREWARNED
FOREWARNER
FOREWARNERS
FOREWARNING
FOREWARNINGLY
FOREWARNINGS
FOREWEIGHED
FOREWEIGHING
FOREWEIGHS
FORFAIRING
FORFAITERS
FORFAITING
FORFAITINGS
FORFEITABLE
FORFEITERS
FORFEITING
FORFEITURE
FORFEITURES
FORFENDING
FORFEUCHEN
FORFICULATE
FORFOUGHEN
FORFOUGHTEN
FORGATHERED
FORGATHERING
FORGATHERS
FORGEABILITIES
FORGEABILITY
FORGETFULLY
FORGETFULNESS
FORGETFULNESSES
FORGETTABLE
FORGETTERIES
FORGETTERS
FORGETTERY
FORGETTING
FORGETTINGLY
FORGETTINGS
FORGIVABLE
FORGIVABLY
FORGIVENESS
FORGIVENESSES
FORGIVINGLY
FORGIVINGNESS
FORGIVINGNESSES
FORGOTTENNESS
FORGOTTENNESSES
FORHAILING
FORHENTING
FORHOOIEING
FORINSECAL
FORISFAMILIATE
FORISFAMILIATED
FORISFAMILIATES
FORJUDGING
FORJUDGMENT
FORJUDGMENTS
FORKEDNESS
FORKEDNESSES
FORKINESSES
FORKLIFTED
FORKLIFTING
FORLENDING
FORLORNEST
FORLORNNESS
FORLORNNESSES
FORMABILITIES
FORMABILITY
FORMALDEHYDE
FORMALDEHYDES
FORMALISABLE
FORMALISATION
FORMALISATIONS
FORMALISED
FORMALISER
FORMALISERS
FORMALISES
FORMALISING
FORMALISMS
FORMALISTIC
FORMALISTICALLY
FORMALISTS
FORMALITER
FORMALITIES
FORMALIZABLE
FORMALIZATION
FORMALIZATIONS
FORMALIZED
FORMALIZER
FORMALIZERS
FORMALIZES
FORMALIZING
FORMALNESS
FORMALNESSES
FORMAMIDES
FORMATIONAL
FORMATIONS
FORMATIVELY
FORMATIVENESS
FORMATIVENESSES
FORMATIVES
FORMATTERS
FORMATTING
FORMFITTING
FORMICARIA
FORMICARIES
FORMICARIUM
FORMICATED
FORMICATES
FORMICATING
FORMICATION
FORMICATIONS
FORMIDABILITIES
FORMIDABILITY
FORMIDABLE
FORMIDABLENESS
FORMIDABLY
FORMLESSLY
FORMLESSNESS
FORMLESSNESSES
FORMULAICALLY
FORMULARIES
FORMULARISATION
FORMULARISE
FORMULARISED
FORMULARISER
FORMULARISERS
FORMULARISES
FORMULARISING
FORMULARISTIC
FORMULARIZATION
FORMULARIZE
FORMULARIZED
FORMULARIZER
FORMULARIZERS
FORMULARIZES
FORMULARIZING
FORMULATED
FORMULATES
FORMULATING
FORMULATION
FORMULATIONS
FORMULATOR
FORMULATORS
FORMULISED
FORMULISES
FORMULISING
FORMULISMS
FORMULISTIC
FORMULISTS
FORMULIZED
FORMULIZES
FORMULIZING
FORNICATED
FORNICATES
FORNICATING
FORNICATION
FORNICATIONS
FORNICATOR
FORNICATORS
FORNICATRESS
FORNICATRESSES
FORSAKENLY
FORSAKENNESS
FORSAKENNESSES
FORSAKINGS
FORSLACKED
FORSLACKING
FORSLOEING
FORSLOWING
FORSPEAKING
FORSPENDING
FORSTERITE
FORSTERITES
FORSWEARER
FORSWEARERS
FORSWEARING
FORSWINKED
FORSWINKING
FORSWORNNESS
FORSWORNNESSES
FORSYTHIAS
FORTALICES
FORTEPIANIST
FORTEPIANISTS
FORTEPIANO
FORTEPIANOS
FORTHCOMES
FORTHCOMING
FORTHCOMINGNESS
FORTHGOING
FORTHGOINGS
FORTHINKING
FORTHOUGHT
FORTHRIGHT
FORTHRIGHTLY
FORTHRIGHTNESS
FORTHRIGHTS
FORTIFIABLE
FORTIFICATION
FORTIFICATIONS
FORTIFIERS
FORTIFYING
FORTIFYINGLY
FORTILAGES
FORTISSIMI
FORTISSIMO
FORTISSIMOS
FORTISSISSIMO
FORTITUDES
FORTITUDINOUS
FORTNIGHTLIES
FORTNIGHTLY
FORTNIGHTS
FORTRESSED
FORTRESSES
FORTRESSING
FORTRESSLIKE
FORTUITIES
FORTUITISM
FORTUITISMS
FORTUITIST
FORTUITISTS
FORTUITOUS
FORTUITOUSLY
FORTUITOUSNESS
FORTUNATELY
FORTUNATENESS
FORTUNATENESSES

FORTUNATES
FORTUNELESS
FORTUNISED
FORTUNISES
FORTUNISING
FORTUNIZED
FORTUNIZES
FORTUNIZING
FORWANDERED
FORWANDERING
FORWANDERS
FORWARDERS
FORWARDEST
FORWARDING
FORWARDINGS
FORWARDNESS
FORWARDNESSES
FORWARNING
FORWASTING
FORWEARIED
FORWEARIES
FORWEARYING
FOSCARNETS
FOSSICKERS
FOSSICKING
FOSSICKINGS
FOSSILIFEROUS
FOSSILISABLE
FOSSILISATION
FOSSILISATIONS
FOSSILISED
FOSSILISES
FOSSILISING
FOSSILIZABLE
FOSSILIZATION
FOSSILIZATIONS
FOSSILIZED
FOSSILIZES
FOSSILIZING
FOSTERAGES
FOSTERINGLY
FOSTERINGS
FOSTERLING
FOSTERLINGS
FOSTRESSES
FOTHERGILLA
FOTHERGILLAS
FOUDROYANT
FOUGHTIEST
FOULBROODS
FOULDERING
FOULMOUTHED
FOULNESSES
FOUNDATION
FOUNDATIONAL
FOUNDATIONALLY
FOUNDATIONARY
FOUNDATIONER
FOUNDATIONERS
FOUNDATIONLESS
FOUNDATIONS
FOUNDERING
FOUNDEROUS
FOUNDLINGS
FOUNDRESSES
FOUNTAINED
FOUNTAINHEAD
FOUNTAINHEADS
FOUNTAINING
FOUNTAINLESS
FOURCHETTE
FOURCHETTES
FOURDRINIER
FOURDRINIERS
FOURFOLDNESS
FOURFOLDNESSES
FOURPENCES
FOURPENNIES
FOURPLEXES
FOURRAGERE
FOURRAGERES
FOURSCORTH
FOURSQUARE
FOURSQUARELY
FOURSQUARENESS
FOURTEENER
FOURTEENERS
FOURTEENTH
FOURTEENTHLY
FOURTEENTHS
FOVEOLATED
FOXBERRIES
FOXHUNTERS
FOXHUNTING
FOXHUNTINGS
FOXINESSES
FOXTROTTED
FOXTROTTING
FOZINESSES
FRABJOUSLY
FRACTALITIES
FRACTALITY
FRACTIONAL
FRACTIONALISE
FRACTIONALISED
FRACTIONALISES
FRACTIONALISING
FRACTIONALISM
FRACTIONALISMS
FRACTIONALIST
FRACTIONALISTS
FRACTIONALIZE
FRACTIONALIZED
FRACTIONALIZES
FRACTIONALIZING
FRACTIONALLY
FRACTIONARY
FRACTIONATE
FRACTIONATED
FRACTIONATES
FRACTIONATING
FRACTIONATION
FRACTIONATIONS
FRACTIONATOR
FRACTIONATORS
FRACTIONED
FRACTIONING
FRACTIONISATION
FRACTIONISE
FRACTIONISED
FRACTIONISES
FRACTIONISING
FRACTIONIZATION
FRACTIONIZE
FRACTIONIZED
FRACTIONIZES
FRACTIONIZING
FRACTIONLET
FRACTIONLETS
FRACTIOUSLY
FRACTIOUSNESS
FRACTIOUSNESSES
FRACTOCUMULI
FRACTOCUMULUS
FRACTOGRAPHIES
FRACTOGRAPHY
FRACTOSTRATI
FRACTOSTRATUS
FRACTURABLE
FRACTURERS
FRACTURING
FRAGILENESS
FRAGILENESSES
FRAGILITIES
FRAGMENTAL
FRAGMENTALLY
FRAGMENTARILY
FRAGMENTARINESS
FRAGMENTARY
FRAGMENTATE
FRAGMENTATED
FRAGMENTATES
FRAGMENTATING
FRAGMENTATION
FRAGMENTATIONS
FRAGMENTED
FRAGMENTING
FRAGMENTISE
FRAGMENTISED
FRAGMENTISES
FRAGMENTISING
FRAGMENTIZE
FRAGMENTIZED
FRAGMENTIZES
FRAGMENTIZING
FRAGRANCED
FRAGRANCES
FRAGRANCIES
FRAGRANCING
FRAGRANTLY
FRAGRANTNESS
FRAGRANTNESSES
FRAICHEURS
FRAILNESSES
FRAMBESIAS
FRAMBOESIA
FRAMBOESIAS
FRAMBOISES
FRAMESHIFT
FRAMESHIFTS
FRAMEWORKS
FRANCHISED
FRANCHISEE
FRANCHISEES
FRANCHISEMENT
FRANCHISEMENTS
FRANCHISER
FRANCHISERS
FRANCHISES
FRANCHISING
FRANCHISOR
FRANCHISORS
FRANCISING
FRANCIZING
FRANCOLINS
FRANCOMANIA
FRANCOMANIAS
FRANCOPHIL
FRANCOPHILE
FRANCOPHILES
FRANCOPHILS
FRANCOPHOBE
FRANCOPHOBES
FRANCOPHOBIA
FRANCOPHOBIAS
FRANCOPHONE
FRANCOPHONES
FRANGIBILITIES
FRANGIBILITY
FRANGIBLENESS
FRANGIBLENESSES
FRANGIPANE
FRANGIPANES
FRANGIPANI
FRANGIPANIS
FRANGIPANNI
FRANKALMOIGN
FRANKALMOIGNS
FRANKFORTS
FRANKFURTER
FRANKFURTERS
FRANKFURTS
FRANKINCENSE
FRANKINCENSES
FRANKLINITE
FRANKLINITES
FRANKNESSES
FRANKPLEDGE
FRANKPLEDGES
FRANSERIAS
FRANTICALLY
FRANTICNESS
FRANTICNESSES
FRATCHIEST
FRATERNALISM
FRATERNALISMS
FRATERNALLY
FRATERNISATION
FRATERNISATIONS
FRATERNISE
FRATERNISED
FRATERNISER
FRATERNISERS
FRATERNISES
FRATERNISING
FRATERNITIES
FRATERNITY
FRATERNIZATION
FRATERNIZATIONS
FRATERNIZE
FRATERNIZED
FRATERNIZER
FRATERNIZERS
FRATERNIZES

FRATERNIZING
FRATRICIDAL
FRATRICIDE
FRATRICIDES
FRAUDFULLY
FRAUDSTERS
FRAUDULENCE
FRAUDULENCES
FRAUDULENCIES
FRAUDULENCY
FRAUDULENT
FRAUDULENTLY
FRAUDULENTNESS
FRAUGHTAGE
FRAUGHTAGES
FRAUGHTEST
FRAUGHTING
FRAXINELLA
FRAXINELLAS
FREAKERIES
FREAKINESS
FREAKINESSES
FREAKISHLY
FREAKISHNESS
FREAKISHNESSES
FRECKLIEST
FRECKLINGS
FREEBASERS
FREEBASING
FREEBOARDS
FREEBOOTED
FREEBOOTER
FREEBOOTERIES
FREEBOOTERS
FREEBOOTERY
FREEBOOTIES
FREEBOOTING
FREEBOOTINGS
FREEDIVING
FREEDIVINGS
FREEDWOMAN
FREEDWOMEN
FREEHANDED
FREEHANDEDLY
FREEHANDEDNESS
FREEHEARTED
FREEHEARTEDLY
FREEHOLDER
FREEHOLDERS
FREELANCED
FREELANCER
FREELANCERS
FREELANCES
FREELANCING
FREELOADED
FREELOADER
FREELOADERS
FREELOADING
FREELOADINGS
FREEMARTIN
FREEMARTINS
FREEMASONIC
FREEMASONRIES
FREEMASONRY
FREEMASONS
FREENESSES
FREEPHONES
FREESHEETS
FREESTANDING
FREESTONES
FREESTYLER
FREESTYLERS
FREESTYLES
FREESTYLING
FREESTYLINGS
FREETHINKER
FREETHINKERS
FREETHINKING
FREETHINKINGS
FREEWHEELED
FREEWHEELER
FREEWHEELERS
FREEWHEELING
FREEWHEELINGLY
FREEWHEELINGS
FREEWHEELS
FREEWRITES
FREEWRITING
FREEWRITINGS
FREEWRITTEN
FREEZINGLY
FREIGHTAGE
FREIGHTAGES
FREIGHTERS
FREIGHTING
FREIGHTLESS
FREMESCENCE
FREMESCENCES
FREMESCENT
FREMITUSES
FRENCHIFICATION
FRENCHIFIED
FRENCHIFIES
FRENCHIFYING
FRENETICAL
FRENETICALLY
FRENETICISM
FRENETICISMS
FRENETICNESS
FRENETICNESSES
FRENZIEDLY
FREQUENCES
FREQUENCIES
FREQUENTABLE
FREQUENTATION
FREQUENTATIONS
FREQUENTATIVE
FREQUENTATIVES
FREQUENTED
FREQUENTER
FREQUENTERS
FREQUENTEST
FREQUENTING
FREQUENTLY
FREQUENTNESS
FREQUENTNESSES
FRESCOINGS
FRESCOISTS
FRESHENERS
FRESHENING
FRESHERDOM
FRESHERDOMS
FRESHMANSHIP
FRESHMANSHIPS
FRESHNESSES
FRESHWATER
FRESHWATERS
FRETBOARDS
FRETFULNESS
FRETFULNESSES
FRIABILITIES
FRIABILITY
FRIABLENESS
FRIABLENESSES
FRIARBIRDS
FRICANDEAU
FRICANDEAUS
FRICANDEAUX
FRICANDOES
FRICASSEED
FRICASSEEING
FRICASSEES
FRICATIVES
FRICTIONAL
FRICTIONALLY
FRICTIONLESS
FRICTIONLESSLY
FRIEDCAKES
FRIENDINGS
FRIENDLESS
FRIENDLESSNESS
FRIENDLIER
FRIENDLIES
FRIENDLIEST
FRIENDLILY
FRIENDLINESS
FRIENDLINESSES
FRIENDSHIP
FRIENDSHIPS
FRIEZELIKE
FRIGATOONS
FRIGHTENABLE
FRIGHTENED
FRIGHTENER
FRIGHTENERS
FRIGHTENING
FRIGHTENINGLY
FRIGHTFULLY
FRIGHTFULNESS
FRIGHTFULNESSES
FRIGHTSOME
FRIGIDARIA
FRIGIDARIUM
FRIGIDITIES
FRIGIDNESS
FRIGIDNESSES
FRIGORIFIC
FRIGORIFICO
FRIGORIFICOS
FRIKKADELS
FRILLINESS
FRILLINESSES
FRINGELESS
FRINGILLACEOUS
FRINGILLID
FRINGILLIFORM
FRINGILLINE
FRIPONNERIE
FRIPONNERIES
FRIPPERERS
FRIPPERIES
FRISKINESS
FRISKINESSES
FRISKINGLY
FRITHBORHS
FRITHSOKEN
FRITHSOKENS
FRITHSTOOL
FRITHSTOOLS
FRITILLARIA
FRITILLARIAS
FRITILLARIES
FRITILLARY
FRITTERERS
FRITTERING
FRIVOLITIES
FRIVOLLERS
FRIVOLLING
FRIVOLOUSLY
FRIVOLOUSNESS
FRIVOLOUSNESSES
FRIZZINESS
FRIZZINESSES
FRIZZLIEST
FRIZZLINESS
FRIZZLINESSES
FROGFISHES
FROGGERIES
FROGHOPPER
FROGHOPPERS
FROGMARCHED
FROGMARCHES
FROGMARCHING
FROGMOUTHS
FROGSPAWNS
FROLICKERS
FROLICKING
FROLICSOME
FROLICSOMELY
FROLICSOMENESS
FROMENTIES
FRONDESCENCE
FRONDESCENCES
FRONDESCENT
FRONDIFEROUS
FRONTAGERS
FRONTALITIES
FRONTALITY
FRONTCOURT
FRONTCOURTS
FRONTENISES
FRONTIERED
FRONTIERING
FRONTIERSMAN
FRONTIERSMEN
FRONTIERSWOMAN
FRONTIERSWOMEN
FRONTISPIECE
FRONTISPIECED
FRONTISPIECES
FRONTISPIECING
FRONTLESSLY
FRONTLINES
FRONTLISTS

RONTOGENESES
RONTOGENESIS
RONTOGENETIC
RONTOLYSES
RONTOLYSIS
RONTPAGED
RONTPAGES
RONTPAGING
RONTRUNNER
RONTRUNNERS
RONTRUNNING
RONTRUNNINGS
RONTWARDS
ROSTBITES
ROSTBITING
ROSTBITINGS
ROSTBITTEN
ROSTBOUND
ROSTFISHES
ROSTINESS
ROSTINESSES
ROSTLINES
ROSTWORKS
ROTHERIES
ROTHINESS
ROTHINESSES
ROUGHIEST
ROUZINESS
ROUZINESSES
ROWARDNESS
ROWARDNESSES
ROWNINGLY
ROWSINESS
ROWSINESSES
ROWSTIEST
ROWSTINESS
ROWSTINESSES
ROWZINESS
ROWZINESSES
ROZENNESS
ROZENNESSES
RUCTIFEROUS
RUCTIFEROUSLY
RUCTIFICATION
RUCTIFICATIONS
RUCTIFIED
RUCTIFIER
RUCTIFIERS
RUCTIFIES
RUCTIFYING
RUCTIVOROUS
RUCTUARIES
RUCTUATED
RUCTUATES
RUCTUATING
RUCTUATION
RUCTUATIONS
RUCTUOUSLY
RUCTUOUSNESS
RUCTUOUSNESSES
RUGALISTS
RUGALITIES
RUGALNESS
RUGALNESSES
RUGIFEROUS
RUGIVORES

FRUGIVOROUS
FRUITARIAN
FRUITARIANISM
FRUITARIANISMS
FRUITARIANS
FRUITCAKED
FRUITCAKES
FRUITERERS
FRUITERESS
FRUITERESSES
FRUITERIES
FRUITFULLER
FRUITFULLEST
FRUITFULLY
FRUITFULNESS
FRUITFULNESSES
FRUITINESS
FRUITINESSES
FRUITLESSLY
FRUITLESSNESS
FRUITLESSNESSES
FRUITWOODS
FRUMENTACEOUS
FRUMENTARIOUS
FRUMENTATION
FRUMENTATIONS
FRUMENTIES
FRUMPINESS
FRUMPINESSES
FRUMPISHLY
FRUMPISHNESS
FRUMPISHNESSES
FRUSEMIDES
FRUSTRATED
FRUSTRATER
FRUSTRATERS
FRUSTRATES
FRUSTRATING
FRUSTRATINGLY
FRUSTRATION
FRUSTRATIONS
FRUTESCENCE
FRUTESCENCES
FRUTESCENT
FRUTIFYING
FUCIVOROUS
FUCOXANTHIN
FUCOXANTHINS
FUGACIOUSLY
FUGACIOUSNESS
FUGACIOUSNESSES
FUGACITIES
FUGITATION
FUGITATIONS
FUGITIVELY
FUGITIVENESS
FUGITIVENESSES
FUGITOMETER
FUGITOMETERS
FULFILLERS
FULFILLING
FULFILLINGS
FULFILLMENT
FULFILLMENTS
FULFILMENT
FULFILMENTS

FULGENCIES
FULGURATED
FULGURATES
FULGURATING
FULGURATION
FULGURATIONS
FULGURITES
FULIGINOSITIES
FULIGINOSITY
FULIGINOUS
FULIGINOUSLY
FULIGINOUSNESS
FULLBLOODS
FULLERENES
FULLERIDES
FULLERITES
FULLMOUTHED
FULLNESSES
FULMINANTS
FULMINATED
FULMINATES
FULMINATING
FULMINATION
FULMINATIONS
FULMINATOR
FULMINATORS
FULMINATORY
FULMINEOUS
FULSOMENESS
FULSOMENESSES
FUMATORIES
FUMATORIUM
FUMATORIUMS
FUMBLINGLY
FUMBLINGNESS
FUMBLINGNESSES
FUMIGATING
FUMIGATION
FUMIGATIONS
FUMIGATORS
FUMIGATORY
FUMITORIES
FUMOSITIES
FUNAMBULATE
FUNAMBULATED
FUNAMBULATES
FUNAMBULATING
FUNAMBULATION
FUNAMBULATIONS
FUNAMBULATOR
FUNAMBULATORS
FUNAMBULATORY
FUNAMBULISM
FUNAMBULISMS
FUNAMBULIST
FUNAMBULISTS
FUNCTIONAL
FUNCTIONALISM
FUNCTIONALISMS
FUNCTIONALIST
FUNCTIONALISTIC
FUNCTIONALISTS
FUNCTIONALITIES
FUNCTIONALITY
FUNCTIONALLY
FUNCTIONALS

FUNCTIONARIES
FUNCTIONARY
FUNCTIONATE
FUNCTIONATED
FUNCTIONATES
FUNCTIONATING
FUNCTIONED
FUNCTIONING
FUNCTIONLESS
FUNDAMENTAL
FUNDAMENTALISM
FUNDAMENTALISMS
FUNDAMENTALIST
FUNDAMENTALISTS
FUNDAMENTALITY
FUNDAMENTALLY
FUNDAMENTALNESS
FUNDAMENTALS
FUNDAMENTS
FUNDHOLDER
FUNDHOLDERS
FUNDHOLDING
FUNDRAISED
FUNDRAISER
FUNDRAISERS
FUNDRAISES
FUNDRAISING
FUNEREALLY
FUNGIBILITIES
FUNGIBILITY
FUNGICIDAL
FUNGICIDALLY
FUNGICIDES
FUNGISTATIC
FUNGISTATICALLY
FUNGISTATS
FUNGOSITIES
FUNICULARS
FUNICULATE
FUNKINESSES
FUNNELFORM
FUNNELLING
FUNNINESSES
FURACIOUSNESS
FURACIOUSNESSES
FURACITIES
FURALDEHYDE
FURALDEHYDES
FURANOSIDE
FURANOSIDES
FURAZOLIDONE
FURAZOLIDONES
FURBEARERS
FURBELOWED
FURBELOWING
FURBISHERS
FURBISHING
FURCATIONS
FURCIFEROUS
FURFURACEOUS
FURFURACEOUSLY
FURFURALDEHYDE
FURFURALDEHYDES
FURFUROLES
FURIOSITIES
FURIOUSNESS

FURIOUSNESSES
FURLOUGHED
FURLOUGHING
FURMENTIES
FURNIMENTS
FURNISHERS
FURNISHING
FURNISHINGS
FURNISHMENT
FURNISHMENTS
FURNITURES
FUROSEMIDE
FUROSEMIDES
FURRIERIES
FURRINESSES
FURROWLESS
FURSHLUGGINER
FURTHCOMING
FURTHCOMINGS
FURTHERANCE
FURTHERANCES
FURTHERERS
FURTHERING
FURTHERMORE
FURTHERMOST
FURTHERSOME
FURTIVENESS
FURTIVENESSES
FURUNCULAR
FURUNCULOSES
FURUNCULOSIS
FURUNCULOUS
FUSHIONLESS
FUSIBILITIES
FUSIBILITY
FUSIBLENESS
FUSIBLENESSES
FUSILLADED
FUSILLADES
FUSILLADING
FUSILLATION
FUSILLATIONS
FUSIONISMS
FUSIONISTS
FUSIONLESS
FUSSBUDGET
FUSSBUDGETS
FUSSBUDGETY
FUSSINESSES
FUSTANELLA
FUSTANELLAS
FUSTANELLE
FUSTANELLES
FUSTIANISE
FUSTIANISED
FUSTIANISES
FUSTIANISING
FUSTIANIST
FUSTIANISTS
FUSTIANIZE
FUSTIANIZED
FUSTIANIZES
FUSTIANIZING
FUSTIGATED
FUSTIGATES
FUSTIGATING
FUSTIGATION
FUSTIGATIONS
FUSTIGATOR
FUSTIGATORS
FUSTIGATORY
FUSTILARIAN
FUSTILARIANS
FUSTILIRIAN
FUSTILIRIANS
FUSTILLIRIAN
FUSTILLIRIANS
FUSTINESSES
FUSULINIDS
FUTILENESS
FUTILENESSES
FUTILITARIAN
FUTILITARIANISM
FUTILITARIANS
FUTILITIES
FUTURELESS
FUTURELESSNESS
FUTURISTIC
FUTURISTICALLY
FUTURISTICS
FUTURITIES
FUTURITION
FUTURITIONS
FUTUROLOGICAL
FUTUROLOGIES
FUTUROLOGIST
FUTUROLOGISTS
FUTUROLOGY
FUZZINESSES

Gg

ABAPENTIN
ABAPENTINS
ABARDINES
ABBINESSES
ABBLEMENT
ABBLEMENTS
ABBROITIC
ABERDINES
ABERLUNZIE
ABERLUNZIES
ABIONADES
ABIONAGES
ABIONNADE
ABIONNADES
ADGETEERS
ADGETRIES
ADOLINITE
ADOLINITES
ADOLINIUM
ADOLINIUMS
ADROONING
ADROONINGS
ADZOOKERIES
ADZOOKERY
AELICISED
AELICISES
AELICISING
AELICISMS
AELICIZED
AELICIZES
AELICIZING
AILLARDIA
AILLARDIAS
AINFULNESS
AINFULNESSES
AINGIVING
AINGIVINGS
AINLESSNESS
GAINLESSNESSES
GAINLINESS
GAINLINESSES
GAINSAYERS
GAINSAYING
GAINSAYINGS
GAINSTRIVE
GAINSTRIVED
GAINSTRIVEN
GAINSTRIVES
GAINSTRIVING
GAINSTROVE
GAITERLESS
GALABIYAHS
GALACTAGOGUE
GALACTAGOGUES
GALACTOMETER
GALACTOMETERS
GALACTOMETRIES
GALACTOMETRY
GALACTOPHOROUS
GALACTOPOIESES
GALACTOPOIESIS
GALACTOPOIETIC
GALACTOPOIETICS
GALACTORRHEA
GALACTORRHEAS
GALACTORRHOEA
GALACTORRHOEAS
GALACTOSAEMIA
GALACTOSAEMIAS
GALACTOSAMINE
GALACTOSAMINES
GALACTOSEMIA
GALACTOSEMIAS
GALACTOSEMIC
GALACTOSES
GALACTOSIDASE
GALACTOSIDASES
GALACTOSIDE
GALACTOSIDES
GALACTOSYL
GALACTOSYLS
GALANTAMINE
GALANTAMINES
GALANTINES
GALAVANTED
GALAVANTING
GALDRAGONS
GALENGALES
GALENICALS
GALEOPITHECINE
GALEOPITHECOID
GALIMATIAS
GALIMATIASES
GALINGALES
GALIONGEES
GALIVANTED
GALIVANTING
GALLABEAHS
GALLABIAHS
GALLABIEHS
GALLABIYAH
GALLABIYAHS
GALLABIYAS
GALLABIYEH
GALLABIYEHS
GALLAMINES
GALLANTEST
GALLANTING
GALLANTNESS
GALLANTNESSES
GALLANTRIES
GALLBLADDER
GALLBLADDERS
GALLEASSES
GALLERISTS
GALLERYGOER
GALLERYGOERS
GALLERYING
GALLERYITE
GALLERYITES
GALLIAMBIC
GALLIAMBICS
GALLIARDISE
GALLIARDISES
GALLIASSES
GALLICISATION
GALLICISATIONS
GALLICISED
GALLICISES
GALLICISING
GALLICISMS
GALLICIZATION
GALLICIZATIONS
GALLICIZED
GALLICIZES
GALLICIZING
GALLIGASKINS
GALLIMAUFRIES
GALLIMAUFRY
GALLINACEAN
GALLINACEANS
GALLINACEOUS
GALLINAZOS
GALLINIPPER
GALLINIPPERS
GALLINULES
GALLISISED
GALLISISES
GALLISISING
GALLISIZED
GALLISIZES
GALLISIZING

GALLIVANTED
GALLIVANTING
GALLIVANTS
GALLIWASPS
GALLOGLASS
GALLOGLASSES
GALLONAGES
GALLOPADED
GALLOPADES
GALLOPADING
GALLOWGLASS
GALLOWGLASSES
GALLOWSNESS
GALLOWSNESSES
GALLSICKNESS
GALLSICKNESSES
GALLSTONES
GALLUMPHED
GALLUMPHING
GALLYGASKINS
GALRAVAGED
GALRAVAGES
GALRAVAGING
GALRAVITCH
GALRAVITCHED
GALRAVITCHES
GALRAVITCHING
GALUMPHERS
GALUMPHING
GALVANICAL
GALVANICALLY
GALVANISATION
GALVANISATIONS
GALVANISED
GALVANISER
GALVANISERS
GALVANISES
GALVANISING
GALVANISMS
GALVANISTS
GALVANIZATION
GALVANIZATIONS
GALVANIZED
GALVANIZER
GALVANIZERS
GALVANIZES
GALVANIZING
GALVANOMETER
GALVANOMETERS
GALVANOMETRIC
GALVANOMETRICAL
GALVANOMETRIES
GALVANOMETRY
GALVANOPLASTIC
GALVANOPLASTIES
GALVANOPLASTY
GALVANOSCOPE
GALVANOSCOPES
GALVANOSCOPIC
GALVANOSCOPIES
GALVANOSCOPY
GALVANOTROPIC
GALVANOTROPISM
GALVANOTROPISMS
GAMAHUCHED
GAMAHUCHES
GAMAHUCHING
GAMARUCHED
GAMARUCHES
GAMARUCHING
GAMBADOING
GAMBOLLING
GAMEBREAKER
GAMEBREAKERS
GAMEKEEPER
GAMEKEEPERS
GAMEKEEPING
GAMEKEEPINGS
GAMENESSES
GAMESMANSHIP
GAMESMANSHIPS
GAMESOMELY
GAMESOMENESS
GAMESOMENESSES
GAMETANGIA
GAMETANGIAL
GAMETANGIUM
GAMETICALLY
GAMETOCYTE
GAMETOCYTES
GAMETOGENESES
GAMETOGENESIS
GAMETOGENIC
GAMETOGENIES
GAMETOGENOUS
GAMETOGENY
GAMETOPHORE
GAMETOPHORES
GAMETOPHORIC
GAMETOPHYTE
GAMETOPHYTES
GAMETOPHYTIC
GAMINERIES
GAMINESQUE
GAMINESSES
GAMMERSTANG
GAMMERSTANGS
GAMMOCKING
GAMMONINGS
GAMOGENESES
GAMOGENESIS
GAMOGENETIC
GAMOGENETICAL
GAMOGENETICALLY
GAMOPETALOUS
GAMOPHYLLOUS
GAMOSEPALOUS
GAMOTROPIC
GAMOTROPISM
GAMOTROPISMS
GAMYNESSES
GANDERISMS
GANGBANGED
GANGBANGER
GANGBANGERS
GANGBANGING
GANGBOARDS
GANGBUSTER
GANGBUSTERS
GANGBUSTING
GANGBUSTINGS
GANGLIATED
GANGLIFORM
GANGLIONATED
GANGLIONIC
GANGLIOSIDE
GANGLIOSIDES
GANGPLANKS
GANGRENING
GANGRENOUS
GANGSHAGGED
GANGSHAGGING
GANGSTERDOM
GANGSTERDOMS
GANGSTERISH
GANGSTERISM
GANGSTERISMS
GANGSTERLAND
GANGSTERLANDS
GANNETRIES
GANNISTERS
GANTELOPES
GANTLETING
GAOLBREAKS
GAOLERESSES
GARAGISTES
GARBAGEMAN
GARBAGEMEN
GARBOLOGIES
GARBOLOGIST
GARBOLOGISTS
GARDENFULS
GARDENINGS
GARDENLESS
GARDEROBES
GARGANTUAN
GARGANTUAS
GARGARISED
GARGARISES
GARGARISING
GARGARISMS
GARGARIZED
GARGARIZES
GARGARIZING
GARGOYLISM
GARGOYLISMS
GARIBALDIS
GARISHNESS
GARISHNESSES
GARLANDAGE
GARLANDAGES
GARLANDING
GARLANDLESS
GARLANDRIES
GARLICKIER
GARLICKIEST
GARLICKING
GARMENTING
GARMENTLESS
GARMENTURE
GARMENTURES
GARNETIFEROUS
GARNIERITE
GARNIERITES
GARNISHEED
GARNISHEEING
GARNISHEEMENT
GARNISHEEMENTS
GARNISHEES
GARNISHERS
GARNISHING
GARNISHINGS
GARNISHMENT
GARNISHMENTS
GARNISHRIES
GARNITURES
GAROTTINGS
GARRETEERS
GARRISONED
GARRISONING
GARROTTERS
GARROTTING
GARROTTINGS
GARRULITIES
GARRULOUSLY
GARRULOUSNESS
GARRULOUSNESSES
GARRYOWENS
GASBAGGING
GASCONADED
GASCONADER
GASCONADERS
GASCONADES
GASCONADING
GASCONISMS
GASEOUSNESS
GASEOUSNESSES
GASHLINESS
GASHLINESSES
GASHOLDERS
GASIFIABLE
GASIFICATION
GASIFICATIONS
GASOMETERS
GASOMETRIC
GASOMETRICAL
GASOMETRIES
GASPEREAUS
GASPEREAUX
GASPINESSES
GASSINESSES
GASTEROPOD
GASTEROPODOUS
GASTEROPODS
GASTIGHTNESS
GASTIGHTNESSES
GASTNESSES
GASTRAEUMS
GASTRALGIA
GASTRALGIAS
GASTRALGIC
GASTRECTOMIES
GASTRECTOMY
GASTRITIDES
GASTRITISES
GASTROCNEMII
GASTROCNEMIUS
GASTROCOLIC
GASTRODUODENAL
GASTROENTERIC
GASTROENTERITIC
GASTROENTERITIS
GASTROLITH
GASTROLITHS

GASTROLOGER
GASTROLOGERS
GASTROLOGICAL
GASTROLOGIES
GASTROLOGIST
GASTROLOGISTS
GASTROLOGY
GASTROMANCIES
GASTROMANCY
GASTRONOME
GASTRONOMER
GASTRONOMERS
GASTRONOMES
GASTRONOMIC
GASTRONOMICAL
GASTRONOMICALLY
GASTRONOMIES
GASTRONOMIST
GASTRONOMISTS
GASTRONOMY
GASTROPODAN
GASTROPODANS
GASTROPODOUS
GASTROPODS
GASTROSCOPE
GASTROSCOPES
GASTROSCOPIC
GASTROSCOPIES
GASTROSCOPIST
GASTROSCOPISTS
GASTROSCOPY
GASTROSOPH
GASTROSOPHER
GASTROSOPHERS
GASTROSOPHIES
GASTROSOPHS
GASTROSOPHY
GASTROSTOMIES
GASTROSTOMY
GASTROTOMIES
GASTROTOMY
GASTROTRICH
GASTROTRICHES
GASTROTRICHS
GASTROVASCULAR
GASTRULATE
GASTRULATED
GASTRULATES
GASTRULATING
GASTRULATION
GASTRULATIONS
GATECRASHED
GATECRASHER
GATECRASHERS
GATECRASHES
GATECRASHING
GATEHOUSES
GATEKEEPER
GATEKEEPERS
GATEKEEPING
GATHERABLE
GATHERINGS
GAUCHENESS
GAUCHENESSES
GAUCHERIES
GAUDEAMUSES
GAUDINESSES
GAUFFERING
GAUFFERINGS
GAULEITERS
GAULTHERIA
GAULTHERIAS
GAUNTLETED
GAUNTLETING
GAUNTNESSES
GAUSSMETER
GAUSSMETERS
GAUZINESSES
GAVELKINDS
GAWKIHOODS
GAWKINESSES
GAWKISHNESS
GAWKISHNESSES
GAZEHOUNDS
GAZETTEERED
GAZETTEERING
GAZETTEERISH
GAZETTEERS
GAZILLIONAIRE
GAZILLIONAIRES
GAZILLIONS
GAZUNDERED
GAZUNDERER
GAZUNDERERS
GAZUNDERING
GEALOUSIES
GEANTICLINAL
GEANTICLINE
GEANTICLINES
GEARCHANGE
GEARCHANGES
GEARSHIFTS
GEARWHEELS
GEEKINESSES
GEEKSPEAKS
GEFUFFLING
GEGENSCHEIN
GEGENSCHEINS
GEHLENITES
GEITONOGAMIES
GEITONOGAMOUS
GEITONOGAMY
GELANDESPRUNG
GELANDESPRUNGS
GELATINATE
GELATINATED
GELATINATES
GELATINATING
GELATINATION
GELATINATIONS
GELATINISATION
GELATINISATIONS
GELATINISE
GELATINISED
GELATINISER
GELATINISERS
GELATINISES
GELATINISING
GELATINIZATION
GELATINIZATIONS
GELATINIZE
GELATINIZED
GELATINIZER
GELATINIZERS
GELATINIZES
GELATINIZING
GELATINOID
GELATINOIDS
GELATINOUS
GELATINOUSLY
GELATINOUSNESS
GELIDITIES
GELIDNESSES
GELIGNITES
GELLIFLOWRE
GELLIFLOWRES
GELSEMINES
GELSEMININE
GELSEMININES
GELSEMIUMS
GEMEINSCHAFT
GEMEINSCHAFTEN
GEMEINSCHAFTS
GEMFIBROZIL
GEMFIBROZILS
GEMINATELY
GEMINATING
GEMINATION
GEMINATIONS
GEMMACEOUS
GEMMATIONS
GEMMIFEROUS
GEMMINESSES
GEMMIPAROUS
GEMMIPAROUSLY
GEMMOLOGICAL
GEMMOLOGIES
GEMMOLOGIST
GEMMOLOGISTS
GEMMULATION
GEMMULATIONS
GEMOLOGICAL
GEMOLOGIES
GEMOLOGIST
GEMOLOGISTS
GEMUTLICHKEIT
GEMUTLICHKEITS
GENDARMERIE
GENDARMERIES
GENDARMERY
GENDERISED
GENDERISES
GENDERISING
GENDERIZED
GENDERIZES
GENDERIZING
GENDERLESS
GENEALOGIC
GENEALOGICAL
GENEALOGICALLY
GENEALOGIES
GENEALOGISE
GENEALOGISED
GENEALOGISES
GENEALOGISING
GENEALOGIST
GENEALOGISTS
GENEALOGIZE
GENEALOGIZED
GENEALOGIZES
GENEALOGIZING
GENECOLOGIES
GENECOLOGY
GENERALATE
GENERALATES
GENERALCIES
GENERALISABLE
GENERALISATION
GENERALISATIONS
GENERALISE
GENERALISED
GENERALISER
GENERALISERS
GENERALISES
GENERALISING
GENERALISSIMO
GENERALISSIMOS
GENERALIST
GENERALISTS
GENERALITIES
GENERALITY
GENERALIZABLE
GENERALIZATION
GENERALIZATIONS
GENERALIZE
GENERALIZED
GENERALIZER
GENERALIZERS
GENERALIZES
GENERALIZING
GENERALLED
GENERALLING
GENERALNESS
GENERALNESSES
GENERALSHIP
GENERALSHIPS
GENERATING
GENERATION
GENERATIONAL
GENERATIONALLY
GENERATIONISM
GENERATIONISMS
GENERATIONS
GENERATIVE
GENERATORS
GENERATRICES
GENERATRIX
GENERICALLY
GENERICNESS
GENERICNESSES
GENEROSITIES
GENEROSITY
GENEROUSLY
GENEROUSNESS
GENEROUSNESSES
GENETHLIAC
GENETHLIACAL
GENETHLIACALLY
GENETHLIACON
GENETHLIACONS
GENETHLIACS
GENETHLIALOGIC
GENETHLIALOGIES
GENETHLIALOGY

GENETICALLY
GENETICIST
GENETICISTS
GENETOTROPHIC
GENETRICES
GENETRIXES
GENEVRETTE
GENEVRETTES
GENIALISED
GENIALISES
GENIALISING
GENIALITIES
GENIALIZED
GENIALIZES
GENIALIZING
GENIALNESS
GENIALNESSES
GENICULATE
GENICULATED
GENICULATELY
GENICULATES
GENICULATING
GENICULATION
GENICULATIONS
GENISTEINS
GENITALIAL
GENITIVALLY
GENITIVELY
GENITOURINARY
GENITRICES
GENITRIXES
GENOPHOBIA
GENOPHOBIAS
GENOTYPICAL
GENOTYPICALLY
GENOTYPICITIES
GENOTYPICITY
GENOUILLERE
GENOUILLERES
GENSDARMES
GENTAMICIN
GENTAMICINS
GENTEELEST
GENTEELISE
GENTEELISED
GENTEELISES
GENTEELISH
GENTEELISING
GENTEELISM
GENTEELISMS
GENTEELIZE
GENTEELIZED
GENTEELIZES
GENTEELIZING
GENTEELNESS
GENTEELNESSES
GENTIANACEOUS
GENTIANELLA
GENTIANELLAS
GENTILESSE
GENTILESSES
GENTILHOMME
GENTILISED
GENTILISES
GENTILISING
GENTILISMS
GENTILITIAL
GENTILITIAN
GENTILITIES
GENTILITIOUS
GENTILIZED
GENTILIZES
GENTILIZING
GENTILSHOMMES
GENTLEFOLK
GENTLEFOLKS
GENTLEHOOD
GENTLEHOODS
GENTLEMANHOOD
GENTLEMANHOODS
GENTLEMANLIKE
GENTLEMANLINESS
GENTLEMANLY
GENTLEMANSHIP
GENTLEMANSHIPS
GENTLENESS
GENTLENESSE
GENTLENESSES
GENTLEPERSON
GENTLEPERSONS
GENTLEWOMAN
GENTLEWOMANLY
GENTLEWOMEN
GENTRIFICATION
GENTRIFICATIONS
GENTRIFIED
GENTRIFIER
GENTRIFIERS
GENTRIFIES
GENTRIFYING
GENUFLECTED
GENUFLECTING
GENUFLECTION
GENUFLECTIONS
GENUFLECTOR
GENUFLECTORS
GENUFLECTS
GENUFLEXION
GENUFLEXIONS
GENUINENESS
GENUINENESSES
GEOBOTANIC
GEOBOTANICAL
GEOBOTANIES
GEOBOTANIST
GEOBOTANISTS
GEOCACHING
GEOCACHINGS
GEOCARPIES
GEOCENTRIC
GEOCENTRICAL
GEOCENTRICALLY
GEOCENTRICISM
GEOCENTRICISMS
GEOCHEMICAL
GEOCHEMICALLY
GEOCHEMIST
GEOCHEMISTRIES
GEOCHEMISTRY
GEOCHEMISTS
GEOCHRONOLOGIC
GEOCHRONOLOGIES
GEOCHRONOLOGIST
GEOCHRONOLOGY
GEOCORONAE
GEOCORONAS
GEODEMOGRAPHICS
GEODESICAL
GEODESISTS
GEODETICAL
GEODETICALLY
GEODYNAMIC
GEODYNAMICAL
GEODYNAMICIST
GEODYNAMICISTS
GEODYNAMICS
GEOGNOSIES
GEOGNOSTIC
GEOGNOSTICAL
GEOGNOSTICALLY
GEOGRAPHER
GEOGRAPHERS
GEOGRAPHIC
GEOGRAPHICAL
GEOGRAPHICALLY
GEOGRAPHIES
GEOHYDROLOGIC
GEOHYDROLOGIES
GEOHYDROLOGIST
GEOHYDROLOGISTS
GEOHYDROLOGY
GEOLATRIES
GEOLINGUISTICS
GEOLOGIANS
GEOLOGICAL
GEOLOGICALLY
GEOLOGISED
GEOLOGISES
GEOLOGISING
GEOLOGISTS
GEOLOGIZED
GEOLOGIZES
GEOLOGIZING
GEOMAGNETIC
GEOMAGNETICALLY
GEOMAGNETISM
GEOMAGNETISMS
GEOMAGNETIST
GEOMAGNETISTS
GEOMANCERS
GEOMANCIES
GEOMECHANICS
GEOMEDICAL
GEOMEDICINE
GEOMEDICINES
GEOMETRICAL
GEOMETRICALLY
GEOMETRICIAN
GEOMETRICIANS
GEOMETRICS
GEOMETRIDS
GEOMETRIES
GEOMETRISATION
GEOMETRISATIONS
GEOMETRISE
GEOMETRISED
GEOMETRISES
GEOMETRISING
GEOMETRIST
GEOMETRISTS
GEOMETRIZATION
GEOMETRIZATIONS
GEOMETRIZE
GEOMETRIZED
GEOMETRIZES
GEOMETRIZING
GEOMORPHIC
GEOMORPHOGENIC
GEOMORPHOGENIES
GEOMORPHOGENIST
GEOMORPHOGENY
GEOMORPHOLOGIC
GEOMORPHOLOGIES
GEOMORPHOLOGIST
GEOMORPHOLOGY
GEOPHAGIAS
GEOPHAGIES
GEOPHAGISM
GEOPHAGISMS
GEOPHAGIST
GEOPHAGISTS
GEOPHAGOUS
GEOPHILOUS
GEOPHYSICAL
GEOPHYSICALLY
GEOPHYSICIST
GEOPHYSICISTS
GEOPHYSICS
GEOPOLITICAL
GEOPOLITICALLY
GEOPOLITICIAN
GEOPOLITICIANS
GEOPOLITICS
GEOPONICAL
GEOPRESSURED
GEORGETTES
GEOSCIENCE
GEOSCIENCES
GEOSCIENTIFIC
GEOSCIENTIST
GEOSCIENTISTS
GEOSPHERES
GEOSTATICS
GEOSTATIONARY
GEOSTRATEGIC
GEOSTRATEGICAL
GEOSTRATEGIES
GEOSTRATEGIST
GEOSTRATEGISTS
GEOSTRATEGY
GEOSTROPHIC
GEOSTROPHICALLY
GEOSYNCHRONOUS
GEOSYNCLINAL
GEOSYNCLINE
GEOSYNCLINES
GEOTACTICAL
GEOTACTICALLY
GEOTECHNIC
GEOTECHNICAL
GEOTECHNICS
GEOTECHNOLOGIES
GEOTECHNOLOGY
GEOTECTONIC

EOTECTONICALLY
EOTECTONICS
EOTEXTILE
EOTEXTILES
EOTHERMAL
EOTHERMALLY
EOTHERMIC
EOTHERMOMETER
EOTHERMOMETERS
EOTROPICALLY
EOTROPISM
EOTROPISMS
ERANIACEOUS
ERATOLOGICAL
ERATOLOGIES
ERATOLOGIST
ERATOLOGISTS
ERATOLOGY
ERFALCONS
ERIATRICIAN
ERIATRICIANS
ERIATRICS
ERIATRIST
ERIATRISTS
ERMANDERS
ERMANENESS
ERMANENESSES
ERMANISATION
ERMANISATIONS
ERMANISED
ERMANISES
ERMANISING
ERMANITES
ERMANIUMS
ERMANIZATION
ERMANIZATIONS
ERMANIZED
ERMANIZES
ERMANIZING
ERMICIDAL
ERMICIDES
ERMINABILITIES
ERMINABILITY
ERMINABLE
ERMINALLY
ERMINATED
ERMINATES
ERMINATING
ERMINATION
ERMINATIONS
ERMINATIVE
ERMINATOR
ERMINATORS
ERMINESSES
ERMPLASMS
ERONTOCRACIES
ERONTOCRACY
ERONTOCRAT
ERONTOCRATIC
ERONTOCRATS
ERONTOLOGIC
ERONTOLOGICAL
ERONTOLOGIES
ERONTOLOGIST
ERONTOLOGISTS
ERONTOLOGY
GERONTOMORPHIC
GERONTOPHIL
GERONTOPHILE
GERONTOPHILES
GERONTOPHILIA
GERONTOPHILIAS
GERONTOPHILS
GERONTOPHOBE
GERONTOPHOBES
GERONTOPHOBIA
GERONTOPHOBIAS
GERRYMANDER
GERRYMANDERED
GERRYMANDERER
GERRYMANDERERS
GERRYMANDERING
GERRYMANDERS
GERUNDIVAL
GERUNDIVELY
GERUNDIVES
GESELLSCHAFT
GESELLSCHAFTEN
GESELLSCHAFTS
GESNERIADS
GESSAMINES
GESTALTISM
GESTALTISMS
GESTALTIST
GESTALTISTS
GESTATIONAL
GESTATIONS
GESTATORIAL
GESTICULANT
GESTICULATE
GESTICULATED
GESTICULATES
GESTICULATING
GESTICULATION
GESTICULATIONS
GESTICULATIVE
GESTICULATOR
GESTICULATORS
GESTICULATORY
GESTURALLY
GESUNDHEIT
GETTERINGS
GEWURZTRAMINER
GEWURZTRAMINERS
GEYSERITES
GHASTFULLY
GHASTLIEST
GHASTLINESS
GHASTLINESSES
GHASTNESSES
GHETTOISATION
GHETTOISATIONS
GHETTOISED
GHETTOISES
GHETTOISING
GHETTOIZATION
GHETTOIZATIONS
GHETTOIZED
GHETTOIZES
GHETTOIZING
GHOSTLIEST
GHOSTLINESS
GHOSTLINESSES
GHOSTWRITE
GHOSTWRITER
GHOSTWRITERS
GHOSTWRITES
GHOSTWRITING
GHOSTWRITTEN
GHOSTWROTE
GHOULISHLY
GHOULISHNESS
GHOULISHNESSES
GIANTESSES
GIANTHOODS
GIANTLIEST
GIANTSHIPS
GIARDIASES
GIARDIASIS
GIBBERELLIC
GIBBERELLIN
GIBBERELLINS
GIBBERISHES
GIBBETTING
GIBBOSITIES
GIBBOUSNESS
GIBBOUSNESSES
GIDDINESSES
GIFTEDNESS
GIFTEDNESSES
GIFTWRAPPED
GIFTWRAPPING
GIGACYCLES
GIGAHERTZES
GIGANTESQUE
GIGANTICALLY
GIGANTICIDE
GIGANTICIDES
GIGANTICNESS
GIGANTICNESSES
GIGANTISMS
GIGANTOLOGIES
GIGANTOLOGY
GIGANTOMACHIA
GIGANTOMACHIAS
GIGANTOMACHIES
GIGANTOMACHY
GIGGLESOME
GIGGLINGLY
GIGMANITIES
GILDSWOMAN
GILDSWOMEN
GILLFLIRTS
GILLIFLOWER
GILLIFLOWERS
GILLNETTED
GILLNETTER
GILLNETTERS
GILLNETTING
GILLRAVAGE
GILLRAVAGED
GILLRAVAGES
GILLRAVAGING
GILLRAVITCH
GILLRAVITCHED
GILLRAVITCHES
GILLRAVITCHING
GILLYFLOWER
GILLYFLOWERS
GILRAVAGED
GILRAVAGER
GILRAVAGERS
GILRAVAGES
GILRAVAGING
GILRAVITCH
GILRAVITCHED
GILRAVITCHES
GILRAVITCHING
GILSONITES
GIMBALLING
GIMCRACKERIES
GIMCRACKERY
GIMMICKIER
GIMMICKIEST
GIMMICKING
GIMMICKRIES
GINGELLIES
GINGERADES
GINGERBREAD
GINGERBREADED
GINGERBREADS
GINGERBREADY
GINGERLINESS
GINGERLINESSES
GINGERROOT
GINGERROOTS
GINGERSNAP
GINGERSNAPS
GINGIVECTOMIES
GINGIVECTOMY
GINGIVITIS
GINGIVITISES
GINGLIMOID
GIPSYHOODS
GIPSYWORTS
GIRANDOLAS
GIRANDOLES
GIRDLECAKE
GIRDLECAKES
GIRDLESCONE
GIRDLESCONES
GIRDLESTEAD
GIRDLESTEADS
GIRLFRIEND
GIRLFRIENDS
GIRLISHNESS
GIRLISHNESSES
GIRTHLINES
GISMOLOGIES
GITTARONES
GITTERNING
GIVENNESSES
GIZMOLOGIES
GLABRESCENT
GLABROUSNESS
GLABROUSNESSES
GLACIALIST
GLACIALISTS
GLACIATING
GLACIATION
GLACIATIONS
GLACIOLOGIC
GLACIOLOGICAL
GLACIOLOGIES

GLACIOLOGIST
GLACIOLOGISTS
GLACIOLOGY
GLADDENERS
GLADDENING
GLADFULNESS
GLADFULNESSES
GLADIATORIAL
GLADIATORIAN
GLADIATORS
GLADIATORSHIP
GLADIATORSHIPS
GLADIATORY
GLADIOLUSES
GLADNESSES
GLADSOMELY
GLADSOMENESS
GLADSOMENESSES
GLADSOMEST
GLADSTONES
GLADWRAPPED
GLADWRAPPING
GLAIKETNESS
GLAIKETNESSES
GLAIKITNESS
GLAIKITNESSES
GLAIRINESS
GLAIRINESSES
GLAMORISATION
GLAMORISATIONS
GLAMORISED
GLAMORISER
GLAMORISERS
GLAMORISES
GLAMORISING
GLAMORIZATION
GLAMORIZATIONS
GLAMORIZED
GLAMORIZER
GLAMORIZERS
GLAMORIZES
GLAMORIZING
GLAMOROUSLY
GLAMOROUSNESS
GLAMOROUSNESSES
GLAMOURING
GLAMOURISE
GLAMOURISED
GLAMOURISES
GLAMOURISING
GLAMOURIZE
GLAMOURIZED
GLAMOURIZES
GLAMOURIZING
GLAMOURLESS
GLAMOUROUS
GLAMOUROUSLY
GLAMOUROUSNESS
GLAMOURPUSS
GLAMOURPUSSES
GLANCINGLY
GLANDEROUS
GLANDIFEROUS
GLANDIFORM
GLANDULARLY
GLANDULIFEROUS
GLANDULOUS
GLANDULOUSLY
GLARINESSES
GLARINGNESS
GLARINGNESSES
GLASNOSTIAN
GLASNOSTIC
GLASSBLOWER
GLASSBLOWERS
GLASSBLOWING
GLASSBLOWINGS
GLASSHOUSE
GLASSHOUSES
GLASSIFIED
GLASSIFIES
GLASSIFYING
GLASSINESS
GLASSINESSES
GLASSMAKER
GLASSMAKERS
GLASSMAKING
GLASSMAKINGS
GLASSPAPER
GLASSPAPERED
GLASSPAPERING
GLASSPAPERS
GLASSWARES
GLASSWORKER
GLASSWORKERS
GLASSWORKS
GLASSWORMS
GLASSWORTS
GLASSYHEADED
GLAUBERITE
GLAUBERITES
GLAUCESCENCE
GLAUCESCENCES
GLAUCESCENT
GLAUCOMATOUS
GLAUCONITE
GLAUCONITES
GLAUCONITIC
GLAUCOUSLY
GLAUCOUSNESS
GLAUCOUSNESSES
GLAZIERIES
GLAZINESSES
GLEEFULNESS
GLEEFULNESSES
GLEEMAIDEN
GLEEMAIDENS
GLEGNESSES
GLEISATION
GLEISATIONS
GLEIZATION
GLEIZATIONS
GLENDOVEER
GLENDOVEERS
GLENGARRIES
GLIBNESSES
GLIDEPATHS
GLIMMERING
GLIMMERINGLY
GLIMMERINGS
GLIOBLASTOMA
GLIOBLASTOMAS
GLIOBLASTOMATA
GLIOMATOSES
GLIOMATOSIS
GLIOMATOUS
GLISSADERS
GLISSADING
GLISSANDOS
GLISTENING
GLISTENINGLY
GLISTERING
GLISTERINGLY
GLITCHIEST
GLITTERAND
GLITTERATI
GLITTERIER
GLITTERIEST
GLITTERING
GLITTERINGLY
GLITTERINGS
GLITZINESS
GLITZINESSES
GLOATINGLY
GLOBALISATION
GLOBALISATIONS
GLOBALISED
GLOBALISES
GLOBALISING
GLOBALISMS
GLOBALISTS
GLOBALIZATION
GLOBALIZATIONS
GLOBALIZED
GLOBALIZES
GLOBALIZING
GLOBEFISHES
GLOBEFLOWER
GLOBEFLOWERS
GLOBESITIES
GLOBETROTS
GLOBETROTTED
GLOBETROTTER
GLOBETROTTERS
GLOBETROTTING
GLOBETROTTINGS
GLOBIGERINA
GLOBIGERINAE
GLOBIGERINAS
GLOBOSENESS
GLOBOSENESSES
GLOBOSITIES
GLOBULARITIES
GLOBULARITY
GLOBULARLY
GLOBULARNESS
GLOBULARNESSES
GLOBULIFEROUS
GLOBULITES
GLOCHIDIATE
GLOCHIDIUM
GLOCKENSPIEL
GLOCKENSPIELS
GLOMERATED
GLOMERATES
GLOMERATING
GLOMERATION
GLOMERATIONS
GLOMERULAR
GLOMERULATE
GLOMERULES
GLOMERULUS
GLOOMFULLY
GLOOMINESS
GLOOMINESSES
GLORIFIABLE
GLORIFICATION
GLORIFICATIONS
GLORIFIERS
GLORIFYING
GLORIOUSLY
GLORIOUSNESS
GLORIOUSNESSES
GLOSSARIAL
GLOSSARIALLY
GLOSSARIES
GLOSSARIST
GLOSSARISTS
GLOSSATORS
GLOSSECTOMIES
GLOSSECTOMY
GLOSSINESS
GLOSSINESSES
GLOSSINGLY
GLOSSITISES
GLOSSODYNIA
GLOSSODYNIAS
GLOSSOGRAPHER
GLOSSOGRAPHERS
GLOSSOGRAPHICAL
GLOSSOGRAPHIES
GLOSSOGRAPHY
GLOSSOLALIA
GLOSSOLALIAS
GLOSSOLALIST
GLOSSOLALISTS
GLOSSOLOGICAL
GLOSSOLOGIES
GLOSSOLOGIST
GLOSSOLOGISTS
GLOSSOLOGY
GLOTTIDEAN
GLOTTOGONIC
GLOTTOLOGIES
GLOTTOLOGY
GLOWERINGLY
GLOWSTICKS
GLUCINIUMS
GLUCOCORTICOID
GLUCOCORTICOIDS
GLUCOKINASE
GLUCOKINASES
GLUCONATES
GLUCONEOGENESES
GLUCONEOGENESIS
GLUCONEOGENIC
GLUCOPHORE
GLUCOPHORES
GLUCOPROTEIN
GLUCOPROTEINS
GLUCOSAMINE
GLUCOSAMINES
GLUCOSIDAL
GLUCOSIDASE

LUCOSIDASES
LUCOSIDES
LUCOSIDIC
LUCOSURIA
LUCOSURIAS
LUCOSURIC
LUCURONIDASE
LUCURONIDASES
LUCURONIDE
LUCURONIDES
LUEYNESSES
LUINESSES
LUMACEOUS
LUMIFEROUS
LUMNESSES
LUTAMATES
LUTAMINASE
LUTAMINASES
LUTAMINES
LUTAMINIC
LUTARALDEHYDE
LUTARALDEHYDES
LUTATHIONE
LUTATHIONES
LUTETHIMIDE
LUTETHIMIDES
LUTINOSITIES
LUTINOSITY
LUTINOUSLY
LUTINOUSNESS
LUTINOUSNESSES
LUTTINGLY
LUTTONIES
LUTTONISE
LUTTONISED
LUTTONISES
LUTTONISH
LUTTONISING
LUTTONIZE
LUTTONIZED
LUTTONIZES
LUTTONIZING
LUTTONOUS
LUTTONOUSLY
LUTTONOUSNESS
LYCAEMIAS
LYCERALDEHYDE
LYCERALDEHYDES
LYCERIDES
LYCERIDIC
LYCERINATE
LYCERINATED
LYCERINATES
LYCERINATING
LYCERINES
LYCOCOLLS
LYCOGENESES
LYCOGENESIS
LYCOGENETIC
LYCOGENIC
LYCOGENOLYSES
LYCOGENOLYSIS
LYCOGENOLYTIC
LYCOLIPID
LYCOLIPIDS
LYCOLYSES

GLYCOLYSIS
GLYCOLYTIC
GLYCONEOGENESES
GLYCONEOGENESIS
GLYCOPEPTIDE
GLYCOPEPTIDES
GLYCOPHYTE
GLYCOPHYTES
GLYCOPHYTIC
GLYCOPROTEIN
GLYCOPROTEINS
GLYCOSIDASE
GLYCOSIDASES
GLYCOSIDES
GLYCOSIDIC
GLYCOSIDICALLY
GLYCOSURIA
GLYCOSURIAS
GLYCOSURIC
GLYCOSYLATE
GLYCOSYLATED
GLYCOSYLATES
GLYCOSYLATING
GLYCOSYLATION
GLYCOSYLATIONS
GLYOXALINE
GLYOXALINES
GLYPHOGRAPH
GLYPHOGRAPHER
GLYPHOGRAPHERS
GLYPHOGRAPHIC
GLYPHOGRAPHICAL
GLYPHOGRAPHIES
GLYPHOGRAPHS
GLYPHOGRAPHY
GLYPTODONT
GLYPTODONTS
GLYPTOGRAPHER
GLYPTOGRAPHERS
GLYPTOGRAPHIC
GLYPTOGRAPHICAL
GLYPTOGRAPHIES
GLYPTOGRAPHY
GLYPTOTHECA
GLYPTOTHECAE
GMELINITES
GNAPHALIUM
GNAPHALIUMS
GNASHINGLY
GNATCATCHER
GNATCATCHERS
GNATHONICAL
GNATHONICALLY
GNATHOSTOMATOUS
GNATHOSTOME
GNATHOSTOMES
GNEISSITIC
GNETOPHYTE
GNETOPHYTES
GNOMICALLY
GNOMONICAL
GNOMONICALLY
GNOMONOLOGIES
GNOMONOLOGY
GNOSEOLOGIES
GNOSEOLOGY

GNOSIOLOGIES
GNOSIOLOGY
GNOSTICALLY
GNOSTICISM
GNOSTICISMS
GNOTOBIOLOGICAL
GNOTOBIOLOGIES
GNOTOBIOLOGY
GNOTOBIOSES
GNOTOBIOSIS
GNOTOBIOTE
GNOTOBIOTES
GNOTOBIOTIC
GNOTOBIOTICALLY
GNOTOBIOTICS
GOALKEEPER
GOALKEEPERS
GOALKEEPING
GOALKEEPINGS
GOALKICKER
GOALKICKERS
GOALKICKING
GOALKICKINGS
GOALMOUTHS
GOALTENDER
GOALTENDERS
GOALTENDING
GOALTENDINGS
GOATFISHES
GOATISHNESS
GOATISHNESSES
GOATSBEARD
GOATSBEARDS
GOATSUCKER
GOATSUCKERS
GOBBELINES
GOBBLEDEGOOK
GOBBLEDEGOOKS
GOBBLEDYGOOK
GOBBLEDYGOOKS
GOBSMACKED
GOBSTOPPER
GOBSTOPPERS
GODAMNDEST
GODCHILDREN
GODDAMMING
GODDAMNEDEST
GODDAMNING
GODDAUGHTER
GODDAUGHTERS
GODDESSHOOD
GODDESSHOODS
GODFATHERED
GODFATHERING
GODFATHERS
GODFORSAKEN
GODLESSNESS
GODLESSNESSES
GODLIKENESS
GODLIKENESSES
GODLINESSES
GODMOTHERED
GODMOTHERING
GODMOTHERS
GODPARENTS
GODROONING

GODROONINGS
GOFFERINGS
GOGGLEBOXES
GOITROGENIC
GOITROGENICITY
GOITROGENS
GOLDBEATER
GOLDBEATERS
GOLDBRICKED
GOLDBRICKING
GOLDBRICKS
GOLDCRESTS
GOLDENBERRIES
GOLDENBERRY
GOLDENEYES
GOLDENNESS
GOLDENNESSES
GOLDENRODS
GOLDENSEAL
GOLDENSEALS
GOLDFIELDS
GOLDFINCHES
GOLDFINNIES
GOLDFISHES
GOLDILOCKS
GOLDILOCKSES
GOLDMINERS
GOLDSINNIES
GOLDSMITHERIES
GOLDSMITHERY
GOLDSMITHRIES
GOLDSMITHRY
GOLDSMITHS
GOLDSPINKS
GOLDSTICKS
GOLDSTONES
GOLDTHREAD
GOLDTHREADS
GOLIARDERIES
GOLIARDERY
GOLIARDIES
GOLIATHISE
GOLIATHISED
GOLIATHISES
GOLIATHISING
GOLIATHIZE
GOLIATHIZED
GOLIATHIZES
GOLIATHIZING
GOLLIWOGGS
GOLOMYNKAS
GOLOPTIOUS
GOLUPTIOUS
GOMBEENISM
GOMBEENISMS
GONADECTOMIES
GONADECTOMISED
GONADECTOMIZED
GONADECTOMY
GONADOTROPHIC
GONADOTROPHIN
GONADOTROPHINS
GONADOTROPIC
GONADOTROPIN
GONADOTROPINS
GONDOLIERS

GONENESSES
GONFALONIER
GONFALONIERS
GONGORISTIC
GONIATITES
GONIATITOID
GONIATITOIDS
GONIMOBLAST
GONIMOBLASTS
GONIOMETER
GONIOMETERS
GONIOMETRIC
GONIOMETRICAL
GONIOMETRICALLY
GONIOMETRIES
GONIOMETRY
GONIOSCOPE
GONIOSCOPES
GONOCOCCAL
GONOCOCCIC
GONOCOCCOID
GONOCOCCUS
GONOPHORES
GONOPHORIC
GONOPHOROUS
GONORRHEAL
GONORRHEAS
GONORRHEIC
GONORRHOEA
GONORRHOEAL
GONORRHOEAS
GONORRHOEIC
GOODFELLOW
GOODFELLOWS
GOODFELLOWSHIP
GOODFELLOWSHIPS
GOODINESSES
GOODLIHEAD
GOODLIHEADS
GOODLINESS
GOODLINESSES
GOODLYHEAD
GOODLYHEADS
GOODNESSES
GOODNIGHTS
GOODWILLED
GOOEYNESSES
GOOFINESSES
GOOGLEWHACK
GOOGLEWHACKS
GOOGOLPLEX
GOOGOLPLEXES
GOONEYBIRD
GOONEYBIRDS
GOOSANDERS
GOOSEBERRIES
GOOSEBERRY
GOOSEFISHES
GOOSEFLESH
GOOSEFLESHES
GOOSEFOOTS
GOOSEGRASS
GOOSEGRASSES
GOOSEHERDS
GOOSENECKED
GOOSENECKS
GOOSINESSES
GOPHERWOOD
GOPHERWOODS
GORBELLIES
GOREHOUNDS
GORGEOUSLY
GORGEOUSNESS
GORGEOUSNESSES
GORGONEION
GORGONIANS
GORGONISED
GORGONISES
GORGONISING
GORGONIZED
GORGONIZES
GORGONIZING
GORILLAGRAM
GORILLAGRAMS
GORINESSES
GORMANDISE
GORMANDISED
GORMANDISER
GORMANDISERS
GORMANDISES
GORMANDISING
GORMANDISINGS
GORMANDISM
GORMANDISMS
GORMANDIZE
GORMANDIZED
GORMANDIZER
GORMANDIZERS
GORMANDIZES
GORMANDIZING
GORMANDIZINGS
GOSLARITES
GOSPELISED
GOSPELISES
GOSPELISING
GOSPELIZED
GOSPELIZES
GOSPELIZING
GOSPELLERS
GOSPELLING
GOSPELLISE
GOSPELLISED
GOSPELLISES
GOSPELLISING
GOSPELLIZE
GOSPELLIZED
GOSPELLIZES
GOSPELLIZING
GOSSIPINGLY
GOSSIPINGS
GOSSIPMONGER
GOSSIPMONGERS
GOSSIPPERS
GOSSIPPING
GOSSIPRIES
GOTHICALLY
GOTHICISED
GOTHICISES
GOTHICISING
GOTHICISMS
GOTHICIZED
GOTHICIZES
GOTHICIZING
GOURDINESS
GOURDINESSES
GOURMANDISE
GOURMANDISED
GOURMANDISES
GOURMANDISING
GOURMANDISM
GOURMANDISMS
GOURMANDIZE
GOURMANDIZED
GOURMANDIZES
GOURMANDIZING
GOUTINESSES
GOUVERNANTE
GOUVERNANTES
GOVERNABILITIES
GOVERNABILITY
GOVERNABLE
GOVERNABLENESS
GOVERNALLS
GOVERNANCE
GOVERNANCES
GOVERNANTE
GOVERNANTES
GOVERNESSED
GOVERNESSES
GOVERNESSING
GOVERNESSY
GOVERNMENT
GOVERNMENTAL
GOVERNMENTALISE
GOVERNMENTALISM
GOVERNMENTALIST
GOVERNMENTALIZE
GOVERNMENTALLY
GOVERNMENTESE
GOVERNMENTESES
GOVERNMENTS
GOVERNORATE
GOVERNORATES
GOVERNORSHIP
GOVERNORSHIPS
GOWDSPINKS
GOWPENFULS
GRACEFULLER
GRACEFULLEST
GRACEFULLY
GRACEFULNESS
GRACEFULNESSES
GRACELESSLY
GRACELESSNESS
GRACELESSNESSES
GRACILENESS
GRACILENESSES
GRACILITIES
GRACIOSITIES
GRACIOSITY
GRACIOUSES
GRACIOUSLY
GRACIOUSNESS
GRACIOUSNESSES
GRADABILITIES
GRADABILITY
GRADABLENESS
GRADABLENESSES
GRADATIONAL
GRADATIONALLY
GRADATIONED
GRADATIONS
GRADDANING
GRADELIEST
GRADIENTER
GRADIENTERS
GRADIOMETER
GRADIOMETERS
GRADUALISM
GRADUALISMS
GRADUALIST
GRADUALISTIC
GRADUALISTS
GRADUALITIES
GRADUALITY
GRADUALNESS
GRADUALNESSES
GRADUATESHIP
GRADUATESHIPS
GRADUATING
GRADUATION
GRADUATIONS
GRADUATORS
GRAECISING
GRAECIZING
GRAFFITIED
GRAFFITIING
GRAFFITING
GRAFFITIST
GRAFFITISTS
GRAINFIELD
GRAINFIELDS
GRAININESS
GRAININESSES
GRALLATORIAL
GRALLOCHED
GRALLOCHING
GRAMERCIES
GRAMICIDIN
GRAMICIDINS
GRAMINACEOUS
GRAMINEOUS
GRAMINICOLOUS
GRAMINIVOROUS
GRAMINOLOGIES
GRAMINOLOGY
GRAMMALOGUE
GRAMMALOGUES
GRAMMARIAN
GRAMMARIANS
GRAMMARLESS
GRAMMATICAL
GRAMMATICALITY
GRAMMATICALLY
GRAMMATICALNESS
GRAMMATICASTER
GRAMMATICASTERS
GRAMMATICISE
GRAMMATICISED
GRAMMATICISES
GRAMMATICISING
GRAMMATICISM
GRAMMATICISMS
GRAMMATICIZE

GRAMMATICIZED
GRAMMATICIZES
GRAMMATICIZING
GRAMMATIST
GRAMMATISTS
GRAMMATOLOGIES
GRAMMATOLOGIST
GRAMMATOLOGISTS
GRAMMATOLOGY
GRAMOPHONE
GRAMOPHONES
GRAMOPHONIC
GRAMOPHONICALLY
GRAMOPHONIES
GRAMOPHONIST
GRAMOPHONISTS
GRAMOPHONY
GRANADILLA
GRANADILLAS
GRANDADDIES
GRANDAUNTS
GRANDBABIES
GRANDCHILD
GRANDCHILDREN
GRANDDADDIES
GRANDDADDY
GRANDDAUGHTER
GRANDDAUGHTERS
GRANDEESHIP
GRANDEESHIPS
GRANDFATHER
GRANDFATHERED
GRANDFATHERING
GRANDFATHERLY
GRANDFATHERS
GRANDIFLORA
GRANDIFLORAS
GRANDILOQUENCE
GRANDILOQUENCES
GRANDILOQUENT
GRANDILOQUENTLY
GRANDILOQUOUS
GRANDIOSELY
GRANDIOSENESS
GRANDIOSENESSES
GRANDIOSITIES
GRANDIOSITY
GRANDMAMAS
GRANDMAMMA
GRANDMAMMAS
GRANDMASTER
GRANDMASTERS
GRANDMOTHER
GRANDMOTHERLY
GRANDMOTHERS
GRANDNEPHEW
GRANDNEPHEWS
GRANDNESSES
GRANDNIECE
GRANDNIECES
GRANDPAPAS
GRANDPARENT
GRANDPARENTAL
GRANDPARENTHOOD
GRANDPARENTS
GRANDSIRES

GRANDSTAND
GRANDSTANDED
GRANDSTANDER
GRANDSTANDERS
GRANDSTANDING
GRANDSTANDS
GRANDSTOOD
GRANDUNCLE
GRANDUNCLES
GRANGERISATION
GRANGERISATIONS
GRANGERISE
GRANGERISED
GRANGERISER
GRANGERISERS
GRANGERISES
GRANGERISING
GRANGERISM
GRANGERISMS
GRANGERIZATION
GRANGERIZATIONS
GRANGERIZE
GRANGERIZED
GRANGERIZER
GRANGERIZERS
GRANGERIZES
GRANGERIZING
GRANITELIKE
GRANITEWARE
GRANITEWARES
GRANITIFICATION
GRANITIFORM
GRANITISATION
GRANITISATIONS
GRANITISED
GRANITISES
GRANITISING
GRANITITES
GRANITIZATION
GRANITIZATIONS
GRANITIZED
GRANITIZES
GRANITIZING
GRANIVORES
GRANIVOROUS
GRANNIEING
GRANODIORITE
GRANODIORITES
GRANODIORITIC
GRANOLITHIC
GRANOLITHICS
GRANOLITHS
GRANOPHYRE
GRANOPHYRES
GRANOPHYRIC
GRANTSMANSHIP
GRANTSMANSHIPS
GRANULARITIES
GRANULARITY
GRANULARLY
GRANULATED
GRANULATER
GRANULATERS
GRANULATES
GRANULATING
GRANULATION

GRANULATIONS
GRANULATIVE
GRANULATOR
GRANULATORS
GRANULIFEROUS
GRANULIFORM
GRANULITES
GRANULITIC
GRANULITISATION
GRANULITIZATION
GRANULOCYTE
GRANULOCYTES
GRANULOCYTIC
GRANULOMAS
GRANULOMATA
GRANULOMATOUS
GRANULOSES
GRANULOSIS
GRAPEFRUIT
GRAPEFRUITS
GRAPESEEDS
GRAPESHOTS
GRAPESTONE
GRAPESTONES
GRAPETREES
GRAPEVINES
GRAPHEMICALLY
GRAPHEMICS
GRAPHICACIES
GRAPHICACY
GRAPHICALLY
GRAPHICALNESS
GRAPHICALNESSES
GRAPHICNESS
GRAPHICNESSES
GRAPHITISABLE
GRAPHITISATION
GRAPHITISATIONS
GRAPHITISE
GRAPHITISED
GRAPHITISES
GRAPHITISING
GRAPHITIZABLE
GRAPHITIZATION
GRAPHITIZATIONS
GRAPHITIZE
GRAPHITIZED
GRAPHITIZES
GRAPHITIZING
GRAPHITOID
GRAPHOLECT
GRAPHOLECTS
GRAPHOLOGIC
GRAPHOLOGICAL
GRAPHOLOGIES
GRAPHOLOGIST
GRAPHOLOGISTS
GRAPHOLOGY
GRAPHOMANIA
GRAPHOMANIAS
GRAPHOMOTOR
GRAPHOPHOBIA
GRAPHOPHOBIAS
GRAPINESSES
GRAPLEMENT
GRAPLEMENTS

GRAPPLINGS
GRAPTOLITE
GRAPTOLITES
GRAPTOLITIC
GRASPINGLY
GRASPINGNESS
GRASPINGNESSES
GRASSFINCH
GRASSFINCHES
GRASSHOOKS
GRASSHOPPER
GRASSHOPPERS
GRASSINESS
GRASSINESSES
GRASSLANDS
GRASSPLOTS
GRASSQUITS
GRASSROOTS
GRASSWRACK
GRASSWRACKS
GRATEFULLER
GRATEFULLEST
GRATEFULLY
GRATEFULNESS
GRATEFULNESSES
GRATICULATION
GRATICULATIONS
GRATICULES
GRATIFICATION
GRATIFICATIONS
GRATIFIERS
GRATIFYING
GRATIFYINGLY
GRATILLITIES
GRATILLITY
GRATINATED
GRATINATES
GRATINATING
GRATINEEING
GRATITUDES
GRATUITIES
GRATUITOUS
GRATUITOUSLY
GRATUITOUSNESS
GRATULATED
GRATULATES
GRATULATING
GRATULATION
GRATULATIONS
GRATULATORY
GRAUNCHERS
GRAUNCHING
GRAVADLAXES
GRAVELLING
GRAVENESSES
GRAVEOLENT
GRAVESIDES
GRAVESITES
GRAVESTONE
GRAVESTONES
GRAVEYARDS
GRAVIDITIES
GRAVIDNESS
GRAVIDNESSES
GRAVIMETER
GRAVIMETERS

GRAVIMETRIC
GRAVIMETRICAL
GRAVIMETRICALLY
GRAVIMETRIES
GRAVIMETRY
GRAVIPERCEPTION
GRAVITASES
GRAVITATED
GRAVITATER
GRAVITATERS
GRAVITATES
GRAVITATING
GRAVITATION
GRAVITATIONAL
GRAVITATIONALLY
GRAVITATIONS
GRAVITATIVE
GRAVITINOS
GRAVITOMETER
GRAVITOMETERS
GRAYBEARDED
GRAYBEARDS
GRAYFISHES
GRAYHOUNDS
GRAYNESSES
GRAYWACKES
GRAYWATERS
GREASEBALL
GREASEBALLS
GREASEBAND
GREASEBANDS
GREASEBUSH
GREASEBUSHES
GREASELESS
GREASEPAINT
GREASEPAINTS
GREASEPROOF
GREASEPROOFS
GREASEWOOD
GREASEWOODS
GREASINESS
GREASINESSES
GREATCOATED
GREATCOATS
GREATENING
GREATHEARTED
GREATHEARTEDLY
GREATNESSES
GRECIANISE
GRECIANISED
GRECIANISES
GRECIANISING
GRECIANIZE
GRECIANIZED
GRECIANIZES
GRECIANIZING
GREEDINESS
GREEDINESSES
GREENBACKER
GREENBACKERS
GREENBACKISM
GREENBACKISMS
GREENBACKS
GREENBELTS
GREENBONES
GREENBOTTLE
GREENBOTTLES
GREENBRIER
GREENBRIERS
GREENCLOTH
GREENCLOTHS
GREENERIES
GREENFIELD
GREENFIELDS
GREENFINCH
GREENFINCHES
GREENFLIES
GREENGAGES
GREENGROCER
GREENGROCERIES
GREENGROCERS
GREENGROCERY
GREENHANDS
GREENHEADS
GREENHEART
GREENHEARTS
GREENHORNS
GREENHOUSE
GREENHOUSES
GREENISHNESS
GREENISHNESSES
GREENKEEPER
GREENKEEPERS
GREENLIGHT
GREENLIGHTED
GREENLIGHTING
GREENLIGHTS
GREENLINGS
GREENMAILED
GREENMAILER
GREENMAILERS
GREENMAILING
GREENMAILS
GREENNESSES
GREENOCKITE
GREENOCKITES
GREENROOMS
GREENSANDS
GREENSHANK
GREENSHANKS
GREENSICKNESS
GREENSICKNESSES
GREENSKEEPER
GREENSKEEPERS
GREENSOMES
GREENSPEAK
GREENSPEAKS
GREENSTICK
GREENSTICKS
GREENSTONE
GREENSTONES
GREENSTUFF
GREENSTUFFS
GREENSWARD
GREENSWARDS
GREENWASHED
GREENWASHES
GREENWASHING
GREENWEEDS
GREENWINGS
GREENWOODS
GREGARIANISM
GREGARIANISMS
GREGARINES
GREGARINIAN
GREGARIOUS
GREGARIOUSLY
GREGARIOUSNESS
GREISENISATION
GREISENISATIONS
GREISENISE
GREISENISED
GREISENISES
GREISENISING
GREISENIZATION
GREISENIZATIONS
GREISENIZE
GREISENIZED
GREISENIZES
GREISENIZING
GREMOLATAS
GRENADIERS
GRENADILLA
GRENADILLAS
GRENADINES
GRESSORIAL
GRESSORIOUS
GREVILLEAS
GREWHOUNDS
GREWSOMEST
GREYBEARDED
GREYBEARDS
GREYHOUNDS
GREYLISTED
GREYLISTING
GREYNESSES
GREYSTONES
GREYWACKES
GREYWETHER
GREYWETHERS
GRIDDLEBREAD
GRIDDLEBREADS
GRIDDLECAKE
GRIDDLECAKES
GRIDIRONED
GRIDIRONING
GRIDLOCKED
GRIDLOCKING
GRIEVANCES
GRIEVINGLY
GRIEVOUSLY
GRIEVOUSNESS
GRIEVOUSNESSES
GRIFFINISH
GRIFFINISM
GRIFFINISMS
GRILLERIES
GRILLROOMS
GRILLSTEAK
GRILLSTEAKS
GRILLWORKS
GRIMACINGLY
GRIMALKINS
GRIMINESSES
GRIMLOOKED
GRIMNESSES
GRINDELIAS
GRINDERIES
GRINDHOUSE
GRINDHOUSES
GRINDINGLY
GRINDSTONE
GRINDSTONES
GRINNINGLY
GRIPPINGLY
GRISAILLES
GRISEOFULVIN
GRISEOFULVINS
GRISLINESS
GRISLINESSES
GRISTLIEST
GRISTLINESS
GRISTLINESSES
GRISTMILLS
GRITSTONES
GRITTINESS
GRITTINESSES
GRIVATIONS
GRIZZLIEST
GROANINGLY
GROATSWORTH
GROATSWORTHS
GROCETERIA
GROCETERIAS
GROGGERIES
GROGGINESS
GROGGINESSES
GROMMETING
GROOVELESS
GROOVELIKE
GROSGRAINS
GROSSIERETE
GROSSIERETES
GROSSNESSES
GROSSULARITE
GROSSULARITES
GROSSULARS
GROTESQUELY
GROTESQUENESS
GROTESQUENESSES
GROTESQUER
GROTESQUERIE
GROTESQUERIES
GROTESQUERY
GROTESQUES
GROTESQUEST
GROUCHIEST
GROUCHINESS
GROUCHINESSES
GROUNDAGES
GROUNDBAIT
GROUNDBAITED
GROUNDBAITING
GROUNDBAITS
GROUNDBREAKER
GROUNDBREAKERS
GROUNDBREAKING
GROUNDBREAKINGS
GROUNDBURST
GROUNDBURSTS
GROUNDEDLY
GROUNDFISH
GROUNDFISHES
GROUNDHOGS

GROUNDINGS
GROUNDLESS
GROUNDLESSLY
GROUNDLESSNESS
GROUNDLING
GROUNDLINGS
GROUNDMASS
GROUNDMASSES
GROUNDNUTS
GROUNDOUTS
GROUNDPLOT
GROUNDPLOTS
GROUNDPROX
GROUNDPROXES
GROUNDSELL
GROUNDSELLS
GROUNDSELS
GROUNDSHARE
GROUNDSHARED
GROUNDSHARES
GROUNDSHARING
GROUNDSHEET
GROUNDSHEETS
GROUNDSILL
GROUNDSILLS
GROUNDSKEEPER
GROUNDSKEEPERS
GROUNDSMAN
GROUNDSMEN
GROUNDSPEED
GROUNDSPEEDS
GROUNDSWELL
GROUNDSWELLS
GROUNDWATER
GROUNDWATERS
GROUNDWOOD
GROUNDWOODS
GROUNDWORK
GROUNDWORKS
GROUPTHINK
GROUPTHINKS
GROUPUSCULE
GROUPUSCULES
GROUPWARES
GROUSELIKE
GROVELINGLY
GROVELLERS
GROVELLING
GROVELLINGLY
GROWLERIES
GROWLINESS
GROWLINESSES
GROWLINGLY
GROWTHIEST
GROWTHINESS
GROWTHINESSES
GROWTHISTS
GRUBBINESS
GRUBBINESSES
GRUBSTAKED
GRUBSTAKER
GRUBSTAKERS
GRUBSTAKES
GRUBSTAKING
GRUDGELESS
GRUDGINGLY
GRUELINGLY
GRUELLINGS
GRUESOMELY
GRUESOMENESS
GRUESOMENESSES
GRUESOMEST
GRUFFNESSES
GRUMBLIEST
GRUMBLINGLY
GRUMBLINGS
GRUMMETING
GRUMNESSES
GRUMPINESS
GRUMPINESSES
GRUMPISHLY
GRUMPISHNESS
GRUMPISHNESSES
GRUNTINGLY
GUACAMOLES
GUACHAMOLE
GUACHAMOLES
GUACHAROES
GUANABANAS
GUANAZOLOS
GUANETHIDINE
GUANETHIDINES
GUANIDINES
GUANIFEROUS
GUANOSINES
GUARANTEED
GUARANTEEING
GUARANTEES
GUARANTIED
GUARANTIES
GUARANTORS
GUARANTYING
GUARDEDNESS
GUARDEDNESSES
GUARDHOUSE
GUARDHOUSES
GUARDIANSHIP
GUARDIANSHIPS
GUARDRAILS
GUARDROOMS
GUARDSHIPS
GUARISHING
GUAYABERAS
GUBERNACULA
GUBERNACULAR
GUBERNACULUM
GUBERNATION
GUBERNATIONS
GUBERNATOR
GUBERNATORIAL
GUBERNATORS
GUBERNIYAS
GUDGEONING
GUERDONERS
GUERDONING
GUERILLAISM
GUERILLAISMS
GUERRILLAISM
GUERRILLAISMS
GUERRILLAS
GUERRILLERO
GUERRILLEROS
GUESSINGLY
GUESSTIMATE
GUESSTIMATED
GUESSTIMATES
GUESSTIMATING
GUESSWORKS
GUESTENING
GUESTHOUSE
GUESTHOUSES
GUESTIMATE
GUESTIMATED
GUESTIMATES
GUESTIMATING
GUIDEBOOKS
GUIDELINES
GUIDEPOSTS
GUIDESHIPS
GUIDEWORDS
GUIDWILLIE
GUILDHALLS
GUILDSHIPS
GUILDSWOMAN
GUILDSWOMEN
GUILEFULLY
GUILEFULNESS
GUILEFULNESSES
GUILELESSLY
GUILELESSNESS
GUILELESSNESSES
GUILLEMETS
GUILLEMOTS
GUILLOCHED
GUILLOCHES
GUILLOCHING
GUILLOTINE
GUILLOTINED
GUILLOTINER
GUILLOTINERS
GUILLOTINES
GUILLOTINING
GUILTINESS
GUILTINESSES
GUILTLESSLY
GUILTLESSNESS
GUILTLESSNESSES
GUITARFISH
GUITARFISHES
GUITARISTS
GULLIBILITIES
GULLIBILITY
GULOSITIES
GUMMIFEROUS
GUMMINESSES
GUMMOSITIES
GUMSHIELDS
GUMSHOEING
GUMSUCKERS
GUNCOTTONS
GUNFIGHTER
GUNFIGHTERS
GUNFIGHTING
GUNKHOLING
GUNMANSHIP
GUNMANSHIPS
GUNNERSHIP
GUNNERSHIPS
GUNNYSACKS
GUNPOWDERS
GUNPOWDERY
GUNRUNNERS
GUNRUNNING
GUNRUNNINGS
GUNSLINGER
GUNSLINGERS
GUNSLINGING
GUNSLINGINGS
GUNSMITHING
GUNSMITHINGS
GURGITATION
GURGITATIONS
GUSHINESSES
GUSTATIONS
GUSTATORILY
GUSTINESSES
GUTBUCKETS
GUTLESSNESS
GUTLESSNESSES
GUTSINESSES
GUTTATIONS
GUTTERBLOOD
GUTTERBLOODS
GUTTERINGS
GUTTERSNIPE
GUTTERSNIPES
GUTTERSNIPISH
GUTTIFEROUS
GUTTURALISATION
GUTTURALISE
GUTTURALISED
GUTTURALISES
GUTTURALISING
GUTTURALISM
GUTTURALISMS
GUTTURALITIES
GUTTURALITY
GUTTURALIZATION
GUTTURALIZE
GUTTURALIZED
GUTTURALIZES
GUTTURALIZING
GUTTURALLY
GUTTURALNESS
GUTTURALNESSES
GYMNASIARCH
GYMNASIARCHS
GYMNASIAST
GYMNASIASTS
GYMNASIUMS
GYMNASTICAL
GYMNASTICALLY
GYMNASTICS
GYMNORHINAL
GYMNOSOPHIES
GYMNOSOPHIST
GYMNOSOPHISTS
GYMNOSOPHS
GYMNOSOPHY
GYMNOSPERM
GYMNOSPERMIES
GYMNOSPERMOUS
GYMNOSPERMS
GYMNOSPERMY

GYNAECEUMS
GYNAECOCRACIES
GYNAECOCRACY
GYNAECOCRATIC
GYNAECOLOGIC
GYNAECOLOGICAL
GYNAECOLOGIES
GYNAECOLOGIST
GYNAECOLOGISTS
GYNAECOLOGY
GYNAECOMAST
GYNAECOMASTIA
GYNAECOMASTIAS
GYNAECOMASTIES
GYNAECOMASTS
GYNAECOMASTY
GYNANDRIES
GYNANDRISM
GYNANDRISMS
GYNANDROMORPH
GYNANDROMORPHIC
GYNANDROMORPHS
GYNANDROMORPHY
GYNANDROUS
GYNARCHIES
GYNECOCRACIES
GYNECOCRACY
GYNECOCRATIC
GYNECOLOGIC
GYNECOLOGICAL
GYNECOLOGIES
GYNECOLOGIST
GYNECOLOGISTS
GYNECOLOGY
GYNECOMASTIA
GYNECOMASTIAS
GYNIATRICS
GYNIATRIES
GYNIOLATRIES
GYNIOLATRY
GYNOCRACIES
GYNOCRATIC
GYNODIOECIOUS
GYNODIOECISM
GYNODIOECISMS
GYNOGENESES
GYNOGENESIS
GYNOGENETIC
GYNOMONOECIOUS
GYNOMONOECISM
GYNOMONOECISMS
GYNOPHOBES
GYNOPHOBIA
GYNOPHOBIAS
GYNOPHOBIC
GYNOPHOBICS
GYNOPHORES
GYNOPHORIC
GYNOSTEMIA
GYNOSTEMIUM
GYPSIFEROUS
GYPSOPHILA
GYPSOPHILAS
GYPSYHOODS
GYPSYWORTS
GYRATIONAL
GYRFALCONS
GYROCOMPASS
GYROCOMPASSES
GYROCOPTER
GYROCOPTERS
GYROFREQUENCIES
GYROFREQUENCY
GYROMAGNETIC
GYROMAGNETISM
GYROMAGNETISMS
GYROMANCIES
GYROPILOTS
GYROPLANES
GYROSCOPES
GYROSCOPIC
GYROSCOPICALLY
GYROSCOPICS
GYROSTABILISER
GYROSTABILISERS
GYROSTABILIZER
GYROSTABILIZERS
GYROSTATIC
GYROSTATICALLY
GYROSTATICS
GYROVAGUES

Hh

HAANEPOOTS
HABERDASHER
HABERDASHERIES
HABERDASHERS
HABERDASHERY
HABERDINES
HABERGEONS
HABILATORY
HABILIMENT
HABILIMENTS
HABILITATE
HABILITATED
HABILITATES
HABILITATING
HABILITATION
HABILITATIONS
HABILITATOR
HABILITATORS
HABITABILITIES
HABITABILITY
HABITABLENESS
HABITABLENESSES
HABITATION
HABITATIONAL
HABITATIONS
HABITAUNCE
HABITAUNCES
HABITUALLY
HABITUALNESS
HABITUALNESSES
HABITUATED
HABITUATES
HABITUATING
HABITUATION
HABITUATIONS
HABITUDINAL
HACENDADOS
HACIENDADO
HACIENDADOS
HACKAMORES
HACKBERRIES
HACKBUTEER
HACKBUTEERS
HACKBUTTER
HACKBUTTERS
HACKMATACK
HACKMATACKS
HACKNEYING
HACKNEYISM
HACKNEYISMS
HACKNEYMAN
HACKNEYMEN
HACKSAWING
HACQUETONS
HADROSAURS
HADROSAURUS
HADROSAURUSES
HAECCEITIES
HAEMACHROME
HAEMACHROMES
HAEMACYTOMETER
HAEMACYTOMETERS
HAEMAGGLUTINATE
HAEMAGGLUTININ
HAEMAGGLUTININS
HAEMAGOGUE
HAEMAGOGUES
HAEMANGIOMA
HAEMANGIOMAS
HAEMANGIOMATA
HAEMATEINS
HAEMATEMESES
HAEMATEMESIS
HAEMATINIC
HAEMATINICS
HAEMATITES
HAEMATITIC
HAEMATOBLAST
HAEMATOBLASTIC
HAEMATOBLASTS
HAEMATOCELE
HAEMATOCELES
HAEMATOCRIT
HAEMATOCRITS
HAEMATOCRYAL
HAEMATOGENESES
HAEMATOGENESIS
HAEMATOGENETIC
HAEMATOGENIC
HAEMATOGENOUS
HAEMATOLOGIC
HAEMATOLOGICAL
HAEMATOLOGIES
HAEMATOLOGIST
HAEMATOLOGISTS
HAEMATOLOGY
HAEMATOLYSES
HAEMATOLYSIS
HAEMATOMAS
HAEMATOMATA
HAEMATOPHAGOUS
HAEMATOPOIESES
HAEMATOPOIESIS
HAEMATOPOIETIC
HAEMATOSES
HAEMATOSIS
HAEMATOTHERMAL
HAEMATOXYLIC
HAEMATOXYLIN
HAEMATOXYLINS
HAEMATOXYLON
HAEMATOXYLONS
HAEMATOZOA
HAEMATOZOON
HAEMATURIA
HAEMATURIAS
HAEMATURIC
HAEMOCHROME
HAEMOCHROMES
HAEMOCOELS
HAEMOCONIA
HAEMOCONIAS
HAEMOCYANIN
HAEMOCYANINS
HAEMOCYTES
HAEMOCYTOMETER
HAEMOCYTOMETERS
HAEMODIALYSES
HAEMODIALYSIS
HAEMOFLAGELLATE
HAEMOGLOBIN
HAEMOGLOBINS
HAEMOGLOBINURIA
HAEMOLYSES
HAEMOLYSIN
HAEMOLYSINS
HAEMOLYSIS
HAEMOLYTIC
HAEMOPHILE
HAEMOPHILES
HAEMOPHILIA
HAEMOPHILIAC
HAEMOPHILIACS
HAEMOPHILIAS
HAEMOPHILIC
HAEMOPHILIOID
HAEMOPOIESES
HAEMOPOIESIS
HAEMOPOIETIC
HAEMOPTYSES
HAEMOPTYSIS
HAEMORRHAGE

HAEMORRHAGED
HAEMORRHAGES
HAEMORRHAGIC
HAEMORRHAGING
HAEMORRHOID
HAEMORRHOIDAL
HAEMORRHOIDS
HAEMOSTASES
HAEMOSTASIA
HAEMOSTASIAS
HAEMOSTASIS
HAEMOSTATIC
HAEMOSTATICS
HAEMOSTATS
HAGBERRIES
HAGBUTEERS
HAGBUTTERS
HAGGADICAL
HAGGADISTIC
HAGGADISTS
HAGGARDNESS
HAGGARDNESSES
HAGGISHNESS
HAGGISHNESSES
HAGIARCHIES
HAGIOCRACIES
HAGIOCRACY
HAGIOGRAPHER
HAGIOGRAPHERS
HAGIOGRAPHIC
HAGIOGRAPHICAL
HAGIOGRAPHIES
HAGIOGRAPHIST
HAGIOGRAPHISTS
HAGIOGRAPHY
HAGIOLATER
HAGIOLATERS
HAGIOLATRIES
HAGIOLATROUS
HAGIOLATRY
HAGIOLOGIC
HAGIOLOGICAL
HAGIOLOGIES
HAGIOLOGIST
HAGIOLOGISTS
HAGIOSCOPE
HAGIOSCOPES
HAGIOSCOPIC
HAILSTONES
HAILSTORMS
HAIRBRAINED
HAIRBREADTH
HAIRBREADTHS
HAIRBRUSHES
HAIRCLOTHS
HAIRCUTTER
HAIRCUTTERS
HAIRCUTTING
HAIRCUTTINGS
HAIRDRESSER
HAIRDRESSERS
HAIRDRESSING
HAIRDRESSINGS
HAIRDRIERS
HAIRDRYERS
HAIRINESSES
HAIRLESSNESS
HAIRLESSNESSES
HAIRPIECES
HAIRSBREADTH
HAIRSBREADTHS
HAIRSPLITTER
HAIRSPLITTERS
HAIRSPLITTING
HAIRSPLITTINGS
HAIRSPRAYS
HAIRSPRING
HAIRSPRINGS
HAIRSTREAK
HAIRSTREAKS
HAIRSTYLES
HAIRSTYLING
HAIRSTYLINGS
HAIRSTYLIST
HAIRSTYLISTS
HAIRWEAVING
HAIRWEAVINGS
HAIRYBACKS
HALACHISTS
HALAKHISTS
HALBERDIER
HALBERDIERS
HALCYONIAN
HALENESSES
HALFENDEALE
HALFHEARTED
HALFHEARTEDLY
HALFHEARTEDNESS
HALFNESSES
HALFPENNIES
HALFPENNYWORTH
HALFPENNYWORTHS
HALFTRACKS
HALFWITTED
HALFWITTEDLY
HALFWITTEDNESS
HALIEUTICS
HALIPLANKTON
HALIPLANKTONS
HALLALLING
HALLEFLINTA
HALLEFLINTAS
HALLELUIAH
HALLELUIAHS
HALLELUJAH
HALLELUJAHS
HALLMARKED
HALLMARKING
HALLOWEDNESS
HALLOWEDNESSES
HALLOYSITE
HALLOYSITES
HALLSTANDS
HALLUCINATE
HALLUCINATED
HALLUCINATES
HALLUCINATING
HALLUCINATION
HALLUCINATIONAL
HALLUCINATIONS
HALLUCINATIVE
HALLUCINATOR
HALLUCINATORS
HALLUCINATORY
HALLUCINOGEN
HALLUCINOGENIC
HALLUCINOGENICS
HALLUCINOGENS
HALLUCINOSES
HALLUCINOSIS
HALOBIONTIC
HALOBIONTS
HALOBIOTIC
HALOCARBON
HALOCARBONS
HALOCLINES
HALOGENATE
HALOGENATED
HALOGENATES
HALOGENATING
HALOGENATION
HALOGENATIONS
HALOGENOID
HALOGENOUS
HALOGETONS
HALOMORPHIC
HALOPERIDOL
HALOPERIDOLS
HALOPHILES
HALOPHILIC
HALOPHILIES
HALOPHILOUS
HALOPHOBES
HALOPHYTES
HALOPHYTIC
HALOPHYTISM
HALOPHYTISMS
HALOTHANES
HALTERBREAK
HALTERBREAKING
HALTERBREAKS
HALTERBROKE
HALTERBROKEN
HALTERNECK
HALTERNECKS
HALTINGNESS
HALTINGNESSES
HAMADRYADES
HAMADRYADS
HAMADRYASES
HAMAMELIDACEOUS
HAMAMELISES
HAMANTASCH
HAMANTASCHEN
HAMARTHRITIS
HAMARTHRITISES
HAMARTIOLOGIES
HAMARTIOLOGY
HAMBURGERS
HAMBURGHER
HAMBURGHERS
HAMESUCKEN
HAMESUCKENS
HAMFATTERED
HAMFATTERING
HAMFATTERS
HAMMERCLOTH
HAMMERCLOTHS
HAMMERHEAD
HAMMERHEADED
HAMMERHEADS
HAMMERINGS
HAMMERKOPS
HAMMERLESS
HAMMERLOCK
HAMMERLOCKS
HAMMERSTONE
HAMMERSTONES
HAMMERTOES
HAMMINESSES
HAMPEREDNESS
HAMPEREDNESSES
HAMSHACKLE
HAMSHACKLED
HAMSHACKLES
HAMSHACKLING
HAMSTRINGED
HAMSTRINGING
HAMSTRINGS
HANDBAGGED
HANDBAGGING
HANDBAGGINGS
HANDBALLED
HANDBALLER
HANDBALLERS
HANDBALLING
HANDBARROW
HANDBARROWS
HANDBASKET
HANDBASKETS
HANDBRAKES
HANDBREADTH
HANDBREADTHS
HANDCLASPS
HANDCRAFTED
HANDCRAFTING
HANDCRAFTS
HANDCRAFTSMAN
HANDCRAFTSMEN
HANDCUFFED
HANDCUFFING
HANDEDNESS
HANDEDNESSES
HANDFASTED
HANDFASTING
HANDFASTINGS
HANDFEEDING
HANDICAPPED
HANDICAPPER
HANDICAPPERS
HANDICAPPING
HANDICRAFT
HANDICRAFTER
HANDICRAFTERS
HANDICRAFTS
HANDICRAFTSMAN
HANDICRAFTSMEN
HANDICUFFS
HANDINESSES
HANDIWORKS
HANDKERCHER
HANDKERCHERS
HANDKERCHIEF
HANDKERCHIEFS

HANDKERCHIEVES
HANDLANGER
HANDLANGERS
HANDLEABLE
HANDLEBARS
HANDLELESS
HANDMAIDEN
HANDMAIDENS
HANDPHONES
HANDPICKED
HANDPICKING
HANDPRESSES
HANDPRINTS
HANDSBREADTH
HANDSBREADTHS
HANDSELING
HANDSELLED
HANDSELLING
HANDSHAKES
HANDSHAKING
HANDSHAKINGS
HANDSOMELY
HANDSOMENESS
HANDSOMENESSES
HANDSOMEST
HANDSPIKES
HANDSPRING
HANDSPRINGS
HANDSTAFFS
HANDSTAMPED
HANDSTAMPING
HANDSTAMPS
HANDSTANDS
HANDSTAVES
HANDSTROKE
HANDSTROKES
HANDSTURNS
HANDTOWELS
HANDWHEELS
HANDWORKED
HANDWORKER
HANDWORKERS
HANDWRINGER
HANDWRINGERS
HANDWRITES
HANDWRITING
HANDWRITINGS
HANDWRITTEN
HANDWROUGHT
HANDYPERSON
HANDYPERSONS
HANDYWORKS
HANGABILITIES
HANGABILITY
HANKERINGS
HANSARDISE
HANSARDISED
HANSARDISES
HANSARDISING
HANSARDIZE
HANSARDIZED
HANSARDIZES
HANSARDIZING
HANSELLING
HANTAVIRUS
HANTAVIRUSES
HAPAXANTHIC
HAPAXANTHOUS
HAPHAZARDLY
HAPHAZARDNESS
HAPHAZARDNESSES
HAPHAZARDRIES
HAPHAZARDRY
HAPHAZARDS
HAPHTARAHS
HAPHTAROTH
HAPLESSNESS
HAPLESSNESSES
HAPLOBIONT
HAPLOBIONTIC
HAPLOBIONTS
HAPLOGRAPHIES
HAPLOGRAPHY
HAPLOIDIES
HAPLOLOGIC
HAPLOLOGIES
HAPLOSTEMONOUS
HAPLOTYPES
HAPPENCHANCE
HAPPENCHANCES
HAPPENINGS
HAPPENSTANCE
HAPPENSTANCES
HAPPINESSES
HAPTOGLOBIN
HAPTOGLOBINS
HAPTOTROPIC
HAPTOTROPISM
HAPTOTROPISMS
HARAMZADAS
HARAMZADIS
HARANGUERS
HARANGUING
HARASSEDLY
HARASSINGLY
HARASSINGS
HARASSMENT
HARASSMENTS
HARBINGERED
HARBINGERING
HARBINGERS
HARBORAGES
HARBORFULS
HARBORLESS
HARBORMASTER
HARBORMASTERS
HARBORSIDE
HARBOURAGE
HARBOURAGES
HARBOURERS
HARBOURING
HARBOURLESS
HARDBACKED
HARDBOARDS
HARDBOUNDS
HARDCOVERS
HARDENINGS
HARDFISTED
HARDGRASSES
HARDHANDED
HARDHANDEDNESS
HARDHEADED
HARDHEADEDLY
HARDHEADEDNESS
HARDHEARTED
HARDHEARTEDLY
HARDHEARTEDNESS
HARDIHEADS
HARDIHOODS
HARDIMENTS
HARDINESSES
HARDINGGRASS
HARDINGGRASSES
HARDLINERS
HARDMOUTHED
HARDNESSES
HARDSCRABBLE
HARDSTANDING
HARDSTANDINGS
HARDSTANDS
HARDWAREMAN
HARDWAREMEN
HARDWIRING
HARDWORKING
HAREBRAINED
HARELIPPED
HARESTAILS
HARIOLATED
HARIOLATES
HARIOLATING
HARIOLATION
HARIOLATIONS
HARLEQUINADE
HARLEQUINADES
HARLEQUINED
HARLEQUINING
HARLEQUINS
HARLOTRIES
HARMALINES
HARMATTANS
HARMDOINGS
HARMFULNESS
HARMFULNESSES
HARMLESSLY
HARMLESSNESS
HARMLESSNESSES
HARMOLODIC
HARMOLODICS
HARMONICAL
HARMONICALLY
HARMONICAS
HARMONICHORD
HARMONICHORDS
HARMONICIST
HARMONICISTS
HARMONICON
HARMONICONS
HARMONIOUS
HARMONIOUSLY
HARMONIOUSNESS
HARMONIPHON
HARMONIPHONE
HARMONIPHONES
HARMONIPHONS
HARMONISABLE
HARMONISATION
HARMONISATIONS
HARMONISED
HARMONISER
HARMONISERS
HARMONISES
HARMONISING
HARMONISTIC
HARMONISTICALLY
HARMONISTS
HARMONIUMIST
HARMONIUMISTS
HARMONIUMS
HARMONIZABLE
HARMONIZATION
HARMONIZATIONS
HARMONIZED
HARMONIZER
HARMONIZERS
HARMONIZES
HARMONIZING
HARMONOGRAM
HARMONOGRAMS
HARMONOGRAPH
HARMONOGRAPHS
HARMONOMETER
HARMONOMETERS
HARMOSTIES
HARMOTOMES
HARNESSERS
HARNESSING
HARNESSLESS
HARPOONEER
HARPOONEERS
HARPOONERS
HARPOONING
HARPSICHORD
HARPSICHORDIST
HARPSICHORDISTS
HARPSICHORDS
HARQUEBUSE
HARQUEBUSES
HARQUEBUSIER
HARQUEBUSIERS
HARQUEBUSS
HARQUEBUSSES
HARROWINGLY
HARROWMENT
HARROWMENTS
HARRUMPHED
HARRUMPHING
HARSHENING
HARSHNESSES
HARTBEESES
HARTBEESTS
HARTEBEEST
HARTEBEESTS
HARTSHORNS
HARUMPHING
HARUSPICAL
HARUSPICATE
HARUSPICATED
HARUSPICATES
HARUSPICATING
HARUSPICATION
HARUSPICATIONS
HARUSPICES
HARUSPICIES
HARVESTABLE

HARVESTERS
HARVESTING
HARVESTINGS
HARVESTLESS
HARVESTMAN
HARVESTMEN
HARVESTTIME
HARVESTTIMES
HASENPFEFFER
HASENPFEFFERS
HASHEESHES
HASTEFULLY
HASTINESSES
HATBRUSHES
HATCHABILITIES
HATCHABILITY
HATCHBACKS
HATCHELING
HATCHELLED
HATCHELLER
HATCHELLERS
HATCHELLING
HATCHERIES
HATCHETTITE
HATCHETTITES
HATCHLINGS
HATCHMENTS
HATEFULNESS
HATEFULNESSES
HATELESSNESS
HATELESSNESSES
HATEWORTHY
HATLESSNESS
HATLESSNESSES
HAUBERGEON
HAUBERGEONS
HAUGHTIEST
HAUGHTINESS
HAUGHTINESSES
HAUNTINGLY
HAUSFRAUEN
HAUSSMANNISE
HAUSSMANNISED
HAUSSMANNISES
HAUSSMANNISING
HAUSSMANNIZE
HAUSSMANNIZED
HAUSSMANNIZES
HAUSSMANNIZING
HAUSTELLATE
HAUSTELLUM
HAUSTORIAL
HAUSTORIUM
HAVERSACKS
HAVERSINES
HAWFINCHES
HAWKISHNESS
HAWKISHNESSES
HAWKSBEARD
HAWKSBEARDS
HAWKSBILLS
HAWSEHOLES
HAWSEPIPES
HAYMAKINGS
HAZARDABLE
HAZARDIZES
HAZARDOUSLY
HAZARDOUSNESS
HAZARDOUSNESSES
HAZARDRIES
HAZINESSES
HEADACHIER
HEADACHIEST
HEADBANGED
HEADBANGING
HEADBOARDS
HEADBOROUGH
HEADBOROUGHS
HEADCHAIRS
HEADCHEESE
HEADCHEESES
HEADCLOTHS
HEADCOUNTS
HEADDRESSES
HEADFISHES
HEADFOREMOST
HEADFRAMES
HEADGUARDS
HEADHUNTED
HEADHUNTER
HEADHUNTERS
HEADHUNTING
HEADHUNTINGS
HEADINESSES
HEADLEASES
HEADLESSNESS
HEADLESSNESSES
HEADLIGHTS
HEADLINERS
HEADLINING
HEADMASTER
HEADMASTERLY
HEADMASTERS
HEADMASTERSHIP
HEADMASTERSHIPS
HEADMISTRESS
HEADMISTRESSES
HEADMISTRESSY
HEADPEACES
HEADPHONES
HEADPIECES
HEADQUARTER
HEADQUARTERED
HEADQUARTERING
HEADQUARTERS
HEADREACHED
HEADREACHES
HEADREACHING
HEADSCARVES
HEADSHAKES
HEADSHEETS
HEADSHRINKER
HEADSHRINKERS
HEADSPACES
HEADSPRING
HEADSPRINGS
HEADSQUARE
HEADSQUARES
HEADSTALLS
HEADSTANDS
HEADSTICKS
HEADSTOCKS
HEADSTONES
HEADSTREAM
HEADSTREAMS
HEADSTRONG
HEADSTRONGLY
HEADSTRONGNESS
HEADWAITER
HEADWAITERS
HEADWATERS
HEADWORKER
HEADWORKERS
HEALTHCARE
HEALTHCARES
HEALTHFULLY
HEALTHFULNESS
HEALTHFULNESSES
HEALTHIEST
HEALTHINESS
HEALTHINESSES
HEALTHISMS
HEALTHLESS
HEALTHLESSNESS
HEALTHSOME
HEAPSTEADS
HEARKENERS
HEARKENING
HEARTACHES
HEARTBEATS
HEARTBREAK
HEARTBREAKER
HEARTBREAKERS
HEARTBREAKING
HEARTBREAKINGLY
HEARTBREAKS
HEARTBROKE
HEARTBROKEN
HEARTBROKENLY
HEARTBROKENNESS
HEARTBURNING
HEARTBURNINGS
HEARTBURNS
HEARTENERS
HEARTENING
HEARTENINGLY
HEARTHRUGS
HEARTHSTONE
HEARTHSTONES
HEARTIKINS
HEARTINESS
HEARTINESSES
HEARTLANDS
HEARTLESSLY
HEARTLESSNESS
HEARTLESSNESSES
HEARTLINGS
HEARTRENDING
HEARTRENDINGLY
HEARTSEASE
HEARTSEASES
HEARTSEEDS
HEARTSICKNESS
HEARTSICKNESSES
HEARTSOMELY
HEARTSOMENESS
HEARTSOMENESSES
HEARTSTRING
HEARTSTRINGS
HEARTTHROB
HEARTTHROBS
HEARTWARMING
HEARTWATER
HEARTWATERS
HEARTWOODS
HEARTWORMS
HEATEDNESS
HEATEDNESSES
HEATHBERRIES
HEATHBERRY
HEATHBIRDS
HEATHCOCKS
HEATHENDOM
HEATHENDOMS
HEATHENESSE
HEATHENESSES
HEATHENISE
HEATHENISED
HEATHENISES
HEATHENISH
HEATHENISHLY
HEATHENISHNESS
HEATHENISING
HEATHENISM
HEATHENISMS
HEATHENIZE
HEATHENIZED
HEATHENIZES
HEATHENIZING
HEATHENNESS
HEATHENNESSES
HEATHENRIES
HEATHERIER
HEATHERIEST
HEATHFOWLS
HEATHLANDS
HEATSTROKE
HEATSTROKES
HEAVENLIER
HEAVENLIEST
HEAVENLINESS
HEAVENLINESSES
HEAVENWARD
HEAVENWARDS
HEAVINESSES
HEAVYHEARTED
HEAVYHEARTEDLY
HEAVYWEIGHT
HEAVYWEIGHTS
HEBDOMADAL
HEBDOMADALLY
HEBDOMADAR
HEBDOMADARIES
HEBDOMADARS
HEBDOMADARY
HEBDOMADER
HEBDOMADERS
HEBEPHRENIA
HEBEPHRENIAC
HEBEPHRENIACS
HEBEPHRENIAS
HEBEPHRENIC
HEBEPHRENICS
HEBETATING

HEBETATION
HEBETATIONS
HEBETATIVE
HEBETUDINOSITY
HEBETUDINOUS
HEBRAISATION
HEBRAISATIONS
HEBRAISING
HEBRAIZATION
HEBRAIZATIONS
HEBRAIZING
HECKELPHONE
HECKELPHONES
HECOGENINS
HECTICALLY
HECTOCOTYLI
HECTOCOTYLUS
HECTOGRAMME
HECTOGRAMMES
HECTOGRAMS
HECTOGRAPH
HECTOGRAPHED
HECTOGRAPHIC
HECTOGRAPHIES
HECTOGRAPHING
HECTOGRAPHS
HECTOGRAPHY
HECTOLITER
HECTOLITERS
HECTOLITRE
HECTOLITRES
HECTOMETER
HECTOMETERS
HECTOMETRE
HECTOMETRES
HECTORINGLY
HECTORINGS
HECTORISMS
HECTORSHIP
HECTORSHIPS
HECTOSTERE
HECTOSTERES
HEDGEBILLS
HEDGEHOPPED
HEDGEHOPPER
HEDGEHOPPERS
HEDGEHOPPING
HEDGEHOPPINGS
HEDONICALLY
HEDONISTIC
HEDONISTICALLY
HEDYPHANES
HEEDFULNESS
HEEDFULNESSES
HEEDINESSES
HEEDLESSLY
HEEDLESSNESS
HEEDLESSNESSES
HEELPIECES
HEELPLATES
HEFTINESSES
HEGEMONIAL
HEGEMONICAL
HEGEMONIES
HEGEMONISM
HEGEMONISMS
HEGEMONIST
HEGEMONISTS
HEGUMENIES
HEGUMENOSES
HEIGHTENED
HEIGHTENER
HEIGHTENERS
HEIGHTENING
HEIGHTISMS
HEINOUSNESS
HEINOUSNESSES
HEKTOGRAMS
HELDENTENOR
HELDENTENORS
HELIACALLY
HELIANTHEMUM
HELIANTHEMUMS
HELIANTHUS
HELIANTHUSES
HELIBUSSES
HELICHRYSUM
HELICHRYSUMS
HELICITIES
HELICLINES
HELICOGRAPH
HELICOGRAPHS
HELICOIDAL
HELICOIDALLY
HELICONIAS
HELICOPTED
HELICOPTER
HELICOPTERED
HELICOPTERING
HELICOPTERS
HELICOPTING
HELICTITES
HELIDROMES
HELILIFTED
HELILIFTING
HELIOCENTRIC
HELIOCENTRICISM
HELIOCENTRICITY
HELIOCHROME
HELIOCHROMES
HELIOCHROMIC
HELIOCHROMIES
HELIOCHROMY
HELIOGRAMS
HELIOGRAPH
HELIOGRAPHED
HELIOGRAPHER
HELIOGRAPHERS
HELIOGRAPHIC
HELIOGRAPHICAL
HELIOGRAPHIES
HELIOGRAPHING
HELIOGRAPHS
HELIOGRAPHY
HELIOGRAVURE
HELIOGRAVURES
HELIOLATER
HELIOLATERS
HELIOLATRIES
HELIOLATROUS
HELIOLATRY
HELIOLITHIC
HELIOLOGIES
HELIOMETER
HELIOMETERS
HELIOMETRIC
HELIOMETRICAL
HELIOMETRICALLY
HELIOMETRIES
HELIOMETRY
HELIOPAUSE
HELIOPAUSES
HELIOPHILOUS
HELIOPHOBIC
HELIOPHYTE
HELIOPHYTES
HELIOSCIOPHYTE
HELIOSCIOPHYTES
HELIOSCOPE
HELIOSCOPES
HELIOSCOPIC
HELIOSPHERE
HELIOSPHERES
HELIOSTATIC
HELIOSTATS
HELIOTACTIC
HELIOTAXES
HELIOTAXIS
HELIOTHERAPIES
HELIOTHERAPY
HELIOTROPE
HELIOTROPES
HELIOTROPIC
HELIOTROPICAL
HELIOTROPICALLY
HELIOTROPIES
HELIOTROPIN
HELIOTROPINS
HELIOTROPISM
HELIOTROPISMS
HELIOTROPY
HELIOTYPED
HELIOTYPES
HELIOTYPIC
HELIOTYPIES
HELIOTYPING
HELIOZOANS
HELIPILOTS
HELISPHERIC
HELISPHERICAL
HELLACIOUS
HELLACIOUSLY
HELLBENDER
HELLBENDERS
HELLBROTHS
HELLDIVERS
HELLEBORES
HELLEBORINE
HELLEBORINES
HELLENISATION
HELLENISATIONS
HELLENISED
HELLENISES
HELLENISING
HELLENIZATION
HELLENIZATIONS
HELLENIZED
HELLENIZES
HELLENIZING
HELLGRAMITE
HELLGRAMITES
HELLGRAMMITE
HELLGRAMMITES
HELLHOUNDS
HELLISHNESS
HELLISHNESSES
HELMETLIKE
HELMINTHIASES
HELMINTHIASIS
HELMINTHIC
HELMINTHICS
HELMINTHOID
HELMINTHOLOGIC
HELMINTHOLOGIES
HELMINTHOLOGIST
HELMINTHOLOGY
HELMINTHOUS
HELMSMANSHIP
HELMSMANSHIPS
HELOPHYTES
HELPFULNESS
HELPFULNESSES
HELPLESSLY
HELPLESSNESS
HELPLESSNESSES
HELVETIUMS
HEMACHROME
HEMACHROMES
HEMACYTOMETER
HEMACYTOMETERS
HEMAGGLUTINATE
HEMAGGLUTINATED
HEMAGGLUTINATES
HEMAGGLUTININ
HEMAGGLUTININS
HEMAGOGUES
HEMANGIOMA
HEMANGIOMAS
HEMANGIOMATA
HEMATEMESES
HEMATEMESIS
HEMATINICS
HEMATOBLAST
HEMATOBLASTIC
HEMATOBLASTS
HEMATOCELE
HEMATOCELES
HEMATOCRIT
HEMATOCRITS
HEMATOCRYAL
HEMATOGENESES
HEMATOGENESIS
HEMATOGENETIC
HEMATOGENIC
HEMATOGENOUS
HEMATOLOGIC
HEMATOLOGICAL
HEMATOLOGIES
HEMATOLOGIST
HEMATOLOGISTS
HEMATOLOGY
HEMATOLYSES
HEMATOLYSIS
HEMATOMATA

HEMATOPHAGOUS
HEMATOPOIESES
HEMATOPOIESIS
HEMATOPOIETIC
HEMATOPORPHYRIN
HEMATOTHERMAL
HEMATOXYLIN
HEMATOXYLINS
HEMATOZOON
HEMATURIAS
HEMELYTRAL
HEMELYTRON
HEMELYTRUM
HEMERALOPIA
HEMERALOPIAS
HEMERALOPIC
HEMEROCALLIS
HEMEROCALLISES
HEMERYTHRIN
HEMERYTHRINS
HEMIACETAL
HEMIACETALS
HEMIALGIAS
HEMIANOPIA
HEMIANOPIAS
HEMIANOPSIA
HEMIANOPSIAS
HEMIANOPTIC
HEMICELLULOSE
HEMICELLULOSES
HEMICHORDATE
HEMICHORDATES
HEMICRANIA
HEMICRANIAS
HEMICRYPTOPHYTE
HEMICRYSTALLINE
HEMICYCLES
HEMICYCLIC
HEMIELYTRA
HEMIELYTRAL
HEMIELYTRON
HEMIHEDRAL
HEMIHEDRIES
HEMIHEDRISM
HEMIHEDRISMS
HEMIHEDRON
HEMIHEDRONS
HEMIHYDRATE
HEMIHYDRATED
HEMIHYDRATES
HEMIMETABOLOUS
HEMIMORPHIC
HEMIMORPHIES
HEMIMORPHISM
HEMIMORPHISMS
HEMIMORPHITE
HEMIMORPHITES
HEMIMORPHY
HEMIONUSES
HEMIOPSIAS
HEMIPARASITE
HEMIPARASITES
HEMIPARASITIC
HEMIPLEGIA
HEMIPLEGIAS
HEMIPLEGIC
HEMIPLEGICS
HEMIPTERAL
HEMIPTERAN
HEMIPTERANS
HEMIPTERON
HEMIPTERONS
HEMIPTEROUS
HEMISPACES
HEMISPHERE
HEMISPHERES
HEMISPHERIC
HEMISPHERICAL
HEMISPHEROID
HEMISPHEROIDAL
HEMISPHEROIDS
HEMISTICHAL
HEMISTICHS
HEMITERPENE
HEMITERPENES
HEMITROPAL
HEMITROPES
HEMITROPIC
HEMITROPIES
HEMITROPISM
HEMITROPISMS
HEMITROPOUS
HEMIZYGOUS
HEMOCHROMATOSES
HEMOCHROMATOSIS
HEMOCHROME
HEMOCHROMES
HEMOCYANIN
HEMOCYANINS
HEMOCYTOMETER
HEMOCYTOMETERS
HEMODIALYSES
HEMODIALYSIS
HEMODILUTION
HEMODILUTIONS
HEMODYNAMIC
HEMODYNAMICALLY
HEMODYNAMICS
HEMOFLAGELLATE
HEMOFLAGELLATES
HEMOGLOBIN
HEMOGLOBINS
HEMOGLOBINURIA
HEMOGLOBINURIAS
HEMOGLOBINURIC
HEMOLYMPHS
HEMOLYSING
HEMOLYSINS
HEMOLYZING
HEMOPHILES
HEMOPHILIA
HEMOPHILIAC
HEMOPHILIACS
HEMOPHILIAS
HEMOPHILIC
HEMOPHILICS
HEMOPHILIOID
HEMOPOIESES
HEMOPOIESIS
HEMOPOIETIC
HEMOPROTEIN
HEMOPROTEINS
HEMOPTYSES
HEMOPTYSIS
HEMORRHAGE
HEMORRHAGED
HEMORRHAGES
HEMORRHAGIC
HEMORRHAGING
HEMORRHOID
HEMORRHOIDAL
HEMORRHOIDALS
HEMORRHOIDS
HEMOSIDERIN
HEMOSIDERINS
HEMOSTASES
HEMOSTASIA
HEMOSTASIAS
HEMOSTASIS
HEMOSTATIC
HEMOSTATICS
HEMOTOXINS
HEMSTITCHED
HEMSTITCHER
HEMSTITCHERS
HEMSTITCHES
HEMSTITCHING
HENCEFORTH
HENCEFORWARD
HENCEFORWARDS
HENCHPERSON
HENCHPERSONS
HENCHWOMAN
HENCHWOMEN
HENDECAGON
HENDECAGONAL
HENDECAGONS
HENDECAHEDRA
HENDECAHEDRON
HENDECAHEDRONS
HENDECASYLLABIC
HENDECASYLLABLE
HENDIADYSES
HENOTHEISM
HENOTHEISMS
HENOTHEIST
HENOTHEISTIC
HENOTHEISTS
HENPECKERIES
HENPECKERY
HENPECKING
HEORTOLOGICAL
HEORTOLOGIES
HEORTOLOGIST
HEORTOLOGISTS
HEORTOLOGY
HEPARINISED
HEPARINIZED
HEPARINOID
HEPATECTOMIES
HEPATECTOMISED
HEPATECTOMIZED
HEPATECTOMY
HEPATICOLOGICAL
HEPATICOLOGIES
HEPATICOLOGIST
HEPATICOLOGISTS
HEPATICOLOGY
HEPATISATION
HEPATISATIONS
HEPATISING
HEPATITIDES
HEPATITISES
HEPATIZATION
HEPATIZATIONS
HEPATIZING
HEPATOCELLULAR
HEPATOCYTE
HEPATOCYTES
HEPATOGENOUS
HEPATOLOGIES
HEPATOLOGIST
HEPATOLOGISTS
HEPATOLOGY
HEPATOMATA
HEPATOMEGALIES
HEPATOMEGALY
HEPATOPANCREAS
HEPATOSCOPIES
HEPATOSCOPY
HEPATOTOXIC
HEPATOTOXICITY
HEPHTHEMIMER
HEPHTHEMIMERAL
HEPHTHEMIMERS
HEPTACHLOR
HEPTACHLORS
HEPTACHORD
HEPTACHORDS
HEPTADECANOIC
HEPTAGLOTS
HEPTAGONAL
HEPTAGYNOUS
HEPTAHEDRA
HEPTAHEDRAL
HEPTAHEDRON
HEPTAHEDRONS
HEPTAMEROUS
HEPTAMETER
HEPTAMETERS
HEPTAMETRICAL
HEPTANDROUS
HEPTANGULAR
HEPTAPODIC
HEPTAPODIES
HEPTARCHAL
HEPTARCHIC
HEPTARCHIES
HEPTARCHIST
HEPTARCHISTS
HEPTASTICH
HEPTASTICHS
HEPTASYLLABIC
HEPTATHLETE
HEPTATHLETES
HEPTATHLON
HEPTATHLONS
HEPTATONIC
HEPTAVALENT
HERALDICALLY
HERALDISTS
HERALDRIES
HERALDSHIP
HERALDSHIPS

ERBACEOUS
ERBACEOUSLY
ERBALISMS
ERBALISTS
ERBARIANS
ERBARIUMS
ERBICIDAL
ERBICIDALLY
ERBICIDES
ERBIVORES
ERBIVORIES
ERBIVOROUS
ERBIVOROUSLY
ERBIVOROUSNESS
ERBOLOGIES
ERBORISATION
ERBORISATIONS
ERBORISED
ERBORISES
ERBORISING
ERBORISTS
ERBORIZATION
ERBORIZATIONS
ERBORIZED
ERBORIZES
ERBORIZING
ERCOGAMIES
ERCOGAMOUS
ERCULESES
ERCYNITES
EREABOUTS
EREAFTERS
EREDITABILITY
EREDITABLE
EREDITABLY
EREDITAMENT
EREDITAMENTS
EREDITARIAN
EREDITARIANISM
EREDITARIANIST
EREDITARIANS
EREDITARILY
EREDITARINESS
EREDITARY
EREDITIES
EREDITIST
EREDITISTS
EREINABOVE
EREINAFTER
EREINBEFORE
EREINBELOW
ERENESSES
ERESIARCH
ERESIARCHS
ERESIOGRAPHER
ERESIOGRAPHERS
ERESIOGRAPHIES
ERESIOGRAPHY
ERESIOLOGIES
ERESIOLOGIST
ERESIOLOGISTS
ERESIOLOGY
ERESTHETIC
ERESTHETICAL
ERESTHETICIAN
ERESTHETICIANS
HERESTHETICS
HERETICALLY
HERETICATE
HERETICATED
HERETICATES
HERETICATING
HERETOFORE
HERETRICES
HERETRIXES
HERIOTABLE
HERITABILITIES
HERITABILITY
HERITRESSES
HERITRICES
HERITRIXES
HERKOGAMIES
HERMANDADS
HERMAPHRODITE
HERMAPHRODITES
HERMAPHRODITIC
HERMAPHRODITISM
HERMATYPIC
HERMENEUTIC
HERMENEUTICAL
HERMENEUTICALLY
HERMENEUTICS
HERMENEUTIST
HERMENEUTISTS
HERMETICAL
HERMETICALLY
HERMETICISM
HERMETICISMS
HERMETICITIES
HERMETICITY
HERMETISMS
HERMETISTS
HERMITAGES
HERMITESSES
HERMITICAL
HERMITICALLY
HERMITISMS
HERMITRIES
HERNIATING
HERNIATION
HERNIATIONS
HERNIORRHAPHIES
HERNIORRHAPHY
HERNIOTOMIES
HERNIOTOMY
HEROICALLY
HEROICALNESS
HEROICALNESSES
HEROICISED
HEROICISES
HEROICISING
HEROICIZED
HEROICIZES
HEROICIZING
HEROICNESS
HEROICNESSES
HEROICOMIC
HEROICOMICAL
HEROINISMS
HERONSHAWS
HERPESVIRUS
HERPESVIRUSES
HERPETOFAUNA
HERPETOFAUNAE
HERPETOFAUNAS
HERPETOLOGIC
HERPETOLOGICAL
HERPETOLOGIES
HERPETOLOGIST
HERPETOLOGISTS
HERPETOLOGY
HERRENVOLK
HERRENVOLKS
HERRIMENTS
HERRINGBONE
HERRINGBONED
HERRINGBONES
HERRINGBONING
HERRINGERS
HERRYMENTS
HERSTORIES
HESITANCES
HESITANCIES
HESITANTLY
HESITATERS
HESITATING
HESITATINGLY
HESITATION
HESITATIONS
HESITATIVE
HESITATORS
HESITATORY
HESPERIDIA
HESPERIDIN
HESPERIDINS
HESPERIDIUM
HESPERIDIUMS
HESSONITES
HETAERISMIC
HETAERISMS
HETAERISTIC
HETAERISTS
HETAIRISMIC
HETAIRISMS
HETAIRISTIC
HETAIRISTS
HETERARCHIES
HETERARCHY
HETERAUXESES
HETERAUXESIS
HETEROATOM
HETEROATOMS
HETEROAUXIN
HETEROAUXINS
HETEROBLASTIC
HETEROBLASTIES
HETEROBLASTY
HETEROCARPOUS
HETEROCERCAL
HETEROCERCALITY
HETEROCERCIES
HETEROCERCY
HETEROCHROMATIC
HETEROCHROMATIN
HETEROCHROMOUS
HETEROCHRONIC
HETEROCHRONIES
HETEROCHRONISM
HETEROCHRONISMS
HETEROCHRONOUS
HETEROCHRONY
HETEROCLITE
HETEROCLITES
HETEROCLITIC
HETEROCLITOUS
HETEROCONT
HETEROCONTS
HETEROCYCLE
HETEROCYCLES
HETEROCYCLIC
HETEROCYCLICS
HETEROCYST
HETEROCYSTOUS
HETEROCYSTS
HETERODACTYL
HETERODACTYLOUS
HETERODACTYLS
HETERODONT
HETERODOXIES
HETERODOXY
HETERODUPLEX
HETERODUPLEXES
HETERODYNE
HETERODYNED
HETERODYNES
HETERODYNING
HETEROECIOUS
HETEROECISM
HETEROECISMS
HETEROFLEXIBLE
HETEROFLEXIBLES
HETEROGAMETE
HETEROGAMETES
HETEROGAMETIC
HETEROGAMETIES
HETEROGAMETY
HETEROGAMIES
HETEROGAMOUS
HETEROGAMY
HETEROGENEITIES
HETEROGENEITY
HETEROGENEOUS
HETEROGENEOUSLY
HETEROGENESES
HETEROGENESIS
HETEROGENETIC
HETEROGENIC
HETEROGENIES
HETEROGENOUS
HETEROGENY
HETEROGONIC
HETEROGONIES
HETEROGONOUS
HETEROGONOUSLY
HETEROGONY
HETEROGRAFT
HETEROGRAFTS
HETEROGRAPHIC
HETEROGRAPHICAL
HETEROGRAPHIES
HETEROGRAPHY
HETEROGYNOUS
HETEROKARYON
HETEROKARYONS

HETEROKARYOSES
HETEROKARYOSIS
HETEROKARYOTIC
HETEROKONT
HETEROKONTAN
HETEROKONTS
HETEROLECITHAL
HETEROLOGIES
HETEROLOGOUS
HETEROLOGOUSLY
HETEROLOGY
HETEROLYSES
HETEROLYSIS
HETEROLYTIC
HETEROMEROUS
HETEROMORPHIC
HETEROMORPHIES
HETEROMORPHISM
HETEROMORPHISMS
HETEROMORPHOUS
HETEROMORPHY
HETERONOMIES
HETERONOMOUS
HETERONOMOUSLY
HETERONOMY
HETERONYMOUS
HETERONYMOUSLY
HETERONYMS
HETEROOUSIAN
HETEROOUSIANS
HETEROPHIL
HETEROPHILE
HETEROPHONIES
HETEROPHONY
HETEROPHYLLIES
HETEROPHYLLOUS
HETEROPHYLLY
HETEROPLASIA
HETEROPLASIAS
HETEROPLASTIC
HETEROPLASTIES
HETEROPLASTY
HETEROPLOID
HETEROPLOIDIES
HETEROPLOIDS
HETEROPLOIDY
HETEROPODS
HETEROPOLAR
HETEROPOLARITY
HETEROPTERAN
HETEROPTEROUS
HETEROSCEDASTIC
HETEROSCIAN
HETEROSCIANS
HETEROSEXISM
HETEROSEXISMS
HETEROSEXIST
HETEROSEXISTS
HETEROSEXUAL
HETEROSEXUALITY
HETEROSEXUALLY
HETEROSEXUALS
HETEROSOCIAL
HETEROSOCIALITY
HETEROSOMATOUS
HETEROSPECIFIC
HETEROSPORIES
HETEROSPOROUS
HETEROSPORY
HETEROSTROPHIC
HETEROSTROPHIES
HETEROSTROPHY
HETEROSTYLED
HETEROSTYLIES
HETEROSTYLISM
HETEROSTYLISMS
HETEROSTYLOUS
HETEROSTYLY
HETEROTACTIC
HETEROTACTOUS
HETEROTAXES
HETEROTAXIA
HETEROTAXIAS
HETEROTAXIC
HETEROTAXIES
HETEROTAXIS
HETEROTAXY
HETEROTHALLIC
HETEROTHALLIES
HETEROTHALLISM
HETEROTHALLISMS
HETEROTHALLY
HETEROTHERMAL
HETEROTOPIA
HETEROTOPIAS
HETEROTOPIC
HETEROTOPIES
HETEROTOPOUS
HETEROTOPY
HETEROTROPH
HETEROTROPHIC
HETEROTROPHIES
HETEROTROPHS
HETEROTROPHY
HETEROTYPIC
HETEROTYPICAL
HETEROUSIAN
HETEROUSIANS
HETEROZYGOSES
HETEROZYGOSIS
HETEROZYGOSITY
HETEROZYGOTE
HETEROZYGOTES
HETEROZYGOUS
HETHERWARD
HETMANATES
HETMANSHIP
HETMANSHIPS
HEULANDITE
HEULANDITES
HEURISTICALLY
HEURISTICS
HEXACHLORETHANE
HEXACHLORIDE
HEXACHLORIDES
HEXACHLOROPHANE
HEXACHLOROPHENE
HEXACHORDS
HEXACOSANOIC
HEXACTINAL
HEXACTINELLID
HEXACTINELLIDS
HEXADACTYLIC
HEXADACTYLOUS
HEXADECANE
HEXADECANES
HEXADECANOIC
HEXADECIMAL
HEXADECIMALS
HEXAEMERIC
HEXAEMERON
HEXAEMERONS
HEXAFLUORIDE
HEXAFLUORIDES
HEXAGONALLY
HEXAGRAMMOID
HEXAGRAMMOIDS
HEXAGYNIAN
HEXAGYNOUS
HEXAHEDRAL
HEXAHEDRON
HEXAHEDRONS
HEXAHEMERIC
HEXAHEMERON
HEXAHEMERONS
HEXAHYDRATE
HEXAHYDRATED
HEXAHYDRATES
HEXAMERISM
HEXAMERISMS
HEXAMEROUS
HEXAMETERS
HEXAMETHONIUM
HEXAMETHONIUMS
HEXAMETRAL
HEXAMETRIC
HEXAMETRICAL
HEXAMETRICALLY
HEXAMETRISE
HEXAMETRISED
HEXAMETRISES
HEXAMETRISING
HEXAMETRIST
HEXAMETRISTS
HEXAMETRIZE
HEXAMETRIZED
HEXAMETRIZES
HEXAMETRIZING
HEXANDRIAN
HEXANDROUS
HEXANGULAR
HEXAPLARIAN
HEXAPLARIC
HEXAPLOIDIES
HEXAPLOIDS
HEXAPLOIDY
HEXAPODIES
HEXARCHIES
HEXASTICHAL
HEXASTICHIC
HEXASTICHON
HEXASTICHONS
HEXASTICHS
HEXASTYLES
HEXATEUCHAL
HEXAVALENT
HEXOBARBITAL
HEXOBARBITALS
HEXOKINASE
HEXOKINASES
HEXOSAMINIDASE
HEXOSAMINIDASES
HEXYLRESORCINOL
HIBAKUSHAS
HIBERNACLE
HIBERNACLES
HIBERNACULA
HIBERNACULUM
HIBERNATED
HIBERNATES
HIBERNATING
HIBERNATION
HIBERNATIONS
HIBERNATOR
HIBERNATORS
HIBERNICISE
HIBERNICISED
HIBERNICISES
HIBERNICISING
HIBERNICIZE
HIBERNICIZED
HIBERNICIZES
HIBERNICIZING
HIBERNISATION
HIBERNISATIONS
HIBERNISED
HIBERNISES
HIBERNISING
HIBERNIZATION
HIBERNIZATIONS
HIBERNIZED
HIBERNIZES
HIBERNIZING
HIBISCUSES
HICCOUGHED
HICCOUGHING
HICCUPPING
HIDALGOISH
HIDALGOISM
HIDALGOISMS
HIDDENITES
HIDDENMOST
HIDDENNESS
HIDDENNESSES
HIDEOSITIES
HIDEOUSNESS
HIDEOUSNESSES
HIERACIUMS
HIERACOSPHINGES
HIERACOSPHINX
HIERACOSPHINXES
HIERARCHAL
HIERARCHIC
HIERARCHICAL
HIERARCHICALLY
HIERARCHIES
HIERARCHISE
HIERARCHISED
HIERARCHISES
HIERARCHISING
HIERARCHISM
HIERARCHISMS
HIERARCHIZE
HIERARCHIZED

HIERARCHIZES
HIERARCHIZING
HIERATICAL
HIERATICALLY
HIERATICAS
HIEROCRACIES
HIEROCRACY
HIEROCRATIC
HIEROCRATICAL
HIEROCRATS
HIERODULES
HIERODULIC
HIEROGLYPH
HIEROGLYPHED
HIEROGLYPHIC
HIEROGLYPHICAL
HIEROGLYPHICS
HIEROGLYPHING
HIEROGLYPHIST
HIEROGLYPHISTS
HIEROGLYPHS
HIEROGRAMMAT
HIEROGRAMMATE
HIEROGRAMMATES
HIEROGRAMMATIC
HIEROGRAMMATIST
HIEROGRAMMATS
HIEROGRAMS
HIEROGRAPH
HIEROGRAPHER
HIEROGRAPHERS
HIEROGRAPHIC
HIEROGRAPHICAL
HIEROGRAPHIES
HIEROGRAPHS
HIEROGRAPHY
HIEROLATRIES
HIEROLATRY
HIEROLOGIC
HIEROLOGICAL
HIEROLOGIES
HIEROLOGIST
HIEROLOGISTS
HIEROMANCIES
HIEROMANCY
HIEROPHANT
HIEROPHANTIC
HIEROPHANTS
HIEROPHOBIA
HIEROPHOBIAS
HIEROPHOBIC
HIEROSCOPIES
HIEROSCOPY
HIERURGICAL
HIERURGIES
HIGHBALLED
HIGHBALLING
HIGHBINDER
HIGHBINDERS
HIGHBLOODED
HIGHBROWED
HIGHBROWISM
HIGHBROWISMS
HIGHCHAIRS
HIGHERMOST
HIGHFALUTIN
HIGHFALUTING
HIGHFALUTINGS
HIGHFALUTINS
HIGHFLIERS
HIGHFLYERS
HIGHJACKED
HIGHJACKER
HIGHJACKERS
HIGHJACKING
HIGHLANDER
HIGHLANDERS
HIGHLIGHTED
HIGHLIGHTER
HIGHLIGHTERS
HIGHLIGHTING
HIGHLIGHTS
HIGHNESSES
HIGHTAILED
HIGHTAILING
HIGHWAYMAN
HIGHWAYMEN
HIGHWROUGHT
HILARIOUSLY
HILARIOUSNESS
HILARIOUSNESSES
HILARITIES
HILLBILLIES
HILLCRESTS
HILLINESSES
HILLSLOPES
HILLWALKER
HILLWALKERS
HILLWALKING
HILLWALKINGS
HINDBERRIES
HINDBRAINS
HINDERANCE
HINDERANCES
HINDERINGLY
HINDERLAND
HINDERLANDS
HINDERLANS
HINDERLINGS
HINDERLINS
HINDERMOST
HINDFOREMOST
HINDQUARTER
HINDQUARTERS
HINDRANCES
HINDSHANKS
HINDSIGHTS
HINTERLAND
HINTERLANDS
HIPPEASTRUM
HIPPEASTRUMS
HIPPIATRIC
HIPPIATRICS
HIPPIATRIES
HIPPIATRIST
HIPPIATRISTS
HIPPIEDOMS
HIPPIENESS
HIPPIENESSES
HIPPINESSES
HIPPOCAMPAL
HIPPOCAMPI
HIPPOCAMPUS
HIPPOCENTAUR
HIPPOCENTAURS
HIPPOCRASES
HIPPOCREPIAN
HIPPODAMES
HIPPODAMIST
HIPPODAMISTS
HIPPODAMOUS
HIPPODROME
HIPPODROMES
HIPPODROMIC
HIPPOGRIFF
HIPPOGRIFFS
HIPPOGRYPH
HIPPOGRYPHS
HIPPOLOGIES
HIPPOLOGIST
HIPPOLOGISTS
HIPPOMANES
HIPPOPHAGIES
HIPPOPHAGIST
HIPPOPHAGISTS
HIPPOPHAGOUS
HIPPOPHAGY
HIPPOPHILE
HIPPOPHILES
HIPPOPHOBE
HIPPOPHOBES
HIPPOPOTAMI
HIPPOPOTAMIAN
HIPPOPOTAMIC
HIPPOPOTAMUS
HIPPOPOTAMUSES
HIPPURITES
HIPPURITIC
HIPSTERISM
HIPSTERISMS
HIRCOCERVUS
HIRCOCERVUSES
HIRCOSITIES
HIRSELLING
HIRSUTENESS
HIRSUTENESSES
HIRSUTISMS
HIRUDINEAN
HIRUDINEANS
HIRUDINOID
HIRUDINOUS
HISPANICISE
HISPANICISED
HISPANICISES
HISPANICISING
HISPANICISM
HISPANICISMS
HISPANICIZE
HISPANICIZED
HISPANICIZES
HISPANICIZING
HISPANIDAD
HISPANIDADS
HISPANIOLISE
HISPANIOLISED
HISPANIOLISES
HISPANIOLISING
HISPANIOLIZE
HISPANIOLIZED
HISPANIOLIZES
HISPANIOLIZING
HISPANISMS
HISPIDITIES
HISTAMINASE
HISTAMINASES
HISTAMINERGIC
HISTAMINES
HISTAMINIC
HISTIDINES
HISTIOCYTE
HISTIOCYTES
HISTIOCYTIC
HISTIOLOGIES
HISTIOLOGY
HISTIOPHOROID
HISTOBLAST
HISTOBLASTS
HISTOCHEMICAL
HISTOCHEMICALLY
HISTOCHEMIST
HISTOCHEMISTRY
HISTOCHEMISTS
HISTOCOMPATIBLE
HISTOGENESES
HISTOGENESIS
HISTOGENETIC
HISTOGENIC
HISTOGENICALLY
HISTOGENIES
HISTOGRAMS
HISTOLOGIC
HISTOLOGICAL
HISTOLOGICALLY
HISTOLOGIES
HISTOLOGIST
HISTOLOGISTS
HISTOLYSES
HISTOLYSIS
HISTOLYTIC
HISTOLYTICALLY
HISTOPATHOLOGIC
HISTOPATHOLOGY
HISTOPHYSIOLOGY
HISTOPLASMOSES
HISTOPLASMOSIS
HISTORIANS
HISTORIATED
HISTORICAL
HISTORICALLY
HISTORICALNESS
HISTORICISE
HISTORICISED
HISTORICISES
HISTORICISING
HISTORICISM
HISTORICISMS
HISTORICIST
HISTORICISTS
HISTORICITIES
HISTORICITY
HISTORICIZE
HISTORICIZED
HISTORICIZES
HISTORICIZING

HISTORIETTE
HISTORIETTES
HISTORIFIED
HISTORIFIES
HISTORIFYING
HISTORIOGRAPHER
HISTORIOGRAPHIC
HISTORIOGRAPHY
HISTORIOLOGIES
HISTORIOLOGY
HISTORISMS
HISTORYING
HISTRIONIC
HISTRIONICAL
HISTRIONICALLY
HISTRIONICISM
HISTRIONICISMS
HISTRIONICS
HISTRIONISM
HISTRIONISMS
HITCHHIKED
HITCHHIKER
HITCHHIKERS
HITCHHIKES
HITCHHIKING
HITHERMOST
HITHERSIDE
HITHERSIDES
HITHERWARD
HITHERWARDS
HOACTZINES
HOARFROSTS
HOARHOUNDS
HOARINESSES
HOARSENESS
HOARSENESSES
HOARSENING
HOBBITRIES
HOBBLEBUSH
HOBBLEBUSHES
HOBBLEDEHOY
HOBBLEDEHOYDOM
HOBBLEDEHOYDOMS
HOBBLEDEHOYHOOD
HOBBLEDEHOYISH
HOBBLEDEHOYISM
HOBBLEDEHOYISMS
HOBBLEDEHOYS
HOBBLINGLY
HOBBYHORSE
HOBBYHORSED
HOBBYHORSES
HOBBYHORSING
HOBGOBLINISM
HOBGOBLINISMS
HOBGOBLINRIES
HOBGOBLINRY
HOBGOBLINS
HOBJOBBERS
HOBJOBBING
HOBJOBBINGS
HOBNAILING
HOBNOBBERS
HOBNOBBING
HOCHMAGANDIES
HOCHMAGANDY
HODGEPODGE
HODGEPODGES
HODMANDODS
HODOGRAPHIC
HODOGRAPHS
HODOMETERS
HODOMETRIES
HODOSCOPES
HOGGISHNESS
HOGGISHNESSES
HOIDENISHNESS
HOIDENISHNESSES
HOJATOLESLAM
HOJATOLESLAMS
HOJATOLISLAM
HOJATOLISLAMS
HOKEYNESSES
HOKEYPOKEY
HOKEYPOKEYS
HOKINESSES
HOKYPOKIES
HOLARCHIES
HOLDERBATS
HOLDERSHIP
HOLDERSHIPS
HOLIDAYERS
HOLIDAYING
HOLIDAYMAKER
HOLIDAYMAKERS
HOLINESSES
HOLISTICALLY
HOLLANDAISE
HOLLANDAISES
HOLLOWARES
HOLLOWNESS
HOLLOWNESSES
HOLLOWWARE
HOLLOWWARES
HOLLYHOCKS
HOLOBENTHIC
HOLOBLASTIC
HOLOBLASTICALLY
HOLOCAUSTAL
HOLOCAUSTIC
HOLOCAUSTS
HOLOCRYSTALLINE
HOLODISCUS
HOLODISCUSES
HOLOENZYME
HOLOENZYMES
HOLOGAMIES
HOLOGRAPHED
HOLOGRAPHER
HOLOGRAPHERS
HOLOGRAPHIC
HOLOGRAPHICALLY
HOLOGRAPHIES
HOLOGRAPHING
HOLOGRAPHS
HOLOGRAPHY
HOLOGYNIES
HOLOHEDRAL
HOLOHEDRISM
HOLOHEDRISMS
HOLOHEDRON
HOLOHEDRONS
HOLOMETABOLIC
HOLOMETABOLISM
HOLOMETABOLISMS
HOLOMETABOLOUS
HOLOMORPHIC
HOLOPHOTAL
HOLOPHOTES
HOLOPHRASE
HOLOPHRASES
HOLOPHRASTIC
HOLOPHYTES
HOLOPHYTIC
HOLOPHYTISM
HOLOPHYTISMS
HOLOPLANKTON
HOLOPLANKTONS
HOLOSTERIC
HOLOTHURIAN
HOLOTHURIANS
HOLSTERING
HOLYSTONED
HOLYSTONES
HOLYSTONING
HOMALOGRAPHIC
HOMALOIDAL
HOMEBIRTHS
HOMEBODIES
HOMEBUYERS
HOMECOMERS
HOMECOMING
HOMECOMINGS
HOMECRAFTS
HOMELESSNESS
HOMELESSNESSES
HOMELINESS
HOMELINESSES
HOMEMAKERS
HOMEMAKING
HOMEMAKINGS
HOMEOBOXES
HOMEOMERIC
HOMEOMERIES
HOMEOMEROUS
HOMEOMORPH
HOMEOMORPHIC
HOMEOMORPHIES
HOMEOMORPHISM
HOMEOMORPHISMS
HOMEOMORPHOUS
HOMEOMORPHS
HOMEOMORPHY
HOMEOPATHIC
HOMEOPATHICALLY
HOMEOPATHIES
HOMEOPATHIST
HOMEOPATHISTS
HOMEOPATHS
HOMEOPATHY
HOMEOSTASES
HOMEOSTASIS
HOMEOSTATIC
HOMEOTELEUTON
HOMEOTELEUTONS
HOMEOTHERM
HOMEOTHERMAL
HOMEOTHERMIC
HOMEOTHERMIES
HOMEOTHERMOUS
HOMEOTHERMS
HOMEOTHERMY
HOMEOTYPIC
HOMEOTYPICAL
HOMEOWNERS
HOMEOWNERSHIP
HOMEOWNERSHIPS
HOMEPLACES
HOMEPORTED
HOMEPORTING
HOMESCHOOL
HOMESCHOOLED
HOMESCHOOLER
HOMESCHOOLERS
HOMESCHOOLING
HOMESCHOOLS
HOMESCREETCH
HOMESCREETCHES
HOMESICKNESS
HOMESICKNESSES
HOMESTALLS
HOMESTANDS
HOMESTEADED
HOMESTEADER
HOMESTEADERS
HOMESTEADING
HOMESTEADINGS
HOMESTEADS
HOMESTRETCH
HOMESTRETCHES
HOMEWORKER
HOMEWORKERS
HOMEWORKING
HOMEWORKINGS
HOMEYNESSES
HOMICIDALLY
HOMILETICAL
HOMILETICALLY
HOMILETICS
HOMINESSES
HOMINISATION
HOMINISATIONS
HOMINISING
HOMINIZATION
HOMINIZATIONS
HOMINIZING
HOMOBLASTIC
HOMOBLASTIES
HOMOBLASTY
HOMOCENTRIC
HOMOCENTRICALLY
HOMOCERCAL
HOMOCERCIES
HOMOCHLAMYDEOUS
HOMOCHROMATIC
HOMOCHROMATISM
HOMOCHROMATISMS
HOMOCHROMIES
HOMOCHROMOUS
HOMOCHROMY
HOMOCYCLIC
HOMOCYSTEINE
HOMOCYSTEINES
HOMOEOMERIC

HOMOEOMERIES
HOMOEOMEROUS
HOMOEOMERY
HOMOEOMORPH
HOMOEOMORPHIC
HOMOEOMORPHIES
HOMOEOMORPHISM
HOMOEOMORPHISMS
HOMOEOMORPHOUS
HOMOEOMORPHS
HOMOEOMORPHY
HOMOEOPATH
HOMOEOPATHIC
HOMOEOPATHIES
HOMOEOPATHIST
HOMOEOPATHISTS
HOMOEOPATHS
HOMOEOPATHY
HOMOEOSTASES
HOMOEOSTASIS
HOMOEOSTATIC
HOMOEOTELEUTON
HOMOEOTELEUTONS
HOMOEOTHERMAL
HOMOEOTHERMIC
HOMOEOTHERMOUS
HOMOEOTYPIC
HOMOEOTYPICAL
HOMOEROTIC
HOMOEROTICISM
HOMOEROTICISMS
HOMOEROTISM
HOMOEROTISMS
HOMOGAMETIC
HOMOGAMIES
HOMOGAMOUS
HOMOGENATE
HOMOGENATES
HOMOGENEITIES
HOMOGENEITY
HOMOGENEOUS
HOMOGENEOUSLY
HOMOGENEOUSNESS
HOMOGENESES
HOMOGENESIS
HOMOGENETIC
HOMOGENETICAL
HOMOGENIES
HOMOGENISATION
HOMOGENISATIONS
HOMOGENISE
HOMOGENISED
HOMOGENISER
HOMOGENISERS
HOMOGENISES
HOMOGENISING
HOMOGENIZATION
HOMOGENIZATIONS
HOMOGENIZE
HOMOGENIZED
HOMOGENIZER
HOMOGENIZERS
HOMOGENIZES
HOMOGENIZING
HOMOGENOUS
HOMOGONIES

HOMOGONOUS
HOMOGONOUSLY
HOMOGRAFTS
HOMOGRAPHIC
HOMOGRAPHS
HOMOIOMEROUS
HOMOIOTHERM
HOMOIOTHERMAL
HOMOIOTHERMIC
HOMOIOTHERMIES
HOMOIOTHERMS
HOMOIOTHERMY
HOMOIOUSIAN
HOMOIOUSIANS
HOMOLOGATE
HOMOLOGATED
HOMOLOGATES
HOMOLOGATING
HOMOLOGATION
HOMOLOGATIONS
HOMOLOGICAL
HOMOLOGICALLY
HOMOLOGIES
HOMOLOGISE
HOMOLOGISED
HOMOLOGISER
HOMOLOGISERS
HOMOLOGISES
HOMOLOGISING
HOMOLOGIZE
HOMOLOGIZED
HOMOLOGIZER
HOMOLOGIZERS
HOMOLOGIZES
HOMOLOGIZING
HOMOLOGOUMENA
HOMOLOGOUS
HOMOLOGRAPHIC
HOMOLOGUES
HOMOLOGUMENA
HOMOLOSINE
HOMOMORPHIC
HOMOMORPHIES
HOMOMORPHISM
HOMOMORPHISMS
HOMOMORPHOSES
HOMOMORPHOSIS
HOMOMORPHOUS
HOMOMORPHS
HOMOMORPHY
HOMONUCLEAR
HOMONYMIES
HOMONYMITIES
HOMONYMITY
HOMONYMOUS
HOMONYMOUSLY
HOMOOUSIAN
HOMOOUSIANS
HOMOPHILES
HOMOPHOBES
HOMOPHOBIA
HOMOPHOBIAS
HOMOPHOBIC
HOMOPHONES
HOMOPHONIC
HOMOPHONICALLY

HOMOPHONIES
HOMOPHONOUS
HOMOPHYLIES
HOMOPHYLLIC
HOMOPLASIES
HOMOPLASMIES
HOMOPLASMY
HOMOPLASTIC
HOMOPLASTICALLY
HOMOPLASTIES
HOMOPLASTY
HOMOPOLARITIES
HOMOPOLARITY
HOMOPOLYMER
HOMOPOLYMERIC
HOMOPOLYMERS
HOMOPTERAN
HOMOPTERANS
HOMOPTEROUS
HOMORGANIC
HOMOSCEDASTIC
HOMOSEXUAL
HOMOSEXUALISM
HOMOSEXUALISMS
HOMOSEXUALIST
HOMOSEXUALISTS
HOMOSEXUALITIES
HOMOSEXUALITY
HOMOSEXUALLY
HOMOSEXUALS
HOMOSOCIAL
HOMOSOCIALITIES
HOMOSOCIALITY
HOMOSPORIES
HOMOSPOROUS
HOMOSTYLIES
HOMOTAXIAL
HOMOTAXIALLY
HOMOTHALLIC
HOMOTHALLIES
HOMOTHALLISM
HOMOTHALLISMS
HOMOTHALLY
HOMOTHERMAL
HOMOTHERMIC
HOMOTHERMIES
HOMOTHERMOUS
HOMOTHERMY
HOMOTONIES
HOMOTONOUS
HOMOTRANSPLANT
HOMOTRANSPLANTS
HOMOTYPIES
HOMOUSIANS
HOMOZYGOSES
HOMOZYGOSIS
HOMOZYGOSITIES
HOMOZYGOSITY
HOMOZYGOTE
HOMOZYGOTES
HOMOZYGOTIC
HOMOZYGOUS
HOMOZYGOUSLY
HOMUNCULAR
HOMUNCULES
HOMUNCULUS

HONESTNESS
HONESTNESSES
HONEYBUNCH
HONEYBUNCHES
HONEYCOMBED
HONEYCOMBING
HONEYCOMBINGS
HONEYCOMBS
HONEYCREEPER
HONEYCREEPERS
HONEYDEWED
HONEYEATER
HONEYEATERS
HONEYGUIDE
HONEYGUIDES
HONEYMONTH
HONEYMONTHED
HONEYMONTHING
HONEYMONTHS
HONEYMOONED
HONEYMOONER
HONEYMOONERS
HONEYMOONING
HONEYMOONS
HONEYSUCKER
HONEYSUCKERS
HONEYSUCKLE
HONEYSUCKLED
HONEYSUCKLES
HONEYTRAPS
HONORABILITIES
HONORABILITY
HONORABLENESS
HONORABLENESSES
HONORARIES
HONORARILY
HONORARIUM
HONORARIUMS
HONORIFICAL
HONORIFICALLY
HONORIFICS
HONOURABLE
HONOURABLENESS
HONOURABLY
HONOURLESS
HOODEDNESS
HOODEDNESSES
HOODLUMISH
HOODLUMISM
HOODLUMISMS
HOODOOISMS
HOODWINKED
HOODWINKER
HOODWINKERS
HOODWINKING
HOOFPRINTS
HOOKCHECKS
HOOKEDNESS
HOOKEDNESSES
HOOLACHANS
HOOLIGANISM
HOOLIGANISMS
HOOPSKIRTS
HOOTANANNIE
HOOTANANNIES
HOOTANANNY

HOOTENANNIE
HOOTENANNIES
HOOTENANNY
HOOTNANNIE
HOOTNANNIES
HOPEFULNESS
HOPEFULNESSES
HOPELESSLY
HOPELESSNESS
HOPELESSNESSES
HOPLOLOGIES
HOPLOLOGIST
HOPLOLOGISTS
HOPPERCARS
HOPSACKING
HOPSACKINGS
HOPSCOTCHED
HOPSCOTCHES
HOPSCOTCHING
HOREHOUNDS
HORIATIKIS
HORIZONLESS
HORIZONTAL
HORIZONTALITIES
HORIZONTALITY
HORIZONTALLY
HORIZONTALNESS
HORIZONTALS
HORMOGONIA
HORMOGONIUM
HORMONALLY
HORMONELIKE
HORNBLENDE
HORNBLENDES
HORNBLENDIC
HORNEDNESS
HORNEDNESSES
HORNINESSES
HORNLESSNESS
HORNLESSNESSES
HORNSTONES
HORNSWOGGLE
HORNSWOGGLED
HORNSWOGGLES
HORNSWOGGLING
HORNWRACKS
HORNYHEADS
HORNYWINKS
HOROGRAPHER
HOROGRAPHERS
HOROGRAPHIES
HOROGRAPHY
HOROLOGERS
HOROLOGICAL
HOROLOGIES
HOROLOGION
HOROLOGIONS
HOROLOGIST
HOROLOGISTS
HOROLOGIUM
HOROLOGIUMS
HOROMETRICAL
HOROMETRIES
HOROSCOPES
HOROSCOPIC
HOROSCOPIES
HOROSCOPIST
HOROSCOPISTS
HORRENDOUS
HORRENDOUSLY
HORRENDOUSNESS
HORRIBLENESS
HORRIBLENESSES
HORRIDNESS
HORRIDNESSES
HORRIFICALLY
HORRIFICATION
HORRIFICATIONS
HORRIFYING
HORRIFYINGLY
HORRIPILANT
HORRIPILATE
HORRIPILATED
HORRIPILATES
HORRIPILATING
HORRIPILATION
HORRIPILATIONS
HORRISONANT
HORRISONOUS
HORSEBACKS
HORSEBEANS
HORSEBOXES
HORSEFEATHERS
HORSEFLESH
HORSEFLESHES
HORSEFLIES
HORSEHAIRS
HORSEHIDES
HORSELAUGH
HORSELAUGHS
HORSELEECH
HORSELEECHES
HORSEMANSHIP
HORSEMANSHIPS
HORSEMEATS
HORSEMINTS
HORSEPLAYER
HORSEPLAYERS
HORSEPLAYS
HORSEPONDS
HORSEPOWER
HORSEPOWERS
HORSEPOXES
HORSERACES
HORSERADISH
HORSERADISHES
HORSESHITS
HORSESHOED
HORSESHOEING
HORSESHOEINGS
HORSESHOER
HORSESHOERS
HORSESHOES
HORSETAILS
HORSEWEEDS
HORSEWHIPPED
HORSEWHIPPER
HORSEWHIPPERS
HORSEWHIPPING
HORSEWHIPS
HORSEWOMAN
HORSEWOMEN
HORSINESSES
HORTATIONS
HORTATIVELY
HORTATORILY
HORTICULTURAL
HORTICULTURALLY
HORTICULTURE
HORTICULTURES
HORTICULTURIST
HORTICULTURISTS
HOSANNAING
HOSPITABLE
HOSPITABLENESS
HOSPITABLY
HOSPITAGES
HOSPITALER
HOSPITALERS
HOSPITALES
HOSPITALISATION
HOSPITALISE
HOSPITALISED
HOSPITALISES
HOSPITALISING
HOSPITALITIES
HOSPITALITY
HOSPITALIZATION
HOSPITALIZE
HOSPITALIZED
HOSPITALIZES
HOSPITALIZING
HOSPITALLER
HOSPITALLERS
HOSTELLERS
HOSTELLING
HOSTELLINGS
HOSTELRIES
HOSTESSING
HOSTILITIES
HOTCHPOTCH
HOTCHPOTCHES
HOTDOGGERS
HOTDOGGING
HOTFOOTING
HOTHEADEDLY
HOTHEADEDNESS
HOTHEADEDNESSES
HOTHOUSING
HOTPRESSED
HOTPRESSES
HOTPRESSING
HOTTENTOTS
HOUGHMAGANDIE
HOUGHMAGANDIES
HOUNDFISHES
HOURGLASSES
HOURPLATES
HOUSEBOATER
HOUSEBOATERS
HOUSEBOATS
HOUSEBOUND
HOUSEBREAK
HOUSEBREAKER
HOUSEBREAKERS
HOUSEBREAKING
HOUSEBREAKINGS
HOUSEBREAKS
HOUSEBROKE
HOUSEBROKEN
HOUSECARLS
HOUSECLEAN
HOUSECLEANED
HOUSECLEANING
HOUSECLEANINGS
HOUSECLEANS
HOUSECOATS
HOUSECRAFT
HOUSECRAFTS
HOUSEDRESS
HOUSEDRESSES
HOUSEFATHER
HOUSEFATHERS
HOUSEFLIES
HOUSEFRONT
HOUSEFRONTS
HOUSEGUEST
HOUSEGUESTS
HOUSEHOLDER
HOUSEHOLDERS
HOUSEHOLDERSHIP
HOUSEHOLDS
HOUSEHUSBAND
HOUSEHUSBANDS
HOUSEKEEPER
HOUSEKEEPERS
HOUSEKEEPING
HOUSEKEEPINGS
HOUSEKEEPS
HOUSELEEKS
HOUSELESSNESS
HOUSELESSNESSES
HOUSELIGHTS
HOUSELINES
HOUSELLING
HOUSELLINGS
HOUSEMAIDS
HOUSEMASTER
HOUSEMASTERS
HOUSEMATES
HOUSEMISTRESS
HOUSEMISTRESSES
HOUSEMOTHER
HOUSEMOTHERS
HOUSEPAINTER
HOUSEPAINTERS
HOUSEPARENT
HOUSEPARENTS
HOUSEPERSON
HOUSEPERSONS
HOUSEPLANT
HOUSEPLANTS
HOUSEROOMS
HOUSESITTING
HOUSEWARES
HOUSEWARMING
HOUSEWARMINGS
HOUSEWIFELINESS
HOUSEWIFELY
HOUSEWIFERIES
HOUSEWIFERY
HOUSEWIFESHIP
HOUSEWIFESHIPS
HOUSEWIFESKEP

HOUSEWIFESKEPS
HOUSEWIFEY
HOUSEWIVES
HOUSEWORKER
HOUSEWORKERS
HOUSEWORKS
HOUSTONIAS
HOVERCRAFT
HOVERCRAFTS
HOVERFLIES
HOVERINGLY
HOVERPORTS
HOVERTRAIN
HOVERTRAINS
HOWLROUNDS
HOWSOMDEVER
HOWSOMEVER
HOWTOWDIES
HOYDENHOOD
HOYDENHOODS
HOYDENISHNESS
HOYDENISHNESSES
HOYDENISMS
HUBRISTICALLY
HUCKABACKS
HUCKLEBERRIES
HUCKLEBERRY
HUCKLEBERRYING
HUCKLEBERRYINGS
HUCKLEBONE
HUCKLEBONES
HUCKSTERAGE
HUCKSTERAGES
HUCKSTERED
HUCKSTERESS
HUCKSTERESSES
HUCKSTERIES
HUCKSTERING
HUCKSTERISM
HUCKSTERISMS
HUCKSTRESS
HUCKSTRESSES
HUDIBRASTIC
HUFFINESSES
HUFFISHNESS
HUFFISHNESSES
HUGENESSES
HUGEOUSNESS
HUGEOUSNESSES
HULLABALLOO
HULLABALLOOS
HULLABALOO
HULLABALOOS
HUMANENESS
HUMANENESSES
HUMANHOODS
HUMANISATION
HUMANISATIONS
HUMANISERS
HUMANISING
HUMANISTIC
HUMANISTICALLY
HUMANITARIAN
HUMANITARIANISM
HUMANITARIANIST
HUMANITARIANS
HUMANITIES
HUMANIZATION
HUMANIZATIONS
HUMANIZERS
HUMANIZING
HUMANKINDS
HUMANNESSES
HUMBLEBEES
HUMBLENESS
HUMBLENESSES
HUMBLESSES
HUMBLINGLY
HUMBUCKERS
HUMBUGGABLE
HUMBUGGERIES
HUMBUGGERS
HUMBUGGERY
HUMBUGGING
HUMDINGERS
HUMDRUMNESS
HUMDRUMNESSES
HUMDUDGEON
HUMDUDGEONS
HUMECTANTS
HUMECTATED
HUMECTATES
HUMECTATING
HUMECTATION
HUMECTATIONS
HUMECTIVES
HUMGRUFFIANS
HUMGRUFFIN
HUMGRUFFINS
HUMICOLOUS
HUMIDIFICATION
HUMIDIFICATIONS
HUMIDIFIED
HUMIDIFIER
HUMIDIFIERS
HUMIDIFIES
HUMIDIFYING
HUMIDISTAT
HUMIDISTATS
HUMIDITIES
HUMIDNESSES
HUMIFICATION
HUMIFICATIONS
HUMILIATED
HUMILIATES
HUMILIATING
HUMILIATINGLY
HUMILIATION
HUMILIATIONS
HUMILIATIVE
HUMILIATOR
HUMILIATORS
HUMILIATORY
HUMILITIES
HUMMELLERS
HUMMELLING
HUMMINGBIRD
HUMMINGBIRDS
HUMMOCKING
HUMORALISM
HUMORALISMS
HUMORALIST
HUMORALISTS
HUMORESQUE
HUMORESQUES
HUMORISTIC
HUMORLESSLY
HUMORLESSNESS
HUMORLESSNESSES
HUMOROUSLY
HUMOROUSNESS
HUMOROUSNESSES
HUMOURLESS
HUMOURLESSNESS
HUMOURSOME
HUMOURSOMENESS
HUMPBACKED
HUMPINESSES
HUNCHBACKED
HUNCHBACKS
HUNDREDERS
HUNDREDFOLD
HUNDREDFOLDS
HUNDREDORS
HUNDREDTHS
HUNDREDWEIGHT
HUNDREDWEIGHTS
HUNGERINGLY
HUNGRINESS
HUNGRINESSES
HUNTIEGOWK
HUNTIEGOWKS
HUNTRESSES
HUNTSMANSHIP
HUNTSMANSHIPS
HUPAITHRIC
HURLBARROW
HURLBARROWS
HURRICANES
HURRICANOES
HURRIEDNESS
HURRIEDNESSES
HURRYINGLY
HURTFULNESS
HURTFULNESSES
HURTLEBERRIES
HURTLEBERRY
HURTLESSLY
HURTLESSNESS
HURTLESSNESSES
HUSBANDAGE
HUSBANDAGES
HUSBANDERS
HUSBANDING
HUSBANDLAND
HUSBANDLANDS
HUSBANDLESS
HUSBANDLIKE
HUSBANDMAN
HUSBANDMEN
HUSBANDRIES
HUSHABYING
HUSHPUPPIES
HUSKINESSES
HYACINTHINE
HYALINISATION
HYALINISATIONS
HYALINISED
HYALINISES
HYALINISING
HYALINIZATION
HYALINIZATIONS
HYALINIZED
HYALINIZES
HYALINIZING
HYALOMELAN
HYALOMELANE
HYALOMELANES
HYALOMELANS
HYALONEMAS
HYALOPHANE
HYALOPHANES
HYALOPLASM
HYALOPLASMIC
HYALOPLASMS
HYALURONIC
HYALURONIDASE
HYALURONIDASES
HYBRIDISABLE
HYBRIDISATION
HYBRIDISATIONS
HYBRIDISED
HYBRIDISER
HYBRIDISERS
HYBRIDISES
HYBRIDISING
HYBRIDISMS
HYBRIDISTS
HYBRIDITIES
HYBRIDIZABLE
HYBRIDIZATION
HYBRIDIZATIONS
HYBRIDIZED
HYBRIDIZER
HYBRIDIZERS
HYBRIDIZES
HYBRIDIZING
HYBRIDOMAS
HYDANTOINS
HYDATHODES
HYDATIDIFORM
HYDNOCARPATE
HYDNOCARPATES
HYDNOCARPIC
HYDRAEMIAS
HYDRAGOGUE
HYDRAGOGUES
HYDRALAZINE
HYDRALAZINES
HYDRANGEAS
HYDRARGYRAL
HYDRARGYRIA
HYDRARGYRIAS
HYDRARGYRIC
HYDRARGYRISM
HYDRARGYRISMS
HYDRARGYRUM
HYDRARGYRUMS
HYDRARTHROSES
HYDRARTHROSIS
HYDRASTINE
HYDRASTINES
HYDRASTININE
HYDRASTININES

HYDRASTISES
HYDRATIONS
HYDRAULICALLY
HYDRAULICKED
HYDRAULICKING
HYDRAULICS
HYDRAZIDES
HYDRAZINES
HYDRICALLY
HYDROACOUSTICS
HYDROBIOLOGICAL
HYDROBIOLOGIES
HYDROBIOLOGIST
HYDROBIOLOGISTS
HYDROBIOLOGY
HYDROBROMIC
HYDROCARBON
HYDROCARBONS
HYDROCASTS
HYDROCELES
HYDROCELLULOSE
HYDROCELLULOSES
HYDROCEPHALIC
HYDROCEPHALICS
HYDROCEPHALIES
HYDROCEPHALOID
HYDROCEPHALOUS
HYDROCEPHALUS
HYDROCEPHALUSES
HYDROCEPHALY
HYDROCHLORIC
HYDROCHLORIDE
HYDROCHLORIDES
HYDROCHORE
HYDROCHORES
HYDROCHORIC
HYDROCOLLOID
HYDROCOLLOIDAL
HYDROCOLLOIDS
HYDROCORAL
HYDROCORALLINE
HYDROCORALLINES
HYDROCORALS
HYDROCORTISONE
HYDROCORTISONES
HYDROCRACK
HYDROCRACKED
HYDROCRACKER
HYDROCRACKERS
HYDROCRACKING
HYDROCRACKINGS
HYDROCRACKS
HYDROCYANIC
HYDRODYNAMIC
HYDRODYNAMICAL
HYDRODYNAMICIST
HYDRODYNAMICS
HYDROELASTIC
HYDROELECTRIC
HYDROEXTRACTOR
HYDROEXTRACTORS
HYDROFLUORIC
HYDROFOILS
HYDROFORMING
HYDROFORMINGS
HYDROGENASE
HYDROGENASES
HYDROGENATE
HYDROGENATED
HYDROGENATES
HYDROGENATING
HYDROGENATION
HYDROGENATIONS
HYDROGENATOR
HYDROGENATORS
HYDROGENISATION
HYDROGENISE
HYDROGENISED
HYDROGENISES
HYDROGENISING
HYDROGENIZATION
HYDROGENIZE
HYDROGENIZED
HYDROGENIZES
HYDROGENIZING
HYDROGENOLYSES
HYDROGENOLYSIS
HYDROGENOUS
HYDROGEOLOGICAL
HYDROGEOLOGIES
HYDROGEOLOGIST
HYDROGEOLOGISTS
HYDROGEOLOGY
HYDROGRAPH
HYDROGRAPHER
HYDROGRAPHERS
HYDROGRAPHIC
HYDROGRAPHICAL
HYDROGRAPHIES
HYDROGRAPHS
HYDROGRAPHY
HYDROKINETIC
HYDROKINETICAL
HYDROKINETICS
HYDROLASES
HYDROLOGIC
HYDROLOGICAL
HYDROLOGICALLY
HYDROLOGIES
HYDROLOGIST
HYDROLOGISTS
HYDROLYSABLE
HYDROLYSATE
HYDROLYSATES
HYDROLYSATION
HYDROLYSATIONS
HYDROLYSED
HYDROLYSER
HYDROLYSERS
HYDROLYSES
HYDROLYSING
HYDROLYSIS
HYDROLYTES
HYDROLYTIC
HYDROLYTICALLY
HYDROLYZABLE
HYDROLYZATE
HYDROLYZATES
HYDROLYZATION
HYDROLYZATIONS
HYDROLYZED
HYDROLYZER
HYDROLYZERS
HYDROLYZES
HYDROLYZING
HYDROMAGNETIC
HYDROMAGNETICS
HYDROMANCER
HYDROMANCERS
HYDROMANCIES
HYDROMANCY
HYDROMANIA
HYDROMANIAS
HYDROMANTIC
HYDROMECHANICAL
HYDROMECHANICS
HYDROMEDUSA
HYDROMEDUSAE
HYDROMEDUSAN
HYDROMEDUSANS
HYDROMEDUSAS
HYDROMEDUSOID
HYDROMEDUSOIDS
HYDROMETALLURGY
HYDROMETEOR
HYDROMETEORS
HYDROMETER
HYDROMETERS
HYDROMETRIC
HYDROMETRICAL
HYDROMETRICALLY
HYDROMETRIES
HYDROMETRY
HYDROMORPHIC
HYDRONAUTS
HYDRONEPHROSES
HYDRONEPHROSIS
HYDRONEPHROTIC
HYDRONICALLY
HYDRONIUMS
HYDROPATHIC
HYDROPATHICAL
HYDROPATHICALLY
HYDROPATHICS
HYDROPATHIES
HYDROPATHIST
HYDROPATHISTS
HYDROPATHS
HYDROPATHY
HYDROPEROXIDE
HYDROPEROXIDES
HYDROPHANE
HYDROPHANES
HYDROPHANOUS
HYDROPHILE
HYDROPHILES
HYDROPHILIC
HYDROPHILICITY
HYDROPHILIES
HYDROPHILITE
HYDROPHILITES
HYDROPHILOUS
HYDROPHILY
HYDROPHOBIA
HYDROPHOBIAS
HYDROPHOBIC
HYDROPHOBICITY
HYDROPHOBOUS
HYDROPHONE
HYDROPHONES
HYDROPHYTE
HYDROPHYTES
HYDROPHYTIC
HYDROPHYTON
HYDROPHYTONS
HYDROPHYTOUS
HYDROPLANE
HYDROPLANED
HYDROPLANES
HYDROPLANING
HYDROPNEUMATIC
HYDROPOLYP
HYDROPOLYPS
HYDROPONIC
HYDROPONICALLY
HYDROPONICS
HYDROPOWER
HYDROPOWERS
HYDROPSIES
HYDROPULTS
HYDROQUINOL
HYDROQUINOLS
HYDROQUINONE
HYDROQUINONES
HYDROSCOPE
HYDROSCOPES
HYDROSCOPIC
HYDROSCOPICAL
HYDROSERES
HYDROSOLIC
HYDROSOMAL
HYDROSOMATA
HYDROSOMATOUS
HYDROSOMES
HYDROSPACE
HYDROSPACES
HYDROSPHERE
HYDROSPHERES
HYDROSPHERIC
HYDROSTATIC
HYDROSTATICAL
HYDROSTATICALLY
HYDROSTATICS
HYDROSTATS
HYDROSULPHATE
HYDROSULPHATES
HYDROSULPHIDE
HYDROSULPHIDES
HYDROSULPHITE
HYDROSULPHITES
HYDROSULPHURIC
HYDROSULPHUROUS
HYDROTACTIC
HYDROTAXES
HYDROTAXIS
HYDROTHECA
HYDROTHECAE
HYDROTHERAPIC
HYDROTHERAPIES
HYDROTHERAPIST
HYDROTHERAPISTS
HYDROTHERAPY
HYDROTHERMAL
HYDROTHERMALLY

HYDROTHORACES
HYDROTHORACIC
HYDROTHORAX
HYDROTHORAXES
HYDROTROPIC
HYDROTROPICALLY
HYDROTROPISM
HYDROTROPISMS
HYDROVANES
HYDROXIDES
HYDROXONIUM
HYDROXONIUMS
HYDROXYAPATITE
HYDROXYAPATITES
HYDROXYBUTYRATE
HYDROXYLAMINE
HYDROXYLAMINES
HYDROXYLAPATITE
HYDROXYLASE
HYDROXYLASES
HYDROXYLATE
HYDROXYLATED
HYDROXYLATES
HYDROXYLATING
HYDROXYLATION
HYDROXYLATIONS
HYDROXYLIC
HYDROXYPROLINE
HYDROXYPROLINES
HYDROXYUREA
HYDROXYUREAS
HYDROXYZINE
HYDROXYZINES
HYDROZINCITE
HYDROZINCITES
HYDROZOANS
HYETOGRAPH
HYETOGRAPHIC
HYETOGRAPHICAL
HYETOGRAPHIES
HYETOGRAPHS
HYETOGRAPHY
HYETOLOGIES
HYETOMETER
HYETOMETERS
HYETOMETROGRAPH
HYGIENICALLY
HYGIENISTS
HYGRISTORS
HYGROCHASIES
HYGROCHASTIC
HYGROCHASY
HYGRODEIKS
HYGROGRAPH
HYGROGRAPHIC
HYGROGRAPHICAL
HYGROGRAPHS
HYGROLOGIES
HYGROMETER
HYGROMETERS
HYGROMETRIC
HYGROMETRICAL
HYGROMETRICALLY
HYGROMETRIES
HYGROMETRY
HYGROPHILE
HYGROPHILES
HYGROPHILOUS
HYGROPHOBE
HYGROPHYTE
HYGROPHYTES
HYGROPHYTIC
HYGROSCOPE
HYGROSCOPES
HYGROSCOPIC
HYGROSCOPICAL
HYGROSCOPICALLY
HYGROSCOPICITY
HYGROSTATS
HYLOGENESES
HYLOGENESIS
HYLOMORPHIC
HYLOMORPHISM
HYLOMORPHISMS
HYLOPATHISM
HYLOPATHISMS
HYLOPATHIST
HYLOPATHISTS
HYLOPHAGOUS
HYLOPHYTES
HYLOTHEISM
HYLOTHEISMS
HYLOTHEIST
HYLOTHEISTS
HYLOTOMOUS
HYLOZOICAL
HYLOZOISMS
HYLOZOISTIC
HYLOZOISTICALLY
HYLOZOISTS
HYMENEALLY
HYMENOPHORE
HYMENOPHORES
HYMENOPTERA
HYMENOPTERAN
HYMENOPTERANS
HYMENOPTERON
HYMENOPTERONS
HYMENOPTEROUS
HYMNODICAL
HYMNODISTS
HYMNOGRAPHER
HYMNOGRAPHERS
HYMNOGRAPHIES
HYMNOGRAPHY
HYMNOLOGIC
HYMNOLOGICAL
HYMNOLOGIES
HYMNOLOGIST
HYMNOLOGISTS
HYOPLASTRA
HYOPLASTRAL
HYOPLASTRON
HYOSCYAMINE
HYOSCYAMINES
HYOSCYAMUS
HYOSCYAMUSES
HYPABYSSAL
HYPABYSSALLY
HYPAESTHESIA
HYPAESTHESIAS
HYPAESTHESIC
HYPAETHRAL
HYPAETHRON
HYPAETHRONS
HYPALGESIA
HYPALGESIAS
HYPALGESIC
HYPALLACTIC
HYPALLAGES
HYPANTHIAL
HYPANTHIUM
HYPERACIDITIES
HYPERACIDITY
HYPERACTION
HYPERACTIONS
HYPERACTIVE
HYPERACTIVES
HYPERACTIVITIES
HYPERACTIVITY
HYPERACUITIES
HYPERACUITY
HYPERACUSES
HYPERACUSIS
HYPERACUTE
HYPERACUTENESS
HYPERADRENALISM
HYPERAEMIA
HYPERAEMIAS
HYPERAEMIC
HYPERAESTHESIA
HYPERAESTHESIAS
HYPERAESTHESIC
HYPERAESTHETIC
HYPERAGGRESSIVE
HYPERALERT
HYPERALGESIA
HYPERALGESIAS
HYPERALGESIC
HYPERAROUSAL
HYPERAROUSALS
HYPERAWARE
HYPERAWARENESS
HYPERBARIC
HYPERBARICALLY
HYPERBATIC
HYPERBATICALLY
HYPERBATON
HYPERBATONS
HYPERBOLAE
HYPERBOLAS
HYPERBOLES
HYPERBOLIC
HYPERBOLICAL
HYPERBOLICALLY
HYPERBOLISE
HYPERBOLISED
HYPERBOLISES
HYPERBOLISING
HYPERBOLISM
HYPERBOLISMS
HYPERBOLIST
HYPERBOLISTS
HYPERBOLIZE
HYPERBOLIZED
HYPERBOLIZES
HYPERBOLIZING
HYPERBOLOID
HYPERBOLOIDAL
HYPERBOLOIDS
HYPERBOREAN
HYPERBOREANS
HYPERCALCAEMIA
HYPERCALCAEMIAS
HYPERCALCEMIA
HYPERCALCEMIAS
HYPERCALCEMIC
HYPERCAPNIA
HYPERCAPNIAS
HYPERCAPNIC
HYPERCARBIA
HYPERCARBIAS
HYPERCATABOLISM
HYPERCATALECTIC
HYPERCATALEXES
HYPERCATALEXIS
HYPERCAUTIOUS
HYPERCHARGE
HYPERCHARGED
HYPERCHARGES
HYPERCHARGING
HYPERCIVILISED
HYPERCIVILIZED
HYPERCOAGULABLE
HYPERCOLOUR
HYPERCOLOURS
HYPERCOMPLEX
HYPERCONSCIOUS
HYPERCORRECT
HYPERCORRECTION
HYPERCORRECTLY
HYPERCRITIC
HYPERCRITICAL
HYPERCRITICALLY
HYPERCRITICISE
HYPERCRITICISED
HYPERCRITICISES
HYPERCRITICISM
HYPERCRITICISMS
HYPERCRITICIZE
HYPERCRITICIZED
HYPERCRITICIZES
HYPERCRITICS
HYPERCUBES
HYPERDACTYL
HYPERDACTYLIES
HYPERDACTYLY
HYPERDORIAN
HYPERDULIA
HYPERDULIAS
HYPERDULIC
HYPERDULICAL
HYPEREFFICIENT
HYPEREMESES
HYPEREMESIS
HYPEREMETIC
HYPEREMIAS
HYPEREMOTIONAL
HYPERENDEMIC
HYPERENERGETIC
HYPERESTHESIA
HYPERESTHESIAS
HYPERESTHETIC
HYPEREUTECTIC

HYPEREUTECTOID
HYPEREXCITABLE
HYPEREXCITED
HYPEREXCITEMENT
HYPEREXCRETION
HYPEREXCRETIONS
HYPEREXTEND
HYPEREXTENDED
HYPEREXTENDING
HYPEREXTENDS
HYPEREXTENSION
HYPEREXTENSIONS
HYPERFASTIDIOUS
HYPERFOCAL
HYPERFUNCTION
HYPERFUNCTIONAL
HYPERFUNCTIONS
HYPERGAMIES
HYPERGAMOUS
HYPERGEOMETRIC
HYPERGLYCAEMIA
HYPERGLYCAEMIAS
HYPERGLYCAEMIC
HYPERGLYCEMIA
HYPERGLYCEMIAS
HYPERGLYCEMIC
HYPERGOLIC
HYPERGOLICALLY
HYPERHIDROSES
HYPERHIDROSIS
HYPERICUMS
HYPERIDROSES
HYPERIDROSIS
HYPERIMMUNE
HYPERIMMUNISE
HYPERIMMUNISED
HYPERIMMUNISES
HYPERIMMUNISING
HYPERIMMUNIZE
HYPERIMMUNIZED
HYPERIMMUNIZES
HYPERIMMUNIZING
HYPERINFLATED
HYPERINFLATION
HYPERINFLATIONS
HYPERINOSES
HYPERINOSIS
HYPERINOTIC
HYPERINSULINISM
HYPERINTENSE
HYPERINVOLUTION
HYPERIRRITABLE
HYPERKERATOSES
HYPERKERATOSIS
HYPERKERATOTIC
HYPERKINESES
HYPERKINESIA
HYPERKINESIAS
HYPERKINESIS
HYPERKINETIC
HYPERLINKED
HYPERLINKING
HYPERLINKS
HYPERLIPEMIA
HYPERLIPEMIAS
HYPERLIPEMIC
HYPERLIPIDAEMIA
HYPERLIPIDEMIA
HYPERLIPIDEMIAS
HYPERLYDIAN
HYPERMANIA
HYPERMANIAS
HYPERMANIC
HYPERMARKET
HYPERMARKETS
HYPERMARTS
HYPERMASCULINE
HYPERMEDIA
HYPERMEDIAS
HYPERMETABOLIC
HYPERMETABOLISM
HYPERMETER
HYPERMETERS
HYPERMETRIC
HYPERMETRICAL
HYPERMETROPIA
HYPERMETROPIAS
HYPERMETROPIC
HYPERMETROPICAL
HYPERMETROPIES
HYPERMETROPY
HYPERMNESIA
HYPERMNESIAS
HYPERMNESIC
HYPERMOBILITIES
HYPERMOBILITY
HYPERMODERN
HYPERMODERNIST
HYPERMODERNISTS
HYPERMUTABILITY
HYPERMUTABLE
HYPERNATRAEMIA
HYPERNATRAEMIAS
HYPERNOVAE
HYPERNOVAS
HYPERNYMIES
HYPEROPIAS
HYPEROREXIA
HYPEROREXIAS
HYPEROSMIA
HYPEROSMIAS
HYPEROSTOSES
HYPEROSTOSIS
HYPEROSTOTIC
HYPERPARASITE
HYPERPARASITES
HYPERPARASITIC
HYPERPARASITISM
HYPERPHAGIA
HYPERPHAGIAS
HYPERPHAGIC
HYPERPHRYGIAN
HYPERPHYSICAL
HYPERPHYSICALLY
HYPERPIGMENTED
HYPERPITUITARY
HYPERPLANE
HYPERPLANES
HYPERPLASIA
HYPERPLASIAS
HYPERPLASTIC
HYPERPLOID
HYPERPLOIDIES
HYPERPLOIDS
HYPERPLOIDY
HYPERPNEAS
HYPERPNEIC
HYPERPNOEA
HYPERPNOEAS
HYPERPOLARISE
HYPERPOLARISED
HYPERPOLARISES
HYPERPOLARISING
HYPERPOLARIZE
HYPERPOLARIZED
HYPERPOLARIZES
HYPERPOLARIZING
HYPERPOWER
HYPERPOWERS
HYPERPRODUCER
HYPERPRODUCERS
HYPERPRODUCTION
HYPERPROSEXIA
HYPERPROSEXIAS
HYPERPYRETIC
HYPERPYREXIA
HYPERPYREXIAL
HYPERPYREXIAS
HYPERRATIONAL
HYPERREACTIVE
HYPERREACTIVITY
HYPERREACTOR
HYPERREACTORS
HYPERREALISM
HYPERREALISMS
HYPERREALIST
HYPERREALISTIC
HYPERREALITIES
HYPERREALITY
HYPERREALS
HYPERRESPONSIVE
HYPERROMANTIC
HYPERROMANTICS
HYPERSALINE
HYPERSALINITIES
HYPERSALINITY
HYPERSALIVATION
HYPERSARCOMA
HYPERSARCOMAS
HYPERSARCOMATA
HYPERSARCOSES
HYPERSARCOSIS
HYPERSECRETION
HYPERSECRETIONS
HYPERSENSITISE
HYPERSENSITISED
HYPERSENSITISES
HYPERSENSITIVE
HYPERSENSITIZE
HYPERSENSITIZED
HYPERSENSITIZES
HYPERSENSUAL
HYPERSEXUAL
HYPERSEXUALITY
HYPERSOMNIA
HYPERSOMNIAS
HYPERSOMNOLENCE
HYPERSONIC
HYPERSONICALLY
HYPERSONICS
HYPERSPACE
HYPERSPACES
HYPERSPATIAL
HYPERSTATIC
HYPERSTHENE
HYPERSTHENES
HYPERSTHENIA
HYPERSTHENIAS
HYPERSTHENIC
HYPERSTHENITE
HYPERSTHENITES
HYPERSTIMULATE
HYPERSTIMULATED
HYPERSTIMULATES
HYPERSTRESS
HYPERSTRESSES
HYPERSURFACE
HYPERSURFACES
HYPERTENSE
HYPERTENSION
HYPERTENSIONS
HYPERTENSIVE
HYPERTENSIVES
HYPERTEXTS
HYPERTHERMAL
HYPERTHERMIA
HYPERTHERMIAS
HYPERTHERMIC
HYPERTHERMIES
HYPERTHERMY
HYPERTHYMIA
HYPERTHYMIAS
HYPERTHYROID
HYPERTHYROIDISM
HYPERTHYROIDS
HYPERTONIA
HYPERTONIAS
HYPERTONIC
HYPERTONICITIES
HYPERTONICITY
HYPERTROPHIC
HYPERTROPHICAL
HYPERTROPHIED
HYPERTROPHIES
HYPERTROPHOUS
HYPERTROPHY
HYPERTROPHYING
HYPERTYPICAL
HYPERURBANISM
HYPERURBANISMS
HYPERURICEMIA
HYPERURICEMIAS
HYPERVELOCITIES
HYPERVELOCITY
HYPERVENTILATE
HYPERVENTILATED
HYPERVENTILATES
HYPERVIGILANCE
HYPERVIGILANCES
HYPERVIGILANT
HYPERVIRULENT
HYPERVISCOSITY
HYPESTHESIA
HYPESTHESIAS

HYPESTHESIC
HYPHENATED
HYPHENATES
HYPHENATING
HYPHENATION
HYPHENATIONS
HYPHENISATION
HYPHENISATIONS
HYPHENISED
HYPHENISES
HYPHENISING
HYPHENISMS
HYPHENIZATION
HYPHENIZATIONS
HYPHENIZED
HYPHENIZES
HYPHENIZING
HYPHENLESS
HYPNAGOGIC
HYPNOANALYSES
HYPNOANALYSIS
HYPNOANALYTIC
HYPNOGENESES
HYPNOGENESIS
HYPNOGENETIC
HYPNOGENIC
HYPNOGENIES
HYPNOGENOUS
HYPNOGOGIC
HYPNOIDISE
HYPNOIDISED
HYPNOIDISES
HYPNOIDISING
HYPNOIDIZE
HYPNOIDIZED
HYPNOIDIZES
HYPNOIDIZING
HYPNOLOGIC
HYPNOLOGICAL
HYPNOLOGIES
HYPNOLOGIST
HYPNOLOGISTS
HYPNOPAEDIA
HYPNOPAEDIAS
HYPNOPOMPIC
HYPNOTHERAPIES
HYPNOTHERAPIST
HYPNOTHERAPISTS
HYPNOTHERAPY
HYPNOTICALLY
HYPNOTISABILITY
HYPNOTISABLE
HYPNOTISATION
HYPNOTISATIONS
HYPNOTISED
HYPNOTISER
HYPNOTISERS
HYPNOTISES
HYPNOTISING
HYPNOTISMS
HYPNOTISTIC
HYPNOTISTS
HYPNOTIZABILITY
HYPNOTIZABLE
HYPNOTIZATION
HYPNOTIZATIONS
HYPNOTIZED
HYPNOTIZER
HYPNOTIZERS
HYPNOTIZES
HYPNOTIZING
HYPOACIDITIES
HYPOACIDITY
HYPOAEOLIAN
HYPOALLERGENIC
HYPOBLASTIC
HYPOBLASTS
HYPOCALCEMIA
HYPOCALCEMIAS
HYPOCALCEMIC
HYPOCAUSTS
HYPOCENTER
HYPOCENTERS
HYPOCENTRAL
HYPOCENTRE
HYPOCENTRES
HYPOCHLORITE
HYPOCHLORITES
HYPOCHLOROUS
HYPOCHONDRIA
HYPOCHONDRIAC
HYPOCHONDRIACAL
HYPOCHONDRIACS
HYPOCHONDRIAS
HYPOCHONDRIASES
HYPOCHONDRIASIS
HYPOCHONDRIASM
HYPOCHONDRIASMS
HYPOCHONDRIAST
HYPOCHONDRIASTS
HYPOCHONDRIUM
HYPOCORISM
HYPOCORISMA
HYPOCORISMAS
HYPOCORISMS
HYPOCORISTIC
HYPOCORISTICAL
HYPOCOTYLOUS
HYPOCOTYLS
HYPOCRISIES
HYPOCRITES
HYPOCRITIC
HYPOCRITICAL
HYPOCRITICALLY
HYPOCRYSTALLINE
HYPOCYCLOID
HYPOCYCLOIDAL
HYPOCYCLOIDS
HYPODERMAL
HYPODERMAS
HYPODERMIC
HYPODERMICALLY
HYPODERMICS
HYPODERMIS
HYPODERMISES
HYPODIPLOID
HYPODIPLOIDIES
HYPODIPLOIDY
HYPODORIAN
HYPOEUTECTIC
HYPOEUTECTOID
HYPOGAEOUS
HYPOGASTRIA
HYPOGASTRIC
HYPOGASTRIUM
HYPOGENOUS
HYPOGLOSSAL
HYPOGLOSSALS
HYPOGLYCAEMIA
HYPOGLYCAEMIAS
HYPOGLYCAEMIC
HYPOGLYCEMIA
HYPOGLYCEMIAS
HYPOGLYCEMIC
HYPOGLYCEMICS
HYPOGNATHISM
HYPOGNATHISMS
HYPOGNATHOUS
HYPOGYNIES
HYPOGYNOUS
HYPOKALEMIA
HYPOKALEMIAS
HYPOKALEMIC
HYPOLIMNIA
HYPOLIMNION
HYPOLIMNIONS
HYPOLYDIAN
HYPOMAGNESAEMIA
HYPOMAGNESEMIA
HYPOMAGNESEMIAS
HYPOMANIAS
HYPOMANICS
HYPOMENORRHEA
HYPOMENORRHEAS
HYPOMENORRHOEA
HYPOMENORRHOEAS
HYPOMIXOLYDIAN
HYPOMORPHIC
HYPOMORPHS
HYPONASTIC
HYPONASTICALLY
HYPONASTIES
HYPONATRAEMIA
HYPONATRAEMIAS
HYPONITRITE
HYPONITRITES
HYPONITROUS
HYPONYMIES
HYPOPHARYNGES
HYPOPHARYNX
HYPOPHARYNXES
HYPOPHOSPHATE
HYPOPHOSPHATES
HYPOPHOSPHITE
HYPOPHOSPHITES
HYPOPHOSPHORIC
HYPOPHOSPHOROUS
HYPOPHRYGIAN
HYPOPHYGES
HYPOPHYSEAL
HYPOPHYSECTOMY
HYPOPHYSES
HYPOPHYSIAL
HYPOPHYSIS
HYPOPITUITARISM
HYPOPITUITARY
HYPOPLASIA
HYPOPLASIAS
HYPOPLASTIC
HYPOPLASTIES
HYPOPLASTRA
HYPOPLASTRON
HYPOPLASTY
HYPOPLOIDIES
HYPOPLOIDS
HYPOPLOIDY
HYPOPNOEAS
HYPOSENSITISE
HYPOSENSITISED
HYPOSENSITISES
HYPOSENSITISING
HYPOSENSITIZE
HYPOSENSITIZED
HYPOSENSITIZES
HYPOSENSITIZING
HYPOSPADIAS
HYPOSPADIASES
HYPOSTASES
HYPOSTASIS
HYPOSTASISATION
HYPOSTASISE
HYPOSTASISED
HYPOSTASISES
HYPOSTASISING
HYPOSTASIZATION
HYPOSTASIZE
HYPOSTASIZED
HYPOSTASIZES
HYPOSTASIZING
HYPOSTATIC
HYPOSTATICAL
HYPOSTATICALLY
HYPOSTATISATION
HYPOSTATISE
HYPOSTATISED
HYPOSTATISES
HYPOSTATISING
HYPOSTATIZATION
HYPOSTATIZE
HYPOSTATIZED
HYPOSTATIZES
HYPOSTATIZING
HYPOSTHENIA
HYPOSTHENIAS
HYPOSTHENIC
HYPOSTOMES
HYPOSTRESS
HYPOSTRESSES
HYPOSTROPHE
HYPOSTROPHES
HYPOSTYLES
HYPOSULPHATE
HYPOSULPHATES
HYPOSULPHITE
HYPOSULPHITES
HYPOSULPHURIC
HYPOSULPHUROUS
HYPOTACTIC
HYPOTENSION
HYPOTENSIONS
HYPOTENSIVE
HYPOTENSIVES
HYPOTENUSE
HYPOTENUSES

HYPOTHALAMI
HYPOTHALAMIC
HYPOTHALAMUS
HYPOTHECAE
HYPOTHECARY
HYPOTHECATE
HYPOTHECATED
HYPOTHECATES
HYPOTHECATING
HYPOTHECATION
HYPOTHECATIONS
HYPOTHECATOR
HYPOTHECATORS
HYPOTHENUSE
HYPOTHENUSES
HYPOTHERMAL
HYPOTHERMIA
HYPOTHERMIAS
HYPOTHERMIC
HYPOTHESES
HYPOTHESIS
HYPOTHESISE
HYPOTHESISED
HYPOTHESISER
HYPOTHESISERS
HYPOTHESISES
HYPOTHESISING
HYPOTHESIST
HYPOTHESISTS
HYPOTHESIZE
HYPOTHESIZED
HYPOTHESIZER
HYPOTHESIZERS
HYPOTHESIZES
HYPOTHESIZING
HYPOTHETIC
HYPOTHETICAL
HYPOTHETICALLY
HYPOTHETISE
HYPOTHETISED
HYPOTHETISES
HYPOTHETISING
HYPOTHETIZE
HYPOTHETIZED
HYPOTHETIZES
HYPOTHETIZING
HYPOTHYMIA
HYPOTHYMIAS
HYPOTHYROID
HYPOTHYROIDISM
HYPOTHYROIDISMS
HYPOTHYROIDS
HYPOTONIAS
HYPOTONICITIES
HYPOTONICITY
HYPOTROCHOID
HYPOTROCHOIDS
HYPOTYPOSES
HYPOTYPOSIS
HYPOVENTILATION
HYPOXAEMIA
HYPOXAEMIAS
HYPOXAEMIC
HYPOXANTHINE
HYPOXANTHINES
HYPOXEMIAS
HYPSOCHROME
HYPSOCHROMES
HYPSOCHROMIC
HYPSOGRAPHIC
HYPSOGRAPHICAL
HYPSOGRAPHIES
HYPSOGRAPHY
HYPSOMETER
HYPSOMETERS
HYPSOMETRIC
HYPSOMETRICAL
HYPSOMETRICALLY
HYPSOMETRIES
HYPSOMETRIST
HYPSOMETRISTS
HYPSOMETRY
HYPSOPHOBE
HYPSOPHOBES
HYPSOPHOBIA
HYPSOPHOBIAS
HYPSOPHYLL
HYPSOPHYLLARY
HYPSOPHYLLS
HYRACOIDEAN
HYRACOIDEANS
HYSTERANTHOUS
HYSTERECTOMIES
HYSTERECTOMISE
HYSTERECTOMISED
HYSTERECTOMISES
HYSTERECTOMIZE
HYSTERECTOMIZED
HYSTERECTOMIZES
HYSTERECTOMY
HYSTERESES
HYSTERESIAL
HYSTERESIS
HYSTERETIC
HYSTERETICALLY
HYSTERICAL
HYSTERICALLY
HYSTERICKY
HYSTERITIS
HYSTERITISES
HYSTEROGENIC
HYSTEROGENIES
HYSTEROGENY
HYSTEROIDAL
HYSTEROMANIA
HYSTEROMANIAS
HYSTEROTOMIES
HYSTEROTOMY
HYSTRICOMORPH
HYSTRICOMORPHIC
HYSTRICOMORPHS

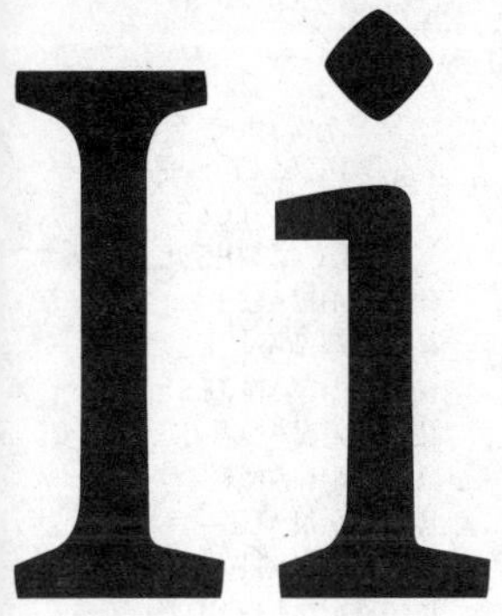

AMBICALLY
AMBOGRAPHER
AMBOGRAPHERS
ATROCHEMICAL
ATROCHEMIST
ATROCHEMISTRY
ATROCHEMISTS
ATROGENIC
ATROGENICALLY
ATROGENICITIES
ATROGENICITY
ATROGENIES
BUPROFENS
CEBOATERS
CEBOATING
CEBOATINGS
CEBREAKER
CEBREAKERS
CEBREAKING
CHNEUMONS
CHNOFOSSIL
CHNOFOSSILS
CHNOGRAPHIC
CHNOGRAPHICAL
CHNOGRAPHIES
CHNOGRAPHY
CHNOLITES
CHNOLOGICAL
CHNOLOGIES
CHTHYOCOLLA
CHTHYOCOLLAS
CHTHYODORULITE
CHTHYODORYLITE
CHTHYOFAUNA
CHTHYOFAUNAE
CHTHYOFAUNAL
CHTHYOFAUNAS
CHTHYOIDAL
ICHTHYOIDS
ICHTHYOLATRIES
ICHTHYOLATROUS
ICHTHYOLATRY
ICHTHYOLITE
ICHTHYOLITES
ICHTHYOLITIC
ICHTHYOLOGIC
ICHTHYOLOGICAL
ICHTHYOLOGIES
ICHTHYOLOGIST
ICHTHYOLOGISTS
ICHTHYOLOGY
ICHTHYOPHAGIES
ICHTHYOPHAGIST
ICHTHYOPHAGISTS
ICHTHYOPHAGOUS
ICHTHYOPHAGY
ICHTHYOPSID
ICHTHYOPSIDAN
ICHTHYOPSIDANS
ICHTHYOPSIDS
ICHTHYORNIS
ICHTHYORNISES
ICHTHYOSAUR
ICHTHYOSAURI
ICHTHYOSAURIAN
ICHTHYOSAURIANS
ICHTHYOSAURS
ICHTHYOSAURUS
ICHTHYOSAURUSES
ICHTHYOSES
ICHTHYOSIS
ICHTHYOTIC
ICKINESSES
ICONICALLY
ICONICITIES
ICONIFYING
ICONOCLASM
ICONOCLASMS
ICONOCLAST
ICONOCLASTIC
ICONOCLASTS
ICONOGRAPHER
ICONOGRAPHERS
ICONOGRAPHIC
ICONOGRAPHICAL
ICONOGRAPHIES
ICONOGRAPHY
ICONOLATER
ICONOLATERS
ICONOLATRIES
ICONOLATROUS
ICONOLATRY
ICONOLOGICAL
ICONOLOGIES
ICONOLOGIST
ICONOLOGISTS
ICONOMACHIES
ICONOMACHIST
ICONOMACHISTS
ICONOMACHY
ICONOMATIC
ICONOMATICISM
ICONOMATICISMS
ICONOMETER
ICONOMETERS
ICONOMETRIES
ICONOMETRY
ICONOPHILISM
ICONOPHILISMS
ICONOPHILIST
ICONOPHILISTS
ICONOSCOPE
ICONOSCOPES
ICONOSTASES
ICONOSTASIS
ICOSAHEDRA
ICOSAHEDRAL
ICOSAHEDRON
ICOSAHEDRONS
ICOSANDRIAN
ICOSANDROUS
ICOSITETRAHEDRA
ICTERICALS
ICTERITIOUS
IDEALISATION
IDEALISATIONS
IDEALISERS
IDEALISING
IDEALISTIC
IDEALISTICALLY
IDEALITIES
IDEALIZATION
IDEALIZATIONS
IDEALIZERS
IDEALIZING
IDEALNESSES
IDEALOGIES
IDEALOGUES
IDEATIONAL
IDEATIONALLY
IDEMPOTENCIES
IDEMPOTENCY
IDEMPOTENT
IDEMPOTENTS
IDENTICALLY
IDENTICALNESS
IDENTICALNESSES
IDENTIFIABLE
IDENTIFIABLY
IDENTIFICATION
IDENTIFICATIONS
IDENTIFIED

IDENTIFIER
IDENTIFIERS
IDENTIFIES
IDENTIFYING
IDENTIKITS
IDENTITIES
IDEOGRAMIC
IDEOGRAMMATIC
IDEOGRAMMIC
IDEOGRAPHIC
IDEOGRAPHICAL
IDEOGRAPHICALLY
IDEOGRAPHIES
IDEOGRAPHS
IDEOGRAPHY
IDEOLOGICAL
IDEOLOGICALLY
IDEOLOGIES
IDEOLOGISE
IDEOLOGISED
IDEOLOGISES
IDEOLOGISING
IDEOLOGIST
IDEOLOGISTS
IDEOLOGIZE
IDEOLOGIZED
IDEOLOGIZES
IDEOLOGIZING
IDEOLOGUES
IDEOPHONES
IDEOPRAXIST
IDEOPRAXISTS
IDIOBLASTIC
IDIOBLASTS
IDIOGLOSSIA
IDIOGLOSSIAS
IDIOGRAPHIC
IDIOGRAPHS
IDIOLECTAL
IDIOLECTIC
IDIOMATICAL
IDIOMATICALLY
IDIOMATICALNESS
IDIOMATICNESS
IDIOMATICNESSES
IDIOMORPHIC
IDIOMORPHICALLY
IDIOMORPHISM
IDIOMORPHISMS
IDIOPATHIC
IDIOPATHICALLY
IDIOPATHIES
IDIOPHONES
IDIOPHONIC
IDIOPLASMATIC
IDIOPLASMIC
IDIOPLASMS
IDIORHYTHMIC
IDIORRHYTHMIC
IDIOSYNCRASIES
IDIOSYNCRASY
IDIOSYNCRATIC
IDIOSYNCRATICAL
IDIOTHERMOUS
IDIOTICALLY
IDIOTICALNESS
IDIOTICALNESSES
IDIOTICONS
IDLENESSES
IDOLATRESS
IDOLATRESSES
IDOLATRIES
IDOLATRISE
IDOLATRISED
IDOLATRISER
IDOLATRISERS
IDOLATRISES
IDOLATRISING
IDOLATRIZE
IDOLATRIZED
IDOLATRIZER
IDOLATRIZERS
IDOLATRIZES
IDOLATRIZING
IDOLATROUS
IDOLATROUSLY
IDOLATROUSNESS
IDOLISATION
IDOLISATIONS
IDOLIZATION
IDOLIZATIONS
IDOLOCLAST
IDOLOCLASTS
IDONEITIES
IDOXURIDINE
IDOXURIDINES
IDYLLICALLY
IFFINESSES
IGNESCENTS
IGNIMBRITE
IGNIMBRITES
IGNIPOTENT
IGNITABILITIES
IGNITABILITY
IGNITIBILITIES
IGNITIBILITY
IGNOBILITIES
IGNOBILITY
IGNOBLENESS
IGNOBLENESSES
IGNOMINIES
IGNOMINIOUS
IGNOMINIOUSLY
IGNOMINIOUSNESS
IGNORAMUSES
IGNORANCES
IGNORANTLY
IGNORANTNESS
IGNORANTNESSES
IGNORATION
IGNORATIONS
IGUANODONS
ILEOSTOMIES
ILLAQUEABLE
ILLAQUEATE
ILLAQUEATED
ILLAQUEATES
ILLAQUEATING
ILLAQUEATION
ILLAQUEATIONS
ILLATIVELY
ILLAUDABLE
ILLAUDABLY
ILLEGALISATION
ILLEGALISATIONS
ILLEGALISE
ILLEGALISED
ILLEGALISES
ILLEGALISING
ILLEGALITIES
ILLEGALITY
ILLEGALIZATION
ILLEGALIZATIONS
ILLEGALIZE
ILLEGALIZED
ILLEGALIZES
ILLEGALIZING
ILLEGIBILITIES
ILLEGIBILITY
ILLEGIBLENESS
ILLEGIBLENESSES
ILLEGITIMACIES
ILLEGITIMACY
ILLEGITIMATE
ILLEGITIMATED
ILLEGITIMATELY
ILLEGITIMATES
ILLEGITIMATING
ILLEGITIMATION
ILLEGITIMATIONS
ILLIBERALISE
ILLIBERALISED
ILLIBERALISES
ILLIBERALISING
ILLIBERALISM
ILLIBERALISMS
ILLIBERALITIES
ILLIBERALITY
ILLIBERALIZE
ILLIBERALIZED
ILLIBERALIZES
ILLIBERALIZING
ILLIBERALLY
ILLIBERALNESS
ILLIBERALNESSES
ILLICITNESS
ILLICITNESSES
ILLIMITABILITY
ILLIMITABLE
ILLIMITABLENESS
ILLIMITABLY
ILLIMITATION
ILLIMITATIONS
ILLIQUATION
ILLIQUATIONS
ILLIQUIDITIES
ILLIQUIDITY
ILLITERACIES
ILLITERACY
ILLITERATE
ILLITERATELY
ILLITERATENESS
ILLITERATES
ILLOCUTION
ILLOCUTIONARY
ILLOCUTIONS
ILLOGICALITIES
ILLOGICALITY
ILLOGICALLY
ILLOGICALNESS
ILLOGICALNESSES
ILLUMINABLE
ILLUMINANCE
ILLUMINANCES
ILLUMINANT
ILLUMINANTS
ILLUMINATE
ILLUMINATED
ILLUMINATES
ILLUMINATI
ILLUMINATING
ILLUMINATINGLY
ILLUMINATION
ILLUMINATIONAL
ILLUMINATIONS
ILLUMINATIVE
ILLUMINATO
ILLUMINATOR
ILLUMINATORS
ILLUMINERS
ILLUMINING
ILLUMINISM
ILLUMINISMS
ILLUMINIST
ILLUMINISTS
ILLUSIONAL
ILLUSIONARY
ILLUSIONED
ILLUSIONISM
ILLUSIONISMS
ILLUSIONIST
ILLUSIONISTIC
ILLUSIONISTS
ILLUSIVELY
ILLUSIVENESS
ILLUSIVENESSES
ILLUSORILY
ILLUSORINESS
ILLUSORINESSES
ILLUSTRATABLE
ILLUSTRATE
ILLUSTRATED
ILLUSTRATEDS
ILLUSTRATES
ILLUSTRATING
ILLUSTRATION
ILLUSTRATIONAL
ILLUSTRATIONS
ILLUSTRATIVE
ILLUSTRATIVELY
ILLUSTRATOR
ILLUSTRATORS
ILLUSTRATORY
ILLUSTRIOUS
ILLUSTRIOUSLY
ILLUSTRIOUSNESS
ILLUSTRISSIMO
ILLUVIATED
ILLUVIATES
ILLUVIATING
ILLUVIATION
ILLUVIATIONS
IMAGINABLE
IMAGINABLENESS

MAGINABLY
MAGINARIES
MAGINARILY
MAGINARINESS
IMAGINARINESSES
IMAGINATION
MAGINATIONAL
MAGINATIONS
IMAGINATIVE
IMAGINATIVELY
IMAGINATIVENESS
IMAGININGS
IMAGINISTS
IMAGISTICALLY
IMBALANCED
IMBALANCES
IMBECILELY
IMBECILICALLY
IMBECILITIES
IMBECILITY
IMBIBITION
IMBIBITIONAL
IMBIBITIONS
IMBITTERED
IMBITTERING
IMBOLDENED
IMBOLDENING
IMBORDERED
IMBORDERING
IMBOSOMING
IMBOWERING
IMBRANGLED
IMBRANGLES
IMBRANGLING
IMBRICATED
IMBRICATELY
IMBRICATES
IMBRICATING
IMBRICATION
IMBRICATIONS
IMBROCCATA
IMBROCCATAS
IMBROGLIOS
IMBROWNING
IMBRUEMENT
IMBRUEMENTS
IMBUEMENTS
IMIDAZOLES
IMINAZOLES
IMINOUREAS
IMIPRAMINE
IMIPRAMINES
IMITABILITIES
IMITABILITY
IMITABLENESS
IMITABLENESSES
IMITANCIES
IMITATIONAL
IMITATIONS
IMITATIVELY
IMITATIVENESS
IMITATIVENESSES
IMMACULACIES
IMMACULACY
IMMACULATE
IMMACULATELY
IMMACULATENESS
IMMANACLED
IMMANACLES
IMMANACLING
IMMANATION
IMMANATIONS
IMMANENCES
IMMANENCIES
IMMANENTAL
IMMANENTISM
IMMANENTISMS
IMMANENTIST
IMMANENTISTIC
IMMANENTISTS
IMMANENTLY
IMMANITIES
IMMANTLING
IMMARCESCIBLE
IMMARGINATE
IMMATERIAL
IMMATERIALISE
IMMATERIALISED
IMMATERIALISES
IMMATERIALISING
IMMATERIALISM
IMMATERIALISMS
IMMATERIALIST
IMMATERIALISTS
IMMATERIALITIES
IMMATERIALITY
IMMATERIALIZE
IMMATERIALIZED
IMMATERIALIZES
IMMATERIALIZING
IMMATERIALLY
IMMATERIALNESS
IMMATURELY
IMMATURENESS
IMMATURENESSES
IMMATURITIES
IMMATURITY
IMMEASURABILITY
IMMEASURABLE
IMMEASURABLY
IMMEASURED
IMMEDIACIES
IMMEDIATELY
IMMEDIATENESS
IMMEDIATENESSES
IMMEDIATISM
IMMEDIATISMS
IMMEDICABLE
IMMEDICABLENESS
IMMEDICABLY
IMMEMORIAL
IMMEMORIALLY
IMMENSENESS
IMMENSENESSES
IMMENSITIES
IMMENSURABILITY
IMMENSURABLE
IMMERGENCE
IMMERGENCES
IMMERITOUS
IMMERSIBLE
IMMERSIONISM
IMMERSIONISMS
IMMERSIONIST
IMMERSIONISTS
IMMERSIONS
IMMETHODICAL
IMMETHODICALLY
IMMIGRANTS
IMMIGRATED
IMMIGRATES
IMMIGRATING
IMMIGRATION
IMMIGRATIONAL
IMMIGRATIONS
IMMIGRATOR
IMMIGRATORS
IMMIGRATORY
IMMINENCES
IMMINENCIES
IMMINENTLY
IMMINENTNESS
IMMINENTNESSES
IMMINGLING
IMMINUTION
IMMINUTIONS
IMMISCIBILITIES
IMMISCIBILITY
IMMISCIBLE
IMMISCIBLY
IMMISERATION
IMMISERATIONS
IMMISERISATION
IMMISERISATIONS
IMMISERISE
IMMISERISED
IMMISERISES
IMMISERISING
IMMISERIZATION
IMMISERIZATIONS
IMMISERIZE
IMMISERIZED
IMMISERIZES
IMMISERIZING
IMMISSIONS
IMMITIGABILITY
IMMITIGABLE
IMMITIGABLY
IMMITTANCE
IMMITTANCES
IMMIXTURES
IMMOBILISATION
IMMOBILISATIONS
IMMOBILISE
IMMOBILISED
IMMOBILISER
IMMOBILISERS
IMMOBILISES
IMMOBILISING
IMMOBILISM
IMMOBILISMS
IMMOBILITIES
IMMOBILITY
IMMOBILIZATION
IMMOBILIZATIONS
IMMOBILIZE
IMMOBILIZED
IMMOBILIZER
IMMOBILIZERS
IMMOBILIZES
IMMOBILIZING
IMMODERACIES
IMMODERACY
IMMODERATE
IMMODERATELY
IMMODERATENESS
IMMODERATION
IMMODERATIONS
IMMODESTIES
IMMODESTLY
IMMOLATING
IMMOLATION
IMMOLATIONS
IMMOLATORS
IMMOMENTOUS
IMMORALISM
IMMORALISMS
IMMORALIST
IMMORALISTS
IMMORALITIES
IMMORALITY
IMMORTALISATION
IMMORTALISE
IMMORTALISED
IMMORTALISER
IMMORTALISERS
IMMORTALISES
IMMORTALISING
IMMORTALITIES
IMMORTALITY
IMMORTALIZATION
IMMORTALIZE
IMMORTALIZED
IMMORTALIZER
IMMORTALIZERS
IMMORTALIZES
IMMORTALIZING
IMMORTALLY
IMMORTELLE
IMMORTELLES
IMMOTILITIES
IMMOTILITY
IMMOVABILITIES
IMMOVABILITY
IMMOVABLENESS
IMMOVABLENESSES
IMMOVABLES
IMMOVEABILITIES
IMMOVEABILITY
IMMOVEABLE
IMMOVEABLENESS
IMMOVEABLES
IMMOVEABLY
IMMUNIFACIENT
IMMUNISATION
IMMUNISATIONS
IMMUNISERS
IMMUNISING
IMMUNITIES
IMMUNIZATION
IMMUNIZATIONS
IMMUNIZERS
IMMUNIZING
IMMUNOASSAY

IMMUNOASSAYABLE
IMMUNOASSAYIST
IMMUNOASSAYISTS
IMMUNOASSAYS
IMMUNOBLOT
IMMUNOBLOTS
IMMUNOBLOTTING
IMMUNOBLOTTINGS
IMMUNOCHEMICAL
IMMUNOCHEMIST
IMMUNOCHEMISTRY
IMMUNOCHEMISTS
IMMUNOCOMPETENT
IMMUNOCOMPLEX
IMMUNOCOMPLEXES
IMMUNODEFICIENT
IMMUNODIAGNOSES
IMMUNODIAGNOSIS
IMMUNODIFFUSION
IMMUNOGENESES
IMMUNOGENESIS
IMMUNOGENETIC
IMMUNOGENETICAL
IMMUNOGENETICS
IMMUNOGENIC
IMMUNOGENICALLY
IMMUNOGENICITY
IMMUNOGENS
IMMUNOGLOBULIN
IMMUNOGLOBULINS
IMMUNOLOGIC
IMMUNOLOGICAL
IMMUNOLOGICALLY
IMMUNOLOGIES
IMMUNOLOGIST
IMMUNOLOGISTS
IMMUNOLOGY
IMMUNOMODULATOR
IMMUNOPATHOLOGY
IMMUNOPHORESES
IMMUNOPHORESIS
IMMUNOREACTION
IMMUNOREACTIONS
IMMUNOREACTIVE
IMMUNOSORBENT
IMMUNOSORBENTS
IMMUNOSUPPRESS
IMMUNOTHERAPIES
IMMUNOTHERAPY
IMMUNOTOXIC
IMMUNOTOXIN
IMMUNOTOXINS
IMMUREMENT
IMMUREMENTS
IMMUTABILITIES
IMMUTABILITY
IMMUTABLENESS
IMMUTABLENESSES
IMPACTIONS
IMPACTITES
IMPAINTING
IMPAIRABLE
IMPAIRINGS
IMPAIRMENT
IMPAIRMENTS
IMPALEMENT
IMPALEMENTS
IMPALPABILITIES
IMPALPABILITY
IMPALPABLE
IMPALPABLY
IMPALUDISM
IMPALUDISMS
IMPANATION
IMPANATIONS
IMPANELING
IMPANELLED
IMPANELLING
IMPANELMENT
IMPANELMENTS
IMPANNELLED
IMPANNELLING
IMPARADISE
IMPARADISED
IMPARADISES
IMPARADISING
IMPARIDIGITATE
IMPARIPINNATE
IMPARISYLLABIC
IMPARITIES
IMPARKATION
IMPARKATIONS
IMPARLANCE
IMPARLANCES
IMPARTABLE
IMPARTATION
IMPARTATIONS
IMPARTIALITIES
IMPARTIALITY
IMPARTIALLY
IMPARTIALNESS
IMPARTIALNESSES
IMPARTIBILITIES
IMPARTIBILITY
IMPARTIBLE
IMPARTIBLY
IMPARTMENT
IMPARTMENTS
IMPASSABILITIES
IMPASSABILITY
IMPASSABLE
IMPASSABLENESS
IMPASSABLY
IMPASSIBILITIES
IMPASSIBILITY
IMPASSIBLE
IMPASSIBLENESS
IMPASSIBLY
IMPASSIONATE
IMPASSIONED
IMPASSIONEDLY
IMPASSIONEDNESS
IMPASSIONING
IMPASSIONS
IMPASSIVELY
IMPASSIVENESS
IMPASSIVENESSES
IMPASSIVITIES
IMPASSIVITY
IMPASTATION
IMPASTATIONS
IMPATIENCE
IMPATIENCES
IMPATIENTLY
IMPEACHABILITY
IMPEACHABLE
IMPEACHERS
IMPEACHING
IMPEACHMENT
IMPEACHMENTS
IMPEARLING
IMPECCABILITIES
IMPECCABILITY
IMPECCABLE
IMPECCABLY
IMPECCANCIES
IMPECCANCY
IMPECUNIOSITIES
IMPECUNIOSITY
IMPECUNIOUS
IMPECUNIOUSLY
IMPECUNIOUSNESS
IMPEDANCES
IMPEDIMENT
IMPEDIMENTA
IMPEDIMENTAL
IMPEDIMENTARY
IMPEDIMENTS
IMPEDINGLY
IMPEDITIVE
IMPELLENTS
IMPENDENCE
IMPENDENCES
IMPENDENCIES
IMPENDENCY
IMPENETRABILITY
IMPENETRABLE
IMPENETRABLY
IMPENETRATE
IMPENETRATED
IMPENETRATES
IMPENETRATING
IMPENETRATION
IMPENETRATIONS
IMPENITENCE
IMPENITENCES
IMPENITENCIES
IMPENITENCY
IMPENITENT
IMPENITENTLY
IMPENITENTNESS
IMPENITENTS
IMPERATIVAL
IMPERATIVE
IMPERATIVELY
IMPERATIVENESS
IMPERATIVES
IMPERATORIAL
IMPERATORIALLY
IMPERATORS
IMPERATORSHIP
IMPERATORSHIPS
IMPERCEABLE
IMPERCEIVABLE
IMPERCEPTIBLE
IMPERCEPTIBLY
IMPERCEPTION
IMPERCEPTIONS
IMPERCEPTIVE
IMPERCEPTIVELY
IMPERCEPTIVITY
IMPERCIPIENCE
IMPERCIPIENCES
IMPERCIPIENT
IMPERFECTIBLE
IMPERFECTION
IMPERFECTIONS
IMPERFECTIVE
IMPERFECTIVELY
IMPERFECTIVES
IMPERFECTLY
IMPERFECTNESS
IMPERFECTNESSES
IMPERFECTS
IMPERFORABLE
IMPERFORATE
IMPERFORATED
IMPERFORATION
IMPERFORATIONS
IMPERIALISE
IMPERIALISED
IMPERIALISES
IMPERIALISING
IMPERIALISM
IMPERIALISMS
IMPERIALIST
IMPERIALISTIC
IMPERIALISTS
IMPERIALITIES
IMPERIALITY
IMPERIALIZE
IMPERIALIZED
IMPERIALIZES
IMPERIALIZING
IMPERIALLY
IMPERIALNESS
IMPERIALNESSES
IMPERILING
IMPERILLED
IMPERILLING
IMPERILMENT
IMPERILMENTS
IMPERIOUSLY
IMPERIOUSNESS
IMPERIOUSNESSES
IMPERISHABILITY
IMPERISHABLE
IMPERISHABLES
IMPERISHABLY
IMPERMANENCE
IMPERMANENCES
IMPERMANENCIES
IMPERMANENCY
IMPERMANENT
IMPERMANENTLY
IMPERMEABILITY
IMPERMEABLE
IMPERMEABLENESS
IMPERMEABLY
IMPERMISSIBLE
IMPERMISSIBLY
IMPERSCRIPTIBLE
IMPERSEVERANT
IMPERSISTENT

IMPERSONAL
IMPERSONALISE
IMPERSONALISED
IMPERSONALISES
IMPERSONALISING
IMPERSONALITIES
IMPERSONALITY
IMPERSONALIZE
IMPERSONALIZED
IMPERSONALIZES
IMPERSONALIZING
IMPERSONALLY
IMPERSONATE
IMPERSONATED
IMPERSONATES
IMPERSONATING
IMPERSONATION
IMPERSONATIONS
IMPERSONATOR
IMPERSONATORS
IMPERTINENCE
IMPERTINENCES
IMPERTINENCIES
IMPERTINENCY
IMPERTINENT
IMPERTINENTLY
IMPERTURBABLE
IMPERTURBABLY
IMPERTURBATION
IMPERTURBATIONS
IMPERVIABILITY
IMPERVIABLE
IMPERVIABLENESS
IMPERVIOUS
IMPERVIOUSLY
IMPERVIOUSNESS
IMPETICOSSED
IMPETICOSSES
IMPETICOSSING
IMPETIGINES
IMPETIGINOUS
IMPETRATED
IMPETRATES
IMPETRATING
IMPETRATION
IMPETRATIONS
IMPETRATIVE
IMPETRATOR
IMPETRATORS
IMPETRATORY
IMPETUOSITIES
IMPETUOSITY
IMPETUOUSLY
IMPETUOUSNESS
IMPETUOUSNESSES
IMPICTURED
IMPIERCEABLE
IMPIGNORATE
IMPIGNORATED
IMPIGNORATES
IMPIGNORATING
IMPIGNORATION
IMPIGNORATIONS
IMPINGEMENT
IMPINGEMENTS
IMPIOUSNESS
IMPIOUSNESSES
IMPISHNESS
IMPISHNESSES
IMPLACABILITIES
IMPLACABILITY
IMPLACABLE
IMPLACABLENESS
IMPLACABLY
IMPLACENTAL
IMPLANTABLE
IMPLANTATION
IMPLANTATIONS
IMPLANTERS
IMPLANTING
IMPLAUSIBILITY
IMPLAUSIBLE
IMPLAUSIBLENESS
IMPLAUSIBLY
IMPLEACHED
IMPLEACHES
IMPLEACHING
IMPLEADABLE
IMPLEADERS
IMPLEADING
IMPLEDGING
IMPLEMENTAL
IMPLEMENTATION
IMPLEMENTATIONS
IMPLEMENTED
IMPLEMENTER
IMPLEMENTERS
IMPLEMENTING
IMPLEMENTOR
IMPLEMENTORS
IMPLEMENTS
IMPLETIONS
IMPLEXIONS
IMPLEXUOUS
IMPLICATED
IMPLICATES
IMPLICATING
IMPLICATION
IMPLICATIONAL
IMPLICATIONS
IMPLICATIVE
IMPLICATIVELY
IMPLICATIVENESS
IMPLICATURE
IMPLICATURES
IMPLICITIES
IMPLICITLY
IMPLICITNESS
IMPLICITNESSES
IMPLODENTS
IMPLORATION
IMPLORATIONS
IMPLORATOR
IMPLORATORS
IMPLORATORY
IMPLORINGLY
IMPLOSIONS
IMPLOSIVELY
IMPLOSIVES
IMPLUNGING
IMPOCKETED
IMPOCKETING
IMPOLDERED
IMPOLDERING
IMPOLICIES
IMPOLITELY
IMPOLITENESS
IMPOLITENESSES
IMPOLITEST
IMPOLITICAL
IMPOLITICALLY
IMPOLITICLY
IMPOLITICNESS
IMPOLITICNESSES
IMPONDERABILIA
IMPONDERABILITY
IMPONDERABLE
IMPONDERABLES
IMPONDERABLY
IMPONDEROUS
IMPORTABILITIES
IMPORTABILITY
IMPORTABLE
IMPORTANCE
IMPORTANCES
IMPORTANCIES
IMPORTANCY
IMPORTANTLY
IMPORTATION
IMPORTATIONS
IMPORTINGS
IMPORTUNACIES
IMPORTUNACY
IMPORTUNATE
IMPORTUNATELY
IMPORTUNATENESS
IMPORTUNED
IMPORTUNELY
IMPORTUNER
IMPORTUNERS
IMPORTUNES
IMPORTUNING
IMPORTUNINGS
IMPORTUNITIES
IMPORTUNITY
IMPOSINGLY
IMPOSINGNESS
IMPOSINGNESSES
IMPOSITION
IMPOSITIONS
IMPOSSIBILISM
IMPOSSIBILISMS
IMPOSSIBILIST
IMPOSSIBILISTS
IMPOSSIBILITIES
IMPOSSIBILITY
IMPOSSIBLE
IMPOSSIBLENESS
IMPOSSIBLES
IMPOSSIBLY
IMPOSTHUMATE
IMPOSTHUMATED
IMPOSTHUMATES
IMPOSTHUMATING
IMPOSTHUMATION
IMPOSTHUMATIONS
IMPOSTHUME
IMPOSTHUMED
IMPOSTHUMES
IMPOSTOROUS
IMPOSTROUS
IMPOSTUMATE
IMPOSTUMATED
IMPOSTUMATES
IMPOSTUMATING
IMPOSTUMATION
IMPOSTUMATIONS
IMPOSTUMED
IMPOSTUMES
IMPOSTURES
IMPOSTUROUS
IMPOTENCES
IMPOTENCIES
IMPOTENTLY
IMPOTENTNESS
IMPOTENTNESSES
IMPOUNDABLE
IMPOUNDAGE
IMPOUNDAGES
IMPOUNDERS
IMPOUNDING
IMPOUNDMENT
IMPOUNDMENTS
IMPOVERISH
IMPOVERISHED
IMPOVERISHER
IMPOVERISHERS
IMPOVERISHES
IMPOVERISHING
IMPOVERISHMENT
IMPOVERISHMENTS
IMPOWERING
IMPRACTICABLE
IMPRACTICABLY
IMPRACTICAL
IMPRACTICALITY
IMPRACTICALLY
IMPRACTICALNESS
IMPRECATED
IMPRECATES
IMPRECATING
IMPRECATION
IMPRECATIONS
IMPRECATORY
IMPRECISELY
IMPRECISENESS
IMPRECISENESSES
IMPRECISION
IMPRECISIONS
IMPREDICATIVE
IMPREGNABILITY
IMPREGNABLE
IMPREGNABLENESS
IMPREGNABLY
IMPREGNANT
IMPREGNANTS
IMPREGNATABLE
IMPREGNATE
IMPREGNATED
IMPREGNATES
IMPREGNATING
IMPREGNATION
IMPREGNATIONS
IMPREGNATOR

IMPREGNATORS
IMPREGNING
IMPRESARIO
IMPRESARIOS
IMPRESCRIPTIBLE
IMPRESCRIPTIBLY
IMPRESSERS
IMPRESSIBILITY
IMPRESSIBLE
IMPRESSING
IMPRESSION
IMPRESSIONABLE
IMPRESSIONAL
IMPRESSIONALLY
IMPRESSIONISM
IMPRESSIONISMS
IMPRESSIONIST
IMPRESSIONISTIC
IMPRESSIONISTS
IMPRESSIONS
IMPRESSIVE
IMPRESSIVELY
IMPRESSIVENESS
IMPRESSMENT
IMPRESSMENTS
IMPRESSURE
IMPRESSURES
IMPRIMATUR
IMPRIMATURS
IMPRINTERS
IMPRINTING
IMPRINTINGS
IMPRISONABLE
IMPRISONED
IMPRISONER
IMPRISONERS
IMPRISONING
IMPRISONMENT
IMPRISONMENTS
IMPROBABILITIES
IMPROBABILITY
IMPROBABLE
IMPROBABLENESS
IMPROBABLY
IMPROBATION
IMPROBATIONS
IMPROBITIES
IMPROMPTUS
IMPROPERLY
IMPROPERNESS
IMPROPERNESSES
IMPROPRIATE
IMPROPRIATED
IMPROPRIATES
IMPROPRIATING
IMPROPRIATION
IMPROPRIATIONS
IMPROPRIATOR
IMPROPRIATORS
IMPROPRIETIES
IMPROPRIETY
IMPROVABILITIES
IMPROVABILITY
IMPROVABLE
IMPROVABLENESS
IMPROVABLY
IMPROVEMENT
IMPROVEMENTS
IMPROVIDENCE
IMPROVIDENCES
IMPROVIDENT
IMPROVIDENTLY
IMPROVINGLY
IMPROVISATE
IMPROVISATED
IMPROVISATES
IMPROVISATING
IMPROVISATION
IMPROVISATIONAL
IMPROVISATIONS
IMPROVISATOR
IMPROVISATORE
IMPROVISATORES
IMPROVISATORI
IMPROVISATORIAL
IMPROVISATORS
IMPROVISATORY
IMPROVISATRICES
IMPROVISATRIX
IMPROVISATRIXES
IMPROVISED
IMPROVISER
IMPROVISERS
IMPROVISES
IMPROVISING
IMPROVISOR
IMPROVISORS
IMPROVVISATORE
IMPROVVISATORES
IMPROVVISATRICE
IMPRUDENCE
IMPRUDENCES
IMPRUDENTLY
IMPSONITES
IMPUDENCES
IMPUDENCIES
IMPUDENTLY
IMPUDENTNESS
IMPUDENTNESSES
IMPUDICITIES
IMPUDICITY
IMPUGNABLE
IMPUGNATION
IMPUGNATIONS
IMPUGNMENT
IMPUGNMENTS
IMPUISSANCE
IMPUISSANCES
IMPUISSANT
IMPULSIONS
IMPULSIVELY
IMPULSIVENESS
IMPULSIVENESSES
IMPULSIVITIES
IMPULSIVITY
IMPUNDULUS
IMPUNITIES
IMPURENESS
IMPURENESSES
IMPURITIES
IMPURPLING
IMPUTABILITIES
IMPUTABILITY
IMPUTABLENESS
IMPUTABLENESSES
IMPUTATION
IMPUTATIONS
IMPUTATIVE
IMPUTATIVELY
INABILITIES
INABSTINENCE
INABSTINENCES
INACCESSIBILITY
INACCESSIBLE
INACCESSIBLY
INACCURACIES
INACCURACY
INACCURATE
INACCURATELY
INACCURATENESS
INACTIVATE
INACTIVATED
INACTIVATES
INACTIVATING
INACTIVATION
INACTIVATIONS
INACTIVELY
INACTIVENESS
INACTIVENESSES
INACTIVITIES
INACTIVITY
INADAPTABLE
INADAPTATION
INADAPTATIONS
INADAPTIVE
INADEQUACIES
INADEQUACY
INADEQUATE
INADEQUATELY
INADEQUATENESS
INADEQUATES
INADMISSIBILITY
INADMISSIBLE
INADMISSIBLY
INADVERTENCE
INADVERTENCES
INADVERTENCIES
INADVERTENCY
INADVERTENT
INADVERTENTLY
INADVISABILITY
INADVISABLE
INADVISABLENESS
INADVISABLY
INALIENABILITY
INALIENABLE
INALIENABLENESS
INALIENABLY
INALTERABILITY
INALTERABLE
INALTERABLENESS
INALTERABLY
INAMORATAS
INAMORATOS
INANENESSES
INANIMATELY
INANIMATENESS
INANIMATENESSES
INANIMATION
INANIMATIONS
INANITIONS
INAPPARENT
INAPPARENTLY
INAPPEASABLE
INAPPELLABLE
INAPPETENCE
INAPPETENCES
INAPPETENCIES
INAPPETENCY
INAPPETENT
INAPPLICABILITY
INAPPLICABLE
INAPPLICABLY
INAPPOSITE
INAPPOSITELY
INAPPOSITENESS
INAPPRECIABLE
INAPPRECIABLY
INAPPRECIATION
INAPPRECIATIONS
INAPPRECIATIVE
INAPPREHENSIBLE
INAPPREHENSION
INAPPREHENSIONS
INAPPREHENSIVE
INAPPROACHABLE
INAPPROACHABLY
INAPPROPRIATE
INAPPROPRIATELY
INAPTITUDE
INAPTITUDES
INAPTNESSES
INARGUABLE
INARGUABLY
INARTICULACIES
INARTICULACY
INARTICULATE
INARTICULATELY
INARTICULATES
INARTICULATION
INARTICULATIONS
INARTIFICIAL
INARTIFICIALLY
INARTISTIC
INARTISTICALLY
INATTENTION
INATTENTIONS
INATTENTIVE
INATTENTIVELY
INATTENTIVENESS
INAUDIBILITIES
INAUDIBILITY
INAUDIBLENESS
INAUDIBLENESSES
INAUGURALS
INAUGURATE
INAUGURATED
INAUGURATES
INAUGURATING
INAUGURATION
INAUGURATIONS
INAUGURATOR
INAUGURATORS
INAUGURATORY

NAUSPICIOUS
NAUSPICIOUSLY
NAUTHENTIC
NAUTHENTICITY
NBOUNDING
NBREATHED
NBREATHES
NBREATHING
NBREEDERS
NBREEDING
NBREEDINGS
NBRINGING
NBRINGINGS
NCALCULABILITY
NCALCULABLE
NCALCULABLY
NCALESCENCE
NCALESCENCES
NCALESCENT
NCANDESCE
NCANDESCED
NCANDESCENCE
NCANDESCENCES
NCANDESCENCIES
NCANDESCENCY
NCANDESCENT
NCANDESCENTLY
NCANDESCENTS
NCANDESCES
NCANDESCING
NCANTATION
NCANTATIONAL
NCANTATIONS
NCANTATOR
NCANTATORS
NCANTATORY
NCAPABILITIES
NCAPABILITY
NCAPABLENESS
NCAPABLENESSES
NCAPABLES
NCAPACIOUS
NCAPACIOUSNESS
NCAPACITANT
NCAPACITANTS
NCAPACITATE
NCAPACITATED
NCAPACITATES
NCAPACITATING
NCAPACITATION
NCAPACITATIONS
NCAPACITIES
NCAPACITY
NCAPSULATE
NCAPSULATED
NCAPSULATES
NCAPSULATING
NCAPSULATION
NCAPSULATIONS
NCARCERATE
NCARCERATED
NCARCERATES
NCARCERATING
NCARCERATION
NCARCERATIONS
NCARCERATOR

INCARCERATORS
INCARDINATE
INCARDINATED
INCARDINATES
INCARDINATING
INCARDINATION
INCARDINATIONS
INCARNADINE
INCARNADINED
INCARNADINES
INCARNADINING
INCARNATED
INCARNATES
INCARNATING
INCARNATION
INCARNATIONS
INCARVILLEA
INCARVILLEAS
INCASEMENT
INCASEMENTS
INCATENATION
INCATENATIONS
INCAUTIONS
INCAUTIOUS
INCAUTIOUSLY
INCAUTIOUSNESS
INCEDINGLY
INCENDIARIES
INCENDIARISM
INCENDIARISMS
INCENDIARY
INCENDIVITIES
INCENDIVITY
INCENSATION
INCENSATIONS
INCENSEMENT
INCENSEMENTS
INCENSORIES
INCENTIVELY
INCENTIVES
INCENTIVISATION
INCENTIVISE
INCENTIVISED
INCENTIVISES
INCENTIVISING
INCENTIVIZATION
INCENTIVIZE
INCENTIVIZED
INCENTIVIZES
INCENTIVIZING
INCEPTIONS
INCEPTIVELY
INCEPTIVES
INCERTAINTIES
INCERTAINTY
INCERTITUDE
INCERTITUDES
INCESSANCIES
INCESSANCY
INCESSANTLY
INCESSANTNESS
INCESSANTNESSES
INCESTUOUS
INCESTUOUSLY
INCESTUOUSNESS
INCHARITABLE

INCHOATELY
INCHOATENESS
INCHOATENESSES
INCHOATING
INCHOATION
INCHOATIONS
INCHOATIVE
INCHOATIVELY
INCHOATIVES
INCIDENCES
INCIDENTAL
INCIDENTALLY
INCIDENTALNESS
INCIDENTALS
INCINERATE
INCINERATED
INCINERATES
INCINERATING
INCINERATION
INCINERATIONS
INCINERATOR
INCINERATORS
INCIPIENCE
INCIPIENCES
INCIPIENCIES
INCIPIENCY
INCIPIENTLY
INCISIFORM
INCISIVELY
INCISIVENESS
INCISIVENESSES
INCISORIAL
INCITATION
INCITATIONS
INCITATIVE
INCITATIVES
INCITEMENT
INCITEMENTS
INCITINGLY
INCIVILITIES
INCIVILITY
INCLASPING
INCLEMENCIES
INCLEMENCY
INCLEMENTLY
INCLEMENTNESS
INCLEMENTNESSES
INCLINABLE
INCLINABLENESS
INCLINATION
INCLINATIONAL
INCLINATIONS
INCLINATORIA
INCLINATORIUM
INCLINATORY
INCLININGS
INCLINOMETER
INCLINOMETERS
INCLIPPING
INCLOSABLE
INCLOSURES
INCLUDABLE
INCLUDEDNESS
INCLUDEDNESSES
INCLUDIBLE
INCLUSIONS

INCLUSIVELY
INCLUSIVENESS
INCLUSIVENESSES
INCLUSIVITIES
INCLUSIVITY
INCOAGULABLE
INCOERCIBLE
INCOGITABILITY
INCOGITABLE
INCOGITANCIES
INCOGITANCY
INCOGITANT
INCOGITATIVE
INCOGNISABLE
INCOGNISANCE
INCOGNISANCES
INCOGNISANT
INCOGNITAS
INCOGNITOS
INCOGNIZABLE
INCOGNIZANCE
INCOGNIZANCES
INCOGNIZANT
INCOHERENCE
INCOHERENCES
INCOHERENCIES
INCOHERENCY
INCOHERENT
INCOHERENTLY
INCOHERENTNESS
INCOMBUSTIBLE
INCOMBUSTIBLES
INCOMBUSTIBLY
INCOMMENSURABLE
INCOMMENSURABLY
INCOMMENSURATE
INCOMMISCIBLE
INCOMMODED
INCOMMODES
INCOMMODING
INCOMMODIOUS
INCOMMODIOUSLY
INCOMMODITIES
INCOMMODITY
INCOMMUNICABLE
INCOMMUNICABLY
INCOMMUNICADO
INCOMMUNICATIVE
INCOMMUTABILITY
INCOMMUTABLE
INCOMMUTABLY
INCOMPARABILITY
INCOMPARABLE
INCOMPARABLY
INCOMPARED
INCOMPATIBILITY
INCOMPATIBLE
INCOMPATIBLES
INCOMPATIBLY
INCOMPETENCE
INCOMPETENCES
INCOMPETENCIES
INCOMPETENCY
INCOMPETENT
INCOMPETENTLY
INCOMPETENTS

INCOMPLETE
INCOMPLETELY
INCOMPLETENESS
INCOMPLETION
INCOMPLETIONS
INCOMPLIANCE
INCOMPLIANCES
INCOMPLIANCIES
INCOMPLIANCY
INCOMPLIANT
INCOMPLIANTLY
INCOMPOSED
INCOMPOSITE
INCOMPOSSIBLE
INCOMPREHENSION
INCOMPREHENSIVE
INCOMPRESSIBLE
INCOMPRESSIBLY
INCOMPUTABILITY
INCOMPUTABLE
INCOMPUTABLY
INCOMUNICADO
INCONCEIVABLE
INCONCEIVABLES
INCONCEIVABLY
INCONCINNITIES
INCONCINNITY
INCONCINNOUS
INCONCLUSION
INCONCLUSIONS
INCONCLUSIVE
INCONCLUSIVELY
INCONDENSABLE
INCONDENSIBLE
INCONDITELY
INCONFORMITIES
INCONFORMITY
INCONGRUENCE
INCONGRUENCES
INCONGRUENT
INCONGRUENTLY
INCONGRUITIES
INCONGRUITY
INCONGRUOUS
INCONGRUOUSLY
INCONGRUOUSNESS
INCONSCIENT
INCONSCIENTLY
INCONSCIONABLE
INCONSCIOUS
INCONSECUTIVE
INCONSECUTIVELY
INCONSEQUENCE
INCONSEQUENCES
INCONSEQUENT
INCONSEQUENTIAL
INCONSEQUENTLY
INCONSIDERABLE
INCONSIDERABLY
INCONSIDERATE
INCONSIDERATELY
INCONSIDERATION
INCONSISTENCE
INCONSISTENCES
INCONSISTENCIES
INCONSISTENCY
INCONSISTENT
INCONSISTENTLY
INCONSOLABILITY
INCONSOLABLE
INCONSOLABLY
INCONSONANCE
INCONSONANCES
INCONSONANT
INCONSONANTLY
INCONSPICUOUS
INCONSPICUOUSLY
INCONSTANCIES
INCONSTANCY
INCONSTANT
INCONSTANTLY
INCONSTRUABLE
INCONSUMABLE
INCONSUMABLY
INCONTESTABLE
INCONTESTABLY
INCONTIGUOUS
INCONTIGUOUSLY
INCONTINENCE
INCONTINENCES
INCONTINENCIES
INCONTINENCY
INCONTINENT
INCONTINENTLY
INCONTROLLABLE
INCONTROLLABLY
INCONVENIENCE
INCONVENIENCED
INCONVENIENCES
INCONVENIENCIES
INCONVENIENCING
INCONVENIENCY
INCONVENIENT
INCONVENIENTLY
INCONVERSABLE
INCONVERSANT
INCONVERTIBLE
INCONVERTIBLY
INCONVINCIBLE
INCONVINCIBLY
INCOORDINATE
INCOORDINATION
INCOORDINATIONS
INCORONATE
INCORONATED
INCORONATION
INCORONATIONS
INCORPORABLE
INCORPORAL
INCORPORALL
INCORPORATE
INCORPORATED
INCORPORATES
INCORPORATING
INCORPORATION
INCORPORATIONS
INCORPORATIVE
INCORPORATOR
INCORPORATORS
INCORPOREAL
INCORPOREALITY
INCORPOREALLY
INCORPOREITIES
INCORPOREITY
INCORPSING
INCORRECTLY
INCORRECTNESS
INCORRECTNESSES
INCORRIGIBILITY
INCORRIGIBLE
INCORRIGIBLES
INCORRIGIBLY
INCORRODIBLE
INCORROSIBLE
INCORRUPTED
INCORRUPTIBLE
INCORRUPTIBLES
INCORRUPTIBLY
INCORRUPTION
INCORRUPTIONS
INCORRUPTIVE
INCORRUPTLY
INCORRUPTNESS
INCORRUPTNESSES
INCRASSATE
INCRASSATED
INCRASSATES
INCRASSATING
INCRASSATION
INCRASSATIONS
INCRASSATIVE
INCREASABLE
INCREASEDLY
INCREASEFUL
INCREASERS
INCREASING
INCREASINGLY
INCREASINGS
INCREATELY
INCREDIBILITIES
INCREDIBILITY
INCREDIBLE
INCREDIBLENESS
INCREDIBLY
INCREDULITIES
INCREDULITY
INCREDULOUS
INCREDULOUSLY
INCREDULOUSNESS
INCREMATED
INCREMATES
INCREMATING
INCREMATION
INCREMATIONS
INCREMENTAL
INCREMENTALISM
INCREMENTALISMS
INCREMENTALIST
INCREMENTALISTS
INCREMENTALLY
INCREMENTALS
INCREMENTED
INCREMENTING
INCREMENTS
INCRESCENT
INCRETIONARY
INCRETIONS
INCRIMINATE
INCRIMINATED
INCRIMINATES
INCRIMINATING
INCRIMINATION
INCRIMINATIONS
INCRIMINATOR
INCRIMINATORS
INCRIMINATORY
INCROSSBRED
INCROSSBREDS
INCROSSBREED
INCROSSBREEDING
INCROSSBREEDS
INCROSSING
INCRUSTANT
INCRUSTANTS
INCRUSTATION
INCRUSTATIONS
INCRUSTING
INCUBATING
INCUBATION
INCUBATIONAL
INCUBATIONS
INCUBATIVE
INCUBATORS
INCUBATORY
INCULCATED
INCULCATES
INCULCATING
INCULCATION
INCULCATIONS
INCULCATIVE
INCULCATOR
INCULCATORS
INCULCATORY
INCULPABILITIES
INCULPABILITY
INCULPABLE
INCULPABLENESS
INCULPABLY
INCULPATED
INCULPATES
INCULPATING
INCULPATION
INCULPATIONS
INCULPATIVE
INCULPATORY
INCUMBENCIES
INCUMBENCY
INCUMBENTLY
INCUMBENTS
INCUMBERED
INCUMBERING
INCUMBERINGLY
INCUMBRANCE
INCUMBRANCES
INCUNABLES
INCUNABULA
INCUNABULAR
INCUNABULIST
INCUNABULISTS
INCUNABULUM
INCURABILITIES
INCURABILITY
INCURABLENESS
INCURABLENESSES

INCURABLES
INCURIOSITIES
INCURIOSITY
INCURIOUSLY
INCURIOUSNESS
INCURIOUSNESSES
INCURRABLE
INCURRENCE
INCURRENCES
INCURSIONS
INCURVATED
INCURVATES
INCURVATING
INCURVATION
INCURVATIONS
INCURVATURE
INCURVATURES
INCURVITIES
INDAGATING
INDAGATION
INDAGATIONS
INDAGATIVE
INDAGATORS
INDAGATORY
INDAPAMIDE
INDAPAMIDES
INDEBTEDNESS
INDEBTEDNESSES
INDECENCIES
INDECENTER
INDECENTEST
INDECENTLY
INDECIDUATE
INDECIDUOUS
INDECIPHERABLE
INDECIPHERABLY
INDECISION
INDECISIONS
INDECISIVE
INDECISIVELY
INDECISIVENESS
INDECLINABLE
INDECLINABLY
INDECOMPOSABLE
INDECOROUS
INDECOROUSLY
INDECOROUSNESS
INDECORUMS
INDEFATIGABLE
INDEFATIGABLY
INDEFEASIBILITY
INDEFEASIBLE
INDEFEASIBLY
INDEFECTIBILITY
INDEFECTIBLE
INDEFECTIBLY
INDEFENSIBILITY
INDEFENSIBLE
INDEFENSIBLY
INDEFINABILITY
INDEFINABLE
INDEFINABLENESS
INDEFINABLES
INDEFINABLY
INDEFINITE
INDEFINITELY
INDEFINITENESS
INDEFINITES
INDEHISCENCE
INDEHISCENCES
INDEHISCENT
INDELIBILITIES
INDELIBILITY
INDELIBLENESS
INDELIBLENESSES
INDELICACIES
INDELICACY
INDELICATE
INDELICATELY
INDELICATENESS
INDEMNIFICATION
INDEMNIFIED
INDEMNIFIER
INDEMNIFIERS
INDEMNIFIES
INDEMNIFYING
INDEMNITIES
INDEMONSTRABLE
INDEMONSTRABLY
INDENTATION
INDENTATIONS
INDENTIONS
INDENTURED
INDENTURES
INDENTURESHIP
INDENTURESHIPS
INDENTURING
INDEPENDENCE
INDEPENDENCES
INDEPENDENCIES
INDEPENDENCY
INDEPENDENT
INDEPENDENTLY
INDEPENDENTS
INDESCRIBABLE
INDESCRIBABLES
INDESCRIBABLY
INDESIGNATE
INDESTRUCTIBLE
INDESTRUCTIBLY
INDETECTABLE
INDETECTIBLE
INDETERMINABLE
INDETERMINABLY
INDETERMINACIES
INDETERMINACY
INDETERMINATE
INDETERMINATELY
INDETERMINATION
INDETERMINED
INDETERMINISM
INDETERMINISMS
INDETERMINIST
INDETERMINISTIC
INDETERMINISTS
INDEXATION
INDEXATIONS
INDEXICALS
INDEXTERITIES
INDEXTERITY
INDICATABLE
INDICATING
INDICATION
INDICATIONAL
INDICATIONS
INDICATIVE
INDICATIVELY
INDICATIVES
INDICATORS
INDICATORY
INDICOLITE
INDICOLITES
INDICTABLE
INDICTABLY
INDICTIONAL
INDICTIONS
INDICTMENT
INDICTMENTS
INDIFFERENCE
INDIFFERENCES
INDIFFERENCIES
INDIFFERENCY
INDIFFERENT
INDIFFERENTISM
INDIFFERENTISMS
INDIFFERENTIST
INDIFFERENTISTS
INDIFFERENTLY
INDIFFERENTS
INDIGENCES
INDIGENCIES
INDIGENISATION
INDIGENISATIONS
INDIGENISE
INDIGENISED
INDIGENISES
INDIGENISING
INDIGENITIES
INDIGENITY
INDIGENIZATION
INDIGENIZATIONS
INDIGENIZE
INDIGENIZED
INDIGENIZES
INDIGENIZING
INDIGENOUS
INDIGENOUSLY
INDIGENOUSNESS
INDIGENTLY
INDIGESTED
INDIGESTIBILITY
INDIGESTIBLE
INDIGESTIBLES
INDIGESTIBLY
INDIGESTION
INDIGESTIONS
INDIGESTIVE
INDIGNANCE
INDIGNANCES
INDIGNANTLY
INDIGNATION
INDIGNATIONS
INDIGNIFIED
INDIGNIFIES
INDIGNIFYING
INDIGNITIES
INDIGOLITE
INDIGOLITES
INDIGOTINS
INDINAVIRS
INDIRECTION
INDIRECTIONS
INDIRECTLY
INDIRECTNESS
INDIRECTNESSES
INDIRUBINS
INDISCERNIBLE
INDISCERNIBLY
INDISCERPTIBLE
INDISCIPLINABLE
INDISCIPLINE
INDISCIPLINED
INDISCIPLINES
INDISCOVERABLE
INDISCREET
INDISCREETLY
INDISCREETNESS
INDISCRETE
INDISCRETELY
INDISCRETENESS
INDISCRETION
INDISCRETIONARY
INDISCRETIONS
INDISCRIMINATE
INDISPENSABLE
INDISPENSABLES
INDISPENSABLY
INDISPOSED
INDISPOSEDNESS
INDISPOSES
INDISPOSING
INDISPOSITION
INDISPOSITIONS
INDISPUTABILITY
INDISPUTABLE
INDISPUTABLY
INDISSOCIABLE
INDISSOCIABLY
INDISSOLUBILITY
INDISSOLUBLE
INDISSOLUBLY
INDISSOLVABLE
INDISSUADABLE
INDISSUADABLY
INDISTINCT
INDISTINCTION
INDISTINCTIONS
INDISTINCTIVE
INDISTINCTIVELY
INDISTINCTLY
INDISTINCTNESS
INDISTRIBUTABLE
INDITEMENT
INDITEMENTS
INDIVERTIBLE
INDIVERTIBLY
INDIVIDABLE
INDIVIDUAL
INDIVIDUALISE
INDIVIDUALISED
INDIVIDUALISER
INDIVIDUALISERS
INDIVIDUALISES
INDIVIDUALISING

INDIVIDUALISM
INDIVIDUALISMS
INDIVIDUALIST
INDIVIDUALISTIC
INDIVIDUALISTS
INDIVIDUALITIES
INDIVIDUALITY
INDIVIDUALIZE
INDIVIDUALIZED
INDIVIDUALIZER
INDIVIDUALIZERS
INDIVIDUALIZES
INDIVIDUALIZING
INDIVIDUALLY
INDIVIDUALS
INDIVIDUATE
INDIVIDUATED
INDIVIDUATES
INDIVIDUATING
INDIVIDUATION
INDIVIDUATIONS
INDIVIDUATOR
INDIVIDUATORS
INDIVIDUUM
INDIVISIBILITY
INDIVISIBLE
INDIVISIBLENESS
INDIVISIBLES
INDIVISIBLY
INDOCILITIES
INDOCILITY
INDOCTRINATE
INDOCTRINATED
INDOCTRINATES
INDOCTRINATING
INDOCTRINATION
INDOCTRINATIONS
INDOCTRINATOR
INDOCTRINATORS
INDOLEACETIC
INDOLEBUTYRIC
INDOLENCES
INDOLENCIES
INDOLENTLY
INDOMETHACIN
INDOMETHACINS
INDOMITABILITY
INDOMITABLE
INDOMITABLENESS
INDOMITABLY
INDOPHENOL
INDOPHENOLS
INDORSABLE
INDORSEMENT
INDORSEMENTS
INDRAUGHTS
INDRENCHED
INDRENCHES
INDRENCHING
INDUBITABILITY
INDUBITABLE
INDUBITABLENESS
INDUBITABLY
INDUCEMENT
INDUCEMENTS
INDUCIBILITIES
INDUCIBILITY
INDUCTANCE
INDUCTANCES
INDUCTILITIES
INDUCTILITY
INDUCTIONAL
INDUCTIONS
INDUCTIVELY
INDUCTIVENESS
INDUCTIVENESSES
INDUCTIVITIES
INDUCTIVITY
INDULGENCE
INDULGENCED
INDULGENCES
INDULGENCIES
INDULGENCING
INDULGENCY
INDULGENTLY
INDULGINGLY
INDUMENTUM
INDUMENTUMS
INDUPLICATE
INDUPLICATED
INDUPLICATION
INDUPLICATIONS
INDURATING
INDURATION
INDURATIONS
INDURATIVE
INDUSTRIAL
INDUSTRIALISE
INDUSTRIALISED
INDUSTRIALISES
INDUSTRIALISING
INDUSTRIALISM
INDUSTRIALISMS
INDUSTRIALIST
INDUSTRIALISTS
INDUSTRIALIZE
INDUSTRIALIZED
INDUSTRIALIZES
INDUSTRIALIZING
INDUSTRIALLY
INDUSTRIALS
INDUSTRIES
INDUSTRIOUS
INDUSTRIOUSLY
INDUSTRIOUSNESS
INDUSTRYWIDE
INDWELLERS
INDWELLING
INDWELLINGS
INEARTHING
INEBRIANTS
INEBRIATED
INEBRIATES
INEBRIATING
INEBRIATION
INEBRIATIONS
INEBRIETIES
INEDIBILITIES
INEDIBILITY
INEDUCABILITIES
INEDUCABILITY
INEDUCABLE
INEFFABILITIES
INEFFABILITY
INEFFABLENESS
INEFFABLENESSES
INEFFACEABILITY
INEFFACEABLE
INEFFACEABLY
INEFFECTIVE
INEFFECTIVELY
INEFFECTIVENESS
INEFFECTUAL
INEFFECTUALITY
INEFFECTUALLY
INEFFECTUALNESS
INEFFICACIES
INEFFICACIOUS
INEFFICACIOUSLY
INEFFICACITIES
INEFFICACITY
INEFFICACY
INEFFICIENCIES
INEFFICIENCY
INEFFICIENT
INEFFICIENTLY
INEFFICIENTS
INEGALITARIAN
INELABORATE
INELABORATELY
INELASTICALLY
INELASTICITIES
INELASTICITY
INELEGANCE
INELEGANCES
INELEGANCIES
INELEGANCY
INELEGANTLY
INELIGIBILITIES
INELIGIBILITY
INELIGIBLE
INELIGIBLENESS
INELIGIBLES
INELIGIBLY
INELOQUENCE
INELOQUENCES
INELOQUENT
INELOQUENTLY
INELUCTABILITY
INELUCTABLE
INELUCTABLY
INELUDIBILITIES
INELUDIBILITY
INELUDIBLE
INELUDIBLY
INENARRABLE
INEPTITUDE
INEPTITUDES
INEPTNESSES
INEQUALITIES
INEQUALITY
INEQUATION
INEQUATIONS
INEQUIPOTENT
INEQUITABLE
INEQUITABLENESS
INEQUITABLY
INEQUITIES
INEQUIVALVE
INEQUIVALVED
INERADICABILITY
INERADICABLE
INERADICABLY
INERASABLE
INERASABLY
INERASIBLE
INERASIBLY
INERRABILITIES
INERRABILITY
INERRABLENESS
INERRABLENESSES
INERRANCIES
INERTIALLY
INERTNESSES
INESCAPABLE
INESCAPABLY
INESCULENT
INESCUTCHEON
INESCUTCHEONS
INESSENTIAL
INESSENTIALITY
INESSENTIALS
INESTIMABILITY
INESTIMABLE
INESTIMABLENESS
INESTIMABLY
INEVITABILITIES
INEVITABILITY
INEVITABLE
INEVITABLENESS
INEVITABLY
INEXACTITUDE
INEXACTITUDES
INEXACTNESS
INEXACTNESSES
INEXCITABLE
INEXCUSABILITY
INEXCUSABLE
INEXCUSABLENESS
INEXCUSABLY
INEXECRABLE
INEXECUTABLE
INEXECUTION
INEXECUTIONS
INEXHAUSTED
INEXHAUSTIBLE
INEXHAUSTIBLY
INEXHAUSTIVE
INEXISTANT
INEXISTENCE
INEXISTENCES
INEXISTENCIES
INEXISTENCY
INEXISTENT
INEXORABILITIES
INEXORABILITY
INEXORABLE
INEXORABLENESS
INEXORABLY
INEXPANSIBLE
INEXPECTANCIES
INEXPECTANCY
INEXPECTANT
INEXPECTATION

NEXPECTATIONS
NEXPEDIENCE
NEXPEDIENCES
NEXPEDIENCIES
NEXPEDIENCY
NEXPEDIENT
NEXPEDIENTLY
NEXPENSIVE
NEXPENSIVELY
NEXPENSIVENESS
NEXPERIENCE
NEXPERIENCED
NEXPERIENCES
NEXPERTLY
NEXPERTNESS
NEXPERTNESSES
NEXPIABLE
NEXPIABLENESS
NEXPIABLY
NEXPLAINABLE
NEXPLAINABLY
NEXPLICABILITY
NEXPLICABLE
NEXPLICABLY
NEXPLICIT
NEXPLICITLY
NEXPLICITNESS
NEXPRESSIBLE
NEXPRESSIBLES
NEXPRESSIBLY
NEXPRESSIVE
NEXPRESSIVELY
NEXPUGNABILITY
NEXPUGNABLE
NEXPUGNABLY
NEXPUNGIBLE
NEXTENDED
NEXTENSIBILITY
NEXTENSIBLE
NEXTENSION
NEXTENSIONS
NEXTIRPABLE
NEXTRICABILITY
NEXTRICABLE
NEXTRICABLY
NFALLIBILISM
NFALLIBILISMS
NFALLIBILIST
NFALLIBILISTS
NFALLIBILITIES
NFALLIBILITY
NFALLIBLE
NFALLIBLENESS
NFALLIBLES
NFALLIBLY
NFAMISING
NFAMIZING
NFAMONISE
NFAMONISED
NFAMONISES
NFAMONISING
NFAMONIZE
NFAMONIZED
NFAMONIZES
NFAMONIZING
NFAMOUSLY
INFAMOUSNESS
INFAMOUSNESSES
INFANGTHIEF
INFANGTHIEFS
INFANTHOOD
INFANTHOODS
INFANTICIDAL
INFANTICIDE
INFANTICIDES
INFANTILISATION
INFANTILISE
INFANTILISED
INFANTILISES
INFANTILISING
INFANTILISM
INFANTILISMS
INFANTILITIES
INFANTILITY
INFANTILIZATION
INFANTILIZE
INFANTILIZED
INFANTILIZES
INFANTILIZING
INFANTIVORE
INFANTIVORES
INFANTRIES
INFANTRYMAN
INFANTRYMEN
INFARCTION
INFARCTIONS
INFATUATED
INFATUATEDLY
INFATUATES
INFATUATING
INFATUATION
INFATUATIONS
INFEASIBILITIES
INFEASIBILITY
INFEASIBLE
INFEASIBLENESS
INFECTIONS
INFECTIOUS
INFECTIOUSLY
INFECTIOUSNESS
INFECTIVELY
INFECTIVENESS
INFECTIVENESSES
INFECTIVITIES
INFECTIVITY
INFECUNDITIES
INFECUNDITY
INFEFTMENT
INFEFTMENTS
INFELICITIES
INFELICITOUS
INFELICITOUSLY
INFELICITY
INFEOFFING
INFERENCES
INFERENCING
INFERENCINGS
INFERENTIAL
INFERENTIALLY
INFERIORITIES
INFERIORITY
INFERIORLY
INFERNALITIES
INFERNALITY
INFERNALLY
INFERRABLE
INFERRIBLE
INFERTILELY
INFERTILITIES
INFERTILITY
INFESTANTS
INFESTATION
INFESTATIONS
INFEUDATION
INFEUDATIONS
INFIBULATE
INFIBULATED
INFIBULATES
INFIBULATING
INFIBULATION
INFIBULATIONS
INFIDELITIES
INFIDELITY
INFIELDERS
INFIELDSMAN
INFIELDSMEN
INFIGHTERS
INFIGHTING
INFIGHTINGS
INFILLINGS
INFILTRATE
INFILTRATED
INFILTRATES
INFILTRATING
INFILTRATION
INFILTRATIONS
INFILTRATIVE
INFILTRATOR
INFILTRATORS
INFINITANT
INFINITARY
INFINITATE
INFINITATED
INFINITATES
INFINITATING
INFINITELY
INFINITENESS
INFINITENESSES
INFINITESIMAL
INFINITESIMALLY
INFINITESIMALS
INFINITIES
INFINITIVAL
INFINITIVALLY
INFINITIVE
INFINITIVELY
INFINITIVES
INFINITUDE
INFINITUDES
INFIRMARER
INFIRMARERS
INFIRMARIAN
INFIRMARIANS
INFIRMARIES
INFIRMITIES
INFIRMNESS
INFIRMNESSES
INFIXATION
INFIXATIONS
INFLAMABLE
INFLAMINGLY
INFLAMMABILITY
INFLAMMABLE
INFLAMMABLENESS
INFLAMMABLES
INFLAMMABLY
INFLAMMATION
INFLAMMATIONS
INFLAMMATORILY
INFLAMMATORY
INFLATABLE
INFLATABLES
INFLATEDLY
INFLATEDNESS
INFLATEDNESSES
INFLATINGLY
INFLATIONARY
INFLATIONISM
INFLATIONISMS
INFLATIONIST
INFLATIONISTS
INFLATIONS
INFLATUSES
INFLECTABLE
INFLECTEDNESS
INFLECTEDNESSES
INFLECTING
INFLECTION
INFLECTIONAL
INFLECTIONALLY
INFLECTIONLESS
INFLECTIONS
INFLECTIVE
INFLECTORS
INFLEXIBILITIES
INFLEXIBILITY
INFLEXIBLE
INFLEXIBLENESS
INFLEXIBLY
INFLEXIONAL
INFLEXIONALLY
INFLEXIONLESS
INFLEXIONS
INFLEXURES
INFLICTABLE
INFLICTERS
INFLICTING
INFLICTION
INFLICTIONS
INFLICTIVE
INFLICTORS
INFLORESCENCE
INFLORESCENCES
INFLORESCENT
INFLOWINGS
INFLUENCEABLE
INFLUENCED
INFLUENCER
INFLUENCERS
INFLUENCES
INFLUENCING
INFLUENTIAL
INFLUENTIALLY
INFLUENTIALS

INFLUENZAL
INFLUENZAS
INFLUXIONS
INFOLDMENT
INFOLDMENTS
INFOMANIAS
INFOMERCIAL
INFOMERCIALS
INFOPRENEURIAL
INFORMABLE
INFORMALITIES
INFORMALITY
INFORMALLY
INFORMANTS
INFORMATICIAN
INFORMATICIANS
INFORMATICS
INFORMATION
INFORMATIONAL
INFORMATIONALLY
INFORMATIONS
INFORMATIVE
INFORMATIVELY
INFORMATIVENESS
INFORMATORILY
INFORMATORY
INFORMEDLY
INFORMIDABLE
INFORMINGLY
INFORTUNES
INFOSPHERE
INFOSPHERES
INFOTAINMENT
INFOTAINMENTS
INFRACOSTAL
INFRACTING
INFRACTION
INFRACTIONS
INFRACTORS
INFRAGRANT
INFRAHUMAN
INFRAHUMANS
INFRALAPSARIAN
INFRALAPSARIANS
INFRAMAXILLARY
INFRANGIBILITY
INFRANGIBLE
INFRANGIBLENESS
INFRANGIBLY
INFRAORBITAL
INFRAPOSED
INFRAPOSITION
INFRAPOSITIONS
INFRASONIC
INFRASOUND
INFRASOUNDS
INFRASPECIFIC
INFRASTRUCTURAL
INFRASTRUCTURE
INFRASTRUCTURES
INFREQUENCE
INFREQUENCES
INFREQUENCIES
INFREQUENCY
INFREQUENT
INFREQUENTLY
INFRINGEMENT
INFRINGEMENTS
INFRINGERS
INFRINGING
INFRUCTUOUS
INFRUCTUOUSLY
INFUNDIBULA
INFUNDIBULAR
INFUNDIBULATE
INFUNDIBULIFORM
INFUNDIBULUM
INFURIATED
INFURIATELY
INFURIATES
INFURIATING
INFURIATINGLY
INFURIATION
INFURIATIONS
INFUSCATED
INFUSIBILITIES
INFUSIBILITY
INFUSIBLENESS
INFUSIBLENESSES
INFUSIONISM
INFUSIONISMS
INFUSIONIST
INFUSIONISTS
INFUSORIAL
INFUSORIAN
INFUSORIANS
INGATHERED
INGATHERER
INGATHERERS
INGATHERING
INGATHERINGS
INGEMINATE
INGEMINATED
INGEMINATES
INGEMINATING
INGEMINATION
INGEMINATIONS
INGENERATE
INGENERATED
INGENERATES
INGENERATING
INGENERATION
INGENERATIONS
INGENIOUSLY
INGENIOUSNESS
INGENIOUSNESSES
INGENUITIES
INGENUOUSLY
INGENUOUSNESS
INGENUOUSNESSES
INGESTIBLE
INGESTIONS
INGLENEUKS
INGLENOOKS
INGLORIOUS
INGLORIOUSLY
INGLORIOUSNESS
INGRAFTATION
INGRAFTATIONS
INGRAFTING
INGRAFTMENT
INGRAFTMENTS
INGRAINEDLY
INGRAINEDNESS
INGRAINEDNESSES
INGRAINING
INGRATEFUL
INGRATIATE
INGRATIATED
INGRATIATES
INGRATIATING
INGRATIATINGLY
INGRATIATION
INGRATIATIONS
INGRATIATORY
INGRATITUDE
INGRATITUDES
INGRAVESCENCE
INGRAVESCENCES
INGRAVESCENT
INGREDIENT
INGREDIENTS
INGRESSION
INGRESSIONS
INGRESSIVE
INGRESSIVENESS
INGRESSIVES
INGROOVING
INGROSSING
INGROWNNESS
INGROWNNESSES
INGULFMENT
INGULFMENTS
INGULPHING
INGURGITATE
INGURGITATED
INGURGITATES
INGURGITATING
INGURGITATION
INGURGITATIONS
INHABITABILITY
INHABITABLE
INHABITANCE
INHABITANCES
INHABITANCIES
INHABITANCY
INHABITANT
INHABITANTS
INHABITATION
INHABITATIONS
INHABITERS
INHABITING
INHABITIVENESS
INHABITORS
INHABITRESS
INHABITRESSES
INHALATION
INHALATIONAL
INHALATIONS
INHALATORIUM
INHALATORIUMS
INHALATORS
INHARMONIC
INHARMONICAL
INHARMONICITIES
INHARMONICITY
INHARMONIES
INHARMONIOUS
INHARMONIOUSLY
INHAUSTING
INHEARSING
INHERENCES
INHERENCIES
INHERENTLY
INHERITABILITY
INHERITABLE
INHERITABLENESS
INHERITABLY
INHERITANCE
INHERITANCES
INHERITING
INHERITORS
INHERITRESS
INHERITRESSES
INHERITRICES
INHERITRIX
INHERITRIXES
INHIBITABLE
INHIBITERS
INHIBITING
INHIBITION
INHIBITIONS
INHIBITIVE
INHIBITORS
INHIBITORY
INHOLDINGS
INHOMOGENEITIES
INHOMOGENEITY
INHOMOGENEOUS
INHOSPITABLE
INHOSPITABLY
INHOSPITALITIES
INHOSPITALITY
INHUMANELY
INHUMANITIES
INHUMANITY
INHUMANNESS
INHUMANNESSES
INHUMATING
INHUMATION
INHUMATIONS
INIMICALITIES
INIMICALITY
INIMICALLY
INIMICALNESS
INIMICALNESSES
INIMICITIOUS
INIMITABILITIES
INIMITABILITY
INIMITABLE
INIMITABLENESS
INIMITABLY
INIQUITIES
INIQUITOUS
INIQUITOUSLY
INIQUITOUSNESS
INITIALERS
INITIALING
INITIALISATION
INITIALISATIONS
INITIALISE
INITIALISED
INITIALISES
INITIALISING

INITIALISM
INITIALISMS
INITIALIZATION
INITIALIZATIONS
INITIALIZE
INITIALIZED
INITIALIZES
INITIALIZING
INITIALLED
INITIALLER
INITIALLERS
INITIALLING
INITIALNESS
INITIALNESSES
INITIATING
INITIATION
INITIATIONS
INITIATIVE
INITIATIVELY
INITIATIVES
INITIATORIES
INITIATORS
INITIATORY
INITIATRESS
INITIATRESSES
INITIATRICES
INITIATRIX
INITIATRIXES
INJECTABLE
INJECTABLES
INJECTANTS
INJECTIONS
INJELLYING
INJOINTING
INJUDICIAL
INJUDICIALLY
INJUDICIOUS
INJUDICIOUSLY
INJUDICIOUSNESS
INJUNCTING
INJUNCTION
INJUNCTIONS
INJUNCTIVE
INJUNCTIVELY
INJURIOUSLY
INJURIOUSNESS
INJURIOUSNESSES
INJUSTICES
INKBERRIES
INKHOLDERS
INKINESSES
INMARRIAGE
INMARRIAGES
INMIGRANTS
INNATENESS
INNATENESSES
INNAVIGABLE
INNAVIGABLY
INNERMOSTS
INNERNESSES
INNERSOLES
INNERSPRING
INNERVATED
INNERVATES
INNERVATING
INNERVATION
INNERVATIONS
INNERWEARS
INNKEEPERS
INNOCENCES
INNOCENCIES
INNOCENTER
INNOCENTEST
INNOCENTLY
INNOCUITIES
INNOCUOUSLY
INNOCUOUSNESS
INNOCUOUSNESSES
INNOMINABLE
INNOMINABLES
INNOMINATE
INNOVATING
INNOVATION
INNOVATIONAL
INNOVATIONIST
INNOVATIONISTS
INNOVATIONS
INNOVATIVE
INNOVATIVELY
INNOVATIVENESS
INNOVATORS
INNOVATORY
INNOXIOUSLY
INNOXIOUSNESS
INNOXIOUSNESSES
INNUENDOED
INNUENDOES
INNUENDOING
INNUMERABILITY
INNUMERABLE
INNUMERABLENESS
INNUMERABLY
INNUMERACIES
INNUMERACY
INNUMERATE
INNUMERATES
INNUMEROUS
INNUTRIENT
INNUTRITION
INNUTRITIONS
INNUTRITIOUS
INOBEDIENCE
INOBEDIENCES
INOBEDIENT
INOBEDIENTLY
INOBSERVABLE
INOBSERVANCE
INOBSERVANCES
INOBSERVANT
INOBSERVANTLY
INOBSERVATION
INOBSERVATIONS
INOBTRUSIVE
INOBTRUSIVELY
INOBTRUSIVENESS
INOCCUPATION
INOCCUPATIONS
INOCULABILITIES
INOCULABILITY
INOCULABLE
INOCULANTS
INOCULATED
INOCULATES
INOCULATING
INOCULATION
INOCULATIONS
INOCULATIVE
INOCULATOR
INOCULATORS
INOCULATORY
INODOROUSLY
INODOROUSNESS
INODOROUSNESSES
INOFFENSIVE
INOFFENSIVELY
INOFFENSIVENESS
INOFFICIOUS
INOFFICIOUSLY
INOFFICIOUSNESS
INOPERABILITIES
INOPERABILITY
INOPERABLE
INOPERABLENESS
INOPERABLY
INOPERATIVE
INOPERATIVENESS
INOPERCULATE
INOPERCULATES
INOPPORTUNE
INOPPORTUNELY
INOPPORTUNENESS
INOPPORTUNITIES
INOPPORTUNITY
INORDINACIES
INORDINACY
INORDINATE
INORDINATELY
INORDINATENESS
INORDINATION
INORDINATIONS
INORGANICALLY
INORGANISATION
INORGANISATIONS
INORGANISED
INORGANIZATION
INORGANIZATIONS
INORGANIZED
INOSCULATE
INOSCULATED
INOSCULATES
INOSCULATING
INOSCULATION
INOSCULATIONS
INPATIENTS
INPAYMENTS
INPOURINGS
INQUIETING
INQUIETUDE
INQUIETUDES
INQUILINES
INQUILINIC
INQUILINICS
INQUILINISM
INQUILINISMS
INQUILINITIES
INQUILINITY
INQUILINOUS
INQUINATED
INQUINATES
INQUINATING
INQUINATION
INQUINATIONS
INQUIRATION
INQUIRATIONS
INQUIRENDO
INQUIRENDOS
INQUIRINGLY
INQUISITION
INQUISITIONAL
INQUISITIONIST
INQUISITIONISTS
INQUISITIONS
INQUISITIVE
INQUISITIVELY
INQUISITIVENESS
INQUISITOR
INQUISITORIAL
INQUISITORIALLY
INQUISITORS
INQUISITRESS
INQUISITRESSES
INQUISITURIENT
INRUSHINGS
INSALIVATE
INSALIVATED
INSALIVATES
INSALIVATING
INSALIVATION
INSALIVATIONS
INSALUBRIOUS
INSALUBRIOUSLY
INSALUBRITIES
INSALUBRITY
INSALUTARY
INSANENESS
INSANENESSES
INSANITARINESS
INSANITARY
INSANITATION
INSANITATIONS
INSANITIES
INSATIABILITIES
INSATIABILITY
INSATIABLE
INSATIABLENESS
INSATIABLY
INSATIATELY
INSATIATENESS
INSATIATENESSES
INSATIETIES
INSCIENCES
INSCONCING
INSCRIBABLE
INSCRIBABLENESS
INSCRIBERS
INSCRIBING
INSCRIPTION
INSCRIPTIONAL
INSCRIPTIONS
INSCRIPTIVE
INSCRIPTIVELY
INSCROLLED
INSCROLLING
INSCRUTABILITY

INSCRUTABLE
INSCRUTABLENESS
INSCRUTABLY
INSCULPING
INSCULPTURE
INSCULPTURED
INSCULPTURES
INSCULPTURING
INSECTARIA
INSECTARIES
INSECTARIUM
INSECTARIUMS
INSECTICIDAL
INSECTICIDALLY
INSECTICIDE
INSECTICIDES
INSECTIFORM
INSECTIFUGE
INSECTIFUGES
INSECTIONS
INSECTIVORE
INSECTIVORES
INSECTIVOROUS
INSECTOLOGIES
INSECTOLOGIST
INSECTOLOGISTS
INSECTOLOGY
INSECURELY
INSECURENESS
INSECURENESSES
INSECURITIES
INSECURITY
INSELBERGE
INSELBERGS
INSEMINATE
INSEMINATED
INSEMINATES
INSEMINATING
INSEMINATION
INSEMINATIONS
INSEMINATOR
INSEMINATORS
INSENSATELY
INSENSATENESS
INSENSATENESSES
INSENSIBILITIES
INSENSIBILITY
INSENSIBLE
INSENSIBLENESS
INSENSIBLY
INSENSITIVE
INSENSITIVELY
INSENSITIVENESS
INSENSITIVITIES
INSENSITIVITY
INSENSUOUS
INSENTIENCE
INSENTIENCES
INSENTIENCIES
INSENTIENCY
INSENTIENT
INSEPARABILITY
INSEPARABLE
INSEPARABLENESS
INSEPARABLES
INSEPARABLY
INSEPARATE
INSERTABLE
INSERTIONAL
INSERTIONS
INSESSORIAL
INSEVERABLE
INSHEATHED
INSHEATHES
INSHEATHING
INSHELLING
INSHELTERED
INSHELTERING
INSHELTERS
INSHIPPING
INSHRINING
INSIDIOUSLY
INSIDIOUSNESS
INSIDIOUSNESSES
INSIGHTFUL
INSIGHTFULLY
INSIGNIFICANCE
INSIGNIFICANCES
INSIGNIFICANCY
INSIGNIFICANT
INSIGNIFICANTLY
INSIGNIFICATIVE
INSINCERELY
INSINCERITIES
INSINCERITY
INSINEWING
INSINUATED
INSINUATES
INSINUATING
INSINUATINGLY
INSINUATION
INSINUATIONS
INSINUATIVE
INSINUATOR
INSINUATORS
INSINUATORY
INSIPIDITIES
INSIPIDITY
INSIPIDNESS
INSIPIDNESSES
INSIPIENCE
INSIPIENCES
INSIPIENTLY
INSISTENCE
INSISTENCES
INSISTENCIES
INSISTENCY
INSISTENTLY
INSISTINGLY
INSNAREMENT
INSNAREMENTS
INSOBRIETIES
INSOBRIETY
INSOCIABILITIES
INSOCIABILITY
INSOCIABLE
INSOCIABLY
INSOLATING
INSOLATION
INSOLATIONS
INSOLENCES
INSOLENTLY
INSOLIDITIES
INSOLIDITY
INSOLUBILISE
INSOLUBILISED
INSOLUBILISES
INSOLUBILISING
INSOLUBILITIES
INSOLUBILITY
INSOLUBILIZE
INSOLUBILIZED
INSOLUBILIZES
INSOLUBILIZING
INSOLUBLENESS
INSOLUBLENESSES
INSOLUBLES
INSOLVABILITIES
INSOLVABILITY
INSOLVABLE
INSOLVABLY
INSOLVENCIES
INSOLVENCY
INSOLVENTS
INSOMNIACS
INSOMNIOUS
INSOMNOLENCE
INSOMNOLENCES
INSOUCIANCE
INSOUCIANCES
INSOUCIANT
INSOUCIANTLY
INSOULMENT
INSOULMENTS
INSPANNING
INSPECTABLE
INSPECTING
INSPECTINGLY
INSPECTION
INSPECTIONAL
INSPECTIONS
INSPECTIVE
INSPECTORAL
INSPECTORATE
INSPECTORATES
INSPECTORIAL
INSPECTORS
INSPECTORSHIP
INSPECTORSHIPS
INSPHERING
INSPIRABLE
INSPIRATION
INSPIRATIONAL
INSPIRATIONALLY
INSPIRATIONISM
INSPIRATIONISMS
INSPIRATIONIST
INSPIRATIONISTS
INSPIRATIONS
INSPIRATIVE
INSPIRATOR
INSPIRATORS
INSPIRATORY
INSPIRINGLY
INSPIRITED
INSPIRITER
INSPIRITERS
INSPIRITING
INSPIRITINGLY
INSPIRITMENT
INSPIRITMENTS
INSPISSATE
INSPISSATED
INSPISSATES
INSPISSATING
INSPISSATION
INSPISSATIONS
INSPISSATOR
INSPISSATORS
INSTABILITIES
INSTABILITY
INSTALLANT
INSTALLANTS
INSTALLATION
INSTALLATIONS
INSTALLERS
INSTALLING
INSTALLMENT
INSTALLMENTS
INSTALMENT
INSTALMENTS
INSTANCIES
INSTANCING
INSTANTANEITIES
INSTANTANEITY
INSTANTANEOUS
INSTANTANEOUSLY
INSTANTIAL
INSTANTIATE
INSTANTIATED
INSTANTIATES
INSTANTIATING
INSTANTIATION
INSTANTIATIONS
INSTANTNESS
INSTANTNESSES
INSTARRING
INSTATEMENT
INSTATEMENTS
INSTAURATION
INSTAURATIONS
INSTAURATOR
INSTAURATORS
INSTIGATED
INSTIGATES
INSTIGATING
INSTIGATINGLY
INSTIGATION
INSTIGATIONS
INSTIGATIVE
INSTIGATOR
INSTIGATORS
INSTILLATION
INSTILLATIONS
INSTILLERS
INSTILLING
INSTILLMENT
INSTILLMENTS
INSTILMENT
INSTILMENTS
INSTINCTIVE
INSTINCTIVELY
INSTINCTIVITIES
INSTINCTIVITY

INSTINCTUAL
INSTINCTUALLY
INSTITORIAL
INSTITUTED
INSTITUTER
INSTITUTERS
INSTITUTES
INSTITUTING
INSTITUTION
INSTITUTIONAL
INSTITUTIONALLY
INSTITUTIONARY
INSTITUTIONS
INSTITUTIST
INSTITUTISTS
INSTITUTIVE
INSTITUTIVELY
INSTITUTOR
INSTITUTORS
INSTREAMING
INSTREAMINGS
INSTRESSED
INSTRESSES
INSTRESSING
INSTRUCTED
INSTRUCTIBLE
INSTRUCTING
INSTRUCTION
INSTRUCTIONAL
INSTRUCTIONS
INSTRUCTIVE
INSTRUCTIVELY
INSTRUCTIVENESS
INSTRUCTOR
INSTRUCTORS
INSTRUCTORSHIP
INSTRUCTORSHIPS
INSTRUCTRESS
INSTRUCTRESSES
INSTRUMENT
INSTRUMENTAL
INSTRUMENTALISM
INSTRUMENTALIST
INSTRUMENTALITY
INSTRUMENTALLY
INSTRUMENTALS
INSTRUMENTATION
INSTRUMENTED
INSTRUMENTING
INSTRUMENTS
INSUBJECTION
INSUBJECTIONS
INSUBORDINATE
INSUBORDINATELY
INSUBORDINATES
INSUBORDINATION
INSUBSTANTIAL
INSUBSTANTIALLY
INSUFFERABLE
INSUFFERABLY
INSUFFICIENCE
INSUFFICIENCES
INSUFFICIENCIES
INSUFFICIENCY
INSUFFICIENT
INSUFFICIENTLY
INSUFFLATE
INSUFFLATED
INSUFFLATES
INSUFFLATING
INSUFFLATION
INSUFFLATIONS
INSUFFLATOR
INSUFFLATORS
INSULARISM
INSULARISMS
INSULARITIES
INSULARITY
INSULATING
INSULATION
INSULATIONS
INSULATORS
INSULINASE
INSULINASES
INSULSITIES
INSULTABLE
INSULTINGLY
INSULTMENT
INSULTMENTS
INSUPERABILITY
INSUPERABLE
INSUPERABLENESS
INSUPERABLY
INSUPPORTABLE
INSUPPORTABLY
INSUPPRESSIBLE
INSUPPRESSIBLY
INSURABILITIES
INSURABILITY
INSURANCER
INSURANCERS
INSURANCES
INSURGENCE
INSURGENCES
INSURGENCIES
INSURGENCY
INSURGENTLY
INSURGENTS
INSURMOUNTABLE
INSURMOUNTABLY
INSURRECTION
INSURRECTIONAL
INSURRECTIONARY
INSURRECTIONISM
INSURRECTIONIST
INSURRECTIONS
INSUSCEPTIBLE
INSUSCEPTIBLY
INSUSCEPTIVE
INSUSCEPTIVELY
INSWATHING
INSWINGERS
INTACTNESS
INTACTNESSES
INTAGLIATED
INTAGLIOED
INTAGLIOING
INTANGIBILITIES
INTANGIBILITY
INTANGIBLE
INTANGIBLENESS
INTANGIBLES
INTANGIBLY
INTEGRABILITIES
INTEGRABILITY
INTEGRABLE
INTEGRALITIES
INTEGRALITY
INTEGRALLY
INTEGRANDS
INTEGRANTS
INTEGRATED
INTEGRATES
INTEGRATING
INTEGRATION
INTEGRATIONIST
INTEGRATIONISTS
INTEGRATIONS
INTEGRATIVE
INTEGRATOR
INTEGRATORS
INTEGRITIES
INTEGUMENT
INTEGUMENTAL
INTEGUMENTARY
INTEGUMENTS
INTELLECTED
INTELLECTION
INTELLECTIONS
INTELLECTIVE
INTELLECTIVELY
INTELLECTS
INTELLECTUAL
INTELLECTUALISE
INTELLECTUALISM
INTELLECTUALIST
INTELLECTUALITY
INTELLECTUALIZE
INTELLECTUALLY
INTELLECTUALS
INTELLIGENCE
INTELLIGENCER
INTELLIGENCERS
INTELLIGENCES
INTELLIGENT
INTELLIGENTIAL
INTELLIGENTLY
INTELLIGENTSIA
INTELLIGENTSIAS
INTELLIGENTZIA
INTELLIGENTZIAS
INTELLIGIBILITY
INTELLIGIBLE
INTELLIGIBLY
INTEMERATE
INTEMERATELY
INTEMERATENESS
INTEMPERANCE
INTEMPERANCES
INTEMPERANT
INTEMPERANTS
INTEMPERATE
INTEMPERATELY
INTEMPERATENESS
INTEMPESTIVE
INTEMPESTIVELY
INTEMPESTIVITY
INTENDANCE
INTENDANCES
INTENDANCIES
INTENDANCY
INTENDANTS
INTENDEDLY
INTENDERED
INTENDERING
INTENDMENT
INTENDMENTS
INTENERATE
INTENERATED
INTENERATES
INTENERATING
INTENERATION
INTENERATIONS
INTENSATED
INTENSATES
INTENSATING
INTENSATIVE
INTENSATIVES
INTENSENESS
INTENSENESSES
INTENSIFICATION
INTENSIFIED
INTENSIFIER
INTENSIFIERS
INTENSIFIES
INTENSIFYING
INTENSIONAL
INTENSIONALITY
INTENSIONALLY
INTENSIONS
INTENSITIES
INTENSITIVE
INTENSITIVES
INTENSIVELY
INTENSIVENESS
INTENSIVENESSES
INTENSIVES
INTENTIONAL
INTENTIONALITY
INTENTIONALLY
INTENTIONED
INTENTIONS
INTENTNESS
INTENTNESSES
INTERABANG
INTERABANGS
INTERACTANT
INTERACTANTS
INTERACTED
INTERACTING
INTERACTION
INTERACTIONAL
INTERACTIONISM
INTERACTIONISMS
INTERACTIONIST
INTERACTIONISTS
INTERACTIONS
INTERACTIVE
INTERACTIVELY
INTERACTIVITIES
INTERACTIVITY
INTERAGENCY
INTERALLELIC
INTERALLIED

INTERAMBULACRA
INTERAMBULACRAL
INTERAMBULACRUM
INTERANIMATION
INTERANIMATIONS
INTERANNUAL
INTERARCHED
INTERARCHES
INTERARCHING
INTERATOMIC
INTERBASIN
INTERBEDDED
INTERBEDDING
INTERBEDDINGS
INTERBEHAVIOR
INTERBEHAVIORAL
INTERBEHAVIORS
INTERBOROUGH
INTERBRAIN
INTERBRAINS
INTERBRANCH
INTERBREED
INTERBREEDING
INTERBREEDINGS
INTERBREEDS
INTERBROKER
INTERCALAR
INTERCALARILY
INTERCALARY
INTERCALATE
INTERCALATED
INTERCALATES
INTERCALATING
INTERCALATION
INTERCALATIONS
INTERCALATIVE
INTERCAMPUS
INTERCASTE
INTERCEDED
INTERCEDENT
INTERCEDER
INTERCEDERS
INTERCEDES
INTERCEDING
INTERCELLULAR
INTERCENSAL
INTERCEPTED
INTERCEPTER
INTERCEPTERS
INTERCEPTING
INTERCEPTION
INTERCEPTIONS
INTERCEPTIVE
INTERCEPTOR
INTERCEPTORS
INTERCEPTS
INTERCESSION
INTERCESSIONAL
INTERCESSIONS
INTERCESSOR
INTERCESSORIAL
INTERCESSORS
INTERCESSORY
INTERCHAIN
INTERCHAINED
INTERCHAINING
INTERCHAINS
INTERCHANGE
INTERCHANGEABLE
INTERCHANGEABLY
INTERCHANGED
INTERCHANGEMENT
INTERCHANGER
INTERCHANGERS
INTERCHANGES
INTERCHANGING
INTERCHANNEL
INTERCHAPTER
INTERCHAPTERS
INTERCHURCH
INTERCIPIENT
INTERCIPIENTS
INTERCLASS
INTERCLAVICLE
INTERCLAVICLES
INTERCLAVICULAR
INTERCLUDE
INTERCLUDED
INTERCLUDES
INTERCLUDING
INTERCLUSION
INTERCLUSIONS
INTERCLUSTER
INTERCOASTAL
INTERCOLLEGIATE
INTERCOLLINE
INTERCOLONIAL
INTERCOLONIALLY
INTERCOLUMNAR
INTERCOMMUNAL
INTERCOMMUNE
INTERCOMMUNED
INTERCOMMUNES
INTERCOMMUNING
INTERCOMMUNION
INTERCOMMUNIONS
INTERCOMMUNITY
INTERCOMPANY
INTERCOMPARE
INTERCOMPARED
INTERCOMPARES
INTERCOMPARING
INTERCOMPARISON
INTERCONNECT
INTERCONNECTED
INTERCONNECTING
INTERCONNECTION
INTERCONNECTOR
INTERCONNECTORS
INTERCONNECTS
INTERCONNEXION
INTERCONNEXIONS
INTERCONVERSION
INTERCONVERT
INTERCONVERTED
INTERCONVERTING
INTERCONVERTS
INTERCOOLED
INTERCOOLER
INTERCOOLERS
INTERCORPORATE
INTERCORRELATE
INTERCORRELATED
INTERCORRELATES
INTERCORTICAL
INTERCOSTAL
INTERCOSTALS
INTERCOUNTRY
INTERCOUNTY
INTERCOUPLE
INTERCOURSE
INTERCOURSES
INTERCRATER
INTERCROPPED
INTERCROPPING
INTERCROPS
INTERCROSS
INTERCROSSED
INTERCROSSES
INTERCROSSING
INTERCRURAL
INTERCULTURAL
INTERCULTURALLY
INTERCULTURE
INTERCURRENCE
INTERCURRENCES
INTERCURRENT
INTERCURRENTLY
INTERCUTTING
INTERDASHED
INTERDASHES
INTERDASHING
INTERDEALER
INTERDEALERS
INTERDEALING
INTERDEALS
INTERDEALT
INTERDENTAL
INTERDENTALLY
INTERDEPEND
INTERDEPENDED
INTERDEPENDENCE
INTERDEPENDENCY
INTERDEPENDENT
INTERDEPENDING
INTERDEPENDS
INTERDIALECTAL
INTERDICTED
INTERDICTING
INTERDICTION
INTERDICTIONS
INTERDICTIVE
INTERDICTIVELY
INTERDICTOR
INTERDICTORS
INTERDICTORY
INTERDICTS
INTERDIFFUSE
INTERDIFFUSED
INTERDIFFUSES
INTERDIFFUSING
INTERDIFFUSION
INTERDIFFUSIONS
INTERDIGITAL
INTERDIGITATE
INTERDIGITATED
INTERDIGITATES
INTERDIGITATING
INTERDIGITATION
INTERDINED
INTERDINES
INTERDINING
INTERDISTRICT
INTERDIVISIONAL
INTERDOMINION
INTERELECTRODE
INTERELECTRON
INTERELECTRONIC
INTEREPIDEMIC
INTERESSED
INTERESSES
INTERESSING
INTERESTED
INTERESTEDLY
INTERESTEDNESS
INTERESTING
INTERESTINGLY
INTERESTINGNESS
INTERETHNIC
INTERFACED
INTERFACES
INTERFACIAL
INTERFACIALLY
INTERFACING
INTERFACINGS
INTERFACULTY
INTERFAITH
INTERFAMILIAL
INTERFAMILY
INTERFASCICULAR
INTERFEMORAL
INTERFERED
INTERFERENCE
INTERFERENCES
INTERFERENTIAL
INTERFERER
INTERFERERS
INTERFERES
INTERFERING
INTERFERINGLY
INTERFEROGRAM
INTERFEROGRAMS
INTERFEROMETER
INTERFEROMETERS
INTERFEROMETRIC
INTERFEROMETRY
INTERFERON
INTERFERONS
INTERFERTILE
INTERFERTILITY
INTERFIBER
INTERFILED
INTERFILES
INTERFILING
INTERFLOWED
INTERFLOWING
INTERFLOWS
INTERFLUENCE
INTERFLUENCES
INTERFLUENT
INTERFLUOUS
INTERFLUVE
INTERFLUVES
INTERFLUVIAL

INTERFOLDED
INTERFOLDING
INTERFOLDS
INTERFOLIATE
INTERFOLIATED
INTERFOLIATES
INTERFOLIATING
INTERFRATERNITY
INTERFRETTED
INTERFRONTAL
INTERFUSED
INTERFUSES
INTERFUSING
INTERFUSION
INTERFUSIONS
INTERGALACTIC
INTERGENERATION
INTERGENERIC
INTERGLACIAL
INTERGLACIALS
INTERGRADATION
INTERGRADATIONS
INTERGRADE
INTERGRADED
INTERGRADES
INTERGRADIENT
INTERGRADING
INTERGRAFT
INTERGRAFTED
INTERGRAFTING
INTERGRAFTS
INTERGRANULAR
INTERGROUP
INTERGROWING
INTERGROWN
INTERGROWS
INTERGROWTH
INTERGROWTHS
INTERINDIVIDUAL
INTERINDUSTRY
INTERINFLUENCE
INTERINFLUENCES
INTERINVOLVE
INTERINVOLVED
INTERINVOLVES
INTERINVOLVING
INTERIONIC
INTERIORISATION
INTERIORISE
INTERIORISED
INTERIORISES
INTERIORISING
INTERIORITIES
INTERIORITY
INTERIORIZATION
INTERIORIZE
INTERIORIZED
INTERIORIZES
INTERIORIZING
INTERIORLY
INTERISLAND
INTERJACENCIES
INTERJACENCY
INTERJACENT
INTERJACULATE
INTERJACULATED
INTERJACULATES
INTERJACULATING
INTERJACULATORY
INTERJECTED
INTERJECTING
INTERJECTION
INTERJECTIONAL
INTERJECTIONARY
INTERJECTIONS
INTERJECTOR
INTERJECTORS
INTERJECTORY
INTERJECTS
INTERJECTURAL
INTERJOINED
INTERJOINING
INTERJOINS
INTERKINESES
INTERKINESIS
INTERKNITS
INTERKNITTED
INTERKNITTING
INTERKNOTS
INTERKNOTTED
INTERKNOTTING
INTERLACED
INTERLACEDLY
INTERLACEMENT
INTERLACEMENTS
INTERLACES
INTERLACING
INTERLACUSTRINE
INTERLAMINAR
INTERLAMINATE
INTERLAMINATED
INTERLAMINATES
INTERLAMINATING
INTERLAMINATION
INTERLAPPED
INTERLAPPING
INTERLARDED
INTERLARDING
INTERLARDS
INTERLAYER
INTERLAYERED
INTERLAYERING
INTERLAYERS
INTERLAYING
INTERLEAVE
INTERLEAVED
INTERLEAVES
INTERLEAVING
INTERLENDING
INTERLENDS
INTERLEUKIN
INTERLEUKINS
INTERLIBRARY
INTERLINEAL
INTERLINEALLY
INTERLINEAR
INTERLINEARLY
INTERLINEARS
INTERLINEATE
INTERLINEATED
INTERLINEATES
INTERLINEATING
INTERLINEATION
INTERLINEATIONS
INTERLINED
INTERLINER
INTERLINERS
INTERLINES
INTERLINGUA
INTERLINGUAL
INTERLINGUALLY
INTERLINGUAS
INTERLINING
INTERLININGS
INTERLINKED
INTERLINKING
INTERLINKS
INTERLOANS
INTERLOBULAR
INTERLOCAL
INTERLOCATION
INTERLOCATIONS
INTERLOCKED
INTERLOCKER
INTERLOCKERS
INTERLOCKING
INTERLOCKS
INTERLOCUTION
INTERLOCUTIONS
INTERLOCUTOR
INTERLOCUTORILY
INTERLOCUTORS
INTERLOCUTORY
INTERLOCUTRESS
INTERLOCUTRICE
INTERLOCUTRICES
INTERLOCUTRIX
INTERLOCUTRIXES
INTERLOOPED
INTERLOOPING
INTERLOOPS
INTERLOPED
INTERLOPER
INTERLOPERS
INTERLOPES
INTERLOPING
INTERLUDED
INTERLUDES
INTERLUDIAL
INTERLUDING
INTERLUNAR
INTERLUNARY
INTERLUNATION
INTERLUNATIONS
INTERMARGINAL
INTERMARRIAGE
INTERMARRIAGES
INTERMARRIED
INTERMARRIES
INTERMARRY
INTERMARRYING
INTERMATTED
INTERMATTING
INTERMAXILLA
INTERMAXILLAE
INTERMAXILLARY
INTERMEDDLE
INTERMEDDLED
INTERMEDDLER
INTERMEDDLERS
INTERMEDDLES
INTERMEDDLING
INTERMEDIA
INTERMEDIACIES
INTERMEDIACY
INTERMEDIAL
INTERMEDIARIES
INTERMEDIARY
INTERMEDIATE
INTERMEDIATED
INTERMEDIATELY
INTERMEDIATES
INTERMEDIATING
INTERMEDIATION
INTERMEDIATIONS
INTERMEDIATOR
INTERMEDIATORS
INTERMEDIATORY
INTERMEDIN
INTERMEDINS
INTERMEDIUM
INTERMEDIUMS
INTERMEMBRANE
INTERMENSTRUAL
INTERMENTS
INTERMESHED
INTERMESHES
INTERMESHING
INTERMETALLIC
INTERMETALLICS
INTERMEZZI
INTERMEZZO
INTERMEZZOS
INTERMIGRATION
INTERMIGRATIONS
INTERMINABILITY
INTERMINABLE
INTERMINABLY
INTERMINGLE
INTERMINGLED
INTERMINGLES
INTERMINGLING
INTERMISSION
INTERMISSIONS
INTERMISSIVE
INTERMITOTIC
INTERMITTED
INTERMITTENCE
INTERMITTENCES
INTERMITTENCIES
INTERMITTENCY
INTERMITTENT
INTERMITTENTLY
INTERMITTER
INTERMITTERS
INTERMITTING
INTERMITTINGLY
INTERMITTOR
INTERMITTORS
INTERMIXED
INTERMIXES
INTERMIXING
INTERMIXTURE
INTERMIXTURES

INTERMODAL
INTERMODULATION
INTERMOLECULAR
INTERMONTANE
INTERMOUNTAIN
INTERMUNDANE
INTERMURED
INTERMURES
INTERMURING
INTERNALISATION
INTERNALISE
INTERNALISED
INTERNALISES
INTERNALISING
INTERNALITIES
INTERNALITY
INTERNALIZATION
INTERNALIZE
INTERNALIZED
INTERNALIZES
INTERNALIZING
INTERNALLY
INTERNALNESS
INTERNALNESSES
INTERNATIONAL
INTERNATIONALLY
INTERNATIONALS
INTERNECINE
INTERNECIVE
INTERNEURAL
INTERNEURON
INTERNEURONAL
INTERNEURONS
INTERNISTS
INTERNMENT
INTERNMENTS
INTERNODAL
INTERNODES
INTERNODIAL
INTERNSHIP
INTERNSHIPS
INTERNUCLEAR
INTERNUCLEON
INTERNUCLEONIC
INTERNUCLEOTIDE
INTERNUNCIAL
INTERNUNCIO
INTERNUNCIOS
INTEROBSERVER
INTEROCEAN
INTEROCEANIC
INTEROCEPTIVE
INTEROCEPTOR
INTEROCEPTORS
INTEROCULAR
INTEROFFICE
INTEROPERABLE
INTEROPERATIVE
INTERORBITAL
INTERORGAN
INTEROSCULANT
INTEROSCULATE
INTEROSCULATED
INTEROSCULATES
INTEROSCULATING
INTEROSCULATION
INTEROSSEAL
INTEROSSEOUS
INTERPAGED
INTERPAGES
INTERPAGING
INTERPANDEMIC
INTERPARIETAL
INTERPARISH
INTERPAROCHIAL
INTERPAROXYSMAL
INTERPARTICLE
INTERPARTY
INTERPELLANT
INTERPELLANTS
INTERPELLATE
INTERPELLATED
INTERPELLATES
INTERPELLATING
INTERPELLATION
INTERPELLATIONS
INTERPELLATOR
INTERPELLATORS
INTERPENETRABLE
INTERPENETRANT
INTERPENETRATE
INTERPENETRATED
INTERPENETRATES
INTERPERCEPTUAL
INTERPERMEATE
INTERPERMEATED
INTERPERMEATES
INTERPERMEATING
INTERPERSONAL
INTERPERSONALLY
INTERPETIOLAR
INTERPHALANGEAL
INTERPHASE
INTERPHASES
INTERPHONE
INTERPHONES
INTERPILASTER
INTERPILASTERS
INTERPLANETARY
INTERPLANT
INTERPLANTED
INTERPLANTING
INTERPLANTS
INTERPLAYED
INTERPLAYING
INTERPLAYS
INTERPLEAD
INTERPLEADED
INTERPLEADER
INTERPLEADERS
INTERPLEADING
INTERPLEADS
INTERPLEURAL
INTERPLUVIAL
INTERPOINT
INTERPOLABLE
INTERPOLAR
INTERPOLATE
INTERPOLATED
INTERPOLATER
INTERPOLATERS
INTERPOLATES
INTERPOLATING
INTERPOLATION
INTERPOLATIONS
INTERPOLATIVE
INTERPOLATOR
INTERPOLATORS
INTERPONED
INTERPONES
INTERPONING
INTERPOPULATION
INTERPOSABLE
INTERPOSAL
INTERPOSALS
INTERPOSED
INTERPOSER
INTERPOSERS
INTERPOSES
INTERPOSING
INTERPOSITION
INTERPOSITIONS
INTERPRETABLE
INTERPRETABLY
INTERPRETATE
INTERPRETATED
INTERPRETATES
INTERPRETATING
INTERPRETATION
INTERPRETATIONS
INTERPRETATIVE
INTERPRETED
INTERPRETER
INTERPRETERS
INTERPRETERSHIP
INTERPRETESS
INTERPRETESSES
INTERPRETING
INTERPRETIVE
INTERPRETIVELY
INTERPRETRESS
INTERPRETRESSES
INTERPRETS
INTERPROVINCIAL
INTERPROXIMAL
INTERPSYCHIC
INTERPUNCTION
INTERPUNCTIONS
INTERPUNCTUATE
INTERPUNCTUATED
INTERPUNCTUATES
INTERPUPILLARY
INTERQUARTILE
INTERRACIAL
INTERRACIALLY
INTERRADIAL
INTERRADIALLY
INTERRADII
INTERRADIUS
INTERRADIUSES
INTERRAILED
INTERRAILER
INTERRAILERS
INTERRAILING
INTERRAILS
INTERRAMAL
INTERREGAL
INTERREGES
INTERREGIONAL
INTERREGNA
INTERREGNAL
INTERREGNUM
INTERREGNUMS
INTERRELATE
INTERRELATED
INTERRELATEDLY
INTERRELATES
INTERRELATING
INTERRELATION
INTERRELATIONS
INTERRELIGIOUS
INTERRENAL
INTERROBANG
INTERROBANGS
INTERROGABLE
INTERROGANT
INTERROGANTS
INTERROGATE
INTERROGATED
INTERROGATEE
INTERROGATEES
INTERROGATES
INTERROGATING
INTERROGATINGLY
INTERROGATION
INTERROGATIONAL
INTERROGATIONS
INTERROGATIVE
INTERROGATIVELY
INTERROGATIVES
INTERROGATOR
INTERROGATORIES
INTERROGATORILY
INTERROGATORS
INTERROGATORY
INTERROGEE
INTERROGEES
INTERRUPTED
INTERRUPTEDLY
INTERRUPTER
INTERRUPTERS
INTERRUPTIBLE
INTERRUPTING
INTERRUPTION
INTERRUPTIONS
INTERRUPTIVE
INTERRUPTIVELY
INTERRUPTOR
INTERRUPTORS
INTERRUPTS
INTERSCAPULAR
INTERSCHOLASTIC
INTERSCHOOL
INTERSCRIBE
INTERSCRIBED
INTERSCRIBES
INTERSCRIBING
INTERSECTED
INTERSECTING
INTERSECTION
INTERSECTIONAL
INTERSECTIONS
INTERSECTS
INTERSEGMENT

NTERSEGMENTAL
NTERSENSORY
NTERSEPTAL
NTERSERTAL
NTERSERTED
NTERSERTING
NTERSERTS
NTERSERVICE
NTERSESSION
NTERSESSIONS
NTERSEXES
NTERSEXUAL
NTERSEXUALISM
NTERSEXUALISMS
NTERSEXUALITY
NTERSEXUALLY
NTERSIDEREAL
NTERSOCIETAL
NTERSOCIETY
NTERSPACE
NTERSPACED
NTERSPACES
NTERSPACING
NTERSPATIAL
NTERSPATIALLY
NTERSPECIES
NTERSPECIFIC
NTERSPERSAL
NTERSPERSALS
NTERSPERSE
NTERSPERSED
NTERSPERSEDLY
NTERSPERSES
NTERSPERSING
NTERSPERSION
NTERSPERSIONS
NTERSPINAL
NTERSPINOUS
NTERSTADIAL
NTERSTADIALS
NTERSTAGE
NTERSTATE
NTERSTATES
NTERSTATION
NTERSTELLAR
NTERSTELLARY
NTERSTERILE
NTERSTERILITY
NTERSTICE
NTERSTICES
NTERSTIMULUS
NTERSTITIAL
NTERSTITIALLY
NTERSTITIALS
NTERSTRAIN
NTERSTRAND
NTERSTRATIFIED
NTERSTRATIFIES
NTERSTRATIFY
NTERSUBJECTIVE
NTERSYSTEM
NTERTANGLE
NTERTANGLED
NTERTANGLEMENT
NTERTANGLES
NTERTANGLING

INTERTARSAL
INTERTENTACULAR
INTERTERMINAL
INTERTEXTS
INTERTEXTUAL
INTERTEXTUALITY
INTERTEXTUALLY
INTERTEXTURE
INTERTEXTURES
INTERTIDAL
INTERTIDALLY
INTERTILLAGE
INTERTILLAGES
INTERTILLED
INTERTILLING
INTERTILLS
INTERTISSUED
INTERTRAFFIC
INTERTRAFFICS
INTERTRIAL
INTERTRIBAL
INTERTRIGO
INTERTRIGOS
INTERTROOP
INTERTROPICAL
INTERTWINE
INTERTWINED
INTERTWINEMENT
INTERTWINEMENTS
INTERTWINES
INTERTWINING
INTERTWININGLY
INTERTWININGS
INTERTWIST
INTERTWISTED
INTERTWISTING
INTERTWISTINGLY
INTERTWISTS
INTERUNION
INTERUNIONS
INTERUNIVERSITY
INTERURBAN
INTERVALES
INTERVALLEY
INTERVALLIC
INTERVALLUM
INTERVALLUMS
INTERVALOMETER
INTERVALOMETERS
INTERVARSITY
INTERVEINED
INTERVEINING
INTERVEINS
INTERVENED
INTERVENER
INTERVENERS
INTERVENES
INTERVENIENT
INTERVENING
INTERVENOR
INTERVENORS
INTERVENTION
INTERVENTIONAL
INTERVENTIONISM
INTERVENTIONIST
INTERVENTIONS

INTERVENTOR
INTERVENTORS
INTERVERTEBRAL
INTERVIEWED
INTERVIEWEE
INTERVIEWEES
INTERVIEWER
INTERVIEWERS
INTERVIEWING
INTERVIEWS
INTERVILLAGE
INTERVISIBILITY
INTERVISIBLE
INTERVISITATION
INTERVITAL
INTERVOCALIC
INTERVOLVE
INTERVOLVED
INTERVOLVES
INTERVOLVING
INTERWEAVE
INTERWEAVED
INTERWEAVEMENT
INTERWEAVEMENTS
INTERWEAVER
INTERWEAVERS
INTERWEAVES
INTERWEAVING
INTERWINDING
INTERWINDS
INTERWORKED
INTERWORKING
INTERWORKINGS
INTERWORKS
INTERWOUND
INTERWOVEN
INTERWREATHE
INTERWREATHED
INTERWREATHES
INTERWREATHING
INTERWROUGHT
INTERZONAL
INTERZONES
INTESTACIES
INTESTATES
INTESTINAL
INTESTINALLY
INTESTINES
INTHRALLED
INTHRALLING
INTHRONING
INTIFADAHS
INTIFADEHS
INTIMACIES
INTIMATELY
INTIMATENESS
INTIMATENESSES
INTIMATERS
INTIMATING
INTIMATION
INTIMATIONS
INTIMIDATE
INTIMIDATED
INTIMIDATES
INTIMIDATING
INTIMIDATINGLY

INTIMIDATION
INTIMIDATIONS
INTIMIDATOR
INTIMIDATORS
INTIMIDATORY
INTIMISTES
INTIMITIES
INTINCTION
INTINCTIONS
INTITULING
INTOLERABILITY
INTOLERABLE
INTOLERABLENESS
INTOLERABLY
INTOLERANCE
INTOLERANCES
INTOLERANT
INTOLERANTLY
INTOLERANTNESS
INTOLERANTS
INTOLERATION
INTOLERATIONS
INTONATING
INTONATION
INTONATIONAL
INTONATIONS
INTONATORS
INTONINGLY
INTORSIONS
INTORTIONS
INTOXICABLE
INTOXICANT
INTOXICANTS
INTOXICATE
INTOXICATED
INTOXICATEDLY
INTOXICATES
INTOXICATING
INTOXICATINGLY
INTOXICATION
INTOXICATIONS
INTOXICATIVE
INTOXICATOR
INTOXICATORS
INTOXIMETER
INTOXIMETERS
INTRACAPSULAR
INTRACARDIAC
INTRACARDIAL
INTRACARDIALLY
INTRACAVITARY
INTRACELLULAR
INTRACELLULARLY
INTRACEREBRAL
INTRACEREBRALLY
INTRACOMPANY
INTRACRANIAL
INTRACRANIALLY
INTRACTABILITY
INTRACTABLE
INTRACTABLENESS
INTRACTABLY
INTRACUTANEOUS
INTRADERMAL
INTRADERMALLY
INTRADERMIC

INTRADERMICALLY
INTRADOSES
INTRAFALLOPIAN
INTRAFASCICULAR
INTRAGALACTIC
INTRAGENIC
INTRAMEDULLARY
INTRAMERCURIAL
INTRAMOLECULAR
INTRAMUNDANE
INTRAMURAL
INTRAMURALLY
INTRAMUSCULAR
INTRAMUSCULARLY
INTRANASAL
INTRANASALLY
INTRANATIONAL
INTRANSIGEANCE
INTRANSIGEANCES
INTRANSIGEANT
INTRANSIGEANTLY
INTRANSIGEANTS
INTRANSIGENCE
INTRANSIGENCES
INTRANSIGENCIES
INTRANSIGENCY
INTRANSIGENT
INTRANSIGENTISM
INTRANSIGENTIST
INTRANSIGENTLY
INTRANSIGENTS
INTRANSITIVE
INTRANSITIVELY
INTRANSITIVITY
INTRANSMISSIBLE
INTRANSMUTABLE
INTRANUCLEAR
INTRAOCULAR
INTRAOCULARLY
INTRAPARIETAL
INTRAPARTUM
INTRAPERITONEAL
INTRAPERSONAL
INTRAPETIOLAR
INTRAPLATE
INTRAPOPULATION
INTRAPRENEUR
INTRAPRENEURIAL
INTRAPRENEURS
INTRAPSYCHIC
INTRASEXUAL
INTRASPECIES
INTRASPECIFIC
INTRASTATE
INTRATELLURIC
INTRATHECAL
INTRATHECALLY
INTRATHORACIC
INTRAUTERINE
INTRAVASATION
INTRAVASATIONS
INTRAVASCULAR
INTRAVASCULARLY
INTRAVENOUS
INTRAVENOUSLY
INTRAVITAL
INTRAVITALLY
INTRAVITAM
INTRAZONAL
INTREATFULL
INTREATING
INTREATINGLY
INTREATMENT
INTREATMENTS
INTRENCHANT
INTRENCHED
INTRENCHER
INTRENCHERS
INTRENCHES
INTRENCHING
INTRENCHMENT
INTRENCHMENTS
INTREPIDITIES
INTREPIDITY
INTREPIDLY
INTREPIDNESS
INTREPIDNESSES
INTRICACIES
INTRICATELY
INTRICATENESS
INTRICATENESSES
INTRIGANTE
INTRIGANTES
INTRIGANTS
INTRIGUANT
INTRIGUANTE
INTRIGUANTES
INTRIGUANTS
INTRIGUERS
INTRIGUING
INTRIGUINGLY
INTRINSICAL
INTRINSICALITY
INTRINSICALLY
INTRINSICALNESS
INTRINSICATE
INTRODUCED
INTRODUCER
INTRODUCERS
INTRODUCES
INTRODUCIBLE
INTRODUCING
INTRODUCTION
INTRODUCTIONS
INTRODUCTIVE
INTRODUCTORILY
INTRODUCTORY
INTROFYING
INTROGRESSANT
INTROGRESSANTS
INTROGRESSION
INTROGRESSIONS
INTROGRESSIVE
INTROITUSES
INTROJECTED
INTROJECTING
INTROJECTION
INTROJECTIONS
INTROJECTIVE
INTROJECTS
INTROMISSIBLE
INTROMISSION
INTROMISSIONS
INTROMISSIVE
INTROMITTED
INTROMITTENT
INTROMITTER
INTROMITTERS
INTROMITTING
INTRORSELY
INTROSPECT
INTROSPECTED
INTROSPECTING
INTROSPECTION
INTROSPECTIONAL
INTROSPECTIONS
INTROSPECTIVE
INTROSPECTIVELY
INTROSPECTS
INTROSUSCEPTION
INTROVERSIBLE
INTROVERSION
INTROVERSIONS
INTROVERSIVE
INTROVERSIVELY
INTROVERTED
INTROVERTING
INTROVERTIVE
INTROVERTS
INTRUDINGLY
INTRUSIONAL
INTRUSIONIST
INTRUSIONISTS
INTRUSIONS
INTRUSIVELY
INTRUSIVENESS
INTRUSIVENESSES
INTRUSIVES
INTRUSTING
INTRUSTMENT
INTRUSTMENTS
INTUBATING
INTUBATION
INTUBATIONS
INTUITABLE
INTUITIONAL
INTUITIONALISM
INTUITIONALISMS
INTUITIONALIST
INTUITIONALISTS
INTUITIONALLY
INTUITIONISM
INTUITIONISMS
INTUITIONIST
INTUITIONISTS
INTUITIONS
INTUITIVELY
INTUITIVENESS
INTUITIVENESSES
INTUITIVISM
INTUITIVISMS
INTUMESCED
INTUMESCENCE
INTUMESCENCES
INTUMESCENCIES
INTUMESCENCY
INTUMESCENT
INTUMESCES
INTUMESCING
INTURBIDATE
INTURBIDATED
INTURBIDATES
INTURBIDATING
INTUSSUSCEPT
INTUSSUSCEPTED
INTUSSUSCEPTING
INTUSSUSCEPTION
INTUSSUSCEPTIVE
INTUSSUSCEPTS
INTWINEMENT
INTWINEMENTS
INTWISTING
INUMBRATED
INUMBRATES
INUMBRATING
INUNCTIONS
INUNDATING
INUNDATION
INUNDATIONS
INUNDATORS
INUNDATORY
INURBANELY
INURBANITIES
INURBANITY
INUREDNESS
INUREDNESSES
INUREMENTS
INURNMENTS
INUSITATION
INUSITATIONS
INUTILITIES
INUTTERABLE
INVAGINABLE
INVAGINATE
INVAGINATED
INVAGINATES
INVAGINATING
INVAGINATION
INVAGINATIONS
INVALIDATE
INVALIDATED
INVALIDATES
INVALIDATING
INVALIDATION
INVALIDATIONS
INVALIDATOR
INVALIDATORS
INVALIDHOOD
INVALIDHOODS
INVALIDING
INVALIDINGS
INVALIDISM
INVALIDISMS
INVALIDITIES
INVALIDITY
INVALIDNESS
INVALIDNESSES
INVALUABLE
INVALUABLENESS
INVALUABLY
INVARIABILITIES
INVARIABILITY
INVARIABLE
INVARIABLENESS

NVARIABLES
NVARIABLY
NVARIANCE
NVARIANCES
NVARIANCIES
NVARIANCY
NVARIANTS
NVASIVENESS
NVASIVENESSES
NVEAGLING
NVECTIVELY
NVECTIVENESS
NVECTIVENESSES
NVECTIVES
NVEIGHERS
NVEIGHING
NVEIGLEMENT
NVEIGLEMENTS
NVEIGLERS
NVEIGLING
NVENDIBILITIES
NVENDIBILITY
NVENDIBLE
NVENTABLE
NVENTIBLE
NVENTIONAL
NVENTIONLESS
NVENTIONS
NVENTIVELY
NVENTIVENESS
NVENTIVENESSES
NVENTORIABLE
NVENTORIAL
NVENTORIALLY
NVENTORIED
NVENTORIES
NVENTORYING
NVENTRESS
NVENTRESSES
NVERACITIES
NVERACITY
NVERITIES
NVERNESSES
NVERSIONS
NVERTASES
NVERTEBRAL
NVERTEBRATE
NVERTEBRATES
NVERTEDLY
NVERTIBILITIES
NVERTIBILITY
NVERTIBLE
NVESTABLE
NVESTIBLE
NVESTIGABLE
NVESTIGATE
NVESTIGATED
NVESTIGATES
NVESTIGATING
NVESTIGATION
NVESTIGATIONAL
NVESTIGATIONS
NVESTIGATIVE
NVESTIGATOR
NVESTIGATORS
NVESTIGATORY
INVESTITIVE
INVESTITURE
INVESTITURES
INVESTMENT
INVESTMENTS
INVETERACIES
INVETERACY
INVETERATE
INVETERATELY
INVETERATENESS
INVIABILITIES
INVIABILITY
INVIABLENESS
INVIABLENESSES
INVIDIOUSLY
INVIDIOUSNESS
INVIDIOUSNESSES
INVIGILATE
INVIGILATED
INVIGILATES
INVIGILATING
INVIGILATION
INVIGILATIONS
INVIGILATOR
INVIGILATORS
INVIGORANT
INVIGORANTS
INVIGORATE
INVIGORATED
INVIGORATES
INVIGORATING
INVIGORATINGLY
INVIGORATION
INVIGORATIONS
INVIGORATIVE
INVIGORATIVELY
INVIGORATOR
INVIGORATORS
INVINCIBILITIES
INVINCIBILITY
INVINCIBLE
INVINCIBLENESS
INVINCIBLY
INVIOLABILITIES
INVIOLABILITY
INVIOLABLE
INVIOLABLENESS
INVIOLABLY
INVIOLACIES
INVIOLATED
INVIOLATELY
INVIOLATENESS
INVIOLATENESSES
INVISIBILITIES
INVISIBILITY
INVISIBLENESS
INVISIBLENESSES
INVISIBLES
INVITATION
INVITATIONAL
INVITATIONALS
INVITATIONS
INVITATORIES
INVITATORY
INVITEMENT
INVITEMENTS
INVITINGLY
INVITINGNESS
INVITINGNESSES
INVOCATING
INVOCATION
INVOCATIONAL
INVOCATIONS
INVOCATIVE
INVOCATORS
INVOCATORY
INVOLUCELLA
INVOLUCELLATE
INVOLUCELLATED
INVOLUCELLUM
INVOLUCELS
INVOLUCRAL
INVOLUCRATE
INVOLUCRES
INVOLUCRUM
INVOLUNTARILY
INVOLUNTARINESS
INVOLUNTARY
INVOLUTEDLY
INVOLUTELY
INVOLUTING
INVOLUTION
INVOLUTIONAL
INVOLUTIONS
INVOLVEDLY
INVOLVEMENT
INVOLVEMENTS
INVULNERABILITY
INVULNERABLE
INVULNERABLY
INVULTUATION
INVULTUATIONS
INWARDNESS
INWARDNESSES
INWORKINGS
INWRAPPING
INWREATHED
INWREATHES
INWREATHING
IODINATING
IODINATION
IODINATIONS
IODISATION
IODISATIONS
IODIZATION
IODIZATIONS
IODOMETRIC
IODOMETRICAL
IODOMETRICALLY
IODOMETRIES
IONICITIES
IONISATION
IONISATIONS
IONIZATION
IONIZATIONS
IONOPAUSES
IONOPHORES
IONOPHORESES
IONOPHORESIS
IONOSONDES
IONOSPHERE
IONOSPHERES
IONOSPHERIC
IONOSPHERICALLY
IONOTROPIC
IONOTROPIES
IONTOPHORESES
IONTOPHORESIS
IONTOPHORETIC
IPECACUANHA
IPECACUANHAS
IPRATROPIUM
IPRATROPIUMS
IPRINDOLES
IPRONIAZID
IPRONIAZIDS
IPSELATERAL
IPSILATERAL
IPSILATERALLY
IRACUNDITIES
IRACUNDITY
IRACUNDULOUS
IRASCIBILITIES
IRASCIBILITY
IRASCIBLENESS
IRASCIBLENESSES
IRATENESSES
IREFULNESS
IREFULNESSES
IRENICALLY
IRENICISMS
IRENOLOGIES
IRIDACEOUS
IRIDECTOMIES
IRIDECTOMY
IRIDESCENCE
IRIDESCENCES
IRIDESCENT
IRIDESCENTLY
IRIDISATION
IRIDISATIONS
IRIDIZATION
IRIDIZATIONS
IRIDOCYTES
IRIDOLOGIES
IRIDOLOGIST
IRIDOLOGISTS
IRIDOSMINE
IRIDOSMINES
IRIDOSMIUM
IRIDOSMIUMS
IRIDOTOMIES
IRISATIONS
IRKSOMENESS
IRKSOMENESSES
IRONFISTED
IRONHANDED
IRONHEARTED
IRONICALLY
IRONICALNESS
IRONICALNESSES
IRONMASTER
IRONMASTERS
IRONMONGER
IRONMONGERIES
IRONMONGERS
IRONMONGERY
IRONNESSES

IRONSMITHS
IRONSTONES
IRONWORKER
IRONWORKERS
IRRADIANCE
IRRADIANCES
IRRADIANCIES
IRRADIANCY
IRRADIATED
IRRADIATES
IRRADIATING
IRRADIATION
IRRADIATIONS
IRRADIATIVE
IRRADIATOR
IRRADIATORS
IRRADICABLE
IRRADICABLY
IRRADICATE
IRRADICATED
IRRADICATES
IRRADICATING
IRRATIONAL
IRRATIONALISE
IRRATIONALISED
IRRATIONALISES
IRRATIONALISING
IRRATIONALISM
IRRATIONALISMS
IRRATIONALIST
IRRATIONALISTIC
IRRATIONALISTS
IRRATIONALITIES
IRRATIONALITY
IRRATIONALIZE
IRRATIONALIZED
IRRATIONALIZES
IRRATIONALIZING
IRRATIONALLY
IRRATIONALNESS
IRRATIONALS
IRREALISABLE
IRREALITIES
IRREALIZABLE
IRREBUTTABLE
IRRECEPTIVE
IRRECIPROCAL
IRRECIPROCITIES
IRRECIPROCITY
IRRECLAIMABLE
IRRECLAIMABLY
IRRECOGNISABLE
IRRECOGNITION
IRRECOGNITIONS
IRRECOGNIZABLE
IRRECONCILABLE
IRRECONCILABLES
IRRECONCILABLY
IRRECONCILED
IRRECONCILEMENT
IRRECOVERABLE
IRRECOVERABLY
IRRECUSABLE
IRRECUSABLY
IRREDEEMABILITY
IRREDEEMABLE
IRREDEEMABLES
IRREDEEMABLY
IRREDENTAS
IRREDENTISM
IRREDENTISMS
IRREDENTIST
IRREDENTISTS
IRREDUCIBILITY
IRREDUCIBLE
IRREDUCIBLENESS
IRREDUCIBLY
IRREDUCTIBILITY
IRREDUCTION
IRREDUCTIONS
IRREFLECTION
IRREFLECTIONS
IRREFLECTIVE
IRREFLEXION
IRREFLEXIONS
IRREFLEXIVE
IRREFORMABILITY
IRREFORMABLE
IRREFORMABLY
IRREFRAGABILITY
IRREFRAGABLE
IRREFRAGABLY
IRREFRANGIBLE
IRREFRANGIBLY
IRREFUTABILITY
IRREFUTABLE
IRREFUTABLENESS
IRREFUTABLY
IRREGARDLESS
IRREGULARITIES
IRREGULARITY
IRREGULARLY
IRREGULARS
IRRELATION
IRRELATIONS
IRRELATIVE
IRRELATIVELY
IRRELATIVENESS
IRRELEVANCE
IRRELEVANCES
IRRELEVANCIES
IRRELEVANCY
IRRELEVANT
IRRELEVANTLY
IRRELIEVABLE
IRRELIGION
IRRELIGIONIST
IRRELIGIONISTS
IRRELIGIONS
IRRELIGIOUS
IRRELIGIOUSLY
IRRELIGIOUSNESS
IRREMEABLE
IRREMEABLY
IRREMEDIABLE
IRREMEDIABLY
IRREMISSIBILITY
IRREMISSIBLE
IRREMISSIBLY
IRREMISSION
IRREMISSIONS
IRREMISSIVE
IRREMOVABILITY
IRREMOVABLE
IRREMOVABLENESS
IRREMOVABLY
IRRENOWNED
IRREPAIRABLE
IRREPARABILITY
IRREPARABLE
IRREPARABLENESS
IRREPARABLY
IRREPEALABILITY
IRREPEALABLE
IRREPEALABLY
IRREPLACEABLE
IRREPLACEABLY
IRREPLEVIABLE
IRREPLEVISABLE
IRREPREHENSIBLE
IRREPREHENSIBLY
IRREPRESSIBLE
IRREPRESSIBLY
IRREPROACHABLE
IRREPROACHABLY
IRREPRODUCIBLE
IRREPROVABLE
IRREPROVABLY
IRRESISTANCE
IRRESISTANCES
IRRESISTIBILITY
IRRESISTIBLE
IRRESISTIBLY
IRRESOLUBILITY
IRRESOLUBLE
IRRESOLUBLY
IRRESOLUTE
IRRESOLUTELY
IRRESOLUTENESS
IRRESOLUTION
IRRESOLUTIONS
IRRESOLVABILITY
IRRESOLVABLE
IRRESOLVABLY
IRRESPECTIVE
IRRESPECTIVELY
IRRESPIRABLE
IRRESPONSIBLE
IRRESPONSIBLES
IRRESPONSIBLY
IRRESPONSIVE
IRRESPONSIVELY
IRRESTRAINABLE
IRRESUSCITABLE
IRRESUSCITABLY
IRRETENTION
IRRETENTIONS
IRRETENTIVE
IRRETENTIVENESS
IRRETRIEVABLE
IRRETRIEVABLY
IRREVERENCE
IRREVERENCES
IRREVERENT
IRREVERENTIAL
IRREVERENTLY
IRREVERSIBILITY
IRREVERSIBLE
IRREVERSIBLY
IRREVOCABILITY
IRREVOCABLE
IRREVOCABLENESS
IRREVOCABLY
IRRIDENTAS
IRRIGATING
IRRIGATION
IRRIGATIONAL
IRRIGATIONS
IRRIGATIVE
IRRIGATORS
IRRITABILITIES
IRRITABILITY
IRRITABLENESS
IRRITABLENESSES
IRRITANCIES
IRRITATING
IRRITATINGLY
IRRITATION
IRRITATIONS
IRRITATIVE
IRRITATORS
IRROTATIONAL
IRRUPTIONS
IRRUPTIVELY
ISABELLINE
ISABELLINES
ISALLOBARIC
ISALLOBARS
ISAPOSTOLIC
ISCHAEMIAS
ISCHURETIC
ISCHURETICS
ISEIKONIAS
ISENTROPIC
ISENTROPICALLY
ISINGLASSES
ISLOMANIAS
ISMATICALNESS
ISMATICALNESSES
ISOAGGLUTININ
ISOAGGLUTININS
ISOALLOXAZINE
ISOALLOXAZINES
ISOAMINILE
ISOAMINILES
ISOANTIBODIES
ISOANTIBODY
ISOANTIGEN
ISOANTIGENIC
ISOANTIGENS
ISOBARISMS
ISOBAROMETRIC
ISOBILATERAL
ISOBUTANES
ISOBUTENES
ISOBUTYLENE
ISOBUTYLENES
ISOCALORIC
ISOCARBOXAZID
ISOCARBOXAZIDS
ISOCHASMIC
ISOCHEIMAL
ISOCHEIMALS
ISOCHEIMENAL

SOCHEIMENALS
SOCHEIMIC
SOCHIMALS
SOCHROMATIC
SOCHROMOSOME
SOCHROMOSOMES
SOCHRONAL
SOCHRONALLY
SOCHRONES
SOCHRONISE
SOCHRONISED
SOCHRONISES
SOCHRONISING
SOCHRONISM
SOCHRONISMS
SOCHRONIZE
SOCHRONIZED
SOCHRONIZES
SOCHRONIZING
SOCHRONOUS
SOCHRONOUSLY
SOCHROOUS
SOCLINALS
SOCLINICS
SOCRACIES
SOCRYMALS
SOCYANATE
SOCYANATES
SOCYANIDE
SOCYANIDES
SODIAMETRIC
SODIAMETRICAL
SODIAPHERE
SODIAPHERES
SODIMORPHIC
SODIMORPHISM
SODIMORPHISMS
SODIMORPHOUS
SODONTALS
SODYNAMIC
SODYNAMICS
SOELECTRIC
SOELECTRONIC
OENZYMATIC
SOENZYMES
SOENZYMIC
SOFLAVONE
SOFLAVONES
SOGAMETES
SOGAMETIC
SOGENETIC
SOGEOTHERM
SOGEOTHERMAL
SOGEOTHERMALS
SOGEOTHERMIC
SOGEOTHERMICS
SOGEOTHERMS
SOGLOSSAL
SOGLOSSES
SOGLOSSIC
SOGLOTTAL
SOGLOTTIC
SOGRAFTED
SOGRAFTING
SOHYETALS
SOIMMUNISATION
ISOIMMUNIZATION
ISOKINETIC
ISOKONTANS
ISOLABILITIES
ISOLABILITY
ISOLATABLE
ISOLATIONISM
ISOLATIONISMS
ISOLATIONIST
ISOLATIONISTS
ISOLATIONS
ISOLECITHAL
ISOLEUCINE
ISOLEUCINES
ISOMAGNETIC
ISOMAGNETICS
ISOMERASES
ISOMERISATION
ISOMERISATIONS
ISOMERISED
ISOMERISES
ISOMERISING
ISOMERISMS
ISOMERIZATION
ISOMERIZATIONS
ISOMERIZED
ISOMERIZES
ISOMERIZING
ISOMETRICAL
ISOMETRICALLY
ISOMETRICS
ISOMETRIES
ISOMETROPIA
ISOMETROPIAS
ISOMORPHIC
ISOMORPHICALLY
ISOMORPHISM
ISOMORPHISMS
ISOMORPHOUS
ISONIAZIDE
ISONIAZIDES
ISONIAZIDS
ISONITRILE
ISONITRILES
ISOOCTANES
ISOPACHYTE
ISOPACHYTES
ISOPERIMETER
ISOPERIMETERS
ISOPERIMETRICAL
ISOPERIMETRIES
ISOPERIMETRY
ISOPIESTIC
ISOPIESTICALLY
ISOPLETHIC
ISOPOLITIES
ISOPRENALINE
ISOPRENALINES
ISOPRENOID
ISOPROPYLS
ISOPROTERENOL
ISOPROTERENOLS
ISOPTEROUS
ISOPYCNALS
ISOPYCNICS
ISORHYTHMIC
ISOSEISMAL
ISOSEISMALS
ISOSEISMIC
ISOSEISMICS
ISOSMOTICALLY
ISOSPONDYLOUS
ISOSPORIES
ISOSPOROUS
ISOSTACIES
ISOSTASIES
ISOSTATICALLY
ISOSTEMONOUS
ISOTENISCOPE
ISOTENISCOPES
ISOTHENURIA
ISOTHENURIAS
ISOTHERALS
ISOTHERMAL
ISOTHERMALLY
ISOTHERMALS
ISOTONICALLY
ISOTONICITIES
ISOTONICITY
ISOTOPICALLY
ISOTRETINOIN
ISOTRETINOINS
ISOTROPICALLY
ISOTROPIES
ISOTROPISM
ISOTROPISMS
ISOTROPOUS
ISOXSUPRINE
ISOXSUPRINES
ISPAGHULAS
ITACOLUMITE
ITACOLUMITES
ITALIANATE
ITALIANATED
ITALIANATES
ITALIANATING
ITALIANISE
ITALIANISED
ITALIANISES
ITALIANISING
ITALIANIZE
ITALIANIZED
ITALIANIZES
ITALIANIZING
ITALICISATION
ITALICISATIONS
ITALICISED
ITALICISES
ITALICISING
ITALICIZATION
ITALICIZATIONS
ITALICIZED
ITALICIZES
ITALICIZING
ITCHINESSES
ITEMISATION
ITEMISATIONS
ITEMIZATION
ITEMIZATIONS
ITERATIONS
ITERATIVELY
ITERATIVENESS
ITERATIVENESSES
ITEROPARITIES
ITEROPARITY
ITEROPAROUS
ITHYPHALLI
ITHYPHALLIC
ITHYPHALLICS
ITHYPHALLUS
ITHYPHALLUSES
ITINERACIES
ITINERANCIES
ITINERANCY
ITINERANTLY
ITINERANTS
ITINERARIES
ITINERATED
ITINERATES
ITINERATING
ITINERATION
ITINERATIONS
IVERMECTIN
IVERMECTINS
IVORYBILLS
IVORYWOODS
IZVESTIYAS

JABBERINGLY
JABBERINGS
JABBERWOCK
JABBERWOCKIES
JABBERWOCKS
JABBERWOCKY
JABORANDIS
JABOTICABA
JABOTICABAS
JACARANDAS
JACKALLING
JACKANAPES
JACKANAPESES
JACKAROOED
JACKAROOING
JACKASSERIES
JACKASSERY
JACKBOOTED
JACKBOOTING
JACKEROOED
JACKEROOING
JACKETLESS
JACKFISHES
JACKFRUITS
JACKHAMMER
JACKHAMMERED
JACKHAMMERING
JACKHAMMERS
JACKKNIFED
JACKKNIFES
JACKKNIFING
JACKKNIVES
JACKLIGHTED
JACKLIGHTING
JACKLIGHTS
JACKPLANES
JACKRABBIT
JACKRABBITS
JACKROLLED
JACKROLLING
JACKSCREWS
JACKSHAFTS
JACKSMELTS
JACKSMITHS
JACKSNIPES
JACKSTONES
JACKSTRAWS
JACQUERIES
JACTATIONS
JACTITATION
JACTITATIONS
JACULATING
JACULATION
JACULATIONS
JACULATORS
JACULATORY
JADEDNESSES
JADISHNESS
JADISHNESSES
JAGGEDNESS
JAGGEDNESSES
JAGGHERIES
JAGHIRDARS
JAGUARONDI
JAGUARONDIS
JAGUARUNDI
JAGUARUNDIS
JAILBREAKS
JAILERESSES
JAILHOUSES
JAILORESSES
JAMAHIRIYA
JAMAHIRIYAS
JAMBALAYAS
JAMBOKKING
JAMBOLANAS
JANISARIES
JANISSARIES
JANITORIAL
JANITORSHIP
JANITORSHIPS
JANITRESSES
JANITRIXES
JANIZARIAN
JANIZARIES
JAPANISING
JAPANIZING
JAPONAISERIE
JAPONAISERIES
JARDINIERE
JARDINIERES
JARGONEERS
JARGONELLE
JARGONELLES
JARGONISATION
JARGONISATIONS
JARGONISED
JARGONISES
JARGONISING
JARGONISTIC
JARGONISTS
JARGONIZATION
JARGONIZATIONS
JARGONIZED
JARGONIZES
JARGONIZING
JARLSBERGS
JAROVISING
JAROVIZING
JASPERISED
JASPERISES
JASPERISING
JASPERIZED
JASPERIZES
JASPERIZING
JASPERWARE
JASPERWARES
JASPIDEOUS
JASPILITES
JAUNDICING
JAUNTINESS
JAUNTINESSES
JAUNTINGLY
JAVELINING
JAWBATIONS
JAWBONINGS
JAWBREAKER
JAWBREAKERS
JAWBREAKING
JAWBREAKINGLY
JAWBREAKINGS
JAWCRUSHER
JAWCRUSHERS
JAWDROPPINGLY
JAYHAWKERS
JAYWALKERS
JAYWALKING
JAYWALKINGS
JAZZINESSES
JEALOUSHOOD
JEALOUSHOODS
JEALOUSIES
JEALOUSING
JEALOUSNESS
JEALOUSNESSES
JEISTIECOR
JEISTIECORS
JEJUNENESS
JEJUNENESSES
JEJUNITIES
JEJUNOSTOMIES
JEJUNOSTOMY

:LLIFICATION
:LLIFICATIONS
:LLIFYING
:LLYBEANS
:LLYFISHES
:LLYGRAPH
:LLYGRAPHED
:LLYGRAPHING
:LLYGRAPHS
:LLYROLLS
:MMINESSES
:NNETINGS
:OPARDERS
:OPARDIED
:OPARDIES
:OPARDING
:OPARDISE
:OPARDISED
:OPARDISES
:OPARDISING
:OPARDIZE
:OPARDIZED
:OPARDIZES
:OPARDIZING
:OPARDOUS
:OPARDOUSLY
:OPARDYING
:QUERITIES
:QUIRITIES
:RFALCONS
:RKINESSES
:RKINHEAD
:RKINHEADS
:RKWATERS
:RRYMANDER
:RRYMANDERED
:RRYMANDERING
:RRYMANDERS
:SSAMINES
:SSERANTS
:SUITICAL
:SUITICALLY
:SUITISMS
:SUITRIES
:TSTREAMS
:TTATURAS
:TTINESSES
:TTISONABLE
:TTISONED
:TTISONING
:WELFISHES
:WELLERIES
:WELWEEDS
CKAJOGGED
CKAJOGGING
GAJIGGED
GAJIGGING
GAJOGGED
GAJOGGING
GAMAREES
GGERMAST
GGERMASTS
GGUMBOBS
GJIGGING
LLFLIRTS
MPNESSES
JIMSONWEED
JIMSONWEEDS
JINGOISTIC
JINGOISTICALLY
JINRICKSHA
JINRICKSHAS
JINRICKSHAW
JINRICKSHAWS
JINRIKISHA
JINRIKISHAS
JINRIKSHAS
JITTERBUGGED
JITTERBUGGING
JITTERBUGS
JITTERIEST
JITTERINESS
JITTERINESSES
JOBCENTRES
JOBERNOWLS
JOBHOLDERS
JOBLESSNESS
JOBLESSNESSES
JOBSEEKERS
JOBSWORTHS
JOCKEYISMS
JOCKEYSHIP
JOCKEYSHIPS
JOCKSTRAPS
JOCKTELEGS
JOCOSENESS
JOCOSENESSES
JOCOSERIOUS
JOCOSITIES
JOCULARITIES
JOCULARITY
JOCULATORS
JOCUNDITIES
JOCUNDNESS
JOCUNDNESSES
JOHANNESES
JOHNNYCAKE
JOHNNYCAKES
JOHNSONGRASS
JOHNSONGRASSES
JOINTEDNESS
JOINTEDNESSES
JOINTNESSES
JOINTRESSES
JOINTURESS
JOINTURESSES
JOINTURING
JOINTWEEDS
JOINTWORMS
JOKESMITHS
JOKINESSES
JOLLEYINGS
JOLLIFICATION
JOLLIFICATIONS
JOLLIFYING
JOLLIMENTS
JOLLINESSES
JOLLYBOATS
JOLLYHEADS
JOLTERHEAD
JOLTERHEADS
JONNYCAKES
JOSEPHINITE
JOSEPHINITES
JOSTLEMENT
JOSTLEMENTS
JOUISANCES
JOURNALESE
JOURNALESES
JOURNALING
JOURNALISATION
JOURNALISATIONS
JOURNALISE
JOURNALISED
JOURNALISER
JOURNALISERS
JOURNALISES
JOURNALISING
JOURNALISM
JOURNALISMS
JOURNALIST
JOURNALISTIC
JOURNALISTS
JOURNALIZATION
JOURNALIZATIONS
JOURNALIZE
JOURNALIZED
JOURNALIZER
JOURNALIZERS
JOURNALIZES
JOURNALIZING
JOURNALLED
JOURNALLING
JOURNEYERS
JOURNEYING
JOURNEYMAN
JOURNEYMEN
JOURNEYWORK
JOURNEYWORKS
JOUYSAUNCE
JOUYSAUNCES
JOVIALITIES
JOVIALNESS
JOVIALNESSES
JOVIALTIES
JOVYSAUNCE
JOVYSAUNCES
JOWLINESSES
JOYFULLEST
JOYFULNESS
JOYFULNESSES
JOYLESSNESS
JOYLESSNESSES
JOYOUSNESS
JOYOUSNESSES
JOYPOPPERS
JOYPOPPING
JOYRIDINGS
JUBILANCES
JUBILANCIES
JUBILANTLY
JUBILARIAN
JUBILARIANS
JUBILATING
JUBILATION
JUBILATIONS
JUDGEMENTAL
JUDGEMENTS
JUDGESHIPS
JUDGMATICAL
JUDGMATICALLY
JUDGMENTAL
JUDGMENTALLY
JUDICATION
JUDICATIONS
JUDICATIVE
JUDICATORIAL
JUDICATORIES
JUDICATORS
JUDICATORY
JUDICATURE
JUDICATURES
JUDICIALLY
JUDICIARIES
JUDICIOUSLY
JUDICIOUSNESS
JUDICIOUSNESSES
JUGGERNAUT
JUGGERNAUTS
JUGGLERIES
JUGGLINGLY
JUGLANDACEOUS
JUGULATING
JUGULATION
JUGULATIONS
JUICEHEADS
JUICINESSES
JULIENNING
JUMBLINGLY
JUMBOISING
JUMBOIZING
JUMHOURIYA
JUMHOURIYAS
JUMPINESSES
JUNCACEOUS
JUNCTIONAL
JUNEATINGS
JUNGLEGYMS
JUNGLELIKE
JUNIORATES
JUNIORITIES
JUNKETEERED
JUNKETEERING
JUNKETEERS
JUNKETINGS
JUNKETTERS
JUNKETTING
JUNKINESSES
JURIDICALLY
JURISCONSULT
JURISCONSULTS
JURISDICTION
JURISDICTIONAL
JURISDICTIONS
JURISDICTIVE
JURISPRUDENCE
JURISPRUDENCES
JURISPRUDENT
JURISPRUDENTIAL
JURISPRUDENTS
JURISTICAL
JURISTICALLY
JUSTICESHIP
JUSTICESHIPS

JUSTICIABILITY
JUSTICIABLE
JUSTICIALISM
JUSTICIALISMS
JUSTICIARIES
JUSTICIARS
JUSTICIARSHIP
JUSTICIARSHIPS
JUSTICIARY
JUSTIFIABILITY
JUSTIFIABLE
JUSTIFIABLENESS
JUSTIFIABLY
JUSTIFICATION
JUSTIFICATIONS
JUSTIFICATIVE
JUSTIFICATOR
JUSTIFICATORS
JUSTIFICATORY
JUSTIFIERS
JUSTIFYING
JUSTNESSES
JUVENESCENCE
JUVENESCENCES
JUVENESCENT
JUVENILELY
JUVENILENESS
JUVENILENESSES
JUVENILITIES
JUVENILITY
JUXTAPOSED
JUXTAPOSES
JUXTAPOSING
JUXTAPOSITION
JUXTAPOSITIONAL
JUXTAPOSITIONS

Kk

ABALISTIC
ABARAGOYA
ABARAGOYAS
ABBALISMS
ABBALISTIC
ABBALISTS
ABELJOUWS
ADAITCHAS
AFFEEKLATSCH
AFFEEKLATSCHES
AFFIRBOOM
AFFIRBOOMS
AHIKATEAS
AILYAIRDS
AINOGENESES
AINOGENESIS
AINOGENETIC
AIROMONES
AISERDOMS
AISERISMS
AISERSHIP
AISERSHIPS
AKISTOCRACIES
AKISTOCRACY
ALAMKARIS
ALANCHOES
ALASHNIKOV
ALASHNIKOVS
ALEIDOPHONE
ALEIDOPHONES
ALEIDOSCOPE
ALEIDOSCOPES
ALEIDOSCOPIC
ALENDARED
ALENDARING
ALIPHATES
ALLIKREIN
ALLIKREINS
KALLITYPES
KALSOMINED
KALSOMINES
KALSOMINING
KAMELAUKION
KAMELAUKIONS
KAMERADING
KANAMYCINS
KANGAROOED
KANGAROOING
KANTIKOYED
KANTIKOYING
KAOLINISED
KAOLINISES
KAOLINISING
KAOLINITES
KAOLINITIC
KAOLINIZED
KAOLINIZES
KAOLINIZING
KAOLINOSES
KAOLINOSIS
KAPELLMEISTER
KAPELLMEISTERS
KARABINERS
KARANGAING
KARATEISTS
KARSTIFICATION
KARSTIFICATIONS
KARSTIFIED
KARSTIFIES
KARSTIFYING
KARUHIRUHI
KARYOGAMIC
KARYOGAMIES
KARYOGRAMS
KARYOKINESES
KARYOKINESIS
KARYOKINETIC
KARYOLOGIC
KARYOLOGICAL
KARYOLOGIES
KARYOLOGIST
KARYOLOGISTS
KARYOLYMPH
KARYOLYMPHS
KARYOLYSES
KARYOLYSIS
KARYOLYTIC
KARYOPLASM
KARYOPLASMIC
KARYOPLASMS
KARYOSOMES
KARYOTYPED
KARYOTYPES
KARYOTYPIC
KARYOTYPICAL
KARYOTYPICALLY
KARYOTYPING
KATABOLICALLY
KATABOLISM
KATABOLISMS
KATABOTHRON
KATABOTHRONS
KATADROMOUS
KATATHERMOMETER
KATAVOTHRON
KATAVOTHRONS
KATHAKALIS
KATHAREVOUSA
KATHAREVOUSAS
KATHAROMETER
KATHAROMETERS
KATZENJAMMER
KATZENJAMMERS
KAWANATANGA
KAWANATANGAS
KAZATSKIES
KAZILLIONS
KEELHALING
KEELHAULED
KEELHAULING
KEELHAULINGS
KEELIVINES
KEELYVINES
KEENNESSES
KEEPERLESS
KEEPERSHIP
KEEPERSHIPS
KEESHONDEN
KEFUFFLING
KELYPHITIC
KENNELLING
KENNETTING
KENOGENESIS
KENOGENETIC
KENOGENETICALLY
KENOPHOBIA
KENOPHOBIAS
KENOTICIST
KENOTICISTS
KENSPECKLE
KENTLEDGES
KERATINISATION
KERATINISATIONS
KERATINISE
KERATINISED
KERATINISES
KERATINISING
KERATINIZATION
KERATINIZATIONS
KERATINIZE
KERATINIZED
KERATINIZES

KERATINIZING
KERATINOPHILIC
KERATINOUS
KERATITIDES
KERATITISES
KERATOGENOUS
KERATOMATA
KERATOMETER
KERATOMETERS
KERATOPHYRE
KERATOPHYRES
KERATOPLASTIC
KERATOPLASTIES
KERATOPLASTY
KERATOTOMIES
KERATOTOMY
KERAUNOGRAPH
KERAUNOGRAPHS
KERBSTONES
KERCHIEFED
KERCHIEFING
KERCHIEVES
KERFUFFLED
KERFUFFLES
KERFUFFLING
KERMESITES
KERNELLING
KERNICTERUS
KERNICTERUSES
KERNMANTEL
KERPLUNKED
KERPLUNKING
KERSANTITE
KERSANTITES
KERSEYMERE
KERSEYMERES
KERYGMATIC
KETOGENESES
KETOGENESIS
KETONAEMIA
KETONAEMIAS
KETONEMIAS
KETONURIAS
KETOSTEROID
KETOSTEROIDS
KETTLEDRUM
KETTLEDRUMMER
KETTLEDRUMMERS
KETTLEDRUMS
KETTLEFULS
KETTLESTITCH
KETTLESTITCHES
KEYBOARDED
KEYBOARDER
KEYBOARDERS
KEYBOARDING
KEYBOARDINGS
KEYBOARDIST
KEYBOARDISTS
KEYBUTTONS
KEYLOGGERS
KEYPUNCHED
KEYPUNCHER
KEYPUNCHERS
KEYPUNCHES
KEYPUNCHING
KEYSTONING
KEYSTROKED
KEYSTROKES
KEYSTROKING
KEYSTROKINGS
KHALIFATES
KHANSAMAHS
KHEDIVATES
KHEDIVIATE
KHEDIVIATES
KHIDMUTGAR
KHIDMUTGARS
KHITMUTGAR
KHITMUTGARS
KHUSKHUSES
KIBBITZERS
KIBBITZING
KIBBUTZNIK
KIBBUTZNIKS
KICKABOUTS
KICKAROUND
KICKAROUNDS
KICKBOARDS
KICKBOXERS
KICKBOXING
KICKBOXINGS
KICKSHAWSES
KICKSORTER
KICKSORTERS
KICKSTANDS
KICKSTARTED
KICKSTARTING
KICKSTARTS
KIDDIEWINK
KIDDIEWINKIE
KIDDIEWINKIES
KIDDIEWINKS
KIDDISHNESS
KIDDISHNESSES
KIDDYWINKS
KIDNAPINGS
KIDNAPPEES
KIDNAPPERS
KIDNAPPING
KIDNAPPINGS
KIDNEYLIKE
KIDOLOGIES
KIDOLOGIST
KIDOLOGISTS
KIESELGUHR
KIESELGUHRS
KIESELGURS
KIESERITES
KILDERKINS
KILLIFISHES
KILLIKINICK
KILLIKINICKS
KILOCALORIE
KILOCALORIES
KILOCURIES
KILOCYCLES
KILOGAUSSES
KILOGRAMME
KILOGRAMMES
KILOHERTZES
KILOJOULES
KILOLITERS
KILOLITRES
KILOMETERS
KILOMETRES
KILOMETRIC
KILOMETRICAL
KILOPARSEC
KILOPARSECS
KILOPASCAL
KILOPASCALS
KIMBERLITE
KIMBERLITES
KINAESTHESES
KINAESTHESIA
KINAESTHESIAS
KINAESTHESIS
KINAESTHETIC
KINDERGARTEN
KINDERGARTENER
KINDERGARTENERS
KINDERGARTENS
KINDERGARTNER
KINDERGARTNERS
KINDERSPIEL
KINDERSPIELS
KINDHEARTED
KINDHEARTEDLY
KINDHEARTEDNESS
KINDLESSLY
KINDLINESS
KINDLINESSES
KINDNESSES
KINDREDNESS
KINDREDNESSES
KINDREDSHIP
KINDREDSHIPS
KINEMATICAL
KINEMATICALLY
KINEMATICS
KINEMATOGRAPH
KINEMATOGRAPHER
KINEMATOGRAPHIC
KINEMATOGRAPHS
KINEMATOGRAPHY
KINESCOPED
KINESCOPES
KINESCOPING
KINESIATRIC
KINESIATRICS
KINESIOLOGIES
KINESIOLOGIST
KINESIOLOGISTS
KINESIOLOGY
KINESIPATH
KINESIPATHIC
KINESIPATHIES
KINESIPATHIST
KINESIPATHISTS
KINESIPATHS
KINESIPATHY
KINESITHERAPIES
KINESITHERAPY
KINESTHESES
KINESTHESIA
KINESTHESIAS
KINESTHESIS
KINESTHETIC
KINESTHETICALLY
KINETHEODOLITE
KINETHEODOLITES
KINETICALLY
KINETICIST
KINETICISTS
KINETOCHORE
KINETOCHORES
KINETOGRAPH
KINETOGRAPHS
KINETONUCLEI
KINETONUCLEUS
KINETONUCLEUSES
KINETOPLAST
KINETOPLASTS
KINETOSCOPE
KINETOSCOPES
KINETOSOME
KINETOSOMES
KINGCRAFTS
KINGDOMLESS
KINGFISHER
KINGFISHERS
KINGFISHES
KINGLIHOOD
KINGLIHOODS
KINGLINESS
KINGLINESSES
KINGMAKERS
KINGSNAKES
KINKINESSES
KINNIKINIC
KINNIKINICK
KINNIKINICKS
KINNIKINICS
KINNIKINNICK
KINNIKINNICKS
KIRBIGRIPS
KIRKYAIRDS
KIRSCHWASSER
KIRSCHWASSERS
KISSAGRAMS
KISSOGRAMS
KITCHENALIA
KITCHENALIAS
KITCHENDOM
KITCHENDOMS
KITCHENERS
KITCHENETS
KITCHENETTE
KITCHENETTES
KITCHENING
KITCHENWARE
KITCHENWARES
KITESURFING
KITESURFINGS
KITSCHIEST
KITSCHIFIED
KITSCHIFIES
KITSCHIFYING
KITSCHNESS
KITSCHNESSES
KITTENISHLY
KITTENISHNESS
KITTENISHNESSES

ITTIWAKES
IWIFRUITS
IWISPORTS
LANGFARBE
LANGFARBES
LEBSIELLA
LEBSIELLAS
LEINHUISIE
LEINHUISIES
LENDUSITIES
LENDUSITY
LEPHTISMS
LEPTOCRACIES
LEPTOCRACY
LEPTOCRATIC
LEPTOMANIA
LEPTOMANIAC
LEPTOMANIACS
LEPTOMANIAS
LETTERSCHUH
LETTERSCHUHE
LINOSTATS
LIPSPRINGER
LIPSPRINGERS
LONDIKERS
LONDIKING
LONDYKERS
LONDYKING
LOOCHMANS
LOOTCHMAN
LOOTCHMANS
LOOTCHMEN
LUTZINESS
LUTZINESSES
NACKERIES
NACKERING
NACKINESS
NACKINESSES
NACKWURST
NACKWURSTS
NAGGINESS
NAGGINESSES
NAPSACKED
NAVESHIPS
NAVISHNESS
NAVISHNESSES
NEECAPPED
NEECAPPING
NEECAPPINGS
NEEPIECES
NEVELLING
NICKERBOCKER
NICKERBOCKERS
NICKKNACK
NICKKNACKS
NICKPOINT
NICKPOINTS
NIFEPOINT
NIFEPOINTS
NIFERESTS
NIGHTAGES
NIGHTHEAD
NIGHTHEADS
NIGHTHOOD
NIGHTHOODS
NIGHTLESS
KNIGHTLIER
KNIGHTLIEST
KNIGHTLINESS
KNIGHTLINESSES
KNIPHOFIAS
KNOBBINESS
KNOBBINESSES
KNOBBLIEST
KNOBKERRIE
KNOBKERRIES
KNOBSTICKS
KNOCKABOUT
KNOCKABOUTS
KNOCKDOWNS
KNOCKWURST
KNOCKWURSTS
KNOTGRASSES
KNOTTINESS
KNOTTINESSES
KNOWABLENESS
KNOWABLENESSES
KNOWINGEST
KNOWINGNESS
KNOWINGNESSES
KNOWLEDGABILITY
KNOWLEDGABLE
KNOWLEDGABLY
KNOWLEDGEABLE
KNOWLEDGEABLY
KNOWLEDGED
KNOWLEDGES
KNOWLEDGING
KNUBBLIEST
KNUCKLEBALL
KNUCKLEBALLER
KNUCKLEBALLERS
KNUCKLEBALLS
KNUCKLEBONE
KNUCKLEBONES
KNUCKLEDUSTER
KNUCKLEDUSTERS
KNUCKLEHEAD
KNUCKLEHEADED
KNUCKLEHEADS
KNUCKLIEST
KOEKSISTER
KOEKSISTERS
KOHLRABIES
KOHUTUHUTU
KOLINSKIES
KOLKHOZNIK
KOLKHOZNIKI
KOLKHOZNIKS
KOMONDOROCK
KOMONDOROK
KONIMETERS
KONIOLOGIES
KONISCOPES
KOOKABURRA
KOOKABURRAS
KOOKINESSES
KOTAHITANGA
KOTAHITANGAS
KOTTABOSES
KOTUKUTUKU
KOULIBIACA
KOULIBIACAS
KOURBASHED
KOURBASHES
KOURBASHING
KOUSKOUSES
KOWHAIWHAI
KOWHAIWHAIS
KRAKOWIAKS
KREASOTING
KREMLINOLOGIES
KREMLINOLOGIST
KREMLINOLOGISTS
KREMLINOLOGY
KREOSOTING
KRIEGSPIEL
KRIEGSPIELS
KRIEGSSPIEL
KRIEGSSPIELS
KROMESKIES
KRUGERRAND
KRUGERRANDS
KRUMMHORNS
KRYOMETERS
KUMARAHOUS
KUMMERBUND
KUMMERBUNDS
KUNDALINIS
KURBASHING
KURCHATOVIUM
KURCHATOVIUMS
KURDAITCHA
KURFUFFLED
KURFUFFLES
KURFUFFLING
KURRAJONGS
KURTOSISES
KVETCHIEST
KVETCHINESS
KVETCHINESSES
KWASHIORKOR
KWASHIORKORS
KYANISATION
KYANISATIONS
KYANIZATION
KYANIZATIONS
KYMOGRAPHIC
KYMOGRAPHIES
KYMOGRAPHS
KYMOGRAPHY

Ll

LABANOTATION
LABANOTATIONS
LABDACISMS
LABEFACTATION
LABEFACTATIONS
LABEFACTION
LABEFACTIONS
LABELLISTS
LABIALISATION
LABIALISATIONS
LABIALISED
LABIALISES
LABIALISING
LABIALISMS
LABIALITIES
LABIALIZATION
LABIALIZATIONS
LABIALIZED
LABIALIZES
LABIALIZING
LABILITIES
LABIODENTAL
LABIODENTALS
LABIONASAL
LABIONASALS
LABIOVELAR
LABIOVELARS
LABORATORIES
LABORATORY
LABOREDNESS
LABOREDNESSES
LABORINGLY
LABORIOUSLY
LABORIOUSNESS
LABORIOUSNESSES
LABORSAVING
LABOUREDLY
LABOUREDNESS
LABOUREDNESSES
LABOURINGLY
LABOURISMS
LABOURISTS
LABOURSOME
LABRADOODLE
LABRADOODLES
LABRADORESCENT
LABRADORITE
LABRADORITES
LABYRINTHAL
LABYRINTHIAN
LABYRINTHIC
LABYRINTHICAL
LABYRINTHICALLY
LABYRINTHINE
LABYRINTHITIS
LABYRINTHITISES
LABYRINTHODONT
LABYRINTHODONTS
LABYRINTHS
LACCOLITES
LACCOLITHIC
LACCOLITHS
LACCOLITIC
LACERABILITIES
LACERABILITY
LACERATING
LACERATION
LACERATIONS
LACERATIVE
LACERTIANS
LACERTILIAN
LACERTILIANS
LACHRYMALS
LACHRYMARIES
LACHRYMARY
LACHRYMATION
LACHRYMATIONS
LACHRYMATOR
LACHRYMATORIES
LACHRYMATORS
LACHRYMATORY
LACHRYMOSE
LACHRYMOSELY
LACHRYMOSITIES
LACHRYMOSITY
LACINESSES
LACINIATED
LACINIATION
LACINIATIONS
LACKADAISICAL
LACKADAISICALLY
LACKADAISY
LACKLUSTER
LACKLUSTERS
LACKLUSTRE
LACKLUSTRES
LACONICALLY
LACONICISM
LACONICISMS
LACQUERERS
LACQUERING
LACQUERINGS
LACQUERWARE
LACQUERWARES
LACQUERWORK
LACQUERWORKS
LACQUEYING
LACRIMATION
LACRIMATIONS
LACRIMATOR
LACRIMATORS
LACRIMATORY
LACRYMATOR
LACRYMATORS
LACRYMATORY
LACTALBUMIN
LACTALBUMINS
LACTARIANS
LACTATIONAL
LACTATIONALLY
LACTATIONS
LACTESCENCE
LACTESCENCES
LACTESCENT
LACTIFEROUS
LACTIFEROUSNESS
LACTIFLUOUS
LACTOBACILLI
LACTOBACILLUS
LACTOFLAVIN
LACTOFLAVINS
LACTOGENIC
LACTOGLOBULIN
LACTOGLOBULINS
LACTOMETER
LACTOMETERS
LACTOPROTEIN
LACTOPROTEINS
LACTOSCOPE
LACTOSCOPES
LACTOSURIA
LACTOSURIAS
LACTOVEGETARIAN
LACUNOSITIES
LACUNOSITY
LACUSTRINE
LADDERLIKE
LADDISHNESS
LADDISHNESSES
LADIESWEAR
LADIESWEARS
LADYFINGER

LADYFINGERS
LADYFISHES
LADYLIKENESS
LADYLIKENESSES
LAEOTROPIC
LAEVIGATED
LAEVIGATES
LAEVIGATING
LAEVOGYRATE
LAEVOROTARY
LAEVOROTATION
LAEVOROTATIONS
LAEVOROTATORY
LAEVULOSES
LAGENIFORM
LAGERPHONE
LAGERPHONES
LAGGARDNESS
LAGGARDNESSES
LAGNIAPPES
LAGOMORPHIC
LAGOMORPHOUS
LAGOMORPHS
LAICISATION
LAICISATIONS
LAICIZATION
LAICIZATIONS
LAIRDSHIPS
LAKEFRONTS
LAKESHORES
LALAPALOOZA
LALAPALOOZAS
LALLAPALOOZA
LALLAPALOOZAS
LALLATIONS
LALLYGAGGED
LALLYGAGGING
LAMASERAIS
LAMASERIES
LAMBASTING
LAMBDACISM
LAMBDACISMS
LAMBDOIDAL
LAMBENCIES
LAMBITIVES
LAMBREQUIN
LAMBREQUINS
LAMBRUSCOS
LAMEBRAINED
LAMEBRAINS
LAMELLARLY
LAMELLATED
LAMELLATELY
LAMELLATION
LAMELLATIONS
LAMELLIBRANCH
LAMELLIBRANCHS
LAMELLICORN
LAMELLICORNS
LAMELLIFORM
LAMELLIROSTRAL
LAMELLIROSTRATE
LAMELLOSITIES
LAMELLOSITY
LAMENESSES
LAMENTABLE

LAMENTABLENESS
LAMENTABLY
LAMENTATION
LAMENTATIONS
LAMENTEDLY
LAMENTINGLY
LAMENTINGS
LAMINARIAN
LAMINARIANS
LAMINARIAS
LAMINARINS
LAMINARISE
LAMINARISED
LAMINARISES
LAMINARISING
LAMINARIZE
LAMINARIZED
LAMINARIZES
LAMINARIZING
LAMINATING
LAMINATION
LAMINATIONS
LAMINATORS
LAMINECTOMIES
LAMINECTOMY
LAMINGTONS
LAMINITISES
LAMMERGEIER
LAMMERGEIERS
LAMMERGEYER
LAMMERGEYERS
LAMPADARIES
LAMPADEDROMIES
LAMPADEDROMY
LAMPADEPHORIA
LAMPADEPHORIAS
LAMPADISTS
LAMPADOMANCIES
LAMPADOMANCY
LAMPBLACKS
LAMPHOLDER
LAMPHOLDERS
LAMPLIGHTER
LAMPLIGHTERS
LAMPLIGHTS
LAMPOONERIES
LAMPOONERS
LAMPOONERY
LAMPOONING
LAMPOONIST
LAMPOONISTS
LAMPROPHYRE
LAMPROPHYRES
LAMPROPHYRIC
LAMPSHADES
LAMPSHELLS
LANCEJACKS
LANCEOLATE
LANCEOLATED
LANCEOLATELY
LANCEWOODS
LANCINATED
LANCINATES
LANCINATING
LANCINATION
LANCINATIONS

LANDAMMANN
LANDAMMANNS
LANDAMMANS
LANDAULETS
LANDAULETTE
LANDAULETTES
LANDBOARDING
LANDBOARDINGS
LANDBOARDS
LANDDAMNED
LANDDAMNES
LANDDAMNING
LANDDROSES
LANDDROSTS
LANDFILLED
LANDFILLING
LANDFILLINGS
LANDFORCES
LANDGRAVATE
LANDGRAVATES
LANDGRAVES
LANDGRAVIATE
LANDGRAVIATES
LANDGRAVINE
LANDGRAVINES
LANDHOLDER
LANDHOLDERS
LANDHOLDING
LANDHOLDINGS
LANDLADIES
LANDLESSNESS
LANDLESSNESSES
LANDLOCKED
LANDLOPERS
LANDLORDISM
LANDLORDISMS
LANDLUBBER
LANDLUBBERLY
LANDLUBBERS
LANDLUBBING
LANDMARKED
LANDMARKING
LANDMASSES
LANDOWNERS
LANDOWNERSHIP
LANDOWNERSHIPS
LANDOWNING
LANDOWNINGS
LANDSCAPED
LANDSCAPER
LANDSCAPERS
LANDSCAPES
LANDSCAPING
LANDSCAPIST
LANDSCAPISTS
LANDSHARKS
LANDSKIPPED
LANDSKIPPING
LANDSKNECHT
LANDSKNECHTS
LANDSLIDDEN
LANDSLIDES
LANDSLIDING
LANDWAITER
LANDWAITERS
LANGBEINITE

LANGBEINITES
LANGLAUFER
LANGLAUFERS
LANGOSTINO
LANGOSTINOS
LANGOUSTES
LANGOUSTINE
LANGOUSTINES
LANGRIDGES
LANGSPIELS
LANGUAGELESS
LANGUAGING
LANGUESCENT
LANGUETTES
LANGUIDNESS
LANGUIDNESSES
LANGUISHED
LANGUISHER
LANGUISHERS
LANGUISHES
LANGUISHING
LANGUISHINGLY
LANGUISHINGS
LANGUISHMENT
LANGUISHMENTS
LANGUOROUS
LANGUOROUSLY
LANGUOROUSNESS
LANIFEROUS
LANIGEROUS
LANKINESSES
LANKNESSES
LANOSITIES
LANSQUENET
LANSQUENETS
LANTERLOOS
LANTERNING
LANTERNIST
LANTERNISTS
LANTHANIDE
LANTHANIDES
LANTHANONS
LANTHANUMS
LANUGINOSE
LANUGINOUS
LANUGINOUSNESS
LANZKNECHT
LANZKNECHTS
LAODICEANS
LAPAROSCOPE
LAPAROSCOPES
LAPAROSCOPIC
LAPAROSCOPIES
LAPAROSCOPIST
LAPAROSCOPISTS
LAPAROSCOPY
LAPAROTOMIES
LAPAROTOMY
LAPIDARIAN
LAPIDARIES
LAPIDARIST
LAPIDARISTS
LAPIDATING
LAPIDATION
LAPIDATIONS
LAPIDESCENCE

LAPIDESCENCES
LAPIDESCENT
LAPIDICOLOUS
LAPIDIFICATION
LAPIDIFICATIONS
LAPIDIFIED
LAPIDIFIES
LAPIDIFYING
LAPILLIFORM
LAPSTRAKES
LAPSTREAKS
LARCENISTS
LARCENOUSLY
LARDACEOUS
LARDALITES
LARGEHEARTED
LARGEMOUTH
LARGEMOUTHS
LARGENESSES
LARGHETTOS
LARGITIONS
LARKINESSES
LARKISHNESS
LARKISHNESSES
LARRIKINISM
LARRIKINISMS
LARRUPPING
LARVICIDAL
LARVICIDES
LARVIKITES
LARVIPAROUS
LARYNGEALLY
LARYNGEALS
LARYNGECTOMEE
LARYNGECTOMEES
LARYNGECTOMIES
LARYNGECTOMISED
LARYNGECTOMIZED
LARYNGECTOMY
LARYNGISMUS
LARYNGISMUSES
LARYNGITIC
LARYNGITIS
LARYNGITISES
LARYNGOLOGIC
LARYNGOLOGICAL
LARYNGOLOGIES
LARYNGOLOGIST
LARYNGOLOGISTS
LARYNGOLOGY
LARYNGOPHONIES
LARYNGOPHONY
LARYNGOSCOPE
LARYNGOSCOPES
LARYNGOSCOPIC
LARYNGOSCOPIES
LARYNGOSCOPIST
LARYNGOSCOPISTS
LARYNGOSCOPY
LARYNGOSPASM
LARYNGOSPASMS
LARYNGOTOMIES
LARYNGOTOMY
LASCIVIOUS
LASCIVIOUSLY
LASCIVIOUSNESS
LASERDISCS
LASERDISKS
LASERWORTS
LASSITUDES
LASTINGNESS
LASTINGNESSES
LATCHSTRING
LATCHSTRINGS
LATECOMERS
LATEENRIGGED
LATENESSES
LATENSIFICATION
LATERALING
LATERALISATION
LATERALISATIONS
LATERALISE
LATERALISED
LATERALISES
LATERALISING
LATERALITIES
LATERALITY
LATERALIZATION
LATERALIZATIONS
LATERALIZE
LATERALIZED
LATERALIZES
LATERALIZING
LATERALLED
LATERALLING
LATERBORNS
LATERIGRADE
LATERISATION
LATERISATIONS
LATERISING
LATERITIOUS
LATERIZATION
LATERIZATIONS
LATERIZING
LATEROVERSION
LATEROVERSIONS
LATESCENCE
LATESCENCES
LATHERIEST
LATHYRISMS
LATHYRITIC
LATHYRUSES
LATICIFEROUS
LATICIFERS
LATICLAVES
LATIFUNDIA
LATIFUNDIO
LATIFUNDIOS
LATIFUNDIUM
LATIMERIAS
LATINISATION
LATINISATIONS
LATINISING
LATINITIES
LATINIZATION
LATINIZATIONS
LATINIZING
LATIROSTRAL
LATIROSTRATE
LATISEPTATE
LATITANCIES
LATITATION
LATITATIONS
LATITUDINAL
LATITUDINALLY
LATITUDINARIAN
LATITUDINARIANS
LATITUDINOUS
LATRATIONS
LATROCINIA
LATROCINIES
LATROCINIUM
LATTERMATH
LATTERMATHS
LATTERMOST
LATTICEWORK
LATTICEWORKS
LATTICINGS
LATTICINIO
LAUDABILITIES
LAUDABILITY
LAUDABLENESS
LAUDABLENESSES
LAUDATIONS
LAUDATIVES
LAUDATORIES
LAUGHABLENESS
LAUGHABLENESSES
LAUGHINGLY
LAUGHINGSTOCK
LAUGHINGSTOCKS
LAUGHLINES
LAUGHWORTHY
LAUNCEGAYE
LAUNCEGAYES
LAUNCHPADS
LAUNDERERS
LAUNDERETTE
LAUNDERETTES
LAUNDERING
LAUNDRESSES
LAUNDRETTE
LAUNDRETTES
LAUNDRYMAN
LAUNDRYMEN
LAUNDRYWOMAN
LAUNDRYWOMEN
LAURACEOUS
LAURDALITE
LAURDALITES
LAUREATESHIP
LAUREATESHIPS
LAUREATING
LAUREATION
LAUREATIONS
LAURELLING
LAURUSTINE
LAURUSTINES
LAURUSTINUS
LAURUSTINUSES
LAURVIKITE
LAURVIKITES
LAVALIERES
LAVALLIERE
LAVALLIERES
LAVATIONAL
LAVATORIAL
LAVATORIES
LAVENDERED
LAVENDERING
LAVERBREAD
LAVERBREADS
LAVEROCKED
LAVEROCKING
LAVISHMENT
LAVISHMENTS
LAVISHNESS
LAVISHNESSES
LAVOLTAING
LAWBREAKER
LAWBREAKERS
LAWBREAKING
LAWBREAKINGS
LAWFULNESS
LAWFULNESSES
LAWGIVINGS
LAWLESSNESS
LAWLESSNESSES
LAWMAKINGS
LAWMONGERS
LAWNMOWERS
LAWRENCIUM
LAWRENCIUMS
LAWYERINGS
LAWYERLIKE
LAXATIVENESS
LAXATIVENESSES
LAYBACKING
LAYPERSONS
LAZARETTES
LAZARETTOS
LAZINESSES
LEACHABILITIES
LEACHABILITY
LEADENNESS
LEADENNESSES
LEADERBOARD
LEADERBOARDS
LEADERENES
LEADERETTE
LEADERETTES
LEADERLESS
LEADERSHIP
LEADERSHIPS
LEADPLANTS
LEADSCREWS
LEAFCUTTER
LEAFHOPPER
LEAFHOPPERS
LEAFINESSES
LEAFLESSNESS
LEAFLESSNESSES
LEAFLETEER
LEAFLETEERS
LEAFLETERS
LEAFLETING
LEAFLETTED
LEAFLETTING
LEAFSTALKS
LEAGUERING
LEAKINESSES
LEANNESSES
LEAPFROGGED
LEAPFROGGING

LEARINESSES
LEARNABILITIES
LEARNABILITY
LEARNEDNESS
LEARNEDNESSES
LEASEBACKS
LEASEHOLDER
LEASEHOLDERS
LEASEHOLDS
LEASTAWAYS
LEATHERBACK
LEATHERBACKS
LEATHERETTE
LEATHERETTES
LEATHERGOODS
LEATHERHEAD
LEATHERHEADS
LEATHERIER
LEATHERIEST
LEATHERINESS
LEATHERINESSES
LEATHERING
LEATHERINGS
LEATHERJACKET
LEATHERJACKETS
LEATHERLEAF
LEATHERLEAVES
LEATHERLIKE
LEATHERNECK
LEATHERNECKS
LEATHERWOOD
LEATHERWOODS
LEAVENINGS
LEBENSRAUM
LEBENSRAUMS
LECHEROUSLY
LECHEROUSNESS
LECHEROUSNESSES
LECITHINASE
LECITHINASES
LECTIONARIES
LECTIONARY
LECTISTERNIA
LECTISTERNIUM
LECTORATES
LECTORSHIP
LECTORSHIPS
LECTOTYPES
LECTRESSES
LECTURESHIP
LECTURESHIPS
LECYTHIDACEOUS
LEDERHOSEN
LEECHCRAFT
LEECHCRAFTS
LEERINESSES
LEFTWARDLY
LEGALISATION
LEGALISATIONS
LEGALISERS
LEGALISING
LEGALISTIC
LEGALISTICALLY
LEGALITIES
LEGALIZATION
LEGALIZATIONS
LEGALIZERS
LEGALIZING
LEGATARIES
LEGATESHIP
LEGATESHIPS
LEGATIONARY
LEGATISSIMO
LEGATORIAL
LEGENDARIES
LEGENDARILY
LEGENDISED
LEGENDISES
LEGENDISING
LEGENDISTS
LEGENDIZED
LEGENDIZES
LEGENDIZING
LEGENDRIES
LEGERDEMAIN
LEGERDEMAINIST
LEGERDEMAINISTS
LEGERDEMAINS
LEGERITIES
LEGGINESSES
LEGIBILITIES
LEGIBILITY
LEGIBLENESS
LEGIBLENESSES
LEGIONARIES
LEGIONELLA
LEGIONELLAE
LEGIONNAIRE
LEGIONNAIRES
LEGISLATED
LEGISLATES
LEGISLATING
LEGISLATION
LEGISLATIONS
LEGISLATIVE
LEGISLATIVELY
LEGISLATIVES
LEGISLATOR
LEGISLATORIAL
LEGISLATORS
LEGISLATORSHIP
LEGISLATORSHIPS
LEGISLATRESS
LEGISLATRESSES
LEGISLATURE
LEGISLATURES
LEGITIMACIES
LEGITIMACY
LEGITIMATE
LEGITIMATED
LEGITIMATELY
LEGITIMATENESS
LEGITIMATES
LEGITIMATING
LEGITIMATION
LEGITIMATIONS
LEGITIMATISE
LEGITIMATISED
LEGITIMATISES
LEGITIMATISING
LEGITIMATIZE
LEGITIMATIZED
LEGITIMATIZES
LEGITIMATIZING
LEGITIMATOR
LEGITIMATORS
LEGITIMISATION
LEGITIMISATIONS
LEGITIMISE
LEGITIMISED
LEGITIMISER
LEGITIMISERS
LEGITIMISES
LEGITIMISING
LEGITIMISM
LEGITIMISMS
LEGITIMIST
LEGITIMISTIC
LEGITIMISTS
LEGITIMIZATION
LEGITIMIZATIONS
LEGITIMIZE
LEGITIMIZED
LEGITIMIZER
LEGITIMIZERS
LEGITIMIZES
LEGITIMIZING
LEGLESSNESS
LEGLESSNESSES
LEGUMINOUS
LEGWARMERS
LEIOMYOMAS
LEIOMYOMATA
LEIOTRICHIES
LEIOTRICHOUS
LEIOTRICHY
LEISHMANIA
LEISHMANIAE
LEISHMANIAL
LEISHMANIAS
LEISHMANIASES
LEISHMANIASIS
LEISHMANIOSES
LEISHMANIOSIS
LEISTERING
LEISURABLE
LEISURABLY
LEISURELINESS
LEISURELINESSES
LEITMOTIFS
LEITMOTIVS
LEMMATISATION
LEMMATISATIONS
LEMMATISED
LEMMATISES
LEMMATISING
LEMMATIZATION
LEMMATIZATIONS
LEMMATIZED
LEMMATIZES
LEMMATIZING
LEMMINGLIKE
LEMNISCATE
LEMNISCATES
LEMONFISHES
LEMONGRASS
LEMONGRASSES
LEMONWOODS
LENGTHENED
LENGTHENER
LENGTHENERS
LENGTHENING
LENGTHIEST
LENGTHINESS
LENGTHINESSES
LENGTHSMAN
LENGTHSMEN
LENGTHWAYS
LENGTHWISE
LENIENCIES
LENITIVELY
LENOCINIUM
LENOCINIUMS
LENTAMENTE
LENTICELLATE
LENTICULAR
LENTICULARLY
LENTICULARS
LENTICULES
LENTIGINES
LENTIGINOSE
LENTIGINOUS
LENTISSIMO
LENTIVIRUS
LENTIVIRUSES
LEONTIASES
LEONTIASIS
LEONTOPODIUM
LEONTOPODIUMS
LEOPARDESS
LEOPARDESSES
LEPIDODENDROID
LEPIDODENDROIDS
LEPIDOLITE
LEPIDOLITES
LEPIDOMELANE
LEPIDOMELANES
LEPIDOPTERA
LEPIDOPTERAN
LEPIDOPTERANS
LEPIDOPTERIST
LEPIDOPTERISTS
LEPIDOPTEROLOGY
LEPIDOPTERON
LEPIDOPTERONS
LEPIDOPTEROUS
LEPIDOSIREN
LEPIDOSIRENS
LEPRECHAUN
LEPRECHAUNISH
LEPRECHAUNS
LEPRECHAWN
LEPRECHAWNS
LEPROMATOUS
LEPROSARIA
LEPROSARIUM
LEPROSARIUMS
LEPROSERIE
LEPROSERIES
LEPROSITIES
LEPROUSNESS
LEPROUSNESSES
LEPTOCEPHALI
LEPTOCEPHALIC

LEPTOCEPHALOUS
LEPTOCEPHALUS
LEPTOCERCAL
LEPTODACTYL
LEPTODACTYLOUS
LEPTODACTYLS
LEPTOKURTIC
LEPTOPHOSES
LEPTOPHYLLOUS
LEPTORRHINE
LEPTOSOMATIC
LEPTOSOMES
LEPTOSOMIC
LEPTOSPIRAL
LEPTOSPIRE
LEPTOSPIRES
LEPTOSPIROSES
LEPTOSPIROSIS
LEPTOTENES
LESBIANISM
LESBIANISMS
LESPEDEZAS
LESSEESHIP
LESSEESHIPS
LESSONINGS
LETHALITIES
LETHARGICAL
LETHARGICALLY
LETHARGIED
LETHARGIES
LETHARGISE
LETHARGISED
LETHARGISES
LETHARGISING
LETHARGIZE
LETHARGIZED
LETHARGIZES
LETHARGIZING
LETHIFEROUS
LETTERBOXED
LETTERBOXES
LETTERBOXING
LETTERBOXINGS
LETTERFORM
LETTERFORMS
LETTERHEAD
LETTERHEADS
LETTERINGS
LETTERLESS
LETTERPRESS
LETTERPRESSES
LETTERSETS
LETTERSPACING
LETTERSPACINGS
LEUCAEMIAS
LEUCAEMOGEN
LEUCAEMOGENIC
LEUCAEMOGENS
LEUCHAEMIA
LEUCHAEMIAS
LEUCITOHEDRA
LEUCITOHEDRON
LEUCITOHEDRONS
LEUCOBLAST
LEUCOBLASTS
LEUCOCIDIN
LEUCOCIDINS
LEUCOCRATIC
LEUCOCYTES
LEUCOCYTHAEMIA
LEUCOCYTHAEMIAS
LEUCOCYTIC
LEUCOCYTOLYSES
LEUCOCYTOLYSIS
LEUCOCYTOPENIA
LEUCOCYTOPENIAS
LEUCOCYTOSES
LEUCOCYTOSIS
LEUCOCYTOTIC
LEUCODEPLETED
LEUCODERMA
LEUCODERMAL
LEUCODERMAS
LEUCODERMIA
LEUCODERMIAS
LEUCODERMIC
LEUCOMAINE
LEUCOMAINES
LEUCOPENIA
LEUCOPENIAS
LEUCOPENIC
LEUCOPLAKIA
LEUCOPLAKIAS
LEUCOPLAST
LEUCOPLASTID
LEUCOPLASTIDS
LEUCOPLASTS
LEUCOPOIESES
LEUCOPOIESIS
LEUCOPOIETIC
LEUCORRHOEA
LEUCORRHOEAL
LEUCORRHOEAS
LEUCOTOMES
LEUCOTOMIES
LEUKAEMIAS
LEUKAEMOGENESES
LEUKAEMOGENESIS
LEUKEMOGENESES
LEUKEMOGENESIS
LEUKEMOGENIC
LEUKOBLAST
LEUKOBLASTS
LEUKOCYTES
LEUKOCYTIC
LEUKOCYTOSES
LEUKOCYTOSIS
LEUKOCYTOTIC
LEUKODERMA
LEUKODERMAL
LEUKODERMAS
LEUKODERMIC
LEUKODYSTROPHY
LEUKOPENIA
LEUKOPENIAS
LEUKOPENIC
LEUKOPLAKIA
LEUKOPLAKIAS
LEUKOPLAKIC
LEUKOPOIESES
LEUKOPOIESIS
LEUKOPOIETIC
LEUKORRHEA
LEUKORRHEAL
LEUKORRHEAS
LEUKOTOMIES
LEUKOTRIENE
LEUKOTRIENES
LEVANTINES
LEVELHEADED
LEVELHEADEDNESS
LEVELLINGS
LEVELNESSES
LEVERAGING
LEVIATHANS
LEVIGATING
LEVIGATION
LEVIGATIONS
LEVIGATORS
LEVIRATICAL
LEVIRATION
LEVIRATIONS
LEVITATING
LEVITATION
LEVITATIONAL
LEVITATIONS
LEVITATORS
LEVITICALLY
LEVOROTARY
LEVOROTATORY
LEWDNESSES
LEXICALISATION
LEXICALISATIONS
LEXICALISE
LEXICALISED
LEXICALISES
LEXICALISING
LEXICALITIES
LEXICALITY
LEXICALIZATION
LEXICALIZATIONS
LEXICALIZE
LEXICALIZED
LEXICALIZES
LEXICALIZING
LEXICOGRAPHER
LEXICOGRAPHERS
LEXICOGRAPHIC
LEXICOGRAPHICAL
LEXICOGRAPHIES
LEXICOGRAPHIST
LEXICOGRAPHISTS
LEXICOGRAPHY
LEXICOLOGICAL
LEXICOLOGICALLY
LEXICOLOGIES
LEXICOLOGIST
LEXICOLOGISTS
LEXICOLOGY
LEXIGRAPHIC
LEXIGRAPHICAL
LEXIGRAPHIES
LEXIGRAPHY
LHERZOLITE
LHERZOLITES
LIABILITIES
LIABLENESS
LIABLENESSES
LIBATIONAL
LIBATIONARY
LIBECCHIOS
LIBELLANTS
LIBELLINGS
LIBELLOUSLY
LIBERALISATION
LIBERALISATIONS
LIBERALISE
LIBERALISED
LIBERALISER
LIBERALISERS
LIBERALISES
LIBERALISING
LIBERALISM
LIBERALISMS
LIBERALIST
LIBERALISTIC
LIBERALISTS
LIBERALITIES
LIBERALITY
LIBERALIZATION
LIBERALIZATIONS
LIBERALIZE
LIBERALIZED
LIBERALIZER
LIBERALIZERS
LIBERALIZES
LIBERALIZING
LIBERALNESS
LIBERALNESSES
LIBERATING
LIBERATION
LIBERATIONISM
LIBERATIONISMS
LIBERATIONIST
LIBERATIONISTS
LIBERATIONS
LIBERATORS
LIBERATORY
LIBERTARIAN
LIBERTARIANISM
LIBERTARIANISMS
LIBERTARIANS
LIBERTICIDAL
LIBERTICIDE
LIBERTICIDES
LIBERTINAGE
LIBERTINAGES
LIBERTINES
LIBERTINISM
LIBERTINISMS
LIBIDINALLY
LIBIDINIST
LIBIDINISTS
LIBIDINOSITIES
LIBIDINOSITY
LIBIDINOUS
LIBIDINOUSLY
LIBIDINOUSNESS
LIBRAIRIES
LIBRARIANS
LIBRARIANSHIP
LIBRARIANSHIPS
LIBRATIONAL
LIBRATIONS

LIBRETTIST
LIBRETTISTS
LICENSABLE
LICENSURES
LICENTIATE
LICENTIATES
LICENTIATESHIP
LICENTIATESHIPS
LICENTIATION
LICENTIATIONS
LICENTIOUS
LICENTIOUSLY
LICENTIOUSNESS
LICHANOSES
LICHENISMS
LICHENISTS
LICHENOLOGICAL
LICHENOLOGIES
LICHENOLOGIST
LICHENOLOGISTS
LICHENOLOGY
LICHTLYING
LICITNESSES
LICKERISHLY
LICKERISHNESS
LICKERISHNESSES
LICKPENNIES
LICKSPITTLE
LICKSPITTLES
LIDOCAINES
LIEBFRAUMILCH
LIEBFRAUMILCHS
LIENTERIES
LIEUTENANCIES
LIEUTENANCY
LIEUTENANT
LIEUTENANTRIES
LIEUTENANTRY
LIEUTENANTS
LIEUTENANTSHIP
LIEUTENANTSHIPS
LIFEBLOODS
LIFEGUARDED
LIFEGUARDING
LIFEGUARDS
LIFELESSLY
LIFELESSNESS
LIFELESSNESSES
LIFELIKENESS
LIFELIKENESSES
LIFEMANSHIP
LIFEMANSHIPS
LIFESAVERS
LIFESAVING
LIFESAVINGS
LIFESTYLER
LIFESTYLERS
LIFESTYLES
LIFEWORLDS
LIGAMENTAL
LIGAMENTARY
LIGAMENTOUS
LIGATURING
LIGHTBULBS
LIGHTENERS
LIGHTENING
LIGHTENINGS
LIGHTERAGE
LIGHTERAGES
LIGHTERING
LIGHTERMAN
LIGHTERMEN
LIGHTFACED
LIGHTFACES
LIGHTFASTNESS
LIGHTFASTNESSES
LIGHTHEARTED
LIGHTHEARTEDLY
LIGHTHOUSE
LIGHTHOUSEMAN
LIGHTHOUSEMEN
LIGHTHOUSES
LIGHTLYING
LIGHTNESSES
LIGHTNINGED
LIGHTNINGS
LIGHTPLANE
LIGHTPLANES
LIGHTPROOF
LIGHTSHIPS
LIGHTSOMELY
LIGHTSOMENESS
LIGHTSOMENESSES
LIGHTTIGHT
LIGHTWEIGHT
LIGHTWEIGHTS
LIGHTWOODS
LIGNICOLOUS
LIGNIFICATION
LIGNIFICATIONS
LIGNIFYING
LIGNIPERDOUS
LIGNIVOROUS
LIGNOCAINE
LIGNOCAINES
LIGNOCELLULOSE
LIGNOCELLULOSES
LIGNOCELLULOSIC
LIGNOSULFONATE
LIGNOSULFONATES
LIGULIFLORAL
LIKABILITIES
LIKABILITY
LIKABLENESS
LIKABLENESSES
LIKEABLENESS
LIKEABLENESSES
LIKELIHOOD
LIKELIHOODS
LIKELINESS
LIKELINESSES
LIKENESSES
LILIACEOUS
LILLIPUTIAN
LILLIPUTIANS
LILTINGNESS
LILTINGNESSES
LIMACIFORM
LIMACOLOGIES
LIMACOLOGIST
LIMACOLOGISTS
LIMACOLOGY
LIMBERNESS
LIMBERNESSES
LIMBURGITE
LIMBURGITES
LIMELIGHTED
LIMELIGHTER
LIMELIGHTERS
LIMELIGHTING
LIMELIGHTS
LIMESCALES
LIMESTONES
LIMEWASHES
LIMEWATERS
LIMICOLINE
LIMICOLOUS
LIMINESSES
LIMITABLENESS
LIMITABLENESSES
LIMITARIAN
LIMITARIANS
LIMITATION
LIMITATIONAL
LIMITATIONS
LIMITATIVE
LIMITEDNESS
LIMITEDNESSES
LIMITINGLY
LIMITLESSLY
LIMITLESSNESS
LIMITLESSNESSES
LIMITROPHE
LIMIVOROUS
LIMNOLOGIC
LIMNOLOGICAL
LIMNOLOGICALLY
LIMNOLOGIES
LIMNOLOGIST
LIMNOLOGISTS
LIMNOPHILOUS
LIMOUSINES
LIMPIDITIES
LIMPIDNESS
LIMPIDNESSES
LIMPNESSES
LINCOMYCIN
LINCOMYCINS
LINCRUSTAS
LINEALITIES
LINEAMENTAL
LINEAMENTS
LINEARISATION
LINEARISATIONS
LINEARISED
LINEARISES
LINEARISING
LINEARITIES
LINEARIZATION
LINEARIZATIONS
LINEARIZED
LINEARIZES
LINEARIZING
LINEATIONS
LINEBACKER
LINEBACKERS
LINEBACKING
LINEBACKINGS
LINEBREEDING
LINEBREEDINGS
LINECASTER
LINECASTERS
LINECASTING
LINECASTINGS
LINEOLATED
LINERBOARD
LINERBOARDS
LINGBERRIES
LINGERINGLY
LINGERINGS
LINGONBERRIES
LINGONBERRY
LINGUIFORM
LINGUISTER
LINGUISTERS
LINGUISTIC
LINGUISTICAL
LINGUISTICALLY
LINGUISTICIAN
LINGUISTICIANS
LINGUISTICS
LINGUISTRIES
LINGUISTRY
LINGULATED
LINISHINGS
LINKSLANDS
LINOLEATES
LINOTYPERS
LINOTYPING
LINTSTOCKS
LINTWHITES
LIONCELLES
LIONFISHES
LIONHEARTED
LIONHEARTEDNESS
LIONISATION
LIONISATIONS
LIONIZATION
LIONIZATIONS
LIPECTOMIES
LIPIDOPLAST
LIPIDOPLASTS
LIPOCHROME
LIPOCHROMES
LIPODYSTROPHIES
LIPODYSTROPHY
LIPOGENESES
LIPOGENESIS
LIPOGRAMMATIC
LIPOGRAMMATISM
LIPOGRAMMATISMS
LIPOGRAMMATIST
LIPOGRAMMATISTS
LIPOGRAPHIES
LIPOGRAPHY
LIPOMATOSES
LIPOMATOSIS
LIPOMATOUS
LIPOPHILIC
LIPOPLASTS
LIPOPROTEIN
LIPOPROTEINS
LIPOSCULPTURE
LIPOSCULPTURES

LIPOSUCKED
LIPOSUCKING
LIPOSUCTION
LIPOSUCTIONS
LIPOTROPIC
LIPOTROPIES
LIPOTROPIN
LIPOTROPINS
LIPPINESSES
LIPPITUDES
LIPREADERS
LIPREADING
LIPREADINGS
LIPSTICKED
LIPSTICKING
LIQUATIONS
LIQUEFACIENT
LIQUEFACIENTS
LIQUEFACTION
LIQUEFACTIONS
LIQUEFACTIVE
LIQUEFIABLE
LIQUEFIERS
LIQUEFYING
LIQUESCENCE
LIQUESCENCES
LIQUESCENCIES
LIQUESCENCY
LIQUESCENT
LIQUESCING
LIQUEURING
LIQUIDAMBAR
LIQUIDAMBARS
LIQUIDATED
LIQUIDATES
LIQUIDATING
LIQUIDATION
LIQUIDATIONS
LIQUIDATOR
LIQUIDATORS
LIQUIDISED
LIQUIDISER
LIQUIDISERS
LIQUIDISES
LIQUIDISING
LIQUIDITIES
LIQUIDIZED
LIQUIDIZER
LIQUIDIZERS
LIQUIDIZES
LIQUIDIZING
LIQUIDNESS
LIQUIDNESSES
LIQUIDUSES
LIQUIFYING
LIQUORICES
LIQUORISHLY
LIQUORISHNESS
LIQUORISHNESSES
LIRIODENDRA
LIRIODENDRON
LIRIODENDRONS
LISSENCEPHALOUS
LISSOMENESS
LISSOMENESSES
LISSOMNESS
LISSOMNESSES
LISSOTRICHOUS
LISTENABILITIES
LISTENABILITY
LISTENABLE
LISTENERSHIP
LISTENERSHIPS
LISTERIOSES
LISTERIOSIS
LISTLESSLY
LISTLESSNESS
LISTLESSNESSES
LITENESSES
LITERACIES
LITERALISATION
LITERALISATIONS
LITERALISE
LITERALISED
LITERALISER
LITERALISERS
LITERALISES
LITERALISING
LITERALISM
LITERALISMS
LITERALIST
LITERALISTIC
LITERALISTS
LITERALITIES
LITERALITY
LITERALIZATION
LITERALIZATIONS
LITERALIZE
LITERALIZED
LITERALIZER
LITERALIZERS
LITERALIZES
LITERALIZING
LITERALNESS
LITERALNESSES
LITERARILY
LITERARINESS
LITERARINESSES
LITERARYISM
LITERARYISMS
LITERATELY
LITERATENESS
LITERATENESSES
LITERATION
LITERATIONS
LITERATORS
LITERATURE
LITERATURED
LITERATURES
LITEROSITIES
LITEROSITY
LITHENESSES
LITHESOMENESS
LITHESOMENESSES
LITHIFICATION
LITHIFICATIONS
LITHIFYING
LITHISTIDS
LITHOCHROMATIC
LITHOCHROMATICS
LITHOCHROMIES
LITHOCHROMY
LITHOCLAST
LITHOCLASTS
LITHOCYSTS
LITHODOMOUS
LITHOGENOUS
LITHOGLYPH
LITHOGLYPHS
LITHOGRAPH
LITHOGRAPHED
LITHOGRAPHER
LITHOGRAPHERS
LITHOGRAPHIC
LITHOGRAPHICAL
LITHOGRAPHIES
LITHOGRAPHING
LITHOGRAPHS
LITHOGRAPHY
LITHOLAPAXIES
LITHOLAPAXY
LITHOLATRIES
LITHOLATROUS
LITHOLATRY
LITHOLOGIC
LITHOLOGICAL
LITHOLOGICALLY
LITHOLOGIES
LITHOLOGIST
LITHOLOGISTS
LITHOMANCIES
LITHOMANCY
LITHOMARGE
LITHOMARGES
LITHOMETEOR
LITHOMETEORS
LITHONTHRYPTIC
LITHONTHRYPTICS
LITHONTRIPTIC
LITHONTRIPTICS
LITHONTRIPTIST
LITHONTRIPTISTS
LITHONTRIPTOR
LITHONTRIPTORS
LITHOPHAGOUS
LITHOPHANE
LITHOPHANES
LITHOPHILOUS
LITHOPHYSA
LITHOPHYSAE
LITHOPHYSE
LITHOPHYSES
LITHOPHYTE
LITHOPHYTES
LITHOPHYTIC
LITHOPONES
LITHOPRINT
LITHOPRINTS
LITHOSPERMUM
LITHOSPERMUMS
LITHOSPHERE
LITHOSPHERES
LITHOSPHERIC
LITHOSTATIC
LITHOTOMES
LITHOTOMIC
LITHOTOMICAL
LITHOTOMIES
LITHOTOMIST
LITHOTOMISTS
LITHOTOMOUS
LITHOTRIPSIES
LITHOTRIPSY
LITHOTRIPTER
LITHOTRIPTERS
LITHOTRIPTIC
LITHOTRIPTICS
LITHOTRIPTIST
LITHOTRIPTISTS
LITHOTRIPTOR
LITHOTRIPTORS
LITHOTRITE
LITHOTRITES
LITHOTRITIC
LITHOTRITICS
LITHOTRITIES
LITHOTRITISE
LITHOTRITISED
LITHOTRITISES
LITHOTRITISING
LITHOTRITIST
LITHOTRITISTS
LITHOTRITIZE
LITHOTRITIZED
LITHOTRITIZES
LITHOTRITIZING
LITHOTRITOR
LITHOTRITORS
LITHOTRITY
LITIGATING
LITIGATION
LITIGATIONS
LITIGATORS
LITIGIOUSLY
LITIGIOUSNESS
LITIGIOUSNESSES
LITTERATEUR
LITTERATEURS
LITTERBAGS
LITTERBUGS
LITTERMATE
LITTERMATES
LITTLENECK
LITTLENECKS
LITTLENESS
LITTLENESSES
LITTLEWORTH
LITURGICAL
LITURGICALLY
LITURGIOLOGIES
LITURGIOLOGIST
LITURGIOLOGISTS
LITURGIOLOGY
LITURGISMS
LITURGISTIC
LITURGISTS
LIVABILITIES
LIVABILITY
LIVABLENESS
LIVABLENESSES
LIVEABILITIES
LIVEABILITY
LIVEABLENESS
LIVEABLENESSES

LIVELIHEAD
LIVELIHEADS
LIVELIHOOD
LIVELIHOODS
LIVELINESS
LIVELINESSES
LIVENESSES
LIVERISHNESS
LIVERISHNESSES
LIVERLEAVES
LIVERWORTS
LIVERWURST
LIVERWURSTS
LIVESTOCKS
LIVETRAPPED
LIVETRAPPING
LIVIDITIES
LIVIDNESSES
LIVINGNESS
LIVINGNESSES
LIVRAISONS
LIXIVIATED
LIXIVIATES
LIXIVIATING
LIXIVIATION
LIXIVIATIONS
LOADMASTER
LOADMASTERS
LOADSAMONEY
LOADSAMONEYS
LOADSAMONIES
LOADSPACES
LOADSTONES
LOAMINESSES
LOANSHIFTS
LOATHEDNESS
LOATHEDNESSES
LOATHFULNESS
LOATHFULNESSES
LOATHINGLY
LOATHLINESS
LOATHLINESSES
LOATHNESSES
LOATHSOMELY
LOATHSOMENESS
LOATHSOMENESSES
LOBECTOMIES
LOBLOLLIES
LOBOTOMIES
LOBOTOMISE
LOBOTOMISED
LOBOTOMISES
LOBOTOMISING
LOBOTOMIZE
LOBOTOMIZED
LOBOTOMIZES
LOBOTOMIZING
LOBSCOUSES
LOBSTERERS
LOBSTERING
LOBSTERINGS
LOBSTERLIKE
LOBSTERMAN
LOBSTERMEN
LOBULATION
LOBULATIONS
LOCALISABILITY
LOCALISABLE
LOCALISATION
LOCALISATIONS
LOCALISERS
LOCALISING
LOCALISTIC
LOCALITIES
LOCALIZABILITY
LOCALIZABLE
LOCALIZATION
LOCALIZATIONS
LOCALIZERS
LOCALIZING
LOCALNESSES
LOCATEABLE
LOCATIONAL
LOCATIONALLY
LOCKHOUSES
LOCKKEEPER
LOCKKEEPERS
LOCKMAKERS
LOCKSMITHERIES
LOCKSMITHERY
LOCKSMITHING
LOCKSMITHINGS
LOCKSMITHS
LOCKSTITCH
LOCKSTITCHED
LOCKSTITCHES
LOCKSTITCHING
LOCOMOBILE
LOCOMOBILES
LOCOMOBILITIES
LOCOMOBILITY
LOCOMOTING
LOCOMOTION
LOCOMOTIONS
LOCOMOTIVE
LOCOMOTIVELY
LOCOMOTIVENESS
LOCOMOTIVES
LOCOMOTIVITIES
LOCOMOTIVITY
LOCOMOTORS
LOCOMOTORY
LOCOPLANTS
LOCORESTIVE
LOCULAMENT
LOCULAMENTS
LOCULATION
LOCULATIONS
LOCULICIDAL
LOCUTIONARY
LOCUTORIES
LODESTONES
LODGEMENTS
LODGEPOLES
LOFTINESSES
LOGAGRAPHIA
LOGAGRAPHIAS
LOGANBERRIES
LOGANBERRY
LOGANIACEOUS
LOGAOEDICS
LOGARITHMIC
LOGARITHMICAL
LOGARITHMICALLY
LOGARITHMS
LOGGERHEAD
LOGGERHEADED
LOGGERHEADS
LOGICALITIES
LOGICALITY
LOGICALNESS
LOGICALNESSES
LOGICISING
LOGICIZING
LOGINESSES
LOGISTICAL
LOGISTICALLY
LOGISTICIAN
LOGISTICIANS
LOGJAMMING
LOGNORMALITIES
LOGNORMALITY
LOGNORMALLY
LOGODAEDALIC
LOGODAEDALIES
LOGODAEDALUS
LOGODAEDALUSES
LOGODAEDALY
LOGOGRAMMATIC
LOGOGRAPHER
LOGOGRAPHERS
LOGOGRAPHIC
LOGOGRAPHICAL
LOGOGRAPHICALLY
LOGOGRAPHIES
LOGOGRAPHS
LOGOGRAPHY
LOGOGRIPHIC
LOGOGRIPHS
LOGOMACHIES
LOGOMACHIST
LOGOMACHISTS
LOGOPAEDIC
LOGOPAEDICS
LOGOPEDICS
LOGOPHILES
LOGORRHEAS
LOGORRHEIC
LOGORRHOEA
LOGORRHOEAS
LOGOTHETES
LOGOTYPIES
LOGROLLERS
LOGROLLING
LOGROLLINGS
LOINCLOTHS
LOITERINGLY
LOITERINGS
LOLLAPALOOZA
LOLLAPALOOZAS
LOLLYGAGGED
LOLLYGAGGING
LOMENTACEOUS
LONELINESS
LONELINESSES
LONENESSES
LONESOMELY
LONESOMENESS
LONESOMENESSES
LONGAEVOUS
LONGANIMITIES
LONGANIMITY
LONGANIMOUS
LONGBOARDS
LONGBOWMAN
LONGBOWMEN
LONGCLOTHS
LONGEVITIES
LONGHAIRED
LONGHEADED
LONGHEADEDNESS
LONGHOUSES
LONGICAUDATE
LONGICORNS
LONGINQUITIES
LONGINQUITY
LONGIPENNATE
LONGIROSTRAL
LONGITUDES
LONGITUDINAL
LONGITUDINALLY
LONGJUMPED
LONGJUMPING
LONGLEAVES
LONGNESSES
LONGPRIMER
LONGPRIMERS
LONGSHOREMAN
LONGSHOREMEN
LONGSHORING
LONGSHORINGS
LONGSIGHTED
LONGSIGHTEDNESS
LONGSOMELY
LONGSOMENESS
LONGSOMENESSES
LONGSUFFERING
LONGSUFFERINGS
LONGWEARING
LOOKALIKES
LOONINESSES
LOOPHOLING
LOOPINESSES
LOOSEBOXES
LOOSENESSES
LOOSESTRIFE
LOOSESTRIFES
LOOYENWORK
LOOYENWORKS
LOPGRASSES
LOPHOBRANCH
LOPHOBRANCHIATE
LOPHOBRANCHS
LOPHOPHORATE
LOPHOPHORE
LOPHOPHORES
LOPSIDEDLY
LOPSIDEDNESS
LOPSIDEDNESSES
LOQUACIOUS
LOQUACIOUSLY
LOQUACIOUSNESS
LOQUACITIES
LORAZEPAMS

LORDLINESS
LORDLINESSES
LORDOLATRIES
LORDOLATRY
LORGNETTES
LORICATING
LORICATION
LORICATIONS
LORNNESSES
LOSABLENESS
LOSABLENESSES
LOSSMAKERS
LOSSMAKING
LOSTNESSES
LOTHNESSES
LOTUSLANDS
LOUDHAILER
LOUDHAILERS
LOUDMOUTHED
LOUDMOUTHS
LOUDNESSES
LOUDSPEAKER
LOUDSPEAKERS
LOUNDERING
LOUNDERINGS
LOUNGEWEAR
LOUNGEWEARS
LOUNGINGLY
LOUSEWORTS
LOUSINESSES
LOUTISHNESS
LOUTISHNESSES
LOVABILITIES
LOVABILITY
LOVABLENESS
LOVABLENESSES
LOVASTATIN
LOVASTATINS
LOVEABILITIES
LOVEABILITY
LOVEABLENESS
LOVEABLENESSES
LOVELESSLY
LOVELESSNESS
LOVELESSNESSES
LOVELIGHTS
LOVELIHEAD
LOVELIHEADS
LOVELINESS
LOVELINESSES
LOVELORNNESS
LOVELORNNESSES
LOVEMAKERS
LOVEMAKING
LOVEMAKINGS
LOVESICKNESS
LOVESICKNESSES
LOVESTRUCK
LOVEWORTHY
LOVINGNESS
LOVINGNESSES
LOWBALLING
LOWBALLINGS
LOWBROWISM
LOWBROWISMS
LOWERCASED
LOWERCASES
LOWERCASING
LOWERCLASSMAN
LOWERCLASSMEN
LOWERINGLY
LOWLANDERS
LOWLIGHTED
LOWLIGHTING
LOWLIHEADS
LOWLINESSES
LOWSENINGS
LOXODROMES
LOXODROMIC
LOXODROMICAL
LOXODROMICALLY
LOXODROMICS
LOXODROMIES
LOYALNESSES
LUBBERLINESS
LUBBERLINESSES
LUBRICANTS
LUBRICATED
LUBRICATES
LUBRICATING
LUBRICATION
LUBRICATIONAL
LUBRICATIONS
LUBRICATIVE
LUBRICATOR
LUBRICATORS
LUBRICIOUS
LUBRICIOUSLY
LUBRICITIES
LUBRICOUSLY
LUBRITORIA
LUBRITORIUM
LUBRITORIUMS
LUCIDITIES
LUCIDNESSES
LUCIFERASE
LUCIFERASES
LUCIFERINS
LUCIFEROUS
LUCIFUGOUS
LUCKENBOOTH
LUCKENBOOTHS
LUCKENGOWAN
LUCKENGOWANS
LUCKINESSES
LUCKLESSLY
LUCKLESSNESS
LUCKLESSNESSES
LUCKPENNIES
LUCRATIVELY
LUCRATIVENESS
LUCRATIVENESSES
LUCTATIONS
LUCUBRATED
LUCUBRATES
LUCUBRATING
LUCUBRATION
LUCUBRATIONS
LUCUBRATOR
LUCUBRATORS
LUCULENTLY
LUDICROUSLY
LUDICROUSNESS
LUDICROUSNESSES
LUETICALLY
LUFTMENSCH
LUFTMENSCHEN
LUGUBRIOUS
LUGUBRIOUSLY
LUGUBRIOUSNESS
LUKEWARMISH
LUKEWARMLY
LUKEWARMNESS
LUKEWARMNESSES
LUKEWARMTH
LUKEWARMTHS
LULLABYING
LUMBAGINOUS
LUMBERINGLY
LUMBERINGNESS
LUMBERINGNESSES
LUMBERINGS
LUMBERJACK
LUMBERJACKET
LUMBERJACKETS
LUMBERJACKS
LUMBERSOME
LUMBERSOMENESS
LUMBERYARD
LUMBERYARDS
LUMBOSACRAL
LUMBRICALES
LUMBRICALIS
LUMBRICALISES
LUMBRICALS
LUMBRICIFORM
LUMBRICOID
LUMBRICUSES
LUMINAIRES
LUMINANCES
LUMINARIAS
LUMINARIES
LUMINARISM
LUMINARISMS
LUMINARIST
LUMINARISTS
LUMINATION
LUMINATIONS
LUMINESCED
LUMINESCENCE
LUMINESCENCES
LUMINESCENT
LUMINESCES
LUMINESCING
LUMINIFEROUS
LUMINOSITIES
LUMINOSITY
LUMINOUSLY
LUMINOUSNESS
LUMINOUSNESSES
LUMISTEROL
LUMISTEROLS
LUMPECTOMIES
LUMPECTOMY
LUMPFISHES
LUMPINESSES
LUMPISHNESS
LUMPISHNESSES
LUMPSUCKER
LUMPSUCKERS
LUNARNAUTS
LUNATICALLY
LUNCHBOXES
LUNCHEONED
LUNCHEONETTE
LUNCHEONETTES
LUNCHEONING
LUNCHMEATS
LUNCHROOMS
LUNCHTIMES
LUNGFISHES
LUNINESSES
LUNKHEADED
LURIDNESSES
LUSCIOUSLY
LUSCIOUSNESS
LUSCIOUSNESSES
LUSHNESSES
LUSKISHNESS
LUSKISHNESSES
LUSTERLESS
LUSTERWARE
LUSTERWARES
LUSTFULNESS
LUSTFULNESSES
LUSTIHEADS
LUSTIHOODS
LUSTINESSES
LUSTRATING
LUSTRATION
LUSTRATIONS
LUSTRATIVE
LUSTRELESS
LUSTREWARE
LUSTREWARES
LUSTROUSLY
LUSTROUSNESS
LUSTROUSNESSES
LUTEINISATION
LUTEINISATIONS
LUTEINISED
LUTEINISES
LUTEINISING
LUTEINIZATION
LUTEINIZATIONS
LUTEINIZED
LUTEINIZES
LUTEINIZING
LUTEOTROPHIC
LUTEOTROPHIN
LUTEOTROPHINS
LUTEOTROPIC
LUTEOTROPIN
LUTEOTROPINS
LUTESTRING
LUTESTRINGS
LUXULIANITE
LUXULIANITES
LUXULLIANITE
LUXULLIANITES
LUXULYANITE
LUXULYANITES
LUXURIANCE
LUXURIANCES

LUXURIANCIES
LUXURIANCY
LUXURIANTLY
LUXURIATED
LUXURIATES
LUXURIATING
LUXURIATION
LUXURIATIONS
LUXURIOUSLY
LUXURIOUSNESS
LUXURIOUSNESSES
LYCANTHROPE
LYCANTHROPES
LYCANTHROPIC
LYCANTHROPIES
LYCANTHROPIST
LYCANTHROPISTS
LYCANTHROPY
LYCHNOSCOPE
LYCHNOSCOPES
LYCOPODIUM
LYCOPODIUMS
LYMPHADENITIS
LYMPHADENITISES
LYMPHADENOPATHY
LYMPHANGIAL
LYMPHANGIOGRAM
LYMPHANGIOGRAMS
LYMPHANGITIC
LYMPHANGITIDES
LYMPHANGITIS
LYMPHANGITISES
LYMPHATICALLY
LYMPHATICS
LYMPHOADENOMA
LYMPHOADENOMAS
LYMPHOADENOMATA
LYMPHOBLAST
LYMPHOBLASTIC
LYMPHOBLASTS
LYMPHOCYTE
LYMPHOCYTES
LYMPHOCYTIC
LYMPHOCYTOPENIA
LYMPHOCYTOSES
LYMPHOCYTOSIS
LYMPHOCYTOTIC
LYMPHOGRAM
LYMPHOGRAMS
LYMPHOGRANULOMA
LYMPHOGRAPHIC
LYMPHOGRAPHIES
LYMPHOGRAPHY
LYMPHOKINE
LYMPHOKINES
LYMPHOMATA
LYMPHOMATOID
LYMPHOMATOSES
LYMPHOMATOSIS
LYMPHOMATOUS
LYMPHOPENIA
LYMPHOPENIAS
LYMPHOPOIESES
LYMPHOPOIESIS
LYMPHOPOIETIC
LYMPHOSARCOMA
LYMPHOSARCOMAS
LYMPHOSARCOMATA
LYMPHOTROPHIC
LYOPHILISATION
LYOPHILISATIONS
LYOPHILISE
LYOPHILISED
LYOPHILISER
LYOPHILISERS
LYOPHILISES
LYOPHILISING
LYOPHILIZATION
LYOPHILIZATIONS
LYOPHILIZE
LYOPHILIZED
LYOPHILIZER
LYOPHILIZERS
LYOPHILIZES
LYOPHILIZING
LYOSORPTION
LYOSORPTIONS
LYRICALNESS
LYRICALNESSES
LYRICISING
LYRICIZING
LYSERGIDES
LYSIGENETIC
LYSIGENOUS
LYSIMETERS
LYSIMETRIC
LYSOGENICITIES
LYSOGENICITY
LYSOGENIES
LYSOGENISATION
LYSOGENISATIONS
LYSOGENISE
LYSOGENISED
LYSOGENISES
LYSOGENISING
LYSOGENIZATION
LYSOGENIZATIONS
LYSOGENIZE
LYSOGENIZED
LYSOGENIZES
LYSOGENIZING
LYSOLECITHIN
LYSOLECITHINS
LYTHRACEOUS

Mm

MACABERESQUE
MACADAMIAS
MACADAMISATION
MACADAMISATIONS
MACADAMISE
MACADAMISED
MACADAMISER
MACADAMISERS
MACADAMISES
MACADAMISING
MACADAMIZATION
MACADAMIZATIONS
MACADAMIZE
MACADAMIZED
MACADAMIZER
MACADAMIZERS
MACADAMIZES
MACADAMIZING
MACARISING
MACARIZING
MACARONICALLY
MACARONICS
MACARONIES
MACCARONIES
MACCARONIS
MACCHERONCINI
MACCHERONCINIS
MACCHIATOS
MACEBEARER
MACEBEARERS
MACEDOINES
MACERANDUBA
MACERANDUBAS
MACERATERS
MACERATING
MACERATION
MACERATIONS
MACERATIVE
MACERATORS
MACHAIRODONT
MACHAIRODONTS
MACHIAVELIAN
MACHIAVELIANS
MACHIAVELLIAN
MACHIAVELLIANS
MACHICOLATE
MACHICOLATED
MACHICOLATES
MACHICOLATING
MACHICOLATION
MACHICOLATIONS
MACHINABILITIES
MACHINABILITY
MACHINABLE
MACHINATED
MACHINATES
MACHINATING
MACHINATION
MACHINATIONS
MACHINATOR
MACHINATORS
MACHINEABILITY
MACHINEABLE
MACHINEGUN
MACHINEGUNNED
MACHINEGUNNING
MACHINEGUNS
MACHINELESS
MACHINELIKE
MACHINEMAN
MACHINEMEN
MACHINERIES
MACHININGS
MACHINISTS
MACHMETERS
MACHTPOLITIK
MACHTPOLITIKS
MACINTOSHES
MACKINTOSH
MACKINTOSHES
MACONOCHIE
MACONOCHIES
MACRENCEPHALIA
MACRENCEPHALIAS
MACRENCEPHALIES
MACRENCEPHALY
MACROAGGREGATE
MACROAGGREGATED
MACROAGGREGATES
MACROBIOTA
MACROBIOTE
MACROBIOTES
MACROBIOTIC
MACROBIOTICS
MACROCARPA
MACROCARPAS
MACROCEPHALIA
MACROCEPHALIAS
MACROCEPHALIC
MACROCEPHALIES
MACROCEPHALOUS
MACROCEPHALY
MACROCLIMATE
MACROCLIMATES
MACROCLIMATIC
MACROCODES
MACROCOPIES
MACROCOSMIC
MACROCOSMICALLY
MACROCOSMS
MACROCYCLE
MACROCYCLES
MACROCYCLIC
MACROCYSTS
MACROCYTES
MACROCYTIC
MACROCYTOSES
MACROCYTOSIS
MACRODACTYL
MACRODACTYLIC
MACRODACTYLIES
MACRODACTYLOUS
MACRODACTYLY
MACRODIAGONAL
MACRODIAGONALS
MACRODOMES
MACROECONOMIC
MACROECONOMICS
MACROEVOLUTION
MACROEVOLUTIONS
MACROFAUNA
MACROFLORA
MACROFOSSIL
MACROFOSSILS
MACROGAMETE
MACROGAMETES
MACROGLIAS
MACROGLOBULIN
MACROGLOBULINS
MACROGRAPH
MACROGRAPHIC
MACROGRAPHS
MACROLOGIES
MACROMERES
MACROMOLECULAR
MACROMOLECULE
MACROMOLECULES
MACROMOLES
MACRONUCLEAR
MACRONUCLEI
MACRONUCLEUS
MACRONUTRIENT

MACRONUTRIENTS
MACROPHAGE
MACROPHAGES
MACROPHAGIC
MACROPHAGOUS
MACROPHOTOGRAPH
MACROPHYLA
MACROPHYLUM
MACROPHYSICS
MACROPHYTE
MACROPHYTES
MACROPHYTIC
MACROPINAKOID
MACROPINAKOIDS
MACROPRISM
MACROPRISMS
MACROPSIAS
MACROPTEROUS
MACROSCALE
MACROSCALES
MACROSCOPIC
MACROSCOPICALLY
MACROSOCIOLOGIES
MACROSOCIOLOGY
MACROSPORANGIA
MACROSPORANGIUM
MACROSPORE
MACROSPORES
MACROSTRUCTURAL
MACROSTRUCTURE
MACROSTRUCTURES
MACROZAMIA
MACROZAMIAS
MACTATIONS
MACULATING
MACULATION
MACULATIONS
MACULATURE
MACULATURES
MADBRAINED
MADDENINGLY
MADDENINGNESS
MADDENINGNESSES
MADEFACTION
MADEFACTIONS
MADELEINES
MADEMOISELLE
MADEMOISELLES
MADERISATION
MADERISATIONS
MADERISING
MADERIZATION
MADERIZATIONS
MADERIZING
MADONNAISH
MADONNAWISE
MADRASSAHS
MADREPORAL
MADREPORES
MADREPORIAN
MADREPORIANS
MADREPORIC
MADREPORITE
MADREPORITES
MADREPORITIC
MADRIGALESQUE
MADRIGALIAN
MADRIGALIST
MADRIGALISTS
MADRILENES
MAELSTROMS
MAENADICALLY
MAENADISMS
MAFFICKERS
MAFFICKING
MAFFICKINGS
MAGALOGUES
MAGAZINIST
MAGAZINISTS
MAGDALENES
MAGGOTIEST
MAGGOTORIA
MAGGOTORIUM
MAGIANISMS
MAGISTERIAL
MAGISTERIALLY
MAGISTERIALNESS
MAGISTERIES
MAGISTERIUM
MAGISTERIUMS
MAGISTRACIES
MAGISTRACY
MAGISTRALITIES
MAGISTRALITY
MAGISTRALLY
MAGISTRALS
MAGISTRAND
MAGISTRANDS
MAGISTRATE
MAGISTRATES
MAGISTRATESHIP
MAGISTRATESHIPS
MAGISTRATIC
MAGISTRATICAL
MAGISTRATICALLY
MAGISTRATURE
MAGISTRATURES
MAGMATISMS
MAGNALIUMS
MAGNANIMITIES
MAGNANIMITY
MAGNANIMOUS
MAGNANIMOUSLY
MAGNANIMOUSNESS
MAGNATESHIP
MAGNESITES
MAGNESIUMS
MAGNESSTONE
MAGNESSTONES
MAGNETICAL
MAGNETICALLY
MAGNETICIAN
MAGNETICIANS
MAGNETISABLE
MAGNETISATION
MAGNETISATIONS
MAGNETISED
MAGNETISER
MAGNETISERS
MAGNETISES
MAGNETISING
MAGNETISMS
MAGNETISTS
MAGNETITES
MAGNETITIC
MAGNETIZABLE
MAGNETIZATION
MAGNETIZATIONS
MAGNETIZED
MAGNETIZER
MAGNETIZERS
MAGNETIZES
MAGNETIZING
MAGNETOCHEMICAL
MAGNETOELECTRIC
MAGNETOGRAPH
MAGNETOGRAPHS
MAGNETOMETER
MAGNETOMETERS
MAGNETOMETRIC
MAGNETOMETRIES
MAGNETOMETRY
MAGNETOMOTIVE
MAGNETOPAUSE
MAGNETOPAUSES
MAGNETOSPHERE
MAGNETOSPHERES
MAGNETOSPHERIC
MAGNETOSTATIC
MAGNETOSTATICS
MAGNETRONS
MAGNIFIABLE
MAGNIFICAL
MAGNIFICALLY
MAGNIFICAT
MAGNIFICATION
MAGNIFICATIONS
MAGNIFICATS
MAGNIFICENCE
MAGNIFICENCES
MAGNIFICENT
MAGNIFICENTLY
MAGNIFICENTNESS
MAGNIFICENTNESSES
MAGNIFICOES
MAGNIFICOS
MAGNIFIERS
MAGNIFYING
MAGNILOQUENCE
MAGNILOQUENCES
MAGNILOQUENT
MAGNILOQUENTLY
MAGNITUDES
MAGNITUDINOUS
MAGNOLIACEOUS
MAHARAJAHS
MAHARANEES
MAHARISHIS
MAHATMAISM
MAHATMAISMS
MAHLSTICKS
MAHOGANIES
MAIASAURAS
MAIDENHAIR
MAIDENHAIRS
MAIDENHEAD
MAIDENHEADS
MAIDENHOOD
MAIDENHOODS
MAIDENLIKE
MAIDENLINESS
MAIDENLINESSES
MAIDENWEED
MAIDENWEEDS
MAIDISHNESS
MAIDISHNESSES
MAIDSERVANT
MAIDSERVANTS
MAIEUTICAL
MAILABILITIES
MAILABILITY
MAILCOACHES
MAILGRAMMED
MAILGRAMMING
MAILMERGED
MAILMERGES
MAILMERGING
MAILPOUCHES
MAILSHOTTED
MAILSHOTTING
MAIMEDNESS
MAIMEDNESSES
MAINBRACES
MAINFRAMES
MAINLANDER
MAINLANDERS
MAINLINERS
MAINLINING
MAINLININGS
MAINPERNOR
MAINPERNORS
MAINPRISES
MAINSHEETS
MAINSPRING
MAINSPRINGS
MAINSTREAM
MAINSTREAMED
MAINSTREAMING
MAINSTREAMS
MAINSTREETING
MAINSTREETINGS
MAINTAINABILITY
MAINTAINABLE
MAINTAINED
MAINTAINER
MAINTAINERS
MAINTAINING
MAINTENANCE
MAINTENANCED
MAINTENANCES
MAINTENANCING
MAINTOPMAST
MAINTOPMASTS
MAINTOPSAIL
MAINTOPSAILS
MAISONETTE
MAISONETTES
MAISONNETTE
MAISONNETTES
MAISTERDOME
MAISTERDOMES
MAISTERING
MAISTRINGS
MAJESTICAL

MAJESTICALLY
MAJESTICALNESS
MAJESTICNESS
MAJESTICNESSES
MAJOLICAWARE
MAJOLICAWARES
MAJORDOMOS
MAJORETTES
MAJORETTING
MAJORETTINGS
MAJORITAIRE
MAJORITAIRES
MAJORITARIAN
MAJORITARIANISM
MAJORITARIANS
MAJORITIES
MAJORSHIPS
MAJUSCULAR
MAJUSCULES
MAKEREADIES
MAKESHIFTS
MAKEWEIGHT
MAKEWEIGHTS
MAKUNOUCHI
MAKUNOUCHIS
MALABSORPTION
MALABSORPTIONS
MALACHITES
MALACOLOGICAL
MALACOLOGIES
MALACOLOGIST
MALACOLOGISTS
MALACOLOGY
MALACOPHILIES
MALACOPHILOUS
MALACOPHILY
MALACOPHYLLOUS
MALACOPTERYGIAN
MALACOSTRACAN
MALACOSTRACANS
MALACOSTRACOUS
MALADAPTATION
MALADAPTATIONS
MALADAPTED
MALADAPTIVE
MALADAPTIVELY
MALADDRESS
MALADDRESSES
MALADJUSTED
MALADJUSTIVE
MALADJUSTMENT
MALADJUSTMENTS
MALADMINISTER
MALADMINISTERED
MALADMINISTERS
MALADROITLY
MALADROITNESS
MALADROITNESSES
MALADROITS
MALAGUENAS
MALAGUETTA
MALAGUETTAS
MALAKATOONE
MALAKATOONES
MALAPERTLY
MALAPERTNESS
MALAPERTNESSES
MALAPPORTIONED
MALAPPROPRIATE
MALAPPROPRIATED
MALAPPROPRIATES
MALAPROPIAN
MALAPROPISM
MALAPROPISMS
MALAPROPIST
MALAPROPISTS
MALAPROPOS
MALARIOLOGIES
MALARIOLOGIST
MALARIOLOGISTS
MALARIOLOGY
MALASSIMILATION
MALATHIONS
MALAXATING
MALAXATION
MALAXATIONS
MALAXATORS
MALCONFORMATION
MALCONTENT
MALCONTENTED
MALCONTENTEDLY
MALCONTENTS
MALDEPLOYMENT
MALDEPLOYMENTS
MALDISTRIBUTION
MALEDICENT
MALEDICTED
MALEDICTING
MALEDICTION
MALEDICTIONS
MALEDICTIVE
MALEDICTORY
MALEFACTION
MALEFACTIONS
MALEFACTOR
MALEFACTORS
MALEFACTORY
MALEFACTRESS
MALEFACTRESSES
MALEFFECTS
MALEFICALLY
MALEFICENCE
MALEFICENCES
MALEFICENT
MALEFICIAL
MALENESSES
MALENGINES
MALENTENDU
MALENTENDUS
MALEVOLENCE
MALEVOLENCES
MALEVOLENT
MALEVOLENTLY
MALFEASANCE
MALFEASANCES
MALFEASANT
MALFEASANTS
MALFORMATION
MALFORMATIONS
MALFUNCTION
MALFUNCTIONED
MALFUNCTIONING
MALFUNCTIONINGS
MALFUNCTIONS
MALICIOUSLY
MALICIOUSNESS
MALICIOUSNESSES
MALIGNANCE
MALIGNANCES
MALIGNANCIES
MALIGNANCY
MALIGNANTLY
MALIGNANTS
MALIGNITIES
MALIGNMENT
MALIGNMENTS
MALIMPRINTED
MALIMPRINTING
MALIMPRINTINGS
MALINGERED
MALINGERER
MALINGERERS
MALINGERIES
MALINGERING
MALLANDERS
MALLEABILITIES
MALLEABILITY
MALLEABLENESS
MALLEABLENESSES
MALLEATING
MALLEATION
MALLEATIONS
MALLEIFORM
MALLEMAROKING
MALLEMAROKINGS
MALLEMUCKS
MALLENDERS
MALLEOLUSES
MALLOPHAGOUS
MALLOWPUFF
MALLOWPUFFS
MALMSTONES
MALNOURISHED
MALNUTRITION
MALNUTRITIONS
MALOCCLUDED
MALOCCLUSION
MALOCCLUSIONS
MALODOROUS
MALODOROUSLY
MALODOROUSNESS
MALOLACTIC
MALONYLUREA
MALONYLUREAS
MALPIGHIACEOUS
MALPOSITION
MALPOSITIONS
MALPRACTICE
MALPRACTICES
MALPRACTITIONER
MALPRESENTATION
MALTALENTS
MALTINESSES
MALTREATED
MALTREATER
MALTREATERS
MALTREATING
MALTREATMENT
MALTREATMENTS
MALVACEOUS
MALVERSATION
MALVERSATIONS
MALVOISIES
MAMAGUYING
MAMILLATED
MAMILLATION
MAMILLATIONS
MAMILLIFORM
MAMMALIANS
MAMMALIFEROUS
MAMMALITIES
MAMMALOGICAL
MAMMALOGIES
MAMMALOGIST
MAMMALOGISTS
MAMMECTOMIES
MAMMECTOMY
MAMMETRIES
MAMMIFEROUS
MAMMILLARIA
MAMMILLARIAS
MAMMILLARY
MAMMILLATE
MAMMILLATED
MAMMITIDES
MAMMOCKING
MAMMOGENIC
MAMMOGRAMS
MAMMOGRAPH
MAMMOGRAPHIC
MAMMOGRAPHIES
MAMMOGRAPHS
MAMMOGRAPHY
MAMMONISMS
MAMMONISTIC
MAMMONISTS
MAMMONITES
MAMMOPLASTIES
MAMMOPLASTY
MANAGEABILITIES
MANAGEABILITY
MANAGEABLE
MANAGEABLENESS
MANAGEABLY
MANAGEMENT
MANAGEMENTAL
MANAGEMENTS
MANAGERESS
MANAGERESSES
MANAGERIAL
MANAGERIALISM
MANAGERIALISMS
MANAGERIALIST
MANAGERIALISTS
MANAGERIALLY
MANAGERSHIP
MANAGERSHIPS
MANCHESTER
MANCHESTERS
MANCHINEEL
MANCHINEELS
MANCIPATED
MANCIPATES
MANCIPATING

MANCIPATION
MANCIPATIONS
MANCIPATORY
MANDAMUSED
MANDAMUSES
MANDAMUSING
MANDARINATE
MANDARINATES
MANDARINES
MANDARINIC
MANDARINISM
MANDARINISMS
MANDATARIES
MANDATORIES
MANDATORILY
MANDIBULAR
MANDIBULATE
MANDIBULATED
MANDILIONS
MANDIOCCAS
MANDOLINES
MANDOLINIST
MANDOLINISTS
MANDRAGORA
MANDRAGORAS
MANDUCABLE
MANDUCATED
MANDUCATES
MANDUCATING
MANDUCATION
MANDUCATIONS
MANDUCATORY
MANDYLIONS
MANEUVERABILITY
MANEUVERABLE
MANEUVERED
MANEUVERER
MANEUVERERS
MANEUVERING
MANEUVERINGS
MANFULNESS
MANFULNESSES
MANGABEIRA
MANGABEIRAS
MANGALSUTRA
MANGALSUTRAS
MANGANATES
MANGANESES
MANGANESIAN
MANGANIFEROUS
MANGANITES
MANGELWURZEL
MANGELWURZELS
MANGEMANGE
MANGETOUTS
MANGINESSES
MANGOLDWURZEL
MANGOLDWURZELS
MANGOSTANS
MANGOSTEEN
MANGOSTEENS
MANGOUSTES
MANGULATED
MANGULATES
MANGULATING
MANHANDLED
MANHANDLES
MANHANDLING
MANHATTANS
MANHUNTERS
MANIACALLY
MANICOTTIS
MANICURING
MANICURIST
MANICURISTS
MANIFESTABLE
MANIFESTANT
MANIFESTANTS
MANIFESTATION
MANIFESTATIONAL
MANIFESTATIONS
MANIFESTATIVE
MANIFESTED
MANIFESTER
MANIFESTERS
MANIFESTIBLE
MANIFESTING
MANIFESTLY
MANIFESTNESS
MANIFESTNESSES
MANIFESTOED
MANIFESTOES
MANIFESTOING
MANIFESTOS
MANIFOLDED
MANIFOLDER
MANIFOLDERS
MANIFOLDING
MANIFOLDLY
MANIFOLDNESS
MANIFOLDNESSES
MANIPULABILITY
MANIPULABLE
MANIPULARS
MANIPULATABLE
MANIPULATE
MANIPULATED
MANIPULATES
MANIPULATING
MANIPULATION
MANIPULATIONS
MANIPULATIVE
MANIPULATIVELY
MANIPULATOR
MANIPULATORS
MANIPULATORY
MANLINESSES
MANNEQUINS
MANNERISMS
MANNERISTIC
MANNERISTICAL
MANNERISTICALLY
MANNERISTS
MANNERLESS
MANNERLESSNESS
MANNERLESSNESSES
MANNERLINESS
MANNERLINESSES
MANNIFEROUS
MANNISHNESS
MANNISHNESSES
MANOEUVRABILITY
MANOEUVRABLE
MANOEUVRED
MANOEUVRER
MANOEUVRERS
MANOEUVRES
MANOEUVRING
MANOEUVRINGS
MANOMETERS
MANOMETRIC
MANOMETRICAL
MANOMETRICALLY
MANOMETRIES
MANORIALISM
MANORIALISMS
MANOSCOPIES
MANSERVANT
MANSIONARIES
MANSIONARY
MANSLAUGHTER
MANSLAUGHTERS
MANSLAYERS
MANSONRIES
MANSUETUDE
MANSUETUDES
MANTELLETTA
MANTELLETTAS
MANTELPIECE
MANTELPIECES
MANTELSHELF
MANTELSHELVES
MANTELTREE
MANTELTREES
MANTICALLY
MANTICORAS
MANTICORES
MANTLETREE
MANTLETREES
MANUBRIUMS
MANUFACTORIES
MANUFACTORY
MANUFACTURABLE
MANUFACTURAL
MANUFACTURE
MANUFACTURED
MANUFACTURER
MANUFACTURERS
MANUFACTURES
MANUFACTURING
MANUFACTURINGS
MANUMISSION
MANUMISSIONS
MANUMITTED
MANUMITTER
MANUMITTERS
MANUMITTING
MANURANCES
MANUSCRIPT
MANUSCRIPTS
MANZANILLA
MANZANILLAS
MANZANITAS
MAPMAKINGS
MAPPEMONDS
MAQUILADORA
MAQUILADORAS
MAQUILLAGE
MAQUILLAGES
MAQUISARDS
MARABUNTAS
MARANATHAS
MARASCHINO
MARASCHINOS
MARASMUSES
MARATHONER
MARATHONERS
MARATHONING
MARATHONINGS
MARBELISED
MARBELISES
MARBELISING
MARBELIZED
MARBELIZES
MARBELIZING
MARBLEISED
MARBLEISES
MARBLEISING
MARBLEIZED
MARBLEIZES
MARBLEIZING
MARBLEWOOD
MARBLEWOODS
MARCANTANT
MARCANTANTS
MARCASITES
MARCASITICAL
MARCATISSIMO
MARCELLERS
MARCELLING
MARCESCENCE
MARCESCENCES
MARCESCENT
MARCESCIBLE
MARCHANTIA
MARCHANTIAS
MARCHIONESS
MARCHIONESSES
MARCHLANDS
MARCHPANES
MARCONIGRAM
MARCONIGRAMS
MARCONIGRAPH
MARCONIGRAPHED
MARCONIGRAPHING
MARCONIGRAPHS
MARCONIING
MARESCHALS
MARGARINES
MARGARITAS
MARGARITES
MARGARITIC
MARGARITIFEROUS
MARGENTING
MARGINALIA
MARGINALISATION
MARGINALISATIONS
MARGINALISE
MARGINALISED
MARGINALISES
MARGINALISING
MARGINALISM
MARGINALISMS
MARGINALIST

MARGINALISTS
MARGINALITIES
MARGINALITY
MARGINALIZATION
MARGINALIZE
MARGINALIZED
MARGINALIZES
MARGINALIZING
MARGINALLY
MARGINATED
MARGINATES
MARGINATING
MARGINATION
MARGINATIONS
MARGRAVATE
MARGRAVATES
MARGRAVIAL
MARGRAVIATE
MARGRAVIATES
MARGRAVINE
MARGRAVINES
MARGUERITE
MARGUERITES
MARIALITES
MARICULTURE
MARICULTURES
MARICULTURIST
MARICULTURISTS
MARIGRAPHS
MARIHUANAS
MARIJUANAS
MARIMBAPHONE
MARIMBAPHONES
MARIMBISTS
MARINADING
MARINATING
MARINATION
MARINATIONS
MARIONBERRIES
MARIONBERRY
MARIONETTE
MARIONETTES
MARISCHALLED
MARISCHALLING
MARISCHALS
MARIVAUDAGE
MARIVAUDAGES
MARKEDNESS
MARKEDNESSES
MARKETABILITIES
MARKETABILITY
MARKETABLE
MARKETABLENESS
MARKETABLY
MARKETEERS
MARKETINGS
MARKETISATION
MARKETISATIONS
MARKETIZATION
MARKETIZATIONS
MARKETPLACE
MARKETPLACES
MARKSMANSHIP
MARKSMANSHIPS
MARKSWOMAN
MARKSWOMEN

MARLACIOUS
MARLINESPIKE
MARLINESPIKES
MARLINGSPIKE
MARLINGSPIKES
MARLINSPIKE
MARLINSPIKES
MARLSTONES
MARMALADES
MARMALISED
MARMALISES
MARMALISING
MARMALIZED
MARMALIZES
MARMALIZING
MARMARISED
MARMARISES
MARMARISING
MARMARIZED
MARMARIZES
MARMARIZING
MARMAROSES
MARMAROSIS
MARMELISED
MARMELISES
MARMELISING
MARMELIZED
MARMELIZES
MARMELIZING
MARMOREALLY
MAROONINGS
MARPRELATE
MARPRELATED
MARPRELATES
MARPRELATING
MARQUESSATE
MARQUESSATES
MARQUESSES
MARQUETERIE
MARQUETERIES
MARQUETRIES
MARQUISATE
MARQUISATES
MARQUISETTE
MARQUISETTES
MARRIAGEABILITY
MARRIAGEABLE
MARROWBONE
MARROWBONES
MARROWFATS
MARROWLESS
MARROWSKIED
MARROWSKIES
MARROWSKYING
MARSEILLES
MARSHALCIES
MARSHALERS
MARSHALING
MARSHALLED
MARSHALLER
MARSHALLERS
MARSHALLING
MARSHALLINGS
MARSHALSHIP
MARSHALSHIPS
MARSHBUCKS

MARSHINESS
MARSHINESSES
MARSHLANDER
MARSHLANDERS
MARSHLANDS
MARSHLOCKS
MARSHLOCKSES
MARSHMALLOW
MARSHMALLOWS
MARSHMALLOWY
MARSHWORTS
MARSIPOBRANCH
MARSIPOBRANCHS
MARSQUAKES
MARSUPIALIAN
MARSUPIALIANS
MARSUPIALS
MARSUPIANS
MARSUPIUMS
MARTELLANDO
MARTELLANDOS
MARTELLATO
MARTELLING
MARTENSITE
MARTENSITES
MARTENSITIC
MARTENSITICALLY
MARTIALISM
MARTIALISMS
MARTIALIST
MARTIALISTS
MARTIALNESS
MARTIALNESSES
MARTINETISH
MARTINETISM
MARTINETISMS
MARTINGALE
MARTINGALES
MARTINGALS
MARTYRDOMS
MARTYRISATION
MARTYRISATIONS
MARTYRISED
MARTYRISES
MARTYRISING
MARTYRIZATION
MARTYRIZATIONS
MARTYRIZED
MARTYRIZES
MARTYRIZING
MARTYROLOGIC
MARTYROLOGICAL
MARTYROLOGIES
MARTYROLOGIST
MARTYROLOGISTS
MARTYROLOGY
MARVELLING
MARVELLOUS
MARVELLOUSLY
MARVELLOUSNESS
MARVELOUSLY
MARVELOUSNESS
MARVELOUSNESSES
MASCARAING
MASCARPONE
MASCARPONES

MASCULINELY
MASCULINENESS
MASCULINENESSES
MASCULINES
MASCULINISATION
MASCULINISATIONS
MASCULINISE
MASCULINISED
MASCULINISES
MASCULINISING
MASCULINIST
MASCULINISTS
MASCULINITIES
MASCULINITY
MASCULINIZATION
MASCULINIZE
MASCULINIZED
MASCULINIZES
MASCULINIZING
MASCULISTS
MASHGICHIM
MASKALLONGE
MASKALLONGES
MASKALONGE
MASKALONGES
MASKANONGE
MASKANONGES
MASKINONGE
MASKINONGES
MASKIROVKA
MASKIROVKAS
MASOCHISMS
MASOCHISTIC
MASOCHISTICALLY
MASOCHISTS
MASONICALLY
MASQUERADE
MASQUERADED
MASQUERADER
MASQUERADERS
MASQUERADES
MASQUERADING
MASSACRERS
MASSACRING
MASSAGISTS
MASSARANDUBA
MASSARANDUBAS
MASSASAUGA
MASSASAUGAS
MASSERANDUBA
MASSERANDUBAS
MASSETERIC
MASSINESSES
MASSIVENESS
MASSIVENESSES
MASSOTHERAPIES
MASSOTHERAPIST
MASSOTHERAPISTS
MASSOTHERAPY
MASSPRIEST
MASSPRIESTS
MASSYMORES
MASTECTOMIES
MASTECTOMY
MASTERATES
MASTERCLASS

MASTERCLASSES
MASTERDOMS
MASTERFULLY
MASTERFULNESS
MASTERFULNESSES
MASTERHOOD
MASTERHOODS
MASTERINGS
MASTERLESS
MASTERLINESS
MASTERLINESSES
MASTERMIND
MASTERMINDED
MASTERMINDING
MASTERMINDS
MASTERPIECE
MASTERPIECES
MASTERSHIP
MASTERSHIPS
MASTERSINGER
MASTERSINGERS
MASTERSTROKE
MASTERSTROKES
MASTERWORK
MASTERWORKS
MASTERWORT
MASTERWORTS
MASTHEADED
MASTHEADING
MASTHOUSES
MASTICABLE
MASTICATED
MASTICATES
MASTICATING
MASTICATION
MASTICATIONS
MASTICATOR
MASTICATORIES
MASTICATORS
MASTICATORY
MASTIGOPHORAN
MASTIGOPHORANS
MASTIGOPHORE
MASTIGOPHORES
MASTIGOPHORIC
MASTIGOPHOROUS
MASTITIDES
MASTITISES
MASTODONIC
MASTODONTIC
MASTODONTS
MASTODYNIA
MASTODYNIAS
MASTOIDECTOMIES
MASTOIDECTOMY
MASTOIDITIS
MASTOIDITISES
MASTOPEXIES
MASTURBATE
MASTURBATED
MASTURBATES
MASTURBATING
MASTURBATION
MASTURBATIONS
MASTURBATOR
MASTURBATORS
MASTURBATORY
MATACHINAS
MATAGOURIS
MATCHBOARD
MATCHBOARDING
MATCHBOARDINGS
MATCHBOARDS
MATCHBOOKS
MATCHBOXES
MATCHLESSLY
MATCHLESSNESS
MATCHLESSNESSES
MATCHLOCKS
MATCHMAKER
MATCHMAKERS
MATCHMAKES
MATCHMAKING
MATCHMAKINGS
MATCHMARKED
MATCHMARKING
MATCHMARKS
MATCHSTICK
MATCHSTICKS
MATCHWOODS
MATELASSES
MATELLASSE
MATELLASSES
MATELOTTES
MATERFAMILIAS
MATERFAMILIASES
MATERIALISATION
MATERIALISE
MATERIALISED
MATERIALISER
MATERIALISERS
MATERIALISES
MATERIALISING
MATERIALISM
MATERIALISMS
MATERIALIST
MATERIALISTIC
MATERIALISTICAL
MATERIALISTS
MATERIALITIES
MATERIALITY
MATERIALIZATION
MATERIALIZE
MATERIALIZED
MATERIALIZER
MATERIALIZERS
MATERIALIZES
MATERIALIZING
MATERIALLY
MATERIALNESS
MATERIALNESSES
MATERNALISM
MATERNALISMS
MATERNALISTIC
MATERNALLY
MATERNITIES
MATEYNESSES
MATGRASSES
MATHEMATIC
MATHEMATICAL
MATHEMATICALLY
MATHEMATICIAN
MATHEMATICIANS
MATHEMATICISE
MATHEMATICISED
MATHEMATICISES
MATHEMATICISING
MATHEMATICISM
MATHEMATICISMS
MATHEMATICIZE
MATHEMATICIZED
MATHEMATICIZES
MATHEMATICIZING
MATHEMATICS
MATHEMATISATION
MATHEMATISE
MATHEMATISED
MATHEMATISES
MATHEMATISING
MATHEMATIZATION
MATHEMATIZE
MATHEMATIZED
MATHEMATIZES
MATHEMATIZING
MATINESSES
MATRESFAMILIAS
MATRIARCHAL
MATRIARCHALISM
MATRIARCHALISMS
MATRIARCHATE
MATRIARCHATES
MATRIARCHIC
MATRIARCHICAL
MATRIARCHIES
MATRIARCHS
MATRIARCHY
MATRICIDAL
MATRICIDES
MATRICLINIC
MATRICLINOUS
MATRICULANT
MATRICULANTS
MATRICULAR
MATRICULAS
MATRICULATE
MATRICULATED
MATRICULATES
MATRICULATING
MATRICULATION
MATRICULATIONS
MATRICULATOR
MATRICULATORS
MATRICULATORY
MATRIFOCAL
MATRIFOCALITIES
MATRIFOCALITY
MATRILINEAL
MATRILINEALLY
MATRILINEAR
MATRILINIES
MATRILOCAL
MATRILOCALITIES
MATRILOCALITY
MATRILOCALLY
MATRIMONIAL
MATRIMONIALLY
MATRIMONIES
MATRIOSHKA
MATRIOSHKI
MATROCLINAL
MATROCLINIC
MATROCLINIES
MATROCLINOUS
MATROCLINY
MATRONAGES
MATRONHOOD
MATRONHOODS
MATRONISED
MATRONISES
MATRONISING
MATRONIZED
MATRONIZES
MATRONIZING
MATRONLINESS
MATRONLINESSES
MATRONSHIP
MATRONSHIPS
MATRONYMIC
MATRONYMICS
MATROYSHKA
MATROYSHKAS
MATRYOSHKA
MATRYOSHKAS
MATRYOSHKI
MATSUTAKES
MATTAMORES
MATTERLESS
MATTIFYING
MATTRASSES
MATTRESSES
MATURATING
MATURATION
MATURATIONAL
MATURATIONS
MATURATIVE
MATURENESS
MATURENESSES
MATURITIES
MATUTINALLY
MAUDLINISM
MAUDLINISMS
MAUDLINNESS
MAUDLINNESSES
MAULSTICKS
MAUMETRIES
MAUNDERERS
MAUNDERING
MAUNDERINGS
MAURIKIGUSARI
MAURIKIGUSARIS
MAUSOLEUMS
MAVERICKED
MAVERICKING
MAVOURNEEN
MAVOURNEENS
MAVOURNINS
MAWKISHNESS
MAWKISHNESSES
MAWMETRIES
MAXILLARIES
MAXILLIPED
MAXILLIPEDARY
MAXILLIPEDE
MAXILLIPEDES

MAXILLIPEDS
MAXILLOFACIAL
MAXILLULAE
MAXIMALIST
MAXIMALISTS
MAXIMAPHILIES
MAXIMAPHILY
MAXIMATION
MAXIMATIONS
MAXIMISATION
MAXIMISATIONS
MAXIMISERS
MAXIMISING
MAXIMIZATION
MAXIMIZATIONS
MAXIMIZERS
MAXIMIZING
MAYFLOWERS
MAYONNAISE
MAYONNAISES
MAYORALTIES
MAYORESSES
MAYORSHIPS
MAYSTERDOME
MAYSTERDOMES
MAZARINADE
MAZARINADES
MAZEDNESSES
MAZINESSES
MEADOWLAND
MEADOWLANDS
MEADOWLARK
MEADOWLARKS
MEADOWSWEET
MEADOWSWEETS
MEAGERNESS
MEAGERNESSES
MEAGRENESS
MEAGRENESSES
MEALINESSES
MEALYMOUTHED
MEANDERERS
MEANDERING
MEANDERINGLY
MEANINGFUL
MEANINGFULLY
MEANINGFULNESS
MEANINGLESS
MEANINGLESSLY
MEANINGLESSNESS
MEANNESSES
MEANWHILES
MEASLINESS
MEASLINESSES
MEASURABILITIES
MEASURABILITY
MEASURABLE
MEASURABLENESS
MEASURABLY
MEASUREDLY
MEASUREDNESS
MEASUREDNESSES
MEASURELESS
MEASURELESSLY
MEASURELESSNESS
MEASURELESSNESSES
MEASUREMENT
MEASUREMENTS
MEASURINGS
MEATINESSES
MEATLOAVES
MEATPACKING
MEATPACKINGS
MEATSCREEN
MEATSCREENS
MEATSPACES
MECAMYLAMINE
MECAMYLAMINES
MECHANICAL
MECHANICALISM
MECHANICALISMS
MECHANICALLY
MECHANICALNESS
MECHANICALNESSES
MECHANICALS
MECHANICIAN
MECHANICIANS
MECHANISABLE
MECHANISATION
MECHANISATIONS
MECHANISED
MECHANISER
MECHANISERS
MECHANISES
MECHANISING
MECHANISMS
MECHANISTIC
MECHANISTICALLY
MECHANISTS
MECHANIZABLE
MECHANIZATION
MECHANIZATIONS
MECHANIZED
MECHANIZER
MECHANIZERS
MECHANIZES
MECHANIZING
MECHANOCHEMICAL
MECHANOMORPHISM
MECHANORECEPTOR
MECHANOTHERAPIES
MECHANOTHERAPY
MECHATRONIC
MECHATRONICS
MECLIZINES
MECONOPSES
MECONOPSIS
MEDAILLONS
MEDALLIONED
MEDALLIONING
MEDALLIONS
MEDALLISTS
MEDDLESOME
MEDDLESOMELY
MEDDLESOMENESS
MEDDLINGLY
MEDEVACING
MEDEVACKED
MEDEVACKING
MEDIAEVALISM
MEDIAEVALISMS
MEDIAEVALIST
MEDIAEVALISTIC
MEDIAEVALISTS
MEDIAEVALLY
MEDIAEVALS
MEDIAGENIC
MEDIASTINA
MEDIASTINAL
MEDIASTINUM
MEDIATENESS
MEDIATENESSES
MEDIATIONAL
MEDIATIONS
MEDIATISATION
MEDIATISATIONS
MEDIATISED
MEDIATISES
MEDIATISING
MEDIATIZATION
MEDIATIZATIONS
MEDIATIZED
MEDIATIZES
MEDIATIZING
MEDIATORIAL
MEDIATORIALLY
MEDIATORSHIP
MEDIATORSHIPS
MEDIATRESS
MEDIATRESSES
MEDIATRICES
MEDIATRIXES
MEDICALISATION
MEDICALISATIONS
MEDICALISE
MEDICALISED
MEDICALISES
MEDICALISING
MEDICALIZATION
MEDICALIZATIONS
MEDICALIZE
MEDICALIZED
MEDICALIZES
MEDICALIZING
MEDICAMENT
MEDICAMENTAL
MEDICAMENTALLY
MEDICAMENTARY
MEDICAMENTED
MEDICAMENTING
MEDICAMENTOUS
MEDICAMENTS
MEDICASTER
MEDICASTERS
MEDICATING
MEDICATION
MEDICATIONS
MEDICATIVE
MEDICINABLE
MEDICINALLY
MEDICINALS
MEDICINERS
MEDICINING
MEDICOLEGAL
MEDIEVALISM
MEDIEVALISMS
MEDIEVALIST
MEDIEVALISTIC
MEDIEVALISTS
MEDIEVALLY
MEDIOCRACIES
MEDIOCRACY
MEDIOCRITIES
MEDIOCRITY
MEDITATING
MEDITATION
MEDITATIONS
MEDITATIVE
MEDITATIVELY
MEDITATIVENESS
MEDITATORS
MEDITERRANEAN
MEDIUMISTIC
MEDIUMSHIP
MEDIUMSHIPS
MEDIVACING
MEDIVACKED
MEDIVACKING
MEDRESSEHS
MEDULLATED
MEDULLOBLASTOMA
MEDUSIFORM
MEEKNESSES
MEERSCHAUM
MEERSCHAUMS
MEETINGHOUSE
MEETINGHOUSES
MEETNESSES
MEFLOQUINE
MEFLOQUINES
MEGACEPHALIC
MEGACEPHALIES
MEGACEPHALOUS
MEGACEPHALY
MEGACITIES
MEGACORPORATION
MEGACURIES
MEGACYCLES
MEGADEATHS
MEGAFARADS
MEGAFAUNAE
MEGAFAUNAL
MEGAFAUNAS
MEGAFLORAE
MEGAFLORAS
MEGAGAMETE
MEGAGAMETES
MEGAGAMETOPHYTE
MEGAGAUSSES
MEGAHERBIVORE
MEGAHERBIVORES
MEGAHERTZES
MEGAJOULES
MEGAKARYOCYTE
MEGAKARYOCYTES
MEGAKARYOCYTIC
MEGALITHIC
MEGALITRES
MEGALOBLAST
MEGALOBLASTIC
MEGALOBLASTS
MEGALOCARDIA
MEGALOCARDIAS
MEGALOCEPHALIC

MEGALOCEPHALIES
MEGALOCEPHALOUS
MEGALOCEPHALY
MEGALOMANIA
MEGALOMANIAC
MEGALOMANIACAL
MEGALOMANIACS
MEGALOMANIAS
MEGALOMANIC
MEGALOPOLIS
MEGALOPOLISES
MEGALOPOLITAN
MEGALOPOLITANS
MEGALOPSES
MEGALOSAUR
MEGALOSAURIAN
MEGALOSAURIANS
MEGALOSAURS
MEGALOSAURUS
MEGALOSAURUSES
MEGANEWTON
MEGANEWTONS
MEGAPARSEC
MEGAPARSECS
MEGAPHONED
MEGAPHONES
MEGAPHONIC
MEGAPHONICALLY
MEGAPHONING
MEGAPHYLLS
MEGAPIXELS
MEGAPLEXES
MEGAPROJECT
MEGAPROJECTS
MEGASCOPES
MEGASCOPIC
MEGASCOPICALLY
MEGASPORANGIA
MEGASPORANGIUM
MEGASPORES
MEGASPORIC
MEGASPOROPHYLL
MEGASPOROPHYLLS
MEGASTORES
MEGASTRUCTURE
MEGASTRUCTURES
MEGATECHNOLOGY
MEGATHERES
MEGATHERIAN
MEGATONNAGE
MEGATONNAGES
MEGAVERTEBRATE
MEGAVERTEBRATES
MEGAVITAMIN
MEGAVITAMINS
MEIOFAUNAL
MEIOSPORES
MEIOTICALLY
MEITNERIUM
MEITNERIUMS
MEKOMETERS
MELACONITE
MELACONITES
MELALEUCAS
MELAMPODES
MELANAEMIA
MELANAEMIAS
MELANCHOLIA
MELANCHOLIAC
MELANCHOLIACS
MELANCHOLIAS
MELANCHOLIC
MELANCHOLICALLY
MELANCHOLICS
MELANCHOLIES
MELANCHOLILY
MELANCHOLINESS
MELANCHOLINESSES
MELANCHOLIOUS
MELANCHOLY
MELANISATION
MELANISATIONS
MELANISING
MELANISTIC
MELANIZATION
MELANIZATIONS
MELANIZING
MELANOBLAST
MELANOBLASTS
MELANOCHROI
MELANOCHROIC
MELANOCHROOUS
MELANOCYTE
MELANOCYTES
MELANOGENESES
MELANOGENESIS
MELANOMATA
MELANOPHORE
MELANOPHORES
MELANOSITIES
MELANOSITY
MELANOSOME
MELANOSOMES
MELANOTROPIN
MELANOTROPINS
MELANTERITE
MELANTERITES
MELANURIAS
MELAPHYRES
MELASTOMACEOUS
MELATONINS
MELIACEOUS
MELICOTTON
MELICOTTONS
MELIORABLE
MELIORATED
MELIORATES
MELIORATING
MELIORATION
MELIORATIONS
MELIORATIVE
MELIORATOR
MELIORATORS
MELIORISMS
MELIORISTIC
MELIORISTS
MELIORITIES
MELIPHAGOUS
MELISMATIC
MELLIFEROUS
MELLIFICATION
MELLIFICATIONS
MELLIFLUENCE
MELLIFLUENCES
MELLIFLUENT
MELLIFLUENTLY
MELLIFLUOUS
MELLIFLUOUSLY
MELLIFLUOUSNESS
MELLIPHAGOUS
MELLIVOROUS
MELLOPHONE
MELLOPHONES
MELLOTRONS
MELLOWNESS
MELLOWNESSES
MELLOWSPEAK
MELLOWSPEAKS
MELOCOTONS
MELOCOTOON
MELOCOTOONS
MELODICALLY
MELODIOUSLY
MELODIOUSNESS
MELODIOUSNESSES
MELODISERS
MELODISING
MELODIZERS
MELODIZING
MELODRAMAS
MELODRAMATIC
MELODRAMATICS
MELODRAMATISE
MELODRAMATISED
MELODRAMATISES
MELODRAMATISING
MELODRAMATIST
MELODRAMATISTS
MELODRAMATIZE
MELODRAMATIZED
MELODRAMATIZES
MELODRAMATIZING
MELODRAMES
MELOMANIAC
MELOMANIACS
MELOMANIAS
MELONGENES
MELPHALANS
MELTABILITIES
MELTABILITY
MELTINGNESS
MELTINGNESSES
MELTWATERS
MELUNGEONS
MEMBERLESS
MEMBERSHIP
MEMBERSHIPS
MEMBRANACEOUS
MEMBRANEOUS
MEMBRANOUS
MEMBRANOUSLY
MEMOIRISMS
MEMOIRISTS
MEMORABILE
MEMORABILIA
MEMORABILITIES
MEMORABILITY
MEMORABLENESS
MEMORABLENESSES
MEMORANDUM
MEMORANDUMS
MEMORATIVE
MEMORIALISATION
MEMORIALISATIONS
MEMORIALISE
MEMORIALISED
MEMORIALISER
MEMORIALISERS
MEMORIALISES
MEMORIALISING
MEMORIALIST
MEMORIALISTS
MEMORIALIZATION
MEMORIALIZATIONS
MEMORIALIZE
MEMORIALIZED
MEMORIALIZER
MEMORIALIZERS
MEMORIALIZES
MEMORIALIZING
MEMORIALLY
MEMORISABLE
MEMORISATION
MEMORISATIONS
MEMORISERS
MEMORISING
MEMORIZABLE
MEMORIZATION
MEMORIZATIONS
MEMORIZERS
MEMORIZING
MENACINGLY
MENADIONES
MENAGERIES
MENAQUINONE
MENAQUINONES
MENARCHEAL
MENARCHIAL
MENDACIOUS
MENDACIOUSLY
MENDACIOUSNESS
MENDACITIES
MENDELEVIUM
MENDELEVIUMS
MENDICANCIES
MENDICANCY
MENDICANTS
MENDICITIES
MENINGIOMA
MENINGIOMAS
MENINGIOMATA
MENINGITIC
MENINGITIDES
MENINGITIS
MENINGITISES
MENINGOCELE
MENINGOCELES
MENINGOCOCCAL
MENINGOCOCCI
MENINGOCOCCIC
MENINGOCOCCUS
MENISCECTOMIES
MENISCECTOMY
MENISCUSES

MENISPERMACEOUS
MENISPERMUM
MENISPERMUMS
MENOLOGIES
MENOMINEES
MENOPAUSAL
MENOPAUSES
MENOPAUSIC
MENOPOLISES
MENORRHAGIA
MENORRHAGIAS
MENORRHAGIC
MENORRHEAS
MENORRHOEA
MENORRHOEAS
MENSERVANTS
MENSTRUALLY
MENSTRUATE
MENSTRUATED
MENSTRUATES
MENSTRUATING
MENSTRUATION
MENSTRUATIONS
MENSTRUOUS
MENSTRUUMS
MENSURABILITIES
MENSURABILITY
MENSURABLE
MENSURATION
MENSURATIONAL
MENSURATIONS
MENSURATIVE
MENTALESES
MENTALISMS
MENTALISTIC
MENTALISTICALLY
MENTALISTS
MENTALITIES
MENTATIONS
MENTHACEOUS
MENTHOLATED
MENTICIDES
MENTIONABLE
MENTIONERS
MENTIONING
MENTONNIERE
MENTONNIERES
MENTORINGS
MENTORSHIP
MENTORSHIPS
MENUISIERS
MEPACRINES
MEPERIDINE
MEPERIDINES
MEPHITICAL
MEPHITICALLY
MEPHITISES
MEPHITISMS
MEPROBAMATE
MEPROBAMATES
MERBROMINS
MERCANTILE
MERCANTILISM
MERCANTILISMS
MERCANTILIST
MERCANTILISTIC
MERCANTILISTS
MERCAPTANS
MERCAPTIDE
MERCAPTIDES
MERCAPTOPURINE
MERCAPTOPURINES
MERCENARIES
MERCENARILY
MERCENARINESS
MERCENARINESSES
MERCENARISM
MERCENARISMS
MERCERISATION
MERCERISATIONS
MERCERISED
MERCERISER
MERCERISERS
MERCERISES
MERCERISING
MERCERIZATION
MERCERIZATIONS
MERCERIZED
MERCERIZER
MERCERIZERS
MERCERIZES
MERCERIZING
MERCHANDISE
MERCHANDISED
MERCHANDISER
MERCHANDISERS
MERCHANDISES
MERCHANDISING
MERCHANDISINGS
MERCHANDIZE
MERCHANDIZED
MERCHANDIZER
MERCHANDIZERS
MERCHANDIZES
MERCHANDIZING
MERCHANDIZINGS
MERCHANTABILITY
MERCHANTABLE
MERCHANTED
MERCHANTING
MERCHANTINGS
MERCHANTLIKE
MERCHANTMAN
MERCHANTMEN
MERCHANTRIES
MERCHANTRY
MERCHILDREN
MERCIFULLY
MERCIFULNESS
MERCIFULNESSES
MERCIFYING
MERCILESSLY
MERCILESSNESS
MERCILESSNESSES
MERCURATED
MERCURATES
MERCURATING
MERCURATION
MERCURATIONS
MERCURIALISE
MERCURIALISED
MERCURIALISES
MERCURIALISING
MERCURIALISM
MERCURIALISMS
MERCURIALIST
MERCURIALISTS
MERCURIALITIES
MERCURIALITY
MERCURIALIZE
MERCURIALIZED
MERCURIALIZES
MERCURIALIZING
MERCURIALLY
MERCURIALNESS
MERCURIALNESSES
MERCURIALS
MERCURISED
MERCURISES
MERCURISING
MERCURIZED
MERCURIZES
MERCURIZING
MERDIVOROUS
MEREOLOGICAL
MEREOLOGIES
MERESTONES
MERETRICIOUS
MERETRICIOUSLY
MERGANSERS
MERIDIONAL
MERIDIONALITIES
MERIDIONALITY
MERIDIONALLY
MERIDIONALS
MERISTEMATIC
MERISTICALLY
MERITOCRACIES
MERITOCRACY
MERITOCRAT
MERITOCRATIC
MERITOCRATS
MERITORIOUS
MERITORIOUSLY
MERITORIOUSNESS
MERMAIDENS
MEROBLASTIC
MEROBLASTICALLY
MEROGENESES
MEROGENESIS
MEROGENETIC
MEROGONIES
MEROMORPHIC
MEROMYOSIN
MEROMYOSINS
MERONYMIES
MEROPIDANS
MEROPLANKTON
MEROPLANKTONS
MEROZOITES
MERPEOPLES
MERRIMENTS
MERRINESSES
MERRYMAKER
MERRYMAKERS
MERRYMAKING
MERRYMAKINGS
MERRYTHOUGHT
MERRYTHOUGHTS
MERVEILLEUSE
MERVEILLEUSES
MERVEILLEUX
MERVEILLEUXES
MESALLIANCE
MESALLIANCES
MESATICEPHALIC
MESATICEPHALIES
MESATICEPHALOUS
MESATICEPHALY
MESCALINES
MESCALISMS
MESDEMOISELLES
MESENCEPHALA
MESENCEPHALIC
MESENCEPHALON
MESENCEPHALONS
MESENCHYMAL
MESENCHYMATOUS
MESENCHYME
MESENCHYMES
MESENTERIAL
MESENTERIC
MESENTERIES
MESENTERITIS
MESENTERITISES
MESENTERON
MESENTERONIC
MESHUGAASEN
MESHUGASEN
MESHUGGENAH
MESHUGGENAHS
MESHUGGENEH
MESHUGGENEHS
MESHUGGENER
MESHUGGENERS
MESITYLENE
MESITYLENES
MESMERICAL
MESMERICALLY
MESMERISATION
MESMERISATIONS
MESMERISED
MESMERISER
MESMERISERS
MESMERISES
MESMERISING
MESMERISMS
MESMERISTS
MESMERIZATION
MESMERIZATIONS
MESMERIZED
MESMERIZER
MESMERIZERS
MESMERIZES
MESMERIZING
MESNALTIES
MESOAMERICAN
MESOBENTHOS
MESOBENTHOSES
MESOBLASTIC
MESOBLASTS
MESOCEPHALIC
MESOCEPHALICS
MESOCEPHALIES

MESOCEPHALISM
MESOCEPHALISMS
MESOCEPHALOUS
MESOCEPHALY
MESOCRANIES
MESOCRATIC
MESOCYCLONE
MESOCYCLONES
MESODERMAL
MESODERMIC
MESOGASTRIA
MESOGASTRIC
MESOGASTRIUM
MESOGLOEAS
MESOGNATHIES
MESOGNATHISM
MESOGNATHISMS
MESOGNATHOUS
MESOGNATHY
MESOHIPPUS
MESOHIPPUSES
MESOKURTIC
MESOMERISM
MESOMERISMS
MESOMORPHIC
MESOMORPHIES
MESOMORPHISM
MESOMORPHISMS
MESOMORPHOUS
MESOMORPHS
MESOMORPHY
MESONEPHRIC
MESONEPHROI
MESONEPHROS
MESONEPHROSES
MESOPAUSES
MESOPELAGIC
MESOPHILES
MESOPHILIC
MESOPHYLLIC
MESOPHYLLOUS
MESOPHYLLS
MESOPHYTES
MESOPHYTIC
MESOSCAPHE
MESOSCAPHES
MESOSPHERE
MESOSPHERES
MESOSPHERIC
MESOTHELIA
MESOTHELIAL
MESOTHELIOMA
MESOTHELIOMAS
MESOTHELIOMATA
MESOTHELIUM
MESOTHELIUMS
MESOTHORACES
MESOTHORACIC
MESOTHORAX
MESOTHORAXES
MESOTHORIUM
MESOTHORIUMS
MESOTROPHIC
MESQUINERIE
MESQUINERIES
MESSAGINGS
MESSALINES
MESSEIGNEURS
MESSENGERED
MESSENGERING
MESSENGERS
MESSIAHSHIP
MESSIAHSHIPS
MESSIANICALLY
MESSIANISM
MESSIANISMS
MESSINESSES
MESTRANOLS
METABOLICALLY
METABOLIES
METABOLISABLE
METABOLISE
METABOLISED
METABOLISES
METABOLISING
METABOLISM
METABOLISMS
METABOLITE
METABOLITES
METABOLIZABLE
METABOLIZE
METABOLIZED
METABOLIZES
METABOLIZING
METABOLOME
METABOLOMES
METABOLOMICS
METABOTROPIC
METACARPAL
METACARPALS
METACARPUS
METACENTER
METACENTERS
METACENTRE
METACENTRES
METACENTRIC
METACENTRICS
METACERCARIA
METACERCARIAE
METACERCARIAL
METACHROMATIC
METACHROMATISM
METACHROMATISMS
METACHRONISM
METACHRONISMS
METACHROSES
METACHROSIS
METACINNABARITE
METACINNABARITES
METACOGNITION
METACOGNITIONS
METACOMPUTER
METACOMPUTERS
METACOMPUTING
METACOMPUTINGS
METAETHICAL
METAETHICS
METAFEMALE
METAFEMALES
METAFICTION
METAFICTIONAL
METAFICTIONIST
METAFICTIONISTS
METAFICTIONS
METAGALACTIC
METAGALAXIES
METAGALAXY
METAGENESES
METAGENESIS
METAGENETIC
METAGENETICALLY
METAGNATHISM
METAGNATHISMS
METAGNATHOUS
METAGRABOLISE
METAGRABOLISED
METAGRABOLISES
METAGRABOLISING
METAGRABOLIZE
METAGRABOLIZED
METAGRABOLIZES
METAGRABOLIZING
METAGROBOLISE
METAGROBOLISED
METAGROBOLISES
METAGROBOLISING
METAGROBOLIZE
METAGROBOLIZED
METAGROBOLIZES
METAGROBOLIZING
METALANGUAGE
METALANGUAGES
METALDEHYDE
METALDEHYDES
METALEPSES
METALEPSIS
METALEPTIC
METALEPTICAL
METALHEADS
METALINGUISTIC
METALINGUISTICS
METALISING
METALIZATION
METALIZATIONS
METALIZING
METALLICALLY
METALLIDING
METALLIDINGS
METALLIFEROUS
METALLINGS
METALLISATION
METALLISATIONS
METALLISED
METALLISES
METALLISING
METALLISTS
METALLIZATION
METALLIZATIONS
METALLIZED
METALLIZES
METALLIZING
METALLOCENE
METALLOCENES
METALLOGENETIC
METALLOGENIC
METALLOGENIES
METALLOGENY
METALLOGRAPHER
METALLOGRAPHERS
METALLOGRAPHIC
METALLOGRAPHIES
METALLOGRAPHIST
METALLOGRAPHISTS
METALLOGRAPHY
METALLOIDAL
METALLOIDS
METALLOPHONE
METALLOPHONES
METALLURGIC
METALLURGICAL
METALLURGICALLY
METALLURGIES
METALLURGIST
METALLURGISTS
METALLURGY
METALMARKS
METALSMITH
METALSMITHS
METALWARES
METALWORKER
METALWORKERS
METALWORKING
METALWORKINGS
METALWORKS
METAMATHEMATICS
METAMERICALLY
METAMERISM
METAMERISMS
METAMICTISATION
METAMICTISATIONS
METAMICTIZATION
METAMICTIZATIONS
METAMORPHIC
METAMORPHICALLY
METAMORPHISM
METAMORPHISMS
METAMORPHIST
METAMORPHISTS
METAMORPHOSE
METAMORPHOSED
METAMORPHOSES
METAMORPHOSING
METAMORPHOSIS
METAMORPHOUS
METANALYSES
METANALYSIS
METANEPHRIC
METANEPHROI
METANEPHROS
METAPHASES
METAPHORIC
METAPHORICAL
METAPHORICALLY
METAPHORIST
METAPHORISTS
METAPHOSPHATE
METAPHOSPHATES
METAPHOSPHORIC
METAPHRASE
METAPHRASED
METAPHRASES
METAPHRASING
METAPHRASIS
METAPHRAST

METAPHRASTIC
METAPHRASTICAL
METAPHRASTS
METAPHYSIC
METAPHYSICAL
METAPHYSICALLY
METAPHYSICIAN
METAPHYSICIANS
METAPHYSICISE
METAPHYSICISED
METAPHYSICISES
METAPHYSICISING
METAPHYSICIST
METAPHYSICISTS
METAPHYSICIZE
METAPHYSICIZED
METAPHYSICIZES
METAPHYSICIZING
METAPHYSICS
METAPLASES
METAPLASIA
METAPLASIAS
METAPLASIS
METAPLASMIC
METAPLASMS
METAPLASTIC
METAPOLITICAL
METAPOLITICS
METAPSYCHIC
METAPSYCHICAL
METAPSYCHICS
METAPSYCHOLOGY
METARCHONS
METASEQUOIA
METASEQUOIAS
METASILICATE
METASILICATES
METASILICIC
METASOMATA
METASOMATIC
METASOMATISM
METASOMATISMS
METASOMATOSES
METASOMATOSIS
METASTABILITIES
METASTABILITY
METASTABLE
METASTABLES
METASTABLY
METASTASES
METASTASIS
METASTASISE
METASTASISED
METASTASISES
METASTASISING
METASTASIZE
METASTASIZED
METASTASIZES
METASTASIZING
METASTATIC
METASTATICALLY
METATARSAL
METATARSALS
METATARSUS
METATHEORETICAL
METATHEORIES
METATHEORY
METATHERIAN
METATHERIANS
METATHESES
METATHESIS
METATHESISE
METATHESISED
METATHESISES
METATHESISING
METATHESIZE
METATHESIZED
METATHESIZES
METATHESIZING
METATHETIC
METATHETICAL
METATHETICALLY
METATHORACES
METATHORACIC
METATHORAX
METATHORAXES
METAXYLEMS
METECDYSES
METECDYSIS
METEMPIRIC
METEMPIRICAL
METEMPIRICALLY
METEMPIRICISM
METEMPIRICISMS
METEMPIRICIST
METEMPIRICISTS
METEMPIRICS
METEMPSYCHOSES
METEMPSYCHOSIS
METEMPSYCHOSIST
METEMPSYCHOSISTS
METENCEPHALA
METENCEPHALIC
METENCEPHALON
METENCEPHALONS
METEORICALLY
METEORISMS
METEORISTS
METEORITAL
METEORITES
METEORITIC
METEORITICAL
METEORITICIST
METEORITICISTS
METEORITICS
METEOROGRAM
METEOROGRAMS
METEOROGRAPH
METEOROGRAPHIC
METEOROGRAPHS
METEOROIDAL
METEOROIDS
METEOROLITE
METEOROLITES
METEOROLOGIC
METEOROLOGICAL
METEOROLOGIES
METEOROLOGIST
METEOROLOGISTS
METEOROLOGY
METESTICKS
METESTROUS
METESTRUSES
METFORMINS
METHACRYLATE
METHACRYLATES
METHACRYLIC
METHADONES
METHAEMOGLOBIN
METHAEMOGLOBINS
METHAMPHETAMINE
METHANATION
METHANATIONS
METHANOMETER
METHANOMETERS
METHAQUALONE
METHAQUALONES
METHEDRINE
METHEDRINES
METHEGLINS
METHEMOGLOBIN
METHEMOGLOBINS
METHENAMINE
METHENAMINES
METHICILLIN
METHICILLINS
METHINKETH
METHIONINE
METHIONINES
METHODICAL
METHODICALLY
METHODICALNESS
METHODISATION
METHODISATIONS
METHODISED
METHODISER
METHODISERS
METHODISES
METHODISING
METHODISMS
METHODISTIC
METHODISTS
METHODIZATION
METHODIZED
METHODIZER
METHODIZERS
METHODIZES
METHODIZING
METHODOLOGICAL
METHODOLOGIES
METHODOLOGIST
METHODOLOGISTS
METHODOLOGY
METHOMANIA
METHOMANIAS
METHOTREXATE
METHOTREXATES
METHOXIDES
METHOXYBENZENE
METHOXYBENZENES
METHOXYCHLOR
METHOXYCHLORS
METHOXYFLURANE
METHOXYFLURANES
METHYLAMINE
METHYLAMINES
METHYLASES
METHYLATED
METHYLATES
METHYLATING
METHYLATION
METHYLATIONS
METHYLATOR
METHYLATORS
METHYLCELLULOSE
METHYLDOPA
METHYLDOPAS
METHYLENES
METHYLMERCURIES
METHYLMERCURY
METHYLPHENIDATE
METHYLPHENOL
METHYLPHENOLS
METHYLTHIONINE
METHYLTHIONINES
METHYLXANTHINE
METHYLXANTHINES
METHYSERGIDE
METHYSERGIDES
METICULOSITIES
METICULOSITY
METICULOUS
METICULOUSLY
METICULOUSNESS
METOESTROUS
METOESTRUS
METOESTRUSES
METONYMICAL
METONYMICALLY
METONYMIES
METOPOSCOPIC
METOPOSCOPICAL
METOPOSCOPIES
METOPOSCOPIST
METOPOSCOPISTS
METOPOSCOPY
METRALGIAS
METRICALLY
METRICATED
METRICATES
METRICATING
METRICATION
METRICATIONS
METRICIANS
METRICISED
METRICISES
METRICISING
METRICISMS
METRICISTS
METRICIZED
METRICIZES
METRICIZING
METRIFICATION
METRIFICATIONS
METRIFIERS
METRIFYING
METRITISES
METROLOGIC
METROLOGICAL
METROLOGICALLY
METROLOGIES
METROLOGIST
METROLOGISTS
METROMANIA

METROMANIAS
METRONIDAZOLE
METRONIDAZOLES
METRONOMES
METRONOMIC
METRONOMICAL
METRONOMICALLY
METRONYMIC
METRONYMICS
METROPLEXES
METROPOLIS
METROPOLISES
METROPOLITAN
METROPOLITANATE
METROPOLITANISE
METROPOLITANISM
METROPOLITANISMS
METROPOLITANIZE
METROPOLITANS
METROPOLITICAL
METRORRHAGIA
METRORRHAGIAS
METROSEXUAL
METROSTYLE
METROSTYLES
METTLESOME
METTLESOMENESS
MEZCALINES
MEZZALUNAS
MEZZANINES
MEZZOTINTED
MEZZOTINTER
MEZZOTINTERS
MEZZOTINTING
MEZZOTINTO
MEZZOTINTOS
MEZZOTINTS
MIAROLITIC
MIASMATICAL
MIASMATOUS
MIASMICALLY
MICRIFYING
MICROAEROPHILE
MICROAEROPHILES
MICROAEROPHILIC
MICROAMPERE
MICROAMPERES
MICROANALYSES
MICROANALYSIS
MICROANALYST
MICROANALYSTS
MICROANALYTIC
MICROANALYTICAL
MICROANATOMICAL
MICROANATOMIES
MICROANATOMY
MICROARRAY
MICROARRAYS
MICROBALANCE
MICROBALANCES
MICROBAROGRAPH
MICROBAROGRAPHS
MICROBEAMS
MICROBIOLOGIC
MICROBIOLOGICAL
MICROBIOLOGIES
MICROBIOLOGIST
MICROBIOLOGISTS
MICROBIOLOGY
MICROBIOTA
MICROBREWER
MICROBREWERIES
MICROBREWERS
MICROBREWERY
MICROBREWING
MICROBREWINGS
MICROBREWS
MICROBUBBLES
MICROBURST
MICROBURSTS
MICROBUSES
MICROBUSSES
MICROCAPSULE
MICROCAPSULES
MICROCARDS
MICROCASSETTE
MICROCASSETTES
MICROCELEBRITIES
MICROCELEBRITY
MICROCEPHAL
MICROCEPHALIC
MICROCEPHALICS
MICROCEPHALIES
MICROCEPHALOUS
MICROCEPHALS
MICROCEPHALY
MICROCHEMICAL
MICROCHEMISTRY
MICROCHIPS
MICROCIRCUIT
MICROCIRCUITRY
MICROCIRCUITS
MICROCLIMATE
MICROCLIMATES
MICROCLIMATIC
MICROCLINE
MICROCLINES
MICROCOCCAL
MICROCOCCI
MICROCOCCUS
MICROCODES
MICROCOMPONENT
MICROCOMPONENTS
MICROCOMPUTER
MICROCOMPUTERS
MICROCOMPUTING
MICROCOMPUTINGS
MICROCOPIED
MICROCOPIES
MICROCOPYING
MICROCOPYINGS
MICROCOSMIC
MICROCOSMICAL
MICROCOSMICALLY
MICROCOSMOS
MICROCOSMOSES
MICROCOSMS
MICROCRACK
MICROCRACKED
MICROCRACKING
MICROCRACKINGS
MICROCRACKS
MICROCRYSTAL
MICROCRYSTALS
MICROCULTURAL
MICROCULTURE
MICROCULTURES
MICROCURIE
MICROCURIES
MICROCYTES
MICROCYTIC
MICRODETECTION
MICRODETECTIONS
MICRODETECTOR
MICRODETECTORS
MICRODISSECTION
MICRODONTOUS
MICRODRIVE
MICRODRIVES
MICROEARTHQUAKE
MICROECONOMIC
MICROECONOMICS
MICROELECTRODE
MICROELECTRODES
MICROELECTRONIC
MICROELEMENT
MICROELEMENTS
MICROEVOLUTION
MICROEVOLUTIONS
MICROFARAD
MICROFARADS
MICROFAUNA
MICROFAUNAE
MICROFAUNAL
MICROFAUNAS
MICROFELSITIC
MICROFIBER
MICROFIBERS
MICROFIBRE
MICROFIBRES
MICROFIBRIL
MICROFIBRILLAR
MICROFIBRILS
MICROFICHE
MICROFICHES
MICROFILAMENT
MICROFILAMENTS
MICROFILARIA
MICROFILARIAE
MICROFILARIAL
MICROFILARIAS
MICROFILING
MICROFILINGS
MICROFILMABLE
MICROFILMED
MICROFILMER
MICROFILMERS
MICROFILMING
MICROFILMS
MICROFILTER
MICROFILTERS
MICROFLOPPIES
MICROFLOPPY
MICROFLORA
MICROFLORAE
MICROFLORAL
MICROFLORAS
MICROFORMS
MICROFOSSIL
MICROFOSSILS
MICROFUNGI
MICROFUNGUS
MICROGAMETE
MICROGAMETES
MICROGAMETOCYTE
MICROGLIAS
MICROGRAMS
MICROGRANITE
MICROGRANITES
MICROGRANITIC
MICROGRAPH
MICROGRAPHED
MICROGRAPHER
MICROGRAPHERS
MICROGRAPHIC
MICROGRAPHICS
MICROGRAPHIES
MICROGRAPHING
MICROGRAPHS
MICROGRAPHY
MICROGRAVITIES
MICROGRAVITY
MICROGROOVE
MICROGROOVES
MICROHABITAT
MICROHABITATS
MICROIMAGE
MICROIMAGES
MICROINCHES
MICROINJECT
MICROINJECTED
MICROINJECTING
MICROINJECTION
MICROINJECTIONS
MICROINJECTS
MICROLIGHT
MICROLIGHTING
MICROLIGHTINGS
MICROLIGHTS
MICROLITER
MICROLITERS
MICROLITES
MICROLITHIC
MICROLITHS
MICROLITIC
MICROLOANS
MICROLOGIC
MICROLOGICAL
MICROLOGICALLY
MICROLOGIES
MICROLOGIST
MICROLOGISTS
MICROLUCES
MICROLUXES
MICROMANAGE
MICROMANAGED
MICROMANAGEMENT
MICROMANAGER
MICROMANAGERS
MICROMANAGES
MICROMANAGING
MICROMARKETING
MICROMARKETINGS
MICROMERES

MICROMESHES
MICROMETEORITE
MICROMETEORITES
MICROMETEORITIC
MICROMETEOROID
MICROMETEOROIDS
MICROMETER
MICROMETERS
MICROMETHOD
MICROMETHODS
MICROMETRE
MICROMETRES
MICROMETRIC
MICROMETRICAL
MICROMETRIES
MICROMETRY
MICROMICROCURIE
MICROMICROFARAD
MICROMILLIMETRE
MICROMINIATURE
MICROMINIS
MICROMOLAR
MICROMOLES
MICROMORPHOLOGY
MICRONEEDLE
MICRONEEDLES
MICRONISATION
MICRONISATIONS
MICRONISED
MICRONISES
MICRONISING
MICRONIZATION
MICRONIZATIONS
MICRONIZED
MICRONIZES
MICRONIZING
MICRONUCLEI
MICRONUCLEUS
MICRONUCLEUSES
MICRONUTRIENT
MICRONUTRIENTS
MICROORGANISM
MICROORGANISMS
MICROPARASITE
MICROPARASITES
MICROPARASITIC
MICROPARTICLE
MICROPARTICLES
MICROPAYMENT
MICROPAYMENTS
MICROPEGMATITE
MICROPEGMATITES
MICROPEGMATITIC
MICROPHAGE
MICROPHAGES
MICROPHAGOUS
MICROPHONE
MICROPHONES
MICROPHONIC
MICROPHONICS
MICROPHOTOGRAPH
MICROPHOTOMETER
MICROPHOTOMETRY
MICROPHYLL
MICROPHYLLOUS
MICROPHYLLS
MICROPHYSICAL
MICROPHYSICALLY
MICROPHYSICS
MICROPHYTE
MICROPHYTES
MICROPHYTIC
MICROPIPET
MICROPIPETS
MICROPIPETTE
MICROPIPETTES
MICROPLANKTON
MICROPLANKTONS
MICROPOLIS
MICROPOLISES
MICROPORES
MICROPOROSITIES
MICROPOROSITY
MICROPOROUS
MICROPOWER
MICROPOWERS
MICROPRINT
MICROPRINTED
MICROPRINTING
MICROPRINTINGS
MICROPRINTS
MICROPRISM
MICROPRISMS
MICROPROBE
MICROPROBES
MICROPROCESSING
MICROPROCESSOR
MICROPROCESSORS
MICROPROGRAM
MICROPROGRAMS
MICROPROJECTION
MICROPROJECTOR
MICROPROJECTORS
MICROPSIAS
MICROPTEROUS
MICROPUBLISHER
MICROPUBLISHERS
MICROPUBLISHING
MICROPULSATION
MICROPULSATIONS
MICROPUMPS
MICROPUNCTURE
MICROPUNCTURES
MICROPYLAR
MICROPYLES
MICROPYROMETER
MICROPYROMETERS
MICROQUAKE
MICROQUAKES
MICRORADIOGRAPH
MICROREADER
MICROREADERS
MICROSATELLITE
MICROSATELLITES
MICROSCALE
MICROSCALES
MICROSCOPE
MICROSCOPES
MICROSCOPIC
MICROSCOPICAL
MICROSCOPICALLY
MICROSCOPIES
MICROSCOPIST
MICROSCOPISTS
MICROSCOPY
MICROSECOND
MICROSECONDS
MICROSEISM
MICROSEISMIC
MICROSEISMICAL
MICROSEISMICITY
MICROSEISMS
MICROSITES
MICROSKIRT
MICROSKIRTS
MICROSLEEP
MICROSLEEPS
MICROSMATIC
MICROSOMAL
MICROSOMES
MICROSPECIES
MICROSPHERE
MICROSPHERES
MICROSPHERICAL
MICROSPORANGIA
MICROSPORANGIUM
MICROSPORE
MICROSPORES
MICROSPORIC
MICROSPOROCYTE
MICROSPOROCYTES
MICROSPOROPHYLL
MICROSPOROUS
MICROSTATE
MICROSTATES
MICROSTOMATOUS
MICROSTOMOUS
MICROSTRUCTURAL
MICROSTRUCTURE
MICROSTRUCTURES
MICROSURGEON
MICROSURGEONS
MICROSURGERIES
MICROSURGERY
MICROSURGICAL
MICROSWITCH
MICROSWITCHES
MICROTECHNIC
MICROTECHNICS
MICROTECHNIQUE
MICROTECHNIQUES
MICROTECHNOLOGY
MICROTOMES
MICROTOMIC
MICROTOMICAL
MICROTOMIES
MICROTOMIST
MICROTOMISTS
MICROTONAL
MICROTONALITIES
MICROTONALITY
MICROTONALLY
MICROTONES
MICROTUBULAR
MICROTUBULE
MICROTUBULES
MICROTUNNELLING
MICROVASCULAR
MICROVILLAR
MICROVILLI
MICROVILLOUS
MICROVILLUS
MICROVOLTS
MICROWATTS
MICROWAVABLE
MICROWAVEABLE
MICROWAVED
MICROWAVES
MICROWAVING
MICROWIRES
MICROWORLD
MICROWORLDS
MICROWRITER
MICROWRITERS
MICRURGIES
MICTURATED
MICTURATES
MICTURATING
MICTURITION
MICTURITIONS
MIDDELMANNETJIE
MIDDELMANNETJIES
MIDDENSTEAD
MIDDENSTEADS
MIDDLEBREAKER
MIDDLEBREAKERS
MIDDLEBROW
MIDDLEBROWED
MIDDLEBROWISM
MIDDLEBROWISMS
MIDDLEBROWS
MIDDLEBUSTER
MIDDLEBUSTERS
MIDDLEMOST
MIDDLEWEIGHT
MIDDLEWEIGHTS
MIDDLINGLY
MIDFIELDER
MIDFIELDERS
MIDINETTES
MIDISKIRTS
MIDLATITUDE
MIDLATITUDES
MIDLITTORAL
MIDLITTORALS
MIDNIGHTLY
MIDRASHOTH
MIDSAGITTAL
MIDSECTION
MIDSECTIONS
MIDSHIPMAN
MIDSHIPMATE
MIDSHIPMATES
MIDSHIPMEN
MIDSTORIES
MIDSTREAMS
MIDSUMMERS
MIDWATCHES
MIDWIFERIES
MIDWINTERS
MIFEPRISTONE
MIFEPRISTONES
MIFFINESSES
MIGHTINESS

MIGHTINESSES
MIGMATITES
MIGNONETTE
MIGNONETTES
MIGRAINEUR
MIGRAINEURS
MIGRAINOUS
MIGRATIONAL
MIGRATIONIST
MIGRATIONISTS
MIGRATIONS
MILATAINMENT
MILATAINMENTS
MILDNESSES
MILEOMETER
MILEOMETERS
MILESTONES
MILITANCES
MILITANCIES
MILITANTLY
MILITANTNESS
MILITANTNESSES
MILITARIES
MILITARILY
MILITARISATION
MILITARISATIONS
MILITARISE
MILITARISED
MILITARISES
MILITARISING
MILITARISM
MILITARISMS
MILITARIST
MILITARISTIC
MILITARISTS
MILITARIZATION
MILITARIZATIONS
MILITARIZE
MILITARIZED
MILITARIZES
MILITARIZING
MILITATING
MILITATION
MILITATIONS
MILITIAMAN
MILITIAMEN
MILKFISHES
MILKINESSES
MILKSHAKES
MILKSOPISM
MILKSOPISMS
MILKSOPPING
MILKTOASTS
MILLBOARDS
MILLEFEUILLE
MILLEFEUILLES
MILLEFIORI
MILLEFIORIS
MILLEFLEUR
MILLEFLEURS
MILLENARIAN
MILLENARIANISM
MILLENARIANISMS
MILLENARIANS
MILLENARIES
MILLENARISM
MILLENARISMS
MILLENNIAL
MILLENNIALISM
MILLENNIALISMS
MILLENNIALIST
MILLENNIALISTS
MILLENNIALLY
MILLENNIANISM
MILLENNIANISMS
MILLENNIARISM
MILLENNIARISMS
MILLENNIUM
MILLENNIUMS
MILLEPEDES
MILLEPORES
MILLERITES
MILLESIMAL
MILLESIMALLY
MILLESIMALS
MILLHOUSES
MILLIAMPERE
MILLIAMPERES
MILLIARIES
MILLICURIE
MILLICURIES
MILLIDEGREE
MILLIDEGREES
MILLIGRAMME
MILLIGRAMMES
MILLIGRAMS
MILLIHENRIES
MILLIHENRY
MILLIHENRYS
MILLILAMBERT
MILLILAMBERTS
MILLILITER
MILLILITERS
MILLILITRE
MILLILITRES
MILLILUCES
MILLILUXES
MILLIMETER
MILLIMETERS
MILLIMETRE
MILLIMETRES
MILLIMICRON
MILLIMICRONS
MILLIMOLAR
MILLIMOLES
MILLINERIES
MILLIONAIRE
MILLIONAIRES
MILLIONAIRESS
MILLIONAIRESSES
MILLIONARY
MILLIONFOLD
MILLIONNAIRE
MILLIONNAIRES
MILLIONNAIRESS
MILLIONNAIRESSES
MILLIONTHS
MILLIOSMOL
MILLIOSMOLS
MILLIPEDES
MILLIPROBE
MILLIPROBES
MILLIRADIAN
MILLIRADIANS
MILLIROENTGEN
MILLIROENTGENS
MILLISECOND
MILLISECONDS
MILLISIEVERT
MILLISIEVERTS
MILLIVOLTS
MILLIWATTS
MILLOCRACIES
MILLOCRACY
MILLOCRATS
MILLSCALES
MILLSTONES
MILLSTREAM
MILLSTREAMS
MILLWHEELS
MILLWRIGHT
MILLWRIGHTS
MILOMETERS
MILQUETOAST
MILQUETOASTS
MIMEOGRAPH
MIMEOGRAPHED
MIMEOGRAPHING
MIMEOGRAPHS
MIMETICALLY
MIMMICKING
MIMOGRAPHER
MIMOGRAPHERS
MIMOGRAPHIES
MIMOGRAPHY
MIMOSACEOUS
MINACIOUSLY
MINACITIES
MINATORIAL
MINATORIALLY
MINATORILY
MINAUDERIE
MINAUDERIES
MINAUDIERE
MINAUDIERES
MINCEMEATS
MINDBLOWER
MINDBLOWERS
MINDEDNESS
MINDEDNESSES
MINDFULNESS
MINDFULNESSES
MINDLESSLY
MINDLESSNESS
MINDLESSNESSES
MINDSHARES
MINEFIELDS
MINEHUNTER
MINEHUNTERS
MINELAYERS
MINERALISABLE
MINERALISATION
MINERALISATIONS
MINERALISE
MINERALISED
MINERALISER
MINERALISERS
MINERALISES
MINERALISING
MINERALIST
MINERALISTS
MINERALIZABLE
MINERALIZATION
MINERALIZATIONS
MINERALIZE
MINERALIZED
MINERALIZER
MINERALIZERS
MINERALIZES
MINERALIZING
MINERALOGIC
MINERALOGICAL
MINERALOGICALLY
MINERALOGIES
MINERALOGISE
MINERALOGISED
MINERALOGISES
MINERALOGISING
MINERALOGIST
MINERALOGISTS
MINERALOGIZE
MINERALOGIZED
MINERALOGIZES
MINERALOGIZING
MINERALOGY
MINESHAFTS
MINESTONES
MINESTRONE
MINESTRONES
MINESWEEPER
MINESWEEPERS
MINESWEEPING
MINESWEEPINGS
MINGIMINGI
MINGIMINGIS
MINGINESSES
MINGLEMENT
MINGLEMENTS
MINGLINGLY
MINIATIONS
MINIATURED
MINIATURES
MINIATURING
MINIATURISATION
MINIATURISE
MINIATURISED
MINIATURISES
MINIATURISING
MINIATURIST
MINIATURISTIC
MINIATURISTS
MINIATURIZATION
MINIATURIZE
MINIATURIZED
MINIATURIZES
MINIATURIZING
MINIBIKERS
MINIBREAKS
MINIBUDGET
MINIBUDGETS
MINIBUSSES
MINICABBING
MINICABBINGS
MINICOMPUTER

MINICOMPUTERS
MINICOURSE
MINICOURSES
MINIDISHES
MINIDRESSES
MINIFICATION
MINIFICATIONS
MINIFLOPPIES
MINIFLOPPY
MINIMALISM
MINIMALISMS
MINIMALIST
MINIMALISTS
MINIMAXING
MINIMISATION
MINIMISATIONS
MINIMISERS
MINIMISING
MINIMIZATION
MINIMIZATIONS
MINIMIZERS
MINIMIZING
MINIRUGBIES
MINISCHOOL
MINISCHOOLS
MINISCULES
MINISERIES
MINISKIRTED
MINISKIRTS
MINISTATES
MINISTERED
MINISTERIA
MINISTERIAL
MINISTERIALIST
MINISTERIALISTS
MINISTERIALLY
MINISTERING
MINISTERIUM
MINISTERSHIP
MINISTERSHIPS
MINISTRANT
MINISTRANTS
MINISTRATION
MINISTRATIONS
MINISTRATIVE
MINISTRESS
MINISTRESSES
MINISTRIES
MINISTROKE
MINISTROKES
MINITOWERS
MINITRACKS
MINIVOLLEY
MINIVOLLEYS
MINNESINGER
MINNESINGERS
MINNICKING
MINNOCKING
MINORITAIRE
MINORITAIRES
MINORITIES
MINORSHIPS
MINOXIDILS
MINSTRELSIES
MINSTRELSY
MINUSCULAR
MINUSCULES
MINUTENESS
MINUTENESSES
MIRABELLES
MIRABILISES
MIRACIDIAL
MIRACIDIUM
MIRACULOUS
MIRACULOUSLY
MIRACULOUSNESS
MIRANDIZED
MIRANDIZES
MIRANDIZING
MIRIFICALLY
MIRINESSES
MIRKINESSES
MIRRORLIKE
MIRRORWISE
MIRTHFULLY
MIRTHFULNESS
MIRTHFULNESSES
MIRTHLESSLY
MIRTHLESSNESS
MIRTHLESSNESSES
MISACCEPTATION
MISACCEPTATIONS
MISADAPTED
MISADAPTING
MISADDRESS
MISADDRESSED
MISADDRESSES
MISADDRESSING
MISADJUSTED
MISADJUSTING
MISADJUSTS
MISADVENTURE
MISADVENTURED
MISADVENTURER
MISADVENTURERS
MISADVENTURES
MISADVENTUROUS
MISADVERTENCE
MISADVERTENCES
MISADVICES
MISADVISED
MISADVISEDLY
MISADVISEDNESS
MISADVISES
MISADVISING
MISALIGNED
MISALIGNING
MISALIGNMENT
MISALIGNMENTS
MISALLEGED
MISALLEGES
MISALLEGING
MISALLIANCE
MISALLIANCES
MISALLOCATE
MISALLOCATED
MISALLOCATES
MISALLOCATING
MISALLOCATION
MISALLOCATIONS
MISALLOTMENT
MISALLOTMENTS
MISALLOTTED
MISALLOTTING
MISALLYING
MISALTERED
MISALTERING
MISANALYSES
MISANALYSIS
MISANDRIES
MISANDRIST
MISANDRISTS
MISANDROUS
MISANTHROPE
MISANTHROPES
MISANTHROPIC
MISANTHROPICAL
MISANTHROPIES
MISANTHROPIST
MISANTHROPISTS
MISANTHROPOS
MISANTHROPOSES
MISANTHROPY
MISAPPLICATION
MISAPPLICATIONS
MISAPPLIED
MISAPPLIES
MISAPPLYING
MISAPPRAISAL
MISAPPRAISALS
MISAPPRECIATE
MISAPPRECIATED
MISAPPRECIATES
MISAPPRECIATING
MISAPPRECIATION
MISAPPRECIATIVE
MISAPPREHEND
MISAPPREHENDED
MISAPPREHENDING
MISAPPREHENDS
MISAPPREHENSION
MISAPPREHENSIVE
MISAPPROPRIATE
MISAPPROPRIATED
MISAPPROPRIATES
MISARRANGE
MISARRANGED
MISARRANGEMENT
MISARRANGEMENTS
MISARRANGES
MISARRANGING
MISARTICULATE
MISARTICULATED
MISARTICULATES
MISARTICULATING
MISASSAYED
MISASSAYING
MISASSEMBLE
MISASSEMBLED
MISASSEMBLES
MISASSEMBLING
MISASSIGNED
MISASSIGNING
MISASSIGNS
MISASSUMPTION
MISASSUMPTIONS
MISATONING
MISATTRIBUTE
MISATTRIBUTED
MISATTRIBUTES
MISATTRIBUTING
MISATTRIBUTION
MISATTRIBUTIONS
MISAUNTERS
MISAVERRED
MISAVERRING
MISAWARDED
MISAWARDING
MISBALANCE
MISBALANCED
MISBALANCES
MISBALANCING
MISBECOMES
MISBECOMING
MISBECOMINGNESS
MISBEGINNING
MISBEGOTTEN
MISBEHAVED
MISBEHAVER
MISBEHAVERS
MISBEHAVES
MISBEHAVING
MISBEHAVIOR
MISBEHAVIORS
MISBEHAVIOUR
MISBEHAVIOURS
MISBELIEFS
MISBELIEVE
MISBELIEVED
MISBELIEVER
MISBELIEVERS
MISBELIEVES
MISBELIEVING
MISBESEEMED
MISBESEEMING
MISBESEEMS
MISBESTOWAL
MISBESTOWALS
MISBESTOWED
MISBESTOWING
MISBESTOWS
MISBIASING
MISBIASSED
MISBIASSES
MISBIASSING
MISBILLING
MISBINDING
MISBRANDED
MISBRANDING
MISBUILDING
MISBUTTONED
MISBUTTONING
MISBUTTONS
MISCALCULATE
MISCALCULATED
MISCALCULATES
MISCALCULATING
MISCALCULATION
MISCALCULATIONS
MISCALCULATOR
MISCALCULATORS
MISCALLERS
MISCALLING
MISCANTHUS

MISCANTHUSES
MISCAPTION
MISCAPTIONED
MISCAPTIONING
MISCAPTIONS
MISCARRIAGE
MISCARRIAGES
MISCARRIED
MISCARRIES
MISCARRYING
MISCASTING
MISCATALOG
MISCATALOGED
MISCATALOGING
MISCATALOGS
MISCEGENATE
MISCEGENATED
MISCEGENATES
MISCEGENATING
MISCEGENATION
MISCEGENATIONAL
MISCEGENATIONS
MISCEGENATOR
MISCEGENATORS
MISCEGENES
MISCEGENETIC
MISCEGENIST
MISCEGENISTS
MISCEGINES
MISCELLANARIAN
MISCELLANARIANS
MISCELLANEA
MISCELLANEOUS
MISCELLANEOUSLY
MISCELLANIES
MISCELLANIST
MISCELLANISTS
MISCELLANY
MISCHALLENGE
MISCHALLENGES
MISCHANCED
MISCHANCEFUL
MISCHANCES
MISCHANCING
MISCHANNEL
MISCHANNELED
MISCHANNELING
MISCHANNELLED
MISCHANNELLING
MISCHANNELS
MISCHANTER
MISCHANTERS
MISCHARACTERISE
MISCHARACTERIZE
MISCHARGED
MISCHARGES
MISCHARGING
MISCHIEFED
MISCHIEFING
MISCHIEVOUS
MISCHIEVOUSLY
MISCHIEVOUSNESS
MISCHMETAL
MISCHMETALS
MISCHOICES
MISCHOOSES
MISCHOOSING
MISCIBILITIES
MISCIBILITY
MISCITATION
MISCITATIONS
MISCLAIMED
MISCLAIMING
MISCLASSED
MISCLASSES
MISCLASSIFIED
MISCLASSIFIES
MISCLASSIFY
MISCLASSIFYING
MISCLASSING
MISCOINING
MISCOLORED
MISCOLORING
MISCOLOURED
MISCOLOURING
MISCOLOURS
MISCOMPREHEND
MISCOMPREHENDED
MISCOMPREHENDS
MISCOMPUTATION
MISCOMPUTATIONS
MISCOMPUTE
MISCOMPUTED
MISCOMPUTES
MISCOMPUTING
MISCONCEIT
MISCONCEITED
MISCONCEITING
MISCONCEITS
MISCONCEIVE
MISCONCEIVED
MISCONCEIVER
MISCONCEIVERS
MISCONCEIVES
MISCONCEIVING
MISCONCEPTION
MISCONCEPTIONS
MISCONDUCT
MISCONDUCTED
MISCONDUCTING
MISCONDUCTS
MISCONJECTURE
MISCONJECTURED
MISCONJECTURES
MISCONJECTURING
MISCONNECT
MISCONNECTED
MISCONNECTING
MISCONNECTION
MISCONNECTIONS
MISCONNECTS
MISCONSTER
MISCONSTERED
MISCONSTERING
MISCONSTERS
MISCONSTRUCT
MISCONSTRUCTED
MISCONSTRUCTING
MISCONSTRUCTION
MISCONSTRUCTS
MISCONSTRUE
MISCONSTRUED
MISCONSTRUES
MISCONSTRUING
MISCONTENT
MISCONTENTED
MISCONTENTING
MISCONTENTMENT
MISCONTENTMENTS
MISCONTENTS
MISCOOKING
MISCOPYING
MISCORRECT
MISCORRECTED
MISCORRECTING
MISCORRECTION
MISCORRECTIONS
MISCORRECTS
MISCORRELATION
MISCORRELATIONS
MISCOUNSEL
MISCOUNSELLED
MISCOUNSELLING
MISCOUNSELS
MISCOUNTED
MISCOUNTING
MISCREANCE
MISCREANCES
MISCREANCIES
MISCREANCY
MISCREANTS
MISCREATED
MISCREATES
MISCREATING
MISCREATION
MISCREATIONS
MISCREATIVE
MISCREATOR
MISCREATORS
MISCREAUNCE
MISCREAUNCES
MISCREDITED
MISCREDITING
MISCREDITS
MISCUTTING
MISDEALERS
MISDEALING
MISDEEMFUL
MISDEEMING
MISDEEMINGS
MISDEFINED
MISDEFINES
MISDEFINING
MISDEMEANANT
MISDEMEANANTS
MISDEMEANED
MISDEMEANING
MISDEMEANOR
MISDEMEANORS
MISDEMEANOUR
MISDEMEANOURS
MISDEMEANS
MISDESCRIBE
MISDESCRIBED
MISDESCRIBES
MISDESCRIBING
MISDESCRIPTION
MISDESCRIPTIONS
MISDESERTS
MISDEVELOP
MISDEVELOPED
MISDEVELOPING
MISDEVELOPS
MISDEVOTION
MISDEVOTIONS
MISDIAGNOSE
MISDIAGNOSED
MISDIAGNOSES
MISDIAGNOSING
MISDIAGNOSIS
MISDIALING
MISDIALLED
MISDIALLING
MISDIRECTED
MISDIRECTING
MISDIRECTION
MISDIRECTIONS
MISDIRECTS
MISDISTRIBUTION
MISDIVIDED
MISDIVIDES
MISDIVIDING
MISDIVISION
MISDIVISIONS
MISDOUBTED
MISDOUBTFUL
MISDOUBTING
MISDRAWING
MISDRAWINGS
MISDRIVING
MISEDITING
MISEDUCATE
MISEDUCATED
MISEDUCATES
MISEDUCATING
MISEDUCATION
MISEDUCATIONS
MISEMPHASES
MISEMPHASIS
MISEMPHASISE
MISEMPHASISED
MISEMPHASISES
MISEMPHASISING
MISEMPHASIZE
MISEMPHASIZED
MISEMPHASIZES
MISEMPHASIZING
MISEMPLOYED
MISEMPLOYING
MISEMPLOYMENT
MISEMPLOYMENTS
MISEMPLOYS
MISENROLLED
MISENROLLING
MISENROLLS
MISENTERED
MISENTERING
MISENTREAT
MISENTREATED
MISENTREATING
MISENTREATS
MISENTRIES
MISERABILISM
MISERABILISMS

MISERABILIST
MISERABILISTS
MISERABLENESS
MISERABLENESSES
MISERABLES
MISERABLISM
MISERABLIST
MISERABLISTS
MISERICORD
MISERICORDE
MISERICORDES
MISERICORDS
MISERLIEST
MISERLINESS
MISERLINESSES
MISESTEEMED
MISESTEEMING
MISESTEEMS
MISESTIMATE
MISESTIMATED
MISESTIMATES
MISESTIMATING
MISESTIMATION
MISESTIMATIONS
MISEVALUATE
MISEVALUATED
MISEVALUATES
MISEVALUATING
MISEVALUATION
MISEVALUATIONS
MISFALLING
MISFARINGS
MISFEASANCE
MISFEASANCES
MISFEASORS
MISFEATURE
MISFEATURED
MISFEATURES
MISFEATURING
MISFEEDING
MISFEIGNED
MISFEIGNING
MISFIELDED
MISFIELDING
MISFITTING
MISFOCUSED
MISFOCUSES
MISFOCUSING
MISFOCUSSED
MISFOCUSSES
MISFOCUSSING
MISFORMATION
MISFORMATIONS
MISFORMING
MISFORTUNE
MISFORTUNED
MISFORTUNES
MISFRAMING
MISFUNCTION
MISFUNCTIONED
MISFUNCTIONING
MISFUNCTIONS
MISGAUGING
MISGIVINGS
MISGOVERNAUNCE
MISGOVERNAUNCES
MISGOVERNED
MISGOVERNING
MISGOVERNMENT
MISGOVERNMENTS
MISGOVERNOR
MISGOVERNORS
MISGOVERNS
MISGRADING
MISGRAFTED
MISGRAFTING
MISGROWING
MISGROWTHS
MISGUESSED
MISGUESSES
MISGUESSING
MISGUGGLED
MISGUGGLES
MISGUGGLING
MISGUIDANCE
MISGUIDANCES
MISGUIDEDLY
MISGUIDEDNESS
MISGUIDEDNESSES
MISGUIDERS
MISGUIDING
MISHALLOWED
MISHANDLED
MISHANDLES
MISHANDLING
MISHANTERS
MISHAPPENED
MISHAPPENING
MISHAPPENS
MISHAPPING
MISHEARING
MISHEGAASEN
MISHGUGGLE
MISHGUGGLED
MISHGUGGLES
MISHGUGGLING
MISHITTING
MISHMASHES
MISHMOSHES
MISIDENTIFIED
MISIDENTIFIES
MISIDENTIFY
MISIDENTIFYING
MISIMPRESSION
MISIMPRESSIONS
MISIMPROVE
MISIMPROVED
MISIMPROVEMENT
MISIMPROVEMENTS
MISIMPROVES
MISIMPROVING
MISINFERRED
MISINFERRING
MISINFORMANT
MISINFORMANTS
MISINFORMATION
MISINFORMATIONS
MISINFORMED
MISINFORMER
MISINFORMERS
MISINFORMING
MISINFORMS
MISINSTRUCT
MISINSTRUCTED
MISINSTRUCTING
MISINSTRUCTION
MISINSTRUCTIONS
MISINSTRUCTS
MISINTELLIGENCE
MISINTENDED
MISINTENDING
MISINTENDS
MISINTERPRET
MISINTERPRETED
MISINTERPRETER
MISINTERPRETERS
MISINTERPRETING
MISINTERPRETS
MISINTERRED
MISINTERRING
MISJOINDER
MISJOINDERS
MISJOINING
MISJUDGEMENT
MISJUDGEMENTS
MISJUDGERS
MISJUDGING
MISJUDGMENT
MISJUDGMENTS
MISKEEPING
MISKENNING
MISKICKING
MISKNOWING
MISKNOWLEDGE
MISKNOWLEDGES
MISLABELED
MISLABELING
MISLABELLED
MISLABELLING
MISLABORED
MISLABORING
MISLEADERS
MISLEADING
MISLEADINGLY
MISLEARNED
MISLEARNING
MISLEEKING
MISLIGHTED
MISLIGHTING
MISLIKINGS
MISLIPPENED
MISLIPPENING
MISLIPPENS
MISLOCATED
MISLOCATES
MISLOCATING
MISLOCATION
MISLOCATIONS
MISLODGING
MISLUCKING
MISMANAGED
MISMANAGEMENT
MISMANAGEMENTS
MISMANAGER
MISMANAGERS
MISMANAGES
MISMANAGING
MISMANNERS
MISMARKING
MISMARRIAGE
MISMARRIAGES
MISMARRIED
MISMARRIES
MISMARRYING
MISMATCHED
MISMATCHES
MISMATCHING
MISMATCHMENT
MISMATCHMENTS
MISMEASURE
MISMEASURED
MISMEASUREMENT
MISMEASUREMENTS
MISMEASURES
MISMEASURING
MISMEETING
MISMETRING
MISNOMERED
MISNOMERING
MISNUMBERED
MISNUMBERING
MISNUMBERS
MISOBSERVANCE
MISOBSERVANCES
MISOBSERVE
MISOBSERVED
MISOBSERVES
MISOBSERVING
MISOCAPNIC
MISOGAMIES
MISOGAMIST
MISOGAMISTS
MISOGYNIES
MISOGYNIST
MISOGYNISTIC
MISOGYNISTICAL
MISOGYNISTS
MISOGYNOUS
MISOLOGIES
MISOLOGIST
MISOLOGISTS
MISONEISMS
MISONEISTIC
MISONEISTS
MISORDERED
MISORDERING
MISORIENTATION
MISORIENTATIONS
MISORIENTED
MISORIENTING
MISORIENTS
MISPACKAGE
MISPACKAGED
MISPACKAGES
MISPACKAGING
MISPAINTED
MISPAINTING
MISPARSING
MISPARTING
MISPATCHED
MISPATCHES
MISPATCHING
MISPENNING
MISPERCEIVE

MISPERCEIVED
MISPERCEIVES
MISPERCEIVING
MISPERCEPTION
MISPERCEPTIONS
MISPERSUADE
MISPERSUADED
MISPERSUADES
MISPERSUADING
MISPERSUASION
MISPERSUASIONS
MISPHRASED
MISPHRASES
MISPHRASING
MISPICKELS
MISPLACEMENT
MISPLACEMENTS
MISPLACING
MISPLANNED
MISPLANNING
MISPLANTED
MISPLANTING
MISPLAYING
MISPLEADED
MISPLEADING
MISPLEADINGS
MISPLEASED
MISPLEASES
MISPLEASING
MISPOINTED
MISPOINTING
MISPOISING
MISPOSITION
MISPOSITIONED
MISPOSITIONING
MISPOSITIONS
MISPRAISED
MISPRAISES
MISPRAISING
MISPRICING
MISPRINTED
MISPRINTING
MISPRISERS
MISPRISING
MISPRISION
MISPRISIONS
MISPRIZERS
MISPRIZING
MISPROGRAM
MISPROGRAMED
MISPROGRAMING
MISPROGRAMMED
MISPROGRAMMING
MISPROGRAMS
MISPRONOUNCE
MISPRONOUNCED
MISPRONOUNCES
MISPRONOUNCING
MISPROPORTION
MISPROPORTIONED
MISPROPORTIONS
MISPUNCTUATE
MISPUNCTUATED
MISPUNCTUATES
MISPUNCTUATING
MISPUNCTUATION
MISPUNCTUATIONS
MISQUOTATION
MISQUOTATIONS
MISQUOTERS
MISQUOTING
MISRAISING
MISREADING
MISREADINGS
MISRECKONED
MISRECKONING
MISRECKONINGS
MISRECKONS
MISRECOLLECTION
MISRECORDED
MISRECORDING
MISRECORDS
MISREFERENCE
MISREFERENCES
MISREFERRED
MISREFERRING
MISREGARDS
MISREGISTER
MISREGISTERED
MISREGISTERING
MISREGISTERS
MISREGISTRATION
MISRELATED
MISRELATES
MISRELATING
MISRELATION
MISRELATIONS
MISRELYING
MISREMEMBER
MISREMEMBERED
MISREMEMBERING
MISREMEMBERS
MISRENDERED
MISRENDERING
MISRENDERS
MISREPORTED
MISREPORTER
MISREPORTERS
MISREPORTING
MISREPORTS
MISREPRESENT
MISREPRESENTED
MISREPRESENTER
MISREPRESENTERS
MISREPRESENTING
MISREPRESENTS
MISROUTEING
MISROUTING
MISSAYINGS
MISSEATING
MISSEEMING
MISSEEMINGS
MISSENDING
MISSETTING
MISSHAPENLY
MISSHAPENNESS
MISSHAPENNESSES
MISSHAPERS
MISSHAPING
MISSHEATHED
MISSILEERS
MISSILEMAN
MISSILEMEN
MISSILERIES
MISSILRIES
MISSIOLOGIES
MISSIOLOGY
MISSIONARIES
MISSIONARISE
MISSIONARISED
MISSIONARISES
MISSIONARISING
MISSIONARIZE
MISSIONARIZED
MISSIONARIZES
MISSIONARIZING
MISSIONARY
MISSIONERS
MISSIONING
MISSIONISATION
MISSIONISATIONS
MISSIONISE
MISSIONISED
MISSIONISER
MISSIONISERS
MISSIONISES
MISSIONISING
MISSIONIZATION
MISSIONIZATIONS
MISSIONIZE
MISSIONIZED
MISSIONIZER
MISSIONIZERS
MISSIONIZES
MISSIONIZING
MISSISHNESS
MISSISHNESSES
MISSORTING
MISSOUNDED
MISSOUNDING
MISSPACING
MISSPEAKING
MISSPELLED
MISSPELLING
MISSPELLINGS
MISSPENDER
MISSPENDERS
MISSPENDING
MISSTAMPED
MISSTAMPING
MISSTARTED
MISSTARTING
MISSTATEMENT
MISSTATEMENTS
MISSTATING
MISSTEERED
MISSTEERING
MISSTEPPED
MISSTEPPING
MISSTOPPED
MISSTOPPING
MISSTRICKEN
MISSTRIKES
MISSTRIKING
MISSTYLING
MISSUITING
MISSUMMATION
MISSUMMATIONS
MISTAKABLE
MISTAKABLY
MISTAKEABLE
MISTAKEABLY
MISTAKENLY
MISTAKENNESS
MISTAKENNESSES
MISTAKINGS
MISTEACHES
MISTEACHING
MISTELLING
MISTEMPERED
MISTEMPERING
MISTEMPERS
MISTENDING
MISTERMING
MISTHINKING
MISTHOUGHT
MISTHOUGHTS
MISTHROWING
MISTIGRISES
MISTINESSES
MISTITLING
MISTLETOES
MISTOUCHED
MISTOUCHES
MISTOUCHING
MISTRACING
MISTRAINED
MISTRAINING
MISTRANSCRIBE
MISTRANSCRIBED
MISTRANSCRIBES
MISTRANSCRIBING
MISTRANSLATE
MISTRANSLATED
MISTRANSLATES
MISTRANSLATING
MISTRANSLATION
MISTRANSLATIONS
MISTRAYNED
MISTREADING
MISTREADINGS
MISTREATED
MISTREATING
MISTREATMENT
MISTREATMENTS
MISTRESSED
MISTRESSES
MISTRESSING
MISTRESSLESS
MISTRESSLY
MISTRUSTED
MISTRUSTER
MISTRUSTERS
MISTRUSTFUL
MISTRUSTFULLY
MISTRUSTFULNESS
MISTRUSTING
MISTRUSTINGLY
MISTRUSTLESS
MISTRYSTED
MISTRYSTING
MISTUTORED
MISTUTORING
MISUNDERSTAND

MISUNDERSTANDS
MISUNDERSTOOD
MISUTILISATION
MISUTILISATIONS
MISUTILIZATION
MISUTILIZATIONS
MISVALUING
MISVENTURE
MISVENTURES
MISVENTUROUS
MISVOCALISATION
MISVOCALIZATION
MISWANDRED
MISWEENING
MISWENDING
MISWORDING
MISWORDINGS
MISWORSHIP
MISWORSHIPPED
MISWORSHIPPING
MISWORSHIPS
MISWRITING
MISWRITTEN
MITERWORTS
MITHRADATIC
MITHRIDATE
MITHRIDATES
MITHRIDATIC
MITHRIDATISE
MITHRIDATISED
MITHRIDATISES
MITHRIDATISING
MITHRIDATISM
MITHRIDATISMS
MITHRIDATIZE
MITHRIDATIZED
MITHRIDATIZES
MITHRIDATIZING
MITIGATING
MITIGATION
MITIGATIONS
MITIGATIVE
MITIGATIVES
MITIGATORS
MITIGATORY
MITOCHONDRIA
MITOCHONDRIAL
MITOCHONDRION
MITOGENETIC
MITOGENICITIES
MITOGENICITY
MITOMYCINS
MITOTICALLY
MITRAILLES
MITRAILLEUR
MITRAILLEURS
MITRAILLEUSE
MITRAILLEUSES
MITREWORTS
MITTIMUSES
MIXABILITIES
MIXABILITY
MIXEDNESSES
MIXMASTERS
MIXOBARBARIC
MIXOLOGIES
MIXOLOGIST
MIXOLOGISTS
MIXOLYDIAN
MIXOTROPHIC
MIZENMASTS
MIZZENMAST
MIZZENMASTS
MIZZONITES
MNEMONICAL
MNEMONICALLY
MNEMONISTS
MNEMOTECHNIC
MNEMOTECHNICS
MNEMOTECHNIST
MNEMOTECHNISTS
MOBILISABLE
MOBILISATION
MOBILISATIONS
MOBILISERS
MOBILISING
MOBILITIES
MOBILIZABLE
MOBILIZATION
MOBILIZATIONS
MOBILIZERS
MOBILIZING
MOBLOGGERS
MOBOCRACIES
MOBOCRATIC
MOBOCRATICAL
MOCHINESSES
MOCKERNUTS
MOCKINGBIRD
MOCKINGBIRDS
MOCKUMENTARIES
MOCKUMENTARY
MODALISTIC
MODALITIES
MODELLINGS
MODERATELY
MODERATENESS
MODERATENESSES
MODERATING
MODERATION
MODERATIONS
MODERATISM
MODERATISMS
MODERATORS
MODERATORSHIP
MODERATORSHIPS
MODERATRICES
MODERATRIX
MODERATRIXES
MODERNISATION
MODERNISATIONS
MODERNISED
MODERNISER
MODERNISERS
MODERNISES
MODERNISING
MODERNISMS
MODERNISTIC
MODERNISTICALLY
MODERNISTS
MODERNITIES
MODERNIZATION
MODERNIZATIONS
MODERNIZED
MODERNIZER
MODERNIZERS
MODERNIZES
MODERNIZING
MODERNNESS
MODERNNESSES
MODIFIABILITIES
MODIFIABILITY
MODIFIABLE
MODIFIABLENESS
MODIFIABLENESSES
MODIFICATION
MODIFICATIONS
MODIFICATIVE
MODIFICATORY
MODILLIONS
MODIOLUSES
MODISHNESS
MODISHNESSES
MODULABILITIES
MODULABILITY
MODULARISED
MODULARITIES
MODULARITY
MODULARIZED
MODULATING
MODULATION
MODULATIONS
MODULATIVE
MODULATORS
MODULATORY
MOISTENERS
MOISTENING
MOISTIFIED
MOISTIFIES
MOISTIFYING
MOISTNESSES
MOISTURELESS
MOISTURISE
MOISTURISED
MOISTURISER
MOISTURISERS
MOISTURISES
MOISTURISING
MOISTURIZE
MOISTURIZED
MOISTURIZER
MOISTURIZERS
MOISTURIZES
MOISTURIZING
MOITHERING
MOLALITIES
MOLARITIES
MOLASSESES
MOLDABILITIES
MOLDABILITY
MOLDAVITES
MOLDBOARDS
MOLDINESSES
MOLECATCHER
MOLECATCHERS
MOLECULARITIES
MOLECULARITY
MOLECULARLY
MOLEHUNTER
MOLEHUNTERS
MOLENDINAR
MOLENDINARIES
MOLENDINARS
MOLENDINARY
MOLESTATION
MOLESTATIONS
MOLIMINOUS
MOLLIFIABLE
MOLLIFICATION
MOLLIFICATIONS
MOLLIFIERS
MOLLIFYING
MOLLITIOUS
MOLLUSCANS
MOLLUSCICIDAL
MOLLUSCICIDE
MOLLUSCICIDES
MOLLUSCOID
MOLLUSCOIDAL
MOLLUSCOIDS
MOLLUSCOUS
MOLLUSKANS
MOLLYCODDLE
MOLLYCODDLED
MOLLYCODDLER
MOLLYCODDLERS
MOLLYCODDLES
MOLLYCODDLING
MOLLYHAWKS
MOLLYMAWKS
MOLOCHISED
MOLOCHISES
MOLOCHISING
MOLOCHIZED
MOLOCHIZES
MOLOCHIZING
MOLYBDATES
MOLYBDENITE
MOLYBDENITES
MOLYBDENOSES
MOLYBDENOSIS
MOLYBDENOUS
MOLYBDENUM
MOLYBDENUMS
MOLYBDOSES
MOLYBDOSIS
MOMENTANEOUS
MOMENTARILY
MOMENTARINESS
MOMENTARINESSES
MOMENTOUSLY
MOMENTOUSNESS
MOMENTOUSNESSES
MONACHISMS
MONACHISTS
MONACTINAL
MONADELPHOUS
MONADICALLY
MONADIFORM
MONADISTIC
MONADNOCKS
MONADOLOGIES
MONADOLOGY
MONANDRIES

MONANDROUS
MONANTHOUS
MONARCHALLY
MONARCHIAL
MONARCHICAL
MONARCHICALLY
MONARCHIES
MONARCHISE
MONARCHISED
MONARCHISES
MONARCHISING
MONARCHISM
MONARCHISMS
MONARCHIST
MONARCHISTIC
MONARCHISTS
MONARCHIZE
MONARCHIZED
MONARCHIZES
MONARCHIZING
MONASTERIAL
MONASTERIES
MONASTICAL
MONASTICALLY
MONASTICISM
MONASTICISMS
MONAURALLY
MONCHIQUITE
MONCHIQUITES
MONDEGREEN
MONDEGREENS
MONECIOUSLY
MONERGISMS
MONESTROUS
MONETARILY
MONETARISM
MONETARISMS
MONETARIST
MONETARISTS
MONETISATION
MONETISATIONS
MONETISING
MONETIZATION
MONETIZATIONS
MONETIZING
MONEYCHANGER
MONEYCHANGERS
MONEYGRUBBING
MONEYGRUBBINGS
MONEYLENDER
MONEYLENDERS
MONEYLENDING
MONEYLENDINGS
MONEYMAKER
MONEYMAKERS
MONEYMAKING
MONEYMAKINGS
MONEYSPINNING
MONEYWORTS
MONGERINGS
MONGOLISMS
MONGOLOIDS
MONGRELISATION
MONGRELISATIONS
MONGRELISE
MONGRELISED
MONGRELISER
MONGRELISERS
MONGRELISES
MONGRELISING
MONGRELISM
MONGRELISMS
MONGRELIZATION
MONGRELIZATIONS
MONGRELIZE
MONGRELIZED
MONGRELIZER
MONGRELIZERS
MONGRELIZES
MONGRELIZING
MONILIASES
MONILIASIS
MONILIFORM
MONISTICAL
MONISTICALLY
MONITORIAL
MONITORIALLY
MONITORIES
MONITORING
MONITORSHIP
MONITORSHIPS
MONITRESSES
MONKEYGLAND
MONKEYISMS
MONKEYPODS
MONKEYPOTS
MONKEYSHINE
MONKEYSHINES
MONKFISHES
MONKISHNESS
MONKISHNESSES
MONKSHOODS
MONOACIDIC
MONOAMINERGIC
MONOAMINES
MONOATOMIC
MONOBLEPSES
MONOBLEPSIS
MONOCARBOXYLIC
MONOCARDIAN
MONOCARPELLARY
MONOCARPIC
MONOCARPOUS
MONOCEROSES
MONOCEROUS
MONOCHASIA
MONOCHASIAL
MONOCHASIUM
MONOCHLAMYDEOUS
MONOCHLORIDE
MONOCHLORIDES
MONOCHORDS
MONOCHROIC
MONOCHROICS
MONOCHROMASIES
MONOCHROMASY
MONOCHROMAT
MONOCHROMATE
MONOCHROMATES
MONOCHROMATIC
MONOCHROMATICS
MONOCHROMATISM
MONOCHROMATISMS
MONOCHROMATOR
MONOCHROMATORS
MONOCHROMATS
MONOCHROME
MONOCHROMES
MONOCHROMIC
MONOCHROMICAL
MONOCHROMIES
MONOCHROMIST
MONOCHROMISTS
MONOCHROMY
MONOCLINAL
MONOCLINALLY
MONOCLINES
MONOCLINIC
MONOCLINISM
MONOCLINISMS
MONOCLINOUS
MONOCLONAL
MONOCLONALS
MONOCOQUES
MONOCOTYLEDON
MONOCOTYLEDONS
MONOCOTYLS
MONOCRACIES
MONOCRATIC
MONOCRYSTAL
MONOCRYSTALLINE
MONOCRYSTALS
MONOCULARLY
MONOCULARS
MONOCULOUS
MONOCULTURAL
MONOCULTURE
MONOCULTURES
MONOCYCLES
MONOCYCLIC
MONOCYTOID
MONODACTYLOUS
MONODELPHIAN
MONODELPHIC
MONODELPHOUS
MONODICALLY
MONODISPERSE
MONODRAMAS
MONODRAMATIC
MONOECIOUS
MONOECIOUSLY
MONOECISMS
MONOESTERS
MONOFILAMENT
MONOFILAMENTS
MONOGAMIES
MONOGAMIST
MONOGAMISTIC
MONOGAMISTS
MONOGAMOUS
MONOGAMOUSLY
MONOGAMOUSNESS
MONOGAMOUSNESSES
MONOGASTRIC
MONOGENEAN
MONOGENEANS
MONOGENESES
MONOGENESIS
MONOGENETIC
MONOGENICALLY
MONOGENIES
MONOGENISM
MONOGENISMS
MONOGENIST
MONOGENISTIC
MONOGENISTS
MONOGENOUS
MONOGLYCERIDE
MONOGLYCERIDES
MONOGONIES
MONOGRAMED
MONOGRAMING
MONOGRAMMATIC
MONOGRAMMED
MONOGRAMMER
MONOGRAMMERS
MONOGRAMMING
MONOGRAPHED
MONOGRAPHER
MONOGRAPHERS
MONOGRAPHIC
MONOGRAPHICAL
MONOGRAPHICALLY
MONOGRAPHIES
MONOGRAPHING
MONOGRAPHIST
MONOGRAPHISTS
MONOGRAPHS
MONOGRAPHY
MONOGYNIAN
MONOGYNIES
MONOGYNIST
MONOGYNISTS
MONOGYNOUS
MONOHYBRID
MONOHYBRIDS
MONOHYDRATE
MONOHYDRATED
MONOHYDRATES
MONOHYDRIC
MONOHYDROXY
MONOICOUSLY
MONOLATERS
MONOLATRIES
MONOLATRIST
MONOLATRISTS
MONOLATROUS
MONOLAYERS
MONOLINGUAL
MONOLINGUALISM
MONOLINGUALISMS
MONOLINGUALS
MONOLINGUIST
MONOLINGUISTS
MONOLITHIC
MONOLITHICALLY
MONOLOGGED
MONOLOGGING
MONOLOGICAL
MONOLOGIES
MONOLOGISE
MONOLOGISED
MONOLOGISES
MONOLOGISING

MONOLOGIST
MONOLOGISTS
MONOLOGIZE
MONOLOGIZED
MONOLOGIZES
MONOLOGIZING
MONOLOGUED
MONOLOGUES
MONOLOGUING
MONOLOGUISE
MONOLOGUISED
MONOLOGUISES
MONOLOGUISING
MONOLOGUIST
MONOLOGUISTS
MONOLOGUIZE
MONOLOGUIZED
MONOLOGUIZES
MONOLOGUIZING
MONOMACHIA
MONOMACHIAS
MONOMACHIES
MONOMANIAC
MONOMANIACAL
MONOMANIACALLY
MONOMANIACS
MONOMANIAS
MONOMEROUS
MONOMETALLIC
MONOMETALLISM
MONOMETALLISMS
MONOMETALLIST
MONOMETALLISTS
MONOMETERS
MONOMETRIC
MONOMETRICAL
MONOMOLECULAR
MONOMOLECULARLY
MONOMORPHEMIC
MONOMORPHIC
MONOMORPHISM
MONOMORPHISMS
MONOMORPHOUS
MONOMYARIAN
MONONUCLEAR
MONONUCLEARS
MONONUCLEATE
MONONUCLEATED
MONONUCLEOSES
MONONUCLEOSIS
MONONUCLEOTIDE
MONONUCLEOTIDES
MONOPETALOUS
MONOPHAGIES
MONOPHAGOUS
MONOPHASIC
MONOPHOBIA
MONOPHOBIAS
MONOPHOBIC
MONOPHOBICS
MONOPHONIC
MONOPHONICALLY
MONOPHONIES
MONOPHOSPHATE
MONOPHOSPHATES
MONOPHTHONG
MONOPHTHONGAL
MONOPHTHONGISE
MONOPHTHONGISED
MONOPHTHONGISES
MONOPHTHONGIZE
MONOPHTHONGIZED
MONOPHTHONGIZES
MONOPHTHONGS
MONOPHYLETIC
MONOPHYLIES
MONOPHYLLOUS
MONOPHYODONT
MONOPHYODONTS
MONOPHYSITE
MONOPHYSITES
MONOPHYSITIC
MONOPHYSITISM
MONOPHYSITISMS
MONOPLANES
MONOPLEGIA
MONOPLEGIAS
MONOPLEGIC
MONOPLOIDS
MONOPODIAL
MONOPODIALLY
MONOPODIES
MONOPODIUM
MONOPOLIES
MONOPOLISATION
MONOPOLISATIONS
MONOPOLISE
MONOPOLISED
MONOPOLISER
MONOPOLISERS
MONOPOLISES
MONOPOLISING
MONOPOLISM
MONOPOLISMS
MONOPOLIST
MONOPOLISTIC
MONOPOLISTS
MONOPOLIZATION
MONOPOLIZATIONS
MONOPOLIZE
MONOPOLIZED
MONOPOLIZER
MONOPOLIZERS
MONOPOLIZES
MONOPOLIZING
MONOPRIONIDIAN
MONOPROPELLANT
MONOPROPELLANTS
MONOPSONIES
MONOPSONIST
MONOPSONISTIC
MONOPSONISTS
MONOPTERAL
MONOPTEROI
MONOPTERON
MONOPTEROS
MONOPTEROSES
MONOPTOTES
MONOPULSES
MONORCHIDISM
MONORCHIDISMS
MONORCHIDS
MONORCHISM
MONORCHISMS
MONORHINAL
MONORHYMED
MONORHYMES
MONOSACCHARIDE
MONOSACCHARIDES
MONOSATURATED
MONOSEMIES
MONOSEPALOUS
MONOSKIERS
MONOSKIING
MONOSKIINGS
MONOSODIUM
MONOSOMICS
MONOSOMIES
MONOSPACED
MONOSPECIFIC
MONOSPECIFICITY
MONOSPERMAL
MONOSPERMOUS
MONOSTABLE
MONOSTELES
MONOSTELIC
MONOSTELIES
MONOSTICHIC
MONOSTICHOUS
MONOSTICHS
MONOSTOMOUS
MONOSTROPHE
MONOSTROPHES
MONOSTROPHIC
MONOSTROPHICS
MONOSTYLAR
MONOSTYLOUS
MONOSYLLABIC
MONOSYLLABICITY
MONOSYLLABISM
MONOSYLLABISMS
MONOSYLLABLE
MONOSYLLABLES
MONOSYMMETRIC
MONOSYMMETRICAL
MONOSYMMETRIES
MONOSYMMETRY
MONOSYNAPTIC
MONOTELEPHONE
MONOTELEPHONES
MONOTERPENE
MONOTERPENES
MONOTHALAMIC
MONOTHALAMOUS
MONOTHECAL
MONOTHECOUS
MONOTHEISM
MONOTHEISMS
MONOTHEIST
MONOTHEISTIC
MONOTHEISTICAL
MONOTHEISTS
MONOTHELETE
MONOTHELETES
MONOTHELETIC
MONOTHELETICAL
MONOTHELETISM
MONOTHELETISMS
MONOTHELISM
MONOTHELISMS
MONOTHELITE
MONOTHELITES
MONOTHELITISM
MONOTHELITISMS
MONOTOCOUS
MONOTONICALLY
MONOTONICITIES
MONOTONICITY
MONOTONIES
MONOTONING
MONOTONISE
MONOTONISED
MONOTONISES
MONOTONISING
MONOTONIZE
MONOTONIZED
MONOTONIZES
MONOTONIZING
MONOTONOUS
MONOTONOUSLY
MONOTONOUSNESS
MONOTREMATOUS
MONOTREMES
MONOTRICHIC
MONOTRICHOUS
MONOTROCHS
MONOUNSATURATE
MONOUNSATURATED
MONOUNSATURATES
MONOVALENCE
MONOVALENCES
MONOVALENCIES
MONOVALENCY
MONOVALENT
MONOXYLONS
MONOXYLOUS
MONOZYGOTIC
MONOZYGOUS
MONSEIGNEUR
MONSIGNORI
MONSIGNORIAL
MONSIGNORS
MONSTERING
MONSTERINGS
MONSTRANCE
MONSTRANCES
MONSTROSITIES
MONSTROSITY
MONSTROUSLY
MONSTROUSNESS
MONSTROUSNESSES
MONSTRUOSITIES
MONSTRUOSITY
MONSTRUOUS
MONTADALES
MONTAGNARD
MONTAGNARDS
MONTBRETIA
MONTBRETIAS
MONTELIMAR
MONTELIMARS
MONTGOLFIER
MONTGOLFIERS
MONTHLINGS

MONTICELLITE
MONTICELLITES
MONTICOLOUS
MONTICULATE
MONTICULES
MONTICULOUS
MONTICULUS
MONTICULUSES
MONTMORILLONITE
MONUMENTAL
MONUMENTALISE
MONUMENTALISED
MONUMENTALISES
MONUMENTALISING
MONUMENTALITIES
MONUMENTALITY
MONUMENTALIZE
MONUMENTALIZED
MONUMENTALIZES
MONUMENTALIZING
MONUMENTALLY
MONUMENTED
MONUMENTING
MONZONITES
MONZONITIC
MOODINESSES
MOONCALVES
MOONCHILDREN
MOONFISHES
MOONFLOWER
MOONFLOWERS
MOONINESSES
MOONLIGHTED
MOONLIGHTER
MOONLIGHTERS
MOONLIGHTING
MOONLIGHTINGS
MOONLIGHTS
MOONPHASES
MOONQUAKES
MOONRAKERS
MOONRAKING
MOONRAKINGS
MOONSCAPES
MOONSHINED
MOONSHINER
MOONSHINERS
MOONSHINES
MOONSHINING
MOONSTONES
MOONSTRICKEN
MOONSTRIKE
MOONSTRIKES
MOONSTRUCK
MOONWALKED
MOONWALKER
MOONWALKERS
MOONWALKING
MOORBUZZARD
MOORBUZZARDS
MOOSEBIRDS
MOOSEWOODS
MOOSEYARDS
MOOTNESSES
MOPINESSES
MOPISHNESS
MOPISHNESSES
MORALISATION
MORALISATIONS
MORALISERS
MORALISING
MORALISTIC
MORALISTICALLY
MORALITIES
MORALIZATION
MORALIZATIONS
MORALIZERS
MORALIZING
MORATORIUM
MORATORIUMS
MORBIDEZZA
MORBIDEZZAS
MORBIDITIES
MORBIDNESS
MORBIDNESSES
MORBIFEROUS
MORBIFICALLY
MORBILLIFORM
MORBILLIVIRUS
MORBILLIVIRUSES
MORBILLOUS
MORDACIOUS
MORDACIOUSLY
MORDACIOUSNESS
MORDACIOUSNESSES
MORDACITIES
MORDANCIES
MORDANTING
MORENESSES
MORGANATIC
MORGANATICALLY
MORGANITES
MORGENSTERN
MORGENSTERNS
MORIBUNDITIES
MORIBUNDITY
MORIBUNDLY
MORIGERATE
MORIGERATION
MORIGERATIONS
MORIGEROUS
MORONICALLY
MORONITIES
MOROSENESS
MOROSENESSES
MOROSITIES
MORPHACTIN
MORPHACTINS
MORPHALLAXES
MORPHALLAXIS
MORPHEMICALLY
MORPHEMICS
MORPHINISM
MORPHINISMS
MORPHINOMANIA
MORPHINOMANIAC
MORPHINOMANIACS
MORPHINOMANIAS
MORPHOGENESES
MORPHOGENESIS
MORPHOGENETIC
MORPHOGENIC
MORPHOGENIES
MORPHOGENS
MORPHOGENY
MORPHOGRAPHER
MORPHOGRAPHERS
MORPHOGRAPHIES
MORPHOGRAPHY
MORPHOLOGIC
MORPHOLOGICAL
MORPHOLOGICALLY
MORPHOLOGIES
MORPHOLOGIST
MORPHOLOGISTS
MORPHOLOGY
MORPHOMETRIC
MORPHOMETRICS
MORPHOMETRIES
MORPHOMETRY
MORPHOPHONEME
MORPHOPHONEMES
MORPHOPHONEMIC
MORPHOPHONEMICS
MORPHOTROPIC
MORPHOTROPIES
MORPHOTROPY
MORSELLING
MORTADELLA
MORTADELLAS
MORTALISED
MORTALISES
MORTALISING
MORTALITIES
MORTALIZED
MORTALIZES
MORTALIZING
MORTARBOARD
MORTARBOARDS
MORTARLESS
MORTCLOTHS
MORTGAGEABLE
MORTGAGEES
MORTGAGERS
MORTGAGING
MORTGAGORS
MORTICIANS
MORTIFEROUS
MORTIFEROUSNESS
MORTIFICATION
MORTIFICATIONS
MORTIFIERS
MORTIFYING
MORTIFYINGLY
MORTIFYINGS
MORTUARIES
MORULATION
MORULATIONS
MOSAICALLY
MOSAICISMS
MOSAICISTS
MOSAICKING
MOSAICLIKE
MOSASAURUS
MOSBOLLETJIE
MOSBOLLETJIES
MOSCHATELS
MOSCHIFEROUS
MOSKONFYTS
MOSQUITOES
MOSQUITOEY
MOSSBACKED
MOSSBLUITER
MOSSBLUITERS
MOSSBUNKER
MOSSBUNKERS
MOSSINESSES
MOSSPLANTS
MOSSTROOPER
MOSSTROOPERS
MOTETTISTS
MOTHBALLED
MOTHBALLING
MOTHERBOARD
MOTHERBOARDS
MOTHERCRAFT
MOTHERCRAFTS
MOTHERESES
MOTHERFUCKER
MOTHERFUCKERS
MOTHERFUCKING
MOTHERHOOD
MOTHERHOODS
MOTHERHOUSE
MOTHERHOUSES
MOTHERINGS
MOTHERLAND
MOTHERLANDS
MOTHERLESS
MOTHERLESSNESS
MOTHERLINESS
MOTHERLINESSES
MOTHERWORT
MOTHERWORTS
MOTHPROOFED
MOTHPROOFER
MOTHPROOFERS
MOTHPROOFING
MOTHPROOFS
MOTILITIES
MOTIONISTS
MOTIONLESS
MOTIONLESSLY
MOTIONLESSNESS
MOTIVATING
MOTIVATION
MOTIVATIONAL
MOTIVATIONALLY
MOTIVATIONS
MOTIVATIVE
MOTIVATORS
MOTIVELESS
MOTIVELESSLY
MOTIVELESSNESS
MOTIVITIES
MOTOCROSSES
MOTONEURON
MOTONEURONAL
MOTONEURONS
MOTORBICYCLE
MOTORBICYCLES
MOTORBIKED
MOTORBIKES
MOTORBIKING

MOTORBOATED
MOTORBOATER
MOTORBOATERS
MOTORBOATING
MOTORBOATINGS
MOTORBOATS
MOTORBUSES
MOTORBUSSES
MOTORCADED
MOTORCADES
MOTORCADING
MOTORCOACH
MOTORCOACHES
MOTORCYCLE
MOTORCYCLED
MOTORCYCLES
MOTORCYCLING
MOTORCYCLIST
MOTORCYCLISTS
MOTORHOMES
MOTORICALLY
MOTORISATION
MOTORISATIONS
MOTORISING
MOTORIZATION
MOTORIZATIONS
MOTORIZING
MOTORMOUTH
MOTORMOUTHS
MOTORSHIPS
MOTORTRUCK
MOTORTRUCKS
MOUCHARABIES
MOUCHARABY
MOUDIEWART
MOUDIEWARTS
MOUDIEWORT
MOUDIEWORTS
MOUDIWARTS
MOUDIWORTS
MOULDABILITIES
MOULDABILITY
MOULDBOARD
MOULDBOARDS
MOULDERING
MOULDINESS
MOULDINESSES
MOULDWARPS
MOULDYWARP
MOULDYWARPS
MOUNDBIRDS
MOUNTAINBOARD
MOUNTAINBOARDER
MOUNTAINBOARDS
MOUNTAINED
MOUNTAINEER
MOUNTAINEERED
MOUNTAINEERING
MOUNTAINEERINGS
MOUNTAINEERS
MOUNTAINOUS
MOUNTAINOUSLY
MOUNTAINOUSNESS
MOUNTAINSIDE
MOUNTAINSIDES
MOUNTAINTOP
MOUNTAINTOPS
MOUNTEBANK
MOUNTEBANKED
MOUNTEBANKERIES
MOUNTEBANKERY
MOUNTEBANKING
MOUNTEBANKINGS
MOUNTEBANKISM
MOUNTEBANKISMS
MOUNTEBANKS
MOUNTENANCE
MOUNTENANCES
MOUNTENAUNCE
MOUNTENAUNCES
MOURNFULLER
MOURNFULLEST
MOURNFULLY
MOURNFULNESS
MOURNFULNESSES
MOURNINGLY
MOURNIVALS
MOUSEBIRDS
MOUSEOVERS
MOUSEPIECE
MOUSEPIECES
MOUSETAILS
MOUSETRAPPED
MOUSETRAPPING
MOUSETRAPS
MOUSINESSES
MOUSQUETAIRE
MOUSQUETAIRES
MOUSSELINE
MOUSSELINES
MOUSTACHED
MOUSTACHES
MOUSTACHIAL
MOUSTACHIO
MOUSTACHIOS
MOUTHBREATHER
MOUTHBREATHERS
MOUTHBREEDER
MOUTHBREEDERS
MOUTHBROODER
MOUTHBROODERS
MOUTHFEELS
MOUTHPARTS
MOUTHPIECE
MOUTHPIECES
MOUTHWASHES
MOUTHWATERING
MOUTHWATERINGLY
MOUVEMENTE
MOVABILITIES
MOVABILITY
MOVABLENESS
MOVABLENESSES
MOVEABILITIES
MOVEABILITY
MOVEABLENESS
MOVEABLENESSES
MOVELESSLY
MOVELESSNESS
MOVELESSNESSES
MOVIEGOERS
MOVIEGOING
MOVIEGOINGS
MOVIELANDS
MOVIEMAKER
MOVIEMAKERS
MOVIEMAKING
MOVIEMAKINGS
MOWBURNING
MOWDIEWART
MOWDIEWARTS
MOWDIEWORT
MOWDIEWORTS
MOXIBUSTION
MOXIBUSTIONS
MOYGASHELS
MOZZARELLA
MOZZARELLAS
MRIDAMGAMS
MRIDANGAMS
MUCEDINOUS
MUCHNESSES
MUCIDITIES
MUCIDNESSES
MUCIFEROUS
MUCILAGINOUS
MUCILAGINOUSLY
MUCINOGENS
MUCKAMUCKED
MUCKAMUCKING
MUCKAMUCKS
MUCKENDERS
MUCKINESSES
MUCKRAKERS
MUCKRAKING
MUCKSPREAD
MUCKSPREADER
MUCKSPREADERS
MUCKSPREADING
MUCKSPREADS
MUCKSWEATS
MUCOCUTANEOUS
MUCOMEMBRANOUS
MUCOPEPTIDE
MUCOPEPTIDES
MUCOPROTEIN
MUCOPROTEINS
MUCOPURULENT
MUCOSANGUINEOUS
MUCOSITIES
MUCOVISCIDOSES
MUCOVISCIDOSIS
MUCRONATED
MUCRONATION
MUCRONATIONS
MUDCAPPING
MUDDINESSES
MUDDLEDNESS
MUDDLEDNESSES
MUDDLEHEAD
MUDDLEHEADED
MUDDLEHEADEDLY
MUDDLEHEADS
MUDDLEMENT
MUDDLEMENTS
MUDDLINGLY
MUDLARKING
MUDLOGGERS
MUDLOGGING
MUDLOGGINGS
MUDPUPPIES
MUDSKIPPER
MUDSKIPPERS
MUDSLINGER
MUDSLINGERS
MUDSLINGING
MUDSLINGINGS
MUFFINEERS
MUGEARITES
MUGGINESSES
MUGWUMPERIES
MUGWUMPERY
MUGWUMPISH
MUGWUMPISM
MUGWUMPISMS
MUJAHEDDIN
MUJAHEDEEN
MUJAHIDEEN
MULATTRESS
MULATTRESSES
MULBERRIES
MULIEBRITIES
MULIEBRITY
MULISHNESS
MULISHNESSES
MULLAHISMS
MULLARKIES
MULLIGATAWNIES
MULLIGATAWNY
MULLIGRUBS
MULLIONING
MULTANGULAR
MULTANIMOUS
MULTARTICULATE
MULTEITIES
MULTIACCESS
MULTIACCESSES
MULTIAGENCY
MULTIANGULAR
MULTIARMED
MULTIARTICULATE
MULTIAUTHOR
MULTIAXIAL
MULTIBARREL
MULTIBARRELED
MULTIBILLION
MULTIBLADED
MULTIBRANCHED
MULTIBUILDING
MULTICAMERATE
MULTICAMPUS
MULTICAPITATE
MULTICARBON
MULTICASTS
MULTICAULINE
MULTICAUSAL
MULTICELLED
MULTICELLULAR
MULTICENTER
MULTICENTRAL
MULTICENTRIC
MULTICHAIN
MULTICHAMBERED
MULTICHANNEL

MULTICHARACTER
MULTICIDES
MULTICIPITAL
MULTICLIENT
MULTICOATED
MULTICOLOR
MULTICOLORED
MULTICOLORS
MULTICOLOUR
MULTICOLOURED
MULTICOLOURS
MULTICOLUMN
MULTICOMPONENT
MULTICONDUCTOR
MULTICOSTATE
MULTICOUNTY
MULTICOURSE
MULTICULTURAL
MULTICURIE
MULTICURRENCIES
MULTICURRENCY
MULTICUSPID
MULTICUSPIDATE
MULTICUSPIDS
MULTICYCLE
MULTICYCLES
MULTIDENTATE
MULTIDIALECTAL
MULTIDIGITATE
MULTIDISCIPLINE
MULTIDIVISIONAL
MULTIDOMAIN
MULTIELECTRODE
MULTIELEMENT
MULTIEMPLOYER
MULTIEMPLOYERS
MULTIENGINE
MULTIENZYME
MULTIETHNIC
MULTIETHNICS
MULTIFACED
MULTIFACETED
MULTIFACTOR
MULTIFACTORIAL
MULTIFAMILY
MULTIFARIOUS
MULTIFARIOUSLY
MULTIFIDLY
MULTIFIDOUS
MULTIFILAMENT
MULTIFILAMENTS
MULTIFLASH
MULTIFLORA
MULTIFLOROUS
MULTIFOCAL
MULTIFOILS
MULTIFOLIATE
MULTIFOLIOLATE
MULTIFORMITIES
MULTIFORMITY
MULTIFORMS
MULTIFREQUENCY
MULTIFUNCTION
MULTIFUNCTIONAL
MULTIGENIC
MULTIGRADE
MULTIGRAIN
MULTIGRAVIDA
MULTIGRAVIDAE
MULTIGRAVIDAS
MULTIGROUP
MULTIHEADED
MULTIHOSPITAL
MULTIHULLS
MULTIJUGATE
MULTIJUGOUS
MULTILANES
MULTILATERAL
MULTILATERALISM
MULTILATERALIST
MULTILATERALLY
MULTILAYER
MULTILAYERED
MULTILEVEL
MULTILEVELED
MULTILINEAL
MULTILINEAR
MULTILINGUAL
MULTILINGUALISM
MULTILINGUALLY
MULTILINGUIST
MULTILINGUISTS
MULTILOBATE
MULTILOBED
MULTILOBES
MULTILOBULAR
MULTILOBULATE
MULTILOCATIONAL
MULTILOCULAR
MULTILOCULATE
MULTILOQUENCE
MULTILOQUENCES
MULTILOQUENT
MULTILOQUIES
MULTILOQUOUS
MULTILOQUY
MULTIMANNED
MULTIMEDIA
MULTIMEDIAS
MULTIMEGATON
MULTIMEGAWATT
MULTIMEGAWATTS
MULTIMEMBER
MULTIMETALLIC
MULTIMETER
MULTIMETERS
MULTIMILLENNIAL
MULTIMILLION
MULTIMODAL
MULTIMOLECULAR
MULTINATION
MULTINATIONAL
MULTINATIONALS
MULTINOMIAL
MULTINOMIALS
MULTINOMINAL
MULTINUCLEAR
MULTINUCLEATE
MULTINUCLEATED
MULTINUCLEOLATE
MULTIORGASMIC
MULTIPACKS
MULTIPANED
MULTIPARAE
MULTIPARAMETER
MULTIPARAS
MULTIPARITIES
MULTIPARITY
MULTIPAROUS
MULTIPARTICLE
MULTIPARTITE
MULTIPARTY
MULTIPARTYISM
MULTIPARTYISMS
MULTIPEDES
MULTIPHASE
MULTIPHASIC
MULTIPHOTON
MULTIPICTURE
MULTIPIECE
MULTIPISTON
MULTIPLANE
MULTIPLANES
MULTIPLANT
MULTIPLAYER
MULTIPLAYERS
MULTIPLETS
MULTIPLEXED
MULTIPLEXER
MULTIPLEXERS
MULTIPLEXES
MULTIPLEXING
MULTIPLEXOR
MULTIPLEXORS
MULTIPLIABLE
MULTIPLICABLE
MULTIPLICAND
MULTIPLICANDS
MULTIPLICATE
MULTIPLICATES
MULTIPLICATION
MULTIPLICATIONS
MULTIPLICATIVE
MULTIPLICATOR
MULTIPLICATORS
MULTIPLICITIES
MULTIPLICITY
MULTIPLIED
MULTIPLIER
MULTIPLIERS
MULTIPLIES
MULTIPLYING
MULTIPOLAR
MULTIPOLARITIES
MULTIPOLARITY
MULTIPOLES
MULTIPOTENT
MULTIPOTENTIAL
MULTIPOWER
MULTIPRESENCE
MULTIPRESENCES
MULTIPRESENT
MULTIPROBLEM
MULTIPROCESSING
MULTIPROCESSOR
MULTIPROCESSORS
MULTIPRODUCT
MULTIPRONGED
MULTIPURPOSE
MULTIRACIAL
MULTIRACIALISM
MULTIRACIALISMS
MULTIRAMIFIED
MULTIRANGE
MULTIREGIONAL
MULTIRELIGIOUS
MULTISCIENCE
MULTISCIENCES
MULTISCREEN
MULTISENSE
MULTISENSORY
MULTISEPTATE
MULTISERIAL
MULTISERIATE
MULTISERVICE
MULTISIDED
MULTISKILL
MULTISKILLED
MULTISKILLING
MULTISKILLINGS
MULTISKILLS
MULTISONANT
MULTISOURCE
MULTISPECIES
MULTISPECTRAL
MULTISPEED
MULTISPIRAL
MULTISPORT
MULTISTAGE
MULTISTATE
MULTISTEMMED
MULTISTOREY
MULTISTOREYS
MULTISTORIED
MULTISTORY
MULTISTRANDED
MULTISTRIKE
MULTISTRIKES
MULTISULCATE
MULTISYLLABIC
MULTISYSTEM
MULTITALENTED
MULTITASKED
MULTITASKING
MULTITASKINGS
MULTITASKS
MULTITERMINAL
MULTITHREADING
MULTITHREADINGS
MULTITIERED
MULTITONES
MULTITOWERED
MULTITRACK
MULTITRILLION
MULTITUDES
MULTITUDINARY
MULTITUDINOUS
MULTITUDINOUSLY
MULTIUNION
MULTIVALENCE
MULTIVALENCES
MULTIVALENCIES
MULTIVALENCY
MULTIVALENT

MULTIVALENTS
MULTIVARIABLE
MULTIVARIATE
MULTIVARIOUS
MULTIVERSE
MULTIVERSES
MULTIVERSITIES
MULTIVERSITY
MULTIVIBRATOR
MULTIVIBRATORS
MULTIVIOUS
MULTIVITAMIN
MULTIVITAMINS
MULTIVOCAL
MULTIVOCALS
MULTIVOLTINE
MULTIVOLUME
MULTIWARHEAD
MULTIWAVELENGTH
MULTIWINDOW
MULTIWINDOWS
MULTOCULAR
MULTUNGULATE
MULTUNGULATES
MUMBLEMENT
MUMBLEMENTS
MUMBLETYPEG
MUMBLETYPEGS
MUMBLINGLY
MUMCHANCES
MUMMICHOGS
MUMMIFICATION
MUMMIFICATIONS
MUMMIFYING
MUMPISHNESS
MUMPISHNESSES
MUMPSIMUSES
MUNDANENESS
MUNDANENESSES
MUNDANITIES
MUNDIFICATION
MUNDIFICATIONS
MUNDIFICATIVE
MUNDIFYING
MUNDUNGUSES
MUNICIPALISE
MUNICIPALISED
MUNICIPALISES
MUNICIPALISING
MUNICIPALISM
MUNICIPALISMS
MUNICIPALIST
MUNICIPALISTS
MUNICIPALITIES
MUNICIPALITY
MUNICIPALIZE
MUNICIPALIZED
MUNICIPALIZES
MUNICIPALIZING
MUNICIPALLY
MUNICIPALS
MUNIFICENCE
MUNIFICENCES
MUNIFICENT
MUNIFICENTLY
MUNIFICENTNESS
MUNIFICENTNESSES
MUNIFIENCE
MUNIFIENCES
MUNITIONED
MUNITIONEER
MUNITIONEERS
MUNITIONER
MUNITIONERS
MUNITIONETTE
MUNITIONETTES
MUNITIONING
MURDERESSES
MURDEROUSLY
MURDEROUSNESS
MURDEROUSNESSES
MURGEONING
MURKINESSES
MURMURATION
MURMURATIONS
MURMURINGLY
MURMURINGS
MURMUROUSLY
MURTHERERS
MURTHERING
MUSCADELLE
MUSCADELLES
MUSCADINES
MUSCARDINE
MUSCARDINES
MUSCARINES
MUSCARINIC
MUSCATORIA
MUSCATORIUM
MUSCAVADOS
MUSCOLOGIES
MUSCOVADOS
MUSCOVITES
MUSCULARITIES
MUSCULARITY
MUSCULARLY
MUSCULATION
MUSCULATIONS
MUSCULATURE
MUSCULATURES
MUSCULOSKELETAL
MUSEOLOGICAL
MUSEOLOGIES
MUSEOLOGIST
MUSEOLOGISTS
MUSHINESSES
MUSHMOUTHS
MUSHROOMED
MUSHROOMER
MUSHROOMERS
MUSHROOMING
MUSICALISATION
MUSICALISATIONS
MUSICALISE
MUSICALISED
MUSICALISES
MUSICALISING
MUSICALITIES
MUSICALITY
MUSICALIZATION
MUSICALIZATIONS
MUSICALIZE
MUSICALIZED
MUSICALIZES
MUSICALIZING
MUSICALNESS
MUSICALNESSES
MUSICIANER
MUSICIANERS
MUSICIANLY
MUSICIANSHIP
MUSICIANSHIPS
MUSICOLOGICAL
MUSICOLOGICALLY
MUSICOLOGIES
MUSICOLOGIST
MUSICOLOGISTS
MUSICOLOGY
MUSICOTHERAPIES
MUSICOTHERAPY
MUSKELLUNGE
MUSKELLUNGES
MUSKETEERS
MUSKETOONS
MUSKETRIES
MUSKINESSES
MUSKMELONS
MUSQUASHES
MUSQUETOON
MUSQUETOONS
MUSSELCRACKER
MUSSELCRACKERS
MUSSINESSES
MUSSITATED
MUSSITATES
MUSSITATING
MUSSITATION
MUSSITATIONS
MUSTACHIOED
MUSTACHIOS
MUSTELINES
MUSTINESSES
MUTABILITIES
MUTABILITY
MUTABLENESS
MUTABLENESSES
MUTAGENESES
MUTAGENESIS
MUTAGENICALLY
MUTAGENICITIES
MUTAGENICITY
MUTAGENISE
MUTAGENISED
MUTAGENISES
MUTAGENISING
MUTAGENIZE
MUTAGENIZED
MUTAGENIZES
MUTAGENIZING
MUTATIONAL
MUTATIONALLY
MUTATIONIST
MUTATIONISTS
MUTENESSES
MUTESSARIF
MUTESSARIFAT
MUTESSARIFATS
MUTESSARIFS
MUTILATING
MUTILATION
MUTILATIONS
MUTILATIVE
MUTILATORS
MUTINEERED
MUTINEERING
MUTINOUSLY
MUTINOUSNESS
MUTINOUSNESSES
MUTOSCOPES
MUTTERATION
MUTTERATIONS
MUTTERINGLY
MUTTERINGS
MUTTONBIRD
MUTTONBIRDS
MUTTONCHOPS
MUTTONFISH
MUTTONFISHES
MUTTONHEAD
MUTTONHEADED
MUTTONHEADS
MUTUALISATION
MUTUALISATIONS
MUTUALISED
MUTUALISES
MUTUALISING
MUTUALISMS
MUTUALISTIC
MUTUALISTS
MUTUALITIES
MUTUALIZATION
MUTUALIZATIONS
MUTUALIZED
MUTUALIZES
MUTUALIZING
MUTUALNESS
MUTUALNESSES
MUZZINESSES
MYASTHENIA
MYASTHENIAS
MYASTHENIC
MYASTHENICS
MYCETOLOGIES
MYCETOLOGY
MYCETOMATA
MYCETOMATOUS
MYCETOPHAGOUS
MYCETOZOAN
MYCETOZOANS
MYCOBACTERIA
MYCOBACTERIAL
MYCOBACTERIUM
MYCOBIONTS
MYCODOMATIA
MYCODOMATIUM
MYCOFLORAE
MYCOFLORAS
MYCOLOGICAL
MYCOLOGICALLY
MYCOLOGIES
MYCOLOGIST
MYCOLOGISTS
MYCOPHAGIES
MYCOPHAGIST

MYCOPHAGISTS
MYCOPHAGOUS
MYCOPHILES
MYCOPLASMA
MYCOPLASMAL
MYCOPLASMAS
MYCOPLASMATA
MYCOPLASMOSES
MYCOPLASMOSIS
MYCORHIZAE
MYCORHIZAL
MYCORHIZAS
MYCORRHIZA
MYCORRHIZAE
MYCORRHIZAL
MYCORRHIZAS
MYCOTOXICOSES
MYCOTOXICOSIS
MYCOTOXINS
MYCOTOXOLOGIES
MYCOTOXOLOGY
MYCOTROPHIC
MYCOVIRUSES
MYDRIATICS
MYELENCEPHALA
MYELENCEPHALIC
MYELENCEPHALON
MYELENCEPHALONS
MYELINATED
MYELITIDES
MYELITISES
MYELOBLAST
MYELOBLASTIC
MYELOBLASTS
MYELOCYTES
MYELOCYTIC
MYELOFIBROSES
MYELOFIBROSIS
MYELOFIBROTIC
MYELOGENOUS
MYELOGRAMS
MYELOGRAPHIES
MYELOGRAPHY
MYELOMATOID
MYELOMATOUS
MYELOPATHIC
MYELOPATHIES
MYELOPATHY
MYIOPHILIES
MYIOPHILOUS
MYLOHYOIDS
MYLONITISATION
MYLONITISATIONS
MYLONITISE
MYLONITISED
MYLONITISES
MYLONITISING
MYLONITIZATION
MYLONITIZATIONS
MYLONITIZE
MYLONITIZED
MYLONITIZES
MYLONITIZING
MYOBLASTIC
MYOCARDIAL
MYOCARDIOGRAPH
MYOCARDIOGRAPHS
MYOCARDIOPATHY
MYOCARDITIS
MYOCARDITISES
MYOCARDIUM
MYOCARDIUMS
MYOCLONUSES
MYOELECTRIC
MYOELECTRICAL
MYOFIBRILLAR
MYOFIBRILS
MYOFILAMENT
MYOFILAMENTS
MYOGLOBINS
MYOGRAPHIC
MYOGRAPHICAL
MYOGRAPHICALLY
MYOGRAPHIES
MYOGRAPHIST
MYOGRAPHISTS
MYOINOSITOL
MYOINOSITOLS
MYOLOGICAL
MYOLOGISTS
MYOMANCIES
MYOMECTOMIES
MYOMECTOMY
MYOPATHIES
MYOPHILIES
MYOPHILOUS
MYOPICALLY
MYOSITISES
MYOSOTISES
MYRIADFOLD
MYRIADFOLDS
MYRIAPODAN
MYRIAPODOUS
MYRINGITIS
MYRINGITISES
MYRINGOSCOPE
MYRINGOSCOPES
MYRINGOTOMIES
MYRINGOTOMY
MYRIORAMAS
MYRIOSCOPE
MYRIOSCOPES
MYRISTICIVOROUS
MYRMECOCHORIES
MYRMECOCHORY
MYRMECOLOGIC
MYRMECOLOGICAL
MYRMECOLOGIES
MYRMECOLOGIST
MYRMECOLOGISTS
MYRMECOLOGY
MYRMECOPHAGOUS
MYRMECOPHILE
MYRMECOPHILES
MYRMECOPHILIES
MYRMECOPHILOUS
MYRMECOPHILY
MYRMIDONES
MYRMIDONIAN
MYROBALANS
MYRTACEOUS
MYSOPHOBIA
MYSOPHOBIAS
MYSTAGOGIC
MYSTAGOGICAL
MYSTAGOGICALLY
MYSTAGOGIES
MYSTAGOGUE
MYSTAGOGUES
MYSTAGOGUS
MYSTAGOGUSES
MYSTERIOUS
MYSTERIOUSLY
MYSTERIOUSNESS
MYSTICALLY
MYSTICALNESS
MYSTICALNESSES
MYSTICETES
MYSTICISMS
MYSTIFICATION
MYSTIFICATIONS
MYSTIFIERS
MYSTIFYING
MYSTIFYINGLY
MYTHICALLY
MYTHICISATION
MYTHICISATIONS
MYTHICISED
MYTHICISER
MYTHICISERS
MYTHICISES
MYTHICISING
MYTHICISMS
MYTHICISTS
MYTHICIZATION
MYTHICIZATIONS
MYTHICIZED
MYTHICIZER
MYTHICIZERS
MYTHICIZES
MYTHICIZING
MYTHMAKERS
MYTHMAKING
MYTHMAKINGS
MYTHOGENESES
MYTHOGENESIS
MYTHOGRAPHER
MYTHOGRAPHERS
MYTHOGRAPHIES
MYTHOGRAPHY
MYTHOLOGER
MYTHOLOGERS
MYTHOLOGIAN
MYTHOLOGIANS
MYTHOLOGIC
MYTHOLOGICAL
MYTHOLOGICALLY
MYTHOLOGIES
MYTHOLOGISATION
MYTHOLOGISE
MYTHOLOGISED
MYTHOLOGISER
MYTHOLOGISERS
MYTHOLOGISES
MYTHOLOGISING
MYTHOLOGIST
MYTHOLOGISTS
MYTHOLOGIZATION
MYTHOLOGIZE
MYTHOLOGIZED
MYTHOLOGIZER
MYTHOLOGIZERS
MYTHOLOGIZES
MYTHOLOGIZING
MYTHOMANES
MYTHOMANIA
MYTHOMANIAC
MYTHOMANIACS
MYTHOMANIAS
MYTHOPOEIA
MYTHOPOEIAS
MYTHOPOEIC
MYTHOPOEISM
MYTHOPOEISMS
MYTHOPOEIST
MYTHOPOEISTS
MYTHOPOESES
MYTHOPOESIS
MYTHOPOETIC
MYTHOPOETICAL
MYTHOPOETS
MYTILIFORM
MYXAMOEBAE
MYXAMOEBAS
MYXEDEMATOUS
MYXOEDEMAS
MYXOEDEMATOUS
MYXOEDEMIC
MYXOMATOSES
MYXOMATOSIS
MYXOMATOUS
MYXOMYCETE
MYXOMYCETES
MYXOMYCETOUS
MYXOVIRUSES

Nn

NABOBERIES
NABOBESSES
NACHTMAALS
NAFFNESSES
NAIFNESSES
NAILBITERS
NAILBRUSHES
NAISSANCES
NAIVENESSES
NAKEDNESSES
NALBUPHINE
NALBUPHINES
NALORPHINE
NALORPHINES
NALTREXONE
NALTREXONES
NAMAYCUSHES
NAMECHECKED
NAMECHECKING
NAMECHECKS
NAMELESSLY
NAMELESSNESS
NAMELESSNESSES
NAMEPLATES
NAMEWORTHY
NANDROLONE
NANDROLONES
NANISATION
NANISATIONS
NANIZATION
NANIZATIONS
NANNOPLANKTON
NANNOPLANKTONS
NANOGRAMME
NANOGRAMMES
NANOMATERIAL
NANOMATERIALS
NANOMETERS
NANOMETRES
NANOPARTICLE
NANOPARTICLES
NANOPHYSICS
NANOPLANKTON
NANOPLANKTONS
NANOSECOND
NANOSECONDS
NANOTECHNOLOGY
NANOTESLAS
NANOWORLDS
NAPHTHALENE
NAPHTHALENES
NAPHTHALIC
NAPHTHALIN
NAPHTHALINE
NAPHTHALINES
NAPHTHALINS
NAPHTHALISE
NAPHTHALISED
NAPHTHALISES
NAPHTHALISING
NAPHTHALIZE
NAPHTHALIZED
NAPHTHALIZES
NAPHTHALIZING
NAPHTHENES
NAPHTHENIC
NAPHTHYLAMINE
NAPHTHYLAMINES
NAPOLEONITE
NAPOLEONITES
NAPPINESSES
NAPRAPATHIES
NAPRAPATHY
NARCISSISM
NARCISSISMS
NARCISSIST
NARCISSISTIC
NARCISSISTS
NARCISSUSES
NARCOANALYSES
NARCOANALYSIS
NARCOCATHARSES
NARCOCATHARSIS
NARCOHYPNOSES
NARCOHYPNOSIS
NARCOLEPSIES
NARCOLEPSY
NARCOLEPTIC
NARCOLEPTICS
NARCOSYNTHESES
NARCOSYNTHESIS
NARCOTERRORISM
NARCOTERRORISMS
NARCOTERRORIST
NARCOTERRORISTS
NARCOTICALLY
NARCOTINES
NARCOTISATION
NARCOTISATIONS
NARCOTISED
NARCOTISES
NARCOTISING
NARCOTISMS
NARCOTISTS
NARCOTIZATION
NARCOTIZATIONS
NARCOTIZED
NARCOTIZES
NARCOTIZING
NARGHILIES
NARGHILLIES
NARRATABLE
NARRATIONAL
NARRATIONS
NARRATIVELY
NARRATIVES
NARRATOLOGICAL
NARRATOLOGIES
NARRATOLOGIST
NARRATOLOGISTS
NARRATOLOGY
NARROWBAND
NARROWBANDS
NARROWCAST
NARROWCASTED
NARROWCASTING
NARROWCASTINGS
NARROWCASTS
NARROWINGS
NARROWNESS
NARROWNESSES
NASALISATION
NASALISATIONS
NASALISING
NASALITIES
NASALIZATION
NASALIZATIONS
NASALIZING
NASCENCIES
NASEBERRIES
NASOFRONTAL
NASOGASTRIC
NASOLACRYMAL
NASOPHARYNGEAL
NASOPHARYNGES
NASOPHARYNX
NASOPHARYNXES
NASTINESSES
NASTURTIUM
NASTURTIUMS
NATALITIAL
NATALITIES

NATATIONAL
NATATORIAL
NATATORIUM
NATATORIUMS
NATHELESSE
NATIONALISATION
NATIONALISE
NATIONALISED
NATIONALISER
NATIONALISERS
NATIONALISES
NATIONALISING
NATIONALISM
NATIONALISMS
NATIONALIST
NATIONALISTIC
NATIONALISTS
NATIONALITIES
NATIONALITY
NATIONALIZATION
NATIONALIZE
NATIONALIZED
NATIONALIZER
NATIONALIZERS
NATIONALIZES
NATIONALIZING
NATIONALLY
NATIONHOOD
NATIONHOODS
NATIONLESS
NATIONWIDE
NATIVENESS
NATIVENESSES
NATIVISTIC
NATIVITIES
NATRIURESES
NATRIURESIS
NATRIURETIC
NATRIURETICS
NATROLITES
NATTERJACK
NATTERJACKS
NATTINESSES
NATURALISATION
NATURALISATIONS
NATURALISE
NATURALISED
NATURALISES
NATURALISING
NATURALISM
NATURALISMS
NATURALIST
NATURALISTIC
NATURALISTS
NATURALIZATION
NATURALIZATIONS
NATURALIZE
NATURALIZED
NATURALIZES
NATURALIZING
NATURALNESS
NATURALNESSES
NATURISTIC
NATUROPATH
NATUROPATHIC
NATUROPATHIES
NATUROPATHS
NATUROPATHY
NAUGAHYDES
NAUGHTIEST
NAUGHTINESS
NAUGHTINESSES
NAUMACHIAE
NAUMACHIAS
NAUMACHIES
NAUPLIIFORM
NAUSEATING
NAUSEATINGLY
NAUSEATION
NAUSEATIONS
NAUSEATIVE
NAUSEOUSLY
NAUSEOUSNESS
NAUSEOUSNESSES
NAUTICALLY
NAUTILOIDS
NAUTILUSES
NAVARCHIES
NAVELWORTS
NAVICULARE
NAVICULARES
NAVICULARS
NAVIGABILITIES
NAVIGABILITY
NAVIGABLENESS
NAVIGABLENESSES
NAVIGATING
NAVIGATION
NAVIGATIONAL
NAVIGATIONALLY
NAVIGATIONS
NAVIGATORS
NAYSAYINGS
NAZIFICATION
NAZIFICATIONS
NEANDERTAL
NEANDERTALER
NEANDERTALERS
NEANDERTALS
NEANDERTHAL
NEANDERTHALER
NEANDERTHALERS
NEANDERTHALOID
NEANDERTHALS
NEAPOLITAN
NEAPOLITANS
NEARNESSES
NEARSIGHTED
NEARSIGHTEDLY
NEARSIGHTEDNESS
NEARTHROSES
NEARTHROSIS
NEATNESSES
NEBBISHERS
NEBENKERNS
NEBUCHADNEZZAR
NEBUCHADNEZZARS
NEBULISATION
NEBULISATIONS
NEBULISERS
NEBULISING
NEBULIZATION
NEBULIZATIONS
NEBULIZERS
NEBULIZING
NEBULOSITIES
NEBULOSITY
NEBULOUSLY
NEBULOUSNESS
NEBULOUSNESSES
NECESSAIRE
NECESSAIRES
NECESSARIAN
NECESSARIANISM
NECESSARIANISMS
NECESSARIANS
NECESSARIES
NECESSARILY
NECESSARINESS
NECESSARINESSES
NECESSITARIAN
NECESSITARIANS
NECESSITATE
NECESSITATED
NECESSITATES
NECESSITATING
NECESSITATION
NECESSITATIONS
NECESSITATIVE
NECESSITIED
NECESSITIES
NECESSITOUS
NECESSITOUSLY
NECESSITOUSNESS
NECKCLOTHS
NECKERCHIEF
NECKERCHIEFS
NECKERCHIEVES
NECKLACING
NECKLACINGS
NECKPIECES
NECKVERSES
NECROBIOSES
NECROBIOSIS
NECROBIOTIC
NECROGRAPHER
NECROGRAPHERS
NECROLATER
NECROLATERS
NECROLATRIES
NECROLATRY
NECROLOGIC
NECROLOGICAL
NECROLOGIES
NECROLOGIST
NECROLOGISTS
NECROMANCER
NECROMANCERS
NECROMANCIES
NECROMANCY
NECROMANIA
NECROMANIAC
NECROMANIACS
NECROMANIAS
NECROMANTIC
NECROMANTICAL
NECROMANTICALLY
NECROPHAGOUS
NECROPHILE
NECROPHILES
NECROPHILIA
NECROPHILIAC
NECROPHILIACS
NECROPHILIAS
NECROPHILIC
NECROPHILIES
NECROPHILISM
NECROPHILISMS
NECROPHILOUS
NECROPHILS
NECROPHILY
NECROPHOBE
NECROPHOBES
NECROPHOBIA
NECROPHOBIAS
NECROPHOBIC
NECROPHOROUS
NECROPOLEIS
NECROPOLES
NECROPOLIS
NECROPOLISES
NECROPSIED
NECROPSIES
NECROPSYING
NECROSCOPIC
NECROSCOPICAL
NECROSCOPIES
NECROSCOPY
NECROTISED
NECROTISES
NECROTISING
NECROTIZED
NECROTIZES
NECROTIZING
NECROTOMIES
NECROTROPH
NECROTROPHIC
NECROTROPHS
NECTAREOUS
NECTAREOUSNESS
NECTARIFEROUS
NECTARINES
NECTARIVOROUS
NECTOCALYCES
NECTOCALYX
NEEDCESSITIES
NEEDCESSITY
NEEDFULNESS
NEEDFULNESSES
NEEDINESSES
NEEDLECORD
NEEDLECORDS
NEEDLECRAFT
NEEDLECRAFTS
NEEDLEFISH
NEEDLEFISHES
NEEDLEFULS
NEEDLELIKE
NEEDLEPOINT
NEEDLEPOINTS
NEEDLESSLY
NEEDLESSNESS
NEEDLESSNESSES
NEEDLESTICK

NEEDLEWOMAN
NEEDLEWOMEN
NEEDLEWORK
NEEDLEWORKER
NEEDLEWORKERS
NEEDLEWORKS
NEESBERRIES
NEFARIOUSLY
NEFARIOUSNESS
NEFARIOUSNESSES
NEGATIONAL
NEGATIONIST
NEGATIONISTS
NEGATIVELY
NEGATIVENESS
NEGATIVENESSES
NEGATIVING
NEGATIVISM
NEGATIVISMS
NEGATIVIST
NEGATIVISTIC
NEGATIVISTS
NEGATIVITIES
NEGATIVITY
NEGLECTABLE
NEGLECTEDNESS
NEGLECTEDNESSES
NEGLECTERS
NEGLECTFUL
NEGLECTFULLY
NEGLECTFULNESS
NEGLECTING
NEGLECTINGLY
NEGLECTION
NEGLECTIONS
NEGLECTIVE
NEGLECTORS
NEGLIGEABLE
NEGLIGENCE
NEGLIGENCES
NEGLIGENTLY
NEGLIGIBILITIES
NEGLIGIBILITY
NEGLIGIBLE
NEGLIGIBLENESS
NEGLIGIBLY
NEGOCIANTS
NEGOTIABILITIES
NEGOTIABILITY
NEGOTIABLE
NEGOTIANTS
NEGOTIATED
NEGOTIATES
NEGOTIATING
NEGOTIATION
NEGOTIATIONS
NEGOTIATOR
NEGOTIATORS
NEGOTIATORY
NEGOTIATRESS
NEGOTIATRESSES
NEGOTIATRICES
NEGOTIATRIX
NEGOTIATRIXES
NEGRITUDES
NEGROHEADS
NEGROPHILE
NEGROPHILES
NEGROPHILISM
NEGROPHILISMS
NEGROPHILIST
NEGROPHILISTS
NEGROPHILS
NEGROPHOBE
NEGROPHOBES
NEGROPHOBIA
NEGROPHOBIAS
NEIGHBORED
NEIGHBORHOOD
NEIGHBORHOODS
NEIGHBORING
NEIGHBORLESS
NEIGHBORLINESS
NEIGHBORLY
NEIGHBOURED
NEIGHBOURHOOD
NEIGHBOURHOODS
NEIGHBOURING
NEIGHBOURLESS
NEIGHBOURLINESS
NEIGHBOURLY
NEIGHBOURS
NELUMBIUMS
NEMATHELMINTH
NEMATHELMINTHIC
NEMATHELMINTHS
NEMATICIDAL
NEMATICIDE
NEMATICIDES
NEMATOBLAST
NEMATOBLASTS
NEMATOCIDAL
NEMATOCIDE
NEMATOCIDES
NEMATOCYST
NEMATOCYSTIC
NEMATOCYSTS
NEMATODIRIASES
NEMATODIRIASIS
NEMATODIRUS
NEMATODIRUSES
NEMATOLOGICAL
NEMATOLOGIES
NEMATOLOGIST
NEMATOLOGISTS
NEMATOLOGY
NEMATOPHORE
NEMATOPHORES
NEMERTEANS
NEMERTIANS
NEMERTINES
NEMOPHILAS
NEOANTHROPIC
NEOARSPHENAMINE
NEOCLASSIC
NEOCLASSICAL
NEOCLASSICISM
NEOCLASSICISMS
NEOCLASSICIST
NEOCLASSICISTS
NEOCOLONIAL
NEOCOLONIALISM
NEOCOLONIALISMS
NEOCOLONIALIST
NEOCOLONIALISTS
NEOCONSERVATISM
NEOCONSERVATIVE
NEOCORTEXES
NEOCORTICAL
NEOCORTICES
NEODYMIUMS
NEOGENESES
NEOGENESIS
NEOGENETIC
NEOGOTHICS
NEOGRAMMARIAN
NEOGRAMMARIANS
NEOLIBERAL
NEOLIBERALISM
NEOLIBERALISMS
NEOLIBERALS
NEOLOGIANS
NEOLOGICAL
NEOLOGICALLY
NEOLOGISED
NEOLOGISES
NEOLOGISING
NEOLOGISMS
NEOLOGISTIC
NEOLOGISTICAL
NEOLOGISTICALLY
NEOLOGISTS
NEOLOGIZED
NEOLOGIZES
NEOLOGIZING
NEONATALLY
NEONATICIDE
NEONATICIDES
NEONATOLOGIES
NEONATOLOGIST
NEONATOLOGISTS
NEONATOLOGY
NEONOMIANISM
NEONOMIANISMS
NEONOMIANS
NEOORTHODOX
NEOORTHODOXIES
NEOORTHODOXY
NEOPAGANISE
NEOPAGANISED
NEOPAGANISES
NEOPAGANISING
NEOPAGANISM
NEOPAGANISMS
NEOPAGANIZE
NEOPAGANIZED
NEOPAGANIZES
NEOPAGANIZING
NEOPHILIAC
NEOPHILIACS
NEOPHILIAS
NEOPHOBIAS
NEOPILINAS
NEOPLASIAS
NEOPLASTIC
NEOPLASTICISM
NEOPLASTICISMS
NEOPLASTICIST
NEOPLASTICISTS
NEOPLASTIES
NEOREALISM
NEOREALISMS
NEOREALIST
NEOREALISTIC
NEOREALISTS
NEOSTIGMINE
NEOSTIGMINES
NEOTEINIAS
NEOTERICAL
NEOTERICALLY
NEOTERICALS
NEOTERISED
NEOTERISES
NEOTERISING
NEOTERISMS
NEOTERISTS
NEOTERIZED
NEOTERIZES
NEOTERIZING
NEOTROPICS
NEOVITALISM
NEOVITALISMS
NEOVITALIST
NEOVITALISTS
NEPENTHEAN
NEPHALISMS
NEPHALISTS
NEPHELINES
NEPHELINIC
NEPHELINITE
NEPHELINITES
NEPHELINITIC
NEPHELITES
NEPHELOMETER
NEPHELOMETERS
NEPHELOMETRIC
NEPHELOMETRIES
NEPHELOMETRY
NEPHOGRAMS
NEPHOGRAPH
NEPHOGRAPHS
NEPHOLOGIC
NEPHOLOGICAL
NEPHOLOGIES
NEPHOLOGIST
NEPHOLOGISTS
NEPHOSCOPE
NEPHOSCOPES
NEPHRALGIA
NEPHRALGIAS
NEPHRALGIC
NEPHRALGIES
NEPHRECTOMIES
NEPHRECTOMISE
NEPHRECTOMISED
NEPHRECTOMISES
NEPHRECTOMISING
NEPHRECTOMIZE
NEPHRECTOMIZED
NEPHRECTOMIZES
NEPHRECTOMIZING
NEPHRECTOMY
NEPHRIDIAL
NEPHRIDIUM

NEPHRITICAL
NEPHRITICS
NEPHRITIDES
NEPHRITISES
NEPHROBLASTOMA
NEPHROBLASTOMAS
NEPHROLEPIS
NEPHROLEPISES
NEPHROLOGICAL
NEPHROLOGIES
NEPHROLOGIST
NEPHROLOGISTS
NEPHROLOGY
NEPHROPATHIC
NEPHROPATHIES
NEPHROPATHY
NEPHROPEXIES
NEPHROPEXY
NEPHROPTOSES
NEPHROPTOSIS
NEPHROSCOPE
NEPHROSCOPES
NEPHROSCOPIES
NEPHROSCOPY
NEPHROSTOME
NEPHROSTOMES
NEPHROTICS
NEPHROTOMIES
NEPHROTOMY
NEPHROTOXIC
NEPHROTOXICITY
NEPOTISTIC
NEPTUNIUMS
NERDINESSES
NERVATIONS
NERVATURES
NERVELESSLY
NERVELESSNESS
NERVELESSNESSES
NERVINESSES
NERVOSITIES
NERVOUSNESS
NERVOUSNESSES
NERVURATION
NERVURATIONS
NESCIENCES
NESHNESSES
NESSELRODE
NESSELRODES
NETBALLERS
NETHERLINGS
NETHERMORE
NETHERMOST
NETHERSTOCK
NETHERSTOCKS
NETHERWARD
NETHERWARDS
NETHERWORLD
NETHERWORLDS
NETIQUETTE
NETIQUETTES
NETMINDERS
NETTLELIKE
NETTLESOME
NETWORKERS
NETWORKING
NETWORKINGS
NEURALGIAS
NEURAMINIDASE
NEURAMINIDASES
NEURASTHENIA
NEURASTHENIAC
NEURASTHENIACS
NEURASTHENIAS
NEURASTHENIC
NEURASTHENICS
NEURATIONS
NEURECTOMIES
NEURECTOMY
NEURILEMMA
NEURILEMMAL
NEURILEMMAS
NEURILITIES
NEURITIDES
NEURITISES
NEUROACTIVE
NEUROANATOMIC
NEUROANATOMICAL
NEUROANATOMIES
NEUROANATOMIST
NEUROANATOMISTS
NEUROANATOMY
NEUROBIOLOGICAL
NEUROBIOLOGIES
NEUROBIOLOGIST
NEUROBIOLOGISTS
NEUROBIOLOGY
NEUROBLAST
NEUROBLASTOMA
NEUROBLASTOMAS
NEUROBLASTOMATA
NEUROBLASTS
NEUROCHEMICAL
NEUROCHEMICALS
NEUROCHEMIST
NEUROCHEMISTRY
NEUROCHEMISTS
NEUROCHIPS
NEUROCOELE
NEUROCOELES
NEUROCOELS
NEUROCOGNITIVE
NEUROCOMPUTER
NEUROCOMPUTERS
NEUROCOMPUTING
NEUROCOMPUTINGS
NEUROENDOCRINE
NEUROETHOLOGIES
NEUROETHOLOGY
NEUROFEEDBACK
NEUROFEEDBACKS
NEUROFIBRIL
NEUROFIBRILAR
NEUROFIBRILLAR
NEUROFIBRILLARY
NEUROFIBRILS
NEUROFIBROMA
NEUROFIBROMAS
NEUROFIBROMATA
NEUROGENESES
NEUROGENESIS
NEUROGENIC
NEUROGENICALLY
NEUROGLIAL
NEUROGLIAS
NEUROGRAMS
NEUROHORMONAL
NEUROHORMONE
NEUROHORMONES
NEUROHUMOR
NEUROHUMORAL
NEUROHUMORS
NEUROHYPNOLOGY
NEUROHYPOPHYSES
NEUROHYPOPHYSIS
NEUROLEMMA
NEUROLEMMAS
NEUROLEPTIC
NEUROLEPTICS
NEUROLINGUIST
NEUROLINGUISTIC
NEUROLINGUISTS
NEUROLOGIC
NEUROLOGICAL
NEUROLOGICALLY
NEUROLOGIES
NEUROLOGIST
NEUROLOGISTS
NEUROLYSES
NEUROLYSIS
NEUROMARKETING
NEUROMARKETINGS
NEUROMASTS
NEUROMATOUS
NEUROMUSCULAR
NEUROPATHIC
NEUROPATHICAL
NEUROPATHICALLY
NEUROPATHIES
NEUROPATHIST
NEUROPATHISTS
NEUROPATHOLOGIC
NEUROPATHOLOGY
NEUROPATHS
NEUROPATHY
NEUROPEPTIDE
NEUROPEPTIDES
NEUROPHYSIOLOGY
NEUROPLASM
NEUROPLASMS
NEUROPSYCHIATRY
NEUROPSYCHOLOGY
NEUROPTERA
NEUROPTERAN
NEUROPTERANS
NEUROPTERIST
NEUROPTERISTS
NEUROPTERON
NEUROPTERONS
NEUROPTEROUS
NEURORADIOLOGY
NEUROSCIENCE
NEUROSCIENCES
NEUROSCIENTIFIC
NEUROSCIENTIST
NEUROSCIENTISTS
NEUROSECRETION
NEUROSECRETIONS
NEUROSECRETORY
NEUROSENSORY
NEUROSPORA
NEUROSPORAS
NEUROSURGEON
NEUROSURGEONS
NEUROSURGERIES
NEUROSURGERY
NEUROSURGICAL
NEUROSURGICALLY
NEUROTICALLY
NEUROTICISM
NEUROTICISMS
NEUROTOMIES
NEUROTOMIST
NEUROTOMISTS
NEUROTOXIC
NEUROTOXICITIES
NEUROTOXICITY
NEUROTOXIN
NEUROTOXINS
NEUROTROPHIC
NEUROTROPHIES
NEUROTROPHY
NEUROTROPIC
NEUROVASCULAR
NEURULATION
NEURULATIONS
NEURYPNOLOGIES
NEURYPNOLOGY
NEUTRALISATION
NEUTRALISATIONS
NEUTRALISE
NEUTRALISED
NEUTRALISER
NEUTRALISERS
NEUTRALISES
NEUTRALISING
NEUTRALISM
NEUTRALISMS
NEUTRALIST
NEUTRALISTIC
NEUTRALISTS
NEUTRALITIES
NEUTRALITY
NEUTRALIZATION
NEUTRALIZATIONS
NEUTRALIZE
NEUTRALIZED
NEUTRALIZER
NEUTRALIZERS
NEUTRALIZES
NEUTRALIZING
NEUTRALNESS
NEUTRALNESSES
NEUTRETTOS
NEUTRINOLESS
NEUTROPENIA
NEUTROPENIAS
NEUTROPHIL
NEUTROPHILE
NEUTROPHILES
NEUTROPHILIC
NEUTROPHILS
NEVERMINDS
NEVERTHELESS

NEVERTHEMORE
NEWFANGLED
NEWFANGLEDLY
NEWFANGLEDNESS
NEWFANGLENESS
NEWFANGLENESSES
NEWISHNESS
NEWISHNESSES
NEWMARKETS
NEWSAGENCIES
NEWSAGENCY
NEWSAGENTS
NEWSBREAKS
NEWSCASTER
NEWSCASTERS
NEWSCASTING
NEWSCASTINGS
NEWSDEALER
NEWSDEALERS
NEWSFLASHES
NEWSGROUPS
NEWSHOUNDS
NEWSINESSES
NEWSLETTER
NEWSLETTERS
NEWSMAGAZINE
NEWSMAGAZINES
NEWSMAKERS
NEWSMONGER
NEWSMONGERS
NEWSPAPERDOM
NEWSPAPERDOMS
NEWSPAPERED
NEWSPAPERING
NEWSPAPERISM
NEWSPAPERISMS
NEWSPAPERMAN
NEWSPAPERMEN
NEWSPAPERS
NEWSPAPERWOMAN
NEWSPAPERWOMEN
NEWSPEOPLE
NEWSPERSON
NEWSPERSONS
NEWSPRINTS
NEWSREADER
NEWSREADERS
NEWSSTANDS
NEWSTRADES
NEWSWEEKLIES
NEWSWEEKLY
NEWSWORTHINESS
NEWSWORTHY
NEWSWRITING
NEWSWRITINGS
NEXTNESSES
NIACINAMIDE
NIACINAMIDES
NIAISERIES
NIALAMIDES
NIBBLINGLY
NICCOLITES
NICENESSES
NICKELIFEROUS
NICKELINES
NICKELISED
NICKELISES
NICKELISING
NICKELIZED
NICKELIZES
NICKELIZING
NICKELLING
NICKELODEON
NICKELODEONS
NICKNAMERS
NICKNAMING
NICKPOINTS
NICKSTICKS
NICKUMPOOP
NICKUMPOOPS
NICOMPOOPS
NICOTIANAS
NICOTINAMIDE
NICOTINAMIDES
NICOTINISM
NICOTINISMS
NICROSILAL
NICROSILALS
NICTATIONS
NICTITATED
NICTITATES
NICTITATING
NICTITATION
NICTITATIONS
NIDAMENTAL
NIDAMENTUM
NIDDERINGS
NIDDERLING
NIDDERLINGS
NIDERLINGS
NIDICOLOUS
NIDIFICATE
NIDIFICATED
NIDIFICATES
NIDIFICATING
NIDIFICATION
NIDIFICATIONS
NIDIFUGOUS
NIDULATION
NIDULATIONS
NIFEDIPINE
NIFEDIPINES
NIFFNAFFED
NIFFNAFFING
NIFTINESSES
NIGGARDING
NIGGARDISE
NIGGARDISES
NIGGARDIZE
NIGGARDIZES
NIGGARDLINESS
NIGGARDLINESSES
NIGGERDOMS
NIGGERHEAD
NIGGERHEADS
NIGGERISMS
NIGGERLING
NIGGERLINGS
NIGGLINGLY
NIGHNESSES
NIGHTBIRDS
NIGHTBLIND
NIGHTBLINDNESS
NIGHTCLASS
NIGHTCLASSES
NIGHTCLOTHES
NIGHTCLUBBED
NIGHTCLUBBER
NIGHTCLUBBERS
NIGHTCLUBBING
NIGHTCLUBBINGS
NIGHTCLUBS
NIGHTDRESS
NIGHTDRESSES
NIGHTFALLS
NIGHTFARING
NIGHTFIRES
NIGHTGEARS
NIGHTGLOWS
NIGHTGOWNS
NIGHTHAWKS
NIGHTINGALE
NIGHTINGALES
NIGHTLIFES
NIGHTLIVES
NIGHTMARES
NIGHTMARISH
NIGHTMARISHLY
NIGHTMARISHNESS
NIGHTPIECE
NIGHTPIECES
NIGHTRIDER
NIGHTRIDERS
NIGHTRIDING
NIGHTRIDINGS
NIGHTSCOPE
NIGHTSCOPES
NIGHTSHADE
NIGHTSHADES
NIGHTSHIRT
NIGHTSHIRTS
NIGHTSIDES
NIGHTSPOTS
NIGHTSTAND
NIGHTSTANDS
NIGHTSTICK
NIGHTSTICKS
NIGHTTIDES
NIGHTTIMES
NIGHTWALKER
NIGHTWALKERS
NIGHTWEARS
NIGRESCENCE
NIGRESCENCES
NIGRESCENT
NIGRIFYING
NIGRITUDES
NIGROMANCIES
NIGROMANCY
NIGROSINES
NIHILISTIC
NIHILITIES
NIKETHAMIDE
NIKETHAMIDES
NILPOTENTS
NIMBLENESS
NIMBLENESSES
NIMBLESSES
NIMBLEWITS
NIMBLEWITTED
NIMBOSTRATI
NIMBOSTRATUS
NIMBYNESSES
NINCOMPOOP
NINCOMPOOPERIES
NINCOMPOOPERY
NINCOMPOOPS
NINEPENCES
NINEPENNIES
NINESCORES
NINETEENTH
NINETEENTHLY
NINETEENTHS
NINETIETHS
NINHYDRINS
NINNYHAMMER
NINNYHAMMERS
NIPCHEESES
NIPPERKINS
NIPPINESSES
NIPPLEWORT
NIPPLEWORTS
NISBERRIES
NITPICKERS
NITPICKIER
NITPICKIEST
NITPICKING
NITRAMINES
NITRANILINE
NITRANILINES
NITRATINES
NITRATIONS
NITRAZEPAM
NITRAZEPAMS
NITRIDINGS
NITRIFIABLE
NITRIFICATION
NITRIFICATIONS
NITRIFIERS
NITRIFYING
NITROBACTERIA
NITROBACTERIUM
NITROBENZENE
NITROBENZENES
NITROCELLULOSE
NITROCELLULOSES
NITROCHLOROFORM
NITROCOTTON
NITROCOTTONS
NITROFURAN
NITROFURANS
NITROGENASE
NITROGENASES
NITROGENISATION
NITROGENISE
NITROGENISED
NITROGENISES
NITROGENISING
NITROGENIZATION
NITROGENIZE
NITROGENIZED
NITROGENIZES
NITROGENIZING
NITROGENOUS

NITROGLYCERIN
NITROGLYCERINE
NITROGLYCERINES
NITROGLYCERINS
NITROMETER
NITROMETERS
NITROMETHANE
NITROMETHANES
NITROMETRIC
NITROPARAFFIN
NITROPARAFFINS
NITROPHILOUS
NITROSAMINE
NITROSAMINES
NITROSATION
NITROSATIONS
NITROTOLUENE
NITROTOLUENES
NITWITTEDNESS
NITWITTEDNESSES
NITWITTERIES
NITWITTERY
NOBBINESSES
NOBILESSES
NOBILITATE
NOBILITATED
NOBILITATES
NOBILITATING
NOBILITATION
NOBILITATIONS
NOBILITIES
NOBLENESSES
NOBLEWOMAN
NOBLEWOMEN
NOCHELLING
NOCICEPTIVE
NOCICEPTOR
NOCICEPTORS
NOCIRECEPTOR
NOCIRECEPTORS
NOCTAMBULATION
NOCTAMBULATIONS
NOCTAMBULISM
NOCTAMBULISMS
NOCTAMBULIST
NOCTAMBULISTS
NOCTILUCAE
NOCTILUCAS
NOCTILUCENCE
NOCTILUCENCES
NOCTILUCENT
NOCTILUCOUS
NOCTIVAGANT
NOCTIVAGATION
NOCTIVAGATIONS
NOCTIVAGOUS
NOCTUARIES
NOCTURNALITIES
NOCTURNALITY
NOCTURNALLY
NOCTURNALS
NOCUOUSNESS
NOCUOUSNESSES
NODALISING
NODALITIES
NODALIZING
NODOSITIES
NODULATION
NODULATIONS
NOEMATICAL
NOEMATICALLY
NOISELESSLY
NOISELESSNESS
NOISELESSNESSES
NOISEMAKER
NOISEMAKERS
NOISEMAKING
NOISEMAKINGS
NOISINESSES
NOISOMENESS
NOISOMENESSES
NOMADICALLY
NOMADISATION
NOMADISATIONS
NOMADISING
NOMADIZATION
NOMADIZATIONS
NOMADIZING
NOMARCHIES
NOMENCLATIVE
NOMENCLATOR
NOMENCLATORIAL
NOMENCLATORS
NOMENCLATURAL
NOMENCLATURE
NOMENCLATURES
NOMENKLATURA
NOMENKLATURAS
NOMINALISATION
NOMINALISATIONS
NOMINALISE
NOMINALISED
NOMINALISES
NOMINALISING
NOMINALISM
NOMINALISMS
NOMINALIST
NOMINALISTIC
NOMINALISTS
NOMINALIZATION
NOMINALIZATIONS
NOMINALIZE
NOMINALIZED
NOMINALIZES
NOMINALIZING
NOMINATELY
NOMINATING
NOMINATION
NOMINATIONS
NOMINATIVAL
NOMINATIVALLY
NOMINATIVE
NOMINATIVELY
NOMINATIVES
NOMINATORS
NOMOCRACIES
NOMOGENIES
NOMOGRAPHER
NOMOGRAPHERS
NOMOGRAPHIC
NOMOGRAPHICAL
NOMOGRAPHICALLY
NOMOGRAPHIES
NOMOGRAPHS
NOMOGRAPHY
NOMOLOGICAL
NOMOLOGICALLY
NOMOLOGIES
NOMOLOGIST
NOMOLOGISTS
NOMOTHETES
NOMOTHETIC
NOMOTHETICAL
NONABRASIVE
NONABSORBABLE
NONABSORBENT
NONABSORPTIVE
NONABSTRACT
NONACADEMIC
NONACADEMICS
NONACCEPTANCE
NONACCEPTANCES
NONACCIDENTAL
NONACCOUNTABLE
NONACCREDITED
NONACCRUAL
NONACHIEVEMENT
NONACHIEVEMENTS
NONACQUISITIVE
NONACTIONS
NONACTIVATED
NONADAPTIVE
NONADDICTIVE
NONADDICTS
NONADDITIVE
NONADDITIVITIES
NONADDITIVITY
NONADHESIVE
NONADIABATIC
NONADJACENT
NONADMIRER
NONADMIRERS
NONADMISSION
NONADMISSIONS
NONAESTHETIC
NONAFFILIATED
NONAFFLUENT
NONAGENARIAN
NONAGENARIANS
NONAGESIMAL
NONAGESIMALS
NONAGGRESSION
NONAGGRESSIONS
NONAGGRESSIVE
NONAGRICULTURAL
NONALCOHOLIC
NONALIGNED
NONALIGNMENT
NONALIGNMENTS
NONALLELIC
NONALLERGENIC
NONALLERGIC
NONALPHABETIC
NONALUMINUM
NONAMBIGUOUS
NONANALYTIC
NONANATOMIC
NONANSWERS
NONANTAGONISTIC
NONANTIBIOTIC
NONANTIBIOTICS
NONANTIGENIC
NONAPPEARANCE
NONAPPEARANCES
NONAQUATIC
NONAQUEOUS
NONARBITRARY
NONARCHITECT
NONARCHITECTS
NONARCHITECTURE
NONARGUMENT
NONARGUMENTS
NONARISTOCRATIC
NONAROMATIC
NONAROMATICS
NONARTISTIC
NONARTISTS
NONASCETIC
NONASPIRIN
NONASSERTIVE
NONASSOCIATED
NONASTRONOMICAL
NONATHLETE
NONATHLETES
NONATHLETIC
NONATTACHED
NONATTACHMENT
NONATTACHMENTS
NONATTENDANCE
NONATTENDANCES
NONATTENDER
NONATTENDERS
NONAUDITORY
NONAUTHORS
NONAUTOMATED
NONAUTOMATIC
NONAUTOMOTIVE
NONAUTONOMOUS
NONAVAILABILITY
NONBACTERIAL
NONBANKING
NONBARBITURATE
NONBARBITURATES
NONBEARING
NONBEHAVIORAL
NONBELIEFS
NONBELIEVER
NONBELIEVERS
NONBELLIGERENCY
NONBELLIGERENT
NONBELLIGERENTS
NONBETTING
NONBINDING
NONBIOGRAPHICAL
NONBIOLOGICAL
NONBIOLOGICALLY
NONBIOLOGIST
NONBIOLOGISTS
NONBONDING
NONBOTANIST
NONBOTANISTS
NONBREAKABLE
NONBREATHING
NONBREEDER

NONBREEDERS
NONBREEDING
NONBROADCAST
NONBUILDING
NONBURNABLE
NONBUSINESS
NONCABINET
NONCALLABLE
NONCALORIC
NONCANCELABLE
NONCANCEROUS
NONCANDIDACIES
NONCANDIDACY
NONCANDIDATE
NONCANDIDATES
NONCAPITAL
NONCAPITALIST
NONCAPITALISTS
NONCARCINOGEN
NONCARCINOGENIC
NONCARCINOGENS
NONCARDIAC
NONCARRIER
NONCARRIERS
NONCELEBRATION
NONCELEBRATIONS
NONCELEBRITIES
NONCELEBRITY
NONCELLULAR
NONCELLULOSIC
NONCENTRAL
NONCERTIFICATED
NONCERTIFIED
NONCHALANCE
NONCHALANCES
NONCHALANT
NONCHALANTLY
NONCHARACTER
NONCHARACTERS
NONCHARISMATIC
NONCHARISMATICS
NONCHAUVINIST
NONCHEMICAL
NONCHEMICALS
NONCHROMOSOMAL
NONCHURCHGOER
NONCHURCHGOERS
NONCIRCULAR
NONCIRCULATING
NONCITIZEN
NONCITIZENS
NONCLANDESTINE
NONCLASSES
NONCLASSICAL
NONCLASSIFIED
NONCLASSROOM
NONCLERICAL
NONCLINICAL
NONCLOGGING
NONCOERCIVE
NONCOGNITIVE
NONCOGNITIVISM
NONCOGNITIVISMS
NONCOHERENT
NONCOINCIDENCE
NONCOINCIDENCES
NONCOLLECTOR
NONCOLLECTORS
NONCOLLEGE
NONCOLLEGIATE
NONCOLLINEAR
NONCOLORED
NONCOLORFAST
NONCOMBATANT
NONCOMBATANTS
NONCOMBATIVE
NONCOMBUSTIBLE
NONCOMMERCIAL
NONCOMMISSIONED
NONCOMMITMENT
NONCOMMITMENTS
NONCOMMITTAL
NONCOMMITTALLY
NONCOMMITTED
NONCOMMUNIST
NONCOMMUNISTS
NONCOMMUNITY
NONCOMMUTATIVE
NONCOMPARABLE
NONCOMPATIBLE
NONCOMPETITION
NONCOMPETITIVE
NONCOMPETITOR
NONCOMPETITORS
NONCOMPLEX
NONCOMPLIANCE
NONCOMPLIANCES
NONCOMPLICATED
NONCOMPLYING
NONCOMPOSER
NONCOMPOSERS
NONCOMPOUND
NONCOMPRESSIBLE
NONCOMPUTER
NONCOMPUTERISED
NONCOMPUTERIZED
NONCONCEPTUAL
NONCONCERN
NONCONCERNS
NONCONCLUSION
NONCONCLUSIONS
NONCONCURRED
NONCONCURRENCE
NONCONCURRENCES
NONCONCURRENT
NONCONCURRING
NONCONCURS
NONCONDENSABLE
NONCONDITIONED
NONCONDUCTING
NONCONDUCTION
NONCONDUCTIVE
NONCONDUCTOR
NONCONDUCTORS
NONCONFERENCE
NONCONFIDENCE
NONCONFIDENCES
NONCONFIDENTIAL
NONCONFLICTING
NONCONFORM
NONCONFORMANCE
NONCONFORMANCES
NONCONFORMED
NONCONFORMER
NONCONFORMERS
NONCONFORMING
NONCONFORMISM
NONCONFORMISMS
NONCONFORMIST
NONCONFORMISTS
NONCONFORMITIES
NONCONFORMITY
NONCONFORMS
NONCONGRUENT
NONCONJUGATED
NONCONNECTION
NONCONNECTIONS
NONCONSCIOUS
NONCONSECUTIVE
NONCONSENSUAL
NONCONSERVATION
NONCONSERVATIVE
NONCONSOLIDATED
NONCONSTANT
NONCONSTRUCTION
NONCONSTRUCTIVE
NONCONSUMER
NONCONSUMERS
NONCONSUMING
NONCONSUMPTION
NONCONSUMPTIONS
NONCONSUMPTIVE
NONCONTACT
NONCONTAGIOUS
NONCONTEMPORARY
NONCONTIGUOUS
NONCONTINGENT
NONCONTINUOUS
NONCONTRACT
NONCONTRACTUAL
NONCONTRIBUTORY
NONCONTROLLABLE
NONCONTROLLED
NONCONTROLLING
NONCONVENTIONAL
NONCONVERTIBLE
NONCOOPERATION
NONCOOPERATIONS
NONCOOPERATIVE
NONCOOPERATOR
NONCOOPERATORS
NONCOPLANAR
NONCORPORATE
NONCORRELATION
NONCORRELATIONS
NONCORRODIBLE
NONCORRODING
NONCORROSIVE
NONCOUNTRY
NONCOVERAGE
NONCOVERAGES
NONCREATIVE
NONCREATIVITIES
NONCREATIVITY
NONCREDENTIALED
NONCRIMINAL
NONCRIMINALS
NONCRITICAL
NONCROSSOVER
NONCRUSHABLE
NONCRYSTALLINE
NONCULINARY
NONCULTIVATED
NONCULTIVATION
NONCULTIVATIONS
NONCULTURAL
NONCUMULATIVE
NONCURRENT
NONCUSTODIAL
NONCUSTOMER
NONCUSTOMERS
NONCYCLICAL
NONDANCERS
NONDECEPTIVE
NONDECISION
NONDECISIONS
NONDECREASING
NONDEDUCTIBLE
NONDEDUCTIVE
NONDEFENSE
NONDEFERRABLE
NONDEFORMING
NONDEGENERATE
NONDEGRADABLE
NONDELEGATE
NONDELEGATES
NONDELIBERATE
NONDELINQUENT
NONDELINQUENTS
NONDELIVERIES
NONDELIVERY
NONDEMANDING
NONDEMANDS
NONDEMOCRATIC
NONDEPARTMENTAL
NONDEPENDENT
NONDEPENDENTS
NONDEPLETABLE
NONDEPLETING
NONDEPOSITION
NONDEPOSITIONS
NONDEPRESSED
NONDERIVATIVE
NONDESCRIPT
NONDESCRIPTIVE
NONDESCRIPTLY
NONDESCRIPTNESS
NONDESCRIPTS
NONDESTRUCTIVE
NONDETACHABLE
NONDEVELOPMENT
NONDEVELOPMENTS
NONDEVIANT
NONDIABETIC
NONDIABETICS
NONDIALYSABLE
NONDIALYZABLE
NONDIAPAUSING
NONDIDACTIC
NONDIFFUSIBLE
NONDIMENSIONAL
NONDIPLOMATIC
NONDIRECTED
NONDIRECTIONAL

NONDIRECTIVE
NONDISABLED
NONDISCLOSURE
NONDISCLOSURES
NONDISCOUNT
NONDISCURSIVE
NONDISJUNCTION
NONDISJUNCTIONS
NONDISPERSIVE
NONDISRUPTIVE
NONDISTINCTIVE
NONDIVERSIFIED
NONDIVIDING
NONDOCTORS
NONDOCTRINAIRE
NONDOCUMENTARY
NONDOGMATIC
NONDOMESTIC
NONDOMICILED
NONDOMINANT
NONDORMANT
NONDRAMATIC
NONDRINKER
NONDRINKERS
NONDRINKING
NONDRIVERS
NONDURABLE
NONEARNING
NONECONOMIC
NONECONOMIST
NONECONOMISTS
NONEDIBLES
NONEDITORIAL
NONEDUCATION
NONEDUCATIONAL
NONEFFECTIVE
NONEFFECTIVES
NONELASTIC
NONELECTED
NONELECTION
NONELECTIONS
NONELECTIVE
NONELECTRIC
NONELECTRICAL
NONELECTROLYTE
NONELECTROLYTES
NONELECTRONIC
NONELEMENTARY
NONEMERGENCIES
NONEMERGENCY
NONEMOTIONAL
NONEMPHATIC
NONEMPIRICAL
NONEMPLOYEE
NONEMPLOYEES
NONEMPLOYMENT
NONEMPLOYMENTS
NONENCAPSULATED
NONENFORCEMENT
NONENFORCEMENTS
NONENGAGEMENT
NONENGAGEMENTS
NONENGINEERING
NONENTITIES
NONENTRIES
NONENZYMATIC
NONENZYMIC
NONEQUILIBRIA
NONEQUILIBRIUM
NONEQUILIBRIUMS
NONEQUIVALENCE
NONEQUIVALENCES
NONEQUIVALENT
NONESSENTIAL
NONESSENTIALS
NONESTABLISHED
NONESTERIFIED
NONESUCHES
NONETHELESS
NONETHICAL
NONETHNICS
NONEVALUATIVE
NONEVIDENCE
NONEVIDENCES
NONEXCLUSIVE
NONEXECUTIVE
NONEXECUTIVES
NONEXEMPTS
NONEXISTENCE
NONEXISTENCES
NONEXISTENT
NONEXISTENTIAL
NONEXPENDABLE
NONEXPERIMENTAL
NONEXPERTS
NONEXPLANATORY
NONEXPLOITATION
NONEXPLOITATIVE
NONEXPLOITIVE
NONEXPLOSIVE
NONEXPOSED
NONFACTORS
NONFACTUAL
NONFACULTY
NONFAMILIAL
NONFAMILIES
NONFARMERS
NONFATTENING
NONFEASANCE
NONFEASANCES
NONFEDERAL
NONFEDERATED
NONFEMINIST
NONFEMINISTS
NONFERROUS
NONFICTION
NONFICTIONAL
NONFICTIONALLY
NONFICTIONS
NONFIGURATIVE
NONFILAMENTOUS
NONFILTERABLE
NONFINANCIAL
NONFISSIONABLE
NONFLAMMABILITY
NONFLAMMABLE
NONFLOWERING
NONFLUENCIES
NONFLUENCY
NONFLUORESCENT
NONFORFEITABLE
NONFORFEITURE
NONFORFEITURES
NONFREEZING
NONFRIVOLOUS
NONFULFILLMENT
NONFULFILLMENTS
NONFUNCTIONAL
NONFUNCTIONING
NONGASEOUS
NONGENETIC
NONGENITAL
NONGEOMETRICAL
NONGLAMOROUS
NONGOLFERS
NONGONOCOCCAL
NONGOVERNMENT
NONGOVERNMENTAL
NONGRADUATE
NONGRADUATES
NONGRAMMATICAL
NONGRANULAR
NONGREGARIOUS
NONGROWING
NONHALOGENATED
NONHANDICAPPED
NONHAPPENING
NONHAPPENINGS
NONHARMONIC
NONHAZARDOUS
NONHEMOLYTIC
NONHEREDITARY
NONHIERARCHICAL
NONHISTONE
NONHISTORICAL
NONHOMOGENEOUS
NONHOMOLOGOUS
NONHOMOSEXUAL
NONHOMOSEXUALS
NONHORMONAL
NONHOSPITAL
NONHOSPITALISED
NONHOSPITALIZED
NONHOSTILE
NONHOUSING
NONHUNTERS
NONHUNTING
NONHYGROSCOPIC
NONHYSTERICAL
NONIDENTICAL
NONIDENTITIES
NONIDENTITY
NONIDEOLOGICAL
NONILLIONS
NONILLIONTH
NONILLIONTHS
NONIMITATIVE
NONIMMIGRANT
NONIMMIGRANTS
NONIMPLICATION
NONIMPLICATIONS
NONIMPORTATION
NONIMPORTATIONS
NONINCLUSION
NONINCLUSIONS
NONINCREASING
NONINCUMBENT
NONINCUMBENTS
NONINDEPENDENCE
NONINDIGENOUS
NONINDIVIDUAL
NONINDUCTIVE
NONINDUSTRIAL
NONINDUSTRY
NONINFECTED
NONINFECTIOUS
NONINFECTIVE
NONINFESTED
NONINFLAMMABLE
NONINFLAMMATORY
NONINFLATIONARY
NONINFLECTIONAL
NONINFLUENCE
NONINFLUENCES
NONINFORMATION
NONINFORMATIONS
NONINFRINGEMENT
NONINITIAL
NONINITIATE
NONINITIATES
NONINSECTICIDAL
NONINSECTS
NONINSTALLMENT
NONINSTALLMENTS
NONINSTRUMENTAL
NONINSURANCE
NONINSURED
NONINTEGRAL
NONINTEGRATED
NONINTELLECTUAL
NONINTERACTING
NONINTERACTIVE
NONINTERCOURSE
NONINTERCOURSES
NONINTEREST
NONINTERFERENCE
NONINTERSECTING
NONINTERVENTION
NONINTIMIDATING
NONINTOXICANT
NONINTOXICANTS
NONINTOXICATING
NONINTRUSIVE
NONINTUITIVE
NONINVASIVE
NONINVOLVED
NONINVOLVEMENT
NONINVOLVEMENTS
NONIONIZING
NONIRRADIATED
NONIRRIGATED
NONIRRITANT
NONIRRITANTS
NONIRRITATING
NONJOINDER
NONJOINDERS
NONJOINERS
NONJUDGEMENTAL
NONJUDGMENTAL
NONJUDICIAL
NONJUSTICIABLE
NONKOSHERS
NONLANDOWNER
NONLANDOWNERS

NONLANGUAGE
NONLANGUAGES
NONLAWYERS
NONLEGUMES
NONLEGUMINOUS
NONLEXICAL
NONLIBRARIAN
NONLIBRARIANS
NONLIBRARY
NONLINEARITIES
NONLINEARITY
NONLINGUISTIC
NONLIQUIDS
NONLITERAL
NONLITERARY
NONLITERATE
NONLITERATES
NONLIVINGS
NONLOGICAL
NONLUMINOUS
NONMAGNETIC
NONMAINSTREAM
NONMALIGNANT
NONMALLEABLE
NONMANAGEMENT
NONMANAGERIAL
NONMARITAL
NONMARKETS
NONMATERIAL
NONMATHEMATICAL
NONMATRICULATED
NONMEANINGFUL
NONMEASURABLE
NONMECHANICAL
NONMECHANISTIC
NONMEDICAL
NONMEETING
NONMEETINGS
NONMEMBERS
NONMEMBERSHIP
NONMEMBERSHIPS
NONMERCURIAL
NONMETALLIC
NONMETAMERIC
NONMETAPHORICAL
NONMETRICAL
NONMETROPOLITAN
NONMICROBIAL
NONMIGRANT
NONMIGRATORY
NONMILITANT
NONMILITANTS
NONMILITARY
NONMIMETIC
NONMINORITIES
NONMINORITY
NONMODERNS
NONMOLECULAR
NONMONETARIST
NONMONETARISTS
NONMONETARY
NONMONOGAMOUS
NONMORTALS
NONMOTILITIES
NONMOTILITY
NONMOTORISED
NONMOTORIZED
NONMUNICIPAL
NONMUSICAL
NONMUSICALS
NONMUSICIAN
NONMUSICIANS
NONMUTANTS
NONMYELINATED
NONMYSTICAL
NONNARRATIVE
NONNATIONAL
NONNATIONALS
NONNATIVES
NONNATURAL
NONNECESSITIES
NONNECESSITY
NONNEGATIVE
NONNEGLIGENT
NONNEGOTIABLE
NONNEGOTIABLES
NONNETWORK
NONNITROGENOUS
NONNORMATIVE
NONNUCLEAR
NONNUCLEATED
NONNUMERICAL
NONNUTRITIOUS
NONNUTRITIVE
NONOBJECTIVE
NONOBJECTIVISM
NONOBJECTIVISMS
NONOBJECTIVIST
NONOBJECTIVISTS
NONOBJECTIVITY
NONOBSCENE
NONOBSERVANCE
NONOBSERVANCES
NONOBSERVANT
NONOBVIOUS
NONOCCUPATIONAL
NONOCCURRENCE
NONOCCURRENCES
NONOFFICIAL
NONOFFICIALS
NONOPERATIC
NONOPERATING
NONOPERATIONAL
NONOPERATIVE
NONOPTIMAL
NONORGANIC
NONORGASMIC
NONORTHODOX
NONOVERLAPPING
NONOXIDISING
NONOXIDIZING
NONPAPISTS
NONPARALLEL
NONPARAMETRIC
NONPARASITIC
NONPAREILS
NONPARENTS
NONPARITIES
NONPARTICIPANT
NONPARTICIPANTS
NONPARTIES
NONPARTISAN
NONPARTISANSHIP
NONPARTIZAN
NONPARTIZANSHIP
NONPASSERINE
NONPASSIVE
NONPATHOGENIC
NONPAYMENT
NONPAYMENTS
NONPERFORMANCE
NONPERFORMANCES
NONPERFORMER
NONPERFORMERS
NONPERFORMING
NONPERISHABLE
NONPERISHABLES
NONPERMANENT
NONPERMISSIVE
NONPERSISTENT
NONPERSONAL
NONPERSONS
NONPETROLEUM
NONPHILOSOPHER
NONPHILOSOPHERS
NONPHONEMIC
NONPHONETIC
NONPHOSPHATE
NONPHOTOGRAPHIC
NONPHYSICAL
NONPHYSICIAN
NONPHYSICIANS
NONPLASTIC
NONPLASTICS
NONPLAYERS
NONPLAYING
NONPLUSING
NONPLUSSED
NONPLUSSES
NONPLUSSING
NONPOISONOUS
NONPOLARISABLE
NONPOLARIZABLE
NONPOLITICAL
NONPOLITICALLY
NONPOLITICIAN
NONPOLITICIANS
NONPOLLUTING
NONPOSSESSION
NONPOSSESSIONS
NONPRACTICAL
NONPRACTICING
NONPRACTISING
NONPREGNANT
NONPRESCRIPTION
NONPROBLEM
NONPROBLEMS
NONPRODUCING
NONPRODUCTIVE
NONPRODUCTIVITY
NONPROFESSIONAL
NONPROFESSORIAL
NONPROFITS
NONPROGRAM
NONPROGRAMMER
NONPROGRAMMERS
NONPROGRESSIVE
NONPROPRIETARY
NONPROSSED
NONPROSSES
NONPROSSING
NONPROTEIN
NONPSYCHIATRIC
NONPSYCHIATRIST
NONPSYCHOTIC
NONPUNITIVE
NONPURPOSIVE
NONQUANTIFIABLE
NONQUANTITATIVE
NONRACIALLY
NONRADIOACTIVE
NONRAILROAD
NONRANDOMNESS
NONRANDOMNESSES
NONRATIONAL
NONREACTIVE
NONREACTOR
NONREACTORS
NONREADERS
NONREADING
NONREALISTIC
NONRECEIPT
NONRECEIPTS
NONRECIPROCAL
NONRECOGNITION
NONRECOGNITIONS
NONRECOMBINANT
NONRECOMBINANTS
NONRECOURSE
NONRECURRENT
NONRECURRING
NONRECYCLABLE
NONRECYCLABLES
NONREDUCING
NONREDUNDANT
NONREFILLABLE
NONREFLECTING
NONREFLEXIVE
NONREFUNDABLE
NONREGULATED
NONREGULATION
NONRELATIVE
NONRELATIVES
NONRELATIVISTIC
NONRELEVANT
NONRELIGIOUS
NONRENEWABLE
NONRENEWAL
NONREPAYABLE
NONREPRODUCTIVE
NONRESIDENCE
NONRESIDENCES
NONRESIDENCIES
NONRESIDENCY
NONRESIDENT
NONRESIDENTIAL
NONRESIDENTS
NONRESISTANCE
NONRESISTANCES
NONRESISTANT
NONRESISTANTS
NONRESONANT
NONRESPONDENT
NONRESPONDENTS

NONRESPONDER
NONRESPONDERS
NONRESPONSE
NONRESPONSES
NONRESPONSIVE
NONRESTRICTED
NONRESTRICTIVE
NONRETRACTILE
NONRETROACTIVE
NONRETURNABLE
NONRETURNABLES
NONREUSABLE
NONREVERSIBLE
NONRHOTICITIES
NONRHOTICITY
NONRIOTERS
NONRIOTING
NONROTATING
NONROUTINE
NONRUMINANT
NONRUMINANTS
NONSALABLE
NONSAPONIFIABLE
NONSCHEDULED
NONSCIENCE
NONSCIENCES
NONSCIENTIFIC
NONSCIENTIST
NONSCIENTISTS
NONSEASONAL
NONSECRETOR
NONSECRETORS
NONSECRETORY
NONSECRETS
NONSECTARIAN
NONSEDIMENTABLE
NONSEGREGATED
NONSEGREGATION
NONSEGREGATIONS
NONSELECTED
NONSELECTIVE
NONSENSATIONAL
NONSENSICAL
NONSENSICALITY
NONSENSICALLY
NONSENSICALNESS
NONSENSITIVE
NONSENSUOUS
NONSENTENCE
NONSENTENCES
NONSEPTATE
NONSEQUENTIAL
NONSERIALS
NONSERIOUS
NONSHRINKABLE
NONSIGNERS
NONSIGNIFICANT
NONSIMULTANEOUS
NONSINKABLE
NONSKATERS
NONSKELETAL
NONSMOKERS
NONSMOKING
NONSOCIALIST
NONSOCIALISTS
NONSOLUTION
NONSOLUTIONS
NONSPATIAL
NONSPEAKER
NONSPEAKERS
NONSPEAKING
NONSPECIALIST
NONSPECIALISTS
NONSPECIFIC
NONSPECIFICALLY
NONSPECTACULAR
NONSPECULAR
NONSPECULATIVE
NONSPHERICAL
NONSPORTING
NONSTANDARD
NONSTAPLES
NONSTARTER
NONSTARTERS
NONSTATIONARY
NONSTATISTICAL
NONSTATIVE
NONSTATIVES
NONSTEROID
NONSTEROIDAL
NONSTEROIDS
NONSTORIES
NONSTRATEGIC
NONSTRIATED
NONSTRUCTURAL
NONSTRUCTURED
NONSTUDENT
NONSTUDENTS
NONSUBJECT
NONSUBJECTIVE
NONSUBJECTS
NONSUBSIDISED
NONSUBSIDIZED
NONSUCCESS
NONSUCCESSES
NONSUITING
NONSUPERVISORY
NONSUPPORT
NONSUPPORTS
NONSURGICAL
NONSWIMMER
NONSWIMMERS
NONSYLLABIC
NONSYMBOLIC
NONSYMMETRIC
NONSYMMETRICAL
NONSYNCHRONOUS
NONSYSTEMATIC
NONSYSTEMIC
NONSYSTEMS
NONTALKERS
NONTAXABLE
NONTEACHING
NONTECHNICAL
NONTEMPORAL
NONTENURED
NONTERMINAL
NONTERMINALS
NONTERMINATING
NONTHEATRICAL
NONTHEISTIC
NONTHEISTS
NONTHEOLOGICAL
NONTHEORETICAL
NONTHERAPEUTIC
NONTHERMAL
NONTHINKING
NONTHREATENING
NONTOBACCO
NONTOTALITARIAN
NONTRADITIONAL
NONTRANSFERABLE
NONTRANSITIVE
NONTREATMENT
NONTREATMENTS
NONTRIVIAL
NONTROPICAL
NONTURBULENT
NONTYPICAL
NONUNANIMOUS
NONUNIFORM
NONUNIFORMITIES
NONUNIFORMITY
NONUNIONISED
NONUNIONISM
NONUNIONIST
NONUNIONISTS
NONUNIONIZED
NONUNIQUENESS
NONUNIQUENESSES
NONUNIVERSAL
NONUNIVERSITY
NONUTILITARIAN
NONUTILITIES
NONUTILITY
NONUTOPIAN
NONVALIDITIES
NONVALIDITY
NONVANISHING
NONVASCULAR
NONVECTORS
NONVEGETARIAN
NONVEGETARIANS
NONVENOMOUS
NONVERBALLY
NONVETERAN
NONVETERANS
NONVIEWERS
NONVINTAGE
NONVIOLENCE
NONVIOLENCES
NONVIOLENT
NONVIOLENTLY
NONVIRGINS
NONVISCOUS
NONVOCATIONAL
NONVOLATILE
NONVOLCANIC
NONVOLUNTARY
NONWINNING
NONWORKERS
NONWORKING
NONWRITERS
NONYELLOWING
NOODLEDOMS
NOOGENESES
NOOGENESIS
NOOMETRIES
NOOSPHERES
NOOTROPICS
NORADRENALIN
NORADRENALINE
NORADRENALINES
NORADRENALINS
NORADRENERGIC
NOREPINEPHRINE
NOREPINEPHRINES
NORETHINDRONE
NORETHINDRONES
NORETHISTERONE
NORETHISTERONES
NORMALCIES
NORMALISABLE
NORMALISATION
NORMALISATIONS
NORMALISED
NORMALISER
NORMALISERS
NORMALISES
NORMALISING
NORMALITIES
NORMALIZABLE
NORMALIZATION
NORMALIZATIONS
NORMALIZED
NORMALIZER
NORMALIZERS
NORMALIZES
NORMALIZING
NORMATIVELY
NORMATIVENESS
NORMATIVENESSES
NORMOTENSIVE
NORMOTENSIVES
NORMOTHERMIA
NORMOTHERMIAS
NORMOTHERMIC
NORSELLERS
NORSELLING
NORTHBOUND
NORTHCOUNTRYMAN
NORTHCOUNTRYMEN
NORTHEASTER
NORTHEASTERLIES
NORTHEASTERLY
NORTHEASTERN
NORTHEASTERS
NORTHEASTS
NORTHEASTWARD
NORTHEASTWARDLY
NORTHEASTWARDS
NORTHERING
NORTHERLIES
NORTHERLINESS
NORTHERLINESSES
NORTHERMOST
NORTHERNER
NORTHERNERS
NORTHERNISE
NORTHERNISED
NORTHERNISES
NORTHERNISING
NORTHERNISM
NORTHERNISMS

NORTHERNIZE
NORTHERNIZED
NORTHERNIZES
NORTHERNIZING
NORTHERNMOST
NORTHLANDS
NORTHWARDLY
NORTHWARDS
NORTHWESTER
NORTHWESTERLIES
NORTHWESTERLY
NORTHWESTERN
NORTHWESTERS
NORTHWESTS
NORTHWESTWARD
NORTHWESTWARDLY
NORTHWESTWARDS
NORTRIPTYLINE
NORTRIPTYLINES
NOSEBANDED
NOSEBLEEDING
NOSEBLEEDINGS
NOSEBLEEDS
NOSEDIVING
NOSEGUARDS
NOSEPIECES
NOSEWHEELS
NOSINESSES
NOSOCOMIAL
NOSOGRAPHER
NOSOGRAPHERS
NOSOGRAPHIC
NOSOGRAPHIES
NOSOGRAPHY
NOSOLOGICAL
NOSOLOGICALLY
NOSOLOGIES
NOSOLOGIST
NOSOLOGISTS
NOSOPHOBIA
NOSOPHOBIAS
NOSTALGIAS
NOSTALGICALLY
NOSTALGICS
NOSTALGIST
NOSTALGISTS
NOSTOLOGIC
NOSTOLOGICAL
NOSTOLOGIES
NOSTOMANIA
NOSTOMANIAS
NOSTOPATHIES
NOSTOPATHY
NOSTRADAMIC
NOTABILITIES
NOTABILITY
NOTABLENESS
NOTABLENESSES
NOTAPHILIC
NOTAPHILIES
NOTAPHILISM
NOTAPHILISMS
NOTAPHILIST
NOTAPHILISTS
NOTARIALLY
NOTARISATION
NOTARISATIONS
NOTARISING
NOTARIZATION
NOTARIZATIONS
NOTARIZING
NOTARYSHIP
NOTARYSHIPS
NOTATIONAL
NOTCHBACKS
NOTCHELLED
NOTCHELLING
NOTEDNESSES
NOTEPAPERS
NOTEWORTHILY
NOTEWORTHINESS
NOTEWORTHY
NOTHINGARIAN
NOTHINGARIANISM
NOTHINGARIANS
NOTHINGISM
NOTHINGISMS
NOTHINGNESS
NOTHINGNESSES
NOTICEABILITIES
NOTICEABILITY
NOTICEABLE
NOTICEABLY
NOTIFIABLE
NOTIFICATION
NOTIFICATIONS
NOTIONALIST
NOTIONALISTS
NOTIONALITIES
NOTIONALITY
NOTIONALLY
NOTIONISTS
NOTOCHORDAL
NOTOCHORDS
NOTODONTID
NOTODONTIDS
NOTONECTAL
NOTORIETIES
NOTORIOUSLY
NOTORIOUSNESS
NOTORIOUSNESSES
NOTORNISES
NOTOTHERIUM
NOTOTHERIUMS
NOTOUNGULATE
NOTOUNGULATES
NOTUNGULATE
NOTUNGULATES
NOTWITHSTANDING
NOUMENALISM
NOUMENALISMS
NOUMENALIST
NOUMENALISTS
NOUMENALITIES
NOUMENALITY
NOUMENALLY
NOURISHABLE
NOURISHERS
NOURISHING
NOURISHINGLY
NOURISHMENT
NOURISHMENTS
NOURITURES
NOURRITURE
NOURRITURES
NOUSELLING
NOVACULITE
NOVACULITES
NOVELETTES
NOVELETTISH
NOVELETTIST
NOVELETTISTS
NOVELISATION
NOVELISATIONS
NOVELISERS
NOVELISING
NOVELISTIC
NOVELISTICALLY
NOVELIZATION
NOVELIZATIONS
NOVELIZERS
NOVELIZING
NOVEMDECILLION
NOVEMDECILLIONS
NOVENARIES
NOVICEHOOD
NOVICEHOODS
NOVICESHIP
NOVICESHIPS
NOVICIATES
NOVITIATES
NOVOBIOCIN
NOVOBIOCINS
NOVOCAINES
NOVOCENTENARIES
NOVOCENTENARY
NOVODAMUSES
NOWCASTING
NOWCASTINGS
NOXIOUSNESS
NOXIOUSNESSES
NUBBINESSES
NUBIFEROUS
NUBIGENOUS
NUBILITIES
NUCIFEROUS
NUCIVOROUS
NUCLEARISATION
NUCLEARISATIONS
NUCLEARISE
NUCLEARISED
NUCLEARISES
NUCLEARISING
NUCLEARIZATION
NUCLEARIZATIONS
NUCLEARIZE
NUCLEARIZED
NUCLEARIZES
NUCLEARIZING
NUCLEATING
NUCLEATION
NUCLEATIONS
NUCLEATORS
NUCLEOCAPSID
NUCLEOCAPSIDS
NUCLEOLATE
NUCLEOLATED
NUCLEONICALLY
NUCLEONICS
NUCLEOPHILE
NUCLEOPHILES
NUCLEOPHILIC
NUCLEOPHILICITY
NUCLEOPLASM
NUCLEOPLASMATIC
NUCLEOPLASMIC
NUCLEOPLASMS
NUCLEOPROTEIN
NUCLEOPROTEINS
NUCLEOSIDE
NUCLEOSIDES
NUCLEOSOMAL
NUCLEOSOME
NUCLEOSOMES
NUCLEOSYNTHESES
NUCLEOSYNTHESIS
NUCLEOSYNTHETIC
NUCLEOTIDASE
NUCLEOTIDASES
NUCLEOTIDE
NUCLEOTIDES
NUDENESSES
NUDIBRANCH
NUDIBRANCHIATE
NUDIBRANCHIATES
NUDIBRANCHS
NUDICAUDATE
NUDICAULOUS
NUGATORINESS
NUGATORINESSES
NUGGETTING
NUISANCERS
NULLIFICATION
NULLIFICATIONS
NULLIFIDIAN
NULLIFIDIANS
NULLIFIERS
NULLIFYING
NULLIPARAE
NULLIPARAS
NULLIPARITIES
NULLIPARITY
NULLIPAROUS
NULLIPORES
NULLNESSES
NUMBERABLE
NUMBERINGS
NUMBERLESS
NUMBERLESSLY
NUMBERLESSNESS
NUMBERPLATE
NUMBERPLATES
NUMBFISHES
NUMBNESSES
NUMBSKULLS
NUMERABILITIES
NUMERABILITY
NUMERACIES
NUMERAIRES
NUMERATING
NUMERATION
NUMERATIONS
NUMERATIVE
NUMERATORS

NUMERICALLY
NUMEROLOGICAL
NUMEROLOGIES
NUMEROLOGIST
NUMEROLOGISTS
NUMEROLOGY
NUMEROSITIES
NUMEROSITY
NUMEROUSLY
NUMEROUSNESS
NUMEROUSNESSES
NUMINOUSES
NUMINOUSNESS
NUMINOUSNESSES
NUMISMATIC
NUMISMATICALLY
NUMISMATICS
NUMISMATIST
NUMISMATISTS
NUMISMATOLOGIES
NUMISMATOLOGIST
NUMISMATOLOGY
NUMMULATED
NUMMULATION
NUMMULATIONS
NUMMULITES
NUMMULITIC
NUMSKULLED
NUNCIATURE
NUNCIATURES
NUNCUPATED
NUNCUPATES
NUNCUPATING
NUNCUPATION
NUNCUPATIONS
NUNCUPATIVE
NUNCUPATORY
NUNNATIONS
NUNNISHNESS
NUNNISHNESSES
NUPTIALITIES
NUPTIALITY
NURSEHOUND
NURSEHOUNDS
NURSELINGS
NURSEMAIDED
NURSEMAIDING
NURSEMAIDS
NURSERYMAID
NURSERYMAIDS
NURSERYMAN
NURSERYMEN
NURTURABLE
NURTURANCE
NURTURANCES
NUTATIONAL
NUTBUTTERS
NUTCRACKER
NUTCRACKERS
NUTGRASSES
NUTHATCHES
NUTJOBBERS
NUTMEGGING
NUTPECKERS
NUTRACEUTICAL
NUTRACEUTICALS
NUTRIMENTAL
NUTRIMENTS
NUTRITIONAL
NUTRITIONALLY
NUTRITIONARY
NUTRITIONIST
NUTRITIONISTS
NUTRITIONS
NUTRITIOUS
NUTRITIOUSLY
NUTRITIOUSNESS
NUTRITIVELY
NUTRITIVES
NUTTINESSES
NYCHTHEMERAL
NYCHTHEMERON
NYCHTHEMERONS
NYCTAGINACEOUS
NYCTALOPES
NYCTALOPIA
NYCTALOPIAS
NYCTALOPIC
NYCTANTHOUS
NYCTINASTIC
NYCTINASTIES
NYCTINASTY
NYCTITROPIC
NYCTITROPISM
NYCTITROPISMS
NYCTOPHOBIA
NYCTOPHOBIAS
NYCTOPHOBIC
NYMPHAEACEOUS
NYMPHAEUMS
NYMPHALIDS
NYMPHETTES
NYMPHOLEPSIES
NYMPHOLEPSY
NYMPHOLEPT
NYMPHOLEPTIC
NYMPHOLEPTS
NYMPHOMANIA
NYMPHOMANIAC
NYMPHOMANIACAL
NYMPHOMANIACS
NYMPHOMANIAS
NYSTAGMOID
NYSTAGMUSES

Oo

OAFISHNESS
OAFISHNESSES
OAKENSHAWS
OARSMANSHIP
OARSMANSHIPS
OASTHOUSES
OBBLIGATOS
OBCOMPRESSED
OBDURACIES
OBDURATELY
OBDURATENESS
OBDURATENESSES
OBDURATING
OBDURATION
OBDURATIONS
OBEDIENCES
OBEDIENTIAL
OBEDIENTIARIES
OBEDIENTIARY
OBEDIENTLY
OBEISANCES
OBEISANTLY
OBELISCOID
OBELISKOID
OBESENESSES
OBFUSCATED
OBFUSCATES
OBFUSCATING
OBFUSCATION
OBFUSCATIONS
OBFUSCATORY
OBITUARIES
OBITUARIST
OBITUARISTS
OBJECTIFICATION
OBJECTIFIED
OBJECTIFIES
OBJECTIFYING
OBJECTIONABLE
OBJECTIONABLY
OBJECTIONS
OBJECTIVAL
OBJECTIVATE
OBJECTIVATED
OBJECTIVATES
OBJECTIVATING
OBJECTIVATION
OBJECTIVATIONS
OBJECTIVELY
OBJECTIVENESS
OBJECTIVENESSES
OBJECTIVES
OBJECTIVISE
OBJECTIVISED
OBJECTIVISES
OBJECTIVISING
OBJECTIVISM
OBJECTIVISMS
OBJECTIVIST
OBJECTIVISTIC
OBJECTIVISTS
OBJECTIVITIES
OBJECTIVITY
OBJECTIVIZE
OBJECTIVIZED
OBJECTIVIZES
OBJECTIVIZING
OBJECTLESS
OBJECTLESSNESS
OBJURATION
OBJURATIONS
OBJURGATED
OBJURGATES
OBJURGATING
OBJURGATION
OBJURGATIONS
OBJURGATIVE
OBJURGATOR
OBJURGATORS
OBJURGATORY
OBLANCEOLATE
OBLATENESS
OBLATENESSES
OBLATIONAL
OBLIGATELY
OBLIGATING
OBLIGATION
OBLIGATIONAL
OBLIGATIONS
OBLIGATIVE
OBLIGATORILY
OBLIGATORINESS
OBLIGATORS
OBLIGATORY
OBLIGEMENT
OBLIGEMENTS
OBLIGINGLY
OBLIGINGNESS
OBLIGINGNESSES
OBLIQUATION
OBLIQUATIONS
OBLIQUENESS
OBLIQUENESSES
OBLIQUITIES
OBLIQUITOUS
OBLITERATE
OBLITERATED
OBLITERATES
OBLITERATING
OBLITERATION
OBLITERATIONS
OBLITERATIVE
OBLITERATOR
OBLITERATORS
OBLIVIOUSLY
OBLIVIOUSNESS
OBLIVIOUSNESSES
OBLIVISCENCE
OBLIVISCENCES
OBMUTESCENCE
OBMUTESCENCES
OBMUTESCENT
OBNOXIOUSLY
OBNOXIOUSNESS
OBNOXIOUSNESSES
OBNUBILATE
OBNUBILATED
OBNUBILATES
OBNUBILATING
OBNUBILATION
OBNUBILATIONS
OBREPTIONS
OBREPTITIOUS
OBSCENENESS
OBSCENENESSES
OBSCENITIES
OBSCURANTIC
OBSCURANTISM
OBSCURANTISMS
OBSCURANTIST
OBSCURANTISTS
OBSCURANTS
OBSCURATION
OBSCURATIONS
OBSCUREMENT
OBSCUREMENTS
OBSCURENESS
OBSCURENESSES
OBSCURITIES
OBSECRATED
OBSECRATES
OBSECRATING

OBSECRATION
OBSECRATIONS
OBSEQUIOUS
OBSEQUIOUSLY
OBSEQUIOUSNESS
OBSERVABILITIES
OBSERVABILITY
OBSERVABLE
OBSERVABLENESS
OBSERVABLES
OBSERVABLY
OBSERVANCE
OBSERVANCES
OBSERVANCIES
OBSERVANCY
OBSERVANTLY
OBSERVANTS
OBSERVATION
OBSERVATIONAL
OBSERVATIONALLY
OBSERVATIONS
OBSERVATIVE
OBSERVATOR
OBSERVATORIES
OBSERVATORS
OBSERVATORY
OBSERVINGLY
OBSESSIONAL
OBSESSIONALLY
OBSESSIONIST
OBSESSIONISTS
OBSESSIONS
OBSESSIVELY
OBSESSIVENESS
OBSESSIVENESSES
OBSESSIVES
OBSIDIONAL
OBSIDIONARY
OBSIGNATED
OBSIGNATES
OBSIGNATING
OBSIGNATION
OBSIGNATIONS
OBSIGNATORY
OBSOLESCED
OBSOLESCENCE
OBSOLESCENCES
OBSOLESCENT
OBSOLESCENTLY
OBSOLESCES
OBSOLESCING
OBSOLETELY
OBSOLETENESS
OBSOLETENESSES
OBSOLETING
OBSOLETION
OBSOLETIONS
OBSOLETISM
OBSOLETISMS
OBSTETRICAL
OBSTETRICALLY
OBSTETRICIAN
OBSTETRICIANS
OBSTETRICS
OBSTINACIES
OBSTINATELY
OBSTINATENESS
OBSTINATENESSES
OBSTIPATION
OBSTIPATIONS
OBSTREPERATE
OBSTREPERATED
OBSTREPERATES
OBSTREPERATING
OBSTREPEROUS
OBSTREPEROUSLY
OBSTRICTION
OBSTRICTIONS
OBSTROPALOUS
OBSTROPULOUS
OBSTRUCTED
OBSTRUCTER
OBSTRUCTERS
OBSTRUCTING
OBSTRUCTION
OBSTRUCTIONAL
OBSTRUCTIONALLY
OBSTRUCTIONISM
OBSTRUCTIONISMS
OBSTRUCTIONIST
OBSTRUCTIONISTS
OBSTRUCTIONS
OBSTRUCTIVE
OBSTRUCTIVELY
OBSTRUCTIVENESS
OBSTRUCTIVES
OBSTRUCTOR
OBSTRUCTORS
OBSTRUENTS
OBTAINABILITIES
OBTAINABILITY
OBTAINABLE
OBTAINMENT
OBTAINMENTS
OBTEMPERATE
OBTEMPERATED
OBTEMPERATES
OBTEMPERATING
OBTEMPERED
OBTEMPERING
OBTENTIONS
OBTESTATION
OBTESTATIONS
OBTRUDINGS
OBTRUNCATE
OBTRUNCATED
OBTRUNCATES
OBTRUNCATING
OBTRUSIONS
OBTRUSIVELY
OBTRUSIVENESS
OBTRUSIVENESSES
OBTUNDENTS
OBTUNDITIES
OBTURATING
OBTURATION
OBTURATIONS
OBTURATORS
OBTUSENESS
OBTUSENESSES
OBTUSITIES
OBUMBRATED
OBUMBRATES
OBUMBRATING
OBUMBRATION
OBUMBRATIONS
OBVENTIONS
OBVERSIONS
OBVIATIONS
OBVIOUSNESS
OBVIOUSNESSES
OBVOLUTION
OBVOLUTIONS
OBVOLUTIVE
OCCASIONAL
OCCASIONALISM
OCCASIONALISMS
OCCASIONALIST
OCCASIONALISTS
OCCASIONALITIES
OCCASIONALITY
OCCASIONALLY
OCCASIONED
OCCASIONER
OCCASIONERS
OCCASIONING
OCCIDENTAL
OCCIDENTALISE
OCCIDENTALISED
OCCIDENTALISES
OCCIDENTALISING
OCCIDENTALISM
OCCIDENTALISMS
OCCIDENTALIST
OCCIDENTALISTS
OCCIDENTALIZE
OCCIDENTALIZED
OCCIDENTALIZES
OCCIDENTALIZING
OCCIDENTALLY
OCCIDENTALS
OCCIPITALLY
OCCIPITALS
OCCLUDENTS
OCCLUSIONS
OCCLUSIVENESS
OCCLUSIVENESSES
OCCLUSIVES
OCCULTATION
OCCULTATIONS
OCCULTISMS
OCCULTISTS
OCCULTNESS
OCCULTNESSES
OCCUPANCES
OCCUPANCIES
OCCUPATING
OCCUPATION
OCCUPATIONAL
OCCUPATIONALLY
OCCUPATIONS
OCCUPATIVE
OCCURRENCE
OCCURRENCES
OCCURRENTS
OCEANARIUM
OCEANARIUMS
OCEANFRONT
OCEANFRONTS
OCEANGOING
OCEANOGRAPHER
OCEANOGRAPHERS
OCEANOGRAPHIC
OCEANOGRAPHICAL
OCEANOGRAPHIES
OCEANOGRAPHY
OCEANOLOGICAL
OCEANOLOGIES
OCEANOLOGIST
OCEANOLOGISTS
OCEANOLOGY
OCELLATION
OCELLATIONS
OCHLOCRACIES
OCHLOCRACY
OCHLOCRATIC
OCHLOCRATICAL
OCHLOCRATICALLY
OCHLOCRATS
OCHLOPHOBIA
OCHLOPHOBIAC
OCHLOPHOBIACS
OCHLOPHOBIAS
OCHLOPHOBIC
OCHRACEOUS
OCHROLEUCOUS
OCTACHORDAL
OCTACHORDS
OCTAGONALLY
OCTAHEDRAL
OCTAHEDRALLY
OCTAHEDRITE
OCTAHEDRITES
OCTAHEDRON
OCTAHEDRONS
OCTAMEROUS
OCTAMETERS
OCTANDRIAN
OCTANDROUS
OCTANEDIOIC
OCTANGULAR
OCTAPEPTIDE
OCTAPEPTIDES
OCTAPLOIDIES
OCTAPLOIDS
OCTAPLOIDY
OCTAPODIES
OCTARCHIES
OCTASTICHON
OCTASTICHONS
OCTASTICHOUS
OCTASTICHS
OCTASTROPHIC
OCTASTYLES
OCTAVALENT
OCTENNIALLY
OCTILLIONS
OCTILLIONTH
OCTILLIONTHS
OCTINGENARIES
OCTINGENARY
OCTINGENTENARY
OCTOCENTENARIES
OCTOCENTENARY

OCTODECILLION
OCTODECILLIONS
OCTODECIMO
OCTODECIMOS
OCTOGENARIAN
OCTOGENARIANS
OCTOGENARIES
OCTOGENARY
OCTOGYNOUS
OCTOHEDRON
OCTOHEDRONS
OCTONARIAN
OCTONARIANS
OCTONARIES
OCTONARIUS
OCTONOCULAR
OCTOPETALOUS
OCTOPLOIDS
OCTOPODANS
OCTOPODOUS
OCTOPUSHER
OCTOPUSHERS
OCTOPUSHES
OCTOSEPALOUS
OCTOSTICHOUS
OCTOSTYLES
OCTOSYLLABIC
OCTOSYLLABICS
OCTOSYLLABLE
OCTOSYLLABLES
OCTOTHORPS
OCTUPLICATE
OCTUPLICATES
OCULARISTS
OCULOMOTOR
ODALISQUES
ODDSMAKERS
ODIOUSNESS
ODIOUSNESSES
ODOMETRIES
ODONATISTS
ODONATOLOGIES
ODONATOLOGIST
ODONATOLOGISTS
ODONATOLOGY
ODONTALGIA
ODONTALGIAS
ODONTALGIC
ODONTALGIES
ODONTOBLAST
ODONTOBLASTIC
ODONTOBLASTS
ODONTOCETE
ODONTOCETES
ODONTOGENIC
ODONTOGENIES
ODONTOGENY
ODONTOGLOSSUM
ODONTOGLOSSUMS
ODONTOGRAPH
ODONTOGRAPHIES
ODONTOGRAPHS
ODONTOGRAPHY
ODONTOLITE
ODONTOLITES
ODONTOLOGIC
ODONTOLOGICAL
ODONTOLOGIES
ODONTOLOGIST
ODONTOLOGISTS
ODONTOLOGY
ODONTOMATA
ODONTOMATOUS
ODONTOPHOBIA
ODONTOPHOBIAS
ODONTOPHORAL
ODONTOPHORAN
ODONTOPHORE
ODONTOPHORES
ODONTOPHOROUS
ODONTORHYNCHOUS
ODONTORNITHES
ODONTOSTOMATOUS
ODORIFEROUS
ODORIFEROUSLY
ODORIFEROUSNESS
ODORIMETRIES
ODORIMETRY
ODORIPHORE
ODORIPHORES
ODOROUSNESS
ODOROUSNESSES
OECOLOGICAL
OECOLOGICALLY
OECOLOGIES
OECOLOGIST
OECOLOGISTS
OECUMENICAL
OECUMENICALLY
OEDEMATOSE
OEDEMATOUS
OEDOMETERS
OENOLOGICAL
OENOLOGIES
OENOLOGIST
OENOLOGISTS
OENOMANCIES
OENOMANIAS
OENOMETERS
OENOPHILES
OENOPHILIES
OENOPHILIST
OENOPHILISTS
OENOTHERAS
OESOPHAGEAL
OESOPHAGITIS
OESOPHAGITISES
OESOPHAGOSCOPE
OESOPHAGOSCOPES
OESOPHAGOSCOPY
OESOPHAGUS
OESTRADIOL
OESTRADIOLS
OESTROGENIC
OESTROGENICALLY
OESTROGENS
OFFENCEFUL
OFFENCELESS
OFFENDEDLY
OFFENDRESS
OFFENDRESSES
OFFENSELESS
OFFENSIVELY
OFFENSIVENESS
OFFENSIVENESSES
OFFENSIVES
OFFERTORIES
OFFHANDEDLY
OFFHANDEDNESS
OFFHANDEDNESSES
OFFICEHOLDER
OFFICEHOLDERS
OFFICERING
OFFICIALDOM
OFFICIALDOMS
OFFICIALESE
OFFICIALESES
OFFICIALISM
OFFICIALISMS
OFFICIALITIES
OFFICIALITY
OFFICIALLY
OFFICIALTIES
OFFICIALTY
OFFICIANTS
OFFICIARIES
OFFICIATED
OFFICIATES
OFFICIATING
OFFICIATION
OFFICIATIONS
OFFICIATOR
OFFICIATORS
OFFICINALLY
OFFICINALS
OFFICIOUSLY
OFFICIOUSNESS
OFFICIOUSNESSES
OFFISHNESS
OFFISHNESSES
OFFLOADING
OFFPRINTED
OFFPRINTING
OFFSADDLED
OFFSADDLES
OFFSADDLING
OFFSCOURING
OFFSCOURINGS
OFFSEASONS
OFFSETABLE
OFFSETTING
OFFSHORING
OFFSHORINGS
OFFSPRINGS
OFTENNESSES
OFTENTIMES
OILINESSES
OINOLOGIES
OLDFANGLED
OLEAGINOUS
OLEAGINOUSLY
OLEAGINOUSNESS
OLEANDOMYCIN
OLEANDOMYCINS
OLECRANONS
OLEIFEROUS
OLEOGRAPHIC
OLEOGRAPHIES
OLEOGRAPHS
OLEOGRAPHY
OLEOMARGARIN
OLEOMARGARINE
OLEOMARGARINES
OLEOMARGARINS
OLEOPHILIC
OLEORESINOUS
OLEORESINS
OLERACEOUS
OLFACTIBLE
OLFACTIONS
OLFACTOLOGIES
OLFACTOLOGIST
OLFACTOLOGISTS
OLFACTOLOGY
OLFACTOMETER
OLFACTOMETERS
OLFACTOMETRIES
OLFACTOMETRY
OLFACTORIES
OLFACTRONICS
OLIGAEMIAS
OLIGARCHAL
OLIGARCHIC
OLIGARCHICAL
OLIGARCHICALLY
OLIGARCHIES
OLIGOCHAETE
OLIGOCHAETES
OLIGOCHROME
OLIGOCHROMES
OLIGOCLASE
OLIGOCLASES
OLIGOCYTHAEMIA
OLIGOCYTHAEMIAS
OLIGODENDROCYTE
OLIGODENDROGLIA
OLIGOGENES
OLIGOMERIC
OLIGOMERISATION
OLIGOMERIZATION
OLIGOMEROUS
OLIGONUCLEOTIDE
OLIGOPEPTIDE
OLIGOPEPTIDES
OLIGOPHAGIES
OLIGOPHAGOUS
OLIGOPHAGY
OLIGOPOLIES
OLIGOPOLISTIC
OLIGOPSONIES
OLIGOPSONISTIC
OLIGOPSONY
OLIGOSACCHARIDE
OLIGOSPERMIA
OLIGOSPERMIAS
OLIGOTROPHIC
OLIGOTROPHIES
OLIGOTROPHY
OLIGURESES
OLIGURESIS
OLIGURETIC
OLIVACEOUS
OLIVENITES
OLIVINITIC

OLOGOANING
OLOLIUQUIS
OMBROGENOUS
OMBROMETER
OMBROMETERS
OMBROPHILE
OMBROPHILES
OMBROPHILOUS
OMBROPHILS
OMBROPHOBE
OMBROPHOBES
OMBROPHOBOUS
OMBUDSMANSHIP
OMBUDSMANSHIPS
OMINOUSNESS
OMINOUSNESSES
OMISSIVENESS
OMISSIVENESSES
OMITTANCES
OMMATIDIAL
OMMATIDIUM
OMMATOPHORE
OMMATOPHORES
OMMATOPHOROUS
OMNIBENEVOLENCE
OMNIBENEVOLENT
OMNIBUSSES
OMNICOMPETENCE
OMNICOMPETENCES
OMNICOMPETENT
OMNIDIRECTIONAL
OMNIFARIOUS
OMNIFARIOUSLY
OMNIFARIOUSNESS
OMNIFEROUS
OMNIFICENCE
OMNIFICENCES
OMNIFICENT
OMNIFORMITIES
OMNIFORMITY
OMNIGENOUS
OMNIPARITIES
OMNIPARITY
OMNIPAROUS
OMNIPATIENT
OMNIPOTENCE
OMNIPOTENCES
OMNIPOTENCIES
OMNIPOTENCY
OMNIPOTENT
OMNIPOTENTLY
OMNIPOTENTS
OMNIPRESENCE
OMNIPRESENCES
OMNIPRESENT
OMNIRANGES
OMNISCIENCE
OMNISCIENCES
OMNISCIENT
OMNISCIENTLY
OMNIVORIES
OMNIVOROUS
OMNIVOROUSLY
OMNIVOROUSNESS
OMOPHAGIAS
OMOPHAGIES
OMOPHAGOUS
OMOPHORION
OMOPLATOSCOPIES
OMOPLATOSCOPY
OMPHACITES
OMPHALOMANCIES
OMPHALOMANCY
OMPHALOSKEPSES
OMPHALOSKEPSIS
ONAGRACEOUS
ONCHOCERCIASES
ONCHOCERCIASIS
ONCOGENESES
ONCOGENESIS
ONCOGENETICIST
ONCOGENETICISTS
ONCOGENICITIES
ONCOGENICITY
ONCOGENOUS
ONCOLOGICAL
ONCOLOGIES
ONCOLOGIST
ONCOLOGISTS
ONCOLYTICS
ONCOMETERS
ONCORNAVIRUS
ONCORNAVIRUSES
ONCOTOMIES
ONCOVIRUSES
ONDOGRAPHS
ONEIRICALLY
ONEIROCRITIC
ONEIROCRITICAL
ONEIROCRITICISM
ONEIROCRITICS
ONEIRODYNIA
ONEIRODYNIAS
ONEIROLOGIES
ONEIROLOGY
ONEIROMANCER
ONEIROMANCERS
ONEIROMANCIES
ONEIROMANCY
ONEIROSCOPIES
ONEIROSCOPIST
ONEIROSCOPISTS
ONEIROSCOPY
ONEROUSNESS
ONEROUSNESSES
ONGOINGNESS
ONGOINGNESSES
ONIONSKINS
ONOCENTAUR
ONOCENTAURS
ONOMASIOLOGIES
ONOMASIOLOGY
ONOMASTICALLY
ONOMASTICIAN
ONOMASTICIANS
ONOMASTICON
ONOMASTICONS
ONOMASTICS
ONOMATOLOGIES
ONOMATOLOGIST
ONOMATOLOGISTS
ONOMATOLOGY
ONOMATOPOEIA
ONOMATOPOEIAS
ONOMATOPOEIC
ONOMATOPOESES
ONOMATOPOESIS
ONOMATOPOETIC
ONOMATOPOIESES
ONOMATOPOIESIS
ONSETTINGS
ONSHORINGS
ONSLAUGHTS
ONTOGENESES
ONTOGENESIS
ONTOGENETIC
ONTOGENETICALLY
ONTOGENICALLY
ONTOGENIES
ONTOLOGICAL
ONTOLOGICALLY
ONTOLOGIES
ONTOLOGIST
ONTOLOGISTS
ONYCHITISES
ONYCHOCRYPTOSES
ONYCHOCRYPTOSIS
ONYCHOMANCIES
ONYCHOMANCY
ONYCHOPHAGIES
ONYCHOPHAGIST
ONYCHOPHAGISTS
ONYCHOPHAGY
ONYCHOPHORAN
ONYCHOPHORANS
OOPHORECTOMIES
OOPHORECTOMISE
OOPHORECTOMISED
OOPHORECTOMISES
OOPHORECTOMIZE
OOPHORECTOMIZED
OOPHORECTOMIZES
OOPHORECTOMY
OOPHORITIC
OOPHORITIS
OOPHORITISES
OOZINESSES
OPACIFIERS
OPACIFYING
OPALESCENCE
OPALESCENCES
OPALESCENT
OPALESCENTLY
OPALESCING
OPAQUENESS
OPAQUENESSES
OPEIDOSCOPE
OPEIDOSCOPES
OPENABILITIES
OPENABILITY
OPENHANDED
OPENHANDEDLY
OPENHANDEDNESS
OPENHEARTED
OPENHEARTEDLY
OPENHEARTEDNESS
OPENMOUTHED
OPENMOUTHEDLY
OPENMOUTHEDNESS
OPENNESSES
OPERABILITIES
OPERABILITY
OPERAGOERS
OPERAGOING
OPERAGOINGS
OPERATICALLY
OPERATIONAL
OPERATIONALISM
OPERATIONALISMS
OPERATIONALIST
OPERATIONALISTS
OPERATIONALLY
OPERATIONISM
OPERATIONISMS
OPERATIONIST
OPERATIONISTS
OPERATIONS
OPERATISED
OPERATISES
OPERATISING
OPERATIVELY
OPERATIVENESS
OPERATIVENESSES
OPERATIVES
OPERATIVITIES
OPERATIVITY
OPERATIZED
OPERATIZES
OPERATIZING
OPERATORLESS
OPERCULARS
OPERCULATE
OPERCULATED
OPERCULUMS
OPERETTIST
OPERETTISTS
OPEROSENESS
OPEROSENESSES
OPEROSITIES
OPHICALCITE
OPHICALCITES
OPHICLEIDE
OPHICLEIDES
OPHIDIARIA
OPHIDIARIUM
OPHIDIARIUMS
OPHIOLATER
OPHIOLATERS
OPHIOLATRIES
OPHIOLATROUS
OPHIOLATRY
OPHIOLITES
OPHIOLITIC
OPHIOLOGIC
OPHIOLOGICAL
OPHIOLOGIES
OPHIOLOGIST
OPHIOLOGISTS
OPHIOMORPH
OPHIOMORPHIC
OPHIOMORPHOUS
OPHIOMORPHS
OPHIOPHAGOUS
OPHIOPHILIST

OPHIOPHILISTS
OPHIUROIDS
OPHTHALMIA
OPHTHALMIAS
OPHTHALMIC
OPHTHALMIST
OPHTHALMISTS
OPHTHALMITIS
OPHTHALMITISES
OPHTHALMOLOGIC
OPHTHALMOLOGIES
OPHTHALMOLOGIST
OPHTHALMOLOGY
OPHTHALMOMETER
OPHTHALMOMETERS
OPHTHALMOMETRY
OPHTHALMOPHOBIA
OPHTHALMOPLEGIA
OPHTHALMOSCOPE
OPHTHALMOSCOPES
OPHTHALMOSCOPIC
OPHTHALMOSCOPY
OPINICUSES
OPINIONATED
OPINIONATEDLY
OPINIONATEDNESS
OPINIONATELY
OPINIONATIVE
OPINIONATIVELY
OPINIONATOR
OPINIONATORS
OPINIONIST
OPINIONISTS
OPISOMETER
OPISOMETERS
OPISTHOBRANCH
OPISTHOBRANCHS
OPISTHOCOELIAN
OPISTHOCOELOUS
OPISTHODOMAI
OPISTHODOMOS
OPISTHOGLOSSAL
OPISTHOGNATHISM
OPISTHOGNATHOUS
OPISTHOGRAPH
OPISTHOGRAPHIC
OPISTHOGRAPHIES
OPISTHOGRAPHS
OPISTHOGRAPHY
OPISTHOSOMA
OPISTHOSOMATA
OPISTHOTONIC
OPISTHOTONOS
OPISTHOTONOSES
OPOBALSAMS
OPODELDOCS
OPOPANAXES
OPOTHERAPIES
OPOTHERAPY
OPPIGNERATE
OPPIGNERATED
OPPIGNERATES
OPPIGNERATING
OPPIGNORATE
OPPIGNORATED
OPPIGNORATES
OPPIGNORATING
OPPIGNORATION
OPPIGNORATIONS
OPPILATING
OPPILATION
OPPILATIONS
OPPILATIVE
OPPONENCIES
OPPORTUNELY
OPPORTUNENESS
OPPORTUNENESSES
OPPORTUNISM
OPPORTUNISMS
OPPORTUNIST
OPPORTUNISTIC
OPPORTUNISTS
OPPORTUNITIES
OPPORTUNITY
OPPOSABILITIES
OPPOSABILITY
OPPOSELESS
OPPOSINGLY
OPPOSITELY
OPPOSITENESS
OPPOSITENESSES
OPPOSITION
OPPOSITIONAL
OPPOSITIONIST
OPPOSITIONISTS
OPPOSITIONLESS
OPPOSITIONS
OPPOSITIVE
OPPRESSING
OPPRESSINGLY
OPPRESSION
OPPRESSIONS
OPPRESSIVE
OPPRESSIVELY
OPPRESSIVENESS
OPPRESSORS
OPPROBRIOUS
OPPROBRIOUSLY
OPPROBRIOUSNESS
OPPROBRIUM
OPPROBRIUMS
OPPUGNANCIES
OPPUGNANCY
OPPUGNANTLY
OPPUGNANTS
OPSIMATHIES
OPSIOMETER
OPSIOMETERS
OPSOMANIAC
OPSOMANIACS
OPSOMANIAS
OPSONIFICATION
OPSONIFICATIONS
OPSONIFIED
OPSONIFIES
OPSONIFYING
OPSONISATION
OPSONISATIONS
OPSONISING
OPSONIZATION
OPSONIZATIONS
OPSONIZING
OPTATIVELY
OPTIMALISATION
OPTIMALISATIONS
OPTIMALISE
OPTIMALISED
OPTIMALISES
OPTIMALISING
OPTIMALITIES
OPTIMALITY
OPTIMALIZATION
OPTIMALIZATIONS
OPTIMALIZE
OPTIMALIZED
OPTIMALIZES
OPTIMALIZING
OPTIMISATION
OPTIMISATIONS
OPTIMISERS
OPTIMISING
OPTIMISTIC
OPTIMISTICAL
OPTIMISTICALLY
OPTIMIZATION
OPTIMIZATIONS
OPTIMIZERS
OPTIMIZING
OPTIONALITIES
OPTIONALITY
OPTIONALLY
OPTOACOUSTIC
OPTOELECTRONIC
OPTOELECTRONICS
OPTOKINETIC
OPTOLOGIES
OPTOLOGIST
OPTOLOGISTS
OPTOMETERS
OPTOMETRIC
OPTOMETRICAL
OPTOMETRIES
OPTOMETRIST
OPTOMETRISTS
OPTOPHONES
OPULENCIES
ORACULARITIES
ORACULARITY
ORACULARLY
ORACULARNESS
ORACULARNESSES
ORACULOUSLY
ORACULOUSNESS
ORACULOUSNESSES
ORANGEADES
ORANGERIES
ORANGEWOOD
ORANGEWOODS
ORANGUTANS
ORATORIANS
ORATORICAL
ORATORICALLY
ORATRESSES
ORBICULARES
ORBICULARIS
ORBICULARITIES
ORBICULARITY
ORBICULARLY
ORBICULATE
ORBICULATED
ORCHARDING
ORCHARDINGS
ORCHARDIST
ORCHARDISTS
ORCHARDMAN
ORCHARDMEN
ORCHESOGRAPHIES
ORCHESOGRAPHY
ORCHESTICS
ORCHESTRAL
ORCHESTRALIST
ORCHESTRALISTS
ORCHESTRALLY
ORCHESTRAS
ORCHESTRATE
ORCHESTRATED
ORCHESTRATER
ORCHESTRATERS
ORCHESTRATES
ORCHESTRATING
ORCHESTRATION
ORCHESTRATIONAL
ORCHESTRATIONS
ORCHESTRATOR
ORCHESTRATORS
ORCHESTRIC
ORCHESTRINA
ORCHESTRINAS
ORCHESTRION
ORCHESTRIONS
ORCHIDACEOUS
ORCHIDECTOMIES
ORCHIDECTOMY
ORCHIDEOUS
ORCHIDISTS
ORCHIDLIKE
ORCHIDOLOGIES
ORCHIDOLOGIST
ORCHIDOLOGISTS
ORCHIDOLOGY
ORCHIDOMANIA
ORCHIDOMANIAC
ORCHIDOMANIACS
ORCHIDOMANIAS
ORCHIECTOMIES
ORCHIECTOMY
ORCHITISES
ORDAINABLE
ORDAINMENT
ORDAINMENTS
ORDERLINESS
ORDERLINESSES
ORDINAIRES
ORDINANCES
ORDINARIER
ORDINARIES
ORDINARIEST
ORDINARILY
ORDINARINESS
ORDINARINESSES
ORDINATELY
ORDINATING
ORDINATION
ORDINATIONS

ORDONNANCE
ORDONNANCES
ORECCHIETTE
ORECCHIETTI
OREOGRAPHIC
OREOGRAPHICAL
OREOGRAPHIES
OREOGRAPHY
OREOLOGICAL
OREOLOGIES
OREOLOGIST
OREOLOGISTS
OREPEARCHED
OREPEARCHES
OREPEARCHING
ORGANELLES
ORGANICALLY
ORGANICISM
ORGANICISMS
ORGANICIST
ORGANICISTIC
ORGANICISTS
ORGANICITIES
ORGANICITY
ORGANISABILITY
ORGANISABLE
ORGANISATION
ORGANISATIONAL
ORGANISATIONS
ORGANISERS
ORGANISING
ORGANISMAL
ORGANISMALLY
ORGANISMIC
ORGANISMICALLY
ORGANISTRUM
ORGANISTRUMS
ORGANITIES
ORGANIZABILITY
ORGANIZABLE
ORGANIZATION
ORGANIZATIONAL
ORGANIZATIONS
ORGANIZERS
ORGANIZING
ORGANOCHLORINE
ORGANOCHLORINES
ORGANOGENESES
ORGANOGENESIS
ORGANOGENETIC
ORGANOGENIES
ORGANOGENY
ORGANOGRAM
ORGANOGRAMS
ORGANOGRAPHIC
ORGANOGRAPHICAL
ORGANOGRAPHIES
ORGANOGRAPHIST
ORGANOGRAPHISTS
ORGANOGRAPHY
ORGANOLEPTIC
ORGANOLOGICAL
ORGANOLOGIES
ORGANOLOGIST
ORGANOLOGISTS
ORGANOLOGY
ORGANOMERCURIAL
ORGANOMETALLIC
ORGANOMETALLICS
ORGANOPHOSPHATE
ORGANOSOLS
ORGANOTHERAPIES
ORGANOTHERAPY
ORGANZINES
ORGIASTICALLY
ORICALCHES
ORICHALCEOUS
ORIENTALISE
ORIENTALISED
ORIENTALISES
ORIENTALISING
ORIENTALISM
ORIENTALISMS
ORIENTALIST
ORIENTALISTS
ORIENTALITIES
ORIENTALITY
ORIENTALIZE
ORIENTALIZED
ORIENTALIZES
ORIENTALIZING
ORIENTALLY
ORIENTATED
ORIENTATES
ORIENTATING
ORIENTATION
ORIENTATIONAL
ORIENTATIONALLY
ORIENTATIONS
ORIENTATOR
ORIENTATORS
ORIENTEERED
ORIENTEERING
ORIENTEERINGS
ORIENTEERS
ORIFLAMMES
ORIGINALITIES
ORIGINALITY
ORIGINALLY
ORIGINATED
ORIGINATES
ORIGINATING
ORIGINATION
ORIGINATIONS
ORIGINATIVE
ORIGINATIVELY
ORIGINATOR
ORIGINATORS
ORINASALLY
ORISMOLOGICAL
ORISMOLOGIES
ORISMOLOGY
ORNAMENTAL
ORNAMENTALLY
ORNAMENTALS
ORNAMENTATION
ORNAMENTATIONS
ORNAMENTED
ORNAMENTER
ORNAMENTERS
ORNAMENTING
ORNAMENTIST
ORNAMENTISTS
ORNATENESS
ORNATENESSES
ORNERINESS
ORNERINESSES
ORNITHICHNITE
ORNITHICHNITES
ORNITHINES
ORNITHISCHIAN
ORNITHISCHIANS
ORNITHODELPHIAN
ORNITHODELPHIC
ORNITHODELPHOUS
ORNITHOGALUM
ORNITHOGALUMS
ORNITHOLOGIC
ORNITHOLOGICAL
ORNITHOLOGIES
ORNITHOLOGIST
ORNITHOLOGISTS
ORNITHOLOGY
ORNITHOMANCIES
ORNITHOMANCY
ORNITHOMANTIC
ORNITHOMORPH
ORNITHOMORPHIC
ORNITHOMORPHS
ORNITHOPHILIES
ORNITHOPHILOUS
ORNITHOPHILY
ORNITHOPHOBIA
ORNITHOPHOBIAS
ORNITHOPOD
ORNITHOPODS
ORNITHOPTER
ORNITHOPTERS
ORNITHORHYNCHUS
ORNITHOSAUR
ORNITHOSAURS
ORNITHOSCOPIES
ORNITHOSCOPY
ORNITHOSES
ORNITHOSIS
OROBANCHACEOUS
OROGENESES
OROGENESIS
OROGENETIC
OROGENETICALLY
OROGENICALLY
OROGRAPHER
OROGRAPHERS
OROGRAPHIC
OROGRAPHICAL
OROGRAPHICALLY
OROGRAPHIES
OROLOGICAL
OROLOGICALLY
OROLOGISTS
OROPHARYNGEAL
OROPHARYNGES
OROPHARYNX
OROPHARYNXES
OROROTUNDITIES
OROROTUNDITY
OROTUNDITIES
OROTUNDITY
ORPHANAGES
ORPHANHOOD
ORPHANHOODS
ORPHANISMS
ORPHARIONS
ORPHEOREON
ORPHEOREONS
ORPHICALLY
ORRISROOTS
ORTANIQUES
ORTHOBORATE
ORTHOBORATES
ORTHOBORIC
ORTHOCAINE
ORTHOCAINES
ORTHOCENTER
ORTHOCENTERS
ORTHOCENTRE
ORTHOCENTRES
ORTHOCEPHALIC
ORTHOCEPHALIES
ORTHOCEPHALOUS
ORTHOCEPHALY
ORTHOCHROMATIC
ORTHOCHROMATISM
ORTHOCLASE
ORTHOCLASES
ORTHOCOUSINS
ORTHODIAGONAL
ORTHODIAGONALS
ORTHODONTIA
ORTHODONTIAS
ORTHODONTIC
ORTHODONTICALLY
ORTHODONTICS
ORTHODONTIST
ORTHODONTISTS
ORTHODOXES
ORTHODOXIES
ORTHODOXLY
ORTHODROMIC
ORTHODROMICS
ORTHODROMIES
ORTHODROMY
ORTHOEPICAL
ORTHOEPICALLY
ORTHOEPIES
ORTHOEPIST
ORTHOEPISTS
ORTHOGENESES
ORTHOGENESIS
ORTHOGENETIC
ORTHOGENIC
ORTHOGENICALLY
ORTHOGENICS
ORTHOGNATHIC
ORTHOGNATHIES
ORTHOGNATHISM
ORTHOGNATHISMS
ORTHOGNATHOUS
ORTHOGNATHY
ORTHOGONAL
ORTHOGONALISE
ORTHOGONALISED
ORTHOGONALISES
ORTHOGONALISING

ORTHOGONALITIES
ORTHOGONALITY
ORTHOGONALIZE
ORTHOGONALIZED
ORTHOGONALIZES
ORTHOGONALIZING
ORTHOGONALLY
ORTHOGRADE
ORTHOGRAPH
ORTHOGRAPHER
ORTHOGRAPHERS
ORTHOGRAPHIC
ORTHOGRAPHICAL
ORTHOGRAPHIES
ORTHOGRAPHIST
ORTHOGRAPHISTS
ORTHOGRAPHS
ORTHOGRAPHY
ORTHOHYDROGEN
ORTHOHYDROGENS
ORTHOMOLECULAR
ORTHOMORPHIC
ORTHONORMAL
ORTHOPAEDIC
ORTHOPAEDICAL
ORTHOPAEDICS
ORTHOPAEDIES
ORTHOPAEDIST
ORTHOPAEDISTS
ORTHOPAEDY
ORTHOPEDIA
ORTHOPEDIAS
ORTHOPEDIC
ORTHOPEDICAL
ORTHOPEDICALLY
ORTHOPEDICS
ORTHOPEDIES
ORTHOPEDIST
ORTHOPEDISTS
ORTHOPHOSPHATE
ORTHOPHOSPHATES
ORTHOPHOSPHORIC
ORTHOPHYRE
ORTHOPHYRES
ORTHOPHYRIC
ORTHOPINAKOID
ORTHOPINAKOIDS
ORTHOPNOEA
ORTHOPNOEAS
ORTHOPRAXES
ORTHOPRAXIES
ORTHOPRAXIS
ORTHOPRAXY
ORTHOPRISM
ORTHOPRISMS
ORTHOPSYCHIATRY
ORTHOPTERA
ORTHOPTERAN
ORTHOPTERANS
ORTHOPTERIST
ORTHOPTERISTS
ORTHOPTEROID
ORTHOPTEROIDS
ORTHOPTEROLOGY
ORTHOPTERON
ORTHOPTEROUS
ORTHOPTERS
ORTHOPTICS
ORTHOPTIST
ORTHOPTISTS
ORTHOPYROXENE
ORTHOPYROXENES
ORTHORHOMBIC
ORTHOSCOPE
ORTHOSCOPES
ORTHOSCOPIC
ORTHOSILICATE
ORTHOSILICATES
ORTHOSTATIC
ORTHOSTICHIES
ORTHOSTICHOUS
ORTHOSTICHY
ORTHOTISTS
ORTHOTONES
ORTHOTONESES
ORTHOTONESIS
ORTHOTONIC
ORTHOTOPIC
ORTHOTROPIC
ORTHOTROPIES
ORTHOTROPISM
ORTHOTROPISMS
ORTHOTROPOUS
ORTHOTROPY
ORYCTOLOGIES
ORYCTOLOGY
OSCILLATED
OSCILLATES
OSCILLATING
OSCILLATION
OSCILLATIONAL
OSCILLATIONS
OSCILLATIVE
OSCILLATOR
OSCILLATORS
OSCILLATORY
OSCILLOGRAM
OSCILLOGRAMS
OSCILLOGRAPH
OSCILLOGRAPHIC
OSCILLOGRAPHIES
OSCILLOGRAPHS
OSCILLOGRAPHY
OSCILLOSCOPE
OSCILLOSCOPES
OSCILLOSCOPIC
OSCITANCES
OSCITANCIES
OSCITANTLY
OSCITATING
OSCITATION
OSCITATIONS
OSCULATING
OSCULATION
OSCULATIONS
OSCULATORIES
OSCULATORY
OSMETERIUM
OSMIDROSES
OSMIDROSIS
OSMIRIDIUM
OSMIRIDIUMS
OSMOLALITIES
OSMOLALITY
OSMOLARITIES
OSMOLARITY
OSMOMETERS
OSMOMETRIC
OSMOMETRICALLY
OSMOMETRIES
OSMOREGULATION
OSMOREGULATIONS
OSMOREGULATORY
OSMOTICALLY
OSMUNDINES
OSSIFEROUS
OSSIFICATION
OSSIFICATIONS
OSSIFRAGAS
OSSIFRAGES
OSSIVOROUS
OSTEICHTHYAN
OSTEICHTHYANS
OSTEITIDES
OSTEITISES
OSTENSIBILITIES
OSTENSIBILITY
OSTENSIBLE
OSTENSIBLY
OSTENSIVELY
OSTENSORIA
OSTENSORIES
OSTENSORIUM
OSTENTATION
OSTENTATIONS
OSTENTATIOUS
OSTENTATIOUSLY
OSTEOARTHRITIC
OSTEOARTHRITICS
OSTEOARTHRITIS
OSTEOARTHROSES
OSTEOARTHROSIS
OSTEOBLAST
OSTEOBLASTIC
OSTEOBLASTS
OSTEOCLASES
OSTEOCLASIS
OSTEOCLAST
OSTEOCLASTIC
OSTEOCLASTS
OSTEOCOLLA
OSTEOCOLLAS
OSTEOCYTES
OSTEODERMAL
OSTEODERMATOUS
OSTEODERMIC
OSTEODERMOUS
OSTEODERMS
OSTEOFIBROSES
OSTEOFIBROSIS
OSTEOGENESES
OSTEOGENESIS
OSTEOGENETIC
OSTEOGENIC
OSTEOGENIES
OSTEOGENOUS
OSTEOGRAPHIES
OSTEOGRAPHY
OSTEOLOGICAL
OSTEOLOGICALLY
OSTEOLOGIES
OSTEOLOGIST
OSTEOLOGISTS
OSTEOMALACIA
OSTEOMALACIAL
OSTEOMALACIAS
OSTEOMALACIC
OSTEOMYELITIS
OSTEOMYELITISES
OSTEOPATHIC
OSTEOPATHICALLY
OSTEOPATHIES
OSTEOPATHIST
OSTEOPATHISTS
OSTEOPATHS
OSTEOPATHY
OSTEOPETROSES
OSTEOPETROSIS
OSTEOPHYTE
OSTEOPHYTES
OSTEOPHYTIC
OSTEOPLASTIC
OSTEOPLASTIES
OSTEOPLASTY
OSTEOPOROSES
OSTEOPOROSIS
OSTEOPOROTIC
OSTEOSARCOMA
OSTEOSARCOMAS
OSTEOSARCOMATA
OSTEOSISES
OSTEOTOMES
OSTEOTOMIES
OSTLERESSES
OSTRACEOUS
OSTRACISABLE
OSTRACISED
OSTRACISER
OSTRACISERS
OSTRACISES
OSTRACISING
OSTRACISMS
OSTRACIZABLE
OSTRACIZED
OSTRACIZER
OSTRACIZERS
OSTRACIZES
OSTRACIZING
OSTRACODAN
OSTRACODERM
OSTRACODERMS
OSTRACODES
OSTRACODOUS
OSTREACEOUS
OSTREICULTURE
OSTREICULTURES
OSTREICULTURIST
OSTREOPHAGE
OSTREOPHAGES
OSTREOPHAGIES
OSTREOPHAGOUS
OSTREOPHAGY
OSTRICHISM
OSTRICHISMS

OSTRICHLIKE
OTHERGATES
OTHERGUESS
OTHERNESSES
OTHERWHERE
OTHERWHILE
OTHERWHILES
OTHERWORLD
OTHERWORLDISH
OTHERWORLDLY
OTHERWORLDS
OTIOSENESS
OTIOSENESSES
OTIOSITIES
OTOLARYNGOLOGY
OTOLOGICAL
OTOLOGISTS
OTOPLASTIES
OTORRHOEAS
OTOSCLEROSES
OTOSCLEROSIS
OTOSCOPIES
OTOTOXICITIES
OTOTOXICITY
OTTRELITES
OUANANICHE
OUANANICHES
OUBLIETTES
OUGHTLINGS
OUGHTNESSES
OUROBOROSES
OUROLOGIES
OUROSCOPIES
OUTACHIEVE
OUTACHIEVED
OUTACHIEVES
OUTACHIEVING
OUTARGUING
OUTBACKERS
OUTBALANCE
OUTBALANCED
OUTBALANCES
OUTBALANCING
OUTBARGAIN
OUTBARGAINED
OUTBARGAINING
OUTBARGAINS
OUTBARKING
OUTBARRING
OUTBAWLING
OUTBEAMING
OUTBEGGING
OUTBIDDERS
OUTBIDDING
OUTBITCHED
OUTBITCHES
OUTBITCHING
OUTBLAZING
OUTBLEATED
OUTBLEATING
OUTBLESSED
OUTBLESSES
OUTBLESSING
OUTBLOOMED
OUTBLOOMING
OUTBLUFFED
OUTBLUFFING
OUTBLUSHED
OUTBLUSHES
OUTBLUSHING
OUTBLUSTER
OUTBLUSTERED
OUTBLUSTERING
OUTBLUSTERS
OUTBOASTED
OUTBOASTING
OUTBRAGGED
OUTBRAGGING
OUTBRAVING
OUTBRAWLED
OUTBRAWLING
OUTBRAZENED
OUTBRAZENING
OUTBRAZENS
OUTBREAKING
OUTBREATHE
OUTBREATHED
OUTBREATHES
OUTBREATHING
OUTBREEDING
OUTBREEDINGS
OUTBRIBING
OUTBUILDING
OUTBUILDINGS
OUTBULGING
OUTBULKING
OUTBULLIED
OUTBULLIES
OUTBULLYING
OUTBURNING
OUTBURSTING
OUTCAPERED
OUTCAPERING
OUTCASTING
OUTCATCHES
OUTCATCHING
OUTCAVILED
OUTCAVILING
OUTCAVILLED
OUTCAVILLING
OUTCHARGED
OUTCHARGES
OUTCHARGING
OUTCHARMED
OUTCHARMING
OUTCHEATED
OUTCHEATING
OUTCHIDDEN
OUTCHIDING
OUTCLASSED
OUTCLASSES
OUTCLASSING
OUTCLIMBED
OUTCLIMBING
OUTCOACHED
OUTCOACHES
OUTCOACHING
OUTCOMPETE
OUTCOMPETED
OUTCOMPETES
OUTCOMPETING
OUTCOOKING
OUTCOUNTED
OUTCOUNTING
OUTCRAFTIED
OUTCRAFTIES
OUTCRAFTYING
OUTCRAWLED
OUTCRAWLING
OUTCROPPED
OUTCROPPING
OUTCROPPINGS
OUTCROSSED
OUTCROSSES
OUTCROSSING
OUTCROSSINGS
OUTCROWDED
OUTCROWDING
OUTCROWING
OUTCURSING
OUTDACIOUS
OUTDANCING
OUTDATEDLY
OUTDATEDNESS
OUTDATEDNESSES
OUTDAZZLED
OUTDAZZLES
OUTDAZZLING
OUTDEBATED
OUTDEBATES
OUTDEBATING
OUTDELIVER
OUTDELIVERED
OUTDELIVERING
OUTDELIVERS
OUTDESIGNED
OUTDESIGNING
OUTDESIGNS
OUTDISTANCE
OUTDISTANCED
OUTDISTANCES
OUTDISTANCING
OUTDODGING
OUTDOORSMAN
OUTDOORSMANSHIP
OUTDOORSMEN
OUTDRAGGED
OUTDRAGGING
OUTDRAWING
OUTDREAMED
OUTDREAMING
OUTDRESSED
OUTDRESSES
OUTDRESSING
OUTDRINKING
OUTDRIVING
OUTDROPPED
OUTDROPPING
OUTDUELING
OUTDUELLED
OUTDUELLING
OUTDWELLED
OUTDWELLING
OUTEARNING
OUTECHOING
OUTERCOATS
OUTERCOURSE
OUTERCOURSES
OUTERWEARS
OUTFABLING
OUTFANGTHIEF
OUTFANGTHIEVES
OUTFASTING
OUTFAWNING
OUTFEASTED
OUTFEASTING
OUTFEELING
OUTFENCING
OUTFIELDER
OUTFIELDERS
OUTFIGHTING
OUTFIGURED
OUTFIGURES
OUTFIGURING
OUTFINDING
OUTFISHING
OUTFITTERS
OUTFITTING
OUTFITTINGS
OUTFLANKED
OUTFLANKING
OUTFLASHED
OUTFLASHES
OUTFLASHING
OUTFLOATED
OUTFLOATING
OUTFLOWING
OUTFLOWINGS
OUTFLUSHED
OUTFLUSHES
OUTFLUSHING
OUTFOOLING
OUTFOOTING
OUTFROWNED
OUTFROWNING
OUTFUMBLED
OUTFUMBLES
OUTFUMBLING
OUTGAINING
OUTGALLOPED
OUTGALLOPING
OUTGALLOPS
OUTGAMBLED
OUTGAMBLES
OUTGAMBLING
OUTGASSING
OUTGASSINGS
OUTGENERAL
OUTGENERALED
OUTGENERALING
OUTGENERALLED
OUTGENERALLING
OUTGENERALS
OUTGIVINGS
OUTGLARING
OUTGLEAMED
OUTGLEAMING
OUTGLITTER
OUTGLITTERED
OUTGLITTERING
OUTGLITTERS
OUTGLOWING
OUTGNAWING
OUTGOINGNESS

OUTGOINGNESSES
OUTGRINNED
OUTGRINNING
OUTGROSSED
OUTGROSSES
OUTGROSSING
OUTGROWING
OUTGROWTHS
OUTGUESSED
OUTGUESSES
OUTGUESSING
OUTGUIDING
OUTGUNNING
OUTGUSHING
OUTHANDLED
OUTHANDLES
OUTHANDLING
OUTHAULERS
OUTHEARING
OUTHITTING
OUTHOMERED
OUTHOMERING
OUTHOWLING
OUTHUMORED
OUTHUMORING
OUTHUNTING
OUTHUSTLED
OUTHUSTLES
OUTHUSTLING
OUTINTRIGUE
OUTINTRIGUED
OUTINTRIGUES
OUTINTRIGUING
OUTJESTING
OUTJETTING
OUTJETTINGS
OUTJINXING
OUTJOCKEYED
OUTJOCKEYING
OUTJOCKEYS
OUTJUGGLED
OUTJUGGLES
OUTJUGGLING
OUTJUMPING
OUTJUTTING
OUTJUTTINGS
OUTKEEPING
OUTKICKING
OUTKILLING
OUTKISSING
OUTLANDERS
OUTLANDISH
OUTLANDISHLY
OUTLANDISHNESS
OUTLASTING
OUTLAUGHED
OUTLAUGHING
OUTLAUNCED
OUTLAUNCES
OUTLAUNCHED
OUTLAUNCHES
OUTLAUNCHING
OUTLAUNCING
OUTLAWRIES
OUTLEADING
OUTLEAPING
OUTLEARNED
OUTLEARNING
OUTLODGING
OUTLODGINGS
OUTLOOKING
OUTLUSTRED
OUTLUSTRES
OUTLUSTRING
OUTMANEUVER
OUTMANEUVERED
OUTMANEUVERING
OUTMANEUVERS
OUTMANIPULATE
OUTMANIPULATED
OUTMANIPULATES
OUTMANIPULATING
OUTMANNING
OUTMANOEUVRE
OUTMANOEUVRED
OUTMANOEUVRES
OUTMANOEUVRING
OUTMANTLED
OUTMANTLES
OUTMANTLING
OUTMARCHED
OUTMARCHES
OUTMARCHING
OUTMARRIAGE
OUTMARRIAGES
OUTMASTERED
OUTMASTERING
OUTMASTERS
OUTMATCHED
OUTMATCHES
OUTMATCHING
OUTMEASURE
OUTMEASURED
OUTMEASURES
OUTMEASURING
OUTMODEDLY
OUTMODEDNESS
OUTMODEDNESSES
OUTMUSCLED
OUTMUSCLES
OUTMUSCLING
OUTNIGHTED
OUTNIGHTING
OUTNUMBERED
OUTNUMBERING
OUTNUMBERS
OUTOFFICES
OUTORGANISE
OUTORGANISED
OUTORGANISES
OUTORGANISING
OUTORGANIZE
OUTORGANIZED
OUTORGANIZES
OUTORGANIZING
OUTPAINTED
OUTPAINTING
OUTPASSING
OUTPASSION
OUTPASSIONED
OUTPASSIONING
OUTPASSIONS
OUTPATIENT
OUTPATIENTS
OUTPEEPING
OUTPEERING
OUTPEOPLED
OUTPEOPLES
OUTPEOPLING
OUTPERFORM
OUTPERFORMED
OUTPERFORMING
OUTPERFORMS
OUTPITCHED
OUTPITCHES
OUTPITCHING
OUTPITYING
OUTPLACEMENT
OUTPLACEMENTS
OUTPLACERS
OUTPLACING
OUTPLANNED
OUTPLANNING
OUTPLAYING
OUTPLODDED
OUTPLODDING
OUTPLOTTED
OUTPLOTTING
OUTPOINTED
OUTPOINTING
OUTPOLITICK
OUTPOLITICKED
OUTPOLITICKING
OUTPOLITICKS
OUTPOLLING
OUTPOPULATE
OUTPOPULATED
OUTPOPULATES
OUTPOPULATING
OUTPORTERS
OUTPOURERS
OUTPOURING
OUTPOURINGS
OUTPOWERED
OUTPOWERING
OUTPRAYING
OUTPREACHED
OUTPREACHES
OUTPREACHING
OUTPREENED
OUTPREENING
OUTPRESSED
OUTPRESSES
OUTPRESSING
OUTPRICING
OUTPRIZING
OUTPRODUCE
OUTPRODUCED
OUTPRODUCES
OUTPRODUCING
OUTPROMISE
OUTPROMISED
OUTPROMISES
OUTPROMISING
OUTPULLING
OUTPUNCHED
OUTPUNCHES
OUTPUNCHING
OUTPURSUED
OUTPURSUES
OUTPURSUING
OUTPUSHING
OUTPUTTING
OUTQUARTERS
OUTQUOTING
OUTRAGEOUS
OUTRAGEOUSLY
OUTRAGEOUSNESS
OUTRAISING
OUTRANGING
OUTRANKING
OUTREACHED
OUTREACHES
OUTREACHING
OUTREADING
OUTREASONED
OUTREASONING
OUTREASONS
OUTREBOUND
OUTREBOUNDED
OUTREBOUNDING
OUTREBOUNDS
OUTRECKONED
OUTRECKONING
OUTRECKONS
OUTRECUIDANCE
OUTRECUIDANCES
OUTREDDENED
OUTREDDENING
OUTREDDENS
OUTREDDING
OUTREIGNED
OUTREIGNING
OUTRELIEFS
OUTREPRODUCE
OUTREPRODUCED
OUTREPRODUCES
OUTREPRODUCING
OUTRIGGERS
OUTRIGGING
OUTRIGHTLY
OUTRINGING
OUTRIVALED
OUTRIVALING
OUTRIVALLED
OUTRIVALLING
OUTROARING
OUTROCKING
OUTROLLING
OUTROOPERS
OUTROOTING
OUTRUNNERS
OUTRUNNING
OUTRUSHING
OUTSAILING
OUTSAVORED
OUTSAVORING
OUTSCHEMED
OUTSCHEMES
OUTSCHEMING
OUTSCOLDED
OUTSCOLDING
OUTSCOOPED
OUTSCOOPING

OUTSCORING
OUTSCORNED
OUTSCORNING
OUTSCREAMED
OUTSCREAMING
OUTSCREAMS
OUTSELLING
OUTSERVING
OUTSETTING
OUTSETTINGS
OUTSETTLEMENT
OUTSETTLEMENTS
OUTSHAMING
OUTSHINING
OUTSHOOTING
OUTSHOUTED
OUTSHOUTING
OUTSIDERNESS
OUTSIDERNESSES
OUTSINGING
OUTSINNING
OUTSITTING
OUTSKATING
OUTSLEEPING
OUTSLICKED
OUTSLICKING
OUTSMARTED
OUTSMARTING
OUTSMELLED
OUTSMELLING
OUTSMILING
OUTSMOKING
OUTSNORING
OUTSOARING
OUTSOURCED
OUTSOURCES
OUTSOURCING
OUTSOURCINGS
OUTSPANNED
OUTSPANNING
OUTSPARKLE
OUTSPARKLED
OUTSPARKLES
OUTSPARKLING
OUTSPEAKING
OUTSPECKLE
OUTSPECKLES
OUTSPEEDED
OUTSPEEDING
OUTSPELLED
OUTSPELLING
OUTSPENDING
OUTSPOKENLY
OUTSPOKENNESS
OUTSPOKENNESSES
OUTSPORTED
OUTSPORTING
OUTSPREADING
OUTSPREADS
OUTSPRINGING
OUTSPRINGS
OUTSPRINTED
OUTSPRINTING
OUTSPRINTS
OUTSTANDING
OUTSTANDINGLY
OUTSTARING
OUTSTARTED
OUTSTARTING
OUTSTATING
OUTSTATION
OUTSTATIONS
OUTSTAYING
OUTSTEERED
OUTSTEERING
OUTSTEPPED
OUTSTEPPING
OUTSTRAINED
OUTSTRAINING
OUTSTRAINS
OUTSTRETCH
OUTSTRETCHED
OUTSTRETCHES
OUTSTRETCHING
OUTSTRIDDEN
OUTSTRIDES
OUTSTRIDING
OUTSTRIKES
OUTSTRIKING
OUTSTRIPPED
OUTSTRIPPING
OUTSTRIVEN
OUTSTRIVES
OUTSTRIVING
OUTSTROKES
OUTSTUDIED
OUTSTUDIES
OUTSTUDYING
OUTSTUNTED
OUTSTUNTING
OUTSULKING
OUTSUMMING
OUTSWEARING
OUTSWEEPING
OUTSWEETEN
OUTSWEETENED
OUTSWEETENING
OUTSWEETENS
OUTSWELLED
OUTSWELLING
OUTSWIMMING
OUTSWINGER
OUTSWINGERS
OUTSWINGING
OUTSWOLLEN
OUTTALKING
OUTTASKING
OUTTELLING
OUTTHANKED
OUTTHANKING
OUTTHIEVED
OUTTHIEVES
OUTTHIEVING
OUTTHINKING
OUTTHOUGHT
OUTTHROBBED
OUTTHROBBING
OUTTHROWING
OUTTHRUSTED
OUTTHRUSTING
OUTTHRUSTS
OUTTONGUED
OUTTONGUES
OUTTONGUING
OUTTOPPING
OUTTOWERED
OUTTOWERING
OUTTRADING
OUTTRAVELED
OUTTRAVELING
OUTTRAVELLED
OUTTRAVELLING
OUTTRAVELS
OUTTRICKED
OUTTRICKING
OUTTROTTED
OUTTROTTING
OUTTRUMPED
OUTTRUMPING
OUTVALUING
OUTVAUNTED
OUTVAUNTING
OUTVENOMED
OUTVENOMING
OUTVILLAIN
OUTVILLAINED
OUTVILLAINING
OUTVILLAINS
OUTVOICING
OUTWAITING
OUTWALKING
OUTWARDNESS
OUTWARDNESSES
OUTWARRING
OUTWASTING
OUTWATCHED
OUTWATCHES
OUTWATCHING
OUTWEARIED
OUTWEARIES
OUTWEARING
OUTWEARYING
OUTWEEDING
OUTWEEPING
OUTWEIGHED
OUTWEIGHING
OUTWELLING
OUTWHIRLED
OUTWHIRLING
OUTWICKING
OUTWILLING
OUTWINDING
OUTWINGING
OUTWINNING
OUTWISHING
OUTWITTING
OUTWORKERS
OUTWORKING
OUTWORTHED
OUTWORTHING
OUTWRESTED
OUTWRESTING
OUTWRESTLE
OUTWRESTLED
OUTWRESTLES
OUTWRESTLING
OUTWRITING
OUTWRITTEN
OUTWROUGHT
OUTYELLING
OUTYELPING
OUTYIELDED
OUTYIELDING
OUVIRANDRA
OUVIRANDRAS
OVALBUMINS
OVALNESSES
OVARIECTOMIES
OVARIECTOMISED
OVARIECTOMIZED
OVARIECTOMY
OVARIOTOMIES
OVARIOTOMIST
OVARIOTOMISTS
OVARIOTOMY
OVARITIDES
OVARITISES
OVERABOUND
OVERABOUNDED
OVERABOUNDING
OVERABOUNDS
OVERABSTRACT
OVERABUNDANCE
OVERABUNDANCES
OVERABUNDANT
OVERACCENTUATE
OVERACCENTUATED
OVERACCENTUATES
OVERACHIEVE
OVERACHIEVED
OVERACHIEVEMENT
OVERACHIEVER
OVERACHIEVERS
OVERACHIEVES
OVERACHIEVING
OVERACTING
OVERACTION
OVERACTIONS
OVERACTIVE
OVERACTIVITIES
OVERACTIVITY
OVERADJUSTMENT
OVERADJUSTMENTS
OVERADVERTISE
OVERADVERTISED
OVERADVERTISES
OVERADVERTISING
OVERAGGRESSIVE
OVERAMBITIOUS
OVERAMPLIFIED
OVERANALYSED
OVERANALYSES
OVERANALYSING
OVERANALYSIS
OVERANALYTICAL
OVERANALYZE
OVERANALYZED
OVERANALYZES
OVERANALYZING
OVERANXIETIES
OVERANXIETY
OVERANXIOUS
OVERAPPLICATION
OVERARCHED

OVERARCHES
OVERARCHING
OVERARMING
OVERAROUSAL
OVERAROUSALS
OVERARRANGE
OVERARRANGED
OVERARRANGES
OVERARRANGING
OVERARTICULATE
OVERARTICULATED
OVERARTICULATES
OVERASSERT
OVERASSERTED
OVERASSERTING
OVERASSERTION
OVERASSERTIONS
OVERASSERTIVE
OVERASSERTS
OVERASSESSMENT
OVERASSESSMENTS
OVERATTENTION
OVERATTENTIONS
OVERATTENTIVE
OVERBAKING
OVERBALANCE
OVERBALANCED
OVERBALANCES
OVERBALANCING
OVERBEARING
OVERBEARINGLY
OVERBEARINGNESS
OVERBEATEN
OVERBEATING
OVERBEJEWELED
OVERBETTED
OVERBETTING
OVERBIDDEN
OVERBIDDER
OVERBIDDERS
OVERBIDDING
OVERBIDDINGS
OVERBILLED
OVERBILLING
OVERBLANKET
OVERBLANKETS
OVERBLEACH
OVERBLEACHED
OVERBLEACHES
OVERBLEACHING
OVERBLOUSE
OVERBLOUSES
OVERBLOWING
OVERBOILED
OVERBOILING
OVERBOLDLY
OVERBOOKED
OVERBOOKING
OVERBORROW
OVERBORROWED
OVERBORROWING
OVERBORROWS
OVERBOUGHT
OVERBOUNDED
OVERBOUNDING
OVERBOUNDS
OVERBRAKED
OVERBRAKES
OVERBRAKING
OVERBREATHING
OVERBREATHINGS
OVERBREEDING
OVERBREEDS
OVERBRIDGE
OVERBRIDGED
OVERBRIDGES
OVERBRIDGING
OVERBRIEFED
OVERBRIEFING
OVERBRIEFS
OVERBRIGHT
OVERBRIMMED
OVERBRIMMING
OVERBROWED
OVERBROWING
OVERBROWSE
OVERBROWSED
OVERBROWSES
OVERBROWSING
OVERBRUTAL
OVERBUILDING
OVERBUILDS
OVERBULKED
OVERBULKING
OVERBURDEN
OVERBURDENED
OVERBURDENING
OVERBURDENS
OVERBURDENSOME
OVERBURNED
OVERBURNING
OVERBURTHEN
OVERBURTHENED
OVERBURTHENING
OVERBURTHENS
OVERBUSIED
OVERBUSIES
OVERBUSYING
OVERBUYING
OVERCALLED
OVERCALLING
OVERCANOPIED
OVERCANOPIES
OVERCANOPY
OVERCANOPYING
OVERCAPACITIES
OVERCAPACITY
OVERCAPITALISE
OVERCAPITALISED
OVERCAPITALISES
OVERCAPITALIZE
OVERCAPITALIZED
OVERCAPITALIZES
OVERCAREFUL
OVERCARRIED
OVERCARRIES
OVERCARRYING
OVERCASTED
OVERCASTING
OVERCASTINGS
OVERCATCHES
OVERCATCHING
OVERCAUGHT
OVERCAUTION
OVERCAUTIONS
OVERCAUTIOUS
OVERCENTRALISE
OVERCENTRALISED
OVERCENTRALISES
OVERCENTRALIZE
OVERCENTRALIZED
OVERCENTRALIZES
OVERCHARGE
OVERCHARGED
OVERCHARGES
OVERCHARGING
OVERCHECKS
OVERCHILLED
OVERCHILLING
OVERCHILLS
OVERCIVILISED
OVERCIVILIZED
OVERCLAIMED
OVERCLAIMING
OVERCLAIMS
OVERCLASSES
OVERCLASSIFIED
OVERCLASSIFIES
OVERCLASSIFY
OVERCLASSIFYING
OVERCLEANED
OVERCLEANING
OVERCLEANS
OVERCLEARED
OVERCLEARING
OVERCLEARS
OVERCLOUDED
OVERCLOUDING
OVERCLOUDS
OVERCLOYED
OVERCLOYING
OVERCOACHED
OVERCOACHES
OVERCOACHING
OVERCOATING
OVERCOATINGS
OVERCOLORED
OVERCOLORING
OVERCOLORS
OVERCOLOUR
OVERCOLOURED
OVERCOLOURING
OVERCOLOURS
OVERCOMERS
OVERCOMING
OVERCOMMIT
OVERCOMMITMENT
OVERCOMMITMENTS
OVERCOMMITS
OVERCOMMITTED
OVERCOMMITTING
OVERCOMMUNICATE
OVERCOMPENSATE
OVERCOMPENSATED
OVERCOMPENSATES
OVERCOMPLEX
OVERCOMPLIANCE
OVERCOMPLIANCES
OVERCOMPLICATE
OVERCOMPLICATED
OVERCOMPLICATES
OVERCOMPRESS
OVERCOMPRESSED
OVERCOMPRESSES
OVERCOMPRESSING
OVERCONCERN
OVERCONCERNED
OVERCONCERNING
OVERCONCERNS
OVERCONFIDENCE
OVERCONFIDENCES
OVERCONFIDENT
OVERCONFIDENTLY
OVERCONSCIOUS
OVERCONSTRUCT
OVERCONSTRUCTED
OVERCONSTRUCTS
OVERCONSUME
OVERCONSUMED
OVERCONSUMES
OVERCONSUMING
OVERCONSUMPTION
OVERCONTROL
OVERCONTROLLED
OVERCONTROLLING
OVERCONTROLS
OVERCOOKED
OVERCOOKING
OVERCOOLED
OVERCOOLING
OVERCORRECT
OVERCORRECTED
OVERCORRECTING
OVERCORRECTION
OVERCORRECTIONS
OVERCORRECTS
OVERCOUNTED
OVERCOUNTING
OVERCOUNTS
OVERCOVERED
OVERCOVERING
OVERCOVERS
OVERCRAMMED
OVERCRAMMING
OVERCRAWED
OVERCRAWING
OVERCREDULITIES
OVERCREDULITY
OVERCREDULOUS
OVERCRITICAL
OVERCROPPED
OVERCROPPING
OVERCROWDED
OVERCROWDING
OVERCROWDINGS
OVERCROWDS
OVERCROWED
OVERCROWING
OVERCULTIVATION
OVERCURING
OVERCUTTING
OVERDARING
OVERDECKED
OVERDECKING

OVERDECORATE
OVERDECORATED
OVERDECORATES
OVERDECORATING
OVERDECORATION
OVERDECORATIONS
OVERDEMANDING
OVERDEPENDENCE
OVERDEPENDENCES
OVERDEPENDENT
OVERDESIGN
OVERDESIGNED
OVERDESIGNING
OVERDESIGNS
OVERDETERMINED
OVERDEVELOP
OVERDEVELOPED
OVERDEVELOPING
OVERDEVELOPMENT
OVERDEVELOPS
OVERDEVIATE
OVERDEVIATED
OVERDEVIATES
OVERDEVIATING
OVERDIRECT
OVERDIRECTED
OVERDIRECTING
OVERDIRECTS
OVERDISCOUNT
OVERDISCOUNTED
OVERDISCOUNTING
OVERDISCOUNTS
OVERDIVERSITIES
OVERDIVERSITY
OVERDOCUMENT
OVERDOCUMENTED
OVERDOCUMENTING
OVERDOCUMENTS
OVERDOMINANCE
OVERDOMINANCES
OVERDOMINANT
OVERDOSAGE
OVERDOSAGES
OVERDOSING
OVERDRAFTS
OVERDRAMATIC
OVERDRAMATISE
OVERDRAMATISED
OVERDRAMATISES
OVERDRAMATISING
OVERDRAMATIZE
OVERDRAMATIZED
OVERDRAMATIZES
OVERDRAMATIZING
OVERDRAUGHT
OVERDRAUGHTS
OVERDRAWING
OVERDRESSED
OVERDRESSES
OVERDRESSING
OVERDRINKING
OVERDRINKS
OVERDRIVEN
OVERDRIVES
OVERDRIVING
OVERDRYING
OVERDUBBED
OVERDUBBING
OVERDUSTED
OVERDUSTING
OVERDYEING
OVEREAGERNESS
OVEREAGERNESSES
OVEREARNEST
OVEREATERS
OVEREATING
OVEREDITED
OVEREDITING
OVEREDUCATE
OVEREDUCATED
OVEREDUCATES
OVEREDUCATING
OVEREDUCATION
OVEREDUCATIONS
OVEREGGING
OVERELABORATE
OVERELABORATED
OVERELABORATES
OVERELABORATING
OVERELABORATION
OVEREMBELLISH
OVEREMBELLISHED
OVEREMBELLISHES
OVEREMOTED
OVEREMOTES
OVEREMOTING
OVEREMOTIONAL
OVEREMPHASES
OVEREMPHASIS
OVEREMPHASISE
OVEREMPHASISED
OVEREMPHASISES
OVEREMPHASISING
OVEREMPHASIZE
OVEREMPHASIZED
OVEREMPHASIZES
OVEREMPHASIZING
OVEREMPHATIC
OVERENAMORED
OVERENCOURAGE
OVERENCOURAGED
OVERENCOURAGES
OVERENCOURAGING
OVERENERGETIC
OVERENGINEER
OVERENGINEERED
OVERENGINEERING
OVERENGINEERS
OVERENROLLED
OVERENTERTAINED
OVERENTHUSIASM
OVERENTHUSIASMS
OVEREQUIPPED
OVERESTIMATE
OVERESTIMATED
OVERESTIMATES
OVERESTIMATING
OVERESTIMATION
OVERESTIMATIONS
OVEREVALUATION
OVEREVALUATIONS
OVEREXAGGERATE
OVEREXAGGERATED
OVEREXAGGERATES
OVEREXCITABLE
OVEREXCITE
OVEREXCITED
OVEREXCITES
OVEREXCITING
OVEREXERCISE
OVEREXERCISED
OVEREXERCISES
OVEREXERCISING
OVEREXERTED
OVEREXERTING
OVEREXERTION
OVEREXERTIONS
OVEREXERTS
OVEREXPAND
OVEREXPANDED
OVEREXPANDING
OVEREXPANDS
OVEREXPANSION
OVEREXPANSIONS
OVEREXPECTATION
OVEREXPLAIN
OVEREXPLAINED
OVEREXPLAINING
OVEREXPLAINS
OVEREXPLICIT
OVEREXPLOIT
OVEREXPLOITED
OVEREXPLOITING
OVEREXPLOITS
OVEREXPOSE
OVEREXPOSED
OVEREXPOSES
OVEREXPOSING
OVEREXPOSURE
OVEREXPOSURES
OVEREXTEND
OVEREXTENDED
OVEREXTENDING
OVEREXTENDS
OVEREXTENSION
OVEREXTENSIONS
OVEREXTRACTION
OVEREXTRACTIONS
OVEREXTRAVAGANT
OVEREXUBERANT
OVEREYEING
OVERFACILE
OVERFALLEN
OVERFALLING
OVERFAMILIAR
OVERFAMILIARITY
OVERFASTIDIOUS
OVERFATIGUE
OVERFATIGUED
OVERFATIGUES
OVERFAVORED
OVERFAVORING
OVERFAVORS
OVERFEARED
OVERFEARING
OVERFEEDING
OVERFERTILISE
OVERFERTILISED
OVERFERTILISES
OVERFERTILISING
OVERFERTILIZE
OVERFERTILIZED
OVERFERTILIZES
OVERFERTILIZING
OVERFILLED
OVERFILLING
OVERFINENESS
OVERFINENESSES
OVERFINISHED
OVERFISHED
OVERFISHES
OVERFISHING
OVERFLIGHT
OVERFLIGHTS
OVERFLOODED
OVERFLOODING
OVERFLOODS
OVERFLOURISH
OVERFLOURISHED
OVERFLOURISHES
OVERFLOURISHING
OVERFLOWED
OVERFLOWING
OVERFLOWINGLY
OVERFLOWINGS
OVERFLUSHES
OVERFLYING
OVERFOCUSED
OVERFOCUSES
OVERFOCUSING
OVERFOCUSSED
OVERFOCUSSES
OVERFOCUSSING
OVERFOLDED
OVERFOLDING
OVERFONDLY
OVERFONDNESS
OVERFONDNESSES
OVERFORWARD
OVERFORWARDNESS
OVERFRAUGHT
OVERFREEDOM
OVERFREEDOMS
OVERFREELY
OVERFREIGHT
OVERFREIGHTING
OVERFREIGHTS
OVERFULFILL
OVERFULFILLED
OVERFULFILLING
OVERFULFILLS
OVERFULLNESS
OVERFULLNESSES
OVERFULNESS
OVERFULNESSES
OVERFUNDED
OVERFUNDING
OVERFUNDINGS
OVERGALLED
OVERGALLING
OVERGANGING
OVERGARMENT
OVERGARMENTS
OVERGEARED

OVERGEARING
OVERGENERALISE
OVERGENERALISED
OVERGENERALISES
OVERGENERALIZE
OVERGENERALIZED
OVERGENERALIZES
OVERGENEROSITY
OVERGENEROUS
OVERGENEROUSLY
OVERGETTING
OVERGILDED
OVERGILDING
OVERGIRDED
OVERGIRDING
OVERGIVING
OVERGLAMORISE
OVERGLAMORISED
OVERGLAMORISES
OVERGLAMORISING
OVERGLAMORIZE
OVERGLAMORIZED
OVERGLAMORIZES
OVERGLAMORIZING
OVERGLANCE
OVERGLANCED
OVERGLANCES
OVERGLANCING
OVERGLAZED
OVERGLAZES
OVERGLAZING
OVERGLOOMED
OVERGLOOMING
OVERGLOOMS
OVERGOADED
OVERGOADING
OVERGOINGS
OVERGORGED
OVERGORGES
OVERGORGING
OVERGOVERN
OVERGOVERNED
OVERGOVERNING
OVERGOVERNS
OVERGRADED
OVERGRADES
OVERGRADING
OVERGRAINED
OVERGRAINER
OVERGRAINERS
OVERGRAINING
OVERGRAINS
OVERGRASSED
OVERGRASSES
OVERGRASSING
OVERGRAZED
OVERGRAZES
OVERGRAZING
OVERGRAZINGS
OVERGREEDY
OVERGREENED
OVERGREENING
OVERGREENS
OVERGROUND
OVERGROWING
OVERGROWTH
OVERGROWTHS
OVERHAILED
OVERHAILES
OVERHAILING
OVERHALING
OVERHANDED
OVERHANDING
OVERHANDLE
OVERHANDLED
OVERHANDLES
OVERHANDLING
OVERHANGING
OVERHARVEST
OVERHARVESTED
OVERHARVESTING
OVERHARVESTS
OVERHASTES
OVERHASTILY
OVERHASTINESS
OVERHASTINESSES
OVERHATING
OVERHAULED
OVERHAULING
OVERHEAPED
OVERHEAPING
OVERHEARING
OVERHEATED
OVERHEATING
OVERHEATINGS
OVERHENTING
OVERHITTING
OVERHOLDING
OVERHOMOGENISE
OVERHOMOGENISED
OVERHOMOGENISES
OVERHOMOGENIZE
OVERHOMOGENIZED
OVERHOMOGENIZES
OVERHONORED
OVERHONORING
OVERHONORS
OVERHOPING
OVERHUNTED
OVERHUNTING
OVERHUNTINGS
OVERHYPING
OVERIDEALISE
OVERIDEALISED
OVERIDEALISES
OVERIDEALISING
OVERIDEALIZE
OVERIDEALIZED
OVERIDEALIZES
OVERIDEALIZING
OVERIDENTIFIED
OVERIDENTIFIES
OVERIDENTIFY
OVERIDENTIFYING
OVERIMAGINATIVE
OVERIMPRESS
OVERIMPRESSED
OVERIMPRESSES
OVERIMPRESSING
OVERINCLINE
OVERINCLINED
OVERINCLINES
OVERINCLINING
OVERINDULGE
OVERINDULGED
OVERINDULGENCE
OVERINDULGENCES
OVERINDULGENT
OVERINDULGES
OVERINDULGING
OVERINFLATE
OVERINFLATED
OVERINFLATES
OVERINFLATING
OVERINFLATION
OVERINFLATIONS
OVERINFORM
OVERINFORMED
OVERINFORMING
OVERINFORMS
OVERINGENIOUS
OVERINGENUITIES
OVERINGENUITY
OVERINSISTENT
OVERINSURANCE
OVERINSURANCES
OVERINSURE
OVERINSURED
OVERINSURES
OVERINSURING
OVERINTENSE
OVERINTENSITIES
OVERINTENSITY
OVERINVESTMENT
OVERINVESTMENTS
OVERISSUANCE
OVERISSUANCES
OVERISSUED
OVERISSUES
OVERISSUING
OVERJOYING
OVERJUMPED
OVERJUMPING
OVERKEEPING
OVERKILLED
OVERKILLING
OVERKINDNESS
OVERKINDNESSES
OVERLABORED
OVERLABORING
OVERLABORS
OVERLABOUR
OVERLABOURED
OVERLABOURING
OVERLABOURS
OVERLADING
OVERLANDED
OVERLANDER
OVERLANDERS
OVERLANDING
OVERLAPPED
OVERLAPPING
OVERLARDED
OVERLARDING
OVERLAUNCH
OVERLAUNCHED
OVERLAUNCHES
OVERLAUNCHING
OVERLAVISH
OVERLAYING
OVERLAYINGS
OVERLEAPED
OVERLEAPING
OVERLEARNED
OVERLEARNING
OVERLEARNS
OVERLEARNT
OVERLEATHER
OVERLEATHERS
OVERLEAVEN
OVERLEAVENED
OVERLEAVENING
OVERLEAVENS
OVERLENDING
OVERLENGTH
OVERLENGTHEN
OVERLENGTHENED
OVERLENGTHENING
OVERLENGTHENS
OVERLENGTHS
OVERLETTING
OVERLIGHTED
OVERLIGHTING
OVERLIGHTS
OVERLITERAL
OVERLITERARY
OVERLIVING
OVERLOADED
OVERLOADING
OVERLOCKED
OVERLOCKER
OVERLOCKERS
OVERLOCKING
OVERLOCKINGS
OVERLOOKED
OVERLOOKER
OVERLOOKERS
OVERLOOKING
OVERLORDED
OVERLORDING
OVERLORDSHIP
OVERLORDSHIPS
OVERLOVING
OVERMANAGE
OVERMANAGED
OVERMANAGES
OVERMANAGING
OVERMANNED
OVERMANNERED
OVERMANNING
OVERMANTEL
OVERMANTELS
OVERMASTED
OVERMASTER
OVERMASTERED
OVERMASTERING
OVERMASTERS
OVERMASTING
OVERMATCHED
OVERMATCHES
OVERMATCHING
OVERMATTER
OVERMATTERS
OVERMATURE

OVERMATURITIES
OVERMATURITY
OVERMEASURE
OVERMEASURED
OVERMEASURES
OVERMEASURING
OVERMEDICATE
OVERMEDICATED
OVERMEDICATES
OVERMEDICATING
OVERMEDICATION
OVERMEDICATIONS
OVERMELTED
OVERMELTING
OVERMIGHTY
OVERMILKED
OVERMILKING
OVERMINING
OVERMIXING
OVERMODEST
OVERMODESTLY
OVERMOUNTED
OVERMOUNTING
OVERMOUNTS
OVERMUCHES
OVERMULTIPLIED
OVERMULTIPLIES
OVERMULTIPLY
OVERMULTIPLYING
OVERMULTITUDE
OVERMULTITUDED
OVERMULTITUDES
OVERMULTITUDING
OVERMUSCLED
OVERNAMING
OVERNETTED
OVERNETTING
OVERNICELY
OVERNICENESS
OVERNICENESSES
OVERNIGHTED
OVERNIGHTER
OVERNIGHTERS
OVERNIGHTING
OVERNIGHTS
OVERNOURISH
OVERNOURISHED
OVERNOURISHES
OVERNOURISHING
OVERNUTRITION
OVERNUTRITIONS
OVEROBVIOUS
OVEROFFICE
OVEROFFICED
OVEROFFICES
OVEROFFICING
OVEROPERATE
OVEROPERATED
OVEROPERATES
OVEROPERATING
OVEROPINIONATED
OVEROPTIMISM
OVEROPTIMISMS
OVEROPTIMIST
OVEROPTIMISTIC
OVEROPTIMISTS
OVERORCHESTRATE
OVERORGANISE
OVERORGANISED
OVERORGANISES
OVERORGANISING
OVERORGANIZE
OVERORGANIZED
OVERORGANIZES
OVERORGANIZING
OVERORNAMENT
OVERORNAMENTED
OVERORNAMENTING
OVERORNAMENTS
OVERPACKAGE
OVERPACKAGED
OVERPACKAGES
OVERPACKAGING
OVERPACKED
OVERPACKING
OVERPAINTED
OVERPAINTING
OVERPAINTS
OVERPARTED
OVERPARTICULAR
OVERPARTING
OVERPASSED
OVERPASSES
OVERPASSING
OVERPAYING
OVERPAYMENT
OVERPAYMENTS
OVERPEDALED
OVERPEDALING
OVERPEDALLED
OVERPEDALLING
OVERPEDALS
OVERPEERED
OVERPEERING
OVERPEOPLE
OVERPEOPLED
OVERPEOPLES
OVERPEOPLING
OVERPERCHED
OVERPERCHES
OVERPERCHING
OVERPERSUADE
OVERPERSUADED
OVERPERSUADES
OVERPERSUADING
OVERPERSUASION
OVERPERSUASIONS
OVERPICTURE
OVERPICTURED
OVERPICTURES
OVERPICTURING
OVERPITCHED
OVERPITCHES
OVERPITCHING
OVERPLACED
OVERPLAIDED
OVERPLAIDS
OVERPLANNED
OVERPLANNING
OVERPLANTED
OVERPLANTING
OVERPLANTS
OVERPLAYED
OVERPLAYING
OVERPLOTTED
OVERPLOTTING
OVERPLUSES
OVERPLUSSES
OVERPLYING
OVERPOISED
OVERPOISES
OVERPOISING
OVERPOPULATE
OVERPOPULATED
OVERPOPULATES
OVERPOPULATING
OVERPOPULATION
OVERPOPULATIONS
OVERPOSTED
OVERPOSTING
OVERPOTENT
OVERPOWERED
OVERPOWERING
OVERPOWERINGLY
OVERPOWERS
OVERPRAISE
OVERPRAISED
OVERPRAISES
OVERPRAISING
OVERPRECISE
OVERPREPARATION
OVERPREPARE
OVERPREPARED
OVERPREPARES
OVERPREPARING
OVERPRESCRIBE
OVERPRESCRIBED
OVERPRESCRIBES
OVERPRESCRIBING
OVERPRESSED
OVERPRESSES
OVERPRESSING
OVERPRESSURE
OVERPRESSURES
OVERPRICED
OVERPRICES
OVERPRICING
OVERPRINTED
OVERPRINTING
OVERPRINTS
OVERPRIVILEGED
OVERPRIZED
OVERPRIZES
OVERPRIZING
OVERPROCESS
OVERPROCESSED
OVERPROCESSES
OVERPROCESSING
OVERPRODUCE
OVERPRODUCED
OVERPRODUCES
OVERPRODUCING
OVERPRODUCTION
OVERPRODUCTIONS
OVERPROGRAM
OVERPROGRAMED
OVERPROGRAMING
OVERPROGRAMMED
OVERPROGRAMMING
OVERPROGRAMS
OVERPROMISE
OVERPROMISED
OVERPROMISES
OVERPROMISING
OVERPROMOTE
OVERPROMOTED
OVERPROMOTES
OVERPROMOTING
OVERPROPORTION
OVERPROPORTIONS
OVERPROTECT
OVERPROTECTED
OVERPROTECTING
OVERPROTECTION
OVERPROTECTIONS
OVERPROTECTIVE
OVERPROTECTS
OVERPUMPED
OVERPUMPING
OVERQUALIFIED
OVERRACKED
OVERRACKING
OVERRAKING
OVERRASHLY
OVERRASHNESS
OVERRASHNESSES
OVERRATING
OVERRAUGHT
OVERREACHED
OVERREACHER
OVERREACHERS
OVERREACHES
OVERREACHING
OVERREACTED
OVERREACTING
OVERREACTION
OVERREACTIONS
OVERREACTS
OVERREADING
OVERRECKON
OVERRECKONED
OVERRECKONING
OVERRECKONS
OVERREDDED
OVERREDDING
OVERREFINE
OVERREFINED
OVERREFINEMENT
OVERREFINEMENTS
OVERREFINES
OVERREFINING
OVERREGULATE
OVERREGULATED
OVERREGULATES
OVERREGULATING
OVERREGULATION
OVERREGULATIONS
OVERRELIANCE
OVERRELIANCES
OVERRENNING
OVERREPORT
OVERREPORTED
OVERREPORTING
OVERREPORTS

OVERREPRESENTED
OVERRESPOND
OVERRESPONDED
OVERRESPONDING
OVERRESPONDS
OVERRIDDEN
OVERRIDERS
OVERRIDING
OVERRIPENED
OVERRIPENESS
OVERRIPENESSES
OVERRIPENING
OVERRIPENS
OVERROASTED
OVERROASTING
OVERROASTS
OVERRUFFED
OVERRUFFING
OVERRULERS
OVERRULING
OVERRULINGS
OVERRUNNER
OVERRUNNERS
OVERRUNNING
OVERSAILED
OVERSAILING
OVERSALTED
OVERSALTING
OVERSANGUINE
OVERSATURATE
OVERSATURATED
OVERSATURATES
OVERSATURATING
OVERSATURATION
OVERSATURATIONS
OVERSAUCED
OVERSAUCES
OVERSAUCING
OVERSAVING
OVERSCALED
OVERSCHUTCHT
OVERSCORED
OVERSCORES
OVERSCORING
OVERSCRUPULOUS
OVERSCUTCHED
OVERSECRETION
OVERSECRETIONS
OVERSEEDED
OVERSEEDING
OVERSEEING
OVERSELLING
OVERSENSITIVE
OVERSENSITIVITY
OVERSERIOUS
OVERSERIOUSLY
OVERSERVICE
OVERSERVICED
OVERSERVICES
OVERSERVICING
OVERSETTING
OVERSEWING
OVERSHADED
OVERSHADES
OVERSHADING
OVERSHADOW
OVERSHADOWED
OVERSHADOWING
OVERSHADOWS
OVERSHINES
OVERSHINING
OVERSHIRTS
OVERSHOOTING
OVERSHOOTS
OVERSHOWER
OVERSHOWERED
OVERSHOWERING
OVERSHOWERS
OVERSIGHTS
OVERSIMPLE
OVERSIMPLIFIED
OVERSIMPLIFIES
OVERSIMPLIFY
OVERSIMPLIFYING
OVERSIMPLISTIC
OVERSIMPLY
OVERSIZING
OVERSKIPPED
OVERSKIPPING
OVERSKIRTS
OVERSLAUGH
OVERSLAUGHED
OVERSLAUGHING
OVERSLAUGHS
OVERSLEEPING
OVERSLEEPS
OVERSLEEVE
OVERSLEEVES
OVERSLIPPED
OVERSLIPPING
OVERSMOKED
OVERSMOKES
OVERSMOKING
OVERSOAKED
OVERSOAKING
OVERSOLICITOUS
OVERSOWING
OVERSPECIALISE
OVERSPECIALISED
OVERSPECIALISES
OVERSPECIALIZE
OVERSPECIALIZED
OVERSPECIALIZES
OVERSPECULATE
OVERSPECULATED
OVERSPECULATES
OVERSPECULATING
OVERSPECULATION
OVERSPENDER
OVERSPENDERS
OVERSPENDING
OVERSPENDS
OVERSPICED
OVERSPICES
OVERSPICING
OVERSPILLED
OVERSPILLING
OVERSPILLS
OVERSPREAD
OVERSPREADING
OVERSPREADS
OVERSTABILITIES
OVERSTABILITY
OVERSTAFFED
OVERSTAFFING
OVERSTAFFS
OVERSTAINED
OVERSTAINING
OVERSTAINS
OVERSTANDING
OVERSTANDS
OVERSTARED
OVERSTARES
OVERSTARING
OVERSTATED
OVERSTATEMENT
OVERSTATEMENTS
OVERSTATES
OVERSTATING
OVERSTAYED
OVERSTAYER
OVERSTAYERS
OVERSTAYING
OVERSTEERED
OVERSTEERING
OVERSTEERS
OVERSTEPPED
OVERSTEPPING
OVERSTIMULATE
OVERSTIMULATED
OVERSTIMULATES
OVERSTIMULATING
OVERSTIMULATION
OVERSTINKING
OVERSTINKS
OVERSTIRRED
OVERSTIRRING
OVERSTOCKED
OVERSTOCKING
OVERSTOCKS
OVERSTORIES
OVERSTRAIN
OVERSTRAINED
OVERSTRAINING
OVERSTRAINS
OVERSTRESS
OVERSTRESSED
OVERSTRESSES
OVERSTRESSING
OVERSTRETCH
OVERSTRETCHED
OVERSTRETCHES
OVERSTRETCHING
OVERSTREWED
OVERSTREWING
OVERSTREWN
OVERSTREWS
OVERSTRIDDEN
OVERSTRIDE
OVERSTRIDES
OVERSTRIDING
OVERSTRIKE
OVERSTRIKES
OVERSTRIKING
OVERSTRODE
OVERSTRONG
OVERSTROOKE
OVERSTRUCK
OVERSTRUCTURED
OVERSTRUNG
OVERSTUDIED
OVERSTUDIES
OVERSTUDYING
OVERSTUFFED
OVERSTUFFING
OVERSTUFFS
OVERSUBSCRIBE
OVERSUBSCRIBED
OVERSUBSCRIBES
OVERSUBSCRIBING
OVERSUBTLE
OVERSUBTLETIES
OVERSUBTLETY
OVERSUDSED
OVERSUDSES
OVERSUDSING
OVERSUPPED
OVERSUPPING
OVERSUPPLIED
OVERSUPPLIES
OVERSUPPLY
OVERSUPPLYING
OVERSUSPICIOUS
OVERSWAYED
OVERSWAYING
OVERSWEARING
OVERSWEARS
OVERSWEETEN
OVERSWEETENED
OVERSWEETENING
OVERSWEETENS
OVERSWEETNESS
OVERSWEETNESSES
OVERSWELLED
OVERSWELLING
OVERSWELLS
OVERSWIMMING
OVERSWINGING
OVERSWINGS
OVERSWOLLEN
OVERTAKING
OVERTALKATIVE
OVERTALKED
OVERTALKING
OVERTASKED
OVERTASKING
OVERTAUGHT
OVERTAXATION
OVERTAXATIONS
OVERTAXING
OVERTEACHES
OVERTEACHING
OVERTEDIOUS
OVERTEEMED
OVERTEEMING
OVERTHINKING
OVERTHINKS
OVERTHOUGHT
OVERTHROWER
OVERTHROWERS
OVERTHROWING
OVERTHROWN
OVERTHROWS
OVERTHRUST

OVERTHRUSTS
OVERTHWART
OVERTHWARTED
OVERTHWARTING
OVERTHWARTS
OVERTIGHTEN
OVERTIGHTENED
OVERTIGHTENING
OVERTIGHTENS
OVERTIMELY
OVERTIMERS
OVERTIMING
OVERTIPPED
OVERTIPPING
OVERTIRING
OVERTNESSES
OVERTOILED
OVERTOILING
OVERTOPPED
OVERTOPPING
OVERTOWERED
OVERTOWERING
OVERTOWERS
OVERTRADED
OVERTRADES
OVERTRADING
OVERTRAINED
OVERTRAINING
OVERTRAINS
OVERTREATED
OVERTREATING
OVERTREATMENT
OVERTREATMENTS
OVERTREATS
OVERTRICKS
OVERTRIMMED
OVERTRIMMING
OVERTRIPPED
OVERTRIPPING
OVERTRUMPED
OVERTRUMPING
OVERTRUMPS
OVERTRUSTED
OVERTRUSTING
OVERTRUSTS
OVERTURING
OVERTURNED
OVERTURNER
OVERTURNERS
OVERTURNING
OVERTYPING
OVERURGING
OVERUTILISATION
OVERUTILISE
OVERUTILISED
OVERUTILISES
OVERUTILISING
OVERUTILIZATION
OVERUTILIZE
OVERUTILIZED
OVERUTILIZES
OVERUTILIZING
OVERVALUATION
OVERVALUATIONS
OVERVALUED
OVERVALUES
OVERVALUING
OVERVEILED
OVERVEILING
OVERVIOLENT
OVERVOLTAGE
OVERVOLTAGES
OVERVOTING
OVERWARMED
OVERWARMING
OVERWASHES
OVERWATCHED
OVERWATCHES
OVERWATCHING
OVERWATERED
OVERWATERING
OVERWATERS
OVERWEARIED
OVERWEARIES
OVERWEARING
OVERWEARYING
OVERWEATHER
OVERWEATHERED
OVERWEATHERING
OVERWEATHERS
OVERWEENED
OVERWEENING
OVERWEENINGLY
OVERWEENINGNESS
OVERWEENINGS
OVERWEIGHED
OVERWEIGHING
OVERWEIGHS
OVERWEIGHT
OVERWEIGHTED
OVERWEIGHTING
OVERWEIGHTS
OVERWETTED
OVERWETTING
OVERWHELMED
OVERWHELMING
OVERWHELMINGLY
OVERWHELMINGS
OVERWHELMS
OVERWINDING
OVERWINGED
OVERWINGING
OVERWINTER
OVERWINTERED
OVERWINTERING
OVERWINTERS
OVERWISELY
OVERWITHHELD
OVERWITHHOLD
OVERWITHHOLDING
OVERWITHHOLDS
OVERWORKED
OVERWORKING
OVERWRESTED
OVERWRESTING
OVERWRESTLE
OVERWRESTLED
OVERWRESTLES
OVERWRESTLING
OVERWRESTS
OVERWRITES
OVERWRITING
OVERWRITTEN
OVERWROUGHT
OVERYEARED
OVERYEARING
OVERZEALOUS
OVERZEALOUSNESS
OVIPARITIES
OVIPAROUSLY
OVIPOSITED
OVIPOSITING
OVIPOSITION
OVIPOSITIONAL
OVIPOSITIONS
OVIPOSITOR
OVIPOSITORS
OVIRAPTORS
OVOVIVIPARITIES
OVOVIVIPARITY
OVOVIVIPAROUS
OVOVIVIPAROUSLY
OVULATIONS
OVULIFEROUS
OWERLOUPEN
OWERLOUPING
OWERLOUPIT
OWLISHNESS
OWLISHNESSES
OWNERSHIPS
OXACILLINS
OXALACETATE
OXALACETATES
OXALOACETATE
OXALOACETATES
OXIDATIONAL
OXIDATIONS
OXIDATIVELY
OXIDIMETRIC
OXIDIMETRIES
OXIDIMETRY
OXIDISABLE
OXIDISATION
OXIDISATIONS
OXIDIZABLE
OXIDIZATION
OXIDIZATIONS
OXIDOREDUCTASE
OXIDOREDUCTASES
OXIMETRIES
OXYACETYLENE
OXYCEPHALIC
OXYCEPHALIES
OXYCEPHALOUS
OXYCEPHALY
OXYCODONES
OXYGENASES
OXYGENATED
OXYGENATES
OXYGENATING
OXYGENATION
OXYGENATIONS
OXYGENATOR
OXYGENATORS
OXYGENISED
OXYGENISER
OXYGENISERS
OXYGENISES
OXYGENISING
OXYGENIZED
OXYGENIZER
OXYGENIZERS
OXYGENIZES
OXYGENIZING
OXYGENLESS
OXYHAEMOGLOBIN
OXYHAEMOGLOBINS
OXYHEMOGLOBIN
OXYHEMOGLOBINS
OXYHYDROGEN
OXYMORONIC
OXYMORONICALLY
OXYPHENBUTAZONE
OXYRHYNCHUS
OXYRHYNCHUSES
OXYSULPHIDE
OXYSULPHIDES
OXYTETRACYCLINE
OXYURIASES
OXYURIASIS
OYSTERCATCHER
OYSTERCATCHERS
OYSTERINGS
OZOCERITES
OZOKERITES
OZONATIONS
OZONIFEROUS
OZONISATION
OZONISATIONS
OZONIZATION
OZONIZATIONS
OZONOLYSES
OZONOLYSIS
OZONOSPHERE
OZONOSPHERES

Pp

PACEMAKERS
PACEMAKING
PACEMAKINGS
PACESETTER
PACESETTERS
PACESETTING
PACESETTINGS
PACHYCARPOUS
PACHYDACTYL
PACHYDACTYLOUS
PACHYDACTYLS
PACHYDERMAL
PACHYDERMATOUS
PACHYDERMIA
PACHYDERMIAS
PACHYDERMIC
PACHYDERMOUS
PACHYDERMS
PACHYMENINGITIS
PACHYMETER
PACHYMETERS
PACHYSANDRA
PACHYSANDRAS
PACHYTENES
PACIFIABLE
PACIFICALLY
PACIFICATE
PACIFICATED
PACIFICATES
PACIFICATING
PACIFICATION
PACIFICATIONS
PACIFICATOR
PACIFICATORS
PACIFICATORY
PACIFICISM
PACIFICISMS
PACIFICIST
PACIFICISTS
PACIFISTIC
PACIFISTICALLY
PACKABILITIES
PACKABILITY
PACKAGINGS
PACKBOARDS
PACKFRAMES
PACKHORSES
PACKINGHOUSE
PACKINGHOUSES
PACKNESSES
PACKSADDLE
PACKSADDLES
PACKSHEETS
PACKSTAFFS
PACKTHREAD
PACKTHREADS
PACLITAXEL
PACLITAXELS
PACTIONING
PADDLEBALL
PADDLEBALLS
PADDLEBOARD
PADDLEBOARDS
PADDLEBOAT
PADDLEBOATS
PADDLEFISH
PADDLEFISHES
PADDOCKING
PADDYMELON
PADDYMELONS
PADDYWACKED
PADDYWACKING
PADDYWACKS
PADDYWHACK
PADDYWHACKS
PADEMELONS
PADEREROES
PADLOCKING
PADRONISMS
PADYMELONS
PAEDAGOGIC
PAEDAGOGUE
PAEDAGOGUES
PAEDERASTIC
PAEDERASTIES
PAEDERASTS
PAEDERASTY
PAEDEUTICS
PAEDIATRIC
PAEDIATRICIAN
PAEDIATRICIANS
PAEDIATRICS
PAEDIATRIES
PAEDIATRIST
PAEDIATRISTS
PAEDOBAPTISM
PAEDOBAPTISMS
PAEDOBAPTIST
PAEDOBAPTISTS
PAEDODONTIC
PAEDODONTICS
PAEDODONTIST
PAEDODONTISTS
PAEDOGENESES
PAEDOGENESIS
PAEDOGENETIC
PAEDOGENIC
PAEDOLOGICAL
PAEDOLOGIES
PAEDOLOGIST
PAEDOLOGISTS
PAEDOMORPHIC
PAEDOMORPHISM
PAEDOMORPHISMS
PAEDOMORPHOSES
PAEDOMORPHOSIS
PAEDOPHILE
PAEDOPHILES
PAEDOPHILIA
PAEDOPHILIAC
PAEDOPHILIACS
PAEDOPHILIAS
PAEDOPHILIC
PAEDOPHILICS
PAEDOTRIBE
PAEDOTRIBES
PAEDOTROPHIES
PAEDOTROPHY
PAGANISATION
PAGANISATIONS
PAGANISERS
PAGANISING
PAGANISTIC
PAGANISTICALLY
PAGANIZATION
PAGANIZATIONS
PAGANIZERS
PAGANIZING
PAGEANTRIES
PAGINATING
PAGINATION
PAGINATIONS
PAIDEUTICS
PAILLASSES
PAILLETTES
PAINFULLER
PAINFULLEST
PAINFULNESS
PAINFULNESSES
PAINKILLER
PAINKILLERS
PAINKILLING

PAINLESSLY
PAINLESSNESS
PAINLESSNESSES
PAINSTAKER
PAINSTAKERS
PAINSTAKING
PAINSTAKINGLY
PAINSTAKINGNESS
PAINSTAKINGS
PAINTBALLS
PAINTBOXES
PAINTBRUSH
PAINTBRUSHES
PAINTERLINESS
PAINTERLINESSES
PAINTINESS
PAINTINESSES
PAINTRESSES
PAINTWORKS
PAKIRIKIRI
PAKIRIKIRIS
PALAEANTHROPIC
PALAEBIOLOGIC
PALAEBIOLOGIES
PALAEBIOLOGIST
PALAEBIOLOGISTS
PALAEBIOLOGY
PALAEETHNOLOGY
PALAEOANTHROPIC
PALAEOBIOLOGIC
PALAEOBIOLOGIES
PALAEOBIOLOGIST
PALAEOBIOLOGY
PALAEOBOTANIC
PALAEOBOTANICAL
PALAEOBOTANIES
PALAEOBOTANIST
PALAEOBOTANISTS
PALAEOBOTANY
PALAEOCLIMATE
PALAEOCLIMATES
PALAEOCLIMATIC
PALAEOCRYSTIC
PALAEOCURRENT
PALAEOCURRENTS
PALAEOECOLOGIC
PALAEOECOLOGIES
PALAEOECOLOGIST
PALAEOECOLOGY
PALAEOETHNOLOGY
PALAEOGAEA
PALAEOGAEAS
PALAEOGEOGRAPHY
PALAEOGRAPHER
PALAEOGRAPHERS
PALAEOGRAPHIC
PALAEOGRAPHICAL
PALAEOGRAPHIES
PALAEOGRAPHIST
PALAEOGRAPHISTS
PALAEOGRAPHY
PALAEOLIMNOLOGY
PALAEOLITH
PALAEOLITHIC
PALAEOLITHS
PALAEOMAGNETIC
PALAEOMAGNETISM
PALAEONTOGRAPHY
PALAEONTOLOGIES
PALAEONTOLOGIST
PALAEONTOLOGY
PALAEOPATHOLOGY
PALAEOPEDOLOGY
PALAEOPHYTOLOGY
PALAEOTYPE
PALAEOTYPES
PALAEOTYPIC
PALAEOZOOLOGIES
PALAEOZOOLOGIST
PALAEOZOOLOGY
PALAESTRAE
PALAESTRAL
PALAESTRAS
PALAESTRIC
PALAESTRICAL
PALAFITTES
PALAGONITE
PALAGONITES
PALAMPORES
PALANKEENS
PALANQUINS
PALATABILITIES
PALATABILITY
PALATABLENESS
PALATABLENESSES
PALATALISATION
PALATALISATIONS
PALATALISE
PALATALISED
PALATALISES
PALATALISING
PALATALIZATION
PALATALIZATIONS
PALATALIZE
PALATALIZED
PALATALIZES
PALATALIZING
PALATIALLY
PALATIALNESS
PALATIALNESSES
PALATINATE
PALATINATES
PALAVERERS
PALAVERING
PALEACEOUS
PALEMPORES
PALENESSES
PALEOBIOLOGIC
PALEOBIOLOGICAL
PALEOBIOLOGIES
PALEOBIOLOGIST
PALEOBIOLOGISTS
PALEOBIOLOGY
PALEOBOTANIC
PALEOBOTANICAL
PALEOBOTANIES
PALEOBOTANIST
PALEOBOTANISTS
PALEOBOTANY
PALEOECOLOGIC
PALEOECOLOGICAL
PALEOECOLOGIES
PALEOECOLOGIST
PALEOECOLOGISTS
PALEOECOLOGY
PALEOGEOGRAPHIC
PALEOGEOGRAPHY
PALEOGRAPHER
PALEOGRAPHERS
PALEOGRAPHIC
PALEOGRAPHICAL
PALEOGRAPHIES
PALEOGRAPHY
PALEOLITHS
PALEOLOGIES
PALEOMAGNETIC
PALEOMAGNETISM
PALEOMAGNETISMS
PALEOMAGNETIST
PALEOMAGNETISTS
PALEONTOLOGIC
PALEONTOLOGICAL
PALEONTOLOGIES
PALEONTOLOGIST
PALEONTOLOGISTS
PALEONTOLOGY
PALEOPATHOLOGY
PALEOZOOLOGICAL
PALEOZOOLOGIES
PALEOZOOLOGIST
PALEOZOOLOGISTS
PALEOZOOLOGY
PALFRENIER
PALFRENIERS
PALFREYING
PALIFICATION
PALIFICATIONS
PALILALIAS
PALILLOGIES
PALIMONIES
PALIMPSEST
PALIMPSESTS
PALINDROME
PALINDROMES
PALINDROMIC
PALINDROMICAL
PALINDROMIST
PALINDROMISTS
PALINGENESES
PALINGENESIA
PALINGENESIAS
PALINGENESIES
PALINGENESIS
PALINGENESIST
PALINGENESISTS
PALINGENESY
PALINGENETIC
PALINGENETICAL
PALINODIES
PALINOPIAS
PALINOPSIA
PALINOPSIAS
PALISADING
PALISADOED
PALISADOES
PALISADOING
PALISANDER
PALISANDERS
PALLADIOUS
PALLADIUMS
PALLBEARER
PALLBEARERS
PALLESCENCE
PALLESCENCES
PALLESCENT
PALLETISATION
PALLETISATIONS
PALLETISED
PALLETISER
PALLETISERS
PALLETISES
PALLETISING
PALLETIZATION
PALLETIZATIONS
PALLETIZED
PALLETIZER
PALLETIZERS
PALLETIZES
PALLETIZING
PALLIAMENT
PALLIAMENTS
PALLIASSES
PALLIATING
PALLIATION
PALLIATIONS
PALLIATIVE
PALLIATIVELY
PALLIATIVES
PALLIATORS
PALLIATORY
PALLIDITIES
PALLIDNESS
PALLIDNESSES
PALMACEOUS
PALMATIFID
PALMATIONS
PALMATIPARTITE
PALMATISECT
PALMCORDER
PALMCORDERS
PALMERWORM
PALMERWORMS
PALMETTOES
PALMHOUSES
PALMIFICATION
PALMIFICATIONS
PALMIPEDES
PALMISTERS
PALMISTRIES
PALMITATES
PALOVERDES
PALPABILITIES
PALPABILITY
PALPABLENESS
PALPABLENESSES
PALPATIONS
PALPEBRATE
PALPEBRATED
PALPEBRATES
PALPEBRATING
PALPITATED
PALPITATES
PALPITATING
PALPITATION

PALPITATIONS
PALSGRAVES
PALSGRAVINE
PALSGRAVINES
PALTRINESS
PALTRINESSES
PALUDAMENT
PALUDAMENTA
PALUDAMENTS
PALUDAMENTUM
PALUDAMENTUMS
PALUDICOLOUS
PALUDINOUS
PALUSTRIAN
PALUSTRINE
PALYNOLOGIC
PALYNOLOGICAL
PALYNOLOGICALLY
PALYNOLOGIES
PALYNOLOGIST
PALYNOLOGISTS
PALYNOLOGY
PAMPELMOOSE
PAMPELMOOSES
PAMPELMOUSE
PAMPELMOUSES
PAMPEREDNESS
PAMPEREDNESSES
PAMPHLETEER
PAMPHLETEERED
PAMPHLETEERING
PAMPHLETEERINGS
PAMPHLETEERS
PAMPOOTIES
PANACHAEAS
PANAESTHESIA
PANAESTHESIAS
PANAESTHETISM
PANAESTHETISMS
PANARITIUM
PANARITIUMS
PANARTHRITIS
PANARTHRITISES
PANATELLAS
PANBROILED
PANBROILING
PANCHAYATS
PANCHROMATIC
PANCHROMATISM
PANCHROMATISMS
PANCOSMISM
PANCOSMISMS
PANCRATIAN
PANCRATIAST
PANCRATIASTS
PANCRATIST
PANCRATISTS
PANCRATIUM
PANCRATIUMS
PANCREASES
PANCREATECTOMY
PANCREATIC
PANCREATIN
PANCREATINS
PANCREATITIDES
PANCREATITIS
PANCREATITISES
PANCREOZYMIN
PANCREOZYMINS
PANCYTOPENIA
PANCYTOPENIAS
PANDAEMONIUM
PANDAEMONIUMS
PANDANACEOUS
PANDANUSES
PANDATIONS
PANDECTIST
PANDECTISTS
PANDEMONIAC
PANDEMONIACAL
PANDEMONIAN
PANDEMONIC
PANDEMONIUM
PANDEMONIUMS
PANDERESSES
PANDERISMS
PANDERMITE
PANDERMITES
PANDICULATION
PANDICULATIONS
PANDOWDIES
PANDURATED
PANDURIFORM
PANEGOISMS
PANEGYRICA
PANEGYRICAL
PANEGYRICALLY
PANEGYRICON
PANEGYRICS
PANEGYRIES
PANEGYRISE
PANEGYRISED
PANEGYRISES
PANEGYRISING
PANEGYRIST
PANEGYRISTS
PANEGYRIZE
PANEGYRIZED
PANEGYRIZES
PANEGYRIZING
PANELLINGS
PANELLISTS
PANENTHEISM
PANENTHEISMS
PANENTHEIST
PANENTHEISTS
PANESTHESIA
PANESTHESIAS
PANETELLAS
PANETTONES
PANGENESES
PANGENESIS
PANGENETIC
PANGENETICALLY
PANGRAMMATIST
PANGRAMMATISTS
PANHANDLED
PANHANDLER
PANHANDLERS
PANHANDLES
PANHANDLING
PANHARMONICON
PANHARMONICONS
PANHELLENIC
PANHELLENION
PANHELLENIONS
PANHELLENIUM
PANHELLENIUMS
PANICKIEST
PANICMONGER
PANICMONGERS
PANICULATE
PANICULATED
PANICULATELY
PANIDIOMORPHIC
PANIFICATION
PANIFICATIONS
PANISLAMIC
PANISLAMISM
PANISLAMISMS
PANISLAMIST
PANISLAMISTS
PANJANDARUM
PANJANDARUMS
PANJANDRUM
PANJANDRUMS
PANLEUCOPENIA
PANLEUCOPENIAS
PANLEUKOPENIA
PANLEUKOPENIAS
PANLOGISMS
PANMIXISES
PANNICULUS
PANNICULUSES
PANNIKELLS
PANOMPHAEAN
PANOPHOBIA
PANOPHOBIAS
PANOPHTHALMIA
PANOPHTHALMIAS
PANOPHTHALMITIS
PANOPTICAL
PANOPTICALLY
PANOPTICON
PANOPTICONS
PANORAMICALLY
PANPHARMACON
PANPHARMACONS
PANPSYCHISM
PANPSYCHISMS
PANPSYCHIST
PANPSYCHISTIC
PANPSYCHISTS
PANRADIOMETER
PANRADIOMETERS
PANSEXUALISM
PANSEXUALISMS
PANSEXUALIST
PANSEXUALISTS
PANSEXUALITIES
PANSEXUALITY
PANSEXUALS
PANSOPHICAL
PANSOPHICALLY
PANSOPHIES
PANSOPHISM
PANSOPHISMS
PANSOPHIST
PANSOPHISTS
PANSPERMATIC
PANSPERMATISM
PANSPERMATISMS
PANSPERMATIST
PANSPERMATISTS
PANSPERMIA
PANSPERMIAS
PANSPERMIC
PANSPERMIES
PANSPERMISM
PANSPERMISMS
PANSPERMIST
PANSPERMISTS
PANTAGAMIES
PANTAGRAPH
PANTAGRAPHS
PANTALEONS
PANTALETTED
PANTALETTES
PANTALONES
PANTALOONED
PANTALOONERIES
PANTALOONERY
PANTALOONS
PANTDRESSES
PANTECHNICON
PANTECHNICONS
PANTHEISMS
PANTHEISTIC
PANTHEISTICAL
PANTHEISTICALLY
PANTHEISTS
PANTHENOLS
PANTHEOLOGIES
PANTHEOLOGIST
PANTHEOLOGISTS
PANTHEOLOGY
PANTHERESS
PANTHERESSES
PANTHERINE
PANTHERISH
PANTILINGS
PANTISOCRACIES
PANTISOCRACY
PANTISOCRAT
PANTISOCRATIC
PANTISOCRATICAL
PANTISOCRATIST
PANTISOCRATISTS
PANTISOCRATS
PANTOFFLES
PANTOGRAPH
PANTOGRAPHER
PANTOGRAPHERS
PANTOGRAPHIC
PANTOGRAPHICAL
PANTOGRAPHIES
PANTOGRAPHS
PANTOGRAPHY
PANTOMIMED
PANTOMIMES
PANTOMIMIC
PANTOMIMICAL
PANTOMIMICALLY
PANTOMIMING

PANTOMIMIST
PANTOMIMISTS
PANTOPHAGIES
PANTOPHAGIST
PANTOPHAGISTS
PANTOPHAGOUS
PANTOPHAGY
PANTOPHOBIA
PANTOPHOBIAS
PANTOPRAGMATIC
PANTOPRAGMATICS
PANTOSCOPE
PANTOSCOPES
PANTOSCOPIC
PANTOTHENATE
PANTOTHENATES
PANTOTHENIC
PANTOUFLES
PANTROPICAL
PANTRYMAID
PANTRYMAIDS
PANTSUITED
PANTYWAIST
PANTYWAISTS
PANZOOTICS
PAPALISING
PAPALIZING
PAPAPRELATIST
PAPAPRELATISTS
PAPAVERACEOUS
PAPAVERINE
PAPAVERINES
PAPAVEROUS
PAPERBACKED
PAPERBACKER
PAPERBACKERS
PAPERBACKING
PAPERBACKS
PAPERBARKS
PAPERBOARD
PAPERBOARDS
PAPERBOUND
PAPERBOUNDS
PAPERCLIPS
PAPERGIRLS
PAPERHANGER
PAPERHANGERS
PAPERHANGING
PAPERHANGINGS
PAPERINESS
PAPERINESSES
PAPERKNIFE
PAPERKNIVES
PAPERMAKER
PAPERMAKERS
PAPERMAKING
PAPERMAKINGS
PAPERWARES
PAPERWEIGHT
PAPERWEIGHTS
PAPERWORKS
PAPETERIES
PAPILIONACEOUS
PAPILLATED
PAPILLIFEROUS
PAPILLIFORM
PAPILLITIS
PAPILLITISES
PAPILLOMAS
PAPILLOMATA
PAPILLOMATOSES
PAPILLOMATOSIS
PAPILLOMATOUS
PAPILLOMAVIRUS
PAPILLOTES
PAPILLULATE
PAPILLULES
PAPISTICAL
PAPISTICALLY
PAPISTRIES
PAPOVAVIRUS
PAPOVAVIRUSES
PAPULATION
PAPULATIONS
PAPULIFEROUS
PAPYRACEOUS
PAPYROLOGICAL
PAPYROLOGIES
PAPYROLOGIST
PAPYROLOGISTS
PAPYROLOGY
PARABAPTISM
PARABAPTISMS
PARABEMATA
PARABEMATIC
PARABIOSES
PARABIOSIS
PARABIOTIC
PARABIOTICALLY
PARABLASTIC
PARABLASTS
PARABLEPSES
PARABLEPSIES
PARABLEPSIS
PARABLEPSY
PARABLEPTIC
PARABOLANUS
PARABOLANUSES
PARABOLICAL
PARABOLICALLY
PARABOLISATION
PARABOLISATIONS
PARABOLISE
PARABOLISED
PARABOLISES
PARABOLISING
PARABOLIST
PARABOLISTS
PARABOLIZATION
PARABOLIZATIONS
PARABOLIZE
PARABOLIZED
PARABOLIZES
PARABOLIZING
PARABOLOID
PARABOLOIDAL
PARABOLOIDS
PARABRAKES
PARACASEIN
PARACASEINS
PARACENTESES
PARACENTESIS
PARACETAMOL
PARACETAMOLS
PARACHRONISM
PARACHRONISMS
PARACHUTED
PARACHUTES
PARACHUTIC
PARACHUTING
PARACHUTIST
PARACHUTISTS
PARACLETES
PARACROSTIC
PARACROSTICS
PARACYANOGEN
PARACYANOGENS
PARADIDDLE
PARADIDDLES
PARADIGMATIC
PARADIGMATICAL
PARADISAIC
PARADISAICAL
PARADISAICALLY
PARADISEAN
PARADISIAC
PARADISIACAL
PARADISIACALLY
PARADISIAL
PARADISIAN
PARADISICAL
PARADOCTOR
PARADOCTORS
PARADOXERS
PARADOXICAL
PARADOXICALITY
PARADOXICALLY
PARADOXICALNESS
PARADOXIDIAN
PARADOXIES
PARADOXIST
PARADOXISTS
PARADOXOLOGIES
PARADOXOLOGY
PARADOXURE
PARADOXURES
PARADOXURINE
PARADROPPED
PARADROPPING
PARAENESES
PARAENESIS
PARAENETIC
PARAENETICAL
PARAESTHESIA
PARAESTHESIAS
PARAESTHETIC
PARAFFINED
PARAFFINES
PARAFFINIC
PARAFFINING
PARAFFINOID
PARAGENESES
PARAGENESIA
PARAGENESIAS
PARAGENESIS
PARAGENETIC
PARAGENETICALLY
PARAGLIDED
PARAGLIDER
PARAGLIDERS
PARAGLIDES
PARAGLIDING
PARAGLIDINGS
PARAGLOSSA
PARAGLOSSAE
PARAGLOSSAL
PARAGLOSSATE
PARAGNATHISM
PARAGNATHISMS
PARAGNATHOUS
PARAGNOSES
PARAGNOSIS
PARAGOGICAL
PARAGOGICALLY
PARAGOGUES
PARAGONING
PARAGONITE
PARAGONITES
PARAGRAMMATIST
PARAGRAMMATISTS
PARAGRAPHED
PARAGRAPHER
PARAGRAPHERS
PARAGRAPHIA
PARAGRAPHIAS
PARAGRAPHIC
PARAGRAPHICAL
PARAGRAPHICALLY
PARAGRAPHING
PARAGRAPHIST
PARAGRAPHISTS
PARAGRAPHS
PARAHELIOTROPIC
PARAHYDROGEN
PARAHYDROGENS
PARAINFLUENZA
PARAINFLUENZAS
PARAJOURNALISM
PARAJOURNALISMS
PARAKEELYA
PARAKEELYAS
PARAKELIAS
PARAKITING
PARAKITINGS
PARALALIAS
PARALANGUAGE
PARALANGUAGES
PARALDEHYDE
PARALDEHYDES
PARALEGALS
PARALEIPOMENA
PARALEIPOMENON
PARALEIPSES
PARALEIPSIS
PARALEXIAS
PARALIMNION
PARALIMNIONS
PARALINGUISTIC
PARALINGUISTICS
PARALIPOMENA
PARALIPOMENON
PARALIPSES
PARALIPSIS
PARALLACTIC

PARALLACTICAL
PARALLACTICALLY
PARALLAXES
PARALLELED
PARALLELEPIPED
PARALLELEPIPEDA
PARALLELEPIPEDS
PARALLELING
PARALLELINGS
PARALLELISE
PARALLELISED
PARALLELISES
PARALLELISING
PARALLELISM
PARALLELISMS
PARALLELIST
PARALLELISTIC
PARALLELISTS
PARALLELIZE
PARALLELIZED
PARALLELIZES
PARALLELIZING
PARALLELLED
PARALLELLING
PARALLELLY
PARALLELOGRAM
PARALLELOGRAMS
PARALLELOPIPED
PARALLELOPIPEDA
PARALLELOPIPEDS
PARALLELWISE
PARALOGIAS
PARALOGIES
PARALOGISE
PARALOGISED
PARALOGISES
PARALOGISING
PARALOGISM
PARALOGISMS
PARALOGIST
PARALOGISTIC
PARALOGISTS
PARALOGIZE
PARALOGIZED
PARALOGIZES
PARALOGIZING
PARALYMPIC
PARALYMPICS
PARALYSATION
PARALYSATIONS
PARALYSERS
PARALYSING
PARALYSINGLY
PARALYTICALLY
PARALYTICS
PARALYZATION
PARALYZATIONS
PARALYZERS
PARALYZING
PARALYZINGLY
PARAMAECIA
PARAMAECIUM
PARAMAGNET
PARAMAGNETIC
PARAMAGNETISM
PARAMAGNETISMS
PARAMAGNETS
PARAMASTOID
PARAMASTOIDS
PARAMATTAS
PARAMECIUM
PARAMECIUMS
PARAMEDICAL
PARAMEDICALS
PARAMEDICO
PARAMEDICOS
PARAMEDICS
PARAMENSTRUA
PARAMENSTRUUM
PARAMENSTRUUMS
PARAMETERISE
PARAMETERISED
PARAMETERISES
PARAMETERISING
PARAMETERIZE
PARAMETERIZED
PARAMETERIZES
PARAMETERIZING
PARAMETERS
PARAMETRAL
PARAMETRIC
PARAMETRICAL
PARAMETRICALLY
PARAMETRISATION
PARAMETRISE
PARAMETRISED
PARAMETRISES
PARAMETRISING
PARAMETRIZATION
PARAMETRIZE
PARAMETRIZED
PARAMETRIZES
PARAMETRIZING
PARAMILITARIES
PARAMILITARY
PARAMNESIA
PARAMNESIAS
PARAMOECIA
PARAMOECIUM
PARAMORPHIC
PARAMORPHINE
PARAMORPHINES
PARAMORPHISM
PARAMORPHISMS
PARAMORPHOUS
PARAMORPHS
PARAMOUNCIES
PARAMOUNCY
PARAMOUNTCIES
PARAMOUNTCY
PARAMOUNTLY
PARAMOUNTS
PARAMYLUMS
PARAMYXOVIRUS
PARAMYXOVIRUSES
PARANEPHRIC
PARANEPHROS
PARANEPHROSES
PARANOEICS
PARANOIACS
PARANOICALLY
PARANOIDAL
PARANORMAL
PARANORMALITIES
PARANORMALITY
PARANORMALLY
PARANORMALS
PARANTHELIA
PARANTHELION
PARANTHROPUS
PARANTHROPUSES
PARANYMPHS
PARAPARESES
PARAPARESIS
PARAPARETIC
PARAPENTES
PARAPENTING
PARAPENTINGS
PARAPHASIA
PARAPHASIAS
PARAPHASIC
PARAPHERNALIA
PARAPHILIA
PARAPHILIAC
PARAPHILIACS
PARAPHILIAS
PARAPHIMOSES
PARAPHIMOSIS
PARAPHONIA
PARAPHONIAS
PARAPHONIC
PARAPHRASABLE
PARAPHRASE
PARAPHRASED
PARAPHRASER
PARAPHRASERS
PARAPHRASES
PARAPHRASING
PARAPHRAST
PARAPHRASTIC
PARAPHRASTICAL
PARAPHRASTS
PARAPHRAXES
PARAPHRAXIA
PARAPHRAXIAS
PARAPHRAXIS
PARAPHRENIA
PARAPHRENIAS
PARAPHYSATE
PARAPHYSES
PARAPHYSIS
PARAPINEAL
PARAPLEGIA
PARAPLEGIAS
PARAPLEGIC
PARAPLEGICS
PARAPODIAL
PARAPODIUM
PARAPOPHYSES
PARAPOPHYSIAL
PARAPOPHYSIS
PARAPRAXES
PARAPRAXIS
PARAPSYCHIC
PARAPSYCHICAL
PARAPSYCHISM
PARAPSYCHISMS
PARAPSYCHOLOGY
PARAPSYCHOSES
PARAPSYCHOSIS
PARAQUADRATE
PARAQUADRATES
PARAQUITOS
PARARHYMES
PARAROSANILINE
PARAROSANILINES
PARARTHRIA
PARARTHRIAS
PARASAILED
PARASAILING
PARASAILINGS
PARASCENDER
PARASCENDERS
PARASCENDING
PARASCENDINGS
PARASCENIA
PARASCENIUM
PARASCEVES
PARASCIENCE
PARASCIENCES
PARASELENAE
PARASELENE
PARASELENIC
PARASEXUAL
PARASEXUALITIES
PARASEXUALITY
PARASHIOTH
PARASITAEMIA
PARASITAEMIAS
PARASITICAL
PARASITICALLY
PARASITICALNESS
PARASITICIDAL
PARASITICIDE
PARASITICIDES
PARASITISATION
PARASITISATIONS
PARASITISE
PARASITISED
PARASITISES
PARASITISING
PARASITISM
PARASITISMS
PARASITIZATION
PARASITIZATIONS
PARASITIZE
PARASITIZED
PARASITIZES
PARASITIZING
PARASITOID
PARASITOIDS
PARASITOLOGIC
PARASITOLOGICAL
PARASITOLOGIES
PARASITOLOGIST
PARASITOLOGISTS
PARASITOLOGY
PARASITOSES
PARASITOSIS
PARASKIING
PARASPHENOID
PARASPHENOIDS
PARASTATAL
PARASTATALS

PARASTICHIES
PARASTICHOUS
PARASTICHY
PARASUICIDE
PARASUICIDES
PARASYMBIONT
PARASYMBIONTS
PARASYMBIOSES
PARASYMBIOSIS
PARASYMBIOTIC
PARASYMPATHETIC
PARASYNAPSES
PARASYNAPSIS
PARASYNAPTIC
PARASYNTHESES
PARASYNTHESIS
PARASYNTHETA
PARASYNTHETIC
PARASYNTHETON
PARATACTIC
PARATACTICAL
PARATACTICALLY
PARATANIWHA
PARATHESES
PARATHESIS
PARATHIONS
PARATHORMONE
PARATHORMONES
PARATHYROID
PARATHYROIDS
PARATROOPER
PARATROOPERS
PARATROOPS
PARATYPHOID
PARATYPHOIDS
PARAWALKER
PARAWALKERS
PARBOILING
PARBREAKED
PARBREAKING
PARBUCKLED
PARBUCKLES
PARBUCKLING
PARCELLING
PARCELWISE
PARCENARIES
PARCHEDNESS
PARCHEDNESSES
PARCHEESIS
PARCHMENTISE
PARCHMENTISED
PARCHMENTISES
PARCHMENTISING
PARCHMENTIZE
PARCHMENTIZED
PARCHMENTIZES
PARCHMENTIZING
PARCHMENTS
PARCHMENTY
PARCIMONIES
PARDALISES
PARDALOTES
PARDONABLE
PARDONABLENESS
PARDONABLY
PARDONINGS
PARDONLESS
PAREGORICS
PARENCEPHALA
PARENCEPHALON
PARENCHYMA
PARENCHYMAL
PARENCHYMAS
PARENCHYMATA
PARENCHYMATOUS
PARENTAGES
PARENTALLY
PARENTERAL
PARENTERALLY
PARENTHESES
PARENTHESIS
PARENTHESISE
PARENTHESISED
PARENTHESISES
PARENTHESISING
PARENTHESIZE
PARENTHESIZED
PARENTHESIZES
PARENTHESIZING
PARENTHETIC
PARENTHETICAL
PARENTHETICALLY
PARENTHOOD
PARENTHOODS
PARENTINGS
PARENTLESS
PARESTHESIA
PARESTHESIAS
PARESTHETIC
PARFLECHES
PARFLESHES
PARFOCALISE
PARFOCALISED
PARFOCALISES
PARFOCALISING
PARFOCALITIES
PARFOCALITY
PARFOCALIZE
PARFOCALIZED
PARFOCALIZES
PARFOCALIZING
PARGASITES
PARGETINGS
PARGETTING
PARGETTINGS
PARGYLINES
PARHELIACAL
PARHYPATES
PARIPINNATE
PARISCHANE
PARISCHANES
PARISCHANS
PARISHIONER
PARISHIONERS
PARISYLLABIC
PARKINSONIAN
PARKINSONISM
PARKINSONISMS
PARKLEAVES
PARLEMENTS
PARLEYVOOED
PARLEYVOOING
PARLEYVOOS
PARLIAMENT
PARLIAMENTARIAN
PARLIAMENTARILY
PARLIAMENTARISM
PARLIAMENTARY
PARLIAMENTING
PARLIAMENTINGS
PARLIAMENTS
PARLOUSNESS
PARLOUSNESSES
PARMACITIE
PARMACITIES
PARMIGIANA
PARMIGIANO
PAROCCIPITAL
PAROCHIALISE
PAROCHIALISED
PAROCHIALISES
PAROCHIALISING
PAROCHIALISM
PAROCHIALISMS
PAROCHIALITIES
PAROCHIALITY
PAROCHIALIZE
PAROCHIALIZED
PAROCHIALIZES
PAROCHIALIZING
PAROCHIALLY
PAROCHINES
PARODISTIC
PAROECIOUS
PAROEMIACS
PAROEMIOGRAPHER
PAROEMIOGRAPHY
PAROEMIOLOGIES
PAROEMIOLOGY
PARONOMASIA
PARONOMASIAS
PARONOMASIES
PARONOMASTIC
PARONOMASTICAL
PARONOMASY
PARONYCHIA
PARONYCHIAL
PARONYCHIAS
PARONYMIES
PARONYMOUS
PARONYMOUSLY
PAROTIDITIC
PAROTIDITIS
PAROTIDITISES
PAROTITISES
PAROXETINE
PAROXETINES
PAROXYSMAL
PAROXYSMALLY
PAROXYSMIC
PAROXYTONE
PAROXYTONES
PAROXYTONIC
PARQUETING
PARQUETRIES
PARQUETTED
PARQUETTING
PARRAKEETS
PARRAMATTA
PARRAMATTAS
PARRHESIAS
PARRICIDAL
PARRICIDES
PARRITCHES
PARROCKING
PARROQUETS
PARROTFISH
PARROTFISHES
PARROTRIES
PARSIMONIES
PARSIMONIOUS
PARSIMONIOUSLY
PARSONAGES
PARSONICAL
PARTAKINGS
PARTHENOCARPIC
PARTHENOCARPIES
PARTHENOCARPOUS
PARTHENOCARPY
PARTHENOGENESES
PARTHENOGENESIS
PARTHENOGENETIC
PARTHENOSPORE
PARTHENOSPORES
PARTIALISE
PARTIALISED
PARTIALISES
PARTIALISING
PARTIALISM
PARTIALISMS
PARTIALIST
PARTIALISTS
PARTIALITIES
PARTIALITY
PARTIALIZE
PARTIALIZED
PARTIALIZES
PARTIALIZING
PARTIALNESS
PARTIALNESSES
PARTIBILITIES
PARTIBILITY
PARTICIPABLE
PARTICIPANT
PARTICIPANTLY
PARTICIPANTS
PARTICIPATE
PARTICIPATED
PARTICIPATES
PARTICIPATING
PARTICIPATION
PARTICIPATIONAL
PARTICIPATIONS
PARTICIPATIVE
PARTICIPATOR
PARTICIPATORS
PARTICIPATORY
PARTICIPIAL
PARTICIPIALLY
PARTICIPLE
PARTICIPLES
PARTICLEBOARD
PARTICLEBOARDS
PARTICULAR

PARTICULARISE
PARTICULARISED
PARTICULARISER
PARTICULARISERS
PARTICULARISES
PARTICULARISING
PARTICULARISM
PARTICULARISMS
PARTICULARIST
PARTICULARISTIC
PARTICULARISTS
PARTICULARITIES
PARTICULARITY
PARTICULARIZE
PARTICULARIZED
PARTICULARIZER
PARTICULARIZERS
PARTICULARIZES
PARTICULARIZING
PARTICULARLY
PARTICULARNESS
PARTICULARS
PARTICULATE
PARTICULATES
PARTISANLY
PARTISANSHIP
PARTISANSHIPS
PARTITIONED
PARTITIONER
PARTITIONERS
PARTITIONING
PARTITIONIST
PARTITIONISTS
PARTITIONMENT
PARTITIONMENTS
PARTITIONS
PARTITIVELY
PARTITIVES
PARTITURAS
PARTIZANSHIP
PARTIZANSHIPS
PARTNERING
PARTNERLESS
PARTNERSHIP
PARTNERSHIPS
PARTRIDGEBERRY
PARTRIDGES
PARTURIENCIES
PARTURIENCY
PARTURIENT
PARTURIENTS
PARTURIFACIENT
PARTURITION
PARTURITIONS
PARTYGOERS
PARVANIMITIES
PARVANIMITY
PARVIFOLIATE
PARVOLINES
PARVOVIRUS
PARVOVIRUSES
PASIGRAPHIC
PASIGRAPHICAL
PASIGRAPHIES
PASIGRAPHY
PASODOBLES
PASQUEFLOWER
PASQUEFLOWERS
PASQUILANT
PASQUILANTS
PASQUILERS
PASQUILLED
PASQUILLING
PASQUINADE
PASQUINADED
PASQUINADER
PASQUINADERS
PASQUINADES
PASQUINADING
PASSABLENESS
PASSABLENESSES
PASSACAGLIA
PASSACAGLIAS
PASSAGEWAY
PASSAGEWAYS
PASSAGEWORK
PASSAGEWORKS
PASSALONGS
PASSAMENTED
PASSAMENTING
PASSAMENTS
PASSAMEZZO
PASSAMEZZOS
PASSEMEASURE
PASSEMEASURES
PASSEMENTED
PASSEMENTERIE
PASSEMENTERIES
PASSEMENTING
PASSEMENTS
PASSENGERS
PASSEPIEDS
PASSERINES
PASSIBILITIES
PASSIBILITY
PASSIBLENESS
PASSIBLENESSES
PASSIFLORA
PASSIFLORACEOUS
PASSIFLORAS
PASSIMETER
PASSIMETERS
PASSIONALS
PASSIONARIES
PASSIONARY
PASSIONATE
PASSIONATED
PASSIONATELY
PASSIONATENESS
PASSIONATES
PASSIONATING
PASSIONFLOWER
PASSIONFLOWERS
PASSIONING
PASSIONLESS
PASSIONLESSLY
PASSIONLESSNESS
PASSIVATED
PASSIVATES
PASSIVATING
PASSIVATION
PASSIVATIONS
PASSIVENESS
PASSIVENESSES
PASSIVISMS
PASSIVISTS
PASSIVITIES
PASSMENTED
PASSMENTING
PASTEBOARD
PASTEBOARDS
PASTEDOWNS
PASTELISTS
PASTELLIST
PASTELLISTS
PASTEURELLA
PASTEURELLAE
PASTEURELLAS
PASTEURISATION
PASTEURISATIONS
PASTEURISE
PASTEURISED
PASTEURISER
PASTEURISERS
PASTEURISES
PASTEURISING
PASTEURISM
PASTEURISMS
PASTEURIZATION
PASTEURIZATIONS
PASTEURIZE
PASTEURIZED
PASTEURIZER
PASTEURIZERS
PASTEURIZES
PASTEURIZING
PASTICCIOS
PASTICHEUR
PASTICHEURS
PASTINESSES
PASTITSIOS
PASTMASTER
PASTMASTERS
PASTNESSES
PASTORALES
PASTORALISM
PASTORALISMS
PASTORALIST
PASTORALISTS
PASTORALLY
PASTORALNESS
PASTORALNESSES
PASTORATES
PASTORIUMS
PASTORSHIP
PASTORSHIPS
PASTOURELLE
PASTOURELLES
PASTRYCOOK
PASTRYCOOKS
PASTURABLE
PASTURAGES
PASTURELAND
PASTURELANDS
PASTURELESS
PATAPHYSICS
PATCHBOARD
PATCHBOARDS
PATCHCOCKE
PATCHCOCKES
PATCHERIES
PATCHINESS
PATCHINESSES
PATCHOCKES
PATCHOULIES
PATCHOULIS
PATCHWORKED
PATCHWORKING
PATCHWORKS
PATELLECTOMIES
PATELLECTOMY
PATELLIFORM
PATENTABILITIES
PATENTABILITY
PATENTABLE
PATERCOVES
PATEREROES
PATERFAMILIAS
PATERFAMILIASES
PATERNALISM
PATERNALISMS
PATERNALIST
PATERNALISTIC
PATERNALISTS
PATERNALLY
PATERNITIES
PATERNOSTER
PATERNOSTERS
PATHBREAKING
PATHETICAL
PATHETICALLY
PATHFINDER
PATHFINDERS
PATHFINDING
PATHFINDINGS
PATHLESSNESS
PATHLESSNESSES
PATHOBIOLOGIES
PATHOBIOLOGY
PATHOGENES
PATHOGENESES
PATHOGENESIS
PATHOGENETIC
PATHOGENIC
PATHOGENICITIES
PATHOGENICITY
PATHOGENIES
PATHOGENOUS
PATHOGNOMIES
PATHOGNOMONIC
PATHOGNOMY
PATHOGRAPHIES
PATHOGRAPHY
PATHOLOGIC
PATHOLOGICAL
PATHOLOGICALLY
PATHOLOGIES
PATHOLOGISE
PATHOLOGIST
PATHOLOGISTS
PATHOLOGIZE
PATHOLOGIZED
PATHOLOGIZES
PATHOLOGIZING

PATHOPHOBIA
PATHOPHOBIAS
PATHOPHYSIOLOGY
PATIBULARY
PATIENTEST
PATIENTING
PATINATING
PATINATION
PATINATIONS
PATINISING
PATINIZING
PATISSERIE
PATISSERIES
PATISSIERS
PATRESFAMILIAS
PATRIALISATION
PATRIALISATIONS
PATRIALISE
PATRIALISED
PATRIALISES
PATRIALISING
PATRIALISM
PATRIALISMS
PATRIALITIES
PATRIALITY
PATRIALIZATION
PATRIALIZATIONS
PATRIALIZE
PATRIALIZED
PATRIALIZES
PATRIALIZING
PATRIARCHAL
PATRIARCHALISM
PATRIARCHALISMS
PATRIARCHALLY
PATRIARCHATE
PATRIARCHATES
PATRIARCHIES
PATRIARCHISM
PATRIARCHISMS
PATRIARCHS
PATRIARCHY
PATRIATING
PATRIATION
PATRIATIONS
PATRICIANLY
PATRICIANS
PATRICIATE
PATRICIATES
PATRICIDAL
PATRICIDES
PATRICLINIC
PATRICLINOUS
PATRIFOCAL
PATRIFOCALITIES
PATRIFOCALITY
PATRILINEAGE
PATRILINEAGES
PATRILINEAL
PATRILINEALLY
PATRILINEAR
PATRILINEARLY
PATRILINIES
PATRILOCAL
PATRILOCALLY
PATRIMONIAL
PATRIMONIALLY
PATRIMONIES
PATRIOTICALLY
PATRIOTISM
PATRIOTISMS
PATRISTICAL
PATRISTICALLY
PATRISTICISM
PATRISTICISMS
PATRISTICS
PATROCLINAL
PATROCLINIC
PATROCLINIES
PATROCLINOUS
PATROCLINY
PATROLLERS
PATROLLING
PATROLOGICAL
PATROLOGIES
PATROLOGIST
PATROLOGISTS
PATROLWOMAN
PATROLWOMEN
PATRONAGED
PATRONAGES
PATRONAGING
PATRONESSES
PATRONISATION
PATRONISATIONS
PATRONISED
PATRONISER
PATRONISERS
PATRONISES
PATRONISING
PATRONISINGLY
PATRONIZATION
PATRONIZATIONS
PATRONIZED
PATRONIZER
PATRONIZERS
PATRONIZES
PATRONIZING
PATRONIZINGLY
PATRONLESS
PATRONYMIC
PATRONYMICS
PATROONSHIP
PATROONSHIPS
PATTERNING
PATTERNINGS
PATTERNLESS
PATULOUSLY
PATULOUSNESS
PATULOUSNESSES
PAUCILOQUENT
PAUGHTIEST
PAULOWNIAS
PAUNCHIEST
PAUNCHINESS
PAUNCHINESSES
PAUPERESSES
PAUPERISATION
PAUPERISATIONS
PAUPERISED
PAUPERISES
PAUPERISING
PAUPERISMS
PAUPERIZATION
PAUPERIZATIONS
PAUPERIZED
PAUPERIZES
PAUPERIZING
PAUPIETTES
PAUSEFULLY
PAUSELESSLY
PAVEMENTED
PAVEMENTING
PAVILIONED
PAVILIONING
PAVONAZZOS
PAWKINESSES
PAWNBROKER
PAWNBROKERS
PAWNBROKING
PAWNBROKINGS
PAWNTICKET
PAWNTICKETS
PAYMASTERS
PAYNIMRIES
PAYROLLING
PAYSAGISTS
PEABERRIES
PEACEABLENESS
PEACEABLENESSES
PEACEFULLER
PEACEFULLEST
PEACEFULLY
PEACEFULNESS
PEACEFULNESSES
PEACEKEEPER
PEACEKEEPERS
PEACEKEEPING
PEACEKEEPINGS
PEACELESSNESS
PEACELESSNESSES
PEACEMAKER
PEACEMAKERS
PEACEMAKING
PEACEMAKINGS
PEACETIMES
PEACHBLOWS
PEACHERINO
PEACHERINOS
PEACHINESS
PEACHINESSES
PEACOCKERIES
PEACOCKERY
PEACOCKIER
PEACOCKIEST
PEACOCKING
PEACOCKISH
PEAKEDNESS
PEAKEDNESSES
PEARLASHES
PEARLESCENCE
PEARLESCENCES
PEARLESCENT
PEARLINESS
PEARLINESSES
PEARLWORTS
PEARMONGER
PEARMONGERS
PEARTNESSES
PEASANTRIES
PEASHOOTER
PEASHOOTERS
PEASOUPERS
PEBBLEDASH
PEBBLEDASHED
PEBBLEDASHES
PEBBLEDASHING
PECCABILITIES
PECCABILITY
PECCADILLO
PECCADILLOES
PECCADILLOS
PECCANCIES
PECKERWOOD
PECKERWOODS
PECKISHNESS
PECKISHNESSES
PECTINACEOUS
PECTINATED
PECTINATELY
PECTINATION
PECTINATIONS
PECTINESTERASE
PECTINESTERASES
PECTISABLE
PECTISATION
PECTISATIONS
PECTIZABLE
PECTIZATION
PECTIZATIONS
PECTOLITES
PECTORALLY
PECTORILOQUIES
PECTORILOQUY
PECULATING
PECULATION
PECULATIONS
PECULATORS
PECULIARISE
PECULIARISED
PECULIARISES
PECULIARISING
PECULIARITIES
PECULIARITY
PECULIARIZE
PECULIARIZED
PECULIARIZES
PECULIARIZING
PECULIARLY
PECUNIARILY
PEDAGOGICAL
PEDAGOGICALLY
PEDAGOGICS
PEDAGOGIES
PEDAGOGISM
PEDAGOGISMS
PEDAGOGUED
PEDAGOGUERIES
PEDAGOGUERY
PEDAGOGUES
PEDAGOGUING
PEDAGOGUISH
PEDAGOGUISHNESS
PEDAGOGUISM

PEDAGOGUISMS
PEDALLINGS
PEDANTICAL
PEDANTICALLY
PEDANTICISE
PEDANTICISED
PEDANTICISES
PEDANTICISING
PEDANTICISM
PEDANTICISMS
PEDANTICIZE
PEDANTICIZED
PEDANTICIZES
PEDANTICIZING
PEDANTISED
PEDANTISES
PEDANTISING
PEDANTISMS
PEDANTIZED
PEDANTIZES
PEDANTIZING
PEDANTOCRACIES
PEDANTOCRACY
PEDANTOCRAT
PEDANTOCRATIC
PEDANTOCRATS
PEDANTRIES
PEDDLERIES
PEDERASTIC
PEDERASTIES
PEDEREROES
PEDESTALED
PEDESTALING
PEDESTALLED
PEDESTALLING
PEDESTRIAN
PEDESTRIANISE
PEDESTRIANISED
PEDESTRIANISES
PEDESTRIANISING
PEDESTRIANISM
PEDESTRIANISMS
PEDESTRIANIZE
PEDESTRIANIZED
PEDESTRIANIZES
PEDESTRIANIZING
PEDESTRIANS
PEDETENTOUS
PEDIATRICIAN
PEDIATRICIANS
PEDIATRICS
PEDIATRIST
PEDIATRISTS
PEDICELLARIA
PEDICELLARIAE
PEDICELLATE
PEDICULATE
PEDICULATED
PEDICULATES
PEDICULATION
PEDICULATIONS
PEDICULOSES
PEDICULOSIS
PEDICULOUS
PEDICURING
PEDICURIST
PEDICURISTS
PEDIMENTAL
PEDIMENTED
PEDIPALPUS
PEDOGENESES
PEDOGENESIS
PEDOGENETIC
PEDOLOGICAL
PEDOLOGIES
PEDOLOGIST
PEDOLOGISTS
PEDOMETERS
PEDOPHILES
PEDOPHILIA
PEDOPHILIAC
PEDOPHILIACS
PEDOPHILIAS
PEDOPHILIC
PEDUNCULAR
PEDUNCULATE
PEDUNCULATED
PEDUNCULATION
PEDUNCULATIONS
PEELGARLIC
PEELGARLICS
PEERLESSLY
PEERLESSNESS
PEERLESSNESSES
PEEVISHNESS
PEEVISHNESSES
PEGMATITES
PEGMATITIC
PEIRASTICALLY
PEJORATING
PEJORATION
PEJORATIONS
PEJORATIVE
PEJORATIVELY
PEJORATIVES
PELARGONIC
PELARGONIUM
PELARGONIUMS
PELECYPODS
PELLAGRINS
PELLAGROUS
PELLETIFIED
PELLETIFIES
PELLETIFYING
PELLETISATION
PELLETISATIONS
PELLETISED
PELLETISER
PELLETISERS
PELLETISES
PELLETISING
PELLETIZATION
PELLETIZATIONS
PELLETIZED
PELLETIZER
PELLETIZERS
PELLETIZES
PELLETIZING
PELLICULAR
PELLITORIES
PELLUCIDITIES
PELLUCIDITY
PELLUCIDLY
PELLUCIDNESS
PELLUCIDNESSES
PELMANISMS
PELOLOGIES
PELOTHERAPIES
PELOTHERAPY
PELTATIONS
PELTMONGER
PELTMONGERS
PELVIMETER
PELVIMETERS
PELVIMETRIES
PELVIMETRY
PELYCOSAUR
PELYCOSAURS
PEMPHIGOID
PEMPHIGOUS
PEMPHIGUSES
PENALISATION
PENALISATIONS
PENALISING
PENALITIES
PENALIZATION
PENALIZATIONS
PENALIZING
PENANNULAR
PENCILINGS
PENCILLERS
PENCILLING
PENCILLINGS
PENDENCIES
PENDENTIVE
PENDENTIVES
PENDICLERS
PENDRAGONS
PENDRAGONSHIP
PENDRAGONSHIPS
PENDULATED
PENDULATES
PENDULATING
PENDULINES
PENDULOSITIES
PENDULOSITY
PENDULOUSLY
PENDULOUSNESS
PENDULOUSNESSES
PENELOPISE
PENELOPISED
PENELOPISES
PENELOPISING
PENELOPIZE
PENELOPIZED
PENELOPIZES
PENELOPIZING
PENEPLAINS
PENEPLANATION
PENEPLANATIONS
PENEPLANES
PENETRABILITIES
PENETRABILITY
PENETRABLE
PENETRABLENESS
PENETRABLY
PENETRALIA
PENETRALIAN
PENETRANCE
PENETRANCES
PENETRANCIES
PENETRANCY
PENETRANTS
PENETRATED
PENETRATES
PENETRATING
PENETRATINGLY
PENETRATION
PENETRATIONS
PENETRATIVE
PENETRATIVELY
PENETRATIVENESS
PENETRATOR
PENETRATORS
PENETROMETER
PENETROMETERS
PENGUINERIES
PENGUINERY
PENGUINRIES
PENHOLDERS
PENICILLAMINE
PENICILLAMINES
PENICILLATE
PENICILLATELY
PENICILLATION
PENICILLATIONS
PENICILLIA
PENICILLIFORM
PENICILLIN
PENICILLINASE
PENICILLINASES
PENICILLINS
PENICILLIUM
PENICILLIUMS
PENINSULAR
PENINSULARITIES
PENINSULARITY
PENINSULAS
PENINSULATE
PENINSULATED
PENINSULATES
PENINSULATING
PENISTONES
PENITENCES
PENITENCIES
PENITENTIAL
PENITENTIALLY
PENITENTIALS
PENITENTIARIES
PENITENTIARY
PENITENTLY
PENMANSHIP
PENMANSHIPS
PENNACEOUS
PENNALISMS
PENNATULACEOUS
PENNATULAE
PENNATULAS
PENNILESSLY
PENNILESSNESS
PENNILESSNESSES
PENNILLION
PENNINITES
PENNONCELLE

PENNONCELLES
PENNONCELS
PENNYCRESS
PENNYCRESSES
PENNYLANDS
PENNYROYAL
PENNYROYALS
PENNYWEIGHT
PENNYWEIGHTS
PENNYWHISTLE
PENNYWHISTLES
PENNYWINKLE
PENNYWINKLES
PENNYWORTH
PENNYWORTHS
PENNYWORTS
PENOLOGICAL
PENOLOGICALLY
PENOLOGIES
PENOLOGIST
PENOLOGISTS
PENONCELLE
PENONCELLES
PENPUSHERS
PENPUSHING
PENSIEROSO
PENSILENESS
PENSILENESSES
PENSILITIES
PENSIONABLE
PENSIONARIES
PENSIONARY
PENSIONEER
PENSIONEERS
PENSIONERS
PENSIONING
PENSIONLESS
PENSIONNAT
PENSIONNATS
PENSIVENESS
PENSIVENESSES
PENSTEMONS
PENTABARBITAL
PENTABARBITALS
PENTACHORD
PENTACHORDS
PENTACRINOID
PENTACRINOIDS
PENTACTINAL
PENTACYCLIC
PENTADACTYL
PENTADACTYLE
PENTADACTYLES
PENTADACTYLIC
PENTADACTYLIES
PENTADACTYLISM
PENTADACTYLISMS
PENTADACTYLOUS
PENTADACTYLS
PENTADACTYLY
PENTADELPHOUS
PENTAGONAL
PENTAGONALLY
PENTAGONALS
PENTAGRAMS
PENTAGRAPH
PENTAGRAPHS
PENTAGYNIAN
PENTAGYNOUS
PENTAHEDRA
PENTAHEDRAL
PENTAHEDRON
PENTAHEDRONS
PENTALOGIES
PENTALPHAS
PENTAMERIES
PENTAMERISM
PENTAMERISMS
PENTAMEROUS
PENTAMETER
PENTAMETERS
PENTAMIDINE
PENTAMIDINES
PENTANDRIAN
PENTANDROUS
PENTANGLES
PENTANGULAR
PENTAPEPTIDE
PENTAPEPTIDES
PENTAPLOID
PENTAPLOIDIES
PENTAPLOIDS
PENTAPLOIDY
PENTAPODIC
PENTAPODIES
PENTAPOLIS
PENTAPOLISES
PENTAPOLITAN
PENTAPRISM
PENTAPRISMS
PENTAQUARK
PENTAQUARKS
PENTARCHICAL
PENTARCHIES
PENTASTICH
PENTASTICHES
PENTASTICHOUS
PENTASTICHS
PENTASTYLE
PENTASTYLES
PENTASYLLABIC
PENTATEUCHAL
PENTATHLETE
PENTATHLETES
PENTATHLON
PENTATHLONS
PENTATHLUM
PENTATHLUMS
PENTATOMIC
PENTATONIC
PENTAVALENT
PENTAZOCINE
PENTAZOCINES
PENTECONTER
PENTECONTERS
PENTETERIC
PENTHEMIMER
PENTHEMIMERAL
PENTHEMIMERS
PENTHOUSED
PENTHOUSES
PENTHOUSING
PENTIMENTI
PENTIMENTO
PENTLANDITE
PENTLANDITES
PENTOBARBITAL
PENTOBARBITALS
PENTOBARBITONE
PENTOBARBITONES
PENTOSANES
PENTOSIDES
PENTOXIDES
PENTSTEMON
PENTSTEMONS
PENTYLENES
PENULTIMAS
PENULTIMATE
PENULTIMATELY
PENULTIMATES
PENUMBROUS
PENURIOUSLY
PENURIOUSNESS
PENURIOUSNESSES
PEOPLEHOOD
PEOPLEHOODS
PEOPLELESS
PEPEROMIAS
PEPPERBOXES
PEPPERCORN
PEPPERCORNS
PEPPERCORNY
PEPPERGRASS
PEPPERGRASSES
PEPPERIDGE
PEPPERIDGES
PEPPERIEST
PEPPERINESS
PEPPERINESSES
PEPPERINGS
PEPPERMILL
PEPPERMILLS
PEPPERMINT
PEPPERMINTS
PEPPERMINTY
PEPPERONIS
PEPPERTREE
PEPPERTREES
PEPPERWORT
PEPPERWORTS
PEPPINESSES
PEPSINATED
PEPSINATES
PEPSINATING
PEPSINOGEN
PEPSINOGENS
PEPTALKING
PEPTICITIES
PEPTIDASES
PEPTIDOGLYCAN
PEPTIDOGLYCANS
PEPTISABLE
PEPTISATION
PEPTISATIONS
PEPTIZABLE
PEPTIZATION
PEPTIZATIONS
PEPTONISATION
PEPTONISATIONS
PEPTONISED
PEPTONISER
PEPTONISERS
PEPTONISES
PEPTONISING
PEPTONIZATION
PEPTONIZATIONS
PEPTONIZED
PEPTONIZER
PEPTONIZERS
PEPTONIZES
PEPTONIZING
PERACIDITIES
PERACIDITY
PERADVENTURE
PERADVENTURES
PERAEOPODS
PERAMBULATE
PERAMBULATED
PERAMBULATES
PERAMBULATING
PERAMBULATION
PERAMBULATIONS
PERAMBULATOR
PERAMBULATORS
PERAMBULATORY
PERBORATES
PERCALINES
PERCEIVABILITY
PERCEIVABLE
PERCEIVABLY
PERCEIVERS
PERCEIVING
PERCEIVINGS
PERCENTAGE
PERCENTAGES
PERCENTILE
PERCENTILES
PERCEPTIBILITY
PERCEPTIBLE
PERCEPTIBLY
PERCEPTION
PERCEPTIONAL
PERCEPTIONS
PERCEPTIVE
PERCEPTIVELY
PERCEPTIVENESS
PERCEPTIVITIES
PERCEPTIVITY
PERCEPTUAL
PERCEPTUALLY
PERCHERIES
PERCHERONS
PERCHLORATE
PERCHLORATES
PERCHLORIC
PERCHLORIDE
PERCHLORIDES
PERCHLOROETHENE
PERCIPIENCE
PERCIPIENCES
PERCIPIENCIES
PERCIPIENCY
PERCIPIENT
PERCIPIENTLY

PERCIPIENTS
PERCOIDEAN
PERCOIDEANS
PERCOLABLE
PERCOLATED
PERCOLATES
PERCOLATING
PERCOLATION
PERCOLATIONS
PERCOLATIVE
PERCOLATOR
PERCOLATORS
PERCURRENT
PERCURSORY
PERCUSSANT
PERCUSSING
PERCUSSION
PERCUSSIONAL
PERCUSSIONIST
PERCUSSIONISTS
PERCUSSIONS
PERCUSSIVE
PERCUSSIVELY
PERCUSSIVENESS
PERCUSSORS
PERCUTANEOUS
PERCUTANEOUSLY
PERCUTIENT
PERCUTIENTS
PERDENDOSI
PERDITIONABLE
PERDITIONS
PERDUELLION
PERDUELLIONS
PERDURABILITIES
PERDURABILITY
PERDURABLE
PERDURABLY
PERDURANCE
PERDURANCES
PERDURATION
PERDURATIONS
PEREGRINATE
PEREGRINATED
PEREGRINATES
PEREGRINATING
PEREGRINATION
PEREGRINATIONS
PEREGRINATOR
PEREGRINATORS
PEREGRINATORY
PEREGRINES
PEREGRINITIES
PEREGRINITY
PEREIOPODS
PEREMPTORILY
PEREMPTORINESS
PEREMPTORY
PERENNATED
PERENNATES
PERENNATING
PERENNATION
PERENNATIONS
PERENNIALITIES
PERENNIALITY
PERENNIALLY
PERENNIALS
PERENNIBRANCH
PERENNIBRANCHS
PERENNITIES
PERESTROIKA
PERESTROIKAS
PERFECTATION
PERFECTATIONS
PERFECTERS
PERFECTEST
PERFECTIBILIAN
PERFECTIBILIANS
PERFECTIBILISM
PERFECTIBILISMS
PERFECTIBILIST
PERFECTIBILISTS
PERFECTIBILITY
PERFECTIBLE
PERFECTING
PERFECTION
PERFECTIONATE
PERFECTIONATED
PERFECTIONATES
PERFECTIONATING
PERFECTIONISM
PERFECTIONISMS
PERFECTIONIST
PERFECTIONISTIC
PERFECTIONISTS
PERFECTIONS
PERFECTIVE
PERFECTIVELY
PERFECTIVENESS
PERFECTIVES
PERFECTIVITIES
PERFECTIVITY
PERFECTNESS
PERFECTNESSES
PERFECTORS
PERFERVIDITIES
PERFERVIDITY
PERFERVIDLY
PERFERVIDNESS
PERFERVIDNESSES
PERFERVORS
PERFERVOUR
PERFERVOURS
PERFICIENT
PERFIDIOUS
PERFIDIOUSLY
PERFIDIOUSNESS
PERFLUOROCARBON
PERFOLIATE
PERFOLIATION
PERFOLIATIONS
PERFORABLE
PERFORANSES
PERFORATED
PERFORATES
PERFORATING
PERFORATION
PERFORATIONS
PERFORATIVE
PERFORATOR
PERFORATORS
PERFORATORY
PERFORATUS
PERFORATUSES
PERFORMABILITY
PERFORMABLE
PERFORMANCE
PERFORMANCES
PERFORMATIVE
PERFORMATIVELY
PERFORMATIVES
PERFORMATORY
PERFORMERS
PERFORMING
PERFORMINGS
PERFUMELESS
PERFUMERIES
PERFUMIERS
PERFUNCTORILY
PERFUNCTORINESS
PERFUNCTORY
PERFUSATES
PERFUSIONIST
PERFUSIONISTS
PERFUSIONS
PERGAMENEOUS
PERGAMENTACEOUS
PERGUNNAHS
PERIASTRON
PERIASTRONS
PERIBLASTS
PERICARDIA
PERICARDIAC
PERICARDIAL
PERICARDIAN
PERICARDITIC
PERICARDITIS
PERICARDITISES
PERICARDIUM
PERICARDIUMS
PERICARPIAL
PERICARPIC
PERICENTER
PERICENTERS
PERICENTRAL
PERICENTRE
PERICENTRES
PERICENTRIC
PERICHAETIA
PERICHAETIAL
PERICHAETIUM
PERICHONDRAL
PERICHONDRIA
PERICHONDRIAL
PERICHONDRIUM
PERICHORESES
PERICHORESIS
PERICHYLOUS
PERICLASES
PERICLASTIC
PERICLINAL
PERICLINES
PERICLITATE
PERICLITATED
PERICLITATES
PERICLITATING
PERICRANIA
PERICRANIAL
PERICRANIUM
PERICRANIUMS
PERICULOUS
PERICYCLES
PERICYCLIC
PERICYNTHIA
PERICYNTHION
PERICYNTHIONS
PERIDERMAL
PERIDERMIC
PERIDESMIA
PERIDESMIUM
PERIDINIAN
PERIDINIANS
PERIDINIUM
PERIDINIUMS
PERIDOTITE
PERIDOTITES
PERIDOTITIC
PERIDROMES
PERIEGESES
PERIEGESIS
PERIGASTRIC
PERIGASTRITIS
PERIGASTRITISES
PERIGENESES
PERIGENESIS
PERIGLACIAL
PERIGONIAL
PERIGONIUM
PERIGYNIES
PERIGYNOUS
PERIHELIAL
PERIHELION
PERIHEPATIC
PERIHEPATITIS
PERIHEPATITISES
PERIKARYAL
PERIKARYON
PERILOUSLY
PERILOUSNESS
PERILOUSNESSES
PERILYMPHS
PERIMENOPAUSAL
PERIMENOPAUSE
PERIMENOPAUSES
PERIMETERS
PERIMETRAL
PERIMETRIC
PERIMETRICAL
PERIMETRICALLY
PERIMETRIES
PERIMORPHIC
PERIMORPHISM
PERIMORPHOUS
PERIMORPHS
PERIMYSIUM
PERIMYSIUMS
PERINAEUMS
PERINATALLY
PERINEPHRIA
PERINEPHRIC
PERINEPHRITIS
PERINEPHRITISES
PERINEPHRIUM
PERINEURAL

PERINEURIA
PERINEURIAL
PERINEURITIC
PERINEURITIS
PERINEURITISES
PERINEURIUM
PERIODATES
PERIODICAL
PERIODICALIST
PERIODICALISTS
PERIODICALLY
PERIODICALS
PERIODICITIES
PERIODICITY
PERIODIDES
PERIODISATION
PERIODISATIONS
PERIODIZATION
PERIODIZATIONS
PERIODONTAL
PERIODONTALLY
PERIODONTIA
PERIODONTIAS
PERIODONTIC
PERIODONTICALLY
PERIODONTICS
PERIODONTIST
PERIODONTISTS
PERIODONTITIS
PERIODONTITISES
PERIODONTOLOGY
PERIONYCHIA
PERIONYCHIUM
PERIOSTEAL
PERIOSTEUM
PERIOSTITIC
PERIOSTITIS
PERIOSTITISES
PERIOSTRACUM
PERIOSTRACUMS
PERIPATETIC
PERIPATETICAL
PERIPATETICALLY
PERIPATETICISM
PERIPATETICISMS
PERIPATETICS
PERIPATUSES
PERIPETEIA
PERIPETEIAN
PERIPETEIAS
PERIPETIAN
PERIPETIAS
PERIPETIES
PERIPHERAL
PERIPHERALITIES
PERIPHERALITY
PERIPHERALLY
PERIPHERALS
PERIPHERIC
PERIPHERICAL
PERIPHERIES
PERIPHONIC
PERIPHRASE
PERIPHRASED
PERIPHRASES
PERIPHRASING
PERIPHRASIS
PERIPHRASTIC
PERIPHRASTICAL
PERIPHYTIC
PERIPHYTON
PERIPHYTONS
PERIPLASMS
PERIPLASTS
PERIPLUSES
PERIPROCTS
PERIPTERAL
PERIPTERIES
PERISARCAL
PERISARCOUS
PERISCIANS
PERISCOPES
PERISCOPIC
PERISCOPICALLY
PERISELENIA
PERISELENIUM
PERISHABILITIES
PERISHABILITY
PERISHABLE
PERISHABLENESS
PERISHABLES
PERISHABLY
PERISHINGLY
PERISPERMAL
PERISPERMIC
PERISPERMS
PERISPOMENON
PERISPOMENONS
PERISSODACTYL
PERISSODACTYLE
PERISSODACTYLES
PERISSODACTYLIC
PERISSODACTYLS
PERISSOLOGIES
PERISSOLOGY
PERISSOSYLLABIC
PERISTALITH
PERISTALITHS
PERISTALSES
PERISTALSIS
PERISTALTIC
PERISTALTICALLY
PERISTERITE
PERISTERITES
PERISTERONIC
PERISTOMAL
PERISTOMATIC
PERISTOMES
PERISTOMIAL
PERISTREPHIC
PERISTYLAR
PERISTYLES
PERITECTIC
PERITHECIA
PERITHECIAL
PERITHECIUM
PERITONAEA
PERITONAEAL
PERITONAEUM
PERITONAEUMS
PERITONEAL
PERITONEALLY
PERITONEOSCOPY
PERITONEUM
PERITONEUMS
PERITONITIC
PERITONITIS
PERITONITISES
PERITRACKS
PERITRICHA
PERITRICHOUS
PERITRICHOUSLY
PERITRICHS
PERITYPHLITIS
PERITYPHLITISES
PERIVITELLINE
PERIWIGGED
PERIWIGGING
PERIWINKLE
PERIWINKLES
PERJINKETY
PERJINKITIES
PERJINKITY
PERJURIOUS
PERJURIOUSLY
PERKINESSES
PERLEMOENS
PERLOCUTION
PERLOCUTIONARY
PERLOCUTIONS
PERLUSTRATE
PERLUSTRATED
PERLUSTRATES
PERLUSTRATING
PERLUSTRATION
PERLUSTRATIONS
PERMACULTURE
PERMACULTURES
PERMAFROST
PERMAFROSTS
PERMALLOYS
PERMANENCE
PERMANENCES
PERMANENCIES
PERMANENCY
PERMANENTLY
PERMANENTNESS
PERMANENTNESSES
PERMANENTS
PERMANGANATE
PERMANGANATES
PERMANGANIC
PERMEABILITIES
PERMEABILITY
PERMEABLENESS
PERMEABLENESSES
PERMEAMETER
PERMEAMETERS
PERMEANCES
PERMEATING
PERMEATION
PERMEATIONS
PERMEATIVE
PERMEATORS
PERMETHRIN
PERMETHRINS
PERMILLAGE
PERMILLAGES
PERMISSIBILITY
PERMISSIBLE
PERMISSIBLENESS
PERMISSIBLY
PERMISSION
PERMISSIONS
PERMISSIVE
PERMISSIVELY
PERMISSIVENESS
PERMITTANCE
PERMITTANCES
PERMITTEES
PERMITTERS
PERMITTING
PERMITTIVITIES
PERMITTIVITY
PERMUTABILITIES
PERMUTABILITY
PERMUTABLE
PERMUTABLENESS
PERMUTABLY
PERMUTATED
PERMUTATES
PERMUTATING
PERMUTATION
PERMUTATIONAL
PERMUTATIONS
PERNANCIES
PERNICIOUS
PERNICIOUSLY
PERNICIOUSNESS
PERNICKETINESS
PERNICKETY
PERNOCTATE
PERNOCTATED
PERNOCTATES
PERNOCTATING
PERNOCTATION
PERNOCTATIONS
PERONEUSES
PERORATING
PERORATION
PERORATIONAL
PERORATIONS
PERORATORS
PEROVSKIAS
PEROVSKITE
PEROVSKITES
PEROXIDASE
PEROXIDASES
PEROXIDATION
PEROXIDATIONS
PEROXIDING
PEROXIDISE
PEROXIDISED
PEROXIDISES
PEROXIDISING
PEROXIDIZE
PEROXIDIZED
PEROXIDIZES
PEROXIDIZING
PEROXISOMAL
PEROXISOME
PEROXISOMES
PEROXYSULPHURIC
PERPENDICULAR

PERPENDICULARLY
PERPENDICULARS
PERPENDING
PERPETRABLE
PERPETRATE
PERPETRATED
PERPETRATES
PERPETRATING
PERPETRATION
PERPETRATIONS
PERPETRATOR
PERPETRATORS
PERPETUABLE
PERPETUALISM
PERPETUALISMS
PERPETUALIST
PERPETUALISTS
PERPETUALITIES
PERPETUALITY
PERPETUALLY
PERPETUALS
PERPETUANCE
PERPETUANCES
PERPETUATE
PERPETUATED
PERPETUATES
PERPETUATING
PERPETUATION
PERPETUATIONS
PERPETUATOR
PERPETUATORS
PERPETUITIES
PERPETUITY
PERPHENAZINE
PERPHENAZINES
PERPLEXEDLY
PERPLEXEDNESS
PERPLEXEDNESSES
PERPLEXERS
PERPLEXING
PERPLEXINGLY
PERPLEXITIES
PERPLEXITY
PERQUISITE
PERQUISITES
PERQUISITION
PERQUISITIONS
PERQUISITOR
PERQUISITORS
PERRUQUIER
PERRUQUIERS
PERSCRUTATION
PERSCRUTATIONS
PERSECUTED
PERSECUTEE
PERSECUTEES
PERSECUTES
PERSECUTING
PERSECUTION
PERSECUTIONS
PERSECUTIVE
PERSECUTOR
PERSECUTORS
PERSECUTORY
PERSEITIES
PERSELINES
PERSEVERANCE
PERSEVERANCES
PERSEVERANT
PERSEVERATE
PERSEVERATED
PERSEVERATES
PERSEVERATING
PERSEVERATION
PERSEVERATIONS
PERSEVERATIVE
PERSEVERATOR
PERSEVERATORS
PERSEVERED
PERSEVERES
PERSEVERING
PERSEVERINGLY
PERSICARIA
PERSICARIAS
PERSIENNES
PERSIFLAGE
PERSIFLAGES
PERSIFLEUR
PERSIFLEURS
PERSIMMONS
PERSISTENCE
PERSISTENCES
PERSISTENCIES
PERSISTENCY
PERSISTENT
PERSISTENTLY
PERSISTENTS
PERSISTERS
PERSISTING
PERSISTINGLY
PERSISTIVE
PERSNICKETINESS
PERSNICKETY
PERSONABLE
PERSONABLENESS
PERSONABLY
PERSONAGES
PERSONALIA
PERSONALISATION
PERSONALISE
PERSONALISED
PERSONALISES
PERSONALISING
PERSONALISM
PERSONALISMS
PERSONALIST
PERSONALISTIC
PERSONALISTS
PERSONALITIES
PERSONALITY
PERSONALIZATION
PERSONALIZE
PERSONALIZED
PERSONALIZES
PERSONALIZING
PERSONALLY
PERSONALTIES
PERSONALTY
PERSONATED
PERSONATES
PERSONATING
PERSONATINGS
PERSONATION
PERSONATIONS
PERSONATIVE
PERSONATOR
PERSONATORS
PERSONHOOD
PERSONHOODS
PERSONIFIABLE
PERSONIFICATION
PERSONIFIED
PERSONIFIER
PERSONIFIERS
PERSONIFIES
PERSONIFYING
PERSONISED
PERSONISES
PERSONISING
PERSONIZED
PERSONIZES
PERSONIZING
PERSONNELS
PERSONPOWER
PERSONPOWERS
PERSPECTIVAL
PERSPECTIVE
PERSPECTIVELY
PERSPECTIVES
PERSPECTIVISM
PERSPECTIVISMS
PERSPECTIVIST
PERSPECTIVISTS
PERSPICACIOUS
PERSPICACIOUSLY
PERSPICACITIES
PERSPICACITY
PERSPICUITIES
PERSPICUITY
PERSPICUOUS
PERSPICUOUSLY
PERSPICUOUSNESS
PERSPIRABLE
PERSPIRATE
PERSPIRATED
PERSPIRATES
PERSPIRATING
PERSPIRATION
PERSPIRATIONS
PERSPIRATORY
PERSPIRING
PERSPIRINGLY
PERSTRINGE
PERSTRINGED
PERSTRINGES
PERSTRINGING
PERSUADABILITY
PERSUADABLE
PERSUADERS
PERSUADING
PERSUASIBILITY
PERSUASIBLE
PERSUASION
PERSUASIONS
PERSUASIVE
PERSUASIVELY
PERSUASIVENESS
PERSUASIVES
PERSUASORY
PERSULFURIC
PERSULPHATE
PERSULPHATES
PERSULPHURIC
PERSWADING
PERTAINING
PERTINACIOUS
PERTINACIOUSLY
PERTINACITIES
PERTINACITY
PERTINENCE
PERTINENCES
PERTINENCIES
PERTINENCY
PERTINENTLY
PERTINENTS
PERTNESSES
PERTURBABLE
PERTURBABLY
PERTURBANCE
PERTURBANCES
PERTURBANT
PERTURBANTS
PERTURBATE
PERTURBATED
PERTURBATES
PERTURBATING
PERTURBATION
PERTURBATIONAL
PERTURBATIONS
PERTURBATIVE
PERTURBATOR
PERTURBATORIES
PERTURBATORS
PERTURBATORY
PERTURBEDLY
PERTURBERS
PERTURBING
PERTURBINGLY
PERTUSIONS
PERTUSSISES
PERVASIONS
PERVASIVELY
PERVASIVENESS
PERVASIVENESSES
PERVERSELY
PERVERSENESS
PERVERSENESSES
PERVERSEST
PERVERSION
PERVERSIONS
PERVERSITIES
PERVERSITY
PERVERSIVE
PERVERTEDLY
PERVERTEDNESS
PERVERTEDNESSES
PERVERTERS
PERVERTIBLE
PERVERTING
PERVIATING
PERVICACIES
PERVICACIOUS
PERVICACITIES
PERVICACITY

PERVIOUSLY
PERVIOUSNESS
PERVIOUSNESSES
PESKINESSES
PESSIMISMS
PESSIMISTIC
PESSIMISTICAL
PESSIMISTICALLY
PESSIMISTS
PESTERINGLY
PESTERMENT
PESTERMENTS
PESTHOUSES
PESTICIDAL
PESTICIDES
PESTIFEROUS
PESTIFEROUSLY
PESTIFEROUSNESS
PESTILENCE
PESTILENCES
PESTILENTIAL
PESTILENTIALLY
PESTILENTLY
PESTOLOGICAL
PESTOLOGIES
PESTOLOGIST
PESTOLOGISTS
PETAHERTZES
PETALIFEROUS
PETALODIES
PETALOMANIA
PETALOMANIAS
PETAURINES
PETAURISTS
PETCHARIES
PETERSHAMS
PETHIDINES
PETIOLATED
PETIOLULES
PETITENESS
PETITENESSES
PETITIONARY
PETITIONED
PETITIONER
PETITIONERS
PETITIONING
PETITIONINGS
PETITIONIST
PETITIONISTS
PETNAPINGS
PETNAPPERS
PETNAPPING
PETRIFACTION
PETRIFACTIONS
PETRIFACTIVE
PETRIFICATION
PETRIFICATIONS
PETRIFIERS
PETRIFYING
PETRISSAGE
PETRISSAGES
PETROCHEMICAL
PETROCHEMICALLY
PETROCHEMICALS
PETROCHEMISTRY
PETROCURRENCIES
PETROCURRENCY
PETRODOLLAR
PETRODOLLARS
PETRODROME
PETRODROMES
PETROGENESES
PETROGENESIS
PETROGENETIC
PETROGENIES
PETROGLYPH
PETROGLYPHIC
PETROGLYPHIES
PETROGLYPHS
PETROGLYPHY
PETROGRAMS
PETROGRAPHER
PETROGRAPHERS
PETROGRAPHIC
PETROGRAPHICAL
PETROGRAPHIES
PETROGRAPHY
PETROLAGES
PETROLATUM
PETROLATUMS
PETROLEOUS
PETROLEUMS
PETROLEURS
PETROLEUSE
PETROLEUSES
PETROLHEAD
PETROLHEADS
PETROLIFEROUS
PETROLLING
PETROLOGIC
PETROLOGICAL
PETROLOGICALLY
PETROLOGIES
PETROLOGIST
PETROLOGISTS
PETROMONEY
PETROMONEYS
PETROMONIES
PETRONELLA
PETRONELLAS
PETROPHYSICAL
PETROPHYSICIST
PETROPHYSICISTS
PETROPHYSICS
PETROPOUNDS
PETTEDNESS
PETTEDNESSES
PETTICHAPS
PETTICHAPSES
PETTICOATED
PETTICOATS
PETTIFOGGED
PETTIFOGGER
PETTIFOGGERIES
PETTIFOGGERS
PETTIFOGGERY
PETTIFOGGING
PETTIFOGGINGS
PETTINESSES
PETTISHNESS
PETTISHNESSES
PETULANCES
PETULANCIES
PETULANTLY
PEWHOLDERS
PHACOLITES
PHACOLITHS
PHAELONION
PHAELONIONS
PHAENOGAMIC
PHAENOGAMOUS
PHAENOGAMS
PHAENOLOGIES
PHAENOLOGY
PHAENOMENA
PHAENOMENON
PHAENOTYPE
PHAENOTYPED
PHAENOTYPES
PHAENOTYPING
PHAEOMELANIN
PHAEOMELANINS
PHAGEDAENA
PHAGEDAENAS
PHAGEDAENIC
PHAGEDENAS
PHAGEDENIC
PHAGOCYTES
PHAGOCYTIC
PHAGOCYTICAL
PHAGOCYTISE
PHAGOCYTISED
PHAGOCYTISES
PHAGOCYTISING
PHAGOCYTISM
PHAGOCYTISMS
PHAGOCYTIZE
PHAGOCYTIZED
PHAGOCYTIZES
PHAGOCYTIZING
PHAGOCYTOSE
PHAGOCYTOSED
PHAGOCYTOSES
PHAGOCYTOSING
PHAGOCYTOSIS
PHAGOCYTOTIC
PHAGOMANIA
PHAGOMANIAC
PHAGOMANIACS
PHAGOMANIAS
PHAGOPHOBIA
PHAGOPHOBIAS
PHAGOSOMES
PHALANGEAL
PHALANGERS
PHALANGIDS
PHALANGIST
PHALANGISTS
PHALANSTERIAN
PHALANSTERIES
PHALANSTERISM
PHALANSTERISMS
PHALANSTERIST
PHALANSTERISTS
PHALANSTERY
PHALAROPES
PHALLICALLY
PHALLICISM
PHALLICISMS
PHALLICIST
PHALLICISTS
PHALLOCENTRIC
PHALLOCENTRISM
PHALLOCENTRISMS
PHALLOCENTRIST
PHALLOCENTRISTS
PHALLOCRAT
PHALLOCRATIC
PHALLOCRATS
PHALLOIDIN
PHALLOIDINS
PHANEROGAM
PHANEROGAMIC
PHANEROGAMOUS
PHANEROGAMS
PHANEROPHYTE
PHANEROPHYTES
PHANSIGARS
PHANTASIAST
PHANTASIASTS
PHANTASIED
PHANTASIES
PHANTASIME
PHANTASIMES
PHANTASIMS
PHANTASMAGORIA
PHANTASMAGORIAL
PHANTASMAGORIAS
PHANTASMAGORIC
PHANTASMAGORIES
PHANTASMAGORY
PHANTASMAL
PHANTASMALIAN
PHANTASMALITIES
PHANTASMALITY
PHANTASMALLY
PHANTASMAS
PHANTASMATA
PHANTASMIC
PHANTASMICAL
PHANTASMICALLY
PHANTASTIC
PHANTASTICS
PHANTASTRIES
PHANTASTRY
PHANTASYING
PHANTOMATIC
PHANTOMISH
PHANTOMLIKE
PHANTOSMES
PHARISAICAL
PHARISAICALLY
PHARISAICALNESS
PHARISAISM
PHARISAISMS
PHARISEEISM
PHARISEEISMS
PHARMACEUTIC
PHARMACEUTICAL
PHARMACEUTICALS
PHARMACEUTICS
PHARMACEUTIST
PHARMACEUTISTS
PHARMACIES

PHARMACIST
PHARMACISTS
PHARMACODYNAMIC
PHARMACOGENOMIC
PHARMACOGNOSIES
PHARMACOGNOSIST
PHARMACOGNOSTIC
PHARMACOGNOSY
PHARMACOKINETIC
PHARMACOLOGIC
PHARMACOLOGICAL
PHARMACOLOGIES
PHARMACOLOGIST
PHARMACOLOGISTS
PHARMACOLOGY
PHARMACOPEIA
PHARMACOPEIAL
PHARMACOPEIAS
PHARMACOPOEIA
PHARMACOPOEIAL
PHARMACOPOEIAN
PHARMACOPOEIAS
PHARMACOPOEIC
PHARMACOPOEIST
PHARMACOPOEISTS
PHARMACOPOLIST
PHARMACOPOLISTS
PHARMACOTHERAPY
PHARYNGALS
PHARYNGEAL
PHARYNGITIC
PHARYNGITIDES
PHARYNGITIS
PHARYNGITISES
PHARYNGOLOGICAL
PHARYNGOLOGIES
PHARYNGOLOGIST
PHARYNGOLOGISTS
PHARYNGOLOGY
PHARYNGOSCOPE
PHARYNGOSCOPES
PHARYNGOSCOPIC
PHARYNGOSCOPIES
PHARYNGOSCOPY
PHARYNGOTOMIES
PHARYNGOTOMY
PHASCOGALE
PHASCOGALES
PHASEDOWNS
PHASEOLINS
PHATICALLY
PHEASANTRIES
PHEASANTRY
PHELLODERM
PHELLODERMAL
PHELLODERMS
PHELLOGENETIC
PHELLOGENIC
PHELLOGENS
PHELLOPLASTIC
PHELLOPLASTICS
PHELONIONS
PHENACAINE
PHENACAINES
PHENACETIN
PHENACETINS
PHENACITES
PHENAKISMS
PHENAKISTOSCOPE
PHENAKITES
PHENANTHRENE
PHENANTHRENES
PHENARSAZINE
PHENARSAZINES
PHENAZINES
PHENCYCLIDINE
PHENCYCLIDINES
PHENETICIST
PHENETICISTS
PHENETIDINE
PHENETIDINES
PHENETOLES
PHENFORMIN
PHENFORMINS
PHENGOPHOBIA
PHENGOPHOBIAS
PHENMETRAZINE
PHENMETRAZINES
PHENOBARBITAL
PHENOBARBITALS
PHENOBARBITONE
PHENOBARBITONES
PHENOCOPIES
PHENOCRYST
PHENOCRYSTIC
PHENOCRYSTS
PHENOLATED
PHENOLATES
PHENOLATING
PHENOLOGICAL
PHENOLOGICALLY
PHENOLOGIES
PHENOLOGIST
PHENOLOGISTS
PHENOLPHTHALEIN
PHENOMENAL
PHENOMENALISE
PHENOMENALISED
PHENOMENALISES
PHENOMENALISING
PHENOMENALISM
PHENOMENALISMS
PHENOMENALIST
PHENOMENALISTIC
PHENOMENALISTS
PHENOMENALITIES
PHENOMENALITY
PHENOMENALIZE
PHENOMENALIZED
PHENOMENALIZES
PHENOMENALIZING
PHENOMENALLY
PHENOMENAS
PHENOMENISE
PHENOMENISED
PHENOMENISES
PHENOMENISING
PHENOMENISM
PHENOMENISMS
PHENOMENIST
PHENOMENISTS
PHENOMENIZE
PHENOMENIZED
PHENOMENIZES
PHENOMENIZING
PHENOMENOLOGIES
PHENOMENOLOGIST
PHENOMENOLOGY
PHENOMENON
PHENOMENONS
PHENOTHIAZINE
PHENOTHIAZINES
PHENOTYPED
PHENOTYPES
PHENOTYPIC
PHENOTYPICAL
PHENOTYPICALLY
PHENOTYPING
PHENOXIDES
PHENTOLAMINE
PHENTOLAMINES
PHENYLALANIN
PHENYLALANINE
PHENYLALANINES
PHENYLALANINS
PHENYLAMINE
PHENYLAMINES
PHENYLBUTAZONE
PHENYLBUTAZONES
PHENYLENES
PHENYLEPHRINE
PHENYLEPHRINES
PHENYLKETONURIA
PHENYLKETONURIC
PHENYLMETHYL
PHENYLMETHYLS
PHENYLTHIOUREA
PHENYLTHIOUREAS
PHENYTOINS
PHEROMONAL
PHEROMONES
PHIALIFORM
PHILADELPHUS
PHILADELPHUSES
PHILANDERED
PHILANDERER
PHILANDERERS
PHILANDERING
PHILANDERS
PHILANTHROPE
PHILANTHROPES
PHILANTHROPIC
PHILANTHROPICAL
PHILANTHROPIES
PHILANTHROPIST
PHILANTHROPISTS
PHILANTHROPOID
PHILANTHROPOIDS
PHILANTHROPY
PHILATELIC
PHILATELICALLY
PHILATELIES
PHILATELIST
PHILATELISTS
PHILHARMONIC
PHILHARMONICS
PHILHELLENE
PHILHELLENES
PHILHELLENIC
PHILHELLENISM
PHILHELLENISMS
PHILHELLENIST
PHILHELLENISTS
PHILHORSES
PHILIPPICS
PHILIPPINA
PHILIPPINAS
PHILIPPINE
PHILIPPINES
PHILISTIAS
PHILISTINE
PHILISTINES
PHILISTINISM
PHILISTINISMS
PHILLABEGS
PHILLIBEGS
PHILLIPSITE
PHILLIPSITES
PHILLUMENIES
PHILLUMENIST
PHILLUMENISTS
PHILLUMENY
PHILODENDRA
PHILODENDRON
PHILODENDRONS
PHILOGYNIES
PHILOGYNIST
PHILOGYNISTS
PHILOGYNOUS
PHILOLOGER
PHILOLOGERS
PHILOLOGIAN
PHILOLOGIANS
PHILOLOGIC
PHILOLOGICAL
PHILOLOGICALLY
PHILOLOGIES
PHILOLOGIST
PHILOLOGISTS
PHILOLOGUE
PHILOLOGUES
PHILOMATHIC
PHILOMATHICAL
PHILOMATHIES
PHILOMATHS
PHILOMATHY
PHILOMELAS
PHILOPENAS
PHILOPOENA
PHILOPOENAS
PHILOSOPHASTER
PHILOSOPHASTERS
PHILOSOPHE
PHILOSOPHER
PHILOSOPHERESS
PHILOSOPHERS
PHILOSOPHES
PHILOSOPHESS
PHILOSOPHESSES
PHILOSOPHIC
PHILOSOPHICAL
PHILOSOPHICALLY
PHILOSOPHIES
PHILOSOPHISE

PHILOSOPHISED
PHILOSOPHISER
PHILOSOPHISERS
PHILOSOPHISES
PHILOSOPHISING
PHILOSOPHISM
PHILOSOPHISMS
PHILOSOPHIST
PHILOSOPHISTIC
PHILOSOPHISTS
PHILOSOPHIZE
PHILOSOPHIZED
PHILOSOPHIZER
PHILOSOPHIZERS
PHILOSOPHIZES
PHILOSOPHIZING
PHILOSOPHY
PHILOXENIA
PHILOXENIAS
PHILTERING
PHISNOMIES
PHLEBECTOMIES
PHLEBECTOMY
PHLEBITIDES
PHLEBITISES
PHLEBOGRAM
PHLEBOGRAMS
PHLEBOGRAPHIC
PHLEBOGRAPHIES
PHLEBOGRAPHY
PHLEBOLITE
PHLEBOLITES
PHLEBOLOGIES
PHLEBOLOGY
PHLEBOSCLEROSES
PHLEBOSCLEROSIS
PHLEBOTOMIC
PHLEBOTOMICAL
PHLEBOTOMIES
PHLEBOTOMISE
PHLEBOTOMISED
PHLEBOTOMISES
PHLEBOTOMISING
PHLEBOTOMIST
PHLEBOTOMISTS
PHLEBOTOMIZE
PHLEBOTOMIZED
PHLEBOTOMIZES
PHLEBOTOMIZING
PHLEBOTOMY
PHLEGMAGOGIC
PHLEGMAGOGUE
PHLEGMAGOGUES
PHLEGMASIA
PHLEGMASIAS
PHLEGMATIC
PHLEGMATICAL
PHLEGMATICALLY
PHLEGMATICNESS
PHLEGMIEST
PHLEGMONIC
PHLEGMONOID
PHLEGMONOUS
PHLOGISTIC
PHLOGISTICATE
PHLOGISTICATED
PHLOGISTICATES
PHLOGISTICATING
PHLOGISTON
PHLOGISTONS
PHLOGOPITE
PHLOGOPITES
PHLORIZINS
PHLYCTAENA
PHLYCTAENAE
PHLYCTENAE
PHOCOMELIA
PHOCOMELIAS
PHOCOMELIC
PHOENIXISM
PHOENIXISMS
PHOENIXLIKE
PHOLIDOSES
PHOLIDOSIS
PHONASTHENIA
PHONASTHENIAS
PHONATHONS
PHONATIONS
PHONAUTOGRAPH
PHONAUTOGRAPHIC
PHONAUTOGRAPHS
PHONECARDS
PHONEMATIC
PHONEMATICALLY
PHONEMICALLY
PHONEMICISATION
PHONEMICISE
PHONEMICISED
PHONEMICISES
PHONEMICISING
PHONEMICIST
PHONEMICISTS
PHONEMICIZATION
PHONEMICIZE
PHONEMICIZED
PHONEMICIZES
PHONEMICIZING
PHONENDOSCOPE
PHONENDOSCOPES
PHONETICAL
PHONETICALLY
PHONETICIAN
PHONETICIANS
PHONETICISATION
PHONETICISE
PHONETICISED
PHONETICISES
PHONETICISING
PHONETICISM
PHONETICISMS
PHONETICIST
PHONETICISTS
PHONETICIZATION
PHONETICIZE
PHONETICIZED
PHONETICIZES
PHONETICIZING
PHONETISATION
PHONETISATIONS
PHONETISED
PHONETISES
PHONETISING
PHONETISMS
PHONETISTS
PHONETIZATION
PHONETIZATIONS
PHONETIZED
PHONETIZES
PHONETIZING
PHONEYNESS
PHONEYNESSES
PHONICALLY
PHONINESSES
PHONMETERS
PHONOCAMPTIC
PHONOCAMPTICS
PHONOCARDIOGRAM
PHONOCHEMISTRY
PHONOFIDDLE
PHONOFIDDLES
PHONOGRAMIC
PHONOGRAMICALLY
PHONOGRAMMIC
PHONOGRAMS
PHONOGRAPH
PHONOGRAPHER
PHONOGRAPHERS
PHONOGRAPHIC
PHONOGRAPHIES
PHONOGRAPHIST
PHONOGRAPHISTS
PHONOGRAPHS
PHONOGRAPHY
PHONOLITES
PHONOLITIC
PHONOLOGIC
PHONOLOGICAL
PHONOLOGICALLY
PHONOLOGIES
PHONOLOGIST
PHONOLOGISTS
PHONOMETER
PHONOMETERS
PHONOMETRIC
PHONOMETRICAL
PHONOPHOBIA
PHONOPHOBIAS
PHONOPHORE
PHONOPHORES
PHONOPORES
PHONOSCOPE
PHONOSCOPES
PHONOTACTIC
PHONOTACTICS
PHONOTYPED
PHONOTYPER
PHONOTYPERS
PHONOTYPES
PHONOTYPIC
PHONOTYPICAL
PHONOTYPIES
PHONOTYPING
PHONOTYPIST
PHONOTYPISTS
PHORMINGES
PHOSGENITE
PHOSGENITES
PHOSPHATASE
PHOSPHATASES
PHOSPHATED
PHOSPHATES
PHOSPHATIC
PHOSPHATIDE
PHOSPHATIDES
PHOSPHATIDIC
PHOSPHATIDYL
PHOSPHATIDYLS
PHOSPHATING
PHOSPHATISATION
PHOSPHATISE
PHOSPHATISED
PHOSPHATISES
PHOSPHATISING
PHOSPHATIZATION
PHOSPHATIZE
PHOSPHATIZED
PHOSPHATIZES
PHOSPHATIZING
PHOSPHATURIA
PHOSPHATURIAS
PHOSPHATURIC
PHOSPHENES
PHOSPHIDES
PHOSPHINES
PHOSPHITES
PHOSPHOCREATIN
PHOSPHOCREATINE
PHOSPHOCREATINS
PHOSPHOKINASE
PHOSPHOKINASES
PHOSPHOLIPASE
PHOSPHOLIPASES
PHOSPHOLIPID
PHOSPHOLIPIDS
PHOSPHONIC
PHOSPHONIUM
PHOSPHONIUMS
PHOSPHOPROTEIN
PHOSPHOPROTEINS
PHOSPHORATE
PHOSPHORATED
PHOSPHORATES
PHOSPHORATING
PHOSPHORES
PHOSPHORESCE
PHOSPHORESCED
PHOSPHORESCENCE
PHOSPHORESCENT
PHOSPHORESCES
PHOSPHORESCING
PHOSPHORET
PHOSPHORETS
PHOSPHORETTED
PHOSPHORIC
PHOSPHORISE
PHOSPHORISED
PHOSPHORISES
PHOSPHORISING
PHOSPHORISM
PHOSPHORISMS
PHOSPHORITE
PHOSPHORITES
PHOSPHORITIC
PHOSPHORIZE

PHOSPHORIZED
PHOSPHORIZES
PHOSPHORIZING
PHOSPHOROLYSES
PHOSPHOROLYSIS
PHOSPHOROLYTIC
PHOSPHOROSCOPE
PHOSPHOROSCOPES
PHOSPHOROUS
PHOSPHORUS
PHOSPHORUSES
PHOSPHORYL
PHOSPHORYLASE
PHOSPHORYLASES
PHOSPHORYLATE
PHOSPHORYLATED
PHOSPHORYLATES
PHOSPHORYLATING
PHOSPHORYLATION
PHOSPHORYLATIVE
PHOSPHORYLS
PHOSPHURET
PHOSPHURETS
PHOSPHURETTED
PHOTICALLY
PHOTOACTINIC
PHOTOACTIVE
PHOTOAUTOTROPH
PHOTOAUTOTROPHS
PHOTOBATHIC
PHOTOBIOLOGIC
PHOTOBIOLOGICAL
PHOTOBIOLOGIES
PHOTOBIOLOGIST
PHOTOBIOLOGISTS
PHOTOBIOLOGY
PHOTOCATALYSES
PHOTOCATALYSIS
PHOTOCATALYTIC
PHOTOCATHODE
PHOTOCATHODES
PHOTOCELLS
PHOTOCHEMICAL
PHOTOCHEMICALLY
PHOTOCHEMIST
PHOTOCHEMISTRY
PHOTOCHEMISTS
PHOTOCHROMIC
PHOTOCHROMICS
PHOTOCHROMIES
PHOTOCHROMISM
PHOTOCHROMISMS
PHOTOCHROMY
PHOTOCOMPOSE
PHOTOCOMPOSED
PHOTOCOMPOSER
PHOTOCOMPOSERS
PHOTOCOMPOSES
PHOTOCOMPOSING
PHOTOCONDUCTING
PHOTOCONDUCTION
PHOTOCONDUCTIVE
PHOTOCONDUCTOR
PHOTOCONDUCTORS
PHOTOCOPIABLE
PHOTOCOPIED
PHOTOCOPIER
PHOTOCOPIERS
PHOTOCOPIES
PHOTOCOPYING
PHOTOCOPYINGS
PHOTOCURRENT
PHOTOCURRENTS
PHOTODEGRADABLE
PHOTODETECTOR
PHOTODETECTORS
PHOTODIODE
PHOTODIODES
PHOTODISSOCIATE
PHOTODUPLICATE
PHOTODUPLICATED
PHOTODUPLICATES
PHOTODYNAMIC
PHOTODYNAMICS
PHOTOELASTIC
PHOTOELASTICITY
PHOTOELECTRIC
PHOTOELECTRICAL
PHOTOELECTRODE
PHOTOELECTRODES
PHOTOELECTRON
PHOTOELECTRONIC
PHOTOELECTRONS
PHOTOEMISSION
PHOTOEMISSIONS
PHOTOEMISSIVE
PHOTOENGRAVE
PHOTOENGRAVED
PHOTOENGRAVER
PHOTOENGRAVERS
PHOTOENGRAVES
PHOTOENGRAVING
PHOTOENGRAVINGS
PHOTOEXCITATION
PHOTOEXCITED
PHOTOFINISHER
PHOTOFINISHERS
PHOTOFINISHING
PHOTOFINISHINGS
PHOTOFISSION
PHOTOFISSIONS
PHOTOFLASH
PHOTOFLASHES
PHOTOFLOOD
PHOTOFLOODS
PHOTOFLUOROGRAM
PHOTOGELATINE
PHOTOGENES
PHOTOGENIC
PHOTOGENICALLY
PHOTOGENIES
PHOTOGEOLOGIC
PHOTOGEOLOGICAL
PHOTOGEOLOGIES
PHOTOGEOLOGIST
PHOTOGEOLOGISTS
PHOTOGEOLOGY
PHOTOGLYPH
PHOTOGLYPHIC
PHOTOGLYPHIES
PHOTOGLYPHS
PHOTOGLYPHY
PHOTOGRAMMETRIC
PHOTOGRAMMETRY
PHOTOGRAMS
PHOTOGRAPH
PHOTOGRAPHED
PHOTOGRAPHER
PHOTOGRAPHERS
PHOTOGRAPHIC
PHOTOGRAPHICAL
PHOTOGRAPHIES
PHOTOGRAPHING
PHOTOGRAPHIST
PHOTOGRAPHISTS
PHOTOGRAPHS
PHOTOGRAPHY
PHOTOGRAVURE
PHOTOGRAVURES
PHOTOINDUCED
PHOTOINDUCTION
PHOTOINDUCTIONS
PHOTOINDUCTIVE
PHOTOIONISATION
PHOTOIONISE
PHOTOIONISED
PHOTOIONISES
PHOTOIONISING
PHOTOIONIZATION
PHOTOIONIZE
PHOTOIONIZED
PHOTOIONIZES
PHOTOIONIZING
PHOTOJOURNALISM
PHOTOJOURNALIST
PHOTOKINESES
PHOTOKINESIS
PHOTOKINETIC
PHOTOLITHO
PHOTOLITHOGRAPH
PHOTOLITHOS
PHOTOLUMINESCE
PHOTOLUMINESCED
PHOTOLUMINESCES
PHOTOLYSABLE
PHOTOLYSED
PHOTOLYSES
PHOTOLYSING
PHOTOLYSIS
PHOTOLYTIC
PHOTOLYTICALLY
PHOTOLYZABLE
PHOTOLYZED
PHOTOLYZES
PHOTOLYZING
PHOTOMACROGRAPH
PHOTOMAPPED
PHOTOMAPPING
PHOTOMASKS
PHOTOMECHANICAL
PHOTOMETER
PHOTOMETERS
PHOTOMETRIC
PHOTOMETRICALLY
PHOTOMETRIES
PHOTOMETRIST
PHOTOMETRISTS
PHOTOMETRY
PHOTOMICROGRAPH
PHOTOMONTAGE
PHOTOMONTAGES
PHOTOMOSAIC
PHOTOMOSAICS
PHOTOMULTIPLIER
PHOTOMURAL
PHOTOMURALS
PHOTONASTIC
PHOTONASTIES
PHOTONASTY
PHOTONEGATIVE
PHOTONEUTRON
PHOTONEUTRONS
PHOTONOVEL
PHOTONOVELS
PHOTONUCLEAR
PHOTOOXIDATION
PHOTOOXIDATIONS
PHOTOOXIDATIVE
PHOTOOXIDISE
PHOTOOXIDISED
PHOTOOXIDISES
PHOTOOXIDISING
PHOTOOXIDIZE
PHOTOOXIDIZED
PHOTOOXIDIZES
PHOTOOXIDIZING
PHOTOPERIOD
PHOTOPERIODIC
PHOTOPERIODISM
PHOTOPERIODISMS
PHOTOPERIODS
PHOTOPHASE
PHOTOPHASES
PHOTOPHILIC
PHOTOPHILIES
PHOTOPHILOUS
PHOTOPHILS
PHOTOPHILY
PHOTOPHOBE
PHOTOPHOBES
PHOTOPHOBIA
PHOTOPHOBIAS
PHOTOPHOBIC
PHOTOPHONE
PHOTOPHONES
PHOTOPHONIC
PHOTOPHONIES
PHOTOPHONY
PHOTOPHORE
PHOTOPHORES
PHOTOPHORESES
PHOTOPHORESIS
PHOTOPLAYS
PHOTOPOLYMER
PHOTOPOLYMERS
PHOTOPOSITIVE
PHOTOPRODUCT
PHOTOPRODUCTION
PHOTOPRODUCTS
PHOTOPSIAS
PHOTOPSIES
PHOTOREACTION
PHOTOREACTIONS
PHOTOREALISM

PHOTOREALISMS
PHOTOREALIST
PHOTOREALISTIC
PHOTOREALISTS
PHOTORECEPTION
PHOTORECEPTIONS
PHOTORECEPTIVE
PHOTORECEPTOR
PHOTORECEPTORS
PHOTOREDUCE
PHOTOREDUCED
PHOTOREDUCES
PHOTOREDUCING
PHOTOREDUCTION
PHOTOREDUCTIONS
PHOTOREFRACTIVE
PHOTORESIST
PHOTORESISTS
PHOTOSCANNED
PHOTOSCANNING
PHOTOSCANS
PHOTOSENSITISE
PHOTOSENSITISED
PHOTOSENSITISER
PHOTOSENSITISES
PHOTOSENSITIVE
PHOTOSENSITIZE
PHOTOSENSITIZED
PHOTOSENSITIZER
PHOTOSENSITIZES
PHOTOSETTER
PHOTOSETTERS
PHOTOSETTING
PHOTOSETTINGS
PHOTOSHOOT
PHOTOSHOOTS
PHOTOSPHERE
PHOTOSPHERES
PHOTOSPHERIC
PHOTOSTATED
PHOTOSTATIC
PHOTOSTATING
PHOTOSTATS
PHOTOSTATTED
PHOTOSTATTING
PHOTOSYNTHATE
PHOTOSYNTHATES
PHOTOSYNTHESES
PHOTOSYNTHESIS
PHOTOSYNTHESISE
PHOTOSYNTHESIZE
PHOTOSYNTHETIC
PHOTOSYSTEM
PHOTOSYSTEMS
PHOTOTACTIC
PHOTOTACTICALLY
PHOTOTAXES
PHOTOTAXIES
PHOTOTAXIS
PHOTOTELEGRAPH
PHOTOTELEGRAPHS
PHOTOTELEGRAPHY
PHOTOTHERAPIES
PHOTOTHERAPY
PHOTOTHERMAL
PHOTOTHERMALLY
PHOTOTHERMIC
PHOTOTONIC
PHOTOTONUS
PHOTOTONUSES
PHOTOTOPOGRAPHY
PHOTOTOXIC
PHOTOTOXICITIES
PHOTOTOXICITY
PHOTOTRANSISTOR
PHOTOTROPE
PHOTOTROPES
PHOTOTROPH
PHOTOTROPHIC
PHOTOTROPHS
PHOTOTROPIC
PHOTOTROPICALLY
PHOTOTROPIES
PHOTOTROPISM
PHOTOTROPISMS
PHOTOTROPY
PHOTOTUBES
PHOTOTYPED
PHOTOTYPES
PHOTOTYPESET
PHOTOTYPESETS
PHOTOTYPESETTER
PHOTOTYPIC
PHOTOTYPICALLY
PHOTOTYPIES
PHOTOTYPING
PHOTOTYPOGRAPHY
PHOTOVOLTAIC
PHOTOVOLTAICS
PHOTOXYLOGRAPHY
PHOTOZINCOGRAPH
PHRAGMOPLAST
PHRAGMOPLASTS
PHRASELESS
PHRASEMAKER
PHRASEMAKERS
PHRASEMAKING
PHRASEMAKINGS
PHRASEMONGER
PHRASEMONGERING
PHRASEMONGERS
PHRASEOGRAM
PHRASEOGRAMS
PHRASEOGRAPH
PHRASEOGRAPHIC
PHRASEOGRAPHIES
PHRASEOGRAPHS
PHRASEOGRAPHY
PHRASEOLOGIC
PHRASEOLOGICAL
PHRASEOLOGIES
PHRASEOLOGIST
PHRASEOLOGISTS
PHRASEOLOGY
PHREAKINGS
PHREATOPHYTE
PHREATOPHYTES
PHREATOPHYTIC
PHRENESIAC
PHRENETICAL
PHRENETICALLY
PHRENETICNESS
PHRENETICNESSES
PHRENETICS
PHRENITIDES
PHRENITISES
PHRENOLOGIC
PHRENOLOGICAL
PHRENOLOGICALLY
PHRENOLOGIES
PHRENOLOGISE
PHRENOLOGISED
PHRENOLOGISES
PHRENOLOGISING
PHRENOLOGIST
PHRENOLOGISTS
PHRENOLOGIZE
PHRENOLOGIZED
PHRENOLOGIZES
PHRENOLOGIZING
PHRENOLOGY
PHRENSICAL
PHRENSYING
PHRONTISTERIES
PHRONTISTERY
PHTHALATES
PHTHALEINS
PHTHALOCYANIN
PHTHALOCYANINE
PHTHALOCYANINES
PHTHALOCYANINS
PHTHIRIASES
PHTHIRIASIS
PHTHISICAL
PHTHISICKY
PHYCOBILIN
PHYCOBILINS
PHYCOBIONT
PHYCOBIONTS
PHYCOCYANIN
PHYCOCYANINS
PHYCOCYANS
PHYCOERYTHRIN
PHYCOERYTHRINS
PHYCOLOGICAL
PHYCOLOGIES
PHYCOLOGIST
PHYCOLOGISTS
PHYCOMYCETE
PHYCOMYCETES
PHYCOMYCETOUS
PHYCOPHAEIN
PHYCOPHAEINS
PHYCOXANTHIN
PHYCOXANTHINS
PHYLACTERIC
PHYLACTERICAL
PHYLACTERIES
PHYLACTERY
PHYLARCHIES
PHYLAXISES
PHYLESISES
PHYLETICALLY
PHYLLARIES
PHYLLOCLAD
PHYLLOCLADE
PHYLLOCLADES
PHYLLOCLADS
PHYLLODIAL
PHYLLODIES
PHYLLODIUM
PHYLLOMANIA
PHYLLOMANIAS
PHYLLOPHAGOUS
PHYLLOPLANE
PHYLLOPLANES
PHYLLOPODS
PHYLLOQUINONE
PHYLLOQUINONES
PHYLLOSILICATE
PHYLLOSILICATES
PHYLLOSPHERE
PHYLLOSPHERES
PHYLLOTACTIC
PHYLLOTACTICAL
PHYLLOTAXES
PHYLLOTAXIES
PHYLLOTAXIS
PHYLLOTAXY
PHYLLOXERA
PHYLLOXERAE
PHYLLOXERAS
PHYLOGENESES
PHYLOGENESIS
PHYLOGENETIC
PHYLOGENIC
PHYLOGENIES
PHYSALISES
PHYSHARMONICA
PHYSHARMONICAS
PHYSIATRIC
PHYSIATRICAL
PHYSIATRICS
PHYSIATRIES
PHYSIATRIST
PHYSIATRISTS
PHYSICALISM
PHYSICALISMS
PHYSICALIST
PHYSICALISTIC
PHYSICALISTS
PHYSICALITIES
PHYSICALITY
PHYSICALLY
PHYSICALNESS
PHYSICALNESSES
PHYSICIANCIES
PHYSICIANCY
PHYSICIANER
PHYSICIANERS
PHYSICIANS
PHYSICIANSHIP
PHYSICIANSHIPS
PHYSICISMS
PHYSICISTS
PHYSICKING
PHYSICOCHEMICAL
PHYSIOCRACIES
PHYSIOCRACY
PHYSIOCRAT
PHYSIOCRATIC
PHYSIOCRATS
PHYSIOGNOMIC
PHYSIOGNOMICAL

PHYSIOGNOMIES
PHYSIOGNOMIST
PHYSIOGNOMISTS
PHYSIOGNOMY
PHYSIOGRAPHER
PHYSIOGRAPHERS
PHYSIOGRAPHIC
PHYSIOGRAPHICAL
PHYSIOGRAPHIES
PHYSIOGRAPHY
PHYSIOLATER
PHYSIOLATERS
PHYSIOLATRIES
PHYSIOLATRY
PHYSIOLOGIC
PHYSIOLOGICAL
PHYSIOLOGICALLY
PHYSIOLOGIES
PHYSIOLOGIST
PHYSIOLOGISTS
PHYSIOLOGUS
PHYSIOLOGUSES
PHYSIOLOGY
PHYSIOPATHOLOGY
PHYSIOTHERAPIES
PHYSIOTHERAPIST
PHYSIOTHERAPY
PHYSITHEISM
PHYSITHEISMS
PHYSITHEISTIC
PHYSOCLISTOUS
PHYSOSTIGMIN
PHYSOSTIGMINE
PHYSOSTIGMINES
PHYSOSTIGMINS
PHYSOSTOMOUS
PHYTOALEXIN
PHYTOALEXINS
PHYTOBENTHOS
PHYTOBENTHOSES
PHYTOCHEMICAL
PHYTOCHEMICALLY
PHYTOCHEMICALS
PHYTOCHEMIST
PHYTOCHEMISTRY
PHYTOCHEMISTS
PHYTOCHROME
PHYTOCHROMES
PHYTOESTROGEN
PHYTOESTROGENS
PHYTOFLAGELLATE
PHYTOGENESES
PHYTOGENESIS
PHYTOGENETIC
PHYTOGENETICAL
PHYTOGENIC
PHYTOGENIES
PHYTOGEOGRAPHER
PHYTOGEOGRAPHIC
PHYTOGEOGRAPHY
PHYTOGRAPHER
PHYTOGRAPHERS
PHYTOGRAPHIC
PHYTOGRAPHIES
PHYTOGRAPHY
PHYTOHORMONE
PHYTOHORMONES
PHYTOLITHS
PHYTOLOGICAL
PHYTOLOGICALLY
PHYTOLOGIES
PHYTOLOGIST
PHYTOLOGISTS
PHYTONADIONE
PHYTONADIONES
PHYTOPATHOGEN
PHYTOPATHOGENIC
PHYTOPATHOGENS
PHYTOPATHOLOGY
PHYTOPHAGIC
PHYTOPHAGIES
PHYTOPHAGOUS
PHYTOPHAGY
PHYTOPLANKTER
PHYTOPLANKTERS
PHYTOPLANKTON
PHYTOPLANKTONIC
PHYTOPLANKTONS
PHYTOSOCIOLOGY
PHYTOSTEROL
PHYTOSTEROLS
PHYTOTHERAPIES
PHYTOTHERAPY
PHYTOTOMIES
PHYTOTOMIST
PHYTOTOMISTS
PHYTOTOXIC
PHYTOTOXICITIES
PHYTOTOXICITY
PHYTOTOXIN
PHYTOTOXINS
PHYTOTRONS
PIACULARITIES
PIACULARITY
PIANISSIMI
PIANISSIMO
PIANISSIMOS
PIANISSISSIMO
PIANISTICALLY
PIANOFORTE
PIANOFORTES
PIANOLISTS
PICADILLOS
PICANINNIES
PICARESQUE
PICARESQUES
PICAROONED
PICAROONING
PICAYUNISH
PICAYUNISHLY
PICAYUNISHNESS
PICCADILLIES
PICCADILLO
PICCADILLOES
PICCADILLS
PICCADILLY
PICCALILLI
PICCALILLIS
PICCANINNIES
PICCANINNY
PICCOLOIST
PICCOLOISTS
PICHICIAGO
PICHICIAGOS
PICHICIEGO
PICHICIEGOS
PICHOLINES
PICKABACKED
PICKABACKING
PICKABACKS
PICKADILLIES
PICKADILLO
PICKADILLOES
PICKADILLS
PICKADILLY
PICKANINNIES
PICKANINNY
PICKAPACKS
PICKAROONS
PICKEDNESS
PICKEDNESSES
PICKEERERS
PICKEERING
PICKELHAUBE
PICKELHAUBES
PICKERELWEED
PICKERELWEEDS
PICKETBOAT
PICKETBOATS
PICKETINGS
PICKINESSES
PICKPOCKET
PICKPOCKETS
PICKTHANKS
PICNICKERS
PICNICKING
PICOCURIES
PICOFARADS
PICOMETERS
PICOMETRES
PICORNAVIRUS
PICORNAVIRUSES
PICOSECOND
PICOSECONDS
PICOWAVING
PICQUETING
PICROCARMINE
PICROCARMINES
PICROTOXIN
PICROTOXINS
PICTARNIES
PICTOGRAMS
PICTOGRAPH
PICTOGRAPHIC
PICTOGRAPHIES
PICTOGRAPHS
PICTOGRAPHY
PICTORIALISE
PICTORIALISED
PICTORIALISES
PICTORIALISING
PICTORIALISM
PICTORIALISMS
PICTORIALIST
PICTORIALISTS
PICTORIALIZE
PICTORIALIZED
PICTORIALIZES
PICTORIALIZING
PICTORIALLY
PICTORIALNESS
PICTORIALNESSES
PICTORIALS
PICTORICAL
PICTORICALLY
PICTUREGOER
PICTUREGOERS
PICTUREPHONE
PICTUREPHONES
PICTURESQUE
PICTURESQUELY
PICTURESQUENESS
PICTURISATION
PICTURISATIONS
PICTURISED
PICTURISES
PICTURISING
PICTURIZATION
PICTURIZATIONS
PICTURIZED
PICTURIZES
PICTURIZING
PIDDLINGLY
PIDGINISATION
PIDGINISATIONS
PIDGINISED
PIDGINISES
PIDGINISING
PIDGINIZATION
PIDGINIZATIONS
PIDGINIZED
PIDGINIZES
PIDGINIZING
PIECEMEALED
PIECEMEALING
PIECEMEALS
PIECEWORKER
PIECEWORKERS
PIECEWORKS
PIEDMONTITE
PIEDMONTITES
PIEDNESSES
PIEMONTITE
PIEMONTITES
PIEPOWDERS
PIERCEABLE
PIERCINGLY
PIERCINGNESS
PIERCINGNESSES
PIERRETTES
PIETISTICAL
PIETISTICALLY
PIEZOCHEMISTRY
PIEZOELECTRIC
PIEZOMAGNETIC
PIEZOMAGNETISM
PIEZOMAGNETISMS
PIEZOMETER
PIEZOMETERS
PIEZOMETRIC
PIEZOMETRICALLY
PIEZOMETRIES
PIEZOMETRY
PIGEONHOLE

PIGEONHOLED
PIGEONHOLER
PIGEONHOLERS
PIGEONHOLES
PIGEONHOLING
PIGEONITES
PIGEONRIES
PIGEONWING
PIGEONWINGS
PIGGINESSES
PIGGISHNESS
PIGGISHNESSES
PIGGYBACKED
PIGGYBACKING
PIGGYBACKS
PIGHEADEDLY
PIGHEADEDNESS
PIGHEADEDNESSES
PIGMENTARY
PIGMENTATION
PIGMENTATIONS
PIGMENTING
PIGNERATED
PIGNERATES
PIGNERATING
PIGNORATED
PIGNORATES
PIGNORATING
PIGNORATION
PIGNORATIONS
PIGSCONCES
PIGSTICKED
PIGSTICKER
PIGSTICKERS
PIGSTICKING
PIGTAILING
PIKEPERCHES
PIKESTAFFS
PIKESTAVES
PILASTERED
PILEORHIZA
PILEORHIZAS
PILFERABLE
PILFERAGES
PILFERINGLY
PILFERINGS
PILFERPROOF
PILGARLICK
PILGARLICKS
PILGARLICKY
PILGARLICS
PILGRIMAGE
PILGRIMAGED
PILGRIMAGER
PILGRIMAGERS
PILGRIMAGES
PILGRIMAGING
PILGRIMERS
PILGRIMISE
PILGRIMISED
PILGRIMISES
PILGRIMISING
PILGRIMIZE
PILGRIMIZED
PILGRIMIZES
PILGRIMIZING
PILIFEROUS
PILLARISTS
PILLARLESS
PILLICOCKS
PILLIONING
PILLIONIST
PILLIONISTS
PILLIWINKS
PILLORISED
PILLORISES
PILLORISING
PILLORIZED
PILLORIZES
PILLORIZING
PILLORYING
PILLOWCASE
PILLOWCASES
PILLOWSLIP
PILLOWSLIPS
PILNIEWINKS
PILOCARPIN
PILOCARPINE
PILOCARPINES
PILOCARPINS
PILOSITIES
PILOTFISHES
PILOTHOUSE
PILOTHOUSES
PIMPERNELS
PIMPLINESS
PIMPLINESSES
PIMPMOBILE
PIMPMOBILES
PINACOIDAL
PINACOTHECA
PINACOTHECAE
PINAFORING
PINAKOIDAL
PINAKOTHEK
PINAKOTHEKS
PINBALLING
PINCERLIKE
PINCHBECKS
PINCHCOCKS
PINCHCOMMONS
PINCHCOMMONSES
PINCHFISTS
PINCHINGLY
PINCHPENNIES
PINCHPENNY
PINCHPOINT
PINCHPOINTS
PINCUSHION
PINCUSHIONS
PINEALECTOMIES
PINEALECTOMISE
PINEALECTOMISED
PINEALECTOMISES
PINEALECTOMIZE
PINEALECTOMIZED
PINEALECTOMIZES
PINEALECTOMY
PINEAPPLES
PINFEATHER
PINFEATHERS
PINFOLDING
PINGRASSES
PINGUEFIED
PINGUEFIES
PINGUEFYING
PINGUIDITIES
PINGUIDITY
PINGUITUDE
PINGUITUDES
PINHEADEDNESS
PINHEADEDNESSES
PINHOOKERS
PINKERTONS
PINKINESSES
PINKISHNESS
PINKISHNESSES
PINKNESSES
PINNACLING
PINNATIFID
PINNATIFIDLY
PINNATIONS
PINNATIPARTITE
PINNATIPED
PINNATISECT
PINNIEWINKLE
PINNIEWINKLES
PINNIPEDES
PINNIPEDIAN
PINNIPEDIANS
PINNULATED
PINNYWINKLE
PINNYWINKLES
PINOCYTOSES
PINOCYTOSIS
PINOCYTOTIC
PINOCYTOTICALLY
PINPOINTED
PINPOINTING
PINPRICKED
PINPRICKING
PINSETTERS
PINSPOTTER
PINSPOTTERS
PINSTRIPES
PINTADERAS
PINWHEELED
PINWHEELING
PINWRENCHES
PIONEERING
PIOUSNESSES
PIPECLAYED
PIPECLAYING
PIPEFISHES
PIPEFITTER
PIPEFITTERS
PIPEFITTING
PIPEFITTINGS
PIPELINING
PIPELININGS
PIPERACEOUS
PIPERAZINE
PIPERAZINES
PIPERIDINE
PIPERIDINES
PIPERONALS
PIPESTONES
PIPINESSES
PIPISTRELLE
PIPISTRELLES
PIPISTRELS
PIPIWHARAUROA
PIPIWHARAUROAS
PIPSISSEWA
PIPSISSEWAS
PIPSQUEAKS
PIQUANCIES
PIQUANTNESS
PIQUANTNESSES
PIRACETAMS
PIRATICALLY
PIRLICUING
PIROPLASMA
PIROPLASMATA
PIROPLASMS
PIROUETTED
PIROUETTER
PIROUETTERS
PIROUETTES
PIROUETTING
PISCATORIAL
PISCATORIALLY
PISCATRIXES
PISCICOLOUS
PISCICULTURAL
PISCICULTURALLY
PISCICULTURE
PISCICULTURES
PISCICULTURIST
PISCICULTURISTS
PISCIFAUNA
PISCIFAUNAE
PISCIFAUNAS
PISCIVORES
PISCIVOROUS
PISSASPHALT
PISSASPHALTS
PISTACHIOS
PISTAREENS
PISTILLARY
PISTILLATE
PISTILLODE
PISTILLODES
PISTOLEERS
PISTOLEROS
PISTOLIERS
PISTOLLING
PITAPATTED
PITAPATTING
PITCHBENDS
PITCHBLENDE
PITCHBLENDES
PITCHERFUL
PITCHERFULS
PITCHERSFUL
PITCHFORKED
PITCHFORKING
PITCHFORKS
PITCHINESS
PITCHINESSES
PITCHOMETER
PITCHOMETERS
PITCHPERSON
PITCHPERSONS

PITCHPINES
PITCHPIPES
PITCHPOLED
PITCHPOLES
PITCHPOLING
PITCHSTONE
PITCHSTONES
PITCHWOMAN
PITCHWOMEN
PITEOUSNESS
PITEOUSNESSES
PITHECANTHROPI
PITHECANTHROPUS
PITHINESSES
PITIABLENESS
PITIABLENESSES
PITIFULLER
PITIFULLEST
PITIFULNESS
PITIFULNESSES
PITILESSLY
PITILESSNESS
PITILESSNESSES
PITTOSPORUM
PITTOSPORUMS
PITUITARIES
PITUITRINS
PITYRIASES
PITYRIASIS
PITYROSPORUM
PITYROSPORUMS
PIWAKAWAKA
PIXELATION
PIXELATIONS
PIXELLATED
PIXILATION
PIXILATIONS
PIXILLATED
PIXILLATION
PIXILLATIONS
PIXINESSES
PIZZAIOLAS
PIZZICATOS
PLACABILITIES
PLACABILITY
PLACABLENESS
PLACABLENESSES
PLACARDING
PLACATINGLY
PLACATIONS
PLACEHOLDER
PLACEHOLDERS
PLACEKICKED
PLACEKICKER
PLACEKICKERS
PLACEKICKING
PLACEKICKS
PLACELESSLY
PLACEMENTS
PLACENTALS
PLACENTATE
PLACENTATION
PLACENTATIONS
PLACENTIFORM
PLACENTOLOGIES
PLACENTOLOGY
PLACIDITIES
PLACIDNESS
PLACIDNESSES
PLACODERMS
PLAGIARIES
PLAGIARISE
PLAGIARISED
PLAGIARISER
PLAGIARISERS
PLAGIARISES
PLAGIARISING
PLAGIARISM
PLAGIARISMS
PLAGIARIST
PLAGIARISTIC
PLAGIARISTS
PLAGIARIZE
PLAGIARIZED
PLAGIARIZER
PLAGIARIZERS
PLAGIARIZES
PLAGIARIZING
PLAGIOCEPHALIES
PLAGIOCEPHALY
PLAGIOCLASE
PLAGIOCLASES
PLAGIOCLASTIC
PLAGIOCLIMAX
PLAGIOCLIMAXES
PLAGIOSTOMATOUS
PLAGIOSTOME
PLAGIOSTOMES
PLAGIOSTOMOUS
PLAGIOTROPIC
PLAGIOTROPISM
PLAGIOTROPISMS
PLAGIOTROPOUS
PLAGUESOME
PLAINCHANT
PLAINCHANTS
PLAINCLOTHES
PLAINCLOTHESMAN
PLAINCLOTHESMEN
PLAINNESSES
PLAINSONGS
PLAINSPOKEN
PLAINSPOKENNESS
PLAINSTANES
PLAINSTONES
PLAINTEXTS
PLAINTIFFS
PLAINTIVELY
PLAINTIVENESS
PLAINTIVENESSES
PLAINTLESS
PLAINWORKS
PLAISTERED
PLAISTERING
PLANARIANS
PLANARITIES
PLANATIONS
PLANCHETTE
PLANCHETTES
PLANELOADS
PLANENESSES
PLANESIDES
PLANETARIA
PLANETARIES
PLANETARIUM
PLANETARIUMS
PLANETESIMAL
PLANETESIMALS
PLANETICAL
PLANETLIKE
PLANETOIDAL
PLANETOIDS
PLANETOLOGICAL
PLANETOLOGIES
PLANETOLOGIST
PLANETOLOGISTS
PLANETOLOGY
PLANETWIDE
PLANGENCIES
PLANGENTLY
PLANIGRAPH
PLANIGRAPHS
PLANIMETER
PLANIMETERS
PLANIMETRIC
PLANIMETRICAL
PLANIMETRICALLY
PLANIMETRIES
PLANIMETRY
PLANISHERS
PLANISHING
PLANISPHERE
PLANISPHERES
PLANISPHERIC
PLANKTONIC
PLANLESSLY
PLANLESSNESS
PLANLESSNESSES
PLANOBLAST
PLANOBLASTS
PLANOGAMETE
PLANOGAMETES
PLANOGRAPHIC
PLANOGRAPHIES
PLANOGRAPHY
PLANOMETER
PLANOMETERS
PLANOMETRIC
PLANOMETRICALLY
PLANOMETRIES
PLANOMETRY
PLANTAGINACEOUS
PLANTATION
PLANTATIONS
PLANTIGRADE
PLANTIGRADES
PLANTLINGS
PLANTOCRACIES
PLANTOCRACY
PLANTSWOMAN
PLANTSWOMEN
PLANULIFORM
PLAQUETTES
PLASMAGELS
PLASMAGENE
PLASMAGENES
PLASMAGENIC
PLASMALEMMA
PLASMALEMMAS
PLASMAPHERESES
PLASMAPHERESIS
PLASMASOLS
PLASMATICAL
PLASMINOGEN
PLASMINOGENS
PLASMODESM
PLASMODESMA
PLASMODESMAS
PLASMODESMATA
PLASMODESMS
PLASMODIAL
PLASMODIUM
PLASMOGAMIES
PLASMOGAMY
PLASMOLYSE
PLASMOLYSED
PLASMOLYSES
PLASMOLYSING
PLASMOLYSIS
PLASMOLYTIC
PLASMOLYTICALLY
PLASMOLYZE
PLASMOLYZED
PLASMOLYZES
PLASMOLYZING
PLASMOSOMA
PLASMOSOMATA
PLASMOSOME
PLASMOSOMES
PLASTERBOARD
PLASTERBOARDS
PLASTERERS
PLASTERINESS
PLASTERINESSES
PLASTERING
PLASTERINGS
PLASTERSTONE
PLASTERSTONES
PLASTERWORK
PLASTERWORKS
PLASTICALLY
PLASTICENE
PLASTICENES
PLASTICINE
PLASTICINES
PLASTICISATION
PLASTICISATIONS
PLASTICISE
PLASTICISED
PLASTICISER
PLASTICISERS
PLASTICISES
PLASTICISING
PLASTICITIES
PLASTICITY
PLASTICIZATION
PLASTICIZATIONS
PLASTICIZE
PLASTICIZED
PLASTICIZER
PLASTICIZERS
PLASTICIZES
PLASTICIZING
PLASTIDIAL

PLASTIDULE
PLASTIDULES
PLASTILINA
PLASTILINAS
PLASTIQUES
PLASTISOLS
PLASTOCYANIN
PLASTOCYANINS
PLASTOGAMIES
PLASTOGAMY
PLASTOMETER
PLASTOMETERS
PLASTOMETRIC
PLASTOMETRIES
PLASTOMETRY
PLASTOQUINONE
PLASTOQUINONES
PLATANACEOUS
PLATEAUING
PLATEGLASS
PLATELAYER
PLATELAYERS
PLATEMAKER
PLATEMAKERS
PLATEMAKING
PLATEMAKINGS
PLATEMARKS
PLATERESQUE
PLATFORMED
PLATFORMING
PLATFORMINGS
PLATINIFEROUS
PLATINIRIDIUM
PLATINIRIDIUMS
PLATINISATION
PLATINISATIONS
PLATINISED
PLATINISES
PLATINISING
PLATINIZATION
PLATINIZATIONS
PLATINIZED
PLATINIZES
PLATINIZING
PLATINOCYANIC
PLATINOCYANIDE
PLATINOCYANIDES
PLATINOIDS
PLATINOTYPE
PLATINOTYPES
PLATITUDES
PLATITUDINAL
PLATITUDINARIAN
PLATITUDINISE
PLATITUDINISED
PLATITUDINISER
PLATITUDINISERS
PLATITUDINISES
PLATITUDINISING
PLATITUDINIZE
PLATITUDINIZED
PLATITUDINIZER
PLATITUDINIZERS
PLATITUDINIZES
PLATITUDINIZING
PLATITUDINOUS
PLATITUDINOUSLY
PLATONICALLY
PLATONISMS
PLATOONING
PLATTELAND
PLATTELANDS
PLATTERFUL
PLATTERFULS
PLATTERSFUL
PLATYCEPHALIC
PLATYCEPHALOUS
PLATYFISHES
PLATYHELMINTH
PLATYHELMINTHIC
PLATYHELMINTHS
PLATYKURTIC
PLATYPUSES
PLATYRRHINE
PLATYRRHINES
PLATYRRHINIAN
PLATYRRHINIANS
PLAUDITORY
PLAUSIBILITIES
PLAUSIBILITY
PLAUSIBLENESS
PLAUSIBLENESSES
PLAYABILITIES
PLAYABILITY
PLAYACTING
PLAYACTINGS
PLAYACTORS
PLAYBUSSES
PLAYFELLOW
PLAYFELLOWS
PLAYFIELDS
PLAYFULNESS
PLAYFULNESSES
PLAYGOINGS
PLAYGROUND
PLAYGROUNDS
PLAYGROUPS
PLAYHOUSES
PLAYLEADER
PLAYLEADERS
PLAYMAKERS
PLAYMAKING
PLAYMAKINGS
PLAYSCHOOL
PLAYSCHOOLS
PLAYTHINGS
PLAYWRIGHT
PLAYWRIGHTING
PLAYWRIGHTINGS
PLAYWRIGHTS
PLAYWRITING
PLAYWRITINGS
PLEADINGLY
PLEASANCES
PLEASANTER
PLEASANTEST
PLEASANTLY
PLEASANTNESS
PLEASANTNESSES
PLEASANTRIES
PLEASANTRY
PLEASINGLY
PLEASINGNESS
PLEASINGNESSES
PLEASURABILITY
PLEASURABLE
PLEASURABLENESS
PLEASURABLY
PLEASUREFUL
PLEASURELESS
PLEASURERS
PLEASURING
PLEBEIANISE
PLEBEIANISED
PLEBEIANISES
PLEBEIANISING
PLEBEIANISM
PLEBEIANISMS
PLEBEIANIZE
PLEBEIANIZED
PLEBEIANIZES
PLEBEIANIZING
PLEBEIANLY
PLEBIFICATION
PLEBIFICATIONS
PLEBIFYING
PLEBISCITARY
PLEBISCITE
PLEBISCITES
PLECOPTERAN
PLECOPTERANS
PLECOPTEROUS
PLECTOGNATH
PLECTOGNATHIC
PLECTOGNATHOUS
PLECTOGNATHS
PLECTOPTEROUS
PLEDGEABLE
PLEINAIRISM
PLEINAIRISMS
PLEINAIRIST
PLEINAIRISTS
PLEIOCHASIA
PLEIOCHASIUM
PLEIOMERIES
PLEIOMEROUS
PLEIOTAXIES
PLEIOTROPIC
PLEIOTROPIES
PLEIOTROPISM
PLEIOTROPISMS
PLEIOTROPY
PLENARTIES
PLENILUNAR
PLENILUNES
PLENIPOTENCE
PLENIPOTENCES
PLENIPOTENCIES
PLENIPOTENCY
PLENIPOTENT
PLENIPOTENTIAL
PLENIPOTENTIARY
PLENISHERS
PLENISHING
PLENISHINGS
PLENISHMENT
PLENISHMENTS
PLENITUDES
PLENITUDINOUS
PLENTEOUSLY
PLENTEOUSNESS
PLENTEOUSNESSES
PLENTIFULLY
PLENTIFULNESS
PLENTIFULNESSES
PLENTITUDE
PLENTITUDES
PLEOCHROIC
PLEOCHROISM
PLEOCHROISMS
PLEOMORPHIC
PLEOMORPHIES
PLEOMORPHISM
PLEOMORPHISMS
PLEOMORPHOUS
PLEOMORPHY
PLEONASTES
PLEONASTIC
PLEONASTICAL
PLEONASTICALLY
PLEONECTIC
PLEONEXIAS
PLEROCERCOID
PLEROCERCOIDS
PLEROMATIC
PLEROPHORIA
PLEROPHORIAS
PLEROPHORIES
PLEROPHORY
PLESIOSAUR
PLESIOSAURIAN
PLESIOSAURS
PLESSIMETER
PLESSIMETERS
PLESSIMETRIC
PLESSIMETRIES
PLESSIMETRY
PLETHORICAL
PLETHORICALLY
PLETHYSMOGRAM
PLETHYSMOGRAMS
PLETHYSMOGRAPH
PLETHYSMOGRAPHS
PLETHYSMOGRAPHY
PLEURAPOPHYSES
PLEURAPOPHYSIS
PLEURISIES
PLEURITICAL
PLEURITICS
PLEURITISES
PLEUROCARPOUS
PLEUROCENTESES
PLEUROCENTESIS
PLEURODONT
PLEURODONTS
PLEURODYNIA
PLEURODYNIAS
PLEUROPNEUMONIA
PLEUROTOMIES
PLEUROTOMY
PLEUSTONIC
PLEXIGLASS
PLEXIGLASSES
PLEXIMETER

PLEXIMETERS
PLEXIMETRIC
PLEXIMETRIES
PLEXIMETRY
PLIABILITIES
PLIABILITY
PLIABLENESS
PLIABLENESSES
PLIANTNESS
PLIANTNESSES
PLICATENESS
PLICATENESSES
PLICATIONS
PLICATURES
PLODDINGLY
PLODDINGNESS
PLODDINGNESSES
PLOTLESSNESS
PLOTLESSNESSES
PLOTTERING
PLOTTINGLY
PLOUGHABLE
PLOUGHBOYS
PLOUGHGATE
PLOUGHGATES
PLOUGHHEAD
PLOUGHHEADS
PLOUGHINGS
PLOUGHLAND
PLOUGHLANDS
PLOUGHMANSHIP
PLOUGHMANSHIPS
PLOUGHSHARE
PLOUGHSHARES
PLOUGHSTAFF
PLOUGHSTAFFS
PLOUGHTAIL
PLOUGHTAILS
PLOUGHWISE
PLOUGHWRIGHT
PLOUGHWRIGHTS
PLOUTERING
PLOWMANSHIP
PLOWMANSHIPS
PLOWSHARES
PLOWSTAFFS
PLOWTERING
PLUCKINESS
PLUCKINESSES
PLUGBOARDS
PLUGUGLIES
PLUMASSIER
PLUMASSIERS
PLUMBAGINACEOUS
PLUMBAGINOUS
PLUMBERIES
PLUMBIFEROUS
PLUMBISOLVENCY
PLUMBISOLVENT
PLUMBNESSES
PLUMBOSOLVENCY
PLUMBOSOLVENT
PLUMDAMASES
PLUMIGEROUS
PLUMMETING
PLUMOSITIES
PLUMPENING
PLUMPNESSES
PLUMULACEOUS
PLUMULARIAN
PLUMULARIANS
PLUNDERABLE
PLUNDERAGE
PLUNDERAGES
PLUNDERERS
PLUNDERING
PLUNDEROUS
PLUPERFECT
PLUPERFECTS
PLURALISATION
PLURALISATIONS
PLURALISED
PLURALISER
PLURALISERS
PLURALISES
PLURALISING
PLURALISMS
PLURALISTIC
PLURALISTICALLY
PLURALISTS
PLURALITIES
PLURALIZATION
PLURALIZATIONS
PLURALIZED
PLURALIZER
PLURALIZERS
PLURALIZES
PLURALIZING
PLURILITERAL
PLURILOCULAR
PLURIPARAE
PLURIPARAS
PLURIPOTENT
PLURIPRESENCE
PLURIPRESENCES
PLURISERIAL
PLURISERIATE
PLUSHINESS
PLUSHINESSES
PLUSHNESSES
PLUTOCRACIES
PLUTOCRACY
PLUTOCRATIC
PLUTOCRATICAL
PLUTOCRATICALLY
PLUTOCRATS
PLUTOLATRIES
PLUTOLATRY
PLUTOLOGIES
PLUTOLOGIST
PLUTOLOGISTS
PLUTONISMS
PLUTONIUMS
PLUTONOMIES
PLUTONOMIST
PLUTONOMISTS
PLUVIOMETER
PLUVIOMETERS
PLUVIOMETRIC
PLUVIOMETRICAL
PLUVIOMETRIES
PLUVIOMETRY
PLYOMETRIC
PLYOMETRICS
PNEUMATHODE
PNEUMATHODES
PNEUMATICAL
PNEUMATICALLY
PNEUMATICITIES
PNEUMATICITY
PNEUMATICS
PNEUMATOLOGICAL
PNEUMATOLOGIES
PNEUMATOLOGIST
PNEUMATOLOGISTS
PNEUMATOLOGY
PNEUMATOLYSES
PNEUMATOLYSIS
PNEUMATOLYTIC
PNEUMATOMETER
PNEUMATOMETERS
PNEUMATOMETRIES
PNEUMATOMETRY
PNEUMATOPHORE
PNEUMATOPHORES
PNEUMECTOMIES
PNEUMECTOMY
PNEUMOBACILLI
PNEUMOBACILLUS
PNEUMOCOCCAL
PNEUMOCOCCI
PNEUMOCOCCUS
PNEUMOCONIOSES
PNEUMOCONIOSIS
PNEUMOCONIOTIC
PNEUMOCONIOTICS
PNEUMOCYSTIS
PNEUMOCYSTISES
PNEUMODYNAMICS
PNEUMOGASTRIC
PNEUMOGASTRICS
PNEUMOGRAM
PNEUMOGRAMS
PNEUMOGRAPH
PNEUMOGRAPHS
PNEUMOKONIOSES
PNEUMOKONIOSIS
PNEUMONECTOMIES
PNEUMONECTOMY
PNEUMONIAS
PNEUMONICS
PNEUMONITIS
PNEUMONITISES
PNEUMOTHORACES
PNEUMOTHORAX
PNEUMOTHORAXES
POACHINESS
POACHINESSES
POCKETABLE
POCKETBIKE
POCKETBIKES
POCKETBOOK
POCKETBOOKS
POCKETFULS
POCKETKNIFE
POCKETKNIVES
POCKETLESS
POCKETPHONE
POCKETPHONES
POCKETSFUL
POCKMANKIES
POCKMANTIE
POCKMANTIES
POCKMARKED
POCKMARKING
POCKPITTED
POCKPITTING
POCOCURANTE
POCOCURANTEISM
POCOCURANTEISMS
POCOCURANTES
POCOCURANTISM
POCOCURANTISMS
POCOCURANTIST
POCOCURANTISTS
POCULIFORM
PODAGRICAL
PODARGUSES
PODCASTERS
PODCASTING
PODCASTINGS
PODGINESSES
PODIATRIES
PODIATRIST
PODIATRISTS
PODOCONIOSES
PODOCONIOSIS
PODOLOGIES
PODOLOGIST
PODOLOGISTS
PODOPHTHALMOUS
PODOPHYLIN
PODOPHYLINS
PODOPHYLLI
PODOPHYLLIN
PODOPHYLLINS
PODOPHYLLUM
PODOPHYLLUMS
PODSOLISATION
PODSOLISATIONS
PODSOLISED
PODSOLISES
PODSOLISING
PODSOLIZATION
PODSOLIZATIONS
PODSOLIZED
PODSOLIZES
PODSOLIZING
PODZOLISATION
PODZOLISATIONS
PODZOLISED
PODZOLISES
PODZOLISING
PODZOLIZATION
PODZOLIZATIONS
PODZOLIZED
PODZOLIZES
PODZOLIZING
POENOLOGIES
POETASTERIES
POETASTERING
POETASTERINGS
POETASTERS
POETASTERY

POETASTRIES
POETICALLY
POETICALNESS
POETICALNESSES
POETICISED
POETICISES
POETICISING
POETICISMS
POETICIZED
POETICIZES
POETICIZING
POETICULES
POETRESSES
POGONOPHORAN
POGONOPHORANS
POGONOTOMIES
POGONOTOMY
POGROMISTS
POHUTUKAWA
POHUTUKAWAS
POIGNADOES
POIGNANCES
POIGNANCIES
POIGNANTLY
POIKILITIC
POIKILOCYTE
POIKILOCYTES
POIKILOTHERM
POIKILOTHERMAL
POIKILOTHERMIC
POIKILOTHERMIES
POIKILOTHERMISM
POIKILOTHERMS
POIKILOTHERMY
POINCIANAS
POINSETTIA
POINSETTIAS
POINTEDNESS
POINTEDNESSES
POINTELLES
POINTILLISM
POINTILLISME
POINTILLISMES
POINTILLISMS
POINTILLIST
POINTILLISTE
POINTILLISTES
POINTILLISTIC
POINTILLISTS
POINTLESSLY
POINTLESSNESS
POINTLESSNESSES
POISONABLE
POISONOUSLY
POISONOUSNESS
POISONOUSNESSES
POISONWOOD
POISONWOODS
POKEBERRIES
POKELOGANS
POKERISHLY
POKERWORKS
POKINESSES
POLARIMETER
POLARIMETERS
POLARIMETRIC
POLARIMETRIES
POLARIMETRY
POLARISABLE
POLARISATION
POLARISATIONS
POLARISCOPE
POLARISCOPES
POLARISCOPIC
POLARISERS
POLARISING
POLARITIES
POLARIZABILITY
POLARIZABLE
POLARIZATION
POLARIZATIONS
POLARIZERS
POLARIZING
POLAROGRAM
POLAROGRAMS
POLAROGRAPH
POLAROGRAPHIC
POLAROGRAPHIES
POLAROGRAPHS
POLAROGRAPHY
POLEMARCHES
POLEMARCHS
POLEMICALLY
POLEMICISE
POLEMICISED
POLEMICISES
POLEMICISING
POLEMICIST
POLEMICISTS
POLEMICIZE
POLEMICIZED
POLEMICIZES
POLEMICIZING
POLEMISING
POLEMIZING
POLEMONIACEOUS
POLEMONIUM
POLEMONIUMS
POLIANITES
POLICEWOMAN
POLICEWOMEN
POLICYHOLDER
POLICYHOLDERS
POLIOMYELITIDES
POLIOMYELITIS
POLIOMYELITISES
POLIORCETIC
POLIORCETICS
POLIOVIRUS
POLIOVIRUSES
POLISHABLE
POLISHINGS
POLISHMENT
POLISHMENTS
POLITBUROS
POLITENESS
POLITENESSES
POLITESSES
POLITICALISE
POLITICALISED
POLITICALISES
POLITICALISING
POLITICALIZE
POLITICALIZED
POLITICALIZES
POLITICALIZING
POLITICALLY
POLITICASTER
POLITICASTERS
POLITICIAN
POLITICIANS
POLITICISATION
POLITICISATIONS
POLITICISE
POLITICISED
POLITICISES
POLITICISING
POLITICIZATION
POLITICIZATIONS
POLITICIZE
POLITICIZED
POLITICIZES
POLITICIZING
POLITICKED
POLITICKER
POLITICKERS
POLITICKING
POLITICKINGS
POLITICOES
POLITIQUES
POLLARDING
POLLENATED
POLLENATES
POLLENATING
POLLENIFEROUS
POLLENISER
POLLENISERS
POLLENIZER
POLLENIZERS
POLLENOSES
POLLENOSIS
POLLICITATION
POLLICITATIONS
POLLINATED
POLLINATES
POLLINATING
POLLINATION
POLLINATIONS
POLLINATOR
POLLINATORS
POLLINIFEROUS
POLLINISED
POLLINISER
POLLINISERS
POLLINISES
POLLINISING
POLLINIZED
POLLINIZER
POLLINIZERS
POLLINIZES
POLLINIZING
POLLINOSES
POLLINOSIS
POLLTAKERS
POLLUCITES
POLLUSIONS
POLLUTANTS
POLLUTEDLY
POLLUTEDNESS
POLLUTEDNESSES
POLLUTIONS
POLLYANNAISH
POLLYANNAISM
POLLYANNAISMS
POLLYANNAS
POLLYANNISH
POLONAISES
POLONISING
POLONIZING
POLTERGEIST
POLTERGEISTS
POLTFOOTED
POLTROONERIES
POLTROONERY
POLVERINES
POLYACRYLAMIDE
POLYACRYLAMIDES
POLYACTINAL
POLYACTINE
POLYADELPHOUS
POLYALCOHOL
POLYALCOHOLS
POLYAMIDES
POLYAMINES
POLYANDRIES
POLYANDROUS
POLYANTHAS
POLYANTHUS
POLYANTHUSES
POLYARCHIES
POLYATOMIC
POLYAXIALS
POLYAXONIC
POLYBASITE
POLYBASITES
POLYBUTADIENE
POLYBUTADIENES
POLYCARBONATE
POLYCARBONATES
POLYCARBOXYLATE
POLYCARBOXYLIC
POLYCARPELLARY
POLYCARPIC
POLYCARPIES
POLYCARPOUS
POLYCENTRIC
POLYCENTRISM
POLYCENTRISMS
POLYCHAETE
POLYCHAETES
POLYCHAETOUS
POLYCHASIA
POLYCHASIUM
POLYCHETES
POLYCHLORINATED
POLYCHLOROPRENE
POLYCHOTOMIES
POLYCHOTOMOUS
POLYCHOTOMY
POLYCHREST
POLYCHRESTS
POLYCHROIC
POLYCHROISM
POLYCHROISMS

POLYCHROMATIC
POLYCHROMATISM
POLYCHROMATISMS
POLYCHROME
POLYCHROMED
POLYCHROMES
POLYCHROMIC
POLYCHROMIES
POLYCHROMING
POLYCHROMOUS
POLYCHROMY
POLYCISTRONIC
POLYCLINIC
POLYCLINICS
POLYCLONAL
POLYCOTTON
POLYCOTTONS
POLYCOTYLEDON
POLYCOTYLEDONS
POLYCROTIC
POLYCROTISM
POLYCROTISMS
POLYCRYSTAL
POLYCRYSTALLINE
POLYCRYSTALS
POLYCULTURE
POLYCULTURES
POLYCYCLIC
POLYCYCLICS
POLYCYSTIC
POLYCYTHAEMIA
POLYCYTHAEMIAS
POLYCYTHEMIA
POLYCYTHEMIAS
POLYCYTHEMIC
POLYDACTYL
POLYDACTYLIES
POLYDACTYLISM
POLYDACTYLISMS
POLYDACTYLOUS
POLYDACTYLS
POLYDACTYLY
POLYDAEMONISM
POLYDAEMONISMS
POLYDEMONISM
POLYDEMONISMS
POLYDIPSIA
POLYDIPSIAS
POLYDIPSIC
POLYDISPERSE
POLYDISPERSITY
POLYELECTROLYTE
POLYEMBRYONATE
POLYEMBRYONIC
POLYEMBRYONIES
POLYEMBRYONY
POLYESTERS
POLYESTROUS
POLYETHENE
POLYETHENES
POLYETHYLENE
POLYETHYLENES
POLYGALACEOUS
POLYGAMIES
POLYGAMISE
POLYGAMISED
POLYGAMISES
POLYGAMISING
POLYGAMIST
POLYGAMISTS
POLYGAMIZE
POLYGAMIZED
POLYGAMIZES
POLYGAMIZING
POLYGAMOUS
POLYGAMOUSLY
POLYGENESES
POLYGENESIS
POLYGENETIC
POLYGENETICALLY
POLYGENIES
POLYGENISM
POLYGENISMS
POLYGENIST
POLYGENISTS
POLYGENOUS
POLYGLOTISM
POLYGLOTISMS
POLYGLOTTAL
POLYGLOTTIC
POLYGLOTTISM
POLYGLOTTISMS
POLYGLOTTOUS
POLYGLOTTS
POLYGONACEOUS
POLYGONALLY
POLYGONATUM
POLYGONATUMS
POLYGONIES
POLYGONUMS
POLYGRAPHED
POLYGRAPHER
POLYGRAPHERS
POLYGRAPHIC
POLYGRAPHICALLY
POLYGRAPHIES
POLYGRAPHING
POLYGRAPHIST
POLYGRAPHISTS
POLYGRAPHS
POLYGRAPHY
POLYGYNIAN
POLYGYNIES
POLYGYNIST
POLYGYNISTS
POLYGYNOUS
POLYHALITE
POLYHALITES
POLYHEDRAL
POLYHEDRIC
POLYHEDRON
POLYHEDRONS
POLYHEDROSES
POLYHEDROSIS
POLYHISTOR
POLYHISTORIAN
POLYHISTORIANS
POLYHISTORIC
POLYHISTORIES
POLYHISTORS
POLYHISTORY
POLYHYBRID
POLYHYBRIDS
POLYHYDRIC
POLYHYDROXY
POLYIMIDES
POLYISOPRENE
POLYISOPRENES
POLYLEMMAS
POLYLYSINE
POLYLYSINES
POLYMASTIA
POLYMASTIAS
POLYMASTIC
POLYMASTIES
POLYMASTISM
POLYMASTISMS
POLYMATHIC
POLYMATHIES
POLYMERASE
POLYMERASES
POLYMERIDE
POLYMERIDES
POLYMERIES
POLYMERISATION
POLYMERISATIONS
POLYMERISE
POLYMERISED
POLYMERISES
POLYMERISING
POLYMERISM
POLYMERISMS
POLYMERIZATION
POLYMERIZATIONS
POLYMERIZE
POLYMERIZED
POLYMERIZES
POLYMERIZING
POLYMEROUS
POLYMORPHIC
POLYMORPHICALLY
POLYMORPHISM
POLYMORPHISMS
POLYMORPHOUS
POLYMORPHOUSLY
POLYMORPHS
POLYMYOSITIS
POLYMYOSITISES
POLYMYXINS
POLYNEURITIS
POLYNEURITISES
POLYNOMIAL
POLYNOMIALISM
POLYNOMIALISMS
POLYNOMIALS
POLYNUCLEAR
POLYNUCLEATE
POLYNUCLEOTIDE
POLYNUCLEOTIDES
POLYOLEFIN
POLYOLEFINS
POLYOMINOS
POLYONYMIC
POLYONYMIES
POLYONYMOUS
POLYPARIES
POLYPARIUM
POLYPEPTIDE
POLYPEPTIDES
POLYPEPTIDIC
POLYPETALOUS
POLYPHAGIA
POLYPHAGIAS
POLYPHAGIES
POLYPHAGOUS
POLYPHARMACIES
POLYPHARMACY
POLYPHASIC
POLYPHENOL
POLYPHENOLIC
POLYPHENOLS
POLYPHLOESBOEAN
POLYPHLOISBIC
POLYPHONES
POLYPHONIC
POLYPHONICALLY
POLYPHONIES
POLYPHONIST
POLYPHONISTS
POLYPHONOUS
POLYPHONOUSLY
POLYPHOSPHORIC
POLYPHYLETIC
POLYPHYLLOUS
POLYPHYODONT
POLYPIDOMS
POLYPLOIDAL
POLYPLOIDIC
POLYPLOIDIES
POLYPLOIDS
POLYPLOIDY
POLYPODIES
POLYPODOUS
POLYPROPENE
POLYPROPENES
POLYPROPYLENE
POLYPROPYLENES
POLYPROTODONT
POLYPROTODONTS
POLYPTYCHS
POLYRHYTHM
POLYRHYTHMIC
POLYRHYTHMS
POLYRIBOSOMAL
POLYRIBOSOME
POLYRIBOSOMES
POLYSACCHARIDE
POLYSACCHARIDES
POLYSACCHAROSE
POLYSACCHAROSES
POLYSEMANT
POLYSEMANTS
POLYSEMIES
POLYSEMOUS
POLYSEPALOUS
POLYSILOXANE
POLYSILOXANES
POLYSOMICS
POLYSOMIES
POLYSORBATE
POLYSORBATES
POLYSTICHOUS
POLYSTYLAR
POLYSTYLES

POLYSTYRENE
POLYSTYRENES
POLYSULFIDE
POLYSULFIDES
POLYSULPHIDE
POLYSULPHIDES
POLYSYLLABIC
POLYSYLLABICAL
POLYSYLLABICISM
POLYSYLLABISM
POLYSYLLABISMS
POLYSYLLABLE
POLYSYLLABLES
POLYSYLLOGISM
POLYSYLLOGISMS
POLYSYNAPTIC
POLYSYNDETON
POLYSYNDETONS
POLYSYNTHESES
POLYSYNTHESIS
POLYSYNTHESISM
POLYSYNTHESISMS
POLYSYNTHETIC
POLYSYNTHETICAL
POLYSYNTHETISM
POLYSYNTHETISMS
POLYTECHNIC
POLYTECHNICAL
POLYTECHNICS
POLYTENIES
POLYTHALAMOUS
POLYTHEISM
POLYTHEISMS
POLYTHEIST
POLYTHEISTIC
POLYTHEISTICAL
POLYTHEISTS
POLYTHENES
POLYTOCOUS
POLYTONALISM
POLYTONALISMS
POLYTONALIST
POLYTONALISTS
POLYTONALITIES
POLYTONALITY
POLYTONALLY
POLYTROPHIC
POLYTUNNEL
POLYTUNNELS
POLYTYPICAL
POLYUNSATURATED
POLYURETHAN
POLYURETHANE
POLYURETHANES
POLYURETHANS
POLYVALENCE
POLYVALENCES
POLYVALENCIES
POLYVALENCY
POLYVALENT
POLYVINYLIDENE
POLYVINYLIDENES
POLYVINYLS
POLYWATERS
POLYZOARIA
POLYZOARIAL
POLYZOARIES
POLYZOARIUM
POMEGRANATE
POMEGRANATES
POMICULTURE
POMICULTURES
POMIFEROUS
POMMELLING
POMOERIUMS
POMOLOGICAL
POMOLOGICALLY
POMOLOGIES
POMOLOGIST
POMOLOGISTS
POMOSEXUAL
POMOSEXUALS
POMPADOURED
POMPADOURS
POMPELMOOSE
POMPELMOOSES
POMPELMOUS
POMPELMOUSE
POMPELMOUSES
POMPHOLYGOUS
POMPHOLYXES
POMPOSITIES
POMPOUSNESS
POMPOUSNESSES
PONDERABILITIES
PONDERABILITY
PONDERABLE
PONDERABLES
PONDERABLY
PONDERANCE
PONDERANCES
PONDERANCIES
PONDERANCY
PONDERATED
PONDERATES
PONDERATING
PONDERATION
PONDERATIONS
PONDERINGLY
PONDERMENT
PONDERMENTS
PONDEROSAS
PONDEROSITIES
PONDEROSITY
PONDEROUSLY
PONDEROUSNESS
PONDEROUSNESSES
PONDOKKIES
PONEROLOGIES
PONEROLOGY
PONIARDING
PONTIANACS
PONTIANAKS
PONTICELLO
PONTICELLOS
PONTIFICAL
PONTIFICALITIES
PONTIFICALITY
PONTIFICALLY
PONTIFICALS
PONTIFICATE
PONTIFICATED
PONTIFICATES
PONTIFICATING
PONTIFICATION
PONTIFICATIONS
PONTIFICATOR
PONTIFICATORS
PONTIFICES
PONTIFYING
PONTLEVISES
PONTONEERS
PONTONIERS
PONTONNIER
PONTONNIERS
PONTOONERS
PONTOONING
PONYTAILED
POORHOUSES
POORMOUTHED
POORMOUTHING
POORMOUTHS
POORNESSES
POPLINETTE
POPLINETTES
POPMOBILITIES
POPMOBILITY
POPPERINGS
POPPYCOCKS
POPPYHEADS
POPULARISATION
POPULARISATIONS
POPULARISE
POPULARISED
POPULARISER
POPULARISERS
POPULARISES
POPULARISING
POPULARITIES
POPULARITY
POPULARIZATION
POPULARIZATIONS
POPULARIZE
POPULARIZED
POPULARIZER
POPULARIZERS
POPULARIZES
POPULARIZING
POPULATING
POPULATION
POPULATIONAL
POPULATIONS
POPULISTIC
POPULOUSLY
POPULOUSNESS
POPULOUSNESSES
PORBEAGLES
PORCELAINEOUS
PORCELAINISE
PORCELAINISED
PORCELAINISES
PORCELAINISING
PORCELAINIZE
PORCELAINIZED
PORCELAINIZES
PORCELAINIZING
PORCELAINLIKE
PORCELAINOUS
PORCELAINS
PORCELANEOUS
PORCELLANEOUS
PORCELLANISE
PORCELLANISED
PORCELLANISES
PORCELLANISING
PORCELLANITE
PORCELLANITES
PORCELLANIZE
PORCELLANIZED
PORCELLANIZES
PORCELLANIZING
PORCELLANOUS
PORCUPINES
PORCUPINISH
PORIFERANS
PORIFEROUS
PORINESSES
PORISMATIC
PORISMATICAL
PORISTICAL
PORKINESSES
PORLOCKING
PORLOCKINGS
PORNOCRACIES
PORNOCRACY
PORNOGRAPHER
PORNOGRAPHERS
PORNOGRAPHIC
PORNOGRAPHIES
PORNOGRAPHY
PORNOTOPIA
PORNOTOPIAN
PORNOTOPIAS
POROGAMIES
POROMERICS
POROSCOPES
POROSCOPIC
POROSCOPIES
POROSITIES
POROUSNESS
POROUSNESSES
PORPENTINE
PORPENTINES
PORPHYRIAS
PORPHYRIES
PORPHYRINS
PORPHYRIOS
PORPHYRITE
PORPHYRITES
PORPHYRITIC
PORPHYROGENITE
PORPHYROGENITES
PORPHYROID
PORPHYROIDS
PORPHYROPSIN
PORPHYROPSINS
PORPHYROUS
PORPOISING
PORRACEOUS
PORRECTING
PORRECTION
PORRECTIONS
PORRENGERS
PORRIGINOUS

PORRINGERS
PORTABELLA
PORTABELLAS
PORTABELLO
PORTABELLOS
PORTABILITIES
PORTABILITY
PORTALLING
PORTAMENTI
PORTAMENTO
PORTAPACKS
PORTATIVES
PORTCULLIS
PORTCULLISED
PORTCULLISES
PORTCULLISING
PORTENDING
PORTENTOUS
PORTENTOUSLY
PORTENTOUSNESS
PORTEOUSES
PORTERAGES
PORTERESSES
PORTERHOUSE
PORTERHOUSES
PORTFOLIOS
PORTHORSES
PORTHOUSES
PORTIONERS
PORTIONING
PORTIONIST
PORTIONISTS
PORTIONLESS
PORTLINESS
PORTLINESSES
PORTMANTEAU
PORTMANTEAUS
PORTMANTEAUX
PORTMANTLE
PORTMANTLES
PORTMANTUA
PORTMANTUAS
PORTOBELLO
PORTOBELLOS
PORTOLANOS
PORTRAITED
PORTRAITING
PORTRAITIST
PORTRAITISTS
PORTRAITURE
PORTRAITURES
PORTRAYABLE
PORTRAYALS
PORTRAYERS
PORTRAYING
PORTREEVES
PORTRESSES
PORTULACACEOUS
PORTULACAS
PORWIGGLES
POSHNESSES
POSIGRADES
POSITIONAL
POSITIONALLY
POSITIONED
POSITIONING
POSITIVELY
POSITIVENESS
POSITIVENESSES
POSITIVEST
POSITIVISM
POSITIVISMS
POSITIVIST
POSITIVISTIC
POSITIVISTS
POSITIVITIES
POSITIVITY
POSITRONIUM
POSITRONIUMS
POSOLOGICAL
POSOLOGIES
POSSESSABLE
POSSESSEDLY
POSSESSEDNESS
POSSESSEDNESSES
POSSESSING
POSSESSION
POSSESSIONAL
POSSESSIONARY
POSSESSIONATE
POSSESSIONATES
POSSESSIONED
POSSESSIONLESS
POSSESSIONS
POSSESSIVE
POSSESSIVELY
POSSESSIVENESS
POSSESSIVES
POSSESSORS
POSSESSORSHIP
POSSESSORSHIPS
POSSESSORY
POSSIBILISM
POSSIBILISMS
POSSIBILIST
POSSIBILISTS
POSSIBILITIES
POSSIBILITY
POSSIBLEST
POSTABORTION
POSTACCIDENT
POSTADOLESCENT
POSTAMPUTATION
POSTAPOCALYPTIC
POSTARREST
POSTATOMIC
POSTATTACK
POSTBELLUM
POSTBIBLICAL
POSTBOURGEOIS
POSTBUSSES
POSTCAPITALIST
POSTCARDED
POSTCARDING
POSTCARDLIKE
POSTCLASSIC
POSTCLASSICAL
POSTCODING
POSTCOITAL
POSTCOLLEGE
POSTCOLLEGIATE
POSTCOLONIAL
POSTCONCEPTION
POSTCONCERT
POSTCONQUEST
POSTCONSONANTAL
POSTCONVENTION
POSTCOPULATORY
POSTCORONARY
POSTCRANIAL
POSTCRANIALLY
POSTCRISIS
POSTDATING
POSTDEADLINE
POSTDEBATE
POSTDEBUTANTE
POSTDELIVERY
POSTDEPRESSION
POSTDEVALUATION
POSTDILUVIAL
POSTDILUVIAN
POSTDILUVIANS
POSTDIVESTITURE
POSTDIVORCE
POSTDOCTORAL
POSTDOCTORATE
POSTEDITING
POSTELECTION
POSTEMBRYONAL
POSTEMBRYONIC
POSTEMERGENCE
POSTEMERGENCY
POSTEPILEPTIC
POSTERIORITIES
POSTERIORITY
POSTERIORLY
POSTERIORS
POSTERISATION
POSTERISATIONS
POSTERITIES
POSTERIZATION
POSTERIZATIONS
POSTEROLATERAL
POSTERUPTIVE
POSTEXERCISE
POSTEXILIAN
POSTEXILIC
POSTEXPERIENCE
POSTEXPOSURE
POSTFEMINISM
POSTFEMINISMS
POSTFEMINIST
POSTFEMINISTS
POSTFIXING
POSTFLIGHT
POSTFORMED
POSTFORMING
POSTFRACTURE
POSTFREEZE
POSTGANGLIONIC
POSTGLACIAL
POSTGRADUATE
POSTGRADUATES
POSTGRADUATION
POSTHARVEST
POSTHASTES
POSTHEMORRHAGIC
POSTHOLDER
POSTHOLDERS
POSTHOLIDAY
POSTHOLOCAUST
POSTHORSES
POSTHOSPITAL
POSTHOUSES
POSTHUMOUS
POSTHUMOUSLY
POSTHUMOUSNESS
POSTHYPNOTIC
POSTICALLY
POSTILIONS
POSTILLATE
POSTILLATED
POSTILLATES
POSTILLATING
POSTILLATION
POSTILLATIONS
POSTILLATOR
POSTILLATORS
POSTILLERS
POSTILLING
POSTILLION
POSTILLIONS
POSTIMPACT
POSTIMPERIAL
POSTINAUGURAL
POSTINDUSTRIAL
POSTINFECTION
POSTINJECTION
POSTINOCULATION
POSTIRRADIATION
POSTISCHEMIC
POSTISOLATION
POSTLANDING
POSTLAPSARIAN
POSTLAUNCH
POSTLIBERATION
POSTLIMINARY
POSTLIMINIA
POSTLIMINIARY
POSTLIMINIES
POSTLIMINIOUS
POSTLIMINIUM
POSTLIMINOUS
POSTLIMINY
POSTLITERATE
POSTMARITAL
POSTMARKED
POSTMARKING
POSTMASTECTOMY
POSTMASTER
POSTMASTERS
POSTMASTERSHIP
POSTMASTERSHIPS
POSTMATING
POSTMEDIEVAL
POSTMENOPAUSAL
POSTMENSTRUAL
POSTMERIDIAN
POSTMIDNIGHT
POSTMILLENARIAN
POSTMILLENNIAL
POSTMISTRESS
POSTMISTRESSES
POSTMODERN

POSTMODERNISM
POSTMODERNISMS
POSTMODERNIST
POSTMODERNISTS
POSTMORTEM
POSTMORTEMS
POSTNATALLY
POSTNEONATAL
POSTNUPTIAL
POSTOCULAR
POSTOPERATIVE
POSTOPERATIVELY
POSTORBITAL
POSTORGASMIC
POSTPARTUM
POSTPERSON
POSTPERSONS
POSTPOLLINATION
POSTPONABLE
POSTPONEMENT
POSTPONEMENTS
POSTPONENCE
POSTPONENCES
POSTPONERS
POSTPONING
POSTPOSING
POSTPOSITION
POSTPOSITIONAL
POSTPOSITIONS
POSTPOSITIVE
POSTPOSITIVELY
POSTPOSITIVES
POSTPRANDIAL
POSTPRIMARY
POSTPRISON
POSTPRODUCTION
POSTPRODUCTIONS
POSTPUBERTY
POSTPUBESCENT
POSTRECESSION
POSTRETIREMENT
POSTRIDERS
POSTROMANTIC
POSTSCENIUM
POSTSCENIUMS
POSTSCRIPT
POSTSCRIPTS
POSTSEASON
POSTSEASONS
POSTSECONDARY
POSTSTIMULATION
POSTSTIMULATORY
POSTSTIMULUS
POSTSTRIKE
POSTSURGICAL
POSTSYNAPTIC
POSTSYNCED
POSTSYNCING
POSTTENSION
POSTTENSIONED
POSTTENSIONING
POSTTENSIONS
POSTTRANSFUSION
POSTTRAUMATIC
POSTTREATMENT
POSTULANCIES
POSTULANCY
POSTULANTS
POSTULANTSHIP
POSTULANTSHIPS
POSTULATED
POSTULATES
POSTULATING
POSTULATION
POSTULATIONAL
POSTULATIONALLY
POSTULATIONS
POSTULATOR
POSTULATORS
POSTULATORY
POSTULATUM
POSTURISED
POSTURISES
POSTURISING
POSTURISTS
POSTURIZED
POSTURIZES
POSTURIZING
POSTVACCINAL
POSTVACCINATION
POSTVAGOTOMY
POSTVASECTOMY
POSTVOCALIC
POSTWEANING
POSTWORKSHOP
POTABILITIES
POTABILITY
POTABLENESS
POTABLENESSES
POTAMOGETON
POTAMOGETONS
POTAMOLOGICAL
POTAMOLOGIES
POTAMOLOGIST
POTAMOLOGISTS
POTAMOLOGY
POTASSIUMS
POTATOBUGS
POTBELLIED
POTBELLIES
POTBOILERS
POTBOILING
POTENTATES
POTENTIALITIES
POTENTIALITY
POTENTIALLY
POTENTIALS
POTENTIARIES
POTENTIARY
POTENTIATE
POTENTIATED
POTENTIATES
POTENTIATING
POTENTIATION
POTENTIATIONS
POTENTIATOR
POTENTIATORS
POTENTILLA
POTENTILLAS
POTENTIOMETER
POTENTIOMETERS
POTENTIOMETRIC
POTENTIOMETRIES
POTENTIOMETRY
POTENTISED
POTENTISES
POTENTISING
POTENTIZED
POTENTIZES
POTENTIZING
POTENTNESS
POTENTNESSES
POTHECARIES
POTHOLDERS
POTHOLINGS
POTHUNTERS
POTHUNTING
POTHUNTINGS
POTICARIES
POTICHOMANIA
POTICHOMANIAS
POTLATCHED
POTLATCHES
POTLATCHING
POTOMETERS
POTPOURRIS
POTSHOTTING
POTTERINGLY
POTTERINGS
POTTINESSES
POTTINGARS
POTTINGERS
POTTYMOUTH
POTTYMOUTHS
POTWALLERS
POULDERING
POULTERERS
POULTICING
POULTROONE
POULTROONES
POULTRYMAN
POULTRYMEN
POUNDCAKES
POURBOIRES
POURPARLER
POURPARLERS
POURPOINTS
POURSEWING
POURTRAHED
POURTRAICT
POURTRAICTS
POURTRAYED
POURTRAYING
POUSOWDIES
POUSSETTED
POUSSETTES
POUSSETTING
POUTHERING
POWDERIEST
POWDERLESS
POWDERLIKE
POWELLISED
POWELLISES
POWELLISING
POWELLITES
POWELLIZED
POWELLIZES
POWELLIZING
POWERBOATING
POWERBOATINGS
POWERBOATS
POWERFULLY
POWERFULNESS
POWERFULNESSES
POWERHOUSE
POWERHOUSES
POWERLESSLY
POWERLESSNESS
POWERLESSNESSES
POWERLIFTER
POWERLIFTERS
POWERLIFTING
POWERLIFTINGS
POWERPLAYS
POWERTRAIN
POWERTRAINS
POWSOWDIES
POXVIRUSES
POZZOLANAS
POZZOLANIC
POZZUOLANA
POZZUOLANAS
PRACHARAKS
PRACTICABILITY
PRACTICABLE
PRACTICABLENESS
PRACTICABLY
PRACTICALISM
PRACTICALISMS
PRACTICALIST
PRACTICALISTS
PRACTICALITIES
PRACTICALITY
PRACTICALLY
PRACTICALNESS
PRACTICALNESSES
PRACTICALS
PRACTICERS
PRACTICIAN
PRACTICIANS
PRACTICING
PRACTICUMS
PRACTIQUES
PRACTISANT
PRACTISANTS
PRACTISERS
PRACTISING
PRACTITIONER
PRACTITIONERS
PRACTIVELY
PRACTOLOLS
PRAEAMBLES
PRAECOCIAL
PRAECORDIAL
PRAEDIALITIES
PRAEDIALITY
PRAEFECTORIAL
PRAELECTED
PRAELECTING
PRAELUDIUM
PRAEMUNIRE
PRAEMUNIRES
PRAENOMENS
PRAENOMINA

PRAENOMINAL
PRAENOMINALLY
PRAEPOSTOR
PRAEPOSTORS
PRAESIDIUM
PRAESIDIUMS
PRAETORIAL
PRAETORIAN
PRAETORIANS
PRAETORIUM
PRAETORIUMS
PRAETORSHIP
PRAETORSHIPS
PRAGMATICAL
PRAGMATICALITY
PRAGMATICALLY
PRAGMATICALNESS
PRAGMATICISM
PRAGMATICISMS
PRAGMATICIST
PRAGMATICISTS
PRAGMATICS
PRAGMATISATION
PRAGMATISATIONS
PRAGMATISE
PRAGMATISED
PRAGMATISER
PRAGMATISERS
PRAGMATISES
PRAGMATISING
PRAGMATISM
PRAGMATISMS
PRAGMATIST
PRAGMATISTIC
PRAGMATISTS
PRAGMATIZATION
PRAGMATIZATIONS
PRAGMATIZE
PRAGMATIZED
PRAGMATIZER
PRAGMATIZERS
PRAGMATIZES
PRAGMATIZING
PRAISEACHS
PRAISELESS
PRAISEWORTHILY
PRAISEWORTHY
PRAISINGLY
PRALLTRILLER
PRALLTRILLERS
PRANAYAMAS
PRANCINGLY
PRANDIALLY
PRANKINGLY
PRANKISHLY
PRANKISHNESS
PRANKISHNESSES
PRANKSTERS
PRASEODYMIUM
PRASEODYMIUMS
PRATFALLEN
PRATFALLING
PRATINCOLE
PRATINCOLES
PRATTLEBOX
PRATTLEBOXES
PRATTLEMENT
PRATTLEMENTS
PRATTLINGLY
PRAXEOLOGICAL
PRAXEOLOGIES
PRAXEOLOGY
PRAXINOSCOPE
PRAXINOSCOPES
PRAYERFULLY
PRAYERFULNESS
PRAYERFULNESSES
PRAYERLESS
PRAYERLESSLY
PRAYERLESSNESS
PREABSORBED
PREABSORBING
PREABSORBS
PREACCUSED
PREACCUSES
PREACCUSING
PREACHABLE
PREACHERSHIP
PREACHERSHIPS
PREACHIEST
PREACHIFIED
PREACHIFIES
PREACHIFYING
PREACHINESS
PREACHINESSES
PREACHINGLY
PREACHINGS
PREACHMENT
PREACHMENTS
PREACQUAINT
PREACQUAINTANCE
PREACQUAINTED
PREACQUAINTING
PREACQUAINTS
PREACQUISITION
PREADAMITE
PREADAMITES
PREADAPTATION
PREADAPTATIONS
PREADAPTED
PREADAPTING
PREADAPTIVE
PREADJUSTED
PREADJUSTING
PREADJUSTS
PREADMISSION
PREADMISSIONS
PREADMITTED
PREADMITTING
PREADMONISH
PREADMONISHED
PREADMONISHES
PREADMONISHING
PREADMONITION
PREADMONITIONS
PREADOLESCENCE
PREADOLESCENCES
PREADOLESCENT
PREADOLESCENTS
PREADOPTED
PREADOPTING
PREAGRICULTURAL
PREALLOTTED
PREALLOTTING
PREALTERED
PREALTERING
PREAMBLING
PREAMBULARY
PREAMBULATE
PREAMBULATED
PREAMBULATES
PREAMBULATING
PREAMBULATORY
PREAMPLIFIER
PREAMPLIFIERS
PREANESTHETIC
PREANNOUNCE
PREANNOUNCED
PREANNOUNCES
PREANNOUNCING
PREAPPLIED
PREAPPLIES
PREAPPLYING
PREAPPOINT
PREAPPOINTED
PREAPPOINTING
PREAPPOINTS
PREAPPROVE
PREAPPROVED
PREAPPROVES
PREAPPROVING
PREARRANGE
PREARRANGED
PREARRANGEMENT
PREARRANGEMENTS
PREARRANGES
PREARRANGING
PREASSEMBLED
PREASSIGNED
PREASSIGNING
PREASSIGNS
PREASSURANCE
PREASSURANCES
PREASSURED
PREASSURES
PREASSURING
PREATTUNED
PREATTUNES
PREATTUNING
PREAUDIENCE
PREAUDIENCES
PREAUDITED
PREAUDITING
PREAVERRED
PREAVERRING
PREAXIALLY
PREBENDARIES
PREBENDARY
PREBIBLICAL
PREBIDDING
PREBILLING
PREBIOLOGIC
PREBIOLOGICAL
PREBLESSED
PREBLESSES
PREBLESSING
PREBOARDED
PREBOARDING
PREBOILING
PREBOOKING
PREBREAKFAST
PREBUDGETS
PREBUILDING
PREBUTTALS
PRECALCULI
PRECALCULUS
PRECALCULUSES
PRECANCELED
PRECANCELING
PRECANCELLATION
PRECANCELLED
PRECANCELLING
PRECANCELS
PRECANCEROUS
PRECANCERS
PRECAPITALIST
PRECARIOUS
PRECARIOUSLY
PRECARIOUSNESS
PRECASTING
PRECAUTION
PRECAUTIONAL
PRECAUTIONARY
PRECAUTIONED
PRECAUTIONING
PRECAUTIONS
PRECAUTIOUS
PRECEDENCE
PRECEDENCES
PRECEDENCIES
PRECEDENCY
PRECEDENTED
PRECEDENTIAL
PRECEDENTIALLY
PRECEDENTLY
PRECEDENTS
PRECENSORED
PRECENSORING
PRECENSORS
PRECENTING
PRECENTORIAL
PRECENTORS
PRECENTORSHIP
PRECENTORSHIPS
PRECENTRESS
PRECENTRESSES
PRECENTRICES
PRECENTRIX
PRECENTRIXES
PRECEPTIAL
PRECEPTIVE
PRECEPTIVELY
PRECEPTORAL
PRECEPTORATE
PRECEPTORATES
PRECEPTORIAL
PRECEPTORIALS
PRECEPTORIES
PRECEPTORS
PRECEPTORSHIP
PRECEPTORSHIPS
PRECEPTORY
PRECEPTRESS
PRECEPTRESSES

PRECESSING
PRECESSION
PRECESSIONAL
PRECESSIONALLY
PRECESSIONS
PRECHARGED
PRECHARGES
PRECHARGING
PRECHECKED
PRECHECKING
PRECHILLED
PRECHILLING
PRECHOOSES
PRECHOOSING
PRECHRISTIAN
PRECIEUSES
PRECIOSITIES
PRECIOSITY
PRECIOUSES
PRECIOUSLY
PRECIOUSNESS
PRECIOUSNESSES
PRECIPICED
PRECIPICES
PRECIPITABILITY
PRECIPITABLE
PRECIPITANCE
PRECIPITANCES
PRECIPITANCIES
PRECIPITANCY
PRECIPITANT
PRECIPITANTLY
PRECIPITANTNESS
PRECIPITANTS
PRECIPITATE
PRECIPITATED
PRECIPITATELY
PRECIPITATENESS
PRECIPITATES
PRECIPITATING
PRECIPITATION
PRECIPITATIONS
PRECIPITATIVE
PRECIPITATOR
PRECIPITATORS
PRECIPITIN
PRECIPITINOGEN
PRECIPITINOGENS
PRECIPITINS
PRECIPITOUS
PRECIPITOUSLY
PRECIPITOUSNESS
PRECISENESS
PRECISENESSES
PRECISIANISM
PRECISIANISMS
PRECISIANIST
PRECISIANISTS
PRECISIANS
PRECISIONISM
PRECISIONISMS
PRECISIONIST
PRECISIONISTS
PRECISIONS
PRECLASSICAL
PRECLEANED
PRECLEANING
PRECLEARANCE
PRECLEARANCES
PRECLEARED
PRECLEARING
PRECLINICAL
PRECLINICALLY
PRECLUDABLE
PRECLUDING
PRECLUSION
PRECLUSIONS
PRECLUSIVE
PRECLUSIVELY
PRECOCIALS
PRECOCIOUS
PRECOCIOUSLY
PRECOCIOUSNESS
PRECOCITIES
PRECOGNISANT
PRECOGNISE
PRECOGNISED
PRECOGNISES
PRECOGNISING
PRECOGNITION
PRECOGNITIONS
PRECOGNITIVE
PRECOGNIZANT
PRECOGNIZE
PRECOGNIZED
PRECOGNIZES
PRECOGNIZING
PRECOGNOSCE
PRECOGNOSCED
PRECOGNOSCES
PRECOGNOSCING
PRECOLLEGE
PRECOLLEGIATE
PRECOLONIAL
PRECOMBUSTION
PRECOMBUSTIONS
PRECOMMITMENT
PRECOMMITMENTS
PRECOMPETITIVE
PRECOMPOSE
PRECOMPOSED
PRECOMPOSES
PRECOMPOSING
PRECOMPUTE
PRECOMPUTED
PRECOMPUTER
PRECOMPUTES
PRECOMPUTING
PRECONCEIT
PRECONCEITS
PRECONCEIVE
PRECONCEIVED
PRECONCEIVES
PRECONCEIVING
PRECONCEPTION
PRECONCEPTIONS
PRECONCERT
PRECONCERTED
PRECONCERTEDLY
PRECONCERTING
PRECONCERTS
PRECONCILIAR
PRECONDEMN
PRECONDEMNED
PRECONDEMNING
PRECONDEMNS
PRECONDITION
PRECONDITIONED
PRECONDITIONING
PRECONDITIONS
PRECONISATION
PRECONISATIONS
PRECONISED
PRECONISES
PRECONISING
PRECONIZATION
PRECONIZATIONS
PRECONIZED
PRECONIZES
PRECONIZING
PRECONQUEST
PRECONSCIOUS
PRECONSCIOUSES
PRECONSCIOUSLY
PRECONSONANTAL
PRECONSTRUCT
PRECONSTRUCTED
PRECONSTRUCTING
PRECONSTRUCTION
PRECONSTRUCTS
PRECONSUME
PRECONSUMED
PRECONSUMES
PRECONSUMING
PRECONTACT
PRECONTRACT
PRECONTRACTED
PRECONTRACTING
PRECONTRACTS
PRECONVENTION
PRECONVICTION
PRECONVICTIONS
PRECOOKERS
PRECOOKING
PRECOOLING
PRECOPULATORY
PRECORDIAL
PRECREASED
PRECREASES
PRECREASING
PRECRITICAL
PRECURRERS
PRECURSIVE
PRECURSORS
PRECURSORY
PRECUTTING
PREDACEOUS
PREDACEOUSNESS
PREDACIOUS
PREDACIOUSNESS
PREDACITIES
PREDATIONS
PREDATISMS
PREDATORILY
PREDATORINESS
PREDATORINESSES
PREDECEASE
PREDECEASED
PREDECEASES
PREDECEASING
PREDECESSOR
PREDECESSORS
PREDEDUCTED
PREDEDUCTING
PREDEDUCTS
PREDEFINED
PREDEFINES
PREDEFINING
PREDEFINITION
PREDEFINITIONS
PREDELIVERY
PREDENTATE
PREDEPARTURE
PREDEPOSIT
PREDEPOSITED
PREDEPOSITING
PREDEPOSITS
PREDESIGNATE
PREDESIGNATED
PREDESIGNATES
PREDESIGNATING
PREDESIGNATION
PREDESIGNATIONS
PREDESIGNATORY
PREDESIGNED
PREDESIGNING
PREDESIGNS
PREDESTINABLE
PREDESTINARIAN
PREDESTINARIANS
PREDESTINATE
PREDESTINATED
PREDESTINATES
PREDESTINATING
PREDESTINATION
PREDESTINATIONS
PREDESTINATIVE
PREDESTINATOR
PREDESTINATORS
PREDESTINE
PREDESTINED
PREDESTINES
PREDESTINIES
PREDESTINING
PREDESTINY
PREDETERMINABLE
PREDETERMINATE
PREDETERMINE
PREDETERMINED
PREDETERMINER
PREDETERMINERS
PREDETERMINES
PREDETERMINING
PREDETERMINISM
PREDETERMINISMS
PREDEVALUATION
PREDEVELOP
PREDEVELOPED
PREDEVELOPING
PREDEVELOPMENT
PREDEVELOPMENTS
PREDEVELOPS
PREDIABETES
PREDIABETESES

PREDIABETIC
PREDIABETICS
PREDIALITIES
PREDIALITY
PREDICABILITIES
PREDICABILITY
PREDICABLE
PREDICABLENESS
PREDICABLES
PREDICAMENT
PREDICAMENTAL
PREDICAMENTS
PREDICANTS
PREDICATED
PREDICATES
PREDICATING
PREDICATION
PREDICATIONS
PREDICATIVE
PREDICATIVELY
PREDICATOR
PREDICATORS
PREDICATORY
PREDICTABILITY
PREDICTABLE
PREDICTABLENESS
PREDICTABLY
PREDICTERS
PREDICTING
PREDICTION
PREDICTIONS
PREDICTIVE
PREDICTIVELY
PREDICTORS
PREDIGESTED
PREDIGESTING
PREDIGESTION
PREDIGESTIONS
PREDIGESTS
PREDIKANTS
PREDILECTED
PREDILECTING
PREDILECTION
PREDILECTIONS
PREDILECTS
PREDINNERS
PREDISCHARGE
PREDISCOVERIES
PREDISCOVERY
PREDISPOSAL
PREDISPOSALS
PREDISPOSE
PREDISPOSED
PREDISPOSES
PREDISPOSING
PREDISPOSITION
PREDISPOSITIONS
PREDNISOLONE
PREDNISOLONES
PREDNISONE
PREDNISONES
PREDOCTORAL
PREDOMINANCE
PREDOMINANCES
PREDOMINANCIES
PREDOMINANCY
PREDOMINANT
PREDOMINANTLY
PREDOMINATE
PREDOMINATED
PREDOMINATELY
PREDOMINATES
PREDOMINATING
PREDOMINATION
PREDOMINATIONS
PREDOMINATOR
PREDOMINATORS
PREDOOMING
PREDRILLED
PREDRILLING
PREDYNASTIC
PREECLAMPSIA
PREECLAMPSIAS
PREECLAMPTIC
PREEDITING
PREELECTED
PREELECTING
PREELECTION
PREELECTRIC
PREEMBARGO
PREEMERGENCE
PREEMERGENT
PREEMINENCE
PREEMINENCES
PREEMINENT
PREEMINENTLY
PREEMPLOYMENT
PREEMPTING
PREEMPTION
PREEMPTIONS
PREEMPTIVE
PREEMPTIVELY
PREEMPTORS
PREENACTED
PREENACTING
PREENROLLMENT
PREERECTED
PREERECTING
PREESTABLISH
PREESTABLISHED
PREESTABLISHES
PREESTABLISHING
PREETHICAL
PREEXCITED
PREEXCITES
PREEXCITING
PREEXEMPTED
PREEXEMPTING
PREEXEMPTS
PREEXISTED
PREEXISTENCE
PREEXISTENCES
PREEXISTENT
PREEXISTING
PREEXPERIMENT
PREEXPOSED
PREEXPOSES
PREEXPOSING
PREFABBING
PREFABRICATE
PREFABRICATED
PREFABRICATES
PREFABRICATING
PREFABRICATION
PREFABRICATIONS
PREFABRICATOR
PREFABRICATORS
PREFASCIST
PREFATORIAL
PREFATORIALLY
PREFATORILY
PREFECTORIAL
PREFECTSHIP
PREFECTSHIPS
PREFECTURAL
PREFECTURE
PREFECTURES
PREFERABILITIES
PREFERABILITY
PREFERABLE
PREFERABLENESS
PREFERABLY
PREFERENCE
PREFERENCES
PREFERENTIAL
PREFERENTIALISM
PREFERENTIALIST
PREFERENTIALITY
PREFERENTIALLY
PREFERMENT
PREFERMENTS
PREFERRABLE
PREFERRERS
PREFERRING
PREFIGURATE
PREFIGURATED
PREFIGURATES
PREFIGURATING
PREFIGURATION
PREFIGURATIONS
PREFIGURATIVE
PREFIGURATIVELY
PREFIGURED
PREFIGUREMENT
PREFIGUREMENTS
PREFIGURES
PREFIGURING
PREFILLING
PREFINANCE
PREFINANCED
PREFINANCES
PREFINANCING
PREFIXALLY
PREFIXIONS
PREFIXTURE
PREFIXTURES
PREFLIGHTED
PREFLIGHTING
PREFLIGHTS
PREFLORATION
PREFLORATIONS
PREFOCUSED
PREFOCUSES
PREFOCUSING
PREFOCUSSED
PREFOCUSSES
PREFOCUSSING
PREFOLIATION
PREFOLIATIONS
PREFORMATION
PREFORMATIONISM
PREFORMATIONIST
PREFORMATIONS
PREFORMATIVE
PREFORMATS
PREFORMATTED
PREFORMATTING
PREFORMING
PREFORMULATE
PREFORMULATED
PREFORMULATES
PREFORMULATING
PREFRANKED
PREFRANKING
PREFREEZES
PREFREEZING
PREFRESHMAN
PREFRONTAL
PREFRONTALS
PREFULGENT
PREFUNDING
PREGANGLIONIC
PREGENITAL
PREGLACIAL
PREGNABILITIES
PREGNABILITY
PREGNANCES
PREGNANCIES
PREGNANTLY
PREGNENOLONE
PREGNENOLONES
PREGROWTHS
PREGUIDING
PREGUSTATION
PREGUSTATIONS
PREHALLUCES
PREHALLUXES
PREHANDLED
PREHANDLES
PREHANDLING
PREHARDENED
PREHARDENING
PREHARDENS
PREHARVEST
PREHEADACHE
PREHEATERS
PREHEATING
PREHEMINENCE
PREHEMINENCES
PREHENDING
PREHENSIBLE
PREHENSILE
PREHENSILITIES
PREHENSILITY
PREHENSION
PREHENSIONS
PREHENSIVE
PREHENSORIAL
PREHENSORS
PREHENSORY
PREHISTORIAN
PREHISTORIANS
PREHISTORIC
PREHISTORICAL

PREHISTORICALLY
PREHISTORIES
PREHISTORY
PREHOLIDAY
PREHOMINID
PREHOMINIDS
PREIGNITION
PREIGNITIONS
PREIMPLANTATION
PREIMPOSED
PREIMPOSES
PREIMPOSING
PREINAUGURAL
PREINDUCTION
PREINDUSTRIAL
PREINFORMED
PREINFORMING
PREINFORMS
PREINSERTED
PREINSERTING
PREINSERTS
PREINTERVIEW
PREINTERVIEWED
PREINTERVIEWING
PREINTERVIEWS
PREINVASION
PREINVITED
PREINVITES
PREINVITING
PREJUDGEMENT
PREJUDGEMENTS
PREJUDGERS
PREJUDGING
PREJUDGMENT
PREJUDGMENTS
PREJUDICANT
PREJUDICATE
PREJUDICATED
PREJUDICATES
PREJUDICATING
PREJUDICATION
PREJUDICATIONS
PREJUDICATIVE
PREJUDICED
PREJUDICES
PREJUDICIAL
PREJUDICIALLY
PREJUDICIALNESS
PREJUDICING
PREKINDERGARTEN
PRELAPSARIAN
PRELATESHIP
PRELATESHIPS
PRELATESSES
PRELATICAL
PRELATICALLY
PRELATIONS
PRELATISED
PRELATISES
PRELATISING
PRELATISMS
PRELATISTS
PRELATIZED
PRELATIZES
PRELATIZING
PRELATURES
PRELAUNCHED
PRELAUNCHES
PRELAUNCHING
PRELECTING
PRELECTION
PRELECTIONS
PRELECTORS
PRELEXICAL
PRELIBATION
PRELIBATIONS
PRELIMINARIES
PRELIMINARILY
PRELIMINARY
PRELIMITED
PRELIMITING
PRELINGUAL
PRELINGUALLY
PRELITERACIES
PRELITERACY
PRELITERARY
PRELITERATE
PRELITERATES
PRELOADING
PRELOCATED
PRELOCATES
PRELOCATING
PRELOGICAL
PRELUDIOUS
PRELUNCHEON
PRELUSIONS
PRELUSIVELY
PRELUSORILY
PREMALIGNANT
PREMANDIBULAR
PREMANDIBULARS
PREMANUFACTURE
PREMANUFACTURED
PREMANUFACTURES
PREMARITAL
PREMARITALLY
PREMARKETED
PREMARKETING
PREMARKETS
PREMARRIAGE
PREMATURELY
PREMATURENESS
PREMATURENESSES
PREMATURES
PREMATURITIES
PREMATURITY
PREMAXILLA
PREMAXILLAE
PREMAXILLARIES
PREMAXILLARY
PREMAXILLAS
PREMEASURE
PREMEASURED
PREMEASURES
PREMEASURING
PREMEDICAL
PREMEDICALLY
PREMEDICATE
PREMEDICATED
PREMEDICATES
PREMEDICATING
PREMEDICATION
PREMEDICATIONS
PREMEDIEVAL
PREMEDITATE
PREMEDITATED
PREMEDITATEDLY
PREMEDITATES
PREMEDITATING
PREMEDITATION
PREMEDITATIONS
PREMEDITATIVE
PREMEDITATOR
PREMEDITATORS
PREMEIOTIC
PREMENOPAUSAL
PREMENSTRUAL
PREMENSTRUALLY
PREMIERING
PREMIERSHIP
PREMIERSHIPS
PREMIGRATION
PREMILLENARIAN
PREMILLENARIANS
PREMILLENNIAL
PREMILLENNIALLY
PREMODIFICATION
PREMODIFIED
PREMODIFIES
PREMODIFYING
PREMOISTEN
PREMOISTENED
PREMOISTENING
PREMOISTENS
PREMOLDING
PREMONISHED
PREMONISHES
PREMONISHING
PREMONISHMENT
PREMONISHMENTS
PREMONITION
PREMONITIONS
PREMONITIVE
PREMONITOR
PREMONITORILY
PREMONITORS
PREMONITORY
PREMOTIONS
PREMOVEMENT
PREMOVEMENTS
PREMUNITION
PREMUNITIONS
PREMYCOTIC
PRENATALLY
PRENEGOTIATE
PRENEGOTIATED
PRENEGOTIATES
PRENEGOTIATING
PRENEGOTIATION
PRENEGOTIATIONS
PRENOMINAL
PRENOMINATE
PRENOMINATED
PRENOMINATES
PRENOMINATING
PRENOMINATION
PRENOMINATIONS
PRENOTIFICATION
PRENOTIFIED
PRENOTIFIES
PRENOTIFYING
PRENOTIONS
PRENTICESHIP
PRENTICESHIPS
PRENTICING
PRENUMBERED
PRENUMBERING
PRENUMBERS
PRENUPTIAL
PREOBTAINED
PREOBTAINING
PREOBTAINS
PREOCCUPANCIES
PREOCCUPANCY
PREOCCUPANT
PREOCCUPANTS
PREOCCUPATE
PREOCCUPATED
PREOCCUPATES
PREOCCUPATING
PREOCCUPATION
PREOCCUPATIONS
PREOCCUPIED
PREOCCUPIES
PREOCCUPYING
PREOCULARS
PREOPENING
PREOPERATIONAL
PREOPERATIVE
PREOPERATIVELY
PREOPTIONS
PREORDAINED
PREORDAINING
PREORDAINMENT
PREORDAINMENTS
PREORDAINS
PREORDERED
PREORDERING
PREORDINANCE
PREORDINANCES
PREORDINATION
PREORDINATIONS
PREOVULATORY
PREPACKAGE
PREPACKAGED
PREPACKAGES
PREPACKAGING
PREPACKING
PREPARATION
PREPARATIONS
PREPARATIVE
PREPARATIVELY
PREPARATIVES
PREPARATOR
PREPARATORILY
PREPARATORS
PREPARATORY
PREPAREDLY
PREPAREDNESS
PREPAREDNESSES
PREPASTING
PREPATELLAR
PREPAYABLE
PREPAYMENT

PREPAYMENTS
PREPENSELY
PREPENSING
PREPENSIVE
PREPERFORMANCE
PREPLACING
PREPLANNED
PREPLANNING
PREPLANTED
PREPLANTING
PREPOLLENCE
PREPOLLENCES
PREPOLLENCIES
PREPOLLENCY
PREPOLLENT
PREPOLLICES
PREPONDERANCE
PREPONDERANCES
PREPONDERANCIES
PREPONDERANCY
PREPONDERANT
PREPONDERANTLY
PREPONDERATE
PREPONDERATED
PREPONDERATELY
PREPONDERATES
PREPONDERATING
PREPONDERATION
PREPONDERATIONS
PREPORTION
PREPORTIONED
PREPORTIONING
PREPORTIONS
PREPOSITION
PREPOSITIONAL
PREPOSITIONALLY
PREPOSITIONS
PREPOSITIVE
PREPOSITIVELY
PREPOSITIVES
PREPOSITOR
PREPOSITORS
PREPOSSESS
PREPOSSESSED
PREPOSSESSES
PREPOSSESSING
PREPOSSESSINGLY
PREPOSSESSION
PREPOSSESSIONS
PREPOSTEROUS
PREPOSTEROUSLY
PREPOSTORS
PREPOTENCE
PREPOTENCES
PREPOTENCIES
PREPOTENCY
PREPOTENTLY
PREPPINESS
PREPPINESSES
PREPRANDIAL
PREPREPARED
PREPRESIDENTIAL
PREPRICING
PREPRIMARIES
PREPRIMARY
PREPRINTED
PREPRINTING
PREPROCESS
PREPROCESSED
PREPROCESSES
PREPROCESSING
PREPROCESSOR
PREPROCESSORS
PREPRODUCTION
PREPRODUCTIONS
PREPROFESSIONAL
PREPROGRAM
PREPROGRAMED
PREPROGRAMING
PREPROGRAMMED
PREPROGRAMMING
PREPROGRAMS
PREPSYCHEDELIC
PREPUBERAL
PREPUBERTAL
PREPUBERTIES
PREPUBERTY
PREPUBESCENCE
PREPUBESCENCES
PREPUBESCENT
PREPUBESCENTS
PREPUBLICATION
PREPUBLICATIONS
PREPUNCHED
PREPUNCHES
PREPUNCHING
PREPUNCTUAL
PREPURCHASE
PREPURCHASED
PREPURCHASES
PREPURCHASING
PREQUALIFIED
PREQUALIFIES
PREQUALIFY
PREQUALIFYING
PREREADING
PRERECESSION
PRERECORDED
PRERECORDING
PRERECORDS
PREREGISTER
PREREGISTERED
PREREGISTERING
PREREGISTERS
PREREGISTRATION
PREREHEARSAL
PRERELEASE
PRERELEASED
PRERELEASES
PRERELEASING
PREREQUIRE
PREREQUIRED
PREREQUIRES
PREREQUIRING
PREREQUISITE
PREREQUISITES
PRERETIREMENT
PREREVISIONIST
PREREVOLUTION
PRERINSING
PREROGATIVE
PREROGATIVED
PREROGATIVELY
PREROGATIVES
PREROMANTIC
PRESAGEFUL
PRESAGEFULLY
PRESAGEMENT
PRESAGEMENTS
PRESANCTIFIED
PRESANCTIFIES
PRESANCTIFY
PRESANCTIFYING
PRESBYACOUSES
PRESBYACOUSIS
PRESBYACUSES
PRESBYACUSIS
PRESBYCOUSES
PRESBYCOUSIS
PRESBYCUSES
PRESBYCUSIS
PRESBYOPES
PRESBYOPIA
PRESBYOPIAS
PRESBYOPIC
PRESBYOPICS
PRESBYOPIES
PRESBYTERAL
PRESBYTERATE
PRESBYTERATES
PRESBYTERIAL
PRESBYTERIALLY
PRESBYTERIALS
PRESBYTERIAN
PRESBYTERIANISE
PRESBYTERIANISM
PRESBYTERIANIZE
PRESBYTERIANS
PRESBYTERIES
PRESBYTERS
PRESBYTERSHIP
PRESBYTERSHIPS
PRESBYTERY
PRESBYTISM
PRESBYTISMS
PRESCHEDULE
PRESCHEDULED
PRESCHEDULES
PRESCHEDULING
PRESCHOOLER
PRESCHOOLERS
PRESCHOOLS
PRESCIENCE
PRESCIENCES
PRESCIENTIFIC
PRESCIENTLY
PRESCINDED
PRESCINDENT
PRESCINDING
PRESCISSION
PRESCISSIONS
PRESCORING
PRESCREENED
PRESCREENING
PRESCREENS
PRESCRIBED
PRESCRIBER
PRESCRIBERS
PRESCRIBES
PRESCRIBING
PRESCRIBINGS
PRESCRIPTIBLE
PRESCRIPTION
PRESCRIPTIONS
PRESCRIPTIVE
PRESCRIPTIVELY
PRESCRIPTIVISM
PRESCRIPTIVISMS
PRESCRIPTIVIST
PRESCRIPTIVISTS
PRESCRIPTS
PRESEASONS
PRESELECTED
PRESELECTING
PRESELECTION
PRESELECTIONS
PRESELECTOR
PRESELECTORS
PRESELECTS
PRESELLING
PRESENSION
PRESENSIONS
PRESENTABILITY
PRESENTABLE
PRESENTABLENESS
PRESENTABLY
PRESENTATION
PRESENTATIONAL
PRESENTATIONISM
PRESENTATIONIST
PRESENTATIONS
PRESENTATIVE
PRESENTEEISM
PRESENTEEISMS
PRESENTEES
PRESENTENCE
PRESENTENCED
PRESENTENCES
PRESENTENCING
PRESENTERS
PRESENTIAL
PRESENTIALITIES
PRESENTIALITY
PRESENTIALLY
PRESENTIENT
PRESENTIMENT
PRESENTIMENTAL
PRESENTIMENTS
PRESENTING
PRESENTISM
PRESENTISMS
PRESENTIST
PRESENTIVE
PRESENTIVENESS
PRESENTMENT
PRESENTMENTS
PRESENTNESS
PRESENTNESSES
PRESERVABILITY
PRESERVABLE
PRESERVABLY
PRESERVATION
PRESERVATIONIST
PRESERVATIONS

PRESERVATIVE
PRESERVATIVES
PRESERVATORIES
PRESERVATORY
PRESERVERS
PRESERVICE
PRESERVING
PRESETTING
PRESETTLED
PRESETTLEMENT
PRESETTLES
PRESETTLING
PRESHAPING
PRESHIPPED
PRESHIPPING
PRESHOWING
PRESHRINKING
PRESHRINKS
PRESHRUNKEN
PRESIDENCIES
PRESIDENCY
PRESIDENTESS
PRESIDENTESSES
PRESIDENTIAL
PRESIDENTIALLY
PRESIDENTS
PRESIDENTSHIP
PRESIDENTSHIPS
PRESIDIARY
PRESIDIUMS
PRESIFTING
PRESIGNALED
PRESIGNALING
PRESIGNALLED
PRESIGNALLING
PRESIGNALS
PRESIGNIFIED
PRESIGNIFIES
PRESIGNIFY
PRESIGNIFYING
PRESLAUGHTER
PRESLICING
PRESOAKING
PRESOLVING
PRESORTING
PRESPECIFIED
PRESPECIFIES
PRESPECIFY
PRESPECIFYING
PRESSBOARD
PRESSBOARDS
PRESSGANGS
PRESSINGLY
PRESSINGNESS
PRESSINGNESSES
PRESSMARKS
PRESSROOMS
PRESSURELESS
PRESSURING
PRESSURISATION
PRESSURISATIONS
PRESSURISE
PRESSURISED
PRESSURISER
PRESSURISERS
PRESSURISES
PRESSURISING
PRESSURIZATION
PRESSURIZATIONS
PRESSURIZE
PRESSURIZED
PRESSURIZER
PRESSURIZERS
PRESSURIZES
PRESSURIZING
PRESSWOMAN
PRESSWOMEN
PRESSWORKS
PRESTAMPED
PRESTAMPING
PRESTATION
PRESTATIONS
PRESTERILISE
PRESTERILISED
PRESTERILISES
PRESTERILISING
PRESTERILIZE
PRESTERILIZED
PRESTERILIZES
PRESTERILIZING
PRESTERNUM
PRESTERNUMS
PRESTIDIGITATOR
PRESTIGEFUL
PRESTIGIATOR
PRESTIGIATORS
PRESTIGIOUS
PRESTIGIOUSLY
PRESTIGIOUSNESS
PRESTISSIMO
PRESTISSIMOS
PRESTORAGE
PRESTORING
PRESTRESSED
PRESTRESSES
PRESTRESSING
PRESTRICTION
PRESTRICTIONS
PRESTRUCTURE
PRESTRUCTURED
PRESTRUCTURES
PRESTRUCTURING
PRESUMABLE
PRESUMABLY
PRESUMEDLY
PRESUMINGLY
PRESUMMITS
PRESUMPTION
PRESUMPTIONS
PRESUMPTIVE
PRESUMPTIVELY
PRESUMPTIVENESS
PRESUMPTUOUS
PRESUMPTUOUSLY
PRESUPPOSE
PRESUPPOSED
PRESUPPOSES
PRESUPPOSING
PRESUPPOSITION
PRESUPPOSITIONS
PRESURGERY
PRESURMISE
PRESURMISES
PRESURVEYED
PRESURVEYING
PRESURVEYS
PRESWEETEN
PRESWEETENED
PRESWEETENING
PRESWEETENS
PRESYMPTOMATIC
PRESYNAPTIC
PRESYNAPTICALLY
PRETASTING
PRETELEVISION
PRETELLING
PRETENCELESS
PRETENDANT
PRETENDANTS
PRETENDEDLY
PRETENDENT
PRETENDENTS
PRETENDERS
PRETENDERSHIP
PRETENDERSHIPS
PRETENDING
PRETENDINGLY
PRETENSION
PRETENSIONED
PRETENSIONING
PRETENSIONLESS
PRETENSIONS
PRETENSIVE
PRETENTIOUS
PRETENTIOUSLY
PRETENTIOUSNESS
PRETERHUMAN
PRETERISTS
PRETERITENESS
PRETERITENESSES
PRETERITES
PRETERITION
PRETERITIONS
PRETERITIVE
PRETERMINAL
PRETERMINATION
PRETERMINATIONS
PRETERMISSION
PRETERMISSIONS
PRETERMITS
PRETERMITTED
PRETERMITTER
PRETERMITTERS
PRETERMITTING
PRETERNATURAL
PRETERNATURALLY
PRETERPERFECT
PRETERPERFECTS
PRETESTING
PRETEXTING
PRETHEATER
PRETORIANS
PRETORSHIP
PRETORSHIPS
PRETOURNAMENT
PRETRAINED
PRETRAINING
PRETREATED
PRETREATING
PRETREATMENT
PRETREATMENTS
PRETRIMMED
PRETRIMMING
PRETTIFICATION
PRETTIFICATIONS
PRETTIFIED
PRETTIFIER
PRETTIFIERS
PRETTIFIES
PRETTIFYING
PRETTINESS
PRETTINESSES
PRETTYISMS
PREUNIFICATION
PREUNITING
PREUNIVERSITY
PREVAILERS
PREVAILING
PREVAILINGLY
PREVAILMENT
PREVAILMENTS
PREVALENCE
PREVALENCES
PREVALENCIES
PREVALENCY
PREVALENTLY
PREVALENTNESS
PREVALENTNESSES
PREVALENTS
PREVALUING
PREVARICATE
PREVARICATED
PREVARICATES
PREVARICATING
PREVARICATION
PREVARICATIONS
PREVARICATOR
PREVARICATORS
PREVENANCIES
PREVENANCY
PREVENIENCE
PREVENIENCES
PREVENIENT
PREVENIENTLY
PREVENTABILITY
PREVENTABLE
PREVENTABLY
PREVENTATIVE
PREVENTATIVES
PREVENTERS
PREVENTIBILITY
PREVENTIBLE
PREVENTIBLY
PREVENTING
PREVENTION
PREVENTIONS
PREVENTIVE
PREVENTIVELY
PREVENTIVENESS
PREVENTIVES
PREVIEWERS
PREVIEWING
PREVIOUSLY
PREVIOUSNESS

PREVIOUSNESSES
PREVISIONAL
PREVISIONARY
PREVISIONED
PREVISIONING
PREVISIONS
PREVISITED
PREVISITING
PREVOCALIC
PREVOCALICALLY
PREVOCATIONAL
PREWARMING
PREWARNING
PREWASHING
PREWEANING
PREWEIGHED
PREWEIGHING
PREWORKING
PREWRAPPED
PREWRAPPING
PREWRITING
PREWRITINGS
PRICELESSLY
PRICELESSNESS
PRICELESSNESSES
PRICINESSES
PRICKLIEST
PRICKLINESS
PRICKLINESSES
PRICKLINGS
PRICKWOODS
PRIDEFULLY
PRIDEFULNESS
PRIDEFULNESSES
PRIESTCRAFT
PRIESTCRAFTS
PRIESTESSES
PRIESTHOOD
PRIESTHOODS
PRIESTLIER
PRIESTLIEST
PRIESTLIKE
PRIESTLINESS
PRIESTLINESSES
PRIESTLING
PRIESTLINGS
PRIESTSHIP
PRIESTSHIPS
PRIGGERIES
PRIGGISHLY
PRIGGISHNESS
PRIGGISHNESSES
PRIMAEVALLY
PRIMALITIES
PRIMAQUINE
PRIMAQUINES
PRIMARINESS
PRIMARINESSES
PRIMATESHIP
PRIMATESHIPS
PRIMATIALS
PRIMATICAL
PRIMATOLOGICAL
PRIMATOLOGIES
PRIMATOLOGIST
PRIMATOLOGISTS
PRIMATOLOGY
PRIMAVERAS
PRIMENESSES
PRIMEVALLY
PRIMIGENIAL
PRIMIGRAVIDA
PRIMIGRAVIDAE
PRIMIGRAVIDAS
PRIMIPARAE
PRIMIPARAS
PRIMIPARITIES
PRIMIPARITY
PRIMIPAROUS
PRIMITIVELY
PRIMITIVENESS
PRIMITIVENESSES
PRIMITIVES
PRIMITIVISM
PRIMITIVISMS
PRIMITIVIST
PRIMITIVISTIC
PRIMITIVISTS
PRIMITIVITIES
PRIMITIVITY
PRIMNESSES
PRIMOGENIAL
PRIMOGENIT
PRIMOGENITAL
PRIMOGENITARY
PRIMOGENITIVE
PRIMOGENITIVES
PRIMOGENITOR
PRIMOGENITORS
PRIMOGENITRICES
PRIMOGENITRIX
PRIMOGENITRIXES
PRIMOGENITS
PRIMOGENITURE
PRIMOGENITURES
PRIMORDIAL
PRIMORDIALISM
PRIMORDIALISMS
PRIMORDIALITIES
PRIMORDIALITY
PRIMORDIALLY
PRIMORDIALS
PRIMORDIUM
PRIMROSING
PRIMULACEOUS
PRIMULINES
PRINCEDOMS
PRINCEHOOD
PRINCEHOODS
PRINCEKINS
PRINCELETS
PRINCELIER
PRINCELIEST
PRINCELIKE
PRINCELINESS
PRINCELINESSES
PRINCELING
PRINCELINGS
PRINCESHIP
PRINCESHIPS
PRINCESSES
PRINCESSLY
PRINCIFIED
PRINCIPALITIES
PRINCIPALITY
PRINCIPALLY
PRINCIPALNESS
PRINCIPALNESSES
PRINCIPALS
PRINCIPALSHIP
PRINCIPALSHIPS
PRINCIPATE
PRINCIPATES
PRINCIPIAL
PRINCIPIUM
PRINCIPLED
PRINCIPLES
PRINCIPLING
PRINTABILITIES
PRINTABILITY
PRINTABLENESS
PRINTABLENESSES
PRINTERIES
PRINTHEADS
PRINTMAKER
PRINTMAKERS
PRINTMAKING
PRINTMAKINGS
PRINTWHEEL
PRINTWHEELS
PRINTWORKS
PRIORESSES
PRIORITIES
PRIORITISATION
PRIORITISATIONS
PRIORITISE
PRIORITISED
PRIORITISES
PRIORITISING
PRIORITIZATION
PRIORITIZATIONS
PRIORITIZE
PRIORITIZED
PRIORITIZES
PRIORITIZING
PRIORSHIPS
PRISMATICAL
PRISMATICALLY
PRISMATOID
PRISMATOIDAL
PRISMATOIDS
PRISMOIDAL
PRISONMENT
PRISONMENTS
PRISSINESS
PRISSINESSES
PRISTINELY
PRIVATDOCENT
PRIVATDOCENTS
PRIVATDOZENT
PRIVATDOZENTS
PRIVATEERED
PRIVATEERING
PRIVATEERINGS
PRIVATEERS
PRIVATEERSMAN
PRIVATEERSMEN
PRIVATENESS
PRIVATENESSES
PRIVATIONS
PRIVATISATION
PRIVATISATIONS
PRIVATISED
PRIVATISER
PRIVATISERS
PRIVATISES
PRIVATISING
PRIVATISMS
PRIVATISTS
PRIVATIVELY
PRIVATIVES
PRIVATIZATION
PRIVATIZATIONS
PRIVATIZED
PRIVATIZER
PRIVATIZERS
PRIVATIZES
PRIVATIZING
PRIVILEGED
PRIVILEGES
PRIVILEGING
PRIZEFIGHT
PRIZEFIGHTER
PRIZEFIGHTERS
PRIZEFIGHTING
PRIZEFIGHTINGS
PRIZEFIGHTS
PRIZEWINNER
PRIZEWINNERS
PRIZEWINNING
PRIZEWOMAN
PRIZEWOMEN
PROABORTION
PROACTIONS
PROAIRESES
PROAIRESIS
PROBABILIORISM
PROBABILIORISMS
PROBABILIORIST
PROBABILIORISTS
PROBABILISM
PROBABILISMS
PROBABILIST
PROBABILISTIC
PROBABILISTS
PROBABILITIES
PROBABILITY
PROBATIONAL
PROBATIONALLY
PROBATIONARIES
PROBATIONARY
PROBATIONER
PROBATIONERS
PROBATIONERSHIP
PROBATIONS
PROBATIVELY
PROBENECID
PROBENECIDS
PROBIOTICS
PROBLEMATIC
PROBLEMATICAL
PROBLEMATICALLY
PROBLEMATICS
PROBLEMIST

PROBLEMISTS
PROBOSCIDEAN
PROBOSCIDEANS
PROBOSCIDES
PROBOSCIDIAN
PROBOSCIDIANS
PROBOSCISES
PROBOULEUTIC
PROBUSINESS
PROCACIOUS
PROCACITIES
PROCAMBIAL
PROCAMBIUM
PROCAMBIUMS
PROCAPITALIST
PROCAPITALISTS
PROCARBAZINE
PROCARBAZINES
PROCARYONS
PROCARYOTE
PROCARYOTES
PROCARYOTIC
PROCATHEDRAL
PROCATHEDRALS
PROCEDURAL
PROCEDURALLY
PROCEDURALS
PROCEDURES
PROCEEDERS
PROCEEDING
PROCEEDINGS
PROCELEUSMATIC
PROCELEUSMATICS
PROCELLARIAN
PROCEPHALIC
PROCERCOID
PROCERCOIDS
PROCEREBRA
PROCEREBRAL
PROCEREBRUM
PROCEREBRUMS
PROCERITIES
PROCESSABILITY
PROCESSABLE
PROCESSERS
PROCESSIBILITY
PROCESSIBLE
PROCESSING
PROCESSINGS
PROCESSION
PROCESSIONAL
PROCESSIONALIST
PROCESSIONALLY
PROCESSIONALS
PROCESSIONARY
PROCESSIONED
PROCESSIONER
PROCESSIONERS
PROCESSIONING
PROCESSIONINGS
PROCESSIONS
PROCESSORS
PROCESSUAL
PROCHRONISM
PROCHRONISMS
PROCIDENCE
PROCIDENCES
PROCLAIMANT
PROCLAIMANTS
PROCLAIMED
PROCLAIMER
PROCLAIMERS
PROCLAIMING
PROCLAMATION
PROCLAMATIONS
PROCLAMATORY
PROCLITICS
PROCLIVITIES
PROCLIVITY
PROCOELOUS
PROCONSULAR
PROCONSULATE
PROCONSULATES
PROCONSULS
PROCONSULSHIP
PROCONSULSHIPS
PROCRASTINATE
PROCRASTINATED
PROCRASTINATES
PROCRASTINATING
PROCRASTINATION
PROCRASTINATIVE
PROCRASTINATOR
PROCRASTINATORS
PROCRASTINATORY
PROCREANTS
PROCREATED
PROCREATES
PROCREATING
PROCREATION
PROCREATIONAL
PROCREATIONS
PROCREATIVE
PROCREATIVENESS
PROCREATOR
PROCREATORS
PROCRUSTEAN
PROCRYPSES
PROCRYPSIS
PROCRYPTIC
PROCRYPTICALLY
PROCTALGIA
PROCTALGIAS
PROCTITIDES
PROCTITISES
PROCTODAEA
PROCTODAEAL
PROCTODAEUM
PROCTODAEUMS
PROCTODEUM
PROCTODEUMS
PROCTOLOGIC
PROCTOLOGICAL
PROCTOLOGIES
PROCTOLOGIST
PROCTOLOGISTS
PROCTOLOGY
PROCTORAGE
PROCTORAGES
PROCTORIAL
PROCTORIALLY
PROCTORING
PROCTORISE
PROCTORISED
PROCTORISES
PROCTORISING
PROCTORIZE
PROCTORIZED
PROCTORIZES
PROCTORIZING
PROCTORSHIP
PROCTORSHIPS
PROCTOSCOPE
PROCTOSCOPES
PROCTOSCOPIC
PROCTOSCOPIES
PROCTOSCOPY
PROCUMBENT
PROCURABLE
PROCURACIES
PROCURANCE
PROCURANCES
PROCURATION
PROCURATIONS
PROCURATOR
PROCURATORIAL
PROCURATORIES
PROCURATORS
PROCURATORSHIP
PROCURATORSHIPS
PROCURATORY
PROCUREMENT
PROCUREMENTS
PROCURESSES
PROCUREURS
PRODIGALISE
PRODIGALISED
PRODIGALISES
PRODIGALISING
PRODIGALITIES
PRODIGALITY
PRODIGALIZE
PRODIGALIZED
PRODIGALIZES
PRODIGALIZING
PRODIGALLY
PRODIGIOSITIES
PRODIGIOSITY
PRODIGIOUS
PRODIGIOUSLY
PRODIGIOUSNESS
PRODITORIOUS
PRODNOSING
PRODROMATA
PRODUCEMENT
PRODUCEMENTS
PRODUCIBILITIES
PRODUCIBILITY
PRODUCIBLE
PRODUCTIBILITY
PRODUCTILE
PRODUCTION
PRODUCTIONAL
PRODUCTIONS
PRODUCTIVE
PRODUCTIVELY
PRODUCTIVENESS
PRODUCTIVITIES
PRODUCTIVITY
PROEMBRYOS
PROENZYMES
PROESTRUSES
PROFANATION
PROFANATIONS
PROFANATORY
PROFANENESS
PROFANENESSES
PROFANITIES
PROFASCIST
PROFECTITIOUS
PROFEMINIST
PROFESSEDLY
PROFESSING
PROFESSION
PROFESSIONAL
PROFESSIONALISE
PROFESSIONALISM
PROFESSIONALIST
PROFESSIONALIZE
PROFESSIONALLY
PROFESSIONALS
PROFESSIONS
PROFESSORATE
PROFESSORATES
PROFESSORESS
PROFESSORESSES
PROFESSORIAL
PROFESSORIALLY
PROFESSORIAT
PROFESSORIATE
PROFESSORIATES
PROFESSORIATS
PROFESSORS
PROFESSORSHIP
PROFESSORSHIPS
PROFFERERS
PROFFERING
PROFICIENCE
PROFICIENCES
PROFICIENCIES
PROFICIENCY
PROFICIENT
PROFICIENTLY
PROFICIENTS
PROFILINGS
PROFILISTS
PROFITABILITIES
PROFITABILITY
PROFITABLE
PROFITABLENESS
PROFITABLY
PROFITEERED
PROFITEERING
PROFITEERINGS
PROFITEERS
PROFITEROLE
PROFITEROLES
PROFITINGS
PROFITLESS
PROFITLESSLY
PROFITWISE
PROFLIGACIES
PROFLIGACY
PROFLIGATE

PROFLIGATELY
PROFLIGATES
PROFLUENCE
PROFLUENCES
PROFOUNDER
PROFOUNDEST
PROFOUNDLY
PROFOUNDNESS
PROFOUNDNESSES
PROFULGENT
PROFUNDITIES
PROFUNDITY
PROFUSENESS
PROFUSENESSES
PROFUSIONS
PROGENITIVE
PROGENITIVENESS
PROGENITOR
PROGENITORIAL
PROGENITORS
PROGENITORSHIP
PROGENITORSHIPS
PROGENITRESS
PROGENITRESSES
PROGENITRICES
PROGENITRIX
PROGENITRIXES
PROGENITURE
PROGENITURES
PROGESTATIONAL
PROGESTERONE
PROGESTERONES
PROGESTINS
PROGESTOGEN
PROGESTOGENIC
PROGESTOGENS
PROGGINSES
PROGLOTTIC
PROGLOTTID
PROGLOTTIDEAN
PROGLOTTIDES
PROGLOTTIDS
PROGLOTTIS
PROGNATHIC
PROGNATHISM
PROGNATHISMS
PROGNATHOUS
PROGNOSING
PROGNOSTIC
PROGNOSTICATE
PROGNOSTICATED
PROGNOSTICATES
PROGNOSTICATING
PROGNOSTICATION
PROGNOSTICATIVE
PROGNOSTICATOR
PROGNOSTICATORS
PROGNOSTICS
PROGRADATION
PROGRADATIONS
PROGRADING
PROGRAMABLE
PROGRAMERS
PROGRAMING
PROGRAMINGS
PROGRAMMABILITY
PROGRAMMABLE
PROGRAMMABLES
PROGRAMMATIC
PROGRAMMED
PROGRAMMER
PROGRAMMERS
PROGRAMMES
PROGRAMMING
PROGRAMMINGS
PROGRESSED
PROGRESSES
PROGRESSING
PROGRESSION
PROGRESSIONAL
PROGRESSIONALLY
PROGRESSIONARY
PROGRESSIONISM
PROGRESSIONISMS
PROGRESSIONIST
PROGRESSIONISTS
PROGRESSIONS
PROGRESSISM
PROGRESSISMS
PROGRESSIST
PROGRESSISTS
PROGRESSIVE
PROGRESSIVELY
PROGRESSIVENESS
PROGRESSIVES
PROGRESSIVISM
PROGRESSIVISMS
PROGRESSIVIST
PROGRESSIVISTIC
PROGRESSIVISTS
PROGRESSIVITIES
PROGRESSIVITY
PROGYMNASIA
PROGYMNASIUM
PROGYMNASIUMS
PROHIBITED
PROHIBITER
PROHIBITERS
PROHIBITING
PROHIBITION
PROHIBITIONARY
PROHIBITIONISM
PROHIBITIONISMS
PROHIBITIONIST
PROHIBITIONISTS
PROHIBITIONS
PROHIBITIVE
PROHIBITIVELY
PROHIBITIVENESS
PROHIBITOR
PROHIBITORS
PROHIBITORY
PROINSULIN
PROINSULINS
PROJECTABLE
PROJECTILE
PROJECTILES
PROJECTING
PROJECTINGS
PROJECTION
PROJECTIONAL
PROJECTIONIST
PROJECTIONISTS
PROJECTIONS
PROJECTISATION
PROJECTISATIONS
PROJECTIVE
PROJECTIVELY
PROJECTIVITIES
PROJECTIVITY
PROJECTIZATION
PROJECTIZATIONS
PROJECTMENT
PROJECTMENTS
PROJECTORS
PROJECTURE
PROJECTURES
PROKARYONS
PROKARYOTE
PROKARYOTES
PROKARYOTIC
PROKARYOTS
PROLACTINS
PROLAMINES
PROLAPSING
PROLAPSUSES
PROLATENESS
PROLATENESSES
PROLATIONS
PROLEGOMENA
PROLEGOMENAL
PROLEGOMENARY
PROLEGOMENON
PROLEGOMENOUS
PROLEPTICAL
PROLEPTICALLY
PROLETARIAN
PROLETARIANISE
PROLETARIANISED
PROLETARIANISES
PROLETARIANISM
PROLETARIANISMS
PROLETARIANIZE
PROLETARIANIZED
PROLETARIANIZES
PROLETARIANNESS
PROLETARIANS
PROLETARIAT
PROLETARIATE
PROLETARIATES
PROLETARIATS
PROLETARIES
PROLICIDAL
PROLICIDES
PROLIFERATE
PROLIFERATED
PROLIFERATES
PROLIFERATING
PROLIFERATION
PROLIFERATIONS
PROLIFERATIVE
PROLIFEROUS
PROLIFEROUSLY
PROLIFICACIES
PROLIFICACY
PROLIFICAL
PROLIFICALLY
PROLIFICATION
PROLIFICATIONS
PROLIFICITIES
PROLIFICITY
PROLIFICNESS
PROLIFICNESSES
PROLIXIOUS
PROLIXITIES
PROLIXNESS
PROLIXNESSES
PROLOCUTION
PROLOCUTIONS
PROLOCUTOR
PROLOCUTORS
PROLOCUTORSHIP
PROLOCUTORSHIPS
PROLOCUTRICES
PROLOCUTRIX
PROLOCUTRIXES
PROLOGISED
PROLOGISES
PROLOGISING
PROLOGISTS
PROLOGIZED
PROLOGIZES
PROLOGIZING
PROLOGUING
PROLOGUISE
PROLOGUISED
PROLOGUISES
PROLOGUISING
PROLOGUIZE
PROLOGUIZED
PROLOGUIZES
PROLOGUIZING
PROLONGABLE
PROLONGATE
PROLONGATED
PROLONGATES
PROLONGATING
PROLONGATION
PROLONGATIONS
PROLONGERS
PROLONGING
PROLONGMENT
PROLONGMENTS
PROLUSIONS
PROMACHOSES
PROMENADED
PROMENADER
PROMENADERS
PROMENADES
PROMENADING
PROMETHAZINE
PROMETHAZINES
PROMETHEUM
PROMETHEUMS
PROMETHIUM
PROMETHIUMS
PROMILITARY
PROMIMENTLY
PROMINENCE
PROMINENCES
PROMINENCIES
PROMINENCY
PROMINENTLY
PROMINENTNESS

PROMINENTNESSES
PROMISCUITIES
PROMISCUITY
PROMISCUOUS
PROMISCUOUSLY
PROMISCUOUSNESS
PROMISEFUL
PROMISELESS
PROMISINGLY
PROMISSIVE
PROMISSORILY
PROMISSORS
PROMISSORY
PROMONARCHIST
PROMONTORIES
PROMONTORY
PROMOTABILITIES
PROMOTABILITY
PROMOTABLE
PROMOTIONAL
PROMOTIONS
PROMOTIVENESS
PROMOTIVENESSES
PROMPTBOOK
PROMPTBOOKS
PROMPTINGS
PROMPTITUDE
PROMPTITUDES
PROMPTNESS
PROMPTNESSES
PROMPTUARIES
PROMPTUARY
PROMPTURES
PROMULGATE
PROMULGATED
PROMULGATES
PROMULGATING
PROMULGATION
PROMULGATIONS
PROMULGATOR
PROMULGATORS
PROMULGING
PROMUSCIDATE
PROMUSCIDES
PROMYCELIA
PROMYCELIAL
PROMYCELIUM
PRONATIONS
PRONATORES
PRONENESSES
PRONEPHRIC
PRONEPHROI
PRONEPHROS
PRONEPHROSES
PRONGBUCKS
PRONGHORNS
PRONOMINAL
PRONOMINALISE
PRONOMINALISED
PRONOMINALISES
PRONOMINALISING
PRONOMINALIZE
PRONOMINALIZED
PRONOMINALIZES
PRONOMINALIZING
PRONOMINALLY
PRONOUNCEABLE
PRONOUNCED
PRONOUNCEDLY
PRONOUNCEMENT
PRONOUNCEMENTS
PRONOUNCER
PRONOUNCERS
PRONOUNCES
PRONOUNCING
PRONOUNCINGS
PRONUCLEAR
PRONUCLEARIST
PRONUCLEARISTS
PRONUCLEUS
PRONUCLEUSES
PRONUNCIAMENTO
PRONUNCIAMENTOS
PRONUNCIATION
PRONUNCIATIONAL
PRONUNCIATIONS
PRONUNCIOS
PROOEMIONS
PROOEMIUMS
PROOFREADER
PROOFREADERS
PROOFREADING
PROOFREADINGS
PROOFREADS
PROOFROOMS
PROPAEDEUTIC
PROPAEDEUTICAL
PROPAEDEUTICS
PROPAGABILITIES
PROPAGABILITY
PROPAGABLE
PROPAGABLENESS
PROPAGANDA
PROPAGANDAS
PROPAGANDISE
PROPAGANDISED
PROPAGANDISER
PROPAGANDISERS
PROPAGANDISES
PROPAGANDISING
PROPAGANDISM
PROPAGANDISMS
PROPAGANDIST
PROPAGANDISTIC
PROPAGANDISTS
PROPAGANDIZE
PROPAGANDIZED
PROPAGANDIZER
PROPAGANDIZERS
PROPAGANDIZES
PROPAGANDIZING
PROPAGATED
PROPAGATES
PROPAGATING
PROPAGATION
PROPAGATIONAL
PROPAGATIONS
PROPAGATIVE
PROPAGATOR
PROPAGATORS
PROPAGULES
PROPAGULUM
PROPANEDIOIC
PROPANONES
PROPAROXYTONE
PROPAROXYTONES
PROPELLANT
PROPELLANTS
PROPELLENT
PROPELLENTS
PROPELLERS
PROPELLING
PROPELLORS
PROPELMENT
PROPELMENTS
PROPENDENT
PROPENDING
PROPENSELY
PROPENSENESS
PROPENSENESSES
PROPENSION
PROPENSIONS
PROPENSITIES
PROPENSITY
PROPENSIVE
PROPERDINS
PROPERISPOMENON
PROPERNESS
PROPERNESSES
PROPERTIED
PROPERTIES
PROPERTYING
PROPERTYLESS
PROPHECIES
PROPHESIABLE
PROPHESIED
PROPHESIER
PROPHESIERS
PROPHESIES
PROPHESYING
PROPHESYINGS
PROPHETESS
PROPHETESSES
PROPHETHOOD
PROPHETHOODS
PROPHETICAL
PROPHETICALLY
PROPHETICISM
PROPHETICISMS
PROPHETISM
PROPHETISMS
PROPHETSHIP
PROPHETSHIPS
PROPHYLACTIC
PROPHYLACTICS
PROPHYLAXES
PROPHYLAXIS
PROPINQUITIES
PROPINQUITY
PROPIONATE
PROPIONATES
PROPITIABLE
PROPITIATE
PROPITIATED
PROPITIATES
PROPITIATING
PROPITIATION
PROPITIATIONS
PROPITIATIOUS
PROPITIATIVE
PROPITIATOR
PROPITIATORIES
PROPITIATORILY
PROPITIATORS
PROPITIATORY
PROPITIOUS
PROPITIOUSLY
PROPITIOUSNESS
PROPLASTID
PROPLASTIDS
PROPODEONS
PROPODEUMS
PROPOLISES
PROPONENTS
PROPORTION
PROPORTIONABLE
PROPORTIONABLY
PROPORTIONAL
PROPORTIONALITY
PROPORTIONALLY
PROPORTIONALS
PROPORTIONATE
PROPORTIONATED
PROPORTIONATELY
PROPORTIONATES
PROPORTIONATING
PROPORTIONED
PROPORTIONING
PROPORTIONINGS
PROPORTIONLESS
PROPORTIONMENT
PROPORTIONMENTS
PROPORTIONS
PROPOSABLE
PROPOSITAE
PROPOSITION
PROPOSITIONAL
PROPOSITIONALLY
PROPOSITIONED
PROPOSITIONING
PROPOSITIONS
PROPOSITUS
PROPOUNDED
PROPOUNDER
PROPOUNDERS
PROPOUNDING
PROPOXYPHENE
PROPOXYPHENES
PROPRAETOR
PROPRAETORIAL
PROPRAETORIAN
PROPRAETORS
PROPRANOLOL
PROPRANOLOLS
PROPRETORS
PROPRIETARIES
PROPRIETARILY
PROPRIETARY
PROPRIETIES
PROPRIETOR
PROPRIETORIAL
PROPRIETORIALLY
PROPRIETORS
PROPRIETORSHIP

PROPRIETORSHIPS
PROPRIETRESS
PROPRIETRESSES
PROPRIETRICES
PROPRIETRIX
PROPRIETRIXES
PROPRIOCEPTION
PROPRIOCEPTIONS
PROPRIOCEPTIVE
PROPRIOCEPTOR
PROPRIOCEPTORS
PROPROCTOR
PROPROCTORS
PROPUGNATION
PROPUGNATIONS
PROPULSION
PROPULSIONS
PROPULSIVE
PROPULSORS
PROPULSORY
PROPYLAEUM
PROPYLAMINE
PROPYLAMINES
PROPYLENES
PROPYLITES
PROPYLITISATION
PROPYLITISE
PROPYLITISED
PROPYLITISES
PROPYLITISING
PROPYLITIZATION
PROPYLITIZE
PROPYLITIZED
PROPYLITIZES
PROPYLITIZING
PRORATABLE
PRORATIONS
PRORECTORS
PROROGATED
PROROGATES
PROROGATING
PROROGATION
PROROGATIONS
PROROGUING
PROSAICALLY
PROSAICALNESS
PROSAICALNESSES
PROSAICISM
PROSAICISMS
PROSAICNESS
PROSAICNESSES
PROSATEURS
PROSAUROPOD
PROSAUROPODS
PROSCENIUM
PROSCENIUMS
PROSCIUTTI
PROSCIUTTO
PROSCIUTTOS
PROSCRIBED
PROSCRIBER
PROSCRIBERS
PROSCRIBES
PROSCRIBING
PROSCRIPTION
PROSCRIPTIONS
PROSCRIPTIVE
PROSCRIPTIVELY
PROSCRIPTS
PROSECTING
PROSECTORIAL
PROSECTORS
PROSECTORSHIP
PROSECTORSHIPS
PROSECUTABLE
PROSECUTED
PROSECUTES
PROSECUTING
PROSECUTION
PROSECUTIONS
PROSECUTOR
PROSECUTORIAL
PROSECUTORS
PROSECUTRICES
PROSECUTRIX
PROSECUTRIXES
PROSELYTED
PROSELYTES
PROSELYTIC
PROSELYTING
PROSELYTISATION
PROSELYTISE
PROSELYTISED
PROSELYTISER
PROSELYTISERS
PROSELYTISES
PROSELYTISING
PROSELYTISM
PROSELYTISMS
PROSELYTIZATION
PROSELYTIZE
PROSELYTIZED
PROSELYTIZER
PROSELYTIZERS
PROSELYTIZES
PROSELYTIZING
PROSEMINAR
PROSEMINARS
PROSENCEPHALA
PROSENCEPHALIC
PROSENCEPHALON
PROSENCHYMA
PROSENCHYMAS
PROSENCHYMATA
PROSENCHYMATOUS
PROSEUCHAE
PROSIFYING
PROSILIENCIES
PROSILIENCY
PROSILIENT
PROSIMIANS
PROSINESSES
PROSLAMBANOMENE
PROSLAVERY
PROSOBRANCH
PROSOBRANCHS
PROSODIANS
PROSODICAL
PROSODICALLY
PROSODISTS
PROSOPAGNOSIA
PROSOPAGNOSIAS
PROSOPOGRAPHER
PROSOPOGRAPHERS
PROSOPOGRAPHIES
PROSOPOGRAPHY
PROSOPOPEIA
PROSOPOPEIAL
PROSOPOPEIAS
PROSOPOPOEIA
PROSOPOPOEIAL
PROSOPOPOEIAS
PROSPECTED
PROSPECTING
PROSPECTINGS
PROSPECTION
PROSPECTIONS
PROSPECTIVE
PROSPECTIVELY
PROSPECTIVENESS
PROSPECTIVES
PROSPECTLESS
PROSPECTOR
PROSPECTORS
PROSPECTUS
PROSPECTUSES
PROSPERING
PROSPERITIES
PROSPERITY
PROSPEROUS
PROSPEROUSLY
PROSPEROUSNESS
PROSTACYCLIN
PROSTACYCLINS
PROSTAGLANDIN
PROSTAGLANDINS
PROSTANTHERA
PROSTANTHERAS
PROSTATECTOMIES
PROSTATECTOMY
PROSTATISM
PROSTATISMS
PROSTATITIS
PROSTATITISES
PROSTERNUM
PROSTERNUMS
PROSTHESES
PROSTHESIS
PROSTHETIC
PROSTHETICALLY
PROSTHETICS
PROSTHETIST
PROSTHETISTS
PROSTHODONTIA
PROSTHODONTIAS
PROSTHODONTICS
PROSTHODONTIST
PROSTHODONTISTS
PROSTITUTE
PROSTITUTED
PROSTITUTES
PROSTITUTING
PROSTITUTION
PROSTITUTIONS
PROSTITUTOR
PROSTITUTORS
PROSTOMIAL
PROSTOMIUM
PROSTOMIUMS
PROSTRATED
PROSTRATES
PROSTRATING
PROSTRATION
PROSTRATIONS
PROSYLLOGISM
PROSYLLOGISMS
PROTACTINIUM
PROTACTINIUMS
PROTAGONISM
PROTAGONISMS
PROTAGONIST
PROTAGONISTS
PROTAMINES
PROTANDRIES
PROTANDROUS
PROTANOMALIES
PROTANOMALOUS
PROTANOMALY
PROTANOPES
PROTANOPIA
PROTANOPIAS
PROTANOPIC
PROTEACEOUS
PROTECTANT
PROTECTANTS
PROTECTERS
PROTECTING
PROTECTINGLY
PROTECTION
PROTECTIONISM
PROTECTIONISMS
PROTECTIONIST
PROTECTIONISTS
PROTECTIONS
PROTECTIVE
PROTECTIVELY
PROTECTIVENESS
PROTECTIVES
PROTECTORAL
PROTECTORATE
PROTECTORATES
PROTECTORIAL
PROTECTORIES
PROTECTORLESS
PROTECTORS
PROTECTORSHIP
PROTECTORSHIPS
PROTECTORY
PROTECTRESS
PROTECTRESSES
PROTECTRICES
PROTECTRIX
PROTECTRIXES
PROTEIFORM
PROTEINACEOUS
PROTEINASE
PROTEINASES
PROTEINOUS
PROTEINURIA
PROTEINURIAS
PROTENDING
PROTENSION
PROTENSIONS
PROTENSITIES

PROTENSITY
PROTENSIVE
PROTENSIVELY
PROTEOCLASTIC
PROTEOGLYCAN
PROTEOGLYCANS
PROTEOLYSE
PROTEOLYSED
PROTEOLYSES
PROTEOLYSING
PROTEOLYSIS
PROTEOLYTIC
PROTEOLYTICALLY
PROTEOMICS
PROTERANDRIES
PROTERANDROUS
PROTERANDRY
PROTEROGYNIES
PROTEROGYNOUS
PROTEROGYNY
PROTERVITIES
PROTERVITY
PROTESTANT
PROTESTANTS
PROTESTATION
PROTESTATIONS
PROTESTERS
PROTESTING
PROTESTINGLY
PROTESTORS
PROTHALAMIA
PROTHALAMION
PROTHALAMIUM
PROTHALLIA
PROTHALLIAL
PROTHALLIC
PROTHALLIUM
PROTHALLOID
PROTHALLUS
PROTHALLUSES
PROTHETICALLY
PROTHONOTARIAL
PROTHONOTARIAT
PROTHONOTARIATS
PROTHONOTARIES
PROTHONOTARY
PROTHORACES
PROTHORACIC
PROTHORAXES
PROTHROMBIN
PROTHROMBINS
PROTISTANS
PROTISTOLOGIES
PROTISTOLOGIST
PROTISTOLOGISTS
PROTISTOLOGY
PROTOACTINIUM
PROTOACTINIUMS
PROTOAVISES
PROTOCHORDATE
PROTOCHORDATES
PROTOCOCCAL
PROTOCOLED
PROTOCOLIC
PROTOCOLING
PROTOCOLISE
PROTOCOLISED
PROTOCOLISES
PROTOCOLISING
PROTOCOLIST
PROTOCOLISTS
PROTOCOLIZE
PROTOCOLIZED
PROTOCOLIZES
PROTOCOLIZING
PROTOCOLLED
PROTOCOLLING
PROTOCTIST
PROTOCTISTS
PROTODERMS
PROTOGALAXIES
PROTOGALAXY
PROTOGENIC
PROTOGINES
PROTOGYNIES
PROTOGYNOUS
PROTOHISTORIAN
PROTOHISTORIANS
PROTOHISTORIC
PROTOHISTORIES
PROTOHISTORY
PROTOHUMAN
PROTOHUMANS
PROTOLANGUAGE
PROTOLANGUAGES
PROTOLITHIC
PROTOMARTYR
PROTOMARTYRS
PROTOMORPHIC
PROTONATED
PROTONATES
PROTONATING
PROTONATION
PROTONATIONS
PROTONEMAL
PROTONEMATA
PROTONEMATAL
PROTONOTARIAL
PROTONOTARIAT
PROTONOTARIATS
PROTONOTARIES
PROTONOTARY
PROTOPATHIC
PROTOPATHIES
PROTOPATHY
PROTOPHILIC
PROTOPHLOEM
PROTOPHLOEMS
PROTOPHYTE
PROTOPHYTES
PROTOPHYTIC
PROTOPLANET
PROTOPLANETARY
PROTOPLANETS
PROTOPLASM
PROTOPLASMAL
PROTOPLASMATIC
PROTOPLASMIC
PROTOPLASMS
PROTOPLAST
PROTOPLASTIC
PROTOPLASTS
PROTOPORPHYRIN
PROTOPORPHYRINS
PROTOSPATAIRE
PROTOSPATAIRES
PROTOSPATHAIRE
PROTOSPATHAIRES
PROTOSPATHARIUS
PROTOSTARS
PROTOSTELE
PROTOSTELES
PROTOSTELIC
PROTOSTOME
PROTOSTOMES
PROTOTHERIAN
PROTOTHERIANS
PROTOTROPH
PROTOTROPHIC
PROTOTROPHIES
PROTOTROPHS
PROTOTROPHY
PROTOTYPAL
PROTOTYPED
PROTOTYPES
PROTOTYPIC
PROTOTYPICAL
PROTOTYPICALLY
PROTOTYPING
PROTOXIDES
PROTOXYLEM
PROTOXYLEMS
PROTOZOANS
PROTOZOOLOGICAL
PROTOZOOLOGIES
PROTOZOOLOGIST
PROTOZOOLOGISTS
PROTOZOOLOGY
PROTOZOONS
PROTRACTED
PROTRACTEDLY
PROTRACTEDNESS
PROTRACTIBLE
PROTRACTILE
PROTRACTING
PROTRACTION
PROTRACTIONS
PROTRACTIVE
PROTRACTOR
PROTRACTORS
PROTREPTIC
PROTREPTICAL
PROTREPTICS
PROTRUDABLE
PROTRUDENT
PROTRUDING
PROTRUSIBLE
PROTRUSILE
PROTRUSION
PROTRUSIONS
PROTRUSIVE
PROTRUSIVELY
PROTRUSIVENESS
PROTUBERANCE
PROTUBERANCES
PROTUBERANCIES
PROTUBERANCY
PROTUBERANT
PROTUBERANTLY
PROTUBERATE
PROTUBERATED
PROTUBERATES
PROTUBERATING
PROTUBERATION
PROTUBERATIONS
PROUDHEARTED
PROUDNESSES
PROUSTITES
PROVABILITIES
PROVABILITY
PROVABLENESS
PROVABLENESSES
PROVANTING
PROVASCULAR
PROVECTION
PROVECTIONS
PROVEDITOR
PROVEDITORE
PROVEDITORES
PROVEDITORS
PROVEDORES
PROVENANCE
PROVENANCES
PROVENDERED
PROVENDERING
PROVENDERS
PROVENIENCE
PROVENIENCES
PROVENTRICULAR
PROVENTRICULI
PROVENTRICULUS
PROVERBIAL
PROVERBIALISE
PROVERBIALISED
PROVERBIALISES
PROVERBIALISING
PROVERBIALISM
PROVERBIALISMS
PROVERBIALIST
PROVERBIALISTS
PROVERBIALIZE
PROVERBIALIZED
PROVERBIALIZES
PROVERBIALIZING
PROVERBIALLY
PROVERBING
PROVIDABLE
PROVIDENCE
PROVIDENCES
PROVIDENTIAL
PROVIDENTIALLY
PROVIDENTLY
PROVINCEWIDE
PROVINCIAL
PROVINCIALISE
PROVINCIALISED
PROVINCIALISES
PROVINCIALISING
PROVINCIALISM
PROVINCIALISMS
PROVINCIALIST
PROVINCIALISTS
PROVINCIALITIES
PROVINCIALITY

PROVINCIALIZE
PROVINCIALIZED
PROVINCIALIZES
PROVINCIALIZING
PROVINCIALLY
PROVINCIALS
PROVIRUSES
PROVISIONAL
PROVISIONALLY
PROVISIONALS
PROVISIONARIES
PROVISIONARY
PROVISIONED
PROVISIONER
PROVISIONERS
PROVISIONING
PROVISIONS
PROVISORILY
PROVITAMIN
PROVITAMINS
PROVOCABLE
PROVOCANTS
PROVOCATEUR
PROVOCATEURS
PROVOCATION
PROVOCATIONS
PROVOCATIVE
PROVOCATIVELY
PROVOCATIVENESS
PROVOCATIVES
PROVOCATOR
PROVOCATORS
PROVOCATORY
PROVOKABLE
PROVOKEMENT
PROVOKEMENTS
PROVOKINGLY
PROVOLONES
PROVOSTRIES
PROVOSTSHIP
PROVOSTSHIPS
PROWLINGLY
PROXIMALLY
PROXIMATELY
PROXIMATENESS
PROXIMATENESSES
PROXIMATION
PROXIMATIONS
PROXIMITIES
PROZYMITES
PRUDENTIAL
PRUDENTIALISM
PRUDENTIALISMS
PRUDENTIALIST
PRUDENTIALISTS
PRUDENTIALITIES
PRUDENTIALITY
PRUDENTIALLY
PRUDENTIALS
PRUDISHNESS
PRUDISHNESSES
PRURIENCES
PRURIENCIES
PRURIENTLY
PRURIGINOUS
PRURITUSES
PRUSSIANISATION
PRUSSIANISE
PRUSSIANISED
PRUSSIANISES
PRUSSIANISING
PRUSSIANIZATION
PRUSSIANIZE
PRUSSIANIZED
PRUSSIANIZES
PRUSSIANIZING
PRUSSIATES
PSALIGRAPHIES
PSALIGRAPHY
PSALMBOOKS
PSALMODICAL
PSALMODIES
PSALMODISE
PSALMODISED
PSALMODISES
PSALMODISING
PSALMODIST
PSALMODISTS
PSALMODIZE
PSALMODIZED
PSALMODIZES
PSALMODIZING
PSALTERIAN
PSALTERIES
PSALTERIUM
PSALTRESSES
PSAMMOPHIL
PSAMMOPHILE
PSAMMOPHILES
PSAMMOPHILOUS
PSAMMOPHILS
PSAMMOPHYTE
PSAMMOPHYTES
PSAMMOPHYTIC
PSELLISMUS
PSELLISMUSES
PSEPHOANALYSES
PSEPHOANALYSIS
PSEPHOLOGICAL
PSEPHOLOGICALLY
PSEPHOLOGIES
PSEPHOLOGIST
PSEPHOLOGISTS
PSEPHOLOGY
PSEUDAESTHESIA
PSEUDAESTHESIAS
PSEUDARTHROSES
PSEUDARTHROSIS
PSEUDEPIGRAPH
PSEUDEPIGRAPHA
PSEUDEPIGRAPHIC
PSEUDEPIGRAPHON
PSEUDEPIGRAPHS
PSEUDEPIGRAPHY
PSEUDERIES
PSEUDIMAGINES
PSEUDIMAGO
PSEUDIMAGOS
PSEUDOACID
PSEUDOACIDS
PSEUDOALLELE
PSEUDOALLELES
PSEUDOBULB
PSEUDOBULBS
PSEUDOCARP
PSEUDOCARPOUS
PSEUDOCARPS
PSEUDOCLASSIC
PSEUDOCLASSICS
PSEUDOCODE
PSEUDOCODES
PSEUDOCOEL
PSEUDOCOELOMATE
PSEUDOCOELS
PSEUDOCYESES
PSEUDOCYESIS
PSEUDOEPHEDRINE
PSEUDOGRAPH
PSEUDOGRAPHIES
PSEUDOGRAPHS
PSEUDOGRAPHY
PSEUDOLOGIA
PSEUDOLOGIAS
PSEUDOLOGIES
PSEUDOLOGUE
PSEUDOLOGUES
PSEUDOLOGY
PSEUDOMARTYR
PSEUDOMARTYRS
PSEUDOMEMBRANE
PSEUDOMEMBRANES
PSEUDOMONAD
PSEUDOMONADES
PSEUDOMONADS
PSEUDOMONAS
PSEUDOMORPH
PSEUDOMORPHIC
PSEUDOMORPHISM
PSEUDOMORPHISMS
PSEUDOMORPHOUS
PSEUDOMORPHS
PSEUDOMUTUALITY
PSEUDONYMITIES
PSEUDONYMITY
PSEUDONYMOUS
PSEUDONYMOUSLY
PSEUDONYMS
PSEUDOPODAL
PSEUDOPODIA
PSEUDOPODIAL
PSEUDOPODIUM
PSEUDOPODS
PSEUDOPREGNANCY
PSEUDOPREGNANT
PSEUDORANDOM
PSEUDOSCALAR
PSEUDOSCALARS
PSEUDOSCHOLARLY
PSEUDOSCIENCE
PSEUDOSCIENCES
PSEUDOSCIENTIST
PSEUDOSCOPE
PSEUDOSCOPES
PSEUDOSCORPION
PSEUDOSCORPIONS
PSEUDOSOLUTION
PSEUDOSOLUTIONS
PSEUDOSYMMETRY
PSEUDOVECTOR
PSEUDOVECTORS
PSILANTHROPIC
PSILANTHROPIES
PSILANTHROPISM
PSILANTHROPISMS
PSILANTHROPIST
PSILANTHROPISTS
PSILANTHROPY
PSILOCYBIN
PSILOCYBINS
PSILOMELANE
PSILOMELANES
PSILOPHYTE
PSILOPHYTES
PSILOPHYTIC
PSITTACINE
PSITTACINES
PSITTACOSES
PSITTACOSIS
PSITTACOTIC
PSORIATICS
PSYCHAGOGUE
PSYCHAGOGUES
PSYCHASTHENIA
PSYCHASTHENIAS
PSYCHASTHENIC
PSYCHASTHENICS
PSYCHEDELIA
PSYCHEDELIAS
PSYCHEDELIC
PSYCHEDELICALLY
PSYCHEDELICS
PSYCHIATER
PSYCHIATERS
PSYCHIATRIC
PSYCHIATRICAL
PSYCHIATRICALLY
PSYCHIATRIES
PSYCHIATRIST
PSYCHIATRISTS
PSYCHIATRY
PSYCHICALLY
PSYCHICISM
PSYCHICISMS
PSYCHICIST
PSYCHICISTS
PSYCHOACOUSTIC
PSYCHOACOUSTICS
PSYCHOACTIVE
PSYCHOANALYSE
PSYCHOANALYSED
PSYCHOANALYSER
PSYCHOANALYSERS
PSYCHOANALYSES
PSYCHOANALYSING
PSYCHOANALYSIS
PSYCHOANALYST
PSYCHOANALYSTS
PSYCHOANALYTIC
PSYCHOANALYZE
PSYCHOANALYZED
PSYCHOANALYZER
PSYCHOANALYZERS
PSYCHOANALYZES
PSYCHOANALYZING

PSYCHOBABBLE
PSYCHOBABBLER
PSYCHOBABBLERS
PSYCHOBABBLES
PSYCHOBILLIES
PSYCHOBILLY
PSYCHOBIOGRAPHY
PSYCHOBIOLOGIC
PSYCHOBIOLOGIES
PSYCHOBIOLOGIST
PSYCHOBIOLOGY
PSYCHOCHEMICAL
PSYCHOCHEMICALS
PSYCHOCHEMISTRY
PSYCHODELIA
PSYCHODELIAS
PSYCHODELIC
PSYCHODELICALLY
PSYCHODRAMA
PSYCHODRAMAS
PSYCHODRAMATIC
PSYCHODYNAMIC
PSYCHODYNAMICS
PSYCHOGALVANIC
PSYCHOGASES
PSYCHOGENESES
PSYCHOGENESIS
PSYCHOGENETIC
PSYCHOGENETICAL
PSYCHOGENETICS
PSYCHOGENIC
PSYCHOGENICALLY
PSYCHOGERIATRIC
PSYCHOGNOSES
PSYCHOGNOSIS
PSYCHOGNOSTIC
PSYCHOGONIES
PSYCHOGONY
PSYCHOGRAM
PSYCHOGRAMS
PSYCHOGRAPH
PSYCHOGRAPHIC
PSYCHOGRAPHICAL
PSYCHOGRAPHICS
PSYCHOGRAPHIES
PSYCHOGRAPHS
PSYCHOGRAPHY
PSYCHOHISTORIAN
PSYCHOHISTORIES
PSYCHOHISTORY
PSYCHOKINESES
PSYCHOKINESIS
PSYCHOKINETIC
PSYCHOLINGUIST
PSYCHOLINGUISTS
PSYCHOLOGIC
PSYCHOLOGICAL
PSYCHOLOGICALLY
PSYCHOLOGIES
PSYCHOLOGISE
PSYCHOLOGISED
PSYCHOLOGISES
PSYCHOLOGISING
PSYCHOLOGISM
PSYCHOLOGISMS
PSYCHOLOGIST
PSYCHOLOGISTIC
PSYCHOLOGISTS
PSYCHOLOGIZE
PSYCHOLOGIZED
PSYCHOLOGIZES
PSYCHOLOGIZING
PSYCHOLOGY
PSYCHOMACHIA
PSYCHOMACHIAS
PSYCHOMACHIES
PSYCHOMACHY
PSYCHOMETER
PSYCHOMETERS
PSYCHOMETRIC
PSYCHOMETRICAL
PSYCHOMETRICIAN
PSYCHOMETRICS
PSYCHOMETRIES
PSYCHOMETRIST
PSYCHOMETRISTS
PSYCHOMETRY
PSYCHOMOTOR
PSYCHONEUROSES
PSYCHONEUROSIS
PSYCHONEUROTIC
PSYCHONEUROTICS
PSYCHONOMIC
PSYCHONOMICS
PSYCHOPATH
PSYCHOPATHIC
PSYCHOPATHICS
PSYCHOPATHIES
PSYCHOPATHIST
PSYCHOPATHISTS
PSYCHOPATHOLOGY
PSYCHOPATHS
PSYCHOPATHY
PSYCHOPHILIES
PSYCHOPHILY
PSYCHOPHYSICAL
PSYCHOPHYSICIST
PSYCHOPHYSICS
PSYCHOPOMP
PSYCHOPOMPS
PSYCHOSEXUAL
PSYCHOSEXUALITY
PSYCHOSEXUALLY
PSYCHOSOCIAL
PSYCHOSOCIALLY
PSYCHOSOMATIC
PSYCHOSOMATICS
PSYCHOSOMIMETIC
PSYCHOSURGEON
PSYCHOSURGEONS
PSYCHOSURGERIES
PSYCHOSURGERY
PSYCHOSURGICAL
PSYCHOSYNTHESES
PSYCHOSYNTHESIS
PSYCHOTECHNICS
PSYCHOTHERAPIES
PSYCHOTHERAPIST
PSYCHOTHERAPY
PSYCHOTICALLY
PSYCHOTICISM
PSYCHOTICISMS
PSYCHOTICS
PSYCHOTOMIMETIC
PSYCHOTOXIC
PSYCHOTROPIC
PSYCHOTROPICS
PSYCHROMETER
PSYCHROMETERS
PSYCHROMETRIC
PSYCHROMETRICAL
PSYCHROMETRIES
PSYCHROMETRY
PSYCHROPHILIC
PTARMIGANS
PTERANODON
PTERANODONS
PTERIDINES
PTERIDOLOGICAL
PTERIDOLOGIES
PTERIDOLOGIST
PTERIDOLOGISTS
PTERIDOLOGY
PTERIDOMANIA
PTERIDOMANIAS
PTERIDOPHILIST
PTERIDOPHILISTS
PTERIDOPHYTE
PTERIDOPHYTES
PTERIDOPHYTIC
PTERIDOPHYTOUS
PTERIDOSPERM
PTERIDOSPERMS
PTERODACTYL
PTERODACTYLE
PTERODACTYLES
PTERODACTYLS
PTEROSAURIAN
PTEROSAURIANS
PTEROSAURS
PTERYGIALS
PTERYGIUMS
PTERYGOIDS
PTERYLOGRAPHIC
PTERYLOGRAPHIES
PTERYLOGRAPHY
PTERYLOSES
PTERYLOSIS
PTOCHOCRACIES
PTOCHOCRACY
PTYALAGOGIC
PTYALAGOGUE
PTYALAGOGUES
PTYALISING
PTYALIZING
PUBERULENT
PUBERULOUS
PUBESCENCE
PUBESCENCES
PUBLICALLY
PUBLICATION
PUBLICATIONS
PUBLICISED
PUBLICISES
PUBLICISING
PUBLICISTS
PUBLICITIES
PUBLICIZED
PUBLICIZES
PUBLICIZING
PUBLICNESS
PUBLICNESSES
PUBLISHABLE
PUBLISHERS
PUBLISHING
PUBLISHINGS
PUBLISHMENT
PUBLISHMENTS
PUCCINIACEOUS
PUCKERIEST
PUCKISHNESS
PUCKISHNESSES
PUDGINESSES
PUDIBUNDITIES
PUDIBUNDITY
PUDICITIES
PUERILISMS
PUERILITIES
PUERPERALLY
PUERPERIUM
PUERPERIUMS
PUFFINESSES
PUFFTALOONAS
PUFTALOONIES
PUFTALOONS
PUGGINESSES
PUGILISTIC
PUGILISTICAL
PUGILISTICALLY
PUGNACIOUS
PUGNACIOUSLY
PUGNACIOUSNESS
PUGNACITIES
PUISSANCES
PUISSANTLY
PUISSAUNCE
PUISSAUNCES
PULCHRITUDE
PULCHRITUDES
PULCHRITUDINOUS
PULLULATED
PULLULATES
PULLULATING
PULLULATION
PULLULATIONS
PULMOBRANCH
PULMOBRANCHIATE
PULMOBRANCHS
PULMONATES
PULPBOARDS
PULPIFYING
PULPINESSES
PULPITEERS
PULPITRIES
PULPSTONES
PULSATANCE
PULSATANCES
PULSATILITIES
PULSATILITY
PULSATILLA
PULSATILLAS
PULSATIONS
PULSATIVELY
PULSELESSNESS

PULSELESSNESSES
PULSIMETER
PULSIMETERS
PULSOMETER
PULSOMETERS
PULTACEOUS
PULTRUSION
PULTRUSIONS
PULVERABLE
PULVERATION
PULVERATIONS
PULVERINES
PULVERISABLE
PULVERISATION
PULVERISATIONS
PULVERISED
PULVERISER
PULVERISERS
PULVERISES
PULVERISING
PULVERIZABLE
PULVERIZATION
PULVERIZATIONS
PULVERIZED
PULVERIZER
PULVERIZERS
PULVERIZES
PULVERIZING
PULVERULENCE
PULVERULENCES
PULVERULENT
PULVILISED
PULVILIZED
PULVILLIFORM
PULVILLING
PULVILLIOS
PULVINATED
PULVINULES
PUMICATING
PUMMELLING
PUMPERNICKEL
PUMPERNICKELS
PUMPKINSEED
PUMPKINSEEDS
PUNCHBALLS
PUNCHBOARD
PUNCHBOARDS
PUNCHBOWLS
PUNCHINELLO
PUNCHINELLOES
PUNCHINELLOS
PUNCHINESS
PUNCHINESSES
PUNCTATION
PUNCTATIONS
PUNCTATORS
PUNCTILIOS
PUNCTILIOUS
PUNCTILIOUSLY
PUNCTILIOUSNESS
PUNCTUALIST
PUNCTUALISTS
PUNCTUALITIES
PUNCTUALITY
PUNCTUALLY
PUNCTUATED
PUNCTUATES
PUNCTUATING
PUNCTUATION
PUNCTUATIONIST
PUNCTUATIONISTS
PUNCTUATIONS
PUNCTUATIVE
PUNCTUATOR
PUNCTUATORS
PUNCTULATE
PUNCTULATED
PUNCTULATION
PUNCTULATIONS
PUNCTURABLE
PUNCTURATION
PUNCTURATIONS
PUNCTURERS
PUNCTURING
PUNDIGRION
PUNDIGRIONS
PUNDITRIES
PUNGENCIES
PUNICACEOUS
PUNINESSES
PUNISHABILITIES
PUNISHABILITY
PUNISHABLE
PUNISHINGLY
PUNISHMENT
PUNISHMENTS
PUNITIVELY
PUNITIVENESS
PUNITIVENESSES
PUNKINESSES
PUPIGEROUS
PUPILABILITIES
PUPILABILITY
PUPILARITIES
PUPILARITY
PUPILLAGES
PUPILLARITIES
PUPILLARITY
PUPILLATED
PUPILLATES
PUPILLATING
PUPILSHIPS
PUPIPAROUS
PUPPETEERED
PUPPETEERING
PUPPETEERS
PUPPETLIKE
PUPPETRIES
PUPPYHOODS
PURBLINDLY
PURBLINDNESS
PURBLINDNESSES
PURCHASABILITY
PURCHASABLE
PURCHASERS
PURCHASING
PURDONIUMS
PUREBLOODS
PURENESSES
PURGATIONS
PURGATIVELY
PURGATIVES
PURGATORIAL
PURGATORIALLY
PURGATORIAN
PURGATORIES
PURIFICATION
PURIFICATIONS
PURIFICATIVE
PURIFICATOR
PURIFICATORS
PURIFICATORY
PURISTICAL
PURISTICALLY
PURITANICAL
PURITANICALLY
PURITANICALNESS
PURITANISE
PURITANISED
PURITANISES
PURITANISING
PURITANISM
PURITANISMS
PURITANIZE
PURITANIZED
PURITANIZES
PURITANIZING
PURLICUING
PURLOINERS
PURLOINING
PUROMYCINS
PURPLEHEART
PURPLEHEARTS
PURPLENESS
PURPLENESSES
PURPLISHNESS
PURPLISHNESSES
PURPORTEDLY
PURPORTING
PURPORTLESS
PURPOSEFUL
PURPOSEFULLY
PURPOSEFULNESS
PURPOSELESS
PURPOSELESSLY
PURPOSELESSNESS
PURPOSIVELY
PURPOSIVENESS
PURPOSIVENESSES
PURPRESTURE
PURPRESTURES
PURSERSHIP
PURSERSHIPS
PURSINESSES
PURSUANCES
PURSUANTLY
PURSUINGLY
PURSUIVANT
PURSUIVANTS
PURTENANCE
PURTENANCES
PURTRAYING
PURULENCES
PURULENCIES
PURULENTLY
PURVEYANCE
PURVEYANCES
PUSCHKINIA
PUSCHKINIAS
PUSHCHAIRS
PUSHFULNESS
PUSHFULNESSES
PUSHINESSES
PUSHINGNESS
PUSHINGNESSES
PUSILLANIMITIES
PUSILLANIMITY
PUSILLANIMOUS
PUSILLANIMOUSLY
PUSSYFOOTED
PUSSYFOOTER
PUSSYFOOTERS
PUSSYFOOTING
PUSSYFOOTS
PUSTULANTS
PUSTULATED
PUSTULATES
PUSTULATING
PUSTULATION
PUSTULATIONS
PUTANGITANGI
PUTATIVELY
PUTONGHUAS
PUTREFACIENT
PUTREFACTION
PUTREFACTIONS
PUTREFACTIVE
PUTREFIABLE
PUTREFIERS
PUTREFYING
PUTRESCENCE
PUTRESCENCES
PUTRESCENT
PUTRESCIBILITY
PUTRESCIBLE
PUTRESCIBLES
PUTRESCINE
PUTRESCINES
PUTRIDITIES
PUTRIDNESS
PUTRIDNESSES
PUTSCHISTS
PUTTYROOTS
PUZZLEDOMS
PUZZLEHEADED
PUZZLEMENT
PUZZLEMENTS
PUZZLINGLY
PUZZOLANAS
PYCNIDIOSPORE
PYCNIDIOSPORES
PYCNOCONIDIA
PYCNOCONIDIUM
PYCNODYSOSTOSES
PYCNODYSOSTOSIS
PYCNOGONID
PYCNOGONIDS
PYCNOGONOID
PYCNOMETER
PYCNOMETERS
PYCNOMETRIC
PYCNOSPORE
PYCNOSPORES
PYCNOSTYLE

PYCNOSTYLES
PYELITISES
PYELOGRAMS
PYELOGRAPHIC
PYELOGRAPHIES
PYELOGRAPHY
PYELONEPHRITIC
PYELONEPHRITIS
PYGOSTYLES
PYKNODYSOSTOSES
PYKNODYSOSTOSIS
PYKNOMETER
PYKNOMETERS
PYKNOSOMES
PYLORECTOMIES
PYLORECTOMY
PYOGENESES
PYOGENESIS
PYORRHOEAL
PYORRHOEAS
PYORRHOEIC
PYRACANTHA
PYRACANTHAS
PYRACANTHS
PYRALIDIDS
PYRAMIDALLY
PYRAMIDICAL
PYRAMIDICALLY
PYRAMIDING
PYRAMIDION
PYRAMIDIONS
PYRAMIDIST
PYRAMIDISTS
PYRAMIDOLOGIES
PYRAMIDOLOGIST
PYRAMIDOLOGISTS
PYRAMIDOLOGY
PYRAMIDONS
PYRANOMETER
PYRANOMETERS
PYRANOSIDE
PYRANOSIDES
PYRARGYRITE
PYRARGYRITES
PYRENEITES
PYRENOCARP
PYRENOCARPS
PYRENOMYCETOUS
PYRETHRINS
PYRETHROID
PYRETHROIDS
PYRETHRUMS
PYRETOLOGIES
PYRETOLOGY
PYRETOTHERAPIES
PYRETOTHERAPY
PYRGEOMETER
PYRGEOMETERS
PYRHELIOMETER
PYRHELIOMETERS
PYRHELIOMETRIC
PYRIDOXALS
PYRIDOXAMINE
PYRIDOXAMINES
PYRIDOXINE
PYRIDOXINES
PYRIDOXINS
PYRIMETHAMINE
PYRIMETHAMINES
PYRIMIDINE
PYRIMIDINES
PYRITHIAMINE
PYRITHIAMINES
PYRITIFEROUS
PYRITISING
PYRITIZING
PYRITOHEDRA
PYRITOHEDRAL
PYRITOHEDRON
PYROBALLOGIES
PYROBALLOGY
PYROCATECHIN
PYROCATECHINS
PYROCATECHOL
PYROCATECHOLS
PYROCERAMS
PYROCHEMICAL
PYROCHEMICALLY
PYROCLASTIC
PYROCLASTICS
PYROCLASTS
PYROELECTRIC
PYROELECTRICITY
PYROELECTRICS
PYROGALLATE
PYROGALLATES
PYROGALLIC
PYROGALLOL
PYROGALLOLS
PYROGENETIC
PYROGENICITIES
PYROGENICITY
PYROGENOUS
PYROGNOSTIC
PYROGNOSTICS
PYROGRAPHER
PYROGRAPHERS
PYROGRAPHIC
PYROGRAPHIES
PYROGRAPHY
PYROGRAVURE
PYROGRAVURES
PYROKINESES
PYROKINESIS
PYROLATERS
PYROLATRIES
PYROLIGNEOUS
PYROLIGNIC
PYROLISING
PYROLIZING
PYROLOGIES
PYROLUSITE
PYROLUSITES
PYROLYSABLE
PYROLYSATE
PYROLYSATES
PYROLYSERS
PYROLYSING
PYROLYTICALLY
PYROLYZABLE
PYROLYZATE
PYROLYZATES
PYROLYZERS
PYROLYZING
PYROMAGNETIC
PYROMANCER
PYROMANCERS
PYROMANCIES
PYROMANIAC
PYROMANIACAL
PYROMANIACS
PYROMANIAS
PYROMANTIC
PYROMERIDE
PYROMERIDES
PYROMETALLURGY
PYROMETERS
PYROMETRIC
PYROMETRICAL
PYROMETRICALLY
PYROMETRIES
PYROMORPHITE
PYROMORPHITES
PYRONINOPHILIC
PYROPHOBIA
PYROPHOBIAS
PYROPHOBIC
PYROPHOBICS
PYROPHONES
PYROPHORIC
PYROPHOROUS
PYROPHORUS
PYROPHORUSES
PYROPHOSPHATE
PYROPHOSPHATES
PYROPHOSPHORIC
PYROPHOTOGRAPH
PYROPHOTOGRAPHS
PYROPHOTOGRAPHY
PYROPHOTOMETER
PYROPHOTOMETERS
PYROPHOTOMETRY
PYROPHYLLITE
PYROPHYLLITES
PYROSCOPES
PYROSTATIC
PYROSULPHATE
PYROSULPHATES
PYROSULPHURIC
PYROTARTRATE
PYROTARTRATES
PYROTECHNIC
PYROTECHNICAL
PYROTECHNICALLY
PYROTECHNICIAN
PYROTECHNICIANS
PYROTECHNICS
PYROTECHNIES
PYROTECHNIST
PYROTECHNISTS
PYROTECHNY
PYROXENITE
PYROXENITES
PYROXENITIC
PYROXENOID
PYROXENOIDS
PYROXYLINE
PYROXYLINES
PYROXYLINS
PYRRHICIST
PYRRHICISTS
PYRRHOTINE
PYRRHOTINES
PYRRHOTITE
PYRRHOTITES
PYRRHULOXIA
PYRRHULOXIAS
PYRROLIDINE
PYRROLIDINES
PYTHOGENIC
PYTHONESSES
PYTHONOMORPH
PYTHONOMORPHS

Qq

QABALISTIC
QINGHAOSUS
QUACKERIES
QUACKSALVER
QUACKSALVERS
QUACKSALVING
QUADPLEXES
QUADRAGENARIAN
QUADRAGENARIANS
QUADRAGESIMAL
QUADRANGLE
QUADRANGLES
QUADRANGULAR
QUADRANGULARLY
QUADRANTAL
QUADRANTES
QUADRAPHONIC
QUADRAPHONICS
QUADRAPHONIES
QUADRAPHONY
QUADRAPLEGIA
QUADRAPLEGIAS
QUADRAPLEGIC
QUADRAPLEGICS
QUADRATICAL
QUADRATICALLY
QUADRATICS
QUADRATING
QUADRATRIX
QUADRATRIXES
QUADRATURA
QUADRATURE
QUADRATURES
QUADRATUSES
QUADRELLAS
QUADRENNIA
QUADRENNIAL
QUADRENNIALLY
QUADRENNIALS
QUADRENNIUM
QUADRENNIUMS
QUADRICEPS
QUADRICEPSES
QUADRICIPITAL
QUADRICONE
QUADRICONES
QUADRIENNIA
QUADRIENNIAL
QUADRIENNIUM
QUADRIFARIOUS
QUADRIFOLIATE
QUADRIFORM
QUADRIGEMINAL
QUADRIGEMINATE
QUADRIGEMINOUS
QUADRILATERAL
QUADRILATERALS
QUADRILINGUAL
QUADRILITERAL
QUADRILITERALS
QUADRILLED
QUADRILLER
QUADRILLERS
QUADRILLES
QUADRILLING
QUADRILLION
QUADRILLIONS
QUADRILLIONTH
QUADRILLIONTHS
QUADRILOCULAR
QUADRINGENARIES
QUADRINGENARY
QUADRINOMIAL
QUADRINOMIALS
QUADRIPARTITE
QUADRIPARTITION
QUADRIPHONIC
QUADRIPHONICS
QUADRIPLEGIA
QUADRIPLEGIAS
QUADRIPLEGIC
QUADRIPLEGICS
QUADRIPOLE
QUADRIPOLES
QUADRIREME
QUADRIREMES
QUADRISECT
QUADRISECTED
QUADRISECTING
QUADRISECTION
QUADRISECTIONS
QUADRISECTS
QUADRISYLLABIC
QUADRISYLLABLE
QUADRISYLLABLES
QUADRIVALENCE
QUADRIVALENCES
QUADRIVALENCIES
QUADRIVALENCY
QUADRIVALENT
QUADRIVALENTS
QUADRIVIAL
QUADRIVIUM
QUADRIVIUMS
QUADROPHONIC
QUADROPHONICS
QUADROPHONIES
QUADROPHONY
QUADRUMANE
QUADRUMANES
QUADRUMANOUS
QUADRUMANS
QUADRUMVIR
QUADRUMVIRATE
QUADRUMVIRATES
QUADRUMVIRS
QUADRUPEDAL
QUADRUPEDS
QUADRUPLED
QUADRUPLES
QUADRUPLET
QUADRUPLETS
QUADRUPLEX
QUADRUPLEXED
QUADRUPLEXES
QUADRUPLEXING
QUADRUPLICATE
QUADRUPLICATED
QUADRUPLICATES
QUADRUPLICATING
QUADRUPLICATION
QUADRUPLICITIES
QUADRUPLICITY
QUADRUPLIES
QUADRUPLING
QUADRUPOLE
QUADRUPOLES
QUAESITUMS
QUAESTIONARIES
QUAESTIONARY
QUAESTORIAL
QUAESTORSHIP
QUAESTORSHIPS
QUAESTUARIES
QUAESTUARY
QUAGGINESS
QUAGGINESSES
QUAGMIRIER
QUAGMIRIEST
QUAGMIRING
QUAINTNESS
QUAINTNESSES

QUAKINESSES
QUALIFIABLE
QUALIFICATION
QUALIFICATIONS
QUALIFICATIVE
QUALIFICATIVES
QUALIFICATOR
QUALIFICATORS
QUALIFICATORY
QUALIFIEDLY
QUALIFIERS
QUALIFYING
QUALIFYINGS
QUALITATIVE
QUALITATIVELY
QUALMISHLY
QUALMISHNESS
QUALMISHNESSES
QUANDARIES
QUANGOCRACIES
QUANGOCRACY
QUANTIFIABLE
QUANTIFICATION
QUANTIFICATIONS
QUANTIFIED
QUANTIFIER
QUANTIFIERS
QUANTIFIES
QUANTIFYING
QUANTISATION
QUANTISATIONS
QUANTISERS
QUANTISING
QUANTITATE
QUANTITATED
QUANTITATES
QUANTITATING
QUANTITATION
QUANTITATIONS
QUANTITATIVE
QUANTITATIVELY
QUANTITIES
QUANTITIVE
QUANTITIVELY
QUANTIVALENCE
QUANTIVALENCES
QUANTIVALENT
QUANTIZATION
QUANTIZATIONS
QUANTIZERS
QUANTIZING
QUANTOMETER
QUANTOMETERS
QUAQUAVERSAL
QUAQUAVERSALLY
QUARANTINE
QUARANTINED
QUARANTINES
QUARANTINING
QUARENDENS
QUARENDERS
QUARRELERS
QUARRELING
QUARRELLED
QUARRELLER
QUARRELLERS
QUARRELLING
QUARRELLINGS
QUARRELLOUS
QUARRELSOME
QUARRELSOMELY
QUARRELSOMENESS
QUARRENDER
QUARRENDERS
QUARRIABLE
QUARRINGTON
QUARRINGTONS
QUARRYINGS
QUARRYMASTER
QUARRYMASTERS
QUARTATION
QUARTATIONS
QUARTERAGE
QUARTERAGES
QUARTERBACK
QUARTERBACKED
QUARTERBACKING
QUARTERBACKS
QUARTERDECK
QUARTERDECKER
QUARTERDECKERS
QUARTERDECKS
QUARTERERS
QUARTERFINAL
QUARTERFINALIST
QUARTERFINALS
QUARTERING
QUARTERINGS
QUARTERLIES
QUARTERLIFE
QUARTERLIGHT
QUARTERLIGHTS
QUARTERMASTER
QUARTERMASTERS
QUARTERMISTRESS
QUARTEROON
QUARTEROONS
QUARTERSAW
QUARTERSAWED
QUARTERSAWING
QUARTERSAWN
QUARTERSAWS
QUARTERSTAFF
QUARTERSTAFFS
QUARTERSTAVES
QUARTETTES
QUARTODECIMAN
QUARTODECIMANS
QUARTZIEST
QUARTZIFEROUS
QUARTZITES
QUARTZITIC
QUASICRYSTAL
QUASICRYSTALS
QUASIPARTICLE
QUASIPARTICLES
QUASIPERIODIC
QUATERCENTENARY
QUATERNARIES
QUATERNARY
QUATERNATE
QUATERNION
QUATERNIONIST
QUATERNIONISTS
QUATERNIONS
QUATERNITIES
QUATERNITY
QUATORZAIN
QUATORZAINS
QUATREFEUILLE
QUATREFEUILLES
QUATREFOIL
QUATREFOILS
QUATTROCENTISM
QUATTROCENTISMS
QUATTROCENTIST
QUATTROCENTISTS
QUATTROCENTO
QUATTROCENTOS
QUAVERIEST
QUAVERINGLY
QUAVERINGS
QUEACHIEST
QUEASINESS
QUEASINESSES
QUEBRACHOS
QUEECHIEST
QUEENCAKES
QUEENCRAFT
QUEENCRAFTS
QUEENHOODS
QUEENLIEST
QUEENLINESS
QUEENLINESSES
QUEENSHIPS
QUEENSIDES
QUEERCORES
QUEERITIES
QUEERNESSES
QUELQUECHOSE
QUELQUECHOSES
QUENCHABLE
QUENCHINGS
QUENCHLESS
QUENCHLESSLY
QUERCETINS
QUERCETUMS
QUERCITINS
QUERCITRON
QUERCITRONS
QUERIMONIES
QUERIMONIOUS
QUERIMONIOUSLY
QUERNSTONE
QUERNSTONES
QUERSPRUNG
QUERSPRUNGS
QUERULOUSLY
QUERULOUSNESS
QUERULOUSNESSES
QUERYINGLY
QUESADILLA
QUESADILLAS
QUESTINGLY
QUESTIONABILITY
QUESTIONABLE
QUESTIONABLY
QUESTIONARIES
QUESTIONARY
QUESTIONED
QUESTIONEE
QUESTIONEES
QUESTIONER
QUESTIONERS
QUESTIONING
QUESTIONINGLY
QUESTIONINGS
QUESTIONIST
QUESTIONISTS
QUESTIONLESS
QUESTIONLESSLY
QUESTIONNAIRE
QUESTIONNAIRES
QUESTORIAL
QUESTORSHIP
QUESTORSHIPS
QUESTRISTS
QUIBBLINGLY
QUIBBLINGS
QUICKBEAMS
QUICKENERS
QUICKENING
QUICKENINGS
QUICKLIMES
QUICKNESSES
QUICKSANDS
QUICKSILVER
QUICKSILVERED
QUICKSILVERING
QUICKSILVERINGS
QUICKSILVERISH
QUICKSILVERS
QUICKSILVERY
QUICKSTEPPED
QUICKSTEPPING
QUICKSTEPS
QUICKTHORN
QUICKTHORNS
QUIDDANIES
QUIDDITATIVE
QUIDDITCHES
QUIDDITIES
QUIESCENCE
QUIESCENCES
QUIESCENCIES
QUIESCENCY
QUIESCENTLY
QUIETENERS
QUIETENING
QUIETENINGS
QUIETISTIC
QUIETNESSES
QUILLBACKS
QUILLWORKS
QUILLWORTS
QUINACRINE
QUINACRINES
QUINAQUINA
QUINAQUINAS
QUINCENTENARIES
QUINCENTENARY
QUINCENTENNIAL
QUINCENTENNIALS
QUINCUNCIAL

QUINCUNCIALLY
QUINCUNXES
QUINCUNXIAL
QUINDECAGON
QUINDECAGONS
QUINDECAPLET
QUINDECAPLETS
QUINDECENNIAL
QUINDECENNIALS
QUINDECILLION
QUINDECILLIONS
QUINGENTENARIES
QUINGENTENARY
QUINIDINES
QUINOLINES
QUINOLONES
QUINQUAGENARIAN
QUINQUAGESIMAL
QUINQUECOSTATE
QUINQUEFARIOUS
QUINQUEFOLIATE
QUINQUENNIA
QUINQUENNIAD
QUINQUENNIADS
QUINQUENNIAL
QUINQUENNIALLY
QUINQUENNIALS
QUINQUENNIUM
QUINQUENNIUMS
QUINQUEPARTITE
QUINQUEREME
QUINQUEREMES
QUINQUEVALENCE
QUINQUEVALENCES
QUINQUEVALENCY
QUINQUEVALENT
QUINQUINAS
QUINQUIVALENT
QUINTESSENCE
QUINTESSENCES
QUINTESSENTIAL
QUINTETTES
QUINTILLION
QUINTILLIONS
QUINTILLIONTH
QUINTILLIONTHS
QUINTROONS
QUINTUPLED
QUINTUPLES
QUINTUPLET
QUINTUPLETS
QUINTUPLICATE
QUINTUPLICATED
QUINTUPLICATES
QUINTUPLICATING
QUINTUPLICATION
QUINTUPLING
QUIRISTERS
QUIRKINESS
QUIRKINESSES
QUISLINGISM
QUISLINGISMS
QUITCLAIMED
QUITCLAIMING
QUITCLAIMS
QUITTANCED
QUITTANCES
QUITTANCING
QUIVERFULS
QUIVERIEST
QUIVERINGLY
QUIVERINGS
QUIXOTICAL
QUIXOTICALLY
QUIXOTISMS
QUIXOTRIES
QUIZMASTER
QUIZMASTERS
QUIZZERIES
QUIZZICALITIES
QUIZZICALITY
QUIZZICALLY
QUIZZIFICATION
QUIZZIFICATIONS
QUIZZIFIED
QUIZZIFIES
QUIZZIFYING
QUIZZINESS
QUIZZINESSES
QUODLIBETARIAN
QUODLIBETARIANS
QUODLIBETIC
QUODLIBETICAL
QUODLIBETICALLY
QUODLIBETS
QUOTABILITIES
QUOTABILITY
QUOTABLENESS
QUOTABLENESSES
QUOTATIONS
QUOTATIOUS
QUOTATIVES
QUOTEWORTHY
QUOTIDIANS
QUOTITIONS

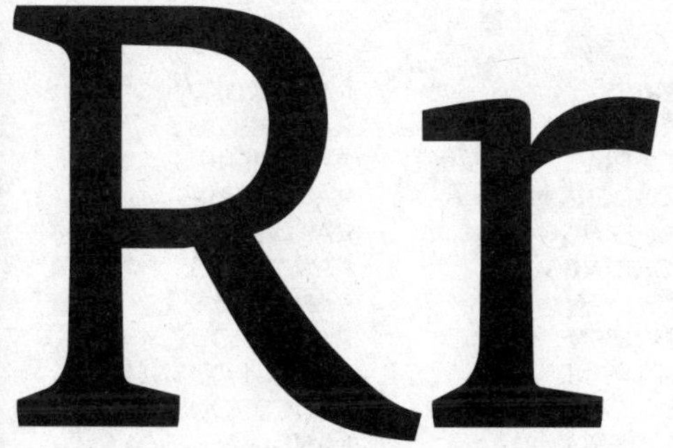

RABATMENTS
RABATTEMENT
RABATTEMENTS
RABATTINGS
RABBINATES
RABBINICAL
RABBINICALLY
RABBINISMS
RABBINISTIC
RABBINISTS
RABBINITES
RABBITBRUSH
RABBITBRUSHES
RABBITFISH
RABBITFISHES
RABBITRIES
RABBLEMENT
RABBLEMENTS
RABIDITIES
RABIDNESSES
RACCAHOUTS
RACECOURSE
RACECOURSES
RACEGOINGS
RACEHORSES
RACEMATION
RACEMATIONS
RACEMISATION
RACEMISATIONS
RACEMISING
RACEMIZATION
RACEMIZATIONS
RACEMIZING
RACEMOSELY
RACEMOUSLY
RACETRACKER
RACETRACKERS
RACETRACKS
RACEWALKED
RACEWALKER
RACEWALKERS
RACEWALKING
RACEWALKINGS
RACHIOTOMIES
RACHIOTOMY
RACHISCHISES
RACHISCHISIS
RACHITIDES
RACHITISES
RACIALISED
RACIALISES
RACIALISING
RACIALISMS
RACIALISTIC
RACIALISTS
RACIALIZED
RACIALIZES
RACIALIZING
RACIATIONS
RACINESSES
RACKABONES
RACKETEERED
RACKETEERING
RACKETEERINGS
RACKETEERS
RACKETIEST
RACKETRIES
RACONTEURING
RACONTEURINGS
RACONTEURS
RACONTEUSE
RACONTEUSES
RACQUETBALL
RACQUETBALLS
RACQUETING
RADARSCOPE
RADARSCOPES
RADIALISATION
RADIALISATIONS
RADIALISED
RADIALISES
RADIALISING
RADIALITIES
RADIALIZATION
RADIALIZATIONS
RADIALIZED
RADIALIZES
RADIALIZING
RADIANCIES
RADIATIONAL
RADIATIONLESS
RADIATIONS
RADICALISATION
RADICALISATIONS
RADICALISE
RADICALISED
RADICALISES
RADICALISING
RADICALISM
RADICALISMS
RADICALISTIC
RADICALITIES
RADICALITY
RADICALIZATION
RADICALIZATIONS
RADICALIZE
RADICALIZED
RADICALIZES
RADICALIZING
RADICALNESS
RADICALNESSES
RADICATING
RADICATION
RADICATIONS
RADICCHIOS
RADICELLOSE
RADICICOLOUS
RADICIFORM
RADICIVOROUS
RADICULOSE
RADIESTHESIA
RADIESTHESIAS
RADIESTHESIST
RADIESTHESISTS
RADIESTHETIC
RADIOACTIVATE
RADIOACTIVATED
RADIOACTIVATES
RADIOACTIVATING
RADIOACTIVATION
RADIOACTIVE
RADIOACTIVELY
RADIOACTIVITIES
RADIOACTIVITY
RADIOAUTOGRAPH
RADIOAUTOGRAPHS
RADIOAUTOGRAPHY
RADIOBIOLOGIC
RADIOBIOLOGICAL
RADIOBIOLOGIES
RADIOBIOLOGIST
RADIOBIOLOGISTS
RADIOBIOLOGY
RADIOCARBON
RADIOCARBONS
RADIOCHEMICAL
RADIOCHEMICALLY
RADIOCHEMIST
RADIOCHEMISTRY
RADIOCHEMISTS
RADIOECOLOGIES
RADIOECOLOGY

RADIOELEMENT
RADIOELEMENTS
RADIOGENIC
RADIOGONIOMETER
RADIOGRAMS
RADIOGRAPH
RADIOGRAPHED
RADIOGRAPHER
RADIOGRAPHERS
RADIOGRAPHIC
RADIOGRAPHIES
RADIOGRAPHING
RADIOGRAPHS
RADIOGRAPHY
RADIOISOTOPE
RADIOISOTOPES
RADIOISOTOPIC
RADIOLABEL
RADIOLABELED
RADIOLABELING
RADIOLABELLED
RADIOLABELLING
RADIOLABELS
RADIOLARIAN
RADIOLARIANS
RADIOLOCATION
RADIOLOCATIONAL
RADIOLOCATIONS
RADIOLOGIC
RADIOLOGICAL
RADIOLOGICALLY
RADIOLOGIES
RADIOLOGIST
RADIOLOGISTS
RADIOLUCENCIES
RADIOLUCENCY
RADIOLUCENT
RADIOLYSES
RADIOLYSIS
RADIOLYTIC
RADIOMETER
RADIOMETERS
RADIOMETRIC
RADIOMETRICALLY
RADIOMETRIES
RADIOMETRY
RADIOMICROMETER
RADIOMIMETIC
RADIONUCLIDE
RADIONUCLIDES
RADIOPACITIES
RADIOPACITY
RADIOPAGER
RADIOPAGERS
RADIOPAGING
RADIOPAGINGS
RADIOPAQUE
RADIOPHONE
RADIOPHONES
RADIOPHONIC
RADIOPHONICALLY
RADIOPHONICS
RADIOPHONIES
RADIOPHONIST
RADIOPHONISTS
RADIOPHONY
RADIOPHOTO
RADIOPHOTOS
RADIOPROTECTION
RADIOPROTECTIVE
RADIORESISTANT
RADIOSCOPE
RADIOSCOPES
RADIOSCOPIC
RADIOSCOPICALLY
RADIOSCOPIES
RADIOSCOPY
RADIOSENSITISE
RADIOSENSITISED
RADIOSENSITISES
RADIOSENSITIVE
RADIOSENSITIZE
RADIOSENSITIZED
RADIOSENSITIZES
RADIOSONDE
RADIOSONDES
RADIOSTRONTIUM
RADIOSTRONTIUMS
RADIOTELEGRAM
RADIOTELEGRAMS
RADIOTELEGRAPH
RADIOTELEGRAPHS
RADIOTELEGRAPHY
RADIOTELEMETER
RADIOTELEMETERS
RADIOTELEMETRIC
RADIOTELEMETRY
RADIOTELEPHONE
RADIOTELEPHONES
RADIOTELEPHONIC
RADIOTELEPHONY
RADIOTELETYPE
RADIOTELETYPES
RADIOTHERAPIES
RADIOTHERAPIST
RADIOTHERAPISTS
RADIOTHERAPY
RADIOTHERMIES
RADIOTHERMY
RADIOTHONS
RADIOTHORIUM
RADIOTHORIUMS
RADIOTOXIC
RADIOTRACER
RADIOTRACERS
RADULIFORM
RAFFINATES
RAFFINOSES
RAFFISHNESS
RAFFISHNESSES
RAFFLESIAS
RAFTERINGS
RAGAMUFFIN
RAGAMUFFINS
RAGGAMUFFIN
RAGGAMUFFINS
RAGGEDIEST
RAGGEDNESS
RAGGEDNESSES
RAGMATICAL
RAGPICKERS
RAILBUSSES
RAILLERIES
RAILROADED
RAILROADER
RAILROADERS
RAILROADING
RAILROADINGS
RAILWAYMAN
RAILWAYMEN
RAINBOWLIKE
RAINCHECKS
RAINFOREST
RAINFORESTS
RAININESSES
RAINMAKERS
RAINMAKING
RAINMAKINGS
RAINPROOFED
RAINPROOFING
RAINPROOFS
RAINSPOUTS
RAINSQUALL
RAINSQUALLS
RAINSTORMS
RAINWASHED
RAINWASHES
RAINWASHING
RAINWATERS
RAISONNEUR
RAISONNEURS
RAIYATWARI
RAIYATWARIS
RAJAHSHIPS
RAJPRAMUKH
RAJPRAMUKHS
RAKESHAMES
RAKISHNESS
RAKISHNESSES
RALLENTANDO
RALLENTANDOS
RALLYCROSS
RALLYCROSSES
RALLYINGLY
RAMAPITHECINE
RAMAPITHECINES
RAMBLINGLY
RAMBOUILLET
RAMBOUILLETS
RAMBUNCTIOUS
RAMBUNCTIOUSLY
RAMENTACEOUS
RAMGUNSHOCH
RAMIFICATION
RAMIFICATIONS
RAMMISHNESS
RAMMISHNESSES
RAMOSITIES
RAMPACIOUS
RAMPAGEOUS
RAMPAGEOUSLY
RAMPAGEOUSNESS
RAMPAGINGS
RAMPALLIAN
RAMPALLIANS
RAMPANCIES
RAMPARTING
RAMPAUGING
RAMRODDING
RAMSHACKLE
RANCHERIAS
RANCHERIES
RANCIDITIES
RANCIDNESS
RANCIDNESSES
RANCOROUSLY
RANCOROUSNESS
RANCOROUSNESSES
RANDINESSES
RANDOMISATION
RANDOMISATIONS
RANDOMISED
RANDOMISER
RANDOMISERS
RANDOMISES
RANDOMISING
RANDOMIZATION
RANDOMIZATIONS
RANDOMIZED
RANDOMIZER
RANDOMIZERS
RANDOMIZES
RANDOMIZING
RANDOMNESS
RANDOMNESSES
RANDOMWISE
RANGATIRAS
RANGATIRATANGA
RANGATIRATANGAS
RANGEFINDER
RANGEFINDERS
RANGEFINDING
RANGEFINDINGS
RANGELANDS
RANGERSHIP
RANGERSHIPS
RANGINESSES
RANIVOROUS
RANKNESSES
RANKSHIFTED
RANKSHIFTING
RANKSHIFTS
RANSACKERS
RANSACKING
RANSHACKLE
RANSHACKLED
RANSHACKLES
RANSHACKLING
RANSHAKLED
RANSHAKLES
RANSHAKLING
RANSOMABLE
RANSOMLESS
RANTERISMS
RANTIPOLED
RANTIPOLES
RANTIPOLING
RANUNCULACEOUS
RANUNCULUS
RANUNCULUSES
RAPACIOUSLY
RAPACIOUSNESS
RAPACIOUSNESSES
RAPACITIES

RAPIDITIES
RAPIDNESSES
RAPPELLING
RAPPELLINGS
RAPPORTAGE
RAPPORTAGES
RAPPORTEUR
RAPPORTEURS
RAPPROCHEMENT
RAPPROCHEMENTS
RAPSCALLION
RAPSCALLIONS
RAPTATORIAL
RAPTNESSES
RAPTURELESS
RAPTURISED
RAPTURISES
RAPTURISING
RAPTURISTS
RAPTURIZED
RAPTURIZES
RAPTURIZING
RAPTUROUSLY
RAPTUROUSNESS
RAPTUROUSNESSES
RAREFACTION
RAREFACTIONAL
RAREFACTIONS
RAREFACTIVE
RAREFIABLE
RAREFICATION
RAREFICATIONAL
RAREFICATIONS
RARENESSES
RASCAILLES
RASCALDOMS
RASCALISMS
RASCALITIES
RASCALLIEST
RASCALLION
RASCALLIONS
RASHNESSES
RASPATORIES
RASPBERRIES
RASPINESSES
RASTAFARIAN
RASTAFARIANS
RASTERISED
RASTERISES
RASTERISING
RASTERIZED
RASTERIZES
RASTERIZING
RATABILITIES
RATABILITY
RATABLENESS
RATABLENESSES
RATAPLANNED
RATAPLANNING
RATATOUILLE
RATATOUILLES
RATBAGGERIES
RATBAGGERY
RATCHETING
RATEABILITIES
RATEABILITY
RATEABLENESS
RATEABLENESSES
RATEMETERS
RATEPAYERS
RATHERIPES
RATHSKELLER
RATHSKELLERS
RATIFIABLE
RATIFICATION
RATIFICATIONS
RATIOCINATE
RATIOCINATED
RATIOCINATES
RATIOCINATING
RATIOCINATION
RATIOCINATIONS
RATIOCINATIVE
RATIOCINATOR
RATIOCINATORS
RATIOCINATORY
RATIONALES
RATIONALISABLE
RATIONALISATION
RATIONALISE
RATIONALISED
RATIONALISER
RATIONALISERS
RATIONALISES
RATIONALISING
RATIONALISM
RATIONALISMS
RATIONALIST
RATIONALISTIC
RATIONALISTS
RATIONALITIES
RATIONALITY
RATIONALIZABLE
RATIONALIZATION
RATIONALIZE
RATIONALIZED
RATIONALIZER
RATIONALIZERS
RATIONALIZES
RATIONALIZING
RATIONALLY
RATIONALNESS
RATIONALNESSES
RATTENINGS
RATTINESSES
RATTLEBAGS
RATTLEBOXES
RATTLEBRAIN
RATTLEBRAINED
RATTLEBRAINS
RATTLESNAKE
RATTLESNAKES
RATTLETRAP
RATTLETRAPS
RATTLINGLY
RATTOONING
RAUCOUSNESS
RAUCOUSNESSES
RAUNCHIEST
RAUNCHINESS
RAUNCHINESSES
RAUWOLFIAS
RAVAGEMENT
RAVAGEMENTS
RAVELLINGS
RAVELMENTS
RAVENINGLY
RAVENOUSLY
RAVENOUSNESS
RAVENOUSNESSES
RAVIGOTTES
RAVISHINGLY
RAVISHMENT
RAVISHMENTS
RAWINSONDE
RAWINSONDES
RAWMAISHES
RAYGRASSES
RAYLESSNESS
RAYLESSNESSES
RAZMATAZES
RAZORBACKS
RAZORBILLS
RAZZAMATAZZ
RAZZAMATAZZES
RAZZBERRIES
RAZZMATAZZ
RAZZMATAZZES
REABSORBED
REABSORBING
REABSORPTION
REABSORPTIONS
REACCEDING
REACCELERATE
REACCELERATED
REACCELERATES
REACCELERATING
REACCENTED
REACCENTING
REACCEPTED
REACCEPTING
REACCESSION
REACCESSIONS
REACCLAIMED
REACCLAIMING
REACCLAIMS
REACCLIMATISE
REACCLIMATISED
REACCLIMATISES
REACCLIMATISING
REACCLIMATIZE
REACCLIMATIZED
REACCLIMATIZES
REACCLIMATIZING
REACCREDIT
REACCREDITATION
REACCREDITED
REACCREDITING
REACCREDITS
REACCUSING
REACCUSTOM
REACCUSTOMED
REACCUSTOMING
REACCUSTOMS
REACQUAINT
REACQUAINTANCE
REACQUAINTANCES
REACQUAINTED
REACQUAINTING
REACQUAINTS
REACQUIRED
REACQUIRES
REACQUIRING
REACQUISITION
REACQUISITIONS
REACTANCES
REACTIONAL
REACTIONARIES
REACTIONARISM
REACTIONARISMS
REACTIONARIST
REACTIONARISTS
REACTIONARY
REACTIONARYISM
REACTIONARYISMS
REACTIONISM
REACTIONISMS
REACTIONIST
REACTIONISTS
REACTIVATE
REACTIVATED
REACTIVATES
REACTIVATING
REACTIVATION
REACTIVATIONS
REACTIVELY
REACTIVENESS
REACTIVENESSES
REACTIVITIES
REACTIVITY
REACTUATED
REACTUATES
REACTUATING
READABILITIES
READABILITY
READABLENESS
READABLENESSES
READAPTATION
READAPTATIONS
READAPTING
READDICTED
READDICTING
READDRESSED
READDRESSES
READDRESSING
READERSHIP
READERSHIPS
READINESSES
READJUSTABLE
READJUSTED
READJUSTER
READJUSTERS
READJUSTING
READJUSTMENT
READJUSTMENTS
READMISSION
READMISSIONS
READMITTANCE
READMITTANCES
READMITTED
READMITTING
READOPTING
READOPTION
READOPTIONS

READORNING
READVANCED
READVANCES
READVANCING
READVERTISE
READVERTISED
READVERTISEMENT
READVERTISES
READVERTISING
READVISING
READYMADES
REAEDIFIED
REAEDIFIES
REAEDIFYED
REAEDIFYES
REAEDIFYING
REAFFIRMATION
REAFFIRMATIONS
REAFFIRMED
REAFFIRMING
REAFFIXING
REAFFOREST
REAFFORESTATION
REAFFORESTED
REAFFORESTING
REAFFORESTS
REAGENCIES
REAGGREGATE
REAGGREGATED
REAGGREGATES
REAGGREGATING
REAGGREGATION
REAGGREGATIONS
REALIGNING
REALIGNMENT
REALIGNMENTS
REALISABILITIES
REALISABILITY
REALISABLE
REALISABLY
REALISATION
REALISATIONS
REALISTICALLY
REALIZABILITIES
REALIZABILITY
REALIZABLE
REALIZABLY
REALIZATION
REALIZATIONS
REALLOCATE
REALLOCATED
REALLOCATES
REALLOCATING
REALLOCATION
REALLOCATIONS
REALLOTMENT
REALLOTMENTS
REALLOTTED
REALLOTTING
REALNESSES
REALPOLITIK
REALPOLITIKER
REALPOLITIKERS
REALPOLITIKS
REALTERING
REAMENDING
REAMENDMENT
REAMENDMENTS
REANALYSED
REANALYSES
REANALYSING
REANALYSIS
REANALYZED
REANALYZES
REANALYZING
REANIMATED
REANIMATES
REANIMATING
REANIMATION
REANIMATIONS
REANNEXATION
REANNEXATIONS
REANNEXING
REANOINTED
REANOINTING
REANSWERED
REANSWERING
REAPPARELLED
REAPPARELLING
REAPPARELS
REAPPEARANCE
REAPPEARANCES
REAPPEARED
REAPPEARING
REAPPLICATION
REAPPLICATIONS
REAPPLYING
REAPPOINTED
REAPPOINTING
REAPPOINTMENT
REAPPOINTMENTS
REAPPOINTS
REAPPORTION
REAPPORTIONED
REAPPORTIONING
REAPPORTIONMENT
REAPPORTIONS
REAPPRAISAL
REAPPRAISALS
REAPPRAISE
REAPPRAISED
REAPPRAISEMENT
REAPPRAISEMENTS
REAPPRAISER
REAPPRAISERS
REAPPRAISES
REAPPRAISING
REAPPROPRIATE
REAPPROPRIATED
REAPPROPRIATES
REAPPROPRIATING
REAPPROVED
REAPPROVES
REAPPROVING
REARGUARDS
REARGUMENT
REARGUMENTS
REARHORSES
REARMAMENT
REARMAMENTS
REAROUSALS
REAROUSING
REARRANGED
REARRANGEMENT
REARRANGEMENTS
REARRANGER
REARRANGERS
REARRANGES
REARRANGING
REARRESTED
REARRESTING
REARTICULATE
REARTICULATED
REARTICULATES
REARTICULATING
REASCENDED
REASCENDING
REASCENSION
REASCENSIONS
REASONABILITIES
REASONABILITY
REASONABLE
REASONABLENESS
REASONABLY
REASONEDLY
REASONINGS
REASONLESS
REASONLESSLY
REASSAILED
REASSAILING
REASSEMBLAGE
REASSEMBLAGES
REASSEMBLE
REASSEMBLED
REASSEMBLES
REASSEMBLIES
REASSEMBLING
REASSEMBLY
REASSERTED
REASSERTING
REASSERTION
REASSERTIONS
REASSESSED
REASSESSES
REASSESSING
REASSESSMENT
REASSESSMENTS
REASSIGNED
REASSIGNING
REASSIGNMENT
REASSIGNMENTS
REASSORTED
REASSORTING
REASSORTMENT
REASSORTMENTS
REASSUMING
REASSUMPTION
REASSUMPTIONS
REASSURANCE
REASSURANCES
REASSURERS
REASSURING
REASSURINGLY
REASTINESS
REASTINESSES
REATTACHED
REATTACHES
REATTACHING
REATTACHMENT
REATTACHMENTS
REATTACKED
REATTACKING
REATTAINED
REATTAINING
REATTEMPTED
REATTEMPTING
REATTEMPTS
REATTRIBUTE
REATTRIBUTED
REATTRIBUTES
REATTRIBUTING
REATTRIBUTION
REATTRIBUTIONS
REAUTHORISATION
REAUTHORISE
REAUTHORISED
REAUTHORISES
REAUTHORISING
REAUTHORIZATION
REAUTHORIZE
REAUTHORIZED
REAUTHORIZES
REAUTHORIZING
REAVAILING
REAWAKENED
REAWAKENING
REAWAKENINGS
REBALANCED
REBALANCES
REBALANCING
REBAPTISED
REBAPTISES
REBAPTISING
REBAPTISMS
REBAPTIZED
REBAPTIZES
REBAPTIZING
REBARBATIVE
REBARBATIVELY
REBATEABLE
REBATEMENT
REBATEMENTS
REBBETZINS
REBEGINNING
REBELLIONS
REBELLIOUS
REBELLIOUSLY
REBELLIOUSNESS
REBELLOWED
REBELLOWING
REBIRTHING
REBIRTHINGS
REBLENDING
REBLOOMING
REBLOSSOMED
REBLOSSOMING
REBLOSSOMS
REBOARDING
REBOATIONS
REBORROWED
REBORROWING
REBOTTLING
REBOUNDERS
REBOUNDING

REBRANCHED
REBRANCHES
REBRANCHING
REBRANDING
REBREEDING
REBROADCAST
REBROADCASTED
REBROADCASTING
REBROADCASTS
REBUILDING
REBUKEFULLY
REBUKINGLY
REBUTMENTS
REBUTTABLE
REBUTTONED
REBUTTONING
RECALCITRANCE
RECALCITRANCES
RECALCITRANCIES
RECALCITRANCY
RECALCITRANT
RECALCITRANTS
RECALCITRATE
RECALCITRATED
RECALCITRATES
RECALCITRATING
RECALCITRATION
RECALCITRATIONS
RECALCULATE
RECALCULATED
RECALCULATES
RECALCULATING
RECALCULATION
RECALCULATIONS
RECALESCED
RECALESCENCE
RECALESCENCES
RECALESCENT
RECALESCES
RECALESCING
RECALIBRATE
RECALIBRATED
RECALIBRATES
RECALIBRATING
RECALIBRATION
RECALIBRATIONS
RECALLABILITIES
RECALLABILITY
RECALLABLE
RECALLMENT
RECALLMENTS
RECALMENTS
RECANALISATION
RECANALISATIONS
RECANALISE
RECANALISED
RECANALISES
RECANALISING
RECANALIZATION
RECANALIZATIONS
RECANALIZE
RECANALIZED
RECANALIZES
RECANALIZING
RECANTATION
RECANTATIONS

RECAPITALISE
RECAPITALISED
RECAPITALISES
RECAPITALISING
RECAPITALIZE
RECAPITALIZED
RECAPITALIZES
RECAPITALIZING
RECAPITULATE
RECAPITULATED
RECAPITULATES
RECAPITULATING
RECAPITULATION
RECAPITULATIONS
RECAPITULATIVE
RECAPITULATORY
RECAPPABLE
RECAPTIONS
RECAPTURED
RECAPTURER
RECAPTURERS
RECAPTURES
RECAPTURING
RECARPETED
RECARPETING
RECARRYING
RECATALOGED
RECATALOGING
RECATALOGS
RECATCHING
RECAUTIONED
RECAUTIONING
RECAUTIONS
RECEIPTING
RECEIPTORS
RECEIVABILITIES
RECEIVABILITY
RECEIVABLE
RECEIVABLENESS
RECEIVABLES
RECEIVERSHIP
RECEIVERSHIPS
RECEIVINGS
RECEMENTED
RECEMENTING
RECENSIONS
RECENSORED
RECENSORING
RECENTNESS
RECENTNESSES
RECENTRIFUGE
RECENTRIFUGED
RECENTRIFUGES
RECENTRIFUGING
RECENTRING
RECEPTACLE
RECEPTACLES
RECEPTACULA
RECEPTACULAR
RECEPTACULUM
RECEPTIBILITIES
RECEPTIBILITY
RECEPTIBLE
RECEPTIONIST
RECEPTIONISTS
RECEPTIONS

RECEPTIVELY
RECEPTIVENESS
RECEPTIVENESSES
RECEPTIVITIES
RECEPTIVITY
RECERTIFICATION
RECERTIFIED
RECERTIFIES
RECERTIFYING
RECESSIONAL
RECESSIONALS
RECESSIONARY
RECESSIONS
RECESSIVELY
RECESSIVENESS
RECESSIVENESSES
RECESSIVES
RECHALLENGE
RECHALLENGED
RECHALLENGES
RECHALLENGING
RECHANGING
RECHANNELED
RECHANNELING
RECHANNELLED
RECHANNELLING
RECHANNELS
RECHARGEABLE
RECHARGERS
RECHARGING
RECHARTERED
RECHARTERING
RECHARTERS
RECHARTING
RECHAUFFES
RECHEATING
RECHECKING
RECHOOSING
RECHOREOGRAPH
RECHOREOGRAPHED
RECHOREOGRAPHS
RECHRISTEN
RECHRISTENED
RECHRISTENING
RECHRISTENS
RECHROMATOGRAPH
RECIDIVISM
RECIDIVISMS
RECIDIVIST
RECIDIVISTIC
RECIDIVISTS
RECIDIVOUS
RECIPIENCE
RECIPIENCES
RECIPIENCIES
RECIPIENCY
RECIPIENTS
RECIPROCAL
RECIPROCALITIES
RECIPROCALITY
RECIPROCALLY
RECIPROCALS
RECIPROCANT
RECIPROCANTS
RECIPROCATE
RECIPROCATED

RECIPROCATES
RECIPROCATING
RECIPROCATION
RECIPROCATIONS
RECIPROCATIVE
RECIPROCATOR
RECIPROCATORS
RECIPROCATORY
RECIPROCITIES
RECIPROCITY
RECIRCLING
RECIRCULATE
RECIRCULATED
RECIRCULATES
RECIRCULATING
RECIRCULATION
RECIRCULATIONS
RECITALIST
RECITALISTS
RECITATION
RECITATIONIST
RECITATIONISTS
RECITATIONS
RECITATIVE
RECITATIVES
RECITATIVI
RECITATIVO
RECITATIVOS
RECKLESSLY
RECKLESSNESS
RECKLESSNESSES
RECKONINGS
RECLAIMABLE
RECLAIMABLY
RECLAIMANT
RECLAIMANTS
RECLAIMERS
RECLAIMING
RECLAMATION
RECLAMATIONS
RECLASPING
RECLASSIFIED
RECLASSIFIES
RECLASSIFY
RECLASSIFYING
RECLEANING
RECLIMBING
RECLINABLE
RECLINATION
RECLINATIONS
RECLOSABLE
RECLOTHING
RECLUSENESS
RECLUSENESSES
RECLUSIONS
RECLUSIVELY
RECLUSIVENESS
RECLUSIVENESSES
RECLUSORIES
RECODIFICATION
RECODIFICATIONS
RECODIFIED
RECODIFIES
RECODIFYING
RECOGNISABILITY
RECOGNISABLE

RECOGNISABLY
RECOGNISANCE
RECOGNISANCES
RECOGNISANT
RECOGNISED
RECOGNISEE
RECOGNISEES
RECOGNISER
RECOGNISERS
RECOGNISES
RECOGNISING
RECOGNISOR
RECOGNISORS
RECOGNITION
RECOGNITIONS
RECOGNITIVE
RECOGNITORY
RECOGNIZABILITY
RECOGNIZABLE
RECOGNIZABLY
RECOGNIZANCE
RECOGNIZANCES
RECOGNIZANT
RECOGNIZED
RECOGNIZEE
RECOGNIZEES
RECOGNIZER
RECOGNIZERS
RECOGNIZES
RECOGNIZING
RECOGNIZOR
RECOGNIZORS
RECOILLESS
RECOINAGES
RECOLLECTED
RECOLLECTEDLY
RECOLLECTEDNESS
RECOLLECTING
RECOLLECTION
RECOLLECTIONS
RECOLLECTIVE
RECOLLECTIVELY
RECOLLECTS
RECOLONISATION
RECOLONISATIONS
RECOLONISE
RECOLONISED
RECOLONISES
RECOLONISING
RECOLONIZATION
RECOLONIZATIONS
RECOLONIZE
RECOLONIZED
RECOLONIZES
RECOLONIZING
RECOLORING
RECOMBINANT
RECOMBINANTS
RECOMBINATION
RECOMBINATIONAL
RECOMBINATIONS
RECOMBINED
RECOMBINES
RECOMBINING
RECOMFORTED
RECOMFORTING
RECOMFORTLESS
RECOMFORTS
RECOMFORTURE
RECOMFORTURES
RECOMMENCE
RECOMMENCED
RECOMMENCEMENT
RECOMMENCEMENTS
RECOMMENCES
RECOMMENCING
RECOMMENDABLE
RECOMMENDABLY
RECOMMENDATION
RECOMMENDATIONS
RECOMMENDATORY
RECOMMENDED
RECOMMENDER
RECOMMENDERS
RECOMMENDING
RECOMMENDS
RECOMMISSION
RECOMMISSIONED
RECOMMISSIONING
RECOMMISSIONS
RECOMMITMENT
RECOMMITMENTS
RECOMMITTAL
RECOMMITTALS
RECOMMITTED
RECOMMITTING
RECOMPACTED
RECOMPACTING
RECOMPACTS
RECOMPENCE
RECOMPENCES
RECOMPENSABLE
RECOMPENSE
RECOMPENSED
RECOMPENSER
RECOMPENSERS
RECOMPENSES
RECOMPENSING
RECOMPILATION
RECOMPILATIONS
RECOMPILED
RECOMPILES
RECOMPILING
RECOMPOSED
RECOMPOSES
RECOMPOSING
RECOMPOSITION
RECOMPOSITIONS
RECOMPRESS
RECOMPRESSED
RECOMPRESSES
RECOMPRESSING
RECOMPRESSION
RECOMPRESSIONS
RECOMPUTATION
RECOMPUTATIONS
RECOMPUTED
RECOMPUTES
RECOMPUTING
RECONCEIVE
RECONCEIVED
RECONCEIVES
RECONCEIVING
RECONCENTRATE
RECONCENTRATED
RECONCENTRATES
RECONCENTRATING
RECONCENTRATION
RECONCEPTION
RECONCEPTIONS
RECONCEPTUALISE
RECONCEPTUALIZE
RECONCILABILITY
RECONCILABLE
RECONCILABLY
RECONCILED
RECONCILEMENT
RECONCILEMENTS
RECONCILER
RECONCILERS
RECONCILES
RECONCILIATION
RECONCILIATIONS
RECONCILIATORY
RECONCILING
RECONDENSATION
RECONDENSATIONS
RECONDENSE
RECONDENSED
RECONDENSES
RECONDENSING
RECONDITELY
RECONDITENESS
RECONDITENESSES
RECONDITION
RECONDITIONED
RECONDITIONING
RECONDITIONS
RECONDUCTED
RECONDUCTING
RECONDUCTS
RECONFERRED
RECONFERRING
RECONFIGURATION
RECONFIGURE
RECONFIGURED
RECONFIGURES
RECONFIGURING
RECONFINED
RECONFINES
RECONFINING
RECONFIRMATION
RECONFIRMATIONS
RECONFIRMED
RECONFIRMING
RECONFIRMS
RECONNAISSANCE
RECONNAISSANCES
RECONNECTED
RECONNECTING
RECONNECTION
RECONNECTIONS
RECONNECTS
RECONNOISSANCE
RECONNOISSANCES
RECONNOITER
RECONNOITERED
RECONNOITERER
RECONNOITERERS
RECONNOITERING
RECONNOITERS
RECONNOITRE
RECONNOITRED
RECONNOITRER
RECONNOITRERS
RECONNOITRES
RECONNOITRING
RECONQUERED
RECONQUERING
RECONQUERS
RECONQUEST
RECONQUESTS
RECONSECRATE
RECONSECRATED
RECONSECRATES
RECONSECRATING
RECONSECRATION
RECONSECRATIONS
RECONSIDER
RECONSIDERATION
RECONSIDERED
RECONSIDERING
RECONSIDERS
RECONSIGNED
RECONSIGNING
RECONSIGNS
RECONSOLED
RECONSOLES
RECONSOLIDATE
RECONSOLIDATED
RECONSOLIDATES
RECONSOLIDATING
RECONSOLIDATION
RECONSOLING
RECONSTITUENT
RECONSTITUENTS
RECONSTITUTABLE
RECONSTITUTE
RECONSTITUTED
RECONSTITUTES
RECONSTITUTING
RECONSTITUTION
RECONSTITUTIONS
RECONSTRUCT
RECONSTRUCTED
RECONSTRUCTIBLE
RECONSTRUCTING
RECONSTRUCTION
RECONSTRUCTIONS
RECONSTRUCTIVE
RECONSTRUCTOR
RECONSTRUCTORS
RECONSTRUCTS
RECONSULTED
RECONSULTING
RECONSULTS
RECONTACTED
RECONTACTING
RECONTACTS
RECONTAMINATE
RECONTAMINATED
RECONTAMINATES
RECONTAMINATING
RECONTAMINATION

RECONTEXTUALISE
RECONTEXTUALIZE
RECONTINUE
RECONTINUED
RECONTINUES
RECONTINUING
RECONTOURED
RECONTOURING
RECONTOURS
RECONVALESCENCE
RECONVENED
RECONVENES
RECONVENING
RECONVERSION
RECONVERSIONS
RECONVERTED
RECONVERTING
RECONVERTS
RECONVEYANCE
RECONVEYANCES
RECONVEYED
RECONVEYING
RECONVICTED
RECONVICTING
RECONVICTION
RECONVICTIONS
RECONVICTS
RECONVINCE
RECONVINCED
RECONVINCES
RECONVINCING
RECORDABLE
RECORDATION
RECORDATIONS
RECORDERSHIP
RECORDERSHIPS
RECORDINGS
RECORDISTS
RECOUNTALS
RECOUNTERS
RECOUNTING
RECOUNTMENT
RECOUNTMENTS
RECOUPABLE
RECOUPLING
RECOUPMENT
RECOUPMENTS
RECOURSING
RECOVERABILITY
RECOVERABLE
RECOVERABLENESS
RECOVEREES
RECOVERERS
RECOVERIES
RECOVERING
RECOVERORS
RECOWERING
RECREANCES
RECREANCIES
RECREANTLY
RECREATING
RECREATION
RECREATIONAL
RECREATIONIST
RECREATIONISTS
RECREATIONS
RECREATIVE
RECREATIVELY
RECREATORS
RECREMENTAL
RECREMENTITIAL
RECREMENTITIOUS
RECREMENTS
RECRIMINATE
RECRIMINATED
RECRIMINATES
RECRIMINATING
RECRIMINATION
RECRIMINATIONS
RECRIMINATIVE
RECRIMINATOR
RECRIMINATORS
RECRIMINATORY
RECROSSING
RECROWNING
RECRUDESCE
RECRUDESCED
RECRUDESCENCE
RECRUDESCENCES
RECRUDESCENCIES
RECRUDESCENCY
RECRUDESCENT
RECRUDESCES
RECRUDESCING
RECRUITABLE
RECRUITALS
RECRUITERS
RECRUITING
RECRUITMENT
RECRUITMENTS
RECRYSTALLISE
RECRYSTALLISED
RECRYSTALLISES
RECRYSTALLISING
RECRYSTALLIZE
RECRYSTALLIZED
RECRYSTALLIZES
RECRYSTALLIZING
RECTANGLED
RECTANGLES
RECTANGULAR
RECTANGULARITY
RECTANGULARLY
RECTIFIABILITY
RECTIFIABLE
RECTIFICATION
RECTIFICATIONS
RECTIFIERS
RECTIFYING
RECTILINEAL
RECTILINEALLY
RECTILINEAR
RECTILINEARITY
RECTILINEARLY
RECTIPETALIES
RECTIPETALITIES
RECTIPETALITY
RECTIPETALY
RECTIROSTRAL
RECTISERIAL
RECTITISES
RECTITUDES
RECTITUDINOUS
RECTOCELES
RECTORATES
RECTORESSES
RECTORIALS
RECTORSHIP
RECTORSHIPS
RECTRESSES
RECTRICIAL
RECULTIVATE
RECULTIVATED
RECULTIVATES
RECULTIVATING
RECUMBENCE
RECUMBENCES
RECUMBENCIES
RECUMBENCY
RECUMBENTLY
RECUPERABLE
RECUPERATE
RECUPERATED
RECUPERATES
RECUPERATING
RECUPERATION
RECUPERATIONS
RECUPERATIVE
RECUPERATOR
RECUPERATORS
RECUPERATORY
RECURELESS
RECURRENCE
RECURRENCES
RECURRENCIES
RECURRENCY
RECURRENTLY
RECURRINGLY
RECURSIONS
RECURSIVELY
RECURSIVENESS
RECURSIVENESSES
RECURVIROSTRAL
RECUSANCES
RECUSANCIES
RECUSATION
RECUSATIONS
RECYCLABLE
RECYCLABLES
RECYCLATES
RECYCLEABLE
RECYCLISTS
REDACTIONAL
REDACTIONS
REDACTORIAL
REDAMAGING
REDARGUING
REDBAITERS
REDBAITING
REDBELLIES
REDBREASTS
REDCURRANT
REDCURRANTS
REDDISHNESS
REDDISHNESSES
REDECIDING
REDECORATE
REDECORATED
REDECORATES
REDECORATING
REDECORATION
REDECORATIONS
REDECORATOR
REDECORATORS
REDECRAFTS
REDEDICATE
REDEDICATED
REDEDICATES
REDEDICATING
REDEDICATION
REDEDICATIONS
REDEEMABILITIES
REDEEMABILITY
REDEEMABLE
REDEEMABLENESS
REDEEMABLY
REDEEMLESS
REDEFEATED
REDEFEATING
REDEFECTED
REDEFECTING
REDEFINING
REDEFINITION
REDEFINITIONS
REDELIVERANCE
REDELIVERANCES
REDELIVERED
REDELIVERER
REDELIVERERS
REDELIVERIES
REDELIVERING
REDELIVERS
REDELIVERY
REDEMANDED
REDEMANDING
REDEMPTIBLE
REDEMPTION
REDEMPTIONAL
REDEMPTIONER
REDEMPTIONERS
REDEMPTIONS
REDEMPTIVE
REDEMPTIVELY
REDEMPTORY
REDEPLOYED
REDEPLOYING
REDEPLOYMENT
REDEPLOYMENTS
REDEPOSITED
REDEPOSITING
REDEPOSITS
REDESCENDED
REDESCENDING
REDESCENDS
REDESCRIBE
REDESCRIBED
REDESCRIBES
REDESCRIBING
REDESCRIPTION
REDESCRIPTIONS
REDESIGNED
REDESIGNING
REDETERMINATION
REDETERMINE

REDETERMINED
REDETERMINES
REDETERMINING
REDEVELOPED
REDEVELOPER
REDEVELOPERS
REDEVELOPING
REDEVELOPMENT
REDEVELOPMENTS
REDEVELOPS
REDIALLING
REDICTATED
REDICTATES
REDICTATING
REDIGESTED
REDIGESTING
REDIGESTION
REDIGESTIONS
REDIGRESSED
REDIGRESSES
REDIGRESSING
REDINGOTES
REDINTEGRATE
REDINTEGRATED
REDINTEGRATES
REDINTEGRATING
REDINTEGRATION
REDINTEGRATIONS
REDINTEGRATIVE
REDIRECTED
REDIRECTING
REDIRECTION
REDIRECTIONS
REDISBURSE
REDISBURSED
REDISBURSES
REDISBURSING
REDISCOUNT
REDISCOUNTABLE
REDISCOUNTED
REDISCOUNTING
REDISCOUNTS
REDISCOVER
REDISCOVERED
REDISCOVERER
REDISCOVERERS
REDISCOVERIES
REDISCOVERING
REDISCOVERS
REDISCOVERY
REDISCUSSED
REDISCUSSES
REDISCUSSING
REDISPLAYED
REDISPLAYING
REDISPLAYS
REDISPOSED
REDISPOSES
REDISPOSING
REDISPOSITION
REDISPOSITIONS
REDISSOLUTION
REDISSOLUTIONS
REDISSOLVE
REDISSOLVED
REDISSOLVES
REDISSOLVING
REDISTILLATION
REDISTILLATIONS
REDISTILLED
REDISTILLING
REDISTILLS
REDISTRIBUTE
REDISTRIBUTED
REDISTRIBUTES
REDISTRIBUTING
REDISTRIBUTION
REDISTRIBUTIONS
REDISTRIBUTIVE
REDISTRICT
REDISTRICTED
REDISTRICTING
REDISTRICTS
REDIVIDING
REDIVISION
REDIVISIONS
REDIVORCED
REDIVORCES
REDIVORCING
REDLININGS
REDOLENCES
REDOLENCIES
REDOLENTLY
REDOUBLEMENT
REDOUBLEMENTS
REDOUBLERS
REDOUBLING
REDOUBTABLE
REDOUBTABLENESS
REDOUBTABLY
REDOUBTING
REDOUNDING
REDOUNDINGS
REDRAFTING
REDREAMING
REDRESSABILITY
REDRESSABLE
REDRESSERS
REDRESSIBLE
REDRESSING
REDRESSIVE
REDRESSORS
REDRILLING
REDRUTHITE
REDRUTHITES
REDSHIFTED
REDSHIRTED
REDSHIRTING
REDSTREAKS
REDUCIBILITIES
REDUCIBILITY
REDUCIBLENESS
REDUCIBLENESSES
REDUCTANTS
REDUCTASES
REDUCTIONAL
REDUCTIONISM
REDUCTIONISMS
REDUCTIONIST
REDUCTIONISTIC
REDUCTIONISTS
REDUCTIONS
REDUCTIVELY
REDUCTIVENESS
REDUCTIVENESSES
REDUNDANCE
REDUNDANCES
REDUNDANCIES
REDUNDANCY
REDUNDANTLY
REDUPLICATE
REDUPLICATED
REDUPLICATES
REDUPLICATING
REDUPLICATION
REDUPLICATIONS
REDUPLICATIVE
REDUPLICATIVELY
REEDIFYING
REEDINESSES
REEDITIONS
REEDUCATED
REEDUCATES
REEDUCATING
REEDUCATION
REEDUCATIONS
REEDUCATIVE
REEJECTING
REELECTING
REELECTION
REELECTIONS
REELEVATED
REELEVATES
REELEVATING
REELIGIBILITIES
REELIGIBILITY
REELIGIBLE
REEMBARKED
REEMBARKING
REEMBODIED
REEMBODIES
REEMBODYING
REEMBRACED
REEMBRACES
REEMBRACING
REEMBROIDER
REEMBROIDERED
REEMBROIDERING
REEMBROIDERS
REEMERGENCE
REEMERGENCES
REEMERGING
REEMISSION
REEMISSIONS
REEMITTING
REEMPHASES
REEMPHASIS
REEMPHASISE
REEMPHASISED
REEMPHASISES
REEMPHASISING
REEMPHASIZE
REEMPHASIZED
REEMPHASIZES
REEMPHASIZING
REEMPLOYED
REEMPLOYING
REEMPLOYMENT
REEMPLOYMENTS
REENACTING
REENACTMENT
REENACTMENTS
REENACTORS
REENCOUNTER
REENCOUNTERED
REENCOUNTERING
REENCOUNTERS
REENDOWING
REENERGISE
REENERGISED
REENERGISES
REENERGISING
REENERGIZE
REENERGIZED
REENERGIZES
REENERGIZING
REENFORCED
REENFORCES
REENFORCING
REENGAGEMENT
REENGAGEMENTS
REENGAGING
REENGINEER
REENGINEERED
REENGINEERING
REENGINEERS
REENGRAVED
REENGRAVES
REENGRAVING
REENJOYING
REENLARGED
REENLARGES
REENLARGING
REENLISTED
REENLISTING
REENLISTMENT
REENLISTMENTS
REENROLLED
REENROLLING
REENSLAVED
REENSLAVES
REENSLAVING
REENTERING
REENTHRONE
REENTHRONED
REENTHRONES
REENTHRONING
REENTRANCE
REENTRANCES
REENTRANTS
REEQUIPMENT
REEQUIPMENTS
REEQUIPPED
REEQUIPPING
REERECTING
REESCALATE
REESCALATED
REESCALATES
REESCALATING
REESCALATION
REESCALATIONS
REESTABLISH
REESTABLISHED
REESTABLISHES

REESTABLISHING
REESTABLISHMENT
REESTIMATE
REESTIMATED
REESTIMATES
REESTIMATING
REEVALUATE
REEVALUATED
REEVALUATES
REEVALUATING
REEVALUATION
REEVALUATIONS
REEXAMINATION
REEXAMINATIONS
REEXAMINED
REEXAMINES
REEXAMINING
REEXECUTED
REEXECUTES
REEXECUTING
REEXHIBITED
REEXHIBITING
REEXHIBITS
REEXPELLED
REEXPELLING
REEXPERIENCE
REEXPERIENCED
REEXPERIENCES
REEXPERIENCING
REEXPLAINED
REEXPLAINING
REEXPLAINS
REEXPLORED
REEXPLORES
REEXPLORING
REEXPORTATION
REEXPORTATIONS
REEXPORTED
REEXPORTING
REEXPOSING
REEXPOSURE
REEXPOSURES
REEXPRESSED
REEXPRESSES
REEXPRESSING
REFASHIONED
REFASHIONING
REFASHIONMENT
REFASHIONMENTS
REFASHIONS
REFASTENED
REFASTENING
REFECTIONER
REFECTIONERS
REFECTIONS
REFECTORIAN
REFECTORIANS
REFECTORIES
REFEREEING
REFERENCED
REFERENCER
REFERENCERS
REFERENCES
REFERENCING
REFERENDARIES
REFERENDARY
REFERENDUM
REFERENDUMS
REFERENTIAL
REFERENTIALITY
REFERENTIALLY
REFERRABLE
REFERRIBLE
REFIGHTING
REFIGURING
REFILLABLE
REFILTERED
REFILTERING
REFINANCED
REFINANCES
REFINANCING
REFINANCINGS
REFINEDNESS
REFINEDNESSES
REFINEMENT
REFINEMENTS
REFINERIES
REFINISHED
REFINISHER
REFINISHERS
REFINISHES
REFINISHING
REFITMENTS
REFITTINGS
REFLAGGING
REFLATIONARY
REFLATIONS
REFLECTANCE
REFLECTANCES
REFLECTERS
REFLECTING
REFLECTINGLY
REFLECTION
REFLECTIONAL
REFLECTIONLESS
REFLECTIONS
REFLECTIVE
REFLECTIVELY
REFLECTIVENESS
REFLECTIVITIES
REFLECTIVITY
REFLECTOGRAM
REFLECTOGRAMS
REFLECTOGRAPH
REFLECTOGRAPHS
REFLECTOGRAPHY
REFLECTOMETER
REFLECTOMETERS
REFLECTOMETRIES
REFLECTOMETRY
REFLECTORISE
REFLECTORISED
REFLECTORISES
REFLECTORISING
REFLECTORIZE
REFLECTORIZED
REFLECTORIZES
REFLECTORIZING
REFLECTORS
REFLEXIBILITIES
REFLEXIBILITY
REFLEXIBLE
REFLEXIONAL
REFLEXIONS
REFLEXIVELY
REFLEXIVENESS
REFLEXIVENESSES
REFLEXIVES
REFLEXIVITIES
REFLEXIVITY
REFLEXOLOGICAL
REFLEXOLOGIES
REFLEXOLOGIST
REFLEXOLOGISTS
REFLEXOLOGY
REFLOATING
REFLOODING
REFLOWERED
REFLOWERING
REFLOWERINGS
REFLOWINGS
REFLUENCES
REFOCILLATE
REFOCILLATED
REFOCILLATES
REFOCILLATING
REFOCILLATION
REFOCILLATIONS
REFOCUSING
REFOCUSSED
REFOCUSSES
REFOCUSSING
REFORESTATION
REFORESTATIONS
REFORESTED
REFORESTING
REFORMABILITIES
REFORMABILITY
REFORMABLE
REFORMADES
REFORMADOES
REFORMADOS
REFORMATES
REFORMATION
REFORMATIONAL
REFORMATIONIST
REFORMATIONISTS
REFORMATIONS
REFORMATIVE
REFORMATORIES
REFORMATORY
REFORMATTED
REFORMATTING
REFORMINGS
REFORMISMS
REFORMISTS
REFORMULATE
REFORMULATED
REFORMULATES
REFORMULATING
REFORMULATION
REFORMULATIONS
REFORTIFICATION
REFORTIFIED
REFORTIFIES
REFORTIFYING
REFOUNDATION
REFOUNDATIONS
REFOUNDERS
REFOUNDING
REFRACTABLE
REFRACTARIES
REFRACTARY
REFRACTILE
REFRACTING
REFRACTION
REFRACTIONS
REFRACTIVE
REFRACTIVELY
REFRACTIVENESS
REFRACTIVITIES
REFRACTIVITY
REFRACTOMETER
REFRACTOMETERS
REFRACTOMETRIC
REFRACTOMETRIES
REFRACTOMETRY
REFRACTORIES
REFRACTORILY
REFRACTORINESS
REFRACTORS
REFRACTORY
REFRACTURE
REFRACTURES
REFRAINERS
REFRAINING
REFRAINMENT
REFRAINMENTS
REFRANGIBILITY
REFRANGIBLE
REFRANGIBLENESS
REFREEZING
REFRESHENED
REFRESHENER
REFRESHENERS
REFRESHENING
REFRESHENS
REFRESHERS
REFRESHFUL
REFRESHFULLY
REFRESHING
REFRESHINGLY
REFRESHMENT
REFRESHMENTS
REFRIGERANT
REFRIGERANTS
REFRIGERATE
REFRIGERATED
REFRIGERATES
REFRIGERATING
REFRIGERATION
REFRIGERATIONS
REFRIGERATIVE
REFRIGERATOR
REFRIGERATORIES
REFRIGERATORS
REFRIGERATORY
REFRINGENCE
REFRINGENCES
REFRINGENCIES
REFRINGENCY
REFRINGENT
REFRINGING
REFRONTING

REFUELABLE
REFUELLABLE
REFUELLING
REFUGEEISM
REFUGEEISMS
REFULGENCE
REFULGENCES
REFULGENCIES
REFULGENCY
REFULGENTLY
REFUNDABILITIES
REFUNDABILITY
REFUNDABLE
REFUNDMENT
REFUNDMENTS
REFURBISHED
REFURBISHER
REFURBISHERS
REFURBISHES
REFURBISHING
REFURBISHINGS
REFURBISHMENT
REFURBISHMENTS
REFURNISHED
REFURNISHES
REFURNISHING
REFUSENIKS
REFUTABILITIES
REFUTABILITY
REFUTATION
REFUTATIONS
REGAINABLE
REGAINMENT
REGAINMENTS
REGALEMENT
REGALEMENTS
REGALITIES
REGALNESSES
REGARDABLE
REGARDFULLY
REGARDFULNESS
REGARDFULNESSES
REGARDLESS
REGARDLESSLY
REGARDLESSNESS
REGATHERED
REGATHERING
REGELATING
REGELATION
REGELATIONS
REGENERABLE
REGENERACIES
REGENERACY
REGENERATE
REGENERATED
REGENERATELY
REGENERATENESS
REGENERATES
REGENERATING
REGENERATION
REGENERATIONS
REGENERATIVE
REGENERATIVELY
REGENERATOR
REGENERATORS
REGENERATORY
REGENTSHIP
REGENTSHIPS
REGIMENTAL
REGIMENTALLY
REGIMENTALS
REGIMENTATION
REGIMENTATIONS
REGIMENTED
REGIMENTING
REGIONALISATION
REGIONALISE
REGIONALISED
REGIONALISES
REGIONALISING
REGIONALISM
REGIONALISMS
REGIONALIST
REGIONALISTIC
REGIONALISTS
REGIONALIZATION
REGIONALIZE
REGIONALIZED
REGIONALIZES
REGIONALIZING
REGIONALLY
REGISSEURS
REGISTERABLE
REGISTERED
REGISTERER
REGISTERERS
REGISTERING
REGISTRABLE
REGISTRANT
REGISTRANTS
REGISTRARIES
REGISTRARS
REGISTRARSHIP
REGISTRARSHIPS
REGISTRARY
REGISTRATION
REGISTRATIONAL
REGISTRATIONS
REGISTRIES
REGLORIFIED
REGLORIFIES
REGLORIFYING
REGLOSSING
REGNANCIES
REGRAFTING
REGRANTING
REGRATINGS
REGREDIENCE
REGREDIENCES
REGREENING
REGREETING
REGRESSING
REGRESSION
REGRESSIONS
REGRESSIVE
REGRESSIVELY
REGRESSIVENESS
REGRESSIVITIES
REGRESSIVITY
REGRESSORS
REGRETFULLY
REGRETFULNESS
REGRETFULNESSES
REGRETTABLE
REGRETTABLY
REGRETTERS
REGRETTING
REGRINDING
REGROOMING
REGROOVING
REGROUPING
REGUERDONED
REGUERDONING
REGUERDONS
REGULARISATION
REGULARISATIONS
REGULARISE
REGULARISED
REGULARISES
REGULARISING
REGULARITIES
REGULARITY
REGULARIZATION
REGULARIZATIONS
REGULARIZE
REGULARIZED
REGULARIZES
REGULARIZING
REGULATING
REGULATION
REGULATIONS
REGULATIVE
REGULATIVELY
REGULATORS
REGULATORY
REGULISING
REGULIZING
REGURGITANT
REGURGITANTS
REGURGITATE
REGURGITATED
REGURGITATES
REGURGITATING
REGURGITATION
REGURGITATIONS
REHABILITANT
REHABILITANTS
REHABILITATE
REHABILITATED
REHABILITATES
REHABILITATING
REHABILITATION
REHABILITATIONS
REHABILITATIVE
REHABILITATOR
REHABILITATORS
REHAMMERED
REHAMMERING
REHANDLING
REHANDLINGS
REHARDENED
REHARDENING
REHEARINGS
REHEARSALS
REHEARSERS
REHEARSING
REHEARSINGS
REHEATINGS
REHOSPITALISE
REHOSPITALISED
REHOSPITALISES
REHOSPITALISING
REHOSPITALIZE
REHOSPITALIZED
REHOSPITALIZES
REHOSPITALIZING
REHOUSINGS
REHUMANISE
REHUMANISED
REHUMANISES
REHUMANISING
REHUMANIZE
REHUMANIZED
REHUMANIZES
REHUMANIZING
REHYDRATABLE
REHYDRATED
REHYDRATES
REHYDRATING
REHYDRATION
REHYDRATIONS
REHYPNOTISE
REHYPNOTISED
REHYPNOTISES
REHYPNOTISING
REHYPNOTIZE
REHYPNOTIZED
REHYPNOTIZES
REHYPNOTIZING
REICHSMARK
REICHSMARKS
REIDENTIFIED
REIDENTIFIES
REIDENTIFY
REIDENTIFYING
REIFICATION
REIFICATIONS
REIFICATORY
REIGNITING
REIGNITION
REIGNITIONS
REILLUMINE
REILLUMINED
REILLUMINES
REILLUMING
REILLUMINING
REIMAGINED
REIMAGINES
REIMAGINING
REIMBURSABLE
REIMBURSED
REIMBURSEMENT
REIMBURSEMENTS
REIMBURSER
REIMBURSERS
REIMBURSES
REIMBURSING
REIMMERSED
REIMMERSES
REIMMERSING
REIMPLANTATION
REIMPLANTATIONS
REIMPLANTED
REIMPLANTING

REIMPLANTS
REIMPORTATION
REIMPORTATIONS
REIMPORTED
REIMPORTER
REIMPORTERS
REIMPORTING
REIMPOSING
REIMPOSITION
REIMPOSITIONS
REIMPRESSION
REIMPRESSIONS
REINCARNATE
REINCARNATED
REINCARNATES
REINCARNATING
REINCARNATION
REINCARNATIONS
REINCITING
REINCORPORATE
REINCORPORATED
REINCORPORATES
REINCORPORATING
REINCORPORATION
REINCREASE
REINCREASED
REINCREASES
REINCREASING
REINCURRED
REINCURRING
REINDEXING
REINDICTED
REINDICTING
REINDICTMENT
REINDICTMENTS
REINDUCING
REINDUCTED
REINDUCTING
REINDUSTRIALISE
REINDUSTRIALIZE
REINFECTED
REINFECTING
REINFECTION
REINFECTIONS
REINFESTATION
REINFESTATIONS
REINFLAMED
REINFLAMES
REINFLAMING
REINFLATED
REINFLATES
REINFLATING
REINFLATION
REINFLATIONS
REINFORCEABLE
REINFORCED
REINFORCEMENT
REINFORCEMENTS
REINFORCER
REINFORCERS
REINFORCES
REINFORCING
REINFORMED
REINFORMING
REINFUNDED
REINFUNDING
REINFUSING
REINHABITED
REINHABITING
REINHABITS
REINITIATE
REINITIATED
REINITIATES
REINITIATING
REINJECTED
REINJECTING
REINJECTION
REINJECTIONS
REINJURIES
REINJURING
REINNERVATE
REINNERVATED
REINNERVATES
REINNERVATING
REINNERVATION
REINNERVATIONS
REINOCULATE
REINOCULATED
REINOCULATES
REINOCULATING
REINOCULATION
REINOCULATIONS
REINSERTED
REINSERTING
REINSERTION
REINSERTIONS
REINSPECTED
REINSPECTING
REINSPECTION
REINSPECTIONS
REINSPECTS
REINSPIRED
REINSPIRES
REINSPIRING
REINSPIRIT
REINSPIRITED
REINSPIRITING
REINSPIRITS
REINSTALLATION
REINSTALLATIONS
REINSTALLED
REINSTALLING
REINSTALLS
REINSTALMENT
REINSTALMENTS
REINSTATED
REINSTATEMENT
REINSTATEMENTS
REINSTATES
REINSTATING
REINSTATION
REINSTATIONS
REINSTATOR
REINSTATORS
REINSTITUTE
REINSTITUTED
REINSTITUTES
REINSTITUTING
REINSURANCE
REINSURANCES
REINSURERS
REINSURING
REINTEGRATE
REINTEGRATED
REINTEGRATES
REINTEGRATING
REINTEGRATION
REINTEGRATIONS
REINTEGRATIVE
REINTERMENT
REINTERMENTS
REINTERPRET
REINTERPRETED
REINTERPRETING
REINTERPRETS
REINTERRED
REINTERRING
REINTERROGATE
REINTERROGATED
REINTERROGATES
REINTERROGATING
REINTERROGATION
REINTERVIEW
REINTERVIEWED
REINTERVIEWING
REINTERVIEWS
REINTRODUCE
REINTRODUCED
REINTRODUCES
REINTRODUCING
REINTRODUCTION
REINTRODUCTIONS
REINVADING
REINVASION
REINVASIONS
REINVENTED
REINVENTING
REINVENTION
REINVENTIONS
REINVESTED
REINVESTIGATE
REINVESTIGATED
REINVESTIGATES
REINVESTIGATING
REINVESTIGATION
REINVESTING
REINVESTMENT
REINVESTMENTS
REINVIGORATE
REINVIGORATED
REINVIGORATES
REINVIGORATING
REINVIGORATION
REINVIGORATIONS
REINVIGORATOR
REINVIGORATORS
REINVITING
REINVOKING
REINVOLVED
REINVOLVES
REINVOLVING
REIOYNDURE
REIOYNDURES
REISSUABLE
REISTAFELS
REITERANCE
REITERANCES
REITERATED
REITERATEDLY
REITERATES
REITERATING
REITERATION
REITERATIONS
REITERATIVE
REITERATIVELY
REITERATIVES
REJACKETED
REJACKETING
REJECTABLE
REJECTAMENTA
REJECTIBLE
REJECTINGLY
REJECTIONIST
REJECTIONISTS
REJECTIONS
REJIGGERED
REJIGGERING
REJOICEFUL
REJOICEMENT
REJOICEMENTS
REJOICINGLY
REJOICINGS
REJOINDERS
REJOINDURE
REJOINDURES
REJONEADOR
REJONEADORA
REJONEADORAS
REJONEADORES
REJOURNING
REJUGGLING
REJUSTIFIED
REJUSTIFIES
REJUSTIFYING
REJUVENATE
REJUVENATED
REJUVENATES
REJUVENATING
REJUVENATION
REJUVENATIONS
REJUVENATOR
REJUVENATORS
REJUVENESCE
REJUVENESCED
REJUVENESCENCE
REJUVENESCENCES
REJUVENESCENT
REJUVENESCES
REJUVENESCING
REJUVENISE
REJUVENISED
REJUVENISES
REJUVENISING
REJUVENIZE
REJUVENIZED
REJUVENIZES
REJUVENIZING
REKEYBOARD
REKEYBOARDED
REKEYBOARDING
REKEYBOARDS
REKINDLING
REKNITTING
REKNOTTING

RELABELING
RELABELLED
RELABELLING
RELACQUERED
RELACQUERING
RELACQUERS
RELANDSCAPE
RELANDSCAPED
RELANDSCAPES
RELANDSCAPING
RELATEDNESS
RELATEDNESSES
RELATIONAL
RELATIONALLY
RELATIONISM
RELATIONISMS
RELATIONIST
RELATIONISTS
RELATIONLESS
RELATIONSHIP
RELATIONSHIPS
RELATIVELY
RELATIVENESS
RELATIVENESSES
RELATIVISATION
RELATIVISATIONS
RELATIVISE
RELATIVISED
RELATIVISES
RELATIVISING
RELATIVISM
RELATIVISMS
RELATIVIST
RELATIVISTIC
RELATIVISTS
RELATIVITIES
RELATIVITIST
RELATIVITISTS
RELATIVITY
RELATIVIZATION
RELATIVIZATIONS
RELATIVIZE
RELATIVIZED
RELATIVIZES
RELATIVIZING
RELAUNCHED
RELAUNCHES
RELAUNCHING
RELAUNDERED
RELAUNDERING
RELAUNDERS
RELAXATION
RELAXATIONS
RELAXATIVE
RELAXEDNESS
RELAXEDNESSES
RELEARNING
RELEASABLE
RELEASEMENT
RELEASEMENTS
RELEGATABLE
RELEGATING
RELEGATION
RELEGATIONS
RELENTINGS
RELENTLESS
RELENTLESSLY
RELENTLESSNESS
RELENTMENT
RELENTMENTS
RELETTERED
RELETTERING
RELEVANCES
RELEVANCIES
RELEVANTLY
RELIABILITIES
RELIABILITY
RELIABLENESS
RELIABLENESSES
RELICENSED
RELICENSES
RELICENSING
RELICENSURE
RELICENSURES
RELICTIONS
RELIEFLESS
RELIEVABLE
RELIEVEDLY
RELIGHTING
RELIGIEUSE
RELIGIEUSES
RELIGIONARIES
RELIGIONARY
RELIGIONER
RELIGIONERS
RELIGIONISE
RELIGIONISED
RELIGIONISES
RELIGIONISING
RELIGIONISM
RELIGIONISMS
RELIGIONIST
RELIGIONISTS
RELIGIONIZE
RELIGIONIZED
RELIGIONIZES
RELIGIONIZING
RELIGIONLESS
RELIGIOSELY
RELIGIOSITIES
RELIGIOSITY
RELIGIOUSES
RELIGIOUSLY
RELIGIOUSNESS
RELIGIOUSNESSES
RELINQUISH
RELINQUISHED
RELINQUISHER
RELINQUISHERS
RELINQUISHES
RELINQUISHING
RELINQUISHMENT
RELINQUISHMENTS
RELIQUAIRE
RELIQUAIRES
RELIQUARIES
RELIQUEFIED
RELIQUEFIES
RELIQUEFYING
RELISHABLE
RELIVERING
RELLISHING
RELOCATABLE
RELOCATEES
RELOCATING
RELOCATION
RELOCATIONS
RELOCATORS
RELUBRICATE
RELUBRICATED
RELUBRICATES
RELUBRICATING
RELUBRICATION
RELUBRICATIONS
RELUCTANCE
RELUCTANCES
RELUCTANCIES
RELUCTANCY
RELUCTANTLY
RELUCTATED
RELUCTATES
RELUCTATING
RELUCTATION
RELUCTATIONS
RELUCTIVITIES
RELUCTIVITY
RELUMINING
REMAINDERED
REMAINDERING
REMAINDERMAN
REMAINDERMEN
REMAINDERS
REMANDMENT
REMANDMENTS
REMANENCES
REMANENCIES
REMANUFACTURE
REMANUFACTURED
REMANUFACTURER
REMANUFACTURERS
REMANUFACTURES
REMANUFACTURING
REMARKABILITIES
REMARKABILITY
REMARKABLE
REMARKABLENESS
REMARKABLES
REMARKABLY
REMARKETED
REMARKETING
REMARRIAGE
REMARRIAGES
REMARRYING
REMASTERED
REMASTERING
REMATCHING
REMATERIALISE
REMATERIALISED
REMATERIALISES
REMATERIALISING
REMATERIALIZE
REMATERIALIZED
REMATERIALIZES
REMATERIALIZING
REMEASURED
REMEASUREMENT
REMEASUREMENTS
REMEASURES
REMEASURING
REMEDIABILITIES
REMEDIABILITY
REMEDIABLE
REMEDIABLY
REMEDIALLY
REMEDIATED
REMEDIATES
REMEDIATING
REMEDIATION
REMEDIATIONS
REMEDILESS
REMEDILESSLY
REMEDILESSNESS
REMEMBERABILITY
REMEMBERABLE
REMEMBERABLY
REMEMBERED
REMEMBERER
REMEMBERERS
REMEMBERING
REMEMBRANCE
REMEMBRANCER
REMEMBRANCERS
REMEMBRANCES
REMERCYING
REMIGATING
REMIGATION
REMIGATIONS
REMIGRATED
REMIGRATES
REMIGRATING
REMIGRATION
REMIGRATIONS
REMILITARISE
REMILITARISED
REMILITARISES
REMILITARISING
REMILITARIZE
REMILITARIZED
REMILITARIZES
REMILITARIZING
REMINERALISE
REMINERALISED
REMINERALISES
REMINERALISING
REMINERALIZE
REMINERALIZED
REMINERALIZES
REMINERALIZING
REMINISCED
REMINISCENCE
REMINISCENCES
REMINISCENT
REMINISCENTIAL
REMINISCENTLY
REMINISCENTS
REMINISCER
REMINISCERS
REMINISCES
REMINISCING
REMISSIBILITIES
REMISSIBILITY
REMISSIBLE
REMISSIBLENESS
REMISSIBLY

REMISSIONS
REMISSIVELY
REMISSNESS
REMISSNESSES
REMITMENTS
REMITTABLE
REMITTANCE
REMITTANCES
REMITTENCE
REMITTENCES
REMITTENCIES
REMITTENCY
REMITTENTLY
REMIXTURES
REMOBILISATION
REMOBILISATIONS
REMOBILISE
REMOBILISED
REMOBILISES
REMOBILISING
REMOBILIZATION
REMOBILIZATIONS
REMOBILIZE
REMOBILIZED
REMOBILIZES
REMOBILIZING
REMODELERS
REMODELING
REMODELLED
REMODELLING
REMODIFIED
REMODIFIES
REMODIFYING
REMOISTENED
REMOISTENING
REMOISTENS
REMONETISATION
REMONETISATIONS
REMONETISE
REMONETISED
REMONETISES
REMONETISING
REMONETIZATION
REMONETIZATIONS
REMONETIZE
REMONETIZED
REMONETIZES
REMONETIZING
REMONSTRANCE
REMONSTRANCES
REMONSTRANT
REMONSTRANTLY
REMONSTRANTS
REMONSTRATE
REMONSTRATED
REMONSTRATES
REMONSTRATING
REMONSTRATINGLY
REMONSTRATION
REMONSTRATIONS
REMONSTRATIVE
REMONSTRATIVELY
REMONSTRATOR
REMONSTRATORS
REMONSTRATORY
REMONTANTS
REMONTOIRE
REMONTOIRES
REMONTOIRS
REMORALISATION
REMORALISATIONS
REMORALISE
REMORALISED
REMORALISES
REMORALISING
REMORALIZATION
REMORALIZATIONS
REMORALIZE
REMORALIZED
REMORALIZES
REMORALIZING
REMORSEFUL
REMORSEFULLY
REMORSEFULNESS
REMORSELESS
REMORSELESSLY
REMORSELESSNESS
REMORTGAGE
REMORTGAGED
REMORTGAGES
REMORTGAGING
REMOTENESS
REMOTENESSES
REMOTIVATE
REMOTIVATED
REMOTIVATES
REMOTIVATING
REMOTIVATION
REMOTIVATIONS
REMOULADES
REMOULDING
REMOUNTING
REMOVABILITIES
REMOVABILITY
REMOVABLENESS
REMOVABLENESSES
REMOVALIST
REMOVALISTS
REMOVEABLE
REMOVEDNESS
REMOVEDNESSES
REMUNERABILITY
REMUNERABLE
REMUNERATE
REMUNERATED
REMUNERATES
REMUNERATING
REMUNERATION
REMUNERATIONS
REMUNERATIVE
REMUNERATIVELY
REMUNERATOR
REMUNERATORS
REMUNERATORY
REMURMURED
REMURMURING
REMYTHOLOGISE
REMYTHOLOGISED
REMYTHOLOGISES
REMYTHOLOGISING
REMYTHOLOGIZE
REMYTHOLOGIZED
REMYTHOLOGIZES
REMYTHOLOGIZING
RENAISSANCE
RENAISSANCES
RENASCENCE
RENASCENCES
RENATIONALISE
RENATIONALISED
RENATIONALISES
RENATIONALISING
RENATIONALIZE
RENATIONALIZED
RENATIONALIZES
RENATIONALIZING
RENATURATION
RENATURATIONS
RENATURING
RENCONTRES
RENCOUNTER
RENCOUNTERED
RENCOUNTERING
RENCOUNTERS
RENDERABLE
RENDERINGS
RENDEZVOUS
RENDEZVOUSED
RENDEZVOUSES
RENDEZVOUSING
RENDITIONS
RENEGADING
RENEGADOES
RENEGATION
RENEGATIONS
RENEGOTIABLE
RENEGOTIATE
RENEGOTIATED
RENEGOTIATES
RENEGOTIATING
RENEGOTIATION
RENEGOTIATIONS
RENEWABILITIES
RENEWABILITY
RENEWABLES
RENEWEDNESS
RENEWEDNESSES
RENFORCING
RENITENCES
RENITENCIES
RENOGRAPHIC
RENOGRAPHIES
RENOGRAPHY
RENOMINATE
RENOMINATED
RENOMINATES
RENOMINATING
RENOMINATION
RENOMINATIONS
RENORMALISATION
RENORMALISE
RENORMALISED
RENORMALISES
RENORMALISING
RENORMALIZATION
RENORMALIZE
RENORMALIZED
RENORMALIZES
RENORMALIZING
RENOSTERVELD
RENOSTERVELDS
RENOTIFIED
RENOTIFIES
RENOTIFYING
RENOUNCEABLE
RENOUNCEMENT
RENOUNCEMENTS
RENOUNCERS
RENOUNCING
RENOVASCULAR
RENOVATING
RENOVATION
RENOVATIONS
RENOVATIVE
RENOVATORS
RENSSELAERITE
RENSSELAERITES
RENTABILITIES
RENTABILITY
RENTALLERS
RENUMBERED
RENUMBERING
RENUNCIATE
RENUNCIATION
RENUNCIATIONS
RENUNCIATIVE
RENUNCIATORY
RENUNICATES
RENVERSEMENT
RENVERSEMENTS
RENVERSING
REOBJECTED
REOBJECTING
REOBSERVED
REOBSERVES
REOBSERVING
REOBTAINED
REOBTAINING
REOCCUPATION
REOCCUPATIONS
REOCCUPIED
REOCCUPIES
REOCCUPYING
REOCCURRED
REOCCURRENCE
REOCCURRENCES
REOCCURRING
REOFFENDED
REOFFENDER
REOFFENDERS
REOFFENDING
REOFFERING
REOPERATED
REOPERATES
REOPERATING
REOPERATION
REOPERATIONS
REOPPOSING
REORCHESTRATE
REORCHESTRATED
REORCHESTRATES
REORCHESTRATING
REORCHESTRATION
REORDAINED

REORDAINING
REORDERING
REORDINATION
REORDINATIONS
REORGANISATION
REORGANISATIONS
REORGANISE
REORGANISED
REORGANISER
REORGANISERS
REORGANISES
REORGANISING
REORGANIZATION
REORGANIZATIONS
REORGANIZE
REORGANIZED
REORGANIZER
REORGANIZERS
REORGANIZES
REORGANIZING
REORIENTATE
REORIENTATED
REORIENTATES
REORIENTATING
REORIENTATION
REORIENTATIONS
REORIENTED
REORIENTING
REOUTFITTED
REOUTFITTING
REOVIRUSES
REOXIDATION
REOXIDATIONS
REOXIDISED
REOXIDISES
REOXIDISING
REOXIDIZED
REOXIDIZES
REOXIDIZING
REPACIFIED
REPACIFIES
REPACIFYING
REPACKAGED
REPACKAGER
REPACKAGERS
REPACKAGES
REPACKAGING
REPAGINATE
REPAGINATED
REPAGINATES
REPAGINATING
REPAGINATION
REPAGINATIONS
REPAINTING
REPAINTINGS
REPAIRABILITIES
REPAIRABILITY
REPAIRABLE
REPANELING
REPANELLED
REPANELLING
REPAPERING
REPARABILITIES
REPARABILITY
REPARATION
REPARATIONS
REPARATIVE
REPARATORY
REPARTEEING
REPARTITION
REPARTITIONED
REPARTITIONING
REPARTITIONS
REPASSAGES
REPASTURES
REPATCHING
REPATRIATE
REPATRIATED
REPATRIATES
REPATRIATING
REPATRIATION
REPATRIATIONS
REPATRIATOR
REPATRIATORS
REPATTERNED
REPATTERNING
REPATTERNS
REPAYMENTS
REPEALABLE
REPEATABILITIES
REPEATABILITY
REPEATABLE
REPEATEDLY
REPEATINGS
REPECHAGES
REPELLANCE
REPELLANCES
REPELLANCIES
REPELLANCY
REPELLANTLY
REPELLANTS
REPELLENCE
REPELLENCES
REPELLENCIES
REPELLENCY
REPELLENTLY
REPELLENTS
REPELLINGLY
REPENTANCE
REPENTANCES
REPENTANTLY
REPENTANTS
REPENTINGLY
REPEOPLING
REPERCUSSED
REPERCUSSES
REPERCUSSING
REPERCUSSION
REPERCUSSIONS
REPERCUSSIVE
REPERTOIRE
REPERTOIRES
REPERTORIAL
REPERTORIES
REPERUSALS
REPERUSING
REPETITEUR
REPETITEURS
REPETITEUSE
REPETITEUSES
REPETITION
REPETITIONAL
REPETITIONARY
REPETITIONS
REPETITIOUS
REPETITIOUSLY
REPETITIOUSNESS
REPETITIVE
REPETITIVELY
REPETITIVENESS
REPHOTOGRAPH
REPHOTOGRAPHED
REPHOTOGRAPHING
REPHOTOGRAPHS
REPHRASING
REPIGMENTED
REPIGMENTING
REPIGMENTS
REPINEMENT
REPINEMENTS
REPININGLY
REPLACEABILITY
REPLACEABLE
REPLACEMENT
REPLACEMENTS
REPLANNING
REPLANTATION
REPLANTATIONS
REPLANTING
REPLASTERED
REPLASTERING
REPLASTERS
REPLEADERS
REPLEADING
REPLEDGING
REPLENISHABLE
REPLENISHED
REPLENISHER
REPLENISHERS
REPLENISHES
REPLENISHING
REPLENISHMENT
REPLENISHMENTS
REPLETENESS
REPLETENESSES
REPLETIONS
REPLEVIABLE
REPLEVINED
REPLEVINING
REPLEVISABLE
REPLEVYING
REPLICABILITIES
REPLICABILITY
REPLICABLE
REPLICASES
REPLICATED
REPLICATES
REPLICATING
REPLICATION
REPLICATIONS
REPLICATIVE
REPLICATOR
REPLICATORS
REPLOTTING
REPLUMBING
REPLUNGING
REPOINTING
REPOLARISATION
REPOLARISATIONS
REPOLARISE
REPOLARISED
REPOLARISES
REPOLARISING
REPOLARIZATION
REPOLARIZATIONS
REPOLARIZE
REPOLARIZED
REPOLARIZES
REPOLARIZING
REPOLISHED
REPOLISHES
REPOLISHING
REPOPULARISE
REPOPULARISED
REPOPULARISES
REPOPULARISING
REPOPULARIZE
REPOPULARIZED
REPOPULARIZES
REPOPULARIZING
REPOPULATE
REPOPULATED
REPOPULATES
REPOPULATING
REPOPULATION
REPOPULATIONS
REPORTABLE
REPORTAGES
REPORTEDLY
REPORTINGLY
REPORTINGS
REPORTORIAL
REPORTORIALLY
REPOSEDNESS
REPOSEDNESSES
REPOSEFULLY
REPOSEFULNESS
REPOSEFULNESSES
REPOSITING
REPOSITION
REPOSITIONED
REPOSITIONING
REPOSITIONS
REPOSITORIES
REPOSITORS
REPOSITORY
REPOSSESSED
REPOSSESSES
REPOSSESSING
REPOSSESSION
REPOSSESSIONS
REPOSSESSOR
REPOSSESSORS
REPOTTINGS
REPOUSSAGE
REPOUSSAGES
REPOUSSOIR
REPOUSSOIRS
REPOWERING
REPREEVING
REPREHENDABLE
REPREHENDED
REPREHENDER
REPREHENDERS

REPREHENDING
REPREHENDS
REPREHENSIBLE
REPREHENSIBLY
REPREHENSION
REPREHENSIONS
REPREHENSIVE
REPREHENSIVELY
REPREHENSORY
REPRESENTABLE
REPRESENTAMEN
REPRESENTAMENS
REPRESENTANT
REPRESENTANTS
REPRESENTATION
REPRESENTATIONS
REPRESENTATIVE
REPRESENTATIVES
REPRESENTED
REPRESENTEE
REPRESENTEES
REPRESENTER
REPRESENTERS
REPRESENTING
REPRESENTMENT
REPRESENTMENTS
REPRESENTOR
REPRESENTORS
REPRESENTS
REPRESSERS
REPRESSIBILITY
REPRESSIBLE
REPRESSIBLY
REPRESSING
REPRESSION
REPRESSIONIST
REPRESSIONS
REPRESSIVE
REPRESSIVELY
REPRESSIVENESS
REPRESSORS
REPRESSURISE
REPRESSURISED
REPRESSURISES
REPRESSURISING
REPRESSURIZE
REPRESSURIZED
REPRESSURIZES
REPRESSURIZING
REPRIEVABLE
REPRIEVALS
REPRIEVERS
REPRIEVING
REPRIMANDED
REPRIMANDING
REPRIMANDS
REPRINTERS
REPRINTING
REPRISTINATE
REPRISTINATED
REPRISTINATES
REPRISTINATING
REPRISTINATION
REPRISTINATIONS
REPRIVATISATION
REPRIVATISE
REPRIVATISED
REPRIVATISES
REPRIVATISING
REPRIVATIZATION
REPRIVATIZE
REPRIVATIZED
REPRIVATIZES
REPRIVATIZING
REPROACHABLE
REPROACHABLY
REPROACHED
REPROACHER
REPROACHERS
REPROACHES
REPROACHFUL
REPROACHFULLY
REPROACHFULNESS
REPROACHING
REPROACHINGLY
REPROACHLESS
REPROBACIES
REPROBANCE
REPROBANCES
REPROBATED
REPROBATER
REPROBATERS
REPROBATES
REPROBATING
REPROBATION
REPROBATIONARY
REPROBATIONS
REPROBATIVE
REPROBATIVELY
REPROBATOR
REPROBATORS
REPROBATORY
REPROCESSED
REPROCESSES
REPROCESSING
REPRODUCED
REPRODUCER
REPRODUCERS
REPRODUCES
REPRODUCIBILITY
REPRODUCIBLE
REPRODUCIBLES
REPRODUCIBLY
REPRODUCING
REPRODUCTION
REPRODUCTIONS
REPRODUCTIVE
REPRODUCTIVELY
REPRODUCTIVES
REPRODUCTIVITY
REPROGRAMED
REPROGRAMING
REPROGRAMMABLE
REPROGRAMME
REPROGRAMMED
REPROGRAMMES
REPROGRAMMING
REPROGRAMS
REPROGRAPHER
REPROGRAPHERS
REPROGRAPHIC
REPROGRAPHICS
REPROGRAPHIES
REPROGRAPHY
REPROOFING
REPROVABLE
REPROVINGLY
REPROVINGS
REPROVISION
REPROVISIONED
REPROVISIONING
REPROVISIONS
REPTATIONS
REPTILIANLY
REPTILIANS
REPTILIFEROUS
REPTILIOUS
REPUBLICAN
REPUBLICANISE
REPUBLICANISED
REPUBLICANISES
REPUBLICANISING
REPUBLICANISM
REPUBLICANISMS
REPUBLICANIZE
REPUBLICANIZED
REPUBLICANIZES
REPUBLICANIZING
REPUBLICANS
REPUBLICATION
REPUBLICATIONS
REPUBLISHED
REPUBLISHER
REPUBLISHERS
REPUBLISHES
REPUBLISHING
REPUDIABLE
REPUDIATED
REPUDIATES
REPUDIATING
REPUDIATION
REPUDIATIONIST
REPUDIATIONISTS
REPUDIATIONS
REPUDIATIVE
REPUDIATOR
REPUDIATORS
REPUGNANCE
REPUGNANCES
REPUGNANCIES
REPUGNANCY
REPUGNANTLY
REPULSIONS
REPULSIVELY
REPULSIVENESS
REPULSIVENESSES
REPUNCTUATION
REPUNCTUATIONS
REPURCHASE
REPURCHASED
REPURCHASES
REPURCHASING
REPURIFIED
REPURIFIES
REPURIFYING
REPURPOSED
REPURPOSES
REPURPOSING
REPURSUING
REPUTABILITIES
REPUTABILITY
REPUTATION
REPUTATIONAL
REPUTATIONLESS
REPUTATIONS
REPUTATIVE
REPUTATIVELY
REPUTELESS
REQUALIFIED
REQUALIFIES
REQUALIFYING
REQUESTERS
REQUESTING
REQUESTORS
REQUICKENED
REQUICKENING
REQUICKENS
REQUIESCAT
REQUIESCATS
REQUIGHTED
REQUIGHTING
REQUIRABLE
REQUIREMENT
REQUIREMENTS
REQUIRINGS
REQUISITELY
REQUISITENESS
REQUISITENESSES
REQUISITES
REQUISITION
REQUISITIONARY
REQUISITIONED
REQUISITIONING
REQUISITIONIST
REQUISITIONISTS
REQUISITIONS
REQUISITOR
REQUISITORS
REQUISITORY
REQUITABLE
REQUITEFUL
REQUITELESS
REQUITEMENT
REQUITEMENTS
REQUITTING
REQUOYLING
RERADIATED
RERADIATES
RERADIATING
RERADIATION
RERADIATIONS
REREADINGS
REREBRACES
RERECORDED
RERECORDING
REREDORTER
REREDORTERS
REREDOSSES
REREGISTER
REREGISTERED
REREGISTERING
REREGISTERS
REREGISTRATION
REREGISTRATIONS

REREGULATE
REREGULATED
REREGULATES
REREGULATING
REREGULATION
REREGULATIONS
RERELEASED
RERELEASES
RERELEASING
REREMINDED
REREMINDING
REREPEATED
REREPEATING
REREVIEWED
REREVIEWING
REREVISING
REROUTEING
RESADDLING
RESALEABLE
RESALUTING
RESAMPLING
RESCHEDULE
RESCHEDULED
RESCHEDULES
RESCHEDULING
RESCHEDULINGS
RESCHOOLED
RESCHOOLING
RESCINDABLE
RESCINDERS
RESCINDING
RESCINDMENT
RESCINDMENTS
RESCISSIBLE
RESCISSION
RESCISSIONS
RESCISSORY
RESCREENED
RESCREENING
RESCRIPTED
RESCRIPTING
RESCULPTED
RESCULPTING
RESEALABLE
RESEARCHABLE
RESEARCHED
RESEARCHER
RESEARCHERS
RESEARCHES
RESEARCHFUL
RESEARCHING
RESEARCHIST
RESEARCHISTS
RESEASONED
RESEASONING
RESECTABILITIES
RESECTABILITY
RESECTABLE
RESECTIONAL
RESECTIONS
RESECURING
RESEGREGATE
RESEGREGATED
RESEGREGATES
RESEGREGATING
RESEGREGATION
RESEGREGATIONS
RESEIZURES
RESELECTED
RESELECTING
RESELECTION
RESELECTIONS
RESEMBLANCE
RESEMBLANCES
RESEMBLANT
RESEMBLERS
RESEMBLING
RESENSITISE
RESENSITISED
RESENSITISES
RESENSITISING
RESENSITIZE
RESENSITIZED
RESENSITIZES
RESENSITIZING
RESENTENCE
RESENTENCED
RESENTENCES
RESENTENCING
RESENTFULLY
RESENTFULNESS
RESENTFULNESSES
RESENTINGLY
RESENTMENT
RESENTMENTS
RESERPINES
RESERVABLE
RESERVATION
RESERVATIONIST
RESERVATIONISTS
RESERVATIONS
RESERVATORIES
RESERVATORY
RESERVEDLY
RESERVEDNESS
RESERVEDNESSES
RESERVICED
RESERVICES
RESERVICING
RESERVISTS
RESERVOIRED
RESERVOIRING
RESERVOIRS
RESETTABLE
RESETTLEMENT
RESETTLEMENTS
RESETTLING
RESHARPENED
RESHARPENING
RESHARPENS
RESHINGLED
RESHINGLES
RESHINGLING
RESHIPMENT
RESHIPMENTS
RESHIPPERS
RESHIPPING
RESHOOTING
RESHOWERED
RESHOWERING
RESHUFFLED
RESHUFFLES
RESHUFFLING
RESIDENCES
RESIDENCIES
RESIDENTER
RESIDENTERS
RESIDENTIAL
RESIDENTIALLY
RESIDENTIARIES
RESIDENTIARY
RESIDENTSHIP
RESIDENTSHIPS
RESIDUALLY
RESIGHTING
RESIGNATION
RESIGNATIONS
RESIGNEDLY
RESIGNEDNESS
RESIGNEDNESSES
RESIGNMENT
RESIGNMENTS
RESILEMENT
RESILEMENTS
RESILIENCE
RESILIENCES
RESILIENCIES
RESILIENCY
RESILIENTLY
RESILVERED
RESILVERING
RESINATING
RESINIFEROUS
RESINIFICATION
RESINIFICATIONS
RESINIFIED
RESINIFIES
RESINIFYING
RESINISING
RESINIZING
RESINOUSLY
RESINOUSNESS
RESINOUSNESSES
RESIPISCENCE
RESIPISCENCES
RESIPISCENCIES
RESIPISCENCY
RESIPISCENT
RESISTANCE
RESISTANCES
RESISTANTS
RESISTENTS
RESISTIBILITIES
RESISTIBILITY
RESISTIBLE
RESISTIBLY
RESISTINGLY
RESISTIVELY
RESISTIVENESS
RESISTIVENESSES
RESISTIVITIES
RESISTIVITY
RESISTLESS
RESISTLESSLY
RESISTLESSNESS
RESITTINGS
RESITUATED
RESITUATES
RESITUATING
RESKETCHED
RESKETCHES
RESKETCHING
RESKILLING
RESKILLINGS
RESMELTING
RESMOOTHED
RESMOOTHING
RESNATRONS
RESOCIALISATION
RESOCIALISE
RESOCIALISED
RESOCIALISES
RESOCIALISING
RESOCIALIZATION
RESOCIALIZE
RESOCIALIZED
RESOCIALIZES
RESOCIALIZING
RESOFTENED
RESOFTENING
RESOLDERED
RESOLDERING
RESOLIDIFIED
RESOLIDIFIES
RESOLIDIFY
RESOLIDIFYING
RESOLUBILITIES
RESOLUBILITY
RESOLUBLENESS
RESOLUBLENESSES
RESOLUTELY
RESOLUTENESS
RESOLUTENESSES
RESOLUTEST
RESOLUTION
RESOLUTIONER
RESOLUTIONERS
RESOLUTIONIST
RESOLUTIONISTS
RESOLUTIONS
RESOLUTIVE
RESOLVABILITIES
RESOLVABILITY
RESOLVABLE
RESOLVABLENESS
RESOLVEDLY
RESOLVEDNESS
RESOLVEDNESSES
RESOLVENTS
RESONANCES
RESONANTLY
RESONATING
RESONATION
RESONATIONS
RESONATORS
RESORBENCE
RESORBENCES
RESORCINAL
RESORCINOL
RESORCINOLS
RESORPTION
RESORPTIONS
RESORPTIVE
RESOUNDING

RESOUNDINGLY
RESOURCEFUL
RESOURCEFULLY
RESOURCEFULNESS
RESOURCELESS
RESOURCING
RESPEAKING
RESPECIFIED
RESPECIFIES
RESPECIFYING
RESPECTABILISE
RESPECTABILISED
RESPECTABILISES
RESPECTABILITY
RESPECTABILIZE
RESPECTABILIZED
RESPECTABILIZES
RESPECTABLE
RESPECTABLENESS
RESPECTABLES
RESPECTABLY
RESPECTANT
RESPECTERS
RESPECTFUL
RESPECTFULLY
RESPECTFULNESS
RESPECTING
RESPECTIVE
RESPECTIVELY
RESPECTIVENESS
RESPECTLESS
RESPELLING
RESPELLINGS
RESPIRABILITIES
RESPIRABILITY
RESPIRABLE
RESPIRATION
RESPIRATIONAL
RESPIRATIONS
RESPIRATOR
RESPIRATORS
RESPIRATORY
RESPIRITUALISE
RESPIRITUALISED
RESPIRITUALISES
RESPIRITUALIZE
RESPIRITUALIZED
RESPIRITUALIZES
RESPIROMETER
RESPIROMETERS
RESPIROMETRIC
RESPIROMETRIES
RESPIROMETRY
RESPITELESS
RESPLENDED
RESPLENDENCE
RESPLENDENCES
RESPLENDENCIES
RESPLENDENCY
RESPLENDENT
RESPLENDENTLY
RESPLENDING
RESPLICING
RESPLITTING
RESPONDENCE
RESPONDENCES
RESPONDENCIES
RESPONDENCY
RESPONDENT
RESPONDENTIA
RESPONDENTIAS
RESPONDENTS
RESPONDERS
RESPONDING
RESPONSELESS
RESPONSERS
RESPONSIBILITY
RESPONSIBLE
RESPONSIBLENESS
RESPONSIBLY
RESPONSIONS
RESPONSIVE
RESPONSIVELY
RESPONSIVENESS
RESPONSORIAL
RESPONSORIALS
RESPONSORIES
RESPONSORS
RESPONSORY
RESPONSUMS
RESPOOLING
RESPOTTING
RESPRAYING
RESPREADING
RESPRINGING
RESPROUTED
RESPROUTING
RESSALDARS
RESSENTIMENT
RESSENTIMENTS
RESTABILISE
RESTABILISED
RESTABILISES
RESTABILISING
RESTABILIZE
RESTABILIZED
RESTABILIZES
RESTABILIZING
RESTABLING
RESTACKING
RESTAFFING
RESTAMPING
RESTARTABLE
RESTARTERS
RESTARTING
RESTATEMENT
RESTATEMENTS
RESTATIONED
RESTATIONING
RESTATIONS
RESTAURANT
RESTAURANTEUR
RESTAURANTEURS
RESTAURANTS
RESTAURATEUR
RESTAURATEURS
RESTAURATION
RESTAURATIONS
RESTEMMING
RESTFULLER
RESTFULLEST
RESTFULNESS
RESTFULNESSES
RESTHARROW
RESTHARROWS
RESTIMULATE
RESTIMULATED
RESTIMULATES
RESTIMULATING
RESTIMULATION
RESTIMULATIONS
RESTITCHED
RESTITCHES
RESTITCHING
RESTITUTED
RESTITUTES
RESTITUTING
RESTITUTION
RESTITUTIONISM
RESTITUTIONISMS
RESTITUTIONIST
RESTITUTIONISTS
RESTITUTIONS
RESTITUTIVE
RESTITUTOR
RESTITUTORS
RESTITUTORY
RESTIVENESS
RESTIVENESSES
RESTLESSLY
RESTLESSNESS
RESTLESSNESSES
RESTOCKING
RESTORABLE
RESTORABLENESS
RESTORATION
RESTORATIONISM
RESTORATIONISMS
RESTORATIONIST
RESTORATIONISTS
RESTORATIONS
RESTORATIVE
RESTORATIVELY
RESTORATIVES
RESTRAINABLE
RESTRAINED
RESTRAINEDLY
RESTRAINEDNESS
RESTRAINER
RESTRAINERS
RESTRAINING
RESTRAININGS
RESTRAINTS
RESTRENGTHEN
RESTRENGTHENED
RESTRENGTHENING
RESTRENGTHENS
RESTRESSED
RESTRESSES
RESTRESSING
RESTRETCHED
RESTRETCHES
RESTRETCHING
RESTRICKEN
RESTRICTED
RESTRICTEDLY
RESTRICTEDNESS
RESTRICTING
RESTRICTION
RESTRICTIONISM
RESTRICTIONISMS
RESTRICTIONIST
RESTRICTIONISTS
RESTRICTIONS
RESTRICTIVE
RESTRICTIVELY
RESTRICTIVENESS
RESTRICTIVES
RESTRIKING
RESTRINGED
RESTRINGEING
RESTRINGENT
RESTRINGENTS
RESTRINGES
RESTRINGING
RESTRIVING
RESTRUCTURE
RESTRUCTURED
RESTRUCTURES
RESTRUCTURING
RESTRUCTURINGS
RESTUDYING
RESTUFFING
RESTUMPING
RESUBJECTED
RESUBJECTING
RESUBJECTS
RESUBMISSION
RESUBMISSIONS
RESUBMITTED
RESUBMITTING
RESULTANTLY
RESULTANTS
RESULTATIVE
RESULTLESS
RESULTLESSNESS
RESUMMONED
RESUMMONING
RESUMPTION
RESUMPTIONS
RESUMPTIVE
RESUMPTIVELY
RESUPINATE
RESUPINATION
RESUPINATIONS
RESUPPLIED
RESUPPLIES
RESUPPLYING
RESURFACED
RESURFACER
RESURFACERS
RESURFACES
RESURFACING
RESURGENCE
RESURGENCES
RESURRECTED
RESURRECTING
RESURRECTION
RESURRECTIONAL
RESURRECTIONARY
RESURRECTIONISE
RESURRECTIONISM
RESURRECTIONIST
RESURRECTIONIZE

RESURRECTIONS
RESURRECTIVE
RESURRECTOR
RESURRECTORS
RESURRECTS
RESURVEYED
RESURVEYING
RESUSCITABLE
RESUSCITANT
RESUSCITANTS
RESUSCITATE
RESUSCITATED
RESUSCITATES
RESUSCITATING
RESUSCITATION
RESUSCITATIONS
RESUSCITATIVE
RESUSCITATOR
RESUSCITATORS
RESUSPENDED
RESUSPENDING
RESUSPENDS
RESVERATROL
RESVERATROLS
RESWALLOWED
RESWALLOWING
RESWALLOWS
RESYNCHRONISE
RESYNCHRONISED
RESYNCHRONISES
RESYNCHRONISING
RESYNCHRONIZE
RESYNCHRONIZED
RESYNCHRONIZES
RESYNCHRONIZING
RESYNTHESES
RESYNTHESIS
RESYNTHESISE
RESYNTHESISED
RESYNTHESISES
RESYNTHESISING
RESYNTHESIZE
RESYNTHESIZED
RESYNTHESIZES
RESYNTHESIZING
RESYSTEMATISE
RESYSTEMATISED
RESYSTEMATISES
RESYSTEMATISING
RESYSTEMATIZE
RESYSTEMATIZED
RESYSTEMATIZES
RESYSTEMATIZING
RETACKLING
RETAILINGS
RETAILMENT
RETAILMENTS
RETAILORED
RETAILORING
RETAINABLE
RETAINERSHIP
RETAINERSHIPS
RETAINMENT
RETAINMENTS
RETALIATED
RETALIATES
RETALIATING
RETALIATION
RETALIATIONIST
RETALIATIONISTS
RETALIATIONS
RETALIATIVE
RETALIATOR
RETALIATORS
RETALIATORY
RETALLYING
RETARDANTS
RETARDATES
RETARDATION
RETARDATIONS
RETARDATIVE
RETARDATORY
RETARDMENT
RETARDMENTS
RETARGETED
RETARGETING
RETEACHING
RETELLINGS
RETEMPERED
RETEMPERING
RETENTIONIST
RETENTIONISTS
RETENTIONS
RETENTIVELY
RETENTIVENESS
RETENTIVENESSES
RETENTIVITIES
RETENTIVITY
RETESTIFIED
RETESTIFIES
RETESTIFYING
RETEXTURED
RETEXTURES
RETEXTURING
RETHINKERS
RETHINKING
RETHREADED
RETHREADING
RETIARIUSES
RETICELLAS
RETICENCES
RETICENCIES
RETICENTLY
RETICULARLY
RETICULARY
RETICULATE
RETICULATED
RETICULATELY
RETICULATES
RETICULATING
RETICULATION
RETICULATIONS
RETICULOCYTE
RETICULOCYTES
RETICULUMS
RETIGHTENED
RETIGHTENING
RETIGHTENS
RETINACULA
RETINACULAR
RETINACULUM
RETINALITE
RETINALITES
RETINISPORA
RETINISPORAS
RETINITIDES
RETINITISES
RETINOBLASTOMA
RETINOBLASTOMAS
RETINOPATHIES
RETINOPATHY
RETINOSCOPE
RETINOSCOPES
RETINOSCOPIC
RETINOSCOPIES
RETINOSCOPIST
RETINOSCOPISTS
RETINOSCOPY
RETINOSPORA
RETINOSPORAS
RETINOTECTAL
RETIRACIES
RETIREDNESS
RETIREDNESSES
RETIREMENT
RETIREMENTS
RETIRINGLY
RETIRINGNESS
RETIRINGNESSES
RETORSIONS
RETORTIONS
RETOTALING
RETOTALLED
RETOTALLING
RETOUCHABLE
RETOUCHERS
RETOUCHING
RETRACEABLE
RETRACEMENT
RETRACEMENTS
RETRACKING
RETRACTABILITY
RETRACTABLE
RETRACTATION
RETRACTATIONS
RETRACTIBILITY
RETRACTIBLE
RETRACTILE
RETRACTILITIES
RETRACTILITY
RETRACTING
RETRACTION
RETRACTIONS
RETRACTIVE
RETRACTIVELY
RETRACTORS
RETRAINABLE
RETRAINEES
RETRAINING
RETRANSFER
RETRANSFERRED
RETRANSFERRING
RETRANSFERS
RETRANSFORM
RETRANSFORMED
RETRANSFORMING
RETRANSFORMS
RETRANSLATE
RETRANSLATED
RETRANSLATES
RETRANSLATING
RETRANSLATION
RETRANSLATIONS
RETRANSMISSION
RETRANSMISSIONS
RETRANSMIT
RETRANSMITS
RETRANSMITTED
RETRANSMITTING
RETREADING
RETREATANT
RETREATANTS
RETREATERS
RETREATING
RETRENCHABLE
RETRENCHED
RETRENCHES
RETRENCHING
RETRENCHMENT
RETRENCHMENTS
RETRIBUTED
RETRIBUTES
RETRIBUTING
RETRIBUTION
RETRIBUTIONS
RETRIBUTIVE
RETRIBUTIVELY
RETRIBUTOR
RETRIBUTORS
RETRIBUTORY
RETRIEVABILITY
RETRIEVABLE
RETRIEVABLENESS
RETRIEVABLY
RETRIEVALS
RETRIEVEMENT
RETRIEVEMENTS
RETRIEVERS
RETRIEVING
RETRIEVINGS
RETRIMMING
RETROACTED
RETROACTING
RETROACTION
RETROACTIONS
RETROACTIVE
RETROACTIVELY
RETROACTIVENESS
RETROACTIVITIES
RETROACTIVITY
RETROBULBAR
RETROCEDED
RETROCEDENCE
RETROCEDENCES
RETROCEDENT
RETROCEDES
RETROCEDING
RETROCESSION
RETROCESSIONS
RETROCESSIVE
RETROCHOIR
RETROCHOIRS
RETROCOGNITION
RETROCOGNITIONS

RETRODICTED
RETRODICTING
RETRODICTION
RETRODICTIONS
RETRODICTIVE
RETRODICTS
RETROFIRED
RETROFIRES
RETROFIRING
RETROFITTED
RETROFITTING
RETROFITTINGS
RETROFLECTED
RETROFLECTION
RETROFLECTIONS
RETROFLEXED
RETROFLEXES
RETROFLEXION
RETROFLEXIONS
RETROGRADATION
RETROGRADATIONS
RETROGRADE
RETROGRADED
RETROGRADELY
RETROGRADES
RETROGRADING
RETROGRESS
RETROGRESSED
RETROGRESSES
RETROGRESSING
RETROGRESSION
RETROGRESSIONAL
RETROGRESSIONS
RETROGRESSIVE
RETROGRESSIVELY
RETROJECTED
RETROJECTING
RETROJECTION
RETROJECTIONS
RETROJECTS
RETROLENTAL
RETROMINGENCIES
RETROMINGENCY
RETROMINGENT
RETROMINGENTS
RETROPACKS
RETROPERITONEAL
RETROPHILIA
RETROPHILIAC
RETROPHILIACS
RETROPHILIAS
RETROPULSION
RETROPULSIONS
RETROPULSIVE
RETROREFLECTION
RETROREFLECTIVE
RETROREFLECTOR
RETROREFLECTORS
RETROROCKET
RETROROCKETS
RETRORSELY
RETROSEXUAL
RETROSEXUALS
RETROSPECT
RETROSPECTED
RETROSPECTING
RETROSPECTION
RETROSPECTIONS
RETROSPECTIVE
RETROSPECTIVELY
RETROSPECTIVES
RETROSPECTS
RETROUSSAGE
RETROUSSAGES
RETROVERSE
RETROVERSION
RETROVERSIONS
RETROVERTED
RETROVERTING
RETROVERTS
RETROVIRAL
RETROVIRUS
RETROVIRUSES
RETURNABILITIES
RETURNABILITY
RETURNABLE
RETURNABLES
RETURNLESS
RETWISTING
REUNIFICATION
REUNIFICATIONS
REUNIFYING
REUNIONISM
REUNIONISMS
REUNIONIST
REUNIONISTIC
REUNIONISTS
REUNITABLE
REUPHOLSTER
REUPHOLSTERED
REUPHOLSTERING
REUPHOLSTERS
REUSABILITIES
REUSABILITY
REUTILISATION
REUTILISATIONS
REUTILISED
REUTILISES
REUTILISING
REUTILIZATION
REUTILIZATIONS
REUTILIZED
REUTILIZES
REUTILIZING
REUTTERING
REVACCINATE
REVACCINATED
REVACCINATES
REVACCINATING
REVACCINATION
REVACCINATIONS
REVALENTAS
REVALIDATE
REVALIDATED
REVALIDATES
REVALIDATING
REVALIDATION
REVALIDATIONS
REVALORISATION
REVALORISATIONS
REVALORISE
REVALORISED
REVALORISES
REVALORISING
REVALORIZATION
REVALORIZATIONS
REVALORIZE
REVALORIZED
REVALORIZES
REVALORIZING
REVALUATED
REVALUATES
REVALUATING
REVALUATION
REVALUATIONS
REVAMPINGS
REVANCHISM
REVANCHISMS
REVANCHIST
REVANCHISTS
REVARNISHED
REVARNISHES
REVARNISHING
REVEALABILITIES
REVEALABILITY
REVEALABLE
REVEALINGLY
REVEALINGNESS
REVEALINGNESSES
REVEALINGS
REVEALMENT
REVEALMENTS
REVEGETATE
REVEGETATED
REVEGETATES
REVEGETATING
REVEGETATION
REVEGETATIONS
REVELATION
REVELATIONAL
REVELATIONIST
REVELATIONISTS
REVELATIONS
REVELATIVE
REVELATORS
REVELATORY
REVELLINGS
REVELMENTS
REVENDICATE
REVENDICATED
REVENDICATES
REVENDICATING
REVENDICATION
REVENDICATIONS
REVENGEFUL
REVENGEFULLY
REVENGEFULNESS
REVENGELESS
REVENGEMENT
REVENGEMENTS
REVENGINGLY
REVENGINGS
REVERBERANT
REVERBERANTLY
REVERBERATE
REVERBERATED
REVERBERATES
REVERBERATING
REVERBERATION
REVERBERATIONS
REVERBERATIVE
REVERBERATOR
REVERBERATORIES
REVERBERATORS
REVERBERATORY
REVERENCED
REVERENCER
REVERENCERS
REVERENCES
REVERENCING
REVERENTIAL
REVERENTIALLY
REVERENTLY
REVERENTNESS
REVERENTNESSES
REVERIFIED
REVERIFIES
REVERIFYING
REVERSEDLY
REVERSELESS
REVERSIBILITIES
REVERSIBILITY
REVERSIBLE
REVERSIBLES
REVERSIBLY
REVERSINGS
REVERSIONAL
REVERSIONALLY
REVERSIONARIES
REVERSIONARY
REVERSIONER
REVERSIONERS
REVERSIONS
REVERSISES
REVERTANTS
REVERTIBLE
REVESTIARIES
REVESTIARY
REVESTRIES
REVETMENTS
REVIBRATED
REVIBRATES
REVIBRATING
REVICTUALED
REVICTUALING
REVICTUALLED
REVICTUALLING
REVICTUALS
REVIEWABLE
REVILEMENT
REVILEMENTS
REVILINGLY
REVINDICATE
REVINDICATED
REVINDICATES
REVINDICATING
REVINDICATION
REVINDICATIONS
REVIOLATED
REVIOLATES
REVIOLATING
REVISIONAL
REVISIONARY
REVISIONISM

REVISIONISMS
REVISIONIST
REVISIONISTS
REVISITANT
REVISITANTS
REVISITATION
REVISITATIONS
REVISITING
REVISUALISATION
REVISUALIZATION
REVITALISATION
REVITALISATIONS
REVITALISE
REVITALISED
REVITALISES
REVITALISING
REVITALIZATION
REVITALIZATIONS
REVITALIZE
REVITALIZED
REVITALIZES
REVITALIZING
REVIVABILITIES
REVIVABILITY
REVIVALISM
REVIVALISMS
REVIVALIST
REVIVALISTIC
REVIVALISTS
REVIVEMENT
REVIVEMENTS
REVIVESCENCE
REVIVESCENCES
REVIVESCENCIES
REVIVESCENCY
REVIVESCENT
REVIVIFICATION
REVIVIFICATIONS
REVIVIFIED
REVIVIFIES
REVIVIFYING
REVIVINGLY
REVIVISCENCE
REVIVISCENCES
REVIVISCENCIES
REVIVISCENCY
REVIVISCENT
REVOCABILITIES
REVOCABILITY
REVOCABLENESS
REVOCABLENESSES
REVOCATION
REVOCATIONS
REVOCATORY
REVOKABILITY
REVOKEMENT
REVOKEMENTS
REVOLTINGLY
REVOLUTION
REVOLUTIONAL
REVOLUTIONARIES
REVOLUTIONARILY
REVOLUTIONARY
REVOLUTIONER
REVOLUTIONERS
REVOLUTIONISE
REVOLUTIONISED
REVOLUTIONISER
REVOLUTIONISERS
REVOLUTIONISES
REVOLUTIONISING
REVOLUTIONISM
REVOLUTIONISMS
REVOLUTIONIST
REVOLUTIONISTS
REVOLUTIONIZE
REVOLUTIONIZED
REVOLUTIONIZER
REVOLUTIONIZERS
REVOLUTIONIZES
REVOLUTIONIZING
REVOLUTIONS
REVOLVABLE
REVOLVABLY
REVOLVENCIES
REVOLVENCY
REVOLVINGLY
REVOLVINGS
REVULSIONARY
REVULSIONS
REVULSIVELY
REVULSIVES
REWAKENING
REWARDABLE
REWARDABLENESS
REWARDINGLY
REWARDLESS
REWEIGHING
REWIDENING
REWRAPPING
RHABDOCOELE
RHABDOCOELES
RHABDOLITH
RHABDOLITHS
RHABDOMANCER
RHABDOMANCERS
RHABDOMANCIES
RHABDOMANCY
RHABDOMANTIST
RHABDOMANTISTS
RHABDOMERE
RHABDOMERES
RHABDOMYOMA
RHABDOMYOMAS
RHABDOMYOMATA
RHABDOSPHERE
RHABDOSPHERES
RHABDOVIRUS
RHABDOVIRUSES
RHACHIDIAL
RHACHILLAS
RHACHITISES
RHADAMANTHINE
RHAGADIFORM
RHAMNACEOUS
RHAMPHOTHECA
RHAMPHOTHECAE
RHAPONTICS
RHAPSODICAL
RHAPSODICALLY
RHAPSODIES
RHAPSODISE
RHAPSODISED
RHAPSODISES
RHAPSODISING
RHAPSODIST
RHAPSODISTIC
RHAPSODISTS
RHAPSODIZE
RHAPSODIZED
RHAPSODIZES
RHAPSODIZING
RHEOCHORDS
RHEOLOGICAL
RHEOLOGICALLY
RHEOLOGIES
RHEOLOGIST
RHEOLOGISTS
RHEOMETERS
RHEOMETRIC
RHEOMETRICAL
RHEOMETRIES
RHEOMORPHIC
RHEOMORPHISM
RHEOMORPHISMS
RHEOPHILES
RHEORECEPTOR
RHEORECEPTORS
RHEOSTATIC
RHEOTACTIC
RHEOTROPES
RHEOTROPIC
RHEOTROPISM
RHEOTROPISMS
RHETORICAL
RHETORICALLY
RHETORICIAN
RHETORICIANS
RHETORISED
RHETORISES
RHETORISING
RHETORIZED
RHETORIZES
RHETORIZING
RHEUMATEESE
RHEUMATEESES
RHEUMATICAL
RHEUMATICALLY
RHEUMATICKY
RHEUMATICS
RHEUMATISE
RHEUMATISES
RHEUMATISM
RHEUMATISMAL
RHEUMATISMS
RHEUMATIZE
RHEUMATIZES
RHEUMATOID
RHEUMATOIDALLY
RHEUMATOLOGICAL
RHEUMATOLOGIES
RHEUMATOLOGIST
RHEUMATOLOGISTS
RHEUMATOLOGY
RHIGOLENES
RHINENCEPHALA
RHINENCEPHALIC
RHINENCEPHALON
RHINENCEPHALONS
RHINESTONE
RHINESTONED
RHINESTONES
RHINITIDES
RHINITISES
RHINOCERICAL
RHINOCEROS
RHINOCEROSES
RHINOCEROT
RHINOCEROTE
RHINOCEROTES
RHINOCEROTIC
RHINOLALIA
RHINOLALIAS
RHINOLITHS
RHINOLOGICAL
RHINOLOGIES
RHINOLOGIST
RHINOLOGISTS
RHINOPHYMA
RHINOPHYMAS
RHINOPLASTIC
RHINOPLASTIES
RHINOPLASTY
RHINORRHAGIA
RHINORRHAGIAS
RHINORRHOEA
RHINORRHOEAL
RHINORRHOEAS
RHINOSCLEROMA
RHINOSCLEROMAS
RHINOSCLEROMATA
RHINOSCOPE
RHINOSCOPES
RHINOSCOPIC
RHINOSCOPIES
RHINOSCOPY
RHINOTHECA
RHINOTHECAE
RHINOVIRUS
RHINOVIRUSES
RHIPIDIONS
RHIPIDIUMS
RHIZANTHOUS
RHIZOCARPIC
RHIZOCARPOUS
RHIZOCARPS
RHIZOCAULS
RHIZOCEPHALAN
RHIZOCEPHALANS
RHIZOCEPHALOUS
RHIZOCTONIA
RHIZOCTONIAS
RHIZOGENETIC
RHIZOGENIC
RHIZOGENOUS
RHIZOMATOUS
RHIZOMORPH
RHIZOMORPHOUS
RHIZOMORPHS
RHIZOPHAGOUS
RHIZOPHILOUS
RHIZOPHORE
RHIZOPHORES
RHIZOPLANE

RHIZOPLANES
RHIZOPODAN
RHIZOPODANS
RHIZOPODOUS
RHIZOPUSES
RHIZOSPHERE
RHIZOSPHERES
RHIZOTOMIES
RHODAMINES
RHODANATES
RHODANISED
RHODANISES
RHODANISING
RHODANIZED
RHODANIZES
RHODANIZING
RHODOCHROSITE
RHODOCHROSITES
RHODODAPHNE
RHODODAPHNES
RHODODENDRON
RHODODENDRONS
RHODOLITES
RHODOMONTADE
RHODOMONTADED
RHODOMONTADES
RHODOMONTADING
RHODONITES
RHODOPHANE
RHODOPHANES
RHODOPSINS
RHOEADINES
RHOICISSUS
RHOICISSUSES
RHOMBENCEPHALA
RHOMBENCEPHALON
RHOMBENPORPHYR
RHOMBENPORPHYRS
RHOMBENPORPHYRY
RHOMBOHEDRA
RHOMBOHEDRAL
RHOMBOHEDRON
RHOMBOHEDRONS
RHOMBOIDAL
RHOMBOIDEI
RHOMBOIDES
RHOMBOIDEUS
RHOMBPORPHYRIES
RHOMBPORPHYRY
RHOPALISMS
RHOPALOCERAL
RHOPALOCEROUS
RHOTACISED
RHOTACISES
RHOTACISING
RHOTACISMS
RHOTACISTIC
RHOTACISTS
RHOTACIZED
RHOTACIZES
RHOTACIZING
RHOTICITIES
RHUBARBING
RHUBARBINGS
RHUMBATRON
RHUMBATRONS

RHYMESTERS
RHYNCHOCOEL
RHYNCHOCOELS
RHYNCHODONT
RHYNCHOPHORE
RHYNCHOPHORES
RHYNCHOPHOROUS
RHYPAROGRAPHER
RHYPAROGRAPHERS
RHYPAROGRAPHIC
RHYPAROGRAPHIES
RHYPAROGRAPHY
RHYTHMICAL
RHYTHMICALLY
RHYTHMICITIES
RHYTHMICITY
RHYTHMISATION
RHYTHMISATIONS
RHYTHMISED
RHYTHMISES
RHYTHMISING
RHYTHMISTS
RHYTHMIZATION
RHYTHMIZATIONS
RHYTHMIZED
RHYTHMIZES
RHYTHMIZING
RHYTHMLESS
RHYTHMOMETER
RHYTHMOMETERS
RHYTHMOPOEIA
RHYTHMOPOEIAS
RHYTHMUSES
RHYTIDECTOMIES
RHYTIDECTOMY
RHYTIDOMES
RIBALDRIES
RIBATTUTAS
RIBAUDRIES
RIBAVIRINS
RIBBONFISH
RIBBONFISHES
RIBBONLIKE
RIBBONRIES
RIBBONWOOD
RIBBONWOODS
RIBGRASSES
RIBOFLAVIN
RIBOFLAVINE
RIBOFLAVINES
RIBOFLAVINS
RIBONUCLEASE
RIBONUCLEASES
RIBONUCLEIC
RIBONUCLEOSIDE
RIBONUCLEOSIDES
RIBONUCLEOTIDE
RIBONUCLEOTIDES
RICERCARES
RICERCATAS
RICHNESSES
RICINOLEIC
RICKBURNER
RICKBURNERS
RICKETIEST
RICKETINESS

RICKETINESSES
RICKETTIER
RICKETTIEST
RICKETTSIA
RICKETTSIAE
RICKETTSIAL
RICKETTSIAS
RICKSTANDS
RICKSTICKS
RICOCHETED
RICOCHETING
RICOCHETTED
RICOCHETTING
RIDABILITIES
RIDABILITY
RIDDLINGLY
RIDERSHIPS
RIDGEBACKS
RIDGELINES
RIDGELINGS
RIDGEPOLES
RIDGETREES
RIDICULERS
RIDICULING
RIDICULOUS
RIDICULOUSLY
RIDICULOUSNESS
RIEBECKITE
RIEBECKITES
RIFACIMENTI
RIFACIMENTO
RIFAMPICIN
RIFAMPICINS
RIFAMYCINS
RIFENESSES
RIFLEBIRDS
RIGAMAROLE
RIGAMAROLES
RIGHTABLENESS
RIGHTABLENESSES
RIGHTENING
RIGHTEOUSLY
RIGHTEOUSNESS
RIGHTEOUSNESSES
RIGHTFULLY
RIGHTFULNESS
RIGHTFULNESSES
RIGHTNESSES
RIGHTSIZED
RIGHTSIZES
RIGHTSIZING
RIGHTWARDS
RIGIDIFICATION
RIGIDIFICATIONS
RIGIDIFIED
RIGIDIFIES
RIGIDIFYING
RIGIDISING
RIGIDITIES
RIGIDIZING
RIGIDNESSES
RIGMAROLES
RIGORISTIC
RIGOROUSLY
RIGOROUSNESS
RIGOROUSNESSES

RIGSDALERS
RIGWIDDIES
RIGWOODIES
RIJKSDAALER
RIJKSDAALERS
RIJSTAFELS
RIJSTTAFEL
RIJSTTAFELS
RIMINESSES
RIMOSITIES
RINDERPEST
RINDERPESTS
RINFORZANDO
RINGBARKED
RINGBARKING
RINGHALSES
RINGLEADER
RINGLEADERS
RINGMASTER
RINGMASTERS
RINGSIDERS
RINGSTANDS
RINGSTRAKED
RINGTOSSES
RINKHALSES
RINSABILITIES
RINSABILITY
RINSIBILITIES
RINSIBILITY
RINTHEREOUT
RINTHEREOUTS
RIOTOUSNESS
RIOTOUSNESSES
RIPENESSES
RIPIDOLITE
RIPIDOLITES
RIPIENISTS
RIPPLINGLY
RIPRAPPING
RIPSNORTER
RIPSNORTERS
RIPSNORTING
RISIBILITIES
RISIBILITY
RISKINESSES
RISORGIMENTO
RISORGIMENTOS
RITARDANDO
RITARDANDOS
RITONAVIRS
RITORNELLE
RITORNELLES
RITORNELLI
RITORNELLO
RITORNELLOS
RITORNELLS
RITOURNELLE
RITOURNELLES
RITUALISATION
RITUALISATIONS
RITUALISED
RITUALISES
RITUALISING
RITUALISMS
RITUALISTIC
RITUALISTICALLY

RITUALISTS
RITUALIZATION
RITUALIZATIONS
RITUALIZED
RITUALIZES
RITUALIZING
RITZINESSES
RIVALESSES
RIVALISING
RIVALITIES
RIVALIZING
RIVALSHIPS
RIVERBANKS
RIVERBOATS
RIVERCRAFT
RIVERCRAFTS
RIVERFRONT
RIVERFRONTS
RIVERHEADS
RIVERSCAPE
RIVERSCAPES
RIVERSIDES
RIVERWARDS
RIVERWEEDS
RIVERWORTHINESS
RIVERWORTHY
RIVETINGLY
ROADABILITIES
ROADABILITY
ROADBLOCKED
ROADBLOCKING
ROADBLOCKS
ROADCRAFTS
ROADHEADER
ROADHEADERS
ROADHOLDING
ROADHOLDINGS
ROADHOUSES
ROADROLLER
ROADROLLERS
ROADRUNNER
ROADRUNNERS
ROADSTEADS
ROADWORTHINESS
ROADWORTHY
ROBERDSMAN
ROBERDSMEN
ROBERTSMAN
ROBERTSMEN
ROBORATING
ROBOTICALLY
ROBOTISATION
ROBOTISATIONS
ROBOTISING
ROBOTIZATION
ROBOTIZATIONS
ROBOTIZING
ROBUSTIOUS
ROBUSTIOUSLY
ROBUSTIOUSNESS
ROBUSTNESS
ROBUSTNESSES
ROCAMBOLES
ROCKABILLIES
ROCKABILLY
ROCKCRESSES
ROCKETEERS
ROCKETRIES
ROCKFISHES
ROCKHOPPER
ROCKHOPPERS
ROCKHOUNDING
ROCKHOUNDINGS
ROCKHOUNDS
ROCKINESSES
ROCKSHAFTS
ROCKSLIDES
ROCKSTEADIES
ROCKSTEADY
ROCKWATERS
RODENTICIDE
RODENTICIDES
RODFISHERS
RODFISHING
RODFISHINGS
RODGERSIAS
RODOMONTADE
RODOMONTADED
RODOMONTADER
RODOMONTADERS
RODOMONTADES
RODOMONTADING
ROENTGENISATION
ROENTGENISE
ROENTGENISED
ROENTGENISES
ROENTGENISING
ROENTGENIZATION
ROENTGENIZE
ROENTGENIZED
ROENTGENIZES
ROENTGENIZING
ROENTGENOGRAM
ROENTGENOGRAMS
ROENTGENOGRAPH
ROENTGENOGRAPHS
ROENTGENOGRAPHY
ROENTGENOLOGIC
ROENTGENOLOGIES
ROENTGENOLOGIST
ROENTGENOLOGY
ROENTGENOPAQUE
ROENTGENOSCOPE
ROENTGENOSCOPES
ROENTGENOSCOPIC
ROENTGENOSCOPY
ROGUESHIPS
ROGUISHNESS
ROGUISHNESSES
ROISTERERS
ROISTERING
ROISTERINGS
ROISTEROUS
ROISTEROUSLY
ROLLCOLLAR
ROLLCOLLARS
ROLLERBALL
ROLLERBALLS
ROLLERBLADE
ROLLERBLADED
ROLLERBLADER
ROLLERBLADERS
ROLLERBLADES
ROLLERBLADING
ROLLERBLADINGS
ROLLERCOASTER
ROLLERCOASTERED
ROLLERCOASTERS
ROLLICKING
ROLLICKINGS
ROLLOCKING
ROLLOCKINGS
ROMANCICAL
ROMANCINGS
ROMANICITE
ROMANICITES
ROMANISATION
ROMANISATIONS
ROMANISING
ROMANIZATION
ROMANIZATIONS
ROMANIZING
ROMANTICAL
ROMANTICALITIES
ROMANTICALITY
ROMANTICALLY
ROMANTICISATION
ROMANTICISE
ROMANTICISED
ROMANTICISES
ROMANTICISING
ROMANTICISM
ROMANTICISMS
ROMANTICIST
ROMANTICISTS
ROMANTICIZATION
ROMANTICIZE
ROMANTICIZED
ROMANTICIZES
ROMANTICIZING
ROMELDALES
ROMPISHNESS
ROMPISHNESSES
RONDOLETTO
RONDOLETTOS
RONTGENISATION
RONTGENISATIONS
RONTGENISE
RONTGENISED
RONTGENISES
RONTGENISING
RONTGENIZATION
RONTGENIZATIONS
RONTGENIZE
RONTGENIZED
RONTGENIZES
RONTGENIZING
RONTGENOGRAM
RONTGENOGRAMS
RONTGENOGRAPH
RONTGENOGRAPHS
RONTGENOGRAPHY
RONTGENOLOGICAL
RONTGENOLOGIES
RONTGENOLOGIST
RONTGENOLOGISTS
RONTGENOLOGY
RONTGENOPAQUE
RONTGENOSCOPE
RONTGENOSCOPES
RONTGENOSCOPIC
RONTGENOSCOPIES
RONTGENOSCOPY
RONTGENOTHERAPY
ROOFLESSNESS
ROOFLESSNESSES
ROOFSCAPES
ROOMINESSES
ROOTEDNESS
ROOTEDNESSES
ROOTINESSES
ROOTLESSNESS
ROOTLESSNESSES
ROOTSERVER
ROOTSERVERS
ROOTSINESS
ROOTSINESSES
ROOTSTALKS
ROOTSTOCKS
ROPEDANCER
ROPEDANCERS
ROPEDANCING
ROPEDANCINGS
ROPEWALKER
ROPEWALKERS
ROPINESSES
ROQUELAURE
ROQUELAURES
ROSANILINE
ROSANILINES
ROSANILINS
ROSEBUSHES
ROSEFINCHES
ROSEFISHES
ROSEMALING
ROSEMALINGS
ROSEMARIES
ROSEWATERS
ROSINESSES
ROSINWEEDS
ROSMARINES
ROSTELLATE
ROSTELLUMS
ROSTERINGS
ROSTROCARINATE
ROSTROCARINATES
ROTACHUTES
ROTAMETERS
ROTAPLANES
ROTATIONAL
ROTATIVELY
ROTAVATING
ROTAVATORS
ROTAVIRUSES
ROTGRASSES
ROTIFERANS
ROTIFEROUS
ROTISSERIE
ROTISSERIES
ROTOGRAPHED
ROTOGRAPHING
ROTOGRAPHS
ROTOGRAVURE
ROTOGRAVURES

ROTORCRAFT
ROTORCRAFTS
ROTOTILLED
ROTOTILLER
ROTOTILLERS
ROTOTILLING
ROTOVATING
ROTOVATORS
ROTTENNESS
ROTTENNESSES
ROTTENSTONE
ROTTENSTONED
ROTTENSTONES
ROTTENSTONING
ROTTWEILER
ROTTWEILERS
ROTUNDITIES
ROTUNDNESS
ROTUNDNESSES
ROUGHBACKS
ROUGHCASTED
ROUGHCASTER
ROUGHCASTERS
ROUGHCASTING
ROUGHCASTS
ROUGHDRIED
ROUGHDRIES
ROUGHDRYING
ROUGHENING
ROUGHHEWED
ROUGHHEWING
ROUGHHOUSE
ROUGHHOUSED
ROUGHHOUSES
ROUGHHOUSING
ROUGHNECKED
ROUGHNECKING
ROUGHNECKS
ROUGHNESSES
ROUGHRIDER
ROUGHRIDERS
ROULETTING
ROUNCEVALS
ROUNDABOUT
ROUNDABOUTATION
ROUNDABOUTED
ROUNDABOUTEDLY
ROUNDABOUTILITY
ROUNDABOUTING
ROUNDABOUTLY
ROUNDABOUTNESS
ROUNDABOUTS
ROUNDARCHED
ROUNDBALLS
ROUNDEDNESS
ROUNDEDNESSES
ROUNDELAYS
ROUNDHANDS
ROUNDHEADED
ROUNDHEADEDNESS
ROUNDHEELS
ROUNDHOUSE
ROUNDHOUSES
ROUNDNESSES
ROUNDTABLE
ROUNDTABLES
ROUNDTRIPPING
ROUNDTRIPPINGS
ROUNDTRIPS
ROUNDWOODS
ROUNDWORMS
ROUSEABOUT
ROUSEABOUTS
ROUSEDNESS
ROUSEDNESSES
ROUSEMENTS
ROUSSETTES
ROUSTABOUT
ROUSTABOUTS
ROUTEMARCH
ROUTEMARCHED
ROUTEMARCHES
ROUTEMARCHING
ROUTINEERS
ROUTINISATION
ROUTINISATIONS
ROUTINISED
ROUTINISES
ROUTINISING
ROUTINISMS
ROUTINISTS
ROUTINIZATION
ROUTINIZATIONS
ROUTINIZED
ROUTINIZES
ROUTINIZING
ROWANBERRIES
ROWANBERRY
ROWDINESSES
ROYALISING
ROYALISTIC
ROYALIZING
ROYALMASTS
ROYSTERERS
ROYSTERING
ROYSTEROUS
RUBBERIEST
RUBBERISED
RUBBERISES
RUBBERISING
RUBBERIZED
RUBBERIZES
RUBBERIZING
RUBBERLIKE
RUBBERNECK
RUBBERNECKED
RUBBERNECKER
RUBBERNECKERS
RUBBERNECKING
RUBBERNECKS
RUBBERWEAR
RUBBERWEARS
RUBBISHING
RUBBLEWORK
RUBBLEWORKS
RUBEFACIENT
RUBEFACIENTS
RUBEFACTION
RUBEFACTIONS
RUBELLITES
RUBESCENCE
RUBESCENCES
RUBIACEOUS
RUBICELLES
RUBICONING
RUBICUNDITIES
RUBICUNDITY
RUBIGINOSE
RUBIGINOUS
RUBRICALLY
RUBRICATED
RUBRICATES
RUBRICATING
RUBRICATION
RUBRICATIONS
RUBRICATOR
RUBRICATORS
RUBRICIANS
RUBYTHROAT
RUBYTHROATS
RUCTATIONS
RUDBECKIAS
RUDDERHEAD
RUDDERHEADS
RUDDERLESS
RUDDERPOST
RUDDERPOSTS
RUDDERSTOCK
RUDDERSTOCKS
RUDDINESSES
RUDENESSES
RUDIMENTAL
RUDIMENTALLY
RUDIMENTARILY
RUDIMENTARINESS
RUDIMENTARY
RUEFULNESS
RUEFULNESSES
RUFESCENCE
RUFESCENCES
RUFFIANING
RUFFIANISH
RUFFIANISM
RUFFIANISMS
RUGGEDISATION
RUGGEDISATIONS
RUGGEDISED
RUGGEDISES
RUGGEDISING
RUGGEDIZATION
RUGGEDIZATIONS
RUGGEDIZED
RUGGEDIZES
RUGGEDIZING
RUGGEDNESS
RUGGEDNESSES
RUGOSITIES
RUINATIONS
RUINOUSNESS
RUINOUSNESSES
RULERSHIPS
RUMBLEDETHUMP
RUMBLEDETHUMPS
RUMBLEGUMPTION
RUMBLEGUMPTIONS
RUMBLINGLY
RUMBULLION
RUMBULLIONS
RUMBUSTICAL
RUMBUSTIOUS
RUMBUSTIOUSLY
RUMBUSTIOUSNESS
RUMELGUMPTION
RUMELGUMPTIONS
RUMFUSTIAN
RUMFUSTIANS
RUMGUMPTION
RUMGUMPTIONS
RUMINANTLY
RUMINATING
RUMINATINGLY
RUMINATION
RUMINATIONS
RUMINATIVE
RUMINATIVELY
RUMINATORS
RUMLEGUMPTION
RUMLEGUMPTIONS
RUMMELGUMPTION
RUMMELGUMPTIONS
RUMMINESSES
RUMMLEGUMPTION
RUMMLEGUMPTIONS
RUMORMONGER
RUMORMONGERING
RUMORMONGERINGS
RUMORMONGERS
RUMRUNNERS
RUNAROUNDS
RUNECRAFTS
RUNNINESSES
RUNTINESSES
RUPESTRIAN
RUPICOLINE
RUPICOLOUS
RUPTURABLE
RUPTUREWORT
RUPTUREWORTS
RURALISATION
RURALISATIONS
RURALISING
RURALITIES
RURALIZATION
RURALIZATIONS
RURALIZING
RURALNESSES
RURIDECANAL
RUSHINESSES
RUSHLIGHTS
RUSSETINGS
RUSSETTING
RUSSETTINGS
RUSSIFYING
RUSTBUCKET
RUSTICALLY
RUSTICATED
RUSTICATES
RUSTICATING
RUSTICATION
RUSTICATIONS
RUSTICATOR
RUSTICATORS
RUSTICISED
RUSTICISES

RUSTICISING
RUSTICISMS
RUSTICITIES
RUSTICIZED
RUSTICIZES
RUSTICIZING
RUSTICWORK
RUSTICWORKS
RUSTINESSES
RUSTLINGLY
RUSTPROOFED
RUSTPROOFING
RUSTPROOFS
RUTHENIOUS
RUTHENIUMS
RUTHERFORD
RUTHERFORDIUM
RUTHERFORDIUMS
RUTHERFORDS
RUTHFULNESS
RUTHFULNESSES
RUTHLESSLY
RUTHLESSNESS
RUTHLESSNESSES
RUTTINESSES
RUTTISHNESS
RUTTISHNESSES
RYBAUDRYES
RYEGRASSES

Ss

SABADILLAS
SABBATARIAN
SABBATICAL
SABBATICALS
SABBATISED
SABBATISES
SABBATISING
SABBATISMS
SABBATIZED
SABBATIZES
SABBATIZING
SABERMETRICIAN
SABERMETRICIANS
SABERMETRICS
SABLEFISHES
SABOTAGING
SABRETACHE
SABRETACHES
SABULOSITIES
SABULOSITY
SABURRATION
SABURRATIONS
SACAHUISTA
SACAHUISTAS
SACAHUISTE
SACAHUISTES
SACCADICALLY
SACCHARASE
SACCHARASES
SACCHARATE
SACCHARATED
SACCHARATES
SACCHARIDE
SACCHARIDES
SACCHARIFEROUS
SACCHARIFIED
SACCHARIFIES
SACCHARIFY
SACCHARIFYING
SACCHARIMETER
SACCHARIMETERS
SACCHARIMETRIES
SACCHARIMETRY
SACCHARINE
SACCHARINELY
SACCHARINES
SACCHARINITIES
SACCHARINITY
SACCHARINS
SACCHARISATION
SACCHARISATIONS
SACCHARISE
SACCHARISED
SACCHARISES
SACCHARISING
SACCHARIZATION
SACCHARIZATIONS
SACCHARIZE
SACCHARIZED
SACCHARIZES
SACCHARIZING
SACCHAROID
SACCHAROIDAL
SACCHAROIDS
SACCHAROMETER
SACCHAROMETERS
SACCHAROMYCES
SACCHAROMYCETES
SACCHAROSE
SACCHAROSES
SACCHARUMS
SACCULATED
SACCULATION
SACCULATIONS
SACCULIFORM
SACERDOTAL
SACERDOTALISE
SACERDOTALISED
SACERDOTALISES
SACERDOTALISING
SACERDOTALISM
SACERDOTALISMS
SACERDOTALIST
SACERDOTALISTS
SACERDOTALIZE
SACERDOTALIZED
SACERDOTALIZES
SACERDOTALIZING
SACERDOTALLY
SACHEMDOMS
SACHEMSHIP
SACHEMSHIPS
SACKCLOTHS
SACRALGIAS
SACRALISATION
SACRALISATIONS
SACRALISED
SACRALISES
SACRALISING
SACRALIZATION
SACRALIZATIONS
SACRALIZED
SACRALIZES
SACRALIZING
SACRAMENTAL
SACRAMENTALISM
SACRAMENTALISMS
SACRAMENTALIST
SACRAMENTALISTS
SACRAMENTALITY
SACRAMENTALLY
SACRAMENTALNESS
SACRAMENTALS
SACRAMENTARIAN
SACRAMENTARIES
SACRAMENTARY
SACRAMENTED
SACRAMENTING
SACRAMENTS
SACREDNESS
SACREDNESSES
SACRIFICEABLE
SACRIFICED
SACRIFICER
SACRIFICERS
SACRIFICES
SACRIFICIAL
SACRIFICIALLY
SACRIFICING
SACRIFYING
SACRILEGES
SACRILEGIOUS
SACRILEGIOUSLY
SACRILEGIST
SACRILEGISTS
SACRISTANS
SACRISTIES
SACROCOCCYGEAL
SACROCOSTAL
SACROCOSTALS
SACROILIAC
SACROILIACS
SACROILIITIS
SACROILIITISES
SACROSANCT
SACROSANCTITIES
SACROSANCTITY
SACROSANCTNESS
SADDLEBACK
SADDLEBACKED
SADDLEBACKS
SADDLEBAGS

SADDLEBILL
SADDLEBILLS
SADDLEBOWS
SADDLEBRED
SADDLEBREDS
SADDLECLOTH
SADDLECLOTHS
SADDLELESS
SADDLERIES
SADDLEROOM
SADDLEROOMS
SADDLETREE
SADDLETREES
SADISTICALLY
SADOMASOCHISM
SADOMASOCHISMS
SADOMASOCHIST
SADOMASOCHISTIC
SADOMASOCHISTS
SAFECRACKER
SAFECRACKERS
SAFECRACKING
SAFECRACKINGS
SAFEGUARDED
SAFEGUARDING
SAFEGUARDS
SAFEKEEPING
SAFEKEEPINGS
SAFELIGHTS
SAFENESSES
SAFFLOWERS
SAFRANINES
SAGACIOUSLY
SAGACIOUSNESS
SAGACIOUSNESSES
SAGACITIES
SAGANASHES
SAGAPENUMS
SAGEBRUSHES
SAGENESSES
SAGINATING
SAGINATION
SAGINATIONS
SAGITTALLY
SAGITTARIAN
SAGITTARIANS
SAGITTARIES
SAGITTIFORM
SAILBOARDED
SAILBOARDER
SAILBOARDERS
SAILBOARDING
SAILBOARDINGS
SAILBOARDS
SAILBOATER
SAILBOATERS
SAILBOATING
SAILBOATINGS
SAILCLOTHS
SAILFISHES
SAILMAKERS
SAILORINGS
SAILORLESS
SAILORLIKE
SAILPLANED
SAILPLANER
SAILPLANERS
SAILPLANES
SAILPLANING
SAINTESSES
SAINTFOINS
SAINTHOODS
SAINTLIEST
SAINTLINESS
SAINTLINESSES
SAINTLINGS
SAINTPAULIA
SAINTPAULIAS
SAINTSHIPS
SALABILITIES
SALABILITY
SALABLENESS
SALABLENESSES
SALACIOUSLY
SALACIOUSNESS
SALACIOUSNESSES
SALACITIES
SALAMANDER
SALAMANDERS
SALAMANDRIAN
SALAMANDRINE
SALAMANDROID
SALAMANDROIDS
SALANGANES
SALBUTAMOL
SALBUTAMOLS
SALEABILITIES
SALEABILITY
SALEABLENESS
SALEABLENESSES
SALERATUSES
SALESCLERK
SALESCLERKS
SALESGIRLS
SALESLADIES
SALESMANSHIP
SALESMANSHIPS
SALESPEOPLE
SALESPERSON
SALESPERSONS
SALESROOMS
SALESWOMAN
SALESWOMEN
SALIAUNCES
SALICACEOUS
SALICETUMS
SALICIONAL
SALICIONALS
SALICORNIA
SALICORNIAS
SALICYLAMIDE
SALICYLAMIDES
SALICYLATE
SALICYLATED
SALICYLATES
SALICYLATING
SALICYLISM
SALICYLISMS
SALIENCIES
SALIENTIAN
SALIENTIANS
SALIFEROUS
SALIFIABLE
SALIFICATION
SALIFICATIONS
SALIMETERS
SALIMETRIC
SALIMETRIES
SALINISATION
SALINISATIONS
SALINISING
SALINITIES
SALINIZATION
SALINIZATIONS
SALINIZING
SALINOMETER
SALINOMETERS
SALINOMETRIC
SALINOMETRIES
SALINOMETRY
SALIVATING
SALIVATION
SALIVATIONS
SALIVATORS
SALLENDERS
SALLOWNESS
SALLOWNESSES
SALLYPORTS
SALMAGUNDI
SALMAGUNDIES
SALMAGUNDIS
SALMAGUNDY
SALMANASER
SALMANASERS
SALMANAZAR
SALMANAZARS
SALMONBERRIES
SALMONBERRY
SALMONELLA
SALMONELLAE
SALMONELLAS
SALMONELLOSES
SALMONELLOSIS
SALMONOIDS
SALOMETERS
SALOPETTES
SALPIGLOSSES
SALPIGLOSSIS
SALPIGLOSSISES
SALPINGECTOMIES
SALPINGECTOMY
SALPINGIAN
SALPINGITIC
SALPINGITIS
SALPINGITISES
SALSOLACEOUS
SALSUGINOUS
SALTARELLI
SALTARELLO
SALTARELLOS
SALTATIONISM
SALTATIONISMS
SALTATIONIST
SALTATIONISTS
SALTATIONS
SALTATORIAL
SALTATORIOUS
SALTBUSHES
SALTCELLAR
SALTCELLARS
SALTCHUCKER
SALTCHUCKERS
SALTCHUCKS
SALTFISHES
SALTIGRADE
SALTIGRADES
SALTIMBANCO
SALTIMBANCOS
SALTIMBOCCA
SALTIMBOCCAS
SALTINESSES
SALTIREWISE
SALTISHNESS
SALTISHNESSES
SALTNESSES
SALTPETERS
SALTPETREMAN
SALTPETREMEN
SALTPETRES
SALTSHAKER
SALTSHAKERS
SALUBRIOUS
SALUBRIOUSLY
SALUBRIOUSNESS
SALUBRITIES
SALURETICS
SALUTARILY
SALUTARINESS
SALUTARINESSES
SALUTATION
SALUTATIONAL
SALUTATIONS
SALUTATORIAN
SALUTATORIANS
SALUTATORIES
SALUTATORILY
SALUTATORY
SALUTIFEROUS
SALVABILITIES
SALVABILITY
SALVABLENESS
SALVABLENESSES
SALVAGEABILITY
SALVAGEABLE
SALVARSANS
SALVATIONAL
SALVATIONISM
SALVATIONISMS
SALVATIONIST
SALVATIONISTS
SALVATIONS
SALVATORIES
SALVERFORM
SALVIFICAL
SALVIFICALLY
SALVINIACEOUS
SAMARIFORM
SAMARITANS
SAMARSKITE
SAMARSKITES
SAMENESSES
SAMNITISES
SAMPLERIES
SANATORIUM

SANATORIUMS
SANBENITOS
SANCTIFIABLE
SANCTIFICATION
SANCTIFICATIONS
SANCTIFIED
SANCTIFIEDLY
SANCTIFIER
SANCTIFIERS
SANCTIFIES
SANCTIFYING
SANCTIFYINGLY
SANCTIFYINGS
SANCTIMONIES
SANCTIMONIOUS
SANCTIMONIOUSLY
SANCTIMONY
SANCTIONABLE
SANCTIONED
SANCTIONEER
SANCTIONEERS
SANCTIONER
SANCTIONERS
SANCTIONING
SANCTIONLESS
SANCTITIES
SANCTITUDE
SANCTITUDES
SANCTUARIES
SANCTUARISE
SANCTUARISED
SANCTUARISES
SANCTUARISING
SANCTUARIZE
SANCTUARIZED
SANCTUARIZES
SANCTUARIZING
SANDALLING
SANDALWOOD
SANDALWOODS
SANDARACHS
SANDBAGGED
SANDBAGGER
SANDBAGGERS
SANDBAGGING
SANDBLASTED
SANDBLASTER
SANDBLASTERS
SANDBLASTING
SANDBLASTINGS
SANDBLASTS
SANDCASTLE
SANDCASTLES
SANDCRACKS
SANDERLING
SANDERLINGS
SANDERSWOOD
SANDERSWOODS
SANDFISHES
SANDGLASSES
SANDGROPER
SANDGROPERS
SANDGROUSE
SANDGROUSES
SANDINESSES
SANDLOTTER
SANDLOTTERS
SANDPAINTING
SANDPAINTINGS
SANDPAPERED
SANDPAPERING
SANDPAPERS
SANDPAPERY
SANDPIPERS
SANDSPOUTS
SANDSTONES
SANDSTORMS
SANDSUCKER
SANDSUCKERS
SANDWICHED
SANDWICHES
SANDWICHING
SANENESSES
SANGFROIDS
SANGUIFEROUS
SANGUIFICATION
SANGUIFICATIONS
SANGUIFIED
SANGUIFIES
SANGUIFYING
SANGUINARIA
SANGUINARIAS
SANGUINARILY
SANGUINARINESS
SANGUINARY
SANGUINELY
SANGUINENESS
SANGUINENESSES
SANGUINEOUS
SANGUINEOUSNESS
SANGUINING
SANGUINITIES
SANGUINITY
SANGUINIVOROUS
SANGUINOLENCIES
SANGUINOLENCY
SANGUINOLENT
SANGUIVOROUS
SANITARIAN
SANITARIANISM
SANITARIANISMS
SANITARIANS
SANITARIES
SANITARILY
SANITARINESS
SANITARINESSES
SANITARIST
SANITARISTS
SANITARIUM
SANITARIUMS
SANITATING
SANITATION
SANITATIONIST
SANITATIONISTS
SANITATIONS
SANITISATION
SANITISATIONS
SANITISERS
SANITISING
SANITIZATION
SANITIZATIONS
SANITIZERS
SANITIZING
SANITORIUM
SANITORIUMS
SANNYASINS
SANSCULOTTE
SANSCULOTTERIE
SANSCULOTTERIES
SANSCULOTTES
SANSCULOTTIC
SANSCULOTTIDES
SANSCULOTTISH
SANSCULOTTISM
SANSCULOTTISMS
SANSCULOTTIST
SANSCULOTTISTS
SANSEVIERIA
SANSEVIERIAS
SANTALACEOUS
SANTOLINAS
SANTONICAS
SAPANWOODS
SAPIDITIES
SAPIDNESSES
SAPIENCIES
SAPIENTIAL
SAPIENTIALLY
SAPINDACEOUS
SAPLESSNESS
SAPLESSNESSES
SAPODILLAS
SAPOGENINS
SAPONACEOUS
SAPONACEOUSNESS
SAPONARIAS
SAPONIFIABLE
SAPONIFICATION
SAPONIFICATIONS
SAPONIFIED
SAPONIFIER
SAPONIFIERS
SAPONIFIES
SAPONIFYING
SAPOTACEOUS
SAPPANWOOD
SAPPANWOODS
SAPPERMENT
SAPPHIRINE
SAPPHIRINES
SAPPINESSES
SAPRAEMIAS
SAPROBIONT
SAPROBIONTS
SAPROBIOTIC
SAPROGENIC
SAPROGENICITIES
SAPROGENICITY
SAPROGENOUS
SAPROLEGNIA
SAPROLEGNIAS
SAPROLITES
SAPROLITIC
SAPROPELIC
SAPROPELITE
SAPROPELITES
SAPROPHAGOUS
SAPROPHYTE
SAPROPHYTES
SAPROPHYTIC
SAPROPHYTICALLY
SAPROPHYTISM
SAPROPHYTISMS
SAPROTROPH
SAPROTROPHIC
SAPROTROPHS
SAPSUCKERS
SARABANDES
SARBACANES
SARCASTICALLY
SARCENCHYMATOUS
SARCENCHYME
SARCENCHYMES
SARCOCARPS
SARCOCOLLA
SARCOCOLLAS
SARCOCYSTIS
SARCOCYSTISES
SARCOIDOSES
SARCOIDOSIS
SARCOLEMMA
SARCOLEMMAL
SARCOLEMMAS
SARCOLEMMATA
SARCOLOGIES
SARCOMATOID
SARCOMATOSES
SARCOMATOSIS
SARCOMATOUS
SARCOMERES
SARCOPHAGAL
SARCOPHAGI
SARCOPHAGOUS
SARCOPHAGUS
SARCOPHAGUSES
SARCOPLASM
SARCOPLASMIC
SARCOPLASMS
SARCOSOMAL
SARCOSOMES
SARDONICAL
SARDONICALLY
SARDONICISM
SARDONICISMS
SARDONYXES
SARGASSUMS
SARMENTACEOUS
SARMENTOSE
SARMENTOUS
SARPANCHES
SARRACENIA
SARRACENIACEOUS
SARRACENIAS
SARRUSOPHONE
SARRUSOPHONES
SARSAPARILLA
SARSAPARILLAS
SARTORIALLY
SARTORIUSES
SASKATOONS
SASQUATCHES
SASSAFRASES
SASSARARAS
SASSINESSES

SASSOLITES
SASSYWOODS
SATANICALLY
SATANICALNESS
SATANICALNESSES
SATANITIES
SATANOLOGIES
SATANOLOGY
SATANOPHANIES
SATANOPHANY
SATANOPHOBIA
SATANOPHOBIAS
SATCHELFUL
SATCHELFULS
SATCHELLED
SATCHELSFUL
SATEDNESSES
SATELLITED
SATELLITES
SATELLITIC
SATELLITING
SATELLITISE
SATELLITISED
SATELLITISES
SATELLITISING
SATELLITIUM
SATELLITIUMS
SATELLITIZE
SATELLITIZED
SATELLITIZES
SATELLITIZING
SATIABILITIES
SATIABILITY
SATIATIONS
SATINETTAS
SATINETTES
SATINFLOWER
SATINFLOWERS
SATINWOODS
SATIRICALLY
SATIRICALNESS
SATIRICALNESSES
SATIRISABLE
SATIRISATION
SATIRISATIONS
SATIRISERS
SATIRISING
SATIRIZABLE
SATIRIZATION
SATIRIZATIONS
SATIRIZERS
SATIRIZING
SATISFACTION
SATISFACTIONS
SATISFACTORILY
SATISFACTORY
SATISFIABLE
SATISFICED
SATISFICER
SATISFICERS
SATISFICES
SATISFICING
SATISFICINGS
SATISFIERS
SATISFYING
SATISFYINGLY
SATURABILITIES
SATURABILITY
SATURATERS
SATURATING
SATURATION
SATURATIONS
SATURATORS
SATURNALIA
SATURNALIAN
SATURNALIANLY
SATURNALIAS
SATURNIIDS
SATURNINELY
SATURNINITIES
SATURNINITY
SATURNISMS
SATURNISTS
SATYAGRAHA
SATYAGRAHAS
SATYAGRAHI
SATYAGRAHIS
SATYRESQUE
SATYRESSES
SATYRIASES
SATYRIASIS
SAUCEBOATS
SAUCEBOXES
SAUCERFULS
SAUCERLESS
SAUCERLIKE
SAUCINESSES
SAUCISSONS
SAUERBRATEN
SAUERBRATENS
SAUERKRAUT
SAUERKRAUTS
SAUNTERERS
SAUNTERING
SAUNTERINGLY
SAUNTERINGS
SAURISCHIAN
SAURISCHIANS
SAUROGNATHOUS
SAUROPODOUS
SAUROPSIDAN
SAUROPSIDANS
SAUROPTERYGIAN
SAUSSURITE
SAUSSURITES
SAUSSURITIC
SAVABLENESS
SAVABLENESSES
SAVAGEDOMS
SAVAGENESS
SAVAGENESSES
SAVAGERIES
SAVEABLENESS
SAVEABLENESSES
SAVEGARDED
SAVEGARDING
SAVINGNESS
SAVINGNESSES
SAVORINESS
SAVORINESSES
SAVOURIEST
SAVOURINESS
SAVOURINESSES
SAVOURLESS
SAVVINESSES
SAWBONESES
SAWDUSTING
SAWTIMBERS
SAXICAVOUS
SAXICOLINE
SAXICOLOUS
SAXIFRAGACEOUS
SAXIFRAGES
SAXITOXINS
SAXOPHONES
SAXOPHONIC
SAXOPHONIST
SAXOPHONISTS
SCABBARDED
SCABBARDING
SCABBARDLESS
SCABBEDNESS
SCABBEDNESSES
SCABBINESS
SCABBINESSES
SCABERULOUS
SCABIOUSES
SCABRIDITIES
SCABRIDITY
SCABROUSLY
SCABROUSNESS
SCABROUSNESSES
SCAFFOLAGE
SCAFFOLAGES
SCAFFOLDAGE
SCAFFOLDAGES
SCAFFOLDED
SCAFFOLDER
SCAFFOLDERS
SCAFFOLDING
SCAFFOLDINGS
SCAGLIOLAS
SCAITHLESS
SCALABILITIES
SCALABILITY
SCALABLENESS
SCALABLENESSES
SCALARIFORM
SCALARIFORMLY
SCALATIONS
SCALDBERRIES
SCALDBERRY
SCALDFISHES
SCALDHEADS
SCALDSHIPS
SCALEBOARD
SCALEBOARDS
SCALENOHEDRA
SCALENOHEDRON
SCALENOHEDRONS
SCALETAILS
SCALEWORKS
SCALINESSES
SCALLAWAGS
SCALLOPERS
SCALLOPING
SCALLOPINI
SCALLOPINIS
SCALLYWAGS
SCALOGRAMS
SCALOPPINE
SCALOPPINES
SCALOPPINI
SCALPELLIC
SCALPELLIFORM
SCALPRIFORM
SCAMBAITING
SCAMBAITINGS
SCAMBLINGLY
SCAMBLINGS
SCAMMONIATE
SCAMMONIES
SCAMPERERS
SCAMPERING
SCAMPISHLY
SCAMPISHNESS
SCAMPISHNESSES
SCANDALING
SCANDALISATION
SCANDALISATIONS
SCANDALISE
SCANDALISED
SCANDALISER
SCANDALISERS
SCANDALISES
SCANDALISING
SCANDALIZATION
SCANDALIZATIONS
SCANDALIZE
SCANDALIZED
SCANDALIZER
SCANDALIZERS
SCANDALIZES
SCANDALIZING
SCANDALLED
SCANDALLING
SCANDALMONGER
SCANDALMONGERS
SCANDALOUS
SCANDALOUSLY
SCANDALOUSNESS
SCANSORIAL
SCANTINESS
SCANTINESSES
SCANTITIES
SCANTLINGS
SCANTNESSES
SCAPEGALLOWS
SCAPEGALLOWSES
SCAPEGOATED
SCAPEGOATING
SCAPEGOATINGS
SCAPEGOATISM
SCAPEGOATISMS
SCAPEGOATS
SCAPEGRACE
SCAPEGRACES
SCAPEMENTS
SCAPEWHEEL
SCAPEWHEELS
SCAPHOCEPHALI
SCAPHOCEPHALIC
SCAPHOCEPHALIES
SCAPHOCEPHALISM

SCAPHOCEPHALOUS
SCAPHOCEPHALUS
SCAPHOCEPHALY
SCAPHOPODS
SCAPIGEROUS
SCAPOLITES
SCAPULARIES
SCAPULATED
SCAPULIMANCIES
SCAPULIMANCY
SCAPULIMANTIC
SCAPULOMANCIES
SCAPULOMANCY
SCAPULOMANTIC
SCARABAEAN
SCARABAEANS
SCARABAEID
SCARABAEIDS
SCARABAEIST
SCARABAEISTS
SCARABAEOID
SCARABAEOIDS
SCARABAEUS
SCARABAEUSES
SCARABOIDS
SCARAMOUCH
SCARAMOUCHE
SCARAMOUCHES
SCARCEMENT
SCARCEMENTS
SCARCENESS
SCARCENESSES
SCARCITIES
SCARECROWS
SCAREHEADS
SCAREMONGER
SCAREMONGERING
SCAREMONGERINGS
SCAREMONGERS
SCARFISHES
SCARFSKINS
SCARIFICATION
SCARIFICATIONS
SCARIFICATOR
SCARIFICATORS
SCARIFIERS
SCARIFYING
SCARIFYINGLY
SCARINESSES
SCARLATINA
SCARLATINAL
SCARLATINAS
SCARLETING
SCARPERING
SCATHEFULNESS
SCATHEFULNESSES
SCATHELESS
SCATHINGLY
SCATOLOGIC
SCATOLOGICAL
SCATOLOGIES
SCATOLOGIST
SCATOLOGISTS
SCATOPHAGIES
SCATOPHAGOUS
SCATOPHAGY
SCATTERABLE
SCATTERATION
SCATTERATIONS
SCATTERBRAIN
SCATTERBRAINED
SCATTERBRAINS
SCATTEREDLY
SCATTERERS
SCATTERGOOD
SCATTERGOODS
SCATTERGRAM
SCATTERGRAMS
SCATTERGUN
SCATTERGUNS
SCATTERING
SCATTERINGLY
SCATTERINGS
SCATTERLING
SCATTERLINGS
SCATTERMOUCH
SCATTERMOUCHES
SCATTERSHOT
SCATTINESS
SCATTINESSES
SCATURIENT
SCAVENGERED
SCAVENGERIES
SCAVENGERING
SCAVENGERINGS
SCAVENGERS
SCAVENGERY
SCAVENGING
SCAVENGINGS
SCAZONTICS
SCELERATES
SCENARISATION
SCENARISATIONS
SCENARISED
SCENARISES
SCENARISING
SCENARISTS
SCENARIZATION
SCENARIZATIONS
SCENARIZED
SCENARIZES
SCENARIZING
SCENESHIFTER
SCENESHIFTERS
SCENICALLY
SCENOGRAPHER
SCENOGRAPHERS
SCENOGRAPHIC
SCENOGRAPHICAL
SCENOGRAPHIES
SCENOGRAPHY
SCENTLESSNESS
SCENTLESSNESSES
SCEPTERING
SCEPTERLESS
SCEPTICALLY
SCEPTICISM
SCEPTICISMS
SCEPTRELESS
SCEUOPHYLACIA
SCEUOPHYLACIUM
SCEUOPHYLAX
SCEUOPHYLAXES
SCHADENFREUDE
SCHADENFREUDES
SCHALSTEIN
SCHALSTEINS
SCHAPPEING
SCHATCHENS
SCHECHITAH
SCHECHITAHS
SCHECHITAS
SCHECKLATON
SCHECKLATONS
SCHEDULERS
SCHEDULING
SCHEELITES
SCHEFFLERA
SCHEFFLERAS
SCHEMATICAL
SCHEMATICALLY
SCHEMATICS
SCHEMATISATION
SCHEMATISATIONS
SCHEMATISE
SCHEMATISED
SCHEMATISES
SCHEMATISING
SCHEMATISM
SCHEMATISMS
SCHEMATIST
SCHEMATISTS
SCHEMATIZATION
SCHEMATIZATIONS
SCHEMATIZE
SCHEMATIZED
SCHEMATIZES
SCHEMATIZING
SCHEMINGLY
SCHEMOZZLE
SCHEMOZZLED
SCHEMOZZLES
SCHEMOZZLING
SCHERZANDI
SCHERZANDO
SCHERZANDOS
SCHIAVONES
SCHILLERISATION
SCHILLERISE
SCHILLERISED
SCHILLERISES
SCHILLERISING
SCHILLERIZATION
SCHILLERIZE
SCHILLERIZED
SCHILLERIZES
SCHILLERIZING
SCHILLINGS
SCHINDYLESES
SCHINDYLESIS
SCHINDYLETIC
SCHIPPERKE
SCHIPPERKES
SCHISMATIC
SCHISMATICAL
SCHISMATICALLY
SCHISMATICALS
SCHISMATICS
SCHISMATISE
SCHISMATISED
SCHISMATISES
SCHISMATISING
SCHISMATIZE
SCHISMATIZED
SCHISMATIZES
SCHISMATIZING
SCHISTOSITIES
SCHISTOSITY
SCHISTOSOMAL
SCHISTOSOME
SCHISTOSOMES
SCHISTOSOMIASES
SCHISTOSOMIASIS
SCHIZAEACEOUS
SCHIZANTHUS
SCHIZANTHUSES
SCHIZOCARP
SCHIZOCARPIC
SCHIZOCARPOUS
SCHIZOCARPS
SCHIZOGENESES
SCHIZOGENESIS
SCHIZOGENETIC
SCHIZOGENIC
SCHIZOGNATHOUS
SCHIZOGONIC
SCHIZOGONIES
SCHIZOGONOUS
SCHIZOGONY
SCHIZOIDAL
SCHIZOMYCETE
SCHIZOMYCETES
SCHIZOMYCETIC
SCHIZOMYCETOUS
SCHIZOPHRENE
SCHIZOPHRENES
SCHIZOPHRENETIC
SCHIZOPHRENIA
SCHIZOPHRENIAS
SCHIZOPHRENIC
SCHIZOPHRENICS
SCHIZOPHYCEOUS
SCHIZOPHYTE
SCHIZOPHYTES
SCHIZOPHYTIC
SCHIZOPODAL
SCHIZOPODOUS
SCHIZOPODS
SCHIZOTHYMIA
SCHIZOTHYMIAS
SCHIZOTHYMIC
SCHIZZIEST
SCHLEMIELS
SCHLEMIHLS
SCHLEPPERS
SCHLEPPIER
SCHLEPPIEST
SCHLEPPING
SCHLIMAZEL
SCHLIMAZELS
SCHLOCKERS
SCHLOCKIER
SCHLOCKIEST
SCHLUMBERGERA

SCHLUMBERGERAS
SCHLUMPIER
SCHLUMPIEST
SCHLUMPING
SCHMALTZES
SCHMALTZIER
SCHMALTZIEST
SCHMALZIER
SCHMALZIEST
SCHMEARING
SCHMEERING
SCHMOOSING
SCHMOOZERS
SCHMOOZIER
SCHMOOZIEST
SCHMOOZING
SCHMUTTERS
SCHNAPPERS
SCHNAPPSES
SCHNAUZERS
SCHNITZELS
SCHNORKELED
SCHNORKELING
SCHNORKELLED
SCHNORKELLER
SCHNORKELLERS
SCHNORKELLING
SCHNORKELS
SCHNORRERS
SCHNORRING
SCHNOZZLES
SCHOLARCHS
SCHOLARLIER
SCHOLARLIEST
SCHOLARLINESS
SCHOLARLINESSES
SCHOLARSHIP
SCHOLARSHIPS
SCHOLASTIC
SCHOLASTICAL
SCHOLASTICALLY
SCHOLASTICATE
SCHOLASTICATES
SCHOLASTICISM
SCHOLASTICISMS
SCHOLASTICS
SCHOLIASTIC
SCHOLIASTS
SCHOOLBAGS
SCHOOLBOOK
SCHOOLBOOKS
SCHOOLBOYISH
SCHOOLBOYS
SCHOOLCHILD
SCHOOLCHILDREN
SCHOOLCRAFT
SCHOOLCRAFTS
SCHOOLDAYS
SCHOOLERIES
SCHOOLFELLOW
SCHOOLFELLOWS
SCHOOLGIRL
SCHOOLGIRLISH
SCHOOLGIRLS
SCHOOLGOING
SCHOOLGOINGS
SCHOOLHOUSE
SCHOOLHOUSES
SCHOOLINGS
SCHOOLKIDS
SCHOOLMAID
SCHOOLMAIDS
SCHOOLMARM
SCHOOLMARMISH
SCHOOLMARMS
SCHOOLMASTER
SCHOOLMASTERED
SCHOOLMASTERING
SCHOOLMASTERISH
SCHOOLMASTERLY
SCHOOLMASTERS
SCHOOLMATE
SCHOOLMATES
SCHOOLMISTRESS
SCHOOLMISTRESSY
SCHOOLROOM
SCHOOLROOMS
SCHOOLTEACHER
SCHOOLTEACHERS
SCHOOLTEACHING
SCHOOLTEACHINGS
SCHOOLTIDE
SCHOOLTIDES
SCHOOLTIME
SCHOOLTIMES
SCHOOLWARD
SCHOOLWARDS
SCHOOLWORK
SCHOOLWORKS
SCHORLACEOUS
SCHORLOMITE
SCHORLOMITES
SCHOTTISCHE
SCHOTTISCHES
SCHRECKLICH
SCHUSSBOOMER
SCHUSSBOOMERS
SCHUTZSTAFFEL
SCHUTZSTAFFELS
SCHVARTZES
SCHWARMEREI
SCHWARMEREIS
SCHWARMERISCH
SCHWARTZES
SCHWARZLOT
SCHWARZLOTS
SCIAENOIDS
SCIAMACHIES
SCIENTIFIC
SCIENTIFICAL
SCIENTIFICALLY
SCIENTISED
SCIENTISES
SCIENTISING
SCIENTISMS
SCIENTISTIC
SCIENTISTS
SCIENTIZED
SCIENTIZES
SCIENTIZING
SCINCOIDIAN
SCINCOIDIANS
SCINDAPSUS
SCINDAPSUSES
SCINTIGRAM
SCINTIGRAMS
SCINTIGRAPHIC
SCINTIGRAPHIES
SCINTIGRAPHY
SCINTILLAE
SCINTILLANT
SCINTILLANTLY
SCINTILLAS
SCINTILLASCOPE
SCINTILLASCOPES
SCINTILLATE
SCINTILLATED
SCINTILLATES
SCINTILLATING
SCINTILLATINGLY
SCINTILLATION
SCINTILLATIONS
SCINTILLATOR
SCINTILLATORS
SCINTILLISCAN
SCINTILLISCANS
SCINTILLOMETER
SCINTILLOMETERS
SCINTILLON
SCINTILLONS
SCINTILLOSCOPE
SCINTILLOSCOPES
SCINTISCAN
SCINTISCANNER
SCINTISCANNERS
SCINTISCANS
SCIOLISTIC
SCIOMACHIES
SCIOMANCER
SCIOMANCERS
SCIOMANCIES
SCIOMANTIC
SCIOPHYTES
SCIOPHYTIC
SCIOSOPHIES
SCIRRHOSITIES
SCIRRHOSITY
SCIRRHUSES
SCISSIPARITIES
SCISSIPARITY
SCISSORERS
SCISSORING
SCISSORTAIL
SCISSORTAILS
SCISSORWISE
SCITAMINEOUS
SCLAUNDERS
SCLEREIDES
SCLERENCHYMA
SCLERENCHYMAS
SCLERENCHYMATA
SCLERIASES
SCLERIASIS
SCLERITISES
SCLEROCAULIES
SCLEROCAULOUS
SCLEROCAULY
SCLERODERM
SCLERODERMA
SCLERODERMAS
SCLERODERMATA
SCLERODERMATOUS
SCLERODERMIA
SCLERODERMIAS
SCLERODERMIC
SCLERODERMITE
SCLERODERMITES
SCLERODERMOUS
SCLERODERMS
SCLEROMALACIA
SCLEROMALACIAS
SCLEROMATA
SCLEROMETER
SCLEROMETERS
SCLEROMETRIC
SCLEROPHYLL
SCLEROPHYLLIES
SCLEROPHYLLOUS
SCLEROPHYLLS
SCLEROPHYLLY
SCLEROPROTEIN
SCLEROPROTEINS
SCLEROSING
SCLEROTALS
SCLEROTIAL
SCLEROTICS
SCLEROTINS
SCLEROTIOID
SCLEROTISATION
SCLEROTISATIONS
SCLEROTISE
SCLEROTISED
SCLEROTISES
SCLEROTISING
SCLEROTITIS
SCLEROTITISES
SCLEROTIUM
SCLEROTIZATION
SCLEROTIZATIONS
SCLEROTIZE
SCLEROTIZED
SCLEROTIZES
SCLEROTIZING
SCLEROTOMIES
SCLEROTOMY
SCOFFINGLY
SCOLDINGLY
SCOLECIFORM
SCOLECITES
SCOLLOPING
SCOLOPACEOUS
SCOLOPENDRA
SCOLOPENDRAS
SCOLOPENDRID
SCOLOPENDRIDS
SCOLOPENDRIFORM
SCOLOPENDRINE
SCOLOPENDRIUM
SCOLOPENDRIUMS
SCOLYTOIDS
SCOMBROIDS
SCOMFISHED
SCOMFISHES
SCOMFISHING

SCONCHEONS
SCOOTCHING
SCOOTERIST
SCOOTERISTS
SCOPELOIDS
SCOPOLAMINE
SCOPOLAMINES
SCOPOLINES
SCOPOPHILIA
SCOPOPHILIAC
SCOPOPHILIACS
SCOPOPHILIAS
SCOPOPHILIC
SCOPOPHOBIA
SCOPOPHOBIAS
SCOPTOPHILIA
SCOPTOPHILIAS
SCOPTOPHOBIA
SCOPTOPHOBIAS
SCORBUTICALLY
SCORCHINGLY
SCORCHINGNESS
SCORCHINGNESSES
SCORCHINGS
SCORDATURA
SCORDATURAS
SCOREBOARD
SCOREBOARDS
SCORECARDS
SCOREKEEPER
SCOREKEEPERS
SCORELINES
SCORESHEET
SCORESHEETS
SCORIACEOUS
SCORIFICATION
SCORIFICATIONS
SCORIFIERS
SCORIFYING
SCORNFULLY
SCORNFULNESS
SCORNFULNESSES
SCORODITES
SCORPAENID
SCORPAENIDS
SCORPAENOID
SCORPAENOIDS
SCORPIOIDS
SCORPIONIC
SCORZONERA
SCORZONERAS
SCOTODINIA
SCOTODINIAS
SCOTOMATOUS
SCOTOMETER
SCOTOMETERS
SCOUNDRELLY
SCOUNDRELS
SCOUTCRAFT
SCOUTCRAFTS
SCOUTHERED
SCOUTHERING
SCOUTHERINGS
SCOUTMASTER
SCOUTMASTERS
SCOWDERING
SCOWDERINGS
SCOWLINGLY
SCOWTHERED
SCOWTHERING
SCRABBLERS
SCRABBLIER
SCRABBLIEST
SCRABBLING
SCRAGGEDNESS
SCRAGGEDNESSES
SCRAGGIEST
SCRAGGINESS
SCRAGGINESSES
SCRAGGLIER
SCRAGGLIEST
SCRAGGLING
SCRAICHING
SCRAIGHING
SCRAMBLERS
SCRAMBLING
SCRAMBLINGLY
SCRAMBLINGS
SCRANCHING
SCRANNIEST
SCRAPBOOKS
SCRAPEGOOD
SCRAPEGOODS
SCRAPEGUTS
SCRAPEPENNIES
SCRAPEPENNY
SCRAPERBOARD
SCRAPERBOARDS
SCRAPHEAPS
SCRAPPAGES
SCRAPPIEST
SCRAPPINESS
SCRAPPINESSES
SCRAPYARDS
SCRATCHBACK
SCRATCHBACKS
SCRATCHBOARD
SCRATCHBOARDS
SCRATCHBUILD
SCRATCHBUILDER
SCRATCHBUILDERS
SCRATCHBUILDING
SCRATCHBUILDS
SCRATCHBUILT
SCRATCHCARD
SCRATCHCARDS
SCRATCHERS
SCRATCHIER
SCRATCHIES
SCRATCHIEST
SCRATCHILY
SCRATCHINESS
SCRATCHINESSES
SCRATCHING
SCRATCHINGLY
SCRATCHINGS
SCRATCHLESS
SCRATCHPLATE
SCRATCHPLATES
SCRATTLING
SCRAUCHING
SCRAUGHING
SCRAWLIEST
SCRAWLINGLY
SCRAWLINGS
SCRAWNIEST
SCRAWNINESS
SCRAWNINESSES
SCREAKIEST
SCREAMINGLY
SCREECHERS
SCREECHIER
SCREECHIEST
SCREECHING
SCREEDINGS
SCREENABLE
SCREENAGER
SCREENAGERS
SCREENCRAFT
SCREENCRAFTS
SCREENFULS
SCREENINGS
SCREENLAND
SCREENLANDS
SCREENLIKE
SCREENPLAY
SCREENPLAYS
SCREENSAVER
SCREENSAVERS
SCREENSHOT
SCREENSHOTS
SCREENWRITER
SCREENWRITERS
SCREEVINGS
SCREICHING
SCREIGHING
SCREWBALLS
SCREWBEANS
SCREWDRIVER
SCREWDRIVERS
SCREWINESS
SCREWINESSES
SCREWWORMS
SCRIBACIOUS
SCRIBACIOUSNESS
SCRIBBLEMENT
SCRIBBLEMENTS
SCRIBBLERS
SCRIBBLIER
SCRIBBLIEST
SCRIBBLING
SCRIBBLINGLY
SCRIBBLINGS
SCRIECHING
SCRIEVEBOARD
SCRIEVEBOARDS
SCRIGGLIER
SCRIGGLIEST
SCRIGGLING
SCRIMMAGED
SCRIMMAGER
SCRIMMAGERS
SCRIMMAGES
SCRIMMAGING
SCRIMPIEST
SCRIMPINESS
SCRIMPINESSES
SCRIMPNESS
SCRIMPNESSES
SCRIMSHANDER
SCRIMSHANDERED
SCRIMSHANDERING
SCRIMSHANDERS
SCRIMSHANDIED
SCRIMSHANDIES
SCRIMSHANDY
SCRIMSHANDYING
SCRIMSHANK
SCRIMSHANKED
SCRIMSHANKING
SCRIMSHANKS
SCRIMSHAWED
SCRIMSHAWING
SCRIMSHAWS
SCRIMSHONER
SCRIMSHONERS
SCRIPOPHILE
SCRIPOPHILES
SCRIPOPHILIES
SCRIPOPHILIST
SCRIPOPHILISTS
SCRIPOPHILY
SCRIPPAGES
SCRIPTORIA
SCRIPTORIAL
SCRIPTORIUM
SCRIPTORIUMS
SCRIPTURAL
SCRIPTURALISM
SCRIPTURALISMS
SCRIPTURALIST
SCRIPTURALISTS
SCRIPTURALLY
SCRIPTURES
SCRIPTURISM
SCRIPTURISMS
SCRIPTURIST
SCRIPTURISTS
SCRIPTWRITER
SCRIPTWRITERS
SCRIPTWRITING
SCRIPTWRITINGS
SCRITCHING
SCRIVEBOARD
SCRIVEBOARDS
SCRIVENERS
SCRIVENERSHIP
SCRIVENERSHIPS
SCRIVENING
SCRIVENINGS
SCROBICULAR
SCROBICULATE
SCROBICULATED
SCROBICULE
SCROBICULES
SCROFULOUS
SCROFULOUSLY
SCROFULOUSNESS
SCROGGIEST
SCROLLABLE
SCROLLWISE
SCROLLWORK
SCROLLWORKS
SCROOCHING

SCROOTCHED
SCROOTCHES
SCROOTCHING
SCROPHULARIA
SCROPHULARIAS
SCROUNGERS
SCROUNGIER
SCROUNGIEST
SCROUNGING
SCROUNGINGS
SCROWDGING
SCRUBBABLE
SCRUBBIEST
SCRUBBINESS
SCRUBBINESSES
SCRUBBINGS
SCRUBLANDS
SCRUBWOMAN
SCRUBWOMEN
SCRUFFIEST
SCRUFFINESS
SCRUFFINESSES
SCRUMDOWNS
SCRUMMAGED
SCRUMMAGER
SCRUMMAGERS
SCRUMMAGES
SCRUMMAGING
SCRUMMIEST
SCRUMPLING
SCRUMPOXES
SCRUMPTIOUS
SCRUMPTIOUSLY
SCRUMPTIOUSNESS
SCRUNCHEON
SCRUNCHEONS
SCRUNCHIER
SCRUNCHIES
SCRUNCHIEST
SCRUNCHING
SCRUNCHION
SCRUNCHIONS
SCRUNTIEST
SCRUPLELESS
SCRUPULOSITIES
SCRUPULOSITY
SCRUPULOUS
SCRUPULOUSLY
SCRUPULOUSNESS
SCRUTABILITIES
SCRUTABILITY
SCRUTATORS
SCRUTINEER
SCRUTINEERS
SCRUTINIES
SCRUTINISE
SCRUTINISED
SCRUTINISER
SCRUTINISERS
SCRUTINISES
SCRUTINISING
SCRUTINISINGLY
SCRUTINIZE
SCRUTINIZED
SCRUTINIZER
SCRUTINIZERS
SCRUTINIZES
SCRUTINIZING
SCRUTINIZINGLY
SCRUTINOUS
SCRUTINOUSLY
SCRUTOIRES
SCUDDALERS
SCULDUDDERIES
SCULDUDDERY
SCULDUDDRIES
SCULDUDDRY
SCULDUGGERIES
SCULDUGGERY
SCULLERIES
SCULPTRESS
SCULPTRESSES
SCULPTURAL
SCULPTURALLY
SCULPTURED
SCULPTURES
SCULPTURESQUE
SCULPTURESQUELY
SCULPTURING
SCULPTURINGS
SCUMBERING
SCUMBLINGS
SCUMFISHED
SCUMFISHES
SCUMFISHING
SCUNCHEONS
SCUNGILLIS
SCUNNERING
SCUPPERING
SCUPPERNONG
SCUPPERNONGS
SCURFINESS
SCURFINESSES
SCURRILITIES
SCURRILITY
SCURRILOUS
SCURRILOUSLY
SCURRILOUSNESS
SCURRIOURS
SCURVINESS
SCURVINESSES
SCUTATIONS
SCUTCHEONLESS
SCUTCHEONS
SCUTCHINGS
SCUTELLATE
SCUTELLATED
SCUTELLATION
SCUTELLATIONS
SCUTTERING
SCUTTLEBUTT
SCUTTLEBUTTS
SCUTTLEFUL
SCUTTLEFULS
SCUZZBALLS
SCYPHIFORM
SCYPHISTOMA
SCYPHISTOMAE
SCYPHISTOMAS
SCYPHOZOAN
SCYPHOZOANS
SCYTHELIKE
SDEIGNFULL
SDEIGNFULLY
SDRUCCIOLA
SEABEACHES
SEABORGIUM
SEABORGIUMS
SEABOTTLES
SEACUNNIES
SEAFARINGS
SEALIFTING
SEALPOINTS
SEAMANLIKE
SEAMANSHIP
SEAMANSHIPS
SEAMINESSES
SEAMLESSLY
SEAMLESSNESS
SEAMLESSNESSES
SEAMSTRESS
SEAMSTRESSES
SEAMSTRESSIES
SEAMSTRESSY
SEANNACHIE
SEANNACHIES
SEAQUARIUM
SEAQUARIUMS
SEARCHABLE
SEARCHINGLY
SEARCHINGNESS
SEARCHINGNESSES
SEARCHLESS
SEARCHLIGHT
SEARCHLIGHTS
SEAREDNESS
SEAREDNESSES
SEARNESSES
SEASICKEST
SEASICKNESS
SEASICKNESSES
SEASONABLE
SEASONABLENESS
SEASONABLY
SEASONALITIES
SEASONALITY
SEASONALLY
SEASONALNESS
SEASONALNESSES
SEASONINGS
SEASONLESS
SEASTRANDS
SEAWORTHIER
SEAWORTHIEST
SEAWORTHINESS
SEAWORTHINESSES
SEBIFEROUS
SEBORRHEAL
SEBORRHEAS
SEBORRHEIC
SEBORRHOEA
SEBORRHOEAL
SEBORRHOEAS
SEBORRHOEIC
SECERNENTS
SECERNMENT
SECERNMENTS
SECESSIONAL
SECESSIONISM
SECESSIONISMS
SECESSIONIST
SECESSIONISTS
SECESSIONS
SECLUDEDLY
SECLUDEDNESS
SECLUDEDNESSES
SECLUSIONIST
SECLUSIONISTS
SECLUSIONS
SECLUSIVELY
SECLUSIVENESS
SECLUSIVENESSES
SECOBARBITAL
SECOBARBITALS
SECONDARIES
SECONDARILY
SECONDARINESS
SECONDARINESSES
SECONDHAND
SECONDMENT
SECONDMENTS
SECRETAGES
SECRETAGOGIC
SECRETAGOGUE
SECRETAGOGUES
SECRETAIRE
SECRETAIRES
SECRETARIAL
SECRETARIAT
SECRETARIATE
SECRETARIATES
SECRETARIATS
SECRETARIES
SECRETARYSHIP
SECRETARYSHIPS
SECRETIONAL
SECRETIONARY
SECRETIONS
SECRETIVELY
SECRETIVENESS
SECRETIVENESSES
SECRETNESS
SECRETNESSES
SECRETORIES
SECTARIANISE
SECTARIANISED
SECTARIANISES
SECTARIANISING
SECTARIANISM
SECTARIANISMS
SECTARIANIZE
SECTARIANIZED
SECTARIANIZES
SECTARIANIZING
SECTARIANS
SECTILITIES
SECTIONALISE
SECTIONALISED
SECTIONALISES
SECTIONALISING
SECTIONALISM
SECTIONALISMS
SECTIONALIST
SECTIONALISTS

SECTIONALIZE
SECTIONALIZED
SECTIONALIZES
SECTIONALIZING
SECTIONALLY
SECTIONALS
SECTIONING
SECTIONISATION
SECTIONISATIONS
SECTIONISE
SECTIONISED
SECTIONISES
SECTIONISING
SECTIONIZATION
SECTIONIZATIONS
SECTIONIZE
SECTIONIZED
SECTIONIZES
SECTIONIZING
SECTORIALS
SECTORISATION
SECTORISATIONS
SECTORISED
SECTORISES
SECTORISING
SECTORIZATION
SECTORIZATIONS
SECTORIZED
SECTORIZES
SECTORIZING
SECULARISATION
SECULARISATIONS
SECULARISE
SECULARISED
SECULARISER
SECULARISERS
SECULARISES
SECULARISING
SECULARISM
SECULARISMS
SECULARIST
SECULARISTIC
SECULARISTS
SECULARITIES
SECULARITY
SECULARIZATION
SECULARIZATIONS
SECULARIZE
SECULARIZED
SECULARIZER
SECULARIZERS
SECULARIZES
SECULARIZING
SECUNDINES
SECUNDOGENITURE
SECURANCES
SECUREMENT
SECUREMENTS
SECURENESS
SECURENESSES
SECURIFORM
SECURITANS
SECURITIES
SECURITISATION
SECURITISATIONS
SECURITISE
SECURITISED
SECURITISES
SECURITISING
SECURITIZATION
SECURITIZATIONS
SECURITIZE
SECURITIZED
SECURITIZES
SECURITIZING
SECUROCRAT
SECUROCRATS
SEDATENESS
SEDATENESSES
SEDENTARILY
SEDENTARINESS
SEDENTARINESSES
SEDGELANDS
SEDIGITATED
SEDIMENTABLE
SEDIMENTARILY
SEDIMENTARY
SEDIMENTATION
SEDIMENTATIONS
SEDIMENTED
SEDIMENTING
SEDIMENTOLOGIC
SEDIMENTOLOGIES
SEDIMENTOLOGIST
SEDIMENTOLOGY
SEDIMENTOUS
SEDITIONARIES
SEDITIONARY
SEDITIOUSLY
SEDITIOUSNESS
SEDITIOUSNESSES
SEDUCEABLE
SEDUCEMENT
SEDUCEMENTS
SEDUCINGLY
SEDUCTIONS
SEDUCTIVELY
SEDUCTIVENESS
SEDUCTIVENESSES
SEDUCTRESS
SEDUCTRESSES
SEDULITIES
SEDULOUSLY
SEDULOUSNESS
SEDULOUSNESSES
SEECATCHIE
SEEDEATERS
SEEDINESSES
SEEDNESSES
SEEDSTOCKS
SEEMELESSE
SEEMINGNESS
SEEMINGNESSES
SEEMLIHEAD
SEEMLIHEADS
SEEMLIHEDS
SEEMLINESS
SEEMLINESSES
SEEMLYHEDS
SEERSUCKER
SEERSUCKERS
SEETHINGLY
SEGHOLATES
SEGMENTALLY
SEGMENTARY
SEGMENTATE
SEGMENTATION
SEGMENTATIONS
SEGMENTING
SEGREGABLE
SEGREGANTS
SEGREGATED
SEGREGATES
SEGREGATING
SEGREGATION
SEGREGATIONAL
SEGREGATIONIST
SEGREGATIONISTS
SEGREGATIONS
SEGREGATIVE
SEGREGATOR
SEGREGATORS
SEGUIDILLA
SEGUIDILLAS
SEIGNEURIAL
SEIGNEURIE
SEIGNEURIES
SEIGNIORAGE
SEIGNIORAGES
SEIGNIORALTIES
SEIGNIORALTY
SEIGNIORIAL
SEIGNIORIES
SEIGNIORSHIP
SEIGNIORSHIPS
SEIGNORAGE
SEIGNORAGES
SEIGNORIAL
SEIGNORIES
SEISMICALLY
SEISMICITIES
SEISMICITY
SEISMOGRAM
SEISMOGRAMS
SEISMOGRAPH
SEISMOGRAPHER
SEISMOGRAPHERS
SEISMOGRAPHIC
SEISMOGRAPHICAL
SEISMOGRAPHIES
SEISMOGRAPHS
SEISMOGRAPHY
SEISMOLOGIC
SEISMOLOGICAL
SEISMOLOGICALLY
SEISMOLOGIES
SEISMOLOGIST
SEISMOLOGISTS
SEISMOLOGY
SEISMOMETER
SEISMOMETERS
SEISMOMETRIC
SEISMOMETRICAL
SEISMOMETRIES
SEISMOMETRY
SEISMONASTIC
SEISMONASTIES
SEISMONASTY
SEISMOSCOPE
SEISMOSCOPES
SEISMOSCOPIC
SELACHIANS
SELAGINELLA
SELAGINELLAS
SELDOMNESS
SELDOMNESSES
SELECTABLE
SELECTIONIST
SELECTIONISTS
SELECTIONS
SELECTIVELY
SELECTIVENESS
SELECTIVENESSES
SELECTIVITIES
SELECTIVITY
SELECTNESS
SELECTNESSES
SELECTORATE
SELECTORATES
SELECTORIAL
SELEGILINE
SELEGILINES
SELENIFEROUS
SELENOCENTRIC
SELENODONT
SELENODONTS
SELENOGRAPH
SELENOGRAPHER
SELENOGRAPHERS
SELENOGRAPHIC
SELENOGRAPHICAL
SELENOGRAPHIES
SELENOGRAPHIST
SELENOGRAPHISTS
SELENOGRAPHS
SELENOGRAPHY
SELENOLOGICAL
SELENOLOGIES
SELENOLOGIST
SELENOLOGISTS
SELENOLOGY
SELFISHNESS
SELFISHNESSES
SELFLESSLY
SELFLESSNESS
SELFLESSNESSES
SELFNESSES
SELFSAMENESS
SELFSAMENESSES
SELLOTAPED
SELLOTAPES
SELLOTAPING
SELTZOGENE
SELTZOGENES
SELVEDGING
SEMAINIERS
SEMANTEMES
SEMANTICAL
SEMANTICALLY
SEMANTICIST
SEMANTICISTS
SEMANTIDES
SEMAPHORED
SEMAPHORES

SEMAPHORIC
SEMAPHORICAL
SEMAPHORICALLY
SEMAPHORING
SEMASIOLOGICAL
SEMASIOLOGIES
SEMASIOLOGIST
SEMASIOLOGISTS
SEMASIOLOGY
SEMATOLOGIES
SEMATOLOGY
SEMBLABLES
SEMBLANCES
SEMBLATIVE
SEMEIOLOGIC
SEMEIOLOGICAL
SEMEIOLOGIES
SEMEIOLOGIST
SEMEIOLOGISTS
SEMEIOLOGY
SEMEIOTICIAN
SEMEIOTICIANS
SEMEIOTICS
SEMELPARITIES
SEMELPARITY
SEMELPAROUS
SEMESTRIAL
SEMIABSTRACT
SEMIABSTRACTION
SEMIANGLES
SEMIANNUAL
SEMIANNUALLY
SEMIAQUATIC
SEMIARBOREAL
SEMIARIDITIES
SEMIARIDITY
SEMIAUTOMATIC
SEMIAUTOMATICS
SEMIAUTONOMOUS
SEMIBREVES
SEMICARBAZIDE
SEMICARBAZIDES
SEMICARBAZONE
SEMICARBAZONES
SEMICENTENNIAL
SEMICENTENNIALS
SEMICHORUS
SEMICHORUSES
SEMICIRCLE
SEMICIRCLED
SEMICIRCLES
SEMICIRCULAR
SEMICIRCULARLY
SEMICIRQUE
SEMICIRQUES
SEMICIVILISED
SEMICIVILIZED
SEMICLASSIC
SEMICLASSICAL
SEMICLASSICS
SEMICOLONIAL
SEMICOLONIALISM
SEMICOLONIES
SEMICOLONS
SEMICOLONY
SEMICOMATOSE
SEMICOMMERCIAL
SEMICONDUCTING
SEMICONDUCTION
SEMICONDUCTIONS
SEMICONDUCTOR
SEMICONDUCTORS
SEMICONSCIOUS
SEMICONSCIOUSLY
SEMICRYSTALLIC
SEMICRYSTALLINE
SEMICYLINDER
SEMICYLINDERS
SEMICYLINDRICAL
SEMIDARKNESS
SEMIDARKNESSES
SEMIDEIFIED
SEMIDEIFIES
SEMIDEIFYING
SEMIDEPONENT
SEMIDEPONENTS
SEMIDESERT
SEMIDESERTS
SEMIDETACHED
SEMIDIAMETER
SEMIDIAMETERS
SEMIDIURNAL
SEMIDIVINE
SEMIDOCUMENTARY
SEMIDOMINANT
SEMIDRYING
SEMIDWARFS
SEMIDWARVES
SEMIELLIPTICAL
SEMIEMPIRICAL
SEMIEVERGREEN
SEMIFEUDAL
SEMIFINALIST
SEMIFINALISTS
SEMIFINALS
SEMIFINISHED
SEMIFITTED
SEMIFLEXIBLE
SEMIFLUIDIC
SEMIFLUIDITIES
SEMIFLUIDITY
SEMIFLUIDS
SEMIFORMAL
SEMIFREDDO
SEMIFREDDOS
SEMIGLOBULAR
SEMIGLOSSES
SEMIGROUPS
SEMIHOBOES
SEMILEGENDARY
SEMILETHAL
SEMILETHALS
SEMILIQUID
SEMILIQUIDS
SEMILITERATE
SEMILITERATES
SEMILOGARITHMIC
SEMILUCENT
SEMILUNATE
SEMILUSTROUS
SEMIMANUFACTURE
SEMIMENSTRUAL
SEMIMETALLIC
SEMIMETALS
SEMIMONASTIC
SEMIMONTHLIES
SEMIMONTHLY
SEMIMYSTICAL
SEMINALITIES
SEMINALITY
SEMINARIAL
SEMINARIAN
SEMINARIANS
SEMINARIES
SEMINARIST
SEMINARISTS
SEMINATING
SEMINATION
SEMINATIONS
SEMINATURAL
SEMINIFEROUS
SEMINOMADIC
SEMINOMADS
SEMINOMATA
SEMINUDITIES
SEMINUDITY
SEMIOCHEMICAL
SEMIOCHEMICALS
SEMIOFFICIAL
SEMIOFFICIALLY
SEMIOLOGIC
SEMIOLOGICAL
SEMIOLOGICALLY
SEMIOLOGIES
SEMIOLOGIST
SEMIOLOGISTS
SEMIOPAQUE
SEMIOTICIAN
SEMIOTICIANS
SEMIOTICIST
SEMIOTICISTS
SEMIOVIPAROUS
SEMIPALMATE
SEMIPALMATED
SEMIPALMATION
SEMIPALMATIONS
SEMIPARASITE
SEMIPARASITES
SEMIPARASITIC
SEMIPARASITISM
SEMIPARASITISMS
SEMIPELLUCID
SEMIPERIMETER
SEMIPERIMETERS
SEMIPERMANENT
SEMIPERMEABLE
SEMIPLUMES
SEMIPOLITICAL
SEMIPOPULAR
SEMIPORCELAIN
SEMIPORCELAINS
SEMIPORNOGRAPHY
SEMIPOSTAL
SEMIPOSTALS
SEMIPRECIOUS
SEMIPRIVATE
SEMIPUBLIC
SEMIQUAVER
SEMIQUAVERS
SEMIRELIGIOUS
SEMIRETIRED
SEMIRETIREMENT
SEMIRETIREMENTS
SEMIROUNDS
SEMISACRED
SEMISECRET
SEMISEDENTARY
SEMISHRUBBY
SEMISKILLED
SEMISOLIDS
SEMISOLUSES
SEMISUBMERSIBLE
SEMISYNTHETIC
SEMITERETE
SEMITERRESTRIAL
SEMITONALLY
SEMITONICALLY
SEMITRAILER
SEMITRAILERS
SEMITRANSLUCENT
SEMITRANSPARENT
SEMITROPIC
SEMITROPICAL
SEMITROPICS
SEMITRUCKS
SEMIVITREOUS
SEMIVOCALIC
SEMIVOWELS
SEMIWEEKLIES
SEMIWEEKLY
SEMIYEARLY
SEMPERVIVUM
SEMPERVIVUMS
SEMPITERNAL
SEMPITERNALLY
SEMPITERNITIES
SEMPITERNITY
SEMPITERNUM
SEMPITERNUMS
SEMPSTERING
SEMPSTERINGS
SEMPSTRESS
SEMPSTRESSES
SEMPSTRESSING
SEMPSTRESSINGS
SENARMONTITE
SENARMONTITES
SENATORIAL
SENATORIALLY
SENATORIAN
SENATORSHIP
SENATORSHIPS
SENECTITUDE
SENECTITUDES
SENESCENCE
SENESCENCES
SENESCHALS
SENESCHALSHIP
SENESCHALSHIPS
SENHORITAS
SENILITIES
SENIORITIES
SENNACHIES
SENSATIONAL

SENSATIONALISE
SENSATIONALISED
SENSATIONALISES
SENSATIONALISM
SENSATIONALISMS
SENSATIONALIST
SENSATIONALISTS
SENSATIONALIZE
SENSATIONALIZED
SENSATIONALIZES
SENSATIONALLY
SENSATIONISM
SENSATIONISMS
SENSATIONIST
SENSATIONISTS
SENSATIONLESS
SENSATIONS
SENSELESSLY
SENSELESSNESS
SENSELESSNESSES
SENSIBILIA
SENSIBILITIES
SENSIBILITY
SENSIBLENESS
SENSIBLENESSES
SENSIBLEST
SENSITISATION
SENSITISATIONS
SENSITISED
SENSITISER
SENSITISERS
SENSITISES
SENSITISING
SENSITIVELY
SENSITIVENESS
SENSITIVENESSES
SENSITIVES
SENSITIVITIES
SENSITIVITY
SENSITIZATION
SENSITIZATIONS
SENSITIZED
SENSITIZER
SENSITIZERS
SENSITIZES
SENSITIZING
SENSITOMETER
SENSITOMETERS
SENSITOMETRIC
SENSITOMETRIES
SENSITOMETRY
SENSOMOTOR
SENSORIALLY
SENSORIMOTOR
SENSORINEURAL
SENSORIUMS
SENSUALISATION
SENSUALISATIONS
SENSUALISE
SENSUALISED
SENSUALISES
SENSUALISING
SENSUALISM
SENSUALISMS
SENSUALIST
SENSUALISTIC
SENSUALISTS
SENSUALITIES
SENSUALITY
SENSUALIZATION
SENSUALIZATIONS
SENSUALIZE
SENSUALIZED
SENSUALIZES
SENSUALIZING
SENSUALNESS
SENSUALNESSES
SENSUOSITIES
SENSUOSITY
SENSUOUSLY
SENSUOUSNESS
SENSUOUSNESSES
SENTENCERS
SENTENCING
SENTENTIAE
SENTENTIAL
SENTENTIALLY
SENTENTIOUS
SENTENTIOUSLY
SENTENTIOUSNESS
SENTIENCES
SENTIENCIES
SENTIENTLY
SENTIMENTAL
SENTIMENTALISE
SENTIMENTALISED
SENTIMENTALISES
SENTIMENTALISM
SENTIMENTALISMS
SENTIMENTALIST
SENTIMENTALISTS
SENTIMENTALITY
SENTIMENTALIZE
SENTIMENTALIZED
SENTIMENTALIZES
SENTIMENTALLY
SENTIMENTS
SENTINELED
SENTINELING
SENTINELLED
SENTINELLING
SEPALODIES
SEPARABILITIES
SEPARABILITY
SEPARABLENESS
SEPARABLENESSES
SEPARATELY
SEPARATENESS
SEPARATENESSES
SEPARATING
SEPARATION
SEPARATIONISM
SEPARATIONISMS
SEPARATIONIST
SEPARATIONISTS
SEPARATIONS
SEPARATISM
SEPARATISMS
SEPARATIST
SEPARATISTIC
SEPARATISTS
SEPARATIVE
SEPARATIVELY
SEPARATIVENESS
SEPARATORIES
SEPARATORS
SEPARATORY
SEPARATRICES
SEPARATRIX
SEPARATUMS
SEPIOLITES
SEPIOSTAIRE
SEPIOSTAIRES
SEPTATIONS
SEPTAVALENT
SEPTEMVIRATE
SEPTEMVIRATES
SEPTEMVIRI
SEPTEMVIRS
SEPTENARIES
SEPTENARII
SEPTENARIUS
SEPTENDECILLION
SEPTENNATE
SEPTENNATES
SEPTENNIAL
SEPTENNIALLY
SEPTENNIUM
SEPTENNIUMS
SEPTENTRIAL
SEPTENTRION
SEPTENTRIONAL
SEPTENTRIONALLY
SEPTENTRIONES
SEPTENTRIONS
SEPTICAEMIA
SEPTICAEMIAS
SEPTICAEMIC
SEPTICALLY
SEPTICEMIA
SEPTICEMIAS
SEPTICEMIC
SEPTICIDAL
SEPTICIDALLY
SEPTICITIES
SEPTIFEROUS
SEPTIFRAGAL
SEPTILATERAL
SEPTILLION
SEPTILLIONS
SEPTILLIONTH
SEPTILLIONTHS
SEPTIMOLES
SEPTIVALENT
SEPTUAGENARIAN
SEPTUAGENARIANS
SEPTUAGENARIES
SEPTUAGENARY
SEPTUPLETS
SEPTUPLICATE
SEPTUPLICATES
SEPTUPLING
SEPULCHERED
SEPULCHERING
SEPULCHERS
SEPULCHRAL
SEPULCHRALLY
SEPULCHRED
SEPULCHRES
SEPULCHRING
SEPULCHROUS
SEPULTURAL
SEPULTURED
SEPULTURES
SEPULTURING
SEQUACIOUS
SEQUACIOUSLY
SEQUACIOUSNESS
SEQUACITIES
SEQUELISED
SEQUELISES
SEQUELISING
SEQUELIZED
SEQUELIZES
SEQUELIZING
SEQUENCERS
SEQUENCIES
SEQUENCING
SEQUENCINGS
SEQUENTIAL
SEQUENTIALITIES
SEQUENTIALITY
SEQUENTIALLY
SEQUESTERED
SEQUESTERING
SEQUESTERS
SEQUESTRABLE
SEQUESTRAL
SEQUESTRANT
SEQUESTRANTS
SEQUESTRATE
SEQUESTRATED
SEQUESTRATES
SEQUESTRATING
SEQUESTRATION
SEQUESTRATIONS
SEQUESTRATOR
SEQUESTRATORS
SEQUESTRUM
SEQUESTRUMS
SERAPHICAL
SERAPHICALLY
SERAPHINES
SERASKIERATE
SERASKIERATES
SERASKIERS
SERENADERS
SERENADING
SERENDIPITIES
SERENDIPITIST
SERENDIPITISTS
SERENDIPITOUS
SERENDIPITOUSLY
SERENDIPITY
SERENENESS
SERENENESSES
SERENITIES
SERGEANCIES
SERGEANTIES
SERGEANTSHIP
SERGEANTSHIPS
SERIALISATION
SERIALISATIONS
SERIALISED

SERIALISES
SERIALISING
SERIALISMS
SERIALISTS
SERIALITIES
SERIALIZATION
SERIALIZATIONS
SERIALIZED
SERIALIZES
SERIALIZING
SERIATIONS
SERICICULTURE
SERICICULTURES
SERICICULTURIST
SERICITISATION
SERICITISATIONS
SERICITIZATION
SERICITIZATIONS
SERICTERIA
SERICTERIUM
SERICULTURAL
SERICULTURE
SERICULTURES
SERICULTURIST
SERICULTURISTS
SERIGRAPHER
SERIGRAPHERS
SERIGRAPHIC
SERIGRAPHIES
SERIGRAPHS
SERIGRAPHY
SERINETTES
SERIOCOMIC
SERIOCOMICAL
SERIOCOMICALLY
SERIOUSNESS
SERIOUSNESSES
SERJEANCIES
SERJEANTIES
SERJEANTRIES
SERJEANTRY
SERJEANTSHIP
SERJEANTSHIPS
SERMONEERS
SERMONETTE
SERMONETTES
SERMONICAL
SERMONINGS
SERMONISED
SERMONISER
SERMONISERS
SERMONISES
SERMONISING
SERMONIZED
SERMONIZER
SERMONIZERS
SERMONIZES
SERMONIZING
SEROCONVERSION
SEROCONVERSIONS
SEROCONVERT
SEROCONVERTED
SEROCONVERTING
SEROCONVERTS
SERODIAGNOSES
SERODIAGNOSIS
SERODIAGNOSTIC
SEROLOGICAL
SEROLOGICALLY
SEROLOGIES
SEROLOGIST
SEROLOGISTS
SERONEGATIVE
SERONEGATIVITY
SEROPOSITIVE
SEROPOSITIVITY
SEROPURULENT
SEROSITIES
SEROTAXONOMIES
SEROTAXONOMY
SEROTHERAPIES
SEROTHERAPY
SEROTINIES
SEROTINOUS
SEROTONERGIC
SEROTONINERGIC
SEROTONINS
SEROTYPING
SEROTYPINGS
SEROUSNESS
SEROUSNESSES
SERPENTIFORM
SERPENTINE
SERPENTINED
SERPENTINELY
SERPENTINES
SERPENTINIC
SERPENTINING
SERPENTININGLY
SERPENTININGS
SERPENTINISE
SERPENTINISED
SERPENTINISES
SERPENTINISING
SERPENTINITE
SERPENTINITES
SERPENTINIZE
SERPENTINIZED
SERPENTINIZES
SERPENTINIZING
SERPENTINOUS
SERPENTISE
SERPENTISED
SERPENTISES
SERPENTISING
SERPENTIZE
SERPENTIZED
SERPENTIZES
SERPENTIZING
SERPENTLIKE
SERPENTRIES
SERPIGINES
SERPIGINOUS
SERPIGINOUSLY
SERPULITES
SERRADELLA
SERRADELLAS
SERRADILLA
SERRADILLAS
SERRANOIDS
SERRASALMO
SERRASALMOS
SERRATIONS
SERRATIROSTRAL
SERRATULATE
SERRATURES
SERRATUSES
SERREFILES
SERRIEDNESS
SERRIEDNESSES
SERRULATED
SERRULATION
SERRULATIONS
SERTULARIAN
SERTULARIANS
SERVANTHOOD
SERVANTHOODS
SERVANTING
SERVANTLESS
SERVANTRIES
SERVANTSHIP
SERVANTSHIPS
SERVICEABILITY
SERVICEABLE
SERVICEABLENESS
SERVICEABLY
SERVICEBERRIES
SERVICEBERRY
SERVICELESS
SERVICEMAN
SERVICEMEN
SERVICEWOMAN
SERVICEWOMEN
SERVIETTES
SERVILENESS
SERVILENESSES
SERVILISMS
SERVILITIES
SERVITORIAL
SERVITORSHIP
SERVITORSHIPS
SERVITRESS
SERVITRESSES
SERVITUDES
SERVOCONTROL
SERVOCONTROLS
SERVOMECHANICAL
SERVOMECHANISM
SERVOMECHANISMS
SERVOMOTOR
SERVOMOTORS
SESQUIALTER
SESQUIALTERA
SESQUIALTERAS
SESQUICARBONATE
SESQUICENTENARY
SESQUIOXIDE
SESQUIOXIDES
SESQUIPEDAL
SESQUIPEDALIAN
SESQUIPEDALITY
SESQUIPLICATE
SESQUISULPHIDE
SESQUISULPHIDES
SESQUITERPENE
SESQUITERPENES
SESQUITERTIA
SESQUITERTIAS
SESSILITIES
SESSIONALLY
SESTERTIUM
SESTERTIUS
SETACEOUSLY
SETIFEROUS
SETIGEROUS
SETTERWORT
SETTERWORTS
SETTLEABLE
SETTLEDNESS
SETTLEDNESSES
SETTLEMENT
SETTLEMENTS
SEVENPENCE
SEVENPENCES
SEVENPENNIES
SEVENPENNY
SEVENTEENS
SEVENTEENTH
SEVENTEENTHLY
SEVENTEENTHS
SEVENTIETH
SEVENTIETHS
SEVERABILITIES
SEVERABILITY
SEVERALFOLD
SEVERALTIES
SEVERANCES
SEVERENESS
SEVERENESSES
SEVERITIES
SEWABILITIES
SEWABILITY
SEXAGENARIAN
SEXAGENARIANS
SEXAGENARIES
SEXAGENARY
SEXAGESIMAL
SEXAGESIMALLY
SEXAGESIMALS
SEXAHOLICS
SEXANGULAR
SEXANGULARLY
SEXAVALENT
SEXCENTENARIES
SEXCENTENARY
SEXDECILLION
SEXDECILLIONS
SEXENNIALLY
SEXENNIALS
SEXERCISES
SEXINESSES
SEXIVALENT
SEXLESSNESS
SEXLESSNESSES
SEXLOCULAR
SEXOLOGICAL
SEXOLOGIES
SEXOLOGIST
SEXOLOGISTS
SEXPARTITE
SEXPLOITATION
SEXPLOITATIONS
SEXTILLION
SEXTILLIONS

SEXTILLIONTH
SEXTILLIONTHS
SEXTODECIMO
SEXTODECIMOS
SEXTONESSES
SEXTONSHIP
SEXTONSHIPS
SEXTUPLETS
SEXTUPLICATE
SEXTUPLICATED
SEXTUPLICATES
SEXTUPLICATING
SEXTUPLING
SEXUALISATION
SEXUALISATIONS
SEXUALISED
SEXUALISES
SEXUALISING
SEXUALISMS
SEXUALISTS
SEXUALITIES
SEXUALIZATION
SEXUALIZATIONS
SEXUALIZED
SEXUALIZES
SEXUALIZING
SFORZANDOS
SHABBINESS
SHABBINESSES
SHABRACQUE
SHABRACQUES
SHACKLEBONE
SHACKLEBONES
SHADBERRIES
SHADBUSHES
SHADCHANIM
SHADINESSES
SHADKHANIM
SHADOWBOXED
SHADOWBOXES
SHADOWBOXING
SHADOWCAST
SHADOWCASTING
SHADOWCASTINGS
SHADOWCASTS
SHADOWGRAPH
SHADOWGRAPHIES
SHADOWGRAPHS
SHADOWGRAPHY
SHADOWIEST
SHADOWINESS
SHADOWINESSES
SHADOWINGS
SHADOWLESS
SHADOWLIKE
SHAGGEDNESS
SHAGGEDNESSES
SHAGGINESS
SHAGGINESSES
SHAGGYMANE
SHAGGYMANES
SHAGREENED
SHAGTASTIC
SHAHTOOSHES
SHAKEDOWNS
SHAKINESSES
SHAKUHACHI
SHAKUHACHIS
SHALLOWEST
SHALLOWING
SHALLOWINGS
SHALLOWNESS
SHALLOWNESSES
SHAMANISMS
SHAMANISTIC
SHAMANISTS
SHAMATEURISM
SHAMATEURISMS
SHAMATEURS
SHAMBLIEST
SHAMBLINGS
SHAMEFACED
SHAMEFACEDLY
SHAMEFACEDNESS
SHAMEFASTNESS
SHAMEFASTNESSES
SHAMEFULLY
SHAMEFULNESS
SHAMEFULNESSES
SHAMELESSLY
SHAMELESSNESS
SHAMELESSNESSES
SHAMEWORTHY
SHAMIANAHS
SHAMIYANAH
SHAMIYANAHS
SHAMMASHIM
SHAMPOOERS
SHAMPOOING
SHANACHIES
SHANDRYDAN
SHANDRYDANS
SHANDYGAFF
SHANDYGAFFS
SHANGHAIED
SHANGHAIER
SHANGHAIERS
SHANGHAIING
SHANKBONES
SHANKPIECE
SHANKPIECES
SHANTYTOWN
SHANTYTOWNS
SHAPELESSLY
SHAPELESSNESS
SHAPELESSNESSES
SHAPELIEST
SHAPELINESS
SHAPELINESSES
SHARAWADGI
SHARAWADGIS
SHARAWAGGI
SHARAWAGGIS
SHAREABILITIES
SHAREABILITY
SHARECROPPED
SHARECROPPER
SHARECROPPERS
SHARECROPPING
SHARECROPS
SHAREFARMER
SHAREFARMERS
SHAREHOLDER
SHAREHOLDERS
SHAREHOLDING
SHAREHOLDINGS
SHAREMILKER
SHAREMILKERS
SHAREWARES
SHARKSKINS
SHARKSUCKER
SHARKSUCKERS
SHARPBENDER
SHARPBENDERS
SHARPENERS
SHARPENING
SHARPNESSES
SHARPSHOOTER
SHARPSHOOTERS
SHARPSHOOTING
SHARPSHOOTINGS
SHASHLICKS
SHATTERERS
SHATTERING
SHATTERINGLY
SHATTERPROOF
SHAUCHLIER
SHAUCHLIEST
SHAUCHLING
SHAVELINGS
SHAVETAILS
SHEARLINGS
SHEARWATER
SHEARWATERS
SHEATFISHES
SHEATHBILL
SHEATHBILLS
SHEATHFISH
SHEATHFISHES
SHEATHIEST
SHEATHINGS
SHEATHLESS
SHEBEENERS
SHEBEENING
SHEBEENINGS
SHECHITAHS
SHECKLATON
SHECKLATONS
SHEEPBERRIES
SHEEPBERRY
SHEEPCOTES
SHEEPFOLDS
SHEEPHEADS
SHEEPHERDER
SHEEPHERDERS
SHEEPHERDING
SHEEPHERDINGS
SHEEPISHLY
SHEEPISHNESS
SHEEPISHNESSES
SHEEPSHANK
SHEEPSHANKS
SHEEPSHEAD
SHEEPSHEADS
SHEEPSHEARER
SHEEPSHEARERS
SHEEPSHEARING
SHEEPSHEARINGS
SHEEPSKINS
SHEEPTRACK
SHEEPTRACKS
SHEEPWALKS
SHEERNESSES
SHEETROCKED
SHEETROCKING
SHEETROCKS
SHEIKHDOMS
SHELDDUCKS
SHELDRAKES
SHELFROOMS
SHELFTALKER
SHELFTALKERS
SHELLACKED
SHELLACKER
SHELLACKERS
SHELLACKING
SHELLACKINGS
SHELLBACKS
SHELLBARKS
SHELLBOUND
SHELLCRACKER
SHELLCRACKERS
SHELLDRAKE
SHELLDRAKES
SHELLDUCKS
SHELLFIRES
SHELLFISHERIES
SHELLFISHERY
SHELLFISHES
SHELLINESS
SHELLINESSES
SHELLPROOF
SHELLSHOCK
SHELLSHOCKED
SHELLSHOCKS
SHELLWORKS
SHELLYCOAT
SHELLYCOATS
SHELTERBELT
SHELTERBELTS
SHELTERERS
SHELTERING
SHELTERINGS
SHELTERLESS
SHEMOZZLED
SHEMOZZLES
SHEMOZZLING
SHENANIGAN
SHENANIGANS
SHEPHERDED
SHEPHERDESS
SHEPHERDESSES
SHEPHERDING
SHEPHERDLESS
SHEPHERDLING
SHEPHERDLINGS
SHERARDISATION
SHERARDISATIONS
SHERARDISE
SHERARDISED
SHERARDISES
SHERARDISING
SHERARDIZATION
SHERARDIZATIONS

SHERARDIZE
SHERARDIZED
SHERARDIZES
SHERARDIZING
SHEREEFIAN
SHERGOTTITE
SHERGOTTITES
SHERIFFALTIES
SHERIFFALTY
SHERIFFDOM
SHERIFFDOMS
SHERIFFSHIP
SHERIFFSHIPS
SHEWBREADS
SHIBBOLETH
SHIBBOLETHS
SHIBUICHIS
SHIDDUCHIM
SHIELDINGS
SHIELDLESS
SHIELDLIKE
SHIELDLING
SHIELDLINGS
SHIELDRAKE
SHIELDRAKES
SHIELDWALL
SHIELDWALLS
SHIFTINESS
SHIFTINESSES
SHIFTLESSLY
SHIFTLESSNESS
SHIFTLESSNESSES
SHIFTWORKS
SHIGELLOSES
SHIGELLOSIS
SHIKARRING
SHILLABERS
SHILLALAHS
SHILLELAGH
SHILLELAGHS
SHILLELAHS
SHILLINGLESS
SHILLINGSWORTH
SHILLINGSWORTHS
SHILLYSHALLIED
SHILLYSHALLIER
SHILLYSHALLIERS
SHILLYSHALLIES
SHILLYSHALLY
SHILLYSHALLYING
SHIMMERING
SHIMMERINGLY
SHIMMERINGS
SHIMOZZLES
SHINGLIEST
SHINGLINGS
SHINGUARDS
SHININESSES
SHININGNESS
SHININGNESSES
SHINLEAVES
SHINNERIES
SHINNEYING
SHINPLASTER
SHINPLASTERS
SHINSPLINTS
SHIPBOARDS
SHIPBROKER
SHIPBROKERS
SHIPBUILDER
SHIPBUILDERS
SHIPBUILDING
SHIPBUILDINGS
SHIPFITTER
SHIPFITTERS
SHIPLAPPED
SHIPLAPPING
SHIPMASTER
SHIPMASTERS
SHIPOWNERS
SHIPPOUNDS
SHIPWRECKED
SHIPWRECKING
SHIPWRECKS
SHIPWRIGHT
SHIPWRIGHTS
SHIRRALEES
SHIRTBANDS
SHIRTDRESS
SHIRTDRESSES
SHIRTFRONT
SHIRTFRONTS
SHIRTINESS
SHIRTINESSES
SHIRTLIFTER
SHIRTLIFTERS
SHIRTMAKER
SHIRTMAKERS
SHIRTSLEEVE
SHIRTSLEEVED
SHIRTSLEEVES
SHIRTTAILED
SHIRTTAILING
SHIRTTAILS
SHIRTWAIST
SHIRTWAISTER
SHIRTWAISTERS
SHIRTWAISTS
SHITTIMWOOD
SHITTIMWOODS
SHITTINESS
SHITTINESSES
SHIVAREEING
SHIVERIEST
SHIVERINGLY
SHIVERINGS
SHLEMIEHLS
SHLEMOZZLE
SHLEMOZZLED
SHLEMOZZLES
SHLEMOZZLING
SHLIMAZELS
SHLOCKIEST
SHMALTZIER
SHMALTZIEST
SHOALINESS
SHOALINESSES
SHOALNESSES
SHOCKABILITIES
SHOCKABILITY
SHOCKHEADED
SHOCKINGLY
SHOCKINGNESS
SHOCKINGNESSES
SHOCKPROOF
SHOCKSTALL
SHOCKSTALLS
SHOCKUMENTARIES
SHOCKUMENTARY
SHODDINESS
SHODDINESSES
SHOEBLACKS
SHOEHORNED
SHOEHORNING
SHOEMAKERS
SHOEMAKING
SHOEMAKINGS
SHOESHINES
SHOESTRING
SHOESTRINGS
SHOGGLIEST
SHOGUNATES
SHONGOLOLO
SHONGOLOLOS
SHOOGIEING
SHOOGLIEST
SHOOTAROUND
SHOOTAROUNDS
SHOOTDOWNS
SHOPAHOLIC
SHOPAHOLICS
SHOPAHOLISM
SHOPAHOLISMS
SHOPBOARDS
SHOPBREAKER
SHOPBREAKERS
SHOPBREAKING
SHOPBREAKINGS
SHOPFRONTS
SHOPKEEPER
SHOPKEEPERS
SHOPKEEPING
SHOPKEEPINGS
SHOPLIFTED
SHOPLIFTER
SHOPLIFTERS
SHOPLIFTING
SHOPSOILED
SHOPWALKER
SHOPWALKERS
SHOPWINDOW
SHOPWINDOWS
SHOREBIRDS
SHOREFRONT
SHOREFRONTS
SHORELINES
SHOREWARDS
SHOREWEEDS
SHORTBOARD
SHORTBOARDS
SHORTBREAD
SHORTBREADS
SHORTCAKES
SHORTCHANGE
SHORTCHANGED
SHORTCHANGER
SHORTCHANGERS
SHORTCHANGES
SHORTCHANGING
SHORTCOMING
SHORTCOMINGS
SHORTCRUST
SHORTCUTTING
SHORTENERS
SHORTENING
SHORTENINGS
SHORTFALLS
SHORTGOWNS
SHORTHAIRED
SHORTHAIRS
SHORTHANDED
SHORTHANDS
SHORTHEADS
SHORTHORNS
SHORTLISTED
SHORTLISTING
SHORTLISTS
SHORTNESSES
SHORTSIGHTED
SHORTSIGHTEDLY
SHORTSTOPS
SHORTSWORD
SHORTSWORDS
SHORTWAVED
SHORTWAVES
SHORTWAVING
SHOTFIRERS
SHOTGUNNED
SHOTGUNNER
SHOTGUNNERS
SHOTGUNNING
SHOTMAKERS
SHOTMAKING
SHOTMAKINGS
SHOULDERED
SHOULDERING
SHOULDERINGS
SHOUTHERED
SHOUTHERING
SHOUTINGLY
SHOUTLINES
SHOVELBOARD
SHOVELBOARDS
SHOVELFULS
SHOVELHEAD
SHOVELHEADS
SHOVELLERS
SHOVELLING
SHOVELNOSE
SHOVELNOSES
SHOVELSFUL
SHOWBIZZES
SHOWBOATED
SHOWBOATER
SHOWBOATERS
SHOWBOATING
SHOWBREADS
SHOWCASING
SHOWERHEAD
SHOWERHEADS
SHOWERIEST
SHOWERINESS
SHOWERINESSES
SHOWERINGS

SHOWERLESS
SHOWERPROOF
SHOWERPROOFED
SHOWERPROOFING
SHOWERPROOFS
SHOWGROUND
SHOWGROUNDS
SHOWINESSES
SHOWJUMPER
SHOWJUMPERS
SHOWJUMPING
SHOWJUMPINGS
SHOWMANSHIP
SHOWMANSHIPS
SHOWPIECES
SHOWPLACES
SHOWSTOPPER
SHOWSTOPPERS
SHOWSTOPPING
SHREDDIEST
SHREDDINGS
SHREWDNESS
SHREWDNESSES
SHREWISHLY
SHREWISHNESS
SHREWISHNESSES
SHREWMOUSE
SHRIECHING
SHRIEKIEST
SHRIEKINGLY
SHRIEKINGS
SHRIEVALTIES
SHRIEVALTY
SHRILLIEST
SHRILLINGS
SHRILLNESS
SHRILLNESSES
SHRIMPIEST
SHRIMPINGS
SHRIMPLIKE
SHRINELIKE
SHRINKABLE
SHRINKAGES
SHRINKINGLY
SHRINKPACK
SHRINKPACKS
SHRITCHING
SHRIVELING
SHRIVELLED
SHRIVELLING
SHROFFAGES
SHROUDIEST
SHROUDINGS
SHROUDLESS
SHRUBBERIED
SHRUBBERIES
SHRUBBIEST
SHRUBBINESS
SHRUBBINESSES
SHRUBLANDS
SHTETELACH
SHTICKIEST
SHUBUNKINS
SHUDDERING
SHUDDERINGLY
SHUDDERINGS
SHUDDERSOME
SHUFFLEBOARD
SHUFFLEBOARDS
SHUFFLINGLY
SHUFFLINGS
SHUNAMITISM
SHUNAMITISMS
SHUNPIKERS
SHUNPIKING
SHUNPIKINGS
SHUTTERBUG
SHUTTERBUGS
SHUTTERING
SHUTTERINGS
SHUTTERLESS
SHUTTLECOCK
SHUTTLECOCKED
SHUTTLECOCKING
SHUTTLECOCKS
SHUTTLELESS
SHUTTLEWISE
SHYLOCKING
SIALAGOGIC
SIALAGOGUE
SIALAGOGUES
SIALOGOGIC
SIALOGOGUE
SIALOGOGUES
SIALOGRAMS
SIALOGRAPHIES
SIALOGRAPHY
SIALOLITHS
SIALORRHOEA
SIALORRHOEAS
SIBILANCES
SIBILANCIES
SIBILANTLY
SIBILATING
SIBILATION
SIBILATIONS
SIBILATORS
SIBILATORY
SICCATIVES
SICILIANOS
SICILIENNE
SICILIENNES
SICKENINGLY
SICKENINGS
SICKERNESS
SICKERNESSES
SICKISHNESS
SICKISHNESSES
SICKLEBILL
SICKLEBILLS
SICKLEMIAS
SICKLINESS
SICKLINESSES
SICKNESSES
SICKNURSES
SICKNURSING
SICKNURSINGS
SIDDHUISMS
SIDEBOARDS
SIDEBURNED
SIDECHECKS
SIDEDNESSES
SIDEDRESSES
SIDELEVERS
SIDELIGHTS
SIDELINERS
SIDELINING
SIDEPIECES
SIDERATING
SIDERATION
SIDERATIONS
SIDEREALLY
SIDEROLITE
SIDEROLITES
SIDEROPENIA
SIDEROPENIAS
SIDEROPHILE
SIDEROPHILES
SIDEROPHILIC
SIDEROPHILIN
SIDEROPHILINS
SIDEROSTAT
SIDEROSTATIC
SIDEROSTATS
SIDESADDLE
SIDESADDLES
SIDESHOOTS
SIDESLIPPED
SIDESLIPPING
SIDESPLITTING
SIDESPLITTINGLY
SIDESTEPPED
SIDESTEPPER
SIDESTEPPERS
SIDESTEPPING
SIDESTREAM
SIDESTREET
SIDESTREETS
SIDESTROKE
SIDESTROKES
SIDESWIPED
SIDESWIPER
SIDESWIPERS
SIDESWIPES
SIDESWIPING
SIDETRACKED
SIDETRACKING
SIDETRACKS
SIDEWHEELER
SIDEWHEELERS
SIDEWHEELS
SIDEWINDER
SIDEWINDERS
SIEGECRAFT
SIEGECRAFTS
SIEGEWORKS
SIFFLEUSES
SIGHTLESSLY
SIGHTLESSNESS
SIGHTLESSNESSES
SIGHTLIEST
SIGHTLINES
SIGHTLINESS
SIGHTLINESSES
SIGHTSCREEN
SIGHTSCREENS
SIGHTSEEING
SIGHTSEEINGS
SIGHTSEERS
SIGHTWORTHY
SIGILLARIAN
SIGILLARIANS
SIGILLARID
SIGILLARIDS
SIGILLATION
SIGILLATIONS
SIGMATIONS
SIGMATISMS
SIGMATRONS
SIGMOIDALLY
SIGMOIDECTOMIES
SIGMOIDECTOMY
SIGMOIDOSCOPE
SIGMOIDOSCOPES
SIGMOIDOSCOPIC
SIGMOIDOSCOPIES
SIGMOIDOSCOPY
SIGNALINGS
SIGNALISATION
SIGNALISATIONS
SIGNALISED
SIGNALISES
SIGNALISING
SIGNALIZATION
SIGNALIZATIONS
SIGNALIZED
SIGNALIZES
SIGNALIZING
SIGNALLERS
SIGNALLING
SIGNALLINGS
SIGNALMENT
SIGNALMENTS
SIGNATORIES
SIGNATURES
SIGNBOARDS
SIGNEURIES
SIGNIFIABLE
SIGNIFICANCE
SIGNIFICANCES
SIGNIFICANCIES
SIGNIFICANCY
SIGNIFICANT
SIGNIFICANTLY
SIGNIFICANTS
SIGNIFICATE
SIGNIFICATES
SIGNIFICATION
SIGNIFICATIONS
SIGNIFICATIVE
SIGNIFICATIVELY
SIGNIFICATOR
SIGNIFICATORS
SIGNIFICATORY
SIGNIFIEDS
SIGNIFIERS
SIGNIFYING
SIGNIFYINGS
SIGNIORIES
SIGNORINAS
SIGNPOSTED
SIGNPOSTING
SIKORSKIES
SILENTIARIES

SILENTIARY
SILENTNESS
SILENTNESSES
SILHOUETTE
SILHOUETTED
SILHOUETTES
SILHOUETTING
SILHOUETTIST
SILHOUETTISTS
SILICATING
SILICICOLOUS
SILICIFEROUS
SILICIFICATION
SILICIFICATIONS
SILICIFIED
SILICIFIES
SILICIFYING
SILICONISED
SILICONIZED
SILICOTICS
SILICULOSE
SILIQUACEOUS
SILKALENES
SILKALINES
SILKGROWER
SILKGROWERS
SILKINESSES
SILKOLINES
SILKSCREEN
SILKSCREENS
SILLIMANITE
SILLIMANITES
SILLINESSES
SILTATIONS
SILTSTONES
SILVERBACK
SILVERBACKS
SILVERBERRIES
SILVERBERRY
SILVERBILL
SILVERBILLS
SILVEREYES
SILVERFISH
SILVERFISHES
SILVERHORN
SILVERHORNS
SILVERIEST
SILVERINESS
SILVERINESSES
SILVERINGS
SILVERISED
SILVERISES
SILVERISING
SILVERIZED
SILVERIZES
SILVERIZING
SILVERLING
SILVERLINGS
SILVERPOINT
SILVERPOINTS
SILVERSIDE
SILVERSIDES
SILVERSIDESES
SILVERSKIN
SILVERSKINS
SILVERSMITH
SILVERSMITHING
SILVERSMITHINGS
SILVERSMITHS
SILVERTAIL
SILVERTAILS
SILVERWARE
SILVERWARES
SILVERWEED
SILVERWEEDS
SILVESTRIAN
SILVICULTURAL
SILVICULTURALLY
SILVICULTURE
SILVICULTURES
SILVICULTURIST
SILVICULTURISTS
SIMAROUBACEOUS
SIMAROUBAS
SIMARUBACEOUS
SIMILARITIES
SIMILARITY
SIMILATIVE
SIMILISING
SIMILITUDE
SIMILITUDES
SIMILIZING
SIMILLIMUM
SIMILLIMUMS
SIMONIACAL
SIMONIACALLY
SIMONISING
SIMONIZING
SIMPERINGLY
SIMPLEMINDED
SIMPLEMINDEDLY
SIMPLENESS
SIMPLENESSES
SIMPLESSES
SIMPLETONS
SIMPLICIAL
SIMPLICIALLY
SIMPLICIDENTATE
SIMPLICITER
SIMPLICITIES
SIMPLICITY
SIMPLIFICATION
SIMPLIFICATIONS
SIMPLIFICATIVE
SIMPLIFICATOR
SIMPLIFICATORS
SIMPLIFIED
SIMPLIFIER
SIMPLIFIERS
SIMPLIFIES
SIMPLIFYING
SIMPLISTIC
SIMPLISTICALLY
SIMULACRES
SIMULACRUM
SIMULACRUMS
SIMULATING
SIMULATION
SIMULATIONS
SIMULATIVE
SIMULATIVELY
SIMULATORS
SIMULATORY
SIMULCASTED
SIMULCASTING
SIMULCASTS
SIMULTANEITIES
SIMULTANEITY
SIMULTANEOUS
SIMULTANEOUSES
SIMULTANEOUSLY
SINANTHROPUS
SINANTHROPUSES
SINARCHISM
SINARCHISMS
SINARCHIST
SINARCHISTS
SINARQUISM
SINARQUISMS
SINARQUIST
SINARQUISTS
SINCERENESS
SINCERENESSES
SINCERITIES
SINCIPITAL
SINDONOLOGIES
SINDONOLOGIST
SINDONOLOGISTS
SINDONOLOGY
SINDONOPHANIES
SINDONOPHANY
SINECURISM
SINECURISMS
SINECURIST
SINECURISTS
SINEWINESS
SINEWINESSES
SINFONIETTA
SINFONIETTAS
SINFULNESS
SINFULNESSES
SINGABLENESS
SINGABLENESSES
SINGALONGS
SINGLEDOMS
SINGLEHOOD
SINGLEHOODS
SINGLENESS
SINGLENESSES
SINGLESTICK
SINGLESTICKS
SINGLETONS
SINGLETREE
SINGLETREES
SINGSONGED
SINGSONGING
SINGSPIELS
SINGULARISATION
SINGULARISE
SINGULARISED
SINGULARISES
SINGULARISING
SINGULARISM
SINGULARISMS
SINGULARIST
SINGULARISTS
SINGULARITIES
SINGULARITY
SINGULARIZATION
SINGULARIZE
SINGULARIZED
SINGULARIZES
SINGULARIZING
SINGULARLY
SINGULARNESS
SINGULARNESSES
SINGULTUSES
SINICISING
SINICIZING
SINISTERITIES
SINISTERITY
SINISTERLY
SINISTERNESS
SINISTERNESSES
SINISTERWISE
SINISTRALITIES
SINISTRALITY
SINISTRALLY
SINISTRALS
SINISTRODEXTRAL
SINISTRORSAL
SINISTRORSALLY
SINISTRORSE
SINISTRORSELY
SINISTROUS
SINISTROUSLY
SINLESSNESS
SINLESSNESSES
SINNINGIAS
SINOATRIAL
SINOLOGICAL
SINOLOGIES
SINOLOGIST
SINOLOGISTS
SINOLOGUES
SINSEMILLA
SINSEMILLAS
SINTERABILITIES
SINTERABILITY
SINUATIONS
SINUITISES
SINUOSITIES
SINUOUSNESS
SINUOUSNESSES
SINUPALLIAL
SINUPALLIATE
SINUSITISES
SINUSOIDAL
SINUSOIDALLY
SIPHONAGES
SIPHONOGAM
SIPHONOGAMIES
SIPHONOGAMS
SIPHONOGAMY
SIPHONOPHORE
SIPHONOPHORES
SIPHONOPHOROUS
SIPHONOSTELE
SIPHONOSTELES
SIPHONOSTELIC
SIPHUNCLES
SIPUNCULID
SIPUNCULIDS
SIPUNCULOID

SIPUNCULOIDS
SIRENISING
SIRENIZING
SIRONISING
SIRONIZING
SISERARIES
SISSINESSES
SISSYNESSES
SISTERHOOD
SISTERHOODS
SISTERLESS
SISTERLIKE
SISTERLINESS
SISTERLINESSES
SITATUNGAS
SITIOLOGIES
SITIOPHOBIA
SITIOPHOBIAS
SITOLOGIES
SITOPHOBIA
SITOPHOBIAS
SITOSTEROL
SITOSTEROLS
SITUATIONAL
SITUATIONALLY
SITUATIONISM
SITUATIONISMS
SITUATIONS
SITUTUNGAS
SITZKRIEGS
SIXPENNIES
SIXTEENERS
SIXTEENMOS
SIXTEENTHLY
SIXTEENTHS
SIZABLENESS
SIZABLENESSES
SIZARSHIPS
SIZEABLENESS
SIZEABLENESSES
SIZINESSES
SIZZLINGLY
SJAMBOKING
SJAMBOKKED
SJAMBOKKING
SKAITHLESS
SKALDSHIPS
SKANKINESS
SKANKINESSES
SKATEBOARD
SKATEBOARDED
SKATEBOARDER
SKATEBOARDERS
SKATEBOARDING
SKATEBOARDINGS
SKATEBOARDS
SKATEPARKS
SKEDADDLED
SKEDADDLER
SKEDADDLERS
SKEDADDLES
SKEDADDLING
SKELDERING
SKELETALLY
SKELETOGENOUS
SKELETONIC
SKELETONISE
SKELETONISED
SKELETONISER
SKELETONISERS
SKELETONISES
SKELETONISING
SKELETONIZE
SKELETONIZED
SKELETONIZER
SKELETONIZERS
SKELETONIZES
SKELETONIZING
SKELLOCHED
SKELLOCHING
SKELTERING
SKEPTICALLY
SKEPTICALNESS
SKEPTICALNESSES
SKEPTICISM
SKEPTICISMS
SKETCHABILITIES
SKETCHABILITY
SKETCHABLE
SKETCHBOOK
SKETCHBOOKS
SKETCHIEST
SKETCHINESS
SKETCHINESSES
SKETCHPADS
SKEUOMORPH
SKEUOMORPHIC
SKEUOMORPHISM
SKEUOMORPHISMS
SKEUOMORPHS
SKEWBACKED
SKEWNESSES
SKIAGRAPHS
SKIAMACHIES
SKIASCOPES
SKIASCOPIES
SKIBOBBERS
SKIBOBBING
SKIBOBBINGS
SKIDDOOING
SKIJORINGS
SKIKJORING
SKIKJORINGS
SKILFULNESS
SKILFULNESSES
SKILLCENTRE
SKILLCENTRES
SKILLESSNESS
SKILLESSNESSES
SKILLFULLY
SKILLFULNESS
SKILLFULNESSES
SKILLIGALEE
SKILLIGALEES
SKILLIGOLEE
SKILLIGOLEES
SKIMBOARDED
SKIMBOARDER
SKIMBOARDERS
SKIMBOARDING
SKIMBOARDINGS
SKIMBOARDS
SKIMMINGLY
SKIMMINGTON
SKIMMINGTONS
SKIMOBILED
SKIMOBILES
SKIMOBILING
SKIMPINESS
SKIMPINESSES
SKIMPINGLY
SKINFLICKS
SKINFLINTS
SKINFLINTY
SKINNINESS
SKINNINESSES
SKIPPERING
SKIPPERINGS
SKIPPINGLY
SKIRMISHED
SKIRMISHER
SKIRMISHERS
SKIRMISHES
SKIRMISHING
SKIRMISHINGS
SKITTERIER
SKITTERIEST
SKITTERING
SKITTISHLY
SKITTISHNESS
SKITTISHNESSES
SKREEGHING
SKREIGHING
SKRIECHING
SKRIEGHING
SKRIMMAGED
SKRIMMAGES
SKRIMMAGING
SKRIMSHANK
SKRIMSHANKED
SKRIMSHANKER
SKRIMSHANKERS
SKRIMSHANKING
SKRIMSHANKS
SKULDUDDERIES
SKULDUDDERY
SKULDUGGERIES
SKULDUGGERY
SKULKINGLY
SKULLDUGGERIES
SKULLDUGGERY
SKUMMERING
SKUNKBIRDS
SKUNKWEEDS
SKUTTERUDITE
SKUTTERUDITES
SKYBRIDGES
SKYDIVINGS
SKYJACKERS
SKYJACKING
SKYJACKINGS
SKYLARKERS
SKYLARKING
SKYLARKINGS
SKYLIGHTED
SKYROCKETED
SKYROCKETING
SKYROCKETS
SKYSCRAPER
SKYSCRAPERS
SKYSURFERS
SKYSURFING
SKYSURFINGS
SKYWRITERS
SKYWRITING
SKYWRITINGS
SKYWRITTEN
SLABBERERS
SLABBERING
SLABBINESS
SLABBINESSES
SLABSTONES
SLACKENERS
SLACKENING
SLACKENINGS
SLACKNESSES
SLAISTERED
SLAISTERIES
SLAISTERING
SLALOMISTS
SLAMDANCED
SLAMDANCES
SLAMDANCING
SLAMMAKINS
SLAMMERKIN
SLAMMERKINS
SLANDERERS
SLANDERING
SLANDEROUS
SLANDEROUSLY
SLANDEROUSNESS
SLANGINESS
SLANGINESSES
SLANGINGLY
SLANGUAGES
SLANTENDICULAR
SLANTINDICULAR
SLANTINGLY
SLANTINGWAYS
SLAPDASHES
SLAPHAPPIER
SLAPHAPPIEST
SLAPSTICKS
SLASHFESTS
SLASHINGLY
SLATHERING
SLATINESSES
SLATTERING
SLATTERNLINESS
SLATTERNLY
SLAUGHTERABLE
SLAUGHTERED
SLAUGHTERER
SLAUGHTERERS
SLAUGHTERHOUSE
SLAUGHTERHOUSES
SLAUGHTERIES
SLAUGHTERING
SLAUGHTERMAN
SLAUGHTERMEN
SLAUGHTEROUS
SLAUGHTEROUSLY
SLAUGHTERS
SLAUGHTERY

SLAVEHOLDER
SLAVEHOLDERS
SLAVEHOLDING
SLAVEHOLDINGS
SLAVERINGLY
SLAVISHNESS
SLAVISHNESSES
SLAVOCRACIES
SLAVOCRACY
SLAVOCRATS
SLAVOPHILE
SLAVOPHILES
SLAVOPHILS
SLEAZEBAGS
SLEAZEBALL
SLEAZEBALLS
SLEAZINESS
SLEAZINESSES
SLEDGEHAMMER
SLEDGEHAMMERED
SLEDGEHAMMERING
SLEDGEHAMMERS
SLEECHIEST
SLEEKENING
SLEEKNESSES
SLEEKSTONE
SLEEKSTONES
SLEEPINESS
SLEEPINESSES
SLEEPLESSLY
SLEEPLESSNESS
SLEEPLESSNESSES
SLEEPOVERS
SLEEPSUITS
SLEEPWALKED
SLEEPWALKER
SLEEPWALKERS
SLEEPWALKING
SLEEPWALKINGS
SLEEPWALKS
SLEEPYHEAD
SLEEPYHEADED
SLEEPYHEADS
SLEETINESS
SLEETINESSES
SLEEVEHAND
SLEEVEHANDS
SLEEVELESS
SLEEVELETS
SLEEVELIKE
SLEIGHINGS
SLENDEREST
SLENDERISE
SLENDERISED
SLENDERISES
SLENDERISING
SLENDERIZE
SLENDERIZED
SLENDERIZES
SLENDERIZING
SLENDERNESS
SLENDERNESSES
SLEUTHHOUND
SLEUTHHOUNDS
SLICKENERS
SLICKENING
SLICKENSIDE
SLICKENSIDED
SLICKENSIDES
SLICKNESSES
SLICKROCKS
SLICKSTERS
SLICKSTONE
SLICKSTONES
SLIDDERING
SLIGHTINGLY
SLIGHTNESS
SLIGHTNESSES
SLIMEBALLS
SLIMINESSES
SLIMNASTICS
SLIMNESSES
SLIMPSIEST
SLINGBACKS
SLINGSHOTS
SLINGSTONE
SLINGSTONES
SLINKINESS
SLINKINESSES
SLINKSKINS
SLINKWEEDS
SLIPCOVERED
SLIPCOVERING
SLIPCOVERS
SLIPDRESSES
SLIPFORMED
SLIPFORMING
SLIPNOOSES
SLIPPERIER
SLIPPERIEST
SLIPPERILY
SLIPPERINESS
SLIPPERINESSES
SLIPPERING
SLIPPERWORT
SLIPPERWORTS
SLIPPINESS
SLIPPINESSES
SLIPSHEETED
SLIPSHEETING
SLIPSHEETS
SLIPSHODDINESS
SLIPSHODNESS
SLIPSHODNESSES
SLIPSLOPPY
SLIPSTREAM
SLIPSTREAMED
SLIPSTREAMING
SLIPSTREAMS
SLITHERIER
SLITHERIEST
SLITHERING
SLIVOVICAS
SLIVOVICES
SLIVOVITZES
SLIVOWITZES
SLOBBERERS
SLOBBERIER
SLOBBERIEST
SLOBBERING
SLOBBISHNESS
SLOBBISHNESSES
SLOCKDOLAGER
SLOCKDOLAGERS
SLOCKDOLIGER
SLOCKDOLIGERS
SLOCKDOLOGER
SLOCKDOLOGERS
SLOCKENING
SLOEBUSHES
SLOETHORNS
SLOGANEERED
SLOGANEERING
SLOGANEERINGS
SLOGANEERS
SLOGANISED
SLOGANISES
SLOGANISING
SLOGANISINGS
SLOGANIZED
SLOGANIZES
SLOGANIZING
SLOGANIZINGS
SLOMMOCKED
SLOMMOCKING
SLOPINGNESS
SLOPINGNESSES
SLOPPINESS
SLOPPINESSES
SLOPWORKER
SLOPWORKERS
SLOTHFULLY
SLOTHFULNESS
SLOTHFULNESSES
SLOUCHIEST
SLOUCHINESS
SLOUCHINESSES
SLOUCHINGLY
SLOUGHIEST
SLOVENLIER
SLOVENLIEST
SLOVENLIKE
SLOVENLINESS
SLOVENLINESSES
SLOVENRIES
SLOWCOACHES
SLOWNESSES
SLUBBERING
SLUBBERINGLY
SLUBBERINGS
SLUGGABEDS
SLUGGARDISE
SLUGGARDISED
SLUGGARDISES
SLUGGARDISING
SLUGGARDIZE
SLUGGARDIZED
SLUGGARDIZES
SLUGGARDIZING
SLUGGARDLINESS
SLUGGARDLY
SLUGGARDNESS
SLUGGARDNESSES
SLUGGISHLY
SLUGGISHNESS
SLUGGISHNESSES
SLUGHORNES
SLUICEGATE
SLUICEGATES
SLUICELIKE
SLUICEWAYS
SLUMBERERS
SLUMBERFUL
SLUMBERING
SLUMBERINGLY
SLUMBERINGS
SLUMBERLAND
SLUMBERLANDS
SLUMBERLESS
SLUMBEROUS
SLUMBEROUSLY
SLUMBEROUSNESS
SLUMBERSOME
SLUMBROUSLY
SLUMGULLION
SLUMGULLIONS
SLUMMOCKED
SLUMMOCKING
SLUMPFLATION
SLUMPFLATIONARY
SLUMPFLATIONS
SLUNGSHOTS
SLUSHINESS
SLUSHINESSES
SLUTCHIEST
SLUTTERIES
SLUTTISHLY
SLUTTISHNESS
SLUTTISHNESSES
SMACKHEADS
SMALLCLOTHES
SMALLHOLDER
SMALLHOLDERS
SMALLHOLDING
SMALLHOLDINGS
SMALLMOUTH
SMALLMOUTHS
SMALLNESSES
SMALLPOXES
SMALLSWORD
SMALLSWORDS
SMALMINESS
SMALMINESSES
SMARAGDINE
SMARAGDITE
SMARAGDITES
SMARMINESS
SMARMINESSES
SMARTARSED
SMARTARSES
SMARTASSES
SMARTENING
SMARTMOUTH
SMARTMOUTHS
SMARTNESSES
SMARTPHONE
SMARTPHONES
SMARTWEEDS
SMARTYPANTS
SMASHEROOS
SMASHINGLY
SMATTERERS
SMATTERING
SMATTERINGLY

SMATTERINGS
SMEARCASES
SMEARINESS
SMEARINESSES
SMELLINESS
SMELLINESSES
SMELTERIES
SMICKERING
SMICKERINGS
SMIERCASES
SMIFLIGATE
SMIFLIGATED
SMIFLIGATES
SMIFLIGATING
SMILACACEOUS
SMILINGNESS
SMILINGNESSES
SMIRKINGLY
SMITHCRAFT
SMITHCRAFTS
SMITHEREEN
SMITHEREENED
SMITHEREENING
SMITHEREENS
SMITHERIES
SMITHSONITE
SMITHSONITES
SMOKEBOARD
SMOKEBOARDS
SMOKEBUSHES
SMOKEHOODS
SMOKEHOUSE
SMOKEHOUSES
SMOKEJACKS
SMOKELESSLY
SMOKELESSNESS
SMOKELESSNESSES
SMOKEPROOF
SMOKESCREEN
SMOKESCREENS
SMOKESTACK
SMOKESTACKS
SMOKETIGHT
SMOKETREES
SMOKINESSES
SMOLDERING
SMOOTHABLE
SMOOTHBORE
SMOOTHBORED
SMOOTHBORES
SMOOTHENED
SMOOTHENING
SMOOTHINGS
SMOOTHNESS
SMOOTHNESSES
SMOOTHPATE
SMOOTHPATES
SMORGASBORD
SMORGASBORDS
SMORREBROD
SMORREBRODS
SMOTHERERS
SMOTHERINESS
SMOTHERINESSES
SMOTHERING
SMOTHERINGLY
SMOTHERINGS
SMOULDERED
SMOULDERING
SMOULDERINGS
SMUDGELESS
SMUDGINESS
SMUDGINESSES
SMUGGERIES
SMUGGLINGS
SMUGNESSES
SMUTCHIEST
SMUTTINESS
SMUTTINESSES
SNACKETTES
SNAGGLETEETH
SNAGGLETOOTH
SNAGGLETOOTHED
SNAILERIES
SNAILFISHES
SNAKEBIRDS
SNAKEBITES
SNAKEBITTEN
SNAKEFISHES
SNAKEHEADS
SNAKEMOUTH
SNAKEMOUTHS
SNAKEROOTS
SNAKESKINS
SNAKESTONE
SNAKESTONES
SNAKEWEEDS
SNAKEWOODS
SNAKINESSES
SNAKISHNESS
SNAKISHNESSES
SNAPDRAGON
SNAPDRAGONS
SNAPHANCES
SNAPHAUNCE
SNAPHAUNCES
SNAPHAUNCH
SNAPHAUNCHES
SNAPPERING
SNAPPINESS
SNAPPINESSES
SNAPPINGLY
SNAPPISHLY
SNAPPISHNESS
SNAPPISHNESSES
SNAPSHOOTER
SNAPSHOOTERS
SNAPSHOOTING
SNAPSHOOTINGS
SNAPSHOTTED
SNAPSHOTTING
SNARLINGLY
SNATCHIEST
SNATCHINGLY
SNATCHINGS
SNAZZINESS
SNAZZINESSES
SNEAKINESS
SNEAKINESSES
SNEAKINGLY
SNEAKINGNESS
SNEAKINGNESSES
SNEAKISHLY
SNEAKISHNESS
SNEAKISHNESSES
SNEAKSBIES
SNEERINGLY
SNEESHINGS
SNEEZELESS
SNEEZEWEED
SNEEZEWEEDS
SNEEZEWOOD
SNEEZEWOODS
SNEEZEWORT
SNEEZEWORTS
SNICKERERS
SNICKERING
SNICKERSNEE
SNICKERSNEED
SNICKERSNEEING
SNICKERSNEES
SNIDENESSES
SNIFFINESS
SNIFFINESSES
SNIFFINGLY
SNIFFISHLY
SNIFFISHNESS
SNIFFISHNESSES
SNIFFLIEST
SNIFTERING
SNIGGERERS
SNIGGERING
SNIGGERINGLY
SNIGGERINGS
SNIGGLINGS
SNIPEFISHES
SNIPERSCOPE
SNIPERSCOPES
SNIPPERSNAPPER
SNIPPERSNAPPERS
SNIPPETIER
SNIPPETIEST
SNIPPETINESS
SNIPPETINESSES
SNIPPINESS
SNIPPINESSES
SNITCHIEST
SNIVELLERS
SNIVELLING
SNOBBERIES
SNOBBISHLY
SNOBBISHNESS
SNOBBISHNESSES
SNOBBOCRACIES
SNOBBOCRACY
SNOBOCRACIES
SNOBOCRACY
SNOBOGRAPHER
SNOBOGRAPHERS
SNOBOGRAPHIES
SNOBOGRAPHY
SNOLLYGOSTER
SNOLLYGOSTERS
SNOOKERING
SNOOPERSCOPE
SNOOPERSCOPES
SNOOTINESS
SNOOTINESSES
SNORKELERS
SNORKELING
SNORKELLED
SNORKELLING
SNORKELLINGS
SNORTINGLY
SNOTTERIES
SNOTTERING
SNOTTINESS
SNOTTINESSES
SNOWBALLED
SNOWBALLING
SNOWBERRIES
SNOWBLADER
SNOWBLADERS
SNOWBLADES
SNOWBLADING
SNOWBLADINGS
SNOWBLINKS
SNOWBLOWER
SNOWBLOWERS
SNOWBOARDED
SNOWBOARDER
SNOWBOARDERS
SNOWBOARDING
SNOWBOARDINGS
SNOWBOARDS
SNOWBRUSHES
SNOWBUSHES
SNOWCAPPED
SNOWDRIFTS
SNOWFIELDS
SNOWFLAKES
SNOWFLECKS
SNOWFLICKS
SNOWINESSES
SNOWMAKERS
SNOWMAKING
SNOWMOBILE
SNOWMOBILER
SNOWMOBILERS
SNOWMOBILES
SNOWMOBILING
SNOWMOBILINGS
SNOWMOBILIST
SNOWMOBILISTS
SNOWPLOUGH
SNOWPLOUGHED
SNOWPLOUGHING
SNOWPLOUGHS
SNOWPLOWED
SNOWPLOWING
SNOWSCAPES
SNOWSHOEING
SNOWSHOERS
SNOWSLIDES
SNOWSTORMS
SNOWSURFING
SNOWSURFINGS
SNOWTUBING
SNOWTUBINGS
SNUBBINESS
SNUBBINESSES
SNUBBINGLY
SNUBNESSES
SNUFFBOXES

SNUFFINESS
SNUFFINESSES
SNUFFLIEST
SNUFFLINGS
SNUGGERIES
SNUGNESSES
SOAPBERRIES
SOAPBOXING
SOAPINESSES
SOAPOLALLIE
SOAPOLALLIES
SOAPSTONES
SOBERINGLY
SOBERISING
SOBERIZING
SOBERNESSES
SOBERSIDED
SOBERSIDEDNESS
SOBERSIDES
SOBOLIFEROUS
SOBRIETIES
SOBRIQUETS
SOCDOLAGER
SOCDOLAGERS
SOCDOLIGER
SOCDOLIGERS
SOCDOLOGER
SOCDOLOGERS
SOCIABILITIES
SOCIABILITY
SOCIABLENESS
SOCIABLENESSES
SOCIALISABLE
SOCIALISATION
SOCIALISATIONS
SOCIALISED
SOCIALISER
SOCIALISERS
SOCIALISES
SOCIALISING
SOCIALISMS
SOCIALISTIC
SOCIALISTICALLY
SOCIALISTS
SOCIALITES
SOCIALITIES
SOCIALIZABLE
SOCIALIZATION
SOCIALIZATIONS
SOCIALIZED
SOCIALIZER
SOCIALIZERS
SOCIALIZES
SOCIALIZING
SOCIALNESS
SOCIALNESSES
SOCIATIONS
SOCIETALLY
SOCIOBIOLOGICAL
SOCIOBIOLOGIES
SOCIOBIOLOGIST
SOCIOBIOLOGISTS
SOCIOBIOLOGY
SOCIOCULTURAL
SOCIOCULTURALLY
SOCIOECONOMIC
SOCIOGRAMS
SOCIOHISTORICAL
SOCIOLECTS
SOCIOLINGUIST
SOCIOLINGUISTIC
SOCIOLINGUISTS
SOCIOLOGESE
SOCIOLOGESES
SOCIOLOGIC
SOCIOLOGICAL
SOCIOLOGICALLY
SOCIOLOGIES
SOCIOLOGISM
SOCIOLOGISMS
SOCIOLOGIST
SOCIOLOGISTIC
SOCIOLOGISTS
SOCIOMETRIC
SOCIOMETRIES
SOCIOMETRIST
SOCIOMETRISTS
SOCIOMETRY
SOCIOPATHIC
SOCIOPATHIES
SOCIOPATHS
SOCIOPATHY
SOCIOPOLITICAL
SOCIORELIGIOUS
SOCIOSEXUAL
SOCKDOLAGER
SOCKDOLAGERS
SOCKDOLIGER
SOCKDOLIGERS
SOCKDOLOGER
SOCKDOLOGERS
SODALITIES
SODBUSTERS
SODDENNESS
SODDENNESSES
SODICITIES
SODOMISING
SODOMITICAL
SODOMITICALLY
SODOMIZING
SOFTBALLER
SOFTBALLERS
SOFTBOUNDS
SOFTCOVERS
SOFTENINGS
SOFTHEADED
SOFTHEADEDLY
SOFTHEADEDNESS
SOFTHEARTED
SOFTHEARTEDLY
SOFTHEARTEDNESS
SOFTNESSES
SOFTSHELLS
SOGDOLAGER
SOGDOLAGERS
SOGDOLIGER
SOGDOLIGERS
SOGDOLOGER
SOGDOLOGERS
SOGGINESSES
SOILINESSES
SOJOURNERS
SOJOURNING
SOJOURNINGS
SOJOURNMENT
SOJOURNMENTS
SOKEMANRIES
SOLACEMENT
SOLACEMENTS
SOLANACEOUS
SOLARIMETER
SOLARIMETERS
SOLARISATION
SOLARISATIONS
SOLARISING
SOLARIZATION
SOLARIZATIONS
SOLARIZING
SOLDATESQUE
SOLDERABILITIES
SOLDERABILITY
SOLDERABLE
SOLDERINGS
SOLDIERIES
SOLDIERING
SOLDIERINGS
SOLDIERLIKE
SOLDIERLINESS
SOLDIERLINESSES
SOLDIERSHIP
SOLDIERSHIPS
SOLECISING
SOLECISTIC
SOLECISTICAL
SOLECISTICALLY
SOLECIZING
SOLEMNESSES
SOLEMNIFICATION
SOLEMNIFIED
SOLEMNIFIES
SOLEMNIFYING
SOLEMNISATION
SOLEMNISATIONS
SOLEMNISED
SOLEMNISER
SOLEMNISERS
SOLEMNISES
SOLEMNISING
SOLEMNITIES
SOLEMNIZATION
SOLEMNIZATIONS
SOLEMNIZED
SOLEMNIZER
SOLEMNIZERS
SOLEMNIZES
SOLEMNIZING
SOLEMNNESS
SOLEMNNESSES
SOLENESSES
SOLENETTES
SOLENODONS
SOLENOIDAL
SOLENOIDALLY
SOLEPLATES
SOLEPRINTS
SOLFATARAS
SOLFATARIC
SOLFEGGIOS
SOLFERINOS
SOLICITANT
SOLICITANTS
SOLICITATION
SOLICITATIONS
SOLICITIES
SOLICITING
SOLICITINGS
SOLICITORS
SOLICITORSHIP
SOLICITORSHIPS
SOLICITOUS
SOLICITOUSLY
SOLICITOUSNESS
SOLICITUDE
SOLICITUDES
SOLIDARISM
SOLIDARISMS
SOLIDARIST
SOLIDARISTIC
SOLIDARISTS
SOLIDARITIES
SOLIDARITY
SOLIDATING
SOLIDIFIABLE
SOLIDIFICATION
SOLIDIFICATIONS
SOLIDIFIED
SOLIDIFIER
SOLIDIFIERS
SOLIDIFIES
SOLIDIFYING
SOLIDITIES
SOLIDNESSES
SOLIDUNGULATE
SOLIDUNGULOUS
SOLIFIDIAN
SOLIFIDIANISM
SOLIFIDIANISMS
SOLIFIDIANS
SOLIFLUCTION
SOLIFLUCTIONS
SOLIFLUXION
SOLIFLUXIONS
SOLILOQUIES
SOLILOQUISE
SOLILOQUISED
SOLILOQUISER
SOLILOQUISERS
SOLILOQUISES
SOLILOQUISING
SOLILOQUIST
SOLILOQUISTS
SOLILOQUIZE
SOLILOQUIZED
SOLILOQUIZER
SOLILOQUIZERS
SOLILOQUIZES
SOLILOQUIZING
SOLIPEDOUS
SOLIPSISMS
SOLIPSISTIC
SOLIPSISTICALLY
SOLIPSISTS
SOLITAIRES
SOLITARIAN

SOLITARIANS
SOLITARIES
SOLITARILY
SOLITARINESS
SOLITARINESSES
SOLITUDINARIAN
SOLITUDINARIANS
SOLITUDINOUS
SOLIVAGANT
SOLIVAGANTS
SOLLICKERS
SOLMISATION
SOLMISATIONS
SOLMIZATION
SOLMIZATIONS
SOLONCHAKS
SOLONETSES
SOLONETZES
SOLONETZIC
SOLONISATION
SOLONISATIONS
SOLONIZATION
SOLONIZATIONS
SOLSTITIAL
SOLSTITIALLY
SOLUBILISATION
SOLUBILISATIONS
SOLUBILISE
SOLUBILISED
SOLUBILISES
SOLUBILISING
SOLUBILITIES
SOLUBILITY
SOLUBILIZATION
SOLUBILIZATIONS
SOLUBILIZE
SOLUBILIZED
SOLUBILIZES
SOLUBILIZING
SOLUBLENESS
SOLUBLENESSES
SOLUTIONAL
SOLUTIONED
SOLUTIONING
SOLUTIONIST
SOLUTIONISTS
SOLVABILITIES
SOLVABILITY
SOLVABLENESS
SOLVABLENESSES
SOLVATIONS
SOLVENCIES
SOLVENTLESS
SOLVOLYSES
SOLVOLYSIS
SOLVOLYTIC
SOMAESTHESIA
SOMAESTHESIAS
SOMAESTHESIS
SOMAESTHESISES
SOMAESTHETIC
SOMASCOPES
SOMATICALLY
SOMATOGENIC
SOMATOLOGIC
SOMATOLOGICAL
SOMATOLOGICALLY
SOMATOLOGIES
SOMATOLOGIST
SOMATOLOGISTS
SOMATOLOGY
SOMATOMEDIN
SOMATOMEDINS
SOMATOPLASM
SOMATOPLASMS
SOMATOPLASTIC
SOMATOPLEURAL
SOMATOPLEURE
SOMATOPLEURES
SOMATOPLEURIC
SOMATOSENSORY
SOMATOSTATIN
SOMATOSTATINS
SOMATOTENSIC
SOMATOTONIA
SOMATOTONIAS
SOMATOTONIC
SOMATOTROPHIC
SOMATOTROPHIN
SOMATOTROPHINS
SOMATOTROPIC
SOMATOTROPIN
SOMATOTROPINS
SOMATOTYPE
SOMATOTYPED
SOMATOTYPES
SOMATOTYPING
SOMBERNESS
SOMBERNESSES
SOMBRENESS
SOMBRENESSES
SOMBRERITE
SOMBRERITES
SOMEBODIES
SOMEPLACES
SOMERSAULT
SOMERSAULTED
SOMERSAULTING
SOMERSAULTS
SOMERSETED
SOMERSETING
SOMERSETTED
SOMERSETTING
SOMESTHESIA
SOMESTHESIAS
SOMESTHESIS
SOMESTHESISES
SOMESTHETIC
SOMETHINGS
SOMEWHENCE
SOMEWHERES
SOMEWHILES
SOMEWHITHER
SOMMELIERS
SOMNAMBULANCE
SOMNAMBULANCES
SOMNAMBULANT
SOMNAMBULANTS
SOMNAMBULAR
SOMNAMBULARY
SOMNAMBULATE
SOMNAMBULATED
SOMNAMBULATES
SOMNAMBULATING
SOMNAMBULATION
SOMNAMBULATIONS
SOMNAMBULATOR
SOMNAMBULATORS
SOMNAMBULE
SOMNAMBULES
SOMNAMBULIC
SOMNAMBULISM
SOMNAMBULISMS
SOMNAMBULIST
SOMNAMBULISTIC
SOMNAMBULISTS
SOMNIATING
SOMNIATIVE
SOMNIATORY
SOMNIFACIENT
SOMNIFACIENTS
SOMNIFEROUS
SOMNIFEROUSLY
SOMNILOQUENCE
SOMNILOQUENCES
SOMNILOQUIES
SOMNILOQUISE
SOMNILOQUISED
SOMNILOQUISES
SOMNILOQUISING
SOMNILOQUISM
SOMNILOQUISMS
SOMNILOQUIST
SOMNILOQUISTS
SOMNILOQUIZE
SOMNILOQUIZED
SOMNILOQUIZES
SOMNILOQUIZING
SOMNILOQUOUS
SOMNILOQUY
SOMNOLENCE
SOMNOLENCES
SOMNOLENCIES
SOMNOLENCY
SOMNOLENTLY
SOMNOLESCENT
SONGCRAFTS
SONGFULNESS
SONGFULNESSES
SONGLESSLY
SONGOLOLOS
SONGSMITHS
SONGSTRESS
SONGSTRESSES
SONGWRITER
SONGWRITERS
SONGWRITING
SONGWRITINGS
SONICATING
SONICATION
SONICATIONS
SONICATORS
SONIFEROUS
SONNETEERING
SONNETEERINGS
SONNETEERS
SONNETISED
SONNETISES
SONNETISING
SONNETIZED
SONNETIZES
SONNETIZING
SONNETTING
SONOFABITCH
SONOGRAPHER
SONOGRAPHERS
SONOGRAPHIES
SONOGRAPHS
SONOGRAPHY
SONOMETERS
SONORITIES
SONOROUSLY
SONOROUSNESS
SONOROUSNESSES
SOOTERKINS
SOOTFLAKES
SOOTHERING
SOOTHFASTLY
SOOTHFASTNESS
SOOTHFASTNESSES
SOOTHINGLY
SOOTHINGNESS
SOOTHINGNESSES
SOOTHSAYER
SOOTHSAYERS
SOOTHSAYING
SOOTHSAYINGS
SOOTINESSES
SOPAIPILLA
SOPAIPILLAS
SOPAPILLAS
SOPHISTERS
SOPHISTICAL
SOPHISTICALLY
SOPHISTICATE
SOPHISTICATED
SOPHISTICATEDLY
SOPHISTICATES
SOPHISTICATING
SOPHISTICATION
SOPHISTICATIONS
SOPHISTICATOR
SOPHISTICATORS
SOPHISTRIES
SOPHOMORES
SOPHOMORIC
SOPHOMORICAL
SOPORIFEROUS
SOPORIFEROUSLY
SOPORIFICALLY
SOPORIFICS
SOPPINESSES
SOPRANINOS
SOPRANISTS
SORBABILITIES
SORBABILITY
SORBEFACIENT
SORBEFACIENTS
SORBITISATION
SORBITISATIONS
SORBITISED
SORBITISES
SORBITISING
SORBITIZATION

SORBITIZATIONS
SORBITIZED
SORBITIZES
SORBITIZING
SORCERESSES
SORDAMENTE
SORDIDNESS
SORDIDNESSES
SOREHEADED
SOREHEADEDLY
SOREHEADEDNESS
SORENESSES
SORICIDENT
SORORIALLY
SORORICIDAL
SORORICIDE
SORORICIDES
SORORISING
SORORITIES
SORORIZING
SORRINESSES
SORROWFULLY
SORROWFULNESS
SORROWFULNESSES
SORROWINGS
SORROWLESS
SORTATIONS
SORTILEGER
SORTILEGERS
SORTILEGES
SORTILEGIES
SORTITIONS
SOSTENUTOS
SOTERIOLOGIC
SOTERIOLOGICAL
SOTERIOLOGIES
SOTERIOLOGY
SOTTISHNESS
SOTTISHNESSES
SOTTISIERS
SOUBRETTES
SOUBRETTISH
SOUBRIQUET
SOUBRIQUETS
SOULDIERED
SOULDIERING
SOULFULNESS
SOULFULNESSES
SOULLESSLY
SOULLESSNESS
SOULLESSNESSES
SOUNDALIKE
SOUNDALIKES
SOUNDBITES
SOUNDBOARD
SOUNDBOARDS
SOUNDBOXES
SOUNDCARDS
SOUNDINGLY
SOUNDLESSLY
SOUNDLESSNESS
SOUNDLESSNESSES
SOUNDNESSES
SOUNDPOSTS
SOUNDPROOF
SOUNDPROOFED
SOUNDPROOFING
SOUNDPROOFINGS
SOUNDPROOFS
SOUNDSCAPE
SOUNDSCAPES
SOUNDSTAGE
SOUNDSTAGES
SOUNDTRACK
SOUNDTRACKS
SOUPSPOONS
SOURCEBOOK
SOURCEBOOKS
SOURCELESS
SOURDELINE
SOURDELINES
SOURDOUGHS
SOURNESSES
SOURPUSSES
SOUSAPHONE
SOUSAPHONES
SOUSAPHONIST
SOUSAPHONISTS
SOUTENEURS
SOUTERRAIN
SOUTERRAINS
SOUTHBOUND
SOUTHEASTER
SOUTHEASTERLIES
SOUTHEASTERLY
SOUTHEASTERN
SOUTHEASTERS
SOUTHEASTS
SOUTHEASTWARD
SOUTHEASTWARDS
SOUTHERING
SOUTHERLIES
SOUTHERLINESS
SOUTHERLINESSES
SOUTHERMOST
SOUTHERNER
SOUTHERNERS
SOUTHERNISE
SOUTHERNISED
SOUTHERNISES
SOUTHERNISING
SOUTHERNISM
SOUTHERNISMS
SOUTHERNIZE
SOUTHERNIZED
SOUTHERNIZES
SOUTHERNIZING
SOUTHERNLY
SOUTHERNMOST
SOUTHERNNESS
SOUTHERNNESSES
SOUTHERNWOOD
SOUTHERNWOODS
SOUTHLANDER
SOUTHLANDERS
SOUTHLANDS
SOUTHSAYING
SOUTHWARDLY
SOUTHWARDS
SOUTHWESTER
SOUTHWESTERLIES
SOUTHWESTERLY
SOUTHWESTERN
SOUTHWESTERS
SOUTHWESTS
SOUTHWESTWARD
SOUTHWESTWARDLY
SOUTHWESTWARDS
SOUVENIRED
SOUVENIRING
SOUVLAKIAS
SOVENANCES
SOVEREIGNLY
SOVEREIGNS
SOVEREIGNTIES
SOVEREIGNTIST
SOVEREIGNTISTS
SOVEREIGNTY
SOVIETISATION
SOVIETISATIONS
SOVIETISED
SOVIETISES
SOVIETISING
SOVIETISMS
SOVIETISTIC
SOVIETISTS
SOVIETIZATION
SOVIETIZATIONS
SOVIETIZED
SOVIETIZES
SOVIETIZING
SOVIETOLOGICAL
SOVIETOLOGIST
SOVIETOLOGISTS
SOVRANTIES
SOWBELLIES
SPACEBANDS
SPACEBORNE
SPACECRAFT
SPACECRAFTS
SPACEFARING
SPACEFARINGS
SPACEFLIGHT
SPACEFLIGHTS
SPACEPLANE
SPACEPLANES
SPACEPORTS
SPACESHIPS
SPACESUITS
SPACEWALKED
SPACEWALKER
SPACEWALKERS
SPACEWALKING
SPACEWALKS
SPACEWOMAN
SPACEWOMEN
SPACINESSES
SPACIOUSLY
SPACIOUSNESS
SPACIOUSNESSES
SPADASSINS
SPADEFISHES
SPADEWORKS
SPADICEOUS
SPADICIFLORAL
SPADILLIOS
SPAGERISTS
SPAGHETTILIKE
SPAGHETTINI
SPAGHETTINIS
SPAGHETTIS
SPAGIRISTS
SPAGYRICAL
SPAGYRICALLY
SPAGYRISTS
SPALLATION
SPALLATIONS
SPANAEMIAS
SPANAKOPITA
SPANAKOPITAS
SPANCELING
SPANCELLED
SPANCELLING
SPANGHEWED
SPANGHEWING
SPANGLIEST
SPANGLINGS
SPANIELLED
SPANIELLING
SPANIOLATE
SPANIOLATED
SPANIOLATES
SPANIOLATING
SPANIOLISE
SPANIOLISED
SPANIOLISES
SPANIOLISING
SPANIOLIZE
SPANIOLIZED
SPANIOLIZES
SPANIOLIZING
SPANKINGLY
SPANOKOPITA
SPANOKOPITAS
SPARAGMATIC
SPARAGRASS
SPARAGRASSES
SPARAXISES
SPARENESSES
SPARGANIUM
SPARGANIUMS
SPARINGNESS
SPARINGNESSES
SPARKISHLY
SPARKLESSLY
SPARKLIEST
SPARKLINGLY
SPARKLINGS
SPARKPLUGGED
SPARKPLUGGING
SPARKPLUGS
SPARROWFART
SPARROWFARTS
SPARROWGRASS
SPARROWGRASSES
SPARROWHAWK
SPARROWHAWKS
SPARROWLIKE
SPARSENESS
SPARSENESSES
SPARSITIES
SPARTEINES
SPARTERIES
SPASMATICAL

SPASMODICAL
SPASMODICALLY
SPASMODIST
SPASMODISTS
SPASMOLYTIC
SPASMOLYTICS
SPASTICALLY
SPASTICITIES
SPASTICITY
SPATANGOID
SPATANGOIDS
SPATCHCOCK
SPATCHCOCKED
SPATCHCOCKING
SPATCHCOCKS
SPATHACEOUS
SPATHIPHYLLUM
SPATHIPHYLLUMS
SPATHULATE
SPATIALITIES
SPATIALITY
SPATIOTEMPORAL
SPATTERDASH
SPATTERDASHES
SPATTERDOCK
SPATTERDOCKS
SPATTERING
SPATTERWORK
SPATTERWORKS
SPEAKEASIES
SPEAKERINE
SPEAKERINES
SPEAKERPHONE
SPEAKERPHONES
SPEAKERSHIP
SPEAKERSHIPS
SPEAKINGLY
SPEARFISHED
SPEARFISHES
SPEARFISHING
SPEARHEADED
SPEARHEADING
SPEARHEADS
SPEARMINTS
SPEARWORTS
SPECIALEST
SPECIALISATION
SPECIALISATIONS
SPECIALISE
SPECIALISED
SPECIALISER
SPECIALISERS
SPECIALISES
SPECIALISING
SPECIALISM
SPECIALISMS
SPECIALIST
SPECIALISTIC
SPECIALISTS
SPECIALITIES
SPECIALITY
SPECIALIZATION
SPECIALIZATIONS
SPECIALIZE
SPECIALIZED
SPECIALIZER
SPECIALIZERS
SPECIALIZES
SPECIALIZING
SPECIALLED
SPECIALLING
SPECIALNESS
SPECIALNESSES
SPECIALOGUE
SPECIALOGUES
SPECIALTIES
SPECIATING
SPECIATION
SPECIATIONAL
SPECIATIONS
SPECIESISM
SPECIESISMS
SPECIESIST
SPECIESISTS
SPECIFIABLE
SPECIFICAL
SPECIFICALLY
SPECIFICATE
SPECIFICATED
SPECIFICATES
SPECIFICATING
SPECIFICATION
SPECIFICATIONS
SPECIFICATIVE
SPECIFICITIES
SPECIFICITY
SPECIFIERS
SPECIFYING
SPECIOCIDE
SPECIOCIDES
SPECIOSITIES
SPECIOSITY
SPECIOUSLY
SPECIOUSNESS
SPECIOUSNESSES
SPECKLEDNESS
SPECKLEDNESSES
SPECKSIONEER
SPECKSIONEERS
SPECKTIONEER
SPECKTIONEERS
SPECTACLED
SPECTACLES
SPECTACULAR
SPECTACULARITY
SPECTACULARLY
SPECTACULARS
SPECTATING
SPECTATORIAL
SPECTATORS
SPECTATORSHIP
SPECTATORSHIPS
SPECTATRESS
SPECTATRESSES
SPECTATRICES
SPECTATRIX
SPECTATRIXES
SPECTINOMYCIN
SPECTINOMYCINS
SPECTRALITIES
SPECTRALITY
SPECTRALLY
SPECTRALNESS
SPECTRALNESSES
SPECTROGRAM
SPECTROGRAMS
SPECTROGRAPH
SPECTROGRAPHIC
SPECTROGRAPHIES
SPECTROGRAPHS
SPECTROGRAPHY
SPECTROLOGICAL
SPECTROLOGIES
SPECTROLOGY
SPECTROMETER
SPECTROMETERS
SPECTROMETRIC
SPECTROMETRIES
SPECTROMETRY
SPECTROSCOPE
SPECTROSCOPES
SPECTROSCOPIC
SPECTROSCOPICAL
SPECTROSCOPIES
SPECTROSCOPIST
SPECTROSCOPISTS
SPECTROSCOPY
SPECULARITIES
SPECULARITY
SPECULARLY
SPECULATED
SPECULATES
SPECULATING
SPECULATION
SPECULATIONS
SPECULATIST
SPECULATISTS
SPECULATIVE
SPECULATIVELY
SPECULATIVENESS
SPECULATOR
SPECULATORS
SPECULATORY
SPECULATRICES
SPECULATRIX
SPECULATRIXES
SPEECHCRAFT
SPEECHCRAFTS
SPEECHFULNESS
SPEECHFULNESSES
SPEECHIFICATION
SPEECHIFIED
SPEECHIFIER
SPEECHIFIERS
SPEECHIFIES
SPEECHIFYING
SPEECHLESS
SPEECHLESSLY
SPEECHLESSNESS
SPEECHMAKER
SPEECHMAKERS
SPEECHMAKING
SPEECHMAKINGS
SPEECHWRITER
SPEECHWRITERS
SPEEDBALLED
SPEEDBALLING
SPEEDBALLINGS
SPEEDBALLS
SPEEDBOATING
SPEEDBOATINGS
SPEEDBOATS
SPEEDFREAK
SPEEDFREAKS
SPEEDFULLY
SPEEDINESS
SPEEDINESSES
SPEEDOMETER
SPEEDOMETERS
SPEEDREADING
SPEEDREADS
SPEEDSKATING
SPEEDSKATINGS
SPEEDSTERS
SPEEDWELLS
SPELAEOLOGICAL
SPELAEOLOGIES
SPELAEOLOGIST
SPELAEOLOGISTS
SPELAEOLOGY
SPELAEOTHEM
SPELAEOTHEMS
SPELDERING
SPELDRINGS
SPELEOLOGICAL
SPELEOLOGIES
SPELEOLOGIST
SPELEOLOGISTS
SPELEOLOGY
SPELEOTHEM
SPELEOTHEMS
SPELEOTHERAPIES
SPELEOTHERAPY
SPELLBINDER
SPELLBINDERS
SPELLBINDING
SPELLBINDINGLY
SPELLBINDS
SPELLBOUND
SPELLCHECK
SPELLCHECKER
SPELLCHECKERS
SPELLCHECKS
SPELLDOWNS
SPELLICANS
SPELLINGLY
SPELLSTOPT
SPELUNKERS
SPELUNKING
SPELUNKINGS
SPENDTHRIFT
SPENDTHRIFTS
SPERMACETI
SPERMACETIS
SPERMADUCT
SPERMADUCTS
SPERMAGONIA
SPERMAGONIUM
SPERMAPHYTE
SPERMAPHYTES
SPERMAPHYTIC
SPERMARIES
SPERMARIUM
SPERMATHECA

SPERMATHECAE
SPERMATHECAL
SPERMATIAL
SPERMATICAL
SPERMATICALLY
SPERMATICS
SPERMATIDS
SPERMATIUM
SPERMATOBLAST
SPERMATOBLASTIC
SPERMATOBLASTS
SPERMATOCELE
SPERMATOCELES
SPERMATOCIDAL
SPERMATOCIDE
SPERMATOCIDES
SPERMATOCYTE
SPERMATOCYTES
SPERMATOGENESES
SPERMATOGENESIS
SPERMATOGENETIC
SPERMATOGENIC
SPERMATOGENIES
SPERMATOGENOUS
SPERMATOGENY
SPERMATOGONIA
SPERMATOGONIAL
SPERMATOGONIUM
SPERMATOPHORAL
SPERMATOPHORE
SPERMATOPHORES
SPERMATOPHYTE
SPERMATOPHYTES
SPERMATOPHYTIC
SPERMATORRHEA
SPERMATORRHEAS
SPERMATORRHOEA
SPERMATORRHOEAS
SPERMATOTHECA
SPERMATOTHECAE
SPERMATOZOA
SPERMATOZOAL
SPERMATOZOAN
SPERMATOZOANS
SPERMATOZOIC
SPERMATOZOID
SPERMATOZOIDS
SPERMATOZOON
SPERMICIDAL
SPERMICIDE
SPERMICIDES
SPERMIDUCT
SPERMIDUCTS
SPERMIOGENESES
SPERMIOGENESIS
SPERMIOGENETIC
SPERMOGONE
SPERMOGONES
SPERMOGONIA
SPERMOGONIUM
SPERMOPHILE
SPERMOPHILES
SPERMOPHYTE
SPERMOPHYTES
SPERMOPHYTIC
SPERRYLITE
SPERRYLITES
SPESSARTINE
SPESSARTINES
SPESSARTITE
SPESSARTITES
SPETSNAZES
SPETZNAZES
SPEWINESSES
SPHACELATE
SPHACELATED
SPHACELATES
SPHACELATING
SPHACELATION
SPHACELATIONS
SPHACELUSES
SPHAERIDIA
SPHAERIDIUM
SPHAERITES
SPHAEROCRYSTAL
SPHAEROCRYSTALS
SPHAEROSIDERITE
SPHAGNICOLOUS
SPHAGNOLOGIES
SPHAGNOLOGIST
SPHAGNOLOGISTS
SPHAGNOLOGY
SPHAIRISTIKE
SPHAIRISTIKES
SPHALERITE
SPHALERITES
SPHENDONES
SPHENODONS
SPHENODONT
SPHENOGRAM
SPHENOGRAMS
SPHENOIDAL
SPHENOPSID
SPHENOPSIDS
SPHERELESS
SPHERELIKE
SPHERICALITIES
SPHERICALITY
SPHERICALLY
SPHERICALNESS
SPHERICALNESSES
SPHERICITIES
SPHERICITY
SPHERISTERION
SPHERISTERIONS
SPHEROCYTE
SPHEROCYTES
SPHEROCYTOSES
SPHEROCYTOSIS
SPHEROIDAL
SPHEROIDALLY
SPHEROIDICALLY
SPHEROIDICITIES
SPHEROIDICITY
SPHEROIDISATION
SPHEROIDISE
SPHEROIDISED
SPHEROIDISES
SPHEROIDISING
SPHEROIDIZATION
SPHEROIDIZE
SPHEROIDIZED
SPHEROIDIZES
SPHEROIDIZING
SPHEROMETER
SPHEROMETERS
SPHEROPLAST
SPHEROPLASTS
SPHERULITE
SPHERULITES
SPHERULITIC
SPHINCTERAL
SPHINCTERIAL
SPHINCTERIC
SPHINCTERS
SPHINGOMYELIN
SPHINGOMYELINS
SPHINGOSINE
SPHINGOSINES
SPHINXLIKE
SPHRAGISTIC
SPHRAGISTICS
SPHYGMOGRAM
SPHYGMOGRAMS
SPHYGMOGRAPH
SPHYGMOGRAPHIC
SPHYGMOGRAPHIES
SPHYGMOGRAPHS
SPHYGMOGRAPHY
SPHYGMOLOGIES
SPHYGMOLOGY
SPHYGMOMETER
SPHYGMOMETERS
SPHYGMOPHONE
SPHYGMOPHONES
SPHYGMOSCOPE
SPHYGMOSCOPES
SPHYGMUSES
SPICEBERRIES
SPICEBERRY
SPICEBUSHES
SPICILEGES
SPICINESSES
SPICULATION
SPICULATIONS
SPIDERIEST
SPIDERLIKE
SPIDERWEBS
SPIDERWOOD
SPIDERWOODS
SPIDERWORK
SPIDERWORKS
SPIDERWORT
SPIDERWORTS
SPIEGELEISEN
SPIEGELEISENS
SPIFFINESS
SPIFFINESSES
SPIFFLICATE
SPIFFLICATED
SPIFFLICATES
SPIFFLICATING
SPIFFLICATION
SPIFFLICATIONS
SPIFLICATE
SPIFLICATED
SPIFLICATES
SPIFLICATING
SPIFLICATION
SPIFLICATIONS
SPIKEFISHES
SPIKENARDS
SPIKINESSES
SPILLIKINS
SPILLOVERS
SPILOSITES
SPINACENES
SPINACEOUS
SPINACHLIKE
SPINDLELEGS
SPINDLESHANKS
SPINDLIEST
SPINDLINGS
SPINDRIFTS
SPINELESSLY
SPINELESSNESS
SPINELESSNESSES
SPINESCENCE
SPINESCENCES
SPINESCENT
SPINIFEROUS
SPINIFEXES
SPINIGEROUS
SPINIGRADE
SPININESSES
SPINMEISTER
SPINMEISTERS
SPINNAKERS
SPINNERETS
SPINNERETTE
SPINNERETTES
SPINNERIES
SPINNERULE
SPINNERULES
SPINOSITIES
SPINSTERDOM
SPINSTERDOMS
SPINSTERHOOD
SPINSTERHOODS
SPINSTERIAL
SPINSTERIAN
SPINSTERISH
SPINSTERLY
SPINSTERSHIP
SPINSTERSHIPS
SPINSTRESS
SPINSTRESSES
SPINTHARISCOPE
SPINTHARISCOPES
SPINULESCENT
SPINULIFEROUS
SPIRACULAR
SPIRACULATE
SPIRACULUM
SPIRALIFORM
SPIRALISMS
SPIRALISTS
SPIRALITIES
SPIRALLING
SPIRASTERS
SPIRATIONS
SPIRIFEROUS
SPIRILLOSES
SPIRILLOSIS

SPIRITEDLY
SPIRITEDNESS
SPIRITEDNESSES
SPIRITINGS
SPIRITISMS
SPIRITISTIC
SPIRITISTS
SPIRITLESS
SPIRITLESSLY
SPIRITLESSNESS
SPIRITOUSNESS
SPIRITOUSNESSES
SPIRITUALISE
SPIRITUALISED
SPIRITUALISER
SPIRITUALISERS
SPIRITUALISES
SPIRITUALISING
SPIRITUALISM
SPIRITUALISMS
SPIRITUALIST
SPIRITUALISTIC
SPIRITUALISTS
SPIRITUALITIES
SPIRITUALITY
SPIRITUALIZE
SPIRITUALIZED
SPIRITUALIZER
SPIRITUALIZERS
SPIRITUALIZES
SPIRITUALIZING
SPIRITUALLY
SPIRITUALNESS
SPIRITUALNESSES
SPIRITUALS
SPIRITUALTIES
SPIRITUALTY
SPIRITUELLE
SPIRITUOSITIES
SPIRITUOSITY
SPIRITUOUS
SPIRITUOUSNESS
SPIRITUSES
SPIRKETTING
SPIRKETTINGS
SPIROCHAETAEMIA
SPIROCHAETE
SPIROCHAETES
SPIROCHAETOSES
SPIROCHAETOSIS
SPIROCHETAL
SPIROCHETE
SPIROCHETES
SPIROCHETOSES
SPIROCHETOSIS
SPIROGRAMS
SPIROGRAPH
SPIROGRAPHIC
SPIROGRAPHIES
SPIROGRAPHS
SPIROGRAPHY
SPIROGYRAS
SPIROMETER
SPIROMETERS
SPIROMETRIC
SPIROMETRIES
SPIROMETRY
SPIRONOLACTONE
SPIRONOLACTONES
SPIROPHORE
SPIROPHORES
SPIRULINAS
SPISSITUDE
SPISSITUDES
SPITCHCOCK
SPITCHCOCKED
SPITCHCOCKING
SPITCHCOCKS
SPITEFULLER
SPITEFULLEST
SPITEFULLY
SPITEFULNESS
SPITEFULNESSES
SPITSTICKER
SPITSTICKERS
SPITTLEBUG
SPITTLEBUGS
SPIVVERIES
SPLANCHNIC
SPLANCHNOCELE
SPLANCHNOCELES
SPLANCHNOLOGIES
SPLANCHNOLOGY
SPLASHBACK
SPLASHBACKS
SPLASHBOARD
SPLASHBOARDS
SPLASHDOWN
SPLASHDOWNS
SPLASHIEST
SPLASHINESS
SPLASHINESSES
SPLASHINGS
SPLASHPROOF
SPLATCHING
SPLATTERED
SPLATTERING
SPLATTERPUNK
SPLATTERPUNKS
SPLATTINGS
SPLAYFOOTED
SPLAYFOOTEDLY
SPLEENFULLY
SPLEENIEST
SPLEENLESS
SPLEENSTONE
SPLEENSTONES
SPLEENWORT
SPLEENWORTS
SPLENATIVE
SPLENDIDER
SPLENDIDEST
SPLENDIDIOUS
SPLENDIDLY
SPLENDIDNESS
SPLENDIDNESSES
SPLENDIDOUS
SPLENDIFEROUS
SPLENDIFEROUSLY
SPLENDOROUS
SPLENDOURS
SPLENDROUS
SPLENECTOMIES
SPLENECTOMISE
SPLENECTOMISED
SPLENECTOMISES
SPLENECTOMISING
SPLENECTOMIZE
SPLENECTOMIZED
SPLENECTOMIZES
SPLENECTOMIZING
SPLENECTOMY
SPLENETICAL
SPLENETICALLY
SPLENETICS
SPLENISATION
SPLENISATIONS
SPLENITISES
SPLENIUSES
SPLENIZATION
SPLENIZATIONS
SPLENOMEGALIES
SPLENOMEGALY
SPLEUCHANS
SPLINTERED
SPLINTERIER
SPLINTERIEST
SPLINTERING
SPLINTLIKE
SPLINTWOOD
SPLINTWOODS
SPLODGIEST
SPLODGINESS
SPLODGINESSES
SPLOOSHING
SPLOTCHIER
SPLOTCHIEST
SPLOTCHILY
SPLOTCHINESS
SPLOTCHINESSES
SPLOTCHING
SPLURGIEST
SPLUTTERED
SPLUTTERER
SPLUTTERERS
SPLUTTERING
SPLUTTERINGLY
SPLUTTERINGS
SPODOGRAMS
SPODOMANCIES
SPODOMANCY
SPODOMANTIC
SPODUMENES
SPOILFIVES
SPOILSPORT
SPOILSPORTS
SPOKESHAVE
SPOKESHAVES
SPOKESMANSHIP
SPOKESMANSHIPS
SPOKESPEOPLE
SPOKESPERSON
SPOKESPERSONS
SPOKESWOMAN
SPOKESWOMEN
SPOLIATING
SPOLIATION
SPOLIATIONS
SPOLIATIVE
SPOLIATORS
SPOLIATORY
SPONDAICAL
SPONDOOLICKS
SPONDULICKS
SPONDYLITIC
SPONDYLITICS
SPONDYLITIS
SPONDYLITISES
SPONDYLOLYSES
SPONDYLOLYSIS
SPONDYLOSES
SPONDYLOSIS
SPONDYLOUS
SPONGEABLE
SPONGEBAGS
SPONGELIKE
SPONGEWARE
SPONGEWARES
SPONGEWOOD
SPONGEWOODS
SPONGICOLOUS
SPONGIFORM
SPONGINESS
SPONGINESSES
SPONGIOBLAST
SPONGIOBLASTIC
SPONGIOBLASTS
SPONGOLOGIES
SPONGOLOGIST
SPONGOLOGISTS
SPONGOLOGY
SPONSIONAL
SPONSORIAL
SPONSORING
SPONSORSHIP
SPONSORSHIPS
SPONTANEITIES
SPONTANEITY
SPONTANEOUS
SPONTANEOUSLY
SPONTANEOUSNESS
SPOOFERIES
SPOOKERIES
SPOOKINESS
SPOOKINESSES
SPOONBAITS
SPOONBILLS
SPOONDRIFT
SPOONDRIFTS
SPOONERISM
SPOONERISMS
SPORADICAL
SPORADICALLY
SPORADICALNESS
SPORANGIAL
SPORANGIOLA
SPORANGIOLE
SPORANGIOLES
SPORANGIOLUM
SPORANGIOPHORE
SPORANGIOPHORES
SPORANGIOSPORE
SPORANGIOSPORES
SPORANGIUM

SPORICIDAL
SPORICIDES
SPORIDESMS
SPOROCARPS
SPOROCYSTIC
SPOROCYSTS
SPOROCYTES
SPOROGENESES
SPOROGENESIS
SPOROGENIC
SPOROGENIES
SPOROGENOUS
SPOROGONIA
SPOROGONIAL
SPOROGONIC
SPOROGONIES
SPOROGONIUM
SPOROPHORE
SPOROPHORES
SPOROPHORIC
SPOROPHOROUS
SPOROPHYLL
SPOROPHYLLS
SPOROPHYLS
SPOROPHYTE
SPOROPHYTES
SPOROPHYTIC
SPOROPOLLENIN
SPOROPOLLENINS
SPOROTRICHOSES
SPOROTRICHOSIS
SPOROZOANS
SPOROZOITE
SPOROZOITES
SPORTABILITIES
SPORTABILITY
SPORTANCES
SPORTCASTER
SPORTCASTERS
SPORTFISHERMAN
SPORTFISHERMEN
SPORTFISHING
SPORTFISHINGS
SPORTFULLY
SPORTFULNESS
SPORTFULNESSES
SPORTINESS
SPORTINESSES
SPORTINGLY
SPORTIVELY
SPORTIVENESS
SPORTIVENESSES
SPORTSCAST
SPORTSCASTER
SPORTSCASTERS
SPORTSCASTS
SPORTSMANLIKE
SPORTSMANLY
SPORTSMANSHIP
SPORTSMANSHIPS
SPORTSPEOPLE
SPORTSPERSON
SPORTSPERSONS
SPORTSWEAR
SPORTSWEARS
SPORTSWOMAN
SPORTSWOMEN
SPORTSWRITER
SPORTSWRITERS
SPORTSWRITING
SPORTSWRITINGS
SPORULATED
SPORULATES
SPORULATING
SPORULATION
SPORULATIONS
SPORULATIVE
SPOTLESSLY
SPOTLESSNESS
SPOTLESSNESSES
SPOTLIGHTED
SPOTLIGHTING
SPOTLIGHTS
SPOTTEDNESS
SPOTTEDNESSES
SPOTTINESS
SPOTTINESSES
SPOUSELESS
SPOYLEFULL
SPRACHGEFUHL
SPRACHGEFUHLS
SPRACKLING
SPRADDLING
SPRANGLING
SPRATTLING
SPRAUCHLED
SPRAUCHLES
SPRAUCHLING
SPRAUNCIER
SPRAUNCIEST
SPRAWLIEST
SPREADABILITIES
SPREADABILITY
SPREADABLE
SPREADINGLY
SPREADINGS
SPREADSHEET
SPREADSHEETS
SPREAGHERIES
SPREAGHERY
SPREATHING
SPRECHERIES
SPRECHGESANG
SPRECHGESANGS
SPRECHSTIMME
SPRECHSTIMMES
SPREETHING
SPREKELIAS
SPRIGGIEST
SPRIGHTFUL
SPRIGHTFULLY
SPRIGHTFULNESS
SPRIGHTING
SPRIGHTLESS
SPRIGHTLIER
SPRIGHTLIEST
SPRIGHTLINESS
SPRIGHTLINESSES
SPRIGTAILS
SPRINGALDS
SPRINGBOARD
SPRINGBOARDS
SPRINGBOKS
SPRINGBUCK
SPRINGBUCKS
SPRINGEING
SPRINGHAAS
SPRINGHALT
SPRINGHALTS
SPRINGHASE
SPRINGHEAD
SPRINGHEADS
SPRINGHOUSE
SPRINGHOUSES
SPRINGIEST
SPRINGINESS
SPRINGINESSES
SPRINGINGS
SPRINGKEEPER
SPRINGKEEPERS
SPRINGLESS
SPRINGLETS
SPRINGLIKE
SPRINGTAIL
SPRINGTAILS
SPRINGTIDE
SPRINGTIDES
SPRINGTIME
SPRINGTIMES
SPRINGWATER
SPRINGWATERS
SPRINGWOOD
SPRINGWOODS
SPRINGWORT
SPRINGWORTS
SPRINKLERED
SPRINKLERING
SPRINKLERS
SPRINKLING
SPRINKLINGS
SPRINTINGS
SPRITELIER
SPRITELIEST
SPRITSAILS
SPROUTINGS
SPRUCENESS
SPRUCENESSES
SPRYNESSES
SPUILZIEING
SPULEBLADE
SPULEBLADES
SPULYIEING
SPULZIEING
SPUMESCENCE
SPUMESCENCES
SPUMESCENT
SPUNBONDED
SPUNKINESS
SPUNKINESSES
SPURGALLED
SPURGALLING
SPURIOSITIES
SPURIOSITY
SPURIOUSLY
SPURIOUSNESS
SPURIOUSNESSES
SPUTTERERS
SPUTTERING
SPUTTERINGLY
SPUTTERINGS
SPYGLASSES
SPYMASTERS
SQUABASHED
SQUABASHER
SQUABASHERS
SQUABASHES
SQUABASHING
SQUABBIEST
SQUABBLERS
SQUABBLING
SQUADRONAL
SQUADRONED
SQUADRONES
SQUADRONING
SQUAILINGS
SQUALIDEST
SQUALIDITIES
SQUALIDITY
SQUALIDNESS
SQUALIDNESSES
SQUALLIEST
SQUALLINGS
SQUAMATION
SQUAMATIONS
SQUAMELLAS
SQUAMIFORM
SQUAMOSALS
SQUAMOSELY
SQUAMOSENESS
SQUAMOSENESSES
SQUAMOSITIES
SQUAMOSITY
SQUAMOUSLY
SQUAMOUSNESS
SQUAMOUSNESSES
SQUAMULOSE
SQUANDERED
SQUANDERER
SQUANDERERS
SQUANDERING
SQUANDERINGLY
SQUANDERINGS
SQUANDERMANIA
SQUANDERMANIAS
SQUAREHEAD
SQUAREHEADS
SQUARENESS
SQUARENESSES
SQUAREWISE
SQUARISHLY
SQUARISHNESS
SQUARISHNESSES
SQUARSONAGE
SQUARSONAGES
SQUASHABLE
SQUASHIEST
SQUASHINESS
SQUASHINESSES
SQUATNESSES
SQUATTERED
SQUATTERING
SQUATTIEST
SQUATTINESS
SQUATTINESSES

SQUATTLING
SQUATTOCRACIES
SQUATTOCRACY
SQUAWBUSHES
SQUAWFISHES
SQUAWKIEST
SQUAWKINGS
SQUAWROOTS
SQUEAKERIES
SQUEAKIEST
SQUEAKINESS
SQUEAKINESSES
SQUEAKINGLY
SQUEAKINGS
SQUEALINGS
SQUEAMISHLY
SQUEAMISHNESS
SQUEAMISHNESSES
SQUEEGEEING
SQUEEZABILITIES
SQUEEZABILITY
SQUEEZABLE
SQUEEZIEST
SQUEEZINGS
SQUEGGINGS
SQUELCHERS
SQUELCHIER
SQUELCHIEST
SQUELCHING
SQUELCHINGS
SQUETEAGUE
SQUETEAGUES
SQUIBBINGS
SQUIDGIEST
SQUIFFIEST
SQUIGGLERS
SQUIGGLIER
SQUIGGLIEST
SQUIGGLING
SQUILGEEING
SQUILLIONS
SQUINANCIES
SQUINCHING
SQUINNIEST
SQUINNYING
SQUINTIEST
SQUINTINGLY
SQUINTINGS
SQUIRALITIES
SQUIRALITY
SQUIRALTIES
SQUIRARCHAL
SQUIRARCHICAL
SQUIRARCHIES
SQUIRARCHS
SQUIRARCHY
SQUIREAGES
SQUIREARCH
SQUIREARCHAL
SQUIREARCHICAL
SQUIREARCHIES
SQUIREARCHS
SQUIREARCHY
SQUIREDOMS
SQUIREHOOD
SQUIREHOODS
SQUIRELIKE
SQUIRELING
SQUIRELINGS
SQUIRESHIP
SQUIRESHIPS
SQUIRESSES
SQUIRMIEST
SQUIRMINGLY
SQUIRRELED
SQUIRRELFISH
SQUIRRELFISHES
SQUIRRELING
SQUIRRELLED
SQUIRRELLING
SQUIRRELLY
SQUIRTINGS
SQUISHIEST
SQUISHINESS
SQUISHINESSES
SQUOOSHIER
SQUOOSHIEST
SQUOOSHING
STABBINGLY
STABILATES
STABILISATION
STABILISATIONS
STABILISATOR
STABILISATORS
STABILISED
STABILISER
STABILISERS
STABILISES
STABILISING
STABILITIES
STABILIZATION
STABILIZATIONS
STABILIZATOR
STABILIZATORS
STABILIZED
STABILIZER
STABILIZERS
STABILIZES
STABILIZING
STABLEBOYS
STABLEMATE
STABLEMATES
STABLENESS
STABLENESSES
STABLISHED
STABLISHES
STABLISHING
STABLISHMENT
STABLISHMENTS
STACCATISSIMO
STACKROOMS
STACKYARDS
STACTOMETER
STACTOMETERS
STADDLESTONE
STADDLESTONES
STADHOLDER
STADHOLDERATE
STADHOLDERATES
STADHOLDERS
STADHOLDERSHIP
STADHOLDERSHIPS
STADIOMETER
STADIOMETERS
STADTHOLDER
STADTHOLDERATE
STADTHOLDERATES
STADTHOLDERS
STADTHOLDERSHIP
STAFFROOMS
STAGECOACH
STAGECOACHES
STAGECOACHING
STAGECOACHINGS
STAGECOACHMAN
STAGECOACHMEN
STAGECRAFT
STAGECRAFTS
STAGEHANDS
STAGESTRUCK
STAGFLATION
STAGFLATIONARY
STAGFLATIONS
STAGGERBUSH
STAGGERBUSHES
STAGGERERS
STAGGERING
STAGGERINGLY
STAGGERINGS
STAGHOUNDS
STAGINESSES
STAGNANCES
STAGNANCIES
STAGNANTLY
STAGNATING
STAGNATION
STAGNATIONS
STAIDNESSES
STAINABILITIES
STAINABILITY
STAINLESSES
STAINLESSLY
STAINLESSNESS
STAINLESSNESSES
STAINPROOF
STAIRCASED
STAIRCASES
STAIRCASING
STAIRCASINGS
STAIRFOOTS
STAIRHEADS
STAIRLIFTS
STAIRSTEPPED
STAIRSTEPPING
STAIRSTEPS
STAIRWELLS
STAIRWORKS
STAKEHOLDER
STAKEHOLDERS
STAKHANOVISM
STAKHANOVISMS
STAKHANOVITE
STAKHANOVITES
STAKTOMETER
STAKTOMETERS
STALACTICAL
STALACTIFORM
STALACTITAL
STALACTITE
STALACTITED
STALACTITES
STALACTITIC
STALACTITICAL
STALACTITICALLY
STALACTITIFORM
STALACTITIOUS
STALAGMITE
STALAGMITES
STALAGMITIC
STALAGMITICAL
STALAGMITICALLY
STALAGMOMETER
STALAGMOMETERS
STALAGMOMETRIES
STALAGMOMETRY
STALEMATED
STALEMATES
STALEMATING
STALENESSES
STALKINESS
STALKINESSES
STALLENGER
STALLENGERS
STALLHOLDER
STALLHOLDERS
STALLINGER
STALLINGERS
STALLMASTER
STALLMASTERS
STALWARTLY
STALWARTNESS
STALWARTNESSES
STALWORTHS
STAMINEOUS
STAMINIFEROUS
STAMINODES
STAMINODIA
STAMINODIES
STAMINODIUM
STAMMERERS
STAMMERING
STAMMERINGLY
STAMMERINGS
STAMPEDERS
STAMPEDING
STAMPEDOED
STAMPEDOING
STANCHABLE
STANCHELLED
STANCHELLING
STANCHERED
STANCHERING
STANCHINGS
STANCHIONED
STANCHIONING
STANCHIONS
STANCHLESS
STANCHNESS
STANCHNESSES
STANDARDBRED
STANDARDBREDS
STANDARDISATION
STANDARDISE
STANDARDISED

STANDARDISER
STANDARDISERS
STANDARDISES
STANDARDISING
STANDARDIZATION
STANDARDIZE
STANDARDIZED
STANDARDIZER
STANDARDIZERS
STANDARDIZES
STANDARDIZING
STANDARDLESS
STANDARDLY
STANDDOWNS
STANDFASTS
STANDFIRST
STANDFIRSTS
STANDGALES
STANDISHES
STANDOFFISH
STANDOFFISHLY
STANDOFFISHNESS
STANDOVERS
STANDPATTER
STANDPATTERS
STANDPATTISM
STANDPATTISMS
STANDPIPES
STANDPOINT
STANDPOINTS
STANDSTILL
STANDSTILLS
STANNARIES
STANNATORS
STANNIFEROUS
STANNOTYPE
STANNOTYPES
STAPEDECTOMIES
STAPEDECTOMY
STAPEDIUSES
STAPHYLINE
STAPHYLINID
STAPHYLINIDS
STAPHYLITIS
STAPHYLITISES
STAPHYLOCOCCAL
STAPHYLOCOCCI
STAPHYLOCOCCIC
STAPHYLOCOCCUS
STAPHYLOMA
STAPHYLOMAS
STAPHYLOMATA
STAPHYLOPLASTIC
STAPHYLOPLASTY
STAPHYLOPLASY
STAPHYLORRHAPHY
STARBOARDED
STARBOARDING
STARBOARDS
STARBURSTS
STARCHEDLY
STARCHEDNESS
STARCHEDNESSES
STARCHIEST
STARCHINESS
STARCHINESSES
STARCHLIKE
STARDRIFTS
STARFISHED
STARFISHES
STARFLOWER
STARFLOWERS
STARFRUITS
STARFUCKER
STARFUCKERS
STARFUCKING
STARFUCKINGS
STARGAZERS
STARGAZING
STARGAZINGS
STARKENING
STARKNESSES
STARLIGHTED
STARLIGHTS
STARMONGER
STARMONGERS
STAROSTIES
STARRINESS
STARRINESSES
STARSHINES
STARSTONES
STARSTRUCK
STARTINGLY
STARTLEMENT
STARTLEMENTS
STARTLINGLY
STARTLINGS
STARVATION
STARVATIONS
STARVELING
STARVELINGS
STASIDIONS
STASIMORPHIES
STASIMORPHY
STATECRAFT
STATECRAFTS
STATEHOODS
STATEHOUSE
STATEHOUSES
STATELESSNESS
STATELESSNESSES
STATELIEST
STATELINESS
STATELINESSES
STATEMENTED
STATEMENTING
STATEMENTINGS
STATEMENTS
STATEROOMS
STATESMANLIKE
STATESMANLY
STATESMANSHIP
STATESMANSHIPS
STATESPEOPLE
STATESPERSON
STATESPERSONS
STATESWOMAN
STATESWOMEN
STATICALLY
STATIONARIES
STATIONARILY
STATIONARINESS
STATIONARY
STATIONERIES
STATIONERS
STATIONERY
STATIONING
STATIONMASTER
STATIONMASTERS
STATISTICAL
STATISTICALLY
STATISTICIAN
STATISTICIANS
STATISTICS
STATOBLAST
STATOBLASTS
STATOCYSTS
STATOLATRIES
STATOLATRY
STATOLITHIC
STATOLITHS
STATOSCOPE
STATOSCOPES
STATUARIES
STATUESQUE
STATUESQUELY
STATUESQUENESS
STATUETTES
STATUTABLE
STATUTABLY
STATUTORILY
STAUNCHABLE
STAUNCHERS
STAUNCHEST
STAUNCHING
STAUNCHINGS
STAUNCHLESS
STAUNCHNESS
STAUNCHNESSES
STAUROLITE
STAUROLITES
STAUROLITIC
STAUROSCOPE
STAUROSCOPES
STAUROSCOPIC
STAVESACRE
STAVESACRES
STAVUDINES
STAYMAKERS
STEADFASTLY
STEADFASTNESS
STEADFASTNESSES
STEADICAMS
STEADINESS
STEADINESSES
STEAKHOUSE
STEAKHOUSES
STEALINGLY
STEALTHFUL
STEALTHIER
STEALTHIEST
STEALTHILY
STEALTHINESS
STEALTHINESSES
STEALTHING
STEALTHINGS
STEAMBOATS
STEAMERING
STEAMFITTER
STEAMFITTERS
STEAMINESS
STEAMINESSES
STEAMROLLED
STEAMROLLER
STEAMROLLERED
STEAMROLLERING
STEAMROLLERS
STEAMROLLING
STEAMROLLS
STEAMSHIPS
STEAMTIGHT
STEAMTIGHTNESS
STEAROPTENE
STEAROPTENES
STEARSMATE
STEARSMATES
STEATOCELE
STEATOCELES
STEATOLYSES
STEATOLYSIS
STEATOMATOUS
STEATOPYGA
STEATOPYGAS
STEATOPYGIA
STEATOPYGIAS
STEATOPYGIC
STEATOPYGOUS
STEATORRHEA
STEATORRHEAS
STEATORRHOEA
STEATORRHOEAS
STEDFASTLY
STEDFASTNESS
STEDFASTNESSES
STEELHEADS
STEELINESS
STEELINESSES
STEELMAKER
STEELMAKERS
STEELMAKING
STEELMAKINGS
STEELWARES
STEELWORKER
STEELWORKERS
STEELWORKING
STEELWORKINGS
STEELWORKS
STEELYARDS
STEENBRASES
STEENBUCKS
STEENKIRKS
STEEPDOWNE
STEEPEDOWNE
STEEPENING
STEEPINESS
STEEPINESSES
STEEPLEBUSH
STEEPLEBUSHES
STEEPLECHASE
STEEPLECHASED
STEEPLECHASER
STEEPLECHASERS
STEEPLECHASES
STEEPLECHASING

STEEPLECHASINGS
STEEPLEJACK
STEEPLEJACKS
STEEPNESSES
STEERAGEWAY
STEERAGEWAYS
STEERLINGS
STEERSMATE
STEERSMATES
STEGANOGRAM
STEGANOGRAMS
STEGANOGRAPH
STEGANOGRAPHER
STEGANOGRAPHERS
STEGANOGRAPHIC
STEGANOGRAPHIES
STEGANOGRAPHIST
STEGANOGRAPHS
STEGANOGRAPHY
STEGANOPOD
STEGANOPODOUS
STEGANOPODS
STEGOCARPOUS
STEGOCEPHALIAN
STEGOCEPHALIANS
STEGOCEPHALOUS
STEGODONTS
STEGOMYIAS
STEGOPHILIST
STEGOPHILISTS
STEGOSAURIAN
STEGOSAURS
STEGOSAURUS
STEGOSAURUSES
STEINBOCKS
STEINKIRKS
STELLARATOR
STELLARATORS
STELLATELY
STELLERIDAN
STELLERIDANS
STELLERIDS
STELLIFEROUS
STELLIFIED
STELLIFIES
STELLIFORM
STELLIFYING
STELLIFYINGS
STELLIONATE
STELLIONATES
STELLULARLY
STELLULATE
STEMMATOUS
STEMMERIES
STEMWINDER
STEMWINDERS
STENCHIEST
STENCILERS
STENCILING
STENCILLED
STENCILLER
STENCILLERS
STENCILLING
STENCILLINGS
STENOBATHIC
STENOBATHS
STENOCARDIA
STENOCARDIAS
STENOCHROME
STENOCHROMES
STENOCHROMIES
STENOCHROMY
STENOGRAPH
STENOGRAPHED
STENOGRAPHER
STENOGRAPHERS
STENOGRAPHIC
STENOGRAPHICAL
STENOGRAPHIES
STENOGRAPHING
STENOGRAPHIST
STENOGRAPHISTS
STENOGRAPHS
STENOGRAPHY
STENOHALINE
STENOPAEIC
STENOPETALOUS
STENOPHAGOUS
STENOPHYLLOUS
STENOTHERM
STENOTHERMAL
STENOTHERMS
STENOTOPIC
STENOTROPIC
STENOTYPED
STENOTYPER
STENOTYPERS
STENOTYPES
STENOTYPIC
STENOTYPIES
STENOTYPING
STENOTYPIST
STENOTYPISTS
STENTMASTER
STENTMASTERS
STENTORIAN
STEPBAIRNS
STEPBROTHER
STEPBROTHERS
STEPCHILDREN
STEPDANCER
STEPDANCERS
STEPDANCING
STEPDANCINGS
STEPDAUGHTER
STEPDAUGHTERS
STEPFAMILIES
STEPFAMILY
STEPFATHER
STEPFATHERS
STEPHANITE
STEPHANITES
STEPHANOTIS
STEPHANOTISES
STEPLADDER
STEPLADDERS
STEPMOTHER
STEPMOTHERLY
STEPMOTHERS
STEPPARENT
STEPPARENTING
STEPPARENTINGS
STEPPARENTS
STEPSISTER
STEPSISTERS
STEPSTOOLS
STERADIANS
STERCORACEOUS
STERCORANISM
STERCORANISMS
STERCORANIST
STERCORANISTS
STERCORARIOUS
STERCORARY
STERCORATE
STERCORATED
STERCORATES
STERCORATING
STERCORICOLOUS
STERCULIACEOUS
STERCULIAS
STEREOACUITIES
STEREOACUITY
STEREOBATE
STEREOBATES
STEREOBATIC
STEREOBLIND
STEREOCARD
STEREOCARDS
STEREOCHEMICAL
STEREOCHEMISTRY
STEREOCHROME
STEREOCHROMED
STEREOCHROMES
STEREOCHROMIES
STEREOCHROMING
STEREOCHROMY
STEREOGNOSES
STEREOGNOSIS
STEREOGRAM
STEREOGRAMS
STEREOGRAPH
STEREOGRAPHED
STEREOGRAPHIC
STEREOGRAPHICAL
STEREOGRAPHIES
STEREOGRAPHING
STEREOGRAPHS
STEREOGRAPHY
STEREOISOMER
STEREOISOMERIC
STEREOISOMERISM
STEREOISOMERS
STEREOISOMETRIC
STEREOLOGICAL
STEREOLOGICALLY
STEREOLOGIES
STEREOLOGY
STEREOMETER
STEREOMETERS
STEREOMETRIC
STEREOMETRICAL
STEREOMETRIES
STEREOMETRY
STEREOPHONIC
STEREOPHONIES
STEREOPHONY
STEREOPSES
STEREOPSIS
STEREOPTICON
STEREOPTICONS
STEREOPTICS
STEREOREGULAR
STEREOSCOPE
STEREOSCOPES
STEREOSCOPIC
STEREOSCOPICAL
STEREOSCOPIES
STEREOSCOPIST
STEREOSCOPISTS
STEREOSCOPY
STEREOSONIC
STEREOSPECIFIC
STEREOTACTIC
STEREOTACTICAL
STEREOTAXES
STEREOTAXIA
STEREOTAXIAS
STEREOTAXIC
STEREOTAXICALLY
STEREOTAXIS
STEREOTOMIES
STEREOTOMY
STEREOTROPIC
STEREOTROPISM
STEREOTROPISMS
STEREOTYPE
STEREOTYPED
STEREOTYPER
STEREOTYPERS
STEREOTYPES
STEREOTYPIC
STEREOTYPICAL
STEREOTYPICALLY
STEREOTYPIES
STEREOTYPING
STEREOTYPINGS
STEREOTYPIST
STEREOTYPISTS
STEREOTYPY
STEREOVISION
STEREOVISIONS
STERICALLY
STERIGMATA
STERILANTS
STERILISABLE
STERILISATION
STERILISATIONS
STERILISED
STERILISER
STERILISERS
STERILISES
STERILISING
STERILITIES
STERILIZABLE
STERILIZATION
STERILIZATIONS
STERILIZED
STERILIZER
STERILIZERS
STERILIZES
STERILIZING
STERLINGLY
STERLINGNESS

STERLINGNESSES
STERNALGIA
STERNALGIAS
STERNALGIC
STERNBOARD
STERNBOARDS
STERNEBRAE
STERNFASTS
STERNFOREMOST
STERNNESSES
STERNOCOSTAL
STERNOTRIBE
STERNPORTS
STERNPOSTS
STERNSHEET
STERNSHEETS
STERNUTATION
STERNUTATIONS
STERNUTATIVE
STERNUTATIVES
STERNUTATOR
STERNUTATORIES
STERNUTATORS
STERNUTATORY
STERNWARDS
STERNWORKS
STEROIDOGENESES
STEROIDOGENESIS
STEROIDOGENIC
STERTOROUS
STERTOROUSLY
STERTOROUSNESS
STETHOSCOPE
STETHOSCOPES
STETHOSCOPIC
STETHOSCOPIES
STETHOSCOPIST
STETHOSCOPISTS
STETHOSCOPY
STEVEDORED
STEVEDORES
STEVEDORING
STEVENGRAPH
STEVENGRAPHS
STEWARDESS
STEWARDESSES
STEWARDING
STEWARDRIES
STEWARDSHIP
STEWARDSHIPS
STEWARTRIES
STIACCIATO
STIACCIATOS
STIBIALISM
STIBIALISMS
STICCADOES
STICCATOES
STICHARION
STICHARIONS
STICHICALLY
STICHIDIUM
STICHOLOGIES
STICHOLOGY
STICHOMETRIC
STICHOMETRICAL
STICHOMETRIES
STICHOMETRY
STICHOMYTHIA
STICHOMYTHIAS
STICHOMYTHIC
STICHOMYTHIES
STICHOMYTHY
STICKABILITIES
STICKABILITY
STICKBALLS
STICKERING
STICKHANDLE
STICKHANDLED
STICKHANDLER
STICKHANDLERS
STICKHANDLES
STICKHANDLING
STICKINESS
STICKINESSES
STICKLEADER
STICKLEADERS
STICKLEBACK
STICKLEBACKS
STICKSEEDS
STICKTIGHT
STICKTIGHTS
STICKWEEDS
STICKWORKS
STICKYBEAK
STICKYBEAKED
STICKYBEAKING
STICKYBEAKS
STIDDIEING
STIFFENERS
STIFFENING
STIFFENINGS
STIFFNESSES
STIFFWARES
STIFLINGLY
STIGMARIAN
STIGMARIANS
STIGMASTEROL
STIGMASTEROLS
STIGMATICAL
STIGMATICALLY
STIGMATICS
STIGMATIFEROUS
STIGMATISATION
STIGMATISATIONS
STIGMATISE
STIGMATISED
STIGMATISER
STIGMATISERS
STIGMATISES
STIGMATISING
STIGMATISM
STIGMATISMS
STIGMATIST
STIGMATISTS
STIGMATIZATION
STIGMATIZATIONS
STIGMATIZE
STIGMATIZED
STIGMATIZER
STIGMATIZERS
STIGMATIZES
STIGMATIZING
STIGMATOPHILIA
STIGMATOPHILIAS
STIGMATOPHILIST
STIGMATOSE
STILBESTROL
STILBESTROLS
STILBOESTROL
STILBOESTROLS
STILETTOED
STILETTOES
STILETTOING
STILLATORIES
STILLATORY
STILLBIRTH
STILLBIRTHS
STILLBORNS
STILLHOUSE
STILLHOUSES
STILLICIDE
STILLICIDES
STILLIFORM
STILLNESSES
STILLROOMS
STILPNOSIDERITE
STILTBIRDS
STILTEDNESS
STILTEDNESSES
STILTINESS
STILTINESSES
STIMPMETER
STIMPMETERS
STIMULABLE
STIMULANCIES
STIMULANCY
STIMULANTS
STIMULATED
STIMULATER
STIMULATERS
STIMULATES
STIMULATING
STIMULATINGLY
STIMULATION
STIMULATIONS
STIMULATIVE
STIMULATIVES
STIMULATOR
STIMULATORS
STIMULATORY
STINGAREES
STINGBULLS
STINGFISHES
STINGINESS
STINGINESSES
STINGINGLY
STINGINGNESS
STINGINGNESSES
STINKEROOS
STINKHORNS
STINKINGLY
STINKINGNESS
STINKINGNESSES
STINKSTONE
STINKSTONES
STINKWEEDS
STINKWOODS
STINTEDNESS
STINTEDNESSES
STINTINGLY
STIPELLATE
STIPENDIARIES
STIPENDIARY
STIPENDIATE
STIPENDIATED
STIPENDIATES
STIPENDIATING
STIPITIFORM
STIPPLINGS
STIPULABLE
STIPULACEOUS
STIPULATED
STIPULATES
STIPULATING
STIPULATION
STIPULATIONS
STIPULATOR
STIPULATORS
STIPULATORY
STIRABOUTS
STIRPICULTURE
STIRPICULTURES
STIRRINGLY
STITCHCRAFT
STITCHCRAFTS
STITCHERIES
STITCHINGS
STITCHWORK
STITCHWORKS
STITCHWORT
STITCHWORTS
STOCHASTIC
STOCHASTICALLY
STOCKADING
STOCKBREEDER
STOCKBREEDERS
STOCKBREEDING
STOCKBREEDINGS
STOCKBROKER
STOCKBROKERAGE
STOCKBROKERAGES
STOCKBROKERS
STOCKBROKING
STOCKBROKINGS
STOCKFISHES
STOCKHOLDER
STOCKHOLDERS
STOCKHOLDING
STOCKHOLDINGS
STOCKHORNS
STOCKHORSE
STOCKHORSES
STOCKINESS
STOCKINESSES
STOCKINETS
STOCKINETTE
STOCKINETTES
STOCKINGED
STOCKINGER
STOCKINGERS
STOCKINGLESS
STOCKISHLY
STOCKISHNESS
STOCKISHNESSES

STOCKJOBBER
STOCKJOBBERIES
STOCKJOBBERS
STOCKJOBBERY
STOCKJOBBING
STOCKJOBBINGS
STOCKKEEPER
STOCKKEEPERS
STOCKLISTS
STOCKLOCKS
STOCKPILED
STOCKPILER
STOCKPILERS
STOCKPILES
STOCKPILING
STOCKPILINGS
STOCKPUNISHT
STOCKROOMS
STOCKROUTE
STOCKROUTES
STOCKTAKEN
STOCKTAKES
STOCKTAKING
STOCKTAKINGS
STOCKWORKS
STOCKYARDS
STODGINESS
STODGINESSES
STOECHIOLOGICAL
STOECHIOLOGIES
STOECHIOLOGY
STOECHIOMETRIC
STOECHIOMETRIES
STOECHIOMETRY
STOICALNESS
STOICALNESSES
STOICHEIOLOGIES
STOICHEIOLOGY
STOICHEIOMETRIC
STOICHEIOMETRY
STOICHIOLOGICAL
STOICHIOLOGIES
STOICHIOLOGY
STOICHIOMETRIC
STOICHIOMETRIES
STOICHIOMETRY
STOITERING
STOKEHOLDS
STOKEHOLES
STOLENWISE
STOLIDITIES
STOLIDNESS
STOLIDNESSES
STOLONIFEROUS
STOMACHACHE
STOMACHACHES
STOMACHERS
STOMACHFUL
STOMACHFULNESS
STOMACHFULS
STOMACHICAL
STOMACHICS
STOMACHING
STOMACHLESS
STOMACHOUS
STOMATITIC
STOMATITIDES
STOMATITIS
STOMATITISES
STOMATODAEA
STOMATODAEUM
STOMATOGASTRIC
STOMATOLOGICAL
STOMATOLOGIES
STOMATOLOGY
STOMATOPLASTIES
STOMATOPLASTY
STOMATOPOD
STOMATOPODS
STOMODAEAL
STOMODAEUM
STOMODAEUMS
STOMODEUMS
STONEBOATS
STONEBORER
STONEBORERS
STONEBRASH
STONEBRASHES
STONEBREAK
STONEBREAKS
STONECASTS
STONECHATS
STONECROPS
STONECUTTER
STONECUTTERS
STONECUTTING
STONECUTTINGS
STONEFISHES
STONEFLIES
STONEGROUND
STONEHANDS
STONEHORSE
STONEHORSES
STONELESSNESS
STONELESSNESSES
STONEMASON
STONEMASONRIES
STONEMASONRY
STONEMASONS
STONESHOTS
STONEWALLED
STONEWALLER
STONEWALLERS
STONEWALLING
STONEWALLINGS
STONEWALLS
STONEWARES
STONEWASHED
STONEWASHES
STONEWASHING
STONEWORKER
STONEWORKERS
STONEWORKS
STONEWORTS
STONINESSES
STONISHING
STONKERING
STONYHEARTED
STOOLBALLS
STOOPBALLS
STOOPINGLY
STOPLIGHTS
STOPPERING
STOPWATCHES
STOREFRONT
STOREFRONTS
STOREHOUSE
STOREHOUSES
STOREKEEPER
STOREKEEPERS
STOREKEEPING
STOREKEEPINGS
STOREROOMS
STORESHIPS
STORIETTES
STORIOLOGIES
STORIOLOGIST
STORIOLOGISTS
STORIOLOGY
STORKSBILL
STORKSBILLS
STORMBIRDS
STORMBOUND
STORMFULLY
STORMFULNESS
STORMFULNESSES
STORMINESS
STORMINESSES
STORMPROOF
STORYBOARD
STORYBOARDED
STORYBOARDING
STORYBOARDS
STORYBOOKS
STORYETTES
STORYLINES
STORYTELLER
STORYTELLERS
STORYTELLING
STORYTELLINGS
STOTTERING
STOUTENING
STOUTHEARTED
STOUTHEARTEDLY
STOUTHERIE
STOUTHERIES
STOUTHRIEF
STOUTHRIEFS
STOUTNESSES
STOVEPIPES
STRABISMAL
STRABISMIC
STRABISMICAL
STRABISMOMETER
STRABISMOMETERS
STRABISMUS
STRABISMUSES
STRABOMETER
STRABOMETERS
STRABOTOMIES
STRABOTOMY
STRACCHINI
STRACCHINO
STRADDLEBACK
STRADDLERS
STRADDLING
STRAGGLERS
STRAGGLIER
STRAGGLIEST
STRAGGLING
STRAGGLINGLY
STRAGGLINGS
STRAICHTER
STRAICHTEST
STRAIGHTAWAY
STRAIGHTAWAYS
STRAIGHTBRED
STRAIGHTBREDS
STRAIGHTED
STRAIGHTEDGE
STRAIGHTEDGED
STRAIGHTEDGES
STRAIGHTEN
STRAIGHTENED
STRAIGHTENER
STRAIGHTENERS
STRAIGHTENING
STRAIGHTENS
STRAIGHTER
STRAIGHTEST
STRAIGHTFORTH
STRAIGHTFORWARD
STRAIGHTING
STRAIGHTISH
STRAIGHTJACKET
STRAIGHTJACKETS
STRAIGHTLACED
STRAIGHTLY
STRAIGHTNESS
STRAIGHTNESSES
STRAIGHTWAY
STRAIGHTWAYS
STRAINEDLY
STRAININGS
STRAITENED
STRAITENING
STRAITJACKET
STRAITJACKETED
STRAITJACKETING
STRAITJACKETS
STRAITLACED
STRAITLACEDLY
STRAITLACEDNESS
STRAITNESS
STRAITNESSES
STRAITWAISTCOAT
STRAMACONS
STRAMASHED
STRAMASHES
STRAMASHING
STRAMAZONS
STRAMINEOUS
STRAMONIES
STRAMONIUM
STRAMONIUMS
STRANDEDNESS
STRANDEDNESSES
STRANDFLAT
STRANDFLATS
STRANDLINE
STRANDLINES
STRANDWOLF
STRANDWOLVES
STRANGENESS

STRANGENESSES
STRANGERED
STRANGERING
STRANGLEHOLD
STRANGLEHOLDS
STRANGLEMENT
STRANGLEMENTS
STRANGLERS
STRANGLING
STRANGULATE
STRANGULATED
STRANGULATES
STRANGULATING
STRANGULATION
STRANGULATIONS
STRANGURIES
STRAPHANGED
STRAPHANGER
STRAPHANGERS
STRAPHANGING
STRAPHANGS
STRAPLESSES
STRAPLINES
STRAPONTIN
STRAPONTINS
STRAPPADOED
STRAPPADOES
STRAPPADOING
STRAPPADOS
STRAPPIEST
STRAPPINGS
STRAPWORTS
STRATAGEMS
STRATEGETIC
STRATEGETICAL
STRATEGICAL
STRATEGICALLY
STRATEGICS
STRATEGIES
STRATEGISE
STRATEGISED
STRATEGISES
STRATEGISING
STRATEGIST
STRATEGISTS
STRATEGIZE
STRATEGIZED
STRATEGIZES
STRATEGIZING
STRATHSPEY
STRATHSPEYS
STRATICULATE
STRATICULATION
STRATICULATIONS
STRATIFICATION
STRATIFICATIONS
STRATIFIED
STRATIFIES
STRATIFORM
STRATIFYING
STRATIGRAPHER
STRATIGRAPHERS
STRATIGRAPHIC
STRATIGRAPHICAL
STRATIGRAPHIES
STRATIGRAPHIST
STRATIGRAPHISTS
STRATIGRAPHY
STRATOCRACIES
STRATOCRACY
STRATOCRAT
STRATOCRATIC
STRATOCRATS
STRATOCUMULI
STRATOCUMULUS
STRATOPAUSE
STRATOPAUSES
STRATOSPHERE
STRATOSPHERES
STRATOSPHERIC
STRATOSPHERICAL
STRATOTANKER
STRATOTANKERS
STRATOVOLCANO
STRATOVOLCANOES
STRATOVOLCANOS
STRAUCHTED
STRAUCHTER
STRAUCHTEST
STRAUCHTING
STRAUGHTED
STRAUGHTER
STRAUGHTEST
STRAUGHTING
STRAVAGING
STRAVAIGED
STRAVAIGER
STRAVAIGERS
STRAVAIGING
STRAWBERRIES
STRAWBERRY
STRAWBOARD
STRAWBOARDS
STRAWFLOWER
STRAWFLOWERS
STRAWWEIGHT
STRAWWEIGHTS
STRAWWORMS
STRAYLINGS
STREAKIEST
STREAKINESS
STREAKINESSES
STREAKINGS
STREAKLIKE
STREAMBEDS
STREAMERED
STREAMIEST
STREAMINESS
STREAMINESSES
STREAMINGLY
STREAMINGS
STREAMLESS
STREAMLETS
STREAMLIKE
STREAMLINE
STREAMLINED
STREAMLINER
STREAMLINERS
STREAMLINES
STREAMLING
STREAMLINGS
STREAMLINING
STREAMSIDE
STREAMSIDES
STREETAGES
STREETBOYS
STREETCARS
STREETFULS
STREETIEST
STREETKEEPER
STREETKEEPERS
STREETLAMP
STREETLAMPS
STREETLIGHT
STREETLIGHTS
STREETROOM
STREETROOMS
STREETSCAPE
STREETSCAPES
STREETSMART
STREETWALKER
STREETWALKERS
STREETWALKING
STREETWALKINGS
STREETWARD
STREETWARDS
STREETWEAR
STREETWEARS
STREETWISE
STREIGNING
STRELITZES
STRELITZIA
STRELITZIAS
STRENGTHEN
STRENGTHENED
STRENGTHENER
STRENGTHENERS
STRENGTHENING
STRENGTHENINGS
STRENGTHENS
STRENGTHFUL
STRENGTHLESS
STRENUITIES
STRENUOSITIES
STRENUOSITY
STRENUOUSLY
STRENUOUSNESS
STRENUOUSNESSES
STREPEROUS
STREPHOSYMBOLIA
STREPITANT
STREPITATION
STREPITATIONS
STREPITOSO
STREPITOUS
STREPSIPTEROUS
STREPTOBACILLI
STREPTOBACILLUS
STREPTOCARPUS
STREPTOCARPUSES
STREPTOCOCCAL
STREPTOCOCCI
STREPTOCOCCIC
STREPTOCOCCUS
STREPTOKINASE
STREPTOKINASES
STREPTOLYSIN
STREPTOLYSINS
STREPTOMYCES
STREPTOMYCETE
STREPTOMYCETES
STREPTOMYCIN
STREPTOMYCINS
STREPTOSOLEN
STREPTOSOLENS
STREPTOTHRICIN
STREPTOTHRICINS
STRESSBUSTER
STRESSBUSTERS
STRESSBUSTING
STRESSFULLY
STRESSFULNESS
STRESSFULNESSES
STRESSLESS
STRESSLESSNESS
STRETCHABILITY
STRETCHABLE
STRETCHERED
STRETCHERING
STRETCHERS
STRETCHIER
STRETCHIEST
STRETCHINESS
STRETCHINESSES
STRETCHING
STRETCHINGS
STRETCHLESS
STRETCHMARKS
STREWMENTS
STRIATIONS
STRIATURES
STRICKENLY
STRICKLING
STRICTIONS
STRICTNESS
STRICTNESSES
STRICTURED
STRICTURES
STRIDDLING
STRIDELEGGED
STRIDELEGS
STRIDENCES
STRIDENCIES
STRIDENTLY
STRIDEWAYS
STRIDULANCE
STRIDULANCES
STRIDULANT
STRIDULANTLY
STRIDULATE
STRIDULATED
STRIDULATES
STRIDULATING
STRIDULATION
STRIDULATIONS
STRIDULATOR
STRIDULATORS
STRIDULATORY
STRIDULOUS
STRIDULOUSLY
STRIDULOUSNESS
STRIFELESS
STRIGIFORM
STRIKEBOUND

STRIKEBREAKER
STRIKEBREAKERS
STRIKEBREAKING
STRIKEBREAKINGS
STRIKELESS
STRIKEOUTS
STRIKEOVER
STRIKEOVERS
STRIKINGLY
STRIKINGNESS
STRIKINGNESSES
STRINGBOARD
STRINGBOARDS
STRINGCOURSE
STRINGCOURSES
STRINGENCIES
STRINGENCY
STRINGENDO
STRINGENTLY
STRINGENTNESS
STRINGENTNESSES
STRINGHALT
STRINGHALTED
STRINGHALTS
STRINGIEST
STRINGINESS
STRINGINESSES
STRINGINGS
STRINGLESS
STRINGLIKE
STRINGPIECE
STRINGPIECES
STRINGYBARK
STRINGYBARKS
STRINKLING
STRINKLINGS
STRIPAGRAM
STRIPAGRAMS
STRIPELESS
STRIPINESS
STRIPINESSES
STRIPLINGS
STRIPPABLE
STRIPPERGRAM
STRIPPERGRAMS
STRIPPINGS
STRIPTEASE
STRIPTEASER
STRIPTEASERS
STRIPTEASES
STRIVINGLY
STROBILACEOUS
STROBILATE
STROBILATED
STROBILATES
STROBILATING
STROBILATION
STROBILATIONS
STROBILIFORM
STROBILINE
STROBILISATION
STROBILISATIONS
STROBILIZATION
STROBILIZATIONS
STROBILOID
STROBILUSES
STROBOSCOPE
STROBOSCOPES
STROBOSCOPIC
STROBOSCOPICAL
STROBOTRON
STROBOTRONS
STRODDLING
STROGANOFF
STROGANOFFS
STROLLINGS
STROMATOLITE
STROMATOLITES
STROMATOLITIC
STROMATOUS
STROMBULIFEROUS
STROMBULIFORM
STROMBUSES
STRONGARMED
STRONGARMING
STRONGARMS
STRONGBOXES
STRONGHOLD
STRONGHOLDS
STRONGNESS
STRONGNESSES
STRONGPOINT
STRONGPOINTS
STRONGROOM
STRONGROOMS
STRONGYLES
STRONGYLOID
STRONGYLOIDOSES
STRONGYLOIDOSIS
STRONGYLOIDS
STRONGYLOSES
STRONGYLOSIS
STRONTIANITE
STRONTIANITES
STRONTIANS
STRONTIUMS
STROPHANTHIN
STROPHANTHINS
STROPHANTHUS
STROPHANTHUSES
STROPHICAL
STROPHIOLATE
STROPHIOLATED
STROPHIOLE
STROPHIOLES
STROPHOIDS
STROPHULUS
STROPPIEST
STROPPINESS
STROPPINESSES
STROUDINGS
STROUPACHS
STRUCTURAL
STRUCTURALISE
STRUCTURALISED
STRUCTURALISES
STRUCTURALISING
STRUCTURALISM
STRUCTURALISMS
STRUCTURALIST
STRUCTURALISTS
STRUCTURALIZE
STRUCTURALIZED
STRUCTURALIZES
STRUCTURALIZING
STRUCTURALLY
STRUCTURATION
STRUCTURATIONS
STRUCTURED
STRUCTURELESS
STRUCTURES
STRUCTURING
STRUGGLERS
STRUGGLING
STRUGGLINGLY
STRUGGLINGS
STRUMITISES
STRUMPETED
STRUMPETING
STRUTHIOID
STRUTHIOIDS
STRUTHIOUS
STRUTTINGLY
STRUTTINGS
STRYCHNIAS
STRYCHNINE
STRYCHNINED
STRYCHNINES
STRYCHNINING
STRYCHNINISM
STRYCHNINISMS
STRYCHNISM
STRYCHNISMS
STUBBINESS
STUBBINESSES
STUBBLIEST
STUBBORNED
STUBBORNER
STUBBORNEST
STUBBORNING
STUBBORNLY
STUBBORNNESS
STUBBORNNESSES
STUCCOWORK
STUCCOWORKS
STUDDINGSAIL
STUDDINGSAILS
STUDENTRIES
STUDENTSHIP
STUDENTSHIPS
STUDFISHES
STUDHORSES
STUDIEDNESS
STUDIEDNESSES
STUDIOUSLY
STUDIOUSNESS
STUDIOUSNESSES
STUFFINESS
STUFFINESSES
STULTIFICATION
STULTIFICATIONS
STULTIFIED
STULTIFIER
STULTIFIERS
STULTIFIES
STULTIFYING
STUMBLEBUM
STUMBLEBUMS
STUMBLIEST
STUMBLINGLY
STUMPINESS
STUMPINESSES
STUMPWORKS
STUNNINGLY
STUNTEDNESS
STUNTEDNESSES
STUNTWOMAN
STUNTWOMEN
STUPEFACIENT
STUPEFACIENTS
STUPEFACTION
STUPEFACTIONS
STUPEFACTIVE
STUPEFIERS
STUPEFYING
STUPEFYINGLY
STUPENDIOUS
STUPENDOUS
STUPENDOUSLY
STUPENDOUSNESS
STUPIDITIES
STUPIDNESS
STUPIDNESSES
STUPRATING
STUPRATION
STUPRATIONS
STURDINESS
STURDINESSES
STUTTERERS
STUTTERING
STUTTERINGLY
STUTTERINGS
STYLEBOOKS
STYLELESSNESS
STYLELESSNESSES
STYLIFEROUS
STYLISATION
STYLISATIONS
STYLISHNESS
STYLISHNESSES
STYLISTICALLY
STYLISTICS
STYLITISMS
STYLIZATION
STYLIZATIONS
STYLOBATES
STYLOGRAPH
STYLOGRAPHIC
STYLOGRAPHICAL
STYLOGRAPHIES
STYLOGRAPHS
STYLOGRAPHY
STYLOLITES
STYLOLITIC
STYLOMETRIES
STYLOMETRY
STYLOPHONE
STYLOPHONES
STYLOPISED
STYLOPISES
STYLOPISING
STYLOPIZED
STYLOPIZES
STYLOPIZING

STYLOPODIA
STYLOPODIUM
STYLOSTIXES
STYLOSTIXIS
STYPTICITIES
STYPTICITY
STYRACACEOUS
STYROFOAMS
SUABILITIES
SUASIVENESS
SUASIVENESSES
SUAVENESSES
SUAVEOLENT
SUBABDOMINAL
SUBACETATE
SUBACETATES
SUBACIDITIES
SUBACIDITY
SUBACIDNESS
SUBACIDNESSES
SUBACTIONS
SUBACUTELY
SUBADOLESCENT
SUBADOLESCENTS
SUBAERIALLY
SUBAFFLUENT
SUBAGENCIES
SUBAGGREGATE
SUBAGGREGATES
SUBAGGREGATION
SUBAGGREGATIONS
SUBAHDARIES
SUBAHSHIPS
SUBALLIANCE
SUBALLIANCES
SUBALLOCATION
SUBALLOCATIONS
SUBALTERNANT
SUBALTERNANTS
SUBALTERNATE
SUBALTERNATES
SUBALTERNATION
SUBALTERNATIONS
SUBALTERNITIES
SUBALTERNITY
SUBALTERNS
SUBANGULAR
SUBANTARCTIC
SUBAPOSTOLIC
SUBAPPEARANCE
SUBAPPEARANCES
SUBAQUATIC
SUBAQUEOUS
SUBARACHNOID
SUBARACHNOIDAL
SUBARBOREAL
SUBARBORESCENT
SUBARCTICS
SUBARCUATE
SUBARCUATION
SUBARCUATIONS
SUBARRATION
SUBARRATIONS
SUBARRHATION
SUBARRHATIONS
SUBARTICLE
SUBARTICLES
SUBASSEMBLE
SUBASSEMBLED
SUBASSEMBLES
SUBASSEMBLIES
SUBASSEMBLING
SUBASSEMBLY
SUBASSOCIATION
SUBASSOCIATIONS
SUBATMOSPHERIC
SUBATOMICS
SUBAUDIBLE
SUBAUDITION
SUBAUDITIONS
SUBAURICULAR
SUBAVERAGE
SUBAXILLARY
SUBBASEMENT
SUBBASEMENTS
SUBBITUMINOUS
SUBBRANCHES
SUBBUREAUS
SUBBUREAUX
SUBCABINET
SUBCABINETS
SUBCALIBER
SUBCALIBRE
SUBCANTORS
SUBCAPSULAR
SUBCARDINAL
SUBCARDINALS
SUBCARRIER
SUBCARRIERS
SUBCATEGORIES
SUBCATEGORISE
SUBCATEGORISED
SUBCATEGORISES
SUBCATEGORISING
SUBCATEGORIZE
SUBCATEGORIZED
SUBCATEGORIZES
SUBCATEGORIZING
SUBCATEGORY
SUBCAVITIES
SUBCEILING
SUBCEILINGS
SUBCELESTIAL
SUBCELESTIALS
SUBCELLARS
SUBCELLULAR
SUBCENTERS
SUBCENTRAL
SUBCENTRALLY
SUBCEPTION
SUBCEPTIONS
SUBCHANTER
SUBCHANTERS
SUBCHAPTER
SUBCHAPTERS
SUBCHARTER
SUBCHARTERS
SUBCHASERS
SUBCHELATE
SUBCHLORIDE
SUBCHLORIDES
SUBCIRCUIT
SUBCIRCUITS
SUBCIVILISATION
SUBCIVILISED
SUBCIVILIZATION
SUBCIVILIZED
SUBCLASSED
SUBCLASSES
SUBCLASSIFIED
SUBCLASSIFIES
SUBCLASSIFY
SUBCLASSIFYING
SUBCLASSING
SUBCLAUSES
SUBCLAVIAN
SUBCLAVIANS
SUBCLAVICULAR
SUBCLIMACTIC
SUBCLIMAXES
SUBCLINICAL
SUBCLINICALLY
SUBCLUSTER
SUBCLUSTERED
SUBCLUSTERING
SUBCLUSTERS
SUBCOLLECTION
SUBCOLLECTIONS
SUBCOLLEGE
SUBCOLLEGIATE
SUBCOLONIES
SUBCOMMISSION
SUBCOMMISSIONED
SUBCOMMISSIONER
SUBCOMMISSIONS
SUBCOMMITTEE
SUBCOMMITTEES
SUBCOMMUNITIES
SUBCOMMUNITY
SUBCOMPACT
SUBCOMPACTS
SUBCOMPONENT
SUBCOMPONENTS
SUBCONSCIOUS
SUBCONSCIOUSES
SUBCONSCIOUSLY
SUBCONSULS
SUBCONTIGUOUS
SUBCONTINENT
SUBCONTINENTAL
SUBCONTINENTS
SUBCONTINUOUS
SUBCONTRACT
SUBCONTRACTED
SUBCONTRACTING
SUBCONTRACTINGS
SUBCONTRACTOR
SUBCONTRACTORS
SUBCONTRACTS
SUBCONTRAOCTAVE
SUBCONTRARIES
SUBCONTRARIETY
SUBCONTRARY
SUBCOOLING
SUBCORDATE
SUBCORIACEOUS
SUBCORTEXES
SUBCORTICAL
SUBCORTICES
SUBCOSTALS
SUBCOUNTIES
SUBCRANIAL
SUBCRITICAL
SUBCRUSTAL
SUBCULTURAL
SUBCULTURALLY
SUBCULTURE
SUBCULTURED
SUBCULTURES
SUBCULTURING
SUBCURATIVE
SUBCUTANEOUS
SUBCUTANEOUSLY
SUBCUTISES
SUBDEACONATE
SUBDEACONATES
SUBDEACONRIES
SUBDEACONRY
SUBDEACONS
SUBDEACONSHIP
SUBDEACONSHIPS
SUBDEALERS
SUBDEANERIES
SUBDEANERY
SUBDEBUTANTE
SUBDEBUTANTES
SUBDECANAL
SUBDECISION
SUBDECISIONS
SUBDELIRIA
SUBDELIRIOUS
SUBDELIRIUM
SUBDELIRIUMS
SUBDEPARTMENT
SUBDEPARTMENTS
SUBDEPUTIES
SUBDERMALLY
SUBDEVELOPMENT
SUBDEVELOPMENTS
SUBDIACONAL
SUBDIACONATE
SUBDIACONATES
SUBDIALECT
SUBDIALECTS
SUBDIRECTOR
SUBDIRECTORS
SUBDISCIPLINE
SUBDISCIPLINES
SUBDISTRICT
SUBDISTRICTS
SUBDIVIDABLE
SUBDIVIDED
SUBDIVIDER
SUBDIVIDERS
SUBDIVIDES
SUBDIVIDING
SUBDIVISIBLE
SUBDIVISION
SUBDIVISIONAL
SUBDIVISIONS
SUBDIVISIVE
SUBDOMINANT
SUBDOMINANTS
SUBDUCTING

SUBDUCTION
SUBDUCTIONS
SUBDUEDNESS
SUBDUEDNESSES
SUBDUEMENT
SUBDUEMENTS
SUBDUPLICATE
SUBECONOMIC
SUBECONOMIES
SUBECONOMY
SUBEDITING
SUBEDITORIAL
SUBEDITORS
SUBEDITORSHIP
SUBEDITORSHIPS
SUBEMPLOYED
SUBEMPLOYMENT
SUBEMPLOYMENTS
SUBENTRIES
SUBEPIDERMAL
SUBEQUATORIAL
SUBERISATION
SUBERISATIONS
SUBERISING
SUBERIZATION
SUBERIZATIONS
SUBERIZING
SUBFACTORIAL
SUBFACTORIALS
SUBFAMILIES
SUBFERTILE
SUBFERTILITIES
SUBFERTILITY
SUBFEUDATION
SUBFEUDATIONS
SUBFEUDATORY
SUBFOSSILS
SUBFREEZING
SUBFUSCOUS
SUBGENERATION
SUBGENERATIONS
SUBGENERIC
SUBGENERICALLY
SUBGENUSES
SUBGLACIAL
SUBGLACIALLY
SUBGLOBOSE
SUBGLOBULAR
SUBGOVERNMENT
SUBGOVERNMENTS
SUBGROUPED
SUBGROUPING
SUBHARMONIC
SUBHARMONICS
SUBHASTATION
SUBHASTATIONS
SUBHEADING
SUBHEADINGS
SUBIMAGINAL
SUBIMAGINES
SUBIMAGOES
SUBINCISED
SUBINCISES
SUBINCISING
SUBINCISION
SUBINCISIONS
SUBINDEXES
SUBINDICATE
SUBINDICATED
SUBINDICATES
SUBINDICATING
SUBINDICATION
SUBINDICATIONS
SUBINDICATIVE
SUBINDICES
SUBINDUSTRIES
SUBINDUSTRY
SUBINFEUDATE
SUBINFEUDATED
SUBINFEUDATES
SUBINFEUDATING
SUBINFEUDATION
SUBINFEUDATIONS
SUBINFEUDATORY
SUBINFEUDED
SUBINFEUDING
SUBINFEUDS
SUBINHIBITORY
SUBINSINUATION
SUBINSINUATIONS
SUBINSPECTOR
SUBINSPECTORS
SUBINTELLECTION
SUBINTELLIGENCE
SUBINTELLIGITUR
SUBINTERVAL
SUBINTERVALS
SUBINTRANT
SUBINTRODUCE
SUBINTRODUCED
SUBINTRODUCES
SUBINTRODUCING
SUBINVOLUTION
SUBINVOLUTIONS
SUBIRRIGATE
SUBIRRIGATED
SUBIRRIGATES
SUBIRRIGATING
SUBIRRIGATION
SUBIRRIGATIONS
SUBITANEOUS
SUBITISING
SUBITIZING
SUBJACENCIES
SUBJACENCY
SUBJACENTLY
SUBJECTABILITY
SUBJECTABLE
SUBJECTIFIED
SUBJECTIFIES
SUBJECTIFY
SUBJECTIFYING
SUBJECTING
SUBJECTION
SUBJECTIONS
SUBJECTIVE
SUBJECTIVELY
SUBJECTIVENESS
SUBJECTIVES
SUBJECTIVISE
SUBJECTIVISED
SUBJECTIVISES
SUBJECTIVISING
SUBJECTIVISM
SUBJECTIVISMS
SUBJECTIVIST
SUBJECTIVISTIC
SUBJECTIVISTS
SUBJECTIVITIES
SUBJECTIVITY
SUBJECTIVIZE
SUBJECTIVIZED
SUBJECTIVIZES
SUBJECTIVIZING
SUBJECTLESS
SUBJECTSHIP
SUBJECTSHIPS
SUBJOINDER
SUBJOINDERS
SUBJOINING
SUBJUGABLE
SUBJUGATED
SUBJUGATES
SUBJUGATING
SUBJUGATION
SUBJUGATIONS
SUBJUGATOR
SUBJUGATORS
SUBJUNCTION
SUBJUNCTIONS
SUBJUNCTIVE
SUBJUNCTIVELY
SUBJUNCTIVES
SUBKINGDOM
SUBKINGDOMS
SUBLANCEOLATE
SUBLANGUAGE
SUBLANGUAGES
SUBLAPSARIAN
SUBLAPSARIANISM
SUBLAPSARIANS
SUBLATIONS
SUBLEASING
SUBLESSEES
SUBLESSORS
SUBLETHALLY
SUBLETTERS
SUBLETTING
SUBLETTINGS
SUBLIBRARIAN
SUBLIBRARIANS
SUBLICENSE
SUBLICENSED
SUBLICENSES
SUBLICENSING
SUBLIEUTENANCY
SUBLIEUTENANT
SUBLIEUTENANTS
SUBLIMABLE
SUBLIMATED
SUBLIMATES
SUBLIMATING
SUBLIMATION
SUBLIMATIONS
SUBLIMENESS
SUBLIMENESSES
SUBLIMINAL
SUBLIMINALLY
SUBLIMINALS
SUBLIMINGS
SUBLIMISED
SUBLIMISES
SUBLIMISING
SUBLIMITIES
SUBLIMIZED
SUBLIMIZES
SUBLIMIZING
SUBLINEATION
SUBLINEATIONS
SUBLINGUAL
SUBLITERACIES
SUBLITERACY
SUBLITERARY
SUBLITERATE
SUBLITERATES
SUBLITERATURE
SUBLITERATURES
SUBLITTORAL
SUBLITTORALS
SUBLUXATED
SUBLUXATES
SUBLUXATING
SUBLUXATION
SUBLUXATIONS
SUBMANAGER
SUBMANAGERS
SUBMANDIBULAR
SUBMANDIBULARS
SUBMARGINAL
SUBMARGINALLY
SUBMARINED
SUBMARINER
SUBMARINERS
SUBMARINES
SUBMARINING
SUBMARKETS
SUBMATRICES
SUBMATRIXES
SUBMAXILLARIES
SUBMAXILLARY
SUBMAXIMAL
SUBMEDIANT
SUBMEDIANTS
SUBMERGEMENT
SUBMERGEMENTS
SUBMERGENCE
SUBMERGENCES
SUBMERGIBILITY
SUBMERGIBLE
SUBMERGIBLES
SUBMERGING
SUBMERSIBILITY
SUBMERSIBLE
SUBMERSIBLES
SUBMERSING
SUBMERSION
SUBMERSIONS
SUBMETACENTRIC
SUBMETACENTRICS
SUBMICROGRAM
SUBMICRONS
SUBMICROSCOPIC
SUBMILLIMETER
SUBMINIATURE

SUBMINIATURES
SUBMINIATURISE
SUBMINIATURISED
SUBMINIATURISES
SUBMINIATURIZE
SUBMINIATURIZED
SUBMINIATURIZES
SUBMINIMAL
SUBMINISTER
SUBMINISTERS
SUBMISSIBLE
SUBMISSION
SUBMISSIONS
SUBMISSIVE
SUBMISSIVELY
SUBMISSIVENESS
SUBMISSNESS
SUBMISSNESSES
SUBMITTABLE
SUBMITTALS
SUBMITTERS
SUBMITTING
SUBMITTINGS
SUBMOLECULE
SUBMOLECULES
SUBMONTANE
SUBMONTANELY
SUBMUCOSAE
SUBMUCOSAL
SUBMUCOSAS
SUBMULTIPLE
SUBMULTIPLES
SUBMUNITION
SUBMUNITIONS
SUBNASCENT
SUBNATIONAL
SUBNATURAL
SUBNETWORK
SUBNETWORKED
SUBNETWORKING
SUBNETWORKS
SUBNORMALITIES
SUBNORMALITY
SUBNORMALLY
SUBNORMALS
SUBNUCLEAR
SUBNUCLEUS
SUBNUCLEUSES
SUBOCCIPITAL
SUBOCEANIC
SUBOCTAVES
SUBOCTUPLE
SUBOFFICER
SUBOFFICERS
SUBOFFICES
SUBOPERCULA
SUBOPERCULAR
SUBOPERCULUM
SUBOPTIMAL
SUBOPTIMISATION
SUBOPTIMISE
SUBOPTIMISED
SUBOPTIMISES
SUBOPTIMISING
SUBOPTIMIZATION
SUBOPTIMIZE
SUBOPTIMIZED
SUBOPTIMIZES
SUBOPTIMIZING
SUBOPTIMUM
SUBORBICULAR
SUBORBITAL
SUBORDINAL
SUBORDINANCIES
SUBORDINANCY
SUBORDINARIES
SUBORDINARY
SUBORDINATE
SUBORDINATED
SUBORDINATELY
SUBORDINATENESS
SUBORDINATES
SUBORDINATING
SUBORDINATION
SUBORDINATIONS
SUBORDINATIVE
SUBORDINATOR
SUBORDINATORS
SUBORGANISATION
SUBORGANIZATION
SUBORNATION
SUBORNATIONS
SUBORNATIVE
SUBOSCINES
SUBPANATION
SUBPANATIONS
SUBPARAGRAPH
SUBPARAGRAPHS
SUBPARALLEL
SUBPENAING
SUBPERIODS
SUBPHRENIC
SUBPOENAED
SUBPOENAING
SUBPOPULATION
SUBPOPULATIONS
SUBPOTENCIES
SUBPOTENCY
SUBPREFECT
SUBPREFECTS
SUBPREFECTURE
SUBPREFECTURES
SUBPRIMATE
SUBPRIMATES
SUBPRINCIPAL
SUBPRINCIPALS
SUBPRIORESS
SUBPRIORESSES
SUBPROBLEM
SUBPROBLEMS
SUBPROCESS
SUBPROCESSES
SUBPRODUCT
SUBPRODUCTS
SUBPROFESSIONAL
SUBPROGRAM
SUBPROGRAMS
SUBPROJECT
SUBPROJECTS
SUBPROLETARIAT
SUBPROLETARIATS
SUBRATIONAL
SUBREFERENCE
SUBREFERENCES
SUBREGIONAL
SUBREGIONS
SUBREPTION
SUBREPTIONS
SUBREPTITIOUS
SUBREPTITIOUSLY
SUBREPTIVE
SUBROGATED
SUBROGATES
SUBROGATING
SUBROGATION
SUBROGATIONS
SUBROUTINE
SUBROUTINES
SUBSAMPLED
SUBSAMPLES
SUBSAMPLING
SUBSATELLITE
SUBSATELLITES
SUBSATURATED
SUBSATURATION
SUBSATURATIONS
SUBSCAPULAR
SUBSCAPULARS
SUBSCHEMATA
SUBSCIENCE
SUBSCIENCES
SUBSCRIBABLE
SUBSCRIBED
SUBSCRIBER
SUBSCRIBERS
SUBSCRIBES
SUBSCRIBING
SUBSCRIBINGS
SUBSCRIPTION
SUBSCRIPTIONS
SUBSCRIPTIVE
SUBSCRIPTS
SUBSECRETARIES
SUBSECRETARY
SUBSECTION
SUBSECTIONS
SUBSECTORS
SUBSEGMENT
SUBSEGMENTS
SUBSEIZURE
SUBSEIZURES
SUBSELLIUM
SUBSENSIBLE
SUBSENTENCE
SUBSENTENCES
SUBSEQUENCE
SUBSEQUENCES
SUBSEQUENT
SUBSEQUENTIAL
SUBSEQUENTLY
SUBSEQUENTNESS
SUBSEQUENTS
SUBSERVIENCE
SUBSERVIENCES
SUBSERVIENCIES
SUBSERVIENCY
SUBSERVIENT
SUBSERVIENTLY
SUBSERVIENTS
SUBSERVING
SUBSESSILE
SUBSHRUBBY
SUBSIDENCE
SUBSIDENCES
SUBSIDENCIES
SUBSIDENCY
SUBSIDIARIES
SUBSIDIARILY
SUBSIDIARINESS
SUBSIDIARITIES
SUBSIDIARITY
SUBSIDIARY
SUBSIDISABLE
SUBSIDISATION
SUBSIDISATIONS
SUBSIDISED
SUBSIDISER
SUBSIDISERS
SUBSIDISES
SUBSIDISING
SUBSIDIZABLE
SUBSIDIZATION
SUBSIDIZATIONS
SUBSIDIZED
SUBSIDIZER
SUBSIDIZERS
SUBSIDIZES
SUBSIDIZING
SUBSISTENCE
SUBSISTENCES
SUBSISTENT
SUBSISTENTIAL
SUBSISTERS
SUBSISTING
SUBSOCIALLY
SUBSOCIETIES
SUBSOCIETY
SUBSOILERS
SUBSOILING
SUBSOILINGS
SUBSONICALLY
SUBSPECIALISE
SUBSPECIALISED
SUBSPECIALISES
SUBSPECIALISING
SUBSPECIALIST
SUBSPECIALISTS
SUBSPECIALITIES
SUBSPECIALITY
SUBSPECIALIZE
SUBSPECIALIZED
SUBSPECIALIZES
SUBSPECIALIZING
SUBSPECIALTIES
SUBSPECIALTY
SUBSPECIES
SUBSPECIFIC
SUBSPECIFICALLY
SUBSPINOUS
SUBSPONTANEOUS
SUBSTANCELESS
SUBSTANCES
SUBSTANDARD
SUBSTANTIAL

SUBSTANTIALISE
SUBSTANTIALISED
SUBSTANTIALISES
SUBSTANTIALISM
SUBSTANTIALISMS
SUBSTANTIALIST
SUBSTANTIALISTS
SUBSTANTIALITY
SUBSTANTIALIZE
SUBSTANTIALIZED
SUBSTANTIALIZES
SUBSTANTIALLY
SUBSTANTIALNESS
SUBSTANTIALS
SUBSTANTIATE
SUBSTANTIATED
SUBSTANTIATES
SUBSTANTIATING
SUBSTANTIATION
SUBSTANTIATIONS
SUBSTANTIATIVE
SUBSTANTIATOR
SUBSTANTIATORS
SUBSTANTIVAL
SUBSTANTIVALLY
SUBSTANTIVE
SUBSTANTIVELY
SUBSTANTIVENESS
SUBSTANTIVES
SUBSTANTIVISE
SUBSTANTIVISED
SUBSTANTIVISES
SUBSTANTIVISING
SUBSTANTIVITIES
SUBSTANTIVITY
SUBSTANTIVIZE
SUBSTANTIVIZED
SUBSTANTIVIZES
SUBSTANTIVIZING
SUBSTATION
SUBSTATIONS
SUBSTELLAR
SUBSTERNAL
SUBSTITUENT
SUBSTITUENTS
SUBSTITUTABLE
SUBSTITUTE
SUBSTITUTED
SUBSTITUTES
SUBSTITUTING
SUBSTITUTION
SUBSTITUTIONAL
SUBSTITUTIONARY
SUBSTITUTIONS
SUBSTITUTIVE
SUBSTITUTIVELY
SUBSTITUTIVITY
SUBSTRACTED
SUBSTRACTING
SUBSTRACTION
SUBSTRACTIONS
SUBSTRACTOR
SUBSTRACTORS
SUBSTRACTS
SUBSTRATAL
SUBSTRATES
SUBSTRATIVE
SUBSTRATOSPHERE
SUBSTRATUM
SUBSTRATUMS
SUBSTRUCTED
SUBSTRUCTING
SUBSTRUCTION
SUBSTRUCTIONS
SUBSTRUCTS
SUBSTRUCTURAL
SUBSTRUCTURE
SUBSTRUCTURES
SUBSULTIVE
SUBSULTORILY
SUBSULTORY
SUBSULTUSES
SUBSUMABLE
SUBSUMPTION
SUBSUMPTIONS
SUBSUMPTIVE
SUBSURFACE
SUBSURFACES
SUBSYSTEMS
SUBTACKSMAN
SUBTACKSMEN
SUBTANGENT
SUBTANGENTS
SUBTEMPERATE
SUBTENANCIES
SUBTENANCY
SUBTENANTS
SUBTENDING
SUBTENURES
SUBTERFUGE
SUBTERFUGES
SUBTERMINAL
SUBTERNATURAL
SUBTERRAIN
SUBTERRAINS
SUBTERRANE
SUBTERRANEAN
SUBTERRANEANLY
SUBTERRANEANS
SUBTERRANEOUS
SUBTERRANEOUSLY
SUBTERRANES
SUBTERRENE
SUBTERRENES
SUBTERRESTRIAL
SUBTERRESTRIALS
SUBTEXTUAL
SUBTHERAPEUTIC
SUBTHRESHOLD
SUBTILENESS
SUBTILENESSES
SUBTILISATION
SUBTILISATIONS
SUBTILISED
SUBTILISER
SUBTILISERS
SUBTILISES
SUBTILISIN
SUBTILISING
SUBTILISINS
SUBTILITIES
SUBTILIZATION
SUBTILIZATIONS
SUBTILIZED
SUBTILIZER
SUBTILIZERS
SUBTILIZES
SUBTILIZING
SUBTILTIES
SUBTITLING
SUBTITULAR
SUBTLENESS
SUBTLENESSES
SUBTLETIES
SUBTOTALED
SUBTOTALING
SUBTOTALLED
SUBTOTALLING
SUBTOTALLY
SUBTRACTED
SUBTRACTER
SUBTRACTERS
SUBTRACTING
SUBTRACTION
SUBTRACTIONS
SUBTRACTIVE
SUBTRACTOR
SUBTRACTORS
SUBTRAHEND
SUBTRAHENDS
SUBTREASURER
SUBTREASURERS
SUBTREASURIES
SUBTREASURY
SUBTRIANGULAR
SUBTRIPLICATE
SUBTROPICAL
SUBTROPICALLY
SUBTROPICS
SUBTRUDING
SUBTYPICAL
SUBUMBRELLA
SUBUMBRELLAR
SUBUMBRELLAS
SUBUNGULATE
SUBUNGULATES
SUBURBANISATION
SUBURBANISE
SUBURBANISED
SUBURBANISES
SUBURBANISING
SUBURBANISM
SUBURBANISMS
SUBURBANITE
SUBURBANITES
SUBURBANITIES
SUBURBANITY
SUBURBANIZATION
SUBURBANIZE
SUBURBANIZED
SUBURBANIZES
SUBURBANIZING
SUBURBICARIAN
SUBVARIETIES
SUBVARIETY
SUBVASSALS
SUBVENTION
SUBVENTIONARY
SUBVENTIONS
SUBVERSALS
SUBVERSING
SUBVERSION
SUBVERSIONARIES
SUBVERSIONARY
SUBVERSIONS
SUBVERSIVE
SUBVERSIVELY
SUBVERSIVENESS
SUBVERSIVES
SUBVERTEBRAL
SUBVERTERS
SUBVERTICAL
SUBVERTING
SUBVIRUSES
SUBVISIBLE
SUBVITREOUS
SUBVOCALISATION
SUBVOCALISE
SUBVOCALISED
SUBVOCALISES
SUBVOCALISING
SUBVOCALIZATION
SUBVOCALIZE
SUBVOCALIZED
SUBVOCALIZES
SUBVOCALIZING
SUBVOCALLY
SUBWARDENS
SUBWOOFERS
SUBWRITERS
SUCCEDANEA
SUCCEDANEOUS
SUCCEDANEUM
SUCCEDANEUMS
SUCCEEDABLE
SUCCEEDERS
SUCCEEDING
SUCCEEDINGLY
SUCCENTORS
SUCCENTORSHIP
SUCCENTORSHIPS
SUCCESSANTLY
SUCCESSFUL
SUCCESSFULLY
SUCCESSFULNESS
SUCCESSION
SUCCESSIONAL
SUCCESSIONALLY
SUCCESSIONIST
SUCCESSIONISTS
SUCCESSIONLESS
SUCCESSIONS
SUCCESSIVE
SUCCESSIVELY
SUCCESSIVENESS
SUCCESSLESS
SUCCESSLESSLY
SUCCESSLESSNESS
SUCCESSORAL
SUCCESSORS
SUCCESSORSHIP
SUCCESSORSHIPS
SUCCINATES
SUCCINCTER

SUCCINCTEST
SUCCINCTLY
SUCCINCTNESS
SUCCINCTNESSES
SUCCINCTORIA
SUCCINCTORIES
SUCCINCTORIUM
SUCCINCTORY
SUCCINITES
SUCCINYLCHOLINE
SUCCORABLE
SUCCORLESS
SUCCOTASHES
SUCCOURABLE
SUCCOURERS
SUCCOURING
SUCCOURLESS
SUCCUBUSES
SUCCULENCE
SUCCULENCES
SUCCULENCIES
SUCCULENCY
SUCCULENTLY
SUCCULENTS
SUCCUMBERS
SUCCUMBING
SUCCURSALE
SUCCURSALES
SUCCURSALS
SUCCUSSATION
SUCCUSSATIONS
SUCCUSSING
SUCCUSSION
SUCCUSSIONS
SUCCUSSIVE
SUCHNESSES
SUCKERFISH
SUCKERFISHES
SUCKFISHES
SUCRALFATE
SUCRALFATES
SUCRALOSES
SUCTIONING
SUCTORIANS
SUDATORIES
SUDATORIUM
SUDATORIUMS
SUDDENNESS
SUDDENNESSES
SUDDENTIES
SUDORIFEROUS
SUDORIFICS
SUDORIPAROUS
SUEABILITIES
SUEABILITY
SUFFERABLE
SUFFERABLENESS
SUFFERABLY
SUFFERANCE
SUFFERANCES
SUFFERINGLY
SUFFERINGS
SUFFICIENCE
SUFFICIENCES
SUFFICIENCIES
SUFFICIENCY
SUFFICIENT
SUFFICIENTLY
SUFFICIENTS
SUFFICINGNESS
SUFFICINGNESSES
SUFFIGANCE
SUFFIGANCES
SUFFISANCE
SUFFISANCES
SUFFIXATION
SUFFIXATIONS
SUFFIXIONS
SUFFLATING
SUFFLATION
SUFFLATIONS
SUFFOCATED
SUFFOCATES
SUFFOCATING
SUFFOCATINGLY
SUFFOCATINGS
SUFFOCATION
SUFFOCATIONS
SUFFOCATIVE
SUFFRAGANS
SUFFRAGANSHIP
SUFFRAGANSHIPS
SUFFRAGETTE
SUFFRAGETTES
SUFFRAGETTISM
SUFFRAGETTISMS
SUFFRAGISM
SUFFRAGISMS
SUFFRAGIST
SUFFRAGISTS
SUFFRUTESCENT
SUFFRUTICOSE
SUFFUMIGATE
SUFFUMIGATED
SUFFUMIGATES
SUFFUMIGATING
SUFFUMIGATION
SUFFUMIGATIONS
SUFFUSIONS
SUGARALLIE
SUGARALLIES
SUGARBERRIES
SUGARBERRY
SUGARBUSHES
SUGARCANES
SUGARCOATED
SUGARCOATING
SUGARCOATS
SUGARHOUSE
SUGARHOUSES
SUGARINESS
SUGARINESSES
SUGARLOAVES
SUGARPLUMS
SUGGESTERS
SUGGESTIBILITY
SUGGESTIBLE
SUGGESTIBLENESS
SUGGESTIBLY
SUGGESTING
SUGGESTION
SUGGESTIONISE
SUGGESTIONISED
SUGGESTIONISES
SUGGESTIONISING
SUGGESTIONISM
SUGGESTIONISMS
SUGGESTIONIST
SUGGESTIONISTS
SUGGESTIONIZE
SUGGESTIONIZED
SUGGESTIONIZES
SUGGESTIONIZING
SUGGESTIONS
SUGGESTIVE
SUGGESTIVELY
SUGGESTIVENESS
SUICIDALLY
SUICIDOLOGIES
SUICIDOLOGIST
SUICIDOLOGISTS
SUICIDOLOGY
SUITABILITIES
SUITABILITY
SUITABLENESS
SUITABLENESSES
SUITRESSES
SULCALISED
SULCALISES
SULCALISING
SULCALIZED
SULCALIZES
SULCALIZING
SULCATIONS
SULFACETAMIDE
SULFACETAMIDES
SULFADIAZINE
SULFADIAZINES
SULFADIMIDINE
SULFADIMIDINES
SULFADOXINE
SULFADOXINES
SULFAMETHAZINE
SULFAMETHAZINES
SULFANILAMIDE
SULFANILAMIDES
SULFATASES
SULFATHIAZOLE
SULFATHIAZOLES
SULFATIONS
SULFHYDRYL
SULFHYDRYLS
SULFINPYRAZONE
SULFINPYRAZONES
SULFONAMIDE
SULFONAMIDES
SULFONATED
SULFONATES
SULFONATING
SULFONATION
SULFONATIONS
SULFONIUMS
SULFONYLUREA
SULFONYLUREAS
SULFOXIDES
SULFURATED
SULFURATES
SULFURATING
SULFURETED
SULFURETING
SULFURETTED
SULFURETTING
SULFURISATION
SULFURISATIONS
SULFURISED
SULFURISES
SULFURISING
SULFURIZED
SULFURIZES
SULFURIZING
SULFUROUSLY
SULFUROUSNESS
SULFUROUSNESSES
SULKINESSES
SULLENNESS
SULLENNESSES
SULPHACETAMIDE
SULPHACETAMIDES
SULPHADIAZINE
SULPHADIAZINES
SULPHANILAMIDE
SULPHANILAMIDES
SULPHATASE
SULPHATASES
SULPHATHIAZOLE
SULPHATHIAZOLES
SULPHATING
SULPHATION
SULPHATIONS
SULPHHYDRYL
SULPHHYDRYLS
SULPHINPYRAZONE
SULPHINYLS
SULPHONAMIDE
SULPHONAMIDES
SULPHONATE
SULPHONATED
SULPHONATES
SULPHONATING
SULPHONATION
SULPHONATIONS
SULPHONIUM
SULPHONIUMS
SULPHONMETHANE
SULPHONMETHANES
SULPHONYLS
SULPHONYLUREA
SULPHONYLUREAS
SULPHURATE
SULPHURATED
SULPHURATES
SULPHURATING
SULPHURATION
SULPHURATIONS
SULPHURATOR
SULPHURATORS
SULPHUREOUS
SULPHUREOUSLY
SULPHUREOUSNESS
SULPHURETED
SULPHURETING
SULPHURETS
SULPHURETTED
SULPHURETTING

SULPHURING
SULPHURISATION
SULPHURISATIONS
SULPHURISE
SULPHURISED
SULPHURISES
SULPHURISING
SULPHURIZATION
SULPHURIZATIONS
SULPHURIZE
SULPHURIZED
SULPHURIZES
SULPHURIZING
SULPHUROUS
SULPHUROUSLY
SULPHUROUSNESS
SULPHURWORT
SULPHURWORTS
SULPHURYLS
SULTANATES
SULTANESSES
SULTANSHIP
SULTANSHIPS
SULTRINESS
SULTRINESSES
SUMMABILITIES
SUMMABILITY
SUMMARINESS
SUMMARINESSES
SUMMARISABLE
SUMMARISATION
SUMMARISATIONS
SUMMARISED
SUMMARISER
SUMMARISERS
SUMMARISES
SUMMARISING
SUMMARISTS
SUMMARIZABLE
SUMMARIZATION
SUMMARIZATIONS
SUMMARIZED
SUMMARIZER
SUMMARIZERS
SUMMARIZES
SUMMARIZING
SUMMATIONAL
SUMMATIONS
SUMMERHOUSE
SUMMERHOUSES
SUMMERIEST
SUMMERINESS
SUMMERINESSES
SUMMERINGS
SUMMERLESS
SUMMERLIKE
SUMMERLONG
SUMMERSAULT
SUMMERSAULTED
SUMMERSAULTING
SUMMERSAULTS
SUMMERSETS
SUMMERSETTED
SUMMERSETTING
SUMMERTIDE
SUMMERTIDES
SUMMERTIME
SUMMERTIMES
SUMMERWEIGHT
SUMMERWOOD
SUMMERWOODS
SUMMITEERS
SUMMITLESS
SUMMITRIES
SUMMONABLE
SUMMONSING
SUMPHISHNESS
SUMPHISHNESSES
SUMPSIMUSES
SUMPTUOSITIES
SUMPTUOSITY
SUMPTUOUSLY
SUMPTUOUSNESS
SUMPTUOUSNESSES
SUNBATHERS
SUNBATHING
SUNBATHINGS
SUNBERRIES
SUNBONNETED
SUNBONNETS
SUNBURNING
SUNDERABLE
SUNDERANCE
SUNDERANCES
SUNDERINGS
SUNDERMENT
SUNDERMENTS
SUNDOWNERS
SUNDOWNING
SUNDRENCHED
SUNDRESSES
SUNFLOWERS
SUNGLASSES
SUNLESSNESS
SUNLESSNESSES
SUNLOUNGER
SUNLOUNGERS
SUNNINESSES
SUNPORCHES
SUNRISINGS
SUNSCREENING
SUNSCREENS
SUNSEEKERS
SUNSETTING
SUNSETTINGS
SUNSPOTTED
SUNSTROKES
SUNTANNING
SUNWORSHIPPER
SUNWORSHIPPERS
SUOVETAURILIA
SUPERABILITIES
SUPERABILITY
SUPERABLENESS
SUPERABLENESSES
SUPERABOUND
SUPERABOUNDED
SUPERABOUNDING
SUPERABOUNDS
SUPERABSORBENT
SUPERABSORBENTS
SUPERABUNDANCE
SUPERABUNDANCES
SUPERABUNDANT
SUPERABUNDANTLY
SUPERACHIEVER
SUPERACHIEVERS
SUPERACTIVE
SUPERACTIVITIES
SUPERACTIVITY
SUPERACUTE
SUPERADDED
SUPERADDING
SUPERADDITION
SUPERADDITIONAL
SUPERADDITIONS
SUPERAGENCIES
SUPERAGENCY
SUPERAGENT
SUPERAGENTS
SUPERALLOY
SUPERALLOYS
SUPERALTAR
SUPERALTARS
SUPERALTERN
SUPERALTERNS
SUPERAMBITIOUS
SUPERANNUABLE
SUPERANNUATE
SUPERANNUATED
SUPERANNUATES
SUPERANNUATING
SUPERANNUATION
SUPERANNUATIONS
SUPERATHLETE
SUPERATHLETES
SUPERATING
SUPERATION
SUPERATIONS
SUPERATOMS
SUPERBANKS
SUPERBAZAAR
SUPERBAZAARS
SUPERBAZAR
SUPERBAZARS
SUPERBIKES
SUPERBITCH
SUPERBITCHES
SUPERBITIES
SUPERBLOCK
SUPERBLOCKS
SUPERBNESS
SUPERBNESSES
SUPERBOARD
SUPERBOARDS
SUPERBOMBER
SUPERBOMBERS
SUPERBOMBS
SUPERBRAIN
SUPERBRAINS
SUPERBRATS
SUPERBRIGHT
SUPERBUREAUCRAT
SUPERCABINET
SUPERCABINETS
SUPERCALENDER
SUPERCALENDERED
SUPERCALENDERS
SUPERCARGO
SUPERCARGOES
SUPERCARGOS
SUPERCARGOSHIP
SUPERCARGOSHIPS
SUPERCARRIER
SUPERCARRIERS
SUPERCAUTIOUS
SUPERCEDED
SUPERCEDES
SUPERCEDING
SUPERCELESTIAL
SUPERCENTER
SUPERCENTERS
SUPERCHARGE
SUPERCHARGED
SUPERCHARGER
SUPERCHARGERS
SUPERCHARGES
SUPERCHARGING
SUPERCHERIE
SUPERCHERIES
SUPERCHURCH
SUPERCHURCHES
SUPERCILIARIES
SUPERCILIARY
SUPERCILIOUS
SUPERCILIOUSLY
SUPERCITIES
SUPERCIVILISED
SUPERCIVILIZED
SUPERCLASS
SUPERCLASSES
SUPERCLEAN
SUPERCLUBS
SUPERCLUSTER
SUPERCLUSTERS
SUPERCOILED
SUPERCOILING
SUPERCOILS
SUPERCOLLIDER
SUPERCOLLIDERS
SUPERCOLOSSAL
SUPERCOLUMNAR
SUPERCOMPUTER
SUPERCOMPUTERS
SUPERCOMPUTING
SUPERCOMPUTINGS
SUPERCONDUCT
SUPERCONDUCTED
SUPERCONDUCTING
SUPERCONDUCTION
SUPERCONDUCTIVE
SUPERCONDUCTOR
SUPERCONDUCTORS
SUPERCONDUCTS
SUPERCONFIDENCE
SUPERCONFIDENT
SUPERCONTINENT
SUPERCONTINENTS
SUPERCONVENIENT
SUPERCOOLED
SUPERCOOLING
SUPERCOOLS
SUPERCRIMINAL
SUPERCRIMINALS

SUPERCRITICAL
SUPERCURRENT
SUPERCURRENTS
SUPERDAINTY
SUPERDELUXE
SUPERDENSE
SUPERDIPLOMAT
SUPERDIPLOMATS
SUPERDOMINANT
SUPERDOMINANTS
SUPEREFFECTIVE
SUPEREFFICIENCY
SUPEREFFICIENT
SUPEREGOIST
SUPEREGOISTS
SUPERELASTIC
SUPERELEVATE
SUPERELEVATED
SUPERELEVATES
SUPERELEVATING
SUPERELEVATION
SUPERELEVATIONS
SUPERELITE
SUPEREMINENCE
SUPEREMINENCES
SUPEREMINENT
SUPEREMINENTLY
SUPEREROGANT
SUPEREROGATE
SUPEREROGATED
SUPEREROGATES
SUPEREROGATING
SUPEREROGATION
SUPEREROGATIONS
SUPEREROGATIVE
SUPEREROGATOR
SUPEREROGATORS
SUPEREROGATORY
SUPERESSENTIAL
SUPERETTES
SUPEREVIDENT
SUPEREXALT
SUPEREXALTATION
SUPEREXALTED
SUPEREXALTING
SUPEREXALTS
SUPEREXCELLENCE
SUPEREXCELLENT
SUPEREXPENSIVE
SUPEREXPRESS
SUPEREXPRESSES
SUPERFAMILIES
SUPERFAMILY
SUPERFARMS
SUPERFATTED
SUPERFECTA
SUPERFECTAS
SUPERFEMALE
SUPERFEMALES
SUPERFETATE
SUPERFETATED
SUPERFETATES
SUPERFETATING
SUPERFETATION
SUPERFETATIONS
SUPERFICIAL
SUPERFICIALISE
SUPERFICIALISED
SUPERFICIALISES
SUPERFICIALITY
SUPERFICIALIZE
SUPERFICIALIZED
SUPERFICIALIZES
SUPERFICIALLY
SUPERFICIALNESS
SUPERFICIALS
SUPERFICIES
SUPERFINENESS
SUPERFINENESSES
SUPERFIRMS
SUPERFIXES
SUPERFLACK
SUPERFLACKS
SUPERFLUID
SUPERFLUIDITIES
SUPERFLUIDITY
SUPERFLUIDS
SUPERFLUITIES
SUPERFLUITY
SUPERFLUOUS
SUPERFLUOUSLY
SUPERFLUOUSNESS
SUPERFLUXES
SUPERFOETATION
SUPERFOETATIONS
SUPERFRONTAL
SUPERFRONTALS
SUPERFUNDS
SUPERFUSED
SUPERFUSES
SUPERFUSING
SUPERFUSION
SUPERFUSIONS
SUPERGENES
SUPERGIANT
SUPERGIANTS
SUPERGLACIAL
SUPERGLUED
SUPERGLUES
SUPERGLUING
SUPERGOVERNMENT
SUPERGRAPHICS
SUPERGRASS
SUPERGRASSES
SUPERGRAVITIES
SUPERGRAVITY
SUPERGROUP
SUPERGROUPS
SUPERGROWTH
SUPERGROWTHS
SUPERHARDEN
SUPERHARDENED
SUPERHARDENING
SUPERHARDENS
SUPERHEATED
SUPERHEATER
SUPERHEATERS
SUPERHEATING
SUPERHEATS
SUPERHEAVIES
SUPERHEAVY
SUPERHELICAL
SUPERHELICES
SUPERHELIX
SUPERHELIXES
SUPERHEROES
SUPERHEROINE
SUPERHEROINES
SUPERHETERODYNE
SUPERHIGHWAY
SUPERHIGHWAYS
SUPERHIVES
SUPERHUMAN
SUPERHUMANISE
SUPERHUMANISED
SUPERHUMANISES
SUPERHUMANISING
SUPERHUMANITIES
SUPERHUMANITY
SUPERHUMANIZE
SUPERHUMANIZED
SUPERHUMANIZES
SUPERHUMANIZING
SUPERHUMANLY
SUPERHUMANNESS
SUPERHUMERAL
SUPERHUMERALS
SUPERHYPED
SUPERHYPES
SUPERHYPING
SUPERIMPORTANT
SUPERIMPOSABLE
SUPERIMPOSE
SUPERIMPOSED
SUPERIMPOSES
SUPERIMPOSING
SUPERIMPOSITION
SUPERINCUMBENCE
SUPERINCUMBENCY
SUPERINCUMBENT
SUPERINDIVIDUAL
SUPERINDUCE
SUPERINDUCED
SUPERINDUCEMENT
SUPERINDUCES
SUPERINDUCING
SUPERINDUCTION
SUPERINDUCTIONS
SUPERINFECT
SUPERINFECTED
SUPERINFECTING
SUPERINFECTION
SUPERINFECTIONS
SUPERINFECTS
SUPERINSULATED
SUPERINTEND
SUPERINTENDED
SUPERINTENDENCE
SUPERINTENDENCY
SUPERINTENDENT
SUPERINTENDENTS
SUPERINTENDING
SUPERINTENDS
SUPERINTENSITY
SUPERIORESS
SUPERIORESSES
SUPERIORITIES
SUPERIORITY
SUPERIORLY
SUPERIORSHIP
SUPERIORSHIPS
SUPERJACENT
SUPERJOCKS
SUPERJUMBO
SUPERJUMBOS
SUPERKINGDOM
SUPERKINGDOMS
SUPERLARGE
SUPERLATIVE
SUPERLATIVELY
SUPERLATIVENESS
SUPERLATIVES
SUPERLAWYER
SUPERLAWYERS
SUPERLIGHT
SUPERLINER
SUPERLINERS
SUPERLOADS
SUPERLOBBYIST
SUPERLOBBYISTS
SUPERLOYALIST
SUPERLOYALISTS
SUPERLUMINAL
SUPERLUNAR
SUPERLUNARY
SUPERLUXURIOUS
SUPERLUXURY
SUPERLYING
SUPERMACHO
SUPERMAJORITIES
SUPERMAJORITY
SUPERMALES
SUPERMARKET
SUPERMARKETS
SUPERMARTS
SUPERMASCULINE
SUPERMASSIVE
SUPERMAXES
SUPERMEMBRANE
SUPERMEMBRANES
SUPERMICRO
SUPERMICROS
SUPERMILITANT
SUPERMILITANTS
SUPERMINDS
SUPERMINIS
SUPERMINISTER
SUPERMINISTERS
SUPERMODEL
SUPERMODELS
SUPERMODERN
SUPERMOTOS
SUPERMUNDANE
SUPERNACULA
SUPERNACULAR
SUPERNACULUM
SUPERNALLY
SUPERNATANT
SUPERNATANTS
SUPERNATATION
SUPERNATATIONS
SUPERNATES
SUPERNATION
SUPERNATIONAL

SUPERNATIONALLY
SUPERNATIONS
SUPERNATURAL
SUPERNATURALISE
SUPERNATURALISM
SUPERNATURALIST
SUPERNATURALIZE
SUPERNATURALLY
SUPERNATURALS
SUPERNATURE
SUPERNATURES
SUPERNORMAL
SUPERNORMALITY
SUPERNORMALLY
SUPERNOVAE
SUPERNOVAS
SUPERNUMERARIES
SUPERNUMERARY
SUPERNURSE
SUPERNURSES
SUPERNUTRIENT
SUPERNUTRIENTS
SUPERNUTRITION
SUPERNUTRITIONS
SUPEROCTAVE
SUPEROCTAVES
SUPERORDER
SUPERORDERS
SUPERORDINAL
SUPERORDINARY
SUPERORDINATE
SUPERORDINATED
SUPERORDINATES
SUPERORDINATING
SUPERORDINATION
SUPERORGANIC
SUPERORGANICISM
SUPERORGANICIST
SUPERORGANISM
SUPERORGANISMS
SUPERORGASM
SUPERORGASMS
SUPEROVULATE
SUPEROVULATED
SUPEROVULATES
SUPEROVULATING
SUPEROVULATION
SUPEROVULATIONS
SUPEROXIDE
SUPEROXIDES
SUPERPARASITISM
SUPERPARTICLE
SUPERPARTICLES
SUPERPATRIOT
SUPERPATRIOTIC
SUPERPATRIOTISM
SUPERPATRIOTS
SUPERPERSON
SUPERPERSONAL
SUPERPERSONS
SUPERPHENOMENA
SUPERPHENOMENON
SUPERPHOSPHATE
SUPERPHOSPHATES
SUPERPHYLA
SUPERPHYLUM
SUPERPHYSICAL
SUPERPIMPS
SUPERPLANE
SUPERPLANES
SUPERPLASTIC
SUPERPLASTICITY
SUPERPLASTICS
SUPERPLAYER
SUPERPLAYERS
SUPERPLUSES
SUPERPOLITE
SUPERPOLYMER
SUPERPOLYMERS
SUPERPORTS
SUPERPOSABLE
SUPERPOSED
SUPERPOSES
SUPERPOSING
SUPERPOSITION
SUPERPOSITIONS
SUPERPOWER
SUPERPOWERED
SUPERPOWERFUL
SUPERPOWERS
SUPERPRAISE
SUPERPRAISED
SUPERPRAISES
SUPERPRAISING
SUPERPREMIUM
SUPERPREMIUMS
SUPERPROFIT
SUPERPROFITS
SUPERQUALITY
SUPERRACES
SUPERREALISM
SUPERREALISMS
SUPERREALIST
SUPERREALISTS
SUPERREFINE
SUPERREFINED
SUPERREFINES
SUPERREFINING
SUPERREGIONAL
SUPERREGIONALS
SUPERROADS
SUPERROMANTIC
SUPERSAFETIES
SUPERSAFETY
SUPERSALES
SUPERSALESMAN
SUPERSALESMEN
SUPERSALTS
SUPERSATURATE
SUPERSATURATED
SUPERSATURATES
SUPERSATURATING
SUPERSATURATION
SUPERSAURS
SUPERSAVER
SUPERSAVERS
SUPERSCALAR
SUPERSCALE
SUPERSCHOOL
SUPERSCHOOLS
SUPERSCOUT
SUPERSCOUTS
SUPERSCREEN
SUPERSCREENS
SUPERSCRIBE
SUPERSCRIBED
SUPERSCRIBES
SUPERSCRIBING
SUPERSCRIPT
SUPERSCRIPTION
SUPERSCRIPTIONS
SUPERSCRIPTS
SUPERSECRECIES
SUPERSECRECY
SUPERSECRET
SUPERSEDABLE
SUPERSEDEAS
SUPERSEDEASES
SUPERSEDED
SUPERSEDENCE
SUPERSEDENCES
SUPERSEDER
SUPERSEDERE
SUPERSEDERES
SUPERSEDERS
SUPERSEDES
SUPERSEDING
SUPERSEDURE
SUPERSEDURES
SUPERSELLER
SUPERSELLERS
SUPERSELLING
SUPERSELLS
SUPERSENSIBLE
SUPERSENSIBLY
SUPERSENSITIVE
SUPERSENSORY
SUPERSENSUAL
SUPERSESSION
SUPERSESSIONS
SUPERSEXES
SUPERSEXUALITY
SUPERSHARP
SUPERSHOWS
SUPERSINGER
SUPERSINGERS
SUPERSIZED
SUPERSIZES
SUPERSIZING
SUPERSLEUTH
SUPERSLEUTHS
SUPERSLICK
SUPERSMART
SUPERSMOOTH
SUPERSONIC
SUPERSONICALLY
SUPERSONICS
SUPERSOUND
SUPERSOUNDS
SUPERSPECIAL
SUPERSPECIALIST
SUPERSPECIALS
SUPERSPECIES
SUPERSPECTACLE
SUPERSPECTACLES
SUPERSPEED
SUPERSPEEDS
SUPERSPIES
SUPERSTARDOM
SUPERSTARDOMS
SUPERSTARS
SUPERSTATE
SUPERSTATES
SUPERSTATION
SUPERSTATIONS
SUPERSTIMULATE
SUPERSTIMULATED
SUPERSTIMULATES
SUPERSTITION
SUPERSTITIONS
SUPERSTITIOUS
SUPERSTITIOUSLY
SUPERSTOCK
SUPERSTOCKS
SUPERSTORE
SUPERSTORES
SUPERSTRATA
SUPERSTRATUM
SUPERSTRATUMS
SUPERSTRENGTH
SUPERSTRENGTHS
SUPERSTRIKE
SUPERSTRIKES
SUPERSTRING
SUPERSTRINGS
SUPERSTRONG
SUPERSTRUCT
SUPERSTRUCTED
SUPERSTRUCTING
SUPERSTRUCTION
SUPERSTRUCTIONS
SUPERSTRUCTIVE
SUPERSTRUCTS
SUPERSTRUCTURAL
SUPERSTRUCTURE
SUPERSTRUCTURES
SUPERSTUDS
SUPERSUBTILE
SUPERSUBTLE
SUPERSUBTLETIES
SUPERSUBTLETY
SUPERSURGEON
SUPERSURGEONS
SUPERSWEET
SUPERSYMMETRIC
SUPERSYMMETRIES
SUPERSYMMETRY
SUPERSYSTEM
SUPERSYSTEMS
SUPERTANKER
SUPERTANKERS
SUPERTAXES
SUPERTEACHER
SUPERTEACHERS
SUPERTERRANEAN
SUPERTERRIFIC
SUPERTHICK
SUPERTHRILLER
SUPERTHRILLERS
SUPERTIGHT
SUPERTITLE
SUPERTITLES
SUPERTONIC
SUPERTONICS

SUPERTRUCK
SUPERTRUCKS
SUPERTWIST
SUPERTWISTS
SUPERVENED
SUPERVENES
SUPERVENIENCE
SUPERVENIENCES
SUPERVENIENT
SUPERVENING
SUPERVENTION
SUPERVENTIONS
SUPERVIRILE
SUPERVIRTUOSI
SUPERVIRTUOSO
SUPERVIRTUOSOS
SUPERVIRULENT
SUPERVISAL
SUPERVISALS
SUPERVISED
SUPERVISEE
SUPERVISEES
SUPERVISES
SUPERVISING
SUPERVISION
SUPERVISIONS
SUPERVISOR
SUPERVISORS
SUPERVISORSHIP
SUPERVISORSHIPS
SUPERVISORY
SUPERVOLUTE
SUPERWAIFS
SUPERWAVES
SUPERWEAPON
SUPERWEAPONS
SUPERWEEDS
SUPERWIDES
SUPERWIVES
SUPERWOMAN
SUPERWOMEN
SUPINATING
SUPINATION
SUPINATIONS
SUPINATORS
SUPINENESS
SUPINENESSES
SUPPEAGOES
SUPPEDANEA
SUPPEDANEUM
SUPPERLESS
SUPPERTIME
SUPPERTIMES
SUPPLANTATION
SUPPLANTATIONS
SUPPLANTED
SUPPLANTER
SUPPLANTERS
SUPPLANTING
SUPPLEJACK
SUPPLEJACKS
SUPPLEMENT
SUPPLEMENTAL
SUPPLEMENTALLY
SUPPLEMENTALS
SUPPLEMENTARIES
SUPPLEMENTARILY
SUPPLEMENTARY
SUPPLEMENTATION
SUPPLEMENTED
SUPPLEMENTER
SUPPLEMENTERS
SUPPLEMENTING
SUPPLEMENTS
SUPPLENESS
SUPPLENESSES
SUPPLETION
SUPPLETIONS
SUPPLETIVE
SUPPLETIVES
SUPPLETORILY
SUPPLETORY
SUPPLIABLE
SUPPLIANCE
SUPPLIANCES
SUPPLIANTLY
SUPPLIANTS
SUPPLICANT
SUPPLICANTS
SUPPLICATE
SUPPLICATED
SUPPLICATES
SUPPLICATING
SUPPLICATINGLY
SUPPLICATION
SUPPLICATIONS
SUPPLICATORY
SUPPLICATS
SUPPLICAVIT
SUPPLICAVITS
SUPPLYMENT
SUPPLYMENTS
SUPPORTABILITY
SUPPORTABLE
SUPPORTABLENESS
SUPPORTABLY
SUPPORTANCE
SUPPORTANCES
SUPPORTERS
SUPPORTING
SUPPORTINGS
SUPPORTIVE
SUPPORTIVELY
SUPPORTIVENESS
SUPPORTLESS
SUPPORTMENT
SUPPORTMENTS
SUPPORTRESS
SUPPORTRESSES
SUPPORTURE
SUPPORTURES
SUPPOSABLE
SUPPOSABLY
SUPPOSEDLY
SUPPOSINGS
SUPPOSITION
SUPPOSITIONAL
SUPPOSITIONALLY
SUPPOSITIONARY
SUPPOSITIONLESS
SUPPOSITIONS
SUPPOSITIOUS
SUPPOSITIOUSLY
SUPPOSITITIOUS
SUPPOSITIVE
SUPPOSITIVELY
SUPPOSITIVES
SUPPOSITORIES
SUPPOSITORY
SUPPRESSANT
SUPPRESSANTS
SUPPRESSED
SUPPRESSEDLY
SUPPRESSER
SUPPRESSERS
SUPPRESSES
SUPPRESSIBILITY
SUPPRESSIBLE
SUPPRESSING
SUPPRESSION
SUPPRESSIONS
SUPPRESSIVE
SUPPRESSIVENESS
SUPPRESSOR
SUPPRESSORS
SUPPURATED
SUPPURATES
SUPPURATING
SUPPURATION
SUPPURATIONS
SUPPURATIVE
SUPPURATIVES
SUPRACHIASMIC
SUPRACILIARY
SUPRACOSTAL
SUPRACRUSTAL
SUPRAGLOTTAL
SUPRALAPSARIAN
SUPRALAPSARIANS
SUPRALIMINAL
SUPRALIMINALLY
SUPRALUNAR
SUPRAMAXILLARY
SUPRAMOLECULAR
SUPRAMOLECULE
SUPRAMOLECULES
SUPRAMUNDANE
SUPRANATIONAL
SUPRANATIONALLY
SUPRAOPTIC
SUPRAORBITAL
SUPRAPUBIC
SUPRARATIONAL
SUPRARENAL
SUPRARENALS
SUPRASEGMENTAL
SUPRASENSIBLE
SUPRATEMPORAL
SUPRAVITAL
SUPRAVITALLY
SUPREMACIES
SUPREMACISM
SUPREMACISMS
SUPREMACIST
SUPREMACISTS
SUPREMATISM
SUPREMATISMS
SUPREMATIST
SUPREMATISTS
SUPREMENESS
SUPREMENESSES
SUPREMITIES
SURADDITION
SURADDITIONS
SURBASEMENT
SURBASEMENTS
SURBEDDING
SURCEASING
SURCHARGED
SURCHARGEMENT
SURCHARGEMENTS
SURCHARGER
SURCHARGERS
SURCHARGES
SURCHARGING
SURCINGLED
SURCINGLES
SURCINGLING
SURCULUSES
SUREFOOTED
SUREFOOTEDLY
SUREFOOTEDNESS
SURENESSES
SURETYSHIP
SURETYSHIPS
SURFACELESS
SURFACEMAN
SURFACEMEN
SURFACINGS
SURFACTANT
SURFACTANTS
SURFBOARDED
SURFBOARDER
SURFBOARDERS
SURFBOARDING
SURFBOARDINGS
SURFBOARDS
SURFCASTER
SURFCASTERS
SURFCASTING
SURFCASTINGS
SURFEITERS
SURFEITING
SURFEITINGS
SURFFISHES
SURFPERCHES
SURFRIDERS
SURGEONCIES
SURGEONFISH
SURGEONFISHES
SURGEONSHIP
SURGEONSHIPS
SURGICALLY
SURJECTION
SURJECTIONS
SURJECTIVE
SURLINESSES
SURMASTERS
SURMISABLE
SURMISINGS
SURMISTRESS
SURMISTRESSES
SURMOUNTABLE
SURMOUNTED

SURMOUNTER
SURMOUNTERS
SURMOUNTING
SURMOUNTINGS
SURMULLETS
SURNOMINAL
SURPASSABLE
SURPASSERS
SURPASSING
SURPASSINGLY
SURPASSINGNESS
SURPLUSAGE
SURPLUSAGES
SURPLUSING
SURPLUSSED
SURPLUSSES
SURPLUSSING
SURPRINTED
SURPRINTING
SURPRISALS
SURPRISEDLY
SURPRISERS
SURPRISING
SURPRISINGLY
SURPRISINGNESS
SURPRISINGS
SURPRIZING
SURQUEDIES
SURQUEDRIES
SURREALISM
SURREALISMS
SURREALIST
SURREALISTIC
SURREALISTS
SURREBUTTAL
SURREBUTTALS
SURREBUTTED
SURREBUTTER
SURREBUTTERS
SURREBUTTING
SURREJOINDER
SURREJOINDERS
SURREJOINED
SURREJOINING
SURREJOINS
SURRENDERED
SURRENDEREE
SURRENDEREES
SURRENDERER
SURRENDERERS
SURRENDERING
SURRENDEROR
SURRENDERORS
SURRENDERS
SURRENDRIES
SURREPTITIOUS
SURREPTITIOUSLY
SURROGACIES
SURROGATED
SURROGATES
SURROGATESHIP
SURROGATESHIPS
SURROGATING
SURROGATION
SURROGATIONS
SURROGATUM
SURROGATUMS
SURROUNDED
SURROUNDING
SURROUNDINGS
SURTARBRAND
SURTARBRANDS
SURTURBRAND
SURTURBRANDS
SURVEILING
SURVEILLANCE
SURVEILLANCES
SURVEILLANT
SURVEILLANTS
SURVEILLED
SURVEILLES
SURVEILLING
SURVEYABLE
SURVEYANCE
SURVEYANCES
SURVEYINGS
SURVEYORSHIP
SURVEYORSHIPS
SURVIEWING
SURVIVABILITIES
SURVIVABILITY
SURVIVABLE
SURVIVALISM
SURVIVALISMS
SURVIVALIST
SURVIVALISTS
SURVIVANCE
SURVIVANCES
SURVIVORSHIP
SURVIVORSHIPS
SUSCEPTANCE
SUSCEPTANCES
SUSCEPTIBILITY
SUSCEPTIBLE
SUSCEPTIBLENESS
SUSCEPTIBLY
SUSCEPTIVE
SUSCEPTIVENESS
SUSCEPTIVITIES
SUSCEPTIVITY
SUSCEPTORS
SUSCIPIENT
SUSCIPIENTS
SUSCITATED
SUSCITATES
SUSCITATING
SUSCITATION
SUSCITATIONS
SUSPECTABLE
SUSPECTEDLY
SUSPECTEDNESS
SUSPECTEDNESSES
SUSPECTERS
SUSPECTFUL
SUSPECTING
SUSPECTLESS
SUSPENDERED
SUSPENDERS
SUSPENDIBILITY
SUSPENDIBLE
SUSPENDING
SUSPENSEFUL
SUSPENSEFULLY
SUSPENSEFULNESS
SUSPENSELESS
SUSPENSERS
SUSPENSIBILITY
SUSPENSIBLE
SUSPENSION
SUSPENSIONS
SUSPENSIVE
SUSPENSIVELY
SUSPENSIVENESS
SUSPENSOID
SUSPENSOIDS
SUSPENSORIA
SUSPENSORIAL
SUSPENSORIES
SUSPENSORIUM
SUSPENSORS
SUSPENSORY
SUSPERCOLLATE
SUSPERCOLLATED
SUSPERCOLLATES
SUSPERCOLLATING
SUSPICIONAL
SUSPICIONED
SUSPICIONING
SUSPICIONLESS
SUSPICIONS
SUSPICIOUS
SUSPICIOUSLY
SUSPICIOUSNESS
SUSPIRATION
SUSPIRATIONS
SUSPIRIOUS
SUSTAINABILITY
SUSTAINABLE
SUSTAINEDLY
SUSTAINERS
SUSTAINING
SUSTAININGLY
SUSTAININGS
SUSTAINMENT
SUSTAINMENTS
SUSTENANCE
SUSTENANCES
SUSTENTACULA
SUSTENTACULAR
SUSTENTACULUM
SUSTENTATE
SUSTENTATED
SUSTENTATES
SUSTENTATING
SUSTENTATION
SUSTENTATIONS
SUSTENTATIVE
SUSTENTATOR
SUSTENTATORS
SUSTENTION
SUSTENTIONS
SUSTENTIVE
SUSURRATED
SUSURRATES
SUSURRATING
SUSURRATION
SUSURRATIONS
SUSURRUSES
SUTLERSHIP
SUTLERSHIPS
SUTTEEISMS
SUTTLETIES
SUTURATION
SUTURATIONS
SUZERAINTIES
SUZERAINTY
SVARABHAKTI
SVARABHAKTIS
SVELTENESS
SVELTENESSES
SWAGGERERS
SWAGGERING
SWAGGERINGLY
SWAGGERINGS
SWAINISHNESS
SWAINISHNESSES
SWALLOWABLE
SWALLOWERS
SWALLOWING
SWALLOWTAIL
SWALLOWTAILS
SWALLOWWORT
SWALLOWWORTS
SWAMPINESS
SWAMPINESSES
SWAMPLANDS
SWANKINESS
SWANKINESSES
SWANNERIES
SWANSDOWNS
SWARAJISMS
SWARAJISTS
SWARTHIEST
SWARTHINESS
SWARTHINESSES
SWARTHNESS
SWARTHNESSES
SWARTNESSES
SWASHBUCKLE
SWASHBUCKLED
SWASHBUCKLER
SWASHBUCKLERS
SWASHBUCKLES
SWASHBUCKLING
SWASHWORKS
SWATCHBOOK
SWATCHBOOKS
SWATHEABLE
SWATTERING
SWAYBACKED
SWEARWORDS
SWEATBANDS
SWEATBOXES
SWEATERDRESS
SWEATERDRESSES
SWEATINESS
SWEATINESSES
SWEATPANTS
SWEATSHIRT
SWEATSHIRTS
SWEATSHOPS
SWEATSUITS
SWEEPBACKS
SWEEPINGLY

SWEEPINGNESS
SWEEPINGNESSES
SWEEPSTAKE
SWEEPSTAKES
SWEETBREAD
SWEETBREADS
SWEETBRIAR
SWEETBRIARS
SWEETBRIER
SWEETBRIERS
SWEETCORNS
SWEETENERS
SWEETENING
SWEETENINGS
SWEETFISHES
SWEETHEART
SWEETHEARTED
SWEETHEARTING
SWEETHEARTS
SWEETIEWIFE
SWEETIEWIVES
SWEETISHLY
SWEETISHNESS
SWEETISHNESSES
SWEETMEATS
SWEETNESSES
SWEETSHOPS
SWEETWATER
SWEETWATERS
SWEETWOODS
SWEIRNESSES
SWELLFISHES
SWELLHEADED
SWELLHEADEDNESS
SWELLHEADS
SWELLINGLY
SWELTERING
SWELTERINGLY
SWELTERINGS
SWELTRIEST
SWEPTWINGS
SWERVELESS
SWIFTNESSES
SWIMFEEDER
SWIMFEEDERS
SWIMMERETS
SWIMMINGLY
SWIMMINGNESS
SWIMMINGNESSES
SWINDLINGS
SWINEHERDS
SWINEHOODS
SWINEPOXES
SWINESTONE
SWINESTONES
SWINGBEATS
SWINGBOATS
SWINGEINGLY
SWINGINGEST
SWINGINGLY
SWINGLETREE
SWINGLETREES
SWINGLINGS
SWINGOMETER
SWINGOMETERS
SWINGTREES
SWINISHNESS
SWINISHNESSES
SWIRLINGLY
SWISHINGLY
SWITCHABLE
SWITCHBACK
SWITCHBACKED
SWITCHBACKING
SWITCHBACKS
SWITCHBLADE
SWITCHBLADES
SWITCHBOARD
SWITCHBOARDS
SWITCHEROO
SWITCHEROOS
SWITCHGEAR
SWITCHGEARS
SWITCHGIRL
SWITCHGIRLS
SWITCHGRASS
SWITCHGRASSES
SWITCHIEST
SWITCHINGS
SWITCHLIKE
SWITCHOVER
SWITCHOVERS
SWITCHYARD
SWITCHYARDS
SWITHERING
SWIVELBLOCK
SWIVELBLOCKS
SWIVELLING
SWOLLENNESS
SWOLLENNESSES
SWOONINGLY
SWOOPSTAKE
SWORDBEARER
SWORDBEARERS
SWORDBILLS
SWORDCRAFT
SWORDCRAFTS
SWORDFISHES
SWORDPLAYER
SWORDPLAYERS
SWORDPLAYS
SWORDPROOF
SWORDSMANSHIP
SWORDSMANSHIPS
SWORDSTICK
SWORDSTICKS
SWORDTAILS
SYBARITICAL
SYBARITICALLY
SYBARITISH
SYBARITISM
SYBARITISMS
SYCOPHANCIES
SYCOPHANCY
SYCOPHANTIC
SYCOPHANTICAL
SYCOPHANTICALLY
SYCOPHANTISE
SYCOPHANTISED
SYCOPHANTISES
SYCOPHANTISH
SYCOPHANTISHLY
SYCOPHANTISING
SYCOPHANTISM
SYCOPHANTISMS
SYCOPHANTIZE
SYCOPHANTIZED
SYCOPHANTIZES
SYCOPHANTIZING
SYCOPHANTLY
SYCOPHANTRIES
SYCOPHANTRY
SYCOPHANTS
SYLLABARIA
SYLLABARIES
SYLLABARIUM
SYLLABICAL
SYLLABICALLY
SYLLABICATE
SYLLABICATED
SYLLABICATES
SYLLABICATING
SYLLABICATION
SYLLABICATIONS
SYLLABICITIES
SYLLABICITY
SYLLABIFICATION
SYLLABIFIED
SYLLABIFIES
SYLLABIFYING
SYLLABISED
SYLLABISES
SYLLABISING
SYLLABISMS
SYLLABIZED
SYLLABIZES
SYLLABIZING
SYLLABLING
SYLLABOGRAM
SYLLABOGRAMS
SYLLABOGRAPHIES
SYLLABOGRAPHY
SYLLABUSES
SYLLEPTICAL
SYLLEPTICALLY
SYLLOGISATION
SYLLOGISATIONS
SYLLOGISED
SYLLOGISER
SYLLOGISERS
SYLLOGISES
SYLLOGISING
SYLLOGISMS
SYLLOGISTIC
SYLLOGISTICAL
SYLLOGISTICALLY
SYLLOGISTICS
SYLLOGISTS
SYLLOGIZATION
SYLLOGIZATIONS
SYLLOGIZED
SYLLOGIZER
SYLLOGIZERS
SYLLOGIZES
SYLLOGIZING
SYLPHIDINE
SYLVANITES
SYLVESTRAL
SYLVESTRIAN
SYLVICULTURAL
SYLVICULTURE
SYLVICULTURES
SYLVINITES
SYMBIONTIC
SYMBIONTICALLY
SYMBIOTICAL
SYMBIOTICALLY
SYMBOLICAL
SYMBOLICALLY
SYMBOLICALNESS
SYMBOLISATION
SYMBOLISATIONS
SYMBOLISED
SYMBOLISER
SYMBOLISERS
SYMBOLISES
SYMBOLISING
SYMBOLISMS
SYMBOLISTIC
SYMBOLISTICAL
SYMBOLISTICALLY
SYMBOLISTS
SYMBOLIZATION
SYMBOLIZATIONS
SYMBOLIZED
SYMBOLIZER
SYMBOLIZERS
SYMBOLIZES
SYMBOLIZING
SYMBOLLING
SYMBOLOGICAL
SYMBOLOGIES
SYMBOLOGIST
SYMBOLOGISTS
SYMBOLOGRAPHIES
SYMBOLOGRAPHY
SYMBOLOLATRIES
SYMBOLOLATRY
SYMBOLOLOGIES
SYMBOLOLOGY
SYMMETALISM
SYMMETALISMS
SYMMETALLIC
SYMMETALLISM
SYMMETALLISMS
SYMMETRIAN
SYMMETRIANS
SYMMETRICAL
SYMMETRICALLY
SYMMETRICALNESS
SYMMETRIES
SYMMETRISATION
SYMMETRISATIONS
SYMMETRISE
SYMMETRISED
SYMMETRISES
SYMMETRISING
SYMMETRIZATION
SYMMETRIZATIONS
SYMMETRIZE
SYMMETRIZED
SYMMETRIZES
SYMMETRIZING
SYMMETROPHOBIA

SYMMETROPHOBIAS
SYMPATHECTOMIES
SYMPATHECTOMY
SYMPATHETIC
SYMPATHETICAL
SYMPATHETICALLY
SYMPATHETICS
SYMPATHIES
SYMPATHINS
SYMPATHIQUE
SYMPATHISE
SYMPATHISED
SYMPATHISER
SYMPATHISERS
SYMPATHISES
SYMPATHISING
SYMPATHIZE
SYMPATHIZED
SYMPATHIZER
SYMPATHIZERS
SYMPATHIZES
SYMPATHIZING
SYMPATHOLYTIC
SYMPATHOLYTICS
SYMPATHOMIMETIC
SYMPATRICALLY
SYMPATRIES
SYMPETALIES
SYMPETALOUS
SYMPHILIES
SYMPHILISM
SYMPHILISMS
SYMPHILOUS
SYMPHONICALLY
SYMPHONIES
SYMPHONION
SYMPHONIONS
SYMPHONIOUS
SYMPHONIOUSLY
SYMPHONIST
SYMPHONISTS
SYMPHYLOUS
SYMPHYSEAL
SYMPHYSEOTOMIES
SYMPHYSEOTOMY
SYMPHYSIAL
SYMPHYSIOTOMIES
SYMPHYSIOTOMY
SYMPHYSTIC
SYMPIESOMETER
SYMPIESOMETERS
SYMPLASTIC
SYMPODIALLY
SYMPOSIACS
SYMPOSIARCH
SYMPOSIARCHS
SYMPOSIAST
SYMPOSIASTS
SYMPOSIUMS
SYMPTOMATIC
SYMPTOMATICAL
SYMPTOMATICALLY
SYMPTOMATISE
SYMPTOMATISED
SYMPTOMATISES
SYMPTOMATISING
SYMPTOMATIZE
SYMPTOMATIZED
SYMPTOMATIZES
SYMPTOMATIZING
SYMPTOMATOLOGIC
SYMPTOMATOLOGY
SYMPTOMLESS
SYMPTOMOLOGICAL
SYMPTOMOLOGIES
SYMPTOMOLOGY
SYNADELPHITE
SYNADELPHITES
SYNAERESES
SYNAERESIS
SYNAESTHESES
SYNAESTHESIA
SYNAESTHESIAS
SYNAESTHESIS
SYNAESTHETIC
SYNAGOGICAL
SYNAGOGUES
SYNALEPHAS
SYNALLAGMATIC
SYNALOEPHA
SYNALOEPHAS
SYNANDRIUM
SYNANDROUS
SYNANTHEROUS
SYNANTHESES
SYNANTHESIS
SYNANTHETIC
SYNANTHIES
SYNANTHOUS
SYNAPHEIAS
SYNAPOSEMATIC
SYNAPOSEMATISM
SYNAPOSEMATISMS
SYNAPTASES
SYNAPTICAL
SYNAPTICALLY
SYNAPTOSOMAL
SYNAPTOSOME
SYNAPTOSOMES
SYNARCHIES
SYNARTHRODIAL
SYNARTHRODIALLY
SYNARTHROSES
SYNARTHROSIS
SYNASTRIES
SYNAXARION
SYNCARPIES
SYNCARPOUS
SYNCHONDROSES
SYNCHONDROSIS
SYNCHORESES
SYNCHORESIS
SYNCHROFLASH
SYNCHROFLASHES
SYNCHROMESH
SYNCHROMESHES
SYNCHRONAL
SYNCHRONEITIES
SYNCHRONEITY
SYNCHRONIC
SYNCHRONICAL
SYNCHRONICALLY
SYNCHRONICITIES
SYNCHRONICITY
SYNCHRONIES
SYNCHRONISATION
SYNCHRONISE
SYNCHRONISED
SYNCHRONISER
SYNCHRONISERS
SYNCHRONISES
SYNCHRONISING
SYNCHRONISM
SYNCHRONISMS
SYNCHRONISTIC
SYNCHRONISTICAL
SYNCHRONIZATION
SYNCHRONIZE
SYNCHRONIZED
SYNCHRONIZER
SYNCHRONIZERS
SYNCHRONIZES
SYNCHRONIZING
SYNCHRONOLOGIES
SYNCHRONOLOGY
SYNCHRONOSCOPE
SYNCHRONOSCOPES
SYNCHRONOUS
SYNCHRONOUSLY
SYNCHRONOUSNESS
SYNCHROSCOPE
SYNCHROSCOPES
SYNCHROTRON
SYNCHROTRONS
SYNCLASTIC
SYNCLINALS
SYNCLINORIA
SYNCLINORIUM
SYNCOPATED
SYNCOPATES
SYNCOPATING
SYNCOPATION
SYNCOPATIONS
SYNCOPATIVE
SYNCOPATOR
SYNCOPATORS
SYNCRETISATION
SYNCRETISATIONS
SYNCRETISE
SYNCRETISED
SYNCRETISES
SYNCRETISING
SYNCRETISM
SYNCRETISMS
SYNCRETIST
SYNCRETISTIC
SYNCRETISTS
SYNCRETIZATION
SYNCRETIZATIONS
SYNCRETIZE
SYNCRETIZED
SYNCRETIZES
SYNCRETIZING
SYNDACTYLIES
SYNDACTYLISM
SYNDACTYLISMS
SYNDACTYLOUS
SYNDACTYLS
SYNDACTYLY
SYNDERESES
SYNDERESIS
SYNDESISES
SYNDESMOSES
SYNDESMOSIS
SYNDESMOTIC
SYNDETICAL
SYNDETICALLY
SYNDICALISM
SYNDICALISMS
SYNDICALIST
SYNDICALISTIC
SYNDICALISTS
SYNDICATED
SYNDICATES
SYNDICATING
SYNDICATION
SYNDICATIONS
SYNDICATOR
SYNDICATORS
SYNDICSHIP
SYNDICSHIPS
SYNDIOTACTIC
SYNDYASMIAN
SYNECDOCHE
SYNECDOCHES
SYNECDOCHIC
SYNECDOCHICAL
SYNECDOCHICALLY
SYNECDOCHISM
SYNECDOCHISMS
SYNECOLOGIC
SYNECOLOGICAL
SYNECOLOGICALLY
SYNECOLOGIES
SYNECOLOGIST
SYNECOLOGISTS
SYNECOLOGY
SYNECPHONESES
SYNECPHONESIS
SYNECTICALLY
SYNEIDESES
SYNEIDESIS
SYNERGETIC
SYNERGETICALLY
SYNERGICALLY
SYNERGISED
SYNERGISES
SYNERGISING
SYNERGISMS
SYNERGISTIC
SYNERGISTICALLY
SYNERGISTS
SYNERGIZED
SYNERGIZES
SYNERGIZING
SYNESTHESIA
SYNESTHESIAS
SYNESTHETIC
SYNGENESES
SYNGENESIOUS
SYNGENESIS
SYNGENETIC
SYNGNATHOUS
SYNKARYONIC

SYNKARYONS
SYNODICALLY
SYNOECETES
SYNOECIOSES
SYNOECIOSIS
SYNOECIOUS
SYNOECISED
SYNOECISES
SYNOECISING
SYNOECISMS
SYNOECIZED
SYNOECIZES
SYNOECIZING
SYNOECOLOGIES
SYNOECOLOGY
SYNOEKETES
SYNONYMATIC
SYNONYMICAL
SYNONYMICON
SYNONYMICONS
SYNONYMIES
SYNONYMISE
SYNONYMISED
SYNONYMISES
SYNONYMISING
SYNONYMIST
SYNONYMISTS
SYNONYMITIES
SYNONYMITY
SYNONYMIZE
SYNONYMIZED
SYNONYMIZES
SYNONYMIZING
SYNONYMOUS
SYNONYMOUSLY
SYNONYMOUSNESS
SYNOPSISED
SYNOPSISES
SYNOPSISING
SYNOPSIZED
SYNOPSIZES
SYNOPSIZING
SYNOPTICAL
SYNOPTICALLY
SYNOPTISTIC
SYNOPTISTS
SYNOSTOSES
SYNOSTOSIS
SYNOVIALLY
SYNOVITISES
SYNSEPALOUS
SYNTACTICAL
SYNTACTICALLY
SYNTACTICS
SYNTAGMATA
SYNTAGMATIC
SYNTAGMATITE
SYNTAGMATITES
SYNTECTICAL
SYNTENOSES
SYNTENOSIS
SYNTERESES
SYNTERESIS
SYNTEXISES
SYNTHESISATION
SYNTHESISATIONS
SYNTHESISE
SYNTHESISED
SYNTHESISER
SYNTHESISERS
SYNTHESISES
SYNTHESISING
SYNTHESIST
SYNTHESISTS
SYNTHESIZATION
SYNTHESIZATIONS
SYNTHESIZE
SYNTHESIZED
SYNTHESIZER
SYNTHESIZERS
SYNTHESIZES
SYNTHESIZING
SYNTHESPIAN
SYNTHESPIANS
SYNTHETASE
SYNTHETASES
SYNTHETICAL
SYNTHETICALLY
SYNTHETICISM
SYNTHETICISMS
SYNTHETICS
SYNTHETISATION
SYNTHETISATIONS
SYNTHETISE
SYNTHETISED
SYNTHETISER
SYNTHETISERS
SYNTHETISES
SYNTHETISING
SYNTHETISM
SYNTHETISMS
SYNTHETIST
SYNTHETISTS
SYNTHETIZATION
SYNTHETIZATIONS
SYNTHETIZE
SYNTHETIZED
SYNTHETIZER
SYNTHETIZERS
SYNTHETIZES
SYNTHETIZING
SYNTHRONUS
SYNTONICALLY
SYNTONISED
SYNTONISES
SYNTONISING
SYNTONIZED
SYNTONIZES
SYNTONIZING
SYPHILISATION
SYPHILISATIONS
SYPHILISED
SYPHILISES
SYPHILISING
SYPHILITIC
SYPHILITICALLY
SYPHILITICS
SYPHILIZATION
SYPHILIZATIONS
SYPHILIZED
SYPHILIZES
SYPHILIZING
SYPHILOLOGIES
SYPHILOLOGIST
SYPHILOLOGISTS
SYPHILOLOGY
SYPHILOMAS
SYPHILOMATA
SYPHILOPHOBIA
SYPHILOPHOBIAS
SYRINGITIS
SYRINGITISES
SYRINGOMYELIA
SYRINGOMYELIAS
SYRINGOMYELIC
SYRINGOTOMIES
SYRINGOTOMY
SYSSARCOSES
SYSSARCOSIS
SYSSARCOTIC
SYSTEMATIC
SYSTEMATICAL
SYSTEMATICALLY
SYSTEMATICIAN
SYSTEMATICIANS
SYSTEMATICNESS
SYSTEMATICS
SYSTEMATISATION
SYSTEMATISE
SYSTEMATISED
SYSTEMATISER
SYSTEMATISERS
SYSTEMATISES
SYSTEMATISING
SYSTEMATISM
SYSTEMATISMS
SYSTEMATIST
SYSTEMATISTS
SYSTEMATIZATION
SYSTEMATIZE
SYSTEMATIZED
SYSTEMATIZER
SYSTEMATIZERS
SYSTEMATIZES
SYSTEMATIZING
SYSTEMATOLOGIES
SYSTEMATOLOGY
SYSTEMICALLY
SYSTEMISATION
SYSTEMISATIONS
SYSTEMISED
SYSTEMISER
SYSTEMISERS
SYSTEMISES
SYSTEMISING
SYSTEMIZATION
SYSTEMIZATIONS
SYSTEMIZED
SYSTEMIZER
SYSTEMIZERS
SYSTEMIZES
SYSTEMIZING
SYSTEMLESS
SYZYGETICALLY

Tt

TABASHEERS
TABBOULEHS
TABBYHOODS
TABEFACTION
TABEFACTIONS
TABELLIONS
TABERNACLE
TABERNACLED
TABERNACLES
TABERNACLING
TABERNACULAR
TABESCENCE
TABESCENCES
TABLANETTE
TABLANETTES
TABLATURES
TABLECLOTH
TABLECLOTHS
TABLELANDS
TABLEMATES
TABLESPOON
TABLESPOONFUL
TABLESPOONFULS
TABLESPOONS
TABLESPOONSFUL
TABLETOPPED
TABLETTING
TABLEWARES
TABOGGANED
TABOGGANING
TABOPARESES
TABOPARESIS
TABULARISATION
TABULARISATIONS
TABULARISE
TABULARISED
TABULARISES
TABULARISING
TABULARIZATION
TABULARIZATIONS
TABULARIZE
TABULARIZED
TABULARIZES
TABULARIZING
TABULATING
TABULATION
TABULATIONS
TABULATORS
TABULATORY
TACAMAHACS
TACHEOMETER
TACHEOMETERS
TACHEOMETRIC
TACHEOMETRICAL
TACHEOMETRIES
TACHEOMETRY
TACHISTOSCOPE
TACHISTOSCOPES
TACHISTOSCOPIC
TACHOGRAMS
TACHOGRAPH
TACHOGRAPHS
TACHOMETER
TACHOMETERS
TACHOMETRIC
TACHOMETRICAL
TACHOMETRICALLY
TACHOMETRIES
TACHOMETRY
TACHYARRHYTHMIA
TACHYCARDIA
TACHYCARDIAC
TACHYCARDIAS
TACHYGRAPH
TACHYGRAPHER
TACHYGRAPHERS
TACHYGRAPHIC
TACHYGRAPHICAL
TACHYGRAPHIES
TACHYGRAPHIST
TACHYGRAPHISTS
TACHYGRAPHS
TACHYGRAPHY
TACHYLITES
TACHYLITIC
TACHYLYTES
TACHYLYTIC
TACHYMETER
TACHYMETERS
TACHYMETRIC
TACHYMETRICAL
TACHYMETRICALLY
TACHYMETRIES
TACHYMETRY
TACHYPHASIA
TACHYPHASIAS
TACHYPHRASIA
TACHYPHRASIAS
TACHYPHYLAXES
TACHYPHYLAXIS
TACHYPNEAS
TACHYPNOEA
TACHYPNOEAS
TACITNESSES
TACITURNITIES
TACITURNITY
TACITURNLY
TACKBOARDS
TACKIFIERS
TACKIFYING
TACKINESSES
TACMAHACKS
TACTFULNESS
TACTFULNESSES
TACTICALLY
TACTICIANS
TACTICITIES
TACTILISTS
TACTILITIES
TACTLESSLY
TACTLESSNESS
TACTLESSNESSES
TACTUALITIES
TACTUALITY
TAEKWONDOS
TAENIACIDE
TAENIACIDES
TAENIAFUGE
TAENIAFUGES
TAFFETASES
TAFFETIZED
TAGLIARINI
TAGLIARINIS
TAGLIATELLE
TAGLIATELLES
TAHSILDARS
TAIKONAUTS
TAILBOARDS
TAILCOATED
TAILENDERS
TAILGATERS
TAILGATING
TAILLESSLY
TAILLESSNESS
TAILLESSNESSES
TAILLIGHTS
TAILORBIRD
TAILORBIRDS
TAILORESSES
TAILORINGS
TAILORMADE
TAILORMAKE

TAILORMAKES
TAILORMAKING
TAILPIECES
TAILPIPING
TAILPLANES
TAILSLIDES
TAILSPINNED
TAILSPINNING
TAILSTOCKS
TAILWATERS
TAILWHEELS
TAINTLESSLY
TAKINGNESS
TAKINGNESSES
TALBOTYPES
TALEBEARER
TALEBEARERS
TALEBEARING
TALEBEARINGS
TALEGALLAS
TALENTLESS
TALISMANIC
TALISMANICAL
TALISMANICALLY
TALKABILITIES
TALKABILITY
TALKATHONS
TALKATIVELY
TALKATIVENESS
TALKATIVENESSES
TALKINESSES
TALLGRASSES
TALLIATING
TALLNESSES
TALLYHOING
TALLYSHOPS
TALLYWOMAN
TALLYWOMEN
TALMUDISMS
TAMABILITIES
TAMABILITY
TAMABLENESS
TAMABLENESSES
TAMARILLOS
TAMBOURERS
TAMBOURINE
TAMBOURINES
TAMBOURING
TAMBOURINIST
TAMBOURINISTS
TAMBOURINS
TAMEABILITIES
TAMEABILITY
TAMEABLENESS
TAMEABLENESSES
TAMELESSNESS
TAMELESSNESSES
TAMENESSES
TAMOXIFENS
TAMPERINGS
TAMPERPROOF
TAMPONADES
TAMPONAGES
TANDEMWISE
TANGENCIES
TANGENTALLY
TANGENTIAL
TANGENTIALITIES
TANGENTIALITY
TANGENTIALLY
TANGERINES
TANGHININS
TANGIBILITIES
TANGIBILITY
TANGIBLENESS
TANGIBLENESSES
TANGINESSES
TANGLEFOOT
TANGLEFOOTS
TANGLEMENT
TANGLEMENTS
TANGLESOME
TANGLEWEED
TANGLEWEEDS
TANGLINGLY
TANISTRIES
TANKBUSTER
TANKBUSTERS
TANKBUSTING
TANKBUSTINGS
TANTALATES
TANTALISATION
TANTALISATIONS
TANTALISED
TANTALISER
TANTALISERS
TANTALISES
TANTALISING
TANTALISINGLY
TANTALISINGS
TANTALISMS
TANTALITES
TANTALIZATION
TANTALIZATIONS
TANTALIZED
TANTALIZER
TANTALIZERS
TANTALIZES
TANTALIZING
TANTALIZINGLY
TANTALIZINGS
TANTALUSES
TANTAMOUNT
TANTARARAS
TANZANITES
TAOISEACHS
TAPERINGLY
TAPERNESSES
TAPERSTICK
TAPERSTICKS
TAPESCRIPT
TAPESCRIPTS
TAPESTRIED
TAPESTRIES
TAPESTRYING
TAPHEPHOBIA
TAPHEPHOBIAS
TAPHEPHOBIC
TAPHONOMIC
TAPHONOMICAL
TAPHONOMIES
TAPHONOMIST
TAPHONOMISTS
TAPHOPHOBIA
TAPHOPHOBIAS
TAPHROGENESES
TAPHROGENESIS
TAPOTEMENT
TAPOTEMENTS
TAPSALTEERIE
TAPSALTEERIES
TAPSIETEERIE
TAPSIETEERIES
TAPSTRESSES
TARADIDDLE
TARADIDDLES
TARAMASALATA
TARAMASALATAS
TARANTARAED
TARANTARAING
TARANTARAS
TARANTASES
TARANTASSES
TARANTELLA
TARANTELLAS
TARANTISMS
TARANTISTS
TARANTULAE
TARANTULAS
TARATANTARA
TARATANTARAED
TARATANTARAING
TARATANTARAS
TARAXACUMS
TARBOGGINED
TARBOGGINING
TARBOGGINS
TARBOOSHES
TARBOUCHES
TARBOUSHES
TARDIGRADE
TARDIGRADES
TARDINESSES
TARGETABLE
TARGETEERS
TARGETITIS
TARGETITISES
TARGETLESS
TARIFFICATION
TARIFFICATIONS
TARIFFLESS
TARMACADAM
TARMACADAMS
TARMACKING
TARNATIONS
TARNISHABLE
TARNISHERS
TARNISHING
TARPAULING
TARPAULINGS
TARPAULINS
TARRADIDDLE
TARRADIDDLES
TARRIANCES
TARRINESSES
TARSALGIAS
TARSOMETATARSAL
TARSOMETATARSI
TARSOMETATARSUS
TARTANALIA
TARTANALIAS
TARTANRIES
TARTAREOUS
TARTARISATION
TARTARISATIONS
TARTARISED
TARTARISES
TARTARISING
TARTARIZATION
TARTARIZATIONS
TARTARIZED
TARTARIZES
TARTARIZING
TARTINESSES
TARTNESSES
TARTRAZINE
TARTRAZINES
TASEOMETER
TASEOMETERS
TASIMETERS
TASIMETRIC
TASIMETRIES
TASKMASTER
TASKMASTERS
TASKMISTRESS
TASKMISTRESSES
TASSELLING
TASSELLINGS
TASTEFULLY
TASTEFULNESS
TASTEFULNESSES
TASTELESSLY
TASTELESSNESS
TASTELESSNESSES
TASTEMAKER
TASTEMAKERS
TASTINESSES
TATAHASHES
TATPURUSHA
TATPURUSHAS
TATTERDEMALION
TATTERDEMALIONS
TATTERDEMALLION
TATTERSALL
TATTERSALLS
TATTINESSES
TATTLETALE
TATTLETALES
TATTLINGLY
TATTOOISTS
TAUNTINGLY
TAUROBOLIA
TAUROBOLIUM
TAUROMACHIAN
TAUROMACHIES
TAUROMACHY
TAUROMORPHOUS
TAUTNESSES
TAUTOCHRONE
TAUTOCHRONES
TAUTOCHRONISM
TAUTOCHRONISMS
TAUTOCHRONOUS
TAUTOLOGIC

TAUTOLOGICAL
TAUTOLOGICALLY
TAUTOLOGIES
TAUTOLOGISE
TAUTOLOGISED
TAUTOLOGISES
TAUTOLOGISING
TAUTOLOGISM
TAUTOLOGISMS
TAUTOLOGIST
TAUTOLOGISTS
TAUTOLOGIZE
TAUTOLOGIZED
TAUTOLOGIZES
TAUTOLOGIZING
TAUTOLOGOUS
TAUTOLOGOUSLY
TAUTOMERIC
TAUTOMERISM
TAUTOMERISMS
TAUTOMETRIC
TAUTOMETRICAL
TAUTONYMIC
TAUTONYMIES
TAUTONYMOUS
TAUTOPHONIC
TAUTOPHONICAL
TAUTOPHONIES
TAUTOPHONY
TAWDRINESS
TAWDRINESSES
TAWHEOWHEO
TAWHEOWHEOS
TAWNINESSES
TAXABILITIES
TAXABILITY
TAXABLENESS
TAXABLENESSES
TAXAMETERS
TAXATIONAL
TAXIDERMAL
TAXIDERMIC
TAXIDERMIES
TAXIDERMISE
TAXIDERMISED
TAXIDERMISES
TAXIDERMISING
TAXIDERMIST
TAXIDERMISTS
TAXIDERMIZE
TAXIDERMIZED
TAXIDERMIZES
TAXIDERMIZING
TAXIMETERS
TAXIPLANES
TAXONOMERS
TAXONOMICAL
TAXONOMICALLY
TAXONOMIES
TAXONOMIST
TAXONOMISTS
TAXPAYINGS
TAYASSUIDS
TAYBERRIES
TCHOTCHKES
TCHOUKBALL
TCHOUKBALLS
TEABERRIES
TEACHABILITIES
TEACHABILITY
TEACHABLENESS
TEACHABLENESSES
TEACHERLESS
TEACHERSHIP
TEACHERSHIPS
TEACUPFULS
TEACUPSFUL
TEAKETTLES
TEARFULNESS
TEARFULNESSES
TEARGASSED
TEARGASSES
TEARGASSING
TEARINESSES
TEARJERKER
TEARJERKERS
TEARSHEETS
TEARSTAINED
TEARSTAINS
TEARSTRIPS
TEASELINGS
TEASELLERS
TEASELLING
TEASELLINGS
TEASPOONFUL
TEASPOONFULS
TEASPOONSFUL
TEATASTERS
TEAZELLING
TECHINESSES
TECHNETIUM
TECHNETIUMS
TECHNETRONIC
TECHNICALISE
TECHNICALISED
TECHNICALISES
TECHNICALISING
TECHNICALITIES
TECHNICALITY
TECHNICALIZE
TECHNICALIZED
TECHNICALIZES
TECHNICALIZING
TECHNICALLY
TECHNICALNESS
TECHNICALNESSES
TECHNICALS
TECHNICIAN
TECHNICIANS
TECHNICISE
TECHNICISED
TECHNICISES
TECHNICISING
TECHNICISM
TECHNICISMS
TECHNICIST
TECHNICISTS
TECHNICIZE
TECHNICIZED
TECHNICIZES
TECHNICIZING
TECHNICOLOUR
TECHNICOLOURED
TECHNIKONS
TECHNIQUES
TECHNOBABBLE
TECHNOBABBLES
TECHNOCRACIES
TECHNOCRACY
TECHNOCRAT
TECHNOCRATIC
TECHNOCRATS
TECHNOFEAR
TECHNOFEARS
TECHNOGRAPHIES
TECHNOGRAPHY
TECHNOJUNKIE
TECHNOJUNKIES
TECHNOLOGIC
TECHNOLOGICAL
TECHNOLOGICALLY
TECHNOLOGIES
TECHNOLOGISE
TECHNOLOGISED
TECHNOLOGISES
TECHNOLOGISING
TECHNOLOGIST
TECHNOLOGISTS
TECHNOLOGIZE
TECHNOLOGIZED
TECHNOLOGIZES
TECHNOLOGIZING
TECHNOLOGY
TECHNOMANIA
TECHNOMANIAC
TECHNOMANIACS
TECHNOMANIAS
TECHNOMUSIC
TECHNOMUSICS
TECHNOPHILE
TECHNOPHILES
TECHNOPHOBE
TECHNOPHOBES
TECHNOPHOBIA
TECHNOPHOBIAS
TECHNOPHOBIC
TECHNOPHOBICS
TECHNOPOLE
TECHNOPOLES
TECHNOPOLIS
TECHNOPOLISES
TECHNOPOLITAN
TECHNOPOLITANS
TECHNOPOPS
TECHNOSPEAK
TECHNOSPEAKS
TECHNOSTRESS
TECHNOSTRESSES
TECHNOSTRUCTURE
TECTIBRANCH
TECTIBRANCHIATE
TECTIBRANCHS
TECTONICALLY
TECTONISMS
TECTRICIAL
TEDIOSITIES
TEDIOUSNESS
TEDIOUSNESSES
TEDIOUSOME
TEEMINGNESS
TEEMINGNESSES
TEENTSIEST
TEENYBOPPER
TEENYBOPPERS
TEETERBOARD
TEETERBOARDS
TEETHRIDGE
TEETHRIDGES
TEETOTALED
TEETOTALER
TEETOTALERS
TEETOTALING
TEETOTALISM
TEETOTALISMS
TEETOTALIST
TEETOTALISTS
TEETOTALLED
TEETOTALLER
TEETOTALLERS
TEETOTALLING
TEETOTALLY
TEGUMENTAL
TEGUMENTARY
TEICHOPSIA
TEICHOPSIAS
TEINOSCOPE
TEINOSCOPES
TEKNONYMIES
TEKNONYMOUS
TELAESTHESIA
TELAESTHESIAS
TELAESTHETIC
TELANGIECTASES
TELANGIECTASIA
TELANGIECTASIAS
TELANGIECTASIS
TELANGIECTATIC
TELAUTOGRAPH
TELAUTOGRAPHIC
TELAUTOGRAPHIES
TELAUTOGRAPHY
TELEARCHICS
TELEBANKING
TELEBANKINGS
TELEBRIDGE
TELEBRIDGES
TELECAMERA
TELECAMERAS
TELECASTED
TELECASTER
TELECASTERS
TELECASTING
TELECHIRIC
TELECOMMAND
TELECOMMANDS
TELECOMMUTE
TELECOMMUTED
TELECOMMUTER
TELECOMMUTERS
TELECOMMUTES
TELECOMMUTING
TELECOMMUTINGS
TELECONFERENCE
TELECONFERENCES

TELECONNECTION
TELECONNECTIONS
TELECONTROL
TELECONTROLS
TELECONVERTER
TELECONVERTERS
TELECOTTAGE
TELECOTTAGES
TELECOTTAGING
TELECOTTAGINGS
TELECOURSE
TELECOURSES
TELEDILDONICS
TELEFACSIMILE
TELEFACSIMILES
TELEFAXING
TELEFERIQUE
TELEFERIQUES
TELEGENICALLY
TELEGNOSES
TELEGNOSIS
TELEGNOSTIC
TELEGONIES
TELEGONOUS
TELEGRAMMATIC
TELEGRAMMED
TELEGRAMMIC
TELEGRAMMING
TELEGRAPHED
TELEGRAPHER
TELEGRAPHERS
TELEGRAPHESE
TELEGRAPHESES
TELEGRAPHIC
TELEGRAPHICALLY
TELEGRAPHIES
TELEGRAPHING
TELEGRAPHIST
TELEGRAPHISTS
TELEGRAPHS
TELEGRAPHY
TELEHEALTH
TELEHEALTHS
TELEJOURNALISM
TELEJOURNALISMS
TELEJOURNALIST
TELEJOURNALISTS
TELEKINESES
TELEKINESIS
TELEKINETIC
TELEKINETICALLY
TELEMARKED
TELEMARKETER
TELEMARKETERS
TELEMARKETING
TELEMARKETINGS
TELEMARKING
TELEMATICS
TELEMEDICINE
TELEMEDICINES
TELEMETERED
TELEMETERING
TELEMETERS
TELEMETRIC
TELEMETRICAL
TELEMETRICALLY
TELEMETRIES
TELENCEPHALA
TELENCEPHALIC
TELENCEPHALON
TELENCEPHALONS
TELEOLOGIC
TELEOLOGICAL
TELEOLOGICALLY
TELEOLOGIES
TELEOLOGISM
TELEOLOGISMS
TELEOLOGIST
TELEOLOGISTS
TELEONOMIC
TELEONOMIES
TELEOSAURIAN
TELEOSAURIANS
TELEOSAURS
TELEOSTEAN
TELEOSTEANS
TELEOSTOME
TELEOSTOMES
TELEOSTOMOUS
TELEPATHED
TELEPATHIC
TELEPATHICALLY
TELEPATHIES
TELEPATHING
TELEPATHISE
TELEPATHISED
TELEPATHISES
TELEPATHISING
TELEPATHIST
TELEPATHISTS
TELEPATHIZE
TELEPATHIZED
TELEPATHIZES
TELEPATHIZING
TELEPHEMES
TELEPHERIQUE
TELEPHERIQUES
TELEPHONED
TELEPHONER
TELEPHONERS
TELEPHONES
TELEPHONIC
TELEPHONICALLY
TELEPHONIES
TELEPHONING
TELEPHONIST
TELEPHONISTS
TELEPHOTOGRAPH
TELEPHOTOGRAPHS
TELEPHOTOGRAPHY
TELEPHOTOS
TELEPOINTS
TELEPORTATION
TELEPORTATIONS
TELEPORTED
TELEPORTING
TELEPRESENCE
TELEPRESENCES
TELEPRINTER
TELEPRINTERS
TELEPROCESSING
TELEPROCESSINGS
TELEPROMPTER
TELEPROMPTERS
TELERECORD
TELERECORDED
TELERECORDING
TELERECORDINGS
TELERECORDS
TELERGICALLY
TELESCIENCE
TELESCIENCES
TELESCOPED
TELESCOPES
TELESCOPIC
TELESCOPICAL
TELESCOPICALLY
TELESCOPIES
TELESCOPIFORM
TELESCOPING
TELESCOPIST
TELESCOPISTS
TELESCREEN
TELESCREENS
TELESELLING
TELESELLINGS
TELESERVICES
TELESHOPPED
TELESHOPPING
TELESHOPPINGS
TELESMATIC
TELESMATICAL
TELESMATICALLY
TELESOFTWARE
TELESOFTWARES
TELESTEREOSCOPE
TELESTHESIA
TELESTHESIAS
TELESTHETIC
TELESTICHS
TELESURGERIES
TELESURGERY
TELETYPESETTING
TELETYPEWRITER
TELETYPEWRITERS
TELETYPING
TELEUTOSPORE
TELEUTOSPORES
TELEUTOSPORIC
TELEVANGELICAL
TELEVANGELISM
TELEVANGELISMS
TELEVANGELIST
TELEVANGELISTS
TELEVERITE
TELEVERITES
TELEVIEWED
TELEVIEWER
TELEVIEWERS
TELEVIEWING
TELEVISERS
TELEVISING
TELEVISION
TELEVISIONAL
TELEVISIONALLY
TELEVISIONARY
TELEVISIONS
TELEVISORS
TELEVISUAL
TELEVISUALLY
TELEWORKER
TELEWORKERS
TELEWORKING
TELEWORKINGS
TELEWRITER
TELEWRITERS
TELFERAGES
TELIOSPORE
TELIOSPORES
TELLERSHIP
TELLERSHIPS
TELLURATES
TELLURETTED
TELLURIANS
TELLURIDES
TELLURIONS
TELLURISED
TELLURISES
TELLURISING
TELLURITES
TELLURIUMS
TELLURIZED
TELLURIZES
TELLURIZING
TELLUROMETER
TELLUROMETERS
TELNETTING
TELOCENTRIC
TELOCENTRICS
TELOMERASE
TELOMERASES
TELOMERISATION
TELOMERISATIONS
TELOMERIZATION
TELOMERIZATIONS
TELOPHASES
TELOPHASIC
TELPHERAGE
TELPHERAGES
TELPHERING
TELPHERLINE
TELPHERLINES
TELPHERMAN
TELPHERMEN
TELPHERWAY
TELPHERWAYS
TEMAZEPAMS
TEMERARIOUS
TEMERARIOUSLY
TEMERARIOUSNESS
TEMERITIES
TEMEROUSLY
TEMPERABILITIES
TEMPERABILITY
TEMPERABLE
TEMPERALITIE
TEMPERALITIES
TEMPERAMENT
TEMPERAMENTAL
TEMPERAMENTALLY
TEMPERAMENTFUL
TEMPERAMENTS
TEMPERANCE
TEMPERANCES

TEMPERATED
TEMPERATELY
TEMPERATENESS
TEMPERATENESSES
TEMPERATES
TEMPERATING
TEMPERATIVE
TEMPERATURE
TEMPERATURES
TEMPERINGS
TEMPESTING
TEMPESTIVE
TEMPESTUOUS
TEMPESTUOUSLY
TEMPESTUOUSNESS
TEMPOLABILE
TEMPORALISE
TEMPORALISED
TEMPORALISES
TEMPORALISING
TEMPORALITIES
TEMPORALITY
TEMPORALIZE
TEMPORALIZED
TEMPORALIZES
TEMPORALIZING
TEMPORALLY
TEMPORALNESS
TEMPORALNESSES
TEMPORALTIES
TEMPORALTY
TEMPORANEOUS
TEMPORARIES
TEMPORARILY
TEMPORARINESS
TEMPORARINESSES
TEMPORISATION
TEMPORISATIONS
TEMPORISED
TEMPORISER
TEMPORISERS
TEMPORISES
TEMPORISING
TEMPORISINGLY
TEMPORISINGS
TEMPORIZATION
TEMPORIZATIONS
TEMPORIZED
TEMPORIZER
TEMPORIZERS
TEMPORIZES
TEMPORIZING
TEMPORIZINGLY
TEMPORIZINGS
TEMPTABILITIES
TEMPTABILITY
TEMPTABLENESS
TEMPTABLENESSES
TEMPTATION
TEMPTATIONS
TEMPTATIOUS
TEMPTINGLY
TEMPTINGNESS
TEMPTINGNESSES
TEMPTRESSES
TEMULENCES
TEMULENCIES
TEMULENTLY
TENABILITIES
TENABILITY
TENABLENESS
TENABLENESSES
TENACIOUSLY
TENACIOUSNESS
TENACIOUSNESSES
TENACITIES
TENACULUMS
TENAILLONS
TENANTABLE
TENANTLESS
TENANTRIES
TENANTSHIP
TENANTSHIPS
TENDENCIALLY
TENDENCIES
TENDENCIOUS
TENDENCIOUSLY
TENDENCIOUSNESS
TENDENTIAL
TENDENTIALLY
TENDENTIOUS
TENDENTIOUSLY
TENDENTIOUSNESS
TENDERABLE
TENDERFEET
TENDERFOOT
TENDERFOOTS
TENDERHEARTED
TENDERHEARTEDLY
TENDERINGS
TENDERISATION
TENDERISATIONS
TENDERISED
TENDERISER
TENDERISERS
TENDERISES
TENDERISING
TENDERIZATION
TENDERIZATIONS
TENDERIZED
TENDERIZER
TENDERIZERS
TENDERIZES
TENDERIZING
TENDERLING
TENDERLINGS
TENDERLOIN
TENDERLOINS
TENDERNESS
TENDERNESSES
TENDEROMETER
TENDEROMETERS
TENDINITIS
TENDINITISES
TENDONITIS
TENDONITISES
TENDOVAGINITIS
TENDRESSES
TENDRILLAR
TENDRILLED
TENDRILLOUS
TENDRILOUS
TENEBRIFIC
TENEBRIONID
TENEBRIONIDS
TENEBRIOUS
TENEBRIOUSNESS
TENEBRISMS
TENEBRISTS
TENEBRITIES
TENEBROSITIES
TENEBROSITY
TENEBROUSNESS
TENEBROUSNESSES
TENEMENTAL
TENEMENTARY
TENEMENTED
TENESMUSES
TENIACIDES
TENIAFUGES
TENNANTITE
TENNANTITES
TENORRHAPHIES
TENORRHAPHY
TENOSYNOVITIS
TENOSYNOVITISES
TENOTOMIES
TENOTOMIST
TENOTOMISTS
TENOVAGINITIS
TENOVAGINITISES
TENPOUNDER
TENPOUNDERS
TENSENESSES
TENSIBILITIES
TENSIBILITY
TENSIBLENESS
TENSIBLENESSES
TENSILENESS
TENSILENESSES
TENSILITIES
TENSIMETER
TENSIMETERS
TENSIOMETER
TENSIOMETERS
TENSIOMETRIC
TENSIOMETRIES
TENSIOMETRY
TENSIONALLY
TENSIONERS
TENSIONING
TENSIONLESS
TENTACULAR
TENTACULATE
TENTACULIFEROUS
TENTACULITE
TENTACULITES
TENTACULOID
TENTACULUM
TENTATIONS
TENTATIVELY
TENTATIVENESS
TENTATIVENESSES
TENTATIVES
TENTERHOOK
TENTERHOOKS
TENTIGINOUS
TENTMAKERS
TENTORIUMS
TENUIROSTRAL
TENUOUSNESS
TENUOUSNESSES
TENURIALLY
TEPEFACTION
TEPEFACTIONS
TEPHIGRAMS
TEPHROITES
TEPHROMANCIES
TEPHROMANCY
TEPIDARIUM
TEPIDITIES
TEPIDNESSES
TERAHERTZES
TERATOCARCINOMA
TERATOGENESES
TERATOGENESIS
TERATOGENIC
TERATOGENICIST
TERATOGENICISTS
TERATOGENICITY
TERATOGENIES
TERATOGENS
TERATOGENY
TERATOLOGIC
TERATOLOGICAL
TERATOLOGIES
TERATOLOGIST
TERATOLOGISTS
TERATOLOGY
TERATOMATA
TERATOMATOUS
TERATOPHOBIA
TERATOPHOBIAS
TERCENTENARIES
TERCENTENARY
TERCENTENNIAL
TERCENTENNIALS
TEREBINTHINE
TEREBINTHS
TEREBRANTS
TEREBRATED
TEREBRATES
TEREBRATING
TEREBRATION
TEREBRATIONS
TEREBRATULA
TEREBRATULAE
TEREBRATULAS
TEREPHTHALATE
TEREPHTHALATES
TEREPHTHALIC
TERGIVERSANT
TERGIVERSANTS
TERGIVERSATE
TERGIVERSATED
TERGIVERSATES
TERGIVERSATING
TERGIVERSATION
TERGIVERSATIONS
TERGIVERSATOR
TERGIVERSATORS
TERGIVERSATORY
TERMAGANCIES
TERMAGANCY

TERMAGANTLY
TERMAGANTS
TERMINABILITIES
TERMINABILITY
TERMINABLE
TERMINABLENESS
TERMINABLY
TERMINALLY
TERMINATED
TERMINATES
TERMINATING
TERMINATION
TERMINATIONAL
TERMINATIONS
TERMINATIVE
TERMINATIVELY
TERMINATOR
TERMINATORS
TERMINATORY
TERMINISMS
TERMINISTS
TERMINOLOGICAL
TERMINOLOGIES
TERMINOLOGIST
TERMINOLOGISTS
TERMINOLOGY
TERMINUSES
TERMITARIA
TERMITARIES
TERMITARIUM
TERMITARIUMS
TERNEPLATE
TERNEPLATES
TEROTECHNOLOGY
TERPENELESS
TERPENOIDS
TERPINEOLS
TERPOLYMER
TERPOLYMERS
TERPSICHOREAL
TERPSICHOREAN
TERRACELESS
TERRACETTE
TERRACETTES
TERRACINGS
TERRACOTTA
TERRACOTTAS
TERRAFORMED
TERRAFORMING
TERRAFORMINGS
TERRAFORMS
TERRAMARES
TERRAQUEOUS
TERRARIUMS
TERREMOTIVE
TERREPLEIN
TERREPLEINS
TERRESTRIAL
TERRESTRIALLY
TERRESTRIALNESS
TERRESTRIALS
TERRIBILITIES
TERRIBILITY
TERRIBLENESS
TERRIBLENESSES
TERRICOLES
TERRICOLOUS
TERRIFICALLY
TERRIFIERS
TERRIFYING
TERRIFYINGLY
TERRIGENOUS
TERRITORIAL
TERRITORIALISE
TERRITORIALISED
TERRITORIALISES
TERRITORIALISM
TERRITORIALISMS
TERRITORIALIST
TERRITORIALISTS
TERRITORIALITY
TERRITORIALIZE
TERRITORIALIZED
TERRITORIALIZES
TERRITORIALLY
TERRITORIALS
TERRITORIED
TERRITORIES
TERRORISATION
TERRORISATIONS
TERRORISED
TERRORISER
TERRORISERS
TERRORISES
TERRORISING
TERRORISMS
TERRORISTIC
TERRORISTS
TERRORIZATION
TERRORIZATIONS
TERRORIZED
TERRORIZER
TERRORIZERS
TERRORIZES
TERRORIZING
TERRORLESS
TERSANCTUS
TERSANCTUSES
TERSENESSES
TERTIARIES
TERVALENCIES
TERVALENCY
TESCHENITE
TESCHENITES
TESSARAGLOT
TESSELATED
TESSELATES
TESSELATING
TESSELLATE
TESSELLATED
TESSELLATES
TESSELLATING
TESSELLATION
TESSELLATIONS
TESSERACTS
TESSITURAS
TESTABILITIES
TESTABILITY
TESTACEANS
TESTACEOUS
TESTAMENTAL
TESTAMENTAR
TESTAMENTARILY
TESTAMENTARY
TESTAMENTS
TESTATIONS
TESTATRICES
TESTATRIXES
TESTCROSSED
TESTCROSSES
TESTCROSSING
TESTERNING
TESTICULAR
TESTICULATE
TESTICULATED
TESTIFICATE
TESTIFICATES
TESTIFICATION
TESTIFICATIONS
TESTIFICATOR
TESTIFICATORS
TESTIFICATORY
TESTIFIERS
TESTIFYING
TESTIMONIAL
TESTIMONIALISE
TESTIMONIALISED
TESTIMONIALISES
TESTIMONIALIZE
TESTIMONIALIZED
TESTIMONIALIZES
TESTIMONIALS
TESTIMONIED
TESTIMONIES
TESTIMONYING
TESTINESSES
TESTOSTERONE
TESTOSTERONES
TESTUDINAL
TESTUDINARY
TESTUDINEOUS
TESTUDINES
TETANICALLY
TETANISATION
TETANISATIONS
TETANISING
TETANIZATION
TETANIZATIONS
TETANIZING
TETARTOHEDRAL
TETARTOHEDRALLY
TETARTOHEDRISM
TETARTOHEDRISMS
TETCHINESS
TETCHINESSES
TETHERBALL
TETHERBALLS
TETRABASIC
TETRABASICITIES
TETRABASICITY
TETRABRACH
TETRABRACHS
TETRABRANCHIATE
TETRACAINE
TETRACAINES
TETRACHLORIDE
TETRACHLORIDES
TETRACHORD
TETRACHORDAL
TETRACHORDS
TETRACHOTOMIES
TETRACHOTOMOUS
TETRACHOTOMY
TETRACTINAL
TETRACTINE
TETRACYCLIC
TETRACYCLINE
TETRACYCLINES
TETRADACTYL
TETRADACTYLIES
TETRADACTYLOUS
TETRADACTYLS
TETRADACTYLY
TETRADITES
TETRADRACHM
TETRADRACHMS
TETRADYMITE
TETRADYMITES
TETRADYNAMOUS
TETRAETHYL
TETRAETHYLS
TETRAFLUORIDE
TETRAFLUORIDES
TETRAGONAL
TETRAGONALLY
TETRAGONALNESS
TETRAGONOUS
TETRAGRAMMATON
TETRAGRAMMATONS
TETRAGRAMS
TETRAGYNIAN
TETRAGYNOUS
TETRAHEDRA
TETRAHEDRAL
TETRAHEDRALLY
TETRAHEDRITE
TETRAHEDRITES
TETRAHEDRON
TETRAHEDRONS
TETRAHYDROFURAN
TETRAHYMENA
TETRAHYMENAS
TETRALOGIES
TETRAMERAL
TETRAMERIC
TETRAMERISM
TETRAMERISMS
TETRAMEROUS
TETRAMETER
TETRAMETERS
TETRAMETHYLLEAD
TETRAMORPHIC
TETRANDRIAN
TETRANDROUS
TETRAPLEGIA
TETRAPLEGIAS
TETRAPLEGIC
TETRAPLOID
TETRAPLOIDIES
TETRAPLOIDS
TETRAPLOIDY
TETRAPODIC
TETRAPODIES
TETRAPODOUS

TETRAPOLIS
TETRAPOLISES
TETRAPOLITAN
TETRAPTERAN
TETRAPTEROUS
TETRAPTOTE
TETRAPTOTES
TETRAPYRROLE
TETRAPYRROLES
TETRARCHATE
TETRARCHATES
TETRARCHIC
TETRARCHICAL
TETRARCHIES
TETRASEMIC
TETRASPORANGIA
TETRASPORANGIUM
TETRASPORE
TETRASPORES
TETRASPORIC
TETRASPOROUS
TETRASTICH
TETRASTICHAL
TETRASTICHIC
TETRASTICHOUS
TETRASTICHS
TETRASTYLE
TETRASTYLES
TETRASYLLABIC
TETRASYLLABICAL
TETRASYLLABLE
TETRASYLLABLES
TETRATHEISM
TETRATHEISMS
TETRATHLON
TETRATHLONS
TETRATOMIC
TETRAVALENCIES
TETRAVALENCY
TETRAVALENT
TETRAVALENTS
TETRAZOLIUM
TETRAZOLIUMS
TETRAZZINI
TETRODOTOXIN
TETRODOTOXINS
TETROTOXIN
TETROTOXINS
TETROXIDES
TEUTONISED
TEUTONISES
TEUTONISING
TEUTONIZED
TEUTONIZES
TEUTONIZING
TEXTBOOKISH
TEXTPHONES
TEXTUALISM
TEXTUALISMS
TEXTUALIST
TEXTUALISTS
TEXTUARIES
TEXTURALLY
TEXTURELESS
TEXTURISED
TEXTURISES
TEXTURISING
TEXTURIZED
TEXTURIZES
TEXTURIZING
THALAMENCEPHALA
THALAMICALLY
THALAMIFLORAL
THALASSAEMIA
THALASSAEMIAS
THALASSAEMIC
THALASSEMIA
THALASSEMIAS
THALASSEMIC
THALASSEMICS
THALASSIAN
THALASSIANS
THALASSOCRACIES
THALASSOCRACY
THALASSOCRAT
THALASSOCRATS
THALASSOGRAPHER
THALASSOGRAPHIC
THALASSOGRAPHY
THALASSOTHERAPY
THALATTOCRACIES
THALATTOCRACY
THALICTRUM
THALICTRUMS
THALIDOMIDE
THALIDOMIDES
THALLIFORM
THALLOPHYTE
THALLOPHYTES
THALLOPHYTIC
THANATISMS
THANATISTS
THANATOGNOMONIC
THANATOGRAPHIES
THANATOGRAPHY
THANATOLOGICAL
THANATOLOGIES
THANATOLOGIST
THANATOLOGISTS
THANATOLOGY
THANATOPHOBIA
THANATOPHOBIAS
THANATOPSES
THANATOPSIS
THANATOSES
THANATOSIS
THANEHOODS
THANESHIPS
THANKFULLER
THANKFULLEST
THANKFULLY
THANKFULNESS
THANKFULNESSES
THANKLESSLY
THANKLESSNESS
THANKLESSNESSES
THANKSGIVER
THANKSGIVERS
THANKSGIVING
THANKSGIVINGS
THANKWORTHILY
THANKWORTHINESS
THANKWORTHY
THARBOROUGH
THARBOROUGHS
THATCHIEST
THATCHINGS
THATCHLESS
THATNESSES
THAUMASITE
THAUMASITES
THAUMATINS
THAUMATOGENIES
THAUMATOGENY
THAUMATOGRAPHY
THAUMATOLATRIES
THAUMATOLATRY
THAUMATOLOGIES
THAUMATOLOGY
THAUMATROPE
THAUMATROPES
THAUMATROPICAL
THAUMATURGE
THAUMATURGES
THAUMATURGIC
THAUMATURGICAL
THAUMATURGICS
THAUMATURGIES
THAUMATURGISM
THAUMATURGISMS
THAUMATURGIST
THAUMATURGISTS
THAUMATURGUS
THAUMATURGUSES
THAUMATURGY
THEANTHROPIC
THEANTHROPIES
THEANTHROPISM
THEANTHROPISMS
THEANTHROPIST
THEANTHROPISTS
THEANTHROPY
THEARCHIES
THEATERGOER
THEATERGOERS
THEATERGOING
THEATERGOINGS
THEATREGOER
THEATREGOERS
THEATREGOING
THEATREGOINGS
THEATRICAL
THEATRICALISE
THEATRICALISED
THEATRICALISES
THEATRICALISING
THEATRICALISM
THEATRICALISMS
THEATRICALITIES
THEATRICALITY
THEATRICALIZE
THEATRICALIZED
THEATRICALIZES
THEATRICALIZING
THEATRICALLY
THEATRICALNESS
THEATRICALS
THEATRICISE
THEATRICISED
THEATRICISES
THEATRICISING
THEATRICISM
THEATRICISMS
THEATRICIZE
THEATRICIZED
THEATRICIZES
THEATRICIZING
THEATROMANIA
THEATROMANIAS
THEATROPHONE
THEATROPHONES
THECODONTS
THEFTUOUSLY
THEIRSELVES
THEISTICAL
THEISTICALLY
THELEMENTS
THELITISES
THELYTOKIES
THELYTOKOUS
THEMATICALLY
THEMATISATION
THEMATISATIONS
THEMATIZATION
THEMATIZATIONS
THEMSELVES
THENABOUTS
THENARDITE
THENARDITES
THENCEFORTH
THENCEFORWARD
THENCEFORWARDS
THEOBROMINE
THEOBROMINES
THEOCENTRIC
THEOCENTRICISM
THEOCENTRICISMS
THEOCENTRICITY
THEOCENTRISM
THEOCENTRISMS
THEOCRACIES
THEOCRASIES
THEOCRATIC
THEOCRATICAL
THEOCRATICALLY
THEODICEAN
THEODICEANS
THEODICIES
THEODOLITE
THEODOLITES
THEODOLITIC
THEOGONICAL
THEOGONIES
THEOGONIST
THEOGONISTS
THEOLOGASTER
THEOLOGASTERS
THEOLOGATE
THEOLOGATES
THEOLOGERS
THEOLOGIAN
THEOLOGIANS
THEOLOGICAL
THEOLOGICALLY

THEOLOGIES
THEOLOGISATION
THEOLOGISATIONS
THEOLOGISE
THEOLOGISED
THEOLOGISER
THEOLOGISERS
THEOLOGISES
THEOLOGISING
THEOLOGIST
THEOLOGISTS
THEOLOGIZATION
THEOLOGIZATIONS
THEOLOGIZE
THEOLOGIZED
THEOLOGIZER
THEOLOGIZERS
THEOLOGIZES
THEOLOGIZING
THEOLOGOUMENA
THEOLOGOUMENON
THEOLOGUES
THEOMACHIES
THEOMACHIST
THEOMACHISTS
THEOMANCIES
THEOMANIAC
THEOMANIACS
THEOMANIAS
THEOMANTIC
THEOMORPHIC
THEOMORPHISM
THEOMORPHISMS
THEONOMIES
THEONOMOUS
THEOPATHETIC
THEOPATHIC
THEOPATHIES
THEOPHAGIES
THEOPHAGOUS
THEOPHANIC
THEOPHANIES
THEOPHANOUS
THEOPHOBIA
THEOPHOBIAC
THEOPHOBIACS
THEOPHOBIAS
THEOPHOBIST
THEOPHOBISTS
THEOPHORIC
THEOPHYLLINE
THEOPHYLLINES
THEOPNEUST
THEOPNEUSTIC
THEOPNEUSTIES
THEOPNEUSTY
THEORBISTS
THEOREMATIC
THEOREMATICAL
THEOREMATICALLY
THEOREMATIST
THEOREMATISTS
THEORETICAL
THEORETICALLY
THEORETICIAN
THEORETICIANS
THEORETICS
THEORIQUES
THEORISATION
THEORISATIONS
THEORISERS
THEORISING
THEORIZATION
THEORIZATIONS
THEORIZERS
THEORIZING
THEOSOPHER
THEOSOPHERS
THEOSOPHIC
THEOSOPHICAL
THEOSOPHICALLY
THEOSOPHIES
THEOSOPHISE
THEOSOPHISED
THEOSOPHISES
THEOSOPHISING
THEOSOPHISM
THEOSOPHISMS
THEOSOPHIST
THEOSOPHISTICAL
THEOSOPHISTS
THEOSOPHIZE
THEOSOPHIZED
THEOSOPHIZES
THEOSOPHIZING
THEOTECHNIC
THEOTECHNIES
THEOTECHNY
THERALITES
THERAPEUSES
THERAPEUSIS
THERAPEUTIC
THERAPEUTICALLY
THERAPEUTICS
THERAPEUTIST
THERAPEUTISTS
THERAPISTS
THERAPSIDS
THEREABOUT
THEREABOUTS
THEREAFTER
THEREAGAINST
THEREAMONG
THEREANENT
THEREBESIDE
THEREINAFTER
THEREINBEFORE
THERENESSES
THERETHROUGH
THERETOFORE
THEREUNDER
THEREWITHAL
THEREWITHIN
THERIANTHROPIC
THERIANTHROPISM
THERIOLATRIES
THERIOLATRY
THERIOMORPH
THERIOMORPHIC
THERIOMORPHISM
THERIOMORPHISMS
THERIOMORPHOSES
THERIOMORPHOSIS
THERIOMORPHOUS
THERIOMORPHS
THERMAESTHESIA
THERMAESTHESIAS
THERMALISATION
THERMALISATIONS
THERMALISE
THERMALISED
THERMALISES
THERMALISING
THERMALIZATION
THERMALIZATIONS
THERMALIZE
THERMALIZED
THERMALIZES
THERMALIZING
THERMESTHESIA
THERMESTHESIAS
THERMETTES
THERMICALLY
THERMIDORS
THERMIONIC
THERMIONICS
THERMISTOR
THERMISTORS
THERMOBALANCE
THERMOBALANCES
THERMOBARIC
THERMOBAROGRAPH
THERMOBAROMETER
THERMOCHEMICAL
THERMOCHEMIST
THERMOCHEMISTRY
THERMOCHEMISTS
THERMOCHROMIC
THERMOCHROMIES
THERMOCHROMISM
THERMOCHROMISMS
THERMOCHROMY
THERMOCLINE
THERMOCLINES
THERMOCOUPLE
THERMOCOUPLES
THERMODURIC
THERMODYNAMIC
THERMODYNAMICAL
THERMODYNAMICS
THERMOELECTRIC
THERMOELECTRON
THERMOELECTRONS
THERMOELEMENT
THERMOELEMENTS
THERMOFORM
THERMOFORMABLE
THERMOFORMED
THERMOFORMING
THERMOFORMS
THERMOGENESES
THERMOGENESIS
THERMOGENETIC
THERMOGENIC
THERMOGENOUS
THERMOGRAM
THERMOGRAMS
THERMOGRAPH
THERMOGRAPHER
THERMOGRAPHERS
THERMOGRAPHIC
THERMOGRAPHIES
THERMOGRAPHS
THERMOGRAPHY
THERMOHALINE
THERMOJUNCTION
THERMOJUNCTIONS
THERMOLABILE
THERMOLABILITY
THERMOLOGIES
THERMOLOGY
THERMOLYSES
THERMOLYSIS
THERMOLYTIC
THERMOMAGNETIC
THERMOMETER
THERMOMETERS
THERMOMETRIC
THERMOMETRICAL
THERMOMETRIES
THERMOMETRY
THERMOMOTOR
THERMOMOTORS
THERMONASTIES
THERMONASTY
THERMONUCLEAR
THERMOPERIODIC
THERMOPERIODISM
THERMOPHIL
THERMOPHILE
THERMOPHILES
THERMOPHILIC
THERMOPHILOUS
THERMOPHILS
THERMOPHYLLOUS
THERMOPILE
THERMOPILES
THERMOPLASTIC
THERMOPLASTICS
THERMORECEPTOR
THERMORECEPTORS
THERMOREGULATE
THERMOREGULATED
THERMOREGULATES
THERMOREGULATOR
THERMOREMANENCE
THERMOREMANENT
THERMOSCOPE
THERMOSCOPES
THERMOSCOPIC
THERMOSCOPICAL
THERMOSETS
THERMOSETTING
THERMOSIPHON
THERMOSIPHONS
THERMOSPHERE
THERMOSPHERES
THERMOSPHERIC
THERMOSTABILITY
THERMOSTABLE
THERMOSTAT
THERMOSTATED
THERMOSTATIC
THERMOSTATICS

THERMOSTATING
THERMOSTATS
THERMOSTATTED
THERMOSTATTING
THERMOTACTIC
THERMOTAXES
THERMOTAXIC
THERMOTAXIS
THERMOTENSILE
THERMOTHERAPIES
THERMOTHERAPY
THERMOTICAL
THERMOTICS
THERMOTOLERANT
THERMOTROPIC
THERMOTROPICS
THERMOTROPISM
THERMOTROPISMS
THEROLOGIES
THEROPHYTE
THEROPHYTES
THEROPODAN
THEROPODANS
THERSITICAL
THESAURUSES
THESMOTHETE
THESMOTHETES
THETICALLY
THEURGICAL
THEURGICALLY
THEURGISTS
THIABENDAZOLE
THIABENDAZOLES
THIAMINASE
THIAMINASES
THICKENERS
THICKENING
THICKENINGS
THICKHEADED
THICKHEADEDNESS
THICKHEADS
THICKLEAVES
THICKNESSES
THICKSKINS
THIEVERIES
THIEVISHLY
THIEVISHNESS
THIEVISHNESSES
THIGHBONES
THIGMOTACTIC
THIGMOTAXES
THIGMOTAXIS
THIGMOTROPIC
THIGMOTROPISM
THIGMOTROPISMS
THIMBLEBERRIES
THIMBLEBERRY
THIMBLEFUL
THIMBLEFULS
THIMBLERIG
THIMBLERIGGED
THIMBLERIGGER
THIMBLERIGGERS
THIMBLERIGGING
THIMBLERIGGINGS
THIMBLERIGS
THIMBLESFUL
THIMBLEWEED
THIMBLEWEEDS
THIMBLEWIT
THIMBLEWITS
THIMBLEWITTED
THIMEROSAL
THIMEROSALS
THINGAMABOB
THINGAMABOBS
THINGAMAJIG
THINGAMAJIGS
THINGAMIES
THINGAMYBOB
THINGAMYBOBS
THINGAMYJIG
THINGAMYJIGS
THINGHOODS
THINGINESS
THINGINESSES
THINGLINESS
THINGLINESSES
THINGNESSES
THINGUMABOB
THINGUMABOBS
THINGUMAJIG
THINGUMAJIGS
THINGUMBOB
THINGUMBOBS
THINGUMMIES
THINGUMMYBOB
THINGUMMYBOBS
THINGUMMYJIG
THINGUMMYJIGS
THINKABLENESS
THINKABLENESSES
THINKINGLY
THINKINGNESS
THINKINGNESSES
THINKPIECE
THINKPIECES
THINNESSES
THIOALCOHOL
THIOALCOHOLS
THIOBACILLI
THIOBACILLUS
THIOBARBITURATE
THIOCARBAMIDE
THIOCARBAMIDES
THIOCYANATE
THIOCYANATES
THIOCYANIC
THIODIGLYCOL
THIODIGLYCOLS
THIOFURANS
THIOPENTAL
THIOPENTALS
THIOPENTONE
THIOPENTONES
THIOPHENES
THIORIDAZINE
THIORIDAZINES
THIOSINAMINE
THIOSINAMINES
THIOSULFATE
THIOSULFATES
THIOSULPHATE
THIOSULPHATES
THIOSULPHURIC
THIOURACIL
THIOURACILS
THIRDBOROUGH
THIRDBOROUGHS
THIRDSTREAM
THIRDSTREAMS
THIRSTIEST
THIRSTINESS
THIRSTINESSES
THIRSTLESS
THIRTEENTH
THIRTEENTHLY
THIRTEENTHS
THIRTIETHS
THIRTYFOLD
THIRTYSOMETHING
THISNESSES
THISTLEDOWN
THISTLEDOWNS
THISTLIEST
THITHERWARD
THITHERWARDS
THIXOTROPE
THIXOTROPES
THIXOTROPIC
THIXOTROPIES
THIXOTROPY
THOLEIITES
THOLEIITIC
THOLOBATES
THORACENTESES
THORACENTESIS
THORACICALLY
THORACOCENTESES
THORACOCENTESIS
THORACOPLASTIES
THORACOPLASTY
THORACOSCOPE
THORACOSCOPES
THORACOSTOMIES
THORACOSTOMY
THORACOTOMIES
THORACOTOMY
THORIANITE
THORIANITES
THORNBACKS
THORNBILLS
THORNBUSHES
THORNHEDGE
THORNHEDGES
THORNINESS
THORNINESSES
THORNPROOFS
THORNTREES
THOROUGHBASS
THOROUGHBASSES
THOROUGHBRACE
THOROUGHBRACED
THOROUGHBRACES
THOROUGHBRED
THOROUGHBREDS
THOROUGHER
THOROUGHEST
THOROUGHFARE
THOROUGHFARES
THOROUGHGOING
THOROUGHGOINGLY
THOROUGHLY
THOROUGHNESS
THOROUGHNESSES
THOROUGHPACED
THOROUGHPIN
THOROUGHPINS
THOROUGHWAX
THOROUGHWAXES
THOROUGHWORT
THOROUGHWORTS
THOUGHTCAST
THOUGHTCASTS
THOUGHTFUL
THOUGHTFULLY
THOUGHTFULNESS
THOUGHTLESS
THOUGHTLESSLY
THOUGHTLESSNESS
THOUGHTWAY
THOUGHTWAYS
THOUSANDFOLD
THOUSANDFOLDS
THOUSANDTH
THOUSANDTHS
THRAIPINGS
THRALLDOMS
THRAPPLING
THRASHINGS
THRASONICAL
THRASONICALLY
THREADBARE
THREADBARENESS
THREADFINS
THREADIEST
THREADINESS
THREADINESSES
THREADLESS
THREADLIKE
THREADMAKER
THREADMAKERS
THREADWORM
THREADWORMS
THREATENED
THREATENER
THREATENERS
THREATENING
THREATENINGLY
THREATENINGS
THREEFOLDNESS
THREEFOLDNESSES
THREENESSES
THREEPENCE
THREEPENCES
THREEPENCEWORTH
THREEPENNIES
THREEPENNY
THREEPENNYWORTH
THREESCORE
THREESCORES
THREESOMES
THREMMATOLOGIES
THREMMATOLOGY

THRENETICAL
THRENODIAL
THRENODIES
THRENODIST
THRENODISTS
THREONINES
THRESHINGS
THRESHOLDS
THRIFTIEST
THRIFTINESS
THRIFTINESSES
THRIFTLESS
THRIFTLESSLY
THRIFTLESSNESS
THRILLIEST
THRILLINGLY
THRILLINGNESS
THRILLINGNESSES
THRIVELESS
THRIVINGLY
THRIVINGNESS
THRIVINGNESSES
THROATIEST
THROATINESS
THROATINESSES
THROATLASH
THROATLASHES
THROATLATCH
THROATLATCHES
THROATWORT
THROATWORTS
THROBBINGLY
THROBBINGS
THROMBOCYTE
THROMBOCYTES
THROMBOCYTIC
THROMBOEMBOLIC
THROMBOEMBOLISM
THROMBOGEN
THROMBOGENS
THROMBOKINASE
THROMBOKINASES
THROMBOLYSES
THROMBOLYSIS
THROMBOLYTIC
THROMBOLYTICS
THROMBOPHILIA
THROMBOPHILIAS
THROMBOPLASTIC
THROMBOPLASTIN
THROMBOPLASTINS
THROMBOSED
THROMBOSES
THROMBOSING
THROMBOSIS
THROMBOTIC
THROMBOXANE
THROMBOXANES
THRONELESS
THRONGINGS
THROPPLING
THROTTLEABLE
THROTTLEHOLD
THROTTLEHOLDS
THROTTLERS
THROTTLING
THROTTLINGS
THROUGHFARE
THROUGHFARES
THROUGHGAUN
THROUGHGAUNS
THROUGHITHER
THROUGHOTHER
THROUGHOUT
THROUGHPUT
THROUGHPUTS
THROUGHWAY
THROUGHWAYS
THROWAWAYS
THROWBACKS
THROWSTERS
THRUMMIEST
THRUMMINGLY
THRUMMINGS
THRUPPENCE
THRUPPENCES
THRUPPENNIES
THRUPPENNY
THRUSTINGS
THRUTCHING
THUDDINGLY
THUGGERIES
THUMBHOLES
THUMBIKINS
THUMBLINGS
THUMBNAILS
THUMBPIECE
THUMBPIECES
THUMBPRINT
THUMBPRINTS
THUMBSCREW
THUMBSCREWS
THUMBSTALL
THUMBSTALLS
THUMBTACKED
THUMBTACKING
THUMBTACKS
THUMBWHEEL
THUMBWHEELS
THUMPINGLY
THUNBERGIA
THUNBERGIAS
THUNDERBIRD
THUNDERBIRDS
THUNDERBOLT
THUNDERBOLTS
THUNDERBOX
THUNDERBOXES
THUNDERCLAP
THUNDERCLAPS
THUNDERCLOUD
THUNDERCLOUDS
THUNDERERS
THUNDERFLASH
THUNDERFLASHES
THUNDERHEAD
THUNDERHEADS
THUNDERIER
THUNDERIEST
THUNDERING
THUNDERINGLY
THUNDERINGS
THUNDERLESS
THUNDEROUS
THUNDEROUSLY
THUNDEROUSNESS
THUNDERSHOWER
THUNDERSHOWERS
THUNDERSTONE
THUNDERSTONES
THUNDERSTORM
THUNDERSTORMS
THUNDERSTRICKEN
THUNDERSTRIKE
THUNDERSTRIKES
THUNDERSTRIKING
THUNDERSTROKE
THUNDERSTROKES
THUNDERSTRUCK
THURIFEROUS
THURIFICATION
THURIFICATIONS
THURIFYING
THUSNESSES
THWACKINGS
THWARTEDLY
THWARTINGLY
THWARTINGS
THWARTSHIP
THWARTSHIPS
THWARTWAYS
THWARTWISE
THYLACINES
THYLAKOIDS
THYMECTOMIES
THYMECTOMISE
THYMECTOMISED
THYMECTOMISES
THYMECTOMISING
THYMECTOMIZE
THYMECTOMIZED
THYMECTOMIZES
THYMECTOMIZING
THYMECTOMY
THYMELAEACEOUS
THYMIDINES
THYMIDYLIC
THYMOCYTES
THYRATRONS
THYRISTORS
THYROCALCITONIN
THYROGLOBULIN
THYROGLOBULINS
THYROIDECTOMIES
THYROIDECTOMY
THYROIDITIS
THYROIDITISES
THYROTOXICOSES
THYROTOXICOSIS
THYROTROPHIC
THYROTROPHIN
THYROTROPHINS
THYROTROPIC
THYROTROPIN
THYROTROPINS
THYROXINES
THYRSOIDAL
THYSANOPTEROUS
THYSANURAN
THYSANURANS
THYSANUROUS
TIBIOFIBULA
TIBIOFIBULAE
TIBIOFIBULAS
TIBIOTARSI
TIBIOTARSUS
TIBOUCHINA
TIBOUCHINAS
TICHORRHINE
TICKETLESS
TICKETTYBOO
TICKLISHLY
TICKLISHNESS
TICKLISHNESSES
TICKTACKED
TICKTACKING
TICKTACKTOE
TICKTACKTOES
TICKTOCKED
TICKTOCKING
TICTACKING
TICTOCKING
TIDDLEDYWINK
TIDDLEDYWINKS
TIDDLEYWINK
TIDDLEYWINKS
TIDDLYWINK
TIDDLYWINKS
TIDEWAITER
TIDEWAITERS
TIDEWATERS
TIDINESSES
TIDIVATING
TIDIVATION
TIDIVATIONS
TIEBREAKER
TIEBREAKERS
TIEMANNITE
TIEMANNITES
TIERCELETS
TIERCERONS
TIGERISHLY
TIGERISHNESS
TIGERISHNESSES
TIGGYWINKLE
TIGGYWINKLES
TIGHTASSED
TIGHTASSES
TIGHTENERS
TIGHTENING
TIGHTFISTED
TIGHTFISTEDNESS
TIGHTISHLY
TIGHTNESSES
TIGHTROPES
TIGHTWIRES
TIGRISHNESS
TIGRISHNESSES
TIKOLOSHES
TILEFISHES
TILIACEOUS
TILLANDSIA
TILLANDSIAS
TILLERLESS

TILTMETERS
TILTROTORS
TIMBERDOODLE
TIMBERDOODLES
TIMBERHEAD
TIMBERHEADS
TIMBERINGS
TIMBERLAND
TIMBERLANDS
TIMBERLINE
TIMBERLINES
TIMBERWORK
TIMBERWORKS
TIMBERYARD
TIMBERYARDS
TIMBRELLED
TIMBROLOGIES
TIMBROLOGIST
TIMBROLOGISTS
TIMBROLOGY
TIMBROMANIA
TIMBROMANIAC
TIMBROMANIACS
TIMBROMANIAS
TIMBROPHILIES
TIMBROPHILIST
TIMBROPHILISTS
TIMBROPHILY
TIMEFRAMES
TIMEKEEPER
TIMEKEEPERS
TIMEKEEPING
TIMEKEEPINGS
TIMELESSLY
TIMELESSNESS
TIMELESSNESSES
TIMELINESS
TIMELINESSES
TIMENOGUYS
TIMEPASSED
TIMEPASSES
TIMEPASSING
TIMEPIECES
TIMEPLEASER
TIMEPLEASERS
TIMESAVERS
TIMESAVING
TIMESCALES
TIMESERVER
TIMESERVERS
TIMESERVING
TIMESERVINGS
TIMETABLED
TIMETABLES
TIMETABLING
TIMEWORKER
TIMEWORKERS
TIMIDITIES
TIMIDNESSES
TIMOCRACIES
TIMOCRATIC
TIMOCRATICAL
TIMOROUSLY
TIMOROUSNESS
TIMOROUSNESSES
TIMPANISTS

TINCTORIAL
TINCTORIALLY
TINCTURING
TINDERBOXES
TINGLINGLY
TINGUAITES
TININESSES
TINKERINGS
TINKERTOYS
TINKLINGLY
TINNINESSES
TINNITUSES
TINPLATING
TINSELLING
TINSELRIES
TINSMITHING
TINSMITHINGS
TINTINESSES
TINTINNABULA
TINTINNABULANT
TINTINNABULAR
TINTINNABULARY
TINTINNABULATE
TINTINNABULATED
TINTINNABULATES
TINTINNABULOUS
TINTINNABULUM
TINTOMETER
TINTOMETERS
TINTOOKIES
TIPPYTOEING
TIPSIFYING
TIPSINESSES
TIPTRONICS
TIRAILLEUR
TIRAILLEURS
TIREDNESSES
TIRELESSLY
TIRELESSNESS
TIRELESSNESSES
TIRESOMELY
TIRESOMENESS
TIRESOMENESSES
TIROCINIUM
TIROCINIUMS
TITANESSES
TITANICALLY
TITANIFEROUS
TITANOSAUR
TITANOSAURS
TITANOTHERE
TITANOTHERES
TITARAKURA
TITARAKURAS
TITHINGMAN
TITHINGMEN
TITILLATED
TITILLATES
TITILLATING
TITILLATINGLY
TITILLATION
TITILLATIONS
TITILLATIVE
TITILLATOR
TITILLATORS
TITIPOUNAMU

TITIVATING
TITIVATION
TITIVATIONS
TITIVATORS
TITLEHOLDER
TITLEHOLDERS
TITLEHOLDING
TITRATABLE
TITRATIONS
TITRIMETRIC
TITTERINGLY
TITTERINGS
TITTIVATED
TITTIVATES
TITTIVATING
TITTIVATION
TITTIVATIONS
TITTIVATOR
TITTIVATORS
TITTLEBATS
TITTUPPING
TITUBANCIES
TITUBATING
TITUBATION
TITUBATIONS
TITULARIES
TITULARITIES
TITULARITY
TOADEATERS
TOADFISHES
TOADFLAXES
TOADGRASSES
TOADRUSHES
TOADSTONES
TOADSTOOLS
TOASTMASTER
TOASTMASTERS
TOASTMISTRESS
TOASTMISTRESSES
TOBACCANALIAN
TOBACCANALIANS
TOBACCOLESS
TOBACCONIST
TOBACCONISTS
TOBOGGANED
TOBOGGANER
TOBOGGANERS
TOBOGGANING
TOBOGGANINGS
TOBOGGANIST
TOBOGGANISTS
TOBOGGINED
TOBOGGINING
TOCCATELLA
TOCCATELLAS
TOCCATINAS
TOCHERLESS
TOCOLOGIES
TOCOPHEROL
TOCOPHEROLS
TODDLERHOOD
TODDLERHOODS
TOENAILING
TOERAGGERS
TOFFISHNESS
TOFFISHNESSES

TOGAVIRUSES
TOGETHERNESS
TOGETHERNESSES
TOILETRIES
TOILFULNESS
TOILFULNESSES
TOILINETTE
TOILINETTES
TOILSOMELY
TOILSOMENESS
TOILSOMENESSES
TOKENISTIC
TOKOLOGIES
TOKOLOSHES
TOKOLOSHIS
TOKTOKKIES
TOLBUTAMIDE
TOLBUTAMIDES
TOLERABILITIES
TOLERABILITY
TOLERABLENESS
TOLERABLENESSES
TOLERANCES
TOLERANTLY
TOLERATING
TOLERATION
TOLERATIONISM
TOLERATIONISMS
TOLERATIONIST
TOLERATIONISTS
TOLERATIONS
TOLERATIVE
TOLERATORS
TOLLBOOTHS
TOLLBRIDGE
TOLLBRIDGES
TOLLDISHES
TOLLHOUSES
TOLUIDIDES
TOLUIDINES
TOMAHAWKED
TOMAHAWKING
TOMATILLOES
TOMATILLOS
TOMBOYISHLY
TOMBOYISHNESS
TOMBOYISHNESSES
TOMBSTONES
TOMCATTING
TOMFOOLERIES
TOMFOOLERY
TOMFOOLING
TOMFOOLISH
TOMFOOLISHNESS
TOMOGRAPHIC
TOMOGRAPHIES
TOMOGRAPHS
TOMOGRAPHY
TONALITIES
TONALITIVE
TONELESSLY
TONELESSNESS
TONELESSNESSES
TONETICALLY
TONGUELESS
TONGUELETS

TONGUELIKE
TONGUESTER
TONGUESTERS
TONICITIES
TONISHNESS
TONISHNESSES
TONNISHNESS
TONNISHNESSES
TONOMETERS
TONOMETRIC
TONOMETRIES
TONOPLASTS
TONSILITIS
TONSILITISES
TONSILLARY
TONSILLECTOMIES
TONSILLECTOMY
TONSILLITIC
TONSILLITIS
TONSILLITISES
TONSILLOTOMIES
TONSILLOTOMY
TOOLHOLDER
TOOLHOLDERS
TOOLHOUSES
TOOLMAKERS
TOOLMAKING
TOOLMAKINGS
TOOLPUSHER
TOOLPUSHERS
TOOTHACHES
TOOTHBRUSH
TOOTHBRUSHES
TOOTHBRUSHING
TOOTHBRUSHINGS
TOOTHCOMBS
TOOTHFISHES
TOOTHINESS
TOOTHINESSES
TOOTHPASTE
TOOTHPASTES
TOOTHPICKS
TOOTHSHELL
TOOTHSHELLS
TOOTHSOMELY
TOOTHSOMENESS
TOOTHSOMENESSES
TOOTHWASHES
TOOTHWORTS
TOPAGNOSES
TOPAGNOSIA
TOPAGNOSIAS
TOPAGNOSIS
TOPARCHIES
TOPAZOLITE
TOPAZOLITES
TOPCROSSES
TOPDRESSING
TOPDRESSINGS
TOPECTOMIES
TOPGALLANT
TOPGALLANTS
TOPHACEOUS
TOPHEAVINESS
TOPHEAVINESSES
TOPIARISTS
TOPICALITIES
TOPICALITY
TOPKNOTTED
TOPLESSNESS
TOPLESSNESSES
TOPLOFTICAL
TOPLOFTIER
TOPLOFTIEST
TOPLOFTILY
TOPLOFTINESS
TOPLOFTINESSES
TOPMAKINGS
TOPMINNOWS
TOPNOTCHER
TOPNOTCHERS
TOPOCENTRIC
TOPOCHEMISTRIES
TOPOCHEMISTRY
TOPOGRAPHER
TOPOGRAPHERS
TOPOGRAPHIC
TOPOGRAPHICAL
TOPOGRAPHICALLY
TOPOGRAPHIES
TOPOGRAPHS
TOPOGRAPHY
TOPOLOGICAL
TOPOLOGICALLY
TOPOLOGIES
TOPOLOGIST
TOPOLOGISTS
TOPONYMICAL
TOPONYMICS
TOPONYMIES
TOPONYMIST
TOPONYMISTS
TOPOPHILIA
TOPOPHILIAS
TOPSOILING
TOPSOILINGS
TOPSTITCHED
TOPSTITCHES
TOPSTITCHING
TOPWORKING
TORBANITES
TORBERNITE
TORBERNITES
TORCHBEARER
TORCHBEARERS
TORCHIERES
TORCHLIGHT
TORCHLIGHTS
TORCHWOODS
TORMENTEDLY
TORMENTERS
TORMENTILS
TORMENTING
TORMENTINGLY
TORMENTINGS
TORMENTORS
TORMENTUMS
TOROIDALLY
TOROSITIES
TORPEDINOUS
TORPEDOERS
TORPEDOING
TORPEDOIST
TORPEDOISTS
TORPEFYING
TORPESCENCE
TORPESCENCES
TORPESCENT
TORPIDITIES
TORPIDNESS
TORPIDNESSES
TORPITUDES
TORPORIFIC
TORREFACTION
TORREFACTIONS
TORREFYING
TORRENTIAL
TORRENTIALITIES
TORRENTIALITY
TORRENTIALLY
TORRENTUOUS
TORRIDITIES
TORRIDNESS
TORRIDNESSES
TORRIFYING
TORSIBILITIES
TORSIBILITY
TORSIOGRAPH
TORSIOGRAPHS
TORSIONALLY
TORTELLINI
TORTELLINIS
TORTFEASOR
TORTFEASORS
TORTICOLLAR
TORTICOLLIS
TORTICOLLISES
TORTILITIES
TORTILLONS
TORTIOUSLY
TORTOISESHELL
TORTOISESHELLS
TORTRICIDS
TORTUOSITIES
TORTUOSITY
TORTUOUSLY
TORTUOUSNESS
TORTUOUSNESSES
TORTUREDLY
TORTURESOME
TORTURINGLY
TORTURINGS
TORTUROUSLY
TOSSICATED
TOSTICATED
TOSTICATION
TOSTICATIONS
TOTALISATION
TOTALISATIONS
TOTALISATOR
TOTALISATORS
TOTALISERS
TOTALISING
TOTALISTIC
TOTALITARIAN
TOTALITARIANISE
TOTALITARIANISM
TOTALITARIANIZE
TOTALITARIANS
TOTALITIES
TOTALIZATION
TOTALIZATIONS
TOTALIZATOR
TOTALIZATORS
TOTALIZERS
TOTALIZING
TOTAQUINES
TOTEMICALLY
TOTEMISTIC
TOTIPALMATE
TOTIPALMATION
TOTIPALMATIONS
TOTIPOTENCIES
TOTIPOTENCY
TOTIPOTENT
TOTTERINGLY
TOTTERINGS
TOUCHABLENESS
TOUCHABLENESSES
TOUCHBACKS
TOUCHDOWNS
TOUCHHOLES
TOUCHINESS
TOUCHINESSES
TOUCHINGLY
TOUCHINGNESS
TOUCHINGNESSES
TOUCHLINES
TOUCHMARKS
TOUCHPAPER
TOUCHPAPERS
TOUCHSTONE
TOUCHSTONES
TOUCHTONES
TOUCHWOODS
TOUGHENERS
TOUGHENING
TOUGHENINGS
TOUGHNESSES
TOURBILLION
TOURBILLIONS
TOURBILLON
TOURBILLONS
TOURISTICALLY
TOURMALINE
TOURMALINES
TOURMALINIC
TOURNAMENT
TOURNAMENTS
TOURNEYERS
TOURNEYING
TOURNIQUET
TOURNIQUETS
TOURTIERES
TOVARICHES
TOVARISCHES
TOVARISHES
TOWARDLINESS
TOWARDLINESSES
TOWARDNESS
TOWARDNESSES
TOWELETTES
TOWELHEADS
TOWELLINGS

TOWERINGLY
TOWNHOUSES
TOWNSCAPED
TOWNSCAPES
TOWNSCAPING
TOWNSCAPINGS
TOWNSFOLKS
TOWNSPEOPLE
TOWNSPEOPLES
TOWNSWOMAN
TOWNSWOMEN
TOXALBUMIN
TOXALBUMINS
TOXAPHENES
TOXICATION
TOXICATIONS
TOXICITIES
TOXICOGENIC
TOXICOLOGIC
TOXICOLOGICAL
TOXICOLOGICALLY
TOXICOLOGIES
TOXICOLOGIST
TOXICOLOGISTS
TOXICOLOGY
TOXICOMANIA
TOXICOMANIAS
TOXICOPHAGOUS
TOXICOPHOBIA
TOXICOPHOBIAS
TOXIGENICITIES
TOXIGENICITY
TOXIPHAGOUS
TOXIPHOBIA
TOXIPHOBIAC
TOXIPHOBIACS
TOXIPHOBIAS
TOXOCARIASES
TOXOCARIASIS
TOXOPHILIES
TOXOPHILITE
TOXOPHILITES
TOXOPHILITIC
TOXOPLASMA
TOXOPLASMAS
TOXOPLASMIC
TOXOPLASMOSES
TOXOPLASMOSIS
TOYISHNESS
TOYISHNESSES
TRABEATION
TRABEATIONS
TRABECULAE
TRABECULAR
TRABECULAS
TRABECULATE
TRABECULATED
TRACASSERIE
TRACASSERIES
TRACEABILITIES
TRACEABILITY
TRACEABLENESS
TRACEABLENESSES
TRACELESSLY
TRACHEARIAN
TRACHEARIANS
TRACHEARIES
TRACHEATED
TRACHEATES
TRACHEIDAL
TRACHEIDES
TRACHEITIS
TRACHEITISES
TRACHELATE
TRACHEOLAR
TRACHEOLES
TRACHEOPHYTE
TRACHEOPHYTES
TRACHEOSCOPIES
TRACHEOSCOPY
TRACHEOSTOMIES
TRACHEOSTOMY
TRACHEOTOMIES
TRACHEOTOMY
TRACHINUSES
TRACHITISES
TRACHOMATOUS
TRACHYPTERUS
TRACHYPTERUSES
TRACHYTOID
TRACKBALLS
TRACKERBALL
TRACKERBALLS
TRACKLAYER
TRACKLAYERS
TRACKLAYING
TRACKLAYINGS
TRACKLEMENT
TRACKLEMENTS
TRACKLESSLY
TRACKLESSNESS
TRACKLESSNESSES
TRACKROADS
TRACKSIDES
TRACKSUITS
TRACKWALKER
TRACKWALKERS
TRACTABILITIES
TRACTABILITY
TRACTABLENESS
TRACTABLENESSES
TRACTARIAN
TRACTARIANS
TRACTATORS
TRACTILITIES
TRACTILITY
TRACTIONAL
TRACTORATION
TRACTORATIONS
TRACTORFEED
TRACTORFEEDS
TRACTRICES
TRADECRAFT
TRADECRAFTS
TRADEMARKED
TRADEMARKING
TRADEMARKS
TRADENAMES
TRADERSHIP
TRADERSHIPS
TRADESCANTIA
TRADESCANTIAS
TRADESFOLK
TRADESFOLKS
TRADESMANLIKE
TRADESPEOPLE
TRADESPEOPLES
TRADESWOMAN
TRADESWOMEN
TRADITIONAL
TRADITIONALISE
TRADITIONALISED
TRADITIONALISES
TRADITIONALISM
TRADITIONALISMS
TRADITIONALIST
TRADITIONALISTS
TRADITIONALITY
TRADITIONALIZE
TRADITIONALIZED
TRADITIONALIZES
TRADITIONALLY
TRADITIONARILY
TRADITIONARY
TRADITIONER
TRADITIONERS
TRADITIONIST
TRADITIONISTS
TRADITIONLESS
TRADITIONS
TRADITORES
TRADUCEMENT
TRADUCEMENTS
TRADUCIANISM
TRADUCIANISMS
TRADUCIANIST
TRADUCIANISTIC
TRADUCIANISTS
TRADUCIANS
TRADUCIBLE
TRADUCINGLY
TRADUCINGS
TRADUCTION
TRADUCTIONS
TRADUCTIVE
TRAFFICABILITY
TRAFFICABLE
TRAFFICATOR
TRAFFICATORS
TRAFFICKED
TRAFFICKER
TRAFFICKERS
TRAFFICKING
TRAFFICKINGS
TRAFFICLESS
TRAGACANTH
TRAGACANTHS
TRAGEDIANS
TRAGEDIENNE
TRAGEDIENNES
TRAGELAPHINE
TRAGELAPHS
TRAGICALLY
TRAGICALNESS
TRAGICALNESSES
TRAGICOMEDIES
TRAGICOMEDY
TRAGICOMIC
TRAGICOMICAL
TRAGICOMICALLY
TRAILBASTON
TRAILBASTONS
TRAILBLAZER
TRAILBLAZERS
TRAILBLAZING
TRAILBREAKER
TRAILBREAKERS
TRAILERABLE
TRAILERING
TRAILERINGS
TRAILERIST
TRAILERISTS
TRAILERITE
TRAILERITES
TRAILHEADS
TRAILINGLY
TRAINABILITIES
TRAINABILITY
TRAINBANDS
TRAINBEARER
TRAINBEARERS
TRAINEESHIP
TRAINEESHIPS
TRAINLOADS
TRAINSPOTTERISH
TRAIPSINGS
TRAITORESS
TRAITORESSES
TRAITORHOOD
TRAITORHOODS
TRAITORISM
TRAITORISMS
TRAITOROUS
TRAITOROUSLY
TRAITOROUSNESS
TRAITORSHIP
TRAITORSHIPS
TRAITRESSES
TRAJECTILE
TRAJECTING
TRAJECTION
TRAJECTIONS
TRAJECTORIES
TRAJECTORY
TRALATICIOUS
TRALATITIOUS
TRAMELLING
TRAMMELERS
TRAMMELING
TRAMMELLED
TRAMMELLER
TRAMMELLERS
TRAMMELLING
TRAMONTANA
TRAMONTANAS
TRAMONTANE
TRAMONTANES
TRAMPETTES
TRAMPLINGS
TRAMPOLINE
TRAMPOLINED
TRAMPOLINER
TRAMPOLINERS
TRAMPOLINES

TRAMPOLINING
TRAMPOLININGS
TRAMPOLINIST
TRAMPOLINISTS
TRAMPOLINS
TRANCELIKE
TRANQUILER
TRANQUILEST
TRANQUILISATION
TRANQUILISE
TRANQUILISED
TRANQUILISER
TRANQUILISERS
TRANQUILISES
TRANQUILISING
TRANQUILISINGLY
TRANQUILITIES
TRANQUILITY
TRANQUILIZATION
TRANQUILIZE
TRANQUILIZED
TRANQUILIZER
TRANQUILIZERS
TRANQUILIZES
TRANQUILIZING
TRANQUILIZINGLY
TRANQUILLER
TRANQUILLEST
TRANQUILLISE
TRANQUILLISED
TRANQUILLISER
TRANQUILLISERS
TRANQUILLISES
TRANQUILLISING
TRANQUILLITIES
TRANQUILLITY
TRANQUILLIZE
TRANQUILLIZED
TRANQUILLIZER
TRANQUILLIZERS
TRANQUILLIZES
TRANQUILLIZING
TRANQUILLY
TRANQUILNESS
TRANQUILNESSES
TRANSACTED
TRANSACTING
TRANSACTINIDE
TRANSACTINIDES
TRANSACTION
TRANSACTIONAL
TRANSACTIONALLY
TRANSACTIONS
TRANSACTOR
TRANSACTORS
TRANSALPINE
TRANSALPINES
TRANSAMINASE
TRANSAMINASES
TRANSAMINATION
TRANSAMINATIONS
TRANSANDEAN
TRANSANDINE
TRANSATLANTIC
TRANSAXLES
TRANSCALENCIES
TRANSCALENCY
TRANSCALENT
TRANSCAUCASIAN
TRANSCEIVER
TRANSCEIVERS
TRANSCENDED
TRANSCENDENCE
TRANSCENDENCES
TRANSCENDENCIES
TRANSCENDENCY
TRANSCENDENT
TRANSCENDENTAL
TRANSCENDENTALS
TRANSCENDENTLY
TRANSCENDENTS
TRANSCENDING
TRANSCENDINGLY
TRANSCENDS
TRANSCRANIAL
TRANSCRIBABLE
TRANSCRIBE
TRANSCRIBED
TRANSCRIBER
TRANSCRIBERS
TRANSCRIBES
TRANSCRIBING
TRANSCRIPT
TRANSCRIPTASE
TRANSCRIPTASES
TRANSCRIPTION
TRANSCRIPTIONAL
TRANSCRIPTIONS
TRANSCRIPTIVE
TRANSCRIPTIVELY
TRANSCRIPTS
TRANSCULTURAL
TRANSCURRENT
TRANSCUTANEOUS
TRANSDERMAL
TRANSDUCED
TRANSDUCER
TRANSDUCERS
TRANSDUCES
TRANSDUCING
TRANSDUCTANT
TRANSDUCTANTS
TRANSDUCTION
TRANSDUCTIONAL
TRANSDUCTIONS
TRANSDUCTOR
TRANSDUCTORS
TRANSECTED
TRANSECTING
TRANSECTION
TRANSECTIONS
TRANSENNAS
TRANSEPTAL
TRANSEPTATE
TRANSEXUAL
TRANSEXUALISM
TRANSEXUALISMS
TRANSEXUALS
TRANSFECTED
TRANSFECTING
TRANSFECTION
TRANSFECTIONS
TRANSFECTS
TRANSFERABILITY
TRANSFERABLE
TRANSFERAL
TRANSFERALS
TRANSFERASE
TRANSFERASES
TRANSFEREE
TRANSFEREES
TRANSFERENCE
TRANSFERENCES
TRANSFERENTIAL
TRANSFEROR
TRANSFERORS
TRANSFERRABLE
TRANSFERRAL
TRANSFERRALS
TRANSFERRED
TRANSFERRER
TRANSFERRERS
TRANSFERRIBLE
TRANSFERRIN
TRANSFERRING
TRANSFERRINS
TRANSFIGURATION
TRANSFIGURE
TRANSFIGURED
TRANSFIGUREMENT
TRANSFIGURES
TRANSFIGURING
TRANSFINITE
TRANSFIXED
TRANSFIXES
TRANSFIXING
TRANSFIXION
TRANSFIXIONS
TRANSFORMABLE
TRANSFORMATION
TRANSFORMATIONS
TRANSFORMATIVE
TRANSFORMED
TRANSFORMER
TRANSFORMERS
TRANSFORMING
TRANSFORMINGS
TRANSFORMISM
TRANSFORMISMS
TRANSFORMIST
TRANSFORMISTIC
TRANSFORMISTS
TRANSFORMS
TRANSFUSABLE
TRANSFUSED
TRANSFUSER
TRANSFUSERS
TRANSFUSES
TRANSFUSIBLE
TRANSFUSING
TRANSFUSION
TRANSFUSIONAL
TRANSFUSIONIST
TRANSFUSIONISTS
TRANSFUSIONS
TRANSFUSIVE
TRANSFUSIVELY
TRANSGENDER
TRANSGENDERED
TRANSGENDERS
TRANSGENES
TRANSGENESES
TRANSGENESIS
TRANSGENIC
TRANSGENICS
TRANSGRESS
TRANSGRESSED
TRANSGRESSES
TRANSGRESSING
TRANSGRESSION
TRANSGRESSIONAL
TRANSGRESSIONS
TRANSGRESSIVE
TRANSGRESSIVELY
TRANSGRESSOR
TRANSGRESSORS
TRANSHIPMENT
TRANSHIPMENTS
TRANSHIPPED
TRANSHIPPER
TRANSHIPPERS
TRANSHIPPING
TRANSHIPPINGS
TRANSHISTORICAL
TRANSHUMANCE
TRANSHUMANCES
TRANSHUMANT
TRANSHUMANTS
TRANSHUMED
TRANSHUMES
TRANSHUMING
TRANSIENCE
TRANSIENCES
TRANSIENCIES
TRANSIENCY
TRANSIENTLY
TRANSIENTNESS
TRANSIENTNESSES
TRANSIENTS
TRANSILIENCE
TRANSILIENCES
TRANSILIENCIES
TRANSILIENCY
TRANSILIENT
TRANSILLUMINATE
TRANSISTHMIAN
TRANSISTOR
TRANSISTORISE
TRANSISTORISED
TRANSISTORISES
TRANSISTORISING
TRANSISTORIZE
TRANSISTORIZED
TRANSISTORIZES
TRANSISTORIZING
TRANSISTORS
TRANSITABLE
TRANSITING
TRANSITION
TRANSITIONAL
TRANSITIONALLY
TRANSITIONALS
TRANSITIONARY
TRANSITIONS

TRANSITIVE
TRANSITIVELY
TRANSITIVENESS
TRANSITIVES
TRANSITIVITIES
TRANSITIVITY
TRANSITORILY
TRANSITORINESS
TRANSITORY
TRANSLATABILITY
TRANSLATABLE
TRANSLATED
TRANSLATES
TRANSLATING
TRANSLATION
TRANSLATIONAL
TRANSLATIONALLY
TRANSLATIONS
TRANSLATIVE
TRANSLATIVES
TRANSLATOR
TRANSLATORIAL
TRANSLATORS
TRANSLATORY
TRANSLEITHAN
TRANSLITERATE
TRANSLITERATED
TRANSLITERATES
TRANSLITERATING
TRANSLITERATION
TRANSLITERATOR
TRANSLITERATORS
TRANSLOCATE
TRANSLOCATED
TRANSLOCATES
TRANSLOCATING
TRANSLOCATION
TRANSLOCATIONS
TRANSLUCENCE
TRANSLUCENCES
TRANSLUCENCIES
TRANSLUCENCY
TRANSLUCENT
TRANSLUCENTLY
TRANSLUCID
TRANSLUCIDITIES
TRANSLUCIDITY
TRANSLUNAR
TRANSLUNARY
TRANSMANCHE
TRANSMARINE
TRANSMEMBRANE
TRANSMEWED
TRANSMEWING
TRANSMIGRANT
TRANSMIGRANTS
TRANSMIGRATE
TRANSMIGRATED
TRANSMIGRATES
TRANSMIGRATING
TRANSMIGRATION
TRANSMIGRATIONS
TRANSMIGRATIVE
TRANSMIGRATOR
TRANSMIGRATORS
TRANSMIGRATORY
TRANSMISSIBLE
TRANSMISSION
TRANSMISSIONAL
TRANSMISSIONS
TRANSMISSIVE
TRANSMISSIVELY
TRANSMISSIVITY
TRANSMISSOMETER
TRANSMITTABLE
TRANSMITTAL
TRANSMITTALS
TRANSMITTANCE
TRANSMITTANCES
TRANSMITTANCIES
TRANSMITTANCY
TRANSMITTED
TRANSMITTER
TRANSMITTERS
TRANSMITTIBLE
TRANSMITTING
TRANSMITTIVITY
TRANSMOGRIFIED
TRANSMOGRIFIES
TRANSMOGRIFY
TRANSMOGRIFYING
TRANSMONTANE
TRANSMONTANES
TRANSMOUNTAIN
TRANSMOVED
TRANSMOVES
TRANSMOVING
TRANSMUNDANE
TRANSMUTABILITY
TRANSMUTABLE
TRANSMUTABLY
TRANSMUTATION
TRANSMUTATIONAL
TRANSMUTATIONS
TRANSMUTATIVE
TRANSMUTED
TRANSMUTER
TRANSMUTERS
TRANSMUTES
TRANSMUTING
TRANSNATIONAL
TRANSNATURAL
TRANSOCEANIC
TRANSONICS
TRANSPACIFIC
TRANSPADANE
TRANSPARENCE
TRANSPARENCES
TRANSPARENCIES
TRANSPARENCY
TRANSPARENT
TRANSPARENTISE
TRANSPARENTISED
TRANSPARENTISES
TRANSPARENTIZE
TRANSPARENTIZED
TRANSPARENTIZES
TRANSPARENTLY
TRANSPARENTNESS
TRANSPERSONAL
TRANSPICUOUS
TRANSPICUOUSLY
TRANSPIERCE
TRANSPIERCED
TRANSPIERCES
TRANSPIERCING
TRANSPIRABLE
TRANSPIRATION
TRANSPIRATIONAL
TRANSPIRATIONS
TRANSPIRATORY
TRANSPIRED
TRANSPIRES
TRANSPIRING
TRANSPLACENTAL
TRANSPLANT
TRANSPLANTABLE
TRANSPLANTATION
TRANSPLANTED
TRANSPLANTER
TRANSPLANTERS
TRANSPLANTING
TRANSPLANTINGS
TRANSPLANTS
TRANSPOLAR
TRANSPONDER
TRANSPONDERS
TRANSPONDOR
TRANSPONDORS
TRANSPONTINE
TRANSPORTABLE
TRANSPORTAL
TRANSPORTALS
TRANSPORTANCE
TRANSPORTANCES
TRANSPORTATION
TRANSPORTATIONS
TRANSPORTED
TRANSPORTEDLY
TRANSPORTEDNESS
TRANSPORTER
TRANSPORTERS
TRANSPORTING
TRANSPORTINGLY
TRANSPORTINGS
TRANSPORTIVE
TRANSPORTS
TRANSPOSABILITY
TRANSPOSABLE
TRANSPOSAL
TRANSPOSALS
TRANSPOSED
TRANSPOSER
TRANSPOSERS
TRANSPOSES
TRANSPOSING
TRANSPOSINGS
TRANSPOSITION
TRANSPOSITIONAL
TRANSPOSITIONS
TRANSPOSITIVE
TRANSPOSON
TRANSPOSONS
TRANSPUTER
TRANSPUTERS
TRANSSEXUAL
TRANSSEXUALISM
TRANSSEXUALISMS
TRANSSEXUALITY
TRANSSEXUALS
TRANSSHAPE
TRANSSHAPED
TRANSSHAPES
TRANSSHAPING
TRANSSHIPMENT
TRANSSHIPMENTS
TRANSSHIPPED
TRANSSHIPPER
TRANSSHIPPERS
TRANSSHIPPING
TRANSSHIPPINGS
TRANSSHIPS
TRANSSONIC
TRANSTHORACIC
TRANSUBSTANTIAL
TRANSUDATE
TRANSUDATES
TRANSUDATION
TRANSUDATIONS
TRANSUDATORY
TRANSUDING
TRANSUMING
TRANSUMPTION
TRANSUMPTIONS
TRANSUMPTIVE
TRANSUMPTS
TRANSURANIAN
TRANSURANIC
TRANSURANICS
TRANSURANIUM
TRANSVAGINAL
TRANSVALUATE
TRANSVALUATED
TRANSVALUATES
TRANSVALUATING
TRANSVALUATION
TRANSVALUATIONS
TRANSVALUE
TRANSVALUED
TRANSVALUER
TRANSVALUERS
TRANSVALUES
TRANSVALUING
TRANSVERSAL
TRANSVERSALITY
TRANSVERSALLY
TRANSVERSALS
TRANSVERSE
TRANSVERSED
TRANSVERSELY
TRANSVERSENESS
TRANSVERSES
TRANSVERSING
TRANSVERSION
TRANSVERSIONS
TRANSVERTER
TRANSVERTERS
TRANSVESTED
TRANSVESTIC
TRANSVESTING
TRANSVESTISM
TRANSVESTISMS
TRANSVESTIST
TRANSVESTISTS

TRANSVESTITE
TRANSVESTITES
TRANSVESTITISM
TRANSVESTITISMS
TRANSVESTS
TRAPANNERS
TRAPANNING
TRAPESINGS
TRAPEZIFORM
TRAPEZISTS
TRAPEZIUMS
TRAPEZIUSES
TRAPEZOHEDRA
TRAPEZOHEDRAL
TRAPEZOHEDRON
TRAPEZOHEDRONS
TRAPEZOIDAL
TRAPEZOIDS
TRAPNESTED
TRAPNESTING
TRAPPINESS
TRAPPINESSES
TRAPSHOOTER
TRAPSHOOTERS
TRAPSHOOTING
TRAPSHOOTINGS
TRASHERIES
TRASHINESS
TRASHINESSES
TRASHTRIES
TRATTORIAS
TRAUCHLING
TRAUMATICALLY
TRAUMATISATION
TRAUMATISATIONS
TRAUMATISE
TRAUMATISED
TRAUMATISES
TRAUMATISING
TRAUMATISM
TRAUMATISMS
TRAUMATIZATION
TRAUMATIZATIONS
TRAUMATIZE
TRAUMATIZED
TRAUMATIZES
TRAUMATIZING
TRAUMATOLOGICAL
TRAUMATOLOGIES
TRAUMATOLOGY
TRAUMATONASTIES
TRAUMATONASTY
TRAVAILING
TRAVELATOR
TRAVELATORS
TRAVELINGS
TRAVELLERS
TRAVELLING
TRAVELLINGS
TRAVELOGUE
TRAVELOGUES
TRAVERSABLE
TRAVERSALS
TRAVERSERS
TRAVERSING
TRAVERSINGS
TRAVERTINE
TRAVERTINES
TRAVERTINS
TRAVESTIED
TRAVESTIES
TRAVESTYING
TRAVOLATOR
TRAVOLATORS
TRAWLERMAN
TRAWLERMEN
TRAYMOBILE
TRAYMOBILES
TRAZODONES
TREACHERER
TREACHERERS
TREACHERIES
TREACHEROUS
TREACHEROUSLY
TREACHEROUSNESS
TREACHETOUR
TREACHETOURS
TREACHOURS
TREACLIEST
TREACLINESS
TREACLINESSES
TREADLINGS
TREADMILLS
TREADWHEEL
TREADWHEELS
TREASONABLE
TREASONABLENESS
TREASONABLY
TREASONOUS
TREASURABLE
TREASURELESS
TREASURERS
TREASURERSHIP
TREASURERSHIPS
TREASURIES
TREASURING
TREATABILITIES
TREATABILITY
TREATMENTS
TREATYLESS
TREBBIANOS
TREBLENESS
TREBLENESSES
TREBUCHETS
TREBUCKETS
TRECENTIST
TRECENTISTS
TREDECILLION
TREDECILLIONS
TREDRILLES
TREEHOPPER
TREEHOPPERS
TREEHOUSES
TREELESSNESS
TREELESSNESSES
TREENWARES
TREGETOURS
TREHALOSES
TREILLAGED
TREILLAGES
TREKSCHUIT
TREKSCHUITS
TRELLISING
TRELLISWORK
TRELLISWORKS
TREMATODES
TREMATOIDS
TREMBLEMENT
TREMBLEMENTS
TREMBLIEST
TREMBLINGLY
TREMBLINGS
TREMENDOUS
TREMENDOUSLY
TREMENDOUSNESS
TREMOLANDI
TREMOLANDO
TREMOLANDOS
TREMOLANTS
TREMOLITES
TREMOLITIC
TREMORLESS
TREMULANTS
TREMULATED
TREMULATES
TREMULATING
TREMULOUSLY
TREMULOUSNESS
TREMULOUSNESSES
TRENCHANCIES
TRENCHANCY
TRENCHANTLY
TRENCHARDS
TRENCHERMAN
TRENCHERMEN
TRENDIFIED
TRENDIFIES
TRENDIFYING
TRENDINESS
TRENDINESSES
TRENDSETTER
TRENDSETTERS
TRENDSETTING
TRENDSETTINGS
TRENDYISMS
TREPANATION
TREPANATIONS
TREPANNERS
TREPANNING
TREPANNINGS
TREPHINATION
TREPHINATIONS
TREPHINERS
TREPHINING
TREPHININGS
TREPIDATION
TREPIDATIONS
TREPIDATORY
TREPONEMAL
TREPONEMAS
TREPONEMATA
TREPONEMATOSES
TREPONEMATOSIS
TREPONEMATOUS
TREPONEMES
TRESPASSED
TRESPASSER
TRESPASSERS
TRESPASSES
TRESPASSING
TRESTLETREE
TRESTLETREES
TRESTLEWORK
TRESTLEWORKS
TRETINOINS
TREVALLIES
TRIABLENESS
TRIABLENESSES
TRIACETATE
TRIACETATES
TRIACONTER
TRIACONTERS
TRIACTINAL
TRIADELPHOUS
TRIADICALLY
TRIALITIES
TRIALLISTS
TRIALOGUES
TRIALWARES
TRIAMCINOLONE
TRIAMCINOLONES
TRIANDRIAN
TRIANDROUS
TRIANGULAR
TRIANGULARITIES
TRIANGULARITY
TRIANGULARLY
TRIANGULATE
TRIANGULATED
TRIANGULATELY
TRIANGULATES
TRIANGULATING
TRIANGULATION
TRIANGULATIONS
TRIAPSIDAL
TRIARCHIES
TRIATHLETE
TRIATHLETES
TRIATHLONS
TRIATOMICALLY
TRIAXIALITIES
TRIAXIALITY
TRIBADISMS
TRIBALISMS
TRIBALISTIC
TRIBALISTS
TRIBESPEOPLE
TRIBESWOMAN
TRIBESWOMEN
TRIBOELECTRIC
TRIBOLOGICAL
TRIBOLOGIES
TRIBOLOGIST
TRIBOLOGISTS
TRIBOMETER
TRIBOMETERS
TRIBRACHIAL
TRIBRACHIC
TRIBROMOETHANOL
TRIBROMOMETHANE
TRIBULATED
TRIBULATES
TRIBULATING
TRIBULATION

TRIBULATIONS
TRIBUNATES
TRIBUNESHIP
TRIBUNESHIPS
TRIBUNICIAL
TRIBUNICIAN
TRIBUNITIAL
TRIBUNITIAN
TRIBUTARIES
TRIBUTARILY
TRIBUTARINESS
TRIBUTARINESSES
TRICAMERAL
TRICARBOXYLIC
TRICARPELLARY
TRICENTENARIES
TRICENTENARY
TRICENTENNIAL
TRICENTENNIALS
TRICEPHALOUS
TRICERATOPS
TRICERATOPSES
TRICERIONS
TRICHIASES
TRICHIASIS
TRICHINELLA
TRICHINELLAE
TRICHINELLAS
TRICHINIASES
TRICHINIASIS
TRICHINISATION
TRICHINISATIONS
TRICHINISE
TRICHINISED
TRICHINISES
TRICHINISING
TRICHINIZATION
TRICHINIZATIONS
TRICHINIZE
TRICHINIZED
TRICHINIZES
TRICHINIZING
TRICHINOSE
TRICHINOSED
TRICHINOSES
TRICHINOSING
TRICHINOSIS
TRICHINOTIC
TRICHINOUS
TRICHLORFON
TRICHLORFONS
TRICHLORIDE
TRICHLORIDES
TRICHLOROACETIC
TRICHLOROETHANE
TRICHLORPHON
TRICHLORPHONS
TRICHOBACTERIA
TRICHOCYST
TRICHOCYSTIC
TRICHOCYSTS
TRICHOGYNE
TRICHOGYNES
TRICHOGYNIAL
TRICHOGYNIC
TRICHOLOGICAL
TRICHOLOGIES
TRICHOLOGIST
TRICHOLOGISTS
TRICHOLOGY
TRICHOMONACIDAL
TRICHOMONACIDE
TRICHOMONACIDES
TRICHOMONAD
TRICHOMONADAL
TRICHOMONADS
TRICHOMONAL
TRICHOMONIASES
TRICHOMONIASIS
TRICHOPHYTON
TRICHOPHYTONS
TRICHOPHYTOSES
TRICHOPHYTOSIS
TRICHOPTERAN
TRICHOPTERANS
TRICHOPTERIST
TRICHOPTERISTS
TRICHOPTEROUS
TRICHOTHECENE
TRICHOTHECENES
TRICHOTOMIC
TRICHOTOMIES
TRICHOTOMISE
TRICHOTOMISED
TRICHOTOMISES
TRICHOTOMISING
TRICHOTOMIZE
TRICHOTOMIZED
TRICHOTOMIZES
TRICHOTOMIZING
TRICHOTOMOUS
TRICHOTOMOUSLY
TRICHOTOMY
TRICHROISM
TRICHROISMS
TRICHROMAT
TRICHROMATIC
TRICHROMATISM
TRICHROMATISMS
TRICHROMATS
TRICHROMIC
TRICHROMICS
TRICHRONOUS
TRICHURIASES
TRICHURIASIS
TRICKERIES
TRICKINESS
TRICKINESSES
TRICKISHLY
TRICKISHNESS
TRICKISHNESSES
TRICKLIEST
TRICKLINGLY
TRICKLINGS
TRICKSIEST
TRICKSINESS
TRICKSINESSES
TRICKSTERING
TRICKSTERINGS
TRICKSTERS
TRICKTRACK
TRICKTRACKS
TRICLINIUM
TRICLOSANS
TRICOLETTE
TRICOLETTES
TRICOLORED
TRICOLOURED
TRICOLOURS
TRICONSONANTAL
TRICONSONANTIC
TRICORNERED
TRICORPORATE
TRICORPORATED
TRICOSTATE
TRICOTEUSE
TRICOTEUSES
TRICOTINES
TRICROTISM
TRICROTISMS
TRICROTOUS
TRICUSPIDAL
TRICUSPIDATE
TRICUSPIDS
TRICYCLERS
TRICYCLICS
TRICYCLING
TRICYCLINGS
TRICYCLIST
TRICYCLISTS
TRIDACTYLOUS
TRIDENTATE
TRIDIMENSIONAL
TRIDOMINIA
TRIDOMINIUM
TRIDYMITES
TRIENNIALLY
TRIENNIALS
TRIENNIUMS
TRIERARCHAL
TRIERARCHIES
TRIERARCHS
TRIERARCHY
TRIETHYLAMINE
TRIETHYLAMINES
TRIFACIALS
TRIFARIOUS
TRIFFIDIAN
TRIFLINGLY
TRIFLINGNESS
TRIFLINGNESSES
TRIFLUOPERAZINE
TRIFLURALIN
TRIFLURALINS
TRIFOLIATE
TRIFOLIATED
TRIFOLIOLATE
TRIFOLIUMS
TRIFURCATE
TRIFURCATED
TRIFURCATES
TRIFURCATING
TRIFURCATION
TRIFURCATIONS
TRIGAMISTS
TRIGEMINAL
TRIGEMINALS
TRIGGERFISH
TRIGGERFISHES
TRIGGERING
TRIGGERLESS
TRIGGERMAN
TRIGGERMEN
TRIGLYCERIDE
TRIGLYCERIDES
TRIGLYPHIC
TRIGLYPHICAL
TRIGNESSES
TRIGONALLY
TRIGONOMETER
TRIGONOMETERS
TRIGONOMETRIC
TRIGONOMETRICAL
TRIGONOMETRIES
TRIGONOMETRY
TRIGRAMMATIC
TRIGRAMMIC
TRIGRAPHIC
TRIHALOMETHANE
TRIHALOMETHANES
TRIHEDRALS
TRIHEDRONS
TRIHYBRIDS
TRIHYDRATE
TRIHYDRATED
TRIHYDRATES
TRIHYDROXY
TRIIODOMETHANE
TRIIODOMETHANES
TRILATERAL
TRILATERALISM
TRILATERALISMS
TRILATERALIST
TRILATERALISTS
TRILATERALLY
TRILATERALS
TRILATERATION
TRILATERATIONS
TRILINEATE
TRILINGUAL
TRILINGUALISM
TRILINGUALISMS
TRILINGUALLY
TRILITERAL
TRILITERALISM
TRILITERALISMS
TRILITERALS
TRILITHONS
TRILLIONAIRE
TRILLIONAIRES
TRILLIONTH
TRILLIONTHS
TRILOBATED
TRILOBITES
TRILOBITIC
TRILOCULAR
TRIMERISMS
TRIMESTERS
TRIMESTRAL
TRIMESTRIAL
TRIMETHADIONE
TRIMETHADIONES
TRIMETHOPRIM
TRIMETHOPRIMS

TRIMETHYLAMINE
TRIMETHYLAMINES
TRIMETHYLENE
TRIMETHYLENES
TRIMETRICAL
TRIMETROGON
TRIMETROGONS
TRIMMINGLY
TRIMNESSES
TRIMOLECULAR
TRIMONTHLY
TRIMORPHIC
TRIMORPHISM
TRIMORPHISMS
TRIMORPHOUS
TRINACRIAN
TRINACRIFORM
TRINISCOPE
TRINISCOPES
TRINITARIAN
TRINITRATE
TRINITRATES
TRINITRINS
TRINITROBENZENE
TRINITROCRESOL
TRINITROCRESOLS
TRINITROPHENOL
TRINITROPHENOLS
TRINITROTOLUENE
TRINITROTOLUOL
TRINITROTOLUOLS
TRINKETERS
TRINKETING
TRINKETINGS
TRINKETRIES
TRINOCULAR
TRINOMIALISM
TRINOMIALISMS
TRINOMIALIST
TRINOMIALISTS
TRINOMIALLY
TRINOMIALS
TRINUCLEOTIDE
TRINUCLEOTIDES
TRIOECIOUS
TRIOXYGENS
TRIPALMITIN
TRIPALMITINS
TRIPARTISM
TRIPARTISMS
TRIPARTITE
TRIPARTITELY
TRIPARTITION
TRIPARTITIONS
TRIPEHOUND
TRIPEHOUNDS
TRIPERSONAL
TRIPERSONALISM
TRIPERSONALISMS
TRIPERSONALIST
TRIPERSONALISTS
TRIPERSONALITY
TRIPETALOUS
TRIPHAMMER
TRIPHAMMERS
TRIPHENYLAMINE
TRIPHENYLAMINES
TRIPHIBIOUS
TRIPHOSPHATE
TRIPHOSPHATES
TRIPHTHONG
TRIPHTHONGAL
TRIPHTHONGS
TRIPHYLITE
TRIPHYLITES
TRIPHYLLOUS
TRIPINNATE
TRIPINNATELY
TRIPITAKAS
TRIPLENESS
TRIPLENESSES
TRIPLETAIL
TRIPLETAILS
TRIPLICATE
TRIPLICATED
TRIPLICATES
TRIPLICATING
TRIPLICATION
TRIPLICATIONS
TRIPLICITIES
TRIPLICITY
TRIPLOBLASTIC
TRIPLOIDIES
TRIPPERISH
TRIPPINGLY
TRIPTEROUS
TRIPTYQUES
TRIPUDIARY
TRIPUDIATE
TRIPUDIATED
TRIPUDIATES
TRIPUDIATING
TRIPUDIATION
TRIPUDIATIONS
TRIPUDIUMS
TRIQUETRAL
TRIQUETRAS
TRIQUETROUS
TRIQUETROUSLY
TRIQUETRUM
TRIRADIATE
TRIRADIATELY
TRISACCHARIDE
TRISACCHARIDES
TRISAGIONS
TRISECTING
TRISECTION
TRISECTIONS
TRISECTORS
TRISECTRICES
TRISECTRIX
TRISKELION
TRISKELIONS
TRISOCTAHEDRA
TRISOCTAHEDRAL
TRISOCTAHEDRON
TRISOCTAHEDRONS
TRISTEARIN
TRISTEARINS
TRISTESSES
TRISTFULLY
TRISTFULNESS
TRISTFULNESSES
TRISTICHIC
TRISTICHOUS
TRISTIMULUS
TRISUBSTITUTED
TRISULCATE
TRISULFIDE
TRISULFIDES
TRISULPHIDE
TRISULPHIDES
TRISYLLABIC
TRISYLLABICAL
TRISYLLABICALLY
TRISYLLABLE
TRISYLLABLES
TRITAGONIST
TRITAGONISTS
TRITANOPIA
TRITANOPIAS
TRITANOPIC
TRITENESSES
TRITERNATE
TRITHEISMS
TRITHEISTIC
TRITHEISTICAL
TRITHEISTS
TRITHIONATE
TRITHIONATES
TRITHIONIC
TRITIATING
TRITIATION
TRITIATIONS
TRITICALES
TRITICALLY
TRITICALNESS
TRITICALNESSES
TRITICEOUS
TRITICISMS
TRITUBERCULAR
TRITUBERCULATE
TRITUBERCULIES
TRITUBERCULISM
TRITUBERCULISMS
TRITUBERCULY
TRITURABLE
TRITURATED
TRITURATES
TRITURATING
TRITURATION
TRITURATIONS
TRITURATOR
TRITURATORS
TRIUMPHALISM
TRIUMPHALISMS
TRIUMPHALIST
TRIUMPHALISTS
TRIUMPHALS
TRIUMPHANT
TRIUMPHANTLY
TRIUMPHERIES
TRIUMPHERS
TRIUMPHERY
TRIUMPHING
TRIUMPHINGS
TRIUMVIRAL
TRIUMVIRATE
TRIUMVIRATES
TRIUMVIRIES
TRIUNITIES
TRIVALENCE
TRIVALENCES
TRIVALENCIES
TRIVALENCY
TRIVALVULAR
TRIVIALISATION
TRIVIALISATIONS
TRIVIALISE
TRIVIALISED
TRIVIALISES
TRIVIALISING
TRIVIALISM
TRIVIALISMS
TRIVIALIST
TRIVIALISTS
TRIVIALITIES
TRIVIALITY
TRIVIALIZATION
TRIVIALIZATIONS
TRIVIALIZE
TRIVIALIZED
TRIVIALIZES
TRIVIALIZING
TRIVIALNESS
TRIVIALNESSES
TRIWEEKLIES
TROCHAICALLY
TROCHANTER
TROCHANTERAL
TROCHANTERIC
TROCHANTERS
TROCHEAMETER
TROCHEAMETERS
TROCHELMINTH
TROCHELMINTHS
TROCHILUSES
TROCHISCUS
TROCHISCUSES
TROCHLEARS
TROCHOIDAL
TROCHOIDALLY
TROCHOMETER
TROCHOMETERS
TROCHOPHORE
TROCHOPHORES
TROCHOSPHERE
TROCHOSPHERES
TROCHOTRON
TROCHOTRONS
TROCTOLITE
TROCTOLITES
TROGLODYTE
TROGLODYTES
TROGLODYTIC
TROGLODYTICAL
TROGLODYTISM
TROGLODYTISMS
TROLLEYBUS
TROLLEYBUSES
TROLLEYBUSSES
TROLLEYING
TROLLIUSES
TROLLOPEES

TROLLOPING
TROLLOPISH
TROMBICULID
TROMBICULIDS
TROMBIDIASES
TROMBIDIASIS
TROMBONIST
TROMBONISTS
TROMOMETER
TROMOMETERS
TROMOMETRIC
TROOPSHIPS
TROOSTITES
TROPAEOLIN
TROPAEOLINS
TROPAEOLUM
TROPAEOLUMS
TROPEOLINS
TROPHALLACTIC
TROPHALLAXES
TROPHALLAXIS
TROPHESIAL
TROPHESIES
TROPHICALLY
TROPHOBIOSES
TROPHOBIOSIS
TROPHOBIOTIC
TROPHOBLAST
TROPHOBLASTIC
TROPHOBLASTS
TROPHOLOGIES
TROPHOLOGY
TROPHONEUROSES
TROPHONEUROSIS
TROPHOPLASM
TROPHOPLASMS
TROPHOTACTIC
TROPHOTAXES
TROPHOTAXIS
TROPHOTROPIC
TROPHOTROPISM
TROPHOTROPISMS
TROPHOZOITE
TROPHOZOITES
TROPICALISATION
TROPICALISE
TROPICALISED
TROPICALISES
TROPICALISING
TROPICALITIES
TROPICALITY
TROPICALIZATION
TROPICALIZE
TROPICALIZED
TROPICALIZES
TROPICALIZING
TROPICALLY
TROPICBIRD
TROPICBIRDS
TROPISMATIC
TROPOCOLLAGEN
TROPOCOLLAGENS
TROPOLOGIC
TROPOLOGICAL
TROPOLOGICALLY
TROPOLOGIES
TROPOMYOSIN
TROPOMYOSINS
TROPOPAUSE
TROPOPAUSES
TROPOPHILOUS
TROPOPHYTE
TROPOPHYTES
TROPOPHYTIC
TROPOSCATTER
TROPOSCATTERS
TROPOSPHERE
TROPOSPHERES
TROPOSPHERIC
TROPOTAXES
TROPOTAXIS
TROTHPLIGHT
TROTHPLIGHTED
TROTHPLIGHTING
TROTHPLIGHTS
TROUBADOUR
TROUBADOURS
TROUBLEDLY
TROUBLEFREE
TROUBLEMAKER
TROUBLEMAKERS
TROUBLEMAKING
TROUBLEMAKINGS
TROUBLESHOOT
TROUBLESHOOTER
TROUBLESHOOTERS
TROUBLESHOOTING
TROUBLESHOOTS
TROUBLESHOT
TROUBLESOME
TROUBLESOMELY
TROUBLESOMENESS
TROUBLINGS
TROUBLOUSLY
TROUBLOUSNESS
TROUBLOUSNESSES
TROUGHLIKE
TROUNCINGS
TROUSERING
TROUSERINGS
TROUSERLESS
TROUSSEAUS
TROUSSEAUX
TROUTLINGS
TROUTSTONE
TROUTSTONES
TROUVAILLE
TROUVAILLES
TROWELLERS
TROWELLING
TRUANTRIES
TRUANTSHIP
TRUANTSHIPS
TRUCKLINES
TRUCKLINGS
TRUCKLOADS
TRUCKMASTER
TRUCKMASTERS
TRUCKSTOPS
TRUCULENCE
TRUCULENCES
TRUCULENCIES
TRUCULENCY
TRUCULENTLY
TRUEHEARTED
TRUEHEARTEDNESS
TRUENESSES
TRUEPENNIES
TRUFFLINGS
TRUMPERIES
TRUMPETERS
TRUMPETING
TRUMPETINGS
TRUMPETLIKE
TRUMPETWEED
TRUMPETWEEDS
TRUNCATELY
TRUNCATING
TRUNCATION
TRUNCATIONS
TRUNCHEONED
TRUNCHEONER
TRUNCHEONERS
TRUNCHEONING
TRUNCHEONS
TRUNKFISHES
TRUNKSLEEVE
TRUNKSLEEVES
TRUNNIONED
TRUSTABILITIES
TRUSTABILITY
TRUSTAFARIAN
TRUSTAFARIANS
TRUSTBUSTER
TRUSTBUSTERS
TRUSTBUSTING
TRUSTBUSTINGS
TRUSTEEING
TRUSTEESHIP
TRUSTEESHIPS
TRUSTFULLY
TRUSTFULNESS
TRUSTFULNESSES
TRUSTINESS
TRUSTINESSES
TRUSTINGLY
TRUSTINGNESS
TRUSTINGNESSES
TRUSTLESSLY
TRUSTLESSNESS
TRUSTLESSNESSES
TRUSTWORTHILY
TRUSTWORTHINESS
TRUSTWORTHY
TRUTHFULLY
TRUTHFULNESS
TRUTHFULNESSES
TRUTHLESSNESS
TRUTHLESSNESSES
TRYINGNESS
TRYINGNESSES
TRYPAFLAVINE
TRYPAFLAVINES
TRYPANOCIDAL
TRYPANOCIDE
TRYPANOCIDES
TRYPANOSOMAL
TRYPANOSOME
TRYPANOSOMES
TRYPANOSOMIASES
TRYPANOSOMIASIS
TRYPANOSOMIC
TRYPARSAMIDE
TRYPARSAMIDES
TRYPSINOGEN
TRYPSINOGENS
TRYPTAMINE
TRYPTAMINES
TRYPTOPHAN
TRYPTOPHANE
TRYPTOPHANES
TRYPTOPHANS
TSAREVICHES
TSAREVITCH
TSAREVITCHES
TSCHERNOSEM
TSCHERNOSEMS
TSESAREVICH
TSESAREVICHES
TSESAREVITCH
TSESAREVITCHES
TSESAREVNA
TSESAREVNAS
TSESAREWICH
TSESAREWICHES
TSESAREWITCH
TSESAREWITCHES
TSOTSITAAL
TSOTSITAALS
TSUTSUGAMUSHI
TSUTSUGAMUSHIS
TUBBINESSES
TUBECTOMIES
TUBERACEOUS
TUBERCULAR
TUBERCULARLY
TUBERCULARS
TUBERCULATE
TUBERCULATED
TUBERCULATELY
TUBERCULATION
TUBERCULATIONS
TUBERCULES
TUBERCULIN
TUBERCULINS
TUBERCULISATION
TUBERCULISE
TUBERCULISED
TUBERCULISES
TUBERCULISING
TUBERCULIZATION
TUBERCULIZE
TUBERCULIZED
TUBERCULIZES
TUBERCULIZING
TUBERCULOID
TUBERCULOMA
TUBERCULOMAS
TUBERCULOMATA
TUBERCULOSE
TUBERCULOSED
TUBERCULOSES
TUBERCULOSIS
TUBERCULOUS

TUBERCULOUSLY
TUBERCULUM
TUBERIFEROUS
TUBERIFORM
TUBEROSITIES
TUBEROSITY
TUBICOLOUS
TUBIFICIDS
TUBIFLOROUS
TUBOCURARINE
TUBOCURARINES
TUBOPLASTIES
TUBOPLASTY
TUBULARIAN
TUBULARIANS
TUBULARITIES
TUBULARITY
TUBULATING
TUBULATION
TUBULATIONS
TUBULATORS
TUBULATURE
TUBULATURES
TUBULIFLORAL
TUBULIFLOROUS
TUBULOUSLY
TUCKERBAGS
TUCKERBOXES
TUFFACEOUS
TUFFTAFFETA
TUFFTAFFETAS
TUFFTAFFETIES
TUFFTAFFETY
TUFTAFFETA
TUFTAFFETAS
TUFTAFFETIES
TUFTAFFETY
TUILLETTES
TUILYIEING
TUILZIEING
TUITIONARY
TULARAEMIA
TULARAEMIAS
TULARAEMIC
TULAREMIAS
TULIPOMANIA
TULIPOMANIAS
TULIPWOODS
TUMATAKURU
TUMBLEBUGS
TUMBLEDOWN
TUMBLEHOME
TUMBLEHOMES
TUMBLERFUL
TUMBLERFULS
TUMBLERSFUL
TUMBLESETS
TUMBLEWEED
TUMBLEWEEDS
TUMEFACIENT
TUMEFACTION
TUMEFACTIONS
TUMESCENCE
TUMESCENCES
TUMIDITIES
TUMIDNESSES
TUMORGENIC
TUMORGENICITIES
TUMORGENICITY
TUMORIGENESES
TUMORIGENESIS
TUMORIGENIC
TUMORIGENICITY
TUMULOSITIES
TUMULOSITY
TUMULTUARY
TUMULTUATE
TUMULTUATED
TUMULTUATES
TUMULTUATING
TUMULTUATION
TUMULTUATIONS
TUMULTUOUS
TUMULTUOUSLY
TUMULTUOUSNESS
TUNABILITIES
TUNABILITY
TUNABLENESS
TUNABLENESSES
TUNBELLIED
TUNBELLIES
TUNEFULNESS
TUNEFULNESSES
TUNELESSLY
TUNELESSNESS
TUNELESSNESSES
TUNESMITHS
TUNGSTATES
TUNGSTITES
TUNNELINGS
TUNNELLERS
TUNNELLIKE
TUNNELLING
TUNNELLINGS
TUPPENNIES
TURACOVERDIN
TURACOVERDINS
TURANGAWAEWAE
TURANGAWAEWAES
TURBELLARIAN
TURBELLARIANS
TURBIDIMETER
TURBIDIMETERS
TURBIDIMETRIC
TURBIDIMETRIES
TURBIDIMETRY
TURBIDITES
TURBIDITIES
TURBIDNESS
TURBIDNESSES
TURBINACIOUS
TURBINATED
TURBINATES
TURBINATION
TURBINATIONS
TURBOCHARGED
TURBOCHARGER
TURBOCHARGERS
TURBOCHARGING
TURBOCHARGINGS
TURBOELECTRIC
TURBOGENERATOR
TURBOGENERATORS
TURBOMACHINERY
TURBOPROPS
TURBOSHAFT
TURBOSHAFTS
TURBULATOR
TURBULATORS
TURBULENCE
TURBULENCES
TURBULENCIES
TURBULENCY
TURBULENTLY
TURCOPOLES
TURCOPOLIER
TURCOPOLIERS
TURFGRASSES
TURFINESSES
TURFSKIING
TURFSKIINGS
TURGENCIES
TURGESCENCE
TURGESCENCES
TURGESCENCIES
TURGESCENCY
TURGESCENT
TURGIDITIES
TURGIDNESS
TURGIDNESSES
TURMOILING
TURNABOUTS
TURNAGAINS
TURNAROUND
TURNAROUNDS
TURNBROACH
TURNBROACHES
TURNBUCKLE
TURNBUCKLES
TURNROUNDS
TURNSTILES
TURNSTONES
TURNTABLES
TURNVEREIN
TURNVEREINS
TUROPHILES
TURPENTINE
TURPENTINED
TURPENTINES
TURPENTINING
TURPENTINY
TURPITUDES
TURQUOISES
TURRIBANTS
TURRICULATE
TURRICULATED
TURTLEBACK
TURTLEBACKS
TURTLEDOVE
TURTLEDOVES
TURTLEHEAD
TURTLEHEADS
TURTLENECK
TURTLENECKED
TURTLENECKS
TUTELARIES
TUTIORISMS
TUTIORISTS
TUTORESSES
TUTORIALLY
TUTORISING
TUTORIZING
TUTORSHIPS
TUTOYERING
TUTWORKERS
TUTWORKMAN
TUTWORKMEN
TWADDLIEST
TWADDLINGS
TWALPENNIES
TWANGINGLY
TWANGLINGLY
TWANGLINGS
TWATTLINGS
TWAYBLADES
TWEEDINESS
TWEEDINESSES
TWEEDLEDEE
TWEEDLEDEED
TWEEDLEDEEING
TWEEDLEDEES
TWEENAGERS
TWEENESSES
TWELVEFOLD
TWELVEMONTH
TWELVEMONTHS
TWENTIETHS
TWENTYFOLD
TWENTYFOLDS
TWICHILDREN
TWIDDLIEST
TWIDDLINGS
TWILIGHTED
TWILIGHTING
TWINBERRIES
TWINFLOWER
TWINFLOWERS
TWINKLINGS
TWISTABILITIES
TWISTABILITY
TWITCHIEST
TWITCHINGS
TWITTERERS
TWITTERING
TWITTERINGLY
TWITTERINGS
TWITTINGLY
TWOFOLDNESS
TWOFOLDNESSES
TWOPENCEWORTH
TWOPENCEWORTHS
TWOPENNIES
TWOSEATERS
TYCOONATES
TYCOONERIES
TYLECTOMIES
TYMPANIFORM
TYMPANISTS
TYMPANITES
TYMPANITESES
TYMPANITIC
TYMPANITIS
TYMPANITISES
TYNDALLIMETRIES

TYNDALLIMETRY
TYPECASTER
TYPECASTERS
TYPECASTING
TYPEFOUNDER
TYPEFOUNDERS
TYPEFOUNDING
TYPEFOUNDINGS
TYPESCRIPT
TYPESCRIPTS
TYPESETTER
TYPESETTERS
TYPESETTING
TYPESETTINGS
TYPESTYLES
TYPEWRITER
TYPEWRITERS
TYPEWRITES
TYPEWRITING
TYPEWRITINGS
TYPEWRITTEN
TYPHACEOUS
TYPHLITISES
TYPHLOLOGIES
TYPHLOLOGY
TYPHLOSOLE
TYPHLOSOLES
TYPHOGENIC
TYPHOIDINS
TYPICALITIES
TYPICALITY
TYPICALNESS
TYPICALNESSES
TYPIFICATION
TYPIFICATIONS
TYPOGRAPHED
TYPOGRAPHER
TYPOGRAPHERS
TYPOGRAPHIA
TYPOGRAPHIC
TYPOGRAPHICAL
TYPOGRAPHICALLY
TYPOGRAPHIES
TYPOGRAPHING
TYPOGRAPHIST
TYPOGRAPHISTS
TYPOGRAPHS
TYPOGRAPHY
TYPOLOGICAL
TYPOLOGICALLY
TYPOLOGIES
TYPOLOGIST
TYPOLOGISTS
TYPOMANIAS
TYPOTHETAE
TYRANNESSES
TYRANNICAL
TYRANNICALLY
TYRANNICALNESS
TYRANNICIDAL
TYRANNICIDE
TYRANNICIDES
TYRANNISED
TYRANNISER
TYRANNISERS
TYRANNISES
TYRANNISING
TYRANNIZED
TYRANNIZER
TYRANNIZERS
TYRANNIZES
TYRANNIZING
TYRANNOSAUR
TYRANNOSAURS
TYRANNOSAURUS
TYRANNOSAURUSES
TYRANNOUSLY
TYRANNOUSNESS
TYRANNOUSNESSES
TYROCIDINE
TYROCIDINES
TYROCIDINS
TYROGLYPHID
TYROGLYPHIDS
TYROPITTAS
TYROSINASE
TYROSINASES
TYROTHRICIN
TYROTHRICINS

Uu

UBIQUARIAN
UBIQUINONE
UBIQUINONES
UBIQUITARIAN
UBIQUITARIANISM
UBIQUITARIANS
UBIQUITARY
UBIQUITIES
UBIQUITINATION
UBIQUITINATIONS
UBIQUITINS
UBIQUITOUS
UBIQUITOUSLY
UBIQUITOUSNESS
UDOMETRIES
UFOLOGICAL
UFOLOGISTS
UGLIFICATION
UGLIFICATIONS
UGLINESSES
UGSOMENESS
UGSOMENESSES
UINTAHITES
UINTATHERE
UINTATHERES
UITLANDERS
ULCERATING
ULCERATION
ULCERATIONS
ULCERATIVE
ULCEROGENIC
ULCEROUSLY
ULCEROUSNESS
ULCEROUSNESSES
ULOTRICHIES
ULOTRICHOUS
ULSTERETTE
ULSTERETTES
ULTERIORLY
ULTIMACIES
ULTIMATELY
ULTIMATENESS
ULTIMATENESSES
ULTIMATING
ULTIMATUMS
ULTIMOGENITURE
ULTIMOGENITURES
ULTRABASIC
ULTRABASICS
ULTRACAREFUL
ULTRACASUAL
ULTRACAUTIOUS
ULTRACENTRIFUGE
ULTRACIVILISED
ULTRACIVILIZED
ULTRACLEAN
ULTRACOMMERCIAL
ULTRACOMPACT
ULTRACOMPETENT
ULTRACONVENIENT
ULTRACREPIDATE
ULTRACREPIDATED
ULTRACREPIDATES
ULTRACRITICAL
ULTRADEMOCRATIC
ULTRADENSE
ULTRADISTANCE
ULTRADISTANT
ULTRAEFFICIENT
ULTRAENERGETIC
ULTRAEXCLUSIVE
ULTRAFAMILIAR
ULTRAFASTIDIOUS
ULTRAFEMININE
ULTRAFICHE
ULTRAFICHES
ULTRAFILTER
ULTRAFILTERED
ULTRAFILTERING
ULTRAFILTERS
ULTRAFILTRATE
ULTRAFILTRATES
ULTRAFILTRATION
ULTRAGLAMOROUS
ULTRAHAZARDOUS
ULTRAHEATED
ULTRAHEATING
ULTRAHEATS
ULTRAHEAVY
ULTRAHUMAN
ULTRAISTIC
ULTRALARGE
ULTRALEFTISM
ULTRALEFTISMS
ULTRALEFTIST
ULTRALEFTISTS
ULTRALIBERAL
ULTRALIBERALISM
ULTRALIBERALS
ULTRALIGHT
ULTRALIGHTS
ULTRAMAFIC
ULTRAMARATHON
ULTRAMARATHONER
ULTRAMARATHONS
ULTRAMARINE
ULTRAMARINES
ULTRAMASCULINE
ULTRAMICRO
ULTRAMICROMETER
ULTRAMICROSCOPE
ULTRAMICROSCOPY
ULTRAMICROTOME
ULTRAMICROTOMES
ULTRAMICROTOMY
ULTRAMILITANT
ULTRAMILITANTS
ULTRAMINIATURE
ULTRAMODERN
ULTRAMODERNISM
ULTRAMODERNISMS
ULTRAMODERNIST
ULTRAMODERNISTS
ULTRAMONTANE
ULTRAMONTANES
ULTRAMONTANISM
ULTRAMONTANISMS
ULTRAMONTANIST
ULTRAMONTANISTS
ULTRAMUNDANE
ULTRANATIONAL
ULTRAORTHODOX
ULTRAPATRIOTIC
ULTRAPHYSICAL
ULTRAPOWERFUL
ULTRAPRACTICAL
ULTRAPRECISE
ULTRAPRECISION
ULTRAQUIET
ULTRARADICAL
ULTRARADICALS
ULTRARAPID
ULTRARAREFIED
ULTRARATIONAL
ULTRAREALISM
ULTRAREALISMS
ULTRAREALIST
ULTRAREALISTIC
ULTRAREALISTS
ULTRAREFINED
ULTRARELIABLE
ULTRARIGHT

ULTRARIGHTIST
ULTRARIGHTISTS
ULTRAROMANTIC
ULTRAROYALIST
ULTRAROYALISTS
ULTRASECRET
ULTRASENSITIVE
ULTRASENSUAL
ULTRASERIOUS
ULTRASHARP
ULTRASHORT
ULTRASIMPLE
ULTRASLICK
ULTRASMALL
ULTRASMART
ULTRASMOOTH
ULTRASONIC
ULTRASONICALLY
ULTRASONICS
ULTRASONOGRAPHY
ULTRASOUND
ULTRASOUNDS
ULTRASTRUCTURAL
ULTRASTRUCTURE
ULTRASTRUCTURES
ULTRAVACUA
ULTRAVACUUM
ULTRAVACUUMS
ULTRAVIOLENCE
ULTRAVIOLENCES
ULTRAVIOLENT
ULTRAVIOLET
ULTRAVIOLETS
ULTRAVIRILE
ULTRAVIRILITIES
ULTRAVIRILITY
ULTRAVIRUS
ULTRAVIRUSES
ULTRAWIDEBAND
ULTRAWIDEBANDS
ULTRONEOUS
ULTRONEOUSLY
ULTRONEOUSNESS
ULULATIONS
UMBELLATED
UMBELLATELY
UMBELLIFER
UMBELLIFEROUS
UMBELLIFERS
UMBELLULATE
UMBELLULES
UMBILICALLY
UMBILICALS
UMBILICATE
UMBILICATED
UMBILICATION
UMBILICATIONS
UMBILICUSES
UMBILIFORM
UMBONATION
UMBONATIONS
UMBRACULATE
UMBRACULIFORM
UMBRACULUM
UMBRAGEOUS
UMBRAGEOUSLY
UMBRAGEOUSNESS
UMBRATICAL
UMBRATILOUS
UMBRELLAED
UMBRELLAING
UMBRELLOES
UMBRIFEROUS
UMPIRESHIP
UMPIRESHIPS
UNABASHEDLY
UNABATEDLY
UNABBREVIATED
UNABOLISHED
UNABRIDGED
UNABROGATED
UNABSOLVED
UNABSORBED
UNABSORBENT
UNACADEMIC
UNACADEMICALLY
UNACCENTED
UNACCENTUATED
UNACCEPTABILITY
UNACCEPTABLE
UNACCEPTABLY
UNACCEPTANCE
UNACCEPTANCES
UNACCEPTED
UNACCLIMATED
UNACCLIMATISED
UNACCLIMATIZED
UNACCOMMODATED
UNACCOMMODATING
UNACCOMPANIED
UNACCOMPLISHED
UNACCOUNTABLE
UNACCOUNTABLY
UNACCOUNTED
UNACCREDITED
UNACCULTURATED
UNACCUSABLE
UNACCUSABLY
UNACCUSTOMED
UNACCUSTOMEDLY
UNACHIEVABLE
UNACHIEVED
UNACKNOWLEDGED
UNACQUAINT
UNACQUAINTANCE
UNACQUAINTANCES
UNACQUAINTED
UNACTORISH
UNACTUATED
UNADAPTABLE
UNADDRESSED
UNADJUDICATED
UNADJUSTED
UNADMIRING
UNADMITTED
UNADMONISHED
UNADOPTABLE
UNADULTERATE
UNADULTERATED
UNADULTERATEDLY
UNADVENTROUS
UNADVENTUROUS
UNADVERTISED
UNADVISABLE
UNADVISABLENESS
UNADVISABLY
UNADVISEDLY
UNADVISEDNESS
UNADVISEDNESSES
UNAESTHETIC
UNAFFECTED
UNAFFECTEDLY
UNAFFECTEDNESS
UNAFFECTING
UNAFFECTIONATE
UNAFFILIATED
UNAFFLUENT
UNAFFORDABLE
UNAGGRESSIVE
UNAGREEABLE
UNALIENABLE
UNALIENABLY
UNALIENATED
UNALLEVIATED
UNALLOCATED
UNALLOTTED
UNALLOWABLE
UNALLURING
UNALTERABILITY
UNALTERABLE
UNALTERABLENESS
UNALTERABLY
UNALTERING
UNAMBIGUOUS
UNAMBIGUOUSLY
UNAMBITIOUS
UNAMBITIOUSLY
UNAMBIVALENT
UNAMBIVALENTLY
UNAMENABLE
UNAMENDABLE
UNAMIABILITIES
UNAMIABILITY
UNAMIABLENESS
UNAMIABLENESSES
UNAMORTISED
UNAMORTIZED
UNAMPLIFIED
UNAMUSABLE
UNAMUSINGLY
UNANALYSABLE
UNANALYSED
UNANALYTIC
UNANALYTICAL
UNANALYZABLE
UNANALYZED
UNANCHORED
UNANCHORING
UNANESTHETISED
UNANESTHETIZED
UNANIMATED
UNANIMITIES
UNANIMOUSLY
UNANIMOUSNESS
UNANIMOUSNESSES
UNANNEALED
UNANNOTATED
UNANNOUNCED
UNANSWERABILITY
UNANSWERABLE
UNANSWERABLY
UNANSWERED
UNANTICIPATED
UNANTICIPATEDLY
UNAPOLOGETIC
UNAPOLOGISING
UNAPOLOGIZING
UNAPOSTOLIC
UNAPOSTOLICAL
UNAPOSTOLICALLY
UNAPPALLED
UNAPPARELLED
UNAPPARELLING
UNAPPARELS
UNAPPARENT
UNAPPEALABLE
UNAPPEALABLY
UNAPPEALING
UNAPPEALINGLY
UNAPPEASABLE
UNAPPEASABLY
UNAPPEASED
UNAPPETISING
UNAPPETISINGLY
UNAPPETIZING
UNAPPETIZINGLY
UNAPPLAUSIVE
UNAPPLICABLE
UNAPPOINTED
UNAPPRECIATED
UNAPPRECIATION
UNAPPRECIATIONS
UNAPPRECIATIVE
UNAPPREHENDED
UNAPPREHENSIBLE
UNAPPREHENSIVE
UNAPPRISED
UNAPPROACHABLE
UNAPPROACHABLY
UNAPPROACHED
UNAPPROPRIATE
UNAPPROPRIATED
UNAPPROVED
UNAPPROVING
UNAPPROVINGLY
UNAPTNESSES
UNARGUABLE
UNARGUABLY
UNARMOURED
UNARRANGED
UNARROGANT
UNARTFULLY
UNARTICULATE
UNARTICULATED
UNARTIFICIAL
UNARTIFICIALLY
UNARTISTIC
UNARTISTLIKE
UNASCENDABLE
UNASCENDED
UNASCENDIBLE
UNASCERTAINABLE
UNASCERTAINED
UNASHAMEDLY

UNASHAMEDNESS
UNASHAMEDNESSES
UNASPIRATED
UNASPIRING
UNASPIRINGLY
UNASPIRINGNESS
UNASSAILABILITY
UNASSAILABLE
UNASSAILABLY
UNASSAILED
UNASSEMBLED
UNASSERTIVE
UNASSERTIVELY
UNASSIGNABLE
UNASSIGNED
UNASSIMILABLE
UNASSIMILATED
UNASSISTED
UNASSISTEDLY
UNASSISTING
UNASSOCIATED
UNASSUAGEABLE
UNASSUAGED
UNASSUMING
UNASSUMINGLY
UNASSUMINGNESS
UNATHLETIC
UNATONABLE
UNATTACHED
UNATTAINABLE
UNATTAINABLY
UNATTAINTED
UNATTEMPTED
UNATTENDED
UNATTENDING
UNATTENTIVE
UNATTENUATED
UNATTESTED
UNATTRACTIVE
UNATTRACTIVELY
UNATTRIBUTABLE
UNATTRIBUTED
UNAUGMENTED
UNAUSPICIOUS
UNAUTHENTIC
UNAUTHENTICATED
UNAUTHENTICITY
UNAUTHORISED
UNAUTHORITATIVE
UNAUTHORIZED
UNAUTOMATED
UNAVAILABILITY
UNAVAILABLE
UNAVAILABLENESS
UNAVAILABLY
UNAVAILING
UNAVAILINGLY
UNAVAILINGNESS
UNAVERTABLE
UNAVERTIBLE
UNAVOIDABILITY
UNAVOIDABLE
UNAVOIDABLENESS
UNAVOIDABLY
UNAVOWEDLY
UNAWAKENED
UNAWAKENING
UNAWARENESS
UNAWARENESSES
UNBAILABLE
UNBALANCED
UNBALANCES
UNBALANCING
UNBALLASTED
UNBANDAGED
UNBANDAGES
UNBANDAGING
UNBAPTISED
UNBAPTISES
UNBAPTISING
UNBAPTIZED
UNBAPTIZES
UNBAPTIZING
UNBARBERED
UNBARRICADE
UNBARRICADED
UNBARRICADES
UNBARRICADING
UNBATTERED
UNBEARABLE
UNBEARABLENESS
UNBEARABLY
UNBEATABLE
UNBEATABLY
UNBEAUTIFUL
UNBEAUTIFULLY
UNBEAVERED
UNBECOMING
UNBECOMINGLY
UNBECOMINGNESS
UNBECOMINGS
UNBEDIMMED
UNBEDINNED
UNBEFITTING
UNBEFRIENDED
UNBEGETTING
UNBEGINNING
UNBEGOTTEN
UNBEGUILED
UNBEGUILES
UNBEGUILING
UNBEHOLDEN
UNBEKNOWNST
UNBELIEVABILITY
UNBELIEVABLE
UNBELIEVABLY
UNBELIEVED
UNBELIEVER
UNBELIEVERS
UNBELIEVES
UNBELIEVING
UNBELIEVINGLY
UNBELIEVINGNESS
UNBELLIGERENT
UNBENDABLE
UNBENDINGLY
UNBENDINGNESS
UNBENDINGNESSES
UNBENDINGS
UNBENEFICED
UNBENEFICIAL
UNBENEFITED
UNBENIGHTED
UNBENIGNANT
UNBENIGNLY
UNBESEEMED
UNBESEEMING
UNBESEEMINGLY
UNBESOUGHT
UNBESPEAKING
UNBESPEAKS
UNBESPOKEN
UNBESTOWED
UNBETRAYED
UNBETTERABLE
UNBETTERED
UNBEWAILED
UNBIASEDLY
UNBIASEDNESS
UNBIASEDNESSES
UNBIASSEDLY
UNBIASSEDNESS
UNBIASSEDNESSES
UNBIASSING
UNBIBLICAL
UNBINDINGS
UNBIRTHDAY
UNBIRTHDAYS
UNBISHOPED
UNBISHOPING
UNBLAMABLE
UNBLAMABLY
UNBLAMEABLE
UNBLAMEABLY
UNBLEACHED
UNBLEMISHED
UNBLENCHED
UNBLENCHING
UNBLESSEDNESS
UNBLESSEDNESSES
UNBLESSING
UNBLINDFOLD
UNBLINDFOLDED
UNBLINDFOLDING
UNBLINDFOLDS
UNBLINDING
UNBLINKING
UNBLINKINGLY
UNBLISSFUL
UNBLOCKING
UNBLOODIED
UNBLUSHING
UNBLUSHINGLY
UNBLUSHINGNESS
UNBOASTFUL
UNBONNETED
UNBONNETING
UNBORROWED
UNBOSOMERS
UNBOSOMING
UNBOTTLING
UNBOTTOMED
UNBOUNDEDLY
UNBOUNDEDNESS
UNBOUNDEDNESSES
UNBOWDLERISED
UNBOWDLERIZED
UNBRACKETED
UNBRAIDING
UNBRANCHED
UNBREACHABLE
UNBREACHED
UNBREAKABLE
UNBREATHABLE
UNBREATHED
UNBREATHING
UNBREECHED
UNBREECHES
UNBREECHING
UNBRIBABLE
UNBRIDGEABLE
UNBRIDLEDLY
UNBRIDLEDNESS
UNBRIDLEDNESSES
UNBRIDLING
UNBRILLIANT
UNBROKENLY
UNBROKENNESS
UNBROKENNESSES
UNBROTHERLIKE
UNBROTHERLY
UNBUCKLING
UNBUDGEABLE
UNBUDGEABLY
UNBUDGETED
UNBUDGINGLY
UNBUFFERED
UNBUILDABLE
UNBUILDING
UNBUNDLERS
UNBUNDLING
UNBUNDLINGS
UNBURDENED
UNBURDENING
UNBUREAUCRATIC
UNBURNABLE
UNBURNISHED
UNBURROWED
UNBURROWING
UNBURTHENED
UNBURTHENING
UNBURTHENS
UNBUSINESSLIKE
UNBUTTERED
UNBUTTONED
UNBUTTONING
UNCALCIFIED
UNCALCINED
UNCALCULATED
UNCALCULATING
UNCALIBRATED
UNCALLOUSED
UNCANCELED
UNCANDIDLY
UNCANDIDNESS
UNCANDIDNESSES
UNCANDOURS
UNCANNIEST
UNCANNINESS
UNCANNINESSES
UNCANONICAL
UNCANONICALNESS
UNCANONISE
UNCANONISED

UNCANONISES
UNCANONISING
UNCANONIZE
UNCANONIZED
UNCANONIZES
UNCANONIZING
UNCAPITALISED
UNCAPITALIZED
UNCAPSIZABLE
UNCAPTIONED
UNCAPTURABLE
UNCARPETED
UNCASTRATED
UNCATALOGED
UNCATALOGUED
UNCATCHABLE
UNCATEGORISABLE
UNCATEGORIZABLE
UNCEASINGLY
UNCEASINGNESS
UNCEASINGNESSES
UNCELEBRATED
UNCENSORED
UNCENSORIOUS
UNCENSURED
UNCEREBRAL
UNCEREMONIOUS
UNCEREMONIOUSLY
UNCERTAINLY
UNCERTAINNESS
UNCERTAINNESSES
UNCERTAINTIES
UNCERTAINTY
UNCERTIFICATED
UNCERTIFIED
UNCHAINING
UNCHAIRING
UNCHALLENGEABLE
UNCHALLENGEABLY
UNCHALLENGED
UNCHALLENGING
UNCHANCIER
UNCHANCIEST
UNCHANGEABILITY
UNCHANGEABLE
UNCHANGEABLY
UNCHANGING
UNCHANGINGLY
UNCHANGINGNESS
UNCHANNELED
UNCHAPERONED
UNCHARGING
UNCHARISMATIC
UNCHARITABLE
UNCHARITABLY
UNCHARITIES
UNCHARMING
UNCHARNELLED
UNCHARNELLING
UNCHARNELS
UNCHARTERED
UNCHASTELY
UNCHASTENED
UNCHASTENESS
UNCHASTENESSES
UNCHASTEST
UNCHASTISABLE
UNCHASTISED
UNCHASTITIES
UNCHASTITY
UNCHASTIZABLE
UNCHASTIZED
UNCHAUVINISTIC
UNCHECKABLE
UNCHECKING
UNCHEERFUL
UNCHEERFULLY
UNCHEERFULNESS
UNCHEWABLE
UNCHILDING
UNCHILDLIKE
UNCHIVALROUS
UNCHIVALROUSLY
UNCHLORINATED
UNCHOREOGRAPHED
UNCHRISTEN
UNCHRISTENED
UNCHRISTENING
UNCHRISTENS
UNCHRISTIAN
UNCHRISTIANED
UNCHRISTIANING
UNCHRISTIANISE
UNCHRISTIANISED
UNCHRISTIANISES
UNCHRISTIANIZE
UNCHRISTIANIZED
UNCHRISTIANIZES
UNCHRISTIANLIKE
UNCHRISTIANLY
UNCHRISTIANS
UNCHRONICLED
UNCHRONOLOGICAL
UNCHURCHED
UNCHURCHES
UNCHURCHING
UNCHURCHLY
UNCILIATED
UNCINARIAS
UNCINARIASES
UNCINARIASIS
UNCINEMATIC
UNCIPHERED
UNCIPHERING
UNCIRCULATED
UNCIRCUMCISED
UNCIRCUMCISION
UNCIRCUMCISIONS
UNCIRCUMSCRIBED
UNCIVILISED
UNCIVILISEDLY
UNCIVILISEDNESS
UNCIVILITIES
UNCIVILITY
UNCIVILIZED
UNCIVILIZEDLY
UNCIVILIZEDNESS
UNCIVILNESS
UNCIVILNESSES
UNCLAMPING
UNCLARIFIED
UNCLARITIES
UNCLASPING
UNCLASSICAL
UNCLASSIFIABLE
UNCLASSIFIED
UNCLEANEST
UNCLEANLIER
UNCLEANLIEST
UNCLEANLINESS
UNCLEANLINESSES
UNCLEANNESS
UNCLEANNESSES
UNCLEANSED
UNCLEAREST
UNCLEARNESS
UNCLEARNESSES
UNCLENCHED
UNCLENCHES
UNCLENCHING
UNCLERICAL
UNCLESHIPS
UNCLIMBABLE
UNCLIMBABLENESS
UNCLINCHED
UNCLINCHES
UNCLINCHING
UNCLIPPING
UNCLOAKING
UNCLOGGING
UNCLOISTER
UNCLOISTERED
UNCLOISTERING
UNCLOISTERS
UNCLOTHING
UNCLOUDEDLY
UNCLOUDEDNESS
UNCLOUDEDNESSES
UNCLOUDING
UNCLUBABLE
UNCLUBBABLE
UNCLUTCHED
UNCLUTCHES
UNCLUTCHING
UNCLUTTERED
UNCLUTTERING
UNCLUTTERS
UNCOALESCE
UNCOALESCED
UNCOALESCES
UNCOALESCING
UNCOATINGS
UNCODIFIED
UNCOERCIVE
UNCOERCIVELY
UNCOFFINED
UNCOFFINING
UNCOLLECTED
UNCOLLECTIBLE
UNCOLLECTIBLES
UNCOLOURED
UNCOMATABLE
UNCOMBATIVE
UNCOMBINED
UNCOMBINES
UNCOMBINING
UNCOMEATABLE
UNCOMELINESS
UNCOMELINESSES
UNCOMFORTABLE
UNCOMFORTABLY
UNCOMFORTED
UNCOMMENDABLE
UNCOMMENDABLY
UNCOMMENDED
UNCOMMERCIAL
UNCOMMITTED
UNCOMMONER
UNCOMMONEST
UNCOMMONLY
UNCOMMONNESS
UNCOMMONNESSES
UNCOMMUNICABLE
UNCOMMUNICATED
UNCOMMUNICATIVE
UNCOMMUTED
UNCOMPACTED
UNCOMPANIED
UNCOMPANIONABLE
UNCOMPANIONED
UNCOMPASSIONATE
UNCOMPELLED
UNCOMPELLING
UNCOMPENSATED
UNCOMPETITIVE
UNCOMPLACENT
UNCOMPLAINING
UNCOMPLAININGLY
UNCOMPLAISANT
UNCOMPLAISANTLY
UNCOMPLETED
UNCOMPLIANT
UNCOMPLICATED
UNCOMPLIMENTARY
UNCOMPLYING
UNCOMPOSABLE
UNCOMPOUNDED
UNCOMPREHENDED
UNCOMPREHENDING
UNCOMPREHENSIVE
UNCOMPROMISABLE
UNCOMPROMISING
UNCOMPUTERISED
UNCOMPUTERIZED
UNCONCEALABLE
UNCONCEALED
UNCONCEALING
UNCONCEIVABLE
UNCONCEIVABLY
UNCONCEIVED
UNCONCERNED
UNCONCERNEDLY
UNCONCERNEDNESS
UNCONCERNING
UNCONCERNMENT
UNCONCERNMENTS
UNCONCERNS
UNCONCERTED
UNCONCILIATORY
UNCONCLUSIVE
UNCONCOCTED
UNCONDITIONAL
UNCONDITIONALLY
UNCONDITIONED

UNCONFEDERATED
UNCONFESSED
UNCONFINABLE
UNCONFINED
UNCONFINEDLY
UNCONFINES
UNCONFINING
UNCONFIRMED
UNCONFORMABLE
UNCONFORMABLY
UNCONFORMING
UNCONFORMITIES
UNCONFORMITY
UNCONFOUNDED
UNCONFUSED
UNCONFUSEDLY
UNCONFUSES
UNCONFUSING
UNCONGEALED
UNCONGEALING
UNCONGEALS
UNCONGENIAL
UNCONGENIALITY
UNCONJECTURED
UNCONJUGAL
UNCONJUGATED
UNCONJUNCTIVE
UNCONNECTED
UNCONNECTEDLY
UNCONNECTEDNESS
UNCONNIVING
UNCONQUERABLE
UNCONQUERABLY
UNCONQUERED
UNCONSCIENTIOUS
UNCONSCIONABLE
UNCONSCIONABLY
UNCONSCIOUS
UNCONSCIOUSES
UNCONSCIOUSLY
UNCONSCIOUSNESS
UNCONSECRATE
UNCONSECRATED
UNCONSECRATES
UNCONSECRATING
UNCONSENTANEOUS
UNCONSENTING
UNCONSIDERED
UNCONSIDERING
UNCONSOLED
UNCONSOLIDATED
UNCONSTANT
UNCONSTRAINABLE
UNCONSTRAINED
UNCONSTRAINEDLY
UNCONSTRAINT
UNCONSTRAINTS
UNCONSTRICTED
UNCONSTRUCTED
UNCONSTRUCTIVE
UNCONSUMED
UNCONSUMMATED
UNCONTAINABLE
UNCONTAMINATED
UNCONTEMNED
UNCONTEMPLATED
UNCONTEMPORARY
UNCONTENTIOUS
UNCONTESTABLE
UNCONTESTED
UNCONTRACTED
UNCONTRADICTED
UNCONTRIVED
UNCONTROLLABLE
UNCONTROLLABLY
UNCONTROLLED
UNCONTROLLEDLY
UNCONTROVERSIAL
UNCONTROVERTED
UNCONVENTIONAL
UNCONVERSABLE
UNCONVERSANT
UNCONVERTED
UNCONVERTIBLE
UNCONVICTED
UNCONVINCED
UNCONVINCING
UNCONVINCINGLY
UNCONVOYED
UNCOOPERATIVE
UNCOOPERATIVELY
UNCOORDINATED
UNCOPYRIGHTABLE
UNCOQUETTISH
UNCORRECTABLE
UNCORRECTED
UNCORRELATED
UNCORROBORATED
UNCORRUPTED
UNCORSETED
UNCOUNSELLED
UNCOUNTABLE
UNCOUPLERS
UNCOUPLING
UNCOURAGEOUS
UNCOURTEOUS
UNCOURTLINESS
UNCOURTLINESSES
UNCOUTHEST
UNCOUTHNESS
UNCOUTHNESSES
UNCOVENANTED
UNCOVERING
UNCREATEDNESS
UNCREATEDNESSES
UNCREATING
UNCREATIVE
UNCREDENTIALED
UNCREDIBLE
UNCREDITABLE
UNCREDITED
UNCRIPPLED
UNCRITICAL
UNCRITICALLY
UNCROSSABLE
UNCROSSING
UNCROWNING
UNCRUMPLED
UNCRUMPLES
UNCRUMPLING
UNCRUSHABLE
UNCRYSTALLISED
UNCRYSTALLIZED
UNCTIONLESS
UNCTUOSITIES
UNCTUOSITY
UNCTUOUSLY
UNCTUOUSNESS
UNCTUOUSNESSES
UNCUCKOLDED
UNCULTIVABLE
UNCULTIVATABLE
UNCULTIVATED
UNCULTURED
UNCUMBERED
UNCURBABLE
UNCURTAILED
UNCURTAINED
UNCURTAINING
UNCURTAINS
UNCUSTOMARILY
UNCUSTOMARY
UNCUSTOMED
UNCYNICALLY
UNDANCEABLE
UNDAUNTABLE
UNDAUNTEDLY
UNDAUNTEDNESS
UNDAUNTEDNESSES
UNDAZZLING
UNDEBARRED
UNDEBATABLE
UNDEBATABLY
UNDEBAUCHED
UNDECADENT
UNDECAGONS
UNDECEIVABLE
UNDECEIVED
UNDECEIVER
UNDECEIVERS
UNDECEIVES
UNDECEIVING
UNDECIDABILITY
UNDECIDABLE
UNDECIDEDLY
UNDECIDEDNESS
UNDECIDEDNESSES
UNDECIDEDS
UNDECILLION
UNDECILLIONS
UNDECIMOLE
UNDECIMOLES
UNDECIPHERABLE
UNDECIPHERED
UNDECISIVE
UNDECLARED
UNDECLINING
UNDECOMPOSABLE
UNDECOMPOSED
UNDECORATED
UNDEDICATED
UNDEFEATED
UNDEFENDED
UNDEFINABLE
UNDEFOLIATED
UNDEFORMED
UNDEIFYING
UNDELAYING
UNDELECTABLE
UNDELEGATED
UNDELIBERATE
UNDELIGHTED
UNDELIGHTFUL
UNDELIGHTS
UNDELIVERABLE
UNDELIVERED
UNDEMANDING
UNDEMOCRATIC
UNDEMONSTRABLE
UNDEMONSTRATIVE
UNDENIABLE
UNDENIABLENESS
UNDENIABLY
UNDEPENDABLE
UNDEPENDING
UNDEPLORED
UNDEPRAVED
UNDEPRECIATED
UNDEPRESSED
UNDEPRIVED
UNDERACHIEVE
UNDERACHIEVED
UNDERACHIEVER
UNDERACHIEVERS
UNDERACHIEVES
UNDERACHIEVING
UNDERACTED
UNDERACTING
UNDERACTION
UNDERACTIONS
UNDERACTIVE
UNDERACTIVITIES
UNDERACTIVITY
UNDERACTOR
UNDERACTORS
UNDERAGENT
UNDERAGENTS
UNDERBAKED
UNDERBAKES
UNDERBAKING
UNDERBEARER
UNDERBEARERS
UNDERBEARING
UNDERBEARINGS
UNDERBEARS
UNDERBELLIES
UNDERBELLY
UNDERBIDDER
UNDERBIDDERS
UNDERBIDDING
UNDERBITES
UNDERBITING
UNDERBITTEN
UNDERBLANKET
UNDERBLANKETS
UNDERBODIES
UNDERBORNE
UNDERBOSSES
UNDERBOUGH
UNDERBOUGHS
UNDERBOUGHT
UNDERBREATH
UNDERBREATHS
UNDERBREEDING

UNDERBREEDINGS
UNDERBRIDGE
UNDERBRIDGES
UNDERBRIMS
UNDERBRUSH
UNDERBRUSHED
UNDERBRUSHES
UNDERBRUSHING
UNDERBUDDED
UNDERBUDDING
UNDERBUDGET
UNDERBUDGETED
UNDERBUDGETING
UNDERBUDGETS
UNDERBUILD
UNDERBUILDER
UNDERBUILDERS
UNDERBUILDING
UNDERBUILDS
UNDERBUILT
UNDERBURNT
UNDERBUSHED
UNDERBUSHES
UNDERBUSHING
UNDERBUYING
UNDERCAPITALISE
UNDERCAPITALIZE
UNDERCARDS
UNDERCARRIAGE
UNDERCARRIAGES
UNDERCARTS
UNDERCASTS
UNDERCHARGE
UNDERCHARGED
UNDERCHARGES
UNDERCHARGING
UNDERCLASS
UNDERCLASSES
UNDERCLASSMAN
UNDERCLASSMEN
UNDERCLAYS
UNDERCLIFF
UNDERCLIFFS
UNDERCLOTHE
UNDERCLOTHED
UNDERCLOTHES
UNDERCLOTHING
UNDERCLOTHINGS
UNDERCLUBBED
UNDERCLUBBING
UNDERCLUBS
UNDERCOATED
UNDERCOATING
UNDERCOATINGS
UNDERCOATS
UNDERCOOKED
UNDERCOOKING
UNDERCOOKS
UNDERCOOLED
UNDERCOOLING
UNDERCOOLS
UNDERCOUNT
UNDERCOUNTED
UNDERCOUNTING
UNDERCOUNTS
UNDERCOVER
UNDERCOVERT
UNDERCOVERTS
UNDERCREST
UNDERCRESTED
UNDERCRESTING
UNDERCRESTS
UNDERCROFT
UNDERCROFTS
UNDERCURRENT
UNDERCURRENTS
UNDERCUTTING
UNDERDAMPER
UNDERDAMPERS
UNDERDECKS
UNDERDEVELOP
UNDERDEVELOPED
UNDERDEVELOPING
UNDERDEVELOPS
UNDERDOERS
UNDERDOING
UNDERDOSED
UNDERDOSES
UNDERDOSING
UNDERDRAIN
UNDERDRAINAGE
UNDERDRAINAGES
UNDERDRAINED
UNDERDRAINING
UNDERDRAINS
UNDERDRAWERS
UNDERDRAWING
UNDERDRAWINGS
UNDERDRAWN
UNDERDRAWS
UNDERDRESS
UNDERDRESSED
UNDERDRESSES
UNDERDRESSING
UNDERDRIVE
UNDERDRIVES
UNDEREARTH
UNDEREATEN
UNDEREATING
UNDEREDUCATED
UNDEREMPHASES
UNDEREMPHASIS
UNDEREMPHASISE
UNDEREMPHASISED
UNDEREMPHASISES
UNDEREMPHASIZE
UNDEREMPHASIZED
UNDEREMPHASIZES
UNDEREMPLOYED
UNDEREMPLOYMENT
UNDERESTIMATE
UNDERESTIMATED
UNDERESTIMATES
UNDERESTIMATING
UNDERESTIMATION
UNDEREXPOSE
UNDEREXPOSED
UNDEREXPOSES
UNDEREXPOSING
UNDEREXPOSURE
UNDEREXPOSURES
UNDERFEEDING
UNDERFEEDS
UNDERFELTS
UNDERFINANCED
UNDERFINISHED
UNDERFIRED
UNDERFIRES
UNDERFIRING
UNDERFISHED
UNDERFISHES
UNDERFISHING
UNDERFLOOR
UNDERFLOWS
UNDERFONGED
UNDERFONGING
UNDERFONGS
UNDERFOOTED
UNDERFOOTING
UNDERFOOTS
UNDERFULFIL
UNDERFULFILLED
UNDERFULFILLING
UNDERFULFILS
UNDERFUNDED
UNDERFUNDING
UNDERFUNDINGS
UNDERFUNDS
UNDERGARMENT
UNDERGARMENTS
UNDERGIRDED
UNDERGIRDING
UNDERGIRDS
UNDERGLAZE
UNDERGLAZES
UNDERGOERS
UNDERGOING
UNDERGOWNS
UNDERGRADS
UNDERGRADUATE
UNDERGRADUATES
UNDERGRADUETTE
UNDERGRADUETTES
UNDERGROUND
UNDERGROUNDER
UNDERGROUNDERS
UNDERGROUNDS
UNDERGROVE
UNDERGROVES
UNDERGROWN
UNDERGROWTH
UNDERGROWTHS
UNDERHAIRS
UNDERHANDED
UNDERHANDEDLY
UNDERHANDEDNESS
UNDERHANDS
UNDERHEATED
UNDERHEATING
UNDERHEATS
UNDERHONEST
UNDERINFLATED
UNDERINFLATION
UNDERINFLATIONS
UNDERINSURED
UNDERINVESTMENT
UNDERJAWED
UNDERKEEPER
UNDERKEEPERS
UNDERKEEPING
UNDERKEEPS
UNDERKILLS
UNDERKINGDOM
UNDERKINGDOMS
UNDERKINGS
UNDERLAPPED
UNDERLAPPING
UNDERLAYER
UNDERLAYERS
UNDERLAYING
UNDERLAYMENT
UNDERLAYMENTS
UNDERLEASE
UNDERLEASED
UNDERLEASES
UNDERLEASING
UNDERLEAVES
UNDERLETTER
UNDERLETTERS
UNDERLETTING
UNDERLETTINGS
UNDERLIERS
UNDERLINED
UNDERLINEN
UNDERLINENS
UNDERLINES
UNDERLINGS
UNDERLINING
UNDERLOADED
UNDERLOADING
UNDERLOADS
UNDERLOOKER
UNDERLOOKERS
UNDERLYING
UNDERLYINGLY
UNDERMANNED
UNDERMANNING
UNDERMASTED
UNDERMEANING
UNDERMEANINGS
UNDERMENTIONED
UNDERMINDE
UNDERMINDED
UNDERMINDES
UNDERMINDING
UNDERMINED
UNDERMINER
UNDERMINERS
UNDERMINES
UNDERMINING
UNDERMININGS
UNDERNAMED
UNDERNEATH
UNDERNEATHS
UNDERNICENESS
UNDERNICENESSES
UNDERNOTED
UNDERNOTES
UNDERNOTING
UNDERNOURISH
UNDERNOURISHED
UNDERNOURISHES
UNDERNOURISHING
UNDERNTIME

UNDERNTIMES
UNDERNUTRITION
UNDERNUTRITIONS
UNDERPAINTING
UNDERPAINTINGS
UNDERPANTS
UNDERPARTS
UNDERPASSES
UNDERPASSION
UNDERPASSIONS
UNDERPAYING
UNDERPAYMENT
UNDERPAYMENTS
UNDERPEEPED
UNDERPEEPING
UNDERPEEPS
UNDERPEOPLED
UNDERPERFORM
UNDERPERFORMED
UNDERPERFORMING
UNDERPERFORMS
UNDERPINNED
UNDERPINNING
UNDERPINNINGS
UNDERPITCH
UNDERPLANT
UNDERPLANTED
UNDERPLANTING
UNDERPLANTS
UNDERPLAYED
UNDERPLAYING
UNDERPLAYS
UNDERPLOTS
UNDERPOPULATED
UNDERPOWERED
UNDERPRAISE
UNDERPRAISED
UNDERPRAISES
UNDERPRAISING
UNDERPREPARED
UNDERPRICE
UNDERPRICED
UNDERPRICES
UNDERPRICING
UNDERPRISE
UNDERPRISED
UNDERPRISES
UNDERPRISING
UNDERPRIVILEGED
UNDERPRIZE
UNDERPRIZED
UNDERPRIZES
UNDERPRIZING
UNDERPRODUCTION
UNDERPROOF
UNDERPROPPED
UNDERPROPPER
UNDERPROPPERS
UNDERPROPPING
UNDERPROPS
UNDERPUBLICISED
UNDERPUBLICIZED
UNDERQUOTE
UNDERQUOTED
UNDERQUOTES
UNDERQUOTING
UNDERRATED
UNDERRATES
UNDERRATING
UNDERREACT
UNDERREACTED
UNDERREACTING
UNDERREACTS
UNDERREPORT
UNDERREPORTED
UNDERREPORTING
UNDERREPORTS
UNDERRUNNING
UNDERRUNNINGS
UNDERSATURATED
UNDERSAYING
UNDERSCORE
UNDERSCORED
UNDERSCORES
UNDERSCORING
UNDERSCRUB
UNDERSCRUBS
UNDERSEALED
UNDERSEALING
UNDERSEALINGS
UNDERSEALS
UNDERSECRETARY
UNDERSELLER
UNDERSELLERS
UNDERSELLING
UNDERSELLS
UNDERSELVES
UNDERSENSE
UNDERSENSES
UNDERSERVED
UNDERSETTING
UNDERSEXED
UNDERSHAPEN
UNDERSHERIFF
UNDERSHERIFFS
UNDERSHIRT
UNDERSHIRTED
UNDERSHIRTS
UNDERSHOOT
UNDERSHOOTING
UNDERSHOOTS
UNDERSHORTS
UNDERSHRUB
UNDERSHRUBS
UNDERSIDES
UNDERSIGNED
UNDERSIGNING
UNDERSIGNS
UNDERSIZED
UNDERSKIES
UNDERSKINKER
UNDERSKINKERS
UNDERSKIRT
UNDERSKIRTS
UNDERSLEEVE
UNDERSLEEVES
UNDERSLUNG
UNDERSOILS
UNDERSONGS
UNDERSPEND
UNDERSPENDING
UNDERSPENDS
UNDERSPENT
UNDERSPINS
UNDERSTAFFED
UNDERSTAFFING
UNDERSTAFFINGS
UNDERSTAND
UNDERSTANDABLE
UNDERSTANDABLY
UNDERSTANDED
UNDERSTANDER
UNDERSTANDERS
UNDERSTANDING
UNDERSTANDINGLY
UNDERSTANDINGS
UNDERSTANDS
UNDERSTATE
UNDERSTATED
UNDERSTATEDLY
UNDERSTATEMENT
UNDERSTATEMENTS
UNDERSTATES
UNDERSTATING
UNDERSTEER
UNDERSTEERED
UNDERSTEERING
UNDERSTEERS
UNDERSTOCK
UNDERSTOCKED
UNDERSTOCKING
UNDERSTOCKS
UNDERSTOOD
UNDERSTOREY
UNDERSTOREYS
UNDERSTORIES
UNDERSTORY
UNDERSTRAPPER
UNDERSTRAPPERS
UNDERSTRAPPING
UNDERSTRATA
UNDERSTRATUM
UNDERSTRENGTH
UNDERSTUDIED
UNDERSTUDIES
UNDERSTUDY
UNDERSTUDYING
UNDERSUPPLIED
UNDERSUPPLIES
UNDERSUPPLY
UNDERSUPPLYING
UNDERSURFACE
UNDERSURFACES
UNDERTAKABLE
UNDERTAKEN
UNDERTAKER
UNDERTAKERS
UNDERTAKES
UNDERTAKING
UNDERTAKINGS
UNDERTAXED
UNDERTAXES
UNDERTAXING
UNDERTENANCIES
UNDERTENANCY
UNDERTENANT
UNDERTENANTS
UNDERTHINGS
UNDERTHIRST
UNDERTHIRSTS
UNDERTHRUST
UNDERTHRUSTING
UNDERTHRUSTS
UNDERTIMED
UNDERTIMES
UNDERTINTS
UNDERTONED
UNDERTONES
UNDERTRICK
UNDERTRICKS
UNDERTRUMP
UNDERTRUMPED
UNDERTRUMPING
UNDERTRUMPS
UNDERUSING
UNDERUTILISE
UNDERUTILISED
UNDERUTILISES
UNDERUTILISING
UNDERUTILIZE
UNDERUTILIZED
UNDERUTILIZES
UNDERUTILIZING
UNDERVALUATION
UNDERVALUATIONS
UNDERVALUE
UNDERVALUED
UNDERVALUER
UNDERVALUERS
UNDERVALUES
UNDERVALUING
UNDERVESTS
UNDERVIEWER
UNDERVIEWERS
UNDERVOICE
UNDERVOICES
UNDERVOTES
UNDERWATER
UNDERWATERS
UNDERWEARS
UNDERWEIGHT
UNDERWEIGHTS
UNDERWHELM
UNDERWHELMED
UNDERWHELMING
UNDERWHELMS
UNDERWINGS
UNDERWIRED
UNDERWIRES
UNDERWIRING
UNDERWIRINGS
UNDERWOODS
UNDERWOOLS
UNDERWORKED
UNDERWORKER
UNDERWORKERS
UNDERWORKING
UNDERWORKS
UNDERWORLD
UNDERWORLDS
UNDERWRITE
UNDERWRITER
UNDERWRITERS
UNDERWRITES

UNDERWRITING
UNDERWRITINGS
UNDERWRITTEN
UNDERWROTE
UNDERWROUGHT
UNDESCENDABLE
UNDESCENDED
UNDESCENDIBLE
UNDESCRIBABLE
UNDESCRIBED
UNDESCRIED
UNDESERVED
UNDESERVEDLY
UNDESERVEDNESS
UNDESERVER
UNDESERVERS
UNDESERVES
UNDESERVING
UNDESERVINGLY
UNDESIGNATED
UNDESIGNED
UNDESIGNEDLY
UNDESIGNEDNESS
UNDESIGNING
UNDESIRABILITY
UNDESIRABLE
UNDESIRABLENESS
UNDESIRABLES
UNDESIRABLY
UNDESIRING
UNDESIROUS
UNDESPAIRING
UNDESPAIRINGLY
UNDESPOILED
UNDESTROYED
UNDETECTABLE
UNDETECTED
UNDETERMINABLE
UNDETERMINATE
UNDETERMINATION
UNDETERMINED
UNDETERRED
UNDEVELOPED
UNDEVIATING
UNDEVIATINGLY
UNDIAGNOSABLE
UNDIAGNOSED
UNDIALECTICAL
UNDIDACTIC
UNDIFFERENCED
UNDIGESTED
UNDIGESTIBLE
UNDIGHTING
UNDIGNIFIED
UNDIGNIFIES
UNDIGNIFYING
UNDIMINISHABLE
UNDIMINISHED
UNDIPLOMATIC
UNDIRECTED
UNDISAPPOINTING
UNDISCERNED
UNDISCERNEDLY
UNDISCERNIBLE
UNDISCERNIBLY
UNDISCERNING
UNDISCERNINGS
UNDISCHARGED
UNDISCIPLINABLE
UNDISCIPLINE
UNDISCIPLINED
UNDISCIPLINES
UNDISCLOSED
UNDISCOMFITED
UNDISCORDANT
UNDISCORDING
UNDISCOURAGED
UNDISCOVERABLE
UNDISCOVERABLY
UNDISCOVERED
UNDISCUSSABLE
UNDISCUSSED
UNDISCUSSIBLE
UNDISGUISABLE
UNDISGUISED
UNDISGUISEDLY
UNDISHONOURED
UNDISMANTLED
UNDISMAYED
UNDISORDERED
UNDISPATCHED
UNDISPENSED
UNDISPOSED
UNDISPUTABLE
UNDISPUTED
UNDISPUTEDLY
UNDISSEMBLED
UNDISSOCIATED
UNDISSOLVED
UNDISSOLVING
UNDISTEMPERED
UNDISTILLED
UNDISTINCTIVE
UNDISTINGUISHED
UNDISTORTED
UNDISTRACTED
UNDISTRACTEDLY
UNDISTRACTING
UNDISTRIBUTED
UNDISTURBED
UNDISTURBEDLY
UNDISTURBING
UNDIVERSIFIED
UNDIVERTED
UNDIVERTING
UNDIVESTED
UNDIVESTEDLY
UNDIVIDABLE
UNDIVIDEDLY
UNDIVIDEDNESS
UNDIVIDEDNESSES
UNDIVORCED
UNDIVULGED
UNDOCTORED
UNDOCTRINAIRE
UNDOCUMENTED
UNDOGMATIC
UNDOGMATICALLY
UNDOMESTIC
UNDOMESTICATE
UNDOMESTICATED
UNDOMESTICATES
UNDOMESTICATING
UNDOUBLING
UNDOUBTABLE
UNDOUBTEDLY
UNDOUBTFUL
UNDOUBTING
UNDOUBTINGLY
UNDRAINABLE
UNDRAMATIC
UNDRAMATICALLY
UNDRAMATISED
UNDRAMATIZED
UNDREADING
UNDREAMING
UNDRESSING
UNDRESSINGS
UNDRINKABLE
UNDRIVEABLE
UNDROOPING
UNDULANCES
UNDULANCIES
UNDULATELY
UNDULATING
UNDULATINGLY
UNDULATION
UNDULATIONIST
UNDULATIONISTS
UNDULATIONS
UNDULATORS
UNDULATORY
UNDUPLICATED
UNDUTIFULLY
UNDUTIFULNESS
UNDUTIFULNESSES
UNDYINGNESS
UNDYINGNESSES
UNEARMARKED
UNEARTHING
UNEARTHLIER
UNEARTHLIEST
UNEARTHLINESS
UNEARTHLINESSES
UNEASINESS
UNEASINESSES
UNEATABLENESS
UNEATABLENESSES
UNECCENTRIC
UNECLIPSED
UNECOLOGICAL
UNECONOMIC
UNECONOMICAL
UNEDIFYING
UNEDUCABLE
UNEDUCATED
UNEFFECTED
UNELABORATE
UNELABORATED
UNELECTABLE
UNELECTRIFIED
UNEMBARRASSED
UNEMBELLISHED
UNEMBITTERED
UNEMBODIED
UNEMOTIONAL
UNEMOTIONALLY
UNEMOTIONED
UNEMPHATIC
UNEMPHATICALLY
UNEMPIRICAL
UNEMPLOYABILITY
UNEMPLOYABLE
UNEMPLOYABLES
UNEMPLOYED
UNEMPLOYEDS
UNEMPLOYMENT
UNEMPLOYMENTS
UNENCHANTED
UNENCLOSED
UNENCOURAGING
UNENCUMBERED
UNENDANGERED
UNENDEARED
UNENDEARING
UNENDINGLY
UNENDINGNESS
UNENDINGNESSES
UNENDURABLE
UNENDURABLENESS
UNENDURABLY
UNENFORCEABLE
UNENFORCED
UNENJOYABLE
UNENLARGED
UNENLIGHTENED
UNENLIGHTENING
UNENQUIRING
UNENRICHED
UNENSLAVED
UNENTAILED
UNENTERPRISING
UNENTERTAINED
UNENTERTAINING
UNENTHRALLED
UNENTHUSIASTIC
UNENTITLED
UNENVIABLE
UNENVIABLY
UNEQUALLED
UNEQUIPPED
UNEQUITABLE
UNEQUIVOCABLY
UNEQUIVOCAL
UNEQUIVOCALLY
UNEQUIVOCALNESS
UNERASABLE
UNERRINGLY
UNERRINGNESS
UNERRINGNESSES
UNESCAPABLE
UNESCORTED
UNESSENCED
UNESSENCES
UNESSENCING
UNESSENTIAL
UNESSENTIALLY
UNESSENTIALS
UNESTABLISHED
UNEVALUATED
UNEVANGELICAL
UNEVENNESS
UNEVENNESSES
UNEVENTFUL

UNEVENTFULLY
UNEVENTFULNESS
UNEVIDENCED
UNEXACTING
UNEXAGGERATED
UNEXAMINED
UNEXAMPLED
UNEXCAVATED
UNEXCELLED
UNEXCEPTIONABLE
UNEXCEPTIONABLY
UNEXCEPTIONAL
UNEXCEPTIONALLY
UNEXCITABLE
UNEXCITING
UNEXCLUDED
UNEXCLUSIVE
UNEXCLUSIVELY
UNEXECUTED
UNEXEMPLIFIED
UNEXERCISED
UNEXHAUSTED
UNEXPANDED
UNEXPECTANT
UNEXPECTED
UNEXPECTEDLY
UNEXPECTEDNESS
UNEXPENDED
UNEXPENSIVE
UNEXPENSIVELY
UNEXPERIENCED
UNEXPERIENT
UNEXPIATED
UNEXPLAINABLE
UNEXPLAINED
UNEXPLODED
UNEXPLOITED
UNEXPLORED
UNEXPRESSED
UNEXPRESSIBLE
UNEXPRESSIVE
UNEXPUGNABLE
UNEXPURGATED
UNEXTENDED
UNEXTENUATED
UNEXTINGUISHED
UNEXTRAORDINARY
UNFADINGLY
UNFADINGNESS
UNFADINGNESSES
UNFAILINGLY
UNFAILINGNESS
UNFAILINGNESSES
UNFAIRNESS
UNFAIRNESSES
UNFAITHFUL
UNFAITHFULLY
UNFAITHFULNESS
UNFALLIBLE
UNFALSIFIABLE
UNFALTERING
UNFALTERINGLY
UNFAMILIAR
UNFAMILIARITIES
UNFAMILIARITY
UNFAMILIARLY
UNFASHIONABLE
UNFASHIONABLY
UNFASHIONED
UNFASTENED
UNFASTENING
UNFASTIDIOUS
UNFATHERED
UNFATHERLY
UNFATHOMABLE
UNFATHOMABLY
UNFATHOMED
UNFAVORABLE
UNFAVORABLENESS
UNFAVORABLY
UNFAVORITE
UNFAVOURABLE
UNFAVOURABLY
UNFAVOURED
UNFEARFULLY
UNFEASIBLE
UNFEATHERED
UNFEATURED
UNFEELINGLY
UNFEELINGNESS
UNFEELINGNESSES
UNFEIGNEDLY
UNFEIGNEDNESS
UNFEIGNEDNESSES
UNFEIGNING
UNFELLOWED
UNFEMININE
UNFERMENTED
UNFERTILISED
UNFERTILIZED
UNFETTERED
UNFETTERING
UNFEUDALISE
UNFEUDALISED
UNFEUDALISES
UNFEUDALISING
UNFEUDALIZE
UNFEUDALIZED
UNFEUDALIZES
UNFEUDALIZING
UNFILIALLY
UNFILLABLE
UNFILLETED
UNFILTERABLE
UNFILTERED
UNFILTRABLE
UNFINDABLE
UNFINISHED
UNFINISHING
UNFINISHINGS
UNFITNESSES
UNFITTEDNESS
UNFITTEDNESSES
UNFITTINGLY
UNFIXEDNESS
UNFIXEDNESSES
UNFIXITIES
UNFLAGGING
UNFLAGGINGLY
UNFLAMBOYANT
UNFLAPPABILITY
UNFLAPPABLE
UNFLAPPABLENESS
UNFLAPPABLY
UNFLATTERING
UNFLATTERINGLY
UNFLAVOURED
UNFLESHING
UNFLINCHING
UNFLINCHINGLY
UNFLUSHING
UNFLUSTERED
UNFOCUSSED
UNFOLDINGS
UNFOLDMENT
UNFOLDMENTS
UNFORBIDDEN
UNFORCEDLY
UNFORCIBLE
UNFORDABLE
UNFOREBODING
UNFOREKNOWABLE
UNFOREKNOWN
UNFORESEEABLE
UNFORESEEING
UNFORESEEN
UNFORESKINNED
UNFORESTED
UNFORETOLD
UNFOREWARNED
UNFORFEITED
UNFORGETTABLE
UNFORGETTABLY
UNFORGIVABLE
UNFORGIVEN
UNFORGIVENESS
UNFORGIVENESSES
UNFORGIVING
UNFORGIVINGNESS
UNFORGOTTEN
UNFORMALISED
UNFORMALIZED
UNFORMATTED
UNFORMIDABLE
UNFORMULATED
UNFORSAKEN
UNFORTHCOMING
UNFORTIFIED
UNFORTUNATE
UNFORTUNATELY
UNFORTUNATENESS
UNFORTUNATES
UNFORTUNED
UNFORTUNES
UNFOSSILIFEROUS
UNFOSSILISED
UNFOSSILIZED
UNFOSTERED
UNFOUGHTEN
UNFOUNDEDLY
UNFOUNDEDNESS
UNFOUNDEDNESSES
UNFRANCHISED
UNFRAUGHTED
UNFRAUGHTING
UNFRAUGHTS
UNFREEDOMS
UNFREEZING
UNFREQUENT
UNFREQUENTED
UNFREQUENTLY
UNFRIENDED
UNFRIENDEDNESS
UNFRIENDLIER
UNFRIENDLIEST
UNFRIENDLILY
UNFRIENDLINESS
UNFRIENDLY
UNFRIENDSHIP
UNFRIENDSHIPS
UNFRIGHTED
UNFRIGHTENED
UNFRIVOLOUS
UNFROCKING
UNFRUCTUOUS
UNFRUITFUL
UNFRUITFULLY
UNFRUITFULNESS
UNFULFILLABLE
UNFULFILLED
UNFURNISHED
UNFURNISHES
UNFURNISHING
UNFURROWED
UNFUSSIEST
UNGAINLIER
UNGAINLIEST
UNGAINLINESS
UNGAINLINESSES
UNGAINSAID
UNGAINSAYABLE
UNGALLANTLY
UNGARMENTED
UNGARNERED
UNGARNISHED
UNGARTERED
UNGATHERED
UNGENEROSITIES
UNGENEROSITY
UNGENEROUS
UNGENEROUSLY
UNGENITURED
UNGENTEELLY
UNGENTILITIES
UNGENTILITY
UNGENTLEMANLIKE
UNGENTLEMANLY
UNGENTLENESS
UNGENTLENESSES
UNGENTRIFIED
UNGENUINENESS
UNGENUINENESSES
UNGERMINATED
UNGETATABLE
UNGIMMICKY
UNGIRTHING
UNGLAMORISED
UNGLAMORIZED
UNGLAMOROUS
UNGODLIEST
UNGODLINESS
UNGODLINESSES
UNGOVERNABLE
UNGOVERNABLY

UNGOVERNED
UNGRACEFUL
UNGRACEFULLY
UNGRACEFULNESS
UNGRACIOUS
UNGRACIOUSLY
UNGRACIOUSNESS
UNGRAMMATIC
UNGRAMMATICAL
UNGRAMMATICALLY
UNGRASPABLE
UNGRATEFUL
UNGRATEFULLY
UNGRATEFULNESS
UNGRATIFIED
UNGROUNDED
UNGROUNDEDLY
UNGROUNDEDNESS
UNGRUDGING
UNGRUDGINGLY
UNGUARDEDLY
UNGUARDEDNESS
UNGUARDEDNESSES
UNGUARDING
UNGUENTARIA
UNGUENTARIES
UNGUENTARIUM
UNGUENTARY
UNGUERDONED
UNGUESSABLE
UNGUICULATE
UNGUICULATED
UNGUICULATES
UNGULIGRADE
UNHABITABLE
UNHABITUATED
UNHACKNEYED
UNHALLOWED
UNHALLOWING
UNHAMPERED
UNHANDIEST
UNHANDINESS
UNHANDINESSES
UNHANDSELED
UNHANDSOME
UNHANDSOMELY
UNHANDSOMENESS
UNHAPPIEST
UNHAPPINESS
UNHAPPINESSES
UNHAPPYING
UNHARBOURED
UNHARBOURING
UNHARBOURS
UNHARDENED
UNHARMFULLY
UNHARMONIOUS
UNHARNESSED
UNHARNESSES
UNHARNESSING
UNHARVESTED
UNHATTINGS
UNHAZARDED
UNHAZARDOUS
UNHEALABLE
UNHEALTHFUL
UNHEALTHFULLY
UNHEALTHFULNESS
UNHEALTHIER
UNHEALTHIEST
UNHEALTHILY
UNHEALTHINESS
UNHEALTHINESSES
UNHEARSING
UNHEARTING
UNHEEDEDLY
UNHEEDFULLY
UNHEEDINGLY
UNHELMETED
UNHELPABLE
UNHELPFULLY
UNHERALDED
UNHEROICAL
UNHEROICALLY
UNHESITATING
UNHESITATINGLY
UNHIDEBOUND
UNHINDERED
UNHINGEMENT
UNHINGEMENTS
UNHISTORIC
UNHISTORICAL
UNHITCHING
UNHOARDING
UNHOLINESS
UNHOLINESSES
UNHOMELIKE
UNHOMOGENISED
UNHOMOGENIZED
UNHONOURED
UNHOPEFULLY
UNHOSPITABLE
UNHOUSELED
UNHOUZZLED
UNHUMANISE
UNHUMANISED
UNHUMANISES
UNHUMANISING
UNHUMANIZE
UNHUMANIZED
UNHUMANIZES
UNHUMANIZING
UNHUMOROUS
UNHURRIEDLY
UNHURRYING
UNHURTFULLY
UNHURTFULNESS
UNHURTFULNESSES
UNHUSBANDED
UNHYDROLYSED
UNHYDROLYZED
UNHYGIENIC
UNHYPHENATED
UNHYSTERICAL
UNHYSTERICALLY
UNIAXIALLY
UNICAMERAL
UNICAMERALISM
UNICAMERALISMS
UNICAMERALIST
UNICAMERALISTS
UNICAMERALLY
UNICELLULAR
UNICELLULARITY
UNICENTRAL
UNICOLORATE
UNICOLOROUS
UNICOLOURED
UNICOSTATE
UNICYCLING
UNICYCLIST
UNICYCLISTS
UNIDEALISM
UNIDEALISMS
UNIDEALISTIC
UNIDENTIFIABLE
UNIDENTIFIED
UNIDEOLOGICAL
UNIDIMENSIONAL
UNIDIOMATIC
UNIDIOMATICALLY
UNIDIRECTIONAL
UNIFICATION
UNIFICATIONS
UNIFLOROUS
UNIFOLIATE
UNIFOLIOLATE
UNIFORMEST
UNIFORMING
UNIFORMITARIAN
UNIFORMITARIANS
UNIFORMITIES
UNIFORMITY
UNIFORMNESS
UNIFORMNESSES
UNIGENITURE
UNIGENITURES
UNIGNORABLE
UNILABIATE
UNILATERAL
UNILATERALISM
UNILATERALISMS
UNILATERALIST
UNILATERALISTS
UNILATERALITIES
UNILATERALITY
UNILATERALLY
UNILINGUAL
UNILINGUALISM
UNILINGUALISMS
UNILINGUALS
UNILITERAL
UNILLUMINATED
UNILLUMINATING
UNILLUMINED
UNILLUSIONED
UNILLUSTRATED
UNILOBULAR
UNILOCULAR
UNIMAGINABLE
UNIMAGINABLY
UNIMAGINATIVE
UNIMAGINATIVELY
UNIMAGINED
UNIMMORTAL
UNIMMUNISED
UNIMMUNIZED
UNIMOLECULAR
UNIMPAIRED
UNIMPARTED
UNIMPASSIONED
UNIMPEACHABLE
UNIMPEACHABLY
UNIMPEACHED
UNIMPEDEDLY
UNIMPLORED
UNIMPORTANCE
UNIMPORTANCES
UNIMPORTANT
UNIMPORTUNED
UNIMPOSING
UNIMPREGNATED
UNIMPRESSED
UNIMPRESSIBLE
UNIMPRESSIVE
UNIMPRISONED
UNIMPROVED
UNIMPUGNABLE
UNINAUGURATED
UNINCHANTED
UNINCLOSED
UNINCORPORATED
UNINCUMBERED
UNINDEARED
UNINDICTED
UNINFECTED
UNINFLAMED
UNINFLAMMABLE
UNINFLATED
UNINFLECTED
UNINFLUENCED
UNINFLUENTIAL
UNINFORCEABLE
UNINFORCED
UNINFORMATIVE
UNINFORMATIVELY
UNINFORMED
UNINFORMING
UNINGRATIATING
UNINHABITABLE
UNINHABITED
UNINHIBITED
UNINHIBITEDLY
UNINHIBITEDNESS
UNINITIATE
UNINITIATED
UNINITIATES
UNINOCULATED
UNINQUIRING
UNINQUISITIVE
UNINSCRIBED
UNINSPECTED
UNINSPIRED
UNINSPIRING
UNINSTALLED
UNINSTALLING
UNINSTALLS
UNINSTRUCTED
UNINSTRUCTIVE
UNINSULATED
UNINSURABLE
UNINSUREDS
UNINTEGRATED
UNINTELLECTUAL

UNINTELLIGENCE
UNINTELLIGENCES
UNINTELLIGENT
UNINTELLIGENTLY
UNINTELLIGIBLE
UNINTELLIGIBLY
UNINTENDED
UNINTENTIONAL
UNINTENTIONALLY
UNINTEREST
UNINTERESTED
UNINTERESTEDLY
UNINTERESTING
UNINTERESTINGLY
UNINTERESTS
UNINTERMITTED
UNINTERMITTEDLY
UNINTERMITTING
UNINTERPRETABLE
UNINTERRUPTED
UNINTERRUPTEDLY
UNINTIMIDATED
UNINTOXICATING
UNINTRODUCED
UNINUCLEAR
UNINUCLEATE
UNINVENTIVE
UNINVESTED
UNINVIDIOUS
UNINVITING
UNINVOLVED
UNIONISATION
UNIONISATIONS
UNIONISERS
UNIONISING
UNIONISTIC
UNIONIZATION
UNIONIZATIONS
UNIONIZERS
UNIONIZING
UNIPARENTAL
UNIPARENTALLY
UNIPARTITE
UNIPERSONAL
UNIPERSONALITY
UNIPOLARITIES
UNIPOLARITY
UNIQUENESS
UNIQUENESSES
UNIRONICALLY
UNIRRADIATED
UNIRRIGATED
UNISEPTATE
UNISERIALLY
UNISERIATE
UNISERIATELY
UNISEXUALITIES
UNISEXUALITY
UNISEXUALLY
UNISONALLY
UNISONANCE
UNISONANCES
UNITARIANISM
UNITARIANISMS
UNITARIANS
UNITEDNESS
UNITEDNESSES
UNITHOLDER
UNITHOLDERS
UNITISATION
UNITISATIONS
UNITIZATION
UNITIZATIONS
UNIVALENCE
UNIVALENCES
UNIVALENCIES
UNIVALENCY
UNIVALENTS
UNIVALVULAR
UNIVARIANT
UNIVARIATE
UNIVERSALISE
UNIVERSALISED
UNIVERSALISES
UNIVERSALISING
UNIVERSALISM
UNIVERSALISMS
UNIVERSALIST
UNIVERSALISTIC
UNIVERSALISTS
UNIVERSALITIES
UNIVERSALITY
UNIVERSALIZE
UNIVERSALIZED
UNIVERSALIZES
UNIVERSALIZING
UNIVERSALLY
UNIVERSALNESS
UNIVERSALNESSES
UNIVERSALS
UNIVERSITARIAN
UNIVERSITIES
UNIVERSITY
UNIVOCALLY
UNIVOLTINE
UNJAUNDICED
UNJOINTING
UNJUSTIFIABLE
UNJUSTIFIABLY
UNJUSTIFIED
UNJUSTNESS
UNJUSTNESSES
UNKEMPTNESS
UNKEMPTNESSES
UNKENNELED
UNKENNELING
UNKENNELLED
UNKENNELLING
UNKINDLIER
UNKINDLIEST
UNKINDLINESS
UNKINDLINESSES
UNKINDNESS
UNKINDNESSES
UNKINGLIER
UNKINGLIEST
UNKINGLIKE
UNKNIGHTED
UNKNIGHTING
UNKNIGHTLINESS
UNKNIGHTLY
UNKNITTING
UNKNOTTING
UNKNOWABILITIES
UNKNOWABILITY
UNKNOWABLE
UNKNOWABLENESS
UNKNOWABLES
UNKNOWABLY
UNKNOWINGLY
UNKNOWINGNESS
UNKNOWINGNESSES
UNKNOWINGS
UNKNOWLEDGEABLE
UNKNOWNNESS
UNKNOWNNESSES
UNLABELLED
UNLABORIOUS
UNLABOURED
UNLABOURING
UNLADYLIKE
UNLAMENTED
UNLATCHING
UNLAUNDERED
UNLAWFULLY
UNLAWFULNESS
UNLAWFULNESSES
UNLEARNABLE
UNLEARNEDLY
UNLEARNEDNESS
UNLEARNEDNESSES
UNLEARNING
UNLEASHING
UNLEAVENED
UNLEISURED
UNLEISURELY
UNLESSONED
UNLETTABLE
UNLETTERED
UNLEVELING
UNLEVELLED
UNLEVELLING
UNLIBERATED
UNLIBIDINOUS
UNLICENSED
UNLIFELIKE
UNLIGHTENED
UNLIGHTSOME
UNLIKEABLE
UNLIKELIER
UNLIKELIEST
UNLIKELIHOOD
UNLIKELIHOODS
UNLIKELINESS
UNLIKELINESSES
UNLIKENESS
UNLIKENESSES
UNLIMBERED
UNLIMBERING
UNLIMITEDLY
UNLIMITEDNESS
UNLIMITEDNESSES
UNLIQUEFIED
UNLIQUIDATED
UNLIQUORED
UNLISTENABLE
UNLISTENED
UNLISTENING
UNLITERARY
UNLIVEABLE
UNLIVELINESS
UNLIVELINESSES
UNLOADINGS
UNLOCALISED
UNLOCALIZED
UNLOCKABLE
UNLOOSENED
UNLOOSENING
UNLOVEABLE
UNLOVELIER
UNLOVELIEST
UNLOVELINESS
UNLOVELINESSES
UNLOVERLIKE
UNLOVINGLY
UNLOVINGNESS
UNLOVINGNESSES
UNLUCKIEST
UNLUCKINESS
UNLUCKINESSES
UNLUXURIANT
UNLUXURIOUS
UNMACADAMISED
UNMACADAMIZED
UNMAGNIFIED
UNMAIDENLY
UNMAILABLE
UNMAINTAINABLE
UNMAINTAINED
UNMALICIOUS
UNMALICIOUSLY
UNMALLEABILITY
UNMALLEABLE
UNMANACLED
UNMANACLES
UNMANACLING
UNMANAGEABLE
UNMANAGEABLY
UNMANFULLY
UNMANIPULATED
UNMANLIEST
UNMANLINESS
UNMANLINESSES
UNMANNERED
UNMANNEREDLY
UNMANNERLINESS
UNMANNERLY
UNMANTLING
UNMANUFACTURED
UNMARKETABLE
UNMARRIABLE
UNMARRIAGEABLE
UNMARRIEDS
UNMARRYING
UNMASCULINE
UNMASKINGS
UNMASTERED
UNMATCHABLE
UNMATERIAL
UNMATERIALISED
UNMATERIALIZED
UNMATERNAL
UNMATHEMATICAL
UNMATRICULATED

UNMEANINGLY
UNMEANINGNESS
UNMEANINGNESSES
UNMEASURABLE
UNMEASURABLY
UNMEASURED
UNMEASUREDLY
UNMECHANIC
UNMECHANICAL
UNMECHANISE
UNMECHANISED
UNMECHANISES
UNMECHANISING
UNMECHANIZE
UNMECHANIZED
UNMECHANIZES
UNMECHANIZING
UNMEDIATED
UNMEDICATED
UNMEDICINABLE
UNMEDITATED
UNMEETNESS
UNMEETNESSES
UNMELLOWED
UNMELODIOUS
UNMELODIOUSNESS
UNMEMORABLE
UNMEMORABLY
UNMENTIONABLE
UNMENTIONABLES
UNMENTIONABLY
UNMENTIONED
UNMERCENARY
UNMERCHANTABLE
UNMERCIFUL
UNMERCIFULLY
UNMERCIFULNESS
UNMERITABLE
UNMERITEDLY
UNMERITING
UNMETABOLISED
UNMETABOLIZED
UNMETALLED
UNMETAPHORICAL
UNMETAPHYSICAL
UNMETHODICAL
UNMETHODISED
UNMETHODIZED
UNMETRICAL
UNMILITARY
UNMINDFULLY
UNMINDFULNESS
UNMINDFULNESSES
UNMINGLING
UNMINISTERIAL
UNMIRACULOUS
UNMISSABLE
UNMISTAKABLE
UNMISTAKABLY
UNMISTAKEABLE
UNMISTAKEABLY
UNMISTRUSTFUL
UNMITERING
UNMITIGABLE
UNMITIGABLY
UNMITIGATED
UNMITIGATEDLY
UNMITIGATEDNESS
UNMODERATED
UNMODERNISED
UNMODERNIZED
UNMODIFIABLE
UNMODIFIED
UNMODULATED
UNMOISTENED
UNMOLESTED
UNMONITORED
UNMORALISED
UNMORALISING
UNMORALITIES
UNMORALITY
UNMORALIZED
UNMORALIZING
UNMORTGAGED
UNMORTIFIED
UNMORTISED
UNMORTISES
UNMORTISING
UNMOTHERLY
UNMOTIVATED
UNMOULDING
UNMOUNTING
UNMOVEABLE
UNMOVEABLY
UNMUFFLING
UNMUNITIONED
UNMURMURING
UNMURMURINGLY
UNMUSICALLY
UNMUSICALNESS
UNMUSICALNESSES
UNMUTILATED
UNMUZZLING
UNMUZZLINGS
UNMYELINATED
UNNAMEABLE
UNNATURALISE
UNNATURALISED
UNNATURALISES
UNNATURALISING
UNNATURALIZE
UNNATURALIZED
UNNATURALIZES
UNNATURALIZING
UNNATURALLY
UNNATURALNESS
UNNATURALNESSES
UNNAVIGABLE
UNNAVIGATED
UNNECESSARILY
UNNECESSARINESS
UNNECESSARY
UNNEEDFULLY
UNNEGOTIABLE
UNNEIGHBOURED
UNNEIGHBOURLY
UNNERVINGLY
UNNEUROTIC
UNNEWSWORTHY
UNNILHEXIUM
UNNILHEXIUMS
UNNILPENTIUM
UNNILPENTIUMS
UNNILQUADIUM
UNNILQUADIUMS
UNNILSEPTIUM
UNNILSEPTIUMS
UNNOTICEABLE
UNNOTICEABLY
UNNOTICING
UNNOURISHED
UNNOURISHING
UNNUMBERED
UNNURTURED
UNOBEDIENT
UNOBJECTIONABLE
UNOBJECTIONABLY
UNOBNOXIOUS
UNOBSCURED
UNOBSERVABLE
UNOBSERVANCE
UNOBSERVANCES
UNOBSERVANT
UNOBSERVED
UNOBSERVEDLY
UNOBSERVING
UNOBSTRUCTED
UNOBSTRUCTIVE
UNOBTAINABLE
UNOBTAINED
UNOBTRUSIVE
UNOBTRUSIVELY
UNOBTRUSIVENESS
UNOCCUPIED
UNOFFENDED
UNOFFENDING
UNOFFENSIVE
UNOFFICERED
UNOFFICIAL
UNOFFICIALLY
UNOFFICIOUS
UNOPENABLE
UNOPERATIVE
UNOPPRESSIVE
UNORDAINED
UNORDERING
UNORDINARY
UNORGANISED
UNORGANIZED
UNORIGINAL
UNORIGINALITIES
UNORIGINALITY
UNORIGINATE
UNORIGINATED
UNORNAMENTAL
UNORNAMENTED
UNORTHODOX
UNORTHODOXIES
UNORTHODOXLY
UNORTHODOXY
UNOSSIFIED
UNOSTENTATIOUS
UNOVERCOME
UNOVERTHROWN
UNOXIDISED
UNOXIDIZED
UNOXYGENATED
UNPACIFIED
UNPACKINGS
UNPAINTABLE
UNPAINTING
UNPALATABILITY
UNPALATABLE
UNPALATABLY
UNPAMPERED
UNPANELLED
UNPANELLING
UNPANNELLED
UNPANNELLING
UNPAPERING
UNPARADISE
UNPARADISED
UNPARADISES
UNPARADISING
UNPARAGONED
UNPARALLEL
UNPARALLELED
UNPARASITISED
UNPARASITIZED
UNPARDONABLE
UNPARDONABLY
UNPARDONED
UNPARDONING
UNPARENTAL
UNPARENTED
UNPARLIAMENTARY
UNPASSABLE
UNPASSABLENESS
UNPASSIONATE
UNPASSIONED
UNPASTEURISED
UNPASTEURIZED
UNPASTORAL
UNPASTURED
UNPATENTABLE
UNPATENTED
UNPATHETIC
UNPATHWAYED
UNPATRIOTIC
UNPATRIOTICALLY
UNPATRONISED
UNPATRONIZED
UNPATTERNED
UNPAVILIONED
UNPEACEABLE
UNPEACEABLENESS
UNPEACEFUL
UNPEACEFULLY
UNPEDANTIC
UNPEDIGREED
UNPEERABLE
UNPENSIONED
UNPEOPLING
UNPEPPERED
UNPERCEIVABLE
UNPERCEIVABLY
UNPERCEIVED
UNPERCEIVEDLY
UNPERCEPTIVE
UNPERCHING
UNPERFECTION
UNPERFECTIONS
UNPERFECTLY
UNPERFECTNESS

UNPERFECTNESSES
UNPERFORATED
UNPERFORMABLE
UNPERFORMED
UNPERFORMING
UNPERFUMED
UNPERILOUS
UNPERISHABLE
UNPERISHED
UNPERISHING
UNPERJURED
UNPERPETRATED
UNPERPLEXED
UNPERPLEXES
UNPERPLEXING
UNPERSECUTED
UNPERSONED
UNPERSONING
UNPERSUADABLE
UNPERSUADED
UNPERSUASIVE
UNPERTURBED
UNPERVERTED
UNPERVERTING
UNPERVERTS
UNPHILOSOPHIC
UNPHILOSOPHICAL
UNPHONETIC
UNPICKABLE
UNPICTURESQUE
UNPILLARED
UNPILLOWED
UNPITIFULLY
UNPITIFULNESS
UNPITIFULNESSES
UNPITYINGLY
UNPLAITING
UNPLASTERED
UNPLAUSIBLE
UNPLAUSIBLY
UNPLAUSIVE
UNPLAYABLE
UNPLEASANT
UNPLEASANTLY
UNPLEASANTNESS
UNPLEASANTRIES
UNPLEASANTRY
UNPLEASING
UNPLEASINGLY
UNPLEASURABLE
UNPLEASURABLY
UNPLOUGHED
UNPLUGGING
UNPLUMBING
UNPOETICAL
UNPOETICALLY
UNPOETICALNESS
UNPOISONED
UNPOISONING
UNPOLARISABLE
UNPOLARISED
UNPOLARIZABLE
UNPOLARIZED
UNPOLICIED
UNPOLISHABLE
UNPOLISHED
UNPOLISHES
UNPOLISHING
UNPOLITELY
UNPOLITENESS
UNPOLITENESSES
UNPOLITICAL
UNPOLLUTED
UNPOPULARITIES
UNPOPULARITY
UNPOPULARLY
UNPOPULATED
UNPOPULOUS
UNPORTIONED
UNPOSSESSED
UNPOSSESSING
UNPOSSIBLE
UNPOWDERED
UNPRACTICABLE
UNPRACTICAL
UNPRACTICALITY
UNPRACTICALLY
UNPRACTICALNESS
UNPRACTICED
UNPRACTISED
UNPRACTISEDNESS
UNPRAISEWORTHY
UNPRAISING
UNPREACHED
UNPREACHES
UNPREACHING
UNPRECEDENTED
UNPRECEDENTEDLY
UNPREDICTABLE
UNPREDICTABLES
UNPREDICTABLY
UNPREDICTED
UNPREDICTING
UNPREDICTS
UNPREFERRED
UNPREGNANT
UNPREJUDICED
UNPREJUDICEDLY
UNPRELATICAL
UNPREMEDITABLE
UNPREMEDITATED
UNPREMEDITATION
UNPREOCCUPIED
UNPREPARED
UNPREPAREDLY
UNPREPAREDNESS
UNPREPARES
UNPREPARING
UNPREPOSSESSED
UNPREPOSSESSING
UNPRESCRIBED
UNPRESENTABLE
UNPRESSURED
UNPRESSURISED
UNPRESSURIZED
UNPRESUMING
UNPRESUMPTUOUS
UNPRETENDING
UNPRETENDINGLY
UNPRETENTIOUS
UNPRETENTIOUSLY
UNPRETTINESS
UNPRETTINESSES
UNPREVAILING
UNPREVENTABLE
UNPREVENTED
UNPRIESTED
UNPRIESTING
UNPRIESTLY
UNPRINCELY
UNPRINCIPLED
UNPRINTABLE
UNPRINTABLENESS
UNPRINTABLY
UNPRISABLE
UNPRISONED
UNPRISONING
UNPRIVILEGED
UNPRIZABLE
UNPROBLEMATIC
UNPROCEDURAL
UNPROCESSED
UNPROCLAIMED
UNPROCURABLE
UNPRODUCED
UNPRODUCTIVE
UNPRODUCTIVELY
UNPRODUCTIVITY
UNPROFANED
UNPROFESSED
UNPROFESSIONAL
UNPROFESSIONALS
UNPROFITABILITY
UNPROFITABLE
UNPROFITABLY
UNPROFITED
UNPROFITING
UNPROGRAMMABLE
UNPROGRAMMED
UNPROGRESSIVE
UNPROGRESSIVELY
UNPROHIBITED
UNPROJECTED
UNPROLIFIC
UNPROMISED
UNPROMISING
UNPROMISINGLY
UNPROMPTED
UNPRONOUNCEABLE
UNPRONOUNCED
UNPROPERLY
UNPROPERTIED
UNPROPHETIC
UNPROPHETICAL
UNPROPITIOUS
UNPROPITIOUSLY
UNPROPORTIONATE
UNPROPORTIONED
UNPROPOSED
UNPROPPING
UNPROSPEROUS
UNPROSPEROUSLY
UNPROTECTED
UNPROTECTEDNESS
UNPROTESTANTISE
UNPROTESTANTIZE
UNPROTESTED
UNPROTESTING
UNPROVABLE
UNPROVIDED
UNPROVIDEDLY
UNPROVIDENT
UNPROVIDES
UNPROVIDING
UNPROVISIONED
UNPROVOCATIVE
UNPROVOKED
UNPROVOKEDLY
UNPROVOKES
UNPROVOKING
UNPUBLICISED
UNPUBLICIZED
UNPUBLISHABLE
UNPUBLISHED
UNPUCKERED
UNPUCKERING
UNPUNCTUAL
UNPUNCTUALITIES
UNPUNCTUALITY
UNPUNCTUATED
UNPUNISHABLE
UNPUNISHABLY
UNPUNISHED
UNPURCHASABLE
UNPURCHASEABLE
UNPURCHASED
UNPURIFIED
UNPURPOSED
UNPURVAIDE
UNPURVEYED
UNPUTDOWNABLE
UNPUZZLING
UNQUALIFIABLE
UNQUALIFIED
UNQUALIFIEDLY
UNQUALIFIEDNESS
UNQUALIFIES
UNQUALIFYING
UNQUALITED
UNQUALITIED
UNQUANTIFIABLE
UNQUANTIFIED
UNQUANTISED
UNQUANTIZED
UNQUARRIED
UNQUEENING
UNQUEENLIER
UNQUEENLIEST
UNQUEENLIKE
UNQUENCHABLE
UNQUENCHABLY
UNQUENCHED
UNQUESTIONABLE
UNQUESTIONABLY
UNQUESTIONED
UNQUESTIONING
UNQUESTIONINGLY
UNQUICKENED
UNQUIETEST
UNQUIETING
UNQUIETNESS
UNQUIETNESSES
UNQUOTABLE
UNRANSOMED

UNRATIFIED
UNRAVELING
UNRAVELLED
UNRAVELLER
UNRAVELLERS
UNRAVELLING
UNRAVELLINGS
UNRAVELMENT
UNRAVELMENTS
UNRAVISHED
UNREACHABLE
UNREACTIVE
UNREADABILITIES
UNREADABILITY
UNREADABLE
UNREADABLENESS
UNREADABLY
UNREADIEST
UNREADINESS
UNREADINESSES
UNREALISABLE
UNREALISED
UNREALISES
UNREALISING
UNREALISMS
UNREALISTIC
UNREALISTICALLY
UNREALITIES
UNREALIZABLE
UNREALIZED
UNREALIZES
UNREALIZING
UNREASONABLE
UNREASONABLY
UNREASONED
UNREASONING
UNREASONINGLY
UNRECALLABLE
UNRECALLED
UNRECALLING
UNRECAPTURABLE
UNRECEIPTED
UNRECEIVED
UNRECEPTIVE
UNRECIPROCATED
UNRECKONABLE
UNRECKONED
UNRECLAIMABLE
UNRECLAIMABLY
UNRECLAIMED
UNRECOGNISABLE
UNRECOGNISABLY
UNRECOGNISED
UNRECOGNISING
UNRECOGNIZABLE
UNRECOGNIZABLY
UNRECOGNIZED
UNRECOGNIZING
UNRECOLLECTED
UNRECOMMENDABLE
UNRECOMMENDED
UNRECOMPENSED
UNRECONCILABLE
UNRECONCILABLY
UNRECONCILED
UNRECONCILIABLE
UNRECONSTRUCTED
UNRECORDED
UNRECOUNTED
UNRECOVERABLE
UNRECOVERABLY
UNRECOVERED
UNRECTIFIED
UNRECURING
UNRECYCLABLE
UNREDEEMABLE
UNREDEEMED
UNREDRESSED
UNREDUCIBLE
UNREFLECTED
UNREFLECTING
UNREFLECTINGLY
UNREFLECTIVE
UNREFLECTIVELY
UNREFORMABLE
UNREFORMED
UNREFRACTED
UNREFRESHED
UNREFRESHING
UNREFRIGERATED
UNREGARDED
UNREGARDING
UNREGENERACIES
UNREGENERACY
UNREGENERATE
UNREGENERATED
UNREGENERATELY
UNREGENERATES
UNREGIMENTED
UNREGISTERED
UNREGULATED
UNREHEARSED
UNREINFORCED
UNREJOICED
UNREJOICING
UNRELATIVE
UNRELENTING
UNRELENTINGLY
UNRELENTINGNESS
UNRELENTOR
UNRELENTORS
UNRELIABILITIES
UNRELIABILITY
UNRELIABLE
UNRELIABLENESS
UNRELIEVABLE
UNRELIEVED
UNRELIEVEDLY
UNRELIGIOUS
UNRELIGIOUSLY
UNRELISHED
UNRELUCTANT
UNREMAINING
UNREMARKABLE
UNREMARKABLY
UNREMARKED
UNREMEDIED
UNREMEMBERED
UNREMEMBERING
UNREMINISCENT
UNREMITTED
UNREMITTEDLY
UNREMITTENT
UNREMITTENTLY
UNREMITTING
UNREMITTINGLY
UNREMITTINGNESS
UNREMORSEFUL
UNREMORSEFULLY
UNREMORSELESS
UNREMOVABLE
UNREMUNERATIVE
UNRENDERED
UNREPAIRABLE
UNREPAIRED
UNREPEALABLE
UNREPEALED
UNREPEATABLE
UNREPEATED
UNREPELLED
UNREPENTANCE
UNREPENTANCES
UNREPENTANT
UNREPENTANTLY
UNREPENTED
UNREPENTING
UNREPENTINGLY
UNREPINING
UNREPININGLY
UNREPLACEABLE
UNREPLENISHED
UNREPORTABLE
UNREPORTED
UNREPOSEFUL
UNREPOSING
UNREPRESENTED
UNREPRESSED
UNREPRIEVABLE
UNREPRIEVED
UNREPRIMANDED
UNREPROACHED
UNREPROACHFUL
UNREPROACHING
UNREPRODUCIBLE
UNREPROVABLE
UNREPROVED
UNREPROVING
UNREPUGNANT
UNREPULSABLE
UNREQUIRED
UNREQUISITE
UNREQUITED
UNREQUITEDLY
UNRESCINDED
UNRESENTED
UNRESENTFUL
UNRESENTING
UNRESERVED
UNRESERVEDLY
UNRESERVEDNESS
UNRESERVES
UNRESISTANT
UNRESISTED
UNRESISTIBLE
UNRESISTING
UNRESISTINGLY
UNRESOLVABLE
UNRESOLVED
UNRESOLVEDNESS
UNRESPECTABLE
UNRESPECTED
UNRESPECTIVE
UNRESPITED
UNRESPONSIVE
UNRESPONSIVELY
UNRESTFULNESS
UNRESTFULNESSES
UNRESTINGLY
UNRESTINGNESS
UNRESTINGNESSES
UNRESTORED
UNRESTRAINABLE
UNRESTRAINED
UNRESTRAINEDLY
UNRESTRAINT
UNRESTRAINTS
UNRESTRICTED
UNRESTRICTEDLY
UNRETARDED
UNRETENTIVE
UNRETIRING
UNRETOUCHED
UNRETURNABLE
UNRETURNED
UNRETURNING
UNRETURNINGLY
UNREVEALABLE
UNREVEALED
UNREVEALING
UNREVENGED
UNREVENGEFUL
UNREVEREND
UNREVERENT
UNREVERSED
UNREVERTED
UNREVIEWABLE
UNREVIEWED
UNREVOLUTIONARY
UNREWARDED
UNREWARDEDLY
UNREWARDING
UNRHETORICAL
UNRHYTHMIC
UNRHYTHMICAL
UNRHYTHMICALLY
UNRIDDLEABLE
UNRIDDLERS
UNRIDDLING
UNRIDEABLE
UNRIGHTEOUS
UNRIGHTEOUSLY
UNRIGHTEOUSNESS
UNRIGHTFUL
UNRIGHTFULLY
UNRIGHTFULNESS
UNRIPENESS
UNRIPENESSES
UNRIPPINGS
UNRIVALLED
UNRIVETING
UNROMANISED
UNROMANIZED
UNROMANTIC
UNROMANTICAL

UNROMANTICALLY
UNROMANTICISED
UNROMANTICIZED
UNROOSTING
UNROUNDING
UNRUFFABLE
UNRUFFLEDNESS
UNRUFFLEDNESSES
UNRUFFLING
UNRULIMENT
UNRULIMENTS
UNRULINESS
UNRULINESSES
UNSADDLING
UNSAFENESS
UNSAFENESSES
UNSAFETIES
UNSAILORLIKE
UNSAINTING
UNSAINTLIER
UNSAINTLIEST
UNSAINTLINESS
UNSAINTLINESSES
UNSALABILITIES
UNSALABILITY
UNSALARIED
UNSALEABILITIES
UNSALEABILITY
UNSALEABLE
UNSALVAGEABLE
UNSANCTIFIED
UNSANCTIFIES
UNSANCTIFY
UNSANCTIFYING
UNSANCTIONED
UNSANDALLED
UNSANITARY
UNSATIABLE
UNSATIATED
UNSATIATING
UNSATIRICAL
UNSATISFACTION
UNSATISFACTIONS
UNSATISFACTORY
UNSATISFIABLE
UNSATISFIED
UNSATISFIEDNESS
UNSATISFYING
UNSATURATE
UNSATURATED
UNSATURATES
UNSATURATION
UNSATURATIONS
UNSAVORILY
UNSAVORINESS
UNSAVORINESSES
UNSAVOURILY
UNSAVOURINESS
UNSAVOURINESSES
UNSAYABLES
UNSCABBARD
UNSCABBARDED
UNSCABBARDING
UNSCABBARDS
UNSCALABLE
UNSCAVENGERED
UNSCEPTRED
UNSCHEDULED
UNSCHOLARLIKE
UNSCHOLARLY
UNSCHOOLED
UNSCIENTIFIC
UNSCISSORED
UNSCORCHED
UNSCOTTIFIED
UNSCRAMBLE
UNSCRAMBLED
UNSCRAMBLER
UNSCRAMBLERS
UNSCRAMBLES
UNSCRAMBLING
UNSCRATCHED
UNSCREENED
UNSCREWING
UNSCRIPTED
UNSCRIPTURAL
UNSCRIPTURALLY
UNSCRUPLED
UNSCRUPULOSITY
UNSCRUPULOUS
UNSCRUPULOUSLY
UNSCRUTINISED
UNSCRUTINIZED
UNSCULPTURED
UNSEALABLE
UNSEARCHABLE
UNSEARCHABLY
UNSEARCHED
UNSEASONABLE
UNSEASONABLY
UNSEASONED
UNSEASONEDNESS
UNSEASONING
UNSEAWORTHINESS
UNSEAWORTHY
UNSECONDED
UNSECTARIAN
UNSECTARIANISM
UNSECTARIANISMS
UNSEEMINGS
UNSEEMLIER
UNSEEMLIEST
UNSEEMLINESS
UNSEEMLINESSES
UNSEGMENTED
UNSEGREGATED
UNSEISABLE
UNSEIZABLE
UNSELECTED
UNSELECTIVE
UNSELECTIVELY
UNSELFCONSCIOUS
UNSELFISHLY
UNSELFISHNESS
UNSELFISHNESSES
UNSELLABLE
UNSEMINARIED
UNSENSATIONAL
UNSENSIBLE
UNSENSIBLY
UNSENSITISED
UNSENSITIVE
UNSENSITIZED
UNSENSUALISE
UNSENSUALISED
UNSENSUALISES
UNSENSUALISING
UNSENSUALIZE
UNSENSUALIZED
UNSENSUALIZES
UNSENSUALIZING
UNSENTENCED
UNSENTIMENTAL
UNSEPARABLE
UNSEPARATED
UNSEPULCHRED
UNSERIOUSNESS
UNSERIOUSNESSES
UNSERVICEABLE
UNSETTLEDLY
UNSETTLEDNESS
UNSETTLEDNESSES
UNSETTLEMENT
UNSETTLEMENTS
UNSETTLING
UNSETTLINGLY
UNSETTLINGS
UNSHACKLED
UNSHACKLES
UNSHACKLING
UNSHADOWABLE
UNSHADOWED
UNSHADOWING
UNSHAKABLE
UNSHAKABLENESS
UNSHAKABLY
UNSHAKEABLE
UNSHAKEABLENESS
UNSHAKEABLY
UNSHAKENLY
UNSHAPELIER
UNSHAPELIEST
UNSHARPENED
UNSHEATHED
UNSHEATHES
UNSHEATHING
UNSHELLING
UNSHELTERED
UNSHIELDED
UNSHIFTING
UNSHINGLED
UNSHIPPING
UNSHOCKABLE
UNSHOOTING
UNSHOUTING
UNSHOWERED
UNSHRINKABLE
UNSHRINKING
UNSHRINKINGLY
UNSHROUDED
UNSHROUDING
UNSHRUBBED
UNSHUNNABLE
UNSHUTTERED
UNSHUTTERING
UNSHUTTERS
UNSHUTTING
UNSIGHTEDLY
UNSIGHTING
UNSIGHTLIER
UNSIGHTLIEST
UNSIGHTLINESS
UNSIGHTLINESSES
UNSINEWING
UNSINKABLE
UNSINNOWED
UNSISTERED
UNSISTERLINESS
UNSISTERLY
UNSIZEABLE
UNSKILFULLY
UNSKILFULNESS
UNSKILFULNESSES
UNSKILLFUL
UNSKILLFULLY
UNSKILLFULNESS
UNSLAKABLE
UNSLEEPING
UNSLINGING
UNSLIPPING
UNSLUICING
UNSLUMBERING
UNSLUMBROUS
UNSMILINGLY
UNSMIRCHED
UNSMOOTHED
UNSMOOTHING
UNSMOTHERABLE
UNSNAGGING
UNSNAPPING
UNSNARLING
UNSNECKING
UNSOCIABILITIES
UNSOCIABILITY
UNSOCIABLE
UNSOCIABLENESS
UNSOCIABLY
UNSOCIALISED
UNSOCIALISM
UNSOCIALISMS
UNSOCIALITIES
UNSOCIALITY
UNSOCIALIZED
UNSOCIALLY
UNSOCKETED
UNSOCKETING
UNSOFTENED
UNSOFTENING
UNSOLDERED
UNSOLDERING
UNSOLDIERLIKE
UNSOLDIERLY
UNSOLICITED
UNSOLICITOUS
UNSOLIDITIES
UNSOLIDITY
UNSOLVABLE
UNSOPHISTICATE
UNSOPHISTICATED
UNSOUNDABLE
UNSOUNDEST
UNSOUNDNESS
UNSOUNDNESSES
UNSPARINGLY

UNSPARINGNESS
UNSPARINGNESSES
UNSPARRING
UNSPEAKABLE
UNSPEAKABLENESS
UNSPEAKABLY
UNSPEAKING
UNSPECIALISED
UNSPECIALIZED
UNSPECIFIABLE
UNSPECIFIC
UNSPECIFIED
UNSPECTACLED
UNSPECTACULAR
UNSPECULATIVE
UNSPELLING
UNSPHERING
UNSPIRITED
UNSPIRITUAL
UNSPIRITUALISE
UNSPIRITUALISED
UNSPIRITUALISES
UNSPIRITUALIZE
UNSPIRITUALIZED
UNSPIRITUALIZES
UNSPIRITUALLY
UNSPLINTERABLE
UNSPOOLING
UNSPORTING
UNSPORTSMANLIKE
UNSPOTTEDNESS
UNSPOTTEDNESSES
UNSPRINKLED
UNSTABLENESS
UNSTABLENESSES
UNSTABLEST
UNSTACKING
UNSTAIDNESS
UNSTAIDNESSES
UNSTAINABLE
UNSTANCHABLE
UNSTANCHED
UNSTANDARDISED
UNSTANDARDIZED
UNSTARCHED
UNSTARCHES
UNSTARCHING
UNSTARTLING
UNSTATESMANLIKE
UNSTATUTABLE
UNSTATUTABLY
UNSTAUNCHABLE
UNSTAUNCHED
UNSTEADFAST
UNSTEADFASTLY
UNSTEADFASTNESS
UNSTEADIED
UNSTEADIER
UNSTEADIES
UNSTEADIEST
UNSTEADILY
UNSTEADINESS
UNSTEADINESSES
UNSTEADYING
UNSTEELING
UNSTEPPING
UNSTERCORATED
UNSTERILISED
UNSTERILIZED
UNSTICKING
UNSTIGMATISED
UNSTIGMATIZED
UNSTIMULATED
UNSTINTING
UNSTINTINGLY
UNSTITCHED
UNSTITCHES
UNSTITCHING
UNSTOCKING
UNSTOCKINGED
UNSTOOPING
UNSTOPPABLE
UNSTOPPABLY
UNSTOPPERED
UNSTOPPERING
UNSTOPPERS
UNSTOPPING
UNSTRAINED
UNSTRAPPED
UNSTRAPPING
UNSTRATIFIED
UNSTREAMED
UNSTRENGTHENED
UNSTRESSED
UNSTRESSES
UNSTRIATED
UNSTRINGED
UNSTRINGING
UNSTRIPPED
UNSTRIPPING
UNSTRUCTURED
UNSUBDUABLE
UNSUBJECTED
UNSUBLIMATED
UNSUBLIMED
UNSUBMERGED
UNSUBMISSIVE
UNSUBMITTING
UNSUBSCRIBE
UNSUBSCRIBED
UNSUBSCRIBES
UNSUBSCRIBING
UNSUBSIDISED
UNSUBSIDIZED
UNSUBSTANTIAL
UNSUBSTANTIALLY
UNSUBSTANTIATED
UNSUCCEEDED
UNSUCCESSES
UNSUCCESSFUL
UNSUCCESSFULLY
UNSUCCESSIVE
UNSUCCOURED
UNSUFFERABLE
UNSUFFICIENT
UNSUITABILITIES
UNSUITABILITY
UNSUITABLE
UNSUITABLENESS
UNSUITABLY
UNSUMMERED
UNSUMMONED
UNSUPERFLUOUS
UNSUPERVISED
UNSUPPLENESS
UNSUPPLENESSES
UNSUPPLIED
UNSUPPORTABLE
UNSUPPORTED
UNSUPPORTEDLY
UNSUPPOSABLE
UNSUPPRESSED
UNSURFACED
UNSURMISED
UNSURMOUNTABLE
UNSURPASSABLE
UNSURPASSABLY
UNSURPASSED
UNSURPRISED
UNSURPRISING
UNSURPRISINGLY
UNSURVEYED
UNSUSCEPTIBLE
UNSUSPECTED
UNSUSPECTEDLY
UNSUSPECTEDNESS
UNSUSPECTING
UNSUSPECTINGLY
UNSUSPENDED
UNSUSPICION
UNSUSPICIONS
UNSUSPICIOUS
UNSUSPICIOUSLY
UNSUSTAINABLE
UNSUSTAINED
UNSUSTAINING
UNSWADDLED
UNSWADDLES
UNSWADDLING
UNSWALLOWED
UNSWATHING
UNSWAYABLE
UNSWEARING
UNSWEARINGS
UNSWEETENED
UNSWERVING
UNSWERVINGLY
UNSYLLABLED
UNSYMMETRICAL
UNSYMMETRICALLY
UNSYMMETRIES
UNSYMMETRISED
UNSYMMETRIZED
UNSYMMETRY
UNSYMPATHETIC
UNSYMPATHIES
UNSYMPATHISING
UNSYMPATHIZING
UNSYMPATHY
UNSYNCHRONISED
UNSYNCHRONIZED
UNSYSTEMATIC
UNSYSTEMATICAL
UNSYSTEMATISED
UNSYSTEMATIZED
UNTACKLING
UNTAINTEDLY
UNTAINTEDNESS
UNTAINTEDNESSES
UNTAINTING
UNTALENTED
UNTAMABLENESS
UNTAMABLENESSES
UNTAMEABLE
UNTAMEABLENESS
UNTAMEABLY
UNTAMEDNESS
UNTAMEDNESSES
UNTANGIBLE
UNTANGLING
UNTARNISHED
UNTASTEFUL
UNTEACHABLE
UNTEACHABLENESS
UNTEACHING
UNTEARABLE
UNTECHNICAL
UNTELLABLE
UNTEMPERED
UNTEMPERING
UNTENABILITIES
UNTENABILITY
UNTENABLENESS
UNTENABLENESSES
UNTENANTABLE
UNTENANTED
UNTENANTING
UNTENDERED
UNTENDERLY
UNTERMINATED
UNTERRESTRIAL
UNTERRIFIED
UNTERRIFYING
UNTESTABLE
UNTETHERED
UNTETHERING
UNTHANKFUL
UNTHANKFULLY
UNTHANKFULNESS
UNTHATCHED
UNTHATCHES
UNTHATCHING
UNTHEOLOGICAL
UNTHEORETICAL
UNTHICKENED
UNTHINKABILITY
UNTHINKABLE
UNTHINKABLENESS
UNTHINKABLY
UNTHINKING
UNTHINKINGLY
UNTHINKINGNESS
UNTHOROUGH
UNTHOUGHTFUL
UNTHOUGHTFULLY
UNTHREADED
UNTHREADING
UNTHREATENED
UNTHREATENING
UNTHRIFTILY
UNTHRIFTINESS
UNTHRIFTINESSES
UNTHRIFTYHEAD
UNTHRIFTYHEADS

UNTHRIFTYHED
UNTHRIFTYHEDS
UNTHRONING
UNTIDINESS
UNTIDINESSES
UNTILLABLE
UNTIMBERED
UNTIMELIER
UNTIMELIEST
UNTIMELINESS
UNTIMELINESSES
UNTIMEOUSLY
UNTINCTURED
UNTIRINGLY
UNTOCHERED
UNTOGETHER
UNTORMENTED
UNTORTURED
UNTOUCHABILITY
UNTOUCHABLE
UNTOUCHABLES
UNTOWARDLINESS
UNTOWARDLY
UNTOWARDNESS
UNTOWARDNESSES
UNTRACEABLE
UNTRACKING
UNTRACTABLE
UNTRACTABLENESS
UNTRADITIONAL
UNTRADITIONALLY
UNTRAMMELED
UNTRAMMELLED
UNTRAMPLED
UNTRANQUIL
UNTRANSFERABLE
UNTRANSFERRABLE
UNTRANSFORMED
UNTRANSLATABLE
UNTRANSLATABLY
UNTRANSLATED
UNTRANSMIGRATED
UNTRANSMISSIBLE
UNTRANSMITTED
UNTRANSMUTABLE
UNTRANSMUTED
UNTRANSPARENT
UNTRAVELED
UNTRAVELLED
UNTRAVERSABLE
UNTRAVERSED
UNTREADING
UNTREASURE
UNTREASURED
UNTREASURES
UNTREASURING
UNTREATABLE
UNTREMBLING
UNTREMBLINGLY
UNTREMENDOUS
UNTREMULOUS
UNTRENCHED
UNTRESPASSING
UNTRIMMING
UNTROUBLED
UNTROUBLEDLY
UNTRUENESS
UNTRUENESSES
UNTRUSSERS
UNTRUSSING
UNTRUSSINGS
UNTRUSTFUL
UNTRUSTINESS
UNTRUSTINESSES
UNTRUSTING
UNTRUSTWORTHILY
UNTRUSTWORTHY
UNTRUTHFUL
UNTRUTHFULLY
UNTRUTHFULNESS
UNTUCKERED
UNTUMULTUOUS
UNTUNABLENESS
UNTUNABLENESSES
UNTUNEABLE
UNTUNEFULLY
UNTUNEFULNESS
UNTUNEFULNESSES
UNTURNABLE
UNTWISTING
UNTWISTINGS
UNTYPICALLY
UNTYREABLE
UNUNUNIUMS
UNUPLIFTED
UNUSEFULLY
UNUSEFULNESS
UNUSEFULNESSES
UNUSUALNESS
UNUSUALNESSES
UNUTILISED
UNUTILIZED
UNUTTERABLE
UNUTTERABLENESS
UNUTTERABLES
UNUTTERABLY
UNVACCINATED
UNVALUABLE
UNVANQUISHABLE
UNVANQUISHED
UNVARIABLE
UNVARIEGATED
UNVARNISHED
UNVEILINGS
UNVENDIBLE
UNVENERABLE
UNVENTILATED
UNVERACIOUS
UNVERACITIES
UNVERACITY
UNVERBALISED
UNVERBALIZED
UNVERIFIABILITY
UNVERIFIABLE
UNVERIFIED
UNVIOLATED
UNVIRTUOUS
UNVIRTUOUSLY
UNVISITABLE
UNVISORING
UNVITIATED
UNVITRIFIABLE
UNVITRIFIED
UNVIZARDED
UNVIZARDING
UNVOCALISED
UNVOCALIZED
UNVOICINGS
UNVOYAGEABLE
UNVULGARISE
UNVULGARISED
UNVULGARISES
UNVULGARISING
UNVULGARIZE
UNVULGARIZED
UNVULGARIZES
UNVULGARIZING
UNVULNERABLE
UNWANDERING
UNWARENESS
UNWARENESSES
UNWARINESS
UNWARINESSES
UNWARRANTABLE
UNWARRANTABLY
UNWARRANTED
UNWARRANTEDLY
UNWASHEDNESS
UNWASHEDNESSES
UNWATCHABLE
UNWATCHFUL
UNWATCHFULLY
UNWATCHFULNESS
UNWATERING
UNWAVERING
UNWAVERINGLY
UNWEAKENED
UNWEAPONED
UNWEAPONING
UNWEARABLE
UNWEARIABLE
UNWEARIABLY
UNWEARIEDLY
UNWEARIEDNESS
UNWEARIEDNESSES
UNWEARYING
UNWEARYINGLY
UNWEATHERED
UNWEDGABLE
UNWEDGEABLE
UNWEETINGLY
UNWEIGHING
UNWEIGHTED
UNWEIGHTING
UNWELCOMED
UNWELCOMELY
UNWELCOMENESS
UNWELCOMENESSES
UNWELLNESS
UNWELLNESSES
UNWHISTLEABLE
UNWHOLESOME
UNWHOLESOMELY
UNWHOLESOMENESS
UNWIELDIER
UNWIELDIEST
UNWIELDILY
UNWIELDINESS
UNWIELDINESSES
UNWIELDLILY
UNWIELDLINESS
UNWIELDLINESSES
UNWIFELIER
UNWIFELIEST
UNWIFELIKE
UNWILLINGLY
UNWILLINGNESS
UNWILLINGNESSES
UNWINDABLE
UNWINDINGS
UNWINKINGLY
UNWINNABLE
UNWINNOWED
UNWISENESS
UNWISENESSES
UNWITCHING
UNWITHDRAWING
UNWITHERED
UNWITHERING
UNWITHHELD
UNWITHHOLDEN
UNWITHHOLDING
UNWITHSTOOD
UNWITNESSED
UNWITTINGLY
UNWITTINGNESS
UNWITTINGNESSES
UNWOMANING
UNWOMANLIER
UNWOMANLIEST
UNWOMANLINESS
UNWOMANLINESSES
UNWONTEDLY
UNWONTEDNESS
UNWONTEDNESSES
UNWORKABILITIES
UNWORKABILITY
UNWORKABLE
UNWORKMANLIKE
UNWORLDLIER
UNWORLDLIEST
UNWORLDLINESS
UNWORLDLINESSES
UNWORSHIPFUL
UNWORSHIPPED
UNWORTHIER
UNWORTHIES
UNWORTHIEST
UNWORTHILY
UNWORTHINESS
UNWORTHINESSES
UNWOUNDABLE
UNWRAPPING
UNWREATHED
UNWREATHES
UNWREATHING
UNWRINKLED
UNWRINKLES
UNWRINKLING
UNYIELDING
UNYIELDINGLY
UNYIELDINGNESS
UPBRAIDERS
UPBRAIDING

UPBRAIDINGLY
UPBRAIDINGS
UPBREAKING
UPBRINGING
UPBRINGINGS
UPBUILDERS
UPBUILDING
UPBUILDINGS
UPBUOYANCE
UPBUOYANCES
UPBURSTING
UPCATCHING
UPCHEERING
UPCHUCKING
UPCLIMBING
UPCOUNTRIES
UPDATEABLE
UPDRAGGING
UPDRAUGHTS
UPFILLINGS
UPFLASHING
UPFLINGING
UPFOLLOWED
UPFOLLOWING
UPGATHERED
UPGATHERING
UPGRADABILITIES
UPGRADABILITY
UPGRADABLE
UPGRADATION
UPGRADATIONS
UPGRADEABILITY
UPGRADEABLE
UPGROWINGS
UPHEAPINGS
UPHILLWARD
UPHOARDING
UPHOISTING
UPHOLDINGS
UPHOLSTERED
UPHOLSTERER
UPHOLSTERERS
UPHOLSTERIES
UPHOLSTERING
UPHOLSTERS
UPHOLSTERY
UPHOLSTRESS
UPHOLSTRESSES
UPHOORDING
UPKNITTING
UPLIFTINGLY
UPLIFTINGS
UPLIGHTERS
UPLIGHTING
UPLINKINGS
UPMANSHIPS
UPPERCASED
UPPERCASES
UPPERCASING
UPPERCLASSMAN
UPPERCLASSMEN
UPPERCUTTING
UPPERPARTS
UPPERWORKS
UPPISHNESS
UPPISHNESSES
UPPITINESS
UPPITINESSES
UPPITYNESS
UPPITYNESSES
UPPROPPING
UPREACHING
UPRIGHTEOUSLY
UPRIGHTING
UPRIGHTNESS
UPRIGHTNESSES
UPROARIOUS
UPROARIOUSLY
UPROARIOUSNESS
UPROOTEDNESS
UPROOTEDNESSES
UPROOTINGS
UPSETTABLE
UPSETTINGLY
UPSETTINGS
UPSHIFTING
UPSHOOTING
UPSIDEDEOWNE
UPSITTINGS
UPSKILLING
UPSPEAKING
UPSPEARING
UPSPRINGING
UPSTANDING
UPSTANDINGNESS
UPSTARTING
UPSTEPPING
UPSTIRRING
UPSTREAMED
UPSTREAMING
UPSTRETCHED
UPSURGENCE
UPSURGENCES
UPSWARMING
UPSWEEPING
UPSWELLING
UPSWINGING
UPTHROWING
UPTHRUSTED
UPTHRUSTING
UPTHUNDERED
UPTHUNDERING
UPTHUNDERS
UPTIGHTEST
UPTIGHTNESS
UPTIGHTNESSES
UPTITLINGS
UPTRAINING
UPTURNINGS
UPVALUATION
UPVALUATIONS
UPWARDNESS
UPWARDNESSES
UPWELLINGS
UPWHIRLING
URALITISATION
URALITISATIONS
URALITISED
URALITISES
URALITISING
URALITIZATION
URALITIZATIONS
URALITIZED
URALITIZES
URALITIZING
URANALYSES
URANALYSIS
URANINITES
URANOGRAPHER
URANOGRAPHERS
URANOGRAPHIC
URANOGRAPHICAL
URANOGRAPHIES
URANOGRAPHIST
URANOGRAPHISTS
URANOGRAPHY
URANOLOGIES
URANOMETRIES
URANOMETRY
URANOPLASTIES
URANOPLASTY
URBANENESS
URBANENESSES
URBANISATION
URBANISATIONS
URBANISING
URBANISTIC
URBANISTICALLY
URBANITIES
URBANIZATION
URBANIZATIONS
URBANIZING
URBANOLOGIES
URBANOLOGIST
URBANOLOGISTS
URBANOLOGY
URCEOLUSES
UREDINIOSPORE
UREDINIOSPORES
UREDIOSPORE
UREDIOSPORES
UREDOSORUS
UREDOSPORE
UREDOSPORES
UREOTELISM
UREOTELISMS
URETERITIS
URETERITISES
URETHRITIC
URETHRITIS
URETHRITISES
URETHROSCOPE
URETHROSCOPES
URETHROSCOPIC
URETHROSCOPIES
URETHROSCOPY
URICOSURIC
URICOTELIC
URICOTELISM
URICOTELISMS
URINALYSES
URINALYSIS
URINATIONS
URINIFEROUS
URINIPAROUS
URINOGENITAL
URINOLOGIES
URINOMETER
URINOMETERS
URINOSCOPIES
URINOSCOPY
UROCHORDAL
UROCHORDATE
UROCHORDATES
UROCHROMES
URODYNAMICS
UROGENITAL
UROGRAPHIC
UROGRAPHIES
UROKINASES
UROLAGNIAS
UROLITHIASES
UROLITHIASIS
UROLOGICAL
UROLOGISTS
UROPOIESES
UROPOIESIS
UROPYGIUMS
UROSCOPIES
UROSCOPIST
UROSCOPISTS
UROSTEGITE
UROSTEGITES
UROSTHENIC
UROSTOMIES
URTICACEOUS
URTICARIAL
URTICARIAS
URTICARIOUS
URTICATING
URTICATION
URTICATIONS
USABILITIES
USABLENESS
USABLENESSES
USEABILITIES
USEABILITY
USEABLENESS
USEABLENESSES
USEFULNESS
USEFULNESSES
USELESSNESS
USELESSNESSES
USHERESSES
USHERETTES
USHERSHIPS
USQUEBAUGH
USQUEBAUGHS
USTILAGINEOUS
USTILAGINOUS
USTULATION
USTULATIONS
USUALNESSES
USUCAPIENT
USUCAPIENTS
USUCAPIONS
USUCAPTIBLE
USUCAPTING
USUCAPTION
USUCAPTIONS
USUFRUCTED
USUFRUCTING
USUFRUCTUARIES
USUFRUCTUARY

USURIOUSLY
USURIOUSNESS
USURIOUSNESSES
USURPATION
USURPATIONS
USURPATIVE
USURPATORY
USURPATURE
USURPATURES
USURPINGLY
UTERECTOMIES
UTERECTOMY
UTERITISES
UTEROGESTATION
UTEROGESTATIONS
UTEROTOMIES
UTILISABLE
UTILISATION
UTILISATIONS
UTILITARIAN
UTILITARIANISE
UTILITARIANISED
UTILITARIANISES
UTILITARIANISM
UTILITARIANISMS
UTILITARIANIZE
UTILITARIANIZED
UTILITARIANIZES
UTILITARIANS
UTILIZABLE
UTILIZATION
UTILIZATIONS
UTOPIANISE
UTOPIANISED
UTOPIANISER
UTOPIANISERS
UTOPIANISES
UTOPIANISING
UTOPIANISM
UTOPIANISMS
UTOPIANIZE
UTOPIANIZED
UTOPIANIZER
UTOPIANIZERS
UTOPIANIZES
UTOPIANIZING
UTRICULARIA
UTRICULARIAS
UTRICULATE
UTRICULITIS
UTRICULITISES
UTTERABLENESS
UTTERABLENESSES
UTTERANCES
UTTERMOSTS
UTTERNESSES
UVAROVITES
UVULITISES
UXORICIDAL
UXORICIDES
UXORILOCAL
UXORIOUSLY
UXORIOUSNESS
UXORIOUSNESSES

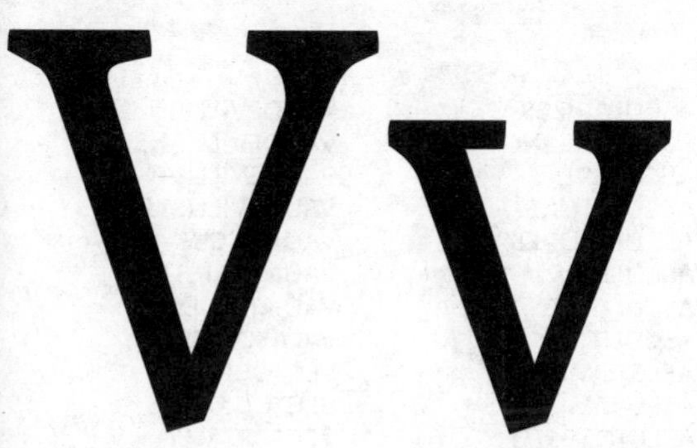

VACANTNESS
VACANTNESSES
VACATIONED
VACATIONER
VACATIONERS
VACATIONING
VACATIONIST
VACATIONISTS
VACATIONLAND
VACATIONLANDS
VACATIONLESS
VACCINATED
VACCINATES
VACCINATING
VACCINATION
VACCINATIONS
VACCINATOR
VACCINATORS
VACCINATORY
VACCINIUMS
VACILLATED
VACILLATES
VACILLATING
VACILLATINGLY
VACILLATION
VACILLATIONS
VACILLATOR
VACILLATORS
VACILLATORY
VACUATIONS
VACUOLATED
VACUOLATION
VACUOLATIONS
VACUOLISATION
VACUOLISATIONS
VACUOLIZATION
VACUOLIZATIONS
VACUOUSNESS
VACUOUSNESSES
VAGABONDAGE
VAGABONDAGES
VAGABONDED
VAGABONDING
VAGABONDISE
VAGABONDISED
VAGABONDISES
VAGABONDISH
VAGABONDISING
VAGABONDISM
VAGABONDISMS
VAGABONDIZE
VAGABONDIZED
VAGABONDIZES
VAGABONDIZING
VAGARIOUSLY
VAGILITIES
VAGINECTOMIES
VAGINECTOMY
VAGINICOLINE
VAGINICOLOUS
VAGINISMUS
VAGINISMUSES
VAGINITISES
VAGOTOMIES
VAGOTONIAS
VAGOTROPIC
VAGRANCIES
VAGRANTNESS
VAGRANTNESSES
VAGUENESSES
VAINGLORIED
VAINGLORIES
VAINGLORIOUS
VAINGLORIOUSLY
VAINGLORYING
VAINNESSES
VAIVODESHIP
VAIVODESHIPS
VALEDICTION
VALEDICTIONS
VALEDICTORIAN
VALEDICTORIANS
VALEDICTORIES
VALEDICTORY
VALENTINES
VALERIANACEOUS
VALETUDINARIAN
VALETUDINARIANS
VALETUDINARIES
VALETUDINARY
VALIANCIES
VALIANTNESS
VALIANTNESSES
VALIDATING
VALIDATION
VALIDATIONS
VALIDATORY
VALIDITIES
VALIDNESSES
VALLATIONS
VALLECULAE
VALLECULAR
VALLECULATE
VALORISATION
VALORISATIONS
VALORISING
VALORIZATION
VALORIZATIONS
VALORIZING
VALOROUSLY
VALPOLICELLA
VALPOLICELLAS
VALPROATES
VALUABLENESS
VALUABLENESSES
VALUATIONAL
VALUATIONALLY
VALUATIONS
VALUELESSNESS
VALUELESSNESSES
VALVASSORS
VALVULITIS
VALVULITISES
VAMPIRISED
VAMPIRISES
VAMPIRISING
VAMPIRISMS
VAMPIRIZED
VAMPIRIZES
VAMPIRIZING
VANADIATES
VANADINITE
VANADINITES
VANASPATIS
VANCOMYCIN
VANCOMYCINS
VANDALISATION
VANDALISATIONS
VANDALISED
VANDALISES
VANDALISING
VANDALISMS
VANDALISTIC
VANDALIZATION
VANDALIZATIONS
VANDALIZED
VANDALIZES
VANDALIZING
VANGUARDISM
VANGUARDISMS
VANGUARDIST
VANGUARDISTS

VANISHINGLY
VANISHINGS
VANISHMENT
VANISHMENTS
VANITORIES
VANPOOLING
VANPOOLINGS
VANQUISHABLE
VANQUISHED
VANQUISHER
VANQUISHERS
VANQUISHES
VANQUISHING
VANQUISHMENT
VANQUISHMENTS
VANTAGELESS
VANTBRACES
VAPIDITIES
VAPIDNESSES
VAPORABILITIES
VAPORABILITY
VAPORESCENCE
VAPORESCENCES
VAPORESCENT
VAPORETTOS
VAPORIFORM
VAPORIMETER
VAPORIMETERS
VAPORISABLE
VAPORISATION
VAPORISATIONS
VAPORISERS
VAPORISHNESS
VAPORISHNESSES
VAPORISING
VAPORIZABLE
VAPORIZATION
VAPORIZATIONS
VAPORIZERS
VAPORIZING
VAPOROSITIES
VAPOROSITY
VAPOROUSLY
VAPOROUSNESS
VAPOROUSNESSES
VAPORWARES
VAPOURABILITIES
VAPOURABILITY
VAPOURABLE
VAPOURINGLY
VAPOURINGS
VAPOURISHNESS
VAPOURISHNESSES
VAPOURLESS
VAPOURWARE
VAPOURWARES
VAPULATING
VAPULATION
VAPULATIONS
VARIABILITIES
VARIABILITY
VARIABLENESS
VARIABLENESSES
VARIATIONAL
VARIATIONALLY
VARIATIONIST
VARIATIONISTS
VARIATIONS
VARICELLAR
VARICELLAS
VARICELLATE
VARICELLOID
VARICELLOUS
VARICOCELE
VARICOCELES
VARICOLORED
VARICOLOURED
VARICOSITIES
VARICOSITY
VARICOTOMIES
VARICOTOMY
VARIEDNESS
VARIEDNESSES
VARIEGATED
VARIEGATES
VARIEGATING
VARIEGATION
VARIEGATIONS
VARIEGATOR
VARIEGATORS
VARIETALLY
VARIFOCALS
VARIFORMLY
VARIOLATED
VARIOLATES
VARIOLATING
VARIOLATION
VARIOLATIONS
VARIOLATOR
VARIOLATORS
VARIOLISATION
VARIOLISATIONS
VARIOLITES
VARIOLITIC
VARIOLIZATION
VARIOLIZATIONS
VARIOLOIDS
VARIOMETER
VARIOMETERS
VARIOUSNESS
VARIOUSNESSES
VARISCITES
VARITYPING
VARITYPIST
VARITYPISTS
VARLETESSES
VARLETRIES
VARNISHERS
VARNISHING
VARNISHINGS
VARSOVIENNE
VARSOVIENNES
VASCULARISATION
VASCULARISE
VASCULARISED
VASCULARISES
VASCULARISING
VASCULARITIES
VASCULARITY
VASCULARIZATION
VASCULARIZE
VASCULARIZED
VASCULARIZES
VASCULARIZING
VASCULARLY
VASCULATURE
VASCULATURES
VASCULIFORM
VASCULITIDES
VASCULITIS
VASECTOMIES
VASECTOMISE
VASECTOMISED
VASECTOMISES
VASECTOMISING
VASECTOMIZE
VASECTOMIZED
VASECTOMIZES
VASECTOMIZING
VASOACTIVE
VASOACTIVITIES
VASOACTIVITY
VASOCONSTRICTOR
VASODILATATION
VASODILATATIONS
VASODILATATORY
VASODILATION
VASODILATIONS
VASODILATOR
VASODILATORS
VASODILATORY
VASOINHIBITOR
VASOINHIBITORS
VASOINHIBITORY
VASOPRESSIN
VASOPRESSINS
VASOPRESSOR
VASOPRESSORS
VASOSPASMS
VASOSPASTIC
VASOTOCINS
VASOTOMIES
VASSALAGES
VASSALESSES
VASSALISED
VASSALISES
VASSALISING
VASSALIZED
VASSALIZES
VASSALIZING
VASSALLING
VASSALRIES
VASTIDITIES
VASTITUDES
VASTNESSES
VATICINATE
VATICINATED
VATICINATES
VATICINATING
VATICINATION
VATICINATIONS
VATICINATOR
VATICINATORS
VATICINATORY
VAUDEVILLE
VAUDEVILLEAN
VAUDEVILLEANS
VAUDEVILLES
VAUDEVILLIAN
VAUDEVILLIANS
VAUDEVILLIST
VAUDEVILLISTS
VAULTINGLY
VAUNTERIES
VAUNTINGLY
VAVASORIES
VECTOGRAPH
VECTOGRAPHS
VECTORIALLY
VECTORINGS
VECTORISATION
VECTORISATIONS
VECTORISED
VECTORISES
VECTORISING
VECTORIZATION
VECTORIZATIONS
VECTORIZED
VECTORIZES
VECTORIZING
VECTORSCOPE
VECTORSCOPES
VEGEBURGER
VEGEBURGERS
VEGETABLES
VEGETARIAN
VEGETARIANISM
VEGETARIANISMS
VEGETARIANS
VEGETATING
VEGETATINGS
VEGETATION
VEGETATIONAL
VEGETATIONS
VEGETATIOUS
VEGETATIVE
VEGETATIVELY
VEGETATIVENESS
VEGGIEBURGER
VEGGIEBURGERS
VEHEMENCES
VEHEMENCIES
VEHEMENTLY
VEILLEUSES
VEINSTONES
VEINSTUFFS
VELARISATION
VELARISATIONS
VELARISING
VELARIZATION
VELARIZATIONS
VELARIZING
VELDSCHOEN
VELDSCHOENS
VELDSKOENS
VELITATION
VELITATIONS
VELLEITIES
VELLENAGES
VELLICATED
VELLICATES
VELLICATING
VELLICATION
VELLICATIONS

VELLICATIVE
VELOCIMETER
VELOCIMETERS
VELOCIMETRIES
VELOCIMETRY
VELOCIPEDE
VELOCIPEDEAN
VELOCIPEDEANS
VELOCIPEDED
VELOCIPEDER
VELOCIPEDERS
VELOCIPEDES
VELOCIPEDIAN
VELOCIPEDIANS
VELOCIPEDING
VELOCIPEDIST
VELOCIPEDISTS
VELOCIRAPTOR
VELOCIRAPTORS
VELOCITIES
VELODROMES
VELOUTINES
VELUTINOUS
VELVETEENED
VELVETEENS
VELVETIEST
VELVETINESS
VELVETINESSES
VELVETINGS
VELVETLIKE
VENALITIES
VENATICALLY
VENATIONAL
VENATORIAL
VENDETTIST
VENDETTISTS
VENDIBILITIES
VENDIBILITY
VENDIBLENESS
VENDIBLENESSES
VENDITATION
VENDITATIONS
VENDITIONS
VENEERINGS
VENEFICALLY
VENEFICIOUS
VENEFICIOUSLY
VENEFICOUS
VENEFICOUSLY
VENENATING
VENEPUNCTURE
VENEPUNCTURES
VENERABILITIES
VENERABILITY
VENERABLENESS
VENERABLENESSES
VENERABLES
VENERATING
VENERATION
VENERATIONAL
VENERATIONS
VENERATIVENESS
VENERATORS
VENEREOLOGICAL
VENEREOLOGIES
VENEREOLOGIST
VENEREOLOGISTS
VENEREOLOGY
VENESECTION
VENESECTIONS
VENGEANCES
VENGEFULLY
VENGEFULNESS
VENGEFULNESSES
VENGEMENTS
VENIALITIES
VENIALNESS
VENIALNESSES
VENIPUNCTURE
VENIPUNCTURES
VENISECTION
VENISECTIONS
VENOGRAPHIC
VENOGRAPHICAL
VENOGRAPHIES
VENOGRAPHY
VENOLOGIES
VENOMOUSLY
VENOMOUSNESS
VENOMOUSNESSES
VENOSCLEROSES
VENOSCLEROSIS
VENOSITIES
VENOUSNESS
VENOUSNESSES
VENTIDUCTS
VENTIFACTS
VENTILABLE
VENTILATED
VENTILATES
VENTILATING
VENTILATION
VENTILATIONS
VENTILATIVE
VENTILATOR
VENTILATORS
VENTILATORY
VENTOSITIES
VENTRICLES
VENTRICOSE
VENTRICOSITIES
VENTRICOSITY
VENTRICOUS
VENTRICULAR
VENTRICULE
VENTRICULES
VENTRICULI
VENTRICULUS
VENTRILOQUAL
VENTRILOQUIAL
VENTRILOQUIALLY
VENTRILOQUIES
VENTRILOQUISE
VENTRILOQUISED
VENTRILOQUISES
VENTRILOQUISING
VENTRILOQUISM
VENTRILOQUISMS
VENTRILOQUIST
VENTRILOQUISTIC
VENTRILOQUISTS
VENTRILOQUIZE
VENTRILOQUIZED
VENTRILOQUIZES
VENTRILOQUIZING
VENTRILOQUOUS
VENTRILOQUY
VENTRIPOTENT
VENTROLATERAL
VENTROMEDIAL
VENTURESOME
VENTURESOMELY
VENTURESOMENESS
VENTURINGLY
VENTURINGS
VENTUROUSLY
VENTUROUSNESS
VENTUROUSNESSES
VERACIOUSLY
VERACIOUSNESS
VERACIOUSNESSES
VERACITIES
VERANDAHED
VERAPAMILS
VERATRIDINE
VERATRIDINES
VERATRINES
VERBALISATION
VERBALISATIONS
VERBALISED
VERBALISER
VERBALISERS
VERBALISES
VERBALISING
VERBALISMS
VERBALISTIC
VERBALISTS
VERBALITIES
VERBALIZATION
VERBALIZATIONS
VERBALIZED
VERBALIZER
VERBALIZERS
VERBALIZES
VERBALIZING
VERBALLING
VERBARIANS
VERBASCUMS
VERBENACEOUS
VERBERATED
VERBERATES
VERBERATING
VERBERATION
VERBERATIONS
VERBICIDES
VERBIFICATION
VERBIFICATIONS
VERBIFYING
VERBIGERATE
VERBIGERATED
VERBIGERATES
VERBIGERATING
VERBIGERATION
VERBIGERATIONS
VERBOSENESS
VERBOSENESSES
VERBOSITIES
VERDANCIES
VERDIGRISED
VERDIGRISES
VERDIGRISING
VERDURELESS
VERGEBOARD
VERGEBOARDS
VERGENCIES
VERGERSHIP
VERGERSHIPS
VERIDICALITIES
VERIDICALITY
VERIDICALLY
VERIDICOUS
VERIFIABILITIES
VERIFIABILITY
VERIFIABLE
VERIFIABLENESS
VERIFIABLY
VERIFICATION
VERIFICATIONS
VERIFICATIVE
VERIFICATORY
VERISIMILAR
VERISIMILARLY
VERISIMILITIES
VERISIMILITUDE
VERISIMILITUDES
VERISIMILITY
VERISIMILOUS
VERITABLENESS
VERITABLENESSES
VERJUICING
VERKRAMPTE
VERKRAMPTES
VERMEILING
VERMEILLED
VERMEILLES
VERMEILLING
VERMICELLI
VERMICELLIS
VERMICIDAL
VERMICIDES
VERMICULAR
VERMICULARLY
VERMICULATE
VERMICULATED
VERMICULATES
VERMICULATING
VERMICULATION
VERMICULATIONS
VERMICULES
VERMICULITE
VERMICULITES
VERMICULOUS
VERMICULTURE
VERMICULTURES
VERMIFUGAL
VERMIFUGES
VERMILIONED
VERMILIONING
VERMILIONS
VERMILLING
VERMILLION
VERMILLIONS
VERMINATED
VERMINATES

VERMINATING
VERMINATION
VERMINATIONS
VERMINOUSLY
VERMINOUSNESS
VERMINOUSNESSES
VERMIVOROUS
VERNACULAR
VERNACULARISE
VERNACULARISED
VERNACULARISES
VERNACULARISING
VERNACULARISM
VERNACULARISMS
VERNACULARIST
VERNACULARISTS
VERNACULARITIES
VERNACULARITY
VERNACULARIZE
VERNACULARIZED
VERNACULARIZES
VERNACULARIZING
VERNACULARLY
VERNACULARS
VERNALISATION
VERNALISATIONS
VERNALISED
VERNALISES
VERNALISING
VERNALITIES
VERNALIZATION
VERNALIZATIONS
VERNALIZED
VERNALIZES
VERNALIZING
VERNATIONS
VERNISSAGE
VERNISSAGES
VERRUCIFORM
VERRUCOSITIES
VERRUCOSITY
VERSABILITIES
VERSABILITY
VERSATILELY
VERSATILENESS
VERSATILENESSES
VERSATILITIES
VERSATILITY
VERSICOLOR
VERSICOLOUR
VERSICOLOURED
VERSICULAR
VERSIFICATION
VERSIFICATIONS
VERSIFICATOR
VERSIFICATORS
VERSIFIERS
VERSIFYING
VERSIONERS
VERSIONING
VERSIONINGS
VERSIONIST
VERSIONISTS
VERSLIBRIST
VERSLIBRISTE
VERSLIBRISTES
VERSLIBRISTS
VERTEBRALLY
VERTEBRATE
VERTEBRATED
VERTEBRATES
VERTEBRATION
VERTEBRATIONS
VERTICALITIES
VERTICALITY
VERTICALLY
VERTICALNESS
VERTICALNESSES
VERTICILLASTER
VERTICILLASTERS
VERTICILLATE
VERTICILLATED
VERTICILLATELY
VERTICILLATION
VERTICILLATIONS
VERTICILLIUM
VERTICILLIUMS
VERTICITIES
VERTIGINES
VERTIGINOUS
VERTIGINOUSLY
VERTIGINOUSNESS
VERTIPORTS
VERUMONTANA
VERUMONTANUM
VERUMONTANUMS
VESICATING
VESICATION
VESICATIONS
VESICATORIES
VESICATORY
VESICULARITIES
VESICULARITY
VESICULARLY
VESICULATE
VESICULATED
VESICULATES
VESICULATING
VESICULATION
VESICULATIONS
VESICULOSE
VESPERTILIAN
VESPERTILIONID
VESPERTILIONIDS
VESPERTILIONINE
VESPERTINAL
VESPERTINE
VESPIARIES
VESTIARIES
VESTIBULAR
VESTIBULED
VESTIBULES
VESTIBULING
VESTIBULITIS
VESTIBULITISES
VESTIBULUM
VESTIGIALLY
VESTIMENTAL
VESTIMENTARY
VESTIMENTS
VESTITURES
VESTMENTAL
VESTMENTED
VESUVIANITE
VESUVIANITES
VETCHLINGS
VETERINARIAN
VETERINARIANS
VETERINARIES
VETERINARY
VEXATIOUSLY
VEXATIOUSNESS
VEXATIOUSNESSES
VEXEDNESSES
VEXILLARIES
VEXILLATION
VEXILLATIONS
VEXILLOLOGIC
VEXILLOLOGICAL
VEXILLOLOGIES
VEXILLOLOGIST
VEXILLOLOGISTS
VEXILLOLOGY
VEXINGNESS
VEXINGNESSES
VIABILITIES
VIBRACULAR
VIBRACULARIA
VIBRACULARIUM
VIBRACULOID
VIBRACULUM
VIBRAHARPIST
VIBRAHARPISTS
VIBRAHARPS
VIBRANCIES
VIBRAPHONE
VIBRAPHONES
VIBRAPHONIST
VIBRAPHONISTS
VIBRATILITIES
VIBRATILITY
VIBRATINGLY
VIBRATIONAL
VIBRATIONLESS
VIBRATIONS
VIBRATIUNCLE
VIBRATIUNCLES
VIBRATOLESS
VIBROFLOTATION
VIBROFLOTATIONS
VIBROGRAPH
VIBROGRAPHS
VIBROMETER
VIBROMETERS
VICARESSES
VICARIANCE
VICARIANCES
VICARIANTS
VICARIATES
VICARIOUSLY
VICARIOUSNESS
VICARIOUSNESSES
VICARSHIPS
VICEGERENCIES
VICEGERENCY
VICEGERENT
VICEGERENTS
VICEREGALLY
VICEREGENT
VICEREGENTS
VICEREINES
VICEROYALTIES
VICEROYALTY
VICEROYSHIP
VICEROYSHIPS
VICHYSSOIS
VICHYSSOISE
VICHYSSOISES
VICINITIES
VICIOSITIES
VICIOUSNESS
VICIOUSNESSES
VICISSITUDE
VICISSITUDES
VICISSITUDINARY
VICISSITUDINOUS
VICOMTESSE
VICOMTESSES
VICTIMHOOD
VICTIMHOODS
VICTIMISATION
VICTIMISATIONS
VICTIMISED
VICTIMISER
VICTIMISERS
VICTIMISES
VICTIMISING
VICTIMIZATION
VICTIMIZATIONS
VICTIMIZED
VICTIMIZER
VICTIMIZERS
VICTIMIZES
VICTIMIZING
VICTIMLESS
VICTIMOLOGIES
VICTIMOLOGIST
VICTIMOLOGISTS
VICTIMOLOGY
VICTORESSES
VICTORIANA
VICTORINES
VICTORIOUS
VICTORIOUSLY
VICTORIOUSNESS
VICTORYLESS
VICTRESSES
VICTROLLAS
VICTUALAGE
VICTUALAGES
VICTUALERS
VICTUALING
VICTUALLAGE
VICTUALLAGES
VICTUALLED
VICTUALLER
VICTUALLERS
VICTUALLESS
VICTUALLING
VIDEOCASSETTE
VIDEOCASSETTES
VIDEOCONFERENCE
VIDEODISCS
VIDEODISKS

VIDEOGRAMS
VIDEOGRAPHER
VIDEOGRAPHERS
VIDEOGRAPHIES
VIDEOGRAPHY
VIDEOLANDS
VIDEOPHILE
VIDEOPHILES
VIDEOPHONE
VIDEOPHONES
VIDEOPHONIC
VIDEOTAPED
VIDEOTAPES
VIDEOTAPING
VIDEOTELEPHONE
VIDEOTELEPHONES
VIDEOTEXES
VIDEOTEXTS
VIEWERSHIP
VIEWERSHIPS
VIEWFINDER
VIEWFINDERS
VIEWINESSES
VIEWLESSLY
VIEWPHONES
VIEWPOINTS
VIGILANCES
VIGILANTES
VIGILANTISM
VIGILANTISMS
VIGILANTLY
VIGILANTNESS
VIGILANTNESSES
VIGINTILLION
VIGINTILLIONS
VIGNETTERS
VIGNETTING
VIGNETTIST
VIGNETTISTS
VIGORISHES
VIGOROUSLY
VIGOROUSNESS
VIGOROUSNESSES
VIKINGISMS
VILDNESSES
VILENESSES
VILIFICATION
VILIFICATIONS
VILIPENDED
VILIPENDER
VILIPENDERS
VILIPENDING
VILLAGERIES
VILLAGIOES
VILLAGISATION
VILLAGISATIONS
VILLAGIZATION
VILLAGIZATIONS
VILLAGREES
VILLAINAGE
VILLAINAGES
VILLAINESS
VILLAINESSES
VILLAINIES
VILLAINOUS
VILLAINOUSLY
VILLAINOUSNESS
VILLANAGES
VILLANELLA
VILLANELLAS
VILLANELLE
VILLANELLES
VILLANOUSLY
VILLEGGIATURA
VILLEGGIATURAS
VILLEINAGE
VILLEINAGES
VILLENAGES
VILLIAGOES
VILLICATION
VILLICATIONS
VILLOSITIES
VINAIGRETTE
VINAIGRETTES
VINBLASTINE
VINBLASTINES
VINCIBILITIES
VINCIBILITY
VINCIBLENESS
VINCIBLENESSES
VINCRISTINE
VINCRISTINES
VINDEMIATE
VINDEMIATED
VINDEMIATES
VINDEMIATING
VINDICABILITIES
VINDICABILITY
VINDICABLE
VINDICATED
VINDICATES
VINDICATING
VINDICATION
VINDICATIONS
VINDICATIVE
VINDICATIVENESS
VINDICATOR
VINDICATORILY
VINDICATORS
VINDICATORY
VINDICATRESS
VINDICATRESSES
VINDICTIVE
VINDICTIVELY
VINDICTIVENESS
VINEDRESSER
VINEDRESSERS
VINEGARETTE
VINEGARETTES
VINEGARING
VINEGARISH
VINEGARRETTE
VINEGARRETTES
VINEGARROON
VINEGARROONS
VINEYARDIST
VINEYARDISTS
VINICULTURAL
VINICULTURE
VINICULTURES
VINICULTURIST
VINICULTURISTS
VINIFEROUS
VINIFICATION
VINIFICATIONS
VINIFICATOR
VINIFICATORS
VINOLOGIES
VINOLOGIST
VINOLOGISTS
VINOSITIES
VINTAGINGS
VINYLCYANIDE
VINYLCYANIDES
VINYLIDENE
VINYLIDENES
VIOLABILITIES
VIOLABILITY
VIOLABLENESS
VIOLABLENESSES
VIOLACEOUS
VIOLATIONS
VIOLENTING
VIOLINISTIC
VIOLINISTICALLY
VIOLINISTS
VIOLONCELLI
VIOLONCELLIST
VIOLONCELLISTS
VIOLONCELLO
VIOLONCELLOS
VIOSTEROLS
VIPERFISHES
VIPERIFORM
VIPERISHLY
VIPEROUSLY
VIRAGINIAN
VIRAGINOUS
VIRESCENCE
VIRESCENCES
VIRGINALIST
VIRGINALISTS
VIRGINALLED
VIRGINALLING
VIRGINALLY
VIRGINHOOD
VIRGINHOODS
VIRGINITIES
VIRGINIUMS
VIRIDESCENCE
VIRIDESCENCES
VIRIDESCENT
VIRIDITIES
VIRILESCENCE
VIRILESCENCES
VIRILESCENT
VIRILISATION
VIRILISATIONS
VIRILISING
VIRILITIES
VIRILIZATION
VIRILIZATIONS
VIRILIZING
VIROLOGICAL
VIROLOGICALLY
VIROLOGIES
VIROLOGIST
VIROLOGISTS
VIRTUALISE
VIRTUALISED
VIRTUALISES
VIRTUALISING
VIRTUALISM
VIRTUALISMS
VIRTUALIST
VIRTUALISTS
VIRTUALITIES
VIRTUALITY
VIRTUALIZE
VIRTUALIZED
VIRTUALIZES
VIRTUALIZING
VIRTUELESS
VIRTUOSITIES
VIRTUOSITY
VIRTUOSOSHIP
VIRTUOSOSHIPS
VIRTUOUSLY
VIRTUOUSNESS
VIRTUOUSNESSES
VIRULENCES
VIRULENCIES
VIRULENTLY
VIRULIFEROUS
VISAGISTES
VISCACHERA
VISCACHERAS
VISCERALLY
VISCERATED
VISCERATES
VISCERATING
VISCEROMOTOR
VISCEROPTOSES
VISCEROPTOSIS
VISCEROTONIA
VISCEROTONIAS
VISCEROTONIC
VISCIDITIES
VISCIDNESS
VISCIDNESSES
VISCOELASTIC
VISCOELASTICITY
VISCOMETER
VISCOMETERS
VISCOMETRIC
VISCOMETRICAL
VISCOMETRIES
VISCOMETRY
VISCOSIMETER
VISCOSIMETERS
VISCOSIMETRIC
VISCOSIMETRICAL
VISCOSIMETRIES
VISCOSIMETRY
VISCOSITIES
VISCOUNTCIES
VISCOUNTCY
VISCOUNTESS
VISCOUNTESSES
VISCOUNTIES
VISCOUNTSHIP
VISCOUNTSHIPS
VISCOUSNESS
VISCOUSNESSES

VISIBILITIES
VISIBILITY
VISIBLENESS
VISIBLENESSES
VISIOGENIC
VISIONALLY
VISIONARIES
VISIONARINESS
VISIONARINESSES
VISIONINGS
VISIONISTS
VISIONLESS
VISIOPHONE
VISIOPHONES
VISITATION
VISITATIONAL
VISITATIONS
VISITATIVE
VISITATORIAL
VISITATORS
VISITORIAL
VISITRESSES
VISUALISATION
VISUALISATIONS
VISUALISED
VISUALISER
VISUALISERS
VISUALISES
VISUALISING
VISUALISTS
VISUALITIES
VISUALIZATION
VISUALIZATIONS
VISUALIZED
VISUALIZER
VISUALIZERS
VISUALIZES
VISUALIZING
VITALISATION
VITALISATIONS
VITALISERS
VITALISING
VITALISTIC
VITALISTICALLY
VITALITIES
VITALIZATION
VITALIZATIONS
VITALIZERS
VITALIZING
VITALNESSES
VITAMINISE
VITAMINISED
VITAMINISES
VITAMINISING
VITAMINIZE
VITAMINIZED
VITAMINIZES
VITAMINIZING
VITASCOPES
VITATIVENESS
VITATIVENESSES
VITELLICLE
VITELLICLES
VITELLIGENOUS
VITELLINES
VITELLOGENESES
VITELLOGENESIS
VITELLOGENIC
VITELLUSES
VITIATIONS
VITICETUMS
VITICOLOUS
VITICULTURAL
VITICULTURALLY
VITICULTURE
VITICULTURER
VITICULTURERS
VITICULTURES
VITICULTURIST
VITICULTURISTS
VITIFEROUS
VITILITIGATE
VITILITIGATED
VITILITIGATES
VITILITIGATING
VITILITIGATION
VITILITIGATIONS
VITIOSITIES
VITRAILLED
VITRAILLIST
VITRAILLISTS
VITRECTOMIES
VITRECTOMY
VITREOSITIES
VITREOSITY
VITREOUSES
VITREOUSLY
VITREOUSNESS
VITREOUSNESSES
VITRESCENCE
VITRESCENCES
VITRESCENT
VITRESCIBILITY
VITRESCIBLE
VITRIFACTION
VITRIFACTIONS
VITRIFACTURE
VITRIFACTURES
VITRIFIABILITY
VITRIFIABLE
VITRIFICATION
VITRIFICATIONS
VITRIFYING
VITRIOLATE
VITRIOLATED
VITRIOLATES
VITRIOLATING
VITRIOLATION
VITRIOLATIONS
VITRIOLING
VITRIOLISATION
VITRIOLISATIONS
VITRIOLISE
VITRIOLISED
VITRIOLISES
VITRIOLISING
VITRIOLIZATION
VITRIOLIZATIONS
VITRIOLIZE
VITRIOLIZED
VITRIOLIZES
VITRIOLIZING
VITRIOLLED
VITRIOLLING
VITUPERABLE
VITUPERATE
VITUPERATED
VITUPERATES
VITUPERATING
VITUPERATION
VITUPERATIONS
VITUPERATIVE
VITUPERATIVELY
VITUPERATOR
VITUPERATORS
VITUPERATORY
VIVACIOUSLY
VIVACIOUSNESS
VIVACIOUSNESSES
VIVACISSIMO
VIVACITIES
VIVANDIERE
VIVANDIERES
VIVANDIERS
VIVERRINES
VIVIANITES
VIVIDITIES
VIVIDNESSES
VIVIFICATION
VIVIFICATIONS
VIVIPARIES
VIVIPARISM
VIVIPARISMS
VIVIPARITIES
VIVIPARITY
VIVIPAROUS
VIVIPAROUSLY
VIVIPAROUSNESS
VIVISECTED
VIVISECTING
VIVISECTION
VIVISECTIONAL
VIVISECTIONALLY
VIVISECTIONIST
VIVISECTIONISTS
VIVISECTIONS
VIVISECTIVE
VIVISECTOR
VIVISECTORIUM
VIVISECTORIUMS
VIVISECTORS
VIVISEPULTURE
VIVISEPULTURES
VIXENISHLY
VIXENISHNESS
VIXENISHNESSES
VIZIERATES
VIZIERSHIP
VIZIERSHIPS
VIZIRSHIPS
VOCABULARIAN
VOCABULARIANS
VOCABULARIED
VOCABULARIES
VOCABULARY
VOCABULIST
VOCABULISTS
VOCALICALLY
VOCALISATION
VOCALISATIONS
VOCALISERS
VOCALISING
VOCALITIES
VOCALIZATION
VOCALIZATIONS
VOCALIZERS
VOCALIZING
VOCALNESSES
VOCATIONAL
VOCATIONALISM
VOCATIONALISMS
VOCATIONALIST
VOCATIONALISTS
VOCATIONALLY
VOCATIVELY
VOCICULTURAL
VOCIFERANCE
VOCIFERANCES
VOCIFERANT
VOCIFERANTS
VOCIFERATE
VOCIFERATED
VOCIFERATES
VOCIFERATING
VOCIFERATION
VOCIFERATIONS
VOCIFERATOR
VOCIFERATORS
VOCIFEROSITIES
VOCIFEROSITY
VOCIFEROUS
VOCIFEROUSLY
VOCIFEROUSNESS
VOETGANGER
VOETGANGERS
VOETSTOETS
VOETSTOOTS
VOGUISHNESS
VOGUISHNESSES
VOICEFULNESS
VOICEFULNESSES
VOICELESSLY
VOICELESSNESS
VOICELESSNESSES
VOICEMAILS
VOICEOVERS
VOICEPRINT
VOICEPRINTS
VOIDABLENESS
VOIDABLENESSES
VOIDNESSES
VOISINAGES
VOITURIERS
VOIVODESHIP
VOIVODESHIPS
VOLATILENESS
VOLATILENESSES
VOLATILISABLE
VOLATILISATION
VOLATILISATIONS
VOLATILISE
VOLATILISED
VOLATILISES
VOLATILISING

VOLATILITIES
VOLATILITY
VOLATILIZABLE
VOLATILIZATION
VOLATILIZATIONS
VOLATILIZE
VOLATILIZED
VOLATILIZES
VOLATILIZING
VOLCANICALLY
VOLCANICITIES
VOLCANICITY
VOLCANISATION
VOLCANISATIONS
VOLCANISED
VOLCANISES
VOLCANISING
VOLCANISMS
VOLCANISTS
VOLCANIZATION
VOLCANIZATIONS
VOLCANIZED
VOLCANIZES
VOLCANIZING
VOLCANOLOGIC
VOLCANOLOGICAL
VOLCANOLOGIES
VOLCANOLOGIST
VOLCANOLOGISTS
VOLCANOLOGY
VOLITATING
VOLITATION
VOLITATIONAL
VOLITATIONS
VOLITIONAL
VOLITIONALLY
VOLITIONARY
VOLITIONLESS
VOLITORIAL
VOLKSLIEDER
VOLKSRAADS
VOLLEYBALL
VOLLEYBALLS
VOLPLANING
VOLTAMETER
VOLTAMETERS
VOLTAMETRIC
VOLTAMMETER
VOLTAMMETERS
VOLTIGEURS
VOLTINISMS
VOLTMETERS
VOLUBILITIES
VOLUBILITY
VOLUBLENESS
VOLUBLENESSES
VOLUMENOMETER
VOLUMENOMETERS
VOLUMETERS
VOLUMETRIC
VOLUMETRICAL
VOLUMETRICALLY
VOLUMETRIES
VOLUMINOSITIES
VOLUMINOSITY
VOLUMINOUS
VOLUMINOUSLY
VOLUMINOUSNESS
VOLUMISING
VOLUMIZING
VOLUMOMETER
VOLUMOMETERS
VOLUNTARIES
VOLUNTARILY
VOLUNTARINESS
VOLUNTARINESSES
VOLUNTARISM
VOLUNTARISMS
VOLUNTARIST
VOLUNTARISTIC
VOLUNTARISTS
VOLUNTARYISM
VOLUNTARYISMS
VOLUNTARYIST
VOLUNTARYISTS
VOLUNTATIVE
VOLUNTEERED
VOLUNTEERING
VOLUNTEERISM
VOLUNTEERISMS
VOLUNTEERS
VOLUPTUARIES
VOLUPTUARY
VOLUPTUOSITIES
VOLUPTUOSITY
VOLUPTUOUS
VOLUPTUOUSLY
VOLUPTUOUSNESS
VOLUTATION
VOLUTATIONS
VOLVULUSES
VOMERONASAL
VOMITORIES
VOMITORIUM
VOMITURITION
VOMITURITIONS
VOODOOISMS
VOODOOISTIC
VOODOOISTS
VOORKAMERS
VOORTREKKER
VOORTREKKERS
VORACIOUSLY
VORACIOUSNESS
VORACIOUSNESSES
VORACITIES
VORAGINOUS
VORTICALLY
VORTICELLA
VORTICELLAE
VORTICELLAS
VORTICISMS
VORTICISTS
VORTICITIES
VORTICULAR
VORTIGINOUS
VOTARESSES
VOTIVENESS
VOTIVENESSES
VOUCHERING
VOUCHSAFED
VOUCHSAFEMENT
VOUCHSAFEMENTS
VOUCHSAFES
VOUCHSAFING
VOUCHSAFINGS
VOUSSOIRED
VOUSSOIRING
VOUTSAFING
VOWELISATION
VOWELISATIONS
VOWELISING
VOWELIZATION
VOWELIZATIONS
VOWELIZING
VOYAGEABLE
VOYEURISMS
VOYEURISTIC
VOYEURISTICALLY
VRAICKINGS
VRAISEMBLANCE
VRAISEMBLANCES
VULCANICITIES
VULCANICITY
VULCANISABLE
VULCANISATE
VULCANISATES
VULCANISATION
VULCANISATIONS
VULCANISED
VULCANISER
VULCANISERS
VULCANISES
VULCANISING
VULCANISMS
VULCANISTS
VULCANITES
VULCANIZABLE
VULCANIZATE
VULCANIZATES
VULCANIZATION
VULCANIZATIONS
VULCANIZED
VULCANIZER
VULCANIZERS
VULCANIZES
VULCANIZING
VULCANOLOGICAL
VULCANOLOGIES
VULCANOLOGIST
VULCANOLOGISTS
VULCANOLOGY
VULGARIANS
VULGARISATION
VULGARISATIONS
VULGARISED
VULGARISER
VULGARISERS
VULGARISES
VULGARISING
VULGARISMS
VULGARITIES
VULGARIZATION
VULGARIZATIONS
VULGARIZED
VULGARIZER
VULGARIZERS
VULGARIZES
VULGARIZING
VULNERABILITIES
VULNERABILITY
VULNERABLE
VULNERABLENESS
VULNERABLY
VULNERARIES
VULNERATED
VULNERATES
VULNERATING
VULNERATION
VULNERATIONS
VULPECULAR
VULPICIDES
VULPINISMS
VULPINITES
VULTURISMS
VULVITISES
VULVOVAGINAL
VULVOVAGINITIS

Ww

WACKINESSES
WADSETTERS
WADSETTING
WAFFLESTOMPER
WAFFLESTOMPERS
WAGELESSNESS
WAGELESSNESSES
WAGENBOOMS
WAGEWORKER
WAGEWORKERS
WAGGISHNESS
WAGGISHNESSES
WAGGLINGLY
WAGGONETTE
WAGGONETTES
WAGGONLESS
WAGGONLOAD
WAGGONLOADS
WAGHALTERS
WAGONETTES
WAGONLOADS
WAGONWRIGHT
WAGONWRIGHTS
WAINSCOTED
WAINSCOTING
WAINSCOTINGS
WAINSCOTTED
WAINSCOTTING
WAINSCOTTINGS
WAINWRIGHT
WAINWRIGHTS
WAISTBANDS
WAISTBELTS
WAISTCLOTH
WAISTCLOTHS
WAISTCOATED
WAISTCOATEER
WAISTCOATEERS
WAISTCOATING
WAISTCOATINGS
WAISTCOATS
WAISTLINES
WAITERAGES
WAITERHOOD
WAITERHOODS
WAITERINGS
WAITLISTED
WAITLISTING
WAITPERSON
WAITPERSONS
WAITRESSED
WAITRESSES
WAITRESSING
WAITRESSINGS
WAITSTAFFS
WAKEBOARDER
WAKEBOARDERS
WAKEBOARDING
WAKEBOARDINGS
WAKEBOARDS
WAKEFULNESS
WAKEFULNESSES
WALDFLUTES
WALDGRAVES
WALDGRAVINE
WALDGRAVINES
WALDSTERBEN
WALDSTERBENS
WALKABOUTS
WALKATHONS
WALKINGSTICK
WALKINGSTICKS
WALKSHORTS
WALLBOARDS
WALLCHARTS
WALLCLIMBER
WALLCLIMBERS
WALLCOVERING
WALLCOVERINGS
WALLFISHES
WALLFLOWER
WALLFLOWERS
WALLOPINGS
WALLOWINGS
WALLPAPERED
WALLPAPERING
WALLPAPERS
WALLPOSTER
WALLPOSTERS
WALLYBALLS
WALLYDRAGS
WALLYDRAIGLE
WALLYDRAIGLES
WALNUTWOOD
WALNUTWOODS
WAMBENGERS
WAMBLINESS
WAMBLINESSES
WAMBLINGLY
WAMPISHING
WAMPUMPEAG
WAMPUMPEAGS
WANCHANCIE
WANDERINGLY
WANDERINGS
WANDERLUST
WANDERLUSTS
WANRESTFUL
WANTHRIVEN
WANTONISED
WANTONISES
WANTONISING
WANTONIZED
WANTONIZES
WANTONIZING
WANTONNESS
WANTONNESSES
WAPENSCHAW
WAPENSCHAWS
WAPENSHAWS
WAPENTAKES
WAPINSCHAW
WAPINSCHAWS
WAPINSHAWS
WAPPENSCHAW
WAPPENSCHAWING
WAPPENSCHAWINGS
WAPPENSCHAWS
WAPPENSHAW
WAPPENSHAWING
WAPPENSHAWINGS
WAPPENSHAWS
WARBLINGLY
WARBONNETS
WARCHALKER
WARCHALKERS
WARCHALKING
WARCHALKINGS
WARDENRIES
WARDENSHIP
WARDENSHIPS
WARDERSHIP
WARDERSHIPS
WARDRESSES
WARDROBERS
WARDROBING
WAREHOUSED
WAREHOUSEMAN
WAREHOUSEMEN
WAREHOUSER
WAREHOUSERS
WAREHOUSES

WAREHOUSING
WAREHOUSINGS
WARFARINGS
WARIBASHIS
WARINESSES
WARLIKENESS
WARLIKENESSES
WARLOCKRIES
WARLORDISM
WARLORDISMS
WARMBLOODS
WARMHEARTED
WARMHEARTEDNESS
WARMNESSES
WARMONGERING
WARMONGERINGS
WARMONGERS
WARRANDICE
WARRANDICES
WARRANDING
WARRANTABILITY
WARRANTABLE
WARRANTABLENESS
WARRANTABLY
WARRANTEES
WARRANTERS
WARRANTIED
WARRANTIES
WARRANTING
WARRANTINGS
WARRANTISE
WARRANTISES
WARRANTLESS
WARRANTORS
WARRANTYING
WARRIORESS
WARRIORESSES
WASHABILITIES
WASHABILITY
WASHATERIA
WASHATERIAS
WASHBASINS
WASHBOARDS
WASHCLOTHS
WASHERWOMAN
WASHERWOMEN
WASHETERIA
WASHETERIAS
WASHHOUSES
WASHINESSES
WASHINGTONIA
WASHINGTONIAS
WASHSTANDS
WASPINESSES
WASPISHNESS
WASPISHNESSES
WASSAILERS
WASSAILING
WASSAILINGS
WASSAILRIES
WASTEBASKET
WASTEBASKETS
WASTEFULLY
WASTEFULNESS
WASTEFULNESSES
WASTELANDS
WASTENESSES
WASTEPAPER
WASTEPAPERS
WASTERFULLY
WASTERFULNESS
WASTERFULNESSES
WASTEWATER
WASTEWATERS
WASTEWEIRS
WASTNESSES
WATCHABLES
WATCHBANDS
WATCHBOXES
WATCHCASES
WATCHCRIES
WATCHDOGGED
WATCHDOGGING
WATCHFULLY
WATCHFULNESS
WATCHFULNESSES
WATCHGLASS
WATCHGLASSES
WATCHGUARD
WATCHGUARDS
WATCHLISTS
WATCHMAKER
WATCHMAKERS
WATCHMAKING
WATCHMAKINGS
WATCHSPRING
WATCHSPRINGS
WATCHSTRAP
WATCHSTRAPS
WATCHTOWER
WATCHTOWERS
WATCHWORDS
WATERBIRDS
WATERBORNE
WATERBRAIN
WATERBRAINS
WATERBUCKS
WATERBUSES
WATERBUSSES
WATERCOLOR
WATERCOLORIST
WATERCOLORISTS
WATERCOLORS
WATERCOLOUR
WATERCOLOURIST
WATERCOLOURISTS
WATERCOLOURS
WATERCOOLER
WATERCOOLERS
WATERCOURSE
WATERCOURSES
WATERCRAFT
WATERCRAFTS
WATERCRESS
WATERCRESSES
WATERDRIVE
WATERDRIVES
WATERFALLS
WATERFINDER
WATERFINDERS
WATERFLOOD
WATERFLOODED
WATERFLOODING
WATERFLOODINGS
WATERFLOODS
WATERFOWLER
WATERFOWLERS
WATERFOWLING
WATERFOWLINGS
WATERFOWLS
WATERFRONT
WATERFRONTS
WATERGLASS
WATERGLASSES
WATERHEADS
WATERINESS
WATERINESSES
WATERISHNESS
WATERISHNESSES
WATERLEAFS
WATERLESSNESS
WATERLESSNESSES
WATERLILIES
WATERLINES
WATERLOGGED
WATERLOGGING
WATERMANSHIP
WATERMANSHIPS
WATERMARKED
WATERMARKING
WATERMARKS
WATERMELON
WATERMELONS
WATERPOWER
WATERPOWERS
WATERPOXES
WATERPROOF
WATERPROOFED
WATERPROOFER
WATERPROOFERS
WATERPROOFING
WATERPROOFINGS
WATERPROOFNESS
WATERPROOFS
WATERQUAKE
WATERQUAKES
WATERSCAPE
WATERSCAPES
WATERSHEDS
WATERSIDER
WATERSIDERS
WATERSIDES
WATERSKIING
WATERSKIINGS
WATERSMEET
WATERSMEETS
WATERSPOUT
WATERSPOUTS
WATERTHRUSH
WATERTHRUSHES
WATERTIGHT
WATERTIGHTNESS
WATERWEEDS
WATERWHEEL
WATERWHEELS
WATERWORKS
WATERZOOIS
WATTLEBARK
WATTLEBARKS
WATTLEBIRD
WATTLEBIRDS
WATTLEWORK
WATTLEWORKS
WATTMETERS
WAULKMILLS
WAVEFRONTS
WAVEGUIDES
WAVELENGTH
WAVELENGTHS
WAVELESSLY
WAVELLITES
WAVEMETERS
WAVERINGLY
WAVERINGNESS
WAVERINGNESSES
WAVESHAPES
WAVINESSES
WAXBERRIES
WAXFLOWERS
WAXINESSES
WAXWORKERS
WAYFARINGS
WAYMARKING
WAYMENTING
WAYWARDNESS
WAYWARDNESSES
WAYZGOOSES
WEAKFISHES
WEAKHEARTED
WEAKISHNESS
WEAKISHNESSES
WEAKLINESS
WEAKLINESSES
WEAKNESSES
WEALTHIEST
WEALTHINESS
WEALTHINESSES
WEALTHLESS
WEAPONEERED
WEAPONEERING
WEAPONEERS
WEAPONISED
WEAPONISES
WEAPONISING
WEAPONIZED
WEAPONIZES
WEAPONIZING
WEAPONLESS
WEAPONRIES
WEARABILITIES
WEARABILITY
WEARIFULLY
WEARIFULNESS
WEARIFULNESSES
WEARILESSLY
WEARINESSES
WEARISOMELY
WEARISOMENESS
WEARISOMENESSES
WEARYINGLY
WEASELLERS
WEASELLING
WEATHERABILITY
WEATHERABLE

WEATHERBOARD
WEATHERBOARDED
WEATHERBOARDING
WEATHERBOARDS
WEATHERCAST
WEATHERCASTER
WEATHERCASTERS
WEATHERCASTS
WEATHERCLOTH
WEATHERCLOTHS
WEATHERCOCK
WEATHERCOCKED
WEATHERCOCKING
WEATHERCOCKS
WEATHERERS
WEATHERGIRL
WEATHERGIRLS
WEATHERGLASS
WEATHERGLASSES
WEATHERING
WEATHERINGS
WEATHERISATION
WEATHERISATIONS
WEATHERISE
WEATHERISED
WEATHERISES
WEATHERISING
WEATHERIZATION
WEATHERIZATIONS
WEATHERIZE
WEATHERIZED
WEATHERIZES
WEATHERIZING
WEATHERLINESS
WEATHERLINESSES
WEATHERMAN
WEATHERMEN
WEATHERMOST
WEATHEROMETER
WEATHEROMETERS
WEATHERPERSON
WEATHERPERSONS
WEATHERPROOF
WEATHERPROOFED
WEATHERPROOFING
WEATHERPROOFS
WEATHERWORN
WEAVERBIRD
WEAVERBIRDS
WEBCASTERS
WEBCASTING
WEBLOGGERS
WEBMASTERS
WEEDICIDES
WEEDINESSES
WEEDKILLER
WEEDKILLERS
WEEKENDERS
WEEKENDING
WEEKENDINGS
WEEKNIGHTS
WEELDLESSE
WEEPINESSES
WEIGHBOARD
WEIGHBOARDS
WEIGHBRIDGE
WEIGHBRIDGES
WEIGHTIEST
WEIGHTINESS
WEIGHTINESSES
WEIGHTINGS
WEIGHTLESS
WEIGHTLESSLY
WEIGHTLESSNESS
WEIGHTLIFTER
WEIGHTLIFTERS
WEIGHTLIFTING
WEIGHTLIFTINGS
WEIMARANER
WEIMARANERS
WEIRDNESSES
WEISENHEIMER
WEISENHEIMERS
WELCOMENESS
WELCOMENESSES
WELCOMINGLY
WELDABILITIES
WELDABILITY
WELDMESHES
WELFARISMS
WELFARISTIC
WELFARISTS
WELLBEINGS
WELLHOUSES
WELLINGTON
WELLINGTONIA
WELLINGTONIAS
WELLINGTONS
WELLNESSES
WELLSPRING
WELLSPRINGS
WELTANSCHAUUNG
WELTANSCHAUUNGS
WELTERWEIGHT
WELTERWEIGHTS
WELTSCHMERZ
WELTSCHMERZES
WELWITSCHIA
WELWITSCHIAS
WENSLEYDALE
WENSLEYDALES
WENTLETRAP
WENTLETRAPS
WEREWOLFERIES
WEREWOLFERY
WEREWOLFISH
WEREWOLFISM
WEREWOLFISMS
WEREWOLVES
WERNERITES
WERWOLFISH
WESTERINGS
WESTERLIES
WESTERLINESS
WESTERLINESSES
WESTERNERS
WESTERNISATION
WESTERNISATIONS
WESTERNISE
WESTERNISED
WESTERNISES
WESTERNISING
WESTERNISM
WESTERNISMS
WESTERNIZATION
WESTERNIZATIONS
WESTERNIZE
WESTERNIZED
WESTERNIZES
WESTERNIZING
WESTERNMOST
WESTWARDLY
WETTABILITIES
WETTABILITY
WHAIKORERO
WHAIKOREROS
WHAKAPAPAS
WHALEBACKS
WHALEBOATS
WHALEBONES
WHAREPUNIS
WHARFINGER
WHARFINGERS
WHARFMASTER
WHARFMASTERS
WHATABOUTS
WHATCHAMACALLIT
WHATNESSES
WHATSHERNAME
WHATSHERNAMES
WHATSHISNAME
WHATSHISNAMES
WHATSITSNAME
WHATSITSNAMES
WHATSOEVER
WHATSOMEVER
WHEATFIELD
WHEATFIELDS
WHEATGRASS
WHEATGRASSES
WHEATLANDS
WHEATMEALS
WHEATSHEAF
WHEATSHEAVES
WHEATWORMS
WHEEDLESOME
WHEEDLINGLY
WHEEDLINGS
WHEELBARROW
WHEELBARROWED
WHEELBARROWING
WHEELBARROWS
WHEELBASES
WHEELCHAIR
WHEELCHAIRS
WHEELHORSE
WHEELHORSES
WHEELHOUSE
WHEELHOUSES
WHEELWORKS
WHEELWRIGHT
WHEELWRIGHTS
WHEESHTING
WHEEZINESS
WHEEZINESSES
WHENCEFORTH
WHENCESOEVER
WHENSOEVER
WHEREABOUT
WHEREABOUTS
WHEREAFTER
WHEREAGAINST
WHEREFORES
WHEREINSOEVER
WHERENESSES
WHERESOEER
WHERESOEVER
WHERETHROUGH
WHEREUNDER
WHEREUNTIL
WHEREWITHAL
WHEREWITHALS
WHEREWITHS
WHERRETING
WHERRITING
WHETSTONES
WHEWELLITE
WHEWELLITES
WHEYISHNESS
WHEYISHNESSES
WHICHSOEVER
WHICKERING
WHIDDERING
WHIFFLERIES
WHIFFLETREE
WHIFFLETREES
WHIFFLINGS
WHIGGAMORE
WHIGGAMORES
WHIGMALEERIE
WHIGMALEERIES
WHIGMALEERY
WHILLYWHAED
WHILLYWHAING
WHILLYWHAS
WHILLYWHAW
WHILLYWHAWED
WHILLYWHAWING
WHILLYWHAWS
WHIMBERRIES
WHIMPERERS
WHIMPERING
WHIMPERINGLY
WHIMPERINGS
WHIMSICALITIES
WHIMSICALITY
WHIMSICALLY
WHIMSICALNESS
WHIMSICALNESSES
WHIMSINESS
WHIMSINESSES
WHINBERRIES
WHINGDINGS
WHINGEINGS
WHININESSES
WHINSTONES
WHIPLASHED
WHIPLASHES
WHIPLASHING
WHIPPERSNAPPER
WHIPPERSNAPPERS
WHIPPETING
WHIPPETINGS
WHIPPINESS

WHIPPINESSES
WHIPPLETREE
WHIPPLETREES
WHIPPOORWILL
WHIPPOORWILLS
WHIPSAWING
WHIPSNAKES
WHIPSTAFFS
WHIPSTALLED
WHIPSTALLING
WHIPSTALLS
WHIPSTITCH
WHIPSTITCHED
WHIPSTITCHES
WHIPSTITCHING
WHIPSTOCKS
WHIPTAILED
WHIRLABOUT
WHIRLABOUTS
WHIRLBLAST
WHIRLBLASTS
WHIRLIGIGS
WHIRLINGLY
WHIRLPOOLS
WHIRLWINDS
WHIRLYBIRD
WHIRLYBIRDS
WHIRRETING
WHISKERANDO
WHISKERANDOED
WHISKERANDOS
WHISKEYFIED
WHISKIFIED
WHISPERERS
WHISPERING
WHISPERINGLY
WHISPERINGS
WHISPEROUSLY
WHISTLEABLE
WHISTLINGLY
WHISTLINGS
WHITEBAITS
WHITEBASSES
WHITEBEAMS
WHITEBEARD
WHITEBEARDS
WHITEBOARD
WHITEBOARDS
WHITEBOYISM
WHITEBOYISMS
WHITECOATS
WHITECOMBS
WHITEDAMPS
WHITEFACES
WHITEFISHES
WHITEFLIES
WHITEHEADS
WHITENESSES
WHITENINGS
WHITESMITH
WHITESMITHS
WHITETAILS
WHITETHORN
WHITETHORNS
WHITETHROAT
WHITETHROATS
WHITEWALLS
WHITEWARES
WHITEWASHED
WHITEWASHER
WHITEWASHERS
WHITEWASHES
WHITEWASHING
WHITEWASHINGS
WHITEWATER
WHITEWINGS
WHITEWOODS
WHITEYWOOD
WHITEYWOODS
WHITHERING
WHITHERSOEVER
WHITHERWARD
WHITHERWARDS
WHITISHNESS
WHITISHNESSES
WHITLEATHER
WHITLEATHERS
WHITTAWERS
WHITTERICK
WHITTERICKS
WHITTERING
WHITTLINGS
WHIZZBANGS
WHIZZINGLY
WHODUNITRIES
WHODUNITRY
WHODUNNITRIES
WHODUNNITRY
WHODUNNITS
WHOLEFOODS
WHOLEGRAIN
WHOLEHEARTED
WHOLEHEARTEDLY
WHOLEMEALS
WHOLENESSES
WHOLESALED
WHOLESALER
WHOLESALERS
WHOLESALES
WHOLESALING
WHOLESOMELY
WHOLESOMENESS
WHOLESOMENESSES
WHOLESOMER
WHOLESOMEST
WHOLESTITCH
WHOLESTITCHES
WHOLEWHEAT
WHOMSOEVER
WHOREHOUSE
WHOREHOUSES
WHOREMASTER
WHOREMASTERIES
WHOREMASTERLY
WHOREMASTERS
WHOREMASTERY
WHOREMISTRESS
WHOREMISTRESSES
WHOREMONGER
WHOREMONGERIES
WHOREMONGERS
WHOREMONGERY
WHORISHNESS
WHORISHNESSES
WHORTLEBERRIES
WHORTLEBERRY
WHOSESOEVER
WHUNSTANES
WHYDUNNITS
WICKEDNESS
WICKEDNESSES
WICKERWORK
WICKERWORKS
WICKETKEEPER
WICKETKEEPERS
WICKTHINGS
WIDDERSHINS
WIDEAWAKES
WIDEBODIES
WIDECHAPPED
WIDEMOUTHED
WIDENESSES
WIDERSHINS
WIDESCREEN
WIDESPREAD
WIDOWBIRDS
WIDOWERHOOD
WIDOWERHOODS
WIDOWHOODS
WIELDINESS
WIELDINESSES
WIENERWURST
WIENERWURSTS
WIFELINESS
WIFELINESSES
WIGWAGGERS
WIGWAGGING
WILDCATTED
WILDCATTER
WILDCATTERS
WILDCATTING
WILDEBEEST
WILDEBEESTS
WILDERMENT
WILDERMENTS
WILDERNESS
WILDERNESSES
WILDFLOWER
WILDFLOWERS
WILDFOWLER
WILDFOWLERS
WILDFOWLING
WILDFOWLINGS
WILDGRAVES
WILDNESSES
WILFULNESS
WILFULNESSES
WILINESSES
WILLEMITES
WILLFULNESS
WILLFULNESSES
WILLIEWAUGHT
WILLIEWAUGHTS
WILLINGEST
WILLINGNESS
WILLINGNESSES
WILLOWHERB
WILLOWHERBS
WILLOWIEST
WILLOWLIKE
WILLOWWARE
WILLOWWARES
WILLPOWERS
WIMPINESSES
WIMPISHNESS
WIMPISHNESSES
WINCEYETTE
WINCEYETTES
WINCHESTER
WINCHESTERS
WINCOPIPES
WINDBAGGERIES
WINDBAGGERY
WINDBLASTS
WINDBREAKER
WINDBREAKERS
WINDBREAKS
WINDBURNED
WINDBURNING
WINDCHEATER
WINDCHEATERS
WINDCHILLS
WINDFALLEN
WINDFLOWER
WINDFLOWERS
WINDGALLED
WINDHOVERS
WINDINESSES
WINDJAMMER
WINDJAMMERS
WINDJAMMING
WINDJAMMINGS
WINDLASSED
WINDLASSES
WINDLASSING
WINDLESSLY
WINDLESSNESS
WINDLESSNESSES
WINDLESTRAE
WINDLESTRAES
WINDLESTRAW
WINDLESTRAWS
WINDMILLED
WINDMILLING
WINDOWINGS
WINDOWLESS
WINDOWPANE
WINDOWPANES
WINDOWSILL
WINDOWSILLS
WINDROWERS
WINDROWING
WINDSCREEN
WINDSCREENS
WINDSHAKES
WINDSHIELD
WINDSHIELDS
WINDSTORMS
WINDSUCKER
WINDSUCKERS
WINDSURFED
WINDSURFER
WINDSURFERS
WINDSURFING

WINDSURFINGS
WINDTHROWS
WINEBERRIES
WINEBIBBER
WINEBIBBERS
WINEBIBBING
WINEBIBBINGS
WINEGLASSES
WINEGLASSFUL
WINEGLASSFULS
WINEGROWER
WINEGROWERS
WINEMAKERS
WINEPRESSES
WINGCHAIRS
WINGLESSNESS
WINGLESSNESSES
WINGSPREAD
WINGSPREADS
WINNABILITIES
WINNABILITY
WINNINGNESS
WINNINGNESSES
WINNOWINGS
WINSOMENESS
WINSOMENESSES
WINTERBERRIES
WINTERBERRY
WINTERBOURNE
WINTERBOURNES
WINTERCRESS
WINTERCRESSES
WINTERFEED
WINTERFEEDING
WINTERFEEDS
WINTERGREEN
WINTERGREENS
WINTERIEST
WINTERINESS
WINTERINESSES
WINTERISATION
WINTERISATIONS
WINTERISED
WINTERISES
WINTERISING
WINTERIZATION
WINTERIZATIONS
WINTERIZED
WINTERIZES
WINTERIZING
WINTERKILL
WINTERKILLED
WINTERKILLING
WINTERKILLS
WINTERLESS
WINTERLINESS
WINTERLINESSES
WINTERTIDE
WINTERTIDES
WINTERTIME
WINTERTIMES
WINTERWEIGHT
WINTRINESS
WINTRINESSES
WIREDRAWER
WIREDRAWERS
WIREDRAWING
WIREDRAWINGS
WIREGRASSES
WIREHAIRED
WIRELESSED
WIRELESSES
WIRELESSING
WIREPHOTOS
WIREPULLER
WIREPULLERS
WIREPULLING
WIREPULLINGS
WIRETAPPED
WIRETAPPER
WIRETAPPERS
WIRETAPPING
WIREWALKER
WIREWALKERS
WIREWORKER
WIREWORKERS
WIREWORKING
WIREWORKINGS
WIRINESSES
WISECRACKED
WISECRACKER
WISECRACKERS
WISECRACKING
WISECRACKS
WISENESSES
WISENHEIMER
WISENHEIMERS
WISHFULNESS
WISHFULNESSES
WISHTONWISH
WISHTONWISHES
WISPINESSES
WISTFULNESS
WISTFULNESSES
WITBLITSES
WITCHBROOM
WITCHBROOMS
WITCHCRAFT
WITCHCRAFTS
WITCHERIES
WITCHETTIES
WITCHGRASS
WITCHGRASSES
WITCHHOODS
WITCHINGLY
WITCHKNOTS
WITCHWEEDS
WITENAGEMOT
WITENAGEMOTE
WITENAGEMOTES
WITENAGEMOTS
WITGATBOOM
WITGATBOOMS
WITHDRAWABLE
WITHDRAWAL
WITHDRAWALS
WITHDRAWER
WITHDRAWERS
WITHDRAWING
WITHDRAWMENT
WITHDRAWMENTS
WITHDRAWNNESS
WITHDRAWNNESSES
WITHEREDNESS
WITHEREDNESSES
WITHERINGLY
WITHERINGS
WITHERITES
WITHERSHINS
WITHHOLDEN
WITHHOLDER
WITHHOLDERS
WITHHOLDING
WITHHOLDMENT
WITHHOLDMENTS
WITHINDOORS
WITHOUTDOORS
WITHSTANDER
WITHSTANDERS
WITHSTANDING
WITHSTANDS
WITHYWINDS
WITLESSNESS
WITLESSNESSES
WITNESSABLE
WITNESSERS
WITNESSING
WITTICISMS
WITTINESSES
WITWANTONED
WITWANTONING
WITWANTONS
WIZARDRIES
WOADWAXENS
WOBBEGONGS
WOBBLINESS
WOBBLINESSES
WOEBEGONENESS
WOEBEGONENESSES
WOEFULLEST
WOEFULNESS
WOEFULNESSES
WOFULNESSES
WOLFBERRIES
WOLFFISHES
WOLFHOUNDS
WOLFISHNESS
WOLFISHNESSES
WOLFRAMITE
WOLFRAMITES
WOLFSBANES
WOLLASTONITE
WOLLASTONITES
WOLVERENES
WOLVERINES
WOMANFULLY
WOMANHOODS
WOMANISERS
WOMANISHLY
WOMANISHNESS
WOMANISHNESSES
WOMANISING
WOMANIZERS
WOMANIZING
WOMANKINDS
WOMANLIEST
WOMANLINESS
WOMANLINESSES
WOMANNESSES
WOMANPOWER
WOMANPOWERS
WOMENFOLKS
WOMENKINDS
WOMENSWEAR
WOMENSWEARS
WONDERFULLY
WONDERFULNESS
WONDERFULNESSES
WONDERINGLY
WONDERINGS
WONDERKIDS
WONDERLAND
WONDERLANDS
WONDERLESS
WONDERMENT
WONDERMENTS
WONDERMONGER
WONDERMONGERING
WONDERMONGERS
WONDERWORK
WONDERWORKS
WONDROUSLY
WONDROUSNESS
WONDROUSNESSES
WONTEDNESS
WONTEDNESSES
WOODBLOCKS
WOODBORERS
WOODBURYTYPE
WOODBURYTYPES
WOODCARVER
WOODCARVERS
WOODCARVING
WOODCARVINGS
WOODCHOPPER
WOODCHOPPERS
WOODCHUCKS
WOODCRAFTS
WOODCRAFTSMAN
WOODCRAFTSMEN
WOODCUTTER
WOODCUTTERS
WOODCUTTING
WOODCUTTINGS
WOODENHEAD
WOODENHEADED
WOODENHEADS
WOODENNESS
WOODENNESSES
WOODENTOPS
WOODENWARE
WOODENWARES
WOODGRAINS
WOODGROUSE
WOODGROUSES
WOODHORSES
WOODHOUSES
WOODINESSES
WOODLANDER
WOODLANDERS
WOODLESSNESS
WOODLESSNESSES
WOODNESSES
WOODPECKER

WOODPECKERS
WOODPIGEON
WOODPIGEONS
WOODPRINTS
WOODREEVES
WOODRUSHES
WOODSCREWS
WOODSHEDDED
WOODSHEDDING
WOODSHEDDINGS
WOODSHOCKS
WOODSHRIKE
WOODSHRIKES
WOODSPITES
WOODSTONES
WOODSTOVES
WOODSWALLOW
WOODSWALLOWS
WOODTHRUSH
WOODTHRUSHES
WOODWAXENS
WOODWORKER
WOODWORKERS
WOODWORKING
WOODWORKINGS
WOOLGATHERER
WOOLGATHERERS
WOOLGATHERING
WOOLGATHERINGS
WOOLGROWER
WOOLGROWERS
WOOLGROWING
WOOLGROWINGS
WOOLINESSES
WOOLLINESS
WOOLLINESSES
WOOLLYBACK
WOOLLYBACKS
WOOLLYBUTT
WOOLLYBUTTS
WOOLLYFOOT
WOOLLYFOOTS
WOOLSORTER
WOOLSORTERS
WOOMERANGS
WOOZINESSES
WORCESTERBERRY
WORCESTERS
WORDBREAKS
WORDINESSES
WORDISHNESS
WORDISHNESSES
WORDLESSLY
WORDLESSNESS
WORDLESSNESSES
WORDMONGER
WORDMONGERS
WORDSEARCH
WORDSEARCHES
WORDSMITHERIES
WORDSMITHERY
WORDSMITHS
WORKABILITIES
WORKABILITY
WORKABLENESS
WORKABLENESSES
WORKAHOLIC
WORKAHOLICS
WORKAHOLISM
WORKAHOLISMS
WORKAROUND
WORKAROUNDS
WORKBASKET
WORKBASKETS
WORKBENCHES
WORKERISTS
WORKERLESS
WORKFELLOW
WORKFELLOWS
WORKFORCES
WORKGROUPS
WORKHORSES
WORKHOUSES
WORKINGMAN
WORKINGMEN
WORKINGWOMAN
WORKINGWOMEN
WORKLESSNESS
WORKLESSNESSES
WORKMANLIKE
WORKMANSHIP
WORKMANSHIPS
WORKMASTER
WORKMASTERS
WORKMISTRESS
WORKMISTRESSES
WORKPEOPLE
WORKPIECES
WORKPLACES
WORKPRINTS
WORKSHEETS
WORKSHOPPED
WORKSHOPPING
WORKSPACES
WORKSTATION
WORKSTATIONS
WORKTABLES
WORKWATCHER
WORKWATCHERS
WORLDBEATS
WORLDLIEST
WORLDLINESS
WORLDLINESSES
WORLDLINGS
WORLDSCALE
WORLDSCALES
WORLDVIEWS
WORMINESSES
WORNNESSES
WORRIMENTS
WORRISOMELY
WORRISOMENESS
WORRISOMENESSES
WORRYINGLY
WORRYWARTS
WORSENESSES
WORSHIPABLE
WORSHIPERS
WORSHIPFUL
WORSHIPFULLY
WORSHIPFULNESS
WORSHIPING
WORSHIPLESS
WORSHIPPED
WORSHIPPER
WORSHIPPERS
WORSHIPPING
WORTHINESS
WORTHINESSES
WORTHLESSLY
WORTHLESSNESS
WORTHLESSNESSES
WORTHWHILE
WORTHWHILENESS
WOUNDINGLY
WOUNDWORTS
WRAITHLIKE
WRANGLERSHIP
WRANGLERSHIPS
WRANGLESOME
WRANGLINGS
WRAPAROUND
WRAPAROUNDS
WRAPPERING
WRAPROUNDS
WRATHFULLY
WRATHFULNESS
WRATHFULNESSES
WRATHINESS
WRATHINESSES
WREATHIEST
WREATHLESS
WREATHLIKE
WRECKFISHES
WRECKMASTER
WRECKMASTERS
WRENCHINGLY
WRENCHINGS
WRESTLINGS
WRETCHEDER
WRETCHEDEST
WRETCHEDLY
WRETCHEDNESS
WRETCHEDNESSES
WRIGGLIEST
WRIGGLINGS
WRINKLELESS
WRINKLIEST
WRISTBANDS
WRISTLOCKS
WRISTWATCH
WRISTWATCHES
WRITERESSES
WRITERSHIP
WRITERSHIPS
WRITHINGLY
WRONGDOERS
WRONGDOING
WRONGDOINGS
WRONGFULLY
WRONGFULNESS
WRONGFULNESSES
WRONGHEADED
WRONGHEADEDLY
WRONGHEADEDNESS
WRONGNESSES
WRONGOUSLY
WULFENITES
WUNDERKIND
WUNDERKINDER
WUNDERKINDS
WYANDOTTES
WYLIECOATS

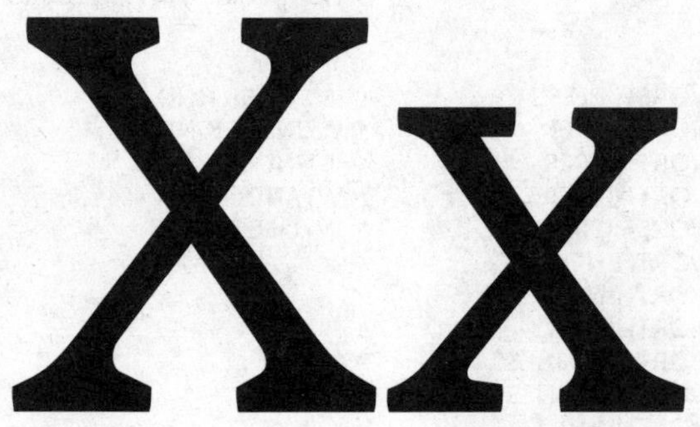

XANTHATION
XANTHATIONS
XANTHOCHROIA
XANTHOCHROIAS
XANTHOCHROIC
XANTHOCHROID
XANTHOCHROIDS
XANTHOCHROISM
XANTHOCHROISMS
XANTHOCHROMIA
XANTHOCHROMIAS
XANTHOCHROOUS
XANTHOMATA
XANTHOMATOUS
XANTHOMELANOUS
XANTHOPHYL
XANTHOPHYLL
XANTHOPHYLLOUS
XANTHOPHYLLS
XANTHOPHYLS
XANTHOPSIA
XANTHOPSIAS
XANTHOPTERIN
XANTHOPTERINE
XANTHOPTERINES
XANTHOPTERINS
XANTHOXYLS
XENARTHRAL
XENOBIOTIC
XENOBIOTICS
XENOBLASTS
XENOCRYSTS
XENODIAGNOSES
XENODIAGNOSIS
XENODIAGNOSTIC
XENODOCHIUM
XENODOCHIUMS
XENOGAMIES
XENOGAMOUS
XENOGENEIC
XENOGENESES
XENOGENESIS
XENOGENETIC
XENOGENIES
XENOGENOUS
XENOGLOSSIA
XENOGLOSSIAS
XENOGLOSSIES
XENOGLOSSY
XENOGRAFTS
XENOLITHIC
XENOMANIAS
XENOMENIAS
XENOMORPHIC
XENOMORPHICALLY
XENOPHILES
XENOPHOBES
XENOPHOBIA
XENOPHOBIAS
XENOPHOBIC
XENOPHOBICALLY
XENOPHOBIES
XENOPLASTIC
XENOTRANSPLANT
XENOTRANSPLANTS
XENOTROPIC
XERANTHEMUM
XERANTHEMUMS
XERISCAPES
XEROCHASIES
XERODERMAE
XERODERMAS
XERODERMATIC
XERODERMATOUS
XERODERMIA
XERODERMIAS
XERODERMIC
XEROGRAPHER
XEROGRAPHERS
XEROGRAPHIC
XEROGRAPHICALLY
XEROGRAPHIES
XEROGRAPHY
XEROMORPHIC
XEROMORPHOUS
XEROMORPHS
XEROPHAGIES
XEROPHILES
XEROPHILIES
XEROPHILOUS
XEROPHTHALMIA
XEROPHTHALMIAS
XEROPHTHALMIC
XEROPHYTES
XEROPHYTIC
XEROPHYTICALLY
XEROPHYTISM
XEROPHYTISMS
XERORADIOGRAPHY
XEROSTOMAS
XEROSTOMATA
XEROSTOMIA
XEROSTOMIAS
XEROTHERMIC
XEROTRIPSES
XEROTRIPSIS
XIPHIHUMERALIS
XIPHIPLASTRA
XIPHIPLASTRAL
XIPHIPLASTRALS
XIPHIPLASTRON
XIPHISTERNA
XIPHISTERNUM
XIPHISTERNUMS
XIPHOPAGIC
XIPHOPAGOUS
XIPHOPAGUS
XIPHOPAGUSES
XIPHOPHYLLOUS
XIPHOSURAN
XIPHOSURANS
XYLOBALSAMUM
XYLOBALSAMUMS
XYLOCARPOUS
XYLOCHROME
XYLOCHROMES
XYLOGENOUS
XYLOGRAPHED
XYLOGRAPHER
XYLOGRAPHERS
XYLOGRAPHIC
XYLOGRAPHICAL
XYLOGRAPHIES
XYLOGRAPHING
XYLOGRAPHS
XYLOGRAPHY
XYLOIDINES
XYLOLOGIES
XYLOMETERS
XYLOPHAGAN
XYLOPHAGANS
XYLOPHAGES
XYLOPHAGOUS
XYLOPHILOUS
XYLOPHONES
XYLOPHONIC
XYLOPHONIST
XYLOPHONISTS
XYLOPYROGRAPHY
XYLORIMBAS
XYLOTOMIES
XYLOTOMIST

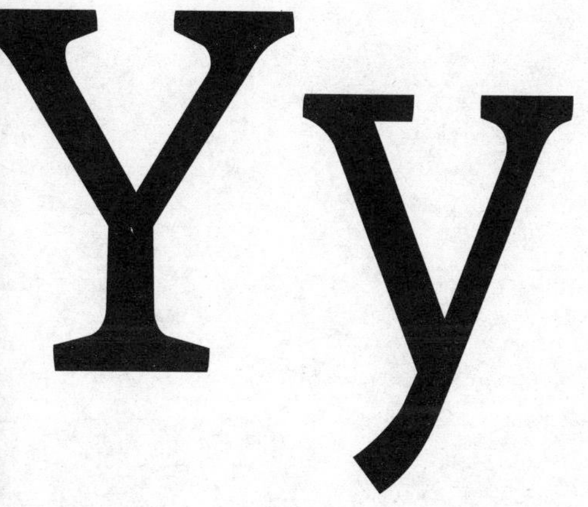

CHTSMANSHIP
CHTSMANSHIPS
CHTSWOMAN
CHTSWOMEN
FFINGALE
FFINGALES
MMERINGS
RBOROUGH
RBOROUGHS
RDMASTER
RDMASTERS
RDSTICKS
TTERINGLY
TTERINGS
ARNINGLY
ASTINESS
ASTINESSES
LLOCHING
LLOWBACK
LLOWBACKS
LLOWBARK
LLOWBARKS
LLOWBIRD
LLOWBIRDS
LLOWCAKE
LLOWCAKES
LLOWFINS
LLOWHAMMER
LLOWHAMMERS
LLOWHEAD
LLOWHEADS
LLOWIEST
LLOWISHNESS
LLOWISHNESSES
LOWLEGS
LOWNESS
LOWNESSES
LOWTAIL
YELLOWTAILS
YELLOWTHROAT
YELLOWTHROATS
YELLOWWARE
YELLOWWARES
YELLOWWEED
YELLOWWEEDS
YELLOWWOOD
YELLOWWOODS
YELLOWWORT
YELLOWWORTS
YEOMANRIES
YERSINIOSES
YERSINIOSIS
YESTERDAYS
YESTEREVEN
YESTEREVENING
YESTEREVENINGS
YESTEREVENS
YESTEREVES
YESTERMORN
YESTERMORNING
YESTERMORNINGS
YESTERMORNS
YESTERNIGHT
YESTERNIGHTS
YESTERYEAR
YESTERYEARS
YIELDABLENESS
YIELDABLENESSES
YIELDINGLY
YIELDINGNESS
YIELDINGNESSES
YOCTOSECOND
YOCTOSECONDS
YOHIMBINES
YOKEFELLOW
YOKEFELLOWS
YOTTABYTES
YOUNGBERRIES
YOUNGBERRY
YOUNGLINGS
YOUNGNESSES
YOUNGSTERS
YOURSELVES
YOUTHENING
YOUTHFULLY
YOUTHFULNESS
YOUTHFULNESSES
YOUTHHEADS
YOUTHHOODS
YOUTHQUAKE
YOUTHQUAKES
YPSILIFORM
YTHUNDERED
YTTERBITES
YTTERBIUMS
YTTRIFEROUS
YUCKINESSES
YUMMINESSES
YUPPIEDOMS
YUPPIFICATION
YUPPIFICATIONS
YUPPIFYING

XYLOTOMISTS
XYLOTOMOUS
XYLOTYPOGRAPHIC
XYLOTYPOGRAPHY
XYRIDACEOUS

Zz

ZABAGLIONE
ZABAGLIONES
ZALAMBDODONT
ZALAMBDODONTS
ZAMBOORAKS
ZAMINDARIES
ZAMINDARIS
ZANINESSES
ZANTEDESCHIA
ZANTEDESCHIAS
ZANTHOXYLS
ZANTHOXYLUM
ZANTHOXYLUMS
ZAPATEADOS
ZAPOTILLAS
ZEALOTISMS
ZEALOTRIES
ZEALOUSNESS
ZEALOUSNESSES
ZEBRAFISHES
ZEBRAWOODS
ZEBRINNIES
ZEITGEBERS
ZEITGEISTS
ZELATRICES
ZELATRIXES
ZELOPHOBIA
ZELOPHOBIAS
ZELOPHOBIC
ZELOPHOBICS
ZELOTYPIAS
ZEMINDARIES
ZEMINDARIS
ZEOLITIFORM
ZEPTOSECOND
ZEPTOSECONDS
ZESTFULNESS
ZESTFULNESSES
ZETTABYTES
ZEUGLODONT
ZEUGLODONTS
ZEUGMATICALLY
ZIBELLINES
ZIDOVUDINE
ZIDOVUDINES
ZIGZAGGEDNESS
ZIGZAGGEDNESSES
ZIGZAGGERIES
ZIGZAGGERS
ZIGZAGGERY
ZIGZAGGING
ZILLIONAIRE
ZILLIONAIRES
ZILLIONTHS
ZINCIFEROUS
ZINCIFICATION
ZINCIFICATIONS
ZINCIFYING
ZINCKENITE
ZINCKENITES
ZINCKIFICATION
ZINCKIFICATIONS
ZINCKIFIED
ZINCKIFIES
ZINCKIFYING
ZINCOGRAPH
ZINCOGRAPHER
ZINCOGRAPHERS
ZINCOGRAPHIC
ZINCOGRAPHICAL
ZINCOGRAPHIES
ZINCOGRAPHS
ZINCOGRAPHY
ZINCOLYSES
ZINCOLYSIS
ZINFANDELS
ZINGIBERACEOUS
ZINJANTHROPI
ZINJANTHROPUS
ZINJANTHROPUSES
ZINKENITES
ZINKIFEROUS
ZINKIFICATION
ZINKIFICATIONS
ZINKIFYING
ZINZIBERACEOUS
ZIRCALLOYS
ZIRCONIUMS
ZITHERISTS
ZIZYPHUSES
ZOANTHARIAN
ZOANTHARIANS
ZOANTHROPIC
ZOANTHROPIES
ZOANTHROPY
ZOECHROMES
ZOMBIELIKE
ZOMBIFICATION
ZOMBIFICATIONS
ZOMBIFYING
ZOOCEPHALIC
ZOOCHEMICAL
ZOOCHEMISTRIES
ZOOCHEMISTRY
ZOOCHORIES
ZOOCHOROUS
ZOOCULTURE
ZOOCULTURES
ZOODENDRIA
ZOODENDRIUM
ZOOGAMETES
ZOOGEOGRAPHER
ZOOGEOGRAPHERS
ZOOGEOGRAPHIC
ZOOGEOGRAPHICAL
ZOOGEOGRAPHIES
ZOOGEOGRAPHY
ZOOGLOEOID
ZOOGONIDIA
ZOOGONIDIUM
ZOOGRAFTING
ZOOGRAFTINGS
ZOOGRAPHER
ZOOGRAPHERS
ZOOGRAPHIC
ZOOGRAPHICAL
ZOOGRAPHIES
ZOOGRAPHIST
ZOOGRAPHISTS
ZOOKEEPERS
ZOOLATRIAS
ZOOLATRIES
ZOOLATROUS
ZOOLOGICAL
ZOOLOGICALLY
ZOOLOGISTS
ZOOMAGNETIC
ZOOMAGNETISM
ZOOMAGNETISMS
ZOOMANCIES
ZOOMETRICAL
ZOOMETRIES
ZOOMORPHIC
ZOOMORPHIES
ZOOMORPHISM
ZOOMORPHISMS
ZOONOMISTS
ZOOPATHIES
ZOOPATHOLOGIES
ZOOPATHOLOGY
ZOOPERISTS
ZOOPHAGANS

ZOOPHAGIES
ZOOPHAGOUS
ZOOPHILIAS
ZOOPHILIES
ZOOPHILISM
ZOOPHILISMS
ZOOPHILIST
ZOOPHILISTS
ZOOPHILOUS
ZOOPHOBIAS
ZOOPHOBOUS
ZOOPHYSIOLOGIES
ZOOPHYSIOLOGIST
ZOOPHYSIOLOGY
ZOOPHYTICAL
ZOOPHYTOID
ZOOPHYTOLOGICAL
ZOOPHYTOLOGIES
ZOOPHYTOLOGIST
ZOOPHYTOLOGISTS
ZOOPHYTOLOGY
ZOOPLANKTER
ZOOPLANKTERS
ZOOPLANKTON
ZOOPLANKTONIC
ZOOPLANKTONS
ZOOPLASTIC
ZOOPLASTIES
ZOOPSYCHOLOGIES
ZOOPSYCHOLOGY
ZOOSCOPIES
ZOOSPERMATIC
ZOOSPERMIA
ZOOSPERMIUM
ZOOSPORANGIA
ZOOSPORANGIAL
ZOOSPORANGIUM
ZOOSPOROUS
ZOOSTEROLS
ZOOTECHNICAL
ZOOTECHNICS
ZOOTECHNIES
ZOOTHAPSES
ZOOTHAPSIS
ZOOTHECIAL
ZOOTHECIUM
ZOOTHEISMS
ZOOTHEISTIC
ZOOTHERAPIES
ZOOTHERAPY
ZOOTOMICAL
ZOOTOMICALLY
ZOOTOMISTS
ZOOTROPHIC
ZOOTROPHIES
ZOOTSUITER
ZOOTSUITERS
ZOOXANTHELLA
ZOOXANTHELLAE
ZORBONAUTS
ZUCCHETTOS
ZUGZWANGED
ZUGZWANGING
ZUMBOORUKS
ZWISCHENZUG
ZWISCHENZUGS
ZWITTERION
ZWITTERIONIC
ZWITTERIONS
ZYGANTRUMS
ZYGAPOPHYSEAL
ZYGAPOPHYSES
ZYGAPOPHYSIAL
ZYGAPOPHYSIS
ZYGOBRANCH
ZYGOBRANCHIATE
ZYGOBRANCHIATES
ZYGOBRANCHS
ZYGOCACTUS
ZYGOCACTUSES
ZYGOCARDIAC
ZYGODACTYL
ZYGODACTYLIC
ZYGODACTYLISM
ZYGODACTYLISMS
ZYGODACTYLOUS
ZYGODACTYLS
ZYGOMATICS
ZYGOMORPHIC
ZYGOMORPHIES
ZYGOMORPHISM
ZYGOMORPHISMS
ZYGOMORPHOUS
ZYGOMORPHY
ZYGOMYCETE
ZYGOMYCETES
ZYGOMYCETOUS
ZYGOPHYLLACEOUS
ZYGOPHYTES
ZYGOPLEURAL
ZYGOSITIES
ZYGOSPERMS
ZYGOSPHENE
ZYGOSPHENES
ZYGOSPORES
ZYGOSPORIC
ZYGOTICALLY
ZYMOGENESES
ZYMOGENESIS
ZYMOLOGICAL
ZYMOLOGIES
ZYMOLOGIST
ZYMOLOGISTS
ZYMOMETERS
ZYMOSIMETER
ZYMOSIMETERS
ZYMOTECHNIC
ZYMOTECHNICAL
ZYMOTECHNICS
ZYMOTICALLY